# INDEX

W9-CPR-010

## —A—

**A.F.L.-C.I.O.** *see American Federation of Labor & Congress of Industrial Organizations*
**Abbreviations—**
  Int'l & Regional Org.
    174, 573-575
  Medical ....................60
  State ......................932
  UN agencies ...174, 571, 574
  U. S. Administrative ......174
**Abrams, Creighton** .........81
**Abyssinia** *see Ethopia*
**Academy Awards** ...........240
**Acadia National Park** ......388
**Acadians (La.)** .............363
**Accidents—**
  1968—by months ....63, 65-92
  Aviation .......67, 663, 765
  Deaths (number, causes) .759
  Grand Canyon air crash ...663
  Home, occupational .......759
  Injuries, types ..........759
  New York air crash (1960) 663
  Railroad .......107, 660, 765
  Ship disasters ......657, 660
  Vehicle accidents ....759, 765
  Wage loss ................759
  *See Disasters*
**Aconcagua Mt.** .......493, 720
**Actors, Actresses—**
  Contemporary ........677-685
  Deceased ............673-685
  Film roles ..........159-160
  Motion picture awards ...240
  Stars of plays ......156-157
  Theatrical awards .......243
**Adak Island (Aleutians)** ...722
**Adams, John (biog.)** .......184
**Adams, John Quincy (biog.)** 186
**Addenda** ....................64
**Address, Forms of** .........351
**Aden** *see Southern Yemen*
**Adenauer, Konrad** ..........515
**Admirals, USN** .............739
**Admiralty Islands** .........495
**Adoption (children)** .......233
**Adventist Churches** ...219, 221
**Aegean Sea** ...........517, 552
**Aero Records, Interntl.** .249-250
**Aeronautics review** ........246
**Afars-Issas, French Terr.** .513
**Afghanistan** .........492, 493
**Africa—**
  Area, dimensions ........736
  Gold production .........140
  Lakes, notable ..........717
  Mountain peaks ..........721
  Petroleum production ....130
  Population ..............224
  —Religious ..............122
  Sugar production ........122
  Trade ...................98
  Waterfalls ..............719
**Africa, Portuguese** ........544
**Africa, South-West** ........547
**African Unity, Org.** *see Org. of African Unity*
**Agencies, Federal** .....174, 175
**Agnew, Spiro T.** ......37, 38, 90
**Agriculture** ...........769-776
  Cooperatives ...........770
  Corn yields ............773
  Crop production ........771
  Egg production .........776
  Elevator capacity ......773
  Employment .............776
  Exports, imports 100, 776, 777
  Farm acreage, value ....769
  Farm income ............770
  Farm population ........604
  Food consumption .......776
  Grain receipts .........776
  Grain supply, visible ..772
  Harvested acreage ......771
  Livestock ..............780
  Loans, mortgages .......777
  Price index numbers ....769

## Agriculture (cont'd)

  Prices received .....769, 770
  Production ...........772, 773
  Wages paid .............769
  Weather service ........288
  Wheat *see Wheat*
**Agriculture, Department of—**
  Administrative personnel .166
  Employees (number) .....145
  Established ............182
  Expenditures ...........131
  Secretaries .......166, 182
**Air—**
  Composition, temperature .260
  Density ............260, 589
**Air Express Service** .......114
**Air Force, Department of the—**
  Administrative personnel .165
  Employees (number) .....145
  Secretaries .......165, 182
**Air Force, U. S.—**
  Academy ...........165, 745
  Capt. convicted .........73
  Civil Air Patrol .......749
  Expenditures ...........131
  Flights (global, ocean) 247-248
  Generals (active duty) ..739
  History ................743
  Library Service ........349
  Major Air Commands .....165
  Military units .........743
  Missiles *see Missiles, rockets*
  Nurse Corps ........743, 748
  Pay scale allowances ..754-755
  SAC plane crash .........67
  Satellites *see Space developments*
  Strength ...............743
  Women's branches ....747-748
  *See Armed forces, U. S.*
**Air Mail—**
  Air-letter .............927
  Domestic rates .........927
  International rates ..929-931
  Parcel Post rates ...927-931
**Air Museum, National** ......444
**Airline distances** .....251-252
**Airlines,** *see Aviation*
**Airports**—*see specific city article*
**Airships,** *see Dirigibles*
**Akron, Ohio** ...............390
  Buildings, tall ........445
  Mayor ..................924
  Museums, attractions ...390
  Population .....604, 625, 652
**Alabama—**
  *See States, U. S.* .......354
  Admission, area cap. .354, 384
  Agriculture ..769-771, 773, 776
  Birmingham (see *Birmingham*) ...............392
  Birth, death statistics 758, 765
  Counties (seats, areas) .635
  Elections ......884, 885, 887
  Lake, largest ..........718
  Marriage, divorce laws 760, 761
  Museums, attractions ...354
  Name, origin of ........383
  Officials, pay .........919
  Population .........593-654
  —Cities and Towns ...604, 605
  —Counties, county seats .635
  —Metropolitan areas ..652-654
  Presidential vote ...884, 887
  Taxes ..............209-218
  Territory ..........354, 384
  Vital statistics ....757-768
**Alabama, ship (1864)** ......657
**Alamo (1836)** ...............302
**Alaska** .................354-355
  *See States, U. S.*
  Accession ..............383
  Admission, area, cap. 354, 384
  Agriculture ..769-771, 772, 773
  Airports ...............355
  Altitudes (high, low) ..738
  Birth, death statistics 758, 765
  Elections ......884, 885, 887
  Farms (statistics) .....769
  Geographic center .......94

## Alaska (cont'd)

  Gold rush (1896-99) ....354
  Highway ................355
  Lake, largest ..........718
  Mountain peaks ....354, 720
  Museums, attractions ...355
  Name, origin of ........383
  Officials, pay .........919
  Population .........593-654
  —Cities and towns ......605
  —Counties, county seats .635
  —Density ...............603
  Presidential vote ...884, 887
  Purchase (1867) .303, 354, 384
  Statehood ..........354, 384
  Taxes ..............209-218
  Territory established .354, 384
  Time zones .............280
  Vital Statistics ....757-768
  Volcanoes ..............716
**Alaska Purchase Treaty** 354 385
**Albania** ....................492
  Area, capital, population .492
  Petroleum production ...130
  President ..............576
  Tirane (population) ....578
**Albany, N. Y.—**
  Buildings, tall ........445
  Mayor ..................924
  Population .........604, 622
**Alberta, Canada** ...........485
**Alcohol—**
  Boiling point ..........589
  Distilled, production ..121
  *See Liquor*
**Aleutian Islands** .....354, 722
  Volcanoes ..............716
**Alexander the Great**
  (356 B.C.) .............295
**Alexandria, Pharos at** .....721
**Algeria** ....................493
  Area, capital, population .493
  Cities (population) ....578
  Peace pact (1962) ......317
  President ..............576
  Trade ..................98
**Aliens—**
  Classes excluded U. S. .701
  Passports, U. S. .......700
  Selective Service Act ..756
**All-America teams, 1968—**
  Basketball .............823
  Lacrosse ...............853
**All-Hallowmas** .............591
**All Saints' Day** ...........591
**All-Star baseball games** ...809
**Allegiance to Flag pledge** .176
**Allegiance, Oath of** .......702
**Allen, Ethan** ..............298
**Almanac, World—**
  Guide to use .............2
  Hawaii song ............42
  Sedition ...............197
**Alofi Island (Fr.)** ........514
**Alps, The** ..................550
  Hannibal crosses, 218 B.C. 295
  Peaks, highest .........720
**Altitudes—**
  Cities, U. S. ..........737
  Highest, lowest ....720-721 738
  Lakes, U. S. (by state) .718
**Aluminum** ...................207
**Amazon River (Brazil)** ..61, 497
**Ambassadors, ministers—**
  Address, form of .......351
  Appointment (law) ......201
  Salute to (artillery) ..746
  U. S. and foreign ...170-171
**Amchitka Island (Aleutians)** 722
**America—**
  Discovery (1492) ...296, 708
  Dutch in (1624, '64) ...298
  Emperor, last (1889) ...306
  English settlement (1607) .297
  Explorations, early ....708
  Name, origin (1497) 175, 296 708
  *See No. & So. America*
**America, Miss** ..............244
**America, Miss Black** .......61
**American Civil Liberties**
  **Union** ................72

3

American Design, Index of ..443
American Federation of Labor
& Congress of Industrial
Organizations (AFL-CIO)
Maritime Union ............ 86
Merger (1955) ............316
Political, Education Comm.173
Steelworkers ............. 86
UAW ..................... 79
Unions ...................245
Amer. Field Service .......346
Amer. Football League .....862
American Indian Mus., NYC 437
American Legion (see Assns.)
Junior baseball champions 804
American Numismatic .......437
American Revolution ...298-299
Boston memorials .........393
Casualties ...............751
Declaration of
Independence .....196-197
Liberty Bell .............198
Military leaders .........665
Monuments, sites ..388, 389
New York City during ....415
Valley Forge State Park .373
American Samoa ............381
Area, capital, population .381
Farms (statistics) .......769
Officials, pay ...........919
Population ...............655
American Stock Exchange
(see Assns.)
Seat prices .............139
Stocks, dividends, yields 51-54
Stocks, prices, symbols .51-54
Transactions .........50, 139
Volume daily ............. 50
American's Creed ..........182
Americans, Dem. Action 79, 173
Americans, noted .....665-685
America's Cup (yachting) ..837
Ampere (electrical unit) ..586
Amritsar, Massacre (1919) .309
Amundsen, Roald ..308, 705, 706
Andamans Islands ......521, 722
Andaman Sea ..............713
Andes Mnts. ....493, 497, 501
Andorra ..................493
Andre, Major John (1780) ..299
Andrea Doria (1956) .......660
Anesthesia (1842) .........302
Angling, see Fish and Fishing
Angola ...................544
Waterfalls ..............719
Anguilla (W. Indies) ......561
Animals ..............779-780
Dogs (breeds) ...........877
Farm see Livestock
Gestation, incubation ....780
Koala ...................494
Names of groups .........780
See Zoological Parks
Annapolis, Naval Academy .744
Anne of Cleves (1509) .....297
Anniversaries, wedding ....760
Antarctica "Ocean" .......713
Antarctica—
Area .....................736
Explorations ..302, 705-707
Mountain peaks ..........721
Volcano .................715
Antarctica, British .......562
Anthem, National ..........171
Anthony, Susan B. (day) ..591
Antic sti Island (Canada) .722
Antigua Is. (Br. W. I.) .561, 722
Antilles, Netherlands .....538
Antipodes Island, N. Z. ...538
Aphelion, perihelion—
Comets ..................256
Meaning of ..............256
Planets .................286
Apogee of Moon ...........283
Apollo exploration ........262
Appalachian Trail ........ 94
Appeals courts, U. S. .....167
Appleton, Jane M. ...183, 185
Appomattox Court House ...377
Appropriations, U. S. .....134
Aquariums ................779
Marine Studios, Fla. ....359
Shedd, Chicago ..........395
Arab League ..............573
Arabia, Saudi .......545, 577
Arabic numerals ..........582
Arbor Day ...........590, 591
Archeology—
Dr. Leakey discoveries ...714
Seven Wonders of World ..721
Archery champions .........829
Archipelagoes—
Bismarck (Australia) .....495
Largest, Indonesia ......522

Architects, Noted ..670, 696, 698
Archives, National ........442
Arctic explorati ns .704-705
Arctic Ocean—
Area, depth .............713
Islands, areas ..........722
Areas—
Circles .................586
Continents ..........651, 736
Earth ...................260
Foreign nations ....485-567
Forests, parks, U. S. 388, 778
Islands .................722
Lakes ..............717, 718
Largest country (USSR) ..553
Measures (units) ....581-584
National memorials .......389
New York City .....653, 654
Oceans ..................713
United States ......94, 655
–Counties, by state 635-651
–States .................384
–Territories ...383, 384, 385
Arenas, sports ...........844
Argentina ............493-494
Area, capital, population .493
Cities, pop. ........578, 651
Gold reserve ............139
Iguazu waterfall ........719
Merchant fleet ..........101
Mountain peaks ..........720
Peron, Juan (1955) ..316, 494
Petroleum production ....130
President ...............576
Revolution (1955) ..316, 494
Sugar production ........122
Trade ................... 98
Weights, measures .......587
Argonne National Lab. ....361
Arithmetic tables ....585-586
Arizona ..................355
See States, U. S.
Admission, area, cap. 355, 384
Agriculture ..769-771, 773, 776
Birth, death statistics 758, 765
Counties (seats, areas) ...635
Elections ..........885, 887
Grand Canyon ...........355
Lake, largest ...........718
Marriage, divorce laws 760, 761
Museums, attractions ....355
Name, Origin of .........383
Officials, pay ..........919
Phoenix (see Phoenix) ...420
Population ..........593-654
–Cities and towns ..604, 605
–Counties, county seats ..635
–Metropolitan areas ..652-654
Presidential vote ...884, 887
Taxes ...............209-218
Vital statistics .....757-768
Vital Statistics .....757-768
Arkansas .................356
See States, U. S.
Admission, area, cap. 356, 384
Agriculture ..769-771, 773, 776
Birth, death statistics 758, 765
Counties (seats, areas) 635-636
Desegregation (1957) ....317
Elections ......884, 885, 888
Lake, largest ...........718
Marriage, divorce laws 760, 761
Museums, attractions ....356
Officials, pay ..........919
Name, Origin of .........383
Population ..........593-654
–Cities and towns ..604, 606
–Counties, county seats 635-636
–Metropolitan areas ..652-654
Presidential vote ...884, 888
Taxes ...............209-218
Territory ..........356, 384
Vital statistics .....757-768
Arkansas River ...........723
Arlington Nat. Cemetery ..441
Kennedy tomb ............441
Tomb, Unknown Soldier ..441
Armed Forces Day .........591
Armed forces, foreign—
World War, I, II ........752
See individual nations
Armed forces, U. S.—
Air Force conviction ... 73
Casualties, see casualties
Cemeteries .........441, 749
Deserters ............... 67
Insignia ...........741, 742
Jets, fighter ...........249
Joint Chiefs of Staff .164, 739
Korea, see Korean War
Medal of Honor (Viet) ...740
Military action (1900-1968) 751
Military pay (1968) ..754-755
Military salute .........739

Armed forces, U. S. (cont'd)
Nurse Corps .........747, 748
Officers on active duty
739, 741, 742
Pay scale, allowances .754-755
Personnel .....739, 741, 742
Reserve call-up ......... 74
Salutes .................746
Selective Service .......756
Sr. enlisted advisers ...742
Social Security .........152
Training centers ........742
Troop strength, wars ....751
Women's branches ...747-748
See specific services and Wars
Armenian SSR .............554
Army, Department of the—
Administrative personnel .165
Employees (number) ......145
Expenditures ............131
Secretaries .......180, 182
Army, U. S.—
Commanding generals .....165
Generals on active duty .739
Insignia ................741
Military units ..........743
Nurse Corps .............747
Officers (form of address) 351
Pay scale, allowances .754-755
Satellites see Space develop-
ments
Time ....................280
West Point ..............744
Women's branches ...747-748
See Armed Forces, U. S.
Arnold, Benedict (1780) ...299
Around World Trips ...247-250
Arrests, by offense, sex ..766
Art—
Awards ..................241
Galleries, Museums, see State
and Cities articles
–New York City .....436-437
–Washington, D. C. ..442-444
Societies ..........339, 340
Artemis, Temple of .......721
Arthur, Chester A. (biog.) .189
Articles of Confederation 199-202
Artillery salutes ........746
Artists, noted .......694-699
Aruba Island (Carib.) .538, 722
Ascension Island .....562, 722
Ash Wednesday (1901-2100) .232
Ashanti, Ghana ...........516
Ashmore, Cartier Islands ..495
Asia—
Area, dimensions ........736
Lakes, notable ..........717
Mountain peaks ..........721
Petroleum production ....130
Population ..............651
–Religious ..............224
Sugar production ........122
Trade ................... 98
U. S. aid ...............580
Waterfalls ..............719
Assassinations—
U. S. Presidents ........662
–Garfield ..........189, 662
–Kennedy, J. F. ..194, 318, 662
–Lincoln .......188, 305, 662
–McKinley ..........190, 662
Kennedy, Robert F. . 80, 662
King, Martin Luther
63, 74, 662
Nixon, alleged plot .... 63
Assemblies of God Churches 219
Associated Press (see Assns.)
Associations, Societies .449-464
or 469-484
College ............339-342
Reporters awards ........242
Astor Place riots (1849) ..303
Astronautics see Space
Developments
Astronomical data .....253-287
Celestial bodies, new ...286
Celestial events ....253-256
Constants ...............281
Eclipses (1969) .........261
Meteorite bombardment ..262
Planetariums ............257
Planets, visible ....258-259
Quasars .................286
Signs and symbols ..256, 282
Star tables .............284
Telescopes ..............257
Time ...............277, 280
Athena torpedoed (1939) ..659
Athletics ...........794-883
See specific sports
Atlanta, Ga. .............390
Buildings, tall .........445
Campaign of 1864 ...305, 391
Mayor ...................924

**Atlanta, Ga. (cont'd)**
Museums, attractions .....391
Population ..........604, 652
Winecoff fire (1946) ......664
**Atlantic Cable** (1858) ......303
Telephone (1956) ........316
**Atlantic Charter** (1941) ....312
**Atlantic City, N. J.—**
Mayor ..................924
Miss America Pageant ..244
Miss Black America ......61
Population ..........621, 652
**Atlantic Coast U. S.—**
Highest point .............94
Ports, cargo volume ......99
Tides ..............786–790
**Atlantic Ocean—**
Area, depth .............713
Crossings, fast ..102, 247–250
First steamer to cross ...102
Islands, areas ..........722
**Atmosphere** ..............260
**Atolls** (Pacific Ocean) ......722
**Atomic Energy—**
Argonne Lab., Ill. .......361
Chain reaction (1942) ...312
Fuchs case (1950) .......315
May, Alan Nunn (1952) ..316
Nautilus (1954) .........316
Reactors ................361
Rosenberg plot (1951) ...315
Savannah, N. S. (1959) ..317
Tests, U. S. (1963) ......317
Submarines *see Submarines*
**Atomic Energy Commission** .175
Power projects ..........361
**Atomic, hydrogen bombs—**
China ....................66
First, atomic (1945) .....313
First hydrogen (1952) ....316
French (1960) ...........317
French tests ......85, 88, 89
Plane crash ..............67
Tests, USSR (1961) ......317
Treaty ..............68, 81
U. S. monopoly ended (1949)
                          314
World War II (1945) .....313
**Atomic weights** .....588–589
**Attorneys General—**
States ..............109–113
United States ......164, 181
**Attu Island** (Aleutians) ....722
**Auckland Island, N. Z.** ....538
**Aunuu Island, Samoa** .....381
**Aurora** ..................283
**Australia** ............494–495
Area, capital, population ..494
Cities (population) .......578
Gold production .........140
Head of State ...........576
Holt drowned .............66
Lakes, notable ..........717
Mountain peaks .........721
Prime Minister .......66, 68
Territories ........494, 495
Trade ..............98, 494
Waterfalls ..............719
**Australian Antarctic** .......495
**Austria** ..............495–496
Area, capital, population ..495
Cities (population) .......578
Germany invades (1938) ..311
Petroleum production .....130
Rulers ............495, 690
Sugar production ........122
Trade ..............98, 495
Waterfalls ..............719
Weights, measures .......587
World War I ........308–309
**Austrians, noted** ......690, 698
**Austro-Hungarian monarchy** .690
**Authors—**
Awards .....234–239, 241–243
Books, 1968 ............155
Noted ..............694–699
**Automobiles—**
Bus statistics .......112, 113
Credit sales (value) ......140
Deaths .............759, 765
Drivers (number by state) .109
—Age ...................115
Exhibit, first (1889) ......306
Exports, imports ........100
First U. S. (1892) ...117, 118
Fuel ...........113, 115, 130
Industry (Mich.) .........402
Injuries ................759
Inventions, noted ....117, 118
Mileage, touring ....110–111
Mobil Economy Run .....113
Mobile homes ...........114
Nascar racing ..........814
Production ..............114

**Automobiles (cont'd)**
Racing records ..........814
Registration, U. S. ...109, 115
Safety laws ............112
Sales ..................114
Speed limits ......108, 109
State taxes .............115
Super highways .........111
Thefts .................768
Travel statistics ........108
Turnpikes ..............109
Used, prices ...........112
*See Roads*
**Auto Racing—**
Amer. road race ........814
Daytona 500 ...........814
Nascar .................814
World Drivers ..........814
**Autumn season** ..........260
**Autumnal Equinox** .......260
**Aviation—**
Accidents ..........663, 765
—Grand Canyon, 1956 ...663
Air Freight .............246
Airports, *see Airports*
Albany-N. Y. flight (1910) .307
Alcock-Brown (1919) ....310
Arnold research ctr. Tenn. .375
Balloons (1783, '84) .....300
Bleriot's flight (1909) ....307
British .................559
Commercial .............246
Corrigan's flight (1938) ...311
Disasters ...............663
Flying distances .....251–252
Hall of Fame ...........250
Helicopters ....246, 250, 316
Inventions, noted .......116
Jet propulsion
—Atlantic, service, first ...317
—Passenger service, first ..316
—Passenger service, U. S.,
                       (1958) 317
Lindbergh (1927) .......310
Maynard-Pearson (1919) .310
N. Y.—Moscow link .....86
Mileage tables ......251–252
Ocean flights ......247–248
Polar flights ...........705
Records, international .249–250
Review (1968) ..........246
Traffic ............246, 250
Transcontinental record
           (1911, '19) ...308, 310
Weather service ........288
Wright Bros. (Ohio) .250, 400
**Avoirdupois measures** ...581, 583
**Awards** .......159–160, 234–244
Academy ...............240
Book ...................241
Income tax on ..........211
Journalism .........236, 241
Lasker ..................64
Medal of Honor .....64, 740
Medicine ..........234–235
Miss America pageant ...244
Miss Black America ......61
Miss Universe ...........61
Motion picture ..........240
Music ..................242
Nobel ..........64, 234–235
Oscar ..................240
Other ..................243
Poetry .................239
Pulitzer ...........236–239
Science ................242
Sports .............794–843
Television, radio ........243
Theater ................243
*See specific awards*
**Axel Heiberg Is.** (Arctic) ...722
**Axis Sally Trial** (1949) .....314
**Axson, Ellen L.** (Wilson) 183, 192
**Azerbaijan, SSR** ..........554
**Azores** (Portugal) .....543, 722

**— B —**

**Baby colors** ..............763
**Babylon, Hanging Gardens** ..721
**Bacon, Nathaniel** (1676) ....298
**Badlands** (No. Dakota) .....371
**Badminton champions** .....829
**Baffin Islands** (Arctic) .....722
**Bahama Islands** .....561, 722
**Bahrain Islands** ......562, 722
**Baker Island** .............382
**Balance of Payments, U. S.**
                         70, 126
**Balboa** (1513) ............297
**Balearic Islands, Spain** .547, 722
**Bali Island** (Indonesia) .522, 722
**Ball, George W.** .......75, 89

**Ballet** ..................687
**Balloon records** ..........250
**Balloons** (1783, '84) .......300
**Baltic Sea** ...............713
**Baltimore, Md.** ...........391
Airport ................391
Buildings, tall ..........445
Chesapeake Bay
—Bridge-Tunnel .......725
Fire (1904) .............664
Mayor .................924
Museums, attractions ...391
Opera ..................157
Population ......604, 616, 641
Port traffic .........96, 99
Public library ..........348
Trolley, first (1885) ..118, 306
**Bancroft Prizes** (writing) ..241
**Bandaranaike, Mrs.** ......501
**Bangka, Indonesia** ........522
**Bank of Canada** ..........490
**Banks—**
Assets, liabilities .......136
Charter, first (1781) .....300
Clearings, U. S. cities ...136
Deposits, largest U. S. ...137
Farm credit ........770, 777
Foreign, largest ........139
France nationalizes (1945) .313
Gold reserve (world) ....139
Inter-Amer. Development .575
Number, U. S. ..........136
Savings by individuals ...137
Suspensions ............144
World (international) 572, 574
*See Currency, U. S.*
**Banks Is.** (Arctic) .........722
**Banks Is.** (New Hebrides) ..563
**Baptist Churches—**
First American ..........223
Headquarters ...........221
History, organization ....223
Membership .......219, 223
**Bar assns.** *see Assns.*
**Barbados** .......496, 576, 722
**Barge, Super** .............98
**Barley—**
Grain center receipts ....773
Prices, farm ...........770
Production .........771, 773
—By state ..............773
**Barnard, Dr. Christiaan** ....66
**Bartholdi, Frederic A.** ..93, 697
**Baseball—**
All-Major League team ...807
All-Star games .........809
American League (1968)
                     802–803
American Legion champ .804
Attendance records .....807
Batting champs .........804
Cy Young Mem. Award ..807
Government .............799
Hall of Fame .......371, 806
Home runs
—Leaders by year ......804
—Leaders, all-time .....798
—Park distances .......810
Little League ...........807
McLain wins 31 games ..810
Minor leagues (1968) .808–809
Player of year ..........808
Most Valuable Players .64, 806
Museum .........371, 806
National League (1968) 800–801
No-hit games ..........805
Parks, capacities .......810
Pennant winners .......799
Perfect games ..........810
Pitching ERA champs ...805
Records ...........794–810
Rookies of the year ..64, 806
RBI leaders ............804
World Series (1968) .794–798
—Gate receipts .........797
—Players' shares .......797
—Records set ..........798
—Series since 1903 .....798
**Basketball, A. B. A.** ......825
**Basketball—**
Biddy .................825
**Basketball, College** ...822, 823
**Basketball Hall of Fame** ...823
**Basketball, N. B. A.** ......824
**Basse-Terre Is., Guadeloupe** .513
**Bastogne battle** ......313, 496
**Basutoland** (Lesotho) ......531
**Bataan death march** (1942) .312
**Bathyscaph** ..............713
**Batista, Fulgencio** .....317, 506
**Battlefield sites, parks** .....388
**Baudouin, King** ......496, 576
**Beamon, Robert** ......878, 879

Beatles, the ............160, 677
Bayonne Bridge ............725
Bechuanaland (Botswana) ..497
Bedloe's Island (Liberty) .. 93
Beef—
  Nutritive value ............774
  Prices, farm ..............770
  Production, consumption ..772
Beer—
  Excise Tax ................218
  Production ................121
Belgian Congo (former)
  *See Congo, Republic of*
Belgians, noted ............698
Belgium ...................496
  Area, capital, population ..496
  Cities (population) ........578
  Gold reserve ..............139
  Govt. ousted .........72, 81
  King Baudouin ......496, 576
  Merchant fleet ............101
  Rulers ........496, 576, 692
  Sugar production ..........122
  Trade ................98, 496
  Weights, Measures ........587
Bell time (shipboard) ......589
Belmont Stakes ............817
Benelux Union .............532
Benes, Eduard (Czech) ..508, 698
Ben-Gurion, David .........526
Berbers (Morocco) .........536
Beria, Lavrenti P. (1953) ..316
Bering Sea ................713
Bering, Vitus (1741) 299, 354, 705
Berlin, Germany—
  Administration ......515, 516
  Blockade airlift ......314, 515
  Population ..........578, 651
  Riots, East sector (1953) ..316
  Wall divides city (1961) ..317
  *See Germany (West*
  *Germany), (East Germany)*
Bermuda Islands ......561, 722
Bernadotte, Count (1948) ..662
Betsy Ross legend .........177
Beverages (consumption) ..776
Bhutan, Kingdom of ...497, 576
Biafra *see Nigeria*
Bible—
  Common Bible ............225
  Early editions (1535) ......297
  Gutenberg (1456) ........296
  King James (1611) ........297
  Ten Commandments ......230
Bicycle Racing—
  Tour de France ............877
Big Bend National Park ....388
Bikini Atoll ................722
Bill of Rights ..........202-206
Billiards ...................829
Biographers, American ..666-668
Birch, John society *see Assns.*
Birds, by State ........354-379
  Dodo (Mauritius) .........535
Birmingham, Ala. .........392
  Buildings, tall ............445
  Mayor ....................924
  Museums, attractions ... 392
  Population ......604, 605, 652
Birth Control .........63, 85
Birth Stones ..............760
Births—
  Certificates, records ..350, 634
  Illegitimate ..............764
  New York State ..........758
  Notable persons, dates 665-699
  Number, rate by state ....758
Bishops—
  Address, form of .........351
  Methodist ................226
  Protestant Episcopal ....225
  Roman Catholic ....228-230
Bismarck Archipelago .....495
Black Friday (1869) .......304
Black Hawk War (1832) ..302
Black Hills, S. Dak. .......375
Black Hole of Calcutta (1756) 300
Black Sea .................713
Black Tom Explosion (1916) 309
Blarney Stone (Ireland) ..524
Blériot, Louis (1909) ......307
Blind *see Assns.*
  Braille, overseas postage . 931
  Income tax exemption ....209
  Social Security aid .......154
Blizzards ..................662
  1888 .....................306
  Descriptive ..............289
Blue Cross hosp. plans ....762
Blue & Gray football games 868
Blue Ridge Mts. (Va.) ....377
Blue Ridge Parkway .......388
Blue Shield medical plans . 762
Boat racing, *see specific sports*
Bobsled racing .........832, 877

Boer War (1899) .......306, 547
Bogota Conference (1948) ..314
Boiling points—
  Alcohol, water ............589
Boleyn, Ann (1509) ........297
Bolivar, Simon (1824)
          302, 505, 693
Bolivia .....................497
  Area, capital, population ..497
  Cities (population) ........578
  Petroleum production ....130
  President ................576
  Trade ................98, 497
  Weights, measures ......587
Bolling, Edith (Wilson) 183, 192
Bombay (India) ......521, 578
Bonaire Island ............538
Bonaparte—
  Napoleon I
  –Birth (1769) ............300
  –Campaigns ........300-301
  –Consul, emperor ....300, 689
  –Empresses (Josephine,
     Marie Louise) ..301, 689
  –Exile, Elba, St. Helena .301
  –Son, King of Rome ..301, 689
  Napoleon III .......303, 689
  –Defeat, surrender .....301
  –Empress Eugenie ........689
Bonds—
  Portraits on U. S. ........144
  Railroad (value) .........107
  Savings, U. S. ............144
  Trading volume ..........139
  World Bank .........572, 574
Bonus march (1932) .......310
Books—
  Awards ...................241
  –Pulitzer Prizes ......236-239
  Best sellers ..............155
  Bible *see Bible*
  Color, first in (1457) ......296
  Copyright law, U. S. ......207
  Dictionary (1755) ........300
  English, first in (1475) ....296
  Gutenberg, Johann (1456) 296
  Postal rates ..............907
  Production ...............155
  U. S. Govt. publications ..346
Booth, John Wilkes ...188, 305
Borneo, North *Sabah* ....533
Borneo, West (Kalimantan) 522
Bornholm Islands (Baltic) ..722
Bosnia-Herzegovina,
    Yugoslavia ............566
Boston, Mass. .............393
  Buildings, tall ............445
  Cocoanut Grove fire (1942) 312
  Logan airport ............393
  Marathon ................861
  Massacre (1770) .........298
  Mayor ....................924
  Mileage to cities ........110
  Museums, attractions 365, 393
  News Letters (1704) .....299
  Opera ....................157
  Pickwick Club (1925) ....310
  Population ......604, 616, 652
  –Jewish ..................602
  Port traffic ..............99
  Postal receipts ...........932
  Tea party (1773) .........298
Botanical Garden, N.Y.C. ..436
Botswana ............497, 576
Bougainville Island ........495
Boundary lines, U. S. Intl. ..174
Bounty Island, N.Z. ........538
Bounty mutiny (1789) .300, 563
Bourbon, House of ........689
Bouvet Island, Norway ....540
Bowl games (football) ....868
Bowling ...............850-853
  Duck pins ...............853
  Lawn ....................853
  Rubberband duckpin ....853
Boxer Insurrection (1900) ..307
Boxing—
  Amateur champions .....841
  Champion by class ....840-841
  Heavyweight champions ..840
  –History of bouts ....843-844
  Major bouts .............842
  Neil Memorial trophy ....844
Boy Scouts of America ....307
Boys Town, Nebr. .........368
Brandy trade, industry ....121
Brandywine, battle (1777) ..298
Brazil .....................497
  Area, capital, population ..497
  Cities (population) ........578
  Coffee exports to U. S. ...777
  Gold reserve .............139
  Merchant fleet ...........101
  Petroleum production ....130
  President ................576

Brazil (cont'd)
  Slavery ends (1889) ......306
  Sugar production .........122
  Trade ....................498
  Waterfalls ...............719
  Weights, measures .......587
Bread (nutritive value) ....775
Breda, Treaty of (Surinam) .538
Brethren Churches ........219
Bridge—
  Contract champions .....848
  Perfect hand odds .......810
Bridges—
  Bronx-Whitestone .......725
  Brooklyn (1883) ......306, 725
  Carquinez Strait (1927) ...725
  Chesapeake Bay .364, 725, 727
  Connecticut Turnpike ....725
  Construction details ......726
  Corpus Christi ...........726
  Eads, St. Louis ..........725
  George Washington .725, 726
  Golden Gate .......725, 726
  Henry Hudson ...........725
  Highest, Royal Gorge,
    Colo. .........357, 725, 726
  Iberville Memorial, Miss. ..366
  Lake Pontchartrain .......725
  Mackinac (Mich.) 365, 725, 726
  New York ............725-726
  Notable (span, date) ..725-726
  Royal Gorge ....357, 725, 726
  San Francisco .......725, 726
  Seaway Skyway ..........726
  Thousand Island .....725, 726
  Verrazano-Narrows ..725, 726
  Woodrow Wilson ....725, 726
Brink's robbery (1950) .....315
Britain *see United Kingdom*
British Antarctica ........562
British Columbia, Canada ..485
British Commonwealth 557-563
British Empire ....557-563, 688
British Guiana (Guyana) ..518
British Honduras .........562
British Isles .........557, 722
British Pacific Islands .....563
British Solomon Islands ...563
British Virgin Islands .381, 561
British West Indies ...561-562
Britons, noted ..686-688, 694-695
Bronx, N. Y. ........416, 436
  Botanic Gardens .........436
  Bridges ..................725
  Population ...........416, 623
  Zoo ......................779
Bronx-Whitestone Bridge ..725
Bronx Zoo, New York City .779
Brooklyn-Battery Tunnel ..727
Brooklyn Bridge ..........725
  Panic (1883) .............306
Brooklyn, N. Y.—
  Botanic Garden ..........437
  Bridges, tunnels ......725, 727
  Museum ..................437
  Plymouth church .........437
  Population ................623
  Public library ............437
  Subway wreck (1918) .309, 660
  Theater fire (1876) .......664
  Verrazano-Narrows Bridge
             725, 726
Broun Memorial Award ....241
Brown, John (raid, 1859) 303, 387
Brown, Rap ...............79
Brunei (British) ...........563
Brussels World's Fair .....61
Bryce Canyon Park .......388
Buchanan, James (biog.) ..187
Buddha, birth (563 B. C.) ..295
Buddhist population .......224
  United States ............224
Budgets—
  Great Britain ............558
  USSR ....................555
  United Nations ..........572
  United States .......131-137
Buenos Aires, Arg. 493, 578, 651
Buffalo, N. Y. ............394
  Buildings, tall ............445
  Mayor ....................924
  Museums, attractions ....394
  Pan-Amer. Exposition
    (1901) .............61, 307
  Population ......604, 623, 652
  Postal receipts ...........932
  Public library ............348
Buildings—
  Empire State Bldg. ..438, 445
  Independence Hall ......198
  New York City .....438, 445
  Office, world's largest ...443
  Oldest public (N. Mex.) ..370
  Rockefeller Center, N. Y. ..438
  Tall, U. S. ............445-448

**Buildings (cont'd)**
Tallest, T. V. ............448
Washington, D. C. ....439-444
*See Construction Housing*
**Buka Island** ..............495
**Bulgaria** ..................498
Area, capital, population. .498
Cities (population) .......578
Merchant fleet ...........101
Premier, Pres. ...........576
**Bunyan, John** (1660) ......298
**Bureau of the Mint** ........144
**Burgesses, House of** (1619) .298
**Burma** ....................499
Area, capital, population .499
Cities (population) .......578
Merchant fleet ...........101
Petroleum production ....130
Premier, Pres. .....499, 576
**Burma Road** ...............499
**Burr, Aaron** (1804, 1807) ...300
**Burundi** .............499, 576
**Buses, motor—**
Operations ..............113
Passengers, revenue ..112, 113
**Business—**
Failures, U. S. ..........146
Finance ............131-137
Financiers, noted ........669
Income, by industry ....134
Index numbers ..........143
Industry statistics ...119-130
Retail sales (value) ......126
*See Corporations, Banks*
**Butter—**
Consumption ............776
Nutritive value .........775
Prices, farm ............770
**Byelorussian SSR** ........554
**Byrd, Richard E.** ....705, 706

**— C —**

**CENTO** *see Central Treaty Org.*
**CIO** *See American Federation
of Labor & Congress of
Industrial Organizations*
**Cabinet members, U. S.** ....164
1789-1968 ..........179-182
Address, form of .........351
Salute (artillery) ........746
**Cable—**
Atlantic (1858) ..........303
—Telephone (1956) ......316
Measurement, unit of ....581
**Cabot, John** (1497) 296, 698, 708
**Caesar, Julius** ....295, 689
**Caicos Islands** ...........561
**Cairo, Egypt** .......556, 578
**Calcium** (foods) .......774-775
**Calendars—**
Ash Wednesday ..........232
Chinese Lunar ..........233
Christian era begins .....295
Dates, day of week ......281
Days between two dates .. 62
Easter Sunday .....232, 591
Eras, cycles .............280
Greek Church ...........233
Gregorian ..............281
Islamic (Mohammedan) ..226
Jewish holidays .........233
Julian .................281
Leap Years .............281
Mayan (300 B.C.) .......295
Monthly (1969-1970) .263-276
–Pascal, dates ...........232
Moon (1969-1970) 263-276, 283
Perpetual (1800-2059) 278-279
Protestant Episcopal ....226
Standard Time 277, 280, 281
Sun. daily (1969-1970) 263-276
Twilight (1969-1970) .263-276
Year ..............278-279
**Calgary** ..................403
**California** .............356-357
*See States, U. S.*
Admission, area, cap. 356, 384
Agriculture .769-772, 773-776
Bear Flag Rep. (1846) ...302
Birth, death statistics 758, 765
Buildings, tall .....447, 448
Counties (seats, areas) ...636
Dams, reservoirs
728, 729, 731, 732
Elections .65, 82, 884, 885, 888
Forest fires .............778
Gold found (1848) .......303
Great cities .408, 425, 429-431
Lake, largest ...........718
Los Angeles (see L.A.) ..408
Marriage, divorce laws 760, 761
Mountains ..............720

**California (cont'd)**
Museums, attractions 356-357
Name, origin of .........383
Officials, pay ...........919
Oakland (*see Oakland*) ...430
Population .........593-654
–Cities and towns 604, 606-607
–Counties, county seats .636
–Metropolitan areas ..652-654
–Voting age .............601
Presidential vote .884, 888-889
Redwood trees ......356, 710
Sacramento (*see
Sacramento*) .........425
San Diego (*see San Diego*) 429
San Francisco (*see S.F.*) ..430
San Jose (*see San Jose*) ...431
Spanish Missions ........357
Taxes ..............209-218
Vital Statistics .....757-768
Water project ...........729
**California, Gulf of** .......713
**Calories** (foods) .......774-775
**Calvin, John** (1534) .......297
**Cambodia** .....67, 499, 576
**Cameroon, Rep. of** ...500, 576
**Campbell Island, N. Z.** ....538
**Canada** ...............485-491
*Canadian readers also see
page 55*
Area, capital, pop. ...485, 578
Armed forces, defense ...487
Assets, debt ............491
Banking statistics ......490
Cabinet ................488
Calgary (*see Calgary*) ....402
Cities (population) 55, 487, 578
Constitutional revision .. 70
Curling ................845
Edmonton (*see Edmonton*) 402
Education ..............490
Electrical power ........123
Figure skating .........834
Fish & Game reg. ....785-786
Football .........865, 877
Francophone ............. 75
French and Indian war ..299
Gold production .........140
Gold reserve ...........139
Golf ..................848
Government .........486-491
Gov. General ......488, 576
Grey Cup .........865, 877
Holidays ...............491
Hospitalization plans ....762
Immigration ............487
Industries ..............490
Insurance in force ......487
Islands (areas) .........722
Medicare .............. 85
Montreal (*see Montreal*) ..413
Mountain peaks .........720
NORAD ................ 71
Ottawa (*see Ottawa*) .....418
Parliament ............. 70
Pearson confidence vote .. 71
Personalities, noted .....676
Petroleum production ....130
Population .....55, 487, 578
Postal rates, new ....... 55
Postal strike ........... 86
Prime Minister,
*see Trudeau, Pierre E.*
Prime Ministers .485, 489, 576
Provinces .............. 55
Quebec Separatists ...... 92
Queens Plate ...........816
Receipts, expenditures ...491
Regina (*see Regina*) .....403
Religious denominations ..490
Rowing ................837
St. Lawrence Seaway
(1959) ..........97, 317
Saskatoon (*see Saskatoon*) 431
Seaway strike .......... 80
Social security .........487
Sugar production ........122
Taxation ..........64, 489
Toronto (*see Toronto*) ....434
Trade ...........98, 491
Unemployment insurance ..487
Universities ............346
Vancouver (*see Vancouver*) 435
Victoria Cross ..........486
Waterfalls .............719
Winnipeg (*see Winnipeg*) .436
**Canadians, noted** .........676
**Canal Zone, Panama**
Accession ..............381
Altitudes ..............738
Area, population ....381, 655
Employees, gov't. .......145
Government .............381
Panama Canal ......97, 381

**Canals—**
Canadian ............... 97
Erie (1825) ............302
Panama ............97, 381
Sault Ste. Marie ....... 97
Suez ..................557
**Canary Islands, Spain** ..548, 722
**Cancer** ................ 59
*See Assns.*
Canoeing ...............845
**Cant in Island, Pacific** .382, 722
**Canyon Diablo, Ariz.** .....355
**Cape Breton Is. Canada** ...722
**Cape of Good Hope (S. Af.)** 548
**Cape Horn, Chile** .........501
**Cape Kennedy, Fla.** .......359
**Cape Verde Islands** ..544, 722
**Capets** (French rulers) ....689
**Capital parks, National** ...389
**Capital punishment** .......767
**Capitals—**
Foreign *see specific nations*
States, U. S. ...........384
Washington, D.C. 435, 439-443
**Capitol of the U. S.** ......439
Statuary Hall ...........439
Visitors, admission of ...440
**Carat** (measure) .....582, 587
**Carbohydrates** (foods) ..774-775
**Cardinals, Roman Cath.** ....228
**Cards, playing** (odds) ......810
**Caribbean Sea—**
Area, depth ............713
Islands, areas ..........722
**Carlsbad Caverns** ....370, 388
**Caroline Islands** ....382, 722
**Carolingians** .......689, 690
**Carow, Edith** (Roosevelt) 183, 191
**Carranza, Venustiano** (1911) 308
**Carthage** (146 B.C.) .......295
**Cartier, Ashmore Islands** ...495
**Cartier, Jacques** (1534) 297, 708
**Cartoonists, American** .....669
**Cascade Mountains, Wash.** .378
**Castle Williams Fort, N. Y.** .438
**Castro, Fidel—**
Assumes power (1959) ...317
Invasion crushed (1961) ..317
Premier, Cuba .......507, 576
**Casualties—**
Boer War (1899) ........306
Civil War, U. S. ....751, 752
Korean War .............751
Merchant Marine ........752
Mexican War ...........751
Revolutionary War ......751
Spanish-American War
307, 751
Vietnam ............... 41
War of 1812 .......301, 751
World War I and II .751, 752
**Catherine of Aragon** (1509) 297
**Catholic Religion—**
*See Roman Catholic*
**Cattle,** *see Agriculture*
**Caucasus Mountains** .......720
**Caves—**
Carlsbad Caverns ....370, 388
Collins, Floyd ..........310
Mammoth, Ky. ..........363
Wind, S. Dak. ..........388
Wyandotte, Ind. ........361
**Caxton, William** (1475) ....296
**Cayman Islands** ...........561
**Celebes, Indonesia** ...522, 722
**Celestial events** (1969) .253-256
**Cemeteries—**
Amer. military, abroad ..749
National ...............749
–Arlington .......441, 749
–Custer Battlefield (Mont.)
367, 389
**Cenozoic era** .............714
**Census, U. S.—**
Bureau of the Census 592-654
Decennial, 1960 .....592-654
Farm population ........604
Population tables ....593-654
*See Population*
**Census, USSR** (1959) .....554
**Center of population, U.S.** .595
**Centigrade** ...............589
**Central African Rep.** ......500
**Central African Union** ..... 75
**Central Intelligence Agency** 175
**Central Treaty Org.** .......573
**Century of Progress Exp.** .. 61
**Century 21 Exp.** (Wash.) ... 61
**Cereals** (consumption) .....776
**Cervera, Adm. Pascual** .....307
**Ceuta, Africa** (Spanish) ...548
**Ceylon** ...............500-501
Area, capital, pop. ......500
Cities (population) .......578

Ceylon (cont'd)
  Gov. General ............576
  Trade ..................98
Chad Republic ........501, 576
Chalmette Historical Park .388
Chambers, Whittaker (1948) 314
Champlain, Samuel de
  (1603-09) ..............708
Chandernagor, India ......520
Channel Islands ......561, 722
Charge of Light Brigade
  (1853) .................303
Charlemagne (800 A.D.) 296, 689
Charles I (1642, '49), Br. 298, 688
Charles II (1660, '64), Br.
                         298, 688
Charleston, S. C. ........374
  Ft. Sumter .......374, 389
  Gardens ...............374
  Mayor .................374
  Population .......630, 647
Charter Oak, Conn. .......358
Chatham Islands, N. Z. 538, 722
Checker Champions ........852
Cheese—
  Consumption ...........776
  Nutritive value .......774
Chemical elements—
  Atomic weights, numbers 588
  Discoverers, symbols ..588
Chemicals—
  Exports ...............100
Chemistry—
  Discoveries ...........116
Chesapeake Bay Bridge 364, 725
Chess champions ..........877
Chessman, Caryl (1960) ...317
Chicago, Ill. ........394-395
  Airports ..............395
  Buildings, tall ...445-446
  Fairs ..................61
  Fires .................664
  Haymarket riot (1886) .306
  Mayor .................924
  Mileage, city-to-city ..110-111
  Museums, attractions ..395
  Population 604, 611, 651, 652
  —Consolidated area ....654
  —Metropolitan area ...652, 654
  Postal receipts .......932
Chickens—
  Consumption ...........776
  Farm income ...........770
  Nutritive value .......774
Child adoption ...........233
Child Health Services ....154
Children's Aid Society see Assns.
Childress, Sarah (Polk) 183, 187
Chile ................501-502
  Area, capital, population .501
  Christ of the Andes ...501
  Cities (population) ....578
  Gold reserve ..........139
  Merchant fleet ........101
  O'Higgins, Liberator ..693
  Petroleum production ..130
  President .............576
  Tierra del Fuego ......501
  Trade .................502
  Volcanoes .............716
  Weights, measures .....587
China (all) ..........502-504
China, People's Republic of
  (Communist) .......503-504
  Agriculture ...........504
  Area, capital, population .503
  Armed forces ..........504
  Cities (population) ....578
  Korean war ............315
  Kwantung ..............504
  Manchuria .............504
  Mongolia, Inner .......504
  Nuclear tests .........66
  Premier, see Chou En-lai
  Sinkiang ..............504
  Tibet revolt (1959) ...504
  U. N. arms embargo (1951) 316
  U. S. bans trade (1950) .315
  U. S. relations .......315
China, Republic of ...502-503
  Area, capital, population .502
  Boxer insurrection (1900) .307
  Cities (population) ....578
  F'loods, 1887, 1911 ....662
  Formosa ..........314, 503
  Genghis Khan (1215) ...296
  Japan, wars ...........502
  Merchant fleet ........101
  Petroleum production ..130
  Sugar production ......122
  Taiwan (Formosa) ......503
  Trade .................503
  U. S. Marines (1927) ..310
  Weights, measures .....587

China Sea ................713
Chinese Lunar Calendar ...233
Chinese Turkestan ........504
Choiseul Is., Solomons ...563
Choreographers ...........687
Chou En-lai .........503, 576
Christ, Jesus ............295
Christ of the Andes ......501
Christian era begins .....295
Christian, Letitia (Tyler)
                         183, 187
Christianity, early 295, 296
Christmas Day ......590, 591
Christmas Island, Austr. 495, 722
Christmas Island, Br. ....563
Chronological era, cycles .280
Chronology (1967-1968) 63, 65-92
Church of Christ, Scientist
                         219, 221
Church of England ....297, 559
Churches—
  Anglican (1558) .......297
  Denomination, data .219-233
  Dutch, Sleepy Hollow ..370
  Fast Days .........227, 233
  Headquarters ......221-222
  Memberships .......219-220
  New York, N. Y. ...437-438
  Natl. Council, Churches of
    Christ in the U. S. A. .232
  Number, U. S. .........219
  Protestant (history) .223-224
  Washington, D. C. .....444
  World Council .........222
  See Religion and specific
    churches
Churchill, Sir Winston—
  Death (1965) ..........694
  Yalta Agreement (1945) ..313
Cincinnati, Ohio .....395-396
  Buildings, tall .......446
  City manager ..........924
  Museums, attractions ..396
  Opera .................156
  Population ......604, 625, 652
Circle (formulas) ........586
Circuit Courts, U. S. ....167
Circulation, periodicals 348, 352
Circus fire, Hartford (1944)
                         312, 664
Citation's record (horse) ..820
Cities, foreign—
  Airline distances ..251-252
  Cost of living ........568
  Population ........578-579
  —Jewish ..............602
  Southernmost (Chile) ..501
  Time differences ......281
  Urban areas, largest ..651
Cities, North Amer. .......64
Cities, U. S. ...64, 390-444
  Altitudes .........737-738
  Bank clearings ........136
  Buildings, tall ...445-448
  Climatological data 288, 290
  Cost of living ...141, 568
  Farthest east, north, south 94
  Income tax ............218
  Largest, area ..........94
  Latitude, longitude 737-738
  Mayor, managers ..924-926
  Metropolitan areas .652-654
  Mileage tables
  —Airline ..........251-252
  —Automobile .......110-111
  —Shipping distances ..103-105
  Murders in major .....768
  Newspapers, circulation .353
  Oldest (Fla.) .........359
  Police ................767
  Population ......604, 605-654
  —Growth ......604, 605-634
  —Jewish ..............602
  —Outlying regions .....655
  Ports .....99-100, 103-105
  Post Office receipts ..932
  Precipitation .....290-292
  Rapid Transit mileage ..107
  Stadiums, arenas 810, 865, 866
  Telephones ............123
  Temperatures ......290-292
  Tides .............786-793
  Time differences ......281
  Wind velocities .......289
  Zip Codes ....605-634, 655
  See specific cities
Citizenship Day ..........591
Citizenship, U. S. .......702
Civil Air Patrol .........749
Civil defense ........748-749
Civil Engineering Awards ..129
Civil rights—
  Civil disorders report .70
Civil Rights Comm. .......175

Civil Service Commission ....175
  Employees (number) .....145
  Expenditures ..........131
Civil War, U. S. (1861-65)
                    304-305, 387
  Appomattox Court House .377
  Battle, leaders ...304-305
  Casualties ...305, 751, 752
  Confederate States ....387
  Lincoln assassination
                    188, 305, 662
  Military leaders ......665
  Secession of states ...387
  Ship losses ...........657
  See Confederate States
Civil, employment,
  Federal .........42, 145-146
Claims, Court, U. S. .....167
Clemens, Samuel L. (Mo.) ..366
Clementis, Vladimir (1952) .316
Clergy (form of address) ..351
Clermont (steamboat, 1807) 301
Cleveland, Grover (biog.) ..190
Cleveland, Ohio ......396-397
  Buildings, tall .......446
  Explosion (1944) ......661
  Hospital fire (1929) ..664
  Mayor .................924
  Mileage to other cities ..110
  Museums, attractions ..397
  Population ......604, 625, 652
  Riot ...................86
Clifford, Clark M....68, 74, 83
Climate, U. S. .......288-294
Climatological Service ...288
  Data (annual) .........290
Cloisters, The (N. Y. C.) .437
Clothing—
  Hosiery production ....124
  Price index ...........141
  Retail sales (value) ..126
Clubs, organizations .449-464
                    or 469-484
Coach of the Year ........868
Coal—
  Production .......127, 128
  Used producing electricity .123
Coast Guard, U. S. .......745
  Academy ..........331, 745
  Insignia ..............742
  Officers .........739, 750
  Pay scale, allowances 754-755
  Personnel .............750
  See Armed Forces, U. S.
Coastlines, U. S. ........712
Coastal warnings .........289
Cobwebs and Spider Webs ..349
Cochin China (Vietnam) ...565
Cocos-Keeling Is. (Austr.) .495
Coffee—
  Crop reports ..........777
  Production (Brazil) ...498
  U. S. imports, by country 777
Cohen, Wilbur, J..........71
Coinage .......135, 141, 144
Coke production, exports ..128
Coliseum, New York .......438
Colleges and Universities—
  American ..........319-342
  Canadian ..............346
  Colors ...........869-875
  Control ...........319-342
  Degrees ...............343
  Endowment .............338
  Enrollment ............344
  —By college .......319-342
  —By type of school ....344
  Faculty, number ...319-342
  Founding dates ....319-342
  Fraternities ......340-342
  Governing officials .319-338
  Journalism, first (Mo.) .367
  Junior ............333-338
  Mexico ................90
  Observatories .........257
  Oldest in U. S. (1636) 298, 323
  Scholarships .....241-243, 347
  Senior ............319-342
  Sororities ........339-342
  Stadiums ..............866
  Student revolts ........75
  Teachers, by college .319-338
  Team nicknames ....869-875
  Tuition fees ..........345
  Yale Univ. ............63
  See Education
Collins, Floyd (1925) ....310
Colombia .............504-505
  Area, capital, population 504
  Bogota conference (1948) .314
  Cities (population) ....578
  Coffee exports ........504
  Merchant fleet ........101
  Petroleum production ..130

Colombia (cont'd)
Pope Paul VI ............88
President ..............576
Sugar production ......122
Tequendama waterfall 504, 719
Trade .................504
Volcano ...............716
Colonial Historical Park ..388
Colorado— ...............357
*See States, U. S.*
Admission, area, cap. 357, 384
Agriculture 769-771, 773, 776
Air Force Acad. ....331, 745
Birth, death statistics 758, 765
Counties (seats, areas) ..636
Denver (*see Denver*) ....400
Elections ........884, 885, 889
Lake, largest ...........718
Marriage, divorce laws 760, 761
Mountains .............357
Museums, attractions 357, 400
Name, origin of .......383
Officials, pay .....919, 920
Opera ............157-158
Population ........593-654
–Cities, towns ..608, 652-654
–Counties, county seats 636
–Metropolitan areas ..652-654
Presidential vote ...884, 889
Taxes .............209-218
Territory ..........357, 384
Vital statistics .....757-768
Colorado River ......708, 723
Dams, reservoirs ..728, 731
Discovered (1540) ..297, 708
Colossus of Rhodes ......721
Columbia River ....708, 723
Columbia Univ. .........75
Columbian Exposition (1893) 61
Columbus, Christopher 296, 708
Columbus Day ..........590
Columbus, Ohio ....397-398
Buildings, tall .......446
Mayor ................924
Museums, attractions ..397
Population ............397
Comets, meteors ...256, 262
Cominform (1948) ......314
Comino Island (Malta) ..534
Commandments, Ten .....230
Commerce *see Shipping, Trade*
Commerce, Department of—
Administrative personnel ..166
Employees (number) ....145
Established ...........182
Expenditures ..........131
Secretaries ....70, 166, 182
Commodities—
Exports, imports .......100
Price indexes ........141
Production .......771-776
Commodity Credit Corp. ....166
Common Market, *see European Economic Community*
Commonwealth (British)
          557-563, 573
Communist Party, U. S.
Arrests, trials (1949) ...314
Communist Party, World—
Albania ..............492
China, People's Rep. ..503-504
Cominform ...........314
Cuba .................506
Czechoslovakia .......508
Estonian .............554
Germany, East ........516
Greek civil war .......517
Hungary .....314, 316, 519
–Brussels (1914) ......308
Korea, North .........530
Latvian ..............554
Lithuanian ...........554
Manifesto (1848) ......303
Mongolian People's Rep. ..536
Poland ...............543
Poznan riots (1956) .316, 543
Romania ..............544
Tibet ................504
USSR ...........316, 556
Yugoslavia ...........567
Comoro Islands ........513
Compass variation .......
Composers ........671-699
Composite number .......589
Compromise of 1850 ......303
Comstock Lode, Nevada ..368
Cone, volume ..........586
Confederate States of America—
Battlefield memorials ..388
Casualties .......751, 752
Civil War ......304-305, 387
Davis, Jefferson ...304, 387
Flags ................387
Jackson, Stonewall 304-305, 665
Leaders ....304-305, 387, 665

Confederate States (cont'd)
Lee, R. E. ......304-305, 665
Secession ............387
Ship losses ..........657
Confucian population ....224
Confucius (551 B. C.) ....295
Congo Rep.-Brazzaville
          87, 89, 505
Congo, Dem. Republic of ..505
Area, capital, population ..505
Congo River ..........505
Gold production .......140
Katanga ..............505
Lumumba, Patrice ..317, 505
President .......505, 576
Congo, Dem. Republic of
Trade ................98
Tshombe, Moise .......505
Volcanoes ............715
Congo River ......61, 505
Congregational Churches 219, 221
Congress, Continental .....298
Congress of Industrial Organizations *see American Federation of Labor & Congress of Industrial Organizations*
Congress, Library of ......441
Congress, United States—
91st, First Session 915, 916-918
Apportionment .........34
First (1789) ..........300
House of Representatives
–Hall of ............439
–Johnson criticism .....65
–Members .......916-918
–Puerto Rican attack ('54) 316
–Revenue bills, originates 200
–Speakers ...........918
Laws passed 1968 ......48
Members
–Address, form of .....351
–Qualifications .......199
–Terms begin .........205
Powers delegated to ....200
Presidents & Congresses ..178
Quorum (defined) ......200
Senate
–Chamber ............439
–Members ............915
–Speech, longest (1957) ..317
Visitors, admission of ...441
Congressional inquiries—
Kefauver, crime (1951) ..315
MacArthur recall (1951) ..315
Tonkin attack ........70
Connecticut .............357
*See States, U. S.*
Admission, area, cap. 357, 384
Agriculture ..769-771, 773, 776
Birth, death statistics 758, 765
Counties (seats, areas) ..636
Elections ......884, 885, 889
Hartford (*see Hartford*) ..403
Industries ............357
Lake, largest .........718
Marriage, divorce laws 760, 761
Museums, attractions 358, 403
Name, origin of .......383
Officials, pay .....919, 920
Population ........593-654
–Cities and towns 604, 608-609
–Counties, county seats ..636
–Metropolitan area ..652-654
Presidential vote ...884, 889
Taxes .............209-218
Vital statistics .....757-768
Conservation—
Definition ...........778
Fish and Game Laws 781-785
Whooping Crane .......780
Conservative Party, N. Y. ...173
Constants, astronomical ...281
Constellation, U.S.S. (1797)
          300, 392
Constitution, U. S. ...199-206
Amendments .......202-206
–Procedure for ......202
Articles, original ..199-202
Bill of Rights ....202-206
Origin ...............199
Poll Tax amendment ...206
Preamble .............199
Ratification dates (states) 199
Constitution, U.S.S. (1797) 300
Construction—
Dwelling units, cost ...654
Employees ...........124
Housing starts, value ..654
New in 1964, '65, '66 ...654
Value, new ...........654
Consumer credit statistics ..140
Consumer price indexes ....143
Consumption—
Commodity imports .....100

Consumption (cont'd)
Foodstuffs ...........776
Gasoline, by state .....115
Personal expenditures ..124
Conterminous ,U. S. ......595
Contests—
Miss Universe .........61
Miss America Pageant ..244
Miss Black America ....61
Miss U. S. A. .........61
Spelling Bee, Nat'l ....350
Continental Congress ..199, 298
Continental Divide ...357, 710
Continental Football League 865
Continental Guinea (Sp.) ..548
Continents—
Altitudes (highest, lowest) 720
Areas, dimensions ....651, 736
Lakes ................717
Mountain peaks .....720-721
Population ............651
–Religious ...........224
Waterfalls ...........719
Contract Bridge ........810, 848
Conventions, political (1968)
Nominations ...........37
Platforms .........38, 39
Sites ................884
Cook Islands, New Zealand ..538
Cooke, Bishop Terence ....72
Coolidge, Calvin (biog.) ...192
Cooper Union, N. Y. C. ....438
Cooperatives—
Denmark ..............509
Farmers .........770, 772
Federal Credit Unions ..150
Finland ..............511
Sweden ...............549
Coplon, Judith (1950) ....315
Copper Production, U. S. ..129
Copyright law, U. S. .....207
Coral Sea battle (1942) ...313
Corfu Island (Greece) ..517, 722
Corn—
Chicago spot prices ....772
Exports ..............776
Grain center receipts ..773
Nutritive value .......774
Prices, farm ..........770
Production ....771, 772, 776
–By state ...........773
Supply in U. S. .......772
Yields ...............773
Corn Islands (area pop.) 381, 655
Coronado, Francisco (1540) ..297
Corporations, Stocks—
Debt .................133
Largest industrial
companies ..........50
Largest U. S. companies ..50
Stock dividends, yields ..51-54
Stock prices, symbols ..51-54
Taxes
–Effect on profit .....120
–Federal law .........212
Widely-held stocks ...50-54
Correctional institutions ....766
Corrections, Addenda ......64
Corregidor (1942) .......312
Corrigan, Douglas G. (1938) 311
Corsica Island (France) 512, 722
Cortes, Hernando (1519) ...297
Cost of living ....141-142, 568
Costa Rica .............506
Area, capital, population ..506
Coffee to U. S. .......777
Merchant fleet .......101
President .......506, 576
San Jose (population) ..578
Volcanoes ............716
Weights, measures .....587
Cotton—
Exports, imports ....100, 125
Industry .............125
Prices, farm .........770
Production .......125, 773
–By state ...........773
–U. S., world .......125
Seed prices ..........770
Cotton Bowl games ......868
Council of Nicaea (325 A.D.) 296
Council of Trent (1545) ...297
Counterfeiting, forgery ....767
Counties, U. S.—
Areas, by state .....635-651
County seats .......635-651
Largest ..............94
Courts—
Arbitration, intl. (1902) ..307
International, (U. N.) ...571
United States .....167-169
Couve de Murville .......85
Coverdale, Miles (1535) ...297

Cowboys, rodeo champs ....834
Coxey, Jacob S. (1894) ......306
Crater, Joseph F., (1930) ...310
Crater Lake Natl. Park 373, 388
Craters, Meteoric ...........262
Credit—
  Consumer statistics ......140
  Farms ...................770
  Foreign (U. S. Aid) ......580
  Credit Unions ...........114
Creed, American's ..........182
Crete (Greece) .......517, 722
Crew racing ............836-837
Crime—
  Arrests by offense, sex ...766
  Assassinations ..........662
  Auto thefts .........765, 766
  Brinks robbery (1950) ....315
  British train robbery ....63
  Brown, Rap .............79
  Burglaries ..........766, 768
  Capital punishment ......767
  Counterfeiting, forgery ..767
  Drugs ..................60
  Eichmann, Adolf ........317
  Electrocution, first (1890) 306
  FBI ....................766
  Kefauver committee (1951) 315
  Kidnapings .............661
  Murders .. 67, 74, 80, 766, 767
  –Penalties, by state ....767
  Prison population .......766
  Robbery, largest U. S.
    (1962) ................317
  Secret Service ..........767
  Spock, Dr. Benjamin ....82
  Summary, 1968 ..........766
  U. S. reports ..........766
  *See espionage*
Crimea, USSR ..............553
Crimean War (1853) ........303
Crippled Children Services ..154
Croatia, Yugoslavia ........566
Cromwell, Oliver (1642, 1658) 298
Crop production ......769-776
  Prices .................769
Crucifixion (29 A.D.) ......295
Crusades, The (1096) ......296
Cuba ..................506-507
  Area, capital, population ..506
  Gas rationing ..........68
  Havana (population) .....578
  Invasion crushed (1961) ...317
  Merchant fleet .........101
  Missile crisis (1962) .....317
  Petroleum production ...130
  President .........506, 576
  Pro-Soviets tried ......70
  Revolts .......317, 506, 507
  Spanish-Amer. War .307, 506
  Sugar production ...122, 506
  U. S. relations ........317
  War of independence .307, 506
  Weights, measures ......587
Cube roots ................585
Cube, volume ..............585
Cubic measures .......581-584
Cumberland Gap Natl. Park 388
Curacao Is. ...........538, 722
Curling champions .........845
Currency, foreign *see specific
  nations*
Currency, U. S.—
  Bureau of the Mint ......144
  Circulation, amount in ..144
  Composite-Type .........144
  Dollar buying power ....141
  Portraits on ...........144
  Silver coinage ....135, 141
  Stock on hand .........135
Curtiss, Glenn H. (1910) ...307
Custer Battlefield, Mont. 367, 389
Custer, Gen. (1876) 306, 367, 372
Custis-Lee Mansion ........441
Custis, Martha ........183, 184
Customs, U. S.—
  Courts .................167
  Duty-free imports ......702
  Receipts ...............140
  Travelers ..............702
Cycles, chronological (1969) 280
Cyclones ..................289
Cyprus ....................507
  Area, capital, pop. ...507, 578
  Crisis settled .........65
  Greek-Turkish strife ....507
  Independence ...........507
  President ..............576
Cyrenaica (Libya) .........532
Czars of Russia ...........692
Czechoslovakia .......507-508
  Area, capital, population
             507, 578
  Benes, Eduard ..........508
  Communist rule (1948) ...314

Czechoslovakia (cont'd)
  Crisis (1967-68)
    65, 68, 72, 75, 84, 89, 91
  German occupation 311, 508
  Hungary, cession to (1938) 311
  Masaryk, Jan (1948) .....314
  Masaryk, Thomas G. ....508
  Merchant fleet .........101
  Novotny, Antonin ....68, 72
  Petroleum production ...130
  President .........508, 576
  Rusk, Dean ............91
  Soviet invasicn ......88, 91
  Sudetenland .......311, 508
  Tito ...................88
Czechs, noted .............698

— D —

D-Day, World War II ......313
Dahomey, Republic..65, 508, 576
Dairy products—
  Consumption ...........776
  Exports ................100
  Price indexes ..........769
Dakota Territory ..........384
Dalai Lama ................504
Dallas, Texas .........398-399
  Buildings, tall ........446
  City manager ..........924
  Johnson speech ........70
  Museums, attractions ...399
  Opera .................158
  Population ...398, 604, 631
Damao, Portug. India ...521
Dams—
  Highest, largest, world 730, 736
  United States .....728-736
  –Hydroelectric power .732-734
Danes—
  English rulers .........688
  Noted .................698
Danzig (Gdansk) .........543
Dardanelies (Turkey) .....553
Dare, Virginia ..(1587) 297, 371
Dartmouth College ........322
Date Line .................280
Dates—
  B.C. and A.D., between ..295
  Days of week, to find 278-279
  Days between two ......62
  Memorable .........295-318
Davis Cup (tennis) ........813
Davis, Jefferson ..........387
Daylight saving time .....280
Days—
  Between two dates ......62
  Degree ................42
  Fast (church) ......227, 233
  Holy (Greek Church) ...233
  Length of .............280
  Public holidays ....590-591
Dayton, Ohio .........399-400
  Buildings, tall ........446
  City manager ..........924
  Museums, attractions ...400
  Population ...604, 625, 652
Death Records, how to get 350
Death Valley, Calif. 356, 389, 720
Deaths—
  Accidental, by type ....759
  Aircraft *see Disasters*
  Assassinations .........662
  Causes .............757, 759
  Keller, Helen ..........82
  Motor vehicles ....759, 765
  New York State ....758, 765
  Noted persons .....665-699
  Number of .....757-759, 765
  Presidents, U. S. (dates) .183
  Railroad accidents ..660, 765
  Ship sinkings ......657-660
  Suicides, world .......60
  Transportation accidents
             759, 765
  United States ....757-759, 765
  Year (1968) ......56-58, 64
  *See Casualties, Disasters*
Debs, Eugene V., 1894, '97 .306
Debts—
  Farms, U. S. ..........777
  Private, U. S. ........133
  Public ................133
  World War I (owed U. S.) 750
Decathlon records
  American record ......858
  National champions ...861
  Olympic games .....878, 882
  World record ..........855
Decatur, Stephen (1801; '12)
             300, 301
Decimals to fractions ....586
Declaration of Independence
        196-197, 298

Declaration of Ind. (cont'd)
  Mecklenburg (1775) .....298
  National Archives ......442
  Signers ...............197
  World Almanac sedition ..197
Decoration Day ...........590
Deepest Oceans ...........713
Defense, Department of—
  Admin. personnel .......164
  Established .......180, 182
  Expenditures ..........131
  Secretaries .....68, 164, 180
  *See Armed Forces, U. S.*
Defense, National—
  Civil Air Patrol .......749
  Civil Defense .......748-749
  Missiles *see Missiles, rockets*
  Mutual defense treaties ..573
  Organizations .........749
  Selective Service Act ...756
  Submarines *see Submarines*
De Galindez, Jesus (1956) ..316
De Gaulle, Charles—
  Elections .............81
  President .......317, 512, 576
  Degree days ...........42
Delaware ..................358
  *See States, U. S.*
  Admission, area, cap. 358, 384
  Agriculture .769-771, 773, 776
  Birth, death statistics 758, 765
  Counties (seats, areas) ...636
  Elections ....884, 885, 890
  Lake, largest .........718
  Marriage, divorce laws 760, 761
  Museums, attractions ...358
  Name, origin of .......383
  Officials, pay .....919, 920
  Population .........593-654
  –Cities and towns .....609
  –Counties, county seats ..636
  –Metropolitan areas .652-654
  Presidential vote ...884, 890
  Taxes .............209-218
  Vital statistics ....757-768
  Wilmington ............358
Democratic party—
  Candidates' Biographies ..38
  Convention sites .......884
  Electoral votes ....884, 886
  Humphrey, Hubert H.
    37, 38, 76, 79, 82, 90, 92
  Kennedy, Edward M. ..38, 86
  Kennedy, Robert F. 45, 73, 82
  McCarthy, Eugene
    37, 45, 71, 73, 76, 79, 82
  McGovern, George S. ..37, 88
  Muskie, Edmund ...37, 38, 90
  National committee ...172-173
  National convention ...37-39
  Nominees ............37-39
  Platform, 1968 ........39
  Popular vote ....884, 887-914
  State chairmen ........173
Demonstrations
  65, 70, 75, 77, 78, 86, 90, 91
Denmark ...................509
  Area, capital, population ..509
  Cities (population) .....578
  Gold Reserve ..........139
  Merchant fleet .........101
  Noted persons .....692, 698
  Rulers ............509, 692
  Sugar production ......122
  Trade .............98, 509
  Weights, measures .....587
Density—
  Air ...............260, 589
  Earth .................260
  Gases .................589
  Population, U. S. .....603
  Sun and Planets ..282, 286
Dent, Julia (Grant) ....183, 189
Dentistry—
  Anaesthesia (1842) .....302
  Selective Service law ..756
Denver, Colo. .............400
  Buildings, tall ........446
  Mayor .................924
  Mint (coinage) ........144
  Museums, attractions ...400
  Population ...604, 608, 652
Department store sales ....126
Department, U. S. Govt.—
  Abbreviations for .....174
  Employees .............145
  Executive personnel ...164-166
  Secretaries .164-166, 179-182
  *See specific departments*
Depression (1929)..........310
Des Moines, Iowa .........401
  Buildings, tall ........446
  City manager ..........924
  Museums, attractions ...401
  Population ...604, 613, 652

**Desegregation—**
Little Rock ...............317
Supreme Court (1954, '55) . .316
**Design, Index of American** . .443
**De Soto, Hernando** (1541) . .297
**Detroit, Mich.** ...........401-402
Buildings, tall ............446
Mayor ...................924
Museums, attractions ....402
Newspaper strike ......... 88
Population ......604, 618, 652
Postal receipts ...........932
**De Valera, Eamon** ..........524
**Devon Island** (Arctic) .......722
**Dewey, George** (USN) .307, 665
**Dewey, Thos. E.** 671, 884, 887-914
**Dew Point** .................288
**Diamonds—**
Only state mines, Ark. ...356
Production
–Republic of Congo ......505
–Republic of South Africa 547
**Diana, Temple of** ..........721
**Diaz Ordaz, Gustavo**
(Mexico) ...............577
**Dice** (odds) ................810
**Diesel engine** ..............117
**Dillinger, John** (1934) .....311
**Dimmock, Mary S. L.** .183, 190
**Diomede Islands,** Pacific 354, 722
**Dionne Quintuplets** (1934) . .311
**Dirigibles—**
Graf Zeppelin .......247, 663
Hindenburg ..............663
Ocean flights ............247
R-34, flight (1919) .......310
Records .................247
**Disasters—**
Aircraft .................663
Coal Mine Explosions ....664
Earthquakes .............661
Explosions ..............681
Fires ...................664
–Causes .................768
*See Fires Chronology*
*and pg. 63*
–Mines, U. S. ............664
Mountain climbing .......707
Railroad accidents .......660
Ships ...............657-660
Volcanic eruptions ...715-716
*See Riots, Chronology and*
*Addenda*
**Disciples of Christ Church—**
Headquarters .............221
History, organization ....223
Membership ........219, 223
**Discoveries—**
Chemical elements .......588
Explorers .........704-708
Inventions .........116-118
Medicine ..............59-60
Science .............116-118
**Discus throw records—**
American ................858
Olympics .........878, 882
World ...................855
**Diseases—**
Death, rates .......757, 759
Mental patients ..........764
*See also Medicine*
**Distance between cities—**
Airline .............251-252
Automobile touring ...110-111
Caribbean-Gulf ports ....104
Great Lakes ports .......105
New York, from ....103, 110
Panama, other ports .....104
San Francisco, from .....104
South American ports ....104
**Distilled Spirits** (production)
121
**District of Columbia** ........379
*See Washington, D. C.*
**District court judges** ...167-169
**Diu, Portuguese India** ......521
**Diving champions** ..........831
**Diving, deepest** ............713
**Division table** ..............586
**Divorce—**
Grounds, by states ......761
Number, rate ..603, 757, 758
**Dixie song composed** (1859) 303
**Documents and laws** ...196-208
**Dodecanese Islands** .........517
**Dodo** (Mauritius) ...........535
**Dogs** (show winners) .......877
**Dollar, purchasing power** ...141
**Dollfuss, E.** (1934) ....311, 662
**Dom Pedro II** (1889) .306, 498
**Dominica Island** (W. Indies)
722
**Dominican Republic** .......509
Area, capital, population 509

**Dominican Republic** (cont'd)
Galindez case (1956) .....316
Merchant fleet ...........101
President ..........509, 576
Santo Domingo ..........509
Sugar production ........122
Trade .............98, 509
**Donelson, Rachel**
(Jackson) ........183, 186
**Doolittle raid, Japan** (1942) 312
**Doud, Mamie** (Eisenhower)
183, 194
**Douglas-Home, Sir Alec** ....558
**Douglas, Stephen** (1858) 303, 387
**Doyle, A. Conan** (1886) 306, 694
**Draft, U. S.** ....65, 71, 72, 756
**Drake, Sir Francis**
(1579) .......297, 695, 708
**Dram** (measure) ....581, 582, 583
**Drama** *see Theater*
**Dred Scott decision** (1857)
303, 387
**Dreyfus trial** (1894, 1906) . .306
**Drownings** (number) .......759
**Drug stores** (retail sales) ..126
**Drugs—**
Addiction ............... 60
Discoveries .........60, 116
**Dry measure** .......581, 582
**Ducie Is.** (Pitcairn group) ..563
**Duck pin bowling** ..........853
**Duff Is.,** Solomons .........563
**Duke of Edinburgh** .........558
**Duke of Windsor** .....311, 558
**Duluth, Minn.** ......604, 618
**Dumbarton Oaks Conference** 569
**Dunkirk, battle of** (1940) . .312
**DuPont de Nemours Co., E. I.—**
Descriptive ..............358
**Duryea automobile** ....116, 118
**Dutch** *see Netherlands*
**Dutch East Indies** *see*
*Indonesia, Republic of*
**Dutch painters,** noted .....699
**Duties** *see Tariff Acts*

— E —

**EEC** *see European*
*Economic Community* •
**EFTA** *see European Free*
*Trade Assn.*
**Eads Bridge, St. Louis** ....725
**Earhart, Amelia** (1937) 247, 311
**Earnings, Needed To Buy** ..142
**Earth, The—**
Atmosphere ..............260
Descriptive ..............260
Dimensions ..............260
Geologic eras ...........714
Life, first recorded ......714
Moon, distance ..........282
Poles ...................261
Rotation ................261
Seasons .................260
Solar system ............286
Sun, distance ...........282
**Earthquakes** .........661, 722
**Earth Science Notes** .......709
**East Africa, Portuguese** ....544
**East Germany** *see Germany,*
*Democratic Republic*
**East Indies, former Dutch** . .522
**Easter Island, Chile** .......722
**Easter Sunday** (1901-2100) . 232
**Eastern Orthodox Churches—**
First in U. S. ...........219
Headquarters .......221-222
Holy Days (Greek) .......233
Membership .............219
Population, world ........224
Rome, break with (1054) . .296
**Easternmost town, U. S.** ... 94
**Eclipses 1969** ..............261
**Economics**
Banking statistics ...136-137
Budget, U. S. .......131-132
Business leaders, noted ..669
Composite-Type coins ....144
Consumer credit statistics 140
Depression (1929) ........310
Discount rates ........... 87
Gold crisis .............. 72
Gold reserves ...........139
Income, national ....133-134
Panics (1873, '84, 1907)
305, 306, 307
Stockholders Equity Rates 121
World Bank ..............574
*See Corporations, Stocks*
**Ecuador** ...................510
Area, capital, pop. ...510, 578
Agoyan Waterfall .........719

**Ecuador** (cont'd)
Merchant fleet ...........101
Petroleum production ....130
President ..........510, 576
Volcanoes ...............716
Weights, measures ......587
**Eddy, Mary Baker** .........223
**Edict of Nantes** (1560) .....297
**Edinburgh, Duke of** .......558
**Edison, Thomas A.—**
Kinetoscope (1894) ...117, 306
National Historic Site ...369
**Edmonton, Canada** .........402
**Education—**
Associations 449-464 or 469-484
Colleges, universities . .319-346
Degrees .................343
–Tuition fees ............345
Day schools, full time ...349
Degrees granted, Canada . .346
Enrollment in schools
–By age, sex .......345, 656
–Colleges .......319-338, 346
–Elementary, high ...344, 349
–Public schools ....345, 349
–Sunday or Sabbath ....219
–Vocational .............351
Expenditures (public) ....345
Federal aid .............344
Ford grants .............347
Foreign nations ....485-567
Medical .......319-338, 346
Scholarships, fellowships,
how to obtain ........347
School prayer ban (1962) 317
Schools
–Attendance (public) ...345
–Catholic students ......231
Teachers strike ......63, 92
Veterans' G. I. Bill .....753
*See Colleges and Universities,*
*Public schools*
**Educators,** noted **American** 670
**Edward VIII,** Eng. .311, 558, 688
**Eggs—**
Consumption ............776
Nutritive value .........774
Price, farm .............770
Production, by state .....776
**Egypt** *see United Arab Republic*
**Eichmann, Adolf** (1960) ....317
**Eiffel Tower** (1889) ........306
**Eire** *see Ireland, Republic of*
**Eisenhower, Dwight D.—**
Abilene museum .........362
Ancestry ..........183, 194
Biography ...............194
Elections .........886, 887-914
Electoral votes ......34, 885
Geneva conference (1955) 316
Health .................. 87
General of the Army ....739
Khrushchev visit (1959) . .317
Panama declaration (1956) 316
Religion, church ...195, 444
Wife, biography ...183, 194
World War II ........312-313
**El Salvador** ................510
Area, capital, population 510
Cities (population).......578
President ...............576
Volcanoes ..............716
Weights, measures ......587
**Elba Island** (Italy) ...526, 722
**Election Day** ...........590, 591
**Election returns—**
Candidates ...........36-39
Congressional 36, 885, 915, 918
Conventions ............ 39
Mayors .............924-926
Platforms ............... 39
Primaries ...73, 76, 79, 80, 82
Returns .............887-914
Senators ...............885
**Electoral College** ..........884
College .................884
Law (Constitution) ......201
Official ................884
President (1920-1968) .884, 886
**Electric Power, U. S.**
123, 318,728-735
World ...................123
**Electrical units** ............586
**Electrocution, first** (1890) ..306
**Elements** .............588-589
**Elephant,** fossil ............714
**Elevations, continental** . .720-721
**Elizabeth, Queen** (1558) 297, 688
**Elizabeth II, Queen** ... 558, 688
**Elizabeth, Queen Mother** ...558
**Ellesmere Island** (Canada) . .722
**Ellice Islands** ..............563
**Emancipation Proc.** ........305
**Emerald Isle** (Ireland) .....524

Emigration *see Immigration*
Emmet, Robert (1803) ........300
Empire State Bldg. ....438, 445
Employment—
  Census report .............143
  Farm ..................... 776
  Government .... 124, 145-146
  Index numbers ............143
  Industry groups ..........124
  Insurance ............149-150
  Manufacturing .......119, 124
  Non-Farm payrolls ........119
  Railroads .................107
  Security ..............152-153
  Service (government) .....152
  *See Unemployment*
Enderbury Island ............382
Endowments—
  Colleges, universities ....345
Engineering—
  Civil wonders of U. S. ....129
  Fraternities ..............341
England .....................557
  Area, capital, population ..557
  Charles I (1642, '49) ..298, 688
  Charles II (1660, '64) 298, 688
  Church of (1558) ...297, 558
  Cities (population) .......579
  Cromwell (1642, '49) .....298
  Edward VIII (1936)
           311, 558, 688
  Elizabeth I (1558) ...297, 688
  Elizabeth II ........558, 688
  Explorers ...695, 704-707
  George V (1936) ..311, 558, 688
  George VI .......311, 558, 688
  Henry VIII (1509) ...297, 688
  Holidays, old .............591
  Magna Carta (1215) .......296
  Margaret, Princess .......558
  Notables .........688, 694-695
  Poet Laureates ...........695
  Pound ....................559
  Rulers ...............558, 688
  Slavery outlawed (1833) ..302
  Trade Unions (1825) ......302
  Victoria, Queen (1837) 302, 688
  *See United Kingdom*
English Channel—
  Bleriot's flight (1909) ....307
English language ............332
English, old holidays .......591
Engravers, noted American ..669
Ephesus, Temple at ..........721
Epiphany ........226, 233, 590
Episcopal Church *see Protestant
    Episcopal Church*
Equatorial Guinea .......64, 548
Equinoxes ...................260
Eras—
  Christian, beginning of ...295
  Chronological (1969) .....280
  Geologic ..................714
Erhard, Ludwig ..............515
Ericsson, Leif (1000 AD) 296, 708
Erie Canal (1825) ...........302
Erie, Lake ..................717
Eritrea .....................511
Espionage—
  Coplon, Judith (1950) ....315
  Fuchs, Dr. Klaus (1950) ..315
  May, Alan Nunn (1952) ....316
  Rosenbergs executed (1951) 315
Estate taxes—
  Federal ...................212
  State .....................212
Estonian SSR ................554
Etchers, noted American ....669
Ethiopia ....................511
  Addis Ababa (population) ..511
  Area, capital, population ..511
  Emperor ...................511
  Eritrea ...................511
  Italy, wars ......311, 511, 526
  Trade .....................98
  Waterfalls ................719
Europe—
  Area, dimensions .........736
  Cities (population) ...578-579
  Common Market ............65
  Heads of State 576-577, 688-693
  Lakes, notable ...........717
  Mountain peaks ...........720
  Petroleum production .....130
  Population ....485-567, 651
  –Religious ...............224
  Sugar production .........122
  Telephone statistics .....123
  Trade .....................101
  U. S. aid to .............580
  Waterfalls ...............719
  Western Union of (1954) ..316
European Economic Commu-
  nity (1957) ..........65, 573

European Free Trade Assn.
  (1960) ...................573
Evangelical Churches—
  Headquarters .............221
  History, organization 223, 224
  Membership .219-220, 223, 224
Evening stars ....256, 263-276
Everest, Mt. .316, 537, 720, 721
Everglades Nat'l Park .359, 388
Evolution trial (1925) ......310
Excise taxes ................218
Executive Agencies, U. S. ..164
Explorations, expeditions—
  America (1492-1842) ......708
  Antarctic (1840) 302, 705-706
  Arctic ................704-705
  Byrd, Richard E. ....670, 705
  Mountain climbing ........707
  National Geographic Soc. 443
  Norse Sagas ..............708
  Northwest Passage ........705
  Oceanographic .........711-712
  Polar .................704-707
Explorers .695-698, 704-707, 736
Explosions *see Disasters*
Expo 67 .....................413
Export-Import Bank—
  Employees (number) .......145
Exports, imports—
  Agricultural Products ....776
  Coal, Coke .......100, 128
  Coffee (U. S. imports) ....777
  Commodities ..............100
  Corn, wheat ..............776
  Duty-free (travelers) ....702
  Economic classes .........96
  Hosiery ..................124
  Manufactures .............100
  Shoes ....................125
  Sugar ....................122
  Textiles .................125
  Tonnage at U. S. ports ...99
  Value ...............96, 98
  –By continent, country .96, 98
  *See Tariff Acts and trade*
Expositions, Fairs ..........61
  Expo 67 ..................413
  HemisFair ................428
Express service (rail, air) ..114

## —F—

FBI *see Federal Bureau of
  Investigation*
Fabric production ...........125
Factors (numbers) ...........589
Faeroe Islands .......509, 722
Fahrenheit scale ............589
Faial Island, Atlantic ......722
Fair, largest state (Tex.) ..376
Fairs, Expositions ..........61
  Expo 67 ..................413
  HemisFair ................428
Faisal II (Iraq) ......523, 662
Falkland Islands, Br. ..562, 722
Fall, Albert B. (1929) ......310
Fall season .................260
Falls, death caused by .....759
Famous personalities ..665-699
Fanning Island (Solomons) .563
Farm Credit Administration 770
Farms, U. S. *see Agriculture*
Farouk I of Egypt ...........557
Fascism *see Italy, Spain*
Fast Days (church) 226, 227, 233
Fastest trips—
  Aircraft .............247-250
  Around the world .........248
  Rail .....................106
  Ships ....................102
  *See Racing*
Father's Day ................591
Fathom (measurement) ........581
Fats and oils—
  Consumption ..............776
  Nutritive values .........775
Federal agencies ......60, 175
Federal Bureau of
  Investigation ............766
Federal Civil Defense Adm. .748
Federal Communications Comm.
                  175
  Employees (number) .......145
Federal courts ..........167-169
Federal Credit Unions ......150
Federal Deposit Insurance,
  Corp. ....................147
Federal Government *see U. S.*
Federal Hall, N. Y. C. ......438
Federal Reserve System ......138
  Created (1913) ...........308
  Discount rates ...........87
  Notes ....................135

Federal taxes *see Taxes, Federal*
Federal Trade Commission ..175
Fellowships *see Scholarships*
Fencing champions ...........825
Ferguson, "Ma" (1924) .......310
Fermi, Enrico ...............116
Fernando Po (Spanish) .......548
Fezzan (Libya) ..............532
Field, Cyrus W. (1858) ......303
Fifty-four, 40 or fight (1846) 302
Figure skating champions ...834
Fiji Islands (Viti Levu) 563, 722
Fillmore, Millard (biog.) ...187
Films *see Motion Pictures*
Finance *see Economics also
  Corporations and stocks*
Fingerprints (FBI file) .....766
Finland .................511-512
  Area, capital, population ..511
  Cities (population) .......578
  Merchant fleet ...........101
  President ...........512, 576
  Soviet War, relations .311, 511
  Trade ................98, 511
Finns, noted ................698
Firearms (accidental deaths) 759
Fires (causes and losses) 664, 768
  Baltimore (1904) .........664
  Chelsea, Mass. (1908) ....307
  Chicago, Ill. (1871) ..304, 664
  Chicago, Ill. (1958) .....664
  Cloquet, Minn. (1918) ....664
  Cocoanut Grove (1942) 312, 664
  Forest fires .........664, 778
  Hartford circus (1944) 312, 664
  Hoboken docks (1900) .....664
  New York City (1835) .....302
  Ohio penitentiary (1930) .664
  San Francisco (1906) .....307
  Triangle, N. Y. C. (1911) .664
Hospitals
  –Cleveland (1929) ........664
  –Effingham, Ill. (1949) ..664
Hotels
  –Gulf, Houston (1943) ....664
  –LaSalle, Chicago (1946) .664
  –Windsor, N. Y. C. (1899) 664
  –Winnicoff, Atlanta (1946) 664
Schools
  –Camden, S. C. (1923) ....664
  –Chicago (1958) ..........664
  –Collinwood, O. (1908) 307, 664
  –Little Rock (1959) ......664
Theaters
  –Boyertown, Pa. (1908) ..664
  –Brooklyn (1876) .........664
  –Iroquois, Chicago (1903)
              307, 664
Fischer quintuplets (1963) .318
Fish and Fishing—
  Angling casting champs ..839
  Consumption ..............776
  Game fish records ....838-839
  Nutritive value ..........774
  Regulations by State .781-785
  Trout, largest (Idaho) ...360
  *See Aquariums*
Fish & Game Laws ....781-786
Fisk, Jr., C. l. James (1872) 305
Fitch, John (1785) ..........300
Flag Day ...............590, 591
Flags—
  Confederate States .......387
  Display of Flag ..........176
  History, U. S. ...........177
  Pledge to ................176
  President, U. S. .........176
  Puerto Rico ..............380
  United States .......176, 177
  World (color) 449-452 or 465-468
  *See specific nations*
Flat racing *see horse racing*
Flaxseed ....................771
Flemish painters ............699
Flights, air *see Aviation*
Flood control projects .728-729
Floods ................289, 662
Florida .....................358
  *See States, U. S.*
  Accession ................383
  Admission, area, cap. 358, 384
  Agriculture .769-771, 773, 776
  Birth, death statistics 758, 765
  Cape Kennedy .............359
  Counties (seats, areas) 636-637
  Elections ......884, 885, 890
  Lake, largest ............718
  Marriage, divorce laws 760, 761
  Miami (*see Miami*) ......411
  Museums, attractions
      359, 411, 418, 428, 434
  Name, origin of ..........383
  Officials, pay ......919, 920
  Orlando (*see Orlando*) ...418

**Florida (cont'd)**
Population ...............593-654
  –Cities and towns 604, 609-610
  –Counties, county seats 636-637
  –Metropolitan areas ..652-654
Presidential vote .....884, 890
St. Petersburg (*see*
  *St. Petersburg*) ........427
Tampa (*see Tampa*) .....433
Taxes ...............209-218
Territory .......359, 383, 384
Vital statistics .......757-768
**Florida Is., Solomons** ......563
**Flour** .....................776
**Flowers—**
  Dutch, tulip bulbs .......537
  Month, of the ...........763
  State .............354-379
**Fluid measures** ........581-582
**Folsom, Frances** ......183, 190
**Food & Drug Adm.** ....174, 175
**Foods—**
  Consumption .............776
  Exports ............100, 776
  Imports ...........100, 777
  Nutritive values ......774-775
  Price indexes ...........142
  Production ..........769-777
**Football, college—**
  Bowl games (records) ....868
  Coach of the year .......868
  Hall of Fame ...........867
  Heisman Trophy ........866
  Scores (1968) ......869-875
  Stadiums ..............865
  Team nicknames, colors 869-875
**Football, professional—**
  Atlantic Coast League ...866
  Canadian ..............865
  Champions .........862-865
  Continental League .....865
  Grey Cup .........865, 877
  Hall of Fame ..........864
  Jim Thorpe Trophy .....862
  Player Draft ...........865
  Stadiums ..............865
  Super Bowl ............862
**Footwear production** .......125
**Ford, Henry—**
  Motor Co. (1903, 1914) 307, 308
**Ford's Theater, Wash.** .....305
**Forefathers' Day** .........591
**Foreign aid, U. S.—**
  By Country ............580
  By type, 1945-1967 .....580
  Truman Doctrine (1947) .314
**Foreign born pop.** ..598-600, 602
**Foreign countries** .....492-567
  *See specific countries*
**Foreign Trade, U. S.** .......98
  By economic classes ......96
**Forest fires** ..............778
**Forests, National** .....388, 778
**Forgery, counterfeiting** ....767
**Formosa (Taiwan)** .........503
**Forms of address** .........351
**Formulas, mathematical** ....586
**Fort Peck Dam** ....730, 732, 736
**Fort Randall Dam** .....730, 736
**Fort Worth, Tex.—**
  Buildings, tall ..........446
  Opera ................158
  Population .....604, 631, 652
**Fortas, Abe** ...........84, 91
**Forts, historic—**
  Castle Williams, N. Y. ..438
  Harrod, Ky. ............363
  Knox, Ky. .............363
  Lincoln, N. Dakota .....372
  Matanzas, Fla. .....359, 389
  McHenry, Md. ......171, 364
  Raleigh, N. C. .........371
  San Marcos, Fla. .......359
  Sumter, S. C. ..........389
**Fossils, prehistoric** .......714
**Four Freedoms (1941)** .....311
**Fox Stakes (harness racing)** 816
**Fractions to decimals** ......586
**France** ...............512-514
  Area, capital, population .512
  Atomic weapons (1960) ...317
  Bank nationalized (1945) 313
  Cities, population ....578, 651
  Common Market .....65, 90
  Community .......513, 573
  Constitution ............512
  Couve de Murville ......85
  De Gaulle, *see De Gaulle,*
    *Chas.*
  Elections ..............81
  Electric power .........123
  Empires ...............689
  Franc crisis ............63
  Gavarnie waterfall ......719

**France (cont'd)**
  German occupation ......512
  Gold crisis ..........63, 72
  Gold reserve ..........139
  Heads of State ..512, 576, 689
  Indo-China war ........565
  Nuclear tests ......85, 88, 89
  Petroleum (oil) ........130
  Pompidou, Georges ......85
  Republics ..........513-514
  Revolution, 1789-1830 300, 302
  Ruhr occupation (1923) ..310
  Shipping
    –Merchant fleet .......101
    –Notable liners ........95
  Sugar production ........122
  Student riots ...........77
  Territories ..........513-514
  Trade .................512
  U. S. relations ..........65
  Weights, measures ......587
  World War I .......308-309
  World War I debt ......750
  World War II ....312-313, 752
**Franco, Francisco** .548, 577, 693
**Franco-Prussian War (1870)** 304
**Franconia, House of** ........690
**Franklin, Benjamin—**
  Declaration of Independ .198
  Flag, U. S. ............177
  Kite, experiment (1752) .299
  Postmaster General .....181
**Franz Josef Land, Arctic** ...722
**Fraternities (College)** ..339-342
  Interfraternity orgs. .....339
  Oldest ................339
**Frederik IX (Denmark)** .....692
**Freedom Fndtn, awards** ....243
**Freedom of the press—**
  Constitution, U. S. ......203
  Zenger victory (1735) ...299
**Freedom of speech (law)** ....203
**Freedom Statue (Capitol)** ..439
**Freedoms, Four (1941)** .....311
**Freer Gallery of Art** .......444
**Freezing points** ...........589
**Freight statistics—**
  Airlines ...............250
  Railroads .............107
  Shipping ..........99-101
**French Antarctica** .........514
**French Community** ........513
**French Guiana** ...........513
**French & Indian War, 1754** 299
**French, noted** ...689, 696-697
**French Polynesia** ..........513
**French Somaliland (Afars-**
  **Issas Terr.)** ...........513
**Frick Collection, N. Y. C.** ..436
**Friendly Isls. (Tongas)** 563, 722
**Friends (Quakers)** .....220, 221
**Frondizi, Arturo** ..........494
**Fruits—**
  Apple prices, farm .......122
  Consumption ...........776
  Exports, imports ........100
  Nutritive values ......774-775
  Price indexes ..........769
  Production .............771
**Fuchs, Dr. Klaus (1950, '59)** 315
**Fujiyama (Japan)** .........528
**Fulton, Robt. (1803, '07)** ..300
**Funafuti Atoll (area)** ......722
**Fundamental Orders (Conn.)** 358
**Furniture (retail sales)** .....126
**Furs, taxes, imports** .......218
**Futuna-Alofi Is. (Fr.)** .....514

**— G —**

**G.I. Bill (veterans)** ........753
**Gabon Republic** .....514, 576
**Gadsden Purchase (1853)** 303, 385
**Gagarin, Yuri (1961)** ......317
**Galapagos Is. (Ecuador)** 510, 722
**Gambia** ................514
**Gambier Islands (Fr.)** ......513
**Game & fish regulations** 781-786
**Gandhi, Mrs. Indira** .......521
**Gandhi, Mohandas K.** ..314, 521
**Ganongga Is., Solomons** ....563
**Gardens—**
  Azalea Trail, Mobile ......354
  Botanical, N. Y. .........436
  Brooklyn botanic ........437
  Charleston, S. C. ........374
  Hanging, Babylon ......721
  Longwood, Pa. .........373
  Peace, N. Dak. .........372
**Gardner, John W.** ..........67
**Gardner, Julia (Tyler)** 183, 187
**Garfield, James A. (biog.)** ..189
**Garibaldi, G. (1860)** ..303, 691

**Gas—**
  Natural (production) 120, 130
  Used producing electricity 123
**Gases (densities)** ...........589
**Gasoline—**
  Consumption by state ...115
  Excise tax rate ..........218
  Exports ...............100
  Mobil economy run .....113
  Production .............130
  Rationing ..............68
  Taxes by state .........115
**Gatun Lake (Canal Zone)** ..381
**Gaza Strip** ...............525
**Gdansk (Danzig)** .........543
**Generals, U. S.** ............739
  Address, form of ........351
  Salute to (artillery) .....746
**Geneva conferences—**
  Disarmament ...........86
  Far Eastern affairs (1954) 316
**Genghis Khan (1215)** ......296
**Geodetic datum point** ......727
**Geographic centers, U. S.** ...94
**Geographic Soc., National** ..443
**Geographic Statistics, U. S.** ..94
**Geological Survey, U. S.** 709-710
**Geology—**
  Eras, periods, epochs ....714
**George, Henry (1879)** .....306
**George V, Eng. (1936)** .....311
**George VI, Eng.** ..311, 558, 688
**George Washington Bridge** .725
**Georgia** .................359
  *See States, U. S.*
  Admission, area, cap. .359, 384
  Agriculture ..769-771, 773, 776
  Andersonville Prison .....360
  Atlanta (*see Atlanta*) .390-391
  Birth, death statistics 758, 765
  Counties (seats, areas) ...637
  Elections ........884, 885, 891
  Kennesaw Mtn. park .....388
  Lake, largest ...........718
  Marriage, divorce laws 760, 761
  Museums, attractions .360, 391
  Name, origin of .........383
  Officials, pay .......919, 920
  Population ..........593-654
    –Cities and towns ...604, 610
    –Counties, county seats ..637
    –Metropolitan areas .652-654
  Presidential vote ....884, 891
  Taxes ...............209-218
  Vital statistics .......757-768
**Georgia Warm Spring Fdn.** ..359
**Georgian SSR** .............554
**Germans, noted** 686-687, 695-696
**Germany: 9 A.D. to 1933** ....513
  Berlin *see Berlin*
  Charlemagne .......689, 690
  Diet of Worms (1517) ...297
  Franco-Prussian war (1870) 304
  Gutenberg, Johann (1456) 296
  Hohenstaufen dynasty ...690
  Hohenzollern dynasty ...690
  Luther, Martin (1517) ...297
  Noted Germans
    686-687, 695-696
  Prussia ..........514, 690
  Romans defeated, 9 A.D. .295
  Rulers .............514, 690
  Weights and measures ...587
  Weimar republic ...515, 690
  Wilhelm I (William)
    304, 515, 690
  World War I ...308-309, 752
**Germany: Federal Republic of**
  **(West Germany)** ....515-516
  Allied zones, postwar .....515
  Area, capital, population .515
  Armed Forces ..........516
  Berlin ................317
  Cities, population ........578
  Elections ..........76, 515
  Erhard, Chancellor ......515
  Exports ...............515
  Gold reserve ..........139
  Helgoland .............516
  Merchant fleet .........101
  Petroleum production ...130
  Sovereignty (1955) ......316
  Sugar production ........122
  Trade .............98, 515
  USSR .................90
**Germany: German Democratic**
  **Republic (E. Germany)** 516
  Area, capital, population .516
  Armed forces ..........516
  Berlin ................317
  Cities, population ........578
  Riots (1953) ...........90
**Germany Third Reich (Nazi)** 515
  Austria taken (1938) 311, 515

**Germany Third Reich (cont'd)**
Belgium invaded .....312, 496
Czechoslovakia (1939) 311, 515
France, conquest of .....312
Hitler *see Hitler, Adolf*
Italy, alliance (1939) .....311
Munich pact (1938) .....515
Poland invaded (1939) .....312
Reichstag fire (1933) .....310
Rhine, occupied (1936) .....311
USSR pact (1939) ...311, 515
World War II ....312-313, 752
–Crimes (1946) .............314
–State of war ends (1951) 316
**Geronimo (surrender, 1886)**.306
**Gestation, incubation** .......780
**Gettysburg Address** .........206
**Ghana** ......................516
**Giant's Causeway (N. Ire.)** .560
**Gibraltar** (1704) ......299, 561
**Gift Taxes, Federal** ........218
**Gilbert and Ellice Islands** .563
**Gillars, Mildred** (1949) .....314
**Girl Scouts of America** *see Assns.*
**Gizo Is., Solomons** .........563
**Glacier National Park** ......388
**Glen Canyon Dam**
   728, 730, 731, 736
**Glenn, John H.** (1962) ......317
**Glider records** (aviation) ...250
**Goa** .........................521
**Goddard, Robert H.** ....118, 310
**Goering, Hermann** (1946) ..314
**Goethals Bridge** (N.Y.-N.J.) 725
**Gold—**
   Black Friday (1869) ......304
   Carats in pure ...........587
   Crisis (1968) .............72
   Discovered U. S. (1848) ..303
   Mine, largest (S. Dakota) 375
   Price ....................140
   Production, by country ...140
   Reserves .................139
**Gold Coast** *see Ghana*
**Gold Cup power boat races**..837
**Goldberg, Arthur** ...........75
**Golden Gate Bridge** ........725
**Golden Number** ......226, 232
**Goldwater, Barry** ..884, 887-914
**Golf** .....................846-848
   Hall of Fame .............846
**Good Friday** .....226, 227, 590
**Goodhue, Grace A.** ....183, 192
**Gordon, Gen. C. G.** (1885) .306
**Gotland Island, Baltic** ......722
**Government, U. S.**
   *See United States*
**Governments, foreign** ..485-567
**Governments, State** ...919-923
**Governors Island** ...........438
**Governors, State** ......919-923
   Address, form of .........351
   New York .............919, 922
   Salaries, terms ..........919
   Women, first (1924) .....310
**Gozo Island** ................534
**Graf Spee** (1939) ...........659
**Grains—**
   Chicago spot prices ......772
   Consumption ..............776
   Elevator capacities ......773
   Exports, imports ....100, 776
   Production, U. S. total ...771
   –By State ...............773
   Receipts at grain centers .773
   Supply in U. S. ..........772
   Wheat seed ...............771
**Gran Canaria Island** .......722
**Grand Canyon** .....355, 388, 389
   Explorer .................306
**Grand Coulee Dam** .728, 730, 731
**Grand Terre Is., Guadeloupe** 513
**Grand Teton Natl. Park** 379, 388
**Grant, Ulysses S.** (biog.) ....189
   Memoirs, death (1884) ....306
   Tomb, New York City 389, 438
   Wife ...............183, 189
**Gravity—**
   Atmosphere, effect on .....260
   Planets (relative) ........286
**Great Britain—**
   *See United Kingdom*
**Great Lakes** .................717
   Distances between ports ..105
   St. Lawrence Seaway
      (1959) ...........97, 317
**Great Salt Lake, Utah** .....376
**Great Seal, U. S.** ...........701
**Great Smoky Mountains** ....388
**Great Stone Face** (N. H.) ...369
**Greece** .....................517
   Ancient and Latins .......685
   Area, capital, population ..517
   Cities (population) .......578

**Greece** (cont'd)
   Constitution ..............90
   Crete ................517, 722
   Cyprus ....................65
   King .................517, 576
   King flees ................65
   Merchant fleet ...........101
   Papandreou, Andreas ......68
   Plotter spared ............63
   Royal family .............517
   Trade ................98, 517
   Weights, measures ........587
**Greek Orthodox Church** *see Eastern Orthodox Church*
**Green Mountain Boys** .......376
**Greenland (Denmark)** .509, 722
**Greenwich meridian** ........280
**Gregorian calendar** (1752)
   278-279, 281, 299
**Grenada Island** (W. Indies) .561
**Grey Cup** ..............865, 877
**Grissom, Capt. Virgil I.** ....317
**Gross National Product** .....133
**Groundhog Day** .............591
**Guadalcanal** .....313, 563, 722
**Guadeloupe Is.** (Fr.) ..513, 722
**Guadelupe-Hidalgo Treaty** ..385
**Guam** ......................382
   Altitudes (high, low) .....738
   Area, capital, population ..382
   Cities (population) .......655
   Farms (statistics) ........769
   Marriage information ......760
   Officials, pay .......919, 923
   Population ..........382, 655
**Guatemala** ..................517
   Area, capital, pop. ...517, 578
   Civil strife ..............518
   Guatemala City (pop.) ....578
   Head of State ............576
   Murders of U. S. aides..67, 87
   Volcano ..................716
   Weights, measures ........587
**Guernsey Is.** (Br.) .....561, 722
**Guggenheim Museum, N.Y.C.** 436
**Guiana, French** .............513
**Guinea, New** (Br.) ..........495
**Guinea, Portuguese** ........544
**Guinea, Rep. of** .......518, 576
**Guinea, Spanish** ...........548
**Gustav VI** (Sweden) ...549, 692
**Gutenberg Bible** (1456) .....296
**Guyana** .....................518
   Waterfalls ...............719
**Gymnastic champions** ......876

**— H —**

**Haile Selassie I.** (Ethiopia)
   (1936) ......311, 511, 576
**Hainan Island** (China) ....722
**Haiti** ......................518
   Area, capital, population ..518
   Cities (population) .......578
   President ................576
**Hale, Nathan** (1776) .......298
**Halifax explosion** (1917) 658, 661
**Hall of Fame—**
   Aviation .................250
   Baseball ...........371, 806
   Basketball ...............823
   Football
   –College .................867
   –Professional ............864
   Golf .....................846
   Madison Square Garden ...845
**Halloween** ..................591
**Hambletonian Stakes** ......816
**Hamilton-Burr duel** (1804) ..300
**Hammarskjold, Dag—**
   Death (1961) .............317
   Library ..................569
   Nobel peace prize ........235
**Hammer throw records—**
   American .................858
   World ....................855
**Hammurabi** (2067 B.C.) .....295
**Handball** ...................877
**Hanging Gardens, Babylon** ..721
**Hannibal** (218 B.C.) ........295
**Hanover, House of** .........688
**Hapsburg Dynasty** .........690
**Harbors,** *see ports*
**Harding, Warren G.** (biog.) .192
**Harness racing** ........815-816
**Harpers Ferry** (1859)
   303, 378, 388
**Harrison, Benjamin** (biog.) .190
**Harrison, Wm. Henry** (biog.) 186
**Hartford, Conn.** ...........403
   Buildings, tall ..........446
   Circus fire (1944) ...312, 664
   City manager ............924

**Hartford, Conn.** (cont'd)
   Museums, attractions .....404
   Population ......604, 608, 652
   Wadsworth Atheneum ....404
**Harvard University—**
   College (1636) ......298, 323
   Rowing, Yale ............836
   Statistics ...........323, 338
**Harvest moon** ..............793
**Hawaii** .....................360
   *See States, U. S.*
   Accession ......383, 384, 385
   Admission, area, cap.
      360, 384, 385
   Agriculture .769-771, 773, 776
   Altitude (highest) .......738
   Birth, death statistics 758, 765
   Bird, state ..............360
   Counties (seats, areas) ...637
   Elections ........884, 885, 892
   Farms (statistics) .......769
   Honolulu (*see Honolulu*) .404
   Lake, largest, highest 360, 718
   Marriage, divorce laws 760, 761
   Mountain peaks ..........360
   Name, origin of ..........383
   Officials, pay .......919, 920
   Population ...........593-655
   –Cities and towns .....604, 610
   –Counties, county seats ..637
   Presidential vote .....884, 892
   Song ......................42
   Statehood (1959) .........360
   Sugar production .........122
   Taxes .................209-218
   Volcanoes .........360, 716
   Wettest spot .............292
**Hay—**
   Prices, farm .............770
   Production ...............771
   –By state ...............773
**Hayden Planetarium, N.Y.C.** 436
**Hayes, Rutherford B.** (biog.) 189
**Haymarket riot** (1886) ......306
**Heads of States** ......64, 576-577
**Health, Education and Welfare Dept.—**
   Administrative personnel ..166
   Established ..............181
   Expenditures ............131
   Secretaries .....67, 71, 181
   Social Security Adm. .....148
**Health Insurance** ...........763
**Health, Medicine** ........59-60
**Heart transplants** ......59, 66
**Heavyweight champions**
   840, 841, 842
**Heavyweight, history** ...843-844
**Hebrides, New** .......514, 563
**Height, weight** (human) ....763
**Heisman Trophy** ............866
**Hejaz, Saudi-Arabia** .......545
**Helgoland** (W. Germany) ...516
**Helicopters** ................250
   Airlines .................246
**Helms World Trophy** .......829
**HemisFair** .............61, 428
**Henderson Island** ..........563
**Henry Hudson Bridge** ......725
**Henry, Lou** ...........183, 193
**Henry, Patrick** (1765) ......298
**Henry VIII, Eng.** (1509) ...297
**Herndon, Ellen** (Arthur) 183, 190
**Hickok, Wild Bill** (1876) ...306
**High schools—**
   Enrollment ..............349
   Sport records ...........856
**Highways** *see Roads*
**Hillary, Sir Edmund** .......707
**Himalaya Mts.** .......537, 707
**Hindenberg** (dirigible) .....663
**Hindenburg, Paul von** (1934) 311
**Hindu population, world** ....224
**Hiroshima bombing** (1945) .313
**Hispanic Society of America** 436
**Hispaniola Island** .....518, 722
**Hiss, Alger** (1948) ..........314
**Historians** ......666-668, 694-699
**Historic dates** ..........295-318
**Historic sites, U. S.** .....383-389
**Historical parks, National** ..388
**Hitler, Adolf** ...............515
   Beer Putsch (1923) ...310, 515
   Chancellor (1933) 310, 515, 690
   Death (1945) ........313, 515
   Reichsfuehrer (1934) .311, 515
   Versailles (1935, '37) ..311, 515
**Ho Chi Minh** ...............566
**Hockey** ..................826-828
**Hoes, Hannah** ........183, 186
**Hogs** (on farms, prices) ....780
**Hohenstaufen, House of** ....690
**Hokkaido Island, Japan** 527, 722
**Holidays—**
   Canadian .................491
   Federal ...................42

**Holidays (cont'd)**
Jewish ..............................233
Legal, public (U. S.) ..590-591
–Flag display ................176
Old English ..................591
Religious ......226, 227, 233
Weeks and months ......591
Holland *see Netherlands*
**Holland Tunnel** .............727
**Holmes, Sherlock (1886)** ...306
**Holt, Harold** ..................66
**Holy Alliance (1815)** ........301
**Holy Days (Greek Church)** .233
**Holy Land (Palestine)** ......525
**Holy Trinity (325 A.D.)** ....296
**Home, Lord** *see Douglas-Home,*
    *Sir Alec*
**Homer's Troy (1184 B.C.)** ...295
**Homestead Act** ...............386
**Honduras, British** ...........562
**Honduras, Republic of** ......519
Area, capital, population ..519
Merchant fleet ..............101
President ................519, 576
Tegucigalpa (pop.) ..........578
Weights, measures ..........587
**Hong Kong** ............563, 578
Trade ..........................98
**Honolulu, Hawaii** ............404
Buildings, tall ..............446
Mayor ........................925
Population ......604, 610, 652
**Honshu Island, Japan** ..527, 722
**Hoover Dam** ...355, 730, 731, 736
**Hoover, Herbert (biog.)** .192-193
**Hoover, J. Edgar** .............766
**Hopkinson, Francis** ...........177
**Horse racing** ............817-880
Belmont Stakes ............817
Citation's record ..........820
Garden State Stakes ........64
Harness stakes winners 815-816
Jockeys, leading ............819
Kentucky Derby ............817
Money winners, leading ....819
Preakness ....................817
Quarter ......................876
Queen's Plate ..............816
Races, major 1968 ..........820
Tax revenues to states ....818
Trainers, leading ..........819
Triple Crown winners ......818
Trotting, pacing ......815-816
**Horsepower** ...................586
**Horses (on farms)** ...........780
**Horseshoe pitching champ** ..853
**Hosiery production** ..........124
**Hospital Insurance Fund** ...151
**Hospitalization plans** .......762
**Hospitals—**
Patients, mental illness ...764
Veterans' benefits ..........753
**Hot Springs Natl. Pk.** .356, 388
**House of Burgesses (1619)** ..298
**House of Commons** ...........558
**House of Lords** ..............558
**House of Representatives**
*See Congress, U. S.*
**Household furnishings—**
Price index ..................143
Retail sales ..................126
**Households—**
Color ..........................593
Size, average ..............593
Type, color, 1967 ..........593
**Housing—**
Construction statistics ....654
Permit valuation ............654
Type ..........................654
*See Construction*
**Housing & Urban Develop-**
**ment, Dept. of—**
Established ..........166, 179
Weaver, Robert C. ........179
**Houston, Tex.** ................405
Buildings, tall ..............446
Gulf Hotel fire (1943) ......664
Mayor ........................925
Museums, attractions ......405
Opera ........................158
Population ......604, 631, 652
Port traffic ..................96
**Howard, Catherine (1509)** ...297
**Howland Island** ..............382
**Hudson Bay** ..................713
**Hudson, Henry (1609)** ......297
**Hudson River** ................723
**Huguenots (1560)** ............297
**Humphrey, Hubert H.**
Presidential campaign 36-38,
    76, 79, 82, 90, 92
**Hundred Years' War (1453)** .296
**Hungarians, noted** ...690, 698-99
**Hungary** ....................519-520
Area, capital, population ..519

**Hungary (cont'd)**
Cities (population) ..........578
Czech land to (1938) ........311
Kadar, Janos ................520
Merchant fleet ..............101
Mindszenty (1948) ..........314
Nagy, Imre ..................519
Petroleum production ......122
Revolt (1956) ........316, 519
Rulers ......519, 520, 576, 690
Weights, measures ..........587
**Hunter's Moon** ...............793
**Hunting—**
Canadian regulations .785-786
Regulations by state ..781-786
**Huon Island (Fr.)** ............514
**Hurdling records—**
American ....................858
Olympic games ......878, 881
World ....................854, 855
**Huron, Lake** .................717
Ship destroyed (1913) ......658
**Hurricanes** ...................662
Descriptive ..................289
Names of ....................294
**Huss, John (1415)** ............296
**Hydroelectric projects** .733-735
Federal power ........728-736
Non-Federal plants ...732-735
USSR ........................555
World's largest ............733
**Hydrogen bomb** *see Atomic,*
    *hydrogen bombs*

— I —

**ILO** *see International Labor Org.*
**INTERPOL** *see Intl. Criminal*
    *Police Org.*
**Iberian Peninsula** ......543, 547
**Iberville Mem. Bridge, Miss.** 366
**Ice hockey** ...............826-828
**Ice skating** ............834, 849
**Iceland** ......................520
Area, capital, population ..520
Merchant fleet ..............101
President ....................576
Reykjavik (population) ....578
Trade ..........................98
U. S. occupied (1941) ......312
Waterfalls ..................719
**Idaho** ........................360
*See States, U. S.*
Admission, area, cap. 360, 384
Agriculture ..769-771, 773, 776
Birth, death statistics 758, 765
Counties (seats, areas) ....638
Elections ........884, 885, 892
Lake, largest ................718
Marriage, divorce laws 760, 761
Museums, attractions ......360
Name, origin of ............383
Officials, pay ........919, 920
Population ..............593-654
–Cities and towns ..........611
–Counties, county seats ....638
Presidential vote †..884, 893
Taxes ....................209-218
Territory ..............360, 384
Vital statistics ........757-768
**Ifni** ....................536, 548
**IJsselmeer** ...................537
**Illinois** ......................360
*See States, U. S.*
Admission, area, cap. 360, 384
Agriculture ..769, 771, 773, 776
Birth, death statistics 758, 765
Chicago (*see Chicago*) ....394
Counties (seats, areas) ....638
Elections ........884, 885, 892
Lake, largest ................718
Marriage, divorce laws 760, 761
Museums, attractions .361, 395
Name, origin of ............383
Officials, pay ........919, 920
Population ..............593-654
–Cities and towns 604, 611-612
–Counties, county seats ....638
–Jewish ......................602
–Metropolitan areas ..652-654
–Non-white ..........596, 597
Presidential vote ....884, 892
Taxes ....................209-218
Territory ....................384
Vital statistics ........757-768
**Illustrators, noted American** 669
**Immigration, emigration—**
Admissions ..........701, 703
Regulations, U. S. ..........701
*Imports see Exports, Imports*
**Income tax, cities** ............218
**Income tax, Federal** ....209-212
Amendment, 16th ..........204
Deductions ......209-212, 218

**Income Tax, Federal (cont'd)**
Filing requirements ........209
Rate schedules ..............210
Returns, types of ..........209
Withholding ................211
*See Taxes*
**Income tax, State** ......213-215
**Incomes—**
Farms (by state) ..........770
National ..............133, 134
Non-Farm Payrolls ........119
Per capita, by state ........138
Poverty, families ..........656
Production workers ........119
Railroads (total) ..........107
*See Salaries*
**Incubation, gestation** ......780
**Independence Day** ..........590
**Independence, Decl. of** .196-198
Almanac, sedition ..........197
**Independence Hall** ..........198
**Index of American Design** .443
**Index Numbers—**
Business ....................143
Consumer prices ..........142
Cost of Living ....141, 143, 568
–By cities ..................568
Employment ................119
Factory earnings ..........119
Farms ........................769
Farm product prices ......770
Food prices ................769
Industrial production ....143
Manufacturers ..............119
Production workers ........119
Wholesale prices ..........143
**India, Republic of** ......520-521
Amritsar massacre (1919) .309
Area, capital, population ..520
Cities (population) ........578
Gandhi (1948) ........314, 521
Goa ..........................521
Gold production ............140
Gold reserve ................139
Kashmir ......................521
Kosygin visit ................68
Languages ..................522
Nagaland ....................521
Petroleum production ......130
Shastri, Lal Bahadur ......521
State (area population) ....521
Sugar production ..........122
Taj Mahal ..................521
Trade ....................98, 521
Waterfalls ..................719
Weights, measures ..........587
**Indian Ocean—**
Area, depth ................713
Islands, areas ..............719
**Indian Territory (Okla.)** 372, 384
**Indiana** ......................361
*See States, U. S.*
Admission, area, cap. 360, 384
Agriculture ..769-771, 773, 776
Birth, death statistics 758, 765
Counties (seats, areas) 638-639
Elections ........884, 885, 893
Indianapolis (*see Indpls*) 405
Lake, largest ................718
Marriage, divorce laws 760, 761
Museums, attractions 361, 406
Name, origin of ............383
Officials, pay ........919, 920
Opera ........................158
Population ..............593-654
–Cities and towns 604, 612-613
–Counties, county seats 638-639
–Metropolitan areas ..652-654
Presidential vote ....884, 000
Taxes ....................209-218
Territory ................361, 384
Vital statistics ........757-768
**Indianapolis, Indiana** ......405
Buildings, tall ..............446
Mayor ........................924
Museums, attractions ......406
Population ......604, 613, 652
**Indianapolis Speedway** ....406
**Indians, American—**
Black Hawk War (1832) ...302
Crazy Horse (1876) ........306
Custer massacre (1876) ....306
French and Indian War ....299
Geronimo surrender (1886) 306
Incas ........................542
Museum, New York City ...417
Navaho art, Santa Fe .....369
New England War (1676) ..298
Oklahoma Exhibits ........372
Population, by state ........597
Sequoya statue ............439
Tippecanoe battle (1811) ..301
**Indo-China** *see Cambodia, Laos,*
    *Vietnam*

**Indonesia, Republic of** ......522
  Area, capital, population ..522
  Cities (population) ........578
  Gold reserve ..............139
  Merchant fleet ............101
  Netherlands union ends ...522
  Petroleum production ......130
  President ............522, 576
  Sugar production ..........122
  Suharto *see* Suharto
  Sukarno *see* Sukarno, Achmed
  Trade ......................98
  Volcanoes ............715-716
**Industries, foreign—**
  *See individual nations*
**Industries, Nationalization—**
  Bulgaria ..................498
  France (1945) .............313
  Great Britain .............559
  Iran (1951) ...............523
  Mexico (1938) ......311, 535
  Poland (1946) .............313
  Romania ...................544
  Yugoslavia ................566
**Industries, U. S.—**
  Agriculture ...........769-778
  Airlines ..................246
  Automotive ...........107, 113
  Business failures .........146
  Employees .................119
  Income ....................134
  Manufacturing .........119-126
  Mineral production ....127-130
  Production index ..........119
  Profit vs. taxes ..........120
  Railroad statistics ...106-107
  States, descriptive ...354-379
  Textile ...................125
  *See Corporations*
**Influenza (1918)** ............309
**Inheritance taxes (state)** ...213
**Inland water area, U. S.** ....384
**Inland waterways, U. S.** .....97
**Inner Mongolia** ..............504
**Insignia, Armed Forces** .741, 742
**Insurance—**
  Health ....................763
  Life *see Life Insurance*
  Savings ...................137
  Social Security .......148-150
  Unemployment
  –United States ......152, 153
  Veterans ..................753
**Insured mail** ................928
**Integration** *see Desegregation*
**Inter-American conferences** .314
**Inter-American Develop-**
  **ment Bank** ...............575
**Intercoastal waterways** ....97
**Intercollegiate Rowing**
  **Records** .................836
**Interest—**
  Laws, rates .........138, 147
  Table of simple ...........585
**Interior, Department of the—**
  Administrative personnel .166
  Employees (number) .......145
  Established ...............182
  Expenditures .............131
  Secretaries .........166, 182
**Internal Revenue Service—**
  Collections ...............131
  Taxes .................209-211
**International Bank** ....572, 574
  *See World Bank*
**Intl. boundary lines, U. S.** ..174
**Intl. Court of Justice**
  *See United Nations*
**Intl. Criminal Police**
  **Org. (INTERPOL)** .......767
**Intl. Labor Org. (ILO)** ....571
**Intl. Monetary Fund** .......574
**Intl. Organizations—**
  Abbreviations ....174, 571-573
**International postage** .929-931
**Interscholastic sport records—**
  National track records ...856
**Interstate Commerce Comm.** 175
**Inventions** ..............116-118
  Inventors, Amer. .116-118, 669
  Patent law ...............208
**Ionosphere** ..................260
**Iowa** ........................361
  *See States, U. S.*
  Admission, area, cap. .361-384
  Agriculture .769-771, 773, 776
  Birth, death statistics 758, 765
  Counties (seats, areas) ..639
  Des Moines
    (see Des Moines)
  Elections ......884, 885, 894
  Lake, largest .............718
  Marriage, divorce laws 760, 761
  Museums, attractions 262, 401

**Iowa (cont'd)**
  Name, origin of ...........383
  Officials, pay ........919, 920
  Population ............593-654
  –Cities and towns 604, 613-614
  –Counties, county seats ..639
  –Metropolitan areas ..652-654
  Presidential vote ....884, 894
  Taxes .................209-213
  Territory .................384
  Vital statistics ......757-768
**Iran** ........................522
  Area, capital, population 522
  Cities (population) .......578
  Gold reserve ..............139
  Great Britain, relations ..523
  Merchant fleet ..........101 *
  Petroleum
  –Nationalization ..........523
  –Production ..........130, 522
  Shah .................523, 576
  Trade ......................98
  Weights, measures ........587
**Iraq** ........................523
  Area, capital, population .523
  Cities (population) .......578
  Coup (1968) ...............86
  King Faisal II (1958) .....317
  Petroleum production ......130
  President ......86, 524, 576
  Revolution (1958) .........317
  Trade .................98, 523
**Ireland, Northern** ...........560
  Area, capital, population 560
  Cities (population) .......579
  *See United Kingdom*
**Ireland, Republic of** ......524
  Area, capital, population .524
  Cities (population) .......578
  De Valera, President 524, 576
  Merchant fleet ...........101
  Presidents, ministers 524, 576
  Sugar production ..........122
  Trade .................98, 524
**Irish authors** ...............699
**Iron—**
  Exports, imports .........100
  Production ..........127, 129
**Irrigation, reclamation** .728-736
**Islam (Moslem) population** ..224
**Islamic calendar** ............226
**Islands (area, ownership)** ..722
**Isle of Man** ...........561, 722
**Isle of Pines, Cuba** ..506, 722
**Isle of Pines (N. Caledonia)** .514
**Isle of Wight (area)** ........722
**Isle Royale National Park** ..388
**Israel** ......................525
  Area, capital, population .525
  Ben-Gurion ...............526
  Cities (population) .......579
  Citizenship (law) .........702
  Egypt, invasion of ........525
  Eichmann, Adolf ..........317
  Formed (1948) .......314, 525
  Gaza Strip ................525
  Jerusalem .................525
  Jerusalem parade ..........78
  Johnson, Lyndon B. ........67
  Jordan ......71, 72, 78, 81, 86
  Merchant fleet ...........101
  Plane Hijacked ............86
  President .................576
  Suez Canal issue .........525
  Trade .................98, 525
  Travel rules .............702
  UAR .......................89
  United Nations ..75, 87, 89, 91
  U. S. jets ................91
  U. S. recognizes (1948) ..314
  Weizmann, Chaim .........525
**Israeli-Arab War** ...........525
**Italians, noted** .......691, 698
**Italy** .......................526
  Area, capital, population .526
  Cities (population) .......579
  Electric power ............123
  Fascist government .......526
  –Ethiopian war ......311, 528
  Gold reserve ..............139
  Islands ..............526, 722
  Merchant fleet ...........101
  –Vessels, notable .........95
  Petroleum production ......130
  Premier resigns ...........81
  Rulers ........526, 576, 691
  Sugar production ..........122
  Toce (Tosa) Waterfall ....719
  Trade .................98, 526
  Trieste ...................527
  Volcanoes ...........526, 716
  World War I 308-309, 750, 752
  World War II ....312-313, 752

**Ivory Coast Rep.** ...527, 552, 579
**Iwo Jima, 1945** .........313, 722

**—J—**

**Jackson, Andrew (biog.)** ....188
  Birthday (legal holiday) ..590
**Jackson, Stonewall** ....304, 665
**Jacksonville, Fla.—**
  Buildings, tall ...........446
  Population ......604, 609, 652
**Jamaica** .....................527
  Area, capital, population .527
  Coffee production .........777
  Gov. Gen. .................576
  Sugar production ..........122
**James, Jesse (birthplace)** ..366
**Jamestown, Va., 1607** .......297
**Jammu-Kashmir** ..............521
**Jan Mayen Is. (Norway)** ....540
**Japan** .......................527
  Area, capital, pop. .......527
  Chinese wars ...306, 502, 528
  Cities (population) ...579,.651
  Elections .................528
  Electric power ............123
  Emperor Hirohito ...528, 576
  Iron-steel industry .......528
  MacArthur in (1945) .313, 528
  Manchuria (1931, '32) 310, 528
  Merchant fleet ......101, 528
  Mikado restored (1867) ...303
  Okinawa .............382, 722
  Peace treaty, U. S. .......528
  Petroleum production ......130
  Premier ..............528, 576
  Railroads .................107
  Russia, war (1904) ........307
  Ryukyu Island ............382
  Shipbuilding ..............528
  Tokyo ..........528, 579, 651
  Trade .................98, 528
  Treaty, U. S. defense .....528
  Treaty, U. S. security ....528
  Undersea tunnel ..........727
  Volcanoes ...........715-716
  Waterfalls ................719
  Weights, measures ........587
  World War I .....308-309, 752
  World War II ....312-313, 752
  –Surrender terms ..........528
**Japan, Sea of** ...............713
**Jarvis Island** ...............382
**Java, Indonesia** .......522, 722
  Volcanoes ...........715-716
**Javelin throw records—**
  American ..................858
  Olympic games ...878, 882, 883
  World .....................855
**Jefferson, Thomas—**
  Biography ............184-185
  Birthday (legal holiday) ..590
  Declaration of Independ. .198
  Memorial, Washington 389, 441
  Mt. Rushmore memorial ...375
  Religion ............185, 195
**Jehovah's Witnesses** ...220, 221
**Jersey City, N. J.—**
  Black Tom explosion (1916) 309
  Buildings, tall ...........446
  Mayor ....................925
  Population ......604, 621, 652
**Jersey Is. (Brit.)** .....561, 722
**Jerusalem (Israel)** .........525
**Jesus Christ** ................295
**Jewelry—**
  Birth stones .............760
  Precious stones (defined) .760
  Wedding anniversaries ...760
**Jewish Congregations—**
  Headquarters .........220, 221
  Membership ...............220
**Jews—**
  Calendar, holidays .......233
  Population statistics .....602
  Zionist movement .........525
**Jim Thorpe Trophy** .........862
**Joan of Arc (1429)** .........296
**Jockeys, leading** ...........819
**Johnson, Andrew (biog.)** ...188
**Johnson, Claudia**
  (Mrs. Lyndon B.) ...183, 195
**Johnson, Louisa**
  (Adams) ............183, 186
**Johnson, Lyndon B.—**
  Ball, George W. ...........75
  Biography ............194-195
  Bombing halt ..............91
  Cabinet .......179-182, 183
  Central American trip .....83
  Civil disorders report ....70
  Crime message ............69

**Johnson, Lyndon B. (cont'd)**
Economic report ......... 9
Education message ........ 69
Eshkol talks ............. 67
Foreign investments .... 67
Fortas, Abe ..........84, 91
Goldberg, Arthur ....... 75
Governors' speech ...... 84
Gun controls ........... 81
Hawaiian trip .......... 84
Israel jets ............. 91
Lynda, daughter ...66, 92
McNamara, Robert ..... 70
Presidents, Vice Presidents,
  Congresses ..........178
Rejects nomination .... 73
Republicans ........... 65
Rights Bill ........... 74
Salary, aides .........164
Shriver, R. Sargent .... 71
State-of-the-Union .... 67
Vance, Cyrus .......... 70
VFW address ........... 87
Vietnam war speech .... 70
Wilson visit .......... 69
**Johnston Island** .......382
**Johnstown flood** (1889) .306, 662
**Joint Chiefs of Staff** ....164, 739
**Jordan** ................529
Amman (population) ...579
Area, capital, population ..529
Israel ....71, 72, 78, 81, 86
King Hussein .......529, 576
United Nations ......75, 87
**Journalism—**
Awards ....236-237, 241-242
College societies .....341, 342
Editors, publishers (noted)
  666-668
First school of (Mo.) ...367
Pulitzer Prizes .......236
*See Newspapers*
**Joyce, William** (1946) ....313
**Judges—**
Address, form of .......351
District courts .....167-169
Supreme court ........169
U. S. courts .......167-169
**Julian Calendar** .........281
**Juliana, Queen** ....538, 577, 692
**Jumping records—**
American ..............858
Olympics .........878-882
World ................855
**Junior colleges** .....333-338
**Jupiter** (planet) 253-256,259, 286
Morning, evening .259, 263-276
Position by months ...253-256
Rises, sets ...........287
**Justice, Department of—**
Administrative personnel ..165
Attorneys General ...165, 181
Employees (number) ...145
Established ...........181
Expenditures .........131
**Jutland, battle of** (1916) 309, 658

**— K —**

**Kalimantan, Indonesia** ....522
**Kansas** ................362
*See States, U. S.*
Admission, area, cap. 362, 384
Agriculture ..769-771,773, 776
Birth, death, statistics 758, 765
Counties (seats, areas) 639-640
Elections .......884, 885, 894
Lake, largest .........718
Marriage, divorce laws 760, 761
Museums, attractions 362, 406
Name, origin of .......383
Officials, pay ......919, 920
Population .........593-654
  –Cities and towns ..604, 614
  –Counties, county seats 639-640
  –Metropolitan areas ..652-654
Presidential vote ....884, 894
Slavery issue (1856) ...303
Taxes ............209-218
Territory .............384
Vital statistics ....757-768
**Kansas City, Mo.** ........406
Buildings, tall .......446
City manager .........925
Museums, attractions ..407
Population ....604, 614, 653
**Kansas-Nebraska Act** (1854) 303
**Karelo-Finnish SSR** ......554
**Kashmir** ...............520
**Kazakh SSR** ............554
**Kefauver crime report** (1951) 315
**Kekkonen, Urho** .....512, 576
**Kelantan, Malaysia** ......533

**Keller, Helen** ........... 82
Birthplace ............354
**Kelly, Grace** (Monaco) ....536
**Kennedy Airport, N. Y.** ..246
**Kennedy, Edward M.** ........86
Eulogy, brother's .... 45
**Kennedy, Jacqueline** *see*
  *Onassis, Mrs. Aristotle*
**Kennedy, John F.** (biog.) ..194
Assassination .......318, 662
Cabinet ..........179-182
Cuba ................317
President ............194
Tomb at Arlington ..194, 441
**Kennedy, Robert F.—**
Assassination ........ 80
Eulogy ............... 45
Presidential campaign ...82
**Kennel clubs, shows** .......877
**Kentucky** ..............362
*See States, U. S.*
Admission, area, cap. 362, 384
Agriculture ..769-771, 773, 776
Birth, death statistics 758, 765
Counties (seats, areas) ...640
Elections .......884, 885, 895
Lake, largest .........718
Lincoln memorial .....363
Louisville (*see Louisville*) 409
Mammoth Cave ........363
Marriage, divorce laws 760, 761
Museums, attractions 363, 409
Name, origin of .......383
Officials, pay ......919, 920
Population .........593-654
  –Cities and towns ..604, 614
  –Counties, county seats ..640
  –Metropolitan areas ..652-654
Presidential vote ...884, 895
Taxes ............209-218
Vital statistics ....757-768
**Kentucky Dam** ...........363
**Kentucky Derby** .........817
**Kenya** (Br. East Africa) 529, 576
**Kermadec Island, N. Z.** ....538
**Kerosene production** .......130
**Key, Francis Scott** ....171, 301
**Khan, Ayub** .........541, 577
**Khrushchev, Nikita S.** .....555
**Kidd, Capt. William** (1696) .299
**Kidnapings, major** ........661
**Kiev, Dukes of** ..........692
**Kilowatt hours** ..........586
**Kingman Reef** ...........382
**King, Dr. Martin Luther—**
  47, 63, 74, 78, 662
**Kings** .............576-577
Form of address .......351
**Kings Canyon Natl. Park** ..388
**Kirghiz SSR** ............554
**Kirkal, India** ...........520
**Kiska Island** (Pacific) ....722
**Kitt, Eartha** ........... 69
**Kling, Florence** (Harding)
  183, 192
**Knickerbocker disaster**
  (1922) ..............310
**Knot** (nautical) .........587
**Knoxville, Tenn.** ........407
Mayor ................925
Population ....604, 630, 653
**Koala** (animal) ..........494
**Koch, Ilse** (sentenced, 1951) 315
**Koch, Robert** (1882) ......306
**Kodiak Island** (Pacific) ...722
**Korea People's Democratic Rep.**
  67, 69, 71, 74, 78, 530, 576
**Korea, Republic of** .......529
Area, capital, population ..529
Cities (population) ....579
Merchant fleet .......101
Occupation (Russo–U. S.) .530
President .............576
Republic established ..530
Rhee, Syngman ........530
Trade ...........98, 529
Vance, Cyrus .......... 70
U. S. forces (1945) ....313
**Korean war** .............315
Armistice ............315
Casualties, U. S. force ...751
MacArthur, Gen. .......315
Veterans G. I. Bill ....753
**Kortwright, Elizabeth**
  (Monroe) ........183, 186
**Kosygin, A.** ............. 68
**Krakatau, volcano** .......716
**Ku Klux Klan** (1866) ......303
**Kuomintang** (China) ......502
**Kuril Islands** ...........527
**Kuwait** ............530, 576

**Kwantung, China** .........504
**Kyushu Island, Japan** ..527, 722

**— L —**

**Labor—**
Employment ...........143
Farm .............143, 776
Haymarket riot (1886) ..306
Occupation groups ....143
Required to buy .......142
Strikes *see Strikes*
Unemployment statistics
  (source) ............153
Union memberships ....245
Women ................143
Workers, by occupation .143
**Labor Day** ..............590
**Labor, Department of—**
Administrative personnel ..166
Employees (number) ...145
Established ...........182
Expenditures .........131
Secretaries ......166, 182
**Labor Unions—**
Memberships ..........245
**Lacrosse records** ........853
**Lafayette, Marquis de** ..302, 696
**Lakes—**
Crater, Oregon ........373
Deepest, U. S. (Ore.) ..373
Gatun (Canal Zone) ....381
Great Lakes
  –Area, depth .........376
  –St. Lawrence Seaway .. 97
Gr. Salt Lake, Utah ..376, 718
Highest in U. S. (Hawaii)
  94, 360
Largest .........717, 718
Managua, Nicaragua ...539
Okeechobee, Fla. ...359, 718
Ports, cargo volume ...105
Reelfoot, Tenn. .......375
Reservoirs ........728-729
St. Clair .............717
Titicaca, Bolivia (highest) 497
U. S., by states (largest) .718
World (notable) .......717
**Lama, Dalai** ............504
**Lama, Panchen** ..........504
**Lamb Production** .........772
Nutritive value .......774
Prices, farm .........770
**Lancaster, House of** ......688
**Land, Public** ............386
Federal owned ........386
**Language, English** .......332
Language societies ....341
**Languages of the world** ...350
**Laos** ..................530
Area, capital, population .530
Cities (population) ....579
Independence (1949) ...531
Souvanna Phouma, Prem. .576
**Lard, produced, consumed** ..772
**La Salle, explorer** (1682) ..299
**Las Vegas, Nevada** .......368
**Lassen Volcanic Park** .....388
**Late News** ............. 63
**Lateran Agreement** .......564
**Latitude, Longitude—**
Cities, U. S. ......737-738
Definitions ..........260
Length of one degree ...260
**Latter-day Saints churches**
Headquarters .........220
History, organiz. .....224
Membership .......221, 224
Utah .................376
**Latvian SSR** ............554
**Lawn bowling** ...........835
**Laws and Documents** ..196-208
**Lazarus, Emma** (poem) .... 93
**Lead Production** ....127, 129
**Leaders, Economic, American** 670
**League of Nations—**
Disbanded (1946) .....314
Established (1920) ....310
Germany (1926, '33) ...310
Italy (1935, '37) ....311
**Leakey, Dr. Louis S. B.** ...714
**Leap years** .............281
**Lebanon** ...............531
Area, capital, population 531
Cities (population) ....579
President ............576
Trade ................ 98
**Lee, Alice** (Roosevelt) ..183, 191
**Lee, Robert E.—**
Birthday (legal holiday) .590
Birthplace, grave, Va. ..377
Civil War ............304
Mansion, Arlington ...441
**Leeward Islands** ........561

Legal holidays .........590-591
 Federal Law ............... 42
Legislation, U. S.—*See Congress,*
 *U. S. and Constitution U. S.*
Legislature, State ......919-923
 New York State ........... 922
Lemnitzer, Gen. L. ........ 739
L'Enfant, Pierre C. (D.C.) . 380
Lenin, Vladimir Ilyich
 (Nikolai) ..........555, 692
Lent ..............226, 232
Leoni, Dr. Raul, Pres. ..... 577
Leopold, King ............ 661
Lesotho (Basutoland) ..531, 576
Lewis and Clark Explor. .... 708
Lewis, John L. (1946) ...... 314
Lexington, Ky. ............ 363
Leyte Gulf battle .......... 313
Leyte Island, Philippines .. 722
Liberal Party of New York . 173
Liberia .................. 531
 Area, capital, population 531
 Merchant fleet ........... 101
 Monrovia (population) ... 579
 President ............532, 576
 Trade .................... 98
Liberty Bell .............. 198
Liberty Island ............ 93
Liberty, Statue of ........ 93
Libraries ................ 348
 Academic ............... 348
 Air Force, U. S. ......... 349
Library of Congress ....... 441
Libya ................... 532
 Area, capital, population 532
 Cities (population) ...... 579
 King ...............532, 576
 U. S. air bases .......... 532
Lick observatory ......... 257
Liechtenstein .....532, 577, 579
Life expectancy, aver. U. S. 763
 Trend by years .......... 763
Life Insurance—
 Income tax, Federal ..... 209
 Purchases ............... 765
Life, start of ............ 714
Light, speed of ........... 281
Lincoln, Abraham (biog.) .. 188
 Birthday (legal holiday) . 590
 Birthplace (Ky.) ...363, 389
 Death ..........188, 305, 662
 Dred Scott decision ..... 303
 Elected 1860 ............ 303
 Emancipation proc. (1863) 305
 Ford's Theater .......... 389
 Gettysburg Address ..... 206
 Indiana memorial ....... 361
 Kentucky memorials ..... 363
 Memorial, Washington 389, 442
 Mt. Rushmore, S. D. 375, 389
 Wife, Mary Todd ....183, 188
Lincoln Center for the
 Performing Arts ....... 438
Lincoln Tunnel (N.Y.C.) ... 727
Lind, Jenny (1850) ....... 303
Lindbergh, Chas. A. ...247, 310
Lindsay, John V. .......... 925
Linear measures .....581, 584
Lipari Islands (Sicily) .... 526
Liquid measures .....581-584
Liquor—
 Drinking age, legal ..... 115
 Excise tax rates ........ 218
 —Duty-free (personal) ... 702
 Production .............. 121
 Prohibition, 1917-33
 205, 309, 311
 Retail sales ............ 126
Liter (measure) .....581-584
Literature—
 Authors, noted .....694-699
 Awards .............234-243
 Best-sellers, 1968 ....... 155
 Holmes, Sherlock (1886) . 306
 Homer's Troy (1184 B.C.) 295
 Walden (1854) .......... 303
 *See Libraries*
Lithuanian SSR ........... 554
Little Brown Jug races .... 816
Little League ............. 807
Livestock *see Agriculture*
Livingstone, David (1871) .. 305
Loans—
 Banks (by state) ........ 136
 Consumer credit ........ 140
 Farm ..............770, 777
 Foreign, by U. S. ........ 580
 Interest rates .......... 147
 Veterans ............... 753
Locarno pact (1926, '36) 310, 311
Logan Airport, Boston .... 393
London, Eng.—
 Area ................... 557
 Plague, 1665, fire, 1666 .. 298
 Plays, long run ......... 157
 Population ......558, 579, 651

London Naval Treaty (1930) 310
Long, Crawford W. (1842) .. 302
Long Island, N. Y. ........ 722
Long Trail, Vt. ........... 377
Longitude *see Latitude*
Longshoremen's Union ..... 245
Lookout Mountain, Tenn. .. 375
Lord Howe Is., Solomons ... 563
Los Angeles, Calif. ....408-409
 Buildings, tall .......... 447
 Mayor .................. 925
 Museums, attractions ... 408
 Population ......604, 607, 653
 Port traffic ............. 99
 Postal receipts .......... 932
 Times dynamited (1910) . 308
Louisiana ................ 363
 *See States, U. S.*
 Acadians ............... 363
 Admission, area, cap. .363, 384
 Agriculture .769-771, 773, 776
 Birth, death statistics 758, 765
 Counties (seat, areas) 640-641
 Elections ............884, 896
 Exposition (1904) ....... 61
 Lake, largest ........... 718
 Mardi Gras ............. 415
 Marriage, divorce laws 760, 761
 Museums, attractions .363, 415
 Name, origin of ........ 383
 New Orleans (*see N. O.*) . 415
 Officials, pay ......919, 920
 Parishes (seats, areas) 640-641
 Population ...........593-654
 —Cities and towns ...604, 615
 —Counties, county seats 640-641
 —Metropolitan areas ..652-654
 Presidential vote .....884, 896
 Taxes ..............209-218
 Territory ...........383, 384
 Vital statistics ......757-768
Louisiana Purchase ...300, 385
Louisville, Ky. ........... 409
 Buildings, tall .......... 447
 Mayor .................. 925
 Museums, attractions ... 409
 Population ......604, 614, 653
Loyalty Is. (New Caledonia) 514
Lumber—
 Mill, largest (Idaho) .... 360
 National forests ........ 778
 Wholesale price index ... 143
Lumumba, Patrice (1961) .. 317
Lunar Calendar .......... 233
Lusitania sunk (1915) ..... 658
Luther, Martin (1517) ..... 297
Lutherans—
 Headquarters .......... 221
 History, organization ... 223
 Membership ......220, 223
Luxembourg ............. 532
 Area, capital, pop. ...... 532
 Duchess abdicates ...... 532
 Head of State .......... 577
 Weights, measures ..... 587
Luzon Isl., Philippines .... 722

—M—

Macao China (Portuguese) ..544
MacArthur, Gen. Douglas—
 Day (holiday) .......... 591
 Japan (1945) ......313, 528
 Korean war ............ 315
 Philippine command .... 313
 Truman recall (1951) .... 315
Macedonia, Yugoslavia .... 566
Machinery (U. S. trade) ... 100
Mackinac Bridge, Mich. 725, 726
Madagascar (Malagasy) 533, 722
Madeira Is. (Portugal) 543, 722
Madison, James (biog.) ... 185
Madison Square Garden ... 438
 Hall of Fame ........... 845
Madura, Indonesia ...522, 722
Magazines—
 Circulation (U. S.) ...... 352
 Mailing rate ........... 927
Magellan (1520) .....297, 708
 Guam, discovers ....... 382
Magna Carta (1215) ...... 296
Magnetic poles of earth ... 261
Mail-order houses (sales) .. 126
Mailing information ...927-932
 Canada ................ 55
Maine ................... 363
 *See States, U. S.*
 Admission, area, cap. 363, 384
 Agriculture .769-771, 773, 776
 Birth, death statistics 758, 765
 Counties (seats, area) ... 641
 Elections ............884, 896
 Lake, largest ........... 718

Maine (cont'd)
 Marriage, divorce laws 760, 761
 Museums, attractions ...364
 Name, origin of ........ 383
 Officials, pay ......919, 921
 Population ...........593-654
 —Cities and towns ...615-616
 —Counties, county seats 641
 —Metropolitan areas ..652-654
 Presidential vote .....884, 896
 Taxes ..............209-218
 Vital statistics ......757-768
Maine, battleship (1898) .. 307
Majorca, Isl. ............. 548
Makarios, Pres. *see Cyprus*
Malacca, Malaya ......... 533
Malagasy Republic ..533, 579
Malaita Is., Solomons ..... 563
Malawi ...........533, 577
Malay Sea (area depth) ... 713
Malaya .................. 533
Malaysia .......90, 533, 577
Malbone St. wreck (1919)
 309, 660
Maldive Islands .......534, 577
Malenkov, Georgi ....555, 692
Mali ...............534, 577
Malta ............534, 577, 722
Mammoth Cave, Ky. ..363, 388
Man, Isle of ..........561, 722
Managua, Lake (Nicaragua) 539
Manchukuo (1932) ....... 310
Manchuria ............... 504
 Flood (1951) ........... 662
 U. S. consul jailed (1949) 314
Manhattan (1624) ...298, 416
Manila, P. I. .....542, 577, 651
Manila Bay—
 Battle of (1898) ........ 307
Manitoba, Canada ....... 485
Manua Islands, Samoa ... 381
Manufactures .........119-126
 Employees, firms (number) 119
 Exports, imports ....... 100
 Index numbers ......... 143
 Profit by industry group . 120
 Workers statistics ...119, 121
 *See Specific Industries*
Maoris (New Zealand) .... 539
Maps .......453-468 or 469-484
Marathon—
 Boston marathon ....... 861
 Olympic record ..878, 881, 883
Marco Polo (1271) ....... 296
Marconi (1896-1901) ..118, 307
Mardi Gras, N. Orleans 415, 590
Margaret, Princess ....... 558
Margarine *see Oleomargarine*
Mariana Islands ......... 382
Marine Corps, U. S. ...742, 746
 China, Nicaragua (1927) . 310
 Drownings (1956) ....... 316
 Generals (active duty) ... 739
 Iceland occupied (1941) . 312
 Insignia ............... 742
 Organization bases ..... 742
 Pay scale, allowances 754-755
 Woman's branch ....... 748
 *See Armed Forces, U. S.*
Marine disasters ......657-660
Marine Life—
 Undersea study of ...... 710
Marine Parkway B'dge, N.Y. 725
Maritime Day, Nat'l. ..... 591
Market price indexes ..... 143
Marquesas Islands (Fr.) 513, 722
Marriage—
 Age, legal, by state ..... 760
 Blood test requirements . 760
 Foreign citizen, to ...... 703
 Number, rate .......... 758
 —New York State ....... 760
 Population statistics ..603, 758
 Records, how to obtain . 350
 Wedding anniversary list 760
Mars (planet) 253-256, 258, 286
 Morning, evening star 253-276
 Positions by months .253-256
 Rising, setting ......... 287
Marshall, Gen. Geo. C. 314, 665
Marshall Islands ......382, 722
Marshall Plan (1947) .... 314
Martha's Vineyard (area) .. 722
Martinique ...........513, 722
 Mt. Pelee ..........513, 716
Martinmas .............. 591
Mary of Scots (1587) ...297, 691
Maryland ................ 364
 *See States, U. S.*
 Admission, area, cap. 364, 384
 Agriculture .769-771, 773, 776
 Baltimore (*see Balt.*) ... 391
 Birth, death statistics 758, 765
 Counties (seats, areas) .. 641
 Elections ........884, 885, 897

**Maryland (cont'd)**
Lake, largest ...........718
Marriage, divorce laws 760, 761
Museums, attractions ......364
Name, origin of .........383
Officials, pay .........919, 921
Population ..........593-654
–Cities and towns .....604, 616
–Counties, county seats .....641
–Metropolitan areas ...652-654
Presidential vote ....884, 897
Taxes ..............209-218
Vital statistics .........757-768
**Masaryk, Thomas G.** ........508
**Mason-Dixon** ...............448
**Mass, unit of** ...........581-584
**Massachusetts** ..............364
*See States, U. S.*
Admission, area, cap. 364, 384
Agriculture . 769-771, 773, 776
Birth, death statistics 758, 765
Boston (*see Boston*) .....393
Counties (seats, areas) .....641
Elections ............884, 897
Harvard U. 323, 338, 345, 364
Lake, largest ............718
Marriage, divorce laws 760, 761
Museums, attractions 365, 393
Name, origin of .........383
Officials, pay .........919, 921
Population ..........593-654
–Cities and towns 604, 616-617
–Counties, county seats .....641
–Metropolitan areas ...652-654
Presidential vote ....884, 897
Taxes ..............209-218
Vital statistics .........757-768
**Masters Bowling Tournament** 850
**Maternal Health Service** ....154
**Mathematical formulas** ....586
**Mathematics—**
Circles, areas of .........586
College fraternities .......341
Division, Multiplication ....586
Formulas ..............586
Fractions, decimals ......586
Multiplication, division ....586
Roots (square, cube) .....585
**Mau Mau** (1953) .......316, 529
**Mauritania, Rep.** .....534, 577
**Mauritius** .........534, 722
**Mausolus, Tomb of** .......721
**May, Alan Nunn** (1952) ....316
**May Day** ................591
**Mayan calendar** (300 B.C.) 295
**Mayas** (731, 1027 A.D.) ....296
**Mayflower** (1620) ..175, 298, 365
**Mayo Foundation** .........366
**Mayors—**
Address, form of .........351
Cities, U. S. .......924-925
New York City .........925
**McCardle, Eliza** ......183, 188
**McCarthy, Eugene—**
37-39, 65, 71, 73, 76, 79, 82
**McGovern, George S.** .. 37, 88
**McIntosh, Caroline C.** ..183, 187
**McKinley, Mt.** 354, 707, 720, 738
**McKinley, Wm.** (biog.)
190, 307, 662
**McNamara, Robert** ........70
**Mead Lake** .............718
**Mean time** ........260, 280
**Measures** ...........581-584
Nautical mile .........587
**Meats—**
Exports, imports ........100
Nutritive values ........774
Price indexes ..........770
Production, consumption 772
**Mecklenburg Decl.** (1775) ..298
**Medal of Honor** ......64, 740
**Medals, prizes** *see Awards*
**Medicare** ..............148
**Medicine** ..............59-60
*See Assns.*
Anesthesia (1842) .......302
Armed forces
–Women's Military ..747-748
Awards .............234-235
College societies ........341
Colleges ...........319-342
Developments, 1968 ....59-60
Diseases (deaths, rates) 759
Drugs ..............59-60
Heart transplants ....66, 59
Hospital statistics .......764
Mayo Assn. ...........366
Research .............59-60
Rockefeller Institute ....329
Sabin vaccine .........116
Salk vaccine (1955) .....116

**Medicine (cont'd)**
Schools of Medicine ..319-346
Signs, abbreviations ......60
Tuberculosis (1882) ......306
Vaccination (1796) .......300
Veterans benefits .......753
**Mediterranean Sea—**
Area, depth ...........713
Islands, areas .........722
**Mein, John G.** .........87
**Mellon art collection** ....443
**Melville Island** (Canadian) 722
**Memorable dates** ....295-318
**Memorial Day** ....176, 304, 590
Confederate .........590
**Memorials, National** .....389
Amer. military overseas ..749
Cemeteries ..........749
**Memphis, Tenn.** .........409
Buildings, tall .........447
Mayor ...............925
Museums, attractions ....410
Population .....604, 630, 653
**Men—**
Births, deaths (U. S.) ....758
Height, weight .........763
per 100 women .........603
**Mennonite churches** ..220, 222
**Mental hospitals** .........764
**Merchant Marine—**
Fleets, by country .......101
Ships, notable ......95-96
W. W. II Casualties 751, 752
**Merchant Marine Acad.** 331, 746
**Mercury** (planet)
253-256, 258, 286
Morning, evening star 263-276
Positions by months ..253-256
**Mercury projects**
*See Space Developments*
**Merovingians** ...........689
**Merrimac, Monitor** ...304, 657
**Mesa Verde National Park** ..388
**Mesopotamia** *see Iraq*
**Mesozoic era** ...........721
**Metals—**
Exports, imports ........100
Price index (wholesale) ..143
Production ........127-128
**Meteors** .........253-256, 262
Bombardment .........262
Chubb crater, Canada ...262
Crater, Ariz. .........262
Paragould, Ark. ........262
**Methodist Churches—**
Bishops ...............226
–Address, form of .......351
Headquarters ......220, 222
History, organization 223-224
Membership ......220, 222
**Metric weights, measures** 581-589
**Metropolitan areas** ....652-654
**Metropolitan Mus. of Art** ..437
Cloisters, The .........437
**Metropolitan Opera** ....157, 438
**Mexican War** (1846) ......302
Casualties ...........751
Guadelupe-Hidalgo Treaty 385
Military leaders, U. S. ...655
**Mexico** .................535
Area, capital, population .535
Cession to U. S. ....383, 385
Cities (population) .......379
Cortes conquers (1519) ..297
Gold production .......140
Gold reserve .........139
Hydroelectric power .....535
Juanacatlan waterfall ...719
Maximilian executed (1867)
303, 535
Merchant fleet .........101
Mexico City ...........410
Mountain peaks .......720
Petroleum production ...130
Ports, mileage ....103-104
President .............577
Revolts (1911) .........308
Student riots ..........91
Sugar production .......122
Trade ...............535
University seized ........90
Volcanoes ...........716
Weights, measures .....587
**Mexico City, Mexico** ......410
Olympics, 1968 ....878-883
**Mexico, Gulf of** .........713
**Miami, Fla.** .............411
Buildings, tall .........447
City manager .........925
Mileage to other cities ..110
Museums, attractions ....411
Population .....604, 609, 653

**Michael of Romania** (1947) 544
**Michaelmas** ..............591
**Michigan** ...............365
*See States, U. S.*
Admission, area, cap. 365, 384
Agriculture .769-771, 773, 776
Birth, death statistics 758, 765
Counties (seats, areas) ...641
Detroit (*see Detroit*) .....401
Elections ........884, 885, 897
Isle Royale ...........388
Lake, largest ..........718
Mackinac Bridge 365, 725, 726
Marriage, divorce laws 760, 761
Museums, attractions 365, 402
Name, origin of .........383
Officials, pay .........919, 921
Population ..........593-654
–Cities and towns 604, 617-618
–Counties, county seats ...641
–Metropolitan areas ...652-654
Presidential vote ....884, 897
Taxes ..............209-218
Territory ..........365, 384
Vital statistics .........757-768
**Michigan Lake** .......717, 718
**Micron** (defined) .........584
**Midnight sun** (Norway) ....540
**Midway Islands** ..........381
**Mikhailovitch, Gen.** (1946) ..314
**Milan, Edict of** (313 A.D.) ..296
**Mileage—**
Between cities
–Airline ..........251-252
–Automobile touring ..110-111
Between ports .......103-105
Roads, rural (U. S.) ......112
**Miles, measurement** ....581, 584
**Military Acad'y U. S.** ...744-746
**Military action, U. S.** ......751
**Military cemeteries** .......749
**Military Commanders** ......739
**Military insignia, U. S.** 741, 742
**Military leaders** .....665-699
**Military parks, National** ....388
**Military Pay Scales** ...754-755
**Military Salute** .......739, 746
**Military time** ...........280
**Military Training Centers** ..742
**Milk—**
Consumption .........776
Nutritive value .........774
**Milwaukee, Wis.** .........412
Buildings, tall .........447
Mayor ...............925
Museums, attractions ....412
Population .....604, 634, 653
**Mindanao, Philippines** .542, 722
**Mindoro, Philippines** ......722
**Mindszenty, Cardinal** (1948) 314
**Mineral production** ....127-128
Distillate oil ..........130
Index numbers .......143
Residual oil ..........130
States, ranking .......128
Value .............127, 128
**Mining—**
Disasters, U. S. .......664
Employees ...........124
Gold, U. S. ..........140
**Ministers, ambassadors** 170-171
Form of address .......351
**Minneapolis, Minn.** ...412-413
Buildings, tall .........447
Mayor ...............925
Museums, attractions ....412
Population .....604, 619, 653
**Minnesota** ...............365
*See States, U. S.*
Admission, area, cap. 365, 384
Agriculture 769, 771, 773, 776
Birth, death statistics 758, 765
Counties (seats, areas) 641-642
Elections ........884, 885, 898
Lake, largest ..........718
Marriage, divorce laws 760, 761
Minneapolis (*see Mpls.*) ..412
Museums, attractions
366, 412, 427
Name, origin of .........383
Officials, pay .........919, 921
Population ..........593-654
–Cities and towns 604, 618-619
–Counties, county seats 641-642
–Metropolitan areas ...652-654
Presidential vote ....884, 898
St. Paul (*see St. Paul*) .....426
Taxes ..............209-218
Territory ..........366, 384
Vital statistics .........757-768
**Minor League Player**
**of Year** ...............808

Minorca Isl. (Spain) .......548
Mint, Bureau of the ........144
Minuit, Peter (1626) ...298, 415
Miquelon Island (Fr.) .......513
Miss America Pageant ......244
Miss Black America ........ 61
Miss United States ........ 61
Miss Universe Pageant .... 61
Missiles, rockets—
  Goddard, Robert H. ..118, 310
  Moon shots, USSR ........317
  USSR, ICBM (1957) .......317
  *See Space Developments*
Mission, UN ............... 48
Mississippi ................366
  *See States, U. S.*
  Admission, area, cap. 366, 384
  Agriculture .769, 771, 773, 776
  Birth, death statistics 758, 765
  Counties (seats, areas) ....642
  Elections ......884, 885, 899
  Lake, largest .............718
  Marriage, divorce laws 760, 761
  Museums, Attractions
  Name, origin of ..........383
  Officials, pay ............921
  Population ............593-654
  –Cities and towns ...604, 619
  –Counties, county seat ...642
  –Metropolitan areas ..652-654
  Presidential vote ....884, 899
  Taxes .................209-218
  Territory ................384
  Vital statistics ......757-768
Mississippi Bubble (1720) ..299
Mississippi River ..........723
  Bridges ..................725
  Discovered (1541) ...297, 708
  First steamboat (1823) ...302
  Floods ...................662
  Tides at New Orleans .....294
Missouri ...................366
  *See States, U. S.*
  Admission, area, cap. 366, 384
  Agriculture .769-771, 773, 776
  Birth, death statistics 758, 765
  Counties (seats, areas) 642-643
  Elections ........884, 885, 900
  Great cities .......407, 426
  Kansas City (*see Kansas*
    *City*) ................406
  Lake, largest .............718
  Marriage, divorce laws 760, 761
  Museums, attractions
        367, 407, 426
  Name, origin of ..........383
  Officials, pay .........919, 921
  Population ............593-654
  –Cities and towns 604, 619-620
  –Counties, county seats 642-643
  –Metropolitan areas ..652-654
  Presidential vote ....884, 900
  St. Louis (*see St. Louis*) ..425
  Taxes .................209-218
  Territory .............367, 384
  Vital statistics ......757-768
Missouri Compromise (1820)
          302, 387
Missouri River .......723, 728
  Bridges spanning .........726
  Dams, reservoirs ....728, 733
Missouri, University of ....326
Mitre Is., Solomons .......563
Mobile economy run ........113
Mobile, Ala. ...............354
Mobile homes ..............114
Modern Art Mus., N. Y. ....437
Mohammed (570 A.D.) .296, 545
Mohammedan Calendar ......226
Mohammedan population ....224
Moldavian SSR .............554
Molly Maguires (1877) .....306
Moluccas, Indonesia ....522, 722
Monaco .............535, 577
Monetary Fund, Intl. ..572  574
Monetary units, foreign *see*
  *specific countries*
Money *see* Currency
Money order fees ..........928
Mongolia, Inner ...........504
Mongolia, Outer ...........536
Monitor, Merrimac ....304, 657
Mono Is., Solomons ........563
Monroe Doctrine (1823) 302, 568
Monroe, James (biog.) .....185
  Law office ...............377
Monsoon, description ......289
Montana ...................367
  *See States, U. S.*
  Admission, area, cap. 367, 384
  Agriculture .769-771, 773, 776
  Birth, death, statistics 758, 765
  Counties (seats, areas) ...643
  Elections ........884, 885, 900

Montana (cont'd)
  Lake, largest .............718
  Marriage, divorce laws 760, 761
  Museums, attractions .....367
  Name, origin of ..........383
  Officials, pay ......919, 921
  Population ............593-654
  –Cities and towns ...604, 620
  –Counties, county seats ..643
  –Metropolitan areas ..652-654
  Presidential vote ....884, 900
  Taxes .................209-218
  Territory ................384
  Vital statistics ......757-768
Monte Carlo (Monaco) ......535
Montenegro, Yugoslavia ....566
Montgomery, Ala. ..........354
  Mayor ....................925
  Population ....604, 605, 653
Montreal, Canada ..........413
  Expo 67 ..................413
  French-Indian War (1754) 299
  Museums, attractions .....413
  Population ..........487, 578
Montserrat Is. (W. Indies) 561
Monuments, national .......389
  Largest, U. S. ............ 94
Moon, The—
  Apogee, perigee ..........283
  Apollo exploration .......262
  Descriptive ..............282
  Diameter .................282
  Eartn, distance from .....282
  Eclipses (1969) ..........261
  Harvest, Hunter's ........793
  Paschal (dates) ..........232
  Phases ... 253-256, 263-276, 283
  Photographs ..............262
  Rises, sets ..........263-276
  Signs and symbols ........256
  Tides, effects on ...282, 294
Moon rockets *see*
  *Space Developments*
Moravian Churches ...220, 222
Morgan Library, N. Y. C. ..437
Mormons *see* Latter-day Saints
Morning stars ......256, 263-276
Morocco ...................536
  Area, capital, population .536
  Cities (population) .......579
  Ifni ................536, 548
  King Hassan II ...........577
  Merchant fleet ...........101
  Tangier ..................536
  Trade ..............98, 536
  Weights, measures ........587
Morristown Historical Park 388
Morse, Samuel F. B. (1884) 302
Mortgages, farm ......770, 777
Morton, Wm. T. G. (1842) ..302
Moses (1450 B.C.) .........297
Moslem (Islamic) Calendar .226
Moslem, population ........224
Mossadegh, Mohammed .....523
Mother's Day ..............591
Motion Pictures—
  Academy awards ..........240
  All-talking (1928) .......310
  Jazz Singer (1927) .......310
  Museum of Modern art .....437
  Principal, 1968 ......159-160
  Sound-on-film, first (1923) 310
  Stars, producers .....677-685
  –Deceased ............673-676
Motor Vehicles, *see* Automobiles
Motto, U. S. Natl. ........195
Mottoes of states .....354-379
Mount Desert Island (Me.) .363
Mount McKinley Natl. Park .388
Mount Rainier Natl. Park ..388
Mount Vernon (Va.) .......377
Mountain Meadows (1857) ..303
Mountaineering ............707
Mountains—
  Andes ....493, 501, 510, 542
  Cascade, Wash. ...........378
  Climbing expeditions .....707
  Etna, Italy ........526, 715
  Everest .......537, 707, 720
  Green, Vermont ...........376
  Highest, by Continents ...720
  Highest, by Countries 720-721
  Highest, U. S. ......720, 738
  Himalayas ...........720, 721
  McKinley, Alaska 354, 720, 738
  Peaks, by country ....720-721
  Rainier, Wash. ..378, 388, 738
  Rushmore, S. D. ...375, 389
  Teton, Wyo. ..............379
  U. S., by states .........738
  Vesuvius, Italy (79 A.D.)
          295, 716
  Volcanoes ...........715-716
  White, N. H. .............368

Mozambique (Portuguese)... 544
Mules (on farms) ..........780
Multiplication table ......586
Munich pact (1938) ........311
Murders *see* Crime
Muscat and Oman .....537, 577
Muscovy Grand Dukes .....692
Museums, attractions *see*
  *specific states and cities*
Music and Musicians—
  Awards ............239, 242
  Composers, works
     671, 685-687, 697-699
  Musicians, singers
     677-685, 698-699
  Opera and artists ...156-158
  Pulitzer Prizes ..........239
  Recordings ...............160
  Symphony orchestras .....161
  Violinists ...............685
Muskie, Edmund .....37, 38, 90
Mussolini, Benito .313, 527, 691
Mutiny on Bounty (1789) ...300
Mystic Seaport, Conn. .....358

      — N —

NAACP *see* Assns.
NAIA Championships ........876
NASCAR ....................814
NATO *see* North Atlantic
  *Treaty Organization*
N.C.A.A. Meets (1968)—
  Basketball ...............823
  –Scoring leaders .........823
  Fencing ..................825
  Track and field (indoor) .860
  Ski ......................849
Nagaland (India) ..........521
Nagasaki atomic bomb (1945) 313
Naguib, Mohammed ..........557
Nantes, Edict of (1598) ...297
Nantucket Island (area) ...722
Napoleon I, III *see* Bonaparte
Narcotics ................. 60
Nashville, Tenn. ..........414
  Buildings, tall ..........447
  Mayor ....................925
  Population .........630, 653
Nassau, Bahamas ...........561
Nasser, Gamal Abdel
     72, 85, 557, 577
Natal, Rep. of South Africa 546
Natchez Trace .............388
Nation, Carry (1900) ......307
National Aeronautics and Space
  Admin. (NASA) *see* Space
  *developments*
National Air Museum ......444
National Anthem ...........171
National Archives .........442
National Baseball Hall of
  Fame .....................806
National battlefield parks ...388
National Book Awards ......241
National capital parks ....388
National Capitol, U. S. ...439
National cemeteries ...441, 749
National Committees ...172-173
Natl. Council, Churches of
  Christ, U. S. A. .........232
National debt *see* Public debt
National defense *see* Defense
National Football League ..862
National forests ..........778
National Gallery of Art ...442
Nat'l Geographic Society ..443
National Guard, U. S. .....743
  Pay scale allowances ..754-755
National historic sites ...389
National historical parks .388
National Income .......131-134
National memorials ........389
National Military Establish-
  ment *see* Defense Dept.
National military parks ...388
National monuments ...489, 444
National Motto, U. S. .....195
National parks, parkways ..388
National Pro. Soccer League 828
National Rifle Assn. *see* Assns.
National salute ...........746
National Science Fdn. .....355
National Spelling Bee .....350
National Statuary Hall ....439
National Trails and Wild
  Rivers ................... 94
Nationalization (industries) *see*
  *Industries, nationalization*
Nations of the World *see*
  *specific nations*
  Wealth ...................567

Natural gas production.....130
Natural History, Museum of 437
Naturalists, noted American 670
Naturalization .................702
Nauru Island (Australia) ...537
Nautical Measures ..........587
Nautilus see Submarines
Naval Academy, U. S.
                    331, 744-745
Naval Treaties (1921) .....310
  London (1930) ..........310
Naval war losses ......657-660
Navassa Is., Caribbean ....381
Navigable Distances ...102-105
Navigation aids, Coast Guard 750
Navy Department—
  Administrative personnel .165
  Employees (number) .....145
  Expenditures .............742
  History .................180
  Secretaries ....165, 180, 182
Navy, U. S.—
  Admirals (active duty) ...739
  Annapolis ..........744-745
  Atomic submarines
    see Submarines
  Commandants ............165
  Expenditures .............742
  Insignia ................742
  Nurse Corps .........747-748
  Officers (form of address) 351
  Pay Scale, allowances 754-755
  Pueblo, U.S.S. .....67, 69, 71
  Satellites see Space
    developments
  Scorpion loss ...........78
  Ship losses .........657-660
  Strength ................742
  Women's branches ...747-748
  See Armed forces, U. S.
Nebraska ...................367
  See States, U. S.
  Admission, area, cap. 367, 384
  Agriculture ..769-771, 773, 776
  Birth, death statistics 758, 765
  Counties (seats, areas) 643-644
  Elections ..........884, 901
  Lake, largest ...........718
  Marriage, divorce laws 760, 761
  Museums, attractions .....368
  Name, origin of .........383
  Officials, pay ......919, 921
  Omaha .................368
  Population .........593-654
  –Cities and towns .....604, 620
  –Counties, county seats 643-644
  –Metropolitan areas ..652-654
  Presidential vote ....884, 901
  Taxes ...............209-218
  Territory .........368, 384
  Vital statistics ......757-768
Necrology (1968) ....56-58, 64
Negri Sembilan (Malaya) ...533
Negroes—
  American history ......46-47
  Apartheid, South Africa ..547
  Desegregation see
    Desegregation
  Equal right (law) ........204
  Miss Black America .....61
  Population, U. S. ....597, 604
  See Civil Rights
Negros Island, P.I. .........722
Nehru, Jawaharlal .........521
Neil Memorial Trophy ......844
Nejd, Saudi-Arabia ........545
Nelson, Lord (1805) ...301, 695
Nepal .....................537
  Area, capital, population .537
  Head of State ..........577
  Himalayas ..............707
  Katmandu (population) .579
Neptune (planet) ...253, 286
Netherland, New (1624) 298, 415
Netherlands ..........537-538
  Area, capital, population 537
  Cities (population) ......579
  Dependencies ...........538
  Gold reserve ...........139
  Head of State .......538, 577
  Indonesia independence ..522
  Merchant fleet ..........101
  Painters, noted ........699
  Petroleum production ...130
  Sugar production .......122
  Trade ..............98, 538
  Weights, measures ......587
Netherlands Antilles ......538
Netherlands Guiana
    (Surinam) ............538
Nevada ....................368
  See States, U. S.
  Admission, area, cap. 368, 384
  Agriculture ..769-771, 773, 776
  Birth, death statistics 758, 765

Nevada (cont'd)
  Counties (seats, areas) ...644
  Elections ........884, 885, 902
  Lake, largest ............718
  Lake Mead ..............368
  Las Vegas ...............368
  Marriage, divorce laws 760, 761
  Museum, attractions .....368
  Name, origin of .........383
  Officials, pay ......919, 921
  Population ........593-654
  –Cities and towns .....604, 620
  –Counties, county seats ..644
  –Metropolitan areas ..652-654
  Presidential vote ....884, 902
  Taxes ...............209-218
  Territory .........368, 384
  Vital statistics ......757-768
Nevis Island (W. Indies) ...561
New Amsterdam (1664) 298, 415
New Britain Island .. 495, 722
New Brunswick, Canada ...485
New Caledonia Is. (Fr.) 514, 722
New Georgia Is. Solomons ..563
New Guinea, Island .......722
New Guinea-Papua .......495
New Hampshire ...........368
  See States, U. S.
  Admission, area, cap. 368, 384
  Agriculture ..769-771, 773, 776
  Birth, death statistics 758, 765
  Counties (seats, areas) ...644
  Elections ........884, 885, 902
  Lake, largest ............718
  Marriage, divorce laws 760, 761
  Museums, attractions .....369
  Name, origin of .........383
  Officials, pay ......919, 921
  Population ........593-654
  –Cities and towns .....604, 621
  –Counties, county seats ..644
  –Metropolitan areas ..652-654
  Presidential vote ....884, 902
  Taxes ...............209-218
  Vital statistics ......757-768
New Hebrides ....514, 563, 722
New Ireland Island ..495, 722
New Jersey .................369
  See States, U. S.
  Admission, area, cap. 369, 384
  Agriculture ..769-771, 773, 776
  Birth, death statistics 758, 765
  Bridges ............725-726
  Counties (seats, areas) ...644
  Elections ...........884, 902
  Lake, largest ............718
  Marriage, divorce laws 760, 761
  Museums, attractions .....369
  Name, origin of .........383
  Officials, pay ......919, 921
  Population ........593-654
  –Cities and towns 604, 621-622
  –Counties, county seats ..644
  –Metropolitan areas ..652-654
  Presidential vote ....884, 902
  Taxes ...............209-218
  Vital statistics ......757-768
New Mexico ...........369-370
  See States, U. S.
  Admission, area, cap. 369, 384
  Agriculture ..769-771, 773, 776
  Birth, death statistics 758, 765
  Carlsbad Caverns .......370
  Counties (seats, areas) ...644
  Elections ........884, 885, 903
  Lake, largest ............718
  Marriage, divorce laws 760, 761
  Museums, attractions .....370
  Name, origin of .........383
  Officials, pay ......919, 921
  Population ........593-654
  –Cities and towns .....604, 622
  –Counties, county seats ..644
  –Metropolitan areas ..652-654
  Presidential vote ....884, 903
  Taxes ...............209-218
  Territory .......370, 383, 384
  Vital statistics ......757-768
New Orleans, La. .........414
  Buildings, tall .........447
  Mardi Gras .......363, 415
  Mayor .................925
  Museums, attractions ...415
  Population ....604, 615, 653
New South Wales .........494
New Year, Jewish (dates) ..233
New Year's Day ..........590
New York City ...415, 436-438
  Avenue numbers .........62
  Bridges, tunnels ....725-727
  Buildings, tall .........445
  Centers of interest ..436-438
  Churches ...........437-438
  City Hall ..............438
  Distances, foreign ports ..103

New York City (cont'd)
  Dutch surrender (1664) ...298
  Latitude, longitude .....737
  Mileage to
  –Cities, U. S. ..........110
  –Foreign ports .........103
  Museums, attractions 436-438
  Police Dept. ...........767
  Population
  –Boroughs .........416, 623
  –City ....604, 623, 651, 653
  –Consolidated areas .....654
  –Growth, rank ....604, 652
  –Jewish ...............602
  –Metropolitan area .....653
  Ports
  –Distances, foreign .....103
  –Traffic ...............96
  Postal receipts .........932
  Precipitation .......290-292
  Presidential vote .......903
  Snowfall ..............290
  Statue of Liberty .......93
  Sun rises, sets .....263-276
  Teachers strike .....63, 92
  Temperature .......290-292
  Theater strike .........82
  Theaters, plays ........156
  Tide tables (1968) ...786-790
  Time differences .......281
  United Nations Hq. .....438
  Verrazano (1524) .297, 725-726
  Wall St. explosion (1920)
                    310, 661
  Winds, extreme .........289
  Zoo ...................778
New York Historical Soc. ..437
New York State .......370-371
  See States, U. S.
  Admission, area, cap. 370, 384
  Agriculture ..769-771, 773, 776
  Birth, death statistics 758, 765
  Buffalo (see Buffalo) ....394
  Counties (seats, areas) ...644
  Elections ...82, 884, 885, 903
  Great Cities 394, 424, 432, 436
  Income, per capita .....138
  Lake, largest ............718
  Marriage, divorce laws 760, 761
  Museums, attractions
                371, 394, 424, 433
  Name, origin of .........383
  New York City (see NYC) 415
  Niagara Falls ..........719
  Officials, pay ......919, 922
  Population ........593-654
  –Cities and towns 604, 622-624
  –Counties, county seats ..644
  –Metropolitan areas ..652-654
  Presidential vote ...884, 903
  Rochester (see Rochester) 424
  Syracuse (see Syracuse) 432
  Taxes ...............209-218
  Vital statistics ......757-768
New York Stock Exchange ..438
  Sales record ...........76
  –Stock, dividends, yields 51-54
  –Stocks, prices, symbols 51-54
  –Transactions ..........139
  –Volume, daily .........50
  –Widely-held stocks ....50
New York University .......327
New Zealand ..............538
  Area, capital, population 538
  Cities (population) ......579
  Gold Reserve ...........139
  Gov. General ...........577
  Merchant fleet ..........101
  Mountain peaks .........721
  Petroleum production ...130
  Trade ..............98, 539
  Volcanoes ..............715
  Waterfalls .............719
Newark, N. J.—
  Airport, terminals ......369
  Buildings, tall .........447
  Mayor .................925
  Museums, attractions ...369
  Population 604, 622, 654, 655
  Truck Terminal .........369
Newark riot report ........71
Newfoundland ............485
Newport, R. I. ......374, 629
Newspapers—
  Boston News Letter (1704) 299
  Circulation .............353
  Daily, first (1784) ......300
  Journalism awards 236-238, 241
  Journalists, noted ......666
  Mailing rate ...........927
  Number in U. S. .......353
  Penn. Gazette (1728) ....299
  Pulitzer Prize winners 236-238
  See Journalism and
    Freedom of the press

News, Late ............... 63
Niagara Falls .......... 719, 738
Niagara power ............... 738
Nicaea, Council of (325 AD) 296
Nicaragua ...............539
　Area, capital, population . . 539
　Gold production ...........140
　Merchant fleet ...........101
　President ...........539, 577
　U. S. Marines in (1927) . .310
　Volcanoes ...............716
　Weights, measures ......587
Nicknames—
　College teams ........869-875
　State .........354-379, 387
Niger Republic, Africa .539, 577
Nigeria ....68, 78, 84, 88, 89
Nigeria, Africa ......539, 577
Nightingale, Florence (1853) 303
Nile River ...........61, 548
Nitrate production (Chile) .501
Niue Island, N. Z. ........538
Nixon, Richard .........36-38
　Assassination plot ........63
　Biography ...............38
　Convention ...............37
　Election statistics . .36, 884-914
　Platform, 1968 ...........39
Nixon, Richard M.
　Presidential campaign,
　　(1968) .....37-38, 71, 73,
　　　　76, 79, 90, 92
　Vice President (1953) ....178
Nkrumah, Kwame ......516
Nobel Prizes .....64, 234-235
NORAD ...............71
Nordic Council 512, 520, 540, 550
Nordaust Landet Is. (Arctic) 722
Norfolk, Va. ...............416
　City manager ...........925
　Museums, attractions ....417
　Population .........633, 653
Norfolk Island, Australia . .495
Normandie, ship (1942) . . .659
Normandy, House of ......688
Norris Dam, Tenn. . .375, 732
North America—
　Area, dimensions . .651, 736
　Explorations . .296, 297, 708
　Geographic center ........94
　Lakes, notable ......717, 718
　Mountain peaks ..........720
　Petroleum production . . . .130
　Population ...............651
　–Religious ...............224
　Sugar production .........122
　Telephone statistics ......123
　Trade ...................98
　Waterfalls ...............719
North Atlantic Treaty Org. .573
　Iceland base ...........520
　International commands . .165
　Similar organizations ....573
　Treaty (1949) .......314, 573
　United Kingdom ..........79
North Borneo (Sabah) ....533
North Carolina ...........371
　*See States, U. S.*
　Admission, area, cap. 371, 384
　Agriculture . .769-771, 773, 776
　Birth, death statistics 758, 765
　Counties (seats, areas) . .645
　Elections .........884, 885
　Lake, largest ...........718
　Marriage, divorce laws 760, 761
　Museums, attractions ....371
　Name, origin of .........383
　Officials, pay .......919, 922
　Population .........593-654
　–Cities and towns 604, 624-625
　–Counties, county seats . .645
　–Metropolitan areas . .652-654
　Presidential vote ....884.
　Taxes ...........209-218
　Vital statistics ......757-768
　Wright Brothers Memorial
　　371, 389
North Dakota ...........371
　*See States, U. S.*
　Admission, area, cap. 371, 384
　Agriculture . .769-771, 773, 776
　Birth, death statistics 758, 765
　Counties (seats, areas) . .645
　Elections .........884, 885
　Lake, largest ...........718
　Marriage, divorce laws 760, 761
　Museums, attractions ....372
　Name, origin of .........383
　Officials, pay .......919, 922
　Population .........593-654
　–Cities and towns ....604, 625
　–Counties, county seats . .645
　–Metropolitan areas . .652-654
　Presidential vote ....884, 904

North Dakota (cont'd)
　Taxes ...........209-218
　Vital statistics ......757-768
North Island, N. Z. . . .538, 722
North Pole—
　Discovery (1909) . . .307, 705
　Explorations .......704-705
North Sea ...............713
North-South games—
　Football (Blue and Gray) 868
　Lacrosse ...............853
Northern Ireland *see*
　*Ireland, Northern*
Northernmost town, U. S. . . 94
Northwest Ordinance (1787) 300
Northwest Terr. (1787) ....300
Northwest Terr., Canada . .485
Norway ...............540
　Antarctic Dependency ....540
　Area, capital, population . .540
　Cities (population) ......579
　Electric power ......123, 540
　Gold reserve ...........139
　Head of State . . . .540, 577
　Merchant fleet . . . .101, 540
　Nordic Council ..........540
　Quisling executed (1945) . .313
　Spitsbergen ...........540
　Sweden, union (1905) 307, 540
　Trade ...................98
　Waterfalls ...............719
　Weights, measures ......587
Norwegian Antarctic ......540
Norwegians, noted . . .692, 699
Noted Personalities ....665-699
　Actors, actresses ....673-685
　Americans
　–Past ...........665-670
　–Present ...............671
　Deaths (1968) . . .56-58, 64
　Negro ...............46-47
Nou Island (New Caledonia) 514
Nova Scotia (Canada) ....485
Novaya Zemlya Is. (Arctic) 722
Novelists, noted .......694-699
Noyd, Capt. Dale E. .......73
Nuclear Energy *see Atomic
　Energy*
Nuclear Power—
　Reactors in U. S. .......735
Numbers (prime composite) 589
Numismatic Soc., Amer. ....437
Numerals (Roman, Arabic) .582
Nurses—
　Armed forces . . .743, 747-748
　College sorority .........342
Nutritive values of food 774-775
Nuts (production) .........771
Nyasaland (former) *see Malawi*

— O —

OAS *see Organization of Amer.
　States*
OAU *see Organization of
　African Unity*
Oakland, Calif. ...........430
　Buildings, tall .........447
　Mayor ...............925
　Population .........604, 607
Oatis, William N. (1951) . .315
Oats—
　Chicago spot prices ......772
　Grain center receipts ....773
　Prices, farm ...........770
　Production ...............771
　Supply in U. S. .........772
Obituaries (1968) . . . .56-58, 64
Observatories, telescopes . .257
Occupation groups ........143
Ocean Islands (Solomons) .563
Oceania—
　Area ...................651
　Petroleum production . . . .130
　Population ...............651
　Sugar production .........122
Oceanography .......711-713
Oceans and seas .........713
　Areas, depths ...........713
　Crossings, notable
　　102, 247-250
　Oceanography .......711-713
Oder-Neisse line . . . .514, 543
Oeno Is. (Pitcairn group) .563
Oregon ...............373
　*See States, U. S.*
Ofu Island, Samoa ......381
Ohio—...............372
　*See States, U. S.*
　Admission, area, cap. 372, 384
　Agriculture . .769-771, 773, 776
　Akron (*see Akron*) ......390
　Altitude .........737-738
　Birth, death statistics 758, 765
　Cincinnati (*see Cinn.*) . . .395

Ohio (cont'd)
　Cities ....390, 395-397, 399
　Cleveland (*see Cleve.*) ....396
　Columbus (*see Columbus*) .397
　Counties (seats, areas)
　　645-646
　Dayton (*see Dayton*) . . . .399
　Elections .........884, 885, 905
　Lake, largest ...........718
　Marriage, divorce laws
　　760, 761
　Museums, attractions
　　372, 390, 396, 397, 398, 400
　Name, origin of .........383
　Officials, pay .......919, 922
　Population .........593-654
　–Cities and towns 604, 625-626
　–Counties, county seats
　　645-646
　–Metropolitan areas . .652-654
　Presidential vote ....884, 905
　Taxes ...........209-218
　Vital statistics ......757-768
Ohio River ...............724
　Flood (1937) ...........662
Ohm (electrical unit) ......586
Oil *see Petroleum*
Okeechobee, Lake (Fla.)
　　359, 718
Okhotsk, Sea of ...........713
Okinawa Island . . . .382, 722
Oklahoma—...............372
　*See States, U. S.*
　Admission, area, cap. 372, 384
　Agriculture . .769-771, 773, 776
　Birth, death statistics 758, 765
　Counties (seats, areas) . .646
　Elections .....884, 885, 906
　Indian territory tribes
　　373, 384
　Lake, largest ...........718
　Marriage, divorce laws
　　760, 761
　Museums, attractions ....372
　Name, origin of .........383
　Officials, pay .......919, 922
　Oklahoma City (*see
　　Okla. City*) ...........417
　Population .........593-654
　–Cities and towns 604, 626-627
　–Counties, county seats . .646
　–Metropolitan areas . .652-654
　Presidential vote ....884, 906
　Taxes ...........209-218
　Territory .........373, 384
　Vital statistics ......757-768
Oklahoma City, Okla. ....417
　Area ...............646
　Buildings, tall .........447
　City manager ...........925
　Museums, attractions ....417
　Population . . . .604, 627, 653
Old age insurance 148-149, 154
Old Catholic Churches, U. S.
　　220
Old Ironsides (1797) ......300
Oleomargarine—
　Consumption ...........776
　Nutritive value .........775
Olesega Island, Samoa . . . .381
Olympic games—
　Beamon's long jump . 878, 879
　History of ...............878
　Records, champions
　　832, 878-883
　Winter ...............832
Olympic Mountains, Wash. 378
Olympic National Park ....388
Omaha, Nebr. ...........368
　Joslyn Art Museum ....368
　Mayor ...............925
　Population . . . .604, 620, 653
Oman (Muscat & Oman) 537, 577
Onassis, Aristotle ..........92
Onassis, Mrs. Aristotle . .183, 194
Ontario, Canada . . . .485, 489
Ontario, Lake ...........717
Opera—
　Composers, works 671, 685-687
　Season of 1967-68 ......157
Orange Bowl Games ......868
Orange Free State (S. Afr.) 546
Orbits, planetary .........286
Orchestras, Symphony ....161
Oregon ...............373
　*See States, U. S.*
　Admission, area, cap. 373, 384
　Agriculture 769-771, 773, 776
　Birth, death statistics 758, 765
　Counties (seats, areas) . .646
　Elections .........884, 885, 906
　Lake, largest ...........718
　Marriage, divorce laws 760, 761
　Museums, attractions ....373

**Oregon** (cont'd)
Name, origin of .........383
Officials, pay .........919, 922
Population .........593-654
-Cities and towns ....604, 627
-Counties, county seats 646
-Metropolitan areas ..652-654
Portland (see Portland) 422
Presidential vote ....884, 906
Redwood trees .........710
Taxes .........209-218
Territory .........383, 384
Vital statistics .........757-768
**Oregon, University of** .........328
Museum of Natural History 373
**Organic Acts** (territories) .384
**Organization of**
African Unity .........573
**Organization of American**
States (OAS) (1948, 1956)
316, 573
**Organizations, clubs** ...339-342
(see also Assns.)
**Orinoco River** .........61, 564
**Orkney Is.** (Scotland) ..560, 722
**Orlando, Fla.** .........418
Mayor .........925
Museums, attractions .....418
Population .........610, 653
**Orleans, House of** .........689
**Orleans, Territory** ....384, 385
**Oswald, Lee Harvey** ..318, 662
**Ottawa, Canada** .........418
**Outer Seven** see
*European Free Trade Assn.*
**Outlying Areas, U. S.** .....655
**Oxford-Cambridge** boat race 836
**Ozone** (in atmosphere) .....260

**— P —**

**Pacific Coast—**
Ports, cargo, volume ..99, 100
**Pacific Islands, disputed** ..382
**Pacific Ocean—**
Area, depth .........713
Crossings, fast ...102, 247-250
Discovery (1513) .........297
Islands, areas .........722
**Pacing, trotting records** ...815
Stakes, winners .........816
**Pago Pago, Samoa** .........381
**Pahang, Malaysia** .........533
**Painted Desert, Ariz.** .....355
**Painters, noted** .........688-699
**Paintings, Famous** .........162
**Pakistan** .........540-541
Area, capital, population ..540
Cities (population) .........579
Defense pacts .........541
Petroleum production ....130
President .........541, 577
Republic formed .........540
Sugar production .........122
Trade .........98, 541
U. S. aid .........580
**Palawan Island, P. I.** .....722
**Paleozoic era** .........714
**Palestine**
*See Israel, Jordan, U. A. R.*
**Pan Am Building** .........438
**Pan-American conference—**
Bogota (1948) .........314
**Pan-American Day** .........591
**Pan-American Expos.** (1901) 61
**Pan American Union**
*See Org. of American States*
**Panama** .........541
Area, capital, pop. ...541, 579
Distances to ports ...103-104
Merchant fleet .........101
President .........577
-Ousted .........72, 91
Treaties, U. S. .........380
**Panama Canal** .........380
Cargo traffic .........97
Employees, Federal .....146
First ship (1914) .........308
**Panama Canal Zone** see
*Canal Zone*
**Panama hats** (Ecuador) .....510
**Panay Is., Philippines** .....722
**Panay, ship** (sunk 1937) 311, 659
**Panchen Lama** (1951) .....504
**Panics** see Riots, panics
**Paper**—exports, imports ....100
**Papua, Br. New Guinea** ....495
**Paraguay** .........541
Area, capital, population ..541
Asuncion (population) .....579
Guaira waterfall .........719
President .........577
Weights, measures .......587

**Parallel bar champs** .........876
**Parcel Post** .........927-932
**Paris, France—**
Eiffel Tower (1889) .........306
Expositions—1889-1900 61, 306
Opera Comique fire (1887)
306, 664
Peace Talks ....78, 83, 87, 89
Population .........578, 651
**Park Place disaster** (1891) ..306
**Parks, parkways** (Nat'l) ...388
**Parliament, oldest** (Iceland) 520
**Parthenon** (438 B.C.) .......295
**Paschal full moon** (dates) ..232
**Passport, U. S.** ...700-701, 703
Issued and Renewed ..700, 703
**Patents—**
Appeals Court .........167
How to apply .........208
**Patton, Gen. George** ...313, 665
Museum, Ky. .........363
**Paul I, Greece** .........517
**Pay scales, U. S. forces** 754-755
**Payne, Dolley** (Madison) 183, 185
**Peabody Awards** .........243
**Peace Corps, U. S.** .........164
**Peace Garden, N. Dak.** .....372
**Peace Prizes, Nobel** ....234-235
**Peace Talks, Paris** ..78, 83, 87, 89
**Peanuts—**
Consumption .........776
Production .........771
**Pearl of the Antilles** (Cuba) 506
**Pearl Harbor** (1941) ...312, 313
**Peary, Adm. R.E.** (1909) 307, 705
**Pemba Island** (Zanzibar) 551, 722
**Penang, Malaya** .........533
**Penghus** (Pescadores) .......503
**Penitentiaries, Federal** .....766
**Penn, William** (1683) .......299
**Pennsylvania** .........373
*See States, U. S.*
Admission, area, cap. 373, 384
Agriculture 769-771, 773, 776
Birth, death statistics 758, 765
Cities .........419, 421
Counties (seats, areas) 646-647
Elections ....76, 884, 885, 907
Harrisburg .........373
Lake, largest .........718
Marriage, divorce laws 760, 761
Museums, attractions
373, 419, 421
Name, origin of .........383
Officials, pay .........919, 922
Philadelphia (see Phila.) ..419
Pittsburgh (see Pitts.) ....421
Population .........593-654
-Cities and towns 604, 627-629
-Counties, county seats 646-647
-Metropolitan areas ..652-654
Presidential vote ....884, 907
Taxes .........209-218
Vital statistics .........757-768
**Pennsylvania Gazette** (1728) 299
**Pensions, veterans** .........753
**Pentagon, Washington** .....443
**Pentathlon—**
American record .........858
National Champions .......861
Olympic games .........878-883
**Pentecostal Churches—**
Headquarters .........222
Membership .........220
**Perak, Malaysia** .........533
**Perigee of Moon** .........283
**Perihelion** see Aphelion
**Perlis, Malaysia** .........533
**Peron, Juan D.** (1955) ..316, 494
**Perpetual Calendar** ...278-279
**Perry Awards** (theater) ....243
**Perry, Matthew C.** (1853) ..303
**Persecution—**
Christians (64 A.D.) ......295
Huguenots (1560) .........297
Jews (Germany) .........515
**Persia** see Iran
**Persian gulf** .........713
**Personal consumption,**
expenditures .........124
**Personalities, noted** ....665-699
**Peru** .........542
Area, capital population ..542
Bolivar, Simon .........542
Cities (population) .........579
Coup .........91
Gold reserve .........139
Incas .........542
Merchant fleet .........101
Petroleum production ....130
Pizarro conquers (1531-1535)
297, 542, 708
President .........91, 577
Sugar production .........122
Weights, measures .......587

**Pescadores** (Penghus) .....503
**Peter I Island** (Norway) ...540
**Petrified Forest, Ariz.** .....355
**Petroleum—**
Canada crude .........130
Distillate Oil .........130
Exports, imports .........100
First well, Pa. (1859) .....303
Gasoline see Gasoline
Industry (La., Tex.) 363, 376
Iranian pact .........523
Nationalization
-Iran (1951) .........523
-Mexico (1938) .........311
Production, by country ....130
-By state (U. S.) .........130
-Crude oil (U. S.) ....127, 130
Residual oil .........130
Used producing electricity 123
**Peugeot, Eric** .........661
**Pharmaceutical Soc.** .......341
**Pharos of Alexandria** .......721
**Phidias statue of Zeus** ....721
**Philadelphia, Pa.** .........419
Buildings, tall .........447
Capital of U.S. (1790-1800) 419
Expositions .........61
Independence Hall .......198
Liberty Bell .........198
Mayor .........925
Mileage to other cities ...110
Mint .........144
Museums, attractions .....419
Opera .........158
Population ..604, 629, 651, 653
Port traffic .........96, 99
Postal receipts .........932
**Philip, Prince** .........558
**Philippines, Republic of** ..542
Accession, U. S. (1898) 385, 543
Area, capital, population .542
Cities (population) ...579, 651
Independence (1945-46) ...543
Insurrection (1899) .......306
MacArthur, Gen. D. ..312, 543
Merchant fleet .........101
President .........577
Sabah .........90
Sugar production .........122
Trade .........98
Volcanoes .........715-716
Weights, measures .......587
World War II .........312-313
**Phoenix, Arizona** .........420
Buildings, tall .........447
Mayor .........925
Museums, attractions ....421
Population ....604, 605, 653
**Phoenix Island** (Solomons) .563
**Phonographs, TV and Radio** 62
**Photography—**
Awards .........237
Eastman House, Rochester 424
Inventions, noted .........117
Pulitzer Prizes .........237
**Physics—**
College fraternity .........342
Discoveries .........116
Nobel awards .........234-235
**Pickwick Club** (1925) .....310
**Pierce, Franklin** (biog.) ...187
**Pig iron production** .........129
**Pike's Peak, Colo.** ....357, 720
**Pilgrims** (1620) .......175, 298
**Pines, Isle of, Cuba** ..506, 722
**Pines, Isle of, N. Caledonia** 514
**Pinochle** (chances, odds) ..810
**Pistol champions** .........876
**Pitcairn Island** .........563
**Pittsburgh, Pa.** .........421
Buildings, tall .........447
Carnegie Institute .......422
Mayor .........925
Opera .........158
Population ....604, 629, 653
**Pizarro, Francisco** (1531)
297, 542
**Planetariums, Major U. S.** ..257
**Planetary configurations** ..285
**Planets—**
Aphelion, perihelion .....286
Events by months ...253-256
Morning, evening stars
256, 263-276
Rise, set (1969) .........287
Signs and symbols .........285
Solar system ....258-259, 286
**Plantagenet, House of** .....688
**Playing cards** (odds) .......810
**Plays** see Theater
**Pledge, allegiance** .........176
**Pluto** (planet) .......253, 286
**Plymouth Pilgrims,** (1620)
175, 298, 364

**Pocket Billiards** see Billiards
**Poe, Edgar A.** ....364, 438, 667
**Poets—**
  Awards ............239, 241
  Laureate ...............695
  Noted ....666-668, 694-698
**Poison gases—**
  Accidental deaths .......759
**Poisons** (deaths, rate) .....759
**Poker hand chances, odds** .810
**Poland** ...................543
  Area, capital, population .543
  Cities (population) ......579
  Electric power ..........123
  Gdansk (Danzig) ........543
  Gomulka (1956) ...316, 543
  Head of State ..........577
  Industry nationalized, 1946 313
  Merchant fleet ..........101
  Oder-Neisse line ........543
  Petroleum production ....130
  Poznan riots (1956) ..316, 543
  Russo-German invasion .543
  Warsaw riots ............72
  Weights, measures ......587
**Polar explorations** ....704-707
**Pole vaulting records—**
  American ...............858
  Olympic games ..878, 881, 883
  World ..................855
**Poles** (notable persons) ....699
**Poles of the Earth** .........261
**Police roster, cities** ........767
**Poliomyelitis—**
  Sabin vaccine ..........116
  Salk vaccine ...........116
  Warm Springs Fdn. .....359
**Political committees** ....172-173
**Political Parties** see
  *specific parties*
**Polk, James K.** (biog.) ....187
**Polo champions** ............817
**Polo, Marco** (1271) ........296
**Polynesia, French** ..........513
**Pompeii destroyed** (79 AD) .85
**Pompidou, Georges** .........85
**Ponce de Leon** (1513) ..297, 708
**Pondicherry, India** .........521
**Pony Express** (1860) ........303
**Poor People's March** ......77, 882
**Popes** see *Roman Catholic*
**Popular vote,** see *Vote, popular*
**Population, U. S.** ..64, 592-654
  Age groups by sex, color .596
  Area (land) .........635-651
  Area, 1790-1960 ........595
  Birth, death statistics 758, 765
  Census of 1960 ....593-654
  Center .................595
  Cities by states .604, 605-634
  Cities, consolidated areas
                652-654
  Cities, largest .....604, 651
  Cities, metropolitan areas
                652-654
  Counties, by state ...635-651
  Density, by state ......603
  Density, 1790-1960 .....594
  Educational attainment .656
  Employment ............143
  Estimates ..............592
  Farm ...........592, 604
  Foreign born ...598-600, 602
  –Cities .................598
  –Country of origin ......598
  –Metropolitan areas .....598
  –States .............599-600
  –White and non-white ..598
  Households (number, type) 593
  Jewish .................602
  Life expectancy, aver. ..763
  Male, female ......596, 601
  Marital status .........603
  Metropolitan areas ..652-654
  Negro .............597, 604
  New York City
    602, 604, 623, 651, 653
  Non-white .593, 596-598, 601
  Occupation groups ......143
  Official by years ..592-595, 604
  Oriental ...............597
  Outlying regions .......655
  Places 2,500 and over 605-634
  Prison .................766
  Regions (1950, 1960) 593, 655
  Religious groups ...219-224
  Rural .............593, 601
  School enrollment ..344, 349
  Sex ratio in U. S.......603
  Sexes ..................506
  SMSA .........398, 652-654
  States .............593-651
  –Census 1790-1880 ......594
  –Census 1890-1960 ......595
  Towns .............605-634

**Population, U. S.** (cont'd)
  Unemployed ............143
  Urban .....593, 601, 605-634
  Urban and rural, by color
              593, 601
  Voting age (number) ....601
  White ..............593-601
  Workers statistics ......143
**Population, World—**
  Area ...................651
  Cities, foreign ....578-579
  Continents .............651
  Jewish .............224, 602
  Religious ..............224
  UN report .............651
  USSR Census (1959) ....554
  Urban areas ...........651
  *See individual nations*
**Pork—**
  Nutritive value ........774
  Prices, farm ...........770
  Production, consumption .776
**Portland, Oregon** ..........422
  Mayor
  Population .....604, 627, 653
**Port of New York** ...........99
**Port of Spain** (Trinidad) ..552
**Portraits on U. S. currency** 144
  On bonds ..............144
**Ports—**
  Distances from......103-105
  United States ...........99
  –Cargo volume (tons) ...99
**Portugal** .................543
  Area, capital, population .543
  Cities (population) ......579
  Colonies ...............544
  Earthquake (1755) .300, 661
  Premier .................90
  President .........544, 577
  Merchant fleet .........101
  Trade ..................98
  U. S. citizens in (law) ..702
  Weights, measures ......587
**Portuguese East Africa** ....544
**Portuguese Guinea** .........544
**Portuguese Timor** ....544, 722
**Portuguese West Africa** ....544
**Possessions, U. S.** ....380-382
**Post Office Department—**
  Administrative personnel ..166
  Employees (number) ....145
  Established .............181
  Expenditures ..........131
  Postmasters General 166, 181
**Post Offices, U. S.** .........926
  Receipts by city ........932
  Santa Claus, Ind. ......361
**Postage Stamps—**
  United Nations .........932
  U. S. issues (1847) .....302
**Postal information** .....927-932
  Air mail .......927, 929-931
  Book rates .........927-931
  Canadian ...............55
  C.O.D. charges .........928
  Domestic rates .....927, 928
  Insured mail ...........928
  International rates ..929-931
  Letter with parcel .....927
  Money order fees .......928
  Parcel post .........927-931
  Registered mail ........928
  Special delivery rates ..927
  State abbreviations .....932
  Zip Code ......605-634, 655
**Potatoes—**
  Consumption ...........776
  Nutritive value ........774
  Prices, farm ...........770
  Production .........771, 773
**Potomac River** ......379, 724
**Potsdam Conf.** (1945) ......313
**Poultry products—**
  Consumption ...........776
  Eggs .........769, 770, 776
  Nutritive value ........774
  Prices, farm .......769, 770
**Pound** (measure) ....581, 582
**Pound, British** ......557, 559
**Poverty**
  Families ...............656
  Welfare ................154
**Power administrations** .....729
**Power boat racing** .........837
**Powers, Abigail** (Fillmore)
              183, 187
**Powers, Francis G.,** (1960) .317
**Preakness Stakes** ..........817
**Precambrian Era** ...........714
**Precipitation—**
  Cities, U. S. ......290, 291
  Wettest spot ...........292
**Prehistoric Man** ...........714

**Presbyterian Churches—**
  Headquarters ..........222
  History, organization ...224
  Membership ......220, 224
  National, Wash., D. C. ..444
**President of the U. S.—**
  Office and Powers
  Address, form of .......351
  Aides ..................164
  Appointments (law) ....201
  Cabinet ................164
  Constitutional powers 199-202
  Disability .........195, 206
  Electoral votes (law) 201, 203
  Flag ...................176
  Inauguration ......205, 439
  Nominees 1968 ....38-39, 885
  Pension ................164
  Salary .................164
  Salute by artillery .....746
  Succession law .........195
  Term begins, limit ..164, 205
  White House .......440-441
**President of the U. S.—**
  Historical and Biographical
  Ancestry, religion ..183, 195
  Biographies .......184-195
  Birth, death dates .....183
  Burial place ...........195
  Cabinets .......164, 179-182
  Children, number .......183
  Election returns (1789-1968) 886
  –By states (1920-1968) 887-914
  –Popular, electoral 34, 884, 886
  Enumeration ...........183
  Inauguration, age at ...183
  Military records .......195
  Native states ..........183
  Politics ................183
  Religious background ...195
  Wives ......183, 184-195
**Presidents, Heads of States**
              576-577
**Presidents, Vice Presidents &**
  their Congresses, U. S. 178
**Press freedom** see *Freedom*
  *of Press*
**Price Indexes** .........142-143
  Farm produce ..........769
**Prices—**
  Farm crops ............770
  Grains (at Chicago) ....772
**Priest** (form of address).....351
**Prime Ministers, Premiers**
         64, 576-577
**Prime numbers** ............589
**Prince Edward Is.** (Canada)
            485, 722
**Prince Patrick Is.** (Canada) 722
**Prince Philip** ...............558
**Prince of Wales** ............560
**Prince of Wales Is.** (Canada) 722
**Princess Margaret** .........558
**Principe Island** (Port.) .....544
**Prism, rectangular** .........586
**Prisons, inmates** ...........766
**Prize fighting** see *Boxing*
**Prizes** see *Awards*
**Product, gross national** .....133
**Production—**
  Aluminum ..............129
  Automobile ............114
  Books .................155
  Coal, Coke .............128
  Coffee .................777
  Copper ................129
  Cotton ................125
  Electric power, by country 123
  Farm crops .........769-780
  Foods .................776
  Gasoline .........126, 130
  Gold ..................140
  Hosiery ...............124
  Index numbers .....142-143
  Iron, steel ............129
  Kerosene ..............130
  Lead ..................129
  Liquor, beer ...........130
  Minerals ..........127-128
  –Distillate oil .........130
  –Natural gas .......129, 130
  –Petroleum .......129, 130
  –Residual oil ..........130
  Rayon .................125
  Rubber ................124
  Shoes and slippers .....125
  Silk ...................125
  Silver .................140
  Sugar .................122
  Textiles ...............125
  Tobacco products .......100
  Wool ..................125
  Zinc ..................129

**Pro, Golf Ass'n**
  championships .........846
**Prohibition—**
  Amendment (1917) ......309
  Mississippi, only dry state 366
  U.S. law, repeal (1933) 205, 311
**Prohibition party** ......887–914
**Protein** (foods) .........774–775
**Protestant Church—**
  Altar Colors, Calendar ....226
  Fast Days .................226
  Headquarters .............222
  History of leading .......224
  Membership ...............220
  National Council .........232
  Oldest in use (Del.) ......358
  Population, world ........222
**Protestant Episcopal Church—**
  Altar colors .............226
  Bishops ..................225
  –Address, form of ........351
  Calendar, fast days ......226
  Headquarters .......222, 224
  Membership .........220, 222
**Prussia, Rulers** ..........690
**Psychiatric patients** .....764
**Public Health Service** ....175
**Public Holidays** .......590–591
**Public Lands** .............386
**Public libraries** .........348
**Public schools—**
  Attendance, expenditures .345
  Desegregation (1955, 1957)
           316, 317
  Enrollment ...........344, 349
  Full time day ............349
  New York State ...........349
  Teachers, salaries .......345
  *See Education*
**Publications, U. S.**
    155, 233, 346, 350
**Pueblo, U. S. S.** .....67, 69, 71
**Puerto Rico** ..............380
  Altitudes (high, low) ....738
  Area, capital, population ..380
  Cities (pop.) ...604, 654, 655
  Commonwealth (1952) 316, 380
  Deaths, motor vehicle ...765
  Marriage information 760, 761
  Nationalist attacks (1950) 315
  Officials, pay ......919, 923
  Resident commissioner ....918
  Sugar production .........122
  Vital statistics ......757–768
**Puget Sound, Wash.** .......378
**Pulitzer Prizes** ......236–239
**Punakha Bhutan** ...........497
**Punic Wars** (264–146 B.C.) .295
**Purchasing power of dollar** .141
**Putnam, Amelia Earhart** 247, 311
**Pyramids** .....295, 556, 721
**Pyramids, volume** .........586
**Pyrenees Mts.** (Spain) .547, 720

**— Q —**

**Qatar, Arabia** ............562
**Quakers** *see Friends*
**Qualifications for voting** ..926
**Quarter horse racing** ......876
**Quasars** ..................286
**Quebec City, Canada** ..487, 578
**Quebec province, Canada** 64, 485
**Queens Borough** ...........416
**Queen's Plate** ............816
**Queens Tunnel (N. Y. C.)** .727
**Queensland, Australia** .....494
**Quemoy** ...................722
**Quintuplets** (1934, 1963) 311, 318
**Quisling, Vidkun** (1945) ...313

**— R —**

**Racial violence—**
  Cleveland ................. 86
  King assassination ....... 74
  Newark report ........... 71
**Racing—**
  Airplane records ......249–250
  Automobile ...............814
  –NASCAR ..................814
  Bobsled ..................877
  Bicycle ..................877
  –Tour de France ..........877
  Harness ..............815–816
  Horse ................817–820
  Ice skating ..............849

**Racing (cont'd)**
  Nascar ...................814
  Power boat ...............837
  Quarter horse ............876
  Roller skating ...........835
  Rowing ...............836–837
  Skiing ...................849
  Swimming .............830–831
  Track (world) ........854–856
  –American ............857–858
  Yacht ....................837
**Radar—**
  Beam to moon (1946) .....314
  Invented .................118
**Radio—**
  Awards ...................243
  Broadcast stations ...... 62
  Inventions, noted ........118
  Marconi (1896, 1901)
         118, 306, 698
  Noted personalities ...673–685
  Sea rescue, first (1909) ..658
  Sets, number ............. 62
  T.V. color ............... 62
**Radio City, New York City** .438
**Radio Free Europe** .........575
**Radio Liberty** .............575
**Radium** (1898) .......116, 306
**Railroads, foreign—**
  British nationalized (1948) 314
  Japanese .................107
  Locomotive invented ......117
  Steam, first (1825) ......302
  Tunnels, world's longest .727
**Railroads, U. S.—**
  Accidents, deaths ....660, 765
  Cog (N. H.) ..............368
  Dividends ................107
  Electric trolley (1885) 118, 306
  Expenses, taxes ..........107
  Fastest runs .........106, 107
  Freight, fast ............106
  High speed trains ....106, 107
  Locomotive, first ........117
  Mileage ..................107
  Passenger, first (1828, '30) 302
  Passenger, freight data ..107
  Rail center, greatest (Ill.) 395
  Rapid Transit ............107
  Retirement ...............211
  Revenue distribution .....107
  Statistics ...............107
  Stocks, bonds, capital ...107
  Tom Thumb engine (Md.) ..364
  Transcontinental (1869) ..304
**Railway Express Service** ...114
**Rainfall** *see Precipitation*
  One inch of .............. 60
**Raleigh, Sir Walter**
  (1587, 1618) .....297, 708
**Rapid Transit—**
  Cities, mileage ..........107
  Passenger traffic ........107
**Rasputin, Gregory** (1916) .309
**Ray, James Earl** .......63, 74
**Rayon production** ..........125
**Reagan, Ronald** .......37, 82
**Recordings** ...............160
**Recreation area (Nat'l)** ...388
**Rectangle, area** ..........586
**Red Sea** ..................713
**Redwood trees** ............710
**Reelfoot Lake, Tenn.** ......375
**Reformatories, Federal** ....766
**Reformed Churches—**
  Headquarters .............222
  Membership ...............220
**Regina, Canada** ...........423
**Registered mail** ..........928
**Relay races—**
  American records .........858
  Interscholastic records ..856
  Olympic games ........878–882
  World records ........854–856
**Religion** ..............219–233
  Breda decl. (1660) .......298
  Calvin, John (1534) ......297
  Common Bible .............225
  Constantine edict (313 AD) 296
  Council of Nicaea (325 AD) 296
  Council of Trent (1545) ..297
  Denominations .........219–233
  Edict of Milan (313 AD) ..296
  Edict of Nantes (1589) ...297
  Fast days ..226, 227, 232, 233
  Foreign countries ....485–567
  Headquarters .........221–222
  Holidays ....227–233, 590–591
  Holy Trinity (325 AD) ..296
  Luther, Martin (1517) ....297
  Membership, U. S. .....219–220
  Persecution
  –Christians (64 AD) .....295
  –Huguenots (1560) .......297

**Religion (cont'd)**
  –Jews (Germany) .........515
  Popes, list of ...........227
  Population, world ........224
  Protestants ..........220–225
  Roman Catholics 220, 225, 227
  School prayer banned .....317
  Ten commandments .....230
  United States .........219–222
  *See Bible, Churches and*
    *Specific denominations*
**Religious leaders of past** 670, 695
**Remington, Wm. W.** (1951) 315
**Rendova Is., Solomons** .....563
**Rennell Is., Solomons** .....563
**Rents—**
  Price index ..............141
**Reporters, newspaper award** 242
**Representatives, U. S.** .916–918
  Address, form of .........351
  House of *see Congress U. S.*
  Salaries, terms ..........916
  Shooting by Puerto Ricans
    (1954) .................316
**Republican party—**
  Agnew, Spiro T. ....37, 38, 90
  Candidates' biographies .. 38
  Convention sites .........884
  Electoral votes ..........884
  First campaign (1856) ....303
  Formed (1854) ............303
  Goldwater, Barry .....887–914
  Johnson criticism ....... 65
  McCloskey, Paul ......... 65
  National committee ...172–173
  National Convention ..37–39
  Nixon, Richard M.
    37, 38, 71, 73, 76, 79, 90, 92
  Nominees ................. 37
  Platform, 1968 ........... 39
  Popular vote .........884–914
  Reagan, Ronald .......37, 82
  Rockefeller, Nelson
    37, 73, 76, 79, 82
  Romney, George ....37, 71, 73
  State chairman ...........173
**Reservoirs—**
  United States ........728–736
  World's largest ..........736
**Restaurant** (retail sales) .126
**Retail price indexes** ......142
**Retail sales** .............126
**Reunion** (Fr.) .......513, 722
**Revenues, U. S.—**
  Bills originate in House ..200
  Customs ..................140
  Receipts .............131–134
  Tax laws .............209–213
**Revere, Paul** (1775) .......298
**Revolutionary War**
  *See American Revolution*
**Rhode Island** .............374
  *See States, U. S.*
  Admission, area, cap. 374, 384
  Agriculture .769–771, 773, 776
  Birth, death statistics 758, 765
  Counties (seats, areas) ..647
  Elections .......884, 885, 907
  Lake, largest ............718
  Marriage, divorce laws 760, 761
  Museums, attractions .....374
  Name, origin of ..........383
  Officials, pay .......919, 922
  Population .............593–654
  –Cities and towns ....604, 629
  Counties (seats, areas) ..647
  –Metropolitan areas ..652–654
  Presidential vote ....884, 907
  Taxes ................209–213
  Vital statistics .....757–768
**Rhodes, Collossus of** ......721
**Rhodes, Island** (Greece) 517, 722
**Rhodesia** .................562
  Executions ............... 72
  United Nations ........... 79
  UK talks ................. 91
**Rice Consumption** ..........776
**Richmond Borough** 623, 416, 623
**Richmond, Va.—** ...........423
  Buildings, tall ..........447
  City manager .............925
  Confederate capital ..377, 387
  Museums, attractions .....424
  Population ....604, 633, 653
**Rifle champions** ..........876
**Rio de Oro** (Spanish) .....548
**Rio Grande** ...............724
  Big Bend Natl. Park ......388
**Riots, panics—**
  Astor Place, N.Y.C. (1849) 303
  Brooklyn Bridge (1883) ..306

Riots, panics (cont'd)
Detroit, Mich. (1943) .....312
Financial (1873, '84,
   19J7, '29) 305, 306, 307, 310
Germany, East (1953)....316
Harlem, N. Y. C. (1943)...312
Haymarket (1886) .........306
Herrin, Ill., strike (1922) 310
New Y.rk school .........303
Poznan (1956) ...........316
Slaves revolt (1712) .....299
Steel strikers (1892) .....306
Rivers—
Dams, reservoirs ....728-734
Foreign .................61
Freight, total ..........105
St. Lawrence Seaway .....97
United States .......723-724
–Longest ................94
*See specific rivers*
Riverside church, N. Y. C. ..437
Roads—
Auto Travel .....108, 110-111
Interstate System .......111
Parkways, National ......388
Rural mileage, U. S. ....112
Speed limits .......108, 109
Touring distances ...110-111
Traffic laws ....108-109, 112
Traffic volume ..........108
Turnpike tolls ..........109
Vehicle registration 1968 .109
Robb, Charles S. .......66, 92
Robles, Marco ...........72
Rochester, N. Y. .........424
Buildings, tall .........447
City manager ...........925
Museums, attractions ....424
Population ....604, 624, 653
Rockefeller Center N. Y. C. 438
Rockefeller, Nelson A.
   .....37, 73, 76, 79, 82
Rockets *see Missiles, rockets*
Rockne, Knute (1931) .....310
Rocky Mountain Natl. Park 388
Rodeo champions .........834
Rogers, Will (death, 1935) .311
Roller skating champions .835
Roman Catholic—
Avignon (1309) .........296
Birth control ........63, 85
College of Cardinals .....228
Common Bible ...........225
Cooke, Bishop ..........72
Dioceses, U. S. ...229-230, 231
Fast days ...............227
Hierarchy ...........228-230
–Address, form of ......351
Laetare Medal ..........243
Membership, U. S. ...220, 231
National Shrine, U. S. ...444
Popes—
–Address, form of ......351
–Avignon Hq. (1309) ....296
–Chronological list ......227
–Italy guarantee (1871) ..305
–Julius II (1506) ........297
–Leo III (800 A.D.) .....296
–Paul III (1545) ........297
–Paul VI .......66, 85, 88
–Urban II, crusade (1096) 296
–Vatican City, State of ...564
Population, world .......224
Schools, enrollment .....231
Spellman, Cardinal .....66
Statistics, U. S. .......231
Roman Numerals ..........582
Roman rulers, emperors ...691
Romania .............544-545
Area, capital, population ..544
Cities (population) ......579
Communism (1947) ......544
Merchant fleet ..........101
Petroleum production ....130
Rome, Ancient .......295, 296
Romney, George ....37, 71, 73
Ronne expedition (1946-48) 707
Roosevelt, Anna Eleanor 183, 193
Roosevelt, Franklin D. ....193
Birthday (holiday) .......590
Congress sessions ......178
Death (1945) .......193, 313
Four Freedoms (1941) ....311
Library, Hyde Park, N. Y. 370
State Park (Warm Spr.) ..359
Wife, family .......183, 193
Yalta Conference (1945) ..313
Roosevelt, Theodore (biog.) .190
Family .............183, 190
Mt. Rushmore Mem., S. D. 375
National Park (N. D.) 371, 389
Roots (square, cube) .....585
Rose Bowl games .........868
Rose Island, Samoa ......381

Rosenberg trial (1951) ....315
Rosenthal, Herman (1912) ..308
Ross, Betsy .............177
Ross, Charley (1874) .....305
Ross Dependency (N. Z.) ...538
Ross, Nellie T. (1924) ....310
Rotation of the Earth .....261
Rothstein, Arnold (1928) ..310
Rowing records .......836-837
Henley Regatta, Canadian 837
Royal Families of Europe 688-693
Address, form of ........351
Royal Gorge, Colo. 357, 725, 726
Ruanda *see Rwanda*
Rubber—Production .......124
Imports, exports ........100
Rubberband Duckpin Bowl'g 853
Ruby, Jack (1963) .......318
Rudolph, Lucretia
   –(Garfield) .......183, 189
Rulers, world .......688-693
Middle Europe .........690
Modern Spain ..........693
Rum production ..........121
Rumsey, James (1778) 118, 300
Runs, walks and marathons—
American records ....857-858
Olympic games ...878, 880-883
World records ..854-856, 876
Rural population, U. S. 593, 601
Rural road mileage, U. S. ..112
Rush-Bagot Treaty (1817) ..302
Rusk, Dean ...........91, 179
Russell Is., Solomons ....563
Russian Empire (Ended 1917)
*For later history see Union of
   Soviet Socialist Republics*
Alaska (1741-1867) ..354, 385
Authors, composers .....697
Crimean War (1853) .....303
Explorers ..............708
Japanese War (1904) .....307
Noted persons ..690, 692, 697
Rasputin killed (1916) ...309
Romanovs killed (1918) ...309
Rulers, czars ..........692
Ships lost in war ....657-658
Turkish War (1877) .....306
World War I .......308-309
Russian Orthodox Church
   .................219, 222
Russian Soviet Federal
   Socialist Republic .....554
Russians, noted ..690, 692, 697
Ruth, Babe .......798, 806
Rwanda .............545, 577
Ryder Cup (golf) .........848
Rye—
Chicago spot prices .....772
Grain center receipts ...773
Production .............771
–By State .............773
Ryukyu Islands .........382

—S—

SEATO *see Southeast Asia
   Treaty Org.*
Saar, The .............516
Saba Island (Neth. Antilles) 538
Sabah, Malaysia .....90, 533
Sacco-Vanzetti case (1920) .310
Sacramento, Calif. .......425
City manager ...........925
Museums, attractions ....425
Population ....607, 636, 653
Sahara, Spanish .........548
St. Augustine, Fla. (1565)
   .................297, 359
St. Bartholomew—1560
   Massacre ............297
St. Christopher Is. (Kitts) .561
St. Clair, Lake .........717
St. Croix, Virgin Is. .....381
St. Eustatius Island (Neth.) 538
St. Helena Island (Br.) 562, 722
St. John the Divine, N.Y.C. 437
St. John, Virgin Is. ......381
St. Kitts (Christopher) Is. .561
St. Lawrence River—
Discovered (1534) .......297
Length outflow ..........61
Power Project ..........738
St. Lawrence Seaway 86, 97, 317
St. Lawrence Waterway ....97
St. Louis, Mo. ..........425
Buildings, tall .........447
Exposition (1904) ........61
Mayor .................925
Museums, attractions ....426
Opera .................158
Population ....604, 620, 653
Tornadoes (1927, 1959) ...664

St. Lucia Island (W. Indies) 561
St. Martin Is. (Maarten) 513, 538
St. Patrick (432 A.D.) ....296
St. Patrick's Cathedral, NYC 437
St. Patrick's Day ........591
St. Paul, Minn. .........426
Buildings, tall .........447
Mayor .................925
Museums, attractions ....427
Opera .................158
Population ....604, 619
St. Petersburg, Fla. ......427
City manager ...........925
Museums, attractions ....428
Population ....604, 610
St. Pierre and Miquelon ...513
St. Thomas, Virgin Is. ....381
St. Valentine's Day ......591
St. Vincent Is., W. Indies .561
Sakhalin Island .......528, 722
Salaries—
Armed forces .......754-755
Cabinet members .......164
Earnings in cities .......121
Federal govt. officials .164-166
Governors (state) .......919
Judges, U. S. ......167-169
Non-farm payroll .......119
President of the U. S. ...164
Queen Elizabeth II ......558
Representatives, U. S. ...916
Senators, U. S. ........915
State officials ......919-923
Supreme Court Justices ..167
Vice president, U. S. ....164
*See Incomes, Wages*
Sales—
Automobile (factory) ....114
Consumer credit ........140
Retail ................126
Sales taxes by states .....216
Salic House (German rulers) 690
Salk polio vaccine (1955, '61) 116
Salt Lake City, Utah .....428
Buildings, tall .........447
Mayor .................925
Population ....604, 632, 653
Salutations, persons of rank 351
Salutes, honors ....739, 746
Salvador *see El Salvador*
Samar Isles, Philippines ..722
Samoa, American *see American
   Samoa*
Samoa, Western *see Western
   Samoa*
San Antonio, Tex. .......428
Buildings, tall .........925
City manager ...........925
HemisFair '68 ....61, 429
Museums, attractions ....428
Opera .................158
Population ....604, 632, 653
San Cristobal Is., Solomons 563
San Diego, Calif. ........429
Buildings, tall .........448
City manager ...........926
Museums, attractions ....429
Opera .................158
Population ....604, 607, 653
San Francisco, Calif. .....430
Bomb explosion (1916) 309, 661
Buildings, tall .........448
Earthquake, fire (1906) 307, 661
Golden Gate Exp. (1939) ..61
Mayor .................926
Mileage to foreign ports .104
Mileage to U. S. cities ...111
Museums, attractions ....430
Opera .................158
Population ....604, 607, 653
Postal receipts ........932
UN conference (1945) ....569
San Jose, Calif. .........431
Mayor .................926
Population ....604, 607, 653
San Marino .............545
Sand Island ............382
Santa Catalina Island ....722
Santa Claus
Yes, Virginia ...........55
Santa Claus, Ind. ........361
Santa Cruz Is., Solomons ..563
Santa Fe, N. M. (1609) 297, 370
Navaho Art Museum .....370
Opera .................158
Sao Miguel Island (area) ..722
Sao Tome Isl. (Portugal) ..544
Saratoga Historical Park ..388
Sarawak, Malaysia .......533
Sardinia (Italy) ......526, 722
Sark Island (area) .......722
Saskatchewan, Canada ....489
Saskatoon, Canada ......431

Satellites, solar system .....286
Satellites, Space *see*
  *Space developments*
Sato, Eisaku (Japan) .....576
Saturn (planet) ...253-256, 259
  Morning, evening star
        256, 263-276
  Position by months ..253-256
  Rises, sets (1969) ........287
Saudi Arabia ..............545
  Area, capital, population ..545
  Cities (population) ......579
  Faisal, Prince ..........545
  Head of State ......545, 577
  Merchant fleet ..........101
  Petroleum production ....130
  Trade ...................98
Savaii Is., W. Samoa .....566
Savannah, Ga.—
  City manager ...........926
  Population .....604, 610, 653
Savannah, N. S. (1959) ...317
Savings in U. S. ..........137
Savings Bonds, U. S. .....218
Savonarola (1498) ........297
Saxe-Coburg, House of ...688
Saxons—
  English rulers ..........688
  German rulers ..........690
Saxton, Ida (McKinley) 183, 190
Scholarships—
  American Academy ......347
  American Field Service ..346
  Fulbright ..............347
  General Motors ........347
  How to obtain ..........347
  Miss America ..........244
  National Merit ........347
  Rhodes ................347
Schools, Public *see Public Schools*
  Catholic students .......231
Science—
  Awards ................242
  Discoveries ........116-118
  Drugs .................116
  Fossil discoveries ......714
Science, Earth .......709-710
Science Service ..........344
Scientists, Noted ..669, 695-699
Scilly Isles (Br.) .........722
Scopes, John T. (1925) ...310
Scorpion, U. S. sub .......78
Scotland .................560
  Area, capital, population .560
  Church ................560
  Cities (population) ..560, 579
  Rulers ................691
  *See United Kingdom*
Scott, Caroline (Harrison)
              183, 190
Scott, Robt. F. (1912) ....308
Scrap Iron (production) ...129
Screen Personalities .673-685
Sculptors, American, Past .669
Sculptures, Famous .......163
Seaborg, Glenn T. ........588
Seal, U. S. ..............701
Seas (area, depth) .......713
Seasons, The ............260
Seattle, Wash. ..........432
  Buildings, tall .........448
  Exposition .............61
  Floating Bridge ........726
  Mayor ................926
  Population ...604, 633, 653
Secession of States ......387
Secret Service ...........767
Secretaries—
  States .........919-923
  U. S. Cabinets ...164, 179-182
Securities & Exchange
  Comm. ...............175
Segregation *see Desegregation*
Sekia el Hamra (Spanish) .548
Selangor, Malaysia .......533
Selective Service System .756
  Employees (number) .....146
Seminole War (1836) ......302
Senate, U. S. *see Congress, U. S.*
Senators, U. S. ..........915
  Address, form of ......351
  Election of (law) .......201
  Salaries, terms ........915
  Speech, longest (1957) ..317
Senegal Republic ....546, 577
Sequoia National Park ...388
Serbia, Yugoslavia .......566
Seven Wonders of the World 721
Seychelles (Br.) ..........563
Seymour, Jane (1509) ....297
Shakespeare, Wm.
  (1564, 1590, 1600) .....297
Shark fishing records .....838

Shastri, Lal Bahadur, Prem. 520
Shays' Rebellion (1787) ....300
Sheep—
  Farm numbers, prices 770, 780
Shenandoah National Park ..388
Shepard, Cmdr. Alan B. ...317
Shereefian Empire (Morocco) 536
Shetland Is. (Scotland) 560, 722
Shikoku Island, Japan .527, 722
Shipping—
  Canal traffic, foreign ....97
  Distances ..........103-105
  Express service (rail, air) 114
  Great Lakes Commerce ..100
  Port of New York ...96, 99
  Tonnage at ports ....99, 100
  U. S. commerce ......99-100
Ships—
  Atlantic, first steam trip ..102
  Barge, super ...........98
  Bell time ..............589
  Bounty mutiny (1789) ...300
  Dimensions of large ....95-96
  Disasters ..........657-660
  First sunk by sub (1864) ..657
  Frigates, famous
  —Constellation (1797) ....300
  —Constitution (1797-1812)
                300, 301
  —Philadelphia (1801) ....300
  —United States (1797) ...300
  Great Western (1838) 102, 302
  Hiroshima bomb carrier ..102
  Liners, new .........95-96
  Mariners' Museum, Va. ...377
  Merchants fleets ........101
  Mystic Seaport, Conn. ...358
  Nautical measures ......587
  Notable ............95-96
  Nuclear merchant (1959) ..317
  Ocean crossings, notable ..102
  Radio rescue, first (1909) .658
  Route distances ....103-104
  Steamboats, early
  —First iron (1825) ......302
  —Fitch's (1785) ........300
  —Fulton's (1803, '07) ...300
  —Inventors ............118
  —Ocean-going (1827) ....302
  —Rumsey's (1787) ......300
  —Stevens (1804, '09) ...301
  Stockholm-Doria (1956) ..660
  Tankers, largest ........95
Shoes and Slippers ........125
Shooting *see pistol, rifle, skeet,*
  *Trapshooting*
Shortland Is., Solomons ...563
Shoshone Falls, Idaho ....360
Shot Put records—
  American ..............858
  Olympic games ..878, 882, 883
  World ................855
Shrine football game .....868
Shriver, R. Sargent ......71
Siam *see Thailand*
Sicily .............61, 526
  Mt. Etna .........526, 715
Side horse champions .....876
Sidereal day, year .......260
Sierra Leone ....76, 546, 577
Sierra Nevada Mts., Nev. ..368
Signs and Symbols—
  Astronomical ..........256
  Chemical elements ..588-589
  Medical ...............60
  Zodiac ...............282
Sikkim .................520
Silk production ..........125
Silver—
  Coinage .........135, 141
  Composite-type coins ...144
  Comstock Lode, Nevada ..368
  Dollars in stock ........135
  Production ............140
  Value in coins .........141
Singapore .........546, 577
Singers, noted—
  Contemporary ....677-685
  Opera (1968-1969) ..156-158
  Stars of the Past ...673-676
Sinkiang, China ..........504
Sioux Indian War (1876) ..306
Sitting Bull, Chief (1876) .306
Skating, ice—
  Championship, speed ...849
  Figure ................834
Skating, roller ..........835
Skeet shooting champions 821
Skiing—
  Championships .........849
  Jumping records .......849
Skye Is. (British) ........560
Slansky, Rudolph (1952) ...316

Slavery—
  America, introduced (1619) 298
  Brazil ends (1889) ........306
  Compromise of 1850 ..303, 387
  Constitutional amend. ....204
  Emancipation procl. (1863) 305
  England outlaws (1833) ...302
  Kansas-Nebr. Act. (1854)
                303, 387
  Mass. outlaws (1783) ....300
  Missouri Compromise (1820)
                302, 387
  New York (1712, 1827) 299, 302
  U. S. abolishes (1865) 204, 305
Slippers and Shoes ........125
Slovenia, Yugoslavia .....566
Smith, Abigail (Adams) 183, 184
Smith, Cyrus R. ..........70
Smith, Capt. John (1607) ...297
Smith, Marg. (Taylor) .183, 187
Smithsonian Institution ....443
Snare Island, N. Z. ......538
Snowfall—
  Blizzard of 1888 ........306
  Cities, U. S. ......290, 292
Snyder-Gray case (1927) ...310
Soap Box Derby .........865
Sobell, Morton (1951) ....315
Soccer ................828
Social Dem. party (1897) ..306
Social Security, U. S.—
  Administration .....148, 154
  Blind, aid to the .......154
  Credit Unions .........114
  Death benefits .....150, 151
  Disability .........148, 150
  Employment security 152, 153
  Employment services ...152
  Farmers ..............149
  Federal Credit Unions ..150
  Hosp. Ins. Trust Fund ..151
  Maternal and child health 154
  Med. Ins. Trust Fund ...151
  Medicare program .....148
  Old age, survivors ..148-149
  Payments .............151
  Self-employed .........149
  Tax rate ..............149
  Unemployment ins. .....152
Socialist Labor party .....173
Socialist party ..........173
Socialist Workers party ...173
Societies, Associations
          449-464 or 469-484
  Colleges .........339-342
Society Islands (Fr.) ......513
Socotra Island (Br. Prot.) .547
Socrates (399 B.C.) ......295
Softball Champions ......799
Solander Island, N. Z. ...538
Solar day ..............260
Solar system ...258-259, 282, 286
Solomon Islands ........563
Solstices ..............260
Somalia (Somali Rep.) 546, 577
Somaliland, French
  (Afars-Issas Terr.) .....513
Somerset Island, Canada ..722
Sorghums (productions) ...771
Sororities (College) ...339-342
  Panhellenic Conference ..339
Sound barrier ..........352
Sound, speed of ........352
South Africa, Rep. of ....546
  Apartheid .............78
  Area, capital, population .546
  Cities (population) ......579
  Gold production .......140
  Gold reserve ..........139
  Heart transplants ...59, 66
  Leaders .........547, 577
  Race policy (apartheid) ..547
  Sugar production ......122
  Trade .............98, 547
  Waterfalls ............719
South African War
  (1899-1902) ..........306
South America—
  Area, dimensions ......736
  Coffee crop ..........777
  Country, largest (Brazil) .497
  Lake, highest (Bolivia) ..497
  Lakes, notable ........717
  Merchant fleet ........101
  Mountain peaks .......720
  Petroleum production ..130
  Population ............651
  —Religion ...........224
  Ports, distances ......104
  Sugar production .....122
  Telephone statistics ...123
  Trade ................98
  Volcanoes ...........716
  Wars of liberation .....693

**South America (cont'd)**
Waterfalls ...............719
**South Arabia** *see Southern Yemen*
**South Carolina** ..............374
*See States, U. S.*
Admission, area, cap. 374, 384
Agriculture . 769-771, 733, 776
Birth, death statistics 758, 765
Counties (seats, areas) ...647
Elections .......884, 885, 907
Lake, largest ..............718
Marriage, divorce laws 760, 761
Name, origin of ...........383
Officials, pay .......919, 922
Population .........593-654
-Cities and towns ....604, 630
-Counties, county seats ...647
-Metropolitan areas ..652-654
Presidential vote ....884, 907
Secession .................387
Tariff protest (1832) ......302
Taxes ...............209-218
Vital statistics ........757-768
**South Dakota** ...............375
*See States, U. S.*
Admission, area, cap. 375, 384
Agriculture . 769-771, 773, 776
Birth, death statistics 758, 765
Counties (seats, areas) ...647
Elections .......884, 885, 908
Lake, largest ..............718
Marriage, divorce laws 760, 761
Mt. Rushmore .......375, 389
Name, origin of ...........383
Officials, pay .......919, 922
Population .........593-654
-Cities and towns ....604, 630
-Counties, county seats ...647
-Metropolitan areas ..652-654
Presidential vote ....884, 908
Taxes ...............209-218
Vital statistics ........757-768
Wind Cave ................388
**South Georgia** (Br.) ........722
**South Island, N. Z.** ...538, 722
**Southampton Island** (area) 722
**Southeast Asia Treaty Org.**
(1954) (SEATO)
75, 81, 316, 573
**Southeastern Power Adm.** ...729
**Southernmost City, Point,**
**Town, U. S.** ............94
**Southern Yemen** ....65, 547, 577
**South-West Africa** ..........547
**Southwestern Power Adm.** ...729
**Soviet Union** *see Union of Soviet Socialist Republics*
**Soy Beans**—
Grain center receipts .....773
Production ................771
**Space developments**—
Apollo exploration ....92, 262
Carpenter, M. Scott (1962) 317
Glenn, John H. (1962) ...317
Highlights of 1968 ....43, 44
Men in space .............317
Missiles *see Missiles, rockets*
Satellite, 1st U. S. (1958) ..317
Schirra, Walter M. (1962) .317
Soviet Union—
-Dog, first in space (1957) 317
-Luniks I, II, III .........317
-Soyuz 3 ..................92
-Sputniks I & II (1957) ...317
-Vostok I, II (1961) ......317
Year 1968 .............43, 44
**Spain** ......................547
Area, capital, population ..547
Cities (population) .......579
Civil war .................548
Electric power ............123
Equatorial Guinea ...64, 548
Franco, Francisco ...548, 577
Gold reserve ..............139
Merchant fleet ............101
Morocco, rule ended .....548
Republic (1931) ......548, 693
Rulers ..........548, 577, 693
Sugar production ..........122
Trade .....................98
Treaties, U. S. ...........307
-Defense agreement .....548
Weights, measures ........587
**Spanish-American War** .....307
Casualties ................751
Military leaders, U. S. 307, 665
Ship losses ...............657
**Spanish Armada** (1588) .....297
**Spanish authors, painters** ..699
**Spanish Guinea** .............548
**Spanish Sahara** .............548
**Speakers, House of**
**Representatives** .........918

**Spearfishing** ...............861
**Special delivery rates** ......927
**Spectrum, colors** ...........352
**Speech, freedom of** (law) ...203
**Speed of light** .............281
**Speed of sound** .............352
**Speed records** *see specific sport*
**Speedboat** *see Power boat*
**Speedway, Indianapolis** .....814
**Spelling Bee, National** ......350
**Spellman, Francis Cardinal**.. 66
**Spenser, Edmund** (1590) ....297
**Sphere** (formulas) ..........586
**Sphinx, Egypt** (2900 B.C.) ..295
**Spiderwebs and Cobwebs** ....343
**Spitsbergen** ...........540, 722
**Spock, Dr. Benjamin** ....69, 82
**Sports arenas** ..............844
**Sports records** ..........794-883
**Spring** (season) ............260
**Sputniks** *see Space developments*
**Square** (area) ..............586
**Square roots** ...............585
**Stadiums** ..............865, 866
Baseball ..................810
Football ..............865, 866
**Stage personalities** .....673-685
**Stalin, Joseph V.** ......555, 692
**Stamps** *see Postage stamps*
**Standard time** .....277, 280, 281
**Stanley Cup** (hockey) .......827
**Stanley, Henry M.** (1871) ...305
**Star-Spangled Banner**—
National Anthem ..........171
**Stars**—
Magnitudes ...............284
Morning, evening .256, 263-276
Polar (1969) .............284
Tables (1969) ............284
**State Department, U. S.**—
Administrative personnel .164
Aides slain .............67, 87
Atomic test ban *see Geneva conferences*
Cambodia ..................67
Employees ................145
Established ...............179
Expenditures .............132
Rusk, Secy. *see Rusk, Dean*
Secretaries ..........164, 179
Shriver, R. Sargent .......71
Treaties, pacts .......65, 573
**State of Vatican City**
*See Vatican City*
**Staten Isl. (Richmond) N. Y.**—
Inst. of Arts, Sciences ...437
Richmond Borough .......416
**States of the U. S.** ......354-379
Admission of new (law) ...202
Admitted to Union ........384
Agriculture ..........769-776
Altitudes (high, low) .737-738
Area, rank .....354-379, 384
Automobile data ....108-115
Banks (assets, liabilities) 136
Birds ................354-379
Births, deaths ......758, 765
Capitals .........354-379, 384
Census ............593-654
Cities ........390-448, 652-654
Climatological data .......290
Coastline, in miles .......712
Congress, Members ..916-918
Constitution, U. S. ...199-206
Counties, county seats 635-651
Deaths, births ......758, 765
Education statistics ..319-351
Election returns ..........886
Electoral votes ...........884
Farm income, crops .769, 770
Flowers ..............354-379
Forest areas ..............778
Geographic centers ........94
Governments ..........919-923
Industries, products ..354-379
Inland water area ........384
Judges, District (U.S.) 167-169
Lakes, largest ............718
Largest, smallest ..........94
Legislatures .........919-923
Liquor, minimum age .....115
Marriage, divorce laws 760, 761
Mineral production ........128
Motor vehicle reg. ........109
Mottoes ..............354-379
Mountain peaks ...........720
Murder, penalties .........767
Names, origin of ..........383
Nicknames ................387
Officials, salaries .....919-923
Original thirteen .........384
Parks, National .......388-389

**States of the U. S. (cont'd)**
Petroleum production ....130
Political chairmen ........173
Population by states ..593-654
Precipitation ........290, 292
Public assistance .........154
Rivers ................723-724
Smallest, largest ..........94
Speed limits, auto ........108
Taxes ................209-218
Telephones ...............123
Temperatures ........292, 293
Trees ................354-379
Vital statistics ......757-768
Voting qualifications .....926
*See specific subjects*
**Statesmen, noted**
671, 672, 694, 698-699
**States' Rights party** ........173
**Statuary Hall, National** ....439
**Statue of Freedom** (Capitol) 439
**Statue of Liberty** ...........93
**Steamboats** *see Ships*
**Steel**—
Discoveries ...............118
Exports, imports .........100
Production ...............129
U. S. price hike ..........86
**Steeplechase** (track and field)—
American record ..........858
Olympic games ...........880
*See Horse Racing*
**Stepinac, Cardinal** (1946) ...314
**Stevens, John** (1804, '09) ...301
**Stewart Island, N. Z.** ...538, 722
**Stock Exchanges**—
American, transactions 50, 139
New York, transactions 50, 139
Seat prices (N. Y.) .......139
**Stockholders**—
Annual rates of equity ...121
**Stockholm-Doria** (1956) ....660
**Stockings** ..................124
**Stocks**—
-Dividends, yields .....51-54
-Market crash (1929) .....310
-Prices, symbols ......51-54
-Railroads (value) ........107
-Shareholders, number ...50
-Widely-held stocks .......50
**Stocks, on exchanges** ...50-54
**Storm warnings** .............289
**Stratosphere** ...............260
**Strikes**—
Britain (1926) ............310
Canadian postal ..........86
Herrin, Ill., 1922 ........310
Homestead steel, 1892 ...306
Miners, UMW (1946) .....314
Newspaper, Detroit .......88
Number, by year ..........245
Pullman, 1894 ............306
Seamen's .................86
Seaway ...................86
Steel seizure (1952) ......316
Teachers, N.Y.C. .....63, 92
Telephone .................76
Theaters, N.Y.C. .........82
**Stuart, House of** ...........688
**Stuyvesant, Peter** ..........415
**Submarines**—
Ballistic missile (1959) ...317
George Washington (1959) 317
Invented .................118
Nautilus (1954) ..........316
Scorpion ..................78
Sinkings .............657-660
Thresher (1963) ..........660
**Subversive activities**—
Immigration law ..........701
**Subways**—
Malbone St. wreck (1918)
309, 660
Opened, New York (1904) 307
Rapid Transit ............107
Times Sq. wreck (1928) 310, 660
Washington, D. C. ........436
**Succession to Presidency** ...195
**Sudan** .....................548
Area, capital, population .548
Cities (population) .......579
Condominium ends .......548
Premier .............549, 577
**Sudanese Republic** *see Mali*
**Suez Canal** (1956) ...316, 557
**Suffrage** *see Voting*
**Sugar**—
Calories ..................775
Consumption ..............776
Govt. subsidy ............770
Imports ..................100
Production, world ........122
-United States .......122, 771
**Sugar Bowl Games** ..........868

Suharto, Gen. .............522
Suicides, World ...........60
Sukarno, Dr. .............522
Sullivan, Arthur, operas ..685
Sullivan Memorial Trophy .856
Sumatra, Indonesia ...522, 722
Volcanoes ...............715
Summer (season) ..........260
Sumter, Fort .............389
Sun Bowl Games ..........868
Sun, The .................282
Diameter ...............282
Earth, distance from .....282
Eclipses (1969) ...253-256, 261
Planets, relation to .....286
Rises, sets .........263-276
Semi-diameter ..........286
Signs and symbols ......256
Solar bombardment ......262
Solar time .............260
Sunrise, correction .....277
Sunspot ................282
Worship, Egypt (1300 B.C.) 295
Zodiac .................282
Super Bowl ...............862
Superior, Lake .......717, 718
Superlative Statistics, U. S. .439
Supreme Court, U. S.—
Appointments, salaries ...169
Created (1789) ..........300
Decisions 1968 ..........49
Dred Scott (1857) ....303, 387
Fortas, Abe ..........84, 91
Justices ...............169
Judicial powers (law) .201-202
–Address, form of ......351
School prayer ban ......317
Segregation in schools
(1954, '55) ...........316
Warren, Earl ......63, 81, 91
Surinam (Netherlands) ....538
Surveyors chain measure ...581
Sutter's sawmill, Calif. ..356
Svalbard Island (Norway) .722
Swain's Island, Samoa ....381
Swan Islands (area, pop.) .381
Swaziland ............64, 549
Sweden ...................549
Area, capital, population .549
Cities (population) ......579
Cooperatives, consumer ..549
Electric power .........123
Gold reserve ..........139
Merchant fleet .........101
Nordic Council .........550
Norway, union (1905) 307, 540
Rulers .........549, 577, 692
Sugar production .......122
Trade ..............98, 549
U.S. deserters ..........67
Waterfalls .............719
Weights, measures ......587
Swedes, noted .......692, 699
Swimming—
Championship, U. S. (1968) 831
Olympic records ..878-879, 883
World records ......830-831
Swiss, noted .............699
Switzerland ..............550
Alps, The .............550
Area, capital, population .550
Cities (population) ......579
Gold reserve ..........139
Merchant fleet .........101
President .............577
Trade .................98
Waterfalls ............719
Symbols *see Signs and symbols*
Symmes, Anna .......183, 186
Symphony orchestras ......161
Syracuse, N. Y. ..........432
Buildings, tall .........448
Mayor ................926
Population ......604, 624, 654
Syria ....................550
Area, capital, population .550
Chief of State .........577
Cities (population) ......579
Egyptian merger .......550
Secession .............550

— T —

Table tennis championships 829
Tadzhik SSR .............554
Taft, Robert A. ..........440
Taft, William H. (biog.) ..191
Taft-Hartley Act (1947) ..314
Tahiti (Fr.) .........513, 722
Taiwan (Formosa) ........503
Tallest
Buildings .........445-448
Trees .................710

T.V. towers .............448
Tampa, Fla. .............433
Mayor ................926
Population .........610, 654
Tanganyika *see Tanzania*
Tangier, North Africa ....536
Tanzania (Tanganyika-
Zanzibar) .........550, 577
Taoist population, world ..224
Tariff Acts—
Exemptions for travelers ..702
Kennedy round ......76, 84
Nullification (1832) .....302
Suspensions (1951) ......316
Tasmania, Australia ......494
Tau Island, Samoa .......381
Tax Court, U. S. ........167
Employees, number ......146
Taxation—
Amer. colonies (1764-73) .298
Canada ...............489
City income tax ........218
Great Britain (income) ..491
Single tax (1879) .......306
Taxes, Federal—
Admissions, entertainment 211
Collections, items ......211
Corporation ...........212
–Profits affected by .....120
Estate ................212
Excise, rate, revenue ....218
Gasoline ..............218
Gift ..................218
Income *see Income tax*
Internal Revenue law 209-211
Life insurance .........209
Liquor ................218
Surcharge table ........210
Taxes, State—
Gasoline ..............218
Horse racing revenue ....818
Income by state .....214-215
Inheritance, estate .....213
Sales (type, rate) ...216-217
Taylor, Claudia .....183, 195
Taylor, Zachary (biog.) ...187
Tea (consumption) ........776
Teachers—
Colleges ...........319-338
Full time day schools ...349
Public school ..........345
Teapot Dome (1929) ......310
Telegraph—
Atlantic cable (1858) .....303
First message (1844) ....302
Inventions, noted ......118
Telephones—
Atlantic cable (1956) ....316
Exchange, first (1878) ...306
Inventions, noted ......118
Strike (1968) ...........76
U. S. cities ...........123
World statistics ........123
Telescopes ...............257
Television—
Actors, actresses ...673-685
Awards ...............243
Color sets .............62
Invented ..............118
Strike (1968) ...........76
Towers, tallest .........448
Transcontinental (1951) ..316
Temperature—
Boiling, melting points ..589
Cities, U. S. normal .....292
Conversion Table .......589
Degree day ............42
Highest, lowest .....292-293
Normal ....289, 291-292
States, normal .........292
Thermometer scales .....589
Temperature-Humidity Index 288
Temple of Artemis .......721
Temple Emanu-el, N. Y. C. 438
Ten Commandments .......230
Tenerife Island, Canaries .722
Tennessee ................375
*See States, U. S.*
Admission, area, cap. 375, 384
Agriculture .769-771, 773, 776
Birth, death statistics 758, 765
Counties (seats, areas) 647-648
Elections ..........884, 904
Knoxville (*see Knoxville*) 407
Lake, largest ..........718
Marriage, divorce laws 760, 761
Memphis (*see Memphis*) .409
Museums, attractions 375, 410
Name, origin of ........383
Nashville (*see Nashville*) 414
Officials, pay ......919, 922
Population .........593-654
–Cities and towns ...604, 630

Tennessee (cont'd)
–Counties, county seats 647-648
–Metropolitan areas ..652-654
Presidential vote ....884, 908
Taxes .............209-218
Vital statistics ......757-768
Tennessee Valley Auth. 146, 729
Tennis champions ......811-813
*See Table Tennis*
Territorial expansion, U. S. 385
Territories, U. S.—
Areas .................383
Chronological list.......384
Tet, festival of ..........233
Teton Mountains, Wyo. ...388
Texas ....................375
*See States, U. S.*
Accession .............383
Admission, area, cap. 375, 384
Agriculture .769-771, 773, 776
Alamo (1836) .......302, 428
Birth, death statistics 758, 765
Cities .........398, 405, 428
Counties (seats, areas) 648-649
Dallas *see Dallas*
Elections ......884, 885, 909
Houston (*see Houston*) ..405
Independence (1835) .....302
Lake, largest ..........718
Marriage, divorce laws 760, 761
Museums, attractions
376, 399, 405, 429
Name, origin of ........383
Officials, pay .....919, 922
Ferguson, Miriam (1924) .310
Population .........593-654
–Cities and towns 604, 631-632
–Counties, county seats 648-649
–Metropolitan areas ..652-654
Presidential vote ....884, 909
San Antonio
(*see San Antonio*) ....428
Taxes .............209-218
Territory .........383, 385
Vital statistics ......757-768
Textiles—
Exports, imports .......100
Industry ..............125
Price Index (wholesale) .143
Thailand (Siam) ..........551
Area, capital, population .551
Bangkok (population) ....579
Guerrillas .............65
King .............551, 577
Merchant fleet .........101
Trade .................98
Weights, measures ......587
Thames River ............61
Thanksgiving Day ........590
Thant, U ...........79, 572
Thaw, Harry K. 1906) .....307
Theater—
Actors, actresses ...673-685
Awards ...............243
Ballet ................687
Dramatists ...694, 696, 698
Long Runs .........156-157
Opera season .......157-158
Plays, stars ........156-157
Pulitzer Prizes .........238
Strike, NYC ...........82
Thermometer scales ......589
Thermopylae Pass (480 B.C.) 295
Thermosphere ............260
Third Party (1968)
36, 38-39, 71, 92, 919
Thirteen Colonies (states) .384
Thirty Years' War (1618) ..297
Three Kings Day .........590
Three Kings' Island, N. Z. .538
Thurmond, Strom (1957) ..317
Tibet ....................504
Dalai Lama ...........504
Panchen Lama .........504
Tidal wave, India (1942) ..662
Tides—
Atlantic coast .........786
Descriptive ...........294
Moon, effect of ...282, 294
New York City .....786-790
Pacific Coast ..........790
Rise and fall, U. S. cities 712
San Francisco .....790-793
Tide Tables .......786-793
Tidewater, Virginia ......377
Tierra del Fuego ...501, 722
Time—
Astronomical .........260
Bell, shipboard ........589
Cities (foreign, U. S.) ...281
Date Line .............280
Daylight saving ........280
Differences for cities ...281
Earth's rotation .......261
Geologic areas .........714

**Time (cont'd)**
Greenwich ................280
Mean, apparent ..........260
Military .................280
Sidereal .................260
Signals broadcast ........280
Standard ........277, 280-281
Twenty-four hour ........280
Zones ...................280
**Times Square subway**
wreck (1928) ......310, 660
**Timor, Portuguese** ....544, 722
**Tin production** ..............127
**Tippecanoe battle** (1811) ...301
**Titanic disaster** (1912) 308, 658
**Titicaca, Lake** (Bolivia) ....497
**Tito, Marshal** .....88, 567, 577
**Titov, Gherman E.** (1961) ..317
**Tobacco—**
Export, imports ..........100
Industry (N. C.) .........371
Production, U. S. ....771, 773
—By state ...............773
Taxes, Excise ...........218
**Tobago** (Trinidad & Tobago)
552, 577, 722
**Todd, Mary** (Lincoln) ..183, 188
**Togo, Republic of** .......551, 577
**Tokelau Is.** (N. Z.) .........538
**Tokyo, Japan** ...............528
Population ...........579, 651
**Tokyo Rose** (1949) ...........314
**Toledo, Ohio** ................372
Buildings, tall ...........448
City manager ............926
Population ......604, 626, 654
**Tomb of Mausolus** ...........721
**Tomb, Unknown Soldier** ....441
**Ton** (measure) .....581, 582, 583
**Tonga Islands** ...........563, 722
**Tornadoes** ....................664
Descriptive ..............289
**Toronto, Canada** .............434
Gr. Lakes Port distance ...105
Population ...........434, 578
**Torres Is.** (New Hebrides) ..563
**Tour de France** ..............877
**Touring mileage, U. S.** ..110-111
**Tourist Attractions—**
Cities .............390-444
Nat'l Pks., Monuments 388-389
New York City .......436-438
States ..............354-379
Washington, D. C. ...439-444
**Towers—Tallest TV** .........448
**Town, easternmost U. S.** ......94
**Town, northernmost U. S.** .....94
**Town, southernmost U. S.** .....94
**Townsend Acts** (1767) .......298
**Track and field—**
American records ....857-861
Beamon's jump ....878, 879
Boston Marathon .......861
Championships ......859-861
Interscholastic records ...856
Olympic games ......878-883
Olympic records ..878, 880-883
One mile run ..........876
Track meets .......859-861
World records ......854-856
**Traffic—**
Foreign Trade U. S.
96-100, 105
Suspensions, U. S. (1951) 316
U. S. statistics ......96, 98
*See Exports, Imports and*
*specific nations*
**Trademark Law** ............208
**Traffic—**
Accidental deaths ...759, 765
Airline .................250
Canal, foreign ...........97
Motor bus ..............113
Panama Canal ...........97
Ports, major U. S. ...96, 99
Railroad ...............107
Truck ..................109
Water-borne .....96-97, 105
**Trails, in U. S.** ...............94
**Training Centers, U. S.** .....742
**Trains** *see Railroads*
**Transportation** ..........95-115
*See Aviation, Automobiles,*
*Railroads, Shipping*
**Transportation, Dept. of**
Secretary ..............166
**Transvaal, South Africa** .....546
**Trapezoid** (area) ............586
**Trapshooting champions** ....821
**Travel, foreign** ..........700-703
**Travel Service, U. S.** .........166
**Treasury Department—**
Administrative personnel 164
Bonds ..................144
Employees (number) ....145

**Treasury Department (cont'd)**
Established ..............179
Expenditures ............131
Secret Service ....164, 767
Secretaries .........164, 179
*See Currency, U. S.*
**Treasury Is., Solomons** ....563
**Treasury U. S.** (reserves) ...135
**Treaties, U. S.—**
Alaska purchase ........385
Arms limits (1921) ......310
—Naval (1921, '30) ......310
Austrian State ..........496
Cuba (1898) ............506
France (1967) ...........65
Germany (1921, '55) 310, 316
Guadelupe-Hidalgo .....385
Japan
—W.W. II peace (1951) 316, 528
Louisiana Purchase (1803)
300, 383, 385
North Atlantic (1949) 314, 573
Oregon boundary (1846) ..302
Panama .......307, 380, 541
Portugal Azores (1951) ...543
Rush-Bagot (1817) ......302
Southeast Asia (SEATO)
(1954) ...............316
Spain
—Defense pact (1953) ...548
—Florida (1819) .........359
—War (1898) ...........307
World War II peace ..312-313
**Treaty of Versailles**
*See Versailles, treaty of*
**Trees**
Oldest ..................356
Tallest .................710
State (official) ......354-379
**Trengganu, Malaya** ..........533
**Trent, Council of** (1545) .....77
**Triangle** (area) ..............586
**Trieste** (Italy) ................527
**Trinidad** (Trinidad & Tobago)
552, 577, 722
**Trinity Church, N. Y. C.** ....438
**Triple Alliance of 1795** ......300
**Triple Crown** (racing) 817, 818
**Tripoli, U. S. war with**
(1801) .................300
**Tripolitania** (Libya) .........532
**Trips, fastest** *see Fastest trips*
**Tristan da Cunha Is.** .........722
**Trolley cars first** (1885) .....306
**Trophies** *see Awards*
**Tropopause, Troposphere** ...260
**Trotsky, Leon** (1940) ........662
**Trotting, pacing records** 815-816
**Trout, largest** (Idaho) .......360
**Troy, Homer's** (1184 B.C.) ..295
**Troy weight** (measure) .......581
**Trucial States** ...............562
**Trudeau, Pierre E.** ...76, 82, 90
**Trujillo Molina, Rafael** .....509
**Truman, Harry S.** (biog.) ....193
Assassination attempt 315, 662
Hydrogen bomb (1950) ...315
MacArthur recall (1951) ..315
Potsdam conference (1945) 313
Railroad seizure (1950) ...315
Steel plant seizure (1952) 316
Taft-Hartley veto (1947) 314
Truman Doctrine (1947) ..314
Wife, biography ....183, 193
**Trust, Territory, U. S.** ......382
**Tsushima Bay Battle** (1905) 657
**Tuamotu Island** (Fr.) .......513
**Tuberculosis—**
Death, rate .............759
Germ discovered (1882) ..306
**Tucopia Is., Solomons** ......563
**Tudor, House of** .............688
**Tuition, major colleges** .....345
**Tulsa, Okla.—**
Buildings, tall ...........448
Mayor ..................926
Opera ..................158
Philbrook Art Center ....372
Population ......604, 627, 654
Thos. Gilcrease Institute ..372
**Tunisia** ......................552
Area, capital, population 552
Constitution .............552
Independence ...........552
President ...........552, 577
**Tunnels** ..................726-727
Land vehicular (U. S.) ...440
World's longest R.R. .....727
Undersea (Japan) ........727
Underwater (U. S.) ......727
**Turkestan, Chinese** ..........504
**Turkey** .......................552
Area, capital, population 552
Cities (population) .......579
Crimean War (1853) .....303

**Turkey (cont'd)**
Cyprus ..................65
Gold reserve ............139
Merchant fleet ..........101
Petroleum production ...130
President ...............577
Russia, war (1877) ......306
Sugar production ........122
Trade ...............98, 553
Weights, measures .......587
**Turkmen SSR** ...............554
**Turks, Caicos Is.** (W. Indies) 561
**Tutankhamen** (1344 B.C.) ..295
**Tutuila Island, Samoa** ......381
**Tweed, Boss W. M.** (1874) ..305
**Twenty-four hour time** .....280
**Twilight** (1969-1970) ....263-276
**Tydings, McDuffie Act** (P.I.) 543
**Tyler, John** (biog.) ......186-187
**Tyndale, William** (1526) .....297
**Typhoons** ....................662

**— U —**

**U-2 flights** (1960) ...........317
**Ubangi-Shari** (former) .....500
**Uganda** ......................553
Area, capital, population .553
Lake Victoria ...........717
Murcheson Falls ........719
President ...............577
**Ukrainian SSR** ..............554
**Ukrainians, noted** ..........697
**Unalaska Island** (Pacific) ..722
**Unemployment—**
Insurance ..........152, 153
—Benefits by state ......153
—Canada ...............487
Statistics (source) .......153
U. S. ...................143
**Union Membership** ........245
**Union of South Africa—**
*See South Africa, Rep. of*
**Union of Soviet Socialist**
**Republics** (USSR) ..553-556
Airlines .................556
Air link to N.Y. .........86
Area, capital, population 553
Armed forces ...........556
Atomic test ban *see*
*Geneva conference*
Austrian treaty ..........496
Beria executed (1953) ...316
Berlin blockade ..........314
Budgets .................555
Census ..................554
Church, Orthodox .......556
Cities (population) ...579, 651
Communist party (1956) .316
Cuban crisis ............317
Czar murdered (1918) ...309
Czechoslovakia 65, 84, 88,
89, 91
East Germany ...........516
Economic system ........554
Education ...............556
Exports and imports .....555
German relations ....515, 516
Hungary, revolt (1956) 316, 520
Hydroelectric projects ...555
Hydrogen bomb (1953) ...316
Islands, areas ...........722
Kosygin *see Kosygin*
Khrushchev, Nikita *see*
*Khrushchev, Nikita S.*
Leaders of the past ..692, 697
Lenin ..............555, 692
Merchant fleet ..........101
Missiles *see Missiles, rockets*
Molotov, V. M. ..........692
Moon shots *see*
*Space developments*
Nasser visit ..............85
Nuclear tests (1963) .....317
Petroleum production ...130
Poland .............312, 543
Population ..............554
Premiers ...............555
Religion ................556
Rockets *see Missiles, rockets*
Rusk, Dean ..............91
Russian Soviet Rep. ....554
Satellites *see*
*Space developments*
Stalin, Joseph V. ....555, 692
Submarines *see Submarines*
Sugar production ........122
Tito, 1948 ..............314
Trade ..............98, 555
Trotsky (1940) ..........662
U. S. recognition (1933) ..311
U. S. jet freed ...........83
U.S. relations ...........83
Volcanoes ..............715

**USSR (cont'd)**
Warning by West ......... 90
Warsaw treaty ............316
Wealth, trade .............555
Weights, measures ........587
World War I ....308-309, 752
World War II ....312-313, 752
 –Casualties, strength .....752
 –Potsdam (1945) ........313
 –Yalta (1945) ...........313
 *See Communist party, World*
Unions, credit ............114
Unions, labor .........79, 245
Unitarian Churches ...220, 222
United Arab Rep. (Egypt) .556
Arab league ..............557
Area, capital, population .556
Aswan dam .........316, 557
Cities (population) ........579
Egypt, Syria (1958) .317, 556
Farouk ousted (1952) .....557
Gold reserve .............139
Invasion (1956) ..........316
Israel ....................89
Merchant fleet ...........101
Nasser, President *see*
 *Nasser, Gamal Abdel*
Petroleum production .....130
Pyramids .....295, 556, 721
Republic (1953) ..........556
Sphinx (2900 B.C.) .......295
Suez Canal (1956) ...316, 557
Sugar production .........122
Sun worship (1360 B.C.) ..295
Trade .................98, 557
U. S. aid ................580
U.S. relations .............72
Weights, measures ........587
**United Church of Christ**
 220, 222, 224
**United Kingdom** ......557-563
 *See England, Scotland, Wales,*
 *Northern Ireland, and*
 *Commonwealth*
Area, capital, population 557
Armed forces .............560
Atomic energy ...........560
Atomic test ban *see*
 *Geneva conferences*
Boer War (1899-1902) ....306
Budgets ..................558
China recognized (1950) .315
Church membership .....559
Churchill, Winston *see*
 *Churchill, Sir Winston*
Cities (population) .......579
Defense ..................560
Common Market .......65, 90
Electric power ...........123
Exports, imports .........559
Gold reserves ............139
Government ..........557-560
Great train robbery ......63
Health Insurance .........559
Hydrogen bomb (1957) ...317
Immigration ...............71
Merchant fleet ...........101
 –Vessels, notable ......95-96
NATO .....................79
Navy .....................560
Parliament ...............558
Pistyll Waterfall (Wales) 719
Prime Minister ....558, 577
Resources, industries ....559
Rhodesia .............72, 91
Rulers .........558, 577, 688
Spending cuts ............68
Suez Canal ..............557
Taxes ....................559
Trade .................98, 559
Weights, measures ........587
Wilson, Prime Minister *see*
 *Wilson, Harold*
World War I ....308-309, 752
World War II ....312-313, 752
Yalta Conference (1945) .313
**United Mine Workers—**
Strike of 1946 ...........314
**United Nations—**
Ball, George ..........75, 89
Budget ...................572
Charter (1945) ...........313
Charter, summary ........569
 *See Geneva conferences*
Disarmament ....68, 81, 86
Dumbarton Oaks ........569
Economic & Social Council
 570-571
Emergency Force (1956) .316
General Assembly, 1st
 (1946) ..........90, 313
Hammarskjold Library ..569
Headquarters ............569
History, 1945 ......313, 569
Information ..............572

**United Nations (cont'd)**
Intl. Finance Corp. .......572
Intl. Labor Org. (ILO) ..571
Israel ...........87, 89, 91
Jerusalem ................79
Intl. (World) Court .......571
Members (*total 126*) 64, 65, 569
Mideast peace (1956) ....316
Officers, committees ..569-572
Postage ..................932
Rhodesia .................79
Secretariat ..............572
Security Council ......75, 570
Southern Yemen ..........65
Specialized agencies ...571-572
Thant, Secy. General
 *See Thant, U*
UNESCO ..................571
United States .............75
U. S. mission to ..........48
 *See Chronology*
**United Nations Day** .......591
**United States Government**
 164-171
**United States of America—**
Accessions ....383, 384, 385
Agency abbreviations ....174
Government ..............175
Altitudes ...........737-738
Ambassadors, ministers 170-171
Areas (in miles) ..94, 384, 651
Boundary line ...........174
Budget ...............131-132
Cabinets .....164, 179-182
Capital ..............439-444
Cities ...............390-436
Civil defense .........748-749
 –Civilian Employment 145-146
Civil Service .............145
Coinage ..............141, 144
Constitution ..........199-206
Construction, new .......654
Courts ...............167-169
Creed ...................182
Customs *see Customs, U. S.*
Decl. of Independence 196-198
Education ............319-351
Election, 1968 ..36-39, 887-914
Engineering wonders ....129
Executive .............164-166
FBI ......................766
Federal agencies ......60, 175
Federal Deposit Ins. Corp. 145
Federal Funds, education 344
Federal Reserve System ..138
Flag ................176-177
Foreign aid, *see*
 *Foreign aid, U. S.*
Foreign relations *see*
 *State Dept., U. S.*
Foreign Trade ...........98
 –By economic class .......96
Geodetic datum point ....727
Geographic centers .......94
Geographic superlatives ..94
Geological survey .....709-710
Government ..........164-171
Holidays .........42, 590-591
Household ...............593
Immigration .......701, 703
Income, national ...133, 134
Income taxes .........209-218
Independent agencies ....175
Information Agency ......175
Island trusteeships ......382
Joint Chiefs of Staff ..164-165
Judiciary .............167-169
Land, Public ............386
 Federal owned .........386
Latitudes, longitudes .737-738
Legislative ...........919-923
Mason-Dixon line .......448
Medal of Honor .........740
Men per 100 females .....603
Merchant fleets ..........101
Military pay 1968 .....754-755
Military training center ..472
Missiles *see Missiles, rockets*
Mission to UN ...........48
Moscow air link ..........86
Motto, national ..........195
Nat'l Guard .............743
Negroes, noted .......46-47
Outlying areas ...380-382, 655
Passports ..........700, 703
Population ...........593-654
Possessions ......380-382, 655
Postal information ....927-932
Zip Code ......605-634, 655
Presidents (Biog.) ....184-195
Public debt ........132, 133
Public lands .............386
Publications, Gov't.
 126, 155, 346, 350
Receipts, expenses ....131-132

**United States of America (cont'd)**
Regions, outlying ....380-382
Savings Bonds ...........218
Seal, The U. S. ..........701
Selective Service ........756
Social Security ......148-154
Soviet Relations ..........83
Space Developments *see*
 *Space developments*
States, individual ....354-379
Statistical information ....126
Superlative statistics .....94
Supreme Court decisions ..49
Telephones ..............123
Territorial expansion ....385
Trade ....................98
Trails ....................94
Treaties *see Treaties, U. S.*
Vital statistics .......757-768
Voice of America ........575
Wars—
 1812 ..................301
 Civil War .........304-305
 Korean .................315
 Spanish Amer. .........307
 Vietnam .............40-42
 World War I ......308-309
 World War II ......312-313
 *See specific subjects*
**Universe, Miss** ............ 61
**Universities** *see Colleges*
**Unknown Soldier, tomb** ....441
**Upolu Is., W. Samoa** ......579
**Upper Volta, Rep. of** ...563, 577
**Uranium—**
Atomic weight ...........589
Congo, Rep. of ..........505
Czechoslovakia ..........508
Fission theory ...........116
U. S. States 355, 357, 376, 379
**Uranus (planet)** ............286
**Urban Affairs, Housing Dept.**
 of ......................179
**Urban area, largest** ........651
**Urban population, U. S.** ....601
**Uruguay** ..................564
Area, capital population .564
Gold reserve ............139
Merchant fleet ..........101
Montevideo (population) .579
President ................577
Weights, measures .......587
**Urundi** *see Burundi*
**Utah** .....................376
 *See States, U. S.*
Admission, area, Cap. 376, 384
Agriculture ..769-771, 773, 776
Birth, death statistics 758, 765
Counties (seats, areas) ..649
Election .........884, 885, 911
Lake, largest ............718
Marriage, divorce laws 760, 761
Mountain Meadows (1857) 303
Museums, attractions 376, 428
Name, origin of .........383
Officials, pay .......919, 923
Population ...........593-654
 –Cities and towns ...604, 632
 –Counties, county seats ..649
 –Metropolitan areas ...652-654
Presidential vote .....884, 911
Salt Lake City (*see Salt*
 *Lake City*) ...........428
Taxes ...............209-218
Territory ...........376, 384
Vital statistics .......757-768
**Uzbek SSR** ................554

**— V —**

**V-E Day, World War II** .....313
**V-J Day, World War II** .....313
**Vaccination (1796)** ........300
**Vaccine—**
Sabin ...................116
Salk ....................116
**Valley of 10,000 Smokes** ...354
**Valois, House of** ...........689
**Van Buren, Martin (biog.)** ..186
**Vance, Cyrus** ..............70
**Vancouver, Canada** ........435
**Vancouver Island (Pacific)** .722
**Vatican City, State of** ......564
Area, population ........564
Lateran Agreement ......564
Law of Guarantees (1871) 305
Popes ........66, 227, 564
**Veal—**
Nutritive value ..........774
Prices, farm .............770
Production, consumption ..776
**Vegetables—**
Consumption ............776
Nutritive value ..........774

**Vegetables (cont'd)**
Price indexes .............769
Production ................771
**Vella Lavella Is., Solomons** .563
**Venezuela** ..................564
Angel Falls ...............564
Area, capital, population ..564
Bolivar, Simon ...........693
Cities (population) .......679
Gold reserve .............139
Merchant fleet ...........101
Petroleum production .....130
President .................577
Quintuplets (1963) .......318
Sugar production .........122
Trade ................98, 565
Waterfall .................564
Weights, measures .......587
**Venus (planet)** ....253-256, 258
Morning, evening star
256, 263-276
Position by months ...253-256
Rises, sets ...............287
**Vermont** ...................376
*See States, U. S.*
Admissions, area, cap. 376, 384
Agriculture ..769-771, 773, 776
Birth, death statistics 758, 765
Counties (seats, areas) ..649
Elections ......884, 885, 911
Lake, largest .............718
Marriage, divorce laws 760, 761
Museums, attractions .....377
Name, origin of ..........383
Officials, pay .......919, 923
Population ...........593-654
−Cities and towns ........632
−Counties, county seats ..649
−Metropolitan areas .652-654
Presidential vote .....884, 911
Taxes .................209-218
Vital statistics .......757, 768
**Vernal Equinox** ............260
**Verrazano, Giovanni da**
(1524) .....297, 415, 708
**Versailles Treaty (1919)** ....309
German cessions .........515
Hitler rejects (1935, '37)
311, 515
**Vespucci, Amerigo (1497)** 175, 296
**Vesuvius, Mt. (Italy)** ..295, 716
**Veterans—**
G.I. Bill ..................753
Insurance .................753
Medical care .............753
New laws, 1968 ...........753
Number in U. S. ..........753
Pension payments ........753
Survivors, orphans benefit 753
**Veterans Administration—**
Employees (number) .....146
Expenditures .............753
Headquarters, functions ..753
**Veterans' Day** ..............590
**Vice Presidents of the U. S.—**
Electoral votes (law) ....
Enumeration .............178
List, with Presidents ....178
Nominees (1968) .......38, 39
Salary ...................164
Succession to Presidency
195, 206
Terms begin .......195, 205
**Victoria, Australia** .........494
**Victoria Cross** ..............486
**Victoria Falls** .......562, 719
**Victoria Island (area)** ......722
**Victoria Lake** ..551, 553, 717
**Victoria, Queen (1837)** .....302
**Vietnam** ....................565
Area, capital, pop. ..565, 579
Casualties ................41
Cities (population) .......579
Dem. Rep. of (North) 566, 577
Leaders ...................577
Medal of Honor ..........740
Peace talks ..78, 83, 87, 89, 91
Republic of (South) ..565, 577
War ......40-42, 65, 68, 69, 70,
73, 77, 79, 80, 81, 83, 84,
87, 89
**Villa, Francisco (1911)** .....308
**Violinists of the Past** .......685
**Virgin Islands, British** .....561
**Virgin Islands, U. S.** .......381
Accession .................383
Altitudes (high, low) .....738
Area, capital, population 381
Cities (population) .......655
Citizenship law, U. S. ....381
Deaths, motor vehicle ....765
Farms (statistics) ........769
Marriage information .....760
Officials, pay .......919, 923

**Virgin Islands U. S. (cont'd)**
Population ..........381, 655
Vital statistics ......757-768
**Virginia** ....................377
*See States, U. S.*
Admissions, area, cap. 377, 384
Agriculture 594-771, 773, 776
Appomattox Court House .377
Birth, death statistics 758, 765
Cities ................416, 423
Counties (seats, areas) 649-650
Elections ..........884, 911
Jamestown (1607) ........297
Lake, largest .............718
Marriage, divorce laws
760, 761
Museums, attractions
377, 417, 424
Name, origin of ..........383
Norfolk (*see Norfolk*) ...416
Officials, pay .......919, 926
Population ...........593-654
−Cities and towns ..604, 633
−Counties, county seats 649-650
−Metropolitan areas .652-654
Presidential vote .....884, 911
Richmond (*see Richmond*) 423
Taxes .................209-218
Vital statistics .......757-768
**Visa regulation, U. S.** ......700
**Vital statistics** .......757-768
**Vitamins in diet value** .774-775
**Viti Levu Island (area)** .....722
**Vladimir, Grand Duke of** ..692
**Vocabulary** .................332
**Vocational education** .......351
Veterans ..................753
**Vogeler, Robert A. (1950)** ..314
**Voice of America** ...........575
**Volcanoes** ..............715-716
**Volstead Act (1917)** .........309
**Volt (electrical unit)** .......586
**Volume—**
Geometric forms .........586
Measures, dry, fluid .581-584
Sun and planets ..........286
**Volunteers of Amer.** ..220, 222
**Vote, electoral—**
Law (constitution) ..201, 203
President (1952-1968) ....884
**Vote, popular—**
President, 1968 ..........884
−By candidate (1789-1968) 885
−By state ......884, 887-914
**Voting—**
Eligible population .......601
Negroes (law) ...........204
Poll taxes, states with ...926
Qualifications, by state ..926
Wash., D.C. residents 205, 379
Woman's suffrage (1920) 205

— W —

**WAC** *see Women's Army Corps*
**WAF** *see Women in Air Force*
**Wages—**
Accidents, loss from .....759
Farm .....................769
Industrial ................119
Railroads .................107
*See Incomes, Salaries*
**Wagner, Richard (composer)** 686
**Wainwright, Gen. J. M.** 312, 665
**Wake Island** ................381
**Wales** ......................560
Area, population .........560
Cities (population) .......579
*See United Kingdom*
**Walker Cup (golf)** ..........848
**Walking** *see track and field items*
**Wall Street, New York City—**
Bomb explosion (1920) 310, 661
Name, origin of ..........415
Stock market crash (1929) 310
**Wallace, Eliz. (Truman)** 183, 193
**Wallace, George C.**
36, 38-39, 71, 72, 98, 919
**Wallis Archipelago** .........514
**Wallis & Futuna Isls. (Fr.)** 514
**War of 1812** .................301
Casualties ................751
Military leaders, U. S.....665
**War Crimes—**
Axis Sally (1949) .........314
Eichmann, Adolf .........317
Japan, trials (1948) ......314
Koch, Ilse (1951) .........315
Lord Haw Haw (1946)...313
Nuremberg trials (1946) ..314
Tokyo Rose (1949) .......314

**War Department—**
Cabinet status ends .....180
History ...................180
Secretaries ...............180
*See Army, Dept. of the*
**Ward, Angus (1949)** .........314
**Warm Springs, Ga.** .........359
**Warren, Earl** ..63, 81, 91, 169
**Wars—**
American Revolution .298-299
Black Hawk (1832) .......302
Boer (1899-1902) .........306
Casualties .............751-752
China-Japan .....306, 312, 313
Civil, U. S. (1861-65)
304-305, 387
Crimean (1853-56) .......303
Cuban revolutions 307, 506, 507
English civil (1642) .......298
Franco-Prussian (1870) ...304
French and Indian (1754) 299
Hundred Years (1338-1453) 296
Indian, New Eng. (1676) ..298
Indo-China ...........531, 565
Israeli-Arab .........525, 557
Italian unity (1870) .......304
Italo-Ethiopian (1934-'36) 311
Korean (1950-'53) ........315
Mexican revolution (1911) 308
Mexico-U. S. (1846-'48) ..302
Napoleonic (1805-'15) ....301
Philippine revolt (1899) ..306
Punic (264-146 BC) .......295
Russo-Japanese (1904-'05) 307
Seminole (1836) ..........302
Ship losses ..........657-660
Sioux war (1876) .........306
Spain, civil (1936-'39) 311, 548
Spanish-American (1898) .307
Thirty Years (1618-'48) ...297
Tripoli-U. S. (1801) .......300
Troop strength, U. S. 751-752
Vietnam ...40-42, 65, 68, 69, 70,
73, 78, 79, 80, 81, 83,
84, 87, 89, 91, 565
War of 1812 ..........301, 751
World *see World War I, II*
**Warsaw Pact (1955)** 88, 316, 573
**Washington Cathedral** ......444
**Washington, D. C.** .435, 439-444
Airlines ..................436
Altitudes (high, low) .....738
Area, population .........435
Automobile statistics ..108-115
Banking statistics ........136
Birth, death statistics 758, 765
Burned (1814) ............301
Centers of interest ...439-444
Education statistics ......349
Federal courts ...........167
Federal workers ......145-146
Government, history ......379
Income, per capita .......138
Marriage, divorce laws 760, 761
Mileage to other cities 110-111
Poor People ...............77
Population ......604, 633, 654
Postal receipts ...........932
Public buildings .....439-444
Seattle (see Seattle) .....432
Subway ...................435
Taxes .................209-218
Vital statistics .......757-768
Vote ...............205, 379
White House ..........440-441
**Washington, George—**
Biography .................184
Birthday (legal holiday) ..590
Birthplace (Va.) .....184, 377
Capitol cornerstone laid ..439
Constitutional convention 199
Farewell Address (1796) ..300
French and Indian War ...299
Mt. Rushmore Memorial ..375
Mount Vernon ...........442
President ........183, 184, 195
Religion, ancestry ........195
Revolution .....184, 298-299
Tomb .....................184
Wife, biography .....183, 184
**Washington Island** ..........563
**Washington Monument** 389, 444
**Washington, Mount, N. H.** 368
**Washington, State of—** ......378
*See States, U. S.*
Admission, area, cap. 378, 384
Agriculture ..769-771, 773, 776
Birth, death statistics 758, 765
Century 21 Expos. ........61
Counties (seats, areas) ...650
Elections ......884, 885, 912
Lake, largest .............718
Marriage, divorce laws 760, 761
Mountains ................720
Museums, attractions 378, 432

**Washington, State of (cont'd)**
Name, origin of ...........383
Officials, pay .........919, 923
Population ...........593-654
-Cities and towns ...604, 633
-Counties, county seats ...650
-Metropolitan areas ..652-654
-Presidential vote ...884, 912
Seattle (*see Seattle*) ......432
Taxes ...............209-218
Territory .............384-385
Vital statistics ......757-768
**Water—**
Area (U. S. inland) ......384
Boiling, freezing points ...589
Calif. project .............729
Oceans, seas ..............703
Resources ................709
Underwater research ......710
Weight ..................584
**Waterfalls, by country** ....719
Highest, U. S. ...........719
Minnehaha Falls .........719
Niagara ................719
**Water Ski Champions** .....835
**Watt** (electrical unit) ......586
**Wayles, Martha** (Jefferson)
183, 185
**Wayne, Anthony** (1794) ...300
**Wealth, Nations** ..........567
**Weather** .............288, 294
1967 Climatological data .290
Blizzard (1888) ....306, 662
Coastal warnings .........289
Degree day ...............42
Dew point ...............288
Forecasts by sattelite ....294
Hurricanes ....289, 294, 662
One inch rain ............60
River and Flood service ..288
States and cities .....290-293
Temperature-Humidity
Index ................288
Temperature normal .....289
Wettest spot .............292
Wind Chill ..............288
Winds, velocities ........289
**Weather Bureau U. S.** ..288-294
**Webb, Lucy** (Hayes) ...183, 189
**Weddings—**
Robb, Lynda Johnson .... 66
Kennedy, Jacqueline .... 92
**Wedding anniversaries** ....760
**Weeks** (observed each year) 591
**Weightlifting** ............848
**Weight throwing records—**
American .................858
Olympic games ..878, 881-883
World ....................855
**Weights and measures** ..581-589
Atomic ..............588-586
Conversion tables 581-584, 589
Electrical units ...........586
Equivalents, table of ..581-584
Foreign ..................587
Gases ...................589
Human (height, weight) .763
Metric system .........581-584
Metric terms .............584
U. S. system ..........581-584
Water ...................584
**Weizmann, Dr. Chaim** ......525
**Welfare services—**
Administration ...........154
**Welland Canal** ............ 97
**West Africa Portuguese** ....544
**West Borneo, Indonesia** ...522
**West Germany** *see Germany,*
*Federal Republic of*
**West Indies, British** ......561
**West Irian** ...............522
**West Point Military Acad.** ..744
**West Virginia** .............378
*See States, U. S.*
Admission, area, cap. 378, 384
Agriculture ..769-771, 773, 776
Birth, death statistics 758, 765
Counties (seats, areas) ...650
Elections ......884, 885, 913
Lake, largest .............718
Marriage, divorce laws 760, 761
Name, origin of ..........383
Officials, pay .........919, 923
Population ...........593-654
-Cities and town ....633-634
-Counties, county seats ..650
-Metropolitan areas ..652-654
Presidential vote ...884, 913
Taxes ...............209-218
Vital statistics ......757-768
**Western Explorations** ......708
**Western Samoa** ......566, 577
**Westernmost point, U. S.** ... 94
**Westminster Kennel Club** ..877

**Westmoreland, Wm. C.** ..71, 81
**Wheat—**
Chicago spot prices ......772
Exports .................776
Grain center receipts ....773
Prices, farm .............770
Production ....771, 772, 773
-By state ...............773
Seed ....................771
Supply in U. S. ..........772
**Whiskey production** ........121
**Whiskey Rebellion** (1794) ..300
**White House** .........440-441
President's staff .........164
Visiting hours ...........441
**White Mountains, N. H.** ..368
**White, Stanford** (1906) ....307
**Whitman, Walt** (1855) ..303, 668
**Whitney Museum, N. Y. C.** 437
**Wholesale price indexes** ...143
**Whooping Crane** ...........780
**Widener art collection** ......443
**Wight, Isle of** (area) .......722
**Wildlife services** ...........781
**Wilhelmina, Queen** ...538, 692
**William I, Germany** ..304, 690
**William II, Germany** .......690
**Williams, Roger** (R. I.) .....374
**Williamsburg, Colonial** .....377
**Wilmington, Del.** ...........358
Art Center ..............358
du Pont industries .......358
Mayor ..................926
Population ...........609, 654
**Wilson, Harold** ..68, 69, 558, 577
**Wilson Is., Solomons** .......563
**Wilson, Woodrow** (biog.) 191-192
**Wimbledon Tennis** ........812
**Wind Cave, So. Dakota** ...388
**Winds—**
Chill ....................288
Designations, force ......289
Velocity, by station ......289
Weather forecasts ....288-290
**Windsor Hotel fire** (1899) ..664
**Windsor, House of** .........688
**Windward Islands** .........561
**Wine—**Excise tax .........218
**Winnipeg, Canada** ..........46
**Winter** (season) ...........260
**Wireless** (1896, 1901) ..306, 307
**Wisconsin—** ..............378
*See States, U. S.*
Admission, area, cap. 378, 384
Agriculture ..769-771, 773, 776
Birth, death statistics 758, 765
Counties (seats, areas) 650-651
Elections ....76, 884, 885, 913
Forest fires (1871) ........664
Lake, largest ............718
Marriage, divorce laws 760, 761
Milwaukee
(*see Milwaukee*) .......412
Museums, attractions 379, 412
Name, origin of ..........383
Officials, pay .........919, 923
Population ...........593-654
-Cities and towns ...604, 634
-Counties, county seats 650-651
-Metropolitan areas ..652-654
Presidential vote ...884, 913
Taxes ...............209-218
Territory ................384
Vital statistics ......757-768
**Witchcraft** (1656, '92) ..298, 299
**Wolfson, Louis B.** ......... 88
**Women—**
Air Force
-History, organization ....748
-Pay scale, allowances 754-755
-Strength ...............743
Army Corps
-History, organization ....747
-Pay scale, allowances 754-755
-Strength ...............741
Aviation records ....247-250
Births, deaths (U. S.) ....758
Coast Guard .............748
Drivers, economy run ....113
Employment .............143
Height, weight ...........763
Illegitimate births .......764
Marines
-History, organization ....748
-Pay scale, allowances 754-755
Marriage, statistics ..758, 760
Nationality effect ........703
Medical Service ......747-748
Men per 100 ............603
Military Service, U. S. 747-748
Navy
-History, organization ....747
-Pay scale, allowances 754-755
Nurses ..............747-748
Population, age, color ....596

**Women** (cont'd)
Social Security .......148-153
Suffrage (1920) ..........205
Wyoming, vote (1869) ....304
**Wonders of World—**
Ancient, Seven ..........721
Engineering of U. S. .....129
**Wool—**
Farm income ............770
Prices, farm .......769, 770
Production (U. S., world) 125
**Woolworth's 5 & 10** (1879) ..306
**Work stoppages** ...........245
**Worktime, required to buy** ..142
**World areas, populations** ...651
**World Bank** .........572, 574
**World Council of Churches** .222
**World Court Internat'l** .....571
**World Health Organization** .572
**World languages** ..........350
**World rulers** ...576-577, 688-693
**World Series** *see Baseball*
**World, Trips around** ...247-250
**World War I—**
Allied nations ...........752
Armed forces, by country .752
Casualties, by country ...752
Cemeteries, U. S., abroad 749
Central powers ..........752
Dawes plan (1924) .......310
Debt owed U. S. .........750
Military leaders, U. S. ...665
Peace treaties
-U. S.-Germany (1921) ...310
-Versailles (1919) ........309
Principal events ......308-309
Ship losses ..............658
Unknown Soldier, tomb ..441
**World War II—**
African campaigns ...312-313
Allied powers ...........752
Ardennes Bulge battle ...313
Armed forces, by country 752
Atomic bombs ......312, 313
Axis powers .............752
Britain, battle of .........312
Casualties, by country ...751
-Merchant Marine .......752
Cemeteries, U. S., abroad 749
Coral Sea battle .........313
D-Day ..................313
Doolittle raids, Japan ....312
Draft *see Selective Service*
Dunkirk, retreat from ....312
German surrender (1945) 313
German war ends .........314
Graf Spee (1939) .........659
Hitler suicide (1945) 313, 515
Iwo Jima, Okinawa ......313
Japan surrenders (1945) ..313
Leyte Gulf battle ........313
Memorial museum, Va. ...377
Military leaders, U. S. ...665
Nazi leaders hanged ......314
Neutral nations ..........752
Patton Museum, Ft. Knox 363
Peace treaties
-Austria (1955) ..........496
-First (1946) ............313
-Japan (1951) .....316, 528
Pearl Harbor attack (1941) 312
Philippine Islands ..312, 543
Rhine, Allies cross the ...313
Ship losses .......312, 313, 659
Soviet-Nazi pact (1939) ..311
Summary of events ...312-313
Treaties ........312, 313, 314
-V-E day, V-J Day .......313
Veterans *see Veterans*
War Crimes *see War Crimes*
**World's Fairs** ............. 61
**World's largest cities**
578-579, 651
**Wrangel Island** (USSR) ...722
**Wrestling, amateur** ........845
**Wright Brothers—**
Flights (1903) ...........307
Hall of Fame ............250
Monument (N. C.) ..371, 307
Smithsonian exhibit ......444
**Writers, noted** *see Authors*
**Wyandotte Cave, Ind.** .....361
**Wycliffe, John** (1382) ......296
**Wyoming** ................379
*See States, U. S.*
Admission, area, cap. 379, 384
Agriculture ..769-771, 773, 776
Birth, death statistics 758, 765
Counties (seats, areas) ...651
Elections .............884, 914
Lake, largest ............718
Marriage, divorce laws 760, 761
Museums, attractions ....379

**Wyoming (cont'd)**
Name, origin of ........ 383
Officials, pay ........919, 923
Ross, Nellie T. (1924) .. 310
Population ..........593-654
–Cities and towns ...604, 634
–Counties, county seats .. 651
–Metropolitan areas . 652-654
Presidential vote ...884, 914
Taxes .............. 209-218
Territory .........379, 384
Vital statistics ......757-768

**— X —**

Xerxes, King (480 B.C.) ... 295
X-ray discovered (1895) 118, 306

**— Y —**

Yacht racing ...............837
Yale University—
Art gallery ..............358
Coed in 1969 ........... 63

**Yale University (cont'd)**
Established (1701) ......358
Peabody Museum .......358
Rowing (Harvard) ......836
Statistics ........332, 345
Yalta Conf. (1945) .......313
Yanaon, India ............520
Year—
Calendars, perpetual ..278-279
Christian era began ..... 295
Chronological eras (1969) 280
Sidereal, tropical .......260
Yellow Fever, 1900 .......307
Yellowstone Natl. Park ....388
Yemen ...................566
Area, capital, population .566
President ............566, 577
Yes, Virginia ............ 55
York, House of ...........688
Yorktown, battle .........299
Yosemite Natl. Park ......388
Ysabel Is., Solomons .....563
Yugoslavia ...............566
Area, capital, population .566
Cities (population) ......579

**Yugoslavia (cont'd)**
Merchant fleet ...........101
Mikhailovitch, Gen. (1946) 314
Petroleum production ....130
Serbia ..................567
Sugar production ........122
Tito *see Tito, Marshal*
Trade ................... 98
Trieste (Italy) ...........527
Yukon River ..............724

**— Z —**

Zambia ..............567, 577
Zanzibar, *see Tanzania*
Zenger, John P. (1735) .....299
Zinc production ..........129
Zion Natl. Park, Utah ....388
Zip Code ..........605-634, 655
Zodiac ..................282
Zoological Parks, U. S. ...779
National ...............444
Natural settings .......779
Zuider Zee (IJsselmeer) ...537

## Electoral Votes for President, 1952-68

The Constitution, Article 2, Section 1 (consult index), provides for the appointment of electors, the counting of the electoral ballots and the procedure in the event of a tie. (*See Electoral College,* page 914.)

| State | 1952 R. | 1952 D. | 1956 R. | 1956 D. | 1960 R. | 1960 D. | 1964 R. | 1964 D. | 1968 R. | 1968 D. | 1968 3d |
|---|---|---|---|---|---|---|---|---|---|---|---|
| Ala.... | | 11 | | [1]11 | | [2]5 10 | 10 | | | | 10 |
| Alaska. | | | 3 | | 3 | | 3 | | 3 | | |
| Ariz... | 4 | | 4 | | 4 | | 5 | | 5 | | |
| Ark.... | | 8 | | 8 | | 8 | | 6 | | 6 | | 6 |
| Calif.. | 32 | | 32 | | 32 | | 40 | 40 | | 40 | |
| Colo.. | 6 | | 6 | | 6 | | 6 | | 6 | | |
| Conn.. | 8 | | 8 | | 8 | | 8 | | 8 | | |
| Del... | 3 | | 3 | | 3 | | 3 | | 3 | | |
| D. of C. | | | | | | | [3]3 | | [2]3 | | |
| Fla... | 10 | | 10 | | 10 | | 14 | 14 | | 14 | |
| Ga.... | | 12 | | 12 | 12 | | 12 | | | | 12 |
| Hawaii. | | | | | [3]3 | | 4 | | 4 | | |
| Idaho.. | 4 | | 4 | | 4 | | 4 | | 4 | | |
| Ill.... | 27 | | 27 | | 27 | | 26 | 26 | | 26 | |
| Ind... | 13 | | 13 | | 13 | | 13 | 13 | | 13 | |
| Iowa... | 10 | | 10 | | 10 | | 9 | | 9 | | |
| Kan... | 8 | | 8 | | 8 | | 7 | | 7 | | |
| Ky.... | | 10 | 10 | | 10 | | 9 | | 9 | | |
| La... | 5 | | 10 | | 5 | | 10 | 10 | | | 10 |
| Me... | 5 | | 5 | | 5 | | 4 | | 4 | | |
| Md... | 9 | | 9 | | 9 | | 10 | | 10 | | |
| Mass.. | 16 | | 16 | | 16 | | 14 | 14 | | 14 | |
| Mich.. | 20 | | 20 | | 20 | | 21 | 21 | | 21 | |
| Minn.. | 11 | | 11 | | 11 | | 10 | | 10 | | |
| Miss.. | | 8 | | 8 | (2) | 7 | 7 | | | | 7 |
| Mo... | 13 | | 13 | | 13 | | 12 | 12 | | | |
| Mont. | 4 | | 4 | | 4 | | 4 | | 4 | | |
| Neb.. | 6 | | 6 | | 6 | | 5 | | 5 | | |
| Nev.. | 3 | | 3 | | 3 | | 3 | | 3 | | |
| N. H. | 4 | | 4 | | 4 | | 4 | | 4 | | |
| N. J. | 16 | | 16 | | 16 | | 17 | | 17 | | |
| N. M. | 4 | | 4 | | 4 | | 4 | | 4 | | |
| N. Y. | 45 | | 45 | | 45 | | 43 | | 43 | | |
| N. C. | | 14 | | 14 | 14 | | 13 | 13 | | 13 | |
| N. D. | 4 | | 4 | | 4 | | 4 | | 4 | | |
| Ohio.. | 25 | | 25 | | 25 | | 26 | 26 | | 26 | |
| Okla.. | 8 | | 8 | | [2]7 | | 8 | | 8 | | |
| Oreg.. | 6 | | 6 | | 6 | | 6 | | 6 | | |
| Penn.. | 32 | | 32 | | | 32 | 29 | | 29 | | |
| R. I. | 4 | | 4 | | 4 | | 4 | | 4 | | |
| S. C. | | 8 | | 8 | | 8 | 8 | | | | 8 |
| S. D. | 4 | | 4 | | 4 | | 4 | | 4 | | |
| Tenn. | 11 | | 11 | | 11 | | 11 | 11 | | 11 | |
| Texas. | 24 | | 24 | | | 24 | 25 | | 25 | | |
| Utah.. | 4 | | 4 | | 4 | | 4 | | 4 | | |
| Vt... | 3 | | 3 | | 3 | | 3 | | 3 | | |
| Va... | 12 | | 12 | | 12 | | 12 | 12 | | | |
| Wash.. | 9 | | 9 | | 9 | | 9 | | 9 | | 9 |
| W. Va. | | 8 | 8 | | | 8 | 7 | | | | 7 |
| Wis... | 12 | | 12 | | 12 | | 12 | 12 | | | |
| Wyo... | 3 | | 3 | | 3 | | 3 | | 3 | | |
| **Totals** | 442 | 89 | 457 | [1]74 | 219 | 303 | 52 | 486 | 302 | 191 | 45 |
| **Plur.** | 353 | | 383 | | | [2]84 | 434 | | 111 | | |

[1]In 1956 in Alabama one Democratic elector refused to vote for Stevenson and cast his ballot for Walter B. Jones, making the Democratic total actually 73.

[2]In 1960 Sen. Harry F. Byrd (D.-Va.) got 15 electoral votes, including those of 8 unpledged Mississippi Democratic electors, 6 unpledged Alabama Democrats and one Oklahoma Republican.

[3]First Presidential election.

## Congressional Apportionment

| State | 1950 Census | 1960 Census | State | 1950 Census | 1960 Census | State | 1950 Census | 1960 Census | State | 1950 Census | 1960 Census |
|---|---|---|---|---|---|---|---|---|---|---|---|
| Ala...... | 9 | 8 | Ind.... | 11 | 11 | Neb.... | 4 | 3 | S. C.... | 6 | 6 |
| Alaska.. | 1 | 1 | Iowa... | 8 | 7 | Nev.... | 1 | 1 | S. D.... | 2 | 2 |
| Ariz.... | 2 | 3 | Kan.... | 6 | 5 | N. H... | 2 | 2 | Tenn.... | 9 | 9 |
| Ark.... | 6 | 4 | Ky..... | 8 | 7 | N. J... | 14 | 15 | Texas... | 22 | 23 |
| Calif... | 30 | 38 | La..... | 8 | 8 | N. M... | 2 | 2 | Utah... | 2 | 2 |
| Colo.... | 4 | 4 | Me..... | 3 | 2 | N. Y... | 43 | 41 | Vt..... | 1 | 1 |
| Conn.... | 6 | 6 | Md..... | 7 | 8 | N. C... | 12 | 11 | Va..... | 10 | 10 |
| Del..... | 1 | 1 | Mass... | 14 | 12 | N. D... | 2 | 2 | Wash... | 7 | 7 |
| Fla..... | 8 | 12 | Mich... | 18 | 19 | Ohio... | 23 | 24 | W. Va.. | 6 | 5 |
| Ga...... | 10 | 10 | Minn... | 9 | 8 | Okla... | 6 | 6 | Wis.... | 10 | 10 |
| Hawaii. | 1 | 2 | Miss... | 6 | 5 | Ore.... | 4 | 4 | Wyo.... | 1 | 1 |
| Idaho.. | 2 | 2 | Mo..... | 11 | 10 | Pa..... | 30 | 27 | | | |
| Ill..... | 25 | 24 | Mont... | 2 | 2 | R. I... | 2 | 2 | **Totals** | 437 | 435 |

The chief reason why the Constitution provided for a census of the population every 10 years was to give a basis for apportionment of Representatives among the states. This apportionment is of added importance because it largely determines how many electoral votes are alloted to each state in Presidential elections. *See Electoral College.*

The number of Representatives of each state in Congress is determined by the state's population, except that each state is entitled to one Representative regardless of population. A Congressional apportionment has been made after each decennial census except that of 1920.

Under provisions of a law that became effective Nov. 15, 1941, apportionment of Representatives is made by the method of equal proportions. In the application of this method, the apportionment is made so that the average population per Representative has the least possible variation between one state and any other. The first House of Representatives, in 1790, had 65 members, or one Representative for each 30,000 of the estimated population, as provided by the Constitution. As the population grew, the number of Representatives was increased but the total membership has been fixed at 435 since 1912 by action of Congress. On the basis of the 1960 census, with 435 Representatives, there was one for each 410,481 persons.

With the admission of Alaska and Hawaii to the Union, the total number of Representatives rose to 437 temporarily. It reverted to 435 with the new apportionment after the 1960 census.

# The World Almanac

## and Book of Facts for 1969

*The 193rd anniversary of the adoption of the Declaration of Independence, 1776, falls on July 4, 1969. The 182nd anniversary of the signing of the Constitution of the United States, 1787, falls on September 17, 1969. The Government declared the Constitution in effect March 4, 1789.*

The first edition of the WORLD ALMANAC, a 120-page hand-set volume containing 12 pages of advertisements, was published by the New York World 101 years ago, in 1868. Annual publication was suspended in 1876. Joseph Pulitzer, publisher of the New York World, revived the WORLD ALMANAC in 1886 with the goal of making it a "compendium of universal knowledge." It has been published annually since. In 1931 it was acquired by Scripps-Howard; until 1951 it bore the imprint of the New York World-Telegram, thereafter until 1967 that of the New York World-Telegram and Sun. It is now published in paper and cloth-bound editions by Newspaper Enterprise Association, Inc.

*President-elect Richard M. Nixon, commenting Nov. 6, 1968, upon his election, said: "I saw many signs in this campaign. Some of them were not friendly and some were very friendly. But the one that touched me most was one that I saw in Deshler, Ohio, at the end of a long day of whistle-stopping, a little town, I suppose five times the population was there in the dark, almost impossible to see—but a teen-ager held up a sign, 'Bring Us Together.' And that will be the great objective of this Administration at the outset, to bring the American people together."*

☞ The Editor acknowledges with thanks the many letters, whether of helpful comment or criticism, that attest the usefulness of the WORLD ALMANAC, and invites suggestions for improvement of its services to readers. Address: 230 Park Avenue, New York, N.Y. 10017.

The WORLD ALMANAC does not decide wagers.

## *1968—THE YEAR THAT WAS*

As the World Almanac enters its second century with this 101st Anniversary Edition, it chronicles the events and developments of a year that was second to none in this long span for surprises, both pleasant and unpleasant, and for shocks, some of which shook not only America but the entire civilized world.

What distinguished 1968 from any of the 100 other years since the establishment of the World Almanac? Here are some of the landmark events, not necessarily in exact order of chronology or importance, which are covered in more detail elsewhere in this edition:

**U.S.S. Pueblo**—First seizure of a U. S. warship on the high seas in 150 years (captured by North Korea).

**Scorpion**—U. S. nuclear submarine lost with 99 men aboard.

**Dr. Benjamin Spock**—Indictment and conviction of famed pediatrician for conspiring to abet draft violations.

**Gov. George Romney**—Surprise withdrawal of Michigan leader from race for Republican Presidential nomination.

**Sen. Eugene McCarthy**—Unprecedentedly successful challenge (on a peace platform) to an incumbent President for the White House nomination by a leader of his own party.

**Assassinations**—The entire world was horrified by the senseless slayings of the Rev. Dr. Martin Luther King, Negro civil rights leader, and Sen. Robert F. Kennedy, brother of the assassinated President John F. Kennedy.

**Student Protests**—A student rebellion that closed Columbia University in New York City was perhaps the most notable in a wave of college disruptions stemming from racial unrest, anti-war sentiment, and revolt against administrative authority.

**Peace Prospects**—Hopes for an end to the war in Vietnam were raised by the opening of preliminary talks in Paris and increased significantly after President Johnson announced the cessation of U. S. bombing of North Vietnam.

**Johnson Withdrawal**—Biggest political bombshell in many years was President Johnson's announcement that he would not seek or accept his party's nomination for another term in the White House.

**Biafra Horror**—The sympathy and outrage of the world were aroused by the plight of the children of Biafra, starving by the hundreds of thousands because of the revolt of that province against parent Nigeria.

**Birth Control**—An encyclical by Pope Paul VI against modern methods of contraception caused widespread controversy and threatened a revolt within the Roman Catholic Church.

**Presidential Election**—The Presidential election year was featured by unprecedented violence in the streets during the Democratic National Convention in Chicago and by the victory of Republican nominee Richard M. Nixon by a razor-thin margin.

**Czechoslovakia Invaded**—The world trembled when the Soviet Union and its Warsaw Pact puppets invaded Czechoslovakia to snuff out a liberalist movement in that country.

**Man to the Moon**—Man's drive to land on the lunar surface received fresh impetus from space achievements by the Soviet Union and the United States. The USSR sent two unmanned vehicles around the moon and back to earth and sent a single-manned vehicle into experimental flight. The United States sent a 3-manned Apollo craft into earth orbit for 11 days and announced plans for another 3-man Apollo to orbit the moon before the end of 1968.

# PRESIDENTIAL ELECTION, 1968

## Republican Richard M. Nixon Victorious in Cliff-Hanger

In one of the most dramatic and suspenseful elections in this century, former Vice President Richard Milhous Nixon was elected the 37th President of the United States Nov. 5, 1968. In his second Presidential bid, the Republican nominee and his Vice Presidential running mate, Maryland's Gov. Spiro T. Agnew, carried 32 states in a 3-way race, garnering 302 of the 538 electoral votes and about 43.4% of the popular vote.

Nixon's proportion of the popular vote was the lowest received by any victorious Presidential candidate since Woodrow Wilson won with 41.9% in a 3-way race in 1912. While the estimated total of 72,000,-000 votes in 1968 set a record, analysis of national totals indicated that only about 60% of the 120,000,000 Americans of voting age cast ballots. This was the lowest proportion since 1956, when 60.5% voted as President Eisenhower was chosen for his second term.

The 1968 Election Night vigil was tense as Nixon ran neck-and-neck with his Democratic opponent, Vice President Hubert H. Humphrey. The suspense was intensified by the breakdown of a computer system assembling the nationwide results for major news media. With 270 electoral votes required for a majority, it was not until the following day that Illinois' 26 were assured to Nixon, putting him over the top. Ironically, it was Illinois that had swung the 1960 election from Nixon to John F. Kennedy when Cook County gave the Democrat a 9,000-vote statewide margin.

In the 3-way 1968 election, Nixon received over 31,000,000 votes—3,000,000 fewer than he did in his two-way contest with Kennedy 8 years earlier.

Despite Nixon's very slight lead over Humphrey in the popular vote, the Republican nominee came in a winner by gaining pluralities in several key states where Kennedy had edged him out in 1960. These included the prize electoral plums of California, Illinois, Indiana, New Jersey and Ohio. Yet, Nixon did not carry one major city in the nation.

### Humphrey, Muskie Win 191 Electoral Votes

Humphrey and the Democratic Vice Presidential candidate, Maine's Sen. Edmund S. Muskie, received slightly over 43% of the popular vote and won 191 electoral votes from 13 states and the District of Columbia.

Opinion polls had indicated early in the campaign that the 3d party vote might bar an electoral majority to either of the two other candidates. But this threat was dispelled as George C. Wallace won only 5 states and their 45 electoral votes, all in the South—Alabama, Arkansas, Georgia, Louisiana and Mississippi.

Wallace and his Vice Presidential running mate, Gen. Curtis E. LeMay, got over 9,500,000 votes, some 13.5% of the popular total. While somewhat less than had been predicted, the Wallace ticket got the highest 3d party popular vote percentage since Robert M. La Follette received almost 17% in 1924. The Wallace popular vote was the largest in history for a 3d party candidate.

There were varying assessments of the effect of the Wallace candidacy on the results achieved by Nixon and Humphrey. But there was general agreement that the Wallace strength faded toward the end of the campaign. This was attributed in some measure to the "don't waste your vote" theme of both major parties and to union campaigns for Humphrey. Much of Humphrey's homestretch surge, which threatened Nixon's early-start advantage, was held due to President Johnson's halting of the bombing of North Vietnam shortly before the election.

Although Humphrey and Muskie won their home states—Minnesota and Maine—Nixon and Agnew lost theirs—New York and Maryland. This was contrary to two political traditions—that no Republican can be elected President without carrying New York and that Minnesota always votes with the winner.

### Democrats Keep Congressional Control

The Democrats kept control of Congress: the House 243 to 192 and the Senate 58 to 42. This made Nixon the first President to begin his first term confronted by the problem of opposition party control of both houses of Congress since Zachary Taylor faced the same situation in 1848. In 1968 the voters cut the Democratic margin in the Senate from 26 seats to 16 seats, and in the House from 58 to 41.

One of the more notable Senate races was in New York, where Republican Sen. Jacob Javits won a 3d term by over 1,000,-000 votes, the biggest margin of his career, while Nixon was losing the state to Humphrey by nearly 400,000. Arizona's former Sen. Barry Goldwater, 1964 GOP Presidential candidate, beat Roy Elson for the seat vacated by retiring Democratic Sen. Carl Hayden. Four-term Sen. Wayne Morse of Oregon, who ran behind Republican State Rep. Robert W. Packwood, demanded a recount.

### GOP Scores Gubernatorial Gains

With 21 governorships on the line, the GOP gained 5 in early and decisive gubernatorial results, taking 7 states from the Democrats and losing two. This gave the Republicans 31 governors, the most they had had since the total of 34 they reached in the 1920 Warren G. Harding landslide. Moreover, after the 1968 votes were counted, the GOP had governorships in 6 of the most populous states—California, Illinois, Michigan, New York, Ohio, and Pennsylvania.

The only one of these important gubernatorial posts contested in 1968 was that of Illinois, where Richard Ogilvie, 45, Cook County Board president and former Federal prosecutor, won a key GOP prize by defeating Democratic incumbent Gov. Samuel Shapiro.

But the Republican cause was jolted when two well known GOP governors lost to unknown Democrats: the casualties were Rhode Island's John Chafee, running for his 4th term, and Montana's Tim Babcock, seeking his 3d.

Vermont and Iowa returned to the traditional Republican column, with Deane C. Davis winning over Vermont Lt. Gov. John J. Daley, and Robert D. Ray victorious over Iowa State Treasurer Paul Franzenburg.

Ticket splitting was the order of 1968 Election Day, and this was evidenced right down to the statehouse level as voters resisted predictable patterns. While Humphrey easily carried New York, for example, Republicans regained control of the State Assembly, which they had lost in 1964. The GOP captured control of the California State Assembly for the first time in a decade, but lost control of the Pennsylvania State House of Representatives and Michigan's lower house.

# Major Nominating Conventions of 1968
## Republican Convention Designates Nixon and Agnew

The Republican National Convention in Miami Beach, Fla., named former Vice President Richard M. Nixon, 54, its Presidential nominee on the first ballot, early Aug. 8, 1968, and later that day ratified his choice of Maryland Gov. Spiro T. Agnew, 49, for Vice President.

The acknowledged front runner in the final weeks before the convention, Nixon defeated New York Gov. Nelson A. Rockefeller and California Gov. Ronald Reagan. Reagan announced his candidacy two days before the balloting, amid speculation of increasing support for him among Southern delegates. Both had worked hard to block a 1st-ballot win for Nixon, with Rockefeller putting strong stock in public opinion polls to boost his image of voter popularity.

Agnew, who made the nomination speech for Nixon, had been one of 3 favorite-son candidates, but had withdrawn in Nixon's favor. No serious threats to Nixon's candidacy were posed by the two others, Michigan's Gov. George W. Romney and Ohio's Gov. James A. Rhodes.

Nixon's choice of Agnew came as a surprise and was attributed to a rumored deal with Sen. Strom Thurmond (S. C.), who was credited largely with winning the Southern delegates for Nixon. Despite a brief liberal Republican flareup of dissent at Agnew's selection, New York Mayor John V. Lindsay of the liberal wing seconded Agnew's nomination, made by Rep. Rogers C. B. Morton (Md.). Both Romney's and Lindsay's names had been placed in nomination—Romney got 186 votes, Lindsay 10—but Romney asked that the nomination be made unanimous, and it was. Agnew received 1,128 votes.

Seconding speeches for Nixon were made by Sens. Howard H. Baker, Jr. (Tenn.) and Mark O. Hatfield (Ore.); Richard Ogilvie, GOP candidate for governor of Illinois, and Gov. John A. Volpe

(Mass.). Nixon's 1st ballot victory came at 1:50 a.m. Aug. 8, when he received all 30 Wisconsin votes which he had won in a primary, giving him more than the 667 votes needed for the nomination. Before switches the 1st ballot total for Nixon was 692; Rockefeller, 277, and Reagan, 182. Nixon's tally went up to 1,238 at the end of the ballot. Reagan, appealing for party unity after Nixon's victory, asked the convention to make it unanimous, but the motion did not come up for a vote. Rockefeller pledged his support to Nixon at an Aug. 8 press conference. Altogether, 12 names were put in nomination.

Ray C. Bliss, chairman of the Republican National Committee, opened the parley at 10 a.m., EST, Aug. 5. The 1,333 delegates heard speeches by ex-Sen. Barry Goldwater (Ariz.), the party's 1964 standard bearer, who called for Republican unity; Sen. Edward Brooke (Mass.), leading GOP Negro spokesman; former President Dwight D. Eisenhower, speaking on closed circuit TV from Walter Reed Army Medical Center in Washington, D. C., where he was recuperating from a 5th heart attack. Mr. Eisenhower, who suffered his 6th attack early the next morning, warned of the dangers of Communism, describing it as "a formidable foe—an expansionist tyranny which respects only toughness and strength."

The keynote address by Washington Gov. Daniel J. Evans reflected the moderate tone of the proposed GOP platform. Blaming the Democratic administration for the frustrations of Vietnam and the urban crisis, he urged that Republicans "unite to rally a great party in the cause of a great nation."

Delegates adopted the platform without controversy. Differences, mostly over the Vietnam plank, on which Nixon and Rockefeller forces compromised, were settled by the committee, headed by Senate GOP leader Everett Dirksen (Ill.).

## Democrats Name Humphrey-Muskie Ticket

In one of the most turbulent parleys in U. S. convention history, the Democrats, meeting in the Chicago International Amphitheater Aug. 26-29, 1968, nominated Vice President Hubert H. Humphrey, 57, for the Presidency shortly before midnight Aug. 28 and Maine Sen. Edmund Sixtus Muskie, 54, for the Vice Presidency on Aug. 29.

Violence erupted intermittently in the streets as police clashed with anti-war demonstrators, and charges of police brutality and "Gestapo tactics" were leveled from the convention floor at the host city's Mayor, Richard J. Daley, whose security precautions had virtually turned the convention hall into a fortress. In a welcoming address, Mayor Daley, who had bolstered the city's police force with National Guardsmen and regular Army troops, defended his action as a requisite to "law and order" in the face of threatened violence, strikes and some 100,000 expected anti-war demonstrators. Actually, some 10,000-15,000 showed up.

Near pandemonium often threatened to end the convention itself and dramatized the deep party split on the Vietnam issue. One of the wildest sessions came when the convention, after an unprecedented 3-hour debate Aug. 28, rejected an anti-war plank fashioned by followers

of Sens. Eugene J. McCarthy (Minn.) and George S. McGovern (S. D.), the two major losing Presidential candidates, in favor of one endorsing President Johnson's policy.

A record number of challenges over seating of delegates came up. Most claimed bias and inadequate Negro representation. Fifteen challenges involving 13 states were settled at the start of the convention, but those of 4 states—Texas, Georgia, Alabama and North Carolina—ran beyond Credential Committee hearings and through a stormy first convention, which did not break up until 2:40 a.m. Aug. 27. Pandemonium broke out after defeat of a move to seat Negro challenger Julian Bond, Georgia state Representative, and his group with all his state's votes. Bond had challenged regular delegates picked by Gov. Lester G. Maddox and state party chairman James H. Gray. At the second session, the convention approved a split-vote compromise suggested by Gov. Richard J. Hughes (N. J.), co-chairman of the Credentials Committee.

John M. Bailey, Democratic party chairman, opened the convention. Hawaii Sen. Daniel K. Inouye, delivering the keynote address, stressed that the party was one of change and challenge which could

deal with problems of America; he lauded the Administration's work in civil rights, disarmament, health and education.

Humphrey's name was put in nomination by San Francisco Mayor Joseph L. Alioto, who described him as a "decisive leader." Gov. Terry Sanford of North Carolina and Cleveland Mayor Carl Stokes seconded the nomination.

There were boos which continued throughout the night when Rep. Carl Albert (Okla.), convention chairman, ordered the roll call for nominations over protests by delegates who wanted to recess the session because of the violence in the streets. More jeers accompanied the yea vote taken by Albert

at 12:03 a.m. Aug. 29, when the Illinois delegation asked that Humphrey's nomination be made unanimous. Humphrey's 1st ballot total was 1,761¾; he attained the required 1,312 votes at 11:47 p.m., when Pennsylvania cast 103¾ for him.

Sen. McCarthy got 601 1st ballot votes and Sen. McGovern 146½. Two other candidates were placed in nomination—the Rev. Channing E. Phillips, of Washington, D. C., the 1st Negro favorite-son for any major party, with 67½ votes, and North Carolina Gov. Dan K. Moore, who withdrew before the end of the 1st ballot, with 17½ votes. Sen. Edward M. Kennedy (Mass.) received 12¾ votes though he had opposed a Kennedy draft.

# Biographies of Principal Candidates in 1968 Campaign

## Republican

**Richard Milhous Nixon**, 55, Republican nominee for President, was elected Vice President in the Eisenhower landslides of 1952 and 1956. Born in Yorba Linda, Calif., Jan. 9, 1913, the son of Francis Anthony and Hannah Milhous Nixon, he attended Whittier College and Duke University Law School, where he finished 3rd in his class. He joined the Navy in 1942; served in the Pacific and was discharged as lieutenant commander. He was elected to the House of Representatives in 1946 and 1948. In 1950 he moved to the Senate after defeating Helen Gahagan Douglas in a bitter campaign in which he accused her of being "soft on communism." Co-author of the Mundt-Nixon Communist-control bill, in 1948, he achieved prominence as the House Un-American Activities Committee member who forced the showdown that resulted in the Alger Hiss perjury conviction. He lost his bid for the Presidency in 1960, trailing John F. Kennedy by 118,550 popular votes. Beaten for California governor by Edmund G. Brown in 1962, he retired to private life and law practice and, in 1963, moved to New York where he became senior partner in the law firm of Nixon, Mudge, Rose, Guthrie, Alexander & Mitchell. Speaking for party unity, he campaigned for Goldwater in 1964 and for Republican Congressional candidates in 1966. He took to the "long hard road of the primaries" to erase his reputation as a "loser," remaining moderately conservative in government spending and internationalist in foreign policy. A more serene and confident figure than he had been in the two previous campaigns, he stressed the need for "black economic power" and eased his hawkish stand on Vietnam. He and his wife, the former Thelma Catherine Patricia Ryan, have two daughters, Patricia, 22, and Julie, 20.

## Republican

**Spiro Theodore Agnew**, 50, candidate for Vice President, elected governor of Maryland in 1966, began his career as county executive of Baltimore County in 1962 after several years of local activities as a member of the zoning board, president of a junior high school PTA and the Kiwanis. The son of a Greek immigrant whose name was Anagnostopolous, he was little known outside Maryland, conceded that his name "is not a household word." Born Nov. 9, 1913, in Maryland, he attended Johns Hopkins University and worked his way through the University of Baltimore law school, graduating in 1947, after serving 4 years in the Army during World War II. He was re-called for a year during the Korean action. Considered a liberal Republican and reformer at the time of his election, Gov. Agnew pushed through progressive legislation, including the 1st local public accommodation law south of the Mason-Dixon line. He disappointed his moderate supporters with criticism of the Kerner report on urban riots, student sit-ins and Resurrection

City. He is married to the former Elinor Isabel Judefind. They have a son, James, 22, serving with the Navy in Vietnam, and 3 daughters.

## Democratic

**Vice President Hubert Horatio Humphrey, Jr.**, 57, was born in Wallace, S. D., May 27, 1911 above his father's drug store. He interrupted his education at the University of Minnesota after two years to return home during the depression of 1931 to help run the family drug store in Huron, S. D. He received a pharmacy degree from the Denver College of Pharmacy in 1933, a bachelor's degree in political science from the University of Minnesota in 1939 and a master's degree from Louisiana State Univ. in 1940. After teaching stints at Minnesota U. and Macalester College, St. Paul, and serving on the regional War Manpower Commission in the early stages of World War II following his rejection by the Army due to a hernia, he was elected Mayor of Minneapolis in 1945 and 1947. He closed gambling houses and brothels, and got enactment of the first municipal Fair Employment Practices law in the country. Elected senator from Minnesota in 1948 and reelected twice, he was considered an overly voluble and intransigent liberal by his colleagues. His eloquence put over the civil rights plank in the 1948 Democratic platform. He was elected majority whip in 1961, after campaigning for the Presidential nomination in 1960 and losing to John F. Kennedy. He became a power in the Senate establishment as his views became gradually more moderate. Chosen by Lyndon B. Johnson to be his running mate in the 1964 election, his support of Johnson's Vietnam policy cost him the loss of much of his former liberal support. He authored two books, "The Cause is Mankind: A Liberal Program for Modern America" and "Moral Crisis: The Case for Civil Rights" in 1964. A member of the United Church of Christ, he is married to the former Muriel Fay Buck and is the father of 4 children.

## Democratic

**Edmund Sixtus Muskie**, 54, Democratic candidate for the Vice Presidency, in 1958 became the first popularly elected Democratic Senator in Maine history. Born Mar. 28, 1914, in Rumford, Me., son of a Polish Catholic tailor whose last name was changed from Marciszewski to Muskie by immigration officials, he worked his way through Bates College, received a law degree from Cornell Law School and was a Navy officer during World War II. He was elected to the Maine House of Representatives in 1946. Before entering the U. S. Senate, he had achieved another record in 1954, when he was the first Democrat to be elected Governor of his state in 20 years, serving two terms. Deemed an expert on urban problems in the Senate, to which he was reelected in 1964, he pushed hard for air and water pollution curbs. He and his wife, the former Jane F. Gray, have 5 children.

# Third Party

**George Corley Wallace**, 49, former Democratic Governor of Alabama, announced his candidacy Feb. 8, 1968, as a 3d party Presidential candidate, pledging he would quell riots with troops and bayonets and work for a change in the "so-called guidelines" on desegregation. A pro-

ponent of states' rights and thought to have mostly sectional and segregationist appeal at first, he drew large audiences of ardent supporters as well as hecklers as he campaigned vigorously throughout the country. This resulted in speculation that he might pull needed votes from

the two major party candidates. On May 7, a slate of Alabama elector candidates won over token opposition to make Wallace the regular Democratic candidate from that state. In 1964, he surprised political observers with the support he drew as Presidential candidate in Democratic state primaries outside his state. Born in Clio, Ala., Aug. 25, 1919, he was state bantamweight champion in high school and boxed professionally to help pay his way through U. of Alabama law school. He served in the Air Force after graduating in 1942. Elected Governor in 1962, he could not succeed himself according to Alabama law. When his wife, Lurleen Burns Wallace, mother of his 4 children, was elected to succeed him in 1966, it was with the understanding that she would be Governor in name only and he would continue to make policies and decisions. She died May 7 while he was on the campaign trail.

**Curtis Emerson LeMay,** 61, retired Air Force Chief of Staff, was named by George C. Wallace Oct. 3, 1968 to be his Vice Presidential running mate. LeMay, father of the Strategic Air Command, had advocated use of atomic weapons against North Vietnam. Before retiring in 1965, Gen. LeMay carved out an outstanding career in 35 years in uniform that included running the Berlin blockade airlift and designing the devastating stacked-plane formation that wrought massive destruction on the enemy in Europe and Japan in World War II. Blunt and gruff, known by the military nickname of "Old Ironpants," he was often the man in the lead plane. Daring as a pilot and thorough as a mechanic, he attained the rank of Major General by the end of the war and became a full general in 1951. He was named Air Force Chief of Staff in 1961. Born in Columbus, Ohio, on Nov. 15, 1906, the son of an ironworker of French-Canadian descent, he attended Ohio State U., enrolled in the ROTC program there and gained a reserve commission in the National Guard. He became a flying cadet at California's March Field in 1928. He married Helen Estelle Maitland of Cleveland in 1938; they have a daughter, Patricia. Gen. LeMay, of Los Angeles, is a former board chairman of Networks Electronics Corp. He has written two books, "Mission with LeMay: My Story" and "America Is in Danger," released shortly before announcement of his candidacy.

# 1968 Platforms of Major Parties

A strong similarity marked the platforms adopted in 1968 by the Democrats and Republicans, especially on 3 key issues—the Vietnam war, the urban crisis, and law and order. Except for GOP criticism and Democratic praise of the Johnson Administration, the parties followed parallel middle-of-the-road paths. Highlights follow:

**Democratic**—Plank indorsing Johnson Administration policy, adopted Aug. 28, declares: "Our most urgent task in Southeast Asia is to end the war in Vietnam by an honorable and lasting settlement which respects the rights of all the people of Vietnam." Proposes end to bombing of North Vietnam "when this action would not endanger the lives of our troops in the field" and depending on "the response from Hanoi;" a cease-fire for withdrawal of U. S. and Hanoi troops; "fair and safeguarded elections" to form a postwar government, and stepped-up training of South Vietnamese army to allow U. S. military cutbacks.

**Republican**—Platform adopted Aug. 7 proposes "a progressive de-Americanization" of war. Pledges development of a "clear and purposeful negotiating position" in its "program for peace in Vietnam—neither peace at any price nor a camouflaged surrender of legitimate United States or Allied interests—but a positive program that will offer a fair and equitable settlement to all, based on the principle of self-determination, our national interests, and the cause of long-range world peace."

### LAW AND ORDER

**Democratic**—Reasserts dedication to "principle that equal justice under law shall remain the American creed." Pledges "a vigorous and sustained campaign against lawlessness in all its forms," combined with an attack on the root causes of crime and disorder." Will "implement" recommendations of the President's National Advisory Commission on Civil Disorders "to wipe out, once and for all, the stain of racial and other discrimination from our national life."

**Republican**—Pledges "all-out" crusade against crime and "vigorous and even-handed administration of justice and enforcement of the law," adding: "We must reestablish the principle that men are accountable for what they do, that criminals are responsible for their crimes." Urges decisive action to suppress civil disorders but advocates measures "to alleviate and remove the frustrations that contribute to riots."

### URBAN CRISIS

**Democratic**—In the framework of Model Cities program will continue attack on poverty in large city slums via "economic development, the rehabilitation or replacement of dilapidated and unsafe housing, job training and placement, and the improvement of education, health, recreation, crime control, welfare and other public services." Steady extension of Model Cities program. Will marshal private enterprise in "attack on slums and poverty." Pledges new Federal banking structure "to provide capital and investment guarantees for urban projects planned and implemented through local initiative."

**Republican**—Cites critical need to stem crisis of decaying urban centers. Terms "deepening misery and limited opportunity" of slum residents "intolerable." Prescribes "new mix of private responsibility and public participation." Will accelerate rural development to stem flow of people from countryside to city. Will revise welfare and poverty programs drastically to "liberate poor from the debilitating dependence which erodes self-respect and discourages family unity and responsibility." Proposes employer tax credits to encourage job training and upgrading for disadvantaged. National Job Opportunity Data Bank to aid unemployed.

### ECONOMIC POLICIES

**Democratic**—"The Democratic economic policies that more than doubled the nation's rate of economic expansion in the past 8 years can double and redouble our national income by the end of this century. Such a rate of economic growth will enable us to win total victory in our wars on ignorance, poverty and the misery of the ghetto." Will continue tax cuts when economy is sluggish and hikes to curb inflation.

**Republican**—Scores Administration "mismanagement." Asserts "inflation robs our paychecks at a present rate of 4½% per year." Cites "crippling" interest rates, declining purchasing power. Will improve management of national debt, reduce heavy interest, seek price stability and tax reform and simplification. Set up Efficiency Commission for the Executive branch and an Office of Executive Management. Will bar "improper Federal competition with private enterprise."

### MILITARY POLICIES

**Democratic**—Calls Soviet invasion of Czechoslovakia a "shocking reminder that we live in a dangerous age" and stresses need to keep U. S.'s "significant lead" in military strength and technology. Asserts "vigilance calls for twin discipline of defense and arms control."

**Republican**—Deplores "humiliating episode" of U.S.S. Pueblo seizure by North Korea. Charges Administration "frittered away superior military capabilities, enabling the Soviets to narrow their defense gap, in some areas to outstrip us." Calls for reinvigorated National Security Council, improved ocean deterrent capability, simplification of "overcentralized" Defense Department.

# The War in Vietnam

## Peace Prospects Brighten; Chronology of Conflict

Hopes for an early peace in Vietnam soared with President Johnson's announcement Oct. 31 that he had ordered all air, naval and artillery bombardment of North Vietnam to cease at 8 a.m. Washington time Nov. 1, 1968. At the same time he said broadened peace talks would begin in Paris Nov. 6, with representatives of the South Vietnam National Liberation Front (Vietcong) participating and those of the South Vietnamese Government "free to participate."

Of the presence of Vietcong representatives, the President emphasized that "their attendance in no way involves recognition of the National Liberation Front in any form." But South Vietnamese President Nguyen Van Thieu said his government would not engage in the Paris talks under the conditions, and the talks were postponed indefinitely. Then Thieu proposed that the talks should be conducted principally between South and North Vietnam, with the U.S. and the National Liberation Front in subsidiary roles. U.S. authorities were hopeful that South Vietnam would join the conference soon.

Meanwhile, the undeclared war in Vietnam became on June 23 the longest ever fought by the United States. It had lasted 6 years, 6 months and one day since the death of the first American service man killed by the Vietcong, Dec. 22, 1961. The American Revolution is generally considered to have lasted 6 years and 6 months, ending with Cornwallis' surrender at Yorktown Oct. 19, 1781.

The present war is a sequel to an earlier war between the French and the forces of Ho Chi Minh (the present leader of North Vietnam). At the end of World War II, Vietnamese nationalist and Communist groups were determined to achieve independence, but the French attempted to re-establish colonial rule over the Indo-Chinese states (Cambodia, Laos and Vietnam). The strongest of the Vietnamese nationalist groups was Ho Chi Minh's Communist-led Vietminh (abbreviated name of the League for the Independence of Vietnam). On Sept. 2, 1945, Ho declared Vietnam independent and announced the creation of the Democratic Republic of Vietnam (DRVN). The French recognized the DRVN Mar. 6, 1946, "as a free state within the French union." However, a series of blunders and misunderstandings by both sides led to armed conflict and the beginning of the French-Vietminh war Dec. 19, 1946.

As the war progressed, the French sought to enlist non-Communist support by turning to ex-Emperor of Vietnam Bao Dai as a rallying-point for the Vietnamese. With French approval, he formed on July 1, 1949, the State of Vietnam with its capital in Saigon.

The U.S. recognized the new state Feb. 7, 1950, and to assist it, President Truman announced June 27 that the U.S. was sending a 35-man Military Assistance Advisory Group (MAAG) to Indo-China to advise the troops there in the use of American weapons. Other assistance measures soon followed. On Dec. 23 the U.S. signed a Mutual Defense Assistance Agreement with Vietnam and on Sept. 7, 1951, the U.S. agreed to provide direct economic assistance to the Saigon government.

The following is a chronological listing of major developments thereafter:

May 8 to July 21, 1954—Geneva Conference on Indo-China attended by France, Britain, Russia, U.S., Democratic Republic of Vietnam, State of Vietnam, Laos, Cambodia and Communist China. France and North Vietnam agreed: to partition of Vietnam along 17th parallel, ban on new troops or bases, scheduling of reunification elections in July 1956, creation of International Control Commission composed of India, Canada and Poland to supervise implementation of the agreement. U.S. and South Vietnam do not sign agreement.

May 8, 1954—French stronghold of Dien Bien Phu in North Vietnam falls to Communist forces.

Oct. 24, 1954—President Eisenhower offers South Vietnam economic aid.

Feb. 12, 1955—U.S. agrees to train South Vietnamese army.

Feb. 19, 1955—SEATO protocol extended to offer protective cover of organization to Vietnam.

Oct. 23, 1955—South Vietnamese national referendum deposes Bao Dai, creates republic with Ngo Dinh Diem as first president. Diem says reunification elections as specified by Geneva Conference impossible because of intimidation by North Vietnam. Reunification elections never held.

Oct. 22, 1957—First injuries of U.S. advisers in Vietnam reported.

July 8, 1959—First U.S. troops killed in combat.

May 5, 1960—Upon request of South Vietnam, U.S. increases number of military advisers from 327 to 685.

Oct. 26, 1960—President Eisenhower pledges continued assistance to South Vietnam.

Dec. 1960—North Vietnam announces formation of the National Liberation Front of South Vietnam. Acts of terrorism in the South increase.

Apr. 3, 1961—Kennedy Administration signs Treaty of Amity and Economic Relations with South Vietnam.

Dec. 14, 1961—President Kennedy declares U.S. prepared to help Republic of South Vietnam "preserve its independence."

June 2, 1962—Majority report of International Control Commission says evidence shows North Vietnam to be supporting, organizing and carrying out hostile acts in South Vietnam.

Dec. 1962—U.S. force in Vietnam stands at 4,000 men.

Nov. 1, 1963—President Diem assassinated. Series of coups follows.

Dec., 1963—U.S. force in Vietnam numbers 15,000.

Aug. 2-4, 1964—U.S. destroyers Maddox and C. Turner Joy attacked by North Vietnamese torpedo boats in Gulf of Tonkin. President Johnson orders immediate retaliatory attacks.

Aug. 7, 1964—Congress approves Gulf of Tonkin Resolution giving President power to "take all necessary measures to repel any armed attack against the forces of the United States and to prevent further aggression."

Dec. 1964—U.S. force in Vietnam numbers 23,000.

Feb. 1965—Continuous U.S. bombing raids over North Vietnam started in effort to force Communists to conference table. Hanoi says negotiations will not be considered until U.S. forces withdraw.

Apr. 17, 1965—President Johnson in speech at Johns Hopkins University offers billion dollar aid program to SE Asia as soon as peace is achieved.

May 13-19, 1965—U. S. halts air raids against North Vietnam. No response from Hanoi.

June 8, 1965—U. S. commanders authorized to send American troops into combat.

July, 1965—President Johnson authorizes increase of U. S. force from 75,000 men to 125,000.

Dec. 24, 1965-Jan. 31, 1966—U. S. again suspends bombing of North Vietnam in hope of bringing foe to conference table. Hanoi rejects all peace feelers.

Feb. 6-7, 1966—President Johnson and South Vietnamese Premier Nguyen Ky meet in Honolulu. "Declaration of Honolulu" issued at end of meeting, declaring the two countries will continue to resist aggression.

June 29, 1966—U. S. bombs major installations near Hanoi and Haiphong for first time.

July 30, 1966—U. S. bombs 6-mile-wide demilitarized zone between North and South Vietnam.

Nov. 1966—U. S. forces in Vietnam number 358,000 men, with 33,000 more stationed in Thailand.

Nov. 12, 1966—U. S. dead killed in action in Vietnam from Jan 1, 1961 to date—4,904.

Dec. 2, 1966—UN Secy. Gen. U Thant pledges new effort to end war.

Dec. 30, 1966—Britain proposes peace conference. Hanoi rejects suggestion Jan. 4, 1967.

Dec. 31, 1966-Jan. 2, 1967—New Year's truce.

Jan. 5, 1967—Defense Dept. announces total U. S. casualties since Jan. 1, 1961 are 6,664 dead, 37,738 wounded.

Feb. 8-12—U. S. suspends air raids during Lunar New Year truce and two days beyond. No response from Hanoi.

Mar. 2, 1967—Sen. Robert F. Kennedy proposes Administration halt bombing as part of 3-point peace plan. Secy. Rusk says there is nothing new in the Kennedy proposals and that Hanoi has already rejected similar peace overtures.

Mar. 20-21, 1967—President Johnson confers with South Vietnamese leaders on Guam. War and election of civilian government in South Vietnam discussed.

Mar. 21, 1967—Ho Chi Minh rejects previously undisclosed proposal by President Johnson in February for peace talks.

Mar. 28, 1967—Peace plan proposal by U Thant calling for stand-still truce, preliminary talks and reconvening of Geneva Conference revealed. Accepted by U. S. and South Vietnam with reservations. Rejected by Hanoi.

Mar. 1967—Total U. S. force in Vietnam stands at 427,000.

Apr. 1, 1967—South Vietnamese constitution goes into effect.

May 2, 1967—U. S. commander in Vietnam, Gen. William C. Westmoreland, urges further buildup of American forces. Domestic debate over war intensifies.

May 11, 1967—U Thant expresses fear Vietnamese war is "initial phase of World War III."

June 23 and 25, 1967—President Johnson and Soviet Premier Kosygin meet in Glassboro, N. J. Discuss Vietnam as well as Mideast crisis. No agreement.

Aug. 3, 1967—President Johnson announces U. S. forces in Vietnam will be increased to 525,000 men by June 1968. Asks for 10% income tax surcharge to finance the war.

Aug. 11, 1967—U. S. extends air raids to within 10 miles of Chinese border.

Aug. 23, 1967—President Johnson appoints 20 Americans to observe South Vietnamese elections.

Sept. 3, 1967—Nguyen Van Thieu elected president, Nguyen Cao Ky, vice president.

Sept. 7, 1967—U. S. announces plans for fortified barrier south of demilitarized zone.

Sept. 29, 1967—In a televised address at San Antonio, President Johnson offers again to stop all bombardment of North Vietnam "when this will lead promptly to

## *U. S. Military Casualties in Vietnam

Source: Secretary of Defense. As of Nov. 2, 1968

| Casualties from hostile forces action Since Jan. 1, 1961 | Army | Navy[1] | Marine | Air force | Total |
|---|---|---|---|---|---|
| 1. Killed | 14,645 | 709 | 8,626 | 311 | 24,291 |
| 2. Wounded or injured: | | | | | |
|   a. Died of wounds | 1,910 | 89 | 1,062 | 27 | 3,088 |
|   b. Nonfatal wounds: | | | | | |
|     Hospital care required | 56,244 | 2,310 | 36,826 | 500 | 95,880 |
|     Hospital care not required | 54,517 | 3,534 | 27,754 | 1,664 | 87,469 |
| 3. Missing: | | | | | |
|   a. Died while missing | 1,404 | 127 | 5 | 259 | 1,795 |
|   b. Returned to control | 45 | 7 | 6 | 23 | 81 |
|   c. Current missing | 162 | 116 | 86 | 522 | 886 |
| 4. Captured or interned: | | | | | |
|   a. Died while captured or interned | 9 | .... | .... | 1 | 10 |
|   b. Returned to control | 11 | 1 | 4 | 5 | 21 |
|   c. Current captured or interned | 42 | 131 | 19 | 139 | 331 |
| 5. Deaths: | | | | | |
|   a. From aircraft accidents/incidents: | | | | | |
|     Fixed Wing | 57 | 138 | 102 | 470 | 767 |
|     Helicopter | 840 | 39 | 272 | 18 | 1,169 |
|   b. From ground action | 17,071 | 748 | 9,319 | 110 | 27,248 |
| †Total deaths | 17,968 | 925 | 9,693 | 598 | 29,184 |
| **Casualties Not the Result of Actions by Hostile Forces** | | | | | |
| 6. Current missing | 80 | 3 | 2 | 2 | 87 |
| 7. Deaths: | | | | | |
|   a. From aircraft accidents/incidents: | | | | | |
|     Fixed Wing | 179 | 84 | 28 | 186 | 477 |
|     Helicopter | 757 | 21 | 160 | 7 | 945 |
|   b. From other causes | 1,992 | 428 | 807 | 158 | 3,385 |
| Total deaths | 2,928 | 533 | 995 | 351 | 4,807 |

| Combat Deaths for Other Forces (Since Jan. 1, 1961) | | | |
|---|---|---|---|
| | S. Vietnam[2] | Other Free World Forces | Enemy |
| Total deaths | 72,202 | 2,581 | 411,358 |

†Sum of lines 1, 2a, 3a and 4a. [1]Navy figures include Coast Guard. [2]Rep. of Vietnam Armed Forces.
*According to military officials, the total of wounded in Vietnam would be less if judged by the standards of World War II and the Korean War.

productive discussion," and says he will send a trusted representative anywhere in the world to talk with a Hanoi spokesman. North Vietnam rejects the offer.

Nov. 2, 1967—Amb. Arthur Goldberg states unequivocally that the U. S. would be willing to have the Vietcong's political arm, the National Liberation Front, participate directly in a reconvened Geneva conference or be present in any discussion of the Vietnam question before the Security Council of the UN.

Nov. 11, 1967—Defense Dept. announces total U. S. casualties since Jan. 1, 1961 are 14,621 dead, 91,971 wounded.

Nov. 17, 1967—President Johnson warns Hanoi not to rely on the 1968 Presidential elections. "I think that whatever interpretation Hanoi might make that would lead them to believe that Uncle Sam, whoever may be President, is going to pull out and it will be easier for them to make an inside deal with another President than will be the present, they'll make a serious misjudgment."

Nov. 19, 1967—Gen. Westmoreland says: "We are winning a war of attrition" and within two years or less we may be able to "phase down the level of our military effort."

Nov. 30, 1967—U. S. casualties since Jan. 1, 1961, reach 15,058 killed, 109,527 wounded, of which some 50,000 required hospitalization, and 914 missing.

Dec. 20, 1967—U. S. troop strength in Vietnam reaches 474,300 men, 1,500 more than American peak strength in Korea during Korean War.

Dec. 24-25, 1967—Allies observe 24-hour Christmas truce.

Jan. 17, 1968—President Johnson, in his State-of-the-Union message, estimates the cost of the war to the U. S. at $25 billion a year.

Jan. 30, 1968—Viet Cong and North Vietnamese attack 30 provincial capitals in South Vietnam in Tet offensive. Record casualties were suffered on both sides, but a few days later President Johnson calls the offensive "a complete failure."

Feb. 24, 1968—UN Secy. Gen. U Thant says after visiting Asia and Europe that if bombing of North Vietnam is halted "meaningful talks . . . will take place much earlier than generally supposed."

Mar. 31, 1968—President Johnson announces the unilateral halting of the bombing of 90% of the territory of North Vietnam as a step toward peace and asks for a response from Hanoi.

Apr. 5, 1968—Some 50,000 American and South Vietnamese troops, in Operation Pegasus, succeed in lifting the 76-day siege of the U. S. Marine base at Khesahn.

Apr. 11, 1968—Defense Secy. Clark M. Clifford announces the call-up of 24,000 Army, Air Force and Navy reservists for active duty in Vietnam and the setting of a new troop ceiling of 549,000 for U. S. strength in Vietnam.

May 5, 1968—Communists launch Round II of their Tet offensive with attacks on Saigon and other cities; less serious than original.

May 10, 1968—Preliminary peace talks between U. S. and North Vietnam open in Paris.

June 10, 1968—Gen. Creighton Abrams takes over command of U. S. forces in Vietnam from Gen. William C. Westmoreland, who becomes Army Chief of Staff.

Aug. 29, 1968—U. S. casualties in Vietnam since Jan. 1, 1961, rise to 27,508 killed and 171,809 wounded.

Sept. 30, 1968—U. S. battleship New Jersey, released from mothball fleet, shells enemy targets in the DMZ.

Oct. 31, 1968—President Johnson orders cessation of U. S. aerial, naval and artillery bombardment of North Vietnam the following day, and plans for broadened peace talks in Paris.

# Hawaii Song Now Official, Thanks to Peggy and the Almanac

Ways in which the World Almanac can prove useful are endless and often surprising. Recently the World Almanac found itself involved in an action by the State Legislature of Hawaii.

Peggy Cooper, pretty, blonde-haired, 12-year-old daughter of Mr. and Mrs. Robert E. Cooper of Kaneohe, Hawaii, had a 5th grade homework assignment that sent her looking for facts in her World Almanac. There she learned that her state's famous song, Hawaii Ponoi (My Hawaii), was only the "unofficial state song."

She was upset. She resolved to have Hawaii Ponoi made the official state song.

"My Daddy and Mommy, who come from Washington and Oregon, were horrified," the Honolulu Advertiser quoted Peggy as saying. "Both their states have official songs."

Peggy's father helped her bring the problem to the attention of George Toyofuku, a member of the state House of Representatives, who sponsored a bill to make the song the official state anthem. It was enthusiastically approved. The House also passed and presented to Peggy a resolution commending her for her efforts.

In due course, Cornelius D. Downes, Information Officer of the Hawaiian Department of Planning and Economic Development, informed the World Almanac of the new status of Hawaii Ponoi. Meanwhile, Peggy was quoted in an Advertiser story as saying she started her campaign "to make Hawaii's song official so the next edition of the Almanac could list it along with the others."

In this edition, Peggy and others who are interested will find that Hawaii Ponoi is now listed as the official state song. (See P. 360.)

# Long Holiday Weekends to Begin in 1971

Beginning Jan. 1, 1971, four major holidays will fall on Mondays every year to provide long weekends. A bill signed by President Johnson June 28, 1968, changes the dates for observances of Washington's Birthday, Memorial Day and Veterans Day and gives Columbus Day legal status as a holiday.

The new law applies only to Federal and District of Columbia employees, but most states are expected to go along with the new holiday line-up, which with Labor Day will produce 5 holiday weekends. Under the new law Washington's birthday will fall on the 3d Monday in February; Memorial Day on the last Monday in May; Columbus Day on the 2d Monday in October, and Veterans Day on the 4th Monday in October. *(See pages 590 and 591 for 1969 holidays.)*

## How Degree Days Are Measured

A degree day is a standard measure used by heating engineers to measure the heating season's coldness. The number of degree days in a calendar day is determined by subtracting the day's average from 65°. If the high on a given day was 60° and the low was 40° the average temperature that day would be 50°. Subtracted from 65°, this would give 15 degree days for that calendar day.

# Space 1968: The Comeback Trail to the Moon

From their earliest days in 1961, when cosmonaut Yuri Gagarin and astronaut Alan Shepard flew through space less than a month apart, the United States and Soviet manned space programs have followed remarkably similar paths—even to their treatment at the hands of fate. In 1967, tragedy stunned both countries, as 3 U.S. astronauts died in a launch pad fire, followed, only three months later, by the fatal crash of the USSR's Soyuz 1, which killed its pilot when its reentry parachutes snarled.

Scarcely two weeks separated the two countries' triumphal returns to space in 1968. The first manned Apollo flight followed an exhaustive redesign of the entire spacecraft, as well as a major overturning of space agency officials. The Soviet Union was believed to have had its own design problems, and caution in trying out solutions may have been why only a single cosmonaut was risked in the presumably multi-man Soyuz capsule.

Triumph was far from all-pervading at the National Aeronautics and Space Administration, however. Congressional disenchantment with the huge cost of the U.S. space program resulted in NASA being given its smallest budget in 6 fiscal years. So great became the pressures that agency head James Webb resigned, only 4 days before the first Apollo astronauts blasted off.

## Americans to Orbit Moon

Nevertheless, the first manned Apollo flight (Apollo 7) put the U. S. squarely back on the path toward the goal of putting men on the moon before 1970. The success of Apollo 7 impelled NASA to schedule Apollo 8 for the end of 1968—to carry 3 astronauts around the moon. The Apollo 8 plan called for 10 orbits around the moon at an altitude of only 70 miles, although an in-flight decision could choose a less ambitious program. Apollo 8 was to get its lunar push from the mighty Saturn 5 booster, which had been tested twice in unmanned flights (Apollo 7 used a smaller rocket, the Saturn 1B).

Apollo 8, called the most ambitious and riskiest space flight to date, was to be manned by Air Force Col. Frank Borman, commander; Navy Capt. James A. Lovell, Jr., and Air Force Maj. William A. Anders.

One major piece of equipment that did not make the grade in 1968 was the tricky and troublesome lunar module, the spidery spacecraft with the job of actually transporting the astronauts from an orbit around the moon down to the lunar surface and back again. Troubles with the craft's weight, engines and electrical system pushed its first manned flight all the way into 1969, leaving planners praying that they could get to the moon in the same year.

As the moon race continued, another area of U.S.-Soviet competition showed signs of developing with the USSR announcement of plans for Intersputnik, a communications satellite network seen as a rival to the U.S.-dominated Intelsat system. Though Intelsat has more than 60 member nations and Intersputnik would initially number only 8, the Soviet network would presumably stymie chances of a single, worldwide "satcom" organization.

Outside of the U.S. and USSR, 1968 was a relatively quiet year for space activity, although several countries did conduct limited research with sounding rockets. In 1967, France, England, Italy and Japan launched satellites (all but Japan's were successful), but the only 1968 contender was the European Space Research Organization, a consortium formed to combine the talents and limited resources of several countries. After a failure in 1967, ESRO (whose members include Great Britain, France, West Germany, Italy, the Netherlands, Belgium, Switzerland, Denmark, Sweden and Spain) came back with a pair of space probes, both of which were still working months later at press time.

Back in the U.S., one marked trend was the turning of the vast aerospace industry away from single-minded devotion to space, and toward the growing problems of aircraft. The remarkable X-15 rocketplane and the giant XB-70 research vehicle were both scheduled for retirement around the end of the year, but overcrowded airports (with poor attendant ground transportation), the supersonic transport, the upcoming generation of giant jets, airbusses to handle a growing volume of flying commuters, and military needs for far-out aircraft of the future provided more than enough problems for the hundreds of thousands of trained scientists and engineers already brought together by the rich promise of space.

---

# 1968 Space Calendar

The following are the principal satellites, spacecraft and probes launched in 1968 through Nov. 13. When pertinent and available, initial orbital distances closest to (perigee) and farthest from (apogee) earth are shown in statute miles. The times represent the periods of the orbits. Unsuccessful launches are not listed.

**SURVEYOR 7 (U. S.)** Jan. 7—Last of the robot moon-landing series, it photographed and analyzed the lunar surface, revealing earth-type basalt and volcanic rock to support the theory that the moon was born either with or from the earth.

**GEOS 2 (U. S.)** Jan. 11—Second in a series of satellites aimed at more accurately measuring earth's size, shape and gravitational field, using, among other instruments, laser beams bounced off it from the ground. 112.2 minutes, 671-976 miles.

**COSMOS 199 (USSR)** Jan. 16—This probable sky-spy was the first of some 50 launches this year in the Soviet all-purpose satellite series, which includes everything from weather-watchers to unmanned checkouts of man-intended spaceships. 90.2 minutes, 127-240 miles.

**APOLLO 5 (U. S.)** Jan. 22—Unmanned earth-orbiting first flight of the lunar module that will actually set two U. S. astronauts down on the moon and lift them off again. 89.5 minutes, 101-138 miles.

**ZOND 4 (USSR)** Mar. 2—If it was, as appears likely, intended to visit the moon, it did not make it, though it was successfully launched outward after first parking in orbit around the earth. 89.5 minutes, 131-180 miles.

**OGO 5 (U. S.)** Mar. 4—With all but one of its two dozen experiments working, the fifth in NASA's most complicated satellite series set out to study a wide range of characteristics of the space surrounding our world. 3,795.9 minutes, 180-91,260 miles.

**SOLAR EXPLORER 2 (U. S.)** Mar. 5—Designed so that any country listening on the proper frequencies could receive its (Space continued on page 44)

(*Space continued from page* 43)
data, this satellite measures X-rays and ultraviolet emissions coming from the sun, though scientists had planned it to end up in a more circular orbit than it did. 98.7 minutes, 324-545 miles.

**COSMOS 206 (USSR)** Mar. 14—Like many U. S. weather satellites, tihs Soviet probe gathered cloud-cover photos both by day and (thanks to infrared cameras) by night. 97 minutes, 391-391 miles.

**Apollo 6 (U. S.)** Apr. 4—The second unmanned test on the huge Saturn 5 booster was considered a success, despite excess vibrations in the first stage, a malfunctioning engine in the second stage and the failure of the third stage to restart in space. 88.2 minutes, 111-226 miles.

**OV-1-13, OV-1-14 (U. S.)** Apr. 6—Of these two Air Force satellites, launched by the same booster, one failed after only a week, leaving the other alone to measure different types of radiation high above earth's atmosphere. OV-1-13: 199.5 minutes, 341-5,792 miles. OV-1-14: 207.8 minutes, 343-6,193 miles.

**LUNA 14 (USSR)** Apr. 7—This Soviet probe settled into orbit around the moon, measuring the lunar gravitational field and its relationship with earth.

**COSMOS 212, 213 (USSR)** Apr. 14, 15—For the second time, a pair of separately launched unmanned Russian satellites met in space, coupled, rode along together and decoupled automatically, demonstrating a maneuvering capability not yet shown by the U. S., although manned U. S. dockings have outstripped the Soviet Union; both spacecraft later landed softly in Soviet territory, a day apart. Orbit while coupled: 89.8 minutes, approximately 123-127 miles.

**COSMOS 215 (USSR)** Apr. 19—The first optical astronomical observatory to be operated successfully in space, it carried 9 telescopes, stayed aloft some six weeks. 91.1 minutes, 162-265 miles.

**MOLNIYA 1-H (USSR)** Apr. 21—Eighth satellite in the USSR's Orbita network for domestic communications. 713 minutes, 286-24,668 miles.

**COSMOS 218 (USSR)** Apr. 25—In orbit for less than one revolution around the earth, this probe was probably a test of the Soviet Fractional Orbital Bombardment System for delivering bombs through space.

**ESRO 2B (E. S. R. O.)** May 17—The first successful satellite launched by the 10-nation European Space Research Organization carried 7 experiments to monitor solar and cosmic radiation. 98.9 minutes, 205-677 miles.

**COSMOS 226 (USSR)** June 12—Thirteenth Soviet weather satellite. 96.9 minutes, 375-404 miles.

**IDSCS 19-26 (U. S.)** June 13—Launched atop a single booster, these 8 satellites added to the Defense Department's Initial Defense Satellite Communications System, largely aimed at keeping the Pentagon in touch with Vietnam and vice versa. Approximate orbits: 1,335 minutes, 20,950-21,150 miles.

**RADIO ASTRONOMY EXPLORER (U. S.)** July 4—Like a huge letter "X" 1,500 feet long, the RAE listens for radio messages from space. 224.3 minutes, 3,626-3,646 miles.

**MOLNIYA 1-I (USSR)** July 5—Ninth addition to the Soviet talk-net. 717.7 minutes, 326-24,751 miles.

**OV-1-15 (U. S.)** July 11—This Air Force research probe carried 9 experiments to study the density of the atmosphere, as well as radiation and other factors which affect it. 95.9 minutes, 91-610 miles. Launched with it was . . .

**OV-1-16 (U. S.)** July 11—the densest satellite ever launched, this 23-inch sphere weighed some 600 pounds, in order to make it resistant to atmospheric disturbances and currents as it, too, made density measurements. 91.5 minutes, 90-345 miles.

**AIR DENSITY EXPLORER C (U. S.)** Aug. 8—This 12-foot balloon was lofted to report on atmospheric densities and temperatures over earth's poles, for correlation with seasonal changes and variations in solar activity. 118 minutes, 430-1,554 miles. Aboard the same booster went . . .

**INJUN 5 (U. S.)** Aug. 8—Designed to study the charged particles in the ionosphere, as well as their effect on low-frequency radio emissions. 118.3 minutes, 423-7,573 miles.

**ATS-4 (U. S.)** Aug. 10—Though the versatile Applications Technology Satellite, designed to try out new ideas for future development, was working fine, a malfunctioning second-stage booster put it in an undesirable orbit, which made most of its data useless. 88.8 minutes, 106-162 miles.

**ESSA 7 (U. S.)** Aug. 16—The seventh of the Environmental Science Services Administration's camera-equipped weather satellites was the fifth in the Tiros Operational Satellite System, taking pictures of the entire world every day. 114.9 minutes, 890-917 miles.

**RAM C-B (U. S.)** Aug. 22—Fired up by one rocket motor and down again by another, this instrumented nose cone was part of the space agency's quest for a way to eliminate the communications blackout that plagues all reentering spacecraft.

**ZOND 5 (USSR)** Sept. 15—This unmanned Soviet probe became the first spacecraft to loop around the moon and return safely to earth.

**OV-2-5, 5-2, 5-4, LES-6 (U. S.)** Sept. 26—Half the satellites in this four-in-one Air Force launch were to investigate radiation and solar flares; another studied the effects of low-gravity on the heat transfer of fluids, and the last was an experimental tactical communications satellite. Three of the 4 in synchronous orbits: approximately 1,430 minutes, 22,240-22,240 miles.

**ESRO 1 (E. S. R. O.)** Oct. 3—A second success for the European Space Research Organization, this time designed to study the northern lights and other phenomena of the ionosphere over the poles. 102.8 minutes, 161-949 miles.

**APOLLO 7 (U. S.)** Oct. 11—The first manned Apollo flight, and the first U. S. manned flight since Gemini 12 flew 23 months before, carried astronauts Walter M. Schirra, Jr., Don F. Eisele and Walter Cunningham for 163 orbits of the earth. 89.9 minutes, 142-160 miles.

**SOYUZ 3 (UUSR)** Oct. 26—The USSR's first manned flight since cosmonaut Vladimir M. Komarov died in the landing crash of his Soyuz 1 spacecraft on Apr. 24, 1967, it carried only one man, Georgy Beregovoi, in a vessel that presumably can hold several; he twice approached, but did not dock with the unmanned Soyuz 2 capsule launched the day before. 88.3 minutes, 109-127 miles.

**PIONEER D (U. S.)** Nov. 8—Launched into an orbit around the sun, the fourth in the Pioneer series will provide the most extensive measurements of the solar corona ever made from a satellite.

**ZOND 6 (USSR)** Nov. 10—Unmanned craft looped around moon and headed back to earth.

**HL-10 (U. S.)** Nov. 13—The first successful powered flight of NASA's manned "lifting body," a "space plane" designed to provide controlled flight from orbit down to earth.

# The Legacy Left by Sen. Robert F. Kennedy

As contained in the eulogy delivered at his funeral services in St. Patrick's Cathedral, New York, June 8, 1968, by his brother, Sen. Edward M. Kennedy.

On behalf of Mrs. Robert Kennedy, her children and the parents and sisters of Robert Kennedy, I want to express what we feel to those who mourn with us today in this cathedral and around the world.

We loved him as a brother and as a father and as a son. From his parents, and from his older brothers and sisters—Joe, Kathleen and Jack—he received an inspiration which he passed on to all of us. He gave us strength in time of trouble, wisd:m in time of uncertainty, and sharing in time of happiness. He was always by our side.

Love is not an easy feeling to put into words. Nor is loyalty, or trust or joy. But he was all of these. He loved life completely and lived it intensely.

A few years back, Robert Kennedy wrote some words about his own father and they expressed the way we in his family feel about him. He said of what his father meant to him:

### His Father's Love

"What it really all adds up to is love—not love as it is described with such facility in popular magazines, but the kind of love that is affection and respect, order, encouragement, and support. Our awareness of this was an incalculable source of strength, and because real love is something unselfish, and involves sacrifice and giving, we could not help but profit from it.

"Beneath it all, he has tried to engender a social conscience. There were wrongs which needed attention. There were people who were poor and who needed help. And we have a responsibility to them and to this country. Through no virtues and accomplishments of our own, we have been fortunate enough to be born in the United States under the most comfortable conditions. We, therefore, have a responsibility to others who are less well off."

This is what Robert Kennedy was given. What he leaves us in what he said, what he did and what he stood for. A speech he made to the young people of South Africa on their Day of Affirmation in 1966 sums it up the best, and I would read it now:

"There is discrimination in this world and slavery and slaughter and starvation. Governments repress their people; and millions are trapped in poverty while the nation grows rich; and wealth is lavished on armaments everywhere.

"These are differing evils, but they are the common works of man. They reflect the imperfection of human justice, the inadequacy of human compassion, our lack of sensibility toward the sufferings of our fellows.

### Human Brotherhood

"But we can perhaps remember—even if only for a time—that those who live with us are our brothers, that they share with us the same short moment of life; that they seek—as we do—nothing but the chance to live out their lives in purpose and happiness, winning what satisfaction and fulfillment they can.

"Surely this bond of common faith, this bond of common goal, can begin to teach us something. Surely we can learn, at least, to look at those around us as fellow men. And surely we can begin to work a little harder to bind up the wounds among us and to become in our own hearts brothers and countrymen once again.

"Our answer is to rely on youth—not a time of life but a state of mind, a temper of the will, a quality of imagination, a predominance of courage over timidity, of the appetite for adventure over the love of ease. The cruelties and obstacles of this swiftly changing planet will not yield to obsolete dogmas and outworn slogans. They cannot be moved by those who cling to a present that is already dying, who prefer the illusion of security to the excitement and danger that come with even the most peaceful progress. It is a revolutionary world we live in; and this generation, at home and around the world, has had thrust upon it a greater burden of responsibility than any generation that has ever lived.

"Some believe there is nothing one man or one woman can do against the enormous array of the world's ills. Yet many of the world's great movements, of thought and action, have flowed from the work of a single man. A young monk began the Protestant Reformation, a young general extended an empire from Macedonia to the borders of the earth, and a young woman reclaimed the territory of France. It was a young Italian explorer who discovered the New World, and the 32-year-old Thomas Jefferson who proclaimed that all men are created equal.

"These moved the world, and so can we all. Few will have the greatness to bend history itself, but each of us can work to change a small portion of events, and in the total of all those acts will be written the history of this generation. It is from numberless diverse acts of courage and belief that human history is shaped.

"Each time a man stands up for an ideal, or acts to improve the lot of others, or strikes out against injustice, he sends forth a tiny ripple of hope, and crossing each other from a million different centers of energy and daring, those ripples build a current that can sweep down the mightiest walls of oppression and resistance.

### Moral Courage

"Few are willing to brave the disapproval of their fellows, the censure of their colleagues, the wrath of their society. Moral courage is a rarer commodity than bravery in battle or great intelligence. Yet it is the one essential, vital quality for those who seek to change a world that yields most painfully to change. And I believe that in this generation those with the courage to enter the moral conflict will find themselves with companions in every corner of the globe.

"For the fortunate among us, there is the temptation to follow the easy and familiar paths of personal ambition and financial success so grandly spread before those who enjoy the privilege of education. But that is not the road history has marked out for us.

"Like it or not, we live in times of danger and uncertainty. But they are also more open to the creative energy of men than any other time in history. All of us will ultimately be judged and as the years pass we will surely judge ourselves, on the effort we have contributed to building a new world society and the extent to which our ideals and goals have shaped that effort.

"The future does not belong to those who are content with today, apathetic toward common problems and their fellow man alike, timid and fearful in the face of new ideas and bold projects. Rather it will belong to those who can blend vision, reason and courage in a personal commitment to the ideals and great enterprises of American society.

### Shaping the Future

"Our future may lie beyond our vision, but it is not completely beyond our control. It is the shaping impulse of America that neither fate nor nature nor the irresistible tides of history, but the work of our own hands, matched to reason and principle, that will determine our destiny. There is pride in that, even arrogance, but there is also experience and truth. In any event, it is the only way we can live."

This is the way he lived. My brother need not be idealized, or enlarged in death beyond what he was in life, to be remembered simply as a good and decent man, who saw wrong and tried to right it, saw suffering and tried to heal it, saw war and tried to stop it.

Those of us who loved him and who take him to his rest today, pray that what he was to us and what he wished for others will some day come to pass for all the world.

As he said many times, in many parts of this nation, to those he touched and who sought to touch him:

"Some men see things as they are and say why. I dream things that never were and say why not."

# The Negro in American History
### By Kenneth C. Johnston, of the World Almanac staff

The contributions made by Negroes to the growth of America have been numerous and varied, but many have gone unmentioned or unstressed in history books.

The names of many of these sometimes forgotten men and women of America's past have appeared in previous editions of the World Almanac, scattered in various sections, but were not singled out and labeled Negro or Black or Afro-American.

With growing interest in this field, with students seeking more knowledge of it, and with schools seeking ways to provide such knowledge, the World Almanac has gathered a list of some of these outstanding Americans of African descent and has briefly noted their contributions.

Among sources for the following facts were the New York Public Library, a series of articles produced by Newspaper Enterprise Association, and several publications sponsored by the B'nai B'rith Anti-Defamation League.

Names of many other notable Negroes, such as entertainers and athletes, are not included. They are well known and have appeared elsewhere in this book.

## EXPLORERS AND SETTLERS

**Pedro Alonzo Nino,** navigator of the Nina, one of Christopher Columbus' three ships on his first voyage of discovery to the New World, 1492.

**Estevanico (also called Esteban)** led the first Spanish explorations into the Arizona and New Mexico area, 1539.

**Francisco,** one of the founders of the town of Bushwick in what is now Brooklyn, N. Y., a landowner who was named by Peter Stuyvesant, with another free Negro, Anton, to a militia company in 1660.

**Jean Baptiste Point du Sable,** fur trader and first settler of Chicago, 1779.

**James P. Beckwourth** (1798-c. 1867), western fur-trader, scout, after whom Beckwourth Pass in northern California is named.

**York,** one of several Negroes in the Lewis & Clark Expedition, 1804-06; a servant, he also served as an interpreter; a "giant" in size, he was admired by Indians for his strength and friendliness.

**Matthew A. Henson** (1866-1955), with Robert E. Peary and 4 Eskimos, discovered the North Pole, 1909; Henson planted the U. S. flag at the Pole.

## SOLDIERS, PATRIOTS

**Crispus Attucks,** (c. 1723-1770), leader of a group fired on by British soldiers in Boston, Mar. 5, 1770, and one of the 5 slain in that action which became known as the "Boston Massacre."

**Peter Salem,** one of the defenders at the Battle of Bunker Hill, June 17, 1775, shot and killed Maj. John Pitcairn, one of the British commanders (who earlier that year had ordered his troops to fire on the Minutemen at Lexington).

**Salem Poor,** commended by the Massachusetts Legislature for performing like "an experienced officer . . . a gallant soldier" at Bunker Hill.

**James Lafayette,** who served as a soldier and spy for the Marquis de Lafayette during the American Revolution.

*(About 5,000 Negroes served in the Continental Army, mostly in integrated units, some in all-Negro combat outfits.)*

**Harriet Tubman,** after escaping from slavery made repeated trips to the South and led more than 300 slaves to freedom as an Underground Railroad conductor; served as nurse and spy for Union Army in the Civil War.

*(Some 200,000 Negroes served in the Union Army during the Civil War; 38,000 gave their lives: 22 won the Medal of Honor, the nation's highest award. Thousands of Negroes helped in the winning of the West; serving after the Civil War in two Negro cavalry and two Negro infantry regiments. In the Spanish-American War, 4 Negro regiments fought at San Juan Hill.)*

**Isaiah Dorman** (19th Century), U. S. Army interpreter, killed with Col. George Custer at Battle of the Little Big Horn (1876).

**Pvt. Henry Johnson** of Albany, N. Y., the first American decorated by France in World War I with the Croix de Guerre.

*(Of 367,000 Negroes in the Armed Forces in World War I, 100,000 served in France. The all-Negro 8th Illinois Regiment received more combat citations than any other American regiment in France; the all-Negro 369th Regiment was the first Allied combat unit to cross the Rhine.)*

**Dorie Miller** of Waco, Tex., a Navy mess attendant on the battleship Arizona during the Pearl Harbor attack, took over an anti-aircraft gun from a dying white sailor and shot down 4 Japanese bombers, Dec. 7, 1941; awarded the Navy Cross by President Franklin D. Roosevelt.

*(More than 1,000,000 Negroes served in the U. S. Armed Forces in World War II; all-Negro fighter and bomber AAF units and infantry divisions gave distinguished service. In 1954 the policy of all-Negro units was finally abolished.)*

**Brig. Gen. Benjamin O. Davis, Sr.,** born 1877, first Negro general (1940) in U. S. Army, rose through ranks to inspector general, retired 1948.

**Lt. Gen. Benjamin O. Davis, Jr.,** b. 1912, first Negro West Point graduate in 20th Century (1936), first Negro Air Force general (1954), had distinguished service as pilot and commander in World War II.

**Brig. Gen. Frederic E. Davison,** b. 1917, 3d Negro to become a general (1968 in Vietnam.)

**Commander Samuel L. Gravely, Jr.,** first Negro to command a Navy ship since the Civil War, became captain of the destroyer Taussig (1966).

*(As of mid-1968, Negroes were 10.5% of the total number of Americans serving in Vietnam; 13.7% of the 25,616 U. S. servicemen killed there between 1961 and June 30, 1968, were Negroes, according to the Defense Department. Further figures show Negroes comprised 14.8% of Army forces in Vietnam, 1961-1965, and suffered 18.3% of Army casualties. Of the total U. S. population, by 1968 Census estimate, 11.1% were Negroes.)*

## SCIENTISTS, INVENTORS

**Benjamin Banneker** (1731-c. 1806), author of annual almanacs (1791-1802) containing tide tables, coming eclipses, medical formulas (called the first scientific publication by an American Negro); built what has been called the first American clock of all American parts (1761); served on commission which surveyed and helped lay out the future city of Washington, D. C.

**Lewis Temple** (1800-1854), invented toggle harpoon for whaling industry (c. 1840).

**Henry Blair** (19th Century), obtained patent (believed the first issued to a Negro) for a corn-planter (1834) and for a cotton-planter (1836).

**Norbert Rillieux** (1806-1894), held many patents; invented a vacuum pan evaporator which revolutionized the sugar-refining industry (1846).

**Elijah McCoy** (1844-c. 1928), held some 75 patents; a pioneer inventor of automatic machinery lubricators; his lubricating cup was in general use for years in locomotives, steamers, factories.

**Lewis H. Latimer** (1848-1928), associate of Thomas Edison, made drawings for Alexander Graham Bell's first telephone, wrote textbook on the Edison Co. lighting system in New York City; supervised installation of first electric street lighting in New York.

**Jan Matzeliger** (1852-1889), invented lasting machine which cut shoe industry costs in half and brought higher wages to shoe workers.

**Granville T. Woods** (1856-1910), held over 50 patents mostly in electric and telegraph fields; one was for "Induction Telegraphy," a system for communicating to and from moving trains.

**Dr. Daniel Hale Williams** (1856-1931), performed one of first two open-heart operations (1893); founded Provident, Chicago's first Negro hospital; first Negro elected a fellow of the American College of Surgeons.

**George Washington Carver** (c. 1864-1943), agricultural scientist, philanthropist; brought about an agricultural revolution in the South, finding ways to enrich the soil, adding to its one-crop cotton economy not only emphasis on peanuts, sweet potatoes and soybeans, but discovering some 300 industrial uses for by-products he synthesized from them; created a school-on-wheels to dem-

onstrate soil-fertilization on farms.

**Andrew J. Beard** (19th Century), invented an automatic coupler for railroad cars (1897).

**Dr. William A. Hinton** (1883-1959), developed the Hinton and Davies-Hinton tests for detection of syphilis; first Negro professor at Harvard Medical School (1949).

**Percy Julian,** b. 1898, chemist; extracted sterols from soybeans, cutting cost of the drugs; synthesized physostigmine (1935) used in treatment of glaucoma.

**Dr. Charles Richard Drew** (1904-1950), pioneer in development of blood banks; director of American Red Cross blood donor project in World War II.

## WRITERS, EDUCATORS

**Amos Fortune** (c. 1710-1801), educator; ex-slave, owned tanning business in Jaffrey, N. H., created a school fund which is still operating.

**Jupiter Hammon** (c. 1720-1800), a Long Island N. Y. poet, the first Negro American to have his works published.

**Phillis Wheatley** (c. 1753-1784), poet, second American woman and first Negro woman to have her works published; b. in Senegal, enslaved, taken to Boston, freed 1773.

**John B. Russwurm** (1799-1851) with **Samuel E. Cornish** (1793-1858), founded the nation's first Negro newspaper, Freedom's Journal (1827) in N. Y. City.

**William Wells Brown** (1815-1884), b. a slave, first American Negro to publish a novel (Clotel), as well as a drama, a travel book, 3 histories.

**Frederick Douglass** (1817-1895), author, editor, orator, diplomat; a runaway slave (b. Frederick Bailey), edited the abolitionist weekly, The North Star, in Rochester, N. Y., before the Civil War; became U. S. Minister and Consul General to Haiti; also was marshal and recorder of deeds for the District of Columbia.

**Booker T. Washington** (1856-1915), founder and first president of Tuskegee Institute (1881); author of a dozen books including Up From Slavery; social reformer.

**Charles Waddell Chesnutt** (1858-1932), novelist; best-known for his short stories including The Conjure Woman.

**William Edward Burghardt Du Bois** (1868-1963), historian, sociologist, a founder of the NAACP (1909) and founding editor of its magazine The Crisis; author of The Souls of Black Folk (1903) and other books.

**James Weldon Johnson** (1871-1938), poet, song-lyricist, novelist; first Negro admitted to Florida bar; a U. S. consul in Venezuela and Nicaragua; a founder of the NAACP.

**Paul Laurence Dunbar** (1872-1906), poet, novelist; won fame with Lyrics of Lowly Life (1896).

**Langston Hughes** (1902-1967), a major American poet; also author of stories and song lyrics.

**Countee Cullen** (1903-1946), poet, winner of numerous literary prizes.

**Richard Wright** (1908-1960), best-selling novels; Native Son (1940), Black Boy (1945), etc.

**Willard Motley** (1912-1965), novelist; wrote Knock on Any Door (1947).

**Ralph Ellison,** b. 1914, novelist, winner of 1952 National Book Award for Invisible Man.

**Frank Yerby,** b. 1916, most successful of American Negro novelists; some 19 novels with over 20,-000,000 copies sold, including The Foxes of Harrow, Vixen, etc.

**Gwendolyn Brooks,** b. 1917, poet, novelist; first Negro to win a Pulitzer Prize (1950), for one of her volumes, Annie Allen.

**James Baldwin,** b. 1924, best-seller author, playwright; Another Country (1962), The Fire Next Time (1963) etc.

**Lorraine Hansberry** (1930-1965), playwright; won N. Y. Drama Critics Circle award with Raisin in the Sun (1959).

**LeRoi Jones,** b. 1934, poet, author of prize-winning off-Broadway plays.

## PUBLIC OFFICIALS

**Hiram R. Revels** (1822-1901), first Negro U. S. Senator, elected in Mississippi, served 1870-1871.

**Blanche Kelso Bruce** (1841-1898), elected U. S. Senator from Mississippi, he served 1875-1881.

**Dr. Mary McCleod Bethune** (1875-1955), adviser to Presidents Franklin D. Roosevelt and Harry Truman; division administrator in National Youth Administration (1935).

**Clifton Wharton,** b. 1899, U. S. Ambassador to Norway (1961-1964).

**James C. Evans,** b. 1900, Director of President Eisenhower's "People to People" program.

**Dr. Ralph Bunche,** b. 1904, first American Negro to win the Nobel Peace Prize (1950); became Undersecretary of the United Nations (1950).

**Dr. Robert C. Weaver,** b. 1907, first Negro member of the U. S. Cabinet: Secretary of the Department of Housing & Urban Development (1966).

**Harold A. Stevens,** b. 1907, first Negro Presiding Justice of the New York State Supreme Court's Appellate Division (1969, First Department).

**Adam Clayton Powell,** b. 1908, became first Negro Congressman since 19th Century Reconstruction days to have legislation passed by both houses of Congress (elected to his first term 1944).

**Thurgood Marshall,** b. 1908, first Negro U. S. Solicitor General (1965); first Negro to be made a Justice of the U. S. Supreme Court (1967); as a lawyer led the legal battery which won the historic decision from the Supreme Court declaring segregation of public schools unconstitutional (1954).

**William H. Hastie,** b. 1904, first Negro Federal Judge (appointed 1937); Governor of Virgin Islands (1946-1949); became Judge, U. S. Circuit Court of Appeals (1949).

**Edward W. Brooke,** b. 1919; Attorney General of Massachusetts (1962); first Negro elected to U. S. Senate since 19th Century Reconstruction (1967).

**Mrs. Constance Baker Motley,** b. 1921; first Negro woman Borough President of Manhattan, N. Y. City (1965); Judge, U. S. District Court (1966).

**Carl T. Rowan,** b. 1925, prize-winning journalist; public official; director of the U. S. Information Agency (1964), making him the first Negro to sit on the National Security Council; U. S. Ambassador to Finland (1963).

**Robert C. Henry,** elected Mayor of Springfield, Ohio (1965), first Negro Mayor of a moderate-sized city in the 20th Century.

**Carl B. Stokes,** b. 1927, elected Mayor of Cleveland (1967).

**Richard G. Hatcher,** b. 1933, elected Mayor of Gary, Ind. (1967).

**Lucius A. Amerson,** b. 1934, elected sheriff of Macon County, Ga. (1966).

## LABOR, CIVIL RIGHTS LEADERS

**Denmark Vesey,** b. in 18th Century, organized a slave revolt in 1822 in Charleston, S.C.; it failed and he and 46 others were executed.

**Nat Turner** (1800-1831), led slave revolt in Virginia in 1831; he and 16 others were hanged.

**Marcus Garvey** (1887-1940), founded Universal Negro Improvement Assn. (1911), sought to promote a Back to Africa movement.

**Willard Townsend** (1895-1957), organized (1935) the United Transport Service Employees (red-caps, etc.); Vice President of AFL-CIO.

**Elijah Muhammad,** b, 1897, founded the Nation of Islam or Black Muslims (1931).

**A. Philip Randolph,** b. 1889, organized the Brotherhood of Sleeping Car Porters (1925); organizer of 1941 and 1963 March on Washington movements; Vice President of AFL-CIO.

**Walter White** (1893-1955), Executive Secretary, NAACP, (1931-1955).

**Roy Wilkins,** b. 1901, became Executive Secretary, NAACP (1955).

**Bayard Rustin,** b. 1910, an organizer of the 1963 March on Washington; Executive Director of the A. Philip Randolph Institute.

**The Rev. Dr. Ralph David Abernathy,** b. 1916, an organizer (1957) of the Southern Christian Leadership Conference; its President (1968).

**James Farmer,** b. 1920, a founder of the Congress of Racial Equality (1942); its National Director (1961-1965).

**Whitney M. Young, Jr.,** b. 1921, Executive Director of the National Urban League (1961); author, lecturer, newspaper columnist.

**Floyd McKissick,** b. 1922, National Director of CORE (1966).

**Malcolm X** (1925-1965), founded the Organization of Afro-American Unity (1963).

**The Rev. Dr. Martin Luther King, Jr.** (1929-1968), led 382-day, Montgomery, Ala., boycott which brought 1956 U. S. Supreme Court decision holding segregation on buses unconstitutional; founder and President of the Southern Christian Leadership Conference (1957); leader of rights marches; won Nobel Peace Prize (1964).

**Roy Innis,** b. 1934, National Director of CORE (1968).

**Stokely Carmichael,** b. 1944, National Chairman of the Student Nonviolent Coordinating Committee (1966-1967).

**H. Rap Brown,** b. 1944, National Chairman of SNCC (1967).

# Laws Passed by 90th Congress, 2nd Session (1968)

The Second Session of the 90th Congress convened Jan. 15, 1968, and adjourned Oct. 14, 1968. The First Session had convened Jan. 10, 1967, and adjourned Dec. 15, 1967.

Together, the two Sessions produced notable legislation in the fields of consumer protection, civil rights, crime control, education and conservation.

President Johnson, despite his "lame duck" status during the Second Session, saw most of his proposals enacted, though many were in altered form.

The President's nomination of Associate Supreme Court Justice Abe Fortas to be Chief Justice of the United States was blocked in the Senate, which also put off a vote on the nuclear non-proliferation treaty.

Important legislation passed by the Second Session and signed by the President included:

**Tax Surcharge.** This was the 10% surcharge on individual and corporate income taxes which had been asked by the President during the First Session. It was finally approved during the Second Session, but Congress coupled the action with a $6 billion mandatory cut in planned spending for the fiscal year.

**Foreign Aid.** Congress appropriated only $1.75 billion, $1.2 billion less than the Administration requested and the smallest sum in the 21-year history of the program.

**Crime Control.** This act authorized $100,-000,000 in the fiscal year 1969 and $300,-000,000 in fiscal 1970 in grants to states and municipalities to improve law enforcement agencies. It also granted Federal, state and local law officers broader rights to use wiretapping and eavesdropping in criminal investigations. It further carried provisions designed to counteract, in part, recent Supreme Court decisions on "voluntary" confessions and on legal representation during police "line-ups."

**Gun Control.** In its crime control bill (above), Congress included bans on the mail order sale of handguns and ammunition to individuals, and over-the-counter sales of handguns to residents of other states and to anyone under 21; it provided for licensing of gun dealers and made it a crime for felons, mental incompetents, illegal aliens, etc., to possess firearms.

In a second gun control act, Congress banned mail order interstate sales of rifles and shotguns and prohibited their sale to persons under 18. But Congress did not act on the President's request for registration of all guns and for licensing of gun owners.

**Consumer Protection.** The Wholesome Poultry Act gave the states two years to develop inspection systems meeting Federal requirements, and provided financial and technical aid to them.

The Truth-in-Lending Act required that beginning July 1, 1969, consumers be informed of the complete cost of credit, requiring disclosure of interest rates in department store and catalogue house revolving charge accounts, disclosure of annual interest rates in credit advertising, disclosure of "true" annual interest rates of first mortgages on housing. It banned loan-sharking.

Congress also passed acts for gas pipeline safety and for protection against radiation from color TV and other appliances.

**Housing.** Congress authorized an ambitious housing program, to spend $5.3 billion to provide 1,700,000 new or rehabilitated housing units over a 3-year period.

**Conservation.** Legislation established the 58,000-acre Redwood National Park in California, the North Cascades Park in Washington, a nationwide system of trails and scenic rivers, and authorized $1.3 billion for the Central Arizona Project to develop a water resource program for the Colorado River basin.

**Drug Control.** This act set penalties for manufacture, sale or possession of LSD and other drugs. Courts were authorized to suspend sentences of first offenders in possession cases.

**Civil Rights.** The open-housing measure imposed a Federal ban on discrimination in the sale and renting of about 80% of the nation's housing. It also set up penalties for persons who cross state lines to incite riots.

**Education.** Congress authorized a $7.3 billion, 3-year extension of Federal aid to higher education; appropriated a record $20,900,000 for the teacher corps; authorized a 4-year vocational education program.

**Defense.** Congress appropriated $71.8 billion for defense.

**Urban Renewal.** Congress appropriated $14.7 billion for Department of Housing and Urban Development programs, making substantial cuts in urban renewal, model cities and rent supplements.

## FIRST SESSION LEGISLATION

In the First Session (1967) of the 90th Congress, legislation included:

**Air Pollution Control.** This authorized a 3-year program, giving HEW the power to shut down factories or immobilize all pollution sources in a city during an emergency; it gave states the initiative in setting clean air standards.

**New GI Benefits.** Congress increased pensions and education and job-training benefits and raised home loan maximums to $25,000.

**Product Safety.** A national commission was created to inform the public of dangerous products.

**Educational TV.** A corporation was established to help finance educational TV and radio programs.

---

# Changes in U. S. Mission to the UN in 1968
### Representatives and Alternates to the 23rd General Assembly, as of Nov. 13, 1968

Arthur J. Goldberg, United States Ambassador to the United Nations since July 20, 1965, resigned that post on April 25, 1968, and was replaced by President Johnson with George W. Ball, former Under Secretary of State. Ambassador Ball resigned Sept. 26, 1968; the President named James Russell Wiggins, editor and executive vice president of the Washington Post, to succeed him.

### REPRESENTATIVES

James R. Wiggins, Sen. Stuart Symington, Sen. John Sherman Cooper, William C. Foster, Brewster C. Denny.

### ALTERNATES

William B. Buffum, Raymond D. Nasher, Jean Picker, Louis Stulberg, Marvin L. Warner.

### PRINCIPAL OFFICERS

Permanent Rep. to the UN—James R. Wiggins. Senior Advisor—Seymour M. Finger.
International Organization Affairs—Joseph J. Sisco.
Legal Advisor—Leonard C. Meeker.
Security Council—Richard F. Pedersen.
Economic and Social Council—Arthur E. Goldschmidt.
Arms Control and Disarmament Agency—Samuel DePalma.

# Major Decisions of the U. S. Supreme Court, 1968

The court affirmed a Federal court ruling that the Texas loyalty oath for teachers and other state employees was an unconstitutional infringement on freedom of association; this was the 6th state loyalty oath law found invalid by the Supreme Court since 1961. (Jan. 15.)

Turned down a 6th appeal by Morton Sobell, convicted as an atom spy in 1951 with Julius and Ethel Rosenberg; Sobell, serving a 30-yr. prison term, contended that the Government had used perjured testimony against him. (Jan. 15.)

Upheld a Federal court decision declaring unconstitutional a 1962 Louisiana law giving state tuition grants for students in private, segregated schools. (Jan. 15.)

Affirmed a lower court ruling upholding the right of the Secy. of Health, Education and Welfare to withhold Federal welfare funds from Alabama because state officials refused to agree to eliminate racial discrimination in the welfare program. (Jan. 15.)

### Kindergarten Prayer Unconstitutional

Upheld a lower court decision that declared unconstitutional a verse prayer recited by kindergarten children in De-Kalb, Ill., even though the word God had been deleted. (Jan. 22.)

Affirmed a Federal court decision upholding the constitutionality of a New York State law requiring teachers in public schools and tax-exempt private schools to swear to uphold the Federal and state constitutions. (Jan. 22.)

### Gambling Stamp Thrown Out

In two related decisions, each by a 7-1 vote with Chief Justice Earl Warren dissenting, declared unconstitutional a Federal law requiring gamblers to buy a $50 gambling stamp annually and to pay a 10% excise tax on their gross wagers, and struck down a section of the National Firearms Act making it a crime to possess an unregistered firearm. (Jan. 29.)

Refused to review the third appeal by James R. Hoffa, Teamsters president, to reach the court, challenging his jury tampering conviction. (Jan. 29.)

Declined to examine an appeal by a Negro citizen group contending that there was racial discrimination in the routing of an interstate highway section through a Negro district of Nashville, Tenn. (Jan. 29.)

Granted an appeal by 3 Des Moines, Iowa, public school children who had been suspended from school because they wore black armbands in protest against the war in Vietnam. (Mar. 4.)

Upheld unanimously a Federal District Court ruling that Alabama could not segregate jail or prison inmates on the ground that such racial separation was necessary to avoid threatened racial violence. (Mar. 11.)

In an 8-0 ruling interpreting the Civil Rights Act of 1964, held that proprietors of public accommodations found guilty of refusing services to Negroes must pay lawyers' fees of the plaintiffs. (Mar. 18.)

### One-Man, One-Vote Extended

In a landmark 5-3 decision, extended its one-man, one-vote doctrine to local governments, holding that if county, city and town governments elect their representatives from single-member districts the districts must be substantially equal in population. (Apr. 1.)

Ruled, 8-0, that the Federal Government must pay more than a century's interest to the Peoria Tribe of Indians of Oklahoma on $172,726 it failed to pay to the tribe in 1857 for land ceded by treaty. (Apr. 1.)

In a 6-2 ruling, declared unconstitutional the death penalty provision of the Federal Kidnapping Law, commonly known as the Lindbergh Law. The court held that the law still can be enforced except for the death penalty provision; the law makes it a Federal crime to transport a kidnapped person across a state line. (Apr. 8.)

Upheld a lower court decision holding that the Los Angeles Times' 1964 purchase of 3 San Bernardino newspapers for $15,-000,000 violated antitrust laws and ordered the Times to divest itself of the newspapers. (Apr. 22.)

### Rights of Criminals

In a series of decisions broadening the rights of criminal defendants and convicted persons, held: that a state prison inmate serving the first of two consecutive sentences may attack the second conviction in Federal habeas corpus proceedings; that state courts must grant defendants jury trials in criminal cases; that defendants in state criminal contempt cases must be granted jury trials except in petty cases; that in joint Federal trials a confession that incriminates one defendant cannot be admitted in evidence if it also incriminates a co-defendant. (May 20.)

In a 7-1 decision on an appeal by David P. O'Brien, who burned his draft card in 1966, upheld a 1965 law that makes it a crime to burn or otherwise destroy or mutilate a draft card. (May 27.)

Struck a blow at capital punishment by holding, 6-3, that persons cannot constitutionally be sentenced to death by juries from which all persons with conscientious scruples against the death penalty have been eliminated. (June 3.)

In a 7-0 decision, upheld the authority of the Federal Communications Commission to regulate community antenna television systems, known as CATV. (June 10.)

### Book Aid to Church Pupils

Upheld, in a 6-3 decision, a 1965 New York State law requiring public school districts to lend textbooks to students in private and parochial schools. (June 10.)

In a 7-2 ruling that prohibits racial discrimination in all sales and rentals of real estate, turned the century-old civil rights law of 1866 into a sweeping fair housing statute. (June 17.)

Over the dissent of Justice William O. Douglas, let stand a lower court ruling that Dallas public schools could constitutionally require long-haired male students to have their hair cut. (Oct. 14.)

Agreed to review a lower court decision that owners of the two daily newspapers in Tucson, Ariz., violated the antitrust laws by sharing a common press and circulation and advertising departments. (Oct. 22.)

Held unconstitutional an Arkansas law that made it a crime to teach the Darwinian theory of evolution in the public schools; the case, the result of the challenge of the law by Mrs. John O. Epperson, a school teacher, was reminiscent of the 1925 Tennessee "monkey trial," in which John T. Scopes was convicted for teaching evolution and which pitted Clearence Darrow against William Jennings Bryan as counsel. (Nov. 12.)

# CORPORATIONS AND STOCKS
## More Than 24,000,000 Persons Own Shares in U. S. Industries

In 1968, more than 24,000,000 persons in the United States owned shares in American industry, as compared to only 8,630,000 in 1956.

The N. Y. Stock Exchange listed 1,750 issues of 1,274 companies—a total of 12.7 billion shares, valued at $668 billion.

Trading activity grew. Average daily volume on the N. Y. Exchange was over 12,600,000 shares in 1968, compared to 9,899,000 in 1967.

The American Exchange listed 1,088 issues of 1,013 companies—totaling 2.04 billion shares, which were valued at $55 billion.

Average daily volume on the American Exchange was over 6,128,000 in 1968; 4,475,000 in 1967.

U. S. corporations boosted their sales volumes. The N. Y. Exchange in 1968 reported 108 of its listed companies had sales or revenues in 1967 of over $1 billion; last year it listed 99 in its "Billionaires Club" for 1966.

## 50 U. S. Companies with Largest Annual Sales or Revenues
As listed in 1968 in The Exchange, magazine of the N. Y. Stock Exchange, for 1967

| Company | Sales or revenues (in millions) | Net profit | Company | Sales or revenues (in millions) | Net profit |
|---|---|---|---|---|---|
| General Motors Corp. | $20,026.3 | $1,627.3 | Penney (J.C.) Co.* | 2,746.0 | 89.5 |
| Standard Oil Co. (N. J.) | 14,409.4 | 1,232.3 | Goodyear Tire & Rubber | 2,637.7 | 127.1 |
| American Tel. & Tel. Co. | 13,009.2 | 2,110.3 | Gen. Tel. & Electronics | 2,622.2 | 213.5 |
| Ford Motor Co. | 10,515.7 | 84.1 | Bethlehem Steel Corp. | 2,594.1 | 130.4 |
| General Electric Co. | 7,741.2 | 361.4 | Union Carbide Corp. | 2,545.6 | 170.7 |
| Sears, Roebuck & Co.* | 7,330.1 | 384.3 | International Harvester* | 2,541.9 | 93.0 |
| Mobil Oil Corp. | 6,345.8 | 385.4 | Procter & Gamble* | 2,438.7 | 174.1 |
| Chrysler Corp. | 6,213.4 | 200.4 | North Amer. Rockwell* | 2,438.5 | 68.3 |
| Great A. & P. Tea Co.* | 5,458.8 | 55.9 | Eastman Kodak Co. | 2,391.5 | 352.3 |
| Int'l. Business Machines | 5,345.3 | 651.5 | Lockheed Aircraft Corp. | 2,335.5 | 54.4 |
| Texaco Inc. | 5,121.4 | 754.4 | National Dairy Products | 2,318.6 | 76.1 |
| Gulf Oil Corp. | 5,109.6 | 578.3 | General Dynamics Corp. | 2,253.3 | 57.0 |
| United States Steel Corp. | 4,067.2 | 172.5 | Continental Oil Co. | 2,233.0 | 149.0 |
| Standard Oil of Calif. | 3,788.9 | 421.7 | United Aircraft Corp. | 2,212.3 | 57.3 |
| Shell Oil Co. | 3,657.7 | 284.8 | Armour & Co.* | 2,156.7 | 22.3 |
| Standard Oil Co. (Ind.) | 3,536.3 | 282.3 | Penn Central Co. | 2,074.3 | 71.4 |
| Safeway Stores, Inc. | 3,360.9 | 50.9 | Phillips Petroleum Co. | 1,981.6 | 164.0 |
| du Pont de Nemours | 3,078.8 | 313.9 | Reynolds (R.J.) Tobacco | 1,911.4 | 151.0 |
| Radio Corp. of America | 3,014.1 | 147.5 | Montgomery Ward* | 1,879.0 | 17.4 |
| McDonnell Douglas Corp. | 2,933.8 | 0.9 | Firestone Tire & Rubber* | 1,875.4 | 102.3 |
| Westinghouse Electric | 2,900.7 | 122.5 | Ling-Temco-Vought | 1,833.3 | 34.0 |
| Boeing Co. | 2,879.7 | 83.9 | Tenneco, Inc. | 1,777.7 | 138.5 |
| Swift & Co.* | 2,834.7 | 26.7 | Sun Oil Co. | 1,765.3 | 163.0 |
| Kroger Co. | 2,806.1 | 25.7 | General Foods Corp.* | 1,739.7 | 103.5 |
| International Tel. & Tel. | 2,760.6 | 122.8 | Union Oil Co. of Calif. | 1,683.7 | 145.0 |

*Fiscal year other than calendar year.

## 30 Largest Industrial Companies Outside the U. S.
As listed for 1967 in the Fortune Directory, © 1968 Time Inc.

| Company | Sales | Net profit (or * loss) | Company | Sales | Net profit (or * loss) |
|---|---|---|---|---|---|
| | (add 000) | (add 000) | | (add 000) | (add 000) |
| Royal Dutch/Shell N-B | $8,376,022 | $742,550 | Renault F | 1,519,123 | 4,557 |
| Unilever B-N | 5,559,950 | 209,275 | Daimler-Benz G | 1,491,000 | 46,082 |
| British Petroleum B | 2,973,575 | 176,550 | Farbenfabriken Bayer G | 1,458,900 | 66,840 |
| ICI (Imperial Chem Ind) B | 2,691,700 | 158,950 | Yawata Iron & Steel J | 1,375,634 | 43,070 |
| National Coal Board B | 2,438,822 | 958 | Cie Francaise des Petroles F | 1,343,310 | 55,968 |
| Philips' Gloeilampenfab N | 2,401,833 | 98,000 | British-American Tobacco B | 1,320,396 | 148,652 |
| Volkswagenwerk G | 2,333,750 | 75,000 | British Motor B | 1,308,182 | *11,130 |
| Montecatini Edison I | 2,092,320 | 74,720 | Ente Naz'le Idrocarburi I | 1,294,880 | 5,760 |
| Siemens G | 1,984,250 | 39,943 | Matsushita Elec Indl J | 1,279,625 | 75,889 |
| Fiat I | 1,910,597 | 51,475 | Nissan Motor J | 1,272,847 | 62,683 |
| Nestle S | 1,795,792 | 37,217 | Badische Anilin & Soda Fabrik G | 1,259,000 | 64,863 |
| Hitachi J | 1,749,125 | 75,039 | Tokyo Shibaura Elec J | 1,258,478 | 38,858 |
| Mitsubishi Heavy Ind J | 1,650,786 | 46,253 | Tokyo Motor J | 1,257,777 | 69,963 |
| Farbwerke Hoechst G | 1,650,250 | 58,938 | Krupp-Konzern G | 1,232,500 | N.A. |
| August Thyssen-Hutte G | 1,637,600 | 23,598 | Finsider I | 1,203,240 | 24,812 |

Nation of Hqs: N Netherlands, B Britain, G Germany, I Italy, S Switzerland, F France, J Japan.

## Stocks Most Widely Held by Investment, Insurance Cos., Trust Funds
As listed in 1968 in Stocks on the Big Board, published by the N. Y. Stock Exchange
*(In order of number of companies etc. which held shares, Sept. 1968)*

| | | | |
|---|---|---|---|
| General Motors | Mobil Oil Corp | Standard Oil (Cal) | General Foods |
| Intnatl Bus Machs | Union Carbide | Dow Chemical | Texas Utilities |
| Standard Oil (NJ) | du Pont Inc | Phillips Petrol | Southern Co |
| Amer Tel & Tel | Sears, Roebuck | Merck & Co | Westinghouse Elec |
| Texaco, Inc. | Ford Motor Co | Amer Elect Power | Commonwealth Ed |
| General Electric | Gen Tel & Elec | Southern Cal Ed | Goodyear Tire & R |
| Eastman Kodak | Xerox Corp | Minn Mng & Mfg | Chase Mnhttn Bnk |
| Gulf Oil Corp | Standard Oil (Ind) | Monsanto Co | Amer Cynamid |

## Selected Common Stocks: Prices, Symbols, Dividends, Yields

As compiled from lists of stocks active on the New York (NY) and American (Am) Stock Exchanges

| Company | Ticker Symbol | Stock Exch. | High and Low 1968 to Oct. 21 | Price Oct. 21 | Indicated Div. $ | Indicated Yield % |
|---|---|---|---|---|---|---|
| ACF Industries | ACF | NY | 68⅜- 39½ | 55⅝ | 2.20 | 4.1 |
| Aerojet-General | AJT | Am | 34¼- 22⅛ | 31 | 1.00 | 3.1 |
| Air Reduction | AN | NY | 36⅞- 28½ | 31¾ | 1.50 | 4.7 |
| Alcan Alum. Ltd. | AL | NY | 27⅜- 21¼ | 26⅝ | 1.10 | 4.3 |
| Allied Artists | AAP | Am | 18⅛- 9¾ | 13½ | ... | ... |
| Allied Chemical | ACD | NY | 43 - 34 | 35¼ | 1.90 | 5.3 |
| Allis-Chalmers | AH | NY | 38⅛- 24 | 30 | .50 | 1.8 |
| Alloys Unlimited | AU | Am | 52⅞- 32⅛ | 49¼ | .07 | 0.2 |
| Alum. Co. Amer. | AA | NY | 81½- 62½ | 74⅞ | 1.80 | 2.5 |
| Amerada Petrolm | ARC | NY | 94⅜- 75 | 87¼ | 3.00 | 3.5 |
| Amer Can Co. | AC | NY | 54½- 45⅞ | 53½ | 2.20 | 4.4 |
| Amer Cyanamid | ACY | NY | 32½- 22¼ | 31⅛ | 1.25 | 4.0 |
| Amer Elec. Power | AEP | NY | 40½- 32½ | 36¾ | 1.52 | 4.1 |
| Amer Home Prods. | AHP | NY | 67½- 50⅝ | 58½ | 1.30 | 2.2 |
| Amer Hosp. Sup. | AHS | NY | 39 - 24⅝ | 30 | .22 | 0.8 |
| Amer Motors | AMO | NY | 15⅛- 10¼ | 13¾ | ... | ... |
| Amer Tel & Tel | T | NY | 55¾- 48 | 55½ | 2.40 | 4.4 |
| Amer Tobacco | AT | NY | 35⅜- 30⅛ | 34½ | 1.90 | 5.5 |
| Ampex | APX | NY | 38 - 26½ | 36⅞ | ... | ... |
| Anaconda Co. | A | NY | 55 - 39 | 53 | 2.50 | 4.9 |
| Arkansas La Gas | AKG | Am | 40¾- 34⅝ | 37¾ | 1.70 | 4.5 |
| Armour & Co. | AM | NY | 54 - 32¼ | 53⅞ | 1.60 | 3.0 |
| Atlas Corp | AZ | NY | 7 - 4¾ | 5⅞ | ... | ... |
| Automatic Radio | ART | Am | 25⅞- 15¾ | 17½ | ... | ... |
| Baxter Labs | BAX | NY | 54⅞- 33¼ | 41¼ | .16 | 0.4 |
| Bendix Corp | BX | NY | 54⅞- 35 | 45½ | 1.40 | 3.0 |
| Benguet Consol | BE | NY | 14¾- 7⅝ | 13 | ... | ... |
| Bethlehem Steel | BS | NY | 34¼- 28⅛ | 32⅞ | 1.60 | 5.0 |
| Boeing Co. | BA | NY | 90¼- 52½ | 58½ | 1.20 | 2.1 |
| Borden Inc. | BN | NY | 36¾- 28⅛ | 31¾ | 1.20 | 3.9 |
| Borg-Warner | BOR | NY | 35 - 25⅞ | 34¼ | 1.25 | 3.6 |
| Boston Edison | BSE | NY | 46⅝- 37¾ | 42¼ | 2.08 | 4.9 |
| Brazilian Lt & P | BL | Am | 20⅛- 12¼ | 18¾ | 1.00 | 5.6 |
| Bristol-Myers | BMY | NY | 83½- 59¼ | 75¾ | 1.20 | 1.6 |
| Brooklyn Union Gas | BU | NY | 32¾- 28 | 31¾ | 1.68 | 5.3 |
| Brown Shoe | BWS | NY | 59½- 40½ | 53⅛ | 1.40 | 2.6 |
| Brunswick Corp | BC | NY | 19⅞- 12½ | 19½ | ... | ... |
| Budd Co. | BF | NY | 37 - 20½ | 32⅜ | .80 | 2.4 |
| Bunker-Ramo | BR | NY | 21⅜- 11¾ | 17⅝ | ... | ... |
| Burroughs Corp | BGH | NY | 239⅝-157 | 222 | 1.00 | 0.4 |
| Campbell Chib | CCH | Am | 11⅝- 7 | 8⅛ | ... | ... |
| Campbell Soup | CPB | NY | 34¾- 26⅛ | 30⅛ | 1.00 | 3.3 |
| Caterpillar Trtr. | CTR | NY | 47⅛- 36⅛ | 46½ | 1.20 | 2.7 |
| Celanese Corp | CZ | NY | 70 - 50½ | 68 | 2.00 | 2.9 |
| Central & S West | CSR | NY | 48 - 39⅛ | 41¼ | 1.70 | 4.2 |
| Chase Mnhtn Bk | CMB | NY | 87½- 61½ | 85 | 2.40 | 2.8 |
| Chesapeake & Ohio | CO | NY | 75 - 60⅛ | 73½ | 4.00 | 5.5 |
| Chesebrough-Pond | CBM | NY | 48½- 34⅛ | 41⅛ | .84 | 2.1 |
| Chock Full O Nut | CHF | NY | 24⅞- 14⅞ | 18½ | .60 | 3.4 |
| Chrysler | C | NY | 72¾- 48 | 71⅝ | 2.00 | 2.9 |
| Cities Service | CS | NY | 65½- 43¼ | 61 | 2.00 | 3.3 |
| Cluett, Peabody | CLU | NY | 38⅞- 22⅞ | 38 | .80 | 2.2 |
| Coca-Cola Co | KO | NY | 81⅜- 61⅞ | 72⅞ | 1.20 | 1.7 |
| Collins Radio | CRI | NY | 101⅛- 53 | 61¼ | .80 | 1.3 |
| Columbia Gas Sys | CG | NY | 30¼- 25⅜ | 30 | 1.52 | 5.0 |
| Commrcl Solvents | CV | NY | 45⅜- 25⅛ | 28¼ | .80 | 2.8 |
| Commonwealth Edison | CWE | NY | 51⅜- 41⅞ | 45⅜ | 2.20 | 4.7 |
| Commonwealth Oil | CWO | NY | 29 - 18½ | 24¾ | .60 | 2.4 |
| Com Sat Corp | CQ | NY | 64¾- 41½ | 55⅛ | ... | ... |
| Computer Aplctns | CPD | Am | 42⅝- 20⅝ | 21¼ | ... | ... |
| Computer Sciencs | CSZ | Am | 64¾- 31⅝ | 56¾ | .10 | 0.2 |
| Consol Edison | ED | NY | 35½- 31⅝ | 33⅝ | 1.80 | 5.4 |
| Consol Oil & G. | CGS | Am | 47 - 11⅞ | 29¼ | ... | ... |
| Consumers Power | CMS | NY | 45¼- 26⅛ | 41¾ | 1.90 | 4.5 |
| Cont Air Lines | CAL | NY | 24¼- 17 | 20⅝ | .50 | 2.4 |
| Cont Can | CCC | NY | 62 - 45⅛ | 61⅜ | 2.20 | 3.8 |
| Cont Oil | CLL | NY | 75 - 63¼ | 73⅝ | 2.80 | 3.8 |
| Control Data | CDA | NY | 156 -124¼ | 141⅝ | ... | ... |
| Corn Products | CFG | NY | 45¾- 36 | 43¾ | 1.70 | 3.8 |
| Curtiss-Wright | CW | NY | 31½- 20⅜ | 28⅛ | 1.00 | 3.6 |
| Daylin | DLN | Am | 43¾- 18 | 29⅜ | .40 | 1.1 |
| Delta Air Lines | DAL | NY | 36⅜- 23 | 35⅜ | .40 | 1.2 |
| Detroit Edison | DTE | NY | 29⅜- 24 | 25⅞ | 1.40 | 5.4 |
| Dictaphone | DC | NY | 28½- 23 | 26⅜ | .51 | 2.0 |
| Diebold | DBD | NY | 45½- 23⅝ | 43½ | .40 | 0.9 |
| Dixilyn | DXL | Am | 39¾- 22 | 30⅛ | ... | ... |
| Dow Chemical | DOW | NY | 87⅝- 70¼ | 84¼ | 2.40 | 2.9 |
| Dreyfus Corp. | DRY | NY | 36¾- 22¾ | 31¾ | .90 | 2.7 |
| du Pont | DD | NY | 177½-148 | 175¼ | 5.00 | 2.9 |
| Dymo Industries | DMO | NY | 26⅞- 17⅛ | 22¼ | ... | ... |
| Dynamics Corp | DCA | NY | 25⅛- 16½ | 22¾ | .40 | 1.7 |
| Eastern Air Lines | EAL | NY | 48 - 26 | 30 | .50 | 1.8 |

| Company | Ticker Symbol | Stock Exch. | High and Low 1968 to Oct. 21 | Price Oct. 21 | Indicated Div. $ | Yield % |
|---|---|---|---|---|---|---|
| Eastman Kodak | EK | NY | 86⅞- 64⅝ | 81¾ | 1.07 | 1.3 |
| El Paso Nat Gas | ELG | NY | 21⅝- 18 | 19¾ | 1.00 | 5.1 |
| Electronic Assoc. | EA | NY | 27¾- 18 | 23½ | ... | ... |
| Emerson Electric | EMR | NY | 104¾- 84 | 95½ | 1.68 | 1.8 |
| Endicott Johnson | EJN | NY | 49¼- 24⅝ | 49¼ | .50 | 1.0 |
| ESB Inc. | ESB | NY | 32 - 24⅜ | 27¾ | 1.20 | 4.1 |
| Ethyl Corp | EY | NY | 37⅞- 27¼ | 35⅛ | .60 | 1.7 |
| Eversharp | EVR | NY | 20⅛- 13¾ | 18⅜ | ... | ... |
| Ex-Cell-O | XLO | NY | 41 - 28½ | 34⅜ | 1.20 | 3.6 |
| Fairchild Camera | FCI | NY | 92⅜- 52 | 81½ | .50 | 0.6 |
| Fairchild Hiller | FEN | NY | 23½- 14⅜ | 17⅞ | ... | ... |
| Fedders Corp. | FJQ | NY | 50½- 19⅛ | 48½ | .60 | 1.3 |
| Federal Resourcs | FDR | Am | 13¼- 8¾ | 11⅞ | ... | ... |
| Federated Dep St | FDS | NY | 42⅜- 34¼ | 37¼ | .95 | 2.6 |
| Firestone Tire | FIR | NY | 65 - 47½ | 64¾ | 1.50 | 2.3 |
| First Chartr Fin. | FCF | NY | 42⅛- 21¾ | 35⅝ | ... | ... |
| First Natl Stors | FST | NY | 38¼- 24 | 37¾ | ... | ... |
| Flintkote Co. | FO | NY | 36⅝- 20⅝ | 32⅝ | 1.00 | 3.2 |
| Flying Tiger Lin. | FLY | NY | 29 - 17½ | 24¾ | .10 | 0.4 |
| Food Fair Stores | FFS | NY | 23¾- 15¾ | 22⅝ | .90 | 4.1 |
| Ford Motor Co. | F | NY | 60⅛- 48 | 59⅝ | 2.40 | 4.2 |
| Foxboro Co | FOX | NY | 64⅜- 37½ | 49¼ | .60 | 1.2 |
| Freeport Sulphur | FT | NY | 77¾- 37 | 40⅝ | 1.40 | 3.6 |
| Fruehauf Corp. | FTR | NY | 42 - 31 | 35⅝ | 1.70 | 4.6 |
| Genl Cigar Co | GCR | NY | 34⅜- 21⅝ | 31¾ | 1.20 | 3.8 |
| Genl Dynamics | GD | NY | 66 - 42⅞ | 43⅜ | 1.00 | 2.2 |
| Genl Electric | GE | NY | 100 - 80¼ | 97¾ | 2.60 | 2.8 |
| Genl Foods | GF | NY | 93⅞- 65 | 87 | 2.40 | 2.7 |
| Genl Instrument | GRL | NY | 63¼- 40½ | 57½ | ... | ... |
| Genl Mills | GIS | NY | 43⅝- 34 | 40 | .80 | 2.1 |
| Genl Motors | GM | NY | 89⅞- 72⅝ | 89 | 4.05 | 4.7 |
| Genl Pub Util. | GPU | NY | 31 - 25 | 29⅛ | 1.60 | 5.5 |
| Genl Tel & Tel | GEN | NY | 46¾- 36⅜ | 43⅝ | 1.48 | 3.5 |
| Genl Time | GLI | NY | 47 - 24½ | 42¼ | .80 | 1.9 |
| Genl Tire & Rub | GY | NY | 33⅞- 23½ | 32¼ | 1.00 | 3.2 |
| Getty Oil | GET | NY | 110¼- 80¼ | 104¾ | .72 | 0.7 |
| Gillette Co. | GS | NY | 61⅞- 44½ | 54½ | 1.20 | 2.2 |
| Goldfield Corp | GV | Am | 14⅛- 7⅛ | 10¼ | ... | ... |
| Goodrich (B.F.) | GR | NY | 47⅞- 38¼ | 42¾ | 1.72 | 4.1 |
| Goodyear Tire | GT | NY | 62½- 45¾ | 61 | 1.50 | 2.5 |
| Grace (W.R.) | GRA | NY | 48⅝- 32½ | 48⅛ | 1.50 | 3.2 |
| Grand Union Co. | GUX | NY | 26¾- 19⅝ | 26¼ | .60 | 2.3 |
| Grant (W.T.) | GTY | NY | 45⅛- 30 | 42 | 1.30 | 3.3 |
| Great A & P Tea | GAP | NY | 33¼- 26⅝ | 32⅜ | 1.60 | 5.0 |
| Great Nrthrn Pap | GPP | NY | 75 - 47¾ | 72⅞ | 1.40 | 1.9 |
| Great Nrthrn Ry | GN | NY | 60¾- 49½ | 59⅞ | 3.00 | 5.3 |
| Great Westrn Fin | GWF | NY | 30⅞- 12⅞ | 27⅛ | ... | ... |
| Greyhound Corp | G | NY | 26⅞- 19⅞ | 26⅜ | 1.00 | 4.1 |
| Grumman Aircft | GQ | NY | 38½- 29⅝ | 29⅜ | 1.00 | 3.2 |
| Gulf Oil | GO | NY | 42¼- 33½ | 40⅞ | 1.50 | 3.6 |
| Gulf & Wstn Inds | GW | NY | 66⅛- 38⅞ | 49½ | .30 | 0.6 |
| Gulf States Utls | GTU | NY | 28 - 20⅞ | 24½ | .88 | 3.7 |
| Harvey Aluminum | HAR | NY | 54¼- 32⅝ | 34½ | 1.20 | 3.4 |
| Heller (W.E.) | HLR | NY | 24⅛- 11⅞ | 24 | .60 | 2.7 |
| Hercules | HPC | NY | 52⅞- 33⅜ | 51¾ | 1.20 | 2.4 |
| Hershey Foods | HSY | NY | 33⅝- 24⅞ | 29⅛ | 1.10 | 3.8 |
| Hess Oil & Chem | HES | NY | 58⅜- 33⅝ | 56⅝ | .30 | 0.5 |
| Hewlett-Packard | HWP | NY | 91⅜- 59⅛ | 80⅞ | .20 | 0.3 |
| Hilton Hotels | HLT | NY | 48¼- 27 | 48 | .80 | 1.8 |
| Hitco | HIT | NY | 49⅞- 30⅛ | 43 | .15 | 0.4 |
| Holiday Inns | HIA | NY | 73¼- 39¼ | 73 | .35 | 0.5 |
| Honeywell Inc. | HON | NY | 139¾- 89⅜ | 125 | 1.10 | 0.9 |
| Hotel Corp Amer | HCA | NY | 19½- 11 | 12¾ | ... | ... |
| Houdaille Inds | HH | NY | 25⅞- 14⅝ | 24⅞ | .80 | 3.1 |
| Household Fin. | HFC | NY | 47¼- 29¾ | 44½ | 1.10 | 2.5 |
| Houston Lt & Pow | HOU | NY | 48⅛- 39⅞ | 42 | 1.12 | 2.7 |
| Howard Johnson | HJ | NY | 53⅝- 33⅝ | 50½ | .40 | 0.3 |
| Illinois Cent In | IL | NY | 72¾- 50⅛ | 67½ | 1.50 | 2.2 |
| Ingersoll-Rand | IR | NY | 51⅞- 39 | 51¼ | 2.00 | 4.1 |
| Inland Steel | IAD | NY | 40¾- 30¾ | 37 | 2.00 | 5.4 |
| Int Bus Machs | IBM | NY | 375 -280 | 327 | 2.60 | 0.8 |
| Int Harvester | HR | NY | 38 - 30⅜ | 37⅛ | 1.80 | 5.0 |
| Int Min & Chem | IGL | NY | 30⅛- 18½ | 22 | .50 | 2.4 |
| Int Nickel, Can | N | NY | 47¼- 36⅜ | 37¾ | 1.24 | 3.2 |
| Int Paper | IP | NY | 36¾- 25⅞ | 36⅜ | 1.35 | 3.8 |
| Int Tel & Tel | ITT | NY | 62 - 44⅞ | 61⅜ | .85 | 1.4 |
| Itek Corp | ITK | NY | 138¼- 77¼ | 99 | ... | ... |
| Jewel Companies | JWL | NY | 47⅝- 31 | 47⅜ | 1.40 | 3.0 |
| Johns-Manville | JM | NY | 81 - 54 | 78¼ | 2.20 | 2.9 |
| Johnson & Jhnsn | JNJ | NY | 97¼- 74½ | 89¼ | .65 | 0.7 |
| Jones & Laughlin | JL | NY | 79⅞- 45⅜ | 71 | 2.70 | 3.9 |
| Joy Mftg | JOY | NY | 36⅜- 28⅝ | 32⅝ | 1.40 | 4.3 |
| Kaiser Alum & Ch. | KLU | NY | 48⅞- 34¼ | 42 | 1.00 | 2.6 |
| Kaiser Inds | KI | Am | 24 - 16¾ | 20⅜ | ... | ... |
| Kayser-Roth | KYR | NY | 37⅞- 27 | 35⅛ | .60 | 1.7 |
| Kelsey-Hayes | KW | NY | 51 - 33 | 51 | 1.30 | 2.7 |
| Kennecott Copper | KN | NY | 47⅞- 37½ | 47¼ | 2.00 | 4.4 |

| Company | Ticker Symbol | Stock Exch. | High and Low 1968 to Oct. 21 | Price Oct. 21 | Indicated Div. $ | Yield % |
|---|---|---|---|---|---|---|
| Kidde (Walter) | KDE | NY | 87 - 53½ | 66½ | ... | ... |
| Kimberly-Clark | KMB | NY | 75⅜- 48⅜ | 73⅝ | 2.20 | 3.1 |
| KLM Airlines | KLM | NY | 75 - 44⅛ | 61 | 1.10 | 1.9 |
| Kresge (S.S.) | KG | NY | 46½- 26 | 42½ | .34 | 0.8 |
| Kroger Co. | KR | NY | 35 - 22⅛ | 34¾ | 1.30 | 3.9 |
| Lear-Siegler | LSI | NY | 53⅛- 31⅛ | 51¾ | .90 | 1.8 |
| Leesona Corp. | LSO | NY | 58½- 28¾ | 53⅞ | .40 | 0.7 |
| Levin Townsend | LTX | Am | 67¾- 27⅝ | 65 | .40 | 0.6 |
| Libby-Owens-Frd | LOF | NY | 70⅜- 46½ | 67 | 2.80 | 4.1 |
| Libby McNll & L | LJ | NY | 19⅛- 14⅛ | 18⅛ | ... | ... |
| Liggett & Myers | LM | NY | 44¾- 35½ | 42½ | 2.50 | 6.0 |
| Ling-Temco-Vgt | LTV | NY | 135¾- 80 | 90¾ | 1.33 | 1.4 |
| Lionel Corp. | LIO | NY | 11⅜- 7⅛ | 10 | ... | ... |
| Litton Inds | LIT | NY | 104¾- 62 | 81⅛ | ... | ... |
| Lockheed Aircft | LK | NY | 60⅝- 40½ | 57 | 2.20 | 3.8 |
| Loews Theatrs | LTR | NY | 135 - 42 | 125¾ | .40 | 0.3 |
| Lone Star Gas | LSG | NY | 32 - 22 | 25⅜ | 1.12 | 4.3 |
| Long Island Ltg | LLT | NY | 29⅞- 24¼ | 27 | 1.24 | 4.5 |
| Lorillard | LL | NY | 70½- 45 | 70 | 2.70 | 3.8 |
| LTV Aerospace | LTA | Am | 45 - 26¾ | 37½ | .80 | 2.0 |
| LTV Electro | LTE | Am | 35⅞- 19¼ | 19⅜ | .50 | 2.5 |
| Magnavox Co. | MAG | NY | 59⅛- 36⅝ | 58¾ | 1.00 | 1.8 |
| Martin Marietta | ML | NY | 29⅝- 17¾ | 27⅝ | 1.00 | 3.8 |
| Massey-Ferguson | MSE | NY | 21¼- 15 | 20⅝ | 1.00 | 4.9 |
| May Dep Stores | MA | NY | 49½- 34¾ | 46⅜ | 1.60 | 3.5 |
| McDonnell Dglass | MD | NY | 59⅝- 43½ | 47⅝ | .40 | 0.9 |
| Melville Shoe | MES | NY | 59½- 39 | 56¾ | 1.10 | 2.0 |
| Merck & Co. | MRK | NY | 96¾- 73¾ | 90 | 1.80 | 2.1 |
| Middle Sth Util | MSU | NY | 26¼- 20¾ | 22½ | .82 | 3.6 |
| Minn Mg & Mfg | MMM | NY | 119¾- 81 | 108½ | 1.45 | 1.4 |
| Miss River | MIS | NY | 26 - 18⅝ | 24 | 1.20 | 5.2 |
| Mobil Oil Corp. | MOB | NY | 59⅜- 42⅛ | 56⅝ | 2.00 | 3.5 |
| Mohasco Inds | MOH | NY | 42¾- 22⅝ | 42 | 1.00 | 2.5 |
| Monsanto Co. | MTC | NY | 54¼- 40½ | 54 | 1.60 | 3.0 |
| Montgomery Ward | M | NY | 43⅞- 22½ | 43⅛ | 1.00 | 2.6 |
| Motorola | MOT | NY | 153¾- 97 | 134¾ | 1.00 | 0.8 |
| Natl Airlines | NAL | NY | 39⅜- 24 | 37 | .30 | 0.8 |
| Natl Biscuit | BI | NY | 53⅜- 43 | 46½ | 2.10 | 4.6 |
| Natl Cash Reg | NCR | NY | 154¼- 99½ | 127 | 1.20 | 0.9 |
| Natl Dairy Prod | ND | NY | 46½- 33¾ | 46 | 1.60 | 3.7 |
| Natl Lead | LT | NY | 74½- 58⅛ | 74 | 3.25 | 4.8 |
| Natl Steel | NS | NY | 50¾- 41¼ | 49¼ | 2.50 | 5.2 |
| New England El | NES | NY | 30⅝- 25½ | 28½ | 1.48 | 5.1 |
| New Park Mg | NKM | Am | 13¼- 8 | 11 | ... | ... |
| Newark Elect | NEC | Am | 18¼- 10¼ | 17½ | .40 | 2.3 |
| Niag Mohwk Pow | NMK | NY | 22½- 19 | 21⅜ | 1.10 | 5.3 |
| Norfolk & Western | NFK | NY | 115½- 87⅛ | 114¾ | 6.00 | 5.2 |
| N Amer Rockwell | NR | NY | 41¾- 32⅝ | 41 | 2.00 | 5.0 |
| Northeast Airlns | NEA | Am | 25½- 16½ | 21 | ... | ... |
| Northeast Utils | NU | NY | 19½- 15⅞ | 17⅝ | .94 | 5.3 |
| Northwest Airlins | NWA | NY | 92¾- 66 | 84 | .80 | 1.0 |
| Occidental Pet | OXY | NY | 55⅜- 28 | 46¼ | .40 | 1.0 |
| Ogden Corp. | OG | NY | 52 - 32 | 38⅛ | .80 | 2.3 |
| Ohio Edison | OEC | NY | 29¾- 25⅛ | 27½ | 1.42 | 5.3 |
| Okla Gas & El | OGE | NY | 27½- 20½ | 23½ | 1.04 | 4.7 |
| Olin Mathieson | OLM | NY | 72¾- 32½ | 40 | 1.20 | 3.0 |
| O'Okiep Copper | OKP | Am | 128½- 89 | 107¾ | 10.89 | 10.1 |
| Otis Elevator | OT | NY | 56⅜- 39 | 55 | 2.00 | 3.6 |
| Owens-Corning | OCF | NY | 87¾- 59½ | 80¾ | 1.40 | 1.8 |
| Owens-Illinois | OI | NY | 71¾- 44½ | 69⅜ | 1.35 | 1.9 |
| Pacific Gas & El | PCG | NY | 36¼- 30¾ | 34¾ | 1.50 | 4.3 |
| Pacific Petrolms | PP | NY | 23⅜- 14⅝ | 21¼ | .15 | 0.7 |
| Pan Amer Sulphur | PAS | NY | 41¼- 27 | 33¼ | 1.50 | 4.7 |
| Pan Am Wld Air | PN | NY | 27½- 19½ | 26 | .40 | 1.5 |
| Parke, Davis | PDC | NY | 33 - 23 | 28⅛ | 1.00 | 3.6 |
| Penney (J.C.) | JCP | NY | 47⅜- 27¾ | 46⅝ | 1.00 | 2.2 |
| Penn Central | PC | NY | 86½- 53½ | 70 | 2.40 | 3.4 |
| Pennsylvania P&L | PPL | NY | 32⅛- 27⅛ | 31 | 1.56 | 5.1 |
| Pepsico Inc | PEP | NY | 52⅛- 36¼ | 48½ | .90 | 1.9 |
| Pfizer (Chas) | PFE | NY | 77¾- 56¾ | 72 | 1.45 | 2.0 |
| Philadelphia El | PE | NY | 32½- 27¼ | 30⅜ | 1.64 | 5.4 |
| Phillips Petrol | P | NY | 70⅜- 53⅛ | 69⅜ | 2.60 | 3.8 |
| Polaroid Corp | PRD | NY | 133⅝- 87½ | 109¾ | .32 | 0.3 |
| Potter Instrumnts | PIC | Am | 38½- 20½ | 28¼ | ... | ... |
| Procter & Gamble | PG | NY | 100½- 81¾ | 88¾ | 2.40 | 2.7 |
| Pub Serv E & G | PEG | NY | 35¾- 29⅞ | 32⅞ | 1.60 | 5.0 |
| Purex Corp | PRX | NY | 38¾- 27½ | 34½ | .78 | 2.3 |
| Quaker Oats | OAT | NY | 53⅝- 34¼ | 53⅛ | 1.30 | 2.6 |
| Radio Corp Amer | RCA | NY | 55 - 44¼ | 47⅞ | 1.00 | 2.0 |
| Ralston Purina | RAL | NY | 27¾- 20½ | 23⅝ | .60 | 2.5 |
| Raytheon Co | RTN | NY | 54 - 33¼ | 46 | .50 | 1.1 |
| Reichhold Chem | RCI | NY | 18½- 13 | 18⅛ | .40 | 2.4 |
| Republic Steel | RS | NY | 46 - 39¾ | 45⅞ | 2.50 | 5.6 |
| Revlon Inc. | REV | NY | 92 - 70¼ | 86¾ | 1.40 | 1.6 |
| Reynolds Metals | RLM | NY | 50¾- 33¼ | 37⅞ | .90 | 2.5 |
| Reynolds Tobacco | RJR | NY | 46½- 39¼ | 40¾ | 2.20 | 5.4 |
| Rheem Mftg | RHE | NY | 63¼- 47¼ | 63 | 1.40 | 2.2 |
| Rheingold Corp. | RG | NY | 22¾- 15¼ | 22 | .20 | 0.9 |
| Roan Slctn Trust | RST | NY | 11¼- 7 | 10½ | 1.06 | 10.0 |
| Rohr Corp. | RHR | NY | 36¾- 26¼ | 30⅝ | .80 | 2.7 |
| Royal Dutch Pet | RD | NY | 55¾- 37⅞ | 55¾ | 1.60 | 2.9 |
| Ryder Systems | RDR | NY | 54½- 28¼ | 54½ | .80 | 1.5 |

| Company | Ticker Symbol | Stock Exch. | High and Low 1968 to Oct. 21 | Price Oct. 21 | Indicated Div. $ | Indicated Yield % |
|---|---|---|---|---|---|---|
| Safeway Stores | SA | NY | 31¼ - 23¼ | 27⅝ | 1.10 | 4.1 |
| Sanders Assoc | SAA | NY | 66½ - 41¾ | 50⅜ | .30 | 0.6 |
| Schenley Inds | SH | NY | 57 - 32⅛ | 46 | 1.30 | 2.7 |
| Scientific Data | SDS | NY | 117½ - 72½ | 80¼ | ... | ... |
| SCM Corp | SCM | NY | 61¼ - 35¾ | 41 | .58 | 1.4 |
| Scott Paper | SPP | NY | 34¾ - 22½ | 34½ | 1.00 | 2.9 |
| Scurry-Rnbow | SRB | Am | 48⅞ - 23⅞ | 36⅝ | ... | ... |
| Sears, Roebuck | S | NY | 72¼ - 56⅛ | 70¼ | 1.30 | 1.9 |
| Seeburg Corp | SBG | NY | 43¼ - 19⅛ | 32 | .60 | 1.5 |
| Shell Oil | SUO | NY | 72⅝ - 56½ | 72⅝ | 2.30 | 3.3 |
| Sinclair Oil | L | NY | 87⅞ - 72 | 79⅝ | 2.80 | 3.4 |
| Singer Co | SMF | NY | 88⅞ - 62¾ | 82⅜ | 2.40 | 3.0 |
| Southern Cal Ed | SCE | NY | 37¾ - 31 | 33⅞ | 1.40 | 4.2 |
| Southern Co | SO | NY | 30⅝ - 24 | 26⅝ | 1.08 | 4.0 |
| Southern Nat Gas | SGA | NY | 54¾ - 39 | 48¼ | 1.40 | 2.8 |
| Southern Pacific | SX | NY | 42⅛ - 26¾ | 40⅝ | 1.60 | 4.1 |
| Spartans Inds | SPT | NY | 28 - 18 | 24½ | ... | ... |
| Sperry Rand | SY | NY | 63⅜ - 41⅞ | 43¾ | .40 | 0.9 |
| Squibb Beech-Nut | SQB | NY | 47⅞ - 35¼ | 43¾ | 1.50 | 3.5 |
| Standard Oil Cal | SD | NY | 68 - 57½ | 67⅜ | 2.70 | 4.0 |
| Standard Oil (Ind) | SN | NY | 60⅜ - 50½ | 59⅝ | 2.10 | 3.6 |
| Standard Oil (NJ) | J | NY | 80⅝ - 66⅝ | 79⅜ | 3.65 | 4.6 |
| Standard Oil (Ohio) | SOH | NY | 71⅝ - 60⅛ | 65⅜ | 2.50 | 4.0 |
| Stauffer Chem | STF | NY | 46¾ - 36¾ | 46⅛ | 1.80 | 3.9 |
| Stevens (J.P.) | STN | NY | 65⅛ - 52 | 61 | 2.25 | 3.7 |
| Struthers Wells | SUW | Am | 29¼ - 15½ | 17¼ | ... | ... |
| Studebaker-Worth | SKW | NY | 72⅛ - 47⅝ | 59 | 1.00 | 1.7 |
| Sun Chemical | SNL | NY | 32¾ - 19⅜ | 30 | .40 | 1.4 |
| Sun Oil | SUN | NY | 76¾ - 60⅛ | 76¾ | 1.00 | 1.3 |
| Sunbeam Corp | SMB | NY | 51⅞ - 35¾ | 44⅛ | 1.16 | 2.6 |
| Sunray DX Oil | SDX | NY | 51⅝ - 37⅛ | 47¼ | 1.50 | 3.1 |
| Swift & Co | SWX | NY | 33¾ - 23¼ | 29 | .60 | 2.0 |
| Syntex Corp | SYN | Am | 79 - 53½ | 68⅝ | .40 | 0.6 |
| Technicolor Inc | TK | Am | 45¼ - 20⅝ | 42¼ | .40 | 0.9 |
| Teledyne | TDY | NY | 143⅞ - 90⅛ | 98 | ... | ... |
| Tenneco Inc | TGT | NY | 30¼ - 24⅝ | 27⅝ | 1.28 | 4.7 |
| Texaco Inc | TX | NY | 86½ - 71½ | 86⅛ | 2.90 | 3.4 |
| Texas Eastn Tran | TET | NY | 30½ - 21¾ | 30⅜ | 1.20 | 4.0 |
| Texas Gulf Sul | TG | NY | 49⅞ - 29 | 31 | .40 | 1.3 |
| Texas Instruments | TXN | NY | 114⅞ - 86¼ | 04⅝ | .80 | 0.8 |
| Texas Utilities | TXU | NY | 61⅞ - 49¼ | 54⅞ | 1.60 | 2.9 |
| Textron Inc | TXT | NY | 57⅞ - 40 | 46 | .80 | 1.8 |
| Thiokol Chem | THI | NY | 21⅜ - 15¼ | 18 | .40 | 2.3 |
| Toledo Edison | TED | NY | 36½ - 29⅞ | 31¾ | 1.48 | 4.6 |
| Transamerica | TA | NY | 77¼ - 43⅞ | 75¼ | 1.00 | 1.3 |
| Transitron Elec | TRN | NY | 21⅝ - 13¼ | 14⅝ | ... | ... |
| Trans World Air | TWA | NY | 50¼ - 35 | 45¾ | 1.00 | 2.2 |
| Tri-Continental | TY | NY | 35 - 27 | 34¼ | .91 | 2.6 |
| Union Carbide | UK | NY | 50⅛ - 40⅛ | 45⅞ | 2.00 | 4.3 |
| Union Oil Cal | UCL | NY | 70 - 49¾ | 67⅜ | 1.40 | 2.1 |
| Union Pacific | UP | NY | 60⅛ - 37⅛ | 58⅛ | 2.00 | 3.4 |
| United Air Lines | UAL | NY | 66½ - 34 | 46⅞ | 1.00 | 2.3 |
| United Aircraft | UA | NY | 83½ - 57⅝ | 65⅝ | 1.80 | 2.8 |
| United Fruit | UF | NY | 76½ - 45⅛ | 75 | 1.40 | 1.9 |
| United Nuclear | UNC | NY | 42¾ - 30⅛ | 31½ | ... | ... |
| US Gypsum | USG | NY | 95¼ - 65⅞ | 86⅞ | 3.20 | 3.7 |
| US Industries | USI | NY | 36¾ - 18¾ | 29⅞ | .40 | 1.3 |
| US Plywood-Cham | UPC | NY | 74½ - 45 | 65⅞ | 1.50 | 2.1 |
| US Smelting | UV | NY | 72 - 53¾ | 65½ | 1.00 | 1.6 |
| US Steel | X | NY | 45 - 38 | 44⅝ | 2.40 | 5.4 |
| Varian Assoc | VAR | NY | 34½ - 22 | 25⅞ | ... | ... |
| Veeder Inds | VR | NY | 42¼ - 31⅞ | 39¾ | 1.45 | 3.8 |
| Vernitron | VRN | Am | 55 - 26¾ | 53¾ | ... | ... |
| Viewlex Inc | VLX | Am | 32⅞ - 14½ | 24¾ | ... | ... |
| Virginia El Pow | VEL | NY | 35 - 26⅜ | 29¼ | 1.08 | 3.6 |
| Vornado Inc | VNO | NY | 37¼ - 20 | 25⅞ | ... | ... |
| Ward Foods | WD | NY | 53⅛ - 33½ | 44⅞ | ... | ... |
| Warner-Lambert | WLA | NY | 55¾ - 39⅛ | 53½ | 1.00 | 1.8 |
| Webb (Del E.) | WBB | NY | 17 - 6¾ | 14⅝ | ... | ... |
| Weil-McLain | WML | Am | 52⅝ - 24½ | 47 | .80 | 1.8 |
| West Va Pulp & P | WP | NY | 32½ - 20½ | 31½ | 1.00 | 3.1 |
| Westates Petrol | WPT | Am | 11¼ - 5¼ | 8⅝ | ... | ... |
| Western Air Lns | WAL | NY | 45 - 24½ | 41½ | 1.00 | 2.4 |
| Western Bancorp | WBC | NY | 42¼ - 27⅝ | 42 | 1.20 | 2.9 |
| Western Union Tel | WU | NY | 50⅛ - 31 | 38½ | 1.40 | 3.7 |
| Westinghouse El | WX | NY | 78⅞ - 59⅝ | 74⅜ | 1.80 | 2.4 |
| Weyerhaeuser | WY | NY | 76⅜ - 36¼ | 71⅞ | 1.40 | 2.0 |
| Wolverine WW | WWW | NY | 23⅜ - 14½ | 20½ | .50 | 2.7 |
| Woolworth | Z | NY | 33¼ - 21⅝ | 32½ | 1.00 | 3.1 |
| Wurlitzer Co | WUR | NY | 25½ - 18⅝ | 24 | .80 | 3.2 |
| Xerox | XRX | NY | 328½ - 229 | 272 | 1.60 | 0.6 |
| Youngstown S & T | YB | NY | 46½ - 28⅞ | 43 | 1.80 | 4.4 |
| Zapata Off-Shore | ZOS | NY | 87 - 36¾ | 72⅛ | ... | ... |
| Zenith Radio | ZE | NY | 65½ - 50⅝ | 57¼ | 1.35 | 2.4 |

## 'Yes, Virginia, There Is a Santa Claus'

(Often called the most famous newspaper editorial ever written, this classic first appeared in the New York Sun Sept. 21, 1897, under the title, "Is There a Santa Claus?")

We take pleasure in answering at once and thus prominently the communication below, expressing at the same time our great gratification that its faithful author is numbered among the friends of The Sun:

*"Dear Editor:*
*I am 8 years old.*
*Some of my little friends say there is no Santa Claus.*
*Papa says 'If you see it in The Sun it's so.'*
*Please tell me the truth, is there a Santa Claus?*

*Virginia O'Hanlon,*
*115 West 95th Street"*

Virginia, your little friends are wrong. They have been affected by the skepticism of a skeptical age. They do not believe except they see. They think that nothing can be which is not comprehensible by their little minds. All minds, Virginia, whether they be men's or children's, are little. In this great universe of ours man is a mere insect, an ant, in his intellect, as compared with the boundless world about him, as measured by the intelligence capable of grasping the whole of truth and knowledge.

Yes, Virginia, there is a Santa Claus. He exists as certainly as love and generosity and devotion exist, and you know that they abound and give to your life its highest beauty and joy. Alas! how dreary would be the world if there were no Santa Claus! It would be as dreary as if there were no Virginias. There would

be no childlike faith then, no poetry, no romance to make tolerable this existence. We should have no enjoyment, except in sense and sight. The eternal light with which childhood fills the world would be extinguished.

Not believe in Santa Claus! You might as well not believe in fairies! You might get your papa to hire men to watch in all the chimneys on Christmas Eve to catch Santa Claus, but even if they did not see Santa Claus coming down, what would that prove? Nobody sees Santa Claus, but that is no sign that there is no Santa Claus. The most real things in the world are those that neither children nor men can see. Did you ever see fairies dancing on the lawn? Of course not, but that's no proof that they are not there. Nobody can conceive or imagine all the wonders there are unseen and unseeable in the world.

You tear apart the baby's rattle and see what makes the noise inside, but there is a veil covering the unseen world which not the strongest man, nor even the united strength of all the strongest men that ever lived, could tear apart. Only faith, fancy, poetry, love, romance, can push aside that curtain and view and picture the supernal beauty and glory beyond. Is it all real? Ah, Virginia, in all this world there is nothing else real and abiding.

No Santa Claus! Thank God he lives, and he lives forever. A thousand years from now, Virginia, nay ten times ten thousand years from now, he will continue to make glad the heart of childhood.

### More About Virginia

**Note:** Virginia O'Hanlon, the little girl who wrote her famous letter to the New York Sun in 1897, became Mrs. Edward M. Douglas. She retired in 1959 as assistant principal of a public school for physically handicapped children in Brooklyn, N. Y. She had been a teacher and administrator in the New York City public school system for more than 48 years.

The man who answered her letter for the Sun was Francis Pharcellus Church (1839-1906), an editorial writer who, according to contemporary accounts, undertook the assignment with considerable reluctance. But the product of his mellow wisdom and sound craftsmanship has been reproduced in every conceivable form, in every quarter of the globe.

The Sun, in which it first appeared, was merged in 1950 into the New York World-Telegram and Sun, a Scripps-Howard newspaper which also was the publisher of the World Almanac. Now published by Newspaper Enterprise Association, the World Almanac is happy to renew its association with "Yes, Virginia," thus making it available to new generations of children and adults.

## Population and Area of Canada by Provinces

| Province, territory | Capital | Area in square miles | | | Population | | |
| | | Land | Fresh water | Total | 1961 Census | 1966 Census | Apr. 1, 1968 est. |
|---|---|---|---|---|---|---|---|
| Newfoundland | St. John's | 143,045 | 13,140 | 156,185 | 457,853 | 493,396 | 505,000 |
| Prince Edward Is. | Charlottetown | 2,184 | | 2,184 | 104,629 | 108,535 | 110,000 |
| Nova Scotia | Halifax | 20,402 | 1,023 | 21,425 | 737,007 | 756,039 | 760,000 |
| New Brunswick | Fredericton | 27,835 | 519 | 28,354 | 597,936 | 616,788 | 624,000 |
| Quebec | Quebec | 523,860 | 71,000 | 594,860 | 5,259,211 | 5,780,845 | 5,923,000 |
| Ontario | Toronto | 344,092 | 68,490 | 412,582 | 6,236,092 | 6,960,870 | 7,283,000 |
| Manitoba | Winnipeg | 211,775 | 39,225 | 251,000 | 921,686 | 963,066 | 969,000 |
| Saskatchewan | Regina | 220,182 | 31,518 | 251,700 | 925,181 | 955,344 | 959,000 |
| Alberta | Edmonton | 248,800 | 6,485 | 255,285 | 1,331,944 | 1,463,203 | 1,520,000 |
| British Columbia | Victoria | 359,279 | 6,976 | 366,255 | 1,629,082 | 1,873,674 | 2,002,000 |
| Yukon Territory | Whitehorse | 205,346 | 1,730 | 207,076 | 14,628 | 14,382 | 15,000 |
| Northwest Territories | Yellowknife | 1,253,438 | 51,465 | 1,304,903 | 22,998 | 28,738 | 30,000 |
| Total | | 3,560,238 | 291,571 | 3,851,809 | 18,238,247 | 20,014,880 | 20,700,000 |

## Late 1968 Revision of Canadian Postal Rates

Canadian postal rates were considerably revised, effective, Nov. 1, 1968; the new rates follow:

**First Class:** Six cents for first ounce, 4¢ each additional ounce. Postcards, 6¢ to Canadian destinations. **Air Mail:** All first class mail goes by air at standard rates where such will speed delivery.

**Printed Matter:** Books, newspapers, magazines, etc., mailed by the public, including unsealed Christmas and other greeting cards, 5¢ first two oz., 3¢ each additional 2 oz. up to 1 lb.

**International:** Surface mail to Great Britain, Northern Ireland and elsewhere in the Commonwealth, Republic of Ireland, France, Spain—Letters 12¢ for first oz., 7¢ each additional oz. Postcards, 6¢. To U. S., North and South America—Letters 7¢. **Air Mail** to U. S., North, Central & South America—Letters 10¢ each oz.

Other rates, registration fees and special delivery fees unchanged from table on Page 489.

## Deaths—Dec. 1, 1967 to Nov. 1, 1968

### A

Alter, Dr. Dinsmore, 80; astronomer; Oakland, Calif., Sept. 20.

Anthony, Norman, 74; editor of Judge and Ballyhoo; Poughkeepsie, N. Y., Jan. 12.

Arana, Lt. Gen. Arturo Ossorio, 65; leader of revolution that overthrew Juan Peron; Buenos Aires, Dec. 6.

Arce, Dr. Jose, 86; Argentine doctor, headed UN Gen. Assembly; Buenos Aires, July 28.

Armour, Thomas Dickson (Tommy), 72; golfer; Larchmont, N.Y., Sept. 11.

Arno, Peter, 64; cartoonist; New Yorker magazine; New York, Feb. 22.

Atkinson, Guy F., 93; built $510,000,000 Mangla Dam in West Pakistan; Los Angeles, Sept. 12.

### B

Bache, Harold, 73; chairman and president Bache & Co.; New York, Mar. 15.

Bainter, Fay, 74; actress; "Auntie Belle in "Jezebel"; Hollywood, Apr. 16.

Baird, Cora, 54; puppeteer; New York, Dec. 6.

Baker, Dorothy, 61; novelist; "Young Man with a Horn"; Terra Bella, Calif., June 17.

Barnes, Henry A., 61; New York Traffic Commissioner; New York, Sept. 16.

Beckett, Scotty, 38; child film star of Our Gang comedies; Hollywood, May 10.

Benaderet, Bea, 62; star of TV series "Petticoat Junction"; Los Angeles, Calif., Oct. 13.

Berman, Stanley, 41; renowned gate crasher; New York, Feb. 25.

Bernstein, Abe, 76; Prohibition era boss of Detroit Purple Gang; Detroit, March 7.

Biddle, Francis, 82; Attorney Gen'l under President F. D. Roosevelt; Cape Cod, Oct. 4.

Boggess, Lynton R. (Dusty), 64; National League umpire; Dallas, Tex., July 8.

Borovsky, Alexander, 79; concert pianist; Waban, Mass., Apr. 20.

Boucher, Anthony, 56; mystery writer and critic; Oakland, Calif., Apr. 29.

Brinton, Crane, 70; educator; author of "The Anatomy of Revolution"; Cambridge, Mass., Sept. 7.

Brookes, Sir Norman, 90; Australian tennis player; Melbourne, Sept. 28.

Brown, Elmer, 66; pres. International Typographical Union; Colorado Springs, Feb. 27.

Brown, Judge Joe, 60; presided in Ruby Oswald case; Dallas, Feb. 20.

Brucker, Wilbur M., 74; Secretary of the Army, 1955-1961; Detroit, Oct. 28.

Burger, Carl, 79; wildlife illustrator and author; Mt. Kisco, N. Y., Dec. 30.

### C

Cadogan, Sir Alexander, 83; wartime adviser to Winston Churchill, former British UN delegate; London, July 9.

Cam, Dr. Helen, 82; historian; first woman professor at Harvard; Orpington, Eng., Feb. 9.

Carroll, Paul Vincent, 68; Irish playwright; "Shadow and Substance"; London, Oct. 20.

Cassidy, Marshall, 76; thoroughbred racing notable; devised starting gate; Glen Cove, N. Y., Oct. 23.

Chaplin, Charles Jr., 42; actor; son of comedian; Hollywood, Mar. 20.

Churchill, Randolph, 57; journalist, son of Winston Churchill, Suffolk, Eng., June 6.

Clark, Jim, 32; twice world auto racing champion; Hockenheim, W. Germany, April 7.

Clifford, Gordon, 65; lyricist; wrote "Paradise" and "I surrender Dear"; Las Vegas, Nev., June 11.

Cluett, Sanford L., 91; inventor of Sanforized cloth; Palm Beach, Fla., May 18.

Coleman, Warren, 67; actor and singer; Crown in 1935 production of Porgy and Bess; West Tisbury, Mass., Jan. 13.

Cominsky, J. R., 69; publisher of Saturday Review; Asbury Park, N. J., Aug. 2.

Conocher, Charlie, 58; hockey player; Toronto, Dec. 30.

Cox, Channing H., 89; governor of Massachusetts, 1921-24; West Harwich, Mass., Aug. 20.

Crawford, Samuel Earl (Wahoo Sam), 88; baseball Hall of Fame outfielder; Los Angeles, Calif., June 15.

Crocker, Edward, 72; diplomat; received formal declaration of WWII from Japanese; New York, Apr. 6.

Culin, Maj. Gen. Frank L. Jr., 75; commander 87th infantry Div. in World War II; Pebble Beach, Calif., Dec. 31.

Currie, Finlay, 90; actor; convict in "Great Expectations"; Gerrards Cross, Eng., May 9.

### D

Daniel, Robert P., 65; president of Virginia State College; Petersburg, Va., Jan. 5.

Davis, Jefferson, 84; hobo king; founded Hobos of America in 1908; Cincinnati, April 5.

Dehn, Adolf, 72; painter-lithographer; New York, May 19.

Dekker, Albert, 62; actor; Hollywood, Calif., May 6.

Desmond, James, 59; N. Y. Daily News political writer; biography of Gov. Nelson A. Rockefeller; New York, July 27.

Dickinson, L. J., 94; former U. S. Senator from Iowa; Des Moines, June 4.

Dimitroff, Dr. George Z., 66; astronomer; former head of Harvard Observatory; Hartland, Vt., Jan. 1.

Dirks, Rudolph, 91; cartoonist, painter; created "Katzenjammer Kids;" New York, Apr. 20.

Dodd, Frank C., 92; book publisher; former head of Dodd, Mead & Co.; New Canaan, Conn., Jan. 4.

Donges, Dr. Eben, 69; president-elect of South Africa; Capetown, Jan. 10.

Duchamp, Marcel, 81; giant of modern art; "Nude Descending a Staircase;" Neuilly, France, Oct. 1.

Dunbar, Dr. Paul D., 86; head of FDA, 1944-51; Rockledge, Fla., Aug. 22.

Duncan, Hank (Henry James), 71; jazz pianist; Jamaica, N. Y., June 7.

Duryea, Dan, 61; actor; played unsavory characters; Hollywood, Calif., June 7.

### E

Edens, Dr. Hollis A., 67; president of Duke University, 1949-60; Atlanta, Ga., Aug. 7.

Egan, the Rev. Joseph, 70; former pres. Loyola University, Chicago; Aurora, Ill., July 18.

Eisler, Gerhart, 71; professional communist revolutionary; Berlin, Mar. 21.

Elman, Harry (Ziggy), 54; jazz trumpeter; "And the Angels Sing;" Los Angeles, Calif., June 26.

Erickson, Frank, 72; "King of the bookmakers"; witness at 1951 Kefauver hearings; New York, Mar. 2.

Erwin, Ray, 62; newspaperman; columnist for Editor & Publisher; New York, Jan. 21.

Erwin, Stuart, 64; actor; "The Stu Erwin Show;" Beverly Hills, Dec. 21.

Eshel, Arieh, 56; Israeli Amb. to Canada; Ottawa, Oct. 9.

Everett, Walker G., 64; artist and president of Art Students League; New York, Sept. 15.

### F

Ferber, Edna, 82; novelist; "So Big," "Show Boat," "Giant;" New York, Apr. 16.

Fernandes, Raul, 90; Brazilian diplomat; last surviving signer of Treaty of Versailles; Rio De Janeiro, Jan. 6.

Fisher, Vardis, 73; won Harper prize for historical novel on Mormons in 1939; Twin Falls, Idaho, July 9.

Fitts, Dudley, 65; literary critic, translator and educator; Lawrence, Mass., July 10.

Flavin, Martin, 84; Pulitzer Prize author and playwright; Carmel, Calif., Dec. 27.

Florey, Lord, 69; Nobel prize for medicine for work on penicillin; London, Feb. 21.

Foley, Clyde Julian (Red), 58; Country singer; Fort Wayne, Ind., Sept. 19.

Francis, Kay, 63; film star; epitome of glamour in 1930s; New York; Aug. 26.

Frauenheim, George, 55; president of American Automobile Assn.; Miami, Apr. 5.

Freeman, Howard, 65; actor; Gen. Bush in "No Time for Sergeants;" New York, Dec. 11.

Fry, Rev. Dr. Franklin Clark, 67; former president of Lutheran Church in America; New Rochelle, N. Y., June 6.

Fry, Dr. William J., 50; inventor of instrument used in bloodless brain surgery and an artificial heart; Urbana, Ill., July 21.

### G

Gagarin, Yuri A., 34; first man to orbit the earth; Moscow, Mar. 27.

Gannon, Archbishop John Mark, 91; dean of U. S. Roman Catholic hierarchy before 1966 retirement; Erie, Pa., Sept. 5.

Gerst, Rev. Francis J., 86; former dean of Loyola U. graduate school; Chicago, Sept. 30.

Gestido, Gen. Oscar Daniel, 66; President of Uruguay; Montevideo, Dec. 6.

Gish, Dorothy, 70; actress; Rapallo, Italy, June 4.

Gitlin, Irving, 49; TV producer; NBC "White Paper" series; New York, Dec. 12.

Gray, Harold, 74; cartoonist; creator of Little Orphan Annie; La Jolla, Calif., May 9.

Grayson, Harry M., 74; N.E.A. sports editor for 30 years; New York, Sept. 30.

Groh, Henry Knight (Heinie), 78; infielder with N. Y. Giants and Cincinnati Reds; famous for "bottle bat;" Cincinnati, Aug. 22.

Guareschi, Giovanni, 60; author of "Don Camillo" books; Cervia, Italy, July 22.

### H

Hackenschmidt, George, 90; world wrestling champion; London, Feb. 19.

Hahn, Dr. Otto, 89; Nobel prize winner for chemistry in 1944; Göttingen, Germany, July 28.

Hall, Alexander, 74; film director; "Little Miss Marker"; San Francisco, July 30.

Hall, Donald A., 69; designed Lindbergh plane, Spirit of St. Louis; San Diego, Calif., May 2.

Hall, Juanita, 66; actress; Bloody Mary of "South Pacific;" Bay Shore, N. Y., Feb. 28.

Hallinan, Archbishop Paul J., 56; head of Roman Catholic

Archdiocese of Atlanta; Atlanta, Mar. 27.

Hammond, Bray, 81; won Pulitzer prize for history in 1958; Middlebury, Vt., July 20.

Harding, Jack, 71; member first round-the-world flight team, 1924; San Diego, Calif., May 26.

Harroun, Ray, 89; first winner of Indianapolis 500 in 1911; Anderson, Ind., Jan. 19.

Hay, George D., 72; originated radio's Grand Ole Opry; Virginia Beach, Va., May 9.

Hines, Gen. John L., 100; oldest West Point graduate; Army chief of staff, 1924-26; Washington, D. C., Oct. 13.

Holt, Harold, 59; Australian Prime Minister; Portsea, Australia, Dec. 17.

Holt, Rev. Dr. Ivan Lee, 81; Methodist bishop, president of World Methodist Conference; Atlanta, Ga., Jan. 12.

Horton, Rev. Dr. Douglas, 77; head of Congregational Christian Churches; dean of Harvard U. Divinity School; Berlin, N. H., Aug. 21.

Hoyt, Henry, 53; diplomat; U. S. Ambassador to Uruguay; Montevideo, Dec. 16.

Humphreys, Dr. Richard F., 57; president of Cooper Union; New York, Aug. 8.

Hurley, Robert, 72; ex-governor of Connecticut; West Hartford, May 3.

Hurst, Fannie, 78; novelist; "Back Street;" New York, Feb. 23.

### I, J

Infeld, Leopold, 69; physicist; collaborator of Einstein; Warsaw, Jan. 16.

Jara, Gen. Heriberto, 88; hero of 1910 Mexican revolution; Mexico City, Apr. 17.

Johnson, Daniel, 53; Premier of Quebec; Manicouagan, Quebec, Sept. 25.

Jones, Dr. Bob, Sr., 84; evangelist and founder of Bob Jones University; Greenville, S. C., Jan. 16.

Judd, Lawrence McCully, 81; former Territorial Governor of Hawaii; Honolulu, Oct. 4.

Kahanamoku, Duke, 77; Olympic swimming champ; Honolulu, Jan. 22.

Kanzler, Ernest, 75; industrialist; adviser of Henry Ford 2d; Dearborn, Mich., Dec. 10.

Keller, Helen, 87; blind and deaf from infancy, overcame handicaps to become accomplished writer and symbol of indomitable human spirit; Westport, Conn., June 1.

Kelton, Pert, 61; character actress; Ridgewood, N. J., Oct. 30.

Kennedy, Sen. Robert F., 42; U. S. Senator from New York; Los Angeles, Calif., June 6.

Kiang, Chipping H. C., 59; retired permanent UN delegate for Republic of China; New Rochelle, N. Y., Sept. 9.

Kimmel, Rear Adm. Husband, 86; commander of Pacific Fleet at time of Pearl Harbor attack; Groton, Conn., May 14.

Kinder, Ellis, 54; former major league pitcher; Memphis, Tenn., Oct. 16.

King, Dr. Martin Luther, 39; Nobel Peace Prize winner; Memphis, Apr. 4.

Knapp, Dr. Arthur Blair, 63; president of Denison University; Granville, Ohio, May 14.

Kurnitz, Harry, 60; playwright and screen writer; "Reclining Figure;" Los Angeles, Mar. 18.

### L

Lahr, Bert, 72; comic actor; Cowardly Lion in "The Wizard of Oz;" New York, Dec. 4.

Lambert, Walter D., 89; geodesist; Washington, Oct. 27.

Larrick, George P.; 66; Commissioner of Food and Drug Administration, 1954-65; Washington, D. C., Aug. 11.

Latzo, Pete, 65; beat Mickey Walker for world's welterweight championship in 1926; Atlantic City, N. J., July 7.

Lawrence, Maj. Robert H. Jr., 31; first U. S. Negro astronaut; Edwards Air Force Base; Calif., Dec. 8.

Leonard, Robert Z., 78; Hollywood film director; "Strange Interlude"; Beverly Hills Calif., Aug. 27.

Lichtenberger, Rt. Rev. Arthur, 68; retired presiding Bishop of the Episcopal Church of U. S.; Bethel, Vt., Sept. 3.

Lillis, Donald C., 66; stockbroker and president of N. Y. Jets football team; Westerly, R. I., July 23.

Lindsay, Howard, 78; playwright; "Life With Father;" New York, Feb. 11.

Little, Lawson, 57; golfing champion; Pebble Beach, Calif., Feb. 1.

Lobert, Hans, 86; major league ball player; manager of Philadelphia Phillies in 1942; Philadelphia, Sept. 14.

Lohr, Lenox R., 76; president, Chicago's Museum of Science and Industry; manager, World's Fair, 1933-34; Chicago, May 28.

Lorne, Marion, 82; comic actress; "Gary Moore Show;" New York, May 9.

Lucas, Scott W., 76; former Dem. senator from Illinois; Rocky Mount, N. C., Feb. 22.

### M

MacNider, Gen. Hanford, 78; hero of 2 World Wars; Sarasota, Fla., Feb. 17.

Macrae, Elliot B., 67; publisher; president E. P. Dutton & Co.; New Canaan, Conn., Feb. 13.

Maney, Richard, 77; theatrical press agent; Norwalk, Conn., June 30.

Marina, Princess, Duchess of Kent, 61; member of Greek royal family and widow of Prince George, Duke of Kent; London, Aug. 27.

Marsh, Mae, 72; movie actress; Little Sister in "The Birth of a Nation;" Hermosa Beach, Calif., Feb. 13.

Martin, Homer, 66; 1st president of the United Auto Workers; Los Angeles, Jan. 22.

Martin, Joseph, 83; former Republican Speaker of the House from Massachusetts; Hollywood, Fla., Mar. 6.

Massey, Vincent, 80; former Gov. General of Canada; London, Dec. 30.

Matthews, Zachariah, 66; Botswana's Ambassador to the U. S.; Washington, May 11.

Mayo, Dr. Charles W., 70; retired surgeon of Mayo Clinic and son of co-founder; Rochester, Minn., July 28.

McAndrew, William R., 53; president of NBC News, Bronxville, N. Y., May 30.

McCord, Jim Nance, 89; twice governor of Tennessee; Nashville, Tenn., Sept. 2.

Michaux, Solomon Lightfoot, 84; Negro founder of Good Neighbor League; Washington, Oct. 20.

Meitner, Lise, 89; pioneer in nuclear physics; Cambridge, England, Oct. 25.

Menke, Capt. Bill, 88; owner of the Goldenrod, last Mississippi River showboat; St. Louis, July 15.

Mennen, William G., 83; chairman, Mennen Co.; Morristown, N. J., Feb. 17.

Menzies, Sir Stewart Graham, 78; headed British Secret Intelligence Service, WWII; London, May 30.

Middleton, George, 87; playwright; former head of Dramatists' Guild; Washington, Dec. 23.

Miller, Rev. Dr. Kenneth Dexter, 81; former president of New York City Mission Society; Livingston, N. J., July 6.

Miller, Max, 68; author; "I Cover the Waterfront;" La Jolla, Calif., Dec. 27.

Millin, Sarah Gertrude, 79; So. African novelist and historian; Johannesburg, July 6.

Molyneux, Robert E., 51; comic art director for Newspaper Enterprise Association; Cleveland, Ohio, Sept. 18.

Montgomery, Wes, 45; jazz guitarist voted first in 1968 Downbeat poll; Indianapolis, Ind., June 15.

Morano, Francesco Cardinal, 96; oldest Cardinal in Roman Catholic Church; Rome, July 12.

Morgan, Dr. Agnes Fay, 84; pioneer in science of nutrition; Berkeley, Calif., July 20.

Morrow, Doretta, 40; soprano; "Kismet;" London, Feb. 28.

Mulholland, Winbert F. (Bert), 84; trainer of thoroughbred horses; Germantown, Pa., July 11.

Mullins, Lawrence A. (Moon), 60; star fullback on Knute Rockne teams at Notre Dame University, 1928-30; Chicago, Aug. 10.

Murch, Walter, 60; painter; noted for his realistic machines; New York, Dec. 11.

Musmanno, Michael A., 72; Nuremburg trial judge; Justice of Pennsylvania Supreme Court; defended Sacco and Vanzetti; Pittsburgh, Oct. 12.

### N

Najmy, Justin, 70; apostolic bishop of Melchite Rite Catholics; Manchester, N. H., June 11.

Nash, Sir Walter, 86; former prime minister of New Zealand; Auckland, N. Z., June 4.

Newman, Bernard, 70; author; "Spy;" London, Feb. 19.

Nordhoff, Heinz, 69; head of Volkswagen Co., Wolfsburg, Germany, Apr. 12.

### O

O'Brien, Donough Edward Foster (Baron of Inchiquin), 71; head of Ireland's O'Brien family, descendant of King Brien Borus; Dublin, Oct. 19.

O'Connor, Edwin, 49; novelist; "The Last Hurrah" Boston, Mar. 23.

O'Keefe, Dennis, 60; star in 1930s and 1940s; Hollywood, Calif., Aug. 31.

Oppenheimer, Fritz, 69; international lawyer; Nairobi, Kenya, Feb. 4.

### P

Pacini, Alfredo Cardinal, 79; member of Roman Curia; Rome, Dec. 23.

Parran, Dr. Thomas, 75; U. S. Surgeon General 1936-48; Pittsburgh, Feb. 15.

Parsons, Adm. Edwin C., 75; last surviving ace of Lafayette Escadrille; Sarasota, Fla., May 2.

Phillippe, Gerald L., 59; chairman of Gen'l Electric Co.; Greenwich, Conn., Oct. 18.

Phillips, William, 89; former U. S. Ambassador to Italy; Sarasota, Fla., Feb. 23.

Pickerill, Elmo, 82; held wireless operator license No. 1, learned to fly from the Wright brothers; Mineola, L. I., Jan. 14.

Pierce, Rear Adm. Maurice R., 80; commanded dirigible Shenandoah; San Diego, Calif., July 22.

Pike, S J Sidney, 68; introduced skywriting to America in 1922; Wyckoff, N. J., Feb. 23.

Pillsbury, John, 90; retired head

of Pillsbury Mills, Inc., West Palm Beach, Jan. 31.

Pitler, Jake, 73; coach for Brooklyn Dodgers; Binghamton, N. Y., Feb. 3.

Poling, Rev. Dr. Daniel A., 83; leader in American Protestantism; Philadelphia, Pa., Feb. 7.

Pool, Joe Richard, 57; Representative (D., Tex.); Houston, July 14.

Power, Sen. Charles G., 80; Canadian legislator for 51 years; Quebec, May 30.

Price, Ellen, 89; dancer; model for Copenhagen's Little Mermaid statue; Copenhagen, Mar. 6.

Proctor, Mortimer, 78; former Gov. of Vermont; Proctor, Vt., Apr. 28.

**Q**

Quasimodo, Salvatore, 66; poet, writer; won 1959 Nobel Prize for literature; Naples, Italy; June 14.

Queeny, Edgar Monsanto, 70; former head of Monsanto Co.; Ladue, Mo., July 7.

**R**

Raboy, Mac, 53; drew "Flash Gordon" comic strip; Mount Kisco, N. Y., Dec. 22.

Rand, James Henry, 81; co-founder, Sperry Rand Corp.; Freeport, Grand Bahama Island, June 3.

Rand, Christopher T. E., 56; writer, roving reporter for The New Yorker; Mexico City, Sept. 26.

Read, Sir Herbert, 74; poet and art critic; Malton, England, June 12.

Reid, Dr. Henry J. E., 72; head of NASA's Langley Research Center; Gloucester, Va., July 30.

Reig, Ben, 72; dress designer; New York, Oct. 17.

Reuther, Roy, 58; organizer of United Auto Workers; Detroit, Jan. 10.

Richter, Conrad, 78; novelist; Pulitzer Prize and National Book Award winner; Pottsville, Pa., Oct. 30.

Robertson, Norman A., 64; Canada's Ambassador to U. S. 1957-58; Ottawa, July 16.

Ryan, Ben (Bennett A.), 77; vaudeville entertainer; wrote Inka-Dinka-Do for Jimmy Durante, other songs; Leonia, N. J., July 5.

**S**

St. Denis, Ruth, 91; pioneer of modern dance; Hollywood, Calif., July 21.

Sande, Earl, 69; jockey; member of Racing Hall of Fame; Jacksonville, Ore., Aug. 20.

Schneirla, Dr. Theodore C., 66; curator of Animal Behavior Dept. of American Museum of Natural History; New York; Aug. 20.

Sanger, Dr. Paul W., 62; heart surgeon; did early work on artificial arteries; Houston, Tex., Sept. 8.

Savage, John, 88; engineer; designed Hoover and Grand Coulee Dams; Englewood, Colo., Dec. 28.

Schick, Dr. Bela, 90; pediatrician; developed Schick diphtheria test; New York, Dec. 6.

Schindler, Dr. Rudolf, 80; gastroentologist; invented flexible gastroscope; Munich, W. Germany, Sept. 7.

Schmidt, Gen. Harry, 81; led Marine attack on Iwo Jima in WWII; San Diego, Feb. 10.

Sears, Eleonora, 87; pioneer sportswoman; Palm Beach, Fla., Mar. 26.

Serafin, Tullio, 89; opera conductor; Rome, Feb. 2.

Shipler, Rev. Dr. Guy Emery, 86; Episcopal clergyman; editor of The Churchman; Ar-

cadia, Calif., April 18.

Silver, Eliezer Rabbi, 87; former pres. of Union of Orthodox Rabbis of the United States and Canada; Cincinnati, Feb. 7.

Sinnott, Edward, 79; plant geneticist; former dean of Yale University's Graduate School; New Haven, Conn., Jan. 6.

Smathers, Rev. Dr. Eugene, 60; headed United Presbyterian Church, U.S.A.; Big Lick, Tenn., Aug. 16.

Smith, Elmo, 58; publisher of Albany Democrat-Herald and former governor of Oregon; Albany, Ore., July 15.

Smith, Howard, 73; actor; Charley in Broadway's "Death of a Salesman"; Hollywood, Jan. 10.

Sorensen, Charles E., 86; Henry Ford's production chief helped turn out 80,000,000 cars; built B-24 bomber assembly line plant; Washington, D.C., Aug. 13.

Spellman, Francis Cardinal, 78; archbishop of New York Archdiocese; New York, Dec. 2.

Stallings, Laurence, 73; co-author "What Price Glory?"; Pacific Palisades, Feb. 28.

Stanton, Edwin F., 67; 1st U. S. Ambassador to Thailand; Devon, Conn., Aug. 29.

Stark, Albert (Dolly), 71; colorful National League umpire of '20s and '30s; New York, Aug. 24.

Steenbock, Dr. Harry, 81; biochemist; discovered value of Vitamin D; Madison, Wisc., Dec. 25.

Sydney, Basil, 73; actor; "Strange Interlude"; London, Jan. 10.

**T**

Talman, William, 51; actor; district attorney in "Perry Mason" TV series; Encino, Calif., Aug. 30.

Thomas, George A., 57; Chief of Iroquois Indian Confederacy; Syracuse, N. Y., Oct. 22.

Tone, Franchot, 63; actor played sophisticates on stage and screen; New York, Sept. 18.

Tooker, John I., 73; New York ship salvage expert; supervised raising of French liner Normandie in 1943; Hialeah, Fla., Sept. 14.

Tower, Oswald, 84; arbiter of amateur basketball rules; West Caldwell, N. J., May 28.

Tracy, Lee, 70; actor; played brash, breezy newspaper types; Santa Monica, Calif., Oct. 18.

Trussell, C. P., 76; N. Y. Times reporter; won 1949 Pulitzer prize for reporting on national affairs; Washington, Oct. 2.

Tryggvadottir, Nina, 55; Icelandic painter, muralist; New York, June 19.

Treneer, J. Maurice, 86; developed Alka-Seltzer for Miles Laboratories; Elkhart, Ind., July 2.

**U**

Upson, Ralph Hazlett, 80; areonautical engineer; balloon racing champion, 1913-21; Burien, Wash., Aug. 13.

Usinger, Dr. Robert L., 55; entomologist; led 1964 expedition to Galapagos Islands; San Francisco, Sept. 30.

**V**

Valli, Virginia, 70; silent screen actress; wife of former film star Charles Farrell; Palm Springs, Calif., Sept. 24.

Van, Gus, 80; vaudeville star; Van and Schenck; Miami Beach, March 12.

Vandenberg, Arthur H., Jr., 60; son of late Michigan Senator; Miami, Jan. 18.

van Paassen, Pierre, 72; author; "Days of Our Years"; New York, Jan. 8.

For later deaths see Page 64

Van Voorhis, Cornelius Westbrook, 64; narrator of radio and movie documentary "The March of Time"; noted for sonorous sign-off: "Time Marches On"; New Milford, Conn., July 13.

Vogt, William, 66; former head of Planned Parenthood Federation of America; author of "Road to Survival"; New York, July 11.

Voris, Dr. John, 87; co-founder of Save the Children Federation; Duarte, Calif., Jan. 12.

**W**

Wallace, Lurleen, 41; governor of Alabama; Montgomery, May 7.

Ward, Marvin (Bud), 54; twice winner of national amateur golf championship; San Mateo, Calif., Jan. 2.

Waring, J. Waties, 87; ex-Federal judge; opened S. C. polls to Negroes in 1947; New York, Jan. 11.

Warner, Milo J., 76; former national commander of the American Legion; Toledo, Ohio, Jan. 1.

Wheeler, Bert, 72; comic of vaudeville, films and theater; New York, Jan. 18.

Wheeler, Elmer, 62; created sales catch-phrases; Mexico, Oct. 2.

White, George, 78; Broadway producer of "Scandals"; Hollywood, Calif., Oct. 10.

Whiteman, Paul, 77; bandleader; "King of Jazz"; Doylestown, Pa., Dec. 29.

Wilfred, Thomas, 79; artist and inventor; pioneer in use of colored light projections as an art medium; Nyack, N. Y., Aug. 15.

Wilhelm, Dr. Richard H., 59; head of Princeton University chemical engineering dept.; Center Harbor, N. H. Aug. 6.

Willan, Dr. Healey, 87; composer; Toronto, Feb. 16.

Williams, R. Norris, 2nd, 77; former national tennis champion; Bryn Mawr, Pa., June 2.

Williamson, George, 70; leading scholar on T. S. Eliot and John Donne; Carmel, Calif., Sept. 8.

Wininger, Bo, 45; professional golfer; Oklahoma City, Dec. 7.

Winters, Yvor, 67; poet; 1960 Bollingen prize winner; Palo Alto, Calif., Jan. 25.

Wismer, Harry, 56; sports broadcaster; helped establish American Football League; New York, Dec. 4.

Wolfit, Sir Donald, 65; actor; "Room at the Top"; London, Feb. 17.

Wood, Craig, 66; golfer; won Masters and U. S. Open; Palm Beach, Fla., May 8.

Woolrich, Cornell (William Irish), 64; writer of mystery stories; New York, Sept. 25.

Wrubel, Dr. Marshal H., 44; astrophysicist; Boulder, Colo., Oct. 26.

Wyatt, Commodore Ben H., 74; mapped Alaska by air for Navy; military governor of Marshall Islands during Bikini Atoll atom bomb testing; Coronado, Calif., Sept. 14.

**Y, Z**

Yashin, Aleksandr, 55; Soviet writer and poet; Moscow, July 11.

Young, Nedrick, 54; once-blacklisted screenwriter won Academy Award under assumed name; Hollywood, Calif., Sept. 16.

Zbyszko, Wladek, 75; wrestler in the 1920s and 1930s; Savannah, Mo., June 10.

Zorach, Marguerite, 80; painter and widow of sculptor William Zorach; B'klyn, N.Y., June 27.

# Medical Developments During 1968

A rapid succession of human heart transplants followed the dramatic success on January 2 of Dr. Philip Blaiberg's surgery in Capetown, South Africa. Dr. Christiaan Barnard, initiator of this specific transplant in December 1967 with Louis Washkansky, who died 18 days afterward, explains Blaiberg's survival as partly due to his younger age and healthier condition; also to the use of anti-lymphocyte globulin in preventing a late rejection.

At the time the World Almanac went to press, 80 heart transplants throughout the world had been reported, the largest number in Houston, Tex., by Dr. Denton A. Cooley of Baylor University. Numerous meetings, attended by the leading transplant surgeons, included discussions of the moment of death and moral issues relating to heart donors. Consensus appeared to be that death occurs when the brain ceases functioning and that the heart is no more than a pump that can be replaced at the discretion of the surgeon. Hope for a perfected artificial heart, now being sponsored by the National Heart Institute, Bethesda, Md., is growing, but awaits testing of materials that will not cause clotting, as well as a better power source and control mechanism among other things. Animal hearts also may be used successfully once the rejection problem is solved.

Liver transplants by Dr. Thomas Starzl in Denver, Colo., kept patients alive for a period of months, the longest for 13½ months as of Nov. 15.

A completely synthetic penicillin was achieved by Dr. Ajay K. Bose, professor of chemistry at Stevens Institute of Technology, Hoboken, N. J., who says the new form can be synthesized by a reasonably short process.

## Drug for Parkinson's Disease

Response of 28 patients with shaking palsy, or Parkinson's disease, to oral doses of the drug, L-dopa, was reported by Dr. George C. Cotzias and his co-workers at the Brookhaven National Laboratory at Upton, N. Y. The therapeutic effect of the drug is believed related to an increase in the compound dopamine, which is deficient in parkinsonian patients. Dr. Cotzias believes there is a possibility that L-dopa may have a beneficial effect on persons with tremors or rigidity from other causes besides parkinsonism.

## Cancer and Chromosomes

An excess of a chromosome called E-16, one of the 46 chromosomes normally found in a cell, was strikingly high in cancer cells studied at Lawrence Radiation Laboratory, Livermore, Calif. Dr. John W. Gofman, who reported the finding, denied that the discovery indicates that cancer can be inherited. Although chromosomes are the mechanism of inheritance, cancer itself could have produced the excess of the E-16 chromosome.

Results of laboratory studies have suggested that venereally transmitted type 2 herpes virus is a prime suspect as a cause of cancer of the cervix, or neck of the womb. The findings confirm evidence that this type of cancer may be fundamentally a venereal disease caused by a virus.

L-asparaginase, an anticancer enzyme that attacks malignant cells while bypassing healthy ones, has been successful in treating some cases of acute leukemia that no longer responded to other drugs. Government support of research brought about increased production of the enzyme, which has been in short supply.

## Syphilis Vaccine Foreseen

A vaccine against syphilis may be several years away, but a beginning has been made by Mexican and United States health officials. They have infected chimpanzees in Mexico with the nonvenereal disease pinta, which is caused by Treponema carateum. Syphilis is caused by the microorganism Treponema pallidum, and patients with pinta appear to have immunity to the venereal infection.

## Hong Kong Flu

Eight pharmaceutical companies were put to work on a new influenza vaccine following a flu epidemic in Hong Kong that reached its peak in the summer of 1968. Considering the amount of travel between the Asian city and the U. S., it was to be expected that the new strain would cross the Pacific. The Division of Biologics Standards of the National Institutes of Health provided seed virus of the Hong Kong 1968 Asian flu strain to aid the drug companies in developing the new vaccine.

## Pooled Blood Plasma Stopped

The risk of hepatitis from pooled human blood plasma was found to be so great that a committee of the National Research Council recommended discontinuing its use.

Warnings also were issued against individual blood transfusions from former servicemen who had had malaria, which can be transmitted in their blood.

## New Anesthetic

A new general anesthetic, ketamine hydrochloride, was recommended as the safest ever developed. It is neither a barbiturate nor a narcotic, and unlike conventional anesthetics, it does not depress all areas of the central nervous system. It leaves the patient with his eyes open but disconnected from his surroundings and unresponsive to pain. It is particularly useful in dental extractions and other types of oral surgery.

## Cost of Drugs

Brand-name drugs cost elderly persons an estimated $41,500,000 more than they would have paid for drugs prescribed by generic name, a Health, Education and Welfare Department task force reported in a study of 175,000,000 prescriptions written for older people in 1966, the last year for which figures were available. Considerable controversy exists on the matter of equivalency, as well as actual cost, however, and the Pharmaceutical Manufacturers Association's officials called the report an illusion without proper documentation. The task force found that 409 drugs were used most frequently by the elderly. Most of these drugs were available from only one supplier and under brand names. The 339-page report, titled The Drug Users, pointed out that of the 10 most frequently used drugs, 8 were still under patent and no equivalent was available under its generic name.

Doctors who prescribed so-called diet pills containing digitalis and thyroid hormone were chastised by the American Medical Association after Senate hearings that included testimony on the dangerous effects and possible death resulting from such prescriptions.

Improvements in treatment of the mentally ill focused on modernization of physical plants such as St. Elizabeth's Hospital, the 113-year-old Federally run hospital, the largest in the U. S. devoted to mental illness. The National Institute of Mental Health took St. Elizabeth's from

the Health, Education and Welfare agency's jurisdiction and placed it under a National Center for Mental Health Services, Training and Research. Improved drugs have made it possible to continue treatment of the mentally ill in their homes rather than keep them for long-term custodial care in huge institutions. The cottage system also has been adopted in many hospitals.

### Army Reports Developments

The Army Medical Department named 9 areas in which there have been major developments since the start of the Vietnamese war. These achievements include: Inflatable hospitals, spray adhesive to control internal bleeding, tissue adhesive called cyanoacrylates, that will enable a physician to repair organs without suturing, shock treatment in the management of shock and wounds, an artificial hand run by rechargeable batteries, improved preservation of blood by the addition of adenine, burn treatment by sulfamylon creme that has been life-saving, a malaria preventive called Diformyl DDS (Diaminodiphenyl sulfone), which when given

once a week kept human volunteers from contracting the disease, and an oral vaccine that has been effective in reducing the occurrence of infectious diseases.

The measles eradication program reduced the number of cases from 203,000 in 1966 to 62,000 at the time of last estimate. The rubella vaccine to prevent German measles was tested to the point that it is expected to be licensed with safety. Isolation of the infectious mononucleosis virus raised hopes that a vaccine will be forthcoming. The development of silastic sheath for nerve repair showed great promise. Synthetic corticotropin showed significant results in asthma treatment. The discovery of the amino acid sequence of thyrocalcitonin was expected to have effects on studies of bone resorption in old age. Some persons were saved from blindness by the glueing of plastic contact lenses directly to the cornea. The Boston arm showed control over an artificial arm by signals from the brain. Cross circulation between a patient and baboon at the Medical College of Virginia saved the patient's life.

## Medical Signs and Abbreviations
### Source: American Medical Association

| | | | |
|---|---|---|---|
| ℞ (Lat. Recipe) .....take | ad.............to, up to | gargarisma......a gargle | q. 3 h...every three hours |
| ℨ............drachm | adde..............add | gr.................grain | q.i.d.....four times daily |
| f ℨ.....fluid drachm | ad libitum...at pleasure | gtt.................drops | q.s. |
| ℥..............ounce | agit.............shake | h.s..........at bedtime | .. as much as is sufficient |
| f ℥.......fluid ounce | aqua.............water | inject .........injection | sig...........sign, write |
| ℥ ss.....half an ounce | b.i.d........twice daily | lb..............pound | solutio.......a solution |
| ℥ i.........one ounce | cap............capsule | m.................mix | ss..............one-half |
| ℥ iss one ounce and a half | cum, or c.........with | non. rep. or n.r. | stat............at once |
| ℥ ij........two ounces | dilute .........dilute | do not repeat | sum.......to be taken |
| ℈.........scruple | e.m.p......as directed | p.c.......after meals | tab.............tablet |
| ℳ.....minim, or drop | fac (mist)........... | pil.............pill | t.i.d....three times daily |
| O...............pint | ...let a mixture be made | p.r.n....as circumstances | ung..........ointment |
| āā..........of each | fiant (ft).......make | may require | ut dict.....as directed |
| a.c........before meals | filtra.............filter | pulvis .........powder | |

## Suicides in Selected Countries
### Source: World Health Organization
### Death rates per 100,000 population, 1964

| MALE | | | | FEMALE | | |
|---|---|---|---|---|---|---|
| West Berlin ....... 56.3 | Puerto Rico ........ 12.3 | West Berlin ....... 30.9 | Israel .............. 5.1 |
| Hungary .......... 40.9 | Bulgaria ........... 12.6 | Hungary ........... 17.1 | Netherlands ....... 4.9 |
| Austria ........... 33.2 | Hong Kong ........ 11.5 | Denmark .......... 15.3 | Puerto Rico ...... 4.5 |
| Finland ........... 30.9 | Norway ........... 11.4 | China Taiwan ..... 14.2 | Panama ........... 4.3 |
| Czechoslovakia ... 29.6 | New Zealand ....... 9.7 | Germany, Fed. Rep. 13.9 | Canada ............ 4.1 |
| Sweden .......... 28.7 | Scotland ........... 9.6 | Austria ........... 13.7 | Northern Ireland .. 4.0 |
| Germany, Fed. Rep. 27.0 | Netherlands ........ 8.2 | Japan ............ 12.9 | Portugal .......... 3.8 |
| Denmark .......... 26.8 | Venezuela .......... 8.1 | Czechoslovakia ... 12.2 | Poland ............ 3.4 |
| Switzerland ...... 24.3 | Italy .............. 7.7 | Sweden .......... 10.9 | Venezuela ......... 3.4 |
| China Taiwan .... 23.9 | Northern Ireland .. 6.9 | Switzerland ...... 10.0 | Norway ........... 3.2 |
| France .......... 22.4 | Panama ............ 6.2 | Australia ......... 9.9 | Italy ............. 3.2 |
| Belgium .......... 20.1 | Israel ............. 5.9 | United Kingdom .. 9.8 | Iceland ........... 2.1 |
| Australia ........ 19.1 | Chile .............. 4.8 | Finland ........... 9.5 | Greece ........... 1.8 |
| Japan ........... 17.5 | Greece ............ 4.7 | Hong Kong ........ 8.1 | Mauritius ......... 1.4 |
| United States .... 16.1 | Mauritius .......... 4.4 | Belgium .......... 8.2 | Chile ............. 1.2 |
| Iceland .......... 15.7 | Mexico ............ 2.8 | France ............ 7.8 | Mexico ............ 0.9 |
| Portugal ......... 15.6 | Nicaragua ......... 2.3 | Scotland ........... 6.8 | Philippines ....... 0.6 |
| Poland ........... 13.9 | Philippines ........ 1.0 | New Zealand ..... 6.2 | Nicaragua ......... 0.1 |
| United Kingdom .. 13.8 | | United States .... 5.6 | Malta and Gozo ... — |
| Canada .......... 12.3 | Malta and Gozo .... 0.6 | Bulgaria .......... 5.4 | |

## New Federal Agency Takes Over Narcotics Fight

Federal narcotic and drug control forces were consolidated Apr. 8, 1968, when Reorganization Plan 1 of 1968 created the Bureau of Narcotics and Dangerous Drugs. Transferred to the new bureau were the functions of two previously existing agencies, the Bureau of Narcotics of the Treasury Dept. and the Bureau of Drug Abuse Control of the Dept. of Health, Education and Welfare.

Meanwhile, latest available Government statistics showed the number of active narcotic addicts in the United States at the end of 1967 as 62,045, an increase of 2,325 over the figure of a year earlier. Nearly 80% of them were reported from 4 states, as follows: New York 32,347, California 7,457, Illinois 6,567, and New Jersey 2,834. Ten cities accounted for 75% of the national total, as follows: New York City 30,543, Chicago 6,489, Los Angeles 1,997, Detroit 1,642, Baltimore 1,348, Philadelphia 1,296, Washington, D. C. 1,106, Newark 1,004, San Diego 587, and Buffalo 550.

## The Meaning of "One Inch of Rain"

An acre of ground contains 43,560 square feet. Consequently, a rainfall of 1 inch over 1 acre of ground would mean a total of 6,272,640 cubic inches of water. This is equivalent of 3,630 cubic feet.

As a cubic foot of pure water weighs about 62.4 pounds, the exact amount varying with the density, it follows that the weight of a uniform coating of 1 inch of rain over 1 acre of surface would be 226,512 pounds, or 113¼ short tons.

The weight of 1 U. S. gallon of pure water is 8.345 pounds. Consequently a rainfall of 1 inch over 1 acre of ground would mean 27,143 gallons of water.

# Principal Foreign Rivers

**Source:** National Geographic Society, Washington, D. C. (Length in miles)

| River | Outflow | Lgth |
|---|---|---|
| Albany | James Bay | 610 |
| Amazon | Atlantic Ocean | 3,900 |
| Amu | Aral Sea | 1,600 |
| Amur | Tartar Strait | 2,700 |
| Angara[1] | Yenisey | 1,150 |
| Athabasca | Lk. Athabasca | 765 |
| Back | Chantrey Inlet of Arctic Ocean | 605 |
| Brahmaputra | Bay of Bengal | 1,800 |
| Bug | Dnieper River | 500 |
| Bug | Wisla River | 450 |
| Churchill | Hudson Bay | 1,000 |
| Congo | Atlantic Ocean | 2,718 |
| Danube | Black Sea | 1,770 |
| Dnieper | Black Sea | 1,420 |
| Dniester | Black Sea | 880 |
| Don | Sea of Azov | 1,210 |
| Drava | Danube River | 450 |
| Dvina, North | White Sea | 800 |
| Ebro | Mediterranean | 577 |
| Elbe | North Sea | 724 |
| Euphrates | Persian Gulf | 1,700 |
| Fraser | Georgia Strait | 850 |
| Gambia | Atlantic Ocean | 700 |
| Ganges | Bay of Bengal | 1,560 |
| Garonne | Bay of Biscay | 402 |
| Hamilton | Atlantic | 208 |
| Huang | Yellow Sea | 3,000 |
| Indus | Arabian Sea | 1,900 |
| Irrawaddy | Bay of Bengal | 1,250 |
| Japurá | Amazon River | 1,500 |
| Jordan | Dead Sea | 200 |
| Kootenay | Columbia Riv. | 407 |
| Lena | Laptev Sea | 2,680 |
| Loire | Bay of Biscay | 625 |
| Mackenzie-Peace | Beaufort Sea | 2,635 |
| Madeira | Amazon River | 2,100 |
| Magdalena | Caribbean Sea | 1,000 |
| Marne | Seine River | 325 |
| Mekong | S. China Sea | 2,600 |
| Meuse | North Sea | 575 |
| Murray-Darling | Indian Ocean | 2,310 |
| Negro | Amazon | 1,400 |
| Nelson | Hudson Bay | 1,600 |
| Niger | Gulf of Guinea | 2,600 |
| Nile | Mediterranean | 4,145 |
| Ob-Irtysh | Gulf of Ob | 3,460 |
| Oder | Baltic Sea | 535 |
| Orange | Atlantic Ocean | 1,300 |
| Orinoco | Atlantic Ocean | 1,700 |
| Ottawa | St. Lawrence R. | 790 |
| Paraguay | Paraná River | 1,500 |
| Parana | Rio de la Plata | 2,500 |
| Peace | Slave River | 1,195 |
| Pilcomayo | Paraguay Riv. | 1,000 |
| Po | Adriatic Sea | 405 |
| Purus | Amazon River | 2,000 |
| Red River N. | Lake Winnipeg | 355 |
| Rhine | North Sea | 820 |
| Rhône | Gulf of Lion | 500 |
| Rio de la Plata[2] | Atlantic Ocean | 150 |
| Rio Grande | Gulf of Mexico | 1,885 |
| Rio Roosevelt or River of Doubt | Madeira River | 950 |
| Saguenay | St. Lawrence | 475 |
| St. John | Bay of Fundy | 418 |
| St. Lawrenc[3] | Gulf of St. Law. | 1,900 |
| St. Maurice | St. Law. River | 325 |
| Salween | Martaban Gulf | 1,750 |
| São Francisco | Atlantic Ocean | 1,800 |
| Saskatchewan | Lake Winnipeg | 1,205 |
| Seine | English Chan. | 482 |
| Shannon | Atlantic Ocean | 224 |
| Si | So. China Sea | 1,250 |
| Sungari | Amur River | 1,150 |
| Syr | Aral Sea | 1,850 |
| Tajo, Tagus | Atlantic Ocean | 565 |
| Thames | North Sea | 215 |
| Tiber | Tyrrhenian Sea | 252 |
| Tigris | Euphrates | 1,150 |
| Tisza | Danube River | 800 |
| Tocantins | Pará River | 1,640 |
| Ural | Caspian Sea | 1,570 |
| Uruguay | Rio de la Plata | 1,000 |
| Usumacinta | Gulf of Mexico | 690 |
| Volga | Caspian Sea | 2,290 |
| Weser | North Sea | 500 |
| Wisla | Bay of Danzig | 665 |
| Yangtze | East China Sea | 3,400 |
| Yapura | Amazon River | 1,500 |
| Yellow (see Huang) | | |
| Yenisey | Kara Sea | 2,080 |
| Yukon | Bering Sea | 1,979 |
| Zambezi | Indian Ocean | 1,600 |

[1]The Angara is the only outlet of Lake Baykal, USSR, and drops 1,140 ft. in 1,150 miles.

[2]The Rio de la Plata is the estuary formed by the Paraná and Uruguay Rivers.

[3]The source of the St. Lawrence River is in the State of Minnesota. The St. Lawrence is viewed as a part of the Great Lakes Waterway and its source is considered the head of the St. Louis River which feeds into Lake Superior. The St. Louis River rises in Minnesota.

**Area (sq. miles) of great river basins**—Amazon (2,053,318); Congo (1,339,923); Nile (1,119,652); Mississippi-Missouri (1,243,700); La Plata (1,198,000); Ob-Irtysh (1,132,000); Yenisey (1,004,000); Lena (934,000); Amur (712,000); Mackenzie-Peace (696,700); Yangtze (666,000); St. Lawrence (565,200); Volga (533,000); Huang (288,000); Danube (315,000); Colorado (246,000); Rio Grande (171,890).

# Famous Fairs and Expositions

1851 May 1 ................ Great Exhibition opened, Crystal Palace, Hyde Park, London.
1853 July 14 ............... New York World's Fair opened, Crystal Palace.
1867 Apr. 1 ................ International Exhibition opened, Paris.
1873 May 1 ................ International Exhibition opened, Vienna
1876 May-Nov ............. Centennial Exposition, Philadelphia.
1889 May 6-Nov. 6 ......... Universal Exposition, Paris.
1893 May 1-Oct. 30 ........ World's Columbian Exposition, Chicago.
1898 June 1-Oct. 31 ....... Trans-Mississippi International Exposition, Omaha.
1900 Apr. 15 .............. International Exposition opened, Paris.
1901 May 1-Nov. 2 ........ Pan-American Exposition, Buffalo.
1904 Apr. 20-Dec. 1 ....... Louisiana Purchase Exposition, St. Louis.
1905 June 1 ............... Lewis and Clark Centennial Exposition opened, Portland, Ore.
1907 Apr. 26 .............. Jamestown, Va., Tercentenary Exposition. opened.
1909 June 1-Oct. 16 ....... Alaska-Yukon-Pacific Exposition, Seattle.
1909 Sept. 25-Oct. 2 ...... Hudson-Fulton Celebration, New York.
1910 Apr. 23 .............. International Exhibition opened, Brussels.
1913 Apr. 26 .............. International Exposition opened, Ghent, Belgium.
1915 Feb. 20-Dec. 4 ....... Panama-Pacific International Exposition, San Francisco.
1915 ...................... Panama-California Exposition, San Diego.
1922-23 ................... Brazilian Exposition, Rio de Janeiro.
1924-25 ................... British Empire Exposition, Wembley.
1926 May 31-Nov. 30 ...... Sesquicentennial Exposition, Philadelphia.
1931 ...................... International Colonial and Overseas Exposition, Paris.
1933 May 27-Nov. 12 ...... Century of Progress Exposition, Chicago.
1934 May 26-Oct. 31 ...... Century of Progress Exposition, Chicago.
1936 ...................... Texas Centennial Exposition, Dallas.
1936-1937 ................. Great Lakes Exposition, Cleveland, Ohio.
1939 Feb. 18-Oct. 29 ...... Golden Gate International Exposition, San Francisco.
1939 Apr. 20-Oct. 31 ...... New York World's Fair.
1940 May 11-Oct. 21 ...... New York World's Fair.
1957 Apr. 26-Oct. 30 ...... Jamestown, Va., 350th Anniversary Festival.
1958 Apr. 17-Oct. 19 ...... World's Fair, Brussels.
1962 Apr. 21-Oct. 21 ...... Century 21 Exposition, Seattle, Wash.
1964 Apr. 22-Oct. 18 ...... New York World's Fair.
1965 Apr. 21-Oct. 17 ...... New York World's Fair.
1967 Apr. 28-Oct. 27 ...... Universal and International Exhibition (Expo. 67), Montreal, Canada.
1968 Apr. 6-Oct. 6 ........ HemisFair 1968, San Antonio, Texas.
1970 ...................... Osaka World's Fair, Osaka, Japan.

# Miss Universe Pageant and Miss U.S.A.

Martha Vasconcellos, of Brazil, was crowned Miss Universe, 1968, at Miami Beach on Saturday, July 13, 1968. She received a $10,000 cash award; a $10,000 service contract; a chinchilla jacket valued at $7,500, plus numerous other prizes.

Dorothy Anstett, of Kirkland, Washington, was elected Miss USA on Saturday, May 18, 1968. She received a $5,000 cash award; a $5,000 service contract and numerous other prizes.

# First Miss Black America

Saundra Williams, 19, of Philadelphia, a student at Maryland State College, was chosen over 7 other contestants as the first Miss Black America in Atlantic City, N. J., Sept. 8. The contest was held in the Ritz Carlton Hotel, to protest what its sponsors termed "the white stereotype" of the Miss America Pageant, held at the same time in nearby Convention Hall. Miss Williams was awarded a trophy, a one-week vacation in Puerto Rico, and a modeling contract.

## Multi-TV Set Homes Double in 6 Years

The number of American households with two or more television sets more than doubled since 1962 as multi-set households reached an estimated 14,700,000 by June 1967, according to the U. S. Department of Commerce.

Sixteen out of 17 homes had television, reaching 96% of the population. Nearly 11,000,000 homes had color sets and more than 23,000,000 had UHF sets. More than one set was most likely to be found in homes with either color or UHF.

## Number of Radio and TV Sets In Use

Source: Electronic Industries Assn.

(In Millions)

| Year | Auto radios | Home radios | Total radios | Television receivers B & W | Television receivers Color | Phono-graphs |
|---|---|---|---|---|---|---|
| 1950...... | 18 | 81 | 99 | 10.6 | .... | 16.8 |
| 1955...... | 29 | 91 | 120 | 37.4 | .... | 24.0 |
| 1960...... | 40 | 116 | 156 | 55.5 | .2 | 34.0 |
| 1961...... | 41 | 127 | 168 | 57.6 | .4 | 35.7 |
| 1962...... | 43 | 140 | 183 | 60.8 | .8 | 37.0 |
| 1963...... | 45 | 151 | 196 | 65.0 | 1.6 | 39.0 |
| 1964...... | 47 | 161 | 208 | 70.0 | 3.0 | 42.0 |
| 1965...... | 55 | 172 | 227 | 75.0 | 5.0 | 45.0 |
| 1966...... | 64 | 188 | 262 | 78.5 | 9.7 | 48.0 |
| 1967...... | 73 | 195 | 268 | 81.5 | 12.7 | 51.0 |

## Commercial Broadcast Stations on the Air

(Includes Puerto Rico, Virgin Islands and Guam)

Source: Federal Communications Commission

| Year | Total on air | AM radio | FM radio | Television |
|---|---|---|---|---|
| 1965............. | 5,814 | 4,040 | 1,270 | 572 |
| 1966............. | 5,986 | 4,004 | 1,393 | 589 |
| 1967............. | 6,253 | 4,085 | 1,560 | 608 |
| 1968............. | 6,708 | 4,203 | 1,850 | 655 |

## Days Between Two Dates

Table covers period of two ordinary years. For leap year, one day must be added after Feb. 28.
**Example**—Days between July 4, 1969, and Dec. 25, 1970, subtract 185 from 724; answer is 539 days.

| Day Mo. | Jan. | Feb. | March | April | May | June | July | Aug. | Sept. | Oct. | Nov. | Dec. | Day Mo. | Jan. | Feb. | Mar. | April | May | June | July | Aug. | Sept. | Oct. | Nov. | Dec. |
|---|---|---|---|---|---|---|---|---|---|---|---|---|---|---|---|---|---|---|---|---|---|---|---|---|---|
| 1 | 1 | 32 | 60 | 91 | 121 | 152 | 182 | 213 | 244 | 274 | 305 | 335 | 1 | 366 | 397 | 425 | 456 | 486 | 517 | 547 | 578 | 609 | 639 | 670 | 700 |
| 2 | 2 | 33 | 61 | 92 | 122 | 153 | 183 | 214 | 245 | 275 | 306 | 336 | 2 | 367 | 398 | 426 | 457 | 487 | 518 | 548 | 579 | 610 | 640 | 671 | 701 |
| 3 | 3 | 34 | 62 | 93 | 123 | 154 | 184 | 215 | 246 | 276 | 307 | 337 | 3 | 368 | 399 | 427 | 458 | 488 | 519 | 549 | 580 | 611 | 641 | 672 | 702 |
| 4 | 4 | 35 | 63 | 94 | 124 | 155 | 185 | 216 | 247 | 277 | 308 | 338 | 4 | 369 | 400 | 428 | 459 | 489 | 520 | 550 | 581 | 612 | 642 | 673 | 703 |
| 5 | 5 | 36 | 64 | 95 | 125 | 156 | 186 | 217 | 248 | 278 | 309 | 339 | 5 | 370 | 401 | 429 | 460 | 490 | 521 | 551 | 582 | 613 | 643 | 674 | 704 |
| 6 | 6 | 37 | 65 | 96 | 126 | 157 | 187 | 218 | 249 | 279 | 310 | 340 | 6 | 371 | 402 | 430 | 461 | 491 | 522 | 552 | 583 | 614 | 644 | 675 | 705 |
| 7 | 7 | 38 | 66 | 97 | 127 | 158 | 188 | 219 | 250 | 280 | 311 | 341 | 7 | 372 | 403 | 431 | 462 | 492 | 523 | 553 | 584 | 615 | 645 | 676 | 706 |
| 8 | 8 | 39 | 67 | 98 | 128 | 159 | 189 | 220 | 251 | 281 | 312 | 342 | 8 | 373 | 404 | 432 | 463 | 493 | 524 | 554 | 585 | 616 | 646 | 677 | 707 |
| 9 | 9 | 40 | 68 | 99 | 129 | 160 | 190 | 221 | 252 | 282 | 313 | 343 | 9 | 374 | 405 | 433 | 464 | 494 | 525 | 555 | 586 | 617 | 647 | 673 | 708 |
| 10 | 10 | 41 | 69 | 100 | 130 | 161 | 191 | 222 | 253 | 283 | 314 | 344 | 10 | 375 | 406 | 434 | 465 | 495 | 526 | 556 | 587 | 618 | 648 | 679 | 709 |
| 11 | 11 | 42 | 70 | 101 | 131 | 162 | 192 | 223 | 254 | 284 | 315 | 345 | 11 | 376 | 407 | 435 | 466 | 496 | 527 | 557 | 588 | 619 | 649 | 680 | 710 |
| 12 | 12 | 43 | 71 | 102 | 132 | 163 | 193 | 224 | 255 | 285 | 316 | 346 | 12 | 377 | 408 | 436 | 467 | 497 | 528 | 558 | 589 | 620 | 650 | 681 | 711 |
| 13 | 13 | 44 | 72 | 103 | 133 | 164 | 194 | 225 | 256 | 286 | 317 | 347 | 13 | 378 | 409 | 437 | 468 | 498 | 529 | 559 | 590 | 621 | 651 | 682 | 712 |
| 14 | 14 | 45 | 73 | 104 | 134 | 165 | 195 | 226 | 257 | 287 | 318 | 348 | 14 | 379 | 410 | 438 | 469 | 499 | 530 | 560 | 591 | 622 | 652 | 683 | 713 |
| 15 | 15 | 46 | 74 | 105 | 135 | 166 | 196 | 227 | 258 | 288 | 319 | 349 | 15 | 380 | 411 | 439 | 470 | 500 | 531 | 561 | 592 | 623 | 653 | 684 | 714 |
| 16 | 16 | 47 | 75 | 106 | 136 | 167 | 197 | 228 | 259 | 289 | 320 | 350 | 16 | 381 | 412 | 440 | 471 | 501 | 532 | 562 | 593 | 624 | 654 | 685 | 715 |
| 17 | 17 | 48 | 76 | 107 | 137 | 168 | 198 | 229 | 260 | 290 | 321 | 351 | 17 | 382 | 413 | 441 | 472 | 502 | 533 | 563 | 594 | 625 | 655 | 686 | 716 |
| 18 | 18 | 49 | 77 | 108 | 138 | 169 | 199 | 230 | 261 | 291 | 322 | 352 | 18 | 383 | 414 | 442 | 473 | 503 | 534 | 564 | 595 | 626 | 656 | 687 | 717 |
| 19 | 19 | 50 | 78 | 109 | 139 | 170 | 200 | 231 | 262 | 292 | 323 | 353 | 19 | 384 | 415 | 443 | 474 | 504 | 535 | 565 | 596 | 627 | 657 | 688 | 718 |
| 20 | 20 | 51 | 79 | 110 | 140 | 171 | 201 | 232 | 263 | 293 | 324 | 354 | 20 | 385 | 416 | 444 | 475 | 505 | 536 | 566 | 597 | 628 | 658 | 689 | 719 |
| 21 | 21 | 52 | 80 | 111 | 141 | 172 | 202 | 233 | 264 | 294 | 325 | 355 | 21 | 386 | 417 | 445 | 476 | 506 | 537 | 567 | 598 | 629 | 659 | 690 | 720 |
| 22 | 22 | 53 | 81 | 112 | 142 | 173 | 203 | 234 | 265 | 295 | 326 | 356 | 22 | 387 | 418 | 446 | 477 | 507 | 538 | 568 | 599 | 630 | 660 | 691 | 721 |
| 23 | 23 | 54 | 82 | 113 | 143 | 174 | 204 | 235 | 266 | 296 | 327 | 357 | 23 | 388 | 419 | 447 | 478 | 508 | 539 | 569 | 600 | 631 | 661 | 692 | 722 |
| 24 | 24 | 55 | 83 | 114 | 144 | 175 | 205 | 236 | 267 | 297 | 328 | 358 | 24 | 389 | 420 | 448 | 479 | 509 | 540 | 570 | 601 | 632 | 662 | 693 | 723 |
| 25 | 25 | 56 | 84 | 115 | 145 | 176 | 206 | 237 | 268 | 298 | 329 | 359 | 25 | 390 | 421 | 449 | 480 | 510 | 541 | 571 | 602 | 633 | 663 | 694 | 724 |
| 26 | 26 | 57 | 85 | 116 | 146 | 177 | 207 | 238 | 269 | 299 | 330 | 360 | 26 | 391 | 422 | 450 | 481 | 511 | 542 | 572 | 603 | 634 | 664 | 695 | 725 |
| 27 | 27 | 58 | 86 | 117 | 147 | 178 | 208 | 239 | 270 | 300 | 331 | 361 | 27 | 392 | 423 | 451 | 482 | 512 | 543 | 573 | 604 | 635 | 665 | 696 | 726 |
| 28 | 28 | 59 | 87 | 118 | 148 | 179 | 209 | 240 | 271 | 301 | 332 | 362 | 28 | 393 | 424 | 452 | 483 | 513 | 544 | 574 | 605 | 636 | 666 | 697 | 727 |
| 29 | 29 | ... | 88 | 119 | 149 | 180 | 210 | 241 | 272 | 302 | 333 | 363 | 29 | 394 | ... | 453 | 484 | 514 | 545 | 575 | 606 | 637 | 667 | 698 | 728 |
| 30 | 30 | ... | 89 | 120 | 150 | 181 | 211 | 242 | 273 | 303 | 334 | 364 | 30 | 395 | ... | 454 | 485 | 515 | 546 | 576 | 607 | 638 | 668 | 699 | 729 |
| 31 | 31 | ... | 90 | ... | 151 | ... | 212 | 243 | ... | 304 | ... | 365 | 31 | 396 | ... | 455 | ... | 516 | ... | 577 | 608 | ... | 669 | ... | 730 |

## A Guide to Avenue Addresses in N.Y.C.

To find the location of a number on the following Avenues of Manhattan, cancel the last figure of the number, divide the remainder by 2 and add the given key number.

Thus: Where is 596 Seventh Avenue? Divide 59 by 2=30, plus 12=42nd Street.

Ave. A ..........add 4
Ave. B ..........add 3
Ave. C ..........add 3
Ave. D ..........add 3
1st Ave..........add 4
2nd Ave..........add 3
3rd Ave..........add 10
4th Ave..........add 8
5th Ave. to 200...add 13
    Up to 400...add 16

Up to 600 ...add 18
Up to 775 ...add 20
From 775 to 1286
    see exception below:
Up to 1500 ......add 45
Up to 2000 Mt. Morris Pk.
    Above 2000...add 24
Ave. of Americas (6th)
    subtract 12 or 13
7th Ave...........add 12

Above 1800...add 20
8th Ave.......add 9
9th Ave.......add 13
10th Ave......add 13
11th Ave......add 13
Amsterdam Ave..add 59
Audubon Ave....add 165
Columbus Ave...add 60
Convent Ave.....add 127
Edgecomb Ave...add 134

Ft. Wash. Ave...add 158
Lenox Ave.......add 110
Lexington Ave...add 22
Madison Ave.....add 27
Manhattan Ave..add 100
Park Ave.........add 34
Pleasant Ave....add 101
St. Nicholas Ave.add 110
Wadsworth Ave..add 175
West End Ave...add 59

### EXCEPTIONS

Broadway: Up to 754 below East 8th St. Above 754, apply above rule but deduct following key numbers:
From 754 to 858 deduct 29.
From 857 to 958 deduct 25.
Above 1000 deduct deduct 31.
Note: From Washington Square North most crosstown streets have 100 numbers to the block. Numbering of these streets starts east and west from Fifth Avenue.

Riverside Drive: Below 567, drop last figure, add 75; do not divide by five.
Above 577, drop last figure, add 78.
Central Park West: Drop last figure, add 60.
5th Avenue: From 775 to 1286, drop last figure and add 18 from remainder.

# Late News Developments
## New York City Teachers End Strike

The New York City school strike, the nation's first major confrontation over the issue of decentralization of a large school system, finally came to an end **Nov. 19.** The United Federation of Teachers voted 6-to-1 to call off the 5-week strike, after the city made new concessions weakening the posture of the experimental local school board and strengthening the protections guaranteed members of the teachers' union. The strike, actually 3 successive strikes, had kept most of the city's 50,000 teachers and 1,100,000 pupils out of classes for 36 of the first 48 days of the fall term.

### Nixon, Humphrey Meet in Florida

Vice President Humphrey, enroute to a Virgin Islands vacation **Nov. 8,** stopped over in Miami for an amiable half-hour airport discussion with vacationing President-elect Nixon, in which he pledged his support of the man who had defeated him 3 days before in the race for the Presidency. Humphrey was accompanied by Maine Sen. Edmund S. Muskie, who had been his Vice Presidential running mate.

### U. S. Bishops Rule on Pill

In an 11,000-word pastoral letter, **Nov. 15,** U. S. Catholic bishops meeting in Washington said Catholic married couples who decide in good conscience to use contraceptives should not feel cut off from the church and its sacraments. The bishops agreed 180-8 that "circumstances may reduce moral guilt," although they described artificial contraception as an "objective evil."

### Greek Plotter Spared

Following worldwide appeals, including one from Pope Paul VI, Greece's army-backed government **Nov. 21** decided to spare the life of Alexandros Panaghoulis, the 30-year-old army deserter who tried to kill Premier George Papadopolous on Aug. 13. He had been sentenced to die **Nov. 17.**

### Assassin Misses Ayub

Pres. Mohammed Ayub Khan of Pakistan escaped an apparent assassination attempt **Nov. 10** when a youth's two pistol shots missed him on the platform on which he was sitting.

### Nip Plot to Kill Nixon

A Yemini Arab, a naturalized citizen of the U. S., and his two sons were arrested **Nov. 9** in Brooklyn, N. Y., for an alleged Arab plot to assassinate President-elect Richard M. Nixon. The father, Ahmed Rageh Namer, 43, and his sons, Hussein Namer, 20, and Abdo Namer, 18, were all described as shipping clerks.

### Warren Firm on Retiring

Chief Justice Earl Warren was firm in his intention to retire, according to reports **Nov. 14.** He was also said by friends to be ready to swear in Richard M. Nixon as 37th President of the United States, and deprecated any talk of ill feeling between him and the President-elect.

### 10 Meet on Money Crisis

With the international monetary system threatened for the 3d time in a year by waves of speculation, top financial officials of the 10 wealthiest non-Communist countries met in Bonn **Nov. 20** to try to resolve the crisis. The French, German, London and Brussels markets were closed down—Brussels "until further notice." With the French franc foundering, it was expected the others would attempt to remedy the situation with massive loans, but that the franc would have to be devalued.

### Ray Trial Delayed

Judge W. Preston Battle **Nov. 12** approved the postponement of James Earl Ray's trial for the murder of the Rev. Dr. Martin Luther King, Jr. until March 3, 1969, to give his new counsel, Perry Foreman of Houston, time to prepare the defense.

### Nixon Names 1st Aide

In his 1st choice of staff aides **Nov. 12,** President-elect Nixon named Bryce Nathaniel Harlow, 52, of Oklahoma, to serve as his assistant for legislative and Congressional affairs. Harlow held a similar job in the Eisenhower administration.

### UK Train Robbery Suspect Seized

After a 5-year search, Bruce Reynolds, last of the suspects in Britain's great train robbery Aug. 8, 1963, was seized **Nov. 8** in Torquay, a fashionable resort town on the Devon coast. Reynolds was a suspected member of the gang that halted a Glasgow-London mail train and made off with bank notes worth more than $7,000,000.

### Yale Going Coed in 1969

Yale University announced **Nov. 14** it would go coed for the first time in its 267-year history with the admission of 500 undergraduate women in September, 1969 to "enhance its contribution to the generations ahead." Ultimate goal was 1,500 girl students, without reducing male undergraduate enrollment, which is now 4,000.

### Gomulka Asks Red Unity

Wladyslaw Gomulka, Poland's Communist chief, **Nov. 11** appealed for unity and urged 37 foreign Red delegations attending the Polish Communist party's 5th congress in Warsaw to openly discuss the "differences existing among us."

## DISASTERS

A cyclone in Orissa State, India, **Nov. 1** killed 35 . . . Twenty-two died in a forest fire west of Algiers, Algeria, **Nov. 1** . . . Seven were killed, two injured when a car carrying Boy Scouts to a weekend canoe trip collided with another car near Grand Ledge, Mich., **Nov. 2** . . . More than 100 perished in floods and landslides in northwestern Italy **Nov. 1-3** . . . One died, 10 were injured in a southwest Yugoslav earthquake **Nov. 3** . . . A fuel tank explosion in Illoilo, Philippines, **Nov. 10** killed 13, injured 57 . . . Some 12 tornadoes along West Florida coast **Nov. 9** killed two, injured 24, caused more than $1,000,000 in damage . . . A bus plunged into a river near Sotik, Kenya, **Nov. 10,** killing 14 . . . Bus-tanker truck crash in Accra, Ghana, **Nov. 12** killed 22 . . . Two French Army helicopters crashed near Dax, France, **Nov. 14,** killing all 5 aboard . . . Brighton, England, hotel fire **Nov. 17** killed 7, injured 4 . . . Coal mine fire trapped 78 of 99 miners in Mannington, W. Va., **Nov. 20.**

# Addenda, Changes

## AWARDS, MEDALS, PRIZES (PP. 234-244)

**Harmon International Aviators Trophy**—Major William J. Knight.

**Louisa Gross Horwitz Prizes**—for research in biochemistry, $12,500 each: Dr. H. Gobind Khorana and Dr. Marshall W. Nirenberg.

**Albert Lasker Medical Research Awards**—Dr. William F. Windle, Dr. John H. Gibbon, Jr., Sen. Lister Hill ($10,000 each); Dr. Marshall W. Nirenberg, Dr. H. Gobind Khorana ($5,000 each).

**National Medal for Literature**—$5,000, Marianne Moore, poet.

**Nobel Prizes for 1968—Peace Prize:** Rene Cassin, France. **Physics:** Luis W. Alvarez, United States. **Chemistry:** Lars Onsager, United States. **Medicine and Physiology:** Robert W. Holley, H. Gobind Khorana and Marshall W. Nirenberg, all United States. **Literature:** Yasunari Kawabata, Japan.

## BASEBALL (P. 806)

**Most Valuable Players**—Bob Gibson, St. Louis Cardinals, was selected as the most valuable player in the National League for the 1968 season. The American League most valuable player was Dennis McLain of the Detroit Tigers.

**Rookies of the Year**—Stan Bahnsen, of the New York Yankees, was chosen rookie of the year in the American League for 1968. The National League rookie of the year was Johnny Bench of the Cincinnati Reds.

## CANADIAN TAXES (P. 489)

Prime Minister Trudeau's government presented its first budget Oct. 22, calling for a 2% increase in income tax levies, limited to a maximum of $120 a year on each taxpayer, taking effect Jan. 1, 1969, and adding new levies on insurance companies.

## DEATHS (PP. 65-92)

**Philby, Mrs. Eleanor Carolyn Kearns,** 54; wife of Harold (Kim) Philby, Soviet spy; Mendocino, Calif., Nov. 14.

**Lewanika, Sr Mwanawina, III,** 78, leader of Lozi of Barotseland, Zambia; Lusaka, Nov. 13.

**Briskin, Samuel,** 71; Hollywood producer; Los Angeles, Nov. 6.

**Bea, Augustin Cardinal,** 87; guided ecumenical decrees; Rome, Nov. 16.

**Clapper, Mrs. Olive Ewing,** 72; widow of Raymond Clapper, Scripps-Howard political columnist; Washington, Nov. 11.

**Wanger, Walter,** 74; film producer; $37,-000,000 "Cleopatra"; New York, Nov. 18.

**Corey, Wendell,** 54; actor; Hollywood, Nov. 8.

**Magnuson, Dr. Paul B.,** 84; former medical director of Veterans Administration; Washington, Nov. 5.

**Munch, Charles,** 77; conductor of Boston Symphony, 1949-1962; Richmond, Va., Nov. 6.

**Mohr, Gerald,** 54; actor; Stockholm, Nov. 10.

**Papandreou, George,** 80; former Premier of Greece; Athens, Nov. 1.

**Gatch, Lee,** 66; artist; Trenton, N. J., Nov. 10.

**Uihlein, Edwin C., Jr.,** 22; heir of Schlitz fortune; Milwaukee, Nov. 12.

## EQUATORIAL GUINEA (P. 548)

**Independence**—Equatorial Guinea, a Spanish province, became independent Oct. 12; Francisco Macias Nguema became president.

## GREAT CITIES OF NORTH AMERICA

**Dayton, Ohio** (P. 399)—The new editor of The Journal Herald is Charles T. Alexander; the new managing editor is Ralph Langer.

**Los Angeles, Calif.** (P. 408)—Telephone number of the Los Angeles Herald-Examiner is 213-748-1212. Circulation daily 667,902; Sunday 687,850.

**Regina, Canada** (P. 423)—The correct spelling is Mackenzie Art Gallery; the CCF is now known as the New Democratic party.

**Tampa, Fla.** (P. 433)—The telephone number of The Tampa Tribune and the Tampa Times has been changed to (813) 224-7711.

## GREECE (P. 517)

Greek voters approved a new Constitution Sept. 29; it took effect Nov. 10; it cut down powers of the King and Parliament and increased those of the Premier; elections and certain rights were left in abeyance until the regime should decide to restore them.

## HEADS OF STATE, PRIME MINISTERS (PP. 576-7)

**Congo-Brazzaville**—Pres. Alphonse Massamba-Debat was ousted Sept. 4; Alfred Raoul was named interim president.

**Italy**—Premier Giovanni Leone resigned Nov. 19.

**Libya**—Wanis el-Geddafi became premier Sept. 4.

**Mali**—Pres. Modibo Keita was ousted Nov. 19.

**Panama**—Pres. Arnulfo Arias was ousted Oct. 11; Col. Jose M. Pinilla was named provisional president.

**Peru**—Pres. Fernando Belaunde Terry was ousted Oct. 3; Gen. Juan Velasco Alvarado became provisional president.

**Portugal**—Premier Salazar suffered a brain hemorrhage and resigned; Marcelo Caetano became premier Sept. 27.

**Syria**—Premier Youssef Zayyin was removed; Chief of State Nureddin al-Attassi took over the post.

## HORSE RACING (P. 820)

**Beau Brummel** won the $125,000 added Garden State Stakes for two year olds.

## MEDAL OF HONOR WINNERS (P. 740)

(*Awarded Posthumously)

Late in 1968 the following additional Medal of Honor winners were announced:

*Pfc. Gary W. Martini, U. S. Marine Corps, of Charleston, W. Va.

*Capt. James A. Graham, U. S. Marine Corps of Forestville, Md.

*First Sgt. Maximo Yabes, U. S. Army, of Lafayette, Colo.

Capt. Angelo J. Liteky, U. S. Army chaplain, of Washington, D. C.

Sgt. Sammy L. Davis, U. S. Army, of Martinsville, Ind.

Capt. James A. Taylor, U. S. Army, of Arcata, Calif.

Specialist 5 Dwight H. Johnson, U. S. Army, of Detroit, Mich.

Specialist 4 Gary G. Wetzel, U. S. Army, of Oak Creek, Wis.

## QUEBEC PREMIER (P. 489)

After the death of Premier Daniel Johnson, a Quebec Legislative Assembly caucus of National Union party members on Oct. 2 chose Jean-Jacques Bertrand, Minister of Justice, to become Premier of the province.

## UNITED NATIONS MEMBERS (P. 569)

**New Members**—The UN roster rose to 126 nations as Swaziland became a member Sept. 24 and Equatorial Africa Nov. 14.

## UNITED STATES POPULATION (P. 592)

**Total estimated population**—As of Oct. 1, 1968, the population of the U. S., including servicemen overseas, was estimated by the Bureau of the Census at 201,750,000.

# Chronology of Year's Events

### Reported Month by Month in 4 Categories:
### National, International, General and Disasters

## December 1, 1967, to November 1, 1968

### December—1967

#### NATIONAL

**McCarthy Called "Stalking Horse"**—Gov. John B. Connally of Texas accused Sen. Eugene McCarthy **Dec. 1** of being "a stalking horse" for the Presidential aspirations of Sen. Robert F. Kennedy. Connally said McCarthy's candidacy for the Democratic nomination, which had been announced the previous day, "can't do anything but result in a greater division in the party." In an apparent answer to Connally's charge, McCarthy declared in a speech in Chicago **Dec. 2** that there was "no conspiracy, collusion or common plan" between himself and Kennedy.

**Draft Demonstrations**—Some 585 anti-draft demonstrators were arrested in New York **Dec. 5-8** as they unsuccessfully sought to close down the Army's induction center at 39 Whitehall St. by marching and blocking the entrance. Among those arrested were Dr. Benjamin Spock and poet Allen Ginsberg. The New York demonstration was part of a national Stop-The-Draft-Week program initiated by some 40 anti-war groups. Anti-war demonstrators also were arrested in Madison, Wis., Manchester, N. H., Cincinnati, O., and New Haven, Conn.

**LBJ Hits House Republicans**—In a nationally televised speech before the AFL-CIO convention in Bal Harbour, Fla., **Dec. 12**, President Johnson accused Republican members of the House of defending the status quo in "vote after vote" like so many "wooden soldiers." The President then ticked off 7 bills that had been opposed by more than a majority of the House Republicans and accused them of voting an enthusiastic "yes" only, ". . . when they could vote to recommit a good bill, to bury it in a blanket of rhetoric beneath the wave of Republican reaction." The GOP received equal TV time to answer the President **Dec. 15** and Senate Republican leader Everett Dirksen (Ill.) said, ". . . the wooden soldiers have not only been sustaining the commander-in-chief, but we have been sustaining the live soldiers in Vietnam, which is infinitely more important."

**McCloskey Wins House Seat**—Republican Paul N. McCloskey, Jr., won election to the House of Representatives from California's 11th Congressional District **Dec. 12**. The previous month, McCloskey had defeated former child screen star Mrs. Shirley Temple Black for the Republican nomination for the seat.

**Vietnam Christmas Truce**—American and Allied forces in Vietnam observed a 24-hour Christmas truce **Dec. 24-25** which they later reported was violated by 108 enemy-initiated incidents. The Viet Cong had declared unilaterally they would observe a 3-day truce **Dec. 24-27**. At the end of the 24-hour period the U. S. resumed air attacks on North Vietnam and reported destroying 23 trucks in a 150-truck convoy 90 miles south of Hanoi.

#### INTERNATIONAL

**Thailand Guerrillas**—Increased Communist guerrilla activity forced the government of Thailand **Dec. 1** to declare martial law in 5 provinces. An estimated 2,000 members of the Communist Patriotic Front were believed operating in the country which previously had imposed martial law in 7 other provinces where the rebels had been particularly active.

**U. S.-France Consular Treaty**—Secy. of State Dean Rusk and French Ambassador to the U. S. Charles Lucet exchanged texts of a new consular treaty in Washington **Dec. 7**. The new treaty between the two countries replaced one in effect for the last 100 years.

**Cyprus Crisis Settled**—The Greek government began removing its troops from the island of Cyprus **Dec. 8** in accordance with a pact signed by Greece, Turkey and Cyprus that averted a war between Greece and Turkey. In mid-November clashes between Greek and Turkish Cypriots had brought the two countries to the brink of war, but mediation efforts by special U. S. envoy Cyrus Vance, the UN and NATO succeeded in heading off the conflict and bringing the principals to the negotiation table.

**Czechoslovakian Unrest**—An unheralded visit to Prague **Dec. 8** by Russian Communist Party Gen. Secy. Leonid Brezhnev reportedly saved Czech President and Communist Party boss Antonin Novotny from being ousted by Slovak dissidents in the Presidium. Novotny was reportedly accused of inept economic and party leadership and anti-Slovakian policies. In the year 3 writers were kicked out of the party in a crackdown by the Central Committee.

**King Flees Greece**—In an attempt to oust the military junta that seized control of Greece in April, King Constantine broadcast **Dec. 13** an appeal to the Greek people to support him in re-establishing a democratic government. Within hours it was apparent that the King had failed to rally the necessary military power to overcome the junta, and **Dec. 14** Constantine flew to exile in Rome with his family and close advisers. In the face of the attempted coup, the junta **Dec. 13** named a new cabinet with Col. George Papadapoulos as Premier and appointed a "regent" and "viceroy" to replace the King. The junta said in a broadcast the same day that "adventurers . . . misled the King." Subsequent negotiations by the junta for Constantine's peaceful return to Greece failed, and in late December Constantine and his entourage remained in Rome.

**New UN Member**—By acclamation the UN Assembly admitted to membership the People's Republic of Southern Yemen **Dec. 14**. Southern Yemen, formerly the British territory of Aden, thus became the 123rd member of the world organization.

**Dahomey Coup**—In a bloodless coup **Dec. 17** a 15-man military junta led by Maj. Maurice Kouandete ousted the Dahomey government of President Christophe Soglo. The coup followed a 5-day general strike that had paralyzed the country the previous week. The junta set up a provisional government **Dec. 18** and announced new elections would be held in 6 months.

**France Opposes Britain**—Opposition by France once again successfully stymied an attempt of Britain to join the European Economic Community or Common Market **Dec. 19**. Though 5 of France's partners in the Common Market favored negotiating Britain's application for mem-

bership, it became apparent that France would not alter its previous position and the issue was not brought to a vote for fear of provoking a French veto. Britain's membership bid "remained on the agenda," the Council said.

**New China A-Test**—Communist China conducted its 7th atmospheric nuclear test **Dec. 24,** the Atomic Energy Commission announced. The test took place in the Lob Nor area of China, the AEC said, and was "in the low yield range." For the first time, the Chinese failed to announce or confirm a nuclear test.

## GENERAL

**Cardinal Spellman Dies**—Francis Cardinal Spellman, archbishop of the New York Archdiocese of the Roman Catholic Church, died in New York **Dec. 2.** The body of the 78-year-old Cardinal, who had headed the New York Archdiocese since 1939, was placed on view in St. Patrick's Cathedral **Dec. 3.** Nine Cardinals took part in a requiem mass **Dec. 7** which was attended by President Johnson and Vice President Humphrey. Cardinal Spellman was interred in a crypt beneath the high altar of St. Patrick's.

**White House Wedding**—President Johnson's daughter Lynda, 23, was married to Marine Capt. Charles Robb, 28, in a White House ceremony **Dec. 9.** It was the first White House marriage of a President's daughter in 53 years.

**Harold Holt Drowns**—Australian Prime Minister Harold Holt disappeared in the surf while swimming off Cheviot Beach, Portsea, Victoria, **Dec. 17.** An air and sea search failed to recover the 59-year-old Holt's body and **Dec. 19,** John McEwen, leader of the Country Party, was sworn in as caretaker prime minister. Funeral services were held in Melbourne **Dec. 22,** and President Johnson attended the rites. President Johnson then went on to visit Thailand, South Vietnam and the Vatican, where he met with Pope Paul **Dec. 23,** before returning to Washington Christmas Eve.

**Vatican Peace Pleas**—Pope Paul VI's Christmas Message, delivered **Dec. 23,** appealed for peace in the world and in Vietnam. In a speech **Dec. 22** the Pontiff called for a halt to the bombing of North Vietnam and seemed to offer his services toward achieving peace. In a message to the heads of government and churches, revealed Dec. 15, the Pope suggested that Jan. 1, 1968, and all future New Year's days be observed as a "Day of Peace."

## DISASTERS

Sixty-seven killed **Dec. 8** when Faucett Airlines plane crashed near Midday, Peru . . . 9 women trampled to death in Vitoria, Brazil, **Dec. 9** in stampede to get free Christmas presents for children . . . Twin-engine plane crashed into Lake Monona, Wis., **Dec. 10,** killing 7 . . . Earthquake in Koyna Nagar, India, reported **Dec. 11** to have killed 172, left 1,000 homeless . . . Collapse of apartment house in Camboriu, Brazil, **Dec. 11** killed 6 . . . 18 persons dead, 15 injured in Iwiny, Poland, **Dec. 13** when small lake broke its bank and flooded community . . . Navy plane with 14 aboard reported missing **Dec. 14** on flight from Alaska to Oak Harbor, Washington . . . 46 killed **Dec. 15** in bridge collapse at Point Pleasant, W. Va. . . . Accidental quarry explosion **Dec. 16** killed 9 near Schaffhausen, Switzerland . . . 4 men burned to death, 30 injured **Dec. 18** when 60,000 pounds of molten metal fell on them in steel mill in Houston, Tex. . . . Tornado killed 4, injured 29 in northern Alabama **Dec. 18** . . . RAF plane crashed near Ft. William, Scotland, **Dec. 21,** killing 13 . . . Father and 4 children burned to death in house fire **Dec. 25** at Lake Winnepaug, Conn. . . . Bus overturned and fell in river near Tafi Del Valle, Argentina **Dec. 25,** killing 16, injuring 20 . . . Apartment house explosion in Moscow **Dec. 25** killed 9 . . . 9 children died in house fire **Dec. 29** in Mont Laurier, Quebec . . . 9 dead, 30,000 homeless reported in flood in Brazil **Dec. 29** . . . Twin-engine Beechcraft crashed into Lake Pontchartrain, La., **Dec. 31,** killing 6.

## First Human Heart Transplant Operations

Shortly before 1 a.m. **Dec. 3,** Denise Ann Darvall, 24, died at Grote Schuur Hospital in Capetown, South Africa, from injuries received in an auto accident. Within 5½ hours the dead woman's heart was beating in the chest of Louis Washkansky, and the world had witnessed the first successful human heart transplant operation.

Washkansky, a 55-year-old grocer whose own heart was damaged beyond repair, lived for 18 days before dying **Dec. 21** from double pneumonia.

The historic operation was performed by a 30-man surgery team led by Prof. Christian N. Barnard, 44. The chief postoperative danger was considered to be rejection of the foreign heart by the body's immunological defense mechanism. To suppress the rejection process, Washkansky was given large doses of steroids to overcome the body's natural defense, a procedure that also seriously weakened his ability to fight off infection.

Dr. Barnard's achievement was hailed by most medical authorities around the world, though some thought the operation upon a human subject to be premature in light of many unanswered questions connected with such an experimental technique.

Nevertheless, Dr. Barnard's pioneering was rapidly followed by an unsuccessful attempt to transplant the heart of an infant who had died of brain damage into a 2½-week-old baby at Maimonides Hospital in Brooklyn **Dec. 6.** The child, born

with a deformed heart, lived 6½ hours after surgery and Dr. Adrian Kantrowitz, who headed the surgical team, said death was not due to rejection.

On **Jan. 2, 1968,** Dr. Barnard performed the world's 3rd heart transplant operation. The recipient this time was Dr. Philip Blaiberg, 58, a retired dentist. In a 5-hour operation, Dr. Blaiberg was given the heart of Clive Haupt, 24, who had died of a stroke. Haupt, under South Africa's policy of apartheid, was classified as a "Cape colored." Dr. Blaiberg is white.

It was **Mar. 16** when Dr. Blaiberg, accompanied by his wife, Eileen, and Dr. Barnard, stepped through the doors of Groote Schuur Hospital and went home. Other transplant recipients were not as fortunate.

Mike Kasperak, a 54-year-old steel worker, was given **Jan. 6** the heart of Virginia Mae White, 43, a housewife who had died of a massive brain hemorrhage. The operation was performed at Stanford University Medical School by a surgical team headed by Dr. Norman Shumway. Kasperak died **Jan. 21** from a variety of medical complications.

By the end of August, 1968, a total of 34 human-to-human heart transplants had been performed and 11 of the recipients were still alive. At that time the longest-surviving recipient was Dr. Blaiberg, who had again shown improvement after sharp setbacks in June and July because of hepatitis and lung complications.

## January—1968

### NATIONAL

**Curtail Foreign Investments**—In an effort to bring the U. S. balance of international payments into line, President Johnson **Jan. 1** placed restrictions upon American investments abroad, and introduced a program to curb American travel to Europe, cut down on government spending in foreign countries and stimulate U. S. export sales. The measures were designed to cut the payments deficit by $3 billion in 1968. The 1967 payments deficit was between $3½ and $4 billion.

**Eshkol-LBJ Confer**—Israeli Premier Levi Eshkol renewed his country's request that the U. S. sell weapons to Israel when he met with President Johnson **Jan. 7-8** at the President's ranch in Texas. In a joint statement **Jan. 8** the President agreed to consider the request in light of Soviet military aid given to Arab countries since the Israeli-Arab war of June 1967.

**Swedes Give GIs Asylum**—Four American sailors who deserted in Japan in 1967 because of their objections to the Vietnam War were given asylum by Sweden **Jan. 9** on "humanitarian grounds." Other American servicemen, reportedly deserters from Army camps in West Germany, were also reported seeking political asylum in Sweden.

**U. S.-Cambodia**—The U. S. and Cambodia agreed **Jan. 12** on a policy to keep Cambodia from becoming embroiled in the Vietnam War. Viet Cong and North Vietnamese troops reportedly had been using Cambodia as a sanctuary for raids into Vietnam. In December reports circulated that a policy of "hot pursuit" by American and South Vietnamese forces was being considered in which the Allied forces would pursue the enemy into Cambodia.

**U. S. Aides Slain in Guatemala**—Two U. S. embassy military attaches were slain and two others wounded **Jan. 16** as part of a terror campaign by the Communist Rebel Armed Forces insurgents. In leaflets distributed in Guatemala City the same day, the Rebel Armed Forces said the shootings were in retaliation for the slaying **Jan. 12** of Rogelia Cruz Martinez, Miss Guatemala of 1950, who was suspected of leftist sympathies.

**State of The Union**—In a televised State-of-the-Union message before a joint session of Congress **Jan. 17**, President Johnson once again called upon Congress to enact a 10% income tax surcharge to reduce an estimated $20 billion budget deficit for 1968 to some $8 billion in 1969. The President also stressed the need for funds to attack the problems of decaying cities, unemployment, poverty and pollution, while continuing to spend $25 billion a year for the war in Vietnam. He outlined many specific areas where he hoped to see legislation, such as gun control, auto insurance and hazardous radiation. He reported that the fiscal budget for 1969 was $186 billion.

**H-Bomb Plane Crashes**—A Strategic Air Command B-52 carrying 4 unarmed hydrogen bombs crashed and exploded **Jan. 22** on frozen North Star Bay near Thule, Greenland, while on an alert flight. Radioactive material was spread over a wide area but there was no nuclear explosion. The wreckage burned through the ice and sank to the bottom of the bay. Six of the 7 crewmen survived after bailing out.

**Cabinet Resignation**—John Gardner, 55, resigned as Secy. of Health, Education

## Pueblo and 83-Man Crew Seized

The U. S. Navy electronic intelligence ship Pueblo and its 83-man crew were seized in the Sea of Japan **Jan. 23** by 4 North Korean patrol boats and taken prisoner to the port of Wonsan.

An early Defense Department report said 4 crewmen had been injured when the 906-ton vessel, loaded with sophisticated radar and electronic intercept equipment, was ordered to surrender or be fired upon by the North Korean boats and two circling MiG planes.

The North Koreans claimed that the Pueblo had violated the 12-mile limit of its territorial waters, but the U. S., initially, insisted it had been in international waters about 30 miles from shore.

In an atmosphere of mounting crisis the U. S. demanded at a meeting of the Mixed Armistice Commission in Panmunjon **Jan. 24** the immediate release of the ship and its crew. This was to be the first of many inconclusive meetings.

The Administration initiated a number of diplomatic and military moves designed to bring pressure on the North Koreans.

Secy. of State Dean Rusk **Jan. 24** said the seizure was "in a category of actions to be construed as an act of war."

President Johnson **Jan. 25** ordered to active duty 14,787 Navy and Air Force reservists to bolster a build-up of American forces in Korea. In a show of force, the nuclear powered aircraft carrier Enterprise and task force were shifted to positions off the North Korean coast in the Sea of Japan.

At the request of the U. S. the UN Security Council convened **Jan. 26** to consider the incident. On **Jan. 24** the American ambassador to the Soviet Union formally requested that the Russians try to persuade North Korea to release the ship and its crew.

Congressional reaction varied, from a demand that the Administration issue an ultimatum to North Korea to warnings against the U. S. taking any rash action.

The war scare crisis peaked **Jan. 26** when President Johnson in a nationwide television report castigated North Korea for recent military incidents along the demilitarized zone between North and South Korea and called the Pueblo seizure a "wanton and aggressive act" which "cannot be accepted." But at the same time, he called upon the world community to dissuade North Korea from its aggressive course and return the ship and crew.

For a short time after this speech it was unclear what the Administration's course would be. But as the days passed it became apparent that diplomatic action, further meetings at Panmunjon and persuasion would be pursued.

The North Koreans used the incident to full propaganda advantage, presenting to the world a series of alleged confessions and apologies by the Pueblo's captain, Comdr. Lloyd M. Bucher and members of the crew; calls for admission of guilt by the U. S., and threats to try the crew members as criminals.

Secy. of Defense Robert McNamara said in a TV interview **Feb. 4** that it was possible the Pueblo had entered North Korean territorial waters before its capture. McNamara said the intrusion could have occurred during a period of radio silence by the Pueblo **Jan. 10-21**, but there was no way of knowing for sure until the crew was questioned.

and Welfare **Jan. 25**, denying that his resignation was prompted by dissatisfaction with the Administration's Vietnam policy. President Johnson accepted the resignation, effective Mar. 1, "with regret." The White House said Gardner's departure "had nothing to do with Vietnam."

**Clifford Defense Secretary**—Clark M. Clifford, 61, was unanimously confirmed by the U. S. Senate to the office of Defense Secretary **Jan. 30**. President Johnson **Jan. 19** nominated Clifford to succeed Robert McNamara whose resignation from the post was announced Nov. 29, 1967. Clifford had been an adviser to both Presidents Truman and Kennedy.

**INTERNATIONAL**

**Cuba Rations Gas**—Cuban Premier Fidel Castro announced **Jan. 2** the imposition of gasoline and fuel oil rationing. Castro said the rationing was necessary because of Cuba's expanding economy and the inability of Russia to supply the growing demand for petroleum. The rationing came upon the 9th anniversary of the Castro regime.

**Nigeria Truce Offer**—The government of Nigeria offered **Jan. 5** to stop all military action against the break-away state of Biafra if the secessionists agreed to "discuss and negotiate" their differences with the Nigerian federal government. On **Jan. 16** the Biafran government accused Britain of planning to send 1,000 troops to aid the federal government. The British denied the charge the same day.

**New Prime Minister**—John Grey Gorton, 56, was sworn in **Jan. 10** as prime minister of Australia. Gorton, a member of the Senate, had been elected Liberal Party leader the previous day. The new prime minister succeeded John McEwen, who headed a caretaker government following the drowning of Harold Holt in December.

**Papandreou Assails Junta**—Andreas Papandreou, freed in a general Christmas amnesty by the ruling Greek military junta, flew to exile in Paris **Jan. 16**. Papandreou, 48, the son of ex-Premier George Papandreou and a former naturalized U. S. citizen, declared in a statement **Jan. 18** that the Greek regime was "oppressive and dictatorial" and said the democratic countries of the world had a moral responsibility to help oust the junta by denying them the weapons from which their power stems.

**British Spending Cuts**—In a series of moves designed to "make devaluation work," British Prime Minister Harold Wilson announced **Jan. 16** the complete withdrawal of British troops from the Far East and Persian Gulf by 1971; cancellation of 50 F-111 jets ordered from the U. S.; a prescription charge of 30 cents in the National Health Service care program; postponement until 1973 of plans to make school attendance mandatory until age 16 instead of the present age 15, and increased welfare payments to those "most in need" only.

**Atom Inspection Pact**—A revised draft of a treaty designed to halt the spread of nuclear weapons was submitted to the 18-member UN Disarmament Committee **Jan. 18** by the U. S. and USSR. The new draft of the treaty included an article providing for international inspection and control systems. The first version of the treaty, submitted in August 1967 by the two countries left the question of inspection and control unsettled.

**Novotny Ousted**—Antonin Novotny was ousted from his post as first secretary of the Czechoslovak Communist Party and replaced by 46-year-old Alexander Dubcek **Jan. 25**. Novotny reportedly lost a power struggle to Dubcek within the 10-member party presidium. The election of Dubcek, a Slovak, was viewed as a victory by the moderates over the Stalinist conservatives. Novotny retained his job as Czech president.

**Kosygin Visits India**—A state visit was paid to India by Soviet Premier Aleksei N. Kosygin **Jan. 25-31**. Kosygin's trip co-

---

## Viet Cong Hits Cities in Tet Offensive

Viet Cong and North Vietnamese forces believed to number 50,000 struck at 30 provincial capitals in South Vietnam **Jan. 30** on what was supposed to be the first day of a mutually agreed upon Tet or lunar New Year truce.

The ferocious Communist attacks caught Allied forces off guard, and Saigon and Hue became major battlefields with the Communists occupying buildings of the U. S. embassy in Saigon for 6 hours before being wiped out. In Hue, block by block fighting continued until **Feb. 24** when the last North Vietnamese troops holed up in the Imperial Palace were finally destroyed. Other cities also fell into Communist hands for a short time.

The attacks against the cities were launched, North Vietnam said **Jan. 30**, "to punish the American aggressors" for unilaterally canceling the Tet cease-fire agreement **Jan. 29** in South Vietnam's 5 northern provinces.

A clandestine Viet Cong broadcast **Jan. 30** urged the South Vietnamese to overthrow their government, saying ". . . the revolution we waited and yearned for has broken out . . ."

**Feb. 2** President Johnson called the enemy offensive "a complete failure" both militarily and psychologically and predicted a new Communist offensive just below the demilitarized zone, particularly at the U. S. Marine base at Khe Sanh, where 5,000 GIs were virtually surrounded by an estimated 20,000 to 40,000 Communists.

U. S. commanders reported **Feb. 8** record American casualties for any single week of the war to date with 416 killed and 2,757 wounded from **Jan. 28 to Feb. 3**. South Vietnamese casualties for the same period were 784 killed and 2,230 wounded with the Communists losing 15,515 men.

Gen. William C. Westmoreland, commander of American forces in South Vietnam, said **Feb. 25** that the enemy had "suffered a military defeat," but had won "some temporary psychological advantage."

The Tet offensive did fail to make any lasting military head-way or to create a popular uprising against the government. But it did create 350,000 new refugees and put a halt, temporarily, to the pacification program.

In addition, the surprising enemy military capability, in areas often said by American military leaders to be secure from such attacks, had a strong psychological impact on much of the American public, which had been led to believe the U. S. had turned the corner in its fight for South Vietnam.

The Administration's conduct of the war came in for much criticism and President Johnson at a press conference **Feb. 16** stressed his continued confidence in Gen. Westmoreland. But **Mar. 22** President Johnson named Westmoreland Army Chief of Staff, an assignment that would bring him home by July.

incided with the 18th anniversary of India's independence. A joint statement by the Soviet Premier and Indian Prime Minister Indira Gandhi was issued **Jan. 31** urging an "unconditional stoppage" of the bombing of North Vietnam. A halt in the bombing would "create conditions for negotiations aimed at a political settlement," the statement said.

### GENERAL

**Dr. Spock Indicted**—Dr. Benjamin Spock, 64, well-known pediatrician and child-care author, was indicted along with four other outspoken critics of the Vietnam war by a Federal grand jury in Boston **Jan. 5.** The four were accused of conspiring to abet, aid and counsel violations of the Selective Service Act. The four indicted with Dr. Spock were the Rev. William Sloane Coffin Jr., 43, chaplain of Yale University; novelist Mitchell Goodman, 44; Marcus Raskin, 33, of the Institute for Policy Studies; and Michael Ferber, 23, a graduate student at Harvard. After the indictment, Dr. Spock told a press conference that resisting the draft was "a very patriotic endeavor requiring enormous amounts of courage—the most effective way of opposing the war."

**Singer Assails Vietnam War**—Singer Eartha Kitt at a White House luncheon and meeting of 50 white and Negro women **Jan. 18** angrily denounced the war in Vietnam and blamed it for the rioting and juvenile delinquency throughout the country. The luncheon given by Mrs. Lyndon B. Johnson, was for the purpose of discussing the Administration's proposals for combating crime on the streets. Miss Kitt told Mrs. Johnson: "You send the best of this country off to be shot and maimed. They rebel in the streets . . . They don't want to go to school because they're going to be snatched off from their mothers to be shot in Vietnam." Mrs. Johnson, in a trembling voice and with tears in her eyes replied: "Because there is a war on—and I pray that there will be a just and honest peace—that still doesn't give us a free ticket not to try to work for better things such as against crime in the streets, better education and better health for our people."

### DISASTERS

Eight killed in head-on auto crash **Jan. 6** near Harrisonburg, Va. . . . Manchester-London express train hit truck near Hixon, England, **Jan. 6,** killing 13, injuring 50 . . . 43 killed **Jan. 7** near Hamyang, S. Korea, when bus plunged into river . . . Brooklyn, N. Y., tenement fire killed 9 children, 4 adults **Jan. 9** . . . Marine Corps C-54 crashed **Jan. 10** near Battle Mountain, Nev., killing 19 . . . 5 dead in house fire near Zebulon, N. C., **Jan. 14** . . . **Jan. 15** earthquakes hit western Sicily, 206 dead, 80,000 homeless . . . 125 mph. winds swept Scotland **Jan. 15,** killing 20 . . . Blizzards in Jordan reported **Jan. 16** to have killed 13 . . . Lebanese storm killed 12, injured 25 **Jan. 16** . . . USAF jet tanker crashed and burned on take-off in Minot, N. D., **Jan. 17,** killing all 13 aboard . . . Pile-up of 18 vehicles in fog near Louisville, Ky., **Jan. 17,** killed 5, injured 15 . . . 7 killed in Chacabuco, Argentina, when 750-ft. TV tower under construction collapsed **Jan. 18** . . . Thai Airways International jet collided in mid-air with Thai army plane near Bangkok **Jan. 21,** 6 aboard army plane killed . . . Boat capsized in Ganges near Benares, India, **Jan. 22,** drowning 40 . . . **Jan. 22** heat wave in Rio de Janeiro, Brazil, reported to have killed 29 . . . 12 reported dead in collision of American freighter and Japanese fishing boat **Jan.**

25 off Kyushu, Japan . . . New quake in Sicily killed 7, injured 55 **Jan. 25** . . . Israeli sub Dakar with 69 aboard reported missing off Cyprus **Jan. 25** . . . French submarine Minerva reported missing in Mediterranean **Jan. 27** with 52 aboard . . . 20 reported killed **Jan. 28** in avalanches in Swiss alps . . . Train crash near General Camara, Brazil, killed 24 **Jan. 28** . . . 7 feared dead in shopping center explosion in Ingram, Pa., **Jan. 30.**

## February—1968

### NATIONAL

**LBJ's Economic Report**—President Johnson submitted to Congress **Feb. 1** his Economic Report on the state of the country's economy. The President warned of the dangers of inflation, stressing the need for his proposed 10% tax surcharge and a tighter rein on wages and prices. The President told Congress we must ". . . put our financial affairs in order . . . slow down the wage-price spiral . . . restore equilibrium in our international accounts . . . deal more effectively with our urban problems . . . expand the opportunities available to every citizen—especially our disadvantaged."

**LBJ On Education**—President Johnson in a special message to Congress **Feb. 5** urged passage of a $3½ billion education program for 1969 to be administered by the Office of Education. The President called his message "The 5th Freedom," which he said was the "freedom from ignorance." Specific bills proposed were an Educational Opportunity Act of 1968 dealing with student loans, scholarship programs and Federal fellowships and a Network for Knowledge Act to spur the pooling of information by colleges through computer networks.

**LBJ On Crime**—In a message to Congress **Feb. 7** President Johnson outlined a series of proposals to deal with crime in the United States and said that $557,000,000 in Federal expenditures would be needed in this area in fiscal 1969. The President's proposals ranged from passage of the Safe Streets & Crime Control Act proposed Feb. 6, 1967, to effective gun control laws and a Right to Privacy Act. The President made it clear that states and cities had the major responsibility for the control and prevention of crime.

**State Visit by Wilson**—On an official state visit to the U. S. **Feb. 8-9,** British Prime Minister Harold Wilson conferred with President Johnson. The two discussed the balance-of-payments deficit, Britain's withdrawal of all its forces from the Far East by 1971, and Wilson's visit to the Soviet Union **Jan. 22-24.** In Moscow, Wilson had talked with the leaders of the Soviet Union, and in a joint statement **Jan. 24** both countries backed a "political settlement" to the Vietnam war.

**Vietnam War**—UN Secy. Gen. U Thant, following his tour of Asian and European capitals **Feb. 7-14,** said **Feb. 24** that if the U. S. bombing of the North was stopped "meaningful talks . . . will take place much earlier than generally supposed . . ." But in South Vietnam Allied forces continued mopping up operations in Hue, and the Communists sustained military pressure by shelling military posts and cities throughout South Vietnam in a coordinated attack **Feb. 18.** The Communists also continued to tighten the siege of the Marine outpost of Khe Sanh.

**Pueblo Meetings**—Meetings between U. S. and North Korean officials at Panmunjom to discuss the Pueblo incident were held **Feb. 14, 15, 19, 20,** and **26.** The question of

the release of the Pueblo and its crew was not resolved and other violations and aspects of the Korean armistice were discussed by the negotiators. The U. S. State Department warned North Korea **Feb. 18** not to punish the Pueblo crew as it had threatened to do.

**Vance Reports to LBJ**—Special envoy Cyrus Vance reported to President Johnson in Washington **Feb. 15** upon his return from South Korea after concluding his special mission there. Before Vance left Seoul **Feb. 15** a joint statement was issued by him and the South Korean government noting the increasing North Korean belligerency. The statement indicated at least a temporary rejection by the U. S. of South Korean demands for major U. S. strikes against any new North Korean aggression.

**Payments Deficit**—The U. S. balance-of-payments deficit totalled $1.832 billion in the final 3 months of 1967, the Commerce Department reported **Feb. 15**. The total deficit for 1967 was $3.572 billion. The last quarter deficit was described by Treasury Secy. Fowler as "the worst . . . since the 3rd quarter of 1950 following the outbreak of the Korean war."

**LBJ On War Talks**—President Johnson in a press conference **Feb. 16** said he did not think the North Vietnamese were any more ready to negotiate today than they had been over the last 2 years. Recent peace probes by the U. S., the President said, had gone "as far as honorable men could go." The following day, **Feb. 17**, the President visited Pope Air Force Base in N. C., and El Toro (Calif.) Marine Corps Naval Station where he talked with combat troops on their way to Vietnam.

**New Commerce Secretary**—The Senate confirmed the nomination of Cyrus Rowlett Smith, 68, as Secretary of Commerce **Feb. 29**. Smith, chairman of the board of American Airlines, was designated for the office by the President **Feb. 16**. He succeeded Alexander B. Trowbridge, 37, who resigned for reasons of health. The new secretary took office Mar. 1.

**Tonkin Attack Hearings**—Administration officials and members of the Senate Foreign Relations committee engaged in a hassle **Feb. 20-26** over the facts concerning the attacks on 2 U. S. destroyers by the North Vietnamese in August, 1964,

which led to the passage by Congress of the Gulf of Tonkin resolution. In its hearings into the matter, the Committee heard closed-door testimony by Secy. of Defense Robert McNamara **Feb. 20**. McNamara issued a public statement after his appearance declaring that intelligence reports of a "highly classified and unimpeachable nature" had established that the 2nd Tonkin attack of Aug. 4 had taken place. Sen. J. W. Fulbright (D.-Ark.) **Feb. 21** accused McNamara of "giving only one side of the story."

**LBJ Dallas Speech**—In a speech in Dallas, Tex., **Feb. 27**, President Johnson declared that the enemy's Tet offensive in Vietnam had failed and told his audience: "There must be no weakening of will that would encourage the enemy and prolong the bloody conflict." The President said U. S. and South Vietnamese forces had "answered aggression's onslaught with one strong voice," declaring, " 'No retreat.' " "That must be our answer, too, here at home. No retreat from responsibility of the hour and the day."

**McNamara's Medal**—The Medal of Freedom was presented to departing Secy. of Defense Robert McNamara by President Johnson in a White House ceremony **Feb. 28**. The President praised the outgoing secretary, named to head the World Bank. McNamara's successor, Clark M. Gifford, was sworn into office at the White House **Mar. 1**.

## INTERNATIONAL

**Pro-Soviet Cubans Tried**—Thirty-five persons were convicted of anti-revolutionary activity in Havana **Feb. 3** and sentenced to terms in jail ranging up to 15 years. The chief defendant was Anibal Escalante, 58, former Cuban Communist Party secretary, who got 15 years for allegedly giving "false information" to Russian, Czechoslovak and East German officials and promulgating "propaganda" unfavorable to Fidel Castro.

**Canadian Constitution**—The long process of revising the Canadian constitution was begun **Feb. 5-7** when a Federal Provincial Constitutional Conference was held in Ottawa. The conference was attended by Prime Minister Lester Pearson and the 10 provincial premiers. The conference agreed that French and English should both be official Canadian languages, and

## Report To The President On Civil Disorders

After 7 months of study the President's National Advisory Commission on Civil Disorders released **Feb. 29** a summary of its 1,400-page report on the summer riots of 1967.

The commission's major findings were:
• The U. S. "is moving toward 2 societies, one black, one white—separate and unequal," but it is still possible to head off this division.
• White racism is the chief cause of the Negro violence and riots.
• To reverse the situation calls for unprecedented levels of "funding and performance" but "there can be no higher priority for national action and no higher claim on the nation's conscience."

The 11-member commission, headed by Gov. Otto Kerner of Illinois, was appointed by President Johnson July 27, 1967, to investigate the nature of the riots, discover their causes and determine how future riots could be avoided.

The commission found that the riots were not organized or part of any conspiracy but happened because of an accumulation of social ills such as unem-

ployment, inadequate housing, discriminatory police practices and various complex social processes.

As to the cause of the riots, the underlying factor was found to be ". . . the racial attitude and behavior of white Americans toward black Americans."

The commission made more than 150 specific recommendations for removing the causes of racial unrest. Some of the recommendations:
• Creation of 2,000,000 new jobs in the next 3 years.
• Decentralization of city governments to make them more responsive to the needs of their people.
• A national system of income supplements based on need.
• New low and moderate income housing.

The commission report received the backing of most of the civil rights leaders in the country.

But there was much adverse reaction, especially to the central findings of the commission that white racism was the root cause of the riots.

it set up a series of committees to draw up a new constitution.

**Israeli-Jordan Fighting**—The Jordan River was the scene of clashes between Israeli and Jordanian forces during the 3 weeks ending **Feb. 16**, with Israeli planes hitting military targets up to 10 miles inside Jordan. **Feb. 1** UN Secy. General U Thant said a clash between Israeli and Egyptian forces could permanently stop the clearing of the Suez Canal. An exchange of gunfire across the canal **Jan. 30** led to the cancellation of an agreement to clear the southern part of the canal.

**Pearson Confidence Vote**—Canadian Prime Minister Lester B. Pierson hurried back to Ottawa from a Jamaican vacation **Feb. 20** following the defeat in the House of Commons **Feb. 19** of a major Liberal tax measure. By **Feb. 28** Pearson had whipped up sufficient support to have the House give his Liberal government a 138-119 vote of confidence.

### GENERAL

**Nixon Enters Race**—Former Vice President Richard Nixon **Feb. 1** formally declared himself a candidate for the Republican nomination for President. Nixon's candidacy was announced in an open letter to New Hampshire voters as an opening shot in his primary election campaign in that state.

**Wallace 3rd Party Candidate**—George C. Wallace, former Democratic Governor of Alabama, announced in Washington **Feb. 8** his candidacy for the Presidency on a 3rd party ticket. If elected, Wallace said, he would keep peace in the streets if it took "30,000 troops . . . with 2-foot-long bayonets." He also said he would change the "so-called civil rights laws" which are in reality "an attack on property rights . . . free enterprise . . . and local government."

**Report On Newark Riot**—A 478-page report on the July, 1967, Newark riot was issued by the Governor's Select Commission on Civil Disorder in New Jersey **Feb. 10**. The report found "excessive and unjustified force" by the National Guard and police and asked for a grand jury probe of charges of corruption in Newark's government. The report contained 100 specific recommendations for change covering the areas of city government, housing, police, municipal courts, welfare, employment, riot procedures and anti-poverty programs.

**ADA Backs McCarthy**—By a vote of 65-47, the national board of Americans for Democratic Action **Feb. 10** endorsed the Presidential candidacy of Sen. Eugene McCarthy (D.-Minn.). Within 3 days after the vote several prominent labor leaders and Administration backers resigned from the ADA board. It was the first time in 20 years that the organization did not support an incumbent Democratic president.

**Draft Deferments Curtailed**—Draft deferments for most graduate students and all occupational deferments were eliminated **Feb. 16** by the National Security Council. Deferments would be granted only to graduate students in critical areas in medicine, optometry, dentistry, veterinary medicine, and those students who will have completed 2 or more years of graduate work by June, 1968, the Council said.

**Romney Quits Race**—In a surprise announcement in Washington **Feb. 28**, Michigan's Gov. George Romney pulled out of the Republican race for the Presidential nomination. The move came just 12 days before the New Hampshire primary and

Romney said he was withdrawing because he had failed to get the broad-based Republican support he had hoped to achieve. There was speculation that private polls had indicated he would do poorly in New Hampshire. The fact that New York's Gov. Rockefeller, one of his main supporters, had said **Feb. 24** that he was himself available for a draft was also thought to be a factor in the decision.

### DISASTERS

Boston hotel fire **Feb. 4** killed 9, injured 15 . . . British fishing trawler with 19 aboard reported lost off Iceland **Feb. 5** . . . 6 killed in head-on crash between pickup truck and tractor trailer near Findlay, Ohio, **Feb. 6** . . . F-100 jet crashed into house in Indianapolis **Feb. 8**, killing pilot and 2 residents . . . Father and 8 children dead in fire **Feb. 11** in Howick, Quebec . . . 11 killed in house fire in Franklin, Pa., **Feb. 11** . . . Fire in Acapulco hotel killed 4 **Feb. 11** . . . 18 dead **Feb. 12** in Hong Kong fire . . . Boeing 727 Chinese Nationalist Civil Air Transport crashed at Taipei International Airport **Feb. 16**, killing 21 . . . Arson blaze in tavern in Moberly, Mo., killed 12 **Feb. 16** . . . Earthquake rocked Greek Islands in Aegean Sea **Feb. 16**, killing 19 . . . Holland, Pa., house fire **Feb. 18** killed 4 . . . House fire **Feb. 21** near Gleichen, Alberta, killed 7 children . . . Bus plunged off cliff near Ponte Nova, Brazil, **Feb. 24**, killing 13 . . . Shrewsbury, Eng., mental hospital fire killed 22, injured 14 **Feb. 26** . . . Gas tank truck exploded in Mexico City **Feb. 26**, 8 killed, 70 injured.

## March—1968

### NATIONAL

**Pueblo Letter**—An open letter, allegedly from the crew of the Pueblo, was received by President Johnson **Mar. 4**. The letter told the President the U. S. must admit the Pueblo had violated North Korean waters, apologize for the act and give promises it would not happen again, before the Pueblo crew would be released.

**Westmoreland to New Post**—Gen. William C. Westmoreland was named by President Johnson **Mar. 22** to the post of Army chief of staff. Following confirmation by the Senate, Westmoreland was scheduled to give up his command in Vietnam and take up his new duties in Washington July 2.

**Shriver Ambassador to France**—R. Sargent Shriver was named ambassador to France by President Johnson **Mar. 22**. The former head of the Peace Corps and Office of Economic Opportunity succeeded Charles E. Bohlen, who was appointed Deputy State Undersecretary for political affairs in December, 1967.

**New HEW Secretary**—Wilbur Joseph Cohen, 55, was named by President Johnson **Mar. 22** to head the department of Health, Education and Welfare. Cohen succeeded John Gardner, who resigned **Mar. 1**.

**NORAD Extended**—The U. S. and Canada agreed **Mar. 30** to extend the 10-year North American Air Defense Command (NORAD) treaty another 5 years. The pact, designed for the defense of North America from long-range bombing attack, would not commit Canada to partake in continental defense against missiles, Canadian External Affairs Min. Paul Martin had told a Parliamentary committee **Mar. 7**.

### INTERNATIONAL

**Britain Curbs Immigration**—A bill drastically restricting the immigration of Asian British citizens to Great Britain became

law **Mar. 1** when the House of Lords rejected by a vote of 109-85 a motion to kill the law. The controversial legislation was approved by the House of Commons **Feb. 27** by a vote of 372-62. The bill was passed to curb the possible immigration by some 200,000 Asians from Kenya, where non-citizens were being deprived of jobs.

**Belgium Government Ousted**—The Belgium parliament was dissolved by King Baudouin **Mar. 1** in anticipation of new elections after several attempts to form a new government had failed. The administration of Premier Paul Vanden Boeynant resigned Feb. 7 after failing to solve a language problem between the Flemish-speaking and French-speaking students at the Roman Catholic University of Louvain. The Flemish students had demanded the ouster of all French-speaking students.

**Nasser Drops War Charge**—President Nasser of the United Arab Republic admitted in an interview published **Mar. 4** that U. S. planes had not aided Israel in the June 1967 war. In an interview printed in Look magazine, Nasser said that the approach of Israeli planes from the Mediterranean had been misinterpreted, since American aircraft carriers were known to be in the same general area.

**Rhodesian Hangings**—The Rhodesian government defied Great Britain and hanged 3 black Africans **Mar. 6** and two others **Mar. 11.** Queen Elizabeth had commuted the sentences of the 5 convicted murderers **Mar. 2**, but Rhodesia's High Court ignored the decree and ordered the executions.

**Warsaw Student Riots**—Apparently inspired by the liberalizing trend in Czechoslovakia, students at Poland's University of Warsaw **Mar. 8-9** clashed with police, shouting: "Down with censorship" and "Long live Czechoslovakia." The student clashes were followed **Mar. 11** by protests by office and factory workers who fought police and militia men in downtown Warsaw. The Communist party blamed the riots on Zionists. Polish Communist anti-Semitism had reportedly been on the rise since the Israeli-Arab war of 1967.

**Panama Crisis**—The National Assembly of Panama **Mar. 14** voted to impeach President Marco Robles for interfering in the political campaign for a scheduled May 12 election. The Assembly accused Robles

of dismissing public employees and misusing state funds in behalf of National Liberation Party candidate David Samudio and against opposition leader Dr. Arnulfo Arias. Robles said **Mar. 15** he would not recognize the Assembly's action and would wait for a Supreme Court ruling on the move. He ordered the country's only military force, the National Guard, to ignore the Assembly vote. The still defiant Assembly **Mar. 24** voted to oust Robles and named Max Delvalle, 57, to succeed him. Robles again refused to recognize the Assembly's action and was backed by the 4,800-man Guard unit. **Mar. 24-29** saw numerous clashes between the Guard and populace as the political stalemate continued.

**Israeli-Arab Clashes**—An Israeli force of 15,000 men crossed into Jordan **Mar. 21** and wiped out guerrilla bases used to stage raids into Israel. The action was unanimously condemned by the UN Security Council **Mar. 24.** A second incident occurred **Mar. 29** when Israeli and Jordanian forces fought an 8-hour artillery duel along the Jordan River in which Israel used airplanes. The UN Security Council met **Mar. 30-Apr. 4** but was unable to decide upon a course of action.

**Novotny Quits**—The democratization of Czechoslovakia increased in tempo **Mar. 22** when President Antonin Novotny resigned his post. The resignation was forced **Mar. 21** by the National Assembly committee, which unanimously recommended that he resign. His ouster was viewed by many as the end of Stalinism in Czechoslovakia.

## GENERAL

**ACLU Reverses Position**—By a vote of 26-20 the national board of the American Civil Liberties Union decided **Mar. 2** to defend persons accused of counseling evasion of the draft. The action reversed a previous stand on the subject taken by the board in January.

**Bishop Cooke Appointed**—The Most Rev. Terence J. Cooke was named auxiliary bishop and vicar general of the New York archdiocese of the Roman Catholic Church by Pope Paul VI, **Mar. 8.** The 47-year-old successor to the late Cardinal Spellman became auxiliary bishop in 1965 and was appointed episcopal vicar for Manhattan and the Bronx in 1966. Bishop Cooke was selected by the Pontiff

---

## Gold Crisis: Two-Price System Emerges

International gold buying fever on a gigantic scale hit the markets of the world **Mar. 1**, fed by the fear and belief that the U. S. would be unable to continue to maintain the $35-an-ounce price of gold.

In just 10 trading days, an estimated 900 tons of gold was sold in the London market, which normally handles 3 to 5 tons daily. By **Mar. 15** speculation had pushed the price of gold in the Paris market to an all-time high of $44.36 an ounce.

At a 2-day meeting in Basel, Switzerland, **Mar 9-10** the U. S. and its 6 European partners in the London Gold Pool stressed their determination to continue to sell gold to all comers at $35 an ounce. But the declaration failed to stem the speculative tide and when 225 tons of gold were sold in London **Mar. 14**, Britain closed the London market until Apr. 11 at the request of the U. S. All other European gold markets, with the exception of Paris, also closed down. France had withdrawn from the London Gold Pool in 1967.

The London Gold Pool members met in Washington **Mar. 17** to face the crisis of

their rapidly dwindling gold reserves and agreed that all gold transactions between governments would continue to be made at $35 an ounce, but that they would no longer sell gold to private investors.

The reasons for the crisis, called by many economists the worst threat to the world's economy since the 1930s depression, seemed obvious to many.

The U. S. balance of payments for 1967 chalked up a $3.572 billion deficit and Congress continued to delay action on President Johnson's proposed tax increases.

Further, speculators had taken off after the U. S. dollar following the devaluation of the British pound Nov. 18, 1967, and even some governments, possibly France, which openly wanted a return to the gold standard, were believed to be behind a large part of the buying.

The new two-price system, many economists believed, was only a temporary answer to the crisis and would have to be followed by U. S. monetary reform and other changes in the international monetary system if a show-down international financial crisis was to be averted.

over many senior prelates, and it was believed he had been singled out by Cardinal Spellman as a possible successor before he died.

**Convict Air Force Captain**—Air Force Capt. Dale E. Noyd was convicted **Mar. 8** in Clovis, N. M., of disobeying an order to train pilots for Vietnam duty. Noyd, 34, a 12-year veteran, said he conscientiously opposed the war in Vietnam but was not a pacifist. He had attempted to resign his commission but the Air Force refused to accept the resignation. **Mar. 9** he was sentenced to a year at hard labor and dismissed from the Air Force.

### DISASTERS

Seven children killed in farmhouse fire **Mar. 1** near Lake City, Mich. . . . Air France Boeing 707 jetliner crashed into mountain **Mar. 5** at Pointe-A-Pitre, Guadeloupe, killing 63 aboard . . . Coal mine fire and blast killed 21 miners in Patterson, La., **Mar. 5** . . . Rooming house fire in Houston, Tex., **Mar. 6** killed 8 . . . 9 servicemen drowned **Mar. 7** when canoe capsized in Potomac near Quantico, Va. . . . Bus and car collided near Baker, Calif. **Mar. 7**, 20 killed, 12 injured . . . 150 feared dead in mountain slide that buried Luhonga, Congo, **Mar. 8** . . . DC-6 crashed at Saint-Denis, Reunion Island, **Mar. 9**, 19 dead . . . Storm in north Congo killed 10 **Mar. 9** . . . Hyderabad, India, express train hit bus **Mar. 9**, killing 9, injuring 44 . . . Private plane crashed into Lake Michigan **Mar. 9** killed 6 . . . Meriden, Conn., apartment house fire killed 5 **Mar. 9** . . . 26 killed, 80 injured **Mar. 15** when a trolley and train collided in Santa Maria De La Alameda, Spain . . . Ship and oil barge collision and fire killed 15, injured 25 **Mar. 16** near Pointe A La Hache, La. . . . Berserk woodsman killed 7, wounded 3 **Mar. 16** in Ironwood, Mich. . . . Bus and truck collided near Lagoas, Nigeria, **Mar. 16**, killing 19, injuring 12 . . . 9 died when twin-engine Beechcraft BE-18 crashed

while landing at Municipal Airport in Rapid City, S. D., **Mar. 17** . . . Car crash in Benson, N. C., **Mar. 17**, killed 6 . . . 27 killed **Mar. 18** when bus left road near Rampur, India . . . 6 women phone operators died in leap from building to escape fire in Pusan, S. Korea. **Mar. 18** . . . 31 killed, 34 injured **Mar. 20** when trains collided at Yalvigi, India . . . Irish International Viscount 4-engine turboprop crashed into Irish Sea **Mar. 24**, killing 61 . . . Omaha, Neb., hotel fire **Mar. 26** killed 5 . . . 60 reported drowned **Mar. 28** when boat capsized near Chapra, India . . . Two-car crash killed 8 **Mar. 29** near Unionville, Mich.

## April—1968

### NATIONAL

**Khesanh Siege Lifted**—Operation Pegasus, launched **Apr. 1** with a force of 30,000 Americans and South Vietnamese to relieve the U. S. Marine base at Khesanh, succeeded in lifting the siege by **Apr. 5**, 76 harrowing days after what had loomed as another Dienbienphu. Much of the 20,000-man North Vietnamese force which had surrounded the 6,000-man garrison since January was believed to have withdrawn to Laos before the Allied drive had started. A relief column from Calu, 15 miles to the east, met little enemy resistance as it moved along the only overland supply road to the base. Maj. Gen. John J. Tolson, commander of the 1st Cavalry Div. (Airmobile), which supplied most of the troops, headed the operation. Until the main relief column arrived **Apr. 8**, armed helicopters attacked North Vietnamese in forward positions as allied forces advanced and nearly 1,000 U. S. relief troops were flown to the base **Apr. 6**.

**Heavy Fighting in Vietnam**—Operation Complete Victory, a 5-nation allied force of 100,000 men, **Apr. 8** launched the biggest drive of the war to clean up Communist forces in the 11 provinces around Saigon,

## Campaign '68: A Year of Political Surprises

"I shall not seek, and I will not accept, the nomination of my party for another term as your President."

With these 20 words, President Lyndon B. Johnson **Mar. 31** climaxed a series of startling domestic political developments which already had turned the Presidential campaign year of 1968 into one of the most unusual on record.

The President dropped his political bombshell toward the end of a 40-minute, nationally televised speech dealing with Vietnam in which he also announced the unilateral halting of the bombing of 90% of the territory of North Vietnam. He asked Hanoi to make some movement toward the peace conference table.

After his speech, it was reported that the President had been thinking of not seeking re-election for some time and that he almost had made the withdrawal announcement in his State-of-the-Union message.

But many political observers saw the surprising showing of Minnesota's Sen. Eugene J. McCarthy in the New Hampshire primary election **Mar. 12** and the subsequent entry of Sen. Robert F. Kennedy into the race for the Democratic presidential nomination as possible contributing factors in the President's decision.

Sen. McCarthy, an avowed foe of the Administration's Vietnam policy, polled a surprising 42% of the Democratic vote in New Hampshire against a 48% organized write-in for President Johnson. On the

Republican side, Richard Nixon got 79% of the vote, and Gov. Nelson Rockefeller 11% on a write-in.

The possible political implications of McCarthy's strength apparently were not lost upon Sen. Robert Kennedy, who **Mar. 16** officially announced his candidacy for the Democratic nomination. Many recalled that just a few months earlier Kennedy had been saying he would support President Johnson for re-election and that he couldn't see himself as a candidate under any circumstances.

The President's withdrawal from the race brought one other candidate into the field, Vice President Hubert Humphrey, who officially announced his candidacy **Apr. 27**.

The developments on the Republican side of the campaign were almost as unusual as the turnabout in the Democratic race.

Michigan's Gov. George Romney in a surprise move **Feb. 28** pulled out of the race, leaving the former Vice President Nixon the only avowed Republican seeking the nomination.

New York's Gov. Rockefeller pulled his own surprise **Mar. 21** by declaring he was not an active candidate at a press conference many believed had been called to announce his active candidacy. But President Johnson's decision apparently also had its influence here, and Gov. Rockefeller held another press conference **Apr. 30** and this time did the expected, entering the race.

but failed to make contact with an estimated force of 18,000-20,000 believed to be there. A ground sweep **Apr. 1** to clear the coastal plain from Hue to Quangtri of North Vietnamese believed to be infiltrating the Ashau Valley was backed by heavy B-52 raids **Apr. 8-13** near the Cambodian border. As of **Apr. 13**, the U. S. Command reported 503 of the enemy and 57 Americans killed in the ground action. **Apr. 10**, a U. S. report said the enemy's Tet offensive had cost $173,633,000 in damage, with 115,276 homes damaged or razed. Operation Delaware in the Ashau Valley, described as one of the enemy's "top logistical support bases," by Gen. Tolson, started **Apr. 19**. Ten U. S. helicopters were reported shot down by enemy antiaircraft, while 20 Americans and 50 North Vietnamese were reported killed the first day. U. S. planes carried out 155 raids over North Vietnam **Apr. 23** and 111 **Apr. 24**.

**Reserve Call-Up**—A major call-up of reservists to active duty in Vietnam by 3 of the armed forces was announced by Defense Secy. Clark M. Clifford **Apr. 11**. It was to affect 24,000 Army, Air Force and Navy Reservists, of whom about 10,000 would go to the war zone in coming weeks to back up the 11,000 combat troops sent in February after the enemy's Tet offensive. The only previous call during the war occurred in the wake of the Pueblo incident, when 14,787 Air and Naval Reservists were ordered to active duty (Jan. 5). But these men had not gone overseas by mid-April. A new troop ceiling of 549,000 for U. S. strength in Vietnam was also announced by Clifford.

**Johnson Signs Rights Bill**—President Johnson **Apr. 11** signed the civil rights bill, banning racial discrimination in the sale or rental of 80% of the nation's housing, a day after the House passed it 250-171, spurred by the assassination of the Rev. Dr. Martin Luther King, Jr. and the widespread riots that followed. The House action was termed "a victory for every American" by the President, having come after "a long, tortuous and difficult road." The measure also made it a Federal crime to harm civil rights workers, to cross a state line to incite a riot or to instruct persons in the use of firearms or Molotov cocktails in riots. It further guaranteed broad rights to American Indians in their dealings with authorities from tribal to state or Federal levels.

**North Korean Raids**—North Korean soldiers ambushed a U. S. Army truck 1,000 yards below the demilitarized zone **Apr. 14**, killing 2 American and 2 South Korean soldiers and wounding 2 from the U. S. **Apr. 18** the Seoul government report-

## Assassin's Bullet Kills Martin Luther King

A sniper's bullet killed the Rev. Dr. Martin Luther King, Jr., 39, Nobel prize winner and leader of the nonviolence civil rights movement, in Memphis, Tenn., **Apr. 4**.

Fear and violence mounted as the shock of the assassination spread across the nation and set off a wave of Negro rioting and looting in U. S. cities.

By **Apr. 14**, at least 46 persons were killed, more than 2,600 were injured and more than 21,270 arrested. In less than 24 hours after King's murder, as rioting spread in Washington, D. C., President Johnson ordered Federal troops to protect the nation's capital. Across the nation, National Guard troops were alerted and the U. S. Army took "precautionary measures." Of the 55,000 troops involved, 21,000 were Federal and 34,000 were National Guardsmen.

**Apr. 4-11** saw racial violence in 125 cities in 29 states and the District of Columbia. Baltimore, Chicago, Kansas City, Mo., and Washington, D. C., were hardest hit. More than 2,600 fires were set. Property damage in assured losses alone was more than $45,000,000

President Johnson, expressing the nation's grief in a TV address lauding the slain Negro leader, urged "every citizen to reject the blind violence that has struck Dr. King, who lived by nonviolence."

Dr. King, who had returned to Memphis to prepare a 2d march in support of a strike by city garbage collectors, most of whom are Negroes, was shot on the balcony of his motel room. The assassin presumably had fired from a nearby rooming house.

Atty. Gen Ramsey Clark flew to Memphis **Apr. 5**, where he said the FBI was hunting the assassin, a white man who was reported to have been seen fleeing the area in a late-model car, in several states. Plans for the Memphis march King was to lead were completed by the Rev. Ralph David Abernathy, 42, named to succeed King as president of the Southern Christian Leadership Conference (SCLC) **Apr. 5**. Mrs. Coretta Scott King, the slain leader's widow, took her husband's place at the head of some 42,000 silent marchers, including thousands of whites, on **Apr. 8**.

On **Apr. 6**, when King's body was put on view at Atlanta's Ebenezer Baptist Church, of which he had been pastor, Mrs. King called for "a creative rather than a destructive way" of solving the racial crisis to fulfill her husband's dream.

The President canceled a Hawaii conference on Vietnam **Apr. 5** and conferred with Negro leaders. He proclaimed Sunday, **Apr. 7**, a day of mourning.

After funeral services at the church **Apr. 9** and memorial services at Morehouse College, dozens of national leaders joined 50,000-100,000 marchers who followed King's coffin on a farm wagon pulled by 2 Georgia mules on its 3½-mile course to South View Cemetery. The American flag was flown at halfstaff at all Federal facilities in the U. S. and abroad until the interment.

The entire nation paused in tribute as television cameras brought the proceedings into homes; memorial services, marches and rallies were held; schools and public facilities as well as businesses and stock exchanges were closed; dockmen and seamen in seaports stopped work; sports events and Hollywood's Oscar awards were postponed, and the Presidential campaign halted. Memorial services also were held abroad.

Shortly after Dr. King's murder, an intensive manhunt was started for Eric Starvo Galt, later revealed to be James Earl Ray, 40, who had escaped from the Missouri State Penitentiary a year earlier after serving 7 years of a 20-yr. term for armed robbery and theft. Ray was arrested at a London airport June 8 under the name of Raymond George Sneyd, an alias he used to get a Canadian passport. He reportedly flew from Toronto to London May 6, on to Lisbon, Portugal, and then back to London. Charged with the slaying of Dr. King, he was extradited and taken to Memphis to await trial.

ed 3 South Korean soldiers missing and presumed dead following an attack **Apr. 17** on an 11-man patrol south of the DMZ by 20 North Koreans. More clashes broke out inside the zone **Apr. 20** and **21**, with one American killed and 3 wounded on the latter day, when a U. S. 2d Infantry Div. patrol was attacked by North Korean troops. A UN Command spokesman said at least 3 North Koreans were killed.

**Ball Succeeds Goldberg**—President Johnson named George W. Ball to succeed Arthur Goldberg as chief representative to the United Nations **Apr. 25**, when he announced Goldberg's resignation. A coolness marked the exchanges between Johnson and Goldberg at the event. According to reports, Goldberg wanted to play a bigger role in Vietnam policy. Later, Goldberg said he could work better for peace in private life. Ball, 58, was former Undersecretary of State.

## INTERNATIONAL

**Francophone Military Units**—Canada announced a program to boost the use of French in its armed forces **Apr. 2**. At the present time about 16,000 of the 103,000 men speak French. Under the program both French- and English-speaking bases would be set up throughout the country. Ultimate goal is to have at least 20% of each unit made up of men whose parent tongue is the other official language. The only all-French speaking unit now is the Royal 22nd Regiment.

**Central African Union**—In a move to join economic and defense forces, 3 African states—Congo (Kinshasa), Chad and the Central African Republic—formed the United States of Central Africa **Apr. 2**.

The new, loosely-knit federation, covering 1,637,757 square miles and a population of 21,400,000, changed its name to the Union of Central African States. **Apr. 3**.

**SEATO Parley**—The 13th annual Ministerial Council meeting of the Southeast Asia Treaty Organization (SEATO) **Apr. 2** and **3** in Wellington, New Zealand, closed with a communique indorsing the limitation of bombing in North Vietnam but warning that Communist aggression in Southeast Asia must be halted.

**UN Council Urges Observers**—The UN Security Council **Apr. 4** urged the stationing of UN observers on the Israeli-Jordanian cease-fire line to prevent further violence. Jordan opposed UN patrols on its territory on the grounds that it could permanently solidify Israel's hold on Jordan's west bank. The Israeli army reported **Apr. 8** that a few dozen Israeli soldiers in helicopters had crossed 18 miles into Jordan to pursue and kill "about half a dozen" Arab infiltrators. The Israelis also destroyed a house used as a base by the terrorists, described as members of the Egyptian 141st Commando Battalion. A Jordan note to the Council **Apr. 8** accused Israel of "new acts of aggression," while an Israeli note, admitting the incursion, explained it was "in pursuit of saboteurs." Thirteen Arab infiltrators were killed by an Israeli patrol on the occupied west bank **Apr. 28**. Defense Min. Moshe Dayan warned **Apr. 26** that the Jordan Valley would become a battlefield if Jordan did not curb the saboteurs.

**Changes in Czechoslovakia**—Gen. Ludvik Svoboda, 72, newly elected president of Czechoslovakia, named Oldrich Cernik premier **Apr. 6**. Among Cernik's new cab-

---

## Students Rebel at Columbia U.

A left-wing led student protest at Columbia University **Apr. 23** grew into a major upheaval marked by bloody clashes with police and virtually paralyzed one of the nation's top educational institutions for two weeks.

Some 150 students met at noon **Apr. 23** to protest the proposed construction of a gymnasium in neighboring Morningside Park, which was opposed by Negroes in nearby Harlem, as well as the school's ties with the Institute of Defense Analyses (IDA). Mark Rudd, president of the campus chapter of Students for a Democratic Society (SDS), led the group which included members of the Students' Afro-American Society and some residents of Harlem.

Afterwards, they invaded Hamilton Hall, headquarters of Columbia College, and held 3 officials hostage for 24 hours. The Negro protesters ordered the others out early **Apr. 24**. The white rebels then marched to Low Library, where they took over and ransacked the office of Dr. Grayson Kirk, president of the university. By now the strike had gone beyond its original aims and "Student Power" had become the battle cry. Asserting their right to partake in the "restructuring of the university," the young rebels demanded complete amnesty, which Dr. Kirk refused **Apr. 25**.

The protesters' number had grown to about 700 when they took over a 5th building **Apr. 26**. Classes were canceled the same day and the campus was sealed off after 250 Negro high school students invaded the area shouting "Black Power."

The administration announced suspension of work on the gym **Apr. 26**.

More than 300 anti-protesters, bolstered by several university athletes, were bent

on removing the rebels and, fearing it might touch off intra-mural violence, Dr. King called on city police **Apr. 29** to clear out the buildings.

At 2 a.m. **Apr. 30**, 1,000 New York policemen moved in with nightsticks and in forcibly removing the white protesters, 132 students, 4 faculty members and 12 policemen were injured. The 85 Negro students in Hamilton Hall departed in orderly fashion. **May 8**, according to a university report, 707 persons had been arrested. Of these 524 were registered students, 181 were not Columbia students and 2 were faculty members. Of the students, 239 arrested were from Columbia College, representing 8.79% of the college's total enrollment. Also, 111 Barnard College students were arrested, representing 6.01% of the undergraduate girls' college total enrollment.

In a **May 1** student rally, the demonstrators and police clashed again, with 5 policemen and 6 students hurt.

Other campuses both large and small were also rocked by revolt. At Northwestern U., in Evanston, Ill., **May 3** Negro students seized the business office for 36 hours, demanding separate housing, more scholarships for Negroes, more Negro faculty and more Negro literature and art taught by teachers they had approved. The school agreed. At Stanford U., California, 200 students stormed and occupied a building **May 6** to protest the suspension of 7 who had led a demonstration November 1967 against Central Intelligence recruiting on campus.

Student turmoil also hit Bowie State College, Bowie, Md.; Cornell U.; Duke U.; Trinity College; U. of Oregon; Ohio State U.; Princeton U.; U. of Chicago; Cheyney State College; Roosevelt U., Southern Illinois U., and others.

inet members were Gen. Josef Pavel, interior minister, one of the victims of Stalinist purges in the 1950s. The Communist Party Central Committee **Apr. 4** announced major chages in the makeup of the party presidium, with membership cut from 14 to 11. The CP **Apr. 9** published its long-awaited "action program" for reforming communism in the country, pledging new guarantees of freedom of speech, press, assembly and religious observance.

**Trudeau Heads Canada Liberals**—Justice Min. Pierre Elliott Trudeau, 48, a French Canadian who opposed the Quebec separatist movement, was elected leader of Canada's Liberal Party **Apr. 6** and succeeded retiring Lester B. Pearson, 70, as prime minister **Apr. 20** in Ottawa. He dissolved Parliament **Apr. 23**, calling for a general election **June 23**. Trudeau **Apr. 30** announced a shift in his 23-member "caretaker" cabinet, sworn in **Apr. 20**, giving decision-making powers to 4 key committees instead of keeping the prior system of 14 standing committees.

**Sierra Leone Coup**—In a successful coup d'etat, non-commissioned Sierra Leone officers replaced the military government of Col. Andrew Juxon-Smith with a 14-member Anti-Corruption Revolutionary Movement **Apr. 18**. Charging that Juxon Smith's National Reform Council had been "more corrupt and selfish" than the civilian regime it had replaced **Mar. 1967**, a Sierra Leone radio broadcast promised restoration of civilian rule. Col. John Bangura, in exile since the 1967 coup, returned to head a 7-man junta **Apr. 19**.

**Rightists Gain**—West Germany's National Democratic Party (NPD) a neo-Nazi party formed in 1964, won 9.8% of the total votes and 12 of the 127 seats in the Landtag (state assembly) elections in Baden-Wurttemberg **Apr. 28**. The NPD's share of the vote was higher than in any previous state election contested by the party. Observers viewed the election as a backlash vote after 5 days of student rioting in several major West German cities as well as an indication of NPD's prospects in the general elections of the Bundestag (federal parliament) in 1969. NPD gains hurt the Social Democratic Party (SPD) most.

### GENERAL

**NYSE Sales Peak**—Trading volume on the N. Y. stock exchange hit a record 17,730,-000 shares **Apr. 1**, the first of 3 new highs **Apr. 1-10** after President Johnson's announcement of North Vietnam bombing curbs. The 2d record was 19,290,000 shares traded **Apr. 3**. A third record day, with 20,410,000 shares sold, came **Apr. 10**. The 3d record was attributed to continued optimism on peace in Vietnam and backlog orders piled up during the exchange's closing in tribute to Martin Luther King **Apr. 9**. An all-time high record to date was established **June 13**, when 21,350,000 shares were traded.

**Wisconsin Primary**—Sen. Eugene J. McCarthy (D., Minn.) won the Wisconsin Democratic Presidential primary **Apr. 2** with 57.6% of the vote to President Johnson's 35.4%. He also won 52 of 60 delegates. Former Vice President Richard M. Nixon, with no major opposition, polled 81.3% of the Republican primary votes and all 30 of the state's GOP delegates.

**Nationwide Phone Strike Ends**—A nationwide telephone strike, started **Apr. 18** by 200,000 members of the AFL-CIO Communications Workers of America, ended **May 5** with a 3-year contract providing wage and fringe benefit hikes totaling 19.58% over 3 years. The highly-automated phone service was near normal during the strike against American Telephone & Telegraph Co.—affiliated Bell Telephone firms in 15 states and Western Electric Co. in 40 states.

**Pennsylvania Primary**—Sen. Eugene J. McCarthy (D., Minn.), the only Presidential candidate of either party in the Pennsylvania primaries **Apr. 23**, polled 76½% of his party's vote. Former Vice President Richard M. Nixon won 76.3% of the GOP write-in vote.

**Humphrey Enters Race**—Vice President Hubert H. Humphrey, 56, entered the Democratic Presidential race **Apr. 27**. Humphrey, who declared his candidacy on a nationally televised program before 1,700 friends and supporters since it was too late to enter the primary races, called for "a new American patriotism." On a TV program **Apr. 28**, Humphrey said he would run on the Administration's record but added that "I am my own man."

**Rockefeller Says He'll Run**—Gov. Nelson A. Rockefeller (R., N.Y.) entered the race for the Republican Presidential nomination **Apr. 30**, 40 days after he had said he would not be an active candidate. He said he had been urged to participate by people of all political persuasions and had finally been moved to change his position by "the gravity of the crisis we face as a people."

### DISASTERS

**Tornadoes in Northern Arkansas Apr. 3** killed 6, caused extensive damage . . . Hotel fire in Shrewsbury, Eng., **Apr. 3** killed 5 . . . Gunpowder explosion and fire in downtown Richmond, Ind., sporting goods store **Apr. 6** destroyed 2 blocks, with 43 dead, 11 missing, 100 injured . . . BOAC Boeing 707 jetliner **Apr. 8** caught fire on takeoff, crash landed, falling apart in air, killing 5; 121 safe . . . 32 dead in Chilean plane crash **Apr. 8** . . . Bus accident killed 6, injured 50 **Apr. 8** in Lahore, W. Pakistan . . . Greek freighter **Apr. 8** struck rock off Orkney Islands, killing 7; 2 missing . . . An interisland ferry with 700 aboard sank in Wellington Harbor, New Zealand, **Apr. 10** after hitting a reef during 120-mph storm, leaving 47 dead and 6 missing . . . The first flight of Aerovias Rojas DC-3 crashed into a mountain 60 miles north of Mexico City, killing 18 **Apr. 10** . . . Five children died in **Apr. 13** house fire in Davisboro, Ga. . . . Faridpur District, East Pakistan, cyclone **Apr. 11** killed 1000, injured 1,000 . . . Eight migrant workers drowned **Apr. 14** when their station wagon fell into creek near Rocky Mount, N. C. . . . Tornado hit Greenwood, Ark., **Apr. 19**, leaving 12 dead, 48 injured . . . South African Airways Boeing 707 crashed on takeoff at Windhoek, South-West Africa, **Apr. 20**; 122 killed, 6 survivors . . . Eleven were killed, 24 injured when bus plunged into ravine at Recife, Brazil, **Apr. 23** . . . Tornadoes along 125-mile stretch of Ohio River **Apr. 23** killed 11, injured 200 in Ohio and Kentucky . . . Biplane in airshow near San Luis Obispo, Calif., **Apr. 27** crashed, killing 4 . . . Pilot and 5 members of Lamar State College of Technology track team and coach died in plane crash **Apr. 28** at Beaumont, Tex. . . . Fifty feared dead when earthquake hit large area of western Iran **Apr. 30.**

## May—1968
### NATIONAL

**Tariff Aid for U.S.**—In a move to aid the U.S. in reducing its balance-of-payments deficit, 16 of its major trading partners

agreed **May 1** to step up the 20% tariff cuts due Jan. 1, 1970, on American exports under the Kennedy Round agreement to Jan. 1, 1969. At the same time, they put off for one year to Jan. 1, 1970, the 20% tariff cut the U.S. was to make Jan. 1, 1969.

**Poor March on Washington**—Nine poor people's caravans from all parts of the country **May 2-17** converged by mule train, bus, cars, railroad and on foot on Washington, where volunteers put up temporary shelters on a 16-acre site dubbed Resurrection City, U.S.A. in West Potomac Park. Sponsored by the Southern Christian Leadership Conference, the poor people's campaign was planned by the late Martin Luther King to prod the Congress and the Administration into taking action on behalf of more than 29,000,000 Americans. The Rev. Ralph D. Abernathy, King's successor as SCLC president, was march leader.

Preceding the poverty pilgrims with a delegation, Abernathy **Apr. 29** met with Cabinet members and Congressmen to present a long list of legislative demands, including 2,000,000 jobs, massive housing programs, larger welfare payments and a guaranteed minimum income for everyone. As demonstrations got under way **May 21**, an air of bedlam often hovered over the camp, with a lack of organization and disunity in staff leadership. There was a shortage of funds, cooking, bathing and sanitation and heavy rains compounded the problems by turning the grassy area into a bog, forcing many to leave the campsite. On **May 15** the local food committee had been able to raise only a third of the $90,000 needed to feed the 3,000 campers for 30 days. Most of the demonstrators were Southern Negroes; some Indians, Mexican Americans and Appalachian whites. There was some racial tension and **May 22** 200 Chicago and

Detroit Negro youth gang members were sent home for "beating whites." Sympathetic officials intervened when some of the demonstrators got out of hand, and **May 23** a bipartisan ad hoc committee of Congressmen was formed to help the marchers present their demands.

Agriculture Secy. Orville Freeman **May 23** promised Abernathy and 200-300 demonstrators that he would enlarge the department's food distribution program. Resurrection City closed down **June 23** when the Interior Dept.'s permit for the campsite expired. The campaign ended far from the dramatic goals of the leaders and 124 persons were arrested after they refused to leave **June 24**. Several hundred others, including Abernathy, were arrested for an illegal demonstration on Capitol grounds.

**Communists Launch Tet II**—Communists launched the expected Round II of their country-wide Tet offensive **May 5**. But it was "a far cry" from the original, a U.S. Command spokesman said. They shelled, mortared and rocketed 122 targets, including 40 cities and towns, 7 air bases and other Allied installations but only about a dozen of the targets struck had ground attacks. Saigon, under heaviest attack through **May 7**, was hit hard only in some areas such as the Chinese Cholon district.

Some 80,000 refugees jammed bridges and streets in flight to safer parts of town as the fight raged fiercely for a week around Saigon's Y bridge and near Tan Son Nhut, where South Vietnam paratroopers fought two days in an old French military cemetery to drive out entrenched troops. Only 5 small portions of the city, with some 2,000 houses and shacks were destroyed. Due to the swift reaction of the city's 500,000 government defenders, civilian dead were a few hundred, less

## Student Riots Precipitate Chaos in France

A protest **May 2** by 6 New Left student militants at the University of Nanterre mushroomed into a movement of civil and economic disobedience by some 10,-000,000 Frenchmen and threatened to end the 10-year regime of President Charles de Gaulle's 5th Republic in chaos.

Led by Daniel Cohn-Bendit, 23, the youthful militants' protest against "imperialism" caused officials to close the suburban campus of the University of Paris. **May 3** Nanterre shutdown protests by 1,000 students at the 715-year-old Sorbonne, heart of the University of Paris, led to its closing after pitched battles with police and precipitated 10 days of fierce Latin Quarter street fighting, with students behind barricades of burned cars tossing paving stones and gasoline bombs. The bloody fighting won the sympathy of France overnight and thousands of students also took to the streets in provincial cities, fired by the deep discontent permeating the country's overcrowded, inadequate and archaic university system.

Communist and Catholic labor groups staged a nationwide 24-hour sympathy strike **May 1**, while in Paris more than half a million workers, students, teachers and opposition leaders marched for 4 hours, singing the Internationale and giving vent to anti-De Gaulle feelings.

By **May 14**, when students occupied the Sorbonne, an epidemic of wildcat strikes started to sweep the country, halting nearly all of the country's industrial production, commerce and transportation.

When De Gaulle rushed back from a state visit to Romania **May 18**, he found

France in a state of economic paralysis not far removed from civil war.

Premier Pompidou's government survived a parliamentary effort to overthrow it **May 22** with 11 votes to spare after a censure motion was introduced by Francois Mitterand, leader of the Federation of the Democratic and Socialist Left.

More than half of France's 19,000,000 workers were on strike by **May 24** and the rest couldn't get to work. The red flag of rebellion flew over factories, mines and shipyards seized by workers. Even after a De Gaulle radio appeal **May 24** for a return to law and order, the violence and rioting continued to spread, with new student-police clashes **May 23-25**. Farmers in southwest France staged a protest **May 24**, demanding price supports and subsidies, banks closed and even the tax collectors walked out.

In his **May 24** appeal, De Gaulle announced he would submit a program of broad reform to the people through a referendum in June and added he would resign if his "mandate for renewal" should be turned down.

Some 200,000 marchers led by Communists chanted "Adieu De Gaulle" when he left suddenly for his country home **May 29** amid speculation that he was resigning. Ex-Premier Pierre Mendez-France declared the same day he was ready to form a "popular government." But De Gaulle returned in a fighting mood, assured of Army support, and dissolved the National Assembly **May 30**. Blaming the Communists for the chaos, he called for new parliamentary elections **June 23** and **30**.

than one-twentieth of those at Tet. At week's end Communist dead were estimated at 2,500. On **May 13** the U. S. and South Vietnam commands said Allied troops had overcome the enemy's main thrust against Saigon and that 5,270 North Vietnam and Viet Cong had been killed, compared to 154 Americans and 362 South Vietnamese slain.

**April Riot Costs**—Using Federal troops in the April riots following the assassination of the Rev. Dr. Martin Luther King Jr. cost $5,375,400, the Defense Dept. reported **May 18**. Altogether, 35,890 soldiers, Marines and National Guardsmen were deployed in Washington, D.C., Baltimore and Chicago, with 22,074 soldiers on standby. Insurance companies would pay $67,-000,000 for losses incurred, the American Insurance Association estimated **May 15**, with biggest damage payments of $24,-000,000 going to Washington, D.C.

**Nuclear Submarine Lost**—The nuclear-powered U.S. submarine Scorpion, two days overdue at Norfolk, Va., after a 3-month training exercise with the 6th Fleet in the Mediterranean, was reported missing **May 29**. The Scorpion, with 99 men aboard, was listed as "presumed lost" **June 5**, after a fruitless search by the Navy.

## INTERNATIONAL

**Israeli Jerusalem Parade**—Israel marked its 20th anniversary **May 2** with an armed forces parade, the biggest in its history, through Jerusalem despite Arab protests and terrorist threats. The parade, featuring equipment captured in the June 1967 war, was scored **May 2** by the UN Security Council which had urged its cancellation **Apr. 27**. Protest demonstrations were held in Damascus, Beirut and Jordan **May 2**. A protest strike by two west-bank Jordan towns was punished **May 5** with Israel travel restrictions for their residents. Eleven Arab women protest marchers in East Jerusalem were detained **Apr. 25** after a clash with police.

**Apartheid Measure Approved**—A bill to abolish Parliamentary representation for South Africa's colored (mixed-race) population was passed in the House of Assembly **May 3**. The measure, one of 3 designed to reinforce the government's apartheid policy, ended colored representation by 4 white deputies at the end of the current Parliament in 1971.

**Israeli-Arab Clashes**—Israeli authorities reported **May 3** that their troops had killed 17 Arab guerrillas in 3 separate clashes **Apr. 30-May 2**. One Israeli soldier was killed in the bloodiest encounter **May 2** at the southern end of the Dead Sea when 12 Arab commandos were killed. Later, two Israeli soldiers and a civilian were killed when their jeeps ran over mines apparently planted by the slain commandos.

**Biafra Talks Start**—After 10 months of fighting between Nigeria and the secessionist government of Biafra, the two sides met in London **May 6** and agreed **May 8** on Kampala, Uganda, as the site for peace negotiations. The civil war had come to an impasse. Fearing genocide at the hands of other tribes if defeated, Biafra's Ibo tribesmen fought on desperately even though Nigeria's well equipped army of 85,000 men had captured all but one of Biafra's major cities, including the capital of Enegu, squeezing the rebel army of about 35,000 into an interior area only a third as large as the 29,000 sq. mi. it originally held. The Federal government had stepped up its bombing, using Russian MiGs and Czechoslovakian Delfin jet planes and bombs, with pilots believed to be Egyptian and Sudanese. Some 200,-000 Ibo refugees had crowded into about 300 camps throughout Biafra, which claimed the bombing raids were aimed at schools and hospitals, killing hundreds of civilians in January and February and about 300 from **Apr. 21-27**. Angered over Britain's alleged military aid to Nigeria, Biafran demonstrators **May 4** burned down 5 British buildings and thousands marched through the streets of 3 towns chanting anti-British slogans. Gabon recognized Biafra **May 8**; Tanzania, the first country to do so, **Apr. 13**, expressed its concern for the slaughter of the Ibos and their struggle for independence.

**North Korean Charges Denied**—North Korea claimed **May 7** its forces had captured a group of U.S. agents sent to its side of the DMZ to commit murder and subversion. The charge was denied by a UN Command spokesman and at a meeting of the Mixed Armistice Commission in Panmunjom **May 17**, U.S. Maj. Gen. Gilbert H. Woodward, senior UN command delegate, warned North Korea was "approaching another serious miscalculation" in a plan to foment a new war. **Apr. 27** North Korean troops had attacked UN command troops near the demilitarized zone, killing 2 South Korean soldiers and wounding 2 Americans.

## Vietnam Preliminary Peace Talks Open in Paris

After a 34-day impasse on selecting a site for preliminary peace negotiations, the U.S. and North Vietnam agreed **May 3** on Paris. Hanoi designated ex-Foreign Min. Xuan Thuy head of its delegation. Hanoi said **May 4** its purpose in the talks was "the unconditional cessation of U.S. bombing raids and other acts of war" against North Vietnam. Secy. of State Dean Rusk declared **May 5** "an honorable peace" in Southeast Asia hinged on a stop to Communist infiltration of South Vietnam and its neighbors.

The parley started **May 10** with Amb.-at-Large Averell Harriman, 76, as U.S. delegation chief and Cyrus R. Vance, 51, his deputy. Thuy, 55, now Min. of State and secretary of the Central Committee of the North Vietnamese Communist party, had as his adviser Col. Ha Van Lau, who had served as liaison officer with the International Control Commission of North Vietnam. After discussing procedure **May 10** and **11**, both sides restated their previous conditions **May 13**. No progress was made at talks **May 15** and **May 18**

as Hanoi still demanded unconditional halt of U.S. bombing and the Americans asked for some military reciprocation in exchange for a halt in raids.

The impasse continued. Amb. Harriman **May 20** denied there was a deadlock, but charged the North Vietnamese had been using the meetings for propaganda purposes. As Thuy continued to press for a halt in U.S. bombing raids **May 22** and **27**, Harriman rejected "the suggestion now urged by you that the only reason for our meetings is to give the hour and date for the cessation of bombing."

Thuy refused to discuss seriously Harriman's suggestion **May 31** that the DMZ be restored as a truly neutral buffer zone although the U.S. diplomat charged the 320th North Vietnam Div. had crossed the DMZ **May 26** to attack the allies at Dongha.

At a press conference **May 29** a Hanoi spokesman berated President Johnson for his charge **May 28** that North Vietnam was obstructing the Paris talks, asserting the Americans were responsible.

**UK Bolsters NATO Force**—A 40% increase of Britain's share in NATO troop strength, announced **May 10**, was made possible by England's planned withdrawal east of Suez by 1971, Defense Min. Denis Healey said. The UK boost included naval forces and vessels for the allied Mediterranean command.

**End of Bombing Urged**—UN Secy. Gen. U Thant, urging "an unconditional end of the bombing of North Vietnam," asserted **May 13** it "had only hardened the determination of the North to prosecute the war and not to negotiate under duress."

**Jerusalem Merger Opposed**—Declaring all Israeli actions in Jerusalem since the capture of the Jordanian area in June, 1967 invalid, the UN Security Council in a resolution **May 21** opposed Israel's administrative unification of the Jordanian and Israeli sectors of the city. Thirteen of the Council's 15 members approved the resolution, while the U.S. and Canada abstained.

**UN Rhodesia Travel Ban**—In another step to isolate the white minority government of Premier Ian D. Smith, the UN Security Council **May 29** unanimously approved a resolution calling on all members to impose a total embargo on all trade with or travel to Rhodesia.

## GENERAL

**Rockefeller Launches Campaign**—Gov. Nelson A. Rockefeller (R., N.Y.) scored the Administration's foreign policy in a speech kicking off his campaign for the GOP Presidential nomination in Philadelphia **May 1**. He termed U.S. policy in Western Europe "sterile" and said the war in Vietnam should be "de-Americanized." At the University of Iowa **May 2** he urged lowering the voting age to 18 and called for a national lottery to end the "inequitable" draft laws.

**Humphrey Starts Campaign**—In his first week as Presidential candidate, Vice President Humphrey told 5,000 delegates to the African Methodist Episcopal Church's quadrennial session in Philadelphia **May 2** he would strive for "a new and complete national commitment to human rights." At Kent (Ohio) State University **May 3** and at Bucknell University in Lewisburg, Pa., **May 4** small groups of students walked out on his speeches, but at the latter school some 3,000 in the audience cheered him when he decried "the censorship of walking out." In Washington **May 7** he told the American Meat institute the Federal role in farm policy was "here to stay." The United Steelworkers of America (AFL-CIO) endorsed him on **May 9**. On **May 10** in Baltimore, Maryland's 49-vote delegation agreed to cast a unit vote for him.

**Nixon on Campaign Trail**—Former Vice President Richard Nixon, the GOP Presidential contender, in a radio address **May 2**, detailed a program for tax incentives and guaranteed loans to bring businesses to urban slums. In Fort Wayne, Ind., **May 3** he stressed the need for a "moratorium" on Vietnam discussion, adding: "Let's not destroy the chance for peace with a mouthful of words from some irresponsible candidate." In a policy paper in New York **May 8**, he asserted the role of poverty as a cause of increased crime "has been grossly exaggerated" and attributed the rise to "the success of the criminals in this country."

**AFL-CIO Suspends UAW**—The United Autoworkers of America was suspended **May 16** by the AFL-CIO for nonpayment of dues for 3 months. The suspension climaxed a bitter feud between AFL-CIO

president George Meany and UAW president Walter P. Reuther. During the UAW convention in Atlantic City **May 4-10**, delegates on **May 9** approved witholding the dues, which were to be put in escrow pending a special convention sought by the UAW to hear the auto union's demands for reform.

**ADA Parley Backs McCarthy**—The Americans for Democratic Action in Washington **May 19** endorsed Sen. Eugene J. McCarthy for the Democratic Presidential nomination, upholding the previous approval of ADA's national board. The group praised "his courage in New Hampshire and Wisconsin," adding that his campaign "forced a change in the Administration's Vietnam policy and induced President Johnson's renunciation of further political activity."

**Rap Brown Convicted**—H. Rap Brown, chairman of the Student Nonviolent Coordinating Committee (SNCC), was convicted in New Orleans Federal Court **May 22** for violating the Federal Firearms Act, sentenced to 5 years in prison and fined $2,000. A jury of 9 whites and 3 Negroes found him guilty of carrying a .30 caliber carbine on a plane trip from New Orleans to New York Aug. 18, 1967. He was released on $15,000 bond.

**McCarthy Wins in Oregon**—Sen. Eugene J. McCarthy (Minn.) defeated Sen. Robert F. Kennedy (N. Y.) in the Oregon Presidential primary **May 28** with 45% of the vote. Kennedy, who had been winner in a pre-primary NBC poll, received 39%. In the GOP primary, Richard M. Nixon won 73% of the vote. Gov. Ronald Reagan (Calif.) received 23% and Gov. Nelson A. Rockefeller (N. Y.) 4% in write-ins.

## DISASTERS

Nineteen members of a wedding party were killed **May 1** when a truck plunged into a ravine near Benares, India . . . All 85 aboard perished when a Braniff International 4-engine turboprop Electra crashed **May 3** during a lightning storm near Dawson, Tex. . . . Coal mine explosion in St. Etienne, France, **May 3** killed 6 . . . Seven teenagers died **May 4** when their car hit a gravel truck near Grand Forks, British Columbia . . . An explosion followed by fire **May 6** destroyed 3 tankers in La Plata harbor, Argentina, killing 10 . . . Four of 25 miners died in flooded coal mine near Hominy Falls, W. Va., **May 6** . . . At least 20 persons died of bubonic plague in Lesotho **May 8** . . . Six died and 30 were injured in passenger express and freight train crash in Vijayavada, India, **May 8** . . . Twelve wedding guests were killed **May 9** when balcony of house in Patna, India, collapsed . . . Earth tremors in Iranian province of Azerbaijan **May 11** killed 40 . . . Ten reported dead and several missing in **May 12** floods in western Algeria . . . Dozens of tornadoes struck 10-state area of Midwest and South, killing at least 72 **May 15** . . . Earthquake hit Japan's northern and eastern seaboard **May 16**, leaving 37 dead, 217 injured, 10 missing and 1,200 houses razed or damaged . . . Five perished in floods near Lake Maracaibo, Venezuela, **May 18** . . . Chartered helicopter crashed in Paramount, Calif., on way to Los Angeles from Disneyland **May 22**, killing 23 . . . Seven schoolchildren and teacher drowned when canoe capsized in Tamaya River near Pucallpa, Peru, **May 22** . . . Ferry sank in Yellow Sea off Kunsan, South Korea, **May 24**, drowning 14 . . . Three of 24 aboard missing when Brazilian cargo ship Fernaodias sank 90 miles from Salvador, Brazil, **May 26** . . . Eight of 9

drowned **May 26** when 15-foot boat capsized off Wells Beach, Me. . . . Four died in light plane crash on Greenwich, Conn., golf course **May 26** . . . U.S. nuclear submarine Scorpion, with 99 men aboard, lost between Azores and Norfolk, Va., **May 27** . . . Gas explosion at nursery school in Hapeville, Ga., **May 29** killed 7 children and 2 adults.

## June—1968

### NATIONAL

**Battle of Saigon**—Communist rockets and snipers continued to punish Saigon **June 3-15**, adding new destruction to the ravages of Tet and making the battle of Saigon one of the Vietnam war's toughest. The mayor's office **June 11** reported that 117,000 persons had left or lost their homes since **May 5**, when the Reds resumed their assault on the city. In the same period, 433 civilians had been killed and 3,660 wounded, while South Vietnamese troops had killed 2,880 Communists and captured 328. Allied forces, mostly American, had slain 2,436 and captured 105. Of South Vietnamese losses, 261 were killed and 1,032 wounded. Besides homes, other civilian targets like schools and hospitals were hit. **June 7**, 25 civilians perished in such a bombardment. The guerrilla warfare was "cheap" for the enemy, said a

## Sen. Robert F. Kennedy Fatally Shot by Assassin

Sen. Robert F. Kennedy, 42, cut down by an assassin's bullet in the Hotel Ambassador, Los Angeles, **June 5** at about 12:16 a.m. PDT, died **June 6** at 1:44 a.m. PDT in Good Samaritan Hospital, where a team of top surgeons had worked for 4 hours to remove bullet fragments from his brain.

His suspected assassin later identified as Sirhan Beshara Sirhan, 24, a slight Jordanian Arab who had lived in the Los Angeles area for 11 years, was seized by members of the Senator's party after a struggle.

The Senator from New York was killed less than 5 years after the assassination of his older brother, President John F. Kennedy, and two months after that of the Rev. Martin Luther King, Jr.

The tragedy, which occurred about 3 minutes after he had left a rally celebrating his victory in the California and South Dakota primaries, brought Presidential campaigning to a standstill. President Johnson, expressing the nation's shocked grief **June 5** ordered Secret Service protection for all Presidential candidates of major parties. Urging "an end to violence," he announced he was creating a commission of distinguished citizens to study the subject. Declaring "our public life is diminished by his loss," the chief Executive **June 6** proclaimed **June 9** a day of mourning and read the **June 5th** statement in which he had called on Congress "in the name of an aroused nation—to give America the gun control law it needs."

An outraged and sad nation kept a close radio and TV vigil during the crucial hours he lay comitose between life and death, with his wife Ethel, expecting their 11th child, at his side. World and national leaders sent condolences to the bereaved Kennedy family, but to grieved Kennedy campaigners who had traveled with him it had not come as a surprise. They had feared for his safety, both from the crush of adoring mobs and from those who hated him, but he had waved the suggestion of extra guards aside, saying: "If anyone wants to kill me it won't be difficult."

It wasn't. As he and a small group of aides passed through a serving kitchen on the way to a press conference, the Senator paused to shake hands when the unobtrusive assassin started shooting a .22 caliber pistol. Of 8 bullets, 3 felled Kennedy, while 5 other persons around him were hit, but not fatally, by the shots. The surgical team, headed by Dr. Henry M. Cuneo of the University of Southern California, found the fatal bullet had entered the cerebellum after penetrating the mastoid bone behind the right ear.

While Kennedy lay on the floor bleeding, his alleged assailant was subdued by 8 men, including Roosevelt Grier, Los Angeles Rams football lineman, and Rafer Johnson, an Olympic champion. Both the athletes and police protected the assassin from the threatening mobs after officials, fearful of "another Lee Oswald case like in Dallas," demanded he be kept alive.

Mayor Samuel W. Yorty revealed that Sirhan, an unemployed clerk, had entered in a notebook found in his home later **June 5** "the necessity to assassinate Sen. Kennedy before **June 5**," the anniversary of the Arab-Israeli war. Yorty said **June 6** the notebook expressed evidence of "Communist sympathies." The release of such information was scored by the Civil Liberties Union and State Atty. Gen Thomas Lynch on the ground that it could affect the legality of the evidence and the course of the trial. Sirhan was indicted **June 7** by a Los Angeles County Grand Jury of 1st degree murder and on 5 counts of assault with intent to kill the other 5 persons shot. With the lesson of Dallas in mind, he was held in strict isolation under heavy guard. His trial was scheduled to start Dec. 9.

On **June 6**, a Presidential jet flew the body of Sen. Kennedy back to New York, where it lay in state in St. Patrick's Cathedral from 5:30 a.m. **June 7** until 5 a.m. **June 8**. More than 151,000 persons, according to a police estimate, stood in in a line stretching for more than a mile and sometimes for as long as 7 hours, for a glimpse of the mahogany coffin. Standing vigil over the bier, 3 at a time, were some 600 men, ranging from New York Gov. Rockefeller, to the Rev. Ralph Abernathy, leader of the Poor People's March. The requiem mass **June 8** was attended by President Johnson, the major Presidential candidates, members of Congress, the Cabinet and other public figures.

In a reading that was unusual at a Roman Catholic funeral, Sen. Edward Kennedy (D., Mass.) said his brother "should be remembered simply as a good and decent man, who saw wrong and tried to right it, saw suffering and tried to heal it, saw war and tried to stop it."

Thousands lined the street to watch the motorcade bringing the body and the funeral party to a 21-car funeral train in Pennsylvania Station for the trip to Washington. Crowds waiting in stations along the way delayed the train 4½ hours and, in the first nighttime burial at Arlington National Cemetery in memory, Robert F. Kennedy was laid to rest near his brother John.

On **June 15**, the late Senator's mother, Mrs. Rose Kennedy, 77, and his brother, Sen. Kennedy, in a brief TV message taped at the Hyannis Port, Mass., home of ex-Amb. Joseph P. Kennedy, thanked Americans for their expressions of sympathy. With the elder Kennedy sitting in a wheelchair beside them, Mrs. Kennedy pledged the family to "carry out the principles for which Bobby stood."

U. S. military official, since he was doing as much damage as in prior battles but with fewer men. Hanoi's aim officials said, was a city in ruins with homeless, unhappy people ripe for an uprising against the government.

**U. S. Hits Saigon Attacks**—No progress was made at the 7th and 8th sessions of the Paris peace talks at North Vietnam continued to demand an end of U. S. bombing in the North **June 5** and U. S. Amb.-at-Large W. Averell Harriman charged 40,-000 Hanoi troops were fighting in Laos in violation of the 1962 Geneva neutralization accord. Harriman **June 12** held the North Vietnamese military responsible for attacks on Saigon with "no military objective" but "to terrorize people." Xuan Thuy, the Hanoi representative, countered: "If the U. S. pulls out of Saigon, the combat will cease around Saigon." The stalemate continued at the **June 19** and **26** sessions, with each side accusing the other of stepping up the war.

**Abrams Succeeds Westmoreland**—Gen. William C. Westmoreland turned over command of U. S. armed forces in Vietnam to Gen. Creighton W. Abrams, his former deputy, **June 10.** Westmoreland left for the U. S. the following day to assume his new duties as Army Chief of Staff.

**LBJ on Gun Controls**—In a message to Congress **June 24,** President Johnson urged registration of every firearm and licensing of every gun owner, with registrations to go into a computer listing at the FBI's National Crime Information Center. Calling for minimal Federal standards, he said licensing should be carried out by the states. However, he added, Federal licensing should be required for states not meeting the standards within two years.

**Chief Justice Resigns**—President Johnson announced the resignation of Earl Warren as Chief Justice of the U. S. **June 26.** At the same time he nominated Associate Supreme Court Justice Abe Fortas, 58, to head the country's highest tribunal and Judge Homer Thornberry of the 5th Circuit Court of Appeals to replace Fortas. Warren, 77, resigned "solely because of age," after 14 years. Often criticized by conservatives, Warren had written the opinion in 3 milestone decisions: 1954, school desegregation; 1964, "one man, one vote," leading to legislative reapportionment; and 1966, outlining of rules for interrogation of criminal suspects.

**U. S. Leaves Khesanh**—In a tactical shift to mobility, to cope with increased Communist strength and activity in the DMZ, the U. S. Command **June 27** announced the Marines were withdrawing from the military base of Khesanh.

## INTERNATIONAL

**Jordan River Clash**—Heavy casualties were reported on both sides when Israeli and Jordanian forces fought all day **June 4** along the northern sector of the Jordan River near the Sea of Galilee. The fighting, with Israeli air attacks on Jordan, was termed their most serious encounter since **Mar. 21** by Amman. The UN Security Council convened **June 5** to consider the outbreak but called off debate because of Sen. Robert F. Kennedy's assassination.

**Italian Premier Resigns**—Premier Aldo Moro and his cabinet resigned **June 5** after the Unified Socialist Party pulled out of Italy's coalition government **June 1.** The party withdrew because it had lost seats in the **May 19** and **20** parliamentary elections, although the other two in the coalition—Moro's Christian Democrats and the reformist Republicans—had scored gains. Many Socialist leaders attributed the losses to such concessions to Moro's more conservative party as delay in reform of the tax and educational systems and governmental organization.

**Southeast Asia Defense Parley**—At the end of a two-day Kuala Lumpur, Malaysia, parley on defenses needed in Southeast Asia after Britain withdraws from that country and Singapore in 1971, 5 nations **June 11** reaffirmed their pledge to maintain the defense of the area. They include Great Britain, Australia, New Zealand, Singapore and Malaysia.

**A-Ban Treaty Signed**—After 4 years of intensive negotiations on measures to halt the proliferation of nuclear weapons, the UN General Assembly **June 12** adopted by a 95-4 vote a resolution commending the draft nuclear non-proliferation treaty submitted by the UN 18-nation Disarmament Committee (ENDC) **Mar. 15.** The endorsement fulfilled a UN General Assembly resolution adopted in 1960 and cleared the way for ratification **July 1,** when 62 nations, including the U. S., Soviet Union and Britain signed.

**New Belgian Cabinet**—Belgium's 132-day political crisis ended **June 17,** when the new premier, Gaston Eyskens, 63, formed a two-party coalition government with a

## De Gaulle Emerges Triumphant Again

As the student and labor revolt which had rocked France in "the days of May" abated and most of the country's 8,000,000-man work force returned to work during the first week of June, there were isolated pockets of resistance. On **June 7,** when the stock exchange reopened, 4,000 striking workers and 200 militant students battled police at the nationalized Renault assembly plant at Flins. The first violent clash between workers and police, it left a dozen injured and was denounced by the Communist-led General Confederation of Labor, which blamed "student agitators."

President De Gaulle jumped the gun **June 7** on the 3-week campaign for the 2-stage national elections, which got under way **June 10.** De Gaulle promised a "society of participation," unlike Communism or Capitalism, which he termed "bad solutions from the human point of view." Premier Georges Pompidou **June 12** opened the government's drive, calling for a clear Gaullist majority to save France from a Communist takeover. Also on **June 12,** as some street fighting continued, 11

extremist student groups were dissolved and protests banned during the campaign. Police cleared the Sorbonne of 200 students without incident **June 16.**

In the relative calm of the campaign, opposition leaders denounced De Gaulle's tactics. Francois Mitterand, leader of the Federation of the Democratic Socialist Left, scoffed: "Two months ago, you would have voted anti-Gaullist, and 2 months from now you would vote anti-Gaullist again." However, De Gaulle won with a grand sweep both on **June 23** and in the runoff **June 30.** Gaullists and their allies won 43.73% of the 22,500,000 votes in the first round, their candidates winning 142 constituencies, thus electing them to the Assembly without undergoing a runoff round. **June 30** they won 294 seats in the 487-seat Assembly, making De Gaulle's party the first in some 100 years to win an outright majority there. The Communists and Mitterand's party lost more than half the seats they had held, their combined total being only 90 votes.

cabinet of 16 Social Christians and 13 Socialists. The two parties had agreed **June 12** on a program for the new center-left government, including the passage of constitutional amendments to give formal recognition to the country's two language regions. The crisis had been precipitated by the demands of each ethnic group, the Dutch-speaking Flemings and the French-speaking Walloons, for greater regional autonomy.

**Trudeau Wins**—With a decisive victory in the House of Commons elections **June 25,** the Liberal Party gave Canada its first majority government since 1962 and assured its leader, Pierre Elliott Trudeau, a solid mandate as prime minister. The Liberals won 155 of the 264 seats in Commons, compared to the 128 they had held. The Conservatives went down from 94 to 72 seats. On **July 5,** Trudeau announced his new 29-man cabinet, including 8 new members, 15 ministers from his interim cabinet who had their portfolios shifted, and 6 key ministers who, like Trudeau, kept their old posts.

## GENERAL

**Helen Keller Dies**—Helen Adams Keller, 87, blind and deaf writer who was an inspiration to others for more than half a century, died **June 1** in Westport, Conn., after a stroke. Miss Keller, born June 27, 1880, in Tuscambia, Ala., lost sight and hearing after serious illness at 19 months. A legend in her lifetime, she corresponded with the poet John Greenleaf Whittier at 9 and was named with Napoleon as one of "the two most interesting characters of the 19th Century" by Mark Twain. Her first book, "The Story of My Life," was published in 1902—two years before she graduated from Radcliffe. Her early years with her teacher, Anne Mansfield Sullivan, who rescued her from what Miss Keller called the "no world," were depicted in a play and film, "The Miracle Worker." A tireless worker for other handicapped people, she traveled extensively to raise money for the American Foundation for the Blind.

**Rockefeller Steps Up Drive**—Convinced "the tide has turned" in his favor at Milwaukee **June 3,** Gov. Nelson A. Rockefeller (R., N. Y.), launched a full-speed-ahead campaign for the GOP Presidential nomination **June 10,** after a campaign moratorium following Sen. Robert F. Kennedy's assassination. At Alleghany College in Meadville, Pa., that day he stressed the need for education for the poor. Later, after a Presidential candidate briefing at the White House, he said candidates must not be deterred by the danger of assassination and must "go to the people." Speaking at the National Press Club in Washington **June 11,** he said "a profoundly new mood" would emerge in America after the assassination, calling for "nothing short of a new government, a new party in power and a new leader at the head of the party." He visited the Watts district in Los Angeles **June 11,** challenged Richard Nixon to a debate **June 13.** Pennsylvania Gov. Raymond P. Shafer **June 15** gave up his favorite-son status to back Rockefeller.

**California Primaries**—Sen. Robert F. Kennedy won California's Democratic Presidential primary and the state's 172 Democratic National Convention delegate votes **June 4,** prior to his assassination. His 46% of the total Democratic vote topped Sen. Eugene J. McCarthy's 42%. State Atty. Gen. Thomas C. Lynch, who headed a 3d slate including supporters of both Senators and Vice President Humphrey, drew 12%. In the GOP primary, unopposed Gov.

Ronald Reagan won as favorite son Presidential candidate.

**McCarthy Challenges Humphrey**—Asserting the "issues remain essentially the same," Sen. Eugene J. McCarthy **June 12** said in resuming his campaigning after Senator Kennedy's assassination that he would find it difficult to support Vice President Humphrey because of Humphrey's "wholehearted" backing of the Administration's Vietnam policy. Denying he would lead a new party, he said he intended to "work this out within the Democratic party." Addressing Idaho Democratic women at the party's state convention **June 14,** McCarthy accused Humphrey of "not dealing with the issues," adding that "our party should take the most difficult issues to the people, even if it destroys the party." He urged **June 15** that the national convention should "withhold final judgment" until the candidates appeared before it to present their views.

**Dr. Spock Convicted**—Dr. Benjamin Spock, 65, noted baby doctor, was found guilty **June 14** in Boston Federal District Court with 3 others of conspiring to counsel young men to evade the draft. Convicted with Dr. Spock were the Rev. William Sloane Coffin, Jr., 43, Yale University chaplain; Michael Ferber, 23, Harvard University graduate student; and Mitchell Goodman, 44, author from Temple, Me. A 5th defendant, Marcus Raskin, 34, of Washington, D. C., was found not guilty. The government indictment had cited 10 "overt acts" it contended one or more of the defendants had committed in the conspiracy. The defendants contended they were concerned over the legality of the Vietnam war and the constitutionality of the draft. After the verdict, asserting he would "press my case," Dr. Spock said: "My main defense was I believed a citizen must work against a war he considers contrary to international law." The 4 were sentenced **July 10** to two years in Federal prison by Judge Francis J. W. Ford, who presided over the case. However, execution of the sentences was waived pending steps for appeal.

**N. Y. Theater Strike**—A 4-day strike, which shut down 19 Broadway shows and 10 touring companies **June 17-20,** ended with a 3-year contract **June 20.** The strike, called by the 15,935-member Actors Equity Association against the League of N. Y. Theaters, idled some 800 performers and several thousand members of other theatrical unions. The new pact called for an increase in weekly pay to $155 over 3 years and banned replacing anyone with a foreign performer.

**New York Primaries**—Sen. Eugene J. McCarthy (D., Minn.) won at least 52 of New York's 123 elected delegates in the state's Democratic primary **June 18,** besting delegates supporting Vice President Humphrey and the late Sen. Robert F. Kennedy for the Presidency. Gov. Nelson A. Rockefeller, GOP contender for the Presidency, won 77 of 82 delegates, the remaining 5 going to Richard M. Nixon.

**End "Fight, Talk"; Humphrey**—Urging an end to "fight and talk," Vice President Humphrey **June 21** called on North Vietnam to join in an immediate cease-fire in Vietnam. The U. S., he said, was "prepared for a cease-fire any hour of the day." Admitting Hanoi "has shown no such interest," he added hopefully: "It may."

## DISASTERS

Four workmen were killed and 4 injured when a 300-ft. crane boom collapsed atop a gas storage tank under construc-

tion in Staten Island, N. Y., **June 5** . . . Three balloonists were killed **June 6,** when their balloon struck an 820-ft. tower in Danube Park, Vienna, Austria . . . Five perished **June 12** in a Hong Kong landslide caused by torrential monsoon rains that buried huts in its wake . . . Tornado killed 7 in Tacy, Minn., **June 13** . . . Twenty perished when landslide **June 17** buried row of slum dwellings under tons of gravel and mud in Salvador, Brazil . . . Seven were killed when their twin-engine plane crashed in a field near Reading, Pa., during a thunderstorm **June 19** . . . A twin-jet Air Force training plane crashed in a dense forest area 24 miles northeast of Alexandria, La., **June 19,** killing the instructor and student . . . Earthquake that rocked a large area of northeast Peru **June 19** left 16 dead and 100 injured . . . A bus carrying students from a girls' school collided with a truck and plunged into a river near Cucuta, Colombia, **June 21,** killing 23 and injuring 25 . . . A stampede of 90,000 fans at a Buenos Aires soccer stadium exit **June 23** killed 71 spectators and injured 130, 40 of them seriously . . . A man fell through the door of a chartered DC-3 airliner carrying 23 passengers when it flew open 8,000 feet over southwest Missouri **June 28;** other passengers and crew of 4 were not injured . . . Four persons were killed and at least 20 injured in the flaming collision of a Greyhound bus and a passenger car 13 miles south of Eugene, Ore., on Interstate 5 **June 28.**

## July—1968

**Intense Fighting After Lull**—U. S. B-52s resumed bombing missions north of the DMZ **July 1** but a lull in ground action **July 1-16,** with most fighting south of the DMZ and around Saigon, was attributed to the Communists' readying of a major new drive on Saigon. Military activity stepped up **July 22-23** when U. S. bases around Danang came under rocket and mortar attack and government administrative centers in Quangngai Province were shelled. In the most widespread concerted bombardments since June, the Communists shelled several cities in the province **July 24.** The Viet Cong carried out a series of attacks on civilians **July 21-26.** U. S. ground and air units anticipating a possible assault on Saigon, **July 25-27** attacked possible infiltration routes to the city. National police **July 16** reported abduction of civilians was up and the Reds were reported to have killed 2,567 civilians, wounded 5,348 and kidnapped 4,241 since Jan 1. Meanwhile, a sharp reduction in Communist shelling of Marine bases in northern Quangtri Province due to recent U. S. air attacks on enemy artillery in the DMZ was reported **July 18,** when B-52s for the first time dropped bombs on North Vietnamese surface-to-air missile sites a few miles north of the DMZ to bolster previous fighter-bomber raids.

**U. S., Soviet A-Talks Due**—Talks on limiting and reducing their arsenals of offensive and defensive nuclear missile systems were planned by the U. S. and Soviets "in the nearest future," President Johnson announced **July 1** during White House ceremonies for signing the nuclear non-proliferation treaty.

**USSR Frees U. S. Jet**—The Soviet Union **July 2** freed a Vietnam-bound U. S. airliner carrying 214 servicemen and a 17-man crew 3 days after two Soviet fighter planes forced it to land on Iturp, one of the Soviet's Kurile Islands north of Japan. The release came after the U. S. acknowl-edged that the Seabord World Airlines DC-8 Super 63, chartered by the Military Airlift Command, had inadvertently intruded on Soviet airspace due to a navigational mistake while en route to a Japanese refueling stop before flying on to Camranh Bay. Capt. Joseph Tosoline, the pilot, **July 3** insisted he had not "strayed off course" as conceded by the State Dept. **June 30.** He said he had signed a statement admitting the violation only to release the plane and those on it. According to reports **July 2,** Japanese radar indicated the plane had been over international waters.

**Paris Peace Talks**—U. S. and North Vietnam peace talks in Paris **July 3, 10** and **17** failed to make any progress as Xuan Thuy, the Hanoi representative, charged that U. S. involvement in Vietnam was contrary to the spirit of the Declaration of Independence and read quotes from U. S. critics of the war, ranging from Black Power advocate Stokely Carmichael to Sen. J. W. Fulbright (D., Ark.), W. Averell Harriman, chief U. S. negotiator, countered that Thuy was distorting American history and should not construe American dissent over the war as a sign of weakness. After talking to both sides in Paris **July 6,** UN Secy. Gen. U Thant said on his return to the U. S. **July 13** he thought the talks would be "a long process," but reiterated his belief that Hanoi would make a "definite move" towards peace if the U. S. were to stop bombing North Vietnam.

**U. S. Viet Deaths Soar**—The U. S. command in Saigon reported **July 4** that U. S. combat deaths for 1968 had reached 9,557 on **June 29,** or 138 more than the 9,419 killed in all of 1967. As of **July 6,** the total American deaths since Jan. 1, 1961, were reported at 25,752. U. S. officials announced **July 13** that 47,411 South Vietnamese civilians had been treated in hospitals during the first 5 months of 1968, as compared to 49,037 for all of 1967. Earlier, the South Vietnamese government reported **July 3** that 7,424 civilians had been killed and another 15,434 had been wounded during the Communist Tct offensive in February. During the week ending **June 29,** 129 Americans died in combat, the lowest weekly toll since Jan. 1.

**LBJ in Central America**—President Johnson assured the people of Central America **July 6** that "we in the U. S. want to help" in promoting economic development and social justice. During a visit to San Salvador, El Salvador, he conferred with the presidents of the 5 countries gathered for the final session of a meeting of the Central American Common Market, the Organization of the States of Central America (ODECA). At the same time he announced he had just approved an additional U. S. contribution of $30,000,-000 to the Central American Bank for Economic Integration for development of regional transport and communication systems, as well as loans totaling $35,-000,000 for distribution among the 5 nations in the market. After touring San Salvador **July 7,** Johnson dropped off the presidents of Nicaragua, Costa Rica, Honduras and Guatemala before returning to Washington **July 8** in his plane.

**Clifford in Vietnam**—In his first visit to South Vietnam as Secretary of Defense, Clark Clifford **July 14-18** conferred with U. S. and South Vietnamese officials and told reporters in Danang **July 17** he ex-

pected the enemy to launch a major new
assault within two months. He termed the
easing of ground fighting at the time "a
lull before the storm" and tied the
enemy's combat plans to "the desire to
make an impression" on the Paris con-
ferees, hoping to affect the negotiations
with "some spectacular accomplishment."

**Senate Unit Quizzes Fortas**—The first
nominee for Chief Justice of the U. S.
ever called upon to do so, Supreme Court
Justice Abe Fortas testified before the
Senate Judiciary Committee **July 16-19** on
his legal philosophy and fitness for confirmation. The longtime friend and adviser of President Johnson admitted he
had continued to counsel the President
while serving on the court, but cited such
precedents as Presidents Washington,
Jackson, Lincoln, Hoover and Roosevelt
having had advisers on the court. Questioned at length and often harshly by
such committee critics of his nomination
as Sens. Sam J. Ervin, Jr. (D., N. C.) and
Strom Thurmond (R., S. C.), Justice Fortas refused to discuss decisions in which
he participated, asserting that to do so
would violate the doctrine of separation
of judicial and legislative power. The
9-day Fortas hearings were put off **July 23**
until after Labor Day and also delayed
the President's nomination of Judge
Homer Thornberry of the U. S. Court of
Appeals as Justice Fortas' successor.

**3 U. S. Pilots Freed**—Three captured
U. S. airmen were freed by Hanoi **July 18**
for "humanitarian" reasons. The 3, shot
down in raids over North Vietnam, were
Maj. James F. Low, 43, of Sausalito, Calif.;
Major Fred N. Thompson, 32, of Taylor,
S. C., and Capt. Joe V. Carpenter, 37, of
Victorville, Calif. Kept in Hanoi until
**Aug. 2**, the 3 were flown to Vientiane, Laos,
in an International Control Commission
plane. From there they arrived in New
York **Aug. 4** via commercial airliner.

**LBJ, Thieu in Hawaii**—Following a 10-
hour conference in Honolulu **July 19** with
South Vietnamese Pres. Nguyen Van
Thieu, President Johnson said he had
affirmed that his Administration was "determined" to defend South Vietnam while
exploring every avenue to peace. Thieu

said he had no doubts about the commitment of both countries to work closely
together in defense of his country and
to keep "aggression" from succeeding.

**LBJ Addresses Governors**—Asserting "we
are doing everything we can to get the
enemy to meet us halfway," President
Johnson at the annual Governors Conference in Cincinnati **July 23** defended the
Administration's Vietnam policies. He also
stressed the need for Federal and state
cooperation in tackling such major domestic problems as crime, unemployment
of the disadvantaged, urban blight and
inadequate health problems.

## INTERNATIONAL

**Soviets Pressure Czechs**—The Kremlin
conducted a 3-prong campaign—military,
propaganda and diplomatic—in July to
pressure the Czechs into backing down
on the liberalization program of Alexander Dubcek's regime, starting with a
reluctance to remove Soviet troops which
should have been out of the country by
**July 1** after a month of Warsaw Pact
troop army games. The Russian and East
bloc press kept up a steady attack on
the "counter-revolutionary" forces which
were trying to make the "people's democracy" more democratic. After a diplomatic cat-and-mouse game, in which
Dubcek, backed solidly by his countrymen, declined a Kremlin summons to a
Warsaw meeting **July 14** and 15 and an
invitation to come to Moscow, the Russians **July 22** made an unprecedented concession: the 11-member Politburo, which
had never left the USSR in a body, would
meet with Czech leaders in their country.
**July 23** the Kremlin announced it would
hold war maneuvers on its western borders up through **Aug. 10**. With troops and
a great show of military strength along
its 1,000-mi. frontier from the Baltic to
North Seas, the meeting was held in
Cierna, just inside Slovakia at the Soviet
border **July 29-Aug. 1** in strictest secrecy.

**Kennedy Round Cuts Start**—Tariff cuts
stipulated under the year-old Kennedy
round agreement to reduce the western
world's tariffs by 35% over a 5-year period
were started **July 1** by the 18 member nations of GATT (General Agreement on

---

## Hunger Joins War on Secessionist Biafra

After 14 months of cruel and bitter
civil war, secessionist Biafra, home of the
Ibo tribe, was outmanned and outgunned
by Nigeria and driven from rich crop-
lands into a landlocked circle of rain forest entirely surrounded by federal troops
and almost completely cut off from food
supplies.

Malnutrition was killing at least 6,000
a day, or 42,000 a week, of the 8,000,000
Ibos crowded into an area one-fourth the
size of Biafra's original territory, according to a July estimate by Dr. Herman
Middlekoop, representative of the World
Council of Churches in Biafra. Pictures
of starving Ibo children touched the conscience of the world but the intransigence
of both sides kept food and medicine
from reaching noncombatants. A Nigerian official said **July 2** that Biafra was
using starvation to win world sympathy.

Tons of food were flown in at great
expense and risk by relief agencies since
Nigeria **July 5** had warned that unau-
thorized planes would be shot down and
offered to set up land mercy routes, insisting on searches for arms in the shipments. Biafrans, fearing the food was
poisoned, refused to touch it.

UN Secy. Gen. U Thant **July 10** urged

Biafran leaders to settle for land routes
and "to cooperate more fully with the
international community in its genuine
endeavors to ameliorate the miserable
plight of the peoples of that region."

Caritas, the international Catholic relief organization, reported **July 15** it had
flown 30 planeloads of food and medicine,
about 315 tons, to Biafra since March.
The World Council of Churches, which
had raised $3,800,000 since March, **July 15**
voted for an additional $3,000,000 for
relief for both Nigeria and Biafra.

Despite reports of food buildups in
nearby Spanish and Portuguese islands
and in Lagos, Dr. Middlekoop said **July 21**
the supply reaching Biafra had actually
been declining. He said that since **July 1**
some 123 tons of food had been brought
in by Caritas, the World Council of
Churches and the Red Cross, and this
amounted to "less than we got in 3 weeks
in April and May."

The U. S. announced **July 12** it was do-
nating $1,300,000 worth of food, bringing
the total of U. S. contributions and supplies to $2,500,000 and the total from all
private and public U. S. sources to $4,300,-
000.

Tariffs and Trade). The cut for most of the members constituted 40% of the total planned in the accord. Those participating included the 6 Common Market nations, Britain, Japan, Norway, Sweden, Denmark, Finland, Spain, Brazil, India, Pakistan, Ceylon and Nigeria. At the same time, the Common Market countries dropped all remaining tariffs among themselves and aligned their common external tariff with Kennedy round cuts. France went along with the cuts, but because of her revolt-weakened economy imposed temporary import quotas and export subsidies.

**Canadian Medicare**—The Canadian Medical Care Insurance Program got under way **July 1,** in British Columbia and Saskatchewan, with the Federal government sharing equally costs for the free medical service. The 1st year's cost of the program was put at $82,000,000 by Health Min. Allen J. MacEachen, who predicted all provinces would be participating in the plan by 1970.

**Nasser in Moscow**—Following conferences with Kremlin leaders during a visit to Moscow **July 4-10,** UAR President Gamal Abdel Nasser, accompanied by Lt. Gen. Abdel Moneim Riad, UAR chief of staff, joined his hosts in a communique condemning "Israel and the imperial forces supporting it." In the communique the Soviets pledged continued economic and political support of the UAR and in "strengthening its defense potential."

**French Pacific A-Tests**—With the explosion of a conventional atomic device one-third of a mile above Mururoa Atoll in the Pacific, France resumed its nuclear testing program **July 7.** The test, the 13th French atmospheric detonation, was the first since July 2, 1967. Fearing radioactive pollution of the atmosphere, Japan, Peru, New Zealand and the Polynesian Territorial Assembly lodged protests against it. A 14th test over the atoll, second in the series believed to be a prelude to a French hydrogen bomb explosion, followed **July 15.**

**De Gaulle Drops Pompidou**—President Charles De Gaulle **July 10** named Maurice Jacques Couve de Murville, 61, to succeed Georges Pompidou, 57, as premier of France. The move spurred wide speculation, coming as it did after the Gaullists' popular sweep in the June elections, much of which was credited to Pompidou. The new premier, who had been finance minister, formed a cabinet two days later, composed largely of members of Pompidou's cabinet, including such key members as Michel Debré, kept on as foreign minister; Andre Malraux, as cultural affairs minister; Pierre Messmer, as armed forces minister, and Raymond

## Pope Paul VI Issues Birth Control Ban

An encyclical condemning all methods of birth control except rhythm as against the will of God was promulgated by Pope Paul VI **July 25.** The pronouncement, "Humanae Vitae" (Of Human Life), made public **July 29,** upheld the doctrine of Pope Pius XI in 1930 proclaiming that "each and every marriage act (of sexual intercourse) must remain open to the transmission of life."

The declaration, coming after a 5-year period in which the Church had indicated it was mulling changes in its traditional stand on contraception, stirred gales of protest from Catholic and non-Catholic clergy and laymen. It rejected the recommendations of the 75-member Commission for the Study of Problems of Population, Family and Birth Control appointed by Pope John XXIII in March 1963 and the Vatican II Ecumenical Council, which had approved the spacing of children by contraception provided a man and wife recognized their obligation to God, to each other and the creation of a family.

Many Catholics declared they would refuse to heed the ban and theologians of other religions joined Catholics in insisting the encyclical was not binding on married Catholics who have reason to practice birth control. Such factors as mutual love and social circumstances should also be considered in guiding the conscience on the morality of contraception, the Dutch hierarchy advised Catholics in refusing to support the encyclical.

Many of the hierarchy were openly disappointed—like Franciscus Cardinal Koenig of Vienna, who tried to keep the Pope from publishing the declaration. Other clerics expressed outrage. "It is incredible that the Pope could even be thinking about issuing such a statement," said the Rev. Charles Curran, vice president of the Catholic Theological Society of America and professor at Catholic U. on **July 27.** Father Curran and 172 U. S. theologians and other Catholics, including all 6 American lay members of the pontifical birth control commission, **July 30** rejected it as outdated and inadequate and urged couples to decide for themselves, "according to their consciences."

"Rome has spoken," Richard Cardinal Cushing of Boston said **July 29** and, according to an old Church proverb, that would have indicated that the case was closed but the protests grew to tidal wave proportions.

At the Lambeth Conference of Anglican bishops **July 30,** the Rt. Rev. J. R. Moorman, a Church of England observer at Vatican II, called it "ecumenically, a disaster for Christianity."

The encyclical also urged world leaders to prevent the use of birth control methods that "allow the morality of your peoples to be degraded" and warned that "directly willed and procured abortion, even if for therapeutic reasons . . . (was) absolutely excluded as licit means of regulating births," adding that sterilization, whether perpetual or temporary, whether of the man or woman was also prohibited. The impact of the edict on population control programs in such areas as Latin America was of special concern to many. A West Berlin paper, Die Zeit, asked: "How is this Papal decree reconcilable with the command to love thy neighbor, when we already know that between now and 1980 approximately 40,-000,000 people will starve to death?" Archbishop Thomas Roberts, a Jesuit pacifist and former Bishop of Bombay, said in London **July 29** that the encyclical "flies in the face of reality."

In a message **July 31,** the National Conference of Catholic Bishops came to the defense of the Pope. Asserting that "we are aware of the difficulty that this teaching lays upon so many of our conscientious married people," the bishops' statement said "we must face the reality that struggling to live out the will of God will often entail sacrifice." Bishop Fulton J. Sheen of Rochester **Aug. 4** praised the Pope's "courage to oppose mass demand for the frustration of life."

Marcellin, as interior minister.

**Seaway Strike Ends**—A pact calling for a 19% wage increase over 3 years **July 14** ended a strike of some 1,250 bridge and lock operators, maintenance men and other workers on the St. Lawrence Seaway. The strike, called by the Canadian Brotherhood of Railway, Transport and General Workers **June 21** tied up 71 ocean-going vessels and about 200 Canadian Lake vessels. It cost shippers, workers and the St. Lawrence Seaway Authority about $15,000,000.

**Geneva Talks Resume**—The UN Disarmament Committee, which had been in recess since **Mar. 4**, reconvened in Geneva **July 16**. William C. Foster, chief U. S. delegate and co-chairman of the 18-nation conference, read a message from President Johnson urging the parley to come up with a "workable" plan to bar "weapons of mass destruction" from the sea bed.

**Coup in Iraq**—A group of Iraq army officers sympathetic with the right wing of the Baath Socialist party toppled the government of Pres. Abdel Rahman Arif **July 17**. The Revolutionary Command Council, with Maj. Gen. Ahmed Hassan al-Bakr, 56, a former premier and defense minister, at its head, called the leftist Arif regime "opportunists, thieves, ignorant, illiterate Zionist spies" and urged liberation of Palestine "now, not tomorrow."

**Canada Postal Strike**—All postal service in Canada came to a halt for 22 days when some 24,000 letter carriers and postal workers went on strike **July 18** after rejecting the government's **July 17** pre-strike pay offer as inadequate. Negotiators reached an accord **Aug. 6** after more than 30 hours of non-stop bargaining. The strikers **Aug. 8** approved a contract retroactive to Aug. 1, 1967, with a pay increase amounting to 15.1% over 26 months on the average hourly wage of $2.57. They returned to work **Aug. 9.**

**Israeli vs. Arab Guerrillas**—Clashes along the west bank of the Jordan River **July 17-22** took a heavy toll of Arab guerrillas, bringing to 59 the number killed since early June, according to Israeli army figures. Seven more, identified as members of Al Fatah, were killed **July 26** in a two-hour clash with Israeli army troops near Jericho. Two Israelis were killed and 10 wounded in the earlier clashes, while two Israeli officers were killed in the Jericho engagement.

**Arabs Hijack Israeli Plane**—Three armed Arab guerrillas **July 23** hijacked an Israeli commercial airliner en route from Rome to Tel Aviv over Italian airspace and forced it to land in Algiers. The 19 non-Israeli passengers were flown to Paris in an Algerian plane later in the day, while 10 Israelis, including 4 women, 3 children and 3 of the plane's hostesses, were released **July 27** and flown to Geneva. However, the Algerian government continued to hold 7 crew members and 5 Israeli passengers, as well as the El Al Boeing 707 jet. Israel **July 23** denounced the act as "airborne hijacking" and **July 28** called on the UN to help negotiate for the release of the plane. Algeria denied being "involved" in the hijacking. The hijackers were members of the Popular Front for the Liberation of Palestine, which claimed **July 23** its members had taken over the plane without any advance knowledge of the Algerian government. **July 24** it said it had asked the International Red Cross to supervise the ex-

change of the Israeli crew and passengers in Algiers for captured Palestinian guerrillas imprisoned in Israel. On **Aug. 31** Algeria freed the 7 crew members and the last 5 passengers, two weeks after the International Federation of Airline Pilots' Association dropped a threatened boycott of Algerian airports on condition that they be released.

## GENERAL

**Seamen Win Wage Hike**—A contract providing a 5% wage hike and 15 more vacation days **July 1** ended the 3-day seamen's strike called by the AFL-CIO Maritime Union against 73 firms bargaining through the Maritime Service Committee and Tanker Service Committee. The strike idled more than 100 freighters and involved some 45,000 seamen.

**N. Y.-Moscow Air Link**—After 7 years of diplomatic and technical delays, direct airline service between New York and Moscow was launched **July 15.** Commercial jets of the two countries were scheduled to make one round trip a week each between the two cities.

**Cleveland Ghetto Riot**—A small band of black nationalists the night of **July 23-24** fired rifles pointblank at two policemen in a squad car on the edge of the city's Glenville ghetto district. With snipers shooting from all sides, the outgunned police called for reinforcements and in the 4-hour pitched battle which followed 7 persons were killed—3 black nationalists, 3 white policemen and a Negro who had tried to help the wounded policeman. The eruption ignited a full scale riot and looters and arsonists rampaged through Glenville and nearby Hough, and 3 more Negroes were killed. Damage on insured property was estimated at $1,500,000. Altogether, 23 persons were wounded—15 in the 1st gunfight. Some 2,700 National Guardsmen brought tenuous order by dawn. Mayor Carl Stokes pointed out that while previous riots had been "a spontaneous reaction to an unresponsive environment," the Glenville conflict had been planned by a few "determined men." Their alleged leader was 37-year-old Fred (Ahmed) Evans, an astrologer in African robe, who had received a summer grant from Stokes' "Cleveland: Now" action group. Evans calmly surrendered to the police, after his gun had jammed. Stokes the 2d night withdrew all white police and National Guard and replaced them with some 100 Negro policemen and about 500 Negro civilian volunteers, most of them militants, who with the aid of heavy rain "cooled it." Some looting continued but the rioting stopped. On the night of **July 25** he brought back the integrated police and some Guards and imposed a 9 p.m.-6 a.m. curfew, having ordered all bars and liquor shops to close. Evans **July 26** was charged with 1st degree murder of the 3 policemen. The 400 Guardsmen were returned to their armories **July 27.**

**Ted Kennedy Says No**—In a statement **July 26**, Sen. Edward M. (Ted) Kennedy (D., Mass.) said he would not accept the Democratic Vice Presidential nomination if it were offered him. His "final decision," given for "personal reasons," ended speculation that he might be Vice President Humphrey's running mate in the hope that his candidacy would have a unifying effect on the party.

**Steel Pact Spurs Price Tiff**—The AFL-CIO United Steelworkers of America (USW) and 11 big steel producers reached accord **July 30** on a 3-year contract providing a package hike of about 6%. The

package, covering about 400,000 workers, was valued at about 90 cents an hour per worker over 3 years by the steel giants and well over $1 billion by USW Pres. I. W. Abel. Bethlehem Steel **July 31** announced a 5% across-the-board steel price rise. The same day the steel firm reported a jump in profits for the 2d quarter and 1st half of 1968, attributing it to consumer steel stockpiling as a hedge against a possible strike. President Johnson **July 31** resisted the price hike as an "inflationary threat." Bethlehem was adamant and later, **July 31** Republic Steel announced 4½% increases and other firms followed suit. The price dispute between the Administration and the industry continued until **Aug. 7,** when U. S. Steel Corp., the largest producer, posted hikes averaging 2½% and others, including many who had slated higher increases, adjusted to that figure.

### DISASTERS

Gas fumes from a sewer line at a Canton, N. C., paper mill killed two **July 3,** hospitalized 4 . . . Seven persons and 8 horses perished **July 3** when a British cargo plane carrying racehorses from France crashed into two parked jet airliners at London airport . . . Five members of a family died in crash of twin-engine plane **July 3** in a field near Gasport, N. Y. . . . Torrential rains in Seoul, South Korea, **July 4** killed 12 persons . . . Two horses perished by fire **July 4** when 125 were led to safety **July 4** when a fire swept through barns at Charlottetown Driving Park, Prince Edward Island . . . A Clyde Beatty-Cole Bros. Circus tent collapsed during a thunder storm in Auburn, N. Y., **July 9,** trapping 300 and injuring at least 110 . . . Thousands were left homeless and 66 perished in Pakistan floods **July 14** . . . Mexicali, Mexico, heat wave **July 12** killed 40 persons, mostly children . . . Torrential rains and floods in 3 states in India swept away hundreds of homes, isolated dozens of villages and left 45 dead **July 14** . . . Nine persons were killed and 6 seriously injured when a truck carrying 20 crashed over a bridge parapet near Beni Mellal, Morocco, **July 15** . . . Fresh areas of the South Indian state of Kerala were swamped by flood waters **July 20,** killing 6 and driving thousands from their homes . . . An emerald mine tunnel cave-in near Bogota, Colombia, **July 20** killed 8 miners, trapped 7 . . . Fire swept through wing of Sahara Hotel, Los Vegas, Nev., **July 20,** routing 400 guests and injuring 29 . . . Seven were badly burned **July 21** when their 19-foot motorboat exploded and burst into flames in Norwalk, Conn. . . . A train collided with a bus carrying 39 migrant farm workers in Newtonville, N. J., **July 23,** killing 9 of the laborers and injuring 16 . . . A typhoon cut across southern Japan **July 28,** leaving 22 victims, most drowned in flood waters . . . About 4,000 refugees fled when Costa Rica's Mt. Arenal volcano erupted for 4 days, **July 29-Aug. 1,** killing 78, injuring more than 100 and leaving many missing.

## August—1968

### NATIONAL

**U. S. Viet Forces Up**—American troops in South Vietnam rose to 541,000, according to a U. S. command announcement **Aug. 1.**

**Vietnam War Intensifies**—Allied forces swept the Ashau Valley **Aug. 4-6** as Vietnam fighting intensified from the Mekong Delta to the demilitarized zone. Heavy civilian and army casualties resulted from accidental ground and air attacks **Aug. 8, 9** and **10.** U. S. and enemy casualties

rose as fighting grew more savage **Aug. 18-31,** especially in the Mekong Delta, the Saigon area and the northern provinces. In the highest weekly combat loss since June 1, 408 Americans died **Aug. 25-31.** Enemy deaths for the week were put at 4,755, most of them in the attack on a U. S. camp at Duclap in the mountains near Cambodia. At month's end, total U. S. casualties reported since 1961 came to 27,508 killed and 171,809 wounded. As of **Aug. 29,** 3,000 civilians had been reported killed in terrorist attacks since **Jan. 1** and the Viet Cong had kidnapped 4,850.

**Paris Peace Talks**—There was no progress in Paris peace talks **Aug. 7, 14, 21,** and **28** as Hanoi representatives continued to press for an unconditional end to U. S. bombing in North Vietnam.

**FRB Discount Rates Cut**—The Federal Reserve Board (FRB) cut its basic discount lending rate from 5½% to 5¼% **Aug. 16.** President Johnson hailed the move as a needed stimulus to homebuilding.

**'Up to Hanoi Now:' LBJ**—The "next move" was up to Hanoi, President Johnson told the Veterans of Foreign Wars at their convention in Detroit **Aug. 19.** He declared the U. S. would take no further steps to de-escalate in Vietnam until Hanoi indicated it would make a serious move toward peace. "We have made a reasonable offer and we have taken first a major step," he said, referring to the **Mar. 31** bombing curtailment and offer to halt bombing in return for "prompt de-escalation" by Hanoi.

**Envoy to Guatemala Slain**—Terrorists shot and killed John Gordon Mein, 54, U. S. Ambassador to Guatemala, **Aug. 28** after stopping his car while he was enroute back to the Embassy after a luncheon. Mein, the first U. S. ambassador murdered at his post, had been in Guatemala since September, 1965. A pro-Communist guerrilla group, the Rebel Armed Forces (FAR) announced **Aug. 29** it had planned to kidnap the envoy in retaliation for the government's capture **Aug. 24** of a FAR leader.

**Eisenhower Rallies**—After suffering two heart attacks, his 6th and 7th, **Aug. 6** and **16,** former President Dwight D. Eisenhower was removed from the critical list **Aug. 29.** His 6th attack came 10 hours after he had addressed the GOP convention by closed circuit TV from his suite at Walter Reed Army Medical Center in the capital. He suffered continual heart spasms known as ventricular fibrillations and cardiac irritability after his 7th attack. An electronic pacer placed in his heart **Aug. 18** was removed later that day as unsuccessful. He suffered new attacks of irritability and spasms **Aug. 21** and **24** but improved steadily, and by **Sept. 3** the hospital stopped issuing daily bulletins.

### INTERNATIONAL

**Congo-Brazzaville Coup**—Coup leaders reversed themselves and called back Pres. Alphonse Massamba-Debat of the Republic of Congo-Brazzaville **Aug. 4,** a day after they had ousted him. Capt. Marien Ngouabi, a paratroop commander who reportedly had led the left-wing Army officers' coup, was named army commander by the returned president on **Aug. 5.**

**UN Raps Israeli Raids**—The UN Security Council met **Aug. 5** to study a new Mideast flareup after a 3-hour Israeli air raid on Arab guerrilla bases 10 mi. inside Jordan **Aug. 4,** during which both countries exchanged tank and artillery fire across the Jordan River. Israeli helicopter-borne troops **Aug. 6** pursued a band of Arab

guerrillas into Jordan, blew up their jeep and a cave believed to have been their base. On **Aug. 16** the Security Council unanimously condemned Israel's **Aug. 4** air attack as a "flagrant violation" of the UN Charter and the Council's Mideast resolution.

**Tito Visits Prague**—Yugoslavia Pres. Tito **Aug. 9-11** visited Prague to indicate his support of Communist chief Dubcek. He was followed **Aug. 15-17** by Romanian Pres. Nicolae Ceausecu, also a sympathizer with the reformist regime.

**Biafra Relief Stalled**—Nigeria **Aug. 15** rejected a plan of the International Committee of the Red Cross in Geneva to fly food to starving Biafra via a neutral airstrip. The Red Cross deplored the rejection **Aug. 17**, asserting in a joint statement with other relief organizations that the civil war was its biggest emergency since World War II. Its relief flights, as well as those of other agencies, had been suspended since Nigerians fired on a Red Cross-chartered plane **Aug. 8-9**. A private U. S. organization, the American Committee to Keep Biafra Alive, focusing on the starving children, demonstrated in front of UN headquarters in New York **Aug. 8** and **18** and called for quick international relief. Other U. S. groups, including several church agencies, also raised funds. Meanwhile, new peace talks, which opened in Addis Ababa, Ethiopia **Aug. 5**, brought neither side closer to agreement on ending the conflict. An **Aug. 14** session on getting relief to victims of the civil war came to naught.

**French Fusion Bomb**—France became the world's 5th thermonuclear nation **Aug. 24** with the explosion of a fusion bomb suspended from a balloon one-third of a mile above its Mururoa Atoll test site. The explosion, after 8 years and 15 atmospheric tests of fission devices, released energy equal to that produced by the blast of 2,000,000 tons of TNT, according to a Paris report **Aug. 27**.

## GENERAL

**Wolfson Convicted**—Louis B. Wolfson, 55, Florida financier, and 3 of his associates were convicted in New York **Aug. 8** of violating the Securities and Exchange Act. They were found guilty by a Federal jury in connection with selling and buying of stock of Merritt-Chapman & Scott Corp., a shipbuilding, construction, chemicals and money-lending firm, currently being liquidated.

**Poor People Demonstrate**—Describing the demonstrators as "representatives of the 51st State—that of poverty," the Poor People's campaign moved to Miami Beach **Aug. 5** to confront the GOP delegates. The Rev. Ralph D. Abernathy, leader of the drive, lauded N. Y. Gov. Nelson A. Rockefeller **Aug. 6** as "one of the last chances for the Republican Party to really win back the black vote." Making the rounds of the major candidates' headquarters **Aug. 7**, the demonstrators were cheered at the Rockefeller hotel, met with a counter-demonstration at Nixon HQ and were barred from a Reagan press conference.

**Detroit News Blackout Ends**—The 267-day news blackout in Detroit ended **Aug. 9** when the city's two daily papers, shut by labor disputes, resumed publication after an agreement on new pacts calling for a $33-a-week pay raise over 34½ months. A strike by the Teamsters Union against the Detroit News had started the shutdown **Nov. 15, 1967**. Two days later, the Detroit Free Press closed.

**McGovern in Presidential Race**—Sen. George S. McGovern (S. D.), 46, announced his entry in the Democratic Presidential race **Aug. 10**, asserting he was committed to the "twin goals for which Robert Kennedy gave his life—an end to the war in Vietnam and a passionate commitment to heal the divisions in our lives here at home."

**Pope Visits Colombia**—In the first Papal visit to South America, Pope Paul VI went to Bogota, Colombia, **Aug. 22-24** for the 39th International Eucharistic Congress of the Roman Catholic Church. Warning against the use of "violence and revolution" as being "contrary to the Christian spirit," he called for social and economic reform on the continent. Welcomed by cheering crowds everywhere,

## Soviet Union Invades Czechoslovakia

More than 200,000 Soviet troops, augmented by token forces from loyal Warsaw Pact puppets, invaded Czechoslovakia **Aug. 20-21**.

The outraged populace staged a stunning nonviolent campaign since physical resistance was useless as Soviet tanks and paratroops took over Prague and other key areas. Their force rose to 650,000 in a week. Throngs of unarmed Czechs gathered, proclaiming their loyalty to Communist Party First Secretary Alexander Dubcek, who with 6 other liberal Czech Communists, had been taken to an unknown destination.

As the invaders solidified their position, 1,200 delegates to the Czech Communist party **Aug. 21-22** held a clandestine meeting and elected a new and liberal presidium which told the Russians to get out or face a general strike. The strike lasted one hour as 20,000 peaceful demonstrators marched in Prague's Wenceslas Square in front of Soviet tanks and soldiers, shouting, "Russian murderers go home."

The world outcry against the invasion included protests from some major Red parties. The U. S. and 6 other nations took the issue to the UN Security Council, demanding condemnation of the invasion. The action met with the Soviet Union's 105th veto after it was approved 10-2 **Aug.**
23; only Hungary voted with the Kremlin.

Concern centered on the fate of Dubcek and there were unconfirmed rumors he had been killed. Vowing he would not bow to a Moscow-imposed puppet regime, Czech Pres. Ludvik Svoboda left for the Kremlin **Aug. 23** to attempt to resolve the crisis.

Dubcek and Svoboda returned to Prague **Aug. 27** and urged their people to remain calm in the face of Soviet demands for reversal of the regime's liberalization of Communism. The people cried betrayal at first, when the price they would have to pay was announced **Aug. 29**: They would have to settle for loss of some of their most precious recent reforms—liberalization of the press and the right to form non-Communist political organizations.

Moscow agreed in turn to send some troops home and to withdraw eventually, but there were no guarantees for that "other than our own wisdom," Natl. Assembly Pres. Josef Smrkovsky said **Aug. 29**. A new 21-member ruling presidium superseding the one chosen at the secret **Aug. 23** meeting was elected **Sept. 1**. The new presidium, again headed by Dubcek, was chosen after a two-day Prague meeting in which plans to reshuffle the government to suit the Soviets were made.

he denounced "the unjust economic inequalities between rich and poor, and abuses of authority and administration against you and the community" in addressing 35,000 peasants **Aug. 23.**

## DISASTERS

At least 307 perished in Manila earthquake **Aug. 2** . . . Seven died in British freighter fire 800 mi. off New Zealand coast **Aug. 5** . . . Mine shaft explosion near Greenville, Ky., **Aug. 7** killed 9 . . . Interstate bus plunged over precipice near Rio De Janiero, Brazil, **Aug. 9**, killing 6, injuring 14 . . . British airliner crash north of Munich **Aug. 9** left 48 dead . . . Thirty-five of 37 aboard died in Piedmont Airlines plane crash **Aug. 10** just short of Charleston, W. Va., airport . . . At least 200 died and 500 disappeared in series of earthquakes and tidal waves starting in Celebes islands, Indonesia, **Aug. 10** and ending with sinking of Tuguan island **Aug. 15** . . . Italian oil tanker explosion off Sicily coast **Aug. 11** killed 7, injured 7 . . . Los Angeles Airways helicopter crash in Compton, Calif., **Aug. 14**, on way to Disneyland, killed all 21 aboard . . . Overflowing dam flooded 3 villages in northeastern Nicaragua **Aug. 14**, leaving 2,000 homeless, 19 missing . . . Floods in GurGujarat and Rajasthan, India, claimed more than 1,000 lives in 7 days, according to Bombay reports **Aug. 14** . . . At least 21 were killed when a factory making explosives for toy pistols blew up **Aug. 16** in Ibi, Spain . . . All 40 aboard perished in Egyptian airliner plunge into Mediterranean north of Port Said **Aug. 18** . . . At least 102 women and children were killed when two sightseeing buses were swept into typhoonrain swollen river during Honshu, Japan, landslide **Aug. 18** . . . Earthquake in Donggala city, Celebes, Indonesia, killed 200 **Aug. 20** . . . All 10 aboard a bus died in collision with a truck near Tarragona, Spain, **Aug. 20** . . . Eight were killed, 3 injured while fighting brush fire in Glendora, Calif., **Aug. 24.**

# September—1968

## NATIONAL

**Paris Talks Stalemate**—U. S.-North Vietnam talks in Paris **Sept. 11, 17** and **25** continued at a stalemate, with both sides airing conflicting battlefield claims.

**Savage Vietnam Battle**—A savage battle **Sept. 11-16** in and around Tayninh, a major invasion route to Saigon, cost the Communists at least 500 men killed. The Allied toll was more than 200 killed or wounded. In one of the longest sustained U. S. thrusts inside the southern half of the DMZ, 2,000 Marines were airlifted to the southern half **Sept. 17** to prevent an expected drive south by two Hanoi Divs. and to neutralize enemy pressure on Allied outposts along the 40-mi. stretch. They were bolstered by 4,000 more **Sept. 27.** The New Jersey, the world's only active battleship, which had arrived from the U. S. after its release from the mothball fleet, shelled enemy targets in the DMZ **Sept. 30.**

**Ball Leaves UN Post**—George W. Ball, chief U. S. representative to the UN, resigned **Sept. 26** to join Vice President Humphrey's Presidential campaign staff as top foreign policy adviser. His resignation after 5 months at the UN was announced by President Johnson, who designated James Russell Wiggins, 64, editor and executive vice president of the Washington Post, as Ball's successor.

## INTERNATIONAL

**Massamba-Debat Ousted**—Congo-Brazzaville Pres. Alphonse Massamba-Debat was ousted again **Sept. 4** for failing to "assure peace and national unity" by the military government following fierce fighting between regular army units and a Cuban-trained militia of some 300 men. The rebels reportedly had resisted incorporation of the militia into the army, which took over their camp late **Aug. 31.** The junta, headed by Capt. Marien Ngouabi, named Alfred Raoul interim president.

**'Final' Nigerian Assault**—Nigeria claimed the capture of the Biafran cities of Aba **Sept. 4** and Owerri **Sept. 16** in what the army described as its "final offensive" against the secessionist state. Federal troops were reported marching on Umuahia, the last remaining city held by the Biafrans and headquarters of their military leader. Lt. Col. Chukwuemeka Odumegwu Ojukwu.

**UN Truce Bid**—The UN Security Council, meeting since **Sept. 4** to study Israeli charges that Egyptians had kidnapped an Israeli soldier after killing two others in an ambush along the Suez Canal, **Sept. 18** called on Israel and the Arab states to respect the Council's cease-fire orders and urged them to cooperate with UN envoy Gunnar V. Jarring's Mideast mission.

**Czechoslovak Crisis Continues**—Soviet 1st Deputy Foreign Min. Vasilly V. Kuznetsov arrived in Prague **Sept. 6** to confer with Czechoslovak leaders for 5 days on the Moscow agreement. In line with that accord, two quasi political clubs formed in the wake of the liberalized Dubcek program were outlawed **Sept. 6.** This followed the banning **Sept. 2** of 3 journals termed "counterrevolutionary" by the Soviets. Premier Oldrich Cernik in an economic mission to Moscow **Sept. 10** signed two trade protocols. One provided for the USSR to build a natural gas pipeline from Kiev. The other was not disclosed. Soviet tank units moved from conspicuous positions in Prague to the surrounding countryside **Sept. 11**, but continued to occupy strategic areas such as the international airport. The National Assembly **Sept. 13** reimposed "preventive censorship." Dubcek appealed for public order **Sept. 14,** urging his people not to provoke clashes with the occupying troops. After intensive Soviet pressure for his dismissal, Foreign Min. Jiri Hajek was ousted **Sept. 19.** Hajek, who had been in Yugoslavia at the time of the invasion, had put his country's case against the occupation before the UN. A Dubcek mission to Moscow authorized by the presidium due to rising disagreement over the interpretation of the Moscow agreement was cancelled **Sept. 24.**

**UAR-Israeli Clashes Continue**—Both Israeli and Egyptian forces suffered heavy casualties in a 4-hour artillery duel across the cease-fire line of the Suez Canal **Sept. 8.** The Israeli reported 10 soldiers killed, 17 wounded; Egypt, 5 soldiers and 6 civilians killed, 12 soldiers and 30 civilians wounded. Three Egyptian towns were reported heavily damaged. Arab saboteurs had carried out damaging explosive attacks in Jerusalem **Aug. 18** and in Tel Aviv **Sept. 4** as part of a stepped-up guerrilla terror drive against Israeli civilians. Sporadic guerrilla and Israeli patrol clashes continued along the cease-fire line and **Sept. 25** Israeli Defense Min. Moshe Dayan said he feared another war was imminent. Israeli Foreign Min. Abba Eban **Sept. 26** rejected a 4-point USSR plan to end the Mideast impasse as identical to a plan presented by the Soviets Nov. 22, 1967, which he said, called for Israeli withdrawal "without the possibility of sure and recognized frontiers."

**2d French H-Bomb**—France exploded its second hydrogen bomb **Sept. 8** over its

Mururoa Atoll testing ground and announced the end of the two-month test series, which had included 3 atomic and two thermonuclear explosions, on **Sept. 9.**

**France Vetoes UK Again**—France for the 3d time vetoed Britain's entry into the European Common Market **Sept. 27,** when it turned down a West German interim plan to give the United Kingdom membership.

**Canadian Parliament Opens**—with a Liberal party majority in the House of Commons, Canada's Parliament opened **Sept. 12.** The traditional opening speech, read by Gov. Gen. Roland Michener to Commons and the Senate, was prepared by Prime Min. Pierre Elliott Trudeau and reiterated his pledge for a "just society."

**West Bars Soviet Force**—The U. S., Britain and France warned Russia **Sept. 17** that carrying out its threats to use military force against West Germany would bring "immediate Allied response" under the North Atlantic Treaty.

**Philippines Claims Sabah**—A law claiming Malaysia's Borneo state of Sabah belonged to the Philippines Republic was signed by Philippine Pres. Ferdinand E. Marcos **Sept. 18,** and precipitated a rupture with Malaysia, which suspended diplomatic relations with the Philippines **Sept. 19.** There were international repercussions as well since the U. S. proclaimed its neutrality, for which it was assailed by Manila legislators **Sept. 20.** Thousands marched in protest against the Philippines in Malaysia **Sept. 20.** In retaliation for British support of Malaysia in the dispute, the Philippines **Sept. 23** said UK and Australian ships could not go through Philippine waters without prior permission. Some 250 students attacked the British Embassy in Manila **Sept. 27.** Another demonstration in the U. S. Embassy grounds **Sept. 27** protested the "insincere neutrality."

**Mexican Army Seizes University**—In a move to end 7 weeks of student agitation in Mexico City an army force of 1,300 seized the National University **Sept. 18.** This precipitated new clashes between students and police, causing at least 17 deaths through **Sept. 24** and the arrest of more than 1,000 students. At least 15 were killed in fierce fighting **Sept. 23-24** when students fired on police from university buildings and surrounding houses. Striking students returned after the army withdrew from the campus **Sept. 30.**

**UN Assembly Opens**—The UN General Assembly gathered at UN headquarters **Sept. 24** for its 23d regular session, after a brief meeting **Sept. 22,** when the issue of Mideast peace was held over for the 23d term. With Guatemalan Foreign Min. Emilio Arenales Catalan presiding, the Assembly **Sept. 24** unanimously elected the new African state of Swaziland as the UN's 125th member.

**New Portugal Premier**—Dr. Marcelo Caetano, 62, was named premier of Portugal **Sept. 27** to succeed Antonio de Oliveira Salazar, 79, who had been in a coma from a brain hemmorhage since **Sept. 16.** Dr. Caetano, a long-time associate of Salazar, who had governed the country since 1932, was a law professor and businessman. He had been assistant premier from 1955 to 1958.

**Greek Junta Charter OKd**—Greek voters **Sept. 29** approved the new constitution submitted by the ruling military junta to replace the 1952 charter. Final figures showed 4,638,543, or 91.7% of the 5,048,981 votes cast under military law were in favor of the constitution.

## GENERAL

**Humphrey Starts Drive**—Vice Pres. Hubert H. Humphrey, Democratic Presidential candidate, launched his drive in a Labor Day parade in New York **Sept. 2,** marching beside AFL-CIO Pres. George Meany. In a sharp attack on Nixon's policy, Humphrey **Sept. 8** said the Republican party had joined "forces with the most reactionary elements" to "exploit the fears and tensions that grip significant portions of our people." He pointed out he had fought reactionaries and extremists on the right for human rights, adding that now he was defending rights against extremism of both left and right. In the early stages of the campaign, crowds were small and mostly sprinkled with anti-war demonstrators. By the 3d week he stepped up his attacks on Nixon, but drew his biggest response in Sioux Falls, S. D., **Sept. 19** and in Louisville, Ky., **Sept. 20** when he pledged the end of the Vietnam war would be his chief goal if elected. While stumping in Ohio, Minnesota, California and Oregon **Sept. 22-28,** he stressed the need to reassess Vietnam issues, proposed a 50% increase in Social Security benefits over 4 years and a river conservation program.

**Nixon Launches Campaign**—Republican Presidential candidate Richard M. Nixon drew a crowd of some 450,000 persons when started his campaign with a Chicago motorcade **Sept. 4.** He was accompanied by Sen. Edward W. Brooke (R., Mass.), who told the crowd Nixon would unite the country, "black and white," and "do everything he can" to end the Vietnam war. Nixon drew large crowds everywhere. In Houston, Tex., **Sept. 6** he said there was "not a dime's worth of difference" between his opponent's policies and "what we've had for the past 4 years." Discussing "law and order" at B'nai B'rith's convention in Washington **Sept. 8,** he declared some "people think it is a code for racism." Actually, he said, "order without progress is tyranny. You cannot have order without progress in a free society." He declared the balance of power in the Mideast "must be tipped in Israel's favor." Polls indicated Nixon was leading as he campaigned in California, Salt Lake City and Philadelphia **Sept. 16-21.** Campaigning in 9 states **Sept. 23-28,** he cited the Administration's high taxes and inflationary prices and said the country "cannot afford Hubert Humphrey as president." In Louisville **Sept. 27** he wrote off Humphrey's attempt to get him to debate as "kid stuff." He described 3d party Presidential candidate George C. Wallace as Humphrey's "secret weapon" to "beat Nixon in the new South."

**Muskie Campaign**—Sen. Edmund S. Muskie (Me.) appealed to voters "to get our emotions under control" and to "start using our heads" in launching his Democratic campaign for Vice President in San Antonio, Tex., **Sept. 8.** Throughout his campaign he accented the issues of Vietnam and crime and scored 3d party Presidential candidate George C. Wallace. He deplored "playing upon the discontent and uneasiness of the voters" by "playing off one group of Americans against another."

**Agnew Apologizes**—Maryland Gov. Spiro T. Agnew put strong stress on "law and order" in his drive as GOP Vice Presidential candidate. In Washington **Sept. 10** he charged Democratic Presidential candidate Hubert H. Humphrey had been soft on Communism. After criticism in his party as well as the opposition he retracted the statement **Sept. 12.** He came under fire again for using the terms "Jap"

and "Polack" in referring to Americans of Japanese or Polish ancestry and apologized for his faux pas **Sept. 23**, asserting it was "ridiculous" to accuse him, "son of a Greek immigrant," of being "insensitive to the national pride and heritage of other people."

### DISASTERS

Death toll after weekend of earthquakes in eastern Iran was put at 10,000 **Sept. 2** . . . Single-engine plane exploded and crashed in thunderstorm near Wilkes-Barre, Pa., **Sept. 2**, killing all 3 aboard . . . Landslides from heavy rains in San Salvador **Sept. 2** killed 14 . . . Three soccer fans were killed in riot when stand collapsed during game in Bhangura, East Pakistan, **Sept. 4** . . . Bulgarian airliner carrying East German tourists to Black Sea coast crashed near Burgas, Bulgaria, **Sept. 4**, killing 50 of 89 aboard . . . All 95 aboard perished **Sept. 12** when an Air France jet en route from Corsica to Nice crashed into stormy waters off the French Riviera . . . Dozens were injured and trapped in their homes when 3 earthquakes rocked Jahrum, Iran, **Sept. 15** . . . One died, 48 were injured in HemisFair monorail train crash **Sept. 15** in San Antonio, Tex. . . . Twenty-eight soldiers perished **Sept. 16** when their truck plunged over a cliff into the Kali River in northern Uttar Pradesh, India . . . Eleven persons were killed and 19 injured **Sept. 17** when their truck plunged into ravine near Bursa, Turkey . . . Diesel fuel-fed explosion and fire on freighter Cerberus, being broken up for scrap in Hong Kong, left 5 dead, 20 injured **Sept. 18** . . . Six children perished in landslide that destroyed their homes in San Jose, Costa Rica, **Sept. 20** . . . Chilean Air Force plane crashed into home in Santiago **Sept. 20**, killing 6 . . . Six died in French experimental plane crash **Sept. 20** in Farnborough, England . . . Head-on collision of two trains near Depok, Indonesia **Sept. 20** killed 30, injured 150 . . . Twenty-three persons were injured **Sept. 21** in 35-vehicle chain collision on fog-shrouded New Jersey Turnpike near Woodbury, N. J. . . . Twin-engined Navy plane crashed on landing at Lakehurst Naval Air Station, N. J., **Sept. 21**, killing 3 . . . One was killed, 11 were hurt in 30-car crash in heavy fog over U. S. 10 Freeway, Midland, Mich., **Sept. 23** . . . Eleven were killed, 23 injured and 22 escaped unhurt when Air Force jet tanker crash landed at Wake Island **Sept. 24** with one engine out . . . Nineteen perished **Sept. 28** in Madras, India, fireworks factory explosion.

## October—1968

### NATIONAL

**LBJ Withdraws Fortas' Name**—President Johnson **Oct. 2** withdrew his nomination of Supreme Court Justice Abe Fortas as Chief Justice of the U. S. after an effort to end a Senate filibuster to block the nomination failed. The withdrawal also voided the nomination of Judge Homer Thornberry to succeed Fortas as Associate Supreme Court Justice.

**U. S. Jets for Israel**—President Johnson **Oct. 9** gave State Secy. Dean Rusk the go-ahead signal to negotiate with Israel on its request to buy U. S. jet fighter-bombers. His directive was in line with a Foreign Aid Authorization Act amendment urging the U. S. to sell planes to Israel to prevent "future Arab aggression by offsetting sophisticated weapons received by the Arab states (from the USSR) and to replace losses suffered by Israel in the 1967 conflict."

**Justice Warren to Stay**—In the aftermath of the filibuster that "prevented the Senate from voting on the nomination" of Justice Abe Fortas, President Johnson **Oct. 10** disclosed that Earl Warren, Chief Justice of the U. S., would stay on "until his successor qualifies."

**LBJ Calls Bombing Halt**—President Johnson **Oct. 31** announced that he was calling a complete halt to all American air, naval and artillery bombardment of North Vietnam as of 8 a.m., (EST) on **Nov. 1**. *See The War in Vietnam, Page 40.*

### INTERNATIONAL

**Mexico Students, Troops Clash**—Women and children were killed when the bloodiest clash between students and troops in the 9-week student strike erupted **Oct. 2** in a Mexico City housing project plaza, where 6,000 had gathered for a march on the National Polytechnic Institute to protest army occupation of the campus. Conflicting reports put the toll at 28 to 200 dead, 200 to 500 wounded. Some 1,500 were jailed.

**Rusk Hits Soviet Invasion**—U. S. State Secy. Dean Rusk **Oct. 2** scored the Soviet invasion of Czechoslovakia in a major address at the UN's 23d General Assembly. He charged the Russians were violating the UN Charter by flouting the occupied country's sovereignty and heating up the cold war. Soviet Foreign Min. Andrei A. Gromyko **Oct. 3** countered that the invasion was "self-defense taken by the Socialist countries against imperialistic intrigue."

**Peru's Belaunde Ousted**—Peruvian military leaders early **Oct. 3** ousted Pres. Fernando Belaunde Terry, 55, in a bloodless coup and put him on a plane to Buenos Aires, Argentina. Gen. Juan Velasco Alvarado, 58, Army chief of staff and president of the joint chiefs of staff, took over as president of the new "Revolutionary Government."

**Prague Yields to Kremlin**—After two postponements and one cancellation, Czechoslovakia's leaders finally went to Moscow **Oct. 3-4** and gave in to Kremlin pressure to abandon the remnants of their 8-month liberalization program and to let Soviet troops stay on. Although press censorship had been reimposed, Czech newspapers **Oct. 5** scored the "lies" in Soviet news media, which leveled a steady propaganda barrage at the Czech "slowness" in "normalization." Soviet Premier Aleksei N. Kosygin and other Russian officials signed in Prague **Oct. 16** a treaty giving the USSR the right to station troops in the country "temporarily."

**Israel Submits Peace Plan**—Israeli Foreign Min. Abba Eban **Oct. 8** detailed a 9-point Mideast peace plan at the UN General Assembly. The program, providing for withdrawal of Israeli troops from Arab territories in exchange for a permanent peace treaty, called for secure boundaries, a mutual nonaggression pact, open frontiers, freedom of navigation, solution of the Arab refugee problem, new arrangements for Jerusalem's religious shrines, mutual recognition of sovereignty and regional cooperation.

**UK-Rhodesia Talks Fail**—British Prime Min. Harold Wilson and Ian D. Smith, his Rhodesian counterpart, met aboard the British warship Fearless in Gibraltar harbor **Oct. 9-13**, but failed to agree on the problem of eventual black majority rule in Rhodesia.

**Junta Ousts Arias**—Arnulfo Arias, 67, inaugurated President of Panama **Oct. 1**, was ousted in a coup by the National

Guard **Oct. 11.** A junta headed by Col. Jose M. Pinilla and Col. Bolivar Urrutia, named President and Vice President, respectively, took over **Oct. 12.** Arias, who took refuge in the U. S.-controlled Canal Zone **Oct. 12,** flew to Washington **Oct. 22** and "symbolically" occupied the Panama Embassy for a day, asserting he was still his country's constitutional president. Pro-junta men moved in again **Oct. 23.**

**New Quebec Separatist Party**—Two Quebec separatist groups merged at a convention in the city of Quebec **Oct. 11-14** to form the Parti Québecois (PQ), dedicated to independence by peaceful, democratic means for a republican Quebec linked in an economic union with Canada. René Lévesque, head of the Mouvement Souveraineté-Association, one of the groups, was elected president and Gilles Gregoire, head of Ralliement National, the other, vice president.

## GENERAL

**Humphrey Campaign Trail**—Vice President Hubert H. Humphrey **Oct. 1** said in a radio address in Nashville, Tenn., he would run thereafter as the Democratic "candidate and leader of my party" and not as Vice President. The previous day, in Salt Lake City, Utah, he pledged he would stop the bombing of North Vietnam "as an acceptable risk for peace" if he should be elected President. He challenged Nixon to TV debates **Oct. 7** and **Oct. 20,** but the GOP candidate would not be drawn into them.

**Wallace Tags LeMay as VP**—At a joint TV press conference in Pittsburgh, Pa., **Oct. 3,** George C. Wallace, 3d party Presidential candidate, introduced Gen. Curtis E. LeMay, 61, former Air Force Chief of Staff, as his Vice Presidential running mate. LeMay's remarks on the use of nuclear weapons stirred controversy and brought expressions of concern from both major party candidates **Oct. 4.** LeMay said he would use nuclear arms "if it was necessary," but he added, "I don't think it's necessary in this case or this war to use" them.

**Nixon Campaign**—GOP Presidential candidate Richard M. Nixon, engaging in a 5-day-a-week campaign schedule across the country and resting weekends in Key Biscayne, Fla., told UPI editors and publishers **Oct. 7** he could accept a Vietnam peace settlement President Johnson could not accept. Anti-war hecklers attempted to disrupt some of his rallies. At one, in Santa Monica, Calif., **Oct. 9,** he shouted: "Those who have had a chance for 4 years and could not produce peace should not be given another chance."

**11-Day Apollo 7 Flight**—Three U. S. astronauts **Oct. 11-22** successfully circled the earth 163 times in an 11-day test flight of the Apollo 7, the space ship designed to carry the first Americans to the moon. Navy Capt. Walter Marty (Wally) Schirra, Jr., 45, the first man to go into orbit for a 3d time, commanded the 260-hour, 4,500,000-mile space journey. It was a 1st flight for the other crew members, Air Force Maj. Donn Fulton Eisele, 38, the navigator, and Ronnie Walter Cunningham, 36, a civilian, who monitored the controls and handled communications. All 3 astronauts had colds during the flight but suffered no ill effects. They started transmitting the 1st of 7 live TV broadcasts from the spaceship **Oct. 14.** In the splashdown 7:11 a.m. EDT **Oct. 22,** some 325 mi. south of Bermuda, the capsule landed upside down, but was quickly righted by inflated balloons. It landed only one-third of a mile from the aiming point. Air Force Lt. Gen. Samuel C. Phillips, Apollo program director, **Oct. 22** declared the flight was "the first space operation that has accomplished more than 100% of its preplanned objectives." *See Space 1968, Page 43.*

**Mrs. Kennedy, Onassis Wed**—Mrs. Jacqueline Kennedy, 39-year-old widow of President John F. Kennedy, was married to Greek shipping magnate Aristotle Socrates Onassis, 62, in a Greek Orthodox ceremony **Oct. 20** on his private island of Skorpios off the Greek coast. The wedding was attended only by relatives, including her two children, Caroline, 10, and John, Jr., 7, and a few close friends.

**Daughter to Lynda Bird**—Mrs. Charles S. Robb, President Johnson's older daughter, gave birth to a 7-pound, 8-ounce girl early **Oct. 25.** The former Lynda Bird Johnson's husband, Marine Capt. Charles S. Robb, was stationed in Danang, South Vietnam.

**4-Day Soviet Space Flight**—A Soviet spacecraft, Soyuz 3, manned by Col. Georgi T. Beregovoi, 47, was launched **Oct. 26** and carried out in its 1st orbit of the earth an approach maneuver with Soyus 2, an unmanned craft sent up the day before. After flying two days in tandem, Soyus 2 landed in the Soviet Union **Oct. 28.** Four days after he was lofted into orbit, Beregovoi brought his craft to a soft landing in the steppes of Kazakhstan **Oct. 30.**

**N. Y. School Strike Continues**—Some 1,-000,000 New York City children were still out of school all through **October** as the strike called by the United Federation of Teachers, headed by Alfred Shanker, continued and threatened to extend throughout the entire term. The strike, against the leaders of a model decentralization program in the predominantly Negro community of Ocean Hill-Brownsville in Brooklyn, brought charges of racial discrimination from both sides.

## DISASTERS

Six crewmen were reported missing but 31 were rescued from a disabled Panamanian vessel **Oct. 2** after it was hit by typhoon Elaine in Taiwan Strait . . . Eleven persons were killed, 7 injured and 32 missing **Oct. 3** when a truck plunged into a river south of Bangkok, Thailand . . . Eight coal miners were killed, 7 missing and two injured **Oct. 4** when a gas explosion wrecked a mine in Lünen, the Ruhr, Germany . . . More than 2,000 perished in 4 days of floods **Oct. 4-7,** caused by torrential rains in the eastern Himalayas . . . Two buses plunged over cliffs in provincial areas of South Korea **Oct. 8,** killing 18 . . . Crash of light plane into a television tower guy wire near Hetlands, S. D., **Oct. 8** left 4 dead . . . Ten perished and 20 were injured when fire swept Hotel Metzerbrau in Zurich, Switzerland, **Oct. 9** . . . Eleven perished in the crash of a Czechoslovak Airlines plane **Oct. 11,** shortly after takeoff . . . At least 300 died **Oct. 10** when an overloaded ferry sank in shark-infested waters off Mindanao island, Philippines . . . A bus plunged into a northern Kashmir ravine **Oct. 14,** killing 21 and injuring 20 . . . Seven died **Oct. 18** when a disabled private plane crashed and exploded in a residential area in Cleveland's West Side . . . Forty persons were missing after a boat capsized while crossing the Koel River near Rourkela, India **Oct. 19.**

## Statue of Liberty National Monument

Since 1886 the Statue of Liberty Enlightening the World has stood on Liberty Island in New York harbor, as a symbol of freedom. It also commemorates Franco-American friendship for it was given by the people of France and designed by Frederic Auguste Bartholdi (1834-1904). A $2,500,000 building housing the American Museum of Immigration is being constructed at the base of the statue. Exhibit halls, a library and study rooms as well as a Hall of Records will be grouped within the star-shaped Fort Wood which encompasses the statue. The statue is a National Monument, administered by the National Park Service.

Edouard de Laboulaye, French historian and admirer of American political institutions, suggested that the French present a monument to the United States, the latter to provide pedestal and site. In June, 1871, Bartholdi, who had defended his native Colmar in Alsace when it was overrun during the Franco-Prussian War, came to the United States to investigate the project. He visualized the idea of a colossal statue at the entrance of New York harbor, welcoming the peoples of the world with the torch of liberty. Bartholdi was then 37 years old.

The French approved the idea and formed the Franco-American Union to raise funds, which eventually reached $250,000. Bartholdi began work about 1874 in Paris. He made several models and one, 36 ft. tall, enabled him to compute the statue in sections. Wooden battens were made and sheets of copper 3-32 of an inch thick were hammered into shape on them by hand. A framework of four steel supports was designed by Gustave Eiffel, creator of the Eiffel tower. When completed the statue was 151 ft., 1 in. tall.

The hand of the statue holding aloft the torch was exhibited at the Centennial exposition in Philadelphia in 1876 and later in Madison Square.

On Washington's birthday, Feb. 22, 1877, Congress approved the use of a site on Bedloe's island suggested by Bartholdi. This island of 12 acres had been owned in the 17th century by a Walloon named Isaac Bedloe, who came to New Amsterdam in 1639. He died in 1673 and his wife sold the island for £80. In later years it was owned by the City of New York and the U. S. Government. It was called Bedloe's until Aug. 3, 1956, when President Eisenhower approved a resolution of Congress changing the name to Liberty Island.

The head was shown at the Paris exposition of 1878. When framework and base were put in place in Paris the American minister, Levi P. Morton, drove the first rivet on Oct. 24, 1881, in honor of the centennial of the battle of Yorktown, in which French and Americans were allies.

The statue was finished May 21, 1884, and formally presented to U. S. Minister Morton July 4, 1884, by Ferdinand de Lesseps then head of the Franco-American Union and promoter of the Panama Canal.

On Aug. 5, 1884, the Americans laid the cornerstone for the pedestal. This was to be built on the foundations of Fort Wood, which had been erected by the Government in 1811. The fort originally mounted 24 heavy guns and had a garrison of from 50 to as many as 600 troops.

The American committee had raised $125,000, but when the pedestal was 15 ft. high, this was found to be inadequate.

Joseph Pulitzer, owner of The World of New York City, on Mar. 16, 1885, called for general subscriptions. By Aug. 11, 1885 he had raised $100,000. The total cost of statue and pedestal was estimated at $500,000.

The statue arrived dismantled, in 214 packing cases, in the steamship Isere, which reached New York from Rouen, France, in June, 1885. The pedestal was made of concrete with granite facing and steel girders were built into it to connect with the framework of the statue. The first rivet of the statue was driven July 12, 1886, and the last on Oct. 28, 1886, when President Grover Cleveland dedicated the statue in the presence of the sculptor.

The torch was originally maintained by the Lighthouse Service. Funds for permanently lighting the statue were raised by subscription by The World of New York in 1916 and President Wilson turned on the lights Dec. 2, 1916. The Island was used by the United States Army until 1937, when the post was given up.

The statue weighs 450,000 lbs. or 225 tons. The copper sheeting weighs 200,000 lbs. There are 167 steps from the land level to the top of the pedestal, 168 steps inside the statue to the head, and 54 rungs on the ladder leading to the arm that holds the torch. Visitors may enter the head, which holds from 30 to 40 persons, but not the torch. The statue is open daily.

| DIMENSIONS OF THE STATUE | Ft. | In. |
|---|---|---|
| Height from base to torch | 151 | 1 |
| Foundation of pedestal to torch | 305 | 1 |
| Heel to top of head | 111 | 1 |
| Length of hand | 16 | 5 |
| Index finger | 8 | 0 |
| Circumference at second joint | 3 | 6 |
| Size of finger nail | 13x10 in. | |
| Head from chin to cranium | 17 | 3 |
| Head, thickness from ear to ear | 10 | 0 |
| Distance across the eye | 2 | 6 |
| Length of nose | 4 | 6 |
| Right arm, length | 42 | 0 |
| Right arm, greatest thickness | 12 | 0 |
| Thickness of waist | 35 | 0 |
| Width of mouth | 3 | 0 |
| Tablet, length | 23 | 7 |
| Tablet, width | 13 | 7 |
| Tablet, thickness | 2 | 0 |

### EMMA LAZARUS' FAMOUS POEM

A poem by Emma Lazarus, which is graven on a tablet within the pedestal on which the Goddess stands, follows:

#### THE NEW COLOSSUS

Not like the brazen giant of Greek fame,
With conquering limbs astride from land to land;
Here at our sea-washed, sunset gates shall stand
A mighty woman with a torch, whose flame
Is the imprisoned lightning, and her name
Mother of Exiles. From her beacon-hand
Glows world-wide welcome; her mild eyes command
The air-bridged harbor that twin cities frame.
"Keep ancient lands, your storied pomp!" cries she
With silent lips. "Give me your tired, your poor.
Your huddled masses yearning to breathe free,
The wretched refuse of your teeming shore.
Send these, the homeless, tempest-tost to me,
I lift my lamp beside the golden door!"

Nearby Ellis Island, abandoned as an immigration center in 1954 after having served as the gateway to America for 16,000,000 was proclaimed by President Johnson in 1965 part of the Statue of Liberty National Monument. Congress authorized $6,000,000 to develop Ellis Island as a park and museum.

## Superlative United States Statistics
### Source: National Geographic Society, Washington, D. C.

Area for Fifty States.................... Total........................................3,615,211 sq. mi.
          Land 3,548,974 sq. mi.......Water 66,237 sq. mi.........
Largest state........................... Alaska........................................586,400 sq. mi.
Smallest state.......................... Rhode Island..................................1,214 sq. mi.
Largest county......................... San Bernardino County, California.............20,119 sq. mi.
Largest city in area.................... Los Angeles, California (see note below)........454.8 sq. mi.
          Oklahoma City, Okla. (see note below)...........647.5 sq. mi.
          Jacksonville, Fla. (see note below)............827 sq. mi.
Northernmost town..................... Barrow, Alaska...............................71° 18′ N.
Northernmost point.................... Point Barrow, Alaska.........................71° 23′ N.
Southernmost city..................... Hilo, Island of Hawaii.......................19° 42′ N.
Southernmost town.................... Naalehu, Island of Hawaii........19° 4′ N. (155° 35′ W.)
Southernmost point................... Ka Lae (South Cape), Island of Hawaii..18° 56′ N. (155° 41′ W.)
Easternmost town..................... Lubec, Maine................................66° 59′ W.
Easternmost point.................... West Quoddy Head, Maine....................66° 57′ W.
Westernmost point.................... Cape Wrangell, Attu Island, Aleutians, Alaska...172° 27′ E.
Highest point on Atlantic coast........ Cadillac Mountain, Mount Desert Isl., Me........1,530 ft.
Largest and oldest national park....... Yellowstone National Park (1872), Wyoming,
          Montana, Idaho..............................3,472 sq. mi.
Largest national monument............ Katmai National Monument, Alaska............4,215 sq. mi.
Highest waterfall...................... Yosemite Falls—Total in three sections..........2,425 ft.
          Upper Yosemite Fall..........................1,430 ft.
          Cascades in middle section.....................675 ft.
          Lower Yosemite Fall..........................320 ft.
Longest river.......................... Mississippi-Missouri..........................3,710 miles
Highest mountain...................... Mount McKinley, Alaska......................20,320 ft.
Lowest point.......................... Death Valley, California.......................−282 ft.
Deepest lake.......................... Crater Lake, Oregon.....................1,932 ft. deep
Highest lake.......................... Lake Waiau, Hawaii..........................13,020 ft.

### THE FORTY-NINE STATES, INCLUDING ALASKA
Area for Forty-nine States............. Total........................................3,608,787 sq. mi.
          Land 3,542,559 sq. mi.......Water 66, 228 sq. mi.

### THE FORTY-EIGHT STATES
Area for Forty-eight States............ Total........................................3,022,387 sq. mi.
          Land 2,971,494 sq. mi.......Water 50,893 sq. mi.
Largest state........................... Texas........................................267,339 sq. mi.
Northernmost town..................... Penasse, Minnesota..........................49° 22′ N.
Northernmost point.................... Lake of the Woods, Minnesota................49° 23′ N.
Southernmost city..................... Key West, Florida............................24° 33′ N.
Southernmost mainland town........... Florida City, Florida.........................25° 27′ N.
Westernmost point.................... Cape Alava, Washington.....................124° 44′ W.
Highest mountain...................... Mt. Whitney, California......................14,494 ft.

The 1960 census officially listed Los Angeles as the United States city with the largest area—454.8 square miles. However, Oklahoma City claimed an area of 647.5 square miles in 1968 after a series of annexation ordinances. And Jacksonville, Fla., topped both of them by a wide margin when most of Duval County was consolidated into the city's borders Oct. 1, 1968, giving the city 827 sq. mi.

## Geographic Centers, United States and States
### Source: U. S. Geological Survey, Department of the Interior

| State | County | Locality |
|---|---|---|
| **United States, including Alaska and Hawaii**—South Dakota; Butte County, 17 miles west of Castle Rock, 14 miles east of junction of borders of South Dakota, Montana and Wyoming. Approx. Lat. 44°58′N, Long. 103°46′W. | | |
| **Continental U. S. (49 States)**—Near Castle Rock, Butte Co., South Dakota. Lat. 44°59′N, Long. 103°38′W. | | |
| **Conterminous U. S. (48 States)**—Near Lebanon, Smith Co., Kansas. Lat. 39°50′N, Long. 98°35′W. | | |
| **North American Continent**—The geographic center is in Pierce County, North Dakota, 6 miles west of Balta, latitude 48°10′, longitude 100°10′W. | | |

#### STATES

| State | County | Locality |
|---|---|---|
| Alabama—Chilton, 12 miles S.W. of Clanton. | | |
| Alaska—Lat. 63°50′N, Long. 152°00′W. Approx. 60 mi. N.W. of Mt. McKinley. | | |
| Arizona—Yavapai, 55 miles E.S.E. of Prescott. | | |
| Arkansas—Pulaski, 12 miles N.W. of Little Rock. | | |
| California—Madera, 35 miles N.E. of Madera. | | |
| Colorado—Park, 30 miles northwest of Pikes Peak. | | |
| Connecticut—Hartford, at East Berlin. | | |
| Delaware—Kent, 11 miles south of Dover. | | |
| District of Columbia—Washington, near Corner of Fourth and "L" Streets. N. W. | | |
| Florida—Hernando, 12 miles N.N.W. of Brooksville. | | |
| Georgia—Twiggs, 18 miles S.E. of Macon. | | |
| Hawaii—Hawaii, 20°15′N; 156°20′W, off Maui Isle. | | |
| Idaho—Custer, at Custer, S.W. of Challis. | | |
| Illinois—Logan, 28 miles N.E. of Springfield. | | |
| Indiana—Boone, 14 miles N.N.W. of Indianapolis. | | |
| Iowa—Story, 5 miles N.E. of Ames. | | |
| Kansas—Barton, 15 miles N.E. of Great Bend. | | |
| Kentucky—Marion, 3 miles N.N.W. of Lebanon. | | |
| Louisiana—Avoyelles, 3 miles S.E. of Marksville. | | |
| Maine—Piscataquis, 18 miles north of Dover. | | |
| Maryland—Prince Georges, 4½ miles N.W. of Davidsonville. | | |
| Massachusetts—Worcester, north part of City. | | |
| Michigan—Wexford, 5 miles N.N.W. of Cadillac. | | |
| Minnesota—Crow Wing, 10 miles S.W. of Brainerd. | | |
| Mississippi—Leake, 9 miles W.N.W. of Carthage. | | |
| Missouri—Miller, 20 miles S.W. of Jefferson City. | | |
| Montana—Fergus, 12 miles west of Lewistown. | | |
| Nebraska—Custer, 10 miles N.W. of Broken Bow. | | |
| Nevada—Lander, 26 miles S.E. of Austin. | | |
| New Hampshire—Belknap, 3 miles east of Ashland. | | |
| New Jersey—Mercer, 5 miles S.E. of Trenton. | | |
| New Mexico—Torrance, 12 miles S.S.W. of Willard. | | |
| New York—Madison, 12 miles south of Oneida and 26 miles S.W. of Utica. | | |
| North Carolina—Chatham, 10 miles N.W. of Sanford. | | |
| North Dakota—Sheridan, 5 miles S.W. of McClusky. | | |
| Ohio—Delaware, 25 miles N.N.E. of Columbus. | | |
| Oklahoma—Oklahoma, 8 miles N. of Oklahoma City. | | |
| Oregon—Crook, 25 miles S.S.E. of Prineville. | | |
| Pennsylvania—Centre, 2½ miles S.W. of Bellefonte. | | |
| Rhode Island—Kent, 1 mile S.S.W. of Crompton. | | |
| South Carolina—Richland, 13 miles S.E. of Columbia. | | |
| South Dakota—Hughes, 8 miles N.E. of Pierre. | | |
| Tennessee—Rutherford, 5 mi. N.E. of Murfreesboro. | | |
| Texas—McCulloch, 15 miles N.E. of Brady. | | |
| Utah—Sanpete, 3 miles north of Manti. | | |
| Vermont—Washington, 3 miles east of Roxbury. | | |
| Virginia—Buckingham, 5 miles S.W. of Buck'ham. | | |
| Washington—Chelan, 10 mi. W.S.W. of Wenatchee. | | |
| West Virginia—Braxton, 4 miles east of Sutton. | | |
| Wisconsin—Wood, 9 miles S.E. of Marshfield. | | |
| Wyoming—Fremont, 58 miles E.N.E. of Lander. | | |

There is no generally accepted definition of geographic center, and no satisfactory method for determining it. The geographic center of an area may be defined as the center of gravity of the surface, or that point on which the surface of the area would balance if it were a plane of uniform thickness.

No marked or monumented point has been established by any government agency as the geographic center of either the 50 states, the conterminous United States, or the North American continent. However, a monument was erected in Lebanon, Kan., by a group of citizens.

## National Trails System and Wild & Scenic Rivers System Established

A National Trails System, established by 1968 Federal legislation, includes initially the Appalachian Trail, extending 2,000 miles generally along the Appalachian Mountains from Maine to Georgia, and the Pacific Crest Trail, running 2,350 miles along western mountain ranges from the Mexico-California border to the Canada-Washington border near Lake Ross. Also established by 1968 legislation was a National Wild & Scenic Rivers System. Named for immediate inclusion were stretches of the Clearwater (middle fork), in Idaho; Eleven Point, in Mo.; Feather, Calif.; Rio Grande, N. M.; Rogue, Ore.; Saint Croix, Minn. and Wis.; Salmon (middle fork), Idaho; and Wolf, Wis.

# TRADE AND TRANSPORTATION

## Notable Steamships and Motorships

Source: Lloyd's Register of Shipping as of June 30, 1968
Gross tonnage is a measurement of enclosed space (1 gross ton=100 cu. ft.)

### WORLD'S LARGEST PASSENGER SHIPS
#### 30,000 gross tons and over

| Name—registry | Gross ton. | Lgth. Ft.-In. | Bdth. Ft.-In. |
|---|---|---|---|
| Queen Elizabeth, Br. | 82,998 | 1031-0 | 118-7 |
| France, Fr. | 66,348 | 1035-2 | 110-11 |
| United States, U.S. | 38,216 | 990-0 | 101-7 |
| Raffaello, It. | 45,933 | 904-7 | 101-10 |
| Michelangelo, It. | 45,911 | 904-11 | 101-10 |
| Canberra, Br. | 45,733 | 818-6 | 102-6 |
| Oriana, Br. | 41,915 | 804-0 | 97-2 |
| Rotterdam, Neth. | 38,621 | 748-7 | 94-2 |
| Windsor Castle, Br. | 33,994 | 783-1 | 92-6 |
| Nieuw Amsterdam, Neth. | 36,982 | 758-6 | 88-4 |
| Colombia, Pan. | 34,274 | 715-0 | 91-5 |
| Leonardo Da Vinci, It. | 33,340 | 767-4 | 92-2 |
| S. A. Vaal, Br. (1) | 30,212 | 760-2 | 90-2 |
| Bremen, Ger. (2) | 32,360 | 696-10 | 90-4 |
| Eugenio C., It. | 30,567 | 713-5 | 90-5 |
| Flandre, Fr. | 20,477 | 599-8 | 80-4 |
| Franconia, Br. | 22,637 | 608-3 | 80-4 |
| Galileo Galilei, It. | 27,907 | 700-11 | 94-2 |
| Giulio Cesare, It. | 27,078 | 680-7 | 87-6 |
| Gripsholm, Sw. | 23,216 | 631-3 | 81-10 |
| Guglielmo Marconi, It. | 27,905 | 700-11 | 94-2 |
| Hanseatic, Ger. (12) | 25,320 | 627-9 | 81-6 |
| Henrietta Latsi, Gr. (13) | 23,580 | 665-1 | 82-3 |
| Himalaya, Br. | 27,989 | 708-8 | 90-10 |
| Iberia, Br. | 29,614 | 718-8 | 90-10 |
| Independence, U. S. | 20,269 | 682-5 | 89-2 |
| Infante Dom Henrique, Port. | 23,306 | 641-8 | 84-5 |
| Joyama Maru, Jap. | 29,139 | 649-8 | 95-4 |
| Jules Verne, Fr. | 22,292 | 659-6 | 81-7 |
| Kazutama Maru, Jap. | 34,529 | n.r. | 103-2 |
| Kungsholm, Sw. | 26,678 | 660-2 | 87-2 |
| Kyokuyo Maru No. 3, Jap. | 20,300 | 555-0 | 77-5 |
| Lenin, Rus. | 14,067 | 439-8 | 90-8 |
| Marianna Latsi, Gr. (14) | 23,732 | 664-6 | 82-2 |
| Methane Princess, Br. | 21,876 | 621-1 | 81-9 |
| Methane Progress, Br. | 21,875 | 621-0 | 81-9 |
| Nevasa, Br. | 20,746 | 609-3 | 78-3 |
| Nisshin Maru No. 2, Jap. | 27,035 | 634-8 | 80-2 |
| Nisshin Maru No. 3, Jap. | 23,406 | 638-6 | 78-2 |
| Northern Star, Br. | 24,756 | 650-0 | 83-8 |
| Oceanic, Pan. | 27,644 | 782-3 | 96-7 |
| Orcades, Br. | 28,399 | 708-8 | 93-6 |
| Oronsay, Br. | 27,632 | 708-8 | 93-6 |
| Orsova, Br. | 28,790 | 722-10 | 90-7 |
| Pendennis Castle, Br. | 28,453 | 763-3 | 83-10 |
| Queen Anna Maria, Gr. (15) | 21,716 | 640-0 | 85-2 |
| Rangitane, Br. | 21,867 | 609-2 | 81-0 |
| Rangitoto, Br. | 21,809 | 609-2 | 81-0 |
| Reina Del Mar, Br. | 20,750 | 600-9 | 78-4 |
| S. A. Oranje, Br. (16) | 27,513 | 747-5 | 84-0 |
| Sagafjord, Nor. | 24,002 | 619-8 | 80-3 |
| Santa Maria, Port. | 20,906 | 608-11 | 75-9 |
| Savannah, U. S. | 15,585 | 595-6 | 78-2 |
| *(world's 1st nuclear-powered merchant vessel)* | | | |
| Sovetsky Sojus, USSR (17) | 23,009 | 673-3 | 72-2 |
| Sovietskaya Rossia, USSR | 33,154 | 714-6 | 94-3 |
| Sovietskaya Ukraina, USSR | 32,024 | 714-6 | 94-3 |
| Statendam, Neth. | 24,294 | 642-6 | 81-0 |
| Tatsuno Maru, Jap. | 31,137 | 663-1 | 98-7 |
| Vera Cruz, Port. | 21,765 | 609-8 | 75-9 |
| Willem Barendsz, S. Af. | 23,155 | 677-6 | 90-6 |
| Yuri Dolgoruky, USSR (19) | 25,377 | 680-0 | 79-0 |

### OTHER PASSENGER AND CARGO SHIPS

| Name—registry | Gross ton. | Lgth. Ft.-In. | Bdth. Ft.-In. |
|---|---|---|---|
| Achille Lauro, It. (3) | 23,629 | 631-2 | 82-0 |
| Adm. Wm. M. Callaghan, U.S. | 24,471 | 694-3 | 92-2 |
| Andes, Br. | 26,435 | 669-4 | 83-6 |
| Angelina Lauro, It. (4) | 24,377 | 656-3 | 83-6 |
| Arcadia, Br. | 29,871 | 721-4 | 90-8 |
| Augustus, It. | 27,090 | 680-5 | 87-6 |
| Australis, Gr. (5) | 26,315 | 723-0 | 93-6 |
| Bridgestone Maru, Jap. | 20,516 | 602-9 | 82-6 |
| Bridgestone Maru No. 2, Jap. | 23,785 | 615-2 | 90-4 |
| Bridgestone Maru No. 3, Jap. | 26,099 | 635-8 | 95-4 |
| Caribia, It. (6) | 24,496 | 629-8 | 79-6 |
| Carla C., It. (11) | 20,477 | 599-8 | 80-4 |
| Carmania, Br. | 22,592 | 608-4 | 80-4 |
| Chusan, Br. | 24,318 | 672-6 | 85-2 |
| Constitution, U. S. | 20,269 | 682-6 | 89-2 |
| Cristoforo Colombo, It. | 29,429 | 700-9 | 89-11 |
| Cruz Del Sur, Lib. (7) | 24,570 | 664-1 | 80-6 |
| Edinburgh Castle, Br. | 27,497 | 747-5 | 84-0 |
| Empress of Canada, Br. | 27,284 | 650-0 | 86-9 |
| Empress of England, Br. | 25,585 | 640-0 | 85-4 |
| Europa, Ger. (8) | 21,514 | 600-0 | 77-1 |
| Fairland, Lib. (10) | 21,947 | 608-3 | 80-4 |
| Fairstar, Lib. (9) | 21,619 | 609-5 | 78-3 |
| Fairwind, Lib. (18) | 22,017 | 608-3 | 80-4 |
| Federico C., It. | 20,416 | 605-8 | 78-11 |

### OIL TANKERS
#### 110,000 tons deadweight and over (June, 1968)

*Deadweight tonnage is the weight (long tons) of cargo, fuel, etc., which a vessel is designed to carry safely.*

| Name—registry | Gross ton. | Lgth. Ft.-In. | Bdth. Ft.-In. |
|---|---|---|---|
| Universe Ireland, Lib. | 312,000 | 1135-2 | 175-2 |
| Universe Kuwait, Lib. | 312,000 | 1135-2 | 175-2 |
| Bulford, Br. | 212,000 | 1067-1 | 158-4 |
| Macoma, Neths. | 210,000 | 1066-6 | 154-11 |
| Magdala, Fr. | 210,000 | 1065-4 | 154-11 |
| Marinula, Br. | 210,000 | 1077-1 | 143-8 |
| Marisa, Br. | 210,000 | 1066-4 | 154-11 |
| Megara, Br. | 210,000 | 1066-4 | 154-11 |
| Metula, Neths. | 210,000 | 1066-5 | 154-11 |
| Murex, Br. | 210,000 | 1067-4 | 154-11 |
| Idemitsu Maru, Jap. | 206,006 | 1122-0 | 163-6 |
| Berghus, Nor. | 202,557 | 1065-4 | 158-11 |
| Berge Commander, Nor. | 202,250 | 1064-2 | 158-11 |
| Hien Maru, Jap. | 192,900 | 1026-0 | 166-10 |
| Myrina, W. Ger. | 192,250 | 1050-0 | 155-2 |
| Esso Malaysia, Pan. | 190,000 | 1062-6 | 155-0 |
| Nicholas J. Goulandris, Lib. | 188,000 | n.r. | n.r. |
| Kiho Maru, Jap. | 182,889 | 1040-0 | 165-6 |
| Esso Mercia, Br. | 175,000 | 1010-2 | 146-3 |
| Kaimon Maru, Jap. | 175,000 | 985-0 | 158-4 |
| Good Hope, Lib. | 167,314 | 1010-2 | 146-2 |
| Jasankoa, Nor. | 157,000 | 984-5 | 158-5 |
| Tenko Maru, Jap. | 157,000 | 984-4 | 158-4 |
| Bergebragd, Nor. | 156,680 | 956-1 | 135-0 |
| Meisen Maru, Jap. | 152,480 | 1036-0 | 144-6 |
| Tokyo Maru, Jap. | 151,258 | 1005-7 | 156-0 |
| Shoyo Maru, Jap. | 150,728 | 964-7 | 151-10 |
| Bergeborg, Nor. | 149,634 | 915-5 | 145-2 |
| Bergehaven, Nor. | 149,556 | 915-5 | 145-2 |
| Bergebig, Nor. | 149,513 | 915-5 | 145-2 |
| Molda, Nor. | 143,620 | 932-5 | 141-8 |
| Tohkosen Maru, Jap. | 139,528 | 961-4 | 144-5 |
| Wilstar, Nor. | 132,700 | 903-8 | 138-2 |
| Nissho Maru, Jap. | 130,250 | 954-8 | 141-4 |
| Japan Hyacinth, Jap. | 129,549 | 889-1 | 139-8 |
| Jingu Maru, Jap. | 129,000 | 964-8 | 142-11 |
| Gekko Maru, Jap. | 128,000 | n.r. | 149-9 |
| Toyama Maru, Jap. | 125,214 | 886-3 | 139-9 |
| Montsoreau, Fr. | 125,000 | 900-0 | n.r. |
| Kinokawa Maru, Jap. | 124,700 | n.r. | 138-0 |
| Hokaku Maru, Jap. | 122,600 | 885-10 | 139-7 |
| Tokushima Maru, Jap. | 122,030 | 886-3 | 139-7 |
| Toba Maru, Jap. | 121,718 | 886-3 | 139-7 |
| Sea Spirit, Sw. | 121,185 | 871-3 | 134-2 |
| Sea Spray, Sw. | 121,185 | 871-3 | 134-2 |
| Japan Jasmin, Jap. | 121,129 | 885-10 | 139-7 |
| Dairyu Maru, Jap. | 121,000 | 912-0 | 145-1 |
| Choja Maru, Jap. | 120,871 | 886-1 | 139-8 |
| Kaho Maru, Jap. | 119,383 | 912-0 | 145-2 |
| Niso, Neths. | 119,378 | 870-0 | 138-0 |
| Yamaju Maru, Jap. | 119,250 | 912-0 | 145-2 |
| Oriental Dragon, Lib. | 118,927 | 949-2 | 126-9 |
| Naticina, Br. | 118,580 | 870-0 | 138-0 |
| Izumigawa Maru, Jap. | 118,400 | 869-7 | 138-0 |
| Lake Palourde, Lib. | 117,966 | 974-5 | 125-5 |
| Dauphine, Lib. | 117,272 | 902-3 | 135-6 |
| Isuzugawa Maru, Jap. | 116,626 | 898-2 | 138-2 |
| Chichiro Maru, Jap. | 115,505 | 886-1 | 139-7 |
| Universe Daphne, Lib. | 115,360 | 949-9 | 135-5 |
| Nacella, W. Ger. | 115,000 | 870-0 | 138-0 |
| Universe Apollo, Lib. | 114,356 | 949-9 | 135-5 |
| Betelgeuse, Fr. | 113,960 | 924-0 | 127-11 |
| British Argosy, Br. | 112,786 | 920-9 | 128-5 |
| Golar Nikko, Lib. | 111,790 | 849-0 | 128-2 |
| British Admiral, Br. | 111,274 | 917-6 | 128-6 |
| Imperial Ottawa, Ber. | 110,187 | 907-2 | 136-3 |

### BULK AND ORE/OIL CARRIERS
#### 45,000 tons gross and over

| Name—registry | Gross ton. | Lgth. Ft.-In. | Bdth. Ft.-In. |
|---|---|---|---|
| Aegir, W. Ger. | 45,796 | 836-8 | n.r. |
| Athenic, Br. | 48,747 | 834-2 | 124-3 |
| Atlantic Maru, Jap. | 51,973 | 817-7 | 126-6 |
| Cedros, Lib. (20) | 85,907 | 995-9 | 142-4 |
| Cetra Colomba, Fr. | 53,448 | 866-11 | 118-4 |
| Chitosegawa Maru, Jap. | 45,796 | 779-2 | 118-4 |
| Daiko Maru, Jap. | 55,692 | 820-3 | 126-6 |
| Fernstar, Nor. | 55,986 | 835-7 | 128-10 |
| Fukuyama Maru, Jap. | 57,000 | n.r. | n.r. |
| Furyu Maru, Jap. | 56,500 | 849-9 | 130-2 |
| Gloric, Lib. | 48,747 | 834-2 | 124-3 |
| Hoegh Rider, Nor. | 57,848 | 820-6 | 127-11 |

*(continued on page 96)*

| Name—registry | Gross ton. | Lgth. Ft.-In. | Bdth. Ft.-In. | Name—registry | Gross ton. | Lgth. Ft.-In. | Bdth. Ft.-In. |
|---|---|---|---|---|---|---|---|
| Hoegh Rover, Nor......... | 57,848 | 820-6 | 127-11 | Rivalta, It................ | 52,000 | 851-5 | 127-11 |
| Horyu Maru, Jap......... | 55,213 | n.r. | 124-9 | Runa, Nor................ | 45,003 | 848-7 | 105-11 |
| Inayama, Nor............ | 48,460 | 820-2 | 120-11 | San Juan Pathfinder, Lib... | 45,513 | 835-0 | 106-5 |
| Jacob Malmros, Sw....... | 60,555 | 870-1 | n.r. | San Juan Prospector, Lib... | 45,513 | 835-0 | 106-5 |
| Jacques Cartier, Fr....... | 51,644 | 823-0 | 120-2 | Santa Valeria, It.......... | 51,579 | 832-6 | 128-0 |
| Japan Wisteria, Jap...... | 56,312 | 830-1 | 127-4 | Sidney Spiro, Lib......... | 52,000 | 820-2 | 124-1 |
| Kaiko Maru, Jap.. ....... | 54,513 | 820-3 | 126-6 | Sigfuji, Lib............... | 46,011 | 820-3 | 128-3 |
| Kofukusan Maru, Jap..... | 55,482 | 825-11 | 124-10 | Sigsilver, Br............. | 57,318 | 802-5 | 134-0 |
| Kokko Maru, Jap......... | 54,600 | 820-2 | 126-5 | Sigtone, Lib.............. | 46,488 | 820-3 | 128-3 |
| Marshall Clark, Lib....... | 47,552 | 820-2 | 120-11 | Tasman Maru, Jap........ | 56,600 | 830-0 | 127-11 |
| Mirafiori, It............. | 51,579 | 832-6 | 128-2 | Tehran, Nor.............. | 46,000 | n.r. | n.r. |
| Nephos, Lib............. | 54,502 | 818-0 | 127-11 | Tsugara Maru, Jap....... | 55,334 | 820-3 | 126-6 |
| Nippon Maru, Jap........ | 53,751 | n.r. | 127-10 | Tsukushi Maru, Jap...... | 45,848 | 779-2 | 118-3 |
| Port Latta Maru, Jap..... | 50,817 | 816-11 | 126-6 | Tsurusaki Maru, Jap..... | 55,320 | 820-2 | 126-6 |
| Rinda, Nor.............. | 45,003 | 848-7 | 106-10 | Vestan, Nor.............. | 55,752 | 827-1 | 128-1 |

Former names: (1) Transvaal Castle, (2) Pasteur, (3) Willem Ruys, (4) Oranje, (5) America, (6) Vulcania, (7) Juan Peron, (8) Kungsholm, (9) Oxfordshire, (10) Carinthia, (11) Frandoe, (12) Shalom, (13) Marianna Latsi, ex Strathmore, (14) Henrietta Latsi, ex Stratheden, (15) Empress of Britain, (16) Pretoria Castle, (17) Hansa, ex Albert Balin, (18) Sylvania, (19) Hamburg, (20), Salt/oil carrier, the tonnage shown is the gross tonnage when ship operates as a salt carrier. NR—Not recorded.

# Maritime Traffic in 11 Major U. S. Seaports

Source: Maritime Assn. of the Port of New York, Wm. F. Giesen, Gen. Mgr.

The total of ocean-going vessels moving through the 11 major U. S. ports (arrivals and sailings) during the first 6 months of 1968 was 52,031, a decrease of 2,124 vessels from the figure of the corresponding period in 1967. The total for the calendar year, 1967, was 106,757, a decrease of 1,548 vessels from the 1966 total.

In the first half of 1968, New York continued to hold top place by a wide margin, although New York's share of the total volume dropped to 20.2%, compared with 22% recorded in the first 6 months of the previous year. Philadelphia continued in second place despite a slight percentage decrease under the corresponding period in 1967. The Los Angeles Long Beach share of the total was 11%, an increase of 1.6% over the 1967 figure.

Total activity (arrivals and sailings) in the 11 major ports during the first half of 1968 and the first half of 1967 was reported as follows:

| | First 6 Months of: | |
|---|---|---|
| | 1968 | 1967 |
| New York | 10,528 | 11,888 |
| Philadelphia | 5,994 | 6,493 |
| Los Angeles-Long Beach | 5,724 | 5,118 |
| San Francisco | 5,137 | 5,126 |
| Hampton Roads | 4,760 | 5,243 |
| New Orleans | 4,646 | 4,643 |
| Baltimore | 4,520 | 4,853 |
| Houston | 4,454 | 4,221 |
| Seattle | 2,428 | 2,483 |
| Portland, Oregon | 2,105 | 2,082 |
| Boston | 1,735 | 2,005 |
| Totals | 52,031 | 54,155 |

# Value of U. S. Merchandise Exports and Imports

Source: International Trade Analysis Division, Dept. of Commerce

Value in millions of dollars (Revised) p—Preliminary

| Year | Total including re-exports | Exports Merchandise U. S. | Exports Merchandise Foreign | Military aid | General[1] | Imports For con- sumption | Excess over imports[2] |
|---|---|---|---|---|---|---|---|
| 1950..... | 10,275 | 10,142 | 133 | [3]282 | 8,874 | 8,765 | 1,119 |
| 1955..... | 15,547 | 15,419 | 128 | 1,256 | 11,495 | 11,448 | 2,796 |
| 1960..... | 20,586 | 20,386 | 200 | 949 | 15,019 | 15,016 | 4,619 |
| 1964..... | 26,489 | 26,136 | 352 | 818 | 18,684 | 18,600 | 6,987 |
| 1965..... | 27,478 | 27,135 | 343 | 779 | 21,366 | 21,283 | 5,334 |
| 1966..... | 30,320 | 29,884 | 436 | 940 | 25,542 | 25,360 | 3,837 |
| 1967..... | 31,534 | 31,147 | 387 | 592 | 26,816 | 26,732 | 4,126 |

[1]General Imports—Include merchandise entered immediately upon arrival into merchandising or consumption channels, plus commodities entered into bonded customs warehouse for storage.
[2]Exports, excluding military grant-aid, less general imports.
[3]Includes data from April 1950 when shipments under the program began.

## U. S. MERCHANDISE EXPORTS AND IMPORTS, BY CONTINENT

Value in millions of dollars

| Year | Exports Western Hemisp. | Exports Europe | Exports Asia & Oceania | Exports Africa | General imports Western Hemisp. | General imports Europe | General imports Asia & Oceania | General imports Africa |
|---|---|---|---|---|---|---|---|---|
| 1961..... | 7,373 | 6,459 | 4,678 | 669 | 6,995 | 4,143 | 2,938 | 636 |
| 1962..... | 7,418 | 6,542 | 4,841 | 747 | 7,591 | 4,623 | 3,426 | 728 |
| 1963..... | 7,704 | 7,116 | 5,553 | 782 | 7,850 | 4,812 | 3,714 | 758 |
| 1964..... | 8,967 | 8,327 | 6,252 | 954 | 8,389 | 5,307 | 4,076 | 900 |
| 1965..... | 9,917 | 9,364 | 7,126 | 1,071 | 9,202 | 6,292 | 4,997 | 861 |
| 1966..... | 11,429 | 10,003 | 7,727 | 1,159 | 10,829 | 7,857 | 5,888 | 961 |
| 1967[1]..... | 11,894 | 10,294 | 8,229 | 1,116 | 11,737 | 8,232 | 5,948 | 890 |

# United States Foreign Trade, by Economic Classes

Source: International Trade Analysis Div., Dept. of Commerce. (Value in millions)

| Year (cal.) | Value of domestic exports Crude Mater'ls | Value of domestic exports Crude Foodst's | Value of domestic exports Manu'd Foodst's | Value of domestic exports Semi- Manuf's | Value of domestic exports Finish. Manuf's | Value of imports [2]Crude Mater'ls | Value of imports Crude Foodst's | Value of imports Manu'd Foodst's | Value of imports [2]Semi- Manuf's | Value of imports Finish. Manuf's |
|---|---|---|---|---|---|---|---|---|---|---|
| 1962.. | 2,234 | 2,010 | 1,366 | 3,067 | 12,754 | 3,087 | 1,776 | 1,792 | 3,641 | 5,957 |
| 1963.. | 2,577 | 2,273 | 1,496 | 3,343 | 13,373 | 3,141 | 1,725 | 1,998 | 3,756 | 6,382 |
| 1964.. | 2,896 | 2,540 | 1,687 | 4,086 | 14,947 | 3,474 | 2,034 | 1,819 | 3,991 | 7,366 |
| 1965.. | 2,886 | 2,587 | 1,590 | 4,063 | 16,008 | 3,653 | 2,008 | 1,877 | 4,957 | 8,871 |
| 1966.. | 3,143 | 3,198 | 1,582 | 4,258 | 17,703 | 3,851 | 2,117 | 2,309 | 5,587 | 11,678 |
| 1967.. | 3,294 | 2,600 | 1,594 | 4,415 | 19,244 | 3,676 | 1,981 | 2,518 | 5,544 | 13,096 |

[1]Preliminary. [2]Revised to reflect transfer of uranium oxide from Crude Materials to Semi-mfrs.
Total agricultural exports were valued as follows (in millions of dollars): 1961—5,084; 1962—5,101; 1963—5,651; 1964—6,439; 1965—6,306; 1966—6,962; 1967—6,451.
Agricultural imports for consumption were valued as follows (in millions of dollars): 1961—3,689; 1962—3,869; 1963—4,020; 1964—4,143; 1965—4,082; 1966—4,530; 1967—4,472.

# Important Waterways and Canals

**The St. Lawrence Waterway**, the largest inland navigation system on the continent, extends from the Atlantic Ocean to Duluth at the western end of Lake Superior, a distance of 2,342 miles. With the deepening of channels and locks to 27 ft., ocean carriers are able to penetrate to ports in the Canadian interior and the American midwest.

The major canals in Canada are those of the St. Lawrence-Great Lakes waterway—the 3 new canals of the St. Lawrence Seaway, with their 7 locks, providing navigation for vessels of 25-foot draught from Montreal to Lake Ontario; the Welland Ship Canal by-passing the Niagara River between Lake Ontario and Lake Erie with its 8 locks, and the Sault Ste. Marie Canal and lock between Lake Huron and Lake Superior. These 16 locks overcome a drop of 580 ft. from the head of the lakes to Montreal. From Montreal to Lake Ontario the former bottleneck of narrow, shallow canals and of slow passage through 22 locks has been overcome, giving faster and safer movement for larger vessels. The new locks and linking channels now accommodate all but the largest ocean-going vessels and the upper St. Lawrence and Great Lakes are open to 80% of the world's saltwater fleet.

Subsidiary Canadian canals or branches include the St. Peters Canal between Bras d'Or Lakes and the Atlantic Ocean in Nova Scotia; the St. Ours and Chambly Canals on the Richelieu River, Quebec; the Ste. Anne, Carillon and Grenville Canals on the Ottawa River; the Rideau Canal between the Ottawa River and Lake Ontario, and the Trent and Murray Canals between Lake Ontario and Georgian Bay in Ontario. The commercial value of these canals is not great but they are maintained to control water levels and permit the passage of small vessels and pleasure craft. The Canso Canal, completed 1957, permits shipping to pass through the causeway connecting Cape Breton Island with the Nova Scotia mainland. During 1966, 111,188,312 tons of freight passed through all Canadian canals in 22,592 vessels.

**The Saint Lawrence Seaway**, opened 1959 set new records for cargo traffic in 1967 with a grand total of 44,028,638 cargo tons. The total for 1968 is estimated at 52,000,000 tons. The general cargo tonnage for 1967 was 5,962,747.

Ship transits amounted to 6,921 in 1967 with an average cargo ton load per transit of 6,361.

Cargo traffic via the Montreal-Lake Ontario section during the 1967 navigation season was 46,178,486 tons.

St. Lawrence Seaway provides a navigational channel with a minimum water depth of 27 ft. to link the Great Lakes to the Atlantic Ocean. A vessel entering the Great Lakes from the Atlantic ascends 20 ft. above sea level in the 1,000-mile long reach up the Gulf of St. Lawrence and St. Lawrence River to Montreal, Quebec. At Montreal, the vessel enters the first of 7 new locks, 5 of which are in Canadian waters and 2 within United States waters, which raise or lower shipping a total of 226 ft. in the 182-mile stretch of the St. Lawrence River between Montreal and Lake Ontario. Crossing Lake Ontario, the vessel enters Canada's 28-mile-long Welland Canal, with 8 locks to compensate for the difference in elevation of 326 ft. between Lake Ontario and Lake Erie.

The Seaway, built and operated jointly by the United States and Canada, is unique in that the statutes of both nations provide that the full costs of construction, operation and maintenance, with interest, be repaid to the federal treasuries within 50 years from revenues by the assessment of tolls levied against Seaway users.

Saint Lawrence Seaway Development Corporation (U.S.), Seaway Circle, Massena, New York. Joseph H. McCann, Administrator.

St. Lawrence Seaway Authority (Canada), Ottawa, Ontario. Dr. Pierre Camu, president.

**The Welland Canal** overcomes the 326-ft. drop of Niagara Falls and the rapids of the Niagara River. It has 8 locks, each 859 ft. long, 80 ft. wide and 30 ft. deep. Regulations permit ships of 730-ft. length and 75-ft. beam to transit with special handling, while largest size for regular handling is 715-ft. length and 72-ft. beam.

In 1967 the Welland Canal carried 52,-809,414 cargo tons; in 1966 59,271,666 cargo tons were carried, a loss of 10.9%. A tie-up of lake shipping due to strike action decreased the traffic in 1967.

**Sault Ste. Marie Canal** reported 89,366,-249 short tons passing through the American locks and 1,037,728 short tons passing through the Canadian canal for a total of 90,403,977 for the season of 1967.

In 1966 the comparable American figure was 102,309,719 and the Canadian figure 1,281,211 for a total of 103,670,930 short tons.

## PANAMA CANAL

Cargo tonnage on the Panama Canal in fiscal 1968 amounted to 105,527,869 compared with 92,983,791 tons in 1967. Transit of oceangoing ships in fiscal 1968 totaled 14,807 compared with 13,385 in fiscal 1967. Toll collections in fiscal 1968 were $93,-154,680 compared with $82,296,638 in 1967.

Improvements have included the widening of the eight-mile long channel through Gaillard Cut from 300 to 500 feet, costing $50,000,000; illumination of Gaillard Cut and installation of new towing locomotives at the locks costing $8,000,000.

**Thatcher Ferry Bridge**, opened 1962, spans Panama Canal 201 ft. above the water level near Balboa. It is a steel-arch bridge, about 1 mi. long, with 3 spans and 4 lanes. It cost $20,000,000 authorized by the U. S. Congress in 1956.

## OTHER FOREIGN CANALS

One of the busiest canals in Europe is the Gota, in Sweden, 115 mi. long. Others: Kiel Canal, Germany, connecting the Baltic with the North Sea, 61 mi.; Elbe, Germany, 41 mi.; Amsterdam, Netherlands, 16 mi. Also the Manchester Ship Canal, England, 35.5 mi.

The Suez Canal is now operated by the government of United Arab Rep. *For its history see page 557.*

# United States Foreign Trade with Leading Countries

Source: Bureau of International Commerce, Dept. of Commerce
(Value in millions of dollars)

| Exports from the U. S. to the following areas and countries and imports into the U. S. from those areas and countries: | Exports, including re-exports | | General Imports | |
|---|---|---|---|---|
| | 1966 | 1967 | 1966 | 1967 |
| Total (including special category) see asterisk ... | 30,320 | 31,534 | 25,542 | 26,816 |
| Western Hemisphere ......................... | 11,429 | 11,894 | 10,829 | 11,737 |
| Canada ................................... | 6,661 | 7,173 | 6,125 | 7,099 |
| 19 American Republics ..................... | 4,231 | 4,126 | 3,970 | 3,853 |
| Central American Common Market ......... | 361 | 357 | 303 | 300 |
| Latin American Free Trade Association[1] ...... | 3,623 | 3,511 | 3,452 | 3,323 |
| Dominican Republic ...................... | 88 | 97 | 128 | 134 |
| Panama ................................. | 138 | 139 | 68 | 76 |
| Bahamas ................................. | 134 | 153 | 24 | 26 |
| Bermuda ................................. | 49 | 57 | 2 | 2 |
| Jamaica ................................. | 115 | 126 | 133 | 144 |
| Netherland Antilles ...................... | 72 | 78 | 304 | 311 |
| Surinam ................................. | 32 | 37 | 50 | 56 |
| Trinidad and Tobago ..................... | 59 | 61 | 163 | 184 |
| Europe .................................. | 10,003 | 10,294 | 7,857 | 8,232 |
| OECD countries, total[2] .................. | 9,556 | 9,932 | 7,503 | 7,871 |
| Western Europe ........................... | 9,805 | 10,099 | 7,678 | 8,055 |
| European Economic Community ......... | 5,504 | 5,646 | 4,125 | 4,457 |
| Belgium and Luxembourg ............. | 690 | 704 | 568 | 584 |
| France ............................. | 1,007 | 1,025 | 698 | 690 |
| Germany, Western ................... | 1,674 | 1,706 | 1,796 | 1,955 |
| Italy ............................... | 909 | 973 | 743 | 856 |
| Netherlands ......................... | 1,224 | 1,238 | 320 | 372 |
| European Free Trade Association ...... | 2,984 | 3,270 | 2,954 | 2,882 |
| Austria* ............................ | 55 | 47 | 80 | 72 |
| Denmark ............................ | 184 | 205 | 202 | 183 |
| Norway* ............................ | 144 | 138 | 129 | 134 |
| Portugal* ........................... | 64 | 75 | 75 | 69 |
| Sweden ............................. | 359 | 385 | 295 | 330 |
| Switzerland ......................... | 414 | 430 | 386 | 383 |
| United Kingdom ..................... | 1,737 | 1,960 | 1,786 | 1,710 |
| Finland* ............................ | 64 | 59 | 97 | 93 |
| Greece ............................. | 180 | 143 | 51 | 68 |
| Ireland ............................. | 86 | 77 | 94 | 130 |
| Spain ............................... | 518 | 521 | 163 | 217 |
| Turkey ............................. | 265 | 252 | 96 | 103 |
| Yugoslavia* ......................... | 173 | 96 | 74 | 87 |
| Eastern Europe[2] ........................ | 198 | 195 | 179 | 177 |

### Asia and Oceania

| | | | | |
|---|---|---|---|---|
| Asia[3] ................................... | 6,922 | 7,213 | 5,294 | 5,367 |
| Near East ............................... | 1,112 | 961 | 403 | 308 |
| Iran ................................. | 230 | 246 | 115 | 83 |
| Israel ............................... | 210 | 196 | 77 | 87 |
| Kuwait .............................. | 89 | 108 | 29 | 22 |
| Lebanon ............................. | 84 | 55 | 9 | 7 |
| Saudi Arabia ........................ | 152 | 169 | 96 | 58 |
| United Arab Republic (Egypt) ........ | 189 | 66 | 18 | 15 |
| Japan ................................... | 2,364 | 2,696 | 2,963 | 2,999 |
| East and South Asia ..................... | 3,447 | 3,557 | 1,925 | 2,058 |
| China, Rep. of (Taiwan) ............. | 237 | 333 | 117 | 166 |
| Hong Kong .......................... | 229 | 255 | 416 | 498 |
| India* ............................... | 929 | 955 | 327 | 298 |
| Indonesia ........................... | 68 | 68 | 179 | 182 |
| Korea, Rep. of ...................... | 342 | 416 | 85 | 117 |
| Malaysia[4] .......................... | 46 | 49 | 177 | 196 |
| Singapore ........................... | 51 | 66 | 15 | 16 |
| Pakistan* ........................... | 239 | 347 | 68 | 55 |
| Philippines ......................... | 348 | 428 | 398 | 380 |
| Thailand* ........................... | 123 | 164 | 76 | 96 |
| South Viet-Nam[5] .................... | 311 | 297 | 2 | 2 |
| Oceania ................................. | 805 | 1,016 | 594 | 581 |
| Australia ........................... | 653 | 891 | 395 | 406 |
| New Zealand and Western Samoa ..... | 127 | 90 | 180 | 156 |
| Africa[6] ................................ | 1,159 | 1,116 | 961 | 890 |
| North Africa, excluding Egypt ......... | 273 | 266 | 126 | 124 |
| Algeria ............................. | 67 | 33 | 3 | 3 |
| Ethiopia ............................ | 24 | 23 | 45 | 51 |
| Libya ............................... | 59 | 86 | 57 | 36 |
| Morocco ............................ | 63 | 51 | 10 | 12 |
| Tunisia ............................. | 44 | 52 | 3 | 5 |
| Western and equatorial Africa ......... | 318 | 281 | 379 | 348 |
| Angola .............................. | 17 | 35 | 53 | 63 |
| Ghana .............................. | 53 | 43 | 46 | 57 |
| Ivory Coast ......................... | 23 | 13 | 65 | 48 |
| Liberia ............................. | 38 | 49 | 60 | 52 |
| Nigeria ............................. | 103 | 64 | 51 | 44 |
| Central and southern Africa ........... | 567 | 570 | 457 | 418 |
| Congo (Kinshasa) .................... | 59 | 49 | 45 | 40 |
| Kenya .............................. | 28 | 20 | 21 | 14 |
| Tanzania ........................... | 8 | 9 | 17 | 14 |
| Uganda ............................. | 2 | 4 | 58 | 44 |
| Sout Africa, Rep. of[7] ............... | 401 | 426 | 249 | 227 |

*Where the asterisk appears the "special category shipments" are excluded.*

[1]Includes Paraguay. [2]Excludes Finland and Yugoslavia. [3]Includes United Arab Republic (Egypt). [4]Includes Sarawak and Sabah. [5]Prior to Jan. 1, 1966 includes North Vietnam. [6]Excludes UAR. [7]Includes SW Africa and British High Commission Territories of Bechuanaland, Basutoland and Swaziland.

## A Super Barge Load of Sugar

The world's largest barge, the Caribbean, carried its largest load Aug. 9-16, 1968. Towed by tug Elizabeth Moran, it brought 17,391 long tons of raw sugar, worth $3,000,000 and enough to fill household needs of 10,000,000 people for a year, from Puerto Rico to N.Y.C.

# Commerce at Principal U. S. Ports

### EXCLUDING GREAT LAKES SHIPPING

Source: Corps of Engineers, Department of the Army

Calendar Year of 1966. In tons of 2,000 pounds.

| Port | Tons | Port | Tons |
|---|---|---|---|
| **TONNAGE SHIPPED AT MAJOR PORTS** | | Natchez, Miss. | 598,318 |
| | | Pascagoula Harbor, Miss. | 9,673,782 |
| Port of New York, N. Y. and N. J. | 157,071,892 | Vicksburg, Miss. | 1,626,141 |
| New Orleans, La. | 99,387,697 | Brownsville, Texas. | 4,355,988 |
| Houston, Texas. | 59,793,312 | Freeport Harbor, Texas. | 4,361,657 |
| Philadelphia Harbor, Pa. | 49,505,860 | Galveston, Texas. | 4,798,764 |
| Baltimore Harbor and Channels, Md. | 43,876,778 | Harbor Island, Texas. | 6,653,066 |
| Norfolk Harbor, Va. | 39,497,670 | Orange, Texas. | 1,408,683 |
| Baton Rouge, La. | 34,104,315 | Palacios, Texas. | 149,099 |
| Beaumont, Texas. | 32,660,280 | Port Isabel, Texas. | 369,699 |
| Port Arthur, Texas. | 26,298,267 | Matagorda Ship Channel (Port Lavaca-Point Comfort, Tex.) | 4,337,074 |
| Tampa Harbor, Fla. | 23,915,622 | Port Mansfield, Texas. | 73,359 |
| Los Angeles Harbor, Calif. | 23,502,611 | Sabine Pass Harbor, Texas. | 103,711 |
| Corpus Christi, Texas. | 22,464,936 | Victoria, Texas. | 927,629 |
| Portland Harbor, Me. | 22,315,086 | Helena, Ark. | 1,958,106 |
| Mobile Harbor, Ala. | 22,307,913 | Chattanooga, Tenn. | 1,417,689 |
| Paulsboro, N. J. and vicinity. | 20,532,333 | Knoxville, Tenn. | 513,522 |
| Boston, Mass. | 20,287,217 | Memphis, Tenn. | 7,614,953 |
| Marcus Hook, Pa. and vicinity. | 19,643,963 | Nashville, Tenn. | 2,717,990 |
| Texas City, Tex. | 17,691,501 | Kansas City, Mo. | 1,695,192 |
| Huntington, W. Va. | 17,035,691 | Cincinnati, Ohio. | 9,133,544 |
| Lake Charles, La. | 16,530,105 | Louisville, Ky. | 8,591,169 |
| Portland, Ore. | 15,590,726 | Mount Vernon, Ind. | 3,365,006 |
| Richmond Harbor, Calif. | 15,149,011 | Minneapolis, Minn. | 1,512,800 |
| Port of Newport News, Va. | 14,108,909 | St. Paul, Minn. | 4,941,242 |
| New Castle, Del. and vicinity. | 13,035,957 | Carpinteria, Calif. | 948,747 |
| St. Louis, Mo. | 9,426,324 | Crescent City Harbor, Calif. | 440,203 |
| | | El Segundo, Calif. | 4,457,740 |
| **OTHER PORTS MAINE TO WASHINGTON** | | Ellwood, Calif. | 111,450 |
| | | Encino, Calif. | 74,787 |
| Rockland Harbor, Maine. | 96,647 | Gaviota, Santa Barbara County, Calif. | 332,276 |
| Searsport Harbor, Maine. | 1,333,579 | Humboldt Harbor and Bay, Calif. | 890,106 |
| Portsmouth Harbor, N. H. | 1,740,119 | Huntington Beach, Calif. | 407,668 |
| Burlington Harbor, Vt. | 539,008 | Long Beach, Calif. | 13,547,600 |
| Beverly Harbor, Mass. | 213,812 | Monterey Harbor, Calif. | 9,185 |
| Fall River Harbor, Mass. | 4,040,441 | Moss Landing Harbor, Calif. | 42,575 |
| Gloucester Harbor, Mass. | 198,340 | Oakland Harbor, Calif. | 5,187,886 |
| New Bedford, Fairhaven Harbor, Mass. | 427,511 | Port Hueneme, Calif. | 72,945 |
| Salem Harbor, Mass. | 1,375,249 | Redwood City Harbor, Calif. | 3,168,467 |
| Newport Harbor, R. I. | 123,423 | San Diego Harbor, Calif. | 1,905,511 |
| Providence River and Harbor, R. I. | 9,206,698 | San Francisco Harbor, Calif. | 4,961,483 |
| Bridgeport Harbor, Conn. | 2,489,475 | San Luis Obispo Harbor, Calif. | 1,242,604 |
| New Haven Harbor, Conn. | 9,530,184 | Stockton, Calif. | 2,635,259 |
| New London Harbor, Conn. | 1,045,970 | Ventura Harbor, Calif. | 557,284 |
| Norwalk Harbor, Conn. | 1,346,050 | Astoria, Ore. | 1,243,081 |
| Stamford Harbor, Conn. | 1,039,506 | Coos Bay, Ore. | 5,265,795 |
| Cold Spring Harbor, N. Y. | 152,646 | Oregon Slough (No. Portland Hbr.), Ore. | 607,140 |
| Hempstead Harbor, N. Y. | 4,293,470 | Port of Bandom, Ore. | 285,969 |
| Huntington Harbor, N. Y. | 553,967 | Port of St. Helens, Ore. | 310,896 |
| Peekskill Harbor, N. Y. | 128,352 | Yaquina Bay and Harbor, Ore. | 286,327 |
| Plattsburg, N. Y. | 477,212 | Anacortes Harbor, Wash. | 5,615,207 |
| Port Chester Harbor, N. Y. | 405,714 | Bellingham Bay and Harbor, Wash. | 2,067,573 |
| Port Jefferson Harbor, N. Y. | 2,002,472 | Everett Harbor, Wash. | 4,241,102 |
| Port of Albany, N. Y. | 8,502,566 | Grays Harbor and Chehalis River, Wash. | 2,737,555 |
| Rondout Harbor, N. Y. | 446,797 | Hammersley Inlet, Wash. (Shelton Hbr.) | 895,042 |
| Tarrytown Harbor, N. Y. | 638,860 | Longview, Wash. | 3,883,423 |
| Camden-Gloucester, N. J. | 5,466,473 | Neah Bay, Wash. | 253,533 |
| Trenton Harbor, N. J. | 2,446,842 | Olympia Harbor, Wash. | 640,060 |
| Aliquippa-Rochester, Pa. | 6,835,517 | Port Angeles Harbor, Wash. | 2,552,220 |
| Chester, Pa. | 805,859 | Port Gamble Harbor, Wash. | 213,484 |
| Clairton-Elizabeth, Pa. | 13,317,500 | Port Townsend Harbor, Wash. | 852,636 |
| Penn Manor, Pa. and vicinity. | 10,252,550 | Seattle Harbor, Wash. | 14,846,806 |
| Pittsburgh, Pa. | 8,369,023 | Tacoma Harbor, Wash. | 5,827,876 |
| Wilmington Harbor, Del. | 2,361,698 | Vancouver, Wash. | 1,825,588 |
| Cambridge Harbor, Md. | 114,149 | Willapa Riv. & Hbr., Naselle Riv., Wash. | 578,460 |
| Washington Harbor, D. C. | 2,102,197 | | |
| Alexandria, Va. | 261,922 | | |
| Port of Hopewell, Va. | 510,694 | **ALASKA, HAWAII, PUERTO RICO** | |
| Port of Richmond, Va. | 1,618,414 | | |
| Morehead City Harbor, N. C. | 655,808 | Anchorage, Alaska. | 1,008,999 |
| Port of Wilmington, N. C. (see also Wilmington Harbor, N. C., for waterway data) | 4,394,457 | Illuluk Harbor, Alaska. | 170,865 |
| | | Juneau Harbor, Alaska. | 133,524 |
| | | Ketchikan Harbor, Alaska. | 1,542,093 |
| Charleston Harbor, S. C. | 5,419,919 | Seward Harbor, Alaska. | 49,326 |
| Georgetown Harbor, S. C. | 1,092,629 | Sitka Harbor, Alaska. | 1,072,382 |
| Brunswick Harbor, Ga. | 870,557 | Skagway Harbor, Alaska. | 296,888 |
| Savannah Harbor, Ga. | 4,756,663 | Whittier Harbor, Alaska. | 114,170 |
| Canaveral Harbor, Fla. | 1,696,458 | Wrangell Harbor, Alaska. | 501,642 |
| Charlotte Harbor, Fla. | 1,359,455 | Barbers Point, Oahu, Hawaii. | 2,469,739 |
| Fernandina Harbor, Fla. | 209,528 | Hilo Harbor, Hawaii, Hawaii. | 835,029 |
| Fort Pierce Harbor, Fla. | 85,623 | Honolulu Harbor, Oahu, Hawaii. | 6,180,798 |
| Jacksonville Harbor, Fla. | 10,295,556 | Kahului Harbor, Maui, Hawaii. | 895,405 |
| Key West Harbor, Fla. | 214,901 | Kaumalapau Harbor, Lanai, Hawaii. | 293,386 |
| Miami Harbor, Fla. | 1,377,514 | Kaunakakai Harbor, Molokai, Hawaii. | 377,827 |
| Palm Beach Harbor, Fla. | 886,556 | Kawaihae Harbor, Hawaii, Hawaii. | 266,894 |
| Panama City Harbor, Fla. | 1,244,067 | Nawiliwili Harbor, Kauai, Hawaii. | 522,286 |
| Pensacola Harbor, Fla. | 730,324 | Pearl Harbor, Oahu, Hawaii. | 1,043,431 |
| Port Everglades Harbor, Fla. | 7,135,333 | Port Allen Harbor, Kauai, Hawaii. | 127,935 |
| Port St. Joe Harbor, Fla. | 301,045 | Wake Island Harbor. | 453,730 |
| St. Petersburg Harbor, Fla. | 282,703 | Guanica Harbor, P. R. | 318,534 |
| Weedon Island, Fla. | 722,484 | Mayaguez Harbor, P. R. | 312,489 |
| Guntersville, Ala. | 1,390,291 | Ponce Harbor, P. R. | 624,910 |
| Biloxi Harbor, Miss. | 152,572 | San Juan Harbor, P. R. | 7,460,810 |
| Greenville, Miss. | 1,262,347 | St. Thomas Harbor, V. I. | 326,890 |
| Gulfport Harbor, Miss. | 534,197 | Guam Island, Pacific Ocean. | 192,339 |

## Commerce at Great Lakes Ports

Source: Corps of Engineers, Dept. of the Army
Calendar Year 1966. In tons of 2,000 pounds

| Port | Tons | Port | Tons |
|---|---|---|---|
| **Duluth-Superior Hbr., Minn. & Wis.** | **46,297,520** | Port Dolomite, Mich | 3,367,645 |
| **Silver Bay, Minn** | **12,099,673** | Port Gypsum, Mich | 266,271 |
| Taconite Harbor, Minn | 9,810,784 | Port Huron, Mich | 990,049 |
| Ashland Harbor, Wis | 411,363 | Port Inland, Mich | 3,875,272 |
| Green Bay Harbor, Wis | 2,664,342 | **Port of Detroit, Mich** | **33,501,647** |
| Kewaunee Harbor, Wis | 1,279,661 | Presque Isle Harbor, Mich | 6,664,442 |
| Manitowoc Harbor, Wis | 2,383,629 | St. Clair, Mich | 3,834,612 |
| Milwaukee Harbor, Wis | 6,387,733 | St. Ignace, Mich | 150,240 |
| Oak Creek, Wis | 2,998,403 | St. Joseph Harbor, Mich | 457,293 |
| Port Washington Harbor, Wis | 871,437 | Sault Ste. Marie, Mich | 321,635 |
| Racine Harbor, Wis | 127,093 | Stoneport, Mich | 6,232,360 |
| Sheboygan Harbor, Wis | 443,539 | Traverse City Harbor, Mich | 180,111 |
| Two Rivers Harbor, Wis | 131,646 | Wells, Mich | 91,602 |
| Alabaster, Mich | 618,735 | **Port of Chicago, Ill** | **44,658,834** |
| Alpena Harbor, Mich | 3,199,105 | Waukegan Harbor, Ill | 457,773 |
| **Calcite, Mich** | **14,266,112** | Buffington Harbor, Ind | 2,352,612 |
| Cheboygan Harbor, Mich | 115,259 | **Gary Harbor, Ind** | **11,007,075** |
| Detour, Mich | 349,036 | **Indiana Harbor, Ind** | **20,706,497** |
| Drummond Island, Mich | 2,772,005 | Michigan City Harbor, Ind | 22,533 |
| Escanaba, Mich | 7,908,331 | Ashtabula Harbor, Ohio | 9,314,794 |
| Frankfort Harbor, Mich | 1,766,757 | **Cleveland Harbor, Ohio** | **24,020,820** |
| Gladstone Harbor, Mich | 282,903 | Conneaut Harbor, Ohio | 12,822,154 |
| Gd. Haven Harbor & Gd. River, Mich | 3,595,210 | Fairport Harbor, Ohio | 2,074,456 |
| Holland Harbor, Mich | 241,426 | Huron Harbor, Ohio | 1,305,995 |
| Lime Island, Mich | 263,102 | Lorain Harbor, Ohio | 6,620,983 |
| Ludington Harbor, Mich | 3,969,311 | Marblehead, Ohio | 1,285,216 |
| Mackinaw City, Mich | 36,625 | Sandusky Harbor, Ohio | 3,805,129 |
| Manistee Harbor, Mich | 628,795 | **Toledo Harbor, Ohio** | **43,932,128** |
| Manistique Harbor, Mich | 257,255 | Erie Harbor, Pa | 975,187 |
| Marquette Harbor, Mich | 2,096,642 | Great Sodus Bay Harbor, N. Y | 407,240 |
| Marysville, Mich | 577,318 | Ogdensburg Harbor, N. Y | 541,197 |
| Menominee Harbor, Mich. & Wis | 453,238 | Oswego Harbor, N. Y | 449,154 |
| Muskegon Harbor, Mich | 3,563,538 | **Port of Buffalo, N. Y** | **18,611,802** |
| Petoskey Penn-Dixie Harbor, Mich | 1 | Rochester (Charlotte) Harbor, N. Y | 839,502 |

# U. S. Exports and Imports of Leading Commodities

Source: Bureau of International Commerce, Dept. of Commerce, May 1968
(Value in millions of dollars)

| Commodity | Exports | | Imports | |
|---|---|---|---|---|
| | 1966 | 1967 | 1966 | 1967 |
| **Total** | **$29,884** | **$31,147** | **$25,542** | **$26,816** |
| **Food and live animals**[1] | **4,562** | **4,064** | **3,948** | **4,003** |
| Meat | 130 | 122 | 600 | 645 |
| Poultry | 46 | 39 | ...... | ...... |
| Dairy products and eggs | 125 | 117 | ...... | ...... |
| Cheese | ...... | ...... | 61 | 65 |
| Fish | 63 | 67 | 553 | 522 |
| Grains and preparation | 3,190 | 2,681 | 43 | 46 |
| Wheat and wheat flour[2] | 1,536 | 1,207 | ...... | ...... |
| Rice | 230 | 319 | ...... | ...... |
| Coarse grains | 1,335 | 1,055 | ...... | ...... |
| Corn | 876 | 704 | ...... | ...... |
| Grain sorghums | 357 | 299 | ...... | ...... |
| Fruits and nuts | 340 | 338 | 369 | 360 |
| Vegetables | 169 | 154 | 170 | 195 |
| Sugar | ...... | ...... | 501 | 588 |
| Coffee, green or roasted | ...... | ...... | 1,069 | 964 |
| **Beverages and Tobacco** | **624** | **649** | **642** | **698** |
| Alcoholic beverages | ...... | ...... | 497 | 528 |
| Tobacco, unmanufactured | 482 | 498 | 137 | 162 |
| Cigarettes | 111 | 116 | ...... | ...... |
| **Crude materials, inedible except fuels** | **3,070** | **3,280** | **3,266** | **2,965** |
| Hides and skins, except fur skins | 155 | 128 | 89 | 61 |
| Soybeans, peanuts other oilseeds | 815 | 827 | ...... | ...... |
| Synthethic rubber | 175 | 170 | 177 | 170 |
| Ores and metal scrap | 422 | 520 | 11,020 | 974 |
| Coal | 468 | 432 | ...... | ...... |
| Petroleum and products | 434 | 539 | 2,127 | 2,088 |
| **Animal and vegetable oils and fats** | **357** | **338** | **146** | **122** |
| Soybean oil | 125 | 143 | ...... | ...... |
| **Chemicals** | **2,675** | **2,803** | **955** | **963** |
| Medicinal and pharmaceutical | 269 | 288 | 75 | 72 |
| **Machinery and transport equipment** | **11,155** | **12,573** | **4,823** | **5,791** |
| Automotive engines | 200 | 225 | 232 | 268 |
| Agricultural machinery | 233 | 237 | 190 | 216 |
| Tractors and parts | 215 | 214 | 106 | 101 |
| Metalworking machinery | 338 | 339 | 135 | 203 |
| Textile and leather machinery | 227 | 205 | 221 | 238 |
| Other nonelectrical machinery | 1,119 | 1,168 | 474 | 495 |
| Electrical apparatus | 1,900 | 2,097 | 1,010 | 1,140 |
| **Transport equipment**[3] | **3,478** | **4,296** | **2,135** | **2,688** |
| Railway vehicles | 116 | 145 | ...... | ...... |
| New motor vehicles | 1,276 | 1,302 | 1,236 | 1,695 |
| Aircraft and parts | 1,097 | 1,518 | 273 | 248 |
| **Other manufactured goods** | **5,278** | **5,376** | **8,635** | **8,963** |
| Rubber manufactures | 168 | 156 | 64 | 69 |
| Paper and manufactures | 443 | 466 | 985 | 962 |
| Diamonds excluding industrial | ...... | ...... | 375 | 389 |
| Metals and manufactures | 1,776 | 1,734 | 3,267 | 3,398 |
| Iron and steel-mill products | 537 | 539 | 1,183 | 1,289 |
| Nonferrous base metals | 582 | 517 | 1,468 | 1,477 |
| Textiles other than clothing | 554 | 531 | 909 | 812 |
| Furniture | 47 | 52 | 81 | 91 |
| Clothing | 125 | 129 | 608 | 649 |
| **Other transactions** | **1,187** | **960** | **866** | **1,060** |

[1]Includes relief shipments. [2]Wheat equivalent. [3]Excludes parts for tractors.

# Merchant Fleets of the World
## OCEANGOING STEAM AND MOTORSHIPS OF 1,000 GROSS TONS AND OVER
### Source: Maritime Administration, U. S. Dept. of Commerce

Excludes ships operating exclusively on the Great Lakes and Inland Waterways and special types such as channel ships, icebreakers, cable ships, etc., and merchant ships owned by any military force.
Gross Tons: Volume, not weight; each gross ton represents 100 cubic ft. of enclosed space. Deadweight Tons: Number of long tons (2,240 lbs. ea.) of cargo, fuel, etc, a ship can carry at maximum draft.

| January 1, 1968 Country of Registry | Total no. | Gross tons | Dwt. tons | Tankers Number | Tankers Dwt. tons |
|---|---|---|---|---|---|
| UnitedStates† | 2,162 | 19,179,000 | 26,079,000 | 316 | 7,293,000 |
| United Kingdom | 1,903 | 20,005,000 | 27,536,000 | 410 | 12,123,000 |
| Australia | 102 | 637,000 | 883,000 | 12 | 212,000 |
| British Colonies | 135 | 1,268,000 | 1,922,000 | 17 | 768,000 |
| Canada | 65 | 266,000 | 314,000 | 16 | 109,000 |
| Cyprus | 64 | 420,000 | 606,000 | 7 | 113,000 |
| Ghana | 14 | 105,000 | 134,000 | | |
| India | 219 | 1,894,000 | 2,774,000 | 10 | 307,000 |
| Jamaica | 3 | 15,000 | 14,000 | 1 | 5,000 |
| Malaysia | 5 | 7,000 | 6,000 | 1 | 2,000 |
| Malta | 8 | 44,000 | 67,000 | 1 | 16,000 |
| New Zealand | 50 | 151,000 | 181,000 | 1 | 3,000 |
| Nigeria | 9 | 53,000 | 89,000 | | |
| Pakistan | 61 | 467,000 | 631,000 | 1 | 16,000 |
| Tonga | 1 | 2,000 | 3,000 | | |
| *Albania | 8 | 33,000 | 45,000 | | |
| Algeria | 4 | 15,000 | 20,000 | | |
| Argentina | 148 | 1,051,000 | 1,421,000 | 54 | 711,000 |
| Belgium | 69 | 847,000 | 1,231,000 | 15 | 464,000 |
| Brazil | 224 | 1,178,000 | 1,656,000 | 50 | 650,000 |
| *Bulgaria | 77 | 494,000 | 717,000 | 13 | 204,000 |
| Burma | 8 | 45,000 | 60,000 | | |
| Burundi | 2 | 16,000 | 21,000 | | |
| Chile | 46 | 262,000 | 355,000 | 5 | 102,000 |
| China (Taiwan) | 126 | 760,000 | 1,081,000 | 9 | 124,000 |
| *China (Communist) | 193 | 863,000 | 1,150,000 | 20 | 137,000 |
| Colombia | 25 | 145,000 | 189,000 | 1 | 16,000 |
| Congolese Republic | 3 | 29,000 | 34,000 | | |
| Costa Rica | 1 | 5,000 | 8,000 | | |
| *Cuba | 40 | 223,000 | 305,000 | 2 | 6,000 |
| *Czechoslovakia | 7 | 75,000 | 109,000 | | |
| Denmark | 342 | 2,842,000 | 4,237,000 | 56 | 1,898,000 |
| Dominican Republic | 5 | 14,000 | 20,000 | | |
| Ecuador | 5 | 26,000 | 33,000 | 1 | 2,000 |
| Ethiopia | 6 | 37,000 | 56,000 | 1 | 33,000 |
| Finland | 221 | 1,012,000 | 1,488,000 | 37 | 560,000 |
| France | 532 | 5,284,000 | 7,220,000 | 154 | 4,112,000 |
| Germany (West) | 886 | 5,870,000 | 8,423,000 | 48 | 1,792,000 |
| *Germany (East) | 114 | 720,000 | 940,000 | 10 | 143,000 |
| Greece | 975 | 7,275,000 | 10,580,000 | 143 | 3,134,000 |
| Guatemala | 2 | 4,000 | 6,000 | | |
| Guinea | 1 | 11,000 | 15,000 | | |
| Haiti | 1 | 7,000 | 9,000 | | |
| Honduras | 13 | 51,000 | 52,000 | 1 | 2,000 |
| *Hungary | 17 | 21,000 | 23,000 | | |
| Iceland | 23 | 51,000 | 67,000 | 2 | 7,000 |
| Indonesia | 154 | 498,000 | 599,000 | 22 | 130,000 |
| Iran | 5 | 58,000 | 87,000 | 2 | 63,000 |
| Iraq | 2 | 12,000 | 17,000 | | |
| Ireland | 15 | 119,000 | 170,000 | | |
| Israel | 92 | 709,000 | 949,000 | 1 | 2,000 |
| Italy | 613 | 5,943,000 | 8,002,000 | 152 | 3,278,000 |
| Ivory Coast | 4 | 20,000 | 26,000 | | |
| Japan | 1,582 | 16,101,000 | 24,738,000 | 275 | 10,238,000 |
| Korea (South) | 60 | 360,000 | 564,000 | 7 | 220,000 |
| *Korea (North) | 2 | 4,000 | 6,000 | | |
| Kuwait | 13 | 144,000 | 216,000 | 3 | 161,000 |
| Lebanon | 105 | 490,000 | 746,000 | | |
| Liberia | 1,496 | 23,881,000 | 39,599,000 | 607 | 22,943,000 |
| Malagasy | 8 | 21,000 | 28,000 | 1 | 2,000 |
| Mexico | 47 | 326,000 | 490,000 | 27 | 391,000 |
| Monaco | 3 | 24,000 | 35,000 | 3 | 35,000 |
| Morocco | 16 | 53,000 | 76,000 | | |
| Netherlands | 456 | 4,531,000 | 6,245,000 | 88 | 2,630,000 |
| Nicaragua | 5 | 14,000 | 21,000 | | |
| Norway | 1,368 | 18,666,000 | 29,238,000 | 459 | 16,742,000 |
| Panama | 585 | 4,691,000 | 7,232,000 | 137 | 4,112,000 |
| Peru | 30 | 165,000 | 244,000 | 6 | 74,000 |
| Philippines | 133 | 707,000 | 987,000 | 10 | 49,000 |
| *Poland | 197 | 1,178,000 | 1,665,000 | 6 | 108,000 |
| Portugal | 92 | 605,000 | 717,000 | 15 | 297,000 |
| *Romania | 34 | 278,000 | 409,000 | 3 | 74,000 |
| Saudi Arabia | 13 | 42,000 | 49,000 | | |
| Senegal | 2 | 6,000 | 6,000 | | |
| Singapore | 13 | 55,000 | 62,000 | | |
| Somalia | 3 | 20,000 | 31,000 | | |
| South Africa | 54 | 350,000 | 476,000 | 1 | 18,000 |
| Spain | 361 | 2,023,000 | 2,811,000 | 86 | 1,419,000 |
| Sudan | 4 | 20,000 | 25,000 | | |
| Sweden | 422 | 4,404,000 | 6,382,000 | 68 | 2,387,000 |
| Switzerland | 28 | 217,000 | 305,000 | | |
| Thailand | 13 | 43,000 | 62,000 | 5 | 13,000 |
| Tunisia | 9 | 19,000 | 25,000 | | |
| Turkey | 101 | 575,000 | 767,000 | 12 | 250,000 |
| United Arab Republic | 44 | 194,000 | 240,000 | 10 | 101,000 |
| Uruguay | 18 | 123,000 | 186,000 | 4 | 64,000 |
| *USSRa | 1,449 | 8,562,000 | 10,958,000 | 283 | 4,148,000 |
| Venezuela | 34 | 293,000 | 419,000 | 14 | 325,000 |
| Vietnam (South) | 2 | 5,000 | 6,000 | | |
| Yugoslavia | 181 | 1,174,000 | 1,655,000 | 17 | 202,000 |
| **Total all Countries** | **18,800** | **171,522,000** | **250,403,000** | **3,740** | **105,542,000** |

*Source material limited and unreliable. †Comprised of ships under general agreement, bareboat charter, and in the custody of the Department of Defense, State and Interior.
aIncludes the following U. S. Government-owned ships transferred to USSR under lend-lease agreements and still remaining under that registry: 76 | 431,000 | 645,000 | 1 | 11,000

# Notable Ocean Passages by Ships

| Time | From | To | Distance naut. mi. | Date | Ship |
|---|---|---|---|---|---|
| **ONE HUNDRED YEARS OF SAILING VESSELS** | | | | | |
| 16d | Liverpool | New York | 3,150 | Nov. 1846 | Yorkshire |
| 76d 6h | San Francisco | Boston | ..... | 1853 | Northern Light |
| 12d 6h | Boston Light | Light Rock | ..... | 1854 | James Baines |
| 89d | New York | San Francisco | 15,091 | 1854 | Flying Cloud |
| 89d 20h | New York | San Francisco | 13,700 | 1860 | Andrew Jackson |
| 63d 18h 15m | Liverpool | Melbourne | ..... | 1868-69 | Thermopylae |
| 13d 1h 25m | New York | Liverpool | 3,150 | ........... | Red Jacket |
| 36d | 50 S. lat. | Golden Gate | ..... | ........... | Starr King |
| 12d 12h | Equator | San Francisco | ..... | ........... | Golden Fleece |
| 12d 4h 1m | Sandy Hook | England | 3,013 | 1905 | Atlantic |
| 23d | England | Sandy Hook | 3,013 | 1928 | Atlantic |
| 22d 6h 7m | Bishop's Rock | Boston Light | ..... | 1936 | Yankee |
| **ATLANTIC CROSSINGS BY POWER VESSELS** | | | | | |
| 29d 4h | Savannah | Liverpool | ..... | May 22, 1819 | Savannah (Amer.)  (a) |
| 15d | Bristol | New York | ..... | Apr., 1838 | Great Western (Br.) |
| 14d 8h | Liverpool | New York | 3,150 | July, 1840 | Britannia (Br.)  (b) |
| 9d 19h 25m | Atlantic | ..... | ..... | May, 1851 | Pacific |
| 9d 13h | Liverpool | New York | 3,054 | Aug., 1852 | Baltic (Amer.) |
| 8d 1h 45m | Queenstown | New York | 2,780 | 1856 | Persia |
| 8d 2h 48m | Queenstown | New York | 2,780 | 1866 | Scotia |
| 7d 4h 1m | Queenstown | New York | ..... | 1867 | City of Paris (Br.) |
| 7d 22h 3m | Queenstown | New York | 2,780 | 1869 | City of Brussels (Br.) |
| 7d 20h 9m | Queenstown | New York | 2,780 | 1873 | Baltic (Br.) |
| 7d 15h 48m | Queenstown | New York | 2,780 | 1875 | City of Berlin (Br.) |
| 7d 11h 37m | Queenstown | New York | 2,780 | 1876 | Germanic (Br.) |
| 7d 10h 53m | Queenstown | New York | 2,780 | 1877 | Britannic (Br.) |
| 7d 8h 0m | New York | Queenstown | ..... | 1879 | Arizona (Br.) |
| 6d 7h 23m | Queenstown | New York | 2,780 | 1880 | Arizona (Br.) |
| 6d 18h 37m | New York | Queenstown | 2,780 | 1882 | Alaska (Br.) |
| 6d 21h 40m | Queenstown | New York | 2,780 | 1883 | Alaska (Br.) |
| 6d 10h 40m | New York | Queenstown | 2,780 | 1884 | Oregon (Br.) |
| 6d 9h 42m | Queenstown | New York | 2,780 | 1884 | Oregon (Br.) |
| 6d 4h 34m | Queenstown | New York | 2,780 | 1887 | Umbria (Br.) |
| 5d 1h 55m | Queenstown | New York | 2,780 | 1888 | Etruria (Br.) |
| 5d 22h 50m | New York | Queenstown | 2,780 | 1889 | City of Paris (Br.) |
| 5d 16h 31m | Queenstown | New York | 2,780 | 1891 | Teutonic (Br.) |
| 5d 14h 24m | Queenstown | New York | 2,780 | 1892 | City of Paris (Br.) |
| 5d 9h 6m | Queenstown | New York | 2,780 | 1893 | Campania (Br.) |
| 5d 7h 23m | Queenstown | New York | 2,780 | 1894 | Lucania (Br.) |
| 5d 15h 25m | New York | Southampton | 3,189 | 1897 | Kaiser Wilhelm Der Grosse (Ger.) |
| 5d 15h 20m | Southampton | New York | 3,189 | 1898 | Kaiser Wilhelm Der Grosse (Ger.) |
| 5d 7h 38m | Sandy Hook | Plymouth | 3,082 | Sept., 1900 | Deutschland (Ger.) |
| 4d 15h | Queenstown | New York | 2,780 | 1908 | Lusitania (Br.) |
| 4d 11h 42m | Queenstown | New York | 2,780 | 1909 | Lusitania (Br.) |
| 4d 10h 41m | Queenstown | New York | 2,780 | 1910 | Mauretania (Br.) |
| 5d 6h 21m | New York | Cherbourg | 3,227 | Oct., 1924 | Leviathan (Amer.) |
| 6d 5h 30m | Cherbourg | Cape Henry | 3,320 | June, 1927 | U.S.S. Memphis  (c) |
| 4d 17h 42m | Cherbourg | Ambrose Lt. | 3,164 | July, 1929 | Bremen (Ger.)* |
| 4d 14h 30m | New York | Plymouth | 3,082 | July, 1929 | Bremen (Ger.) |
| 4d 17h 06m | Cherbourg | Ambrose Lt. | 3,157 | March, 1930 | Europa (Ger.)* |
| 4d 19h 57m | Ambrose Lt. | Cherbourg | 3,196 | June, 1933 | Europa (Ger.) |
| 4d 16h 48m | Cherbourg | New York | 3,149 | July, 1933 | Europa (Ger.) |
| 4d 13h 58m | Gibraltar | Ambrose Lt. | 3,181 | Aug., 1933 | Rex (Ital.) |
| 4d 14h 27m | Cherbourg | Ambrose Lt. | 3,092 | Nov., 1934 | Bremen (Ger.) |
| 4d 3h 13m | Cherbourg | New York | 2,971 | May-June, '35 | Normandie (Fr.)* |
| 4d 3h 25m | New York | Cherbourg | 3,015 | June, 1935 | Normandie (Fr.) |
| 4d 12h 24m | Cherbourg | Ambrose Lt. | 3,158 | May-June, '36 | Queen Mary (Br.)* |
| 3d 23h 02m | Bishop's Rock | Ambrose Lt. | 2,906 | July-Aug., '37 | Normandie (Fr.) |
| 3d 22h 07m | New York | Southampton | 2,936 | Aug., 1937 | Normandie (Fr.) |
| 3d 20h 42m | Ambrose Lt. | Bishop's Rock | 3,120 | Aug., 10-14, 1938 | Queen Mary (Br.) |
| 3d 21h 48m | Bishop's Rock | Ambrose Lt. | 3,120 | Aug., 1948 | Queen Mary (Br.) |
| 3d 10h 40m | Ambrose Lt. | Bishop's Rock | 2,942 | July, 3-7, 1952 | United States (U.S.)*  (e) |
| 3d 12h 12m | Bishop's Rock | Ambrose Lt. | 2,902 | July, 11-14, 1952 | United States (U.S.)  (e) |
| 4d 23h 25m | Quebec | Le Havre | 2,630 | Aug., 1956 | Homeric (Pan.) |
| 4d 20h 50m | Ambrose Lt. | Bishop's Rock | 2,853 | Sept., 1962 | American Challenger (Amer.) (j) |
| **OTHER OCEAN PASSAGES** | | | | | |
| 3d 00h 36m | San Pedro | Honolulu | 2,226 | June, 1928 | U.S.S. Lexington |
| 3d 2h 30m | San Francisco | Oahu, T. H. | 2,091 | July, 16-19, '45 | U.S.S. Indianapolis  (d) |
| 4d 8h 51m | Gibraltar | Newp't News | 3,360 | Nov., 26, 1945 | U.S.S. Lake Champlain |
| 7d 18h 36m | Japan | San Francisco | 5,000 | July-Aug. 4, '50 | U.S.S. Boxer |
| 7d 13h | Yokosuka | Alameda | 5,000 | June 1-9, 1951 | U.S.S. Philippine Sea |
| 8d 11h | Nantucket | Portland, Eng | 3,161 | Feb.25-Mar4,'58 | U.S.S. Skate (f) |
| 7d 5h | Lizard Head | Nantucket | ..... | Mar. 23-20, '58 | U.S.S. Skate (f) |
| 15d | Pearl Harbor, Hawaii | Iceland (via North Pole) | ..... | July 23-Aug. 7, 1958 | U.S.S. Nautilus  (g) |
| 84d | New London, Conn. | Rehoboth, Del. | 41,500 | Feb. 16-May 10, 1960 | S.S. Triton  (h) |
| 9d 6h 53m | Yokohama | San Francisco | ..... | Aug., 1960 | Brooklyn Maru (Jap.)* |
| 6d | Baffin Bay | Pacific Ocean, N.W. Passage | 850 | Aug. 15-20, 1960 | U.S.S. Seadragon  (i) |
| 12d 16h 22m | New York | Cape Town | 6,786 | Oct. 30-Nov. 11, 1962— | African Comet* |

*Maiden voyage. (a) The Savannah, a fully rigged sailing vessel with steam auxiliary (over 300 tons, 98.5 ft. long, beam 25.8 ft., deptn 12.9 ft.), was launched in the East River in 1818. It was the first ship to use steam in crossing any ocean. It was supplied with engines and detachable iron paddle wheels. On its famous voyage it used steam 105 hours during parts of 12 days. The world's first nuclear-powered merchant ship, the N.S. Savannah, was named for the old steamship. (b) First Cunard liner. (c) Carried Charles A. Lindberg back to the United States after his flight from New York to Paris. (d) Carried Hiroshima atomic bomb in World War II. (e) Set world speed record; average speed eastbound on maiden voyage 35.59 knots (about 41 m.p.h.); westbound, 34.51 knots. (f) First atomic submarine to cross Atlantic both ways submerged. (g) World's first atomic submarine, also first to make undersea voyage under polar ice cap, 1,830 mi. from Point Barrow, Alaska, to Atlantic Ocean, Aug. 1-4, 1958, reaching North Pole Aug. 3. Second undersea transit of the North Pole made by submarine USS Skate Aug. 11, 1958, during trip from New London, Conn., and return. (h) World's largest submarine. Nuclear-powered Triton was submerged during nearly all its voyage around the globe. It duplicated the route of Ferdinand Magellan's circuit (1519-1952), 30,708 mi., starting from St. Paul Rocks off the NE coast of Brazil, Feb. 24-Apr. 25, 1960, then sailed to Cadiz, Spain, before returning home. (i) First underwater transit of Northwest Passage. (j) Fastest freighter crossing of Atlantic.

## Navigable Distances Between Ports

**Source:** Distances between ports, U. S. Naval Oceanographic Office
Distances between U. S. ports, Coast and Geodetic Survey ESSA

**One nautical mile:** International Nautical Mile (INM) is equivalent to 1,852 meters, or approximately 6,076.11549 feet.
**One statute mile** = 5,280 ft. Distances shown are in nautical miles. For statute miles, multiply by 1.151.

## Navigable Distances from New York City

The distances from New York to European ports and Straits of Gibraltar are based on Track "C" (North Atlantic Track Agreement 1950), which is used from July 1 through April 10.

| Port | Naut. Miles | Port | Naut. Miles |
|---|---|---|---|
| Acajutla, El Salvador—via Panama | 2,851 | Manila, P. I.—via Panama | 11,365 |
| Acapulco, Mexico—via Panama | 3,444 | Maracaibo, Venezuela | 1,890 |
| Accra, Ghana | 4,660 | Mare Island, Calif.—via Panama | 5,285 |
| Aden, Arabia | 6,523 | Marseille, France | 3,891 |
| Ajaccio, Corsica | 3,962 | Mazatlan, Mexico—via Panama | 4,024 |
| Algiers, Algeria | 3,617 | Mobile, Alabama | 1,655 |
| Amapala, Honduras—via Panama | 2,763 | Mollendo, Peru—via Panama | 3,814 |
| Amsterdam, Netherlands | 3,438 | Monrovia, Liberia | 3,965 |
| Angra, Azores | 2,179 | Murmansk, U. S. S. R.—via south of Iceland | 3,948 |
| Antarctica (McMurdo Sound) | 8,302 | —via north of Iceland | 3,844 |
| Antofagasta, Chile—via Panama | 4,158 | Naples, Italy | 4,181 |
| Antwerp, Belgium | 3,406 | Nassau, Bahamas | 962 |
| Argentia, Newfoundland | 1,009 | New London, Connecticut | 104 |
| Baltimore, Maryland | 417 | New Orleans, Louisiana | 1,708 |
| Barcelona, Spain | 3,714 | Newport News, Virginia | 291 |
| Basse Terre, Guadeloupe | 1,624 | Odessa, U. S. S. R. | 5,349 |
| Basseterre, St. Christopher Island | 1,531 | Oslo, Norway | 3,644 |
| Belize, British Honduras | 1,703 | Pago Pago, Samoa—via Panama | 7,674 |
| Bluefields, Nicaragua | 2,001 | Palermo, Sicily | 4,120 |
| Bombay, India | 8,172 | Panama | 2,018 |
| Bordeaux, France | 3,258 | Paramaribo, Surinam | 2,334 |
| Boston, Mass.—via Cape Cod Canal | 234 | Philadelphia, Pennsylvania | 240 |
| —via Pollock Rip Channel | 234 | Piraeus, Greece | 4,688 |
| —via Nantucket Shoals Lightship | 284 | Plymouth, England | 3,042 |
| Bremen, Germany | 386 | Ponce, Puerto Rico | 1,462 |
| Brest, France | 3,648 | Port Arthur, Texas | 1,846 |
| Bridgetown, Barbados | 3,049 | Port-au-Prince, Haiti | 1,372 |
| Brisbane, Australia | 1,829 | Port of Spain, Trinidad | 1,939 |
| Brunswick, Georgia | 9,705 | Port Said, United Arab Rep. | 5,123 |
| Buenaventura, Colombia—via Panama | 755 | Port Townsend, Washington—via Panama | 6,092 |
| Buenos Aires, Argentina | 2,370 | Portland, Oregon—via Panama | 5,887 |
| Cadiz, Spain | 5,871 | Portsmouth, New Hampshire | 403 |
| Calcutta, India—via Suez | 3,146 | Progreso, Mexico | 1,609 |
| Cape of Good Hope, South Africa | 9,835 | Puerto Barrios, Guatemala | 1,804 |
| Cape Town, South Africa | 6,801 | Puerto Colombia, Colombia | 1,800 |
| Cartagena, Colombia | 6,786 | Puerto Cortes, Honduras | 1,764 |
| Carupano, Venezuela | 1,853 | Puerto Plata, Dominican Republic | 1,270 |
| Castries, St. Lucia | 1,893 | Puntarenas, Costa Rica—via Panama | 2,489 |
| Cayenne, French Guiana | 1,747 | Pusan, Korea | 10,222 |
| Charleston, South Carolina | 2,447 | Quebec, Canada | 1,381 |
| Charlotte Amalie, Virgin Islands | 630 | Recife, Brazil | 3,698 |
| Charlottetown, Prince Edward Island | 1,434 | Reykjavik, Iceland | 2,495 |
| Cherbourg, France | 832 | Rijeka, Yugoslavia | 4,828 |
| Coatzacoalcos, Mexico | 3,154 | Rio de Janeiro, Brazil | 4,770 |
| Cobh, Ireland | 1,991 | Rotterdam, Netherlands | 3,411 |
| Colombo, Ceylon—via Suez | 2,901 | | |
| Copenhagen, Denmark | 8,617 | Saigon, South Vietnam | 12,035 |
| Corinto, Nicaragua—via Panama | 3,958 | —via Suez Canal | 10,790 |
| Dakar, Senegal | 2,701 | St. Georges, Grenada | 1,842 |
| Dover, England | 3,335 | St. Johns, Antigua | 1,572 |
| Durban, South Africa | 3,280 | St. John's, Newfoundland | 1,093 |
| Ensenada Honda, Culebra Island | 7,565 | St. Nazaire, France | 3,128 |
| Famagusta, Cyprus | 1,422 | St. Pierre, Martinique | 1,705 |
| Fernandina, Florida | 5,175 | Salaverry, Peru—via Panama | 3,127 |
| Fort de France, Martinique | 761 | Salvador, Brazil | 4,089 |
| Freetown, Sierra Leone | 1,717 | San Francisco, Calif.—via Panama | 5,263 |
| Galveston, Texas | 3,757 | San Jose, Guatemala—via Panama | 2,904 |
| Galway, Ireland | 1,882 | San Juan, Puerto Rico | 1,399 |
| Gdynia, Poland (via Kiel Canal) | 2,872 | San Juan del Norte, Nicaragua | 2,032 |
| Genoa, Italy | 4,023 | Sanchez, Dominican Republic | 1,350 |
| Georgetown, British Guiana | 4,048 | Santa Cruz, Teneriffe Is., Canary Islands | 2,936 |
| Georgetown, South Carolina | 2,317 | Santa Marta, Colombia | 1,783 |
| Gibraltar | 593 | Santiago, Cuba | 1,362 |
| Glasgow, Scotland | 3,204 | Santo Domingo, Dominican Rep. | 1,489 |
| Goteborg, Sweden | 3,072 | Santos, Brazil | 4,957 |
| Guam, Mariana Islands | 3,612 | Savannah, Georgia | 704 |
| Guantanamo, Cuba | 10,006 | Shanghai, China—via Panama | 10,584 |
| Haiphong, North Vietnam | 1,312 | Singapore, Malaysia—via Suez | 10,141 |
| —via Suez Canal | 12,324 | Sitka, Alaska—via Panama | 6,542 |
| Havana, Cuba | 11,496 | Southampton, England | 3,189 |
| Halifax, Nova Scotia | 1,186 | Stanley, Falkland Islands | 6,547 |
| Hamburg, Germany | 600 | Strait of Gibraltar | 3,180 |
| Hamilton, Bermuda | 3,674 | Straits of Florida—outside | 1,184 |
| Hong Kong—via Panama | 697 | —inside | 1,237 |
| Honolulu, Hawaii—via Panama | 11,213 | Sydney, Australia—via Panama | 9,692 |
| Istanbul, Turkey | 6,703 | Sydney, Nova Scotia | 808 |
| | 5,001 | | |
| Jacksonville, Florida | 788 | Tacoma, Washington—via Panama | 6,059 |
| Julianehab, Greenland | 1,911 | Tahiti, Society Islands—via Panama(Papeete) | 6,511 |
| Key West, Florida | 1,109 | Thule, Greenland | 2,913 |
| Kingston, Jamaica | 1,474 | Truk, Caroline Island—via Panama | 9,703 |
| Kodiak, Alaska | 6,925 | Tsingtao, China—via Panama | 10,593 |
| La Guaira, Venezuela | 1,848 | Valletta, Malta | 4,185 |
| Las Palmas, Canary Islands | 2,965 | Veracruz, Mexico | 1,973 |
| Le Havre, France | 3,220 | Vladivostok, U. S. S. R.—via Panama | 9,757 |
| Limon, Costa Rica | 2,047 | Wake Island, Pacific | 8,691 |
| Lisbon, Portugal | 2,972 | Washington, D. C. | 430 |
| Liverpool, England | 3,132 | Willemstad, Curacao | 1,771 |
| London, England | 3,370 | Wilmington, North Carolina | 564 |
| Los Angeles, Calif.—via Panama | 4,931 | Yucatan Channel, Central America | 1,366 |

## Navigable Distances from Panama Canal (Pacific) to:

| Port | Miles | Port | Miles |
|---|---|---|---|
| Apia, Samoa Is. | 5,710 | Le Havre, France | 4,651 |
| Arica, Chile | 1,921 | Liverpool, Nova Scotia | 2,288 |
| Auckland, N. Z. | 6,516 | Los Angeles, Calif. | 2,913 |
| Baltimore, Md. | 1,944 | Manila, P. I. | 9,347 |
| Belem, Brazil | 2,447 | Melbourne, Australia | 7,928 |
| Bombay, India | 9,343 | Mobile, Ala. | 1,413 |
| Bordeaux, France | 4,641 | Montevideo, Uruguay | 5,379 |
| Boston, Mass. | 2,200 | New Orleans, La. | 1,433 |
| Buenos Aires, Argentina | 5,523 | New York | 2,018 |
| Calcutta, India | 10,989 | Norfolk, Va. | 1,822 |
| Callao, Peru | 1,350 | Pensacola, Fla | 1,412 |
| Charleston, S. C. | 1,607 | Philadelphia, Pa. | 1,989 |
| Colombo, Ceylon. | 9,775 | Plymouth, England | 4,473 |
| Colon, Pan. (Atlantic entrance of Canal) | 44 | Punta Arenas, via west of South America | 3,932 |
| Galveston, Tex. | 1,536 | via east of South America | 6,587 |
| Glasgow, Scotland. | 4,538 | Recife, Brazil | 3,339 |
| Guam, Mariana Islands. | 7,988 | Rio de Janeiro, Brazil | 4,411 |
| Guayaquil, Ecuador. | 824 | San Francisco, Calif. | 3,245 |
| Havana, Cuba | 1,042 | Seattle, Wash. | 4,020 |
| Halifax, Nova Scotia. | 2,338 | Shanghai, China | 8,566 |
| Hamburg, Germany. | 5,105 | Singapore, Malaysia | 10,505 |
| Hong Kong. | 9,195 | Straits of Gibraltar | 4,351 |
| Honolulu, Hawaii. | 4,685 | Valpariso, Chile. | 2,616 |
| Jacksonville, Fla. | 1,559 | Vancouver, British Columbia. | 4,032 |
| Key West, Fla. | 1,108 | Wellington, New Zealand | 6,505 |
| Kingston, Jamaica. | 594 | Yokohama, Japan. | 7,682 |

## Navigable Distances from San Francisco to:

| Port | Miles | Port | Miles |
|---|---|---|---|
| Acapulco, Mexico. | 1,833 | Melbourne, Australia | 6,970 |
| Aleksandrovsk-Sakhalinsky (on Sakhalin) USSR | 4,372 | Midway Island | 2,792 |
| | | Nome, Alaska. | 2,636 |
| Amoy, China (Hsia-men) | 5,788 | Nonouti, Gilbert Islands | 4,185 |
| Anchorage, Alaska. | 1,872 | Pago Pago, Samoa Islands | 4,150 |
| Antofagasta, Chile. | 4,762 | Punta Arenas, Chile | 6,188 |
| Arica, Chile | 4,551 | Pusan, Korea | 4,914 |
| Auckland, N. Z. | 5,680 | Rabaul, New Britain. | 5,396 |
| Brisbane, Australia. | 6,193 | Saigon, Vietnam | 6,878 |
| Buenaventura, Colombia. | 3,383 | San Jose, Guatemala. | 2,395 |
| Callao, Peru. | 3,989 | Shanghai, China. | 5,395 |
| Colon, Panama. | 3,289 | Singapore, Malaysia | 7,353 |
| Darwin, Australia. | 6,984 | Sitka, Alaska. | 1,302 |
| Djakarta, Indonesia. | 7,642 | Suva, Fiji Islands. | 4,749 |
| Dutch Harbor, Alaska. | 2,051 | Sydney, Australia. | 6,448 |
| Guam. | 5,053 | Talara, Peru. | 3,494 |
| Guayaquil, Ecuador. | 3,548 | Tan-shui, Taiwan (Formosa) | 5,611 |
| Hong Kong | 6,044 | Valparaiso, Chile. | 5,140 |
| Honolulu, Hawaii. | 2,091 | Vancouver, B. C. | 812 |
| Jaluit, Marshall Islands. | 4,150 | Vladivostok, U.S.S.R. | 4,563 |
| Kiska Harbor, Kiska Island, Alaska. | 2,629 | Wake Island. | 3,821 |
| Kobe, Japan. | 4,819 | Wellington, N. Z. | 5,900 |
| Kodiak, Alaska. | 1,693 | Yokohama, Japan. | 4,536 |
| Manila, P. I. | 6,221 | | |

## DISTANCES BETWEEN WEST INDIES, CARIBBEAN AND GULF PORTS

| City From: | Cap-Haitien | Carta- gena | Charlotte Amalie | Colon | Galves- ton | Havana | Key West | La Guaira | New Orleans | Pensacola | Port of Spain | Port Royal | Veracruz | Willem- stad |
|---|---|---|---|---|---|---|---|---|---|---|---|---|---|---|
| Cap-Haitien | | 697 | 442 | 817 | 1302 | 631 | 619 | 750 | 1128 | 1035 | 888 | 321 | 1396 | 674 |
| Cartagena | 697 | | 811 | 281 | 1583 | 1142 | 1130 | 612 | 1468 | 1422 | 932 | 474 | 1510 | 471 |
| Charlotte Amalie | 442 | 811 | | 1029 | 1785 | 1048 | 1036 | 479 | 1611 | 1518 | 518 | 700 | 1854 | 457 |
| Colon | 817 | 281 | 1029 | | 1508 | 998 | 1065 | 841 | 1389 | 1369 | 1159 | 546 | 1420 | 698 |
| Galveston | 1302 | 1583 | 1785 | 1508 | | 769 | 775 | 1938 | 395 | 446 | 2213 | 1241 | 623 | 1790 |
| Havana | 631 | 1142 | 1048 | 998 | 769 | | 92 | 1292 | 602 | 515 | 1494 | 732 | 814 | 1144 |
| Key West | 619 | 1130 | 1036 | 1065 | 775 | 92 | | 1280 | 613 | 504 | 1484 | 747 | 869 | 1134 |
| La Guaira | 750 | 612 | 479 | 841 | 1938 | 1292 | 1280 | | 1819 | 1773 | 329 | 727 | 1888 | 150 |
| New Orleans | 1128 | 1468 | 1611 | 1389 | 395 | 602 | 613 | 1819 | | 255 | 2057 | 1122 | 789 | 1671 |
| Pensacola | 1035 | 1422 | 1518 | 1369 | 446 | 515 | 504 | 1773 | 255 | | 1964 | 1076 | 831 | 1625 |
| Port of Spain | 888 | 932 | 518 | 1159 | 2213 | 1494 | 1484 | 329 | 2057 | 1964 | | 998 | 2182 | 456 |
| Port Royal | 321 | 474 | 700 | 546 | 1241 | 732 | 747 | 727 | 1122 | 1076 | 998 | | 1205 | 581 |
| Veracruz | 1396 | 1510 | 1854 | 1420 | 623 | 814 | 869 | 1888 | 789 | 831 | 2182 | 1205 | | 1756 |
| Willemstad | 674 | 471 | 457 | 698 | 1790 | 1144 | 1134 | 150 | 1671 | 1625 | 456 | 581 | 1756 | |

## DISTANCES BETWEEN SOUTH AMERICAN PACIFIC PORTS

| City From: | Anto- fagasta | Arica | Caldera | Callao | Coquim- bo | Esme- raldas | Guaya- quil | Iquique | Lota | Mollendo | Pacas- mayo | Paita | Pisco | Punta Arenas | Valpa- raiso |
|---|---|---|---|---|---|---|---|---|---|---|---|---|---|---|---|
| Antofagasta | | 325 | 215 | 813 | 396 | 1703 | 1470 | 224 | 828 | 417 | 1119 | 1299 | 713 | 1996 | 576 |
| Arica | 325 | | 522 | 593 | 702 | 1484 | 1251 | 110 | 1134 | 137 | 899 | 1080 | 492 | 2301 | 882 |
| Caldera | 215 | 522 | | 980 | 196 | 1865 | 1632 | 420 | 628 | 606 | 1285 | 1461 | 880 | 1795 | 376 |
| Callao | 813 | 593 | 980 | | 1136 | 909 | 712 | 659 | 1530 | 468 | 323 | 505 | 128 | 2671 | 1306 |
| Coquimbo | 396 | 702 | 196 | 1136 | | 2014 | 1781 | 602 | 455 | 782 | 1437 | 1609 | 1036 | 1623 | 203 |
| Esmeraldas | 1703 | 1484 | 1865 | 909 | 2014 | | 356 | 1550 | 2388 | 1359 | 603 | 420 | 1021 | 3486 | 2179 |
| Guayaquil | 1470 | 1251 | 1632 | 712 | 1781 | 356 | | 1317 | 2155 | 1126 | 370 | 187 | 788 | 3307 | 1980 |
| Iquique | 224 | 110 | 420 | 659 | 602 | 1550 | 1317 | | 1033 | 220 | 965 | 1146 | 560 | 2201 | 782 |
| Lota | 828 | 1134 | 628 | 1530 | 455 | 2388 | 2155 | 1033 | | 1209 | 1821 | 1983 | 1432 | 1191 | 268 |
| Mollendo | 417 | 137 | 606 | 468 | 782 | 1359 | 1126 | 220 | 1209 | | 774 | 955 | 367 | 2374 | 962 |
| Pacasmayo | 1119 | 899 | 1285 | 323 | 1437 | 603 | 370 | 965 | 1821 | 774 | | 201 | 435 | 2949 | 1605 |
| Paita | 1299 | 1080 | 1461 | 505 | 1609 | 420 | 187 | 1146 | 1983 | 955 | 201 | | 617 | 3101 | 1774 |
| Pisco | 713 | 492 | 880 | 128 | 1036 | 1021 | 788 | 560 | 1432 | 367 | 435 | 617 | | 2578 | 1207 |
| Punta Arenas | 1996 | 2301 | 1795 | 2671 | 1623 | 3486 | 3307 | 2201 | 1191 | 2374 | 2949 | 3101 | 2578 | | 1432 |
| Valparaiso | 576 | 882 | 376 | 1306 | 203 | 2179 | 1980 | 782 | 268 | 962 | 1605 | 1774 | 1207 | 1432 | |

## Distances Between Great Lakes Ports
### Source: Coast and Geodetic Survey, ESSA

| In Statute Miles | St. Lawrence | | | | | Erie | | | | St. Clair and Huron | | | | |
|---|---|---|---|---|---|---|---|---|---|---|---|---|---|---|
| | Quebec | Montreal | Ogdensburg | Kingston | Buffalo | Port Colborne | Erie | Cleveland | Toledo | Detroit | Port Huron | Bay City | Alpena | Collingwood |
| Quebec, Canada | | 157 | 283 | 346 | 553 | 531 | 596 | 691 | 768 | 775 | 837 | 999 | 994 | 1095 |
| Montreal, Canada | 157 | | 126 | 189 | 396 | 374 | 439 | 534 | 611 | 618 | 680 | 842 | 837 | 938 |
| Ogdensburg, New York | 283 | 126 | | 63 | 270 | 248 | 313 | 408 | 485 | 492 | 554 | 716 | 711 | 812 |
| Kingston, Canada | 346 | 189 | 63 | | 208 | 186 | 251 | 346 | 423 | 430 | 492 | 654 | 649 | 750 |
| Buffalo, New York | 553 | 396 | 270 | 208 | | 22 | 78 | 176 | 254 | 261 | 322 | 484 | 479 | 580 |
| Port Colborne, Canada | 531 | 374 | 248 | 186 | 22 | | 65 | 160 | 237 | 244 | 306 | 468 | 463 | 564 |
| Erie, Pennsylvania | 596 | 439 | 313 | 251 | 78 | 65 | | 102 | 185 | 191 | 253 | 415 | 410 | 511 |
| Cleveland, Ohio | 691 | 534 | 408 | 346 | 176 | 160 | 102 | | 96 | 108 | 170 | 331 | 326 | 427 |
| Toledo, Ohio | 768 | 611 | 485 | 423 | 254 | 237 | 185 | 96 | | 54 | 116 | 278 | 273 | 374 |
| Detroit, Michigan | 775 | 618 | 492 | 430 | 261 | 244 | 191 | 108 | 54 | | 62 | 224 | 219 | 320 |
| Port Huron, Michigan | 837 | 680 | 554 | 492 | 322 | 306 | 253 | 170 | 116 | 62 | | 162 | 157 | 258 |
| Bay City, Michigan | 999 | 842 | 716 | 654 | 484 | 468 | 415 | 331 | 278 | 224 | 162 | | 116 | 257 |
| Alpena, Michigan | 994 | 837 | 711 | 649 | 479 | 463 | 410 | 326 | 273 | 219 | 157 | 116 | | 185 |
| Collingwood, Canada | 1095 | 938 | 812 | 750 | 580 | 564 | 511 | 427 | 374 | 320 | 258 | 257 | 185 | |
| Oswego, New York | 391 | 234 | 108 | 55 | 190 | 168 | 233 | 328 | 405 | 412 | 474 | 636 | 631 | 732 |
| Rochester, New York | 432 | 275 | 149 | 89 | 139 | 117 | 182 | 277 | 354 | 361 | 423 | 585 | 580 | 681 |
| Toronto, Canada | 506 | 349 | 223 | 161 | 77 | 55 | 120 | 215 | 292 | 299 | 361 | 523 | 518 | 619 |
| Sault Ste. Marie | 1106 | 949 | 823 | 761 | 592 | 575 | 522 | 438 | 385 | 331 | 269 | 232 | 137 | 259 |
| Marquette, Michigan | 1266 | 1109 | 983 | 921 | 751 | 735 | 682 | 598 | 545 | 491 | 429 | 391 | 297 | 418 |
| Houghton, Michigan | 1327 | 1170 | 1044 | 982 | 813 | 796 | 743 | 659 | 606 | 552 | 490 | 453 | 358 | 480 |
| Ashland, Wisconsin | 1455 | 1298 | 1172 | 1110 | 941 | 924 | 871 | 788 | 734 | 680 | 618 | 581 | 486 | 608 |
| Duluth, Minnesota | 1501 | 1344 | 1218 | 1156 | 986 | 970 | 917 | 833 | 781 | 726 | 664 | 627 | 532 | 653 |
| Port Arthur, Canada | 1379 | 1222 | 1096 | 1034 | 864 | 848 | 795 | 711 | 658 | 604 | 542 | 505 | 410 | 531 |
| Escanaba, Michigan | 1213 | 1056 | 930 | 868 | 699 | 682 | 629 | 545 | 492 | 438 | 376 | 339 | 244 | 376 |
| Green Bay, Wisconsin | 1282 | 1125 | 999 | 937 | 767 | 751 | 698 | 614 | 561 | 507 | 445 | 407 | 313 | 444 |
| Muskegon, Michigan | 1308 | 1151 | 1025 | 963 | 794 | 777 | 724 | 640 | 587 | 533 | 471 | 434 | 339 | 471 |
| Milwaukee, Wisconsin | 1343 | 1186 | 1060 | 998 | 828 | 812 | 759 | 675 | 622 | 568 | 506 | 468 | 374 | 505 |
| Chicago, Illinois | 1408 | 1251 | 1125 | 1063 | 893 | 877 | 824 | 740 | 688 | 633 | 571 | 534 | 439 | 570 |

| In Statute Miles | Ontario | | | | Superior | | | | | Michigan | | | | |
|---|---|---|---|---|---|---|---|---|---|---|---|---|---|---|
| | Oswego | Rochester | Toronto | Sault Ste. Marie | Marquette | Houghton | Ashland | Duluth | Port Arthur | Escanaba | Green Bay | Muskegon | Milwaukee | Chicago |
| Quebec, Canada | 391 | 432 | 506 | 1106 | 1266 | 1327 | 1455 | 1501 | 1379 | 1213 | 1282 | 1308 | 1343 | 1408 |
| Montreal, Canada | 234 | 275 | 349 | 949 | 1109 | 1170 | 1298 | 1344 | 1222 | 1056 | 1125 | 1151 | 1186 | 1251 |
| Ogdensburg, New York | 108 | 149 | 223 | 823 | 983 | 1044 | 1172 | 1218 | 1096 | 930 | 999 | 1025 | 1060 | 1125 |
| Kingston, Canada | 55 | 89 | 161 | 761 | 921 | 982 | 1110 | 1156 | 1034 | 868 | 937 | 963 | 998 | 1063 |
| Buffalo, New York | 190 | 139 | 77 | 592 | 751 | 813 | 941 | 986 | 864 | 699 | 767 | 794 | 828 | 893 |
| Port Colborne, Canada | 168 | 117 | 55 | 575 | 735 | 796 | 924 | 970 | 848 | 682 | 751 | 777 | 812 | 877 |
| Erie, Pennsylvania | 233 | 182 | 120 | 522 | 682 | 743 | 871 | 917 | 795 | 629 | 698 | 724 | 759 | 824 |
| Cleveland, Ohio | 328 | 277 | 215 | 438 | 598 | 659 | 788 | 833 | 711 | 545 | 614 | 640 | 675 | 740 |
| Toledo, Ohio | 405 | 354 | 292 | 385 | 545 | 606 | 734 | 781 | 658 | 492 | 561 | 587 | 622 | 688 |
| Detroit, Michigan | 412 | 361 | 299 | 331 | 491 | 552 | 680 | 726 | 604 | 438 | 507 | 533 | 568 | 633 |
| Port Huron, Michigan | 474 | 423 | 361 | 269 | 429 | 490 | 618 | 664 | 542 | 376 | 445 | 471 | 506 | 571 |
| Bay City, Michigan | 636 | 585 | 523 | 232 | 391 | 453 | 581 | 627 | 505 | 339 | 407 | 434 | 468 | 534 |
| Alpena, Michigan | 631 | 580 | 518 | 137 | 297 | 358 | 486 | 532 | 410 | 244 | 313 | 339 | 374 | 439 |
| Collingwood, Canada | 732 | 681 | 619 | 259 | 418 | 480 | 608 | 653 | 531 | 376 | 444 | 471 | 505 | 570 |
| Oswego, New York | | 59 | 145 | 743 | 900 | 964 | 1092 | 1138 | 1016 | 850 | 919 | 945 | 980 | 1045 |
| Rochester, New York | 59 | | 95 | 692 | 852 | 913 | 1041 | 1087 | 965 | 799 | 868 | 894 | 929 | 994 |
| Toronto, Canada | 145 | 95 | | 630 | 790 | 851 | 979 | 1025 | 903 | 737 | 806 | 832 | 867 | 932 |
| Sault Ste. Marie | 743 | 692 | 630 | | 159 | 221 | 349 | 394 | 273 | 219 | 288 | 314 | 349 | 414 |
| Marquette, Michigan | 903 | 852 | 790 | 159 | | 84 | 213 | 261 | 171 | 378 | 447 | 474 | 508 | 573 |
| Houghton, Michigan | 964 | 913 | 851 | 221 | 84 | | 131 | 179 | 116 | 440 | 509 | 535 | 570 | 635 |
| Ashland, Wisconsin | 1092 | 1041 | 979 | 349 | 213 | 131 | | 93 | 93 | 164 | 568 | 637 | 663 | 698 | 763 |
| Duluth, Minnesota | 1138 | 1087 | 1025 | 394 | 261 | 179 | 93 | | 195 | 614 | 682 | 709 | 743 | 808 |
| Port Arthur, Canada | 1016 | 965 | 903 | 273 | 171 | 116 | 164 | 195 | | 492 | 560 | 587 | 621 | 686 |
| Escanaba, Michigan | 850 | 799 | 737 | 219 | 378 | 440 | 568 | 614 | 492 | | 101 | 181 | 201 | 274 |
| Green Bay, Wisconsin | 919 | 868 | 806 | 288 | 447 | 509 | 637 | 682 | 560 | 101 | | 171 | 180 | 255 |
| Muskegon, Michigan | 945 | 894 | 832 | 314 | 474 | 535 | 663 | 709 | 587 | 181 | 171 | | 80 | 114 |
| Milwaukee, Wisconsin | 980 | 929 | 867 | 349 | 508 | 570 | 698 | 743 | 621 | 201 | 180 | 80 | | 85 |
| Chicago, Illinois | 1045 | 994 | 932 | 414 | 573 | 635 | 763 | 808 | 686 | 274 | 255 | 114 | 85 | |

## Net Total Water-Borne Commerce of the United States
### Source: Corps of Engineers, Department of the Army, Calendar Years. In tons of 2,000 pounds

| Type of traffic | 1965 | 1966 | Type of traffic | 1965 | 1966 |
|---|---|---|---|---|---|
| Net total water-borne commerce of the U. S. | 1,272,896,243 | 1,334,116,078 | **Foreign** | | |
| **Domestic** | | | Imports | 269,834,819 | 283,847,300 |
| Coastwise | 201,508,107 | 208,374,966 | Coastal ports | 244,874,087 | 257,173,478 |
| Lakewise | 153,695,242 | 164,036,995 | Gt. Lakes, Canada | 21,059,701 | 22,585,271 |
| Internal | 369,615,461 | 389,851,631 | Gt. Lakes, overseas | 3,901,031 | 4,088,551 |
| Local | 102,875,022 | 99,214,579 | Exports | 173,891,990 | 187,543,783 |
| Intraterritory | 1,485,602 | 1,246,824 | Coastal ports | 142,121,011 | 155,759,371 |
| | | | Gt. Lakes to Canada | 25,692,770 | 24,905,662 |
| | | | Gt. Lakes to overseas | 6,078,209 | 6,878,750 |
| **Total domestic** | 829,169,434 | 862,724,995 | **Total foreign** | 443,726,809 | 471,391,083 |

### TON-MILEAGE OF FREIGHT CARRIED ON INLAND WATERWAYS

| System | 1965 | 1966 |
|---|---|---|
| Atlantic coast waterways | 27,781,436,000 | 28,109,299,000 |
| Gulf coast waterways | 21,807,792,000 | 23,618,876,000 |
| Pacific coast waterways | 6,629,670,000 | 6,424,661,000 |
| Mississippi River system, including Ohio River and tributaries | 96,593,337,000 | 106,375,962,000 |
| Great Lakes system. Includes Alaskan waterways | 109,608,579,000 | 115,998,018,000 |
| **Total** | 262,420,814,000 | 280,526,816,000 |

# Fastest Scheduled Train Runs in United States and Canada

**Source:** Donald M. Steffee and Association of American Railroads; figures are based on 1968 timetables

| Railroad | Train | From | To | Dis. miles | Time min. | Speed m.p.h. |
|---|---|---|---|---|---|---|
| **DIESEL TRACTION—PASSENGER—(76 m.p.h. and over)** | | | | | | |
| Burlington | Morning Zephyr | Aurora | Rochelle | 45.25 | 32 | 84.8 |
| Santa Fe | Grand Canyon | Holbrook | Gallup | 94.9 | 70 | 81.3 |
| Illinois Central | City of N. O. Mid American | Champaign | Mattoon | 44.6 | 33 | 81.8 |
| Santa Fe | Grand Canyon | Gallup | Holbrook | 94.9 | 71 | 80.2 |
| Illinois Central | Panama Ltd.-Magnolia Star | McComb | Hammond | 52.1 | 39 | 80.2 |
| Canadian National | Rapido (2) | Dorval | Brockville | 115.3 | 87 | 79.5 |
| Canadian National | Rapido (2) | Guildwood | Belleville | 100.5 | 76 | 79.4 |
| Milwaukee | Morning Hiawatha | Tomah | Portage | 62.9 | 47 | 79.0 |
| Santa Fe | Super Chief-El Capitan | Garden City | Lamar | 99.9 | 76 | 78.8 |
| Burlington | Morning Zephyr; North Coast Limited | Prairie du Chien | La Crosse | 57.7 | 44 | 78.7 |
| Illinois Central | City of Miami; Panama; Limited-Magnolia Star | Champaign | Mattoon | 44.6 | 34 | 78.7 |
| Santa Fe | San Francisco Chief | Wasco | Corcoran | 37.9 | 29 | 78.4 |
| Santa Fe | San Francisco Chief | Corcoran | Wasco | 37.9 | 29 | 78.4 |
| Milwaukee | Afternoon Hiawatha | Portage | New Lisbon | 43.1 | 33 | 78.4 |
| Canadian National | Railiner | Trenton | Cobourg | 31.2 | 24 | 78.0 |
| Milwaukee | Number 16 | Webster | Millbrook | 46.1 | 35½ | 77.8 |
| Illinois Central | Campus; City of N. O. | Centralia | Effingham | 53.2 | 41 | 77.8 |
| Burlington | Denver Zephyr | Hastings | Crete | 76.4 | 59 | 77.7 |
| Milwaukee | Number 15 | Montevideo | Ortonville | 45.8 | 35½ | 77.4 |
| Seaboard Coast | Sunland | Thalmann | Yulee | 47.6 | 37 | 77.2 |
| Penn-Central | Empire Service (4) | Syracuse | Utica | 47.5 | 37 | 77.0 |
| Burlington | Afternoon Zephyr | La Crosse | Prairie du Chien | 57.7 | 45 | 76.9 |
| Burlington | California Zephyr | Wray | Benkelman | 38.4 | 30 | 76.8 |
| Santa Fe | Super Chief-El Capitan | Lamar | Garden City | 99.9 | 78 | 76.8 |
| Santa Fe | Super Chief-El Capitan | Dodge City | Hutchinson | 120.2 | 94 | 76.7 |
| Illinois Central | Four trains | Mattoon | Effingham | 26.8 | 21 | 76.6 |
| Burlington | Afternoon Zephyr | St. Paul | Winona Junc. | 100.8 | 79 | 76.6 |
| Canadian National | Railiner | Prescott | Cornwall | 45.8 | 36 | 76.3 |
| Canadian National | Rapido (2) | Belleville | Guildwood | 100.5 | 79 | 76.3 |
| Illinois Central | City of N. O. Mid American | Homewood | Kankakee | 32.4 | 25½ | 76.2 |
| Burlington | Morning Zephyr; North Coast Limited | East Dubuque | Prairie du Chien | 54.6 | 43 | 76.2 |
| Illinois Central | Campus | Centralia | Effingham | 53.2 | 42 | 76.0 |
| Illinois Central | City of New Orleans | Effingham | Centralia | 53.2 | 42 | 76.0 |
| **DIESEL TRACTION—FREIGHT—(63 m.p.h. and over)** | | | | | | |
| Santa Fe | Super-C | Gallup | Winslow | 127.2 | 110 | 69.4 |
| Santa Fe | Super-C | Winslow | Gallup | 127.2 | 110 | 69.4 |
| Santa Fe | Super-C | Wellington | Waynoka | 106.6 | 95 | 67.2 |
| Santa Fe | Super-C | Amarillo | Waynoka | 205.2 | 185 | 66.6 |
| Santa Fe | Super-C | Amarillo | Clovis | 103.7 | 95 | 65.5 |
| Santa Fe | Super-C | Waynoka | Amarillo | 205.2 | 190 | 64.9 |
| Southern Pacific | Blue Streak Merchandise | East Yard | Del Rio | 171.2 | 159 | 64.6 |
| Santa Fe | Super-C | Gallup | Belen | 144.0 | 135 | 64.0 |
| Santa Fe | Super-C | Waynoka | Wellington | 106.6 | 100 | 64.0 |
| Rock Island | Number 23 | Liberal | Dalhart | 111.2 | 105 | 63.5 |
| **ELECTRIC TRACTION—PASSENGER—(70 m.p.h. and over)** | | | | | | |
| Penn-Central | Afternoon Congressional | Baltimore | Wilmington | 68.4 | 48 | 85.5* |
| Penn-Central | Afternoon Congressional | Wilmington | Baltimore | 68.4 | 51 | 80.5* |
| Penn-Central | Afternoon Congressional | Newark | North Phila. | 76.0 | 57 | 80.0* |
| Penn-Central | Afternoon Congressional | Newark | North Phila. | 76.0 | 64 | 71.3† |
| Penn-Central | Number 191 | Wilmington | Baltimore | 68.4 | 58 | 70.8 |
| Penn-Central | Juniata | Lancaster | Paoli | 48.3 | 41 | 70.7 |
| CSS & SB | Number 12 | Hudson Lake | Michigan City | 17.6 | 15 | 70.4 |
| Penn-Central | Afternoon Congressional | North Phila. | Newark | 76.0 | 65 | 70.1† |

*Under experimental schedule operated until Apr. 27, 1968.

†Under schedule effective Apr. 28, 1968.

# Some Fast Railway Runs in the United States

| Date | Railroad | Run | Miles | Time H. M. S. | M. P. Hour |
|---|---|---|---|---|---|
| May, 1905 | Atlantic City Boardwalk Flyer | Camden—Atlantic City | 55.5 | 42 33 | 78.3 |
| Apr. 1911 | N. Y. Central-Lake Shore | Toledo—Elkhart, Ind.—20th Cent. | 133 | 1 46 | 75.28 |
| June, 1927 | Pennsylvania | Washington D.C.—N.Y. City | 224.5 | 3 7 | 72.1 |
| May, 1934 | Chicago, Burlington & Quincy | Denver—Chicago | 1015.31 | 13 5 44 | 77.6 |
| July, 1934 | Chicago, Milwaukee & St. Paul | Chicago—Milwaukee | 85.0 | 1 7 35 | 75.46 |
| Oct., 1934 | Union Pacific | Cheyenne—Omaha | 506.7 | 6 00 | 84.45 |
| Oct., 1934 | Chicago & N.W. N. Y. Central | Los Angeles—New York | 3257.6 | 56 55 | 57.2 |
| Jan., 1935 | Pennsylvania | Philadelphia—Washington | 134.2 | 1 50 | 73.2 |
| Apr., 1935 | New Haven | Providence—Boston | 43.8 | 32 35 | 86.65 |
| Oct., 1936 | Chicago, Burlington & Quincy | Chicago—Denver | 1017.23 | 12 12 27 | 83.3 |
| May, 1937 | Santa Fe | Los Angeles, Calif.—Chicago | 2228.6 | 36 49 | 60.5 |
| May, 1937 | Santa Fe | LaJunta, Colo.—Dodge City, Kan. | 202.4 | 2 19 | 87.3 |
| May, 1955 | Baltimore & Ohio | Washington, D. C.—Chicago (Train consisted of 3 Budd Rail Diesel cars) | 768.0 | 12 29 30 | 61.5 |
| July, 1966 | New York Central | Byran, Ohio (MP 350-345) | 5.0 | 1 39¾ | 181.00* |
| May, 1967 | Pennsylvania | County—Milham Tower | 21.2 | 11† | 115.66† |
| Jan., 1968 | ATSF Super-C (FastFreight) | Corwith—Hobart Yard | 2202.1 | 34 35 40 | 63.6 |

*The official speed measured by ground instruments was 183.85 in passing mile post 347 + 13 over an accurately measured 300 feet of track. This is the highest speed on rails ever recorded in the United States. The run was made by a single Budd Rail Diesel car fitted with two turbo-jet J-47 aircraft engines mounted on the forward end. †Time and speed calculated from standing start at County to passing Milham Tower (end of test track) at 80 mph, after which time was gradually braked down on regular track to a stop in Trenton passenger station. Between mileposts 46 and 51 speed was 150 mph or over, a momentary peak of 156 mph was reached in the vicinity of milepost 47.

¹All runs listed above are in the "start-to-stop" category, several including intermediate stops as well. The several "pass-to-pass" runs (where train passed both starting and finishing points at speed) such as the 1 mile in 32 seconds—112.5 claimed for the "Empire State Express" in 1893 which did appear in this listing are now eliminated. Some of these runs were actually segments of some of the longer runs listed above while others border on the fantastic, having little supporting testimony as to their authenticity.

## Japanese Trains Average Over 100 Miles per Hour

Service between Tokyo and Osaka via the standard-gauged New Tokaido Line is headed by 25 "Hikari" superexpress trains daily in each direction which make the 320.1-mile run, inclusive of stops at Nagoya and Kyoto, in 3 hrs. 10 mins.—at an average overall speed of 101.1 mph. Twenty-one "Kodama" or limited express trains in each direction make the run in 4 hours, inclusive of 10 intermediate stops, averaging just 80 mph. overall

## First High-Speed Trains Under U. S. Federal Program in Service

First results of the Federal Government's 3-year $90,000,000 program for mass transportation research and development may be seen in the current timetable of the Pennsylvania Railroad under which service between New York and Washington has been greatly expanded and schedules speeded up. New self-propelled electric trains make the 224.6-mile run in 2 hr. 59 min.—averaging 75.3 mph overall.

## Rapid Transit Service in Cities Over 500,000

Source: American Transit Association
Miles of Main Track

| Year | N. Y. C. | Chicago | Phila. | Boston | Cleve. | N.Y.-N.J.[1] | Total |
|---|---|---|---|---|---|---|---|
| 1940 | 247.3 | 82.15 | 26.43 | 23.32 | ......... | 8.47 | 387.40 |
| 1945 | 236.89 | 86.98 | 26.43 | 21.04 | ......... | 8.47 | 379.81 |
| 1950 | 239.07 | 82.10 | 26.43 | 21.04 | ......... | 8.47 | 377.11 |
| 1955 | 228.71 | 72.89 | *28.12 | 25.06 | 13.16 | 8.47 | 376.41 |
| 1960 | 236.70 | 68.23 | *32.13 | 25.06 | 14.92 | 8.47 | 385.51 |
| 1962 | 236.70 | 68.23 | *32.08 | 25.04 | 14.92 | 8.47 | 385.45 |
| 1963 | 236.70 | 68.24 | *32.08 | 25.04 | 14.92 | 8.47 | 385.42 |
| 1964 | 236.70 | 68.21 | *32.08 | 25.04 | 14.92 | 8.47 | 390.42 |
| 1965 | 236.70 | 73.21 | *32.08 | 25.04 | 14.92 | 8.47 | 390.79 |
| 1966 | 236.70 | 73.58 | *32.08 | 25.04 | 14.92 | 8.47 | 390.79 |

*Estimate. [1]Port Authority Trans-Hudson Corp., operates between points in N. J. and N. Y. C.

## Passenger Traffic

1967

**N. Y. C.**
Transit Authority
Rapid Transit ........... 1,302,527,478
Surface ........... 431,911,431
Manhattan-Bronx
Surface ........... 398,244,239
**Chicago Transit Authority**
Rapid Transit ........... 120,808,456
Surface ........... 390,089,027
**Los Angeles Rapid Transit** ........... 135,912,209
**Philadelphia Transit Co.**
Rapid Transit ........... 68,473,013
Surface ........... 209,048,000
**Detroit Street Railways** ........... 128,811,331
**Baltimore Transit Co.** ........... 97,195,650

**Cleveland Transit System**
Rapid Transit ........... 16,286,942
Surface ........... N.A.
**Washington, D. C. Transit** ........... 133,646,024
**San Francisco Mun. Railway** ........... 148,412,488
**Milwaukee Transport Co.** ........... 76,359,871
**Boston Transportation Auth.** ........... 285,465,650
**Dallas Transit Co.** ........... 32,518,235
**New Orleans Public Ser.** ........... 93,638,444
**Pittsburgh Authority** ........... 91,176,211
**San Antonio Transit System** ........... 24,098,504
**San Diego Transit System** ........... 15,393,202
**Seattle Transit System** ........... 35,704,277
**Buffalo, Niagara Transit** ........... 51,940,023
**Cincinnati Transit Co.** ........... 28,607,523

## American Railway Statistics

Source: Interstate Commerce Commission

| Year | Mileage Owned | Miles Built | Loco-mo'es in use | Freight Cars in use | Pass. Cars in use | Passengers Carried | Freight Carried | Em-ployees | Employees Wages |
|---|---|---|---|---|---|---|---|---|---|
| | Miles | Miles | No. | No. | No. | No. | Tons | No. | Dollars |
| 1950 | 223,779 | 33 | 42,951 | 1,745,778 | 37,359 | 488,019,000 | 2,710,909,000 | 1,237,000 | 4,644,890,000 |
| 1955 | 220,670 | 105 | 33,533 | 1,723,747 | 32,118 | 433,307,627 | 2,745,378,713 | 1,071,393 | 5,044,278,278 |
| 1960 | 217,552 | 21 | 31,178 | 1,690,396 | 25,746 | 327,171,745 | 2,409,039,608 | 793,071 | 4,956,902,360 |
| 1965 | 211,384 | 59 | 30,061 | 1,515,169 | 20,022 | 305,825,407 | 2,741,706,964 | 654,670 | 4,886,739,954 |
| 1966 | 210,573 | 89 | 30,124 | 1,523,741 | 18,974 | 307,529,553 | 2,850,756,332 | 645,336 | 4,974,510,066 |

### PASSENGER AND FREIGHT DATA

| Year | Passenger Revenue | Freight Revenue | Miles Traveled by Passenger | Rev. per Mile Pas. | Ave. Trip per Pas. | Fre. Rev. a ton Mile | Miles Traveled by Pass. Trains | Miles Traveled by Freight Trains | Casualties Kill'd | Inj. |
|---|---|---|---|---|---|---|---|---|---|---|
| | Dollars | Dollars | Thousands | Cts. | Miles | Cts. | Miles | Miles | No. | No. |
| 1950 | 814,741,000 | 7,933,764,000 | 31,790,470 | 2.56 | 65.14 | 1.34 | 329,055,000 | 522,816,000 | 3,398 | 33,255 |
| 1955 | 743,688,009 | 8,665,379,045 | 28,547,877 | 2.61 | 65.88 | 1.38 | 299,234,930 | 483,393,077 | 2,667 | 27,832 |
| 1960 | 641,495,655 | 8,151,706,391 | 21,284,084 | 3.01 | 65.05 | 1.42 | 209,676,995 | 411,173,556 | 2,248 | 19,577 |
| 1965 | 555,985,653 | 9,036,540,448 | 17,453,919 | 3.19 | 57.07 | 1.28 | 173,579,220 | 430,716,900 | 2,399 | 25,789 |
| 1966 | 547,138,828 | 9,487,412,599 | 17,161,775 | 3.19 | 55.72 | 1.27 | 165,439,185 | 447,187,648 | 2,684 | 25,552 |

### REVENUES, EXPENSES AND DIVIDENDS

| Year | Total Operating Revenues | Operating Expenses | Tax Accruals | Net Railway Operating Income | Net Income | Dividends Declared | Ratio Opp. Exp. to Oper. Rev. |
|---|---|---|---|---|---|---|---|
| | Dollars | Dollars | Dollars | Dollars | Dollars | Dollars | Pct. |
| 1950 | 9,587,000,000 | 7,135,055,000 | 1,212,084,000 | 1,055,309,000 | 854,951,000 | 348,811,000 | 74.42 |
| 1955 | 10,229,600,486 | 7,724,496,197 | 1,100,919,579 | 1,144,347,404 | 958,849,372 | 476,206,666 | 75.51 |
| 1960 | 9,641,592,812 | 7,657,328,712 | 1,020,471,011 | 594,618,250 | 449,174,842 | 411,649,958 | 79.42 |
| 1963 | 9,684,635,915 | 7,542,306,287 | 906,455,966 | 815,952,374 | 681,325,268 | 412,814,754 | 77.88 |
| 1965 | 10,425,052,359 | 8,002,684,949 | 949,215,638 | 980,065,623 | 865,898,587 | 532,649,374 | 76.76 |
| 1966 | 10,880,466,665 | 8,277,293,918 | 1,001,510,016 | 1,065,232,256 | 957,359,346 | 547,566,882 | 76.07 |

### VALUES, STOCKS, BONDS AND CAPITAL

| Yr. | Investment In Road and Equipment | Common Stock Outstand.[1] | Preferred Stock Outstand.[1] | Funded Debt Outstand.[1] | Tot. Railway Capital Outstand.[1] | Amount of Stock Pay Dividends |
|---|---|---|---|---|---|---|
| | Dollars | Dollars | Dollars | Dollars | Dollars | Dollars |
| 1950 | 30,174,312,000 | 7,207,461,852 | 1,976,670,404 | 9,089,499,251 | 18,273,631,507 | 6,768,638,000 |
| 1955 | 33,034,952,366 | 7,341,246,103 | 1,309,481,678 | 8,771,315,107 | 17,422,042,888 | 7,300,385,953 |
| 1960 | 35,513,350,796 | 6,185,117,735 | 1,218,060,497 | 8,730,551,088 | 16,133,729,320 | 5,617,239,155 |
| 1963 | 34,519,308,492 | 5,591,821,051 | 1,189,239,111 | 8,230,049,552 | 15,011,109,714 | 4,462,474,424 |
| 1965 | 35,489,328,198 | 5,579,833,608 | 1,115,727,381 | 8,161,792,077 | 14,857,353,066 | 4,845,089,904 |
| 1966 | 36,618,069,410 | 5,639,238,709 | 1,090,631,611 | 8,070,298,765 | 14,800,169,085 | 4,709,176,813 |

[1]Data for years prior to 1964 have been revised to represent amounts actually outstanding in order that they may be comparable to those shown for the year 1964.

# State Automobile Speed Limits

### (Except as otherwise posted)
#### Source: American Automobile Assn., Digest of Motor Laws 1967

**Alabama:** Interstate highways, 70 mph. daytime, 60 mph. nighttime; open highways, 60 mph. daytime, 50 mph. nighttime; residential districts, 25 mph.; business districts, school zones, etc., 15 mph.

**Alaska:** Open highways, 50 mph.; urban area, 35 mph.; residential and business districts, 30 mph.

**Arizona:** State highways, 65 mph. daytime, 60 mph. nighttime; other state highways, 50 mph. daytime, 45 mph. nighttime; residential areas, business districts, 25 mph.; school zones, 15 mph.

**Arkansas:** Interstate highways, 70 mph.; controlled access highways, 60 mph.; urban districts, 30 mph.; other locations, 60 mph.

**California:** Statewide limit, 65 mph. (except freeways posted for 70 mph.); residential and business districts, school zones, 25 mph.

**Colorado:** Open highways, 60 mph.; residential districts, 30 mph.; business districts, 25 mph.; open mountain highway, 40 mph.; winding mountain highway, 20 mph.

**Connecticut:** Super highways, 70 mph.; other highways, 60 mph.; residential and business, reasonable rate.

**Delaware:** Open highways, 4-lane, 60 mph., 2-lane, 50 mph.; residential and business districts, 25 mph.

**District of Columbia:** Expressways, 45 mph.; school and playground areas, 15 mph.; other roads, 25 mph.

**Florida:** Interstate highways, 70 mph. day, 65 mph. night; open highway, 65 mph. day, 55 mph. night; residential & business districts, 30 mph.

**Georgia:** Interstate highways, 70 mph. daytime, 65 mph. nighttime; open highway, 60 mph. daytime, 50 mph. nighttime; residential, business and school areas, 25 mph.

**Hawaii:** Open highways, 45 mph.; residential and business districts, local ordinances govern.

**Idaho:** Interstate highways, 70 mph.; open highway, 60 mph. daytime, 55 mph. nighttime; urban and business districts, 35 mph.

**Illinois:** Expressways, 70 mph.; open highways, 65 mph.; urban areas, 30 mph.; school zones, 20 mph.

**Indiana:** Open highways, 65 mph.; residential district, 30 mph.; business district, 20 mph.; Interstate highways, 70 mph.

**Iowa:** Interstate limited access roads, 75 mph. daytime, 65 mph. nighttime; open highways, 70 mph. daytime, 60 mph. nighttime; suburban, 45 mph.; residential and school districts, 25 mph.; business districts, 20 mph.; secondary roads, 60 mph. daytime, 50 mph. nighttime.

**Kansas:** Interstate highways, 75 mph. daytime, 70 nighttime; open highways, 70 mph. daytime, 60 mph. nighttime; residential districts, 30 mph.; business districts, 20 mph.; Kansas Turnpike, 80 mph.

**Kentucky:** Interstate highways, 70 mph.; open highways, 60 mph. daytime, 50 mph. nighttime; residential and business districts, 35 mph.

**Louisiana:** Open highways 4-lane, 70 mph.; other open highways, 60 mph.

**Maine:** Turnpikes, 70 mph. daytime, 65 mph. nighttime; open highways, 45 mph.; residential and business districts, 25 mph.; school zones at recess and when children going to and from school, 15 mph.

**Maryland:** Open country, expressways, 60 mph.; dual lane highways, 55 mph.; other highways, 50 mph.; residential and business districts, 30 mph.; thinly settled areas, 35 mph., other highways 30 mph.

**Massachusetts:** Turnpike, 65 mph.; divided highway, 50 mph.; other highways, 40 mph.; residential and business districts, 30 mph.; school zones, 20 mph.

**Michigan:** Freeways, 70 mph.; open highways, 65 mph. daytime, 55 mph. nighttime; residential and business districts, 25 mph.

**Minnesota:** Open highways, 65 mph. daytime, 55 mph. nighttime; all speeds in urban districts, 30 mph.

**Mississippi:** Open highways, 65 mph.; residential districts, 25 mph.; business districts, 20 mph.; school zones, 15 mph.

**Missouri:** Dual lane U. S. routes, 70 mph.; undivided U. S. routes, 70 mph. daytime, 65 mph.

**Montana:** Open highways, day, reasonable and prudent unless posted, 55 mph. night, except Interstate highways 65 mph. nights; residential and business districts, 25 mph.

**Nebraska:** Interstate highways, 75 mph.; open highways, 65 mph. daytime, 60 mph. nighttime; residential districts, 25 mph.; business districts, 20 mph.; on non-hard surfaced roads, 50 mph.

**Nevada:** Careful and prudent; residential and business, posted.

**New Hampshire:** Turnpike, 70 mph.; open highways, 60 mph.; rural residential districts, 35 mph.; urban and business districts, 30 mph.; school zones, 20 mph.

**New Jersey:** Turnpike, 60 mph.; open highways, 50 mph.; residential and business districts, 25 mph.

**New Mexico:** Open highways, 70 mph. daytime, 60 mph. nighttime; other highways, 60 mph. daytime, 50 mph. nighttime; residential and business districts, 25 mph.; school zones, 15 mph.

**New York:** New York State Thruway, 65 mph.; open highways, 50 mph.; school zones when children going to and from school, 15 mph.

**North Carolina:** Open highways, 55 mph.; residential districts, 35 mph.; business districts, 20 mph.

**North Dakota:** Interstate highways, 75 mph. day, 65 mph. night; all other highways, 60 mph.; residential and business districts, 25 mph.; school zones, 20 mph.

**Ohio:** Ohio Turnpike and expressways, 70 mph.; open highways, 60 mph. daytime, 50 mph. nighttime; within municipal corporations, 25 mph; school zones, 20 mph.

**Oklahoma:** Turnpikes and Interstate highways, 70 mph.; open highways, 65 mph. daytime, 55 mph. nighttime; school zones, 25 mph.

**Oregon:** Open highways, 55 mph.; freeways up to 70 mph; residential districts, 25 mph.; business and school zones, 20 mph.

**Pennsylvania:** Turnpike, 65 mph.; open highways 55 mph.; residential and business districts, 25 to 35 mph.; school zones, 15 mph.

**Rhode Island:** Residential and business districts, 25 mph.; elsewhere, 50 mph. daytime, 45 mph. nighttime.

**South Carolina:** Interstate System 70 mph. daytime, 65 mph. night; State highways 60 mph. daytime, 55 mph. night; urban districts 30 mph.

**South Dakota:** Interstate highways, 75 mph. daytime, 70 mph. nighttime; open highways, 70 mph. daytime, 60 mph. nighttime; residential and business districts, 30 mph.; school zones, 15 mph.

**Tennessee:** Open highways, 65 mph. day, 55 mph. night; school zones, 15 mph; Interstate highways 75 mph.

**Texas:** Federal or State roads, 70 mph. daytime, 65 mph. nighttime; other rural roads, 60 mph, daytime, 55 mph. nighttime; in urban districts, 30 mph.

**Utah:** Open highways, as posted; residential and business districts, 25 mph; school zones, 20 mph.

**Vermont:** Interstate highways, 65 mph.; open highways, 50 mph.

**Virginia:** Open highways, 55 mph.; residential, business and school areas, 25 mph.

**Washington:** County roads, 50 mph.; cities and towns, 25 mph.; school zones, 20 mph.; Interstate highways 70 mph.; in other locations, 60 mph.

**West Virginia:** Interstate highways, 70 mph.; Turnpike, 60 mph.; open highways, 55 mph.; residential districts, 25 mph.; school zones, 15 mph.

**Wisconsin:** Interstate highways, 70 mph. daytime, 60 mph. nighttime; open highways, 65 mph. daytime, 55 mph. nighttime; residential and business districts, 25 mph.; school zone, 15 mph.

**Wyoming:** Open highways 4-lane divided, 70 mph.; open highways, 65 mph.; residential districts, 30 mph.; business and school districts, 20 mph.

**Canal Zone:** Outside town limits, 40 mph.; within town limits, 25 mph.

**Guam:** Roads, 45 mph.; school zones when children at recess or going to and from school, 10 mph.

**Puerto Rico:** Open highways, 45 mph.; urban districts and school zones, 20 mph.

# Another New Record in Automobile Traffic Volume in U. S.

Some 105,000,000 Americans took to the highways within their own country for at least one vacation or pleasure trip by automobile during 1968, establishing a new record. They spent $29 billion and traveled an estimated 195 billion miles. The total mileage traveled by the over 84,000,000 passenger cars registered in this country in 1968 amounted to 780 billion miles. In addition, more than 200 billion miles were driven by the nearly 17,000,000 trucks and buses. It is estimated that private passenger automobiles are used for 90% of all vacation and recreation trips in the U. S.

# Major Turnpikes; Passenger Car Tolls and Speed Limits
### Source: American Automobile Association, Washington, D. C. 20006

**Airport Expressway:** Miami International Airport Airport to North-South Expressway interchange, 4.4 miles. Speed limit 60 mph. Toll 5¢ per axle.

**Atlantic City Expressway:** N. J. Freeway at Turnersville to Atlantic City, N. J. 44 miles. Speed limit 70 mph. Maximum toll $1.15.

**Bluegrass Parkway:** Fort Springs to Elizabethtown, Ky. 72 miles. Maximum toll $1.30.

**Connecticut Turnpike:** N. Y. State line near Greenwich, Conn., to R. I. State line at Killingly, Conn., 129 miles. Speed limit 60 mph. Maximum toll $2.

**Eastern Townships Autoroute:** Montreal to Magog, Quebec. 72 miles. Speed limit 70 mph. (50 minimum). Maximum toll $1.50.

**Ensenada-Tijuana Tollway:** Ensenada to Tiajuana, Mexico, 63 miles. Speed limit 68 mph. Maximum toll $2.40.

**Everett Turnpike:** Mass.-N. H. state line to Concord, N. H. 40 miles. Speed limit 60 mph. Toll maximum 50¢.

**Garden State Parkway:** Montvale, N. J., to Cape May, N. J., 173 miles. Speed limit 60-65 mph. Maximum toll $2.75.

**H. E. Bailey Turnpike:** Oklahoma City to Randlett, Okla., 86.4 miles. Speed limit 70 mph. Toll maximum $1.70.

**Hutchinson River Parkway:** N.Y.C. to Conn. state line, 15 miles. Speed limit 50 mph. Toll 25¢.

**Illinois Tollway:** Includes Tri-State Tollway from Indiana state line to Deerfield; Northwest Tollway from the Tri-State to Wisconsin state line at So. Beloit, Ill., and East-West Tollway between Chicago and Aurora. 187 miles. Maximum tolls, Tri-State $2.10, Northwest $1.55 and East-West 50¢.

**Indian Nation Turnpike:** Henryetta to McAlester, Okla. 41 miles. Speed limit 70 mph (40 minimum). Maximum toll 70¢.

**Indiana Toll Road:** Eastpoint (Ohio line) to Westpoint (Illinois line), 157 miles. Speed limit 70 mph. (40 minimum). Maximum toll $2.80.

**John F. Kennedy Memorial Highway:** Baltimore, Md., to Wilmington, Del., 60 miles. Speed limit 60 mph. Maximum toll $1.30.

**Kansas Turnpike:** Kansas City to South Haven, Kan. 236 miles. Speed limit 80 mph. 40 mph minimum. Maximum toll $4.95.

**Kentucky Turnpike:** Louisville to Elizabethtown, Ky. 40 miles. Speed limit 70 mph, 40 minimum. Maximum toll 60¢.

**Maine Turnpike:** Kittery, Me., to Augusta, Me., 106 miles. Speed limit 70 mph. (65 at night). Maximum toll $2.15.

**Massachusetts Turnpike:** Downtown Boston to State Line, Mass., (N. Y. border), 135 miles. Speed limit 65 mph. (40 mph. minimum). Maximum toll $3.

**Merritt Parkway:** New York-Conn. State line to Housatonic River, Stratford, Conn., 37½ miles. Speed limit 60 mph. Toll 20¢.

**Montreal-Laurentian Autoroute:** Montreal to Ste. Adele. 45 miles. Speed limit 70 mph. Maximum toll $1.

**Mountain Parkway:** Winchester to Salyersville, Ky. 76 miles. Speed limit 70 mph. Maximum toll $1.60.

**New Hampshire Turnpike:** Mass.-N. H. State line to Portsmouth, N. H., 14.7 miles. Speed limit 60 mph. Toll 15¢ to 25¢.

**New Jersey Turnpike:** Deepwater, N. J., to Ridgefield Park, N. J., 131 miles including extensions. Speed limit 60 mph. (50 mph. on Hudson County extension). Maximum toll $1.75.

**New York Thruway** (Thomas E. Dewey Thruway): Pennsylvania border near Erie to New York City, 559 miles including extensions. Speed limit 65 mph Maximum toll $8.20.

**Ohio Turnpike:** Ohio-Pennsylvania line to Ohio-Indiana line, 241 miles. Speed limit 70 mph. Maximum toll $3.50.

**Pennsylvania Turnpike:** Gateway (state line near Youngstown, Ohio) to New Jersey line near Norristown, Pa., then to Scranton. 470 miles. Speed limit 65 mph. Maximum toll $4.80.

**Richmond-Petersburg Turnpike:** North of Richmond, Va., to south of Petersburg, Va., 34.7 miles, speed 65 mph. (minimum 40 mph.) Maximum toll 95¢.

**Saw Mill River Parkway:** New York City to Katonah, N. Y. 30.4 miles. Speed limit 50 mph. Maximum toll 25¢. Trailers not permitted.

**Seventeen-Mile Drive:** Pacific Grove through Pebble Beach, Monterey, Calif. Maximum toll $2.

**Spaulding Turnpike:** Portsmouth, N. H., to Rochester, N. H., 22.8 miles. Speed limit 60 mph. Maximum toll 10¢ to 25¢.

**Sunshine State Parkway:** Miami, Fla., to Wildwood, Fla., 265 miles. Speed limit 70 mph. (40 mph. minimum). Maximum toll $4.80.

**Turner Turnpike:** Oklahoma City to Tulsa, Okla., 86 miles. Speed limit 70 mph. Maximum toll $1.40.

**Western Kentucky Parkway:** Elizabethtown to Princeton, Ky., 127 miles. Speed limit 70 mph. Maximum toll $2.

**West Virginia Turnpike:** Princeton, W. Va., to Charleston, W. Va., 88 miles. Speed limit 60 mph. Maximum toll $2.25.

**Wilbur Cross Parkway:** Milford to Meriden, Conn. 29.5 miles. Speed limit 60 mph. Maximum toll 35¢.

**Will Rogers Turnpike:** Tulsa, Okla., to Joplin, Mo., 88 miles. Speed limit 70 mph. Maximum toll $1.50.

## Motor-Vehicle Registrations in U. S. Near 100,000,000

Motor-vehicle registrations in the United States will reach 99,958,000 by Jan. 1, 1969, according to estimates by the Federal Highway Administration of the U. S. Dept. of Transportation. This represents an expected increase of more than 3,000,000 over the total registered a year earlier. Passenger car registration will reach 82,821,000, a 3% increase over year-earlier figures, while trucks and buses will total 17,137,000, a 3.7% increase. California's estimated 11,200,000 registrations are followed by 6,200,000 in New York and nearly 6,000,000 in Texas. Ohio and Pennsylvania will have 5,500,000 motor vehicles each by the beginning of 1969. Illinois and Michigan will have more than 4,000,000 each, Florida and New Jersey more than 3,000,000 each, and Minnesota, Indiana, North Carolina, Massachusetts, Missouri, Wisconsin, Virginia and Georgia in the 2,000,000 registration class. There will be 15 additional states with registrations of more than 1,000,000 each.

## CAR, TRUCK AND BUS DRIVERS IN THE U.S.A.
### Source: Bureau of Public Roads, estimated total licenses in force during 1967

| State | No. of drivers | State | No. of drivers | State | No. of drivers | State | No. of drivers |
|---|---|---|---|---|---|---|---|
| Alabama..... | 1,598,288 | Iowa...... | 1,584,015 | N. Hampshire | 371,412 | Texas...... | 5,600,749 |
| Alaska..... | 114,563 | Kansas...... | 1,409,730 | New Jersey.. | 3,596,637 | Utah........ | 557,933 |
| Arizona..... | 964,336 | Kentucky.... | 1,441,985 | New Mexico.. | 548,684 | Vermont.... | 219,299 |
| Arkansas.... | 1,012,907 | Louisiana.... | 1,621,822 | New York.... | 7,903,004 | Virginia.... | 2,229,546 |
| California... | 10,688,074 | Maine...... | 484,748 | N. Carolina.. | 2,511,867 | Washington.. | 1,705,157 |
| Colorado.... | 1,261,386 | Maryland.... | 1,867,273 | N. Dakota... | 333,432 | West Virginia | 855,055 |
| Connecticut.. | 1,897,875 | Massachusetts | 2,790,546 | Ohio........ | 5,726,270 | Wisconsin.... | 2,280,544 |
| Delaware.... | 295,086 | Michigan.... | 4,513,847 | Oklahoma.... | 1,465,389 | Wyoming.... | 220,926 |
| Florida...... | 3,335,861 | Minnesota.... | 2,073,939 | Oregon...... | 1,100,002 | Dist. of Col... | 343,549 |
| Georgia...... | 2,152,911 | Mississippi... | 971,762 | Pennsylvania. | 5,913,029 | | |
| Hawaii....... | 392,800 | Missouri..... | 2,499,627 | Rhode Island. | 468,984 | **Total...** | **103,171,641** |
| Idaho....... | 429,233 | Montana..... | 391,198 | S. Carolina.. | 1,243,991 | | |
| Illinois...... | 5,801,527 | Nebraska.... | 917,197 | S. Dakota... | 404,099 | | |
| Indiana...... | 2,661,091 | Nevada...... | 337,856 | Tennessee... | 2,060,000 | | |

### U. S. MOTOR VEHICLE REGISTRATIONS BY YEARS

| | | | | | | | | | |
|---|---|---|---|---|---|---|---|---|---|
| 1900.... | 8,000 | 1920.... | 9,239,161 | 1940....32,453,233 | 1959*....71,354,420 | 1965....90,357,667 |
| 1905.... | 78,800 | 1925....20,068,543 | 1945....31,035,420 | 1960....73,868,682 | 1966....93,962,030 |
| 1910.... | 468,500 | 1930....26,749,853 | 1950....49,161,691 | 1963....82,713,717 | 1967....96,944,896 |
| 1915.... | 2,490,932 | 1935....26,546,126 | 1955....62,688,792 | 1964....86,301,207 | 1968....99,958,000[1] |

*Beginning with 1959 Alaska and Hawaii are included. [1]Estimated.

# Highway Mileage Between Selected Cities

**Source:** American Automobile Association and Others

*Mileage is approximate and based on limited access highways and favorable commonly traveled routes.*

## CITIES IN THE EAST*

| | Albany, N. Y. | Atlanta, Ga. | Baltimore, Md. | Bangor, Me. | Birmingham, Ala. | Boston, Mass. | Buffalo, N. Y. | Charleston, W. Va. | Chicago, Ill. | Cincinnati, Ohio | Cleveland, Ohio | Detroit, Mich. | Hartford, Conn. | Indianapolis, Ind. | Jackson, Miss. |
|---|---|---|---|---|---|---|---|---|---|---|---|---|---|---|---|
| Albany | | 1013 | 341 | 403 | 1239 | 169 | 299 | 749 | 830 | 742 | 486 | 641 | 105 | 795 | 1460 |
| Atlanta | 1013 | | 676 | 1313 | 155 | 1079 | 912 | 499 | 708 | 461 | 725 | 738 | 977 | 549 | 402 |
| Baltimore | 341 | 676 | | 641 | 787 | 407 | 350 | 403 | 741 | 494 | 409 | 586 | 305 | 574 | 1065 |
| Bangor | 403 | 1313 | 641 | | 1656 | 234 | 702 | 1044 | 1192 | 1132 | 889 | 913 | 336 | 1208 | 1903 |
| Birmingham | 1239 | 155 | 787 | 1656 | | 1185 | 940 | 612 | 656 | 497 | 753 | 767 | 1090 | 496 | 247 |
| Boston | 169 | 1079 | 407 | 234 | 1185 | | 468 | 809 | 990 | 898 | 646 | 711 | 102 | 955 | 1668 |
| Buffalo | 299 | 912 | 350 | 702 | 940 | 468 | | 450 | 621 | 443 | 187 | 342 | 404 | 537 | 1161 |
| Charleston | 749 | 499 | 403 | 1044 | 612 | 809 | 450 | | 514 | 210 | 263 | 480 | 708 | 321 | 833 |
| Chicago | 830 | 708 | 741 | 1192 | 656 | 990 | 621 | 514 | | 304 | 344 | 279 | 970 | 193 | 799 |
| Cincinnati | 742 | 461 | 494 | 1132 | 497 | 898 | 443 | 210 | 304 | | 256 | 270 | 796 | 111 | 744 |
| Cleveland | 486 | 725 | 409 | 889 | 753 | 646 | 187 | 263 | 344 | 256 | | 177 | 626 | 309 | 974 |
| Detroit | 641 | 738 | 586 | 913 | 767 | 711 | 342 | 480 | 279 | 270 | 177 | | 754 | 295 | 988 |
| Hartford | 105 | 977 | 305 | 336 | 1090 | 102 | 404 | 708 | 970 | 796 | 626 | 754 | | 835 | 741 |
| Indianapolis | 795 | 549 | 574 | 1208 | 496 | 955 | 537 | 321 | 193 | 111 | 309 | 295 | 835 | | 650 |
| Jackson | 1460 | 402 | 1065 | 1903 | 247 | 1665 | 1161 | 833 | 799 | 744 | 974 | 988 | 741 | 650 | |
| Jacksonville | 1333 | 320 | 827 | 1468 | 464 | 1187 | 1132 | 782 | 1053 | 777 | 1045 | 996 | 1129 | 869 | 589 |
| Memphis | 1246 | 366 | 1022 | 1663 | 244 | 1428 | 947 | 619 | 585 | 504 | 760 | 774 | 1327 | 436 | 214 |
| Miami | 1688 | 675 | 1146 | 1824 | 789 | 1543 | 1588 | 1138 | 1383 | 1226 | 1400 | 1408 | 1485 | 1224 | 919 |
| Nashville | 1036 | 256 | 812 | 1453 | 203 | 1218 | 743 | 409 | 486 | 294 | 550 | 564 | 1117 | 293 | 424 |
| New Orleans | 1637 | 500 | 1145 | 2013 | 357 | 1549 | 1338 | 999 | 976 | 854 | 1096 | 1058 | 1470 | 927 | 177 |
| New York | 153 | 860 | 188 | 543 | 974 | 219 | 445 | 501 | 840 | 679 | 509 | 637 | 117 | 729 | 1223 |
| Norfolk | 575 | 559 | 229 | 875 | 714 | 640 | 967 | 402 | 916 | 612 | 560 | 882 | 536 | 723 | 1006 |
| Philadelphia | 243 | 774 | 98 | 633 | 884 | 309 | 473 | 501 | 779 | 602 | 435 | 612 | 207 | 648 | 1163 |
| Pittsburgh | 531 | 714 | 283 | 921 | 798 | 597 | 217 | 215 | 478 | 301 | 134 | 311 | 495 | 354 | 934 |
| Portland, Me. | 275 | 1185 | 513 | 128 | 1527 | 106 | 574 | 915 | 1105 | 1004 | 752 | 817 | 208 | 1061 | 1774 |
| Richmond | 488 | 529 | 147 | 788 | 684 | 553 | 468 | 315 | 829 | 525 | 486 | 695 | 449 | 636 | 919 |
| St. Louis | 1038 | 565 | 879 | 1451 | 537 | 1208 | 880 | 531 | 292 | 377 | 554 | 537 | 1178 | 243 | 507 |
| Tampa | 1524 | 467 | 981 | 1663 | 542 | 1382 | 1248 | 977 | 1171 | 1061 | 1236 | 1249 | 1324 | 1060 | 672 |
| Trenton | 223 | 806 | 130 | 613 | 1045 | 289 | 358 | 533 | 811 | 634 | 467 | 603 | 187 | 680 | 1195 |
| Washington | 380 | 633 | 39 | 680 | 776 | 445 | 359 | 364 | 702 | 500 | 370 | 535 | 341 | 564 | 1027 |

| | Jacksonville, Fla. | Memphis, Tenn. | Miami, Fla. | Nashville, Tenn. | New Orleans, La. | New York, N. Y. | Norfolk, Va. | Philadelphia, Pa. | Pittsburgh, Pa. | Portland, Me. | Richmond, Va. | St. Louis, Mo. | Tampa, Fla. | Trenton, N. J. | Washington, D. C. |
|---|---|---|---|---|---|---|---|---|---|---|---|---|---|---|---|
| Albany | 1333 | 1246 | 1688 | 1036 | 1637 | 153 | 575 | 243 | 531 | 275 | 488 | 1038 | 1524 | 223 | 380 |
| Atlanta | 320 | 366 | 675 | 256 | 500 | 860 | 559 | 774 | 714 | 1185 | 529 | 565 | 467 | 806 | 633 |
| Baltimore | 827 | 1022 | 1146 | 812 | 1145 | 188 | 229 | 98 | 283 | 513 | 147 | 879 | 981 | 130 | 39 |
| Bangor | 1468 | 1663 | 1824 | 1453 | 2013 | 543 | 875 | 633 | 921 | 128 | 788 | 1451 | 1663 | 613 | 680 |
| Birmingham | 464 | 244 | 789 | 203 | 357 | 974 | 714 | 884 | 798 | 1527 | 684 | 537 | 542 | 1045 | 776 |
| Boston | 1187 | 1428 | 1543 | 1218 | 1549 | 219 | 640 | 309 | 597 | 106 | 553 | 1208 | 1382 | 289 | 445 |
| Buffalo | 1132 | 947 | 1588 | 737 | 1338 | 445 | 967 | 473 | 217 | 574 | 468 | 880 | 1248 | 358 | 359 |
| Charleston | 782 | 619 | 1138 | 409 | 999 | 591 | 402 | 501 | 215 | 915 | 315 | 531 | 977 | 533 | 364 |
| Chicago | 1053 | 585 | 1383 | 486 | 976 | 840 | 916 | 779 | 478 | 1105 | 829 | 292 | 1171 | 811 | 702 |
| Cincinnati | 777 | 504 | 1226 | 294 | 854 | 679 | 612 | 602 | 301 | 1004 | 525 | 377 | 1061 | 634 | 500 |
| Cleveland | 1045 | 760 | 1400 | 550 | 1096 | 509 | 560 | 435 | 134 | 752 | 486 | 554 | 1236 | 467 | 370 |
| Detroit | 996 | 774 | 1408 | 564 | 1058 | 637 | 882 | 612 | 311 | 817 | 695 | 537 | 1249 | 603 | 535 |
| Hartford | 1129 | 1327 | 1485 | 1117 | 1470 | 117 | 536 | 207 | 495 | 208 | 449 | 1178 | 1324 | 187 | 341 |
| Indianapolis | 869 | 436 | 1224 | 293 | 927 | 729 | 723 | 648 | 354 | 1061 | 636 | 243 | 1060 | 680 | 564 |
| Jackson | 589 | 214 | 919 | 424 | 177 | 1223 | 1006 | 1163 | 934 | 1774 | 919 | 507 | 672 | 1195 | 1027 |
| Jacksonville | | 708 | 356 | 576 | 574 | 1012 | 678 | 925 | 897 | 1293 | 680 | 885 | 195 | 957 | 788 |
| Memphis | 708 | | 1033 | 210 | 391 | 1138 | 1021 | 1120 | 834 | 1534 | 904 | 293 | 786 | 1152 | 983 |
| Miami | 356 | 1033 | | 932 | 877 | 1331 | 1034 | 1244 | 1289 | 1649 | 1036 | 1235 | 247 | 1276 | 1107 |
| Nashville | 576 | 210 | 932 | | 560 | 1000 | 811 | 910 | 624 | 1324 | 624 | 309 | 767 | 942 | 686 |
| New Orleans | 574 | 391 | 877 | 560 | | 1330 | 1059 | 1243 | 1114 | 1655 | 1029 | 684 | 652 | 1275 | 1106 |
| New York | 1012 | 1138 | 1331 | 1000 | 1330 | | 419 | 90 | 378 | 325 | 332 | 985 | 1167 | 70 | 224 |
| Norfolk | 678 | 1021 | 1034 | 811 | 1059 | 419 | | 327 | 434 | 739 | 87 | 933 | 873 | 359 | 195 |
| Philadelphia | 925 | 1120 | 1244 | 910 | 1243 | 90 | 327 | | 301 | 415 | 245 | 885 | 1120 | 32 | 137 |
| Pittsburgh | 897 | 834 | 1289 | 624 | 1114 | 378 | 434 | 301 | | 703 | 352 | 678 | 1102 | 233 | 244 |
| Portland, Me. | 1293 | 1534 | 1649 | 1324 | 1655 | 325 | 739 | 415 | 703 | | 657 | 1381 | 1488 | 395 | 549 |
| Richmond | 680 | 904 | 1036 | 642 | 1029 | 332 | 87 | 245 | 352 | 657 | | 846 | 875 | 277 | 108 |
| St. Louis | 885 | 293 | 1235 | 309 | 684 | 985 | 933 | 885 | 678 | 1381 | 846 | | 1076 | 1064 | 840 |
| Tampa | 195 | 786 | 247 | 767 | 652 | 1167 | 873 | 1120 | 1102 | 1488 | 875 | 1076 | | 1152 | 983 |
| Trenton | 957 | 1152 | 1276 | 942 | 1275 | 70 | 359 | 32 | 233 | 395 | 277 | 1064 | 1152 | | 169 |
| Washington | 788 | 983 | 1107 | 686 | 1106 | 224 | 195 | 137 | 244 | 549 | 108 | 840 | 983 | 169 | |

## *Directions for Use of Mileage Charts

To measure mileage between the east and west charts there are 5 key cities: Chicago, Jackson (Miss.), Memphis, New Orleans and St. Louis.

Plot your course between the city listed nearest your home town and whichever of the 5 key cities you desire to pass through to the city of your destination. Add the mileage shown and this will give you the approximate total mileage.

For example: The mileage between Cheyenne and Philadelphia through St. Louis. Philadelphia to St. Louis = 885 miles, St. Louis to Cheyenne = 898; the total is 1,783 miles.

# Highway Mileage Between Selected Cities

### Source: American Automobile Association and Others

*Mileage is approximate and based on limited access highways and favorable commonly traveled routes.*

## CITIES IN THE WEST†

| | Albuquerque, N. M. | Bismarck, N.D. | Boise, Idaho | Cheyenne, Wyo. | Chicago, Ill. | Dallas, Texas | Denver, Colo. | Des Moines, Iowa | Helena, Mont. | Houston, Texas | Jackson, Miss. | Kansas City, Mo. | Little Rock, Ark. | Los Angeles, Calif. | Louisville, Ky. |
|---|---|---|---|---|---|---|---|---|---|---|---|---|---|---|---|
| Albuquerque | | 1105 | 994 | 522 | 1350 | 651 | 421 | 994 | 1111 | 829 | 1046 | 790 | 900 | 830 | 1306 |
| Bismarck | 1105 | | 1182 | 652 | 850 | 1175 | 685 | 672 | 617 | 1417 | 1479 | 930 | 1188 | 1649 | 1146 |
| Boise | 994 | 1182 | | 762 | 1731 | 1607 | 842 | 1394 | 494 | 1797 | 2014 | 1410 | 1798 | 962 | 1929 |
| Cheyenne | 522 | 652 | 762 | | 969 | 875 | 102 | 632 | 700 | 1117 | 1282 | 648 | 1040 | 1169 | 1162 |
| Chicago | 1350 | 850 | 1731 | 969 | | 925 | 1008 | 338 | 1478 | 1085 | 764 | 499 | 644 | 2166 | 301 |
| Dallas | 651 | 1175 | 1607 | 875 | 925 | | 780 | 704 | 1571 | 242 | 407 | 566 | 325 | 1405 | 833 |
| Denver | 421 | 685 | 842 | 102 | 1008 | 780 | | 679 | 792 | 1026 | 1191 | 604 | 957 | 1132 | 1120 |
| Des Moines | 994 | 672 | 1394 | 632 | 338 | 704 | 679 | | 1162 | 946 | 828 | 213 | 573 | 1801 | 569 |
| Helena | 1111 | 617 | 494 | 700 | 1478 | 1571 | 792 | 1162 | | 1813 | 1922 | 1261 | 1666 | 1234 | 1777 |
| Houston | 829 | 1417 | 1797 | 1117 | 1085 | 242 | 1026 | 946 | 1813 | | 429 | 741 | 441 | 1553 | 930 |
| Jackson | 1046 | 1479 | 2014 | 1282 | 764 | 407 | 1191 | 828 | 1922 | 429 | | 661 | 256 | 1810 | 512 |
| Kansas City | 790 | 930 | 1410 | 648 | 499 | 566 | 604 | 213 | 1261 | 741 | 661 | | 405 | 1596 | 516 |
| Little Rock | 900 | 1188 | 1798 | 1040 | 644 | 325 | 957 | 573 | 1666 | 441 | 256 | 405 | | 1701 | 508 |
| Los Angeles | 830 | 1649 | 962 | 1169 | 2166 | 1405 | 1132 | 1801 | 1234 | 1553 | 1810 | 1596 | 1701 | | 2107 |
| Louisville | 1306 | 1146 | 1929 | 1162 | 301 | 833 | 1120 | 569 | 1777 | 930 | 512 | 516 | 508 | 2107 | |
| Memphis | 1030 | 1266 | 1869 | 1107 | 544 | 464 | 1035 | 608 | 1720 | 561 | 220 | 459 | 139 | 1831 | 369 |
| Milwaukee | 1370 | 764 | 1700 | 988 | 91 | 1015 | 1040 | 361 | 1392 | 1174 | 844 | 580 | 723 | 2176 | 390 |
| Minneapolis | 1276 | 428 | 1422 | 794 | 407 | 966 | 855 | 252 | 1056 | 1198 | 1060 | 457 | 825 | 1940 | 711 |
| New Orleans | 1155 | 1604 | 2105 | 1373 | 976 | 504 | 1282 | 989 | 2070 | 359 | 181 | 821 | 416 | 1901 | 710 |
| Oklahoma City | 550 | 1377 | 1502 | 692 | 800 | 215 | 615 | 560 | 1392 | 457 | 578 | 347 | 349 | 1357 | 770 |
| Omaha | 895 | 581 | 1255 | 493 | 476 | 656 | 540 | 139 | 1056 | 898 | 866 | 205 | 610 | 1662 | 689 |
| Phoenix | 454 | 1501 | 978 | 918 | 1722 | 1005 | 818 | 1430 | 1147 | 1153 | 1412 | 1226 | 1330 | 398 | 1757 |
| Portland, Ore. | 1413 | 1607 | 436 | 1198 | 2112 | 2043 | 1278 | 1819 | 657 | 2233 | 2450 | 1846 | 2234 | 970 | 2412 |
| Reno | 1136 | 980 | 425 | 985 | 1956 | 1677 | 1041 | 1623 | 905 | 1867 | 2084 | 1784 | 1938 | 477 | 2154 |
| St. Louis | 1058 | 960 | 1660 | 898 | 292 | 633 | 865 | 336 | 1498 | 794 | 514 | 252 | 353 | 1888 | 264 |
| Salt Lake City | 625 | 1633 | 366 | 462 | 1439 | 1260 | 507 | 1094 | 500 | 1431 | 1648 | 1116 | 1456 | 730 | 1632 |
| San Francisco | 1138 | 1213 | 658 | 1220 | 2198 | 1789 | 1266 | 1852 | 1134 | 1955 | 2212 | 1874 | 2027 | 412 | 2390 |
| Seattle | 1487 | 505 | 505 | 1267 | 2076 | 2150 | 1370 | 1773 | 611 | 2302 | 2519 | 1872 | 2277 | 1143 | 2362 |
| Sioux Falls | 1166 | 531 | 1614 | 654 | 659 | 856 | 720 | 329 | 960 | 1099 | 1166 | 405 | 1019 | 2021 | 927 |
| Wichita | 596 | 791 | 1348 | 590 | 697 | 384 | 507 | 403 | 1241 | 612 | 733 | 198 | 473 | 1402 | 714 |

| | Memphis, Tenn. | Milwaukee, Wisc. | Minneapolis, Minn. | New Orleans, La. | Oklahoma City, Okla. | Omaha, Nebr. | Phoenix, Ariz. | Portland, Ore. | Reno, Nev. | St. Louis, Mo. | Salt Lake City, Utah | San Francisco, Calif. | Seattle, Wash. | Sioux Falls, S. D. | Wichita, Kansas |
|---|---|---|---|---|---|---|---|---|---|---|---|---|---|---|---|
| Albuquerque | 1030 | 1370 | 1276 | 1155 | 550 | 895 | 454 | 1413 | 1136 | 1058 | 625 | 1138 | 1487 | 1166 | 596 |
| Bismarck | 1266 | 764 | 428 | 1604 | 1377 | 581 | 1501 | 1607 | 980 | 960 | 1633 | 1213 | 505 | 531 | 791 |
| Boise | 1869 | 1700 | 1422 | 2105 | 1502 | 1255 | 978 | 436 | 425 | 1660 | 366 | 658 | 505 | 1614 | 1348 |
| Cheyenne | 1107 | 988 | 794 | 1373 | 692 | 493 | 918 | 1198 | 985 | 898 | 462 | 1220 | 1267 | 654 | 590 |
| Chicago | 544 | 91 | 407 | 976 | 800 | 476 | 1722 | 2112 | 1956 | 292 | 1439 | 2198 | 2076 | 659 | 697 |
| Dallas | 464 | 1015 | 966 | 504 | 215 | 656 | 1005 | 2043 | 1677 | 633 | 1260 | 1789 | 2150 | 856 | 384 |
| Denver | 1035 | 1040 | 855 | 1282 | 615 | 540 | 818 | 1278 | 1041 | 865 | 507 | 1266 | 1370 | 720 | 507 |
| Des Moines | 608 | 361 | 252 | 989 | 560 | 139 | 1430 | 1819 | 1623 | 336 | 1094 | 1852 | 1773 | 329 | 403 |
| Helena | 1720 | 1392 | 1056 | 2070 | 1392 | 1056 | 1147 | 657 | 905 | 1498 | 500 | 1134 | 611 | 960 | 1241 |
| Houston | 561 | 1174 | 1198 | 359 | 457 | 898 | 1153 | 2233 | 1867 | 794 | 1431 | 1955 | 2302 | 1099 | 612 |
| Jackson | 220 | 844 | 1060 | 181 | 578 | 866 | 1412 | 2450 | 2084 | 514 | 1648 | 2212 | 2519 | 1166 | 733 |
| Kansas City | 459 | 580 | 457 | 821 | 347 | 205 | 1226 | 1846 | 1784 | 252 | 1116 | 1874 | 1872 | 405 | 198 |
| Little Rock | 139 | 723 | 825 | 416 | 349 | 610 | 1330 | 2234 | 1938 | 353 | 1456 | 2027 | 2277 | 1019 | 473 |
| Los Angeles | 1831 | 2176 | 1940 | 1901 | 1357 | 1662 | 398 | 970 | 477 | 1888 | 730 | 412 | 1143 | 2021 | 1402 |
| Louisville | 369 | 390 | 711 | 710 | 770 | 689 | 1757 | 2412 | 2154 | 264 | 1632 | 2390 | 2362 | 927 | 714 |
| Albuquerque | 1030 | 1370 | 1276 | 1155 | 550 | 895 | 454 | 1413 | 1136 | 1058 | 625 | 1138 | 1487 | 1166 | 596 |
| Memphis | | 624 | 840 | 401 | 479 | 664 | 1466 | 2305 | 2041 | 294 | 1534 | 2157 | 2331 | 952 | 529 |
| Milwaukee | 624 | | 326 | 1013 | 876 | 500 | 1806 | 2026 | 1979 | 370 | 1455 | 2231 | 1977 | 578 | 778 |
| Minneapolis | 840 | 326 | | 1251 | 813 | 358 | 1630 | 1690 | 1773 | 567 | 1245 | 2004 | 1669 | 252 | 655 |
| New Orleans | 401 | 1013 | 1251 | | 678 | 1026 | 1503 | 2541 | 2175 | 684 | 1764 | 2283 | 2626 | 1343 | 833 |
| Oklahoma City | 479 | 876 | 813 | 678 | | 454 | 987 | 1893 | 1660 | 606 | 1108 | 1578 | 1962 | 645 | 157 |
| Omaha | 664 | 500 | 358 | 1026 | 454 | | 1335 | 1666 | 1484 | 451 | 955 | 1713 | 1667 | 190 | 303 |
| Phoenix | 1466 | 1806 | 1630 | 1503 | 987 | 1335 | | 1305 | 738 | 1478 | 653 | 800 | 1541 | 1625 | 1032 |
| Portland, Ore. | 2305 | 2026 | 1690 | 2541 | 1893 | 1666 | 1305 | | 567 | 2096 | 802 | 652 | 175 | 1784 | 1784 |
| Reno | 2041 | 1979 | 1773 | 2175 | 1660 | 1484 | 738 | 567 | | 1890 | 567 | 221 | 742 | 1559 | 1512 |
| St. Louis | 294 | 370 | 567 | 684 | 606 | 451 | 1478 | 2096 | 1890 | | 1370 | 2134 | 2226 | 659 | 450 |
| Salt Lake City | 1534 | 1455 | 1245 | 1764 | 1108 | 955 | 653 | 802 | 567 | 1370 | | 759 | 864 | 1032 | 1005 |
| San Francisco | 2157 | 2231 | 2004 | 2283 | 1578 | 1713 | 800 | 652 | 221 | 2134 | 759 | | 821 | 1791 | 1721 |
| Seattle | 2331 | 1977 | 1669 | 2626 | 1962 | 1667 | 1541 | 175 | 742 | 2226 | 864 | 821 | | 1567 | 1852 |
| Sioux Falls | 952 | 578 | 252 | 1343 | 645 | 190 | 1625 | 1784 | 1559 | 659 | 1032 | 1791 | 1567 | | 493 |
| Wichita | 529 | 778 | 655 | 833 | 157 | 303 | 1032 | 1784 | 1512 | 450 | 1005 | 1721 | 1852 | 493 | |

†See preceding page for explanation.

## National Interstate Highway System Nearly 70% Completed

The National System of Interstate and Defense Highways was more than 68% completed at the end of 1968, with approximately 28,000 miles open to traffic. The total cost of this 41,000-mile network of high-speed, super roads is currently estimated at $56.5 billion, of which the Federal Government will pay 90% and the states 10%.

The Interstate System will span the nation and link more than 90% of all cities of over 50,000 population and thousands of smaller cities and towns. It is predicted that by 1975 the system will be carrying nearly 25% of the total 1.3 trillion vehicle miles of travel projected for that year. The system is expected to cut driving time drastically, to save at least 8,000 lives annually because of its safety design, and to enable motorists to cross the United States on non-stop highways with no traffic lights.

## Average Retail Prices of Used Automobiles

Listed below are average prices that a buyer may expect to pay for various American-made automobiles, of model years 1965 through 1968. They are NOT the prices one might expect to receive from a dealer. The prices listed are average retail values based upon reports of actual transactions by dealers. They are derived chiefly from the N.A.D.A. Official Used Car Guide, Eastern Edition for October, 1968, published by Automobile Dealers Used Car Guide Co., 2000 K St., N.W., Washington, D. C. 20006. The table is intended only as a guide for used-car buyers; actual prices may vary throughout the country. The listed values are for cars in average condition with average mileage (15,000 miles per year); values will vary according to condition and mileage.

All cars 4-door sedans with automatic transmission, power steering, radio and heater except where otherwise designated.

| Car (Cylinders) | 1968 | 1967 | 1966 | 1965 | Car (Cylinders) | 1968 | 1967 | 1966 | 1965 |
|---|---|---|---|---|---|---|---|---|---|
| Buick Spl. Deluxe (6) ... | $2185 | $1780 | $1445 | $1100 | ¹Imperial Crown (8) ... .... | | 3930 | 3060 | 2250 |
| Buick Le Sabre (8) ...... | 2675 | 2185 | 1690 | 1335 | (hardtop) | | | | |
| ¹Buick Electra (8) ...... | 3630 | 2990 | 2270 | 1730 | ¹Imperial Le Baron (8) .. .. .... | | 4190 | 3295 | 2400 |
| ¹Cadillac Calais (8) .... | 5185 | 4230 | 3265 | 2415 | (hardtop) | | | | |
| ¹Cadillac De Ville (8) .. | 5430 | 4480 | 3510 | 2615 | ¹Lincoln Continental .... .... | | 4055 | 3205 | 2350 |
| ²Chevrolet Chevy II (6) . | 1935 | 1395 | 1110 | 810 | ²Mercury Comet (6) ....... | 1980 | 1385 | 1065 | 825 |
| Chevrolet Biscayne (8) .. | 2155 | 1620 | 1250 | 1000 | Mercury Monterey (8) ... | 2405 | 1860 | 1460 | 1035 |
| Chevrolet Impala (8) .... | 2330 | 1930 | 1525 | 1190 | Mercury Park Lane (8) .. | 2705 | 2105 | 1710 | 1305 |
| Chrysler Newport (8) .... | 2710 | 2180 | 1695 | 1285 | Oldsmobile F-85 (6) .... | 2080 | 1625 | 1270 | 1000 |
| Chrysler 300 (8) ....... | 3185 | 2530 | 1990 | 1520 | Oldsmobile Delta 88 (8) . | 2800 | 2250 | 1755 | 1410 |
| (hardtop) | | | | | ²Plymouth Valiant (6) ... | 1815 | 1455 | 1155 | 865 |
| ¹Chrysler New Yorker (8) .. | 3740 | 2900 | 2195 | 1675 | ²Plymouth Belvedere (8) . | 2040 | 1620 | 1235 | 990 |
| ²Dodge Dart 270 (6) .... | 1950 | 1615 | 1220 | 960 | Plymouth Fury III (8) .. | 2355 | 1940 | 1545 | 1185 |
| Dodge Coronet 500 (8) ... | 2380 | 1850 | 1440 | .... | Pontiac Tempest (6) .... | 2090 | 1640 | 1300 | 1060 |
| Dodge Polara (8) ....... | 2425 | 1920 | 1525 | 1110 | Pontiac Catalina (8) ... | 2555 | 2065 | 1645 | 1295 |
| ²Ford Falcon Std. (6) ... | 1745 | 1365 | 1070 | 765 | Pontiac Bonneville (8) . | 3060 | 2455 | 1960 | 1535 |
| ²Ford Fairlane (8) ...... | 2045 | 1580 | 1205 | 950 | (hardtop) | | | | |
| Ford Galaxie 500 (8) .... | 2350 | 1875 | 1425 | 1135 | ²Rambler American (6) ... | 1710 | 1345 | 1075 | 830 |
| | | | | | ³Rambler Ambassador (8) . | 2410 | 1765 | 1375 | 1145 |

¹Air conditioning included. ²Power steering not included. ³Air conditioning included 1968 model only.

## Additional Auto Safety Requirements Go Into Effect

New safety standards and requirements which must be met by all autos manufactured after Jan. 1, 1969, for sale or use in the United States were issued in 1968 by the Department of Transportation's Federal Highway Administration.

These were in addition to a longer list of such safety rules which took effect Jan. 1, 1968.

The new rules included:

Head restraints (head-rests) to reduce the severity of whiplash injuries, on two front seats.

Two latches, or a double latch, on front-opening hoods to reduce the danger of them opening while car is in motion.

Vehicle identification numbers to be installed inside all cars, near the driver but visible from outside the car, as an aid to reducing auto thefts.

Fail-safe devices for cars with concealed headlights, designed so the shielding covers cannot close while the lights are on, and, if they should fail, they would fail in open position.

An amendment to earlier rules which will extend to passenger cars (as of Jan. 1, 1969) requirements for 4-way flashing signal lights, back-up lights and 4 side reflectors or side lights.

## Total Road and Street Mileage in United States

Source: Bureau of Public Roads, Dept. of Transportation 1966

| State | Rural | Municipal | Surfaced | Total | State | Rural | Municipal | Surfaced | Total |
|---|---|---|---|---|---|---|---|---|---|
| Alabama.... | 66,186 | 10,579 | 68,483 | 76,765 | Nebraska... | 97,097 | 6,098 | 68,783 | 103,195 |
| Alaska...... | 6,020 | 542 | 2,663 | 6,562 | Nevada...... | 45,050 | 1,728 | 14,697 | 46,778 |
| Arizona..... | 34,336 | 5,434 | 18,896 | 39,770 | N. Hamp.... | 12,904 | 1,624 | 11,818 | 14,528 |
| Arkansas.... | 72,665 | 8,427 | 54,382 | 81,092 | New Jersey.. | 17,051 | 16,110 | 30,462 | 33,161 |
| California... | 130,284 | 40,723 | 116,859 | 171,007 | New Mexico. | 62,906 | 3,913 | 19,341 | 66,819 |
| Colorado.... | 74,185 | 6,175 | 46,506 | 80,360 | New York... | 85,276 | 16,856 | 91,964 | 102,132 |
| Connecticut. | 5,256 | 12,604 | 17,699 | 17,860 | N. Carolina.. | 71,649 | 12,756 | 74,600 | 84,405 |
| Delaware.... | 3,444 | 1,369 | 4,792 | 4,813 | N. Dakota.. | 103,874 | 3,010 | 65,638 | 106,884 |
| Florida..... | 61,924 | 18,223 | 54,740 | 80,147 | Ohio........ | 85,020 | 22,733 | 105,941 | 107,753 |
| Georgia..... | 83,392 | 13,581 | 63,480 | 96,973 | Oklahoma... | 94,094 | 12,675 | 75,066 | 106,769 |
| Hawaii...... | 2,469 | 904 | 3,193 | 3,373 | Oregon...... | 79,881 | 5,709 | 53,140 | 85,590 |
| Idaho....... | 50,808 | 2,783 | 28,895 | 53,591 | Penn........ | 90,043 | 22,815 | 94,475 | 112,858 |
| Illinois.... | 102,506 | 25,883 | 119,051 | 128,389 | R. I........ | 823 | 3,831 | 4,383 | 4,654 |
| Indiana..... | 78,123 | 12,626 | 85,747 | 90,749 | S. Carolina. | 52,666 | 6,074 | 36,540 | 58,740 |
| Iowa........ | 99,692 | 12,616 | 103,837 | 112,308 | S. Dakota... | 80,994 | 2,870 | 67,244 | 83,864 |
| Kansas...... | 123,491 | 9,805 | 92,881 | 133,296 | Tennessee... | 67,894 | 8,966 | 75,016 | 76,860 |
| Kentucky.... | 65,263 | 4,822 | 55,391 | 70,085 | Texas....... | 197,166 | 40,744 | 168,901 | 237,910 |
| Louisiana... | 41,093 | 9,686 | 45,271 | 50,779 | Utah ....... | 34,123 | 4,229 | 21,274 | 38,352 |
| Maine....... | 18,888 | 2,304 | 19,235 | 21,192 | Vermont.... | 13,062 | 918 | 12,006 | 13,980 |
| Maryland... | 21,427 | 3,898 | 25,245 | 25,325 | Virginia..... | 51,628 | 7,691 | 58,101 | 59,319 |
| Mass........ | 7,444 | 19,957 | 25,803 | 27,401 | Washington. | 63,323 | 9,632 | 59,679 | 72,955 |
| Michigan.... | 95,204 | 18,566 | 94,542 | 113,590 | W. Virginia.. | 32,109 | 3,550 | 25,993 | 35,659 |
| Minnesota... | 110,554 | 15,831 | 113,499 | 126,385 | Wisconsin... | 87,511 | 13,269 | 94,805 | 100,780 |
| Mississippi.. | 59,252 | 6,164 | 62,283 | 65,416 | Wyoming... | 75,754 | 1,202 | 60,996 | 76,956 |
| Missouri.... | 99,636 | 14,518 | 101,938 | 114,154 | D. C........ | | 1,083 | 1,071 | 1,083 |
| Montana.... | 72,455 | 2,129 | 38,274 | 74,584 | **Total.....** | **3,187,715** | **510,235** | **2,800,481** | **3,697,950** |

## Intercity Bus Operations

Source: National Association of Motor Bus Owners

| | 1965 | 1966 | 1967 |
|---|---|---|---|
| Number of operating companies............ | 1,100 | 1,100 | 1,100 |
| Number of buses........................ | 20,522 | 21,200 | 21,400 |
| Miles of highway served¹................ | 262,000 | 263,000 | 263,000 |
| Number of employees²................... | 44,000 | 46,200 | 46,600 |
| Total bus miles......................... | 1,165,000,000 | 1,200,000,000 | 1,210,000,000 |
| Revenue passengers..................... | 369,800,000 | 383,900,000 | 384,000,000 |
| Revenue passenger miles................ | 23,300,000,000 | 24,600,000,000 | 24,600,000,000 |
| Operating revenue, (all services)......... | $702,600,000 | $739,800,000 | $772,800,000 |
| Operating expenses..................... | $602,400,000 | $637,200,000 | $684,900,000 |
| Net operating revenue (Before income taxes) ... | $100,200,000 | $102,600,000 | $87,900,000 |
| Taxes assignable to operations³............ | $58,500,000 | $64,500,000 | $67,000,000 |

¹Includes duplication between carriers. ²Operating companies only. ³Excludes income taxes.

## Women Defeat Men in 1968 Mobil Economy Run

Ice, snow, heavy winds and torrential rains in the Rockies, plus higher average speeds, all combined to lower the average gasoline economy of the late-model American stock cars competing in the 1968 Mobile Economy Run. Over-all fuel mileage was 19.1671 mi. per gallon compared to 19.9884 in 1967. Average speed was 55.03 m.p.h. compared to 51.36 in 1967. Women drivers again scored better with an average of 19.9203 compared to 19.0073 for the men. The run was ended in Indianapolis on Apr. 5 after the 40 competing cars had covered 2,272.25 mi. The event which started in Los Angeles Apr. 2 was scheduled to have ended in New York Apr. 7. The early ending was made because Apr. 7 had been declared a day of mourning in memory of Dr. Martin Luther King. The run is conducted under the supervision of the U. S. Auto Club.

| Make and model (all automatic transmissions) | Miles per gallon | Driver | Make and model (all automatic transmissions) | Miles per gallon | Driver |
|---|---|---|---|---|---|
| **CLASS A—COMPACT 6-CYLINDER** | | | **CLASS D (Contd.)** | | |
| Rambler Rogue | 24.0917 | Les Viland | Buick Special | 18.5357 | John Rich |
| Barracuda | 23.3179 | Jerry Gross | Chevelle Malibu | 17.8811 | Dr. Tom Evans |
| Corvair 500 | 22.8535 | Gordon Madison | Olds F-85 | 17.0889 | Mel Alsbury, Jr. |
| Valiant | 22.7058 | Bob Cahill | Pontiac Tempest | 16.8924 | Don Francisco |
| Mustang 2 + 2 | 22.6487 | Kay Kimes | **CLASS E—STANDARD SIZE,** | | |
| Dodge Dart 170 | 21.9158 | Mary Ann Foss | **LOW-PRICE 8-CYLINDER** | | |
| Falcon 170 | 21.1303 | Bill Levy | Chevy Impala SS | 18.8162 | Don Royer |
| **CLASS B—COMPACT 8-CYLINDER** | | | Plymouth Fury III | 18.3332 | Bill Keller |
| Barracuda 318 | 20.0078 | Jack Kirkpatrick | Ford Custom | 17.9562 | John Allen |
| Chevy II Nova | 19.6260 | Mary Hauser | Chevy Caprice | 17.3699 | C. K. Enoch |
| Mustang 2 + 2 | 19.5429 | Fran Foster | **CLASS F—STANDARD SIZE,** | | |
| Valiant | 19.5408 | Bob Checkley | **MEDIUM PRICE 8-CYLINDER** | | |
| Javelin | 13.6720 | Tommy Thomas | Buick LeSabre | 18.4883 | Marta Retzlaff |
| **CLASS C—INTERMEDIATE** | | | Dodge Polara 318 | 18.4639 | Jim Wright |
| **6-CYLINDER** | | | Pontiac Catalina | 17.9815 | Ted Block |
| Fairlane | 22.7680 | Ginny Sims | Chrysler Newport | 17.3538 | Jim Latham |
| Mercury Montego | 22.6601 | Al Johnson | Mercury Monterey | 16.9084 | Byron Froelich |
| Plymouth Belvedere | 21.9822 | Carl Diehl | Olds Delta 88 | 16.3248 | Stan Raymond |
| Chevelle 300 | 19.2543 | Ed Miller | **CLASS G—LUXURY CARS** | | |
| **CLASS C—INTERMEDIATE** | | | Chrysler New Yorker | 17.1340 | Hart Fullerton |
| **8-CYLINDER CARS** | | | Olds 98 | 16.7003 | Mandy Williams |
| Dodge Coronet | 20.5744 | Shirley Shahan | Thunderbird | 16.5735 | Nelson Stacy |
| Plymouth Belvedere | 20.4154 | Scott Harvey | Buick Electra 225 | 16.5270 | Paula Murphy |
| Mercury Montego | 19.4283 | Ronnie Duman | Olds Toronado | 15.9898 | Tom Gillum, Jr. |
| Ford Torino GT | 19.0656 | Darrell Droke | Cadillac | 15.4621 | Pete Novotny |

## Passenger Car Production, U. S. Plants

Source: Automobile Manufacturers Association

| | 1966 | 1967 | 1968 6 Mos. | | 1966 | 1967 | 1968 6 Mos. |
|---|---|---|---|---|---|---|---|
| **American Motors Corp.** | 279,225 | 229,057 | 149,307 | **General Motors Corp.** | | | |
| | | | | Chevrolet | 1,431,022 | 1,150,264 | 644,898 |
| **Chrysler Corp.** | | | | Corvette | 24,939 | 23,775 | 16,056 |
| Plymouth | 640,450 | 610,098 | 368,486 | Chevelle | 423,317 | 375,831 | 231,121 |
| Dodge | 532,026 | 497,380 | 316,081 | Camaro | 94,426 | 216,210 | 118,394 |
| Chrysler | 255,487 | 240,712 | 130,484 | Chevy II | 155,726 | 135,884 | 113,116 |
| Imperial | 17,653 | 15,506 | 5,281 | Corvair | 73,362 | 18,701 | 7,440 |
| **Total Chrysler Corp.** | 1,445,616 | 1,363,696 | 820,332 | **Total Chevrolet** | 2,202,792 | 1,920,665 | 1,131,025 |
| | | | | Pontiac | 481,591 | 445,956 | 238,323 |
| **Ford Motor Co.** | | | | Tempest | 384,794 | 288,924 | 201,933 |
| Ford | 948,462 | 699,356 | 556,933 | Firebird | | 122,291 | 58,197 |
| Fairlane | 304,659 | 190,383 | 284,981 | **Total Pontiac** | 866,385 | 857,171 | 498,453 |
| Falcon | 131,793 | 33,527 | 34,858 | Oldsmobile | 318,667 | 277,910 | 164,230 |
| Mustang | 580,767 | 394,482 | 197,677 | Toronado | 37,420 | 18,444 | 16,177 |
| Thunderbird | 72,734 | 59,640 | 44,131 | F-85 | 237,982 | 256,643 | 163,216 |
| **Total Ford** | 2,038,415 | 1,377,388 | 1,118,580 | **Total Oldsmobile** | 594,069 | 552,997 | 343,623 |
| Mercury | 153,680 | 96,309 | 77,930 | Buick | 315,639 | 336,366 | 212,484 |
| Montego-Comet | 133,165 | 56,451 | 93,822 | Riviera | 48,073 | 43,145 | 29,358 |
| Cougar | 48.013 | 131,743 | 75,232 | Special | 216,709 | 194,355 | 132,544 |
| **Total Mercury** | 334,858 | 284,503 | 246,984 | **Total Buick** | 580,421 | 573,866 | 374,386 |
| Lincoln | 52,169 | 34,333 | 31,415 | Cadillac | 205,001 | 213,161 | 126,820 |
| **Total Ford Motor Co.** | 2,425,442 | 1,696,224 | 1,396,979 | **Total General Motors Corp.** | 4,448,668 | 4,117,860 | 2,474,307 |
| | | | | Checker Motors Corp. | 5,761 | 5,822 | 2,485 |
| | | | | Total passenger cars. | 8,604,712 | 7,412,659 | 4,843,410 |

## Motor Bus Passenger Operations, Intercity Class I Carriers

Source: Interstate Commerce Commission

| Year ended December 31 | 1964 | 1965 | 1966 | 1967 |
|---|---|---|---|---|
| Number of carriers reporting | 158 | 147 | 156 | 161 |
| Miles of line, regular route | 211,621 | 211 131 | 216,580 | 219,260 |
| Regular route intercity service revenue (dollars) | 442,098,685 | 452,302,408 | 475,280,834 | 478,411,327 |
| Local and suburban service revenue (dollars) | 79,654,963 | 13,664,810 | 13,149,293 | 15,905,174 |
| Charter or special service bus (dollars) | 63,829,994 | 61,172,462 | 69,743,934 | 80,007,681 |
| Total operating revenue (dollars) | 656,485,751 | 604,677,139 | 640,990,577 | 663,851,245 |
| Total expenses (dollars) | 570,882,528 | 511,470,607 | 545,753,076 | 586,002,062 |
| Net operating revenue (dollars) | 85,603,223 | 93,206,532 | 95,237,501 | 77,829,183 |
| Bus-miles in intercity line service | 834,041,327 | 815,579,656 | 844,445,549 | 837,403,930 |
| Bus-miles in local and suburban service | 117,954,966 | 24,397,719 | 22,407,474 | 25,008,586 |
| Bus-miles in charter or special service | 103,643,274 | 98,821,490 | 112,258,094 | 124,891,316 |
| Intercity revenue passengers carried (line service) | 180,516,753 | 162,992,836 | 169,323,447 | 166,285,070 |
| Local and suburban revenue passengers carried | 296,511,245 | 29,475,279 | 26,956,727 | 30,815,509 |
| Charter or special revenue passengers carried | 29,861,540 | 20,714,320 | 26,969,666 | 26,483,225 |

## Mobile Homes and Travel Trailers—Manufacturers' Shipments

Source: Dept. of Commerce, Business and Defense Services Administration; *Construction Review*

A mobile home, or housing-type trailer, is a vehicular portable structure built on a chassis and designed to be used without a permanent foundation as a year-round dwelling when connected to utilities. Mobile homes are defined as units 29 feet or longer and weighing over 4,500 pounds; travel trailers, as units less than 29 feet long, regardless of weight, *or* weighing less than 4,500 pounds, regardless of length. Excludes units designed for commercial uses, pickup cabs, folding campers, and amphibious units.

| Year and month | Total | Mobile homes | Travel trailers | Mobile homes as percent of total shipments |
|---|---|---|---|---|
| 1960 | 144,000 | 103,700 | 40,300 | 72.0 |
| 1963 | 223,010 | 150,840 | 72,170 | 67.6 |
| 1964 | 281,690 | 191,320 | 90,370 | 67.9 |
| 1965 | 324,050 | 216,470 | 107,580 | 66.8 |
| 1966 | 340,000 | 217,300 | 122,700 | 63.9 |
| 1967 | 370,780 | 240,360 | 130,420 | 64.8 |
| 1968 Jan. | 25,820 | 18,970 | 6,850 | 73.5 |
| Feb. | 29,710 | 21,100 | 8,610 | 71.0 |
| Mar. | 39,090 | 23,880 | 15,210 | 61.1 |
| Apr. | 45,490 | 26,990 | 18,500 | 59.3 |
| May | 47,570 | 27,470 | 20,100 | 57.7 |
| June | 46,000 | 26,370 | 19,630 | 57.3 |

## Automobile Factory Sales

Source: Automobile Manufacturers Association, Detroit, Mich.—Values, Wholesale

| Year | Passenger Cars | | Motor Trucks, Buses | | Total | |
|---|---|---|---|---|---|---|
| | Number | Value | Number | Value | Number | Value |
| 1900 | 4,192 | $4,899,443 | .......... | .......... | 4,192 | $4,899,443 |
| 1905 | 24,250 | 38,670,000 | 750 | $1,330,000 | 25,000 | 40,000,000 |
| 1910 | 181,000 | 215,340,000 | 6,000 | 9,660,000 | 187,000 | 225,000,000 |
| 1915 | 895,930 | 575,978,000 | 74,000 | 125,800,000 | 969,930 | 701,778,000 |
| 1920 | 1,905,560 | 1,809,170,963 | 321,789 | 423,249,410 | 2,227,349 | 2,232,420,373 |
| 1925 | 3,735,171 | 2,458,370,026 | 530,659 | 458,400,277 | 4,265,830 | 2,916,770,303 |
| 1930 | 2,787,456 | 1,644,083,152 | 575,364 | 390,752,061 | 3,362,820 | 2,034,835,213 |
| 1935 | 3,273,874 | 1,707,836,325 | 697,367 | 380,997,330 | 3,971,241 | 2,088,833,655 |
| 1940 | 3,717,385 | 2,370,654,083 | 754,901 | 567,820,414 | 4,472,286 | 2,938,474,497 |
| 1945 | 69,532 | 57,254,655 | 655,683 | 1,181,955,532 | 725,215 | 1,239,210,187 |
| 1950 | 6,665,863 | 8,468,137,000 | 1,337,193 | 1,707,748,000 | 8,003,056 | 10,175,885,000 |
| 1955 | 7,920,186 | 12,452,871,000 | 1,249,106 | 2,020,973,000 | 9,169,292 | 14,473,844,000 |
| 1960 | 6,674,796 | 12,164,234,000 | 1,194,475 | 2,350,680,000 | 7,869,271 | 14,514,914,000 |
| 1965 | 9,305,561 | 18,380,036,000 | 1,751,805 | 3,733,664,000 | 11,057,366 | 22,113,700,000 |
| 1966 | 8,598,326 | 17,554,326,000 | 1,731,084 | 3,953,472,900 | 10,329,410 | 21,507,798,900 |
| 1967 | *7,436,764 | 15,600,000,000 | 1,539,462 | 3,600,000,000 | 8,976,226 | 19,200,000,000 |

After July 1, 1964 all tactical vehicles are excluded. Federal excise taxes are excluded in all years.
*Preliminary.

## Automotive Exports from United States

Source: Bureau of Census, Dept. of Commerce
(in thousands)

| | Vehicles | | | Vehicles | | | Vehicles | |
|---|---|---|---|---|---|---|---|---|
| | Total | Value* | | Total | Value* | | Total | Value* |
| 1940 | $155,091 | $ 299,785 | 1960 | $616,881 | $1,411,418 | 1964 | $ 694,289 | $1,900,096 |
| 1945 | 233,179 | 387,667 | 1961 | 520,514 | 1,300,200 | 1965 | 721,294 | 2,197,515 |
| 1950 | 396,571 | 793,802 | 1962 | 499,069 | 1,400,990 | 1966 | 924,717 | 2,474,423 |
| 1955 | 719,754 | 1,367,151 | 1963 | 548,530 | 1,566,866 | 1967 | 1,219,318 | 2,887,362 |

*Includes used passenger cars and trucks, trailers, parts for assembly, and garage equipment.

## Domestic and International Express Service

Source: REA Express

Domestic surface and air express service extends throughout the U. S., Puerto Rico and points in Canada. The company operates an international shipping service by surface transportation between the U. S. and 112 countries. Agents in the countries operate in a manner similar to REA Express in the U. S. The company also operates a worldwide air shipping service via connections with International (IATA) airlines.

Express service was inaugurated March 4, 1839. Air express service was inaugurated September 1, 1927.

| Year | Surface shipments | Revenue | Air shipments | Revenue |
|---|---|---|---|---|
| 1955 | 78,251,300 | $381,444,436 | 5,223,454 | $40,316,233 |
| 1960 | 59,853,687 | 315,863,193 | 6,533,023 | 49,861,000 |
| 1962 | 59,312,291 | 325,011,239 | 7,480,094 | 57,607,445 |
| 1963 | 58,350,917 | 322,588,085 | 7,674,877 | 59,955,803 |
| 1964 | 59,417,824 | 344,674,007 | 8,336,627 | 66,762,408 |
| 1965 | 57,707,696 | 352,479,354 | 9,211,339 | 78,080,340 |
| 1966 | 53,263,136 | 343,643,830 | 9,517,773 | 86,293,468 |
| 1967 | 46,736,424 | 334,918,673 | 9,274,034 | 86,954,235 |

## Credit Unions Are World Wide

There are about 52,000 credit unions in the world with more than 30,800,000 members. At the end of 1967 in the United States and its territories, there were 23,210 credit unions with 19,100,000 members who had savings of $11.3 billion and assets of $12.7 billion.

Credit unions are financial self-help groups whose members save their money together and make loans to each other at low interest. They are nonprofit corporations. All credit unions are chartered by Federal or state governments and regulated by law. They are entirely owned by their members, and their operations are restricted to their membership.

Credit unions are found throughout the free world. In the United States and Canada, where the majority are located, they are usually formed by groups who share the same employment, such as factory workers, government employees and school teachers. Other groups that have formed credit unions include members of the same church congregation, fraternal organizations and residents of the same community.

*(For Bureau of Federal Credit Unions see Social Security.)*

## Auto Registrations, Taxes, Gasoline, Drivers' Ages

Source: Bureau of Public Roads

| State | Minimum age* | Registered automobiles, buses & trucks[1] | State Gasoline Tax per gallon | Motor Fuel Gross Tax collections | Motor fuel consumption (1967[2]) | | |
|---|---|---|---|---|---|---|---|
| | | | | | Highway | Non-highway | Total[3] |
| | (1968) | (1967) | (1968) | 1,000 | 1,000 | 1,000 | 1,000 |
| | | Number | Cents | Dollars | Gallons | Gallons | Gallons |
| Alabama ....... | 16 | 1,735,179 | 7 | 99,972 | 1,390,040 | 39,741 | 1,429,781 |
| Alaska ........ | 18 (14) | 110,382 | 8 | 8,022 | 72,927 | 56,730 | 129,657 |
| Arizona ....... | 18 | 889,615 | 7 | 53,821 | 723,646 | 42,484 | 766,130 |
| Arkansas ...... | 18 | 982,936 | 7.5 | 65,489 | 844,044 | 46,273 | 890,317 |
| California ..... | 18 (14) | 10,849,514 | 7 | 574,706 | 8,008,678 | 245,019 | 8,253,697 |
| Colorado ...... | 18 | 1,241,870 | 6 | 54,923 | 877,428 | 72,876 | 950,304 |
| Connecticut .... | 21 | 1,544,761 | 4[7] | 72,468 | 1,076,857 | 20,356 | 1,097,213 |
| Delaware ...... | 18 | 267,660 | 7 | 16,618 | 230,227 | 8,732 | 238,959 |
| Florida ........ | 18 | 3,392,661 | 7 | 183,461 | 2,561,698 | 135,851 | 2,697,549 |
| Georgia ....... | 16 | 2,164,367 | 6.5 | 130,246 | 1,953,292 | 57,659 | 2,010,951 |
| Hawaii ........ | 20 | 336,498 | 5[5] | 10,947 | 189,736 | 26,708 | 216,444 |
| Idaho ......... | 18 (14) | 454,572 | 6 | 21,915 | 332,865 | 40,211 | 373,076 |
| Illinois ........ | 21 (15) | 4,818,259 | 4[6] | 222,294 | 3,998,771 | 260,730 | 4,259,501 |
| Indiana ....... | 21 | 2,631,944 | 6 | 138,460 | 2,233,650 | 112,838 | 2,346,488 |
| Iowa .......... | 18 (14) | 1,651,549 | 7 | 104,642 | 1,235,515 | 289,424 | 1,524,939 |
| Kansas ........ | 16 (14) | 1,440,595 | 5 | 60,607 | 1,041,470 | 153,253 | 1,194,723 |
| Kentucky ...... | 18 | 1,632,380 | 6[7] | 92,520 | 1,248,482 | 44,817 | 1,293,299 |
| Louisiana ...... | 21 | 1,633,802 | 7 | 94,549 | 1,306,286 | 54,729 | 1,361,015 |
| Maine ......... | 18 (15) | 452,083 | 7 | 29,833 | 413,878 | 13,082 | 426,960 |
| Maryland ...... | 21 | 1,611,986 | 7 | 95,761 | 1,328,139 | 33,291 | 1,361,430 |
| Massachusetts.. | 18 (16½) | 2,223,472 | 6.5 | 118,161 | 1,844,203 | 31,102 | 1,875,305 |
| Michigan ...... | 18 (14) | 4,133,428 | 6 | 209,505 | 3,527,133 | 245,921 | 3,773,054 |
| Minnesota ..... | 18 (15) | 1,996,926 | 4[7] | 107,146 | 1,521,373 | 179,933 | 1,701,306 |
| Mississippi .... | 17 | 1,012,166 | 7 | 68,834 | 918,780 | 37,266 | 956,046 |
| Missouri ....... | 16 | 2,211,187 | 5 | 105,784 | 2,019,013 | 153,975 | 2,172,988 |
| Montana ...... | 18 (13) | 451,337 | 4[6.5] | 24,556 | 340,860 | 44,078 | 384,938 |
| Nebraska ...... | 16 (14) | 887,809 | 7.5 | 56,483 | 677,564 | 88,069 | 765,633 |
| Nevada ........ | 18 (14) | 286,637 | 6 | 18,044 | 261,478 | 16,030 | 277,508 |
| New Hampshire. | 18 (16) | 348,717 | 7 | 19,850 | 276,225 | 5,639 | 281,864 |
| New Jersey .... | 17 (16) | 3,200,454 | 6 | 157,031 | 2,550,052 | 68,736 | 2,618,788 |
| New Mexico .... | 18 | 571,239 | 4[7] | 34,173 | 525,761 | 15,530 | 541,291 |
| New York ...... | 18 (16) | 6,060,491 | 6 | 290,520 | 4,841,102 | 216,528 | 5,057,630 |
| North Carolina. | 18 | 2,433,241 | 7 | 147,946 | 2,072,717 | 81,303 | 2,154,020 |
| North Dakota .. | 18 (13) | 404,886 | 6 | 22,078 | 257,952 | 113,979 | 371,931 |
| Ohio .......... | 21 (14) | 5,305,391 | 7 | 285,519 | 4,054,699 | 153,650 | 4,208,349 |
| Oklahoma ..... | 16 | 1,541,907 | 6.5 | 80,285 | 1,215,084 | 55,177 | 1,270,261 |
| Oregon ........ | 18 (14) | 1,190,006 | 4[7] | 55,873 | 933,421 | 51,977 | 985,398 |
| Pennsylvania .. | 18 (16) | 5,335,237 | 7 | 285,338 | 4,010,141 | 190,652 | 4,200,793 |
| Rhode Island .. | 18 | 434,362 | 7 | 21,718 | 300,778 | 5,866 | 306,644 |
| South Carolina. | 21 (15) | 1,180,392 | 7 | 74,840 | 1,026,233 | 39,692 | 1,065,925 |
| South Dakota .. | 18 (14) | 406,961 | 6 | 25,118 | 305,490 | 106,090 | 411,580 |
| Tennessee ..... | 21 | 1,869,918 | 7 | 116,074 | 1,606,355 | 50,725 | 1,657,080 |
| Texas ......... | 18 | 5,893,582 | 5 | 272,529 | 5,168,740 | 194,269 | 5,363,009 |
| Utah .......... | 18 | 561,585 | 6 | 28,167 | 430,666 | 27,293 | 457,959 |
| Vermont ....... | 21 (16) | 194,120 | 6.5 | 11,745 | 180,399 | 6,807 | 187,206 |
| Virginia ....... | 18 | 1,932,478 | 6[7] | 128,617 | 1,748,407 | 65,258 | 1,813,665 |
| Washington .... | 21 | 1,851,761 | 4[9] | 116,023 | 1,331,999 | 46,735 | 1,388,734 |
| West Virginia.. | 18 | 765,347 | 7 | 44,187 | 621,868 | 13,604 | 635,472 |
| Wisconsin ..... | 18 (14) | 1,954,112 | 7 | 119,874 | 1,596,723 | 129,557 | 1,726,280 |
| Wyoming ...... | 21 | 226,403 | 4[6] | 13,777 | 217,659 | 26,142 | 243,801 |
| Dist. of Col. ... | 18 | 246,712 | 7 | 16,095 | 242,146 | 3,471 | 245,617 |
| **Totals** ................ | | **96,944,876** | 7[6.47] | **5,206,734** | **77,692,650** | 8[4,229,858] | **81,922,508** |

*Figures in parentheses are age limits for junior permits, school permits or in other special situations. [1]Registrations include: Automobiles, private and commercial (including taxicabs) 80,013,724; publicly owned 400,456. Buses, private and commercial 164,670, publicly owned 839,798. Total private and commercial motor vehicles 95,531,372, publicly owned 1,413,504. Total commercial 1,934,413, publicly owned 18,609. [2]Total motor fuel consumed includes (in gallons) for private and commercial use, 80,059,523,000; for public use, 1,862,985,000. [3]Losses allowed for evaporation, handling, etc., not included in total are 677,834,000. [4]Tax rate changes in 1967 were as follows: Conn., Minn., and N. M., 6 to 7¢, July 1; Ill. 5 to 6¢, Aug. 1; Mont. 6 to 6.5¢, July 1; Ore. 6 to 7¢, Oct. 1; Wash. 7.5 to 9¢, May 1; Wyo. 5 to 6¢, May 20. [5]The state tax rate is 8¢ per gal. in Hawaii County and 5¢ in the other counties. [6]Trucks or combinations of more than two axles pay motor-fuel tax at rate of 9¢ per gallon in Kentucky and Virginia. [7]Weighted average tax rate. (For motor-fuel was 6.45¢ per gallon.) [8]Does not include an estimated 5.7 billion gallons of aviation jet fuel.

## Minimum Legal Age for Purchase of Alcoholic Beverages

Source: Distilled Spirits Institute, Inc., Washington, D. C. 20004

| State | Years | State | Years | State | Years |
|---|---|---|---|---|---|
| Alabama.......... | 21 | Kentucky............. | 21 | North Dakota........... | 21 |
| Alaska........... | 21 | Louisiana............ | 18 | Ohio (c)............... | 21 |
| Arizona.......... | 21 | Maine............... | 21 | Oklahoma (d)........... | 21 |
| Arkansas......... | 21 | Maryland............ | 21 | Oregon................ | 21 |
| California........ | 21 | Massachusetts........ | 21 | Pennsylvania.......... | 21 |
| Colorado (c)...... | 21 | Michigan............ | 21 | Rhode Island.......... | 21 |
| Connecticut...... | 21 | Minnesota........... | 21 | South Carolina (e)...... | 21 |
| Delaware......... | 21 | Mississippi (h)....... | 21 | South Dakota (g)....... | 21 |
| Dist. of Col. (b).. | 21 | Missouri............ | 21 | Tennessee............. | 21 |
| Florida.......... | 21 | Montana............ | 21 | Texas................. | 21 |
| Georgia.......... | 21 | Nebraska............ | 21 | Utah.................. | 21 |
| Hawaii........... | 20 | Nevada.............. | 21 | Vermont.............. | 21 |
| Idaho (a)........ | 21 | New Hampshire....... | 21 | Virginia (c)........... | 21 |
| Illinois.......... | 21 | New Jersey.......... | 21 | Washington........... | 21 |
| Indiana.......... | 21 | New Mexico.......... | 21 | West Virginia (c)....... | 21 |
| Iowa............ | 21 | New York............ | 18 | Wisconsin (f).......... | 21 |
| Kansas (c)....... | 21 | North Carolina (b).... | 21 | Wyoming............. | 21 |

**(a)** Beer 20. **(b)** Light wine, beer 18. **(c)** 3.2 beer 18. **(d)** 3.2 beer: male 21; female 18 off-sale, 21. **(e)** Beer and wine 18. **(f)** Beer 18. **(g)** 3.2 beer 19. **(h)** Beer not over 4% by wt. 18.

# Discoveries and Innovations in Chemistry, Physics, Biology and Medicine

| Product | Date | Discoverer | Nation |
|---|---|---|---|
| Acetylene gas | 1892 | Wilson | U. S. |
| ACTH | 1949 | Armour & Co. | U. S. |
| Adrenalin | 1901 | Takamine | Japan |
| Aluminum, electrolytic process | 1886 | Hall | U. S. |
| Analine dye | 1856 | Perkin | English |
| Aneathesia, ether | 1842 | Long | U. S. |
| Anesthesia, local | 1885 | Koller | Austria |
| Anesthesia, spinal | 1898 | Bier | German |
| Anti-rabies | 1885 | Pasteur | French |
| Antitoxin, diphtheria | 1891 | Von Behring | German |
| Antiseptic surgery | 1867 | Lister | English |
| Argyrol | | Barnes | U. S. |
| Arsphenamine | 1910 | Ehrlich | German |
| Aspirin | 1889 | Dreser | German |
| Atomic theory | 1803 | Dalton | English |
| Atom-smashing theory | 1919 | Rutherford | English |
| Atabrine | | Mietzsch, et al | German |
| Aureomycin | 1948 | Duggar | U. S. |
| Azo dyes | | Mietzsch, Klarer | German |
| Bacitracin | 1945 | Johnson et al. | U. S. |
| Barbital | 1903 | Fischer | German |
| BCG | 1920 | Calmette, Guerin | French |
| Beatron | 1940 | Kerst, D. W. | U. S. |
| Biotin | 1936 | Kogl, Tonnies | German |
| Bleaching powder | 1798 | Tennant | English |
| Bordeaux mixture | 1885 | Millardet | French |
| Bromine from sea | 1924 | Edgar-Kramer | U. S. |
| Calcium carbide | 1888 | Wilson | U. S. |
| Carbon oxides | 1925 | Fisher | German |
| Carbomycin | 1952 | Tanner | U. S. |
| Camphor synthetic | 1896 | Haller | French |
| Chlorine | 1810 | Davy | English |
| Chloroform | 1831 | Guthrie, S. | U. S. |
| Chloromycetin | 1947 | Burkholder | U. S |
| Cocaine | 1860 | Niemann | German |
| Contebea | 1950 | Behmisch, Mietzsch, Domagh | German |
| Cortisone | 1936 | Kendall | U. S. |
| Cortisone, synthesis | 1946 | Sarett | U. S. |
| Cyanide | 1905 | Caro, Frank | German |
| Cyclotron | 1930 | Lawrence | U. S. |
| DDT | 1874 | Zeidler | German |
| (Not applied as insecticide until 1939) | | | |
| Deuterium (heavy hydrogen) | 1932 | Urey, Brickwedde, Murphy | U. S. |
| DNA (structure) | 1951 | Crick | English |
| | | Watson | U. S. |
| | | Wilkins | English |
| Electric waves | 1888 | Hertz | German |
| Electrolysis | 1852 | Faraday | English |
| Electron | 1897 | Thomson, J. | English |
| Electron diffraction | 1936 | Thomson, G. | English |
| | | Davisson | U. S. |
| Electron spectrometer | 1944 | Deutsch, Elliott, Evans | U. S. |
| Electroshock treatment | 1938 | Cerletti, Bini. | Italy |
| Electrostatic generator | 1929 | VanGraff, de | U. S. |
| Erythromycin | 1952 | McGuire | U. S. |
| Evolution, natural selection | 1858 | Darwin | English |
| Gold (cyanide process for extraction) | 1887 | MacArthur-Forest | British |
| Gravitation, law | 1687 | Newton | English |
| Human heart transplant | 1967 | Barnard | S. Africa |
| Indigo, synthesis of | 1880 | Baeyer | German |
| Insulin | 1922 | Banting, Best, MacLeod | Canada |

| Product | Date | Discoverer | Nation |
|---|---|---|---|
| Isoniazid | 1952 | Hoffman-La-Roche | U. S. |
| | | Domagh | German |
| Laser (light amplification by stimulated emission of radiation) | 1958 | Townes, Schawlow | U. S. |
| Lithography | 1796 | Senefelder | Bohemia |
| Lobotomy | 1935 | Egas Moniz | Portugal |
| LSD-25 | 1943 | Hoffman | Swiss |
| Methanol | 1925 | Patard | French |
| Milk condensation | 1853 | Borden | U. S. |
| Motion, laws of | 1687 | Newton | English |
| Neomycin | 1949 | Waksman & Lechevalier | U. S. |
| Neutron | 1932 | Chadwick | English |
| Nitric acid | 1648 | Glauber | German |
| Nitric oxide | 1772 | Priestley | English |
| Nitroglycerin | 1846 | Sobrero | Italian |
| Oil cracking process | 1891 | Dewar | English |
| Oxygen | 1774 | Priestley | English |
| Paper, from wood pulp, sulfate process | 1884 | Dahl | German |
| Paper, sulfite process | 1867 | Tilghman | U. S. |
| Penicillin | 1929 | Alex. Fleming | English |
| Practical use | 1941 | Florey-Chain | English |
| Plutonium fission | 1940 | Kennedy, J.W. | U. S. |
| | | Wahl, A. C. | U. S. |
| | | Seaborg, G.T. | U. S. |
| | | Segre, Emilio | U. S. |
| Polymixin | 1947 | Ainsworth | English |
| Protargol | 1882 | Neisser | German |
| Proton | 1919 | Rutherford | English |
| Quantum theory | 1900 | Planck | German |
| Quinine-synthetic | 1918 | Rabe | German |
| Radioactivity | 1896 | Becquerel | French |
| Radioactivity counter | 1908 | Rutherford, Geiger | English |
| Radium | 1898 | Curie, Pierre | French |
| Radium | 1898 | Curie, Marie | Polish |
| Relativity theory | 1905 | Einstein | German |
| Reserpine | 1949 | Jal Vakil | India |
| Salvarsan (606) | 1910 | Ehrlich | German |
| Streptomycin | 1945 | Waksman | U. S. |
| Sulfanilamide theory | 1908 | Gelmo | German |
| Sulfanilamide | 1934 | Domagh | German |
| Sulfadiazine | 1940 | Roblin | U. S. |
| Sulfapyridine | 1938 | Ewins Phelps | English |
| Sulfathiazole | | Fosbinder, Walter | U. S. |
| Sulfuric acid | 1831 | Phillips | English |
| Sulfuric acid, lead | 1746 | Roebuck | English |
| Terramycin | 1950 | Finlay, et al | U. S. |
| Tuberculin | 1890 | Koch | German |
| Uranium fission (theory) | 1939 | Hahn, Strassmann | German |
| | | Bohr | Danish |
| | | Einstein | Italian |
| | | Fermi | Italian |
| | | Pegram | U. S. |
| | | Wheeler | U. S. |
| Uranium fission, atomic reactor | 1942 | Enrico Fermi | Italian |
| | | Leo Szilard | U. S. |
| Vaccine, measles | 1954 | Enders, John | U. S. |
| | | Peebles, T. | U. S. |
| Vaccine, polio | 1955 | Sabin, Alb. E. | U. S. |
| Vaccine, polio | 1953 | Salk, Jonas E. | U. S. |
| Vaccine, smallpox | 1796 | Jenner, Edw. | English |
| Vaccine, typhus | 1909 | Nicolle, J. | French |
| Vitamin A | 1913 | McCollum | |
| | | Davis | U. S. |
| Vitamin B | 1916 | McCollum | U. S. |
| Vitamin C | 1912 | Holst, Froelich | Norway |
| Vitamin D | 1922 | McCollum | U. S. |
| Xerography | 1938 | Carlson | U. S. |

# Great Inventions and Scientific Discoveries

| Invention | Date | Inventor | Nation |
|---|---|---|---|
| Adding machine | 1642 | Pascal | French |
| Adding machine | 1885 | Burroughs | U. S. |
| Addressograph | 1892 | Duncan | U. S. |
| Air brake | 1868 | Westinghouse | U. S. |
| Air conditioning | 1911 | Carrier | U. S. |
| Airplane, experim'tal | 1896 | Langley | U. S. |
| Airplane, jet engine | 1930 | Whittle | British |
| Airplane with motor | 1903 | Orville and Wilbur Wright | U. S. |
| Airplane, hydro | 1910 | Fabre, Henri | French |
| Airplane, hydro | 1911 | Curtiss | U S |
| Airplane engine, super-charger | 1917 | Moss | U. S |
| Airship | 1852 | Giffard | French |
| Airship, non-rigid dirigible | 1898 | Santos Dumont | Brazil |

| Invention | Date | Inventor | Nation |
|---|---|---|---|
| Airship, rigid dirigible | 1900 | Zeppelin | German |
| Arc tube | 1923 | Alexanderson Sleplan-Ludwig | U. S. |
| Arc tube, immersion igniter | 1932 | | U. S. |
| Autogyro | 1920 | de la Cierva | Spanish |
| Automatic ry motors | 1904 | Westinghouse | U. S. |
| Automobile, differential gear | 1885 | Benz | German |
| Automobile, electric | 1892 | Morrison | U. S. |
| Automobile, exper | 1875 | Marcus | Austrian |
| Automobile, gasoline | 1887 | Daimler | German |
| Automobile, gasoline | 1892-1893 | Duryea, C. E. (See note) | U. S. |
| Automobile, gasoline | 1894 | Krebs | German |
| Automobile, gasoline | 1895 | Selden | U S |
| Automobile, magneto | 1899 | Daimler | German |

| Invention | Date | Inventor | Nation |
|---|---|---|---|
| Automobile, muffler | .... | Maxim, H. P. | U. S. |
| Automobile, self-star. | 1911 | Kettering.... | U. S. |
| Automobile, steam... | 1889 | Roper....... | U. S. |
| Babbitt metal....... | 1839 | Babbitt...... | U. S. |
| Bakelite........... | 1907 | Baekeland... | Belg. U.S. |
| Balloon............ | 1783 | Montgolfier.. | French |
| Barometer.......... | 1643 | Torricelli.... | Italian |
| Bicycle, modern.... | 1884 | Starley...... | English |
| Bicycle, safety..... | 1886 | Pope........ | U. S. |
| Bifocal lens........ | 1780 | Franklin..... | U. S. |
| Block signals, railway | 1867 | Hall........ | U. S. |
| Bomb, depth........ | 1903 | Unge ....... | Swedish |
| Bomb, depth........ | 1916 | Tait........ | U. S. |
| Bottle machine..... | 1903 | Owens...... | U. S. |
| Braille printing...... | 1829 | Braille...... | French |
| Burner, gas........ | 1855 | Bunsen..... | German |
| Camera, Polaroid Land | 1948 | Land....... | U. S. |
| Car coupler........ | 1873 | Janney..... | U. S. |
| Carburetor, gasoline.. | 1876 | Daimler..... | German |
| Card time recorder... | 1894 | Cooper...... | U. S. |
| Carding machine.... | 1797 | Whittemore.. | U. S. |
| Carpet sweeper...... | 1876 | Bissell...... | U. S. |
| Cash register....... | 1879 | Ritty....... | U. S. |
| Cellophane.......... | 1900 | Brandenberger | Swiss |
| Celluloid........... | 1870 | Hyatt....... | U. S. |
| Cement, Portland.... | 1845 | Aspdin...... | English |
| Circuit breaker...... | 1925 | Hilliard..... | U. S. |
| Clock, pendulum.... | 1657 | Huygens.... | Dutch |
| Coaxial cable system. | 1929 | Affel & Espenched. | U. S. |
| Coke oven.......... | 1893 | Hoffman.... | Austrian |
| Collar, paper....... | 1854 | Hunt....... | U. S. |
| Comptometer....... | 1887 | Felt........ | U. S. |
| Computer, automatic sequence......... | 1939 | Aiken et al. | U. S. |
| Condenser microphone (telephone).. | 1920 | Wente...... | U. S. |
| Cotton gin......... | 1793 | Whitney.... | U. S. |
| Cream separator.... | 1880 | DeLaval.... | Swedish |
| Cultivator, disc.... | 1878 | Mallon..... | U. S. |
| Cystoscope......... | 1877 | Nitze....... | German |
| Dental plate, rubber. | 1855 | Goodyear.... | U. S. |
| Dial recorder....... | 1889 | Day........ | U. S. |
| Diesel engine....... | 1895 | Diesel...... | German |
| Dynamite.......... | 1866 | Nobel....... | Swedish |
| Dynamo, continuous current | 1860 | Picinotti.... | Italian |
| Dynamo, cont. cur... | 1870 | Gramme.... | Belgian |
| Dynamo, hydrogen cooled | 1915 | Schuler..... | U. S. |
| Dynamo, electric machine modulator | 1939 | Alexanderson Edwards.... | U. S. |
| Dynamo, high freq.... | .... | Thomson.... | English |
| Electric battery.... | 1800 | Volta...... | Italian |
| Electric ship power... | 1913 | Emmet..... | U. S. |
| Electrocardiograph.. | 1903 | Einthoven.. | Dutch |
| Electroencephalograph. | 1929 | Berger..... | German |
| Electromagnet...... | 1824 | Sturgeon.... | English |
| Electron tube multigrid.. | 1913 | Langmuir.... | U. S. |
| Electroplating...... | 1805 | Brugnatelli.. | Italian |
| Elevator, brake..... | 1852 | Otis........ | U. S. |
| Elevator, push button | 1922 | Larson...... | U. S. |
| Engine, automobile.. | 1879 | Benz....... | German |
| Engine, coal-gas.... | 1867 | Otto....... | German |
| Engine, gasoline.... | 1872 | Brayton, Geo | U. S. |
| Engine, gasoline.... | 1891 | Levassor.... | French |
| Engine, gas, compound | 1926 | Eickemeyer... | U. S. |
| Engine, coal-gas 4 cycle | 1877 | Otto....... | German |
| Engine, compression ignition........ | 1883 | Daimler.... | German |
| Engine, electric igni. | 1880 | Benz....... | German |
| Engine, gasoline.... | 1886 | Daimler.... | German |
| Engine, gas vacuum.. | 1823 | Brown...... | English |
| Engine, steam, piston | 1705 | Newcomen... | English |
| Engine, steam, piston | 1769 | Watt....... | Scottish |
| Engine, steam, comp'd | 1781 | Hornblower.. | English |
| Engine, high pressure. | 1799 | Evans...... | U. S. |
| Engraving, half-tone. | 1893 | Ives....... | U. S. |
| Filament, tungsten... | 1915 | Langmuir.... | U. S. |
| Furnace, for steel.... | 1861 | Siemens.... | German |
| Galvanometer...... | 1820 | Swelgger.... | German |
| Gas discharge tube... | 1922 | Hull........ | U. S. |
| Gas lighting........ | 1792 | Murdoch.... | Scottish |
| Gas mantle......... | 1885 | Welsbach.... | Austrian |
| Gasoline, (lead ethyl) | 1922 | Midgley..... | U. S. |
| Gasoline cracked.... | 1913 | Burton, W.M. | U. S. |
| Gasoline, high octane. | 1930 | Ipatieff..... | Russian |
| Geiger counter...... | 1913 | Geiger...... | German |
| Glass, laminated.... | 1909 | Benedictus... | French |
| Gun, breechloader.... | 1811 | Thornton.... | U. S. |
| Gun, Browning...... | 1916 | Browning.... | U. S. |
| Gun, magazine...... | 1875 | Hotchkiss.... | U. S. |
| Gun sight, telescopic. | 1891 | Fiske....... | U. S. |
| Gun, silencer....... | 1909 | Maxim, H. P. | U. S. |
| Guncotton.......... | 1846 | Schoenbein.. | German |
| Gyroscope.......... | 1852 | Foucault.... | French |
| Gyrocompass....... | 1911 | Sperry...... | U. S. |
| Harvester.......... | 1836 | Moore...... | U. S. |
| Harvester-Thresher.. | 1888 | Matteson.... | U. S. |
| Helicopter.......... | 1916 | Brennan.... | English |
| Helicopter.......... | 1939 | Sikorsky.... | U. S. |
| Ice-making machine.. | 1851 | Gorrie...... | U. S. |
| Kaleidoscope........ | 1817 | Brewster.... | English |
| Kinetoscope......... | 1887 | Edison...... | U. S. |
| Kodak............. | 1888 | Eastman-Walker... | U. S. |
| Lacquer, nitrocellu... | 1921 | Flaherty.... | U. S. |
| Lamp, arc......... | 1879 | Brush...... | U. S. |
| Lamp, incandescent. | 1879 | Edison...... | U. S. |
| Lamp, incand., frosted | 1924 | Pipkin...... | U. S. |
| Lamp, incand., gas.. | 1916 | Langmuir.... | U. S. |
| Lamp, Kliez...... | 1911 | Kliegl, A.& J. | U. S. |
| Lamp, mercury vapor | 1912 | Hewitt...... | U. S. |
| Lamp, miner's safety. | 1816 | Davy....... | English |
| Lamp, Neon........ | 1915 | Claude...... | French |
| Lathe, turret....... | 1845 | Fitch....... | U. S. |
| Launderette........ | 1934 | Cantrell..... | U. S. |
| Lens, achromatic.... | 1758 | Dolland..... | English |
| Lens, fused bifocal... | 1924 | Drescher.... | U. S. |
| Lens, fused bifocal... | 1908 | Borsch..... | U. S. |
| Leydenjar (condenser) | 1745 | von Kleist... | German |
| Lightning rod....... | 1752 | Franklin.... | U. S. |
| Linoleum.......... | 1860 | Walton..... | English |
| Linotype.......... | 1885 | Mergenthaler | U. S. |
| Locomotive, electric.. | 1851 | Vail........ | U. S. |
| Locomotive, exper... | 1801 | Trevithick... | English |
| Locomotive, exper... | 1812 | Fenton et al. | English |
| Locomotive, exper... | 1813 | Hedley...... | English |
| Locomotive, exper... | 1814 | Stephenson.. | English |
| Locomotive, prac'l... | 1829 | Stephenson.. | English |
| Locomotive, 1st U.S. | 1830 | Cooper, P.... | U. S. |
| Loom, power....... | 1785 | Cartwright.. | English |
| Loudspeaker, dynamic | 1924 | Rice-Kellogg. | U. S. |
| Machine gun....... | 1861 | Gatling..... | U. S. |
| Machine gun, imprvd | 1872 | Hotchkiss.... | U. S. |
| Machine gun (Maxim) | 1883 | Maxim, H. S. | Eng.-U.S. |
| Magnet, electro.... | 1828 | Henry...... | U. S. |
| Mantle, gas........ | 1885 | Welsbach.... | Austrian |
| Mason jar......... | 1858 | Mason, J.... | U. S. |
| Match, friction..... | 1827 | John Walker. | English |
| Match, phosphorus.. | 1831 | Sauria...... | French |
| Match, phosphorus.. | 1836 | Phillips..... | U. S. |
| Mercerized textiles.. | 1843 | Mercer, J.... | English |
| Meter, induction.... | 1888 | Shallenberger | U. S. |
| Meter, parking..... | 1935 | Magee...... | U. S. |
| Micrometer........ | 1636 | Gascoigne... | English |
| Microphone........ | 1877 | Berliner..... | U. S. |
| Microscope compound | 1590 | Janssen..... | Dutch |
| Microscope, electron. | 1931 | Knoll-Ruska. | German |
| Monitor, warship... | 1861 | Ericsson..... | U. S. |
| Monotype......... | 1887 | Lanston..... | U. S. |
| Motor, AC......... | 1892 | Tesla....... | U. S. |
| Motor, induction.... | 1888 | Tesla....... | U. S. |
| Motor, AC, railway.. | 1933 | Jungk...... | U. S. |
| Motor, rotary...... | 1907 | Ocenasek ... | Czech |
| Motor, induction.... | 1887 | Tesla....... | U. S. |
| Motorcycle......... | 1885 | Daimler..... | German |
| Movie machine..... | 1893 | Edison...... | U. S. |
| Movie machine..... | 1895 | Lumière,.... | French |
| Movie machine..... | 1894 | Jenkins..... | U. S. |
| Movie, panoramic .. | 1952 | Waller...... | U. S. |
| Movie, talking..... | 1927 | Warner Bros. | U. S. |
| Mower, lawn....... | 1868 | Hills....... | U. S. |
| Mowing machine.... | 1831 | Manning.... | U. S. |
| Neoprene.......... | 1930 | Carothers.... | U. S. |
| Nylon synthetic.... | 1930 | Carothers.... | U. S. |
| Nylon............. | 1937 | Du Pont lab. | U. S. |
| Oil cracking furnace.. | 1891 | Gavrilov.... | Russian |
| Oil filled power cable. | 1921 | Emanueli.... | Italian |
| Oleomargarine..... | 1868 | Mege-Mouriès | French |
| Ophthalmoscope.... | 1851 | Helmholtz... | German |
| Paper machine..... | 1809 | Dickinson.... | U. S. |
| Parachute......... | 1785 | Blanchard... | French |
| Pen, ballpoint..... | 1888 | Loud....... | U. S. |
| Pen, fountain...... | 1884 | Waterman... | U. S. |
| Pen, fountain...... | 1885 | Wirt....... | U. S. |
| Pen, steel......... | 1780 | Harrison.... | English |
| Pendulum......... | 1581 | Galileo..... | Italian |
| Phonograph....... | 1877 | Edison...... | U. S. |
| Photo, color....... | 1892 | Ives....... | U. S. |
| Photo, color, controlled penetration. | 1928 | Mannes-Godowsky. | U. S. |
| Photo, 3-color screen.. | 1904 | Lumière, L.. | French |
| Photo film, celluloid. | 1887 | Goodwin.... | U. S. |
| Photo film, transparent.......... | 1888 | Eastman-Goodwin.. | U. S. |
| Photographic paper.. | 1898 | Baekeland... | U. S. |
| Photography....... | 1826 | Niepce, Sr... | French |
| Photography....... | 1835 | Fox-Talbot.. | English |
| Photography....... | 1837 | Daguerre.... | French |
| Photography....... | 1839 | Niepce, Jr.. | French |
| Photophone........ | 1880 | Bell........ | U. S. |
| Phototelegraphy.... | 1925 | Bell lab..... | U. S. |
| Piano............. | 1709 | Cristofori... | Italian |
| Piano player....... | 1863 | Fourneaux... | French |
| Pin, safety........ | 1849 | Hunt....... | U. S. |
| Pistol (revolver).... | 1835 | Colt....... | U. S. |
| Plow, cast iron..... | 1797 | Newbold.... | U. S. |
| Plow, disc........ | 1896 | Hardy...... | U. S. |
| Plow, standard..... | 1819 | Wood...... | U. S. |
| Pneumatic hammer.. | 1890 | King....... | U. S. |
| Powder, smokeless... | 1863 | Schultze.... | German |
| Powder, smokeless... | 1884 | Vieille..... | French |
| Printing, color...... | 1457 | J. Fust, P. Schoeffer.. | German |
| Printing press, rotary | 1846 | Hoe........ | U. S. |
| Printing press, web.. | 1865 | Bullock..... | U. S. |

| Invention | Date | Inventor | Nation | Invention | Date | Inventor | Nation |
|---|---|---|---|---|---|---|---|
| Propeller, screw.... | 1804 | Stevens..... | U. S. | Steel, manganese.... | 1884 | Hadfield.... | English |
| Propeller, screw.... | 1837 | Ericsson.... | Swedish | Steel, stainless...... | 1916 | Brearley.... | English |
| Punch card account'g. | 1884 | Hollerith.... | U. S. | Stereoscope........ | 1838 | Wheatstone.. | English |
| Radar............. | 1922 | Taylor and Young.... | U. S. | Stethoscope....... | 1819 | Laennec.... | French |
| Radio amplifier...... | 1907 | De Forest.... | U. S. | Stethoscope, binaural. | 1840 | Cammann.... | U. S. |
| Radio beacon....... | 1928 | Donovan.... | U. S. | Submarine........ | 1891 | Holland..... | U. S. |
| Radio broadcaster... | 1902 | Stubblefield... | U. S. | Submarine, even keel. | 1894 | Lake...... | U. S. |
| Radio crystal oscillat. | 1918 | Nicolson.... | U. S. | Submarine, torpedo.. | 1776 | Bushnell.... | U. S. |
| Radiometer........ | | Crookes..... | English | Tank, military...... | 1914 | Swinton.... | English |
| Radio receiver cascade tuning....... | 1913 | Alexanderson | U. S. | Telegraph, duplex.... | 1853 | Ginti..... | Austrian |
| | | | | Telegraph,electromag. | 1836 | Wheatstone.. | English |
| Radio receiver, heterodyne......... | 1913 | Fessenden.. | U. S. | Telegraph, magnetic.. | 1837 | Morse..... | U. S. |
| Radio transmitter triode modulation.. | 1914 | Alexanderson. | U. S. | Telegraph,quadruplex | 1874 | Edison..... | U. S. |
| Radio tube-diode.... | 1905 | Fleming.... | English | Telegraph, wireless, high frequency.... | 1896 | Marconi..... | Italian |
| Radio tube oscillator. | 1915 | De Forest... | U. S. | Telegraph, wireless, low frequency..... | 1895 | Preece..... | English |
| Radio tube triode... | 1907 | De Forest... | U. S. | Telephone........ | 1876 | Bell...... | U. S. |
| Radio, signals...... | 1895 | Marconi.... | Italian | Telephone amplifier.. | 1912 | De Forest... | U. S. |
| Radio, magnetic detector........ | 1902 | Marconi..... | Italian | Telephone, automatic | 1891 | Strowger.... | U. S. |
| | | | | Telephone, filter..... | 1911 | Campbell.... | U. S. |
| Radio, horizontal direction aerial.... | 1905 | Marconi..... | Italian | Telephone, radio.... | 1902 | Poulsen and Fessenden. | U. S. |
| Radio FM 2-path.... | 1929 | Armstrong.... | U. S. | Telephone, radio..... | 1906 | De Forest... | U. S. |
| Radio FM phase shift | 1930 | Armstrong.... | U. S. | Telephone, radio, l. d. | 1915 | Am. T. & T.. | U. S. |
| Radio FM wide band. | 1932 | Armstrong.... | U. S. | Telephone, recording. | 1898 | Poulson.... | Danish |
| Radio FM multiplex. | 1934 | Armstrong.... | U. S. | Telephone, wireless... | 1899 | Collins..... | U. S. |
| Radio HF transmitter | 1903 | Poulson..... | Danish | Telescope......... | 1608 | Lippershey... | Neth. |
| Rayon............ | 1883 | Swan...... | English | Telescope......... | 1609 | Galileo..... | Italian |
| Rayon acetate....... | 1895 | Cross-Bevan. | English | Telescope, Astron.... | 1611 | Kepler..... | German |
| Rayon cuprammonia. | 1890 | Duplesses... | French | Teletype......... | 1928 | Morkrum-Kleinschmidt | U. S. |
| Rayon (introcellulose) | 1884 | Chardonnet.. | French | Television......... | 1926 | Baird...... | Scottish |
| Rayon (viscose).... | 1892 | Cross-Bevan. | English | Television......... | 1934 | V. Zworykin.. | U. S. |
| Razor, electric...... | 1895 | Schick..... | U. S. | Television, iconoscope | 1934 | P. Farnsworth | U. S. |
| Razor, safety....... | 1895 | Gillette.... | U. S. | Television......... | 1944 | Baird...... | Scottish |
| Reaper.......... | 1834 | McCormick.. | U. S. | Thermometer....... | 1593 | Galileo..... | Italian |
| Record, cylinder.... | 1887 | Bell-Tainter.. | U. S. | Thermometer....... | 1710 | Reaumur.... | French |
| Record, disc....... | 1887 | Berliner.... | U. S. | Thermometer, merc.. | 1714 | Fahrenheit.. | German |
| Record, long playing. | 1948 | Goldmark... | U. S. | Time recorder...... | 1890 | Bundy..... | U. S. |
| Record, wax cylinder | 1888 | Edison..... | U. S. | Time,self-regulator.. | 1918 | Bryce..... | U. S. |
| Refrigerants, low-boiling fluorine comp.. | 1930 | Midgeley and co-workers. | U. S. | Tire, bicycle....... | 1889 | Dunlop..... | Irish |
| | | | | Tire, double-tube.... | 1845 | Thompson... | English |
| Refrigerator car.... | 1868 | David..... | U. S. | Tire, pneumatic..... | 1888 | Dunlop..... | Irish |
| Resin, synthetic.... | 1931 | Hill...... | English | Tool, pneumatic..... | 1865 | Law...... | English |
| Rocket engine...... | 1929 | R.H.Goddard | U. S. | Torpedo.......... | 1866 | Whitehead... | English |
| Rubber, vulcanized.. | 1839 | Goodyear.... | U. S. | Torpedo, dirigible.... | 1876 | Brennan.... | English |
| Saw, band........ | 1808 | Newberry.... | English | Torpedo, marine.... | 1804 | Fulton..... | U. S. |
| Saw, circular...... | 1777 | Miller...... | English | Torpedo, radio...... | 1897 | Fiske..... | U. S. |
| Searchlight, arc..... | 1915 | Sperry..... | U. S. | Torpedo, remote cont. | 1895 | Hammond.... | U. S. |
| Sewing machine..... | 1846 | Howe...... | U. S. | Torpedo, self-propell. | 1868 | Whitehead... | English |
| Shoe-sewing machine | 1860 | McKay..... | U. S. | Tractor, caterpillar.. | 1900 | Holt...... | U. S. |
| Shuttle, flying..... | 1733 | Kay...... | English | Transformer, A.C.... | 1885 | Stanley.... | U. S. |
| Sleeping-car....... | 1858 | Pullman.... | U. S. | Transistor......... | 1947 | Shockley, Brattain, Bardeen... | U. S. |
| Folding upper berth, 1864; diner; 1868; chair car. 1875; vestibule, 1887 | | | | | | | |
| Soap, hardwater.... | 1928 | Bertsch..... | German | Trolley car, electric.. | 1884 -87 | Van Depoel & Sprague. | U. S. |
| Spectroscope....... | 1859 | Kirchoff-Bunsen.... | German | Tungsten (drawn) filament lamp....... | 1913 | Coolidge.... | U. S. |
| Spectroscope (mass).. | 1918 | Dempster.... | U. S. | Tungsten, ductile.... | 1912 | Coolidge.... | U. S. |
| Spinning jenny..... | 1767 | Hargreaves.. | English | Turbine, gas....... | 1899 | C. G. Curtis.. | U. S. |
| Steamboat, exp'mt'l. | 1783 | Jouffroy.... | French | Turbine, hydraulic... | 1849 | Francis..... | U. S. |
| Steamboat, exp'mt'l. | 1785 | Fitch...... | U. S. | Turbine, steam..... | 1896 | C. G. Curtis.. | U. S. |
| Steamboat, exp'mt'l. | 1787 | Rumsey..... | U. S. | Type, movable..... | 1450 | Gutenberg... | German |
| Steamboat, exp'mt'l. | 1788 | Miller...... | Scot. | Typewriter........ | 1868 | Sholes and Gidden... | U. S. |
| Steamboat, exp'mt'l. | 1803 | Fulton..... | U. S. | Welding, atomic hydrogen........ | 1924 | Langmuir-Palmer.... | U. S. |
| Steamboat, exp'mt'l. | 1804 | Stevens..... | U. S. | Welding, electric.... | 1877 | Thomson.... | U. S. |
| Steamboat, practical. | 1802 | Symington... | Scot. | Wind tunnel....... | 1923 | Munk...... | U. S. |
| Steamboat, practical. | 1807 | Fulton..... | U. S. | Wire, barbed...... | 1874 | Gidden.... | U. S. |
| Steam car........ | 1770 | Cugnot..... | French | Wire, barbed...... | 1875 | Haish..... | U. S. |
| Steam turbine...... | 1884 | Parsons..... | English | X-ray........... | 1895 | Roentgen... | German |
| Steel........... | 1856 | Bessemer.... | English | X-ray tube........ | 1916 | Coolidge.... | U. S. |
| Steel........... | 1857 | Kelly...... | U. S. | Zipper.......... | 1891 | Judson..... | U. S. |
| Steel alloy........ | 1891 | Harvey..... | U. S. | | | | |
| Steel alloy, high-speed | 1901 | Taylor-White. | U. S. | | | | |
| Steel, electric...... | 1900 | Heroult..... | French | | | | |

## Details of Famous Inventions

**Automobile.** Charles E. Duryea declared he operated the first successful American automobile in Springfield, Mass., Apr. 19, 1892. His brother, J. Frank Duryea, said he made essential contributions to the car and that it did not run until Sept., 1893. Practical patent was granted to C. E. Duryea June 11, 1895. Supplementary patents were granted to Charles and also to J. Frank Duryea.

**Broadcasting.** A plaque at the Univ. of Wisconsin, Madison, Wis., says the oldest broadcasting station is WHA, which as 9XM began scheduled broadcasts in 1919. Originator was Earle M. Terry (1879-1929).

**Radar.** Principle recognized in 1922 by Dr. A. Hoyt Taylor and Leo C. Young, U. S. Naval Research Aircraft Laboratory, Washington, D. C. The Navy ordered radar for ships, 1936. First vessel to use it was U. S. S. New York, 1938. Radar recorded coming of Japanese planes at Pearl Harbor, but no hostile mission was suspected. During the 1930s the British, alerted by the Taylor-Young experiments, independently developed radar, which they called radio-location.

**Rockets.** Dr. Robert H. Goddard (1882-1945) proved practicality of rockets Mar. 16, 1926, at Auburn, Mass. He obtained 20 patents on rockets and missiles and the U. S. Government Aug. 5, 1960 paid his heir, Mrs. Goddard, and the D. & F. Guggenheim Foundation, $1,000,000 for patent infringements. He was first to launch a liquid-fuel rocket. Two of his engine inventions are in use. Rocket invention also is credited to Hermann Oberth, German, and Konstantin Tsiolkovski, Russian.

**Television.** Developed in the 1930s in laboratories, principal patents going to Vladimir Zworykin and Philo Farnsworth, who developed it independently. Authorized by Federal Communications Commission, July 1, 1941. There were five months of telecasting to about 10,000 sets before Pearl Harbor. First commercial TV from Empire State Bldg., New York, 1941. First stations were WNBT (NBC, New York), WCBW (CBS, New York) and Dumont. The image orthicon pick-up tube was developed by RCA in 1946. J. L. Baird, British inventor, completed his telechrome for color television in 1944. In the United States Peter C. Goldmark made contributions to color TV. CBS demonstrated a color system in 1946. RCA in 1947. The first color broadcast of any duration was a one-hour program by CBS June 25, 1951, over a network. Alfred C. Schroeder, of RCA laboratory at Penns Neck, N. J., received a patent for a tri-color tube in March, 1952, and assigned it to RCA.

# MANUFACTURES AND MINERALS
## General Statistics for Major Industry Groups
### Source: Bureau of the Census

The estimates for 1966 in the following table are based upon reports from a representative sample of about 60,000 manufacturing establishments.

| Industry | All employees | | Production workers | | | Value added by mf'r adjusted $1,000 |
|---|---|---|---|---|---|---|
| | Number | Payroll $1,000 | Number | Man-hours 1,000 | Wages $1,000 | |
| Food and kindred products.......... | 1,642,145 | 9,542,146 | 1,097,657 | 2,239,475 | 5,675,932 | 24,895,940 |
| Tobacco manufactures............... | 72,363 | 356,171 | 64,092 | 122,284 | 289,448 | 1,871,980 |
| Textile mill products............... | 927,339 | 4,243,454 | 827,992 | 1,728,234 | 3,445,904 | 8,028,374 |
| Apparel and related products........ | 1,359,833 | 5,177,084 | 1,202,187 | 2,213,143 | 4,037,772 | 9,220,536 |
| Lumber and wood products.......... | 569,837 | 2,688,677 | 504,183 | 1,012,959 | 2,210,641 | 4,788,595 |
| Furniture and fixtures.............. | 428,125 | 2,185,959 | 360,298 | 734,026 | 1,619,659 | 3,978,170 |
| Paper and allied products.......... | 633,939 | 4,235,900 | 503,173 | 1,075,645 | 3,070,801 | 9,417,167 |
| Printing and publishing............ | 1,017,581 | 6,751,066 | 619,129 | 1,208,749 | 3,831,543 | 13,264,493 |
| Chemicals and allied products....... | 822,491 | 6,130,407 | 528,551 | 1,077,548 | 3,400,854 | 22,812,263 |
| Petroleum and coal products........ | 140,765 | 1,128,036 | 99,900 | 198,001 | 741,676 | 4,736,880 |
| Rubber and plastics products,[3]..... | 491,823 | 3,072,031 | 390,587 | 802,939 | 2,174,282 | 6,277,082 |
| Leather and leather products........ | 341,078 | 1,426,049 | 303,116 | 574,402 | 1,125,309 | 2,480,757 |
| Stone, clay and glass products....... | 618,550 | 3,837,514 | 491,924 | 998,856 | 2,811,708 | 8,494,586 |
| Primary metal industries............ | 1,296,541 | 9,913,533 | 1,065,737 | 2,191,793 | 7,650,316 | 20,907,888 |
| Fabricated metal products.......... | 1,252,294 | 8,244,878 | 984,127 | 2,077,026 | 5,762,428 | 15,791,932 |
| Machinery, except electrical........ | 1,804,255 | 13,473,873 | 1,310,228 | 2,796,547 | 8,846,358 | 27,040,990 |
| Electrical machinery............... | 1,814,302 | 11,988,113 | 1,298,291 | 2,648,286 | 7,249,270 | 23,543,922 |
| Transportation equipment.......... | 1,890,397 | 15,454,072 | 1,406,012 | 3,032,838 | 10,314,801 | 29,250,179 |
| Instruments and related products.... | 362,504 | 2,521,401 | 249,278 | 491,863 | 1,437,594 | 5,844,992 |
| Miscellaneous manufacturing........ | 418,563 | 2,152,714 | 342,769 | 665,693 | 1,463,329 | 4,394,390 |
| Ordnance and accessories[1]......... | 300,528 | 2,395,173 | 161,162 | 329,979 | 1,123,761 | 3,972,787 |
| Administrative and auxiliary[2]...... | 860,744 | 8,540,533 | — | — | — | — |
| **All industries total............** | **19,065,997** | **125,458,784** | **13,810,393** | **28,220,286** | **78,283,386** | **251,013,903** |

[1]Includes data for privately owned or operated establishments. Government-owned and operated establishments are excluded.

[2]In addition to the employment and payroll for operating manufacturing establishments, manufacturing concerns reported separately for central administrative offices or auxiliary units (e.g., research laboratories, storage warehouses, power plants, garages, repair shops, etc.) which serve the manufacturing establishments of a company rather than the general public.

[3]Not elsewhere classified.

## Manufacturing Production Worker Statistics
### Source: Bureau of Labor Statistics, U. S. Dept. of Labor

| Year and month | All Employees number | Production and related workers | | | | |
|---|---|---|---|---|---|---|
| | | Number | Payroll Index 1957-59=100 | Average weekly earnings | Average weekly hours | Average hourly earnings |
| 1950................. | 15,241,000 | 12,523,000 | 69.9 | $58.32 | 45.5 | $1.44 |
| 1955................. | 16,882,000 | 13,288,000 | 94.8 | 75.70 | 40.7 | 1.86 |
| 1960................. | 16,796,000 | 12,586,000 | 106.7 | 89.72 | 39.7 | 2.26 |
| 1961................. | 16,326,000 | 12,083,000 | 105.4 | 92.34 | 39.8 | 2.32 |
| 1962................. | 16,853,000 | 12,488,000 | 113.8 | 96.56 | 40.4 | 2.39 |
| 1963................. | 16,995,000 | 12,555,000 | 117.9 | 99.63 | 40.5 | 2.46 |
| 1964................. | 17,274,000 | 12,781,000 | 124.3 | 102.97 | 40.7 | 2.53 |
| 1965................. | 18,062,000 | 13,434,000 | 136.6 | 107.53 | 41.2 | 2.61 |
| 1966................. | 19,214,000 | 14,297,000 | 151.7 | 112.34 | 41.3 | 2.72 |
| 1967................. | 19,434,000 | 14,300,000 | 155.0 | 114.90 | 40.6 | 2.83 |
| 1968[1] Jan........... | 19,398,000 | 14,213,000 | 158.1 | 117.60 | 40.0 | 2.94 |
| Feb........... | 19,425,000 | 14,231,000 | 160.5 | 119.36 | 40.6 | 2.94 |
| Mar........... | 19,447,000 | 14,248,000 | 161.8 | 120.18 | 40.6 | 2.96 |
| Apr........... | 19,507,000 | 14,303,000 | 159.5 | 118.21 | 39.8 | 2.97 |
| May........... | 19,569,000 | 14,352,000 | 165.9 | 122.29 | 40.9 | 2.99 |
| June........... | 19,897,000 | 14,622,000 | 170.0 | 123.30 | 41.1 | 3.00 |

[1]Preliminary.

## Hourly Earnings in Manufacturing Industries
### Source: Bureau of Labor Statistics, U. S. Dept. of Labor

| Year and month (annual average) | Manufacturing | | Durable goods | | Nondurable goods | |
|---|---|---|---|---|---|---|
| | Gross | Excluding overtime | Gross | Excluding overtime | Gross | Excluding overtime |
| 1950................. | $1.440 | $1.39 | $1.519 | $1.46 | $1.347 | $1.31 |
| 1955................. | 1.86 | 1.79 | 1.99 | 1.91 | 1.67 | 1.62 |
| 1959................. | 2.19 | 2.12 | 2.36 | 2.28 | 1.98 | 1.92 |
| 1960................. | 2.26 | 2.20 | 2.43 | 2.36 | 2.05 | 1.99 |
| 1961................. | 2.32 | 2.25 | 2.49 | 2.42 | 2.11 | 2.05 |
| 1962................. | 2.39 | 2.31 | 2.56 | 2.48 | 2.17 | 2.09 |
| 1963................. | 2.46 | 2.37 | 2.63 | 2.54 | 2.22 | 2.15 |
| 1964................. | 2.53 | 2.44 | 2.71 | 2.60 | 2.29 | 2.21 |
| 1965................. | 2.61 | 2.51 | 2.79 | 2.67 | 2.36 | 2.27 |
| 1966................. | 2.72 | 2.59 | 2.90 | 2.76 | 2.45 | 2.35 |
| 1967................. | 2.83 | 2.72 | 3.00 | 2.88 | 2.57 | 2.47 |
| 1968 Jan............. | 2.94 | 2.83 | 3.13 | 3.00 | 2.67 | 2.57 |
| Feb............. | 2.94 | 2.83 | 3.12 | 3.00 | 2.68 | 2.58 |
| Mar............. | 2.96 | 2.85 | 3.14 | 3.02 | 2.69 | 2.59 |
| Apr............. | 2.97 | 2.86 | 3.15 | 3.03 | 2.70 | 2.61 |
| May............. | 2.99 | 2.87 | 3.18 | 3.04 | 2.72 | 2.62 |
| June............. | 3.00 | 2.87 | 3.18 | 3.04 | 2.73 | 2.62 |

## Employees on Non-farm Payrolls Continue Upward

The Bureau of Labor Statistics reported Sept. 11, 1968, that non-farm payroll employment reached a record high of 68,724,000 in June, 1968. The figure dipped to 68,358,000 in July but edged up to 68,596,000 in August.

# General Manufacturing Statistics for States

Source: Bureau of the Census, 1966. Census of Manufactures.

| Divisions, Regions and States | All employees | | Production workers | | | Value by manu-facture | Capital expend-itures |
| --- | --- | --- | --- | --- | --- | --- | --- |
| | Number (1,000) | Payroll (millions) | Number (1,000) | Man-hrs. (millions) | Wages (millions) | (millions) | (millions) |
| New England | 1,550 | $ 9,707 | 1,134 | 2,306 | $ 6,008 | $ 18,307 | $ 1,197 |
| Maine | 107 | 533 | 90 | 184 | 406 | 980 | 131 |
| New Hampshire | 96 | 483 | 78 | 156 | 345 | 869 | 72 |
| Vermont | 42 | 247 | 32 | 67 | 160 | 576 | 34 |
| Massachusetts | 707 | 4,417 | 505 | 1,005 | 2,619 | 8,367 | 483 |
| Rhode Island | 128 | 686 | 101 | 200 | 467 | 1,341 | 75 |
| Connecticut | 470 | 3,340 | 328 | 694 | 2,011 | 6,173 | 401 |
| Middle Atlantic | 4,387 | 29,394 | 3,069 | 6,072 | 16,972 | 55,741 | 3,432 |
| New York | 1,956 | 13,303 | 1,310 | 2,555 | 7,025 | 24,714 | 1,178 |
| New Jersey | 876 | 6,027 | 606 | 1,223 | 3,499 | 12,287 | 845 |
| Pennsylvania | 1,555 | 10,064 | 1,153 | 2,294 | 6,448 | 18,741 | 1,410 |
| East North Central | 5,181 | 37,794 | 3,783 | 7,952 | 24,824 | 74,677 | 6,050 |
| Ohio | 1,410 | 10,455 | 1,016 | 2,221 | 6,888 | 20,307 | 1,585 |
| Indiana | 708 | 4,922 | 543 | 1,115 | 3,422 | 10,102 | 1,075 |
| Illinois | 1,401 | 9,704 | 1,009 | 2,048 | 6,138 | 19,819 | 1,429 |
| Michigan | 1,146 | 9,221 | 835 | 1,779 | 6,066 | 17,609 | 1,489 |
| Wisconsin | 516 | 3,492 | 381 | 790 | 2,310 | 6,839 | 471 |
| West North Central | 1,172 | 7,626 | 834 | 1,698 | 4,770 | 15,862 | 954 |
| Minnesota | 286 | 1,908 | 196 | 394 | 1,112 | 3,799 | 212 |
| Iowa | 206 | 1,377 | 150 | 309 | 912 | 3,014 | 221 |
| Missouri | 451 | 2,923 | 317 | 640 | 1,774 | 5,821 | 317 |
| North Dakota | 7 | 37 | 4 | 9 | 23 | 101 | 7 |
| South Dakota | 14 | 81 | 10 | 21 | 55 | 166 | 8 |
| Nebraska | 71 | 419 | 53 | 110 | 284 | 993 | 76 |
| Kansas | 136 | 881 | 103 | 214 | 610 | 1,968 | 113 |
| South Atlantic | 2,421 | 12,995 | 1,887 | 3,872 | 8,561 | 27,556 | 2,781 |
| Delaware | 69 | 577 | 36 | 72 | 212 | 956 | 91 |
| Maryland | 288 | 1,876 | 207 | 417 | 1,157 | 3,588 | 271 |
| District of Columbia | 26 | 196 | 12 | 23 | 79 | 303 | 11 |
| Virginia | 336 | 1,807 | 264 | 540 | 1,224 | 3,945 | 374 |
| West Virginia | 126 | 825 | 99 | 196 | 574 | 2,134 | 249 |
| North Carolina | 612 | 2,813 | 511 | 1,048 | 2,025 | 6,135 | 714 |
| South Carolina | 298 | 1,410 | 249 | 530 | 1,054 | 2,987 | 400 |
| Georgia | 414 | 2,040 | 336 | 693 | 1,422 | 4,572 | 367 |
| Florida | 252 | 1,451 | 172 | 353 | 813 | 2,934 | 304 |
| East South Central | 1,082 | 5,631 | 872 | 1,756 | 3,935 | 13,273 | 1,404 |
| Kentucky | 218 | 1,266 | 172 | 355 | 879 | 3,462 | 290 |
| Tennessee | 411 | 2,100 | 326 | 653 | 1,421 | 4,654 | 511 |
| Alabama | 295 | 1,580 | 241 | 477 | 1,122 | 3,668 | 424 |
| Mississippi | 158 | 685 | 134 | 271 | 513 | 1,488 | 180 |
| West South Central | 1,009 | 5,983 | 733 | 1,526 | 3,766 | 14,892 | 1,856 |
| Arkansas | 136 | 591 | 115 | 238 | 451 | 1,410 | 122 |
| Louisiana | 152 | 934 | 113 | 232 | 617 | 2,533 | 476 |
| Oklahoma | 110 | 678 | 74 | 152 | 381 | 1,248 | 71 |
| Texas | 610 | 3,781 | 431 | 905 | 2,317 | 9,702 | 1,188 |
| Mountain | 314 | 2,045 | 221 | 444 | 1,275 | 4,291 | 382 |
| Montana | 22 | 133 | 17 | 33 | 99 | 315 | 28 |
| Idaho | 36 | 205 | 28 | 55 | 144 | 496 | 58 |
| Wyoming | 7 | 38 | 5 | 9 | 25 | 93 | 17 |
| Colorado | 105 | 710 | 74 | 148 | 444 | 1,453 | 130 |
| New Mexico | 17 | 94 | 12 | 23 | 54 | 169 | 14 |
| Arizona | 73 | 504 | 48 | 100 | 292 | 939 | 75 |
| Utah | 47 | 311 | 32 | 65 | 185 | 705 | 53 |
| Nevada | 7 | 50 | 5 | 10 | 32 | 121 | 6 |
| Pacific | 1,958 | 14,477 | 1,313 | 2,616 | 8,273 | 27,039 | 2,201 |
| Washington | 253 | 1,936 | 172 | 333 | 1,113 | 3,311 | 418 |
| Oregon | 162 | 1,033 | 129 | 253 | 770 | 1,999 | 277 |
| California | 1,509 | 11,313 | 987 | 1,984 | 6,269 | 21,288 | 1,469 |
| Alaska | 7 | 51 | 6 | 12 | 41 | 129 | 12 |
| Hawaii | 28 | 143 | 19 | 35 | 79 | 312 | 24 |
| Total | 19,066 | $125,459 | 13,808 | 28,224 | $78,253 | $251,014 | $20,239 |

# Profits of Manufacturing Corporations by Industry Groups

Source: Federal Trade Commission and the Securities and Exchange Commission

| Industry Group (Amounts estimated in millions of dollars) | Before Income Taxes | | | Profits after taxes | | |
| --- | --- | --- | --- | --- | --- | --- |
| | 1967 | Pct. of sales 1966 | 1967 | 1967 | Pct. of sales 1966 | 1967 |
| Durable goods | 25,724 | 10.0 | 8.6 | 14,579 | 5.6 | 4.8 |
| Transportation equipment | 5,641 | 9.4 | 7.4 | 3,165 | 5.2 | 4.1 |
| Motor vehicles and equipment[1] | 4,180 | 11.2 | 8.7 | 2,356 | 6.2 | 4.9 |
| Electrical machinery, equipment and supplies | 4,216 | 9.0 | 8.0 | 2,297 | 4.8 | 4.4 |
| Other machinery | 5,339 | 11.7 | 10.5 | 2,893 | 6.4 | 5.7 |
| Other fabricated metal products | 2,332 | 8.5 | 7.9 | 1,316 | 4.9 | 4.5 |
| Primary iron and steel | 1,816 | 9.8 | 7.5 | 1,165 | 5.8 | 4.8 |
| Primary nonferrous metals | 1,714 | 13.7 | 11.0 | 1,061 | 8.2 | 6.8 |
| Stone, clay and glass products | 1,129 | 9.6 | 8.1 | 672 | 5.6 | 4.8 |
| Furniture and fixtures | 443 | 6.8 | 6.4 | 245 | 3.9 | 3.5 |
| Other lumber and wood products | 508 | 6.0 | 5.2 | 333 | 3.8 | 3.4 |
| Instruments and related products | 1,944 | 17.4 | 15.5 | 1,064 | 9.5 | 8.5 |
| Miscellaneous manufacturing and ordnance | 642 | 8.0 | 7.2 | 370 | 4.9 | 4.2 |
| Nondurable goods | 22,050 | 8.6 | 8.0 | 14,429 | 5.5 | 5.3 |
| Food and kindred products | 3,853 | 4.8 | 4.7 | 2,130 | 2.7 | 2.6 |
| Tobacco manufacturers | 794 | 11.1 | 11.2 | 420 | 5.9 | 5.9 |
| Textile mill products | 982 | 6.5 | 5.3 | 540 | 3.6 | 2.9 |
| Apparel and other finished products | 728 | 4.1 | 4.0 | 420 | 2.4 | 2.3 |
| Paper and allied products | 1,316 | 9.1 | 7.8 | 796 | 5.4 | 4.7 |
| Printing and publishing, except newspapers | 1,098 | 9.1 | 7.9 | 613 | 5.1 | 4.4 |
| Chemicals and allied products | 5,657 | 13.6 | 11.9 | 3,261 | 7.8 | 6.9 |
| Petroleum refining and related products | 6,363 | 12.9 | 12.5 | 5,528 | 11.0 | 10.9 |
| Petroleum refining[1] | 6,311 | 13.0 | 12.7 | 5,497 | 11.2 | 11.0 |
| Rubber products | 926 | 7.7 | 6.8 | 538 | 4.4 | 3.9 |
| Leather and leather products | 331 | 5.4 | 5.4 | 183 | 3.0 | 3.0 |
| All Manufacturing Corps., except newspapers | 47,772 | 9.3 | 8.3 | 29,008 | 5.6 | 5.0 |

[1]Included in major industry above.

## Annual Rates of Profit on Stockholders' Equity
Source: Federal Trade Commission
(Each rate is the arithmetic mean of four quarterly rates, each on an annual basis.)

| By industry after taxes: by percent | 1950 | 1955 | 1960 | 1963 | 1964 | 1965 | 1966 | 1967 |
|---|---|---|---|---|---|---|---|---|
| **All manufacturing corporations, except newspapers.** | 15.4 | 12.6 | 9.2 | 10.2 | 11.6 | 13.0 | 13.4 | 11.7 |
| **Durable goods industries** | 16.8 | 13.8 | 8.6 | 10.1 | 11.8 | 13.8 | 14.2 | 11.7 |
| Metals and metal fabricating industries | 16.9 | 14.1 | 8.6 | 10.4 | 12.0 | 14.2 | 14.3 | 11.7 |
| Transportation equipment | 21.5 | 20.2 | 11.7 | 15.2 | 15.8 | 18.5 | 15.6 | 11.9 |
| Motor vehicles and equipment | 25.2 | 21.7 | 13.5 | 16.7 | 16.9 | 19.5 | 15.9 | 11.7 |
| Aircraft and parts | N.A. | N.A. | 7.4 | 11.3 | 12.2 | 15.1 | 14.4 | 12.8 |
| Electrical machinery, equipment and supplies | 20.8 | 12.3 | 9.5 | 10.0 | 11.2 | 13.5 | 14.8 | 12.8 |
| Machinery, except electrical | 14.0 | 10.3 | 7.6 | 9.6 | 12.4 | 14.1 | 15.0 | 12.9 |
| Metalworking machinery and equipment | N.A. | N.A. | 5.3 | 8.6 | 12.4 | 14.4 | 17.1 | 14.0 |
| Other fabricated metal products | 15.9 | 10.0 | 5.6 | 8.3 | 10.1 | 13.2 | 14.7 | 12.7 |
| Primary metal industries | 14.5 | 14.1 | 7.2 | 7.2 | 9.2 | 10.6 | 12.0 | 9.0 |
| Blast furnaces, steel works and foundries | 14.3 | 13.5 | 7.2 | 7.0 | 8.8 | 9.8 | 10.2 | 7.7 |
| Nonferrous metals | 15.0 | 15.4 | 7.1 | 7.6 | 9.8 | 11.9 | 14.8 | 11.0 |
| **Other durable goods industries** | 16.3 | 12.3 | 8.6 | 9.2 | 10.6 | 12.2 | 13.6 | 11.7 |
| Lumber and wood products, except furniture | 17.4 | 11.1 | 3.6 | 8.2 | 10.0 | 10.0 | 10.0 | 8.6 |
| Furniture and fixtures | 15.1 | 9.2 | 6.5 | 8.2 | 10.1 | 13.3 | 14.2 | 12.1 |
| Stone, clay and glass products | 17.6 | 15.6 | 9.9 | 8.6 | 9.6 | 10.2 | 9.9 | 8.2 |
| Instruments and related products | 16.7 | 12.5 | 11.6 | 12.0 | 14.4 | 17.5 | 20.8 | 17.9 |
| Miscellaneous manufacturing and ordnance | 12.2 | 8.6 | 9.2 | 8.8 | 9.5 | 10.7 | 15.2 | 13.1 |
| **Nondurable goods industries** | 14.0 | 11.4 | 9.8 | 10.4 | 11.5 | 12.2 | 12.7 | 11.8 |
| Chemicals: petroleum, rubber and plastics | 15.4 | 13.7 | 10.8 | 11.6 | 12.4 | 13.0 | 13.3 | 12.6 |
| Chemicals and allied products | 17.8 | 14.7 | 12.2 | 12.9 | 14.4 | 15.2 | 15.1 | 13.0 |
| Basic chemicals and related products | N.A. | N.A. | 11.1 | 12.3 | 14.0 | 14.3 | 14.0 | 10.9 |
| Drugs | N.A. | N.A. | 16.8 | 16.8 | 18.2 | 20.3 | 20.3 | 18.7 |
| Petroleum refining and related industries | 13.8 | 13.2 | 10.1 | 11.2 | 11.4 | 11.8 | 12.4 | 12.5 |
| Petroleum refining | N.A. | 13.3 | 10.1 | 11.3 | 11.4 | 11.8 | 12.4 | 12.5 |
| Rubber and miscellaneous plastics products | 16.7 | 13.2 | 9.1 | 9.2 | 10.6 | 11.7 | 12.2 | 10.3 |
| **Other nondurable goods industries** | 12.8 | 8.8 | 8.5 | 8.5 | 10.2 | 11.1 | 11.7 | 10.6 |
| Food and kindred products | 12.3 | 8.9 | 8.7 | 9.0 | 10.0 | 10.7 | 11.2 | 10.8 |
| Dairy products | N.A. | N.A. | N.A. | 8.5 | 9.6 | 10.6 | 11.0 | 10.2 |
| Bakery products | N.A. | N.A. | N.A. | 9.2 | 9.0 | 9.3 | 11.1 | 12.0 |
| Alcoholic beverages | N.A. | N.A. | 7.1 | 7.9 | 8.8 | 9.3 | 10.4 | 10.2 |
| Tobacco manufactures | 11.5 | 11.4 | 13.4 | 13.4 | 13.4 | 13.5 | 14.0 | 14.4 |
| Textile mill products | 12.6 | 5.7 | 5.8 | 6.0 | 8.4 | 10.8 | 10.0 | 7.6 |
| Apparel and other fabricated textile products | 10.1 | 6.2 | 7.7 | 7.7 | 11.7 | 12.6 | 13.2 | 11.9 |
| Paper and allied products | 16.1 | 11.5 | 8.5 | 8.1 | 9.1 | 9.4 | 10.6 | 9.1 |
| Printing and publishing, except newspapers | 11.5 | 10.2 | 10.6 | 9.1 | 12.6 | 14.1 | 15.6 | 13.0 |
| Leather and leather products | 10.9 | 8.5 | 6.3 | 6.9 | 10.5 | 11.6 | 12.9 | 11.8 |

N.A.—Not available.

## Occupational Earnings in Selected Cities
Source: Bureau of Labor Statistics, Dept. of Labor
(Average earnings[1] for selected occupations studied in 6 broad industry divisions, manufacturing, transportation, communication and other public utilities; wholesale trade; retail trade; finance, insurance and real estate; and services. March—June 1968)

| Occupation | N. Y. | Worcester, Mass. | Atlanta, Ga. | Houston, Texas (Per week[1]) | Chicago | Phoenix, Ariz. | Spokane, Wash. |
|---|---|---|---|---|---|---|---|
| **Office Workers—Men** | | | | | | | |
| Accounting clerks[2] | $129.50 | $135.50 | $125.50 | $134.50 | $132.50 | $110.50 | $144.00 |
| Draftsmen[2] | 181.50 | 159.50 | 175.00 | 182.00 | 166.00 | 163.50 | ......... |
| Office boys | 77.00 | 69.00 | 76.50 | 75.00 | 82.00 | 70.50 | ......... |
| Tabulating operators[2] | 133.50 | ......... | 136.00 | 136.50 | 135.50 | ......... | ......... |
| **Office Workers—Women** | | | | | | | |
| Accounting clerks[2] | 112.50 | 111.00 | 112.00 | 109.00 | 112.50 | 108.50 | 106.50 |
| Billers (machine) | 98.50 | 82.50 | 88.00 | 82.50 | 97.50 | 70.50 | 82.00 |
| Bookkeeping (machine)[2] | 109.00 | 102.50 | 93.00 | 108.00 | 108.00 | 110.50 | ......... |
| Keypunch operators[2] | 101.00 | 94.50 | 105.00 | 97.50 | 102.00 | 94.50 | 111.00 |
| Nurses | 134.00 | 119.50 | 128.00 | 132.00 | 130.50 | 128.00 | ......... |
| office girls | 74.00 | 70.00 | 75.00 | 72.50 | 78.00 | ......... | 77.50 |
| Payroll clerks | 107.50 | 92.00 | 97.00 | 101.50 | 106.00 | 96.50 | 111.50 |
| Secretaries | 123.00 | 110.00 | 113.00 | 117.00 | 118.00 | 107.00 | 105.50 |
| Stenographers (general) | 96.00 | 88.00 | 95.50 | 94.00 | 101.00 | 88.50 | 91.00 |
| Switchboard operators[2] | 105.00 | 91.00 | 102.00 | 98.50 | 103.00 | 96.00 | ......... |
| Typists[2] | 94.50 | 82.00 | 88.50 | 90.00 | 96.00 | 98.50 | 87.50 |
| **Maintenance, Custodial, and Material Handling Workers—Men** | | | | (Per hour[1]) | | | |
| Carpenters | 3.71 | 3.34 | 3.72 | 3.75 | 4.10 | 3.63 | 3.72 |
| Electricians | 3.75 | 3.62 | 3.98 | 3.89 | 4.03 | 3.87 | 4.23 |
| Engineers (stationary) | 4.01 | 3.40 | 3.60 | 3.23 | 4.16 | 3.29 | 3.62 |
| Helpers, trades | 3.11 | 2.69 | 2.53 | 2.78 | 2.90 | 2.64 | 3.07 |
| Machinists | 4.04 | 3.36 | 3.60 | 3.90 | 3.97 | 3.89 | 4.21 |
| Mechanics, automotive | 3.76 | 3.38 | 3.46 | 3.27 | 3.97 | 3.47 | 3.93 |
| Painters | 3.43 | ......... | 3.38 | 3.66 | 4.29 | ......... | 3.88 |
| Plumbers | 3.59 | ......... | ......... | ......... | 4.42 | ......... | ......... |
| Guards and watchmen | 2.32 | 2.30 | 1.97 | 2.01 | 2.31 | 2.22 | 2.90 |
| Janitors, porters, cleaners | 2.38 | 2.19 | 1.88 | 1.82 | 2.38 | 1.85 | 2.37 |
| Laborers, material handling | 2.90 | 2.62 | 2.20 | 2.19 | 2.90 | 2.49 | 2.96 |
| Shipping packers | 2.45 | 2.90 | 2.18 | 2.16 | 2.68 | 2.51 | 3.09 |
| Shipping clerks | 3.04 | 2.68 | 2.65 | 2.75 | 3.10 | 2.46 | 3.24 |
| Truckdrivers (local) | 3.56 | 3.11 | 2.94 | 2.71 | 3.71 | 3.07 | 3.61 |

[1]Weekly earnings relate to regular straight-time salaries that are paid for standard workweeks. Hourly earnings exclude premium pay for overtime, weekends, holidays, or late shifts. [2]More than one skill level surveyed. Earnings are for highest level surveyed.

## Distilled Spirits and Beer Production
Source: Internal Revenue Service. (Figures show thousands of tax gallons or barrels)

| Year fiscal | Distilled Spirits | | | | | Beer | Year fiscal | Distilled Spirits | | | | | Beer |
|---|---|---|---|---|---|---|---|---|---|---|---|---|---|
| | Whky. | Rm. | Bdy. | Alcoh. | Total* | Tot. | | Whky. | Rm. | Bdy. | Alcoh. | Total* | Tot. |
| | Gals. | Gals. | Gals. | Gals. | Gals. | Bbls. | | Gals. | Gals. | Gals. | Gals. | Gals. | Bbls. |
| 1940 | 98,993 | 2,478 | 18,427 | 261,022 | 387,183 | 54,892 | 1960 | 149,545 | 1,866 | 10,114 | 613,924 | 803,751 | 94,541 |
| 1945 | 41,562 | 2,888 | 26,596 | 1,101,286 | 1,174,391 | 86,609 | 1965 | 117,930 | 2,274 | 11,522 | 695,332 | 865,240 | 108,015 |
| 1950 | 118,760 | 1,781 | 5,364 | 391,129 | 521,770 | 88,807 | 1966 | 140,186 | 2,637 | 17,858 | 687,287 | 889,352 | 109,736 |
| 1955 | 103,927 | 2,005 | 4,008 | 465,069 | 593,982 | 89,791 | 1967 | 132,192 | 1,710 | 18,024 | 679,258 | 873,010 | 116,564 |

*Includes gin, vodka and Okelehao.

# Centrifugal Raw Sugar Production

**Source:** Office of Foreign Agricultural Service, Dept. of Agriculture

Centrifugal sugar, as distinguished from non-centrifugal, includes cane and beet sugar produced by the centrifugal process, which is the principal kind moving in international trade. (In short tons)

| Continent and country | Ave. 1960-61 Thru 1964-65 | 1965-66 | 1966-67 (revised) | 1967-68 (prelim.) |
|---|---|---|---|---|
| North America (cane and beet) | 16,223,000 | 16,194,000 | 18,102,000 | 17,221,000 |
| South America (cane and beet) | 7,169,000 | 9,431,000 | 8,736,000 | 8,877,000 |
| Europe, West (cane and beet) | 9,308,000 | 9,552,000 | 9,784,000 | 10,631,000 |
| Europe, East (beet) | 5,166,000 | 5,072,000 | 5,713,000 | 5,949,000 |
| U.S.S.R. (Europe and Asia) | 7,623,000 | 10,700,000 | 10,100,000 | 11,500,000 |
| Africa (cane) | 3,411,000 | 3,754,000 | 4,875,000 | 5,163,000 |
| Asia (cane and beet) | 9,941,000 | 12,054,000 | 10,811,000 | 11,661,000 |
| Oceania (cane) | 2,072,000 | 2,526,000 | 2,877,000 | 3,108,000 |
| **World total (cane)** | **34,354,000** | **39,130,000** | **40,157,000** | **40,663,000** |
| **World total (beet)** | **26,559,000** | **30,153,000** | **30,841,000** | **33,447,000** |

| NON-CENTRIFUGAL SUGAR PRODUCTION | | | | |
|---|---|---|---|---|
| North America | 300,000 | 255,000 | 259,000 | 251,000 |
| South America | 800,000 | 768,000 | 768,000 | 770,000 |
| Asia | 6,975,000 | 7,634,000 | 7,661,000 | 7,315,000 |

| CENTRIFUGAL RAW SUGAR PRODUCTION (OVER 100,000 SHORT TONS) | | | | |
|---|---|---|---|---|
| Argentina | 950,000 | 1,422,000 | 1,125,000 | 855,000 |
| Australia | 1,806,000 | 2,187,000 | 2,527,000 | 2,708,000 |
| Austria | 312,000 | 260,000 | 393,000 | 331,000 |
| Barbados | 194,000 | 193,000 | 225,000 | 190,000 |
| Belgium-Luxembourg | 497,000 | 464,000 | 459,000 | 634,000 |
| Bolivia | 66,000 | 100,000 | 100,000 | 120,000 |
| Brazil | 3,815,000 | 5,324,000 | 4,807,000 | 5,075,000 |
| Bulgaria | 207,000 | 235,000 | 375,000 | 338,000 |
| Canada | 155,000 | 145,000 | 163,000 | 149,000 |
| Chile | 88,000 | 114,000 | 131,000 | 178,000 |
| China, mainland | 1,026,000 | 1,750,000 | 1,800,000 | 2,000,000 |
| China, Taiwan | 991,000 | 1,081,000 | 850,000 | 950,000 |
| Colombia | 421,000 | 482,000 | 635,000 | 724,000 |
| Costa Rica | 91,000 | 139,000 | 135,000 | 150,000 |
| Cuba | 5,596,000 | 4,950,000 | 6,200,000 | 5,700,000 |
| Czechoslovakia | 1,160,000 | 963,000 | 1,021,000 | 1,136,000 |
| Denmark | 341,000 | 265,000 | 352,000 | 365,000 |
| Dominican Republic | 852,000 | 739,000 | 893,000 | 805,000 |
| Ecuador | 162,000 | 210,000 | 185,000 | 205,000 |
| El Salvador | 79,000 | 122,000 | 138,000 | 142,000 |
| Fiji | 266,000 | 339,000 | 350,000 | 400,000 |
| France | 2,309,000 | 2,585,000 | 1,967,000 | 1,904,000 |
| Germany, East | 869,000 | 864,000 | 748,000 | 900,000 |
| Germany, West | 1,980,000 | 1,722,000 | 2,108,000 | 2,270,000 |
| Greece | 30,000 | 126,000 | 133,000 | 140,000 |
| Guadeloupe | 165,000 | 184,000 | 151,000 | 171,000 |
| Guatemala | 137,000 | 174,000 | 200,000 | 160,000 |
| Guyana | 344,000 | 324,000 | 386,000 | 400,000 |
| Hawaii | 1,122,000 | 1,234,000 | 1,235,000 | 1,191,000 |
| Hungary | 492,000 | 495,000 | 528,000 | 419,000 |
| India | 3,694,000 | 4,514,000 | 3,029,000 | 3,095,000 |
| Indonesia | 708,000 | 671,000 | 661,000 | 716,000 |
| Iran | 185,000 | 239,000 | 389,000 | 550,000 |
| Ireland | 156,000 | 130,000 | 123,000 | 161,000 |
| Italy | 1,082,000 | 1,356,000 | 1,507,000 | 1,805,000 |
| Jamaica | 524,000 | 560,000 | 502,000 | 530,000 |
| Japan | 229,000 | 418,000 | 380,000 | 428,000 |
| Malagasy Republic | 110,000 | 126,000 | 117,000 | 120,000 |
| Mauritius | 559,000 | 619,000 | 704,000 | 784,000 |
| Mexico | 1,899,000 | 2,320,000 | 2,679,000 | 2,530,000 |
| Mozambique | 183,000 | 197,000 | 231,000 | 276,000 |
| Netherlands | 620,000 | 657,000 | 631,000 | 815,000 |
| Nicaragua | 97,000 | 74,000 | 113,000 | 118,000 |
| Pakistan | 225,000 | 490,000 | 511,000 | 579,000 |
| Peru | 878,000 | 928,000 | 823,000 | 805,000 |
| Philippines | 1,704,000 | 1,590,000 | 1,718,000 | 1,783,000 |
| Poland | 1,693,000 | 1,620,000 | 1,853,000 | 2,100,000 |
| Puerto Rico | 999,000 | 883,000 | 818,000 | 650,000 |
| Reunion | 246,000 | 255,000 | 212,000 | 230,000 |
| Rhodesia | 95,000 | 292,000 | 290,000 | 150,000 |
| Rumania | 408,000 | 481,000 | 536,000 | 500,000 |
| Ryukyu Islands | 161,000 | 161,000 | 215,000 | 243,000 |
| Spain | 560,000 | 620,000 | 679,000 | 694,000 |
| South Africa, Rep. of | 1,233,000 | 1,002,000 | 1,794,000 | 2,009,000 |
| Swaziland | 105,000 | 131,000 | 165,000 | 175,000 |
| Sweden | 312,000 | 222,000 | 252,000 | 285,000 |
| Thailand | 212,000 | 315,000 | 272,000 | 242,000 |
| Trinidad and Tobago | 258,000 | 236,000 | 222,000 | 269,000 |
| Turkey (Europe and Asia) | 639,000 | 625,000 | 773,000 | 872,000 |
| Uganda | 128,000 | 148,000 | 161,000 | 178,000 |
| United Arab Republic | 401,000 | 446,000 | 399,000 | 400,000 |
| U.S.S.R. (Europe and Asia) | 7,623,000 | 10,700,000 | 10,100,000 | 11,500,000 |
| United Kingdom | 988,000 | 1,032,000 | 1,030,000 | 1,075,000 |
| United States, Continental (beet) | 2,744,000 | 2,820,000 | 2,860,000 | 2,665,000 |
| United States, Continental (cane) | 934,000 | 1,104,000 | 1,215,000 | 1,457,000 |
| Venezuela | 325,000 | 397,000 | 410,000 | 415,000 |
| Yugoslavia | 323,000 | 400,000 | 634,000 | 539,000 |

## Total Exports and Exports Financed by Foreign Aid

**Source:** Bureau of International Commerce, Dept. of Commerce

| (In millions of dollars) | 1960 | 1964 | 1965 | 1966 | 1967 |
|---|---|---|---|---|---|
| **Total exports** | 20,584 | 26,508 | 27,478 | 30,320 | 31,534 |
| Exports financed by foreign aid | 2,685 | 3,588 | 3,406 | 3,586 | 3,368 |
| Loans and grants (AID) | 432 | 1,063 | 1,117 | 1,129 | 1,272 |
| Military grant-aid | 949 | 818 | 779 | 940 | 592 |
| Agricultural aid | 1,304 | 1,707 | 1,510 | 1,517 | 1,504 |
| Sales for foreign currencies | 1,014 | 1,239 | 926 | 820 | 716 |
| Donations | 173 | 248 | 253 | 211 | 287 |
| Barter | 117 | 123 | 188 | 260 | 314 |
| Long term dollar credit sales | — | 97 | 143 | 226 | 187 |

# World Telephone Statistics
## TELEPHONES IN CONTINENTAL AREAS
Source: American Telephone and Telegraph Company

| Continent | Total in service Number 1967 | Percent of world | Per 100 Population | Privately operated[1] Number 1967 | Percent of total | Automatic Number 1967 | Percent of total | Connecting with Bell system Number 1967 | Percent of total |
|---|---|---|---|---|---|---|---|---|---|
| No. Am.... | 106,329,000 | 51.0 | 48.8 | 104,939,000 | 98.7 | 105,837,000 | 99.5 | 106,327,000 | 100.0 |
| M. Am.... | 1,810,000 | 0.9 | 2.2 | 1,328,000 | 73.4 | 1,635,000 | 90.3 | 1,805,000 | 99.7 |
| So. Am.... | 4,469,000 | 2.1 | 2.6 | 2,237,000 | 50.1 | 3,999,000 | 89.5 | 4,370,000 | 97.8 |
| Europe.... | 66,976,000 | 32.1 | 10.6 | 11,825,000 | 17.7 | 61,275,000 | 91.5 | 64,171,000 | 95.8 |
| Africa..... | 2,618,000 | 1.3 | 0.8 | 23,000 | 0.9 | 2,034,000 | 77.7 | 2,448,000 | 93.5 |
| Asia[2]..... | 21,758,000 | 10.4 | 1.1 | 15,229,000 | 70.0 | 16,518,000 | 75.9 | 17,399,000 | 80.0 |
| Oceania.. | 4,540,000 | 2.2 | 24.4 | 345,000 | 7.6 | 3,878,000 | 85.4 | 4,535,000 | 99.9 |
| **World..** | **208,500,000** | **100.0** | **6.2** | **135,926,000** | **65.2** | **195,176,000** | **93.6** | **201,055,000** | **96.4** |

[1]This applies to operation rather than ownership. Systems which are government-owned in whole or in part may be privately operated (e.g., Italy and Japan). The word "government" refers to nations, states or municipalities. [2]These data include allowances for the Asiatic parts of Turkey and the USSR.

## TELEPHONES IN U. S. CITIES WITH OVER 100,000 TELEPHONES (1968)

| City | Number | City | Number | City | Number | City | Number |
|---|---|---|---|---|---|---|---|
| Akron, Ohio... | 280,382 | East Orange... | 103,628 | Madison, Wisc.. | 132,663 | Sacramento.... | 334,071 |
| Albany, N. Y.. | 141,539 | El Paso...... | 159,076 | Memphis...... | 338,018 | St. Louis, Mo. | 547,253 |
| Albuquerque.. | 163,792 | Flint, Mich... | 162,968 | Miami, Fla.... | 610,652 | St. Petersburg | 163,629 |
| Alexandria.... | 143,320 | Ft. Lauderdale.. | 153,151 | Milwaukee.... | 635,330 | Salt Lake City | 262,871 |
| Allentown, Pa. | 102,088 | Ft. Wayne..... | 127,509 | Minneapolis- | | San Antonio.. | 303,118 |
| Anaheim, Cal.. | 140,376 | Ft. Worth..... | 245,040 | St. Paul..... | 961,226 | San Diego | |
| Atlanta, Ga... | 573,409 | Fresno, Cal..... | 161,438 | Mobile, Ala... | 135,851 | (ext. area).. | 601,259 |
| Austin, Texas. | 144,398 | Grand Rapids.. | 207,126 | Nashville..... | 237,720 | San Francisco. | 671,801 |
| Bakersfield ... | 112,255 | Greensboro .... | 105,061 | New Haven.... | 214,819 | San Jose, Cal.. | 310,748 |
| Baltimore .... | 530,897 | Harrisburg .... | 143,919 | New Orleans... | 474,372 | Santa Ana.... | 171,522 |
| Baton Rouge.. | 153,087 | Hartford ..... | 259,982 | New York .... | 5,534,008 | Seattle, Wash.. | 499,283 |
| Birmingham .. | 274,514 | Haywood, Cal.. | 100,518 | Newark, N. J.. | 288,391 | Shreveport.... | 136,019 |
| Boston Mass.. | NA | Honolulu..... | 213,076 | Norfolk, Va... | 220,254 | Skokie, Ill..... | 121,525 |
| Bridgeport.... | 148,837 | Houston...... | 784,134 | Oakland, Cal... | 471,102 | Spokane...... | 140,060 |
| Buffalo, N. Y.. | 410,981 | Huntsville .... | 111,722 | Oklahoma City. | 204,620 | Springfield.... | NA |
| Canton, Ohio.. | 101,977 | Indianapolis .. | 452,888 | Omaha, Nebr.. | 272,035 | Syracuse ..... | 224,275 |
| Charleston.... | 113,765 | Jackson, Miss.. | 109,774 | Orlando, Fla... | 132,411 | Tacoma, Wash.. | 163,358 |
| Charlotte..... | 193,843 | Jacksonville... | 244,898 | Palo Alto..... | 113,874 | Tampa, Fla... | 189,758 |
| Chattanooga .. | 147,072 | Jersey City ... | 147,745 | Passaic, N. J... | 111,158 | Toledo, Ohio.. | 247,075 |
| Chicago, Ill... | 2,260,782 | Kansas City, | | Peoria, Ill..... | 128,754 | Tucson, Ariz... | 153,766 |
| Cincinnati.... | 404,054 | Kans........ | 126,422 | Philadelphia .. | 1,376,299 | Tulsa, Okla.... | 220,912 |
| Cleveland.... | 872,247 | Kansas City, | | Phoenix, Ariz.. | 431,190 | Warren, Mich.. | 203,397 |
| Colo. Springs.. | 116,777 | Mo......... | 310,544 | Pittsburgh, Pa. | 653,610 | Wash., D. C... | 882,667 |
| Columbia, S. C. | 129,381 | Knoxville..... | 124,673 | Pomona, Cal... | 111,400 | West Palm | |
| Columbus, Ga.. | 105,823 | Lansing...... | 148,388 | Portland, Ore.. | 356,286 | Beach...... | 129,827 |
| Columbus, Ohio | 381,413 | Las Vegas .... | 126,761 | Providence .... | NA | Wichita ...... | 166,023 |
| Dallas, Texas.. | 535,447 | Little Rock.... | 129,720 | Reading, Pa... | 120,839 | Wilmington, | |
| Dayton, Ohio.. | 313,056 | Livonia...... | 112,362 | Richmond, Va.. | 245,576 | Del......... | 161,508 |
| Denver, Colo... | 674,333 | Los Angeles | | Rochester .... | 310,260 | Worcester .... | NA |
| Des Moines.... | 183,468 | (ext. area).. | 4,468,457 | Rockford, Ill... | 129,926 | Youngstown .. | 144,931 |
| Detroit...... | 1,323,118 | Louisville..... | 353,474 | Royal Oak..... | 161,849 | | |

# Production of Electric Energy in the U. S.
Source: The Federal Power Commission
These amounts include both the privately-owned and publicly-owned utilities.

| Calendar Year | Electric Energy Produced Total 1,000 Kw. hrs. | Hydro 1,000 Kw. hrs. | Steam 1,000 Kw. hrs. | Internal Comb't'n 1,000 Kw. hrs. | Fuel Consumed in the Year Coal Short tons | Oil 42 Gal. Barrels | Gas 1,000 Cu. ft. |
|---|---|---|---|---|---|---|---|
| 1930........... | 91,111,548 | 31,189,554 | 59,293,363 | 628,631 | 40,277,989 | 8,804,530 | 119,552,711 |
| 1935........... | 95,287,390 | 38,372,154 | 56,144,412 | 770,824 | 32,714,761 | 11,256,565 | 124,117,769 |
| 1940........... | 141,837,010 | 47,321,278 | 93,001,735 | 1,531,997 | 51,321,881 | 16,325,122 | 180,096,185 |
| 1945........... | 222,486,283 | 79,970,312 | 140,435,268 | 2,080,703 | 74,724,956 | 20,225,215 | 326,211,996 |
| 1950........... | 329,141,343 | 95,938,317 | 229,543,366 | 3,659,660 | 91,870,770 | 75,420,490 | 628,918,834 |
| 1955........... | 547,037,985 | 112,975,069 | 430,119,086 | 3,943,830 | 143,759,195 | 75,273,862 | 1,153,279,586 |
| 1960........... | 753,350,271 | 145,516,253 | 603,341,840 | 4,692,178 | 176,233,789 | 85,340,108 | 1,734,762,374 |
| 1965........... | 1,055,251,929 | 193,850,603 | 856,312,128 | 5,089,198 | 244,788,119 | 115,202,583 | 2,321,100,937 |
| 1966........... | 1,144,350,518 | 194,755,781 | 944,430,145 | 5,164,212 | 266,476,823 | 140,948,854 | 2,609,948,660 |
| 1967........... | 1,211,749,276 | 220,043,018 | 986,782,770 | 4,923,488 | 273,972,576 | 161,274,680 | 2,743,251,360 |

Preliminary figures on installed capacity of electric generating plants as of Dec. 31, 1967 are (kilowatts): hydro 47,349,685; steam 215,910,457; int. comb. 3,814,545. Total 267,074,687.
Preliminary data on combined utility and industrial production of electric energy for 1967 show a total of 1,314,298,521,000 kilowatt-hours; combined capacity was 285,916,300 kw.
Electric operating revenues of the larger privately owned utilities were $14,363,930,000 as indicated by the preliminary total for 1966, this includes Alaska and Hawaii.

# World Electric Power
Source: Federal Power Commission
Electric generating capacity as of Jan. 1, 1967; electric energy production for 1966[1]
Kilowatts in thousands; Kilowatt-hours in millions.

| Country | Kw | Kwhrs | Country | Kw | Kwhrs |
|---|---|---|---|---|---|
| United States[2]........... | 266,816 | 1,249,444 | India[3]................. | 12,540 | 38,400 |
| USSR................ | 123,007 | 516,480 | Sweden............. | 12,300 | 49,930 |
| United Kingdom......... | 51,814 | 189,985 | Germany (East)....... | 11,067 | 54,066 |
| Japan[3]............. | 44,814 | 210,098 | Spain............... | 10,650 | 36,530 |
| Germany (West)......... | 42,679 | 166,287 | Norway............. | 10,272 | 48,348 |
| Canada............. | 30,785 | 157,371 | Poland............. | 9,920 | 42,963 |
| France.............. | 30,217 | 106,111 | Other countries...... | 138,704 | 510,120 |
| Italy............... | 26,756 | 87,121 | | | |
| China (Mainland)........ | 14,000 | 40,000 | World total.......... | 836,341 | 3,503,254 |

[1]Preliminary data; year-end except as noted. [2]Including Alaska and Hawaii. [3]Year ending Mar. 31, 1967.

## Hosiery Production by Major Types

Source: National Ass'n of Hosiery Manufacturers, Charlotte, N. C. 28202

| Types of Hosiery | Dozens of pairs | | Employment (monthly average) | | | |
|---|---|---|---|---|---|---|
| | 1966 | 1967 | Year | Total | Women's | Seamless |
| Women's | 105,047,703 | 119,159,389 | 1966 | 100,844 | 52,675 | 48,169 |
| Men's | 54,949,297 | 54,412,481 | 1967 | 98,353 | 56,435 | 41,918 |
| Boys', infants', children's | 58,140,426 | 56,737,606 | | | | |
| Total | 218,137,426 | 230,309,476 | | | | |

| | Hosiery plants | | Seamless | Full fash. | Other |
|---|---|---|---|---|---|
| | | | | Women's | |
| 1966 | 750 | | 266 | 79 | 405 |
| 1967 | 746 | | 270 | 65 | 411 |

### Production by States

(Percentage for all types of hosiery)

| Year | Total | North | Pa. | Other | South | N. C. | Tenn. | Ga. | Other |
|---|---|---|---|---|---|---|---|---|---|
| 1967 | 100% | 7.5% | 4.0% | 3.5% | 92.5% | 55.4% | 13.4% | 7.2% | 16.5% |
| 1966 | 100% | 8.8% | 4.7% | 4.1% | 91.2% | 53.0% | 14.3% | 7.0% | 16.9% |

### Exports and Imports 1967

| Types by fibers | Exports | | Imports | |
|---|---|---|---|---|
| | Dozens | Value | Dozens | Value |
| Cotton | 337,419 | $1,294,245 | 18,926 | $ 150,346 |
| Man-made fibers | 1,001,731 | 5,587,723 | 899,357 | 1,868,211 |
| Wool | 23,812 | 92,292 | 243,475 | 1,648,659 |
| Silk | | | 312 | 6,436 |
| Textile fibers NEC | 39,520 | 193,382 | | |
| Total | 1,402,482 | $7,167,642 | 1,162,070 | $3,673,652 |

| Exports | By 5 Largest Countries | | Imports |
|---|---|---|---|
| Dozens of pairs | | Dozens of pairs | |
| Mexico | 131,194 | Yugoslavia | 340,075 |
| Panama | 118,618 | Rep. of Korea | 290,790 |
| Canada | 116,946 | United Kingdom | 219,805 |
| France | 100,929 | Hong Kong | 67,248 |
| Hong Kong | 77,046 | Spain | 40,785 |

## Employees in Non-Agricultural Establishments

### ANNUAL AVERAGE BY INDUSTRY DIVISION
Source: Bureau of Labor Statistics, U. S. Dept. of Labor
(In thousands)

| Year | Total | Mining | Contract construction | Manufacturing | Transportation and public utilities | Wholesale and retail trade | Finance, insurance, and real estate | Service, and miscellaneous | Government |
|---|---|---|---|---|---|---|---|---|---|
| 1950 | 45,222 | 901 | 2,333 | 15,241 | 4,034 | 9,386 | 1,919 | 5,382 | 6,026 |
| 1955 | 50,675 | 792 | 2,802 | 16,882 | 4,141 | 10,535 | 2,335 | 6,274 | 6,914 |
| 1960 | 54,234 | 712 | 2,885 | 16,796 | 4,004 | 11,391 | 2,669 | 7,423 | 8,353 |
| 1961 | 54,042 | 672 | 2,816 | 16,326 | 3,903 | 11,337 | 2,731 | 7,664 | 8,594 |
| 1962 | 55,596 | 650 | 2,902 | 16,853 | 3,906 | 11,566 | 2,800 | 8,028 | 8,890 |
| 1963 | 56,702 | 635 | 2,963 | 16,995 | 3,903 | 11,778 | 2,877 | 8,325 | 9,225 |
| 1964 | 58,332 | 634 | 3,050 | 17,274 | 3,951 | 12,160 | 2,957 | 8,709 | 9,596 |
| 1965 | 60,832 | 632 | 3,186 | 18,062 | 4,036 | 12,716 | 3,023 | 9,087 | 10,091 |
| 1966 | 64,034 | 627 | 3,275 | 19,214 | 4,151 | 13,245 | 3,100 | 9,551 | 10,871 |
| 1967 | 66,030 | 616 | 3,203 | 19,434 | 4,271 | 13,613 | 3,217 | 10,060 | 11,616 |

## Personal Consumption Expenditures for the U. S.

Source: Office of Business Economics, U. S. Department of Commerce.
(In millions of dollars) *Revised

| | 1940 | 1945 | 1950 | 1955 | 1960 | 1965* | 1966* | 1967 |
|---|---|---|---|---|---|---|---|---|
| Food and tobacco | 22,032 | 43,520 | 58,120 | 72,236 | 87,510 | 107,183 | 115,203 | 118,555 |
| Clothing, accessories and jewelry | 8,852 | 19,645 | 23,709 | 27,982 | 33,032 | 43,318 | 47,953 | 50,677 |
| Personal care | 1,036 | 1,982 | 2,438 | 3,461 | 5,324 | 7,578 | 7,952 | 8,514 |
| Housing | 9,446 | 12,479 | 21,286 | 33,738 | 46,305 | 63,509 | 67,265 | 70,902 |
| Household operation | 10,479 | 15,530 | 29,461 | 37,322 | 46,906 | 61,789 | 66,418 | 69,940 |
| Medical care | 3,018 | 5,042 | 8,788 | 12,755 | 19,116 | 28,082 | 30,851 | 34,035 |
| Personal business | 3,326 | 4,656 | 6,858 | 10,049 | 14,974 | 21,879 | 24,158 | 26,675 |
| Transportation | 7,143 | 6,845 | 24,672 | 35,574 | 43,154 | 58,154 | 60,505 | 63,547 |
| Recreation | 3,761 | 6,139 | 11,147 | 14,078 | 18,295 | 26,298 | 28,591 | 30,603 |
| Private education and research | 632 | 936 | 1,618 | 2,339 | 3,718 | 5,927 | 6,711 | 7,851 |
| Religious and welfare activities | 1,012 | 1,735 | 2,282 | 3,257 | 4,748 | 5,972 | 6,509 | 6,898 |
| Foreign travel and remittances—net | 87 | 1,192 | 630 | 1,590 | 2,179 | 3,150 | 3,368 | 4,035 |
| Total personal consumption expenditures | 70,824 | 119,701 | 191,009 | 254,381 | 325,241 | 432,839 | 465,487 | 492,232 |

## World Production of Natural Rubber

Long Tons—Estimated
Source: Business and Defense Services Administration, U. S. Dept. of Commerce

| Year | Far East | Tropical America | Africa | Total | Year | Far East | Tropical America | Africa | Total |
|---|---|---|---|---|---|---|---|---|---|
| 1940 | 1,357,000 | 26,000 | 16,000 | 1,399,000 | 1961 | 1,923,623 | 29,377 | 142,000 | 2,095,000 |
| 1945 | 170,500 | 48,000 | 53,500 | 272,000 | 1962 | 1,950,961 | 28,289 | 150,750 | 2,130,000 |
| 1950 | 1,760,500 | 27,000 | 55,000 | 1,842,500 | 1963 | 1,888,517 | 27,233 | 151,750 | 2,067,500 |
| 1955 | 1,787,000 | 27,500 | 98,000 | 1,912,500 | 1964 | 2,041,374 | 34,876 | 158,750 | 2,235,000 |
| 1958 | 1,807,500 | 26,250 | 123,750 | 1,957,500 | 1965 | 2,149,673 | 35,827 | 157,000 | 2,342,500 |
| 1959 | 1,870,900 | 28,100 | 141,000 | 2,040,000 | 1966 | 2,195,038 | 30,962 | 174,000 | 2,400,000 |
| 1960 | 1,813,267 | 29,733 | 147,000 | 1,990,000 | 1967 | 2,261,417 | 27,833 | 163,250 | 2,452,500 |

# Cotton, Synthetics, Wool and Silk Textiles

Source: American Textile Manufacturers Inst., Inc., Market Division, N. Y.

## COTTON TEXTILES
### (Including cotton tire cord and fabrics)

| | 1966 | 1967 |
|---|---|---|
| | (1,000 square yds.) | |
| Production | 10,870,211 | 10,179,089 |
| Exports | 336,632 | 288,031 |
| Imports | 682,967 | 611,900 |
| Available for U. S. consumption | 11,216,546 | 10,502,958 |
| Available per capita sq. yds. | 56.96 | 52.75 |

## PRODUCTION OF BROAD WOVEN FABRICS
### (Except tire cord and fabrics)
#### COTTON BROAD WOVEN GOODS

| Fabric | (1,000 linear yards) | |
|---|---|---|
| Duck and allied fabrics | 284,707 | 278,149 |
| Sheetings and allied coarse and medium yard fabrics | 2,654,504 | 2,549,397 |
| Print cloth yard fabrics | 3,063,023 | 2,871,523 |
| Colored yard fabrics | 425,133 | 380,632 |
| Fine cotton fabrics | 1,151,282 | 944,051 |
| Napped fabrics, blankets, blanketing | 153,875 | 154,463 |
| Towels, toweling and dish cloths | 655,896 | 624,509 |
| Other woven cotton fabrics specialties | 451,443 | 481,115 |
| **Total** | **8,839,863** | **8,283,839** |

## WOOLEN AND WORSTED WOVEN GOODS

| | | |
|---|---|---|
| Woolen and worsted woven goods | 264,874 | 233,592 |
| Total production of broad, woven goods (cotton, rayon, acetate, other man-made fiber, woolen and worsted) silk, except tire fabric | 13,338,799 | 12,757,223 |

## TIRE CORD AND FABRICS

| | (1,000 of pounds) | |
|---|---|---|
| Cotton | 7,722 | 4,464 |
| Man-made fiber | 518,517 | 440,040 |
| **Total** | **526,239** | **444,504** |

## MAN-MADE FIBER AND SILK BROAD WOVEN FABRICS

| | 1967 |
|---|---|
| | (1,000 linear yds.) |
| 100% filament | 1,625,645 |
| Chiefly rayon and/or acetate | 761,100 |
| Chiefly nylon | 317,438 |
| Other filament | 547,107 |
| 100% spun (except blanketing) | 1,977,931 |
| 100% rayon or acetate | 291,167 |
| Rayon/acetate blends with other fiber | 309,781 |
| Polyester blends with cotton | 1,163,086 |
| All other spun | 213,897 |
| Filament and spun combin., mixtures | 411,489 |
| Blanketing, silk, paper specialty fabrics | 219,727 |
| **Total** | **4,234,792** |

## COTTON INDUSTRY

| | 1967 |
|---|---|
| Spindles in place Jan. 1, 1967 | 20,046,000 |
| (Includes cotton system spindles on other fibers) | |
| Average spindles active consuming cotton only | 14,918,000 |
| Consuming fibers other than cotton or blends | 4,976,000 |
| Spindle hours on 100% cotton | 94,613,000,000 |
| On other fibers, blends | 31,626,000,000 |
| Production in square yards | 10,179,089,000 |
| Exports in square yards | 288,031,000 |
| Imports in square yards | 611,900,000 |
| Loom hours operated 1966 | 1,996,015,000 |
| Loom hours operated 1967 | 1,707,991,000 |

## COTTON SYSTEM SPINDLES IN PLACE
### Jan. 1, 1968

**Cotton Growing States:** Ala., 1,690,000; Ga., 2,901,000; N. C., 6,834,000; S. C., 7,061,000; Tenn., 451,000; Tex., 238,000; Va., 552,000; Other states, 105,000; total 19,832,000.

**New England States:** Conn., 91,000; Me., 221,100; Mass., 209,000; R. I., 62,000; other states, 119,000; total 702,000.

**Rest of United States:** 73,000.
**Total United States:** 20,607,000.

# Cotton, Wool, Silk, and Man-Made Fibers Production

Source: Economic Research Service, U. S. Dept. of Agriculture

Cotton and wool from reports of the Dept. of Agriculture; silk, rayon and non-cellulosic man-made fibers from Textile Organon, a publication of the Textile Economics Bureau, Inc.

| | Cotton[1] | | Wool[2] | | Silk | Man-made fibers[3] | | | |
|---|---|---|---|---|---|---|---|---|---|
| | | | | | | Rayon&Acetate | | Non-Cellulosic[4] | |
| Year | U. S. | World | U. S. | World | World | U. S. | World | U. S. | World |
| | [5] | Mil. bales | Mil. lb. | Mil. lb. | Mil. lb. | Mil. lb. | Mil. lb. | Mil. lb. | Mil. lb. |
| 1940 | 12.6 | 31.2 | 434.0 | 4,180 | 130 | 471.2 | 2,485.3 | 4.6 | 4.6 |
| 1945 | 9.0 | 21.4 | 378.5 | 3,790 | 24 | 792.1 | 1,325.3 | 50.1 | 50.1 |
| 1950 | 10.0 | 31.1 | 249.3 | 4,000 | 42 | 1,259.4 | 3,552.8 | 145.9 | 177.4 |
| 1955 | 14.7 | 43.6 | 282.9 | 4,685 | 64 | 1,260.7 | 5,023.3 | 455.1 | 670.0 |
| 1960 | 14.3 | 46.5 | 298.9 | 5,640 | 68 | 1,028.5 | 5,731.6 | 854.2 | 1,779.1 |
| 1962 | 14.9 | 47.8 | 276.5 | 5,700 | 73 | 1,272.1 | 6,294.4 | 1,163.2 | 2,638.8 |
| 1963 | 15.3 | 50.2 | 261.2 | 5,820 | 68 | 1,348.8 | 6,725.5 | 1,347.9 | 3,213.7 |
| 1964 | 15.2 | 52.5 | 237.4 | 5,777 | 72 | 1,431.8 | 7,229.2 | 1,646.2 | 4,068.9 |
| 1965 | 15.0 | 53.9 | 224.8 | 5,805 | 73 | 1,527.0 | 7,330.8 | 2,059.2 | 4,946.6 |
| 1966 | 9.6 | 48.3 | 219.2 | 6,001 | 72 | 1,519.0 | 7,359.4 | 2,401.1 | 5,986.5 |
| 1967 (pre.) | 7.5 | 47.3 | 212.2 | 6,094 | 71 | 1,388.1 | 7,269.2 | 2,641.7 | 6,806.2 |

[1]Year beginning Aug. 1. [2]Grease basis. [3]Includes filament yarn and staple & tow fiber. [4]Includes textile glass fiber. [5]500-pound gross weight bales.

# Production of Shoes and Slippers, Except Rubber

Source: National Footwear Manufacturers Assn., New York, N. Y.

In thousands of pairs

| Footwear | 1967 | 1966 |
|---|---|---|
| Men's | 125,605 | 126,903 |
| Youths' and boys' | 21,807 | 24,616 |
| Women's | 264,966 | 284,170 |
| Misses' | 32,767 | 35,912 |
| Children's | 29,361 | 33,581 |
| Infants' and babies' | 22,910 | 32,499 |
| Athletic shoes | 6,834 | 7,268 |
| Slippers | 96,931 | 93,823 |
| Other footwear | 2,156 | 2,924 |
| **Shoes and Slippers, except rubber, grand total** | **603,338** | **641,696** |

**Principal producing states, 1967:** Pennsylvania, 82,448,000; Massachusetts, 80,264,000; New York, 68,745,000; Maine, 54,676,000; Missouri, 53,119,000; New Hampshire, 44,504,000; Tennessee, 37,564,000; and Illinois, 19,906,000.

**Imports of footwear, 1967:** 129,137,000 pairs worth $217,595,000. Largest imports from Japan, 56,768,000 pairs worth $34,231,000; from Italy, 41,555,000 pairs worth $102,731,000.

**Exports of footwear, 1967:** 2,217,057 pairs worth $8,227,065. Principal market: Canada, 391,302; Mexico, 302,863; Netherland Antilles, 201,870; Bahamas, 268,571; Bermuda, 105,827; Hong Kong, 82,282.

**Employees 1967** (average): production workers, 200,600; hours worked weekly 38.0; weekly wages $76.38.

## Retail Store Sales, by Kinds of Business

Source: Office of Business Economics, U. S. Dept. of Commerce. In millions of dollars

| Kinds of business | 1966 | 1967 | Kinds of business | 1966 | 1967 |
|---|---|---|---|---|---|
| **All retail stores**[1] | **303,672** | **313,503** | Apparel group | 17,276 | 18,105 |
| **Durable goods stores**[1] | **97,812** | **99,669** | Men's and boys' wear stores | 3,537 | 3,822 |
| Automotive group | 57,414 | 57,556 | Women's apparel, accessory | | |
| Motor vehicle, other automotive | | | stores | 6,913 | 6,994 |
| dealers | 53,875 | 53,695 | Shoe stores | 2,811 | 2,947 |
| Tire, battery, accessory dealers | 3,539 | 3,861 | Food group[1] | 71,125 | 72,137 |
| Furniture and appliance group | 14,978 | 15,700 | Grocery stores | 65,105 | 66,146 |
| Furniture, home furnishings | | | General merchandise group | 39,811 | 42,174 |
| stores | 9,089 | 9,384 | Department stores, excl. mail | | |
| Household appliance, radio | | | order | 26,094 | 27,703 |
| stores | 4,905 | 5,245 | Mail order (catalog sales) | 2,691 | 2,767 |
| Lumber, building, hardware group | 12,307 | 12,411 | Variety stores | 5,727 | 6,078 |
| Lumber, building materials | | | Eating and drinking places | 23,431 | 24,887 |
| dealers | 9,340 | 9,350 | Gasoline service stations | 23,012 | 24,011 |
| Hardware stores | 2,967 | 3,061 | Drug and proprietary stores | 10,148 | 10,894 |
| **Nondurable goods stores**[1] | **205,860** | **213,834** | Liquor stores | 6,758 | 7,120 |

[1]Sales by jewelry stores, other durable goods stores, other general merchandise stores, and other nondurable goods stores are not shown separately but are included in the totals.
**Total Retail Stores Sales** (In millions of dollars)—(1955) 183,851; (1957) 200,002; (1958) 200,353; (1959) 215,413; (1960) 219,529; (1961) 218,811; (1962) 235,351; (1963) 246,435; (1964) 261,630; (1965) 283,852; (1966) 303,672; (1967) 303,672.

## U. S. Balance of Payments

Source: Office of Business Economics, Dept. of Commerce
(In millions of dollars. Excludes military transfers under grants. Revised)

| | 1955 | 1960 | 1962 | 1963 | 1964 | 1965 | 1966 | 1967 |
|---|---|---|---|---|---|---|---|---|
| **Recorded receipts** | **20,517** | **28,327** | **32,649** | **34,109** | **38,504** | **40,339** | **46,906** | **49,922** |
| Exports of goods and services | 19,804 | 27,325 | 30,343 | 32,432 | 37,098 | 39,196 | 43,142 | 45,756 |
| Merchandise | 14,280 | 19,487 | 20,606 | 22,071 | 25,297 | 26,244 | 29,176 | 30,468 |
| Transportation | 1,406 | 1,782 | 1,965 | 2,115 | 2,324 | 2,413 | 2,608 | 2,701 |
| Foreign travel in U. S. | 654 | 919 | 957 | 1,015 | 1,207 | 1,380 | 1,590 | 1,646 |
| Miscellaneous services | 820 | 1,454 | 1,739 | 1,925 | 2,135 | 2,436 | 2,687 | 2,843 |
| Military transactions | 200 | 335 | 656 | 657 | 747 | 830 | 829 | 1,240 |
| Income on investments | 2,444 | 3,349 | 4,419 | 4,649 | 5,386 | 5,893 | 6,252 | 6,859 |
| Repayments on Government loans | 416 | 637 | 1,279 | 987 | 717 | 872 | 1,232 | 981 |
| Foreign capital other than liquid funds | 297 | 365 | 1,027 | 690 | 689 | 271 | 2,532 | 3,185 |
| **Recorded payments** | **22,274** | **31,335** | **33,856** | **36,535** | **40,444** | **41,358** | **48,052** | **52,960** |
| Imports of goods and services | 17,795 | 23,355 | 25,358 | 26,620 | 28,688 | 32,295 | 38,063 | 40,989 |
| Merchandise | 11,527 | 14,744 | 16,219 | 17,014 | 18,648 | 21,516 | 25,541 | 26,991 |
| Transportation | 1,204 | 1,915 | 2,128 | 2,316 | 2,462 | 2,679 | 2,923 | 2,982 |
| U. S. travel abroad | 1,153 | 1,750 | 1,939 | 2,114 | 2,211 | 2,438 | 2,657 | 3,195 |
| Miscellaneous services | 521 | 795 | 858 | 892 | 1,035 | 989 | 1,132 | 1,189 |
| Military expenditures | 2,901 | 3,087 | 3,105 | 2,961 | 2,876 | 2,945 | 3,735 | 4,340 |
| Income on investments | 489 | 1,063 | 1,110 | 1,325 | 1,456 | 1,729 | 2,074 | 2,293 |
| Private remittances | 456 | 483 | 534 | 629 | 617 | 658 | 648 | 835 |
| Private capital outflow | 1,255 | 3,878 | 3,426 | 4,459 | 6,578 | 3,794 | 4,298 | 5,504 |
| Government pensions and other transfers | 141 | 214 | 245 | 262 | 279 | 369 | 367 | 441 |
| Government grants and capital outflow | 2,627 | 3,405 | 4,293 | 4,565 | 4,282 | 4,242 | 4,676 | 5,191 |
| **Unrecorded transactions, net**[1] | **515** | **−892** | **−997** | **−244** | **−860** | **−315** | **−210** | **−532** |
| Balance of payments | −1,242 | −3,901 | −2,204 | −2,670 | −2,800 | −1,335 | −1,357 | −3,571 |
| Balanced by— | | | | | | | | |
| Monetary reserve assets (increase [−])[2] | | 2,145 | 1,533 | 377 | 171 | 1,222 | 568 | 52 |
| Foreign holdings of liquid dollar assets | | | | | | | | |
| (decrease [−])[3] | 1,060 | 1,756 | 671 | 2,293 | 2,629 | 113 | 789 | 3,519 |

[1]Also called "errors and omissions." Believed to consist largely of unreported short-term capital flows.
[2]Includes gold, convertible currencies, and International Monetary Fund position.
[3]Includes U. S. Government nonmarketable medium-term convertible securities in the amount of $703 million in 1963, $376 million in 1964, $122 million in 1965, $945 million in 1966 and $455 million in 1967.

## Statistical Information About the United States

In the *Statistical Abstract of the United States* the Bureau of the Census of the U. S. Dept. of Commerce annually publishes a summary of social, political and economic information. A book of more than 1,000 pages, it presents in 33 sections comprehensive data on population, housing, health, education, employment, income, prices, business, banking, science, defense, trade, and other subjects. A special section includes comprehensive data for metropolitan areas. The book is prepared under the direction of Edwin D. Goldfield, chief statistical information division, Bureau of the Census Supplements to the *Statistical Abstract* are *Pocket Data Book, USA, 1967* (1969 edition in preparation); *County and City Data Book, 1967; Congressional District Data Book (Districts of the 88th Congress)* and its supplements for states that redistricted for the 89th and 90th Congresses; *Historical Statistics of the United States, Colonial Times to 1957* and its supplement . . . *Continuation to 1962 and Revisions.* Information concerning these and other publications may be obtained from the Supt. of Documents, Government Printing Office, Washington, D. C. 20402.

## Motor Fuel Supply[1] and Demand

Source: Bureau of Mines (Figures in 42-gallon barrels)

| Year | Supply Production | Supply Daily average | Demand Domestic | Demand Export | Year | Supply Production | Supply Daily average | Demand Domestic | Demand Export |
|---|---|---|---|---|---|---|---|---|---|
| | (1,000) | (1,000) | (1,000) | (1,000) | | (1,000) | (1,000) | (1,000) | (1,000) |
| 1940 | 616,314 | 1,684 | 589,490 | 25,377 | 1960 | 1,522,497 | 4,160 | 1,511,670 | 13,456 |
| 1945 | 793,431 | 2,174 | 696,333 | 88,059 | 1964 | 1,687,445 | 4,610 | 1,685,457 | 8,039 |
| 1950 | 1,024,181 | 2,806 | 994,290 | 24,721 | 1965 | 1,733,258 | 4,749 | 1,750,028 | 6,391 |
| 1955 | 1,373,950 | 3,764 | 1,329,788 | 34,521 | 1966 | 1,822,388 | 4,993 | 1,823,642 | 5,796 |
| 1959* | 1,488,860 | 4,079 | 1,485,277 | 16,743 | 1967 | 1,872,849 | 5,131 | 1,867,878 | 6,864 |

*Beginning with 1959 Alaska and Hawaii are included. [1]Includes special naphtha.

# Mineral Production in United States[1]
## INCLUDING ALASKA AND HAWAII
### Source: Bureau of Mines (r-Revised)

| Mineral | 1966 Quantity | 1966 Value (thousands) | 1967 Quantity | 1967 Value (thousands) |
|---|---|---|---|---|
| **MINERAL FUELS** | | | | |
| Asphalt and related bitumens (native): | | | | |
| Bituminous limestone & sandstone and gilsonite.............................short tons | 2,041,271 | $8,438 | 1,866,666 | $8,136 |
| Carbon dioxide, natural (est.)....1,000 cu. ft. | 1,140,907 | 153 | 1,142,374 | 165 |
| Coal: | | | | |
| Bituminous and lignite[2]..thous. short tons | 533,881 | 2,421,293 | 552,626 | 2,555,377 |
| Pennsylvania anthracite..thous. short tons | 12,941 | 100,663 | 12,256 | 96,160 |
| Helium...............thousand cubic feet | 4,606,100 | 74,097 | 4,712,300 | 72,457 |
| Natural gas..........million cubic feet | 17,232,134 | 2,721,875 | 18,171,325 | 2,898,741 |
| Natural gas liquids: | | | | |
| Gasoline and cycle products....1,000 gals. | [3]7,591,658 | [3]524,167 | [3]7,919,831 | [3]549,429 |
| LP gases..................1,000 gals. | 12,134,294 | 527,223 | 13,717,861 | 632,994 |
| Peat..........................short tons | 605,858 | 6,501 | 619,687 | 6,768 |
| Petroleum (crude).......1,000 42-gal. bbls. | 3,028,084 | 8,727,387 | [3]3,216,715 | [3]9,377,516 |
| **Total mineral fuels.................** | ............ | r15,112,000 | ............ | 16,198,000 |
| **NONMETALS (except fuels)** | | | | |
| Abrasive stone[4]...............short tons | 3,806 | $515 | 2,701 | $574 |
| Asbestos.....................short tons | 125,928 | 11,056 | 123,189 | 11,102 |
| Barite.............thousand short tons | 947 | 11,259 | 962 | 11,605 |
| Boron minerals................short tons | 866 | 68,209 | 955 | 74,130 |
| Bromine..............thousand pounds | 326,498 | 78,883 | 349,757 | 85,391 |
| Calcite (optical grade) pounds............ | [5] | [5] | | |
| Cement: | | | | |
| Portland.........thousand 376-lb. bbls. | 373,091 | 1,162,984 | 608,965 | 11,983 |
| Masonry.........thousand 280-lb. bbls. | 22,367 | 63,407 | 365,570 | 1,148,208 |
| Natural and slag...thousand 376-lb. bbls. | r109 | r415 | 21,700 | 62,168 |
| Clays...............thousand short tons | r56,713 | r221,714 | 94 | 360 |
| Emery.......................short tons | 11,102 | 210 | 54,664 | 223,989 |
| Feldspar.....................long tons | r655,452 | r7,020 | [5] | [5] |
| Fluorspar.....................short tons | 253,068 | 10,841 | 615,397 | 7,086 |
| Garnet (abrasive)...............short tons | 21,952 | 2,092 | 295,643 | 13,164 |
| Gem stones (estimate)................... | NA | 2,437 | 20,494 | 1,849 |
| Gypsum..............thousand short tons | 9,647 | 35,681 | NA | 2,430 |
| Lime...............thousand short tons | 18,057 | 239,588 | 9,393 | 34,383 |
| Magnesium compounds from sea water and brine short tons, MgO equivalent...... | r651,187 | r46,690 | 17,974 | 241,137 |
| Mica: | | | | |
| Scrap.......................short tons | 113,133 | 3,733 | 544,428 | 41,414 |
| Sheet..........................pounds | 4,500 | 1 | 118,503 | 2,876 |
| Perlite.......................short tons | 404,160 | 3,907 | 20,500 | [5] |
| Phosphate rock........thousand short tons | r39,044 | r261,092 | 413,001 | 3,973 |
| Potassium salts thousand short tons, K₂O equivalent | 3,320 | 122,210 | 39,770 | 265,947 |
| Pumice...............thousand short tons | 3,218 | 6,765 | 3,299 | 105,313 |
| Pyrites...............thousand long tons | 873 | 5,088 | 3,446 | 5,131 |
| Salt........................thousand short tons | 36,463 | 229,985 | 861 | 7,943 |
| Sand and gravel......thousand short tons | 934,481 | 984,982 | 38,946 | 251,210 |
| Sodium carbonate (natural)......short tons | 1,737,511 | 40,674 | 905,162 | 980,356 |
| Sodium sulfate (natural).........short tons | 640,329 | 11,271 | 1,727,977 | 40,539 |
| Stone[6]...............thousand short tons | 813,374 | 1,260,715 | 636,843 | 10,710 |
| Sulfur: | | | 785,592 | 1,240,244 |
| Frasch process mines...thousand long tons | 7,721 | 201,292 | 7,682 | 251,670 |
| Other mines................long tons | 557 | 5 | 568 | 3 |
| Talc, soapstone, and pyrophyllite..short tons | 895,045 | 6,479 | 902,512 | 6,871 |
| Tripoli.......................short tons | 66,163 | 328 | 70,984 | 377 |
| Vermiculite..........thousand short tons | 262 | 4,955 | 255 | 4,974 |
| Value of items that cannot be disclosed[5].... | ............ | 69,911 | ............ | 55,734 |
| **Total nonmetals..................** | ............ | r$5,176,000 | ............ | $5,205,000 |
| **METALS** | | | | |
| Antimony ore and concentrate....short tons | 927 | [5] | 892 | [5] |
| Bauxite........long tons, dried equivalent | 1,796 | $20,095 | 1,654 | $19,079 |
| Copper (recoverable content).....short tons | 1,429,152 | 1,033,850 | 954,064 | 729,401 |
| Gold (recoverable content of ores)...troy ozs. | 1,803,412 | 63,119 | 1,584,187 | 55,447 |
| Iron ore, usable (excl. byproduct iron sinter) thousand long tons, gross weight | 90,040 | 854,134 | 82,415 | 817,511 |
| Lead (recoverable content of ores)..short tons | 327,368 | 98,964 | 316,931 | 88,741 |
| Manganese ore (35 percent or more Mn) short tons, gross weight | 14,406 | [5] | 12,585 | [5] |
| Manganiferous ore (5 to 35 percent Mn) short tons, gross weight | 324,926 | [5] | 289,160 | [5] |
| Mercury.................76-pound flasks | 22,008 | 9,722 | 23,784 | 11,639 |
| Molybdenum (concentrate) thousand pds.. | 91,670 | 144,327 | 81,596 | 133,604 |
| Nickel (ore and concentrate) short tons..... | 15,036 | [5] | 15,287 | [5] |
| Silver (content of ores, etc.) thousand troy ounces | 43,669 | 56,463 | 32,119 | 49,784 |
| Tin.........................long tons | 97 | 265 | [5] | [5] |
| Titanium concentrate: | | | | |
| Ilmenite........short tons, gross weight | 868,436 | 17,608 | 882,414 | 18,519 |
| Rutile.........short tons, gross weight | [5] | [5] | [5] | [5] |
| Tungsten ore and concentrate short tons, 60-percent WO₃ basis | 8,912 | 17,620 | 9,088 | 20,895 |
| Uranium (recoverable in ore & concentrates) 1,000 pds. | 19,037 | 152,281 | 20,655 | 165,239 |
| Vanadium (recoverable in ore and concentrate)................short tons | 5,166 | 22,210 | 4,963 | 21,331 |
| Zinc (recoverable content of ores, etc.) short tons | 572,558 | 166,044 | 549,413 | 151,562 |
| Value of items that cannot be disclosed[7].... | ............ | r46,605 | ............ | 50,190 |
| **Total metals....................** | ............ | r$2,703,000 | ............ | $2,333,000 |
| **Grand total mineral production.....** | ............ | r$22,991,000 | ............ | $23,736,000 |

[1]Production as measured by mine shipments, sales, or marketable production. [2]Includes small quantity of anthracite mined in states other than Pa. [3]Final figure. [4]Grindstones, pulpstone, millstones, grinding pebbles, sharpening stones, and tube-mill liners. [5]Figure withheld to avoid disclosing confidential data; value included with "Nonmetal items that cannot be disclosed." [6]Excludes abrasive stone, bituminous limestone, bituminous sandstone and ground soapstone.

## Value of Mineral Production in U. S.

Source: Bureau of Mines (data are for 1967)

| State | Value ($1,000) | Rank | Percent of U. S. total | Principal minerals in order of value |
|---|---|---|---|---|
| Alabama...... | $251,391 | 21 | 1.06 | Coal, cement, petroleum, stone. |
| Alaska........ | 134,066 | 29 | .56 | Petroleum, sand and gravel, coal, natural gas. |
| Arizona....... | 463,863 | 15 | 1.95 | Copper, sand and gravel, molybdenum, cement |
| Arkansas..... | 179,453 | 27 | .76 | Petroleum, stone, bauxite, cement. |
| California..... | 1,696,233 | 3 | 7.15 | Petroleum, natural gas, sand and gravel, cement. |
| Colorado..... | 346,235 | 17 | 1.46 | Petroleum, molybdenum, coal, sand and gravel. |
| Connecticut.... | 20,619 | 45 | .09 | Stone, sand and gravel, feldspar, lime. |
| Delaware..... | 2,383 | 50 | .01 | Sand and gravel, stone, clays, gem stones. |
| Dist. of Col.... | .......... | ...... | ...... | |
| Florida....... | 309,797 | 18 | 1.31 | Phosphate rock, stone, cement, clays. |
| Georgia....... | 153,458 | 28 | .65 | Clays, stone, cement, sand and gravel. |
| Hawaii........ | 16,936 | 46 | .07 | Cement, stone, sand and gravel, pumice. |
| Idaho........ | 109,408 | 31 | .46 | Silver, phosphate rock, lead, zinc. |
| Illinois....... | 636,801 | 8 | 2.68 | Coal, petroleum, stone, sand and gravel. |
| Indiana....... | 244,921 | 22 | 1.03 | Coal, cement, stone, petroleum. |
| Iowa.......... | 113,222 | 30 | .48 | Cement, stone, sand and gravel, gypsum. |
| Kansas....... | 574,068 | 10 | 2.42 | Petroleum, natural gas, natural gas liquids, helium. |
| Kentucky..... | 535,705 | 11 | 2.26 | Coal, petroleum stone, natural gas. |
| Louisiana..... | 3,961,750 | 2 | 16.69 | Petroleum, natural gas, natural gas liquids, sulfur. |
| Maine........ | 14,882 | 47 | .06 | Cement, sands and gravel, stone, peat. |
| Maryland..... | 72,819 | 37 | .31 | Stone, cement, sand and gravel, coal. |
| Massachusetts.. | 40,612 | 43 | .17 | Sand and gravel, stone, lime, clays. |
| Michigan..... | 610,204 | 9 | 2.57 | Iron ore, cement, sand and gravel, bromine. |
| Minnesota..... | 523,326 | 13 | 2.20 | Iron ore, sand and gravel, stone, cement. |
| Mississippi..... | 217,010 | 24 | .91 | Petroleum, natural gas, sand and gravel, clays. |
| Missouri...... | 236,659 | 23 | 1.00 | Stone, cement, lead, iron ore. |
| Montana...... | 186,524 | 26 | .79 | Petroleum, copper, sand and gravel, phosphate rock. |
| Nebraska.... | 70,868 | 39 | .30 | Petroleum, cement, sand and gravel, stone. |
| Nevada...... | 90,883 | 33 | .38 | Copper, gold, sand and gravel, diatomite. |
| New Hampshire | 8,117 | 48 | .03 | Sand and gravel, stone, clays, feldspar. |
| New Jersey... | 72,747 | 38 | .31 | Sand and gravel, stone, zinc, magnesium compounds. |
| New Mexico... | 874,106 | 7 | 3.68 | Petroleum, natural gas, potassium salts, uranium. |
| New York..... | 299,318 | 19 | 1.26 | Cement, stone, sand and gravel, salt... |
| North Carolina. | 77,094 | 36 | .32 | Stone, sand and gravel, cement, phosphate rock. |
| North Dakota.. | 97,538 | 32 | .41 | Petroleum, sand and gravel, coal, natural gas. |
| Ohio........ | 498,888 | 14 | 2.10 | Coal, stone, sand and gravel, cement. |
| Oklahoma.... | 1,032,126 | 4 | 4.35 | Petroleum, natural gas, natural gas liquids, cement. |
| Oregon...... | 66,560 | 40 | .28 | Sand and gravel, stone, cement nickel. |
| Pennsylvania... | 898,398 | 6 | 3.78 | Coal, cement, stone, sand and gravel. |
| Rhode Island.. | 4,035 | 49 | .02 | Sand and gravel, stone. |
| South Carolina. | 48,274 | 42 | .20 | Cement, stone clays, sand and gravel. |
| South Dakota.. | 52,618 | 41 | .22 | Gold, sand and gravel, stone, cement. |
| Tennessee..... | 189,572 | 25 | .80 | Stone, zinc, cement, coal. |
| Texas........ | 5,406,371 | 1 | 22.78 | Petroleum, natural gas, natural gas liquids, cement. |
| Utah........ | 354,477 | 16 | 1.49 | Copper, petroleum, coal, molybdenum. |
| Vermont..... | 27,268 | 44 | .11 | Stone, asbestos, sand and gravel, talc. |
| Virginia...... | 283,685 | 20 | 1.20 | Coal, stone, cement, sand and gravel. |
| Washington... | 82,067 | 34 | .35 | Sand and gravel, cement, stone, zinc. |
| West Virginia.. | 937,858 | 5 | 3.95 | Coal, natural gas, natural gas liquids, stone. |
| Wisconsin..... | 79,612 | 35 | .34 | Sand and gravel, stone, cement, zinc. |
| Wyoming..... | 530,696 | 12 | 2.24 | Petroleum, uranium, natural gas, sodium salts. |
| **Total.......** | **23,736,000** | ...... | **100.00** | Petroleum, natural gas, coal, stone. |

## Value of Mineral Production in the United States[2]

Source: Bureau of Mines (r-Revised)
(In millions of dollars)

| Year[1] | Fuels | Nonmetallic (except fuels) | Metals | Total | Year[1] | Fuels | Nonmetallic Metals fuels) | Metals | Total |
|---|---|---|---|---|---|---|---|---|---|
| 1925.... | 2,910 | 1,187 | 715 | 4,812 | 1958.... | 11,589 | 3,466 | 1,594 | 10,649 |
| 1930.... | 2,500 | 973 | 501 | 3,980 | 1959.... | 11,950 | 3,861 | 1,570 | 17,381 |
| 1935.... | 2,013 | 564 | 365 | 2,942 | 1960.... | 12,142 | 3,568 | 2,022 | 18,032 |
| 1940.... | 2,662 | 784 | 752 | 4,198 | 1961.... | 12,357 | 3,946 | 1,927 | 18,230 |
| 1945.... | 4,569 | 888 | 774 | 6,231 | 1962.... | 12,784 | 4,117 | 1,937 | 18,838 |
| 1950.... | 8,689 | 1,882 | 1,351 | 11,862 | 1963.... | 13,317 | 4,316 | 2,002 | 19,635 |
| 1954.... | 9,919 | 2,733 | 1,518 | 14,170 | 1964.... | 13,623 | 4,623 | r2,366 | r20,612 |
| 1955.... | 10,780 | 3,076 | 2,005 | 15,911 | 1965.... | 14,047 | 4,933 | r2,544 | r21,524 |
| 1956.... | 11,741 | 3,391 | 2,358 | 17,490 | 1966.... | 15,112 | 5,176 | 2,703 | 22,991 |
| 1957.... | 12,709 | 3,387 | 2,134 | 18,233 | 1967.... | 16,198 | 5,205 | 2,333 | 23,736 |

[1]Excludes Alaska and Hawaii, 1925-53. Data for 1925-46 are not strictly comparable with those for subsequent years, since for the earlier years the value of heavy clay products has not been replaced by the value of raw clays used for such products. [2]Production as measured by mine shipments sales, or marketable production.

## Coal and Coke Production in the United States

Source: Bureau of Mines (NA-not available)

| Year | Penn. Anthracite Production | Value | Bituminous Production | Value | Year | Penn. Anthracite Production | Value | Bituminous Production | Value |
|---|---|---|---|---|---|---|---|---|---|
| | Net tons | $1,000 | 1,000 net tons | $1,000 | | Net tons | $1,000 | 1,000 net tons | $1,000 |
| 1925... | 61,817,149 | 327,665 | 520,053 | 1,060,402 | 1959... | 20,649,000 | 172,320 | 412,028 | 1,965,606 |
| 1930... | 69,384,837 | 354,574 | 467,526 | 795,483 | 1960... | 18,817,000 | 147,116 | 415,512 | 1,950,421 |
| 1935... | 52,158,783 | 210,131 | 372,373 | 658,063 | 1961... | 17,446,000 | 140,338 | 402,977 | 1,844,567 |
| 1940... | 51,484,640 | 205,490 | 460,772 | 879,327 | 1962... | 16,894,000 | 134,094 | 422,149 | 1,891,555 |
| 1945... | 54,933,909 | 323,944 | 577,617 | 1,768,204 | 1963... | 18,267,000 | 153,503 | 458,928 | 2,013,390 |
| 1950... | 44,076,703 | 392,398 | 516,311 | 2,500,374 | 1964... | 17,184,000 | 148,648 | 486,998 | 2,165,582 |
| 1955... | 26,204,544 | 206,097 | 464,633 | 2,092,383 | 1965... | 14,866,000 | 122,021 | 512,088 | 2,276,022 |
| 1957... | 25,338,321 | 227,754 | 492,704 | 2,504,403 | 1966... | 12,941,000 | 100,663 | 533,881 | 2,421,293 |
| 1958... | 21,171,142 | 187,898 | 410,446 | 1,996,283 | 1967... | 12,256 | 96,160 | 552,626 | 2,555,377 |

**Coke production** (net tons—Value in $1,000)—(1963) 54,278,307, $951,892,000; (1964) 62,144,078, $1,102,468; (1965) 66,854,461, $1,125,756; (1966) 67,402, $1,166,049; (1967) 64,580, $1,123,173.
**Coke exports** (net tons)—(1963) 451,241; (1964) 523,695; (1965) 833,668; (1966) 1,102,166; (1967) 710,380. **Imports**—(1963) 152,595; (1964) 103,286; (1965) 89,620; (1966) 95,721; (1967) 92,001.
**Anthracite exports** (net tons)—(1964) 1,575,097; (1965) 850,630; (1966) 766,025; (1967) 594,797.

# United States Pig Iron and Steel Output

**Source: American Iron and Steel Institute; figures show net tons**

| Year | Total pig iron | Total pig iron and ferro-alloys | Raw Steel | Year | Total pig iron | Total pig iron and ferro-alloys | Raw Steel |
|------|----------|----------|----------|------|----------|----------|----------|
| 1940..... | 46,071,666 | 47,398,529 | 66,982,686 | 1962..... | 65,640,824 | 67,595,338 | 98,327,785 |
| 1945..... | 53,223,169 | 54,919,029 | 79,701,648 | 1963..... | 71,844,054 | 73,715,227 | 109,260,949 |
| 1950..... | 64,586,907 | 66,400,311 | 96,836,075 | 1964..... | 85,600,483 | 87,932,444 | 127,075,767 |
| 1955..... | 76,857,417 | 79,263,865 | 117,036,085 | 1965..... | 88,184,901 | 90,918,040 | 131,461,601 |
| 1960..... | 66,480,648 | 68,566,364 | 99,281,601 | 1966..... | 91,500,000 | 94,003,000 | 134,101,000 |
| 1961..... | 64,630,687 | 66,565,063 | 98,014,492 | 1967..... | 86,984,000 | 89,472,000 | 127,213,000 |

Steel figures include only that portion of the capacity and production of steel for castings used by foundries which were operated by companies producing steel ingots.

## RAW STEEL PRODUCTION
### (Net Tons)

| State | 1967 |
|-------|------|
| New York.......................... | 7,298 |
| Pennsylvania........\........... | 29,881 |
| R. I., Conn., N. J., Del., Md...... | 8,132 |
| Va., W. Va., Ga., Fla., N. C...... | 4,268 |
| Kentucky.......................... | 2,410 |
| Ala., Tenn., Miss................. | 4,444 |
| Ohio.............................. | 20,378 |
| Indiana........................... | 17,610 |
| Illinois........................... | 10,649 |
| Michigan.......................... | 9,245 |
| Minn., Mo., Okla., Texas......... | 4,644 |
| Ariz., Colo., Utah, Wash., Ore, Hawaii. | 4,154 |
| California......................... | 4,100 |
| **Total................** | **127,213** |

### 1967 Scrap Iron Production and Export

**Source: Institute of Scrap Iron & Steel**
(net tons 2,000 pounds each)

The United States generated an estimated 42,-400,000 tons of ferrous scrap. Of this total, 14,000,-000 tons is attributed to "prompt industrial" scrap, the leftovers from the fabrication of new iron and steel products.
Consumption of mill revert and purchased scrap .............. 85,361,000 tons
Consumption of purchased scrap only ............. 35,127,000 tons (est.)
Value of exports .................. $245,300,000
Sales of scrap amounted to ...... $2,500,000,000
Exports of iron and steel scraps .. 7,504,000 tons
Imports of iron and steel scrap.. 229,000,000 tons
(Export and Import figures are from Dept. of Commerce.)

# Copper, Lead and Zinc Production in the U. S.

**Source: Bureau of Mines**

| Year | Copper Mil. lbs. | $1,000 | Lead[1] Short tons | $1,000 | Zinc Short tons | Mil. dol. | Year | Copper Mil. lbs. | $1,000 | Lead[1] Short tons | $1,000 | Zinc Short tons | Mil. dol. |
|------|------|--------|------|--------|------|------|------|------|--------|------|--------|------|------|
| 1925. | 1,675 | 237,832 | 654,921 | 113,956 | 555,631 | 84 | 1959. | 1,599 | 490,788 | 225,270 | 51,812 | 348,443 | 80 |
| 1930. | 1,394 | 181,271 | 573,740 | 57,374 | 489,361 | 47 | 1960. | 2,236 | 733,708 | 228,899 | 53,562 | 334,101 | 87 |
| 1935. | 763 | 63,295 | 310,505 | 24,840 | 412,184 | 36 | 1961. | 2,325 | 697,488 | 288,078 | 59,344 | 413,282 | 95 |
| 1940. | 1,818 | 205,453 | 433,065 | 43,307 | 589,988 | 74 | 1962. | 2,564 | 794,918 | 245,645 | 45,690 | 448,095 | 104 |
| 1945. | 1,565 | 184,723 | 336,535 | 45,636 | 574,453 | 90 | 1963. | 2,426 | 747,310 | 253,369 | 54,727 | 529,254 | 123 |
| 1950. | 1,823 | 379,122 | 418,809 | 113,078 | 591,454 | 167 | 1964. | 2,494 | 812,901 | 286,010 | 74,935 | 574,858 | 156 |
| 1955. | 2,015 | 751,454 | 321,132 | 95,697 | 582,913 | 143 | 1965. | 2,703 | 957,028 | 301,147 | 93,959 | 611,153 | 178 |
| 1957. | 2,162 | 650,825 | 347,675 | 99,435 | 539,692 | 129 | 1966. | 2,858 | 1,033,850 | 327,368 | 98,964 | 572,558 | 166 |
| 1958. | 1,986 | 522,275 | 269,082 | 62,965 | 346,240 | 71 | 1967. | 1,908 | 729,401 | 316,931 | 88,741 | 549,413 | 151 |

[1]Production from domestic ores.

# U. S. Primary Aluminum Production

**Source: U. S. Bureau of Mines and Aluminum Company of America**

| Year | Short tons | Year | Short tons | Year | Short tons | Year | Short tons |
|------|-----------|------|-----------|------|-----------|------|-----------|
| 1883-1902. | 13,981 | 1930..... | 114,518 | 1960..... | 2,014,498 | 1964...... | 2,552,747 |
| 1903-1912. | 108,412 | 1940..... | 206,280 | 1961..... | 1,903,711 | 1965...... | 2,754,478 |
| 1913-1923. | 282,722 | 1950..... | 718,622 | 1962..... | 2,117,929 | 1966...... | 2,968,366 |
| 1924-1925. | 145,340 | 1955...... | 565,721 | 1963..... | 2,312,528 | 1967...... | 3,267,259 |

### ESTIMATED MARKETS FOR TOTAL U. S. ALUMINUM SHIPMENTS (Data for 1967)

| Market | Percent | Market | Percent |
|--------|---------|--------|---------|
| Transportation...................... | 21.4 | Other domestic markets............ | 9.7 |
| Building and construction........... | 20.8 | Containers and Packaging.......... | 9.4 |
| Electrical.......................... | 13.9 | Machinery & Equipment........... | 7.0 |
| Consumer durable foods............. | 10.5 | Exports........................... | 7.3 |

# Crude Oil and Natural Gas Production

**Source: Bureau of Mines (r-Revised)**

| Production (includes Alaska and Hawaii) | 1966 | 1967 | Increase |
|------|------|------|------|
| | (Thousands of barrels of 42 gallons) | | |
| Crude oil............................. | r3,028,084 | 3,216,715 | +188,631 |
| Natural gas liquids.................. | r469,666 | 515,183 | +45,517 |
| **Total liquid hydrocarbona....** | r3,497,750 | 3,731,898 | +234,148 |
| Natural gas, marketed production (in millions of cubic ft.). | 17,232,134 | 18,171,325 | +939,191 |

# Engineering Wonders of the U. S.

### Selected by American Society of Civil Engineers

In 1954 the American Society of Civil Engineers, after several years of research, selected the seven modern civil engineering wonders in the United States (shown listed in alphabetical order) and then selected one each year from 1960 on.

1968—San Mateo-Hayward Bridge over San Francisco Bay, Calif.
1967—The Gateway Arch at St. Louis, Mo.
1966—NASA Complex 39, Appollo-Saturn V assembly.
1965—Chesapeake Bay Bridge-Tunnel.
1964—Glen Canyon Dam on Colorado River.
1963—Ohio River Valley Clean Streams Program.
1962—Intercontinental Ballastic Missiles Program.
1961—John F. Kennedy (N.Y.) Internatl. Airport.
1960—St. Lawrence Power and Seaway Project.

**1954 Awards**

1. Chicago's sewage disposal system.
2. Colorado River Aqueduct.
3. Empire State Building.
4. Grand Coulee Dam and Columbia Basin Project.
5. Hoover Dam.
6. Panama Canal.
7. San Francisco-Oakland Bay Bridge.

# World Production of Crude Petroleum[1]

Source: Bureau of Mines; in thousands of 42-gallon barrels

| Country | 1966 | 1967 | Country | 1966 | 1967 |
|---|---|---|---|---|---|
| **North America:** | | | China e (mainland)...... | 95,000 | 86,300 |
| Canada................ | r320,543 | 352,526 | India................... | 34,228 | 42,190 |
| Cuba[2]e.............. | r460 | 756 | Indonesia.............. | 5r108,429 | 5185,000 |
| Mexico................ | 121,149 | 133,042 | Iran................... | 771,234 | e952,413 |
| Trinidad.............. | 55,603 | 64,995 | Iraq................... | 505,428 | 445,821 |
| United States......... | 3,027,763 | 3,215,742 | Israel................. | r1,359 | 4956 |
| | | | Japan................. | r5,463 | 5,539 |
| **South America:** | | | Kuwait................ | 830,537 | 836,719 |
| Argentina............. | r104,754 | 114,739 | Kuwait-Neutral Zone...... | 153,419 | 152,862 |
| Bolivia............... | 6,085 | 14,527 | Mongolia e............. | r89 | e90 |
| Brazil................ | 42,446 | 53,515 | Muscat and Oman........ | ....... | 23,030 |
| Chile................. | 12,428 | 12,369 | Pakistan............... | 2,502 | 3,700 |
| Colombia............. | r71,430 | 68,377 | Qatar................. | 105,945 | 118,085 |
| Ecuador.............. | 2,660 | 2,198 | Sarawak and Brunei...... | r35,232 | 38,289 |
| Peru................. | 23,027 | 25,857 | Saudi Arabia........... | 873,349 | 948,110 |
| Venezuela............ | 1,230,464 | 1,292,876 | Taiwan (Formosa)....... | 226 | 246 |
| | | | Thailand e............. | 40 | 45 |
| **Europe:** | | | Trucial States......... | 131,531 | 139,467 |
| Albania............... | r5,840 | 7,300 | Turkey................ | r18,062 | 17,459 |
| Austria............... | 19,228 | 18,725 | | | |
| Bulgaria.............. | 2,920 | 3,642 | **Africa:** | | |
| Czechoslovakia........ | r1,288 | 1,424 | Algeria[4]............... | r257,122 | e282,200 |
| France............... | 21,365 | 20,639 | Angola................ | 4,560 | 3,880 |
| Germany, West........ | 56,832 | 57,257 | Congo, Rep. of (Brazzaville) | 467 | 380 |
| Hungary.............. | 13,009 | 12,864 | Gabon, Republic of...... | 10,484 | 25,203 |
| Italy................. | 11,974 | 11,595 | Libya................. | r552,712 | 636,504 |
| Netherlands........... | 16,438 | 15,438 | Morocco.............. | 783 | 732 |
| Poland............... | 2,971 | 3,335 | Nigeria............... | 152,438 | 116,519 |
| Romania............. | 95,588 | 98,379 | Tunisia............... | r4,741 | 17,068 |
| Spain................ | 197 | 560 | UAR (Egypt)........... | r43,300 | 4e42,000 |
| USSR[3]............... | 1,948,000 | 2,116,000 | | | |
| United Kingdom....... | r568 | 648 | **Oceania:** | | |
| Yugoslavia............ | 16,460 | 17,655 | Australia.............. | 3,390 | 7,594 |
| | | | New Zealand.......... | 4 | e4 |
| **Asia:** | | | West Irian............ | 5 | 6 |
| Bahrain............... | 22,521 | 25,370 | | | |
| Burma................ | r4,255 | 4,446 | **World total........** | r12,015,830 | 12,889,705 |

e-Estimate. r-Revised. [1]Compiled mostly from data available May 1968. [2]Natural naphtha and gas oil. [3]USSR in Asia (including Sakhalin) included with USSR in Europe. [4]Excludes Israeli production of Egyptian oilfield. [5]Beginning May 1, 1963, West Irian transferred to Indonesia, production data for West Irian included for the years 1964, 1965, 1966 and 1967 under Indonesia.

## CRUDE PETROLEUM PRODUCTION BY CHIEF STATES

(Figures represent thousands of 42-gallon barrels)

| Year | Ark. | Calif. | Ill. | Kans. | La. | Miss. | N. M. | N. D. | Okla. | Texas | Wyo. |
|---|---|---|---|---|---|---|---|---|---|---|---|
| 1940......... | 25,775 | 223,881 | 147,647 | 66,139 | 103,584 | 4,400 | 39,129 | .... | 156,164 | 493,209 | 25,711 |
| 1945......... | 28,613 | 326,482 | 75,094 | 96,415 | 131,051 | 19,062 | 37,351 | .... | 139,299 | 754,710 | 36,219 |
| 1950......... | 31,108 | 327,607 | 62,028 | 107,586 | 208,965 | 38,236 | 47,367 | .... | 164,599 | 829,874 | 61,631 |
| 1955......... | 28,369 | 354,812 | 81,423 | 121,669 | 271,010 | 37,741 | 82,958 | 11,143 | 202,817 | 1,053,297 | 99,483 |
| 1960......... | 30,117 | 305,352 | 77,341 | 113,453 | 400,832 | 51,673 | 107,380 | 21,992 | 192,913 | 927,479 | 133,910 |
| 1965......... | 25,930 | 316,428 | 63,708 | 104,733 | 594,853 | 56,183 | 119,166 | 26,350 | 203,441 | 1,000,749 | 138,314 |
| 1966[1]....... | 23,824 | 345,295 | 61,661 | 103,738 | 674,318 | 55,227 | 124,154 | 27,126 | 224,839 | 1,057,706 | 134,470 |
| 1967......... | 21,075 | 359,219 | 59,142 | 99,200 | 774,527 | 57,147 | 126,144 | 25,315 | 230,749 | 1,119,762 | 136,312 |

[1]Revised.

## U. S. Petroleum and Natural Gas Production

| Year | Crude oil | | Natural gas liquids | | | | Natural gas | |
|---|---|---|---|---|---|---|---|---|
| | Production | Value | Production | Value | Benzol | Total | Marketed | Value |
| | 1,000 bbls. | $1,000 | 1,000 bbls. | $1,000 | 1,000 42 gal. | bbls. | Mil. cu. ft. | $1,000 |
| 1940...... | 1,353,214 | 1,385,440 | 55,700 | 68,261 | 3,167 | 1,412,081 | 2,660,222 | 120,493 |
| 1945...... | 1,713,655 | 2,094,250 | 112,004 | 145,570 | 2,880 | 1,828,539 | 3,918,686 | 191,006 |
| 1950...... | 1,973,574 | 4,963,380 | 181,961 | 321,832 | 158 | 2,155,693 | 6,282,060 | 408,521 |
| 1955...... | 2,484,428 | 6,870,380 | 281,371 | 423,775 | 526 | 2,766,325 | 9,405,351 | 978,357 |
| 1960...... | 2,574,933 | 7,420,181 | 340,157 | 416,819 | 275 | 2,915,365 | 12,771,038 | 1,789,970 |
| 1965...... | 2,848,514 | 8,158,298 | 441,556 | 494,354 | 13 | 3,290,083 | 16,039,753 | 2,494,542 |
| 1966[1]..... | 3,027,763 | 8,726,423 | 468,635 | 520,138 | 30 | 3,496,428 | 17,206,628 | 2,702,759 |
| 1967...... | 3,215,742 | 9,375,727 | 514,456 | 2 | 87 | 3,730,999 | 18,380,838 | 2 |

[1]Revised. [2]Not available.

## Total Fuel Supply and Demand[1]

In thousands of 42-gallon barrels. *Includes special naphtha production.

| Year | Gasoline* | | Kerosene | | Distillate fuel oil | | Residual fuel oil | |
|---|---|---|---|---|---|---|---|---|
| | Production | Demand | Production | Demand | Production | Demand | Production | Demand |
| 1940.... | 616,314 | 614,867 | 73,882 | 72,150 | 183,304 | 33,718 | 316,221 | 356,272 |
| 1945.... | 793,431 | 784,392 | 81,024 | 81,753 | 249,224 | 38,333 | 469,492 | 535,092 |
| 1950.... | 1,024,181 | 1,019,011 | 118,512 | 119,922 | 398,912 | 75,435 | 425,217 | 570,021 |
| 1955.... | 1,373,950 | 1,364,309 | 117,137 | 120,143 | 602,547 | 108,144 | 420,331 | 590,856 |
| 1960[2].... | 1,522,497 | 1,525,126 | 136,842 | 133,188 | 667,050 | 695,165 | 332,147 | 577,934 |
| 1965.... | 1,733,258 | 1,756,419 | 201,788 | 219,932 | 765,071 | 779,644 | 268,567 | 601,893 |
| 1966[3].... | 1,822,388 | 1,829,438 | 226,822 | 244,329 | 784,717 | 801,757 | 263,961 | 639,325 |
| 1967[3].... | 1,872,849 | 1,874,742 | 262,596 | 289,675 | 804,429 | 821,035 | 275,956 | 674,081 |

[1]Demand in some cases exceeds the production; in these cases the difference is made up by dipping into stocks or by imports. [2]In the years prior to 1960 figures are on a 48-state basis. [3]Preliminary.

# ECONOMICS
## United States Budget Receipts and Expenditures—1967-1968
**Source:** Treasury Department; each fiscal year ends June 30 (data preliminary)
*This report incorporates for the first time the changes recommended by the President's Commission on Budget Concepts which have been adopted and put in use.*

| Classification | Fiscal year 1968 | Fiscal year 1967 |
|---|---|---|
| **GROSS RECEIPTS** | (in thousands) | |
| **Internal Revenue:** | | |
| Individual income taxes: | | |
| Withheld | $ 57,267,620 | $ 50,520,874 |
| Other | 20,950,634 | 18,849,721 |
| Total individual Income taxes | 78,218,254 | 69,379,595 |
| Corporation income taxes | 29,889,415 | 34,917,825 |
| Employment taxes: | | |
| Federal Insurance Contributions Act | 24,566,796 | 23,311,660 |
| Self-Employment Contributions Act | 1,543,852 | 1,775,978 |
| Railroad Retirement Tax Act | 858,517 | 792,858 |
| Federal Unemployment Tax Act | 606,811 | 602,745 |
| Total Employment taxes | 27,575,976 | 26,483,241 |
| Excise taxes | 14,312,551 | 14,113,748 |
| Estate and gift taxes | 3,076,336 | 3,014,406 |
| Total internal Revenue | 153,072,533 | 147,899,815 |
| Customs duties | 2,113,475 | 1,971,800 |
| Railroad Unemployment Trust Fund | 139,595 | 145,666 |
| Deposits by states | 5,175,584 | 5,173,670 |
| Federal Medical Insurance for aged, trust fund | 645,462 | 614,546 |
| Federal employees retirement contributions | 1,340,745 | 1,209,125 |
| Total Miscellaneous receipts | 2,373,235 | 2,121,881 |
| Total Budget receipts | $164,860,627 | $159,136,502 |
| **EXPENDITURES** | | |
| Legislative Branch | $ 268,513 | $ 251,293 |
| The Judiciary | 93,991 | 87,638 |
| Executive Office of the President | 28,083 | 27,767 |
| Funds appropriated to the President: | | |
| Alaska programs | .... | 2,601 |
| Appalachian development programs | 108,163 | .... |
| Disaster relief | 31,760 | 53,472 |
| Emergency fund for the President | 122 | 254 |
| Expansion of defense production | 82,335 | 33,975 |
| Expenses of management improvement | 231 | 28 |
| International Financial Institutions | 201,446 | 170,000 |
| Office of Economic Opportunity | 1,872,176 | 1,485,575 |
| Peace Corps | 110,228 | 112,189 |
| Philippine education programs | 15,364 | 3,400 |
| Public works acceleration | 4,957 | 21,133 |
| Special foreign currency activities | 201 | 226 |
| Southeast hurricane disaster | 590 | 10,408 |
| Military assistance: | | |
| Office of Secretary of Defense | 25,418 | 59,144 |
| Department of the Army | 329,829 | 388,297 |
| Department of the Navy | 35,538 | 130,033 |
| Department of the Air Force | 177,387 | 331,175 |
| All other agencies | 3,050 | −5,630 |
| Foreign military sales fund | 175,131 | 161,068 |
| Total Military assistance | 1,810,605 | 2,134,037 |
| Economic assistance | 2,091,144 | 2,483,374 |
| Total Funds appropriated to the President | 6,329,324 | 6,510,673 |
| Agriculture Department | 13,411,479 | 10,619,860 |
| Commerce Department | 1,030,999 | 973,946 |
| Defense Department: | | |
| Military personnel | 21,931,589 | 19,786,720 |
| Operation and maintenance | 20,485,623 | 19,000,253 |
| Procurement | 23,297,616 | 19,011,857 |
| Research, development, test and evaluation | 7,718,944 | 7,159,668 |
| Military construction | 1,280,739 | 1,535,579 |
| Family housing | 495,171 | 485,300 |
| Civil Defense | 107,637 | 100,058 |
| Revolving and management funds | 2,136,639 | 512,978 |
| Total Military | 77,454,038 | 67,588,396 |
| Corps of Engineers, Dept. of the Army | 1,287,585 | 1,303,130 |
| Panama Canal Zone | 197,820 | 169,134 |
| Other | 41,774 | 39,075 |
| Navy—Wildlife conservation | 12 | 12 |
| Air Force—Wildlife conservation | 45 | 48 |
| Total Civil | 1,521,513 | 1,501,543 |
| Total Defense Department | 78,975,551 | 69,089,939 |
| Health, Education and Welfare Department | 41,162,756 | 34,890,430 |
| Housing and Urban Development Department | 1,847,014 | 1,641,285 |
| Interior Department | 1,813,203 | 1,725,986 |
| Justice Department | 437,756 | 411,398 |
| Labor Department | 3,383,328 | 3,175,476 |
| Post Office Department | 6,793,912 | 6,467,613 |
| State Department | 428,839 | 423,891 |
| Transportation Department | 5,781,572 | 5,475,583 |
| Treasury Department | 15,115,203 | 13,818,534 |
| Interest on the public debt | 14,584,839 | 13,391,068 |
| Atomic Energy Commission | 2,468,578 | 2,264,488 |
| General Services Administration | 591,492 | 655,293 |
| National Aeronautics and Space Administration | 4,724,901 | 5,425,815 |
| Veterans Administration | 7,804,188 | 7,350,794 |
| Other Independent Agencies: | | |
| American Battle Monuments Commission | 2,182 | 2,134 |
| Arms Control Disarmament Agency | 10,740 | 9,509 |
| Central Intelligence Agency (construction) | 41 | 1,432 |
| Civil Aeronautics Board | 64,073 | 73,858 |
| Civil Service Commission | 3,203,459 | 2,829,306 |
| Commission of Fine Arts | 101 | 117 |
| Commission on Civil Rights | 2,530 | 2,450 |
| District of Columbia federal payment | 78,853 | 61,394 |
| Equal Employment Opportunity Commission | 6,179 | 4,631 |

| Classification | Fiscal year 1968 | Fiscal year 1967 |
|---|---|---|
| | (in thousands) | |
| Export-Import Bank of the United States | 179,282 | 155,579 |
| Farm Credit Administration | −34,606 | −11,583 |
| Federal Coal Mine Safety Board of Review | 97 | 76 |
| Federal Communications Commission | 19,261 | 18,253 |
| Federal Deposit Insurance Corporation | −259,174 | −238,859 |
| Federal Field Committee for Development Plan in Alaska | 225 | 181 |
| Federal Home Loan Bank Board | 137,892 | 63,164 |
| Federal Maritime Commission | 3,578 | 3,454 |
| Federal Mediation and Conciliation Service | 7,336 | 7,079 |
| Federal Power Commission | 14,576 | 14,081 |
| Federal Radiation Council | 97 | 107 |
| Federal Trade Commission | 15,221 | 14,108 |
| Foreign Claims Settlement Commission | 198,063 | 20,997 |
| Historical and Memorial Commission | 27 | 124 |
| Indians Claims Commission | 446 | 336 |
| Intergovernment agencies | 4,294 | 1,659 |
| Interstate Commerce Commission | 23,690 | 27,107 |
| National Capital Housing Authority | ..... | 44 |
| National Capital Planning Commission | 872 | 1,245 |
| National Capital Transportation Agency | 1,871 | 2,977 |
| National Labor Relations Board | 31,863 | 30,197 |
| National Mediation Board | 2,014 | 1,981 |
| National Science Foundation | 448,293 | 414,886 |
| President's Advisory Comm. on Labor-Management | ..... | 1 |
| Railroad Retirement Board | 936,288 | 722,165 |
| Renegotiation Board | 2,640 | 2,519 |
| Securities and Exchange Commission | 17,642 | 16,681 |
| Selective Service System | 56,764 | 58,036 |
| Small Business Administration | 238,275 | 156,721 |
| Tennessee Valley Authority | 537,268 | 468,532 |
| U. S. Information Agency | 187,378 | 187,958 |
| Water Resources Council | 2,929 | 1,972 |
| Total Other independent agencies | 6,213,818 | 5,182,353 |
| Undistributed interfund receipt transactions | −4,596,388 | −4,027,920 |
| Total expenditures (excluding net lending) | $194,108,115 | $172,442,136 |
| Receipt-expenditure account surplus (+) or deficit (−) | −19,470,638 | −3,629,071 |

## United States Net Receipts and Expenditures

Source: Treasury Department; annual statements for year ending June 30

| Yearly average | Receipts | Expenditures | Yearly average | Receipts | Expenditures | Yearly average | Receipts | Expenditures |
|---|---|---|---|---|---|---|---|---|
| | $1,000 | $1,000 | | $1,000 | $1,000 | | $1,000 | $1,000 |
| 1789-1800[1]... | 5,717 | 5,776 | 1871-1875.... | 336,830 | 287,460 | 1908........ | 601,862 | 659,196 |
| 1801-1810[2]... | 13,056 | 9,086 | 1876-1880.... | 288,124 | 255,598 | 1909........ | 604,320 | 693,744 |
| 1811-1820[2]... | 21,052 | 23,943 | 1881-1885.... | 366,961 | 257,691 | 1910........ | 675,512 | 693,617 |
| 1821-1830[2]... | 21,923 | 16,162 | 1886-1890.... | 375,448 | 279,134 | 1911........ | 701,833 | 691,202 |
| 1831-1840[2]... | 30,461 | 24,495 | 1891-1895.... | 352,891 | 363,599 | 1912........ | 692,609 | 689,881 |
| 1841-1850[2]... | 28,545 | 34,097 | 1896-1900.... | 434,877 | 457,451 | 1913........ | 724,111 | 724,512 |
| 1851-1860.... | 60,237 | 60,163 | 1901-1905.... | 559,481 | 535,559 | 1914........ | 734,673 | 735,081 |
| 1861-1865.... | 160,907 | 683,785 | 1906........ | 594,984 | 570,202 | 1915........ | 697,910 | 760,586 |
| 1866-1870.... | 447,301 | 377,642 | 1907........ | 665,860 | 579 129 | 1916........ | 782,534 | 734,056 |

| Yearly Average | Receipts | Expenditures | Yearly Average | Receipts | Expenditures |
|---|---|---|---|---|---|
| 1917........... | $1,124,324,795 | $1,977,681,751 | 1943*......... | $21,986,700,787 | $79,407,131,152 |
| 1918........... | 3,664,582,865 | [6]12,696,702,471 | 1944*......... | 43,635,315,356 | 95,058,707,898 |
| 1919........... | 5,152,257,136 | 18,514,879,955 | 1945*......... | 44,475,303,665 | 98,416,219,788 |
| 1920........... | 6,694,565,389 | 6,403,343,841 | 1946*......... | 39,771,403,710 | 60,447,574,319 |
| 1921........... | 5,624,932,961 | 5,115,927,690 | 1947*......... | 39,786,811,936 | 39,032,393,376 |
| 1922........... | 4,109,104,151 | 3,372,607,900 | 1948*......... | 41,488,178,842 | [7]33,068,708,998 |
| 1923........... | 4,007,135,481 | 3,294,627,529 | 1949*......... | 37,695,549,449 | 39,506,989,497 |
| 1924........... | 4,012,044,702 | 3,048,677,965 | 1950*......... | 36,494,900,837 | [8]39,617,003,195 |
| 1925........... | 3,780,148,685 | 3,063,105,332 | 1951*......... | 47,567,613,484 | 44,057,830,859 |
| 1926........... | 3,962,755,690 | 3,097,611,823 | 1952*......... | 61,390,944,552 | 65,407,584,930 |
| 1927........... | 4,129,394,441 | 2,974,029,674 | 1953......... | 64,825,044,026 | 74,274,257,484 |
| 1928........... | 4,042,348,156 | 3,103,264,855 | 1954......... | 64,655,386,989 | 67,772,353,245 |
| 1929........... | 4,033,250,225 | 3,298,859,486 | 1955......... | 60,389,743,895 | 64,569,972,817 |
| 1930........... | 4,177,941,702 | 3,440,268,884 | 1956......... | 68,165,329,582 | 69,539,776,178 |
| 1931........... | [5]3,115,556,923 | [5]3,577,434,003 | 1957......... | 71,028,649,978 | 69,433,078,427 |
| 1932........... | 1,923,913,117 | 4,659,202,825 | 1958......... | 69,116,717,311 | 71,936,171,353 |
| 1933........... | 2,021,212,943 | 4,622,865,028 | 1959......... | 67,915,348,624 | 80,342,335,375 |
| 1934........... | 3,064,267,912 | 6,693,899,854 | 1960......... | 77,763,460,220 | 76,539,412,798 |
| 1935........... | 3,729,913,845 | 6,520,965,945 | 1961......... | 77,659,424,905 | 81,515,167,453 |
| 1936........... | 4,068,936,689 | 8,493,485,919 | 1962......... | 81,409,092,072 | 87,786,766,580 |
| 1937........... | [4]4,978,600,695 | 7,756,021,409 | 1963......... | 86,357,020,251 | 92,589,764,920 |
| 1938*.......... | 5,615,221,162 | 6,791,837,760 | 1964......... | 89,458,664,071 | 97,684,374,794 |
| 1939*.......... | 4,996,299,530 | 18,858,457,570 | 1965......... | 93,071,796,891 | 96,506,904,210 |
| 1940*.......... | 5,144,013,044 | 9,062,032,204 | 1966......... | 106,978,344,155 | 104,727,263,667 |
| 1941*.......... | 7,102,931,383 | 13,262,203,742 | 1967......... | 149,554,815,000 | 153,183,886,000 |
| 1 42*......... | 12,555,436,084 | 44,045,678,816 | 1968 (prel.)... | 153,485,067,000 | 172,955,705,000 |

*Revised to exclude from both net budget receipts and budget expenditures the appropriations of receipts to the Railroad Retirement Account.

(1) Average for period March 4, 1789, to Dec. 1, 1800.

(2) Years ended Dec. 31, 1801, to 1842; average for 1841-1850 is for the period Jan. 1, 1841, to June 30, 1850.

(3) Receipts from 1937 on have deducted appropriations to Federal old-age and survivors insurance trust fund.

(4) Expenditures for years 1932 through 1946 have been revised to include Government Corporations (wholly owned) etc. (net).

(5) Effective January 3, 1949, amounts refunded by the Government, principally for the overpayment of taxes, are being reported as deductions from total receipts rather than as expenditures. Also, effective July 1, 1948, payments to the Treasury, principally by wholly owned Government corporations for retirement of capital stock and for disposition of earnings, are excluded in reporting both budget receipts and expenditures. Neither of these changes affects the size of the budget surplus or deficit. Beginning 1931 figures in each case have been adjusted accordingly for comparative purposes.

(6) Figures for 1918 through 1946 are revised to exclude statutory debt retirement (sinking fund, etc.).

(7) Excludes $3 billion transferred to Foreign Economics Corporation Trust Fund.

(8) Includes $3 billion representing expenditures made from the FEC Trust Fund.

## Net Public and Private Debt
### Sources: Office of Business Economics, U. S. Dept. of Commerce
(In billions of dollars)

| End of year | Public and private total | Total public | Federal[1] | State and Local[2] | Total private | Corporate | Farm Production | Farm Mortgage | Private Individual and noncorporate Nonfarm mortgage 1-4 family residential | Multifamily residential & commercial | Other nonfarm Commercial | Financial | Consumer |
|---|---|---|---|---|---|---|---|---|---|---|---|---|---|
| 1950 | 490.3 | 239.4 | 218.7 | 20.7 | 250.9 | 142.1 | 6.2 | 6.1 | 42.9 | 16.5 | 8.9 | 6.9 | 21.4 |
| 1955 | 672.3 | 269.8 | 231.5 | 38.4 | 402.5 | 212.1 | 9.7 | 9.1 | 83.8 | 24.9 | 12.4 | 11.6 | 38.9 |
| 1959 | 846.2 | 298.8 | 243.2 | 55.6 | 547.4 | 283.3 | 11.7 | 11.3 | 124.3 | 36.5 | 15.3 | 13.4 | 51.5 |
| 1960 | 800.3 | 301.0 | 241.0 | 60.0 | 589.2 | 302.8 | 12.3 | 12.8 | 134.2 | 40.2 | 16.6 | 14.2 | 56.0 |
| 1962[3] | 1,016.7 | 331.2 | 257.5 | 73.7 | 685.5 | 348.2 | 15.0 | 15.2 | 158.3 | 48.0 | 19.3 | 18.3 | 63.2 |
| 1963[3] | 1,068.5 | 348.2 | 258.7 | 82.0 | 720.7 | 376.1 | 16.4 | 16.8 | 177.1 | 21.5 | 21.5 | 20.8 | 70.5 |
| 1964[3] | 1,151.8 | 363.3 | 265.0 | 89.3 | 788.5 | 409.9 | 17.1 | 18.9 | 193.1 | 25.7 | 23.9 | 21.5 | 78.4 |
| 1965[3] | 1,240.2 | 373.7 | 267.9 | 96.4 | 866.5 | 452.3 | 18.1 | 21.2 | 208.7 | 28.0 | 27.6 | 22.7 | 87.9 |
| 1966[3] | 1,331.7 | 388.6 | 274.0 | 102.7 | 943.1 | 498.3 | 18.7 | 23.3 | 221.0 | 30.8 | 32.0 | 24.2 | 94.8 |
| 1967 | 1,419.1 | 410.7 | 287.7 | 113.4 | 1,008.4 | 534.4 | 20.6 | 25.1 | 232.2 | 33.5 | 34.4 | 29.0 | 99.2 |

[1]Net Federal Government debt is the outstanding debt held by the public, as defined in the Budget of the U. S. Govt., Fiscal Year 1969.
[2]Data for State and local governments are for June 30 of each year.
[3]Figures for 1962 thru 1966 have been revised.

## Public Debt of the United States
### Source: Treasury Department
p Preliminary subject to revision. r Revised

| Fiscal Year | Gross Debt | Per Cap. | Fiscal Year | Gross Debt | Per Cap. | Fiscal Year | Gross Debt | Per Cap. |
|---|---|---|---|---|---|---|---|---|
| | Dollars | Dollars | | Dollars | Dollars | | Dollars | Dollars |
| 1870 | 2,436,453,269 | 61.06 | 1930 | 16,185,309,831 | 131.51 | 1963 | 305,859,633,996 | 1,614.74 |
| 1880 | 2,090,908,872 | 41.60 | 1940 | 42,967,531,038 | 367.48 | 1964 | 311,531,973,313 | r 1,621.55 |
| 1890 | 1,132,396,584 | 17.80 | 1950 | 257,357,352,351 | 1,696.67 | 1965 | 317,273,898,984 | r 1,630.46 |
| 1900 | 1,263,416,913 | 16.60 | 1960 | 286,330,760,848 | 1,584.70 | 1966 | 319,907,087,795 | 1,624.55 |
| 1910 | 1,146,939,969 | 12.41 | 1961 | 288,970,938,610 | 1,572.58 | 1967 | 326,220,937,795 | 1,638.33 |
| 1920 | 24,299,321,467 | 228.23 | 1962 | 298,200,822,721 | 1,597.60 | 1968 | 347,578,406,426 | p 1,727.82 |

## National Income by Type of Income
(Millions of dollars)

| | 1959 | 1960 | 1962* | 1963* | 1964 | 1965[1] | 1966[1] | 1967 |
|---|---|---|---|---|---|---|---|---|
| Compensation of employees | 279,093 | 294,226 | 323,632 | 341,004 | 365,720 | 393,844 | 435,611 | 468,163 |
| Wage and salaries | 258,187 | 270,844 | 296,091 | 311,095 | 333,683 | 358,885 | 394,560 | 423,382 |
| Private | 212,538 | 222,108 | 241,632 | 251,616 | 269,355 | 289,621 | 316,865 | 337,100 |
| Military | 9,873 | 9,894 | 10,756 | 10,849 | 11,692 | 12,143 | 14,560 | 16,255 |
| Government civilian | 35,776 | 38,842 | 45,203 | 48,630 | 52,636 | 57,121 | 63,135 | 70,027 |
| Supplements to wages, sal. | 20,906 | 23,382 | 27,541 | 29,909 | 32,037 | 34,959 | 41,051 | 44,781 |
| Empl. contrib. soc. ins. | 9,650 | 11,380 | 13,657 | 15,045 | 15,411 | 16,217 | 20,212 | 21,522 |
| Other labor income | 11,256 | 12,002 | 13,884 | 14,864 | 16,626 | 18,742 | 20,839 | 23,259 |
| Empl. contrib. priv. pen. | 9,064 | 9,684 | 11,356 | 12,165 | 13,670 | 15,623 | 17,355 | 19,462 |
| Other | 2,192 | 2,318 | 2,528 | 2,699 | 2,956 | 3,119 | 3,484 | 3,797 |
| Proprietors' income | 46,550 | 46,209 | 50,111 | 51,013 | 52,315 | 57,253 | 60,665 | 60,715 |
| Business and professional | 35,129 | 34,244 | 37,093 | 37,910 | 40,180 | 42,416 | 44,775 | 46,305 |
| Income unic. enterprises | 35,269 | 34,263 | 37,076 | 37,944 | 40,259 | 42,796 | 45,112 | 46,646 |
| Invent. valu. adjustment | −140 | −19 | 17 | −34 | −79 | −380 | −337 | −341 |
| Farm | 11,421 | 11,965 | 13,018 | 13,103 | 12,135 | 14,837 | 15,890 | 14,410 |
| Rental income of persons | 15,596 | 15,822 | 16,691 | 17,139 | 17,963 | 18,952 | 19,793 | 20,322 |
| Corp. prof., inv. adjust | 51,676 | 49,904 | 55,660 | 58,933 | 66,276 | 76,070 | 83,900 | 80,410 |
| Corp. profits before tax | 52,141 | 49,712 | 55,408 | 59,401 | 66,789 | 77,787 | 85,643 | 81,598 |
| Corp. profits tax liability | 23,679 | 23,032 | 24,179 | 26,324 | 28,345 | 31,326 | 34,629 | 33,499 |
| Corp. profits after tax | 28,462 | 26,680 | 31,229 | 33,077 | 38,444 | 46,461 | 51,014 | 48,099 |
| Dividends | 12,580 | 13,437 | 15,183 | 16,434 | 17,811 | 19,808 | 21,748 | 22,922 |
| Undistributed profits | 15,882 | 13,243 | 16,046 | 16,623 | 20,633 | 26,653 | 29,266 | 25,171 |
| Inventory valuation adj. | −465 | 192 | 252 | −468 | −513 | −1,717 | −1,743 | −1,188 |
| Net interest | 7,110 | 8,361 | 11,593 | 13,838 | 15,794 | 18,217 | 20,791 | 23,257 |
| National income | 400,025 | 414,522 | 457,687 | 481,927 | 518,068 | 564,336 | 620,760 | 652,867 |

*The figures for 1962 and 1963 reflect the new depreciation guidelines issued by the Treasury Department July 11, 1962, and the investment tax credit provided in the Revenue act of 1962. [1]Revised.

## Gross National Product, National Income, and Personal Income
### Source: Department of Commerce. Office of Business Economics
(In millions of dollars) Includes Alaska and Hawaii beginning in 1960

| | 1950 | 1955 | 1960 | 1964 | 1965 | 1966 | 1967 |
|---|---|---|---|---|---|---|---|
| Gross national product | 284,769 | 397,960 | 503,734 | 632,410 | 684,884 | 747,568 | 789,663 |
| Less: Capital consumption allowances | 18,342 | 31,474 | 43,408 | 56,030 | 59,765 | 64,093 | 69,166 |
| Equals: Net national product | 266,427 | 366,486 | 460,326 | 576,330 | 625,119 | 683,475 | 720,497 |
| Less: Indirect business tax and nontax liability | 23,334 | 32,067 | 45,200 | 58,411 | 62,457 | 65,342 | 69,565 |
| Business transfer payments | 778 | 1,245 | 1,878 | 2,489 | 2,737 | 2,981 | 3,138 |
| Statistical discrepancy | 1,488 | 2,093 | −1,031 | −1,310 | −3,121 | −3,318 | −3,522 |
| Plus: Subsidies minus current surplus of government enterprises | 247 | −63 | 243 | 1,328 | 1,290 | 2,290 | 1,551 |
| Equals: National income | 241,074 | 331,018 | 414,522 | 518,068 | 564,336 | 620,760 | 652,867 |
| Less: Corporate profits and inventory valuation adjustment | 37,669 | 46,871 | 49,904 | 66,276 | 76,070 | 83,900 | 80,410 |
| Contributions for social insurance | 6,870 | 11,135 | 20,672 | 27,945 | 29,621 | 37,980 | 41,885 |
| Wage accruals less disbursement | 24 | 0 | 0 | 0 | 0 | 0 | 0 |
| Plus: Government transfer payments to persons | 14,294 | 16,065 | 26,609 | 34,246 | 37,185 | 40,950 | 48,599 |
| Net Interest paid by gov't and consumers | 7,198 | 10,089 | 15,303 | 19,079 | 20,518 | 22,286 | 23,578 |
| Dividends | 8,838 | 10,478 | 13,437 | 17,811 | 19,808 | 21,748 | 22,928 |
| Business transfer payments | 778 | 1,245 | 1,878 | 2,489 | 2,737 | 2,981 | 3,138 |
| Equals: Personal income | 227,619 | 310,889 | 400,953 | 97,462 | 538,893 | 586,845 | 628,815 |

# National Income by Industry

**Source:** Department of Commerce, Office of Business Economics
(Millions of dollars) Beginning with 1960 data includes Alaska and Hawaii. [1]Revised.

| | 1959 | 1960 | 1962 | 1963[1] | 1964[1] | 1965[1] | 1966[1] | 1967 |
|---|---|---|---|---|---|---|---|---|
| **Agricul., forestry, fisheries...** | **16,035** | **16,852** | **18,455** | **18,587** | **17,973** | **21,047** | **22,510** | **21,417** |
| Farms.................... | 15,070 | 15,857 | 17,301 | 17,404 | 16,653 | 19,630 | 20,997 | 19,812 |
| Agri. services, forestry, fisheries | 965 | 995 | 1,154 | 1,183 | 1,320 | 1,417 | 1,513 | 1,605 |
| **Mining................** | **5,523** | **5,732** | **5,653** | **5,954** | **5,924** | **6,116** | **6,511** | **6,435** |
| Metal mining............... | 587 | 817 | 758 | 785 | 861 | 908 | 1,183 | 912 |
| Coal mining............... | 1,306 | 1,253 | 1,141 | 1,212 | 1,307 | 1,332 | 1,391 | 1,443 |
| Crude petroleum, natural gas... | 2,772 | 2,734 | 2,811 | 2,917 | 2,638 | 2,754 | 2,744 | 2,824 |
| Nonmetallic min. & quar..... | 858 | 928 | 943 | 1,040 | 1,118 | 1,122 | 1,193 | 1,256 |
| **Contract construction......** | **20,476** | **20,810** | **24,084** | **24,198** | **26,455** | **29,116** | **32,023** | **33,249** |
| **Manufacturing............** | **124,040** | **125,822** | **136,988** | **143,839** | **155,558** | **172,572** | **191,798** | **196,613** |
| **Nondurable goods..........** | **51,103** | **52,208** | **55,609** | **57,508** | **61,918** | **66,482** | **73,190** | **75,831** |
| Food, kindred products........ | 11,943 | 12,225 | 12,832 | 13,409 | 14,279 | 14,495 | 15,580 | 16,324 |
| Tobacco manufactures......... | 981 | 1,017 | 1,130 | 1,216 | 1,196 | 1,111 | 1,313 | 1,418 |
| Textile mill products........ | 4,477 | 4,488 | 4,664 | 4,713 | 5,237 | 5,837 | 6,502 | 6,252 |
| Appa'l, other fabric prod...... | 4,732 | 4,953 | 5,489 | 5,672 | 6,072 | 6,556 | 7,263 | 7,561 |
| Paper, allied products........ | 4,602 | 4,707 | 5,112 | 5,163 | 5,517 | 5,929 | 6,637 | 6,804 |
| Ptg., pub., allied indust...... | 6,277 | 6,655 | 7,119 | 7,312 | 8,255 | 8,746 | 9,669 | 10,097 |
| Chemicals, allied products.... | 9,172 | 9,159 | 9,910 | 10,402 | 11,225 | 12,648 | 13,752 | 14,511 |
| Petroleum refining, related ind.. | 4,597 | 4,586 | 4,489 | 4,597 | 4,785 | 5,381 | 5,839 | 6,028 |
| Rubber, misc. plastic products.. | 2,766 | 2,809 | 3,172 | 3,286 | 3,576 | 3,949 | 4,553 | 4,646 |
| Leather, leather products...... | 1,556 | 1,609 | 1,686 | 1,738 | 1,776 | 1,830 | 2,082 | 2,190 |
| **Durable goods.............** | **72,937** | **73,614** | **81,379** | **86,331** | **93,640** | **106,090** | **118,608** | **120,782** |
| Lumber, wood, except furn.... | 3,454 | 3,255 | 3,289 | 3,549 | 3,862 | 4,212 | 4,375 | 4,337 |
| Furniture and fixtures........ | 2,067 | 2,092 | 2,260 | 2,363 | 2,574 | 2,870 | 3,226 | 3,308 |
| Stone, clay, glass products..... | 4,765 | 4,640 | 4,748 | 5,062 | 5,443 | 5,713 | 5,965 | 5,857 |
| Primary metal industries...... | 10,895 | 11,103 | 10,937 | 11,521 | 13,100 | 14,735 | 16,148 | 15,194 |
| Fabricated metal products...... | 8,088 | 8,113 | 8,798 | 9,184 | 10,151 | 11,518 | 13,066 | 13,444 |
| Machinery, except electrical.... | 11,765 | 11,861 | 13,307 | 14,016 | 16,182 | 18,357 | 21,259 | 22,238 |
| Electrical machinery......... | 10,160 | 10,469 | 12,066 | 12,326 | 12,760 | 14,530 | 17,509 | 18,811 |
| Trans. equip. exc. autos...... | 8,459 | 8,270 | 9,828 | 10,411 | 10,759 | 11,381 | 13,781 | 15,318 |
| Motor vehicles equipment..... | 8,069 | 8,532 | 10,314 | 11,848 | 12,504 | 15,432 | 15,188 | 13,837 |
| Instruments................ | 2,902 | 2,954 | 3,265 | 3,507 | 3,650 | 4,170 | 4,951 | 5,197 |
| Misc. manufacturing......... | 2,342 | 2,325 | 2,547 | 2,544 | 2,675 | 2,872 | 3,140 | 3,241 |
| **Transportation..............** | **17,903** | **18,177** | **19,060** | **20,025** | **21,226** | **23,150** | **24,996** | **26,096** |
| Railroad................... | 6,941 | 6,718 | 6,438 | 6,634 | 6,710 | 7,047 | 7,295 | 7,215 |
| Local suburban highway pass... | 1,598 | 1,639 | 1,703 | 1,716 | 1,770 | 1,897 | 1,977 | 2,086 |
| Motor freight trans., warehous'g. | 5,697 | 5,840 | 6,588 | 6,913 | 7,420 | 8,317 | 9,031 | 9,338 |
| Water transportation......... | 1,522 | 1,654 | 1,724 | 1,815 | 1,978 | 1,990 | 2,334 | 2,361 |
| Air transportation........... | 1,283 | 1,400 | 1,664 | 1,881 | 2,257 | 2,697 | 3,042 | 3,681 |
| Pipeline transportation........ | 357 | 355 | 340 | 426 | 404 | 401 | 431 | 448 |
| Transportation service........ | 505 | 571 | 603 | 640 | 687 | 801 | 859 | 967 |
| **Communication** | **7,709** | **8,237** | **9,284** | **9,820** | **10,507** | **11,241** | **12,469** | **13,141** |
| Telephone and telegraph...... | 6,857 | 7,304 | 8,253 | 8,717 | 9,380 | 9,991 | 11,056 | 11,753 |
| Radio broadcasting, television.. | 852 | 933 | 1,031 | 1,103 | 1,127 | 1,250 | 1,413 | 1,388 |
| **Electric, gas, sanitary services** | **8,135** | **8,934** | **9,739** | **10,344** | **10,989** | **11,447** | **12,155** | **12,934** |
| **Wholesale and retail trade...** | **63,332** | **64,396** | **70,328** | **73,414** | **79,319** | **84,302** | **91,496** | **96,845** |
| Wholesale trade............. | 22,710 | 23,126 | 25,505 | 26,768 | 28,656 | 30,341 | 33,543 | 35,591 |
| Retail trade................ | 40,622 | 41,270 | 44,823 | 46,646 | 50,663 | 53,961 | 57,953 | 61,254 |
| **Finance, ins. and real estate.** | **43,771** | **45,940** | **50,730** | **53,567** | **57,086** | **61,857** | **67,128** | **70,928** |
| Banking................... | 6,640 | 7,276 | 7,320 | 7,977 | 8,495 | 8,989 | 9,911 | 10,662 |
| Credit agencies, holding, other investment co........... | −402 | −435 | −333 | −361 | −741 | 505 | −259 | −303 |
| Security, commodity brokers.... | 1,391 | 1,243 | 1,513 | 1,397 | 1,627 | 1,903 | 2,260 | 2,730 |
| Insurance carriers........... | 4,299 | 4,641 | 5,064 | 4,903 | 4,994 | 5,186 | 5,947 | 5,944 |
| Insurance agents, brokers, service | 1,838 | 1,948 | 2,175 | 2,268 | 2,490 | 2,671 | 2,851 | 3,018 |
| Real estate................ | 30,005 | 31,267 | 34,991 | 37,383 | 40,221 | 43,613 | 46,418 | 48,877 |
| **Services..................** | **41,664** | **44,371** | **50,678** | **54,134** | **59,080** | **64,076** | **70,975** | **77,015** |
| Hotels, other lodging places.... | 2,048 | 2,111 | 2,270 | 2,423 | 2,577 | 2,788 | 3,217 | 3,416 |
| Personal services........... | 4,462 | 4,608 | 5,036 | 5,282 | 5,691 | 5,993 | 6,564 | 6,991 |
| Misc. business services....... | 4,735 | 5,093 | 6,122 | 6,614 | 7,490 | 8,413 | 9,558 | 10,501 |
| Automobile repair, serv., garages | 1,616 | 1,762 | 2,017 | 2,174 | 2,368 | 2,450 | 2,611 | 2,781 |
| Misc. repair services......... | 1,072 | 1,105 | 1,227 | 1,315 | 1,378 | 1,501 | 1,695 | 1,839 |
| Motion pictures............. | 908 | 894 | 890 | 910 | 1,053 | 1,205 | 1,360 | 1,472 |
| Amusement, recreation services.. | 1,492 | 1,661 | 1,849 | 1,970 | 2,120 | 2,221 | 2,478 | 2,634 |
| Medical, other health services.. | 9,967 | 10,724 | 12,609 | 13,519 | 14,865 | 16,256 | 17,946 | 19,563 |
| Legal services.............. | 2,488 | 2,636 | 3,162 | 3,424 | 3,724 | 4,069 | 4,438 | 4,679 |
| Educational services.......... | 2,163 | 2,402 | 3,010 | 3,574 | 3,768 | 4,191 | 4,722 | 5,313 |
| Nonprofit membership org...... | 3,567 | 3,815 | 4,298 | 4,562 | 4,907 | 5,306 | 5,790 | 6,370 |
| Misc. professional services..... | 3,593 | 3,761 | 3,803 | 4,385 | 4,743 | 5,231 | 5,719 | 6,568 | 7,164 |
| Private households.......... | 3,553 | 3,799 | 3,803 | 3,824 | 3,908 | 3,964 | 4,028 | 4,292 |
| **Govt., govt. enterprises....** | **49,266** | **52,891** | **60,670** | **64,681** | **69,992** | **75,233** | **84,554** | **93,614** |
| Federal—general govt....... | 21,030 | 21,868 | 24,277 | 29,676 | 27,148 | 33,458 | 38,061 | 41,719 |
| Federal................... | 24,380 | 25,524 | 28,347 | 25,261 | 31,850 | 28,450 | 32,589 | 35,841 |
| Govt. enterprises........... | 3,350 | 3,656 | 4,070 | 4,415 | 4,702 | 5,008 | 5,472 | 5,878 |
| State & local—gen. govt...... | 23,280 | 25,615 | 30,391 | 35,005 | 35,873 | 41,775 | 46,493 | 51,895 |
| State and local............. | 24,886 | 27,367 | 32,323 | 32,859 | 38,142 | 39,345 | 43,927 | 49,000 |
| Government enterprises........ | 1,606 | 1,752 | 1,932 | 2,146 | 2,269 | 2,430 | 2,566 | 2,892 |
| **Rest of the world...........** | **2,171** | **2,360** | **3,268** | **3,364** | **3,959** | **4,179** | **4,172** | **4,580** |
| **All industries, total........** | **400,025** | **414,522** | **457,687** | **481,927** | **518,068** | **564,336** | **620,760** | **652,867** |

# Appropriations by the Federal Government

Source: Treasury Department (Fiscal Year)

| Year | Appropriations | Year | Appropriations | Year | Appropriations | Year | Appropriations |
|---|---|---|---|---|---|---|---|
| 1885.. | $306,077,469.58 | 1932.. | $5,181,973,000.95 | 1944.. | $118,411,173,965.24 | 1956.. | $63,837,721,203.86 |
| 1890.. | 395,430,284.26 | 1933.. | 5,785,252,641.95 | 1945.. | 73,067,712,071.39 | 1957.. | 70,717,305,080.55 |
| 1895.. | 492,477,759.97 | 1934.. | 7,692,447,339.17 | 1946.. | 76,597,999,662.67 | 1958.. | 77,145,934,082.25 |
| 1900.. | 698,912,982.83 | 1935.. | 7,527,559,327.66 | 1947.. | 40,823,734,061.18 | 1959.. | 82,055,863,758.58 |
| 1905.. | 781,288,215.95 | 1936.. | 9,306,520,504.31 | 1948.. | 42,098,608,820.40 | 1960.. | 80,169,728,902.87 |
| 1910.. | 1,044,433,622.64 | 1937.. | 10,380,975,796.61 | 1949.. | 47,357,993,957.59 | 1961.. | 89,229,575,129.94 |
| 1915.. | 1,122,471,919.12 | 1938.. | 10,192,826,025.92 | 1950.. | 52,867,672,466.21 | 1962.. | 91,447,827,731.04 |
| 1920.. | 6,454,596,649.56 | 1939.. | 12,118,036,335.68 | 1951.. | 67,966,083,088.46 | 1963.. | 102,149,886,566.52 |
| 1925.. | 3,748,651,750.35 | 1940.. | 13,349,202,681.93 | 1952.. | 127,788,153,262.97 | 1964.. | 101,978,886,034.43 |
| 1929.. | 4,633,577,973.85 | 1941.. | 19,072,003,450.61 | 1953.. | 94,916,821,231.67 | 1965.. | 107,555,087,622.62 |
| 1930.. | 4,665,236,678.04 | 1942.. | 60,294,585,348.60 | 1954.. | 74,744,844,304.80 | 1966.. | 125,998,173,095.19 |
| 1931.. | 4,897,877,825.56 | 1943.. | 150,766,672,723.94 | 1955.. | 54,761,172,461.58 | 1967.. | 140,861,235,376.56 |

# U. S. Currency and Coin—June 30, 1968

Source: Treasury Department

## Amounts Outstanding and In Circulation

| | Currency Being Issued[1] | | | Coin | | |
|---|---|---|---|---|---|---|
| | Total | Federal Reserve Notes[2] | U. S. Notes | Total | Silver Dollars | Fractional Coin |
| Outstanding ..... | $44,753,668,777 | $44,431,129,761 | $322,539,016 | $6,061,783,000 | $484,719,600 | $5,577,063,400 |
| Held by: | | | | | | |
| The Treasury | 156,480,991 | 139,908,679 | 16,572,312 | 339,082,103 | 3,015,476 | 336,066,627 |
| Fed. Res. Banks | 2,575,508,284 | 2,568,729,374 | 6,778,910 | 413,593,967 | 14,963 | 413,579,004 |
| In circulation .... | $42,021,679,502 | $41,722,491,708 | $299,187,794 | $5,309,106,930 | $481,689,161 | $4,827,417,769 |

### Currencies No Longer Issued

| | Total | Federal Reserve Notes[2] | Fed. Res. Bank Notes | National Bank Notes | Certificates | | Treas. Notes of 1890 |
|---|---|---|---|---|---|---|---|
| | | | | | Gold[4] | Silver | |
| Outstanding ....... | $323,363,566 | $1,022,785 | $59,048,002 | $20,700,720 | $4,010,754 | $238,570,771 | $10,534 |
| Held by: | | | | | | | |
| The Treasury .... | 1,299,611 | 8,155 | 149,258 | 34,661 | 142,750 | 964,787 | ........ |
| Fed. Res. Banks | 12,387,097 | ......... | 44,580 | 2,270 | ......... | 12,340,247 | ........ |
| In circulation ...... | $309,676,858 | $1,014,630 | $58,854,164 | $20,663,789 | $3,868,004 | $225,265,737 | $10,534 |

### Currency by Denomination and Coin, In Circulation

| Denomination | Federal Reserve[2] | U. S. Notes | No Longer Issued | Total |
|---|---|---|---|---|
| $1 ............. | $1,697,462,663 | $145,408 | $162,765,764 | $1,860,373,835 |
| 2 ............. | ............. | 136,127,176 | 14,001 | 136,141,177 |
| 5 ............. | 2,515,959,605 | 162,892,675 | 49,303,462 | 2,728,155,742 |
| 10 ............. | 8,258,236,920 | 12,165 | 29,168,260 | 8,287,417,345 |
| 20 ............. | 15,401,966,170 | 4,770 | 21,970,234 | 15,423,941,174 |
| 50 ............. | 3,916,969,000 | 800 | 15,318,500 | 3,932,288,300 |
| 100 ............. | 9,399,615,850 | 2,300 | 30,307,150 | 9,429,925,300 |
| 500 ............. | 239,856,500 | 2,500 | 268,000 | 240,127,000 |
| 1,000 ............. | 285,685,000 | ............. | 346,000 | 286,031,000 |
| 5,000 ............. | 2,970,000 | ............. | 75,000 | 3,045,000 |
| 10,000 ............. | 3,770,000 | ............. | 140,000 | 3,910,000 |
| Fractional Parts... | ............. | ............. | 487 | 487 |
| Total Currency ..... | $41,722,491,708 | $299,187,794 | $309,676,858 | $42,331,356,360 |
| Total Coin ......... | | | | 5,309,106,930 |
| Total currency and Coin | | | | $47,640,463,290 |

### Comparative Totals of Money in Circulation (Selected Dates)

| Date | Amounts (millions) | Per capita[5] | Date | Amounts (millions) | Per capita[6] |
|---|---|---|---|---|---|
| June 30, 1968............. | [6]$47,640.4 | 236.82 | June 30, 1940... | 7,847.5 | $59.40 |
| June 30, 1967............. | 44,712.4 | 224.56 | June 30, 1935... | 5,567.1 | 43.75 |
| June 30, 1965............. | 39,719.8 | 204.14 | June 30, 1930... | 4,522.0 | 36.74 |
| June 30, 1960............. | 32,064.6 | 177.47 | June 30, 1925... | 4,815.2 | 41.56 |
| June 30, 1955............. | 30,229.3 | 182.90 | June 30, 1920... | 5,467.6 | 51.36 |
| June 30, 1950............. | 27,156.3 | 179.03 | June 30, 1915... | 3,319.6 | 33.01 |
| June 30, 1945............. | 26,746.4 | 191.14 | June 30, 1910... | 3,148.7 | 34.07 |

Total currency and coin outstanding, $48,126,692,699; less amounts held by the Treasury, $799,071,286 and the Federal Reserve banks, $2,615,178,217; amounts in circulation, $44,712,443,196.

[1]Excludes gold certificates, Series of 1934, which are issued only to Federal Reserve banks and do not appear in circulation. [2]Issued on and after July 1, 1929. [3]Issued before July 1, 1929. [4]Issued before Series of 1934. [5]Based on Census Bureau estimates of population. [6]Highest amount to date.

There is maintained in the Treasury—(i) as a reserve for United States notes—$156,039,431 in gold bullion; (ii) as security for outstanding silver certificates issued after June 30, 1929 silver in bullion and standard silver dollars of a monetary value equal to the face amount of such silver certificates; and (iii) as security for gold certificates of Series of 1934—gold, bullion of a value at the legal standard equal to the face amount of such gold certificates. Treasury notes of 1890, silver certificates issued before July 1, 1929, and gold certificates prior to Series of 1934 are redeemable from the general fund of the Treasury and upon redemption will be retired. Federal reserve notes are contingent liabilities of the United States. Funds have been deposited in the Treasury for the retirement of Federal Reserve notes of all series prior to the series of 1928. Federal Reserve notes, except those for which such payment has been made to the Treasury, are a first lien on all assets of the issuing Federal Reserve Bank and secured by the deposit by the Federal Reserve Bank concerned with its Federal Reserve Agent, of a like amount of collateral consisting of such discounted or purchased paper as is eligible under the terms of the Federal Reserve Act, or gold certificates, or securities issued by the United States. Each Federal Reserve Bank must maintain reserves in gold certificates of not less than 25 percent against its Federal Reserve notes in actual circulation. Gold certificates deposited with Federal Reserve Agents as collateral, and those deposited with the Treasurer of the United States as a redemption fund, are counted as part of the required reserve. "Gold certificates" as herein used includes credits with the Treasurer of the United States payable in gold certificates. Federal Reserve bank notes and National bank notes are in process of retirement.

# U. S. Money in Circulation, by Denominations

Source: Federal Reserve System

Outside Treasury and Federal Reserve Banks. (In millions of dollars)

| End of year | Total in circula. | Coin and small denomination | | | | | | | Large denomination currency | | | | | | | Unassorted |
|---|---|---|---|---|---|---|---|---|---|---|---|---|---|---|---|---|
| | | Total | Coin | $1 | $2 | $5 | $10 | $20 | Total | $50 | $100 | $500 | $1,000 | $5,000 | $10,000 | |
| 1945 | 28,515 | 20,683 | 1,274 | 1,039 | 73 | 2,313 | 6,782 | 9,201 | 7,834 | 2,327 | 4,220 | 454 | 801 | 7 | 24 | 2 |
| 1950 | 27,741 | 19,305 | 1,554 | 1,113 | 64 | 2,049 | 5,998 | 8,529 | 8,438 | 2,422 | 5,043 | 368 | 588 | 4 | 12 | 2 |
| 1955 | 31,155 | 22,021 | 1,927 | 1,312 | 75 | 2,151 | 6,617 | 9,940 | 9,136 | 2,736 | 5,641 | 307 | 438 | 3 | 12 | ...... |
| 1960 | 32,869 | 23,521 | 2,427 | 1,533 | 88 | 2,246 | 6,691 | 10,536 | 9,348 | 2,815 | 5,954 | 249 | 316 | 3 | 10 | ...... |
| 1965 | 42,056 | 29,842 | 4,027 | 1,908 | 127 | 2,618 | 7,794 | 13,369 | 12,214 | 3,540 | 8,135 | 245 | 288 | 3 | 4 | ...... |
| 1966 | 44,663 | 31,695 | 4,480 | 2,051 | 137 | 2,756 | 8,070 | 14,201 | 12,969 | 3,700 | 8,735 | 241 | 286 | 3 | [1]4 | ...... |
| 1967 | 47,226 | 33,468 | 4,918 | 2,035 | 136 | 2,850 | 8,366 | 15,162 | 13,758 | 3,915 | 9,311 | 240 | 285 | 4 | 4 | ...... |

## Principal Assets and Liabilities of all U. S. Banks
### As of Dec. 30, 1967
Source: Federal Deposit Insurance Corporation, Washington, D. C. (In thousands of dollars)

| States | Net total | Invest-ments* | Deposits | States | Net total | Invest-ments* | Deposits |
|---|---|---|---|---|---|---|---|
| Alabama...... | 2,031,907 | 742,516 | 3,871,399 | Ohio......... | 10,648,342 | 3,618,051 | 18,623,689 |
| Alaska....... | 235,282 | 77,757 | 423,415 | Oklahoma.... | 2,354,436 | 841,170 | 4,537,617 |
| Arizona...... | 1,715,969 | 314,866 | 2,504,362 | Oregon....... | 2,099,900 | 542,860 | 3,472,773 |
| Arkansas..... | 1,257,902 | 416,752 | 2,394,036 | Pennsylvania.. | 17,569,563 | 3,893,266 | 27,120,897 |
| California.... | 26,765,636 | 4,768,816 | 41,254,076 | Rhode Island.. | 1,770,656 | 248,191 | 2,421,790 |
| Colorado..... | 2,097,964 | 582,087 | 3,472,695 | South Carolina. | 1,002,217 | 299,923 | 1,759,047 |
| Connecticut.. | 6,293,265 | 777,877 | 8,453,448 | South Dakota.. | 652,176 | 319,198 | 1,214,406 |
| Delaware..... | 808,428 | 235,937 | 1,341,002 | Tennessee..... | 3,434,718 | 949,171 | 5,850,609 |
| Dist. of Col... | 1,482,135 | 605,229 | 2,591,401 | Texas........ | 11,590,301 | 3,067,810 | 20,854,898 |
| Florida...... | 4,782,399 | 2,084,515 | 9,708,565 | Utah........ | 955,083 | 208,478 | 1,541,102 |
| Georgia...... | 3,364,553 | 852,873 | 5,737,443 | Vermont...... | 675,191 | 130,630 | 890,005 |
| Hawaii...... | 776,118 | 150,354 | 1,174,662 | Virginia...... | 3,843,088 | 1,002,914 | 6,126,754 |
| Idaho....... | 652,107 | 172,315 | 1,053,332 | Washington... | 3,556,893 | 746,406 | 5,573,281 |
| Illinois...... | 17,021,811 | 5,479,537 | 29,464,047 | West Virginia.. | 1,118,736 | 594,346 | 2,131,388 |
| Indiana...... | 4,583,509 | 1,999,328 | 8,410,023 | Wisconsin.... | 4,275,947 | 1,774,738 | 7,812,775 |
| Iowa........ | 2,890,475 | 1,103,491 | 5,246,446 | Wyoming..... | 346,262 | 150,181 | 638,517 |
| Kansas...... | 2,053,284 | 929,140 | 4,052,623 | Other areas | | | |
| Kentucky.... | 2,212,828 | 933,435 | 4,227,745 | Pacific Islands.. | 45,759 | 1,154 | 66,369 |
| Louisiana.... | 2,723,669 | 1,161,370 | 5,285,540 | Panama Canal | | | |
| Maine....... | 1,176,177 | 238,305 | 1,706,397 | Zone........ | 3,264 | ......... | 34,924 |
| Maryland.... | 3,220,074 | 864,610 | 5,063,456 | Puerto Rico... | 1,320,446 | 203,053 | 1,717,350 |
| Massachusetts. | 13,224,020 | 2,699,246 | 18,422,836 | Virgin Islands.. | 83,729 | 3,397 | 141,834 |
| Michigan..... | 10,659,417 | 2,784,372 | 17,398,760 | | | | |
| Minnesota.... | 4,535,005 | 1,414,976 | 7,863,179 | Tot. U. S... | 290,252,700 | 66,956,584 | 458,701,119 |
| Mississippi... | 1,350,540 | 427,921 | 2,435,295 | 50 states and | | | |
| Missouri..... | 5,275,516 | 1,949,630 | 10,024,244 | D. C... | 288,799,502 | 66,748,980 | 456,740,642 |
| Montana..... | 708,625 | 291,818 | 1,292,391 | Other areas... | 1,453,198 | 207,604 | 1,960,477 |
| Nebraska.... | 1,565,043 | 469,914 | 2,793,323 | | | | |
| Nevada...... | 508,801 | 170,705 | 838,602 | *Investment figures above are for U. S. Govern- |
| N. Hampshire. | 1,343,998 | 223,245 | 1,684,284 | ment securities, direct and guaranteed obligations. |
| New Jersey... | 8,999,736 | 2,120,102 | 14,253,246 | Other investment totals follow: Obligations of |
| New Mexico.. | 612,357 | 210,799 | 1,102,735 | States and political subdivisions, $50,340,975. |
| New York.... | 82,032,530 | 10,139,607 | 113,791,842 | Securities of Federal agencies and corporations |
| North Carolina. | 3,342,923 | 730,556 | 5,607,802 | (not guaranteed by the U. S.), $10,208,523. Other |
| North Dakota.. | 601,985 | 297,646 | 1,226,442 | securities, $9,468,092. |

## All Banks in United States—Number, Deposits
### Source: Federal Reserve System
Comprises all national banks in the United States and all state commercial banks, trust companies, mutual and stock savings banks and private and industrial banks and special types of institutions that are treated as banks by the Federal bank supervisory agencies.

| Date June 30 | Number of Banks | | | | | Total Deposits (in millions of dollars) | | | | |
|---|---|---|---|---|---|---|---|---|---|---|
| | Total all banks | Member banks | | | Nonmember banks | Total all banks | Member banks | | | Nonmember banks |
| | | Total | Na-tional | State | Mu-tual sav-ings | Other | | Total | Na-tional | State | Mu-tual sav-ings | Other |
| 1920.... | 29,715 | 9,399 | 8,025 | 1,374 | 628 | 19,688 | 41,282 | 25,401 | 17,159 | 8,242 | 5,168 | 10,713 |
| 1925.... | 28,479 | 9,538 | 8,066 | 1,472 | 621 | 18,320 | 51,641 | 32,457 | 19,912 | 12,546 | 7,089 | 12,095 |
| 1930.... | 23,855 | 8,315 | 7,247 | 1,068 | 604 | 14,936 | 59,828 | 38,069 | 23,235 | 14,834 | 9,117 | 12,642 |
| 1935.... | 16,047 | 6,410 | 5,425 | 985 | 569 | 9,068 | 51,149 | 34,938 | 22,477 | 12,461 | 9,830 | 6,381 |
| 1940.... | 14,955 | 6,398 | 5,164 | 1,234 | 551 | 8,006 | 70,770 | 51,729 | 33,014 | 18,715 | 10,631 | 8,410 |
| 1945.... | 14,542 | 6,840 | 5,015 | 1,825 | 539 | 7,163 | 151,033 | 118,378 | 76,534 | 41,844 | 14,413 | 18,242 |
| 1950.... | 14,674 | 6,885 | 4,971 | 1,914 | 527 | 7,262 | 163,770 | 122,707 | 82,430 | 40,277 | 19,927 | 21,137 |
| 1955.... | 14,309 | 6,611 | 4,744 | 1,867 | 525 | 7,173 | 208,850 | 154,670 | 98,636 | 56,034 | 27,310 | 26,870 |
| 1960.... | 14,006 | 6,217 | 4,542 | 1,675 | 513 | 7,276 | 249,163 | 179,519 | 116,178 | 63,341 | 35,316 | 34,328 |
| 1963.... | 13,993 | 6,058 | 4,537 | 1,521 | 511 | 7,424 | 309,428 | 222,619 | 145,513 | 77,106 | 43,248 | 43,560 |
| 1964.... | 14,175 | 6,180 | 4,702 | 1,478 | 506 | 7,489 | 331,843 | 238,052 | 155,978 | 82,074 | 46,940 | 46,850 |
| 1965.... | 14,295 | 6,235 | 4,803 | 1,432 | 504 | 7,556 | 362,611 | 259,743 | 171,528 | 88,215 | 50,980 | 51,889 |
| 1966.... | 14,307 | 6,194 | 4,811 | 1,383 | 505 | 7,608 | 392,881 | 281,209 | 197,792 | 83,417 | 53,727 | 57,946 |
| 1967.... | 14,247 | 6,108 | 4,780 | 1,328 | 503 | 7,636 | 419,062 | 297,529 | 211,098 | 86,431 | 58,259 | 63,274 |
| 1968*... | 14,223 | 6,071 | 4,758 | 1,313 | 501 | 7,651 | 456,784 | 327,011 | 231,374 | 95,637 | 60,494 | 69,279 |

*First 6 months of fiscal year—to Dec. 31, 1966.

## Bank Clearings in Chief United States Cities
Source: Except as to Los Angeles, the Commercial and Financial Chronicle, N. Y.

| Yr. (Cal.) | New York | Chicago | Phila. | Los Ang. | Boston | San Fran. | Detroit | Dallas |
|---|---|---|---|---|---|---|---|---|
| | $1,000 | $1,000 | $1,000 | $1,000 | $1,000 | $1,000 | $1,000 | $1,000 |
| 1935... | 181,551,008 | 13,194,988 | 16,909,000 | 5,852,244 | 6,455,822 | 6,478,835 | 4,523,167 | 1,969,290 |
| 1940... | 160,878,038 | 16,684,672 | 21,455,000 | 7,543,880 | 11,943,665 | 6,773,877 | 6,312,233 | 2,986,774 |
| 1945... | 334,432,654 | 27,279,588 | 34,710,000 | 17,144,078 | 19,589,725 | 15,743,086 | 16,472,971 | 6,634,514 |
| 1950... | 399,308,634 | 40,674,988 | 51,102,000 | 26,504,731 | 25,348,336 | 21,982,689 | 22,855,273 | 14,451,332 |
| 1955... | 530,883,498 | 52,818,527 | 59,962,000 | 42,818,633 | 32,472,726 | 31,492,157 | 36,364,754 | 21,678,567 |
| 1960... | 738,604,276 | 66,651,600 | 56,716,000 | 53,635,826 | 40,759,040 | 39,787,147 | 39,101,854 | 27,811,939 |
| 1965... | 1,280,402,568 | 82,507,560 | 69,116,728 | 111,587,481 | 60,318,717 | 87,095,481 | 56,068,833 | 42,414,327 |
| 1966... | 1,507,369,953 | 88,299,485 | 71,082,213 | 121,384,391 | 76,638,480 | 91,469,642 | 60,812,774 | 31,155,892 |
| 1967... | 1,831,058,135 | 93,786,895 | 74,860,517 | 134,453,200 | 88,058,364 | 94,497,459 | 60,793,356 | 47,492,822 |

| Yr. (Cal.) | Kan. City | Houston | Pittsb'rgh | Cleveland | St. Louis | Minneap. | Baltimore | Cincin. |
|---|---|---|---|---|---|---|---|---|
| | $1,000 | $1,000 | $1,000 | $1,000 | $1,000 | $1,000 | $1,000 | $1,000 |
| 1935... | 4,348,113 | 1,420,404 | 5,245,718 | 3,417,055 | 3,940,654 | 3,044,735 | 2,910,637 | 2,466,319 |
| 1940... | 4,997,593 | 2,568,518 | 7,074,775 | 5,734,407 | 4,822,016 | 3,787,088 | 4,201,985 | 3,245,329 |
| 1945... | 10,856,497 | 5,982,318 | 12,978,668 | 11,529,428 | 9,723,815 | 8,196,279 | 8,315,468 | 6,305,149 |
| 1950... | 16,707,120 | 11,922,307 | 16,782,419 | 17,683,829 | 14,896,444 | 14,113,814 | 12,154,904 | 9,928,712 |
| 1955... | 20,057,800 | 19,199,929 | 21,142,527 | 26,426,614 | 18,481,105 | 18,496,865 | 17,071,914 | 13,589,421 |
| 1960... | 24,967,582 | 21,887,839 | 23,913,706 | 32,364,009 | 21,138,861 | 25,129,318 | 20,423,684 | 16,213,720 |
| 1965... | 33,938,377 | 33,938,170 | 29,070,474 | 44,600,090 | 28,399,392 | 34,029,120 | 25,893,740 | 21,694,976 |
| 1966... | 37,682,248 | 37,600,344 | 28,124,834 | 45,152,163 | 30,808,218 | 37,685,326 | 28,932,194 | 21,232,144 |
| 1967... | 38,405,791 | 40,699,741 | 28,386,870 | 45,494,403 | 32,085,929 | 39,692,234 | 27,819,851 | 20,011,092 |

## Savings by Individuals in the United States[1]
### Source: Securities and Exchange Commission
(Billions of Dollars) *Indicates less than $50 million.

| Type of savings | 1963 | 1964 | 1965 | 1966 | 1967 | 1968 Jan.-Mar. |
|---|---|---|---|---|---|---|
| Currency and demand deposits............... | 6.8 | 7.0 | 7.3 | * | 9.3 | −6.2 |
| Time and savings deposits................... | 11.6 | 12.3 | 16.0 | 12.5 | 20.2 | 6.4 |
| Savings shares[2]................................ | 11.7 | 11.4 | 9.4 | 4.5 | 11.5 | 1.6 |
| Securities.................................... | .5 | 6.1 | 3.9 | 14.5 | 1.5 | 3.4 |
| U. S. savings bonds | | | | | | |
| Series E & H........................ | 1.6 | 1.2 | .9 | 1.0 | 1.1 | .1 |
| Other.............................. | −.4 | −.3 | −.2 | −.4 | −.2 | * |
| Other U. S. government[3]................. | .6 | 3.2 | 1.6 | 8.2 | −1.2 | 3.2 |
| State and local government.............. | 1.0 | 1.9 | 2.0 | 4.1 | 1.3 | .1 |
| Corporate and other.................... | −2.4 | .1 | −.4 | 1.7 | .5 | .1 |
| Bonds and notes................... | 1.8 | .6 | 1.9 | 2.7 | 4.8 | .2 |
| Investment company shares[4]........ | 1.6 | 2.1 | 2.2 | 4.5 | 4.6 | 1.6 |
| Other preferred and common stock... | −4.2 | −2.6 | −4.5 | −5.5 | −8.8 | −1.8 |
| Private insurance and pension reserves...... | 10.7 | 11.6 | 13.2 | 13.0 | 14.5 | 3.9 |
| Insurance reserves.................... | 4.5 | 4.8 | 5.5 | 4.7 | 5.4 | 1.3 |
| Insured pension reserves.............. | 1.7 | 2.0 | 2.1 | 2.1 | 2.2 | .7 |
| Noninsured pension reserves[5]......... | 4.5 | 4.9 | 5.6 | 6.2 | 6.9 | 1.9 |
| Government insurance and pension reserve[6]..... | 4.0 | 4.5 | 4.8 | 5.0 | 5.5 | 1.5 |
| Increase in debt (8 +9 +10)............ | 22.3 | 23.1 | 25.0 | 19.8 | 14.8 | .9 |
| Mortgage debt[7]..................... | 14.5 | 15.5 | 15.9 | 12.7 | 9.5 | 3.4 |
| Consumer debt[8]..................... | 6.9 | 7.5 | 9.0 | 6.5 | 4.1 | −1.0 |
| Securities loans[9]..................... | .9 | .1 | .1 | .5 | 1.2 | −1.5 |
| Net financial saving (1+2+3+4+5+6−7)..... | 23.0 | 30.0 | 29.8 | 29.8 | 47.6 | 9.8 |

[1]Includes unincorporated business savings of the types specified. Figures are rounded and will not necessarily add to totals. The foregoing data have been compiled by the Commission from many different sources. Because of the nature of the figures, current data are necessarily estimates and, therefore, are subject to revision.
[2]Includes shares in savings and loan associations and shares and deposits in credit unions.
[3]Includes non-guaranteed Federal agency securities.
[4]Includes closed-end investment companies as well as mutual funds.
[5]In addition to corporate funds, includes reserves of nonprofit organizations and multi-employer plans.
[6]Includes civil service, railroad retirement and state and local retirement funds.
[7]Mortgage debt to institutions on one-to-four-family non-farm dwellings.
[8]Consumer debt owed to corporations. Policy loans on life insurance have been deducted from those items of saving.
[9]Change in bank loans to brokers and dealers and others made for the purpose of purchasing or carrying securities.

## U. S. Commercial Banks With Deposits Over One Billion

A compilation of the 300 largest commercial banks in the United States is made twice a year by the American Banker, daily banking newspaper, 67 Pearl St., New York, N. Y. Of these the first 45 banks had deposits of more than 1 billion on Jan. 1, 1968. They are listed below. (Copyright 1968, by American Banker.)

| Rank | Deposits (in $1,000) | Rank | Deposits (in $1,000) |
|---|---|---|---|
| 1 Bank of America NT&SA, San Fran. | $19,099,938 | 25 Harris Trust & Sav. Bank, Chicago | 1,545,479 |
| 2 Chase Manhattan Bank, N. Y. | 15,760,249 | 26 Philadelphia National Bank | 1,543,606 |
| 3 First National City Bank, N. Y. | 15,201,192 | 27 First Nat'l Bank of Oregon, Portland | 1,438,767 |
| 4 Mfrs. Hanover Trust Co., N. Y. | 8,026,564 | 28 Bank of Calif. NA, San Francisco | 1,409,635 |
| 5 Morgan Guaranty Trust Co., N. Y. | 7,284,075 | 29 Pittsburgh National Bank | 1,403,669 |
| 6 Chemical Bank N. Y. Trust Co., N. Y. | 7,091,763 | 30 Nat'l Bank of N. A., Jamaica, N. Y. | 1,392,986 |
| 7 Bankers Trust Co., N. Y. | 6,016,142 | 31 Republic National Bank, Dallas | 1,364,202 |
| 8 Continental Ill. Nat'l B&T Co., Chi. | 5,419,388 | 32 U. S. Nat'l Bank of Oregon, Portland | 1,354,929 |
| 9 Security Pac. Nat'l Bank, L. A. | 5,128,941 | 33 First National Bank, Dallas | 1,313,171 |
| 10 First National Bank, Chicago | 5,119,398 | 34 Bank of New York | 1,301,863 |
| 11 Wells Fargo Bank, San Francisco | 4,064,757 | 35 Girard Trust Bank, Philadelphia | 1,289,941 |
| 12 Crocker-Citizens Nat'l Bank, San Fran. | 3,769,454 | 36 Union Bank, Los Angeles | 1,233,387 |
| 13 Irving Trust Co., New York | 3,523,345 | 37 National City Bank, Cleveland | 1,208,280 |
| 14 United Calif. Bank, Los Angeles | 3,426,527 | 38 Marine Midland Trust Co. of | |
| 15 Mellon Nat'l Bank & Trust Co., Pitts. | 3,281,753 | Western N. Y., Buffalo | 1,202,509 |
| 16 National Bank of Detroit | 3,145,903 | 39 Wachovia Bank & Trust Co., | |
| 17 First National Bank, Boston | 2,923,361 | Winston-Salem, N. C. | 1,183,085 |
| 18 Franklin Nat'l Bank, Mineola, N. Y. | 2,171,455 | 40 Northern Trust Co., Chicago | 1,177,490 |
| 19 Cleveland Trust Co. | 2,025,148 | 41 Citizens & Southern National Bank, | |
| 20 First Penn. Bank. & Trust Co., Phila. | 1,896,916 | Savannah, Ga. | 1,140,514 |
| 21 Detroit Bank & Trust Co. | 1,726,215 | 42 Valley Nat'l Bank of Ariz. Phoenix | 1,134,054 |
| 22 Manufacturers Nat'l Bank Detroit | 1,670,967 | 43 Fidelity Bank, Philadelphia | 1,057,891 |
| 23 Marine Midl'd Grace Trust Co., N. Y. | 1,637,664 | 44 Central National Bank, Cleveland | 1,026,085 |
| 24 Seattle-First National Bank, Wash. | 1,553,602 | 45 Mercantile Tr. Co. NA, St. Louis, Mo. | 1,008,384 |

## Bank Rates on Short-Term Business Loans*
### Source: Federal Reserve System

Percent per annum. Estimates based on reports from large banks in 19 leading cities. Short-term loans comprise loans maturing in one year or less.

| Year | Ave. 19 Cities | N.Y.C. | 7 N. & E. Cities | 11 S. & W. Cities | Size of Loans ($1,000) | | | |
|---|---|---|---|---|---|---|---|---|
| | | | | | $1-9 | $10-99 | $100-199 | over $200 |
| 1940................ | 2.1 | 1.8 | 2.0 | 2.5 | 4.3 | 3.0 | 2.0 | 1.8 |
| 1950................ | 2.7 | 2.4 | 2.7 | 3.2 | 4.5 | 3.6 | 3.0 | 2.4 |
| 1960................ | 5.2 | 5.0 | 5.2 | 5.5 | 6.0 | 5.7 | 5.4 | 5.0 |
| 1965................ | 5.1 | 4.8 | 5.1 | 5.3 | 5.9 | 5.6 | 5.4 | 4.9 |
| 1966................ | 6.0 | 5.8 | 6.1 | 6.2 | 6.5 | 6.4 | 6.2 | 5.9 |

*Starting with the first quarter of 1967 the Survey has been revised. The reporting periods have been shifted from the last month of each calendar quarter to the middle month of the quarter. Consequently it will preclude precise comparability between the old and the revised series.

| | Ave. 35 Cities | N. Y. C. | 8 Other N. E. | 7 No.Cent. Cities | 7 S. E. Cities | 8 S. W. Cities | 4 West Cities | $1-9 | $10-99 | $100 to 499 | $500 to 999 | $1,000 and over |
|---|---|---|---|---|---|---|---|---|---|---|---|---|
| *1967 Feb. 1-15 | 6.13 | 5.86 | 6.45 | 6.12 | 6.07 | 6.18 | 6.26 | 6.73 | 6.64 | 6.33 | 6.17 | 5.90 |
| May 1-15 | 5.95 | 5.67 | 6.32 | 5.91 | 5.93 | 6.04 | 6.05 | 6.61 | 6.48 | 6.16 | 5.89 | 5.73 |
| Aug. 1-15 | 5.95 | 5.66 | 6.29 | 5.92 | 5.92 | 6.01 | 6.02 | 6.58 | 6.46 | 6.16 | 5.89 | 5.72 |
| | 5.96 | 5.71 | 6.29 | 5.91 | 5.94 | 6.03 | 6.03 | 6.60 | 6.48 | 6.17 | 5.90 | 5.73 |
| 1968 Feb. 1-15 | 6.36 | 6.14 | 6.73 | 6.35 | 6.21 | 6.41 | 6.31 | 6.82 | 6.76 | 6.56 | 6.31 | 6.19 |
| May 1-15 | 6.84 | 6.60 | 7.18 | 6.89 | 6.61 | 6.87 | 6.76 | 7.18 | 7.21 | 7.00 | 6.81 | 6.68 |

# Federal Reserve System

The Federal Reserve System, central banking system of the United States, was established Dec. 23, 1913, by an Act of Congress to give the country an elastic currency, to provide facilities for discounting commercial paper, and to improve supervision of banking. Today it is generally recognized that the primary function of the System is to foster a flow of credit and money that will facilitate orderly economic growth, a stable dollar, and a long-run balance in international payments.

The Federal Reserve System consists of the (1) Board of Governors of the Federal Reserve System; (2) Federal Open Market Committee; (3) 12 Fed. Reserve Banks and 24 branches; (4) member banks; and (5) Fed. Advisory Council.

The 7 members of the Board of Governors in Washington are appointed by the President with advice and consent of the Senate; Wm. McC. Martin, Jr., is chairman. One of the Board's principal functions is in the area of monetary policy. The Board has authority to approve changes in discount rates, to change member bank reserve requirements within specified limits, to set margin requirements for certain kinds of stock transactions, and to set maximum interest rates payable on member banks' savings and time deposits. Another important duty of the Board relates to supervision of Federal Reserve Banks and member banks. Expenses of the Board of Governors are paid out of assessments upon the Reserve Banks.

The Federal Open Market Committee is composed of the 7 members of the Board of Governors and 5 Federal Reserve Bank representatives

elected annually. The Committee establishes System open market policy for the purchases and sales of securities and for operations in foreign currencies.

Rather than having one central bank in the political capital, as in central banking systems of most countries, the Federal Reserve System is divided into 12 districts, each with a Federal Reserve Bank—in Boston, New York, Philadelphia, Cleveland, Richmond, Atlanta, Chicago, St. Louis, Minneapolis, Kansas City, Dallas, and San Francisco. Reserve Banks are operated for public service. By statute, their stock is held entirely by member banks, which include all national banks and such state banks and trust companies as have been admitted to membership. Ownership of Reserve Bank stock is in the nature of an obligation incident to membership in the System and does not carry with it the attributes of control and financial interest ordinarily attached to stock ownership in corporations that are operated for profit. The amount of stock that member banks own is specified by law and dividends are limited to 6% per annum. In case of the liquidation of any Reserve Bank, its surplus would be paid entirely to the United States. Each Reserve Bank has 9 directors, 6 of whom are chosen by member banks and 3 by the Board of Governors.

The 12-member Federal Advisory Council is composed of one member selected annually by the directors of each Federal Reserve Bank. The Council meets in Washington at least 4 times a year and advises the Board of Governors on matters within the Board's jurisdiction.

# Per Capita Personal Income, by States and Regions

Source: Department of Commerce. Office of Business Economics

| State and region | Per capita income[1] (dollars) | | | | State and region | Per capita income[1] (dollars) | | | |
|---|---|---|---|---|---|---|---|---|---|
| | 1964 | 1965 | 1966 | 1967 | | 1964 | 1965 | 1966 | 1967 |
| **United States........** | 2,586 | 2,765 | 2,978 | 3,159 | Southeast............ | 1,954 | 2,103 | 2,294 | 2,456 |
| | | | | | Virginia............ | 2,267 | 2,422 | 2,619 | 2,804 |
| **New England........** | 2,853 | 3,027 | 3,267 | 3,503 | West Virginia...... | 1,895 | 2,029 | 2,174 | 2,334 |
| Maine.............. | 2,134 | 2,309 | 2,500 | 2,657 | Kentucky.......... | 1,891 | 2,058 | 2,243 | 2,426 |
| New Hampshire.... | 2,440 | 2,581 | 2,845 | 3,053 | Tennessee.......... | 1,877 | 2,047 | 2,242 | 2,394 |
| Vermont........... | 2,150 | 2,377 | 2,651 | 2,825 | North Carolina.... | 1,919 | 2,054 | 2,278 | 2,439 |
| Massachusetts...... | 2,919 | 3,072 | 3,290 | 3,541 | South Carolina.... | 1,692 | 1,852 | 2,060 | 2,213 |
| Rhode Island...... | 2,660 | 2,819 | 3,075 | 3,328 | Georgia............ | 2,009 | 2,171 | 2,373 | 2,541 |
| Connecticut........ | 3,244 | 3,455 | 3,732 | 3,969 | Florida............ | 2,296 | 2,450 | 2,647 | 2,853 |
| | | | | | Alabama.......... | 1,778 | 1,923 | 2,062 | 2,163 |
| **Mideast............** | 2,958 | 3,124 | 3,347 | 3,561 | Mississippi........ | 1,486 | 1,615 | 1,763 | 1,896 |
| New York.......... | 3,138 | 3,296 | 3,519 | 3,759 | Louisiana.......... | 1,943 | 2,084 | 2,281 | 2,456 |
| New Jersey........ | 3,076 | 3,260 | 3,466 | 3,668 | Arkansas.......... | 1,746 | 1,839 | 2,031 | 2,099 |
| Pennsylvania...... | 2,599 | 2,755 | 2,998 | 3,187 | | | | | |
| Delaware.......... | 3,139 | 3,346 | 3,482 | 3,642 | **Southwest..........** | 2,200 | 2,348 | 2,533 | 2,709 |
| Maryland.......... | 2,834 | 3,027 | 3,235 | 3,421 | Oklahoma........ | 2,121 | 2,303 | 2,462 | 2,643 |
| Dist. of Col........ | 3,549 | 3,694 | 3,853 | 4,123 | Texas............ | 2,216 | 2,360 | 2,559 | 2,744 |
| | | | | | New Mexico...... | 2,100 | 2,240 | 2,370 | 2,477 |
| **Great Lakes........** | 2,775 | 3,011 | 3,243 | 3,395 | Arizona.......... | 2,281 | 2,400 | 2,568 | 2,720 |
| Michigan.......... | 2,782 | 3,052 | 3,280 | 3,396 | | | | | |
| Ohio.............. | 2,649 | 2,859 | 3,081 | 3,213 | **Rocky Mountain....** | 2,386 | 2,552 | 2,705 | 2,873 |
| Indiana............ | 2,603 | 2,860 | 3,056 | 3,196 | Montana.......... | 2,266 | 2,455 | 2,662 | 2,765 |
| Illinois............ | 3,060 | 3,304 | 3,554 | 3,750 | Idaho............ | 2,128 | 2,409 | 2,415 | 2,575 |
| Wisconsin.......... | 2,546 | 2,733 | 2,991 | 3,156 | Wyoming.......... | 2,435 | 2,570 | 2,779 | 3,002 |
| | | | | | Colorado.......... | 2,570 | 2,723 | 2,919 | 3,135 |
| **Plains............** | 2,399 | 2,647 | 2,862 | 3,021 | Utah.............. | 2,270 | 2,379 | 2,495 | 2,604 |
| Minnesota.......... | 2,443 | 2,683 | 2,908 | 3,116 | | | | | |
| Iowa.............. | 2,406 | 2,741 | 3,024 | 3,109 | **Far West..........** | 3,047 | 3,188 | 3,400 | 3,597 |
| Missouri.......... | 2,466 | 2,662 | 2,811 | 2,993 | Washington........ | 2,722 | 2,913 | 3,270 | 3,521 |
| North Dakota...... | 1,981 | 2,311 | 2,412 | 2,487 | Oregon............ | 2,609 | 2,771 | 2,933 | 3,063 |
| South Dakota...... | 1,885 | 2,220 | 2,469 | 2,590 | Nevada............ | 3,246 | 3,320 | 3,499 | 3,583 |
| Nebraska.......... | 2,369 | 2,643 | 2,951 | 3,081 | California.......... | 3,142 | 3,274 | 3,468 | 3,665 |
| Kansas............ | 2,491 | 2,678 | 2,884 | 3,060 | Alaska............ | 3,088 | 3,214 | 3,452 | 3,738 |
| | | | | | Hawaii............ | 2,771 | 2,863 | 3,117 | 3,331 |

[1]Per capita personal income for each state is derived by the division of total personal income by total population. Personal income is a measure of the income received from all sources during the calendar year by the residents of each state. It comprises income received by individuals in the form of wages and salaries, net income of proprietors (including farmers), dividends, interest, net rents, and other items such as social insurance benefits, relief, veterans pensions and benefits, and allotment payments to dependents of military personnel.

# Truth-in-Lending Becomes Federal Law

The Consumer Credit Protection Act, better known as the Truth-in-Lending law, was enacted by Congress in 1968 and signed by President Johnson on May 29.

The law provides that consumers must be given comprehensive and easily understandable information on what they pay in finance charges on both loans and credit purchases.

Effective July 1, 1969, the law requires banks, finance companies and other lenders, and also retailers, to provide borrowers and credit customers

the amount, in writing, of finance charges, in terms of dollars and cents and in annual percentages as well.

In addition, the law puts restrictions, effective July 1, 1970, on the garnishment of wages.

The law further is designed to protect home owners from mortgaging their properties, without realizing they are doing so, in order to finance repairs. It also makes extortionate lending and collection practices a Federal crime.

# N. Y. Stock Exchange Transactions and Seat Prices

Source: New York Stock Exchange

| Year (Cal.) | Stocks Shares | Bonds Par Value | Seats High | Low | Year (Cal.) | Stocks Shares | Bonds Par Value | Seats High | Low |
|---|---|---|---|---|---|---|---|---|---|
| | No. | Dollars | Dollars | Dollars | | No. | Dollars | Dollars | Dollars |
| 1900... | 138,981,000 | 579,293,000 | 47,500 | 37,500 | 1935... | 381,635,752 | 3,339,458,000 | 145,000 | 70,000 |
| 1905... | 260,569,000 | 1,026,254,000 | 85,000 | 72,000 | 1940... | 207,599,749 | 1,669,438,000 | 60,000 | 33,000 |
| 1910... | 163,705,000 | 634,863,000 | 94,000 | 65,000 | 1945... | 377,563,575 | 2,261,985,110 | 95,000 | 49,000 |
| 1915... | 172,497,000 | 961,700,000 | 74,000 | 38,000 | 1950... | 524,799,621 | 1,112,425,170 | 54,000 | 46,000 |
| 1920... | 227,636,000 | 3,868,422,000 | 115,000 | 85,000 | 1955... | 649,602,291 | 1,045,949,100 | 90,000 | 80,000 |
| 1925... | 459,717,623 | 3,427,042,210 | 150,000 | 99,000 | 1960... | 766,693,818 | 1,346,419,750 | 162,000 | 135,000 |
| 1929... | 1,124,800,410 | 2,996,398,000 | 625,000 | 525,000 | 1966... | 1,899,495,014 | 3,092,789,700 | 270,000 | 197,000 |
| 1930... | 810,632,546 | 2,720,301,800 | 480,000 | 205,000 | 1967*... | 2,529,962,472 | 3,955,538,100 | 450,000 | 220,000 |

*Record high for trading in stocks.
As of the close of business Dec. 31, 1967, there was 1,700 stock issues aggregating 11,622,496,614 shares listed on the New York Stock Exchange, with a total value of $605,816,849,182.

# American Stock Exchange Transactions and Seat Prices

Source: American Stock Exchange

| Date | Yearly volumes Stocks | Bonds | Seat price ranges High | Low | Date | Yearly volumes Stocks | Bonds | Seat price ranges High | Low |
|---|---|---|---|---|---|---|---|---|---|
| 1929... | 476,140,375 | $513,551,000 | $254,000 | $150,000 | 1955... | 228,955,915 | $35,330,000 | $22,000 | $17,500 |
| 1930... | 222,270,065 | 863,541,000 | 225,000 | 70,000 | 1960.. | 286,039,982 | 32,670,000 | 60,000 | 51,000 |
| 1935... | 75,747,764 | 1,171,440,000 | 33,000 | 12,000 | 1964... | 374,133,342 | 103,886,000 | 63,000 | 52,000 |
| 1940... | 42,928,377 | 303,902,000 | 7,250 | 6,900 | 1965... | 534,221,999 | 146,927,000 | 80,000 | 55,000 |
| 1945... | 143,309,392 | 167,333,000 | 32,000 | 12,000 | 1966... | 690,762,585 | 159,724,000 | 120,000 | 90,000 |
| 1950... | 107,792,340 | 47,549,000 | 11,000 | 6,500 | 1967... | 1,145,090,300 | 554,824,000 | 230,000 | 90,000 |

Change of name from New York Curb Exchange was effected January 5, 1953.

# Largest Banks in Foreign Countries

Source: 500 Largest Banks in the Free World, compiled by the American Banker, New York (Copyright, 1968) Based on deposits Jan. 1, 1968, or nearest fiscal year-end.

| Bank and Country (in $1,000) | Deposits in U. S. $ | Bank and Country (in $1,000) | Deposits in U. S. $ |
|---|---|---|---|
| England—Barclays Bank Limited, London | $9,742,593 | Australia—Commonwealth Banking Corporation, Sydney ... | 4,307,471 |
| France—Banque Nationale de Paris | 7,694,839 | England—Westminster Bank Limited, London ...... | 4,211,782 |
| England—Midland Bank Limited, London | 6,710,767 | England—National Provincial Bank Limited, London ...... | 4,098,044 |
| Canada—Royal Bank of Canada, Montreal | 6,535,898 | Germany—Dresdner Bank, Frankfurt/Main ...... | 3,763,922 |
| France—Credit Lyonnais, Paris ... | 6,505,765 | Japan—Tokai Bank Limited, Nagoya | 3,719,975 |
| Canada—Canadian Imperial Bank of Commerce, Toronto.. | 6,353,480 | Brazil—Banco do Brasil, Brasilia .. | 3,651,904 |
| Italy—Banca Nazionale del Lavoro, Rome | 6,338,842 | Japan—Dai-Ichi Bank Limited, Tokyo | 3,622,324 |
| France—Societe Generale, Paris ... | 5,984,906 | Italy—Banco di Roma, Rome ...... | 3,574,605 |
| England—Lloyds Bank Limited, London | 5,508,295 | Canada—Bank of Nova Scotia, Toronto | 3,528,830 |
| Japan—Fuji Bank Limited, Tokyo.. | 5,504,762 | Japan—Long-Term Credit Bank of Japan Limited, Tokyo.. | 3,498,303 |
| Japan—Sumitomo Bank Limited, Osaka ... | 5,312,029 | Japan—Mitsui Bank Limited, Tokyo | 3,477,546 |
| Canada—Bank of Montreal ........ | 5,187,853 | Germany—Rheinische Giro. und Provinzialbank, Duesseldorf | 3,349,612 |
| Japan—Mitsubishi Bank Limited, Tokyo | 5,148,318 | Japan—Nippon Kangyo Bank Limited, Tokyo ...... | 3,316,735 |
| Japan—Sanwa Bank Limited, Osaka | 5,084,337 | Japan—Daiwa Bank Limited, Osaka | 3,200,079 |
| Germany—Deutsche Bank, Frankfurt/Main ...... | 4,879,115 | England—Barclays Bank D.C.O., London | 3,081,151 |
| Italy—Banca Commerciale Italiana, Milan | 4,721,249 | Germany—Commerzbank, Duesseldorf | 3,073,800 |
| Japan—Industrial Bank of Japan Limited, Tokyo ....... | 4,676,936 | Canada—Toronto-Dominion Bank, Toronto .......... | 2,935,057 |
| Italy—Credito Italiano, Milan ..... | 4,339,027 | | |

# Gold Reserves of Central Banks and Governments

Source: Federal Reserve Board
Millions of dollars; at par of exchange.

| Dec. | (Est.) total world[1] | Int'l Monetary Fund | United States | (Est.) rest of world | Belgium | France | Germany Fed. Rep. of | Italy | Netherlands | Switzerland | United Kingdom |
|---|---|---|---|---|---|---|---|---|---|---|---|
| 1955......... | 37,585 | 1,808 | 21,753 | 14,025 | 928 | 942 | 920 | 352 | 865 | 1,597 | 2,012 |
| 1960......... | 40,540 | 2,439 | 17,804 | 20,295 | 1,170 | 1,641 | 2,971 | 2,203 | 1,451 | 2,185 | 2,800 |
| 1963......... | 42,305 | 2,312 | 15,596 | 24,395 | 1,371 | 3,175 | 3,843 | 2,343 | 1,601 | 2,820 | 2,484 |
| 1964......... | 43,015 | 2,179 | 15,471 | 25,365 | 1,451 | 3,729 | 4,248 | 2,107 | 1,688 | 2,725 | 2,136 |
| 1965......... | 43,225 | 1,869 | 13,806 | 27,280 | 1,558 | 4,706 | 4,410 | 2,404 | 1,756 | 3,042 | 2,265 |
| 1966......... | 43,180 | 2,652 | 13,235 | 27,295 | 1,525 | 5,238 | 4,292 | 2,414 | 1,730 | 2,842 | 1,940 |
| 1967......... | 41,600 | 2,682 | 12,065 | 26,855 | 1,480 | 5,234 | 4,228 | 2,400 | 1,711 | 3,089 | 1,291 |

[1]Excludes USSR, other Eastern European countries, and China Mainland.

Argentina 84, Australia 231, Austria 701, Brazil 45, Canada 1,015, Chile 45, Colombia 31, Denmark 107, Dominican Rep. 3, Ecuador 17, El Salvador 18, Finland 45, Greece 130, Guatemala 20, India 243, Iran 144, Iraq 115, Ireland 25, Lebanon 193, Mexico 166, Norway 18, Pakistan 53, Peru 20, Philippines 60, Portugal 699, So. Africa 583, Spain 785, Sweden 203, Thailand 92, Turkey 97, UAR (Egypt) 93, Uruguay 140, Venezuela 401, Yugoslavia 22, B. I. S. (net) 624, European Fund 42.

## Consumer Credit Statistics

Source: Federal Reserve System (Estimated amounts outstanding. In millions of dollars.)

| End of year or month | Total | Instalment credit | | | | | Noninstalment credit | | | |
|---|---|---|---|---|---|---|---|---|---|---|
| | | Total | Automobile paper[1] | Other consumer goods paper[1] | Repair and modernization loans[2] | Personal loans | Total | Single payment loans | Charge accounts | Service credit |
| 1945........ | $5,665 | $2,462 | $455 | $816 | $182 | $1,009 | $3,203 | $746 | $1,612 | $845 |
| 1950........ | 21,471 | 14,703 | 6,074 | 4,799 | 1,016 | 2,814 | 6,768 | 1,821 | 3,367 | 1,580 |
| 1955........ | 38,830 | 28,906 | 13,460 | 7,641 | 1,693 | 6,112 | 9,924 | 3,002 | 4,795 | 2,127 |
| 1957........ | 44,970 | 33,867 | 15,340 | 8,844 | 2,101 | 7,582 | 11,103 | 3,364 | 5,146 | 2,593 |
| 1958........ | 45,129 | 33,642 | 14,152 | 9,028 | 2,346 | 8,116 | 11,487 | 3,627 | 5,060 | 2,800 |
| 1959........ | 51,542 | 39,245 | 16,420 | 10,630 | 2,809 | 9,386 | 12,297 | 4,129 | 5,104 | 3,064 |
| 1960........ | 56,028 | 42,832 | 17,688 | 11,525 | 3,139 | 10,480 | 13,196 | 4,507 | 5,329 | 3,360 |
| 1961........ | 57,678 | 43,527 | 17,223 | 11,857 | 3,191 | 11,256 | 14,151 | 5,136 | 5,324 | 3,691 |
| 1962........ | 63,164 | 48,034 | 19,540 | 12,605 | 3,246 | 12,643 | 15,130 | 5,456 | 5,684 | 3,990 |
| 1963........ | 70,461 | 54,158 | 22,453 | 13,356 | 3,405 | 14,464 | 16,303 | 6,117 | 5,871 | 4,315 |
| 1964........ | 78,442 | 60,548 | 25,195 | 15,593 | 3,532 | 16,228 | 17,894 | 6,954 | 6,300 | 4,640 |
| 1965........ | 87,884 | 68,565 | 28,843 | 17,693 | 3,675 | 18,354 | 19,319 | 7,682 | 6,746 | 4,891 |
| 1966........ | 94,786 | 74,656 | 30,961 | 19,834 | 3,751 | 20,110 | 20,130 | 7,844 | 7,144 | 5,142 |
| 1967........ | 99,228 | 77,946 | 31,197 | 21,328 | 3,731 | 21,690 | 21,282 | 8,267 | 7,595 | 5,420 |
| 1968 Jan.... | 98,225 | 77,467 | 31,061 | 21,097 | 3,678 | 21,631 | 20,758 | 8,288 | 6,970 | 5,500 |
| Feb.... | 97,672 | 77,327 | 31,137 | 20,785 | 3,653 | 21,752 | 20,345 | 8,325 | 6,386 | 5,634 |
| Mar.... | 97,875 | 77,581 | 31,380 | 20,692 | 3,636 | 21,873 | 20,294 | 8,370 | 6,263 | 5,661 |
| Apr.... | 99,142 | 78,345 | 31,766 | 20,802 | 3,649 | 22,128 | 20,797 | 8,488 | 6,559 | 5,750 |
| May.... | 100,275 | 79,270 | 32,240 | 20,953 | 3,699 | 22,378 | 21,005 | 8,508 | 6,830 | 5,667 |
| June... | 101,467 | 80,363 | 32,774 | 21,176 | 3,727 | 22,686 | 21,104 | 8,519 | 6,912 | 5,673 |

[1]Includes all consumer instalment credit extended for the purpose of purchasing automobiles and other consumer goods, whether held by retail outlets or financial institutions. Includes credit on purchases by individuals of automobiles or other consumer goods that may be used in part for business. [2]Includes only repair and modernization loans held by financial institutions; such loans held by retail outlets are included in "other consumer goods paper."

## World Gold Production

Source: Federal Reserve System. In millions of dollars at $35 per fine troy ounce.

| Year or month | Estimated world prod. | Africa | | | | North and South America | | | | | | Other | | |
|---|---|---|---|---|---|---|---|---|---|---|---|---|---|---|
| | | South Africa | Rhodesia | Ghana | Congo (Kinshasa) | United States | Canada | Mexico | Nicaragua | Colombia | Australia | India | Philippines | All other[1] |
| 1959........ | 1,125.0 | 702.2 | 19.8 | 32.0 | 12.2 | 57.2 | 156.9 | 11.0 | 7.3 | 13.9 | 38.1 | 5.8 | 14.1 | 54.5 |
| 1960........ | 1,175.0 | 748.4 | 19.6 | 30.8 | 11.1 | 58.8 | 162.0 | 10.5 | 7.0 | 15.2 | 38.0 | 5.6 | 14.4 | 53.6 |
| 1962........ | 1,295.0 | 892.2 | 19.4 | 31.1 | 7.1 | 54.5 | 146.2 | 8.3 | 7.8 | 13.9 | 37.4 | 5.7 | 14.8 | 56.6 |
| 1963........ | 1,355.0 | 960.1 | 19.8 | 32.2 | 7.5 | 51.4 | 139.0 | 8.3 | 7.2 | 11.4 | 35.8 | 4.8 | 13.2 | 64.3 |
| 1964........ | 1,395.0 | 1,018.9 | 20.1 | 30.3 | 6.6 | 51.4 | 133.0 | 7.4 | 7.9 | 12.8 | 33.7 | 5.2 | 14.9 | 62.8 |
| 1965........ | 1,440.0 | 1,069.4 | 19.0 | 26.4 | 2.3 | 58.6 | 125.6 | 7.6 | 6.9 | 11.2 | 30.7 | 4.6 | 15.3 | 61.5 |
| 1966........ | 1,445.0 | 1,080.8 | 19.3 | 24.0 | 5.6 | 63.1 | 114.6 | 7.5 | 7.0 | 9.8 | 32.1 | 4.2 | 15.8 | 61.2 |
| 1967........ | 1,410.0 | 1,068.7 | 18.0 | 26.7 | 5.4 | 55.4 | 103.7 | 6.4 | 6.2 | 9.0 | 3.4 | 17.5 | 28.4 | 61.2 |
| 1968 Jan... | | 90.3 | | | | | 7.7 | .6 | | .9 | | | 2.0 | |
| Feb... | | 90.0 | | | | | 7.7 | | | .7 | | | 2.0 | |
| Mar... | | 91.8 | | | | | 8.3 | | | .7 | | | 2.8 | |
| Apr... | | 91.8 | | | | | 8.2 | | | .7 | | | | |
| May... | | 93.1 | | | | | 8.4 | | | .7 | | | | |
| June... | | 91.5 | | | | | | | | | | | | |

[1]Estimated; excludes U.S.S.R., other Eastern European countries, China Mainland, and North Korea.

## U. S. and World Silver Production

Source: Director of the Mint

Largest production of silver in the United States in 1915—74,961,075 fine ounces.

| Year (Cal.) | United States | | World | Year (Cal.) | United States | | World |
|---|---|---|---|---|---|---|---|
| | Fine ozs. | Value | Fine ozs. | | Fine ozs. | Value | Fine ozs. |
| 1925.... | 66,155,424 | $45,911,000 | 245,213,993 | 1960.... | 36,000,000 | $33,305,858 | 241,300,000 |
| 1930.... | 50,748,127 | 19,538,000 | 248,708,426 | 1962.... | 36,345,000 | 39,481,574 | 245,800,000 |
| 1935.... | 45,924,454 | 33,008,000 | 220,704,231 | 1963.... | 35,000,000 | 44,814,000 | 249,700,000 |
| 1940.... | 69,585,734 | 49,483,000 | 275,387,000 | 1964.... | 37,000,000 | 47,888,730 | 246,600,000 |
| 1945.... | 29,063,255 | 20,667,200 | 162,000,000 | 1965.... | 39,000,000 | 50,477,310 | 254,100,000 |
| 1950.... | 42,308,739 | 38,291,545 | 203,300,000 | 1966.... | 42,500,000 | 55,007,325 | 253,000,000 |
| 1955.... | 36,469,610 | 33,006,839 | 224,000,000 | 1967.... | 31,000,000 | 40,080,800 | ......... |

## United States Customs and Internal Revenue Receipts

Source: Treasury Department

Gross. Not reduced by appropriations to Federal old-age and survivors insurance trust fund, or refunds or receipts. Data are for fiscal years; for 1966 preliminary.

| Year | Customs | Internal Revenue | Year | Customs | Internal Revenue | Year | Customs | Internal Revenue |
|---|---|---|---|---|---|---|---|---|
| | Dollars | Dollars | | Dollars | Dollars | | Dollars | Dollars |
| 1930. | 587,000,903 | 3,039,295,014 | 1954. | 562,020,618 | 70,299,651,501 | 1962. | 1,171,205,973 | 99,440,839,244 |
| 1935. | 343,353,034 | 3,277,690,028 | 1955. | 606,396,634 | 66,288,691,586 | 1963. | 1,240,537,884 | 105,925,395,281 |
| 1940. | 348,590,635 | 5,303,133,988 | 1956. | 704,897,615 | 75,109,083,197 | 1964. | 1,284,176,379 | 112,206,115,000 |
| 1945. | 354,775,542 | 43,902,001,929 | 1957. | 754,461,446 | 80,171,970,804 | 1965. | 1,477,548,820 | 114,428,991,753 |
| 1950. | 422,650,329 | 39,448,607,109 | 1958. | 799,504,808 | 79,978,476,483 | 1966. | 1,811,170,211 | 128,842,531,268 |
| 1951. | 624,008,052 | 51,106,094,995 | 1959. | 948,412,215 | 79,797,972,808 | 1967. | 1,971,799,790 | 147,899,815,000 |
| 1952. | 550,696,379 | 65,634,894,258 | 1960. | 1,123,037,579 | 91,774,802,823 | 1968. | 2,113,475,000 | 153,072,533,000 |
| 1953. | 613,419,582 | 70,170,973,876 | 1961. | 1,007,755,214 | 94,401,086,397 | | | |

# How to Determine the Value of Silver in Coins
### Source: Treasury Department

To figure the value of the silver contained in the silver coins issued by the U. S. Treasury prior to the clad or copper sandwiched coins it is necessary to find the value of pure silver. This may be accomplished by taking the market price as listed and dividing by .999 (the fineness of commercial grade silver) to arrive at the price for silver 1.000 fine. Then multiply by the fraction shown under the table beneath. This will give you the value of the silver content in each coin.

| | Fine Troy Weight | | | | Fine Troy Weight | |
|---|---|---|---|---|---|---|
| | Oz. | Grain | | | Oz. | Grain |
| Dollar | .7734375 | 371.25 | | Quarter | .18084375 | 86.805 |
| Half-Dollar | .3616875 | 173.61 | | Dime | .0723375 | 34.722 |

**For example:** If the market price is $2.30 per troy ounce, then divide $2.30 by .999 the fineness of commercial grade silver = $2.3023 per troy ounce 1.000 fine. For dollars, then multiply .7734375 by $2.3023 = $1.78. For half dollars .3616875 × $2.3023 = 83 cents. For quarters .18084375 × $2.3023 = 41.6 cents. For dimes .0723375 × $2.3023 = 16.6 cents.

The silver content of the new silver-copper half dollar is .14789341504 of a fine troy ounce and this multiplied by the selling price of $2.3023 gives a value for the silver content of 34 cents.

The Secretary of the Treasury by the authority of the Coinage Act of 1965 issued an order effective May 18, 1967, prohibiting the melting of silver coins of the United States; exportation (with certain exceptions), or the treatment of any such coins.

# Average Consumer Price Indexes
### Source: Bureau of Labor Statistics, United States Department of Labor

The Consumer Price Index measures the average change in prices of goods and services purchased by urban wage-earner and clerical-worker families and single workers living alone. Data for 56 large, medium size, and small cities are combined for the all-city average.

### (1957-59=100)

| Year and month | All items | Food | Housing | | | | | Apparel and Upkeep | Transportation | Medical care | Personal care | Reading and recreation | Other goods and services |
|---|---|---|---|---|---|---|---|---|---|---|---|---|---|
| | | | Total | Rent | Gas and electricity | Fuel and Utilities | Household furnishings & operation | | | | | | |
| 1964 Avg | 108.1 | 106.4 | 107.2 | 107.8 | 107.9 | 107.3 | 102.8 | 105.7 | 109.3 | 119.4 | 109.2 | 114.1 | 108.8 |
| 1965 Avg | 109.9 | 108.8 | 108.5 | 108.9 | 107.8 | 107.2 | 103.1 | 106.8 | 111.1 | 122.3 | 109.9 | 115.2 | 111.4 |
| 1966 Avg | 113.1 | 114.2 | 111.1 | 110.4 | 108.1 | 107.7 | 105.0 | 109.6 | 112.7 | 127.7 | 112.2 | 117.1 | 114.9 |
| 1967 Avg | 116.3 | 115.2 | 114.3 | 112.4 | 108.5 | 109.0 | 108.2 | 114.0 | 115.9 | 136.7 | 115.5 | 120.1 | 118.2 |
| 1968 Jan | 118.6 | 117.0 | 116.4 | 113.7 | 108.9 | 109.5 | 110.6 | 115.9 | 118.7 | 141.2 | 117.6 | 122.7 | 121.9 |
| Feb | 119.0 | 117.4 | 116.9 | 113.9 | 109.3 | 109.8 | 111.2 | 116.6 | 118.6 | 141.9 | 117.6 | 123.0 | 122.1 |
| Mar | 119.5 | 117.9 | 117.2 | 114.2 | 109.3 | 109.9 | 111.8 | 117.6 | 119.0 | 142.9 | 118.4 | 124.2 | 122.4 |
| Apr | 119.9 | 118.3 | 117.5 | 114.4 | 109.5 | 110.0 | 112.2 | 118.4 | 119.0 | 143.5 | 119.0 | 124.9 | 122.5 |
| May | 120.3 | 118.8 | 117.8 | 114.6 | 109.5 | 110.3 | 112.5 | 119.5 | 119.1 | 144.0 | 119.6 | 125.3 | 122.6 |
| June | 120.9 | 119.1 | 118.7 | 114.9 | 109.4 | 110.3 | 112.9 | 119.9 | 119.9 | 144.4 | 120.1 | 125.6 | 123.5 |
| July | 121.5 | 120.0 | 119.5 | 115.1 | 109.5 | 110.6 | 113.1 | 119.7 | 119.8 | 145.1 | 120.4 | 125.9 | 123.9 |
| Aug | 121.9 | 120.5 | 120.1 | 115.4 | 109.7 | 110.7 | 113.3 | 120.3 | 120.0 | 145.5 | 120.9 | 126.3 | 124.2 |

## INDEXES BY CITIES, ALL ITEMS AND FOOD (1957-59=100)

| City | Annual Average | | | | City | Annual Average | | | |
|---|---|---|---|---|---|---|---|---|---|
| | All Items | | Food | | | All Items | | Food | |
| | 1966 | 1967 | 1966 | 1967 | | 1966 | 1967 | 1966 | 1967 |
| Average of 56 Cities | 113.1 | 116.3 | 114.2 | 115.2 | Los Angeles, Calif | 114.7 | 117.6 | 113.3 | 114.1 |
| Atlanta, Ga | 111.5 | 115.0 | 112.9 | 114.2 | Milwaukee, Wis | 110.6 | 112.9 | 114.0 | 114.5 |
| Baltimore, Md | 113.4 | 116.1 | 115.9 | 116.3 | Minneapolis, Minn | 112.2 | 115.9 | 112.4 | 113.0 |
| Boston, Mass | 117.0 | 119.8 | 117.0 | 119.4 | New York, N. Y | 116.0 | 119.0 | 115.1 | 115.7 |
| Buffalo, N. Y | 107.0 | 109.9 | 108.8 | 110.0 | Philadelphia, Pa | 113.7 | 116.8 | 113.1 | 114.5 |
| Chicago, Ill | 110.7 | 113.6 | 114.6 | 115.4 | Pittsburgh, Pa | 113.0 | 115.0 | 111.8 | 111.2 |
| Cincinnati, Ohio | 110.3 | 113.5 | 111.8 | 112.5 | Portland, Ore | 115.3 | 118.2 | 114.7 | 115.4 |
| Cleveland, Ohio | 109.7 | 112.9 | 110.9 | 111.4 | St. Louis, Mo | 113.5 | 116.8 | 117.8 | 119.0 |
| Dallas, Texas | 105.0 | 108.1 | 110.0 | 109.7 | San Diego, Calif | 102.1 | 105.1 | 106.5 | 107.6 |
| Detroit, Mich | 111.1 | 114.9 | 112.2 | 114.1 | San Francisco, Calif | 115.6 | 119.0 | 114.2 | 114.7 |
| Honolulu, Hawaii | 104.9 | 107.8 | 106.3 | 108.3 | Scranton, Pa | 114.9 | 118.0 | 112.8 | 113.6 |
| Houston, Tex | 111.5 | 114.4 | 115.4 | 115.8 | Seattle, Wash | 114.1 | 117.5 | 114.1 | 114.6 |
| Kansas City, Mo | 116.3 | 118.7 | 117.2 | 117.9 | Washington, D. C | 113.3 | 116.5 | 114.0 | 115.9 |

# Purchasing Power of the Dollar
### Source: U. S. Department of Labor, Bureau of Labor Statistics
### 1957-59=$1.00

Beginning 1961, wholesale prices include data for Alaska and Hawaii; and, beginning 1964 consumer prices include them. Obtained by dividing the average price index for 1957-59 base period (100.0) by the price index for a given period and expressing the result in dollars and cents.

| Year | Monthly average as measured by— | | Year | Monthly average as measured by— | |
|---|---|---|---|---|---|
| | Whole-sale prices | Con-sumer prices | | Whole-sale prices | Con-sumer prices |
| 1940 | $2.326 | $2.048 | 1957 | $1.010 | $1.021 |
| 1945 | 1.727 | 1.595 | 1958 | .996 | .994 |
| 1947 | 1.232 | 1.285 | 1959 | .994 | .985 |
| 1948 | 1.138 | 1.194 | 1960 | .993 | .971 |
| 1949 | 1.198 | 1.205 | 1961 | .997 | .969 |
| 1950 | 1.152 | 1.194 | 1962 | .994 | .949 |
| 1951 | 1.034 | 1.106 | 1963 | .997 | .937 |
| 1952 | 1.064 | 1.081 | 1964 | .995 | .925 |
| 1953 | 1.079 | 1.072 | 1965 | .976 | .910 |
| 1954 | 1.076 | 1.069 | 1966 | .944 | .884 |
| 1955 | 1.073 | 1.071 | 1967 | .942 | .864 |
| 1956 | 1.040 | 1.056 | | | |

# Worktime Required to Buy Food and Other Articles

**Source: Bureau of Labor Statistics, U. S. Dept. of Labor**

Production workers in manufacturing in the United States in Sept. 1967, earned an average of $2.85 per hour, including overtime. At this rate, with average prices as they were at that time, he worked 13 minutes to earn enough to buy one pound of ground beef, 19 minutes for one pound of butter, and corresponding lengths of time for other articles, as shown below. A month's rent for a dwelling unit of average cost would be earned in about 3 working days. Prices of automobiles and equipment vary widely throughout the United States; roughly, however, a good used car could be bought for about 9¾ weeks' work, and a new car of one of the popular makes for about 26⅖ weeks' work.

| Article | Aver. retail price | Worktime Hrs. | Worktime Mins. | Article | Aver. retail price | Worktime Hrs. | Worktime Mins. |
|---|---|---|---|---|---|---|---|
| **FOOD** | | | | Nylon stockings, 1 pr...... | .98 | | 21 |
| White flour......1 pd | $ 0.119 | | 3 | Man's work shoes, high... | 12.46 | 4 | 22 |
| White wheat bread...1 pd | .221 | | 5 | Man's street shoes, oxford... | 19.87 | 6 | 58 |
| Rice, short grain....1 pd | .187 | | 4 | Boy's sneakers, oxford...... | 5.46 | 1 | 55 |
| Beef: Round steak | | | | Printed cotton percale cloth, | | | |
| (best grade)......1 pd | 1.125 | | 24 | 36 inches wide, 1 yard... | .44 | | 9 |
| Chuck roast | | | | **Medical** | | | |
| (best grade)......1 pd | .621 | | 13 | Penicillin prescription, 12 | | | |
| Hamburger | | | | tablets...... | 2.14 | | 45 |
| (ground beef)....1 pd | .552 | | 12 | Hospital, semiprivate room, | | | |
| Pork: Chops, center | | | | per day...... | 36.05 | 12 | 39 |
| cut.............1 pd | 1.059 | | 22 | Physician, house visit...... | 10.43 | 3 | 40 |
| Bacon (sliced, best | | | | Dentist, extraction...... | 7.76 | 2 | 43 |
| grade)..........1 pd | .859 | | 18 | Dentist, filling...... | 6.79 | 2 | 23 |
| Ham (whole, | | | | Eyeglasses, with examina- | | | |
| smoked)........1 pd | .698 | | 15 | tion...... | 34.47 | 12 | 6 |
| Fish: Frozen filet of | | | | **MISCELLANEOUS** | | | |
| haddock........1 pd | .672 | | 14 | Toothpaste, per oz....... | .17 | | 4 |
| Canned tuna......6½ oz. | .342 | | 7 | Man's haircut...... | 2.22 | | 47 |
| Chicken (ready-to- | | | | Permanent wave...... | 13.59 | 4 | 46 |
| cook)..........1 pd | .391 | | 8 | Washing machine, | | | |
| Butter, 92 score.....1 pd | .833 | | 18 | automatic...... | 212.41 | 74 | 32 |
| Oleomargarine, | | | | Gas cooking stove...... | 196.79 | 69 | 3 |
| colored........1 pd | .280 | | 6 | Refrigerator freezer...... | 276.58 | 97 | 3 |
| Shortening, hydrog- | | | | Vacuum cleaner, electric... | 44.75 | 15 | 42 |
| enated.........3 pds | .864 | | 18 | Television set, 19-inch | | | |
| Cheese (American | | | | portable...... | 141.12 | 49 | 31 |
| Cheddar).......1 pd | .864 | | 18 | Radio, 4 tubes, table model | 16.59 | 5 | 49 |
| Fresh milk, at grocery | | | | Movies, admission, adult... | 1.51 | | 32 |
| store..........½ gal. | .519 | | 11 | Cigarettes, pack of 20 ... | .36 | | 8 |
| Eggs (large, grade A).1 doz | .499 | | 11 | Cigarettes, carton (200) | 3.01 | 1 | 3 |
| Oranges, (size, ap- | | | | Beer, per 6 12-ounce cans | | | |
| proximately 5 pds | | | | or bottles...... | 1.20 | | 25 |
| per dozen).......1 doz | .835 | | 18 | Spirit blended whiskey, ⅘ | | | |
| Potatoes..........1 pd | .074 | | 2 | gallon...... | 4.79 | 1 | 41 |
| Cabbage..........1 pd | .097 | | 2 | Sheet, percale, 81 x 108 | | | |
| Dried beans.......1 pd | .183 | | 4 | inches...... | 3.20 | 1 | 7 |
| Canned tomatoes....1 pd | .199 | | 4 | Detergent, 20 ounces...... | .34 | | 7 |
| Sugar............1 pd | .122 | | 3 | Paper napkins, pkg of 80 | .16 | | 3 |
| Coffee, can.......1 pd | .761 | | 16 | Laundry service: 10-pd | | | |
| Teabags.......pkg. of 48 | .608 | | 13 | bundle finished...... | 2.58 | | 54 |
| **CLOTHES** | | | | Dry cleaning: Man's 2-piece | | | |
| Man's 2-piece suit, wool, | | | | suit, cash and carry..... | 1.46 | | 31 |
| hard-finished worsted, | | | | Domestic service: general | | | |
| medium grade......... | 65.31 | 22 | 55 | housework, 8-hour day... | 11.22 | 3 | 56 |
| Man's work pants, cotton.. | 4.73 | 1 | 40 | Gas, 25 therms...... | 4.11 | 1 | 27 |
| Man's business shirt, | | | | Electricity, 250 kilowatt | | | |
| broadcloth........... | 4.92 | 1 | 44 | hours...... | 7.41 | 2 | 36 |
| Man's socks, dress, | | | | Automobile tires, (7.50 x 15) | 27.80 | 9 | 45 |
| cotton............ | .90 | | 19 | Gasoline, premium, gallon | | | |
| Boy's undershirts........ | .75 | | 16 | (3.785 liters)...... | .38 | | 8 |
| Woman's skirt, wool...... | 6.61 | 2 | 19 | Bus fare, one...... | .25 | | 5 |
| Woman's slip, nylon, tricot, | | | | | | | |
| plain............ | 4.00 | 1 | 24 | | | | |

## Indexes of Retail Prices of Foods

**Source: Bureau of Labor Statistics, United States Department of Labor (1957-59=100)**

| Year and month | Total food | Food at home | Cereals, bakery products | Meats, poultry, fish | Dairy products | Fruits, vegetables | Other foods |
|---|---|---|---|---|---|---|---|
| 1963 Avg........ | 105.1 | 103.5 | 109.1 | 100.2 | 103.8 | 111.0 | 97.8 |
| 1964 Avg........ | 106.4 | 104.7 | 109.6 | 98.6 | 104.7 | 115.3 | 101.6 |
| 1965 Avg........ | 108.8 | 107.2 | 111.2 | 105.1 | 105.0 | 115.2 | 101.8 |
| 1966 Avg........ | 114.2 | 112.6 | 115.5 | 114.1 | 114.5 | 117.6 | 103.9 |
| 1967 Avg........ | 115.2 | 112.3 | 118.5 | 111.2 | 116.7 | 117.5 | 101.9 |
| 1968 Jan........ | 117.0 | 113.8 | 118.3 | 111.6 | 118.5 | 124.1 | 101.9 |
| Feb........ | 117.4 | 114.2 | 118.2 | 112.0 | 118.5 | 124.9 | 102.6 |
| Apr........ | 118.3 | 115.1 | 118.3 | 112.7 | 118.8 | 128.3 | 103.0 |
| June........ | 119.1 | 115.8 | 118.6 | 113.2 | 120.9 | 130.0 | 102.5 |
| July........ | 120.0 | 116.7 | 119.2 | 114.0 | 121.0 | 132.2 | 103.3 |
| Aug........ | 120.5 | 117.1 | 119.6 | 115.3 | 121.5 | 128.2 | 105.5 |

## Average Percent Increase in Earnings

**Source: Bureau of Labor Statistics, United States Department of Labor**

| Period and area Feb. 1966 to Nov. 1967 | All industries | | | | Manufacturing | | | |
|---|---|---|---|---|---|---|---|---|
| | Clerical men and women | Indus- trial nurses | Skilled main- tenance trades | Un- skilled plant workers | Clerical men and women | Indus- trial nurses | Skilled main- tenance trades | Un- skilled plant workers |
| United States......... | 4.6 | 7.0 | 5.1 | 5.1 | 3.9 | 6.9 | 5.2 | 4.9 |
| Northeast.......... | 4.5 | 6.3 | 4.6 | 4.5 | 3.8 | 5.6 | 4.7 | 4.1 |
| South............. | 4.6 | 7.2 | 4.4 | 6.9 | 4.4 | 7.1 | 4.3 | 5.8 |
| North Central...... | 4.9 | 7.4 | 6.0 | 5.0 | 3.9 | 7.5 | 6.2 | 5.3 |
| West.............. | 4.2 | 7.3 | 4.2 | 4.5 | 3.9 | 8.3 | 4.0 | 4.3 |

# U.S. Business Indexes

Source: Federal Reserve System

| Year | Industrial production (physical volume) 1957-59=100 | | | | | | Construct'n contracts (value)[1] 1957-59=100 | | | Employment[2] 1957-59=100 | | | | Freight carloadings 1957-1959=100 | Prices 1957-59=100 | |
|---|---|---|---|---|---|---|---|---|---|---|---|---|---|---|---|---|
| | Total | Manufactures | | | Minerals | Utilities | Total | Residential | All other | Non-agricultural | Manuf. production workers | | | | Consumer | Wholesale commodity |
| | | Total | Durable | Non-durable | | | | | | | Employment | Payrolls | | | | |
| 1955.... | 97 | 97 | 102 | 92 | 99 | 80 | 91 | 95 | 89 | 96.5 | 105.5 | 94.8 | | 115 | 93.3 | 93.2 |
| 1960.... | 109 | 109 | 109 | 119 | 102 | 116 | 106 | 102 | 109 | 103.3 | 99.9 | 106.8 | | 95 | 103.1 | 100.7 |
| 1961.... | 110 | 110 | 107 | 113 | 103 | 122 | 108 | 108 | 108 | 102.9 | 95.9 | 105.4 | | 91 | 104.2 | 100.3 |
| 1962.... | 118 | 119 | 118 | 120 | 105 | 131 | 119 | 121 | 119 | 105.9 | 99.2 | 113.8 | | 92 | 105.4 | 100.6 |
| 1963.... | 124 | 125 | 125 | 125 | 108 | 140 | 132 | 137 | 128 | 108.0 | 99.7 | 117.9 | | 93 | 106.7 | 100.3 |
| 1964.... | 132 | 133 | 134 | 133 | 111 | 151 | 137 | 137 | 137 | 111.1 | 101.5 | 124.3 | | 95 | 108.1 | 100.5 |
| 1965.... | 143 | 145 | 148 | 141 | 115 | 161 | 143 | 142 | 143 | 115.8 | 106.5 | 136.6 | | 97 | 109.9 | 102.5 |
| 1966.... | 156 | 159 | 165 | 151 | 121 | 174 | 145 | 119 | 165 | 121.9 | 113.5 | 151.7 | | 97 | 113.1 | 105.9 |
| 1967.... | 158p | 160p | 164p | 154p | 124p | 184p | 153 | 131 | 170 | 125.7p | 113.5p | 155.0p | | 92 | 116.3 | 106.1 |

[1]Indexes for 1955 are estimated for 37 States only. Indexes beginning 1956 are based on data from 48 states. [2]Revisions have been made in some figures. pPreliminary.

## Employed Persons by Major Occupation Groups and Sex

Source: Bureau of Labor Statistics: Estimates in thousands of persons 16 years old and over

| Annual average, 1967 | Both sexes | Male | Female | Percent distribution | | |
|---|---|---|---|---|---|---|
| | | | | Both sexes | Male | Female |
| Professional, technical and kindred workers..... | 9,879 | 6,183 | 3,697 | 13.3 | 13.0 | 13.7 |
| Farmers and farm managers................. | 1,970 | 1,871 | 98 | 2.6 | 3.9 | .4 |
| Managers, officials and proprietors, except farm | 7,495 | 6,318 | 1,177 | 10.1 | 13.3 | 4.4 |
| Clerical and kindred workers................ | 12,333 | 3,406 | 8,928 | 16.6 | 7.2 | 33.2 |
| Sales workers........................... | 4,525 | 2,621 | 1,904 | 6.1 | 5.5 | 7.1 |
| Craftsmen, foremen and kindred workers...... | 9,845 | 9,560 | 285 | 13.2 | 20.1 | 1.1 |
| Operatives and kindred workers............. | 13,884 | 9,706 | 4,178 | 18.7 | 20.4 | 15.5 |
| Private household workers................. | 1,769 | 33 | 1,737 | 2.4 | .1 | 6.5 |
| Service workers, except private household..... | 7,556 | 3,301 | 4,255 | 10.2 | 7.0 | 15.8 |
| Farm laborers and foremen................. | 1,584 | 1,065 | 520 | 2.1 | 2.2 | 1.9 |
| Laborers, except farm and mine............. | 3,533 | 3,417 | 117 | 4.8 | 7.2 | .4 |
| **Total employed.................** | **74,372** | **47,479** | **26,893** | **100.0** | **100.0** | **100.0** |

## Employment and Unemployment in the United States

CIVILIAN LABOR FORCE. PERSONS 16 YEARS OF AGE AND OVER
Source: Bureau of Labor Statistics

| Year | Civilian Labor Force | Employed | Unemployed | Year | Civilian Labor Force | Employed | Unemployed |
|---|---|---|---|---|---|---|---|
| 1955...... | 65,023,000 | 62,171,000 | 2,852,000 | 1965...... | 74,455,000 | 71,088,000 | 3,366,000 |
| 1956...... | 66,552,000 | 63,802,000 | 2,750,000 | 1966...... | 75,770,000 | 72,895,000 | 2,875,000 |
| 1957...... | 66,929,000 | 64,071,000 | 2,859,000 | 1967...... | 78,402,000 | 75,460,000 | 2,942,000 |
| 1958...... | 67,639,000 | 63,036,000 | 4,602,000 | First Half Average | | | |
| 1959...... | 68,369,000 | 64,630,000 | 3,740,000 | | | | |
| 1960*..... | 69,628,000 | 65,778,000 | 3,852,000 | 1965...... | 73,780,000 | 70,017,000 | 3,763,000 |
| 1961...... | 70,459,000 | 65,746,000 | 4,714,000 | 1966...... | 74,888,000 | 71,811,000 | 3,076,000 |
| 1962...... | 70,614,000 | 66,702,000 | 3,911,000 | 1967...... | 76,291,000 | 73,283,000 | 3,008,000 |
| 1963...... | 71,833,000 | 67,762,000 | 4,070,000 | 1968...... | 77,992,000 | 75,042,000 | 2,950,000 |
| 1964...... | 73,091,000 | 69,305,000 | 3,786,000 | | | | |

*Figures beginning with 1960 include Alaska and Hawaii.

## Wholesale Price Indexes

Source: Bureau of Labor Statistics, United States Department of Labor

The Wholesale Primary Market Price Index is designed to show the rate and direction of the composite of price movements, and to measure price changes not influenced by quality, quantity, terms of sale, etc. Wholesale refers to sales in quantities, not to prices received or paid by wholesalers.

| Commodity group (1957-59=100) | 1968[1] July | June | Jan. | 1967 Avg. |
|---|---|---|---|---|
| All commodities................ | 109.1 | 108.7 | 107.2 | 106.1 |
| **Farm products and processed foods**........ | 109.4 | 108.0 | 105.3 | 105.2 |
| Farm products................ | 103.9 | 102.5 | 99.0 | 99.7 |
| Processed foods and feeds........ | 115.9 | 114.6 | 112.4 | 111.7 |
| All commodities except farm products...... | 109.6 | 109.3 | 108.1 | 106.8 |
| **Industrial commodities**........... | 108.9 | 108.8 | 107.8 | 106.3 |
| Textile products and apparel...... | 105.8 | 105.2 | 104.3 | 102.1 |
| Hides, skins, leather and related products... | 119.5 | 118.7 | 116.5 | 115.8 |
| Fuel, related products and power.... | 103.3 | 103.7 | 101.8 | 103.6 |
| Chemicals and allied products...... | 98.2 | 98.5 | 98.2 | 98.4 |
| Rubber and rubber products........ | 100.7 | 99.9 | 99.5 | 97.0 |
| Lumber and wood products........ | 119.2 | 117.2 | 108.6 | 105.4 |
| Pulp, paper and allied products...... | 104.9 | 104.7 | 105.2 | 104.0 |
| Metals and metal products........ | 111.4 | 111.7 | 111.7 | 109.6 |
| Machinery and equipment........ | 115.2 | 115.0 | 113.9 | 111.8 |
| Furniture and household durables..... | 104.1 | 103.9 | 103.0 | 101.0 |
| Nonmetallic minerals products...... | 108.4 | 108.3 | 106.0 | 104.3 |
| Miscellaneous products.......... | 111.5 | 111.8 | 111.0 | 109.2 |

[1]Preliminary

# Bureau of the Mint

Source: Bureau of the Mint

The first United States Mint was established in Philadelphia, Pa., then the nation's capital, by the Act of April 2, 1792 which provided for gold, silver and copper coinage. Originally, supervision of the Mint was a function of the Secretary of State, but it became (1799) an independent agency reporting directly to the President. When the Coinage Act of 1873 was passed, all mint and assay office activities were placed under a newly organized Bureau of the Mint in the Department of the Treasury.

The Bureau of the Mint manufactures all domestic coins, receives and disburses gold and silver bullion and safeguards the Government's holdings of monetary metals. Other activities include the refining of gold and silver, coinage for foreign governments, manufacture of medals for the armed services, manufacture of coinage dies and platinum assay utensils, and special assays of bullion and ores. Coinage production for the calendar year 1967 is shown as follows:

### Production of U. S. coins by the Philadelphia and Denver Mints, and the San Francisco Assay Office[1], calendar year 1967

| Denomination | Number of pieces[2] | Face value | Weight (short tons) |
|---|---|---|---|
| **SUBSIDARY** | | | |
| Half dollars | 296,910,322 | $148,455,161.00 | 3,764 |
| Quarters | 1,525,895,192 | 381,473,798.00 | 9,537 |
| Dimes | 2,245,870,664 | 224,587,066.40 | 5,615 |
| Five cent pieces | 109,189,144 | 5,459,457.20 | 602 |
| One cent pieces | 3,050,530,444 | 30,505,304.44 | 10,457 |
| Total | 7,228,395,766 | 790,480,787.04 | 29,975 |

[1]Coinage operations authorized by Public Law 89-81, approved July 23, 1965. [2]Includes 1,863,344 special Mint Sets.

## New U. S. Composite-Type Coins in Circulation

The Coinage Act of 1965 (Public Law 89-81, approved July 23, 1965) authorized a change in the metallic composition of the three subsidiary denominations to clad or composite-type coins. The clad dimes and quarters are composed of an outer layer of 75% copper and 25% nickel metallurgically bonded to a center core of pure copper. The clad half dollars, with an overall silver content of 40%, contain an outer layer of 80% silver and 20% copper bonded to an inner core of approximately 20% silver and 80% copper. The new quarters were placed in circulation Nov. 1, 1965, and the dimes and half dollars in Mar. 1966. Subsidiary coins of 90% silver and 10% copper circulate alongside the clad coins. The Coinage Act of 1965, first basic change in U. S. coinage since the nation's monetary system was established in 1792, left the composition of one and five cent coins and silver dollars unchanged. One cent coins are 95% copper and 5% zinc, and five cent coins, 75% copper and 25% nickel. Standard silver dollars are 90% silver and 10% copper.

## Portraits on U. S. Currency

| Amt. | Portrait on Face | Embellishment on Back | Amt. | Portrait on Face | Embellishment on Back |
|---|---|---|---|---|---|
| $1 | Washington | Great Seal of U. S. | $100 | Franklin | Independence Hall |
| 2 | Jefferson | Monticello | 500 | McKinley | Ornate denominational marking |
| 5 | Lincoln | Lincoln Memorial | 1,000 | Cleveland | Ornate denominational marking |
| 10 | Hamilton | U. S. Treasury | 5,000 | Madison | Ornate denominational marking |
| 20 | Jackson | White House | 10,000 | Chase | Ornate denominational marking |
| 50 | Grant | U. S. Capitol | *100,000 | Wilson | Ornate denominational marking |

*For use only in transactions between Federal Reserve System and Treasury Department.

## Portraits on U. S. Treasury Bills, Bonds, Notes and Savings Bonds

| Denomination | Savings bonds | Treas. bills | Treas. bonds | Treas. notes |
|---|---|---|---|---|
| 25 | Washington | | | |
| 50 | Jefferson | | Jefferson | |
| 75 | Kennedy | | | |
| 100 | Cleveland | | Jackson | |
| 200 | F. D. Roosevelt | | | |
| 500 | Wilson | | Washington | |
| 1,000 | Lincoln | H. McCulloch | Lincoln | Lincoln |
| 5,000 | | J. G. Carlisle | Monroe | Monroe |
| 10,000 | T. Roosevelt | J. Sherman | Cleveland | Cleveland |
| 50,000 | | C. Glass | | |
| 100,000 | | A. Gallatin | Grant | Grant |
| 1,000,000 | | O. Wolcott | T. Roosevelt | T. Roosevelt |
| 100,000,000 | | | | Madison |
| 500,000,000 | | | | McKinley |

# Bank Suspensions

Source: Federal Reserve System. The figures for bank suspensions represent banks which during the periods shown, closed temporarily or permanently on account of financial difficulties; does not include banks whose deposit liabilities were assumed by other banks at the time of closing (in some instances with the aid of Federal Deposit Insurance Corporation loans).

| Year | Suspensions | Deposits | Year | Suspensions | Deposits | Year | Suspensions | Deposits |
|---|---|---|---|---|---|---|---|---|
| 1929 | 659 | 230,643,000 | 1941 | 8 | 3,726,000 | 1956 | 3 | 11,881,000 |
| 1930 | 1,352 | 853,363,000 | 1942 | 9 | 1,702,000 | 1957 | 3 | 12,869,000 |
| 1931 | 2,294 | 1,690,669,000 | 1943 | 4 | 6,223,000 | 1958 | 8 | 6,287,000 |
| 1932 | 1,456 | 715,626,000 | 1944 (a) | 1 | 405,000 | 1959 | 3 | 2,048,000 |
| 1933* | 4,004 | 3,598,975,000 | 1947 | 1 | 167,000 | 1960 | 2 | 7,987,000 |
| 1934 | 57 | 36,937,000 | 1949 | 4 | 2,443,000 | 1961 | 9 | 7,527,000 |
| 1935 | 34 | 10,015,000 | 1950 | 1 | 42,000 | 1962 | 2 | 1,201,000 |
| 1936 | 44 | 11,306,000 | 1951 | 3 | 3,113,000 | 1963 | 2 | 23,256,000 |
| 1937 | 59 | 19,723,000 | 1952 | 3 | 1,414,000 | 1964 | 8 | 22,022,000 |
| 1938 | 55 | 13,012,000 | 1953 | 4 | 44,412,000 | 1965 | 7 | 44,857,000 |
| 1939 | 42 | 34,998,000 | 1954 | 3 | 2,880,000 | 1966 | 1 | 699,000 |
| 1940 | 22 | 5,943,000 | 1955 | 4 | 6,498,000 | 1967 | 4 | 10,802,000 |

*Figures for 1933 comprise 628 banks with deposits of $360,413,000 suspended before or after the banking holiday (the holiday began March 6 and closed March 15) or placed in receivership during the holiday; 2,124 banks with deposits of $2,520,391,000 which were not licensed following the banking holiday and were placed in liquidation or receivership; and 1,252 banks with deposits of $718,171,000 which had not been licensed by June 30, 1933. (a) No suspensions in years 1945, 1946 and 1948.

# Civilian Employment of the Federal Government

Source: U. S. Civil Service Commission, Statistics Section, data as of June 30, 1968
Includes all paid employees of agencies listed; excludes employees of Central Intelligence Agency,
National Security Agency (not reported to Civil Service Commission) and uncompensated employees.

| Agency | Total all areas | United States | | | Outside United States | | |
| --- | --- | --- | --- | --- | --- | --- | --- |
| | | Total | Full-time | Part-time | Total | Terr. | Foreign |
| **Total, all agencies (a)** | 3,055,201 | 2,815,723 | 2,665,115 | 150,608 | 239,478 | 36,531 | 202,947 |
| Percent distribution | 100 | 92 | 87 | 5 | 8 | 1 | 7 |
| **Legislative Branch:** | | | | | | | |
| Congress | 10,670 | 10,670 | 10,670 | | | | |
| Architect of the Capitol | 1,542 | 1,542 | 1,201 | 332 | | | |
| Botanic Garden | 56 | 56 | 56 | | | | |
| General Accounting Office | 4,300 | 4,241 | 4,229 | 12 | 59 | | 59 |
| Government Printing Office | 7,902 | 7,902 | 7,387 | 515 | | | |
| Library of Congress | 4,205 | 4,189 | 3,933 | 256 | 16 | | |
| **Judicial Branch** | 6,561 | 6,505 | 6,347 | 158 | 56 | 56 | 16 |
| **Executive Branch:** | | | | | | | |
| **Executive Office of the President:** | | | | | | | |
| White House Office | 273 | 273 | 251 | 22 | | | |
| Bureau of the Budget | 594 | 594 | 569 | 25 | | | |
| Comm. on Marine Science, Engineering and Resources | 38 | 38 | 15 | 23 | | | |
| Council of Economic Advisers | 78 | 78 | 62 | 16 | | | |
| Executive Mansion and Grounds | 73 | 73 | 73 | | | | |
| National Advisory Commission on Civil Disorders | 5 | 5 | 4 | 1 | | | |
| National Aeronautics and Space Council | 26 | 26 | 26 | | | | |
| Natl. Council on Marine Resources and Engineering Development | 34 | 34 | 30 | 4 | | | |
| National Security Council | 35 | 35 | 34 | 1 | | | |
| Office of Economic Opportunity | 3,455 | 3,455 | 3,426 | 29 | | | |
| Office of Emergency Planning | 467 | 467 | 383 | 84 | | | |
| Office of Science and Technology | 83 | 83 | 54 | 29 | | | |
| Office of Special Representative for Trade Negotiations | 27 | 27 | 27 | | | | |
| President's Commission on Income Maintenance Programs | 31 | 31 | 29 | 2 | | | |
| President's Committee on Consumer Interests | 17 | 17 | 17 | | | | |
| President's Committee on Urban Housing | 12 | 12 | 12 | | | | |
| Pres.'s Council on Youth Opportunity | 48 | 48 | 37 | 11 | | | |
| U. S.-Mexico Comm. for Border Development and Friendship | 10 | 10 | 10 | | | | |
| **Executive departments:** | | | | | | | |
| State (b) | 46,761 | 12,613 | 12,113 | 500 | 34,148 | 19 | 34,129 |
| Treasury | 89,125 | 88,406 | 87,506 | 900 | 719 | 418 | 301 |
| Defense: | | | | | | | |
| Office of the Secretary | 2,731 | 2,638 | 2,546 | 92 | 93 | | 93 |
| Army | 486,859 | 401,819 | 399,564 | 2,255 | 85,040 | 3,852 | 81,188 |
| Navy | 430,205 | 387,322 | 383,490 | 3,832 | 42,883 | 7,410 | 35,473 |
| Air Force | 322,661 | 280,969 | 279,859 | 1,110 | 41,692 | 2,626 | 39,066 |
| Other Defense Activities | 74,521 | 73,777 | 73,505 | 272 | 744 | 16 | 728 |
| Justice | 35,811 | 35,353 | 34,930 | 423 | 458 | 231 | 227 |
| Post Office | 730,977 | 728,724 | 639,203 | 89,521 | 2,253 | 2,243 | 10 |
| Interior | 77,534 | 76,881 | 73,007 | 3,874 | 653 | 172 | 481 |
| Agriculture | 122,715 | 121,282 | 103,043 | 18,239 | 1,433 | 601 | 832 |
| Commerce | 38,611 | 38,183 | 35,492 | 2,691 | 428 | 95 | 333 |
| Labor | 10,594 | 10,511 | 10,178 | 333 | 83 | 58 | 25 |
| Health, Education, and Welfare | 117,113 | 116,134 | 113,104 | 3,030 | 979 | 534 | 445 |
| Housing and Urban Development | 15,686 | 15,445 | 15,333 | 112 | 214 | 240 | 1 |
| Transportation | 61,972 | 60,597 | 59,549 | 1,048 | 1,375 | 967 | 408 |
| **Independent Agencies:** | | | | | | | |
| Adm. Conf. of the U. S. | 5 | 5 | 5 | | | | |
| Advisory Commission on Intergovernmental Relations | 34 | 34 | 28 | 6 | | | |
| American Battle Monuments Comm. | 438 | 8 | 8 | | 430 | | 430 |
| Appalachian Region Commission | 8 | 8 | 8 | | | | |
| Arms Control and Disarmament Agency | 186 | 186 | 181 | 5 | | | |
| Atlantic-Pacific Interoceanic Canal Study Commission | 5 | 5 | 3 | 2 | | | |
| Atomic Energy Commission | 7,665 | 7,630 | 7,463 | 167 | 35 | 11 | 24 |
| Board of Governors, Federal Reserve System | 808 | 808 | 790 | 18 | | | |
| Canal Zone Government | 3,255 | | | | 3,255 | 3,255 | |
| Civil Aeronautics Board | 670 | 670 | 667 | 3 | | | |
| Civil Service Commission | 5,577 | 5,566 | 5,365 | 201 | 11 | 11 | |
| Coastal Plains Regional Comm. | 8 | 8 | 7 | 1 | | | |
| Commission of Fine Arts | 8 | 8 | 8 | | | | |
| Commission on Civil Rights | 186 | 186 | 175 | 11 | | | |
| Delaware River Basin Commission | 2 | 2 | 2 | | | | |
| Equal Employment Opportunity Commission | 476 | 476 | 462 | 14 | | | |
| Export-Import Bank | 332 | 332 | 331 | 1 | | | |
| Farm Credit Administration | 233 | 232 | 215 | 17 | 1 | | 1 |
| Federal Coal Mine Safety Board of Review | 9 | 9 | 4 | 5 | | | |
| Federal Communications Commission | 1,453 | 1,446 | 1,444 | 2 | 7 | 7 | |
| Federal Deposit Insurance Corporation | 2,025 | 2,023 | 1,964 | 59 | 2 | 2 | |
| Federal Field Committee for Development Planning in Alaska | 18 | 18 | 10 | 8 | | | |
| Federal Home Loan Bank Board | 1,341 | 1,341 | 1,329 | 12 | | | |
| Federal Maritime Commission | 245 | 245 | 244 | 1 | | | |
| Federal Mediation and Conciliation Service | 458 | 458 | 454 | 4 | | | |
| Federal Power Commission | 1,110 | 1,110 | 1,110 | | | | |
| Federal Radiation Council | 4 | 4 | 4 | | | | |

| Agency | Total all areas | United States | | | Outside United States | | |
|---|---|---|---|---|---|---|---|
| | | Total | Full-time | Part-time | Total | Terr. | Foreign |
| Federal Trade Commission......... | 1,235 | 1,235 | 1,228 | 7 | | | |
| Foreign Claims Settlement Commission................... | 98 | 98 | 98 | | | | |
| Four Corner Regional Comm....... | 7 | 7 | 7 | | | | |
| General Services Administration..... | 39,925 | 39,872 | 39,292 | 580 | 53 | 39 | 14 |
| Indian Claims Commission......... | 42 | 42 | 42 | | | | |
| Information Agency............... | 11,603 | 3,638 | 3,610 | 28 | 7,965 | | 7,965 |
| Interagency Comm. on Mexican-American Affairs............... | 28 | 28 | 28 | | | | |
| Interstate Commerce Commission.... | 1,893 | 1,893 | 1,891 | 2 | | | |
| National Aeronautics and Space Administration................. | 34,641 | 34,615 | 34,352 | 263 | 26 | 2 | 24 |
| National Capital Housing Authority | 653 | 653 | 649 | 4 | | | |
| National Capital Planning Commission.................... | 84 | 84 | 83 | 1 | | | |
| National Commission, Reform of Federal Criminal Laws......... | 15 | 15 | 11 | 4 | | | |
| National Foundation on the Arts and the Humanities............. | 127 | 127 | 86 | 41 | | | |
| National Labor Relations Board..... | 2,433 | 2,404 | 2,389 | 15 | 29 | 29 | |
| National Mediation Board......... | 143 | 143 | 101 | 42 | | | |
| National Science Foundation....... | 1,464 | 1,132 | 982 | 150 | 332 | | 332 |
| New England Regional Commission.. | 5 | 5 | 5 | | | | |
| Ozarks Regional Commission....... | 5 | 5 | 5 | | | | |
| Panama Canal Company.......... | 12,805 | 157 | 157 | | 12,648 | 12,638 | 10 |
| Public Land Law Review Commission. | 46 | 46 | 46 | | | | |
| Railroad Retirement Board........ | 1,824 | 1,824 | 1,816 | 8 | | | |
| Renegotiation Board............. | 184 | 184 | 184 | | | | |
| Securities and Exchange Commission | 1,388 | 1,388 | 1,381 | 7 | | | |
| Selective Service System........... | 9,027 | 8,849 | 6,960 | 1,889 | 178 | 178 | |
| Small Business Administration..... | 4,667 | 4,577 | 4,527 | 50 | 90 | 90 | |
| Smithsonian Institution........... | 2,617 | 2,580 | 2,454 | 126 | 37 | 35 | 2 |
| Soldiers' Home................. | 1,143 | 1,143 | 1,093 | 50 | | | |
| Subversive Activities Control Board.. | 13 | 13 | 13 | | | | |
| Tariff Commission............... | 286 | 286 | 283 | 3 | | | |
| Tax Court of the United States..... | 156 | 156 | 156 | | | | |
| Tennessee Valley Authority........ | 19,958 | 19,954 | 19,720 | 234 | 4 | | 4 |
| Upper Great Lakes Regional Commission................... | 8 | 8 | 8 | | | | |
| Veterans Administration: (c)....... | 175,668 | 174,646 | 157,834 | 16,812 | 1,022 | 696 | 326 |
| Water Resources Council.......... | 33 | 33 | 30 | 3 | | | |

(a)Includes approximately 61,900 participants in furtherance of the President's Youth Opportunity Campaign program. (b)Includes 1,570 employees in the Peace Corps of whom 894 were in Washington; and 18,030 employees in the Agency for International Development, of whom 3,833 were in Washington; employees in foreign countries include 6,506 paid from local currency trust funds established by foreign governments. (c)Includes resident physicians and interns. Civilian employment of the Federal Government—total as of June 30—(1930) 601,319; (1935) 780,582; (1940) 1,042,420; (1945) 3,816,310; (1950) 1,960,708; (1955) 2,397,309; (1956) 2,398,736; (1957) 2,417,565; (1958) 2,382,491; (1959) 2,282,807; (1960) 2,398,704; (1961) 2,435,804; (1962) 2,514,197; (1963) 2,527,960; (1964) 2,500,503; (1965) 2,527,915; (1966) 2,759,019; (1967) 3,002,461; (1968) 3,055,201.

## Federal Civilian Employment

Source: U. S. Civil Service Commission, Statistics Section

| Year and month | United States[1] | | | | Washington, D. C.[2] | | | |
|---|---|---|---|---|---|---|---|---|
| | Total[1] | Executive[3] | Legislative | Judicial | Total | Executive[3] | Legislative | Judicial |
| 1955 Average..... | 2,187,000 | 2,161,500 | 21,600 | 4,100 | 230,000 | 209,500 | 19,800 | 700 |
| 1964 Average..... | 2,347,800 | 2,317,500 | 24,500 | 5,800 | 267,200 | 243,600 | 22,700 | 900 |
| 1965 Average..... | 2,377,900 | 2,346,600 | 25,400 | 5,900 | 274,900 | 250,500 | 23,500 | 900 |
| 1966 Average ..... | 2,563,900 | 2,531,900 | 26,000 | 6,000 | 290,200 | 265,100 | 24,200 | 900 |
| 1967 Average...... | 2,719,000 | 2,685,300 | 27,400 | 6,300 | 309,900 | 283,400 | 25,500 | 900 |
| 1968 June (actual).. | 2,815,700 | 2,780,600 | 28,600 | 6,500 | 329,900 | 302,300 | 26,700 | 900 |

[1]Beginning 1959 includes Alaska and Hawaii.
[2]Includes all Federal civilian employment in the Wash., D. C. Standard Metropolitan Statistical Area which includes the District of Columbia; Alexandria, Falls Church, and Fairfax cities, Arlington and Fairfax Counties, Virginia; and Montgomery and Prince Georges Counties, Maryland. Since July 1967 includes Loudoun and Prince William Counties in Virginia.
[3]Includes all executive agencies except Central Intelligence Agency and National Security Agencies.

## Commercial and Industrial Failures in the United States

Source: Dun & Bradstreet, Inc.; data do not include banks

| Year* | Number | Liabilities | Year* | Number | Liabilities | Year* | Number | Liabilities |
|---|---|---|---|---|---|---|---|---|
| | | ($1,000) | | | ($1.000) | | | ($1.000) |
| 1940.... | 13,619 | 166,684 | 1954.... | 11,086 | 462,628 | 1961.... | 17,075 | 1,090.123 |
| 1945.... | 809 | 30,225 | 1955.... | 10,969 | 449,380 | 1962.... | 15,782 | 1,213,601 |
| 1949.... | 9,246 | 308,109 | 1956.... | 12,686 | 562,697 | 1963.... | 14,374 | 1,352,593 |
| 1950.... | 9,162 | 248,283 | 1957.... | 13,739 | 615,293 | 1964.... | 13,501 | 1,329,223 |
| 1951.... | 8,058 | 259,547 | 1958.... | 14,964 | 728,258 | 1965.... | 13,514 | 1,321,666 |
| 1952.... | 7,611 | 283,314 | 1959.... | 14,053 | 692,808 | 1966.... | 13,061 | 1,385,659 |
| 1953.... | 8,862 | 394,153 | 1960.... | 15,445 | 938,630 | 1967.... | 12,364 | 1,265,227 |

*Data exclude Alaska and Hawaii.

A business failure, as defined for this record, occurs when a commercial or industrial enterprise is envolved in a court proceeding or a voluntary action which is likely to end in loss to creditors. Specifically, the Dun and Bradstreet record of failure includes discontinuances following assignment, voluntary or involuntary petition in bankruptcy, attachment, execution, foreclosure, etc.; voluntary withdrawals from business with known loss to creditors; also enterprises involved in court action, such as receivership, and since June, 1943, reorganization, or arrangement, which may or may not lead to disturbances; as well as businesses making voluntary compromises with creditors out of court. Comparison of this series with the bankruptcy reports of the Attorney General of the United States is not possible. The latter give complete coverage of all types of cases, including farmers, employees, professional men and others not in business, all which are excluded from the Dun & Bradstreet statistics.

# Interest Laws and Consumer Finance Loan Rates

Source: Revised by Roger S Barrett of Chicago, Editor Consumer Finance Law Bulletin

Most states have laws regulating interest rates. These laws fix a legal or conventional rate which applies when there is no contract for interest. They also fix a general maximum contract rate, but there are exceptions for particular purposes including consumer finance loan laws. In many states there are so many exceptions that the general contract maximum actually applies only to exceptional cases.

**1. Legal rate of interest.** The legal or conventional rate of interest applies to money obligations when no interest rate is contracted for and also to judgments. The rate is usually 6% a year, but in some states it is 5% or 7%.

**2. General maximum contract rates.** All states, except Colorado, Massachusetts, and New Hampshire have general laws fixing the maximum rate of interest which may be contracted for, unless another law authorizes a higher rate. The general maximum is fixed by the state constitution in Arkansas, California, Oklahoma, Tennessee, and Texas. The most common maximum rates are 6% and 8% a year, but some states permit 10% or 12%. Rhode Island permits 21%. Penalties for infraction range from forfeiture of interest to loss of the entire principal and even imprisonment. Loans to corporations are frequently exempted or subject to a higher maximum. Courts generally hold that installment sale charges are not interest, but installment sale charges are limited by laws in many states.

**3. Specific enabling acts.** In many states special statutes permit industrial loan companies and banks to charge interest and fees without regard to installment payments which yield 1½% a month or more. Credit unions may generally charge 1% a month. Pawnbrokers' rates vary widely. Building and loan associations, loans insured by the Federal Housing Administration, and frequently retail charge account credit are also specially regulated.

**4. Consumer finance loan statutes.** Consumer finance loan statutes are based on early models drafted by the Russell Sage Foundation (1916-42) to provide small loans to wage earners under license and other protective regulations. In general, licensed lenders may charge 2½% or 3% a month for $300 or less and reduced rates for additional amounts up to $1,000, $1,500 or more. A number of states permit add-on rates of 17% to 20% ($17 to $20 per $100) a year of the original principal for $300 and lower rates for additional amounts. An add-on of 17% ($17 per $100) per year yields about 2½% per month when the loan is paid in equal monthly installments. In the table below unless otherwise stated, monthly rates are based on reducing principal balances, annual add-on rates are based on the original principal for the full term, and two or more rates apply to different portions of balance or original principal.

**The states with consumer finance loan laws and the rates of charge as of October 1, 1968, are as follows:**

| State | Maximum rate |
|---|---|
| | **Monthly unless otherwise stated** |
| Ala. | 3% to $200, 2% to $300. Special rate up to $75 |
| Alaska | 4% to $300, 2½% to $600, 2% to $1,000; 5% for loans up to $50 |
| Ariz. | 3% to $300, 2% to $600, 1% to $1,000 |
| Calif. | 2½% to $200, 2% to $500, 1½% to $700, 1% to $5,000. |
| Colo. | 3% to $300, 1½% to $500, 1% to $1,500 |
| Conn. | Annual Add-on: 17% to $300, 9% to $1,000 |
| D. of C. | 1% to $200 |
| Fla. | 3% to $300, 2% to $600 |
| Hawaii | 3½% to $100, 2½% to $300 |
| Idaho | 3% to $300, 2% to $500, 1% to $1,000 |
| Ill. | 3% to $150, 2% to $300, 1% to $800. |
| Ind. | 3% to $150, 2% to $300, 1½% to $1,000. |
| Ia. | 3% to $150, 2% to $300, 1½% to $700, 1% to $1,000 |
| Kan. | 3% to $300, 5/6% to $2.100 |
| Ky. | 3% to $150, 2% to $600, 1% to 800; or annual add-on of 20% to $150; 15% to $600, 11% to $800 |
| La. | 3½% to $150, 2½% to $300 |
| Me. | 2½% to $300, 1½% to $2,000; 25c minimum |
| Md. | 3% to $300, 2% to $500. |
| Mass. | 2½% to $200, 2% to $600; 1¾% to $1,000, ¾% to $3,000 |
| Mich. | 2½% to $300, 1¼% to $1,000 |
| Minn. | 2¾% to $300, 1½% to $600, 1¼% to $900 |
| Miss. | Interest and service charges combined exceed 3% per month |
| Mo. | 2.218% to $500, 8% per annum on any remainder |
| Mont. | Annual Add-on: 20% to $300, 16% to $500, 12% to $1,000. Special rate to $90 |
| Nebr. | 30% per annum to $300, 24% to $500, 18% to $1,000, 12% to $3,000 |
| Nev. | Annual Add-on: 9% to $1,000, 8% to $2,500; monthly fee of 1% on first $200 and ½% on next $200 |
| N. H. | 2% to $600, 1½% to $1,500, 1½% on larger loans to $5,000 |
| N. J. | 24% per annum to $500, 22% to $1,000 |
| N. M. | 3% to $150, 2½% to $300, 1% to $1,000 |
| N. Y. | 2½% to $100, 2% to $300, ¾% to $800 |
| N. C. | Annual Add-on: 20% to $100, 18% to $200, 15% to $300, 6% to $600. Special rate up to $75 |
| N. D. | 2½% to $250, 2% to $500, 1¾% to $750, 1½% to $1,000 |
| Ohio | Annual Add-on: 16% to $500, 9% to $1,000, 7% to $2,000; or equivalent simple interest rate |
| Okla. | 10% per annum plus various fees to $300 |
| Ore. | 3% to $300, 2% to $500, 1% to $1,500 |
| Penna. | 3% to $150, 2% to $300, 1% to $600 |
| P. Rico | Annual Add-on: 20% to $300, 7% to $600 |
| R. I. | 3% to $300; 2½% for loans between $300 and $800; 2% for larger loans to $2,500 |
| S. C. | Annual Add-on: 20% to $100, 18% to $300, 9% to $1,000; 7% for larger loans to $7,500, plus service fee. Special rate to $150 |
| S. D. | 3% to $300, ¾% to $2,500; $2 minimum |
| Tenn. | 6% per annum plus 4% fee; no size limit. |
| Texas | Annual Add-on: 18% to $300, 8% to $2,500. Special rates to $100 |
| Utah | 3% to $300, 1% to $600 |
| Vt. | 2½% to $125. 2¼% to $300. 1% to $600 |
| Va. | 2½% to $300. 1½% to $1,000; or annual add-on of 17% to $300, 12% to $1,000. |
| Wash. | 3% to $300, 1½% to $500, 1% to $1,000; $1 minimum |
| W. Va. | 3% to $200, 2% to $600, 1½% to $800; or annual add-on of 19% to $200, 16% to $600, 12% to $800 |
| Wisc. | 2½% to $100, 2% to $200, 1% to $300 |
| Wyo. | 3½% to $150, 2½% to $300, 1% to $1,000; plus $1 for loans up to $50 |

# Federal Deposit Insurance Corporation (FDIC)

The primary purpose of the Federal Deposit Insurance Corporation (FDIC) is to insure the deposits of all banks entitled to insurance benefits under the Federal Deposit Insurance Act. The major functions of the FDIC are to pay off depositors of insured banks closed without adequate provision having been made to pay depositors' claims, to act as receiver for all national banks placed in receivership and for state banks placed in receivership when appointed receiver by state authorities, and to prevent the continuance or development of unsafe and unsound banking practices. The FDIC's entire income consists of assessments on insured banks and income from investments; it receives no appropriations from Congress. It may borrow from the U. S. Treasury not to exceed $3 billion outstanding at any one time, but has made no such borrowings since it was organized in 1933. The FDIC surplus (Deposit Insurance Fund) as of Dec. 31, 1967, was $3,485,486,215.

# SOCIAL SECURITY PROGRAMS

## Medicare; Old-Age, Survivors and Disability Insurance

### Legislation Signed in 1968 Increases Old-Age, Survivors and Disability Benefits by 13%; Tax Base Changed

Source: Office of Research and Statistics, Social Security Administration,
Dept. of Health, Education and Welfare

The Social Security Amendments of 1967, signed Jan. 2, 1968, included changes that raised old-age, survivors, and disability benefits 13% beginning with the check for February, 1968, raised the taxable and creditable earnings base, revised the contribution schedule, raised the amount a worker may earn and still get benefits, provided benefits for disabled widows and widowers at reduced rates at age 50, and made it possible for workers disabled before age 31 to qualify for benefits. Changes in Medicare included coverage of added days of hospital care, coverage of physical therapy services and certain podiatrists' services under medical insurance, and transfer of all outpatient hospital services to medical insurance.

The Social Security Act provides that the Secretary of Health, Education, and Welfare is to determine and promulgate each year between July 1 and October 1 the deductible (the amount paid by the patient) for inpatient hospital services under Medicare for the next calendar year. In 1968, the Secretary announced that the patient must pay the first $44 (instead of the first $40) for the first 60 days' hospital care in 1969.

The Commissioner of Social Security is Robert M. Ball. There are 642 district offices (with 117 branch offices) in the country, where the public may obtain information about its right to benefits.

## MEDICARE
### HEALTH INSURANCE FOR AGED

Beginning July 1966, most Americans aged 65 and over became eligible for hospital insurance and if they choose to take it, for voluntary medical insurance, in addition.

Hospital Insurance—In the second year of operation (July 1967-June 1968) about $3.7 billion was paid in hospital benefits. About 19,700,000 persons were enrolled as of June 1968. There were 5,600,000 hospital admissions, 450,000 admissions to extended-care facilities, and 260,000 start-of-care notices for home health services recorded under the program in the 12-month period.

The hospital insurance program pays the cost of covered services for hospital and posthospital care as follows:

● Up to 90 days of hospital care during a benefit period (spell of illness, starting on the 1st day of care as a bedpatient is received in a hospital or extended-care facility and ending when the individual has not been a bedpatient for 60 consecutive days). For the first 60 days, the hospital insurance pays for all but the first $44 of expenses; for the 61st to 90th day, the program pays all but $10 a day for covered services. In addition, each person has a 60-day lifetime reserve that can be used after the 90 days of hospital care in a benefit period are exhausted, and all but $20 a day of expenses during the reserve days are paid. Once used the reserve days are not replaced. (Payment for care in a mental hospital is limited to 190 days.)

● Up to 100 days' care in an extended-care facility (skilled nursing home) in each benefit period. Hospital insurance pays for all covered services for the first 20 days and all but $5 daily for the next 80 days. At least 3 days' hospital stay must precede these services, and the extended-care facility must be entered within 14 days after leaving the hospital.

● Up to 100 visits by nurses or other health workers (not doctors) from a home health agency in the 365 days after release from a hospital or extended-care facility.

Money to pay these benefits comes from a spe-

cial contribution paid by workers and by their employers and by the self-employed. In 1968 and for 1969 through 1972, it is 1/6 of 1% (0.6%) on earnings up to $7,800 (the maximum taxable amount under the 1967 amendments). The tax gradually increases then by steps stated in the law. The contributions are placed in a separate Hospital Insurance Trust Fund from which benefits and administrative expenses are paid. These contributions are made at the same time as those for social security cash benefits.

**Medical insurance**—Aged persons can receive benefits under this supplementary program **only** if they sign up for them and agree to pay a monthly premium ($4, beginning April 1968). The Federal Government pays a matching amount.

The medical insurance program pays 80% of the reasonable charges (after the first $50 in each calendar year) for the following services:

● Physicians' and surgeons' services, whether in the doctor's office, a clinic, or hospital or at home.

● Home health services even without a hospital stay—up to 100 visits in a year.

● Other medical and health services, such as diagnostic tests, surgical dressings and splints, and rental or purchase of medical equipment.

● Physical therapy services furnished under the supervision of a participating hospital, clinic, extended-care facility, or agency.

● Certain services by podiatrists.

● All outpatient services of a participating hospital (including diagnostic tests).

Beginning April 1968, X-ray or laboratory services of physicians for hospital bedpatients are paid on the basis of full reasonable charges without the need to meet the $50 deductible.

To get medical insurance protection, persons approaching age 65 may enroll in the 7-month period that includes 3 months before the 65th birthday, the month of the birthday, and 3 months after the birthday, but if they wish coverage to begin in the month they reach 65 they must enroll in the 3 months **before** their birthday. Persons not enrolling within their 7-month enrollment period may enroll during the first 3 months of each year, provided this period begins within 3 years after the first chance to enroll.

The monthly premium is deducted from the cash benefit for persons receiving social security, railroad retirement, or civil service retirement benefits. Income from the medical premiums and the Federal matching payments are put in a Supplementary Medical Insurance Trust Fund, from which benefits and administrative expenses will be paid.

Persons qualifying for hospital insurance under social security receive a health insurance card similar to the cards now used by Blue Cross and other health agencies. The card indicates whether the individual has taken out medical insurance protection. It is to be shown to the hospital, extended care facility, home health agency, doctor, or whoever provides the covered services. The part of the bill for which payment can be made is taken care of by the program. Payments are made only in the 50 States, Puerto Rico, the Virgin Islands, Guam, and American Samoa, **except that** hospital services may be provided in border areas immediately outside the U. S. if comparable services are not accessible in the U. S. for a beneficiary who becomes ill or is injured in the U. S.

The health insurance programs do not pay the entire costs of medical care. Those unable to pay medical bills not covered by the health insurance programs may qualify for aid from the public welfare agency. Most States have programs to help persons who cannot pay their medical bills. Some of these programs provide aid only for the aged; others help the medically needy, regardless of age.

## OLD-AGE, SURVIVORS, AND DISABILITY INSURANCE

Retired and disabled workers and their families and the survivors of deceased workers received $22.5 billion in social security cash benefits in the 12 months ended in June 1968. In that month the

148

average benefit being received by a retired worker was $98; for retired workers just coming on the rolls, the average benefit award was about $103. For a disabled worker, the June check was $112, and new disabled-worker beneficiaries were awarded $115, on the average.

Old-age, survivors, and disability insurance covers almost all jobs in which people work for wages or salaries, as well as most work of self-employed persons, whether in a city job, or in business, or on a farm.

Old-age, survivors, and disability insurance is paid for by a tax on earnings (beginning Jan. 1, 1968, up to $7,800). The employed worker and his employer share the tax equally. (Beginning 1966, cash tips count as covered wages if they amount to $20 or more from one place of employment. The worker reports them to his employer, who includes them in his social security tax reports, but only the worker pays contributions on the amount of the tips.)

The employer deducts the tax each payday and sends it, with an equal amount as his own share, to the District Director of Internal Revenue. The collected taxes are deposited in the Federal Old-Age and Survivors Insurance Trust Fund and the Federal Disability Insurance Trust Fund; they can be used only to pay benefits and administrative expenses.

The contribution rates on the first $7,800 of covered earnings and the schedule of increases to come are shown in the 2nd table on page 151 for the old-age, survivors, and disability insurance program and for the new hospital insurance program.

## AMOUNT OF WORK REQUIRED

To qualify for benefits for himself and his family, the worker must have been in covered employment long enough to become insured. Just how long depends on his date of birth (or if he dies or becomes disabled, the date of his death or disability).

A person is fully covered if he has one quarter of coverage for every year after 1950 up to but not including the year in which he reaches age 65 (62 for women), dies, or becomes disabled. Under a special 1965 provision a person who reached retirement age before 1957 can qualify for benefits at age 72 with less than 6 quarters of coverage, and his wife or widow (if he was living in 1965) may also receive a benefit at 72 ($40 benefit for the worker or the widow, $20 for the wife).

To get disability benefits, the worker must also have credit for 5 out of 10 years before he becomes disabled. Under the 1965 amendments, persons disabled before age 31 because of blindness as defined in the law can qualify with a briefer period of coverage.

The following table shows the number of work years required to be fully insured for old-age benefits, according to the year worker reaches retirement age or dies.

| Retirement age* or death | Years of credit |
|---|---|
| In 1957 | 1½ |
| 1958 | 1¾ |
| 1959 | 2 |
| 1960 | 2¼ |
| 1961 | 2½ |
| 1962 | 2¾ |
| 1963 | 3 |
| 1964 | 3¼ |
| 1965 | 3½ |
| 1966 | 3¾ |
| 1967 | 4 |
| 1968 | 4¼ |
| 1969 | 4½ |
| 1970 | 4¾ |
| 1971 | 5 |
| 1975 | 6 |
| 1979 | 7 |
| 1983 | 8 |
| 1987 | 9 |
| 1991 or later | 10 |

*Age 62 for women, age 65 for men. Men may actually retire at age 62 and receive a reduced benefit, but age 65 is used for men in determining the minimum number of quarters of coverage needed.

## AGED 72 OR OVER

A 1966 provision made special benefits payable, beginning Oct. 1966, to non-insured persons aged 72 or over or reaching that age before 1968 and residing in the 50 states or the District of Columbia, even if they have no quarters of coverage. Persons reaching 72 after 1967 can also qualify for special benefits, but they must have at least 3 quarters of coverage for each calendar year after 1966 and before the year they become 72.

## SELF-EMPLOYED

A self-employed person who has earnings of $400 or more in a year must report his earnings for income-tax and social security tax purposes. If he is not a farmer he reports only net returns from his business. He need not add income from real estate, savings, dividends, loans, pensions or insurance policies if these are not part of his business.

A self-employed person who has net earnings of $400 or more in a year gets 4 quarters of coverage for that year. If his earnings are less than $400 in a year, they do not count toward social security credits.

Under a 1966 law, the nonfarm self-employed person must make estimated payments of his social security taxes, on a quarterly basis, for taxable years after Dec. 31, 1966, if combined estimated income tax and social security tax amount to at least $40.

When a person has both taxable wages and earnings from self-employment, only as much of the self-employment income as will bring total earnings to $7,800 is subject to tax for social security purposes. A self-employed person pays the tax at a lower rate than the combined rate for an employee and his employer, 1½ times what the employee alone pays.

Before the 1967 amendments, the religious work of ministers and members of religious orders was covered on an individual elective basis. Under the 1967 amendments, services of ministers and members of religious orders who have not taken a vow of poverty are covered automatically unless, within specified time limits, an exemption is obtained from the Internal Revenue Service on the grounds of religious principles or conscience. Once an exemption is obtained it cannot be withdrawn.

## FARM OWNERS AND HANDS

Self-employed farmers whose gross annual earnings from farming are under $2,400 may report ⅔ of their gross earnings instead of net earnings for social security purposes. Cash or crop shares received from a tenant or share farmer count if the owner participated materially in production or management. The self-employed farmer pays contributions at the same rate as other self-employed, but he may make his tax returns annually.

**Farm Workers.** Earnings from farm work count toward benefits (1) if the employer pays $150 or more in cash during the year; (2) if the employee works on 20 or more days for cash pay figured on a time basis. Under these rules a person gets credit for one calendar quarter for each $100 in cash pay in a year but no more than four quarters in any one year.

Foreign farm workers admitted to the United States on a temporary basis will not be covered.

## HOUSEHOLD WORKERS

Anyone working as maid, cook, laundress, nursemaid, baby-sitter, chauffeur, gardener and at other household tasks in the house of another, is covered by social security if he or she earns $50 or more in cash in three months from any one employer. Room and board do not count, but carfare counts if paid in cash. The job does not have to be regular or fulltime. The employee should get a card at the social security office and show it to the employer.

The employer deducts the amount of the social security tax from the worker's pay, adds an identical amount as his own tax and sends the total amount to the Federal Government, with the number of the employee's social security card.

## WHAT AGED WORKERS GET

When a person has enough work in covered employment and reaches retirement age (65 for full benefit, 62 for reduced benefit), he may retire and get monthly old-age benefits. If he continues to work and has earnings of more than $1,680, some benefits are withheld. But only $1 in benefits will be withheld for every $2 of earnings between $1,680 and $2,880 and $1 in benefits for every $1 in earnings above $2,880. The eligible worker who is 72 receives the full amount of benefit, regardless of earnings.

When a person receives old-age benefits, payments can also be made to certain of his dependents including a wife 62 or over, dependent children under 18 or who became totally disabled before that age or who is a full-time student not yet aged 22, a wife (regardless of age) if caring for an eligible child, and a dependent husband 62 or over.

The special benefit for persons aged 72 or over who do not meet the regular coverage requirements is $40 a month ($60 for a couple if both members are eligible). It is not paid to persons on the public assistance rolls.

Social Security benefits are not subject to income taxes.

A woman worker is eligible for a full old-age benefit at age 65, but she may retire at 62 and get 80% of her full benefit for the rest of her life; the nearer she is to 65 when she begins collecting her benefit, the larger it will be. (Benefits for men retiring before 65 are reduced at the same rate as benefits for women retiring before 65.)

Under the 1967 amendments, a child can get benefits based on his mother's earnings on the same conditions as those entitling a child to benefits based on his father's earnings record.

## BENEFITS FOR WORKER'S WIFE (OR HUSBAND)

The wife of a man who is getting social security retirement or disability payments may become entitled to wife's insurance benefits in a reduced amount when she reaches 62, or she may wait until she reaches 65 and get the entire amount of the wife's benefit, which is one-half of the husband's benefits (but not more than $105). Benefits are also payable to the divorced wife of an insured worker if she was married to him for at least 20 years and he was contributing to or was ordered by a court to contribute to her support.

If a woman worker entitled to old-age benefit has a dependent husband aged 65 or over, he may draw a benefit similar to a wife's benefit at 65 (or a reduced benefit at age 62).

## BENEFITS FOR CHILDREN OF RETIRED OR DISABLED WORKERS

If a worker has children under 18 when he retires for age or disability they will get a benefit that is half his benefit, and so will his wife, even if she is under 62. Total benefits based on his earnings up to $6,600 cannot be more than $395.60. (Eventually, as workers earnings records reflect more closely the new $7,800 taxable earnings limit, the maximum family benefit will be $434.40.)

When his children reach 18, their benefits will stop, except that a child permanently and totally disabled before 18 may get a benefit as long as his disability meets the definition in the law. In addition, child's benefits are payable until the child reaches his 22nd birthday if he is attending school as a full-time student.

## SURVIVOR BENEFITS

If a worker should die while insured, one or more types of survivor benefits would be payable to his survivors.

1. A cash payment to cover burial expenses that amounts to 3 times the basic benefit but not more than $255, paid at the death of every insured worker.

2. A benefit for each child until the child reaches 18. The monthly benefit of each child of a worker who has died is three-quarters of the amount the worker would have received if he had lived and drawn retirement benefits. A child with a permanent disability that began before age 18 may receive his benefit after that age (or up to age 22, if he is attending school).

3. A mother's benefit for the widow, if children under 18 are left in her care. Her benefit is 75% of the basic benefit and she draws it until the youngest child reaches 18. Payments stop then even if the child's benefit continues because he is attending school. They will start again when she is 62 (or 60), unless she marries. If she marries and the marriage is ended, she regains benefit rights. If she has a disabled child beneficiary aged 18 or over in her care, her benefits also continue.

The 1967 amendments provide that disabled widows and widowers will be eligible for benefits at age 50 at reduced rates depending on the age of entitlement. The widow or widower must have become totally disabled before or within 7 years after the spouse's death.

4. If there are no children entitled to receive benefits, the widow will get a benefit at 62 that is 82½% of the basic benefit amount. She may choose to start getting benefits at age 60; if she makes this choice, her benefit is reduced by 5/9 of 1% for each month she receives a benefit before she is 62.

5. Dependent parents may be eligible for benefits, if they have been receiving at least half their support from the worker before his death, have reached retirement age (62) and are not eligible for an old-age benefit based on their own earnings. Each parent receives 75% of the basic benefit except that, if tnere is only one surviving parent, the benefit is 82% of the basic benefit.

The survivors of a woman worker receive benefits on the same basis as those of men workers.

## WHAT DISABLED WORKER GETS

If a worker becomes so severely disabled that he is unable to work, he may be eligible to receive a monthly disability benefit that is the same amount he would receive as an old-age benefit if he were 65 at the start of his disability. When he reaches 65, his disability benefit becomes an old-age benefit.

Benefits like those provided for dependents of retired-worker beneficiaries may be paid to dependents of disabled beneficiaries.

## FEDERAL CREDIT UNION

The Bureau of Federal Credit Unions is responsible for chartering, examining, and supervising Federal credit unions. These are voluntary cooperative associations to promote thrift among members and provide loans. Large numbers of credit unions are found among employee groups in commerce, industry, and government At the end of June 1968 there were 12,500 Federal credit unions with about 10,163,000 members and assets of $6,555 billion. The Bureau of Federal Credit Unions is a part of the Social Security Administration.

## OLD-AGE AND SURVIVORS AND DISABILITY INSURANCE TRUST FUNDS
[In thousands]

| Period and fiscal year | Receipts | | | Expenditures | | Total assets at period end |
| --- | --- | --- | --- | --- | --- | --- |
| | Net contribution income and transfers | Net interest received | Financial Transfers | Benefit payments | Administrative expenses | |
| 1936-37.......... | $265,000 | $2,262 | ............ | $27 | ............ | $267,235 |
| 1940-41.......... | 688,141 | 55,958 | ............ | 64,342 | $26,840 | 2,397,615 |
| 1945-46.......... | 1,238,218 | 147,766 | ............ | 320,510 | 37,427 | 7,641,428 |
| 1950-51.......... | 3,124,098 | 287,392 | ............ | 1,498,088 | 70,447 | 14,735,567 |
| 1955-56.......... | 6,442,370 | 487,450 | $7,439 | 5,360,813 | 124,339 | 22,593,109 |
| 1958-59.......... | 8,460,081 | 576,713 | −124,441 | 9,388,377 | 227,504 | 23,208,045 |
| 1959-60.......... | 10,829,764 | 564,040 | −573,606 | 10,798,013 | 234,291 | 22,995,939 |
| 1960-61.......... | 12,314,678 | 591,713 | −336,882 | 11,888,527 | 272,188 | 23,404,734 |
| 1961-62.......... | 12,475,509 | 609,006 | −371,818 | 13,669,211 | 315,417 | 21,132,803 |
| 1962-63.......... | 14,404,383 | 582,043 | −442,132 | 15,015,262 | 329,040 | 21,332,795 |
| 1963-64.......... | 16,645,887 | 606,704 | −421,775 | 15,830,373 | 370,400 | 21,962,838 |
| 1964-65.......... | 17,032,456 | 648,372 | −459,253 | 16,618,084 | 379,145 | 22,187,184 |
| 1965-66.......... | 19,422,599 | 648,635 | −468,782 | 19,792,586 | 437,159 | 21,878,935 |
| 1966-67.......... | ¹24,816,399 | 792,741 | −538,680 | 20,753,125 | 432,735 | 25,536,995 |
| 1967-1968p....... | 25,361,794 | 984,392 | −458,022 | 22,840,888 | 559,559 | 28,118,691 |
| **Cumulative * to July 1968......** | ²$218,896,566 | $11,621,801 | −$4,160,020 | $193,606,683 | $4,836,359 | $28,118,691 |

¹Beginning 1966, includes amounts for rehabilitative services, authorized by 1965 amendments (a total of $23,785,000 from 1965-66 to 1967-68).

²Includes $203,386,000 transferred from general funds for benefits for certain World War II veterans and, beginning 1966, for military service wage credits.

pPreliminary.

*Cumulative totals are not totals of columns for several years are omitted.

# Examples of Monthly OASDI Cash Payments

(Old-Age, Survivors, and Disability Insurance)

| Average yearly earnings after 1950[1] | $899 or less | $1800 | $3000 | $4200 | $5400 | $6600 | $7800 |
|---|---|---|---|---|---|---|---|
| Retired worker—65 or older } Disabled worker—under 65 } | $55.00 | $ 88.40 | $115.00 | $140.40 | $165.00 | $189.90 | $218.00 |
| Wife 65 or older | 27.50 | 44.20 | 57.50 | 70.20 | 82.50 | 95.00 | 105.00 |
| Retired worker at 62 | 44.00 | 70.80 | 92.00 | 112.40 | 132.00 | 152.00 | 174.40 |
| Wife at 62, no child | 20.70 | 33.20 | 43.20 | 52.70 | 61.90 | 71.30 | 78.80 |
| Widow at 62 or older | 55.00 | 73.00 | 94.90 | 115.90 | 136.20 | 156.70 | 179.90 |
| Widow at 60, no child | 47.70 | 63.30 | 82.30 | 100.50 | 118.10 | 135.90 | 156.00 |
| Disabled widow at 50, no child | 33.40 | 44.30 | 57.60 | 70.30 | 82.70 | 95.10 | 109.20 |
| Wife under 65 and one child | 27.50 | 44.20 | 87.40 | 140.40 | 165.00 | 190.00 | 214.00 |
| Widow under 62 and one child | 82.50 | 132.60 | 172.60 | 210.60 | 247.60 | 285.00 | 327.00 |
| Widow under 62 and two children | 82.50 | 132.60 | 202.40 | 280.80 | 354.40 | 395.60 | 434.40 |
| One child of retired or disabled worker | 27.50 | 44.20 | 57.50 | 70.20 | 82.50 | 95.00 | 109.00 |
| One surviving child | 55.00 | 66.30 | 86.30 | 105.30 | 123.80 | 142.50 | 163.50 |
| Maximum family payment | 82.50 | 132.60 | 202.40 | 280.80 | 354.40 | 395.60 | 434.40 |

[1]Generally, average earnings are figured over the period from 1950 until the worker reaches retirement age, becomes disabled, or dies. Up to 5 years of low earnings can be excluded. The maximum earnings creditable for social security are $3,600 for 1951-1954; $4,200 for 1955-1958; $4,800 for 1959-1965; and $6,600 for 1966-1967. The maximum creditable in 1968 and after is $7,800, but average earnings cannot reach this amount until later. Because of this, the benefits shown in the last two columns on the right generally will not be payable until later. When a person is entitled to more than one benefit, the amount actually payable is limited to the larger of the benefits.

## CONTRIBUTION RATE FOR EMPLOYEES, EMPLOYERS, AND SELF-EMPLOYED

### Percent of Covered Earnings

| Years | Employees and employers | | | Self-employed | | |
|---|---|---|---|---|---|---|
| | OASDI Benefits | Hospital Insurance | Total | OASDI Benefits | Hospital Insurance | Total |
| 1968 | 3.8 | 0.6 | 4.4 | 5.8 | 0.6 | 6.4 |
| 1969-70 | 4.2 | .6 | 4.8 | 6.3 | .6 | 6.9 |
| 1971-72 | 4.6 | .6 | 5.2 | 6.9 | .6 | 7.5 |
| 1973-75 | 5.0 | .65 | 5.65 | 7.0 | .65 | 7.65 |
| 1976-79 | 5.0 | .7 | 5.7 | 7.0 | .7 | 7.7 |
| 1980-86 | 5.0 | .8 | 5.8 | 7.0 | .8 | 7.8 |
| 1987 and after | 5.0 | .9 | 5.9 | 7.0 | .9 | 7.9 |

## Hospital insurance trust fund: Status, 1966-68

### [IN THOUSANDS]

| Period | Receipts | | | | Expenditures | | Total assets |
|---|---|---|---|---|---|---|---|
| | Net contribution income[1] | Transfers from general revenues[2] | Transfers from railroad retirement account[3] | Net interest[4] | Net hospital and related service benefits[5] | Administrative expenses[6] | |
| Jan. 1966-June 1968[7] | $7,111,531 | $621,481 | $60,354 | $112,423 | $6,244,095 | $231,058 | $1,430,636 |
| Fiscal years: | | | | | | | |
| 1965-66 | 908,797 | | | 5,970 | | 63,564 | 851,204 |
| 1966-67 | 2,688,684 | 337,850 | 16,305 | 45,798 | 2,507,773 | 88,848 | 1,343,221 |
| 1967-68[7] | 3,514,049 | 283,631 | 44,049 | 60,655 | 3,736,322 | 78,647 | 1,430,000 |

[1]Represents amounts appropriated (estimated tax collections with suitable subsequent adjustments), after deductions for refund of estimated amount of employee-tax overpayment.
[2]Represents Federal Government transfers from general funds appropriations to meet costs of benefits for persons not insured for cash benefits under OASDHI or railroad retirement and for costs of benefits arising from military wage credits.
[3]Represents receipts under the financial interchange with railroad retirement account with respect to contributions for hospital insurance coverage of railroad workers.
[4]Represents interest and profit on investments after transfers of interest on administrative expenses reimbursed to the OASI trust fund.
[5]Represents (1) payment vouchers on letters of credit issued to fiscal intermediaries under sec. 1816 and (2) direct payments to providers of services under sec. 1815 of the Social Security Act.
[6]Subject to subsequent adjustment among all 4 social security trust funds, for allocated cost of each operation.
[7]Preliminary.

## Supplementary medical insurance trust fund: Status, 1966-68

### [IN THOUSANDS]

| Period | Receipts | | | Expenditures | | Total assets |
|---|---|---|---|---|---|---|
| | Premium income[1] | Transfers from general revenues[2] | Net interest[3] | Net medical service benefits[4] | Administrative expenses[5] | |
| July 1966-June 1968[6] | $1,345,170 | $1,257,000 | $34,729 | $2,053,883 | $276,290 | $306,727 |
| Fiscal years: | | | | | | |
| 1966-67 | 646,682 | 623,000 | 14,052 | 664,261 | 133,682 | 485,791 |
| 1967-68[6] | 698,488 | 634,000 | 20,677 | 1,389,622 | 142,608 | 306,727 |

[1]Represents voluntary premium payments from and in behalf of insured persons.
[2]Represent Federal Government transfers from general funds approprations to match aggregate premums paid.
[3]Represents interest and profit on investments after transfers of interest on administrative expenses reimbursed to the OASI trust fund (see footnote 5).
[4]Represents payment vouchers on letters of credit issued to carriers under section 1842 of the Social Security Act.
[5]Subject to subsequent adjustment among all 4 social security trust funds for allocated cost of each operation.
[6]Preliminary.

# Employment Services and Unemployment Insurance

**Source:** Bureau of Employment Security, Manpower Administration. U. S. Department of Labor.
Robert C. Goodwin, Administrator

## EMPLOYMENT SERVICES

The Federal-State Employment Service consists of the U. S. Employment Service in the Bureau of Employment Security and affiliated state employment services with their network of some 2,400 local offices, including 171 youth opportunity centers. During the fiscal year ended June 30, 1968, these local offices recorded 5,759,923 placements in nonfarm jobs and 4,601,501 in year-round seasonal farm jobs. There were 2,099,955 job tests given, and applicants received almost 2,599,022 job counseling interviews. Since the beginning of the training program under the Manpower Development and Training Act in Sept. 1962 through June 30, 1968, enrollees to institutional training have numbered 739,500 and to on-the-job training 295,900.

The Federal-State employment service is concerned with utilizing to the fullest the human resources of the nation; with referring those who are employable to job openings utilizing their highest skills; with reaching out and finding those who are unemployed or underemployed and providing or arranging for necessary service or training to make them employable; with counseling and testing as necessary; with developing appropriate job openings; with referral for employment; and with followup to insure placement.

Special services are provided for those with employment problems—older workers, the young and inexperienced, members of minorities, migrant workers, the handicapped, and the disadvantaged. Veterans are provided with special services in accordance with their needs for employment counseling, job development, and placement and there are Veterans Employment Service representatives in the Bureau's national, state and local offices. Since August 1967, at the direction of the President, the public employment service has been contacting all individuals discharged from military service, to assure that they find jobs rapidly.

The public employment service assists employers in meeting their labor needs and provides appropriate employment-related personnel services. It insures, before an immigrant worker may receive a visa, that there are insufficient workers available for the employment and that there will be no adverse effect upon wages and working conditions of similarly employed U. S. workers. In the case of supplementary seasonal foreign farmworkers, the employment service provides a special program of local and interstate recruitment to insure that domestic farmworkers are given preference in employment. The public employment service assists in development and utilization of civilian manpower capability for meeting national emergencies and disaster needs, and assists other countries to improve their manpower programs.

The human resources development concept was introduced in 1965 and by the end of fiscal year 1967 had been adopted as the operating policy of all public employment service offices. The goal of this effort is to provide total employment and related service to meet needs of the disadvantaged. Human resources development involves outreach—the sending of employment service staff into disadvantaged neighborhoods to seek out and help those who may become employable. Close cooperation with other agencies, such as local community action agencies, is basic to the program.

During the fiscal 1968, 1,236,000 applicants were reached by Youth Opportunity Centers for job placement, training, or other manpower services. Most applicants were between 16 and 22 years of age. These centers and other local employment service offices recorded 4,322,100 registrations of youth, 683,500 initial counseling interviews, and 2,784,400 placements in farm and nonfarm jobs. Employment service offices also referred 63,762 applicants to the Job Corps and 127,200 to the Neighborhood Youth Corps for work-training experience, and provided job placement and other related services to many of those completing or leaving these programs.

## UNEMPLOYMENT INSURANCE

Unlike old-age and survivors insurance, entirely a Federal program, unemployment insurance is a Federal-State program which provides insured wage earners with partial replacement of wages lost during involuntary unemployment. The program protects most workers in industry but few in agriculture. The amount of weekly benefits is determined by State laws, prior wages, and length of employment. Some 56,000,000 jobs in commerce, industry, and government, including the Armed Forces, were covered under the Federal-State system in fiscal year 1968. Another 700,000 railroad workers were insured against unemployment under a system administered by the Railroad Retirement Board.

Each state, as well as the District of Columbia and Puerto Rico, has its own law and operates its own program. The Federal Unemployment Tax Act levies an excise tax of 3.1% on the first $3,600 of payrolls of employers with four employees or more in 20 weeks in a year. Although the Federal tax is limited to employers with four or more workers more than half of the state laws cover firms with fewer than four. Against that tax a credit of up to 2.7% is allowed for taxes paid under State unemployment insurance laws which meet certain criteria, leaving the Federal share at 0.4% of taxable wages from which the Federal Government grants to the states funds to cover the administrative cost of the unemployment insurance and employment service programs. The Social Security Act requires as a condition of such grants, prompt payment of benefits when due to unemployed workers under a state law, and provides safeguards for workers' rights to benefits if they do not take jobs that fail to meet certain labor standards. Through the Unemployment Insurance Service of the Bureau of Employment Security, the Secretary of Labor determines whether states qualify for grants for unemployment insurance administration, and for purposes of tax offset credit for employers.

Benefits are financed solely by employer contributions except in Alaska, Alabama, and New Jersey, where employees also contribute. Employers subject to state unemployment insurance taxes paid about $2.6 billion in fiscal year 1968. Benefits are paid through state public employment offices at which unemployed workers must register for work and to which they must report regularly for referral to a possible job during the time when they are drawing weekly benefit payments. During the 1968 fiscal year, $2,054,970,554 in benefits were paid under the state UI programs to 4,300,000 beneficiaries representing compensation for 50,-858,504 weeks of unemployment. They received an average weekly payment of $41.25 for total unemployment for an average duration of 11.7 weeks. See table on page 153 for data by states.

### For Federal Services

Title 5, chapter 85 of the U. S. code provides unemployment insurance protection to about 2,-950,000 Federal civilian employees and about 3,550,000 members of the armed forces. Benefits for unemployed Federal workers and ex-servicemen are financed through direct Federal appropriations but are paid by the state employment security agencies as agents of the Federal Government on the basis of each state's law.

During fiscal year 1968, a total of $47,300,000 was paid to some 70,806 unemployed Federal civilian workers for a total of 1,086,354 weeks of unemployment. The average weekly payment was $42.41 and was paid for an average of 15.3 weeks. A total of $58,500,000 was paid to 148,161 unemployed ex-servicemen for 1,357,733 weeks of unemployment. The average weekly benefit was $42.69 and was paid for an average of 9.2 weeks.

In fiscal year 1968, under arrangements made with state employment security agencies, weekly training allowances, including subsistence and transportation in certain cases, totaling about $151,000,000 were paid to some 165,000 persons taking basic education or vocational training under sections 203 and 241 of the Manpower Development and Training Act. Arrangements were also in effect with state employment security agencies for payment of $1,649,000 in readjustment allowances to 1,619 workers found to have been affected adversely under the Trade Expansion Act of 1962 or the Automotive Products Trade Act of 1965.

# Employment Security
## SELECTED UNEMPLOYMENT INSURANCE DATA BY STATE
### Fiscal year 1967-68. State Program Only

| State | Insured claim- ants[1] | Bene- ficiaries[2] | Exhaus- tions[3] | Initial claims[4] | Benefit payments | | Funds available for bene- fits, June 30, 1968[6] | Employ- ers sub- ject to State law March 31, 1968 |
|---|---|---|---|---|---|---|---|---|
| | | | | | Total amount[5] | Average weekly benefit for total unem- ployment | | |
| | (1,000) | (1,000) | (1,000) | (1,000) | ($1,000) | (dollars) | (millions) | (1,000) |
| Alabama..... | 75 | 56 | 17 | 141 | $22,653 | $32.25 | $117 | 24 |
| Alaska....... | 12 | 11 | 2 | 24 | 8,375 | 45.37 | 20 | 5 |
| Arizona...... | 39 | 29 | 7 | 82 | 12,224 | 37.97 | 85 | 18 |
| Arkansas..... | 51 | 39 | 9 | 98 | 13,471 | 31.64 | 44 | 36 |
| California.... | 832 | 641 | 156 | 1,698 | 419,286 | 50.24 | 1,010 | 345 |
| Colorado..... | 23 | 16 | 3 | 50 | 7,555 | 47.70 | 73 | 19 |
| Connecticut... | 128 | 109 | 15 | 207 | 47,016 | 48.23 | 280 | 37 |
| Delaware..... | 18 | 15 | 2 | 30 | 6,580 | 44.44 | 24 | 10 |
| Dist. of Col... | 17 | 13 | 3 | 28 | 7,988 | 45.60 | 73 | 18 |
| Florida....... | 81 | 67 | 23 | 181 | 21,937 | 31.24 | 231 | 55 |
| Georgia....... | 91 | 62 | 18 | 124 | 18,957 | 35.68 | 266 | 34 |
| Hawaii....... | 23 | 14 | 3 | 31 | 8,713 | 49.30 | 31 | 13 |
| Idaho........ | 24 | 18 | 4 | 40 | 7,347 | 42.87 | 39 | 14 |
| Illinois...... | 263 | 203 | 42 | 436 | 94,131 | 44.01 | 530 | 94 |
| Indiana...... | 138 | 105 | 25 | 242 | 34,364 | 37.27 | 267 | 38 |
| Iowa......... | 40 | 30 | 7 | 62 | 13,798 | 44.83 | 128 | 25 |
| Kansas....... | 31 | 24 | 5 | 51 | 10,551 | 42.22 | 88 | 21 |
| Kentucky.... | 66 | 53 | 12 | 110 | 21,426 | 37.29 | 152 | 25 |
| Louisiana..... | 77 | 61 | 18 | 146 | 30,742 | 37.25 | 161 | 29 |
| Maine....... | 29 | 30 | 5 | 58 | 8,582 | 36.49 | 42 | 9 |
| Maryland..... | 86 | 73 | 8 | 155 | 27,214 | 40.75 | 224 | 54 |
| Massachusetts. | 220 | 178 | 38 | 423 | 93,072 | 44.51 | 346 | 106 |
| Michigan..... | 366 | 250 | 44 | 604 | 118,529 | 48.71 | 571 | 129 |
| Minnesota.... | 63 | 50 | 14 | 108 | 26,361 | 42.16 | 75 | 45 |
| Mississippi.... | 37 | 29 | 6 | 71 | 8,432 | 26.76 | 80 | 15 |
| Missouri..... | 132 | 100 | 15 | 302 | 35,906 | 39.75 | 269 | 39 |
| Montana..... | 20 | 14 | 4 | 33 | 5,295 | 31.81 | 22 | 16 |
| Nebraska..... | 19 | 15 | 4 | 28 | 6,146 | 37.21 | 50 | 14 |
| Nevada...... | 22 | 19 | 5 | 48 | 9,839 | 43.22 | 30 | 10 |
| N. Hampshire. | 15 | 9 | 0 | 25 | 2,423 | 39.82 | 44 | 8 |
| New Jersey... | 320 | 239 | 55 | 545 | 128,934 | 45.32 | 431 | 69 |
| New Mexico... | 20 | 17 | 3 | 44 | 7,529 | 33.76 | 38 | 18 |
| New York.... | 640 | 526 | 80 | 1,567 | 285,754 | 43.95 | 1,620 | 379 |
| N. Carolina... | 125 | 94 | 15 | 241 | 26,799 | 28.57 | 326 | 41 |
| N. Dakota.... | 8 | 7 | 1 | 13 | 3,953 | 41.23 | 7 | 6 |
| Ohio......... | 189 | 157 | 20 | 388 | 63,931 | 41.53 | 618 | 103 |
| Oklahoma.... | 33 | 27 | 9 | 73 | 12,353 | 30.16 | 58 | 20 |
| Oregon...... | 68 | 57 | 11 | 179 | 27,946 | 39.08 | 121 | 41 |
| Pennsylvania.. | 338 | 272 | 30 | 773 | 112,296 | 39.02 | 771 | 185 |
| Puerto Rico... | 78 | 75 | 44 | 208 | 21,766 | 22.49 | 77 | 12 |
| Rhode Island.. | 50 | 37 | 6 | 105 | 14,971 | 41.92 | 76 | 22 |
| S. Carolina... | 63 | 43 | 14 | 104 | 15,601 | 32.99 | 131 | 17 |
| S. Dakota.... | 5 | 4 | 1 | 8 | 2,915 | 34.11 | 18 | 7 |
| Tennessee.... | 111 | 88 | 21 | 169 | 30,753 | 32.29 | 167 | 27 |
| Texas........ | 112 | 75 | 21 | 200 | 26,938 | 33.66 | 334 | 84 |
| Utah........ | 25 | 20 | 6 | 45 | 10,661 | 40.43 | 42 | 18 |
| Vermont..... | 11 | 9 | 1 | 22 | 4,635 | 41.02 | 21 | 6 |
| Virginia...... | 46 | 32 | 7 | 78 | 9,027 | 33.10 | 189 | 33 |
| Washington... | 115 | 94 | 17 | 249 | 39,524 | 33.48 | 308 | 64 |
| West Virginia. | 56 | 48 | 6 | 93 | 14,330 | 29.95 | 84 | 14 |
| Wisconsin.... | 96 | 79 | 13 | 205 | 43,684 | 48.57 | 274 | 39 |
| Wyoming.... | 5 | 4 | 1 | 9 | 1,783 | 40.79 | 15 | 9 |
| **Total 1967-68.** | **5,549** | **4,336** | **894** | **10,960** | **$2,054,971** | **$42.10** | **$11,093** | **2,518** |

[1]Claimants whose base-period earnings or whose employment—covered by the unemployment insurance program—was sufficient to make them eligible for unemployment insurance benefits as provided by State law. [2]Based on number of first payments.

[3]Based on final payments. Some claimants shown, therefore, actually experienced their final week of compensable unemployment toward the end of the previous fiscal year but received their final payments in the current fiscal year. Similarly, some claimants who served their last week of compensable unemployment toward the end of the current fiscal year did not receive their final payment in this fiscal year and hence are not shown. A final week of compensable unemployment in a benefit year results in the exhaustion of benefit rights for the benefit year. Claimants who exhaust their benefit rights in one benefit year may be entitled to further benefits in the following benefit year.

[4]Excludes intrastate transitional claims to reflect more nearly instances of new unemployment. Includes claims filed by interstate claimants in the Virgin Islands.

[5]Adjusted for voided benefit checks and transfers under interstate combined wage plan.

[6]Sum of balance in State clearing accounts, benefit-payment accounts, and unemployment trust fund accounts maintained in the U. S. Treasury.

## How Unemployment Statistics Are Obtained
### Source: Bureau of Labor Statistics, U. S. Department of Labor

The main source of unemployment statistics in the United States is the Current Population Survey, a sample survey of households, conducted monthly since 1940. The material is collected and tabulated by the Bureau of the Census under contract with the Bureau of Labor Statistics, which analyzes and publishes the data in *Employment and Earnings and Monthly Report on the Labor Force.*

In this survey trained interviewers obtain information from approximately 50,000 households each month; the households form a probability sample representative of the entire civilian noninstitutional population. Sufficient information is obtained to classify persons 16 years of age and over as (1) employed (2) unemployed or (3) not in the labor force. The labor force is simply the total of the employed and the unemployed, and is com- monly referred to as the civilian labor force since it excludes the Armed Forces.

Under this system the unemployed consist of all civilians 16 years of age or older who did not work during the survey week (the week including the 12th of the month) but who looked for work in the previous 4 weeks, and were available for work during the survey week. Persons who never had a job are counted among the unemployed if they meet these criteria. Persons with jobs but on lay- off and those planning to start new jobs within 30 days are also classified as unemployed. The data on the unemployed are analyzed by sex, age, previous occupation and industry, duration of unemployment, and other characteristics. The unemployment rate is the percent of the labor force who are unemployed.

## Social and Rehabilitation Service

Source: Dept. of Health, Education and Welfare

A new agency, the Social and Rehabilitation Service, was established in the Department of Health, Education, and Welfare, Aug. 15, 1967, to strengthen and realign the former functions of the Vocational Rehabilitation Administration, the Administration on Aging, the Welfare Administration, and the Mental Retardation Division of the Bureau of Health Service, Public Health Service. Miss Mary E. Switzer, former Commissioner of Vocational Rehabilitation, was appointed Administrator.

The reorganization is designed to make possible a more unified attack on the problems of needy Americans, with special emphasis on the family and with a more concerted effort toward rehabilitation in the Department's social and welfare programs. A major goal is to give people who receive public assistance the help, the skills, and the incentives they need to become independent.

A Social and Rehabilitation Service Commissioner has been assigned to each of the 9 HEW regions and will supervise all programs and activities of the Service in his region and give approval to all state plans. This will enable states, communities, and voluntary private groups to establish closer working relationships with the Federal government on all SRS programs.

A large number of persons will benefit by the range of services now merged in SRS:

—About 7,600,000 persons (4% of the population) receive cash assistance at any given time under Federally-aided programs. These payments total $7.8 billion annually; 58% ($4.5 billion) comes from the Federal Government and the remainder from state and local governments.

—In 1967 200,000 persons were rehabilitated for gainful employment through vocational rehabilitation programs.

—Over 6,000,000 needy persons receive medical services each year through Federally-assisted programs, including the new Title XIX Medicaid program.

—Over 600,000 children receive child welfare services related to adoption, foster care, or neglect. An additional 4,000,000 dependent children of public assistance families will receive the same quality of child welfare services under the 1967 amendments to the Social Securities Act.

—Over 450,000 crippled children receive medical services each year with Federal assistance.

—More than 250,000 women received family planning help last year through Childrens Bureau programs.

—More than 700 projects assisted by the Administration on Aging provide services for many of the 19,000,000 Americans over 65.

The combined 1968 appropriations of the HEW components joined in the Social and Rehabilitation Service totalled $6.05 billion in Federal funds. The new agency is staffed by about 1,900 employees in the following 5 major program units:

**Rehabilitation Services Administration:** responsible for programs aiding the handicapped, disabled Social Security applicants, crippled children, the mentally retarded, and for services for the blind and the permanently and totally disabled.

**Children's Bureau:** responsible for studies and investigations of the status of children, and for Federal-State child welfare, maternal and child health and juvenile delinquency programs, for health services to school children, and for family and child welfare services.

**Administration on Aging:** responsible for administration of the Older Americans Act, and for collecting and disseminating information on the status of Older Americans, for services for the aged (including insurance and assistance beneficiaries), for maintaining standards for services to OAA beneficiaries and for the Foster Grandparent program.

**Medical Services Administration:** responsible for medical assistance services by State and local agencies, including Title XIX programs (Medicaid).

**Assistance Payments Administration:** responsible for the money payment aspects of public assistance programs (Aid to Families with Dependent Children, Old Age Assistance, Aid to the Blind, and Aid to the Permanently and Totally Disabled) and for the administration of Work Experience and Community Work Training programs.

A significant aspect of the new SRS is the separation of cash payments and social service functions in public assistance. This was done to offer greater opportunities for recipients to obtain social and other rehabilitation services which could lead them to self support and terminate their need for public financial aid.

## Recipients of Public Assistance and Money Payments

| Year | Old Age | Blind | Dis-abled | Families Head | Families Total | Children | General | Total Money Payments (in 1,000) |
|---|---|---|---|---|---|---|---|---|
| 1936–49......... | 28,949 | 1,023 | ... | 4,736 | 15,977 | 11,810 | 31,056 | $15,882,659 |
| 1950........... | 2,786 | 97 | 69 | 651 | 2,233 | 1,661 | 866 | 2,354,485 |
| 1951........... | 2,701 | 97 | 124 | 592 | 2,041 | 1,523 | 664 | 2,279,612 |
| 1952........... | 2,635 | 98 | 161 | 596 | 1,991 | 1,495 | 587 | 2,311,540 |
| 1953........... | 2,582 | 100 | 192 | 547 | 1,941 | 1,464 | 618 | 2,374,158 |
| 1954........... | 2,553 | 102 | 222 | 604 | 2,173 | 1,639 | 880 | 2,451,785 |
| 1955........... | 2,538 | 104 | 241 | 602 | 2,192 | 1,661 | 743 | 2,516,590 |
| 1956........... | 2,499 | 107 | 266 | 615 | 2,270 | 1,731 | 731 | 2,584,204 |
| 1957........... | 2,480 | 108 | 290 | 667 | 2,497 | 1,912 | 907 | 2,788,161 |
| 1958........... | 2,438 | 110 | 325 | 755 | 2,486 | 2,181 | 1,246 | 3,068,701 |
| 1959........... | 2,370 | 108 | 346 | 776 | 2,946 | 2,265 | 1,107 | 3,200,768 |
| 1960........... | 2,305 | 107 | 369 | 803 | 3,073 | 2,370 | 1,244 | 3,262,449 |
| 1961........... | 2,229 | 103 | 389 | 916 | 3,566 | 2,753 | 1,069 | 3,409,371 |
| 1962........... | 2,183 | 99 | 428 | 932 | 3,789 | 2,844 | 900 | 3,510,456 |
| 1963........... | 2,152 | 97 | 464 | 954 | 3,930 | 2,951 | 872 | 3,646,058 |
| 1964........... | 2,120 | 95 | 509 | 1,012 | 4,219 | 3,170 | 779 | 3,815,178 |
| 1965........... | 2,087 | 85 | 557 | 1,054 | 4,396 | 3,316 | 677 | 3,992,964 |
| 1966........... | 2,073 | 84 | 588 | 1,127 | 4,666 | 3,526 | 663 | 4,303,814 |

# BEST SELLING BOOKS IN 1968

(Listed according to frequency of citation in best-seller reports)

## General

1. *Our Crowd: The Great Jewish Families of New York*, Stephen Birmingham
2. *Between Parent and Child*, Dr. Haim G. Ginott
3. *Nicholas and Alexandra*, R. K. Massie
4. *The Naked Ape*, Desmond Morris
5. *The New Industrial State*, John Kenneth Galbraith
6. *At Ease: Stories I Tell to Friends*, Dwight David Eisenhower
7. *Rickenbacker*, Eddie Rickenbacker
8. *Iberia*, James A. Michener
9. *The Right People*, Stephen Birmingham
10. *The Double Helix*, James D. Watson
11. *The Money Game*, "Adam Smith"
12. *Memoirs, 1925-1950*, Geo. F. Kennan
13. *The Doctor's Quick Weight Loss Diet*, Erwin M. Stillman & Samm S. Baker
14. *Tolstoy*, Henri Troyat
15. *Or I'll Dress You In Mourning*, Larry Collins & Dominique Lapierre
16. *Gipsy Moth Circles the World*, Sir Francis Chichester
17. *The Rich and the Super-Rich*, Ferdinand Lundberg
18. *The French Chef Cookbook*, Julia Child
19. *The American Challenge*, J.-J. Servan Schreiber
20. *The Way Things Work: An Illustrated Encyclopedia of Technology*
21. *The Center*, Stewart Alsop
22. *The English*, David Frost, Antony Jay
23. *Kennedy & Johnson*, Evelyn Lincoln
24. *Report From Iron Mountain*, Lester Lewin
25. *The Electric Kool-Aid Acid Test*, Tom Wolfe
26. *The Case Against Congress*, Drew Pearson & Jack Anderson
27. *The Economics of Crisis*, Eliot Janeway
28. *Soul On Ice*, Eldridge Cleaver
29. *Thomas Wolfe*, Andrew Turnbull
30. *The Essence of Security*, Robert S. McNamara
31. *Black Rage*, William H. Grier & Price M. Cobbs
32. *A Mass For the Dead*, Wm. Gibson

## Fiction

1. *Topaz*, Leon Uris
2. *The Confessions of Nat Turner*, William Styron
3. *Rosemary's Baby*, Ira Levin
4. *The Chosen*, Chaim Potok
5. *Christy*, Catherine Marshall
6. *Vanished*, Fletcher Knebel
7. *Myra Breckinridge*, Gore Vidal
8. *Airport*, Arthur Hailey
9. *Couples*, John Updike
10. *The President's Plane is Missing*, Robert J. Serling
11. *The Gabriel Hounds*, Mary Stewart
12. *Testimony of Two Men*, Taylor Caldwell
13. *The Exhibitionist*, Henry Sutton
14. *The Tower of Babel*, Morris L. West
15. *True Grit*, Charles Portis
16. *Red Sky at Morning*, Richard Bradford
17. *The Instrument*, John O'Hara
18. *Heaven Help Us!*, Herbert Tarr
19. *Tunc*, Lawrence Durrell
20. *Where Eagles Dare*, Alistair MacLean
21. *The Queen's Confession*, Victoria Holt
22. *The Triumph*, John Kenneth Galbraith
23. *The Senator*, Drew Pearson
24. *The Salzburg Connection*, Helen MacInnes
25. *Preserve and Protect*, Allen Drury
26. *Tell Me How Long the Train's Been Gone*, James Baldwin

*One of 10 best-sellers in 1967 according to Publishers' Weekly.

## STATISTICS OF BOOK TRADE

The number of new books (titles) published in the U. S. fell from 30,050 in 1966 to 28,762 in 1967, (21,877 new books and 6,885 new editions) according to Publishers' Weekly. The lower figure, however, did not necessarily mean a decline in U. S. book publishing, but is accounted for, at least in part, by new counting procedures initiated by PW at the beginning of 1967. For example, multi-volume sets are now counted as individual books only if each volume in the set has a different title. Also, imported books are counted in the yearly total of new titles only if there is no more than a year's time between their publication abroad and the time they are available in the U. S. Accordingly, the number of imported books fell from 6,347 in 1966 to 4,852 in 1967 (4,107 new books and 745 new editions).

In 1966, the last year for which complete statistics were available, sales of all publishers totaled $2,295,000,000, an increase of about 13% over 1965. Hardcover book prices have risen 51% since the base period 1957-59, but rose only about 6 tenths of 1% during 1966-67.

By far the best selling book of 1967 was William Manchester's *Death of a President*, with over 500,000 copies sold. The best selling work of fiction in 1967 was a first novel, Elia Kazan's *The Arrangement*, which sold about 212,500 copies in bookstores.

*The Long Short Cut*, a suspense novel by Andrew Garve, published in 1967 by Harper & Row, was purported to be the first book (other than directories) set into type by a computer. Using the R.C.A. Videocomp and computer system, up to 600 characters a second were set, a speed 60 times greater than the fastest earlier methods of book type setting.

## Best Sellers of Government Printing Office

Of the 24,000 publications available at the Government Printing Office, Washington, D. C. 20402, these are the 15 best sellers. The 70,000,000 publications sold annually bring in $17,000,000 and net $7,000,000 for the Treasury.

| Title | Cost | Total | Title | Cost | Total |
|---|---|---|---|---|---|
| Infant Care | $0.20 | 14,308,789 | Your Social Security | $0.10 | 2,074,520 |
| Your Federal Income Tax | .60 | 10,923,036 | Rescue Breathing | .05 | 1,842,025 |
| Prenatal Care | .20 | 8,372,972 | Syphilis & Gonorrhea | .05 | 1,669,760 |
| Your Child From 1 to 6 | .20 | 6,389,722 | Postage Stamps of U. S. | 1.25 | 1,438,002 |
| Your Child from 6 to 12 | .25 | 3,015,815 | Breast Feeding | .10 | 1,428,011 |
| Tax Guide for Small Business | .60 | 2,606,056 | Septic Tank Care | .05 | 1,351,090 |
| Strictly for Teenagers | .05 | 2,446,350 | Food for Fitness | .05 | 1,178,057 |
| | | | Adolescent in Your Family | .25 | 1,154,772 |

# THEATER—OPERA—FILMS
## Broadway's Principal Events of 1967-68

**PLAYS PRODUCED BEFORE OCT. 1, 1967, CLOSED BEFORE OCT. 15, 1968; OR CONTINUING**
*Still running Oct. 15, 1968; M designates musicals; stars listed appeared in original cast*

| Production | Stars | Opened | Closed | Run |
|---|---|---|---|---|
| Hello Dolly (M) | Carol Channing, David Burns | Jan. 16, 1964 | | 1,964* |
| Fiddler on the Roof (M) | Zero Mostel, Maria Karnilova | Sept. 22, 1964 | | 1,694* |
| Man of La Mancha (M) | Richard Kiley, Joan Diener | Nov. 22, 1965 | | 1,206* |
| Cactus Flower | Lauren Bacall, Barry Nelson | Dec. 8, 1965 | | 1,188* |
| Mame (M) | Angela Lansbury, Frankie Michaels | May 24, 1966 | | 998* |
| The Apple Tree (M) | Barbara Harris, Larry Blyden | Oct. 20, 1966 | Nov. 25, 1967 | 463 |
| Don't Drink the Water | Kay Medford, Lou Jacobi | Nov. 17, 1966 | Apr. 20, 1968 | 588 |
| Cabaret (M) | Jill Haworth, Jack Gilford, Joel Grey | Nov. 20, 1966 | | 792* |
| I Do! I Do! (M) | Mary Martin, Robert Preston | Dec. 5, 1966 | June 15, 1968 | 584 |
| Black Comedy | Geraldine Page, Lynn Redgrave | Jan. 12, 1967 | Dec. 2, 1967 | 337 |
| You Know I Can't Hear You... | Martin Balsam, Eileen Heckart | Mar. 13, 1967 | | 662* |
| Ilya Darling (M) | Melina Mercouri, Orson Bean | Apr. 11, 1967 | Jan. 13, 1968 | 319 |
| Hallelujah Baby (M) | Leslie Uggams, Robert Hooks | Apr. 26, 1967 | Jan. 13, 1968 | 293 |

## PLAYS PRODUCED OCT. 1, 1967 TO OCT. 15, 1968

| Play | Stars | Opened | Run |
|---|---|---|---|
| **1967** | | | |
| The Birthday Party | Ruth White, Henderson Forsythe | Oct. 3 | 126 |
| A Minor Adjustment | William Redfield, Austin Willis, Joan Darling | Oct. 6 | 3 |
| Johnny No-Trump | Pat Hingle, Don Scardino | Oct. 8 | 1 |
| After the Rain | Alec McCowen, Nancy Marchand | Oct. 9 | 64 |
| By George | Max Adrian | Oct. 12 | 13 |
| Daphne in Cottage D | Sandy Dennis, William Daniels | Oct. 15 | 40 |
| Rosencrantz and Guildenstern etc. | Brian Murray, John Wood | Oct. 16 | 414* |
| There's a Girl in My Soup | Gig Young, Barbara Ferris, Rita Gam | Oct. 18 | 322 |
| What Did We Do Wrong? | Paul Ford, Phillipa Bevans | Oct. 22 | 48 |
| Henry, Sweet Henry (M) | Don Ameche, Carol Bruce | Oct. 24 | 80 |
| More Stately Mansions | Ingrid Bergman, Arthur Hill, Colleen Dewhurst | Nov. 1 | 143 |
| The Trial of Lee Harvey Oswald | Peter Masterson, Dan Priest | Nov. 5 | 9 |
| The 90-Day Mistress | Dyan Cannon, Ruth Ford, Walter Abel | Nov. 6 | 24 |
| Halfway Up the Tree | Anthony Quayle, Eileen Herlie | Nov. 7 | 64 |
| The Promise | Ian McShane, Eileen Atkins | Nov. 14 | 20 |
| Something Different | Bob Dishy, Claudia McNeil | Nov. 28 | 99 |
| Everything in the Garden | Barry Nelson, Barbara Bel Geddes | Nov. 29 | 84 |
| How Now, Dow Jones (M) | Marlyn Mason, Anthony Roberts | Dec. 7 | 213 |
| Spofford | Melvyn Douglas, Pert Kelton, Barbara Britton | Dec. 14 | 202 |
| Brief Lives | Roy Dotrice | Dec. 20 | 16 |
| How to Be a Jewish Mother | Molly Picon, Godfrey Cambridge | Dec. 28 | 21 |
| **1968** | | | |
| Staircase | Eli Wallach, Milo O'Shea | Jan. 10 | 61 |
| Before You Go | Marian Seldes, Gene Troobnick | Jan. 11 | 29 |
| The Prime of Miss Jean Brodie | Zoe Caldwell, Lennox Milne | Jan. 16 | 309* |
| The Happy Time (M) | Robert Goulet, David Wayne | Jan. 18 | 286 |
| I Never Sang for My Father | Hal Holbrook, Lillian Gish, Teresa Wright | Jan. 25 | 124 |
| Darling of the Day (M) | Vincent Price, Patricia Routledge | Jan. 27 | 32 |
| Avanti! | Robert Reed, Betty von Furstenberg | Jan. 31 | 21 |
| A Day in the Death of Joe Egg | Albert Finney, Zena Walker | Feb. 1 | 154 |
| Golden Rainbow (M) | Steve Lawrence, Eydie Gorme | Feb. 4 | 283* |
| The Price | Pat Hingle, Arthur Kennedy, Kate Reid | Feb. 7 | 284* |
| Plaza Suite | George C. Scott, Maureen Stapleton | Feb. 14 | 278* |
| Carry Me Back to Morningside Hgts. | Louis Gossett, Cicely Tyson | Feb. 27 | 7 |
| Portrait Of A Queen | Dorothy Tutin, Dennis King | Feb. 28 | 61 |
| Here's Where I Belong (M) | Paul Rogers, Walter McGinn | Mar. 3 | 1 |
| The Guide | Zia Mohyeddin, Titos Vandis | Mar. 7 | 5 |
| Weekend | John Forsythe, Kim Hunter, Carol Cole, Rosemary Murphy | Mar. 13 | 21 |
| Loot | Liam Redmond, George Rose | Mar. 18 | 23 |
| The Seven Descents of Myrtle | Harry Guardino, Estelle Parsons, Brian Bedford | Mar. 28 | 29 |
| The Education of Hyman Kaplan (M) | Tom Bosley, Gary Krawford, Hal Linden, Barbara Minkus | Apr. 4 | 28 |
| George M! (M) | Joel Grey, Jerry Dodge | Apr. 10 | 214* |
| Mike Downstairs | Dane Clark, Tom Pedi | Apr. 18 | 4 |
| I'm Solomon (M) | Dick Shawn, Karen Morrow, Salome Jens | Apr. 23 | 7 |
| The Exercise | Stephen Joyce, Anne Jackson | Apr. 24 | 5 |
| Hair (M) | James Rado, Gerome Ragni | Apr. 29 | 194* |
| Soldiers | John Colicos, Tony Church | May 1 | 21 |
| New Faces '68 (revue) | Madeline Kahn, Robert Klein | May 2 | 52 |
| Happiness is Just a Little Thing Called a Rolls-Royce | Pat Harrington, John McGiver | May 11 | 1 |
| The Only Game in Town | Barry Nelson, Tammy Grimes, Leo Genn | May 20 | 16 |
| Lovers | Art Carney, Anna Manahan | July 25 | 93* |
| Lovers & Other Strangers | Renee Taylor | Sept. 18 | 30* |
| The Cuban Thing | Rip Torn, Jane White | Sept. 24 | 1 |
| Woman Is My Idea | John Heffernan, Hugh Marlowe | Sept. 25 | 5 |
| The Man in the Glass Booth | Donald Pleasence | Sept. 26 | 21* |
| Noel Coward's Sweet Potato (M) | Dorothy Loudon, George Grizzard | Sept. 29 | 18* |
| The Great White Hope | James Earl Jones, Jane Alexander | Oct. 3 | 13* |
| The Flip Side | David McCallum, Monica Evans | Oct. 10 | 6* |

## Long Run Plays

### PLAYS IN NEW YORK
*Still running Oct. 15, 1968*

| | | |
|---|---|---|
| Life With Father | 3,213 | |
| Tobacco Road | 3,182 | |
| My Fair Lady | 2,717 | |
| Abie's Irish Rose | 2,327 | |
| Oklahoma! | 2,246 | |
| *Hello Dolly | 1,964 | |
| South Pacific | 1,925 | |
| Harvey | 1,775 | |
| *Fiddler on the Roof | 1,694 | |
| Born Yesterday | 1,643 | |
| Mary, Mary | 1,572 | |
| Voice of the Turtle | 1,558 | |

| | | |
|---|---|---|
| Barefoot in the Park | 1,532 |
| Arsenic and Old Lace | 1,444 |
| The Sound of Music | 1,442 |
| How to Succeed in Business Without Really Trying | 1,416 |
| Hellzapoppin | 1,404 |
| The Music Man | 1,376 |
| Funny Girl | 1,348 |
| Angel Street | 1,295 |
| Lightnin' | 1,291 |
| The King and I | 1,246 |

| | | |
|---|---|---|
| *Man of La Mancha | 1,206 |
| Guys and Dolls | 1,200 |
| *Cactus Flower | 1,188 |
| Mister Roberts | 1,157 |
| Annie Get Your Gun | 1,147 |
| The Seven Year Itch | 1,141 |
| Pins and Needles | 1,108 |
| Kiss Me Kate | 1,077 |
| The Pajama Game | 1,061 |
| Teahouse of August Moon | 1,027 |
| Damn Yankees | 1,019 |
| Never Too Late | 1,007 |

## PLAYS IN LONDON
### *Still running Oct. 10, 1968

| | | | | | |
|---|---|---|---|---|---|
| *The Mousetrap | 6,594 | Boeing-Boeing | 2,036 | Our Boys | 1,362 |
| *Black and White | | Blithe Spirit | 1,997 | Knights of Madness | 1,361 |
| Minstrels | 3,978 | Worm's Eye View | 1,745 | Maid of the Mountains | 1,352 |
| Oliver | 2,811 | Me and My Girl | 1,646 | Arsenic and Old Lace | 1,337 |
| Sound of Music | 2,383 | Together Again | 1,566 | The Farmer's Wife | 1,329 |
| Salad Days | 2,282 | Seagulls over Sorrento | 1,551 | Annie Get Your Gun | 1,304 |
| My Fair Lady | 2,281 | Oklahoma! | 1,543 | One for the Pot | 1,151 |
| Chu Chin Chow | 2,238 | Charley's Aunt | 1,466 | | |
| The Boy Friend | 2,082 | The Beggar's Opera | 1,463 | | |

# U. S. Opera Survey
### Reviews of Activities of Opera Companies in Twenty-One U. S. Cities

The number of operatic performances in the U. S. held fairly steady in the 1967-1968 season with 5,222 performances of 348 works, as against 5,487 performances of 335 works in the 1966-1967 season, according to Opera News and Central Opera Service. The most performed opera was The Barber of Seville with 299 performances; Hansel and Gretel had 156 and La Boheme had 143. However, the most performed opera by all groups, including high schools and church groups, was, for the 15th consecutive year, Menotti's Amahl and the Night Visitors with 368 performances.

The U. S. had 297 opera companies and 325 colleges with productive opera departments in 1967-68. Colleges continued to pioneer the production of less well known works of intrinsic value which would rarely, if ever, get a hearing in the commercial or civic theater. For instance, Virginia's Lynchburg College performed Monteverdi's Orfeo, Northern Illinois Univ. gave Telemann's Pimpinone and Cornell produced Cesti's Oronthea.

**METROPOLITAN OPERA ASSN.,** New York, opened its 84th season Sept. 16, 1968, and was scheduled to close Apr. 19, 1969. The season, the third at the Metropolitan Opera House in Lincoln Center, was highlighted by the presentation of 4 new productions: Puccini's Tosca, Strauss' Der Rosenkavalier, Verdi's Il Trovatore, and Wagner's Das Rheingold, the second installment in a new Ring Cycle, conducted by Herbert von Karajan. The repertory also included: La Sonnambula, Wozzeck, Carmen, Peter Grimes, Adriana Lecouvreur, Lucia di Lammermoor, Faust, Romeo et Juliette, Don Giovanni, La Boheme, Turandot, Il Barbiere di Siviglia, Die Frau ohne Schatten, Don Carlo, Rigoletto, Simon Boccanegra, Die Meistersinger and Die Walkure. Rudolf Bing is general manager. Singers and conductors (*designates new artist): SOPRANOS: Karola Agay*, Lucine Amara, Karan Armstrong, Martina Arroyo, Radmila Bakocevic, Colette Boky, Phyllis Brill, Montserrat Caballé, Clarice Carson, Joy Clements, Régine Crespin, Phyllis Curtin, Mary Curtis-Verna, Gianna d'Angelo, Ina Delcampo, Judith DePaul, Loretta Di Franco, Jean Fenn, Mirella Freni, Reri Grist, Gundula Janowitz, Raina Kabaivanska, Margaret Kalil, Dorothy Kirsten, Evelyn Lear, Brenda Lewis, *Marion Lippert, Pilar Lorengar, *Simone Mangelsdorff, Anna Moffo, *Edda Moser, Birgit Nilsson, Carlotta Ordassy, *Rita Orlandi, Roberta Peters, Jeannette Pilou, Mary Ellen Pracht, Leontyne Price, Judith Raskin, *Liselotte Rebmann, Leonie Rysanek, Milka Stojanovic, Teresa Stratas, Lilian Sukis, Joan Sutherland, Renata Tebaldi, Gabriella Tucci, Patricia Welting, *Teresa Zylis-Gara. MEZZO-SOPRANOS AND CONTRALTOS: Marcia Baldwin, Teresa Berganza, Grace Bumbry, Nedda Casei, Elena Cernei, Lili Chookasian, Fiorenza Cossotto, Irene Dalis, Mignon Dunn, Rosalind Elias, *Judith Forst, Joann Grillo, Rosalind Hupp, Gwendolyn Killebrew, Shirley Love, Christa Ludwig, Jean Madeira, Mildred Miller, Louise Pearl, Nell Rankin, Regina Resnik, *Anna Reynolds, *Josephine Veasey, *Shirley Verrett. TENORS: John Alexander, Luigi Alva, Charles Anthony, Giacomo Aragall*, Carlo Bergonzi, Gabor Carelli, Mariano Caruso, William Cochran*, Franco Corelli, Enrico DiGiuseppe*, Placido Domingo*, Loren Driscoll, Paul Franke, Nicolai Gedda, James King, Sándor Kónya, Flaviano Labò, Karl Liebl, *Jerome LoMonaco, *Rod MacWherter, James McCracken, Barry Morell, Robert Nagy, William Olvis, *Luciano Pavarotti, Bruno Prevedi, Gianni Raimondi, Robt. Schmorr, Peter Schreier, Geo. Shirley, *Gerhard Stolze, Richard Tucker, Andrea Velis, Jon Vickers, *Erwin Wohlfahrt. BARITONES: Gabriel Bacquier, Walter Berry, Ron Bottcher, Gene Boucher, Russell Christopher, Anselmo Colzani, Karl Dönch, William Dooley, Otto Edelmann, Geraint Evans, Robert Goodloe, Frank Guarrera, Clifford Harvout, *Zoltán Kelemen, *Rudolf Knoll, Tom Krause, Theodore Lambrinos, Cornell MacNeil, Morley Meredith, Robert Merrill, Sherrill Milnes, John Reardon, Mario Sereni, Thomas Stewart, Theo. Uppman, Wm. Walker.

BASSES: Theo Adam*, Lorenzo Alvary, Fernando Corena, Justino Díaz, Ezio Flagello, Nicolai Ghiauroy, Bonaldo Giaiotti, Donald Gramm, Jerome Hines, John Macurdy, Raymond Michalski, Paul Plishka, Karl Ridderbusch, Norman Scott, Louis Sgarro, Cesare Siepi, *Martti Talvela, Giorgio Tozzi, Ernst Wiemann. CONDUCTORS: Claudio Abbado*, Kurt Adler, Franz Allers, Karl Böhm, Richard Bonynge, Fausto Cleva, Colin Davis, *Carlo Franci, Herbert von Karajan, Alain Lombard, Zubin Mehta, Francesco Molinari-Pradelli, Joseph Rosenstock, George Schick, Silvio Variso.

**METROPOLITAN OPERA NATIONAL AUDITIONS,** New York. Nine National Finalists were to compete for a Metropolitan Opera contract and a number of other awards at the Metropolitan Opera House, Nov. 17, 1968. The 9 finalists were winners of regional contests held throughout the U. S. and Canada, Puerto Rico and Australia in which approximately 2,000 singers were auditioned. The finalists were Jacquelyn Benson, Patricia Craig, Helen-Kay Eberley, Glenys Fowles, Jesye Norman, Nancy Shade, Ruth Weltin, Loretta Ziskin (all sopranos) and Gwen Jones, mezzo-soprano.

**NEW YORK CITY OPERA CO.,** New York State Theater, Lincoln Center, N. Y., opened its third season at Lincoln Center (after 41 seasons at the City Center) with Puccini's Il Trittico on Sept. 19. The 1968 repertory included a new production of Gounod's Faust and the world premiere of Weisgall's Nine Rivers From Jordan. Other operas included Barber of Seville, Bomarzo, La Boheme, Cavalleria Rusticana, Pagliacci, Julius Caesar, Le Coq D'Or, Magic Flute, Manon, Tosca and La Traviata. The fall season was to conclude on Nov. 17. The winter season (Feb. 17-Apr. 20, 1969) had scheduled The Turn of the Screw, Madama Butterfly and The Ballad of Baby Doe. Julius Rudel is general director and John S. White is associate director.

**BALTIMORE CIVIC OPERA CO.,** Baltimore, Md., presented 3 operas in its 1968-69 season. Opening night, Oct. 24, featured Verdi's Otello with Robert Nagy, Mary Curtis Verna and Louis Quilico. Other operas scheduled were: Puccini's Manon Lescaut with Raina Kabaivanski and John Reardon; and Puccini's Tosca with Jeannine Crader, Chester Ludgin and Bernabe Marti. Rosa Ponselle is artistic director and the Baltimore Symphony Orchestra accompanies each performance. The season was to be concluded Apr. 28, 1969.

**OPERA COMPANY OF BOSTON,** Boston, Mass., scheduled 4 American premieres for its 11th season: The original versions of Strauss' Ariadne Auf Naxos and Verdi's Macbeth; Bartok's ballet The Wooden Prince performed with his Bluebeard's Castle and Miraculous Mandarin; and Roger Sessions' Montezuma. A fifth production was to be Mozart's The Marriage of Figaro. Sarah Caldwell is artistic director.

**CENTRAL CITY OPERA HOUSE ASSN.,** Central City, Colo., a summer operation, presented 5 weeks

of Gilbert and Sullivan performed by the D'Oyly Carte Co. from June to Aug., 1968.

**CINCINNATI SUMMER OPERA,** Cincinnati, Ohio, presented, during summer 1968, 10 operas for its 48th annual season. Opening June 26 with Il Trovatore, the repertory also included The Elixir of Love, Madama Butterfly, Manon, Salome, Don Pasquale, Lucia di Lammermoor, Carmen, La Traviata, and The Tales of Hoffmann, which closed July 28, 1968. Styrk Orwoll is general manager.

**DALLAS CIVIC OPERA,** Dallas, Tex., scheduled the opening of its 1968 season Nov. 8 with Offenbach's Orpheus in the Underworld with Graziella Porretta and Loren Driscoll singing the leading roles and Jacques d'Amboise and Melissa Hayden the ballet soloists. Otello was to follow on Nov. 15, starring John Vickers and Victoria de los Angeles. The regular season concluded with Donizetti's Anna Bolena, featuring Elena Suliotis and Ezio Flagello. A special Dorothy Kirsten Concert was scheduled for Nov. 30. Lawrence Kelly is general manager.

**FORT WORTH OPERA ASSN.** was to open its 1968-69 season Nov. 21 with La Traviata with Maralin Niska and Dominic Cossa. Three other operas scheduled were Don Pasquale with Spiro Malas and Joy Clements; Turandot with Elinor Ross and Flaviano Labo; and Romeo and Juliet with John Alexander and Karan Armstrong, which was scheduled to close the season Apr. 20, 1969. Rudolph Kruger is musical director.

**HOUSTON GRAND OPERA,** Houston Tex., scheduled 26 performances of 5 operas, 11 of them student matinees, for its 1968-1969 season. The season was to open Oct. 29 with La Boheme, featuring Teresa Stratas and Maralin Niska. Also to be presented were Salome with Nell Rankin, The Barber of Seville with Sherrill Milnes and Anne Elgar, Don Carlo with Placido Domingo and Raina Kabaivanska, and to conclude the season on May 12, 1969, Don Quixote with Norman Treigle. Walter Herbert is the conductor and director.

**INDIANA UNIV. OPERA THEATER,** Bloomington, Ind., opened its 1968-1969 season Oct. 12 with Rossini's The Italian Girl in Algiers. This was to be followed by Verdi's La Traviata, Mozart's The Marriage of Figaro, Stravinsky's The Rake's Progress, Tchaikovsky's The Queen of Spades and Wagner's Parsifal, which was to close the season Mar. 23.

**LYRIC OPERA OF CHICAGO,** Chicago, Ill., scheduled 9 operas, including a double-bill of Stravinsky operas, Le Rossignol and Oedipus Rex, for its 1968 season. Salome was presented opening night Sept. 27, followed by Norma, Tosca, Falstaff, A Masked Ball, Don Pasquale and Manon Lescaut starring Renata Tebaldi, which was to close the season Dec. 14.

**PHILADELPHIA GRAND OPERA CO.,** Philadelphia, Pa., scheduled 8 operas for the 1968-1969 season including the world premiere of Jericho Road by Pietro Aria on Mar. 12, 1969. Carmen was performed opening evening, Oct. 10, with Rosalind Elias and Richard Tucker. Other operas billed were Aida, La Boheme, Lucia di Lammermoor with Roberta Peters, La Traviata with Gabriella Tucci, I Pagliacci, and Il Trovatore, both with Richard Tucker, which was to close the season Apr. 18, 1969.

**PHILADELPHIA LYRIC OPERA CO.,** Philadelphia, Pa., opened its 1968-1969 season Oct. 22 with Bellini's I Capuletti E Montecchi, with Renata Scotto. The repertory also included: La Boheme, Lakme with Joan Sutherland, Madama Butterfly with Martina Arroyo, Lucrezia Borgia with Montserrat Caballe and John Alexander, and Tosca with Dorothy Kirsten, which was scheduled to close the season Mar. 25, 1969.

**PITTSBURGH OPERA CO.,** Pittsburgh, Pa., scheduled 6 operas for its 30th season, 1968-1969. The season opened Oct. 24 with Rigoletto. This was to be followed by Samson Et Dalila with Mignon Dunn, La Boheme with Heather Thomson, Cavalleria Rusticana with Edith Lang, Pagliacci with Gianni Savelli; Le Nozze Di Figaro starring Roberta Peters was to close the season Apr. 12, 1969. Richard Karp is general and musical director.

**SAN ANTONIO SYMPHONY SOCIETY,** San Antonio, Tex., was to celebrate its 25th anniversary with its annual Grand Opera Festival in March, 1969. The Festival scheduled 4 operas: Faust with Norman Treigle, Placido Domingo and Beverly Sills; Il Trovatore with Montserrat Caballe; Turandot with Birgit Nilsson and Richard Tucker; and Lucia di Lammermoor with Roberta Peters.

**SAN DIEGO OPERA,** San Diego, Calif., presented Rigoletto Oct. 17, as the first of 3 operas scheduled for its 1968-1969 season. The leading roles were sung by Peter Glossop and Anne Elgar. Remaining productions were La Boheme with John Stewart and Lee Venora and Massenet's Don Quixote with Norman Treigle and Nedda Casei, which was to close the season Apr. 26, 1969. Walter Herbert is artistic director and conductor.

**SAN FRANCISCO OPERA,** San Francisco, Calif., opened its 46th season Sept. 13, 1968, with Verdi's Ernani, starring Leontyne Price. Other productions included Il Barbiere di Siviglia, Les Troyens, Die Walkure, Madama Butterfly, Schoenberg's, Erwartung, Weill's Royal Palace, Milhaud's Christopher Columbus, Il Travatore, Wozzeck, Lucia di Lammermoor, Salome, Don Giovanni, Turandot, and Fra Diavolo. The fall season was scheduled to end Dec. 1, 1968. From Mar. 1 to 29, 1969, the Music Center Opera Assn. of Los Angeles, in conjunction with the San Francisco Opera, scheduled 10 operas. This is the first season in a plan to merge eventually the operatic operations of both cities. Kurt Herbert Adler is general director and Howard K. Skinner is manager.

**SANTA FE OPERA,** Santa Fe, N. M., was destroyed by fire July 27, 1967. A new open-air opera house was scheduled for completion in time for the opening of the 1968 season on July 2, 1968, with a production of Madama Butterfly. The repertory included two American premieres, The Bassarids by Hans Werner Henze and Die Jacobsleiter by Arnold Schoenberg, in addition to Persephone, The Magic Flute, La Traviata, The Elixir of Love and Der Rosenkavalier. John Crosby is the general director.

**ST. LOUIS MUNICIPAL OPERA,** St. Louis, Mo., one of America's most famous summer theaters, presented a varied repertory for the 1968 season. The first evening opened with My Fair Lady. This was followed by The Pajama Game, Annie Get Your Gun, The Merry Widow, Brigadoon, Carousel, Call Me Madam, Show Boat, The Wizard of Oz, The Sound of Music and Hello Dolly. America's oldest summer musical theater, the St. Louis Municipal Opera presented its first performance June 15, 1919. Since that time, the theater has given over 230 different comic and light operas, operettas and musical comedies. The group that founded the theater believed that it should belong to all the people of St. Louis and thus they decided not to charge admission for a portion of the seats. Today, approximately 1,500 seats are free of charge. The total seating capacity of the outdoor amphitheater in Forest Park is 12,000.

**ST. PAUL CIVIC OPERA ASSN.,** St. Paul, Minn., was scheduled to open its 1968-1969 season Dec. 14, with Hansel and Gretel. The second half of the season was to present Manon Lescaut, and conclude on May 3 with a double-bill consisting of De Falla's two-act opera La Vida Breve and his two-act ballet El Sombrero De Tres Picos.

**SEATTLE OPERA ASSN.,** Seattle, Wash., opened its 1968-1969 season with Aida Sept. 11 and continued with Giordano's Andrea Chenier starring Franco Corelli; Der Rosenkavalier featuring Regine Crespin and Regina Sarfaty; Tosca presenting Dorothy Kirsten and Cornell MacNeil in the leading roles; and L'Elisir d'Amore, which was to close the season May 3, 1969. Glynn Ross is gen. dir.

**SHREVEPORT SYMPHONY SOCIETY,** Shreveport, La., scheduled 3 operas for its 1968-1969 season. La Traviata, was performed opening night, Nov. 26, Poulenc's La Voix Humaine to follow in Feb. and the season was to close with the Barber of Seville Apr. 16, 1969. John Shenaut is musical director and Joe V. Graber is manager.

**TULSA OPERA,** Tulsa, Okla., opened its 1968-1969 season Nov. 7 with Rigoletto starring Roberta Peters as Gilda and Sesto Bruscantini as Rigoletto. As a Christmas delight, Hansel and Gretel was to be performed with Marija Kova and Lee Venora in the title roles. The season was scheduled to close Mar. 13, 1969, with Die Fledermaus featuring Eileen Schauler as Rosalinda.

# Movies of the Year (Oct. 1, 1967, to Oct. 1, 1968)

## Selected and Rated by the New York Daily News Film Critics

While movie fans have complained bitterly, justifiably, of pornography and violence on the screen, there are still many fine films that have eschewed these two undesirable elements.

The fiscal year, October 1967 to October 1968, has flourished at the box office, as good or better financially as the previous year, the record breaker in motion picture history. Available are clean films of various types that make paying customers glad they spent their money for appealing entertainment.

*The Odd Couple* has made millions of movie goers happy. And is still doing so everywhere it is shown. *The Graduate*, a more sophisticated comedy, may, as a money maker, come just under the big two of all times, *Sound of Music* and *Gone With the Wind*. A phenomenal success all over the world is *2001—A Space Odyssey*, a grand spectacle that appeals especially to men and boys.

*Planet of the Apes* was the big surprise of the year, popular with all ages. *Guess Who's Coming to Dinner*, an important contribution to motion pictures, is among the year's successes. Sidney Poitier, one of its stars, who has since made his own film, *For Love of Ivy*, is the actor of the year. Paul Newman with the public here and abroad. Katharine Hepburn, Oscar winner for *Guess Who's Coming to Dinner*, is the actress of the year. And watch out for Joanne Woodward with the same distinction next year.

*Doctor Doolittle*, a splendid musical made primarily for children, is a financial disappointment while, on the other side of the coin, the sordid melodrama, *Valley of the Dolls*, torn to shreds by the New York Film Critics, is in the big money class. Three foreign films worth mentioning are *Closely Watched Trains*, from Czechoslovakia, *The Two of Us*, from France and *War and Peace*, a magnificent production of Tolstoy's classic, from Russia.

The Fall season started off in New York City with a unique drama, *Rachel, Rachel* and the stunning, wonderful musical, *Funny Girl*. And the greatest of them all, *Gone With the Wind*, is being released all over the country, every scene re-colored and for the first time on wide screen with stereophonic sound.

Listed below, alphabetically, are films rated by The New York Daily News star system. ★★★★ is for excellent; ★★★½★, very good; ★★★, good; ★★½★, mediocre; ★★, fair; ★½★, poor; ★ very poor. Documentaries, such as *Survival 1967*, do not receive stars because they are photographic records of people and places, not fictional stories with actors playing the roles. Included are foreign films of merit.

Wanda Hale
N. Y. Daily News
Movie Editor and Critic

| Movie | Star rating | Stars | Director |
|---|---|---|---|
| Anniversary, The | ★★★ | Bette Davis | Roy Ward Baker |
| Bedazzled | ★★★ | Peter Cook, Dudley Moore | Stanley Donen |
| Camelot | ★★★½★ | Richard Harris, Vanessa Redgrave | Joshua Logan |
| Chappaqua | ★★½★ | Jean-Louis Barrault | Conrad Rooks |
| Charly | ★★★½★ | Cliff Robertson, Claire Bloom | Ralph Nelson |
| Charlie Bubbles | ★★★½★ | Albert Finney | Albert Finney |
| Closely Watched Trains | ★★★ | Vaclav Neckar, Jitka Bendova | Jiri Menzel |
| Comedians, The | ★★½★ | Elizabeth Taylor, Richard Burton | Peter Glenville |
| Cool Hand Luke | ★★★½★ | Paul Newman, George Kennedy | Stuart Rosenberg |
| Devil's Brigade, The | ★★★½★ | William Holden, Cliff Robertson | Andrew McLaglen |
| Dr. Doolittle | ★★★★ | Rex Harrison, Samantha Eggar | Richard Fleischer |
| Dr. Faustus | ★★★ | Elizabeth Taylor, Richard Burton | R. Burton and Nevill Coghill |
| Duffy | ★★★ | James Coburn, James Mason | Robert Parrish |
| Elvira Madigan | ★★★ | Pia Degermark, Thommy Berggren | Bo Wilderberg |
| Far From the Madding Crowd | ★★★★ | Julie Christie, Terence Stamp | Schlesinger |
| For Love of Ivy | ★★★ | Sidney Poitier, Abbey Lincoln | Daniel Mann |
| Fox, The | ★★★★ | Sandy Dennis, Keir Dullea | Mark Rydell |
| Funny Girl | ★★★★ | Barbra Streisand, Omar Sharif | William Wyler |
| Gone With the Wind | ★★★★ | Clark Gable, Vivien Leigh | Victor Fleming |
| Graduate, The | ★★★½★ | Anne Bancroft, Dustin Hoffman | Mike Nichols |
| Green Berets, The | ★★★ | John Wayne, David Janssen | John Wayne & Ray Kellogg |
| Guess Who's Coming to Dinner | ★★★★ | Spencer Tracy, Katharine Hepburn, Sidney Poitier | Stanley Kramer |
| Hagbard and Signe | ★★★ | Gitte Haenning, Oleg Vidov | Gabriel Axel |
| Half a Sixpence | ★★½★ | Tommy Steele, Julia Foster | George Sidney |
| Happiest Millionaire, The | ★★★★ | Fred MacMurray, Tommy Steele | Norman Tokar |
| Heart Is a Lonely Hunter, The | ★★★★ | Alan Arkin, Sondra Locke | Robert Ellis Miller |
| Here We Go 'Round the Mulberry Bush | ★★★½★ | Barry Evans, Judy Geeson | Clive Donner |
| Hot Millions | ★★★★ | Peter Ustinov, Maggie Smith | Eric Till |
| Hour of the Wolf | ★★★ | Liv Ullmann, Max Von Sydow | Ingmar Bergman |
| I'll Never Forget What's 'Isname | ★★½★ | Orson Welles, Oliver Reed | Michael Winner |
| In Cold Blood | ★★★★ | Robert Blake, Scott Wilson | Richard Brooks |
| Interlude | ★★★ | Oskar Werner, Barbara Ferris | Kevin Billington |
| Isabel | ★★★½★ | Beneviev Bujold | Paul Almond |
| Jungle Book, The | ★★★ | Phil Harris, Sebastian Cabot | Wolfgang Reitherman |
| Legend of Lylah Clare, The | ★ | Elsa Brinkmann, Kim Novak | Robert Aldrich |
| Lemmonade Joe | ★★★ | Carl Fiala, Olinka Berova | Oldrich Lipsky |
| Les Carabiniers | ★★★ | Genevieve Galea | Jean-Luc Godard |
| Live for Life | ★★½★ | Yves Montand, Candice Bergen | Claude Lelouch |
| Long Day's Dying, The | ★★★½★ | David Hemmings, Tom Bell | Peter Collinson |
| Madigan | ★★★½★ | Richard Widmark, Henry Fonda | Donald Siegel |
| Matter of Innocence, A | ★★★★ | Hayley Mills, Trevor Howard | Guy Green |
| No Way to Treat a Lady | ★★★½★ | Rod Steiger, Lee Remick | Jack Smight |
| Odd Couple, The | ★★★★ | Jack Lemmon, Walter Matthau | Gene Sacks |
| Our Mother's House | ★★★½★ | Dirk Bogarde, Susannah York | Jack Clayton |
| Planet of the Apes | ★★★½★ | Charlton Heston, Roddy McDowall | Franklin Schaffner |

| Movie | Star rating | Stars | Director |
|---|---|---|---|
| Poor Cow | ★★★½★ | Terence Stamp, Carol White | Kenneth Loach |
| Producers, The | ★★★★ | Zero Mostel, Gene Wilder | Mel Brooks |
| Prudence and the Pill | ★★★★ | Deborah Kerr, David Niven | Fielder Cook |
| Rachel, Rachel | ★★★★ | Joanne Woodward, Estelle Parsons | Paul Newman |
| Reflections In A Golden Eye | ★★½★ | Elizabeth Taylor, Marlon Brando | John Huston |
| Rosemary's Baby | ★★★½★ | Mia Farrow, John Cassavetes | Roman Polanski |
| Rough Night In Jericho, A | ★★★½★ | Dean Martin, George Peppard | Arnold Laven |
| Scalphunters, The | ★★★★ | Burt Lancaster, Shelley Winters | Sydney Pollack |
| Sebastian | ★★★½★ | Dirk Bogarde, Susannah York | David Greene |
| Secret War of Harry Frigg, The | ★★★★ | Paul Newman, Sylva Koscina | Jack Smight |
| Smashing Time | ★★★½★ | Rita Tushingham, Lynn Redgrave | Desmond Davis |
| Stranger Returns, The | ★ | Tony Anthony, Dan Vadis | Vance Lewis |
| Survival 1967 | doc. | Israel | Jules Dassin |
| Tony Rome | ★★★½★ | Frank Sinatra, Jill St. John | Gordon Douglas |
| Trans-Europe Express | ★★★½★ | Jean-Louis Trintignant | Alain Robbe-Grillet |
| Two of Us, The | ★★★★ | Michel Simon, Luce Fabiole | Claude Berri |
| Valley of the Dolls, The | ★½★ | Barbara Parkins, Patty Duke | Mark Robson |
| Venom | | Soeren Stromberg | Knud Leif Thomsen |
| Wait Until Dark | ★★★½★ | Audrey Hepburn, Alan Arkin | Terence Young |
| War and Peace | ★★★★ | Ludmilia Savelyeva | Sergei Bondarchuk |
| Where Were You When the Lights Went Out? | ★★½★ | Doris Day, Robert Morse | Hy Averback |
| Who's Minding the Mint? | ★★★ | Jim Hutton, Dorothy Provine | Howard Morris |
| Yours, Mine and Ours | ★★½★ | Lucille Ball, Henry Fonda | Melville Shavelson |
| Zita | ★★★ | Joanna Shimkus, Katina Paxinou | Robert Enrico |

# RECORDINGS

## Sales of Discs Pass the Billion Dollar Mark in 1968

U. S. record producers, blessed with an ever-growing market for recordings of music both new and classical, set a "record" of their own in 1968, reaching and passing a billion dollars in sales.

The **Beatles** claimed worldwide sales of more than 210,000,000 records, a figure keeping them in the lead, ahead of that long-time popularity king, **Bing Crosby**, whose total output was reckoned at "over 200,000,000."

*In an industry where sales statistics are not readily available to the public, the Record Industry Assn. of America kept count of new top-selling recordings. It regularly presents Gold Record Awards in two categories: for single records it certifies as having sold 1,000,000 copies, and for long-play (LP) albums it certifies as having $1,-000,000 in sales (reckoned in manufacturers' sales figured at 50% of list prices). The RIAA certified awards, it should be noted, did not begin until 1958; many artists sold millions of records before that year.*

Under the certification system, the **Beatles** have been credited with 16 singles with sales of 1,000,000 each, and 12 LP albums with over $1,000,000 in sales each. Their top-selling single was reportedly "I Want to Hold Your Hand," with 5,300,000 copies.

### Bing's Mark Still Stands

**Bing Crosby,** with most of his sales in the days of singles, before the age of the LP album and the RIAA certification, still was tops in individual record sales with 16,000,000 of "White Christmas," over 10,000,000 of "Silent Night" and over 7,000,-000 of "Jingle Bells."

**Crosby** had a total of 20 singles which sold a million copies each. His "Merry Christmas" album, having sold over 5,000,000 copies in various speeds and sizes, racked up new sales annually.

**Elvis Presley** is credited with 45 singles which sold more than 1,000,000 each, including "Hound Dog" with 6,485,000 copies. His total sales have reached well over 100,000,000; those of his singles alone were put at 81,450,000; he also has sold 11 LP albums which won Gold Record awards.

### Sinatra Ranks High

**Frank Sinatra** has made 11 such LP albums, as well as 5 singles with over a million copies each, and a great number of singles with lesser sales.

**Fats Domino** made 22 singles that sold over a million each, including "Blueberry Hill," with total sales (in the '50s and '60s) of 27,000,000 records. **Eddy Arnold,** though credited with only one single in the over-a-million class, "Bouquet of Roses" (1948), and two albums with $1,000,000 in sales, reportedly has sold over 49,000,000 discs.

Artists ranking high in numbers of Gold Record LP albums include:

**The Beatles,** 12; **Frank Sinatra, Elvis Presley, Andy Williams, Mitch Miller,** 11 each; **The Beach Boys, Herb Alpert & the Tijuana Brass,** 10; **Kingston Trio,** 9; **Dean Martin, Rolling Stones, Johnny Mather,** 8; **Barbra Streisand, Bill Cosby,**

**Ray Conniff,** 7; **Mantovani, Harry Belafonte, Roger Williams,** 6; **Bob Dylan, The Monkees,** and **Peter, Paul & Mary,** 5. **Simon & Garfunkel** have sold 3 LP albums and 2 singles which won Gold Record awards.

Top mark for sales of an LP album was the 8,000,000 copies claimed for of the movie soundtrack of "The Sound of Music," followed by the original cast recording of "My Fair Lady," 6,000,000.

The only LP classical to sell a million copies was the **Van Cliburn** rendition of Tchaikovsky's "Piano Concerto No. 1," with nearly 2,000,000.

**Leopold Stokowski** hit a million copies with both "Tales from the Vienna Woods" and "Blue Danube Waltz." **Arthur Fiedler** did it with "Jalousie," **Jose Iturbi** hit the magic number with two singles, "Clair de Lune" and Chopin's "Polonaise in A-Flat." **Percy Faith** joined the club with "Song from Moulin Rouge" and "Theme from a Summer Place."

### No Figures on Caruso

Among the top recording artists of all times were **Enrico Caruso** and **Arturo Toscanini,** but figures on their sales are not available.

Only a half-dozen records sold the magic number of a million in the 1920s. Technical improvements and a tremendous growth in the number of phonographs and record players helped bring the industry to its present peak.

Artists ranking high in singles which had sales of more than 1,000,000 each include:

**Perry Como, Connie Francis,** 13; **Pat Boone,** 12; **Glenn Miller,** 10; **Artie Shaw, Frankie Laine,** 8; **Patti Page, Harry James, Kay Kyser, Little Richard, Ricky Nelson,** 7; **Aretha Franklin, The Monkees, Guy Mitchell, Everly Brothers,** 6; **Nat King Cole, Al Jolson, Gene Autry, Chubby Checkers, Bobby Darin, The Platters, Bobby Rydel, Dean Martin, The Weavers, Doris Day, The Drifters, Hank Ballard & The Midnighters,** 5.

Those who have sold at least 4 singles over a million each include: **Guy Lombardo, Les Paul and Mary Ford, Ames Brothers, Paul Anka, Tony Bennett, Jimmy Dorsey, Tommy Dorsey, Eddie Fisher, Joni James, Vaughan Monroe, Jimmy Rodgers, Four Aces, The Coasters, Bill Black's Combo.**

Among those who sold singles of a million each in the '30s and are not among those named above were: **Rudy Vallee,** "Stein Song," 1930; **Jeanette MacDonald** and **Nelson Eddy,** "Indian Love Call," 1935; **Ella Fitzgerald,** "A-Tisket, A-Tasket," 1938; **Will Glahe,** "Beer Barrel Polka," 1938; **Cab Calloway,** "Jumpin' Jive," 1939; **Orrin Tucker,** "Oh, Johnny," 1939.

The recorders who managed to sell a million copies in the '20s were **Paul Whiteman,** "Whispering," 1920, and "Three O'Clock in the Morning," 1922; **Clyde McCoy,** "Sugar Blues," 1923 (in 1946 McCoy again sold over a million copies of "Sugar Blues"); **Vernon Dalhart,** "Prisoner's Song," 1924; **Gene Austin,** "My Blue Heaven," 1927, and "Ramona," 1928.

# Symphony Orchestras of the United States and Canada
### (As of September 1968)
**Source:** American Symphony Orchestra League Inc.
*Classifications are based on annual budgets of orchestras.*

## Major Symphony Orchestras (Conductors)

| | | |
|---|---|---|
| American Symphony Orch. | 200 W. 57th St., New York, N. Y. 10019 | Leopold Stokowski |
| Atlanta Symphony | Peachtree Center, Atlanta, Ga. 30303 | Robert Shaw |
| Baltimore Symphony | 120 Mount Royal Ave., Baltimore, Md. 21201 | Sergiu Comissiona |
| Boston Symphony | Symphony Hall, Boston, Mass. 02115 | Erich Leinsdorf |
| Buffalo Philharmonic | Kleinhans Music Hall, Buffalo, N. Y. 14201 | Lukas Foss |
| Chicago Symphony | 220 S. Michigan Ave., Chicago, Ill. 60604 | Irwin Hoffman, Act. Music Dir. |
| Cincinnati Symphony | Central Trust Bk. Tower, Cincinnati, Ohio 45202 | Max Rudolf |
| Cleveland Orchestra | 11001 Euclid Ave., Cleveland, Ohio 44106 | George Szell |
| Dallas Symphony | P.O. Box 8472, Dallas, Tev. 75205 | Donald Johanos |
| Denver Symphony | 1615 California St., Denver, Colo. 80202 | V. Golschmann |
| Detroit Symphony | 20 E. Jefferson Ave., Detroit Mich. 48226 | Sixten Ehrling |
| Houston Symphony | Music Hall, Houston, Tex. 77002 | Andre Previn |
| Indianapolis Symphony | 4600 Sunset Ave., Indianapolis, Ind. 46207 | Izler Solomon |
| Kansas City Philharmonic | 210 W. 10th St., Kansas City, Mo. 64105 | Hans Schwieger |
| Los Angeles Philharmonic | 135 North Grand, Los Angeles, Calif. 90012 | Zubin Mehta |
| Milwaukee Symphony Orch. | 161 W. Wisconsin Ave., Milwaukee, Wis. 53202 | Ken. Schermerhorn |
| Minneapolis Symphony | Cyrus Northrop Mem. Aud., Minneapolis, Minn. 55455 | S. Skrowaczewski |
| Montreal Symphony | 200 Ontario St., West Montreal, Quebec, Can. | Franz-Paul Decker |
| New Orleans Philharmonic | 333 St. Charles Ave., New Orleans, La. 70130 | W. Torkanowsky |
| New York Philharmonic | Broadway at 65th St., New York, N. Y. 10023 | Leonard Bernstein |
| Philadelphia Orchestra | 230 S. 15th St. Philadelphia, Pa. 19102 | Eugene Ormandy |
| Pittsburgh Symphony | Rockwell Standard Bldg., Pittsburgh, Pa. 15222 | William Steinberg |
| Rochester Philharmonic | 60 Gibbs St., Rochester, N. Y. 14604 | Laszlo Somogyi |
| St. Louis Symphony | Powell Hall, St. Louis, Mo. 63101 | Walter Susskind |
| San Antonio Symphony | Suite 414, S. Texas Bldg., San Antonio, Tex. 78205 | Victor Alessandro |
| San Francisco Symphony | Veteran's Memorial Bldg., San Francisco, Calif. 94102 | Joseph Krips |
| Seattle Symphony | Fourth & Pike Bldg., Seattle, Wash. 98101 | Milton Katims |
| Toronto Symphony | 215 Victoria St., Toronto 2, Ontario, Can. | Seiji Ozawa |
| Utah Symphony | 55 W. 1st So. St., Salt Lake City, Utah 84101 | Maurice Abravanel |
| Washington Nat. Symphony | Roosevelt Hotel, Washington, D.C. 20009 | Howard Mitchell |

## Metropolitan Orchestras (Conductors)

| | | |
|---|---|---|
| Birmingham Symphony | 710 N. 20th St., Birmingham, Ala. 35203 | Amerigo Marino |
| Brooklyn Philharmonia | 30 Lafayette Ave., Brooklyn, N. Y. 11217 | Siegried Landau |
| Calgary Philharmonic | Allied Arts Center, Calgary, Alberta, Can. | Irwin Hoffman |
| Columbus Symphony | 100 E. Broad St., Columbus, Ohio 43215 | Evan Whallon |
| Dayton Philharmonic | Sheraton-Dayton Hotel, Dayton, Ohio 45402 | Paul Katz |
| Duluth Symphony | 704 Alworth Bldg., Duluth, Minn. 55802 | Joseph Hawthorne |
| Edmonton Symphony | The Bay, Edmonton, Alberta, Can. | Lawrence Leonard |
| Fort Wayne Philharmonic | 201 W. Jefferson St., Fort Wayne, Ind. 46802 | James Sample |
| Florida Gulf Coast Orch. | P. O. Box 449, Tampa, Fla. 33601 | Irwin Hoffman |
| Florida Symphony | P. O. Box 782, Orlando, Fla. 32802 | Hermann Herz |
| Fort Worth Symphony | 3505 W. Lancaster, Fort Worth, Tex. 76107 | Ezra Rachlin |
| Fresno Philharmonic | 1632 N. Fresno St., Fresno, Calif. 93703 | Thomas Griswold |
| Glendale Symphony | 121 W. Lexington Dr., Glendale, Calif. 91203 | Carmen Dragon |
| Grand Rapids Symphony | Auditorium Center, Grand Rapids, Mich. 49502 | Gregory Millar |
| Hartford Symphony | 15 Lewis St., Room 316, Hartford, Conn. 06103 | Arthur Winograd |
| Hofstra University Pro Arte Symphony Orchestra da Camera | Hofstra University, Hempstead, N. Y. 11550 | Eleazar de Carvalho |
| Honolulu Symphony | Merchandise Mart Bldg., Honolulu, Hawaii 96813 | Robt. LaMarchina |
| Hudson Valley Symphony | 54 Noxon St., Poughkeepsie, N. Y. 12601 | Claude Monteux |
| Jacksonville Symphony | 46 W. Duval St., Jacksonville, Fla. 32202 | John Canarina |
| Kalamazoo Symphony Soc. | 426 S. Park St., Kalamazoo, Mich. 49007 | Pierre Etu |
| Little Orchestra Soc. | 1860 Broadway, New York, N. Y. 10023 | Thomas Scherman |
| Louisville Orchestra | 321 W Broadway, Louisville Ky. 40202 | Jorge Mester |
| Memphis Symphony | Crosstown Sta., Box 4682, Memphis, Tenn. 38104 | Vincent DeFrank |
| Miami Philharmonic | P. O. Box 97, Coral Gables, Fla. 33134 | Alain Lombard |
| Midland Odessa Symphony | P. O. Box 6266, Air Terminal Sta., Midland, Tex. 79701 | Robert G. Mann |
| Mobile Symphony | P. O. Box 1403, Mobile, Ala. 36601 | James Yestadt |
| Nashville Symphony | Bennie Dillon Bldg., Nashville, Tenn. 37203 | Thor Johnson |
| New Haven Symphony | 254 College St., New Haven, Conn. 06510 | Frank Brieff |
| New Jersey Symphony | 1020 Broad St., Newark, N. J. 07102 | Henry Lewis |
| North Carolina Symphony | Box 1211, Chapel Hill, N. C. 27514 | Benjamin Swalin |
| Oakland Symphony | Latham Sq. Bldg., Oakland, Calif. 94612 | Gerhard Samuel |
| Oklahoma City Symphony | Municipal Auditorium, Oklahoma City, Okla. 73102 | Guy F. Harrison |
| Omaha Symphony | W.O.W. Bldg., Omaha, Neb. 68102 | Joseph Levine |
| Orange County Symphony | 777 South Main St., Orange, Calif. | Guests |
| Oregon Symphony | 729 W.S. Alder, Portland, Ore. 97205 | Jacques Singer |
| Pasadena Symphony | 301 E. Colorado Blvd., Pasedena, Calif. 91101 | Richard Lert |
| Phoenix Symphony | 1515 E. Osborn Rd., Phoenix, Ariz. | Guy Taylor |
| Portland Maine Symphony | City Hall, Portland, Me. 04101 | Paul Vermel |
| Quebec Symphony | 978 Rue St. Jean, Quebec 4, Can. | Wilfred Pelletier |
| Rhode Island Philharmonic | The Arcade, Providence, R. I. 02903 | Francis Madeira |
| Richmond Symphony | 112 E. Franklin St., Richmond, Va. 23219 | Edgar Schenkman |
| Sacramento Symphony | P. O. Box 2249, Sacramento, Calif. 95804 | Harry Newsone |
| San Diego Symphony | P. O. Box, 3175, San Diego, Calif. 92103 | Zoltan Rozsnyai |
| Savannah Symphony | P. O. Box 217, Savannah, Ga. 31401 | Chauncey Kelley |
| Shreveport Symphony | 2803 Woodlawn Ave., Shreveport, La. | John Shenaut |
| Spokane Symphony | Peyton Building, Spokane, Wash. 99201 | Donald Thulean |
| Springfield Symphony | 49 Chestnut St., Springfield, Mass. | Robt. L. Staffanson |
| Syracuse Symphony | 113 E. Onondaga St., Syracuse, N. Y. 13202 | Karl Kritz |
| Toledo Orchestra | 323 Huron St., Toledo, Ohio 43604 | Serge Fournier |
| Tucson Symphony | 2719 E. Broadway, Tucson, Ariz. 85716 | Gregory Millar |
| Tulsa Philharmonic | 1579 E. 21st St., Tulsa, Okla. 74114 | Franco Autori |
| Vancouver Symphony | 566 Hornby St., Vancouver 2, B. C., Can. | Meredith Davies |
| Victoria Symphony | 613 Pandora Ave., Victoria, B. C., Can. | Laszlo Gati |
| Wichita Symphony | 105 W. Second St., Wichita, Kan. 67202 | James Robertson |
| Winnipeg Symphony | Hudson's Bay, Portage Ave., Winnipeg 1, Manitoba, Can. | George Cleve |
| Youngstown Symphony | 35 S. Phelps St., Youngstown, Ohio 44503 | Franz Bibo |

## Chamber Orchestras

| | | |
|---|---|---|
| Chamber Symphony of Phil. | 1405 Locust St., Philadelphia, Pa. 19102 | Anshel Brusilow |
| Princeton Chamber Orch. | P. O. Box 455, Princeton, N. J. | Nicholas Harsanyi |

## Famous Paintings and Where You Can See Them

The paintings in this list have been chosen because of the fame they have achieved (for various reasons, not necessarily their individual artistic merit) and because of their being viewable in public, rather than private collections. They are listed chronologically. Some are representative of a famed artist, several of whose works are equally well-known. A few of these paintings may not be on view at a particular time in the museum listed because of being on loan elsewhere.

Giotto, Pieta, 1305, Arena Chapel, Padua.

Fra Filippo Lippi, Adoration of the Child, c. 1435, Staatliches Museum, Berlin.

Piero Della Francesca, Duke of Urbino, 1465, Uffizi Gallery, Florence.

Giovanni Bellini, Pieta, c. 1466, Brera, Milan.

Botticelli, The Birth of Venus, c. 1480, Uffizi Gallery, Florence.

Hieronymus Bosch, Christ Crowned with Thorns, c. 1500, National Gallery, London.

Leonardo da Vinci, Mona Lisa (La Gioconda), c. 1505, Louvre, Paris.

Michelangelo, Creation of Adam, 1508-12, Sistine Chapel, Vatican, Rome.

Giorgione, Sleeping Venus, c. 1508, Gemaldegalerie, Dresden.

Raphael, The Sistine Madonna, 1515-19, Gemaldegalerie, Dresden.

Titian, The Tribute Money, 1516, Gemaldegalerie, Dresden.

Durer, The Four Apostles, 1523-26, Alte Pinakothek, Munich.

Holbein, Henry VIII, 1540, National Gallery, Rome.

Pieter Brueghel the Elder, Massacre of the Innocents, 1566, Kunsthistorisches Museum, Vienna.

El Greco, The Burial of Count Orgaz, 1586, Santo Tome, Toledo, Spain.

Rubens, Venus and Adonis, c. 1620, Metropolitan Museum of Art, N. Y.

Frans Hals, Laughing Cavalier, 1624, Wallace Collection, London.

Van Dyck, Charles I of England, c. 1635, Louvre, Paris.

Ribera, The Martyrdom of St. Bartholomew, 1630-39, Prado, Madrid.

Rembrandt, The Night Watch, 1642, Rijksmuseum, Amsterdam.

Velasquez, Maids of Honor, 1656, Prado, Madrid.

Vermeer, Young Woman with a Water Jug, c. 1658-64, Metropolitan, N. Y.

Ruisdael, View of Haarlem, c. 1670, Rijksmuseum, Amsterdam.

Murillo, Virgin and Child, c. 1672, Metropolitan, N. Y.

Watteau, The Embarkation for Cythera, c. 1712, Louvre, Paris.

Hogarth, The Orgy (Rake's Progress), c. 1734, Soane's Museum, London.

Fragonard, The Love Letter, c. 1769-70, Metropolitan, N. Y.

Gainsborough, The Blue Boy, c. 1770, Huntington Gallery, San Marino, Calif.

John Singleton Copley, Watson and the Shark, 1778, Museum of Fine Arts, Boston.

Joshua Reynolds, Mrs. Siddons as the Tragic Muse, 1784, Huntington Gallery, San Marino, Cal.

John Trumbull, The Declaration of Independence, 1786-94, Capitol, Washington, D. C.

Gilbert Stuart, George Washington, c. 1795, Museum of Fine Arts, Boston. (Others in Metropolitan, N. Y., etc.)

David, The Rape of the Sabines, 1799, Louvre, Paris.

Goya, The Naked Maja, 1799, Prado, Madrid.

Ingres, Odalisque, 1814, Louvre, Paris.

John Constable, The Hay Wain, 1821, National Gallery, London.

Thomas Lawrence, The Calmady Children, 1823, Metropolitan, N. Y.

John James Audubon, Birds of America (433 of the original 435 paintings), early 19th Century, New York Historical Society.

Joseph M. W. Turner, The Grand Canal, Venice, early 19th Century, Metropolitan, N. Y.

George Caleb Bingham, Fur Traders Descending the Missouri, 1845, Metropolitan, N. Y.

Emanuel Leutze, Washington Crossing the Delaware, 1851, Washington Crossing State Park, Pa.

Rosa Bonheur, The Horse Fair, 1853-55, Metropolitan, N. Y.

Jean-Baptiste Corot, Le Lac de Terni, 1861, Corcoran Gallery, Washington.

Honore Daumier, The Third-Class Carriage, c. 1862, Metropolitan, N. Y.

Jean-Francois Millet, Man with the Hoe, 1863, San Francisco Museum.

James McNeill Whistler, Arrangement in Black and Gray—The Artist's Mother, c. 1872, Louvre, Paris.

Thomas Eakins, The Gross Clinic, 1875, Jefferson Medical College, Philadelphia.

A. M. Willard Spirit of '76, 1876 (3 versions): Cleveland City Hall; Western Reserve Historical Society, Cleveland; Abbot Hall, Marblehead, Mass.

Edgar Degas, La Danseuse au Bouquet, 1878, Rhode Island School of Design Museum, Providence.

Edouard Manet, In a Boat, 1879, Metropolitan, N. Y.

Pierre Auguste Renoir, Luncheon of the Boating Party, 1881, Phillips Collection, Washington.

Georges Seurat, Sunday Afternoon on the Grande Jatte, 1884-86, Art Institute of Chicago.

Paul Cezanne, Mont Sainte-Victoire, 1885-87, Metropolitan, N. Y.

Vincent Van Gogh, Wheat Field and Cypress Trees, 1889, National Gallery, London.

Albert Pinkham Ryder, Toilers of the Sea, c. 1890, Addison Gallery, Andover, Mass.

Paul Gauguin, Ia Orana Maria (Hail Mary), 1891, Metropolitan, N. Y.

Henri de Toulouse-Lautrec, At the Moulin Rouge, 1892, Art Institute of Chicago.

Claude Monet, Rouen Cathedral, 1894, Metropolitan, N. Y.

Winslow Homer, Gulf Stream, 1899, Art Institute of Chicago.

John Singer Sargent, The Wyndham Sisters, 1900, Metropolitan, N. Y.

Frederic Remington, Cavalry Charge on the Southern Plains, 1907, Metropolitan, N. Y.

Georges Braque, Head of a Woman, 1909, Musee d'Art Moderne, Paris.

Henri Rousseau, The Dream, 1910, Museum of Modern Art, N. Y.

Marc Chagall, I and the Village, 1911, Museum of Modern Art, N. Y.

Marcel Duchamp, Nude Descending a Staircase, 1912, Philadelphia Museum of Art.

Paul Chabas, September Morn, 1912, Metropolitan, N. Y.

Amadeo Modigliani, Portrait of Madame Zboroski, 1917-18, Rhode Island School of Design Museum, Providence.

Piet Mondrian, Composition, 1921, Kunstmuseum, Basel, Switzerland.

Paul Klee, Twittering Machine, 1922, Museum of Modern Art, N. Y.

George Bellows, The Dempsey-Firpo Fight, 1924, Whitney Museum of American Art, N. Y.

Vasily Kandinsky, Several Circles, 1926, Guggenheim Museum, N. Y.

Henri Matisse, Odalisque, 1928, Musee d'Art Moderne, Paris.

Grant Wood, American Gothic, 1930, Art Institute of Chicago.

Joan Miro, Man, Woman and Child, 1931, Philadelphia Museum of Art.

Jose Clemente Orozco, Zapatistas, 1931, Museum of Modern Art, N. Y.

Maurice Utrillo, Sacred-Heart and Montmartre Square, 1932, Musee d'Art et d'Histoire, Geneva.

William Gropper, The Senate, 1935, Museum of Modern Art, N. Y.

Pablo Picasso, Guernica, 1937, Museum of Modern Art, N. Y.

Georges Rouault, The Old King, 1937, Carnegie Institute Museum, Pittsburgh.

Thomas Hart Benton, Threshing Wheat, 1939, Swope Gallery, Terre Haute, Ind.

John Steuart Curry, John Brown, 1939, Metropolitan, N. Y.

Anna (Grandma) Moses, The Thanksgiving Turkey, 1943, Metropolitan, N. Y.

Andrew Wyeth, Christina's World, 1948, Museum of Modern Art, N. Y.

Jackson Pollock, Autumn Rhythm, 1950, Metropolitan, N. Y.

Salvador Dali, Crucifixion, 1954, Metropolitan, N. Y.

Raphael Soyer, Portrait of Hugo Kastor, 1957, Metropolitan, N. Y.

# Famous Sculptures and Where You Can See Them

The statues, monuments and other sculptures in the following list have been chosen because of the fame they have won, independent of the question of their individual artistic merit, and because they are on public view. They are listed chronologically, except for the group titled Non-Western. In a few cases, two works by the same artist have been listed. Some of the works are representative of a famed artist, many of whose works are equally well-known. The creators of some of the earliest works are unknown.

## ANCIENT EGYPT

**The Great Sphinx,** c. 2900 B.C., limestone and masonry, Giza, United Arab Republic.

**Queen Nofretete,** c. 1365 B.C., painted limestone, State Museum, West Berlin.

**Colossi of Ramses II,** c. 1230 B.C., sandstone, Abu Simbel, United Arab Republic.

## ANCIENT GREECE

**Charioteer of Delphi,** c. 470 B.C., bronze, Museum, Delphi, Greece.

**Myron: Discobolus** (Discus Thrower), marble Roman copy of Myron's bronze original of c. 450 B.C., Terme Museum, Rome.

**Phidias: Parthenon Sculptures,** c. 438 B.C., marble (by or under direction of Phidias), British Museum, London.

**Polyclitus: Doryphorus** (Spear Bearer), marble Roman copy of Polyclitus' original of late 5th Century B.C., National Museum, Naples.

**Praxiteles: Hermes with the Infant Dionysus,** c. 350 B.C., Museum, Olympia; **Aphrodite of Cnidus,** marble Roman copy of Praxiteles' original of 330 B.C., Vatican, Rome.

**Scopas: Head from the Temple at Tegea,** c. 350 B.C., National Museum, Athens.

**Lysippus: Apoxyomenos** (athlete cleansing himself with a scraper), marble Roman copy of Lysippus' bronze original of 330 B.C., Vatican, Rome.

**Nike of Samothrace** (Winged Victory), c. 300 B.C., marble, Louvre, Paris.

**Aphrodite of Melos** (Venus de Milo), 2nd Century B.C., marble, Louvre, Paris.

**Laocoön,** 2nd Century B.C., marble, by Agesander, Athenodorus and Polydorus of Rhodes, Vatican, Rome.

## ANCIENT ROME

**Augustus,** c. 20 B.C., marble, Vatican, Rome.

**Caracalla,** 211-217 A.D., marble, National Museum, Naples.

## GOTHIC

**Virgin of Paris,** early 14th Century, stone, Notre Dame Cathedral, Paris.

**Claus Sluter: Moses,** c. 1400, stone, Champmol Monastery, near Dijon.

**Tomb of Philippe Pot,** c. 1480, painted stone, Louvre, Paris.

## RENAISSANCE

**Donatello: St. George,** c. 1415, marble, National Museum, Florence; **Gattamelata,** 1445-50, bronze, Piazza del Santo, Padua.

**Andrea del Verrocchio: Colleoni,** c. 1485, bronze, Campo SS. Giovanni e Paolo, Venice.

**Michelangelo Buonarroti: David,** 1501-04, marble, Academy, Florence; **Pieta,** 1498-99, marble, St. Peter's, Rome.

**Benvenuto Cellini: Perseus with the Head of Medusa,** 16th Century, marble, Loggia dei Lanzi, Florence.

**Gianlorenzo Bernini: Ecstasy of St. Theresa,** 1645-52, marble, Church of Santa Maria della Vittoria, Rome.

## NON-WESTERN

**Buddha Vairocana,** 8th Century A.D., bronze, Nara, Japan.

**Tlaloc (Toltec Rain God),** 900 A.D. or earlier, stone, Anthropology Museum, Mexico City.

**Amida Buddha,** 1252, bronze, Kamakura, Japan.

**Aztec Calendar Stone,** 1427-29, painted volcanic rock, Anthropology Museum, Mexico City.

**Stone Heads,** 17th Century or earlier, Easter Island.

**Mask with Horns,** 19th Century, wood, from southeast Congo (Baluba), Royal Museum of Central Africa, Tervuren, Belgium.

**Buddha,** 1960, concrete, Changhua, Taiwan.

## 18th-19th CENTURIES

**Jean Antoine Houdon: George Washington,** 1788-92, marble, State Capitol, Richmond, Va.

**Thomas Crawford: Statue of Freedom,** bronze, 1863, atop the Capitol dome, Washington, D. C.

**Frederic Auguste Bartholdi: Liberty Enlightening the World,** 1886, copper on steel frame, Liberty Is., N. Y.

**Auguste Rodin: The Thinker,** 1879-89, bronze, Metropolitan Museum of Art, N. Y.

**Augustus St. Gaudens: Abraham Lincoln,** 1887, bronze, Lincoln Park, Chicago.

**John Quincy Adams Ward: Henry Ward Beecher,** bronze, 1891, Cadman Plaza, Brooklyn, N. Y.

## 20th CENTURY

**Aristide Maillol: The Mediterranean,** 1902-05, bronze, Museum of Modern Art, N. Y.

**Mateo Alonso: Christ of the Andes,** 1904, bronze, Uspallata Pass, Chile-Argentina border.

**Ivan Mestrovic: My Mother,** 1908, marble, State Museum, Belgrade.

**Constantin Brancusi: The Kiss,** 1908, stone, Philadelphia Museum of Art; **Bird in Space,** 1927, bronze, Museum of Modern Art, N. Y.

**Wilhelm Lehmbruck: Kneeling Woman,** 1911, cast stone, Museum of Modern Art, N. Y.

**Edvard Erichsen: The Little Mermaid,** 1913, bronze, Copenhagen harbor.

**Daniel Chester French: Abraham Lincoln,** 1922, marble, Lincoln Memorial, Washington, D. C.

**William Zorach: Child with Cat,** 1926, marble, Museum of Modern Art, N. Y.

**Gaston Lachaise: Standing Woman,** 1912-27, bronze, Albright Art Gallery, Buffalo.

**Ernst Barlach: Hovering Angel,** 1927, bronze, Antoniter Church, Cologne.

**Jacob Epstein: Madonna and Child,** 1927, bronze, Riverside Church, N. Y.

**Heitor da Silva Costa and Paul Landowski: Christ the Redeemer,** 1931, reinforced concrete, Corcovado Mtn., Rio de Janeiro.

**Vernon March: Canadian War Memorial,** 1926-32 (dedicated 1939), bronze, Confederation Sq., Ottawa.

**Paul Manship: Prometheus,** 1934, bronze and gold-leaf, Rockefeller Center, N. Y.

**Alexander Calder: Lobster Trap and Fish Tail,** 1939, steel wire and aluminum, Museum of Modern Art, N. Y.

**Carl Milles: Meeting of the Waters Fountain,** 1940, Aloe Plaza, St. Louis; **Millesgarden Sculptures,** Stockholm.

**Gutzon Borglum: Mt. Rushmore Natl. Memorial,** 1927-41, granite, near Keystone, S. D.

**Gustav Vigeland: Sculpture Park,** 1906-43, stone and bronze, Oslo.

**Pablo Picasso: She-Goat,** bronze, 1950, Museum of Modern Art, N. Y.

**Felix de Weldon: Marine Corps War Memorial** (Iwo Jima Flag-Raising), 1954, bronze, near Arlington Natl. Cemetery, Va.

**Jose de Creeft: Alice in Wonderland,** 1959, bronze, Conservatory Lake, Central Park, N. Y.

**Henry Moore: Reclining Figure,** 1963-65, bronze, Lincoln Center, N. Y.

# Sculpture Carves Its Niche in the News

Sculpture, both ancient and modern, made news during 1968.

There were new, and paradoxical, activities underwater. At the eastern end of the Mediterranean, divers used suction pumps, underwater phones and a submerged decompression chamber in a search near Greece for ancient statues and other relics of sunken ships. At the western end of the same sea, modern artist Joan Miro, with the aid of other divers and a sea-going crane, deposited his statue Sea Venus in an underwater grotto on the Mediterranean's floor near Juan-les-Pins, France.

Rising in the wake of the New York Metropolitan Museum's denunciation of its own long-revered ancient Bronze Greek horse as a fake and a forgery, two world-renowned art experts declared it was genuine. They cited technical reasons to back their opinions, just as the Metropolitan's expert had done in denouncing the statue.

In England, the dean of British sculptors, Henry Moore, was feted with an unprecedented round of tributes on his 70th birthday, July 30. There were testimonial dinners, full-page articles in newspapers (including Britain's biggest-circulation tabloid), and exhibits of his works. An American collector donated $30,000 to the famed Tate Gallery in Moore's honor.

For new PRESIDENT and VICE PRESIDENT see Index
under ELECTION RETURNS and ELECTIONS (1968)

# UNITED STATES GOVERNMENT
## THE JOHNSON ADMINISTRATION
### As of October 1, 1968

Terms of office of the President and Vice President, from January 20, 1965 to January 20, 1969.
No person may be elected President of the United States for more than two four-year terms.

PRESIDENT—Lyndon B. Johnson of Texas. Receives salary of $100,000 a year, taxable, and in addition an expense allowance, also taxable, of $50,000 to assist in defraying expenses resulting from his official duties. Also there may be expended not exceeding $40,000, nontaxable, a year for travel expenses and official entertainment. Congress in 1958 provided lifetime pensions of $25,000 a year, free mailing privileges, free office space, and up to $65,000 a year for office help for ex-Presidents and $10,000 annually for their widows.

VICE PRESIDENT—Hubert H. Humphrey of Minnesota. Salary $43,000 a year and $10,000 for expenses, all of which is taxable.

Order of succession to Presidency See P. 195.

## The Cabinet

(Salaries $35,000 each)

Secretary of State—Dean Rusk, of New York.
Secretary of Treasury—Henry H. Fowler, Va.
Secretary of Defense—Clark M. Clifford, Md.
Attorney General—Ramsey Clark, Tex.
Postmaster General—W. Marvin Watson, Tex.
Secretary of the Interior—Stewart L. Udall, of Arizona.
Secretary of Agriculture—Orville L. Freeman, of Minnesota.
Secretary of Commerce—C. R. Smith, New York.
Secretary of Labor—William Willard Wirtz, Ill.
Secretary of Health, Education and Welfare—Wilbur J. Cohen, Michigan.
Secretary of Housing and Urban Development—Robert C. Weaver, New York.
Secretary of Transportation—Alan S. Boyd, Fla.

## The White House Staff

Special Assistants to the President—Joseph A. Califano, Jr., S. Douglass Cater, Jr., George E. Christian, E. Ernest Goldstein, Donald F. Hornig, Walt Whitman Rostow, James R. Jones.
Special Assistant to the President for Consumer Affairs—Betty Furness.
Special Consultant to the President—Gen. Maxwell D. Taylor, USA, Retired.
Special Consultant to the President—George E. Reedy.
Special Counsel to the President—Harry C. McPherson, Jr., Larry E. Temple.
Counselor to the President—Charles S. Murphy.
Deputy Special Counsel to the President—Lawrence E. Levinson.
Associate Special Counsel to the President—W. DeVier Pierson.
Deputy Press Secretary to the President—Wyatt T. Johnson, Jr.
Administrative Assistant to the President—Mike N. Manatos.
Physician to the President—Vice Adm. George G. Burkley (MC), USN.
Armed Forces Aide to the President—Col. Haywood R. Smith, USMC.
Personal Secretary to the President—Mrs. Juanita Duggan Roberts.
Press Secretary and Staff Director for the First Lady—Mrs. Elizabeth S. Carpenter.
Social Secretary—Mrs. Bess Abell.

## EXECUTIVE AGENCIES

National Security Council—Members are the President, the Vice President, the Secretary of State, the Secretary of Defense, the Director of the Office of Emergency Planning, Walt Whitman Rostow, special assistant to the President, and Bromley Smith, exec. secy.
Bureau of the Budget—Charles J. Zwick, dir.
Council of Econ. Advisers—Arthur M. Okun, chmn.
Central Intelligence Agency—Richard Helms, dir.
Natl. Aeronautics & Space Council—Edward C Welsh, exec. secy.
Of. of Economic Opportunity—Bertram M. Harding, act. dir.
Office of Science & Tech.—Donald F. Hornig, dir.
Office of Emergency Planning—Price Daniel, dir.
Special Representative for Trade Negotiations—William M. Roth.
Marine Resources and Engineering Devel.—Edward Wenk Jr., exec. secy.

## Department of State

Secretary of State—Dean Rusk.
Under Secretary—Nicholas deB. Katzenbach.
Under Sec. for Political Affairs—Eugene V. Rostow.
Deputy Under Secretaries—Charles E. Bohlen (for political affairs), Idar Rimestad (for administration).
Ambassadors at Large—W. Averell Harriman, George C. McGhee.
Chmn. of Policy Planning Council—Henry D. Owen.
Assistant Secretaries for:
African Affairs—Joseph Palmer, II.
Congressional Relations—W. B. Macomber, Jr.
Economic Affairs—Anthony M. Solomon.
European Affairs—John M. Leddy.
East Asian & Pacific Affairs—William P. Bundy.
Internatl. Organiz. Affairs—Joseph J. Sisco.
Inter-American Affairs—Covey T. Oliver.
Near-Eastern & So. Asian Affairs—L. D. Battle.
Public Affairs—Dixon Donnelley.
Bureau of Security & Consular Affairs—Barbara M. Watson (admin.).
Inspector Gen., For. Assistance—J. K. Mansfield.
Chief of Protocol—Tyler Abell.
Dir. General, Foreign Service—John M. Steeves.
Director of Intelligence & Research—Thomas L. Hughes.
Director of Internatl. Scientific and Technological Affairs—Herman Pollack.
Insp. Gen. Foreign Service—Fraser Wilkins.
Foreign Service Inst.—George V. Allen.
Agency for Internatl. Development—William S. Gaud, administrator.
Advisory Committee on Foreign Aid—Charles P. Taft, chmn.
Peace Corps—Jack H. Vaughn, dir.
U. S. Rep. to the UN and Rep. in the Security Council—James Russell Wiggins, ambassador.

## Treasury Department

Secretary of the Treasury—Henry H. Fowler.
Under Sec. of the Treasury—Joseph W. Barr.
Under Sec. for Monetary Affairs—Frederick L. Deming.
Assistant Secretaries—Joseph M. Bowman, Jr., John R. Petty, Stanley S. Surrey, Robert A. Wallace.
Deputy Under Sec. for Monetary Affairs—Frank W. Schiff.
Fiscal Assistant Secretary—John K. Carlock.
Asst. Sec. for Adm.—Artemus E. Weatherbee.
Assistants to the Sec.—Raymond J. Albright, R. Duane Saunders, John F. Kane.
Office of Budget and Finance—E. C. Betts, Jr., dir.
Bureaus of:
Accounts—Sidney S. Sokol, commissioner.
Customs—Lester D. Johnson, commissioner.
Engraving & Printing—James A. Conlon, dir.
Mint—Eva B. Adams, dir.
Public Debt—Donald M. Merritt, commissioner.
Internal Revenue Service—Sheldon S. Cohen, commissioner.
Comptroller of the Currency—William B. Camp
Treasurer of the U. S.—Vacant.
U. S. Savings Bonds—Glen R. Johnson, dir.
U. S. Secret Service—James J. Rowley, dir.

## Department of Defense

Secretary of Defense—Clark M. Clifford.
Deputy Sec. of Defense—Paul H. Nitze.
Armed Forces Policy Council—Sec. of Defense Clark M. Clifford, chmn.
Dir. of Def. Research & Eng.—John S. Foster, Jr.
Assistant Secretaries of Defense:
Administration—Solis Horwitz.
Comptroller—Robert C. Moot.
Installations & Logistics—Thomas D. Morris.
Intl. Security Affairs—Paul C. Warneke.
Manpower and Reserve Affairs—Alfred B. Fitt.
Public Affairs—Phil G. Goulding.
Systems Analysis—Alain C. Enthoven.
Joint Chiefs of Staff:
Chairman—Gen. Earle G. Wheeler, USA.
Chief of Staff, Army—Gen. William C. Westmoreland, USA.
Chief of Naval Operations—Adm. Thomas H. Moorer, USN.
Chief of Staff, Air Force—Gen, John P. McConnell, USAF.

**Commandant of the Marine Corps**—Gen. Leonard F. Chapman Jr., USMC.
**Joint Staff**—V. Adm. Nels E. Johnson, USN, dir.
**Spec. Asst. to Joint Chiefs of Staff for Arms Control**—Maj. Gen. B. F. Evans, USA.
**Joint Command & Control Requirements Group**—R. Adm. L. H. Sell, USN, chief.
**Defense Atomic Support Agency**—V. Adm. Lloyd M. Mustin, USN, dir.
**Defense Communications Agency**—Lt. Gen. Richard P. Klocko, USAF, dir.
**Defense Contract Audit Agency**—W. B. Petty, dir.
**Defense Intelligence Agency**—Lt. Gen. Joseph F. Carroll, USAF, dir.
**Defense Supply Agency**—Lt. Gen. Earl C. Hedlund, USAF, dir.

## U. S. UNIFIED AND SPECIFIED COMMANDS

**Alaskan Command**—Lt. Gen. Robert A. Breitweiser, USAF.
**Atlantic Command**—Adm. E. P. Holmes, USN.
**Continental Air Defense Command**—Lt. Gen. Raymond J. Reeves, USAF.
**European Command**—Gen. Lyman L. Lemnitzer, USA.
**Pacific Command**—Adm. John S. McCain Jr., USN.
**Southern Command**—Gen. R. W. Porter, Jr., USA.
**Strat. Air Command**—Gen. Bruce K. Holloway, USAF.
**Strike Command**—Gen. T. J. Conway, USA.

### INTERNATIONAL COMMANDS
#### Under North Atlantic Treaty Organization

**Supr. Allied Commander, Europe (SACEUR)**—Gen. Lyman L. Lemnitzer, USA.
**Deputy SACEUR**—Sir Robert Bray (Britain).
**Air Deputy to SACEUR**—Gen. William B. Stone, USAF.
**C-in-C, Allied Forces, Northern Europe**—Gen. Sir Kenneth Darling (Britain).
**C-in-C Allied Force, Central Europe**—Gen. J. Bennecke (Germany).
**C-in-C Allied Forces, Southern Europe**—Adm. H. Rivero Jr., USN.
**C-in-C, Allied Forces, Mediterranean**—Adm. L. Sotgiu (Italy).
**Supr. Allied Comdr., Atlantic (SACLANT)**—Adm. Ephraim P. Holmes, USN.
**Deputy SACLANT**—V. Adm. Peter M. Compston (Britain).
**Comdr. Striking Fleet Atlantic**—V. Adm. Benedict J. Semmes Jr., USN.
**Allied Comdr. in Chief, Channel**—Adm. Sir John Bush (Britain).

### DEPARTMENT OF THE ARMY

**Secretary of the Army**—Stanley R. Resor.
**Under Secretary**—David E. McGiffert.
**Assistant Secretaries for:**
  Financial Management—Eugene M. Becker.
  Installations & Logistics—Robert A. Brooks.
  Research & Development—Russell D. O'Neal.
  Manpower & Reserve Affairs—W. K. Brehm.
**Chief of Public Information**—Maj. Gen. Wendell J. Coats.
**Civil Defense**—Joseph Romm, dir.
**Chief of Staff**—Gen. William C. Westmoreland.
**Surgeon General**—Lt. Gen. Leonard D. Heaton.
**Adjutant General**—Maj. Gen. K. G. Wickham.
  **Chief of Engineers**—Lt. Gen. William F. Cassidy.
**U. S. Women's Army Corps**—Col. Elizabeth P. Hoisington.
**Natl. Guard Bureau**—Maj. Gen. Winston P. Wilson.
**Chief, Army Reserve**—Maj. Gen. William J. Sutton.
**U. S. Army Materiel Command**—Gen. Frank S. Besson, Jr.
**U. S. Army Combat Developments Command**—Lt. Gen. Harry W. O. Kinnard.
**U. S. Continental Army Command**—Gen. James K. Woolnough.
**Commanding Generals, U. S. Armies:**
  **1st, Fort Meade, Md.**—Lt. Gen. J. O. Seaman.
  **3rd, Ft. McPherson, Ga.**—Lt. Gen. John L. Throckmorton.
  **4th, Ft. Sam Houston, Tex.**—Lt. Gen. Harry H. Critz.
  **5th, Chicago, Ill.**—Lt. Gen. John H. Michaelis.
  **6th, Presidio of San Francisco, Calif.**—Lt. Gen. Stanley R. Larsen.
  **Military Dist. of Washington**—Maj. Gen. Charles S. O'Malley, Jr.

### DEPARTMENT OF THE NAVY

**Secretary of the Navy**—Paul R. Ignatius.
**Under Secretary**—Charles F. Baird.
**Assistant Secretaries for:**
  Financial Management—Charles A. Bowsher.
  Installations & Logistics—Barry J. Shillito.
  Manpower & Reserve Affairs—R. S. Driver.
  Research & Development—Robert A. Frosch.
**Judge Advocate Gen.**—R. Adm. J. B. McDevitt.
**Chief of Naval Operations**—Adm. Thomas H. Moorer.
**Chief Naval Material Command**—Adm. I. J. Galantin.

**Bureau Chiefs:**
  **Medicine & Surgery**—V. Adm., Robert B. Brown.
  **Naval Personnel**—V. Adm. C. K. Duncan.
**Military Sea Tranport Serv.**—V. Adm. Lawson P. Ramage, Comdr.
**U. S. Marine Corps:**
  **Commandant**—Gen. Leonard F. Chapman Jr.
  **Asst. Commandant**—Lt. Gen. Lewis W. Walt Jr.
  **Quartermaster Gen.**—Maj. Gen. Paul R. Tyler.
  **Dir. of Women Marines**—Col. B. J. Bishop.
**Commandants, Naval Districts:**
  **1st, Boston, Mass.**—R. Adm. R. S. Benson.
  **3rd, New York, N. Y.**—R. Adm. F. D. Foley.
  **4th, Philadelphia, Pa.**—R. Adm. Robt. H. Speck.
  **5th, Norfolk, Va.**—R. Adm. J. C. Dempsey.
  **6th, Charleston, S. C.**—R. Adm. H. J. Kossler.
  **8th, New Orleans, La.**—R. Adm. R. A. MacPherson.
  **9th, Great Lakes, Ill.**—R. Adm. H. A. Renken.
  **10th, New York, N. Y.**—R. Adm. A. R. Matter.
  **11th, San Diego, Calif.**—R. Adm. M. E. Dornin.
  **12th, San Francisco, Calif.**—R. Adm. L. B. McCuddin.
  **13th, Seattle, Wash.**—R. Adm. F. L. Johnson.
  **14th, San Francisco, Calif.**—R. Adm. F. E. Bakutis.
  **15th, New York, N. Y.**—R. Adm. E. P. Koch.
  **17th, Seattle, Wash.**—R. Adm. D. M. White.
**Naval District, Washington, D. C.**—R. Adm. D. G. Irvine.

### DEPARTMENT OF THE AIR FORCE

**Secretary of the Air Force**—Dr. Harold Brown.
**Under Secretary**—Townsend W. Hoopes.
**Assistant Secretaries for:**
  Financial Management—Thomas H. Nielsen.
  Research & Development—Alexander H. Flax.
  Installations & Logistics—Robert H. Charles.
**Dir. of Info.**—Maj. Gen. William C. Garland.
**Dir. of Space Systems**—Brig. Gen. W. R. Hedrick.
**Chief of Staff**—Gen. John P. McConnell.
**Vice Chief of Staff**—Gen. B. K. Holloway.
**Secretary of the Air Staff**—Col. James H. Watkins.
**Scientific Advisory Board**—Dr. H. G. Stever.
**Surgeon General**—Lt. Gen. Kenneth E. Pletcher.
**Inspector General**—Lt. Gen. Joseph H. Moore.
**Judge Advocate**—Maj. Gen. Robert W. Manss.
**Major Air Commands:**
  **U. S. Air Force Academy**—Lt. Gen. Thomas S. Moorman.
  **Ar Force Accounting and Finance**—Col. James O. Gross.
  **Office of Aero. Research**—Brig. Gen. L. Kiley.
  **Air National Guard**—Maj. Gen. Winston P. Wilson.
  **Air Defense, Ent. AFB, Colo.**—Lt. Gen. Arthur C. Agan.
  **Air Force Logistics, Wright-Patterson AFB, Ohio**—Gen. Jack G. Merrell.
  **Air Force Systems, Andrews AFB, Md.**—Gen. James Ferguson.
  **Air Training, Randolph AFB, Tex.**—Lt. Gen. Sam Maddux, Jr.
  **Air University, Maxwell AFB, Ala.**—Lt. Gen. John W. Carpenter III.
  **Continental Air Command, Robins AFB, Ga.**—Lt. Gen. Henry Viccellio.
  **Headquarters Command, Bolling AFB, D. C.**—Maj. Gen. Milton B. Adams.
  **Military Airlift, Scott AFB, Ill.**—Gen. Howell M. Estes, Jr.
  **Strategic Air, Offutt AFB, Neb.**—Gen. Joseph J. Nazzaro.
  **Tactical Air, Langley AFB, Va.**—Gen. Gabriel P. Disosway.
  **Alaskan Air, Elmendorf AFB, Alaska**—Maj. Gen. Thomas E. Moore.
  **U.S.A.F. Southern Command AT Albrook AFB, Balboa, Canal Zone**—Maj. Gen. R. J. Clizbe.
  **Pacific Air Forces, Hickam AFB, Hawaii**—Gen. John D. Ryan.
  **U. S. Air Forces in Europe, Wiesbaden, Germany**—Gen. Maurice A. Preston.
  **U. S. Air Force Security Service, San Antonio, Tex.**—Maj. Gen. Louis E. Coira.
  **Air Force Communications Service, Scott AFB, Ill.**—Maj. Gen. Robert W. Paulson.

## Department of Justice

**Attorney General**—Ramsey Clark.
**Solicitor General**—Erwin N. Griswold.
**Assistant Attorneys General:**
  Administrative—Leo M. Pellerzi.
  Antitrust Div.—Edwin M. Zimmerman.
  Civil Div.—Edwin L. Weisl, Jr.
  Civil Rights Div.—Stephen J. Pollak.
  Criminal Div.—Fred M. Vinson, Jr.
  Internal Security Div.—J. Walter Yeagley.
  Lands Div.—Clyde O. Mertz.
  Legal Counsel—Frank Wozencraft.
  Tax Div.—Mitchell Rogovin.
**Fed. Bureau of Investigation**—J. Edgar Hoover, dir.
**Bureau of Prisons**—Myrl Alexander.
**Federal Prison Industries, Inc.**—Myrl E. Alexander, assoc. chairman.

Board of Parole—Walter Dunbar, chmn.
Immigration and Naturalization Service—Raymond F. Farrell, commissioner.
Board of Immigration Appeals—Maurice A. Roberts, chmn.
Pardon Attorney—T. Oscar Smith.

## Post Office Department

Postmaster General—W. Marvin Watson.
Deputy Postmaster General—Frederick C. Belen.
Exec. Asst. to Postmaster Gen.—Lloyd H. Taylor, Jr., Doug R. Nobles.
Spec. Asst. to the Postmaster Gen. (Public Info.)—Bill McSweeny.
Assistant Postmasters General:
    Bureau of Facilities—John L. O'Marra.
    Bureau of Finance—Ralph W. Nicholson.
    Bureau of Operations—William M. McMillan.
    Bureau of Personnel—Richard J. Murphy.
    Bureau of Transportation—Frederick E. Batrus.
    Bureau of Research & Engineering—Leo S. Packer.
    General Counsel—Timothy J. May.
Chief Postal Inspector—H. B. Montague.

## Department of the Interior

Secretary of the Interior—Stewart L. Udall.
Under Secretary—David S. Black.
Assistant Secretaries for:
    Fish & Wildlife—Vacant.
    Mineral Resources—J. Cordell Moore.
    Public Land Management—Harry R. Anderson.
    Water & Power—Kenneth Holum.
    Water Pollution Control—Max N. Edwards.
    Administration—Robert C. McConnell.
Bureau of Indian Affairs—Robert L. Bennett.
Bur. of Land Management—B. L. Rassmussen, dir.
Bur. of Mines—Vacant.
Bur. of Outdoor Recreation—Edward C. Crafts, dir.
Bur. of Reclamation—Floyd E. Dominy, comm.
Fish & Wildlife Service—Clarence F. Pautzke.
Bur. of Commercial Fisheries—Harold E. Crowther (act.), dir.
Bur. of Sport Fisheries & Wildlife—John S. Gottschalk, dir.
Geological Survey—William T. Pecora, dir.
National Park Service—George B. Hartzog, Jr., dir.
Office of Coal Research—George Fumich, Jr., dir.
Office of Information—Charles K. Boatner, dir.
Office of Minerals & Solid Fuels—William E. S. Flory, dir.
Office of Oil & Gas—Onnie P. Lattu.
Office of Saline Water—Jack A. Hunter, dir.
Office of Solicitor—Edward Weinberg.
Office of Territories—Ruth G. VanCleve, dir.
Office of Water Resources Research—Roland R. Renne, dir.
Oil Import Administration—Elmer L. Hoehn.
Water Pollution Control Admn.—J. G. Moore Jr.

## Department of Agriculture

Secretary of Agriculture—Orville L. Freeman.
Under Secretary—John A. Schnittker.
Agric. Economics—Walter W. Wilcox, dir.
Assistant Secretaries—John A. Baker, Dorothy H. Jacobson, Joseph M. Robertson.
Consumer & Mktg. Service—R. E. Leonard, admin.
Agric. Research Service—G. W. Irving, Jr., admin.
Agric. Stabilization & Conserv. Service—Horace D. Godfrey, admin.
Commodity Credit Corp.—John A. Schnittker, pres.
Commodity Exch. Auth.—Alex C. Caldwell, admin.
Cooperative State Research Service—T. C. Byerly, admin.
Econ. Research Service—Melvin L. Upchurch.
Farmer Coop. Service—David W. Angevine, admin.
Farmers Home Admin.—Howard Bertsch, admin.
Fed. Crop Insurance Corp.—John N. Luft, mgr.
Fed. Extension Service—Lloyd Davis, admin.
Foreign Agric. Service—Raymond A. Ioanes, admin.
Forest Service—Edward P. Cliff, chief.
Rural Community Development Service—R. D. Matthews, act. admin.
Rural Electrific. Admin.—Norman Clapp, admin.
Soil Conservation Service—D. A. Williams, admin.
Statistical Reporting Service—Harry C. Trelogan.
Office of Information—Harold R. Lewis, dir.
International Agric. Development Service—Lester R. Brown, admin.

## Department of Commerce

Secretary of Commerce—C. R. Smith.
Under Secy. of Commerce—Joseph W. Bartlett.
Asst. Secretaries—John F. Kincaid, Lawrence C. McQuade, David R. Baldwin, William H. Chartener, Ross D. Davis.
General Counsel—Frederick Simpich.
Bureau of the Census—A. Ross Eckler, dir.
Bureau of Internat. Commerce—L. A. Fox, dir.
Business & Defense Services Admin.—Rodney L. Borum, admin.
Environmental Science Services Admin.—Robert M. White, admin.
Econ. Develop. Admin.—Ross D. Davis, asst. sec.

Maritime Administrator—James W. Gulick (act.).
Natl. Bureau of Standards—A. V. Astin, dir.
Office of Administration, Domestic and International Business—Richard M. Gottfried, dir.
Office of Business Econ.—George Jaszi, dir.
Office of Field Services—Charles F. Boehm, dir.
Office of Foreign Commercial Services—Donald S. Gilpatrick, dir.
U. S. Patent Office—Edward J. Brenner.
U. S. Travel Service—William G. Arey, act. dir.
Office of Publications and Information, Domestic and International Business—Dean Smith, dir.
Economic Development—Ross D. Davis, asst. sec.
Office of State Technical Services—Philip K. Reily.

## Department of Labor

Secretary of Labor—Willard Wirtz.
Under Secretary—James J. Reynolds.
Assistant Secretary for Manpower—Stanley H. Ruttenberg.
    Bur. of Employment Security—Robert C. Goodwin, adm.
    Bur. of Apprenticeship & Training—Hugh C. Murphy, adm.
    Bureau of Work-Training Programs—Mark Battle, admin.
    Bureau of Work Programs—Mark Battle, admin.
Asst. Secy. for Labor-Management Relations—Thomas R. Donahue.
    Office of Labor-Management and Welfare-Pension Reports—Frank M. Kleiler, dir.
    Office of Veterans' Reemployment Rights—Hugh W. Bradley, dir.
    Office of Labor—Management Relations Services—Beatrice M. Burgoon, dir.
Wage and Hour and Public Contracts Div.—Clarence T. Lundquist, adm.
Asst. Secy. for Intl. Affairs—George L-P Weaver
    Bureau of Intl. Affairs—H. N. Blackman.
Asst. Secy. for Wage and Labor Standards—Esther Peterson.
    Women's Bur.—Mary Dublin Keyserling, dir
    Bur. of Labor Standards—David M. Swankin.
    Bur. of Employees' Compensation—Thomas A. Tinsley, dir.
    Employees' Compensation Appeals Board—Theodore M. Schwartz, chmn.
Office of Federal Contract Compliance—Ward McCreedy, act. dir.
Office of Policy Planning and Research—Philip Arnow, dir.
Office of Legislative Liaison—H. Floyd Sherrod.
Solicitor of Labor—Charles Donahue.
Bur. of Labor Statistics—Ben Burdetsky, Comm.
Asst. Secy. for Administration—Leo R. Werts.
Office of Information, Publications & Reports—John W. Leslie, dir.

## Department of Health, Education, and Welfare

Secretary of Health, Education, and Welfare—Wilbur J. Cohen.
Under Secretary—James H. McCrocklin.
Assistant Secretaries—Ralph K. Huitt, Dr. Philip R. Lee, Lynn M. Bartlett, Alice M. Rivlin, Edward C. Sylvester Jr., D. F. Simpson, J. F. Kelly.
General Counsel—Alanson W. Willcox.
Surgeon General, Public Health Service—William H. Stewart, M.D.
Consumer Protection & Environmental Health Service—Charles C. Johnson Jr.
Social and Rehabilitation Service—Mary E. Switzer.
Commissioners of:
    Education—Harold Howe, II.
    Social Security—Robert M. Ball.
    Health Services & Mental Health Admin.—Vacant.
Natl. Institute of Health—R. Q. Marston, M. D., dir.

## Department of Housing and Urban Development

Secretary of Housing & Urban Development—Robert C. Weaver.
Under Secretary—Robert C. Wood.
Assistant Secretaries:
    Administration—Dwight A. Ink.
    Renewal and Housing Assistance—Don Hummel.
    Metropolitan Development—Charles M. Haar.
    Demonstrations and Intergovernmental Relations—N. Ralph Taylor.
    Mortgage Credit and Federal Housing Commissioner—Philip N. Brownstein.
    President Federal National Mortgage Assn.—Raymond H. Lapin.
Division of Public Affairs—Gerald Huard, dir.
Office of Equal Opportunity—Walter B. Lewis, dir.
Division of International Affairs—James A. Moore.
Inspection Division—William H. T. Smith, dir.

## Department of Transportation

Secretary—Alan S. Boyd.
Under Secretary—John Robson.
Nat'l Trans. Safety Board—Joseph O'Connell, Jr.
U. S. Coast Guard—Adm. Willard J. Smith.

# JUDICIARY OF THE UNITED STATES

## AS OF SEPTEMBER 1968
**Source:** Administrative Office of the United States Courts, Washington, D. C.

### SUPREME COURT
For roster of Supreme Court, past and present, see page 169.

**Clerk**—John F. Davis. **Marshal**—T. Perry Lippitt. **Reporter of Decisions**—Henry Putzel, Jr. **Librarian**—H. Charles Hallam, Jr. **Press Information**—Banning E. Whittington.—Washington, D. C.

### UNITED STATES COURT OF CUSTOMS AND PATENT APPEALS
**Chief Judge**—Eugene Worley, Tex.

**Associate Judges**—Giles S. Rich, N. Y.; Arthur M. Smith, Mich.; J. Lindsay Almond, Jr., Va.; Phillip B. Baldwin. ($33,000 each.)

**Clerk**—George E. Hutchinson. **Addres of Court** —717 Madison Pl., N.W., Washington, D. C. 20439.

### UNITED STATES CUSTOMS COURT
**Chief Judge**—Paul P. Rao, N. Y.

**Judges**—Webster J. Oliver, N. Y. Morgan Ford, N. D.; Scovel Richardson, Mo.; Edward D. Re; Frederick Landis; James L. Watson; Herbert N. Maletz; Bernard Newman; Samuel M. Rosenstein. (30,000 each.)

**Clerk**—Howard Basler. **Address of Court**—One Federal Pl., New York, N. Y. 10007.

### UNITED STATES COURT OF CLAIMS
**Chief Judge**—Wilson Cowen. **Associate Judges**—Don N. Laramore, Ind.; James R. Durfee, Wis.; Oscar H. Davis, N. Y.; Linton M. Collins, Ga. B. G. Skelton; Philip Nichols, Jr. ($33,000 each.)

**Clerk**—Frank T. Peartree. **Address of Court**—717 Madison Pl., N.W., Washington, D. C. 20005.

### TAX COURT OF THE UNITED STATES
**Chief Judge**—William M. Drennen, W. Va.

**Judges**—Norman O. Tietjens, Ohio; Arnold Raum, Mass.; Graydon G. Withey, Mich.; Craig S. Atkins, Md.; Bruce M. Forrester, Mo.; Irene F. Scott, Ala.; William M. Fay, Pa.; Howard A. Dawson, Jr., Ark.; Austin Hoyt, Colo.; Theodore Tannenwald, Jr., N. Y.; Charles R. Simpson, Ill.; C. Moxley Featherston, Va.; Leo H. Erwin, N. C. (two vacancies). ($30,000 each.)

**Retired Judges Recalled for Duty**—J. Gregory Bruce, Ky.; Marion J. Harron, Calif.; John W. Kern, Ind.; John E. Mulroney, Iowa; J. Edgar Murdock, Pa.; B. B. Turner, Ark. ($30,000 each.)

**Administrative Officer**—Otto W. Schoenfelder. **Clerk**—Randolph F. Caldwell, Jr. **Address of Court** —1111 Constitution Ave., N.W., Wash. D. C.

### U. S. COURTS OF APPEALS
Where no address other than city and state is given, office is in the U. S. Courthouse. Salaries, $33,000 each.

**District of Columbia Circuit**—David L. Bazelon, Chief Judge; John A. Danaher, Warren E. Burger, J. Skelly Wright, Carl McGowan, Edward Allen Tamm, Harold Leventhal, Spottswood W. Robinson, III. **Clerk**—N. J. Paulson, all Wash., D. C. 20001.

**First Circuit** (Maine, Massachusetts, New Hampshire, Rhode Island, Puerto Rico)—Bailey Aldrich, Chief Judge, Boston, Mass.; Edward M. McEntee, Providence, R. I.; Frank M. Coffin, 156 Federal St., Portland, Me. **Clerk**—Roger A. Stinchfield, Boston, Mass. 02109.

**Second Circuit** (Connecticut, New York, Vermont) (Room 2401, U. S. Courthouse, Foley Square, New York, N. Y. 10007, unless otherwise indicated.)—J. Edward Lumbard, Chief Judge; Sterry R. Waterman, St. Johnsbury, Vt.; Leonard P. Moore, Henry J. Friendly, J. Joseph Smith, Hartford, Conn.; Irving R. Kaufman, Paul R. Hays, Robert P. Anderson, Hartford, Conn.; Wilfred Feinberg. **Clerk**—A. Daniel Fusaro, New York, N. Y. 10007.

**Third Circuit** (Delaware, New Jersey, Pennsylvania, Virgin Islands)—William Henry Hastie, Chief Judge, Philadelphia, Pa.; Harry E. Kalodner, Philadelphia, Pa.; Gerald McLaughlin, Newark, N. J.; Ruggero J. Aldisert, Pittsburgh, Pa.; Abraham L. Freedman, Philadelphia, Pa.; Collins J. Seitz, Wilmington, Del.; Francis L. Van Dusen, Philadelphia, Pa. **Clerk**—Thomas F. Quinn, Phila., Pa. 19107.

**Fourth Circuit** (Maryland, North Carolina, South Carolina, Virginia, West Virginia)—Clement F. Haynsworth, Jr., Chief Judge, Greenville, S. C.; Simon E. Sobeloff, Baltimore, Md.; Herbert S. Boreman, Parkersburg, W. Va.; Albert V. Bryan, Alexandria, Va.; John D. Butzner, Jr., Richmond, Va.; Harrison L. Winter, Baltimore, Md.; J. Braxton Craven, Jr., Shelby, N. C. **Clerk**—Samuel W. Phillips, Richmond, Va. 23219.

**Fifth Circuit** (Alabama, Florida, Georgia, Louisiana, Mississippi, Texas, Canal Zone)—Elbert Parr Tuttle, Atlanta, Ga.; John R. Brown, Chief Judge, Houston, Tex.; John Minor Wisdom, New Orleans, La.; Walter Pettus Gewin, Tuscaloosa, Ala.; Griffin B. Bell, Atlanta, Ga.; Homer Thornberry, Austin, Tex.; James P. Coleman, Ackerman, Miss.; John Godbold, Montgomery, Ala.; Robert A. Ainsworth, Jr., New Orleans, La.; Irving L. Goldberg, Dallas, Tex.; David W. Dyer, Miami, Fla.; Bryan

Simpson, Jacksonville, Fla.; Claude F. Clayton, Aberdeen, Miss.; Lewis R. Morgan, Newnan, Ga. **Clerk**—Edward W. Wadsworth, 400 Royal St., New Orleans, La. 70130.

**Sixth Circuit** (Kentucky, Michigan, Ohio, Tennessee)—Paul C. Weick, Chief Judge, Akron, Ohio; Clifford O' Sullivan, Port Huron, Mich.; Harry Phillips, Nashville, Tenn.; George Clifton Edwards, Jr., Detroit, Mich.; Anthony J. Celebrezze, Cleveland, Ohio; John W. Peck, Cincinnati, Ohio; Wade Hampton McCree. Jr., Detroit, Mich.; Bert T. Combs, Louisville, Ky. **Clerk**—Carl W. Reuss, Cinn., Ohio 45202.

**Seventh Circuit** (Illinois, Indiana, Wisconsin)—Latham Castle, Chief Judge; John S. Hastings, Roger Kiley, Luther M. Swygert, Walter J. Cummings, Jr., Otto Kerner (all Chicago, Ill.); Thomas E. Fairchild, Milwaukee, Wis. **Clerk**—Kenneth J. Carrick, 219 S. Dearborn St., Chicago, Ill. 60604.

**Eighth Circuit** (Arkansas, Iowa, Minnesota, Missouri, Nebraska, North Dakota, South Dakota)—Martin D. Van Oosterhout, Chief Judge, Sioux City, Ia.; M. C. Matthes, St. Louis, Mo.; Harry A. Blackmun, Winona, Minn.; Pat Mehaffy, Little Rock, Ark.; Floyd R. Gibson, Kansas City, Mo.; Donald P. Lay, Omaha, Neb.; Gerald W. Heaney, Duluth, Minn.; Myron H. Bright, Fargo, N. D. **Clerk**—R. C. Tucker, St. Louis., Mo. 63101.

**Ninth Circuit** (Arizona, California, Idaho, Montana, Nevada, Oregon, Washington, Alaska, Hawaii, Guam)—Richard H. Chambers, Chief Judge, Tucson, Ariz.; Stanley N. Barnes, Los Angeles, Calif.; Frederick G. Hamley, San Francisco, Calif.; Charles M. Merrill, M. Oliver Koelsch, both San Francisco, Calif.; James R. Browning, Great Falls, Mont.; Ben C. Duniway, San Francisco, Calif.; Walter Ely, Los Angeles, Calif.; James C. Carter, San Diego, Calif. **Clerk**—William B. Luck, P. O. Box 547, San Francisco, Calif. 94101.

**Tenth Circuit** (Colorado, Kansas, New Mexico, Oklahoma, Utah, Wyoming)—Alfred P. Murrah, Chief Judge, P. O. Box 1554, Oklahoma City, Okla.; David T. Lewis, Salt Lake City, Utah; Jean S. Breitenstein, Denver, Colo.; Delmas C. Hill, Wichita, Kan., Oliver Seth, Santa Fe, N. M.; John J. Hickey, Cheyenne, Wyo. **Clerk**—William L. Whittaker, Denver, Colo. 80202.

### UNITED STATES DISTRICT JUDGES
Districts in parentheses. Salaries, $30,000 each.

**Alabama**—(**Northern**) Seybourn H. Lynne, Chief Judge; Harlan Hobart Grooms, Clarence W. Allgood. **Clerk**—William E. Davis, all Birmingham 35202. (**Middle**) Frank M. Johnson, Jr., Chief Judge, Montgomery; Virgil Pittman, Mobile. **Clerk** —Robert C. Dobson, Montgomery 36101. (**Southern**) Daniel Holcombe Thomas, Chief Judge; Virgil Pittman, both Mobile. **Clerk**—W. J. O'Connor, Mobile 36602.

**Alaska**—Raymond Plummer, Chief Judge; James von der Heydt. **Clerk**—John M. Kroninger, all Anchorage 99501.

**Arizona**—James A. Walsh, Chief Judge, Tucson; Walter Early Craig, C. A. Muecke, William P. Copple, all Phoenix. **Clerk**—William H. Loveless, Phoenix 85001.

**Arkansas**—(**Eastern**) J. Smith Henley, Chief Judge; Gordon E. Young, both Little Rock; Oren Harris, El Dorado. **Clerk**—Woodrow McClellan, Little Rock 72203. (**Western**) Oren Harris, Chief Judge, El Dorado; J. Smith Henley, Little Rock; Paul X. Williams, Fort Smith. **Clerk**—E. A. Riddle, Fort Smith 72902.

**California**—(**Northern**) George B. Harris, Chief Judge; Oliver J. Carter, Albert C. Wollenberg, William T. Sweigert, Lloyd H. Burke, Alfonso J. Zirpoli, and Stanley A. Weigel, all San Francisco; Robert F. Peckham, San Jose. **Clerk**—James P. Welsh, San Francisco 94102. (**Central**) Thurmond Clarke, Chief Judge; Peirson M. Hall, Albert L. Stephens, Jr., Charles H. Carr, Jesse W. Curtis, E. Avery Crary, Francis C. Whelan, Irving Hill. A. Andrew Hauk, Wm. P. Gray, Warren J. Ferguson, Manuel L. Real, Harry Pregerson. **Clerk**—John A. Childress, all Los Angeles 90012. (**Eastern**) M. D. Crocker, Fresno; Sherrill Halbert, Thomas J. McBride, Chief Judge, both Sacramento. **Clerk** —William C. Robb, Sacramento 95814. (**Southern**) Fred Kunzel, Chief Judge; Edward Schwartz. **Clerk** —William W. Luddy, all San Diego 92101.

**Colorado**—Alfred A. Arraj, Chief Judge; Olin Hatfield Chilson, William E. Doyle. **Clerk**—G. Walter Bowman, all Denver 80201.

**Connecticut**—William H. Timbers, Chief Judge, Bridgeport; M. Joseph Blumenfeld, T. Emmett Clarie, both Hartford; Robert C. Zampano, New Haven. **Clerk**—Gilbert C. Earl, New Haven 06505.

**Delaware**—Caleb M. Wright, Chief Judge; James L. Latchum, Edwin D. Steel, Jr. **Clerk**—E. G. Pollard, all Wilmington 19899.

**District of Columbia**—Edward M. Curran, Chief Judge ($30,500) John H. Pratt, June L. Green,

Gerhard Gesell, John J. Sirica, George L. Hart, Jr., Leonard P. Walsh, William B. Jones, Howard F. Corcoran, Oliver Gasch, William B. Bryant, John Lewis Smith, Jr., Aubrey E. Robinson, Jr., Joseph C. Waddy. **Clerk**—Robert M. Stearns, all Washington, D. C. 20001.

**Florida**—(**Northern**) George H. Carswell, Chief Judge, Tallahassee; Winston Arnow, Pensacola. **Clerk**—Marvin S. Waits, Tallahassee 32302. (**Middle**) Joseph P. Lieb, Chief Judge, Tampa; William A. McRae, Jr., Jacksonville; George C. Young, Orlando; Ben Krentzman, Tampa; Charles F. Scott, Jacksonville. **Clerk**—Wesley R. Theis, Jacksonville 32201. (**Southern**) Charles B. Fulton, Chief Judge; W. O. Mehrtens, C. Clyde Atkins, T. Cabot, Joe Eaton, all Miami. **Clerk**—J. I. Bogart, Miami 33101.

**Georgia**—(**Northern**) Sidney O. Smith, Jr., Chief Judge, Gainesville; Newell Edenfield, Atlanta. **Clerk**—Claude L. Goza, Atlanta 30301. (**Middle**) William A. Bootle, Chief Judge, Macon; J. Robert Elliott, Columbus. **Clerk**—John P. Cowart, Macon 31202. (**Southern**) Alexander A. Lawrence, Savannah. **Clerk**—E. F. Edwards, Savannah 31402.

**Hawaii**—Martin Pence, Chief Judge; C. Nils Tavares. **Clerk**—Walter Chinn, all Honolulu 96801.

**Idaho**—Fred M. Taylor, Chief Judge; Ray McNichols. **Clerk**—Edward M. Bryan, all Boise 83702.

**Illinois**—(**Northern**) William J. Campbell, Chief Judge; J. Sam Perry, Julius J. Hoffman, Edwin A. Robson, Richard B. Austin, James B. Parsons, Hubert L. Will, Bernard M. Decker, Abraham L. Marovitz, William J. Lynch, Alexander J. Napoli. **Clerk**—Elbert A. Wagner, Jr., all Chicago 60604. (**Eastern**) William G. Juergens, Chief Judge, Benton; Henry S. Wise, Danville. **Clerk**—Thomas S. Mefford, E. St. Louis. (**Southern**) Omer Poos, Chief Judge, Springfield; Robert D. Morgan, Peoria. **Clerk**—Wm. J. Littell, Peoria 61601.

**Indiana**—(**Northern**) Robert A. Grant, Chief Judge. South Bend; George N. Beamer, Hammond; Jesse E. Eschbach, Fort Wayne. **Clerk**—Francis T. Grandys, Hammond 46325. (**Southern**) W. E. Steckler, Chief Judge; C. J. Holder, S. H. Dillin, J. E. Noland. **Clerk**—R. G. Newbold, Indianapolis 46204.

**Iowa**—(**Northern**) Edward J. McManus, Chief Judge, Cedar Rapids; William C. Hanson, Ft. Dodge. **Clerk**—John J. O'Connor, Cedar Rapids 52401. (**Southern**) Roy L. Stephenson, Chief Judge, Des Moines; William C. Hanson, Ft. Dodge. **Clerk**—Ronald E. Longstaff, Des Moines 50309.

**Kansas**—Arthur J. Stanley, Jr., Chief Judge, Kansas City; Wesley E. Brown, Wichita; G. Templar, Topeka; Frank G. Theis, Wichita. **Clerk**—C. W. Cahill, Wichita 67201.

**Kentucky**—(**Eastern**) Mac Swinford, Chief Judge; Bernard T. Moynahan, Jr. **Clerk**—Davis T. McGarvey, all Lexington 40501. (**Western**) Henry L. Brooks, Chief Judge, Louisville; Mac Swinford, Lexington, James F. Gordon, Louisville. **Clerk**—August Winkenhofer, Jr., Louisville 40202.

**Louisiana**—(**Eastern**) E. Gordon West, Chief Judge, Baton Rouge; Herbert Christenberry, New Orleans, Frederick J. R. Heebe, Edward J. Boyle Sr., Lansing L. Mitchell, Fred J. Cassibry, Alvin B. Rubin, James A. Comiskey. **Clerk**—A. Dallam O'Brien, Jr., all New Orleans 70130. (**Western**) Benjamin C. Dawkins, Jr., Chief Judge, Shreveport; Edwin F. Hunter, Jr., Lake Charles; Richard J. Putnam, Lafayette. **Clerk**—Alton L. Curtis, Shreveport 71102.

**Maine**—Edward T. Gignoux. **Clerk**—Morris Cox, both Portand 04112.

**Maryland**—Roszel C. Thomsen, Chief Judge; R. Dorsey Watkins, Edward S. Northrop, Frank A. Kaufman, Alexander Harvey II. **Clerk**—Wilfred W. Butschky, all Baltimore 21202.

**Massachusetts**—Charles E. Wyzanski, Jr., Chief Judge; Frank J. Murray, Francis J. W. Ford, Anthony Julian, Andrew A. Caffrey, A. Arthur Garrity Jr. **Clerk**—R. H. Peck, all Boston 02109.

**Michigan**—(**Eastern**) Ralph M. Freeman, Chief Judge; Theodore Levin, Frederick W. Kaess, Thaddeus M. Machrowicz, Talbot Smith, Damon Keith, all Detroit; Stephen J. Roth, Flint. **Clerk**—Frederick W. Johnson, Detroit 48226. (**Western**) W. W. Kent, Chief Judge, Kalamazoo; N. P. Fox, Grand Rapids. **Clerk**—H. T. Ziel, Grand Rapids 49502.

**Minnesota**—Edward J. Devitt, Chief Judge, St. Paul; Earl R. Larson, Miles W. Lord, both Minneapolis; Philip Neville, St. Paul. **Clerk**—Frank A. Massey, St. Paul 55101.

**Mississippi**—(**Northern**) William C. Keady, Chief Judge; Orma R. Smith, both Aberdeen. **Clerk**—William T. Robertson, Oxford 38655. (**Southern**) William H. Cox, Chief Judge, Jackson; Dan M. Russell, Jr., Walter L. Nixon, Jr., both Biloxi. **Clerk**—R. C. Thomas, P. O. Box 769, Jackson 39205.

**Missouri**—(**Eastern**) Roy W. Harper, Chief Judge; James H. Meredith, John K. Regan, all St. Louis; William R. Collinson, Kansas City. **Clerk**—Harold G. Pryce, St. Louis 63101. (**Western**) William H. Becker, Chief Judge; John W. Oliver, William R. Collinson, Elmo B. Hunter, all Kansas City; Roy W. Harper, St. Louis. **Clerk**—John C.

Truman, Kansas City 64106.

**Montana**—William J. Jameson, Billings; Russell E. Smith, Chief Judge, Missoula. **Clerk**—John J. Parker, Butte 59701.

**Nebraska**—Richard E. Robinson, Chief Judge, Omaha; Robert Van Pelt, Lincoln. **Clerk**—Richard C. Peck, Omaha 68101.

**Nevada**—Roger D. Foley, Chief Judge, Las Vegas; Bruce R. Thompson, Reno. **Clerk**—Bernard Supera, Jr., 300 Booth St., Reno 89502.

**New Hampshire**—Hugh H. Bownes. **Clerk**—Mrs. Elizabeth M. Hoyt, both Concord 03302.

**New Jersey**—Anthony T. Augelli, Chief Judge; Reynier J. Wortendyke, Jr., James A. Coolahan, Robert Shaw, Lawrence Whipple, all Newark; M. H. Cohen, Camden. **Clerk**—M. Keller, Jr., Trenton 08605.

**New Mexico**—H. Vearle Payne, Chief Judge; Howard C. Bratton. **Clerk**—Eugene E. Greeson, all Albuquerque 87103.

**New York**—(**Northern**) James T. Foley, Chief Judge, Albany; Edmund Port, Auburn. **Clerk**—W. Arthur Dwyer, Utica 13503 (**Southern**) Sidney Sugarman, Chief Judge, Sylvester J. Ryan, John F. X. McGohey, Edward Weinfeld, Thomas F. Murphy, David N. Edelstein, Edmund L. Palmieri, William B. Herlands, Frederick van Pelt Bryan, Charles M. Metzner, Lloyd F. MacMahon, Thomas F. Croake, Dudley B. Bonsal, Irving Ben Cooper, Harold R. Tyler, Jr., Edward C. McLean, Inzer B. Wyatt, John M. Cannella, Charles H. Tenney, Marvin E. Frankel, Walter R. Mansfield, Constance Baker Motley, Milton Pollack. **Clerk**—John J. Olear, Jr., all New York City 10007. (**Eastern**) Joseph C. Zavatt, Chief Judge; John R. Bartels, Jacob Mishler, John F. Dooling, Jr., George Rosling, Jack B. Weinstein, Anthony J. Travia, Orrin G. Judd. **Clerk**—Lewis Orgel, all Brooklyn 11201. (**Western**) Harold P. Burke, Rochester; John O. Henderson, Chief Judge; John T. Curtain, both Buffalo. **Clerk**—R. E. Logel, Buffalo 14202.

**North Carolina**—(**Eastern**) Algernon L. Butler, Chief Judge, Clinton; John D. Larkins, Jr., New Bern. **Clerk**—Samuel A. Howard, Raleigh 27602. (**Middle**) Edwin M. Stanley, Chief Judge, Greensboro; Eugene A. Gordon, Winston-Salem. **Clerk**—Herman A. Smith, Greensboro 27402. (**Western**) Woodrow Wilson Jones, Chief Judge, Shelby; James B. McMillan, Charlotte. **Clerk**—Thomas E. Rhodes, Asheville 28802.

**North Dakota**—George S. Register, Chief Judge, Bismarck; Ronald N. Davies, Fargo. **Clerk**—Miss Florence Williams, Fargo 58103.

**Ohio**—(**Northern**) Girard E. Kalbfleisch, Chief Judge; James C. Connell, Ben C. Green, William K. Thomas, Thomas D. Lambros, Frank Battisti, all Cleveland; Don J. Young, Toledo. **Clerk**—James Green, Cleveland 44144. (**Southern**) Carl A. Weinman, Chief Judge, Dayton; J. P. Kinneary, Columbus; Timothy S. Hogan, David S. Porter, both Cincinnati. **Clerk**—J. D. Lyter, Columbus 43216.

**Oklahoma**—(**Eastern**) Edwin Langley, Chief Judge, Muskogee; Luther L. Bohanon, Fredrick A. Daugherty, both Oklahoma City. **Clerk**—John B. Fink, Muskogee 74402. (**Western**) Stephen S. Chandler, Chief Judge; Rose Rizley, Luther L. Bohanon, Fredrick A. Daugherty, Luther B. Eubanks. **Clerk**—Miss Vera L. Howard, all Oklahoma City 73102. (**Northern**) Allen E. Barrow, Chief Judge, Tulsa; Luther L. Bohanon, Fredrick A. Daugherty, both Oklahoma City. **Clerk**—Milam M. Ewing, Tulsa 74103.

**Oregon**—Gus J. Solomon, Chief Judge; John F. Kilkenny, Robert C. Belloni. **Clerk**—D. D. Sullivan, all Portland 97207.

**Pennsylvania**—(**Eastern**) Thomas J. Clary, Chief Judge; John W. Lord, Jr., C. William Kraft, Jr., Harold K. Wood, Joseph S. Lord, 3rd, Alfred L. Luongo, John Morgan Davis, A. Leon Higginbotham, Jr., John P. Fullam, Charles R. Weiner, Thomas A. Masterson, all Philadelphia; E. Mac Troutman, Ralph C. Body, both Easton. **Clerk**—John J. Harding, Philadelphia 19107. (**Middle**) Michael H. Sheridan, Chief Judge; William J. Nealon, Jr. **Clerk**—Thomas H. Campion, all Scranton 18501. (**Western**) Wallace S. Gourley, Chief Judge; Rabe Ferguson Marsh, Joseph P. Wilson, John L. Miller, Herbert P. Sorg, Edward Dumbauld, Louis Rosenberg, all Pittsburgh; G. J. Weber, Erie. **Clerk**—J. Wallace, Pittsburgh 15230.

**Rhode Island**—Edward William Day, Chief Judge, Raymond J. Pettine. **Clerk**—N. D. Murphy, all Providence 02901.

**South Carolina**—J. Robert Martin, Jr., Chief Judge, Greenville; Robert W. Hamphill, Columbia. Charles E. Simons, Jr., Charleston; Donald Russell, Spartanburg. **Clerk**—Miller C. Foster, Jr., Columbia 29201.

**South Dakota**—Fred J. Nichol, Chief Judge, Sioux Falls; Axel J. Beck, Aberdeen. **Clerk**—William J. Srstka, Sioux Falls 57101.

**Tennessee**—(**Eastern**) Robert L. Taylor, Chief Judge, Knoxville; Frank W. Wilson, Chattanooga; C. G. Neese, Greeneville. **Clerk**—Karl D. Saulpaw, Jr., P. O. Box 2348, Knoxville 37901. (**Middle**) William E. Miller, Chief Judge; Frank Gray, Jr.

**Clerk**—Brandon Lewis, all Nashville 37203. **(Western)** Bailey Brown, Chief Judge, Robert M. McRae, Jr. **Clerk**—W. Lloyd Johnson. All Memphis 38103.

**Texas**—**(Northern)** Joe Ewing Estes, Chief Judge; Sarah T. Hughes, both Dallas; Leo Brewster, Ft. Worth; William M. Taylor, Jr., Dallas; Halbert O. Woodward, Lubbock. **Clerk**—Bailey F. Rankin, P. O. Box 929, Dallas 75221. **(Southern)** Ben C. Connally, Chief Judge; Allen B. Hannay, Joe M. Ingraham, James L. Noel, Jr., all Houston; Reynaldo G. Garza, Brownsville, Woodrow B. Seals, John V. Singleton, Jr., both Houston. **Clerk**—W. Bailey Thomas, Houston 77061. **(Eastern)** Joe J. Fisher, Chief Judge, Beaumont; William W. Justice, Tyler. **Clerk**—James R. Cooney, Beaumont 77704. **(Western)** Adrian A. Spears, Chief Judge, San Antonio; Dorwin W. Suttle, Ernest Guinn, both El Paso; Jack Roberts, Austin. **Clerk**—Daniel Benedict; San Antonio 78206.

**Utah**—Willis W. Ritter, Chief Judge; A. Sherman Christensen, both Salt Lake City. **Clerk**—Andrew J. Brennan, Salt Lake City 84101.

**Vermont**—Ernest W. Gibson, Chief Judge, Brattleboro; Bernard J. Leddy, Burlington. **Clerk**—Edward J. Trudell, Burlington 05402.

**Virginia**—**(Eastern)** Walter E. Hoffman, Chief Judge, Norfolk; Oren R. Lewis, Alexandria; Robert R. Merhige, Jr., Richmond; Richard B. Kellam, John A. MacKenzie, both Norfolk. **Clerk**—W. Farley Powers, Jr., Norfolk 23510. **(Western)** Ted Dalton, Chief Judge, Roanoke; T. J. Michie, Charlottesville. **Clerk**—L. B. Hanes, Jr., Roanoke 24006.

**Washington**—**(Eastern)** Charles L. Powell, Chief Judge, Spokane, William N. Goodwin, Yakima.

**Clerk**—Miss Dorothy E. Moulton, P. O. Box 1493, Spokane 99210. **(Western)** William J. Lindberg, Chief Judge, William T. Beeks, both Seattle; George H. Boldt, Tacoma, William N. Goodwin, Yakima. **Clerk**—Harold W. Anderson, 308 U. S. Courthouse, Seattle 98104.

**West Virginia**—**(Northern)** Robert Earl Maxwell, Chief Judge, Elkins; Sidney L. Christie, Bluefield. **Clerk**—Thomas F. Stafford, Elkins 26241. **(Southern)** John A. Field, Jr., Chief Judge, Charleston: Sidney L. Christie, Bluefield. **Clerk**—Virgil F. Frizzell, Charleston 25329.

**Wisconsin**—**(Eastern)** Robert E. Tehan, Chief Judge; John W. Reynolds, Myron L. Gordon. **Clerk**—Mrs. Ruth La Fave, all Milwaukee 53202. **(Western)** J. E. Doyle, Madison. **Clerk**—J. R. Adams, Madison 53701.

**Wyoming**—Ewing T. Kerr, Cheyenne. **Clerk**—A. Marvin Helart, P. O. Box 727, Cheyenne 82001.

### TERRITORIAL JUDGES

**Canal Zone**—**District Judge,** Guthrie F. Crowe ($30,000). Box 2006, Balboa Hts. **Clerk**—Mrs. Lois Harrison, Ancon.

**Guam**—**District Judge,** Paul D. Shriver, Agana 96910. ($30,000). **Clerk**—Edward Aguon, P. O. Box DC. Agana 96910.

**Puerto Rico**—**District Judge,** Hiram R. Cancio, Chief Judge: Juan Fernandez-Badillo ($30,000). **Clerk**—Miss Carmen A. Carreras, all San Juan 00904.

**Virgin Islands**—**District Judge,** Walter A. Gordon ($30,000). **Clerk**—Leo Penha, both Charlotte Amalie, St. Thomas 00801.

# Justices of the United States Supreme Court

The Supreme Court comprises the Chief Justice of the United States and such number of Associate Justices as may be fixed by Congress. By virtue of an act of June 25, 1948, the number of Associate Justices is eight. Power to nominate is vested in the President and appointments are made by and with the advice and consent of the Senate. Judges of the Federal courts hold office during good behavior and their compensation may not be diminished while they are in office. A Justice may retire at 70 after serving 10 years as a Federal judge or at 65 after 15 years of service. Salary of the Chief Justice is $40,000 annually, that of each Associate Justice $39,500.

| Name and residence *Chief Justices in italics* | Service Term | Yrs | Born | Died | Name and residence *Chief Justices in italics* | Service Term | Yrs | Born | Died |
|---|---|---|---|---|---|---|---|---|---|
| John Jay, N. Y. | 1789–1795 | 5 | 1745 | 1829 | Melville W. Fuller, Ill. | 1888–1910 | 21 | 1833 | 1910 |
| John Rutledge, S. C. | 1789–1791 | 1 | 1739 | 1800 | David J. Brewer, Kan. | 1890–1910 | 20 | 1837 | 1910 |
| William Cushing, Mass. | 1789–1810 | 20 | 1732 | 1810 | Henry B. Brown, Mich. | 1891–1906 | 15 | 1836 | 1913 |
| James Wilson Pa. | 1789–1798 | 8 | 1742 | 1798 | George Shiras, Jr., Pa. | 1892–1903 | 10 | 1832 | 1924 |
| John Blair, Va. | 1789–1796 | 6 | 1732 | 1800 | Howell E. Jackson, Tenn. | 1893–1895 | 2 | 1832 | 1895 |
| Robert H. Harrison, Md. | 1789–1790 | .. | 1745 | 1790 | Edward D. White, La. | 1894–1910 | 16 | 1845 | 1921 |
| James Iredell, N. C. | 1790–1799 | 9 | 1751 | 1799 | Rufus W. Peckham, N. Y. | 1896–1909 | 13 | 1838 | 1906 |
| Thomas Johnson, Md. | 1791–1793 | 1 | 1732 | 1819 | Joseph McKenna, Cal. | 1898–1925 | 26 | 1843 | 1926 |
| William Paterson, N. J. | 1793–1806 | 13 | 1745 | 1806 | Oliver W. Holmes, Mass. | 1902–1932 | 29 | 1841 | 1935 |
| John Rutledge, S. C. | 1795–(a) | .. | 1739 | 1800 | William R. Day, Ohio | 1903–1922 | 19 | 1849 | 1923 |
| Samuel Chase, Md. | 1796–1811 | 15 | 1741 | 1811 | William H. Moody, Mass. | 1906–1910 | 3 | 1853 | 1917 |
| Oliver Ellsworth, Conn. | 1796–1799 | 4 | 1745 | 1807 | Horace H. Lurton, Tenn. | 1910–1914 | 4 | 1844 | 1914 |
| Bushrod Washington, Va. | 1798–1829 | 31 | 1762 | 1829 | Charles E. Hughes, N. Y. | 1910–1916 | 5 | 1862 | 1948 |
| Alfred Moore, N. C. | 1799–1804 | 4 | 1755 | 1810 | Willis Van Devanter, Wy. | 1911–1937 | 26 | 1859 | 1941 |
| John Marshall, Va. | 1801–1835 | 34 | 1755 | 1835 | Joseph R. Lamar, Ga. | 1911–1916 | 5 | 1857 | 1916 |
| William Johnson, S. C. | 1804–1834 | 30 | 1771 | 1834 | Edward D. White, La. | 1910–1921 | 10 | 1845 | 1921 |
| Brockholst Livingston, N.Y. | 1806–1823 | 16 | 1757 | 1823 | Mahlon Pitney, N. J. | 1912–1922 | 10 | 1858 | 1924 |
| Thomas Todd, Ky. | 1807–1826 | 18 | 1765 | 1826 | Jas. C. McReynolds, Tenn. | 1914–1941 | 26 | 1862 | 1946 |
| Joseph Story, Mass. | 1811–1845 | 33 | 1779 | 1845 | Louis D. Brandeis, Mass. | 1916–1939 | 22 | 1856 | 1941 |
| Gabriel Duval, Md. | 1812–1835 | 22 | 1752 | 1844 | John H. Clarke, Ohio | 1916–1922 | 5 | 1857 | 1945 |
| Smith Thompson, N. Y. | 1823–1843 | 20 | 1768 | 1843 | William H. Taft, Conn. | 1921–1930 | 8 | 1857 | 1930 |
| Robert Trimble, Ky. | 1826–1828 | 2 | 1777 | 1828 | George Sutherland, Utah | 1922–1938 | 15 | 1862 | 1942 |
| John McLean, Ohio | 1829–1861 | 32 | 1785 | 1861 | Pierce Butler, Minn. | 1922–1939 | 16 | 1866 | 1939 |
| Henry Baldwin, Pa. | 1830–1844 | 14 | 1780 | 1844 | Edward T. Sanford, Tenn. | 1923–1930 | 7 | 1865 | 1930 |
| James M. Wayne, Ga. | 1835–1867 | 32 | 1790 | 1867 | Harlan F. Stone, N. Y. | 1925–1941 | 16 | 1872 | 1946 |
| Roger B. Taney, Md. | 1836–1864 | 28 | 1777 | 1864 | Charles E. Hughes, N. Y. | 1930–1941 | 11 | 1862 | 1948 |
| Philip P. Barbour, Va. | 1836–1841 | 4 | 1783 | 1841 | Owen J. Roberts, Penn. | 1930–1945 | 15 | 1875 | 1955 |
| John Catron, Tenn. | 1837–1865 | 28 | 1786 | 1865 | Benjamin N. Cardozo, N.Y. | 1932–1938 | 6 | 1870 | 1938 |
| John McKinley, Ala. | 1837–1852 | 15 | 1780 | 1852 | Hugo L. Black, Ala. | 1937– | .. | 1886 | .... |
| Peter V. Daniel, Va. | 1841–1860 | 19 | 1784 | 1860 | *Stanley F. Reed, Ky. | 1938–1957 | 19 | 1884 | .... |
| Samuel Nelson, N. Y. | 1845–1872 | 27 | 1792 | 1873 | Felix Frankfurter, Mass. | 1939–1962 | 23 | 1882 | 1965 |
| Levi Woodbury, N. H. | 1845–1851 | 5 | 1789 | 1851 | William O. Douglas, Conn. | 1939– | .. | 1898 | .... |
| Robert C. Grier, Pa. | 1846–1870 | 23 | 1794 | 1870 | Frank Murphy, Michigan | 1940–1949 | 9 | 1890 | 1949 |
| Benj. R. Curtis, Mass. | 1851–1857 | 6 | 1809 | 1874 | Harlan F. Stone, N. Y. | 1941–1946 | 5 | 1872 | 1946 |
| John A. Campbell, Ala. | 1853–1861 | 8 | 1811 | 1889 | James F. Byrnes, S. C. (b) | 1941–1942 | 1 | 1879 | .... |
| Nathan Clifford, Me. | 1858–1881 | 23 | 1803 | 1881 | Robert H. Jackson, N. Y. | 1941–1954 | 12 | 1892 | 1954 |
| Noah H. Swayne, Ohio. | 1862–1881 | 18 | 1804 | 1884 | Wiley B. Rutledge, Iowa. | 1943–1949 | 6 | 1894 | 1949 |
| Samuel F. Miller, Iowa. | 1862–1890 | 28 | 1816 | 1890 | Harold H. Burton, Ohio. | 1945–1958 | 13 | 1888 | 1964 |
| David Davis, Ill. | 1862–1877 | 14 | 1815 | 1886 | Fred M. Vinson, Kentucky | 1946–1953 | 7 | 1890 | 1953 |
| Stephen J. Field, Cal. | 1863–1897 | 34 | 1816 | 1899 | *Tom C. Clark, Texas | 1949–1967 | 18 | 1899 | .... |
| Salmon P. Chase, Ohio. | 1864–1873 | 8 | 1808 | 1873 | Sherman Minton, Indiana. | 1949–1956 | 7 | 1890 | 1965 |
| William Strong, Pa. | 1870–1880 | 10 | 1808 | 1895 | Earl Warren, Calif. | 1953– | .. | 1891 | .... |
| Joseph P. Bradley, N. J. | 1870–1892 | 21 | 1813 | 1892 | John Marshall Harlan, N.J. | 1955– | .. | 1899 | .... |
| Ward Hunt, N. Y. | 1873–1882 | 9 | 1810 | 1886 | William J. Brennan, Jr., N.J. | 1956– | .. | 1906 | .... |
| Morrison R. Waite, Ohio. | 1874–1888 | 14 | 1816 | 1888 | *Charles E. Whittaker, Mo. | 1957–1962 | 5 | 1901 | .... |
| John M. Harlan, Ky. | 1877–1911 | 34 | 1833 | 1911 | Potter Stewart, Ohio. | 1958– | .. | 1915 | .... |
| William B. Woods, Ga. | 1881–1887 | 6 | 1824 | 1887 | Byron R. White, Colo. | 1962– | .. | 1917 | .... |
| Stanley Matthews, Ohio. | 1881–1889 | 7 | 1824 | 1889 | Arthur J. Goldberg, Ill. (c) | 1962–1965 | 3 | 1908 | .... |
| Horace Gray, Mass. | 1882–1902 | 20 | 1828 | 1902 | Abe Fortas, Tenn. | 1965– | .. | 1910 | .... |
| Samuel Blatchford, N. Y. | 1882–1893 | 11 | 1820 | 1893 | Thurgood Marshall, N. Y. | 1967– | .. | 1908 | .... |
| Lucius Q. C. Lamar, Miss. | 1888–1893 | 5 | 1825 | 1893 | | | | | |

*Retired. (a) Rejected Dec. 15, 1795; (b) Resigned Oct. 3, 1942, to assume new post as chairman of Economic Stabilization Board. (c) Resigned court, appointed UN Ambassador July 20, 1965.

Robert H. Harrison, who is listed above as an Associate Justice of the Court, was nominated Sept. 24, 1789; confirmed by the Senate, September 26, 1789; and commissioned September 28, 1789. There is nothing affirmative to show that he ever accepted the commission or took the oath. Justice Iredell was nominated February 9, 1790, "vice Harrison, resigned." Under date of Jan. 1790, Harrison wrote to the President saying, "I cannot accept the appointment."

## Ambassadors and Ministers
### AS OF OCTOBER 1, 1968
The address of foreign embassies to the United States is Washington, D. C.

*Embassy has been closed and personnel withdrawn. Limited staffs remain in Algeria, Sudan, and UAR but no ambassadors are assigned.

| Countries | Envoys from United States | Envoys to United States |
|---|---|---|
| Afghanistan | Robert G. Neuman, Amb. | Abdullah Malikyar, Amb. |
| Algeria | *Vacant. | Vacant |
| Argentina | Carter L. Burgess, Amb. | Alvaro C. Alsogaray, Amb. |
| Australia | William H. Crook, Amb. | Sir Keith Waller, Amb. |
| Austria | Douglas MacArthur, II | Dr. Ernst Lemberger, Amb. |
| Barbados | Frederick R. Mann, Amb. | Hilton Augustus Vaughen, Amb. |
| Belgium | Ridgway B. Knight, Amb. | Baron Scheyven, Amb. |
| Bolivia | Raul H. Castro, Amb. | Julio Sanjines-Goytia, Amb. |
| Botswana | Vacant. | Phineas Phokoje Makepe, Amb. |
| Brazil | John W. Tuthill, Amb. | Jorge de Sá Almeida, Amb. |
| Bulgaria | John M. McSweeney, Amb. | Dr. Luben N. Guerassimov, Amb. |
| Burma | Arthur W. Hummel, Jr., Amb. | U Ula Maung, Amb. |
| Burundi | George W. Renchard, Amb. | Terence Nsanze, Amb. |
| Cameroon | Robert L. Payton, Amb. | Joseph N. Owono, Amb. |
| Canada | Harold Francis Linder, Amb. | A. Edgar Ritchie, Amb. |
| Centr. Afr. Rep. | Geoffroy W. Lewis, Amb. | Michel Gallin-Douathe, Amb. |
| Ceylon | Andrew V. Corry, Amb. (also Maldive Is.) | Oliver Weerasinghe, Amb. |
| Chad | Sheldon B. Vance, Amb. | Boukar Abdoul, Amb. |
| Chile | Edward M. Korry, Amb. | Domingo Santa Maria, Amb. |
| China (Taiwan) | Walter P. McConaughy, Amb. | Chow Shu-kai, Amb. |
| Colombia | Reynold E. Carlson, Amb. | Dr. Hernan Echavarria, Amb. |
| Congo (Braz'vil.) | *Vacant. | Vacant |
| Congo (Kinshasa) | Robert H. McBride, Amb. | Cyrille Adoula, Amb. |
| Costa Rica | Clarence A. Boonstra, Amb. | Luis Demetrio Tinoco, Amb. |
| Cyprus | Taylor G. Belcher, Amb. | Zenon Rossides, Amb. |
| Czechoslovakia | Jacob D. Beam, Amb. | Dr. Karel Duda, Amb. |
| Dahomey | Clinton E. Knox, Amb. | Maxime-Leopold Zollner, Amb. |
| Denmark | Angier Biddle Duke, Amb. | Torben Ronne, Amb. |
| Dominican Rep. | John Hugh Crimmins, Amb. | Dr. Hector Garcia-Godoy, Amb. |
| Ecuador | Edson O. Sessions, Amb. | Carlos Mantilla-Ortega, Amb. |
| Egypt | (See United Arab Republic) | |
| El Salvador | William G. Bowdler, Amb. | Col. Julio A. Rivera, Amb. |
| Estonia | | Ernst Jaakson, Consul General |
| Ethiopia | William O. Hall | Dr. Getachew Abdi, Chargé d'Affaires |
| Finland | Tyler Thompson, Amb. | Olavi Munkki, Amb. |
| France | Robert Sargent Shriver, Jr., Amb. | Charles E. Lucet, Amb. |
| Gabon | David M. Bane, Amb. | Leonard Antoine Badinga, Amb. |
| Gambia, The | L. Dean Brown (also Senegal) | Vacant |
| Germany | Henry Cabot Lodge, Amb. | Karl Heinrich Knappstein, Amb. |
| Ghana | Thomas W. McElhiney, Amb. | Ebenezer Moses Debrah, Amb. |
| Great Britain | David K. E. Bruce, Amb. | Sir Patrick Dean, Amb. |
| Greece | Phillips Talbot, Amb. | Christian Xanthopoulos-Palamas, Amb. |
| Guatemala | Vacant. | Dr. Francisco Linares Aranda, Amb. |
| Guinea | Robinson McIlvaine, Amb. | Karim Bangoura, Amb. |
| Guyana | Delmar R. Carlson, Amb. | Sir John Carter, Amb. |
| Haiti | Claude G. Ross, Amb. | Arthur Bonhomme, Amb. |
| Honduras | Joseph J. Jova, Amb. | Ricardo Midence Soto, Amb. |
| Hungary | Martin J. Hillenbrand, Amb. | Sandor Jozan, Chargé d'Affaires |
| Iceland | Karl F. Rolvaag, Amb. | Petur Thorsteinsson, Amb. |
| India | Chester Bowles, Amb. | Nawab Ali Yavar Jung, Amb. |
| Indonesia | Marshall Green, Amb. | Soedjatmoko, Amb. |
| Iran | Armin H. Meyer, Amb. | Hushang Ansary, Amb. |
| Iraq | *Vacant. | Vacant |
| Ireland | Leo J. Sheridan, Amb. | William P. Fay, Amb. |
| Israel | Walworth Barbour, Amb. | Lt. Gen. Yitzhak Rabin, Amb. |
| Italy | H. Gardner Ackley, Amb. | Egidio Ortona, Amb. |
| Ivory Coast | George A. Morgan, Amb. | Timothee N'Guetta Ahoua, Amb. |
| Jamaica | Walter N. Tobriner, Amb. | Egerton R. Richardson, Amb. |
| Japan | U. Alexis Johnson, Amb. | Takeso Shimoda, Amb. |
| Jordan | Harrison M. Symmes, Amb. | Abdul-Hamid Sharaf, Amb. |
| Kenya | Glenn W. Ferguson, Amb. | Burudi Nabwera, Amb. |
| Korea | William J. Porter | Dong Jo Kim, Amb. |
| Kuwait | Howard Rex Cottam, Amb. | Talat Al-Ghoussein, Amb. |
| Laos | William Healy Sullivan, Amb. | Khamking Souvanlasy, Amb. |
| Latvia | | Dr. Arnolds Spekke, Chargé d'Affaires |
| Lebanon | Dwight J. Porter, Amb. | Soleiman Farah, Chargé d'Affaires |
| Lesotho | Vacant. | Albert Steerforth Mohale, Amb. |
| Liberia | Ben Hill Brown, Jr., Amb. | S. Edward Peal, Amb. |
| Libya | David D. Newsom, Amb. | Fathi Abidia, Amb. |
| Lithuania | | Joseph Kajeckas, Chargé d'Affaires |
| Luxembourg | George J. Feldman, Amb. | Maurice Steinmetz, Amb. |
| Malagasy Rep. | David S. King, Amb. (also Mauritius) | René Gilbert Rolison, Chargé d'Affaires |
| Malawi | Marshall P. Jones, Amb. | Nyemba Wales Mbekeani, Amb. |
| Malaysia | James D. Bell, Amb. | Tan Sri Ong Yoke Lin, Amb. |
| Maldive Islands | Andrew V. Corry, Amb. (also Ceylon) | Abdul Sattar, Amb. |
| Mali | G. Edward Clark, Amb. | Moussa Leo Keita, Amb. |
| Malta | Hugh H. Smythe, Amb. | Dr. Arvid Pardo, Amb. |
| Mauritania | *Vacant. | Vacant |
| Mauritius | David S. King, Amb. (also Malagasy Rep.) | Pierre Guy Girald Balancy, Amb. |
| Mexico | Fulton Freeman, Amb. | Hugo B. Margáin, Amb. |
| Morocco | Henry J. Tasca, Amb. | Ahmed Osman, Amb. |
| Nepal | Miss Carol C. Laise, Amb. | Maj. Gen. Padma Bahadur Khatri, Amb. |
| Netherlands | William R. Tyler, Amb. | Carl W. A. Schurmann, Amb. |
| New Zealand | John F. Henning, Amb. | Frank Corner, Amb. |
| Nicaragua | Kennedy M. Crockett, Amb. | Dr. Guillermo Sevilla-Sacasa, Amb. |
| Niger | Samuel C. Adams, Jr., Amb. | Adamou Mayaki, Amb. |
| Nigeria | Elbert G. Mathews, Amb. | Joe Iyalla, Amb. |
| Norway | Miss Margaret Joy Tibbetts, Amb. | Arne Gunneng, Amb. |
| Pakistan | Benjamin H. Oehlert, Jr. | Agha Hilaly, Amb. |
| Panama | Charles W. Adair, Jr., Amb. | Jorge T. Velasquez, Amb. |
| Paraguay | Benigno C. Hernandez, Amb. | Dr. Rogue J. Avila, Amb. |
| Peru | J. Wesley Jones, Amb. | Celso Pastor, Amb. |
| Philippines | G. Mennen Williams, Amb. | Salvador P. Lopez, *Amb. |
| Poland | Walter J. Stoessel, Jr., Amb. | Jerzy Michalowski, Amb. |
| Portugal | W. Tapley Bennett, Jr., Amb. | Vasco Vieira Garin, Amb. |
| Romania | Richard H. Davis, Amb. | Corneliu Bogdan, Amb. |
| Rwanda | Leo G. Cyr, Amb. | Celestin Kabanda, Amb. |

| Countries | Envoys from United States | Envoys to United States |
|---|---|---|
| Saudi Arabia.... | Hermann F. Eilts, Amb................ | Ibrahim Al-Sowayel, Amb. |
| Senegal........ | L. Dean Brown (also The Gambia)......... | Cheikh Ibrahima Fall, Amb. |
| Sierra Leone.... | Robert G. Miner, Amb................. | Adesanya K. Hyde, Amb. |
| Singapore...... | Francis J. Galbraith, Amb................ | Prof. Wong Lin Ken, Amb. |
| Somali Rep..... | Raymond L. Thurston, Amb........... | Yusuf O. Azhari, Amb. |
| South Africa.... | William M. Rountree, Amb........... | H. L. T. Taswell, Amb. |
| Spain.......... | Robert F. Wagner, Amb............... | Marquis de Merry Del Val, Amb. |
| Sudan.......... | *Vacant......................... | *Vacant* |
| Sweden........ | William W. Heath, Amb.............. | Hubert de Besche, Amb. |
| Switzerland..... | John S. Hayes, Amb................ | Felix Schnyder, Amb. |
| Syrian Arab Rep.. | *Vacant......................... | *Vacant* |
| Tanzania........ | John H. Burns, Amb................ | Chief Michael Lukumbuzya, Amb. |
| Thailand........ | Leonard Unger, Amb................ | Bunchana Atthakor, Amb. |
| Togo.......... | Albert W. Sherer, Jr., Amb........... | Dr. Alexandre Ohin, Amb. |
| Trinidad and Tobago......... | William A. Costello, Amb........... | Sir Ellis Emmanuel Innocent Clarke, Amb. |
| Tunisia........ | Francis H. Russell, Amb........... | Rachid Driss, Amb. |
| Turkey........ | *Vacant* | Melih Esenbel, Amb. |
| Uganda........ | Henry E. Stebbins, Amb........... | E. Otema Allimadi, Amb. |
| U.S.S.R....... | Llewellyn E. Thompson, Amb........... | Anatoliy F. Dobrynin, Amb. |
| United Arab. Rep............ | *Vacant......................... | *Vacant* |
| Upper Volta..... | Elliott P. Skinner, Amb........... | Paul Rouamba, Amb. |
| Uruguay....... | Robert M. Sayre, Amb........... | Juan F. Yriart, Amb. |
| Venezuela...... | Maurice M. Bernbaum, Amb........... | Dr. Enrique Tejera-Paris, Amb. |
| Viet Nam...... | Ellsworth Bunker, Amb........... | Bui Diem, Amb. |
| Yemen........ | *Vacant......................... | *Vacant* |
| Yugoslavia..... | C. Burke Elbrick, Amb........... | Bogdan Crnobrnja, Amb. |
| Zambia........ | Robert C. Good, Amb........... | Rupiah B. Banda, Amb. |
| Ambassadors at Large........ | W. Averell Harriman............... | |
| | George C. McGhee.................. | |

## SPECIAL MISSIONS

U. S. Mission to the N. Atlantic Treaty Org., Brussels—Harlan Cleveland.
U. S. Mission to the European Communities, Brussels—J. Robert Schaetzel.
U. S. Mission to the Internatl. Atomic Energy Agency, Vienna—Henry DeWolf Smyth.
U. S. Mission to the Organization of American States, Washington—Sol M. Linowitz.
U. S. Mission to the United Nations, New York—James Russell Wiggins.
U. S. Mission to the European Office of the United Nations and other International Organizations, Geneva—Roger W. Tubby.
U. S. Mission to the Organization for Economic Cooperation and Development, Paris—Philip H. Trezise.

# The National Anthem—The Star-Spangled Banner

The Star-Spangled Banner was ordered played by the military and naval services by President Woodrow Wilson in 1916. It was designated the National Anthem by Act of Congress, March 3, 1931. It was written by Francis Scott Key, of Georgetown, D. C., during the bombardment of Fort McHenry, Baltimore, Md., Sept. 13-14, 1814. Key was a lawyer, a graduate of St. John's College, Annapolis, and a volunteer in a light artillery company. When a friend, Dr. Beanes, a physician of Upper Marlborough, Md., was taken aboard Admiral Cockburn's British squadron for interfering with ground troops, Key and J. S. Skinner, carrying a note from President Madison, went to the fleet under a flag of truce on a cartel ship to ask Beanes' release. Admiral Cockburn consented, but as the fleet was about to sail up the Patapsco to bombard Fort McHenry he detained them, first on H. M. S. Surprise, and then on a supply ship.

Key witnessed the bombardment from his own vessel. It began at 7 a.m., Sept. 13, 1814, and lasted, with intermissions, for 25 hours. The British fired over 1,500 shells, each weighing as much as 220 lbs. They were unable to approach closely because the Americans had sunk 22 vessels in the channel. Only four Americans were killed and 24 wounded. A British bomb-ship was disabled.

During the bombardment Key wrote a stanza on the back of an envelope. Next day at Indian Queen Inn, Baltimore, he wrote out the poem and gave it to his brother-in-law, Judge J. H. Nicholson. Nicholson suggested the tune, Anacreon in Heaven, and had the poem printed on broadsides, of which two survive. On Sept. 20 it appeared in the Baltimore American. Later Key made 3 copies; one is in the Library of Congress and one in the Pennsylvania Historical Society.

The copy that Key wrote in his hotel Sept. 14, 1814, remained in the Nicholson family for 93 years. In 1907 it was sold to Henry Walters of Baltimore. In 1934 it was bought at auction in New York from the Walters estate by the Walters Art Gallery, Baltimore, for $26,400. The Walters Gallery in 1953 sold the manuscript to the Maryland Historical Society for the same price.

The flag that Key saw during the bombardment is preserved in Smithsonian Institution, Washington. It is 30 by 42 ft., and has 15 alternate red and white stripes and 15 stars, for the original 13 states plus Kentucky and Vermont. It was made by Mary Young Pickersgill. The Baltimore Flag house, a museum, occupies her premises, which were restored in 1953.

## I
### THE STAR-SPANGLED BANNER

Oh, say can you see by the dawn's early light
  What so proudly we hailed at the twilight's last gleaming?
Whose broad stripes and bright stars, thru the perilous fight.
  O'er the ramparts we watched were so gallantly streaming?
And the rocket's red glare, the bombs bursting in air,
  Gave proof through the night that our flag was still there.
Oh, say does that star-spangled banner yet wave
  O'er the land of the free and the home of the brave?

## II

On the shore, dimly seen through the mists of the deep.
Where the foe's haughty host in dread silence reposes,
What is that which the breeze, o'er the towering steep,
As it fitfully blows, half conceals, half discloses?
Now it catches the gleam of the morning's first beam.
In full glory reflected now shines on the stream:
'Tis the star-spangled banner! O long may it wave
  O'er the land of the free and the home of the brave!

## III

And where is that band who so vauntingly swore
  That the havoc of war and the battle's confusion,
A home and a country should leave us no more!
  Their blood has washed out their foul footsteps' pollution
No refuge could save the hireling and slave
  From the terror of flight, or the gloom of the grave:
And the star-spangled banner in triumph doth wave
  O'er the land of the free and the home of the brave!

## IV

Oh! thus be it ever, when freemen shall stand
  Between their loved homes and the war's desolation!
Blest with victory and peace, may the heav'n rescued land
  Praise the Power that hath made and preserved us a nation.
Then conquer we must, when our cause it is just,
  And this be our motto: "In God is our trust."
And the star-spangled banner in triumph shall wave
  O'er the land of the free and the home of the brave!

# National Political Committees
### As of Sept., 1968

| DEMOCRATIC OFFICERS | REPUBLICAN OFFICERS |
|---|---|
| Chairman—Lawrence O'Brien | Chairman—Ray C. Bliss |
| Vice Chairman—Mrs. Geri Joseph | Assistant Chairman—Mrs. C. Wayland Brooks |
| Secretary—Mrs. Dorothy Vredenburgh Bush | Vice Chairmen—Donald R. Ross, Mrs. J. W. Marriott, J. Drake Edens, Jr., Mrs. Collis P. Moore. |
| Treasurer—Robert Short (act.) | Secretary—Consuelo Northrop Bailey |
| National Headquarters—2600 Virginia Ave. N.W., Washington, D. C. 20037 | Treasurer—J. William Middendorf, 2nd. |
| | National Headquarters—1625 Eye Street, N.W., Washington, D. C. 20006 |

|  | DEMOCRATIC MEMBERS | | REPUBLICAN MEMBERS | |
|---|---|---|---|---|
| **State** | **Name** | **City** | **Name** | **City** |
| Alabama... | Earl Goodwin | Selma | James Martin | Gadsden |
| | Mrs. Ruth Johnson Owens | Birmingham | Mrs. Bobbie Ames | Marion |
| Alaska..... | Alex Miller | Fairbanks | Lloyd Burgess | Fairbanks |
| | Mrs. Alice Harrigan | Sitka | Mrs. Margee Fitzpatrick | Anchorage |
| Arizona.... | Guy Stillman | Phoenix | John Haugh | Tucson |
| | Mrs. Mildred Larson | Phoenix | Mrs. Forrest Braden | Yuma |
| Arkansas... | Thomas Harper | Ft. Smith | Winthrop A. Rockefeller | Little Rock |
| | Mrs. Jack Carnes | Camden | Mrs. Frank McGillicuddy | Little Rock |
| California... | Stephen Reinhart | Los Angeles | Thomas C. Reed | Ross |
| | Mrs. Carmen Warschaw | Los Angeles | Mrs. Eleanor R. Ring | Coronado |
| Colorado... | Arnold Alperstein | Lakewood | William S. Powers | Denver |
| | Mrs. Doris Banks | Denver | Mrs. Daniel Grey | Denver |
| Conn... | John M. Golden | New Haven | John Alsop | Hartford |
| | Mrs. H. B. Rosenthal | Waterford | Mrs. Norman Harrower, Jr. | New Haven |
| Delaware... | William S. Potter | Wilmington | Harry G. Haskell, Jr. | Wilmington |
| | Mrs. Belle Everett | Kenton | Mrs. C. W. Theobald | Wilmington |
| D. of C.... | Channing E. Philips | Washington | Carl L. Shipley | Washington |
| | Miss Flaxie Pinkett | Washington | Mrs. J. Willard Marriott | Washington |
| Florida..... | William Turnbull | Orlando | William C. Cramer | St. Petersburg |
| | Mrs. Hazel Talley | St. Petersburg | Mrs. Paula F. Hawkins | Maitland |
| Georgia.... | William P. Trotter | La Grange | Howard H. Callaway | Pine Mountain |
| | Mrs. Marge Thurman | Atlanta | Mrs. John A. Cauble | Canton |
| Hawaii..... | Leo B. Rodby, Jr. | Wahiawa | Randolph Crossley | Honolulu |
| | Mrs. Moni Minn | Honolulu | Mrs. George Kellerman | Honolulu |
| Idaho... | Harry Wall | Lewiston | David Little | Emmett |
| | Miss Ellen Healy | Coeur d'alene | Mrs. Gwen Barnett | Boise |
| Illinois..... | Jacob M. Arvey | Chicago | Robert D. Stuart, Jr. | Chicago |
| | Mrs. Dorothy G. O'Brien | De Kalb | Mrs. Hope McCormick | Warrenville |
| Indiana.... | Richard B. Stoner | Columbus | L. Keith Bulen | Indianapolis |
| | Mrs. Katie Wolf | Reynolds | Mrs. Cecil M. Harden | Covington |
| Iowa....... | Robert Fulton | Waterloo | Charles E. Wittenmeyer | Davenport |
| | Mrs. Minette Doderer | Iowa City | Mrs. Elmer M. Smith | Des Moines |
| Kansas..... | Tom Corcoran | Topeka | McDill Boyd | Phillipsburg |
| | Mrs. Neil Blangers | Salina | Mrs. Richard Rogers | Manhattan |
| Kentucky.. | Edward Breathitt | Hopkinsville | Edwin G. Middleton | Louisville |
| | Mrs. Mary Helen Byck | Louisville | Mrs. Harold Barton | Corbin |
| Louisiana.. | J. Marshall Brown | New Orleans | Tom Stagg | Shreveport |
| | Mrs. Blanche Long | Baton Rouge | Mrs. Jean Boese | Alexandria |
| Maine..... | George J. Mitchell | Falmouth | Robert A. Marden | Waterville |
| | Mrs. Faye Broderick | Lincoln | Mrs. Brooks Brown, Jr. | York |
| Maryland.. | J. Millard Tawes | Crisfield | D. Eldred Rinehart | Smithsburg |
| | Dr. Mildred Otenasek | Baltimore | Mrs. K. B. Massenburg | Baltimore |
| Mass...... | John E. Powers | So. Boston | Bruce Crane | Dalton |
| | Mrs. Mary Fantasia | Somerville | Mrs. H. Dunster Howe | Brookline |
| Michigan.. | Coleman A. Young | Detroit | Harold McClure | Alma |
| | Mrs. Mildred Jeffrey | Detroit | Mrs. Elly Peterson | Lansing |
| Minnesota.. | John A. Blatnik | Washington, D.C. | George F. Etzell | Clarissa |
| | Mrs. Geri Joseph | Minneapolis | Mrs. Russell T. Lund | Minneaoplis |
| Mississippi.. | Charles Evers | Fayette | James M. Moye | Laurel |
| | Mrs. Paul S. Derian | Jackson | Mrs. James F. Hooper | Columbus |
| Missouri... | Sidney Salomon, Jr. | Frontenac | Gene Taylor | Sarcoxie |
| | Mrs. Shirley Butters | Bowling Green | Mrs. M. Stanley Ginn | Columbia |
| Montana... | Leif Erickson | Helena | James Murphy | Kalispell |
| | Mrs. Norma Kell | Ledger | Mrs. Isabel C. Moberly | Shelby |
| Nebraska.. | James Exon | Lincoln | Donald R. Ross | Omaha |
| | Mrs. Maurine Biegert | Shickley | Mrs. Clifton B. Batchelder | Omaha |
| Nevada..... | Grant Sawyer | Las Vegas | William Laub | Las Vegas |
| | Mrs. Wilma Moody | Hawthorne | Mrs. Lucie Humphrey | Reno |
| N. Hamp... | John Holland | Bedford | David A. Sterling | Hillsboro |
| | Mrs. Jean Wallin | Nashua | Mrs. Mildred K. Perkins | Concord |
| N. Jersey.. | David T. Wilentz | Perth Amboy | Bernard M. Shanley | Newark |
| | Mrs. Thelma P. Sharp | Vineland | Mrs. K. K. Neuberger | Lincroft |
| N. Mexico.. | Tom E. Brown, Sr. | Artesia | Robert Anderson | Roswell |
| | Mrs. U. D. Sawyer | Crossroads | Mrs. Floyd W. Lee | San Mateo |
| New York.. | John F. English | Syosset | George L. Hinman | New York |
| | Mrs. Shirley Chisholm | Brooklyn | Mrs. Keith McHugh | New York |
| N. Car..... | Jack Kirksey | Morganton | J. E. Broyhill | Lenoir |
| | Mrs. John Winfield | Pinetown | Mrs. Louis G. Rogers | Charlotte |
| N. Dak..... | Mark F. Purdy | Minot | Ben J. Clayburgh | Grand Forks |
| | Mrs. Liv. Bjorlie | Valley City | Mrs. Joe Burgum | Arthur |
| Ohio....... | Albert S. Porter | Pepper Pike | Ray C. Bliss | Akron |
| | Mrs. Betty Jane Gaffney. | Toledo | Mrs. Martha C. Moore | Cambridge |
| Oklahoma.. | J. C. Cobb | Oshtomingo | Bud Wilkinson | Norman |
| | Mrs. Daphine Shear | Duncan | Mrs. Dorothy Stanislaus | Vinita |
| Oregon..... | Blaine Whipple | Portland | George P. Stadelman | The Dalles |
| | Mrs. Alice Corbett | Portland | Mrs. Collis P. Moore | Moro |
| Penn...... | Joseph M. Barr | Pittsburgh | Thomas B. McCabe | Philadelphia |
| | Mrs. Emma G. Miller | Slippery Rock | Mrs. Sarah A. Stauffer | Lancaster Co, |
| Rhode Isl.. | Joseph A. Doorley, Jr. | Providence | Frederick Lippitt | Providence |
| | Mrs. Annette Cusson | Providence | Mrs. D. E. Jackson, Jr. | Providence |
| So. Car.... | Robert McNair | Columbia | J. Drake Edens, Jr. | Columbia |
| | Mrs. Barbara Sylvester | Florence | Mrs. Alice Wilder | Aiken |
| So. Dak.... | William Daugherty | Sioux Falls | D. Jack Gibson | Sioux Falls |
| | Mrs. Mary Wallner | Sioux Falls | Mrs. Louise B. Humphrey | White River |
| Tenn...... | Herbert S. Walters | Morristown | George E. Wilson, Jr. | Harriman |
| | Mrs. Ruth Russell | Gallatin | Mrs. Keith Spurrier | Memphis |
| Texas...... | Robert S. Strauss | Dallas | Albert B. Fay | Houston |
| | Mrs. Lloyd M. Bentsen, Jr. | Houston | Mrs. Tobin Armstrong | Armstrong |
| Utah...... | Wayne L. Black | Salt Lake City | Kendall D. Garff | Salt Lake City |
| | Mrs. Jean Westwood | West Jordan | Mrs. Madge Fairbanks | Salt Lake City |

| State | DEMOCRATIC MEMBERS | | REPUBLICAN MEMBERS | |
|---|---|---|---|---|
| | Name | City | Name | City |
| Vermont... | Daniel O'Brien | S. Burlington | Edward G. Janeway | So. Londonderry |
| | Mrs. Margaret Hartigan.. | Burlington | Mrs. C. N. Bailey | Burlington |
| Virginia.... | William Hopkins, Jr. | Roanoke | I. Lee Potter | Arlington |
| | Mrs. A. Stuart Bolling | Portsmouth | Mrs. Cynthia Newman | Falls Church |
| Washington. | Lloyd K. Graham | Seattle | Robert D. Timm | Olympia |
| | Mrs. Mary Weber | Quincy | Mrs. Harlan Anderson | Kennewick |
| West Va.... | Hulett C. Smith | Beckley | Arch A. Moore, Jr. | Moudsville |
| | Mrs. Hilda Long | Huntington | Mrs. Irvin Humphreys | Huntington |
| Wisconsin.. | Robert T. Huber | West Allis | John E. Hough | Janesville |
| | Miss Mary Lou Berg | West Bend | Mrs. Byron Ising | Oshkosh |
| Wyoming... | William A. Norris, Jr. | Cheyenne | Robert Gosman | Casper |
| | Mrs. June Boyle | Laramie | Mrs. Jack L. Stacy | Douglas |

## OTHER CHIEF POLITICAL COMMITTEES

**AMERICANS FOR DEMOCRATIC ACTION**
(1424 16th St., N.W., Washington, D. C. 20036)
National Chairman—John Kenneth Galbraith
National Director—Leon Shull
Chairman, Exec. Comm.—Jack T. Conway

**COMM. ON POLITICAL EDUCATION, AFL-CIO**
(AFL-CIO Building, 815 16th St.,
Washington, D. C. 20006)
Chairman—George Meany
Secretary-Treasurer—William F. Schnitzler
National Director—Alexander E. Barkan

**CONSERVATIVE PARTY OF THE STATE OF NEW YORK**
(468 Park Ave. So., New York, N. Y. 10016)
Chairman—J. Daniel Mahoney
Secretary—C. Charles Burns

**GREENBACK PARTY**
(1522 Northwest 58th St., Seattle 7, Wash.)
National Chairman—Fred C. Proehl

**LIBERAL PARTY OF NEW YORK STATE**
(1560 Broadway, New York, N. Y. 10036)
Chairman—Donald S. Harrington
First Vice Chairman—David Dubinsky

Exec. Director—Ben Davidson
Treasurer—Harry Uviller

**NATIONAL STATES' RIGHTS PARTY**
(P. O. Box 6263, Savannah, Ga. 31405)
Chairman—Ned Dupes
Secretary-Treasurer—Bernice Settle

**PROHIBITION NATIONAL COMMITTEE**
(P. O. Box 2255, Kalamazoo, Mich.)
National Chairman—E. H. Munn, Sr.
Executive Secretary—Earl F. Dodge
National Secretary—Julia B. Kohler

**SOCIALIST LABOR PARTY**
In Minnesota: Socialist Industrial Gov't. Party
(116 Nassau St., Brooklyn, N. Y. 11201)
National Secretary—Arnold Petersen

**SOCIALIST PARTY**
(1182 Broadway, New York, N. Y. 10001)
National Chairman—Darlington Hoopes
National Honorary Chairman—Norman Thomas
National Secretary—George W. Woywod

**SOCIALIST WORKERS PARTY**
(873 Broadway, New York, N. Y. 10003)
National Chairman—James P. Cannon
National Secretary—Farrell Dobbs

## Chairmen of State Political Committees

| State | DEMOCRATIC | | REPUBLICAN | |
|---|---|---|---|---|
| | Name | City | Name | City |
| Alabama... | Robert S. Vance | Birmingham | Alfred W. Goldthwaite | Montgomery |
| Alaska.... | Jalmar M. Kerttula | Palmer | Robert A. Davenny | Anchorage |
| Arizona.... | Richard Duffield | Tucson | Harry Rosenzweig | Phoenix |
| Arkansas... | Leon Catlett | Little Rock | Odell Pollard | Searcy |
| California.. | Roger Boas | San Francisco | James W. Halley | San Francisco |
| Colorado... | William Grant | Denver | Howard B. Propst | Denver |
| Conn...... | John M. Bailey | Hartford.. | Howard E. Hausman | Hartford |
| Delaware... | Alexis I. Du Pont Bayard.. | Wilmington | Clayton S. Harrison | Wilmington |
| D. of C.... | Bruce Terris | Washington | Carl L. Shipley | Washington |
| Florida.... | Pat Thomas | Tallahassee | William F. Murfin | Ft. Lauderdale |
| Georgia.... | James Grey | Atlanta | G. Paul Jones, Jr. | Macon |
| Hawaii..... | David C. McClung | Honolulu | Edward E. Johnston | Honolulu |
| Idaho...... | E. T. Waters | Boise | Roland Wilber | Lewiston |
| Illinois..... | James A. Ronan | Chicago | Victor L. Smith | Robinson |
| Indiana.... | Gordon St. Angelo | Indianapolis | Buena Chaney | Indianapolis |
| Iowa....... | Clark Rasmussen | Des Moines | John E. Warren | Des Moines |
| Kansas..... | Norbert Dreling | Hays | George E. Nettels, Jr. | Topeka |
| Kentucky... | J. R. Miller | Frankfort | John H. Kerr | Lexington |
| Louisiana... | Arthur C. Watson | Natchitoches | Charles de Gravelles | Lafayette |
| Maine...... | Severin Beliveau | Rumford | Cyril M. Joly, Jr. | Waterville |
| Maryland... | Marvin Mandel | Baltimore | Joseph M. Dukert | Washington, D.C. |
| Mass....... | Lester S. Hyman | Boston | J. A. Spaulding | Boston |
| Michigan... | Sander Levin | Lansing | Mrs. Elly M. Peterson | Lansing |
| Minnesota.. | Warren R. Spannaus | Minneapolis | George Thiss | Minneapolis |
| Mississippi.. | Aaron Henry | Jackson | Clarke Reed | Greenville |
| Missouri.... | Delton L. Houtchens | Clinton | Dorman L. Steelman | Jefferson City |
| Montana.... | Chet Blaylock | Laurel | M. F. (Millett) Keller | Great Falls |
| Nebraska... | John C. Mitchell | Kearney | Mrs. Lorraine Orr | No. Platte |
| Nevada..... | Robert E. Ross | Reno | George W. Abbott | Minden |
| N. Hamp.... | William Craig | Manchester | John Palazzi | Concord |
| N. Jersey... | Robert J. Burkhardt | Trenton | Webster B. Todd | Trenton |
| N. Mexico.. | *Vacant* | | Rex Mattingly | Albuquerque |
| N. York.... | John J. Burns | Binghamton | Charles A. Schoeneck, Jr. | Albany |
| N. Car..... | James V. Johnson | Charlotte | James E. Holshouser, Jr. | Boone |
| N. Dak..... | Larry Erickson | Minot | Thomas L. Secrest | Hettinger |
| Ohio....... | Eugene P. O'Grady | Columbus | John S. Andrews | Columbus |
| Oklahoma.. | William G. Kerr | Oklahoma City | E. L. (Bud) Steward, Jr. | Oklahoma City |
| Oregon..... | Joe Allen | Portland | Irving Enna | Portland |
| Penn...... | Thomas Z. Minehart | Harrisburg | Jack Jordan | Harrisburg |
| Rhode Isl.. | Anthony A. Giannini | Providence | C. George DeStefano | Providence |
| So. Car.... | E. Crosby Lewis | Columbia | Harry S. Dent | Columbia |
| So. Dak.... | Peder K. Ecker | Sioux Falls | Charles A. Howard, Jr. | Aberdeen |
| Tenn...... | James Peeler | Covington | Claude K. Robertson | Knoxville |
| Texas...... | Will Davis | Austin | Peter O'Donnell, Jr. | Dallas |
| Utah....... | A. Wally Sandack | Salt Lake City | Richard Richards | Ogden |
| Vermont.... | William Hunter | Burlington | Elbert G. Moulton | Montpelier |
| Virginia.... | Watkins M. Abbitt | Washington, D. C. | Samuel E. Carpenter | McLean |
| Washington. | Robert E. Kull | Seattle | C. Montgomery Johnson.. | Olympia |
| West Va.... | Rudolph L. DiTrapano | Charleston | Thomas E. Potter | Charleston |
| Wisconsin.. | James W. Wimmer, Jr. | Madison | Ody J. Fish | Hartland |
| Wyoming... | John Rooney | Cheyenne | Clarence A. Brimmer | Casper |

## U. S. Administrative Abbreviations Commonly Used

ACDA.... Arms Control and Disarmament Agency.
ADP ..... Automatic Date Processing.
AEC...... Atomic Energy Commission.
AID...... Agency for International Development.
ARC...... American Red Cross.
ARPA.... Advanced Research Projects Agency
ARS...... Agricultural Research Service.
EDSA.... Business and Defense Services Adm.
BEC...... Bureau of Employees' Compensation.
BLS...... Bureau of Labor Statistics.
CAB...... Civil Aeronautics Board.
CAP...... Civil Air Patrol.
CCC...... Commodity Credit Corporation.
CEA...... Council of Economic Advisers.
CIA...... Central Intelligence Agency.
CMS...... Consumer and Marketing Service.
CONUS .. Continental United States.
CRC...... Civil Rights Commission.
CSC...... Civil Service Commission.
DASA.... Defense Atomic Support Agency.
DOD .... Department of Defense.
DOT .... Department of Transportation.
ESSA .... Environmental Science Services Administration.
FAA...... Federal Aviation Agency.
FAS...... Foreign Agricultural Service.
FBI...... Federal Bureau of Investigation.
FCA...... Farm Credit Administration.
FCC...... Federal Communications Commission.
FDA...... Food and Drug Administration.
FDIC..... Federal Deposit Insurance Corporation.
FHA...... Federal Housing Administration.
FHLBB... Federal Home Loan Bank Board.
FMC...... Federal Maritime Commission.
FMCS..... Federal Mediation and Conciliation Service.
FNMA.... Federal National Mortgage Association.
FPC...... Federal Power Commission.
FRS...... Federal Reserve System.
FTC...... Federal Trade Commission.
GAO...... General Accounting Office.
GPO...... Government Printing Office.
GSA...... General Services Administration.
HEW..... Dept of Health, Education and Welfare.
HHFA.... Housing and Home Finance Agency.
HUD..... Dept. of Housing & Urban Development
IADB.... Inter-American Defense Board.

ICC...... Interstate Commerce Commission or Indian Claims Commission.
IRS...... Internal Revenue Service.
LORAN .. Long-range navigation.
MA....... Maritime Administration.
MAC..... Military Airlift Command.
NARS .... National Archives and Records Service.
NASA..... National Aeronautics and Space Administration.
NATO.... North Atlantic Treaty Organization.
NBS...... National Bureau of Standards.
NIH ..... National Institutes of Health.
NLRB.... National Labor Relations Board.
NSA...... National Shipping Authority.
NSC...... National Security Council.
NSF...... National Science Foundation.
NYC..... Neighborhood Youth Corps.
OECD.... Organization for Economic Cooperation and Development
OEO...... Office of Economic Opportunity.
OEP...... Office of Emergency Planning.
PBS...... Public Buildings Service.
PHA..... Public Housing Administration.
PHS...... Public Health Service.
RB....... Renegotiation Board.
REA...... Rural Electrification Administration.
RRB...... Railroad Retirement Board.
SBA...... Small Business Administration.
SEC...... Securities and Exchange Commission.
SPARS .. Women's Coast Guard Reserves (From Coast Guard motto "Semper-Paratus —Always Ready")
SSA...... Social Security Administration.
SSS...... Selective Service System.
TVA...... Tennessee Valley Authority.
USCG.... United States Coast Guard.
USES..... United States Employment Service.
USIA..... United States Information Agency.
USIS .... United States Information Service.
USMC.... United States Marine Corps.
VA....... Veterans Administration.
VISTA... Volunteers in Service to America.
WAC..... Women's Army Corps.
WAVES.. Women Accepted for Volunteer Emergency Service (Women's Reserve. USNR).

# Abbreviations Commonly Used for International and Regional Organizations

ADB     Asian Development Bank
ADELA     Atlantic Community Development Group for Latin America
AL     Arab League
ANZUS     Australia-New Zealand-United States Defense Treaty and Council
ASPAC     Asian and Pacific Council
BIS     Bank for Intl. Settlements
CABEI     Central American Bank for Economic Integration
CARE     Cooperative for American Relief Everywhere
CB     Casablanca Bloc
CE     Council of Europe
CENTO     Central Treaty Org.
CERN     European Org. for Nuclear Research
CMEA     Council for Mutual Economic Assistance
CMN     Common Market Nations
CN     Commonwealth of Nations
COMECON     Council for Mutual Economic Assistance (Communist Nations)
ECSC     European Coal and Steel Community
ECOSOC     Economic and Social Council
EEC     European Economic Community (European Common Market)
EFTA     European Free Trade Assn. (Outer Seven)
ELDO     European Launcher Development Org.
EURATOM     European Atomic Energy Community
FAO     Food and Agricultural Org.
GATT     General Agreement on Tariffs and Trade
IAEA     Intl. Atomic Energy Agency
IATA     Intl. Air Transport Assn.
IBEC     Intl. Bank for Economic Cooperation
IBRD     Intl. Bank for Reconstruction and Development (World Bank)
ICAO     Intl. Civil Aviation Org.
ICFTU     Intl. Confederation of Free Trade Unions

ICJ     Intl. Court of Justice
IDA     Intl. Development Assn.
IDB     Inter-American Development Bank
IFC     Intl. Finance Corporation
ILO     Intl. Labor Org.
IMCO     Intergovernmental Maritime Consultative Org.
IMF     Intl. Monetary Fund
INTERPOL     Intl. Criminal Police Org.
IOC     Intergovernmental Oceanographic Commission
ITU     Intl. Telecommunicative Union
LAFTA     Latin American Free Trade Assn.
NATO     North Atlantic Treaty Org.
NC     Nordic Council
OAS     Org. of American States
OAU     Org. of African Unity
ODECA     Org. of Central American States (C. A. Common Market)
OECD     Org. for Economic Cooperation and Development
SEATO     Southeast Asia Treaty Org.
SHAPE     Supreme Hdqts., Allied Powers, Europe
UCAR     Union of Central African Republics
UDEAC     Central African Customs and Economic Union
UDEAO     Customs Union of West African States
UN     United Nations
UNCTAD     United Nations Conference on Trade and Development
UNDP     United Nations Development Program
UNESCO     United Nations Educational, Scientific & Cultural Org.
UNICEF     United Nations Children's Fund
UNIDO     United Nations Industrial Development Organization
UPU     Universal Postal Union
WHO     World Health Org.
WMO     World Meteorological Org.
WP     Warsaw Pact

## International Boundary Lines of the United States

The length of the northern boundary of the conterminous United States—the U.S.-Canadian border, excluding Alaska—is 3,987 miles according to the U. S. Geological Survey, Dept. of the Interior. The length of the Alaskan-Canadian border is 1,538 miles. The length of the U.S.-Mexican border, from the Gulf of Mexico to the Pacific Ocean, is approximately 1,933 miles (1963 boundary agreement).

# United States Government Independent Agencies

**Address:** Washington, D. C. Location and zip codes of agencies in parentheses, as of September, 1968

**Appalachian Regional Commission**—Federal cochairman: Joe W. Fleming, 2nd. State cochairman: Gov. Mills Godwin. (1666 Conn. Ave., Wash., D. C. 20235)

**Arms Control & Disarmament Agency**—Director: William C. Foster. (Department of State Bldg., 20451)

**Atomic Energy Commission**—The Commission: Glenn T. Seaborg, chmn., Wilfred E. Johnson, James T. Ramey, Gerald F. Tape. (Wash., D. C., 20545)

**Central Intelligence Agency**—Richard M. Helms, Director. (Wash., D. C. 20505)

**Civil Aeronautics Board—Chairman:** John H. Crooker, Jr. (1825 Connecticut Ave. 20428)

**Commission on Civil Rights**—Staff Dir., William L. Taylor. (801 19th St., 20425)

**Commission of Fine Arts**—William Walton, chmn. (7000 Interior Department Bldg., 20240)

**Civil Service Commission**—John W. Macy, Jr., chmn., L. J. Andolsek, vice chmn. (1900 E St., 20415)

**Consumer Advisory Council**—Betty Furness, exec. secy. (100 Executive Office Bldg., 20506)

**Economic Opportunity, Office of**—Bertrand Harding (act.) Dir. (1200 19th St., 20506)

**Emergency Planning, Office of**—Price Daniel, Dir. (Winder Bldg., 20504)

**Equal Employment Opportunity Commission**—Clifford L. Alexander, Jr., chmn. (1800 G St., 20506)

**Farm Credit Administration**—Lorin Bice, chmn. (So. Agriculture Bldg., 20578)

**Federal Aviation Administration**—Administrator: Gen. William F. McKee. (800 Independence Ave., 20590)

**Federal Communications Commission**—Commissioners: Rosel H. Hyde, chmn., Lee Loevinger, Nicholas Johnson, James J. Wadsworth, Robert T. Bartley, Robert E. Lee, Kenneth A. Cox. (1919 M St., 20554)

**Federal Deposit Insurance Corporation**—Chairman: K. A. Randall. (550 17th St., 20429)

**Federal Home Loan Bank Board**—Chairman: John E. Horne. (101 Indiana Ave., 20552)

**Federal Maritime Commission**—John Harllee, chmn.; (1321 H St., 20573)

**Federal Mediation and Counciliation Service**—Director: William F. Simkin. (Dept. of Labor Bldg., 20427)

**Federal Power Commission**—Lee C. White, chmn., Lawrence J. O'Connor, Jr., vice chmn. (441 G St., 20426)

**Federal Reserve System**—Chairman, Board of Governors: William McC. Martin, Jr. (20th St. & Constitution Ave., 20551)

**Federal Trade Commission** — Commissioners: Paul Rand Dixon, chmn., Philip Elman, Everette

MacIntyre, Mary Gardiner Jones, James M. Nicholson. (Pennsylvania Ave. at 6th St., 20580)

**Food and Drug Administration**—J. L. Goddard, comm. (200 C St., 20204)

**General Accounting Office**—Comptroller General of the U.S.: Elmer B. Staats. (441 G St., 20548)

**General Services Administration**—Administrator: Lawson B. Knott, Jr. (General Services Bldg., 20405)

**Government Printing Office**—Public Printer: James L. Harrison. (North Capitol and H Sts., 20401)

**Indian Claims Commission**—John T. Vance, chmn. (726 Jackson Place, Wash., D. C. 20506)

**Interstate Commerce Commission**—Commissioners: Paul J. Tierney, chmn., Mrs. Virginia Mae Brown, Willard Deason, John Bush, George M. Stafford, Kenneth H. Tuggle, Rupert L. Murphy, Laurence K. Walrath, Dale Hardin. (12th St. and Constitution Ave., 20423)

**National Academy of Sciences and National Research Council**—President: Dr. Frederick Seitz. (2101 Constitution Ave., 20418)

**National Aeronautics and Space Administration**—Administrator: *Vacant.* (Washington, D. C. 20546)

**National Labor Relations Board**—Chairman: F. W. McCulloch. (1717 Pennsylvania Ave., 20570)

**National Mediation Board**—Members: Howard G. Gamser, chmn.; Francis A. O'Neill, Jr., Leverett Edwards, Thomas A. Tracy. (1230 16th St., 20572)

**National Science Foundation**—Director: Leland J. Haworth. (1800 G St., 20550)

**Ozarks Regional Commission**—Federal cochairman: William M. McCandless. State cochairman: Gov. Winthrop Rockefeller. (2001 Wisc. Ave. 20235)

**Public Health Service**—Surgeon General: William H. Stewart. (330 Independence Ave., 20201)

**Railroad Retirement Board**—Chairman: Howard W. Habermeyer. (Rm. 444, 425 13th St., 20004), Main Office, 844 Rush St., Chicago, Ill. 60611)

**Securities and Exchange Commission**—Commissioners: Manuel F. Cohen, chmn., Hamer H. Budge, Hugh F. Owens, Francis M. Wheat, Richard B. Smith. (500 N. Capitol St., 20549)

**Selective Service System**—Director: Lt. Gen. Lewis B. Hershey. (1724 F St., 20435)

**Small Business Administration**—Administrator: Robert C. Moot. (1441 L St., 20416)

**Tariff Commission, United States**—Chairman: Stanley Metzger. (8th and E Sts., 20436)

**Tennessee Valley Authority**—Directors: Aubrey J. Wagner, chmn. (New Sprankle Bldg., Knoxville, Tenn. 37901 and Woodward Bldg., Washington, D. C. 20444)

**United States Information Agency**—Director: *Vacant.* (1750 Pennsylvania Ave., 20547)

**Veterans Administration**—Administrator: W. J. Driver. (Vermont Ave. at H St., 20420)

# The Mayflower Compact

The Mayflower Compact, regarded by some historians as marking the beginning of democracy in America, was signed by 41 adult male members of the Pilgrims aboard the Mayflower as it lay alongside the present site of Provincetown, Mass., in 1620. Because the Pilgrims' patent from the Virginia Company gave them no right to settle so far north, there was grumbling among some members of the company who said abandonment of the Virginia patent left their leaders with no authority over them. To prevent disorder, the Mayflower Compact was signed, binding the Pilgrims to form a government and to abide by its laws. *See Index for other details.*

The text of the compact follows:

In the Name of God, Amen. We whose names are underwritten, the loyal subjects of our dread sovereign Lord, King James, by the grace of God, of Great Britain, France and Ireland; King, Defender of the Faith, etc.

Having undertaken, for the glory of God, and advancement of the Christian faith and honor or our King and Country, a voyage to plant the first colony in the northern parts of Virginia, do by these presents solemnly and mutually in the presence of God and one of another, covenant and combine ourselves together into a civil body politic, for our better ordering and preservation and furtherance of the ends aforesaid; and by virtue hereof enact constitute and frame such just and equal laws, ordinances, acts, constitutions and offices, from time to time, as shall be

thought most meet and convenient for the general good of the Colony; unto which we promise all due submission and obedience.

In witness whereof we have hereunder subscribed our names at Cape Cod the 11 of November, (Nov. 21 new style calendar), in the year of the reign of our sovereign Lord, King James of England, France and Ireland the eighteenth, and of Scotland the fifty-fourth. Ano Dom. 1620.

| | |
|---|---|
| John Carver | Edward Fuller |
| William Bradford | John Turner |
| Edward Winslow | Francis Eaton |
| William Brewster | James Chilton |
| Isaac Allerton | John Craxton |
| Miles Standish | John Billington |
| John Alden (*) | Moses Fletcher |
| Samuel Fuller | John Goodman |
| Christopher Martin | Digery Priest |
| William Mullins | Thomas Williams |
| William White | Gilbert Winslow |
| Richard Warren | Edmund Margesson |
| John Howland | Peter Brown |
| Steven Hopkins | Richard Bitteridge |
| Edward Tilly | George Soule |
| John Tilly | Richard Clark |
| Francis Cooke | Richard Gardiner |
| Thomas Rogers | John Allerton |
| Thomas Tinker | Thomas English |
| John Ridgdale | Edward Doten |
| | Edward Liester |

*Last male survivor, died Sept. 12, 1687.

## How America Was Named

America was named for Amerigo Vespucci (1454-1512), an Italian reputed to have made 4 voyages to the New World for Spain (1497-1503). The German geographer, Martin Waldseemüller, first used the name to honor Vespucci in a book published in 1507.

# Proper Display and Use of the United States Flag

President Johnson signed July 5, 1968, a bill providing penalties of up to a year's imprisonment or a $1,000 fine, or both, for burning publicly or otherwise deliberately desecrating the United States flag. All the states and the District of Columbia already had laws against flag desecration, with varying penalties, but the 1968 legislation provided the first Federal penalties.

A flag code for civilians was adopted June 14, 1923, by a conference of patriotic organizations in Washington. A joint resolution of Congress to codify display of the flag was approved June 22, 1942, for the use of civilians.

**When to Display the Flag**—The flag should be displayed on all days when the weather permits, especially on legal holidays and other special occasions, on official buildings when in use, in or near polling places on election days, and in or near schools when in session. A citizen may fly the flag at any time he wishes. It is customary to display the flag only from sunrise to sunset on buildings and on stationary flagstaffs in the open. However, it may be displayed at night on special occasions, preferably lighted. In Washington, the flag flies over the White House from sunrise to sunset. It flies over the Senate wing of the Capitol when the Senate is in session and over the House wing when that body is in session. It flies day and night over the east and west fronts of the Capitol, without floodlights at night but receiving light from the illuminated Capitol dome. It flies 24 hours a day at several other places, including the Fort McHenry National Monument in Baltimore, where it inspired Francis Scott Key to write The Star Spangled Banner.

**How to Fly the Flag**—The flag should be hoisted briskly and lowered ceremoniously, and should never be allowed to touch the ground or the floor. When hung over a sidewalk from a rope extending from a building to a pole, the union should be away from the building. When hung over the center of a street it should have the union to the north in an east-west street and to the east in a north-south street. No other flag may be flown above or, if on the same level, to the right of the United States flag, except that at the United Nations Headquarters the UN flag may be placed above flags of all member nations and other national flags may be flown with equal prominence or honor with the flag of the United States. Also, at services conducted by Navy chaplains at sea, the church pennant may be flown above the flag.

When two flags are placed against a wall with crossed staffs, the U. S. flag should be at right—its own right, and its staff should be in front of the staff of the other flag; when a number of flags are grouped and displayed from staffs, it should be at the center and at the highest point of the group.

**Church and Platform Use**—In an auditorium, the flag may be displayed flat, above and behind the speaker. If on a staff in a church chancel or on a speaker's platform, it should be in the position of honor at the clergyman's or speaker's right as he faces the congregation or audience. Any other flag in the chancel or on the platform should be displayed at the clergyman's or speaker's left. If elsewhere than in chancel or on platform, the flag should be displayed at the right of the congregation or audience as they face the speaker. The flag should not cover a speaker's desk or be draped in front of a platform.

When the flag is displayed horizontally or vertically against a wall, the stars should be at the observer's left.

**When to Salute the Flag**—All persons present should face the flag, stand at attention and salute on the following occasions: (1) When the flag is passing in a parade or in a review, (2) During the ceremony of hoisting or lowering, (3) When the National Anthem is played and the flag is displayed, and (4) During the Pledge of Allegiance. Those present in uniform should render the military salute. When not in uniform, men should remove the hat with the right hand holding it at the left shoulder, the hand being over the heart. Men without hats should salute in the same manner. Aliens should stand at attention. Women should salute by placing the right hand over the heart.

On Memorial Day, May 30, the flag should fly at half-staff until noon, then be raised to the peak.

As proclaimed by President Eisenhower in 1954, the flag should fly at half-staff for 30 days from the day of a death of a President or former President; for 10 days from the day of death of a Vice President, Chief Justice or retired Chief Justice of the U.S., or Speaker of the House of Representatives; from day of death until burial of an Associate Justice of the Supreme Court, Cabinet member, former Vice President, or Secretary of the Army, Navy or Air Force; for a U. S. Senator, Representative, Territorial Delegate, or the Resident Commissioner of Puerto Rico, on day of death and the following day within the metropolitan area of the District of Columbia and from day of death until burial within the decedent's state, Congressional district, territory or commonwealth; and for the death of the governor of a state, territory or possession of the United States, the flag should fly at half-staff from day of death until burial within that state, territory or possession.

When used to cover a casket, the flag should be placed so that the union is at the head and over the left shoulder. The flag should not be lowered into the grave nor touch the ground.

**Prohibited Uses of the Flag**—The flag should not be dipped to any person or thing. It should never be displayed with the union down save as a signal of distress. It should never be carried flat or horizontally, but always aloft and free.

It should not be displayed on a float, motor car or boat except from a staff.

It should never be used as a covering for a ceiling, nor have placed upon it any word, design, or drawing. It should never be used as a receptacle for carrying anything. It should not be used to cover a statue or a monument.

The flag should never be used for advertising purposes, nor be embroidered on such articles as cushions or handkerchiefs, printed or otherwise impressed on boxes or used as a costume or athletic uniform. Advertising signs should not be fastened to its staff or halyard.

The flag should never be used as drapery of any sort, never festooned, drawn back, nor up, in folds, but always allowed to fall free. Bunting of blue, white and red always arranged with the blue above and the white in the middle, should be used for covering a speaker's desk, draping the front of a platform, and for decoration in general.

**How to Dispose of Worn Flags**—The flag, when it is in such condition that it is no longer a fitting emblem for display, should be destroyed in a dignified way, preferably by burning. Because of the dignity and reverence due the flag, it should be burned in private.

**The President's Flag**—It has a dark blue rectangular background on which appears the coat of arms of the President surrounded by a circle of 50 white stars.

When the President visits a vessel of the United States, the President's flag is broken at the main the moment he reaches the deck and is kept flying as long as he is on board.

## Pledge of Allegiance to the Flag

*I pledge allegiance to the flag of the United States of America and to the republic for which it stands, one nation under God, indivisible, with liberty and justice for all.*

This, the current official version of the Pledge of Allegiance, has developed from the original pledge, which was first published in the Sept. 8, 1892, issue of the Youth's Companion, a weekly magazine then published in Boston. The original pledge contained the phrase "my flag," which was changed more than 30 years later to "flag of the United States of America." An act of Congress in 1954 added the words "under God."

The authorship of the pledge has been in dispute for many years. The Youth's Companion stated in 1917 that the original draft was written by James B. Upham, an executive of the magazine who died in 1910. A leaflet circulated by the magazine later named Upham as the originator of the draft "afterwards condensed and perfected by him and his associates of the Companion force."

Francis Bellamy, a former member of the Youth's Companion editorial staff, publicly claimed authorship of the pledge in 1923. The United States Flag Assn., acting on the advice of a committee named to study the controversy, upheld in 1939 the claim of Bellamy, who had died 8 years earlier. The Library of Congress issued in 1957 a report attributing the authorship to Bellamy.

# The Flag of the United States—The Stars and Stripes

The 50-star flag of the United States was raised for the first time officially at 12:01 a.m. on July 4, 1960, at Fort McHenry National Monument in Baltimore, Md. The 50th star had been added for Hawaii; a year earlier the 49th, for Alaska. Before that, no star had been added since 1912, when New Mexico and Arizona were admitted to the Union.

In the 50-star flag, the stars are arranged in alternate rows of 6 and 5, staggered; there are 5 rows of 6 and 4 rows of 5 stars.

## HISTORY OF THE FLAG

The true history of the Stars and Stripes has become so cluttered by a volume of myth and tradition that the facts are difficult, and in some cases impossible, to establish. For example, it is not certain who designed the Stars and Stripes, who made the first such flag, or even whether it ever flew in any sea fight or land battle of the American Revolution. Historians disagree on many details of the history of the Stars and Stripes and the flags that preceded it in the American colonies.

One thing all agree on is that the Stars and Stripes originated as the result of a resolution offered by the Marine Committee of the Second Continental Congress at Philadelphia and adopted June 14, 1777. It read:

> Resolved: that the flag of the United States be made of thirteen stripes, alternate red and white; that the union be thirteen stars, white in a blue field, representing a new constellation.

Congress gave no hint as to the designer of the flag, no instructions as to the arrangement of the stars, and no information on its appropriate uses. Historians have been unable to find anything to reveal what provided the basis of the resolution —the original flag law.

The resolution establishing the flag was not even published until Sept. 2, 1777, more than 11 weeks after its passage. Despite repeated requests by the American commander, Gen. George Washington, for the "Standard of the United States" for his army, he did not get the flags until 1783, after the Revolutionary War was over. And there is no certainty that the flags were indeed the Stars and Stripes.

## EARLY FLAGS

Although it was never officially adopted by the Continental Congress, many historians consider the first flag of the United States to have been the Grand Union (sometimes called Great Union) flag. This was a modification of the British Meteor flag, which had the red cross of St. George and the white cross of St. Andrew combined in the blue canton. For the Grand Union flag, 6 horizontal stripes were imposed on the red field, dividing it into 13 alternate red and white stripes. On Jan. 1, 1776, when the Continental Army came into formal existence, this flag was unfurled on Prospect Hill, Somerville, Mass. Washington wrote that "we hoisted the Union Flag in compliment to the United Colonies."

Citizens of Easton, Pa., started in 1968 a movement to have the Post Office Department include in a series of U. S. flag commemorative stamps a red, white and blue flag that has been in the public library at Easton for almost 150 years. Supporters of the movement contend that this flag was actually the first Stars and Stripes, and that it was first displayed on July 8, 1776, on the occasion of the public reading of the Declaration of Independence at the court house in Easton. This flag has 13 red and white stripes in the canton, 13 white stars centered in a blue field.

A flag was hastily improvised from garments by the defenders of Fort Schuyler at Rome, N. Y., Aug. 3-22, and this has led to the assumption that it was the Stars and Stripes. Historians believe it was the Grand Union Flag.

The Sons of Liberty had a flag of 9 red and white stripes, to signify 9 colonies, when they met in New York in 1765 to oppose the Stamp Tax. By 1775 the flag had grown to 13 red and white stripes, with a rattlesnake on it.

At Concord, Apr. 19, 1775, the minute men from Bedford, Mass., are said to have carried a flag having a silver arm with sword on a red field.

At Cambridge, Mass., the Sons of Liberty used a plain red flag with a green pine tree on it.

In June, 1775, Washington went from Philadelphia to Boston to take command of the army, escorted to New York by the Philadelphia Light Horse Troop. It carried a yellow flag which had an elaborate coat of arms—the shield charged with 13 knots, the motto "For These We Strive"—and a canton of 13 blue and silver stripes.

In February, 1776, Col. Cristopher Gadsden, member of the Continental Congress, gave the South Carolina Provincial Congress a flag "such as is to be used by the commander-in-chief of the American Navy." It had a yellow field, with a rattlesnake about to strike and the words Don't Tread on Me. Benjamin Franklin's paper, the Pennsylvania Gazette, had suggested sending a cargo of rattlesnakes to London parks to retaliate for British injustice.

At the battle of Bennington, Aug. 16, 1777, patriots used a flag of 7 white and 6 red stripes with a blue canton extending down 9 stripes and showing an arch of 11 white stars over the figure 76 and a star in each of the upper corners. The stars are seven-pointed. This flag is preserved in the Historical Museum at Bennington, Vt.

At the battle of Cowpens, Jan. 17, 1781, the 3rd Maryland Regt. is said to have carried a flag of 13 red and white stripes, with a blue canton containing 12 stars in a circle around one star.

## LEGENDS ABOUT THE FLAG

**Who Designed the Flag?** No one knows for a certainty. Francis Hopkinson, a signer of the Declaration of Independence and designer of seals for the State Department, the Treasury Board and of a naval flag, declared he also had designed the flag and in 1781 asked Congress to reimburse him for his services. Congress did not do so. Dumas Malone of Columbia Univ. wrote: "This talented man . . . designed the American flag."

**Who Called the Flag Old Glory?** The flag is said to have been named Old Glory by William Driver, a sea captain of Salem, Mass. One legend has it that when he raised the flag on his brig, the Charles Doggett, in 1824, he said: "I name thee Old Glory." But his daughter, who presented the flag to the Smithsonian Institution, said he named it at his 21st birthday celebration Mar. 17, 1824, when his mother and some neighbors presented the homemade flag to him.

**Washington Coat-of-Arms Legend**—The idea that the flag was suggested by Washington's coat of arms was publicized by Martin F. Tupper, an English writer, in a play in the 1870s. It rests on a coincidence and has no connection with the flag.

**Washington's Invocation Legend**—Circulation has been given to this speech attributed to General Washington: "We take the stars from heaven, the red from our mother country, separating it by white stripes, thus showing that we have separated from her, and the white stripes shall go down to posterity representing liberty." There is no proof that Washington ever said this.

**The Betsy Ross Legend**—The widely publicized legend that Mrs. Betsy Ross made the first Stars and Stripes in June, 1776, at the request of a committee composed of George Washington, Robert Morris and George Ross, an uncle, was first made public in 1870 by a grandson of Mrs. Ross. Historians have been unable to find a historical record of such a meeting or committee. Dr. Milo Milton Quaife wrote: "No record has ever been found of the creation by Mrs. Ross of the first Stars and Stripes." The New Century Cyclopedia of Names (1954) says: "There is documentary evidence that she was paid in May, 1777, for 'making ships colours, etc.' but no direct documentary evidence has been found to link her with the flag adopted by the Continental Congress on June 14, 1777, as the national emblem, and most historians now doubt if she made it."

## ADDING NEW STARS

The flag of 1777 was used until 1795. Then, on the admission of Vermont and Kentucky to the Union, Congress passed and President Washington signed an act that after May 1, 1795, the flag should have 15 stripes, alternate red and white, and 15 white stars on a blue field in the union.

When new states were admitted it became evident that the flag would become burdened with stripes. Congress thereupon ordered that after July 4, 1818, the flag should have 13 stripes, symbolizing the 13 original states; that the union have 20 stars, and that whenever a new state was admitted a new star should be added on the July 4 following admission. No law designates the permanent arrangement of the stars. However, since 1912 when a new state has been admitted, the new design has been announced by executive order. No star in the flag is specifically identified with any state.

# Presidents, Vice Presidents, Congresses

| # | President | # | Vice President | Service | Congress |
|---|-----------|---|----------------|---------|----------|
| 1 | George Washington....... | 1 | John Adams............. | Apr. 30, 1789–Mar. 3, 1797 | 1, 2, 3, 4. |
| 2 | John Adams............. | 2 | Thomas Jefferson......... | Mar. 4, 1797–Mar. 3, 1801 | 5, 6. |
| 3 | Thomas Jefferson....... | 3 | Aaron Burr.......... | Mar. 4, 1801–Mar. 3, 1805 | 7, 8. |
| do. | | 4 | George Clinton......... | Mar. 4, 1805–Mar. 3, 1809 | 9, 10. |
| 4 | James Madison........... | | do[1] | Mar. 4, 1809–Mar. 3, 1813 | 11, 12. |
| do. | | 5 | Elbridge Gerry[2] | Mar. 4, 1813–Mar. 3, 1817 | 13, 14. |
| 5 | James Monroe.......... | 6 | Daniel D. Tompkins...... | Mar. 4, 1817–Mar. 3, 1825 | 15, 16, 17, 18. |
| 6 | John Quincy Adams...... | 7 | John C. Calhoun......... | Mar. 4, 1825–Mar. 3, 1829 | 19, 20. |
| 7 | Andrew Jackson......... | | do[3] | Mar. 4, 1829–Mar. 3, 1833 | 21, 22. |
| do. | | 8 | Martin Van Buren........ | Mar. 4, 1833–Mar. 3, 1837 | 23, 24. |
| 8 | Martin Van Buren....... | 9 | Richard M. Johnson...... | Mar. 4, 1837–Mar. 3, 1841 | 25, 26. |
| 9 | William Henry Harrison[4].... | 10 | John Tyler........... | Mar. 4, 1841–Apr. 4, 1841 | 27. |
| 10 | John Tyler............ | | | Apr. 6, 1841–Mar. 3, 1845 | 27, 28. |
| 11 | James K. Polk.......... | 11 | George M. Dallas........ | Mar. 4, 1845–Mar. 3, 1849 | 29, 30. |
| 12 | Zachary Taylor[4]........ | 12 | Millard Fillmore........ | Mar. 5, 1849–July 9, 1850 | 31. |
| 13 | Millard Fillmore....... | | | July 10, 1850–Mar. 3, 1853 | 31, 32. |
| 14 | Franklin Pierce........ | 13 | William R. King[5]........ | Mar. 4, 1853–Mar. 3, 1857 | 33, 34. |
| 15 | James Buchanan......... | 14 | John C. Breckinridge.... | Mar. 4, 1857–Mar. 3, 1861 | 35, 36. |
| 16 | Abraham Lincoln........ | 15 | Hannibal Hamlin........ | Mar. 4, 1861–Mar. 3, 1865 | 37, 38. |
| do[4]. | | 16 | Andrew Johnson........ | Mar. 4, 1865–Apr. 15, 1865 | 39. |
| 17 | Andrew Johnson........ | | | Apr. 15, 1865–Mar. 3, 1869 | 39, 40. |
| 18 | Ulysses S. Grant....... | 17 | Schuyler Colfax........ | Mar. 4, 1869–Mar. 3, 1873 | 41, 42. |
| do. | | 18 | Henry Wilson[6]......... | Mar. 4, 1873–Mar. 3, 1877 | 43, 44. |
| 19 | Rutherford B. Hayes.... | 19 | William A. Wheeler...... | Mar. 4, 1877–Mar. 3, 1881 | 45, 46. |
| 20 | James A. Garfield[4]...... | 20 | Chester A. Arthur....... | Mar. 4, 1881–Sept. 19, 1881 | 47. |
| 21 | Chester A. Arthur...... | | | Sept. 20, 1881–Mar. 3, 1885 | 47, 48. |
| 22 | Grover Cleveland[7]...... | 21 | Thomas A. Hendricks[8].... | Mar. 4, 1885–Mar. 3, 1889 | 49, 50. |
| 23 | Benjamin Harrison..... | 22 | Levi P. Morton......... | Mar. 4, 1889–Mar. 3, 1893 | 51, 52. |
| 24 | Grover Cleveland[7]...... | 23 | Adlai E. Stevenson...... | Mar. 4, 1893–Mar. 3, 1897 | 53, 54. |
| 25 | William McKinley....... | 24 | Garret A. Hobart[9]....... | Mar. 4, 1897–Mar. 3, 1901 | 55, 56. |
| do[4]. | | 25 | Theodore Roosevelt..... | Mar. 4, 1901–Sept. 14, 1901 | 57. |
| 26 | Theodore Roosevelt..... | | | Sept. 14, 1901–Mar. 3, 1905 | 57, 58. |
| do. | | 26 | Charles W. Fairbanks... | Mar. 4, 1905–Mar. 3, 1909 | 59, 60. |
| 27 | William H. Taft........ | 27 | James S. Sherman[10]...... | Mar. 4, 1909–Mar. 3, 1913 | 61, 62. |
| 28 | Woodrow Wilson........ | 28 | Thomas R. Marshall..... | Mar. 4, 1913–Mar. 3, 1921 | 63, 64, 65, 66. |
| 29 | Warren G. Harding[4].... | 29 | Calvin Coolidge........ | Mar. 4, 1921–Aug. 2, 1923 | 67. |
| 30 | Calvin Coolidge....... | | | Aug. 3, 1923–Mar. 3, 1925 | 68. |
| do. | | 30 | Charles G. Dawes....... | Mar. 4, 1925–Mar. 3, 1929 | 69, 70. |
| 31 | Herbert C. Hoover...... | 31 | Charles Curtis......... | Mar. 4, 1929–Mar. 3, 1933 | 71, 72. |
| 32 | Franklin D. Roosevelt.. | 32 | John N. Garner........ | Mar. 4, 1933–Jan. 20, 1941 | 73, 74, 75, 76. |
| do. | | 33 | Henry A. Wallace....... | Jan. 20, 1941–Jan. 20, 1945 | 77, 78. |
| do[4]. | | 34 | Harry S. Truman....... | Jan. 20, 1945–Apr. 12, 1945 | 79. |
| 33 | Harry S. Truman....... | | | Apr. 12, 1945–Jan. 20, 1949 | 79, 80. |
| do. | | 35 | Alben W. Barkley....... | Jan. 20, 1949–Jan. 20, 1953 | 81, 82. |
| 34 | Dwight D. Eisenhower... | 36 | Richard M. Nixon...... | Jan. 20, 1953–Jan. 20, 1961 | 83, 84, 85, 86. |
| 35 | John F. Kennedy[4]...... | 37 | Lyndon B. Johnson...... | Jan. 20, 1961–Nov. 22, 1963 | 87, 88. |
| 36 | Lyndon B. Johnson..... | | | Nov. 22, 1963–Jan. 20, 1965 | 88. |
| do. | | 38 | Hubert H. Humphrey.... | Jan. 20, 1965 | 89, 90 |

[1]Died Apr. 30, 1812. [2]Died Nov. 23, 1814. [3]Resigned Dec. 28, 1832, to become United States Senator. [4]Died in office. [5]Died Apr. 18, 1853. [6]Died Nov. 23, 1875. [7]Terms not consecutive. [8]Died Nov. 25, 1885. [9]Died Nov. 21, 1899. [10]Died Oct. 30, 1912.

## Vice Presidents of the United States

The numerals given Vice Presidents do not coincide with those given Presidents, because some Presidents had none and some had more than one.

| # | Name | Birthplace | Yr. | Resi-dence | Quali-fied | Poli-tics | Place of Death | Yr. | Age. |
|---|------|-----------|-----|------------|-----------|-----------|----------------|-----|------|
| 1 | John Adams........ | Quincy, Mass. | 1735 | Mass.. | 1789 | Fed... | Quincy, Mass...... | 1826 | 90 |
| 2 | Thomas Jefferson.... | Shadwell, Va. | 1743 | Va... | 1797 | Rep... | Monticello, Va..... | 1826 | 83 |
| 3 | Aaron Burr........ | Newark, N. J.... | 1756 | N. Y.. | 1801 | Rep... | Staten Island, N. Y. | 1836 | 80 |
| 4 | George Clinton..... | Ulster Co., N.Y | 1739 | N. Y.. | 1805 | Rep... | Washington, D. C... | 1812 | 73 |
| 5 | Elbridge Gerry..... | Marblehead, Mass. | 1744 | Mass.. | 1813 | Rep... | Washington, D. C... | 1814 | 70 |
| 6 | Daniel D. Tompkins. | Scarsdale, N. Y. | 1774 | N. Y.. | 1817 | Rep... | Staten Island, N. Y. | 1825 | 51 |
| 7 | *John C. Calhoun... | Abbeville, S. C.. | 1782 | S. C.. | 1825 | Rep... | Washington, D. C... | 1850 | 68 |
| 8 | Martin Van Buren.. | Kinderhook, N. Y.. | 1782 | N. Y.. | 1833 | Dem.. | Kinderhook, N. Y... | 1862 | 79 |
| 9 | Richard M. Johnson. | Louisville, Ky... | 1780 | Ky... | 1837 | Dem.. | Frankfort, Ky...... | 1850 | 70 |
| 10 | John Tyler......... | Greenway, Va.... | 1790 | Va... | 1841 | Whig. | Richmond, Va...... | 1862 | 71 |
| 11 | George M. Dallas... | Philadelphia, Pa... | 1792 | Pa... | 1845 | Dem.. | Philadelphia, Pa... | 1864 | 72 |
| 12 | Millard Fillmore... | Summerhill, N. Y. | 1800 | N. Y.. | 1849 | Whig. | Buffalo, N. Y...... | 1874 | 74 |
| 13 | William R. King.... | Sampson Co., N. C.. | 1786 | Ala.. | 1853 | Dem.. | Dallas Co., Ala.... | 1853 | 67 |
| 14 | John C. Breckinridge | Lexington, Ky.... | 1821 | Ky... | 1857 | Dem.. | Lexington, Ky..... | 1875 | 54 |
| 15 | Hannibal Hamlin... | Paris, Me....... | 1809 | Me... | 1861 | Rep... | Bangor, Me....... | 1891 | 81 |
| 16 | Andrew Johnson.... | Raleigh, N. C.... | 1808 | Tenn. | 1865 | (x).. | Carter Co., Tenn... | 1875 | 66 |
| 17 | Schuyler Colfax.... | New York City, N.Y. | 1823 | Ind... | 1869 | Rep... | Mankato, Minn..... | 1885 | 62 |
| 18 | Henry Wilson...... | Farmington, N. H.. | 1812 | Mass.. | 1873 | Rep... | Washington, D. C... | 1875 | 63 |
| 19 | William A. Wheeler. | Malone, N. Y..... | 1819 | N. Y.. | 1877 | Rep... | Malone, N. Y...... | 1887 | 68 |
| 20 | Chester A. Arthur.. | Fairfield, Vt..... | 1830 | N. Y.. | 1881 | Rep... | New York City, N.Y. | 1886 | 56 |
| 21 | Thomas A. Hendricks | Muskingum Co., Ohio | 1819 | Ind... | 1885 | Dem.. | Indianapolis, Ind... | 1885 | 66 |
| 22 | Levi P. Morton.... | Shoreham, Vt.... | 1824 | N. Y.. | 1889 | Rep... | Rhinebeck, N. Y.... | 1920 | 96 |
| 23 | Adlai E. Stevenson[1].. | Christian Co., Ky. | 1835 | Ill... | 1893 | Dem.. | Chicago, Ill....... | 1914 | 78 |
| 24 | Garret A. Hobart... | Long Branch, N. J.. | 1844 | N. J.. | 1897 | Rep... | Paterson, N. J .... | 1899 | 55 |
| 25 | Theodore Roosevelt. | New York City, N.Y. | 1858 | N. Y.. | 1901 | Rep... | Oyster Bay, N. Y... | 1919 | 60 |
| 26 | Charles W. Fairbanks | Unionville Centre, Ohio | 1852 | Ind... | 1905 | Rep... | Indianapolis, Ind... | 1918 | 66 |
| 27 | James S. Sherman.. | Utica, N. Y...... | 1855 | N. Y.. | 1909 | Rep... | Utica, N. Y....... | 1912 | 57 |
| 28 | Thomas R. Marshall | No. Manchester, Ind. | 1854 | Ind... | 1913 | Dem.. | Washington, D. C... | 1925 | 71 |
| 29 | Calvin Coolidge.... | Plymouth, Vt..... | 1872 | Mass.. | 1921 | Rep... | Northampton, Mass. | 1933 | 60 |
| 30 | Charles G. Dawes... | Marietta, Ohio.... | 1865 | Ill... | 1925 | Rep... | Evanston, Ill...... | 1951 | 85 |
| 31 | Charles Curtis..... | Topeka, Kan..... | 1860 | Kan.. | 1929 | Rep... | Washington, D. C... | 1936 | 76 |
| 32 | John Nance Garner. | Red River Co., Tex. | 1868 | Tex.. | 1933 | Dem.. | Uvalde, Tex....... | 1967 | 98 |
| 33 | Henry Agard Wallace | Adair County, Ia... | 1888 | Iowa. | 1941 | Dem.. | Danbury, Conn.... | 1965 | 77 |
| 34 | Harry S. Truman... | Lamar, Mo...... | 1884 | Mo... | 1945 | Dem.. | ................. | ... | .. |
| 35 | Alben W. Barkley... | Graves County, Ky. | 1877 | Ky... | 1949 | Dem.. | Lexington, Va...... | 1956 | 78 |
| 36 | Richard M. Nixon.. | Yorba Linda, Calif. | 1913 | Calif. | 1953 | Rep... | ................. | ... | .. |
| 37 | Lyndon B. Johnson. | Johnson City, Tex.. | 1908 | Tex.. | 1961 | Dem.. | ................. | ... | .. |
| 38 | Hubert H. Humphrey | Wallace, S. D..... | 1911 | Minn. | 1965 | Dem.. | ................. | ... | .. |

(*) John C. Calhoun resigned Dec. 28, 1832, having been elected to the U. S. Senate (Dec. 12, 1832) to fill vacancy caused by the resignation of Robert Y. Hayne. (x) Andrew Johnson—A Democrat nominated by Republicans and elected with Lincoln on the Nation Union ticket. [1]Adlai E. Stevenson, 23rd Vice President, was grandfather of Democratic candidate for President, 1952 and 1956.

# CABINETS OF THE UNITED STATES
## Secretaries of State

The Department of Foreign Affairs was created by Act of Congress July 27, 1789, and the name changed to Department of State on Sept. 15. Thomas Jefferson, the minister to France, was appointed Secretary of State by President Washington Sept. 26, and took office March 21, 1790. John Jay, who had held the office of Secretary for Foreign Affairs since his appointment by the Ninth Continental Congress in March 1784, in place of Robert R. Livingston (appointed Jan. 1781), left it in September 1789, when the U. S. Supreme Court was established with him as Chief Justice.

The Secretary of State is charged, under the direction of the President, with the duties appertaining to correspondence with the public ministers and the consuls of the United States and with the representatives of foreign powers accredited to the United States, and to negotiations of whatever character relating to the foreign affairs of the United States.

| Presidents | Cabinet Officers | Home | Apptd. | Presidents | Cabinet Officers | Home | Apptd. |
|---|---|---|---|---|---|---|---|
| Washington.. | Thomas Jefferson..... | Va.... | 1789 | Arthur...... | James G. Blaine...... | Me... | 1881 |
| " | Edmund Randolph.... | " | 1794 | " | F. T. Frelinghuysen... | N. J.. | 1881 |
| " | Timothy Pickering... | Pa.... | 1795 | Cleveland.... | " | " | 1885 |
| J. Adams... | " | " | 1795 | " | Thomas F. Bayard.... | Del... | 1885 |
| " | John Marshall...... | Va.... | 1800 | B. Harrison.. | " | " | 1889 |
| Jefferson... | James Madison...... | " | 1801 | " | James G. Blaine...... | Me.. | 1889 |
| Madison.... | Robert Smith....... | Md... | 1809 | " | John W. Foster...... | Ind... | 1892 |
| " | James Monroe...... | Va.... | 1811 | Cleveland.... | Walter Q. Gresham... | Ill.... | 1893 |
| Monroe..... | John Quincy Adams... | Mass.. | 1817 | " | Richard Olney...... | Mass.. | 1895 |
| J. Q. Adams. | Henry Clay........ | Ky... | 1825 | McKinley.... | " | " | 1897 |
| Jackson..... | Martin Van Buren... | N. Y.. | 1829 | " | John Sherman...... | Ohio.. | 1897 |
| " | Edward Livingston... | La.... | 1831 | " | William R. Day..... | " | 1898 |
| " | Louis McLane..... | Del... | 1833 | " | John Hay......... | D. C.. | 1898 |
| " | John Forsyth...... | Ga.... | 1834 | T. Roosevelt. | " | " | 1901 |
| Van Buren.. | " | " | 1837 | " | Elihu Root........ | N. Y. | 1905 |
| W.H.Harrison | Daniel Webster..... | Mass.. | 1841 | " | Robert Bacon...... | " | 1909 |
| Tyler...... | " | " | 1841 | Taft........ | " | " | 1909 |
| " | Abel P. Upshur..... | Va.... | 1843 | " | Philander C. Knox... | Pa. | 1909 |
| " | John C. Calhoun.... | S. C.. | 1844 | Wilson...... | " | " | 1913 |
| Polk....... | " | " | 1845 | " | William J. Bryan.... | Neb... | 1913 |
| " | James Buchanan.... | Pa.... | 1845 | " | Robert Lansing..... | N. Y.. | 1915 |
| Taylor..... | " | " | 1849 | " | Bainbridge Colby.... | " | 1920 |
| " | John M. Clayton.... | Del... | 1849 | Harding..... | Charles E. Hughes.... | " | 1921 |
| Fillmore.... | " | " | 1850 | Coolidge.... | " | " | 1923 |
| " | Daniel Webster..... | Mass.. | 1850 | " | Frank B. Kellogg.... | Minn. | 1925 |
| " | Edward Everett..... | " | 1852 | Hoover...... | " | " | 1929 |
| Pierce...... | William L. Marcy.... | N. Y.. | 1853 | " | Henry L. Stimson.... | N. Y.. | 1929 |
| Buchanan... | " | " | 1857 | F.D.Roosevelt | Cordell Hull....... | Tenn. | 1933 |
| " | Lewis Cass....... | Mich.. | 1857 | " | E. R. Stettinius, Jr... | Va.... | 1944 |
| " | Jeremiah S. Black... | Pa.... | 1860 | Truman..... | " | " | 1945 |
| Lincoln..... | " | " | 1861 | " | James F. Byrnes.... | S. C. | 1945 |
| " | William H. Seward... | N. Y.. | 1861 | " | George C. Marshall... | Pa... | 1947 |
| Johnson, A.. | " | " | 1865 | " | Dean G. Acheson.... | Conn.. | 1949 |
| Grant...... | Elihu B. Washburne.. | Ill... | 1869 | Eisenhower.. | John Foster Dulles... | N. Y.. | 1953 |
| " | Hamilton Fish..... | N. Y.. | 1869 | " | Christian A. Herter... | Mass.. | 1959 |
| Hayes...... | " | " | 1877 | Kennedy.... | Dean Rusk......... | N. Y.. | 1961 |
| " | William M. Evarts... | " | 1877 | Johnson, L.B. | " | " | 1963 |
| Garfield.... | " | " | 1881 | | | | |
| " | James G. Blaine..... | Me.. | 1881 | | | | |

## Secretaries of the Treasury

The second Continental Congress on July 29, 1775, appointed Michael Hillegas and George Clymer, Esqs., as "joint treasurers of the United Colonies." Francis Hopkinson was elected Treasurer of Loans July 27, 1778. Robert Morris was appointed Superintendent of Finances by the Seventh Continental Congress on Feb. 20, 1781. The Treasury Department was organized by Act of Congress on Sept. 2, 1789, and President Washington commissioned Alexander Hamilton Secretary of the Treasury on Sept. 11.

| Presidents | Cabinet Officers | Home | Apptd. | Presidents | Cabinet Officers | Home | Apptd. |
|---|---|---|---|---|---|---|---|
| Washington.. | Alexander Hamilton.. | N. Y.. | 1789 | Grant...... | William A. Richardson | Mass.. | 1873 |
| " | Oliver Wolcott...... | Conn.. | 1795 | " | Benjamin H. Bristow. | Ky... | 1874 |
| J. Adams.... | " | " | 1797 | " | Lot M. Morrill..... | Me... | 1876 |
| " | Samuel Dexter...... | Mass. | 1801 | Hayes...... | John Sherman...... | Ohio.. | 1877 |
| Jefferson.... | " | " | 1801 | Garfield.... | William Windom..... | Minn. | 1881 |
| " | Albert Gallatin..... | Pa.... | 1801 | Arthur...... | Charles J. Folger.... | N. Y. | 1881 |
| Madison..... | " | " | 1809 | " | Walter Q. Gresham... | Ind... | 1884 |
| " | George W. Campbell. | Tenn. | 1814 | " | Hugh McCulloch..... | " | 1884 |
| " | Alexander J. Dallas.. | Pa.... | 1814 | Cleveland.... | Daniel Manning..... | N. Y.. | 1885 |
| " | William H. Crawford. | Ga.... | 1816 | " | Charles S. Fairchild... | " | 1887 |
| Monroe..... | " | " | 1817 | B. Harrison. | William Windom..... | Minn. | 1889 |
| J. Q. Adams. | Richard Rush...... | Pa.... | 1825 | " | Charles Foster...... | Ohio.. | 1891 |
| Jackson..... | Samuel D. Ingham... | " | 1829 | Cleveland.... | John G. Carlisle.... | Ky... | 1893 |
| " | Louis McLane..... | Del... | 1831 | McKinley.... | Lyman J. Gage..... | Ill... | 1897 |
| " | William J. Duane... | Pa.... | 1833 | T. Roosevelt.. | " | " | 1901 |
| " | Roger B. Taney..... | Md... | 1833 | " | Leslie M. Shaw..... | Ia.... | 1902 |
| " | Levi Woodbury..... | N. H.. | 1834 | " | George B. Cortelyou.. | N. Y. | 1907 |
| Van Buren.. | " | " | 1837 | Taft........ | Franklin MacVeagh... | Ill... | 1909 |
| W.H.Harrison | Thomas Ewing..... | Ohio.. | 1841 | Wilson...... | William G. McAdoo... | N. Y.. | 1913 |
| Tyler...... | " | " | 1841 | " | Carter Glass....... | Va.... | 1918 |
| " | Walter Forward.... | Pa.... | 1841 | " | David F. Houston.... | Mo.... | 1920 |
| " | John C. Spencer.... | N. Y.. | 1843 | Harding..... | Andrew W. Mellon... | Pa... | 1921 |
| " | George M. Bibb..... | Ky... | 1844 | Coolidge.... | " | " | 1923 |
| Polk....... | Robert J. Walker.... | Miss.. | 1845 | Hoover...... | " | " | 1929 |
| Taylor..... | William M. Meredith. | Pa... | 1849 | " | Ogden L. Mills..... | N. Y. | 1932 |
| Fillmore.... | Thomas Corwin.... | Ohio.. | 1850 | F.D.Roosevelt | William H. Woodin... | " | 1933 |
| Pierce...... | James Guthrie..... | Ky... | 1853 | " | Henry Morgenthau,Jr. | " | 1934 |
| Buchanan... | Howell Cobb....... | Ga.... | 1857 | Truman..... | Fred M. Vinson.... | Ky... | 1945 |
| " | Philip F. Thomas.... | Md... | 1860 | " | John W. Snyder..... | Mo... | 1946 |
| " | John A. Dix....... | N. Y. | 1861 | Eisenhower.. | George M. Humphrey | Ohio.. | 1953 |
| Lincoln..... | Salmon P. Chase.... | Ohio.. | 1861 | " | Robert B. Anderson.. | Conn. | 1957 |
| " | William P. Fessenden | Me... | 1864 | Kennedy.... | C. Douglas Dillon... | N. J.. | 1961 |
| " | Hugh McCulloch.... | Ind... | 1865 | Johnson, L. B. | " | " | 1963 |
| Johnson A... | " | " | 1865 | " | Henry H. Fowler.... | Va.... | 1965 |
| Grant...... | George S. Boutwell.. | Mass. | 1869 | | | | |

## Secretaries of Housing and Urban Development

The Department of Housing and Urban Development was created by Act of Congress Sept. 9, 1965.

| President | Cabinet Officer | Home | Apptd. | President | Cabinet Officer | Home | Apptd. |
|---|---|---|---|---|---|---|---|
| Johnson, L. B. | Robert C. Weaver... | Wash. | 1966 | | | | |

## Secretaries of Defense

The Department of Defense, originally designated the National Military Establishment, was created Sept. 18, 1947. It is headed by the Secretary of Defense, who is a member of the President's cabinet. The Departments of the Army, of the Navy and of the Air Force function within the Department of Defense, and their respective secretaries are no longer members of the President's cabinet.

| Presidents | Cabinet Officers | Home | Apptd. | Presidents | Cabinet Officers | Home | Apptd. |
|---|---|---|---|---|---|---|---|
| Truman | James V. Forrestal | N. Y. | 1947 | Eisenhower | Neil H. McElroy | Ohio | 1957 |
| " | Louis A. Johnson | W. Va. | 1949 | " | Thomas S. Gates, Jr. | Pa. | 1959 |
| " | George C. Marshall | Pa. | 1950 | Kennedy | Robert S. McNamara | Mich. | 1961 |
| " | Robert A. Lovett | N. Y. | 1951 | Johnson, L. B. | " | | 1963 |
| Eisenhower | Charles E. Wilson | Mich. | 1953 | " | Clark M. Clifford | Md. | 1968 |

## Secretaries of War

The Second Continental Congress set up in June, 1776, a board of War and Ordnance consisting of five members: John Adams, Roger Sherman, Benjamin Harrison, James Wilson and Edward Rutledge. Richard Peters was elected Secretary on June 12. This Board, several times changed, continued until Oct. 30, 1781, when Congress appointed Benjamin Lincoln Secretary of War, a position created by Act of Congress the previous February. The Eleventh Continental Congress on March 8, 1785, appointed Gen. Henry Knox to succeed him with the added duties of the Navy. The War (and Navy) Department was created by Act of Congress Aug. 7, 1789, and Gen. Henry Knox was commissioned Secretary of War under that Act Sept. 12, 1789.

| Presidents | Cabinet Officers | Home | Apptd. | Presidents | Cabinet Officers | Home | Apptd. |
|---|---|---|---|---|---|---|---|
| Washington | Henry Knox | Mass. | 1789 | Grant | John A. Rawlins | Ill. | 1869 |
| " | Timothy Pickering | Pa. | 1795 | " | William T. Sherman | Ohio | 1869 |
| " | James McHenry | Md. | 1796 | " | William W. Belknap | Iowa | 1869 |
| J. Adams | " | " | 1797 | " | Alphonso Taft | Ohio | 1876 |
| " | Samuel Dexter | Mass. | 1800 | " | James Don. Cameron | Pa. | 1876 |
| Jefferson | Henry Dearborn | " | 1801 | Hayes | George W. McCrary | Iowa | 1877 |
| Madison | William Eustis | Mass. | 1809 | " | Alexander Ramsey | Minn. | 1879 |
| " | John Armstrong | N. Y. | 1813 | Garfield | Robert T. Lincoln | Ill. | 1881 |
| " | James Monroe | Va. | 1814 | Arthur | " | " | 1881 |
| " | William H. Crawford | Ga. | 1815 | Cleveland | William C. Endicott | Mass. | 1885 |
| Monroe | John C. Calhoun | S. C. | 1817 | B. Harrison | Redfield Proctor | Vt. | 1890 |
| J. Q. Adams | James Barbour | Va. | 1825 | " | Stephen B. Elkins | W. Va. | 1891 |
| " | Peter B. Porter | N. Y. | 1828 | Cleveland | Daniel S. Lamont | N. Y. | 1893 |
| Jackson | John H. Eaton | Tenn. | 1829 | McKinley | Russel A. Alger | Mich. | 1897 |
| " | Lewis Cass | Ohio | 1831 | " | Elihu Root | N. Y. | 1899 |
| " | Benjamin F. Butler | N. Y. | 1837 | T. Roosevelt | " | " | 1901 |
| Van Buren | Joel R. Poinsett | S. C. | 1837 | " | William H. Taft | Ohio | 1904 |
| W.H. Harrison | John Bell | Tenn. | 1841 | " | Luke E. Wright | Tenn. | 1908 |
| Tyler | " | " | 1841 | Taft | Jacob M. Dickinson | " | 1909 |
| " | John C. Spencer | N. Y. | 1841 | " | Henry L. Stimson | N. Y. | 1911 |
| " | James M. Porter | Pa. | 1843 | Wilson | Lindley M. Garrison | N. J. | 1913 |
| " | William Wilkins | " | 1844 | " | Newton D. Baker | Ohio | 1916 |
| Polk | William L. Marcy | N. Y. | 1845 | Harding | John W. Weeks | Mass. | 1921 |
| Taylor | George W. Crawford | Ga. | 1849 | Coolidge | " | " | 1923 |
| Fillmore | Charles M. Conrad | La. | 1850 | " | Dwight F. Davis | Mo. | 1925 |
| Pierce | Jefferson Davis | Miss. | 1853 | Hoover | James W. Good | Ill. | 1929 |
| Buchanan | John B. Floyd | Va. | 1857 | " | Patrick J. Hurley | Okla. | 1929 |
| " | Joseph Holt | Ky. | 1861 | F.D. Roosevelt | George H. Dern | Utah | 1933 |
| Lincoln | Simon Cameron | Pa. | 1861 | " | Harry H. Woodring | Kan. | 1937 |
| " | Edwin M. Stanton | Pa. | 1862 | " | Henry L. Stimson | N. Y. | 1940 |
| Johnson, A. | " | " | 1865 | Truman | Robert P. Patterson | N. Y. | 1945 |
| " | John M. Schofield | Ill. | 1868 | " | *Kenneth C. Royall | N. C. | 1947 |

(*) Last member of the President's Cabinet. The War Dept. became the Dept. of the Army and is now a branch of the Dept. of Defense, created September 18, 1947.

## Secretaries of the Navy

The Navy Department was created by Act of Congress April 30, 1798, which made the Secretary a member of the Cabinet. President Adams appointed George Cabot of Beverly, Mass., the first Secretary of the Navy, May 3, 1798, but he declined the office. Benjamin Stoddert was appointed the same day.

| Presidents | Cabinet Officers | Home | Apptd. | Presidents | Cabinet Officers | Home | Apptd. |
|---|---|---|---|---|---|---|---|
| J. Adams | Benjamin Stoddert | Md. | 1798 | Lincoln | Gideon Welles | Conn. | 1861 |
| Jefferson | " | " | 1801 | Johnson, A. | " | " | 1865 |
| " | Robert Smith | " | 1801 | Grant | Adolph E. Borie | Pa. | 1869 |
| Madison | Paul Hamilton | S. C. | 1809 | " | George M. Robeson | N. J. | 1869 |
| " | William Jones | Pa. | 1813 | Hayes | Richard W. Thompson | Ind. | 1877 |
| " | Benjamin Williams Crownshield | Mass. | 1814 | " | Nathan Goff, Jr. | W. Va. | 1881 |
| " | " | " | 1817 | Garfield | William H. Hunt | La. | 1881 |
| Monroe | " | " | 1817 | Arthur | William E. Chandler | N. H. | 1882 |
| " | Smith Thompson | N. Y. | 1818 | Cleveland | William C. Whitney | N. Y. | 1885 |
| " | Samuel L. Southard | N. J. | 1823 | B. Harrison | Benjamin F. Tracy | N. Y. | 1889 |
| J. Q. Adams | " | " | 1825 | Cleveland | Hilary A. Herbert | Ala. | 1893 |
| Jackson | John Branch | N. C. | 1829 | McKinley | John D. Long | Mass. | 1897 |
| " | Levi Woodbury | N. H. | 1831 | T. Roosevelt | " | " | 1901 |
| " | Mahlon Dickerson | N. J. | 1834 | " | William H. Moody | " | 1902 |
| Van Buren | " | " | 1837 | " | Paul Morton | Ill. | 1904 |
| " | James K. Paulding | N. Y. | 1838 | " | Charles J. Bonaparte | Md. | 1905 |
| W.H. Harrison | George E. Badger | N. C. | 1841 | " | Victor H. Metcalf | Cal. | 1906 |
| Tyler | " | " | 1841 | " | Truman H. Newberry | Mich. | 1908 |
| " | Abel P. Upshur | Va. | 1841 | Taft | George von L. Meyer | Mass. | 1909 |
| " | David Henshaw | Mass. | 1843 | Wilson | Josephus Daniels | N. C. | 1913 |
| " | Thomas W. Gilmer | Va. | 1844 | Harding | Edwin Denby | Mich. | 1921 |
| " | John Y. Mason | " | 1844 | Coolidge | " | " | 1923 |
| Polk | George Bancroft | Mass. | 1845 | " | Curtis D. Wilbur | Cal. | 1924 |
| " | John Y. Mason | Va. | 1846 | Hoover | Charles Francis Adams | Mass. | 1929 |
| Taylor | William B. Preston | " | 1849 | F.D. Roosevelt | Claude A. Swanson | Va. | 1933 |
| Fillmore | William A. Graham | N. C. | 1850 | " | Charles Edison | N. J. | 1940 |
| " | John P. Kennedy | Md. | 1852 | " | Frank Knox | Ill. | 1940 |
| Pierce | James C. Dobbin | N. C. | 1853 | " | *James V. Forrestal | N. Y. | 1944 |
| Buchanan | Isaac Toucey | Conn. | 1857 | Truman | " | " | 1945 |

(*) Last member of the President's Cabinet. The Navy Department is now a branch of the Dept. of Defense, created September 18, 1947.

## Secretaries of Transportation

The Department of Transportation was created by Act of Congress Oct. 15, 1966.

| President | Cabinet Officer | Home | Apptd. | President | Cabinet Officer | Home | Apptd. |
|---|---|---|---|---|---|---|---|
| Johnson, L. B. | Alan S. Boyd | Fla. | 1966 | | | | |

# Postmasters General

Benjamin Franklin had been Deputy Postmaster in America (1737), and Postmaster General for the Colonies (1753) under the King until summarily dismissed by him Jan. 30, 1774. The Second Continental Congress created the Post Office Department with headquarters in Philadelphia and on July 26, 1775, elected Benjamin Franklin Postmaster General for one year. On his sailing later for France as one of the ambassadors, Richard Bache succeeded him on Nov. 7, 1776. Ebenezer Hazard was appointed Postmaster General Jan. 28, 1782. Congress temporarily established the Post Office Department as a branch of the Treasury, on Sept. 22, 1789, and Washington commissioned Samuel Osgood Postmaster General on Sept. 26. The Postmaster General was made a member of the Cabinet March 9, 1829. His is the only portfolio in the Cabinet that expires every four years. The Post Office Department was established as an executive department June 8, 1872.

| Presidents | Cabinet Officers | Home | Apptd. | Presidents | Cabinet Officers | Home | Apptd. |
|---|---|---|---|---|---|---|---|
| Washington.. | Samuel Osgood..... | Mass.. | 1789 | Hayes...... | David McK. Key.... | Tenn.. | 1877 |
| " .. | Timothy Pickering... | Pa.... | 1791 | " | Horace Maynard.... | Tenn.. | 1880 |
| " .. | Joseph Habersham... | Ga.... | 1795 | Garfield.... | Thomas L. James.... | N. Y.. | 1881 |
| J. Adams.... | | | 1797 | Arthur...... | Timothy O. Howe... | Wis... | 1881 |
| Jefferson.... | | " | 1801 | " | Walter Q. Gresham.. | Ind.... | 1883 |
| " | Gideon Granger..... | Conn.. | 1801 | " | Frank Hatton...... | Iowa. | 1884 |
| Madison.... | | " | 1809 | Cleveland... | William F. Vilas... | Wis... | 1885 |
| " | Return J. Meigs, Jr.. | Ohio | 1814 | " | Don M. Dickinson... | Mich.. | 1888 |
| Monroe...... | | " | 1817 | B. Harrison.. | John Wanamaker... | Pa.... | 1889 |
| " | John McLean...... | " | 1823 | Cleveland... | Wilson S. Bissel.... | N. Y.. | 1893 |
| J. Q. Adams.. | | " | 1825 | " | William L. Wilson... | W. Va. | 1895 |
| Jackson..... | William T. Barry.... | Ky... | 1829 | McKinley... | James A. Gary..... | Md... | 1897 |
| " | Amos Kendall...... | " | 1835 | " | Charles E. Smith... | Pa.... | 1898 |
| Van Buren... | | " | 1837 | T. Roosevelt. | | " | 1901 |
| " | John M. Niles..... | Conn.. | 1840 | " | Henry C. Payne.... | Wis... | 1902 |
| W.H.Harrison | Francis Granger.... | N. Y.. | 1841 | " | Robert J. Wynne... | Pa.... | 1904 |
| Tyler....... | Francis Granger.... | N. Y.. | 1841 | " | George B. Cortelyou. | N. Y.. | 1905 |
| " | Charles A. Wickliffe. | Ky.... | 1841 | " | George von L. Meyer | Mass.. | 1907 |
| Polk........ | Cave Johnson..... | Tenn. | 1845 | Taft........ | Frank H. Hitchcock. | | 1909 |
| Taylor...... | Jacob Collamer.... | Vt.... | 1849 | Wilson..... | Albert S. Burleson.. | Tex... | 1913 |
| Fillmore.... | Nathan K. Hall.... | N. Y.. | 1850 | Harding.... | Will H. Hays..... | Ind... | 1921 |
| " | Samuel D. Hubbard. | Conn.. | 1852 | " | Hubert Work...... | Colo.. | 1922 |
| Pierce...... | James Campbell.... | Pa.... | 1853 | " | Harry S. New..... | Ind... | 1923 |
| Buchanan... | Aaron V. Brown.... | Tenn. | 1857 | Coolidge.... | | " | 1923 |
| " | Joseph Holt....... | Ky.... | 1859 | Hoover..... | Walter F. Brown... | Ohio.. | 1929 |
| " | Horatio King...... | Me... | 1861 | F.D.Roosevelt | James A. Farley.... | N. Y.. | 1933 |
| Lincoln..... | Montgomery Blair... | D. C.. | 1861 | " | Frank C. Walker... | Pa.... | 1940 |
| " | William Dennison... | Ohio. | 1864 | Truman..... | Robt. E. Hannegan.. | Mo... | 1945 |
| Johnson, A... | | " | 1865 | " | Jesse M. Donaldson. | Mo... | 1947 |
| " | Alex. W. Randall... | Wis... | 1866 | Eisenhower.. | A. E. Summerfield... | Mich.. | 1953 |
| Grant...... | John A. J. Creswell. | Md... | 1869 | Kennedy.... | J. Edward Day..... | Calif. | 1961 |
| " | James W. Marshall.. | Va.... | 1874 | " | John A. Gronouski... | Wis... | 1963 |
| " | Marshall Jewell.... | Conn. | 1874 | Johnson, L. B. | | " | 1963 |
| " | James N. Tyner..... | Ind... | 1876 | " | Lawrence F. O'Brien. | Mass.. | 1965 |
| | | | | " | W. Marvin Watson... | Texas. | 1968 |

# Attorneys General

The office of Attorney General was organized by Act of Congress Sept. 24, 1789. Washington appointed Edmund Randolph to the post. The Attorney General was made a member of the Cabinet in 1814. The Dept. of Justice was created June 22, 1870, and the Attorney General was placed at its head.

| Presidents | Cabinet Officers | Home | Apptd. | Presidents | Cabinet Officers | Home | Apptd. |
|---|---|---|---|---|---|---|---|
| Washington.. | Edmund Randolph... | Va.... | 1789 | Grant...... | Alphonso Taft..... | Ohio.. | 1876 |
| " .. | William Bradford... | Pa.... | 1794 | Hayes...... | Charles Devens.... | Mass.. | 1877 |
| " .. | Charles Lee........ | Va.... | 1795 | Garfield.... | Wayne MacVeagh... | Pa.... | 1881 |
| J. Adams.... | | | 1797 | Arthur...... | Benjamin H. Brewster | | 1881 |
| Jefferson.... | Levi Lincoln....... | Mass.. | 1801 | Cleveland... | Augustus Garland... | Ark... | 1885 |
| " | John Breckenridge... | Ky.... | 1805 | B. Harrison.. | William H. H. | | |
| " | Caesar A. Rodney... | Del... | 1807 | | Miller......... | Ind... | 1889 |
| Madison.... | | " | 1809 | Cleveland... | Richard Olney..... | Mass.. | 1893 |
| " | William Pinkney.... | Md... | 1801 | " | Judson Harmon.... | Ohio.. | 1895 |
| " | Richard Rush....... | Pa.... | 1814 | McKinley... | Joseph McKenna.... | Cal... | 1897 |
| Monroe...... | | " | 1817 | " | John W. Griggs.... | N. J.. | 1898 |
| " | William Wirt...... | Va.... | 1817 | " | Philander C. Knox... | Pa.... | 1901 |
| J. Q. Adams.. | | " | 1825 | T. Roosevelt. | | " | 1901 |
| Jackson..... | John McP. Berrien... | Ga.... | 1829 | " | William H. Moody... | Mass.. | 1904 |
| " | Roger B. Taney.... | Md... | 1831 | " .. | Charles J. Bona- | | |
| " | Benjamin F. Butler.. | N. Y.. | 1833 | | parte.......... | Md... | 1906 |
| Van Buren... | | " | 1837 | Taft........ | George W. Wicker- | | |
| " | Felix Grundy...... | Tenn. | 1838 | | sham......... | N. Y.. | 1909 |
| " | Henry D. Gilpin.... | Pa.... | 1840 | Wilson..... | J. C. McReynolds... | Tenn.. | 1913 |
| W.H.Harrison | John J. Crittenden... | Ky.... | 1841 | " | Thomas W. Gregory. | Tex... | 1914 |
| Tyler....... | | " | 1841 | " | A. Mitchell Palmer.. | Pa.... | 1919 |
| " | Hugh S. Legare.... | S. C.. | 1841 | Harding.... | Harry M. Daugh- | | |
| " | John Nelson....... | Md... | 1843 | | erty.......... | Ohio.. | 1921 |
| Polk........ | John Y. Mason..... | Va.... | 1845 | Coolidge.... | | " | 1923 |
| " | Nathan Clifford.... | Me... | 1946 | " | Harlan F. Stone.... | N. Y.. | 1924 |
| " | Isaac Toucey...... | Conn. | 1848 | " | John G. Sargent.... | Vt.... | 1925 |
| Taylor...... | Reverdy Johnson.... | Md... | 1849 | Hoover..... | William D. Mitchell.. | Minn. | 1929 |
| Fillmore.... | John J. Crittenden... | Ky.... | 1850 | F.D.Roosevelt | Homer S. Cummings. | Conn. | 1933 |
| Pierce...... | Caleb Cushing..... | Mass.. | 1853 | " | Frank Murphy..... | Mich.. | 1939 |
| Buchanan... | Jeremiah S. Black... | Pa.... | 1857 | " | Robert H. Jackson.. | N. Y.. | 1940 |
| " | Edwin M. Stanton... | Pa.... | 1860 | " | Francis Biddle..... | Pa.... | 1941 |
| Lincoln..... | Edward Bates...... | Mo... | 1861 | Truman..... | Tom C. Clark...... | Tex... | 1945 |
| " | James Speed....... | Ky.... | 1864 | " | J. Howard McGrath.. | R. I.. | 1949 |
| Johnson, A... | | " | 1865 | " | J. P. McGranery.... | Pa.... | 1952 |
| " | Henry Stanbery..... | Ohio.. | 1866 | Eisenhower.. | H. Brownell, Jr..... | N. Y.. | 1953 |
| " | William M. Evarts... | N. Y.. | 1868 | " | William P. Rogers... | Md... | 1957 |
| Grant...... | Ebenezer R. Hoar... | Mass.. | 1869 | Kennedy.... | Robert F. Kennedy.. | Mass.. | 1961 |
| " | Amos T. Akerman... | Ga.... | 1870 | Johnson, L. B. | | " | 1963 |
| " | George H. Williams.. | Ore... | 1871 | " | N. deB. Katzenbach. | Ill.... | 1965 |
| " | Edwards Pierrepont.. | N. Y.. | 1875 | " | Ramsey Clark...... | Tex... | 1967 |

# Secretaries of Health, Education and Welfare

The Department of Health, Education and Welfare was created by Act of Congress April 11, 1953.

| Presidents | Cabinet Officers | Home | Apptd. | Presidents | Cabinet Officers | Home | Apptd. |
|---|---|---|---|---|---|---|---|
| Eisenhower... | Oveta Culp Hobby... | Texas. | 1953 | Kennedy.... | Anthony J. Celebrezze | Ohio.. | 1962 |
| " | Marion B. Folsom... | N. Y.. | 1955 | Johnson, L. B. | | " | 1963 |
| " | Arthur S. Flemming. | Ohio.. | 1958 | " | John W. Gardner.... | N. Y.. | 1965 |
| Kennedy..... | Abraham A. Ribicoff.. | Conn.. | 1961 | " | Wilbur J. Cohen.... | Mich.. | 1968 |

## Secretaries of the Interior

The Department of Interior was created by Act of Congress March 3, 1849.

| Presidents | Cabinet Officers | Home | Apptd. | Presidents | Cabinet Officers | Home | Apptd. |
|---|---|---|---|---|---|---|---|
| Taylor...... | Thomas Ewing...... | Ohio.. | 1849 | McKinley.... | Cornelius N. Bliss.... | N. Y.. | 1897 |
| Fillmore..... | Thomas M. T. Mc- | | | " .... | Ethan A. Hitchcock.. | Mo... | 1898 |
| | Kennan.......... | Pa.... | 1850 | T. Roosevelt. | " | " | 1901 |
| " .... | Alex. H. H. Stuart... | Va.... | 1850 | " .... | James R. Garfield.... | Ohio.. | 1907 |
| Pierce...... | Robert McClelland.. | Mich.. | 1853 | Taft........ | Richard A. Ballinger. | Wash.. | 1909 |
| Buchanan... | Jacob Thompson.... | Miss.. | 1857 | " .... | Walter L. Fisher.... | Ill.... | 1911 |
| Lincoln...... | Caleb B. Smith..... | Ind... | 1861 | Wilson..... | Franklin K. Lane.... | Cal... | 1913 |
| " .... | John P. Usher...... | " | 1863 | " .... | John B. Payne...... | Ill.... | 1920 |
| Johnson, A... | " | " | 1865 | Harding..... | Albert B. Fall....... | N. M. | 1921 |
| " .... | James Harlan...... | Iowa.. | 1865 | " .... | Hubert Work....... | Colo.. | 1923 |
| " .... | Orville H. Browning. | Ill.... | 1866 | Coolidge..... | " | Colo.. | 1923 |
| Grant....... | Jacob D. Cox...... | Ohio.. | 1869 | " .... | Roy O. West....... | Ill.... | 1929 |
| " .... | Columbus Delano... | " | 1870 | Hoover...... | Ray Lyman Wilbur.. | Cal... | 1929 |
| " .... | Zachariah Chandler.. | Mich.. | 1875 | F.D.Roosevelt | Harold L. Ickes..... | Ia.... | 1933 |
| Hayes...... | Carl Schurz....... | Mo.... | 1877 | Truman..... | " | Ill.... | 1945 |
| Garfield..... | Sam. J. Kirkwood... | Iowa.. | 1881 | " .... | Julius A. Krug...... | Wis... | 1946 |
| Arthur...... | Henry M. Teller.... | Colo.. | 1882 | " .... | Oscar L. Chapman... | Colo.. | 1950 |
| Cleveland... | Lucius Q. C. Lamar.. | Miss.. | 1885 | Eisenhower... | Douglas McKay..... | Oreg.. | 1953 |
| " .... | William F. Vilas.... | Wis... | 1888 | " .... | Fred A. Seaton...... | Nebr.. | 1956 |
| B. Harrison.. | John W. Noble..... | Mo... | 1889 | Kennedy.... | Stewart L. Udall..... | Ariz.. | 1961 |
| Cleveland... | Hoke Smith........ | Ga.... | 1893 | Johnson, L. B. | " | " | 1963 |
| " .... | David R. Francis... | Mo... | 1890 | | | | |

## Secretaries of Agriculture

The Department of Agriculture was created by Act of Congress, May 15, 1862. On Feb. 8, 1889, its Commissioner was renamed Secretary of Agriculture and became a member of the Cabinet.

| Presidents | Cabinet Officers | Home | Apptd. | Presidents | Cabinet Officers | Home | Apptd. |
|---|---|---|---|---|---|---|---|
| Cleveland... | Norman J. Colman.. | Mo.... | 1889 | Coolidge | Howard M Gore.... | W Va.. | 1924 |
| B. Harrison.. | Jeremiah M. Rusk... | Wis... | 1889 | Coolidge..... | W. M. Jardine...... | Kan... | 1925 |
| Cleveland... | J. Sterling Morton.. | Neb... | 1893 | Hoover...... | Arthur M. Hyde.... | Mo... | 1929 |
| McKinley.... | James Wilson....... | Ia..... | 1897 | F.D.Roosevelt | Henry A. Wallace.... | Iowa.. | 1933 |
| T. Roosevelt. | " | " | 1901 | " .... | Claude R. Wickard... | Ind... | 1940 |
| Taft........ | " | " | 1909 | Truman..... | Clinton P. Anderson. | N. M. | 1945 |
| Wilson...... | David F. Houston... | Mo.... | 1913 | " .... | Charles F. Brannan.. | Colo.. | 1948 |
| " .... | Edward T. Meredith. | Ia..... | 1920 | Eisenhower... | Ezra Taft Benson.... | Utah.. | 1953 |
| Harding..... | Henry C. Wallace... | Ia..... | 1921 | Kennedy.... | Orville L. Freeman.. | Minn.. | 1961 |
| Coolidge..... | " | " | 1923 | Johnson, L. B. | " | " | 1963 |

## Secretaries of Commerce and Labor

The Dept. of Commerce & Labor, created by Congress Feb. 14, 1903, was divided by Congress Mar. 4, 1913, into separate Depts. of Commerce and Labor, the Secretary of each made a Cabinet member.

### Secretaries of Commerce and Labor

| Presidents | Cabinet Officers | Home | Apptd. |
|---|---|---|---|
| T. Roosevelt | Geo. B. Cortelyou... | N. Y.. | 1903 |
| " | Victor H. Metcalf... | Cal... | 1904 |
| " | Oscar S. Straus..... | N. Y.. | 1906 |
| Taft........ | Charles Nagel...... | Mo... | 1909 |

### Secretaries of Labor

| Presidents | Cabinet Officers | Home | Apptd. |
|---|---|---|---|
| Wilson...... | William B. Wilson... | Pa.... | 1913 |
| Harding..... | James J. Davis...... | Pa.... | 1921 |
| Coolidge..... | " | " | 1923 |
| Hoover..... | " | " | 1929 |
| | William N. Doak.... | Va.... | 1930 |
| F.D.Roosevelt | Frances Perkins.... | N. Y.. | 1933 |
| Truman..... | L. B. Schwellenbach. | Wash. | 1945 |
| " | Maurice J. Tobin... | Mass.. | 1949 |
| Eisenhower... | Martin P. Durkin... | Ill.... | 1953 |
| " | James P. Mitchell... | N. J... | 1953 |
| Kennedy.... | Arthur J. Goldberg... | Ill.... | 1961 |
| " | W. Willard Wirtz... | Ill.... | 1962 |
| Johnson, L. B. | " | .... | 1963 |

### Secretaries of Commerce

| Presidents | Cabinet Officers | Home | Apptd. |
|---|---|---|---|
| Wilson...... | William C. Redfield.. | N. Y.. | 1913 |
| " | Josh. W. Alexander.. | Mo... | 1919 |
| Harding..... | Herbert C. Hoover... | Cal... | 1921 |
| Coolidge..... | " | " | 1923 |
| " | William F. Whiting.. | Mass.. | 1928 |
| Hoover...... | Robert P. Lamont.... | Ill.... | 1929 |
| " | Roy D. Chapin..... | Mich.. | 1932 |
| F.D.Roosevelt | Daniel C. Roper.... | S. C.. | 1933 |
| " | Harry L. Hopkins... | N. Y.. | 1939 |
| " | Jesse Jones........ | Texas. | 1940 |
| " | Henry A. Wallace... | Ia..... | 1945 |
| Truman..... | " | .... | 1945 |
| " | W. Averell Harriman. | N. Y.. | 1947 |
| " | Charles Sawyer..... | Ohio.. | 1948 |
| Eisenhower... | Sinclair Weeks..... | Mass.. | 1953 |
| " | Lewis L. Strauss.... | N. Y.. | 1958 |
| " | Frederick H. Mueller. | Mich.. | 1959 |
| Kennedy.... | Luther H. Hodges... | N. C.. | 1961 |
| Johnson, L. B. | John T. Connor.... | N. J.. | 1965 |
| " | Alex. B. Trowbridge,. | N. J.. | 1967 |
| " | C. R. Smith....... | N. Y.. | 1968 |

## Secretaries of the U. S. Air Force, Army and Navy

### Not Members of the President's Cabinet

The Department of Defense created September 18, 1947, consolidated the Departments of the Navy, Army, Air Force into a single executive department.

| Secretaries of the Air Force | Appointed |
|---|---|
| W. Stuart Symington........... | Sept. 18, 1947 |
| Thomas K. Finletter........... | Apr. 24, 1950 |
| Harold E. Talbot............. | Feb. 4, 1953 |
| Donald A. Quarles............ | Aug. 12, 1955 |
| James H. Douglas............. | Mar. 26, 1957 |
| Dudley C. Sharpe............. | Dec. 10, 1959 |
| Eugene M. Zuckert............ | Jan. 23, 1961 |
| Dr. Harold Brown............. | July 10, 1965 |

| Secretaries of the Army | |
|---|---|
| Kenneth C. Royall........... | Sept. 18, 1947 |
| Gordon Gray*............... | June 20, 1949 |
| Frank Pace, Jr.............. | Apr. 12, 1950 |
| Earl D. Johnson (Acting)...... | Jan. 20, 1953 |
| Robert T. Stevens........... | Feb. 4, 1953 |
| Wilber M. Brucker........... | July 21, 1955 |
| Elvis J. Stahr, Jr........... | Jan. 23, 1961 |

| | |
|---|---|
| Cyrus R. Vance................ | May. 21, 1962 |
| Stephen Ailes................ | Jan. 20, 1964 |
| Stanley R. Resor.............. | June 17, 1965 |

*In addition, Gordon Gray was Acting Secretary of the Army from Apr. 28, 1949, and Under Secretary from May 25, 1949, until June 20, 1949.

| Secretaries of the Navy | Appointed |
|---|---|
| John L. Sullivan............. | Sept. 18, 1947 |
| Francis P. Matthews.......... | May 25, 1949 |
| Dan A. Kimball.............. | July 31, 1951 |
| Robert B. Anderson.......... | Feb. 4, 1953 |
| Charles S. Thomas........... | May 3, 1954 |
| Thomas S. Gates, Jr......... | Apr. 1, 1957 |
| William B. Franke........... | June 1, 1958 |
| John B. Connally, Jr......... | Jan. 23, 1961 |
| Fred Korth................. | Dec. 11, 1961 |
| Paul H. Nitze.............. | Oct. 14, 1963 |
| Paul R. Ignatius............ | Aug. 4, 1967 |

## The American's Creed

Written by William Tyler Page, clerk of the U. S. House of Representatives, in 1917.

I believe in the United States of America as a government of the people, by the people, for the people; whose just powers are derived from the consent of the governed; a democracy in a republic; a sovereign nation of many sovereign states, a perfect union, one and inseparable; established upon those principles of freedom, equality, justice and humanity for which American patriots sacrificed their lives and fortunes. I therefore believe it is my duty to my country to love it; to support its Constitution; to obey its laws; to respect its flag, and to defend it against all enemies.

# Presidents of the United States

According to a ruling of the State Dept., Grover Cleveland is counted twice, as the 22nd and the 24th President, because his two terms were not consecutive. Only 35 individuals have been President.

| No. | Name | Politics | Native State | Born | | Inau. | Age at Inau. | Date of Death | | Age at Death |
|-----|------|----------|--------------|------|---|-------|--------------|---------------|---|--------------|
| 1.. | George Washington...... | Fed...... | Va...... | 1732, Feb. | 22 | 1789 | 57 | 1799, Dec. | 14 | 67 |
| 2.. | John Adams............. | Fed...... | Mass.... | 1735, Oct. | 30 | 1797 | 61 | 1826, July | 4 | 90 |
| 3.. | Thomas Jefferson........ | Dem.-Rep. | Va...... | 1743, April | 13 | 1801 | 57 | 1826, July | 4 | 83 |
| 4.. | James Madison.......... | Dem.-Rep. | Va...... | 1751, March | 16 | 1809 | 57 | 1836, June | 28 | 85 |
| 5.. | James Monroe........... | Dem.-Rep. | Va...... | 1758, April | 28 | 1817 | 58 | 1831, July | 4 | 73 |
| 6.. | John Quincy Adams....... | Dem.-Rep. | Mass.... | 1767, July | 11 | 1825 | 57 | 1848, Feb. | 23 | 80 |
| 7.. | Andrew Jackson.......... | Dem..... | S. C.... | 1767, March | 15 | 1829 | 61 | 1845, June | 8 | 78 |
| 8.. | Martin Van Buren........ | Dem..... | N. Y.... | 1782, Dec. | 5 | 1837 | 54 | 1862, July | 24 | 79 |
| 9.. | William Henry Harrison... | Whig..... | Va...... | 1773, Feb. | 9 | 1841 | 68 | 1841, April | 4 | 68 |
| 10.. | John Tyler.............. | Whig..... | Va...... | 1790, March | 29 | 1841 | 51 | 1862, Jan. | 18 | 71 |
| 11.. | James Knox Polk........ | Dem..... | N. C.... | 1795, Nov. | 2 | 1845 | 49 | 1849, June | 15 | 53 |
| 12.. | Zachary Taylor.......... | Whig..... | Va...... | 1784, Nov. | 24 | 1849 | 64 | 1850, July | 9 | 65 |
| 13.. | Millard Fillmore........ | Whig..... | N. Y.... | 1800, Jan. | 7 | 1850 | 50 | 1874, March | 8 | 74 |
| 14.. | Franklin Pierce......... | Dem..... | N. H.... | 1804, Nov. | 23 | 1853 | 48 | 1869, Oct. | 8 | 64 |
| 15.. | James Buchanan......... | Dem..... | Pa..... | 1791, April | 23 | 1857 | 65 | 1868, June | 1 | 77 |
| 16.. | Abraham Lincoln........ | Rep...... | Ky..... | 1809, Feb. | 12 | 1861 | 52 | 1865, April | 15 | 56 |
| 17.. | Andrew Johnson......... | (see note).. | N. C.... | 1808, Dec. | 29 | 1865 | 56 | 1875, July | 31 | 66 |
| 18.. | Ulysses Simpson Grant.... | Rep...... | Ohio.... | 1822, April | 27 | 1869 | 46 | 1885, July | 23 | 63 |
| 19.. | Rutherford Birchard Hayes | Rep...... | Ohio.... | 1822, Oct. | 4 | 1877 | 54 | 1893, Jan. | 17 | 70 |
| 20.. | James Abram Garfield.... | Rep...... | Ohio.... | 1831, Nov. | 19 | 1881 | 49 | 1881, Sept. | 19 | 49 |
| 21.. | Chester Alan Arthur...... | Rep...... | Vt..... | 1830, Oct. | 5 | 1881 | 50 | 1886, Nov. | 18 | 56 |
| 22.. | Grover Cleveland........ | Dem..... | N. J.... | 1837, March | 18 | 1885 | 47 | 1908, June | 24 | 71 |
| 23.. | Benjamin Harrison....... | Rep...... | Ohio.... | 1833, Aug. | 20 | 1889 | 55 | 1901, March | 13 | 67 |
| 24.. | Grover Cleveland........ | Dem..... | N. J.... | 1837, March | 18 | 1893 | 55 | 1908, June | 24 | 71 |
| 25.. | William McKinley........ | Rep...... | Ohio.... | 1843, Jan. | 29 | 1897 | 54 | 1901, Sept. | 14 | 58 |
| 26.. | Theodore Roosevelt...... | Rep...... | N. Y.... | 1858, Oct. | 27 | 1901 | 42 | 1919, Jan. | 6 | 60 |
| 27.. | William Howard Taft..... | Rep...... | Ohio.... | 1857, Sept. | 15 | 1909 | 51 | 1930, March | 8 | 72 |
| 28.. | Woodrow Wilson........ | Dem..... | Va..... | 1856, Dec. | 28 | 1913 | 56 | 1924, Feb. | 3 | 67 |
| 29.. | Warren Gamaliel Harding.. | Rep...... | Ohio.... | 1865, Nov. | 2 | 1921 | 55 | 1923, Aug. | 2 | 57 |
| 30.. | Calvin Coolidge......... | Rep...... | Vt..... | 1872, July | 4 | 1923 | 51 | 1933, Jan. | 5 | 60 |
| 31.. | Herbert Clark Hoover..... | Rep...... | Iowa.... | 1874, Aug. | 10 | 1929 | 54 | 1964, Oct. | 20 | 90 |
| 32.. | Franklin Delano Roosevelt. | Dem..... | N. Y.... | 1882, Jan. | 30 | 1933 | 51 | 1945, April | 12 | 63 |
| 33.. | Harry S. Truman........ | Dem..... | Mo..... | 1884, May | 8 | 1945 | 60 | ............ | | ...... |
| 34.. | Dwight David Eisenhower.. | Rep...... | Texas... | 1890, Oct. | 14 | 1953 | 62 | ............ | | ...... |
| 35.. | John F. Kennedy........ | Dem..... | Mass.... | 1917, May | 29 | 1961 | 43 | 1963, Nov. | 22 | 46 |
| 36.. | Lyndon Baines Johnson... | Dem..... | Texas... | 1908, Aug. | 27 | 1963 | 55 | ............ | | ...... |

Andrew Johnson—a Democrat, nominated vice president by Republicans and elected with Lincoln.

## ORIGINAL PATERNAL ANCESTRY

**Dutch**—Van Buren, Theodore Roosevelt, Franklin D. Roosevelt. **German**—Eisenhower. **Swiss and Palatinate German**—Hoover.

**English**—Washington, John Adams, Madison, John Quincy Adams, William Henry Harrison, Tyler, Taylor, Fillmore, Pierce, Lincoln, Andrew Johnson, Garfield, Cleveland, Benjamin Harrison, Taft, Harding, Coolidge. **English-French-German**—L. B. Johnson. **English-Scotch-Irish**—Truman.

**Irish**—Kennedy.

**Scottish**—Monroe, Grant, Hayes. **Scotch-Irish**—Jackson, Polk, Buchanan, Arthur, McKinley, Wilson. **Welsh**—Jefferson (a family tradition).

## Wives and Children of the Presidents

| Presidents* | Wife's Name | Nativity | Born | Mar'ed | Died | Sons | Dau'ers |
|-------------|-------------|----------|------|--------|------|------|---------|
| Washington........ | Martha (Dandridge) Custis..... | Va...... | 1732 | 1759 | 1802 | ...... | ...... |
| John Adams........ | Abigail Smith................ | Mass.... | 1744 | 1764 | 1818 | 3 | 2 |
| Jefferson.......... | Martha (Wayles) Skelton...... | Va...... | 1748 | 1772 | 1782 | 1 | 5 |
| Madison........... | Dorothea("Dolley")(Payne)Todd | N. Car.. | 1768 | 1794 | 1849 | ...... | ...... |
| Monroe........... | Elizabeth Kortwright.......... | N. Y.... | 1768 | 1786 | 1830 | ...... | 2 |
| J. Q. Adams....... | Louisa Catherine Johnson[1].... | Md..... | 1775 | 1797 | 1852 | 3 | 1 |
| Jackson........... | Rachel (Donelson) Robards..... | Va...... | 1767 | 1791 | 1828 | ...... | ...... |
| Van Buren........ | Hannah Hoes................ | N. Y.... | 1783 | 1807 | 1819 | 4 | ...... |
| William H. Harrison. | Anna Symmes............... | N. J.... | 1775 | 1795 | 1864 | 6 | 4 |
| Tyler............. | Letitia Christian............. | Va...... | 1790 | 1813 | 1842 | 3 | 4 |
| | Julia Gardiner............... | N. Y.... | 1820 | 1844 | 1889 | 5 | 2 |
| Polk.............. | Sarah Childress.............. | Tenn.... | 1803 | 1824 | 1891 | ...... | ...... |
| Taylor............ | Margaret Smith.............. | Md..... | 1788 | 1810 | 1852 | 1 | 5 |
| Fillmore.......... | Abigail Powers............... | N. Y.... | 1798 | 1826 | 1853 | 1 | 1 |
| | Caroline (Carmichael) McIntosh | N. J.... | 1813 | 1858 | 1881 | ...... | ...... |
| Pierce............ | Jane Means Appleton......... | N. H.... | 1806 | 1834 | 1863 | 3 | ...... |
| Lincoln........... | Mary Todd.................. | Ky..... | 1818 | 1842 | 1882 | 4 | ...... |
| Johnson, Andrew... | Eliza McCardle.............. | Tenn.... | 1810 | 1827 | 1876 | 3 | 2 |
| Grant............ | Julia Dent.................. | Mo..... | 1826 | 1848 | 1902 | 3 | 1 |
| Hayes............ | Lucy Ware Webb............. | Ohio.... | 1831 | 1852 | 1889 | 7 | 1 |
| Garfield.......... | Lucretia Rudolph............. | Ohio.... | 1832 | 1858 | 1918 | 4 | 1 |
| Arthur........... | Ellen Lewis Herndon.......... | Va...... | 1837 | 1859 | 1880 | 2 | 1 |
| Cleveland......... | Frances Folsom.............. | N. Y.... | 1864 | 1886 | 1947 | 2 | 3 |
| Benjamin Harrison.. | Caroline Lavinia Scott......... | Ohio.... | 1832 | 1853 | 1892 | 1 | 1 |
| | Mary Scott (Lord) Dimmock... | Pa..... | 1858 | 1896 | 1948 | ...... | 1 |
| McKinley......... | Ida Saxton................. | Ohio.... | 1847 | 1871 | 1907 | ...... | 2 |
| Theodore Roosevelt.. | Alice Hathaway Lee.......... | Mass.... | 1861 | 1880 | 1884 | ...... | 1 |
| | Edith Kermit Carow.......... | Conn.... | 1861 | 1886 | 1948 | 4 | 1 |
| Taft.............. | Helen Herron............... | Ohio.... | 1861 | 1886 | 1943 | 2 | 1 |
| Wilson........... | Ellen Louise Axson........... | Ga...... | 1860 | 1885 | 1914 | ...... | 3 |
| | Edith (Bolling) Galt.......... | Va...... | 1872 | 1915 | 1961 | ...... | ...... |
| Harding.......... | Florence (Kling) De Wolfe..... | Ohio.... | 1860 | 1891 | 1924 | ...... | ...... |
| Coolidge.......... | Grace Anna Goodhue.......... | Vt...... | 1879 | 1905 | 1957 | 2 | ...... |
| Hoover........... | Lou Henry.................. | Iowa.... | 1875 | 1899 | 1944 | 2 | ...... |
| F. D. Roosevelt.... | Anna Eleanor Roosevelt[3]...... | N. Y.... | 1884 | 1905 | 1962 | 4 | 1 |
| Truman........... | Bess Wallace............... | Mo..... | 1885 | 1919 | ...... | ...... | 1 |
| Eisenhower........ | Mamie Geneva Doud[3]........ | Iowa.... | 1896 | 1916 | ...... | 1 | ...... |
| Kennedy.......... | Jacqueline Lee Bouvier[3]...... | N. Y.... | 1929 | 1953 | ...... | 1 | 1 |
| Johnson, Lyndon... | Claudia Alta Taylor........... | Texas... | 1912 | 1934 | ...... | ...... | 2 |

*James Buchanan, 15th president, was unmarried. [1]Born London, father a Maryland citizen. [2]Plus 2 infants, dec'd. [3]Plus 1 infant, dec'd.

# BIOGRAPHIES OF THE PRESIDENTS AND THEIR WIVES

## George Washington

**George Washington**, first President, was born Friday, Feb. 22, 1732 (Feb. 11, Old Style), the son of Augustine Washington and Mary Ball, at Wakefield on Pope's creek, Westmoreland Co., Va. Col. John Washington, George's great-grandfather, came from Northamptonshire in 1657 or 1658; in 1665 he and an associate named Spencer bought 5,000 acres on the Potomac. George's father took the north 2,500 acres near Hunting creek in 1735 and built a house in which George lived from 3 to 6 years of age; when 6 the family moved to Ferry farm, near Fredericksburg. His father died in 1743 when he was 11. He studied mathematics and surveying and when 16 went to live with his half-brother Lawrence, who had inherited the Potomac farm and built Mount Vernon, the original house having burned. George surveyed the lands of William Fairfax on the Shenandoah, keeping a diary. He accompanied Lawrence to Barbados, West Indies, contracted smallpox and was deeply scarred. Lawrence died in 1752 and George acquired his property by inheritance and purchase and added the 2,500 acres held by the Spencers. He valued land and when he died owned 70,000 acres in Virginia and 40,000 acres on the Great Kanawa and environs.

Washington's military service began in 1753 when Gov. Dinwiddie of Virginia made him lieut. colonel of militia. He clashed with the French and had to surrender Fort Necessity July 3, 1754. He was an aide to Braddock and helped organize the retreat after the fatal ambuscade of July 9, 1755. He helped take Fort DuQuesne from the French in 1758.

After his marriage to Martha Dandridge Custis, 1759, Washington lived at Mount Vernon, bred horses and cattle, raised fruit and practiced crop rotation. In 1773 he enlarged the house. During the stamp act agitation, 1765, he supported the protesting Virginians. Although not at first for independence, he stood out against British exactions and took charge of the Virginia troops before war broke out. He was made commander-in-chief by the Continental Congress June 15, 1775 and took command at Cambridge July 3.

The successful issue of a war filled with hardships was largely due to his leadership. He was resourceful, a stern disciplinarian, and the one strong, dependable force for unity. He favored a federal government and became chairman of the Constitutional convention of 1787. He helped get the Constitution ratified and was unanimously elected President and inaugurated, April 30, 1789, on the balcony of New York's Federal hall at Broad and Wall Sts., now marked by his statue. In New York his mansion, near Franklin Sq., was the scene of formal dinners and levees. His pew in St. Paul's chapel is preserved.

His birthplace, Wakefield, was burned in 1780. On Feb. 22, 1932, a new Wakefield, built by donations, was dedicated as the George Washington Birthplace Monument, administered by the National Parks Service. The older Washingtons are buried there. It is 34 miles from Fredericksburg, Va., on State road 3, and five miles from Stratford Hall, birthplace of Robert E. Lee.

Although a Federalist, Washington made Thomas Jefferson secretary of state (resigned 1793). He was reelected 1792, but refused to consider a third term and retired to Mount Vernon, 1797. He suffered acute laryngitis after a ride in snow and rain around his estate, was bled profusely, and died Dec. 14, 1799, aged 67. He was mourned here and abroad as one of the great men of his time. He was buried in a vault at Mount Vernon. (*See article on Mount Vernon.*) He willed Mount Vernon to his nephew, Bushrod Washington (1762-1829), associate justice, U. S. Supreme Court.

### MARTHA WASHINGTON

**Mrs. Martha Dandridge Custis Washington** was born June 2, 1732, in New Kent Co., Va. In 1749 she married Daniel Parke Custis, wealthy planter, who died in 1757. She lived in the White House on the Pamunkey, site of McClellan's supply depot in 1862. (Her house had burned down and been replaced before the Civil War.) In 1758 Washington, hurrying to Williamsburg, was invited by the owner of Poplar Grove to meet "the prettiest and richest widow in Virginia." She was plump, small, had dark hair and hazel eyes. Washington fell, and on his return from taking Fort DuQuesne they were

married, Jan. 6, 1759. Martha had two children living, two having died in infancy. Her daughter Martha died at 17. Her son, Col. John Parke Custis, bought the 1,100 acres of Arlington in 1778, but died 1781, from wounds received at Yorktown. Washington adopted John's son, George Washington Parke Custis, who inherited Arlington and built the present house; his daughter Mary married Robert E. Lee there in 1831. Martha Washington managed her husband's plantations in his absence and in winter visited him at Valley Forge, Newburgh and other camps. She presided gracefully at official levees as Lady Washington. She died in 1802 and was buried at Mount Vernon.

## John Adams

**John Adams**, 2nd President, Federalist, was born in Braintree (Quincy), Mass., Oct. 30, 1735 (Oct. 19, O. S.), the son of John Adams, a farmer and Susanna Boylston of Brookline. He was a great-grandson of Henry Adams who came from England in 1636. He was graduated from Harvard, 1755, taught school, studied law. In 1765 he argued against taxation without representation before the royal governor. In 1770 he defended the British soldiers who fired on civilians in the "Boston Massacre." He took part in the Provincial Congress of Massachusetts and the Continental Congress, seconded the independence resolution presented by Richard Henry Lee and with his cousin, Samuel Adams, signed the Declaration of Independence. He was a commissioner to France, 1778, with Benjamin Franklin and Arthur Lee; won recognition of the United States by The Hague, 1782; was first American minister to England, 1785-1788, and elected vice president with Washington, 1788 and 1792.

In 1796 Adams was chosen President by the electors, 71 to 68 so that opponents called him "president by 3 votes." The candidate with the second highest number of votes became vice president; this was Thomas Jefferson, his opponent. Intense antagonism to America by France caused agitation for war, led by Alexander Hamilton. Adams, breaking with Hamilton, opposed war but put the Navy on a fighting basis. The U.S.S. Constitution, the United States, both 44 guns, and the Constellation, 36 guns, and armed merchantmen bagged 84 French ships in an undeclared war. To fight alien influence and muzzle criticism Adams supported the Alien and Sedition acts of 1798, which led to his defeat for reelection. He died July 4, 1826, on the same day as Jefferson, and was buried in the First Unitarian church in Quincy, Mass.

### ABIGAIL ADAMS

**Mrs. Abigail Smith Adams** was born at Weymouth, Mass., Nov. 23, 1744 (Nov. 12, O. S.), daughter of a Congregational minister and descendant of the Puritan divine, Thomas Shepard of Cambridge, Mass. She died at Quincy, Oct. 28, 1818. She had two daughters and three sons, one of whom, John Quincy Adams, became the sixth President. Often separated from John Adams during the Revolution, she joined him in Paris in 1784, and from 1785 to 1788 endured social slights at the court of St. James's, where Adams was our first minister. When New York was the seat of Washington's administration she lived at Richmond Hill, a manor house located where Charlton crosses Varick St. She was known for her sharp criticism of Adams' opponents.

## Thomas Jefferson

**Thomas Jefferson**, 3rd President, was born April 13, 1743 (Apr. 2, O. S.) at Shadwell, Va., the son of Peter Jefferson, a civil engineer of Welsh descent who raised tobacco, and Jane Randolph. Jefferson was an agrarian, an expansionist; because he opposed the Federalists and centralization he was called a Republican, now synonymous with Democrat. His father died when he was 14, leaving him 2,750 acres and his slaves. Jefferson attended the College of William and Mary, 1760-1762, read classics in Greek and Latin; studied law with George Wythe in Williamsburg; played the violin and rode horses. In 1769 he was elected to the House of Burgesses. In 1770 Shadwell burned and he began Monticello, near Charlottesville. In 1772 he married Martha Wayles Skelton. He was a member of the Virginia Committee of Correspondence and the Continental Congress and denied Britain's right to tax. Named a member of the committee to draw up a Declaration of Independence, he wrote the basic draft, 1776. He was a member of the Virginia House of Delegates, 1776-79, elected

governor to succeed Patrick Henry, 1779, re-elected 1780, resigned, June 1781, amid charges of ineffectual military preparation. During his term he wrote the statute on religious freedom. In the Continental Congress, 1783, he drew up an ordinance for the Northwest Territory, forbidding slavery after 1800; its terms were put into the Ordinance of 1787. He was sent to Paris with Benjamin Franklin and John Adams to negotiate treaties of commerce, 1784; made minister to France, 1785, he made treaties with France and Prussia, studied architecture, gardening and the French Revolution, whose leaders consulted him.

Washington appointed him secretary of state, 1789. Jefferson's strong faith in the consent of the governed, as opposed to executive control favored by Hamilton, secretary of the treasury, often led to conflict: Dec. 31, 1793, he resigned. He was the Republican candidate for President in 1796; beaten by John Adams, he became vice president. He opposed Adams' alien and sedition laws with the Kentucky and Virginia resolutions, reiterating the basic rights of states. In 1800 Jefferson and Aaron Burr received equal votes for President, so the House of Representatives, with Hamilton's help, elected Jefferson, the first President to be inaugurated in Washington. Adams left town before the ceremony, but when Jefferson was re-elected in 1804 he voted for him. Jefferson cancelled levees and titles and ignored diplomatic precedence. He turned Federalists out of office. He opposed a strong navy. By fighting those who feared to give power to the people he made democracy work. He considered John Marshall's Supreme Court reactionary. Big events of his administration were the Louisiana Purchase, 1803, and the Lewis and Clark Expedition. He established the University of Virginia and designed its buildings. After the Library of Congress was burned by the British he sold Congress 13,000 vols. for $23,950. He was 6 ft. 2, temperate in debate, a deist in religion. He died July 4, 1826, on the same day as John Adams and was buried at Monticello, which, after various vicissitudes, passed to the Thomas Jefferson Memorial Foundation in 1923.

### MRS. THOMAS JEFFERSON

Mrs. Martha Wayles Jefferson, daughter of John Wayles, was 23 and the widow of Bathurst Skelton when she married Jefferson Jan. 1, 1772. She bore Jefferson six children at Monticello, two of whom lived to maturity. Martha, 1772-1836, married Thomas Mann Randolph, Jr.; Mary (Marie) 1778-1804, married her cousin, J. W. Eppes. Mrs. Jefferson's father's large farm and slaves became part of the estate. She died Sept. 6, 1782.

## James Madison

James Madison, 4th President, Republican, was born Mar. 16, 1751 (Mar. 5, O. S.) at Port Conway, King George Co., Va., the eldest of 12 children of James Madison and Eleanor Rose Conway. His great-grandfather, James Taylor (1674-1729), was also the great-grandfather of Zachary Taylor. Madison was graduated from Princeton, 1771, studied theology, 1772, sat in the Virginia Constitutional Convention, 1776, where his resolution on religious freedom was voted down; was a member of the Continental Congress and of the Annapolis convention, 1786, where he and Hamilton proposed the Constitutional Convention. He was chief recorder at that convention in 1787, and supported ratification in the Federalist papers, written with Hamilton and Jay. In 1785 he carried Jefferson's statute on religious liberty through the Virginia assembly. He was elected to the House of Representatives in 1789, helped adopt the Bill of Rights and fought John Adams' alien and sedition laws. He favored agrarian policies with Jefferson and in 1801 became Jefferson's secretary of state. In 1803, when the Louisiana Purchase was consummated, he insisted on free navigation of the Mississippi, which he had already urged on Jay in 1780.

Elected President in 1808, Madison was a "strict constructionist," opposed to the free interpretation of the Constitution by the Federalists; he vetoed federal funds for state improvements, but changed in his second term. Madison inherited the conflict with Britain over its orders in council and impressment of American seamen, which had led to Jefferson's embargo act and injured American commerce. He was reelected in 1812 by the votes of the agrarian South and recently admitted western states. Caught between British and French maritime restrictions, Madison drifted into war, declared June 18, 1812, unaware that Britain had cancelled the orders two days before. While the war was inconclusive, it opened the way to peaceful negotiations. Madison successfully advocated a

tariff to protect industry, a national system of roads and canals and a strong military organization. He retired in 1817 to his estate at Montpellier (now Montpelier), Va., built 1760, with a portico suggested by Jefferson. There he edited his famous papers on the Constitutional Convention. He became rector of the Univ. of Virginia, 1826. He died June 28, 1836, and was buried near his home.

### DOLLEY MADISON

Mrs. Dorothea (Dolley) Payne Madison, was born May 12, 1768, in North Carolina, daughter of John Payne, a Virginia Quaker, who freed his slaves. She grew up in Hanover County, Va. Her first husband, John Todd, died in 1793. She married Madison Sept. 15, 1794, and when he became secretary of state in 1801, became hostess for Jefferson in the White House. She presided at the first inaugural ball in 1809. She is supposed to have rescued Gilbert Stuart's portrait of Washington from the White House when the British came Aug. 24, 1814. She helped edit Madison's records of the Constitutional Convention. From 1817 to 1837 she lived at Montpellier, Orange Co., Va. (now Montpelier, privately owned). She returned to Washington as a welcome, but impecunious, social leader, in 1837. Congress bought her husband's records in 1837 for $30,000, and other papers in 1848, for $25,000. She took part in the dedication of the Washington monument and sent the first personal message over S. F. B. Morse's telegraph wire. She was respected for her tact and intelligence by presidents from Washington to Polk. In old age she suffered from the wastefulness of a son. She died July 12, 1849, aged 81, and is buried beside Madison near Montpelier.

## James Monroe

James Monroe, 5th President, Republican, was born April 28, 1758, in Westmoreland Co., Va., the son of Spence Monroe and Eliza Jones, who were of Scottish and Welsh descent, respectively. He attended the College of William and Mary, fought in the 3rd Virginia regiment at White Plains, Brandywine, Monmouth, and was wounded at Trenton. He studied law with Thomas Jefferson, 1780, was a member of the Virginia house of delegates and of Congress, 1783-86. He opposed ratification of the Constitution because it lacked a bill of rights; was U. S. Senator, 1790; minister to France, 1794-96, during which he improved relations with France, Spain and Algiers; four times governor of Virginia, 1799-1802, and 1811, Jefferson sent him to France as minister, 1803, to join R. R. Livingston in buying the isle of New Orleans from France and East and West Florida from Spain. Exceeding instructions, he signed a treaty for all of Louisiana. (Navigation of the Mississippi was one of his demands as early as 1783.) He was also sent to Madrid, 1804, and London, 1805, to settle disputes. He ran against Madison for President in 1808. He was chosen member of the Virginia Assembly, 1810-1811; secretary of state under Madison, 1811-1817; also secretary of war Sept. 1814-Mar., 1815.

In 1816 Monroe was elected President; in 1820 reelected with all but one vote, this being cast for John Quincy Adams by William Plumer, Sr., of New Hampshire. Although many historians have held that Plumer withheld his vote from Monroe so that only Washington would have been elected unanimously, Plumer himself said he voted for Adams because he had "discovered a want of foresight" in Monroe. Monroe's administration became the Era of Good Feeling. He obtained the Floridas from Spain and suppressed the Seminoles; settled boundaries with Canada and eliminated border forts; supported the anti-slavery position that led to the Missouri Compromise. (In 1801 he had proposed settling Negro slaves in Africa. Monrovia, Liberia, was named for him.) In July, 1823, the U. S. served notice on Russia that it would oppose any Russian colony on this continent, after Russia had prohibited fishing on the northwest coasts. On Dec. 2, 1823, Monroe announced the Doctrine that the U. S. would consider its safety endangered if European powers had authority on this hemisphere or attempted colonization. First half had been suggested by George Canning, British foreign minister, to curb Spain; U. S., rejecting proposal for joint declaration, issued it also as warning to Russia. Monroe owned Ash Lawn, 5 mi. from Charlottesville, Va., 1799-1825; inherited Oak Hill, Loudon Co., Va., from his uncle Jos. Jones, 1806. The mansion, replacing Jones' cottage, was designed by Jefferson and executed by Jas. Hoban, White House architect. He moved to New York, 1830, to be with his daughters, and died there July 4, 1831, and was buried in

Marble cemetery. In 1858 his remains were removed to Richmond.

### MRS. JAMES MONROE

Mrs. Elizabeth Kortwright Monroe was born in New York, 1768, the daughter of Lawrence Kortwright, formerly British army officer. She married Monroe in 1786. They had two daughters, who married and lived in New York. She died 1830 at Oak Hill.

## John Quincy Adams

John Quincy Adams, 6th President, independent Federalist, was born July 11, 1767, at Braintree (Quincy), Mass., the son of John and Abigail Adams. He was educated in Paris, Leyden, and Harvard, graduating in 1787. He served as American minister in the Netherlands, Berlin, St. Petersburg and London and helped draft the peace treaty of 1814. He had served as senator from 1803 to 1808 and his support of the Republican administration alienated the Federalists. President Monroe made him secretary of state, 1817, and he negotiated the cession of the Floridas from Spain, supported exclusion of slavery in the Missouri Compromise, and laid the base for the Monroe Doctrine, of which he, as much as Monroe, was the creator. In 1824 he was elected President by the House after he failed to win an Electoral College majority over Henry Clay and Andrew Jackson. His expansion of executive powers was strongly opposed and he was beaten in 1828 by Jackson. In 1831 he was sent to Congress as representative and served nine terms with distinction and independence. He fought slavery, opposed the annexation of Texas and the war with Mexico; was responsible for the Smithsonian Institution. He had a stroke in the House and died in the Speaker's room, Feb. 23, 1848.

### MRS. JOHN QUINCY ADAMS

Mrs. Louisa Catherine Johnson Adams was born in London, Feb. 12, 1775, the daughter of Joshua Johnson, a Marylander who acted as American fiscal agent there. She married Adams July 26, 1797. Of their four children, George Washington Adams, John Q. Adams, Jr., Charles Francis Adams and Louisa Catherine Adams, Charles Francis became Free Soil candidate for vice president in 1848, member of Congress, minister to England during the Civil War and president of the Geneva Board of Arbitration. He was father of Charles Francis Adams, Henry Adams and Brooks Adams.

## Andrew Jackson

Andrew Jackson, 7th President, originally Jeffersonian-Republican, later first Democrat, was born in the Waxhaws district, New Lancaster Co., S. C., Mar. 15, 1767, the posthumous son of Andrew Jackson, who came from County Antrim, Ireland, with his wife, Elizabeth Hutchinson, and two sons, in 1765. At 13 he joined the militia in the Revolution and when captured a British officer struck Andrew with his sword when the boy refused to shine his boots. He read law in Salisbury, N. C., moved to Nashville, Tenn., speculated in land, married and raised cotton at the Hermitage, originally a log house. In 1796 he helped draft the Constitution of Tennessee and for one year occupied its one seat in the national House. He was in the Senate in 1797, and again in 1823. He defeated the Creek Indians at Horseshoe Bend, Ala., 1814, and as major general, U. S. A., drove the British out of Pensacola. With 6,000 backwoods fighters he defeated Packenham's 12,000 British troops at Chalmette, outside New Orleans, Jan. 8, 1815, losing only seven to the British loss of 2,000. In 1818 he fought so recklessly against the Seminoles in Florida that he endangered foreign relations. In 1824 he ran for President against John Quincy Adams and was voted down by the House, though he had the most votes; in 1828 he carried everything, the West rising to support "Old Hickory" and a liberal land policy. He was a noisy debater and duellist and introduced rotation in office or "spoils system." He was suspicious of privilege; ruined the Bank of the United States by depositing federal funds with state banks. Though "Let the people rule" was his slogan, he at times supported strict constructionist policies against the expansionist West. He killed the Congressional caucus for nominating presidential candidates and substituted the national convention, 1832, when he was reelected, with Martin Van Buren vice president. When South Carolina refused to collect imports under his protective tariff he ordered army and naval forces to Charleston. At the Jefferson Day dinner, 1830, he offered the toast: "Our Federal Union; it must be preserved." Vice President John C. Calhoun, exponent of state sovereignty, gave in reply the toast: "The Union—next to our liberty, most dear." Jackson recognized the Republic of Texas, 1836. His party took the name of Democrat. He died at the Hermitage, June 8, 1845, and is buried there.

### MRS. ANDREW JACKSON

Mrs. Rachel Jackson was the daughter of Col. John Donelson, a surveyor at Nashville, and first married Capt. Lewis Robards. Under the impression that Robards had obtained a divorce she married Jackson in Natchez in 1791. Robards did not get a divorce until 1793, when the Jacksons were remarried, but the ordeal affected her spirits. She died in 1828 after Jackson's election and never lived in the White House. Jackson adopted her sister's son, named him Andrew Jackson, Jr. White House hostesses were his wife's niece, Mrs. Emily Donelson, and the adopted son's wife, Mrs. Sarah York Jackson, a Philadelphia Quaker.

## Martin Van Buren

Martin Van Buren, 8th President, Democrat, was born Dec. 5, 1782, at Kinderhook, N. Y., the son of Abraham Van Buren, a Dutch farmer, and Mary Hoes. He was surrogate of Columbia county, New York, state senator and attorney general and a law partner of Benj. F. Butler in Albany. He was U. S. senator, 1821, re-elected, 1827, elected governor of New York, 1828. He helped swing eastern support to Andrew Jackson in 1828 and was his secretary of state, 1829-31. In 1832 he was elected vice president. He was a consummate politician, known as "the little magician," and influenced Jackson's policies. In 1836 he defeated William Henry Harrison for President by 170 to 73 electoral votes. He inaugurated the independent treasury system, and was the first advocate of mutual insurance of deposits by banks. He advocated tariff for revenue only and opposed internal improvements at national expense. His refusal to spend land revenues led to his defeat by Harrison in 1840. He lost the Democratic nomination of 1844 to Polk because he opposed annexation of Texas. In 1848 he ran for President on the Free Soil ticket and lost. Thus he ran three times. He died July 24, 1862 at Kinderhook, N. Y.

### MRS. MARTIN VAN BUREN

Mrs. Hannah Hoes Van Buren, born 1783, was a relative of Van Buren's mother and his classmate in school. She married in 1807, died 1819. Their son Abraham, 1807-1873, a West Pointer, was secretary to the President, an officer in the Mexican war and a New York resident. His wife, Angelica Singleton, cousin of Dolley Madison, was White House hostess during Van Buren's term. Another son, John Van Buren (1810-1866), was elected attorney general of New York, 1845.

## William Henry Harrison

William Henry Harrison, 9th President, Whig, who served only 31 days, was born in Berkeley, Charles City Co., Va., Feb. 9, 1773, the third son of Benjamin Harrison, signer of the Declaration of Independence. Educated at Hampden Sydney college, he later studied medicine under Dr. Benjamin Rush. Commissioned by Washington, he fought under Gen. Anthony Wayne at Fallen Timbers, 1794. He was secretary of Northwest Terr., 1798; its delegate in Congress, 1799; first governor of Indiana Terr., and supt. of Indian affairs. With 900 men he routed Tecumseh's Indians at Tippecanoe, Nov. 7, 1811. A major general, he defeated British and Indians at Battle of the Thames, Oct. 5, 1813. He served Ohio in Congress, 1816; as senator, 1824; was minister to Colombia. In 1840, when 68, he was elected President with John Tyler, 234 to 60, on a "log cabin and hard cider" slogan. He caught pneumonia during the inauguration and died April 4, 1841. He was buried in North Bend, O.

### MRS. WILLIAM HENRY HARRISON

Mrs. Anna Symmes Harrison, daughter of Col. John Cleves Symmes, chief justice of the New Jersey Supreme Court and Revolutionary veteran, was born in Morristown, N. J., 1775 and died 1864. She did not leave her North Bend, O., home for Washington and Mrs. Jane Findlay Irwin Harrison, wife of her son, Col. W. H. Harrison, Jr., stayed in the White House during Harrison's illness. Another son, John Scott Harrison, 1804-1878, was member of Congress and father of Benjamin Harrison, 23rd President.

## John Tyler

John Tyler, 10th President, independent Whig, was born Mar. 29, 1790, in Greenway, Charles City

Co., Va., son of John Tyler and Mary Armistead. His father was governor of Virginia, 1808-11. Tyler was graduated from William and Mary, 1807; member of the House of Delegates, 1811; in Congress, 1816-21; in Virginia legislature, 1823-25; governor of Virginia, 1825-26; U. S. senator, 1827-36. In 1836 he was defeated for vice president on a states' rights Whig ticket. In 1840 he was elected vice president on a Whig ticket with Harrison and succeeded him. He favored pre-emption, allowing settlers to get government land; rejected a new bank bill and thus alienated Whig supporters except Daniel Webster, his secretary of state; refused to honor the spoils system. He signed the resolution annexing Texas, Mar. 1, 1845. He accepted renomination, 1844, but withdrew before election. He condemned South Carolina's nullification and secession and as Virginia's commissioner to Buchanan tried to keep Fort Sumter neutralized. He was president of the peace congress called in Washington by Virginia, 1861. After its failure he supported secession, sat in the provisional Confederate congress, became a member of the Confederate House, but died, Jan. 18, 1862, before it met. He is buried in Richmond.

### MARRIAGES OF JOHN TYLER

When 23 John Tyler married **Letitia Christian** of Cedar Grove, Va., born 1790, daughter of a planter. She was an invalid and died in the White House, 1842. She was an Episcopalian. Of her children Robert Tyler, 1818-1877, married Priscilla Cooper, daughter of a tragedian; presided in the White House. On June 28, 1844, in New York, Tyler married **Julia Gardiner**, born 1820, daughter of David Gardiner of Gardiner's Island, N. Y., She became a Catholic, 1872; died, 1889. Her son Lyon Gardiner Tyler became president of William and Mary, 1888; died 1935. Another, David Gardiner Tyler, judge, member of Congress and Confederate veteran, died 1927. A third son, Robert Fitzwalter Tyler, died 1927 at Richmond, aged 70.

## James Knox Polk

**James Knox Polk**, 11th President, Democrat, was born in Mecklenburg Co., N. C., Nov. 2, 1795, the son of Samuel Polk, farmer and surveyor of Scotch-Irish descent, and Jane Knox. He went to Maury Co., Tenn., 1806; was graduated from the University of North Carolina, 1818; member of the Tenn. state legislature, 1823-25, known as "Napoleon of the Stump." He served in Congress 1825-39 and as speaker 1835-39. He supported Jackson and Van Buren, but was always expansionist. He was governor of Tennessee, 1839-41, being defeated 1841, '43. In 1844, when both Clay and Van Buren announced opposition to annexing Texas, the Democrats made Polk the first dark horse nominee because he demanded control of all Oregon and annexation of Texas. He won 170 to 105. James Buchanan was his secretary of state. He re-established the independent treasury system originated by Van Buren. His expansionist policy was opposed by Clay, Webster, Calhoun; he sent Zachary Taylor and an army to the Mexican border and when Mexicans attacked declared war existed. Abraham Lincoln, a Whig in Congress, opposed his war policy. Polk approved the acquisition of California, Utah and New Mexico (522,568 square miles) as part of America's "manifest destiny," but opposed retaining Mexico by force. He compromised on the Oregon boundary ("54-40 or fight!") by accepting the 49th parallel and giving Vancouver to the British. The Wilmot Proviso, outlawing slavery in new states, was debated in his term. Polk died in Nashville, June 15, 1849, and is buried on the capitol grounds there.

### MRS. JAMES K. POLK

**Mrs. Sarah Childress Polk** was born in 1803 and married Polk Jan. 1, 1824. Her father was a wealthy planter near Murfreesboro, Tenn. She was educated by the Moravians. The Polks were Methodists and Mrs. Polk prohibited liquor and dancing in the White House. They had no children.

## Zachary Taylor

**Zachary Taylor**, 12th President, Whig, who served only 16 months, was born Nov. 24, 1784, in Orange Co., Va., the son of Richard Taylor, later collector of the port of Louisville. His grandfather and James Madison's paternal grandmother were brother and sister. Taylor enlisted 1806; was commissioned lieutenant by Jefferson, 1808; fought in the War of 1812, the Black Hawk War, 1832, and the Seminole war, 1837. He became known as Old Rough and Ready. He settled on a plantation near Baton Rouge, La. in 1845 Polk sent him to the Rio Grande; when the Mexicans attacked him, Polk declared war. Taylor was successful at Palo Alto and Resaca de la Palma, May 8 and 9, 1846; occupied Monterey. Polk made him major general but gave many of his troops to Gen. Winfield Scott at Vera Cruz. Taylor, with 5,000 men, defeated Santa Anna's 20.000 at Buena Vista, Feb. 22, 1847. He defeated Scott at the Whig convention, 1848; was elected President over Martin Van Buren (Free Soil) with Millard Fillmore vice pres. He resumed the spoils system and though once a slave-holder worked to have California admitted as a free state. He died of typhus July 9, 1850, and was buried near Louisville.

### MRS. ZACHARY TAYLOR

**Mrs. Margaret Smith Taylor** was born in 1788, the daughter of Walter Smith, Maryland planter. She married Taylor, 1810, died 1852. Of their daughters Elizabeth, Mrs. W. W. S. Bliss, was hostess of the White House; Ann married Dr. Robert Wood, asst. surgeon general, U. S. A.; Sarah Knox married Jefferson Davis, 1835, and died three months later. A son, Richard, 1826-79, served under Stonewall Jackson and became a Confederate general. He died in New York.

## Millard Fillmore

**Millard Fillmore**, 13th President, Whig, was born Jan. 7, 1800, in a log cabin on a farm in Cayuga Co., N. Y., cleared in 1795 by his father, Nathaniel. He was apprenticed to a fuller and dyer; bought his freedom for $30 to study and became a teacher and postmaster in Buffalo, N. Y. He was counsellor of the state supreme court, 1829; in the state assembly, 1829-32; in Congress, 1833-35 and again 1837-43. He opposed the entrance of Texas as slave territory and voted for a protective tariff. He supported the appropriation of $30,000 for Morse's telegraph. In 1844 he was defeated for governor of New York. In 1848 he was elected vice president and succeeded as President July 10, 1850. Daniel Webster was secretary of state until he died, 1852; then Edward Everett. Fillmore favored the compromise of 1850 and signed the Fugitive Slave Law. His policies pleased neither expansionists nor slave-holders and he was not renominated. In 1856 he was nominated by the American (Know-Nothing) party and accepted by the Whigs, but defeated by Buchanan. He was chancellor of the University of Buffalo. He died in Buffalo, Mar. 8, 1874.

### FILLMORE'S TWO MARRIAGES

The first Mrs. Fillmore, 1798-1853, was **Abigail Powers**, the daughter of Lemuel Powers, a Baptist clergyman of Stillwater, N. Y., and taught school in Cayuga Co. Owing to her poor health her daughter, Mary Abigail (1832-54) was the White House hostess. Their other child was Millard Powers Fillmore (1828-89). The second Mrs. Fillmore was **Mrs. Caroline Carmichael McIntosh**, born in Morristown, N. J., and widow of an Albany merchant. They had no children.

## Franklin Pierce

**Franklin Pierce**, 14th President, Democrat, was born in Hillsboro, N. H., Nov. 23, 1804, the son of Benjamin Pierce, veteran of the Revolution and governor of New Hampshire, 1827. He attended Exeter and was graduated from Bowdoin, 1824. A lawyer, he served in the New Hampshire House, 1829-32; in Congress, supporting Jackson, 1833; U. S. Senator, 1837-42. He enlisted in the Mexican war, became brigadier general of volunteers and was wounded at Contreras. In 1852 Pierce was nominated on the 49th ballot over Cass, Douglas and Buchanan, defeating Gen. Winfield Scott, Whig. Though against slavery, Pierce was influenced by southern pro-slavery men (Jefferson Davis was his secy. of war) but he ignored the Ostend Manifesto that the U. S. either buy or take Cuba. He approved the Kansas-Nebraska act, leaving slavery to popular vote ("squatter sovereignty"), 1854, and named a pro-slavery governor of Kansas. He signed a reciprocity treaty with Canada and approved the Gadsden Purchase from Mexico, 1853. He supported Commodore Matthew Perry's opening of Japan, 1854. Pierce died at Concord, N.H., Oct. 8, 1869.

### MRS. FRANKLIN PIERCE

**Mrs. Jane Means Appleton Pierce** was born at Hampton, N. H., 1806, daughter of the Rev. Jesse A. Appleton, president of Bowdoin. The Pierces had three children; one died in infancy, one at 4 and one was killed in a railroad accident at 11. Mrs. Pierce died in 1863.

## James Buchanan

**James Buchanan**, 15th President, Federalist, later Democrat, was born of Scottish descent near Mercersburg, Pa., Apr. 23, 1791. He was a volunteer in the War of 1812; graduated from Dickinson,

1809; member Pa. legislature, 1814-16, Congress, 1820-31; Jackson's minister to Russia, 1831-33; senator, 1834-45. As Polk's secy. of state, 1845-49, he ended Oregon dispute with Britain, supported Mexican war and annexation of Texas. As minister to Britain, 1853, he signed the Ostend Manifesto, 1854, urging U. S. to take Cuba. Nominated by Democrats over Pierce and Stephen A. Douglas, he was elected, 1856, over John C. Fremont (Republican) and Millard Fillmore (American Know-Nothing and Whig tickets). On slavery he favored popular sovereignty and choice by state constitutions; he accepted the pro-slavery Dred Scott decision as binding. His support of the pro-slavery Lecompton constitution for Kansas caused a break with Douglas Democrats. He denied the right of states to secede but wanted U. S. constitutional recognition of property rights in slaves and Federal action against fugitives. Buchanan refused demands of South Carolina for Federal property, but also refused to reinforce forts there until too late to help Fort Sumter. A strict constructionist, he desired to keep peace and found no authority for using force. He died at Wheatland, near Lancaster, Pa., June 1, 1868, aged 77.

Buchanan was a bachelor. The mistress of the White House was the daughter of Buchanan's sister Jane, Harriet Lane, whose parents had died when she was a child. The major social event was the visit in 1860 of the Prince of Wales, later Edward VII.

## Abraham Lincoln

Abraham Lincoln, 16th President, Republican, was born Feb. 12, 1809, in a log cabin on a farm then in Hardin Co., Ky., now in Larue. He was the son of Thomas Lincoln (1778-1851), a descendant of Samuel Lincoln, who came with his wife Martha from Hingham, England, 1635, settled at Salem and Hingham, Mass., and had 11 children. Thomas, a carpenter, married Nancy Hanks, June 12, 1806. She was the natural daughter of Lucy Hanks, whose ancestor, Thomas Hanks, came from England to Virginia, 1644. Abe had a sister, Sarah, born 1807, died 1828, and a brother, Thomas, who died in infancy.

The Lincolns moved to Spencer Co., Ind., near Gentryville, when Abe was 7. His mother died Oct. 5, 1818, aged 35. His father married Mrs. Sarah Bush Johnston, 1819; she had a favorable influence on Abe. He was 6 ft., 3 in. tall. Abe made two trips on flatboats to New Orleans, one via the Ohio-Mississippi, 1828, and one via the Illinois-Mississippi, 1831. In 1830 the family moved to Macon County, Ill., where Abe and a cousin split 3,000 fence rails. In 1831 they moved to Coles County. In New Salem, 1831-1837, Lincoln lost election to the Illinois General Assembly, 1832, but won four times later, beginning in 1834. He enlisted in the militia for the Black Hawk War, 1832. In New Salem he ran a store, 1833, surveyed land, 1834-36, was postmaster, 1833-36. Ann Rutledge, whom he is said to have loved, died near New Salem, 1835, aged 19.

In 1837 Lincoln was admitted to the bar and became partner in a Springfield law office. He began practice on 8th Judicial Circuit, 1839. He was a presidential elector, 1839, 1844, 1852, 1856. He failed of nomination for representative, 1843, but was elected to the 30th Congress, 1847. He opposed the Mexican war. He stumped New England for Zachary Taylor, 1848. He refused offices of secretary and governor of Oregon Terr., 1849. He opposed the Kansas-Nebraska Act and extension of slavery, 1854. When elected to the Ill. legislature, 1854, he declined in order to try for the Senate, but failed of election, 1855. He was proposed but not chosen for vice president at the first Republican convention, 1856, and he made 50 speeches for John C. Fremont, presidential nominee.

In 1858 Lincoln had Republican support in the Ill. legisiature for the Senate but was defeated by Stephen A. Douglas, Dem., who sponsored the Kansas-Nebraska Act. The issues were debated by Lincoln and Douglas Aug. 21-Oct. 15 at Ottawa, Freeport, Jonesboro, Charleston, Galesburg, Quincy and Alton, Ill.

Lincoln was nominated for President by the Republican party over Wm. H. Seward, on an anti-slavery platform, at Chicago, May 18, 1860. He ran against Stephen A. Douglas, northern Democrat; John C. Breckinridge, southern pro-slavery Democrat; John Bell, Constitutional Union party. Lincoln got only 40% of the votes, but 180 electoral votes to 123. South Carolina seceded from the Union Dec. 20, 1860, followed in 1861 by 10 southern states.

Lincoln was inaugurated Mar. 4, 1861. Fort Sumter was attacked Apr. 12-14, and surrendered. Lincoln called for 75,000 volunteers Apr. 15, and 500,000 May 3. On Sept. 22, 1862, 5 days after the battle of Antietam, he announced that slaves in territory then in rebellion would be free Jan. 1, 1863, date of the Emancipation Proclamation. He reached the highest degree of eloquence at Gettysburg National Cemetery, Nov. 19, 1863.

Lincoln was re-elected, 1864, over Gen. Geo. B. McClellan, Democrat. Lee surrendered April 9, 1865. On April 14 (Good Friday) Lincoln was shot by John Wilkes Booth, actor, in Ford's Theater, Washington. He died the next day. His body lay in state in New York, Chicago and other cities before burial in Springfield, Ill. His estate reached $110,974, most of it saved from his annual salary of $25,000. His humanity, lofty concept of office and generous spirit made him the hero of the common man the world over.

### MRS. LINCOLN AND FAMILY

Mrs. Mary Todd Lincoln was born in Lexington, Ky., 1818, daughter of a pioneer; moved to Springfield, Ill., 1837, where she married Lincoln Nov. 4, 1842. Her half-sister, Emily, became the wife of Brig. Gen. Ben Hardin Helm of the Confederate Army, who was killed at Chickamauga. Mrs. Lincoln was accused of undue extravagance while in the White House. In 1875 she was temporarily in a mental hospital in Batavia, Ill. She died 1882.

The Lincolns had four sons. Edward Baker died 1850; Wm. Wallace, 1862; Thomas ("Tad"), 1871. Robert Todd Lincoln, born Aug. 1, 1843, in Springfield, attended Ill. State Univ., Phillips Exeter Acad., A. B. Harvard, 1864, in Harvard Law School, 1864. Captain, USA, on staff of Grant, 1865. Secy. of War, 1881-85; minister to Great Britain, 1889-93; later pres. Pullman Co. Married Mary Harlan, dau. Sen. Jas. Harlan (Iowa) 1868; children, since deceased, were Abraham (d at 17), Mrs. Chas. Isham, Mrs. Robt. J. Randolph. Robert Todd Lincoln died July 26, 1926, at Manchester Vt., was buried at Arlington, Va. Gave Library of Congress 18,350 letters and documents of Lincoln's tenure, opened July 26, 1947. The Lincoln family Bible and Bible on which Lincoln took oath of office were given to library by Mrs. Robert Lincoln (d. 1937).

## Andrew Johnson

Andrew Johnson, 17th President, Democrat, was born in Raleigh, N. C., Dec. 29, 1808, the son of Jacob Johnson, porter at an inn and church sexton, and Mary McDonough Johnson, who had been a maid at the inn. His father died when he was 5. At 10 he was apprenticed to a tailor. At 16 he ran off to Greenville, Tenn. He became an alderman, 1828; mayor, 1830; state representative and senator, 1835-43: member of Congress, 1843-53; governor of Tennessee, 1853-57; U. S. Senator, 1857-62. He supported John C. Breckinridge against Lincoln in 1860. He had held slaves, but opposed secession and refused to follow Tennessee out of the Union. In March, 1862, Lincoln appointed him military governor of occupied Tennessee. In 1864 he was nominated for vice president with Lincoln on the National Union ticket to win Democratic support. He succeeded Lincoln as President April 15, 1865. In a controversy with Congress over the president's power over the South, he proclaimed, May 26, 1865, an amnesty to all Confederates except certain leaders if they would abolish slavery and ratify the 13th amendment. States doing so added anti-Negro provisions that enraged Congress, which intended to enfranchise all Negroes and disenfranchise former Confederates. Congress restored military control over the South. When Johnson removed Edwin M. Stanton, secretary of war, without notifying the Senate, thus repudiating the Tenure of Office Act, the House impeached him for this and other reasons. He was tried by the Senate, which voted 35 for conviction, 19 for acquittal, lacking the two-thirds necessary to convict, May 26, 1868. He was a candidate before the next Democratic convention, but not nominated. He returned to the Senate in 1875, and in a strong speech defended his course. He supported the Lincoln policies, but his conciliatory attitude toward the South was fought by the radical Republicans. Johnson died July 31, 1875, and was buried at Greenville (now Greeneville), where his log-cabin tailor shop and home are museums.

### MRS. ANDREW JOHNSON

Mrs. Eliza McCardle Johnson was born in Leesburg, Tenn., in 1810, the only daughter of a widow in a mountain hamlet when Johnson married her. She helped him get an education. Their daughter Martha, born 1828, educated in Georgetown, D. C., was often a guest at the White House in Polk's

administration. In 1857 she married Judge D. T. Patterson. She was mistress of the White House in place of her invalid mother. Another daughter, Mary, married Daniel Stover of Carter Co., Tenn., and had three children; after Stover's death she married W. R. Bacon of Greeneville. Mrs. Johnson died in 1876.

## Ulysses S. Grant

Ulysses Simpson Grant, 18th President, Republican, was born at Point Pleasant, O., Apr. 27, 1822, son of Jesse R. Grant, a tanner. The next year the family moved to Georgetown, O. Grant's mother was Hannah Simpson. Grant was named Hiram Ulysses, but on entering West Point, 1839, his name was entered as Ulysses Simpson and he adopted it. He was graduated in 1843; was 1st lieut. and captain under Gens. Taylor and Scott in the Mexican War; resigned, 1854, worked in St. Louis until 1860, then went to Galena, Ill., where his father sold leather and hardware. He became colonel of the 21st Illinois Vols., 1861, then brigadier general; took Forts Henry and Donelson; made maj. gen. of volunteers; fought at Shiloh. Took Vicksburg, became maj. gen. USA., and in Mar., 1864, lieut. gen. He accepted Lee's surrender at Appomattox. In 1866 he was named General of the Army. President Johnson appointed Grant secretary of war when he suspended Stanton in defiance of the Senate, but Grant was not confirmed. He was nominated on the first ballot, May 30, 1868, and elected over Horatio Seymour, Democrat, 214 vs. 80 electoral votes. The 15th amendment, amnesty bill and civil service reform were events of his administration. The Liberal Republicans opposed him with Horace Greeley, also Democratic nominee, 1872, but he was re-elected. He vetoed the inflation bill, 1874. An attempt by the Stalwarts (Old Guard) to nominate him in 1880 failed. In 1884 the collapse of Grant & Ward, investment house, left him penniless. He began his *Personal Memoirs*, writing while ill of cancer and completing them four days before his death at Mt. McGregor, N. Y., July 23, 1885. The book realized over $450,000. Grant was buried in an imposing tomb on Riverside Drive, New York, where his wife also lies.

### MRS. ULYSSES S. GRANT

Mrs. Julia Dent Grant (1826-1902) was the daughter of Judge Frederick Dent of St. Louis, son of a Revolutionary officer. She married Grant, Aug. 1848. Their children were Frederick Dent Grant (1850-1912), minister to Austria-Hungary, police commissioner of New York, major general, Spanish-American War; Ulysses, Jr. (1852-1929); Jesse R. (1858-1934); Nellie (1857-1922), who was married in the White House to Capt. Algernon Sartoris, 1874, and in 1912, a widow, married Frank H. Jones. Cleveland's assistant postmaster general.

## Rutherford Birchard Hayes

Rutherford Birchard Hayes, 19th President, Republican, was born in Delaware, O., Oct. 4, 1822, the posthumous son of Rutherford Hayes, a farmer, and Sophia Birchard. He was descended from George Hayes, a Scot who reached Windsor, Conn., in 1680. He was raised by his uncle Sardis Birchard, educated in Norwalk, O., and Middletown, Conn., and graduated from Kenyon College, 1842, and Harvard Law School, 1845. He practiced law in Lower Sandusky, O., now Fremont; was city solicitor of Cincinnati, 1858-61. He was major of the 23d Ohio Vols., wounded at South Mountain; became brigadier general and major general by brevet, 1864. He served in Congress 1864-67, supporting Reconstruction and Johnson's impeachment. He was elected governor of Ohio, 1867 and 1869; beaten for Congress 1872; re-elected governor, 1875. He supported the merit principle in appointments, economy, prison reform and public libraries. In 1876 he was nominated for President over James G. Blaine and believed he had lost to Samuel J. Tilden, Democrat, 184 to 163 electoral votes. But Zachariah Chandler, chairman of the Republican National Committee, relying on Republican domination of the South, urged the validity of contesting 22 electoral returns from Florida, South Carolina, Louisiana; also Oregon. Frauds in Louisiana injuring Tilden were permitted to stand. Promises to withdraw troops from the South were reported used to suborn Democrats. The election was judged by an Electoral Commission, appointed by Congress, 8 Republicans and 7 Democrats, who refused to "go behind state returns" and by strict party vote elected Hayes by 185 over 184. Tilden's refusal to fight back was blamed by his party. The withdrawal of troops followed, but handicapped Republican rule, and as Hayes proceeded to reform civil service he alienated political spoilsmen. He advocated repeal of the Tenure of Office Act that had led to Johnson's impeachment. He supported sound money and specie payments. Hayes died in Fremont, O., Jan. 17, 1893.

### MRS. RUTHERFORD B. HAYES

Mrs. Lucy Webb Hayes, born 1831, was the daughter of Dr. James Webb of Chillicothe, O. She married Hayes Dec. 30, 1852. She was an advocate of temperance, as was Hayes, and did not permit alcoholic beverages in the White House. The Hayeses had eight children: Birchard A. (1853-1926); Webb C. (1856-1934); Rutherford P. (1858-1927); Joseph T. (1861-1863); George C. (1864-66); Frances (1867-1950); Scott R. (1871-1923); Manning F. (1873-74). Mrs. Hayes died June, 1889.

## James Abram Garfield

James A. Garfield, 20th President, Republican, was born Nov. 19, 1831, in a log cabin at Orange, Cuyahoga Co., Ohio., the son of Abram and Eliza Ballou Garfield. His father, a canal contractor and farmer from New York, was descended from Edward Garfield, who reached Massachusetts Bay Colony in 1630 and helped found Watertown, Mass.; his mother was a descendant of an owner of Providence Plantation. James was the youngest of four children; his father died in 1833 and his mother supported them. He worked as canal bargeman, farmer and carpenter; got an education at Western Reserve Eclectic, later Hiram College, and was graduated from Williams in 1856. He became professor of ancient languages and literature at Hiram, then principal. He was in the Ohio senate in 1859. Anti-slavery and anti-secession, he volunteered for the war, became colonel of the 42nd Ohio Infantry and brigadier general in 1862. He fought at Shiloh, was chief of staff for Rosecrans and was made major general for gallantry at Chickamauga. He entered Congress as a radical Republican in 1863; supported specie payment as against paper money (greenbacks). On the electoral commission in 1876 he voted for Hayes against Tilden on strict party lines. He was senator-elect in 1880 when he became the Republican nominee for President. He was chosen on the 36th ballot as a compromise between Gen. Grant, James G. Blaine and John Sherman. This alienated the Grant following but Garfield was elected and Blaine became his secretary of state. On July 2, 1881, Garfield was shot by an unbalanced officeseeker, Charles J. Guiteau, while entering the old Baltimore & Potomac station in Washington. He died Sept. 19, 1881, at Elberon, N. J., and was buried in Cleveland, O. Guiteau was hanged June 30, 1882.

### MRS. JAMES A. GARFIELD

Mrs. Lucretia Rudolph Garfield was born in 1832, daughter of an Ohio farmer. Her mother was a descendant of Gen. Nathaniel Greene. She and Garfield were schoolmates and were married Nov. 11, 1858, when he was principal at Hiram, O. Cyrus W. Field and friends raised a trust fund of $360,000 for the family. She died March 13, 1918. Five children survived. James R. became secretary of the interior, 1907-09; Harry A. was president of Williams College; Irvin M. became a Boston lawyer and Abram G. a Cleveland architect; a daughter, Mrs. Mary Stanley-Brown, died Dec. 30, 1947.

## Chester Alan Arthur

Chester A. Arthur, 21st President, Republican, was born at Fairfield, Vt., Oct. 5, 1830, the son of the Rev. William Arthur, from County Antrim, Ireland, and Malvina Stone Arthur, member of a New Hampshire family. He was graduated at Union College, 1848, taught school at Pownall, Vt., studied law in New York. In 1853 he argued in a fugitive slave case that slaves transported through New York state were thereby freed; in 1855 he obtained a ruling that Negroes were to be treated the same as whites on street cars. He helped organize the New York State militia, 1861; was made quartermaster general and equipped troops for the front. He was made collector of the port of New York, 1871. In 1877 President Hayes, reforming the civil service, ordered Arthur's resignation; he refused because he was not personally culpable, but was removed, 1879. This made Senators Conkling, Platt and the New York machine stalwarts enemies of Hayes. Arthur and the stalwarts tried to nominate Grant for a third term, 1880; when Garfield was nominated, Arthur received second place in the interests of harmony. On Sept. 19, 1881, he succeeded Garfield as President. He supported civil service reform and the tariff

of 1883; arranged an unratified canal treaty with Nicaragua. He was defeated for renomination by James G. Blaine, 1884, but supported Blaine. He died Nov. 18, 1886, and was buried in Albany, N. Y.

### MRS. CHESTER A. ARTHUR

Mrs. Ellen Lewis Herndon Arthur was born in Fredericksburg, Va., in 1837, the daughter of Commander William Lewis Herndon, U. S. N. She died in 1880. The Arthurs had three children, W. L. H. Arthur, who died in infancy; Chester Alan Arthur, Jr., (1865-1937) and Ella Herndon Arthur, born 1871 (Mrs. Charles Pinkerton). The mistress of the White House was Arthur's sister, Mary, Mrs. John E. McElroy of Albany, N. Y.

## Grover Cleveland

*According to a ruling of the State Dept. Grover Cleveland is both the 22nd and the 24th president, because his two terms were not consecutive. By individuals, he is only the 22nd.*

Grover Cleveland, 22nd and 24th President, Democrat, was born in Caldwell, N. J., Mar. 18, 1837, the son of Richard F. Cleveland, a Presbyterian minister, and Ann Neale, daughter of a Baltimore merchant who had come from Ireland. He was named Stephen Grover, but dropped Stephen. He clerked in Clinton and Buffalo, N. Y., taught in the New York City Institution for the Blind; was admitted to the bar in Buffalo, 1859; ass't district attorney, 1863; sheriff, 1869; mayor, 1881; governor of New York, 1882. He was an independent, honest administrator who hated corruption. He was nominated for President over Tammany opposition, 1884, defeating James G. Blaine, 219 to 182. He enlarged the civil service, vetoed many pension raids on Treasury. In 1888 he was defeated by Benjamin Harrison, although his popular vote was larger. Re-elected over Harrison, 1892, by 277 to 145, he faced a money crisis brought about by lowering of the gold reserve, circulation of paper and exorbitant silver purchases under the Sherman act; he obtained repeal of the latter and a reduced tariff. An income tax was passed but declared unconstitutional by the Supreme Court, 1895. A severe depression and labor troubles racked his administration but he refused to interfere in business matters and rejected as crackpot theory, Jacob Coxey's demand for work relief of $20,000,000 monthly. He broke the Pullman strike with troops to move the mails, 1894. He rejected the platform of W. J. Bryan's silver Democrats, 1896, and supported the gold Democrats, Palmer & Buckner. He had part in the reorganization of the Equitable Life Assurance Assn. He died in Princeton, N. J., June 24, 1908.

### MRS. GROVER CLEVELAND

Mrs. Frances Folsom Cleveland was born in 1864, the daughter of Cleveland's law partner in Buffalo, Oscar Folsom and Emma C. Harmon. She married Cleveland in the White House, June 2, 1886. They had five children, Ruth, Esther, Marion, Richard Folsom and Francis Grover. Mrs. Cleveland married, Feb. 10, 1913, Thomas J. Preston, Jr., an archaeologist in Princeton, N. J. She died Oct. 29, 1947.

## Benjamin Harrison

Benjamin Harrison, 23rd President, Republican, was born at North Bend, O., Aug. 20, 1833. His great-grandfather, Benjamin Harrison, was a signer of the Declaration of Independence; his grandfather, William Henry Harrison, was 9th President; his father John Scott Harrison was a Member of Congress, 1853-57. His mother was Elizabeth F. Irwin. He attended school in a log cabin on his father's farm; was graduated from Miami Univ. 1852; admitted to the bar, 1853 and practiced in Indianapolis, Ind. As 2nd lieut. he raised recruits and became colonel of the 70th Indiana Volunteer Infantry. He fought at Kenesaw Mountain, Peachtree Creek, Nashville, and in the Atlanta campaign. In 1865 he was made brigadier general by brevet. He failed to be elected governor of Indiana, 1876; but became Senator, 1881, and worked for the G. A. R. pensions vetoed by Cleveland. In 1888 he defeated Cleveland for president, 233 to 168. He expanded the pension list greatly; suppressed the Louisiana lottery; signed the McKinley high tariff bill and the Sherman silver purchase act. He helped the admission of North and South Dakota, Montana, Washington, Idaho and Wyoming, Republican states. He was defeated for reelection, 1892. He represented Venezuela in arbitration with Great Britain in Paris, 1899. He died at Indianapolis, Mar. 13, 1901, and was buried there.

### HARRISON'S TWO MARRIAGES

Mrs. Caroline Lavinia Scott Harrison was born

in 1832 in Oxford, O., the daughter of Prof. John W. Scott of Miami Univ. She married Harrison Oct. 29, 1853. She was the first head of the Daughters of the American Revolution. She died in the White House, 1892. Her son Russell B. became a mining engineer. Her daughter Mary married an Indianapolis merchant, James R. McKee; Mary's child, "Baby McKee," was a White House favorite and became a New York businessman. Mary died in Greenwich in 1930. Harrison's second wife was Mrs. Harrison's niece, Mrs. Mary Scott Lord Dimmock, whom he married in 1896. She was born in Honesdale, Pa., 1858, and died in New York, Jan. 5, 1948. She spent two years in the White House during her aunt's lifetime. She had one daughter, Elizabeth Harrison, born 1897, who married James Blaine Walker, Jr., great-nephew of Blaine.

## William McKinley

William McKinley, 25th President, Republican, was born in Niles, O., Jan. 29, 1843, the son of William McKinley, an iron manufacturer, and Nancy Allison McKinley, and was the seventh of nine children. His father's family was Scotch-Irish from County Antrim; his great-grandfather fought in the American Revolution. McKinley attended school in Poland, O., and Alleghany College, Meadville, Pa., and enlisted for the Civil War at 18 in the 23rd Ohio, in which R. B. Hayes was a major. He was a commissary sergeant at Antietam, where the state of Ohio honored him with the tallest monument. He rose to captain and in 1865 was made major by brevet. He studied law in the Albany, N. Y., law school; opened an office in Canton, O., in 1867, and campaigned for Grant and Hayes. From 1876 to 1890, excepting 1882, he served in the House of Representatives and led the fight for a high tariff to protect "infant industries," with reciprocal trade agreements (McKinley bill, enacted Oct. 1, 1890). Defeated on this issue in 1890, he was elected governor of Ohio, 1891 and 1893. He received 182 ballots for President in the Republican convention that nominated Benjamin Harrison in 1892. In 1896 he was elected President on a protective tariff, sound money (gold standard) platform over William J. Bryan, Democratic proponent of free silver. Chief factor was the astute vote-getting of Senator Marcus A. Hanna. McKinley was reluctant to intervene in Cuba on grounds of humanity, but the loss of the battleship Maine at Havana crystallized opinion. He demanded Spain's withdrawal from Cuba; Spain agreed to arbitration and armistice but Congress announced state of war as of Apr. 21. (Peace signed Dec. 10.) In the 1900 campaign he defeated Bryan's anti-imperialist arguments with the prestige of prosperity, "the full dinner pail" and the vigorous campaigning of Theodore Roosevelt, vice presidential nominee. McKinley was a Methodist, beloved for his conciliatory nature, but conservative (stand-pat) on business issues. He abhorred violence. The need to regulate the Philippines is believed to have inspired John Hay's Open Door Policy in Asia. On Sept. 6, 1901, while welcoming citizens at the Pan-American exposition, Buffalo, N. Y., he was shot by Leon Czolgosz, an anarchist terrorist. He died Sept. 14. His last words were: "It is God's way. His will, not ours, be done." McKinley, his wife and infant daughters rest in an imposing tomb in Canton. His favorite flower, the red carnation, was made the state flower.

### MRS. WILLIAM McKINLEY

Mrs. Ida Saxton McKinley, born 1847, was the daughter of James A. Saxton and Katherine De-Walt. She was cashier in her father's bank in Canton, O., when she married McKinley. Their two children died in childhood. Mrs. McKinley became an invalid through a nervous ailment, but presided in the White House and was with her husband when he was assassinated. She died in 1907.

## Theodore Roosevelt

Theodore Roosevelt, 26th President, Republican, was born in New York City, Oct. 27, 1858, the son of Theodore Roosevelt, Collector of the Port, and Martha Bulloch, daughter of Maj. Jas. S. Bulloch, Roswell, Ga. He was descended from Claes Martenszan van Rosenvelt, and his wife Janette, who reached New Netherland from Holland about 1650. Theodore was a fifth cousin of Franklin D. Roosevelt and an uncle of Mrs. Eleanor Roosevelt. His mother was of Scotch-Irish, Huguenot stock and a Southern sympathizer. Roosevelt was graduated from Harvard, 1880, attended Columbia Law School briefly; sat in the New York State Assembly, 1882-84; ranched in North Dakota, 1884-86; failed

of election as mayor of New York, 1886; member of U. S. Civil Service Comm. 1889; president, New York Police Board, 1895, supporting the merit system; Asst. Secy. of the Navy under McKinley, Apr. 19, 1897—May 10, 1898, during which he instituted naval target practice and instructed Commodore George Dewey to take Manila in the event of war with Spain. He organized the 1st U. S. Volunteer Cavalry (Rough Riders) as lieut. col., Leonard Wood, col.; led the charge up Kettle Hill at San Juan and was made colonel by brevet. Elected governor, New York, 1898-1900, he fought the spoils system and achieved taxation of corporation franchises. Drafted for vice president, 1900, he became nation's youngest President at 42 years, 10 mos., 18 days, when McKinley died at Buffalo, Sept. 14, 1901. As President he fought corruption of politics by big business; dissolved Northern Securities Co. and others for violating anti-trust laws; intervened in coal strike on behalf of the public, 1902; instituted Dept. of Commerce and Labor; obtained Elkins law forbidding rebates to favored corporations, 1903; Hepburn law regulating railroad rates, 1906; Pure Food and Drugs Act, 1906, Reclamation Act and employers' liability laws. He organized Conservation, mediated the peace between Japan and Russia, 1905; won the Nobel peace prize. He was the first to use the Hague Court of International Arbitration. By recognizing the new Republic of Panama he made Panama Canal possible, appointed Col. Geo. W. Goethals head commissioner and began canal. He was re-elected 1904, with 336 electoral votes vs. 140.

In 1908 he obtained the nomination of William H. Taft, who was elected; considering Taft inimical to liberal policies he organized the Progressive party, June 22, 1912, and ran for President against Taft and Woodrow Wilson, splitting the Republicans and causing Wilson's election. He was shot during the campaign but recovered. He advocated recall of elected officials, referendum on legislation and recall of judicial decisions, which alienated conservatives. In 1916 he left the Progressives and supported Charles A. Hughes, Republican. A strong friend of Britain, he fought American isolation. In 1917 President Wilson refused to let him organize a division. His four sons served in World War I; two were wounded, one killed. He wrote on many topics—his Winning of the West is best known—was a naturalist and hunter and traced the River of Doubt in Brazil, 1913, now Rio Roosevelt. He was looked upon as certain nominee of the Republicans in 1920. He died Jan. 6, 1919, at Sagamore Hill, Oyster Bay, Long Island, N. Y., now a national shrine, and was buried near the Roosevelt bird refuge there.

### THEODORE ROOSEVELT'S FAMILY

Mrs. Alice Hathaway Lee Roosevelt, daughter of George Cabot Lee and Caroline Haskell Lee, of Boston, married Roosevelt Oct. 27, 1880, in Boston. She and Roosevelt's mother died in New York Feb. 14, 1884. She was the mother of Alice Lee Roosevelt, who married Nicholas Longworth, of Cincinnati, Member of Congress, in the White House, 1906. Their daughter, Paulina, was born Feb. 14, 1925. Longworth, Republican Speaker of the House, died April 9, 1931.

Roosevelt's second wife, Edith Kermit Carow, married him Dec. 2, 1886, in London. She was born in Norwich, Conn., Aug. 16, 1861, daughter of Charles and Gertrude Tyler Carow, and survived her husband 29 years, dying Sept. 30, 1948, aged 87. Of their five children Theodore Roosevelt, Jr., was lieut. col. in World War I, assistant secretary of the Navy, governor of Puerto Rico and governor general of the Philippines. He failed of election as governor of New York. A brigadier general, he served in North Africa, Italy and in Normandy with the 1st Army, and died there July 12, 1944, aged 56. Kermit, major in World War II, died on active duty in Alaska, June 4, 1943, aged 53. Ethel Carow is Mrs. Richard Derby. Archibald Bulloch was a lieut. colonel in World War II. Quentin, aviator in World War I, was killed in action and buried where he fell in France.

## William Howard Taft

William Howard Taft, 27th President, Republican, was born in Cincinnati, O., Sept. 15, 1857, the son of Alphonso Taft and Louisa Maria Torrey. His father was secretary of war and attorney general in Grant's cabinet; minister to Austria and Russia under Arthur. Taft was graduated from Yale, 1878, Cincinnati Law School, 1880, became law reporter for Cincinnati newspapers; was ass't prosecuting attorney, 1881-83; ass't county solicitor, 1885; judge, Superior Court, 1887; U. S. solicitor-general,

1890; federal circuit judge, 1892. In 1900 he became head of the U. S. Philippine Comm. and was first civil governor of the Philippines, 1901-04. Secretary of war, 1904; provisional governor of Cuba, 1906. He was groomed for President by Theodore Roosevelt as an exemplary public servant and elected over W. J. Bryan, 1908. His administration dissolved Standard Oil and tobacco trusts; instituted Department of Labor; drafted direct election of senators and income tax amendments. His tariff and conservation policies angered progressives; though renominated he was fought by Theodore Roosevelt; the result was Wilson's election. Taft was president League to Enforce Peace, supporting the League of Nations. He was professor of constitutional law, Yale, 1913-21; Chief Justice of the United States, 1921-30, when illness forced him to resign. He died in Washington, Mar. 8, 1930, and was buried in Arlington National cemetery.

### MRS. WILLIAM H. TAFT

Mrs. Helen Herron Taft (1861-1943) was born in Cincinnati, daughter of John W. Herron and Harriet Collins. She was a musician and a founder of the Cincinnati orchestra. The Taft children are Helen (Mrs. Frederick J. Manning), born 1891, prof. of history and former dean and acting president at Bryn Mawr; Robert Alphonso Taft, born 1889, U. S. Senator from Ohio 1938-1953, died July 31, 1953, and Charles Phelps Taft, born 1897, lawyer, former mayor of Cincinnati. Mrs. Taft introduced musicales at White House dinners and instigated planting cherry trees along the Tidewater basin.

## Woodrow Wilson

Woodrow Wilson, 28th President, Democrat, was born at Staunton, Va., Dec. 28, 1856, as Thomas Woodrow Wilson, son of a Presbyterian minister, the Rev. Joseph Ruggles and Janet (Jessie) Woodrow, daughter of a Scotch Presbyterian minister. He was a grandson of James Wilson, a Presbyterian of Ulster who reached Philadelphia in 1807, became a printer and in 1808 married an Ulster Presbyterian girl, a shipmate. In his youth Wilson lived in Augusta, Ga., Columbia, S. C., and Wilmington, N. C. He attended Davidson College, 1873-74; was graduated from Princeton, A.B., 1879; A.M., 1882; read law at the Univ. of Virginia, 1881; practiced law, Atlanta, 1882-83; Ph.D., Johns Hopkins, 1886 with "Congressional Government." He taught history and political economy at Bryn Mawr, 1885-88; at Wesleyan, 1888-90; was professor of jurisprudence and political economy at Princeton, 1890-1910; president of Princeton, 1902-1910, during which he tried to introduce innovations of organization that were fought by the graduate dean and alumni; governor of New Jersey, 1911-13, during which he obtained a primary election law, an employers' liability law and other reforms. In 1912 he was nominated for President by the strategy of Wm. J. Bryan, who was out to defeat Champ Clark and Tammany. He won because the Republican vote for Taft was split by the Progressives under Theodore Roosevelt.

Wilson protected American interests in revolutionary Mexico and fought for American rights on the high seas as the first World War opened. His sharp warnings to Germany led to the resignation of his secretary of state, Wm. J. Bryan, pacifist, while his protests against British interference with American ships disturbed the Allies. In 1916 he was re-elected by a slim margin with the slogan, "He kept us out of war," over Charles Evans Hughes, who was strongly supported by Theodore Roosevelt. Wilson's offer to mediate in the war (Dec. 18, 1916) was rejected. When the Germans started unrestricted submarine warfare, contrary to pledges, he broke diplomatic relations. After four American ships had been sunk he asked a declaration of war; it was voted April 6, 1917.

Wilson kept tight personal control over all phases of diplomatic and military activity. He relied more on reports of his confidential agent in Europe, Col. E. M. House, than on Secretary of State Robert Lansing and the U. S. ambassadors. However, he backed Gen. John J. Pershing, U. S. commander in chief, Herbert Hoover, food administrator, and others who had his confidence.

Wilson proposed peace Jan. 8, 1918, on the basis of the Fourteen Points, a state paper with worldwide influence. Basic was his doctrine of self-determination, or consent of the governed, in which he opposed handing peoples from one sovereignty to another. He also demanded a league to enforce peace. The Germans overturned the monarchy and a new republic accepted his terms and

an armistice, Nov. 11. At the November elections the Democrats lost control of Congress.

Wilson went to Paris to help negotiate the peace treaty, the crux of which he considered the League of Nations, also urged by Gen. J. C. Smuts, Lord Robert Cecil, Lord Phillimore, William H. Taft and Elihu Root. In the U. S. Senate Henry Cabot Lodge, William E. Borah and Hiram Johnson demanded reservations that would not make the United States subordinate to the votes of other nations in case of war. Wilson refused to consider any reservations and toured the country to get support. At Pueblo, Colo., Sept. 25, 1919, he broke down and several days later suffered a stroke that made him an invalid. The treaty was rejected, Mar. 1920, by 49 to 35 (29 being sufficient to kill it). He made a public appearance on the day of Harding's inauguration, and formed a law partnership with Bainbridge Colby, but did not practice. He won the Nobel peace prize, 1919. During invalidism of 17 months he was confined to his home, seeing few members of his administration, but holding on to the executive powers. He died Feb. 3, 1924, and was buried in Washington Cathedral.

### WILSON'S TWO MARRIAGES

**Mrs. Ellen Louise Axson Wilson** was born in Rome, Ga., in 1860, the daughter of the Rev. S. E. Axson and Margaret Hoyt. She married Wilson June 28, 1885, and died in the White House Aug. 6, 1914. They had three daughters: Margaret W., born 1886, member of a religious colony in Pondicherry, India, when she died in 1944; Eleanor B., second wife of William G. McAdoo, Wilson's secretary of the treasury, later divorced; Jessie W., who married Francis B. Sayre in the White House Nov. 25, 1913 and died Jan. 15, 1933.

**Mrs. Edith Bolling Wilson** was born in Wytheville, Va., 1872, and was the widow of Norman Galt, a Washington jeweler, when she married Wilson, Dec. 18, 1915. She died in Washington Dec. 28, 1961. During the President's illness Mrs. Wilson conveyed his wishes to members of the government and instituted what she called "a workable system of handling matters of state." She was a director of the Woodrow Wilson Foundation and bequeathed her house to the National Trust for Historic Preservation.

## Warren Gamaliel Harding

**Warren Gamaliel Harding**, 29th President, Republican, was born near Blooming Grove, now Corsica, O., Nov. 2, 1865, the son of Dr. Geo. Tyron Harding, a country doctor, and Phoebe Elizabeth Dickerson. He attended Ohio Central College, Iberia, O., 1879-82; worked on the Star, Marion, O., 1884, and a few years later bought the paper with a friend's help for a reported sum of $300. He was state senator, 1900-04; lieut. governor, 1904-06; defeated for governor, 1910; chosen U. S. Senator, 1915. He was a regular, Old Guard Republican; supported Taft, opposed Federal control of food and fuel, voted for anti-strike legislation, woman's suffrage, Volstead prohibition enforcement act over President Wilson's veto and opposed the League of Nations. In 1920 he was nominated for President on the tenth ballot with Calvin Coolidge. The Republicans capitalized war weariness and fear that Wilson's League of Nations would curtail U. S. sovereignty. They defeated the Democrats, James M. Cox and Franklin D. Roosevelt, 16,152,000 to 9,147,000. Harding stressed a return to "normalcy"; worked for repeal of excess profits and high income taxes and a revision of tariff. On announcing ratification of treaties with Germany, Austro-Hungary, Nov. 14, 1921, he declared war officially ended July 2, 1921. His cabinet included Charles Evans Hughes (State); Herbert Hoover (Commerce); Andrew S. Mellon (Treasury). Two appointees, Albert B. Fall (Interior) and Harry Daugherty (Atty. General), became involved in the Teapot Dome scandal that embittered Harding's last days. He called the International Conference on Limitation of Armaments, Nov. 11, 1921-Feb. 1, 1922, and dedicated the Lincoln Memorial. He left for Alaska June 20, 1923; became ill on his return and died in San Francisco, Aug. 2, 1923. He was buried in Marion, Ohio.

### MRS. WARREN GAMALIEL HARDING

**Mrs. Florence Kling Harding** was born Aug. 15, 1860, the daughter of Amos O. Kling, a Marion, O., hardware merchant and later banker. She married, first, Henry De Wolfe, and had a son, Marshall Eugene De Wolfe. She divorced De Wolfe and in

1891 married Harding. For 14 years she was his associate in managing the Star. She died in Marion, Nov. 21, 1924. The Hardings had no children.

## Calvin Coolidge

**Calvin Coolidge**, 30th President, Republican, was born in Plymouth, Vt., July 4, 1872, the son of John Calvin Coolidge, a storekeeper, and Victoria J. Moor, and named John Calvin Coolidge. His paternal ancestors came from England to Watertown, later Cambridge, Massachusetts Bay Colony, in 1630. Coolidge was graduated at Amherst, 1895; admitted to the bar in Northampton, 1897; city councilman, 1889; city solicitor, 1900-01; clerk of the courts, 1904; member of the lower Massachusetts house, 1907-08; mayor of Northampton, 1910-11; State Senator, 1912-15; and president of Senate, 1914-15; lieut. governor, 1916-18; governor, 1919; re-elected, 1920. In Sept., 1919, Coolidge attained national prominence by his action in the Boston police strike, during which he wired Samuel Gompers of the A. F. of L.: "There is no right to strike against the public safety by anybody, anywhere, anytime." This brought his name before the Republican convention of 1920, where he received 34 votes for President and was nominated for vice president by 674¼ votes. He succeeded to the presidency on Harding's death, Aug. 2, 1923, the oath being administered by his father, a justice of the peace, in his home in Plymouth, Aug. 3, and again Aug. 17 before Justice A. A. Hoehling of the Supreme Court of the District of Columbia. He opposed the League of Nations; approved the World Court; vetoed the soldiers' bonus bill, which was passed over his veto. In 1924 he was re-elected by a huge majority with 15,725,016 over John W. Davis. Dem., 8,385,586, and Robert M. LaFollette, Prog., 4,822,856. He reduced the national debt by $2,000,000,000 in three years. He opposed the McNary-Haugen farm bill and price fixing, and supported his secretary of state, Frank B. Kellogg, in the Kellogg-Briand treaties outlawing war. His dry, laconic remarks are often quoted: opposing reduction of Europe's war debt. "They hired the money, didn't they?" With Republicans eager to renominate him he announced, Aug. 2, 1927: "I do not choose to run for President in 1928." He became a life insurance director, wrote syndicated articles and died of a heart attack in Northampton, Jan. 5, 1933. He was buried on a Plymouth hillside.

### MRS. CALVIN COOLIDGE

**Mrs. Grace Anne Goodhue Coolidge** was born in Burlington, Vt., Jan. 3, 1879, the daughter of Andrew I. Goodhue, a steamboat inspector under Cleveland. She was graduated from the Univ. of Vermont, 1902; taught in the Clarke School for the Deaf, 1902-1905, and became president of its board. She married Coolidge Oct. 4, 1905. She died July 8, 1957, in Northampton, Mass.; aged 78. The Coolidges had two sons: John, born 1906, and Calvin (1908-1924).

## Herbert Hoover

**Herbert Clark Hoover**, 31st President, Republican, was born at West Branch, Iowa, Aug. 10, 1874, son of Jesse Clark Hoover, a blacksmith (1847-1880) and Hulda Randall Minthorn (1848-83). Ancestor Andrew Hoover came to Penn. from Palatinate, 1738; great-grandfather reached West Branch, 1854. Hoover grew up in Indian Terr. and Oregon, won A.B. in engineering, Stanford, 1891. Briefly with U. S. Geological Survey and western mines; then mining engineer in western Australia, Asia, Europe, Africa, America. While chief engineer, imperial mines, China, he directed food relief for victims of Boxer Rebellion, 1900. He became a world figure in relief work, distributing over $5 billion worth during 1914-1923. He directed American Relief Committee, London, 1914-15; U. S. Comm. for Relief in Belgium, 1915-1919; U. S. Food Administrator, 1917-1919; American Relief Admin., 1918-1923, feeding children in defeated nations; Russian Relief, 1918-1923; Interallied Food Council; Supreme Economic Council; Comm. on Industrial Relations. As Secy. of Commerce, 1921-28, he began regulation of radio and aviation, pushed research program for Natl. Academy of Science; organized 7-state pact for Colorado River irrigation and Hoover (Boulder) Dam. Elected President over Alfred E. Smith, 1928, he started White House Conferences on child health and protection, and housing; supported conservation of forests, oil, resources; initiated Naval Conference, 1930; organized RFC, Home Loan Banks, expanded Farm Loan Banks; called WEC.

He gave his official salary to charities and underpaid help. President Truman made him coordinator of European Food Program, 1947, and ch. of Comm. for Reorganization of the Executive Branch, 1947-49, and ch. of the 2nd Comm. on Reorganization, 1953-55. He founded the Hoover Institution on War, Revolution & Peace at Stanford Univ., Calif. In his final years he lived at Waldorf Towers, New York, N. Y. He died there Oct. 20, 1964, and was buried at West Branch, Iowa, where his birthplace is now a memorial.

### MRS. HERBERT HOOVER

**Mrs. Lou Henry Hoover** was born in Waterloo, Ia., Mar. 29, 1875, daughter of Charles D. Henry, a banker. The family moved to Monterey, Calif. She was graduated from Stanford University 1898 and married Hoover in 1899. She died Jan. 7, 1944.

Sons: Herbert Hoover, Jr., b. 1903; Allan Henry Hoover, b. 1907.

## Franklin D. Roosevelt

**Franklin Delano Roosevelt**, 32nd President, Democrat, was born near Hyde Park, N. Y., Jan. 30, 1882, the son of James Roosevelt (died 1900) and Sara Delano (died 1941). His ancestor, Claes Martenszan van Rosenvelt, came to New Amsterdam from Holland in 1649. Claes' son Nicholas, a New York alderman in 1700 and 1715, had a son Johannes, from whom Theodore Roosevelt was descended, and a son Jacobus, from whom Franklin D. Roosevelt was descended. Roosevelt was graduated at Harvard, 1904; attended Columbia Law school, was admitted to the bar. He went to the New York Senate from his Dutchess county district 1910 and 1913. He voted for Woodrow Wilson at the 1912 Democratic convention; in 1913 Wilson made him assistant secretary of the Navy.

Roosevelt ran for vice president, 1920, with Jas. M. Cox and was defeated. From 1920 to 1928 he was a New York lawyer and v.p. of Fidelity & Deposit Co. In Aug., 1921, infantile paralysis paralyzed his legs. He learned to walk with leg braces and a cane and established the Warm Springs, Ga., Foundation, for helping those so afflicted.

Roosevelt presented the name of Alfred E. Smith to the Democratic convention of 1924 in New York, and 1928 in Houston, Texas, calling Smith the Happy Warrior. Smith was nominated in 1928 and defeated. Roosevelt was elected governor of New York, 1928 and 1930. In 1932 at Chicago W. G. McAdoo, pledged to John N. Garner, threw his votes to Roosevelt, who was chosen, alienating Smith. The financial crash, unemployment and the Democratic promise to repeal prohibition made his victory inevitable. He asked emergency powers, proclaimed the New Deal, and put into effect a vast number of administrative changes. Foremost was "pump priming," or use of public funds for relief and public works, resulting in deficit financing. He greatly expanded the controls of the central government over business and by an excess profits tax and pyramiding income taxes produced a redistribution of earnings on an unprecedented scale. The Wagner act gave labor many advantages in organizing and collective bargaining, at the same time denying equal privileges to employers. He was the last President inaugurated on Mar. 4 (1933) and the first inaugurated on Jan. 20 (1937).

Roosevelt was a tremendous worker and traveler despite physical handicaps. He was the first President to use radio for "fireside chats." When the Supreme Court voided his measures he demanded additional judges of Congress. It refused, but resignations soon enabled him to replace conservatives who had opposed him. He was the first President to break the third term tradition and was elected to a fourth term, 1944, despite failing health. The culminating event of his career was World War II. He was openly hostile to fascist governments before the war and gave Britain substantial support, such as exchanging 50 destroyers for air bases, before Pearl Harbor made the United States a belligerent. He wrote the principles of fair dealing into the Atlantic Charter, Aug. 14, 1941 (with Winston Churchill) and in the Four Freedoms (Freedom of speech, of worship, from want, from fear) Jan. 6, 1941. He conferred with the heads of state at Casablanca, Jan., 1943; Quebec, Aug., 1943; Teheran, Nov.-Dec., 1943; Cairo, Dec., 1943; Yalta, Feb., 1945. He died at Warm Springs, Ga., April 12, 1945, aged 63, and was buried on his Hyde Park estate, where his house and library are in the national care.

### ELEANOR ROOSEVELT

**Mrs. Anna Eleanor Roosevelt** was born Oct. 11, 1884, the daughter of Elliott Roosevelt, a younger brother of Theodore Roosevelt, and Anna Hall. She was educated in private schools. She married Franklin D. Roosevelt Mar. 17, 1905. In 1924-28 she was finance chairman of the New York Democratic State committee. She was asst. director, Office of Civilian Defense, 1941-42; U. S. representative, General Assembly, U. N., 1945-53 and ch. of its Human Rights Commission. In 1961 President Kennedy appointed her to General Assembly, U. N. Mrs. Roosevelt died Nov. 7, 1962, in New York, N. Y., and was buried beside her husband at Hyde Park, N. Y. President Kennedy and former Presidents Eisenhower and Truman were present. The Roosevelts had 6 children. one dying in infancy. The others: Anna Eleanor (Mrs. James H. Halsted), b. 1906; James, b. Dec. 23, 1907; Elliott, b. Sept. 23, 1910; Franklin Delano, Jr., b. Aug. 17, 1914; John A., b. Mar. 13, 1916.

## Harry S. Truman

**Harry S. Truman**, 33rd President, Democrat, was born at Lamar, Mo., May 8, 1884, the son of John Anderson Truman and Martha Ellen Young. Four grandparents were born in Kentucky and moved to Missouri in the 1840s. The Trumans came from England and the President's mother's grandmother from Northern Ireland, while an ancestor of his maternal grandfather, Solomon Young came from Germany. A family disagreement on whether Harry Truman's middle name was Shippe or Solomon, after names of two grandfathers, resulted in his using only S. for his middle initial. He is a Baptist.

He attended public schools in Independence, Mo., worked for the Kansas City Star, 1901, and as railroad timekeeper, and helper in Kansas City banks up to 1905. He joined the Missouri National Guard, 1905, and was rejected by West Point for defective eyesight. He ran his family's farm, 1906-17. He entered the Field Artillery school at Fort Sill, Okla., 1917; became 1st lieut., Battery F and capt., Battery D, 129th Field Artillery, 35th Div., A. E. F. He served in the Vosges, Meuse-Argonne and St. Mihiel actions and was discharged as major, 1919. He is a colonel in the Field Artillery Reserve. After the war he ran a haberdashery, became judge of Jackson Co. Court, 1922-24; attended Kansas City School of Law, 1923-25. He was defeated, then elected presiding judge.

Truman was chosen senator Nov. 6, 1934; reelected Nov. 5, 1940. In 1944 with President Roosevelt's approval he was nominated for vice president, and elected. On Roosevelt's death Apr. 12, 1945, Truman was sworn in as President by Chief Justice Harlan F. Stone. In 1948 he was elected President as polls predicted his defeat.

Truman supported the Marshall Plan, ECA, the rehabilitation of Greece and arming of Turkey, and NATO, naming Gen. of the Army Eisenhower to the supreme command in Europe. He opened the United Nations conference by radio and participated with Stalin and Attlee in the Potsdam Agreement. He authorized the first use of an atomic bomb (Hiroshima, Aug. 6; Nagasaki, Aug. 9, 1945). He supported a policy of compromise between Chiang Kai-shek and the Chinese Communists. When the Communists attacked in Korea, June, 1950, and the UN asked for armed aid he ordered Gen. of the Army MacArthur to give it, but when MacArthur opposed his policy of limited objectives he removed him.

Truman established the Office of Defense Mobilization in 1950, instituted controls of materials and prices. He won a higher minimum wage, increased social security and aid for housing. In 1952 he ordered seizure of steel companies, which had refused demands of CIO and WSB, and when overruled by the U. S. Supreme Court refused to use the Taft-Hartley law. He rebuilt the White House. He retired to Independence, Mo., and wrote his memoirs. The Harry S. Truman Library, containing his letters and documents, was given by the city of Independence and friends to National Archives, 1957. It has offices for Mr. Truman.

### MRS. HARRY S. TRUMAN

**Mrs. Elizabeth Virginia Wallace Truman** was born Feb. 13, 1885, in Independence, Mo., the eldest of four children and the only daughter of David Willock Wallace. She and Mr. Truman attended the same grade and high schools in Independence, both being graduated in 1901. She attended Barstow, a girls' preparatory school in Kansas City, Mo., and is an Episcopalian. She married Mr. Truman June 28, 1919. They have one daughter, Margaret, born 1924, a concert and radio artist, who married Clifton Daniel, a New York newspaper editor, April 21, 1956. The Daniels have 4 sons: Clifton Truman, William Wallace, Harrison Gates, and Thomas Washington.

## Dwight David Eisenhower

Dwight David Eisenhower, 34th President, Republican, was born Oct. 14, 1890, at Denison, Tex., the son of David Jacob Eisenhower and Ida Elizabeth Stover Eisenhower. His paternal grandfather descended from German Mennonites who left the Rhineland for Pennsylvania in the 1730s, moved to Kansas in 1878. His father met his mother at Lane University, a United Brethren college at Lecompton, Kan. When Dwight was 1 year old his parents moved to Abilene, Kan. He attended high school and in 1915 was graduated at West Point. He became 2nd lieut., 19th U. S. Infantry, at Fort Sam Houston, Tex. He was a lieutenant colonel in charge of a tank corps at Camp Colt, Gettysburg, Pa., in 1918. He was graduated from Infantry Tank School, 1922; Command and General Staff Sch., 1926; Army War College, 1928; Army Industrial College, 1933. He was asst. executive officer of the Asst. Secy. of War, 1929-1933, and in the office of the Chief of Staff, 1933-35. He was on the American Military Mission to the Philippines, 1935-39 and during 4 of those years on the staff of Gen. MacArthur. He was chief of staff, 3rd Div., later 9th Corps, 1940-41, and of the 3rd Army, 1941 as brigadier general. After the Louisiana maneuvers he was made chief of the War Plans Div., War Dept. General Staff, and then became asst. chief of staff, Operations Div. and in June, 1942, lieutenant general. He was made Commander of Allied forces landing in North Africa Nov. 8, 1942, and advanced to full general in Feb., 1943, and Commander in Chief of Allied Forces in North Africa. He became Supreme Commander, Allied Expeditionary Forces Dec. 31, 1943, and as such led the Normandy invasion June 6, 1944. He was given the temporary rank of General of the Army Dec. 19, 1944, which was made permanent in 1946. On May 7, 1945, he received the surrender of the Germans at Rheims. He was in command of the U. S. Occupation Force in Germany in 1945, and returned to serve as Chief of Staff, Nov. 19, 1945, to Feb. 7, 1948. From June 7, 1948, to Jan. 19, 1953, he was president of Columbia Univ., but he took leave of absence Dec. 16, 1950, to serve as Supreme Allied Commander in Europe to organize NATO forces.

Eisenhower resigned from the Army in June, 1952, and was nominated for President by the Republicans at Chicago July 11, 1952. He defeated Adlai E. Stevenson by 442 to 89 electoral votes, was inaugurated Jan. 20, 1953. He was renominated unanimously in San Francisco Aug. 22, 1956, and defeated Stevenson 457 to 74. He called himself a moderate, favored "free market system" vs. government price and wage controls; kept government out of labor disputes; reorganized defense establishment; promoted missile programs, including Polaris. With strong aid of John Foster Dulles, his Secy. of State, he continued foreign aid; demanded unification of Germany by free elections; sped end of Korean fighting; supplied planes to anti-communist Guatemalan govt.; endorsed Formosa and SE Asia defense treaties; backed U.N. in condemning Anglo-French raid on Egypt; advocated "open skies" policy of mutual inspection to USSR. He sent U. S. troops into Little Rock, Ark., Sept., 1957, during the segregation crisis and ordered Marines into Lebanon July-Aug., 1958. Eisenhower's rank as General of the Army was restored by Congress and signed by President Kennedy Mar. 22, 1961. He farms near Gettysburg, Pa.

### MRS. DWIGHT D. EISENHOWER

Mrs. Dwight D. Eisenhower was born Mamie Geneva Doud in Boone, Ia., Nov. 14, 1896. Her home was in Denver when Eisenhower, then a 1st lieutenant of infantry at Fort Sam Houston, met her. They were married July 1, 1916. Their first son, Dwight Doud, died in infancy; their second is John Sheldon Doud Eisenhower, lt. colonel, USA, ret., left the Army 1963. He is married to Barbara Jean Thompson, and they have four children.

## John F. Kennedy

John Fitzgerald Kennedy, 35th President, Democrat, was born May 29, 1917, in Brookline, Mass., the second of 9 children of Joseph P. Kennedy, financier who later became ambassador to Great Britain, and Rose Fitzgerald Kennedy. He entered Harvard, attended the London School of Economics briefly in 1935, received a B.S. *cum laude* from Harvard in 1940. He served in the U. S. Navy, 1941-1945, commanded a PT boat in the Solomons and won Navy and Marine Corps medals and the Purple Heart. He covered the Potsdam Conference and the start of the U. N. at San Francisco for International News Service. He served as Representative in Congress from Massachusetts, 1947-1953, defeated Henry Cabot Lodge for the Senate in 1952, was re-elected 1958. He nearly won the vice presidential nomination in 1956.

Kennedy won the Democratic nomination for President at Los Angeles, July 14, 1960. Sen. Lyndon B. Johnson (Tex.), was named for vice president. Kennedy defeated Richard M. Nixon, Republican, by the slim margin of 118,550 popular votes and an electoral vote of 303 to 219. He was the first Roman Catholic to be elected President.

President Kennedy's most important act was his successful demand Oct. 22, 1962, that the Soviet Union dismantle all missile bases in Cuba. He established a quarantine of arms shipments to Cuba and continued surveillance by air. He defied Soviet attempts to force the Allies out of Berlin. He made the steel industry rescind its price rise. He backed civil rights, a mental health program, arbitration of railroad disputes and larger medical care for the aged. Astronaut flights and satellite orbiting were greatly developed during his less than 3-yrs. tenure. Cape Canaveral was renamed Cape Kennedy later. He wrote *Profiles in Courage*, which won a Pulitzer prize, and *Why England Slept*. He turned the White House spotlight on the cultural arts.

On Nov. 22, 1963, Kennedy was assassinated in Dallas, Texas. On Nov. 25, a national day of mourning, he was buried in Arlington National Cemetery, Va.

### MRS. JOHN F. KENNEDY

Mrs. Jacqueline Bouvier Kennedy was born July 28, 1929, in Southampton, N. Y., daughter of John Vernon Bouvier, a New York Banker, and Janet Lee Bouvier (Mrs. Hugh D. Auchincloss). She attended private schools for girls and Vassar, and studied the history of art at the Sorbonne, Paris, during one year. She was graduated from George Washington Univ., 1951, afterward studying American history there. She was on the reporting staff of Washington Times-Herald, 1952. She married John F. Kennedy at Newport, Sept. 12, 1953, when she was 24 and Sen. Kennedy 36. They had three children: Caroline, born Nov. 27, 1957; John F., Jr., Nov. 25, 1960 and Patrick Bouvier, Aug. 7, 1963 (deceased). Mrs. Kennedy supervised the complete refurnishing of the White House. She moved to New York City in 1964.

## Lyndon Baines Johnson

Lyndon Baines Johnson, 36th President, Democrat, was born on a farm near Stonewall, Tex., Aug. 27, 1908, son of Sam Ealy and Rebekah Baines Johnson. His father and grandfather had served in the Texas legislature. His family moved to Johnson City in 1913, where he was graduated from the high school in 1924. He received a B.S. degree at Southwest Texas State Teachers College, 1930, attended Georgetown Univ., Law School, Washington, 1935. He taught public speaking in Houston high school, 1930-32; served as secretary to Rep. R. M. Kleberg, 1932-35. In 1935 President Roosevelt appointed Johnson Texas state administrator of the National Youth Admin. In 1937 Johnson won a contest to fill the vacancy caused by the death of a Representative, and in 1938 was elected to the full term, after which he returned for four terms. A member of the Naval Reserve, he was lieut. commander, U. S. Navy, 1941-42, winning the Silver Star for a flight over Japanese positions at New Guinea. He was elected Senator 1948 by only 87 votes margin over Gov. Coke Stevenson of Texas; in 1954 he was reelected by a large majority. He became Democratic whip, 1951, and leader, 1953, at 44. Johnson was Texas' favorite son for the Democratic presidential nomination in 1956 and had strong support in the 1960 convention, when the nominee, John F. Kennedy, asked him to run for Vice President. His campaigning helped overcome religious bias against Kennedy in the South. As Vice President he proved to be a tireless worker. He represented Kennedy abroad, was ch. of the President's Committee on Equal Employment Opportunity and member of advisory bodies dealing with security, space and the Peace Corps. Johnson took the oath of office as President at 2:30 p.m., CST, on November 22, 1963, 99 min. after the death of President Kennedy. In filling out the Kennedy term Johnson worked hard for welfare legislation and signed acts for civil rights, anti-poverty and tax reduction and averted strikes on railroads. He was nominated for President and elected Nov. 3, 1964, by 486 electoral votes to 52. Overshadowing

other developments during Johnson's first full term in the White House were the expansion of the war in Vietnam, the committing of more than 500,000 American servicemen to the conflict, intensive bombing by U. S. planes, mounting U. S. casualties, and attempts to achieve peace.

In a nationally televised speech Mar. 31, 1968, Johnson announced that he had ordered a halt to air and naval bombardment of most of North Vietnam. In a surprise statement at the close of the address he said: "I shall not seek, and I will not accept, the nomination of my party for another term as your President." Johnson withdrew in the name of national unity after acknowledging that there was "division in the American house."

**MRS. LYNDON B. JOHNSON**
Mrs. Claudia Alta Taylor Johnson, affectionately called Lady Bird by family and friends, is the daughter of a Marshall, Texas, rancher and was born Dec. 22, 1912. Her mother, dying when Claudia was a little girl, left her $67,000, which she multiplied by careful investment. She was graduated from the Univ. of Texas, 1933, and married Johnson Nov. 17, 1934. An able business woman, she became owner of radio-television station KTBC in Austin, Tex., since placed in a trust. The Johnsons have two daughters, Lynda Bird, born Mar. 19, 1944 and Luci Baines, born July 2, 1947. The Johnson ranch of 400 acres is near Johnson City, Texas. President Johnson is a member of the Christian Church (Disciples of Christ). Mrs. Johnson and Lynda are Episcopalians; Luci became a Roman Catholic July 2, 1965. Luci was married to Patrick Nugent Aug. 6, 1966. She gave birth in Austin, Tex., June 21, 1967, to the President's first grandchild, Patrick Lyndon Nugent. On Dec. 9, 1967, Lynda was married to Marine Capt. Charles S. Robb in the first White House marriage of a President's daughter in 53 years.

## Religious Background of Presidents

**Baptist**—Harding, Truman.
**Christian Church (Disciples of Christ)**—Garfield, Lyndon B. Johnson.
**Congregationalist**—Coolidge.
**Episcopalian**—Washington, Madison, Monroe, William Henry Harrison, Tyler, Taylor, Pierce, Arthur, and Franklin D. Roosevelt.
Jefferson, an Episcopal Church member, later became a deist, said he was a "disciple of the doctrines of Jesus," and commended Unitarianism.
**Friends (Quakers)**—Hoover.

**Methodist**—Polk, Andrew Johnson, Grant, McKinley.
**Presbyterian**—Jackson, Buchanan, Cleveland, Benjamin Harrison, Wilson, Eisenhower.
Lincoln attended Presbyterian services in Washington but was not a member. Hayes attended the Methodist Church, but never joined.
**Reformed Dutch**—Van Buren, Theodore Roosevelt.
**Roman Catholic**—Kennedy.
**Unitarian**—John Adams, John Quincy Adams, Fillmore, Taft.

## Law on Succession to the Presidency

If by reason of death, resignation, removal from office, inability, or failure to qualify there is neither a President nor Vice President to discharge the powers and duties of the office of President, then the Speaker of the House of Representatives shall upon his resignation as Speaker and as Representative, act as President. The same rule shall apply in the case of the death, resignation, removal from office, or inability of an individual acting as President.

If at the time when a Speaker is to begin the discharge of the powers and duties of the office of President there is no Speaker, or the Speaker fails to qualify as Acting President, then the President pro tempore of the Senate, upon his resignation as President pro tempore and as Senator, shall act as President.

An individual acting as President shall continue to act until the expiration of the then current Presidential term, except that (1) if his discharge of the powers and duties of the office is founded in whole or in part in the failure of both the President-elect and the Vice President-elect to qualify, then he shall act only until a President or Vice President qualifies, and (2) if his discharge of the powers and duties of the office is founded in whole or in part on the inability of the President or Vice President, then he shall act only until the removal of the disability of one of such individuals.

If, by reason of death, resignation, removal from office, or failure to qualify, there is no President pro tempore to act as President, then the officer of the United States who is highest on the following list, and who is not under disability to discharge the powers and duties of President, shall act as President: Secy. of State, Secy. of the Treasury, Secy. of Defense, Attorney General, Postmaster General, Secy. of the Interior, Secy. of Agriculture, Secy. of Commerce, Secy. of Labor, Secy. of Health, Education and Welfare, Secy. Housing and Urban Development and Secy. of Transportation. *Approved July 18, 1947; amended Sept. 9, 1965, and Oct. 15, 1966.*

### Presidents Who Wore Military Uniforms

Washington—French and Indian War; Revolution.
Monroe—Revolution.
Jackson—Revolution, Creek, 1812, and Seminole wars.
Harrison, W. H.—Indian wars, Ohio and Indiana, 1812.
Tyler—1812.

Taylor—1812, Black Hawk, Seminole and Mexican.
Pierce—Mexican.
Buchanan—1812.
Lincoln—Black Hawk.
Johnson, Andrew—Military Gov. Tennessee, Civil War.
Grant—Mexican, Civil War.
Hayes—Civil War.

Garfield—Civil War.
Arthur—Q. M. Gen., N. Y. State.
Harrison, B.—Civil War.
McKinley—Civil War.
Roosevelt, T.—Spanish War.
Truman—World War I.
Eisenhower—World War I and II.
Kennedy—World War II.
Johnson, Lyndon—World War II.

## Burial Places of the Presidents

G. Washington.. 1732-1799 Mt. Vernon, Va.
John Adams.... 1735-1826 Quincy, Mass.
T. Jefferson..... 1743-1826 Charlottesville, Va.
James Madison. 1751-1836 Montpelier, Va.
James Monroe.. 1758-1831 Richmond, Va.
John Q. Adams.. 1767-1848 Quincy, Mass.
Andrew Jackson. 1767-1845 Nashville, Tenn.
M. Van Buren.. 1782-1862 Kinderhook, N. Y.
W. H. Harrison. 1773-1841 North Bend, Ohio
John Tyler...... 1790-1862 Richmond, Va.
James Knox Polk 1795-1849 Nashville, Tenn.
Zachary Taylor. 1784-1850 Louisville, Ky.
Millard Fillmore 1800-1874 Buffalo, N. Y.
Franklin Pierce. 1804-1869 Concord, N. H.
James Buchanan 1791-1868 Lancaster, Pa.
A. Lincoln...... 1809-1865 Springfield, Ill.

Andrew Johnson 1808-1875 Greeneville, Tenn.
Ulysses S. Grant 1822-1885 New York City
R. B. Hayes.... 1822-1893 Fremont, Ohio
J. A. Garfield... 1831-1881 Cleveland, Ohio
C. A. Arthur.... 1830-1886 Albany, N. Y.
Grover Cleveland 1837-1908 Princeton, N. J.
B. Harrison.... 1833-1901 Indianapolis, Ind.
W. McKinley.... 1843-1901 Canton, Ohio
T. Roosevelt.... 1858-1919 Oyster Bay, N. Y.
William H. Taft 1857-1930 Arlington Nat'l Cem'y
Woodrow Wilson 1856-1924 Washington Cathedral
W. G. Harding.. 1865-1923 Marion, Ohio
Calvin Coolidge. 1872-1933 Plymouth, Vt.
Herbert Hoover.. 1874-1964 West Branch, Iowa
F. D. Roosevelt.. 1882-1945 Hyde Park, N. Y.
J. F. Kennedy... 1917-1963 Arlington Nat'l Cem'y

## Origin of the United States National Motto

*In God We Trust*, designated as the U. S. National Motto by Congress in 1956, originated during the Civil War as an inscription for U. S. coins, although it was used by Francis Scott Key in a slightly different form when he wrote The Star-Spangled Banner in 1814. On Nov. 13, 1861, when Union morale had been shaken by battlefield defeats, the Rev. M. R. Watkinson, of Ridleyville, Pa., wrote to Secy. of the Treasury Salmon P. Chase. "From my heart I have felt our national shame in disowning God as not the least of our present national disasters," the minister wrote, suggesting "recognition of the Almighty God in some form on our coins." Secy. Chase ordered designs prepared with the inscription *In God We Trust* and backed coinage legislation which authorized use of this slogan. It first appeared on some U. S. coins in 1864, disappeared and reappeared on various coins until 1955, when Congress ordered it placed on all paper money and all coins.

# LAWS AND DOCUMENTS
## DECLARATION OF INDEPENDENCE

*The Declaration of Independence was adopted by the Continental Congress, in Philadelphia, on July 4, 1776. John Hancock was president of the Congress and Charles Thomson was secretary. A copy of the Declaration, engrossed on parchment, was signed by Members of Congress on and after August 2, 1776. On January 18, 1777, Congress ordered that "authenticated copies, with the names of the Members of Congress subscribed the same, be sent to each of the United States, and that they be desired to have same put upon record." Authenticated copies were printed in broadside form in Baltimore, where the Continental Congress was then in session. The following text is that of the original printed by John Dunlap at Philadelphia for the Continental Congress.*

## In CONGRESS, July 4, 1776.
## A DECLARATION
### By the REPRESENTATIVES of the
# UNITED STATES OF AMERICA,
### In GENERAL CONGRESS assembled

WHEN in the Course of human Events, it becomes necessary for one People to dissolve the Political Bands which have connected them with another, and to assume among the Powers of the Earth, the separate and equal Station to which the Laws of Nature and of Nature's God entitle them, a decent Respect to the Opinions of Mankind requires that they should declare the causes which impel them to the Separation.

We hold these Truths to be self-evident, that all Men are created equal, that they are endowed by their Creator with certain unalienable Rights, that among these are Life, Liberty, and the Pursuit of Happiness—That to secure these Rights, Governments are instituted among Men, deriving their just Powers from the Consent of the Governed, that whenever any Form of Government becomes destructive of these Ends, it is the Right of the People to alter or to abolish it, and to institute new Government, laying its Foundation on such Principles, and organizing its Powers in such Form, as to them shall seem most likely to effect their Safety and Happiness. Prudence, indeed, will dictate that Governments long established should not be changed for light and transient Causes; and accordingly all Experience hath shewn, that Mankind are more disposed to suffer, while Evils are sufferable, than to right themselves by abolishing the Forms to which they are accustomed. But when a long Train of Abuses and Usurpations, pursuing invariably the same Object, evinces a Design to reduce them under absolute Despotism, it is their Right, it is their Duty, to throw off such Government, and to provide new Guards for their future Security. Such has been the patient Sufferance of these Colonies; and such is now the Necessity which constrains them to alter their former Systems of Government. The History of the present King of Great-Britain is a History of repeated Injuries and Usurpations, all having in direct Object the Establishment of an absolute Tyranny over these States. To prove this, let Facts be submitted to a candid World.

He has refused his Assent to Laws, the most wholesome and necessary for the public Good.

He has forbidden his Governors to pass Laws of immediate and pressing Importance, unless suspended in their Operation till his Assent should be obtained; and when so suspended, he has utterly neglected to attend to them.

He has refused to pass other Laws for the Accommodation of large Districts of People, unless those People would relinquish the Right of Representation in the Legislature, a Right inestimable to them, and formidable to Tyrants only.

He has called together Legislative Bodies at Places unusual, uncomfortable, and distant from the Depository of their public Records, for the sole Purpose of fatiguing them into Compliance with his Measures.

He has dissolved Representative Houses repeatedly, for opposing with manly Firmness his Invasions on the Rights of the People.

He has refused for a long Time, after such Dissolutions, to cause others to be elected; whereby the Legislative Powers, incapable of Annihilation, have returned to the People at large for their exercise; the State remaining in the mean time exposed to all the Dangers of Invasion from without, and Convulsions within.

He has endeavoured to prevent the Population of these States; for that Purpose obstructing the Laws for Naturalization of Foreigners; refusing to pass others to encourage their Migrations hither, and raising the Conditions of new Appropriations of Lands.

He has obstructed the Administration of Justice, by refusing his Assent to Laws for establishing Judiciary Powers.

He has made Judges dependent on his Will alone, for the Tenure of their Offices, and the Amount and Payment of their Salaries.

He has erected a Multitude of new Offices, and sent hither Swarms of Officers to harrass our People, and eat out their Substance.

He has kept among us, in Times of Peace, Standing Armies, without the consent of our Legislatures.

He has affected to render the Military independent of and superior to the Civil Power.

He has combined with others to subject us to a Jurisdiction foreign to our Constitution, and unacknowledged by our Laws; giving his Assent to their Acts of pretended Legislation:

For quartering large Bodies of Armed Troops among us:

For protecting them, by a mock Trial, from Punishment for any Murders which they should commit on the Inhabitants of these States:

For cutting off our Trade with all Parts of the World:

For imposing Taxes on us without our Consent:

For depriving us, in many Cases, of the Benefits of Trial by Jury:

For transporting us beyond Seas to be tried for pretended Offences:

For abolishing the free System of English Laws in a neighbouring Province, establishing therein an arbitrary Government, and enlarging its Boundaries, so as to render it at once an Example and fit Instrument for introducing the same absolute Rule into these Colonies:

For taking away our Charters, abolishing our most valuable Laws, and altering fundamentally the Forms of our Governments:

For suspending our own Legislatures, and declaring themselves invested with Power to legislate for us in all Cases whatsoever.

He has abdicated Government here, by declaring us out of his Protection and waging War against us.

He has plundered our Seas, ravaged our Coasts, burnt our Towns, and destroyed the Lives of our People.

He is, at this Time, transporting large Armies of foreign Mercenaries to compleat the Works of Death, Desolation, and Tyranny, already begun with circumstances of Cruelty and Perfidy, scarcely paralleled in the most barbarous Ages, and totally unworthy the Head of a civilized Nation.

He has constrained our fellow Citizens taken Captive on the high Seas to bear Arms against their Country, to become the Executioners of their Friends and Brethren, or to fall themselves by their Hands.

He has excited domestic Insurrections amongst us, and has endeavoured to bring on the Inhabitants of our Frontiers, the merciless Indian Savages, whose known Rule of Warfare, is an undistinguished Destruction, of all Ages, Sexes and Conditions.

In every stage of these Oppressions we have Petitioned for Redress in the most humble Terms: Our repeated Petitions have been answered only by repeated Injury. A Prince, whose Character is thus marked by every act which may define a Tyrant, is unfit to be the Ruler of a free People.

Nor have we been wanting in Attentions to our British Brethren. We have warned them from Time to Time of Attempts by their Legislature to extend an unwarrantable Jurisdiction over us. We have reminded them of the Circumstances of our

Emigration and Settlement here. We have appealed to their native Justice and Magnanimity, and we have conjured them by the Ties of our common Kindred to disavow these Usurpations, which, would inevitably interrupt our Connections and Correspondence. They too have been deaf to the Voice of Justice and of Consanguinity. We must, therefore, acquiesce in the Necessity, which denounces our Separation, and hold them, as we hold the rest of Mankind, Enemies in War, in Peace, Friends.

We, therefore, the Representatives of the UNITED STATES OF AMERICA, in GENERAL CONGRESS, Assembled, appealing to the Supreme Judge of the World for the Rectitude of our Intentions, do, in the Name, and by Authority of the good People of these Colonies, solemnly Publish and Declare, That these United Colonies are, and of Right ought to be, FREE AND INDEPENDENT STATES; that they are absolved from all Allegiance to the British Crown, and that all political Connection between them and the State of Great-Britain, is and ought to be totally dissolved; and that as FREE AND INDEPENDENT STATES, they have full Power to levy War, conclude Peace, contract Alliances, establish Commerce, and to do all other Acts and Things which INDEPENDENT STATES may of right do. And for the support of this Declaration, with a firm Reliance on the Protection of divine Providence, we mutually pledge to each other our Lives, our Fortunes, and our sacred Honor.

*Signed by* ORDER *and in* BEHALF *of the* CONGRESS,
**JOHN HANCOCK, President.**
ATTEST.
**CHARLES THOMSON, Secretary.**

## World Almanac Guilty of the Crime of Sedition*

*(Excerpts from an editorial in the New York World, former publisher of the World Almanac, dated Jan. 13, 1920, and reprinted in the American Heritage of June, 1968.)*

The World Almanac for 1920 has already been printed and tens of thousands of copies have been distributed and cannot be recalled; but the Almanac once again contains the Declaration of Independence, and the new Sedition Bill as agreed to by the House Judiciary Committee provides that any person shall be deemed guilty of a felony "who either orally or by writing, printing or . . . shall otherwise teach, incite, advocate, propose or advise, or aid, abet or encourage forcible resistance to, or destruction of the Government of the United States. . . ."

Now, unfortunately, the second paragraph of the Declaration of Independence is defiantly seditious . . . The World can easily suppress the Declaration of Independence in all future editions of the Almanac, but in the mean time the mischief has been done for 1920 and the seditious utterances of Thomas Jefferson have been scattered to the four corners of the country.

For any evil consequences that may ensue . . . we can only beg for mercy and for such consideration as the Department of Justice may graciously grant. . . .

*Sedition is conduct which tends to treason, but which falls short of it for want of an overt act.

## Signers of the Declaration of Independence

| Delegate and State | Vocation | Birthplace | Born | | Died | |
|---|---|---|---|---|---|---|
| Adams, John (Mass.) | Lawyer | Braintree (Quincy), Mass. | 1735, Oct. | 30 | 1826, July | 4 |
| Adams, Samuel (Mass.) | Politician | Boston, Mass. | 1722, Sept. | 27 | 1803, Oct. | 2 |
| Bartlett, Josiah (N. H.) | Phys., Law. | Amesbury, Mass. | 1729, Nov. | 21 | 1795, May | 19 |
| Braxton, Carter (Va.) | Farmer | King & Queen C. H., Va. | 1736, Sept. | 10 | 1797, Oct. | 10 |
| Carroll, Chas. of Carrollton (Md.) | Lawyer | Annapolis, Md. | 1737, Sept. | 19 | 1832, Nov. | 14 |
| Chase, Samuel (Md.) | Jurist | Princess Anne, Md. | 1741, April | 17 | 1811, June | 19 |
| Clark, Abram (N. J.) | Law., Fin. | Elizabeth, N. J. | 1726, Feb. | 15 | 1794, Sept. | 15 |
| Clymer, George (Pa.) | Merchant | Philadelphia, Pa. | 1739, March | 16 | 1813, Jan. | 23 |
| Ellery, William (R. I.) | Jurist | Newport, R. I. | 1727, Dec. | 22 | 1820, Feb. | 15 |
| Floyd, William (N. Y.) | Soldier | Brookhaven, N. Y. | 1734, Dec. | 17 | 1821, Aug. | 4 |
| Franklin, Benjamin (Pa.) | Print., Pub. | Boston, Mass. | 1706, Jan. | 17 | 1790, April | 17 |
| Gerry, Elbridge (Mass.) | Merchant | Marblehead, Mass. | 1744, July | 17 | 1814, Nov. | 23 |
| Gwinnett, Button (Ga.) | Merchant | Down Hatherly, Eng. | 1732 | | 1777, May | 19 |
| Hall, Lyman (Ga.) | Phys., Jurist | Wallingford, Conn. | 1724, April | 12 | 1790, Oct. | 19 |
| Hancock, John (Mass.) | Merchant | Braintree (Quincy), Mass. | 1737, Jan. | 12 | 1793, Oct. | 8 |
| Harrison, Benjamin (Va.) | Farmer | Berkeley, Va. | 1726, April | 5 | 1791, April | 24 |
| Hart, John (N. J.) | Farmer | Stonington, Conn. | (1707–1711?) | | 1779, May | 11 |
| Hewes, Joseph (N. C.) | Merchant | Kingston, N. J. | 1730, Jan. | 23 | 1779, Nov. | 10 |
| Heyward, Thos. Jr. (S. C.) | Law., Farm. | St. Luke's Parish, S. C. | 1746, July | 28 | 1809, March | 6 |
| Hooper, William (N. C.) | Lawyer | Boston, Mass. | 1742, June | 28 | 1790, Oct. | 14 |
| Hopkins, Stephen (R. I.) | Mer., Judge. | Providence, R. I. | 1707, March | 7 | 1785, July | 13 |
| Hopkinson, Francis (N. J.) | Jur., Music. | Philadelphia, Pa. | 1737, Sept. | 21 | 1791, May | 9 |
| Huntington, Samuel (Conn.) | Jurist | Windham County, Conn. | 1731, July | 3 | 1796, Jan. | 5 |
| Jefferson, Thomas (Va.) | Lawyer | Old Shadwell, Va. | 1743, April | 13 | 1826, July | 4 |
| Lee, Richard Henry (Va.) | Farmer | Stratford, Va. | 1732, Jan. | 20 | 1794, June | 19 |
| Lee, Francis Lightfoot (Va.) | Farmer | Stratford, Va. | 1734, Oct. | 14 | 1797, Jan. | 11 |
| Lewis, Francis (N. Y.) | Merchant | Landaff, Wales | 1713, March | | 1803, Dec. | 30 |
| Livingston, Philip (N. Y.) | Merchant | Albany, N. Y. | 1716, Jan. | 15 | 1778, June | 12 |
| Lynch, Thomas, Jr. (S. C.) | Farmer | Winyah, S. C. | 1749, Aug. | 5 | 1779, (at sea) | |
| McKean, Thomas (Del.) | Lawyer | New London, Pa. | 1734, March | 19 | 1817, June | 24 |
| Middleton, Arthur (S. C.) | Farmer | Charleston, S. C. | 1742, June | 26 | 1787, Jan. | 1 |
| Morris, Lewis (N. Y.) | Farmer | Morrisania, N. Y. (N.Y.C.) | 1726, April | 8 | 1798, Jan. | 22 |
| Morris, Robert (Pa.) | Merchant | Liverpool, Eng. | 1734, Jan. | 20 | 1806, May | 8 |
| Morton, John (Pa.) | Jurist | Ridley, Pa. | 1724 | | 1777, April | |
| Nelson, Thos., Jr. (Va.) | Soldier | Yorktown, Va. | 1738, Dec. | 26 | 1789, Jan. | 4 |
| Paca, William (Md.) | Jurist | Abingdon, Md. | 1740, Oct. | 31 | 1799, Oct. | 23 |
| Paine, Robert Treat (Mass.) | Rev., Jurist. | Boston, Mass. | 1731, March | 11 | 1814, May | 12 |
| Penn, John (N. C.) | Lawyer | Near Port Royal, Va. | 1741, May | 17 | 1788, Sept. | 14 |
| Read, George (Del.) | Jurist | Near North East, Md. | 1733, Sept. | 18 | 1798, Sept. | 21 |
| Rodney, Caesar (Del.) | Jurist | Dover, Del. | 1728, Oct. | 7 | 1784, June | 29 |
| Ross, George (Pa.) | Jurist | New Castle, Del. | 1730, May | 10 | 1779, July | 14 |
| Rush, Benjamin (Pa.) | Physician | Byberry, Pa. (Philadelphia) | 1745, Dec. | 24 | 1813, April | 19 |
| Rutledge, Edward (S. C.) | Lawyer | Charleston, S. C. | 1749, Nov. | 23 | 1800, Jan. | 23 |
| Sherman, Roger (Conn.) | Lawyer | Newton, Mass. | 1721, April | 19 | 1793, July | 23 |
| Smith, James (Pa.) | Lawyer | Dublin, Ireland. | 1713 | | 1806, July | 11 |
| Stockton, Richard (N. J.) | Lawyer | Near Princeton, N. J. | 1730, Oct. | 1 | 1781, Feb. | 28 |
| Stone, Thomas (Md.) | Lawyer | Charles County, Md. | 1743 | | 1787, Oct. | 5 |
| Taylor, George (Pa.) | Ironmonger | Ireland. | 1716 | | 1781, Feb. | 23 |
| Thornton, Matthew (N. H.) | Phys., Jurist. | Ireland. | 1741 | | 1803, June | 24 |
| Walton, George (Ga.) | Jurist | Prince Edward County, Va. | 1740, Jan. | 14 | 1804, Feb. | 2 |
| Whipple, William (N. H.) | Mer., Jurist. | Kittery, Maine. | 1730, Jan. | 14 | 1785, Nov. | 28 |
| Williams, William (Conn.) | Mer., Jurist. | Lebanon, Conn. | 1731, April | 23 | 1811, Aug. | 2 |
| Wilson, James (Pa.) | Jurist | Carskerdo, Scotland. | 1742, Sept. | 14 | 1798, Aug. | 28 |
| Witherspoon, John (N. J.) | Educator | Gifford, Scotland. | 1723, Feb. | 5 | 1794, Nov. | 15 |
| Wolcott, Oliver (Conn.) | Jurist | Windsor, Conn. | 1726, Dec. | 1 | 1797, Dec. | 1 |
| Wythe, George (Va.) | Lawyer | Elizabeth City, Va. | 1726 | | 1806, June | 8 |

## How the Declaration of Independence Was Adopted

On June 7, 1776, Richard Henry Lee, who had issued the first call for a congress of the colonies, introduced in the Continental Congress at Philadelphia a resolution declaring "that these United Colonies are, and of right ought to be, free and independent states, that they are absolved from all allegiance to the British Crown, and that all political connection between them and the state of Great Britain is, and ought to be, totally dissolved."

The resolution, seconded by John Adams on behalf of the Massachusetts delegation, came up again June 10 when a committee of five, headed by Thomas Jefferson, was appointed to express the purpose of the resolution in a declaration of independence. The others on the committee were John Adams, Benjamin Franklin, Robert R. Livingston, and Roger Sherman.

Drafting the Declaration was assigned to Jefferson, who worked on a portable desk of his own construction in a room at Market and 7th Sts. The committee reported the result June 28, 1776. The members of the Congress suggested a number of changes, which Jefferson called "deplorable." They didn't approve Jefferson's arraignment of the British people and King George III for encouraging and fostering the slave trade, which Jefferson called "an execrable commerce." They made 86 changes, eliminating 480 words and leaving 1,337. In the final form capitalization was erratic. Jefferson had written that men were endowed with "inalienable" rights; in the final copy it came out as "unalienable" and has been thus ever since.

The Lee-Adams resolution of independence was adopted by 12 yeas July 2—the actual date of the act of independence. The Declaration, which explains the act, was adopted the evening of July 4.

After the Declaration was adopted, July 4, 1776, it was turned over to John Dunlap, printer, to be printed on broadsides. The original copy was lost and one of his broadsides was attached to a page in the journal of the Congress. It was read aloud July 8 in Philadelphia, Easton, Pa. and Trenton, N. J. On July 9 at 6 p.m. it was read by order of Gen. George Washington to the troops assembled on the Common in New York City (City Hall Park).

The Continental Congress on July 19, 1776, adopted the following resolution:

"Resolved, That the Declaration passed on the 4th, be fairly engrossed on parchment with the title and stile of 'The unanimous Declaration of the thirteen united States of America' and that the same, when engrossed, be signed by every member of Congress."

Not all delegates who signed the engrossed Declaration were present on July 4. Robert Morris (Pa.), William Williams (Conn.) and Samuel Chase (Md.) signed on Aug. 2. Oliver Wolcott (Conn.), George Wythe (Va.), Richard Henry Lee (Va.) and Elbridge Gerry (Mass.) signed in August and September. Matthew Thornton (N.H.) joined the Congress Nov. 4 and signed later. Thomas McKean (Del.) rejoined Washington's Army before signing and said later that he signed in 1781.

Charles Carroll of Carrollton was appointed a delegate by Maryland on July 4, 1776, presented his credentials July 18, and signed the engrossed Declaration Aug. 2. Born Sept. 19, 1737, he was 95 years old and the last surviving signer when he died Nov. 14, 1832.

Two Pennsylvania delegates who did not support the Declaration on July 4 were replaced.

The four New York delegates did not have authority from their state to vote on July 4. On July 9 the New York state convention authorized its delegates to approve the Declaration and the Congress was so notified on July 15, 1776. The four signed the engrossed Declaration on Aug. 2.

The original engrossed Declaration is preserved in the National Archives Building in Washington.

## The Liberty Bell; Its History and Significance

The Liberty Bell, in Independence Hall, Philadelphia, is an object of great reverence to Americans because of its association with the historic events of the War of Independence.

The original Province bell, ordered to commemorate the 50th anniversary of the Commonwealth of Pennsylvania, was cast by Thomas Lister, Whitechapel, London, and reached Philadelphia in August, 1752. It bore an inscription from Leviticus XXV, 10: "Proclaim liberty throughout all the land unto all the inhabitants thereof."

The bell was cracked by a stroke of its clapper in September, 1752, while it hung on a truss in the State House yard for testing. Pass & Stow, Philadelphia founders, recast the bell, adding 1½ ounces of copper to a pound of the original metal to reduce brittleness. It was found that the bell contained too much copper, injuring its tone, so Pass & Stow recast it again, this time successfully.

In June, 1753, the bell was hung in the wooden steeple of the State House, erected on top of the brick tower. In use while the Continental Congress was in session in the State House, it rang out in defiance of British tax and trade restrictions, and proclaimed the Boston Tea Party and the first public reading of the Declaration of Independence.

On Sept. 18, 1777, when the British Army was about to occupy Philadelphia, the bell was moved in a baggage train of the American Army to Allentown, Pa., where it was hidden in Zion's Church until June 27, 1778. It was moved back to Philadelphia after the British left.

In July, 1781, the wooden steeple became insecure and had to be taken down. The bell was lowered into the brick section of the tower. Here it was hanging in July, 1835, when it cracked while tolling for the funeral of John Marshall, Chief Justice of the United States. Because of its association with the War of Independence it was not recast but remained mute in this location until 1846, the year of the Mexican War, when it was placed on exhibition in the Declaration Chamber of Independence Hall.

In 1876, when many thousands of Americans visited Philadelphia for the Centennial Exposition, it was placed in its old walnut frame in the tower hallway. In 1877 it was hung from the ceiling of the tower by a chain of 13 links. It was returned again to the Declaration Chamber and in 1896 taken back to the tower hall, where it occupied a glass case. In 1915 the case was removed so that the public might touch it. It remains there today.

The measurements of the bell follow: Circumference around the lip, 12 ft.; circumference around the crown, 7 ft. 6 in.; lip to the crown, 3 ft.; height over the crown, 2 ft. 3 in.; thickness at lip, 3 in.; thickness at crown, 1¼ in.; weight, 2080 lbs.; length of clapper, 3 ft. 2 in.; cost, £60 14s 5d.

## Independence Hall, American Patriotic Shrine

Independence Hall is the central and main building of a group in Philadelphia, located in Independence Square and facing Chestnut St. It is connected by arcades with two 2-story buildings, the East and West Wings, and two separate corner buildings. Of the latter Congress Hall is at Sixth St., and Old City Hall at Fifth St.

Independence Hall originally was the State House. It was begun in 1732, and completed in 1759. The East and West Wings were intended to house offices. Tower and spire were completed by June 1753.

The Pennsylvania Assembly occupied Assembly Hall in 1735, before the whole structure was completed. In 1775 it gave the use of the room to the Second Continental Congress. Here, on June 16, 1775, George Washington accepted command of the Continental Army. Here the Declaration of Independence was adopted on July 4, 1776; the Articles of Confederation and Perpetual Union were signed beginning on July 9, 1778, and the Constitution of the United States was framed by the Constitutional Convention in 1787.

Congress Hall, at the west end of the group, was erected in 1787 and was the seat of the United States Congress from 1790 to 1800, when the Congress moved to Washington, D. C. The Court House, or Old City Hall, at the east end, was built in 1790 for the municipal courts, and was the first seat of the United States Supreme Court.

Independence Hall and the other buildings in Independence Square form the nucleus around which has been developed the Independence National Historical Park, established in 1956. Much restoration work has been done on the buildings.

# CONSTITUTION OF THE UNITED STATES
## The Original Seven Articles

### PREAMBLE

We, the people of the United States, in order to form a more perfect Union, establish justice, insure domestic tranquility, provide for the common defense, promote the general welfare, and secure the blessings of liberty to ourselves and our posterity, do ordain and establish this Constitution for the United States of America.

### ARTICLE I.

**Section 1—Legislative powers; in whom vested:**

All legislative powers herein granted shall be vested in a Congress of the United States, which shall consist of a Senate and House of Representatives.

**Section 2—House of Representatives, how and by whom chosen. Qualifications of a Representative. Representatives and direct taxes, how apportioned. Enumeration. Vacancies to be filled. Power of choosing officers, and of impeachment.**

1. The House of Representatives shall be composed of members chosen every second year by the people of the several States, and the electors in each State shall have the qualifications requisite for electors of the most numerous branch of the State Legislature.

2. No person shall be a Representative who shall not have attained to the age of twenty-five years and been seven years a citizen of the United States, and who shall not, when elected, be an inhabitant of that State in which he shall be chosen.

3. Representatives and direct taxes shall be apportioned among the several States which may be included within this Union according to their respective numbers, which shall be determined by adding to the whole number of free persons, including those bound to service for a term of years, and excluding Indians not taxed, three-fifths of all other persons. The actual enumeration shall be made within three years after the first meeting of the Congress of the United States, and within every subsequent term of ten years, in such manner as they shall by law direct. The number of Representatives shall not exceed one for every thirty thousand, but each State shall have at least one Representative; and until such enumeration shall be made, the State of New Hampshire shall be entitled to choose 3; Massachusetts, 8; Rhode Island and Providence Plantations, 1; Connecticut, 5; New York, 6; New Jersey, 4; Pennsylvania, 8; Delaware, 1; Maryland, 6; Virginia, 10; North Carolina, 5; South Carolina, 5; and Georgia, 3.

4. When vacancies happen in the representation from any State, the Executive Authority thereof shall issue writs of election to fill such vacancies.

5. The House of Representatives shall choose their Speaker and other officers, and shall have the sole power of impeachment.

**Section 3—Senators, how and by whom chosen. How classified. State Executive, when to make temporary appointments, in case, etc. Qualifications of a Senator. President of the Senate, his right to vote. President pro tem., and other officers of the Senate, how chosen. Power to try impeachments. When President is tried, Chief Justice to preside. Sentence.**

1. The Senate of the United States shall be composed of two Senators from each State, chosen by the Legislature thereof, for six years; and each Senator shall have one vote.

2. Immediately after they shall be assembled in consequence of the first election, they shall be divided as equally as may be into three classes. The seats of the Senators of the first class shall be vacated at the expiration of the second year, of the second class at the expiration of the fourth year, and of the third class at the expiration of the sixth year, so that one-third may be chosen every second year; and if vacancies happen by resignation or otherwise during the recess of the

---

## Origin of the Constitution

The War of Independence was conducted by delegates from the original 13 states, called the Congress of the United States of America and generally known as the Continental Congress. In 1777 the Congress submitted to the legislatures of the states the Articles of Confederation and Perpetual Union, which were ratified by New Hampshire, Massachusetts, Rhode Island, Connecticut, New York, New Jersey, Pennsylvania, Delaware, Virginia, North Carolina, South Carolina and Georgia, and finally, in 1781, by Maryland.

The first article of the instrument read: "The stile of this confederacy shall be the United States of America." This did not signify a sovereign nation, because the states delegated only those powers they could not handle individually, such as power to wage war, establish a uniform currency, make treaties with foreign nations and contract debts for general expenses, such as paying the army. Taxes for the payment of such debts were levied by the individual states. The president under the Articles signed himself "President of the United States in Congress assembled," but here the United States were considered in the plural, a cooperating group. Canada was invited to join the union on equal terms but did not act.

When the war was won it became evident that a stronger federal union was needed to protect the mutual interests of the states. The Congress left the initiative to the legislatures. Virginia in January, 1786, appointed commissioners to meet with representatives of other states, with the result that delegates from Virginia, Delaware, New York, New Jersey and Pennsylvania met at Annapolis. Alexander Hamilton prepared their call asking delegates from all states to meet in Philadelpiha in May, 1787, "to render the Constitution of the Federal government adequate to the exigencies of the union." Congress endorsed the plan Feb. 21, 1787. Delegates were appointed by all states except Rhode Island.

The convention met May 14, 1787. George Washington was chosen president (presiding officer). The states certified 65 delegates, but 10 did not attend. The work was done by 55, not all of whom were present at all sessions. Of the 65 qualified delegates, 16 failed to sign, and 39 actually signed Sept. 17, 1787, some with reservations. Some historians have said 74 delegates were named and 19 failed to attend. These 9 additional persons refused the appointment, were never delegates and never counted as absentees. Washington sent the Constitution to Congress with a covering letter and that body, Sept. 28, 1787, ordered it sent to the legislatures, "in order to be submitted to a convention of delegates chosen in each state by the people thereof."

The Constitution was ratified by votes of state conventions as follows: Delaware, Dec. 7, 1787, unanimous; Pennsylvania, Dec. 12, 1787, 43 to 23; New Jersey, Dec. 18, 1787, unanimous; Georgia, Jan. 2, 1788, unanimous; Connecticut, Jan. 9, 1788, 128 to 40; Massachusetts, Feb. 6, 1788, 187 to 168; Maryland, April 28, 1788, 63 to 11; South Carolina, May 23, 1788, 149 to 73; New Hampshire, June 21, 1788, 57 to 46; Virginia, June 26, 1788, 89 to 79; New York, July 26, 1788, 30 to 27. Nine states were needed to establish the operation of the Constitution "between the states so ratifying the same" and New Hampshire was the ninth state. The government did not declare the Constitution in effect until the first Wednesday in March, 1789, which was March 4. After that North Carolina ratified it Nov. 21, 1789, 197 to 77; and Rhode Island May 29, 1790, 34 to 32. Vermont in convention ratified it Jan. 10, 1791, and by act of Congress approved Feb. 19, 1791, was admitted into the Union as the 14th state, Mar. 4, 1791.

Legislature of any State, the Executive thereof may make temporary appointment until the next meeting of the Legislature which shall then fill such vacancies.

3. No person shall be a Senator who shall not have attained to the age of thirty years, and been nine years a citizen of the United States, and who shall not, when elected, be an inhabitant of that State for which he shall be chosen.

**4. The Vice-President of the United States shall** be President of the Senate, but shall have no vote unless they be equally divided.

5. The Senate shall choose their other officers, and also a President pro tempore, in the absence of the Vice-President, or when he shall exercise the office of the President of the United States.

6. The Senate shall have the sole power to try all impeachments. When sitting for that purpose, they shall be on oath or affirmation. When the President of the United States is tried, the Chief Justice shall preside; and no person shall be convicted without the concurrence of two-thirds of the members present.

7. Judgment in cases of impeachment shall not extend further than to removal from office, and disqualification to hold and enjoy any office of honor, trust, or profit under the United States; but the party convicted shall nevertheless be liable and subject to indictment, trial, judgment, and punishment, according to law.

**Section 4—Times, etc., of holding elections, how prescribed. One session in each year.**

1. The times, places and manner of holding elections for Senators and Representatives shall be prescribed in each State by the Legislature thereof; but the Congress may at any time by law make or alter such regulations, except as to places of choosing Senators.

2. The Congress shall assemble at least once in every year, and such meetings shall be on the first Monday in December, unless they shall by law appoint a different day.

**Section 5—Membership, Quorum, Adjournments, Rules. Power to punish or expel. Journal. Time of adjournments, how limited, etc.**

1. Each House shall be the judge of the elections, returns, and qualifications of its own members, and a majority of each shall constitute a quorum to do business; but a smaller number may adjourn from day to day, and may be authorized to compel the attendance of absent members in such manner and under such penalties as each House may provide.

2. Each House may determine the rules of its proceedings, punish its members for disorderly behavior, and with the concurrence of two-thirds expel a member.

3. Each House shall keep a journal of its proceedings, and from time to time publish the same, excepting such parts as may in their judgment require secrecy; and the yeas and nays of the members of either House on any question shall, at the desire of one-fifth of those present, be entered on the journal.

4. Neither House, during the session on Congress shall, without the consent of the other, adjourn for more than three days, nor to any other place than that in which the two Houses shall be sitting.

**Section 6—Compensation, Privileges, Disqualifications in certain cases.**

1. The Senators and Representatives shall receive a compensation for their services to be ascertained by law, and paid out of the Treasury of the United States. They shall in all cases, except treason, felony, and breach of the peace, be privileged from arrest during their attendance at the session of their respective Houses, and in going to and returning from the same; and for any speech or debate in either House they shall not be questioned in any other place.

2. No Senator or Representative shall, during the time for which he was elected, be appointed to any civil office under the authority of the United States which shall have been created, or the emoluments whereof shall have been increased during such time; and no person holding any office under the United States shall be a member of either House during his continuance in office.

**Section 7—House to originate all revenue bills. Veto. Bill may be passed by two-thirds of each House, notwithstanding, etc. Bill, not returned in ten days, to become a law. Provisions as to orders, concurrent resolutions, etc.**

1. All bills for raising revenue shall originate in the House of Representatives, but the Senate may propose or concur with amendments, as on other bills.

2. Every bill which shall have passed the House of Representatives and the Senate shall, before it becomes a law, be presented to the President of the United States; if he approve, he shall sign it, but if not, he shall return it, with his objections, to that House in which it shall have originated, who shall enter the objections at large on their journal, and proceed to reconsider it. If after such reconsideration two-thirds of that House shall agree to pass the bill, it shall be sent, together with the objections, to the other House, by which it shall likewise

be reconsidered; and if approved by two-thirds of that House it shall become a law. But in all such cases the votes of both Houses shall be determined by yeas and nays, and the names of the persons voting for and against the bill shall be entered on the journal of each House respectively. If any bill shall not be returned by the President within ten days (Sundays excepted) after it shall have been presented to him, the same shall be a law in like manner as if he had signed it, unless the Congress by their adjournment prevent its return; in which case it shall not be a law.

3. Every order, resolution, or vote to which the concurrence of the Senate and House of Representatives may be necessary (except on a question of adjournment) shall be presented to the President of the United States, and before the same shall take effect shall be approved by him, or being disapproved by him, shall be repassed by two-thirds of the Senate and the House of Representatives, according to the rules and limitations prescribed in the case of a bill.

**Section 8—Powers of Congress.**

1. The Congress shall have power

To lay and collect taxes, duties, imposts, and excises, to pay the debts and provide for the common defense and general welfare of the United States; but all duties, imposts, and excises shall be uniform throughout the United States;

2. To borrow money on the credit of the United States.

3. To regulate commerce with foreign nations, and among the several States and with the Indian tribes.

4. To establish a uniform rule of naturalization and uniform laws on the subject of bankruptcies throughout the United States.

5. To coin money, regulate the value thereof, and of foreign coin, and fix the standard of weights and measures.

6. To provide for the punishment of counterfeiting the securities and current coin of the United States.

7. To establish post-offices and post-roads.

8. To promote the progress of science and useful arts by securing for limited times to authors and inventors the exclusive rights to their respective writings and discoveries.

9. To constitute tribunals inferior to the Supreme Court.

10. To define and punish piracies and felonies committed on the high seas, and offenses against the law of nations.

11. To declare war, grant letters of marque and reprisal, and make rules concerning captures on land and water.

12. To raise and support armies, but no appropriation of money to that use shall be for a longer term than two years.

13. To provide and maintain a navy.

14. To make rules for the government and regulation of the land and naval forces.

15. To provide for calling forth the militia to execute the laws of the Union, suppress insurrections, and repel invasions.

16. To provide for organizing, arming, and disciplining the militia, and for governing such part of them as may be employed in the service of the United States, reserving to the States respectively the appointment of the officers, and the authority of training the militia according to the discipline prescribed by Congress.

17. To exercise exclusive legislation in all cases whatsoever over such district (not exceeding ten miles square) as may, by cession of particular States and the acceptance of Congress, become the seat of Government of the United States, and to exercise like authority over all places purchased by the consent of the Legislature of the State in which the same shall be, for the erection of forts, magazines, arsenals, dockyards, and other needful buildings;—And

18. To make all laws which shall be necessary and proper for carrying into execution the foregoing powers and all other powers vested by this Constitution in the Government of the United States, or in any department or officer thereof.

**Section 9—Provision as to migration or importation of certain persons. Habeas Corpus, Bills of attainder, etc. Taxes, how apportioned. No export duty. No commercial preference. Money, how drawn from Treasury, etc. No titular nobility. Officers not to receive presents, etc.**

1. The migration or importation of such persons as any of the States now existing shall think proper to admit shall not be prohibited by the Congress prior to the year one thousand eight hundred and eight, but a tax or duty may be imposed on such importation, not exceeding ten dollars for each person.

2. The privilege of the writ of habeas corpus shall not be suspended, unless when in cases of rebellion or invasion the public safety may require it.

3. No bill of attainder or ex post facto law shall be passed.

4. No capitation or other direct tax shall be laid

unless in proportion to the census or enumeration hereinbefore directed to be taken.

5. No tax or duty shall be laid on articles exported from any State.

6. No preference shall be given by any regulation of commerce or revenue to the ports of one State over those of another, nor shall vessels bound to or from one State be obliged to enter, clear, or pay duties to another.

7. No money shall be drawn from the Treasury but in consequence of appropriations made by law; and a regular statement and account of the receipts and expenditures of all public money shall be published from time to time.

8. No title of nobility shall be granted by the United States. And no person holding any office of profit or trust under them shall, without the consent of the Congress, accept any present, emolument, office, or title of any kind whatever from any king, prince, or foreign state.

Section 10—(States prohibited from the exercise of certain powers.)

1. No State shall enter into any treaty, alliance, or confederation, grant letters of marque and reprisal, coin money, emit bills of credit, make anything but gold and silver coin a tender in payment of debts, pass any bill of attainder, ex post facto law, or law impairing the obligation of contracts, or grant any title of nobility.

2. No State shall, without the consent of the Congress, lay any impost or duties on imports or exports, except what may be absolutely necessary for executing its inspection laws, and the net produce of all duties and imposts, laid by any State on imports or exports, shall be for the use of the Treasury of the United States; and all such laws shall be subject to the revision and control of the Congress.

3. No State shall, without the consent of Congress, lay any duty of tonnage, keep troops or ships of war in time of peace, enter into agreement or compact with another State, or with a foreign power, or engage in war, unless actually invaded, or in such imminent danger as will not admit of delay.

### ARTICLE II.

Section 1—President: his term of office. Electors of President: number and how appointed. Electors to vote on same day. Qualification of President. On whom his duties devolve in case of his removal, death, etc. President's compensation. His oath of office.

1. The Executive power shall be vested in a President of the United States of America. He shall hold his office during the term of four years, and together with the Vice President, chosen for the same term, be elected as follows:

2. Each State shall appoint, in such manner as the Legislature thereof may direct, a number of electors equal to the whole number of Senators and Representatives to which the State may be entitled in the Congress; but no Senator or Representative or person holding an office of trust or profit under the United States shall be appointed an elector.

(*The electors shall meet in their respective States and vote by ballot for two persons, of whom one at least shall not be an inhabitant of the same State with themselves. And they shall make a list of all the persons voted for, and of the number of votes for each, which list they shall sign and certify and transmit, sealed, to the seat of the Government of the United States, directed to the President of the Senate. The President of the Senate shall, in the presence of the Senate and House of Representatives, open all the certificates, and the votes shall then be counted. The person having the greatest number of votes shall be the President, if such number be a majority of the whole number of electors appointed, and if there be more than one who have such a majority, and have an equal number of votes, then the House of Representatives shall immediately choose by ballot one of them for President; and if no person have a majority, then from the five highest on the list the said House shall in like manner choose the President. But in choosing the President, the vote shall be taken by States, the representation from each State having one vote. A quorum, for this purpose, shall consist of a member or members from two-thirds of the States, and a majority of all the States shall be necessary to a choice. In every case, after the choice of the President, the person having the greatest number of votes of the electors shall be the Vice President. But if there should remain two or more who have equal votes, the Senate shall choose from them by ballot the Vice President.)

(*This clause has been superseded by the 12th amendment.)

3. The Congress may determine the time of choosing the electors and the day on which they shall give their votes, which day shall be the same throughout the United States.

4. No person except a natural born citizen, or a citizen of the United States at the time of the adoption of this Constitution, shall be eligible to the office of President; neither shall any person be eligible to that office who shall not have attained

to the age of thirty-five years and been fourteen years a resident within the United States.

(For qualification of the Vice President, see Article XII of the amendments.)

5. In case of the removal of the President from office, or of his death, resignation, or inability to discharge the powers and duties of the said office, the same shall devolve on the Vice President, and the Congress may by law provide for the case of removal, death, resignation, or inability, both of the President and Vice-President, declaring what officer shall then act as President, and such officer shall act accordingly until the disability be removed or a President shall be elected.

(This clause has been amended by Article XX, sections 3 and 4, of the amendments.)

6. The President shall, at stated times, receive for his services a compensation which shall neither be increased nor diminished during the period for which he shall have been elected, and he shall not receive within that period any other emolument from the United States or any of them.

7. Before he enter on the execution of his office he shall take the following oath or affirmation:

"I do solemnly swear (or affirm) that I will faithfully execute the office of President of the United States, and will, to the best of my ability, preserve, protect, and defend the Constitution of the United States."

Section 2—President to be Commander-in-Chief. He may require opinions of Cabinet Officers, etc., may pardon. Treaty-making power. Nomination of certain officers. When President may fill vacancies.

1. The President shall be Commander-in-Chief of the Army and Navy of the United States, and of the militia of the several States when called into the actual service of the United States; he may require the opinion, in writing, of the principal officer in each of the executive departments upon any subject relating to the duties of their respective offices, and he shall have power to grant reprieves and pardons for offenses against the United States except in cases of impeachment.

2. He shall have power by and with the advice and consent of the Senate to make treaties, provided two-thirds of the Senators present concur; and he shall nominate and by and with the advice and consent of the Senate shall appoint ambassadors, other public ministers and consuls, judges of the Supreme Court, and all other officers of the United States whose appointments are not herein otherwise provided for, and which shall be established by law: but the Congress may by law vest the appointment of such inferior officers as they think proper in the President alone, in the courts of law, or in the heads of departments.

3. The President shall have power to fill up all vacancies that may happen during the recess of the Senate by granting commissions, which shall expire at the end of their next session.

Section 3—(President shall communicate to Congress. He may convene and adjourn Congress, in case of disagreement, etc. Shall receive Ambassadors, execute laws, and commission officers.)

He shall from time to time give to the Congress information of the state of the Union, and recommend to their consideration such measures as he shall judge necessary and expedient; he may on extraordinary occasions, convene both Houses, or either of them, and in case of disagreement between them with respect to the time of adjournment, he may adjourn them to such time as he shall think proper; he shall receive ambassadors and other public ministers; he shall take care that the laws be faithfully executed, and shall commission all the officers of the United States.

Section 4—(All civil offices forfeited for certain crimes.)

The President, Vice President, and all civil officers of the United States shall be removed from office on impeachment for and conviction of treason, bribery or other high crimes and misdemeanors.

### ARTICLE III

Section 1—Judicial powers. Tenure. Compensation.

The judicial power of the United States shall be vested in one Supreme Court, and in such inferior courts as the Congress may from time to time ordain and establish. The judges, both of the Supreme and inferior courts, shall hold their offices during good behavior, and shall at stated times receive for their services a compensation which shall not be diminished during their continuance in office.

Section 2—Judicial power; to what cases it extends. Original jurisdiction of Supreme Court Appellate. Trial by jury, etc. Trial, where.

1. The judicial power shall extend to all cases in law and equity arising under this Constitution, the laws of the United States, and treaties made, or which shall be made, under their authority; to all cases affecting ambassadors, other public ministers and consuls; to all cases of admiralty and maritime jurisdiction; to controversies to which the United

States shall be a party; to controversies between two or more States, between a State and citizens of another State, between citizens of different States, between citizens of the same State claiming lands under grants of different States, and between a State, or the citizens thereof, and foreign states, citizens, or subjects.

**(This section is abridged by Article XI of the amendments.)**

2. In all cases affecting ambassadors, other public ministers, and consuls, and those in which a State shall be party, the Supreme Court shall have original jurisdiction. In all the other cases before mentioned the Supreme Court shall have appellate jurisdiction both as to law and fact, with such exceptions and under such regulations as the Congress shall make.

3. The trial of all crimes, except in cases of impeachment, shall be by jury, and such trial shall be held in the State where the said crimes shall have been committed; but when not committed within any State the trial shall be at such place or places as the Congress may by law have directed.

**Section 3—Treason defined. Proof of. Punishment of.**

1. Treason against the United States shall consist only in levying war against them, or in adhering to their enemies, giving them aid and comfort. No person shall be convicted of treason unless on the testimony of two witnesses to the same overt act, or on confession in open court.

2. The Congress shall have power to declare the punishment of treason, but no attainder of treason shall work corruption of blood or forfeiture except during the life of the person attainted.

**ARTICLE IV.**

**Section 1—Each State to give credit to the public acts, etc., of every other State.**

Full faith and credit shall be given in each State to the public acts, records, and judicial proceedings of every other State. And the Congress may by general laws prescribe the manner in which such acts, records, and proceedings shall be proved, and the effect therof.

**Section 2—Privileges of citizens of each State. Fugitives from justice to be delivered up. Persons held to service having escaped, to be delivered up.**

1. The citizens of each State shall be entitled to all privileges and immunities of citizens in the several States.

2. A person charged in any State with treason, felony, or other crime, who shall flee from justice, and be found in another State, shall, on demand of the Executive authority of the State from which he fled, be delivered up, to be removed to the State having jurisdiction of the crime.

3. No person held to service or labor in one State, under the laws thereof, escaping into another shall in consequence of any law or regulation therein, be discharged from such service or labor, but shall be delivered up on claim of the party to whom such service or labor may be due. (See 13th amendment.)

**Section 3—Admission of new States. Power of Congress over territory and other property.**

1. New States may be admitted by the Congress into this Union; but no new State shall be formed or erected within the jurisdiction of any other State, nor any State be formed by the junction of two or more States or parts of States, without the consent of the Legislatures of the States concerned, as well as of the Congress.

2. The Congress shall have power to dispose of and make all needful rules and regulations respecting the territory or other property belonging to the United States; and nothing in this Constitution shall be so construed as to prejudice any claims of the United States, or of any particular State.

**Section 4—Republican form of government guaranteed. Each State to be protected.**

The United States shall guarantee to every State in this Union a Republican form of government, and shall protect each of them against invasion, and, on application of the Legislature, or of the Executive (when the Legislature cannot be convened) against domestic violence.

**ARTICLE V.**

**Constitution: how amended, Proviso.**

The Congress, whenever two-thirds of both Houses shall deem it necessary, shall propose amendments to this Constitution, or, on the application of the Legislatures of two-thirds of the several States, shall call a convention for proposing amendments, which in either case, shall be valid to all intents and purposes, as part of this Constitution, when ratified by the Legislatures of three-fourths of the several States, or by conventions in three-fourths thereof, as the one or the other mode of ratification may be proposed by the Congress, provided that no amendment which may be made prior to the year one thousand eight hundred and eight shall in any manner affect the first and fourth clauses in the Ninth Section of the First Article; and that no State, without its consent, shall be deprived of its equal suffrage in the Senate.

**ARTICLE VI.**

**Certain debts, etc., declared valid, Supremacy of Constitution, treaties, and laws of the United States. Oath to support Constitution, by whom taken. No religious test.**

1. All debts contracted and engagements entered into before the adoption of this Constitution shall be as valid against the United States under this Constitution as under the Confederation.

2. This Constitution and the laws of the United States which shall be made in pursuance thereof and all treaties made, or which shall be made, under the authority of the United States, shall be the supreme law of the land, and the judges in every State shall be bound thereby, anything in the Constitution or laws of any State to the contrary notwithstanding.

3. The Senators and Representatives before mentioned and the members of the several State Legislatures, and all executive and judicial officers, both of the United States and of the several States, shall be bound by oath or affirmation to support this Constitution; but no religious test shall ever be required as a qualification to any office or public trust under the United States.

**ARTICLE VII.**

**What ratification shall establish Constitution.**

The ratification of the Conventions of nine States shall be sufficient for the establishment of this Constitution between the States so ratifying the same.

Done in convention by the unanimous consent of the States present the 17th day of September in the year of our Lord 1787, and of the independence of the United States of America the 12th. In witness whereof we have hereunto subscribed our names.

George Washington, President and deputy from Virginia.

New Hampshire—John Langdon, Nicholas Gilman.

Massachusetts—Nathaniel Gorham, Rufus King.

Connecticut—Wm. Saml. Johnson, Roger Sherman.

New York—Alexander Hamilton.

New Jersey—Wil: Livingston, David Brearley, Wm. Paterson, Jona: Dayton.

Pennsylvania—B. Franklin, Thomas Mifflin, Robt. Morris, Geo. Clymer, Thos. Fitzsimons, Jared Ingersoll, James Wilson, Gouv. Morris.

Delaware—Geo: Read, Gunning Bedford, Jun., John Dickinson, Richard Bassett; Jaco: Broom.

Maryland—James McHenry, Daniel of Saint Thomas Jenifer, Danl. Carroll.

Virginia—John Blair, James Madison, Jr.

North Carolina—Wm. Blount, Rich'd Dobbs Speight, Hugh Williamson.

South Carolina—J. Rutledge, Charles Cotesworth Pinckney, Charles Pinckney, Pierce Butler.

Georgia—William Few, Abr. Baldwin.

Attest: William Jackson, Secretary.

# Ten Original Amendments—The Bill of Rights

## In force December 15, 1791

The First Congress, at its first session in the City of New York, Sept. 25, 1789, submitted to the states 12 amendments to clarify certain individual and state rights not named in the Constitution. They are generally called the Bill of Rights.

Influential in framing these amendments was the Declaration of Rights of Virginia, written by George Mason (1725-1792) in 1776. Mason, a Virginia delegate to the Constitutional Convention, did not sign the Constitution and opposed its ratification on the ground that it did not sufficiently oppose slavery or safeguard individual rights.

In the preamble to the resolution offering the proposed amendments, Congress said: "The conventions of a number of the States having at the time of their adopting the Constitution, expressed a desire, in order to prevent misconstruction or abuse of its powers, that further declaratory and restrictive clauses should be added, and as extending the ground of public confidence in the government will best insure the beneficent ends of its institution, be it resolved," etc.

Ten of these amendments now commonly known as one to 10 inclusive, but in reality three to 12 inclusive were ratified by the states as follows: New Jersey, Nov. 20, 1789; Maryland, December 19, 1789; North Carolina, Dec. 22, 1789; South Carolina, Jan. 19, 1790; New Hampshire, Jan. 25, 1790; Delaware, Jan. 28, 1790; New York, Feb. 24, 1790; Pennsylvania, March 10, 1790; Rhode Island, June 11, 1790; Vermont, Nov. 3, 1791; Virginia, Dec. 15, 1791; Massachusetts, March 2, 1939; Georgia, March 18, 1939; Connecticut, April 19, 1939. These original 10 ratified amendments appear in order on the next page as Article I to X inclusive.

The two of the original proposed amendments which were not ratified by the necessary number of States related, the first to apportionment of Representatives; the second, to compensation of members.

## ARTICLE I.
### Religious Establishment Prohibited. Freedom of Speech, of the Press, and Right to Petition.

Congress shall make no law respecting an establishment of religion, or prohibiting the free exercise thereof; or abridging the freedom of speech or of the press; or the right of the people peaceably to assemble and to petition the Government for a redress of grievances.

## ARTICLE II.
### Right to Keep and Bear Arms.

A well-regulated militia being necessary to the security of a free State, the right of the people to keep and bear arms shall not be infringed.

## ARTICLE III.
### Conditions for Quarters for Soldiers.

No soldier shall, in time of peace, be quartered in any house without the consent of the owner, nor in time of war but in a manner to be prescribed by law.

## ARTICLE IV.
### Right of Search and Seizure Regulated.

The right of the people to be secure in their persons, houses, papers, and effects, against unreasonable searches and seizures, shall not be violated, and no warrants shall issue but upon probable cause, supported by oath or affirmation, and particularly describing the place to be searched, and the persons or things to be seized.

## ARTICLE V.
### Provisions Concerning Prosecution. Trial and Punishment—Private Property Not to Be Taken for Public Use Without Compensation.

No person shall be held to answer for a capital or other infamous crime unless on a presentment or indictment of a Grand Jury, except in cases arising in the land or naval forces, or in the militia, when in actual service, in time of war or public danger; nor shall any person be subject for the same offense to be twice put in jeopardy of life or limb; nor shall be compelled in any criminal case to be a witness against himself, nor be deprived of life, liberty, or property, without due process of law; nor shall private property be taken for public use without just compensation.

## ARTICLE VI.
### Right to Speedy Trial, Witnesses, etc.

In all criminal prosecutions, the accused shall enjoy the right to a speedy and public trial, by an impartial jury of the State and district wherein the crime shall have been committed, which districts shall have been previously ascertained by law, and to be informed of the nature and cause of the accusation; to be confronted with the witnesses against him; to have compulsory process for obtaining witnesses in his favor, and to have the assistance of counsel for his defense.

## ARTICLE VII.
### Right of Trial by Jury.

In suits at common law, where the value in controversy shall exceed twenty dollars, the right of trial by jury shall be preserved, and no fact tried by a jury shall be otherwise re-examined in any court of the United States than according to the rules of the common law.

## ARTICLE VIII.
### Excessive Bail or Fines and Cruel Punishment Prohibited.

Excessive bail shall not be required, nor excessive fines imposed, nor cruel and unusual punishments inflicted.

## ARTICLE IX.
### Rule of Construction of Constitution.

The enumeration in the Constitution of certain rights shall not be construed to deny or disparage others retained by the people.

## ARTICLE X.
### Rights of States Under Constitution.

The powers not delegated to the United States by the Constitution, nor prohibited by it to the States, are reserved to the States respectively, or to the people.

# Amendments Since the Bill of Rights

## ARTICLE XI.
### Judicial Powers Construed.

*The following amendment was proposed to the Legislature of the several States by the Third Congress on the 5th of March 1794, and was declared to have been ratified in a message from the President to Congress, dated Jan. 8, 1798.*

The judicial power of the United States shall not be construed to extend to any suit in law or equity, commenced or prosecuted against one of the United States, by citizens of another State, or by citizens or subjects of any foreign state.

(It was on Jan. 5, 1798, that Secretary of State Pickering received from 12 of the States authenticated ratifications, and informed President John Adams of that fact.)

As a result of recent research in the Department of State, it is now established that the Eleventh Amendment became part of the Constitution on Feb. 7, 1795, for on that date it had been ratified by twelve States as follows:

(1) New York, (March 27, 1794); (2) Rhode Island, (March 31, 1794); (3) Connecticut, (May 8, 1794); (4) New Hampshire, (June 16, 1794); (5) Massachusetts, (June 25, 1794); (6) Vermont, (between Oct. 9, 1794 and Nov. 9, 1794); (7) Virginia, (Nov. 18, 1794); (8) Georgia, (Nov. 29, 1794); (9) Kentucky, (Dec. 7, 1794); (10) Maryland, (Dec. 26, 1794); (11) Delaware, (Jan. 23, 1795); (12) North Carolina, (Feb. 7, 1795).

On June 1, 1796, more than a year after the Eleventh Amendment had become part of the Constitution (but before anyone was officially aware of this), Tennessee had been admitted as a State; but not until Oct. 16, 1797, was a certified copy of the resolution of Congress proposing the amendment sent to the Governor of Tennessee (John Sevier) by Secretary of State Pickering, whose office was then at Trenton, New Jersey, because of the epidemic of yellow fever at Philadelphia; it seems, however, that the Legislature of Tennessee took no action on the Eleventh Amendment, owing doubtless to the fact that public announcement of its adoption was made soon thereafter.

Besides the necessary twelve States, one other, South Carolina, ratified the Eleventh Amendment, but this action was not taken until Dec. 4, 1797; the two remaining States, New Jersey and Pennsylvania, failed to ratify.

## ARTICLE XII.
### Manner of Choosing President and Vice-President.

*The following amendment was proposed to the Legislatures of the several States by the Eighth Congress Dec. 12, 1803, and was declared to have been ratified in a proclamation by the Secretary of State September 25, 1804.*

The Electors shall meet in their respective States, and vote by ballot for President and Vice-President one of whom at least shall not be an inhabitant of the same State with themselves; they shall name in their ballots the person voted for as President, and in distinct ballots the person voted for as Vice-President; and they shall make distinct lists of all persons voted for as President and of all persons voted for as Vice-President, and of the number of votes for each, which lists they shall sign and certify, and transmit, sealed, to the seat of the Government of the United States, directed to the President of the Senate; the President of the Senate shall, in the presence of the Senate and House of Representatives, open all the certificates and the votes shall then be counted—The person having the greatest number of votes for President shall be the President, if such number be a majority of the whole number of Electors appointed; and if no person have such majority, then from the persons having the highest numbers, not exceeding three, on the list of those voted for as President, the House of Representatives shall choose immediately, by ballot the President. But in choosing the President, the votes shall be taken by States, the representation from each State having one vote; a quorum for this purpose shall consist of a member or members from two-thirds of the States and a majority of all the States shall be necessary to a choice. And if the House of Representatives shall not choose a President, whenever the right of choice shall devolve upon them, before the fourth day of March next following, then the Vice-President shall act as President, as in case of the death or other constitutional disability of the President. The person having the greatest number of votes as Vice-President shall be the Vice-President if such number be a majority of the whole number of Electors appointed, and if no person have a majority, then, from the two highest numbers on the list the Senate shall choose the Vice-President; a quorum for the purpose shall consist of two-thirds of the whole number of Senators, and a majority of the whole number shall be necessary to a choice. But no person constitutionally ineligible to the office of President shall be eligible to that of Vice-President of the United States.

### TITLES OF NOBILITY—*Not Ratified*

Congress, May 1, 1810, proposed to the States the following Amendment to the Constitution:

"If any citizen of the United States shall accept, claim, receive, or retain any title of nobility or honor, or shall, without the consent of Congress, accept and retain any present, pension, office, or emolument of any kind whatever, from any emperor, king, prince or foreign power, such person shall cease to be a citizen of the United States and shall be incapable of holding any office of trust or profit under them or either of them."

It was ratified by Maryland, (Dec. 25, 1810); Kentucky, (Jan. 31, 1811); Ohio, (Jan. 31, 1811); Delaware, (Feb. 2, 1811); Pennsylvania, (Feb. 6, 1811); New Jersey, (Feb. 13, 1811); Vermont, (Oct. 24, 1811); Tennessee, (Nov. 21, 1811); Georgia, (Dec. 13, 1811); North Carolina, (Dec. 23, 1811); Massachusetts, (Feb. 27, 1812); New Hampshire, (Dec. 10, 1812).

Rejected by New York (Senate), (March 12, 1811); Connecticut, (May session, 1813); South Carolina approved by Senate Nov. 28, 1811, reported unfavorably in House and not further considered Dec. 7, 1813; Rhode Island (Sept. 15, 1814). The amendment failed, not having sufficient ratifications.

**THE CORWIN AMENDMENT**—*Not Ratified*
Congress March 2, 1861, in a joint resolution signed by President James Buchanan, proposed to the States the following Amendments to the Constitution:

"No amendment shall be made to the Constitution which will authorize or give to Congress the power to abolish or interfere, within any State, with the domestic institutions thereof, including that of persons held to labor or service by the laws of said State."

Ratified by Ohio, (March 13, 1861); Maryland, (Jan. 10, 1862); Illinois (convention), (Feb. 14, 1862). The amendment failed, for lack of a sufficient number of ratifications.

---

## THE RECONSTRUCTION AMENDMENTS

The 13th, 14th and 15th Amendments to the Constitution are commonly known as the Reconstruction Amendments, inasmuch as they followed the Civil War, and were drafted by Republicans who were bent on imposing their own policy of reconstruction on the South. Post-bellum legislatures there—Mississippi, South Carolina, Georgia, for example—had set up laws which, it was charged, were contrived to perpetuate Negro slavery under other names.

### ARTICLE XIII.
#### Slavery Abolished.

*The following amendment was proposed to the Legislatures of the several states by the Thirty-eighth Congress (Feb. 1, 1865), and was declared to have been ratified in a proclamation by the Secretary of State (Dec. 18, 1865).*

The Amendment when first proposed by a resolution in Congress, was passed by the Senate, 38 to 6, on April 8, 1864, but was defeated in the House, 95 to 66 on June 15, 1864. On reconsideration by the House, on Jan. 31, 1865, the resolution passed, 119 to 56. It was approved by President Lincoln on Feb. 1, 1865, although the Supreme Court had decided, in 1798, that the President has nothing to do with the proposing of amendments to the Constitution, or their adoption.

1. Neither slavery nor involuntary servitude, except as a punishment for crime whereof the party shall have been duly convicted, shall exist within the United States, or any place subject to their jurisdiction.

2. Congress shall have power by appropriate legislation, to enforce the provisions of this article.

### ARTICLE XIV
#### Citizenship Rights Not to Be Abridged.

*The following amendment was proposed to the Legislatures of the several States by the Thirty-ninth Congress (June 16, 1866), and was declared to have been ratified in a proclamation by the Secretary of State (July 28, 1868).*

The 14th amendment was adopted only by virtue of ratification subsequent to earlier rejections. Newly constituted legislatures in both North Carolina and South Carolina, respectively (July 4 and 9, 1868), ratified the proposed amendment, although earlier legislatures had rejected the proposal. The Secretary of State issued a proclamation, which, though doubtful as to the effect of attempted withdrawals by Ohio and New Jersey, entertained no doubt as to the validity of the ratification by North and South Carolina. The following day (July 21, 1868), Congress passed a resolution which declared the 14th Amendment to be a part of the Constitution and directed the Secretary of State so to promulgate it. The Secretary waited, however, until the newly constituted legislature of Georgia had ratified the amendment, subsequent to an earlier rejection, before the promulgation of the ratification of the new amendment.

1. All persons born or naturalized in the United States, and subject to the jurisdiction thereof, are citizens of the United States and of the State wherein they reside. No State shall make or enforce any law which shall abridge the privileges or immunities of citizens of the United States, nor shall any State deprive any person of life, liberty, or property without due process of law, nor deny to any person within its jurisdiction the equal protection of the laws.

Apportionment of Representatives in Congress.
2. Representatives shall be apportioned among the several States according to their respective numbers, counting the whole number of persons in each State excluding Indians not taxed. But when the right to vote at any election for the choice of Electors for President and Vice-President of the United States, Representatives in Congress, the executive and judicial officers of a State, or the members of the Legislature thereof, is denied to any of the male inhabitants of such State, being twenty-one years of age, and citizens of the United States, or in any way abridged, except for participation in rebellion, or other crime, the basis of representation therein shall be reduced in the proportion which the number of such male citizens shall bear to the whole number of male citizens twenty-one years of age in such State.

Power of Congress to Remove Disabilities of United States Officials for Rebellion.
3. No person shall be a Senator or Representative in Congress, or Elector of President and Vice-President or hold any office, civil or military, under the United States, or under any State, who having previously taken an oath, as a member of Congress, or as an officer of the United States, executive or judicial officer of any Sate, to support or as a member of any State Legislature or as an the Constitution of the United States, shall have engaged in insurrection or rebellion against the same, or given aid or comfort to the enemies thereof. But Congress may, by a vote of two-thirds of each House, remove such disability.

What Public Debts Are Valid.
4. The validity of the public debt of the United States, authorized by law, including debts incurred for payment of pensions and bounties for services in suppressing insurrection and rebellion, shall not be questioned. But neither the United States nor any State shall assume or pay any debt or obligation incurred in aid of insurrection or rebellion against the Unted States, or any claim for the loss or emancipation of any slave; but all such debts, obligations, and claims shall be held illegal and void.

5. The Congress shall have power to enforce by appropriate legislation the provisions of this article.

### ARTICLE XV.
#### Equal Rights for White and Colored Citizens.

*The following amendment was proposed to the Legislatures of the several States by the Fortieth Congress (Feb. 26, 1869), and was declared to have been ratified in a proclamation by the Secretary of State (March 30, 1870).*

1. The right of the citizens of the United States to vote shall not be denied or abridged by the United States or by any State on account of race, color, or previous condition of servitude.

2. The Congress shall have power to enforce this article by appropriate legislation.

### ARTICLE XVI.
#### Income Taxes Authorized.

*The following amendment was proposed to the Legislatures of the several States by the Sixty-first Congress (July 12, 1909) and was declared to have been ratified in a proclamation by the Secretary of State (Feb. 25, 1913).*

The Congress shall have power to lay and collect taxes on incomes, from whatever sources derived, without apportionment among the several States, and without regard to any census or enumeration.

### ARTICLE XVII.
#### United States Senators to Be Elected by Direct Popular Vote.

*The following amendment was proposed to the Legislatures of the several States by the Sixty-second Congress (May 16, 1912) and was declared to have been ratified in a proclamation by the Secretary of State (May 31, 1913).*

1. The Senate of the United States shall be composed of two Senators from each State, elected by the people thereof, for six years and each Senator shall have one vote. The electors in each State shall have the qualifications requisite for electors of the most numerous branch of the State Legislatures.

2. When vacancies happen in the representation of any State in the Senate, the executive authority of such State shall issue writs of election to fill such vacancies: Provided, That the Legislature of any State may empower the Executive thereof to make temporary appointment until the people fill the vacancies by election as the Legislature may direct.

3. This amendment shall not be so construed as to affect the election or term of any Senator chosen before it becomes valid as part of the Constitution.

### ARTICLE XVIII.
#### Liquor Prohibition Amendment.

*The following amendment was proposed to the*

Legislatures of the several States by the Sixty-fifth Congress (Dec. 18, 1917), and (Jan. 29, 1919) the United States Secretary of State proclaimed its adoption by 36 States, and declared it in effect (Jan. 16, 1920).

1. After one year from the ratification of this article the manufacture, sale, or transportation of intoxicating liquors within, the importation thereof into, or the exportation therof from the United States and all territory subject to the jurisdiction thereof for beverage purposes is hereby prohibited.

2. The Congress and the several States shall have concurrent power to enforce this article by appropriate legislation.

3. This article shall be inoperative unless it shall have been ratified as an amendment to the Constitution by the Legislatures of the several States, as provided in the Constitution, within seven years from the date of the submission hereof to the States by the Congress.

The total vote in the Senates of the various States was 1,310 for, 237 against—84.6% dry. In the lower houses of the States the vote was, 3,782 for, 1,035 against—78.5% dry.

The amendment ultimately was adopted by all the States except Connecticut and Rhode Island.

**Repealed by Article XXI effective Dec. 5, 1933.**

### ARTICLE XIX.
#### Giving Nation-Wide Suffrage to Women.

*The following amendment was presented to the Legislatures of the several States by the Sixty-sixth Congress, having been adopted by the House of Representatives (May 21, 1919) and by the Senate (June 4, 1919). The Secretary of State (Aug. 26, 1920) proclaimed it in effect, having been adopted (June 10, 1919-August 18, 1920) by three-quarters of the States.*

1. The right of citizens of the United States to vote shall not be denied or abridged by the United States or by any State on account of sex.

2. Congress shall have power to enforce this Article by appropriate legislation.

### CHILD LABOR—*Not Ratified*

Congress, in a joint resolution passed by the House of Representatives Apr. 26, 1924, and by the Senate June 2, 1924, submitted to the states the following proposed amendment:

1. The Congress shall have power to limit, regulate and prohibit the labor of persons under 18 years of age.

2. The power of the several States is unimpaired by this article except that the operation of State laws shall be suspended to the extent necessary to give effect to legislation enacted by the Congress.

It was ratified by Arizona (1925), Arkansas (1924), California (1925), Colorado (1931), Idaho (1935), Illinois (1933), Indiana (1935), Iowa (1933), Kansas (1937), Kentucky (1937), Maine (1933), Michigan (1933), Minnesota (1933), Montana (1927), Nevada (1937), New Hampshire (1933), New Jersey (1933), New Mexico (1937), North Dakota (1933), Ohio (1933), Oklahoma (1933), Oregon (1933), Pennsylvania (1933), Utah (1935), Washington (1933), West Virginia (1933), Wisconsin (1925), Wyoming (1925). With ratification by 36 states necessary, only these 28 had ratified it by 1938, when Congress passed the Fair Labor Standards Act, prohibiting labor of children under 16 in industries whose products entered interstate commerce. When the constitutionality of this act was upheld the proposed child labor amendment became virtually a dead issue.

### ARTICLE XX.
#### Terms of President and Vice-President to Begin on Jan. 20; Those of Senators and Representatives, on Jan. 3.

*The following amendment was proposed to the Legislatures of the several States by the Seventy-second Congress (March, 1932), a joint resolution to that effect having been adopted, first by the House, and then (March 2) by the Senate. The Secretary of State (Feb. 6, 1933) proclaimed it in effect, 39 of the 48 States having ratified. By Oct. 15, 1933, it had been ratified by all of the 48 States.*

1. The terms of the President and Vice-President shall end at noon on the 20th day of January, and the terms of Senators and Representatives at noon on the 3rd day of January, of the years in which such terms would have ended if this article had not been ratified; and the terms of their successors shall then begin.

2. The Congress shall assemble at least once in every year, and such meeting shall begin at noon on the 3rd day of January, unless they shall by law appoint a different day.

3. If, at the time fixed for the beginning of the term of the President, the President elect shall have died, the Vice-President elect shall become President. If a President shall not have been chosen before the time fixed for the beginning of his term, or if the President elect shall have failed to qualify, then the Vice-President elect shall act as President until a President shall have qualified; and the Congress may by law provide for the case wherein neither a President nor a Vice-President shall have qualified, declaring who shall then act as President, or the manner in which one who is to act shall be selected, and such person shall act accordingly until a President or Vice-President shall have qualified.

4. The Congress may by law provide for the case of the death of any of the persons from whom the House of Representatives may choose a President whenever the right of choice shall have devolved upon them, and for the case of the death of any of the persons from whom the Senate may choose a Vice-President whenever the right of choice shall have devolved upon them.

5. Sections 1 and 2 shall take effect on the 15th day of October following the ratification of this article (Oct., 1933).

6. This article shall be inoperative unless it shall have been ratified as an amendment to the Constitution by the Legislatures of three-fourths of the several States within seven years from the date of its submission.

### ARTICLE XXI.
#### Repeal of the Eighteenth (Prohibition) Amendment by Conventions in the States.

*The following proposed amendment in the Constitution, embodied in a joint resolution of the 72nd Congress (Senate, Feb. 16, 1933, by 63 to 23; House, Feb. 20, 1933, by 289 to 121), was transmitted to the Secretary of State on Feb. 21 and he at once sent to the governors of the States copies of the resolution. The amendment went into effect on Dec. 5, 1933, having been adopted by 36 of the 48 States— Utah was the 36th State to ratify.*

1. The eighteenth article of amendment to the Constitution of the United States is hereby repealed.

2. The transportation or importation into any State, Territory, or Possession of the United States for delivery or use therein of intoxicating liquors, in violation of the laws thereof, is hereby prohibited.

3. This article shall be inoperative unless it shall have been ratified as an amendment to the Constitution by convention in the several States, as provided in the Constitution, within seven years from the date of the submission hereof to the States by the Congress.

### ARTICLE XXII.
#### Limiting Presidential Terms of Office.

*The following proposed amendment in the Constitution, embodied in a joint resolution of the 80th Congress (House, Feb. 6, 1947, by 285 to 121; Senate, March 12, 1947, by 59 to 23). Signed by the Speaker of the House, Mar. 24, 1947, and by the President pro tempore of the Senate, Mar. 24, 1947. Presented to the Secretary of State, Mar. 24, 1947. Went into effect Feb. 26, 1951, when Nevada became the 36th State to ratify. Utah had ratified earlier the same day, and Minnesota, Feb. 27th.*

1. No person shall be elected to the office of the President more than twice, and no person who has held the office of President, or acted as President, for more than two years of a term to which some other person was elected President shall be elected to the office of the President more than once. But this Article shall not apply to any person holding the office of President when this Article was proposed by the Congress, and shall not prevent any person who may be holding the office of President, or acting as President, during the term within which this Article becomes operative from holding the office of President or acting as President during the remainder of such term.

2. This article shall be inoperative unless it shall have been ratified as an amendment to the Constitution by the Legislatures of three-fourths of the several States within seven years from the date of its submission to the States by the Congress.

### ARTICLE XXIII.
#### Presidential Vote for District of Columbia.

*The following amendment was submitted to the Legislatures of the 50 states following approval by voice votes in both houses of the 87th Congress (House June 14, 1960; Senate June 16, 1960). Ratification by the required three-fourths majority of the states was completed Mar. 29, 1961, when Kansas became the 38th state to ratify, 42 minutes before approval by the Ohio Legislature. Arkansas was the only state to reject the amendment. The amendment was formally declared a part of the Constitution Apr. 3, 1961.*

1. The District constituting the seat of Government of the United States shall appoint in such manner as the Congress may direct:

A number of electors of President and Vice President equal to the whole number of Senators and Representatives in Congress to which the District would be entitled if it were a State, but in no event more than the least populous State; they shall be in addition to those appointed by the States, but they shall be considered, for the purposes of the election of President and Vice President, to be electors appointed by a State; and they shall meet in the District and perform such duties as provided by the twelfth article of amendment.

2. The Congress shall have power to enforce this article by appropriate legislation.

### ARTICLE XXIV
#### Barring Poll Tax in Federal Elections

*The following amendment was submitted to the Legislatures of the 50 states Sept. 14, 1962, after approval by both houses of the 87th Congress. It became a part of the Constitution after ratification by the required 38 states was completed Jan. 23, 1964; South Dakota was the 38th state to ratify.*

1. The right of citizens of the United States to vote in any primary or other election for President or Vice President, for electors for President or Vice President, or for Senator or Representative in Congress, shall not be denied or abridged by the United States or any State by reason of failure to pay any poll tax or other tax.

2. The Congress shall have the power to enforce this article by appropriate legislation.

### ARTICLE XXV
#### Presidential Disability and Succession

*The following amendment was submitted to the Legislatures of the 50 states July 6, 1965, after approval by both houses of the 89th Congress. It became a part of the Constitution Feb. 10, 1967, after ratification by the required 38 states. Nevada was the 38th state to ratify.*

1. In case of the removal of the President from office or his death or resignation, the Vice President shall become President.

2. Whenever there is a vacancy in the office of the Vice President, the President shall nominate a Vice President who shall take the office upon confirmation by a majority vote of both houses of Congress.

3. Whenever the President transmits to the President pro tempore of the Senate and the Speaker of the House of Representatives his written declaration that he is unable to discharge the powers and duties of his office, and until he transmits to them a written declaration to the contrary, such powers and duties shall be discharged by the Vice President as Acting President.

4. Whenever the Vice President and a majority of either the principal officers of the executive departments or of such other body as Congress may by law provide, transmit to the President pro tempore of the Senate and the Speaker of the House of Representatives their written declaration that the President is unable to discharge the powers and duties of his office, the Vice President shall immediately assume the powers and duties of the office as Acting President.

Thereafter, when the President transmits to the President pro tempore of the Senate and the Speaker of the House of Representatives his written declaration that no inability exists, he shall resume the powers and duties of his office unless the Vice President and a majority of either the principal officers of the executive department or of such other body as Congress may by law provide, transmit within four days to the President pro tempore of the Senate and the Speaker of the House of Representatives their written declaration that the President is unable to discharge the powers and duties of his office. Thereupon Congress shall decide the issue, assembling within 48 hours for that purpose if not in session. If the Congress, within 21 days after receipt of the latter written declaration, or, if Congress is not in session, within 21 days after Congress is required to assemble, determines by two-thirds vote of both houses that the President is unable to discharge the powers and duties of his office, the Vice President shall continue to discharge the same as Acting President; otherwise, the President shall resume the powers and duties of his office.

---

# Lincoln's Address at Gettysburg, 1863

Fourscore and seven years ago our fathers brought forth on this continent a new nation, conceived in liberty and dedicated to the proposition that all men are created equal.

Now we are engaged in a great civil war, testing whether that nation or any nation so conceived and so dedicated can long endure. We are met on a great battle field of that war. We have come to dedicate a portion of that field, as a final resting-place for those who here gave their lives that that nation might live. It is altogether fitting and proper that we should do this.

But, in a larger sense, we can not dedicate—we can not consecrate—we can not hallow—this ground. The brave men, living and dead, who struggled here, have consecrated it, far above our poor power to add or detract. The world will little note, nor long remember, what we say here, but it can never forget what they did here. It is for us the living, rather, to be dedicated here to the unfinished work which they who fought here have thus far so nobly advanced. It is rather for us to be here dedicated to the great task remaining before us—that from these honored dead we take increased devotion to that cause for which they gave the last full measure of devotion—that we here highly resolve that these dead shall not have died in vain—that this nation, under God, shall have a new birth of freedom—and that government of the people, by the people, for the people, shall not perish from the earth.

---

President Lincoln delivered his address at the dedication of the military cemetery at Gettysburg, Pa., Nov. 19, 1863. The battle had been fought July 1-3, 1863. He was preceded by Edward Everett, former president of Harvard, secretary of state and senator from Massachusetts, then 69 and one of the nation's great orators. Everett gave a full resume of the battle, Lincoln's speech was so short that the photographer did not get his camera adjusted in time. The report that newspapers ignored Lincoln's address is not entirely accurate; Everett's address swamped their columns, but the greatness of Lincoln's speech was immediately recognized. Everett wrote him: "I should be glad if I could flatter myself that I came as near the central idea of the occasion in two hours as you did in two minutes."

Five copies of the Gettysburg address in Lincoln's hand are extant. The first and second draft, prepared in Washington and Gettysburg just before delivery, are in the Library of Congress. The third draft, written at the request of Everett to be sold at a fair in New York for the benefit of soldiers, was given the Illinois State Historical Library by popular subscription.

The fourth copy was written out by Lincoln for George Bancroft, the historian, and remained in custody of the Bancroft family until 1929, when it was acquired by Mrs. Nicholas H. Noyes, of Indianapolis, Ind. In 1949 Mrs. Noyes presented this copy to the Cornell University Library, Ithaca, N.Y. The fifth copy, usually described as the clearest and best, was also written by Lincoln for George Bancroft, for facsimile reproduction in a volume to be sold for the benefit of soldiers and sailors in Baltimore, where Bancroft lived. It is the second Bancroft copy. It passed to Bancroft's stepchildren, named Bliss, and was sold for $54,000 by the estate of Dr. William J. A. Bliss in New York April 27, 1949, to Oscar B. Cintas, former Cuban ambassador to the United States. He died in May, 1957, and willed it to the Lincoln room of the White House, where it was placed in March, 1959. Lincoln's spelling of battle field and can not as separated words in that version is reproduced above.

Sen. John Sherman Cooper (R.-Ky.) president of the Lincoln Sesquicentennial Commission, on June 17, 1959 presented a Latin translation of Lincoln's Gettysburg Address to the Apostolic Delegation of the Roman Catholic Church, in Washington, D. C. It was engrossed on vellum and was to be sent to Pope John XXIII for deposit in the Vatican Library. The presentation took place in the presence of Government officials and members of the Diplomatic Corps. The translation was made by the Rt. Rev. Edwin Ryan of White Plains, N. Y. The Latin Version was ordered printed in the Congressional Record.

# Copyright Law of the United States

Source: Copyright Office, Library of Congress

An author or proprietor may obtain statutory copyright protection by complying with the provisions of Title 17 of the United States Code. Applications for registration of claims to copyright are filed with the Register of Copyrights, Library of Congress, Washington, D. C. 20540. Application forms as well as information circulars covering various subjects are furnished free upon request to the Register of Copyrights.

A bill providing the first major revision of the copyright law in 58 years was passed by the House of Representatives in 1967 and sent to the Senate. *Any Senate action on the bill will be found in the Work of Congress, for which see Index.*

## CATEGORIES OF WORKS

The copyright law provides that the application for registration of any work shall specify to which of the following classes the work in which copyright is claimed belongs:

(a) Books, including composite and cyclopaedic works, directories, gazetteers and other compilations; (b) periodicals, including newspapers; (c) lectures, sermons, addresses, prepared for oral delivery; (d) dramatic or dramatico-musical compositions; (e) musical compositions; (f) maps; (g) works of art, models or designs for works of art; (h) reproductions of a work of art; (i) drawings or plastic works of a scientific or technical character; (j) photographs; (k) prints and pictorial illustrations including prints or labels used for articles of merchandise; (l) motion-picture photoplays; (m) motion pictures other than photoplays.

**Works reproduced in copies for sale or public distribution.** 1. The notice of copyright should appear on all copies of the work at the time of printing and shall consist either of the word "Copyright" or the abbreviation "Copr.," or the symbol "©" accompanied by the name of the copyright proprietor, and if the work be a printed literary, musical, or dramatic work, the notice shall include also the year in which the copyright was secured by publication. For example: "© John Doe 19—." In the case, however, of copies of works specified above—(f) to (k)—the notice may consist of the letter C inclosed in a circle © accompanied by the initials, monogram, mark or symbol of the proprietor—provided that his name shall appear on some accessible part of the copies. 2. Promptly after publication send to the Copyright Office, Library of Congress, Washington, D. C. 20540, two copies (or if the work is by a foreign citizen and is first published in a foreign country, one copy only) of the best edition of the work, with an application for registration and $6 fee.

**The notice of copyright** shall be applied in the case of a book or other printed publication, upon its title page or the page immediately following, or if a periodical, either upon the title page, or upon the first page of text of each separate number or under the title heading, or if a musical work either upon its title page or the first page of music.

**Books by American authors, or alien authors domiciled within the United States at the time of first publication of the work.** The copies deposited must be accompanied by an affidavit, under the official seal of an officer authorized to administer oaths, stating that the typesetting, printing and binding of the book have been performed within the United States. Affidavit and application forms will be supplied on request.

**Works published outside of the United States.** Foreign authors have an alternative to the requirements of the deposit of one copy of the work, an application for registration and a $6 fee. The alternative is the deposit of two copies of the book, musical composition or other work, an application and a catalog card, but no fee. The alternative can be availed of only if the required items reach the Copyright Office in acceptable form within 6 months after first publication. A book or periodical in the English language must be registered within six months from first publication abroad if an ad interim copyright, which lasts for five years, is sought. An author who obtains an ad interim registration is permitted the importation into the United States of 1500 copies, in one or more shipments, of a book or periodical in the English language during the 5 years after first publication abroad. Books or periodicals so imported must bear a U.S. copyright notice.

**Works not reproduced in copies for sale.** Copyright may also be had of certain classes of works of which copies are not reproduced for sale, by filing in the Copyright Office an application for registration, with the statutory fee of $6, sending therewith: (1) In the case of lectures or other oral addresses or of dramatic or musical compositions, one complete copy of the work. (2) In the case of photographs, one photographic print. (3) In the case of works of art (paintings, drawings, sculptures), or of drawings or plastic works of a scientific or technical character, one photograph or other identifying reproduction of the work. (4) In the case of motion-picture photoplays, a title and description, with one print taken from each scene or act. (5) In the case of motion pictures other than photoplays, a title and description, with not less than two prints taken from different sections of a complete motion picture.

## FEES

A new fee schedule, reflecting the first increase since 1948, became effective Nov. 26, 1965. The fee schedule follows:

Registration of copyright claims (including a certificate bearing the Copyright Office seal) for all classes of works, $6.

For registration of a claim to renewal, during the 28th year of the first term of copyright, $4.

Each additional certificate; typewritten, certified copy of the record of registration, $2.

Other certifications, including certifications of photocopies of Copyright Office records, $3.

For recording each assignment, agreement or other document of 6 pages or less, listing no more than one title, $5. For each page over 6 and each title over one, 50 cents.

For recording a notice of use of copyrighted music on mechanical instruments such as phonograph records, where the notice contains 5 titles or less, $3. For each title over 5 in a single notice, 50 cents.

For recording a notice of intention to use copyrighted music on mechanical instruments such as phonograph records, where the notice contains 5 titles or less, $3. For each title over 5 in a single notice of intention to use, 50 cents.

Searches: for each hour or fraction thereof spent by the Copyright Office staff in searching the official records, $5.

**Terms of Copyright.** The original term of copyright runs for 28 years. Within one year prior to the expiration of the original term, the author or, if he is not living, certain specified representatives, may secure a renewal for a further term of protection. In case of composite works, posthumous work or works made for hire, the proprietor may secure the renewal.

## UNIVERSAL COPYRIGHT

The United States is a party to the Universal Copyright Convention which became effective on Sept. 16, 1955.

Under terms of the convention each state will provide for protection of the rights of authors and other copyright owners in literary, scientific and artistic works, including writings, music, drama, cinematographic works, paintings, engravings and sculpture. Works first published in any member nation will generally get the same protection in other member nations as they afford their own nationals. The letter "c" in a circle accompanied by name of copyright owner and date of publication in a reasonable location on a work at first publication will obtain protection for the work in any member country.

One of the amendments to U. S. law was modification of the clause requiring books in English by foreign authors to be manufactured here in order to get copyright protection. Foreign works need not be subject to the U. S. requirement of deposit and registration, if they are first published in a Universal Convention country or are written by nationals of any contracting state.

# Trademarks: How to Obtain and Protect Them

U. S. Government bureaus have adopted trademark as a single word compounded from the former trade mark.

A trademark, as defined by Act of Congress, "includes any word, name, symbol, or device, or any combination thereof, adopted and used by a manufacturer or merchant to identify his goods and distinguish them from those manufactured or sold by others." Rights in trademarks are acquired only by use, which must continue if those rights are to be preserved. In order to be eligible for registration a mark must be in use in commerce which may be lawfully regulated by Congress.

Trademarks are registered on the Principal Register and the Supplemental Register of the U. S. Patent Office. "Coined, arbitrary, fanciful or suggestive marks, usually called technical marks, if otherwise qualified," may be registered on the Principal Register. A trademark that is merely descriptive of goods, or their regional origin, or is primarily a surname, is placed on the Supplemental Register.

The Trademark Act of 1946 provides that "For the purposes of registration on the supplemental register, a mark may consist of any trademark, symbol, label package, configuration of goods, name, word, slogan, phrase, surname, geographical name, numeral, or device, or any combination of any of the foregoing, but such mark must be capable of distinguishing the applicant's goods or services."

A trademark cannot be registered if it comprises immoral, deceptive or scandalous matter, or matter that may disparage or falsely suggest a connection with persons living or dead, institutions, beliefs, or national symbols. It cannot use the flag or coat of arms or other insignia of the United States, any state, municipality or foreign nation. It cannot use a portrait, signature or name of a living individual without his consent, or those of a deceased President of the United States without consent of his widow.

An application for registration must be filed in the name of the owner of the mark, who may submit his case or be represented by an attorney at law, or other person authorized to practice in trademark matters. A complete application comprises a written application, a drawing of the mark, five specimens or facsimiles and the required filing fee.

The Patent Office publishes a pamphlet, General Information Concerning Trademarks, which describes the way applications and drawings are to be prepared and gives sample forms for applications. The Patent Office, upon request, will supply forms for the registration of a trademark in the name of (1) an individual; (2) a firm, and (3) a corporation. If facilities permit, the Office will make drawings from the applicant's direction and at his expense. If the application is allowed, the trademark will be published in the Official Gazette so that anyone who considers that he will be damaged by the new mark may file his opposition in 30 days.

The Trademark Act of 1946 also provides for the registration of service marks, certification marks and collective marks. A service mark is a title, symbol or name used in sale or advertising of services to identify them. A certification mark is used by others than the owner to certify origin or quality, such as work by a union. A collective mark is used by members of a cooperative, an association or other group and indicates membership in a union or other organization. A digest of registered trademarks may be inspected at the Patent Office.

A trademark is registered for 20 years and may be renewed for periods of 20 years if still in use in commerce regulated by Congress, or if nonuse is due to special circumstances which excuse nonuse and is not due to any intention to abandon the mark. The fee for the original application is $35, and for the renewal is $25, with lesser fees for corrections, amendments, abstracts of title and other services.

The pamphlet, General Information Concerning Trademarks, is a general guide. Pamphlet copies of the Trademark Laws and the Trademark Rules of Practice of the Patent Office also are published. The Official Gazette, issued weekly, contains information concerning trademarks published for opposition, registered, and renewed. The first pamphlet is available at the U. S. Patent Office, Washington, D. C. For the others inquiries may be addressed to the Supt. of Documents, Government Printing Office, Washington, D. C.

# Patents and How to Apply for Them

A patent for an invention is granted by the United States Patent Office to the inventor of any new and useful process, machine, manufacture, or composition of matter, or any new and useful improvements in these categories. The grant to the patentee is of "the right to exclude others from making, using or selling the invention throughout the United States" for the term of 17 years. A patent is also granted for certain distinct and new varieties of plants, also for 17 years.

Patents for new, original and ornamental designs for articles of manufacture may be obtained for 3½, 7 and 14 years, as requested by the inventor. The filing fee on each design application is $20; the issue fee is $10 for a 3½-yr. term, $20 for 7 years and $30 for 14 years.

Except in special circumstances, an application must be made by the inventor; if two are associated in the invention both must apply; if the inventor is mentally ill or dead, application may be made by the guardian or administrator of the estate. The specification must include a written description of the invention and of the manner and process of making and using it, and is required to be in such full, clear, concise, and exact terms as to enable any person skilled in the art to which the invention pertains, or with which it is most nearly connected, to make and use the same. The claims are full descriptions of the subject matter of the invention reciting all essential features necessary to distinguish the invention. A drawing is required by the statute in all cases which admit of drawings. The filing fee is $65, with $2 additional for each claim in excess of 10, and $10 additional for each claim in independent form in excess of one.

The Patent Office examines the application to determine whether the invention is new and useful and whether the application otherwise complies with the law. If the application is allowed, a notice is sent the applicant and the final fee of $100, plus $10 for each page or portion thereof of specification as printed and $2 for each sheet of drawing, is due within 3 months. The patent is in force on the date it is granted. The terms "patent applied for" and "patent pending" have no legal significance but serve notice that a patent is being sought. Falsely using this marking is punishable by a fine.

If the Patent Office rejects an application, the applicant may ask for reconsideration, giving reason; if rejected again he may appeal to the Board of Appeals of the Patent Office, and if rejected there, may go to the Court of Customs and Patent Appeals or file a civil action in the U. S. District Court for the District of Columbia.

A patent will not be granted for a mere idea or suggestion, or a machine that will not operate, or an invention that lacks utility, or printed matter, or methods of doing business, or medicines that are merely mixtures of known ingredients, like physicians' prescriptions. So-called patent medicines are not protected by patents. So-called perpetual 'motion machines cannot be patented.

A patent cannot be obtained if the invention has been described in a printed publication or has been in public use or on sale before the date the invention was made or more than one year prior to the filing of the application. When two or more applications for patenting identical inventions are received, or when the applicant claims the invention for which a patent has been issued, the Patent Office begins "interference proceedings" to determine prior rights. The decision of the Patent Office may be reviewed by the courts.

Under certain conditions a license must be obtained before an application for a patent can be filed in a foreign country. The Commissioner of Patents may order an invention kept secret if publication would hurt the national safety or defense. Pamphlet copies of the Patent Laws, the Rules of Practice of the U. S. Patent Office in Patent Cases, and General Information Concerning Patents, can be obtained from the Superintendent of Documents, Government Printing Office, Washington, D. C.

The final report of the President's Commission on the Patent System was released by President Johnson Dec. 2, 1966. Bills based upon and incorporating many of the recommendations have been introduced in Congress and were under consideration in 1968.

# TAXATION

## Federal Individual Income Tax

Source: Internal Revenue Service, Treasury Dept.: Tax Foundation

### WHO MUST FILE

Every individual under 65 years of age who resided in the United States and had a gross income of $600 or more during the year, must file a Federal income tax return. Anyone 65 or older on the last day of the tax year is not required to file a return unless he had gross income of $1,200 or more during the year.

A taxpayer with gross income of less than $600 (or less than $1,200 if 65 or older) should file a return to claim the refund of any taxes withheld, even if he is listed as a dependent by another taxpayer.

### FORMS TO USE

**Form 1040A** may be filed by the taxpayer if his income is less than $10,000 and consisted entirely of wages reported on withholding statements, or such wages and not more than $200 income from other wages, dividends and interest. His accounting must be for the calendar year.

On this form the taxpayer does not itemize his deductions but takes the standard deduction. If his total income is $5,000 or more, he can take the higher of the standard deduction of 10% or the minimum standard deduction. Both are limited to $1,000 for all except a married taxpayer filing a separate return, who is limited to $500.

If the adjusted gross income is under $5,000, the taxpayer may not deduct the standard deductions, but must compute his tax fom the tax table, which makes allowances for exemptions and standard deductions. If he wishes to itemize, he must use Form 1040.

Taxpayers are entitled to a minimum standard deduction of $200 for a single individual, $200 for a married couple filing jointly, plus $100 for each exemption up to a total of $1,000.

**Form 1040** may be filed by an individual regardless of the source or amount of his income.

### DATES FOR FILING RETURNS

For individuals using the calendar year, Apr. 15 is final date for filing income tax returns and for payment of any tax due, and the first quarterly installment of the estimated tax. Other installments of estimated tax to be paid June 15, Sept. 15 and Jan. 15.

Apr. 15 is final date for filing declaration of estimated tax. Amended declarations may be filed June 16, Sept. 15, and Jan. 15.

Instead of paying the 4th installment a final income return may be filed Feb. 2. Farmers may file a final return Feb. 16 to satisfy estimated tax requirements.

### JOINT RETURN

A husband and wife may make a return jointly, even if one has no income personally. Their tax will be twice the tax imposed if the income were cut in half and taxed at the single rate.

One provision stipulates that if one spouse dies, the survivor may compute his tax using joint return rates for the first two taxable years following, provided he or she also was entitled to file a joint return the year of the death, and maintains in the household a home for a dependent child or stepchild. If the taxpayer remarries before the end of the taxable year these privileges are lost but he is permitted to file a joint return with his new spouse. An individual legally separated or divorced from spouse is not considered married. The survivor may file a joint return with the decedent for the year of death, if he does not remarry by the end of the tax year.

### ESTIMATED TAX

If total estimated tax exceeds withheld tax by at least $40, declarations of estimated income are required from (1) every single individual not head of a household or married individual not eligible to file a joint return with his spouse who expects over $5,000 gross income; (2) every head of a household or surviving spouse who expects a gross income over $10,000; (3) every married individual with over $5,000 who is entitled to file a joint declaration with his spouse and their aggregate gross income can reasonably be expected to exceed $10,000; and (4) every individual whose gross income can reasonably be expected to include more than $200 from sources other than wages subject to withholding.

### EXEMPTIONS

Personal exemption is $600.

Every individual has an exemption of $600, to be deducted from gross income. A husband and a wife are each entitled to a $600 exemption. A taxpayer 65 or over gets another exemption of $600. A blind person gets another exemption of $600.

Exemption for dependents, over one-half of whose support comes from the taxpayer, is $600. This applies to a child, stepchild or adopted child as well as certain other relatives with less than $600 gross income; also to a child, stepchild, or adopted child of the taxpayer who is under 19 or full-time student even if he makes $600 or more. A dependent can be a non-relative if a member of the taxpayer's household and living there all year.

Taxpayer gets the exemption for his child a student regardless of the student's age or earnings, provided the taxpayer provides over half of the student's total support. If the student gets a scholarship, this is not counted as support.

### CHILD AND DISABLED DEPENDENT CARE

A woman, a widower, a man whose wife is in an institution or unable to care for herself, or a man legally separated or divorced who has the care of a dependent child under 13 or a disabled dependent ragardless of age, may deduct not more than $600 for one child or dependent and $900 for two or more children or dependents for expenses incurred for care of dependent if taxpayer has to work. No deduction is allowed for payments to another dependent.

If a wife is working, the deduction is allowed only if she and her husband file a joint return. If their total income exceeds $6,000, the allowance will be reduced by the amount above $6,000. If the husband is incapable of self-support because handicapped, limitation and joint return requirement do not apply.

### LIFE INSURANCE

Life insurance paid to survivors is not taxed as income. Interest on life insurance left with the insurance company and paid to survivors at intervals is taxable when available. Surviving spouse (husband or wife )has an exclusion of the pro-rata amount of principal payable at death plus up to $1,000 per year of interest earned where life insurance proceeds are payable in installments.

Payments received as social security, and under the Railroad Retirement Act, are exempt.

### DIVIDENDS

The first $100 in dividends can be excluded from income. If husband and wife can both receive $100 on their joint return they can exclude $200.

The exclusion does not apply to dividends from tax-exempt corporations, mutual savings banks, building and loan associations and several others.

Dividends paid in stock or in stock rights are generally exempt from tax, except when paid in place of preferred stock dividends of the current or preceding year, or when the stockholder has an option to take stock or property.

## 1968 Income Tax Rate Schedules*

**I. (A) SINGLE TAXPAYERS WHO DO NOT QUALIFY IN TABLES II AND III, AND (B) MARRIED PERSONS FILING SEPARATE RETURNS.**

If taxable income is:—The tax is:

Not over $500.........14% of the taxable income

| Over | But not over | | Of excess over |
|------|------|------|------|
| $500 | $1,000 | $70, plus 15% | $500 |
| $1,000 | $1,500 | $145, plus 16% | $1,000 |
| $1,500 | $2,000 | $225, plus 17% | $1,500 |
| $2,000 | $4,000 | $310, plus 19% | $2,000 |
| $4,000 | $6,000 | $690, plus 22% | $4,000 |
| $6,000 | $8,000 | $1,130, plus 25% | $6,000 |
| $8,000 | $10,000 | $1,630, plus 28% | $8,000 |
| $10,000 | $12,000 | $2,190, plus 32% | $10,000 |
| $12,000 | $14,000 | $2,830, plus 36% | $12,000 |
| $14,000 | $16,000 | $3,550, plus 39% | $14,000 |
| $16,000 | $18,000 | $4,330, plus 42% | $16,000 |
| $18,000 | $20,000 | $5,170, plus 45% | $18,000 |
| $20,000 | $22,000 | $6,070, plus 48% | $20,000 |
| $22,000 | $26,000 | $7,030, plus 50% | $22,000 |
| $26,000 | $32,000 | $9,030, plus 53% | $26,000 |
| $32,000 | $38,000 | $12,210, plus 55% | $32,000 |
| $38,000 | $44,000 | $15,510, plus 58% | $38,000 |
| $44,000 | $50,000 | $18,990, plus 60% | $44,000 |
| $50,000 | $60,000 | $22,590, plus 62% | $50,000 |
| $60,000 | $70,000 | $28,700, plus 64% | $60,000 |
| $70,000 | $80,000 | $35,190, plus 66% | $70,000 |
| $80,000 | $90,000 | $41,790, plus 68% | $80,000 |
| $90,000 | $100,000 | $48,590, plus 69% | $90,000 |
| $100,000 | | $55,490, plus 70% | $100,000 |

**II. (A) MARRIED TAXPAYERS FILING JOINT RETURNS, AND (B) CERTAIN WIDOWS AND WIDOWERS.**

If taxable income is:—The tax is:

Not over $1,000............14% of taxable income

| Over | But not over | | Of excess over |
|------|------|------|------|
| $1,000 | $2,000 | $140, plus 15% | $1,000 |
| $2,000 | $3,000 | $290, plus 16% | $2,000 |
| $3,000 | $4,000 | $450, plus 17% | $3,000 |
| $4,000 | $8,000 | $620, plus 19% | $4,000 |
| $8,000 | $12,000 | $1,380, plus 22% | $8,000 |
| $12,000 | $16,000 | $2,260, plus 25% | $12,000 |
| $16,000 | $20,000 | $3,260, plus 28% | $16,000 |
| $20,000 | $24,000 | $4,380, plus 32% | $20,000 |
| $24,000 | $28,000 | $5,660, plus 36% | $24,000 |
| $28,000 | $32,000 | $7,100, plus 39% | $28,000 |
| $32,000 | $36,000 | $8,660, plus 42% | $32,000 |
| $36,000 | $40,000 | $10,340, plus 45% | $36,000 |
| $40,000 | $44,000 | $12,140, plus 48% | $40,000 |
| $44,000 | $52,000 | $14,060, plus 50% | $44,000 |
| $52,000 | $64,000 | $18,060, plus 53% | $52,000 |
| $64,000 | $76,000 | $24,420, plus 55% | $64,000 |
| $76,000 | $88,000 | $31,020, plus 58% | $76,000 |
| $88,000 | $100,000 | $37,980, plus 60% | $88,000 |
| $100,000 | $120,000 | $45,180, plus 62% | $100,000 |
| $120,000 | $140,000 | $57,580, plus 64% | $120,000 |
| $140,000 | $160,000 | $70,380, plus 66% | $140,000 |
| $160,000 | $180,000 | $83,580, plus 68% | $160,000 |
| $180,000 | $200,000 | $97,180, plus 69% | $180,000 |
| $200,000 | | $110,980, plus 70% | $200,000 |

**III. UNMARRIED (OR LEGALLY SEPARATED) TAXPAYERS WHO QUALIFY AS HEAD OF HOUSEHOLD.**

If taxable income is:—The tax is:

Not over $1,000............14% of taxable income

| Over | But not over | | Of excess over |
|------|------|------|------|
| $1,000 | $2,000 | $140, plus 16% | $1,000 |
| $2,000 | $4,000 | $300, plus 18% | $2,000 |
| $4,000 | $6,000 | $660, plus 20% | $4,000 |
| $6,000 | $8,000 | $1,060, plus 22% | $6,000 |
| $8,000 | $10,000 | $1,500, plus 25% | $8,000 |
| $10,000 | $12,000 | $2,000, plus 27% | $10,000 |
| $12,000 | $14,000 | $2,540, plus 31% | $12,000 |
| $14,000 | $16,000 | $3,160, plus 32% | $14,000 |
| $16,000 | $18,000 | $3,800, plus 35% | $16,000 |
| $18,000 | $20,000 | $4,500, plus 36% | $18,000 |
| $20,000 | $22,000 | $5,220, plus 40% | $20,000 |
| $22,000 | $24,000 | $6,020, plus 41% | $22,000 |
| $24,000 | $26,000 | $6,840, plus 43% | $24,000 |
| $26,000 | $28,000 | $7,700, plus 45% | $26,000 |
| $28,000 | $32,000 | $8,600, plus 46% | $28,000 |
| $32,000 | $36,000 | $10,440, plus 48% | $32,000 |
| $36,000 | $38,000 | $12,360, plus 50% | $36,000 |
| $38,000 | $40,000 | $13,360, plus 52% | $38,000 |
| $40,000 | $44,000 | $14,400, plus 53% | $40,000 |
| $44,000 | $50,000 | $16,520, plus 55% | $44,000 |
| $50,000 | $52,000 | $19,820, plus 56% | $50,000 |
| $52,000 | $64,000 | $20,940, plus 58% | $52,000 |
| $64,000 | $70,000 | $27,900, plus 59% | $64,000 |
| $70,000 | $76,000 | $31,440, plus 61% | $70,000 |
| $76,000 | $80,000 | $35,100, plus 62% | $76,000 |
| $80,000 | $88,000 | $37,580, plus 63% | $80,000 |
| $88,000 | $100,000 | $42,620, plus 64% | $88,000 |
| $100,000 | $120,000 | $50,300, plus 66% | $100,000 |
| $120,000 | $140,000 | $63,500, plus 67% | $120,000 |
| $140,000 | $160,000 | $76,900, plus 68% | $140,000 |
| $160,000 | $180,000 | $90,500, plus 69% | $160,000 |
| $180,000 | | $104,300, plus 70% | $180,000 |

*Beginning Apr. 1, 1968 individual taxpayers were subject to a surcharge on income tax. For additional tax due see Surcharge Table.

## DEDUCTIBLE MEDICAL EXPENSES

Expenses for medical care, not compensated for by insurance or other payment for taxpayer, spouse, and dependents, in excess of 3% of total income are deductible. This rule also applies to taxpayers 65 or over and dependent parents 65 or over. Previously these persons were not subject to the percentage limitations. There is no limit to the maximum amount of medical expense that can be deducted.

Medical care includes diagnosis, treatment and prevention of disease or for the purpose of affecting any structure or function of the body, and amounts paid for insurance to reimburse for hospitalization, surgical fees and other medical expenses.

Only medicine and drugs in excess of 1% of total income may be included with other medical expenses.

One-half the cost of medical care insurance premiums up to $150 can be deducted without regard to the 3% limitation. The other half plus any excess over $150 is included with other medical expenses subject to the 3% limitation.

Medical expenses for a decedent paid by his estate within one year after his death may be treated as expenses of the decedent taxpayer.

Medical and hospital benefits provided by the employer may be exempt from individual income tax. Wages paid as "sick pay" are exempt up to $100 a week after a certain waiting period.

# Surcharge Table
## Calendar Year 1968

| Single[1] | | | Head of Household | | | Married[2] | | |
|---|---|---|---|---|---|---|---|---|
| If the adjusted tax is: | | | | | | | | |
| At least | less than | tax is— | At least | less than | tax is— | At least | less than | tax is— |
| 0 | $148 | 0 | 0 | $223 | 0 | 0 | $293 | 0 |
| $148 | 155 | $1 | $223 | 230 | $1 | $293 | 300 | $1 |
| 155 | 162 | 2 | 230 | 237 | 2 | 300 | 307 | 2 |
| 162 | 168 | 3 | 237 | 243 | 3 | 307 | 313 | 3 |
| 168 | 175 | 4 | 243 | 250 | 4 | 313 | 320 | 4 |
| 175 | 182 | 5 | 250 | 257 | 5 | 320 | 327 | 5 |
| 182 | 188 | 6 | 257 | 263 | 6 | 327 | 333 | 6 |
| 188 | 195 | 7 | 263 | 270 | 7 | 333 | 340 | 7 |
| 195 | 202 | 8 | 270 | 277 | 8 | 340 | 347 | 8 |
| 202 | 208 | 9 | 277 | 283 | 9 | 347 | 353 | 9 |
| 208 | 215 | 10 | 283 | 290 | 10 | 353 | 360 | 10 |
| 215 | 222 | 11 | 290 | 297 | 11 | 360 | 367 | 11 |
| 222 | 228 | 12 | 297 | 303 | 12 | 367 | 373 | 12 |
| 228 | 235 | 13 | 303 | 310 | 13 | 373 | 380 | 13 |
| 235 | 242 | 14 | 310 | 317 | 14 | 380 | 387 | 14 |
| 242 | 248 | 15 | 317 | 323 | 15 | 387 | 393 | 15 |
| 248 | 255 | 16 | 323 | 330 | 16 | 393 | 400 | 16 |
| 255 | 262 | 17 | 330 | 337 | 17 | 400 | 407 | 17 |
| 262 | 268 | 18 | 337 | 343 | 18 | 407 | 413 | 18 |
| 268 | 275 | 19 | 343 | 350 | 19 | 413 | 420 | 19 |
| 275 | 282 | 20 | 350 | 357 | 20 | 420 | 427 | 20 |
| 282 | 288 | 21 | 357 | 363 | 21 | 427 | 433 | 21 |
| 288 | 298 | 22 | 363 | 370 | 22 | 433 | 440 | 22 |
| 298 | 313 | 23 | 370 | 377 | 23 | 440 | 447 | 23 |
| 313 | 327 | 24 | 377 | 383 | 24 | 447 | 453 | 24 |
| 327 | 340 | 25 | 383 | 390 | 25 | 453 | 460 | 25 |
| 340 | 353 | 26 | 390 | 397 | 26 | 460 | 467 | 26 |
| 353 | 367 | 27 | 397 | 403 | 27 | 467 | 473 | 27 |
| 367 | 380 | 28 | 403 | 410 | 28 | 473 | 480 | 28 |
| 380 | 393 | 29 | 410 | 417 | 29 | 480 | 487 | 29 |
| 393 | 407 | 30 | 417 | 423 | 30 | 487 | 493 | 30 |
| 407 | 420 | 31 | 423 | 430 | 31 | 493 | 500 | 31 |
| 420 | 433 | 32 | 430 | 437 | 32 | 500 | 507 | 32 |
| 433 | 447 | 33 | 437 | 447 | 33 | 507 | 513 | 33 |
| 447 | 460 | 34 | 447 | 460 | 34 | 513 | 520 | 34 |
| 460 | 473 | 35 | 460 | 473 | 35 | 520 | 527 | 35 |
| 473 | 487 | 36 | 473 | 487 | 36 | 527 | 533 | 36 |
| 487 | 500 | 37 | 487 | 500 | 37 | 533 | 540 | 37 |
| 500 | 513 | 38 | 500 | 513 | 38 | 540 | 547 | 38 |
| 513 | 527 | 39 | 513 | 527 | 39 | 547 | 553 | 39 |
| 527 | 540 | 40 | 527 | 540 | 40 | 553 | 560 | 40 |
| 540 | 553 | 41 | 540 | 553 | 41 | 560 | 567 | 41 |
| 553 | 567 | 42 | 553 | 567 | 42 | 567 | 573 | 42 |
| 567 | 580 | 43 | 567 | 580 | 43 | 573 | 580 | 43 |
| 580 | 593 | 44 | 580 | 593 | 44 | 580 | 593 | 44 |
| 593 | 607 | 45 | 593 | 607 | 45 | 593 | 607 | 45 |
| 607 | 620 | 46 | 607 | 620 | 46 | 607 | 620 | 46 |
| 620 | 633 | 47 | 620 | 633 | 47 | 620 | 633 | 47 |
| 633 | 647 | 48 | 633 | 647 | 48 | 633 | 647 | 48 |
| 647 | 660 | 49 | 647 | 660 | 49 | 647 | 660 | 49 |
| 660 | 673 | 50 | 660 | 673 | 50 | 660 | 673 | 50 |
| 673 | 687 | 51 | 673 | 687 | 51 | 673 | 687 | 51 |
| 687 | 700 | 52 | 687 | 700 | 52 | 687 | 700 | 52 |
| 700 | 713 | 53 | 700 | 713 | 53 | 700 | 713 | 53 |
| 713 | 727 | 54 | 713 | 727 | 54 | 713 | 727 | 54 |
| 727 | 734 | 55 | 727 | 734 | 55 | 727 | 734 | 55 |

$734 and over 7.5% of the adjusted tax.
[1]Single person (other than Head of household) and married person filing separate return.
[2]Married persons or surviving spouse filing joint return.

## DEDUCTIONS FOR CONTRIBUTIONS

Deductions up to 30% of taxpayers total income may be taken for contribution to most publicly supported charitable organizations, including churches or associations of churches, tax-exempt educational institutions, tax-exempt hospitals, and medical research organizations associated with a hospital, and nonprofit cemeteries. The deduction is limited to 20% for such organizations as private foundations.

Taxpayers also are permitted to carry over for five years certain contributions, generally to publicly supported organizations, which exceed the 30% allowable deduction the year the contribution was made.

Also permissible is the deduction as a charitable contribution of unreimbursed amounts up to $50 a month spent to maintain an elementary or high school student, other than a dependent or relative, in taxpayer's home. The arrangement must be covered by a written agreement with an organization to which contributions are deductible.

## DEDUCTION FOR INTEREST PAID

Interest paid by the taxpayer is deductible.

If personal property is bought under a contract providing for payment by installments, and in which carrying charges are stated but interest is not ascertainable, then subject to limitation payments are held to include interest equal to 6% on average unpaid balance.

## PRIZES AND AWARDS

All prizes and awards must be reported in gross income, except when received without action by the recipient. To be exempt, awards must be received primarily in recognition of religious, charitable, scientific, educational, artistic, literary, or civic achievement. (Nobel and Pulitzer prizes exempt.)

Also excluded from gross income is any amount received as a scholarship at an educational institution, or a fellowship grant with money for research and clerical expense. The exclusion for those not candidates for a degree is limited to $300 per month for 36 months.

## DEDUCTIONS FOR EMPLOYEES

An employee may take the standard deduction and deduct as well the following if in connection with his employment: transportation, except commuting; automobile expense, including gas, oil and depreciation; however, meals and lodging are deductible as traveling expense only if the employee is away from home overnight.

An outside salesman—a salesman who works full-time outside the office, using the latter only

for incidentals—may deduct both the standard deduction and all his business expenses.

An employee who is reimbursed and is required to account to his employer for his business expenses will not be required to report either the reimbursed or the expenses on his tax return. Any allowance to the employee in excess of his expenses must be included in gross income. If he claims a deduction for an excess of expenses over reimbursement he will have to report the reimbursement and claim actual expenses.

An employee who is not required to account to his employer must report on his return the total amounts of reimbursements and expenses for travel, transportation, entertainment, etc., that he incurs under a reimbursement arrangement with his employer.

The expense of moving to a new place of employment may be deducted under certain circumstances regardless of whether the taxpayer is a new or continuing employee, or whether he pays his own expenses or is reimbursed by his employer if he reports the reimbursement as income.

## RETIREMENT INCOME CREDIT

A credit against the tax, otherwise due of 15% of retirement income up to $1,524 included in gross income is allowed to persons 65 and over. Persons under 65 and retired under a public retirement system (firemen, policemen, teachers, Federal employees) are allowed the same credit on income from pensions and annuities paid under the system, but not on dividends, interest and rent. Included in public systems are funds for members of the Armed Forces for 1955 and subsequent years. Any pension or annuity received under the Social Security Act or the Railroad Retirement Act reduces the $1,524. Compensation in excess of $900 received by an individual under 62 and compensation in excess of $1,200 for one 62 or over but under 72 will reduce the $1,524 by varying amounts.

## NET CAPITAL LOSSES

An individual taxpayer may deduct up to $1,000 against his ordinary income if his capital losses exceed his capital gains in the year of the loss. He may carry the rest over to subsequent years at the same rate. The law places no limit on the number of years.

## INCOME AVERAGING

Individuals with large fluctuations in their annual income may be able to take advantage of averaging provisions available to taxpayers whose income for a particular year exceeds 133⅓% of their average income for the prior 4 years, if the excess is more than $3,000.

## WITHHOLDING

Every employer paying wages is required to withhold a tax based on a graduated scale which allows deductions for exemptions.

Employers may use either the percentage method or wage-bracket tables to determine the amount of tax to be withheld. The percentage method usually gives a result closer to actual tax liability.

Under the percentage method, a sum related to the taxpayers' exemptions is subtracted from his wage, and the tax is computed on the remainder, using tables with rates for married and single persons.

For example, the employer subtracts from a weekly wage $13.50 times the number of exemptions claimed (i.e., $13.50 for the taxpayer alone; $27.00 for a married couple, $54.00 for a couple with two children, etc.) to obtain the amount of taxable wages, and then uses the table shown below:

For a semimonthly pay period, $29.20 times the number of exemptions is deducted from the semimonthly wage (i.e., $29.20 for taxpayer alone; $58.40 for a married couple; $101.80 for a couple with 2 children, etc.), and then the tax is computed from the following table:

## TABLE FOR PERCENTAGE METHOD OF WITHHOLDING

### Weekly Payroll Period

(a) Single person

| Wages after exemption allowance: | | Tax to be withheld: |
|---|---|---|
| Not over $4 | | 0 |
| Over—But not over | | of excess over |
| $4 —$13 | 14% | $4 |
| $13 —$23 | $ 1.26, plus 15%— | $13 |
| $23 —$85 | $ 2.76, plus 19%— | $23 |
| $85 —$169 | $14.54, plus 22%— | $85 |
| $169—$212 | $33.02, plus 28%— | $169 |
| $212 | $45.06, plus 33%— | $212 |

(b) Married person

| | | |
|---|---|---|
| Not over $4 | | 0 |
| Over—But not over | | of excess over |
| $4 —$23 | 14% | $4 |
| $23 —$58 | $ 2.66, plus 15%— | $23 |
| $58 —$169 | $ 7.91, plus 19%— | $58 |
| $169—$340 | $29.00, plus 22%— | $169 |
| $340—$423 | $66.62, plus 28%— | $340 |
| $423 | $89.86, plus 33%— | $423 |

### Semimonthly Payroll Period

(a) Single person

| Wages after exemption allowance: | | Tax to be withheld: |
|---|---|---|
| Not over $8 | | 0 |
| Over—But not over | | of excess over |
| $8 —$29 | 14% | $8 |
| $29 —$50 | $ 2.94, plus 15%— | $29 |
| $50 —$183 | $ 6.09, plus 19%— | $50 |
| $183—$367 | $31.36, plus 22%— | $183 |
| $367—$458 | $71.84, plus 28%— | $367 |
| $458 | $97.32, plus 33%— | $458 |

(b) Married person

| | | |
|---|---|---|
| Not over $8 | | 0 |
| Over—But not over | | of excess over |
| $8 —$50 | 14% | $8 |
| $50 —$125 | $ 5.88, plus 15%— | $50 |
| $125—$367 | $ 17.13, plus 19%— | $125 |
| $367—$738 | $63.11, plus 22%— | $367 |
| $738—$917 | $144.73, plus 28%— | $738 |
| $917 | $194.85, plus 33%— | $917 |

# Federal Estate Tax

**Source:** Tax Foundation

An estate tax return must be filed for every citizen or resident of the United States whose gross estate exceeds $60,000 in value at the time of his death. In general, the tax must be paid within 15 mos. from the date of death. Extensions may be granted in hardship cases. A return must be filed for a non-resident, not a citizen, if his gross estate in the U. S. exceeds $2,000 in value.

An estate gets credit for state death taxes, according to a graduated table; also deductions for funeral expenses, administration, claims, and bequests to religious, charitable and fraternal organizations or government welfare agencies.

Life insurance payable to named beneficiaries is not to be included in the gross estate if the insured retained no incidents of ownership in the policy. A reversionary interest which exceeds 5

per cent of the value of the policy is considered an incident of ownership in the policy.

The marital deduction provides that the value of the taxable estate "shall be determined by deducting from the value of the gross estate an amount equal to the value of any interest in property which passes or has passed from the decedent to his surviving spouse." Thus the deduction applies when the surviving spouse has a right to the income for life from all or only a part of the property, as well as power to appoint all, or the part in which the survivor has income rights, whether or not the property is held in trust. If the spouse has control only over part, the deduction is limited proportionately. The deduction is limited, however, to the value of one-half of the adjusted gross estate.

## ESTATE TAX RATE

The tax is computed under the rates listed below on the net taxable estate of the decedent, citizen or resident of the United States after allowing for the specific exemption of $60,000 and deduction for debts, expenses, charitable, marital deductions. There is a credit allowance for state death taxes.

| If the taxable estate is: | The tax shall be: |
|---|---|
| Not over $5,000 | 3% of the taxable estate |
| Over $5,000 but not over $10,000 | $150, plus 7% of excess over $5,000 |
| Over $10,000 but not over $20,000 | $500, plus 11% of excess over $10,000 |
| Over $20,000 but not over $30,000 | $1,600, plus 14% of excess over $20,000 |
| Over $30,000 but not over $40,000 | $3,000, plus 18% of excess over $30,000 |
| Over $40,000 but not over $50,000 | $4,800, plus 22% of excess over $40,000 |
| Over $50,000 but not over $60,000 | $7,000, plus 25% of excess over $50,000 |
| Over $60,000 but not over $100,000 | $9,500, plus 28% of excess over $60,000 |
| Over $100,000 but not over $250,000 | $20,700, plus 30% of excess over $100,000 |
| Over $250,000 but not over $500,000 | $65,700, plus 32% of excess over $250,000 |
| Over $500,000 but not over $750,000 | $145,700, plus 35% of excess over $500,000 |
| Over $750,000 but not over $1,000,000 | $233,200, plus 37% of excess over $750,000 |
| Over $1,000,000 but not over $1,250,000 | $325,700, plus 39% of excess over $1,000,000 |
| Over $1,250,000 but not over $1,500,000 | $423,200, plus 42% of excess over $1,250,000 |
| Over $1,500,000 but not over $2,000,000 | $528,200, plus 45% of excess over $1,500,000 |
| Over $2,000,000 but not over $2,500,000 | $753,200, plus 49% of excess over $2,000,000 |
| Over $2,500,000 but not over $3,000,000 | $998,200, plus 53% of excess over $2,500,000 |
| Over $3,000,000 but not over $3,500,000 | $1,263,200, plus 56% of excess over $3,000,000 |
| Over $3,500,000 but not over $4,000,000 | $1,543,200, plus 59% of excess over $3,500,000 |
| Over $4,000,000 but not over $5,000,000 | $1,838,200, plus 63% of excess over $4,000,000 |
| Over $5,000,000 but not over $6,000,000 | $2,468,200, plus 67% of excess over $5,000,000 |
| Over $6,000,000 but not over $7,000,000 | $3,138,200, plus 70% of excess over $6,000,000 |
| Over $7,000,000 but not over $8,000,000 | $3,838,200, plus 73% of excess over $7,000,000 |
| Over $8,000,000 but not over $10,000,000 | $4,568,200, plus 76% of excess over $8,000,000 |
| Over $10,000,000 | $6,088,200, plus 77% of excess over $10,000,000 |

# State Estate Tax Rates and Exemptions*

**Source:** Compiled by Tax Foundation from Commerce Clearing House Data
As of October 21, 1968. *See page 213 for state inheritance tax rates and exemptions.*

| State (a) | Rates (on net estate after exemptions) | Maximum rate applies above | Exemption |
|---|---|---|---|
| Alabama | Maximum Federal Credit (c, d) | $10,040,000 | $60,000 |
| Arizona | 0.8% on first $50,000 to 16% (e) | 10,000,000 | 100,000 (f, g) |
| Arkansas | Maximum Federal Credit (c, d) | 10,040,000 | 60,000 (g) |
| Florida | Maximum Federal Credit (c, d) | 10,040,000 | 60,000 |
| Georgia | Maximum Federal Credit (c, d) | 10,040,000 | 60,000 |
| Mississippi | 1% on first $60,000 to 16% | 10,000,000 | 60,000 (f, g) |
| New York | 2% on first $50,000 to 21% (e, h) | 10,100,000 | (f, g, i) |
| North Dakota | 2% on first $25,000 to 23% | 1,500,000 | 20,000 (g, j) |
| Ohio | 2% on first $40,000 to 7% (e) | 500,000 | 5,000 (g, k) |
| Oklahoma | 1% on first $10,000 to 10% (e) | 10,000,000 | 15,000 (g, l) |
| South Carolina | 4% on first $40,000 to 6% (e) | 100,000 | 60,000 (g) |
| Utah | 3% of first $10,000 to 10% | 125,000 | 10,000 (g, m) |

(a) Excludes states shown in table on page 213 which levy an estate tax, in addition to their inheritance taxes, to assure a full absorption of the Federal credit.

(b) The rates generally are in addition to graduated absolute amounts.

(c) Maximum Federal credit allowed under the 1954 code for state estate taxes paid is expressed as a percentage of the taxable estate (after $60,-000 exemption) in excess of $40,000, plus a graduated absolute amount.

(d) A tax on nonresident estates is imposed on the proportionate share of the net estate which the property located in the state bears to the entire estate wherever situated.

(e) An additional estate tax is imposed to assure full absorption of the Federal credit.

(f) Insurance receives special treatment.

(g) Transfers to religious, charitable, educational, and municipal corporations are fully exempt. Limited in Mississippi to those located in

U. S.; does not extend to governmental (municipal) corporations in North Dakota.

(h) On net estate before exemption.

(i) The specific exemptions ($20,000 of the net estate transferred to spouse and $5,000 to lineal ancestors and descendants and certain other named relatives) are taken out of the first bracket which is fixed at $50,000. Net estates which do not exceed $2,000, after deducting the applicable exemptions, are not taxed.

(j) A marital deduction of 50% of adjusted gross estate is allowed instead, if larger. Exemption for a lineal descendant, if a minor, is $5,000; for other lineal descendants and ancestors, $2,000.

(k) Property is exempt to the extent transferred to surviving spouse not exceeding $20,000; for a child under 21, $7,000 and for each child over 21, $3,000.

(l) An estate valued at $100 or less is exempt.

(m) Transfers not exceeding $40,000, if made to surviving spouse or children, are exempt from tax.

# Corporation Taxes

**Normal Tax:** The normal tax rate on all net income is 22%.

**Surtax:** Surtax net income tax rate on net income over $25,000 is 26%.

**Surcharge:** A tax equal to 10% of the normal tax and surtax is imposed on corporations for the period Jan. 1, 1968 to July 1, 1969.

**Pay-as-you-go Tax:** Corporations which expect to pay over $75,600 tax must file an estimated tax

report by Apr. 15, June 15, Sept. 15, and Jan. 15, depending on when they first meet the requirements, while those on a fiscal-year basis must file a report on the 15th day of their 4th, 6th, 9th and 12th month. In 1968 the tax liability is 25% of the tax in excess of $75,600 during each quarter.

Net operating losses may be applied against profits for 8 years. The carry-back provision allows losses to be carried back to 3 preceding years and forward to 5 succeeding years. *Tax Foundation.*

# State Inheritance Tax Rates and Exemptions

**Source:** Compiled by Tax Foundation from Commerce Clearing House data

As of October 21, 1968

| State (c) | Rates (per cent) (a) | | | Max. Rate applies above ($1,000) | Exemptions (b) ($1,000) | | | |
|---|---|---|---|---|---|---|---|---|
| | Spouse Child or parent | Brother or sister | Other than relative | | Spouse | Child or parent | Brother or sister | Other than relative |
| Alaska........ | 1-5.25 | 3-10.5 | 5-17.5 | $100 | $10 | 3 (d) | $1 | None |
| California...... | 3-14 | 6-20 | 10-24 | 400 | 5 (e) | 5 (d) | 2 | (f) |
| Colorado (g)..... | 2-8 | 3-10 | 10-19 | 500 | 35 (h) | 10 (a) | 2 | $.5 (i) |
| Connecticut (j).... | 2-8 | 4-10 | 8-14 | 1,000 | 50 | 10 | 3 | .5 |
| Delaware........ | 1-4 | 2-5 | 5-8 | 200 (k) | 20 | 3 | 1 | None |
| Dist. of Columbia.. | 1-5 | 3-10 | 5-15 | 1,000 | 5 | 5 | 2 | 1 |
| Hawaii.......... | 2-75 | 3.5-9 | 3.5-9 | 250 | 20 | 5 | .5 | .5 |
| Idaho.......... | 2-15 | 4-20 | 8-30 | 500 | 10 (e, h) | 4 (d) | 1 | None |
| Illinois......... | 2-14 | 2-14 | 10-30 | 500 | 20 | 20 | 10 | .1 |
| Indiana........ | 1-10 | 5-15 | 7-20 | 1,500 | 15 | 2 (a) | .5 | .1 |
| Iowa........... | 1-8 | 5-10 | 10-15 | 150 | 40 | 10 (d) | None | None |
| Kansas......... | .5-5 | 3-12.5 | 10-15 | 500 | 75 | 15 | 5 | .2 (i) |
| Kentucky....... | 2-10 | 4-16 | 6-16 | 500 (i) | 10 (h) | 5 (d) | 1 | .5 |
| Louisiana...... | 2-3 | 5-7 | 5-10 | 25 | 5 | 5 | 1 | .5 |
| Maine.......... | 2-6 | 8-12 | 10-18 | 250 | 15 | 10 | .5 | .5 |
| Maryland....... | 1 | 7.5 | 7.5 | (m) | .15 (l) | 0.15 (h) | .15 (l) | .15 (l) |
| Massachusetts..... | 1.25-11.25 | 5-18.75 | 7.5-18.75 | 1,000 | 10 (n) | 10 (n) | 1 (n) | 1 (n) |
| Michigan........ | 2,8 (o) | 2-8 (o) | 10-15 | 750 | 30 | 5 | 5 | none |
| Minnesota....... | 1.5-10 | 6-25 | 8-30 | 1,000 (p) | 30 (h) | 6 (d) | 1.5 | .5 |
| Missouri........ | 1-6 | 3-18 | 5-30 | 400 | 20 (q) | 5 | .5 | .1 (l) |
| Montana........ | 2-8 | 4-16 | 8-32 | 100 | 20 (n) | 2 | .5 | Non |
| Nebraska........ | 1 | 1 | 6-18 | 60 | 10 | 10 | 10 | .5 |
| New Hampshire... | (r) | 10 | 10 | (m) | (r) | (r) | None | None |
| New Jersey...... | 1-16 | 11-16 | 15-16 | 3,200 | 5 | 5 | .5 (l) | .5 (l) |
| New Mexico...... | 1 (s) | 5 (s) | 5 (s) | (m) | (t) | (t) | (t) | .5 |
| North Carolina.... | 1-12 | 4-16 | 8-17 | 3,000 | 10 (h) | 2 (d) | None | None |
| Oregon (a)...... | 1-10 | 1-10 (u) | 1.10 (u) | 500 | None | None | 1 (u) | .5 (u) |
| Pennsylvania..... | 6 | 15 | 15 | (m) | 1 | None (x) | None | None |
| Rhode Island..... | 2-9 | 3-10 | 8-15 | 1,000 | 10 | 10 | 5 | 1 |
| South Dakota (a).. | 1-8 | 3-20 | 5-20 | 500 | 15 | 3 (d) | .5 | .1 |
| Tennessee........ | 1.4-9.5 | 6.5-8 | 6.5-20 | 500 | (v) | (v) | (v) | (v) |
| Texas........... | 1-6 | 3-10 | 5-20 | 1,000 | 25 (e) | 25 | 10 | .5 |
| Vermont........ | 2-6 | 2-6 | 12 | 250 | 15 | 15 | 15 | None |
| Virginia........ | 1-5 | 2-10 | 5-15 | 1,000 | 5 | 5 | 2 | 1 |
| Washington...... | 1-10 | 3-20 | 10-25 | 500 | 10 (e) | 10 | 1 | None |
| West Virginia (a).. | 3-13 | 4-18 | 10-30 | 1,000 | 15 | 5 | None | None |
| Wisconsin....... | 2-10 (w) | 2-10 (w) | 8-40 (w) | 500 | 15 (h) | 2 | .5 | .1 |
| Wyoming........ | 2 | 2 | 6 | (m) | 10 | 10 | 10 | None |

(a) In addition to an inheritance tax all states listed also levy an estate tax, generally to assure full absorption of the Federal credit. Exceptions are Oregon, South Dakota and West Virginia. *See page 212 for taxes not listed here.*

(b) Rates generally apply to excess above graduated absolute amounts.

(c) Generally, transfers to governments or to solely charitable (educational, scientific, religious, literary, public, and other similar organizations in the United States are wholly exempt. Some states grant additional exemptions either for insurance, homestead, joint deposits, support allowance, disinherited minor children, orphaned, incompetent or blind children, and for previously or later taxed transfers. In many states, exemptions are deducted from the first bracket only. Adopted children generally receive the same consideration as natural children.

(d) Exemption for child is (in thousands): $10 in South Dakota and $15 in Iowa. Exemption for minor child is (in thousands): $12 in California; $10 in Idaho; $5 in Indiana; $10 in Kentucky; $15 in Colorado and Minnesota; $10 in Ohio, and $5 in North Carolina.

(e) Community property state in which, in general, either all community property to the surviving spouse is exempt or only one-half of the community property is taxable on the death of either spouse.

(f) Exemption is $300.

(g) Additional tax: Colorado—10% on the amount of tax computed at above rates; Massachusetts—20% of inheritance tax of decedents dying before July 1, 1967, and a second tax of 3% of inheritance tax.

(h) Exemption for widower differs in the following states (thousands): Colorado, $10; Idaho, $4; Kentucky, $5; Minnesota, $6; Montana, $10; North Carolina, $2; Wisconsin, $5.

(i) No exemption if share exceeds amount stated.

(j) On estates of decedents dying on or after June 8, 1961 an additional inheritance tax equal to 30% of the basic tax is imposed.

(k) Maximum rate applies above $100,000 for other than husband, wife, lineal descendants or ancestors, wife or widow of son, and husband or widower of daughter.

(l) Estates over $3,000,000 are not subject to the inheritance tax but are subject to an estate tax equal to the amount of the Federal credit.

(m) Entire share.

(n) No exemption if share exceeds amount stated except that the tax shall not reduce the share below the amount of the exemption. In addition there are certain exemptions to spouse for home.

(o) Transfers of real estate are taxable at 75% of specified rates.

(p) Maximum tax is 35% of value of transfer in excess of exemption.

(q) In addition, an exemption of one-half decedent's estate or one-third if decedent is survived by lineal descendants.

(r) Entirely exempt.

(s) An additional tax of 1.5-3% is also applied depending upon beneficiary.

(t) Only one exemption is allowed upon aggregate of property passing to each class of beneficiaries: $10,000 for parents, spouse, lineal descendants, brothers, and sisters; $500 for all others. Amount of exemption for each class is proportionate to the respective shares of the estate and shared proportionately by the beneficiaries within the class.

(u) An additional tax of 1-20% is also levied. The exemptions apply to the additional tax only.

(v) A single exemption of $10,000 is granted against that portion of the estate distributed to the spouse, children, lineal ancestors and lineal descendants. A single exemption of $1,000 is granted to that portion of the estate distributed to all other beneficiaries.

(w) An additional tax of 30% on the amount of tax computed at rates shown is imposed; however, there is a statutory limitation that the total tax shall not exceed 15% of property transferred to the beneficiary

(x) In the absence of a spouse, the children may claim the $1,000 exemption.

# State Individual Income Taxes; Rates, Exemptions

**Source:** Analysis Staff, Tax Division, Treasury Dept. Data as of July 1, 1968

| State | Net income after personal exemption | Percentage rates | Net income after personal exemption | Percentage rates | Personal Exemp. Single | Personal Exemp. Married or head of family | Credit for dependents |
|---|---|---|---|---|---|---|---|
| Alabama[1] | First $1,000<br>1,001- 3,000 | 1.5<br>3 | $3,001-$5,000<br>Over 5,000 | 4.5<br>5 | $1,500 | $3,000 | $300 |
| Alaska[1-6] | 16% of Federal income tax | | | | 600 | 1,200 | 600 |
| Arizona[1-7] | First 1,000<br>1,001- 2,000<br>2,001- 3,000<br>3,001- 4,000 | 2<br>3<br>4<br>5 | 4,001- 5,000<br>5,001- 6,000<br>6,001- 7,000<br>Over 7,000 | 6<br>7<br>8<br>9 | 1,000 | 2,000 | 600 |

Resident taxpayers have the option of using as a tax base Federal net income less Federal income tax and certain Federal credits.

| State | Net income after personal exemption | Percentage rates | Net income after personal exemption | Percentage rates | Personal Exemp. Single | Personal Exemp. Married or head of family | Credit for dependents |
|---|---|---|---|---|---|---|---|
| Arkansas[2-3] | First 3,000<br>3,001- 6,000<br>6,001-11,000 | 1<br>2<br>3 | 11,001-25,000<br>Over 25,000 | 4<br>5 | 17.50<br>(1,750) | 50<br>(3,250) | 6<br>(333) |
| California[1-3-6-7] | First 2,000<br>2,001- 3,500<br>3,501- 5,000<br>5,001- 6,500<br>6,501- 8,000 | 1<br>2<br>3<br>4<br>5 | 8,001- 9,500<br>9,501-11,000<br>11,001-12,500<br>12,501-14,000<br>Over 14,000 | 6<br>7<br>8<br>9<br>10 | 25<br>(2,250) | 50<br>(4,500) | 400 |
| Colorado[1-6-8-9] | First 1,000<br>1,001- 2,000<br>2,001- 3,000<br>3,001- 4,000<br>4,001- 5,000<br>5,001- 6,000 | 3<br>3.5<br>4<br>4.5<br>5<br>5.5 | 6,001- 7,000<br>7,001- 8,000<br>8,001- 9,000<br>9,001-10,000<br>Over 10,000 | 6<br>6.5<br>7<br>7.5<br>8 | 750 | 1,500<br>Surtax on intangible income over $5,000, 2%. A credit of ½ of 1% in each bracket rate is allowed for income under $9,000. | 750 |
| Delaware[1-6] | First 1,000<br>1,001- 2,000<br>2,001- 3,000<br>3,001- 4,000<br>4,001- 5,000<br>5,001- 6,000 | 1.5<br>2<br>3<br>4<br>5<br>6 | 6,001- 8,000<br>8,001-30,000<br>30,001-50,000<br>50,001-100,000<br>Over 100,000 | 7<br>8<br>9<br>10<br>11 | 600 | 1,200 | 600 |
| Georgia[2-6] | First 1,000<br>1,001- 3,000<br>3,001- 5,000 | 1<br>2<br>3 | 5,001- 7,000<br>7,001-10,000<br>Over 10,000 | 4<br>5<br>6 | 1,500 | 3,000<br>Students above high school level and handicapped or retarded children under age 21 are allowed a $1,200 exemption. | 600 |
| Hawaii[1-4-6-8-9] | First 500<br>501- 1,000<br>1,001- 1,500<br>1,501- 2,000<br>2,001- 3,000<br>3,001- 5,000 | 2.25<br>3.25<br>4.5<br>5<br>6.5<br>7.5 | 5,001-10,000<br>10,001-14,000<br>14,001-20,000<br>20,001-30,000<br>Over-30,000 | 8.5<br>9.5<br>10<br>10.5<br>11 | 600 | 1,200 | 600 |
| Idaho[2-6-7] | First 1,000<br>1,001- 2,000<br>2,001- 3,000 | 2.5<br>5<br>6 | 3,001- 4,000<br>4,001- 5,000<br>Over 5,000 | 7<br>8<br>9 | 600<br>A $10 filing fee is imposed. A credit of $10 is allowed for each personal exemption. | 1,200 | 600 |
| Indiana[6-8-9] | | | | | 1,000 | * | 500 |

*Lesser of $1,000 or adjusted gross income of each spouse, but not less than $500.

| State | Net income after personal exemption | Percentage rates | Net income after personal exemption | Percentage rates | Personal Exemp. Single | Personal Exemp. Married or head of family | Credit for dependents |
|---|---|---|---|---|---|---|---|
| Iowa[2-3-6-8-9] | First 1,000<br>1,001- 2,000<br>2,001- 3,000 | .75<br>1.5<br>2.25 | 3,001- 4,000<br>4,001- 7,000<br>7,001- 9,000<br>Over 9,000 | 3<br>3.75<br>4.5<br>5.25 | 15<br>(1,500) | 30<br>(2,333) | 10<br>(467) |
| Kansas[1-6] | First 2,000<br>2,001- 3,000<br>3,001- 5,000 | 2<br>3.5<br>4 | 5,001- 7,000<br>Over 7,000 | 5<br>6.5 | 600 | 1,200 | 600 |
| Kentucky[1-3-6] | First 3,000<br>3,001- 4,000<br>4,001- 5,000 | 2<br>3<br>4 | 5,001- 8,000<br>Over 8,000 | 5<br>6 | 20<br>(1,000) | 40<br>(2,000) | 20<br>(1,111) |
| Louisiana[2-6-7] | First 10,000<br>10,001-50,000 | 2<br>4 | Over 50,000 | 6 | 2,500<br>(50) | 5,000<br>(100) | 400<br>(8) |

The exemptions and credits for dependents are deductible from the lowest income bracket and are equivalent to the tax credits shown in parentheses. A $1,000 additional exemption for blindness is also allowed for dependents.

| State | Net income after personal exemption | Percentage rates | Net income after personal exemption | Percentage rates | Personal Exemp. Single | Personal Exemp. Married or head of family | Credit for dependents |
|---|---|---|---|---|---|---|---|
| Maryland[1-6-8] | First 1,001<br>1,001- 2,000 | 2<br>3 | 2,001- 3,000<br>Over 3,000 | 4<br>5 | 800 | 1,600<br>An additional credit of $800 is allowed for each dependent 65 years of age or over. | 800 |
| Massachusetts[6-8-9] | Earned and business income:<br>divs., capital gains on intangibles:<br>Annuities: | 4<br><br>8<br>2 | | | 2,000 | 2,500<br>4,000 | 400 |

The exemptions shown are those allowed against business income, including salaries and wages. A specific exemption of $2,000 is allowed for each taxpayer. In addition, a dependency exemption of $600 is allowed for a dependent spouse who has income from all sources of less than $2,000. In the case of a joint return, the exemption is the smaller of (1) $4,000 or (2) $2,000 plus the income of the spouse having the smaller income. The exemption allowed against annuity income is the amount of any unused business income exemptions. Married persons must file a joint return in order to obtain any nonbusiness income exemption.

| State | Net income after personal exemption | Percentage rates | Net income after personal exemption | Percentage rates | Personal Exemp. Single | Personal Exemp. Married or head of family | Credit for dependents |
|---|---|---|---|---|---|---|---|
| Michigan[6-8-9] | All Taxable Income | | | 2.6 | 1,200 | 2,400 | 1,200 |
| Minnesota[1-3-6-8-9] | First 500<br>501- 1,000<br>1,001- 2,000<br>2,001- 3,000<br>3,001- 4,000<br>4,001- 5,000 | 1.5<br>2<br>3<br>5<br>6<br>7 | 5,001- 7,000<br>7,001- 9,000<br>9,001-12,500<br>12,501-20,000<br>Over 20,000 | 8<br>9<br>10<br>11<br>12 | 19<br>(1,050) | 38<br>(1,683)<br>An additional tax credit of $20 for single persons aged 65 or over or blind. Married $25. | 19<br>(507) |
| Mississippi[2] | First 5,000 | 1 | Over 5,000 | 4 | 4,000 | 6,000 | |
| Missouri[1] | First 1,000<br>1,001- 2,000<br>2,001- 3,000<br>3,001- 5,000 | 1<br>1.5-Less $5<br>2 -Less $15<br>2.5- $30 | 5,001- 7,000<br>7,001- 9,000<br>Over 9,000 | 3 - $55<br>3.5 - $90<br>4 - $135 | 1,200<br>The rates apply to total income. | 2,400 | 400 |

| State | Net income after exemption | Percentage rates | Net income after exemption | Percentage rates | Personal Exemp. | | Credit deps. |
|---|---|---|---|---|---|---|---|
| | | | | | Single | Married or head of family | |
| Montana[2-6] | First 1,000<br>1,001- 2,000<br>2,001- 4,000<br>4,001- 6,000 | 2<br>3<br>4<br>5 | 6,001-8,000<br>8,001-10,000<br>10,001-25,000<br>Over 25,000 | 6<br>7<br>8<br>10 | 600<br>The tax computed under these rates is reduced by 5%. | 1,200 | 600 |
| | | | | | Minimum tax for all taxable individuals $1. | | |
| Nebraska[6] | The tax is imposed as a percentage of taxpayer's Federal income tax before credits. The rate will be determined by the State Board of Equalization by Nov. 15 each year. | | | | 600 | 1,200 | 600 |
| New Hampshire[5] | Interest & dividends (except interest on savings deposits). | 4.25 | | | 600 | 600 | |
| New Jersey[2-6] | First 1,000<br>1,001- 3,000<br>3,001- 5,000<br>5,001- 7,000<br>7,001- 9,000 | 2<br>3<br>4<br>5<br>6 | 9,001-11,000<br>11,001-13,000<br>13,001-15,000<br>Over -15,000 | 7<br>8<br>9<br>10 | 600 | 1,200 | 600 |
| | The tax is imposed on net income and net capital gain derived from N. Y. sources by N. J. resident individuals and from N. J. sources by N. Y. resident individuals. A statutory credit of $10 for a single person and $25 for a married person living with spouse or a head of household is provided. | | | | | | |
| New Mexico[1-6-7] | First 10,000<br>10,001-20,000 | 1.5<br>3.0 | 20,001-100,000<br>Over 100,000 | 4.5<br>6.0 | 600 | 1,200 | 600 |
| | No tax is imposed on married taxpayers eligible to file joint returns and individual taxpayers who have one or more dependents and net income of $1,500 or less. | | | | | | |
| New York[1-6] | First 1,000<br>1,001- 3,000<br>3,001- 5,000<br>5,001- 7,000<br>7,001- 9,000 | 2<br>3<br>4<br>5<br>6 | 9,001-11,000<br>11,001-13,000<br>13,001-15,000<br>Over 15,000 | 7<br>8<br>9<br>10 | 600<br>Tax credits of $10 for single persons, $12.50 for married persons filing separately, and $25 for married persons filing jointly and heads of households are allowed. Income from unincorporated business is taxed at 5½%. The following credit is allowed: $100 or less-full amount; $100-200-difference between $200 and amount of tax; $200 or more, no credit. | 1,200 | 600 |
| North Carolina[2-6] | First 2,000<br>2,001- 4,000<br>4,001- 6,000 | 3<br>4<br>5 | 6,001-10,000<br>Over 10,000 | 6<br>7 | 1,000<br>An add'l exemption of $1,000 is allowed a married woman with separate income. | 2,000 | 600 |
| North Dakota[1-6] | First 3,000<br>3,001- 4,000<br>4,001- 5,000<br>5,001- 6,000 | 1<br>2<br>3<br>5 | 6,001- 8,000<br>8,001-15,000<br>Over 15,000 | 7.5<br>10<br>11 | 600 | 1,500 | 600 |
| Oklahoma[1] | First 1,500<br>1,501- 3,000<br>3,001- 4,500 | 1<br>2<br>3 | 4,501- 6,000<br>6,001- 7,500<br>Over 7,500 | 4<br>5<br>6 | 1,000 | 2,000 | 500 |
| Oregon[1-6] | First $500<br>501- 1,000<br>1,001- 1,500<br>1,501- 2,000 | 3<br>4<br>5<br>6 | 2,001- 4,000<br>4,001- 8,000<br>Over 8,000 | 7<br>9<br>9.5 | 600<br>A credit of $1 is allowed for each $100 actually contributed by a taxpayer as partial support of a person who would qualify as a dependent except for the chief support provision. The credit shall not exceed $6. Taxpayers and their spouses aged 65 or over receive a $12 tax credit each. Blind taxpayers and their spouses receive a tax credit of $18 each. | 1200 | 600 |
| South Carolina[1-6] | First 2,000<br>2,001- 4,000<br>4,001- 6,000 | 2<br>3<br>4 | 6,001- 8,000<br>8,001-10,000<br>Over 10,000 | 5<br>6<br>7 | 800 | 1,600 | 800 |
| Tennessee | Interest and dividends | 6 | Dividends from corporations, 75% of whose property is taxable in Tenn., are taxed at 4%. | | | | |
| Utah[2-6] | First 1,000<br>1,001- 2,000<br>2,001- 3,000 | 2<br>3<br>4 | 3,001- 4,000<br>4,001- 5,000<br>Over 5,000 | 5<br>6<br>6.5 | 600<br>An additional exemption of $400 in 1969 and $600 for 1970 and thereafter will be allowed taxpayers and their spouses aged 65 and over. | 1,200 | 600 |
| Vermont[1-6] | First 1,000<br>1,001- 3,000 | 2<br>4 | 3,001- 5,000<br>Over 5,000 | 6<br>7.5 | 600<br>The tax is imposed at a rate of 25% of the Federal income tax liability after certain credits (retirement income, investment, foreign tax and tax-free covenant bonds), reduced by the percentage of gross income not Vermont income. | 600 | 600 |
| Virginia[2-6] | First 3,000<br>3,001- 5,000 | 2<br>3 | Over 5,000 | 5 | 1,000 | 2,000 | 300 |
| West Virginia[1-6] | First $2,000<br>2,001- 4,000<br>4,001- 6,000<br>6,001- 8,000<br>8,001-10,000<br>10,001-12,000<br>12,001-14,000<br>14,001-16,000 | 1.2<br>1.3<br>1.6<br>1.8<br>2.0<br>2.3<br>2.6<br>2.8 | 16,001-18,000<br>18,001-20,000<br>20,001-22,000<br>22,001-26,000<br>26,001-32,000<br>32,001-38,000<br>38,001-44,000<br>44,001-50,000 | 3.0<br>3.1<br>3.4<br>3.5<br>3.7<br>3.9<br>4.1<br>4.3 | 600<br>For married persons filing joint returns, the size of the brackets is doubled. | 600 | 600 |
| | | | 50,000- 60,000<br>60,001- 70,000<br>70,001- 80,000<br>80,001- 90,000<br>90,001-100,000<br>100,001-150,000<br>150,001-200,000<br>Over 200,000 | 4.5<br>4.7<br>4.9<br>5.0<br>5.2<br>5.3<br>5.4<br>5.5 | | | |
| Wisconsin[1-3-6-8-9] | First 1,000<br>1,001- 2,000<br>2,001- 3,000<br>3,001- 4,000<br>4,001- 5,000 | 2.7<br>2.95<br>3.2<br>4.2<br>4.7 | 5,001- 6,000<br>6,001- 7,000<br>7,001- 8,000<br>8,001- 9,000<br>9,001-10,000<br>10,001-11,000 | 5.2<br>5.7<br>6.7<br>7.2<br>7.7<br>8.2 | 10<br>(370) | 20<br>(740) | 10<br>(361) |
| | | | 11,001-12,000<br>12,001-13,000<br>13,001-14,000<br>Over 14,000 | 8.7<br>9.2<br>9.7<br>10 | | | |
| Dist. of Col.[1-6] | First 1,000<br>1,001- 3,000<br>3,001- 5,000 | 2<br>3<br>4 | 5,001-10,000<br>Over 10,000 | 5<br>6 | 1,000<br>Income from unincorporated business is taxed at 6%. | 2,000 | 500 |

[1]A standard deduction and an optional tax table are provided. [2]A standard deduction is allowed. [3]Personal exemptions and credits for dependents are allowed in the form of tax credits which are deductible from the amount of tax. With personal exemptions, the sum in parentheses is the exemption equivalent of the tax credit assuming that the exemption is deducted from the lowest brackets. With respect to the credits for dependents, the sum in parentheses is the amount by which the first dependent raises the level at which a married couple becomes taxable. [4]A $5,000 exemption for blindness is allowed in lieu of the personal exemption. [5]The tax applies only to interest and dividends. [6]Exemptions are made for age (over 65) and/or blindness. [7]Community property state in which, in general, one-half of the community income is taxable to each spouse. [8]A limited tax credit is allowed for sales taxes; for property taxes on homesteads of the elderly in Minn. and Wisc., for property taxes and city income taxes in Mich.; for personal property taxes in Md. [9]In addition to exemption deductions, a sales tax credit or cash rebate is provided.

# State Sales Taxes; Types and Rates

Source: Analysis Staff, Tax Division, Treasury Dept. Data as of July 1, 1968

| State | Type of tax[1] | Rates on retail sales | | | | Rates on other services and nonretail businesses |
| --- | --- | --- | --- | --- | --- | --- |
| | | Tangible pers'l prop. | Selected service | | | |
| | | | Admissions | Rest. meals | Public utilities | |
| Alabama[5] | Retail sales | [2]4% | 4% | 4% | ...... | Gross receipts of amusement operators, 4%. Agriculture machinery and equipment and mining and manufacturing machinery, farm machines, 1.5%; transient lodging, 4%; closed circuit TV, 10%. |
| Arizona[3-4] | Retail sales | 3 | 3 | 3 | 1½ | Leasing, renting of tangible personal property, 3%; producing, processing natural resources, 2%; timbering, 1½%; storage, apartment and office rentals, 3%; meat packing and wholesale sales of feed to poultrymen and stockmen, ⅜%; amusement operators, 3%. |
| Arkansas[4] | Retail sales | 3 | 3 | 3 | 3 | Printing and photography, transient lodging, coin-operated devices, 3%. |
| California[4] | Retail sales | 4 | ...... | | 4 | Renting, leasing, producing, fabricating, processing, printing, 4%. |
| Colorado[4] | Retail sales | 3 | ...... | 3 | 3 | Transient lodging, 3%. |
| Connecticut | Retail sales | 3½ | ...... | [5]3½ | | Transient lodging, 3½%. |
| Florida | Retail sales | [2]4 | 4 | 4 | ...... | Rental, storage or furnishing services, altering, remodeling or repairing personal property and rental income of amusement machines, 4%. Fishing, hunting, camping, swimming and diving equipment, 5% of wholesale price. Transient lodging, 4%. |
| Georgia[3] | Retail sales | 3 | 3 | 3 | 3 | Transient lodging, 3%; lease or rental of tangible personal property, charges on amusements and amusement devices, 3%. |
| Hawaii | Multiple-stage sales | 4 | 4 | 4 | 4 | Manufacturers, producers, wholesalers, sugar processors and pineapple canners and selected service businesses ½%; insurance solicitors 2%; contractors, sales representatives, professions, radio broadcasting stations, service businesses and other businesses not otherwise specified, transient lodging 4%. |
| Idaho | Retail sales | 3 | | 3 | 3 | Renting, leasing, producing, fabricating, processing, printing, gross receipts of amusement operators, 3%. (Closed circuit TV on boxing and wrestling matches, 5%.) |
| Illinois[4] | Retail sales | 4¼ | | 4¼ | | Remodeling, repairing and reconditioning tangible personal property, 4¼%. A special hotel occupancy tax of 3% of 97% of gross receipts from rental of rooms to transients. |
| Indiana | Retail sales | 2 | | 2 | 2 | Transient lodging 2%. |
| Iowa[4] | Retail sales | 3 | 3 | 3 | 3 | Laundry, drycleaning, automobile and cold storage, photography, printing, repairs, barber and beauty parlor services, advertising, drycleaning equipment rentals and gross receipts from amusement devices and commercial amusement enterprises, 3%. |
| Kansas | Retail sales | 3 | 3 | 3 | 3 | Transient lodging and coin-operated devices and commercial amusements 3%. |
| Kentucky | Retail sales | 5 | 5 | 5 | 5 | Transient lodging, photographic services and sewer services, 5%. |
| Louisiana[4] | Retail sales | 2 | 2 | 2 | | Leasing, renting, repairing tangible personal property, laundry, drycleaning, automobile and cold storage, printing, transient lodging, 2%. |
| Maine | Retail sales | 4½ | | 4½ | 4½ | Transient lodging 4½%; proceeds from closed circuit TV, 4½%. |
| Maryland | Retail sales | [2]3 | | [5]3 | 3 | Lease or rental of tangible personal property, production, fabrication, or printing on special order, 3%; farm equipment, 2%; manufacturing equipment and machinery used in electricity, research and development, 2%. |
| Massachusetts[6] | Retail sales | 3 | ...... | [5]5 | | Transient lodging, 5%[7]. Renting, leasing, producing, fabricating, processing, printing, 3%. |
| Michigan | Retail sales | 4 | | 4 | 4 | Transient lodging 4%. |
| Minnesota | Retail sales | 3 | 3 | 3 | 3 | Renting, leasing, processing, producing, fabricating or printing tangible personal property, transient lodging, 3%. |
| Mississippi[3] | Multiple-stage sales | [2]5 | | 5 | [3]3½ | Wholesaling ⅛% (beer and motor fuel 5%); farm tractors, 1%; contracts exceeding $10,000, 2½%; extracting or mining, specified businesses including warehouses, laundry and drycleaning, photo finishing, storage, termites or pest control services, specified repair services, 5%; cotton ginning 15c per bale. Transient lodging 5%. |
| Missouri | Retail sales | 3 | 3 | 3 | 3 | Transient lodging, trailer camp rentals, rental or lease of tangible personal property, 3%. |
| Nebraska | Retail sales | 2½ | 2½ | 2½ | 2½ | Renting, leasing, producing, fabricating, processing, printing, storage, 2½%. |
| Nevada[4] | Retail sales | 3 | | 3 | | Renting, leasing, producing, fabricating, processing, printing, storage, 3%. |
| New Jersey[6] | Retail sales | 3 | 3 | 3 | | Producing, fabricating, storing, processing, installing maintenance and repair 3%. Transient lodging[7] 3%. |
| New Mexico[4] | Retail sales | [2]3 | 3 | 3 | 3 | Leasing of tangible personal property, gross receipts of services (excluding wages), 3%; contracting, 1½%; sales of farm implements and vehicles, 1½%; originating and servicing real property loans, ¾%. |

| State | Type of tax[1] | Rates on retail sales | | | | Rates on other services and nonretail businesses |
|---|---|---|---|---|---|---|
| | | Tangible pers'l prop. | Selected service | | | |
| | | | Admissions | Rest. meals | Public utilities | |
| New York [4-6] | Retail sales | 2 | 2 | [4]2 | ·2 | Leasing, renting, laundry, dry-cleaning, 3%; airplanes, boats, railway locomotives and cars, 1½%; sales of horses, mules and industrial fuels, 1%; farm and industrial machinery, 1%. |
| North Carolina | Retail sales | [2]3 | ........ | 3 | ...... | Farm and industrial machinery, 1% ($80 maximum); boats ($120 maximum), air planes, 1½%; laundry and dry cleaning 3%; transient lodging 3%. |
| North Dakota | ............. | [2]3 | 3 | 3 | 3 | Transient lodging, leasing, renting, fabricating, storing tangible personal property, proceeds from coin-operated amusement machinery, severance of sand or gravel from the soil, 3%. |
| Ohio | Retail sales | 4 | 3 | 3 | ........ | Transient lodging, printing and reproducing, production and fabrication, 3%. |
| Oklahoma [3-4] | Retail sales | [2]2 | 2 | 2 | | Advertising (exclusive of newspapers, periodicals and billboards), printing, automobile storage, transient lodging, 2% |
| Pennsylvania | Retail sales | 6 | ........ | [5]6 | 6 | Repairing, altering, laundering and cleaning of tangible personal property, cleaning, polishing, lubricating and inspection of motor vehicles, rental income of coin-operated amusement devices and transient lodging 6%. |
| Rhode Island | Retail sales | 5 | ........ | 5 | 5 | Producing, processing, fabricating, printing, transient lodging, 5%. |
| South Carolina | Retail sales | 3 | ........ | 3 | 3 | Transient lodging, laundry and dry cleaning, 3%. |
| South Dakota | Retail sales | [2]3 | 3 | 3 | 3 | Amusement devices, transient lodging, 3%. Farm machinery, 2%. Professional fees (other than medical) 3%. |
| Tennessee [4] | Retail sales | 3 | ........ | 3 | 3 | Transient lodging, parking lots and storage of motor vehicles, repair service, installations, laundry and dry cleaning, 3%; industrial machinery, farm equipment and machinery, 1%; vending machines, 1½%, except tobacco products, 2½%; lease or rental of tangible personal property, 3%. |
| Texas [4] | Retail sales | [2]2 | | 2 | 2 | Lease or rental of tangible personal property, producing, processing and storage, 2%. |
| Utah [3-4] | Retail sales | 3 | 3 | 3 | | Lease or rental of tangible personal property, repairing, renovating, installing transient lodging, laundry, dry cleaning, 3%. |
| Virginia [4] | Retail sales | [2]3 | ........ | 3 | ........ | Transient lodging, storage, contracting, fabricating of tangible personal property, 3%. |
| Washington | Retail sales | 4.5 | 4.5 | 4.5 | ........ | Transient lodging, auto parking and storage, other specified services, selected amusement and recreation activities 4.5%. |
| West Virginia | Retail sales | [2]3 | | 3 | ........ | All services except personal, professional and public utilities, transient lodging 3%. |
| Wisconsin | Retail services | 3 | 3 | 3 | ........ | Lease or rental of tangible personal property, laundry, dry cleaning, repair services, photography, transient lodging, 3%. |
| Wyoming | Retail sales | 3 | 3 | 3 | 3 | Lease or rental of tangible personal property, laundry, drycleaning, fabricating, repairing, altering, printing, garage, other services, 3%. |
| Dist. of Col. | Retail sales | [2]4 | ........ | 4 | 4 | Transient lodging, 5%; food for off-premises consumption, 1%, leasing, renting, producing, fabricating, printing 4%. |

[1]All but a few states levy sales taxes of the single-stage retail type. Hawaii and Mississippi levy multiple-stage sales taxes. The New Mexico and South Dakota taxes have broad bases with respect to taxable services but they are not multiple-stage taxes. Washington and West Virginia levy gross receipts taxes on all businesses, distinct from their sales taxes. Alaska also levies a gross receipts tax on businesses. The rates applicable to retailers (with exceptions) under these gross receipts taxes are as follows: Alaska, ½%, on gross receipts of $20,000-$100,000 and ¼% on gross receipts in excess of $100,000; Washington, 44/100%; and West Virginia, ½%. In Indiana, an additional tax of ½% is imposed on retailers under the gross income tax. New Jersey imposes a tax of 1/20 of 1% on retail stores with income in excess of $150,000.

[2]Motor vehicles are taxed at the general sales tax rates with the following exemptions. Alabama 1½%; Florida 3%; Mississippi 3% and North Carolina 1½% ($120 maximum). The following states exempt motor vehicles from their general sales and use taxes but are taxed under motor vehicle tax laws: Maryland 3%; New Mexico 1½%; North Dakota 2%; Oklahoma 2%; South Dakota 3%; Texas and Virginia 2%; West Virginia and the District of Columbia 2%.

[3]Ariz. and Miss. also tax the transportation of oil and gas by pipeline. Ga., Okla. and Utah do not tax transportation of property. Miss. taxes taxicabs transportation 2%.

[4]In addition to the state tax, sales taxes are also levied by certain cities and/or counties.

[5]Restaurant meals below a specified price are exempt; Connecticut, Maryland and New York, less than $1; Pennsylvania 10 cents or less.

[6]Rooms which rent for $2 a day or less are exempt.

## City Income Tax in Cities Over 50,000

| City | Rates % Now | Rates % Orig. | Year start | City | Rates % Now | Rates % Orig. | Year start |
|---|---|---|---|---|---|---|---|
| **Cities with 500,000 or more inhabitants** | | | | **Cities with 50,000 to 99,000 inhabitants** | | | |
| Baltimore, Md. | 1.0 | 1.0 | 1966 | Altoona, Pa. | 1.0 | 1.0 | 1948 |
| Cleveland, Ohio | 1.0 | .5 | 1967 | Bethlehem, Pa. | 1.0 | 1.0 | 1957 |
| Cincinnati, Ohio | 1.0 | 1.0 | 1954 | Chester, Pa. | 1.0 | 1.0 | 1956 |
| Detroit, Mich. | 1.0 | 1.0 | 1962 | Covington, Ky. | 1.5 | 1.0 | 1956 |
| New York, N.Y. | .4-2.0 | .4-2.0 | 1966 | Euclid, Ohio | .5 | .5 | 1967 |
| Pittsburgh, Pa. | 1.0 | 1.0 | 1954 | Gadsden, Ala. | 2.0 | 1.0 | 1956 |
| Philadelphia, Pa. | 2.0 | 1.5 | 1939 | Hamilton, Ohio | 1.0 | .8 | 1960 |
| St. Louis, Mo. | 1.0 | .25 | 1948 | Harrisburg, Pa. | 1.0 | 1.0 | 1966 |
| **Cities with 100,000 to 499,000 inhabitants** | | | | Johnstown, Pa. | 1.0 | 1.0 | 1948 |
| Akron, Ohio | 1.0 | 1.0 | 1962 | Kettering, Ohio | 1.0 | 1.0 | 1968 |
| Allentown, Pa. | 1.0 | 1.0 | 1958 | Lakewood, Ohio | 1.0 | 1.0 | 1968 |
| Canton, Ohio | 1.4 | .6 | 1954 | Lancaster, Pa. | .5 | .5 | 1959 |
| Columbus, Ohio | 1.0 | .5 | 1947 | Lexington, Ky. | 1.5 | 1.0 | 1952 |
| Dayton, Ohio | 1.0 | .5 | 1949 | Lima, Ohio | 1.0 | .75 | 1959 |
| Erie, Pa. | 1.0 | 1.0 | 1948 | Lorain, Ohio | .5 | .5 | 1967 |
| Flint, Mich. | 1.0 | 1.0 | 1965 | Parma City, Ohio | .5 | .5 | 1967 |
| Grand Rapids, Mich. | 1.0 | 1.0 | 1967 | Pontiac, Mich. | 1.0 | 1.0 | 1968 |
| Kansas City, Mo. | .5 | .5 | 1964 | Saginaw, Mich. | 1.0 | 1.0 | 1965 |
| Lansing, Mich. | 1.0 | 1.0 | 1968 | Springfield, Ohio | 1.0 | 1.0 | 1948 |
| Louisville, Ky. | 1.25 | 1.0 | 1948 | Warren, Ohio | 1.0 | .5 | 1952 |
| Scranton, Pa. | 1.0 | 1.0 | 1948 | Wilkes-Barre, Pa. | 1.0 | 1.0 | 1966 |
| Toledo, Ohio | 1.5 | 1.0 | 1946 | York, Pa. | 1.0 | 1.0 | 1965 |
| Youngstown, Ohio | 1.0 | .3 | 1948 | | | | |

## Excise Taxes on Selected Items

**Source: Tax Foundation (As of July 15, 1968)**

Gasoline, diesel fuel, benzol, naphtha, for vehicle propulsion are taxed at 4¢ a gallon scheduled through Sept. 30, 1972, and at 1.5¢ thereafter.

Liquor taxes:
Distilled spirits..........$10.50 per proof gallon
Perfumed, imported (containing distilled spirits).......$10.50 per wine gallon
Still wines (including vermouth and artificial or imitation wines)
  Not over 14% alcohol....17¢ per wine gallon
  Not over 21% alcohol....67¢ per wine gallon
  Not over 24% alcohol ..$2.25 per wine gallon
Champagnes, sparkling wines, liqueurs and cordials:
  Champagne or sparkling wine....................$3.40 per wine gallon
  Artificially carbonated wine................$2.40 per wine gallon
  Liqueurs and cordials

(containing wine)....$1.92 per wine gallon
Beer and fermented liquors:
  (Beer, ale, porter, etc., containing 1% or more of alcohol) $9.00 per barrel
Passenger car chassis or body (Mfg's sales) 7% to be reduced to 5% Jan. 1, 1970; 3%, Jan. 1, 1971; 1% Jan. 1, 1972.
  Tires and tubes (per lb.) .....................10¢
Pistols, revolvers (Mfg's sales) ..............10%
Slot machines, $250 a year each. This applies to all gaming devices.
Sugar (per lb.) ( *To be repealed July 1, 1972*) 0.53¢
Fishing equipment (Mfg's sales) ..............10%
Telephone calls (toll). To be reduced Jan. 1, 1970 to 5%; Jan. 1, 1971 to 3%; Jan. 1, 1972 to 1%.
Tobacco–small cigarettes weighing less than 3 lbs. per thousand, $4.00 per thousand.
Air travel tickets...........................5%

## Federal Gift Tax

Any citizen or resident who within the calendar year makes gifts in excess of $3,000 to any one individual, or any gift of a future interest regardless of value, must file a gift tax return on or before April 15 of the following year. In addition to the annual $3,000 exclusion for each person to whom gifts are made, each donor also has a lifetime exemption of $30,000, and this may be taken all at one time or spread over years.

When a husband and wife transfers by gift interest in property to his or her spouse a deduction in computing gift tax will be allowed to the extent of one-half of the value of the gift. Also gifts to a third party by either husband or wife may be treated as made one-half by each. *Tax Foundation*

| If the taxable gifts are: | The tax will be: |
|---|---|
| Not over $5,000 .......................... | 2¼% of the taxable gifts |
| Over $5,000 but not over $10,000 ........... | $112.50, plus 5¼% of excess over $5,000 |
| Over $10,000 but not over $20,000 ........... | $375, plus 8¼% of excess over $10,000 |
| Over $20,000 but not over $30,000 ........... | $1,200, plus 10½% of excess over $20,000 |
| Over $30,000 but not over $40,000 ........... | $2,250, plus 13½% of excess over $30,000 |
| Over $40,000 but not over $50,000 ........... | $3,600, plus 16½% of excess over $40,000 |
| Over $50,000 but not over $60,000 ........... | $5,250, plus 18¾% of excess over $50,000 |
| Over $60,000 but not over $100,000 ........... | $7,125, plus 21 % of excess over $60,000 |
| Over $100,000 but not over $250,000 ........... | $15,525, plus 22½% of excess over $100,000 |
| Over $250,000 but not over $500,000 ........... | $49,275, plus 24 % of excess over $250,000 |
| Over $500,000 but not over $750,000 ........... | $109,275, plus 26¼% of excess over $500,000 |
| Over $750,000 but not over $1,000,000 ........... | $174,900, plus 27¾% of excess over $750,000 |
| Over $1,000,000 but not over $1,250,000 ........... | $244,275, plus 29¼% of excess over $1,000,000 |
| Over $1,250,000 but not over $1,500,000 ........... | $317,400, plus 31½% of excess over $1,250,000 |
| Over $1,500,000 but not over $2,000,000 ........... | $396,150, plus 33¾% of excess over $1,500,000 |
| Over $2,000,000 but not over $2,500,000 ........... | $564,900, plus 36¾% of excess over $2,000,000 |
| Over $2,500,000 but not over $3,000,000 ........... | $748,650, plus 39¾% of excess over $2,500,000 |
| Over $3,000,000 but not over $3,500,000 ........... | $947,400, plus 42 % of excess over $3,000,000 |
| Over $3,500,000 but not over $4,000,000 ........... | $1,157,400, plus 44¼% of excess over $3,500,000 |
| Over $4,000,000 but not over $5,000,000 ........... | $1,378,650, plus 47¼% of excess over $4,000,000 |
| Over $5,000,000 but not over $6,000,000 ........... | $1,851,150, plus 50¼% of excess over $5,000,000 |
| Over $6,000,000 but not over $7,000,000 ........... | $2,353,650, plus 52½% of excess over $6,000,000 |
| Over $7,000,000 but not over $8,000,000 ........... | $2,878,650, plus 54¾% of excess over $7,000,000 |
| Over $8,000,000 but not over $10,000,000 ........... | $3,426,150, plus 57 % of excess over $8,000,000 |
| Over $10,000,000 .......................... | $4,566,150, plus 57¾% of excess over $10,000,000 |

## U. S. Savings Bonds

**Source: Treasury Department**
**(in millions As of December 31)**

| Year | Amounts outstanding[1] | Funds received from sale | Accrued discounts | Redemption[2] | Year | Amounts outstanding[1] | Funds received from sale | Accrued discounts | Redemption[2] |
|---|---|---|---|---|---|---|---|---|---|
| 1935-41... | 6,140 | 6,486 | 201 | 547 | 1955.... | 57,924 | 6,276 | 1,216 | 7,301 |
| 1943.... | 27,363 | 13,729 | 169 | 1,585 | 1960.... | 47,159 | 4,350 | 1,262 | 6,732 |
| 1944.... | 40,361 | 16,044 | 295 | 3,341 | 1965.... | 50,324 | 4,486 | 1,527 | 5,441 |
| 1945.... | 48,183 | 12,937 | 484 | 5,558 | 1966.... | 50,752 | 4,860 | 1,591 | 6,000 |
| 1950.... | 58,019 | 6,074 | 1,104 | 5,840 | 1967.... | 51,581 | 4,898 | 1,686 | 5,793 |

[1]Interest-bearing debt only.    [2]Comprises both matured and unmatured bonds.

# RELIGIOUS INFORMATION

## Census of Religious Bodies in the United States

Source: The WORLD ALMANAC Questionnaire and Yearbook of American Churches

The Yearbook of American Churches for 1969, Lauris B. Whitman, editor, published by Natl. Council of the Churches of Christ in the U. S. A., reports the following statistics compiled from figures, mainly for 1967, that were furnished by the religious bodies in the United States:

**Religious Bodies Reporting**—238. **Total Membership**—126,445,110 in the 50 states and the District of Columbia. Total membership exceeds that reported a year earlier by 666,454, a gain of .44%. There are 321,079 churches staffed by 360,092 clergymen. Church membership in the U. S. is 63.2% of the population.

Membership figures in the following table are the latest available. They come from different sources, and totals may be at variance with the figures quoted above. Some denominations submitted carefully compiled data while others approached the task more casually. Some membership figures were obtained by WORLD ALMANAC Questionnaire, others from the Yearbook of American Churches for 1968. The number of churches is given in parentheses.

| Denomination | Members | Denomination | Members |
|---|---|---|---|
| **Adventist Bodies:** | **426,632** | Church of God in Christ (4,500)...... | **425,000** |
| Advent Christian Church (403)....... | 29,838 | Ch. of God & Saints of Christ (217).. | 38,127 |
| Church of God (Abrahamic Faith) (121) | 6,500 | Church of Illumination (14)........... | 9,000 |
| Primitive Advent Christian Ch. (10)... | 578 | Church of the Nazarene (4,652)....... | 358,346 |
| Seventh-day Adventists (3,180)....... | 389,716 | Church of Our Lord Jesus Christ of | |
| **African Orthodox Church** (24)....... | 6,000 | the Apostolic Faith (155).......... | 45,000 |
| **Amana Church Society** (7)............ | 737 | Church of Revelation (5)............ | 750 |
| **Amer. Evang. Christian Chs.** | | Church of Scientology (15)........... | 55,000 |
| (no report) | | Churches of Christ (16,500)......... | 2,260,000 |
| **American Rescue Workers** (46)....... | 5,580 | Chs. of Christ in Christn. Union (240). | 7,928 |
| **Apostolic Faith** (43)................. | 4,764 | **Churches of God:** | **542,990** |
| **Apostolic Overcoming Holy Church** | | Ch. of God (Anderson, Ind.) (2,247).. | 144,243 |
| **Of God** (300)....................... | **75,000** | Ch. of God (Cleveland, Tenn.) (3,727). | 220,405 |
| **Armenian Church of America** (56)... | 196,000 | Church of God of Prophecy (1,469)... | 43,441 |
| **Assemblies of God** (8,510)........... | 595,231 | Ch. of God, Seventh Day (7)......... | 2,000 |
| | | Ch. of God, Seventh Day (Denver, | |
| **Baha'i Faith** (no statistics available) | | Colo.) (56)........................ | 5,500 |
| **Baptist Bodies:** | **25,896,250** | Churches of God in N. A. (Gen. Elder- | |
| American Baptist Assn. (3,262)...... | 745,620 | ship) (300)........................ | 30,000 |
| American Baptist Convention (6,085).. | 1,555,460 | The Church of God (1,925)........... | 74,101 |
| Baptist General Conference (589).... | 96,041 | The (Original) Ch. of God (75)....... | 18,000 |
| Bethel Baptist Assembly (22)........ | 5,147 | The Church of God by Faith (105).... | 5,300 |
| Christian Unity Baptist Assn. (11).... | 645 | **Churches of God, Holiness** (32)...... | 25,600 |
| Conserv. Baptist Assn. of Amer. (1,160) | 325,000 | **Churches of the Living God:** | **45,922** |
| Duck River (and Kindred) Assns. of | | Church of the Living God, Christian | |
| Baptist (69)....................... | 6,841 | Workers for Fellowship (276)...... | 47,670 |
| Evang. Baptist Ch. Gen. Conf. of (31) | 2,200 | House of God, which is the Church | |
| Free Will Baptists (2,200)........... | 250,000 | of the Living God, the Pillar and | |
| General Assn. of Regular Baptist Chs. | | Ground of Truth (107)............. | 2,350 |
| (1,244)........................... | 170,299 | **Churches of the New Jerusalem:** | **5,771** |
| General Baptists (844)............... | 64,498 | General Ch. of the New Jerusalem (35) | 2,028 |
| General Six-Principle Baptist (5).... | 190 | General Convention of the New Jeru- | |
| Natl. Baptist Conv. of Amer. (11,398). | 2,668,799 | salem in the U.S.A. (35)............ | 3,743 |
| Natl. Baptist Conv., U.S.A. (27,233).. | 6,300,000 | **Congregational Christian Churches,** | |
| Natl. Bapt. Evangelical Life & Soul | | **Natl Assn. of** (341).................. | **110,000** |
| Saving Assembly of U.S.A. (264).... | 57,674 | **Congregational Holiness Ch.** (147).... | 4,859 |
| Natl. Primitive Baptist Convention of | | **Conservative Congregational** | |
| the U.S.A. (18,076)............... | 1,225,000 | **Christian Conf.** (80)................ | **13,513** |
| No. American Baptist Assn. (1,750).... | 275,000 | | |
| No. American Baptist Gen. Conf. (337) | 54,358 | **Disciples of Christ** (see Christian | |
| Primitive Baptists (1,000)........... | 72,000 | Churches—Disciples of Christ) | |
| Progressive Natl. Baptist Conv. (655). | 521,692 | | |
| Regular Bapt. Chs. Gen. Assn. of | | **Eastern Orthodox Churches:** | **3,280,315** |
| (1,316)........................... | 180,000 | Albanian Orthodox Archdiocese in | |
| Separate Baptists in Christ (84) .... | 7,496 | Am. (12)........................... | 17,000 |
| Seventh Day Bapt. Gen. Conf. (165).. | 5,773 | American Carpatho-Russian Orthodox | |
| Seventh Day Bapts. (German 1728) (3) | 150 | Greek Catholic Church (66)........ | 104,500 |
| Southern Baptist Convention (34,147).. | 11,142,726 | American Catholic Church (Syro- | |
| United Baptists (586)............... | 63,641 | Antiochean) (1).................. | 450 |
| United Free Will Baptist Ch. (836).... | 100,000 | Antiochian Orthodox Archdiocese | |
| **Berean Fundamental Church** (37)..... | 1,982 | of Toledo, O. (21)................. | 35,000 |
| **Bible Protestant Church** (42) ....... | 2,388 | Orthodox Catholic | |
| **Bible Way Chs. of Our Lord Jesus** | | Patriarchate of America (30)...... | 2,850 |
| **Christ World Wide** (347).......... | 25,010 | Bulgarian Eastern Orthodox Ch. (19).. | 80,000 |
| **Brethren (German Baptists):** | **238,256** | Church of the East and of the | |
| Brethren Ch. (Ashland, Ohio) (120)... | 18,013 | Assyrians (12)..................... | 5,000 |
| Brethren Church (Progressive) (180).. | 26,402 | Greek Archdiocese of North and South | |
| Church of the Brethren (1,054)....... | 189,616 | America (406)..................... | 1,770,000 |
| Old German Baptist Brethren (54).... | 4,225 | Holy Orthodox Church in America | |
| **Brethren, Plymouth** (665)........... | 33,250 | (Eastern Cath. & Apostolic) (4)... | 260 |
| **Brethren (River):** | **9,473** | Holy Ukrainian Autocephalic Orthodox | |
| Brethren in Christ (159)............. | 8,593 | Ch. in Exile (15).................. | 4,800 |
| United Zion Church (16)............. | 880 | Romanian Orthod. Episc. of Amer. (49) | 50,000 |
| **Buddhist Churches of America** (60).. | 200,000 | Russian Orthodox Catholic Ch. in | |
| | | America Patriarchal Exarchate (67) | 152,973 |
| **Catholic Apostolic Church** (no data) | | Russian Orthodox Church Outside | |
| **Catholic Churches** (other than Roman, | | Russia (102)...................... | 85,000 |
| see Eastern Orthodox, Liberal Catholic | | Russian Orthodox Greek Catholic | |
| and Old Catholics) | | Church of America (350)........... | 500,000 |
| **Christadelphians** (850)............. | 15,800 | Serbian Eastern Orthodox Church (49) | 200,000 |
| **Christian Catholic Church** (5)........ | 1,555 | Syrian Antiochian Orthodox Ch. (82).. | 120,000 |
| **Christian Church of N. A.** (108) ..... | 8,000 | Syrian Orthodox Church of Antioch | |
| **Christian Churches, Internat'l Conv.** | | (Archdiocese of the U.S.A. & Canada) | |
| **of (Disciples of Christ)** (7,964) .... | 1,883,263 | (7)............................... | 25,000 |
| **Christian & Missionary Alliance** | | Ukrainian Orthodox Ch. of Amer. (37) | 40,250 |
| (1,110)............................ | 68,679 | Ukrainian Orthodox Ch. of U.S.A. (125) | 87,232 |
| **Christian Nation Church, U. S. A.** (16) | 3,300 | **Ethical Union, American** (30).......... | 6,000 |
| **Christian Scientists** (see Church of | | **Evangelical Christian Churches** (71).. | 11,201 |
| Christ, Scientist) | | **Evangelical Congregational Ch.** (163) | 29,744 |
| **Christian Union** (130)............... | 5,821 | **Evangelical Covenant Church of** | |
| **Christ's Sanctified Holy Church** (30). | 600 | **America** (517)..................... | 65,496 |
| **Ch. of Christ (Holiness) U. S. A.** (159) | 9,289 | **Evangelical Free Ch. of America** (517) | 50,312 |
| **Church of Christ, Scientist** (2,461) | | **Evangelical United Brethren Church** | |
| (membership data not published) | | (3,970)............................ | 732,377 |

| Denomination | Members | Denomination | Members |
|---|---:|---|---:|
| **Evangelistic Associations:** | **74,864** | Holiness Methodist Church (23)...... | 1,000 |
| Apostolic Christian Ch. of Amer. (72).. | 8,740 | Lumber River Annual Conference of | |
| Apostolic Christian Church | | the Holiness Methodist Ch. (7)...... | 360 |
| (Nazarean) (51)................ | 2,347 | The Methodist Church (42,165)...... | 11,035,313 |
| The Christian Congregation (256)..... | 45,767 | New Cong. Methodist Ch. (11)...... | 518 |
| Church of Daniel's Band (4)......... | 200 | Primitive Method. Ch., U.S.A. (86)... | 11,945 |
| The Church of God (Apostolic) (22)... | 600 | Reformed Meth. Union Episc. Ch. (21) | 16,198 |
| Ch. of God as Organized by Christ (14) | 2,192 | Reform, Zion Union Apostolic Ch. (50) | 16,000 |
| Metropolitan Church Assn. (15)....... | 443 | Southern Methodist Church (52)..... | 4,025 |
| Missionary Church Assn. (137)....... | 9,475 | Union Amer. Methodist Episcopal | |
| Pillar of Fire (61).................. | 5,100 | Church (256)................ | 27,560 |
| | | Wesleyan Meth. Ch. of Amer. (1,195).. | 48,861 |
| **Fire Baptized Holiness Ch. (53)**...... | **988** | **Moravian Bodies:** | **66,742** |
| **Fire Baptized Holiness Church** | | Moravian Church (Unitas Fratrum) | |
| **(Wesleyan) (53)**............ | **1,007** | (140)................ | 60,600 |
| **Free Christn. Zion Ch. of Christ (742)**. | **22,260** | Unity of the Brethren (32)............ | 6,142 |
| **Friends:** | **126,982** | **Mormons (see Latter-Day Saints)** | |
| Central Yearly Meeting of Friends (12) | 534 | **Moslems (no statistics available)** | |
| Friends United Meeting (509)....... | 69,353 | | |
| Ohio Yearly Meeting of the Friends... | | **Natl. David Spiritual Temple of Christ** | |
| Church (Independent) (87)....... | 7,059 | **Church Union (66)**............ | **40,816** |
| Oregon Yearly Meeting of the Friends | | **New Apostolic Church of N.A. (176)**.. | **19,867** |
| Church (63)............ | 6,055 | | |
| Pacific Yearly Meeting of Friends (36). | 2,227 | **Old Catholic Churches:** | **99,283** |
| Religious Society of Friends (Conserva- | | American Catholic Church, Arch- | |
| tive) (21)............ | 1,696 | diocese of N. Y. (20)............ | 8,437 |
| Religious Society of Friends (General | | No. Amer. Catholic Ch. (50)...... | 62,575 |
| Conference) (306)........ | 31,831 | No. Amer. Old R. C. Church (32)..... | 18,954 |
| Religious Society of Friends (Kansas | | Old Cath. Archdiocese of Americas & | |
| Yearly Meeting) (89)............ | 8,227 | Europe (24)............ | 7,100 |
| | | Reformed Catholic Church (Utrecht | |
| **Greek Orthodox (see Eastern Orthodox** | | Confession), Prov. of No. Am. (20).. | 2,217 |
| **Churches)** | | **Open Bible Standard Churches (262)** | **30,000** |
| | | | |
| **Holiness Church of God (28)**........ | **884** | **Pentecostal Assemblies:** | **458,606** |
| | | Calvary Pentecostal Church (22)...... | 8,000 |
| **Independent Fundamental Churches** | | Elim Missionary Assemblies (64)...... | 3,000 |
| **of America (899)**................ | **119,970** | Emmanuel Holiness Church (56)...... | 1,200 |
| **Independent Negro Churches (50)**... | **12,337** | Internatl. Pentecostal Assemblies (60).. | 7,500 |
| **International Church of the Four-** | | Pent. Assemblies of the World (550)... | 45,000 |
| **square Gospel (749)**........ | **94,788** | Pentecostal Church of Christ (42)..... | 1,150 |
| | | Pentecostal Ch. of God of Amer. (975). | 115,000 |
| **Jehovah's Witnesses (5,317)**.......... | **328,648** | Pentecostal Evang. Ch. of God, Natl. & | |
| **Jewish Congregations:** | **5,650,000** | Internal. (4)............ | 229 |
| Union of Amer. Hebrew Cong. (690) | 1,000,000 | Pentecostal Fire-Baptized Holiness | |
| Union of Orthod. Jewish Cong. of Amer. | | Church (41)............ | 500 |
| (3,000)............ | 3,000,000 | Pentecostal Free Will Baptist Ch. (176) | 10,000 |
| United Synagogue of Amer. (850)..... | 1,650,000 | Pentecostal Holiness Church (1,388).. | 67,027 |
| | | United Pentecostal Church (2,167).... | 200,000 |
| **Latter-Day Saints:** | **2,063,522** | **Pilgrim Holiness Church (953)**...... | **32,765** |
| Church of Jesus Christ (Bickertonites) | | **Polish Natl. Catholic Ch. of Amer.** | |
| (46)............ | 2,309 | **(162)**............ | **282,411** |
| Church of Jesus Christ of Latter-Day | | **Presbyterian Bodies:** | **4,406,411** |
| Saints (Mormon) (4,413)....... | 1,891,965 | Associate Presbyterian Ch., of N. A. (4) | 650 |
| Reorganized Church of Jesus Christ | | Associate Reformed Presbyt. Church | |
| of Latter Day Saints (1,008)....... | 169,248 | (General Synod) (143)............ | 28,302 |
| **Liberal Catholic Church (8)**............ | **4,000** | Cumberland Presbyterian Ch. (914).. | 86,729 |
| **Lithuanian Nat'l Catholic Ch. (4)**..... | **3,950** | Second Cumberland Presbyt. Ch. in the | |
| **Lutheran Bodies:** | **8,999,007** | U. S. (121)............ | 30,000 |
| **The Evangelical Lutheran** | | Orthodox Presbyterian Ch. (124)..... | 13,823 |
| **Synodical Conf. of N. America:** | **2,868,878** | Presbyterian Ch. in the U. S. (3,987).. | 960,776 |
| Lutheran Church-Mo. Synod (5,427).. | 2,759,308 | Reformed Presbyterian Ch. Evan- | |
| Synod of Evangel. Lutheran Chs. (65) | 21,656 | gelical Synod (115)............ | 11,835 |
| **U. S. A. National Committee of the** | | Reformed Presbyterian Church of N. A. | |
| **Lutheran World Federation** | | (Old School) (69)............ | 5,535 |
| **Constituents:**............ | **5,741,593** | United Presbyt. Ch. in the U.S.A. | |
| The American Lutheran Church (4,906) | 2,576,027 | (8,877)............ | 3,268,761 |
| The Lutheran Ch. in America (5,892).. | 3,165,566 | **Protestant Episcopal Church (7,180)**.. | **3,420,297** |
| **Other Lutheran Churches:** | | | |
| Church of the Lutheran Brethren of | | **Quakers (see Friends)** | |
| America (71)............ | 7,768 | | |
| Evangelical Lutheran Church in | | **Reformed Bodies:** | **688,814** |
| America (Eielsen Synod) (44)...... | 4,220 | Christian Reformed Church (635)..... | 278,969 |
| Evangelical Lutheran Synod (Nor- | | Hungarian Reformed Ch. in Am. (40).. | 11,110 |
| welgan Synod) (84)............ | 15,632 | Netherlands Ref. Congregations (14).. | 2,500 |
| Protestant Conference (Lutheran) (7).. | 2,400 | Protestant Reformed Chs. of Amer. (19) | 3,061 |
| Wisconsin Evangelical Lutheran Synod | | Reformed Church in America (939) | 389,751 |
| (869)............ | 358,466 | Reformed Church in the U.S. (20).... | 3,423 |
| | | **Reformed Episcopal Church (65)**..... | **7,085** |
| **Mennonite Bodies:** | **198,888** | **Roman Catholic Church (23,814)**.. | **47,468,333** |
| Beachy Amish Mennonite Chs. (47).. | 3,689 | **Russian Orthodox (see Eastern Ortho-** | |
| Ch. of God in Christ (Mennonite) (38) | 5,000 | **dox Churches)** | |
| Conference of the Evangelical Men- | | | |
| nonite Church (21) | 2,516 | **Salvation Army (1,121)**............ | **324,911** |
| Evangelical Mennonite Brethren (36).. | 3,591 | **The Schwenkfelder Church (5)**...... | **2,550** |
| General Conf. Mennonite Ch. (284)... | 53,584 | **Social Brethren (31)**................ | **1,540** |
| Hutterian Brethren (28)............ | 2,835 | **Spiritualists:** | **24,174** |
| Mennonite Brethren Ch. of N. A. (81).. | 13,171 | Int. Gen. Assembly of Spiritualist (84).. | 16,000 |
| Mennonite Church (1,055)............ | 83,627 | Natl. Spiritual Alliance of the U.S.A. (30) | 3,212 |
| Old Order Amish Mennonite Ch. (301).. | 21,023 | Natl. Spiritualist Assn. of Chs. (183).. | 4,962 |
| Old Order (Wisler) Mennonite Ch. (55) | 7,512 | | |
| Reformed Mennonite Church (14)..... | 500 | **Triumph the Church and Kingdom of** | |
| Unaffiliated Conservative and Amish | | **God in Christ (420)**............ | **45,000** |
| Mennonite Churches (42) | 1,840 | | |
| **Methodist Bodies:** | **13,693,322** | **Unitarian Universalist Assn. (1,135)**.. | **177,431** |
| African Meth. Episcopal Ch. (5,878).. | 1,166,301 | **United Brethren:** | **25,057** |
| African M. E. Zion Ch. (3,800)...... | 805,000 | United Brethren in Christ (340)...... | 24,457 |
| African Union First Colored Methodist | | United Christian Church (12)...... | 600 |
| Protestant Church (41) | 8,000 | **United Church of Christ (6,909)**..... | **2,052,857** |
| Christian Meth. Episcopal Ch. (2,598).. | 466,718 | **United Holy Ch. of America (470)**.... | **28,980** |
| Congregational Methodist Ch. (223).. | 14,274 | **United Missionary Church (141)**.... | **8,381** |
| Cong. Meth. Ch. of U.S.A. (100)..... | 7,500 | | |
| Evangelical Methodist Church (153).. | 1,085 | **Vedanta Societies (11)**................ | **1,000** |
| Free Methodist Ch., of N. A. (1,124).. | 62,090 | **Volunteers of America (219)**........ | **32,760** |
| Fundamental Methodist Church (12).. | 574 | | |

# Headquarters of Religious Bodies

(Year organized in parentheses)

**Advent Christian Church** (1854)—Pres. Rev. Joe Tom Tate. Exec. Sec., Rev. J. Howard Shaw, 917 Hardin St., Aurora, Ill. 60506.

**Adventists, Seventh-day, General Conference of** (1863)—Pres., Robert H. Pierson. Secretary, W. R. Beach, Takoma Park, Washington, D. C. 20012.

**African Methodist Episcopal Zion Church** (1796) —Senior Bishop, Bishop R. L. Jones, 741 S. 44th St., Louisville, Ky. 40211; Sec., Board of Bishops, Bishop F. S. Anderson.

**Antiochian Orthodox Archdiocese of Toledo, Ohio** (1936), Archbishop Metropolitan Michael G. Shaheen, 532 Bush St., Toledo, Ohio 43604.

**Armenian Church of America, Diocese** (1889)— Primate, Most Rev. Archbishop Torkom Manoogian. Sec., Rev. Arten Ashjian, 630 Second Ave., New York, N. Y. 10016.

**Assemblies of God** (1914)—Gen. Supt., Thomas F. Zimmerman. Gen. Sec., Bartlett Peterson, 1445 Boonville Ave., Springfield, Mo. 65802.

**Augustana Evangelical Lutheran Church.** *See The Lutheran Church in America.*

**Baha'i Faith**—About 2,300 communities, groups and isolated centers in the U. S. Sec., Natl. Spiritual Assembly. Glenford E. Mitchell, 536 Sheridan Rd., Wilmette, Ill. 60091.

**Baptist Association, American** (1905)—Pres., Martin Canavan. Corr. Sec., Dr. A. L. Patterson, 214 E. Broad St., Texarkana, Tex.

**Baptist Association. North American** (1950)— Pres., Rev. W. R. Speer, Dir. Publ. Rel., Dr. D. N. Jackson, P. O. Box 19099, Oklahoma City, Okla. 73119.

**Baptist Association of America, Conservative** (1947)—Pres., Dr. Lester Thompson. Corr. Sec., Rev. Richard P. Camp Jr., P. O. Box 66, Wheaton, Ill. 60187.

**Baptist Convention, American** (1907)—Pres. Rev. Dr. Culbert G. Rutenber. Gen. Sec., Rev. Edwin H. Tuller, Valley Forge, Pa. 19481.

**Baptist Convention Southern** (1845)—Pres. Dr. W. A. Criswell. Exec. Sec., Dr. Porter Routh, 460 James Robertson Parkway, Nashville, Tenn. 37219.

**Baptists, General** (1611)—Moderator, Glen Lashley. Clerk, Vern Whitten, 1629 Stinson Ave., Evansville, Ind. 47712.

**Baptist General Conference** (1879)—Gen. Sec. Lloyd W. Dahlquist. 5750 No. Ashland Ave., Chicago, Ill. 60626.

**Baptist General Conference, North American** (1865)—Moderator, Stanley C. Johnson. Exec. Sec., Rev. G. K. Zimmerman, 7308 Madison St., Forest Park, Ill. 60130.

**Baptists, Free Will** (1727)—Moderator, Dr. Robert Picirilli. Exec. Sec., Rufus Coffey, P. O. Box 1088, Nashville, Tenn. 37202.

**Buddhist Churches of America** (1914)—Bishop Takashi Tsuji, 1710 Octavia St., San Francisco, Calif. 94109.

**Bulgarian Eastern Orthodox Church** (1909)— Most Rev. Metropolitan Andrey, Archbishop. 312 West 101st St., New York, N. Y. 10025.

**Calvary Grace Christian Churches of Faith** (1961)—Internatl. Gen. Supt., Rev. Dr. Herman Keck, Jr., P. O. Box 1674, Ft. Lauderdale, Fla.

**Calvary Grace Church of Faith** (1954)—Rev. A. C. Spern, Internatl. Gen. Supt., P. O. Box 333, Rillton, Pa. 15678.

**Christian Churches (Disciples of Christ)** (1809) —Exec. Sec., Dr. A. Dale Fiers, 221 Ohmer Ave., Indianapolis, Ind. 46219.

**Christian Endeavor, International Society of** (1881)—Pres., Elwood Dunn. Gen. Sec., Rev. Christian A. Tirre, 1221 East Broad St., Columbus, Ohio 43216.

**Christian and Missionary Alliance** (1887)—President, Dr. Nathan Bailey. Secretary, Rev. W. F. Smalley, 260 West 44th St., New York, N. Y. 10036.

**Christian Reformed Church** (1857)—Stated Clerk, Dr. R. J. Danhof, 2850 Kalamazoo Ave., S.E., Grand Rapids, Mich. 49508.

**Church of the Brethren** (1719)—Sec. Gen. General Board, S. Loren Bowman, 1451 Dundee Ave., Elgin, Ill. 60120.

**Church of Christ, Scientist,** (1879)—Christian Science Mother Church. The First Church of Christ, Scientist, in Boston, Mass. Pres., Gordon V. Comer. First Reader, William B. Waite. Clerk, Charles Henry Gabriel, 107 Falmouth St., Boston, Mass. 02115.

**Church of God (Anderson, Ind.)** (1880)—Exec. Secy., Charles V. Weber, Box 2420, Anderson, Ind. 46011.

**Church of God, The** (1903) General Overseer, Bishop Homer A. Tomlinson, 9305 224th St., Queens Village. N. Y. 11428.

**Church of Jesus Christ of Latter Day Saints, Mormon)** (1830)—Pres., David O. McKay. Presi-

dent of the Council of Twelve Apostles, Joseph Fielding Smitn. 47 East South Temple St., Salt Lake City, Utah 84111.

**Church of Jesus Christ of Latter Day Saints, Reorganized** (1830)—Pres. W. Wallace Smith. President of the Council of Twelve Apostles, Clifford A. Cole. The Auditorium, Independence, Mo. 64051.

**Church of the Nazarene** (1908)—Gen. Sec., B. Edgar Johnson, 6401 The Paseo, Kansas City, Mo. 64131.

**Church of Scientology of California** (1954)— Pres., Julia L. Salmen. Sec., William Banka, 2005 9th St., Los Angeles, Calif.

**Churches of Christ**—No central organization. B. C. Goodpasture, editor, the Gospel Advocate, 1113 Eighth Ave. So., Nashville, Tenn. 372 4.

**Churches of God in North America, General Eldership** (1825)—Pres., Dr. G. Marion Smith, Sec., Dr. Arthur Eakin, R. D. 2, Box 1063A, Ellwood City, Pa. 16117.

**Congregational Christian Churches, General Council.** *See United Church of Christ.*

**Congregational Christian Churches, Natl. Assn. of** (1955)—Moderator, Rev. Malcolm K. Burton. Exec. Sec., A. Vaughan Abercrombie, 176 W. Wisconsin Ave., Milwaukee, Wis. 53203.

**Disciples of Christ.** *See Christian Churches, International Convention of.*

**Ethical Union, American (Ethical Culture Movement)**—Pres., Werner Klugman. Exec. Dir., H. B. Radest, 2 West 64th St., New York, N. Y. 10023. Member of Int. Humanist and Ethical Union.

**Evangelical Christian Churches** (1966)—Dir., Dr. Richard W. Hart, P. O. Box 742, Fontana, Calif. 92335.

**Evangelical Lutheran Synod (Norwegian Synod)** (1918)—Pres., Rev. J. B. Madson. Sec., Rev. W. C. Gullixson, Princeton, Minn. 55371.

**Evangelical Lutheran Synodical Conference of North America** (1872)—Pres., John Daniel, D.D., 1240 E. 4th St., Bethlehem, Pa. 18015.

**Evangelical Methodist Church** (1946)—Gen. Supt. Dr. Ralph A. Vanderwood. Gen. Sec., Rev. R. D. Driggers, 3036 N. Meridian, Wichita, Kan. 67204.

**Evangelical and Reformed Church.** *See United Church of Christ.*

**Finnish Evangelical Lutheran Church (Suomi Synod)** *See The Lutheran Church in America.*

**Foursquare Gospel, International Church of the** (1927)—Pres., Dr. Rolf K. McPherson. Sec., Dr. Herman D. Mitzner. 1100 Glendale Blvd., Los Angeles, Calif. 90026.

**Free Methodist Church of North America** (1860) —Sec., Board of Bishops, Bishop Paul N. Ellis, Winona Lake, Ind. 46590.

**Friends, General Conference of the Religious Society of** (1900)—Chmn., William Hubben. Gen. Sec., Lawrence McK. Miller, Jr., 1520 Race St., Philadelphia, Pa. 19102.

**Friends United Meeting (formerly, Five Years Meeting of Friends)** (1902)—Presiding Clerk, Byron Haworth. Gen. Sec., Lorton Heusel, 101 Quaker Hill Dr., Richmond, Ind. 47374.

**Greek Orthodox Church of North and South America** (1864)—Primate, the Most Rev. Archbishop Iakovos. Chan.. V. Rev. George J. Bacopulos, 10 East 79th St., New York, N. Y. 10021.

**Hebrew Congregations, Union of American**— Pres., Rabbi Maurice N. Eisendrath. 838 Fifth Ave., New York, N. Y. 10021.

**Independent Fundamental Churches of America** (1930)—Pres., Rev. Tunis Mouw. Exec. Sec., Rev. Glen A. Lehman, 145 N. Washington St., Wheaton, Ill. 60187.

**Jehovah's Witness** (1884)—Pres. Nathan H. Knorr, 124 Columbia Heights, Brooklyn, N. Y. 11201.

**Jewish Congregations of America, Union of Orthodox**—Pres., Joseph Karasick. Exec. Vice Pres., Dr. Samson R. Weiss, 84 Fifth Ave., New York, N. Y. 10011.

**Latter-day Saints.** *See Church of Jesus Christ.*

**Lutheran Church, The American** (1961)—Pres., Dr. F. A. Schiotz. Sec., A. R. Mickelson, 422 So. 5th St., Minneapolis, Minn. 55415.

**Lutheran Church in America, The** (estab. June 28, 1962 by merging Am. Evangelical Lutheran Ch., Augustana Evangelical Lutheran Ch., Finnish Evangelical Lutheran Ch., and The United Lutheran Ch. in Am.)—Pres., Rev. Robert J. Marshall. Sec., Rev. George F. Harkins, 231 Madison Ave., New York, N. Y. 10016.

**Lutheran Church-Missouri Synod** (1847)—Pres., Dr. Oliver R. Harms. Sec., Dr. Herbert A. Mueller, 210 No. Broadway, St. Louis, Mo. 60118.

**Lutheran World Federation, U. S. A. National**

**Committee of the** (formed Jan. 1, 1967, former National Lutheran Council)—Gen. Sec., Rev. Dr. Paul C. Empie, 315 Park Ave. South, N. Y., N. Y. 10010.

**Mennonite Church** (1863)—Moderator, John R. Mumaw. Exec. Sec., Howard J. Zehr, Mennonite Bldg., Scottdale, Pa. 15683.

**Methodist Church, The United** (1784)—Pres., Bishop Eugene M. Frank; Vice Pres., Bishop Rueben H. Mueller; Sec., Bishop Roy H. Short, 1115 S. Fourth St., Louisville, Ky. 40203.

**Moravian Church in America** (Unitas Fratrum) (1740)—**Northern Province:** Hq., 69 West Church St., Bethlehem, Pa. 18018; Pres., Provincial Elders' Conf., Dr. J. S. Groenfeldt. **Southern Province:** Hq., 500 So. Church St., Winston-Salem, N. C. 27101; Pres., Provincial Elders' Conf., Dr. R. Gordon Spaugh.

**New Jerusalem in the U. S. A., General Convention of the** (1782)—Pres., Rev. Ernest O. Martin. Rec. Sec., Mrs. Wilfred G. Rice, 31 Poole St., Brockton, Mass. 02401.

**Open Bible Standard Churches** (1919)—Gen. Supt., Raymond E. Smith, Sec.-Treas., O. Ralph Isbill, P. O. Box 1737, Des Moines, Ia. 50306.

**Pentecostal Church of God of America** (1919)—Gen. Supt., Rev. R. D. Heard, 316 Joplin Ave., Joplin, Mo. 64801.

**Pentecostal Church, United** (1945)—Gen. Supt., Stanley W. Chambers. Gen. Sec., Cleveland M. Becton, 3654 So. Grand Blvd., St. Louis, Mo. 63118.

**Presbyterian Church, Cumberland** (1810)—Moderator, Loyce S. Estes. Stated Clerk, H. Shaw Scates. Box 4149, Memphis, Tenn. 38104.

**Presbyterian Church in the U. S.** (1861)—Moderator, Rev. Patrick D. Miller. Stated Clerk, Dr. James A. Millard, Jr. 341 Ponce de Leon Ave., N.E., Atlanta, Ga. 30308.

**Presbyterian Church in the U.S.A., United** (formed 1958 through merger of the Presbyterian Ch. in the U. S. A. and the United Presbyt. Ch. of No. America)—Moderator, Rev. John C. Smith. Stated Clerk, Ruling Elder William P. Thompson. 510 Witherspoon Bldg., Philadelphia Pa. 19107.

**Primitive Baptist Convention of the U. S. A.** Natl. (1907)—Pres. of Natl. Convention, Rev. P. D. Brantley, 1795 N.W. 58th St., Miami, Fla.

**Protestant Episcopal Church, The** (1789)—Presiding Bishop, Pres. of Exec. Council, Rt. Rev. John E. Hines; Sec., Gen. Convention, Exec. Council, Rev. Canon Charles M. Guilbert, 815 Second Ave., New York, N. Y. 10017.

**Rabbinical Alliance of America**—Pres., Rabbi Bernard Weinberger, 156 5th Ave., New York, N. Y.

**Rabbinical Assembly, The**—Pres., Ralph Simon. Exec. Vice Pres., Rabbi Wolfe Kelman, 3080 Broadway, New York, N. Y. 10027.

**Rabbinical Council of America**—Pres., Rabbi Zev Segal. Exec. V. P., Rabbi Israel Klavan, 84 Fifth Ave., New York, N. Y. 10011.

**Rabbis, Central Conference of American**—Pres. Rabbi Levi A. Olan. Exec. Vice Pres., Rabbi Sidney L. Regner, 790 Madison Ave., New York, N. Y. 10021.

**Reformed Church in America** (1628)—Pres., Dr. Raymond R. Van Heukelom. Gen. Sec., Rev. Marion de Velder, D.D., 475 Riverside Dr., N. Y., N. Y. 10027.

**Reformed Episcopal Church** (1873)—President and Presiding Bishop, Rev. Howard D. Higgins. Sec., Rev. D. Ellsworth Raudenbush, 560 Fountain St., Havre de Grace, Md.

**Reformed Presbyterian Church, Evangelical Synod** (April 6, 1965, union of the **Reformed Presbyterian Church, General Synod** and the **Evangelical Presbyterian Church**)—Moderator, Mr. Wesley G. Vannoy, Ph.D. Stated Clerk, Rev. Harry H. Meiners, Jr., 1918 Missouri Avenue, Las Cruces, N. M. 88001.

**Regular Baptist Churches, General Assn. of** (1932)—Natl. Rep., Dr. Paul R. Jackson, 1800 Oakton Boulevard, Des Plaines, Ill. 60018.

**Romanian Orthodox Episcopate of America** (1929)—Bishop, His Grace Valerian D. Trifa. Sec. Rev. Eugene Lazar, 1465 Brown St., Akron, O. 44301.

**Russian Orthodox Church Outside Russia** (1920) —Pres., Council of Bishops, Most Rev. Metropolitan Philaret Voznesensky, 75 East 93rd St., New York, N. Y. 10028.

**Russian Orthodox Greek Catholic Church of America** (1792)—Ruling Bishop, Metropolitan—Archbishop Ireney. Chancellor, Rt. Rev. Joseph Pishtey, 59 East 2nd St., New York 3, N. Y.

**Salvation Army, The** (1865 in England, 1880 in America)—Natl. Cmdr., Commissioner Samuel Hepburn. Natl. Chief Sec., Lt. Comr. John Grace, National Headquarters, 120-130 West 14th St., New York, N. Y. 10011.

**Seamen's Church Institute of N. Y.** (1834)—Director, Rev. John M. Mulligan. Sec., Clifford M. Carver, 15 State St., New York, N. Y. 10004.

**Serbian Eastern Orthodox Church**—Diocese for U. S., Canada, and Europe. Bishops: Most Rev. Dionisije and Iriney. Sec., Very Rev. Aleksandar Ivanovich, St. Sava Monastery, Libertyville, Ill.

**Serbian Orthodox Church in U. S. and Canada**—Bishops: Rt. Rev. Firmilian, Midwest Diocese, 8347 W. Summerdale Ave., Chicago, Ill. 60656; Rt. Rev. Gregory, Western Diocese, 2511 W. Garvey, Alhambra, Calif. 91803; Rt. Rev. Sava, Eastern U. S. and Canadian Diocese, 5847 Broadview Rd., Cleveland, O. 44134.

**Serbian Orthodox Church, Free**—Diocese for Australia and New Zealand. Bishop Most Rev. Dimitrie, Austral, N.S.W. 2171, Australia.

**Spiritualists, International General Assembly** of (1936)—Pres., Fred Jordan. Sec.-Treas., Harold R. Levy, 1809 Bayview Blvd., Norfolk, Va. 23503.

**Synagogue Council of America**—Pres., Rabbi Jacob P. Rudin. Exec. V. P. Rabbi Henry Siegman, 235 Fifth Ave., New York, N. Y. 10016.

**Syrian Antiochian Orthodox Church** (1894)—Head of Archdiocese, Metropn. Archbishop Philip (Saliba), 239 85th St., Brooklyn, N. Y. 10009.

**Ukrainian Orthodox Church of U. S. A.** (1919)—President of Consistory, Archbishop Mstyslaw S. Skrypnyk. Sec., Very Rev. Bohdan Zelechiwsky, Box 595, South Bound Brook, N. J. 08880.

**Unitarian Universalist Assn.** (formed May 11, 1961 by merger of the American Unitarian Assn. and the Universalist Church of America)—Pres., Rev. Dana McLean Greeley. Moderator, Dr. Joseph L. Fisher. Sec., Mrs. J. Robert Reynolds, 25 Beacon St., Boston, Mass. 02108.

**United Church of Christ** (formed June 25, 1957, through union of the General Council of the Congregational Christian Churches with the Evangelical and Reformed Church)—President, Rev. Dr. Ben M. Herbster. Sec., Rev. Joseph H. Evans, 297 Park Ave. South, New York, N. Y. 10010.

**United Israel World Union**—Pres. & Chmn. of the Board, David Horowitz. Sec., Peter-Shimon Olin Moyle, 507 Fifth Ave., New York 17, N. Y.

**United Sons & Daughters of True Holiness Assn.**, (1912)—Gen. Secy., Rev. Edward R. Everette, 2132A Fulton St., Bklyn, N. Y.

**United Synagogue of America**—Pres., Henry N. Rapaport. Exec. Dir., Dr. Bernard Segal, 3080 Broadway, New York, N. Y. 10027.

**Volunteers of America** (1896)—Commander-in-Chief, Gen. John F. McMahon. Natl. Field Sec., Col. E. R. Coleman. Hq., 340 West 85th St., New York, N. Y. 10024. (*See page 162.*)

**Wesleyan Methodist Church of America, The** (1843)—General Superintendents, Dr. B. H. Phaup, Dr. Harold K. Sheets, Dr. Virgil A. Mitchell. Gen. Conf. Sec., Rev. Garl Beaver, P. O. Box 2000, Marion, Ind.

**Wisconsin Evangelical Lutheran Synod** (1850)—Pres., Rev. Oscar Naumann. Sec., Paul R. Hanke, 425 West Mulberry, Box 32, St. Peter, Minn. 56082.

**World Council of Christian Education**—Gen. Sec., Rev. Ralph Mould, 150 Route de Ferney, 1211 Geneva 20, Switzerland.

**World Council of Churches, U. S. Conference for** the—Chmn., Dr. John Coventry Smith. Exec. Sec., Dr. Eugene L. Smith, 475 Riverside Dr., New York, N. Y. 10027.

---

# The World Council of Churches

The World Council of Churches is a fellowship of 232 Protestant, Anglican, Orthodox and Old Catholic churches from 90 countries and territories throughout the world. It was founded in Amsterdam in 1948 and stresses evangelical projects, the study of Christian doctrine and inter-church cooperation in philanthropic undertakings such as aid and service to refugees. The Council has no judicial powers over its member churches. Denominations belonging to the Council have an estimated 400,000,000 members. The Roman Catholic Church is not a Council member. Every 5 or 6 years a world Assembly of member churches is held. The Fourth Assembly was held in Uppsala, Sweden, July 4-20, 1968. The Central Committee, policy making body of the WCC between assemblies, will meet in Kent, England, Aug. 12-23, 1969. World headquarters of the Council are in Geneva, Switzerland where the offices of General Secy. Dr. Eugene Blake are located. The Council's New York office is located at 475 Riverside Drive, New York, N. Y. 10027.

# Leading Protestant Bodies in the United States

## Baptists

The Baptist church was formed in Europe during the Protestant Reformation.

The first Baptist Church in America was founded in 1638 in Providence, R. I., by Roger Williams. National Organization began in 1814, and a Missionary Convention was formed to permit followers to express themselves in terms of missionary activities. Baptist bodies throughout the United States have a membership of 26,386,262.

**American Baptist Convention** (formerly Northern Baptist Convention) was organized in 1907. Renamed in 1950. Churches, 6,085, membership, 1,555,460. Headquarters at Valley Forge, Pa. 19481, with regional offices at 475 Riverside Dr., New York, N. Y. 10027, and 2855 Telegraph Ave., Berkeley, Calif. 94705. Agencies operating under this convention of Baptists include the American Baptist Foreign Mission Society, American Baptist Board of Education and Publication, and Ministers and Missionaries Benefit Board, all at Valley Forge, Pa. 19481.

**National Baptist Convention of America**, org. 1880. Churches, 11,398; membership, 2,668,799. The General Organization and 11 others. Pres., Dr. C. D. Pettaway, 714 West 10th St., Little Rock, Ark.

**National Baptist Convention, U. S. A., Inc.,** founded in 1880, in Montgomery, Alabama, is the oldest and parent convention of Negro Baptists. Churches, 27,369; membership, 6,410,017. Pres. Dr. J. H. Jackson; Gen. Sec., Dr. T. J. Jemison, 915 Spain St., Baton Rouge, La. 70802.

**Southern Baptist Convention.** In 1845 Southern Baptists withdrew from the General Missionary Convention over the question of slavery and other matters and formed the Southern Baptist Convention, largest of Baptist bodies. Churches in all 50 states are related to the Convention. 2,277 missionaries serve in 66 countries. Churches, 34,147; membership, 11,142,726. Executive Committee, 460 James Robertson Parkway, Nashville, Tenn. 37219. Exec. Sec., Dr. Porter Routh. Boards include Sunday School Board, Nashville, Tenn.; Foreign Mission Board, Richmond, Va.; Home Mission Board, Atlanta, Ga.; Annuity Board, Dallas, Tex.

## Church of Christ, Scientist

First organized in 1879, under the direction of Mary Baker Eddy, the Christian Science Church took its present form in 1892 as the Mother Church, the First Church of Christ, Scientist, in Boston, Mass. Today there are 3,272 branches in 58 countries. There are 2,438 Christian Science churches in the United States. Christian Science regards the Bible as its ultimate authority and includes spiritual healing as part of its teachings.

The denomination supports radio and television programs, charitable institutions, and a worldwide Board of Lectureship. It also maintains the Christian Science Publishing Society which publishes the Christian Science Monitor and various religious periodicals. The affairs of the denomination are administered by the Christian Science Board of Directors, 107 Falmouth St., Boston, Mass. 02115. Pres., Mrs. Beatrice Thayer Pittman.

## Disciples of Christ

The Christian Churches (Disciples of Christ) is an American communion arising out of a concern for Christian unity expressed by Barton W. Stone in 1804 and by Thomas Campbell and his son Alexander, in 1809. The first churches were Cane Ridge in Ky. and Brush Run near Washington, Pa. The "Christians" of Kentucky and the "Disciples" of Pennsylvania and Virginia united in 1832. The first General Convention was held in 1849. A missionary society was formed. The movement is congregational in government. Churches in the United States and Canada number 8,046; membership is 1,883,263. The communion is served by the International Convention, 16 member bodies, 40 state societies and 34 educational institutions. Exec. Sec., Dr. A. Dale Fiers, 221 Ohmer Ave., Indianapolis, Ind. 46219.

## Evangelical Churches

**The Evangelical and Reformed Church.** *See United Church of Christ.*

**The Evangelical United Brethren Church.** *See United Methodist Church.*

## Lutherans

The church was started in Europe during the Protestant Reformation by the followers of Martin Luther.

Lutheranism was introduced into the United States by Dutch colonists on Manhattan, later by Swedes on the Delaware, by Palatines in Pennsylvania and New York and by Salzburgers in Georgia.

**The American Lutheran Church** was organized during a constituting convention at Minneapolis, Minn., in April 1960, merging the American Lutheran Church, The Evangelical Lutheran Church, and United Evangelical Lutheran Church. The merger brought together Lutherans of Danish, German and Norwegian heritage. A fourth body, The Lutheran Free Church, joined with The American Lutheran Church in February 1963. The American Lutheran Church has 2,576,027 members. Headquarters at 422 So. 5th St., Minneapolis. Dr. F. A. Schiotz is president. Regional offices in Chicago, Dallas, Minneapolis, Palo Alto and Washington, D. C. The 4,906 congregations are divided territorially into 18 districts in the U. S. The foreign mission program involves 670 missionaries (including wives) on 12 fields in South America, Africa and Asia. The church's Board of Publication operates the Augsburg Publishing House, 426 So. 5th St., Minneapolis 55415.

**Augustana Evangelical Lutheran Church.** *See The Lutheran Church in America.*

**The Lutheran Church-Missouri Synod** was organized in 1847. It is the leader in the conservative group among the Lutherans with 6,774 churches and a membership of 3,009,189. The Synod is divided into 37 districts (32 in the U. S.; 3 in Canada; 2 in South America). The Synod conducts a worldwide mission program and fosters a system of ministerial and teacher training to staff its congregations and its 1,326 parochial schools. Affiliated are the Lutheran Laymen's League, Lutheran Women's Missionary League, and Walther League (a young people's organization). Valparaiso University, Valparaiso, Ind., is supported and controlled by the Lutheran University Assn. Headq. for the Synod; 210 No. Broadway, St. Louis, Mo.

**The Lutheran Church in America** was organized June 28, 1962 by the consolidation of the American Evangelical Lutheran Church, the Augustana Evangelical Lutheran Church, the Finnish Evangelical Lutheran Church and The United Lutheran Church in America. With 3,288,037 baptized members, the new body is the largest of the Lutheran churches in the United States. The Lutheran Church in America has 6,242 congregations, organized in 33 constituent synods. The headquarters of the denomination is at 231 Madison Ave., New York, N. Y. 10016, and principal agencies are located at 2900 Queen Lane, Philadelphia, Pa., 327 South LaSalle St., Chicago, Ill., and the Pillsbury Building, Minneapolis, Minn.

**Wisconsin Evangelical Lutheran Synod,** organized in 1850. It has 908 congregations, 368,000 members. Formerly the second largest body of the Synodical Conference, Wisconsin withdrew from the Conference in August 1963.

## Methodists

The name Methodist was originally given to Charles and John Wesley and several other Oxford students, in 1729. It is thought that the term was selected due to the exact and "methodical" manner in which they performed various engagements which a sense of Christian duty induced them to undertake. The Methodist movement was carried to America in 1760 by emigrants from Ireland. Methodist bodies in the United States (20) have a membership of 13,273,417.

**The United Methodist Church** has 42,165 churches and 11,035,313 members. The present organization of The United Methodist Church was formed Apr. 23, 1968, in Dallas, Tex., by the union of The Methodist Church and The Evangelical United Brethren Church. The two churches shared a common historical and spiritual heritage. The Methodist Church resulted in 1939 from the unification of three branches of Methodism—the Methodist Episcopal Church, the Methodist Episcopal Church, South, and the Methodist Protestant Church. The Methodist movement began in 18th Century England under the preaching of John Wesley, but the

so-called Christmas Conference of 1784 in Baltimore is regarded as the date on which the organized Methodist Church was founded as an ecclesiastical organization. It was there that Francis Asbury was elected the first bishop in this country. The Evangelical United Brethren Church was formed in 1946 with the merger of the Evangelical Church and the Church of the United Brethren in Christ, both of which had their beginnings in Pennsylvania in the evangelistic movement of the 18th and early 19th centuries. Philip William Otterbein and Jacob Albright were early leaders of this movement among German-speaking settlers of the Middle Colonies.

The supreme policy-making body of The United Methodist Church is the quadrennial General Conference. Principal agencies are in the following cities: New York, N. Y., Evanston, Ill., Nashville, Tenn., Washington, D. C., Dayton, O., and Lake Junaluska, N. C.

**African Methodist Episcopal Church,** incorporated 1816 under Pennsylvania laws, is second largest of the Methodist bodies. Churches, 6,105, membership, 1,405,000. President, Council of Bishops, Bishop H. Thomas Primm, 1724 Villa Place, Nashville, Tenn.

## Presbyterians

Presbyterianism is a system of representative church government by presbyters, or elders. John Calvin (1509-1564) has been regarded as the founder of Presbyterianism. Presbyterians were among the earliest colonists of America. Their first church was established about 1640 and the first presbytery in 1706. Nine Presbyterian bodies in the United States have a membership of 4,410,000.

**The United Presbyterian Church in the U.S.A.,** largest of the Presbyterian bodies, was formed on May 28, 1958 by a merger of the Presbyterian Church in the U.S.A. and the United Presbyterian Church of North America. It has 8,877 churches and 3,268,761 members. Offices of the General Assembly, Board of Christian Education and Board of Pensions, Witherspoon Bldg., Philadelphia, Pa. 19107. Offices of the General Council, Board of Nat'l. Missions, Commission on Ecumenical Mission and Relations and Council on Theological Education, 475 Riverside Dr., New York, N. Y. 10027.

**Presbyterian Church in the United States,** which established a separate existence in 1861, is sometimes miscalled the Southern Church. Churches, 3,987, membership, 960,776. Office of the Gen. Assembly, 341 Ponce de Leon Ave., N.E., Atlanta, Ga. 30308. Moderator, Rev. Dr. Patrick D. Miller; Stated Clerk, Rev. Dr. James A. Millard, Jr.

## Protestant Episcopal Church

An American religious denomination directly descended from the Church of England. Brought to America by the Jamestown colonists in 1607. Separated from English church and adopted present name in 1789. Constitutional amendment to recognize "The Episcopal Church" as an alternative name was adopted in 1967. Churches, 7,546; membership, 3,588,435. Headquarters of the Exec. Council, 815 Second Ave., N. Y., N. Y. Presiding Bishop, Rt. Rev. John E. Hines; Sec. of Gen. Convention and Exec. Council, Rev. Canon Charles M. Guilbert.

## United Church of Christ

Formed in 1957 by a union of the General Council of the Congregational Christian Church and the Evangelical and Reformed Church. It is the first union in the United States of churches with different forms of church government—congregational and modified presbyterian—and different historical backgrounds. Congregationalism was brought to America by both the Pilgrims of the "Mayflower" and the Puritans of the Mass. Bay Colony. Eventually it became the dominant form of church organization in New England. The Evangelical and Reformed Church was started in 1934 with the union of the Evangelical Synod of North America and the Reformed Church in the U. S.

A constitution for the United Church of Christ was declared in force in July, 1961. The denomination has 2,052,857 members in 6,909 local congregations. The United Church Board for World Ministries has 450 missionaries and other personnel at work in 30 countries. In the United States, the United Church of Christ is active in Christian education, church extension, health and welfare, mass communication, race relations, and social action. Headquarters of United Church of Christ, 297 Park Ave. So., New York, N. Y. 10010; Office of Communication, 289 Park Ave. So., New York, N. Y. United Church Board for Homeland Ministries, 287 Park Ave. So. United Church Board for World Ministries, 475 Riverside Dr., New York, N. Y. 10027.

## Latter-Day Saints

The churches of the Latter-Day Saints do not consider themselves Protestants because they had no part in the 16th century Protestant Reformation.

**The Church of Jesus Christ of Latter-Day Saints,** often called the "Mormon" church, regards the Bible, the Book of Mormon, the Doctrine and Covenants, and the Pearl of Great Price as the word of God. The church was organized Apr. 6, 1830, at Fayette, Seneca Co., N. Y., by Joseph Smith, first president. After settling in Kirtland, O., and Independence, Mo., the members located in Nauvoo, Ill., in 1839 to escape persecution. Attacks by a mob led to the fatal shooting of Joseph Smith and his brother Hyrum while they were in the Carthage, Ill., jail for protection from the mob, June 27, 1844. Beginning in 1847 many members under the leadership of Brigham Young, moved by covered wagons across the Plains to Utah.

The church is divided into stakes, wards, branches and missions. Highest authority is the First Presidency, consisting of the President and 5 counselors, assisted by 12 apostles. David O. McKay is the 9th and current President. Total membership, 2,614,340. Headq. at 47 East South Temple St., Salt Lake City, Utah.

Following the death of Joseph Smith in 1844, the scattered congregations that did not leave for the Far West formed the **Reorganized Church of Jesus Christ of Latter-Day Saints,** with the founder's son, Joseph Smith, as president. Churches, 1,100 (U. S. and Canada); membership, 196,512 (U. S., Canada and 18 foreign missions). Hq., the Auditorium, Independence, Mo. 64051.

# Religious Population of the World

**Source:** The Encyclopedia Britannica's 1968 Book of the Year. 1967 estimated memberships.

| Religion | North America[1] | South America | Europe | Asia | Africa | Oceania[2] | Total |
|---|---|---|---|---|---|---|---|
| Total Christian | 208,018,000 | 148,937,000 | 502,280,000 | 60,864,000 | 44,238,000 | 13,646,000 | 977,383,000 |
| Roman Cath. | 121,604,000 | 146,017,000 | 251,453,000 | 47,151,000 | 30,556,000 | 3,987,000 | 600,768,000 |
| East Orth. | 3,639,000 | 47,000 | 134,233,000 | 2,805,000 | 5,272,000 | 84,000 | 146,080,000 |
| Protestant | 82,775,000 | 2,873,000 | 116,594,000 | 10,908,000 | 8,410,000 | 8,975,000 | 230,535,000 |
| Jewish[3] | 6,035,000 | 705,000 | 4,025,000 | 2,460,000 | 238,000 | 74,000 | 13,537,000 |
| Moslem[4] | 41,000 | 416,000 | 13,576,000 | 359,776,000 | 100,382,000 | 118,000 | 474,309,000 |
| Zoroastrian | .......... | .......... | .......... | 150,000 | .......... | .......... | 150,000 |
| Shinto | 31,000 | 115,000 | 2,000 | 70,215,000 | .......... | .......... | 70,363,000 |
| Taoist | 16,000 | 19,000 | 12,000 | 54,277,000 | .......... | .......... | 54,324,000 |
| Confucian | 96,000 | 109,000 | 55,000 | 371,261,000 | 9,000 | 57,000 | 371,587,000 |
| Buddhist[5] | 182,000 | 157,000 | .......... | 171,425,000 | .......... | .......... | 171,764,000 |
| Hindu | 54,000 | 623,000 | 160,000 | 421,869,000 | 1,455,000 | 218,000 | 424,379,000 |
| Others or none.. | 81,619,000 | 19,138,000 | 101,191,000 | 462,185,000 | 165,743,000 | 4,182,000 | 834,058,000 |
| **Grand total** | **296,092,000** | **170,219,000** | **621,301,000** | **1,974,482,000** | **312,065,000** | **17,695,000** | **3,391,854,000** |

[1]Includes Central America and the West Indies. [2]Includes Australia, New Zealand. [3]Includes total Jewish population whether or not related to the synagogue. [4]Moslem figures for China are unknown; estimates vary from 12,000,000 to 50,000,000. [5]No one knows how many Buddhists there are; estimates vary greatly as many are in China and any accurate count is impossible.

# Active Bishops of the Protestant Episcopal Church

Source: Rt. Rev. Scott Field Bailey, Sec., House of Bishops, 520 San Jacinto St., Houston, Tex. 77002
**PRESIDING BISHOP: Rt. Rev. John Elbridge Hines**, 815 Second Ave., N. Y. C. 10017

(M) Missionary Bishop; (C) Coadjutor; (S) Suffragan

**Alabama:** Charles C. J. Carpenter, George M. Murray (C), Birmingham.
**Alaska:** William J. Gordon, Jr. (M), Fairbanks.
**Albany (N. Y.):** Allen W. Brown, Charles B. Persell (S).
**Arizona:** Joseph M. Harte, Phoenix.
**Arkansas:** Robert R. Brown, Little Rock, Christoph Keller (S).
**Atlanta (Ga.):** Randolph R. Claiborne, Milton L. Wood (S).
**Bethlehem (Pa.):** Frederick J. Warnecke.
**California:** C. Kilmer Myers, George R. Millard (S), San Francisco.
**Costa Rica:** David E. Richards (M), San Jose, Costa Rica.
**Central New York:** Walter M. Higley, Ned Cole, Jr. (C), Syracuse.
**Chicago:** Gerald F. Burrill, J. W. Montgomery (C).
**Colombia, South America:** David B. Reed (M), Bogota.
**Colorado:** Edwin B. Thayer (M), Denver.
**Connecticut:** Walter H. Gray, John H. Esquirol (C), Joseph Warren Hutchens (S), Hartford.
**Dallas (Tex.):** C. Avery Mason, Theodore H. McCrea (S). William P. Barnds (S).
**Delaware:** J. Brooke Mosley, Wilmington.
**Dominican Republic:** Paul A. Kellogg (M), Santo Domingo.
**East Carolina:** Thomas H. Wright, Hunley A. Elebash (C), Wilmington, N. C.
**Eastern Oregon:** Lane W. Barton (M), Bend.
**Easton (Md.):** George A. Taylor.
**Eau Claire (Wis.):** William W. Horstick.
**Erie (Pa.):** William Crittenden.
**Executive Council:** Stephen F. Bayne Jr., First Vice-President of Executive Council; Daniel Corrigan, Director of Home Dept., N. Y. C.; Arnold M. Lewis, Suffragan Bishop to Armed Forces.
**Florida:** Hamilton West, Jacksonville.
**Fond du Lac (Wis.):** William H. Brady.
**Georgia:** Albert R. Stuart, Savannah.
**Guatemala:** William C. Fry.
**Haiti:** C. A. Voegeli (M).
**Harrisburg (Pa.):** Dean T. Stevenson, Harrisburg; Earl M. Honaman (S), Williamsport.
**Honolulu:** Harry S. Kennedy (M), Edwin L. Hancherr (S).
**Idaho:** Norman L. Foote (M), Boise.
**Indianapolis:** John P. Craine.
**Iowa:** Gordon V. Smith, Des Moines.
**Kansas:** Edward C Turner, Topeka.
**Kentucky:** C. Gresham Marmion Jr., Louisville.
**Lexington (Ky.):** William R. Moody.
**Liberia:** Dillard Houston Brown, Jr. (M), Monrovia.
**Long Island:** Jonathan G. Sherman, Charles W. MacLean (S), R. B. Martin (S), Garden City, N. Y.
**Los Angeles:** Francis Bloy, Robert C. Rusack (S).
**Louisiana:** Girault M. Jones, New Orleans; Iveson B. Noland (C), Baton Rouge.
**Maine:** Frederick B. Wolf, Portland.
**Maryland:** Harry L. Doll, Baltimore.
**Massachusetts:** Anson Phelps Stokes, Jr., Boston, John M. Burgess (S).
**Mexico:** Jose G. Saucedo (M), Mexico City; Leonardo Romero (S), Monterey; Melchor Saucedo (S), Guadalajara.
**Michigan:** Richard S. Emrich, Archie H. Crowley (S), Detroit.
**Milwaukee:** Donald H. V. Hallock.
**Minnesota:** Hamilton H. Kellogg, Phillip F. McNairy (S), Minneapolis.
**Mississippi:** John Maury Allin.
**Missouri:** George L. Cadigan, St. Louis.

**Montana:** Jackson E. Gilliam, Helena.
**Nebraska:** Russell T. Rauscher, Omaha.
**Nevada:** William G. Wright (M), Reno.
**New Hampshire:** Charles F. Hall, Concord.
**New Jersey:** Alfred L. Banyard, Albert W. Van Duzer (S), Trenton.
**New Mexico and Southwest Texas:** Charles J. Kinsolving III, Santa Fe, N. M.
**New York:** Horace W. B. Donegan, Charles F. Boynton (S), J. Stuart Wetmore (S), N. Y. C.
**Newark (N. J.):** Leland Stark, George E. Rath (S).
**North Carolina:** Thomas A. Fraser, Jr., Raleigh.
**North Dakota:** George T. Masuda (M), Fargo.
**Northern California:** Clarence R. Haden, Jr., Edward M. McNair (S), Sacramento.
**Northern Indiana:** Walter C. Klein, South Bend.
**Northern Michigan:** George R. Selway, Menominee
**Northwest Texas:** George H. Quarterman, Amarillo.
**Ohio:** Nelson M. Burroughs, John H. Burt (C), Cleveland.
**Oklahoma:** Chilton Powell, Frederick W. Putnam, Jr. (S), Oklahoma City.
**Olympia, Wash.:** Ivol I. Curtis, Seattle.
**Oregon:** James W. F. Carman, Portland; Hal R. Gross (S), Portland.
**Panama Canal Zone:** Reginald H. Gooden (M), Balboa.
**Pennsylvania:** Robert L. DeWitt, Philadelphia.
**Philippines:** Benito C. Cabanban (M), Edward G. Longid (S), Mt. Province.
**Pittsburgh:** Robert Appleyard.
**Puerto Rico:** Francisco Reus-Froylan, Santurce.
**Quincy (Ill.):** William Lickfield.
**Rhode Island:** John S. Higgins, Providence.
**Rochester (N. Y.):** George W. Barrett.
**San Joaquin (Calif.):** Victor M. Rivera, Stockton.
**South Carolina:** Gray Temple, Charleston.
**South Dakota:** Conrad H. Gesner (M), Lyman C. Ogilby (C), Sioux Falls.
**South Florida:** Henry I. Louttit, Winter Park; James L. Duncan (S), Miami; William L. Hargrave (S). St. Petersburg.
**Southern Ohio:** Roger W. Blanchard, Cincinnati.
**Southern Virginia:** George P. Gunn, Norfolk; David S. Rose (C), Petersburg.
**Southwestern Virginia:** William H. Marmion, Roanoke.
**Spokane (Wash.):** John R. Wyatt.
**Springfield (Ill.):** Albert A. Chambers.
**Taiwan:** James C. Wong (M), Taipei.
**Tennessee:** John Vander Horst, Memphis; William E. Sanders (C), Knoxville, William F. Gates Jr., (S), Memphis.
**Texas:** J. Milton Richardson, Houston; Percy Goddard (S), Tyler; Scott F. Bailey (S).
**Upper South Carolina:** John Pinckney, Columbia.
**Utah:** Richard S. Watson (M), Salt Lake City.
**Vermont:** Harvey D. Butterfield, Burlington.
**Virgin Islands:** Cedric E. Mills (M), St. Thomas.
**Virginia:** Robert F. Gibson, Jr., Samuel B. Chilton (S), Robert B. Hall (C), Richmond.
**Washington (D. C.):** William F. Creighton, Paul Moore, Jr. (S).
**West Missouri:** Edward R. Welles, Robert R. Spears Jr., (S), Kansas City.
**West Texas:** Everett H. Jones, Harold C. Gosnell (C), R. Earl Dicus (S), San Antonio.
**West Virginia:** Wilburn C. Campbell, Charleston.
**Western Kansas:** William Davidson (M), Salina.
**Western Mass.:** Robert M. Hatch, Springfield.
**Western Michigan:** Charles E. Bennison, Kalamazoo.
**Western New York:** Lauriston L. Scaife, Harold B. Robinson (C), Buffalo.
**Western North Carolina:** M. George Henry, Asheville, N. C.
**Wyoming:** James W. Hunter (M), Laramie.

The three Missionary Districts of Central, Southern, and Southwestern Brazil became an independent branch of the Anglican Communion in 1965 fulfilling the action of the General Convention of 1964.

# Catholics, Protestants Prepare for a Common Bible

A major step toward publication of a common Christian Bible was taken in 1968 by the Roman Catholic Church and the United Bible Societies, a mostly Protestant organization.

Experts of the two bodies culminated nearly 5 years of work with publication on June 1 of a set of guiding principles for interfaith cooperation in translating the Bible.

The document prepared the way for a Bible which will include new translations of ancient basic texts with analyses, to be published in all the world's languages and dialects.

The project followed a decision of the United Bible Societies to produce Bibles which would meet the canonical requirements of all churches, and a recommendation by the Ecumenical Council Vatican II, for considering cooperation with other Christians in a new Bible translation.

## Protestant Episcopal Calendar and Altar Colors

**White**—From the First Service (First Vespers) of Christmas Day to the Octave of Epiphany, inclusive (except on the Feasts of Martyrs); on Maundy Thursday (for the celebration); from the First Service of Easter Day to the Vigil of Pentecost (except on Feasts of Martyrs and Rogation Days); on Trinity Sunday, Conversion of St. Paul, Purification, Annunciation, St. John Baptist, St. Michael, All Saints, Saints not Martyrs, and Patron Saints (Transfiguration and Dedication of Church).

**Red**—From First Vespers of Pentecost to the First Vespers of Trinity Sunday (which includes Ember Days); Holy Innocents, and Feasts of all Martyrs, Apostles and Evangelists.

**Violet**—From Septuagesima to Maundy Thursday; Easter Even; Advent Sunday to Christmas Eve, Vigils, Ember Days (except in Whitsun Week); and Rogation Days.

An alternate Lenten color scheme: **Violet**—from Septuagesima to the Tuesday before Ash Wednesday; **Lenten White**—from Ash Wednesday to the Saturday after Fourth Lent; and **Crimson**—from Passion Sunday (Fifth Lent) to Easter Even (all inclusive).

**Black**—Good Friday and at funerals. **Green**—All other days.

| Days, Etc. | 1969 | 1970 | 1971 | 1972 | 1973 | 1974 | 1975 |
|---|---|---|---|---|---|---|---|
| Golden Number | 13 | 14 | 15 | 16 | 17 | 18 | O |
| Sunday Letter | E | D | C | BA | G | F | E |
| Sundays after Epiphany | 3 | 2 | 4 | 3 | 6 | 4 | 2 |
| Septuagesima | Feb. 2 | Jan. 25 | Feb. 6 | Jan. 30 | Feb. 18 | Feb. 10 | Jan. 26 |
| Ash Wednesday | Feb. 19 | Feb. 11 | Feb. 24 | Feb. 16 | Mar. 7 | Feb. 27 | Feb. 12 |
| First Sunday in Lent | Feb. 23 | Feb. 15 | Feb. 28 | Feb. 20 | Mar. 11 | Mar. 3 | Feb. 16 |
| Passion Sunday | Mar. 23 | Mar. 15 | Mar. 28 | Mar. 19 | Apr. 8 | Mar. 31 | Mar. 16 |
| Palm Sunday | Mar. 30 | Mar. 22 | Apr. 4 | Mar. 26 | Apr. 15 | Apr. 7 | Mar. 23 |
| Good Friday | Apr. 4 | Mar. 27 | Apr. 9 | Mar. 31 | Apr. 20 | Apr. 12 | Mar. 28 |
| Easter Day | Apr. 6 | Mar. 29 | Apr. 11 | Apr. 2 | Apr. 22 | Apr. 14 | Mar. 30 |
| Rogation Sunday | May 11 | May 3 | May 16 | May 7 | May 27 | May 19 | May 4 |
| Ascension Day | May 15 | May 7 | May 20 | May 11 | May 31 | May 23 | May 8 |
| Whitsunday | May 25 | May 17 | May 30 | May 21 | June 10 | June 2 | May 18 |
| Trinity Sunday | June 1 | May 24 | June 6 | May 28 | June 17 | June 9 | May 25 |
| Sundays after Trinity | 25 | 26 | 24 | 26 | 23 | 24 | 26 |
| First Sunday in Advent | Nov. 30 | Nov. 29 | Nov. 28 | Dec. 3 | Dec. 2 | Dec. 1 | Nov. 30 |

In the Protestant Episcopal Church the days of fasting are Ash Wednesday and Good Friday. Other days of abstinence are the 40 days of Lent, the Ember Days, and all Fridays of the year except Christmas Day and the Epiphany and any Friday which may fall between them. Ember Days (12 annually at about the beginning of the four seasons) are days of abstinence and prayer for ordinands and the increase of the ministry. They fall on the Wednesday, Friday, and Saturday after the first Sunday in Lent, the Feast of Pentecost (Whitsunday), September 14, and December 13. Rogation Days are the three days from Rogation Sunday (the fifth after Easter) to Ascension Day, and are days of solemn supplication for God's blessing upon the fields and harvests of the world.

## Bishops of the United Methodist Church

**Source:** United Methodist Information, 777 United Nations Plaza, New York, N. Y. 10017
President: Bishop Eugene M. Frank, St. Louis, Mo. (to April 1969). President-designate: Bishop Reuben H. Mueller, Indianapolis, Ind. Secretary: Bishop Roy H. Short, 1115 So. Fourth St., Louisville, Ky. 40203

Allen, L. Scott, Knoxville, Tenn.
Alton, Ralph T., Madison, Wis.
Andreassen, Harry P., Luanda, Angola
Armstrong, A. James, Aberdeen, S. C.
Barbieri, Sante Uberto, Buenos Aires
Cannon, William R., Raleigh, N. C.
Carleton, Alsie H., Albuquerque, N. M.
Chen, W. Y.
Copeland, Kenneth W., Houston, Tex.
Ensley, F. Gerald, Columbus, Ohio
Finger, Jr., H. Ellis, Nashville, Tenn.
Frank, Eugene M., St. Louis, Mo.
Galloway, Paul V., Little Rock, Ark.
Golden, Charles F., San Francisco, Cal.
Goodson, W. Kenneth, Birmingham, Ala.
Hagen, Odd, Stockholm, Sweden
Hardin, Jr., Paul, Columbia, S. C.
Henley, James W., Lakeland, Fla.
Herrick, Paul M., Richmond, Va.
Howard, J. Gordon, Philadelphia, Pa.
Hunt, Jr., Earl G., Charlotte, N. C.
Kaebnick, Hermann W., Harrisburg, Pa.
Kearns, Francis E., Canton, Ohio
Kennedy, Gerald, Los Angeles, Cal.
Loder, Dwight E., Detroit, Mich.
Lord, John Wesley, Washington, D. C.
Mathews, James K., Boston, Mass.
Milhouse, Paul W., Oklahoma City, Okla.
Moore, Jr., Noah W., Lincoln, Neb.
Mueller, Reuben H., Indianapolis, Ind.
Muzorewa, Abel, Salisbury, Rhodesia

Nagbe, Stephen Trowen, Monrovia, Liberia
Nall, T. Otto, Hong Kong
Nichols, Roy C., Pittsburgh, Pa.
Palmer, Everett W., Portland, Ore.
Pendergrass, Edward J., Jackson, Miss.
Pope, W. Kenneth, Dallas, Tex.
Pryor, Thomas M., Chicago, Ill.
Schafer, Franz, Zurich, Switzerland
Shaw, Alfred J., Bombay, India
Short, Roy H., Louisville, Ky.
Shungu, John Wesley, Luluabourg, Congo
Singh, Mangal, Delhi, India
Slater, O. Eugene, San Antonio, Tex.
Smith, John Owen, Atlanta, Ga.
Sommer, Carl E., Frankfurt, Germany
Sparks, W. Maynard, Seattle, Wash.
Stowe, W. McFerrin, Topeka, Kans.
Stuart, R. Marvin, Denver, Colo.
Sundaram, Gabriel, Hyderabad, India
Taylor, Jr., Prince A., Princeton, N. J.
Thomas, James S., Des Moines, Iowa
Valencia, Jose L., Baguio City, Philippines
Walton, Aubrey G., New Orleans, La.
Ward, W. Ralph, Syracuse, N. Y.
Washburn, Paul, Minneapolis, Minn.
Webb, Lance, Springfield, Ill.
Wertz, D. Frederick, Charleston, W. Va.
Wicke, Lloyd C., Rye, N. Y.
Zottele, Pedro, Santiago, Chile
Zunguze, Escrivao A., Loureco Marques, Mozambique

## Islamic (Moslem) Calendar 1969-1970

The Islamic calendar, often referred to as Mohammedan, is a lunar reckoning from the year of the hegira, 622 A.D., when Mohammed fled from Mecca. It runs in cycles of 30 years, of which the second, 5th, 7th, 10th, 13th, 16th, 18th, 21st, 24th, 26th and 29th are leap years. Common years have 354 days, leap years 355, the extra day being added to the last month, Zu'lhijjah. Except for this case, the 12 months beginning with Muharram have alternately 30 and 29 days. The month begins at sunset on the day before that given in the tables. *Leap year, 30 days.

| Year | Name of the Month | Month Begins | Year | Name of the Month | Month Begins |
|---|---|---|---|---|---|
| 1388 | Zu'lkadah | Jan. 20, 1969 | 1389 | Rajab | Sept. 13, 1969 |
| 1388 | Zu'lhijjah | Feb. 19, 1969 | 1389 | Shaban | Oct. 13, 1969 |
| 1389 | Muharram (New Year) | Mar. 20, 1969 | 1389 | Ramadan | Nov. 11, 1969 |
| 1389 | Safar | Apr. 19, 1969 | 1389 | Shawwal | Dec. 11, 1969 |
| 1389 | Rabia I | May 18, 1969 | 1389 | Zu'lkadah | Jan. 9, 1970 |
| 1389 | Rabia II | June 17, 1969 | 1389 | Zu'lhijjah | Feb. 8, 1970 |
| 1389 | Jumada I | July 16, 1969 | 1390 | Muharram (New Year) | Mar. 9, 1970 |
| 1389 | Jumada II | Aug. 15, 1969 | | | |

# Chronological List of Popes

**Source:** Annuario Pontificio. Table lists year of consecration of each Pope.

The Roman Catholic Church names the Apostle Peter as founder of the Church in Rome. He arrived there c. 42, was martyred there c. 67, and raised to sainthood.

The Pope's temporal title is: Sovereign of the State of Vatican City.

The Pope's spiritual titles are: Bishop of Rome, Vicar of Jesus Christ, Successor of St. Peter, Prince of the Apostles, Supreme Pontiff of the Universal Church, Patriarch of the West, Primate of Italy, Archbishop and Metropolitan of the Roman Province and Sovereign of the State of Vatican City.

Anti-Popes are in *Italics*. Anti-Popes were illegitimate claimants of or pretenders to the papal throne.

| Year | Name of Pope | Year | Name of Pope | Year | Name of Pope | Year | Name of Pope |
|---|---|---|---|---|---|---|---|
| See above | St. Peter | 615 | St. Deusdedit or Adeodatus I | 974 | Benedict VII | 1305 | Clement V |
| 67 | St. Linus | 619 | Boniface V | 983 | John XIV | 1316 | John XXII |
| 76 | St. Anacletus or Cletus | 625 | Honorius I | 985 | John XV | *1328* | *Nicholas V* |
| 88 | St. Clement I | 640 | Severinus | 996 | Gregory V | 1334 | Benedict XII |
| 97 | St. Evaristus | 640 | John IV | *997* | *John XVI* | 1342 | Clement VI |
| 105 | St. Alexander I | 642 | Theodore I | 999 | Sylvester II | 1352 | Innocent VI |
| 115 | St. Sixtus I | 649 | St. Martin I | 1003 | John XVII | 1362 | Urban V |
| 125 | St. Telesphorus | 654 | St. Eugene I | 1004 | John XVIII | 1370 | Gregory XI |
| 136 | St. Hyginus | 657 | St. Vitalian | 1009 | Sergius IV | 1378 | Urban VI |
| 140 | St. Pius I | 672 | Adeodatus II | 1012 | Benedict VIII | *1378* | *Clement VII* |
| 155 | St. Anicetus | 676 | Donus I | *1012* | *Gregory* | 1389 | Boniface IX |
| 166 | St. Soterus | 678 | St. Agatho | 1024 | John XIX | *1394* | *Benedict XIII* |
| 175 | St. Eleutherius | 682 | St. Leo II | 1032 | Benedict IX | 1404 | Innocent VII |
| 189 | St. Victor I | 684 | St. Benedict II | 1045 | Sylvester III | 1406 | Gregory XII |
| 199 | St. Zephyrinus | 685 | John V | 1045 | Benedict IX | *1409* | *Alexander V* |
| 217 | St. Callistus I | 686 | Conon | 1045 | Gregory VI | *1410* | *John XXIII* |
| *217* | *St. Hippolytus* | *687* | *Theodore* | 1046 | Clement II | 1417 | Martin V |
| 222 | St. Urban I | *687* | *Paschal* | 1047 | Benedict IX | 1431 | Eugene IV |
| 230 | St. Pontian | 687 | St. Sergius I | 1048 | Damasus II | *1440* | *Felix V* |
| 235 | St. Anterus | 701 | John VI | 1049 | St. Leo IX | 1447 | Nicholas V |
| 236 | St. Fabian | 705 | John VII | 1055 | Victor II | 1455 | Callistus III |
| 251 | St. Cornelius | 708 | Sisinnius | 1057 | Stephen IX | 1458 | Pius II |
| *251* | *Novatian* | 708 | Constantine | *1058* | *Benedict X* | 1464 | Paul II |
| 253 | St. Lucius I | 715 | St. Gregory II | 1059 | Nicholas II | 1471 | Sixtus IV |
| 254 | St. Stephen I | 731 | St. Gregory III | 1061 | Alexander II | 1484 | Innocent VIII |
| 257 | St. Sixtus II | 741 | St. Zachary | *1061* | *Honorius II* | 1492 | Alexander VI |
| 259 | St. Dionysius | 752 | Stephen II | 1073 | St. Gregory VII | 1503 | Pius III |
| 269 | St. Felix I | 757 | St. Paul I | *1080* | *Clement III* | 1503 | Julius II |
| 275 | St. Eutychian | *767* | *Constantine* | 1086 | Victor III | 1513 | Leo X |
| 283 | St. Caius | *768* | *Philip* | 1088 | Urban II | 1522 | Adrian VI |
| 296 | St. Marcellinus | 768 | Stephen III | 1099 | Paschal II | 1523 | Clement VII |
| 308 | St. Marcellus I | 772 | Adrian I | *1100* | *Theodore* | 1534 | Paul III |
| 309 | St. Eusebius | 795 | St. Leo III | *1102* | *Albert* | 1550 | Julius III |
| 311 | St. Melchiades | 816 | Stephen IV | *1105* | *Sylvester IV* | 1555 | Marcellus II |
| 314 | St. Sylvester I | 817 | St. Paschal I | 1118 | Gelasius II | 1555 | Paul IV |
| 336 | St. Mark | 824 | Eugene II | *1118* | *Gregory VIII* | 1559 | Pius IV |
| 337 | St. Julius I | 827 | Valentine | 1119 | Callistus II | 1566 | St. Pius V |
| 352 | Liberius | 827 | Gregory IV | 1124 | Honorius II | 1572 | Gregory XIII |
| *355* | *Felix II* | *843* | *John* | *1124* | *Celestine II* | 1585 | Sixtus V |
| 366 | St. Damasus I | 844 | Sergius II | 1130 | Innocent II | 1590 | Urban VII |
| *366* | *Ursinus* | 847 | St. Leo IV | *1130* | *Anacletus II* | 1590 | Gregory XIV |
| 384 | St. Siricius | 855 | Benedict III | *1138* | *Victor IV* | 1591 | Innocent IX |
| 399 | St. Anastasius I | *855* | *Anastasius* | 1143 | Celestine II | 1592 | Clement VIII |
| 401 | St. Innocent I | 858 | St. Nicholas I | 1144 | Lucius II | 1605 | Leo XI |
| 417 | St. Zozimus | 867 | Adrian II | 1145 | Eugene III | 1605 | Paul V |
| 418 | St. Boniface I | 872 | John VIII | 1153 | Anastasius IV | 1621 | Gregory XV |
| *418* | *Eulalius* | 882 | Marinus I | 1154 | Adrian IV | 1623 | Urban VIII |
| 422 | St. Celestine I | 884 | St. Adrian III | 1159 | Alexander III | 1644 | Innocent X |
| 432 | St. Sixtus III | 885 | Stephen V | *1159* | *Victor IV* | 1655 | Alexander VII |
| 440 | St. Leo I | 891 | Formosus | *1164* | *Paschal III* | 1667 | Clement IX |
| 461 | St. Hilary | 896 | Boniface VI | *1168* | *Callistus III* | 1670 | Clement X |
| 468 | St. Simplicius | 896 | Stephen VI | *1179* | *Innocent III* | 1676 | Innocent XI |
| 483 | St. Felix III or II | 897 | Romanus | 1181 | Lucius III | 1689 | Alexander VIII |
| 492 | St. Gelasius I | 897 | Theodore II | 1185 | Urban III | 1691 | Innocent XII |
| 496 | Anastasius II | 898 | John IX | 1187 | Gregory VIII | 1700 | Clement XI |
| 498 | St. Symmachus | 900 | Benedict IV | 1187 | Clement III | 1721 | Innocent XIII |
| *498* | *Lawrence* | 903 | Leo V | 1191 | Celestine III | 1724 | Benedict XIII |
| | *(501-505)* | *903* | *Christopher* | 1198 | Innocent III | 1730 | Clement XII |
| 514 | St. Hormisdas | 904 | Sergius III | 1216 | Honorius III | 1740 | Benedict XIV |
| 523 | St. John I | 911 | Anastasius III | 1227 | Gregory IX | 1758 | Clement XIII |
| 526 | St. Felix IV or III | 913 | Landus | 1241 | Celestine IV | 1769 | Clement XIV |
| 530 | Boniface II | 914 | John X | 1243 | Innocent IV | 1775 | Pius VI |
| *530* | *Dioscorus* | 928 | Leo VI | 1254 | Alexander IV | 1800 | Pius VII |
| 533 | John II | 928 | Stephen VII | 1261 | Urban IV | 1823 | Leo XII |
| 535 | St. Agapitus | 931 | John XI | 1265 | Clement IV | 1829 | Pius VIII |
| 536 | St. Silverius | 936 | Leo VII | 1271 | Gregory X | 1831 | Gregory XVI |
| 537 | Vigilius | 939 | Stephen VIII | 1276 | Innocent V | 1846 | Pius IX |
| 556 | Pelagius I | 942 | Marinus II | 1276 | Adrian V | 1878 | Leo XIII |
| 561 | John III | 946 | Agapitus II | 1276 | John XXI | 1903 | St. Pius X |
| 575 | Benedict I | 955 | John XII | 1277 | Nicholas III | 1914 | Benedict XV |
| 579 | Pelagius II | 963 | Leo VIII | 1281 | Martin IV | 1922 | Pius XI |
| 590 | St. Gregory I | 964 | Benedict V | 1285 | Honorius IV | 1939 | Pius XII |
| 604 | Sabinianus | 965 | John XIII | 1288 | Nicholas IV | 1958 | John XXIII |
| 607 | Boniface III | 973 | Benedict VI | 1294 | St. Celestine V | 1963 | Paul VI |
| 608 | St. Boniface IV | *974* | *Boniface VII* | 1294 | Boniface VIII | | |
| | | | | 1303 | Benedict XI | | |

# Roman Catholic Days of Obligation, Fast and Abstinence, 1969

**Days of Obligation** in the United States are Octave of the Birth of Our Lord, January 1; Ascension Day, May 15; Assumption of the Blessed Virgin Mary, August 15; All Saints' Day, November 1; Immaculate Conception of the Blessed Virgin Mary, December 8; Christmas Day, December 25. Also all Sundays.

**Days of Fast.** Ash Wednesday, Feb. 19, and Good Friday, April 4. The law binds Catholics from the completion of their 21st year to the beginning of their 60th; i.e., from the ages of 21 to 59.

**Days of Abstinence:** Ash Wednesday, Good Friday and other Fridays in Lent. The law binds Catholics 14 years of age and older.

# Roman Catholic Hierarchy

**Source: Apostolic Delegation, Washington, D. C.**

## SUPREME PONTIFF

At the head of the Roman Catholic Church is the Supreme Pontiff, Paul VI, Giovanni Battista Montini, born at Concesio, Italy, Sept. 26, 1897, ordained priest May 29, 1920, enthroned archbishop of Milan Jan. 6, 1955, proclaimed cardinal Dec. 15, 1958; elected Pope as successor of John XXIII, June 21, 1963; crowned June 30, 1963.

### CARDINAL BISHOPS

| | | Nation | Born | Chosen |
|---|---|---|---|---|
| Eugene Tisserant | Bishop of Ostia and Porto and Santa Rufina; Dean of the Sacred College | French | 1884 | 1936 |
| Giuseppe Pizzardo | Bishop of Albano | Italian | 1877 | 1937 |
| Benedetto Aloisi Masella | Bishop of Palestrina | Italian | 1870 | 1946 |
| Amleto G. Cicognani | Titular Bishop of Frascati, Sec. of State of His Holiness | Italian | 1883 | 1958 |
| Giuseppe Ferretto | Titular Bishop of Sabina and Poggio Mirteto; Major Penitentiary | Italian | 1889 | 1961 |
| Fernando Cento | Titular Bishop of Velletri | Italian | 1883 | 1958 |
| Paul Pierre Meouchi | Maronite Patriarch of Antioch | Lebanese | 1894 | 1965 |
| Stephanos I Sidarouss | Coptic Patriarch of Alexandria | Untd. Arab Republic | 1904 | 1965 |

### CARDINAL PRIESTS

| | | Nation | Born | Chosen |
|---|---|---|---|---|
| Emmanuel G. Cereleira | Patriarch of Lisbon | Portuguese | 1888 | 1929 |
| Gregory Peter XV Agagianian | Prefect of the Sacred Congregation for the Evangelization of the Nations | Armenian | 1894 | 1946 |
| James C. McGuigan | Archbishop of Toronto | Canadian | 1894 | 1946 |
| Carlos Carmelo de Vasconcellos Motta | Archbishop of Aparecida | Brazilian | 1890 | 1946 |
| Norman Gilroy | Archbishop of Sydney | Australian | 1896 | 1946 |
| Giacomo de Barros Camara | Archbishop of Rio de Janeiro | Brazilian | 1894 | 1946 |
| Josef Frings | Archbishop of Cologne | German | 1887 | 1946 |
| Joseph Mindszenty | Archbishop of Esztergom | Hungarian | 1892 | 1946 |
| Antonio Caggiano | Archbishop of Buenos Aires | Argentinian | 1889 | 1946 |
| Maurice Feltin | | French | 1883 | 1953 |
| Carlos Maria de la Torre | Archbishop of Quito | Ecuadorean | 1873 | 1953 |
| Giuseppe Siri | Archbishop of Genoa | Italian | 1906 | 1953 |
| James Francis McIntyre | Archbishop of Los Angeles | American | 1886 | 1953 |
| Giacomo Lercaro | | Italian | 1891 | 1953 |
| Stefan Wyszynski | Archbishop of Gniezno and Warsaw | Polish | 1901 | 1953 |
| Benjamin de Arriba y Castro | Archbishop of Tarragona | Spanish | 1886 | 1953 |
| Fernando Quiroga y Palacios | Archbishop of Santiago de Compostela | Spanish | 1900 | 1953 |
| Paul-Emile Leger | | Canadian | 1904 | 1953 |
| Valerian Gracias | Archbishop of Bombay | Indian | 1900 | 1953 |
| Alfredo Ottaviani | | Italian | 1890 | 1953 |
| Giovanni Urbani | Patriarch of Venice | Italian | 1900 | 1958 |
| Paolo Giobbe | | Italian | 1880 | 1958 |
| José Garibi y Rivera | Archbishop of Guadalajara | Mexican | 1889 | 1958 |
| Antonio Barbieri | Archbishop of Montevideo | Uruguayan | 1892 | 1958 |
| Carlo Confalonieri | Prefect of Sacred Cong. for Bishops | Italian | 1893 | 1958 |
| Richard Cushing | Archbishop of Boston | American | 1895 | 1958 |
| José Bueno y Monreal | Archbishop of Seville | Spanish | 1904 | 1958 |
| Franz Koenig | Archbishop of Vienna | Austrian | 1905 | 1958 |
| Julius Doepfner | Archbishop of Munich | German | 1913 | 1958 |
| Alberto Di Jorio | | Italian | 1884 | 1958 |
| Francesco Roberti | | Italian | 1889 | 1958 |
| Gustavo Testa | | Italian | 1886 | 1959 |
| Paolo Marella | Praeses of Secretariat for non-christians | Italian | 1895 | 1959 |
| Luigi Traglia | Chancellor of the Holy Roman Church | Italian | 1895 | 1960 |
| Peter Doi | Archbishop of Tokyo | Japanese | 1892 | 1960 |
| Joseph Lefebvre | Archbishop of Bourges | French | 1892 | 1960 |
| Bernard Alfrink | Archbishop of Utrecht | Dutch | 1900 | 1960 |
| Rufino Santos | Archbishop of Manila | Filipino | 1908 | 1960 |
| Laurian Rugambwa | Bishop of Bukoba | African | 1912 | 1960 |
| Jose Quintero | Archbishop of Caracas | Venezuelan | 1902 | 1961 |
| Luis Concha | | Columbian | 1891 | 1961 |
| Jose da Costa Nunes | | Portuguese | 1880 | 1962 |
| Ildebrando Antoniutti | Prefect of the Sacred Cong. for Religious and Secular Institutes | Italian | 1898 | 1962 |
| Efrem Forni | | Italian | 1889 | 1962 |
| Juan Landazuri Ricketts | Archbishop of Lima | Peruvian | 1913 | 1962 |
| Raul Silva Henriquez | Archbishop of Santiago | Chilean | 1907 | 1962 |
| Leo Joseph Suenens | Archbishop of Malines—Brussels | Belgian | 1904 | 1962 |
| Josyf Slipyi | Ukrainian Archbishop of Lwow | Ukrainian | 1892 | 1965 |
| Lorenz Jaeger | Archbishop of Paderborn | German | 1892 | 1965 |
| Thomas B. Cooray | Archbishop of Colombo | Ceylonese | 1901 | 1965 |
| Josef Beran | Archbishop of Prague | Czechoslovakian | 1888 | 1965 |
| Maurice Roy | Archbishop of Quebec | Canadian | 1905 | 1965 |
| Joseph Marie Martin | | French | 1891 | 1965 |
| Owen McCann | Archbishop of Cape Town | So. African | 1907 | 1965 |
| Leon-Etienne Duval | Archbishop of Algiers | Algerian | 1903 | 1965 |
| Ermenegildo Florit | Archbishop of Florence | Italian | 1901 | 1965 |
| Franjo Seper | Prefect of Sacred Congregation for the Doctrine of the Faith | Yugoslav | 1905 | 1965 |
| John C. Heenan | Archbishop of Westminster | English | 1905 | 1965 |
| Jean Villot | Prefect of the Sacred Cong. for the Clergy | French | 1905 | 1965 |
| Paul Zoungrana | Archbishop of Ouagadougou | Up. Volta | 1917 | 1965 |
| Lawrence J. Shehan | Archbishop of Baltimore | American | 1898 | 1965 |
| Cesare Zerba | | Italian | 1892 | 1965 |
| Agnello Rossi | Archbishop of Sao Paulo | Brazilian | 1913 | 1965 |
| Giovanni Colombo | Archbishop of Milan | Italian | 1902 | 1965 |
| William Conway | Archbishop of Armagh | Irish | 1913 | 1965 |
| Nicholas Fasolino | Archbishop of Santa Fe in Argentina | Argentinian | 1887 | 1967 |
| Giuseppe Beltrami | | Italian | 1889 | 1967 |
| Gabriel Garrone | Prefect of Sacred Congregation for Catholic Education | French | 1901 | 1967 |
| Patrick O'Boyle | Archbishop of Washington | American | 1896 | 1967 |
| Maximilian De Furstenberg | Prefect of the Sacred Congregation for the Oriental churches | Belgian | 1904 | 1967 |
| Antonio Samore | President of Pontifical commission for Latin America | Italian | 1905 | 1967 |

## CARDINAL PRIESTS

| | | Nation | Born | Chosen |
|---|---|---|---|---|
| Francesco Carpino........ | Archbishop of Palermo................. | Italian.... | 1905 | 1967 |
| Joseph Maurer............ | Archbishop of Sucre................... | Bolivian... | 1900 | 1967 |
| Pietro Parente............ | | Italian.... | 1891 | 1967 |
| Carlo Grano.............. | | Italian.... | 1887 | 1967 |
| Angelo Dell'Acqua........ | Vicar General of Rome................ | Italian.... | 1903 | 1967 |
| Dino Staffa.............. | Prefect of the Sup. Tribunal of the Apostolic Signatura................. | Italian.... | 1906 | 1967 |
| John Krol............../... | Archbishop of Philadelphia........... | American.. | 1910 | 1967 |
| John Cody............... | Archbishop of Chicago................ | American.. | 1907 | 1967 |
| Corrado Ursi............ | Archbishop of Naples................. | Italian.... | 1908 | 1967 |
| Alfred Bengsch........... | Archbishop-Bishop of Berlin.......... | German... | 1921 | 1967 |
| Justin Darmajuwana...... | Archbishop of Semarang.............. | Indonesian | 1914 | 1967 |
| Karl Wojtyla............. | Archbishop of Krakow................ | Polish.... | 1920 | 1967 |
| Michele Pellegrino....... | Archbishop of Turin.................. | Italian.... | 1903 | 1967 |
| Alexandre Renard........ | Archbishop of Lyon.................. | French... | 1906 | 1967 |

## CARDINAL DEACONS

| | | Nation | Born | Chosen |
|---|---|---|---|---|
| Arcadio Larraona........ | | Spanish... | 1887 | 1959 |
| Francesco Morano........ | | Italian.... | 1872 | 1959 |
| William Heard........... | Praeses of Sec. for Prom. Christian Unity... | Scottish... | 1884 | 1959 |
| Augustine Bea........... | | German... | 1881 | 1959 |
| Antonio Bacci........... | | Italian.... | 1885 | 1960 |
| Michael Browne.......... | | Irish.... | 1887 | 1962 |
| Federico Callori di Vignale. | | Italian.... | 1890 | 1965 |
| Charles Journet.......... | President of the Prefecture of the Holy See's Economic Affairs............... | Swiss.... | 1891 | 1965 |
| Egidio Vagnozzi.......... | | Italian.... | 1906 | 1967 |
| Pericle Felici............ | Pres. of Pontifical Commission for the Revision of the Code of Canon Law:.... | Italian.... | 1911 | 1967 |
| Francis Brennan.......... | Prefect of the Sacred Cong. of the Sacraments | American.. | 1894 | 1967 |
| Benno Gut.............. | Prefect of the Sacred Congregation of Rites.. | Swiss.... | 1897 | 1967 |

# Roman Catholic Hierarchy of the United States

Source: Apostolic Delegation, Washington, D. C.

## ARCHDIOCESES

| See | Archbishops | Cons. |
|---|---|---|
| Anchorage....... | Joseph T. Ryan. | 1966 |
| Atlanta, Ga.... | Thomas A. Donnellan. | 1964 |
| Baltimore, Md.... | Lawrence Shehan (Card.). | 1945 |
| | Thomas A. Murphy (Aux.) | 1962 |
| Boston, Mass.... | Richard J. Cushing, (Card.) | 1939 |
| | Eric F. Mackenzie (Aux.) | 1950 |
| | Jeremiah F. Minihan (Aux.) | 1954 |
| | Thomas J. Riley (Aux.) | 1960 |
| Chicago, Ill...... | John Cody (Card.) | 1947 |
| | Bernard J. Shell (Aux.) | 1928 |
| | Raymond Hillinger (Aux.) | 1953 |
| | Thomas J. Grady (Aux.) | 1967 |
| | William McManus (Aux.) | 1967 |
| | John L. May (Aux.) | 1967 |
| | Michael R. Dempsey (Aux.) | 1968 |
| | Alfred Abramowicz (Aux.) | 1968 |
| Cincinnati, Ohio.. | Karl J. Alter | 1931 |
| | E. A. McCarthy (Aux.) | 1965 |
| Denver, Colo..... | James V. Casey | 1957 |
| Detroit, Mich.... | John F. Dearden | 1948 |
| | Joseph M. Brietenbeck | 1965 |
| | Walter J. Schoenherr (Aux.) | 1968 |
| | Thomas J. Gumbleton (Aux.) | 1968 |
| Dubuque, Iowa.. | James J. Byrne | 1947 |
| | Loras J. Watters (Aux.) | 1965 |
| Hartford, Conn.. | Henry J. O'Brien | 1940 |
| | John F. Hackett (Aux.) | 1952 |
| | Joseph Donnelly (Aux.) | 1965 |
| Kansas City, Kan. | Edward J. Hunkeler | 1945 |
| Indianapolis, Ind. | Paul C. Schulte | 1937 |
| | George J. Biskup (Coad.) | 1957 |
| Los Angeles, Calif. | J. Francis McIntyre, Card. | 1941 |
| | John J. Ward (Aux.) | 1963 |
| Louisville, Ky.... | Thomas J. McDonough | 1947 |
| | Charles G. Maloney (Aux.) | 1955 |
| Miami, Fla....... | Coleman F. Carroll | 1953 |
| Milwaukee, Wis... | William E. Cousins | 1952 |
| | Roman Atkielski (Aux.) | 1940 |

| See | Archbishops | Cons. |
|---|---|---|
| Newark, N. J.... | Thomas A. Boland | 1947 |
| | Martin W. Stanton (Aux.) | 1957 |
| | John J. Dougherty (Aux.) | 1962 |
| | Joseph A. Costello (Aux.) | 1962 |
| New Orleans, La.. | Philip M. Hannan | 1956 |
| | Louis A. Caillouet (Aux.) | 1947 |
| | Harold R. Perry (Aux.) | 1965 |
| New York, N. Y.. | Terence J. Cooke | 1965 |
| | John J. Maguire (Coad.) | 1959 |
| | Stephen J. Donahue (Aux.), 1934; Joseph F. Flannelly (Aux.), 1948; Edward V. Dargin (Aux.) 1953; J. M. Pernicone (Aux.), 1954; John M. A. Fearns (Aux.), 1957; Edward E. Swanstrom (Aux.), 1960; James E. McManus (Aux.), 1947; Edwin Broderick (Aux.)....1967 | |
| Omaha, Nebr.... | Gerald T. Bergan | 1934 |
| | Daniel E. Sheehan (Aux.) | 1964 |
| Philadelphia, Pa... | John J. Krol (Card.) | 1953 |
| | Gerald V. McDevitt (Aux.) | 1962 |
| | John J. Graham (Aux.) | 1964 |
| Portland, Ore.... | Robert P. Dwyer | 1952 |
| St. Louis, Mo.... | John J. Carberry | 1956 |
| | George Gottwald (Aux.) | 1961 |
| St. Paul, Minn... | Leo Binz | 1942 |
| | Leo C. Byrne (Coad.) | 1954 |
| | Leonard Cowley (Aux.) | 1958 |
| | James P. Shannon (Aux.) | 1965 |
| San Antonio, Tex. | Robert E. Lucey | 1934 |
| | Stephen A. Leven (Aux.) | 1956 |
| San Francisco, Cal. | Joseph T. McGucken | 1941 |
| | Merlin Guilfoyle (Aux.) | 1950 |
| | William McDonald (Aux.) | 1964 |
| | Mark J. Hurley (Aux.) | 1967 |
| Santa Fe, N. Mex. | James Peter Davis | 1943 |
| Seattle, Wash.... | Thomas A. Connolly | 1939 |
| | Thomas E. Gill (Aux.) | 1956 |
| Washington, D. C. | Patrick A. O'Boyle (Card.) | 1948 |
| | John S. Spence (Aux.) | 1964 |
| | Edward J. Herrmann (Aux.) | 1966 |

## DIOCESES

| Bishops | | |
|---|---|---|
| Agana, Guam.... | Apollinaris Baumgartner | 1945 |
| Albany, N. Y..... | William A. Scully | 1945 |
| | Edward J.Maginn(Ap.Adm) | 1957 |
| Alexandria, La... | Charles F. Greco | 1946 |
| Allentown, Pa.... | Joseph M. McShea | 1952 |
| Altoona-Johns- town, Pa....... | James J. Hogan | 1959 |
| Amarillo, Tex.... | Lawrence DeFalco | 1963 |
| Arecibo, P. R.... | Alfred Mendez | 1960 |
| Austin, Texas.... | Louis J. Reicher | 1948 |
| Baker, Oreg...... | Francis P. Leipzig | 1950 |
| Baton Rouge, La.. | Robert E. Tracy | 1959 |
| Beaumont....... | Vincent Harris | 1966 |
| Belleville, Ill..... | A. R. Zuroweste | 1948 |
| Belm't Abbey, N.C. | Walter Coggin | 1960 |
| Bismarck, N. Dak. | Hilary Hacker | 1957 |
| Boise, Idaho...... | Sylvester, W. Treinen | 1962 |
| Bridgeport, Conn.. | Walter W. Curtis | 1959 |
| Brooklyn, N. Y... | Francis J. Mugavero | 1940 |
| | John J. Boardman (Aux.) | 1952 |
| | Joseph P. Denning (Aux.) | 1959 |
| | Chas. R. Mulrooney (Aux.) | 1959 |
| Brownsville, Tex.. | Humberto Medeiros | 1966 |
| Buffalo, N. Y..... | James A. McNulty | 1947 |
| | Pius A. Benincasa (Aux.) | 1964 |

| Bishops | | |
|---|---|---|
| Burlington, Vt.... | Robert F. Joyce | 1954 |
| Camden, N. J.... | George H. Guilfoyle | 1964 |
| | James L. Schad (Aux.) | 1966 |
| Charleston, S. C... | Ernest L. Unterkoefler | 1962 |
| Cheyenne, Wyo... | Hubert M. Newell | 1947 |
| Cleveland, Ohio... | Clarence Issenmann | 1954 |
| Columbus, Ohio... | Clarence E. Elwell | 1962 |
| | Edw. G. Hettinger (Aux.) | 1942 |
| Corpus Christi, Tex. | Thomas J. Drury | 1962 |
| Covington, Ky.... | Richard Henry Ackerman | 1956 |
| Crookston, Minn.. | Laurence Glenn | 1956 |
| Dallas-Ft. Worth.. | Thomas K. Gorman | 1931 |
| | A. Danglmayr | 1942 |
| | John J. Cassata (Aux.) | 1968 |
| Davenport, Iowa.. | Gerald F. O'Keefe | 1966 |
| Des Moines, Iowa | Maurice Dingman | 1968 |
| Dodge City, Kan.. | Marion F. Forst | 1960 |
| Duluth, Minn..... | Francis J. Schenk | 1945 |
| El Paso, Tex..... | S. M. Metzger | 1940 |
| Erie, Pa........ | John F. Whealon | 1961 |
| | Alfred M. Watson | 1965 |
| Evansville, Ind.... | Paul F. Leibold | 1958 |
| Fairbanks........ | Francis D. Gleeson | 1948 |
| | Robert L. Whelan (Coad) | 1968 |
| Fall River, Mass.. | James Louis Connolly | 1945 |
| | James J. Gerrard (Aux.) | 1959 |

Fargo, N. Dak....Leo F. Dworschak........1946
Fort Wayne-South
  Bend, Ind......Leo A. Pursley...........1950
Fresno, Calif....Timothy Manning.........1940
Gallup, N. Mex...Bernard Espelage.........1940
Galveston-      Wendelin J. Nold........1948
  Houston........J. L. Morkovsky (Ap Adm.)1956
Gary, Ind.....Andrew Gregory Grutka....1957
Grand Isl., Nebr..John L. Paschang........1952
GrandRapids,Mich.Allan J. Babcock.........1947
Great Falls, Mont..Aloysius J. Wycislo......1960
    Eldon B. Schuster (Aux.).....1961
Green Bay, Wis...Stanislaus V. Bona........1932
    John B. Grellinger (Aux.)....1949
Greensburg, Pa....William Connare........1960
Harrisburg, Pa...George L. Leech.........1935
    Joseph T. Daley (Coad.).....1964
Helena, Mont...Raymond G. Hunthausen..1962
Honolulu, Hawaii .John J. Scanlan.........1954
Jefferson City, Mo.Joseph Marling..........1947
Joliet, Ill.......Romeo Blanchette.......1965
    Raymond J. Vonesh (Aux.)...1968
Juneau, Alaska...Robert D. O'Flanagan....1951
Kan.C.-St. Joseph.Charles Helmsing........1949
    Jos. Sullivan (Aux.).........1967
La Crosse, Wis...Frederick Freking.......1957
Lafayette, Ind...Raymond J. Gallagher....1965
Lafayette, La....M. Schexnayder.........1951
    Warren L. Boudreaux (Aux)..1962
Lansing, Mich....Alex. M. Zaleski........1950
Lincoln, Nebr....Glennon P. Flavin.......1957
Little Rock, Ark...A. L. Fletcher.........1940
Madison, Wis....Cletus F. O'Donnell.....1960
    Jerome J. Hastrich (Aux.)...1963
Manchester, N. H..Ernest J. Primeau......1959
Marquette, Mich..Charles A. Salatka......1962
Miami, Fla......Coleman F. Carroll......1953
Mobile-Bir'ham,
  Alabama......Thomas Toolen (Abp.)...1927
    Joseph G. Vath (Aux.).....1966
Monterey, Calif..Harry A. Clinch........1956
Nashville, Tenn...William L. Adrian......1936
    Joseph M. Durick (Ap. Adm.)1955
Natchez-Jackson
  Miss..........J. B. Brunini..........1956
New Ulm, Minn...Alphonse Schladweiler....1958
Norwich, Conn...Vincent J. Hines.......1959
Oakland, Calif...Floyd L. Begin.........1947
Ogdensburg, N. Y.Stanislaus J. Brzana.....1964
Oklahoma City and
  Tulsa, Okla....Victor Reed...........1958
Orlando, Fla....William Borders........1968
Owensboro, Ky...Henry Soenneker.......1961
Paterson, N. J....Lawrence Casey........1953
Peoria, Ill......John B. Franz.........1951
Pittsburgh, Pa....John J. Wright.........1947
    Vincent M. Leonard (Aux.)..1964
    John B. McDowell (Aux)....1966
Ponce, P. R......Juan Fremito Torres Oliver.1964
Portland, Maine...Daniel J. Feeney.......1946
    Peter L. Gerety (Coad.).....1966
Providence, R. I..Russell R. McVinney....1948
    Bernard M. Kelly (Aux.)....1964
Pueblo, Colo......Charles A. Buswell......1959

Raleigh, N. C....Vincent S. Waters........1945
Rapid City, S. Dak.William T. McCarty.....1943
Reno, Nev......Joseph Green.........1962
Richmond, Va....John J. Russell.........1950
    J. Louis Flaherty (Aux.)....1966
Rochester, N. Y...Fulton J. Sheen........1951
    Dennis W. Hickey (Aux.)....1968
    John E. McCafferty (Aux.)..1968
Rockford, Ill....Loras T. Lane..........1951
Rockville Centre...Walter Kellenberg.......1953
    Vincent J. Baldwin (Aux.)...1962
Sacramento, Calif..Alden J. Bell.........1956
Saginaw, Mich....Stephen S. Woznicki.....1938
    James A. Hickey.........1967
Salina, Kansas...Cyril J. Vogel.........1965
St. Augustine, Fla..Paul F. Tanner.......1965
St. Cloud, Minn...George Speltz.........1963
St. Petersburg, Fla.Charles B. McLaughlin...1964
Salt Lake C., Utah.Joseph Lennox Federal...1951
San Angelo.......Thomas Tschoepe.......1966
San Diego, Calif..Francis J. Furey.......1960
    John R. Quinn (Aux.).....1967
San Juan, P. R...Luis Aponte Martinez....1960
Santa Rosa, Calif..Leo T. Maher.........1962
Savannah, Ga....Gerard Frey..........1967
Scranton, Pa....J. Carroll McCormick....1947
    Henry Klonowski (Aux.)...1943
Sioux City, Iowa...Joseph M. Mueller......1947
    Frank Greteman (Aux.).....1965
Sioux Falls, S. Dak.Lambert A. Hoch.......1952
Spokane, Wash...Bernard J. Topel.......1955
Springfield, Ill...William A. O'Connor.....1949
Springfield, Mass..Christopher J. Weldon...1950
Springfield-Cape
  Girardeau, Mo..Ignatius J. Strecker......1962
Stockton, Calif...Hugh A. Donohoe.......1947
Steubenville, Ohio.John K. Mussio........1945
Superior, Wis....George A. Hammes.....1960
Syracuse, N. Y...Walter A. Foery.......1937
    D. F. Cunningham (Coad.)..1950
Toledo, Ohio.....John A. Donovan.......1954
Trenton, N. J....George W. Ahr.........1950
    John C. Reiss (Aux.).......1967
Tucson, Ariz....Francis S. Green.......1953
Wheeling, W. Va..Joseph H. Hodges......1952
Wichita, Kans....David Maloney.........1961
Wilmington, Del...Thomas A. Mardaga.....1966
Winona, Minn....Edward J. Fitzgerald....1946
Worcester, Mass..Bernard J. Flanagan....1953
    Timothy Harrington (Aux.)1968
Yakima, Wash....Joseph P. Dougherty....1953
Youngstown, Ohio.James W. Malone.......1960
Military Vicar.....Terence J. Cooke........1965
    Philip J. Furlong (Aux.)....1955
    William Moran (Aux.).....1965

**Byzantine Rite:**

Philadelphia......A. Senyshyn............1942
Pittsburgh.......Stephen Kocisko........1959
Passaic..........Vacant.
St. Nicholas......Jaroslav Gabbo........1961
Stamford........Joseph Schmondiuk.......1956
**Maronite Rite:**..Francis Zayek............1962
**Melchite Rite:**..Vacant...................

# The Ten Commandments

The Ten Commandments are an integral part of the Judaeo-Christian ethical system and represent the divine law, engraved on two stone tablets and given to Moses by God atop Mt. Sinai. Two varying versions of the Ten Commandments, or Decalogue, appear in the Bible. One is in Exodus 20, the other in Deuteronomy 5. The numbering of the Commandments differs in various religions. The following text is that of Exodus 20 as it appears in the Holy Bible, Revised Standard Version:

1—I am the Lord your God, who brought you out of the land of Egypt, out of the house of bondage. You shall have no other gods before me.

2—You shall not make for yourself a graven image, or any likeness of anything that is in heaven above, or that is in the earth beneath, or that is in the water under the earth; you shall not bow down to them or serve them; for I the Lord your God am a jealous God, visiting the iniquity of the fathers upon the children to the third and the fourth generation of those who hate me, but showing steadfast love to thousands of those who love me and keep my commandments.

3—You shall not take the name of the Lord your God in vain; for the Lord will not hold him guiltless who takes his name in vain.

4—Remember the sabbath day, to keep it holy. Six days you shall labor, and do all your work; but the seventh day is a sabbath to the Lord your God; in it you shall not do any work, you, or your son, or your daughter, or your manservant, or your maidservant, or your cattle, or the sojourner who is within your gates; for in six days the Lord made heaven and earth, the sea, and all that is in them, and rested the seventh day; therefore the Lord blessed the sabbath day and hallowed it.

5—Honor your father and your mother, that your days may be long in the land which the Lord your God gives you.

6—You shall not kill.

7—You shall not commit adultery.

8—You shall not steal.

9—You shall not bear false witness against your neighbor.

10—You shall not covet your neighbor's house; you shall not covet your neighbor's wife, or his manservant, or his maidservant, or his ox, or his ass, or anything that is your neighbor's.

# Roman Catholic Statistics for the United States

**Source:** Official Catholic Directory copyright 1968 by P. J. Kedenay & Sons
All data in the tables, including population, are for the archdioceses and the dioceses named (1968)

| ARCH-DIOCESES | Clergy | Parishes | Students | Catholic Pop.* |
|---|---|---|---|---|
| Anchorage | 24 | 11 | 3,090 | 34,937 |
| Atlanta | 146 | 33 | 16,418 | 48,982 |
| Baltimore | 746 | 145 | 107,100 | 475,745 |
| Boston | 2,549 | 401 | 462,153 | 1,871,408 |
| Chicago | 2,616 | 461 | 573,844 | 2,342,000 |
| Cincinnati | 938 | 260 | 157,930 | 523,608 |
| Denver | 367 | 111 | 79,561 | 274,260 |
| Detroit | 1,455 | 331 | 372,624 | 1,548,594 |
| Dubuque | 559 | 201 | 71,113 | 222,598 |
| Hartford | 768 | 207 | 179,396 | 812,011 |
| Indianapolis | 483 | 165 | 55,676 | 210,515 |
| Kan.City,Kan. | 334 | 104 | 40,964 | 136,750 |
| Los Angeles | 1,438 | 313 | 416,858 | 1,662,242 |
| Louisville | 454 | 121 | 63,795 | 196,135 |
| Milwaukee | 1,204 | 264 | 208,236 | 699,728 |
| Newark | 1,333 | 253 | 287,730 | 1,637,634 |
| New Orleans | 541 | 154 | 141,874 | 629,403 |
| New York | 2,235 | 407 | 357,780 | 1,870,000 |
| Omaha | 405 | 143 | 60,498 | 186,981 |
| Philadelphia | 1,745 | 312 | 345,673 | 1,353,024 |
| Portland, Ore. | 402 | 114 | 52,096 | 200,509 |
| St. Louis | 1,098 | 249 | 144,827 | 511,669 |
| St. Paul | 660 | 215 | 159,936 | 523,938 |
| San Antonio | 448 | 144 | 97,889 | 512,894 |
| San Francisco | 815 | 145 | 156,167 | 849,190 |
| Santa Fe | 356 | 90 | 58,236 | 257,675 |
| Seattle | 473 | 118 | 80,460 | 311,426 |
| Washington | 1,223 | 123 | 119,067 | 384,400 |
| Ukr. of Phila. | 142 | 101 | 19,822 | 223,923 |

**DIOCESES**

| DIOCESES | Clergy | Parishes | Students | Catholic Pop.* |
|---|---|---|---|---|
| Albany | 746 | 209 | 97,204 | 421,112 |
| Alexandria, La. | 184 | 87 | 23,377 | 95,405 |
| Allentown | 394 | 151 | 53,698 | 245,700 |
| Altoona-Johnstn | 320 | 119 | 39,259 | 146,181 |
| Amarillo | 104 | 56 | 15,691 | 85,658 |
| Austin | 160 | 78 | 21,456 | 136,110 |
| Baker, Ore. | 53 | 31 | 7,528 | 24,530 |
| Baton Rouge | 153 | 64 | 41,563 | 178,000 |
| Beaumont | 84 | 32 | 17,250 | 89,191 |
| Belleville | 250 | 132 | 33,824 | 118,503 |
| Belmont Abbey | 51 | 1 | 806 | 656 |
| Bismarck | 161 | 88 | 24,536 | 76,557 |
| Boise | 104 | 56 | 15,013 | 52,970 |
| Bridgeport | 359 | 84 | 80,251 | 310,574 |
| Brooklyn | 1,394 | 228 | 305,870 | 1,551,264 |
| Brownsville | 101 | 167 | 33,888 | 248,000 |
| Buffalo | 1,208 | 272 | 210,786 | 937,567 |
| Burlington | 414 | 150 | 41,859 | 139,758 |
| Camden | 434 | 121 | 76,581 | 299,769 |
| Charleston | 153 | 66 | 15,711 | 41,561 |
| Cheyenne | 64 | 39 | 12,050 | 48,000 |
| Cleveland | 923 | 232 | 225,034 | 868,871 |
| Columbus | 311 | 110 | 49,438 | 182,000 |
| Corpus Christi | 156 | 66 | 41,070 | 202,806 |
| Covington | 236 | 84 | 31,440 | 95,000 |
| Crookston | 80 | 55 | 13,626 | 40,647 |
| Dallas-Ft.Worth | 287 | 99 | 47,480 | 166,081 |
| Davenport | 251 | 124 | 31,832 | 102,563 |
| Des Moines | 142 | 71 | 23,040 | 80,351 |
| Dodge City | 76 | 50 | 11,209 | 32,043 |
| Duluth | 144 | 90 | 26,670 | 108,940 |
| El Paso | 161 | 67 | 48,706 | 187,500 |
| Erie | 357 | 125 | 67,898 | 217,755 |
| Evansville | 152 | 74 | 33,248 | 84,886 |
| Fairbanks | 39 | 18 | 3,504 | 12,205 |
| Fall River | 413 | 109 | 69,185 | 290,904 |
| Fargo | 192 | 127 | 28,711 | 100,034 |
| Ft. Wayne-S. Bend | 485 | 86 | 50,798 | 157,411 |
| Fresno | 177 | 79 | 38,134 | 324,586 |
| Gallup | 108 | 53 | 20,009 | 79,260 |
| Galveston-Houston | 372 | 104 | 74,287 | 305,000 |
| Gary | 259 | 86 | 47,666 | 198,480 |
| Grand Island | 93 | 59 | 13,730 | 49,707 |
| Grand Rapids | 286 | 130 | 61,775 | 195,461 |
| Great Falls | 134 | 71 | 9,038 | 83,120 |
| Green Bay | 487 | 192 | 95,588 | 317,527 |
| Greensburg | 280 | 120 | 43,701 | 221,732 |
| Harrisburg | 259 | 100 | 47,716 | 183,468 |
| Helena | 156 | 57 | 18,877 | 75,500 |
| Honolulu | 176 | 62 | 35,929 | 239,000 |
| Jefferson City | 201 | 93 | 18,632 | 62,900 |
| Joliet | 434 | 105 | 75,507 | 290,226 |
| Juneau | 10 | 6 | 1,198 | 3,500 |
| Kansas City-St. Joseph | 364 | 96 | 39,976 | 136,634 |
| La Crosse | 404 | 175 | 57,690 | 181,875 |
| Lafayette Ind. | 182 | 61 | 20,016 | 75,600 |
| Lafayette, La. | 302 | 147 | 86,268 | 398,086 |
| Lansing | 233 | 96 | 68,527 | 249,504 |
| Lincoln | 175 | 139 | 15,569 | 58,382 |
| Little Rock | 203 | 86 | 13,664 | 53,234 |
| Madison | 277 | 139 | 51,914 | 184,253 |
| Manchester | 421 | 122 | 65,224 | 261,644 |
| Marquette | 175 | 95 | 28,675 | 104,290 |
| Miami | 326 | 99 | 70,211 | 453,470 |
| Mobile-B'ham | 414 | 150 | 37,874 | 134,685 |
| Monterey | 124 | 38 | 28,298 | 125,000 |
| Nashville | 167 | 76 | 30,243 | 93,029 |
| Natchez-Jackson | 217 | 98 | 24,221 | 77,635 |
| New Ulm | 131 | 91 | 23,354 | 70,245 |
| Norwich | 265 | 70 | 50,124 | 189,634 |
| Oakland | 338 | 82 | 74,972 | 358,730 |
| Ogdensburg | 256 | 118 | 47,493 | 165,987 |
| Okla. City-Tulsa | 281 | 123 | 29,600 | 112,127 |
| Owensboro | 83 | 73 | 13,752 | 46,070 |
| Paterson | 453 | 99 | 77,376 | 320,831 |
| Peoria | 416 | 170 | 62,026 | 217,013 |
| Pittsburgh | 830 | 318 | 217,786 | 926,879 |
| Portland, Me. | 378 | 138 | 73,629 | 275,118 |
| Providence | 613 | 155 | 117,275 | 577,460 |
| Pueblo | 170 | 61 | 29,424 | 107,173 |
| Raleigh | 169 | 110 | 22,682 | 59,400 |
| Rapid City | 108 | 60 | 13,996 | 40,580 |
| Reno | 85 | 38 | 14,970 | 82,000 |
| Richmond | 380 | 121 | 73,745 | 257,199 |
| Rochester | 589 | 157 | 89,997 | 361,790 |
| Rockford | 354 | 97 | 53,251 | 195,146 |
| Rockville C'tr. | 512 | 124 | 263,959 | 878,810 |
| Sacramento | 267 | 88 | 50,927 | 221,085 |
| Saginaw | 202 | 116 | 50,393 | 173,632 |
| St. Augustine | 275 | 131 | 61,973 | 209,241 |
| St. Cloud | 359 | 146 | 44,243 | 140,089 |
| Salina | 147 | 100 | 18,820 | 60,287 |
| Salt Lake City | 101 | 35 | 15,398 | 52,695 |
| San Angelo | 73 | 37 | 15,925 | 60,067 |
| San Diego | 474 | 163 | 110,087 | 345,558 |
| Santa Rosa | 104 | 36 | 13,994 | 61,659 |
| Savannah | 96 | 38 | 13,260 | 35,050 |
| Scranton | 620 | 236 | 92,172 | 358,270 |
| Sioux City | 232 | 140 | 35,701 | 108,016 |
| Sioux Falls | 216 | 123 | 34,423 | 103,000 |
| Spokane | 211 | 57 | 21,342 | 68,663 |
| Springfield, Ill. | 369 | 143 | 48,044 | 182,340 |
| Springfield, Mass. | 480 | 135 | 98,181 | 385,241 |
| Springfield-Cape Girardeau | 123 | 58 | 11,056 | 36,608 |
| Steubenville | 194 | 73 | 15,932 | 55,000 |
| Stockton | 82 | 30 | 18,071 | 90,000 |
| Superior | 154 | 89 | 24,055 | 82,536 |
| Syracuse | 530 | 165 | 119,120 | 397,325 |
| Toledo | 412 | 162 | 87,775 | 304,289 |
| Trenton | 482 | 188 | 163,162 | 655,016 |
| Tucson | 323 | 83 | 157,382 | 413,100 |
| Wheeling | 216 | 102 | 25,276 | 257,199 |
| Wichita | 211 | 98 | 23,559 | 87,215 |
| Wilmington | 198 | 52 | 31,330 | 124,107 |
| Winona | 261 | 131 | 34,062 | 115,019 |
| Worcester | 514 | 129 | 91,290 | 352,309 |
| Yakima | 78 | 38 | 12,431 | 47,042 |
| Youngstown | 355 | 117 | 74,565 | 312,708 |
| **Eastern Rite:** | | | | |
| Byzan Pitts. | 151 | 119 | 19,822 | 223,923 |
| Uk. Gk., Chi. | 46 | 25 | 1,754 | 29,785 |
| Passaic | 108 | 77 | 10,426 | 96,415 |
| Stamford | 102 | 57 | 5,218 | 87,625 |
| Maronite | 59 | 45 | 421 | 151,252 |
| Melkite | 41 | 23 | 3 | 55,000 |
| Military Ordinariate** | | | | 2,000,000 |
| **Total 1968** | 59,803 | 18,064 | 11,093,024 | 47,468,333 |
| **Total 1967** | 59,193 | 17,765 | 11,006,687 | 46,864,910 |

*Archdiocese of New York includes the boroughs of Manhattan, Bronx and Richmond, and 7 counties of eastern New York. Cities and dioceses of the same name do not have the same areas and in some cases the population of the diocese is greater than that of the city because of its greater area.

**Military Ordinariate under jurisdiction of His Excellency Archbishop Cooke (N. Y.) as Military Vicar.

The first 29 dioceses are archdioceses; there are 125 other dioceses.

Cardinals 6 (Baltimore, Boston, Chicago, Los Angeles, Philadelphia, and Washington). Archbishops 26, Bishops 235, Abbots 53, Priests 59,803, Brothers 12,261, Sisters 176,341, and 18,064 parishes with 17,500 pastors. There are 437 religious order seminaries with 39,838 seminarians; 305 colleges with 433,-960 students; 1,407 high schools with 694,996 students; 868 private high schools with 394,276 students; 10,375 elementary schools with 4,089,826 students; 362 private elementary schools with 75,678 students; 103 protective institutes with 8,110 students; full time teachers 206,959; 239 orphanages and infant asylums with 46,425 dependent children; 788 general hospitals, 142 special hospitals, 19,180,735 patients treated annually; 420 homes for the aged. Converts (1967) 110,717.

## Ash Wednesday and Easter Sunday

| Year | Ash Wed. | Easter Sunday | Year | Ash Wed. | Easter Sunday | Year | Ash Wed. | Easter Sunday | Year | Ash Wed. | Easter Sunday |
|---|---|---|---|---|---|---|---|---|---|---|---|
| 1901 | Feb. 20 | April 7 | 1951 | Feb. 7 | Mar. 25 | 2001 | Feb. 28 | Apr. 15 | 2051 | Feb. 15 | Apr. 2 |
| 1902 | Feb. 12 | Mar. 30 | 1952 | Feb. 27 | April 13 | 2002 | Feb. 13 | Mar. 31 | 2052 | Mar. 6 | Apr. 21 |
| 1903 | Feb. 25 | April 12 | 1953 | Feb. 18 | April 5 | 2003 | Mar. 5 | Apr. 20 | 2053 | Feb. 19 | Apr. 6 |
| 1904 | Feb. 17 | April 3 | 1954 | Mar. 3 | April 18 | 2004 | Feb. 25 | Apr. 11 | 2054 | Feb. 11 | Mar. 29 |
| 1905 | Mar. 8 | April 23 | 1955 | Feb. 23 | April 10 | 2005 | Feb. 9 | Mar. 27 | 2055 | Mar. 3 | Apr. 18 |
| 1906 | Feb. 28 | April 15 | 1956 | Feb. 15 | April 1 | 2006 | Mar. 1 | Apr. 16 | 2056 | Feb. 16 | Apr. 2 |
| 1907 | Feb. 13 | Mar. 31 | 1957 | Mar. 6 | April 21 | 2007 | Feb. 21 | Apr. 8 | 2057 | Mar. 7 | Apr. 22 |
| 1908 | Mar. 4 | April 19 | 1958 | Feb. 19 | April 6 | 2008 | Feb. 6 | Mar. 23 | 2058 | Feb. 27 | Apr. 14 |
| 1909 | Feb. 24 | April 11 | 1959 | Feb. 11 | Mar. 29 | 2009 | Feb. 25 | Apr. 12 | 2059 | Feb. 12 | Mar. 30 |
| 1910 | Feb. 9 | Mar. 27 | 1960 | Mar. 2 | April 17 | 2010 | Feb. 17 | Apr. 4 | 2060 | Mar. 3 | Apr. 18 |
| 1911 | Mar. 1 | April 16 | 1961 | Feb. 15 | April 2 | 2011 | Mar. 9 | Apr. 24 | 2061 | Feb. 23 | Apr. 10 |
| 1912 | Feb. 21 | April 7 | 1962 | Mar. 7 | April 22 | 2012 | Feb. 22 | Apr. 8 | 2062 | Feb. 8 | Mar. 26 |
| 1913 | Feb. 5 | Mar. 23 | 1963 | Feb. 27 | April 14 | 2013 | Feb. 13 | Mar. 31 | 2063 | Feb. 28 | Apr. 15 |
| 1914 | Feb. 25 | April 12 | 1964 | Feb. 12 | Mar. 29 | 2014 | Mar. 5 | Apr. 20 | 2064 | Feb. 20 | Apr. 6 |
| 1915 | Feb. 17 | April 4 | 1965 | Mar. 3 | April 18 | 2015 | Feb. 18 | Apr. 5 | 2065 | Feb. 11 | Mar. 29 |
| 1916 | Mar. 8 | April 23 | 1966 | Feb. 23 | April 10 | 2016 | Feb. 10 | Mar. 27 | 2066 | Feb. 24 | Apr. 11 |
| 1917 | Feb. 21 | April 8 | 1967 | Feb. 8 | Mar. 26 | 2017 | Mar. 1 | Apr. 16 | 2067 | Feb. 16 | Apr. 3 |
| 1918 | Feb. 13 | Mar. 31 | 1968 | Feb. 28 | April 14 | 2018 | Feb. 14 | Apr. 1 | 2068 | Mar. 7 | Apr. 22 |
| 1919 | Mar. 5 | April 20 | 1969 | Feb. 19 | April 6 | 2019 | Mar. 6 | Apr. 21 | 2069 | Feb. 27 | Apr. 14 |
| 1920 | Feb. 18 | April 4 | 1970 | Feb. 11 | Mar. 29 | 2020 | Feb. 26 | Apr. 12 | 2070 | Feb. 12 | Mar. 30 |
| 1921 | Feb. 9 | Mar. 27 | 1971 | Feb. 24 | April 11 | 2021 | Feb. 17 | Apr. 4 | 2071 | Mar. 4 | Apr. 19 |
| 1922 | Mar. 1 | April 16 | 1972 | Feb. 16 | April 2 | 2022 | Mar. 2 | Apr. 17 | 2072 | Feb. 24 | Apr. 10 |
| 1923 | Feb. 14 | April 1 | 1973 | Mar. 7 | April 22 | 2023 | Feb. 22 | Apr. 9 | 2073 | Feb. 8 | Mar. 26 |
| 1924 | Mar. 5 | April 20 | 1974 | Feb. 27 | April 14 | 2024 | Feb. 14 | Mar. 31 | 2074 | Feb. 28 | Apr. 15 |
| 1925 | Feb. 25 | April 12 | 1975 | Feb. 12 | Mar. 30 | 2025 | Mar. 5 | Apr. 20 | 2075 | Feb. 20 | Apr. 7 |
| 1926 | Feb. 17 | April 4 | 1976 | Mar. 3 | April 18 | 2026 | Feb. 18 | Apr. 5 | 2076 | Mar. 4 | Apr. 19 |
| 1927 | Mar. 2 | April 17 | 1977 | Feb. 23 | April 10 | 2027 | Feb. 10 | Mar. 28 | 2077 | Feb. 24 | Apr. 11 |
| 1928 | Feb. 22 | April 8 | 1978 | Feb. 8 | Mar. 26 | 2028 | Mar. 1 | Apr. 16 | 2078 | Feb. 16 | Apr. 3 |
| 1929 | Feb. 13 | Mar. 31 | 1979 | Feb. 28 | April 15 | 2029 | Feb. 14 | Apr. 1 | 2079 | Mar. 8 | Apr. 23 |
| 1930 | Mar. 5 | April 20 | 1980 | Feb. 20 | April 6 | 2030 | Mar. 6 | Apr. 21 | 2080 | Feb. 21 | Apr. 7 |
| 1931 | Feb. 18 | April 5 | 1981 | Mar. 4 | April 19 | 2031 | Feb. 26 | Apr. 13 | 2081 | Feb. 12 | Mar. 30 |
| 1932 | Feb. 10 | Mar. 27 | 1982 | Feb. 24 | April 11 | 2032 | Feb. 11 | Mar. 28 | 2082 | Mar. 4 | Apr. 19 |
| 1933 | Mar. 1 | April 16 | 1983 | Feb. 16 | April 3 | 2033 | Mar. 2 | Apr. 17 | 2083 | Feb. 17 | Apr. 4 |
| 1934 | Feb. 14 | April 1 | 1984 | Mar. 7 | April 22 | 2034 | Feb. 22 | Apr. 9 | 2084 | Feb. 9 | Mar. 26 |
| 1935 | Mar. 6 | April 21 | 1985 | Feb. 20 | April 7 | 2035 | Feb. 7 | Mar. 25 | 2085 | Feb. 28 | Apr. 15 |
| 1936 | Feb. 26 | April 12 | 1986 | Feb. 12 | Mar. 30 | 2036 | Feb. 27 | Apr. 13 | 2086 | Feb. 13 | Mar. 31 |
| 1937 | Feb. 10 | Mar. 28 | 1987 | Mar. 4 | April 19 | 2037 | Feb. 18 | Apr. 5 | 2087 | Mar. 5 | Apr. 20 |
| 1938 | Mar. 2 | April 17 | 1988 | Feb. 17 | April 3 | 2038 | Mar. 10 | Apr. 25 | 2088 | Feb. 25 | Apr. 11 |
| 1939 | Feb. 22 | April 9 | 1989 | Feb. 8 | Mar. 26 | 2039 | Feb. 23 | Apr. 10 | 2089 | Feb. 16 | Apr. 3 |
| 1940 | Feb. 7 | Mar. 24 | 1990 | Feb. 28 | April 15 | 2040 | Feb. 15 | Apr. 1 | 2090 | Mar. 1 | Apr. 16 |
| 1941 | Feb. 26 | April 13 | 1991 | Feb. 13 | Mar. 31 | 2041 | Mar. 6 | Apr. 21 | 2091 | Feb. 21 | Apr. 8 |
| 1942 | Feb. 18 | April 5 | 1992 | Mar. 4 | April 19 | 2042 | Feb. 19 | Apr. 6 | 2092 | Feb. 13 | Mar. 30 |
| 1943 | Mar. 10 | April 25 | 1993 | Feb. 24 | April 11 | 2043 | Feb. 11 | Mar. 29 | 2093 | Feb. 25 | Apr. 12 |
| 1944 | Feb. 23 | April 9 | 1994 | Feb. 16 | April 3 | 2044 | Mar. 2 | Apr. 17 | 2094 | Feb. 17 | Apr. 4 |
| 1945 | Feb. 14 | April 1 | 1995 | Mar. 1 | April 16 | 2045 | Feb. 22 | Apr. 9 | 2095 | Mar. 9 | Apr. 24 |
| 1946 | Mar. 6 | April 21 | 1996 | Feb. 21 | April 7 | 2046 | Feb. 7 | Mar. 25 | 2096 | Feb. 29 | Apr. 15 |
| 1947 | Feb. 19 | April 6 | 1997 | Feb. 12 | Mar. 30 | 2047 | Feb. 27 | Apr. 14 | 2097 | Feb. 13 | Mar. 31 |
| 1948 | Feb. 11 | Mar. 28 | 1998 | Feb. 25 | April 12 | 2048 | Feb. 19 | Apr. 5 | 2098 | Mar. 5 | Apr. 20 |
| 1949 | Mar. 2 | April 17 | 1999 | Feb. 17 | April 4 | 2049 | Mar. 3 | Apr. 18 | 2099 | Feb. 25 | Apr. 12 |
| 1950 | Feb. 22 | April 9 | 2000 | Mar. 8 | April 23 | 2050 | Feb. 23 | Apr. 10 | 2100 | Feb. 10 | Mar. 28 |

A lengthy dispute over the date for the celebration of Easter was settled by the first Council of the Christian Churches at Nicaea, in Asia Minor, in 325 A.D. The council ruled that Easter would be observed on the first Sunday following the 14th day of the Paschal Moon, referred to as the Paschal Full Moon. The Paschal Moon is the first moon whose 14th day comes on or after March 21. Dates of the Paschal Full Moon, which are not necessarily the same as those of the real or astronomical full moon, are listed in the table below with an explanation of how to compute the date of Easter.

If the Paschal Full Moon falls on a Sunday, then Easter is the following Sunday. The earliest date on which Easter can fall is March 22; it fell on that date in 1761 and 1818 but will not do so in any year in the 20th Century. The latest possible date for Easter is April 25; it fell on that date in 1943 and so next in 2038.

Lent begins on Ash Wednesday, which comes 40 days previous to Easter Sunday, not counting Sundays. Originally it was a period of but 40 hours. Later it comprised 30 days of fasting, omitting all the Sundays and also all the Saturdays except one. Pope Gregory added Ash Wednesday to the fast, together with the remainder of that week.

The last seven days of Lent constitute Holy Week, beginning with Palm Sunday. Passion Week precedes Holy Week. The last Thursday—Maundy Thursday—commemorates the institution of the Eucharist.

The following day, Good Friday, commemorates the day of the crucifixion. Mohammedans celebrate Friday as the day of Adam's creation.

Easter is the chief festival of the Christian year, commemorating the resurrection of Christ. It occurs about the same time as the ancient heathen Roman celebration of the Vernal Equinox, the arrival of Spring. In the second century, A.D., Easter Day was among Christians in Asia Minor, the 14th of Nisan, the seventh month of the Jewish calendar. The Christians in Europe observed the nearest Sunday.

---

## Date of Paschal Full Moon, 1900-2199

The Golden Number, used in table, is greater by unity (one) than the remainder obtained upon dividing the given year by 19; for example: 13 is the Golden Number for the year 1969, from the table the date of Paschal Full Moon is Apr. 2 and this being Wednesday, Easter Sunday is on Apr. 6.

| Golden Number | Date | Golden Number | Date | Golden Number | Date | Golden Number | Date |
|---|---|---|---|---|---|---|---|
| 1 | April 14 | 6 | April 18 | 11 | Mar. 25 | 16 | Mar. 30 |
| 2 | April 3 | 7 | April 8 | 12 | April 13 | 17 | April 17 |
| 3 | Mar. 23 | 8 | Mar. 28 | 13 | April 2 | 18 | April 7 |
| 4 | April 11 | 9 | April 16 | 14 | Mar. 22 | 19 | Mar. 27 |
| 5 | Mar. 31 | 10 | April 5 | 15 | April 10 | | |

## National Council of Churches

The National Council of the Churches of Christ in the U. S. A. is a cooperative federation of 33 Protestant and Orthodox churches which seeks to advance programs and policies of mutual interest to its members. The NCC was formed in 1950 by the merger of 12 inter-denominational agencies. The Council's member churches now have an aggregate congregation totaling approximately 42,000,000. The NCC is not a governing body and has no control over the policies or operations of any church belonging to it. The Southern Baptist Convention and the Lutheran Church-Missouri Synod have chosen not to join the NCC. The work of the Council is divided into 4 Divisions—Christian Life and Mission, Christian Education, Overseas Ministries and Christian Unity. The chief administrative officer of the NCC is Dr. R. H. Edwin Espy. The president is Dr. Arthur S. Flemming. The main office is located at 475 Riverside Drive, New York, N. Y. 10027.

# Greek Orthodox Church Calendar, 1969

| Date | Holy Days | Date | Holy Days |
|---|---|---|---|
| Jan. 1 | The Circumcision of Christ—The Feastday of St. Basil New Year's Day | June 29 | Feastday of Saints Peter and Paul |
| | | June 30 | Feastday of the Twelve Holy Apostles |
| Jan. 6 | The Epiphany, The Baptism of Jesus Christ The Sanctification of the Waters | Aug. 6 | The Transfiguration |
| | | Aug. 15 | The Dormition of the Virgin Mary |
| Jan. 7 | Feastday of St. John the Baptist | Aug. 29 | Beheading of St. John The Baptist |
| Jan. 30 | Feastday of Three Hierachs: St. Basil, St. Gregory and St. John Chrysostom | Sept. 1 | Beginning of the Church Year |
| | | Sept. 8 | Nativity of the Virgin Mary |
| Feb. 24 | Beginning of Easter lenten period | Sept. 14 | The Elevation of the Holy Cross |
| Mar. 25 | The Annunication of the Virgin Mary | Oct. 23 | The Feast of St. James (Iakovos) |
| Apr. 6 | Palm Sunday | Nov. 15 | The beginning of the Christmas Lent |
| Apr. 7-13 | Holy Easter Week | Nov. 21 | Presentation of Blessed Virgin Mary |
| Apr. 11 | Holy Friday—The Burial of Christ | Nov. 30 | The Feast of St. Andrew, Founder Ecumenical Patriarchate of Constantinople. |
| Apr. 13 | Easter Sunday—The Resurrection of Christ | | |
| May 22 | The Ascension | Dec. 25 | Christmas Day: The Birth of Jesus Christ. |
| June 1 | Pentecost Sunday | | |

The dates above are according to the Gregorian calendar, adopted by the Greek Church in 1923. First Greek Orthodox church in U. S. founded 1864, in New Orleans, La.

# Jewish Holidays, Festivals and Fasts

### Source: Synagogue Council of America

**All Jewish holidays, etc., begin at sunset on the day previous. *Also observed the following day.**

| Festivals and Fasts | Hebrew Date | 1968-1969 (5729) | 1969-1970 (5730) | 1970-1971 (5731) | 1971-1972 (5732) | 1972-1973 (5733) |
|---|---|---|---|---|---|---|
| New Year* (Rosh Hashanah)..... | Tishri 1 | Sept. 23 M | Sept. 13 S | Oct. 1 Th | Sept. 20 M | Sept. 9 S |
| Fast of Gedalia......... | Tishri 3 | Sept. 25 W | Sept. 15 M | Oct. 4 Su | Sept. 22 W | Sept. 11 M |
| Fast of Gedalia......... | Tishri 4 | ........... | ........... | ........... | ........... | ........... |
| Day of Atonement (Yom Kippur)....... | Tishri 10 | Oct. 2 W | Sept. 22 M | Oct. 10 S | Sept. 29 W | Sept. 18 M |
| Tabernacles, 1st Day*.... | Tishri 15 | Oct. 7 M | Sept. 27 S | Oct. 15 Th | Oct. 4 M | Sept. 23 S |
| Tabernacles, 8th Day.... | Tishri 22 | Oct. 14 M | Oct. 4 S | Oct. 22 Th | Oct. 11 M | Sept. 30 S |
| Rejoicing of the Law.... | Tishri 23 | Oct. 15 Tu | Oct. 5 Su | Oct. 23 F | Oct. 12 T | Oct. 1 Su |
| Hanukah......... | Kislev 25 | Dec. 16 M | Dec. 5 F | Dec. 23 W | Dec. 13 M | Dec. 1 F |
| Fast of Tebet......... | Tebet 10 | Dec. 31 Tu | Dec. 19 F | Jan. 7 Th | Dec. 28 T | Dec. 15 F |
| Purim......... | Adar 14 | Mar. 4 Tu | ........... | ........... | Feb. 29 T | ........... |
| Purim......... | Adar II 14 | ........... | Mar. 22 Su | Mar. 11 Th | ........... | Mar. 18 Su |
| Passover, 1st Day*..... | Nisan 15 | Apr. 3 Th | Apr. 21 T | Apr. 10 S | Mar. 30 Th | Apr. 17 T |
| Passover, 7th Day..... | Nisan 21 | Apr. 9 W | Apr. 27 M | Apr. 16 F | Apr. 5 W | Apr. 23 M |
| Passover, Last Day..... | Nisan 22 | Apr. 10 Th | Apr. 28 T | Apr. 17 S | Apr. 6 Th | Apr. 24 T |
| Shebuoth (Feast of Weeks)..... | Sivan 6 | May 23 F | June 10 W | May 30 Su | May 19 F | June 6 W |
| Fast of Tammuz....... | Tammuz 17 | July 3 Th | July 21 T | ........... | June 29 Th | July 17 T |
| Fast of Tammuz....... | Tammuz 18 | ........... | ........... | July 11 Su | ........... | ........... |
| Fast of Av............ | Av 9 | July 24 Th | Aug. 11 T | Aug. 1 Su | July 20 Th | Aug. 7 T |
| Fast of Av............ | Av *10 | ........... | ........... | ........... | ........... | ........... |

The months of the Jewish year are: 1 Tishri; 2 Chesvan (Also Marchesvan); 3 Kislev; 4 Tebet (Also Tebeth); 5 Sebat (Also Shebhat); 6 Adar; 6a, added month some years, Adar Sheni (II); 7 Nisan; 8 Iyar; 9 Sivan; 10 Tammuz; 11 Av (also Abh); 12 Elul.

# Lunar Calendar, Chinese New Year's, Vietnamese Tet

The ancient Chinese lunar calendar is divided into 12 months of either 29 or 30 days (compensating for the fact that the mean duration of the lunar month is 29 days, 12 hrs., 44.05 mins.). Every 30 months the calendar is further adjusted by the addition of an extra month.

The Chinese calendar runs on a sexagenary cycle, i.e., 60 years. The cycles 1864-1923 and 1924-1983, with the years grouped under their 12 animal designations, are printed below. The year 1969 is found in the 10th column, under Fowl or Chicken, and is known as a "Year of the Chicken." Similarly, readers can find the animal name for the year of their birth, marriage, etc., in the same chart.

The lunar calendar is still used to set the dates for traditional festivals in the Republic of China (Taiwan), in Chinese communities around the world, and also in Vietnam where the old Chinese calendar was in use for many centuries.

The Chinese New Year, Hsin Nien, and the 3-day Vietnamese New Year festival, Tet, begin at the first new moon after the sun enters Aquarius. The day may fall, therefore, between Jan. 21 and Feb. 19 of the Gregorian calendar. The old-style Chinese year 4667 begins Feb. 17, 1969. The year 4668 begins Feb. 6, 1970. (The date is fixed according to the date of the new moon in Taiwan and Vietnam. Since both are west of the International Date Line, the date may be one day later than that of the new moon in New York.)

Except for marking such traditional festivals, both Vietnam and the Republic of China use the western, Gregorian calendar.

| Rat | Ox | Tiger | Hare (Rabbit) | Dragon | Snake | Horse | Sheep (Goat) | Monkey | Fowl Chicken | Dog | Pig |
|---|---|---|---|---|---|---|---|---|---|---|---|
| 1864 | 1865 | 1866 | 1867 | 1868 | 1869 | 1870 | 1871 | 1872 | 1873 | 1874 | 1875 |
| 1876 | 1877 | 1878 | 1879 | 1880 | 1881 | 1882 | 1883 | 1884 | 1885 | 1886 | 1887 |
| 1888 | 1889 | 1890 | 1891 | 1892 | 1893 | 1894 | 1895 | 1896 | 1897 | 1898 | 1899 |
| 1900 | 1901 | 1902 | 1903 | 1904 | 1905 | 1906 | 1907 | 1908 | 1909 | 1910 | 1911 |
| 1912 | 1913 | 1914 | 1915 | 1916 | 1917 | 1918 | 1919 | 1920 | 1921 | 1922 | 1923 |
| 1924 | 1925 | 1926 | 1927 | 1928 | 1929 | 1930 | 1931 | 1932 | 1933 | 1934 | 1935 |
| 1936 | 1937 | 1938 | 1939 | 1940 | 1941 | 1942 | 1943 | 1944 | 1945 | 1946 | 1947 |
| 1948 | 1949 | 1950 | 1951 | 1952 | 1953 | 1954 | 1955 | 1956 | 1957 | 1958 | 1959 |
| 1960 | 1961 | 1962 | 1963 | 1964 | 1965 | 1966 | 1967 | 1968 | 1969 | 1970 | 1971 |
| 1972 | 1973 | 1974 | 1975 | 1976 | 1977 | 1978 | 1979 | 1980 | 1981 | 1982 | 1983 |

## Procedures for Adopting a Child

The United States Government has published factual reports on procedures for adopting a child. They are entitled The Physician's Part in Adoption; The Social Worker's Part in Adoption; The Attorney's Part in Adoption; Social Workers Look at Adoption and Manual on Intercountry Adoption; When You Adopt a Child; Legislative Guides for the Termination of Parental Rights and Responsibilities and the Adoption of Children. The Supt. of Documents, Government Printing Office, Washington, D. C. 20402, supplies information on how to procure these issues.

# AWARDS—MEDALS—PRIZES
## The Alfred B. Nobel Prize Winners

Alfred B. Nobel, inventor of dynamite, who died Dec. 10, 1896, bequeathed $9,000,000, the interest to be distributed yearly to those who had most benefited mankind during the preceding year.

Awards for physics and chemistry are made by the Swedish Academy of Science; medicine or physiology by the Stockholm Faculty of Medicine; literature by the Swedish Academy of Literature; peace by five persons elected by the Norwegian Parliament (Storting). The Fund is managed by a board of directors, the head of which is appointed by the Swedish Government.

A., American; Arg., Argentine; Austl., Australian; Aus., Austrian; B., Belgian; Br., British; Can., Canadian; Ch., Chilean; Chin., Chinese; Cz., Czechoslovak; D., Dutch; Dn., Danish; F., French; Fin., Finnish; G., German; Gr., Greek; Guat., Guatemala; Hun., Hungarian; Ice., Iceland; Ind., Indian; Ir., Irish; Is., Israel; I., Italian; J., Japanese; N., Norwegian; Nl., Netherlands; P., Polish; Port., Portuguese; R., Russian; So. A., South Africa; Sp., Spanish; Swe., Swedish; Swi., Swiss; Y., Yugoslav.

| Year | Physics | Chemistry | Medicine and Physiology | Literature | Peace |
|---|---|---|---|---|---|
| 1901.. | Wilhelm K. Röntgen (G.) | Jacobus H. van't Hoff (D.) | Emil A. von Behring (G.) | René F. A. Sully Prudhomme (F.) | H. Dunant (Swi.); Fred. Passy (F.) |
| 1902.. | H. A. Lorentz & P. Zeeman (D.) | Emil Fischer (G.) | Sir Ronald Ross (Br.) | Theodor Mommsen (G.) | E. Ducommun & A. Gobat (Swi.) |
| 1903.. | H. A. Becquerel (F.); Pierre and Marie Curie (F.), born Poland | Svante A. Arrhenius (Swe.) | Niels R. Finsen (Dn.) | Björnstjerne Björnson (N.) | Sir William R. Cremer (Br.) |
| 1904.. | Lord Rayleigh (Br.) | Sir William Ramsay (Br.) | Ivan P. Pavlov (R.) | F. Mistral (F.); J. Echegaray (Sp.) | Institute of International Law |
| 1905.. | Phillipp Lenard (G.) | Adolf von Baeyer (G.) | Robert Koch (G.) | Henryk Sienkiewicz (P.) | Bertha von Suttner (Aus.) |
| 1906.. | Joseph J. Thomson (Br.) | Henri Moissan (F.) | C. Golgi (I.); S. Ramon y Cajal (Sp.) | Giosuè Carducci (I.) | Theodore Roosevelt (A.) |
| 1907.. | Albert A. Michelson (A.) | Eduard Buchner (G.) | Charles L. A. Laveran (F.) | Rudyard Kipling (Br.) | E. T. Moneta (I.); L. Renault (F.) |
| 1908.. | Gabriel Lippmann (F.) | Ernest Rutherford (Br.) | Paul Ehrlich (G.); E. Metchnikoff (F.), born Russia | Rudolf Eucken (G.) | Klas P. Arnoldson (Swe.); Frederik Bajer (Dn.) |
| 1909.. | Guglielmo Marconi (I.); Ferdinand Braun (G.) | Wilhelm Ostwald (G.) | Theodor Kocher (Swi.) | Selma Lagerlöf (Swe.) | Aug. M. E. Beernaert (B.); Baron de Constant de Rebecque d' Estournelles (F.) |
| 1910.. | Johannes D. van der Waals (D.) | Otto Wallach (G.) | Albrecht Kossel (G.) | Paul Heyse (G.) | International Peace Bureau (Swi.) |
| 1911.. | Wilhelm Wien (G.) | Marie Curie (F.), born Poland | Allvar Gullstrand (Swe.) | Maurice Maeterlinck (B.) | T. M. C. Asser (D); A. H. Fried (Aus.) |
| 1912.. | Gustaf Dalén (Swe.) | V. Grignard & P. Sabatier (F.) | Alexis Carrel (A.), born France | Gerhart Hauptmann (G.) | Elihu Root (A.) |
| 1913.. | H. Kamerlingh-Onnes (D.) | Alfred Werner (Swi.) | Charles Richet (F.) | Rabindranath Tagore (Ind.) | Henri La Fontaine (B.) |
| 1914.. | M. von Laue (G.) | T. W. Richards (A.) | R. Bárány (Aus.) | Not awarded | Not awarded |
| 1915.. | W. H. Bragg & W. L. Bragg (Br.) | Richard Willstätter (G.) | Not awarded | Romain Rolland (F.) | Not awarded |
| 1916.. | Not awarded | Not awarded | Not awarded | Verner von Heidenstam (Swe.) | Not awarded |
| 1917.. | Charles G. Barkla (Br.) | Not awarded | Not awarded | K. Gjellerup & H. Pontoppidan (Dn.) | International Red Cross of Geneva |
| 1918.. | Max Planck (G.) | Fritz Haber (G.) | Not awarded | Not awarded | Not awarded |
| 1919.. | Johannes Stark (G.) | Not awarded | Jules Bordet (B.) | Carl Spitteler (Swi.) | Woodrow Wilson (A.) |
| 1920.. | C. Guillaume (Swi.) | Walther Nernst (G.) | A. Krogh (Dn.) | Knut Hamsun (N.) | L. Bourgeois (F.) |
| 1921.. | Albert Einstein (G.) | Frederick Soddy (Br.) | Not awarded | Anatole France (F.) | K. H. Branting (Swe) Chr. Lange (N.) |
| 1922.. | Niels Bohr (Dn.) | Francis W. Aston (Br.) | A. V. Hill (Br.); O. Meyerhof (G.) | Jacinto Benavente (Sp.) | Fridtjof Nansen (N.) |
| 1923.. | Robert A. Millikan (A.) | Fritz Pregl (Aus.) | Frederick G. Banting & John J. R. Macleod (Can.) | William B. Yeats (Ir.) | Not awarded |
| 1924.. | Karl M. G. Siegbahn (Swe.) | Not awarded | Willem Einthoven (D.) | Wladislaw Reymont (P.) | Not awarded |
| 1925.. | James Franck & Gustav Hertz (G.) | Richard Zsigmondy (G.), born in Austria | Not awarded | George Bernard Shaw (Br.) | C. G. Dawes (A.); Sir Austen Chamberlain (Br.) |
| 1926.. | Jean B. Perrin (F.) | Theodor Svedberg (Swe.) | Johan Fibiger (Dn.) | Grazia Deledda (I.) | Arist. Briand (F.); G. Stresemann (G.) |
| 1927.. | Arthur Compton (A.); Chas. T. R. Wilson (Br.) | Heinrich Wieland (G.) | J. Wagner Jauregg (Aus.) | Henri Bergson (F.) | Ferdinand Buisson (F.); Ludwig Quidde (G.) |
| 1928.. | Owen W. Richardson (Br.) | Adolf Windaus (G.) | Charles Nicolle (F.) | Sigrid Undset (N.) | Not awarded |
| 1929.. | Prince Louis V. de Broglie (F.) | Arth. Harden (Br.) H. von Euler-Chelpin (Swe.), German born | Sir Frederick G Hopkins (Br.); Christiaan Eijkman (D.) | Thomas Mann (G.) | Frank B. Kellogg (A.) |
| 1930.. | Sir Chandrasekhara V. Raman (Ind.) | Hans Fischer (G.) | Karl Landsteiner (A.), born Austria | Sinclair Lewis (A.) | Nathan Söderblom (Swe.) |
| 1931.. | Not awarded | Carl Bosch & Friedrich Bergius (G.) | Otto Warburg (G.) | Erik A. Karlfeldt (Swe.) | N. M. Butler & Jane Addams (A.) |
| 1932.. | Werner Heisenberg (G.) | Irving Langmuir (A.) | Sir Charles S. Sherrington & E. D. Adrian (Br.) | John Galsworthy (Br.) | Not awarded |
| 1933.. | P. A. M. Dirac (Br.); Erwin Schroedinger (Aus.) | Not awarded | Thomas H. Morgan (A.) | Ivan Bunin (F.), born Russia | Sir Norman Angell (Br.) |
| 1934.. | Not awarded | Harold C. Urey (A.) | G. H. Whipple, G. R. Minot & W. P. Murphy (A.) | Luigi Pirandello (I.) | Arthur Henderson (Br.) |
| 1935.. | James Chadwick (Br.) | Frédéric and Irène Joliot-Curie (F.) | Hans Spemann (G.) | Not awarded | Carl von Ossietzky (G.) |
| 1936.. | Carl D. Anderson (A.); Victor F. Hess (Aus.) | Peter J. W. Debye (Nl.) | Sir Henry H. Dale (Br.); Otto Loewi (Aus.) | Eugene O'Neill (A.) | Carlos deS. Lamas (Arg.) |
| 1937.. | Clinton J. Davisson (A.); G. P. Thomson (Br.) | Walter N. Haworth (Br.); Paul Karrer (Swi.) | Albert von Szent-Györgyi (Hun.) | Roger Martin du Gard (F.) | Viscount Cecil of Chelwood (Br.) |

| Year | Physics | Chemistry | Medicine and Physiology | Literature | Peace |
|---|---|---|---|---|---|
| 1938.. | Enrico Fermi (I.) | Richard Kuhn (G.)* | Cornelie Heymans (B.) | Pearl Buck (A.) | Nansen Internat'l Office for Refugees at Geneva |
| 1939.. (**) | E. O. Lawrence (A.) | A. Butenandt (G.)*; L. Ruzicka (Swi.) | Gerhard Domagk (G.)* | Frans Eemil Sillanpaa (Fin.) | Not awarded |
| 1943.. | Otto Stern (A.) | Georg von Hevesy (Hun.) | Edward Doisy (A.); Henrik Dam (Dn.) | Not awarded | Not awarded |
| 1944.. | Isador Isaac Rabi (A.) | Otto Hahn (G.) | Joseph Erlanger & Herb. Gasser (A.) | Johannes V. Jensen (Dn.) | International Red Cross of Geneva |
| 1945.. | Wolfgang Pauli (Aus.) | Artturi Virtanen (Fin.) | Sir Alexander Fleming & Sir Howard W. Florey (Br.); Ernst Boris Chain (G.) | Gabriela Mistral (Lucila Godoy y Alcayaga) (Ch.) | Cordell Hull (A.) |
| 1946.. | Percy W. Bridgman (A.) | James B. Sumner, John H. Northrop & Wendell M. Stanley (A.) | Herman J. Muller (A.) | Herman Hesse (Swi.), born in Germany | John R. Mott & Emily G. Balch (A.) |
| 1947.. | Sir Edward Appleton (Br.) | Sir Robert Robinson (Br.) | Carl F. and Gerty T. Cori (A.), born in Czechoslovakia; Bernardo Houssay (Arg.) | Andre P. G. Gide (F.) | American Friends Service Committee (Quakers) & Friends Service Council, London |
| 1948.. | Patrick M. S. Blackett (Br.) | Arne Tiselius (Swe.) | Paul Mueller (Swi.) | Thomas Stearns Eliot (Br.), American-born | Not awarded |
| 1949.. | Hideki Yukawa (J.) | William F. Giauque (A.) | Walter R. Hess (Swi.); Antonio C. A. F. E. Moniz (Port.) | William Faulkner (A.) | Lord Boyd Orr (Br.) |
| 1950.. | Cecil Frank Powell (Br.) | Otto Diels & Kurt Alder (G.) | Philip S. Hench & Edward C. Kendall (A.); Tadeus Reichstein (Swi.) | Bertrand Russell (Br.) | Ralph J. Bunche (A.) |
| 1951.. | Sir John Cockcroft (Br.); Ernest T. S. Walton (Ir.) | Edwin M. McMillan & Glenn T. Seaborg (A.) | Max Theiler (So. A.) | Par Lagerkvist (Swe.) | Leon Jouhaux (F.) |
| 1952.. | Felix Bloch & Edward Mills Purcell (A.) | Archer J. P. Martin & Richard L. M. Synge (Br.) | Selman A. Waksman (A.), born in Ukraine | Franco Mauriac (F.) | Albert Schweitzer (F.) |
| 1953.. | Fritz Zernike (D.) | Herman Staudinger (G.) | Fritz A. Lipmann (A.) & Hans A. Krebs (Br.), both German born | Winston Churchill (Br.) | Gen. George C. Marshall (A.) |
| 1954.. | Max Born (Br.), German-born & Walter Bothe (G.) | Linus Pauling (A.) | Thomas H. Weller, Frederick C. Robbins & John F. Enders (A.) | Ernest Hemingway (A.) | The office of the United Nations Commissioner for Refugees |
| 1955.. | Polykarp Kusch & Willis E. Lamb (A.) | Vincent du Vigneaud (A.) | Hugo Theorell (Swe.) | Halldor K. Laxness (Ice.) | Not awarded |
| 1956.. | William Shockley, Walter H. Brattain & John Bardeen (A.) | Sir Cyril N. Hinshelwood (Br.); Nikolai N. Semenov (R.) | Dickinson W. Richards, Jr. (A.); André F. Cournand (A.), born in France; Werner Forssmann (G.) | Juan Ramon Jiménez (Puerto Rico), born in Spain | Not awarded |
| 1957.. | Chen Ning Yang & Tsung Dao Lee (Chin) | Sir Alexander Todd (Br.) | Daniel Bovet (I.), born in Switzerland | Albert Camus (F) | Lester B. Pearson (Can.) |
| 1958.. | Pavel A. Cherenkov, Igor E. Tamm & Ilya M. Frank (R.) | Frederick Sanger (Br.) | George W. Beadle, Edward L. Tatum & Joshua Lederberg (A.) | Boris Pasternak (R.)* | Rev. Dominique Georges Pire (B.) |
| 1959.. | Emilio Segre (A.), born Italy; Owen Chamberlain (A.) | Jaroslav Heyrovsky (Cz.) | Severo Ochoa (A.), born Sp.; Arthur Kornberg (A.) | Salvatore Quasimodo (I.) | Philip John Noel-Baker (Br.) |
| 1960.. | Donald A. Glaser (A.) | Willard F. Libby (A.) | Sir Macfarlane Burnet (Austl.); Peter Brian Medawar (Br.) | Alexis Léger (St.-John Perse) (F.) | Albert John Luthuli (So. A.) |
| 1961.. | Robert Hofstadter (A); Rudolf L. Mössbauer (G.) | Melvin Calvin (A.) | George von Bekesy (A.), Hungarian-born | Ivo Andric (Y) | Dag Hammarskjold (Swe.) *Posthumously* |
| 1962.. | Lev Davidovich Landau (R.) | John C. Kendrew (Br.); Max F. Perutz (Br.), Austrian-born | Francis H. C. Crick (Br.); James D. Watson (A.); Maurice H. F. Wilkins (Br.) | John Steinbeck (A.) | Linus C. Pauling (A.) |
| 1963.. | Eugene B. Wigner (A.), Hungarian born; Maria Goeppert Mayer (A.) & J. Hans D. Jensen (G.) | Karl Ziegler (G.) & Giulio Natta (I.) | Alan Lloyd Hodgkin (Br.); Andrew Fielding Huxley (Br.) & John C. Eccles (Austl.) | Giorgos Seferis (Gr.) | International Red Cross & League of Red Cross Societies |
| 1964.. | Charles H. Townes (A.); Nikolai Basov (R.) & Alexander Prochorov (R.) | Dorothy Crowfoot Hodgkin (Br.) | Konrad E. Bloch (A.); Feodor Lynen (G.) | Jean-Paul C. A. Sartre (F.)* | Dr. Martin Luther King (A.) |
| 1965.. | Richard P. Feynman (A.); Julian S. Schwinger (A.); Shinichero Tomonaga (J.) | Robert Burns Woodward (A.) | Francois Jacob; Andre Lwoff & Jacques Monod, all French | Mikhail Sholokhov (R.) | United Nations Children's Fund |
| 1966.. | Alfred Kastler (F.) | Robert S. Mulliken (A.) | Charles B. Huggins (A.); Francis Peyton Rous (A.) | Shmuel Yosef Agnon (Is.) & Nelly Sachs (Swe.) | Not awarded |
| 1967.. | Hans Albrecht Bethe (A.) | Manfred Eigen (G). Ronald G. W. Norrish (Br.) George Porter (Br.) | Haldan Keffer Hartline (A.) George Wald (A.) Ragnar Granit (Swe.) | Miguel Angel Asturias (Guat.) | Not awarded |

*(See Index for 1968 awards.)*

*Declined. **No prizes announced in 1940, 1941 and 1942.

# Pulitzer Prizes in Journalism, Letters and Music

The Pulitzer Prizes were endowed by Joseph Pulitzer (1847-1911), publisher of The World, New York, N. Y., in a bequest to Columbia University, New York, N. Y., and are awarded annually by the trustees of the university on recommendation of the Advisory Board on Pulitzer Prizes for work done during the preceding year. Secretary of the Advisory Board is John Hohenberg of Columbia Univ.

Prizes in Journalism are $1,000 (originally $500) in each category, except Meritorious Public Service for which a gold medal is given. Prizes in Letters, in each category, and Prize in Music are $500.

No awards given for years omitted.

## PULITZER PRIZES IN JOURNALISM
### MERITORIOUS PUBLIC SERVICE

For disinterested and meritorious public service by a United States newspaper.

1918—The New York Times. Also special award to Minna Lewinson and Henry Beetle Hough.
1919—Milwaukee Journal
1921—Boston Post.
1922—The World, New York.
1923—Memphis (Tenn.) Commercial Appeal.
1924—The World, New York.
1926—Enquirer-Sun, Columbus, Ga.
1927—Canton (O.) Daily News.
1928—Indianapolis Times.
1929—Evening World, New York.
1931—Atlanta (Ga.) Constitution.
1932—Indianapolis (Ind.) News.
1933—New York World-Telegram.
1934—Medford (Ore.) Mail-Tribune.
1935—Sacramento (Calif.) Bee.
1936—Cedar Rapids (Iowa) Gazette.
1937—St. Louis Post-Dispatch.
1938—Bismarck (N. D.) Tribune.
1939—Miami (Fla.) Daily News.
1940—Waterbury (Conn.) Republican and American.
1941—St. Louis Post-Dispatch.
1942—Los Angeles Times.
1943—Omaha World Herald.
1944—The New York Times.
1945—Detroit Free Press.
1946—The Scranton (Pa.) Times.
1947—Baltimore Sun.
1948—St. Louis Post-Dispatch.
1949—Nebraska State Journal.
1950—Chicago Daily News; St. Louis Post-Dispatch.
1951—Miami (Fla.) Herald and Brooklyn Eagle.
1952—St. Louis Post-Dispatch.
1953—Whiteville (N. C.) News Reporter; Tabor City (N. C.) Tribune.
1954—Newsday, Garden City, N. Y.
1955—Columbus (Ga.) Ledger and Sunday Ledger-Enquirer.
1956—Watsonville (Calif.) Register-Pajaronian.
1957—Chicago Daily News.
1958—Arkansas Gazette, Little Rock.
1959—Utica (N. Y.) Observer-Dispatch and Utica Daily Press.
1960—Los Angeles Times.
1961—Amarillo (Tex.) Globe-Times.
1962—Panama City (Fla.) News-Herald.
1963—Chicago Daily News.
1964—St. Petersburg (Fla.) Times.
1965—The Hutchinson (Kans.) News.
1966—Boston Globe.
1967—The Louisville Courier-Journal and The Milwaukee Journal.
1968—The Riverside (Calif.) Press-Enterprise.

### REPORTING

This category originally embraced all fields, local, national, and international. Later separate categories were created for the different fields of reporting.

1917—Herbert Bayard Swope, The World, N. Y.
1918—Harold A. Littledale, New York Evening Post.
1920—John J. Leary, Jr., The World, New York.
1921—Louis Seibold, The World, New York.
1922—Kirke L. Simpson, Associated Press.
1923—Alva Johnston, New York Times.
1924—Magner White, San Diego (Calif.) Sun.
1925—James W. Mulroy and Alvin H. Goldstein, Chicago Daily News.
1926—William Burke Miller, Louisville Courier-Journal.
1927—John T. Rogers, St. Louis Post-Dispatch.
1929—Paul Y. Anderson, St. Louis Post-Dispatch.
1930—Russell D. Owens, New York Times. Also $500 to W. O. Dapping, Auburn (N. Y.) Citizen.
1931—A. B. MacDonald, Kansas City (Mo.) Star.
1932—W. C. Richards, D. D. Martin, J. S. Pooler, F. D. Webb, J. N. W. Sloan, Detroit Free Press.
1933—Francis A. Jamieson, Associated Press.
1934—Royce Brier, San Francisco Chronicle.
1935—William H. Taylor, New York Herald Tribune
1936—Lauren D. Lyman, New York Times.
1937—John J. O'Neill, N. Y. Herald Tribune; William L. Laurence, N. Y. Times; Howard W. Blakeslee, A. P.; Gobind Behari Lal, Universal Service and David Dietz, Scripps-Howard Newspapers.
1938—Raymond Sprigle, Pittsburgh Post-Gazette.
1939—Thomas L. Stokes, Scripps-Howard Newspaper Alliance.
1940—S. Burton Heath, New York World-Telegram.
1941—Westbrook Pegler, New York World-Telegram.
1942—Stanton Delaplane, San Francisco Chronicle.

1943—George Weller, Chicago Daily News.
1944—Paul Schoenstein, N. Y. Journal-American.
1945—Jack S. McDowell, San Francisco Call-Bulletin.
1946—William L. Laurence, New York Times.
1947—Frederick Woltman, N. Y. World-Telegram.
1948—George E. Goodwin, Atlanta (Ga.) Journal.
1949—Malcolm Johnson, The Sun, New York.
1950—Meyer Berger, New York Times.
1951—Edward S. Montgomery, San Francisco Examiner.
1952—Geo. de Carvalho, San Francisco Chronicle.
*Since 1953 two prizes are given for local reporting: (1) to meet a deadline; (2) free of deadline.*
1953—(1) Providence (R. I.) Journal and Evening Bulletin; (2) Edward J. Mowery, N. Y. World-Telegram & Sun.
1954—(1) Vicksburg (Miss.) Sunday Post-Herald; (2) Alvin Scott McCoy, Kansas City (Mo.) Star.
1955—(1) Mrs. Caro Brown, Alice (Tex.) Daily Echo; (2) Roland K. Towery, Cuero (Tex.) Record.
1956—(1) Lee Hills, Detroit Free Press; (2) Arthur Daley, New York Times.
1957—(1) Salt Lake Tribune, Salt Lake City, Utah; (2) Wallace Turner and William Lambert, Portland Oregonian ($1,000 each).
1958—(1) Fargo (N. D.) Forum; (2) George Beveridge, Evening Star, Washington, D. C.
1959—(1) Miss Mary Lou Werner, Evening Star, Washington, D. C.; (2) John Harold Brislin, Scranton (Pa.) Tribune and The Scrantonian.
1960—(1) Jack Nelson, Atlanta (Ga.) Constitution; (2) Miriam Ottenberg, Evening Star, Washington, D. C.
1961—(1) Sanche de Gramont, N. Y. Herald Tribune; (2) Edgar May, Buffalo Evening News.
1962—(1) Robert D. Mullins, Desert News, Salt Lake City; (2) George Bliss, Chicago Tribune.
1963—(1) Shared by Sylvan Fox, William Longgood, and Anthony Shannon, N. Y. World-Telegram & Sun; (2) Oscar Griffin, Jr., Pecos (Tex.) Independent and Enterprise.
1964—(1) Norman C. Miller, Wall Street Journal; (2) Shared by James V. Magee, Albert V. Gaudiosi, and Frederick A. Meyer, Philadelphia Bulletin.
1965—(1) Melvin H. Ruder, Hungry Horse News (Columbia Falls, Mont.); (2) Gene Goltz, Houston, Post.
1966—(1) Los Angeles Times staff; (2) John A. Frasca, Tampa (Fla.) Tribune.
1967—(1) Robert V. Cox, Chambersburg (Pa.) Public Opinion; (2) Gene Miller, Miami Herald.
1968—Detroit Free Press; (2) J. Anthony Lukas, N. Y. Times.

### NATIONAL REPORTING

1942—Louis Stark, New York Times.
1944—Dewey L. Fleming, Baltimore Sun.
1945—James B. Reston, New York Times.
1946—Edward A. Harris, St. Louis Post-Dispatch.
1947—Edward T. Folliard, Washington Post.
1948—Bert Andrews, New York Herald Tribune; Nat S. Finney, Minneapolis Tribune.
1949—Charles P. Trussell, New York Times.
1950—Edwin O. Guthman, Seattle (Wash.) Times.
1952—Anthony Leviero, New York Times.
1953—Don Whitehead, Associated Press.
1954—Richard Wilson, Cowles Newspapers.
1955—Anthony Lewis, Washington Daily News.
1956—Charles L. Bartlett, Chattanooga Times.
1957—James Reston, New York Times.
1958—Relman Morin, A. P.; Clark Mollenhoff, Des Moines Register & Tribune ($1,000 each).
1959—Howard Van Smith, Miami (Fla.) News.
1960—Vance Trimble, Scripps-Howard, Washington, D. C.
1961—Edward R. Cony, Wall Street Journal.
1962—Nathan G. Caldwell and Gene S. Graham, Nashville Tennessean.
1963—Anthony Lewis, New York Times.
1964—Merriman Smith, U.P.I.
1965—Louis M. Kohlmeier, Wall Street Journal.
1966—Haynes Johnson, Evening Star, Washington, D. C.
1967—Monroe W. Karmin and Stanley W. Penn, Wall Street Journal.
1968—Howard James, Christian Science Monitor; Nathan K. Kotz, Des Moines Register.

### INTERNATIONAL REPORTING

1942—Laurence Edmund Allen, Associated Press
1943—Ira Wolfert, No. Am. Newspaper Alliance.
1944—Daniel DeLuce, Associated Press.
1945—Mark S. Watson, Baltimore Sun.

1946—Homer W. Bigart, New York Herald Tribune.
1947—Eddy Gilmore, Associated Press.
1948—Paul W. Ward, Baltimore Sun.
1949—Price Day, Baltimore Sun.
1950—Edmund Stevens, Christian Science Monitor.
1951—Keyes Beech, Chicago Daily News; Homer Bigart and Marguerite Higgins, New York Herald Tribune; Relman Morin and Don Whitehead. A. P.; Fred Sparks, Chicago Daily News.
1952—John M. Hightower, Associated Press.
1953—Austin C. Wehrwein, Milwaukee Journal.
1954—Jim G. Lucas, Scripps-Howard Newspapers.
1955—Harrison Salisbury, New York Times.
1956—William Randolph Hearst, Jr., J. Kingsbury Smith, Frank Conniff, Hearst Newspapers.
1957—Russell Jones, United Press.
1958—The New York Times.
1959—Joseph Martin and Philip Santora, N. Y. Daily News.
1960—A. M. Rosenthal, New York Times.
1961—Lynn Heinzerling, Associated Press.
1962—Walter Lippman, N. Y. Herald Tribune Synd.
1963—Hal Hendrix, Miami (Fla.) News.
1964—Malcolm W. Browne, A.P.; David Halberstam, N.Y. Times.
1965—J. A. Livingston, Philadelphia Bulletin.
1966—Peter Arnett, A.P.
1967—R. John Hughes, Christian Science Monitor.
1968—Alfred Friendly, Washington Post.

## CORRESPONDENCE

For Washington or foreign correspondence. Category was merged with those in national and international reporting in 1948.
1929—Paul Scott Mowrer, Chicago Daily News.
1930—Leland Stowe, New York Herald Tribune.
1931—H. R. Knickerbocker, Philadelphia Public Ledger and New York Evening Post.
1932—Walter Duranty, New York Times, and Charles G. Ross, St. Louis Post-Dispatch.
1933—Edgar Ansel Mowrer, Chicago Daily News.
1934—Frederick T. Birchall, New York Times.
1935—Arthur Krock, New York Times.
1936—Wilfred C. Barber, Chicago Tribune.
1937—Anne O'Hare McCormick, New York Times.
1938—Arthur Krock, New York Times.
1939—Louis P. Lochner, Associated Press.
1940—Otto D. Tolischus, New York Times.
1941—Bronze plaque to commemorate work of American correspondents on war fronts.
1942—Carlos P. Romulo, Philippines Herald.
1943—Hanson W. Baldwin, New York Times.
1944—Ernest Taylor Pyle, Scripps-Howard Newspaper Alliance.
1945—Harold V. (Hal) Boyle, Associated Press.
1946—Arnaldo Cortesi, New York Times.
1947—Brooks Atkinson. New York Times.

## EDITORIAL WRITING

The test of excellence is clearness of style, moral purpose, sound reasoning and power to influence public opinion.
1917—New York Tribune.
1918—Louisville (Ky.) Courier-Journal.
1920—Harvey E. Newbranch, Omaha Evening World-Herald.
1922—Frank M. O'Brien, New York Herald.
1923—William Allen White, Emporia Gazette.
1924—Boston Herald, Frank Buxton. Special prize. Frank I. Cobb, The World, New York.
1925—Charleston (S. C.) News and Courier.
1926—The New York Times, Edward M. Kingsbury.
1927—Boston Herald, F. Lauriston Bullard.
1928—Grover C. Hall, Montgomery Advertiser.
1929—Louis Isaac Jaffe, Norfolk Virginian-Pilot.
1931—Chas. Ryckman, Fremont (Nebr.) Tribune
1933—Kansas City (Mo.) Star.
1934—E. P. Chase, Atlantic (Ia.) News Telegraph.
1936—Felix Morley, Washington Post. George B. Parker, Scripps-Howard Newspapers.
1937—John W. Owens, Baltimore (Md.) Sun.
1938—W. W. Waymack, Des Moines (Ia.) Register and Tribune.
1939—Ronald G. Callvert, Portland Oregonian.
1940—Bart Howard, St. Louis (Mo.) Post-Dispatch.
1941—Reuben Maury, Daily News, N. Y.
1942—Geoffrey Parsons, New York Herald Tribune.
1943—Forrest W. Seymour, Des Moines (Ia.) Register and Tribune.
1944—Kansas City (Mo.) Star, Henry J. Haskell.
1945—George W. Potter, Providence (R. I.) Journal-Bulletin.
1946—Hodding Carter, Greenville (Miss.) Delta Democrat-Times.
1947—William H. Grimes, Wall Street Journal, N. Y.
1948—Virginius Dabney, Richmond (Va.) Times-Dispatch.
1949—John H. Crider, Boston (Mass.) Herald, Herbert Elliston, Washington (D.C.) Post.
1950—Carl M. Saunders, Jackson Citizen-Patriot.
1951—William H. Fitzpatrick, New Orleans States.
1952—Louis LaCoss, St. Louis Globe Democrat.
1953—Vermont C. Royster, Wall Street Journal.
1954—Boston Herald, Don Murray.
1955—Detroit Free Press, Royce Howes.
1956—Lauren K. Soth, Des Moines (Ia.) Register and Tribune.

1957—Buford Boone, Tuscaloosa (Ala.) News.
1958—Harry S. Ashmore, Arkansas Gazette.
1959—Ralph McGill, Atlanta (Ga.) Constitution.
1960—Lenoir Chambers, Norfolk Virginian-Pilot.
1961—William J. Dorvillier. San Juan (Puerto Rico) Star.
1962—Thomas M. Storke, Santa Barbara (Calif.) News-Press.
1963—Ira B. Harkey, Jr., Pascagoula (Miss.) Chronicle.
1964—Hazel Brannon Smith, Lexington (Miss.) Advertiser.
1965—John R. Harrison, The Gainesville (Fla.) Sun.
1966—Robert Lasch. St. Louis Post-Dispatch.
1967—Eugene C. Patterson, Atlanta Constitution.
1968—John S. Knight, Knight Newspapers.

## CARTOON

1922—Rollin Kirby, The World, New York.
1924—J. N. Darling, New York Herald Tribune.
1925—Rollin Kirby, The World, New York.
1926—D. R. Fitzpatrick, St. Louis Post-Dispatch
1927—Nelson Harding, Brooklyn Eagle.
1928—Nelson Harding, Brooklyn Eagle.
1929—Rollin Kirby, The World, New York.
1930—Charles Macauley, Brooklyn Eagle.
1931—Edmund Duffy, Baltimore Sun.
1932—John T. McCutcheon, Chicago Tribune.
1933—H. M. Talburt, Washington Daily News.
1934—Edmund Duffy, Baltimore Sun.
1935—Ross A. Lewis, Milwaukee Journal.
1937—C. D. Batchelor, Daily News, New York.
1938—Vaughn Shoemaker, Chicago Daily News.
1939—Charles G. Werner, Daily Oklahoman.
1940—Edmund Duffy, Baltimore Sun.
1941—Jacob Burck, Chicago Times.
1942—H. L. Block, Newspaper Enterprise Assn.
1943—Jay N. Darling, New York Herald Tribune.
1944—Clifford K. Berryman, Washington Star.
1945—Bill Mauldin, United Feature Syndicate.
1946—Bruce Alexander Russell, Los Angeles Times.
1947—Vaughn Shoemaker, Chicago Daily News.
1948—Reuben L. (Rube) Goldberg, The Sun, N. Y.
1949—Lute Pease, Newark (N. J.) Evening News.
1950—James T. Berryman, Washington Star.
1951—Reginald W. Manning, Arizona Republic.
1952—Fred L. Packer, New York Mirror.
1953—Edward D. Kuekes, Cleveland Plain Dealer.
1954—Herbert L. Block, Washington Post & Times-Herald.
1955—Daniel R. Fitzpatrick. St. Louis Post-Dispatch.
1956—Robert York, Louisville (Ky.) Times.
1957—Tom Little, Nashville Tennessean.
1958—Bruce M. Shanks, Buffalo Evening News.
1959—Bill Mauldin, St. Louis Post-Dispatch.
1961—Carey Orr, Chicago Tribune.
1962—Edmund S. Valtman, Hartford Times.
1963—Frank Miller, Des Moines Register.
1964—Paul Conrad, Denver Post.
1966—Don Wright, Miami News.
1967—Patrick B. Oliphant, Denver Post
1968—Eugene Gray Payne, Charlotte Observer.

## FEATURE PHOTOGRAPHY

1968—Toshio Sakai, UPI.

## NEWS PHOTOGRAPHY

1942—Milton Brooks. Detroit News.
1943—Frank Noel, Associated Press.
1944—Frank Filan, Associated Press; Earle L. Bunker, Omaha World-Herald.
1945—Joe Rosenthal, Associated Press, for photograph of planting American flag on Iwo Jima.
1947—Arnold Hardy, amateur, Atlanta, Ga.
1948—Frank Cushing, Boston Traveler.
1949—Nathaniel Fein, New York Herald Tribune.
1950—Bill Crouch. Oakland (Calif.) Tribune.
1951—Max Desfor. Associated Press.
1952—John Robinson and Don Ultang, Des Moines. Register and Tribune.
1953—William M. Gallagher, Flint (Mich.) Journal.
1954—Mrs. Walter M. Schau, amateur (Calif.).
1955—John L. Gaunt, Jr., Los Angeles Times.
1956—New York Daily News.
1957—Harry A. Trask, Boston Traveler.
1958—William C. Beall, Washington Daily News.
1959—William Seaman, Minneapolis Star.
1960—Andrew Lopez, United Press Intl.
1961—Yasushi Nagao, Mainichi Newspapers, Tokyo.
1962—Paul Vathis, Associated Press.
1963—Hector Rondon, La Republica, Caracas, Venezuela.
1964—Robert H. Jackson, Dallas Times-Herald.
1965—Horst Faas, Associated Press.
1966—Kyoichi Sawada, U.P.I.
1967—Jack R. Thornell, Associated Press.
1968—Rocco Morabito, Jacksonville Journal.

## SPECIAL CITATION

1938—Edmonton (Alberta) Journal, bronze plaque.
1941—New York Times.
1944—Byron Price and Mrs. William Allen White. Also to Richard Rodgers and Oscar Hammerstein, 2nd, for musical, Oklahoma!

1945—Press cartographers for war maps.
1947—(Pulitzer centennial year.) Columbia University and the Graduate School of Journalism, and the St. Louis Post-Dispatch.
1948—Dr. Frank Diehl Fackenthal.
1951—Cyrus L. Sulzberger, New York Times.
1952—Max Kase, New York Journal-American, and Kansas City (Mo.) Star.
1953—The New York Times, for Review of the Week section and Lester Markel, its founder.
1957—Kenneth Roberts, for his historical novels.
1958—Walter Lippmann, New York Herald Tribune.
1960—Garrett Mattingly, for The Armada.
1961—American Heritage Picture History of the Civil War.
1964—The Gannett Newspapers.

## PULITZER PRIZES IN LETTERS
### FICTION

For fiction in book form by an American author, preferably dealing with American life.
1918—Ernest Poole, His Family.
1919—Booth Tarkington, The Magnificent Ambersons.
1921—Edith Wharton, The Age of Innocence.
1922—Booth Tarkington, Alice Adams.
1923—Willa Cather, One of Ours.
1924—Margaret Wilson, The Able McLaughlins.
1925—Edna Ferber, So Big.
1926—Sinclair Lewis, Arrowsmith. (Refused prize.)
1927—Louis Bromfield, Early Autumn.
1928—Thornton Wilder, Bridge of San Luis Rey.
1929—Julia M. Peterkin, Scarlet Sister Mary.
1930—Oliver La Farge, Laughing Boy.
1931—Margaret Ayer Barnes, Years of Grace.
1932—Pearl S. Buck, The Good Earth.
1933—T. S. Stribling, The Store.
1934—Caroline Miller, Lamb in His Bosom.
1935—Josephine W. Johnson, Now in November.
1936—Harold L. Davis, Honey in the Horn.
1937—Margaret Mitchell, Gone With the Wind.
1938—John P. Marquand, The Late George Apley.
1939—Marjorie Kinnan Rawlings, The Yearling.
1940—John Steinbeck, The Grapes of Wrath.
1942—Ellen Glasgow, In This Our Life.
1943—Upton Sinclair, Dragon's Teeth.
1944—Martin Flavin, Journey in the Dark.
1945—John Hersey, A Bell for Adano.
1947—Robert Penn Warren, All the King's Men.
1948—James A. Michener, Tales of the South Pacific.
1949—James Gould Cozzens, Guard of Honor.
1950—A. B. Guthrie, Jr., The Way West.
1951—Conrad Richter, The Town.
1952—Herman Wouk, The Caine Mutiny.
1953—Ernest Hemingway, The Old Man and the Sea.
1955—William Faulkner, A Fable.
1956—MacKinlay Kantor, Andersonville.
1958—James Agee, A Death in the Family.
1959—Robert Lewis Taylor, The Travels of Jaimie McPheeters.
1960—Allen Drury, Advise and Consent.
1961—Harper Lee, To Kill a Mockingbird.
1962—Edwin O'Connor, The Edge of Sadness.
1963—William Faulkner, The Reivers.
1965—Shirley Ann Grau, The Keepers of the House.
1966—Katherine Anne Porter, Collected Stories of Katherine Anne Porter.
1967—Bernard Malamud, The Fixer.
1968—William Styron, The Confessions of Nat Turner.

### DRAMA

For an American play, preferably original and dealing with American life.
1918—Jesse Lynch Williams, Why Marry?
1920—Eugene O'Neill, Beyond the Horizon.
1921—Zona Gale, Miss Lulu Bett.
1922—Eugene O'Neill, Anna Christie.
1923—Owen Davis, Icebound.
1924—Hatcher Hughes, Hell-Bent fer Heaven.
1925—Sidney Howard, They Knew What They Wanted.
1926—George Kelly, Craig's Wife.
1927—Paul Green. In Abraham's Bosom.
1928—Eugene O'Neill, Strange Interlude.
1929—Elmer Rice, Street Scene.
1930—Marc Connelly, The Green Pastures.
1931—Susan Glaspell, Alison's House.
1932—George S. Kaufman, Morrie Ryskind and Ira Gershwin, Of Thee I Sing.
1933—Maxwell Anderson, Both Your Houses.
1934—Sidney Kingsley, Men in White.
1935—Zoe Akins, The Old Maid.
1936—Robert E. Sherwood, Idiot's Delight.
1937—George S. Kaufman and Moss Hart, You Can't Take It With You.
1938—Thornton Wilder, Our Town.
1939—Robert E. Sherwood, Abe Lincoln in Illinois.
1940—William Saroyan, The Time of Your Life.
1941—Robert E. Sherwood, There Shall Be No Night.
1943—Thornton Wilder, The Skin of Our Teeth.
1945—Mary Chase, Harvey.
1946—Russel Crouse and Howard Lindsay, State of the Union.

1948—Tennessee Williams, A Streetcar Named Desire.
1949—Arthur Miller. Death of a Salesman.
1950—Richard Rodgers, Oscar Hammerstein II, and Joshua Logan, South Pacific, based on James A. Michener's 1948 prize-winning book, Tales of the South Pacific.
1952—Joseph Kramm, The Shrike.
1953—William Inge, Picnic.
1954—John Patrick, Teahouse of the August Moon.
1955—Tennessee Williams, Cat on A Hot Tin Roof.
1956—Frances Goodrich and Albert Hackett, The Diary of Anne Frank.
1957—Eugene O'Neill, Long Day's Journey Into Night.
1958—Ketti Frings, Look Homeward, Angel.
1959—Archibald MacLeish, J. B.
1960—George Abbott, Jerome Weidman, Sheldon Harnick and Jerry Bock, Fiorello.
1961—Tad Mosel, All the Way Home.
1962—Frank Loesser and Abe Burrows, How To Succeed In Business Without Really Trying.
1965—Frank D. Gilroy, The Subject Was Roses.
1967—Edward Albee, A Delicate Balance.

### HISTORY

1917—J. J. Jusserand, With Americans of Past and Present Days.
1918—James Ford Rhodes, History of the Civil War.
1920—Justin H. Smith, The War with Mexico.
1921—William Sowden Sims, The Victory at Sea.
1922—James Truslow Adams. The Founding of New England.
1923—Charles Warren, The Supreme Court in United States History.
1924—Charles Howard McIlwain, The American Revolution: A Constitutional Interpretation.
1925—Frederick L. Paxton, A History of the American Frontier.
1926—Edward Channing, History of the U. S.
1927—Samuel Flagg Bemis, Pinckney's Treaty.
1928—Vernon Louis Parrington, Main Currents in American Thought.
1929—Fred A. Shannon, The Organization and Administration of the Union Army, 1861-65.
1930—Claude H. Van Tyne. The War of Independence.
1931—Bernadotte E. Schmitt, The Coming of the War, 1914.
1932—Gen. John J. Pershing, My Experiences in the World War.
1933—Frederick J. Turner, The Significance of Sections in American History.
1934—Herbert Agar. The People's Choice.
1935—Charles McLean Andrews, The Colonial Period of American History.
1936—Andrew C. McLaughlin, A Constitutional History of the United States.
1937—Van Wyck Brooks, The Flowering of New England.
1938—Paul Herman Buck, The Road to Reunion.
1939—Frank Luther Mott, A History of American Magazines.
1940—Carl Sandburg, Abraham Lincoln: The War Years.
1941—Marcus Lee Hansen, The Atlantic Migration.
1942—Margaret Leech, Reveille in Washington.
1943—Esther Forbes, Paul Revere and the World He Lived In.
1944—Merle Curti, The Growth of American Thought.
1945—Stephen Bonsal, Unfinished Business.
1946—Arthur M. Schlesinger. Jr., The Age of Jackson.
1947—Dr. James Phinney Baxter 3d, Scientists Against Time.
1948—Bernard De Voto, Across the Wide Missouri.
1949—Roy F. Nichols. The Disruption of American Democracy.
1950—O. W. Larkin, Art and Life in America.
1951—R. Carlyle Buley, The Old Northwest, Pioneer Period 1815-1840.
1952—Oscar Handlin, The Uprooted.
1953—George Dangerfield, The Era of Good Feelings.
1954—Bruce Catton—A Stillness at Appomattox.
1955—Paul Horgan, Great River: The Rio Grande in North American History.
1956—Richard Hofstadter, The Age of Reform.
1957—George F. Kennan. Russia Leaves the War.
1958—Bray Hammond, Banks and Politics in America—From the Revolution to the Civil War.
1959—Leonard D. White and Jean Schneider, The Republican Era: 1869-1901.
1960—Margaret Leech, In the Days of McKinley.
1961—Herbert Feis, Between War and Peace: The Potsdam Conference.
1962—Lawrence H. Gipson, The Triumphant Empire, Thunder-Clouds Gather in the West.
1963—Constance McLaughlin Green, Washington, Village and Capital. 1800-1878.
1964—Sumner Chilton Powell, Puritan Village: The Formation of A New England Town.
1965—Irwin Unger, The Greenback Era.
1966—Perry Miller, Life of the Mind in America.
1967—William H. Goetzmann, Exploration and Empire: the Explorer and Scientist in the Winning of the American West.

1968—Bernard Bailyn, The Ideological Origins of the American Revolution.

## BIOGRAPHY OR AUTOBIOGRAPHY

For a distinguished biography or autobiography by an American author, preferably on an American subject.

1917—Laura E. Richards and Maude Howe Elliott, assisted by Florence Howe Hall, Julia Ward Howe.
1918—William Cabell Bruce, Benjamin Franklin, Self-Revealed.
1919—Henry Adams, The Education of Henry Adams.
1920—Albert J. Beveridge, The Life of John Marshall.
1921—Edward Bok, The Americanization of Edward Bok.
1922—Hamlin Garland, A Daughter of the Middle Border.
1923—Burton J. Hendrick, The Life and Letters of Walter H. Page.
1924—Michael Pupin, From Immigrant to Inventor.
1925—M. A. DeWolfe Howe, Barrett Wendell and His Letters.
1926—Harvey Cushing, Life of Sir William Osler.
1927—Emory Holloway, Whitman, An Interpretation in Narrative.
1928—Charles Edward Russell, The American Orchestra and Theodore Thomas.
1929—Burton J. Hendrick, The Training of an American: The Earlier Life and Letters of Walter H. Page.
1930—Marquis James, The Raven. (Sam Houston).
1931—Henry James, Charles W. Eliot.
1932—Henry F. Pringle, Theodore Roosevelt.
1933—Allan Nevins, Grover Cleveland.
1934—Tyler Dennett, John Hay.
1935—Douglas Southall Freeman, R. E. Lee.
1936—Ralph Barton Perry, The Thought and Character of William James.
1937—Allan Nevins, Hamilton Fish, the Inner History of the Great Administration.
1938—Divided between Odell Shepard, Pedlar's Progress; Marquis James, Andrew Jackson.
1939—Carl Van Doren, Benjamin Franklin.
1940—Ray Stannard Baker, Woodrow Wilson, Life and Letters.
1941—Ola Elizabeth Winslow, Jonathan Edwards.
1942—Forrest Wilson, Crusader in Crinoline.
1943—Samuel Eliot Morison, Admiral of the Ocean Sea (Columbus).
1944—Carleton Mabee, The American Leonardo: The Life of Samuel F. B. Morse.
1945—Russel Blaine Nye, George Bancroft: Brahmin Rebel.
1946—Linny Marsh Wolfe, Son of the Wilderness.
1947—William Allen White, The Autobiography of William Allen White.
1948—Margaret Clapp, Forgotten First Citizen, John Bigelow.
1949—Robert E. Sherwood, Roosevelt and Hopkins.
1950—Samuel Flag Bemis, John Quincy Adams and the Foundations of American Foreign Policy.
1951—Margaret Louise Colt, John C. Calhoun: American Portrait.
1952—Merlo J. Pusey, Charles Evans Hughes.
1953—David J. Mays, Edmund Pendleton 1721-1803.
1954—Charles A. Lindbergh, The Spirit of St. Louis.
1955—William S. White, The Taft Story.
1956—Talbot F. Hamlin, Benjamin Henry Latrobe.
1957—John F. Kennedy, Profiles in Courage.
1958—Douglas Southall Freeman (decd. 1953), George Washington, vols. I-VI; John Alexander Carroll and Mary Wells Ashworth, vol. VII.
1959—Arthur Walworth, Woodrow Wilson, American Prophet.
1960—Samuel Eliot Morison, John Paul Jones.
1961—David Donald, Charles Sumner and The Coming of the Civil War.
1963—Leon Edel, Henry James: Vol. II, The Conquest of London, 1870-1881; Vol. III, The Middle Years, 1881-1895.
1964—Walter Jackson Bate, John Keats.
1965—Ernest Samuels, Henry Adams.
1966—Arthur M. Schlesinger, Jr., A Thousand Days.
1967—Justin Kaplan, Mr. Clemens and Mark Twain.
1968—George F. Kennan, Memoirs (1925-1950).

## AMERICAN POETRY

Before this prize was established in 1922, the following awards were made from gifts provided by the Poetry Society. 1918—Love Songs, by Sara Teasdale. 1919—Old Road to Paradise, by Margaret Widdemer; Corn Huskers, by Carl Sandburg.
1922—Edwin Arlington Robinson, Collected Poems.
1923—Edna St. Vincent Millay, The Ballad of the Harp-Weaver; A Few Figs from Thistles: Eight Sonnets in American Poetry, 1922; A Miscellany.

1924—Robert Frost, New Hampshire: A Poem with Notes and Grace Notes.
1925—Edwin Arlington Robinson, The Man Who Died Twice.
1926—Amy Lowell, What's O'Clock.
1927—Leonora Speyer, Fiddler's Farewell.
1928—Edwin Arlington Robinson, Tristram.
1929—Stephen Vincent Benét, John Brown's Body.
1930—Conrad Aiken, Selected Poems.
1931—Robert Frost, Collected Poems.
1932—George Dillon, The Flowering Stone.
1933—Archibald MacLeish, Conquistador.
1934—Robert Hillyer, Collected Verse.
1935—Audrey Wurdemann, Bright Ambush.
1936—Robert P. Tristram Coffin, Strange Holiness.
1937—Robert Frost, A Further Range.
1938—Marya Zaturenska, Cold Morning Sky.
1939—John Gould Fletcher, Selected Poems.
1940—Mark Van Doren, Collected Poems.
1941—Leonard Bacon, Sunderland Capture.
1942—William Rose Benet, The Dust Which Is God.
1943—Robert Frost, A Witness Tree.
1944—Stephen Vincent Benet, Western Star.
1945—Karl Shapiro, V-Letter and Other Poems.
1947—Robert Lowell, Lord Weary's Castle.
1948—W. H. Auden, The Age of Anxiety.
1949—Peter Viereck, Terror and Decorum.
1950—Gwendolyn Brooks, Annie Allen.
1951—Carl Sandburg, Complete Poems.
1952—Marianne Moore, Collected Poems.
1953—Archibald MacLeish, Collected Poems.
1954—Theodore Roethke, The Waking.
1955—Wallace Stevens, Collected Poems.
1956—Elizabeth Bishop, Poems, North and South.
1957—Richard Wilbur, Things of This World.
1958—Robert Penn Warren, Promises: Poems 1954-1956.
1959—Stanley Kunitz, Selected Poems 1928-1958.
1960—W. D. Snodgrass, Heart's Needle.
1961—Phyllis McGinley, Times Three: Selected Verse from Three Decades.
1962—Alan Dugan, Poems.
1963—William Carlos Williams, Pictures From Breughel.
1964—Louis Simpson, At the End of the Open Road.
1965—John Berryman, 77 Dream Songs.
1966—Richard Eberhart, Selected Poems.
1967—Anne Sexton, Live or Die.
1968—Anthony Hecht, The Hard Hours.

## GENERAL NON-FICTION

For best book by an American, not eligible in any other category.
1962—Theodore H. White, The Making of the President 1960.
1963—Barbara W. Tuchman, The Guns of August.
1964—Richard Hofstadter, Anti-Intellectualism in American Life.
1965—Howard Mumford Jones, O Strange New World.
1966—Edwin Way Teale, Wandering Through Winter.
1967—David Brion Davis, The Problem of Slavery in Western Culture.
1968—Will and Ariel Durant, the Story of Civilization (Vol. 10).

## PULITZER PRIZE IN MUSIC

For composition in the larger forms of chamber, orchestral or choral music or for an operatic work including ballet, performed or published by a composer resident in the United States.
1943—William Schuman, Secular Cantata No. 2, A Free Song.
1944—Howard Hanson, Symphony No. 4, Op. 34.
1945—Aaron Copland, Appalachian Spring.
1946—Leo Sowerby, The Canticle of the Sun.
1947—Charles E. Ives, Symphony No. 3.
1948—Walter Piston, Symphony No. 3.
1949—Virgil Thomson, Louisiana Story.
1950—Gian-Carlo Menotti, The Consul.
1951—Douglas Moore, Giants in the Earth.
1952—Gail Kubik, Symphony Concertante.
1954—Quincy Porter, Concerto for Two Pianos and Orchestra.
1955—Gian-Carlo Menotti, The Saint of Bleecker Street.
1956—Ernest Toch, Symphony No. 3.
1957—Norman Dello Joio, Meditations on Ecclesiastes.
1958—Samuel Barber, Vanessa.
1959—John La-Montaine, Concerto for Piano and Orchestra.
1960—Elliott Carter, Second String Quartet.
1961—Walter Piston, Symphony No. 7.
1962—Robert Ward, The Crucible.
1963—Samuel Barber, Piano Concerto No. 1.
1966—Leslie Bassett, Variations for Orchestra.
1967—Leon Kirchner, Quartet No. 3.
1968—George Crumb, Echoes of Time and the River.

# Academy Awards in Motion Pictures

## Source: Academy of Motion Picture Arts and Sciences

**1927-28**
Actor: Emil Jannings, Way of All Flesh.
Actress: Janet Gaynor, Seventh Heaven.
Picture: Wings, Paramount.
**1928-29**
Actor: Warner Baxter, In Old Arizona.
Actress: Mary Pickford, Coquette.
Picture: Broadway Melody, MGM.
**1929-30**
Actor: George Arliss, Disraeli.
Actress: Norma Shearer, The Divorcee.
Picture: All Quiet on the Western Front, Univ.
**1930-31**
Actor: Lionel Barrymore, Free Soul.
Actresss: Marie Dressler, Min and Bill.
Picture: Cimarron, RKO.
**1931-32**
Actor: Fredric March, Dr. Jekyll and Mr. Hyde.
Actress: Heyen Hayes, Sin of Madelon Claudet.
Picture: Grand Hotel, MGM.
Special: Walt Disney, Mickey Mouse.
**1931-32**
Actor: Chas. Laughton, Private Life of Henry VIII.
Actress: Katharine Hepburn, Morning Glory.
Picture: Cavalcade, Fox.
**1934**
Actor: Clark Gable. It Happened One Night.
Actress: Claudette Colbert, same.
Picture: It Happened One Night, Columbia.
**1935**
Actor: Victor McLaglen, The Informer.
Actress: Bette Davis, Dangerous.
Picture: Mutiny on the Bounty, MGM.
**1936**
Actor: Paul Muni, Story of Louis Pasteur.
Actress: Luise Rainer, The Great Ziegfeld.
Picture: The Great Ziegfeld, MGM.
**1937**
Actor: Spencer Tracy, Captains Courageous.
Actress: Luise Rainer, The Good Earth.
Picture: Life of Emile Zola, Warner.
**1938**
Actor: Spencer Tracy, Boys Town.
Actress: Bette Davis, Jezebel.
Picture: You Can't Take It With You, Columbia.
**1939**
Actor: Robert Donat, Goodbye Mr. Chips.
Actress: Vivien Leigh, Gone With the Wind.
Picture: Gone With the Wind, Selznick International.
**1940**
Actor: James Stewart, The Philadelphia Story.
Actress: Ginger Rogers, Kitty Foyle.
Picture: Rebecca, Selznick International.
**1941**
Actor: Gary Cooper, Sergeant York.
Actress: Joan Fontaine, Suspicion.
Picture: How Green Was My Valley, 20th Cnt.-Fox.
**1942**
Actor: James Cagney, Yankee Doodle Dandy.
Actress: Greer Garson, Mrs. Miniver.
Picture: Mrs. Miniver, MGM.
**1943**
Actor: Paul Lukas, Watch on the Rhine.
Actress: Jennifer Jones, The Song of Bernadette.
Picture: Casablanca, Warner.
**1944**
Actor: Bing Crosby, Going My Way.
Actress: Ingrid Bergman, Gaslight.
Picture: Going My Way, Paramount.
**1945**
Actor: Ray Milland, The Lost Weekend.
Actresss: Joan Crawford, Mildred Pierce.
Picture: The Lost Weekend, Paramount.
**1946**
Actor: Fredric March, Best Years of Our Lives.
Actress: Olivia de Havilland, To Each His Own.
Picture: The Best Years of Our Lives, Saml.
Goldwyn, RKO.
**1947**
Actor: Ronald Colman, A Double Life.
Actress: Loretta Young, The Farmer's Daughter.
Picture: Gentleman's Agreement, 20th Cent.-Fox.
**1948**
Actor: Laurence Olivier, Hamlet.
Actress: Jane Wyman, Johnny Belinda.
Picture: Hamlet, Two Cities Film, Universal
International.
**1949**
Actor: Broderick Crawford, All the King's Men.
Actress: Olivia de Havilland, The Heiress.
Picture: All the King's Men, Columbia.
**1950**
Actor: Jose Ferrer, Cyrano de Bergerac.
Actress: Judy Holliday, Born Yesterday.
Picture: All About Eve, 20th Century-Fox.
**1951**
Actor: Humphrey Bogart, The African Queen.
Actress: Vivien Leigh, A Streetcar Named Desire.
Picture: An American in Paris, MGM.

**1952**
Actor: Gary Cooper, High Noon.
Actress: Shirley Booth, Come Back, Little Sheba.
Picture: Greatest Show on Earth, Cecil B. De-
Mille, Paramount.
**1953**
Actor: William Holden, Stalag 17.
Actress: Audrey Hepburn, Roman Holiday.
Picture: From Here to Eternity, Columbia.
**1954**
Actor: Marlon Brando, On the Waterfront.
Actress: Grace Kelly, The Country Girl.
Picture: On the Waterfront, Horizon-American
Corp., Columbia.
**1955**
Actor: Ernest Borgnine, Marty.
Actress: Anna Magnani, The Rose Tattoo.
Picture: Marty, Hecht and Lancaster's Steven
Productions, U.A.
**1956**
Actor: Yul Brynner, The King and I.
Actress: Ingrid Bergman, Anastasia.
Picture: Around The World in 80 Days, Michael
Todd Co., U.A.
**1957**
Actor: Alec Guinness, The Bridge on the River
Kwai.
Actress: Joanne Woodward, The Three Faces of Eve.
Picture: The Bridge on the River Kwai, Horizon
Picture, Columbia.
**1958**
Actor: David Niven, Separate Tables.
Actress: Susan Hayward, I Want to Live.
Picture: Gigi, Arthur Freed Production, MGM.
**1959**
Actor: Charlton Heston, Ben-Hur.
Actress: Simone Signoret, Room at the Top.
Picture: Ben-Hur, MGM.
**1960**
Actor: Burt Lancaster, Elmer Gantry.
Actress: Elizabeth Taylor, Butterfield 8.
Picture: The Apartment, Mirisch Co., U.A.
**1961**
Actor: Maximilian Schell, Judgment at Nuremberg.
Actress: Sophia Loren, Two Women.
Picture: West Side Story, Mirisch Pictures, Inc.
and B & P Enterprises, Inc., United Artists.
**1962**
Actor: Gregory Peck, To Kill a Mockingbird.
Actress: Anne Bancroft, The Miracle Worker.
Picture: Lawrence of Arabia, Horizon Pictures
Ltd.—Sam Spiegel-David Lean prod., Columbia.
**1963**
Actor: Sidney Poitier, Lillies of the Field.
Actress: Patricia Neal, Hud.
Picture: Tom Jones, Woodfall Prod., UA-Lopert
Pictures.
**1964**
Actor: Rex Harrison, My Fair Lady.
Actress: Julie Andrews, Mary Poppins.
Picture: My Fair Lady, Warner Bros.
**1965**
Actor: Lee Marvin, Cat Ballou.
Actress: Julie Christie, Darling.
Picture: The Sound of Music, 20th Century-Fox.
**1966**
Actor: Paul Scofield, A Man for All Seasons.
Actress: Elizabeth Taylor, Who's Afraid of Vir-
ginia Woolf?
Picture: A Man for All Seasons, Columbia.
**1967**
Actor: Rod Steiger, In the Heat of the Night.
Supporting Actor: George Kennedy, Cool Hand
Luke.
Actress: Katharine Hepburn, Guess Who's Coming
to Dinner.
Supporting Actress: Estelle Parsons, Bonnie and
Clyde.
Picture: In the Heat of the Night.
Foreign Language Film: Closely Watched Trains,
Czechoslovakia.
Documentary: (feature) Pierre Schoendorffer, The
Anderson Platoon; (short subject) Mark Harris
& Trevor Greenwood, The Redwoods.
Costume Design: John Truscott, Camelot.
Short Subjects: (cartoon) Fred Wolf, The Box;
(live action) Christopher Chapman, A Place to
Stand.
Music: (substantially original) Elmer Bernstein,
Thoroughly Modern Millie; (adaptation or treat-
ment) Alfred Newman & Ken Darby, Camelot;
(song) Leslie Brisusse, Talk to the Animals from
Dr. Dolittle.
Cinematography: Burnett Guffey, Bonnie and
Clyde.
Writing: (screenplay adapted) Stirling Silliphant,
In the Heat of the Night; (directly for screen)
William Rose, Guess Who's Coming to Dinner.
Irving Thalberg Memorial Award: Alfred Hitch-
cock.
Jean Hersholt Award: Gregory Peck.

# SPECIAL AWARDS, GRANTS, FELLOWSHIPS
All awards in 1968, unless otherwise designated

## Books, Allied Arts

**Jane Addams Children's Book Award,** for the children's book best combining literary merit, themes of brotherhood and creative solutions to problems: Erik Christian Haugaard for *The Little Fishes.*

**American Revolution Round Table Book Award,** for a contribution to a better understanding of the history of the American Revolution: Lt. Col. John R. Galvin for *The Minute Men: A Compact History of the Defenders of the American Colonies, 1645-1775.*

**Anisfield-Wolf Awards,** by the Saturday Review for contribution to intergroup understanding, $750 each: Raul Hilberg for *The Destruction of the European Jews*; Erich Kahler for *The Jews Among the Nations*; Robert Coles for *Children of Crisis: A Study of Courage and Fear*; and Norman Cohn for *Warrant for Genocide: The Myth of the Jewish World-Conspiracy and the Protocols of the Elders of Zion.*

**Aviation/Space Writers Assn. Awards:** Martin Caidin for *No Man's World*; Don Dwiggins for *Hollywood Pilot*; and Lt. Col. Gene Gurney and Lt. Col. James C. Elliott for *The Private Pilot's Handbook of Navigation.*

**Emily Clark Balch Prizes,** by the Virginia Quarterly Review, First Prize, $500: John Berryman for *Eleven Dream Songs.*

**Bancroft Prizes,** by Columbia Univ. for books in American history, diplomacy and international relations, $4,000 each: Bernard Bailyn for *The Ideological Origins of the American Revolution*; Dr. Henry Allen Bullock for *A History of Negro Education in the South from 1619 to the Present*; and Dr. Richard L. Bushman for *From Puritan to Yankee: Character and the Social Order in Connecticut, 1690-1765.*

**Henry Bellamann Award,** for contribution to literature, $1,000: Elizabeth Spencer.

**B'nai B'rith Jewish Heritage Award,** for excellence in Jewish literature, $1,000: Saul Bellow.

**Brandeis Univ. Creative Arts Awards,** $1,000 each: Lionel Trilling, Elizabeth Thomas, Joseph Cornell and Richard Rodgers.

**John Burroughs Medal,** for book on natural history: Hal Borland for *Hill Country Harvest.*

**National Conference on Christianity and Literature Book Award:** Dr. Nathan A. Scott, Jr. for *The Broken Center: Studies in the Theological Horizon of Modern Literature.*

**The Civil War Round Table, Fletcher Pratt Award,** for best nonfiction book about the civil war: Glyndon G. Van Deusen for *William Henry Seward.*

**Commonwealth Club of California,** gold medals for best books by California authors: Fiction, Wallace Stegner for *All the Little Live Things*; nonfiction, Margaret Sanborn for *Robert E. Lee: The Complete Man, 1861-1870.*

**John O'Hara Cosgrave Gold Medal for Literature,** by the Dutch Treat Club of New York for services to American writing: Ben Lucien Burman.

**Dutton Junior Animal Book Award:** Walt Morey for *Kavik the Wolf Dog.*

**Educator's Award,** by the Delta Kappa Gamma Society, for the book by a woman which best deals with interests and aspects of education, $1,500: Maya Pines for *Revolution in Learning.*

**William Faulkner Foundation Award,** for the best first novel of the year: Robert Stone for *A Hall of Mirrors.*

**Friends of American Writers Award,** $1,000: Allan W. Eckert for two books, *The Frontiersman* and *Wild Season.*

**Eva L. Gordon Award,** by the American Nature Study Society: Robert M. McClung for *Redbird: The Story of a Cardinal.*

**Joseph Henry Jackson Award,** by the San Francisco Foundation, $1,500: Stanley T. Rice, Jr., for 48 poems collected under the title *Eye.*

**John F. Kennedy Memorial Award,** by Harper & Row, $10,000: Louis Heren for *The New American Commonwealth.*

**Otto Kinkeldy Award,** by the American Musicological Society for excellence in a musicological book: William Austin for *Music in the Twentieth Century.*

**Frederic G. Melcher Award,** by the Unitarian Universalist Assn. for book judged to be the most significant contribution to religious liberalism, $1,000: Alan Westin for *Privacy and Freedom.*

**National Book Awards,** by the American Booksellers Assn., American Book Publishers Council and the Book Manufacturers Institute, $1,000 each: Thornton Wilder for *The Eighth Day*; Johnathan Kozel for *Death at an Early Age*; George F. Kennan for *Memoirs*; Robert Bly for *The Light Around the Body*; William Troy for *Selected Essays.*

**National Institute of Arts and Letters, Richard and Hilda Rosenthal Foundation Awards,** $2,000 each: Joyce Carol Oates, author; and Elizabeth Osborne, painter. **Arnold W. Brunner Memorial Prize in Architecture,** $1,000: John M. Johansen. **Gold Medals,** poetry: Wystan Hugh Auden; architecture: Buckminster Fuller. **Marc Blitzstein Award for the Musical Theatre,** $2,500: Jack Beeson. **Marjorie Peabody Waite Award,** $1,500: Abraham Harriton, painter. **Loines Award for Poetry,** $2,500: Anthony Hecht. **Arts and Letters Grants,** $2,500 each, **Art:** A Robert Birmelin, Kenneth Callahan, Leon Goldin, Joe Lasker, Vincent Smith, Elbert Weinberg, and Charles Wilson. **Literature:** John Malcolm Brinnin, Fred Chappell, Reuel Denney, Howard Moss, John Frederick Nims, Julia Randall, Richard G. Stern, and Eleanor Ross Taylor. **Music:** David Del Tredici, William Flanagan, Ned Rorem, and Francis Thorne. **Award of Merit,** $1,000: Joseph Cornell, artist.

**Nebula Awards,** by the Science Fiction Writers of America. Samuel R. Dalany won an award for the best novel *The Einstein Intersection*, and for the best short story *Aye and Gomorrah*; Novelette: Fritz Leiber for *Gonna Roll the Bones.*

**John Newbery Medal,** by the American Library Assn. for contribution to American literature for children: E. L. Konigsburg for *From the Mixed-up Files of Mrs. Basil E. Frankweiler.*

**P.E.N. Translation Award,** $1,000: Vladimir Marov and Merrill Sparks for *Modern Russian Poetry.*

**Edgar Allan Poe Awards,** by the Mystery Writers of America. Mystery Novel: Donald Westlake for *God Save the Mark*; First Mystery Novel: Michael Collins for *Act of Fear*; Fact Crime Book: Victoria Lincoln for *A Private Disgrace*; Juvenile Mystery: Gretchen Sprague for *Signpost to Terror.*

**Academy of American Poets Fellowship Award,** $5,000: Stanley Kunitz.

**John Gilmary Shea Prize,** by the American Catholic Historical Assn. for contributions to literature in history & biography: Rev. Robert Burns for *The Crusader Kingdom of Valencia: Reconstruction of a Thirteenth-Century Frontier.*

**The Texas Institute of Letters,** for best Texas books. **Carr P. Collins Award,** for non-fiction, $1,000: Willie Morris for *North Toward Home.* **Jesse H. Jones Award** for fiction, $1,000: Robert Flynn for *North to Yesterday.* **Friends of the Dallas Public Library Award,** for best book in the field of general knowledge, $500: W. W. Newcomb for *Rock Art of Texas Indians.* **Amon G. Carter Award,** for book on Southwest history, $500: Pauline A. Pinckney for *Painting in Texas.* **Voertman Poetry Award,** $200: Frederic Will for *Planets.*

**Western Heritage Awards,** by the National Cowboy Hall of Fame: Robert Flynn for *North to Yesterday*; Eric Scott for *Down the Rivers, Westward Ho!*; E. Maurice Bloch for *George Caleb Bingham: Evolution of an Artist*; John Hawgood for *America's Western Frontiers*; and Carolyn Woirhaye for *The Snows of Rimrock Ridge.*

## Journalism Awards

**American Institute of Physics—United States Steel Foundation Science Writing Award,** $1,500: William J. Perkinson, The Baltimore Evening Sun.

**Meyer Berger Award,** by Columbia Univ. Graduate School of Journalism for distinguished local reporting in a New York daily, $500 each: J. Anthony Lukas, N. Y. Times; and Felix Kessler, The Wall Street Journal.

**Heywood Broun Memorial Award,** By the American Newspaper Guild, $1,000: Robert Wyrick, Today, Cocoa, Fla.

**National Cartoonist Society Awards.** Cartoonist of the Year (Reuben Award): Rube Goldberg. Humor strip: John Hart, Wizard of Id, B.C., Publishers-Hall Syndicate. Advertising and illustration: Roy Doty. Editorial cartoon: Karl Hubenthal, Los Angeles Herald Examiner. Sports cartoon: Lou Darvas, Cleveland Press. Syndicated panel: Bil Keane, Family Circus, Channel Chuckles, Register and Tribune Syndicate. Comic books: Will Eisner. Magazine gag cartoons: Orlando Busino. Special features: Hal Foster, Prince Valiant, King Features Syndicate. Story strip: John Prentice, Rip Kirby, King Features.

**Raymond Clapper Memorial Award:** Nathan K. Kotz, The Des Moines Register.

**Grenville Clark Editorial Page Award,** sponsored by the Stanley Foundation: Joe Lersky, Celina (Ohio) Daily Standard, and Jack Bender, Waterloo (Iowa) Daily Courier.

**Fourth Estate Award,** for distinguished public service in communications: William S. White, United Features Syndicate.

**Albert Lasker Medical Journalism Awards:** Carl M. Cobb, The Boston Globe; Matt Clark, Newsweek magazine; and CBS News.

**Loeb Awards,** for excellence in business and

financial writing, $1,000 each: Richard A. Nenneman, Christian Science Monitor; and Michael Laurence, Playboy Magazine.

**Edward J. Meeman Conservation Awards,** by Scripps-Howard Foundation, for work in the cause of conservation: First Prize, $1,000: James Ryan, St. Petersburg Times. **Other Awards,** cash prizes as indicated: Neva S. Flaherty, Perth Amboy (N. J.) Evening News ($750); Fred Garretson, Oakland Tribune ($750); Guernsey Le Peller, Christian Science Monitor ($500); James Robey, Dayton, Ohio, Journal Herald ($500); Julian Morrison, Washington Daily News ($500); John G. Warren, Moline, Ill., Daily Dispatch ($500); Ralph Thornton, Minneapolis Star ($250); and Ward Sinclair, Louisville Times ($250).

**University of Missouri Awards:** Honor awards for distinguished service in journalism to Seymour Topping, foreign news editor of the New York Times; Ben F. Weir, Sr., publisher of the Nevada (Mo.) Daily Mail; NBC's Today Show; the New York Daily News; the Newspaper Fund; the Encyclopaedia Britannica; and the Saturday Review.

**National Magazine Award:** Newsweek magazine, for development of a new form of editorial analysis and advocacy in its major effort to present American racial problems.

**Newspaper Reporters Assn. of New York City,** plaques for excellence in writing, reporting and public service: Lawrence Van Gelder, William Pedercii, Edward O'Neill, Patrick Doyle and Joseph Modzelowski, all New York Daily News; J. Anthony Lukas and Milton Esterow, both New York Times; Cy Egan, New York Post; Ralph Penza, WCBS-TV; and Joe Famm, WABC.

**Overseas Press Club Awards,** for distinguished service in foreign journalism. **George Polk Memorial Award,** for best reporting in any medium requiring exceptional courage and enterprise abroad, $500: Eric Pace, The New York Times. **Vision Magazine—Ed Stout Award,** for a report on Latin America, $500: Laura Bergquist. Look magazine. **E. W. Fairchild Award,** for best business reporting, $500: Ray Vicker, The Wall Street Journal. **Asia Magazine Award,** for a report on that region, $500: Horace Sutton, Saturday Review. **Robert Capa Medal for Photography,** David Douglas Duncan, Life Magazine & ABC. **Other Award Winners:** Joe Alex Morris, Jr., Los Angeles Times; Michael R. McGrady, Newsday; R. W. Apple, Jr., The New York Times; Linda Grant Martin; Frances FitzGerald, Atlantic Monthly; Catherine Leroy, Associated Press; Jack Smith, Saturday Evening Post; Peter Skingley, United Press International; Don North; James Robinson, Wells Hangen, both NBC; Eric Sevareid, CBS; Ted Yates, NBC; George F. Kennan; and William Attwood, Look magazine.

**Page One Awards,** by the Newspaper Guild of New York: Local Reporting, William Rice, Daily News; Crusading Journalism, Leonard Victor, Long Island Press; National Reporting, Louis Cassels, UPI; Feature Writing J. Anthony Lukas, Times, and Bernard Bard, Post; News Photo, Frank Hurley, Daily News; Feature Photo, Bill Quinn, Daily News; Sports Photo, Robert Walker, Times; Editorial Cartoon, John Pierotti, Post; Sports Cartoon, Bill Gallo, Daily News; Magazine photography, Stanley Tretick, Look magazine.

**George Polk Memorial Awards,** by Long Island Univ. for achievement in journalism: Foreign Reporting, R. W. Apple, Jr., The New York Times; National Reporting, Clayton Fritchey, Newsday; Local Reporting, J. Anthony Lukas, The New York Times; Community Service, Newsday; News Photography, Catherine Leroy, The Associated Press; Magazine Reporting, The Paris Review; Criticism, Saul Maloff, Newsweek.

**Ernie Pyle Memorial Award,** by Scripps-Howard Newspapers, to the newspaperman most nearly exemplifying the style and craftsmanship of Ernie Pyle, $1,000: Martin Gershen, The Newark Star-Ledger; and William Thomas, The Memphis Commercial Appeal.

**Richard Reid Memorial Award,** by the Catholic Institute of the Press: Victor L. Ridder, publisher, The Catholic News.

**John Russwurm Awards,** by the N. Y. Urban League to members of the news media whose material has contributed to improving the plight of the unfortunate in the New York community: C. Gerald Fraser, New York Times; Ponchitta Pierce, Ebony Magazine; George Barner, The Amsterdam News; Layhmond Robinson, ABC-TV; Hugh L. Simpson, WMCA; Nat Hentoff, Village Voice; Nancy Hicks, New York Post.

**Sigma Delta Chi Awards.** General reporting: Charles Nicodemus, Chicago Daily News. Editorial writing: Robert E. Fisher, Crossett (Ark.) News Observer. Washington correspondence: Jack. C. Landau, Newhouse News Service. Foreign correspondence: Peter Arnett, Associated Press. News photography: Catherine Leroy, free-lance, Paris. Editorial cartooning: Eugene C. Payne, Charlotte (N. C.) Observer. Public service: Newsday, Garden

City, N. Y. Magazine reporting: William Lambert, Life. Magazine public service: Philadelphia Magazine. Radio reporting: WJR, Detroit. Radio editorializing: WSBA, York, Pa. Radio public service: Westinghouse Broadcasting Co. TV reporting: John Laurence, CBS. TV public service: NBC. TV editorializing: KWTV, Oklahoma City, Okla. Research about journalism: Prof. John Hohenberg, Columbia University Graduate School of Journalism.

**Silurian Awards,** by the Silurians, a society of present and former New York newspapermen: Spot News, The Morning Call of Paterson, N. J.; Feature Story, Milton Esterow, New York Times; Public Service, Newsday; Spot News Photo, Mel Finkelstein, The Daily News; Feature Photo, Jim Garrett, The Daily News; Editorial Writing, Joseph E. Evans, The Wall Street Journal; Cartoon, John Pierotti, New York Post.

**Mark Watson Memorial Award,** for distinguished news writing on military subjects: Jim G. Lucas, Scripps-Howard Newspaper Alliance.

**William Allen White Foundation Citation for Journalistic Merit:** Erwin D. Canham, The Christian Science Monitor.

**John Peter Zenger Freedom of the Press Award:** John S. Knight, editor and publisher.

# Music Awards

**Chopin Competition,** by the Kosciuszko Foundation, $1,000: Alan David Marks, pianist.

**Kirsten Flagstad Memorial Awards,** for young people preparing for careers in opera: Richard Daren Evans, St. Louis, Mo., and David Stone, Indiana Univ.

**Dimitri Mitropoulos International Music Competition,** $5,000 and a gold medal each: Boris Brott, Canada; Gaetano Delogu, Italy; Francois Huybrechts, Belgium, and Farhad Mechkat, Iran. Other awards, cash prizes as indicated: Catherine Comet, France ($2,500); Akira Endo, Japan ($1,000).

# Science Awards

**Arches of Science Award,** for contributions to public understanding of science, $25,000: Dr. Glenn T. Seaborg.

**Enrico Fermi Award,** by the Atomic Energy Comm., $25,000: Dr. John A. Wheeler, Princeton Univ.

**Robert H. Goddard Memorial Trophy,** by the National Space Club: Dr. Robert C. Seamans.

**Haley Astronautics Award,** by the American Institute of Aeronautics and Astronautics: Lt. Col. Virgil I. Grissom, posthumously, for meritorious service and outstanding contributions to the advancement of manned space flight.

**The National Academy of Sciences Awards,** $5,000 to Dr. Jack L. Strominger, Univ. of Wisconsin, for his work with bacterial cells. **U. S. Steel Foundation Award,** $5,000: Dr. Walter Gilbert, Harvard Univ., for research in the field of genetics. **John J. Carty Medal,** $3,000: Dr. Murray Gell-Mann, Calif. Inst. of Technology. **Comstock Prize,** $2,000 each: Dr. Leon N. Cooper, Brown Univ., and Dr. J. Robert Schrieffer, Univ. of Penn., for research in the field of electricity.

**National Medal of Science,** established by Congress to be awarded by the President to individuals who are deserving of special recognition by reason of their contribution to knowledge in the physical, biological, mathematical or engineering sciences: Kenneth Cole, National Institutes of Health; Harry F. Harlow, Univ. of Wisconsin; Alfred H. Sturtevant, Calif. Inst. of Technology; Michael Heidelberger, New York Univ.; Edwin H. Land, Polaroid Corp.; Igor I. Sikorsky, Sikorsky Aircraft; Paul J. Cohen, Sanford Univ.; Jesse W. Beams, Univ. of Virginia; Francis Birch, Harvard Univ.; Gregory Breit, Yale Univ.; Louis P. Hammett, Columbia Univ.; and George Kistiakowsky, Harvard Univ.

**Smithsonian Institution Research Awards,** provides postdoctoral scientists with opportunities for independent research in the various areas of investigation pursued at the Smithsonian Institution. The stipends ranged from $12,000 to $15,000: Krishna Apparao, India; Philippa Black, New Zealand; Vagn Buchwald, Denmark; Walter Cernohorsky, Fiji Islands; Elias R. de la Sota, Argentina; Dennis Devaney, Hawaii; Leo J. Hickey, Philadelphia, Pa.; Hui Lin Li, Philadelphia, Pa.; Philip Malone, Louisville, Ky.; Bruce Runnegar, Australia.

**Stouffer Prize,** for contribution to the understanding of blood pressure, $12,500 each: Dr. Leonard T. Skeggs, Western Reserve Univ.; Dr. Merlin Bumpus, Cleveland Clinic Fdn.; Dr. William S. Peart, London; Prof. Robert Schwyzer, Zurich.

**Westinghouse Science Talent Search,** annual high school student science talent competition for scholarships conducted by Science Service through its Science Clubs of America. First Prize, $10,000: Roger Y. Tsien, Livingston, N.J. Three students from Forest Hills High School in Queens, N.Y.,

won the following: John Gomori ($8,000); Perrin White ($8,000), and John Goldsmith ($4,000). **Other winners,** scholarship awards as indicated: Bruce L. Frostick, Jr., Richmond, Va. ($6,000); Robert W. Guth, Eureka, Ill. ($6,000); William L. Spence, Farmington, Mich. ($6,000); Penelope Jo Parsons, San Diego, Calif. ($4,000); Jonathan Rosenberg, Pittsburgh, Pa. ($4,000); and Bruce Waddington, Long Beach, Calif. ($4,000).

## Television & Radio Awards

**Emmy Awards** by the Academy of Television Arts and Sciences. **Actors Awards:** Continued performance in a dramatic series, Bill Cosby, I Spy (NBC); Continued performance in a comedy series, Don Adams, Get Smart (NBC); Single performance in a drama, Melvyn Douglas, Do Not Go Gentle Into That Good Night (CBS Playhouse); Supporting role in a dramatic series, Milburn Stone, Gunsmoke (CBS); Supporting role in a comedy series, Werner Klemperer, Hogan's Heroes (CBS); **Actress Awards:** Continued performance in a dramatic series, Barbara Bain, Mission: Impossible (CBS); Continued performance in a comedy series, Lucille Ball, The Lucy Show (CBS); Single performance in a drama, Maureen Stapleton, Among the Paths to Eden (ABC Special); Supporting role in a drama, Barbara Anderson, Ironside (NBC); Supporting role in a comedy, Marion Lorne, Bewitched (ABC). **Best Musical or Variety Program:** Rowan & Martin Laugh-In (NBC). **Dramatic Programs:** (special) Elizabeth the Queen (NBC); (series) Mission: Impossible (CBS). **Writing Awards:** (comedy) Allan Burns & Chris Hayward, He & She (CBS); (music or variety) Chris Beard, Phil Hahn, Jack Hanrahan, Coslough Johnson, Paul Keyes, Marc London, Allan Manings, David Panich, Hugh Wedlock and Digby Wolfe, Rowan and Martin's Laugh-In (NBC); (drama) Loring Mandel, Do Not Go Gentle Into That Good Night (CBS). **Directing Awards:** (comedy) Bruce Bilson, Get Smart; (drama) Paul Bogart, Dear Friends (CBS Playhouse).

**George Foster Peabody Awards,** for achievement in television and radio. **Television:** Entertainment Award: CBS Playhouse; and An Evening at Tanglewood (NBC). **Education Award:** The Eternal Light (NBC); and Africa (ABC). **Youth and Children's Programs:** The Children's Film Festival (CBS); and Mr. Knozit (WIS-TV), Columbia, (S. C.). **Public Service:** The Opportunity Line (WBBM-TV, Chicago). **Special Awards:** Bob Hope, Ed Sullivan, Eric Sevareid and James R. Killian, Jr. **Radio-Television Special Award:** Meet the Press (NBC). **Radio News Award:** Elie Abel, The World and Washington (NBC).

## Theater Awards

**American Society of Composers Award,** for contributions to American theater music, $1,250: Walter Marks.

**Clarence Derwent Awards,** for performance in nonfeatured roles, $500 each: David Birney, for Summertree, and Catherine Burns for The Prime of Miss Jean Brodie.

**Margo Jones Award,** presented to producers who have done the most to stimulate the production of new plays, $500: Paul Baker, managing director of the Dallas Theater Center.

**Joseph Maharam Foundation Awards,** for stage design, $500: Peter Wexler for The Happy Time; Ming Cho Lee for Ergo; and Nancy Potts, designer for the APA-Phoenix's The Show-Off, The Cherry Orchard, Pantegleize, and Exit the King.

**New York Drama Critics Circle Award,** for best productions during the season: Play, Rosencrantz and Guildenstern Are Dead. Musical, Your Own Thing.

**Antoinette Perry Awards (Tonys).** By the League of New York Theaters, 1967-68 season. Hallelujah, Baby! won the following awards: Best Musical; Musical Score, Jule Styne, Betty Comden and Adolph Green; Supporting Actress, Lillian Hayman; Actress (co-winner), Leslie Uggams. **Other Awards, Drama:** Best Play, Rosencrantz and Guildenstern Are Dead. Actor, Martin Balsam, You Know I Can't Hear You When the Water's Running. Actress, Zoe Caldwell, The Prime of Miss Jean Brodie. Supporting Actor, James Patterson, The Birthday Party. Supporting Actress, Zena Walker, Joe Egg. Director, Mike Nichols, Plaza Suite. **Musical:** Best Actor, Robert Goulet, The Happy Time. Actress, Patricia Routledge (co-winner) Darling of the Day. Supporting Actor, Hiram Sherman, How Now, Dow Jones. Director, Gower Champion, The Happy Time. Choreographer, Gower Champion, The Happy Time.

**Vernon Rice Awards,** by the Drama Desk, an organization of drama editors and reporters, for outstanding achievement in the Off-Broadway theater: Israel Horwitz, Bruce Jay Friedman, Ron Cowen and Ed Bullins, playwrights. Donald Driver, Tom O'Horgan and Robert Moore, directors. Galt MacDermot and Al Carmines, composers. Helen Hayes, actress.

**Sang Prize for Critics of the Fine Arts,** by Knox College. $5,000: Harold Clurman.

**Sam S. Shubert Foundation Award,** for outstanding contribution to the American theater: Neil Simon.

## Other Awards

**American Homemaker of Tomorrow,** conducted annually by General Mills, Inc., for senior class high school girls; $5,000 first prize to Irene Lindley, Honolulu, Hawaii.

**American Institute of Architects Gold Medal:** Marcel Breuer.

**Aspen Award,** $30,000 tax free to the individual anywhere in the world judged to have made the greatest contribution to the advancement of the humanities: Edmund Wilson.

**Atoms for Peace Award,** $30,000 each: Sigvard Eklund, Sweden; Abdus Salam, Pakistan; and Henry DeWolf Smyth, United States.

**Bernard M. Baruch Prize,** for contributions in the field of conservation, $2,000 each: Rep. John P. Saylor and Rep. John A. Blatnik.

**Frederick Douglas Awards,** by the New York Urban League: Robert Mangum; Rev. Gregory L. Mooney; and Mr. and Mrs. Stephen Currier. **Special Citation:** W. Willard Wirtz.

**Albert Einstein Commemorative Awards,** for contributions to man's betterment: Henry S. Moore; Dr. Harry Eagle; James Reston; Robert C. Weaver and Jack D. Weiler.

**Federal Woman's Award,** for outstanding service to the nation: Dr. Ruth Rogan Benerito, Dr. Mabel Kunce Gibby, Frances M. James, Mrs. Ruby Grant Martin, Dr. Lucille F. Stickel, Rogene L. Thompson, and Dr. Nina Bencich Woodside.

**Freedoms Foundation Awards,** given annually by the Freedoms Foundation at Valley Forge for contribution toward a better understanding and greater appreciation of the American Way of Life. **George Washington Award,** $5,000: Frank J. Mrkva. **National Service Medal:** Martha Raye. **American Statesman Medal:** James F. Byrnes. **Defender of Freedom Award,** $1,000: Mark A. White. Creston, Iowa. **Freedom Leadership Medals:** Dr. William B. Walsh, Washington, D. C.; Dr. Kenneth McFarland, Topeka, Kansas; and Mr. and Mrs. Walter Knott, Buena Park, Calif. **National Recognition Awards:** Ernest Crain, Sheriff Donald S. Genung, Lt. Col. Samuel R. Loboda, and Mr. and Mrs. Ken Magner. **Other Awards, George Washington Medals,** cash prizes as indicated: Rev. John F. Sammon, Tustim, Calif. ($500); Carl R. Terzian, Los Angeles, Calif. ($500); Louis Goodwin, Columbus, Ohio ($500); Jim Wright, Dallas, Tex. ($500); Mary Jo Payne, Tulsa, Okla. ($500).

**Sidney Hillman Awards,** by the Sidney Hillman Fdn. for achievement in mass communications, $500 each: Dr. Alan Westin, Ronald Steel, Howard James, and Jay L. McMullen. **Special Citation:** Harold and Lynne Mayer.

**Human Relations Awards,** by the National Conference of Christians and Jews: John Cardinal Krol, Archbishop of Philadelphia.

**Thomas Jefferson Memorial Medal in Architecture,** by the Univ. of Virginia, $5,000: Marcel Breuer.

**Joseph P. Kennedy Jr. International Awards,** for work in mental retardation, $20,000 each: Dr. Neils Erik Bank-Mikkelsen, Copenhagen, Denmark; Dr. Maria Egg, Zurich, Switzerland; Dr. Robert Cooke, Johns Hopkins Univ.; Harvey A. Stevens, Univ. of Wisconsin; Dr. Harold M. Skells, Balboa, Calif.; Dr. Maria Skodak, Swartz Creek, Mich.; Dr. Jack Tizard and Dr. Neil O'Connor, both London.

**Laetare Medal,** by the Univ. of Notre Dame to an outstanding Catholic layman: Sargent Shriver.

**Lawman of the Year,** by the National Sheriff's Assn.: Sheriff William R. Heidtman, Palm Beach County, Fla.

**Herbert H. Lehman Human Relations Award,** by the American Jewish Committee: Gustave L. Levy.

**Frances Lehman Loeb Award,** from the American Field Service for contributions toward understanding among people of different nations, $5,000; Yves-Louis Demeer.

**Jawaharlal Nehru Award for International Understanding,** $13,000: Dr. Martin Luther King, posthumously.

**Philadelphia Fellowship Commission's National Fellowship Award,** for contributions to human rights: Mayor Carl B. Stokes of Cleveland and Mayor Richard G. Hatcher of Gary, Indiana.

**Sylvanus Thayer Medal,** by the Association of Graduates, U. S. Military Academy: Bob Hope, for outstanding service to the nation.

**Thomas D. White National Defense Award,** by the Air Force Academy for contribution to the national defense and security of the country: Gen. Carl Spaatz.

# Miss America Pageant of Atlantic City, N. J.

The Miss America Pageant of Atlantic City, N. J., is a resort-promotion device developed since 1921, attracting thousands of visitors and getting national newspaper, radio and television coverage. Miss Ruth McCandliss is Executive Secretary. Local and state contestants are chosen by civic, educational and service organizations. A contestant must have a high school education and may come from any of the 50 states. The Scholarship Foundation, supported by industrial leaders, supplies $58,000 at the national finals, while $500,000 is awarded at 3,500 local and state pageants leading up to the finals. The 1968 finals were held at Atlantic City Sept. 2-8.

## MISS AMERICA PAGEANT CONTESTANTS

**MISS AMERICA OF 1969 ($10,000 Scholarship)**
Miss Illinois—Judith Anne Ford, Belvidere.

### RUNNERS UP

**Miss Massachusetts**—Catherine Monroe, Lynnfield, 1st—$6,000 scholarship.
**Miss Iowa**—Susan Alane Thompson, Des Moines, 2nd—$3,000 scholarship.
**Miss Oregon**—Marjean Kay Langley, Milton-Freewater, 3rd—$2,500 scholarship.
**Miss Indiana**—Katherine Virginia Field, Indianapolis, 4th—$2,0000 scholarship.

### SEMI-FINALISTS ($1,500 Scholarship)

**Miss Alabama**—Dellynne Cole Catching, Birmingham.
**Miss Florida**—Linda Fitts, Panama City.
**Miss New York**—Patricia Joy Burmeister, Portville.
**Miss Tennessee**—Brenda Joan Seal, Kingsport.
**Miss Virginia**—Cherie Suzanne Davis, Clifton Forge.

### TALENT AWARDS ($1,000 Scholarship)

**Most Talented in All Other Fields**—Miss California, Sharon Kay Terrill, Torrance.
**Most Talented Classical Singer**—Miss Connecticut, Gunnel L. Ragone, West Hartford.
**Most Talented Popular Singer**—Miss North Carolina, Elisa Annette Johnson, New Bern.
**Most Talented Actress (Serious)**—Miss South Dakota, Charlotte Ann McKay, Vermillion.
**Most Talented Dancer**—Miss Vermont, Elizabeth Ann Sackler, Putney.
**Most Talented Musician**—Miss Wyoming, Carol Ann Ross, Burns.
**Miss Congeniality**—Miss New Mexico, Karen Jan Maciolek, Albuquerque.
**Judges Special Award**—Miss Idaho, Karen Renee Ryder, Weiser.
**Preliminary Talent Winners**—Misses Florida, Illinois and Virginia.
**Preliminary Swimsuit Winners**—Misses Alabama, Illinois and Iowa.

### ALL OTHER CONTESTANTS ($500.00 Scholarships)

**Miss Alaska**—Jane Allison Haycraft, Fairbanks.
**Miss Arizona**—Linda Johnson, Warren.
**Miss Arkansas**—Helen Rose Gennings, Batesville.
**Miss Colorado**—Pamela Sue Kerker, Sterling.
**Miss Delaware**—Gayle Freeman, Wilmington.
**Miss Georgia**—Burma Ann Davis, Warner Robbins.
**Miss Hawaii**—Deborah Ynez Gima, Kailua, Oahu.
**Miss Kansas**—Jane Kathryn Bair, Parsons.
**Miss Kentucky**—Janet Sue Hatfield, Jeffersontown.
**Miss Louisiana**—Susanne Gail Saunders, Shreveport.
**Miss Maine**—Brenda Renee Verceles, Bangor.
**Miss Maryland**—Karen Ann Hansen, College Park.
**Miss Michigan**—Darlene Joyce Kurant, Muskegon.
**Miss Minnesota**—Mary Louise Williams, Minneapolis.
**Miss Mississippi**—Mary Linda Mills, Hattiesburg.
**Miss Missouri**—Kathleen Paulette Goff, DeSoto.
**Miss Montana**—Karen Sue Frank, Park City.
**Miss Nebraska**—Diane Lorraine Boldt, Omaha.
**Miss Nevada**—Sharon Jane Davis, Reno.
**Miss New Hampshire**—Michelle Sharon Godfrey, Pease A.F.B.
**Miss New Jersey**—Linda Ann Wilmer, Laurel Springs.
**Miss North Dakota**—Virginia Lee Hansen, Bismark.
**Miss Ohio**—Leslyn Anita Hiple, Louisville.
**Miss Oklahoma**—Beverly Jeanne Drew, Harrah.
**Miss Pennsylvania**—Susan Robinson, Hershey.
**Miss Rhode Island**—Arlene Lois Pinto, Warwick.
**Miss South Carolina**—Rebecca Louise Smith, Clover.
**Miss Texas**—Shirley Diane Hugghins, Tyler.
**Miss Utah**—Kathleen Frances Wood, Salt Lake City.
**Miss Washington**—Joyce Kay Stepanek, Issaquah.
**Miss West Virginia**—Charlotte Delana Warwick, Charleston.
**Miss Wisconsin**—Marilyn Kay Brahmstaedt, Wisc. Rapids.

---

# Miss America Winners of Yesterday and Today

| | | Height | Bust | Waist | Hips | Wgt. | Age | Hair | Eyes |
|---|---|---|---|---|---|---|---|---|---|
| 1921 | Margaret Gorman, Washington, D. C. | 5-1 | 30 | 25 | 32 | 108 | 16 | Blonde | Blue |
| 1922-23 | Mary Campbell, Columbus, Ohio | 5-7 | 35 | 26 | 34 | 140 | 16 | Brown | Blue |
| 1924 | Ruth Malcolmson, Philadelphia, Pa. | 5-6 | 34 | 25 | 34 | 137 | 18 | Brown | Blue |
| 1925 | Fay Lanphier, Oakland, California | 5-8 | 35 | 26 | 37 | 138 | 19 | Blonde | Hazel |
| 1926 | Norma Smallwood, Tulsa, Oklahoma | 5-4 | 33 | 25 | 34 | 118 | 18 | Brown | Blue |
| 1927 | Lois Delander, Joliet, Illinois | 5-5½ | 33 | 25 | 34 | 115 | 17 | Brown | Blue |
| 1933 | Marion Bergeron, West Haven, Conn. | 5-4½ | 32 | 26½ | 37½ | 112 | 16 | Blonde | Blue |
| 1935 | Henrietta Leaver, Pittsburgh, Pa. | 5-6½ | 33 | 23 | 35½ | 120 | 19 | Brown | Blue |
| 1936 | Rose Coyle, Philadelphia, Pa. | 5-6 | 34 | 23½ | 34½ | 114 | 22 | Black | Brown |
| 1937 | Bette Cooper, Bertrand Island, N. J. | 5-6 | 32 | 26 | 36 | 120 | 17 | Blonde | Blue |
| 1938 | Marilyn Meseke, Marion, Ohio | 5-7 | 34¾ | 26 | 35½ | 128 | 20 | Blonde | Blue |
| 1939 | Patricia Donnelly, Detroit, Michigan | 5-7 | 36 | 25 | 34 | 126 | 19 | Brown | Brown |
| 1940 | Frances Marie Burke, Philadelphia, Pa. | 5-9 | 34 | 23 | 35 | 120 | 19 | Brown | Green |
| 1941 | Rosemary LaPlanche, Los Angeles, Calif. | 5-5½ | 34 | 24 | 36 | 120 | 18 | Blonde | Hazel |
| 1942 | Jo-Carroll Dennison, Tyler, Texas | 5-5 | 34 | 22 | 34½ | 118 | 18 | Brown | Brown |
| 1943 | Jean Bartel, Los Angeles, Calif. | 5-8 | 36 | 23 | 35 | 130 | 19 | Brown | Blue |
| 1944 | Venus Ramey, Washington, D. C. | 5-7 | 37½ | 25 | 36½ | 125 | 19 | Auburn | Blue |
| 1945 | Bess Myerson, New York City, N. Y. | 5-10 | 35½ | 25 | 35 | 135 | 21 | Black | Hazel |
| 1946 | Marilyn Buferd, Los Angeles, Calif. | 5-8 | 35½ | 25½ | 36 | 123 | 21 | Brown | Blue |
| 1947 | Barbara Walker, Memphis, Tennessee | 5-7 | 35 | 25 | 35 | 130 | 21 | Black | Hazel |
| 1948 | BeBe Shopp, Hopkins, Minnesota | 5-9 | 37 | 27 | 36 | 140 | 18 | Brown | Hazel |
| 1949 | Jacque Mercer, Litchfield, Arizona | 5-4 | 34 | 22 | 34 | 106 | 18 | Black | Brown |
| 1951 | Yolande Betbeze, Mobile, Alabama (Postdated) | 5-5½ | 35 | 24 | 35 | 119 | 21 | Brown | Brown |
| 1952 | Colleen Kay Hutchins, Salt Lake City, Utah | 5-10 | 36 | 24 | 36 | 143 | 25 | Blonde | Blue |
| 1953 | Neva Jane Langley, Macon, Ga. | 5-6¼ | 35 | 23 | 35 | 118 | 19 | Brown | Green |
| 1954 | Evelyn Margaret Ay, Ephrata, Pa. | 5-8 | 37 | 24 | 36 | 132 | 20 | Blonde | Green |
| 1955 | Lee Meriwether, San Francisco, Calif. | 5-8½ | 34½ | 22 | 35 | 124 | 19 | Brown | Blue |
| 1956 | Sharon Ritchie, Denver, Colorado | 5-6 | 35 | 23 | 35 | 116 | 18 | Brown | Blue |
| 1957 | Marian McKnight, Manning, S. C. | 5-5 | 35 | 23 | 35 | 120 | 19 | Blonde | Blue |
| 1958 | Marilyn Van Derbur, Denver, Colorado | 5-8¼ | 35 | 25 | 36 | 130 | 20 | Blonde | Green |
| 1959 | Mary Ann Mobley, Brandon, Miss. | 5-5 | 34½ | 22 | 35 | 114 | 21 | Brown | Brown |
| 1960 | Lynda Lee Mead, Natchez, Miss. | 5-7 | 36 | 24 | 36 | 120 | 20 | Brown | Green |
| 1961 | Nancy Fleming, Montague, Michigan | 5-6 | 35 | 22 | 35 | 116 | 18 | Brown | Green |
| 1962 | Maria Fletcher, Asheville, N. C. | 5-5½ | 35 | 24 | 35 | 118 | 19 | Brown | Hazel |
| 1963 | Jacquelyn Mayer, Sandusky, Ohio | 5-6 | 36 | 22 | 36 | 115 | 20 | Brown | Hazel |
| 1964 | Donna Axum, El Dorado, Arkansas | 5-6½ | 35 | 23 | 35 | 124 | 21 | Brown | Brown |
| 1965 | Vonda Kay Van Dyke, Phoenix, Ariz. | 5-6 | 36 | 24 | 36 | 124 | 21 | Brown | Brown |
| 1966 | Deborah Irene Bryant, Overland Park, Kansas | 5-7 | 36 | 23 | 36 | 115 | 19 | Brown | Blue |
| 1967 | Jane Anne Jayroe, Laverne, Oklahoma | 5-6 | 36 | 24 | 35 | 116 | 19 | Brown | Green |
| 1968 | Debra Dene Barnes, Moran, Kansas | 5-9 | 36½ | 24 | 36½ | 135 | 20 | Brown | Blue |
| 1969 | Judith Anne Ford, Belvidere, Ill. | 5-7 | 36 | 24½ | 36 | 125 | 18 | Blonde | Blue |

Prior to 1950 the selection of Miss America was for the year in which she was selected. Starting with 1950 she became Miss America of the following year; as a result there was no Miss America for 1950.

# Labor Union Memberships

Source: AFL-CIO and World Almanac Questionnaire
**UNIONS WITH A MEMBERSHIP OF 25,000 OR OVER**
As of Sept. 1, 1968

| AFL-CIO UNIONS | MEMBERS | AFL-CIO UNIONS | MEMBERS |
|---|---|---|---|
| Actors and Artistes of America, Associated | 68,000 | Office & Professional Employees Int'l Union | 61,000 |
| Air Line Pilots Assn. | 28,000 | Oil, Chemical and Atomic Workers Int'l Union | 147,000 |
| Aluminum Workers Intl. Union | 27,000 | Painters, Decorators and Paperhangers of America, Brotherhood of | 160,000 |
| Bakery and Confectionery Workers Int'l Union, American | 82,000 | Papermakers and Paperworkers, United | 121,000 |
| Barbers, Hairdressers and Cosmetologists' Int'l Union of America, Journeymen | 66,000 | Plasterers' and Cement Masons' Int'l Ass'n of the United States and Canada, Operative | 68,000 |
| Boilermakers, Iron Ship Builders, Blacksmiths, Forgers and Helpers, Int'l Brotherhood of | 123,000 | Plumbing and Pipe Fitting Industry of the United States and Canada, United Ass'n of Journeymen and Apprentices of the | 225,000 |
| Bookbinders, Int'l Brotherhood of | 61,000 | Postal Clerks, United Federation of | 152,000 |
| Boot and Shoe Workers' Union | 40,000 | Printing Pressmen's and Assistants' Union of North America, Int'l | 106,000 |
| Brewery, Flour, Cereal, Soft Drink and Distillery Workers, Int'l Union of United | 40,000 | Pulp Sulphite and Paper Mill Workers of the United States and Canada, Int'l Brotherhood of | 141,000 |
| Bricklayers, Masons and Plasters Int'l Union of America | 120,000 | Railroad Trainmen, Brotherhood of | 96,000 |
| Carpenters and Joiners of America, United Brotherhood of | 700,000 | Railway Carmen of America, Brotherhood | 76,000 |
| Cement, Lime and Gypsum Workers Int'l Union, United | 28,000 | Railway, Airline, and Steamship Clerks, Freight Handlers, Express and Station Employees, Brotherhood of | 175,000 |
| Chemical Workers Union, Int'l | 88,000 | Retail Clerks Int'l Ass'n | 510,000 |
| Clothing Workers of America Amalgamated | 288,000 | Retail, Wholesale and Department Store Union | 119,000 |
| Communications Workers of America | 329,000 | Rubber, Cork, Linoleum and Plastic Workers of America, United | 174,000 |
| Distillery, Rectifying, Wine & Allied Workers' Int'l Union of America | 27,000 | Seafarers Int'l Union of North America | 80,000 |
| Dolls, Toys, Playthings, Novelties and Allied Products of the United States and Canada, International Union of | 26,000 | Service Employees Intl. Union | 344,000 |
| Electrical, Radio and Machine Workers Int'l Union of | 312,000 | Sheet Metal Workers Intl. Union | 100,000 |
| Electrical Workers, Int'l Brotherhood of | 724,000 | Shoe Workers of America, United | 44,000 |
| Engineers, Int'l Union of Operating | 300,000 | Stage Employees and Moving Picture Machine Operators of the United States and Canada, Int'l Alliance of Theatrical | 50,000 |
| Fire Fighters, Int'l Ass'n of | 87,000 | State, County and Municipal Employees, American Federation of | 350,000 |
| Firemen and Oilers, Int'l Brotherhood of | 41,000 | Steelworkers of America, United | 943,000 |
| Furniture Workers of America, United | 34,000 | Teachers, American Federation of | 143,000 |
| Garment Workers of America, United | 35,000 | Textile Workers of America, United | 37,000 |
| Garment Workers Union, Int'l Ladies | 363,000 | Textile Workers Union of America | 122,000 |
| Glass and Ceramic Workers of North America, United | 32,000 | Transit Union Amalgamated | 89,000 |
| Glass Bottle Blowers' Ass'n of the United States and Canada | 70,000 | Transportation-Communication Employees Union | 27,000 |
| Glass Workers Union, American Flint | 34,000 | Transport Workers Union of America | 80,000 |
| Government Employees, American Federation of | 249,000 | Typographical Union, Int'l | 90,000 |
| Hatters, Cap and Millinery Workers Int'l Union, United | 28,000 | Upholsters' Int'l Union of North America | 50,000 |
| Hotel and Restaurant Employees' and Bartenders' Int'l. Union | 300,000 | Utility Workers Union of America | 52,000 |
| Industrial Workers of America, Int'l Union, Allied | 86,000 | Woodworkers of America, Int'l | 49,000 |
| Iron Workers, International Association of Bridge and Structural | 150,000 | **INDEPENDENT UNIONS** | |
| Laborers' International Union of North America | 453,000 | Automobile, Aerospace and Agricultural Implement Workers of America, Intl. Union, United | 1,339,000 |
| Leather Goods, Plastics and Novelty Workers Union, International | 39,000 | Bakery and Confectionery Workers' Int'l Union of America | 62,000 |
| Letter Carriers, National Association of | 130,000 | Electrical, Radio and Machine Workers of America, United | 165,000 |
| Lithographers and Photoengravers Int'l Union | 44,000 | Federal Employees, Nat'l Federation of | 90,000 |
| Locomotive Firemen and Enginemen, Brotherhood of | 33,000 | Government Employees, Natl. Assn. | 151,000 |
| Longshoremen's Ass'n, Int'l | 50,000 | Internal Revenue Employees, Nat'l Ass'n of | 27,000 |
| Machinists & Aerospace Workers Int'l Ass'n of | 800,000 | Letter Carriers Ass'n, Nat'l Rural | 42,500 |
| Maintenance of Way Employees, Brotherhood of | 63,000 | Locomotive Engineers, Brotherhood of | 61,000 |
| Marine and Shipbuilding Workers of America, Industrial Union of | 32,000 | Longshoremen's Union, Int'l | 65,000 |
| Maritime Union of America, Nat'l | 45,000 | Mine, Mill and Smelter Workers, Int'l Union of | 75,000 |
| Meat Cutters & Butcher Workmen of No. America | 429,000 | Mine Workers of America, United | 450,000 |
| Mechanics Educational Society of America | 37,000 | Postal Union, National | 80,000 |
| Molders and Allied Workers Union, Int'l | 50,000 | Teamsters, Chauffeurs, Warehousemen and Helpers of America, Int'l Brotherhood of | 1,666,230 |
| Musicians, American Federation of | 233,000 | Telephone Unions, Alliance of Independent | 72,036 |
| Newspaper Guild, American | 25,000 | | |

# Work Stoppages (Strikes) in the United States

Source: Bureau of Labor Statistics, U. S. Department of Labor

| Year | Number stoppages | Workers involved | Man days idle | Year | Number stoppages | Workers involved | Man days idle |
|---|---|---|---|---|---|---|---|
| Average 1935 to 1939 | 2,862 | 1,130,000 | 16,900,000 | 1959 | 3,708 | 1,880,000 | 69,000,000 |
| | | | | 1960 | 3,333 | 1,320,000 | 19,100,000 |
| War Period Dec. 8, 1941- | | | | 1961 | 3,367 | 1,450,000 | 16,300,000 |
| Aug. 14, 1945. | 14,371 | 6,744,000 | 36,300,000 | 1962 | 3,614 | 1,230,000 | 18,600,000 |
| | | | | 1964 | 3,655 | 1,640,000 | 22,900,000 |
| 1946 | 4,985 | 4,600,000 | 116,000,000 | 1965 | 3,963 | 1,550,000 | 23,300,000 |
| 1947 | 3,693 | 2,170,000 | 34,600,000 | 1966 | 4,115 | 1,791,700 | 25,105,000 |
| 1948 | 3,419 | 1,960,000 | 34,100,000 | 1967 prelim. | 4,495 | 2,870,700 | 40,520,000 |
| 1949 | 3,606 | 3,030,000 | 50,500,000 | 1968 Jan. | 316 | 135,000 | 2,520,000 |
| | | | | Feb. | 330 | 232,000 | 3,780,000 |
| Average 1947-49 | 3,573 | 2,380,000 | 39,700,000 | Mar. | 330 | 130,000 | 3,550,000 |
| 1950 | 4,843 | 2,410,000 | 38,800,000 | Apr. | 490 | 438,000 | 4,910,000 |
| 1955 | 4,320 | 2,650,000 | 28,200,000 | May | 600 | 252,000 | 5,650,000 |
| | | | | June | 500 | 167,000 | 4,260,000 |

# AVIATION

## Huge Aviation Increase by 1979 Forecast by Federal Agency

The Federal Aviation Administration, in its latest multiyear projections, forecast a doubling, tripling, and even quadrupling of major indicators of aviation activity in the United States by 1979.

According to the FAA, airline passengers will more than triple, from 126,000,-000 in fiscal 1967 to 444,000,000 in 1979. Revenue passenger miles flown by the airlines will nearly quadruple, from 86 billion in 1967 to 342 billion in 1979. The airline fleet will increase from 2,272 aircraft to 3,860.

General aviation (non-airline) flying will show similar increases. The general aviation fleet will almost double from 104,706 aircraft as of Jan. 1, 1967, to 203,000 at the beginning of 1979. General aviation flying hours will increase from 21,900,000 hours to 40,500,000.

Use of jet fuel and aviation gasoline in the United States will more than triple, increasing from a total of 5.403 billion gallons in 1967 to 17.7 billion gallons in 1979. Jet fuel consumption will increase from 4.697 billion gallons to 16.890 billion. Use of aviation gasoline will increase from 706,000,000 gallons to 810,000,000.

Civil aircraft production will more than double from 15,171 aircraft in 1967 to 32,480 in 1979. Airline transport production will decrease from 372 to 280 aircraft, while general aviation aircraft production will increase from 14,799 aircraft to 32,200 by 1979. Aircraft engine production will increase from 20,812 units to 46,300 in the same time period.

### Busiest Control Towers

The 10 busiest FAA control towers all reported more than 400,000 operations during 1967. The top 10 were: O'Hare International, Chicago—643,787 operations; Opa Locka, Fla.—634,799; Van Nuys, Calif. —496,564; Ft. Lauderdale, Fla.—495,874; Long Beach, Calif.—484,863; Los Angeles International—482,774; Kennedy International—481,458; Miami International—446,-867; Denver International (Stapleton)— 444,910; San Jose Municipal (Calif.)— 410,311.

The annual FAA Air Traffic Activity report, released in 1968, showed that flying nearly doubled during the 1957-1967 period, with yearly increases varying from 2% to 19%. In 1967 the FAA's 313 airport traffic control towers (108 more than in 1957) reported a record 49,900,000 takeoffs and landings, nearly twice as many as the 25,100,000 operations reported by 205 FAA towers in 1957. IFR (instrument flight rules) aircraft handled by FAA air route traffic control centers jumped from 8,000,000 in 1957 to 16,600,000 in 1967.

By 1979, according to FAA projections, landings and takeoffs at airports with FAA air traffic control towers are expected to more than triple, jumping to 167,-000,000. Part of the huge gain will stem from increased airline and general aviation flying and part from installation of more airport traffic control towers. Currently there are 311 control towers in operation.

### Domestic Air Traffic Increases

During the first half of 1968, scheduled domestic airline passenger traffic increased 17.4% compared with the corresponding period in 1967, according to the Air Transport Assn. of America. The 11 trunk, 10 local service and 3 helicopter airlines flew 41,385,618,000 revenue passenger miles compared with the 35,262,-945,000 flown in the same part of 1967. Available seat miles flown totaled 77,909,-621,000, up 25.6% from the 62,027,938,000 of 1967's corresponding period. Passenger load factor (percentage of available seats sold) was 53.1%, down from the 56.9% of the first 6 months of the previous year.

Domestic air cargo carried by U. S. scheduled airlines gained 21.9% during the first half of 1968, compared with the corresponding period of 1967. The 11 trunk, 10 local service and 3 all-cargo carriers carried 1,077,614,000 revenue ton miles of air freight, mail and express service compared with their total of 883,-803,000 during the first half of 1967 (a ton mile is one ton flown one mile).

### Record Number of U. S. Airports

At the beginning of 1968, U. S. airports numbered a record 9,276, an increase of almost 400 over the total of a year earlier, according to the Federal Aviation Administration. In addition, 452 heliports and 398 seaplane bases brought the total number of landing facilities to a record 10,126. Included were 19 airports in Puerto Rico, 3 in the Virgin Islands, and 5 in the South Pacific. Over 62% of the national total were privately owned.

Texas continued to lead all the states with 900 landing facilities, followed by California with 684. Alaska 626, Pennsylvania 443, Illinois 433, Ohio 397, New York 338, Florida 281, Kansas 266, and Missouri 265. Of the total, 3,149 airports had lighted runways and 3,109 paved runways.

In 1968 the FAA presented its Air Traffic Facility of the Year Awards to the Washington National Airport Tower, the Denver Flight Service Station, and the Oakland Air Route Traffic Control Center for exhibiting "the highest degree of operational efficiency in rendering professional air traffic services" during 1967. The FAA's Director of Air Traffic Service, William M. Flener, said the winning facilities had made important contributions to operational efficiency, community relations and training of personnel, as well as meeting the agency's high standards of air safety.

### 50th Anniversary of U. S. Air Mail

The 50th anniversary of the beginning of United States Air Mail service was commemorated in Washington, D. C., May 15, 1968. A new 10¢ air mail stamp was issued that day to mark the anniversary. The stamp depicted a Curtiss "Jenny," the same plane pictured on the first air mail stamp of 1918, a 24-cent denomination stamp, 10 cents of the charge being for special delivery.

## Notable Ocean and Intercontinental Flights

| Pilot, Plane | From | To | Mi. | Time | Date |
|---|---|---|---|---|---|
| **DIRIGIBLE BALLOONS** | | | | | |
| British R-34 (1) | East Fortune, Scot. | Mineola, N. Y. | | 108 hrs. | July 2-6, 1919 |
| | Mineola, N. Y. | Pulham, Eng. | | 75 hr. | July 9-13, 1919 |
| Amundsen-Ellsworth-Noble expedition | Spitsbergen | Teller, Alaska | | | May 1926 |
| Graf Zeppelin (4) | Friedrichshafen | Lakehurst, N. J. | 6,630 | 4d 15h 46m | Oct. 11-15, 1928 |
| | Germany | Lakehurst, N. J. | | 51h 17m | June 30-July 2, 1936 |
| Hindenburg Zeppelin | Lakehurst, N. J. | Frankfort, Ger. | | 42h 53m | Aug. 9-11, 1936 |
| USN ZPG-2 Blimp | S. Weymouth, Mass. | Africa | } 7,000 | 275h | Mar. 4-16, 1957 |
| | Africa | Key West, Fla. | | | |
| **AIRPLANES** | | | | | |
| USN NC-4 | Newfoundland | Lisbon, Port. | | | May 16-27, 1919 |
| John Alcock-A. W. Brown (2) | St. John's, Nfld | Clifden, Ireland | 1,960 | 16h 12m | June 14-15, 1919 |
| Richard E. Byrd (3) | Spitsbergen | North Pole | 1,545 | 15h 30m | May 9, 1926 |
| Chas. A. Lindbergh (4) | Mineola, N. Y. | Paris | 3,610 | 33h 29m 30s | May 20-21, 1927 |
| Chas. A. Levine-Clarence D. Chamberlin (5) | Roosevelt Field, Mineola, N. Y. | Eisleben, Ger | 3,911 | 42h 31m | June 4-6, 1927 |
| Baron G. von Huenefeld, crew (6) | Dublin | Greenly Isl., Lab. | | 37 hrs. | Apr. 12-13, 1928 |
| Sir Hubert Wilkins (8) | Point Barrow, Alaska | Spitsbergen | | | April 16, 1928 |
| Sir Chas. Kingsford-Smith, crew (7) | Oakland, Calif. | Brisbane, Aust. | | | May 31-June 8 1928 |
| Amelia Earhart Putnam, W. Stultz, L. Gordon | Trepassy, Nfld. | Burry Port, Wales | | 20h 40m | June 17-18, 1928 |
| Richard E. Byrd (9) | Bay of Wales | South Pole | | | Nov. 28-29, 1929 |
| Capt. D. Coste-M. Bellonte | Paris | Valley Stream, N. Y. | 4,100 | 37h 18m 30s | Sept. 1-2, 1930 |
| Lt. L. Challe-Lt. T. L. Borres | Seville, Spain | Natal, Brazil | 3,600 | | Dec. 15-17, 1930 |
| Wiley Post-Harold Gatty | Harbor Grace, Nfld | England | 2,200 | 16h 17m | June 23-24, 1931 |
| Clyde Pangborn-Hugh Herndon, Jr. (10) | Tokyo | Wenatchee, Wash. | 4,458 | 41h 34m | Oct. 3-5, 1931 |
| Amelia Earhart Putnam (11) | Harbor Grace, Nfld | Ireland | 2,026½ | 14h 56m | May 20-21, 1932 |
| James A. Mollison (12) | Portmarnock, Ire. | Pennfield, N. B. | | | Aug. 18, 1932 |
| Amelia Earhart Putnam (11) | Honolulu, T. H. | Oakland, Calif. | 2,408 | 18h 16m | Jan. 11-12, 1935 |
| China Clipper (Pan Am. Airways) (13) | San Francisco | Manila, P. I. | | | Nov. 22-28, 1935 |
| | Manila, P. I. | San Francisco | | | Dec. 1-6, 1935 |
| Gromoff, Yumasheff, Danilin (USSR) | Moscow, USSR | San Jacinto, Calif. | 6,262 | 62h 02m | July 12-14, 1937 |
| Douglas C. Corrigan | Floyd Bennett Field | Dublin, Ire. | | 28h 13m | July 17-18, 1938 |
| B-29 (Lt. Col. C. J. Miller) | Honolulu, T. H. | Washington, D. C. | 4,640 | 17h 21m | Sept. 1, 1945 |
| C-54 (Maj. G. E. Cain) | Tokyo | Washington, D. C. | | 31h 25m | Sept. 3, 1945 |
| William P. Odom | Honolulu, T. H. | Teterboro, N. J. | 5,300 | 36 hrs. | Mar. 8, 1949 |
| USN Caroline Mars | Honolulu, T. H. | San Diego, Calif. | | 14h 17m | June 17-18, 1950 |
| Col. David C. Schilling, USAF (14) | England | Limestone, Me. | 3,300 | 10h 01m | Sept. 22, 1950 |
| Chas. F. Blair, Jr. | New York | London | 3,500 | 7h 48m | Jan. 31, 1951 |
| Canberra Bomber | Aldergrove, Belfast, N. I. | Gander, Nfld. | | 4h 40m | Feb. 21, 1951 |
| Chas. F. Blair, Jr. (15) | Bardufoss, Nor. | Fairbanks, Alaska | 3,300 | 10h 29m | May 29, 1951 |
| Chas. F. Blair, Jr. | Fairbanks, Alaska | New York | 3,450 | 9h 31m | May 30, 1951 |
| Canberra Bomber | England | Australia | | 20h 20m | Mar. 16, 1952 |
| British Comet | London | Johannesburg, S. Af. | | 23h 38m | May 2-3, 1952 |
| Two U. S. S-55 Helicopters (16) | Westover AFB, Mass. | Prestwick, Scot. | 3,410 | 42h 30m | July 15-31, 1952 |
| RB-45 Tornado (17) | Anchorage, Alaska. | Yokoto AFB, Japan. | 3,460 | 9h 50m | July 29, 1952 |
| Canberra Bomber (18) | Aldergrove, N. I. | Gander, Nfld. | 2,073 | 4h 34m | Aug. 26, 1952 |
| | Gander, Nfld | Aldergrove, N. I. | 2,073 | 3h 25m | Aug. 26, 1952 |
| B-47B | California | Hawaii | 2,463 | 4h 52m | Sept. 20, 1952 |
| British Comet | London-Tokyo | Tokyo-London | 20,400 | 74h 52m | April 3-7, 1953 |
| U.S. B-47 | Limestone AFB, Me. | Fairford, Eng. | 2,925 | 4h 45m | July 28, 1953 |
| U.S. B-47 | Fairford, Eng. | Tampa, Fla. | 4,450 | 9h 53m | Aug. 4, 1953 |
| British Comet | London | Rio de Janeiro | 6,000 | 12h 30m | Sept. 13-14, 1953 |
| Flt. Lieut. Roland Burton (Canberra PR-3 bomber in race) | England | New Zealand | 12,270 | 23h 51m | Oct. 8-9, 1953 |
| Comet II | London | Khartoum, Egypt. | 3,064 | 6h 22m | Jan. 22, 1954 |
| Max Conrad (solo) | New York | Paris, France | | 22h 23m | Nov. 7, 1954 |
| 10 U. S. F-84's | Stugate AFB, Eng. | Bergstrom AFB, Austin, Texas | 5,118 | 10h 48m | Aug. 17, 1955 |
| Canberra Bomber | London (round trip) | New York | 6,920 | 14h21m45.4s | Aug. 23, 1955 |
| Capt. William F. Judd | New York | Paris | | 24h 11m | Jan. 29-30, 1956 |
| Pan American DC-7 | New York | Shannon, Ire. | | 7h 45m | Dec. 10, 1956 |
| Bristol Britannia | New York | Rome | 4,700 | 12h 20m | Mar. 8, 1957 |
| Three USAF F-100 Cs | London | Los Angeles, Calif. | 6,710 | 14h 5m | May 13, 1957 |
| Spirit of St. Louis II (USAF F-100F jet) | McGuire AFB, N. J. | Le Bourget, Paris. | | 6h 38m | May 21, 1957 |
| Air France | Los Angeles | Paris | 6,102 | 16h 21m | Aug. 25, 1957 |
| Soviet TU-104 | Vnukovo Airport, Moscow | McGuire AFB, N. J. | 5,570 | 21h 54m | Sept. 3-4, 1957 |
| | McGuire AFB, N. J. | Moscow | 5,570 | 11h 13m | Sept. 7, 1957 |
| Soviet TU-104 | Moscow | McGuire AFB, N. J. | 5,570 | 18h 30m | Sept. 13-14, 1957 |
| Lockheed Super Starliner (19) | New York | Athens, Greece | 5,000 | 14h 38m | Sept. 26, 1957 |
| TWA Jetstream (20) | London | San Francisco | 5,900 | 23h 19m | Oct. 1-2, 1957 |
| 6 USAF B-52 bombers | U.S.-Argentina (no-stp) | Argentina-U. S. | 10,425 | 21h 42m | Nov. 16-17, 1957 |
| 4 USAF RF-101s (21). | Tokyo | Honolulu | 3,850 | 6h 35m | Dec. 2, 1957 |
| El Al Britannia | New York | London | | 7h 44m | Jan. 9, 1958 |
| USAF KC-135 | Tokyo | Lajes AFB, Azores. | 10,230 | 18h 48m | Apr. 7-8, 1958 |
| Max Conrad (solo) | New York | Palermo, Sicily | 4,440 | 33h 55m | June 22-23, 1958 |
| USAF KC-135 | New York | London | 3,442 | 5h 27m 42.8s | June 27, 1958 |
| USAF KC-135 | London | New York | 3,460 | 5h 51m 24.5s | June 29, 1958 |

| Pilot, Plane | From | To | Mi. | Time | Date |
|---|---|---|---|---|---|
| Capt. Mairon Boling | Manila, P. I | Pendleton, Oreg | 6,979 | 45h 42m | Jy. 31-Au. 1/58 |
| Comet IV jet airliner | New York | London | 3,496 | 6h 27m | Aug. 12, 1958 |
| Boeing 707 Clipper | New York | London | | 7h 28m | Sept. 8, 1958 |
| USAF KC-135 | Yokota AB, Japan | Washington, D. C. | 7,100 | 12h 28m | Sept. 12, 1958 |
| Comet IV jet airliner | New York | London | 3,650 | 6h 12m | Oct. 4, 1958 |
| Boeing 707 Clipper | New York | Paris | | 8h 41m | Nov. 4-5, 1958 |
| Boeing 707 | London | New York | 3,700 | 7h 17m | Jan. 10, 1959 |
| Max Conrad (solo) | Chicago | Rome | 5,000 | 34h 3m | Mar. 5-6, 1959 |
| Boeing 707-320 | Seattle, Wash. | Rome | 5,800 | 11h 6m | May 29, 1959 |
| Max Conrad (solo) | Casablanca, Africa | Los Angeles | 7,700 | 58h 36m | June 2-4, 1959 |
| USSR TU-114 (22) | Moscow | New York | 5,092 | 11h 6m | June 28, 1959 |
| Boeing 707 airliner | San Francisco | Sydney, Australia | 7,630 | 16h10m | July 2, 1959 |
| Boeing 707-320 | Honolulu, Hawaii | Moscow | c.5,090 | 8h 54m | July 23, 1959 |
| Pan Amer. Clipper | Honolulu, Hawaii | San Francisco | 2,410 | 4h 25m | Aug. 25, 1959 |
| USAF F-100 (group) | Darwin, Australia | Itazuke, Japan | c.3,000 | 6h 35m | Nov. 4, 1959 |
| Boeing 707 | New York | Paris | | 5h 44m | Nov. 10, 1959 |
| Boeing 707 | New York | Shannon, Ireland | | 5h 5m | Nov. 11, 1959 |
| Max Conrad (solo) | Casablanca, Mor. | El Paso, Texas | 6,911 | 56h 26m | Nov. 22-26, 1959 |
| USAF B-58 | New York | Paris | | 3h 10m 58s | May 26, 1961 |
| Col. J. B. Swindal | Washington, D. C. | Moscow | 5,004 | 8h 39m 02.2s | May 19, 1963 |
| Mrs. Jerrie Mock (23) | Columbus, Ohio | Columbus, Ohio | 23,206 | 29d 11h 59m | Mr. 19-Ap. 18/64 |
| Joan Merriam (24) | Oakland, Calif. | Oakland, Calif. | 27,750 | 56d | Mr. 17-Ma. 12/64 |

**Notable first flights: 1,** Atlantic aerial round trip. **2,** Non-stop transatlantic flight. **3,** Polar flight. **4,** Solo transatlantic flight in the Ryan monoplane the "Spirit of St. Louis." **5,** Transatlantic passenger flight. **6,** East-West transatlantic crossing. **7,** U. S. to Australia flight. **8,** Trans-Arctic flight. **9,** South Pole flight. **10,** Non-stop Pacific flight. **11,** Woman's transoceanic solo flight. **12,** Westbound transatlantic solo flight. **13,** Pacific airmail and U. S. to Philippines crossing. **14,** Non-stop jet transatlantic flight. **15,** Solo across North Pole. **16,** Transatlantic helicopter flight. **17,** Non-stop jet Pacific flight. **18,** Transatlantic round trip on same day. **19,** Non-stop between New York and Athens; carried 59 persons. **20,** Non-stop London to San Francisco via polar route; carried 32 passengers. **21,** Non-stop jet flight from Tokyo to Honolulu. **22,** Non-stop between Moscow and New York. **23,** First woman pilot to circle globe; first woman to fly both North Atlantic and Pacific. **24,** Followed route Amelia Earhart partly completed in 1937.

## Fastest Trips Around the World

Fast circuits of the earth have been a subject of wide interest since Jules Verne, French novelist, described an imaginary trip by Phileas Fogg in Around the World in 80 Days, assertedly occurring Oct. 2 to Dec. 20, 1872. Notable actual such events follow:

| Craft, pilot | Terminal | (Mi.) | Time | Date |
|---|---|---|---|---|
| Nellie Bly | New York, N. Y. | | 72d 6h 11m | 1889 |
| George Francis Train | New York, N. Y. | | 67d 12h 03m | 1890 |
| Charles Fitzmorris | Chicago | | 60d 13h 29m | 1901 |
| J. W. Willis Sayre | Seattle | | 54d 09h 42m | 1903 |
| Henry Frederick | | | 54d 07h 02m | 1903 |
| Col. Burnlay-Campbell | | | 40d 19h 30m | 1907 |
| Andre Jaeger-Schmidt | | | 39d 19h 42m 38s | 1911 |
| John Henry Mears | | | 35d 21h 36m | 1913 |
| Two U.S. Army airplanes | Seattle (57 hops, 21 countries) | 26,103 | 351h 11m | 1924 |
| Edward S. Evans and Linton Wells (New York World) (1) | New York | 18,400 | 28d 14h 36m 05s | June 16-July 14, 1926 |
| John H. Mears and Capt. C. B. D. Collyer | New York | | 23d 15h 21m 03s | June 29-July 22, 1928 |
| Graf Zeppelin | Friedrichshafen, Ger. via Tokyo, Los Angeles, Lakehurst, N. J. | 21,700 | 20d 04h | Aug. 8-Sept. 4, 1929 |
| Wiley Post and Harold Gatty (Monoplane Winnie Mae) | Roosevelt Field, via Artic Circle | 15,474 | 8d 15h 51m | June 23-July 1, 1931 |
| Wiley Post (Monoplane Winnie Mae) (2) | Floyd Bennett Field, via Arctic Circle | 15,596 | 115h 36m 30s | July 15-22, 1933 |
| H. R. Ekins (Scripps-Howard Newspapers in race) (Zeppelin Hindenburg to Germany, airplanes from Frankfort) | Lakehurst, N. J., via Frankfort, Ger. | 25,654 | 18d 11h 14m 33s | Sept. 30-Oct. 19, 1936 |
| Howard Hughes and 4 assistants | New York, Paris, Moscow, Siberia, Fairbanks, Alaska | 14,824 | 3d 19h 08m 10s | July 10-13, 1938 |
| Mrs. Clara Adams (Pan American Clipper) | Port Washington, N. Y., ret. Newark, N. J. | | 16d 19h 04m | June 28-July 15, 1939 |
| Globester, U. S. Air Transport Command | Washington, D. C. | 23,279 | 149h 44m | Sept. 28-Oct. 4, 1945 |
| Capt. William P. Odom (A-26 Reynold Bombshell) | New York, via Paris, Cairo, Tokyo, Alaska | 20,000 | 78h 55m 12s | Apr. 12-16, 1947 |
| America, Pan American 4-engine Lockheed Constellation (3) | New York, eastward | 22,219 | 101h 32m | June 17-30, 1947 |
| Col. Edward P. F. Eagan | New York | 20,559 | 147h 15m | Dec. 13, 1948 |
| USAF B-50, Lucky Lady II (Capt. James Gallagher) (4) | Fort Worth, Texas | 23,452 | 94h 01m | Feb. 26-Mar. 2, 1949 |
| Thos. G. Lapphier, Jr. | New York | 22,180 | 119h 47m | Dec. 2-7, 1949 |
| Jean-Marie Audibert | Paris | | 4d 19h 38m | Dec. 11-15, 1952 |
| Horace C. Boren | Idlewild Airport, New York | | 99h 16m | June 21-25, 1953 |
| Pamela Martin | Midway Airport, Chicago | | 90h 59m | Dec. 5-8, 1953 |
| Three USAF B-52 Stratofortresses (5) | Castle AFB, Merced, Calif., via Nfld., Morocco, Saudi Araba, India, Ceylon, P. I., Guam, Riverside, Calif. | 24,325 | 45h 19m | Jan. 15-18, 1957 |
| Joseph Cavoli | Cleveland, Ohio | | 89h 13m 37s | Jan. 31-Feb. 4, 1958 |
| Miss K. Kanetake | Tokyo, via Bangkok, Karachi, Rome, Anchorage | 18,580 | 73h 9m | July 28-31, 1958 |
| Peter Gluckmann (solo) | San Francisco | 22,800 | 29d | Aug. 22-Sept. 20 1959 |
| Milton Reynolds | San Francisco | | 51h 45m 22s | Jan. 12-14, 1960 |
| Sue Snyder | Chicago | 21,219 | 62h 59m | June 22-24, 1960 |
| Max Conrad (solo) | Miami, Fla. | 25,946 | 8d 18h 35m 57s | Feb. 28-Mar. 8, 1961 |
| Sam Miller & Louis Fodor | New York | | 46h 28m | Aug. 3-4, 1963 |
| Henry G. Beaird | Wichita, Kans. | 22,992 | 65h 38m 49s | May 23-26, 1966 |
| Robert & Joan Wallick (6) | Manila, Philippines | 23,557 | 5d 6h 17m 10s | June 1-7, 1966 |
| Arthur Godfrey, Richard Merrill, Fred Austin, Karl Keller | New York | 23,333 | 86h 9m 1s | June 4-7, 1966 |

**1,** Mileage by train and auto, 4,100; by plane, 6,300; by steamship, 8,000. **2,** First to fly solo around northern circumference of the world, also first to fly twice around the world. **3,** Inception of regular commercial global air service. **4,** First non-stop round-the-world flight, refueled 4 times in flight. **5,** First non-stop global flight by jet planes; refueled in flight by KC-97 aerial tankers; average speed, approx. 525 m.p.h. **6,** Official world record for light planes.

# INTERNATIONAL AERONAUTICAL RECORDS

**Source:** The National Aeronautics Association, 806 15th St., N.W., Washington, D.C. 20005, representative in the United States of the Federation Aeronautique Internationale, certifying agency for world aviation and space records. The International Aeronautical Federation was formed in 1905 by representatives from Belgium, France, Germany, Great Britain, Spain, Italy, Switzerland and the United States, with headquarters in Paris. Regulations for the control of official records were signed Oct. 14, 1905. World records are defined as maximum performance, regardless of class or type of aircraft used. Records to Nov. 1, 1965.

## WORLD AIR RECORDS—MAXIMUM PERFORMANCE IN ANY CLASS

**Speed Over a Straight Course**—3,331.507 km.p.h. (2,070.101 m.p.h.)—Col. R. L. Stephens, USAF, United States; Lockheed YF-12A; Edwards Air Force Base, Calif., May 1, 1965.

**Speed Over a Closed Circuit**—2,981.5 km.p.m. (1,850.61 m.p.h.)—Mikhail Komarov, USSR; E-266 Jet; Oct. 5, 1967.

**Distance in a Straight Line**—20,168.75 kms. (12,532.28 mi.)—Maj. Clyde P. Evely, USAF, United States; Boeing B52-H; Kadena, Okinawa, to Madrid, Spain, Jan. 11, 1962.

**Distance Over a Closed Circuit**—18,245.5 kms. (11,336.92 mi.)—Capt. William Stevenson, USAF, United States; Boeing B52-H; Seymour-Johnson, N. C.; Kindley, Bermuda; Sondrestrom, Greenland; Anchorage, Alaska; March AFB, Calif.; Key West, Fla.; Seymour-Johnson, N. C., June 6-7, 1962.

**Altitude**—95,935.99 meters (314,750 feet)—Maj. Robert M. White, USAF, United States; North American X-15-1; Edwards AFB, Calif., July 17, 1962.

**Altitude in Horizontal Flight**—24,462.596 meters (80,257.86 ft.)—Col. R. L. Stephens, USAF, United States; Lockheed YF-12A; Edwards Air Force Base, Calif., May 1, 1965.

## MANNED SPACE CRAFT

**Duration With Earth Orbit**—330 hrs. 35 mins. 00 secs.—Lt. Col. Frank Borman, USAF and Cdr. James A. Lovell, Jr., USN, United States; Spacecraft Gemini 7; Dec. 4-18, 1965.

**Distance With Earth Orbit**—9,204,575 kms. ((5,719,457 miles))—Lt. Col. Frank Borman, USAF and Cdr. James A. Lovell, Jr., USN, United States; Spacecraft Gemini 7; Dec. 4-18, 1965.

**Greatest Altitude With Earth Orbit**—1,369 kms. (850.65 miles)—Cdr. Charles Conrad Jr. and Lt. Cdr. Richard Gordon, United States; Spacecraft Gemini 11; Sept. 13-15, 1966.

**Greatest Mass Lifted With Earth Orbit**—5,320 kgs. (11,728.59 lbs.)—V. M. Komarov and K. P. Feoktistov, USSR; Spacecraft "Voskhod"; Oct. 12-13, 1964.

**Greatest Altitude Without Earth Orbit**—187.5 kms. (116.5 mi.)—Comdr. Alan B. Shepard, USN, United States; McDonnell Spacecraft Freedom 7; Cape Kennedy, Fla., to 27° 13' 7" N., 75° 51' 14" W., May 5, 1961.

**Greatest Mass Lifted Without Earth Orbit**—1,832.51 kgs. (4,040 lbs.)—Comdr. Alan B. Shepard, USN, United States; McDonnell Spacecraft Freedom 7; Cape Kennedy, Fla., to 27° 13' 7" N., 75° 51' 14" W., May 5, 1961.

All other records, international in scope, are termed World "Class" records and are divided into classes: Airships, free balloons, airplanes, seaplanes, amphibians, gliders, and rotorplanes. Airplanes (Class C) are sub-divided into four groups: Group I—Piston Engine Aircraft, Group II—Turbo-prop Aircraft, Group III—Jet Aircraft, Group IV—Rocket Powered Aircraft. A partial listing of world records follows:

## WORLD "CLASS" RECORDS
### AIRPLANES (Class C, Group I—Piston Engine)

**Distance, Closed Circuit**—14,249.656 kms. (8,854.308 miles)—Lt. Col. O. F. Lassiter, USAF, United States; Boeing B-29; Tampa, Fla., Aug. 1, 1947.

**Distance, airline (International)**—18,081.990 kms. (11,235.6 miles)—Comdr. Thomas D. Davies, USN; Comdr. Eugene P. Rankin, USN; Comdr. Walter S. Reid, USN, and Lt. Comdr. Ray A. Tabeling, USN; United States; Lockheed P2V-1; from Pearce Field, Perth, Australia, to Port Columbus, Columbus, Ohio, Sept. 29-Oct. 1, 1946. (United States)—same.

**Maximum speed over 3-kilometer measured course (International)**—755.138 km.p.h. (469.220 m.p.h.)—Fritz Wendel, Germany, Messerschmitt B. F. 109R, Augsburg, April 26, 1939. (United States)—663.054 km.p.h. (412.002 m.p.h.)—Jacqueline Cochran, United States; North American F-51, Thermal, Calif., Dec. 17, 1947.

**Speed for 100 kilometers (62.137 miles) without payload (International)**—755.668 km.p.h. (469.549 m.p.h.)—Jacqueline Cochran, United States; North American F-51, Coachella Valley, Calif., Dec. 10, 1947. (United States)—same.

**Speed for 1,000 Kilometers (621.369 miles) without payload**—693.78 km.p.h. (431.09 m.p.h.)—Jacqueline Cochran, United States; North American P-51; Santa Rosasummit, Calif.—Flagstaff, Arizona course, May 24, 1948.

**Speed for 5,000 Kilometers (3,106.849 miles) without payload**—544.59 km.p.h. (338.39 m.p.h.)—Capt. James Bauer, USAF, United States; Boeing B-29; Dayton, Ohio, June 28, 1946.

**Speed Around the World**—300.20 km.p.h. (186-53 m.p.h.)—Robert Wallick and Joan Wallick, United States; Beechcraft Baron C55, 2 Continental 10-520 engines; Manila, Philippines; June 2-7, 1966. Distance: 23,129.29 miles. Time: 5 days 6 hours 17 min. 10 sec.

### AIRPLANES (Class C, Group II—Turbo-prop)

**Altitude**—13,513 meters (44,334 ft.)—Loubov Ulanova, USSR; IL-18 Aircraft; Oct. 20, 1967.

**Speed for 1,000 kilometers (621.369 miles) without payload (International)**—871.38 km.p.h. (541.449 m.p.h.)—Ivan Soukhomline, Boris Timochok and crew, USSR; TU-114 Swept Wing Monoplane, 4 turbo-prop TB-12 engines; Sternberg Course, Mar. 24, 1960.

**Speed for 5,000 kilometers (3,106.849 miles) without payload (International)**—877.212 km.p.h. (545.072 m.p.h.)—Ivan Soukhomline, K. Sapielkine and crew, USSR; TU-114 Swept Wing Monoplane, 4 turbo-prop TB-12 engines; Sternberg-Sverdlovsk-Sebastopol-Sternberg, Apr. 9, 1960.

### AIRPLANES (Class C, Group III—Jet-powered)

**Distance in a Straight Line**—20,168.78 kms. (12,532.28 mi.)—Maj. Clyde P. Evely, USAF, United States; Boeing B52-H, 8 Pratt & Whitney TF-33P-3 engines; Kadena, Okinawa, to Madrid, Spain, Jan. 10-11, 1962.

**Distance in a Closed Circuit**—18,245.05 kms. (11,336.92 miles)—Capt. William Stevenson, USAF, United States; Boeing B52-H, 8 Pratt & Whitney TF-33P-3 engines; terminal: Seymour-Johnson, N. C., June 6-7, 1962.

**Altitude**—34,714 meters (113,890.848 feet)—Gueorgui Mossolov, USSR; E-66A jet monoplane, triangular wing, T.R.D. and G.R.D. engines; Podmoskovnoe, USSR. Apr. 28, 1961.

**Speed Over a 3-Kilometer Course**—1,452.777 km.p.h. (902.769 m.p.h.)—Lt. Hunt Hardisty, USN, United States; McDonnell F4H Phantom, 2 GE J-79 jet engines; White Sands, N. M., Aug. 29, 1961.

**Speed over 15-25 Kilometer Course**—3,331.507 km.p.h. (2,070.101 m.p.h.)—Col. R. L. Stephens, USAF, United States; Lockheed YF-12A; Edwards Air Force Base, Calif., May 1, 1965.

**Speed for 100 Kilometers**—2,401 km.p.h. (1,491.9 m.p.h.)—A. Fedotov, USSR; triangular-wing aircraft, P-166 jet engine; Sidorovo Course, USSR, Oct. 7, 1961.

**Speed for 500 Kilometers in a Closed Circuit**—2,981.5 km.p.h. (1,852.61 m.p.h.)—Mikhail Komarov, USSR; E-266 Airplane, 2 RD jet engines; Oct. 5, 1967.

**Speed for 1,000 Kilometers in a Closed Circuit**—2,920.67 km.p.h. (1,814.81 m.p.h.)—Pyotr Ostapenko, USSR; E-266 Airplane, 2 RD jet engines; Oct. 27, 1967.

**Speed for 2,000 Kilometers in Closed Circuit**—1,708.817 km.p.h. (1,061.808 m.p.h.)—Maj. H. J. Deutchendorf, Jr., USAF, United States; Convair B-58 Hustler Bomber; Desert, Stoval, Boundary, Morris, Desert, Edwards AFB, Calif. Course; Jan. 12, 1961.

### LIGHT AIRPLANES—Class C-1.d

**Distance Airline (International)**—12,341.26 kms. (7,668.48 miles)—Max Conrad, United States; Piper Comanche 250, Lycoming 0-540-AIA5 250 hp.; Casablanca, Morocco to Los Angeles, June 2-4, 1959.

**Speed for 100 Kilometers (62.137 miles) in a Closed Circuit (International)**—519.480 km.p.h. (322.789 m.p.h.)—Miss R. M. Sharpe, Great Britain; Vickers Supermarine Spitfire 5-B; Wolverhampton, June 17, 1950.

## GLIDERS (Class D—Single-place)

**Distance, Straight Line**—1,041.52 kms. (647.17 miles)—Alvin Parker, United States; SISU 1-A sailplane; Odessa, Texas, to Kimball, Nebr., July 31, 1964.

**Altitude above sea level**—14,102 meters (46,267 feet)—Paul F. Bikle, United States; Sailplane Schweizer SGS 123E; Mojave, Lancaster, Calif., Feb. 25, 1961.

## HELICOPTERS (Class E-1)

**Distance in a Straight Line** 3,561.55 kms. (2,213.04 miles)—Robert G. Ferry, United States; Hughes YOH-6A Helicopter; Culver City, Calif., to Daytona, Fla., Apr. 6-7, 1966.

**Speed Over 3-Km. Course**—341.23 km.p.h. (212.029 m.p.h.)—Jean Boulet, France; Superfrelon SA 3210/01 helicopter; Istres Airport, France, July 19, 1963.

## FREE BALLOONS (Tenth category, 4001 cu. meters or more)

**Altitude**—34,668 meters (113,739.9 feet)—Cmdr. Malcolm D. Ross, USNR, United States; Lee Lewis Memorial Winzen Research Balloon; Gulf of Mexico, May 4, 1961.

## F. A. I. COURSE RECORDS

**Los Angeles to New York**—1,954.79 km.p.h. (1,214.65 m.p.h.)—Capt. Robert G. Sowers, USAF, United States; Convair B-58 Hustler, 4 GE-J-79-5B engines. Elapsed time: 2 hrs. 58.71 secs., Mar. 5, 1962.

**New York to Los Angeles**—1,741 km.p.h. (1,081.80 m.p.h.)—Capt. Robert G. Sowers, USAF, United States; Convair B-58 Hustler. Elapsed time: 2 hrs. 15 min. 50.08 sec., Mar. 5, 1962.

**Los Angeles-New York-Los Angeles**—1,681.71 km.p.h. (1,044.46 m.p.h.) Capt. Robert G. Sowers, USAF, United States; Convair B-58 Hustler; Elapsed time: 4 hrs. 41 min. 14.98 sec., Mar. 5, 1962.

**New York to Paris**—1,753.068 km.p.h. (1,089.36 m.p.h.)—Maj. W. R. Payne, United States; Convair B58 Hustler; elapsed time, 3 hrs. 10 min. 58 sec., May 26, 1961.

**Anchorage to Chicago**—843.49 km.p.h. (524.12 m.p.h.)—Lt. Col. G. A. Andrews, USAF. United States; Convair B-58A Hustler. Elapsed time: 5 hours 26 minutes 33.9 seconds, Oct. 16, 1963.

**Anchorage to London**—1,330.80 km.p.h. (826.91 m.p.h.)—Maj. S. J. Kubesch, USAF, United States; Convair B-58A Hustler. Elapsed time: 5 hours 24 minutes 54 seconds, Oct. 16, 1963.

**New York to London: (International)**—1,014.248 km.p.h. (630.223 m.p.h.)—Maj. Burl B. Davenport, Lt. James J. Jones, and crew, USAF; Boeing KC-135 Stratotanker, 4 Pratt & Whitney J-57-P-43W turbo-jet engines; Idlewild International Airport, Long Island, to London International Airport, June 27, 1958. Elapsed time: 5 hours 29 minutes 14.64 seconds.

**London to New York (International)**—945.423 km.p.h. (587.457 m.p.h.)—Maj. Burl B. Davenport, Lt. James J. Jones, and crew USAF, United States; Boeing KC-135 Stratotanker; London International Airport to Idlewild International Airport, Long Island, June 27, 1958. Elapsed time: 5 hours 29 minutes 14.64 seconds.

**Baltimore to Moscow, USSR**—906.64 km.p.h. (563.36 m.p.h.)—Col. James B. Swindal, USAF, United States; Boeing VC-137 (707). Elapsed time: 8 hours 33 minutes 45.4 seconds.

**Moscow to Washington, D. C.**—788.67 km.p.h. (490.06 m.p.h.)—Col. James B. Swindal, USAF, United States; Boeing VC-137 (707). Elapsed time: 9 hrs. 54 min., 48.5 sec. May 20-21, 1963.

**Belfast to Gander, Newfoundland (International)**—774.255 km.p.h. (481.099 m.p.h.)—Wing Commander R. P. Beamont and crew, Great Britain; Canberra bomber, two Rolls-Royce turbo-jet engines. Aug. 31, 1951. Elapsed time: 4 hours 18 minutes 24.4 seconds.

# Aviation Hall of Fame

The Aviation Hall of Fame at Dayton, Ohio, is dedicated to honoring aviation's outstanding pioneers. It operates as a non-profit, privately supported organization under a charter granted in 1964 by the Congress of the United States.

**1962**

**Orville Wright and Wilbur Wright** for co-invention of the first successful man-carrying airplane and for the first powered flights in Dec., 1903.

**1963**

**Octave Chanute,** for successful man-carrying glider flights and experiments; **Samuel Pierpont Langley,** for studies of air and space and demonstrations of practicability of mechanical flight; **Frank Purdy Lahm,** first Army airplane and dirigible pilot; and **Benjamin Delahauf Foulois,** first Army Signal Corps pilot.

**1964**

**Thomas Scott Baldwin,** early balloon and dirigible builder and pilot; **Theodore Gordon Ellyson,** first U. S. Navy pilot, pilot of first plane successfully launched by catapult; **Henry W. Walden,** inventor of first American monoplane; **Glenn Hammond Curtiss,** holder of first pilot's license issued by Aero Club of America (1911), inventor, builder; **Calbraith Perry Rodgers,** pilot of first transcontinental flight, New York to Pasadena, Calif., Sept. 17-Nov., 1911; and **John J. Montgomery,** maker of first American glider flight (1884).

**1965**

**Alexander Graham Bell,** inventor of the telephone, for research on aerodynamic lift, propulsion and control; **Alfred Austell Cunningham,** first Marine Corps aviator; **Albert Cushing Read,** a participant in first successful transatlantic flight; **Eugene Burton Ely,** pilot of first plane to fly from a ship, whose work led to practical use of aircraft carriers; **A. Roy Knabenshue,** pioneer in building and flying steerable balloons; **Thomas Etholen Selfridge,** first American killed testing an experimental aircraft; **Charles Edward Taylor,** builder of engine for first successful airplane; and **Edward Vernon Rickenbacker,** World War I ace and later president of Eastern Airlines.

**1966**

**Lincoln Beachey,** early dirigible and airplane exhibitionist, who made the first inside loop in America; **William Edward Boeing,** developer of first airline network and producer of vitally important military and commercial aircraft; **Robert Hutchings Goddard,** pioneer in rocket technology who laid the foundation for space travel; **Glenn Luther Martin,** pioneer in aircraft design and mass manufacturing techniques; **William "Billy" Mitchell,** visionary proponent of an independent air force and a martyr to the cause of airpower; **John Henry Towers,** pioneering naval aviator who promoted airpower as a vital naval doctrine.

**1967**

**Henry Harley "Hap" Arnold,** student of Wright Brothers who later became first five-star general of Air Force; **James Harold Doolittle,** who performed first outside loop, made first blind landing, and led famous Tokyo raid in World War II; **Charles Augustus Lindbergh,** who made first solo trans-Atlantic flight and promoted many facets of aviation; and **Carl A. Spaatz,** World War I pilot, air commander of World War II, and first Chief of Staff of independent Air Force.

**1968**

**Richard Evelyn Byrd,** naval aviator who developed aerial navigation instruments, made flight over North Pole 1926, transatlantic flight 1927, and flight over South Pole in 1929; **Amelia Earhart,** first woman to fly across Atlantic as passenger, later made solo flight across Atlantic, holder of many records, disappeared on flight across Pacific; **John A. MacReady,** Army Air Service pilot who made pioneering high altitude and endurance flights in 1920s, participated in first nonstop transcontinental flight 1923; and **Igor I. Sikorsky,** for development of long-range flying boats in 1930s that opened commercial transoceanic flights, and successful development of the helicopter in 1939.

# Consolidated Airline Traffic

|  | 1966 | 1967 | 1967 (6 mo.) | 1968 (6 mo.) |
|---|---|---|---|---|
| Revenue passenger miles* | 79,889,246,000 | 98,746,641,000 | 45,793,552,000 | 53,620,183,000 |
| Revenue ton-miles traffic: |  |  |  |  |
|    Passenger | 7,736,469,000 | 9,560,623,000 | 4,434,233,000 | 5,183,183,000 |
|    U. S. Mail (priority) | 542,772,000 | 567,728,000 | 271,416,000 | 281,121,000 |
|    U. S. Mail (non-priority) | 207,746,000 | 407,757,000 | 148,729,000 | 305,302,000 |
|    Express | 99,690,000 | 2,351,108,000 | 49,297,000 | 1,302,930,000 |
|    Freight | 2,050,735,000 | 98,883,000 | 1,128,402,000 | 48,788,000 |
|    Charter | 1,754,930,000 | 2,648,005,000 | 1,245,103,000 | 1,411,201,000 |
|    Excess baggage & foreign mail | 48,514,000 | 49,132,000 | 22,800,000 | 28,052,000 |
| **Total revenue ton-miles** | **12,440,856,000** | **15,683,236,000** | **7,299,980,000** | **8,560,577,000** |

# Air Line Distances Between Principal Cities of the World

Source: USAF Aeronautical Chart & Information Center (Statute Miles)
Point-to-point measurements are usually from City Hall.

| Statute miles from/to | Azores | Baghdad | Berlin | Bombay | Buenos Aires | Cairo | Capetown | Chicago | Guam | Honolulu |
|---|---|---|---|---|---|---|---|---|---|---|
| Azores | | 3,852 | 2,142 | 5,865 | 5,376 | 3,225 | 5,621 | 3,295 | 8,904 | 7,389 |
| Baghdad | 3,825 | | 2,029 | 2,015 | 8,135 | 798 | 4,924 | 6,430 | 6,300 | 8,399 |
| Berlin | 2,142 | 2,029 | | 3,915 | 7,395 | 1,768 | 5,958 | 4,415 | 7,052 | 7,323 |
| Bombay | 5,865 | 2,015 | 3,915 | | 9,283 | 2,717 | 5,103 | 8,066 | 4,765 | 8,036 |
| Buenos Aires | 5,376 | 8,135 | 7,395 | 9,283 | | 7,360 | 4,285 | 5,582 | 10,377 | 7,554 |
| Cairo | 3,225 | 798 | 1,768 | 2,717 | 7,360 | | 4,510 | 6,116 | 7,092 | 8,818 |
| Capetown | 5,621 | 4,924 | 5,958 | 5,103 | 4,285 | 4,510 | | 8,489 | 8,810 | 11,534 |
| Chicago | 3,295 | 6,430 | 4,415 | 8,066 | 5,582 | 6,116 | 8,489 | | 7,379 | 4,256 |
| Guam | 8,904 | 6,300 | 7,052 | 4,765 | 10,377 | 7,092 | 8,810 | 7,379 | | 3,808 |
| Honolulu | 7,389 | 8,399 | 7,323 | 8,036 | 7,554 | 8,818 | 11,534 | 4,256 | 3,808 | |
| Istanbul | 2,872 | 1,006 | 1,075 | 3,000 | 7,608 | 741 | 5,204 | 5,485 | 6,892 | 8,118 |
| Juneau | 4,724 | 6,121 | 4,586 | 6,890 | 7,743 | 6,259 | 10,334 | 2,306 | 5,101 | 2,810 |
| London | 1,583 | 2,547 | 580 | 4,478 | 6,907 | 2,158 | 5,988 | 3,960 | 7,489 | 7,241 |
| Manila | 8,258 | 4,910 | 6,139 | 3,195 | 11,048 | 5,704 | 7,488 | 8,142 | 1,599 | 5,308 |
| Melbourne | 11,898 | 8,105 | 9,929 | 6,101 | 7,219 | 8,700 | 6,428 | 9,667 | 3,528 | 5,501 |
| Mexico City | 4,569 | 8,082 | 6,054 | 9,739 | 4,580 | 7,677 | 8,516 | 1,688 | 7,544 | 3,791 |
| Montreal | 2,559 | 5,768 | 3,740 | 7,524 | 5,597 | 5,403 | 7,920 | 746 | 7,723 | 4,919 |
| Moscow | 3,136 | 1,583 | 1,001 | 3,132 | 8,369 | 1,770 | 6,277 | 4,984 | 6,106 | 7,049 |
| New Orleans | 3,718 | 7,161 | 5,132 | 8,881 | 4,902 | 6,764 | 8,324 | 831 | 7,723 | 4,213 |
| New York | 3,623 | 6,007 | 3,980 | 7,811 | 5,279 | 5,598 | 7,801 | 714 | 7,959 | 4,969 |
| Panama City | 3,906 | 7,752 | 5,856 | 9,753 | 3,301 | 7,118 | 7,021 | 2,321 | 9,037 | 5,254 |
| Paris | 1,601 | 2,405 | 549 | 4,367 | 6,857 | 1,973 | 3,782 | 4,145 | 7,571 | 7,452 |
| Rio de Janeiro | 4,283 | 6,938 | 6,207 | 8,334 | 1,231 | 6,153 | 3,773 | 5,288 | 11,604 | 8,295 |
| Rome | 2,021 | 1,836 | 735 | 3,846 | 6,925 | 1,305 | 5,231 | 4,823 | 7,568 | 8,040 |
| San Francisco | 5,081 | 7,466 | 5,673 | 8,406 | 6,455 | 7,436 | 10,248 | 1,860 | 5,809 | 2,397 |
| Santiago | 5,665 | 8,756 | 7,772 | 9,983 | 702 | 7,967 | 4,947 | 5,295 | 9,826 | 6,861 |
| Seattle | 4,708 | 6,799 | 5,060 | 7,756 | 6,903 | 6,809 | 10,205 | 1,737 | 5,675 | 2,681 |
| Shanghai | 7,269 | 4,404 | 5,231 | 3,140 | 12,667 | 5,188 | 8,062 | 7,071 | 1,921 | 4,947 |
| Sydney | 12,138 | 8,319 | 9,997 | 6,304 | 7,341 | 8,969 | 6,856 | 9,242 | 3,282 | 5,065 |
| Tokyo | 7,342 | 5,199 | 5,557 | 4,196 | 11,411 | 5,937 | 9,155 | 6,313 | 1,563 | 3,860 |

| Statute miles from/to | Istanbul | Juneau | London | Manila | Melbourne | Mexico City | Montreal | Moscow | New Orleans | New York |
|---|---|---|---|---|---|---|---|---|---|---|
| Azores | 2,872 | 4,724 | 1,583 | 8,258 | 11,898 | 4,569 | 2,559 | 3,136 | 3,718 | 2,623 |
| Baghdad | 1,006 | 6,121 | 2,547 | 4,910 | 8,105 | 8,082 | 5,768 | 1,583 | 7,161 | 6,007 |
| Berlin | 1,075 | 4,586 | 580 | 6,139 | 9,929 | 6,054 | 3,740 | 1,001 | 5,132 | 3,980 |
| Bombay | 3,000 | 6,890 | 4,478 | 3,195 | 6,101 | 9,739 | 7,524 | 3,132 | 8,881 | 7,811 |
| Buenos Aires | 7,608 | 7,743 | 6,907 | 11,048 | 7,219 | 4,580 | 5,597 | 8,369 | 4,902 | 5,279 |
| Cairo | 741 | 6,259 | 2,158 | 5,704 | 8,700 | 7,677 | 5,403 | 1,770 | 6,764 | 5,598 |
| Capetown | 5,204 | 10,334 | 5,988 | 7,488 | 6,428 | 8,516 | 7,920 | 6,277 | 8,324 | 7,801 |
| Chicago | 5,485 | 2,306 | 3,960 | 8,142 | 9,667 | 1,688 | 746 | 4,984 | 831 | 714 |
| Guam | 6,892 | 5,101 | 7,489 | 1,599 | 3,528 | 7,544 | 7,723 | 6,106 | 7,723 | 7,959 |
| Honolulu | 8,118 | 2,810 | 7,241 | 5,308 | 5,501 | 3,791 | 4,919 | 7,049 | 4,213 | 4,969 |
| Istanbul | | 5,519 | 1,551 | 5,674 | 9,100 | 7,106 | 4,798 | 1,087 | 6,184 | 5,022 |
| Juneau | 5,519 | | 4,441 | 5,885 | 8,067 | 3,217 | 2,644 | 4,560 | 2,859 | 2,859 |
| London | 1,551 | 4,441 | | 6,680 | 10,508 | 5,558 | 3,256 | 1,556 | 4,636 | 3,473 |
| Manila | 5,674 | 5,885 | 6,680 | | 3,932 | 8,849 | 8,198 | 5,139 | 8,737 | 8,509 |
| Melbourne | 9,100 | 8,067 | 10,508 | 3,932 | | 8,420 | 10,390 | 8,965 | 9,271 | 10,352 |
| Mexico City | 7,106 | 3,217 | 5,558 | 8,849 | 8,420 | | 2,315 | 6,671 | 923 | 2,086 |
| Montreal | 4,798 | 2,644 | 3,256 | 8,198 | 10,390 | 2,315 | | 4,397 | 1,394 | 333 |
| Moscow | 1,087 | 4,560 | 1,556 | 5,139 | 8,965 | 6,671 | 4,397 | | 5,773 | 4,665 |
| New Orleans | 6,184 | 2,859 | 4,636 | 8,737 | 9,271 | 923 | 1,394 | 5,773 | | 1,167 |
| New York | 5,022 | 2,859 | 3,473 | 8,509 | 10,352 | 2,086 | 333 | 4,665 | 1,167 | |
| Panama City | 6,756 | 4,453 | 5,285 | 10,296 | 9,027 | 1,496 | 2,542 | 6,720 | 1,601 | 2,213 |
| Paris | 1,400 | 4,654 | 215 | 6,688 | 10,442 | 5,723 | 3,432 | 1,550 | 4,804 | 3,638 |
| Rio de Janeiro | 6,378 | 7,591 | 5,751 | 11,260 | 8,217 | 4,102 | 5,082 | 7,162 | 4,792 | 4,805 |
| Rome | 853 | 5,272 | 892 | 6,466 | 9,940 | 6,374 | 4,102 | 1,477 | 5,460 | 4,292 |
| San Francisco | 6,711 | 1,517 | 5,369 | 6,978 | 7,850 | 1,889 | 2,340 | 5,884 | 1,925 | 2,574 |
| Santiago | 8,135 | 7,307 | 7,241 | 10,945 | 7,017 | 4,094 | 5,436 | 8,770 | 4,546 | 5,106 |
| Seattle | 6,077 | 892 | 4,799 | 6,653 | 8,176 | 2,340 | 2,289 | 5,217 | 2,098 | 2,409 |
| Shanghai | 4,975 | 4,891 | 5,728 | 1,147 | 4,991 | 8,033 | 7,067 | 4,248 | 7,739 | 7,384 |
| Sydney | 9,289 | 7,649 | 10,556 | 3,882 | 437 | 8,064 | 7,959 | 9,002 | 8,887 | 9,936 |
| Tokyo | 5,574 | 4,030 | 5,956 | 1,862 | 5,070 | 7,036 | 6,470 | 4,663 | 6,877 | 6,757 |

| Statute miles from/to | Panama City | Paris | Rio de Janeiro | Rome | San Francisco | Santiago | Seattle | Shanghai | Sydney | Tokyo |
|---|---|---|---|---|---|---|---|---|---|---|
| Azores | 3,906 | 1,601 | 4,283 | 2,021 | 5,081 | 5,665 | 4,708 | 7,269 | 12,138 | 7,342 |
| Baghdad | 7,752 | 2,405 | 6,938 | 1,836 | 7,466 | 8,756 | 6,799 | 4,404 | 8,319 | 5,199 |
| Berlin | 5,856 | 549 | 6,207 | 735 | 5,673 | 7,772 | 5,060 | 5,231 | 9,997 | 5,557 |
| Bombay | 9,753 | 4,367 | 8,334 | 3,846 | 8,406 | 9,982 | 7,756 | 3,140 | 6,304 | 4,196 |
| Buenos Aires | 3,301 | 6,857 | 1,231 | 6,925 | 6,455 | 702 | 6,903 | 12,667 | 7,341 | 11,411 |
| Cairo | 7,118 | 1,973 | 6,153 | 1,305 | 7,436 | 7,967 | 6,809 | 5,188 | 8,969 | 5,937 |
| Capetown | 7,021 | 5,782 | 3,773 | 5,231 | 10,248 | 4,947 | 10,205 | 8,062 | 6,856 | 9,155 |
| Chicago | 2,321 | 4,145 | 5,288 | 4,823 | 1,860 | 5,295 | 1,737 | 7,071 | 9,242 | 6,313 |
| Guam | 9,037 | 7,571 | 11,604 | 7,568 | 5,809 | 9,826 | 5,675 | 1,921 | 3,282 | 1,563 |
| Honolulu | 5,254 | 7,452 | 8,295 | 8,040 | 2,397 | 6,861 | 2,681 | 4,947 | 5,065 | 3,860 |
| Istanbul | 6,756 | 1,400 | 6,378 | 853 | 6,711 | 8,135 | 6,077 | 4,975 | 9,289 | 5,574 |
| Juneau | 4,453 | 4,654 | 7,591 | 5,272 | 1,517 | 7,307 | 892 | 4,891 | 7,649 | 4,030 |
| London | 5,285 | 215 | 5,751 | 892 | 5,369 | 7,241 | 4,799 | 5,728 | 10,556 | 5,956 |
| Manila | 10,296 | 6,688 | 11,260 | 6,466 | 6,978 | 10,945 | 6,653 | 1,147 | 3,882 | 1,862 |
| Melbourne | 9,027 | 10,442 | 8,217 | 9,940 | 7,850 | 7,017 | 8,176 | 4,991 | 437 | 5,070 |
| Mexico City | 1,496 | 5,723 | 4,102 | 6,374 | 1,889 | 4,094 | 2,340 | 8,033 | 8,064 | 7,036 |
| Montreal | 2,542 | 3,432 | 5,082 | 4,102 | 2,340 | 5,436 | 2,289 | 7,067 | 7,959 | 6,470 |
| Moscow | 6,720 | 1,550 | 7,162 | 1,477 | 5,884 | 8,770 | 5,217 | 4,248 | 9,002 | 4,663 |
| New Orleans | 1,601 | 4,804 | 4,792 | 5,460 | 1,925 | 4,546 | 2,098 | 7,739 | 8,887 | 6,877 |
| New York | 2,213 | 3,638 | 4,805 | 4,292 | 2,574 | 5,106 | 2,409 | 7,384 | 9,936 | 6,757 |
| Panama City | | 5,388 | 3,296 | 5,916 | 3,326 | 2,974 | 3,651 | 9,340 | 8,801 | 8,441 |
| Paris | 5,388 | | 5,681 | 688 | 5,579 | 7,224 | 5,012 | 5,772 | 10,539 | 6,054 |
| Rio de Janeiro | 3,296 | 5,681 | | 5,704 | 6,621 | 1,820 | 6,890 | 11,339 | 8,414 | 11,535 |
| Rome | 5,916 | 688 | 5,704 | | 6,259 | 7,391 | 5,680 | 5,679 | 10,141 | 6,140 |
| San Francisco | 3,326 | 5,579 | 6,621 | 6,259 | | 5,926 | 679 | 6,150 | 7,416 | 5,148 |
| Santiago | 2,974 | 7,224 | 1,820 | 7,391 | 5,926 | | 6,433 | 11,718 | 7,066 | 10,711 |
| Seattle | 3,651 | 5,012 | 6,890 | 5,680 | 679 | 6,433 | | 5,721 | 7,740 | 4,793 |
| Shanghai | 9,340 | 5,772 | 11,339 | 5,679 | 6,150 | 11,718 | 5,721 | | 4,879 | 1,097 |
| Sydney | 8,801 | 10,539 | 8,414 | 10,141 | 7,416 | 7,066 | 7,740 | 4,879 | | 4,842 |
| Tokyo | 8,441 | 6,054 | 11,535 | 6,140 | 5,148 | 10,711 | 4,793 | 1,097 | 4,842 | |

# Air Line Distances Between Principal Cities in the United States

Source: Coast and Geodetic Survey, U. S. Dept. of Commerce (Statute Miles)

*Distances are measured from a central point in each city.*

| Statutemiles from/to | Atlanta | Boston | Chicago | Cincinnati | Cleveland | Dallas | Denver | Detroit | Houston | Indianapolis |
|---|---|---|---|---|---|---|---|---|---|---|
| Atlanta, Ga.. | ...... | 937 | 587 | 369 | 554 | 721 | 1,212 | 596 | 701 | 426 |
| Boston, Mass. | 937 | ...... | 851 | 740 | 551 | 1,551 | 1,769 | 613 | 1,605 | 807 |
| Chicago, Ill.. | 587 | 851 | ...... | 252 | 308 | 803 | 920 | 238 | 940 | 165 |
| Cincinnati, O. | 369 | 740 | 252 | ...... | 222 | 814 | 1,094 | 235 | 892 | 100 |
| Cleveland, O. | 554 | 551 | 308 | 222 | ...... | 1,025 | 1,227 | 90 | 1,114 | 263 |
| Dallas, Texas. | 721 | 1,551 | 803 | 814 | 1,025 | ...... | 663 | 999 | 225 | 763 |
| Denver, Colo. | 1,212 | 1,769 | 920 | 1,094 | 1,227 | 663 | ...... | 1,156 | 879 | 1,000 |
| Detroit, Mich. | 596 | 613 | 238 | 235 | 90 | 999 | 1,156 | ...... | 1,105 | 240 |
| Houston, Tex. | 701 | 1,605 | 940 | 892 | 1,114 | 225 | 879 | 1,105 | ...... | 865 |
| Indianapolis.. | 426 | 807 | 165 | 100 | 263 | 763 | 1,000 | 240 | 865 | ...... |
| Jacksonville.. | 285 | 1,017 | 863 | 626 | 770 | 908 | 1,467 | 831 | 821 | 699 |
| Kansas City.. | 676 | 1,251 | 414 | 541 | 700 | 451 | 558 | 645 | 644 | 453 |
| Los Angeles.. | 1,936 | 2,596 | 1,745 | 1,897 | 2,049 | 1,240 | 831 | 1,983 | 1,374 | 1,809 |
| Louisville, Ky. | 319 | 826 | 269 | 90 | 311 | 726 | 1,038 | 316 | 803 | 107 |
| Memphis..... | 337 | 1,137 | 482 | 410 | 630 | 420 | 579 | 623 | 484 | 384 |
| Minneapolis.. | 907 | 1,123 | 355 | 605 | 630 | 862 | 700 | 543 | 1,056 | 511 |
| Nashville.... | 214 | 943 | 397 | 238 | 459 | 617 | 1,023 | 470 | 665 | 251 |
| New Orleans.. | 424 | 1,359 | 833 | 706 | 924 | 443 | 1,082 | 939 | 318 | 712 |
| New York.... | 748 | 188 | 713 | 570 | 405 | 1,374 | 1,631 | 482 | 1,420 | 646 |
| Oklahoma C'y | 757 | 1,495 | 692 | 758 | 951 | 190 | 505 | 910 | 413 | 689 |
| Omaha, Nebr. | 817 | 1,282 | 432 | 622 | 739 | 586 | 488 | 669 | 794 | 525 |
| Philadelphia.. | 666 | 271 | 666 | 503 | 360 | 1,299 | 1,579 | 443 | 1,341 | 585 |
| Pittsburgh... | 521 | 483 | 410 | 257 | 115 | 1,070 | 1,320 | 205 | 1,137 | 330 |
| Portland, Ore. | 2,172 | 2,540 | 1,758 | 1,985 | 2,055 | 1,633 | 982 | 1,969 | 1,836 | 1,885 |
| St. Louis, Mo. | 467 | 1,038 | 262 | 309 | 492 | 547 | 796 | 455 | 679 | 231 |
| Salt Lake C'y. | 1,583 | 2,099 | 1,260 | 1,453 | 1,568 | 999 | 371 | 1,492 | 1,200 | 1,356 |
| San Francisco. | 2,139 | 2,699 | 1,858 | 2,043 | 2,166 | 1,483 | 949 | 2,091 | 1,645 | 1,949 |
| Seattle, Wash. | 2,182 | 2,493 | 1,737 | 1,972 | 2,026 | 1,681 | 1,021 | 1,938 | 1,891 | 1,872 |
| Washington.. | 543 | 393 | 597 | 404 | 306 | 1,185 | 1,494 | 396 | 1,220 | 494 |

| Statutemiles from/to | Jacksonville | Kansas City | Los Angeles | Louisville | Memphis | Miami | Minneapolis | Nashville | New Orleans | New York |
|---|---|---|---|---|---|---|---|---|---|---|
| Atlanta, Ga... | 285 | 676 | 1,936 | 319 | 337 | 604 | 907 | 214 | 424 | 748 |
| Boston, Mass. | 1,017 | 1,251 | 2,596 | 826 | 1,137 | 1,255 | 1,123 | 943 | 1,359 | 188 |
| Chicago, Ill.. | 863 | 414 | 1,745 | 269 | 482 | 1,188 | 355 | 397 | 833 | 713 |
| Cincinnati, O. | 626 | 541 | 1,897 | 90 | 410 | 952 | 605 | 238 | 706 | 570 |
| Cleveland, O. | 770 | 700 | 2,049 | 311 | 630 | 1,087 | 630 | 459 | 924 | 405 |
| Dallas, Texas. | 908 | 451 | 1,240 | 726 | 420 | 1,111 | 862 | 617 | 443 | 1,374 |
| Denver, Colo. | 1,467 | 558 | 831 | 1,038 | 879 | 1,726 | 700 | 1,023 | 1,082 | 1,631 |
| Detroit, Mich. | 831 | 645 | 1,983 | 316 | 623 | 1,152 | 543 | 470 | 939 | 482 |
| Houston, Tex. | 821 | 644 | 1,374 | 803 | 484 | 968 | 1,056 | 665 | 318 | 1,420 |
| Indianapolis.. | 699 | 453 | 1,809 | 107 | 384 | 1,024 | 511 | 251 | 712 | 646 |
| Jacksonville.. | ...... | 950 | 2,147 | 594 | 590 | 326 | 1,191 | 499 | 504 | 838 |
| Kansas City.. | 950 | ...... | 1,356 | 480 | 369 | 1,241 | 413 | 473 | 680 | 1,097 |
| Los Angeles.. | 2,147 | 1,356 | ...... | 1,829 | 1,603 | 2,339 | 1,524 | 1,780 | 1,673 | 2,451 |
| Louisville, Ky. | 594 | 480 | 1,829 | ...... | 320 | 919 | 605 | 154 | 623 | 652 |
| Memphis.... | 590 | 369 | 1,603 | 320 | ...... | 872 | 699 | 197 | 358 | 957 |
| Miami, Fla.. | 326 | 1,241 | 2,339 | 919 | 872 | ...... | 1,511 | 815 | 669 | 1,092 |
| Minneapolis.. | 1,191 | 413 | 1,524 | 605 | 699 | 1,511 | ...... | 697 | 1,051 | 1,018 |
| Nashville.... | 499 | 473 | 1,780 | 154 | 197 | 815 | 697 | ...... | 469 | 761 |
| New Orleans.. | 504 | 680 | 1,673 | 623 | 358 | 669 | 1,051 | 469 | ...... | 1,171 |
| New York.... | 838 | 1,097 | 2,451 | 652 | 957 | 1,092 | 1,018 | 761 | 1,171 | ...... |
| Oklahoma C'y | 986 | 296 | 1,181 | 678 | 422 | 1,226 | 693 | 605 | 577 | 1,328 |
| Omaha, Nebr. | 1,098 | 166 | 1,315 | 580 | 529 | 1,397 | 290 | 607 | 847 | 1,144 |
| Philadelphia.. | 758 | 1,038 | 2,394 | 582 | 881 | 1,019 | 985 | 685 | 1,089 | 83 |
| Pittsburgh... | 703 | 781 | 2,136 | 344 | 660 | 1,010 | 743 | 472 | 919 | 317 |
| Portland, Ore. | 2,439 | 1,497 | 825 | 1,950 | 1,849 | 2,708 | 1,427 | 1,969 | 2,063 | 2,445 |
| St. Louis, Mo. | 751 | 238 | 1,589 | 242 | 240 | 1,061 | 466 | 254 | 598 | 875 |
| Salt Lake C'y. | 1,837 | 925 | 579 | 1,402 | 1,250 | 2,089 | 987 | 1,393 | 1,434 | 1,972 |
| San Francisco. | 2,374 | 1,506 | 347 | 1,986 | 1,802 | 2,594 | 1,584 | 1,963 | 1,926 | 2,571 |
| Seattle, Wash. | 2,455 | 1,506 | 959 | 1,943 | 1,867 | 2,734 | 1,395 | 1,975 | 2,101 | 2,408 |
| Washington.. | 647 | 945 | 2,300 | 476 | 765 | 923 | 934 | 569 | 966 | 205 |

| Statutemiles from/to | Okla. City | Omaha | Phila. | Pittsburgh | P'tland, Ore. | St. Louis | Salt Lake | San Fran. | Seattle | Wash., D.C. |
|---|---|---|---|---|---|---|---|---|---|---|
| Atlanta, Ga... | 757 | 817 | 666 | 521 | 2,172 | 467 | 1,583 | 2,139 | 2,182 | 543 |
| Boston, Mass. | 1,495 | 1,282 | 271 | 483 | 2,540 | 1,038 | 2,099 | 2,699 | 2,493 | 393 |
| Chicago, Ill.. | 692 | 432 | 666 | 410 | 1,758 | 262 | 1,260 | 1,858 | 1,737 | 597 |
| Cincinnati, O. | 758 | 622 | 503 | 257 | 1,985 | 309 | 1,453 | 2,043 | 1,972 | 404 |
| Cleveland, O.. | 951 | 739 | 360 | 115 | 2,055 | 492 | 1,568 | 2,166 | 2,026 | 306 |
| Dallas, Texas. | 190 | 586 | 1,299 | 1,070 | 1,633 | 547 | 999 | 1,483 | 1,681 | 1,185 |
| Denver, Colo. | 505 | 488 | 1,579 | 1,320 | 982 | 796 | 371 | 949 | 1,021 | 1,494 |
| Detroit, Mich. | 910 | 669 | 443 | 205 | 1,969 | 455 | 1,492 | 2,091 | 1,938 | 396 |
| Houston, Tex. | 413 | 794 | 1,341 | 1,137 | 1,836 | 679 | 1,200 | 1,645 | 1,891 | 1,220 |
| Indianapolis.. | 689 | 525 | 585 | 330 | 1,885 | 231 | 1,356 | 1,949 | 1,872 | 494 |
| Jacksonville.. | 986 | 1,098 | 758 | 703 | 2,439 | 751 | 1,837 | 2,374 | 2,455 | 647 |
| Kansas City.. | 296 | 166 | 1,038 | 781 | 1,497 | 238 | 925 | 1,506 | 1,506 | 945 |
| Los Angeles.. | 1,181 | 1,315 | 2,394 | 2,136 | 825 | 1,589 | 579 | 347 | 959 | 2,300 |
| Louisville, Ky. | 678 | 580 | 582 | 344 | 1,950 | 242 | 1,402 | 1,986 | 1,943 | 476 |
| Memphis.... | 422 | 529 | 881 | 660 | 1,849 | 240 | 1,250 | 1,802 | 1,867 | 765 |
| Miami, Fla.. | 1,226 | 1,397 | 1,019 | 1,010 | 2,708 | 1,061 | 2,089 | 2,594 | 2,734 | 923 |
| Minneapolis.. | 693 | 290 | 985 | 743 | 1,427 | 466 | 987 | 1,584 | 1,395 | 934 |
| Nashville.... | 605 | 607 | 685 | 472 | 1,969 | 254 | 1,393 | 1,963 | 1,975 | 569 |
| New Orleans.. | 577 | 847 | 1,089 | 919 | 2,063 | 598 | 1,434 | 1,926 | 2,101 | 966 |
| New York.... | 1,328 | 1,144 | 83 | 317 | 2,445 | 875 | 1,972 | 2,571 | 2,408 | 205 |
| Oklahoma C'y | ...... | 408 | 1,260 | 1,014 | 1,486 | 459 | 862 | 1,388 | 1,524 | 1,153 |
| Omaha, Nebr. | 408 | ...... | 1,094 | 836 | 1,371 | 354 | 833 | 1,429 | 1,369 | 1,014 |
| Philadelphia.. | 1,260 | 1,094 | ...... | 259 | 2,412 | 811 | 1,925 | 2,523 | 2,380 | 123 |
| Pittsburgh... | 1,014 | 836 | 259 | ...... | 2,165 | 559 | 1,668 | 2,264 | 2,138 | 192 |
| Portland, Ore. | 1,486 | 1,371 | 2,412 | 2,165 | ...... | 1,723 | 636 | 534 | 145 | 2,354 |
| St. Louis, Mo. | 459 | 354 | 811 | 559 | 1,723 | ...... | 1,162 | 1,744 | 1,724 | 712 |
| Salt Lake C'y. | 862 | 833 | 1,925 | 1,668 | 636 | 1,162 | ...... | 600 | 701 | 1,848 |
| San Francisco. | 1,388 | 1,429 | 2,523 | 2,264 | 534 | 1,744 | 600 | ...... | 678 | 2,442 |
| Seattle, Wash. | 1,524 | 1,369 | 2,380 | 2,138 | 145 | 1,724 | 701 | 678 | ...... | 2,329 |
| Washington.. | 1,153 | 1,014 | 123 | 192 | 2,354 | 712 | 1,848 | 2,442 | 2,329 | ...... |

# ASTRONOMY AND CALENDAR

## Edited by James S. Pickering
### ASTRONOMER EMERITUS, AMERICAN MUSEUM-HAYDEN PLANETARIUM

## Celestial Events for 1969

Since the planets of the solar system are in constant motion about the sun and thus change their positions continually in the sky, they cannot be shown on conventional star charts. The locations of these planets during 1969 are given in the paragraphs below, either by the constellations which are the backgrounds for their positions or by the time they rise or set with relation to the sun. Also given below are other predictable astronomical phenomena such as meteor showers, phases of the moon, eclipses and the dates of the beginnings of the seasons.

### PLANETS AND THE SUN

The planets of the solar system, in order of their distance from the sun are Mercury, Venus, Earth, Mars, Jupiter, Saturn, Uranus, Neptune and Pluto. Uranus, Neptune and Pluto are not included in the celestial list because they are too faint to be seen without optical aid. Both Uranus and Neptune are visible through good field glasses, but Pluto is so distant and so small that only large telescopes or long exposure photographs can make it visible.

Since Mercury and Venus are nearer to the sun than is the earth, their motions about the sun are seen from the earth as wide swings first to one side of the sun and then to the other, although they are both passing continuously around the sun in orbits that are almost but not quite circular. When their passage takes them either between the earth and the sun, or beyond the sun as seen from the earth, they are invisible to us. Because of the laws which govern the motions of planets about the sun, both Mercury and Venus require much less time to pass between the earth and the sun than around the far side of the sun, so their periods of invisibility are unequal.

The planets that lie farther from the sun than does the earth may be seen for longer periods of time and are invisible only when they are so located in our sky that they rise and set about the same time as the sun when, of course, they are overwhelmed by the sun's great brilliance. None of the planets have any light or exterior heat of their own and shine only by reflecting sunlight from their surfaces. Mercury and Venus, because they are between the earth and the sun, show phases very much as the moon does. The planets farther from the sun are always seen as full, although Mars does occasionally present a slightly gibbous phase—like the moon when not quite full.

The planets move rapidly among the stars because they are very much nearer to us than the stars are. The stars are also in motion, some of them at tremendous speeds, but they are so far away that their motion does not change their apparent positions in the heavens sufficiently for anyone to perceive that change in a single lifetime. The very nearest star is more than 7,000 times as far away as the most distant planet.

### January

**Mercury** reaches greatest angular distance east of the sun—greatest eastern elongation—on Jan. 13 and may be seen in the southwest for about an hour after sunset. It moves rapidly toward interior conjunction—between the earth and the sun—on Jan. 19, when it cannot be seen.

**Venus** is in the western sky after sunset, farther north than Mercury. It reaches greatest eastern elongation Jan. 26, and sets about 3 hours after the sun. On Jan. 21, the crescent moon after new passes 1 degree below Venus, causing an occultation of Venus in Australia and South Africa.

**Mars** rises from 5 to 6 hours before the sun in the southeast in Virgo. On Jan. 12, the last quarter moon passes 5 degrees below Mars early in the morning.

**Jupiter** rises before midnight and is visible most of the night in Virgo, near Mars. On Jan. 10, the moon, approaching last quarter, passes 2 degrees below Jupiter.

**Saturn** is just east of the meridian at sunset and sets about midnight in Pisces. On Jan. 24, the moon, nearly at first quarter, passes 4 degrees above Saturn.

**Moon**—Full moon, Jan. 3; last quarter, Jan. 11; new moon, Jan. 17; first quarter, Jan. 25. Moon at apogee, Jan. 1, at perigee, Jan. 16; again at apogee, Jan. 28. The moon is said to be at perigee when it passes nearest to the earth for the month, and at apogee when it is most distant from the earth. The nearest possible approach of the moon to the earth is 221,463 miles, and the greatest possible distance between the moon and the earth is 252,710 miles. The moon does not reach these extreme distances each month. Note that the moon reaches apogee twice during January. The period between successive returns of the moon to either perigee or apogee is the anomalistic month, which is a few hours shorter than 28 days. Thus, if a perigee or apogee passage occurs during the first days of a calendar month, a second may occur before the end of the month. Because of its proximity to the earth, the moon has a strong tidal effect on the earth which increases as the distance between the earth and the moon decreases. The gravitational pull of the sun also affects the tides, and when the sun and the moon are in line with the earth, as at new moon or full moon, their tide-raising effects are combined and produce spring tides—higher and lower than average. The combination of a perigee position of the full or new moon may produce unusually high and low tides for a short time. The moon reaches perigee this month one day before new moon Jan. 17. This year, the moon passes close before several planets and bright stars, causing occultations of these objects as seen from the earth. When these conjunctions and occultations involve the planets, they are discussed under the heading for that planet. Conjunctions and occultations of the invisible planets and bright stars are mentioned under the heading of the moon.

**Jan. 10.** The moon, nearly at last quarter, passes 1 degree below the planet Uranus. This causes an occultation of Uranus in South America. Uranus is just below naked-eye visibility and may be seen with binoculars. This conjunction at 4 a.m., EST, will help to locate Uranus. Jan. 11, the last quarter moon passes close above the bright star Spica in Virgo. This conjunction occurs during daylight, but will bring Spica close west of the moon in the early morning sky. This is an occultation of Spica over eastern Asia. Jan. 14, at 2 a.m., EST, the moon passes 6 degrees below the planet Neptune. Neptune is only one-fifth as bright as Uranus and a small telescope may be required to make it visible. On the evening of Jan 14, at 7 p.m., EST, the moon passes close below the red star Antares in Scorpius. This causes an occultation of Antares over southern Asia and Australia and brings the crescent moon before new close west of Antares in the morning sky.

**Jan. 3.** The earth reaches perihelion, that point in its orbit when it is nearest the sun for the year. This brings the earth to slightly more than 91,000,000 miles from the sun, about 3,000,000 nearer than in July when it reaches aphelion, its greatest distance from the sun.

### February

**Mercury** is now in the morning sky. It reaches greatest western elongation Feb. 23, when it rises

about 1½ hours before the sun.

**Venus** sets about 4 hours after the sun in Pisces, increasing slightly in brilliance during the month.

**Mars** rises about 1 a.m. in Libra. On Feb. 10, the last quarter moon passes 6 degrees below Mars. On Feb. 22, Mars passes close below the planet Neptune, but a small telescope will be needed to see Neptune.

**Jupiter** rises late in the evening in Virgo. On Feb. 6, the moon, nearing first quarter, passes below Jupiter.

**Saturn** sets a few hours after the sun in Pisces. On Feb. 20, the crescent moon after new passes 5 degrees above Saturn.

**Moon**—Full moon, Feb. 2; last quarter, Feb. 9; new moon, Feb. 16; first quarter, Feb. 23. Moon at perigee, Feb. 13; at apogee, Feb. 25. On Feb. 6 the moon, 4 days past full, is in conjunction with Uranus at 8 a.m. EST. This causes an occultation of Uranus in New Zealand and Antarctica. Observers in the U. S. may see Uranus with binoculars to the west of the moon that evening. On Feb. 7, the moon is in close conjunction with Spica in Virgo. This produces an occultation of Spica in southeast Europe, north Africa, Asia Minor and Australia. On Feb. 11 at 2 a.m. the moon is in close conjunction with Antares in Scorpius, causing an occultation of Antares over South America and south Africa.

## March

**Mercury** is in the morning sky, rising about 1½ hours before the sun early in the month. It is moving toward superior conjunction—beyond the sun from the earth—later in the month when it will no longer be visible. On Mar. 16 at 11 p.m., the moon occults Mercury over western Africa and South America.

**Venus** sets about 3 hours after the sun. It reaches its greatest brilliancy Mar. 3, when it is about 15 times as bright as Sirius, the brightest star. On Mar. 20, Venus and the crescent moon are near each other in the evening sky.

**Mars** rises about midnight in Scorpius and is visible for the last half of the night. On Mar. 10 the moon, nearly at last quarter, passes 6 degrees below Mars.

**Jupiter** reaches opposition on Mar. 21, rising as the sun sets, and is visible in the sky all night in Virgo. On Mar. 5, the moon passes 2 degrees below Jupiter. On Mar. 15, Jupiter will reveal the position of Uranus as the two planets are in conjunction at 6 p.m. Uranus may be seen with binoculars close west of Jupiter.

**Saturn** is approaching conjunction with the sun in Pisces and is far to the west at sunset.

**Moon**—Full moon, Mar. 4; last quarter, Mar. 11; new moon, Mar. 17; first quarter, Mar. 25. Moon at perigee, Mar. 12; at apogee, Mar. 25. At midnight between Mar. 6 and 7, the moon, 3 days past full, occults Spica in Virgo. This occultation is visible in North and South America. On Mar. 10, the moon is in close conjunction with Antares in Scorpius. This occurs by daylight in North America, but causes an occultation of Antares in South America.

**Mar. 18.** An annular eclipse of the sun is visible over the Indian Ocean and Indonesia.

**Mar. 20.** At 2:08 p.m. EST, the sun appears to cross the equator on its way north. This crossing is at the vernal equinox and spring begins in the northern hemisphere while autumn commences south of the equator.

## April

**Mercury** reaches superior conjunction Apr. 8, beyond the sun from the earth, and moves into the evening sky, where it sets about an hour after the sun by the end of the month.

**Venus** reaches inferior conjunction, between the earth and the sun, also Apr. 8 and moves into the morning sky, but is too much in line with the sun to be seen.

**Mars** rises late in the evening in Scorpius. On Apr. 7, the gibbous moon passes 6 degrees below Mars at 11 p.m. EST.

**Jupiter** is in the eastern sky at sunset in Virgo. On Apr. 1, the moon nearing full phase, passes 2 degrees below Jupiter and again Apr. 28, the waning crescent moon is 1 degree below Jupiter.

**Saturn** reaches conjunction with the sun in Pisces Apr. 18 and moves into the morning sky, but is too much in line with the sun all month to be seen.

**Moon**—Full moon, Apr. 2; last quarter, Apr. 9; new moon, Apr. 16; first quarter, Apr. 24. Moon at perigee, Apr. 6; at apogee, Apr. 22. On Apr. 3, the moon is again in close conjunction with Spica in Virgo at 9 p.m. EST. This causes an occultation of Spica over southeast Asia. On Apr. 6, the moon is in close conjunction with Antares in Scorpius. This conjunction occurs during daylight in North America but causes an occultation of Antares over Australia. On Apr. 29, the moon passes 1 degree below Uranus, which may be seen close east of the moon during the evening. On Apr. 30, the moon again occults Spica in Virgo for observers in west and south Africa. This may be seen as an extremely close conjunction early in the evening from the U. S.

**Apr. 2.** The full moon passes through the outer region of the earth's shadow. This eclipse occurs during daylight over North America, but a penumbral eclipse cannot be easily observed without special equipment.

**Apr. 23.** The Lyrid meteor shower occurs. The moon sets early in the evening and does not interfere with observation of the few more than normal number of meteors this shower produces.

## May

**Mercury** reaches greatest eastern elongation May 5 and sets about 1½ hours after the sun. It may be seen in the northwest during the first half of the month. On May 11, Mercury will be near the red star Aldebaran in Taurus, but will rapidly fade from view into inferior conjunction between the earth and the sun May 29.

**Venus** rises from 2 to 3 hours before the sun and reaches greatest brilliancy May 14. On May 12, the waning crescent moon is in conjunction with Venus. This causes an occultation of Venus over eastern Europe and Asia, and brings Venus close west of the moon in the U. S. in the early morning hours.

**Mars** reaches opposition on May 31, rising as the sun sets and visible in the sky all night in Ophiuchus. On May 4, the moon, two days past full, passes close below Mars and on May 31, the full moon is 2 degrees below Mars at 9 p.m. EST.

**Jupiter** is well up in the east at sunset before the stars of Virgo.

**Saturn** is too much in line beyond the sun to be seen, in Pisces.

**Moon**—Full moon, May 2; last quarter, May 8; new moon, May 16; first quarter, May 24; full moon, May 31. Note that the moon reaches full phase twice in May. The period of time for the moon to progress from any given phase to the corresponding phase in its next cycle—in this case, from full moon to the next full moon—is the synodical month, which is slightly more than 29 days. Hence, when a given phase occurs on the 1st or 2nd day of most months, that phase may be reached again before the end of the calendar month. Moon at perigee, May 4; at apogee May 20. The moon passes through two close conjunctions with Antares in Scorpius this month. On May 3, the conjunction occults Antares over South America and southern Africa. On May 31, the conjunction occults Antares over Indonesia and Australasia. On May 28, the moon is in close conjunction with Spica in Virgo, occulting Spica over New Zealand.

**May 1-4.** The Eta Aquarid meteor shower reaches its climax about midnight May 4. The moon, just past full, makes observation of the meteors of this shower difficult.

## June

**Mercury** emerges from inferior conjunction and moves into the morning sky where it reaches greatest western elongation June 23, rising about 1½ hours before the sun.

**Venus** reaches greatest western elongation June 17, rising about 3 hours before the sun and about 1½ hours before Mercury. Venus will be to the south and west of Mercury and near Saturn during the first part of the month. Venus and Saturn are in close conjunction during daylight June 11 and the waning crescent moon passes close above both that morning.

**Mars**, just past opposition, is up in the east in Scorpius and Ophiuchus. On June 3, Mars is 2 degrees above Antares in Scorpius. The name Antares is Greek for "The Rival of Mars," and this conjunction of Mars and the red star will demonstrate the origin of the star's name. On June 8, Mars reaches that point in its orbit near-

est the earth for this passage, bringing it slightly more than 43,000,000 miles from the earth. On June 27, the nearly full moon passes 2 degrees below Mars at 9 p.m. EST.

**Jupiter** is east of the meridian at sunset and is in the sky for the first half of the night in Virgo. On June 18 at 1 a.m. EST, Jupiter is in close conjunction with Uranus, which may be seen with good binoculars.

**Saturn** is in the morning sky near Venus and Mercury. On June 8, the waning crescent moon passes 6 degrees above Saturn.

**Moon**—Last quarter, June 6; new moon, June 14; first quarter, June 22; full moon, June 29. Moon at perigee, June 1; at apogee, June 16; at perigee, June 29. The combination of perigee full moon on June 29 may produce extreme tides. Note that the moon returns to perigee twice in June, which occurs when the first perigee falls on the 1st or 2nd day of the month. *See notes for January.* On June 24, the moon's close conjunction with Spica, the seventh such conjunction this year, occults Spica over South America and south Africa. On June 17, the moon also reaches its seventh close conjunction with Antares in Scorpius. This is also an occultation over South America and south Africa.

**June 21.** At 8:55 a.m., EST (9:55 a.m. EDT) the summer solstice occurs. The earth reaches that point in its orbit where, because of the inclination of the earth's axis, the sun appears highest in the northern sky and summer begins. For the southern hemisphere, this is the beginning of winter.

## July

**Mercury** moves toward superior conjunction July 22 when it changes from the morning to the evening sky, but is too much in line with the sun to be seen.

**Venus** rises from 3 to 4 hours before the sun and is bright in the morning sky. On July 10, the waning crescent moon passes near Venus.

**Mars** is near the meridian at sunset and is visible for the first half of the night in Scorpius. On July 24, the waxing crescent moon passes 2 degrees below Mars at 7 p.m. EST.

**Jupiter** is far to the west at sunset in Virgo. On July 20, the moon, nearly at first quarter, passes Jupiter after setting from the U. S. and appears east of the planet the following evening.

**Saturn** is in the morning sky rising about midnight ahead of Venus in Aries. On July 8, Saturn is close south and west of the waning crescent moon.

**Moon**—Last quarter, July 6; new moon, July 14; first quarter, July 22; full moon, July 28. Moon at apogee, July 13; at perigee, July 28. The combination of perigee and full moon could cause extreme tides at this time. On July 21, the moon near first quarter occults Spica in Virgo for the eighth time this year. This occultation is over New Zealand and South America. On July 25, Antares in Scorpius is occulted for the eighth time this year. This occultation occurs over Indonesia and Australasia.

**July 5.** The earth reaches aphelion, that point in its orbit which brings it farthest from the sun for the year. The earth is now about 3,000,000 miles more distant from the sun than it was at perihelion in January.

**July 29.** The Delta Aquarid meteor shower begins and provides more than the average number of meteors for about 3 weeks. This annual summer display is strikingly augmented by the August Perseid shower whose forerunners may begin to appear late this month. The full moon will handicap observers of this shower for the first few nights.

## August

**Mercury** is too much in line with the sun to be visible this month.

**Venus** rises 3 to 4 hours ahead of the sun. On Aug. 9 the waning crescent moon is near Venus, and Aug. 24 Venus is below the star Pollux in Gemini.

**Mars** is on the meridian at sunset in Ophiuchus and is visible for the first half of the night. On Aug. 11, Mars and Antares, in Scorpius, are again in close association. On Aug. 21 the moon, just past first quarter, passes 2 degrees below Mars at 7 p.m. EST.

**Jupiter** sets from 3 to 2 hours after the sun

in Virgo. On Aug. 16, the early crescent moon passes 3 degrees below Jupiter at 5 p.m., just above the western horizon.

**Saturn** rises about 10 p.m. in Aries.

**Moon**—Last quarter, Aug. 4; new moon, Aug. 13; first quarter, Aug. 20; full moon, Aug. 27. Moon at apogee, Aug. 9; at perigee, Aug. 25. On Aug. 18, the moon again occults Spica in Virgo for the ninth consecutive time this year, but this occultation cannot be seen from North America. On Aug. 21, Antares is occulted by the moon, also for the ninth time this year. This occultation occurs over southwest Australia and South America.

**Aug. 11-12.** The Perseid meteor shower reaches its climax after midnight between these two dates. This is the most dependable and one of the most spectacular meteor showers and there is no interference by the moon with observation of the 50 or more meteors an hour which one observer may see.

**Aug. 27.** The full moon passes through the penumbra, the outer fringe of the earth's shadow. This part of the shadow is faint and makes little or no impression to the casual observer.

## September

**Mercury** reaches greatest eastern elongation Sept. 3 and sets about 1½ hours after the sun during the first part of the month. It moves rapidly to inferior conjunction—between the earth and the sun—on Sept. 29 and is not then visible.

**Venus** is in the morning sky, rising 2 to 3 hours before the sun in Cancer and Leo. On Sept. 8, the waning crescent moon passes 3 degrees above Venus as the moon and planet rise. On Sept. 22, Venus is near the bright star Regulus in Leo.

**Mars** is far to the west at sunset and sets about 3 hours after the sun in Ophiuchus and Sagittarius. On Sept. 19, Mars is close north of the first quarter moon.

**Jupiter** is moving toward conjunction with the sun in early October and is too much in line with the sun to be seen easily. On Sept. 7, Jupiter and Mercury are near each other in the western sky, with Jupiter the more northern and brighter of the two planets.

**Saturn** rises early in the evening in Aries, and is in the sky most of the night. On Sept. 1 the moon, just past full, passes above Saturn; it repeats this performance Sept. 28.

**Moon**—Last quarter, Sept. 3; new moon, Sept. 11; first quarter, Sept. 18; full moon, Sept. 25. Moon at apogee, Sept. 6; at perigee, Sept. 22. On Sept. 14, the moon continues its monthly occultation of Spica in Virgo. This occurs at 8 p.m. EST and is not visible from North America. On Sept. 17, the moon again occults Antares in Scorpius, but this occultation is also invisible from North America.

**Sept. 11.** There is an annular eclipse of the sun, visible over the Pacific Ocean west of North America and over the western portion of South America. The eclipse is partial over all but the northeastern U. S. In an annular eclipse, the moon, at central eclipse, does not completely cover the sun and there is a narrow ring of sun visible around the black silhouette of the moon.

**Sept. 23.** At 12:07 a.m. EST (1:07 a.m. EDT), the sun crosses the equator at the autumnal equinox on its apparent journey south. Autumn commences in the northern hemisphere and spring begins south of the equator.

**Sept. 25.** The full moon passes through the outer fringe of the earth's shadow, causing a penumbral eclipse of the moon. This eclipse, which is not visible except with special methods, affects only the extreme northeast part of North America.

## October

**Mercury** reaches greatest western elongation on Oct. 14, and is visible for a few mornings near that date in the eastern sky for about an hour before sunrise.

**Venus** is also in the eastern sky at sunrise. Venus rises ahead of Mercury and is much the brighter of the two. On Oct. 9, the moon passes close below Venus at 2 a.m., but the moon is so near new that it is difficult to see.

**Mars** is about 3 hours after the sun in Sagittarius, and is difficult to see.

**Jupiter** reaches conjunction with the sun Oct. 9 and cannot be seen.

**Saturn** is in opposition on Oct. 28, rising as

the sun sets and in the sky all night before the stars of Aries. On Oct. 25, the full moon passes 7 degrees above Saturn as the two objects rise.

**Moon**—Last quarter, Oct. 3; new moon, Oct. 11; first quarter, Oct. 18; full moon, Oct. 25. Moon at apogee, Oct. 4; at perigee Oct. 17. Consistent with its performance this year, the moon again occults Antares in Scorpius. This occultation occurs at 11 p.m. EST Oct. 18 and is over Australasia. There is no occultation of Spica in Virgo this month.

**Oct. 18-23.** The Orionid meteor shower occurs, reaching a climax in the early morning hours of Oct. 20. The moon, past first quarter and far to the west, will not interfere greatly with observation.

## November

**Mercury** reaches superior conjunction, beyond the sun from the earth, Nov. 11, and is not visible.

**Venus** rises about an hour before the sun in Virgo and may be seen during morning twilight.

**Mars** sets soon after the sun in Capricornus and is not easy to see close above the western horizon.

**Jupiter** is in the morning sky not far from Venus. The two planets are in conjunction about ½ a degree apart before they rise on Nov. 4. Both planets are near Spica in Virgo.

**Saturn**, just past opposition in Aries, is in the east at sunset. On Nov. 21, the nearly full moon passes above Saturn.

**Moon**—Last quarter, Nov. 2; new moon, Nov. 9; first quarter, Nov. 16; full moon, Nov. 23. Moon at apogee, Nov. 1; at perigee, Nov. 12; at apogee, Nov. 29. For explanation of the moon's return to apogee, *see notes for January.* On Nov. 8, the moon, less than 2 days before new, occults Spica in Virgo, but this occultation occurs during daylight. On Nov. 11, the moon occults Antares in Scorpius, but this occultation also occurs during daylight.

**Nov. 16.** The Leonid meteor shower occurs. This shower has produced spectacular displays in the

past and should be watched. Look to the northeast from 10 p.m. on. The first quarter moon will not interfere with observation.

## December

**Mercury** reaches greatest eastern elongation Dec. 27, but is still too much in line with the sun to be seen easily.

**Venus** is also too much in line with the sun to be seen.

**Mars** is far to the west, setting soon after the sun in Sagittarius. On Oct. 14, the early morning Mars, but this occultation is not visible from North America.

**Jupiter** rises about 5 hours before the sun in Virgo.

**Saturn**, in Aries, is west of the meridian at sunset and is in the sky for the first part of the night. On Dec. 18 at 11 P.M. EST, the gibbous moon passes above Saturn.

**Moon**—Last quarter, Dec. 1; new moon, Dec. 9; first quarter, Dec. 15; full moon, Dec. 23; last quarter, Dec. 31. For explanation of the recurrence of the last quarter moon, *see note for May.* Moon at perigee, Dec. 10; at apogee, Dec. 26. The perigee new moon of Dec. 9-10 may cause extreme tides. On Dec. 1 at 1 a.m. EST, the moon is in close conjunction with the bright star Regulus in Leo, causing occultation of Regulus over eastern Europe. Again on Dec. 28, the moon occults Regulus, but this occultation occurs during daylight in North America. The moon occults Spica in Virgo for the 12th time this year on Dec. 5, but this is also a daylight occultation.

**Dec. 13.** The Geminid meteor shower occurs. This shower has produced many bright meteors and fireballs in the past. The moon, not yet at first quarter, will not interfere with observation.

**Dec. 21.** At 7:44 p.m. EST, the sun reaches its lowest point in northern skies. This is the winter solstice and marks the beginning of winter in the northern hemisphere and of summer south of the equator.

## COMET TABLE 1969

| Name | Due to Return | Period in Years | Year of Disc. | Peri- helion Dist. | Aphe- lion Dist. | Inclina- tion to Ecliptic | Long. of Asc. Node on Ecliptic | From Asc. Node to Perihelion |
|---|---|---|---|---|---|---|---|---|
| | | | | | | Degree | Degree | Degree |
| Perrine | Jan. 1969 | 6.58 | 1896 | 1.19 | 4.59 | 16 | 242 | 167 |
| Dutoit-Neujmin | Mar.1969 | 5.58 | 1941 | 1.34 | 4.95 | 3 | 229 | 70 |
| Pons-Winnecke | July 1969 | 6.15 | 1819 | 1.08 | 5.56 | 22 | 94 | 170 |
| Whipple | Dec.1969 | 7.42 | 1933 | 2.45 | 5.16 | 10 | 189 | 190 |
| Neujmin II | Aug. 1970 | 5.45 | 1916 | 1.34 | 4.84 | 11 | 328 | 194 |
| Encke | Jan. 1971 | 3.31 | 1786 | 0.34 | 4.10 | 12 | 355 | 185 |
| Tempel-Swift | Jan. 1971 | 5.68 | 1809 | 1.15 | 5.21 | 5 | 290 | 114 |
| Grigg-Skellerup | Aug. 1971 | 4.90 | 1902 | 0.86 | 4.91 | 18 | 215 | 359 |
| Tempel II | Jan. 1973 | 5.27 | 1873 | 1.36 | 4.68 | 12 | 119 | 191 |
| Taylor | Sep. 1973 | 6.73 | 1915 | 1.56 | 3.52 | 16 | 114 | 355 |
| Finlay | Apr. 1974 | 6.81 | 1886 | 1.04 | 6.16 | 3 | 45 | 321 |
| Encke | Apr. 1974 | 3.31 | 1786 | 0.34 | 4.10 | 12 | 355 | 185 |
| Forbes | Apr. 1974 | 6.44 | 1929 | 1.55 | 5.40 | 5 | 260 | 25 |
| Brooks II | May 1974 | 6.93 | 1889 | 1.87 | 5.41 | 6 | 178 | 196 |
| Borrelly | July 1974 | 7.01 | 1905 | 1.45 | 5.88 | 31 | 76 | 351 |
| Schwassmann-Wachmann | Aug. 1974 | 6.53 | 1929 | 2.16 | 4.83 | 4 | 126 | 358 |
| Perrine | July 1975 | 6.58 | 1896 | 1.19 | 4.59 | 16 | 242 | 167 |
| Pons-Winnecke | Aug. 1975 | 6.15 | 1819 | 1.08 | 5.56 | 22 | 94 | 170 |
| Dutoit-Neujmin | Aug. 1975 | 5.58 | 1941 | 1.34 | 4.95 | 3 | 229 | 70 |
| Halley | 1986 | 76.02 | 240 B.C. | 0.59 | 35.32 | 162 | 57 | 112 |

## Morning and Evening Stars of 1969

### MORNING

**Mercury**—Jan. 29-Apr. 8; May 29-July 22; Sept. 29-Nov. 16.
**Venus**—Apr. 8-Dec. 31.
**Mars**—Jan. 1-May 31.
**Jupiter**—Jan. 1-Mar. 21; Oct. 9-Dec. 31.
**Saturn**—Apr. 18-Oct. 29.

### EVENING

**Mercury**—Jan. 1-Jan. 29; Apr. 8-May 29; Jul. 22-Sept. 29; Nov. 16-Dec. 31.
**Venus**—Jan. 1-Apr. 8.
**Mars**—May 31-Dec. 31.
**Jupiter**—Mar. 21-Oct. 9.
**Saturn**—Jan. 1-Apr. 18; Oct. 29-Dec. 31.

## Astronomical Signs and Symbols

| | | | | | |
|---|---|---|---|---|---|
| ☉ | The Sun. | ⊕ | The Earth. | ♅ | Uranus. | ⊔ | Quadrature. |
| ☾ | The Moon. | ♂ | Mars. | ♆ | Neptune. | ♂ | Opposition. |
| ☿ | Mercury. | ♃ | Jupiter. | ♇ | Pluto. | ☊ | Ascending Node. |
| ♀ | Venus. | ♄ | Saturn. | ♂ | Conjunction. | ☋ | Descending Node. |

Two heavenly bodies are in "conjunction" (♂) when they have the same Right Ascension, or are on the same meridian, i.e., when one is due north or south of the other; if the bodies are near each other as seen from the earth, they will rise and set at the same time; they are in "opposition" (♂) when in opposite quarters of the heavens, or when one rises as the other is setting. "Quadrature" (⊔) is half way between conjunction and opposition. By "greatest elongation" is meant the greatest apparent angular distance from the sun, the planet is then generally most favorably situated for observation. Mercury can be seen with the naked eye only at this time. When a planet is in its "ascending" (☊) or "descending" (☋) node it is passing through the plane of the earth's orbit. The term "Perihelion" means nearest to the sun, and "Aphelion" farthest from the sun. An "occultation" of a planet or star is an eclipse of it by some other body, usually the moon.

# Giant Telescopes Planned for Southern Hemisphere

For many years astronomers have been aware of a serious deficiency in optical observation. All of the world's larger telescopes are in the northern hemisphere and thus cannot be used to study southern skies. The 200-inch Hale reflector is at Mt. Palomar in California. The 120-inch reflector is at the Lick Observatory in California. Mt. Wilson in California and the Crimean Astrophysical Observatory in the USSR have telescopes with 100-inch and 104-inch mirrors, respectively, and Russia is constructing a reflector with a mirror 236 inches in diameter. The largest telescopes at present in the southern hemisphere, however, are 74-inch reflectors in Pretoria, South Africa and Mt. Stromlo, Australia.

Two telescopes are being planned for South America which will remedy this situation. The U. S. is erecting a 150-inch reflector at Cerro Tololo in Chile, and a 140-inch mirror at La Silla Mountain will be administered by the European Observatory Group. Australia is planning a telescope with an aperture of 150 inches at Siding Spring. Tremendous advances in the study of the central region of the Milky Way and of the Magellanic Clouds, as well as more detailed studies of many other regions hitherto unavailable to giant telescopes, will be made through the use of these planned instruments.

## OPTICAL TELESCOPES

Optical astronomical telescopes are of two kinds, refracting and reflecting. In the first, light passes through a lens which brings the light rays to a focus, where the image may be examined after being magnified by a second lens, the eye-piece, or directly photographed.

The reflector consists of a concave parabolic mirror, generally of Pyrex, coated with silver or aluminum, which reflects the light rays back toward the upper end of the telescope, where they are either magnified and observed by the eye-piece or, as in the case of the refractors, photographed. In most reflecting telescopes, the light is reflected again by a secondary mirror and comes to a focus after passing through a hole in the side of the telescope, where the eye-piece or camera is located, or after passing through a hole in the center of the primary mirror.

The Schmidt Telescopes are strictly cameras and cannot be used for visual observation. Light enters the upper end of the telescope tube, is refracted slightly by a correcting lens and is then reflected from a spherical mirror with a short focus. A camera, placed inside the telescope at the focus of the mirror can photograph large areas of the sky without distortion at the edges of the photograph. The diameters of Schmidt telescopes are given in two figures; first, the diameter of the correcting lens, followed by the diameter of the mirror.

### WORLD'S LARGEST REFRACTORS
Location and diameter in inches.

| | |
|---|---:|
| Yerkes Observatory, Williams Bay, Wisconsin | 40.0 |
| Lick Observatory, Mt. Hamilton, Calif. | 36.0 |
| Paris Observatory, Meudon, France | 32.7 |
| Astrophysical Obs., Potsdam, Germany | 31.5 |
| Allegheny Observatory, Pittsburgh, Pa. | 30.0 |
| Univ. of Paris, Nice, France | 30.0 |
| Pulkovo Observatory, U.S.S.R. | 30.0 |
| U.S. Naval Obs., Washington, D.C. | 26.0 |
| University of Virginia | 26.0 |
| Yale University, Canberra, Australia | 26.0 |

### WORLD'S LARGEST REFLECTORS
*This is a partial list including most reflectors of 40-inches aperture or larger.*

| | |
|---|---:|
| Mt. Palomar, Calif. Inst. of Tech., California | 200.0 |
| Lick Observatory, Mt. Hamilton, Calif. | 120.0 |
| Crimean Astrophysical Obs., Russia | 104.0 |
| Mt. Wilson Obs., California | 100.0 |
| Herstmonceaux, England | 98.0 |
| Kitt Peak Nat'l Obs., Arizona | 84.0 |
| McDonald Obs., Texas | 82.0 |
| Tautenberg, Germany (Schmidt) | 80-54 |
| Haute-Provence Obs., France | 77.0 |
| David Dunlap Obs., Ontario, Can. | 74.0 |
| Radcliffe Obs., Pretoria, So. Africa | 74.0 |
| Mt. Stromlo, Canberra, Australia | 74.0 |
| Helwan Obs., Egypt | 74.0 |
| Tokyo Obs., Japan | 74.0 |
| Mt. Palomar, Calif. | |
| Inst. of Tech., Calif. (Schmidt) | 72-48 |
| Perkins Obs., Arizona | 69.0 |
| Harvard Obs., Oak Ridge, Mass. | 61.0 |
| U. S. Naval Obs., Ariz. | 61.0 |
| Arizona Un. Obs., Tucson, Ariz. | 60.0 |
| Harvard Obs., Bloemfontein, So. Africa | 60.0 |
| Cordoba Obs., Bosque Alegre, Argentina | 60.0 |
| Mt. Wilson Obs., Calif. | 60.0 |
| Uppsala U. Obs., Sweden (Schmidt) | 54-40 |
| Mt. Stromlo, Canberra, Australia | 50.0 |
| Sternberg Inst., Moscow, Russia | 50.0 |
| Merate Obs., Italy | 50.0 |
| Berlin-Babelsberg Obs., Germany | 49.0 |
| Dominion Astrophysical Obs., Canada | 48.0 |
| Melbourne, Australia | 48.0 |
| Crimean Astrophysical Obs., Russia | 48.0 |
| Nizamiah Obs., Hyderabad, India | 48.0 |
| Hamburg Obs., Germany (Schmidt) | 48-32 |
| Paris Obs., St. Michel, France | 47.0 |
| Uccle Obs., Belgium (Schmidt) | 46-33 |
| Lowell Obs., Flagstaff, Ariz. | 44.0 |
| U. S. Naval Obs., Washington, D. C. | 40.0 |
| Merate Obs., Italy | 40.0 |
| Pulkovo Obs., Russia | 40.0 |
| Stockholm Obs., Sweden (Schmidt) | 40-26 |
| U. S. Naval Obs., Flagstaff, Ariz. | 40.0 |
| Royal Cape Obs., So. Africa | 40.0 |
| Mt. Stromlo, Canberra, Australia | 40.0 |

# Major Planetariums in the United States

A planetarium projector is perhaps the most complicated instructional device ever made. The first modern planetarium projector was designed and built in 1923 by Walter Bauersfeld of the Zeiss Optical Company. Other instruments had been attempted with only fair success before this time and modern projectors have developed from this beginning. There are now several manufacturers who make elaborate planetarium projectors.

A typical projector for a large auditorium can project the images of nearly 9,000 stars against the reflective surface of a hemispherical dome. In addition, the Milky Way, star clusters, nebulae and other objects sufficiently bright to be seen under ideal conditions by the unaided eye are shown.

Planetarium projectors are usually in the form of two globes, one at either end of a latticed cylinder. The globes contain projectors for the stars, one for the northern hemisphere and the other for the south. In the latticed cylinder are projectors for the sun, the moon and the five planets visible to the eye. The motions of all of these objects are duplicated by the projector with amazing fidelity. First of all, the projector can be set in latitude so that it will produce the sky as it might be seen from any location on earth. The daily motion of the earth which moves the sky throughout the day and night is the first and simplest effect produced. Then there is annual motion, the progress of the sun, moon and planets through the year, including the phasing of the moon. Finally, the precession of the equinoxes, the slow swing of the poles

of the earth which is accomplished in 25,800 years and which slowly changes our view of the sky are also built into the complicated mechanism of these instruments.

The effects of the projector itself are usually supplemented by auxiliary projectors mounted around the edges of the auditorium to produce the color effects of sunrise and sunset, the aurora, clouds, rainbows, eclipses and many other phenomena. Most of the functions of the projector are controlled by the lecturer, who produces them from an array of switches and rheostats mounted in a control console usually situated near the north side of the auditorium. Appropriate music, pre-recorded on tape and played on signal adds to the dramatic effect of a planetarium presentation.

There are literally hundreds of small planetarium projectors in schools and museums in the United States and several planetariums whose auditoriums will seat hundreds. The major planetariums in the United States are listed below.

Academy Planetarium, U. S. Air Force Academy.
Adler Planetarium, Chicago, Ill.
American Museum-Hayden Planetarium, N. Y. C.
Buhl Planetarium, Pittsburgh, Pa.
Charles Hayden Planetarium, Boston, Mass.
Fels Planetarium, Philadelphia, Pa.
Griffith Planetarium, Los Angeles, Calif.
McDonnell Planetarium, St. Louis, Mo.
Morehead Planetarium, Chapel Hill, N. C.
Morrison Planetarium, San Francisco, Calif.
Robert T. Longway Planetarium, Flint, Mich.

# Visible Planets of the Solar System
## Mercury, Venus, Mars, Jupiter and Saturn

### MERCURY

Mercury, nearest planet to the sun, is also the smallest of the nine planets known to be orbiting the sun. Its diameter is 3,100 miles and its mean distance from the sun is 39,000,000 miles.

Mercury moves with great speed in its journey about the sun, averaging about 30 miles a second to complete its circuit of the sun in 88 of our days. Radar observations of Mercury by the 1,000-foot radio telescope at Arecibo, Puerto Rico, disclosed that Mercury rotates upon its axis over a period of nearly 59 days, thus exposing all of its surface periodically to the sun. For nearly 100 years, astronomy had accepted a rotational period for Mercury of 88 earth-days, synchronous with its period of revolution. A synchronous rotation-revolution period would have caused the same side of Mercury to face the sun constantly and would have produced a temperature of between 750° and 1,000° on the sun-facing surface, while the perpetually dark side would have had a temperature of about −450° Fahrenheit.

Now, while it is believed that the surface passing before the sun may have a temperature of about 800° F., the temperature on the side turned temporarily away from the sun does not fall as low as might be expected. This night temperature has been described by Russian astronomers as "room temperature"—possibly about 70°. This would contradict the former belief that Mercury did not possess an atmosphere, for some sort of atmosphere would be needed to retain some of the fierce solar radiation that must strike Mercury at its small distance from the sun. A shallow but dense layer of carbon dioxide would produce the "greenhouse" effect in which heat accumulated during exposure to the sun, would not completely escape at night.

This uncertainty about conditions upon Mercury and its motion arise from its short angular distance from the sun as seen from the earth, for Mercury is always too much in line with the sun to be observed against a dark sky, but is always seen during either morning or evening twilight.

### VENUS

Venus is slightly smaller than the earth. Its diameter is about 200 miles less than the earth's diameter. Venus moves about the sun at a mean distance of 67,000,000 miles in 225 of our days. Its synodical revolution—its return to the same relationship with the earth and the sun, which is a result of the combination of its own motion and that of the earth—is 584 days. Venus will, then, be nearer to the earth every 19 months than any of the other planets of the solar system. We have never been able to see the surface of Venus because the planet is covered with a dense, white cloudy atmosphere that conceals whatever is below it. This same cloud reflects sunlight efficiently so that when Venus is favorably situated, it is the third brightest object in the sky, exceeded only by the sun and the moon.

Telescopic observation of Venus has not been able to disclose the rate of rotation of the planet and, until late in 1962, there was nothing more than speculation about the temperatures on its surface, the nature of its atmosphere and the inclination of its axis of rotation which would produce seasonal changes there. Latest authorities now state that the polar axis of Venus is tilted away from the vertical by about 32°, so that Venus does have seasons. Opinions as to its period of rotation ranged from about the same as that of the earth—about 24 hours—to a longer intermediate period of about 30 earth days and then to one in which its period of rotation corresponded with its period of revolution, 225 days. This would keep the same side of Venus always facing the sun, and would produce high temperatures on that side. Observation appeared to confirm a high temperature on the sunlighted face of Venus and the longer rotation period was generally accepted. Traces of what appeared to be carbon dioxide were found in the atmosphere and no water vapor or free oxygen appeared to exist there.

In 1959, a spectroscope sent in a balloon to a height of about 100,000 feet did indicate the presence of both these commodities in the atmosphere of Venus and our conception of the planet underwent certain changes. Where Venus had earlier been considered a waterless desert, water vapor and oxygen indicated a planet whose surface must be a steaming caldron because of a possible high temperature, at least upon the sunward side. Estimates of this temperature ran as high as 600° and seemed to inhibit the possibility of organic life on Venus and to support the theory that Venus rotated in the same period as it revolved.

In 1966, the Russian space probe, Venus 4, landed upon the surface of the planet and a few days later, the American space probe, Mariner V, made a close fly-by of Venus. Readings from the instruments of both these vehicles confirmed the 1962 findings of Mariner II, which then passed within 25,000 miles of Venus. The temperature on the surface of Venus, below its atmosphere, is extremely high—perhaps 800 degrees F. No breaks in the cloudy atmosphere were reported. The temperature on the upper surface of the clouds was about 30° below zero. An extremely weak magnetic field or none at all appeared to be indicated by other instruments in the space probe. This would indicate that Venus did not rotate at all or had an extremely slow rotation. Further studies of Venus by radio astronomy indicate a retrograde rotation—in the opposite direction to the rotation of the Earth, for example—with a period of 247 earth days. This, combined with the period of revolution of Venus of 225 earth days, would give a specific point on Venus a period of sunlight 118 earth days in length during which the sun would rise in what would be west on earth, move slowly eastward and set in the east.

Venus also appears to be subjected to fierce blasts of solar plasma which produce conditions dangerous to living organisms in its vicinity. The mysteries of Venus have only been intensified by the knowledge we have recently gained about it.

### MARS

Mars is the first planet beyond the earth, away from the sun. Mars's diameter is about 4,200 miles, although a determination of the radius and mass of Mars by the space-probe, Mariner IV, which flew by Mars on July 14, 1965 at a distance of less than 6,000 miles, indicated that these dimensions were slightly larger than had been previously estimated. While Mars's orbit is also nearly circular, it is not as nearly centered on the sun as are the orbits of many of the other planets, and Mars is more than 30 million miles farther from the sun in some parts of its year than it is at others. Mars takes 687 of our days to make one circuit of the sun, traveling at about 15 miles a second. Mars rotates upon its axis in almost the same period of time that the earth does—24 hours and 37 minutes. Mars's mean distance from the sun is 141 million miles, so that the temperature on Mars would be lower than that on the earth even if Mars's atmosphere were about the same as ours. This is far from being the case, however, for Mariner IV reported that atmospheric pressure on Mars as between 1% and 2% of the earth's atmospheric pressure. This thin atmosphere appears to be largely carbon dioxide with traces of nitrogen and argon. No evidence of free water was found.

There appears to be no magnetic field about Mars. This would eliminate the previous conception of a dangerous radiation belt around Mars similar to the Van Allen Belt around the earth. The same lack of a magnetic field would expose the surface of Mars to an influx of cosmic radiation about 100 times as intense as that on earth.

Five-eighths of the surface of Mars is a desert of reddish rock, sand and soil. The rest of Mars is covered by irregular patches that appear generally green in hues that change through the Martian year. These were formerly held to be some sort of primitive vegetation, but with the findings of Mariner IV of a complete lack of water and oxygen, such growth does not appear possible. The nature of the green areas is now unknown, but two theories about them have been advanced. They may be regions covered with volcanic salts whose color changes with changing temperatures and atmospheric conditions, or they may be gray, rather than green. Optical experiments show that when large gray areas are placed beside large red areas, the gray areas will

appear green to the eye.

Mars is inclined from a vertical to the plane of its orbit about the sun by about 25° and therefore has seasons as does the earth, except that the Martian seasons are longer because Mars's year is longer. White caps form about the winter pole of Mars, growing through the winter and shrinking in summer. These polar caps were thought to be frozen water which when it melted, nourished the green areas. In view of the negative findings of Mariner IV, however, the caps are thought to be carbon dioxide.

The canals of Mars have become more of a mystery than they were before the voyage of Mariner IV. Markings forming a network of fine lines crossing much of the surface of Mars have been seen there by men who have devoted much of their professional time to the study of the planet, but no canals have shown clearly enough upon previous photographs to be universally accepted. A few of the 21 photographs sent back to earth by Mariner IV covered areas crossed by canals. The pictures show faint, ill-defined, broad, dark markings, but no positive identification of the nature of the markings has been made. The photographs show that the surface of Mars bears a marked resemblance to the surface of the moon. There are craters in most of the pictures, which appear identical with lunar craters.

Mars's position in its orbit and its speed around that orbit in relation to the earth's position and speed bring Mars fairly close to the earth on two occasions about two years apart and then move Mars and the earth too far apart for accurate observation and photography for about 15 years. In September, 1956, Mars paid the second of the current series of close visits to the earth, when it came to a little more than 35 million miles from us. It had not been as close as this since 1924 and it will be even closer in 1971.

When Mars is favorably situated it is brighter than most of the stars and is definitely red and not difficult to locate. The polar caps may be seen with a small telescope under good conditions and the differences in color of the various regions of the surface can sometimes be perceived. To bring out any surface detail, however, requires a large instrument and the cooperation of the atmosphere of the earth and Mars.

Mars has two satellites. They are small, about 5 and 10 miles in diameter. They were discovered in 1877 by Asaph Hall. The outer satellite is named Deimos and it revolves around Mars in about 31 hours. The inner satellite, Phobos, whips around Mars in a little more than 7 hours, making three trips around the planet each Martian day. While these tiny satellites were not discovered until 1877, they were described with uncanny accuracy by Johnathan Swift in "Gulliver's Travels," published in 1726.

## JUPITER

Jupiter is the largest of the planets. Its equatorial diameter is 88,000 miles, 11 times the diameter of the earth. Its polar diameter is about 6,000 miles shorter. This is caused by the almost fluid condition of its atmosphere and its extremely rapid rate of rotation. Jupiter's day is just under 10 hours long. For a planet of this size, this rotational speed is amazing, and it carries a point on Jupiter's equator along at a speed of 22,000 miles an hour, as compared with 1,000 miles an hour for a point on the earth's equator. Jupiter is at an average distance of 480 million miles from the sun and takes almost 12 of our years to make one complete circuit of the sun. This makes its apparent motion through our skies very slow. Jupiter moves through one of the 12 zodiacal constellations in about a year.

Much of Jupiter's diameter is atmosphere. The question of whether or not the giant planet has any solid core at all has recently been re-opened, but the current widely accepted picture of the planet provides a small, heavy, solid center, covered with a sheath of ice about 10,000 miles thick. This all lies at the bottom of an atmosphere about 25,000 miles deep. This atmosphere is made up of hydrogen, helium, methane and ammonia and, since the temperature on the surface of Jupiter is about 200° below zero F., these gases must be of the consistency of slush. Jupiter's cloudy atmosphere is a fairly good reflector of sunlight and makes it far brighter than any of the stars among which it wanders. An extremely heavy radioactive belt has also been discovered surrounding Jupiter, similar to the earth's Van Allen Belt.

Jupiter has 12 satellites. Four of these are large and bright, rivalling our own moon and the planet Mercury in diameter, and may be seen through a field glass. They move rapidly around Jupiter and their change of position from night to night is extremely interesting to watch. The eight additional satellites are much smaller and, in all but one instance, much farther from Jupiter, and cannot be seen except through powerful telescopes. The 4 outermost satellites are revolving around Jupiter from east to west, contrary to the motions of the great majority of the satellites in the solar system and to the direction of revolution of the planets around the sun. The reason for this retrograde motion is not known, but one theory is that Jupiter's tremendous gravitational power may have captured 4 of the minor planets or asteroids, that move about the sun between Mars and Jupiter, and that these 4 may be running backwards. Jupiter's mass is more than twice the mass of all the other planets put together, and accounts for Jupiter's tremendous gravitational field and so, probably, for its numerous satellites and its dense atmosphere.

## SATURN

Saturn, last of the planets visible to the unaided eye, is almost twice as far from the sun as is Jupiter, almost 900 million miles. It is second in size to Jupiter but its mass is much smaller. Saturn's specific gravity is less than that of water, and if an ocean big enough could be found, Saturn would float in it. Its diameter is about 71,000 miles at the equator; its rotational speed spins it completely around in a little more than 10 hours, and its atmosphere is much like that of Jupiter, except that at its greater distance from the sun, its temperature is at least 100° colder. At about 300° F. below zero, the ammonia would be frozen out of Saturn's clouds. The theoretical construction of Saturn resembles that of Jupiter, it is either all gas, or it has a small heavy center surrounded by a layer of ice and a deep atmosphere.

Saturn has ten satellites, the 10th having been discovered by the French astronomer Audouin Dollfus in December, 1966. The newly found satellite is a few thousand miles outside of the edge of Saturn's ring system and its discovery was made possible by the edge-on presentation of the rings which is caused by the inclinations of the polar axes of Saturn and the earth. At such times, the rings virtually disappear to observers on earth. This aspect of the rings reduces their brilliance and would permit the hitherto unknown satellite to be seen.

Saturn's ring system begins about 7,000 miles above the visible disk of Saturn, lying above its equator and is a flat ring that extends about 35,000 miles into space around the planet. Although the diameter of the ring system, including Saturn itself, is about 170,000 miles, the rings are estimated to be no more than 10 miles in depth—from top to bottom. This makes them among the flattest things in nature, considering depth in proportion to width. The rings are probably made of billions of tiny particles, undoubtedly including ice, each of which follows its own individual orbit about Saturn. One theory of the origin of this system is that the material in it was once consolidated into an eleventh satellite which, because of some gravitational aberration ages ago, was drawn so close to Saturn that the great planet's gravitational stresses shattered it to bits, scattering the fragments as rings around the destroying planet.

The rings cannot be seen except in a telescope of at least 3-inch aperture. Because of Saturn's inclination, as stated above, there are two periods during Saturn's journey around the sun when the rings are presented to us edge-on. At these times, the rings disappear. Nothing that is only 10 miles wide can be seen from a distance of nearly 900 million miles. The rings are not now in a favorable position to be seen. They were edge-on in 1966 and will reach maximum visibility again in 1973, when we will see the lower or southern face of the rings.

Saturn takes 29½ years to go around the sun. It thus moves very slowly among the constellations of the zodiac, remaining in each one for more than two years.

# The Earth; Size; Computation of Time; Seasons

## SIZE AND DIMENSIONS

The earth is the fifth largest planet and the third from the sun. Its mass is 6 sextillion, 588 quintillion short tons. Using the parameter of an ellipsoid adopted by the International Astronomical Union in 1964 and recognized by the International Union of Geodesy and Geophysics in 1967, the length of the equator is 24,901.55 miles, the length of a meridian is 24,859.82 miles, the equatorial diameter is 7,926.41 miles, and the area of this reference ellipsoid is approximately 196,938,800 square miles.

The earth is considered a solid, rigid mass with a dense core of magnetic, probably metallic material. The outer part of the core is probably liquid. Around the core is a thick shell or mantle of heavy crystalline rock which in turn is covered by a thin crust forming the solid granite and basalt base of the continents and ocean basins. Over broad areas of the earth's surface the crust has a thin cover of sedimentary rock such as sandstone, shale, and limestone formed by weathering of the earth's surface and deposition of sands, clays, and plant and animal remains.

The temperature in the earth increases about 1°F. with every 100 to 200 feet in depth, in the upper 100 kilometers of the earth, and the temperature near the core is believed to be near the melting point of the core materials under the conditions at that depth. The heat of the earth is believed to be derived from radioactivity in the rocks, pressures developed within the earth, and original heat (if the earth in fact was formed at high temperature).

## ATMOSPHERE OF THE EARTH

The earth's atmosphere is a blanket composed of gases and some water vapor. The principal gases are nitrogen, oxygen and argon, in amounts of about 78, 21 and 1% by volume. Also present in minute quantities are carbon dioxide, hydrogen, neon, helium, krypton and xenon.

Water vapor occupies space independent of other gases and varies from nearly zero to about 4% by volume. The height of the **ozone** layer varies from approximately 12 to 21 miles above the earth. Traces exist as low as 6 miles and as high as 35 miles. Bits of methane have been found.

The atmosphere rests on the earth's surface with the weight equivalent to a layer of water 34 ft. deep. For about 300,000 ft. upward the gases remain in the proportions stated. Gravity holds the gases to the earth. The weight of the air compresses it at the bottom, so that the greatest density is at the earth's surface. Pressure, as well as density, decreases as height increases because the weight pressing upon any layer is always less than that pressing upon the layers below.

The temperature of the air drops with increased height, until the **tropopause** is reached. This may vary from 25,000 to 60,000 ft. The atmosphere below the tropopause is the **troposphere**; the atmosphere for about twenty miles above the tropopause is the **stratosphere**, where the temperature generally increases with height except at high latitudes in winter. A temperature maximum near the 30-mile level is called the **stratopause**. Above this boundary is the **mesosphere** where the temperature decreases with height to a minimum, the **mesopause**, at a height of 50 miles. Extending above the mesosphere to the outer fringes of the atmosphere is the **thermosphere**, a region where temperature increases with height to a value measured in thousands of degrees Fahrenheit. The lower portion of this region, extending from 50 to about 400 miles in altitude, is characterized by a high ion density, and is thus called the **ionosphere**. The outer region is called **exosphere**, this is the region where gas molecules traveling at high speed may escape into outer space. Above 600 miles.

## LATITUDE, LONGITUDE

Position on the globe is measured by means of meridians and parallels. Meridians, which are imaginary lines drawn around the earth through the poles, determine **longitude**. The meridian running through Greenwich, England, is the **prime meridian of longitude**, and all others are either east or west. Parallels, which are imaginary circles parallel with the equator, determine **latitude**. The length of a degree of longitude varies as the cosine of the latitude. At the equator a degree is 69.171 statute miles; this is gradually reduced toward the poles. Value of a longitude degree at the poles is zero.

**Latitude** is reckoned by the number of degrees north or south of the equator, an imaginary circle on the earth's surface everywhere equidistant between the two poles. According to the IAU Ellipsoid of 1964, the length of a degree of latitude is 68.708 statute miles at the equator and varies slightly north and south because of the oblate form of the globe; at the poles it is 69.403 statute miles.

## COMPUTATION OF TIME

The earth rotates on its axis and follows an elliptical orbit around the sun. The rotation makes the sun appear to move across the sky from East to West. It determines day and night and the complete rotation, in relation to the sun, is called the **apparent** or **true solar day**. This varies but an average determines the **mean solar day** of 24 hours.

The mean solar day is in universal use for civil purposes. It may be obtained from apparent solar time by correcting observations of the sun for the equation of time, but when high precision is required, the mean solar time is calculated from its relation to sidereal time.

**Sidereal time** is the measure of time defined by the diurnal motion of the vernal equinox, and is determined from observation of the meridian transits of stars. One complete rotation of the earth relative to the equinox is called the **sidereal day**. The **mean sidereal day** is 23 hours, 56 minutes, 4.091 seconds of mean solar time.

The **Calendar Year** begins at 12 o'clock precisely local clock time, on the night of Dec. 31–Jan. 1. The day and the calendar month also begin at midnight by the clock. The interval required for the earth to make one absolute revolution around the sun is a **sidereal year**; it consists of 365 days. 6 hours, 9 minutes, and 9.5 seconds in 1900, and is increasing at the rate of 0.0001 second annually.

The **Tropical Year**, on which the return of the seasons depends, is the interval between two consecutive returns of the sun to the vernal equinox. The tropical year consisted of 365 days, 5 hours, 48 minutes, and 46 seconds. It is decreasing at the rate of 0.530 seconds per century.

In 1956 the unit of time interval was defined to be identical with the second of the tropical year for 1900 January 0d 12th hour E. T. A physical definition of the second based on a quantum transition of cesium (atomic second) was adopted in 1964. The atomic second is equal to 9,192,631,770 cycles of the emitted radiation. In 1967 this atomic second was adopted as the unit of time interval for the Intern'l System of units.

## THE ZONES AND SEASONS

The five zones of the earth's surface are the Torrid, lying between the Tropics of Cancer and Capricorn; North Temperate, between Cancer and the Arctic Circle; South Temperate, between Capricorn and the Antarctic Circle; the Frigid Zones, between the polar Circles and the Poles.

The inclination or tilt of the earth's axis with respect to the sun determines the seasons. These are best marked in the North Temperate Zone, where spring begins at the vernal equinox, summer at the summer solstice, autumn at the autumnal equinox and winter at the winter solstice.

In the South Temperate Zone, the seasons are reversed. Spring begins at the autumnal equinox, summer at the winter solstice, etc.

If the earth's axis were perpendicular to the plane of the earth's orbit around the sun there would be no change of seasons. Day and night would be of equal length and there would be equable conditions of temperature. But the axis is tilted 23° 27′ away from a perpendicular to the orbit and only in March and September is the axis at right angles to the sun.

The points at which the sun crosses the equator are the equinoxes, when day and night are most nearly equal. The points at which the sun is at a maximum distance from the equator are the solstices. Days and nights are then most unequal.

In June the North Pole is tilted 23° 27′ toward the sun and the days in the northern hemisphere are longer than the nights, while the days in the southern hemisphere are shorter than the nights. In December the North Pole is tilted 23° 27′ away from the sun and the situation is reversed.

## THE SEASONS IN 1969

In 1969 the 4 seasons will begin as follows according to EST; add one hour for Atlantic Time; subtract one hour for Central, two hours for Mountain, 3 hours for Pacific; 4 hours for Yukon; 5 hours for Alaska-Hawaii and 6 hours for Bering Time.

| | | |
|---|---|---|
| Vernal Equinox | (Spring) | March 20, 2:08 p.m. |
| Summer Solstice | (Summer) | June 21, 8:55 a.m. |
| Autumnal Equinox | (Autumn) | Sept. 23, 12:07 a.m. |
| Winter Solstice | (Winter) | Dec. 21, 7:44 p.m. |

# Poles and Rotation of the Earth

## POLES OF THE EARTH

**Source:** Coast and Geodetic Survey, ESSA

The geographic (rotation) poles, or points where the earth's axis of rotation cuts the surface, are not absolutely fixed in the body of the earth. The pole of rotation describes an irregular curve about its mean position.

Two periods have been detected in this motion: (1) an annual period due to seasonal changes in barometric pressure, load of ice and snow on the surface and to other phenomena of seasonal character; (2) a period of about 14 months due to the shape and constitution of the Earth.

In addition there are small but as yet unpredictable irregularities. The whole motion is so small that the actual pole at any time remains within a circle of 30 or 40 feet in radius centered at the mean position of the pole.

The pole of rotation for the time being is of course the pole having a latitude of 90° and an indeterminate longitude.

## MAGNETIC POLES

The **north magnetic pole** of the earth is that region where the magnetic force is vertically downward and the **south magnetic pole** that region where the magnetic force is vertically upward. A compass placed at the magnetic poles experiences no directive force.

There are slow changes in the distribution of the earth's magnetic field. These changes were at one time attributed in part to a periodic movement of the magnetic poles around the geographical poles, but later evidence refutes this theory and points, rather, to a slow migration of "disturbance" foci over the earth.

There appear shifts in position of the magnetic poles due to the changes in the earth's magnetic field. The center of the area designated as the north magnetic pole was estimated to be in about latitude 70.5° N and longitude 96° W in 1905; from recent nearby measurements and studies of the secular changes, the position in 1965 is estimated as latitude 75.5° N and longitude 100.5° W. Improved data rather than actual motion account for at least part of the change.

The position of the south magnetic pole in 1912 was near 71° S and longitude 150° E; the position in 1965 is estimated at latitude 66.5° S. and longitude 139.9° E.

The direction of the horizontal components of the magnetic field at any point is known as magnetic north at that point, and the angle by which it deviates east or west of true north is known as the magnetic declination, or in the mariner's terminology the **variation of the compass.**

A compass without error points in the direction of magnetic north. (In general this is *not* the direction of the magnetic north pole.) If one follows the direction indicated by the north end of the compass, he will travel along a rather irregular curve which eventually reaches the north magnetic pole (though not usually by a great-circle route). However, the action of the compass should not be thought of as due to any influence of the distant pole, but simply as an indication of the distribution of the earth's magnetism at the place of observation.

## ROTATION OF THE EARTH

**Source:** U. S. Naval Observatory

The speed of rotation of the earth about its axis has been found to be slightly variable. The variations may be classified as:

(a) **Secular.** Tidal friction acts as a brake on the rotation and causes a slow secular increase in the length of the day, about 1 millisecond per century.

(b) **Irregular.** The speed of rotation may increase for a number of years, about 5 to 10, and then start decreasing. The maximum difference from the mean in the length of the day during a century is about 5 milliseconds. The accumulated difference in time has amounted to approximately 40 seconds since 1900. The cause is probably turbulent motion in the core of the earth.

(c) **Periodic.** Seasonal variations exist with periods of one year and six months. The cumulative effect is such that each year the earth is late about 30 milliseconds near June 1 and is ahead about 30 milliseconds near Oct. 1. The maximum seasonal variation in the length of the day is about 0.5 millisecond. It is believed that the principal cause of the annual variation is the seasonal change in the wind patterns of the Northern and Southern Hemispheres. The semi-annual variation is due chiefly to tidal action of the sun, which distorts the shape of the earth slightly.

The secular and irregular variations were discovered by comparing time based on the rotation of the earth with time based on the orbital motion of the moon about the earth and of the planets about the sun. The periodic variation was determined largely with the aid of quartz-crystal clocks. The introduction of the cesium-beam atomic clock in 1955 made it possible to determine in greater detail than before the nature of the irregular and periodic variations.

---

# Five Eclipses in 1969

The time used in these tables is Eastern Standard Time. To obtain Central Standard Time, subtract 1 hour; Mountain Standard Time, subtract 2 hours; Pacific Standard Time, subtract 3 hours. A.M. light figures; **P.M. black;** 0 designates midnight, 12 designates noon.

## FIRST ECLIPSE

An Annular Eclipse of the Sun, March 17-18, 1969. The eclipse is visible over the Indian Ocean, the Malay Peninsula, Indonesia, the Phillipines, part of Southeast Asia and Japan, Australia, the western Pacific Ocean, and part of Antarctica.

### CIRCUMSTANCES OF THE ECLIPSE

|  | d | h | m |
|---|---|---|---|
| Eclipse begins | March 17 | 09 | 06.5 |
| Central eclipse begins | March 17 | 10 | 08.7 |
| Central eclipse at local apparent noon | March 17 | 11 | 37.8 |
| Central eclipse ends | March 18 | 01 | 40.2 |
| Eclipse ends | March 18 | 02 | 42.4 |

## SECOND ECLIPSE

A **Penumbral Eclipse of the Moon,** April 2, 1969. The beginning of the eclipse is visible in the western part of the Pacific Ocean, Asia, eastern Europe, the eastern half of Africa, the Indian Ocean, Australia, New Zealand, and Antarctica; the end of the eclipse is visible in Asia except the extreme northeastern part, most of Australia, the Indian Ocean, Africa, Europe, the Atlantic Ocean except the western part, and Antarctica.

### CIRCUMSTANCES OF THE ECLIPSE

|  | d | h | m |
|---|---|---|---|
| Moon enters penumbra | April 2 | 11 | 38.4 |
| Middle of the eclipse | April 2 | 01 | 32.5 |
| Moon leaves penumbra | April 2 | 03 | 26.6 |
| Penumbral magnitude of the eclipse 0.728 |  |  |  |

## THIRD ECLIPSE

A Penumbral Eclipse of the Moon, August 27, 1969. The beginning of the eclipse is visible in North America except the extreme northeastern part, the western half of South America, the Pacific Ocean, the northeastern coast of Asia, Australia, New Zealand, and Antarctica; the end visible in North America except the northeastern part, the Pacific Ocean, the east coast of Asia, New Zealand and Antarctica.

### CIRCUMSTANCES OF THE ECLIPSE

|  | d | h | m |
|---|---|---|---|
| Moon enters penumbra | August 27 | 05 | 21.0 |
| Middle of the eclipse | August 27 | 05 | 47.7 |
| Moon leaves penumbra | August 27 | 06 | 14.7 |
| Penumbral magnitude of the eclipse 0.038 |  |  |  |

## FOURTH ECLIPSE

An Annular Eclipse of the Sun, September 11, 1969. The eclipse is visible over the central Pacific Ocean and the western half of South America.

### CIRCUMSTANCES OF THE ECLIPSE

|  | d | h | m |
|---|---|---|---|
| Eclipse begins | September 11 | 12 | 01.5 |
| Central eclipse begins | September 11 | 01 | 06.7 |
| Central eclipse at local apparent noon | September 11 | 02 | 44.6 |
| Central eclipse ends | September 11 | 04 | 50.1 |
| Eclipse ends | September 11 | 05 | 55.1 |

## FIFTH ECLIPSE

A Penumbral Eclipse of the Moon, September 25, 1969. The beginning of the eclipse is visible in Asia, the western Pacific Ocean, Australia, New Zealand, the Indian Ocean, Africa except the western part, Europe except the western part, and the Arctic regions; the end is visible in Asia except the eastern part, the Indian Ocean, Africa, Europe, the Atlantic Ocean, South America except the western part, the extreme northeastern part of North America and the Arctic regions.

### CIRCUMSTANCES OF THE ECLIPSE

|  | d | h | m |
|---|---|---|---|
| Moon enters penumbra | September 25 | 01 | 05.0 |
| Middle of the eclipse | September 25 | 03 | 09.7 |
| Moon leaves penumbra | September 25 | 05 | 14.3 |
| Penumbral magnitude of the eclipse 0.926 |  |  |  |

# Meteor Showers Are Numerous Every Year

About a dozen meteor showers occur each year and the dates on which they take place may be found in the Calendar of Celestial Events. These showers are caused by the earth's passage through streams of meteoroids left in space by comets, of which they were a part. The meteoroids orbit the sun along the path originally followed by the comet and are encountered annually by the earth as it moves about the sun.

Canadian and American researchers have found evidence that the earth has been subjected to heavy bombardment from space on several occasions from 34,000,000 to 700,000 years ago.

The oldest of these catastrophes covered the eastern half of North America, the Atlantic Ocean and the northern half of Africa. Scars in the form of circular pits, sometimes a score of yards in diameter and often filled with water, have been located in northern Quebec, and fragments of metallic, stony and glassy objects define the area.

Central Europe received a fall of similar objects about 15,000,000 years ago and the most recent fall, about 700,000 years ago, struck the region including Australia and southeastern Asia.

The stony-metallic fragments are thought to originate in the asteroid belt, a region in space roughly between Mars and Jupiter in which travel thousands of minor planets ranging in size from 480 miles in diameter down to flying mountains a few miles across. Gravitational upheavals and collisions among asteroids are believed to provide fragments, some of which may reach the earth.

The glassy fragments, called tektites, are thought to be material resulting from collisions of large objects with the earth or the moon, scattered originally in liquid form and cooling after impact into drop-shaped, glassy particles.

## METEORS

Meteoroids are celestial bodies, possibly associated with comets, that move through space with velocities up to 40 miles per second. Upon reaching the earth's atmosphere, they are vaporized by the heat of the friction of their passage into the atmosphere and are seen as meteors. An unusual number in a short period of time is called a meteor shower. Meteors are popularly known as falling stars or shooting stars. While most of them are consumed, a few fall to earth as fused metal or stone, and are called meteorites.

Many meteorites have been picked up in the United States, most of them small. A huge meteorite may lie embedded in the earth at Meteor Crater on U. S. 6 near Canyon Diablo in Arizona. The crater is 1 mi. in diameter at the surface and over 500 feet deep, and is surrounded by a wall of earth filled with pyrites presumably originating with the meteor. A lake in the Ungava region of northern Quebec fills the Chubb Crater, discovered 1943, which is 7½ mi. around. Vast destruction of timber was caused by a meteorite that hit in the vicinity of Lake Baikal, in Siberia, June 30, 1908. A large meteor that split into fragments of 80 to 820 pounds fell Feb. 17, 1930, 14 mi. sw of Paragould, Ark.

On display in the American Museum-Hayden Planetarium, New York, N. Y. are three meteorites; a 34 ton 85 pound iron-nickel meteorite and another 3-ton one brought from Cape York, Greenland, by Robert E. Peary in 1907 and a 14½ ton meteorite found in the Willamette region of Oregon in 1902.

## COMETS

The origin of comets is not known. Dr. Jan Oort, a Dutch astronomer, presents the hypothesis that there is a wide, irregular cloud of comets around the outskirts of the solar system. From this cloud single comets may be drawn, from time to time, by the gravitational pull of one of the large outer planets and started on journeys through the solar system on long elliptical orbits about the sun.

Comets sufficiently bright to be seen without a telescope are rare. In October and November, 1965, a new comet, Ikeya-Seki, was visible in the morning skies before sunrise as the most spectacular comet since Halley's in 1910. Barring the unexpected appearance of an as yet unknown bright comet, possible at any time, the next certain bright comet due to appear is Halley's Comet, expected in 1986.

On page 256 are listed a few of the short-period comets that make fairly regular visits to the region of the earth.

# Landing Sites for Apollo Exploration of Moon Chosen

From a series of unmanned explorations, the National Aeronautics and Space Administration has selected 5 possible landing sites for the first manned mission to the moon. This choice may be reduced to 3 by the time the 3-man Apollo Space Craft is ready for launching.

All 5 landing sites are in relatively smooth areas, which, nevertheless, contain features of scientific interest such as small craters, rilles, faults, ray material and ridges. All the sites are near the lunar equator on the side of the moon that perpetually faces the earth.

One is almost in the center of the visible side of the moon, in the Sinus Medii, "The Central Bay." It is south of the small crater Bruce. Two are in the Oceanus Procellarum, "The Ocean of Storms," the great plain that covers half of the west side of the moon. One of these is near the bright crater Kepler, north and west of the great crater Copernicus. The other is farther east, near the crater Flamsteed.

The remaining two sites are on the lunar east, not far from each other, in the Mare Tranquilitatis, "The Sea of Tranquility." The first of these is north of the small crater Moltke, and the other farther east near the crater Censorius.

The location of these sites on the face of the moon visible from the earth makes continuous radio communication possible, although the two members of the Apollo team on the moon will be able to communicate with the third member, in orbit about the Apollo is above their horizon.

United States space probes, in both hard and soft landings on the moon, and other U. S. space vehicles orbiting the moon have found valuable new material for studies of the lunar surface.

During 1964 and 1965, three successful landings on the moon were made by moon probes of the Ranger series, designed to photograph the surface of the moon at close range. These three Ranger vehicles sent back nearly 18,000 pictures of the surface of the moon before crashing. These pictures were taken at distances ranging from 300 miles to less than 2,000 feet from the moon.

On June 2, 1966, the first of the Surveyor vehicles made a soft landing on the moon near the crater Flamsteed in the Oceanus Procellarum, on the eastern side of the moon slightly north of the lunar equator. Its cameras took photographs from a height of about four feet.

Surveyor III duplicated this feat on April 19, 1967, by landing gently on the moon after some heart-stopping bounces which evidently did no damage to its instruments. It landed in the Oceanus Procellarum, not far from Surveyor I, apparently on the slope of a shallow crater so that its cameras saw the moon at a slight angle.

Meanwhile, three Lunar Orbiters are revolving about the moon, securing and transmitting photographs of much of the moon's surface in order to find the best landing place for the manned Apollo flight to take place in the future. Orbiter II is placed at a much greater distance from the moon than its two orbiting companions so that its cameras can secure pictures of large areas for making detailed lunar maps.

The Ranger vehicles revealed that there is hardly any of the moon's surface unmarked by craters, from the enormous depression visible in telescopes from the earth to tiny holes inches across. There does not appear to be any overall cover of dust on the moon. The pictures sent back by Surveyor I show the surface strewn with small, loose rocks and rubble and the instruments on the vehicle registered a temperature of 280 degrees below zero, Fahrenheit, during the two-week lunar night through which it passed before its communication systems ceased to operate. One of the Orbiter pictures shows Surveyor I on the moon.

Surveyor III was equipped with a small metal claw with which it could dig into the surface material of the moon. The amount of current required to move this claw through the surface gave a measure of the density of this material and its composition. It appears to be dry and fine-grained, resembling silt or closely packed sand. Surveyor III took photographs during an eclipse of the moon which showed the reverse of that phenomenon from the lunar viewpoint—an eclipse of the sun by the earth. Its instruments registered a 400-degree temperature drop as the moon passed through the earth's shadow.

**1st Month**  **JANUARY, 1969**  **31 Days**

**Local Mean Time, A.M., light figures; P.M., black** (0 designates midnight; 12 designates noon)
**CAUTION—Must be converted to ordinary clock time (STANDARD TIME)—See page 277.**

**45° N. Latitude** — Idaho, Iowa (No.), Me., Mich. (except Far So.), Minn., Mont., N. H., N. Y. (upstate), N. D., Ore., S. D., Vt., Wash., Wis., Wyo. (No. & Cent.)

**40° N. Latitude** — Calif. (No.), Colo., Conn., Del., D.C., Ill., Ind., Iowa (So. & Cent.), Kans., Ky. (No. & Cent.), Mass., Md., Mich. (Far So.), Mo. (No. & Cent.), Nebr., Nev. (No. & Cent.), N.J., N.Y. City, N.Y. (So.), Ohio, Pa., R.I., Utah, W.Va., Wyo. (So.).

**35° N. Latitude** — Alabama (No.), Ariz. (Except Far So.), Ark., Calif. (So.), Georgia (No.), Missouri (So.), N. Mex. (Except Far So.), Nevada (So.), N.C., Okla., S.C., Tenn., Tex. (No.), Va. (So.).

**30° N. Latitude** — Alabama (So.), Ariz. (Far So.), Fla., Georgia (So.), La., Miss. (So.), N. Mex. (Far So.), Tex. (So. & Cent.).

| Day of the Month | Day of the Week | 45° Sun Rises | 45° Sun Sets | 45° Moon R.&S. | 40° Sun Rises | 40° Sun Sets | 40° Moon R.&S. | 35° Sun Rises | 35° Sun Sets | 35° Moon R.&S. | 30° Sun Rises | 30° Sun Sets | 30° Moon R.&S. |
|---|---|---|---|---|---|---|---|---|---|---|---|---|---|
| | | h. m. | h. m. | h. m. sets | h. m. | h. m. | h. m. sets | h. m. | h. m. | h. m. sets | h. m. | h. m. | h. m. sets |
| 1 | W | 7 38 | 4 29 | 6 19 | 7 22 | 4 45 | 5 55 | 7 08 | 4 59 | 5 36 | 6 56 | 5 11 | 5 20 |
| 2 | Th | 7 38 | 4 30 | 7 15 | 7 22 | 4 46 | 6 51 | 7 08 | 5 00 | 6 32 | 6 56 | 5 12 | 6 14 |
| 3 | Fr | 7 38 | 4 31 | 8 05 | 7 22 | 4 47 | 7 41 | 7 09 | 5 00 | 7 22 | 6 57 | 5 12 | 7 06 |
| | | | | rises | | | rises | | | rises | | | rises |
| 4 | Sa | 7 38 | 4 32 | 5 11 | 7 22 | 4 48 | 5 30 | 7 09 | 5 01 | 5 48 | 6 57 | 5 13 | 6 02 |
| 5 | S | 7 38 | 4 33 | 6 19 | 7 22 | 4 49 | 6 35 | 7 09 | 5 02 | 6 50 | 6 57 | 5 14 | 7 01 |
| 6 | M | 7 38 | 4 34 | 7 28 | 7 22 | 4 50 | 7 41 | 7 09 | 5 03 | 7 51 | 6 57 | 5 15 | 8 00 |
| 7 | Tu | 7 38 | 4 35 | 8 37 | 7 22 | 4 51 | 8 44 | 7 09 | 5 04 | 8 52 | 6 57 | 5 16 | 8 58 |
| 8 | W | 7 37 | 4 36 | 9 45 | 7 22 | 4 52 | 9 50 | 7 09 | 5 05 | 9 53 | 6 57 | 5 16 | 9 55 |
| 9 | Th | 7 37 | 4 37 | 10 54 | 7 22 | 4 53 | 10 55 | 7 09 | 5 06 | 10 54 | 6 57 | 5 17 | 10 53 |
| 10 | Fr | 7 37 | 4 38 | ..... | 7 22 | 4 54 | ..... | 7 09 | 5 07 | 11 57 | 6 57 | 5 18 | 11 52 |
| 11 | Sa | 7 37 | 4 39 | 0 06 | 7 22 | 4 55 | 0 01 | 7 09 | 5 08 | ..... | 6 57 | 5 19 | ..... |
| 12 | S | 7 36 | 4 40 | 1 22 | 7 21 | 4 56 | 1 12 | 7 09 | 5 09 | 1 03 | 6 57 | 5 20 | 0 56 |
| 13 | M | 7 36 | 4 42 | 2 40 | 7 21 | 4 57 | 2 25 | 7 08 | 5 10 | 2 14 | 6 57 | 5 20 | 2 03 |
| 14 | Tu | 7 35 | 4 43 | 4 03 | 7 20 | 4 58 | 3 44 | 7 08 | 5 11 | 3 27 | 6 57 | 5 21 | 3 14 |
| 15 | W | 7 35 | 4 44 | 5 26 | 7 20 | 4 59 | 5 02 | 7 08 | 5 12 | 4 43 | 6 57 | 5 22 | 4 26 |
| 16 | Th | 7 34 | 4 45 | 6 40 | 7 20 | 5 00 | 6 15 | 7 08 | 5 13 | 5 55 | 6 57 | 5 23 | 5 38 |
| 17 | Fr | 7 34 | 4 47 | 7 39 | 7 19 | 5 01 | 7 16 | 7 07 | 5 14 | 6 57 | 6 57 | 5 24 | 6 40 |
| | | | | sets | | | sets | | | sets | | | sets |
| 18 | Sa | 7 33 | 4 48 | 5 19 | 7 19 | 5 03 | 5 38 | 7 07 | 5 15 | 5 51 | 6 56 | 5 25 | 6 05 |
| 19 | S | 7 33 | 4 50 | 6 45 | 7 18 | 5 04 | 6 56 | 7 06 | 5 16 | 7 07 | 6 56 | 5 26 | 7 16 |
| 20 | M | 7 32 | 4 51 | 8 05 | 7 18 | 5 05 | 8 12 | 7 06 | 5 17 | 8 18 | 6 56 | 5 27 | 8 23 |
| 21 | Tu | 7 31 | 4 52 | 9 20 | 7 17 | 5 06 | 9 22 | 7 06 | 5 18 | 9 24 | 6 56 | 5 28 | 9 25 |
| 22 | W | 7 30 | 4 54 | 10 31 | 7 17 | 5 07 | 10 29 | 7 05 | 5 19 | 10 27 | 6 55 | 5 29 | 10 26 |
| 23 | Th | 7 30 | 4 55 | 11 41 | 7 16 | 5 09 | 11 34 | 7 05 | 5 19 | 11 28 | 6 55 | 5 29 | 11 23 |
| 24 | Fr | 7 29 | 4 57 | ..... | 7 16 | 5 10 | ..... | 7 04 | 5 20 | ..... | 6 54 | 5 30 | ..... |
| 25 | Sa | 7 28 | 4 58 | 0 48 | 7 15 | 5 11 | 0 37 | 7 04 | 5 21 | 0 29 | 6 54 | 5 31 | 0 20 |
| 26 | S | 7 27 | 4 59 | 1 56 | 7 14 | 5 12 | 1 41 | 7 03 | 5 22 | 1 28 | 6 54 | 5 32 | 1 18 |
| 27 | M | 7 26 | 5 01 | 3 04 | 7 13 | 5 13 | 2 45 | 7 02 | 5 23 | 2 28 | 6 53 | 5 33 | 2 15 |
| 28 | Tu | 7 25 | 5 02 | 4 09 | 7 12 | 5 15 | 3 47 | 7 02 | 5 25 | 3 28 | 6 53 | 5 33 | 3 13 |
| 29 | W | 7 24 | 5 04 | 5 09 | 7 12 | 5 16 | 4 45 | 7 01 | 5 26 | 4 25 | 6 52 | 5 34 | 4 09 |
| 30 | Th | 7 23 | 5 05 | 6 10 | 7 11 | 5 17 | 5 37 | 7 01 | 5 27 | 5 37 | 6 52 | 5 35 | 5 01 |
| 31 | Fr | 7 22 | 5 06 | 6 44 | 7 10 | 5 18 | 6 22 | 7 00 | 5 28 | 6 04 | 6 51 | 5 36 | 5 48 |

## Sun on 75th Meridian (Local Mean Time)

| Day | h. m. s. | Day | h. m. s. | Day | h. m. s. | Day | h. m. s. | Day | h. m. s. |
|---|---|---|---|---|---|---|---|---|---|
| 1 | 12 03 23 | 8 | 12 06 33 | 14 | 12 08 56 | 20 | 12 10 57 | 26 | 12 12 31 |
| 2 | 12 03 52 | 9 | 12 06 58 | 15 | 12 09 18 | 21 | 12 11 15 | 27 | 12 12 44 |
| 3 | 12 04 19 | 10 | 12 07 22 | 16 | 12 09 39 | 22 | 12 11 32 | 28 | 12 12 56 |
| 4 | 12 04 47 | 11 | 12 07 47 | 17 | 12 10 00 | 23 | 12 11 48 | 29 | 12 13 07 |
| 5 | 12 05 14 | 12 | 12 08 11 | 18 | 12 10 20 | 24 | 12 12 03 | 30 | 12 13 17 |
| 6 | 12 05 41 | 13 | 12 08 34 | 19 | 12 10 39 | 25 | 12 12 17 | 31 | 12 13 27 |
| 7 | 12 06 07 | | | | | | | | |

## Twilight (Local Mean Time)

| Place | Jan. | Begins h. m. | Ends h. m. | Jan. | Begins h. m. | Ends h. m. | Jan. | Begins h. m. | Ends h. m. |
|---|---|---|---|---|---|---|---|---|---|
| 45° N. Lat. | 1 | 5 52 | 6 15 | 11 | 5 53 | 6 24 | 21 | 5 48 | 6 34 |
| 40° N. Lat. | 1 | 5 44 | 6 22 | 11 | 5 46 | 6 31 | 21 | 5 43 | 6 40 |
| 35° N. Lat. | 1 | 5 37 | 6 29 | 11 | 5 39 | 6 37 | 21 | 5 37 | 6 45 |
| 30° N. Lat. | 1 | 5 30 | 6 36 | 11 | 5 32 | 6 43 | 21 | 5 32 | 6 50 |

## Moon Phases, 1969 (Eastern Standard Time)

| Moon | day | hour | min. | a.m. or p.m. | Moon | day | hour | min. | a.m. or p.m. |
|---|---|---|---|---|---|---|---|---|---|
| Full Moon | 3 | 1 | 28 | P.M. | New Moon | 17 | 11 | 59 | P.M. |
| Last Quarter | 11 | 9 | 00 | A.M. | First Quarter | 25 | 3 | 23 | A.M. |

**Morning Stars**—Mercury (Jan. 29-31); Mars; Jupiter.  **Evening Stars**—Mercury (Jan. 1-29); Venus; Saturn.

**2nd Month**     **FEBRUARY, 1969**     **28 Days**

Local Mean Time, A.M., light figures; **P.M., black** (0 designates midnight; 12 designates noon)
CAUTION—Must be converted to ordinary clock time (**STANDARD TIME**)—See page 277.

| Day of the Month | Day of the Week | 45° N. Latitude<br>Idaho, Iowa (No.), Me., Mich. (except Far So.), Minn., Mont., N. H., N. Y. (upstate), N. D., Ore., S. D., Vt., Wash., Wis., Wyo. (No. & Cent.). | | | 40° N. Latitude<br>Calif. (No.), Colo., Conn., Del., D.C., Ill., Ind., Iowa (So. & Cent.), Kans., Ky. (No. & Cent.), Mass., Md., Mich. (Far So.), Mo. (No. & Cent.), Nebr., Nev. (No. & Cent.), N.J., N.Y. City, N.Y. (So.), Ohio, Pa., R.I., Utah, W.Va., Wyo. (So.). | | | 35° N. Latitude<br>Alabama (No.), Ariz. (Except Far So.), Ark., Calif. (So.), Georgia (No.), Missouri (So.), N. Mex. (Except Far So.), Nevada (So.), N.C., Okla., S.C., Tenn., Tex. (No.), Va. (So.). | | | 30° N. Latitude<br>Alabama (So.), Ariz. (Far So.), Fla., Georgia (So.), La., Miss. (So.), N. Mex. (Far So.), Tex. (So. & Cent.). | | |
|---|---|---|---|---|---|---|---|---|---|---|---|---|---|
| | | Sun Rises | Sun Sets | Moon R. & S. | Sun Rises | Sun Sets | Moon R. & S. | Sun Rises | Sun Sets | Moon R. & S. | Sun Rises | Sun Sets | Moon R. & S. |
| | | h. m. | h. m. | h. m.<br>sets | h. m. | h. m. | h. m.<br>sets | h. m. | h. m. | h. m.<br>sets | h. m. | h. m. | h. m.<br>sets |
| 1 | Sa | 7 21 | 5 08 | 7 18<br>rises | 7 09 | 5 19 | 6 59<br>rises | 6 59 | 5 29 | 6 44<br>rises | 6 51 | 5 37 | 6 30<br>rises |
| 2 | S | 7 19 | 5 09 | 5 17 | 7 08 | 5 21 | 5 32 | 6 59 | 5 30 | 5 43 | 6 50 | 5 38 | 5 53 |
| 3 | M | 7 18 | 5 11 | 6 28 | 7 07 | 5 22 | 6 37 | 6 58 | 5 31 | 6 45 | 6 50 | 5 39 | 6 52 |
| 4 | Tu | 7 17 | 5 12 | 7 38 | 7 05 | 5 23 | 7 49 | 6 57 | 5 32 | 7 47 | 6 49 | 5 40 | 7 50 |
| 5 | W | 7 16 | 5 13 | 8 46 | 7 05 | 5 24 | 8 48 | 6 56 | 5 33 | 8 48 | 6 48 | 5 41 | 8 48 |
| 6 | Th | 7 14 | 5 15 | 9 58 | 7 04 | 5 25 | 9 54 | 6 55 | 5 34 | 9 49 | 6 47 | 5 42 | 9 47 |
| 7 | Fr | 7 13 | 5 16 | 11 11 | 7 03 | 5 27 | 11 02 | 6 54 | 5 35 | 10 56 | 6 47 | 5 42 | 10 49 |
| 8 | Sa | 7 11 | 5 18 | . . . . | 7 02 | 5 28 | . . . . | 6 53 | 5 36 | . . . . | 6 46 | 5 43 | 11 53 |
| 9 | S | 7 10 | 5 19 | 0 27 | 7 01 | 5 29 | 0 14 | 6 52 | 5 37 | 0 03 | 6 45 | 5 44 | . . . . |
| 10 | M | 7 09 | 5 20 | 1 46 | 7 00 | 5 30 | 1 28 | 6 51 | 5 38 | 1 14 | 6 44 | 5 45 | 1 01 |
| 11 | Tu | 7 07 | 5 22 | 3 07 | 6 59 | 5 31 | 2 45 | 6 50 | 5 39 | 2 26 | 6 43 | 5 46 | 2 10 |
| 12 | W | 7 06 | 5 23 | 4 23 | 6 57 | 5 32 | 3 59 | 6 50 | 5 40 | 3 38 | 6 43 | 5 46 | 3 21 |
| 13 | Th | 7 04 | 5 25 | 5 26 | 6 56 | 5 33 | 5 02 | 6 49 | 5 41 | 4 42 | 6 42 | 4 47 | 4 25 |
| 14 | Fr | 7 03 | 5 26 | 6 15 | 6 55 | 5 34 | 5 53 | 6 48 | 5 42 | 5 37 | 6 41 | 5 48 | 5 21 |
| 15 | Sa | 7 01 | 5 27 | 6 50<br>sets | 6 54 | 5 35 | 6 34<br>sets | 6 47 | 5 43 | 6 21<br>sets | 6 40 | 5 49 | 6 08<br>sets |
| 16 | S | 7 00 | 5 29 | 5 35 | 6 52 | 5 36 | 5 45 | 6 46 | 5 44 | 5 53 | 6 39 | 5 50 | 6 01 |
| 17 | M | 6 59 | 5 30 | 6 53 | 6 51 | 5 38 | 6 58 | 6 44 | 5 44 | 7 03 | 6 39 | 5 50 | 7 06 |
| 18 | Tu | 6 57 | 5 32 | 8 08 | 6 49 | 5 39 | 8 08 | 6 43 | 5 45 | 8 08 | 6 38 | 5 51 | 8 08 |
| 19 | W | 6 55 | 5 33 | 9 20 | 6 48 | 5 40 | 9 15 | 6 42 | 5 46 | 9 11 | 6 37 | 5 52 | 9 07 |
| 20 | Th | 6 53 | 5 34 | 10 31 | 6 47 | 5 41 | 10 22 | 6 41 | 5 47 | 10 14 | 6 36 | 5 53 | 10 07 |
| 21 | Fr | 6 52 | 5 36 | 11 41 | 6 45 | 5 42 | 11 27 | 6 40 | 5 48 | 11 16 | 6 35 | 5 53 | 11 04 |
| 22 | Sa | 6 51 | 5 37 | . . . . | 6 44 | 5 44 | . . . . | 6 38 | 5 49 | . . . . | 6 34 | 5 54 | . . . . |
| 23 | S | 6 49 | 5 39 | 0 49 | 6 42 | 5 45 | 0 32 | 6 37 | 5 50 | 0 17 | 6 33 | 5 55 | 0 04 |
| 24 | M | 6 47 | 5 40 | 1 57 | 6 41 | 5 46 | 1 35 | 6 36 | 5 51 | 1 18 | 6 32 | 5 55 | 1 03 |
| 25 | Tu | 6 45 | 5 41 | 2 59 | 6 40 | 5 47 | 2 36 | 6 35 | 5 52 | 2 16 | 6 31 | 5 56 | 2 00 |
| 26 | W | 6 44 | 5 43 | 3 55 | 6 38 | 5 48 | 3 31 | 6 34 | 5 53 | 3 10 | 6 30 | 5 57 | 2 54 |
| 27 | Th | 6 43 | 5 44 | 4 41 | 6 37 | 5 50 | 4 18 | 6 32 | 5 54 | 3 59 | 6 28 | 5 57 | 3 42 |
| 28 | Fr | 6 41 | 5 46 | 5 18 | 6 35 | 5 51 | 4 59 | 6 31 | 5 55 | 4 41 | 6 27 | 5 58 | 4 26 |

## Sun on 75th Meridian (Local Mean Time)

| Day | h. m. s. | Day | h. m. s. | Day | h. m. s. | Day | h. m. s. | Day | h. m. s. |
|---|---|---|---|---|---|---|---|---|---|
| 1 | 12 13 35 | 7 | 12 14 10 | 13 | 12 14 17 | 19 | 12 13 58 | 25 | 12 13 15 |
| 2 | 12 13 43 | 8 | 12 14 13 | 14 | 12 14 16 | 20 | 12 13 52 | 26 | 12 13 04 |
| 3 | 12 13 50 | 9 | 12 14 16 | 15 | 12 14 14 | 21 | 12 13 45 | 27 | 12 12 53 |
| 4 | 12 13 57 | 10 | 12 14 17 | 16 | 12 14 11 | 22 | 12 13 38 | 28 | 12 12 43 |
| 5 | 12 14 02 | 11 | 12 14 18 | 17 | 12 14 07 | 23 | 12 13 31 | | |
| 6 | 12 14 07 | 12 | 12 14 18 | 18 | 12 14 03 | 24 | 12 13 22 | | |

## Twilight (Local Mean Time)

| Place | Feb. | Begins | Ends | Feb. | Begins | Ends | Feb. | Begins | Ends |
|---|---|---|---|---|---|---|---|---|---|
| 45° N. Lat. | 1 | 5 40 | 6 48 | 11 | 5 29 | 7 00 | 21 | 5 16 | 7 15 |
| 40° N. Lat. | 1 | 5 37 | 6 51 | 11 | 5 28 | 7 02 | 21 | 5 15 | 7 14 |
| 35° N. Lat. | 1 | 5 34 | 6 55 | 11 | 5 26 | 7 04 | 21 | 5 15 | 7 13 |
| 30° N. Lat. | 1 | 5 30 | 6 59 | 11 | 5 24 | 7 06 | 21 | 5 15 | 7 13 |

## Moon Phases, 1969 (Eastern Standard Time)

| Moon | day | hour | min. a.m. or p.m. | Moon | day | hour | min. a.m. or p.m. |
|---|---|---|---|---|---|---|---|
| Full Moon | 2 | 7 | 56 A.M. | New Moon | 16 | 11 | 25 A.M. |
| Last Quarter | 9 | 7 | 08 P.M. | First Quarter | 23 | 11 | 30 P.M. |

**Morning Stars**—Mercury; Mars; Jupiter.     **Evening Stars**—Venus; Saturn.

# 3rd Month  MARCH, 1969  31 Days

Local Mean Time, A.M., light figures: **P.M.**, black (0 designates midnight; 12 designates noon)
CAUTION—Must be converted to ordinary clock time (**STANDARD TIME**)—See page 277.

| Day of the Month | Day of the Week | 45° N. Latitude Idaho, Iowa (No.), Me., Mich.(Except Far So.), Minn., Mont., N. H., N. Y. (upstate), N. D., Ore., S. D., Vt., Wash., Wis., Wyo. (No. & Cent.). | | | 40° N. Latitude Calif. (No.), Colo., Conn Del., D.C., Ill., Ind Iowa (So. & Cent.), Kans. Ky. (No. & Cent.), Mass., Md., Mich. (Far So.), Mo. (No. & Cent.), Nebr. Nev. (No. & Cent.), N.J., N.Y. City, N.Y. (So.), Ohio, Pa., R.I., Utah, W.Va., Wyo. (So.). | | | 35° N. Latitude Alabama (No.), Ariz. (Except Far So.), Ark., Calif. (So.), Georgia (No.) Missouri (So.), N. Mex. (Except Far So.), Nevada (So.), N.C., Okla., S.C., Tenn., Tex. (No.), Va. (So.). | | | 30° N. Latitude Alabama (So.), Ariz. (Far So.), Fla., Georgia (So.), La., Miss. (So.), N. Mex. (Far So.), Tex. (So. & Cent.). | | |
|---|---|---|---|---|---|---|---|---|---|---|---|---|---|
| | | Sun Rises | Sun Sets | Moon R. & S. | Sun Rises | Sun Sets | Moon R. & S. | Sun Rises | Sun Sets | Moon R.&S. | Sun Rises | Sun Sets | Moon R.&S. |
| | | h. m. | h. m. | h. m. sets | h. m. | h. m. | h. m. sets | h. m. | h. m. | h. m. sets | h. m. | h. m. | h. m. sets |
| 1 | Sa | 6 39 | 5 47 | 5 40 | 6 34 | 5 52 | 5 31 | 6 30 | 5 56 | 5 18 | 6 26 | 5 59 | 5 05 |
| 2 | S | 6 37 | 5 48 | 6 12 | 6 32 | 5 53 | 6 00 | 6 29 | 5 57 | 5 49 | 6 25 | 6 00 | 5 39 |
| 3 | M | 6 35 | 5 50 | 6 32 | 6 31 | 5 54 | 6 24 | 6 27 | 5 58 | 6 17 | 6 24 | 6 00 | 6 11 |
| | | | | rises | | | rises | | | rises | | | rises |
| 4 | Tu | 6 34 | 5 51 | 6 35 | 6 30 | 5 55 | 6 37 | 6 26 | 5 58 | 6 38 | 6 23 | 6 01 | 6 40 |
| 5 | W | 6 32 | 5 53 | 7 46 | 6 28 | 5 56 | 7 44 | 6 24 | 5 59 | 7 42 | 6 22 | 6 01 | 7 39 |
| 6 | Th | 6 30 | 5 54 | 9 00 | 6 26 | 5 57 | 8 53 | 6 23 | 6 00 | 8 46 | 6 21 | 6 02 | 8 42 |
| 7 | Fr | 6 28 | 5 55 | 10 17 | 6 25 | 5 58 | 10 05 | 6 22 | 6 01 | 9 55 | 6 20 | 6 03 | 9 45 |
| 8 | Sa | 6 26 | 5 56 | 11 36 | 6 23 | 5 59 | 11 19 | 6 21 | 6 02 | 11 06 | 6 19 | 6 04 | 10 53 |
| 9 | S | 6 25 | 5 58 | . . . . | 6 22 | 6 00 | . . . . | 6 19 | 6 02 | . . . . | 6 17 | 6 04 | . . . . |
| 10 | M | 6 23 | 5 59 | 0 57 | 6 20 | 6 01 | 0 35 | 6 18 | 6 03 | 0 18 | 6 16 | 6 05 | 0 02 |
| 11 | Tu | 6 21 | 6 00 | 2 13 | 6 19 | 6 02 | 1 48 | 6 17 | 6 04 | 1 29 | 6 15 | 6 06 | 1 11 |
| 12 | W | 6 19 | 6 01 | 3 19 | 6 17 | 6 03 | 2 54 | 6 16 | 6 05 | 2 34 | 6 14 | 6 07 | 2 17 |
| 13 | Th | 6 17 | 6 03 | 4 10 | 6 16 | 6 04 | 3 49 | 6 14 | 6 06 | 3 30 | 6 13 | 6 07 | 3 14 |
| 14 | Fr | 6 15 | 6 04 | 4 50 | 6 15 | 6 06 | 4 31 | 6 13 | 6 06 | 4 16 | 6 11 | 6 08 | 4 02 |
| 15 | Sa | 6 13 | 6 06 | 5 18 | 6 13 | 6 07 | 5 05 | 6 11 | 6 07 | 4 54 | 6 10 | 6 08 | 4 44 |
| 16 | S | 6 11 | 6 07 | 5 43 | 6 11 | 6 08 | 5 33 | 6 10 | 6 08 | 5 26 | 6 09 | 6 09 | 5 20 |
| 17 | M | 6 09 | 6 08 | 6 01 | 6 09 | 6 09 | 5 57 | 6 09 | 6 09 | 5 54 | 6 08 | 6 10 | 5 51 |
| | | | | sets | | | sets | | | sets | | | sets |
| 18 | Tu | 6 07 | 6 09 | 6 58 | 6 07 | 6 10 | 6 55 | 6 07 | 6 10 | 6 54 | 6 07 | 6 10 | 6 52 |
| 19 | W | 6 06 | 6 11 | 8 10 | 6 06 | 6 11 | 8 03 | 6 06 | 6 10 | 7 56 | 6 05 | 6 11 | 7 51 |
| 20 | Th | 6 04 | 6 12 | 9 21 | 6 04 | 6 12 | 9 09 | 6 04 | 6 11 | 8 59 | 6 04 | 6 11 | 8 50 |
| 21 | Fr | 6 02 | 6 13 | 10 32 | 6 02 | 6 13 | 10 16 | 6 03 | 6 12 | 10 02 | 6 03 | 6 12 | 9 50 |
| 22 | Sa | 6 00 | 6 14 | 11 40 | 6 00 | 6 14 | 11 21 | 6 02 | 6 13 | 11 04 | 6 02 | 6 13 | 10 50 |
| 23 | S | 5 58 | 6 16 | . . . . | 5 59 | 6 15 | . . . . | 6 00 | 6 14 | . . . . | 6 01 | 6 13 | 11 48 |
| 24 | M | 5 57 | 6 17 | 0 47 | 5 58 | 6 16 | 0 23 | 5 59 | 6 14 | 0 05 | 5 59 | 6 14 | . . . . |
| 25 | Tu | 5 55 | 6 19 | 1 45 | 5 56 | 6 17 | 1 21 | 5 57 | 6 15 | 1 01 | 5 58 | 6 14 | 0 44 |
| 26 | W | 5 53 | 6 20 | 2 36 | 5 54 | 6 18 | 2 12 | 5 56 | 6 16 | 1 52 | 5 57 | 6 15 | 1 35 |
| 27 | Th | 5 51 | 6 21 | 3 16 | 5 52 | 6 19 | 2 54 | 5 55 | 6 17 | 2 37 | 5 56 | 6 16 | 2 21 |
| 28 | Fr | 5 49 | 6 22 | 3 48 | 5 51 | 6 20 | 3 31 | 5 53 | 6 18 | 3 15 | 5 55 | 6 16 | 3 02 |
| 29 | Sa | 5 47 | 6 24 | 4 15 | 5 50 | 6 21 | 4 00 | 5 52 | 6 18 | 3 48 | 5 53 | 6 17 | 3 38 |
| 30 | S | 5 45 | 6 25 | 4 36 | 5 48 | 6 22 | 4 25 | 5 50 | 6 19 | 4 17 | 5 52 | 6 17 | 4 10 |
| 31 | M | 5 43 | 6 26 | 4 55 | 5 46 | 6 23 | 4 49 | 5 49 | 6 20 | 4 44 | 5 51 | 6 18 | 4 39 |

## Sun on 75th Meridian (Local Mean Time)

| Day | h. m. s. | Day | h. m. s. | Day | h. m. s. | Day | h. m. s. | Day | h. m. s. |
|---|---|---|---|---|---|---|---|---|---|
| 1 | 12 12 31 | 8 | 12 10 59 | 14 | 12 09 25 | 20 | 12 07 42 | 26 | 12 05 54 |
| 2 | 12 12 20 | 9 | 12 10 44 | 15 | 12 09 08 | 21 | 12 07 24 | 27 | 12 05 35 |
| 3 | 12 12 07 | 10 | 12 10 29 | 16 | 12 08 51 | 22 | 12 07 06 | 28 | 12 05 17 |
| 4 | 12 11 54 | 11 | 12 10 13 | 17 | 12 08 34 | 23 | 12 06 48 | 29 | 12 04 59 |
| 5 | 12 11 41 | 12 | 12 09 57 | 18 | 12 08 17 | 24 | 12 06 30 | 30 | 12 04 41 |
| 6 | 12 11 27 | 13 | 12 09 41 | 19 | 12 08 00 | 25 | 12 06 12 | 31 | 12 04 22 |
| 7 | 12 11 13 | | | | | | | | |

## Twilight (Local Mean Time)

| Place | Mar. | Begins | Ends | Mar. | Begins | Ends | Mar. | Begins | Ends |
|---|---|---|---|---|---|---|---|---|---|
| | | h. m. | h. m. | | h. m. | h. m. | | h. m. | h. m. |
| 45° N. Lat.. | 1 | 5 02 | 7 25 | 11 | 4 44 | 7 38 | 21 | 4 25 | 7 52 |
| 40° N. Lat.. | 1 | 5 05 | 7 22 | 11 | 4 50 | 7 32 | 21 | 4 33 | 7 44 |
| 35° N. Lat.. | 1 | 5 07 | 7 20 | 11 | 4 54 | 7 28 | 21 | 4 39 | 7 37 |
| 30° N. Lat.. | 1 | 5 08 | 7 19 | 11 | 4 57 | 7 26 | 21 | 4 44 | 7 32 |

## Moon Phases, 1969 (Eastern Standard Time)

| Moon | day | hour | min. a.m. or p.m. | Moon | day | hour | min. a.m. or p.m. |
|---|---|---|---|---|---|---|---|
| Full Moon | 4 | 0 | 17 A.M. | New Moon | 17 | 11 | 51 P.M. |
| Last Quarter | 11 | 2 | 44 A.M. | First Quarter | 25 | 7 | 48 P.M. |

**Morning Stars**—Mercury; Mars; Jupiter (Mar. 1-21).　**Evening Stars**—Venus; Saturn; Jupiter (Mar. 21-31).

## 4th Month　　　APRIL, 1969　　　30 Days

Local Mean Time, A.M., light figures: **P.M.**, black (0 designates midnight; 12 designates noon)
CAUTION—Must be converted to ordinary clock time (**STANDARD TIME**)—See page 277.

| Day of the Month | Day of the Week | 45° N. Latitude<br>Idaho, Iowa (No.), Me., Mich. (Except Far So.), Minn., Mont., N. H., N. Y. (upstate), N. D., Ore., S. D., Vt., Wash., Wis., Wyo. (No. & Cent.). | | | 40° N. Latitude<br>Calif. (No.), Colo., Conn., Del., D.C., Ill., Ind., Iowa (So. & Cent.), Kans., Ky. (No. & Cent.), Mass., Md., Mich. (Far So.), Mo. (No. & Cent.), Nebr., Nev. (No. & Cent.), N.J., N.Y. City, N.Y. (So.), Ohio, Pa., R.I., Utah, W.Va., Wyo. (So.). | | | 35° N. Latitude<br>Alabama (No.), Ariz. (Except Far So.), Ark., Calif. (So.), Georgia (No.), Missouri (So.), N. Mex. (Except Far So.), Nevada (So.), N.C., Okla., S.C., Tenn., Tex. (No.), Va. (So.). | | | 30° N. Latitude<br>Alabama (So.), Ariz. (Far So.), Fla., Georgia (So.), La., Miss. (So.), N. Mex. (Far So.), Tex. (So. & Cent.). | | |
|---|---|---|---|---|---|---|---|---|---|---|---|---|---|
| | | Sun Rises | Sun Sets | Moon R. & S. | Sun Rises | Sun Sets | Moon R. & S. | Sun Rises | Sun Sets | Moon R. & S. | Sun Rises | Sun Sets | Moon R. & S. |
| | | h. m. | h. m. | h. m. | h. m. | h. m. | h. m. | h. m. | h. m. | h. m. | h. m. | h. m. | h. m. |
| 1 | Tu | 5 41 | 6 27 | sets<br>5 12 | 5 44 | 6 24 | sets<br>5 11 | 5 48 | 6 21 | sets<br>5 09 | 5 50 | 6 19 | sets<br>5 08 |
| 2 | W | 5 39 | 6 29 | rises<br>6 41 | 5 43 | 6 25 | rises<br>6 36 | 5 46 | 6 22 | rises<br>6 33 | 5 49 | 6 19 | rises<br>6 28 |
| 3 | Th | 5 38 | 6 30 | 7 59 | 5 42 | 6 26 | 7 49 | 5 45 | 6 22 | 7 40 | 5 47 | 6 20 | 7 34 |
| 4 | Fr | 5 36 | 6 31 | 9 20 | 5 40 | 6 27 | 9 05 | 5 43 | 6 23 | 8 50 | 5 46 | 6 20 | 8 41 |
| 5 | Sa | 5 34 | 6 33 | 10 43 | 5 38 | 6 28 | 10 23 | 5 42 | 6 24 | 10 06 | 5 45 | 6 21 | 9 52 |
| 6 | S | 5 32 | 6 34 | ..... | 5 36 | 6 29 | 11 39 | 5 40 | 6 25 | 11 19 | 5 44 | 6 22 | 11 03 |
| 7 | M | 5 30 | 6 35 | 0 03 | 5 35 | 6 30 | ..... | 5 39 | 6 26 | ..... | 5 43 | 6 22 | ..... |
| 8 | Tu | 5 29 | 6 37 | 1 13 | 5 34 | 6 31 | 0 49 | 5 38 | 6 26 | 0 27 | 5 41 | 6 23 | 0 11 |
| 9 | W | 5 27 | 6 38 | 2 09 | 5 32 | 6 32 | 1 46 | 5 36 | 6 27 | 1 27 | 5 40 | 6 23 | 1 11 |
| 10 | Th | 5 25 | 6 39 | 2 51 | 5 30 | 6 33 | 2 32 | 5 35 | 6 28 | 2 16 | 5 39 | 6 24 | 2 01 |
| 11 | Fr | 5 23 | 6 40 | 3 22 | 5 29 | 6 34 | 3 08 | 5 33 | 6 29 | 2 55 | 5 38 | 6 25 | 2 44 |
| 12 | Sa | 5 21 | 6 41 | 3 46 | 5 27 | 6 35 | 3 36 | 5 32 | 6 30 | 3 28 | 5 37 | 6 25 | 3 20 |
| 13 | S | 5 20 | 6 43 | 4 06 | 5 26 | 6 36 | 4 01 | 5 31 | 6 30 | 3 56 | 5 36 | 6 26 | 3 52 |
| 14 | M | 5 18 | 6 44 | 4 25 | 5 24 | 6 37 | 4 23 | 5 29 | 6 31 | 4 21 | 5 35 | 6 26 | 4 21 |
| 15 | Tu | 5 16 | 6 45 | 4 42 | 5 23 | 6 38 | 4 45 | 5 28 | 6 32 | 4 47 | 5 34 | 6 27 | 4 49 |
| 16 | W | 5 14 | 6 46 | sets<br>7 03 | 5 21 | 6 39 | sets<br>6 53 | 5 27 | 6 33 | sets<br>6 45 | 5 33 | 6 28 | sets<br>6 37 |
| 17 | Th | 5 12 | 6 47 | 8 14 | 5 20 | 6 40 | 8 00 | 5 26 | 6 34 | 7 48 | 5 32 | 6 28 | 7 37 |
| 18 | Fr | 5 11 | 6 49 | 9 24 | 5 19 | 6 41 | 9 06 | 5 24 | 6 34 | 8 50 | 5 30 | 6 29 | 8 37 |
| 19 | Sa | 5 09 | 6 50 | 10 31 | 5 17 | 6 42 | 10 11 | 5 23 | 6 35 | 9 52 | 5 29 | 6 29 | 9 36 |
| 20 | S | 5 07 | 6 51 | 11 34 | 5 15 | 6 43 | 11 11 | 5 22 | 6 36 | 10 50 | 5 28 | 6 30 | 10 34 |
| 21 | M | 5 05 | 6 52 | ..... | 5 14 | 6 44 | ..... | 5 21 | 6 37 | 11 44 | 5 27 | 6 31 | 11 27 |
| 22 | Tu | 5 04 | 6 54 | 0 29 | 5 12 | 6 45 | 0 04 | 5 20 | 6 38 | ..... | 5 26 | 6 31 | ..... |
| 23 | W | 5 03 | 6 55 | 1 13 | 5 11 | 6 46 | 0 50 | 5 18 | 6 38 | 0 31 | 5 25 | 6 32 | 0 15 |
| 24 | Th | 5 01 | 6 57 | 1 48 | 5 09 | 6 47 | 1 28 | 5 17 | 6 39 | 1 12 | 5 24 | 6 32 | 0 57 |
| 25 | Fr | 4 59 | 6 58 | 2 15 | 5 08 | 6 48 | 2 00 | 5 16 | 6 40 | 1 46 | 5 23 | 6 33 | 1 34 |
| 26 | Sa | 4 57 | 6 59 | 2 38 | 5 07 | 6 49 | 2 27 | 5 15 | 6 41 | 2 16 | 5 22 | 6 34 | 2 07 |
| 27 | S | 4 56 | 7 00 | 2 58 | 5 06 | 6 50 | 2 50 | 5 14 | 6 42 | 2 44 | 5 21 | 6 35 | 2 37 |
| 28 | M | 4 55 | 7 02 | 3 16 | 5 04 | 6 51 | 3 12 | 5 13 | 6 42 | 3 09 | 5 20 | 6 35 | 3 06 |
| 29 | Tu | 4 53 | 7 03 | 3 33 | 5 03 | 6 52 | 3 34 | 5 12 | 6 43 | 3 34 | 5 19 | 6 36 | 3 35 |
| 30 | W | 4 51 | 7 04 | 3 52 | 5 02 | 6 53 | 3 57 | 5 11 | 6 44 | 4 00 | 5 18 | 6 37 | 4 04 |

### Sun on 75th Meridian (Local Mean Time)

| Day | h. m. s. | Day | h. m. s. | Day | h. m. s. | Day | h. m. s. | Day | h. m. s. |
|---|---|---|---|---|---|---|---|---|---|
| 1 | 12 04 04 | 7 | 12 02 18 | 13 | 12 00 40 | 19 | 11 59 14 | 25 | 11 58 02 |
| 2 | 12 03 46 | 8 | 12 02 01 | 14 | 12 00 25 | 20 | 11 59 01 | 26 | 11 57 52 |
| 3 | 12 03 28 | 9 | 12 01 45 | 15 | 12 00 10 | 21 | 11 58 49 | 27 | 11 57 43 |
| 4 | 12 03 11 | 10 | 12 01 28 | 16 | 11 59 56 | 22 | 11 58 36 | 28 | 11 57 33 |
| 5 | 12 02 53 | 11 | 12 01 12 | 17 | 11 59 42 | 23 | 11 58 25 | 29 | 11 57 24 |
| 6 | 12 02 36 | 12 | 12 00 56 | 18 | 11 59 28 | 24 | 11 58 13 | 30 | 11 57 15 |

### Twilight (Local Mean Time)

| Place | Apr. | Begins | Ends | Apr. | Begins | Ends | Apr. | Begins | Ends |
|---|---|---|---|---|---|---|---|---|---|
| | | h. m. | h. m. | | h. m. | h. m. | | h. m. | h. m. |
| 45° N. Lat.. | 1 | 4 03 | 8 09 | 11 | 3 40 | 8 26 | 21 | 3 17 | 8 44 |
| 40° N. Lat.. | 1 | 4 13 | 7 57 | 11 | 3 55 | 8 09 | 21 | 3 36 | 8 24 |
| 35° N. Lat.. | 1 | 4 22 | 7 47 | 11 | 4 06 | 7 57 | 21 | 3 51 | 8 08 |
| 30° N. Lat.. | 1 | 4 30 | 7 39 | 11 | 4 16 | 7 46 | 21 | 4 04 | 7 54 |

### Moon Phases, 1969 (Eastern Standard Time)

| Moon | day | hour | min. a.m. or p.m. | Moon | day | hour | min. a.m. or p.m. |
|---|---|---|---|---|---|---|---|
| Full Moon ....... | 2 | 1 | 45 | P.M. | New Moon ....... | 16 | 1 | 16 | P.M. |
| Last Quarter ... | 9 | 8 | 58 | A.M. | First Quarter ... | 24 | 2 | 45 | P.M. |

**Morning Stars**—Mercury (Apr. 1-8); Venus (Apr. 8-30); Mars; Saturn (Apr. 18-30).　　**Evening Stars**—Mercury (Apr. 8-30); Venus (Apr. 1-8); Jupiter; Saturn (Apr. 1-18).

## 5th Month     MAY, 1969     31 Days

Local Mean Time, A.M., light figures: P.M., black (0 designates midnight; 12 designates noon)
CAUTION—Must be converted to ordinary clock time (STANDARD TIME)—See page 277.

| Day of the Month | Day of the Week | 45° N. Latitude Idaho, Iowa (No.), Me., Mich. (Except Far So.), Minn., Mont., N. H., N. Y. (upstate), N. D., Ore., S. D., Vt., Wash., Wis., Wyo. (No. & Cent.). | | | 40° N. Latitude Calif. (No.), Colo., Conn., Del., D. C., Ill., Ind., Iowa (So. & Cent.), Kans., Ky. (No. & Cent.), Mass., Md., Mich. (Far So.), Mo. (No. & Cent.), Nebr., Nev. (No. & Cent.), N. J., N. Y. City, N. Y. (So.), Ohio, Pa., R. I., Utah, W. Va., Wyo. (So.) | | | 35° N. Latitude Alabama (No.), Ariz. (Except Far So.), Ark., Calif. (So.), Georgia (No.), Missouri (So.), N. Mex. (Except Far So.), Nevada (So.), N. C., Okla., S. C., Tenn., Tex. (No.), Va. (So.). | | | 30° N. Latitude Alabama (So.), Ariz. (Far So.), Fla., Georgia (So.), La., Miss. (So.), N. Mex. (Far So.), Tex. (So. & Cent.) | | |
|---|---|---|---|---|---|---|---|---|---|---|---|---|---|
| | | Sun Rises | Sun Sets | Moon R. & S. | Sun Rises | Sun Sets | Moon R. & S. | Sun Rises | Sun Sets | Moon R. & S. | Sun Rises | Sun Sets | Moon R. & S. |
| | | h. m. | h. m. | h. m. | h. m. | h. m. | h. m. | h. m. | h. m. | h. m. | h. m. | h. m. | h. m. |
| | | | | sets | | | sets | | | sets | | | sets |
| 1 | Th | 4 50 | 7 05 | 4 12 | 5 01 | 6 54 | 4 21 | 5 10 | 6 45 | 4 30 | 5 17 | 6 38 | 4 37 |
| | | | | rises | | | rises | | | rises | | | rises |
| 2 | Fr | 4 48 | 7 06 | 8 18 | 5 00 | 6 55 | 8 00 | 5 09 | 6 46 | 7 45 | 5 16 | 6 38 | 7 33 |
| 3 | Sa | 4 47 | 7 08 | 9 42 | 4 58 | 6 56 | 9 21 | 5 07 | 6 46 | 9 02 | 5 16 | 6 39 | 8 46 |
| 4 | S | 4 45 | 7 09 | 11 00 | 4 57 | 6 57 | 10 36 | 5 06 | 6 47 | 10 15 | 5 15 | 6 39 | 9 58 |
| 5 | M | 4 44 | 7 10 | .... | 4 56 | 6 58 | 11 40 | 5 05 | 6 48 | 11 20 | 5 14 | 6 40 | 11 03 |
| 6 | Tu | 4 43 | 7 11 | 0 04 | 4 55 | 6 59 | .... | 5 04 | 6 49 | .... | 5 13 | 6 41 | 11 58 |
| 7 | W | 4 41 | 7 12 | 0 52 | 4 54 | 7 00 | 0 30 | 5 03 | 6 50 | 0 14 | 5 12 | 6 41 | .... |
| 8 | Th | 4 40 | 7 14 | 1 26 | 4 52 | 7 01 | 1 10 | 5 03 | 6 50 | 0 56 | 5 12 | 6 42 | 0 44 |
| 9 | Fr | 4 38 | 7 15 | 1 52 | 4 51 | 7 02 | 1 41 | 5 02 | 6 51 | 1 30 | 5 11 | 6 42 | 1 22 |
| 10 | Sa | 4 37 | 7 16 | 2 13 | 4 50 | 7 03 | 2 05 | 5 01 | 6 52 | 2 00 | 5 10 | 6 43 | 1 55 |
| 11 | S | 4 36 | 7 17 | 2 31 | 4 49 | 7 04 | 2 29 | 5 00 | 6 53 | 2 27 | 5 09 | 6 44 | 2 24 |
| 12 | M | 4 35 | 7 18 | 2 49 | 4 48 | 7 05 | 2 49 | 4 59 | 6 54 | 2 51 | 5 09 | 6 44 | 2 52 |
| 13 | Tu | 4 33 | 7 20 | 3 06 | 4 47 | 7 06 | 3 12 | 4 59 | 6 54 | 3 16 | 5 08 | 6 45 | 3 20 |
| 14 | W | 4 32 | 7 21 | 3 24 | 4 46 | 7 07 | 3 34 | 4 58 | 6 55 | 3 43 | 5 08 | 6 45 | 3 49 |
| 15 | Th | 4 31 | 7 22 | 3 45 | 4 45 | 7 08 | 3 59 | 4 57 | 6 56 | 4 11 | 5 07 | 6 46 | 4 22 |
| | | | | sets | | | sets | | | sets | | | sets |
| 16 | Fr | 4 30 | 7 23 | 8 18 | 4 44 | 7 09 | 7 59 | 4 56 | 6 57 | 7 40 | 5 06 | 6 47 | 7 26 |
| 17 | Sa | 4 29 | 7 24 | 9 24 | 4 43 | 7 10 | 9 00 | 4 55 | 6 58 | 8 42 | 5 06 | 6 47 | 8 25 |
| 18 | S | 4 28 | 7 26 | 10 20 | 4 43 | 7 11 | 9 56 | 4 55 | 6 58 | 9 37 | 5 05 | 6 48 | 9 19 |
| 19 | M | 4 27 | 7 27 | 11 08 | 4 42 | 7 12 | 10 46 | 4 54 | 6 59 | 10 25 | 5 05 | 6 48 | 10 10 |
| 20 | Tu | 4 26 | 7 28 | 11 46 | 4 41 | 7 13 | 11 26 | 4 53 | 7 00 | 11 08 | 5 04 | 6 49 | 10 53 |
| 21 | W | 4 25 | 7 29 | .... | 4 40 | 7 14 | 11 59 | 4 52 | 7 01 | 11 45 | 5 04 | 6 50 | 11 32 |
| 22 | Th | 4 24 | 7 30 | 0 17 | 4 39 | 7 15 | .... | 4 52 | 7 02 | .... | 5 03 | 6 50 | .... |
| 23 | Fr | 4 23 | 7 31 | 0 41 | 4 39 | 7 15 | 0 27 | 4 51 | 7 02 | 0 16 | 5 03 | 6 51 | 0 06 |
| 24 | Sa | 4 22 | 7 32 | 1 01 | 4 38 | 7 16 | 0 52 | 4 51 | 7 03 | 0 44 | 5 02 | 6 51 | 0 36 |
| 25 | S | 4 21 | 7 33 | 1 19 | 4 37 | 7 17 | 1 14 | 4 50 | 7 04 | 1 09 | 5 02 | 6 52 | 1 05 |
| 26 | M | 4 20 | 7 34 | 1 37 | 4 36 | 7 18 | 1 36 | 4 50 | 7 05 | 1 34 | 5 02 | 6 53 | 1 33 |
| 27 | Tu | 4 20 | 7 35 | 1 54 | 4 36 | 7 19 | 1 56 | 4 49 | 7 05 | 1 59 | 5 01 | 6 53 | 2 01 |
| 28 | W | 4 19 | 7 36 | 2 13 | 4 35 | 7 19 | 2 20 | 4 49 | 7 06 | 2 27 | 5 01 | 6 54 | 2 31 |
| 29 | Th | 4 19 | 7 37 | 2 36 | 4 35 | 7 20 | 2 47 | 4 48 | 7 06 | 2 57 | 5 00 | 6 54 | 3 06 |
| 30 | Fr | 4 18 | 7 38 | 3 04 | 4 34 | 7 21 | 3 21 | 4 48 | 7 07 | 3 34 | 5 00 | 6 55 | 3 47 |
| | | | | rises | | | rises | | | rises | | | rises |
| 31 | Sa | 4 17 | 7 39 | 8 36 | 4 33 | 7 22 | 8 13 | 4 48 | 7 08 | 7 53 | 5 00 | 6 56 | 7 35 |

## Sun on 75th Meridian (Local Mean Time)

| Day | h. m. s. | Day | h. m. s. | Day | h. m. s. | Day | h. m. s. | Day | h. m. s. |
|---|---|---|---|---|---|---|---|---|---|
| 1 | 11 57 07 | 8 | 11 56 27 | 14 | 11 56 15 | 20 | 11 56 24 | 26 | 11 56 52 |
| 2 | 11 57 00 | 9 | 11 56 24 | 15 | 11 56 15 | 21 | 11 56 28 | 27 | 11 56 59 |
| 3 | 11 56 53 | 10 | 11 56 21 | 16 | 11 56 16 | 22 | 11 56 32 | 28 | 11 57 06 |
| 4 | 11 56 47 | 11 | 11 56 19 | 17 | 11 56 16 | 23 | 11 56 36 | 29 | 11 57 13 |
| 5 | 11 56 41 | 12 | 11 56 17 | 18 | 11 56 19 | 24 | 11 56 41 | 30 | 11 57 21 |
| 6 | 11 56 36 | 13 | 11 56 16 | 19 | 11 56 21 | 25 | 11 56 47 | 31 | 11 57 29 |
| 7 | 11 56 31 | | | | | | | | |

## Twilight (Local Mean Time)

| Place | May | Begins | Ends | May | Begins | Ends | May | Begins | Ends |
|---|---|---|---|---|---|---|---|---|---|
| | | h. m. | h. m. | | h. m. | h. m. | | h. m. | h. m. |
| 45° N. Lat.. | 1 | 2 55 | 9 03 | 11 | 2 33 | 9 23 | 21 | 2 12 | 9 44 |
| 40° N. Lat.. | 1 | 3 18 | 8 38 | 11 | 3 02 | 8 53 | 21 | 2 48 | 9 08 |
| 35° N. Lat.. | 1 | 3 37 | 8 19 | 11 | 3 24 | 8 30 | 21 | 3 13 | 8 42 |
| 30° N. Lat.. | 1 | 3 51 | 8 04 | 11 | 3 41 | 8 13 | 21 | 3 32 | 8 22 |

## Moon Phases, 1969 (Eastern Standard Time)

| Moon | day | hour | min. | a.m. or p.m. | Moon | day | hour | min. | a.m. or p.m. |
|---|---|---|---|---|---|---|---|---|---|
| Full Moon | 2 | 0 | 13 | A.M. | New Moon | 16 | 3 | 26 | A.M. |
| Last Quarter | 8 | 3 | 12 | P.M. | First Quarter | 24 | 7 | 15 | A.M. |
| | | | | | Full Moon | 31 | 8 | 18 | A.M. |

**Morning Stars**—Mercury (May 29-31); Venus; Mars (May 1-31); Saturn.

**Evening Stars**—Mercury (May 1-29); Mars (May 31); Jupiter.

## 6th Month                JUNE, 1969                30 Days

Local Mean Time, A.M., light figures: **P.M., black** (0 designates midnight; 12 designates noon)
**CAUTION**—Must be converted to ordinary clock time (**STANDARD TIME**)—See page 277.

| Day of the Month | Day of the Week | 45° N. Latitude<br>Idaho, Iowa (No.), Me.,<br>Mich.(Except Far So.),<br>Minn., Mont., N. H.,<br>N. Y. (upstate),<br>N. D., Ore., S. D.,<br>Vt., Wash., Wis.,<br>Wyo. (No. & Cent.). | | | 40° N. Latitude<br>Calif. (No.), Colo., Conn.,<br>Del., D.C., Ill., Ind.,<br>Iowa (So. & Cent.), Kans.,<br>Ky. (No. & Cent.), Mass.,<br>Md., Mich. (Far So.),<br>Mo. (No. & Cent.), Nebr.,<br>Nev. (No. & Cent.), N.J.,<br>N.Y. City, N.Y. (So.),<br>Ohio, Pa., R.I., Utah,<br>W.Va., Wyo. (So.). | | | 35° N. Latitude<br>Alabama (No.), Ariz.<br>(Except Far So.), Ark.,<br>Calif. (So.), Georgia<br>(No.), Missouri (So.), N.<br>Mex. (Except Far So.),<br>Nevada (So.), N.C.,<br>Okla., S.C., Tenn., Tex.<br>(No.), Va. (So.). | | | 30° N. Latitude<br>Alabama (So.),<br>Ariz. (Far So.),<br>Fla., Georgia (So.)<br>La., Miss. (So.),<br>N. Mex. (Far So.),<br>Tex. (So. & Cent.) | | |
|---|---|---|---|---|---|---|---|---|---|---|---|---|---|
| | | Sun Rises | Sun Sets | Moon R. & S. | Sun Rises | Sun Sets | Moon R. & S. | Sun Rises | Sun Sets | Moon R. & S. | Sun Rises | Sun Sets | Moon R. & S. |
| | | h. m. | h. m. | h. m. | h. m. | h. m. | h. m. | h. m. | h. m. | h. m. | h. m. | h. m. | h. m. |
| | | | | rises | | | rises | | | rises | | | rises |
| 1 | S | 4 17 | 7 39 | 9 48 | 4 33 | 7 22 | 9 24 | 4 47 | 7 08 | 9 04 | 5 00 | 6 56 | 8 47 |
| 2 | M | 4 16 | 7 40 | 10 42 | 4 33 | 7 23 | 10 23 | 4 47 | 7 09 | 10 04 | 4 59 | 6 57 | 9 48 |
| 3 | Tu | 4 16 | 7 41 | 11 25 | 4 32 | 7 24 | 11 07 | 4 46 | 7 09 | 10 52 | 4 59 | 6 57 | 10 39 |
| 4 | W | 4 15 | 7 42 | 11 55 | 4 32 | 7 25 | 11 42 | 4 46 | 7 10 | 11 30 | 4 59 | 6 58 | 11 21 |
| 5 | Th | 4 15 | 7 43 | . . . . | 4 32 | 7 26 | . . . . | 4 46 | 7 11 | . . . . | 4 59 | 6 58 | 11 57 |
| 6 | Fr | 4 14 | 7 43 | 0 18 | 4 32 | 7 26 | 0 09 | 4 46 | 7 12 | 0 03 | 4 59 | 6 59 | . . . . |
| 7 | Sa | 4 14 | 7 44 | 0 37 | 4 31 | 7 27 | 0 33 | 4 46 | 7 12 | 0 30 | 4 58 | 6 59 | 0 26 |
| 8 | S | 4 13 | 7 44 | 0 55 | 4 31 | 7 27 | 0 55 | 4 46 | 7 13 | 0 55 | 4 58 | 7 00 | 0 56 |
| 9 | M | 4 13 | 7 45 | 1 12 | 4 31 | 7 28 | 1 17 | 4 46 | 7 13 | 1 20 | 4 58 | 7 00 | 1 24 |
| 10 | Tu | 4 13 | 7 46 | 1 30 | 4 31 | 7 28 | 1 39 | 4 46 | 7 13 | 1 45 | 4 58 | 7 00 | 1 52 |
| 11 | W | 4 13 | 7 46 | 1 50 | 4 31 | 7 29 | 2 03 | 4 46 | 7 14 | 2 14 | 4 58 | 7 01 | 2 23 |
| 12 | Th | 4 13 | 7 47 | 2 15 | 4 30 | 7 29 | 2 31 | 4 45 | 7 14 | 2 45 | 4 58 | 7 01 | 2 57 |
| 13 | Fr | 4 13 | 7 47 | 2 44 | 4 30 | 7 30 | 3 05 | 4 45 | 7 15 | 3 21 | 4 58 | 7 02 | 3 36 |
| 14 | Sa | 4 13 | 7 48 | 3 21 | 4 30 | 7 30 | 3 45 | 4 45 | 7 15 | 4 04 | 4 58 | 7 02 | 4 20 |
| | | | | sets | | | sets | | | sets | | | sets |
| 15 | S | 4 13 | 7 48 | 9 05 | 4 30 | 7 30 | 8 41 | 4 45 | 7 15 | 8 22 | 4 58 | 7 02 | 8 05 |
| 16 | M | 4 13 | 7 49 | 9 46 | 4 30 | 7 31 | 9 24 | 4 45 | 7 16 | 9 07 | 4 58 | 7 03 | 8 51 |
| 17 | Tu | 4 13 | 7 49 | 10 18 | 4 31 | 7 31 | 10 00 | 4 46 | 7 16 | 9 45 | 4 59 | 7 03 | 9 32 |
| 18 | W | 4 13 | 7 50 | 10 45 | 4 31 | 7 32 | 10 29 | 4 46 | 7 17 | 10 17 | 4 59 | 7 04 | 10 07 |
| 19 | Th | 4 13 | 7 50 | 11 06 | 4 31 | 7 32 | 10 56 | 4 46 | 7 17 | 10 46 | 4 59 | 7 04 | 10 38 |
| 20 | Fr | 4 13 | 7 50 | 11 24 | 4 32 | 7 32 | 11 17 | 4 46 | 7 17 | 11 11 | 4 59 | 7 04 | 11 06 |
| 21 | Sa | 4 13 | 7 50 | 11 41 | 4 31 | 7 32 | 11 39 | 4 46 | 7 17 | 11 36 | 4 59 | 7 04 | 11 34 |
| 22 | S | 4 14 | 7 51 | 11 58 | 4 32 | 7 33 | 11 58 | 4 47 | 7 18 | . . . . | 5 00 | 7 05 | . . . . |
| 23 | M | 4 14 | 7 51 | . . . . | 4 32 | 7 33 | . . . . | 4 47 | 7 18 | 0 00 | 5 00 | 7 05 | 0 01 |
| 24 | Tu | 4 14 | 7 51 | 0 15 | 4 32 | 7 33 | 0 21 | 4 47 | 7 18 | 0 25 | 5 00 | 7 05 | 0 29 |
| 25 | W | 4 14 | 7 51 | 0 35 | 4 32 | 7 33 | 0 45 | 4 47 | 7 18 | 0 53 | 5 00 | 7 05 | 1 01 |
| 26 | Th | 4 15 | 7 51 | 1 00 | 4 33 | 7 33 | 1 14 | 4 48 | 7 18 | 1 27 | 5 01 | 7 05 | 1 37 |
| 27 | Fr | 4 15 | 7 51 | 1 32 | 4 33 | 7 33 | 1 51 | 4 48 | 7 18 | 2 07 | 5 01 | 7 05 | 2 22 |
| 28 | Sa | 4 16 | 7 51 | 2 17 | 4 34 | 7 33 | 2 40 | 4 49 | 7 18 | 2 59 | 5 02 | 7 05 | 3 16 |
| | | | | rises | | | rises | | | rises | | | rises |
| 29 | S | 4 16 | 7 51 | 8 29 | 4 34 | 7 33 | 8 06 | 4 49 | 7 18 | 7 46 | 5 02 | 7 05 | 7 29 |
| 30 | M | 4 17 | 7 51 | 9 18 | 4 34 | 7 33 | 8 58 | 4 49 | 7 18 | 8 42 | 5 02 | 7 05 | 8 27 |

## Sun on 75th Meridian (Local Mean Time)

| Day | h. m. s. | Day | h. m. s. | Day | h. m. s. | Day | h. m. s. | Day | h. m. s. |
|---|---|---|---|---|---|---|---|---|---|
| 1 | 11 57 38 | 7 | 11 58 37 | 13 | 11 59 48 | 19 | 12 01 06 | 25 | 12 02 24 |
| 2 | 11 57 47 | 8 | 11 58 48 | 14 | 12 00 01 | 20 | 12 01 19 | 26 | 12 02 36 |
| 3 | 11 57 56 | 9 | 11 59 00 | 15 | 12 00 14 | 21 | 12 01 32 | 27 | 12 02 49 |
| 4 | 11 58 06 | 10 | 11 59 12 | 16 | 12 00 27 | 22 | 12 01 45 | 28 | 12 03 01 |
| 5 | 11 58 16 | 11 | 11 59 24 | 17 | 12 00 39 | 23 | 12 01 58 | 29 | 12 03 13 |
| 6 | 11 58 26 | 12 | 11 59 36 | 18 | 12 00 53 | 24 | 12 02 11 | 30 | 12 03 25 |

## Twilight (Local Mean Time)

| Place | June | Begins | Ends | June | Begins | Ends | June | Begins | Ends |
|---|---|---|---|---|---|---|---|---|---|
| | | h. m. | h. m. | | h. m. | h. m. | | h. m. | h. m. |
| 45° N. Lat.. | 1 | 1 54 | 10 05 | 11 | 1 43 | 10 18 | 21 | 1 40 | 10 21 |
| 40° N. Lat.. | 1 | 2 35 | 9 22 | 11 | 2 29 | 9 31 | 21 | 2 28 | 9 35 |
| 35° N. Lat.. | 1 | 3 03 | 8 53 | 11 | 2 59 | 9 00 | 21 | 3 00 | 9 05 |
| 30° N. Lat.. | 1 | 3 25 | 8 31 | 11 | 3 22 | 8 37 | 21 | 3 22 | 8 41 |

## Moon Phases, 1969 (Eastern Standard Time)

| Moon | day | hour | min. | a.m. or p.m. | Moon | day | hour | min. | a.m. or p.m. |
|---|---|---|---|---|---|---|---|---|---|
| Last Quarter | 6 | 10 | 39 | P.M. | First Quarter | 22 | 8 | 44 | P.M. |
| New Moon | 14 | 6 | 09 | P.M. | Full Moon | 29 | 3 | 04 | P.M. |

**Morning Stars**—Mercury; Venus; Saturn.          **Evening Stars**—Mars; Jupiter.

## 7th Month     JULY, 1969     31 Days

**Local Mean Time**, A.M., light figures: **P.M.**, black (0 designates midnight; 12 designates noon)
CAUTION—Must be converted to ordinary clock time (**STANDARD TIME**)—See page 277.

| Day of the Month | Day of the Week | 45° N. Latitude Idaho, Iowa (No.), Me., Mich. (Except Far So.), Minn., Mont., N. H., N. Y. (upstate), N. D., Ore., S. D., Vt., Wash., Wis., Wyo. (No. & Cent.). | | | 40° N. Latitude Calif. (No.), Colo., Conn., Del., D.C., Ill., Ind., Iowa (So. & Cent.), Kans., Ky. (No. & Cent.), Mass., Md., Mich. (Far So.), Mo. (No. & Cent.), Nebr., Nev. (No. & Cent.), N.J., N.Y. City, N.Y. (So.), Ohio, Pa., R.I., Utah, W.Va., Wyo. (So.). | | | 35° N. Latitude Alabama (No.), Ariz. (Except Far So.), Ark., Calif. (So.), Georgia (No.), Missouri (So.), N. Mex. (Except Far So.), Nevada (So.), N.C., Okla., S.C., Tenn., Tex. (No.), Va. (So.). | | | 30° N. Latitude Alabama (So.), Ariz. (Far So.), Fla., Georgia (So.), La., Miss. (So.), N. Mex. (Far So.) Tex. (So. & Cent.) | | |
|---|---|---|---|---|---|---|---|---|---|---|---|---|---|
| | | Sun Rises | Sun Sets | Moon R.&S. | Sun Rises | Sun Sets | Moon R.&S. | Sun Rises | Sun Sets | Moon R.&S. | Sun Rises | Sun Sets | Moon R.&S. |
| | | h. m. | h. m. | h. m. rises | h. m. | h. m. | h. m. rises | h. m. | h. m. | h. m. rises | h. m. | h. m. | h. m. rises |
| 1 | Tu | 4 17 | 7 51 | 9 53 | 4 35 | 7 33 | 9 38 | 4 50 | 7 18 | 9 26 | 5 02 | 7 05 | 9 14 |
| 2 | W | 4 18 | 7 50 | 10 20 | 4 35 | 7 32 | 10 10 | 4 50 | 7 18 | 10 01 | 5 03 | 7 05 | 9 54 |
| 3 | Th | 4 18 | 7 50 | 10 41 | 4 36 | 7 32 | 10 36 | 4 51 | 7 18 | 10 30 | 5 03 | 7 05 | 10 27 |
| 4 | Fr | 4 19 | 7 50 | 11 00 | 4 36 | 7 32 | 10 59 | 4 51 | 7 18 | 10 58 | 5 03 | 7 05 | 10 57 |
| 5 | Sa | 4 20 | 7 50 | 11 18 | 4 37 | 7 32 | 11 21 | 4 51 | 7 18 | 11 23 | 5 04 | 7 05 | 11 26 |
| 6 | S | 4 20 | 7 49 | 11 36 | 4 37 | 7 32 | 11 43 | 4 52 | 7 18 | 11 49 | 5 04 | 7 05 | 11 55 |
| 7 | M | 4 21 | 7 49 | 11 55 | 4 38 | 7 31 | .... | 4 52 | 7 17 | .... | 5 05 | 7 04 | .... |
| 8 | Tu | 4 21 | 7 48 | .... | 4 38 | 7 31 | 0 07 | 4 53 | 7 17 | 0 17 | 5 05 | 7 04 | 0 25 |
| 9 | W | 4 22 | 7 48 | 0 18 | 4 39 | 7 31 | 0 34 | 4 53 | 7 17 | 0 46 | 5 06 | 7 04 | 0 58 |
| 10 | Th | 4 23 | 7 47 | 0 46 | 4 40 | 7 31 | 1 05 | 4 54 | 7 17 | 1 21 | 5 06 | 7 04 | 1 36 |
| 11 | Fr | 4 24 | 7 47 | 1 21 | 4 41 | 7 30 | 1 42 | 4 54 | 7 16 | 2 01 | 5 07 | 7 04 | 2 18 |
| 12 | Sa | 4 24 | 7 46 | 2 05 | 4 41 | 7 30 | 2 28 | 4 55 | 7 16 | 2 49 | 5 07 | 7 03 | 3 05 |
| 13 | S | 4 25 | 7 46 | 2 58 | 4 42 | 7 29 | 3 22 | 4 55 | 7 15 | 3 41 | 5 08 | 7 03 | 3 58 |
| | | | | sets | | | sets | | | sets | | | sets |
| 14 | M | 4 26 | 7 45 | 8 20 | 4 43 | 7 29 | 8 02 | 4 56 | 7 15 | 7 46 | 5 08 | 7 03 | 7 31 |
| 15 | Tu | 4 27 | 7 44 | 8 48 | 4 44 | 7 28 | 8 33 | 4 57 | 7 14 | 8 19 | 5 09 | 7 03 | 8 08 |
| 16 | W | 4 28 | 7 43 | 9 11 | 4 45 | 7 27 | 9 00 | 4 58 | 7 14 | 8 49 | 5 10 | 7 02 | 8 40 |
| 17 | Th | 4 29 | 7 43 | 9 30 | 4 45 | 7 27 | 9 22 | 4 58 | 7 13 | 9 16 | 5 10 | 7 02 | 9 09 |
| 18 | Fr | 4 30 | 7 42 | 9 47 | 4 46 | 7 26 | 9 44 | 4 59 | 7 13 | 9 39 | 5 11 | 7 01 | 9 37 |
| 19 | Sa | 4 31 | 7 41 | 10 04 | 4 47 | 7 25 | 10 03 | 5 00 | 7 12 | 10 03 | 5 11 | 7 01 | 10 04 |
| 20 | S | 4 32 | 7 40 | 10 19 | 4 48 | 7 24 | 10 23 | 5 01 | 7 11 | 10 27 | 5 12 | 7 01 | 10 31 |
| 21 | M | 4 33 | 7 39 | 10 38 | 4 49 | 7 24 | 10 47 | 5 01 | 7 11 | 10 53 | 5 12 | 7 00 | 11 00 |
| 22 | Tu | 4 34 | 7 38 | 10 59 | 4 49 | 7 23 | 11 12 | 5 02 | 7 10 | 11 23 | 5 13 | 7 00 | 11 33 |
| 23 | W | 4 35 | 7 37 | 11 28 | 4 50 | 7 23 | 11 44 | 5 02 | 7 10 | 11 59 | 5 13 | 6 59 | .... |
| 24 | Th | 4 36 | 7 36 | .... | 4 51 | 7 22 | .... | 5 03 | 7 09 | .... | 5 14 | 6 59 | 0 12 |
| 25 | Fr | 4 37 | 7 35 | 0 06 | 4 52 | 7 21 | 0 26 | 5 04 | 7 08 | 0 45 | 5 15 | 6 58 | 1 00 |
| 26 | Sa | 4 38 | 7 34 | 0 57 | 4 53 | 7 20 | 1 21 | 5 05 | 7 08 | 1 41 | 5 15 | 6 58 | 1 59 |
| 27 | S | 4 39 | 7 33 | 2 06 | 4 53 | 7 19 | 2 30 | 5 05 | 7 07 | 2 50 | 5 16 | 6 57 | 3 07 |
| 28 | M | 4 40 | 7 32 | 3 27 | 4 54 | 7 18 | 3 49 | 5 06 | 7 07 | 4 06 | 5 16 | 6 57 | 4 21 |
| | | | | rises | | | rises | | | rises | | | rises |
| 29 | Tu | 4 41 | 7 31 | 8 18 | 4 55 | 7 17 | 8 06 | 5 07 | 7 06 | 7 55 | 5 17 | 6 56 | 7 45 |
| 30 | W | 4 42 | 7 30 | 8 43 | 4 56 | 7 16 | 8 34 | 5 08 | 7 05 | 8 28 | 5 18 | 6 55 | 8 23 |
| 31 | Th | 4 43 | 7 28 | 9 02 | 4 57 | 7 15 | 8 59 | 5 09 | 7 04 | 8 57 | 5 18 | 6 54 | 8 55 |

### Sun on 75th Meridian (Local Mean Time)

| Day | h. m. s. | Day | h. m. s. | Day | h. m. s. | Day | h. m. s. | Day | h. m. s. |
|---|---|---|---|---|---|---|---|---|---|
| 1 | 12 03 37 | 8 | 12 04 52 | 14 | 12 05 41 | 20 | 12 06 14 | 26 | 12 06 26 |
| 2 | 12 03 49 | 9 | 12 05 01 | 15 | 12 05 48 | 21 | 12 06 17 | 27 | 12 06 26 |
| 3 | 12 04 00 | 10 | 12 05 10 | 16 | 12 05 54 | 22 | 12 06 20 | 28 | 12 06 25 |
| 4 | 12 04 11 | 11 | 12 05 18 | 17 | 12 06 00 | 23 | 12 06 23 | 29 | 12 06 24 |
| 5 | 12 04 21 | 12 | 12 05 26 | 18 | 12 06 05 | 24 | 12 06 25 | 30 | 12 06 22 |
| 6 | 12 04 32 | 13 | 12 05 34 | 19 | 12 06 10 | 25 | 12 06 25 | 31 | 12 06 19 |
| 7 | 12 04 42 | | | | | | | | |

### Twilight (Local Mean Time)

| Place | July | Begins | Ends | July | Begins | Ends | July | Begins | Ends |
|---|---|---|---|---|---|---|---|---|---|
| | | h. m. | h. m. | | h. m. | h. m. | | h. m. | h. m. |
| 45° N. Lat.. | 1 | 1 45 | 10 22 | 11 | 1 59 | 10 11 | 21 | 2 17 | 9 53 |
| 40° N. Lat.. | 1 | 2 31 | 9 35 | 11 | 2 38 | 9 29 | 21 | 2 53 | 9 18 |
| 35° N. Lat.. | 1 | 3 02 | 9 05 | 11 | 3 09 | 9 00 | 21 | 3 19 | 8 52 |
| 30° N. Lat.. | 1 | 3 26 | 8 41 | 11 | 3 31 | 8 38 | 21 | 3 38 | 8 33 |

### Moon Phases, 1969 (Eastern Standard Time)

| Moon | day | hour | min. a.m. or p.m. | Moon | day | hour | min. a.m. or p.m. |
|---|---|---|---|---|---|---|---|
| Last Quarter .... | 6 | 8 | 17   A.M. | First Quarter .. | 22 | 7 | 10   A.M. |
| New Moon ....... | 14 | 9 | 11   A.M. | Full Moon ....... | 28 | 9 | 45   P.M. |

**Morning Stars**—Mercury (Jul. 1-22); Venus; Saturn.
**Evening Stars**—Mercury (Jul. 22-31); Mars; Jupiter.

## 8th Month          AUGUST, 1969          31 Days

**Local Mean Time, A.M., light figures: P.M., black** (0 designates midnight; 12 designates noon)
**CAUTION**—Must be converted to ordinary clock time (**STANDARD TIME**)—See page 277.

| Day of the Month | Day of the Week | 45° N. Latitude — Idaho, Iowa (No.), Me., Mich. (Except Far So.), Minn., Mont., N. H., N. Y. (Upstate), N. D., Ore., S. D., Vt., Wash., Wis., Wyo. (No. & Cent.). | | | 40° N. Latitude — Calif. (No.), Colo., Conn., Del., D. C., Ill., Ind., Iowa (So. & Cent.), Kans., Ky. (No. & Cent.), Mass., Md., Mich. (Far So.), Mo. (No. & Cent.), Nebr., Nev. (No. & Cent.), N. J., N. Y. City, N. Y. (So.), Ohio, Pa., R. I., Utah, W. Va., Wyo. (So.). | | | 35° N. Latitude — Alabama (No.), Ariz. (Except Far So.), Ark., Calif. (So.), Georgia (No.), Missouri (So.), N. Mex. (Except Far So.), Nevada (So.), N. C., Okla., S. C., Tenn., Tex. (No.), Va. (So.). | | | 30° N. Latitude — Alabama (So.), Ariz. (Far So.), Fla., Georgia (So.), La., Miss. (So.), N. Mex. (Far So.), Tex. (So. & Cent.). | | |
|---|---|---|---|---|---|---|---|---|---|---|---|---|---|
| | | Sun Rises | Sun Sets | Moon R. & S. | Sun Rises | Sun Sets | Moon R. & S. | Sun Rises | Sun Sets | Moon R. & S. | Sun Rises | Sun Sets | Moon R. & S. |
| | | h. m. | h. m. | h. m. | h. m. | h. m. | h. m. | h. m. | h. m. | h. m. | h. m. | h. m. | h. m. |
| | | | | *rises* | | | *rises* | | | *rises* | | | *rises* |
| 1 | Fr | 4 45 | 7 27 | 9 21 | 4 58 | 7 14 | 9 23 | 5 09 | 7 03 | 9 24 | 5 19 | 6 54 | 9 25 |
| 2 | Sa | 4 46 | 7 25 | 9 39 | 4 59 | 7 13 | 9 45 | 5 10 | 7 02 | 9 51 | 5 19 | 6 53 | 9 54 |
| 3 | S | 4 47 | 7 24 | 9 59 | 5 00 | 7 12 | 10 09 | 5 11 | 7 01 | 10 18 | 5 20 | 6 52 | 10 25 |
| 4 | M | 4 48 | 7 23 | 10 20 | 5 01 | 7 11 | 10 35 | 5 12 | 7 00 | 10 47 | 5 21 | 6 51 | 10 58 |
| 5 | Tu | 4 49 | 7 22 | 10 47 | 5 02 | 7 10 | 11 05 | 5 12 | 6 59 | 11 21 | 5 21 | 6 50 | 11 33 |
| 6 | W | 4 51 | 7 20 | 11 19 | 5 03 | 7 08 | 11 41 | 5 13 | 6 58 | 11 59 | 5 22 | 6 50 | .... |
| 7 | Th | 4 52 | 7 19 | .... | 5 04 | 7 07 | .... | 5 13 | 6 57 | .... | 5 22 | 6 49 | 0 14 |
| 8 | Fr | 4 53 | 7 18 | 0 01 | 5 05 | 7 06 | 0 25 | 5 14 | 6 56 | 0 44 | 5 23 | 6 48 | 1 00 |
| 9 | Sa | 4 54 | 7 16 | 0 51 | 5 06 | 7 05 | 1 15 | 5 15 | 6 55 | 1 35 | 5 24 | 6 47 | 1 53 |
| 10 | S | 4 55 | 7 15 | 1 50 | 5 07 | 7 04 | 2 13 | 5 16 | 6 54 | 2 31 | 5 24 | 6 46 | 2 47 |
| 11 | M | 4 57 | 7 14 | 2 54 | 5 07 | 7 02 | 3 15 | 5 16 | 6 53 | 3 30 | 5 25 | 6 45 | 3 45 |
| 12 | Tu | 4 58 | 7 12 | 4 01 | 5 08 | 7 01 | 4 18 | 5 17 | 6 52 | 4 30 | 5 25 | 6 44 | 4 43 |
| | | | | *sets* | | | *sets* | | | *sets* | | | *sets* |
| 13 | W | 4 59 | 7 10 | 7 36 | 5 09 | 7 00 | 7 27 | 5 18 | 6 51 | 7 20 | 5 26 | 6 43 | 7 12 |
| 14 | Th | 5 00 | 7 08 | 7 54 | 5 10 | 6 59 | 7 49 | 5 19 | 6 50 | 7 44 | 5 27 | 6 42 | 7 41 |
| 15 | Fr | 5 01 | 7 07 | 8 11 | 5 11 | 6 57 | 8 09 | 5 20 | 6 49 | 8 08 | 5 27 | 6 41 | 8 08 |
| 16 | Sa | 5 03 | 7 06 | 8 27 | 5 12 | 6 56 | 8 29 | 5 20 | 6 47 | 8 32 | 5 28 | 6 40 | 8 35 |
| 17 | S | 5 04 | 7 04 | 8 44 | 5 13 | 6 54 | 8 50 | 5 21 | 6 46 | 8 57 | 5 28 | 6 39 | 9 03 |
| 18 | M | 5 05 | 7 02 | 9 04 | 5 14 | 6 53 | 9 15 | 5 22 | 6 45 | 9 25 | 5 29 | 6 38 | 9 33 |
| 19 | Tu | 5 06 | 7 00 | 9 29 | 5 15 | 6 52 | 9 45 | 5 23 | 6 44 | 9 58 | 5 30 | 6 37 | 10 10 |
| 20 | W | 5 07 | 6 59 | 10 01 | 5 16 | 6 50 | 10 21 | 5 24 | 6 43 | 10 38 | 5 30 | 6 36 | 10 53 |
| 21 | Th | 5 09 | 6 58 | 10 46 | 5 17 | 6 49 | 11 10 | 5 24 | 6 41 | 11 29 | 5 31 | 6 35 | 11 46 |
| 22 | Fr | 5 10 | 6 56 | 11 45 | 5 18 | 6 47 | .... | 5 25 | 6 40 | .... | 5 31 | 6 34 | .... |
| 23 | Sa | 5 11 | 6 54 | .... | 5 19 | 6 46 | 0 10 | 5 26 | 6 39 | 0 30 | 5 32 | 6 33 | 0 47 |
| 24 | S | 5 12 | 6 52 | 1 00 | 5 20 | 6 44 | 1 23 | 5 27 | 6 38 | 1 41 | 5 33 | 6 32 | 1 57 |
| 25 | M | 5 13 | 6 50 | 2 24 | 5 21 | 6 43 | 2 42 | 5 27 | 6 37 | 2 59 | 5 33 | 6 31 | 3 12 |
| 26 | Tu | 5 15 | 6 49 | 3 51 | 5 22 | 6 42 | 4 05 | 5 28 | 6 35 | 4 16 | 5 34 | 6 29 | 4 26 |
| | | | | *rises* | | | *rises* | | | *rises* | | | *rises* |
| 27 | W | 5 16 | 6 47 | 7 04 | 5 23 | 6 40 | 6 59 | 5 28 | 6 34 | 6 55 | 5 34 | 6 28 | 6 50 |
| 28 | Th | 5 17 | 6 45 | 7 23 | 5 24 | 6 38 | 7 23 | 5 29 | 6 33 | 7 22 | 5 35 | 6 27 | 7 22 |
| 29 | Fr | 5 18 | 6 43 | 7 42 | 5 25 | 6 36 | 7 46 | 5 30 | 6 32 | 7 49 | 5 35 | 6 26 | 7 52 |
| 30 | Sa | 5 19 | 6 41 | 8 01 | 5 26 | 6 35 | 8 09 | 5 30 | 6 30 | 8 17 | 5 36 | 6 25 | 8 22 |
| 31 | S | 5 21 | 6 40 | 8 22 | 5 26 | 6 34 | 8 35 | 5 31 | 6 29 | 8 46 | 5 36 | 6 24 | 8 55 |

## Sun on 75th Meridian (Local Mean Time)

| Day | h. m. s. | Day | h. m. s. | Day | h. m. s. | Day | h. m. s. | Day | h. m. s. |
|---|---|---|---|---|---|---|---|---|---|
| 1 | 12 06 16 | 8 | 12 05 38 | 14 | 12 04 43 | 20 | 12 03 28 | 26 | 12 01 56 |
| 2 | 12 06 13 | 9 | 12 05 30 | 15 | 12 04 32 | 21 | 12 03 14 | 27 | 12 01 39 |
| 3 | 12 06 08 | 10 | 12 05 22 | 16 | 12 04 20 | 22 | 12 02 59 | 28 | 12 01 21 |
| 4 | 12 06 03 | 11 | 12 05 13 | 17 | 12 04 08 | 23 | 12 02 44 | 29 | 12 01 04 |
| 5 | 12 05 58 | 12 | 12 05 04 | 18 | 12 03 55 | 24 | 12 02 28 | 30 | 12 00 46 |
| 6 | 12 05 52 | 13 | 12 04 54 | 19 | 12 03 42 | 25 | 12 02 12 | 31 | 12 00 27 |
| 7 | 12 05 45 | | | | | | | | |

## Twilight (Local Mean Time)

| Place | Aug. | Begins h. m. | Ends h. m. | Aug. | Begins h. m. | Ends h. m. | Aug. | Begins h. m. | Ends h. m. |
|---|---|---|---|---|---|---|---|---|---|
| 45° N. Lat.. | 1 | 2 36 | 9 33 | 11 | 2 58 | 9 11 | 21 | 3 16 | 8 47 |
| 40° N. Lat.. | 1 | 3 08 | 9 03 | 11 | 3 23 | 8 46 | 21 | 3 36 | 8 28 |
| 35° N. Lat.. | 1 | 3 30 | 8 41 | 11 | 3 42 | 8 26 | 21 | 3 52 | 8 12 |
| 30° N. Lat.. | 1 | 3 47 | 8 23 | 11 | 3 56 | 8 12 | 21 | 4 05 | 7 59 |

## Moon Phases, 1969 (Eastern Standard Time)

| Moon | day | hour | min. a.m. or p.m. | Moon | day | hour | min. a.m. or p.m. |
|---|---|---|---|---|---|---|---|
| Last Quarter ..... | 4 | 8 | 38 P.M. | First Quarter .. | 20 | 3 | 03 P.M. |
| New Moon ....... | 13 | 0 | 17 A.M. | Full Moon ...... | 27 | 5 | 32 A.M. |

**Morning Stars**—Venus; Saturn.    **Evening Stars**—Mercury; Mars; Jupiter.

## 9th Month     SEPTEMBER, 1969     30 Days

Local Mean Time, A.M., light figures: **P.M.**, black (0 designates midnight; 12 designates noon)
CAUTION—Must be converted to ordinary clock time (STANDARD TIME)—See page 277.

| Day of the Month | Day of the Week | 45° N. Latitude Idaho, Iowa (No.), Me., Mich. (Except Far So.), Minn., Mont., N. H., N. Y. (upstate), N. D., Ore., S. D., Vt., Wash., Wis., Wyo. (No. & Cent.). | | | 40° N. Latitude Calif. (No.), Colo., Conn. Del., D.C., Ill., Ind., Iowa (So. & Cent.), Kans., Ky. (No. & Cent.), Mass., Md., Mich. (Far So.), Mo. (No. & Cent.), Nebr., Nev. (No. & Cent.), N.J., N.Y. City, N.Y. (So.), Ohio, Pa., R.I., Utah, W.Va., Wyo. (So.). | | | 35° N. Latitude Alabama (No.), Ariz (Except Far So.), Ark., Calif. (So.), Georgia (No.), Missouri (So.), N. Mex. (Except Far So.), Nevada (So.), N.C., Okla., S.C., Tenn., Tex (No.), Va. (So.). | | | 30° N. Latitude Alabama (So.), Ariz. (Far So.), Fla., Georgia (So.), La., Miss. (So.), N. Mex. (Far So.), Tex. (So. & Cent.). | | |
|---|---|---|---|---|---|---|---|---|---|---|---|---|---|
| | | Sun Rises | Sun Sets | Moon R. & S. | Sun Rises | Sun Sets | Moon R. & S. | Sun Rises | Sun Sets | Moon R. & S. | Sun Rises | Sun Sets | Moon R. & S. |
| | | h. m. | h. m. | h. m. rises | h. m. | h. m. | h. m. rises | h. m. | h. m. | h. m. rises | h. m. | h. m. | h. m. rises |
| 1 | M | 5 22 | 6 38 | 8 47 | 5 27 | 6 32 | 9 04 | 5 32 | 6 27 | 9 19 | 5 37 | 6 23 | 9 30 |
| 2 | Tu | 5 23 | 6 36 | 9 18 | 5 28 | 6 30 | 9 38 | 5 33 | 6 26 | 9 55 | 5 37 | 6 22 | 10 10 |
| 3 | W | 5 24 | 6 34 | 9 57 | 5 29 | 6 28 | 10 19 | 5 34 | 6 25 | 10 39 | 5 38 | 6 21 | 10 55 |
| 4 | Th | 5 25 | 6 32 | 10 43 | 5 30 | 6 27 | 11 08 | 5 35 | 6 23 | 11 28 | 5 38 | 6 20 | 11 45 |
| 5 | Fr | 5 27 | 6 31 | 11 39 | 5 31 | 6 26 | .... | 5 35 | 6 22 | .... | 5 39 | 6 18 | .... |
| 6 | Sa | 5 28 | 6 29 | .... | 5 32 | 6 24 | 0 03 | 5 36 | 6 20 | 0 22 | 5 39 | 6 17 | 0 39 |
| 7 | S | 5 29 | 6 27 | 0 43 | 5 33 | 6 22 | 1 03 | 5 37 | 6 19 | 1 21 | 5 40 | 6 16 | 1 36 |
| 8 | M | 5 30 | 6 25 | 1 50 | 5 34 | 6 20 | 2 07 | 5 38 | 6 18 | 2 21 | 5 41 | 6 15 | 2 34 |
| 9 | Tu | 5 31 | 6 23 | 2 57 | 5 35 | 6 19 | 3 10 | 5 38 | 6 16 | 3 21 | 5 41 | 6 14 | 3 32 |
| 10 | W | 5 33 | 6 21 | 4 05 | 5 36 | 6 18 | 4 14 | 5 39 | 6 15 | 4 21 | 5 42 | 6 12 | 4 29 |
| | | | | sets | | | sets | | | sets | | | sets |
| 11 | Th | 5 34 | 6 19 | 6 17 | 5 37 | 6 16 | 6 14 | 5 39 | 6 13 | 6 12 | 3 42 | 6 11 | 6 11 |
| 12 | Fr | 5 35 | 6 17 | 6 34 | 5 38 | 6 14 | 6 35 | 5 40 | 6 12 | 6 36 | 5 43 | 6 10 | 6 38 |
| 13 | Sa | 5 36 | 6 15 | 6 51 | 5 39 | 6 12 | 6 56 | 5 41 | 6 11 | 7 01 | 5 43 | 6 09 | 7 06 |
| 14 | S | 5 37 | 6 13 | 7 10 | 5 40 | 6 11 | 7 20 | 5 42 | 6 09 | 7 29 | 5 44 | 6 07 | 7 36 |
| 15 | M | 5 39 | 6 12 | 7 34 | 5 40 | 6 10 | 7 48 | 5 42 | 6 08 | 8 00 | 5 44 | 6 06 | 8 11 |
| 16 | Tu | 5 40 | 6 10 | 8 03 | 5 41 | 6 08 | 8 22 | 5 43 | 6 06 | 8 37 | 5 45 | 6 04 | 8 51 |
| 17 | W | 5 41 | 6 08 | 8 43 | 5 42 | 6 06 | 9 06 | 5 44 | 6 05 | 9 24 | 5 45 | 6 03 | 9 41 |
| 18 | Th | 5 42 | 6 06 | 9 35 | 5 43 | 6 04 | 10 00 | 5 45 | 6 03 | 10 20 | 5 46 | 6 02 | 10 37 |
| 19 | Fr | 5 43 | 6 04 | 10 43 | 5 44 | 6 03 | 11 07 | 5 46 | 6 02 | 11 28 | 5 46 | 6 01 | 11 45 |
| 20 | Sa | 5 45 | 6 02 | .... | 5 45 | 6 02 | .... | 5 46 | 6 01 | .... | 5 47 | 5 59 | .... |
| 21 | S | 5 46 | 6 00 | 0 02 | 5 46 | 6 00 | 0 22 | 5 47 | 5 59 | 0 40 | 5 47 | 5 58 | 0 54 |
| 22 | M | 5 47 | 5 58 | 1 23 | 5 47 | 5 58 | 1 42 | 5 48 | 5 57 | 1 56 | 5 48 | 5 57 | 2 07 |
| 23 | Tu | 5 48 | 5 56 | 2 50 | 5 48 | 5 56 | 3 00 | 5 49 | 5 56 | 3 08 | 5 49 | 5 56 | 3 17 |
| 24 | W | 5 49 | 5 54 | 4 10 | 5 49 | 5 54 | 4 15 | 5 49 | 5 54 | 4 20 | 5 49 | 5 55 | 4 24 |
| | | | | rises | | | rises | | | rises | | | rises |
| 25 | Th | 5 51 | 5 53 | 5 45 | 5 50 | 5 53 | 5 46 | 5 50 | 5 53 | 5 48 | 5 50 | 5 53 | 5 49 |
| 26 | Fr | 5 52 | 5 51 | 6 04 | 5 51 | 5 51 | 6 10 | 5 50 | 5 51 | 6 15 | 5 50 | 5 52 | 6 19 |
| 27 | Sa | 5 53 | 5 49 | 6 24 | 5 52 | 5 49 | 6 34 | 5 51 | 5 50 | 6 44 | 5 51 | 5 51 | 6 52 |
| 28 | S | 5 54 | 5 47 | 6 48 | 5 53 | 5 47 | 7 03 | 5 52 | 5 49 | 7 14 | 5 52 | 5 50 | 7 26 |
| 29 | M | 5 55 | 5 45 | 7 16 | 5 54 | 5 46 | 7 34 | 5 53 | 5 47 | 7 50 | 5 52 | 5 49 | 8 05 |
| 30 | Tu | 5 57 | 5 43 | 7 51 | 5 55 | 5 45 | 8 14 | 5 53 | 5 46 | 8 31 | 5 53 | 5 47 | 8 48 |

### Sun on 75th Meridian (Local Mean Time)

| Day | h. m. s. | Day | h. m. s. | Day | h. m. s. | Day | h. m. s. | Day | h. m. s. |
|---|---|---|---|---|---|---|---|---|---|
| 1 | 12 00 09 | 7 | 11 58 11 | 13 | 11 56 07 | 19 | 11 53 59 | 25 | 11 51 52 |
| 2 | 11 59 50 | 8 | 11 57 51 | 14 | 11 55 46 | 20 | 11 53 38 | 26 | 11 51 32 |
| 3 | 11 59 30 | 9 | 11 57 30 | 15 | 11 55 24 | 21 | 11 53 17 | 27 | 11 51 11 |
| 4 | 11 59 11 | 10 | 11 57 09 | 16 | 11 55 03 | 22 | 11 52 55 | 28 | 11 50 51 |
| 5 | 11 58 51 | 11 | 11 56 49 | 17 | 11 54 42 | 23 | 11 52 34 | 29 | 11 50 31 |
| 6 | 11 58 31 | 12 | 11 56 28 | 18 | 11 54 21 | 24 | 11 52 13 | 30 | 11 50 11 |

### Twilight (Local Mean Time)

| Place | Sept. | Begins | Ends | Sept. | Begins | Ends | Sept. | Begins | Ends |
|---|---|---|---|---|---|---|---|---|---|
| | | h. m. | h. m. | | h. m. | h. m. | | h. m. | h. m. |
| 45° N. Lat.. | 1 | 3 35 | 8 23 | 11 | 3 49 | 8 00 | 21 | 4 05 | 7 35 |
| 40° N. Lat.. | 1 | 3 51 | 8 07 | 11 | 4 03 | 7 49 | 21 | 4 14 | 7 27 |
| 35° N. Lat.. | 1 | 4 04 | 7 56 | 11 | 4 13 | 7 36 | 21 | 4 22 | 7 24 |
| 30° N. Lat.. | 1 | 4 15 | 7 46 | 11 | 4 21 | 7 32 | 21 | 4 28 | 7 18 |

### Moon Phases, 1969 (Eastern Standard Time)

| Moon | day | hour | min. a.m. or p.m. | Moon | day | hour | min. a.m. or p.m. |
|---|---|---|---|---|---|---|---|
| Last Quarter .... | 3 | 11 | 58 A.M. | First Quarter .. | 18 | 9 | 25 P.M. |
| New Moon ....... | 11 | 2 | 56 P.M. | Full Moon ..... | 25 | 3 | 21 P.M. |

Morning Stars—Mercury (Sept. 29-30); Venus; Saturn.     Evening Stars—Mercury (Sept. 1-29); Mars; Jupiter.

## 10th Month        OCTOBER, 1969       31 Days

Local Mean Time. A.M., light figures: **P.M., black** (0 designates midnight: 12 designates noon)
CAUTION—Must be converted to ordinary clock time (STANDARD TIME)—See page 277.

| Day of the Month | Day of the Week | 45° N. Latitude Idaho, Iowa (No.), Me. Mich (Except Far So.) Minn., Mont., N. H., N. Y. (upstate), N. D., Ore., S. D., Vt., Wash., Wis., Wyo. (No. & Cent.). | | | 40° N. Latitude Calif. (No.), Colo., Conn., Del., D.C., Ill., Ind., Iowa (So. & Cent.), Kans., Ky. (No. & Cent.), Mass., Md., Mich. (Far So.), Mo. (No. & Cent.), Nebr., Nev. (No. & Cent.), N.J., N.Y. City, N.Y. (So.), Ohio, Pa., R.I., Utah, W.Va., Wyo. (So.). | | | 35° N. Latitude Alabama (No.), Ariz (Except Far So.), Ark., Calif. (So.), Georgia (No.), Missouri (So.), N. Mex. (Except Far So.), Nevada (So.), N.C., Okla., S.C., Tenn., Tex. (No.), Va. (So.). | | | 30° N. Latitude Alabama (So.), Ariz, (Far So.), Fla., Georgia (So.), La., Miss. (So.), N. Mex. (Far So.), Tex. (So. & Cent.). | | |
|---|---|---|---|---|---|---|---|---|---|---|---|---|---|
| | | Sun Rises | Sun Sets | Moon R. & S. | Sun Rises | Sun Sets | Moon R. & S. | Sun Rises | Sun Sets | Moon R. & S. | Sun Rises | Sun Sets | Moon R. & S. |
| | | h. m. | h. m. | h. m. rises | h. m. | h. m. | h. m. rises | h. m. | h. m. | h. m. rises | h. m. | h. m. | h. m. rises |
| 1 | W | 5 58 | 5 41 | 8 35 | 5 56 | 5 43 | 8 59 | 5 54 | 5 44 | 9 20 | 5 53 | 5 46 | 9 36 |
| 2 | Th | 5 59 | 5 39 | 9 29 | 5 57 | 5 41 | 9 53 | 5 55 | 5 43 | 10 13 | 5 54 | 5 45 | 10 29 |
| 3 | Fr | 6 00 | 5 37 | 10 29 | 5 58 | 5 39 | 10 51 | 5 56 | 5 42 | 11 10 | 5 55 | 5 44 | 11 28 |
| 4 | Sa | 6 01 | 5 35 | 11 34 | 5 59 | 5 38 | 11 54 | 5 57 | 5 40 | ..... | 5 55 | 5 43 | ..... |
| 5 | S | 6 03 | 5 34 | ..... | 6 00 | 5 37 | ..... | 5 57 | 5 39 | 0 09 | 5 56 | 5 41 | 0 23 |
| 6 | M | 6 04 | 5 32 | 0 42 | 6 01 | 5 35 | 0 57 | 5 58 | 5 37 | 1 09 | 5 56 | 5 40 | 1 21 |
| 7 | Tu | 6 05 | 5 30 | 1 50 | 6 02 | 5 33 | 2 00 | 5 59 | 5 36 | 2 09 | 5 57 | 5 39 | 2 18 |
| 8 | W | 6 06 | 5 28 | 2 57 | 6 03 | 5 32 | 3 04 | 6 00 | 5 35 | 3 09 | 5 58 | 5 38 | 3 15 |
| 9 | Th | 6 07 | 5 26 | 4 05 | 6 04 | 5 30 | 4 07 | 6 01 | 5 33 | 4 09 | 5 58 | 5 37 | 4 11 |
| 10 | Fr | 6 09 | 5 25 | 5 14 | 6 05 | 5 29 | 5 13 | 6 01 | 5 32 | 5 11 | 5 59 | 5 35 | 5 09 |
| 11 | Sa | 6 10 | 5 23 | 6 25 | 6 06 | 5 27 | 6 19 | 6 02 | 5 30 | 6 14 | 5 59 | 5 34 | 6 08 |
| | | | | sets | | | sets | | | sets | | | sets |
| 12 | S | 6 11 | 5 21 | 5 40 | 6 07 | 5 26 | 5 50 | 6 03 | 5 29 | 6 01 | 6 00 | 5 33 | 6 11 |
| 13 | M | 6 12 | 5 19 | 6 05 | 6 08 | 5 24 | 6 22 | 6 04 | 5 28 | 6 37 | 6 01 | 5 32 | 6 50 |
| 14 | Tu | 6 14 | 5 17 | 6 42 | 6 09 | 5 23 | 7 03 | 6 05 | 5 27 | 7 22 | 6 01 | 5 31 | 7 38 |
| 15 | W | 6 15 | 5 16 | 7 32 | 6 10 | 5 22 | 7 55 | 6 05 | 5 25 | 8 16 | 6 02 | 5 30 | 8 33 |
| 16 | Th | 6 17 | 5 14 | 8 34 | 6 11 | 5 20 | 9 00 | 6 06 | 5 24 | 9 20 | 6 02 | 5 29 | 9 37 |
| 17 | Fr | 6 18 | 5 12 | 9 50 | 6 12 | 5 18 | 10 12 | 6 07 | 5 23 | 10 30 | 6 03 | 5 28 | 10 45 |
| 18 | Sa | 6 19 | 5 10 | 11 12 | 6 13 | 5 17 | 11 29 | 6 08 | 5 22 | 11 43 | 6 04 | 5 27 | 11 56 |
| 19 | S | 6 21 | 5 09 | ..... | 6 14 | 5 15 | ..... | 6 09 | 5 21 | ..... | 6 04 | 5 26 | ..... |
| 20 | M | 6 22 | 5 08 | 0 33 | 6 16 | 5 14 | 0 45 | 6 10 | 5 19 | 0 56 | 6 05 | 5 24 | 1 04 |
| 21 | Tu | 6 24 | 5 06 | 1 51 | 6 17 | 5 12 | 2 00 | 6 11 | 5 18 | 2 06 | 6 05 | 5 23 | 2 11 |
| 22 | W | 6 25 | 5 04 | 3 08 | 6 18 | 5 11 | 3 11 | 6 12 | 5 17 | 3 13 | 6 06 | 5 22 | 3 16 |
| 23 | Th | 6 26 | 5 02 | 4 23 | 6 19 | 5 10 | 4 21 | 6 13 | 5 16 | 4 19 | 6 07 | 5 21 | 4 17 |
| 24 | Fr | 6 27 | 5 01 | 5 36 | 6 20 | 5 08 | 5 31 | 6 14 | 5 15 | 5 25 | 6 08 | 5 20 | 5 19 |
| 25 | Sa | 6 29 | 5 00 | 6 41 | 6 21 | 5 07 | 6 40 | 6 14 | 5 13 | 6 30 | 6 08 | 5 20 | 6 21 |
| | | | | rises | | | rises | | | rises | | | rises |
| 26 | S | 6 30 | 4 58 | 5 14 | 6 22 | 5 05 | 5 32 | 6 15 | 5 12 | 5 46 | 6 09 | 5 19 | 5 58 |
| 27 | M | 6 31 | 4 56 | 5 48 | 6 23 | 5 04 | 6 08 | 6 16 | 5 11 | 6 25 | 6 10 | 5 18 | 6 41 |
| 28 | Tu | 6 32 | 4 55 | 6 28 | 6 24 | 5 03 | 6 52 | 6 17 | 5 10 | 7 11 | 6 11 | 5 17 | 7 28 |
| 29 | W | 6 34 | 4 53 | 7 18 | 6 25 | 5 02 | 7 42 | 6 18 | 5 09 | 8 02 | 6 12 | 5 16 | 8 18 |
| 30 | Th | 6 35 | 5 52 | 8 17 | 6 27 | 5 00 | 8 40 | 6 19 | 5 08 | 8 58 | 6 12 | 5 15 | 9 14 |
| 31 | Fr | 6 37 | 4 50 | 9 20 | 6 28 | 4 59 | 9 40 | 6 20 | 5 07 | 9 57 | 6 13 | 5 14 | 10 12 |

### Sun on 75th Meridian (Local Mean Time)

| Day | h. m. s. | Day | h. m. s. | Day | h. m. s. | Day | h. m. s. | Day | h. m. s. |
|---|---|---|---|---|---|---|---|---|---|
| 1 | 11 49 51 | 8 | 11 47 44 | 14 | 11 46 10 | 20 | 11 44 56 | 26 | 11 44 04 |
| 2 | 11 49 32 | 9 | 11 47 27 | 15 | 11 45 56 | 21 | 11 44 46 | 27 | 11 43 58 |
| 3 | 11 49 13 | 10 | 11 47 10 | 16 | 11 45 42 | 22 | 11 44 36 | 28 | 11 43 53 |
| 4 | 11 48 54 | 11 | 11 46 55 | 17 | 11 45 36 | 23 | 11 44 27 | 29 | 11 43 48 |
| 5 | 11 48 36 | 12 | 11 46 39 | 18 | 11 45 19 | 24 | 11 44 18 | 30 | 11 43 44 |
| 6 | 11 48 18 | 13 | 11 46 25 | 19 | 11 45 07 | 25 | 11 44 11 | 31 | 11 43 41 |
| 7 | 11 48 00 | | | | | | | | |

### Twilight (Local Mean Time)

| Place | Oct. | Begins | Ends | Oct. | Begins | Ends | Oct. | Begins | Ends |
|---|---|---|---|---|---|---|---|---|---|
| | | h. m. | h. m. | | h. m. | h. m. | | h. m. | h. m. |
| 45° N. Lat.. | 1 | 4 19 | 7 19 | 11 | 4 32 | 7 00 | 21 | 4 44 | 6 44 |
| 40° N. Lat.. | 1 | 4 25 | 7 13 | 11 | 4 35 | 6 58 | 21 | 4 46 | 6 43 |
| 35° N. Lat.. | 1 | 4 30 | 7 08 | 11 | 4 37 | 6 55 | 21 | 4 46 | 6 44 |
| 30° N. Lat.. | 1 | 4 34 | 7 05 | 11 | 4 39 | 6 54 | 21 | 4 45 | 6 44 |

### Moon Phases, 1969 (Eastern Standard Time)

| Moon | day | hour | min. a.m. or p.m. | Moon | day | hour | min. a.m. or p.m. |
|---|---|---|---|---|---|---|---|
| Last Quarter | 3 | 6 | 05 A.M. | First Quarter | 18 | 3 | 32 A.M. |
| New Moon | 11 | 4 | 39 A.M. | Full Moon | 25 | 3 | 44 A.M. |

**Morning Stars**—Mercury; Venus; Jupiter (Oct. 9-31); Saturn (Oct. 1-29).     **Evening Stars**—Mars; Jupiter (Oct. 1-9); Saturn (Oct. 29-31).

# 11th Month          NOVEMBER, 1969          30 Days

**Local Mean Time, A.M.,** light figure: **P.M.,** black (0 designates midnight; 12 designates noon)
**CAUTION**—Must be converted to ordinary clock time (**STANDARD TIME**)—See page 277.

| Day of the Month | Day of the Week | 45° N. Latitude Idaho, Iowa (No.), Me., Mich. (Except Far So.), Minn., Mont., N. H., N. Y. (upstate) N. D., Ore., S. D., Vt., Wash., Wis., Wyo. (No. & Cent.). | | | 40° N. Latitude Calif. (No.), Colo., Conn., Del., D. C., Ill., Ind., Iowa (So. & Cent.), Kans., Ky. (No. & Cent.), Mass., Md., Mich. (Far So.), Mo. (No. & Cent.), Nebr., Nev. (No. & Cent.), N. J., N. Y. (So.), N. Y. (So.), Ohio, Pa., R. I., Utah, W. Va., Wyo. (So.). | | | 35° N. Latitude Alabama (No.), Ariz. (Except Far So.), Ark., Calif. (So.), Georgia (No.), Missouri (So.), N. Mex. (Except Far So.), Nevada (So.), N. C., Okla., S. C., Tenn., Tex. (No.), Va. (So.). | | | 30° N. Latitude Alabama (So.), Ariz. (Far So.), Fla., Georgia (So.), La., Miss. (So.), N. Mex. (Far So.), Tex. (So. & Cent.). | | |
|---|---|---|---|---|---|---|---|---|---|---|---|---|
| | | Sun Rises | Sun Sets | Moon R.&S. | Sun Rises | Sun Sets | Moon R.&S. | Sun Rises | Sun Sets | Moon R.&S. | Sun Rises | Sun Sets | Moon R.&S. |
| | | h. m. | h. m. | h. m. rises | h. m. | h. m. | h. m. rises | h. m. | h. m. | h. m. rises | h. m. | h. m. | h. m. rises |
| 1 | Sa | 6 38 | 4 49 | 10 27 | 6 29 | 4 58 | 10 43 | 6 21 | 5 06 | 10 57 | 6 14 | 5 13 | 11 09 |
| 2 | S | 6 39 | 4 48 | 11 34 | 6 30 | 4 57 | 11 46 | 6 22 | 5 05 | 11 56 | 6 15 | 5 12 | .... |
| 3 | M | 6 41 | 4 46 | .... | 6 31 | 4 56 | .... | 6 23 | 5 04 | .... | 6 16 | 5 12 | 0 06 |
| 4 | Tu | 6 42 | 4 45 | 0 41 | 6 33 | 4 54 | 0 49 | 6 24 | 5 04 | 0 55 | 6 16 | 5 11 | 1 02 |
| 5 | W | 6 44 | 4 43 | 1 47 | 6 34 | 4 53 | 1 51 | 6 25 | 5 03 | 1 54 | 6 17 | 5 11 | 1 58 |
| 6 | Th | 6 45 | 4 42 | 2 55 | 6 35 | 4 52 | 2 54 | 6 26 | 5 02 | 2 54 | 6 18 | 5 10 | 2 55 |
| 7 | Fr | 6 46 | 4 41 | 4 04 | 6 36 | 4 51 | 4 01 | 6 27 | 5 01 | 3 57 | 6 19 | 5 09 | 3 53 |
| 8 | Sa | 6 48 | 4 40 | 5 18 | 6 37 | 4 50 | 5 09 | 6 28 | 5 00 | 5 01 | 6 20 | 5 08 | 4 55 |
| 9 | S | 6 49 | 4 38 | 6 37 | 6 38 | 4 50 | 6 22 | 6 28 | 4 59 | 6 10 | 6 20 | 5 08 | 6 01 |
| | | | | sets | | | sets | | | sets | | | sets |
| 10 | M | 6 51 | 4 37 | 4 39 | 6 39 | 4 49 | 4 59 | 6 29 | 4 58 | 5 16 | 6 21 | 5 07 | 5 30 |
| 11 | Tu | 6 52 | 4 36 | 5 24 | 6 40 | 4 48 | 5 48 | 6 30 | 4 57 | 6 07 | 6 22 | 5 06 | 6 24 |
| 12 | W | 6 53 | 4 35 | 6 25 | 6 41 | 4 47 | 6 49 | 6 31 | 4 56 | 7 09 | 6 23 | 5 06 | 7 27 |
| 13 | Th | 6 55 | 4 34 | 7 39 | 6 42 | 4 46 | 8 02 | 6 32 | 4 56 | 8 20 | 6 24 | 5 05 | 8 36 |
| 14 | Fr | 6 56 | 4 33 | 9 01 | 6 44 | 4 45 | 9 19 | 6 33 | 4 55 | 9 34 | 6 24 | 5 05 | 9 48 |
| 15 | Sa | 6 58 | 4 32 | 10 22 | 6 45 | 4 44 | 10 36 | 6 34 | 4 55 | 10 47 | 6 25 | 5 04 | 10 58 |
| 16 | S | 6 59 | 4 31 | 11 42 | 6 46 | 4 43 | 11 57 | 6 35 | 4 54 | 11 58 | 6 26 | 5 04 | .... |
| 17 | M | 7 00 | 4 30 | .... | 6 47 | 4 42 | .... | 6 36 | 4 53 | .... | 6 27 | 5 04 | 0 04 |
| 18 | Tu | 7 01 | 4 29 | 0 58 | 6 48 | 4 42 | 1 01 | 6 37 | 4 53 | 1 05 | 6 28 | 5 03 | 1 07 |
| 19 | W | 7 03 | 4 28 | 2 11 | 6 50 | 4 41 | 2 11 | 6 38 | 4 52 | 2 10 | 6 28 | 5 03 | 2 09 |
| 20 | Th | 7 04 | 4 27 | 3 23 | 6 51 | 4 41 | 3 18 | 6 39 | 4 52 | 3 13 | 6 29 | 5 02 | 3 10 |
| 21 | Fr | 7 05 | 4 26 | 4 35 | 6 52 | 4 40 | 4 26 | 6 40 | 4 51 | 4 17 | 6 30 | 5 02 | 4 11 |
| 22 | Sa | 7 06 | 4 25 | 5 48 | 6 53 | 4 39 | 5 34 | 6 41 | 4 51 | 5 23 | 6 31 | 5 02 | 5 12 |
| 23 | S | 7 08 | 4 25 | 7 01 | 6 54 | 4 39 | 6 42 | 6 42 | 4 51 | 6 26 | 6 32 | 5 02 | 6 14 |
| | | | | rises | | | rises | | | rises | | | rises |
| 24 | M | 7 09 | 4 23 | 4 23 | 6 55 | 4 38 | 4 45 | 6 43 | 4 50 | 5 04 | 6 32 | 5 01 | 5 20 |
| 25 | Tu | 7 11 | 4 24 | 5 09 | 6 56 | 4 38 | 5 34 | 6 44 | 4 50 | 5 53 | 6 33 | 5 01 | 6 10 |
| 26 | W | 7 12 | 4 23 | 6 05 | 6 57 | 4 37 | 6 29 | 6 45 | 4 50 | 6 48 | 6 34 | 5 00 | 7 04 |
| 27 | Th | 7 13 | 4 22 | 7 08 | 6 58 | 4 37 | 7 29 | 6 46 | 4 50 | 7 46 | 6 35 | 5 00 | 8 02 |
| 28 | Fr | 7 14 | 4 22 | 8 14 | 6 59 | 4 36 | 8 30 | 6 47 | 4 50 | 8 46 | 6 36 | 5 00 | 8 59 |
| 29 | Sa | 7 16 | 4 21 | 9 20 | 7 00 | 4 36 | 9 34 | 6 47 | 4 49 | 9 45 | 6 36 | 5 00 | 9 56 |
| 30 | S | 7 17 | 4 21 | 10 26 | 7 01 | 4 35 | 10 36 | 6 48 | 4 49 | 10 44 | 6 37 | 5 00 | 10 50 |

## Sun on 75th Meridian (Local Mean Time)

| Day | h. m. s. | Day | h. m. s. | Day | h. m. s. | Day | h. m. s. | Day | h. m. s. |
|---|---|---|---|---|---|---|---|---|---|
| 1 | 11 43 39 | 7 | 11 43 42 | 13 | 11 44 16 | 19 | 11 45 19 | 25 | 11 46 52 |
| 2 | 11 43 37 | 8 | 11 43 45 | 14 | 11 44 24 | 20 | 11 45 33 | 26 | 11 47 10 |
| 3 | 11 43 36 | 9 | 11 43 50 | 15 | 11 44 33 | 21 | 11 45 47 | 27 | 11 47 29 |
| 4 | 11 43 35 | 10 | 11 43 55 | 16 | 11 44 44 | 22 | 11 46 02 | 28 | 11 47 48 |
| 5 | 11 43 37 | 11 | 11 44 01 | 17 | 11 44 55 | 23 | 11 46 18 | 29 | 11 48 09 |
| 6 | 11 43 39 | 12 | 11 44 08 | 18 | 11 45 07 | 24 | 11 46 35 | 30 | 11 48 30 |

## Twilight (Local Mean Time)

| Place | Nov. | Begins | Ends | Nov. | Begins | Ends | Nov. | Begins | Ends |
|---|---|---|---|---|---|---|---|---|---|
| | | h. m. | h. m. | | h. m. | h. m. | | h. m. | h. m. |
| 45° N. Lat. | 1 | 4 58 | 6 28 | 11 | 5 09 | 6 17 | 21 | 5 21 | 6 09 |
| 40° N. Lat. | 1 | 4 56 | 6 30 | 11 | 5 06 | 6 21 | 21 | 5 16 | 6 15 |
| 35° N. Lat. | 1 | 4 54 | 6 32 | 11 | 5 02 | 6 24 | 21 | 5 11 | 6 19 |
| 30° N. Lat. | 1 | 4 52 | 6 34 | 11 | 4 59 | 6 28 | 21 | 5 06 | 6 25 |

## Moon Phases, 1969 (Eastern Standard Time)

| Moon | day | hour | min. a.m. or p.m. | Moon | day | hour | min. a.m. or p.m. |
|---|---|---|---|---|---|---|---|
| Last Quarter | 2 | 2 | 14 A.M. | First Quarter | 16 | 10 | 45 A.M. |
| New Moon | 9 | 5 | 11 P.M. | Full Moon | 23 | 6 | 54 P.M. |

**Morning Stars**—Mercury (Nov. 1-16); Venus; Ju- | **Evening Stars**—Mercury (Nov. 16-30); Mars; Saturn.

## 12th Month     DECEMBER, 1969     31 Days

**Local Mean Time, A.M., light figures: P.M., black (0 designates midnight; 12 designates noon)**
**CAUTION—Must be converted to ordinary clock time (STANDARD TIME)—See page 277.**

| Day of the Month | Day of the Week | 45° N. Latitude Idaho, Iowa (No.), Me., Mich. (Except Far So.), Minn., Mont., N. H., N. Y. (upstate), N. D., Ore., S. D., Vt., Wash., Wis., Wyo. (No. & Cent.). | | | 40° N. Latitude Calif. (No.), Colo., Conn., Del., D.C., Ill., Ind., Iowa (So. & Cent.), Kans., Ky. (No. & Cent.), Mass., Md., Mich. (Far So.), Mo. (No. & Cent.), Nebr., Nev. (No. & Cent.), N.J., N.Y. City, N.Y. (So.), Ohio, Pa., R.I., Utah, W.Va., Wyo. (So.). | | | 35° N. Latitude Alabama (No.), Ariz. (Except Far So.), Ark., Ky. (So.), Georgia (No.), Missouri (So.), N. Mex. (Except Far So.), Nevada (So.), N.C., Okla., S.C. Tenn., Tex. (No.), Va. (So.). | | | 30° N. Latitude Alabama (So.), Ariz. (Far So.), Fla., Georgia (So.), La., Miss. (So.), N. Mex. (Far So.), Tex. (So. & Cent.). | | |
|---|---|---|---|---|---|---|---|---|---|---|---|---|
| | | Sun Rises | Sun Sets | Moon R. & S. | Sun Rises | Sun Sets | Moon R. & S. | Sun Rises | Sun Sets | Moon R. & S. | Sun Rises | Sun Sets | Moon R. & S. |
| | | h. m. | h. m. | h. m. rises | h. m. | h. m. | h. m. rises | h. m. | h. m. | h. m. rises | h. m. | h. m. | h. m. rises |
| 1 | M | 7 18 | 4 20 | 11 31 | 7 02 | 4 35 | 11 37 | 6 49 | 4 49 | 11 41 | 6 38 | 5 00 | 11 45 |
| 2 | Tu | 7 19 | 4 20 | .... | 7 03 | 4 35 | .... | 6 50 | 4 49 | .... | 6 39 | 5 00 | .... |
| 3 | W | 7 20 | 4 20 | 0 37 | 7 04 | 4 35 | 0 38 | 6 51 | 4 49 | 0 39 | 6 40 | 5 00 | 0 40 |
| 4 | Th | 7 21 | 4 19 | 1 44 | 7 05 | 4 35 | 1 42 | 6 52 | 4 48 | 1 39 | 6 40 | 5 00 | 1 37 |
| 5 | Fr | 7 22 | 4 19 | 2 55 | 7 06 | 4 35 | 2 48 | 6 53 | 4 48 | 2 41 | 6 41 | 5 00 | 2 36 |
| 6 | Sa | 7 23 | 4 19 | 4 09 | 7 07 | 4 35 | 3 57 | 6 54 | 4 48 | 3 48 | 6 42 | 5 00 | 3 39 |
| 7 | S | 7 24 | 4 19 | 5 28 | 7 08 | 4 35 | 5 12 | 6 55 | 4 48 | 4 57 | 6 43 | 5 00 | 4 46 |
| 8 | M | 7 25 | 4 19 | 6 51 | 7 09 | 4 35 | 6 30 | 6 56 | 4 48 | 6 12 | 6 44 | 5 00 | 6 07 |
| | | | | sets | | | sets | | | sets | | | sets |
| 9 | Tu | 7 26 | 4 18 | 4 07 | 7 10 | 4 35 | 4 31 | 6 56 | 4 49 | 4 51 | 6 44 | 5 01 | 5 08 |
| 10 | W | 7 27 | 4 18 | 5 18 | 7 11 | 4 35 | 5 42 | 6 57 | 4 49 | 6 01 | 6 45 | 5 01 | 6 18 |
| 11 | Th | 7 28 | 4 18 | 6 41 | 7 12 | 4 35 | 7 01 | 6 58 | 4 49 | 7 18 | 6 46 | 5 01 | 7 32 |
| 12 | Fr | 7 29 | 4 18 | 8 05 | 7 13 | 4 35 | 8 22 | 6 59 | 4 49 | 8 34 | 6 47 | 5 01 | 8 45 |
| 13 | Sa | 7 30 | 4 18 | 9 29 | 7 13 | 4 35 | 9 39 | 6 59 | 4 49 | 9 47 | 6 48 | 5 01 | 9 56 |
| 14 | S | 7 30 | 4 19 | 10 47 | 7 14 | 4 36 | 10 52 | 7 00 | 4 50 | 10 58 | 6 48 | 5 02 | 11 03 |
| 15 | M | 7 31 | 4 19 | .... | 7 14 | 4 36 | .... | 7 00 | 4 50 | .... | 6 49 | 5 02 | .... |
| 16 | Tu | 7 32 | 4 19 | 0 03 | 7 15 | 4 36 | 0 03 | 7 01 | 4 50 | 0 03 | 6 49 | 5 02 | 0 06 |
| 17 | W | 7 33 | 4 19 | 1 15 | 7 16 | 4 36 | 1 11 | 7 02 | 4 50 | 1 08 | 6 50 | 5 03 | 1 06 |
| 18 | Th | 7 33 | 4 20 | 2 27 | 7 17 | 4 37 | 2 18 | 7 03 | 4 51 | 2 11 | 6 50 | 5 03 | 2 04 |
| 19 | Fr | 7 34 | 4 20 | 3 38 | 7 17 | 4 37 | 3 25 | 7 03 | 4 51 | 3 14 | 6 51 | 5 04 | 3 04 |
| 20 | Sa | 7 34 | 4 21 | 4 50 | 7 18 | 4 38 | 4 32 | 7 04 | 4 52 | 4 18 | 6 51 | 5 04 | 4 06 |
| 21 | S | 7 35 | 4 21 | 6 00 | 7 18 | 4 38 | 5 39 | 7 04 | 4 52 | 5 21 | 6 52 | 5 05 | 5 07 |
| 22 | M | 7 35 | 4 22 | 7 04 | 7 18 | 4 39 | 6 41 | 7 04 | 4 53 | 6 22 | 6 52 | 5 05 | 6 05 |
| | | | | rises | | | rises | | | rises | | | rises |
| 23 | Tu | 7 36 | 4 22 | 3 56 | 7 19 | 4 39 | 4 21 | 7 05 | 4 54 | 4 40 | 6 53 | 5 06 | 4 57 |
| 24 | W | 7 36 | 4 23 | 4 57 | 7 19 | 4 40 | 5 19 | 7 05 | 4 54 | 5 38 | 6 53 | 5 06 | 5 54 |
| 25 | Th | 7 37 | 4 23 | 6 02 | 7 20 | 4 40 | 6 21 | 7 06 | 4 55 | 6 37 | 6 54 | 5 07 | 6 51 |
| 26 | Fr | 7 37 | 4 24 | 7 09 | 7 20 | 4 41 | 7 24 | 7 06 | 4 55 | 7 36 | 6 54 | 5 07 | 7 48 |
| 27 | Sa | 7 37 | 4 25 | 8 15 | 7 20 | 4 42 | 8 26 | 7 06 | 4 56 | 8 35 | 6 54 | 5 08 | 8 44 |
| 28 | S | 7 37 | 4 26 | 9 20 | 7 21 | 4 42 | 9 27 | 7 07 | 4 57 | 9 33 | 6 55 | 5 09 | 9 38 |
| 29 | M | 7 38 | 4 26 | 10 25 | 7 21 | 4 43 | 10 26 | 7 07 | 4 57 | 10 30 | 6 55 | 5 09 | 10 32 |
| 30 | Tu | 7 38 | 4 27 | 11 29 | 7 22 | 4 43 | 11 28 | 7 08 | 4 58 | 11 27 | 6 56 | 5 10 | 11 26 |
| 31 | W | 7 38 | 4 28 | .... | 7 22 | 4 44 | .... | 7 08 | 4 58 | .... | 6 56 | 5 10 | .... |

### Sun on 75th Meridian (Local Mean Time)

| Day | h. m. s. | Day | h. m. s. | Day | h. m. s. | Day | h. m. s. | Day | h. m. s. |
|---|---|---|---|---|---|---|---|---|---|
| 1 | 11 48 52 | 8 | 11 51 42 | 14 | 11 54 27 | 20 | 11 57 23 | 26 | 12 00 21 |
| 2 | 11 49 15 | 9 | 11 52 09 | 15 | 11 54 56 | 21 | 11 57 52 | 27 | 12 00 51 |
| 3 | 11 49 38 | 10 | 11 52 36 | 16 | 11 55 25 | 22 | 11 58 21 | 28 | 12 01 20 |
| 4 | 11 50 01 | 11 | 11 53 03 | 17 | 11 55 54 | 23 | 11 58 52 | 29 | 12 01 50 |
| 5 | 11 50 26 | 12 | 11 53 31 | 18 | 11 56 23 | 24 | 11 59 22 | 30 | 12 02 19 |
| 6 | 11 50 51 | 13 | 11 53 59 | 19 | 11 56 53 | 25 | 11 59 53 | 31 | 12 02 48 |
| 7 | 11 51 16 | | | | | | | | |

### Twilight (Local Mean Time)

| Place | Dec. | Begins | Ends | Dec. | Begins | Ends | Dec. | Begins | Ends |
|---|---|---|---|---|---|---|---|---|---|
| | | h. m. | h. m. | | h. m. | h. m. | | h. m. | h. m. |
| 45° N. Lat. | 1 | 5 32 | 6 05 | 11 | 5 41 | 6 04 | 21 | 5 47 | 6 08 |
| 40° N. Lat. | 1 | 5 25 | 6 11 | 11 | 5 34 | 6 12 | 21 | 5 40 | 6 16 |
| 35° N. Lat. | 1 | 5 20 | 6 19 | 11 | 5 27 | 6 19 | 21 | 5 32 | 6 23 |
| 30° N. Lat. | 1 | 5 13 | 6 25 | 11 | 5 20 | 6 26 | 21 | 5 25 | 6 31 |

### Moon Phases, 1969 (Eastern Standard Time)

| Moon | day | hour | min. a.m. or p.m. | Moon | day | hour | min. a.m. or p.m. |
|---|---|---|---|---|---|---|---|
| Last Quarter | 1 | 10 | 50 P.M. | First Quarter | 15 | 8 | 09 P.M. |
| New Moon | 9 | 4 | 42 A.M. | Full Moon | 23 | 12 | 35 P.M. |
| | | | | Last Quarter | 31 | 5 | 52 P.M. |

**Morning Stars—Venus; Jupiter.**     **Evening Stars—Mercury; Mars; Saturn.**

**1st Month**     **JANUARY, 1970**     **31 Days**

Local Mean Time, A.M., light figures: **P.M.**, black (0 designates midnight; 12 designates noon)
**CAUTION**—Must be converted to ordinary clock time (**STANDARD TIME**)—See page 277.

| Day of the Month | Day of the Week | 45° N. Latitude — Idaho, Iowa (No.), Me., Mich. (Except Far So.), Minn., Mont., N. H., N. Y. (upstate), N. D., Ore., S. D., Vt., Wash., Wis., Wyo. (No. & Cent.). | | | 40° N. Latitude — Calif. (No.), Colo., Conn., Del., D.C., Ill., Ind., Iowa (So. & Cent.), Kans., Ky. (No. & Cent.), Mass., Md., Mich. (Far So.), Mo. (No. & Cent.), Nebr., Nev. (No. & Cent.), N.J., New York City, N.Y. (So.), Ohio, Pa., R.I., Utah, W.Va., Wyo. (So.). | | | 35° N. Latitude — Alabama (No.), Ariz. (Except Far So.), Ark., Calif. (So.), Georgia (No.), Missouri (So.), N. Mex. (Except Far So.), Nevada (So.), N.C., Okla., S.C., Tenn., Tex. (No.), Va. (So.). | | | 30° N. Latitude — Alabama (So.), Ariz. (Far So.), Fla., Georgia (So.), La., Miss. (So.), N. Mex. (Far So.), Tex. (So. & Cent.). | | |
|---|---|---|---|---|---|---|---|---|---|---|---|---|---|
| | | Sun Rises | Sun Sets | Moon R. & S. | Sun Rises | Sun Sets | Moon R. & S. | Sun Rises | Sun Sets | Moon R. & S. | Sun Rises | Sun Sets | Moon R. & S. |
| | | h. m. | h. m. | h. m. | h. m. | h. m. | h. m. | h. m. | h. m. | h. m. | h. m. | h. m. | h. m. |
| 1 | Th | 7 38 | 4 29 | rises 0 36 | 7 22 | 4 45 | rises 0 31 | 7 08 | 4 59 | rises 0 26 | 6 56 | 5 11 | rises 0 21 |
| 2 | Fr | 7 38 | 4 30 | 1 47 | 7 22 | 4 46 | 1 37 | 7 08 | 5 00 | 1 28 | 6 56 | 5 12 | 1 21 |
| 3 | Sa | 7 38 | 4 31 | 3 01 | 7 22 | 4 47 | 2 48 | 7 09 | 5 00 | 2 35 | 6 57 | 5 12 | 2 24 |
| 4 | S | 7 38 | 4 32 | 4 20 | 7 22 | 4 48 | 4 01 | 7 09 | 5 01 | 3 46 | 6 57 | 5 13 | 2 32 |
| 5 | M | 7 38 | 4 33 | 5 41 | 7 22 | 4 49 | 5 18 | 7 09 | 5 02 | 4 58 | 6 57 | 5 14 | 4 43 |
| 6 | Tu | 7 38 | 4 34 | 6 55 | 7 22 | 4 50 | 6 30 | 7 09 | 5 03 | 6 10 | 6 57 | 5 15 | 5 53 |
| 7 | W | 7 38 | 4 35 | 7 56 | 7 22 | 4 51 | 7 30 | 7 09 | 5 04 | 7 14 | 6 57 | 5 16 | 6 58 |
| 8 | Th | 7 37 | 4 36 | sets 5 36 | 7 22 | 4 52 | sets 5 53 | 7 09 | 5 05 | sets 6 08 | 6 57 | 5 16 | sets 6 21 |
| 9 | Fr | 7 37 | 4 37 | 7 03 | 7 22 | 4 53 | 7 16 | 7 09 | 5 06 | 7 26 | 6 57 | 5 17 | 7 36 |
| 10 | Sa | 7 37 | 4 38 | 8 28 | 7 22 | 4 54 | 8 34 | 7 09 | 5 07 | 8 41 | 6 57 | 5 18 | 8 46 |
| 11 | S | 7 37 | 4 39 | 9 47 | 7 22 | 4 55 | 9 49 | 7 09 | 5 08 | 9 51 | 6 57 | 5 19 | 9 54 |
| 12 | M | 7 36 | 4 40 | 11 03 | 7 21 | 4 56 | 11 00 | 7 09 | 5 09 | 10 58 | 6 57 | 5 20 | 10 56 |
| 13 | Tu | 7 36 | 4 42 | . . . . | 7 21 | 4 57 | . . . . | 7 08 | 5 09 | . . . . | 6 57 | 5 20 | 11 58 |
| 14 | W | 7 35 | 4 43 | 0 16 | 7 20 | 4 58 | 0 16 | 7 08 | 5 10 | 0 03 | 6 57 | 5 21 | . . . . |
| 15 | Th | 7 35 | 4 44 | 1 29 | 7 20 | 4 59 | 1 17 | 7 08 | 5 11 | 1 08 | 6 57 | 5 22 | 0 59 |
| 16 | Fr | 7 34 | 4 45 | 2 41 | 7 20 | 5 00 | 2 25 | 7 08 | 5 12 | 2 11 | 6 57 | 5 23 | 2 00 |
| 17 | Sa | 7 34 | 4 46 | 3 52 | 7 19 | 5 01 | 3 32 | 7 07 | 5 13 | 3 15 | 6 57 | 5 24 | 3 01 |
| 18 | S | 7 33 | 4 48 | 4 58 | 7 19 | 5 02 | 4 34 | 7 07 | 5 14 | 4 16 | 6 56 | 5 25 | 3 59 |
| 19 | M | 7 33 | 4 49 | 5 56 | 7 18 | 5 03 | 5 32 | 7 06 | 5 15 | 5 13 | 6 56 | 5 26 | 4 56 |
| 20 | Tu | 7 32 | 4 50 | 6 46 | 7 18 | 5 04 | 6 23 | 7 06 | 5 16 | 6 03 | 6 56 | 5 27 | 5 47 |
| 21 | W | 7 31 | 4 51 | 7 25 | 7 17 | 5 05 | 7 04 | 7 06 | 5 17 | 6 46 | 6 56 | 5 28 | 6 32 |
| 22 | Th | 7 30 | 4 53 | rises 4 56 | 7 17 | 5 06 | rises 5 15 | 7 05 | 5 18 | rises 5 29 | 6 55 | 5 28 | rises 5 41 |
| 23 | Fr | 7 30 | 4 54 | 6 06 | 7 16 | 5 08 | 6 18 | 7 05 | 5 19 | 6 28 | 6 55 | 5 29 | 6 38 |
| 24 | Sa | 7 29 | 4 56 | 7 11 | 7 16 | 5 09 | 7 19 | 7 04 | 5 20 | 7 26 | 6 54 | 5 30 | 7 32 |
| 25 | S | 7 28 | 4 57 | 8 16 | 7 15 | 5 10 | 8 20 | 7 04 | 5 21 | 8 23 | 6 54 | 5 31 | 8 26 |
| 26 | M | 7 27 | 4 58 | 9 19 | 7 14 | 5 11 | 9 19 | 7 03 | 5 22 | 9 20 | 6 54 | 5 32 | 9 20 |
| 27 | Tu | 7 26 | 5 00 | 10 25 | 7 13 | 5 12 | 10 21 | 7 03 | 5 23 | 10 18 | 6 53 | 5 33 | 10 14 |
| 28 | W | 7 25 | 5 01 | 11 32 | 7 13 | 5 14 | 11 24 | 7 02 | 5 24 | 11 17 | 6 53 | 5 33 | 11 12 |
| 29 | Th | 7 24 | 5 03 | . . . . | 7 12 | 5 15 | . . . . | 7 02 | 5 25 | . . . . | 6 52 | 5 34 | . . . . |
| 30 | Fr | 7 23 | 5 04 | 0 44 | 7 11 | 5 16 | 0 31 | 7 01 | 5 26 | 0 20 | 6 52 | 5 35 | 0 11 |
| 31 | Sa | 7 22 | 5 06 | 1 58 | 7 10 | 5 17 | 0 42 | 7 00 | 5 27 | 1 27 | 6 52 | 5 36 | 1 14 |

## Sun on 75th Meridian (Local Mean Time)

| Day | h. m. s. | Day | h. m. s. | Day | h. m. s. | Day | h. m. s. | Day | h. m. s. |
|---|---|---|---|---|---|---|---|---|---|
| 1 | 12 03 16 | 8 | 12 06 27 | 14 | 12 08 52 | 20 | 12 10 53 | 26 | 12 12 27 |
| 2 | 12 03 45 | 9 | 12 06 53 | 15 | 12 09 14 | 21 | 12 11 11 | 27 | 12 12 40 |
| 3 | 12 04 13 | 10 | 12 07 18 | 16 | 12 09 35 | 22 | 12 11 27 | 28 | 12 12 52 |
| 4 | 12 04 40 | 11 | 12 07 42 | 17 | 12 09 56 | 23 | 12 11 44 | 29 | 12 13 04 |
| 5 | 12 05 08 | 12 | 12 08 06 | 18 | 12 10 15 | 24 | 12 11 59 | 30 | 12 13 14 |
| 6 | 12 05 35 | 13 | 12 08 29 | 19 | 12 10 35 | 25 | 12 12 13 | 31 | 12 13 24 |
| 7 | 12 06 01 | | | | | | | | |

## Twilight (Local Mean Time)

| Place | Jan. | Begins | Ends | Jan. | Begins | Ends | Jan. | Begins | Ends |
|---|---|---|---|---|---|---|---|---|---|
| | | h. m. | h. m. | | h. m. | h. m. | | h. m. | h. m. |
| 45° N. Lat.. | 1 | 5 51 | 6 15 | 11 | 5 53 | 6 24 | 21 | 5 49 | 6 34 |
| 40° N. Lat.. | 1 | 5 45 | 6 22 | 11 | 5 46 | 6 31 | 21 | 5 44 | 6 40 |
| 35° N. Lat.. | 1 | 5 37 | 6 29 | 11 | 5 39 | 6 37 | 21 | 5 38 | 6 45 |
| 30° N. Lat.. | 1 | 5 30 | 6 35 | 11 | 5 32 | 6 43 | 21 | 5 32 | 6 51 |

## Moon Phases, 1970 (Eastern Standard Time)

| Moon | day | hour | min. a.m. or p.m. | Moon | day | hour | min. a.m. or p.m. |
|---|---|---|---|---|---|---|---|
| New Moon | 7 | 3 | 36 P.M. | Full Moon | 22 | 7 | 55 A.M. |
| First Quarter | 14 | 8 | 18 A.M. | Last Quarter | 30 | 9 | 39 A.M. |

**Morning Stars**—Mercury (Jan. 13-31); Venus (Jan. 1-24); Jupiter.    **Evening Stars**—Mercury (Jan. 1-13); Venus (Jan. 24-31); Mars; Saturn.

## 2nd Month     FEBRUARY, 1970     28 Days

Local Mean Time, A.M., light figures: **P.M.**, black (0 designates midnight; 12 designates noon)
CAUTION—Must be converted to ordinary clock time (**STANDARD TIME**)—See page 277.

| Day of the Month | Day of the Week | 45° N. Latitude Idaho, Iowa (No.), Me., Mich. (Except Far So.), Minn., Mont., N. H., N. Y. (upstate), N. D., Ore., S. D., Vt., Wash., Wis., Wyo. (No. & Cent.). | | | 40° N. Latitude Calif. (No.), Colo., Conn., Del., D.C., Ill., Ind., Iowa (So. & Cent.), Kans., Ky. (No. & Cent.) Mass., Md., Mich. (Far So.), Mo. (No. & Cent.), Nebr., Nev. (No. & Cent.), N.J., N.Y. City, N.Y. (So.), Ohio, Pa., R.I., Utah, W.Va., Wyo. (So.). | | | 35° N. Latitude Alabama (No.), Ariz. (Except Far So.), Ark., Calif. (So.), Georgia (No.), Missouri (So.), Mex. (Except Far So.), Nevada (So.), N.C., Okla., S.C., Tenn., Tex. (No.), Va. (So.). | | | 30° N. Latitude Alabama (So), Ariz. (Far So.), Fla., Georgia (So.), La., Miss. (So.), N. Mex. (Far So.), Tex. (So. & Cent.). | | |
|---|---|---|---|---|---|---|---|---|---|---|---|---|---|
| | | Sun Rises | Sun Sets | Moon R. & S. | Sun Rises | Sun Sets | Moon R. & S. | Sun Rises | Sun Sets | Moon R. & S. | Sun Rises | Sun Sets | Moon R. & S. |
| | | h. m. | h. m. | h. m. rises | h. m. | h. m. | h. m. rises | h. m. | h. m. | h. m. rises | h. m. | h. m. | h. m. rises |
| 1 | S | 7 21 | 5 07 | 3 16 | 7 09 | 5 18 | 2 54 | 6 59 | 5 28 | 2 36 | 6 51 | 5 37 | 2 21 |
| 2 | M | 7 20 | 5 08 | 4 31 | 7 08 | 5 20 | 4 07 | 6 59 | 5 29 | 3 47 | 6 50 | 5 37 | 3 30 |
| 3 | Tu | 7 18 | 5 10 | 5 37 | 7 07 | 5 21 | 5 13 | 6 58 | 5 30 | 4 53 | 6 50 | 5 38 | 4 36 |
| 4 | W | 7 17 | 5 12 | 6 32 | 7 06 | 5 22 | 6 09 | 6 57 | 5 31 | 5 50 | 6 49 | 5 39 | 5 36 |
| 5 | Th | 7 16 | 5 13 | 7 10 | 7 05 | 5 23 | 6 53 | 6 56 | 5 32 | 6 38 | 6 48 | 5 40 | 6 26 |
| | | | | sets | | | sets | | | sets | | | sets |
| 6 | Fr | 7 14 | 5 15 | 5 52 | 7 04 | 5 24 | 6 04 | 6 55 | 5 33 | 6 13 | 6 47 | 5 41 | 6 20 |
| 7 | Sa | 7 13 | 5 16 | 7 19 | 7 03 | 5 26 | 7 24 | 6 55 | 5 34 | 7 28 | 6 47 | 5 42 | 7 31 |
| 8 | S | 7 11 | 5 18 | 8 39 | 7 02 | 5 27 | 8 39 | 6 54 | 5 35 | 8 39 | 6 46 | 5 43 | 8 38 |
| 9 | M | 7 10 | 5 19 | 9 57 | 7 01 | 5 28 | 9 51 | 6 53 | 5 36 | 9 47 | 6 45 | 5 44 | 9 43 |
| 10 | Tu | 7 09 | 5 20 | 11 13 | 7 00 | 5 29 | 11 03 | 6 52 | 5 37 | 10 54 | 6 44 | 5 45 | 10 46 |
| 11 | W | 7 07 | 5 22 | .... | 6 59 | 5 30 | .... | 6 51 | 5 38 | .... | 6 43 | 5 46 | 11 50 |
| 12 | Th | 7 06 | 5 23 | 0 29 | 6 57 | 5 32 | 0 13 | 6 50 | 5 39 | 0 01 | 6 43 | 5 46 | .... |
| 13 | Fr | 7 04 | 5 25 | 1 40 | 6 56 | 5 33 | 1 21 | 6 49 | 5 40 | 1 06 | 6 42 | 5 47 | 0 52 |
| 14 | Sa | 7 03 | 5 26 | 2 50 | 6 55 | 5 34 | 2 28 | 6 48 | 5 41 | 2 09 | 6 41 | 5 48 | 1 55 |
| 15 | S | 7 02 | 5 27 | 3 51 | 6 54 | 5 35 | 3 28 | 6 47 | 5 42 | 3 07 | 6 40 | 5 49 | 2 51 |
| 16 | M | 7 00 | 5 29 | 4 43 | 6 52 | 5 36 | 4 20 | 6 46 | 5 43 | 4 00 | 6 39 | 5 50 | 3 43 |
| 17 | Tu | 6 59 | 5 30 | 5 26 | 6 51 | 5 38 | 5 05 | 6 44 | 5 44 | 4 46 | 6 39 | 5 50 | 4 30 |
| 18 | W | 6 57 | 5 32 | 5 58 | 6 49 | 5 39 | 5 40 | 6 43 | 5 45 | 5 24 | 6 38 | 5 51 | 5 11 |
| 19 | Th | 6 56 | 5 33 | 6 25 | 6 48 | 5 40 | 6 09 | 6 42 | 5 46 | 5 57 | 6 37 | 5 52 | 5 47 |
| 20 | Fr | 6 54 | 5 34 | 6 46 | 6 47 | 5 41 | 6 36 | 6 41 | 5 47 | 6 26 | 6 36 | 5 53 | 6 18 |
| | | | | rises | | | rises | | | rises | | | rises |
| 21 | Sa | 6 52 | 5 36 | 6 08 | 6 46 | 5 42 | 6 13 | 6 40 | 5 48 | 6 17 | 6 35 | 5 53 | 6 21 |
| 22 | S | 6 51 | 5 37 | 7 11 | 6 44 | 5 44 | 7 14 | 6 38 | 5 49 | 7 15 | 6 34 | 5 54 | 7 15 |
| 23 | M | 6 49 | 5 39 | 8 17 | 6 43 | 5 45 | 8 15 | 6 37 | 5 50 | 8 12 | 6 33 | 5 54 | 8 10 |
| 24 | Tu | 6 47 | 5 40 | 9 24 | 6 42 | 5 46 | 9 17 | 6 36 | 5 51 | 9 11 | 6 32 | 5 55 | 9 05 |
| 25 | W | 6 45 | 5 41 | 10 43 | 6 40 | 5 47 | 10 23 | 6 35 | 5 52 | 10 13 | 6 31 | 5 56 | 10 04 |
| 26 | Th | 6 44 | 5 43 | 11 46 | 6 39 | 5 48 | 11 30 | 6 34 | 5 53 | 11 17 | 6 30 | 5 57 | 11 06 |
| 27 | Fr | 6 43 | 5 44 | .... | 6 38 | 5 49 | .... | 6 32 | 5 53 | .... | 6 29 | 5 57 | .... |
| 28 | Sa | 6 41 | 5 46 | 1 00 | 6 36 | 5 50 | 0 41 | 6 31 | 5 54 | 0 24 | 6 28 | 5 58 | 0 10 |

## Sun on 75th Meridian (Local Mean Time)

| Day | h. m. s. | Day | h. m. s. | Day | h. m. s. | Day | h. m. s. | Day | h. m. s. |
|---|---|---|---|---|---|---|---|---|---|
| 1 | 12 13 33 | 7 | 12 14 10 | 13 | 12 14 18 | 19 | 12 13 59 | 25 | 12 13 15 |
| 2 | 12 13 41 | 8 | 12 14 13 | 14 | 12 14 17 | 20 | 12 13 53 | 26 | 12 13 05 |
| 3 | 12 13 49 | 9 | 12 14 16 | 15 | 12 14 15 | 21 | 12 13 47 | 27 | 12 12 55 |
| 4 | 12 13 55 | 10 | 12 14 18 | 16 | 12 14 12 | 22 | 12 13 39 | 28 | 12 12 44 |
| 5 | 12 14 01 | 11 | 12 14 19 | 17 | 12 14 08 | 23 | 12 13 32 | | |
| 6 | 12 14 06 | 12 | 12 14 19 | 18 | 12 14 04 | 24 | 12 13 23 | | |

## Twilight (Local Mean Time)

| Place | Feb. | Begins | Ends | Feb. | Begins | Ends | Feb. | Begins | Ends |
|---|---|---|---|---|---|---|---|---|---|
| | | h. m. | h. m. | | h. m. | h. m. | | h. m. | h. m. |
| 45° N. Lat.. | 1 | 5 44 | 6 44 | 11 | 5 30 | 7 01 | 21 | 5 16 | 7 15 |
| 40° N. Lat.. | 1 | 5 38 | 6 51 | 11 | 5 28 | 7 02 | 21 | 5 17 | 7 14 |
| 35° N. Lat.. | 1 | 5 33 | 6 54 | 11 | 5 26 | 7 02 | 21 | 5 17 | 7 13 |
| 30° N. Lat.. | 1 | 5 29 | 6 58 | 11 | 5 24 | 7 06 | 21 | 5 16 | 7 12 |

## Moon Phases, 1970 (Eastern Standard Time)

| Moon | day | hour | min. a.m. or p.m. | Moon | day | hour | min. a.m. or p.m. |
|---|---|---|---|---|---|---|---|
| New Moon | 6 | 2 | 13 A.M. | Full Moon | 21 | 3 | 19 A.M. |
| First Quarter | 12 | 11 | 10 P.M. | Last Quarter | 28 | 9 | 33 P.M. |

**Morning Stars**—Mercury; Jupiter.     **Evening Stars**—Venus; Mars; Saturn.

# Standard Time Calendar for U. S. Cities

**How to find the ordinary clock time (STANDARD TIME) in various U. S. cities corresponding to the LOCAL MEAN TIME on daily calendar of each month, pages 263-276.**

**Example:** To find time of sunrise at New York City Jan. 1, 1969, see page 263, column headed 40° N. Latitude, where sunrise on that date is 7:22 a.m., Local Mean Time. Now turn to page 277, which you are now reading.

In the 40° column below you find New York City sub 4Ea. This means to subtract 4 minutes, the result being 7:18 a.m. The "E" means Eastern Standard Time. The small "a" means that a correction for latitude is advisable. In the table at the bottom of this page under the column headed by small "a" you find that between Jan. 1 and Jan. 16 you should add 2 minutes. Thus sunrise at New York City Jan. 1, 1969, is at 7:20 a.m. EST. *A conversion to Standard Time must also be made for sunset, etc.*

A similar procedure is followed for other cities, but the **Correction for Latitude** table is used only where a small letter appears with that city. Example below: Springfield, Ill., "sub 1C." Sunrise there on Jan. 1, 1969, is at 7:21 a.m. CST; no further correction is needed.

*E designates Eastern Standard Time, C Central, M Mountain, and P Pacific.*

| Use Calendar for 45° N. Latitude | Use Calendar for 40° N. (Continued) | Use Calendar for 40° N. (Continued) | Use Calendar for 35° N. (Continued) |
|---|---|---|---|
| **Idaho** | **Connecticut** | Columbus....add 32 E | Winston- |
| Boise.....add 45 Mg | Bridgeport...sub 7 Eb | Dayton......add 37 E | Salem.....add 21 Ea |
| Idaho Falls..add 28 Mh | Hartford.....sub 9 Ec | Toledo.....add 34 Ec | **Oklahoma** |
| **Maine** | **Delaware** | **Pennsylvania** | Oklahoma Cy.add 30 Ca |
| Bangor.....sub 25 E | Wilmington..add 2 E | Allentown...add 2 Ea | Tulsa.......add 24 Cb |
| Portland.....sub 19 Eg | **Dist. of Col.** | Altoona.....add 14 Ea | **South Carolina** |
| **Mich. (except Far So.)** | Washington..add 8 Eg | Erie.......add 20 Ec | Charleston...add 20 Eh |
| Flint.......add 35 Ei | **Illinois** | Harrisburg...add 8 E | Columbia....add 24 Ef |
| GrandRapids.add 43 Ei | Chicago.....sub 9 Cc | Philadelphia..add 1 E | **Tennessee** |
| Lansing.....add 38 Ei | Peoria......sub 2 Ca | Pittsburgh...add 20 Ea | Chattanooga..add 41 E |
| Saginaw.....add 36 Eh | Rockford....sub 4 Cd | Scranton.....add 3 Eb | Knoxville.....add 36 Ea |
| **Minnesota** | Springfield...sub 1 C | **Rhode Island** | Memphis.......0 C |
| Duluth......add 8 Cc | **Indiana** | Providence...sub 14 Ec | Nashville....sub 13 Cb |
| Minneapolis..add 13 C | Evansville...sub 10 Ch | **Utah** | **Texas (No.)** |
| **Montana** | Fort Wayne..add 41 Eb | Ogden.......add 28 Mb | Amarillo.....add 47 C |
| Billings.....add 14 Ma | Indianapolis..add 45 E | Salt Lake Cy.add 28 Ma | Fort Worth..add 29 Ch |
| Great Falls..add 25 Me | South Bend..sub 15 Cc | **West Virginia** | Lubbock.....add 47 Cg |
| **New Hampshire** | **Iowa (So. & Cent.)** | Charleston...add 27 Eg | Wichita Falls add 34 Cf |
| Manchester..sub 14 Ei | Cedar Rapids add 7 Cc | Huntington...add 30 Eg | **Virginia (So.)** |
| **New York (Upstate)** | Davenport...add 2 Cb | **Wyoming (So.)** | Norfolk......add 5 Eb |
| Albany.....add 5 Ei | Des Moines..add 14 Cb | Cheyenne.....sub 1 Mb | Richmond....add 10 Ec |
| Buffalo.....add 15 Ei | Sioux City...add 26 Cd | | Roanoke....add 20 Ec |
| Syracuse.....add 5 Eh | **Kansas** | | |
| Utica.......add 1 Eh | Topeka......add 23 Cf | **Use Calendar for 35° N. Latitude** | **Use Calendar for 30° N. Latitude** |
| **North Dakota** | Wichita.....add 29 Ch | | |
| Bismarck....add 43 Ce | **Kentucky (No. & Cent.)** | **Alabama (No.)** | **Alabama (So.)** |
| Fargo.......add 27 Cd | Lexington...add 38 Eh | Birmingham..sub 13 Cg | Mobile.......sub 8 Ca |
| **Oregon** | Louisville...add 43 Eh | **Ariz. (Except Far So.)** | Montgomery.sub 15 Cc |
| Eugene......add 12 Pg | **Massachusetts** | Phoenix.....add 28 Mg | **Arizona (Far So.)** |
| Portland.....add 11 Pa | Boston......sub 16 Ed | | Tucson.......add 24 Mc |
| **South Dakota** | Springfield...sub 10 Ec | **Arkansas** | **Florida** |
| Rapid City...sub 7 Mg | Worcester....sub 13 Ed | Fort Smith...add 18 Ca | Jacksonville..add 27 E |
| Sioux Falls...add 27 Ch | **Maryland** | Little Rock...add 9 C | Miami.......add 21 Ej |
| **Vermont** | Baltimore....add 6 Ef | **California (So.)** | Tampa.......add 30 Eg |
| Burlington...sub 7 Ef | **Michigan (Far So.)** | Fresno......sub 1 Pb | **West Palm** |
| **Washington** | Detroit.....add 32 Ed | Los Angeles..sub 7 Pf | Beach......add 20 Ei |
| Seattle......add 9 Pe | **Missouri (No. & Cent.)** | San Bernar- | **Georgia (So.)** |
| Spokane.....sub 10 Pe | Kansas City..add 18 Cf | dino.......sub 11 Ph | Columbus....add 40 Ec |
| Yakima......add 2 Pc | St. Joseph...add 19 C | San Diego...sub 11 Ph | Savannah....add 24 Eb |
| **Wisconsin** | St. Louis.....add 1 Cg | San Jose....add 8 Pc | **Louisiana** |
| Green Bay...sub 8 Cf | **Nebraska** | **Georgia (No.)** | Baton Rouge.add 5 Ca |
| Madison.....sub 8 Ch | Lincoln.....add 27 Ca | Atlanta.....add 38 Eg | New Orleans..0 C |
| Milwaukee...sub 8 Ch | Omaha.......add 24 Cb | Augusta.....add 28 Eg | Shreveport...add 15 Cc |
| Wyoming (No. & Cent.) | **Nevada (No. & Cent.)** | **Missouri (So.)** | **Mississippi (So.)** |
| Casper.....add 5 Mi | Reno.......sub 1 Pf | Springfield...add 13 Cc | Gulfport.....sub 4 C |
| | **New Jersey** | **N. Mex. (Except Far So.)** | Jackson......add 1 Cc |
| **Use Calendar for 40° N. Latitude** | Trenton.....sub 1 E | Albuquerque.add 7 M | **Texas (So. & Cent.)** |
| | **New York (So.)** | Roswell......sub 2 Mg | Austin......add 31 C |
| **California (Northern)** | Binghamton..add 4 Ec | | Beaumont....add 16 C |
| Sacramento..add 6 Pg | **New York** | **Nevada (So.)** | Corp. Christi.add 30 Cg |
| San Fran....add 10 Ph | City.......sub 4 Ea | Las Vegas...sub 19 Pb | El Paso......add 6 Mb |
| Stockton.....add 5 Ph | **Ohio** | **North Carolina** | Houston.....add 21 C |
| **Colorado** | Akron......add 26 Eb | Charlotte....add 23 E | San Antonio..add 34 Cf |
| Denver......0 M | Cincinnati...add 38 Ef | Greensboro...add 19 Ea | Waco.......add 29 Cb |
| Pueblo......sub 2 Mh | Cleveland...add 27 Eb | Raleigh......add 15 Ea | |

## CORRECTION FOR LATITUDE

For cities with which a small letter appears, greater accuracy can be obtained by using the corresponding table below. The directions below are for corrections to sunrise; for sunset the figures should be used in the opposite way, subtracted instead of added and vice versa.

| Date | | a | b | c | d | e | f | g | h | i | j |
|---|---|---|---|---|---|---|---|---|---|---|---|
| Jan. | 1 | add 2 | add 4 | add 6 | add 8 | add 10 | sub 2 | sub 4 | sub 6 | sub 8 | sub 10 |
| | 16 | add 2 | add 4 | add 5 | add 7 | add 9 | sub 2 | sub 4 | sub 5 | sub 7 | sub 9 |
| Feb. | 1 | add 1 | add 3 | add 4 | add 6 | add 7 | sub 1 | sub 3 | sub 4 | sub 6 | sub 7 |
| | 15 | add 1 | add 2 | add 3 | add 4 | add 5 | sub 1 | sub 2 | sub 3 | sub 4 | sub 5 |
| Mar. | 1 | add 1 | add 1 | add 2 | add 2 | add 3 | sub 1 | sub 1 | sub 2 | sub 2 | sub 3 |
| | 16 | 0 | 0 | 0 | 0 | 0 | 0 | 0 | 0 | 0 | 0 |
| Apr. | 1 | 0 | sub 1 | sub 1 | sub 2 | sub 2 | 0 | add 1 | add 1 | add 2 | add 2 |
| | 16 | sub 1 | sub 2 | sub 3 | sub 4 | sub 4 | add 1 | add 2 | add 3 | add 3 | add 4 |
| May | 1 | sub 1 | sub 3 | sub 4 | sub 5 | sub 6 | add 1 | add 3 | add 4 | add 5 | add 6 |
| | 16 | sub 2 | sub 3 | sub 5 | sub 7 | sub 8 | add 2 | add 3 | add 5 | add 6 | add 8 |
| June | 1 | sub 2 | sub 4 | sub 6 | sub 8 | sub 9 | add 2 | add 4 | add 6 | add 8 | add 10 |
| | 16 | sub 2 | sub 4 | sub 6 | sub 8 | sub 11 | add 2 | add 4 | add 6 | add 9 | add 11 |
| July | 1 | sub 2 | sub 4 | sub 6 | sub 8 | sub 11 | add 2 | add 4 | add 6 | add 8 | add 11 |
| | 16 | sub 2 | sub 4 | sub 6 | sub 8 | sub 10 | add 2 | add 4 | add 6 | add 8 | add 10 |
| Aug. | 1 | sub 2 | sub 3 | sub 5 | sub 6 | sub 8 | add 2 | add 3 | add 5 | add 6 | add 8 |
| | 16 | sub 1 | sub 2 | sub 3 | sub 5 | sub 6 | add 1 | add 2 | add 3 | add 5 | add 6 |
| Sept. | 1 | sub 1 | sub 1 | sub 2 | sub 3 | sub 4 | add 1 | add 1 | add 2 | add 3 | add 4 |
| | 16 | 0 | 0 | sub 1 | sub 1 | sub 1 | 0 | 0 | add 1 | add 1 | add 1 |
| Oct. | 1 | 0 | 0 | 0 | add 1 | add 1 | 0 | 0 | sub 1 | sub 1 | sub 1 |
| | 16 | add 1 | add 1 | add 2 | add 3 | add 4 | sub 1 | sub 1 | sub 2 | sub 3 | sub 4 |
| Nov. | 1 | add 1 | add 2 | add 4 | add 5 | add 6 | sub 1 | sub 2 | sub 3 | sub 5 | sub 6 |
| | 16 | add 2 | add 3 | add 5 | add 6 | add 8 | sub 2 | sub 3 | sub 5 | sub 6 | sub 8 |
| Dec. | 1 | add 2 | add 4 | add 5 | add 7 | add 9 | sub 2 | sub 4 | sub 5 | sub 7 | sub 9 |
| | 16 | add 2 | add 4 | add 6 | add 8 | add 10 | sub 2 | sub 4 | sub 6 | sub 8 | sub 10 |

# PERPETUAL CALENDAR

## (1800-2059)

### Year-to-Calendar Index

| Year |  | Year |  | Year |  | Year |  | Year |  |
|---|---|---|---|---|---|---|---|---|---|
| 1800 | 4 | 1826 | 1 | 1852 | 12 | 1878 | 3 | 1904 | 13 |
| 1801 | 5 | 1827 | 2 | 1853 | 7 | 1879 | 4 | 1905 | 1 |
| 1802 | 6 | 1828 | 10 | 1854 | 1 | 1880 | 12 | 1906 | 2 |
| 1803 | 7 | 1829 | 5 | 1855 | 2 | 1881 | 7 | 1907 | 3 |
| 1804 | 8 | 1830 | 6 | 1856 | 10 | 1882 | 1 | 1908 | 11 |
| 1805 | 3 | 1831 | 7 | 1857 | 5 | 1883 | 2 | 1909 | 6 |
| 1806 | 4 | 1832 | 8 | 1858 | 6 | 1884 | 10 | 1910 | 7 |
| 1807 | 5 | 1833 | 3 | 1859 | 7 | 1885 | 5 | 1911 | 1 |
| 1808 | 13 | 1834 | 4 | 1860 | 8 | 1886 | 6 | 1912 | 9 |
| 1809 | 1 | 1835 | 5 | 1861 | 3 | 1887 | 7 | 1913 | 4 |
| 1810 | 2 | 1836 | 13 | 1862 | 4 | 1888 | 8 | 1914 | 5 |
| 1811 | 3 | 1837 | 1 | 1863 | 5 | 1889 | 3 | 1915 | 6 |
| 1812 | 11 | 1838 | 2 | 1864 | 13 | 1890 | 4 | 1916 | 14 |
| 1813 | 6 | 1839 | 3 | 1865 | 1 | 1891 | 5 | 1917 | 2 |
| 1814 | 7 | 1840 | 11 | 1866 | 2 | 1892 | 13 | 1918 | 3 |
| 1815 | 1 | 1841 | 6 | 1867 | 3 | 1893 | 1 | 1919 | 4 |
| 1816 | 9 | 1842 | 7 | 1868 | 11 | 1894 | 2 | 1920 | 12 |
| 1817 | 4 | 1843 | 1 | 1869 | 6 | 1895 | 3 | 1921 | 7 |
| 1818 | 5 | 1844 | 9 | 1870 | 7 | 1896 | 11 | 1922 | 1 |
| 1819 | 6 | 1845 | 4 | 1871 | 1 | 1897 | 6 | 1923 | 2 |
| 1820 | 14 | 1846 | 5 | 1872 | 9 | 1898 | 7 | 1924 | 10 |
| 1821 | 2 | 1847 | 6 | 1873 | 4 | 1899 | 1 | 1925 | 5 |
| 1822 | 3 | 1848 | 14 | 1874 | 5 | 1900 | 2 | 1926 | 6 |
| 1823 | 4 | 1849 | 2 | 1875 | 6 | 1901 | 4 | 1927 | 7 |
| 1824 | 12 | 1850 | 3 | 1876 | 14 | 1902 | 5 | 1928 | 8 |
| 1825 | 7 | 1851 | 4 | 1877 | 2 | 1903 | 6 | 1929 | 3 |

| Year |  | Year |  | Year |  | Year |  | Year |  |
|---|---|---|---|---|---|---|---|---|---|
| 1930 | 4 | 1956 | 8 | 1982 | 6 | 2008 | 10 | 2034 | 1 |
| 1931 | 5 | 1957 | 3 | 1983 | 7 | 2009 | 5 | 2035 | 2 |
| 1932 | 13 | 1958 | 4 | 1984 | 8 | 2010 | 6 | 2036 | 10 |
| 1933 | 1 | 1959 | 5 | 1985 | 3 | 2011 | 7 | 2037 | 5 |
| 1934 | 2 | 1960 | 13 | 1986 | 4 | 2012 | 8 | 2038 | 6 |
| 1935 | 3 | 1961 | 1 | 1987 | 5 | 2013 | 3 | 2039 | 7 |
| 1936 | 11 | 1962 | 2 | 1988 | 13 | 2014 | 4 | 2040 | 8 |
| 1937 | 6 | 1963 | 3 | 1989 | 1 | 2015 | 5 | 2041 | 3 |
| 1938 | 7 | 1964 | 11 | 1990 | 2 | 2016 | 13 | 2042 | 4 |
| 1939 | 1 | 1965 | 6 | 1991 | 3 | 2017 | 1 | 2043 | 5 |
| 1940 | 9 | 1966 | 7 | 1992 | 11 | 2018 | 2 | 2044 | 13 |
| 1941 | 4 | 1967 | 1 | 1993 | 6 | 2019 | 3 | 2045 | 1 |
| 1942 | 5 | 1968 | 9 | 1994 | 7 | 2020 | 11 | 2046 | 2 |
| 1943 | 6 | 1969 | 4 | 1995 | 1 | 2021 | 6 | 2047 | 3 |
| 1944 | 14 | 1970 | 5 | 1996 | 9 | 2022 | 7 | 2048 | 11 |
| 1945 | 2 | 1971 | 6 | 1997 | 4 | 2023 | 1 | 2049 | 6 |
| 1946 | 3 | 1972 | 14 | 1998 | 5 | 2024 | 9 | 2050 | 7 |
| 1947 | 4 | 1973 | 2 | 1999 | 6 | 2025 | 4 | 2051 | 1 |
| 1948 | 12 | 1974 | 3 | 2000 | 14 | 2026 | 5 | 2052 | 9 |
| 1949 | 7 | 1975 | 4 | 2001 | 2 | 2027 | 6 | 2053 | 4 |
| 1950 | 1 | 1976 | 12 | 2002 | 3 | 2028 | 14 | 2054 | 5 |
| 1951 | 2 | 1977 | 7 | 2003 | 4 | 2029 | 2 | 2055 | 6 |
| 1952 | 10 | 1978 | 1 | 2004 | 12 | 2030 | 3 | 2056 | 14 |
| 1953 | 5 | 1979 | 2 | 2005 | 7 | 2031 | 4 | 2057 | 2 |
| 1954 | 6 | 1980 | 10 | 2006 | 1 | 2032 | 12 | 2058 | 3 |
| 1955 | 7 | 1981 | 5 | 2007 | 2 | 2033 | 7 | 2059 | 7 |

The page contains 14 numbered reference calendars (keyed 1 through 14), each showing the twelve months JANUARY, FEBRUARY, MARCH, APRIL, MAY, JUNE, JULY, AUGUST, SEPTEMBER, OCTOBER, NOVEMBER and DECEMBER with day grids headed S M T W T F S. Example years 1969 and 1970 are marked alongside calendars 4 and 5.

| 7 | 8 | 9 | 1968 | 10 |
| 11 | 12 | 13 | | 14 |

DIRECTIONS: Pick desired year from box at top left. The number shown with each year indicates what calendar to use for that year.

# Standard Time, Daylight Saving Time and Others

**Source: U. S. Naval Oceanographic Office; Department of Transportation; National Bureau of Standards and U. S. Naval Observatory**

## STANDARD TIME

Standard time is reckoned from Greenwich, England, recognized as the Prime Meridian of Longitude. The world is divided into 24 zones, each 15° of arc, or one hour in time apart. The meridian of Greenwich (0°) extends through the center of the initial zone, and the zones to the eastward are numbered from 1 to 12 with the prefix "minus" indicating the number of hours to be subtracted to obtain Greenwich Time.

Zones westward are similarly numbered, but prefixed "plus" showing the number of hours that must be added to get Greenwich time. While these zones apply generally to sea areas, it should be noted that the Standard Time maintained in many countries does not coincide with zone time. A graphical representation of the zones is shown on the Standard Time Chart of the World (Chart 5192) published by the U. S. Naval Oceanographic Office, Washington, D. C.

The United States and possessions are divided into eight Standard Time zones, as set forth by the Uniform Time Act of 1966, which also provides for the use of Daylight Saving Time therein. Each zone is approximately 15° of longitude in width. All places in each zone use, instead of their own local time, the time counted from the transit of the "mean sun" across the Standard Time meridian which passes near the middle of that zone.

These time zones are designated as Atlantic, Eastern, Central, Mountain, Pacific, Yukon, Alaska-Hawaii, and Bering and the time in these zones is basically reckoned from the 60th, 75th, 90th, 105th, 137th, 141st, 157th meridians west of Greenwich. The line wanders to conform to local geographical reasons. The time in the various zones is slower than Greenwich Time by 4, 5, 6, 7, 8, 9, 10, and 11 hours respectively.

High Precision Time and Frequency are broadcast by U. S. Navy Stations which are maintained on frequency with the aid of Atomic Clocks (Cesium beam and atomic hydrogen masers). The stations are as follows: NBA: NSS: NLK/NPG. NAA: NPM: Omega.

Loran-C navigational transmissions at 100 KC/S of the East Coast, Hawaiian, North Atlantic, North Pacific and the Norwegian sea chains may be used for time and frequency comparisons. These can be made to one microsecond.

## STANDARD FREQUENCY STATIONS

The National Bureau of Standards' radio stations WWV at Fort Collins, Colo., and WWVH on the island of Maui, Hawaii, broadcast six technical services continuously night and day. The services are: (1) standard radio frequencies, 2.5, 5, 10, 15, 20 and 25 MHz (WWV) and 2.5, 5, 10 and 15 MHz (WWVH), (2) standard audio frequencies 440 and 600 cycles per second (3) standard musical pitch, A above middle C (4) standard time intervals of 1 second, 1 minute and longer (5) time signals in voice and telegraphic code each 5 minutes (6) radio propagation forecasts, in telegraph code, every 5 minutes from WWV just preceding the voice announcement for the North Atlantic Area.

WWV is interrupted for about 4 minutes each hour commencing at approximately 45 minutes past the hour. . . . WWVH broadcast is interrupted about four minutes each hour commencing approximately 15 minutes past the hour.

WWV and WWVH have no tone modulation during the last two minutes of each five-minute period commencing on the hour. During the third minute of each five-minute period, except the first and tenth, WWV transmits a special 36-bit, binary coded, 100-pulse/sec. time code, carried on 1,000 c/s modulation which contains time-of-year information (Universal Time) in seconds, minutes, hours, and day of year.

WWVL (20kHz), Fort Collins, Colo., and WWVB (60kNz), Fort Collins, Colo., also transmit standard frequency signals that provide accuracies one to three parts better than is possible at HF (WWV/WWVH).

The reference standard for the broadcast is the frequency provided by a carefully built and tested atomic beam machine (atomic clock) whose accuracy is plus or minus 1.1 parts in 100,000 million.

Inquiries concerning WWV, WWVH, WWVL and WWVB should be addressed Frequency-Time Broadcast Services, National Bureau of Standards, Boulder, Colo.

## DAYLIGHT SAVING TIME

Under the Uniform Time Act, which became effective in 1967, all states, the District of Columbia and U. S. possessions must observe Daylight Saving Time beginning at 2 a.m. on the last Sunday in April and ending at 2 a.m. on the last Sunday in October. Any state, by legislative action, can exempt itself from the law; Hawaii did so in 1967 and Arizona in 1968. The Dept. of Transportation, which oversees the act, is planning to modify some boundaries due to local problems. Daylight Saving Time is achieved by advancing the clock one hour.

Since 1916 the British had moved their clocks ahead an hour in the spring for British summer time and back an hour in the fall for Greenwich Mean Time. On Feb. 18, 1968, however, the British moved their clocks ahead an hour to stay permanently. Thus what was British summer time will extend throughout the year and be known as British standard time. Greenwich Mean Time will live on only as a standard for navigators, geographers and astronomers.

## 24-HOUR TIME

24-hour time is widely used in scientific work throughout the world. In the United States it is used also in operations of the Armed Forces. In Europe it is used in preference to the 12-hour a.m. and p.m. system. With the 24-hour system the day begins at midnight and hours are numbered consecutively through 24. Thus 8 a.m. is 0800, and 8:25 a.m. is 0825; 4 p.m. is 1600, and 7:52 p.m. is 1952, or 19 hours and 52 minutes past midnight.

## DATE LINE

The Date Line is a zig-zag line that approximately coincides with the 180th meridian, and it is where each calendar day begins. The date must be advanced one day when crossing in a westerly direction and set back one day when crossing in an easterly direction. The line is deflected between north latitude 45° and 80°, so that all Asia lies to the west of it and all North America, including the Aleutian Islands, to the east; between south latitude 12° and 56° the line is deflected so that Chatham Island and the Tongo group lie to the west.

# Chronological Eras, 1969

The year 1969 of the Christian Era comprises the latter part of the 193rd and the beginning of the 194th year of the independence of the United States of America.

Corresponding years of various ancient chronological eras are shown in the table below, together with the date in 1969 on which each year begins according to the Gregorian calendar.

| Era | Year | Begins in 1969 | Era | Year | Begins in 1969 |
|---|---|---|---|---|---|
| Byzantine | 7478 | Sept. 14 | Grecian (Seleucidae) | 2281 | Sept. 14 or Oct. 14 (different sects) |
| Jewish | 5730 | Sept. 13 | | | |
| Olympiads | 2745 | July 1 | Indian (Saka) | 1891 | Mar. 22 |
| (First year of Olympiad 687) | | | Diocletian | 1686 | Sept. 11 |
| Roman (Ab Urbe Condita) | 2722 | Jan. 14 | Mohammedan (Hegira) | 1389 | Mar. 20 |
| Nabonassar (Babylonian) | 2718 | May 1 | | | |
| Japanese (44th year of Showa) | 2629 | Jan. 1 | | | |

# Chronological Cycles, 1969

| | | | | |
|---|---|---|---|---|
| Dominical letter | E | Solar Cycle | | 18 |
| Epact | 11 | Roman Indiction | | 7 |
| Lunar Cycle or Golden Number | 13 | Julian Period | | 6682 |

# Standard Time Differences—United States Cities

Source: Dept. of Transportation

**At 12 o'clock noon Eastern Standard Time, the standard time in U. S. cities is as follows:**

| | | |
|---|---|---|
| Akron, Ohio......... 12.00 NOON | Fort Worth, Texas... 11.00 A.M. | Philadelphia, Pa...... 12.00 NOON |
| Albuquerque, N. Mex. 10.00 A.M. | Frankfort, Ky...... 12.00 NOON | Phoenix, Ariz...... 10.00 A.M. |
| Atlanta, Ga....... 12.00 NOON | Galveston, Tex...... 11.00 A.M. | Pierre, S. Dak...... 11.00 A.M. |
| Austin, Tex....... 11.00 A.M. | Grand Rapids, Mich.. 12.00 NOON | Pittsburgh, Pa...... 12.00 NOON |
| Baltimore, Md...... 12.00 NOON | Hartford, Conn...... 12.00 NOON | Portland, Me...... 12.00 NOON |
| Birmingham, Ala.... 11.00 A.M. | Helena, Mont...... 10.00 A.M. | Portland, Oreg...... 9.00 A.M. |
| Bismarck, N. Dak.... 11.00 A.M. | Honolulu, Hawaii.... 7.00 A.M. | Providence, R. I...... 12.00 NOON |
| Boise, Idaho....... 10.00 A.M. | Houston, Tex ...... 11.00 A.M. | Reno, Nev...... 9.00 A.M. |
| Boston, Mass....... 12.00 NOON | Indianapolis, Ind.... 12.00 NOON | Richmond, Va...... 12.00 NOON |
| Buffalo, N. Y....... 12.00 NOON | Jacksonville, Fla...... 12.00 NOON | Rochester, N. Y...... 12.00 NOON |
| Butte, Mont....... 10.00 A.M. | Juneau, Alaska...... 9.00 A.M. | Sacramento, Calif... 9.00 A.M. |
| Charleston, S. C...... 12.00 NOON | Kansas City, Mo...... 11.00 A.M. | St. Louis, Mo...... 11.00 A.M. |
| Charleston, W. Va.... 12.00 NOON | Knoxville, Tenn...... 12.00 NOON | St. Paul, Minn...... 11.00 A.M. |
| Charlotte, N. C...... 12.00 NOON | Lexington, Ky...... 12.00 NOON | Salt Lake City, Utah.. 10.00 A.M. |
| Chattanooga, Tenn... 12.00 NOON | Lincoln, Nebr...... 11.00 A.M. | San Antonio, Tex..... 11.00 A.M. |
| Cheyenne, Wyo...... 10.00 A.M. | Little Rock, Ark...... 11.00 A.M. | San Diego, Calif...... 9.00 A.M. |
| Chicago, Ill....... 11.00 A.M. | Los Angeles, Calif... 9.00 A.M. | San Francisco, Calif.. 9.00 A.M. |
| Cincinnati, Ohio...... 12.00 NOON | Louisville, Ky...... 12.00 NOON | Santa Fe, N. M...... 10.00 A.M. |
| Cleveland, Ohio...... 12.00 NOON | Memphis, Tenn...... 11.00 A.M. | Savannah, Ga...... 12.00 NOON |
| Colorado Springs, Colo 10.00 A.M. | Miami, Fla...... 12.00 NOON | Seattle, Wash...... 9.00 A.M. |
| Columbus, Ohio...... 12.00 NOON | Milwaukee, Wis...... 11.00 A.M. | Shreveport, La...... 11.00 A.M. |
| Dallas, Tex....... 11.00 A.M. | Minneapolis, Minn... 11.00 A.M. | Sioux Falls, S. Dak... 11.00 A.M. |
| Dayton, Ohio...... 12.00 NOON | Mobile, Ala...... 11.00 A.M. | Spokane, Wash...... 9.00 A.M. |
| Denver, Colo....... 10.00 A.M. | Nashville, Tenn...... 11.00 A.M. | Tacoma, Wash...... 9.00 A.M. |
| Des Moines, Iowa.... 11.00 A.M. | Newark, N. J...... 12.00 NOON | Tampa, Fla...... 12.00 NOON |
| Detroit, Mich...... 12.00 NOON | New Haven, Conn... 12.00 NOON | Toledo, Ohio...... 12.00 NOON |
| Duluth, Minn....... 11.00 A.M. | New Orleans, La..... 11.00 A.M. | Topeka, Kan...... 11.00 A.M. |
| El Paso, Tex.*...... 11.00 A.M. | New York, N. Y... 12.00 NOON | Tucson, Ariz...... 10.00 A.M. |
| Erie, Pa....... 12.00 NOON | Nome, Alaska...... 7.00 A.M. | Tulsa, Okla...... 11.00 A.M. |
| Evansville, Ind....... 11.00 A.M. | Norfolk, Va...... 12.00 NOON | Washington, D. C..... 12.00 NOON |
| Fairbanks, Alaska ... 7.00 A.M. | Okla. City, Okla...... 11.00 A.M. | Wichita, Kan...... 11.00 A.M. |
| Flint, Mich....... 12.00 NOON | Omaha, Nebr...... 11.00 A.M. | Wilmington, Del...... 12.00 NOON |
| Fort Wayne, Ind...... 12.00 NOON | Peoria, Ill...... 11.00 A.M. | |

*Actual local observance differs from the official time given above as follows: El Paso, 10:00 A.M.

# Standard Time Differences—Foreign Cities

Source: U. S. Naval Oceanographic Office

By government decree or proclamation Great Britain, Ireland, Spain, France, Netherlands, and Belgium have advanced their time from the standard meridian by one hour throughout the year. The time indicated in table is fixed by law and is called the legal time, or, more generally, Standard Time.

**At 12 o'clock noon Eastern Standard Time, the standard time in foreign cities is as follows:**

| | | |
|---|---|---|
| Alexandria.. 7.00 P.M. | Copenhagen.. 6.00 P.M. | Liverpool.... 6.00 P.M. | Seoul...... 2.00 A.M.* |
| Amsterdam.. 6.00 P.M. | Dawson | London.... 6.00 P.M. | Shanghai ... 1.00 A.M.* |
| Athens...... 7.00 P.M. | (Yukon). . 8.00 A.M. | Madrid...... 6.00 P.M. | Singapore... 12.30 A.M.* |
| Auckland.... 5.00 A.M.* | Delhi...... 10.30 P.M. | Manila...... 1.00 A.M.* | Stockholm... 6.00 P.M. |
| Bagdad...... 8.00 P.M. | Djakarta.... 12.00 MID. | Melbourne... 3.00 A.M.* | Sydney |
| Bangkok.... 12.00 MID. | Dublin...... 6.00 P.M. | Mexico City 11.00 A.M. | (Australia) 3.00 A.M.* |
| Belfast...... 6.00 P.M. | Gdansk...... 6.00 P.M. | Montevideo... 2.00 P.M. | Teheran..... 8-30 P.M. |
| Berlin...... 6.00 P.M. | Geneva...... 6.00 P.M. | Montreal.... 12.00 NOON | Tel Aviv..... 7:00 P.M. |
| Bogota...... 12.00 NOON | Halifax...... 1.00 P.M. | Moscow..... 8.00 P.M. | Tokyo...... 2.00 A.M.* |
| Bombay.... 10.30 P.M. | Havana...... 12.00 NOON | Oslo...... 6.00 P.M. | Valparaiso... 1.00 P.M. |
| Bremen...... 6.00 P.M. | Hong Kong.. 1.00 A.M.* | Paris...... 6.00 P.M. | Vancouver... 9.00 A.M. |
| Brussels..... 6.00 P.M | Istanbul.... 7.00 P.M. | Peking..... 1.00 A.M.* | Vienna...... 6.00 P.M. |
| Bucharest ... 7.00 P.M. | Jerusalem... 7:00 P.M. | Rangoon.... 11.30 P.M. | Warsaw.... 6.00 P.M. |
| Budapest.... 6.00 P.M. | Johannesburg 7.00 P.M. | Rio de Janeiro 2.00 P.M. | Wellington |
| Buenos Aires. 1.00 P.M. | Le Havre.... 6.00 P.M. | Rome...... 6.00 P.M. | (N. Z.).... 5.00 A.M.* |
| Calcutta.... 10.30 P.M. | Leningrad... 8.00 P.M. | Saigon...... 1:00 A.M.* | Winnipeg.... 11.00 A.M. |
| Cape Town.. 7.00 P.M. | Lima...... 12.00 NOON | Santiago | Yokohama... 2.00 A.M.* |
| Caracas..... 1.00 P.M. | Lisbon...... 6.00 P.M. | (Chile).... 1.00 P.M. | Zurich...... 6.00 P.M. |

*Indicates morning of the following day.

## Julian and Gregorian Calendars; Leap Year

Calendars based on the movements of sun and moon have been used since ancient times, but none has been perfect. The Julian calendar, under which western nations measured time until 1582 A. D., was authorized by Julius Caesar in 46 B.C., the year 709 of Rome. His expert was a Greek, Sosigenes. The Julian calendar, on the assumption that the true year was 365¼ days long, gave every fourth year 366 days. The Venerable Bede, an Anglo-Saxon monk, announced in 730 A.D. that the 365¼-day Julian year was 11 min. 14 sec. too long, making a cumulative error of about a day every 128 years, but nothing was done about it for over 800 years.

By 1582 the accumulated error was estimated to have amounted to 10 days. In that year Pope Gregory XIII decreed that the day following Oct. 4, 1582, should be called Oct. 15, thus dropping 10 days.

However, with common years 365 days and a 366-day leap year every fourth year, the error in the length of the year would have recurred at the rate of a little more than 3 days every 400 years. So 3 of every 4 centesimal years (ending in 00) were made common years, not leap years. Thus 1600 was a leap year, 1700 was not. Leap years are those divisible by 4 except centesimal years, which are common unless divisible by 400.

The Gregorian calendar was adopted at once by most predominantly Roman Catholic countries, but many Protestant countries did not accept it until the 18th Century.

The British Government imposed the Gregorian calendar on all its possessions, including the American colonies, in 1752. The British decreed that the day following Sept. 2, 1752, should be called Sept. 14, a loss of 11 days. All dates preceding were marked O.S., for Old Style. George Washington was born Feb. 11, 1732, O.S., and after 1752 his birthday fell on Feb. 22.

In 1793 the French Revolutionary Government adopted a calendar of 12 months of 30 days each, with 5 extra days in September of each common year and a 6th extra day every 4th year. Napoleon reinstated the Gregorian calendar in 1806.

Japan adopted the Gregorian calendar in 1873, the Chinese Republic in 1912, Greece and Greek Orthodox communities in 1924, and Turkey (predominantly Moslem) in 1927.

To change from the Julian calendar to the Gregorian calendar, add 10 days to dates Oct. 5, 1582, through Feb. 28, 1700; 11 days from Feb. 29, 1700, through Feb. 28, 1800; 12 days from Feb. 29, 1800, through Feb. 28, 1900; and 13 days from Feb. 29, 1900, through Feb. 28, 2100.

## Astronomical Constants; Speed of Light

The following astronomical constants were adopted in 1968, in accordance with the resolutions and recommendations of the International Astronomical Union (Hamburg 1964): Velocity of light, 299,792.5 kilometers per second, or about 186,282 statute miles per second; solar parallax, 8".794; constant of nutation, 9".210; and constant of aberration, 20".496.

# The Sun; Project Stratoscope Adds to Knowledge

Telescopic cameras have been sent to heights between 80,000 and 100,000 feet above the surface of the earth to photograph the sun without interference from the densest level of the earth's atmosphere. This was called Project Stratoscope. Many photographs were thus obtained which are the clearest and best ever taken of the detail of the sun's surface. These pictures showed plainly the complicated and turbulent structure of the sun's surface, where small islands of superheated gases, called granules, rise from the interior, radiate their energy into space, cool and sink. These granules, only a few hundred miles in diameter, have lifetimes of only a few minutes. They are surrounded by cooler borders and where several granules touch each other, these borders form more extensive cooler areas called oases. Much was also learned about the appearance and structure of sun-spots, although the causes of sun-spots is still not certainly known.

The sun, the controlling body of our solar system, is a star whose dimensions cause it to be classified among stars as average in size, temperature and brightness. Its proximity to the earth makes it appear to us as tremendously large and bright, and a series of thermo-nuclear reactions involving the atoms of the elements of which it is composed produces the heat and light that make life possible on the earth.

The sun has a diameter of 864,000 miles and is distant, on the average, 92,900,000 miles from the earth. It is 1.41 times as dense as water. The light of the sun reaches the earth in 498.6 seconds or slightly more than 8 minutes. The average solar surface temperature has been measured by several indirect methods which agree closely on a value of 6,000° Centigrade or about 10,000° Fahrenheit. The interior temperature of the sun is about 35,000,000° Fahrenheit.

When sunlight is analyzed with a spectroscope, it is found to consist of a continuous spectrum composed of all the colors of the rainbow in order, crossed by many dark lines. The "absorption lines" are produced by gaseous materials in the atmosphere of the sun. Of these materials, almost all have been identified. More than 60 of the natural terrestrial elements have been thus identified in the sun, all in vaporous form because of the intense heat of the sun.

## SPHERES AND CORONA

The radiating surface of the sun is called the **photosphere**, and just above it is the **chromosphere**, which is a layer of solar atmosphere in a constant state of agitation as if stirred by spouting gases. The chromosphere is visible to the naked eye only at times of total solar eclipses, appearing then to be a pinkish-violet layer with great, swiftly-moving spoutings called prominences projecting above its general level. With proper instruments the chromosphere can be seen or photographed whenever the sun is visible without waiting for a total eclipse. Above the chromosphere is the **corona**, also visible to the naked eye only at times of total eclipse. Instruments also permit the brighter portions of the corona to be studied whenever conditions are favorable. The pearly light of the corona surges millions of miles from the sun. Iron, nickel and calcium are believed to be principal contributors to the composition of the corona, all in a state of extreme attenuation and high excitation that indicates temperatures on the order of a million degrees, Fahrenheit.

## SUN SPOTS

There is an intimate connection between sunspots and the corona. At times of low sunspot activity, the fine streamers of the corona will be much longer above the sun's equator than over the polar regions of the sun, while during high sunspot activity, the corona extends fairly evenly outward from all regions of the sun, but to a much greater distance in space. Sunspots are dark, irregularly-shaped regions whose diameters may reach hundreds of thousands of miles. The average life of a sunspot group is from two to three weeks, but there have been spots that have lasted for more than a year, being carried repeatedly around as the sun rotated upon its axis. The record for the duration of a sunspot is 18 months. Sunspots reach a low point every 11.3 years, with a peak of activity occurring irregularly between two successive minima.

The sun is 400,000 times as bright as the full moon and gives the earth 6 million times as much light as do all the other stars put together. Actually, most of the stars that can be easily seen on any clear night are brighter than the sun.

# The Zodiac

The sun's apparent yearly path among the stars is known as the **ecliptic**. The zone 16° wide, 8° on each side of the ecliptic, is known as the **zodiac**. Inside of this zone are the apparent paths of the sun, moon, earth and major planets. Beginning at the point on the ecliptic which marks the position of the sun at the vernal equinox, and thence proceeding eastward, the zodiac is divided into twelve signs of 30° each, as shown herewith.

These signs are named from the twelve constellations of the zodiac with which the signs coincided in the time of the astronomer Hipparchus, about 2,000 years ago. Owing to the precession of the equinoxes, that is to say, to the retrograde motion of the equinoxes along the ecliptic, each sign in the zodiac has, in the course of 2,000 years, moved backward 30° into the constellation west of it; so that the sign Aries is now in the constellation Pisces, and so on. The signs of the zodiac with their Latin and English names are as follows:

Spring Signs.
1. ♈ Aries. The Ram.
2. ♉ Taurus. The Bull.
3. ♊ Gemini. The Twins.

Summer Signs.
4. ♋ Cancer. The Crab.
5. ♌ Leo. The Lion.
6. ♍ Virgo. The Virgin.

Autumn Signs.
7. ♎ Libra. The Balance.
8. ♏ Scorpius. The Scorpion.
9. ♐ Sagittarius. The Archer.

Winter Signs.
10. ♑ Capricornus. The Goat.
11. ♒ Aquarius. The Water Bearer.
12. ♓ Pisces. The Fishes.

# The Moon

The moon completes a circuit around the earth in a period whose mean or average duration is 27 days 7 hours 43.2 minutes. This is the moon's sidereal period. Because of the motion of the moon in common with the earth around the sun, the mean duration of the lunar month—the period from one new moon to the next new moon—is 29 days 12 hours 44.05 minutes. This is the moon's synodical period.

The mean distance of the moon from the earth according to the American Ephemeris is 238,857 miles. Because the orbit of the moon about the earth is not circular but elliptical, however, the maximum distance from the earth that the moon may reach is 252,710 miles and the least distance is 221,463 miles.

All distances are from the center of one object to the center of the other. The moon's diameter is 2,160 miles. If we deduct the radius of the moon, 1,080 miles, and the radius of the earth, 3,963 miles from the minimum distance, or perigee, given above, we shall have for the nearest approach of the bodies' surfaces 216,420 miles.

The moon rotates on its axis in a period of time exactly equal to its sidereal revolution about the earth—27.321666 days. The moon's revolution about the earth is irregular because of its elliptical orbit. The moon's rotation, however, is regular and this produces what is called "libration in longitude" which permits us to see first farther around the east side and then farther around the west side of the moon. The moon's variation in altitude from season to season permits us to see farther over first one pole and then the other of the moon and this is "libration in latitude." These two libration effects permit us to see a total of about 60% of the moon's surface over a period of time. The hidden side of the moon was photographed in 1959 by the Soviet space vehicle Lunik III. Since then many excellent pictures of this portion of the moon's surface have been transmitted to earth by Lunar Orbiters launched by the U. S.

The tides are caused mainly by the moon, because of its proximity to the earth. The ratio of the tide-raising power of the moon to that of the sun is 11 to 5.

# The Moon's Phases, 1969 (Standard Time)

A.M. light figures; P.M. black (0 designates midnight; 12 designates noon)

| 1969 | Phase | Day | Eastern Std. Time Boston, New York, Etc. | Central Std. Time St. Louis, New Orleans, Etc. | Mountain Std. Time Denver, Salt Lake City, Etc. | Pacific Std. Time San Francisco, L. Angeles, Etc. | Alaska-Hawaii Std. Time Fairbanks Etc. |
|---|---|---|---|---|---|---|---|
| | | | h. m. | h. m. | h. m. | h. m. | h. m. |
| Jan. | Full Moon | 3 | 1 28 | 12 28 | 11 28 | 10 28 | 8 28 |
| | Last Quarter | 11 | 9 00 | 8 00 | 7 00 | 6 00 | 4 00 |
| | New Moon | 17 | 11 59 | 10 59 | 9 59 | 8 59 | 6 59 |
| | First Quarter | 25 | 3 23 | 2 23 | 1 23 | 0 23 | 24d 10 23 |
| Feb. | Full Moon | 2 | 7 56 | 6 56 | 5 56 | 4 56 | 2 56 |
| | Last Quarter | 9 | 7 08 | 6 08 | 5 08 | 4 08 | 2 08 |
| | New Moon | 16 | 11 25 | 10 25 | 9 25 | 8 25 | 6 25 |
| | First Quarter | 23 | 11 30 | 10 30 | 9 30 | 8 30 | 6 30 |
| Mar. | Full Moon | 4 | 0 17 | 3d 11 17 | 10 17 | 9 17 | 7 17 |
| | Last Quarter | 11 | 2 44 | 1 44 | 0 44 | 10d 11 44 | 9 44 |
| | New Moon | 17 | 11 51 | 10 51 | 9 51 | 8 51 | 6 51 |
| | First Quarter | 25 | 7 48 | 6 48 | 5 48 | 4 48 | 2 48 |
| Apr. | Full Moon | 2 | 1 45 | 12 45 | 11 45 | 10 45 | 8 45 |
| | Last Quarter | 9 | 8 58 | 7 58 | 6 58 | 5 58 | 3 58 |
| | New Moon | 16 | 1 16 | 12 16 | 11 16 | 10 16 | 8 16 |
| | First Quarter | 24 | 2 45 | 1 45 | 12 45 | 11 45 | 9 45 |
| May | Full Moon | 2 | 0 13 | 1d 11 13 | 10 13 | 9 13 | 7 13 |
| | Last Quarter | 8 | 3 12 | 2 12 | 1 12 | 12 12 | 10 12 |
| | New Moon | 16 | 3 26 | 2 26 | 1 26 | 0 26 | 10 26 |
| | First Quarter | 24 | 7 15 | 6 15 | 5 15 | 4 15 | 2 15 |
| | Full Moon | 31 | 8 18 | 7 18 | 6 18 | 5 18 | 3 18 |
| June | Last Quarter | 6 | 10 39 | 9 39 | 8 39 | 7 39 | 5 39 |
| | New Moon | 14 | 6 09 | 5 09 | 4 09 | 3 09 | 1 09 |
| | First Quarter | 22 | 8 44 | 7 44 | 6 44 | 5 44 | 4 44 |
| | Full Moon | 29 | 3 04 | 2 04 | 1 04 | 12 04 | 10 04 |
| July | Last Quarter | 6 | 8 17 | 7 17 | 6 17 | 5 17 | 3 17 |
| | New Moon | 14 | 9 11 | 8 11 | 7 11 | 6 11 | 4 11 |
| | First Quarter | 22 | 7 10 | 6 10 | 5 10 | 4 10 | 2 10 |
| | Full Moon | 28 | 9 45 | 8 45 | 7 45 | 6 45 | 4 45 |
| Aug. | Last Quarter | 4 | 8 38 | 7 38 | 6 38 | 5 38 | 3 38 |
| | New Moon | 13 | 0 17 | 12d 11 17 | 10 17 | 9 17 | 7 17 |
| | First Quarter | 20 | 3 03 | 2 03 | 1 03 | 12 03 | 10 03 |
| | Full Moon | 27 | 5 32 | 4 32 | 3 32 | 2 32 | 0 32 |
| Sept. | Last Quarter | 3 | 11 58 | 10 58 | 9 58 | 8 58 | 6 58 |
| | New Moon | 11 | 2 56 | 1 56 | 12 56 | 11 56 | 9 56 |
| | First Quarter | 18 | 9 25 | 8 25 | 7 25 | 6 25 | 4 25 |
| | Full Moon | 25 | 3 21 | 2 21 | 1 21 | 12 21 | 10 21 |
| Oct. | Last Quarter | 3 | 6 05 | 5 05 | 4 05 | 3 05 | 1 05 |
| | New Moon | 11 | 4 39 | 3 39 | 2 39 | 1 39 | 10d 11 39 |
| | First Quarter | 18 | 3 32 | 2 32 | 1 32 | 0 32 | 17d 10 32 |
| | Full Moon | 25 | 3 44 | 2 44 | 1 44 | 0 44 | 24d 10 44 |
| Nov. | Last Quarter | 2 | 2 14 | 1 14 | 0 14 | 1d 11 14 | 9 14 |
| | New Moon | 9 | 5 11 | 4 11 | 3 11 | 2 11 | 12 11 |
| | First Quarter | 16 | 10 45 | 9 45 | 8 45 | 7 45 | 5 45 |
| | Full Moon | 23 | 6 54 | 5 54 | 4 54 | 3 54 | 1 54 |
| Dec. | Last Quarter | 1 | 10 50 | 9 50 | 8 50 | 7 50 | 5 50 |
| | New Moon | 9 | 4 42 | 3 42 | 2 42 | 1 42 | 8d 11 42 |
| | First Quarter | 15 | 8 09 | 7 09 | 6 09 | 5 09 | 3 09 |
| | Full Moon | 23 | 12 35 | 11 35 | 10 35 | 9 35 | 7 35 |
| | Last Quarter | 31 | 5 52 | 4 52 | 3 52 | 2 52 | 12 52 |

## Moon's Perigee and Apogee, 1969

Eastern Standard Time (M is midnight; N is noon)

| Perigee 1969 | | | | Apogee 1969 | | | |
|---|---|---|---|---|---|---|---|
| Day | Hour | Day | Hour | Day | Hour | Day | Hour |
| January....16 | 7 P.M. | July.......28 | 4 A.M. | January.... 1 | 10 A.M. | July.......13 | 1 P.M. |
| February..13 | 11 P.M. | August....25 | 10 A.M. | January....28 | 10 A.M. | August.... 9 | 8 P.M. |
| March....12 | 9 P.M. | September.22 | 6 A.M. | February..25 | 5 P.M. | September. 6 | 10 A.M. |
| April.... 6 | 7 P.M. | October....17 | 11 P.M. | March....25 | 1 P.M. | October.... 4 | 4 A.M. |
| May....... 4 | 6 A.M. | November..12 | 9 P.M. | April.......22 | 9 A.M. | November.. 1 | 1 A.M. |
| June....... 1 | 10 A.M. | December..10 | 7 P.M. | May.......20 | 12 M. | November..29 | 8 P.M. |
| June.......29 | 7 P.M. | | | June.......16 | 10 A.M. | December..26 | 12 N. |

Each month the Moon is said to be in perigee when nearest to the Earth and in apogee when farthest from the Earth. The average time from perigee to perigee or from apogee to apogee is 27d. 13h. 18m. 33s., known as the anomalistic month.

## Aurora Borealis and Aurora Australis

The Aurora Borealis, also called the Northern Lights, is a broad display of rather faint light in the northern skies at night. The Aurora Australis, a similar phenomenon, appears at the same time in southern skies. The aurora appears in a wide variety of forms. Sometimes it is seen as a quiet glow, almost foglike in character; sometimes as vertical streamers in which there may be considerable motion; sometimes as a luminous series of expanding arcs. There are many colors, with white, yellow and red predominating.

The auroras are most vivid and most frequently seen at about 20 degrees from the magnetic poles, along the northern coast of the North American continent and the eastern part of the northern coast of Europe. They have been seen as far south as Key West and as far north as Australia and New Zealand, but such occasions are rare.

While the cause of the auroras is not known beyond question, there does seem to be a definite correlation between auroral displays and the sun-spot activity. Is it thought that atomic or sub-atomic particles expelled from the sun by the forces that cause solar flares speed through space at velocities of 400 to 600 miles per second. If and when such streams of particles reach the earth, their impact upon the atmosphere excites the gases in the upper regions of the atmosphere into the activity we see as the aurora. The earth is a tiny target as compared to the sun and receives only a minute fraction of the material thus expelled. These particles are deflected from their original course by the lines of force of the earth's magnetic field and are guided around the earth in such a way as to account for their appearance. They are most vivid where these lines of forces converge near the magnetic poles.

The auroral displays appear at heights ranging from 50 to about 600 miles and have given us a means of estimating the extent of the earth's atmosphere.

The auroras are often accompanied by magnetic storms whose forces, also guided by the lines of force of the earth's magnetic field, cut across and disrupt electric and radio communication.

# Star Tables, 1969

These tables include stars of visual magnitude 2.5 and brighter. Co-ordinates are for the epoch June 28.0, 1969. Where no parallax figures are given, the trigonometric parallax figure is smaller than the margin for error and the distance given is obtained by indirect methods. Stars of variable magnitude designated by var.

To find the time when star is on meridian, subtract R. A. M. S. of the sun table on page 285 from the star's right ascension, first adding 24h to the latter, if necessary; mark this result P. M., if less than 12h, but if greater than 12h subtract 12h and mark the remainder A. M.

| Star | Magnitude | Parallax | Light Yrs. | Right Ascen. | Declination | Star | Magnitude | Parallax | Light Yrs. | Right Ascen. | Declination |
|---|---|---|---|---|---|---|---|---|---|---|---|
| | | " | | h. m. | ° ' | | | " | | h. m. | ° ' |
| α Andromedae (Alpheratz) | 2.06 | 0.02 | 90 | 0 06.8 | +28 55 | γ Leonis...... | 1.99 | 0.03 | 90 | 10 18.3 | +20 00 |
| β Cassiopeiae.. | 2.26 | 0.07 | 45 | 0 07.6 | +58 59 | β Ursae Majoris | 2.37 | 0.04 | 78 | 11 00.0 | +56 33 |
| α Phoenicis | 2.39 | 0.03 | 93 | 0 24.8 | -42 28 | α Ursae Majoris | 1.81 | 0.03 | 105 | 11 01.9 | +61 55 |
| α Cassiopeiae (Schedir)... | 2.16 | 0.01 | 150 | 0 38.8 | +56 22 | β Leonis (Denebola). | 2.14 | 0.08 | 43 | 11 47.5 | +41 44 |
| β Ceti......... | 2.02 | 0.06 | 57 | 0 42.1 | -18 09 | γ Ursae Majoris | 2.44 | 0.02 | 90 | 11 52.2 | +53 52 |
| γ Cassiopeiae.. | var. | | | | | α Crucis...... | 1.39 | | 370 | 12 24.9 | -62 56 |
| | 2.13 | 0.03 | 96 | 0 54.9 | +60 33 | γ Crucis...... | 1.69 | | 220 | 12 26.5 | -56 57 |
| β Andromedae.. | 2.02 | 0.04 | 76 | 1 08.0 | +35 28 | γ Centauri.... | 2.17 | | 160 | 12 39.9 | -48 48 |
| α Eridani (Achernar).. | 0.51 | 0.02 | 118 | 1 36.6 | -57 23 | β Crucis...... | 1.28 | | 490 | 12 46.0 | -59 32 |
| γ Andromedae.. | 2.14 | | 260 | 2 02.1 | +42 11 | ε Ursae Majoris (Alioth).... | 1.79 | 0.04 | 68 | 12 52.7 | +56 07 |
| α Ursae Min... (Pole Star) | var. | | | | | ζ Ursae Majoris (Mizar)... | 2.26 | 0.04 | 88 | 13 22.7 | +55 05 |
| | 2.12 | | 680 | 2 02.5 | +89 08 | α Virginis..... | var. | | | | |
| α Arietis...... | 2.00 | 0.04 | 76 | 2 05.5 | +23 19 | (Spica) | 0.91 | | 220 | 13 23.6 | -11 00 |
| β Persei...... | var. | | | | | ε Centauri.... | 2.33 | | 570 | 13 38.0 | -53 19 |
| (Algol) | 2.06 | 0.03 | 105 | 3 06.0 | +40 50 | η Ursae Majoris (Alkaid).... | 1.87 | | 210 | 13 46.4 | +49 28 |
| α Persei........ | 1.80 | | 570 | 3 22.2 | +49 45 | β Centauri.... | 0.63 | | 490 | 14 01.7 | -60 13 |
| α Tauri...... | var. | | | | | θ Centauri.... | 2.04 | 0.06 | 55 | 14 04.9 | -36 14 |
| (Aldebaran).. | 0.86 | 0.05 | 68 | 4 34.2 | +16 27 | α Bootis (Arcturus)... | -0.06 | 0.09 | 36 | 14 14.3 | +19 20 |
| β Orionis..... | var. | | | | | γ Centauri.... | var. | | | | |
| (Betelgeuse) | 0.14 | | 900 | 5 13.1 | - 8 14 | | 2.30 | | 390 | 14 33.5 | -42 01 |
| α Aurigae (Capella)... | 0.05 | 0.07 | 45 | 5 14.5 | +45 58 | α Centauri.... | 0.01 | 0.75 | 4.3 | 14 37.1 | -60 43 |
| γ Orionis (Bellatrix).. | 1.64 | | 470 | 5 23.5 | + 6 19 | α Lupi........ | 2.32 | | 430 | 14 39.8 | -47 16 |
| β Tauri (El Nath).. | 1.65 | | 300 | 5 24.4 | +28 35 | β UrsaeMinoris | 2.04 | 0.03 | 105 | 14 50.8 | +74 16 |
| δ Orionis..... | var. | | | | | α Coronae Borealis... | 2.23 | 0.04 | 76 | 15 33.4 | +26 49 |
| | 2.20 | | 1500 | 5 30.5 | -0 19 | δ Scorpii..... | 2.34 | | 590 | 15 58.6 | -22 32 |
| ε Orionis..... | 1.70 | | 1600 | 5 34.7 | - 1 13 | α Scorpii..... | var. | | | | |
| ζ Orionis..... | 1.79 | | 1600 | 5 39.2 | - 1 57 | (Antares) | 0.92 | | 520 | 16 27.5 | -26 22 |
| κ Orionis..... | 2.06 | | 2100 | 5 46.3 | - 9 41 | α Trianguli Australis... | 1.93 | 0.02 | 82 | 16 45.5 | -68 59 |
| α Orionis..... | var. | | | | | ε Scorpii..... | 2.28 | 0.05 | 66 | 16 48.2 | -34 15 |
| (Betelgeuse) | 0.41 | | 520 | 5 53.5 | + 7 24 | η Ophiuchi.... | 2.46 | 0.05 | 69 | 17 08.7 | -15 41 |
| β Aurigae..... | 1.86 | 0.04 | 88 | 5 57.3 | +44 57 | λ Scorpii..... | 1.60 | | 310 | 17 31.5 | -37 05 |
| β Canis Majoris | 1.96 | | 750 | 6 21.4 | -17 56 | α Ophiuchi.... | 2.09 | 0.06 | 58 | 17 33.5 | +12 35 |
| α Carinae (Canopus).. | -0.72 | 0.02 | 98 | 6 23.3 | -52 41 | θ Scorpii..... | 1.86 | | 650 | 17 35.2 | -42 59 |
| γ Geminorum . | 1.93 | 0.03 | 105 | 6 35.9 | +16 26 | κ Scorpii..... | 2.39 | | 470 | 17 40.4 | -39 01 |
| α Canis Majoris (Sirius).. | -1.42 | 0.37 | 8.7 | 6 43.8 | -16 41 | γ Draconis.... | 2.21 | 0.02 | 108 | 17 55.9 | +51 20 |
| ε CanisMajoris | 1.48 | | 680 | 6 57.4 | -28 56 | ε Sagittarii.. | 1.81 | 0.01 | 124 | 18 22.2 | -34 24 |
| δ Canis Majoris | 1.85 | | 2100 | 7 07.2 | -26 21 | α Lyrae (Vega).. | 0.04 | 0.12 | 26.5 | 18 35.9 | +38 45 |
| η Canis Majoris | 2.46 | | 2700 | 7 22.9 | -29 14 | δ Sagittarii... | 2.12 | | 300 | 18 53.4 | -26 20 |
| α Geminorum (Castor).... | 1.97 | 0.07 | 45 | 7 32.7 | +31 57 | α Aquilae (Altair).. | 0.77 | 0.20 | 16.5 | 19 49.3 | + 8 47 |
| α Canis Majoris (Procyon).. | 0.37 | 0.29 | 11.3 | 7 37.7 | + 5 18 | γ Cygni....... | 2.22 | | 750 | 20 21.1 | +40 09 |
| β Geminorum (Pollux).... | 1.16 | 0.09 | 35 | 7 43.5 | +28 06 | α Pavonis..... | 1.95 | | 310 | 20 23.3 | -56 50 |
| ζ Puppis...... | 2.23 | | 2400 | 8 02.5 | -39 55 | α Cygni (Deneb)... | 1.26 | | 1600 | 20 40.4 | +45 10 |
| γ Velorum..... | 1.88 | | 520 | 8 08.6 | -47 16 | ε Cygni....... | 2.46 | 0.04 | 74 | 20 44.9 | +33 51 |
| ε Carinae..... | 1.97 | | 340 | 8 21.9 | -59 27 | α Cephei...... | 2.44 | 0.06 | 52 | 21 17.9 | +62 28 |
| δ Velorum..... | 1.95 | 0.04 | 76 | 8 43.9 | -54 36 | ε Pegasi...... | 2.31 | | 780 | 21 42.7 | + 9 45 |
| λ Velorum..... | 2.24 | | 750 | 9 01.9 | -43 19 | α Gruis....... | 1.76 | 0.05 | 64 | 22 06.3 | -47 07 |
| β Carinae..... | 1.67 | 0.04 | 86 | 9 12.9 | -69 36 | β Gruis....... | var. | | | | |
| ι Carinae..... | 2.25 | | 750 | 9 16.3 | -59 08 | | 2.17 | | 280 | 22 40.9 | -47 02 |
| κ Velorum..... | 2.45 | | 470 | 9 21.2 | -54 53 | αPiscis Austrinis (Fomalhaut) | 1.19 | 0.14 | 22.6 | 22 55.9 | -29 47 |
| α Hydrae..... | 1.98 | 0.02 | 94 | 9 26.1 | - 8 32 | β Pegasi...... | var. | | | | |
| α Leonis (Regulus).. | 1.36 | 0.04 | 84 | 10 06.8 | +12 07 | | 2.50 | 0.01 | 210 | 23 02.3 | +27 55 |
| | | | | | | α Pegasi...... | 2.50 | 0.03 | 109 | 23 03.3 | +15 02 |

## POLAR STAR, 1969

Mean time of upper transit (at 75° W. Longitude) and Polar Distance of Polaris

| Date | Upper Transit | Pole Dist. | Date | Upper Transit | Pole Dist. | Date | Upper Transit | Pole Dist. |
|---|---|---|---|---|---|---|---|---|
| | h. m. s. | ° ' " | | h. m. s. | ° ' " | | h. m. s. | ° ' " |
| Jan....1 | 7 16 38 P.M. | 0 52 20 | May....1 | 11 12 08 A.M. | 0 52 37 | Sept...1 | 3 22 02 A.M. | 0 52 41 |
| Feb....1 | 5 14 03 P.M. | 0 52 17 | June...1 | 9 21 40 A.M. | 0 52 45 | Oct....1 | 1 24 35 A.M. | 0 52 31 |
| Mar....1 | 3 23 22 P.M. | 0 52 20 | July...1 | 7 24 21 A.M. | 0 52 48 | Nov....1 | 11 18 59 P.M. | 0 52 20 |
| Apr....1 | 1 21 25 P.M. | 0 52 28 | Aug....1 | 5 23 12 A.M. | 0 52 45 | Dec....1 | 9 20 52 P.M. | 0 52 09 |

Upper transit of Polaris occurs, on the average, 3m. 56s. earlier each day. The interval between lower and upper transit of Polaris is 11h. 58m. 2s. The greatest Eastern elongation of Polaris occurs 5h. 56m. before upper transit and 6h. 2m. after lower transit, while the greatest Western elongation occurs 5h. 56m. after upper transit and 6h. 2m. before lower transit.

## Planetary Configurations, 1969

**Eastern Standard Time. A.M., light figures; P.M., black figures**
(0 designates midnight; 12 designates noon)

| | d. | h. | m. | | |
|---|---|---|---|---|---|
| Jan. | 3 | — | — | | ⊕ in perihelion |
| | 10 | 07 | — | ☌♃☾ | ♃ 2° N. |
| | 12 | **05** | — | ☌♂☾ | ♂ 5° N. |
| | 13 | 10 | — | | ☿ gr. elong. E. 19° |
| | 19 | 03 | — | ☌☿☾ | ☿ 5° N. |
| | | **06** | — | | ☿ stationary in R. A. |
| | 20 | **10** | — | | ♃ stationary in R. A. |
| | 21 | 11 | — | ☌♀☾ | ♀ 1° N. Occn. |
| | 24 | 01 | — | ☌♄☾ | ♄ 4° S. |
| | 26 | 05 | — | | ♀ gr. elong. E. 47° |
| | 29 | 04 | — | ☌☿☉ | inferior |
| Feb. | 6 | **12** | — | ☌♃☾ | ♃ 2° N. |
| | 9 | **09** | — | | ☿ stationary in R. A. |
| | 10 | 01 | — | ☌♂☾ | ♂ 6° N. |
| | 14 | **01** | — | ☌☿☾ | ☿ 6° N. |
| | 19 | **09** | — | ☌♀☾ | ♀ 2° N. |
| | 20 | **02** | — | ☌♄☾ | ♄ 5° S. |
| | 23 | 06 | — | | ☿ gr. elong. W. 27° |
| Mar. | 3 | 05 | — | | ♀ gr. brilliancy |
| | 5 | **02** | — | ☌♃☾ | ♃ 2° N. |
| | 10 | 03 | — | ☌♂☾ | ♂ 6° N. |
| | 16 | 11 | — | ☌☿☾ | ☿ 0°05′ S. Occn. |
| | 17 | 02 | — | | ♀ stationary in R. A. |
| | 18 | 00 | — | | ☉ eclipse |
| | 20 | 02 | — | ☌♀☾ | ♀ 6° N. |
| | | 05 | — | ☌♄☾ | ♄ 5° S. |
| | | **02** | **08** | | ☉ enters ♈ spring com. |
| | 21 | **06** | — | ☍♃☉ | |
| Apr. | 1 | **04** | — | ☌♃☾ | ♃ 2° N. |
| | 2 | **02** | — | | ☾ eclipse |
| | 6 | **11** | — | ☌♂☾ | ♂ 6° N. |
| | 8 | 10 | — | ☌♀☉ | inferior |
| | | **06** | — | ☌☿☉ | superior |
| | 15 | 11 | — | ☌♀☾ | ♀ 5° N. |
| | 18 | **03** | — | ☌♄☉ | |
| | 26 | **11** | — | | ♂ stationary in R. A. |
| | 27 | 02 | — | | ♀ stationary in R. A. |
| | 28 | **08** | — | ☌♃☾ | ♃ 1° N. |
| May | 4 | 10 | — | ☌♂☾ | ♂ 4° N. |
| | 5 | **06** | — | | ☿ gr. elong. E. 21° |
| | 12 | **08** | — | ☌♀☾ | ♀ 1° S. Occn. |
| | 14 | 04 | — | | ♀ gr. brilliancy |
| | | 10 | — | ☌♄☾ | ♄ 5° S. |
| | 17 | **01** | — | ☌☿☾ | ☿ 4° S. |
| | 18 | 00 | — | | ☿ stationary in R. A. |
| | 23 | **05** | — | | ♃ stationary in R. A. |
| | 26 | 04 | — | ☌♃☾ | ♃ 1° N. |
| | 29 | 05 | — | ☌☿☉ | inferior |
| | 31 | 09 | — | ☌♂☾ | ♂ 3° N. |
| | | 11 | — | ☍♂☉ | |
| June | 10 | 08 | — | | ☿ stationary in R. A. |
| | | **09** | — | ☌♀☾ | ♀ 6° S. |
| | | **09** | — | ☌♃☾ | ♃ 6° S. |
| | 11 | 09 | — | ☌♀♃ | ♀ 0°3′ S. |
| | 13 | 05 | — | ☌☿☾ | ☿ 9° S. |
| | 17 | **12** | — | | ♀ gr. elong. W. 46° |
| | 21 | 08 | 55 | | ☉ enters ♋ summer com. |
| | 22 | **03** | — | ☌♃☾ | ♃ 2° N. |
| | 23 | 05 | — | | ☿ gr. elong. W. 23° |
| | 27 | 08 | — | ☌♂☾ | ♂ 2° N. |
| July | 5 | — | — | | ⊕ in aphelion |
| | 8 | 05 | — | | ♂ stationary in R. A. |
| | | 08 | — | ☌♄☾ | ♄ 6° S. |
| | 10 | 11 | — | ☌♀☾ | ♀ 8° S. |
| | 13 | 09 | — | ☌☿☾ | ☿ 4° S. |
| | 20 | 03 | — | ☌♃☾ | ♃ 2° N. |
| | 22 | 10 | — | ☌☿☉ | superior |
| | 24 | **07** | — | ☌♂☾ | ♂ 2° N. |
| Aug. | 4 | **06** | — | ☌♄☾ | ♄ 7° S. |
| | 9 | 09 | — | ☌♀☾ | ♀ 7° S. |
| | 14 | **09** | — | ☌☿☾ | ☿ 0°3′ S. Occn. |
| | 16 | **06** | — | ☌♃☾ | ♃ 3° N. |
| | 21 | **07** | — | ☌♂☾ | ♂ 2° N. |
| | | **08** | — | | ♄ stationary in R. A. |
| | 27 | 06 | — | | ☾ eclipse |
| Sept. | 1 | 02 | — | ☌♄☾ | ♄ 7° S. |
| | 2 | **11** | — | | ☿ gr. elong. E. 27° |
| | 7 | 11 | — | ☌♃☿ | ☿ 5° S. |
| | 8 | **02** | — | ☌♀☾ | ♀ 3° S. |
| | 11 | **03** | — | | ☉ eclipse |
| | 13 | 11 | — | ☌♃☾ | ♃ 3° N. |
| | | **02** | — | ☌☿☾ | ☿ 2° S. |
| | 16 | 03 | — | | ☿ stationary in R. A. |
| | 19 | 02 | — | ☌♂☾ | ♂ 2° N. |
| | | **03** | — | ☌♃☿ | ☿ 6° S. |
| | 23 | 00 | 07 | | ☉ enters ♎ autumn com. |
| | 25 | **03** | — | | ☾ eclipse |
| | 28 | 10 | — | ☌♄☾ | ♄ 7° S. |
| | 29 | 05 | — | ☌☿☉ | inferior |
| Oct. | 7 | **12** | — | | ☿ stationary in R. A. |
| | 9 | 02 | — | ☌♀☾ | ♀ 1° N. |
| | 9 | **05** | — | ☌♃☉ | |
| | | **09** | — | ☌☿☾ | ☿ 2° N. |
| | 14 | **05** | — | | ☿ gr. elong. W. 18° |
| | 17 | **02** | — | ☌♂☾ | ♂ 2° N. |
| | 25 | **03** | — | ☌♄☾ | ♄ 7° S. |
| | 26 | 05 | — | ☌☿♃ | ☿ 0°8′ N. |
| | 28 | **09** | — | ☍♄☉ | |
| Nov. | 3 | **07** | — | ☌♀♃ | ♀ 0°5′ N. |
| | 8 | 01 | — | ☌♃☾ | ♃ 4° N. |
| | | 10 | — | ☌♀☾ | ♀ 5° N. |
| | 15 | 06 | — | ☌♂☾ | ♂ 2° N. |
| | 16 | 03 | — | ☌☿☉ | superior |
| | 21 | **07** | — | ☌♄☾ | ♄ 7° S. |
| Dec. | 5 | **09** | — | ☌♃☾ | ♃ 5° N. |
| | 14 | 01 | — | ☌♂☾ | ♂ 0°3′ N. Occn. |
| | 18 | **10** | — | ☌♄☾ | ♄ 7° S. |
| | 21 | **08** | **44** | | ☉ enters ♑ winter com. |
| | 27 | **04** | — | | ☿ gr. elong. E. 20° |

## Planetary Configurations, 1970

As a service to those who consult the planetary configurations for early 1970 in the preceding fall, the WORLD ALMANAC publishes the configurations for January, February, March and April 1970.

| | d. | h. | m. | | |
|---|---|---|---|---|---|
| Jan. | 1 | — | — | | ⊕ at perihelion |
| | 3 | **07** | — | | ☿ stationary in R. A. |
| | 4 | **03** | — | | ♄ stationary in R. A. |
| | 13 | 04 | — | ☌☿☉ | inferior |
| | 24 | 09 | — | | ☿ stationary in R. A. |
| | | **03** | — | ☌♀☉ | superior |
| Feb. | 5 | **03** | — | | ☿ gr. elong. W. 26° |
| | 20 | 02 | — | | ♃ stationary in R. A. |
| | | 03 | — | | ☾ eclipse |
| Mar. | 7 | 11 | — | | ☉ eclipse |
| | 17 | 03 | — | ☌♂♄ | ♂ 3° N. |
| | 20 | **07** | **57** | | ☉ enters ♈ spring com. |
| | 23 | 10 | — | ☌☿☉ | superior |
| Apr. | 11 | 08 | — | ☌♀♄ | ♀ 2° N. |
| | 12 | **05** | — | ☌☿♄ | ☿ 5° N. |
| | 18 | 03 | — | | ☿ gr. elong. E. 20° |
| | 21 | **10** | — | ☍♃☉ | |
| | 28 | **04** | — | | ☿ stationary in R. A. |

## Right Ascension of Mean Sun, 1969

**75° West Longitude—Noon—E.S.T.**

| Date | h. | m. | Date | h. | m. | Date | h. | m. | Date | h. | m. | Date | h. | m. | Date | h. | m. |
|---|---|---|---|---|---|---|---|---|---|---|---|---|---|---|---|---|---|
| Jan. 1 | 18 | 44.2 | Mar. 1 | 22 | 36.7 | May 10 | 3 | 12.6 | July 9 | 7 | 09.4 | Sept. 7 | 11 | 05.9 | Nov. 6 | 15 | 02.2 |
| 11 | 19 | 23.9 | 11 | 23 | 16.2 | 20 | 3 | 52.0 | 19 | 7 | 48.4 | 17 | 11 | 45.3 | 16 | 15 | 41.6 |
| 21 | 20 | 02.7 | 21 | 23 | 55.6 | 30 | 4 | 30.7 | 29 | 8 | 28.0 | 27 | 12 | 24.7 | 26 | 16 | 21.0 |
| 31 | 20 | 42.2 | 31 | 0 | 35.0 | | | | | | | | | | | | |
| | | | Apr. 10 | 1 | 14.4 | June 9 | 5 | 10.6 | Aug. 8 | 9 | 07.5 | Oct. 7 | 13 | 04.1 | Dec. 6 | 17 | 00.3 |
| Feb. 10 | 21 | 21.7 | 20 | 1 | 53.8 | 19 | 5 | 50.2 | 18 | 9 | 46.9 | 17 | 13 | 43.5 | 16 | 17 | 39.7 |
| 20 | 22 | 01.2 | 30 | 2 | 33.2 | 29 | 6 | 29.6 | 28 | 10 | 26.4 | 27 | 14 | 22.9 | 26 | 18 | 19.1 |

The Right Ascension of Mean Sun increases 3.943 minutes daily.

## The Planets and the Solar System

| Name of Planet | Mean Daily Motion | Sidereal Revolution Days | Dist. from Sun in Miles Maximum | Minimum | Approx. Dist. from Earth Millions of Miles Maximum | Minimum |
|---|---|---|---|---|---|---|
| Mercury | 14732.420 | 87.9686 | 43,355,000 | 28,566,000 | 136 | 50 |
| Venus | 5767.668 | 224.7007 | 67,653,000 | 66,738,000 | 161 | 25 |
| Earth | 3548.193 | 365.2564 | 94,452,000 | 91,342,000 | .... | .... |
| Mars | 1886.519 | 686.9804 | 154,760,000 | 128,830,000 | 248 | 35 |
| Jupiter | 298.122 | 4332.5870 | 506,710,000 | 459,940,000 | 600 | 367 |
| Saturn | 119.683 | 10759.2025 | 935,570,000 | 836,700,000 | 1028 | 744 |
| Uranus | 42.382 | 30685.93 | 1,866,800,000 | 1,698,800,000 | 1960 | 1606 |
| Neptune | 21.562 | 60187.64 | 2,817,400,000 | 2,769,600,000 | 2910 | 2677 |
| Pluto | 14.432 | 90737. | 4,600,000,000 | 2,760,000,000 | 4700 | 2670 |

Jupiter has 4 large and 8 small satellites, or moons, revolving around it; Saturn has 10; Uranus, 5; Neptune, 2; Mars, 2; the Earth, 1.

| Name of Planet | Eccentricity of Orbit* | Synodical Revolution— Days | Inclination of Orbit to Ecliptic* | Orbital Velocity Miles per Second |
|---|---|---|---|---|
| Mercury | 0.205 628 | 116 | 7 00 14.4 | 29.73 |
| Venus | 0.006 788 | 584 | 3 23 39.6 | 21.75 |
| Earth | 0.016 730 | .... | 0 00 00.0 | 18.50 |
| Mars | 0.093 377 | 780 | 1 56 25.7 | 14.98 |
| Jupiter | 0.048 161 | 399 | 1 18 31.9 | 8.11 |
| Saturn | 0.053 921 | 378 | 2 29 18.8 | 5.99 |
| Uranus | 0.051 373 | 370 | 0 46 21.4 | 4.22 |
| Neptune | 0.004 978 | 367 | 1 46 22.8 | 3.40 |
| Pluto | 0.253 265 | 367 | 17 08 09.7 | 3.00 |

| Name of Planet | Mean Longitude at the Epoch* | Mean Longitude of the Peri'el'n* | Annual Sidereal Motion | Mean Long. of the Ascending Node | Annual Sidereal Motion | Light at Perihelion | Aphelion |
|---|---|---|---|---|---|---|---|
| | ° ' " | ° ' " | " | ° ' " | " | | |
| Mercury | 341 15 58.8 | 76 58 50.6 | + 5.7 | 47 58 10.6 | − 7.5 | 10.58 | 4.59 |
| Venus | 326 22 05.3 | 131 08 30.4 | + 0.5 | 76 24 18.5 | −17.8 | 1.94 | 1.91 |
| Earth | 276 07 13.7 | 102 26 45.3 | +11.7 | ......... | ..... | 1.03 | 0.97 |
| Mars | 265 04 54.1 | 335 29 50.5 | +10.1 | 49 19 19.9 | −22.5 | 0.52 | 0.36 |
| Jupiter | 188 34 02.9 | 13 41 06.0 | + 7.7 | 100 08 20.8 | −13.8 | 0.41 | 0.034 |
| Saturn | 31 04 52.1 | 93 49 41.2 | +20.4 | 113 20 27.6 | −18.8 | 0.012 | 0.010 |
| Uranus | 183 13 35.7 | 171 30 45.7 | + 8.0 | 73 54 56.2 | −31.8 | 0.003 | 0.0025 |
| Neptune | 237 34 50.3 | 52 16 29.3 | +18.8 | 131 23 50.3 | −10.4 | 0.001 | 0.001 |
| Pluto | 174 25 42.6 | 222 53 38.0 | + 3.0 | 109 52 12.7 | 0.0 | 0.001 | 0.001 |

*Epoch—1969, June 28. 0 hours, Greenwich Mean Time.

| Sun and Planets | Semi-Diameter At Unit Distance | At Mean Least Dist. | In Miles (Mean S.-D.) | Volume ⊕=1. | Mass. ⊕=1 | Density ⊕=1 | Axial Rotation | Gravity at Surface ⊕=1. | Reflecting Power | Probable Temperature |
|---|---|---|---|---|---|---|---|---|---|---|
| | ' " | " | " | | | | d. h. m. s. | | Pct. | F |
| Sun | 15 59.63 | | 432000. | 1300000. | 332000. | 0.26 | 24 16 48 | 27. 9 | | +10,000 |
| Mercury | 3.34 | 5.45 | 1505 | 0.056 | 0.0543 | 0.68 | 59 | 0.38 | 0.07 | − 600 |
| Venus | 8.41 | 30.40 | 3805 | 0.910 | 0.8136 | 0.94 | 247 (R) | 0.88 | 0.76 | + 100 |
| Earth | ..... | ..... | 3959 | 1.000 | 1.000 | 1.00 | 23 56 4 | 1.00 | 0.39 | + 50 |
| Moon | 15 32.58 | | 1080 | 0.020 | 0.0120 | 0.60 | 27 7 43 12 | 0.16 | 0.07 | + 215 |
| Mars | 4.68 | 8.94 | 2070 | 0.150 | 0.1069 | 0.71 | 24 37 23 | 0.39 | 0.15 | 0 |
| Jupiter | 1 35.19 | 22.60 | 43450 | 1312. | 318.35 | 0.24 | 9 50 | 2.65 | 0.51 | − 150 |
| Saturn | 1 18.95 | 9.24 | 35750 | 763. | 95.3 | 0.12 | 10 02 | 1.17 | 0.50 | − 250 |
| Uranus | 34.28 | 1.88 | 14750 | 53. | 14.54 | 0.28 | 10 45 | 1.05 | 0.66 | − 350 |
| Neptune | 36.56 | 1.26 | 13400 | 34. | 17.2 | 0.45 | 15 48 | 1.23 | 0.62 | − 400 |

The planet Pluto was located by C. W. Tombaugh of Lowell Observatory March 13, 1930. Its mass is about 0.06 of the mass of the earth. Its average distance from the sun is 3,664,000 miles. On June 1, 1969, its predicted position in the sky will be 12 hours 06 minutes 30 seconds of astrometric right ascension and +16 degrees 18 minutes astrometric declination, in Leo. (R) Venus is in retrograde motion, rotating in opposite direction from other planets.

---

# New Astronomical Enigma Found by Radio Astronomy

Radio telescopes in recent years have picked up signals from space of such a nature that the forces producing them from stellar distances must have been incredibly powerful. In photographs obtained by optical telescopes these objects appear to be ordinary stars. Because they produce energy impossible in ordinary stars they are called "quasi-stellar objects," or "quasars." They remain a puzzle.

More recently, another baffling phenomenon has been added to the many unknowns of astronomy. British radio astronomers have detected 4 sources of radiation of such a nature that they were first thought to be signals originating in highly advanced civilizations on planets around stars other than the sun at vast distances. One of these sources has been examined by the 1,000-foot radio telescope at Arecibo in Puerto Rico. The radio emanations from this object occur at intervals measured at 1.337 seconds, continue for about one minute and then vanish for about 3 minutes. This source is in the small constellation of Vulpecula, The Little Fox, in late summer. These objects have been named "pulsars" in analogy to quasars.

The first theory of artificially produced radiation is not fully accepted because of the tremendous power which would be needed to broadcast such signals. They were also believed to come from

stars in the final stages of stellar evolution. When the hydrogen content of a star is virtually exhausted, internal pressure ceases. It is this internal pressure which combats the never-ceasing force of gravity and maintains the volume of the stars, keeping them distended sometimes to hundreds of times the volume of the sun. When internal pressure ceases, the star collapses to the smallest possible compass, ending its career as an object smaller than a planet, so condensed that one cubic inch of its material would weigh thousands of tons. The sub-atomic particles of such a star would be smashed together until only neutrons were left. This could produce the strange pulsations.

Astronomers also believe that the pulsars may be neutron stars, tiny bodies of densely packed neutrons which are atomic particles having no electrical charge. They are planet size and seem to be as close as 50 to 400 light years.

Both quasars and pulsars, together with other so-called "radio stars," emit x-radiation—energy in waves far shorter than ultra-violet radiation. Quasars radiate incredible energy from objects which appear to be relatively small. Pulsars, smaller than the earth, are keeping time in a sort of syncopation with their radio pulses and their light. Astronomers declare that it will be hard to make any theory of physics and cosmology fill the bill.

# Rising and Setting of Planets, 1969

Local Mean Time. A.M., light figures; P.M., black
(0 designates midnight; 12 designates noon)

| | 45° N. Latitude | | 40° N. Latitude | | 35° N. Latitude | | 30° N. Latitude | |
|---|---|---|---|---|---|---|---|---|
| | Rise h.m. | Set h.m. | Rise h.m. | Set h.m. | Rise h.m. | Set h.m. | Rise h.m. | Set h.m. |
| **VENUS** | | | | | | | | |
| Jan. 1 | 10 13 | 8 13 | 10 03 | 8 23 | 9 55 | 8 31 | 9 48 | 8 38 |
| 15 | 9 47 | 8 41 | 9 41 | 8 47 | 9 36 | 8 52 | 9 33 | 8 55 |
| Feb. 1 | 9 08 | 9 08 | 9 06 | 9 10 | 9 07 | 9 09 | 9 07 | 9 09 |
| 15 | 8 28 | 9 24 | 8 32 | 9 20 | 8 36 | 9 16 | 8 40 | 9 12 |
| Mar. 1 | 7 44 | 9 28 | 7 52 | 9 20 | 8 00 | 9 12 | 8 06 | 9 06 |
| 15 | 6 46 | 9 08 | 6 58 | 8 54 | 7 08 | 8 44 | 7 16 | 8 36 |
| Apr. 1 | 5 25 | 7 41 | 5 36 | 7 30 | 5 46 | 7 20 | 5 53 | 7 13 |
| 15 | 4 21 | 5 55 | 4 29 | 5 47 | 4 36 | 5 40 | 4 41 | 5 35 |
| May 1 | 3 31 | 4 23 | 3 35 | 4 19 | 3 39 | 4 15 | 3 42 | 4 12 |
| 15 | 2 59 | 3 45 | 3 02 | 3 42 | 3 06 | 3 38 | 3 08 | 3 36 |
| June 1 | 2 28 | 3 34 | 2 34 | 3 28 | 2 39 | 3 23 | 2 42 | 3 20 |
| 15 | 2 07 | 3 41 | 2 15 | 3 33 | 2 23 | 3 26 | 2 27 | 3 21 |
| July 1 | 1 46 | 4 00 | 1 57 | 3 49 | 2 08 | 3 38 | 2 14 | 3 32 |
| 15 | 1 39 | 4 19 | 1 52 | 4 16 | 2 03 | 4 13 | 2 13 | 3 45 |
| Aug. 1 | 1 39 | 4 45 | 1 55 | 4 29 | 2 08 | 4 16 | 2 19 | 4 05 |
| 15 | 1 53 | 4 59 | 2 09 | 4 43 | 2 22 | 4 40 | 2 33 | 4 19 |
| Sept. 1 | 2 24 | 5 04 | 2 37 | 4 51 | 2 45 | 4 40 | 2 58 | 4 30 |
| 15 | 2 53 | 4 59 | 3 03 | 4 49 | 3 12 | 4 40 | 3 20 | 4 32 |
| Oct. 1 | 3 32 | 4 46 | 3 38 | 4 40 | 3 44 | 4 34 | 3 48 | 4 30 |
| 15 | 4 08 | 4 28 | 4 10 | 4 26 | 4 11 | 4 25 | 4 12 | 4 24 |
| Nov. 1 | 4 50 | 4 06 | 4 47 | 4 07 | 4 43 | 4 13 | 4 41 | 4 15 |
| 15 | 5 28 | 3 50 | 5 20 | 3 58 | 5 13 | 4 05 | 5 07 | 4 11 |
| Dec. 1 | 6 13 | 3 39 | 6 00 | 3 52 | 5 49 | 4 03 | 5 39 | 4 13 |
| 15 | 6 49 | 3 39 | 6 33 | 3 55 | 6 20 | 4 08 | 6 08 | 4 20 |
| **MARS** | | | | | | | | |
| Jan. 1 | 1 57 | 12 21 | 1 50 | 12 38 | 1 44 | 12 44 | 1 38 | 12 50 |
| 15 | 1 44 | 11 54 | 1 34 | 12 04 | 1 26 | 12 12 | 1 20 | 12 18 |
| Feb. 1 | 1 25 | 11 11 | 1 14 | 11 22 | 1 04 | 11 32 | 0 57 | 11 39 |
| 15 | 1 06 | 10 36 | 0 54 | 10 48 | 0 44 | 10 58 | 0 35 | 11 07 |
| Mar. 1 | 0 46 | 10 00 | 0 32 | 10 14 | 0 20 | 10 26 | 0 11 | 10 35 |
| 15 | 0 18 | 9 24 | 0 04 | 9 38 | 11 52 | 9 50 | 11 41 | 10 01 |
| Apr. 1 | 11 41 | 8 35 | 11 26 | 8 50 | 11 12 | 9 04 | 11 02 | 9 14 |
| 15 | 11 02 | 7 46 | 10 46 | 8 02 | 10 32 | 8 16 | 10 20 | 8 28 |
| May 1 | 10 04 | 6 44 | 9 48 | 7 00 | 9 33 | 7 15 | 9 21 | 7 27 |
| 15 | 9 04 | 5 38 | 8 47 | 5 56 | 8 32 | 6 10 | 8 19 | 6 23 |
| June 1 | 7 32 | 4 02 | 7 15 | 4 19 | 7 00 | 4 34 | 6 46 | 4 48 |
| 15 | 6 17 | 2 47 | 6 00 | 3 02 | 5 45 | 3 14 | 5 31 | 3 33 |
| July 1 | 4 59 | 1 31 | 4 42 | 1 48 | 4 28 | 2 02 | 4 14 | 2 16 |
| 15 | 4 06 | 0 36 | 3 49 | 0 53 | 3 34 | 1 08 | 3 20 | 1 22 |
| Aug. 1 | 3 18 | 11 42 | 3 00 | 0 00 | 2 44 | 0 16 | 2 31 | 0 29 |
| 15 | 2 49 | 11 05 | 2 30 | 11 24 | 2 14 | 11 40 | 2 00 | 11 51 |
| Sept. 1 | 2 22 | 10 30 | 2 03 | 10 49 | 1 46 | 11 06 | 1 31 | 11 21 |
| 15 | 2 05 | 10 09 | 1 45 | 10 29 | 1 28 | 10 46 | 1 13 | 11 01 |
| Oct. 1 | 1 43 | 9 51 | 1 34 | 10 10 | 1 07 | 10 27 | 12 52 | 10 42 |
| 15 | 1 25 | 9 43 | 1 06 | 10 02 | 12 50 | 10 18 | 12 36 | 10 32 |
| Nov. 1 | 12 57 | 9 39 | 12 41 | 9 55 | 12 26 | 10 10 | 12 15 | 10 21 |
| 15 | 12 29 | 9 39 | 12 15 | 9 53 | 12 03 | 10 05 | 11 53 | 10 15 |
| Dec. 1 | 11 57 | 9 39 | 11 46 | 9 50 | 11 36 | 10 00 | 11 28 | 10 08 |
| 15 | 11 26 | 9 40 | 11 17 | 9 49 | 11 10 | 9 56 | 11 04 | 10 02 |
| **JUPITER** | | | | | | | | |
| Jan. 1 | 11 42 | 11 34 | 11 41 | 11 35 | 11 41 | 11 35 | 11 40 | 11 28 |
| 15 | 10 39 | 10 41 | 10 38 | 10 42 | 10 38 | 10 42 | 10 37 | 10 43 |
| Feb. 1 | 9 42 | 9 34 | 9 41 | 9 35 | 9 41 | 9 35 | 9 40 | 9 36 |
| 15 | 8 42 | 8 38 | 8 42 | 8 38 | 8 41 | 8 39 | 8 41 | 8 39 |
| Mar. 1 | 7 40 | 7 40 | 7 40 | 7 40 | 7 40 | 7 40 | 7 40 | 7 40 |
| 15 | 6 37 | 6 41 | 6 37 | 6 41 | 6 38 | 6 40 | 6 38 | 6 40 |
| Apr. 1 | 5 14 | 5 26 | 5 15 | 5 25 | 5 16 | 5 24 | 5 16 | 5 24 |
| 15 | 4 11 | 4 27 | 4 12 | 4 26 | 4 13 | 4 25 | 4 14 | 4 24 |
| May 1 | 3 01 | 3 21 | 3 03 | 3 19 | 3 04 | 3 18 | 3 05 | 3 17 |
| 15 | 2 01 | 2 25 | 2 03 | 2 23 | 2 05 | 2 21 | 2 06 | 2 20 |
| June 1 | 12 55 | 1 19 | 12 58 | 1 16 | 12 59 | 1 15 | 1 00 | 1 14 |
| 15 | 12 04 | 0 24 | 12 06 | 0 22 | 12 07 | 0 21 | 12 08 | 0 20 |
| July 1 | 11 08 | 11 24 | 11 09 | 11 23 | 11 10 | 11 22 | 11 11 | 11 21 |
| 15 | 10 23 | 10 31 | 10 24 | 10 30 | 10 24 | 10 30 | 10 25 | 10 29 |
| Aug. 1 | 9 30 | 9 30 | 9 30 | 9 30 | 9 30 | 9 30 | 9 30 | 9 30 |
| 15 | 8 48 | 8 40 | 8 47 | 8 41 | 8 47 | 8 41 | 8 46 | 8 42 |
| Sept. 1 | 7 58 | 7 40 | 7 57 | 7 41 | 7 55 | 7 43 | 7 54 | 7 44 |
| 15 | 7 17 | 6 55 | 7 15 | 6 53 | 7 13 | 6 55 | 7 12 | 6 56 |
| Oct. 1 | 6 33 | 5 55 | 6 30 | 5 58 | 6 29 | 5 59 | 6 25 | 6 03 |
| 15 | 5 54 | 5 06 | 5 50 | 5 10 | 5 47 | 5 13 | 5 44 | 5 16 |
| Nov. 1 | 5 06 | 4 08 | 5 02 | 4 12 | 4 57 | 4 17 | 4 54 | 4 20 |
| 15 | 4 27 | 3 19 | 4 21 | 3 25 | 4 15 | 3 31 | 4 13 | 3 33 |
| Dec. 1 | 3 41 | 2 23 | 3 34 | 2 30 | 3 29 | 2 35 | 3 29 | 2 40 |
| 15 | 2 58 | 1 34 | 2 51 | 1 41 | 2 49 | 1 48 | 2 40 | 1 52 |
| **SATURN** | | | | | | | | |
| Jan. 1 | 12 07 | 0 47 | 12 10 | 0 44 | 12 13 | 0 41 | 12 15 | 0 39 |
| 15 | 11 13 | 11 54 | 11 16 | 11 52 | 11 20 | 11 48 | 11 22 | 11 46 |
| Feb. 1 | 10 12 | 10 52 | 10 10 | 10 50 | 10 14 | 10 46 | 10 16 | 10 44 |
| 15 | 9 16 | 10 04 | 9 20 | 10 00 | 9 23 | 9 57 | 9 36 | 9 54 |
| Mar. 1 | 8 23 | 9 17 | 8 27 | 9 13 | 8 31 | 9 09 | 8 34 | 9 06 |
| 15 | 7 32 | 8 30 | 7 36 | 8 26 | 7 40 | 8 22 | 7 44 | 8 18 |
| Apr. 1 | 6 28 | 7 34 | 6 34 | 7 28 | 6 39 | 7 23 | 6 42 | 7 20 |
| 15 | 5 37 | 6 49 | 5 43 | 6 43 | 5 48 | 6 38 | 5 52 | 6 34 |
| May 1 | 4 39 | 5 57 | 4 46 | 5 50 | 4 51 | 5 45 | 5 56 | 5 40 |
| 15 | 3 48 | 5 10 | 3 55 | 5 03 | 4 01 | 4 57 | 4 06 | 4 52 |
| June 1 | 2 47 | 4 13 | 2 53 | 4 07 | 3 00 | 4 00 | 3 05 | 3 55 |
| 15 | 1 56 | 3 26 | 2 03 | 3 19 | 2 10 | 3 12 | 2 15 | 3 07 |
| July 1 | 0 54 | 2 30 | 1 04 | 2 22 | 1 11 | 2 15 | 1 16 | 2 10 |
| 15 | 0 03 | 1 41 | 0 11 | 1 33 | 0 18 | 1 26 | 0 24 | 1 20 |
| Aug. 1 | 10 59 | 12 37 | 11 07 | 12 29 | 11 14 | 12 22 | 11 20 | 12 16 |
| 15 | 10 06 | 11 44 | 10 14 | 11 36 | 10 21 | 11 29 | 10 27 | 11 23 |
| Sept. 1 | 8 58 | 10 36 | 9 06 | 10 28 | 9 13 | 10 21 | 9 19 | 10 15 |
| 15 | 8 03 | 9 39 | 8 11 | 9 31 | 8 18 | 9 24 | 8 23 | 9 19 |
| Oct. 1 | 6 58 | 8 32 | 7 06 | 8 24 | 7 13 | 8 17 | 7 18 | 8 12 |
| 15 | 6 01 | 7 31 | 6 08 | 7 24 | 6 15 | 7 17 | 6 20 | 7 12 |
| Nov. 1 | 4 46 | 6 14 | 4 53 | 6 07 | 5 00 | 6 00 | 5 05 | 5 55 |
| 15 | 3 49 | 5 11 | 3 56 | 5 06 | 4 02 | 5 00 | 4 07 | 4 55 |
| Dec. 1 | 2 43 | 4 04 | 2 50 | 3 59 | 3 01 | 3 57 | 3 01 | 3 47 |
| 15 | 1 45 | 3 07 | 1 52 | 3 00 | 1 58 | 2 54 | 2 03 | 2 49 |

## U. S. Weather Bureau: Environmental Science Services Administration

The Weather Bureau is now a component of the Environmental Science Services Administration (ESSA), an agency of the U. S. Department of Commerce. Created in 1965 by merging the Weather Bureau, the Coast and Geodetic Survey, and the Central Radio Propagation Laboratory, ESSA provides a single focus for national efforts to describe, understand, and predict man's natural environment.

Some former Weather Bureau activities have been transferred to other parts of ESSA, but the Weather Bureau continues to provide meteorological service to the nation.

Weather service for the public safety, welfare, recreation, and convenience consists of current weather information, warnings of hurricanes, tornadoes, winter storms, and other weather hazards, regularly scheduled weather forecasts up to 48 hours, extended forecasts up to five days, and outlook for 30 days. This information reaches the general public through the cooperation of radio, television, and the newspapers. *See also Weather Bureau Watches and Warnings, page 289.*

The River and Flood Forecasting Service is conducted through 82 river district offices and 11 river forecasting centers and issues river stage and flood warnings for all the principal rivers and tributaries of the United States. The Water Supply Forecasting Service is conducted through 6 Water Supply Forecasting Centers for the Western and Northeastern United States on a water year or seasonal basis. Rainfall studies conducted in cooperation with the Army Corps of Engineers and the Department of Agriculture Soil Conservation Service assist in planning engineering works for flood control, water utilization, water-shed protection and local drainage design.

Weather Service to aviation involves the responsibilities of providing current measurements and of forecasting conditions pertinent to conducting safe and efficient flight operations at airport terminals and along flight routes. Aviation weather forecasts and briefings are provided for transoceanic and domestic operations extending upward from the surface to include operational levels of civil jet aircraft.

The agricultural weather service program provides weather observations from representative agricultural areas, specialized forecasts of weather factors directly affecting agricultural production and a teletypewriter network for rapid and efficient dissemination of weather information to the farmers. In addition, technical studies of the influence of weather on agriculture are coordinated jointly with agricultural experiment station personnel.

U. S. Department of Agriculture and the Weather Bureau cooperate in issuing local weather-crop bulletins on an area basis.

The Fruit-frost Service provides detailed and localized forecasts and warnings to fruit growers on a cooperative basis in those states where winter and spring fruit and vegetable production is a major activity. The Fire-Weather Service warns against atmospheric conditions conducive to disastrous fires in the forest areas of the nation.

The marine weather service provides specialized weather forecasts, warnings, and data essential to the conduct of marine operations on the high seas and on coastal and inland waterways. In addition, it supplies forecasts for related phenomena, such as seiches and storm surges, for the protection of life and property.

The Weather Bureau also provides weather support for the U. S. manned space flight program and assists in the weather support to the Nation's other space programs.

The climatological service for the United States, Puerto Rico, and the oceans, is managed by the ESSA Environmental Data Service. In the field, climatologists are responsible for applications of climatology to problems of the national economy in their geographical areas. This work is supported in each state by State Climatologists who (a) direct liaison with state interests and (b) carry out certain state responsibilities such as those of Crop-Weather Services and severe storm investigation. The work depends basically on observations taken at about 12,000 substations (mostly manned by unpaid cooperative observers) and about 300 regular Weather Bureau stations. The repository for all American weather records and facilities for large-scale tabulation, processing, and publication are maintained in the National Weather Records Center, Asheville, N. C.

## Wind Chill Table

Source: Environmental Science Services Administration

| Degrees (Fahrenheit) | 35 | 30 | 25 | 20 | 15 | 10 | 5 | 0 | −5 | −10 | −15 | −20 | −25 | −30 | −35 | −40 | −45 |
|---|---|---|---|---|---|---|---|---|---|---|---|---|---|---|---|---|---|
| MPH | Wind Chill Index: (Equivalent temperature) Equivalent in cooling power on exposed flesh under calm conditions. | | | | | | | | | | | | | | | | |
| 0 | 35 | 30 | 25 | 20 | 15 | 10 | 5 | 0 | −5 | −10 | −15 | −20 | −25 | −30 | −35 | −40 | −45 |
| 5 | 33 | 27 | 21 | 16 | 12 | 7 | 1 | −6 | −11 | −15 | −20 | −26 | −31 | −35 | −41 | −47 | −54 |
| 10 | 21 | 16 | 9 | 2 | −2 | −9 | −15 | −22 | −27 | −31 | −38 | −45 | −52 | −58 | −64 | −70 | −77 |
| 15 | 16 | 11 | 1 | −6 | −11 | −18 | −25 | −33 | −40 | −45 | −51 | −60 | −65 | −70 | −78 | −85 | −90 |
| 20 | 12 | 3 | −4 | −9 | −17 | −24 | −32 | −40 | −46 | −52 | −60 | −68 | −76 | −81 | −88 | −96 | −103 |
| 25 | 7 | 0 | −7 | −15 | −22 | −29 | −37 | −45 | −52 | −58 | −67 | −75 | −83 | −89 | −96 | −104 | −112 |
| 30 | 5 | −2 | −11 | −18 | −26 | −33 | −41 | −49 | −56 | −63 | −70 | −78 | −87 | −94 | −101 | −109 | −117 |
| 35 | 3 | −4 | −13 | −20 | −27 | −35 | −43 | −52 | −60 | −67 | −72 | −83 | −90 | −98 | −105 | −113 | −123 |
| 40 | 1 | −4 | −15 | −22 | −29 | −36 | −45 | −54 | −62 | −69 | −76 | −87 | −94 | −101 | −107 | −116 | −128 |
| 45 | 1 | −6 | −17 | −24 | −31 | −38 | −46 | −54 | −63 | −70 | −78 | −87 | −94 | −101 | −108 | −118 | −128 |
| 50 | 0 | −7 | −17 | −24 | −31 | −38 | −47 | −56 | −63 | −70 | −79 | −88 | −96 | −103 | −110 | −120 | −128 |

*(Wind speeds greater than 40 mph have little additional chilling effect)*

How Cold is Cold? Temperature and wind both affect the heat loss from the surface of the body. The effect of these two factors is expressed as an "equivalent temperature," which approximates the still-air temperature which would have the same cooling effect as the wind and temperature combination. For example, from the table above, with a temperature of 20°F. and a wind of 20 mph., the effect on exposed flesh is the same as -9°F. with no wind.

## Dew Point Explained

The dew point is the temperature to which air must be cooled to become saturated. When this temperature is below freezing, it is sometimes called the frost point.

The higher the air temperature, the more water vapor air can hold before saturation is reached and condensation occurs (fog, snow or rain). Thus, unsaturated air containing a given amount of water vapor will become saturated if its temperature decreases sufficiently.

The difference between the actual air temperature and the dew point temperature is an indication of how close the air is to saturation. Relative humidity increases as this difference decreases, reaching 100% when the spread is zero degrees.

### Temperature-Humidity Index

The purpose of the temperature-humidity index (THI) is to measure or estimate human discomfort in the summertime resulting from the combined effects of temperature and humidity. The THI is calculated by adding wet bulb and dry bulb temperature readings, multiplying the sum by 0.4 and adding 15. The theory is that more than half the people will be uncomfortable when the THI passes 75. Almost all will be uncomfortable when it reaches 80 or above, and many will be miserable.

# Weather Bureau Watches and Warnings

Weather Bureau forecasters issue a TORNADO WATCH for a specific area where it is reasonably possible that tornadoes may occur during the next several hours. A WATCH is to alert people to watch for tornado activity and listen for a TORNADO WARNING. A TORNADO WARNING means that a tornado has been sighted and that safety precautions should be taken at once. The terms HURRICANE WATCH and HURRICANE WARNING are used similarly during hurricane season.

## Definitions

**Tornado**—A violent twisting column of air pendant from a thundercloud, usually recognized as a funnel-shaped vortex accompanied by a loud roar. With rotating winds est. over 200 mph., it is the most destructive storm. Tornado paths have varied in length from a few feet to nearly 300 miles (avg. 13 mi.); diameter 9 feet to over a mile (avg. 250 yds.); forward speed up to 68 mph. (avg. 25-40 mph.). Persisting from a few minutes to a few hours, they usually move from SW to NE, but can come from any direction.

**Cyclone**—An atmospheric circulation of winds rotating counterclockwise in the northern hemisphere and clockwise in the southern hemisphere. Tornadoes, hurricanes and the LOWS shown on weather maps are all examples of cyclones having various sizes and intensities. Cyclones are usually accompanied by precipitation or stormy weather.

**Hurricane**—A severe cyclone originating over tropical ocean waters and having winds over 73 miles an hour. (In the western Pacific, such storms are known as typhoons.) The area of strong winds takes the form of a circle or an oval, sometimes as much as 500 miles in diameter. Hurricanes usually move toward the west or northwest at 10 to 15 m.p.h. When the center approaches 25° to 30° North Latitude, direction of motion often changes to northeast, with increased forward speed.

**Blizzard**—A severe weather condition characterized by low temperatures and by strong winds bearing a great amount of snow (mostly fine, dry snow picked up from the ground). The U. S. Weather Bureau specifies, for blizzard, a wind of 35 miles an hour or higher, low temperatures, and sufficient snow in the air to reduce visibility to less than 500 feet; and for "severe blizzard" wind speeds of 45 miles an hour or more, temperature near or below 10°F., and visibility reduced by snow to near zero.

**Monsoon**—A name for seasonal winds (derived from Arabic "mausim," a season). It was first applied to the winds over the Arabian Sea, which blow for six months from northeast and six months from southwest, but it has been extended to similar winds in other parts of the world. The monsoons are strongest on the southern and eastern sides of Asia.

**Flood**—The condition that occurs when water overflows the natural or artificial confines of a stream or other body of water, or accumulates by drainage over low-lying areas.

# Weather Bureau Coastal Warnings

**Source:** Weather Bureau, National Weather Records, ESSA; Dept. of Commerce

**Small Craft Warning:** One red pennant displayed by day and a red light over a white light at night to indicate winds up to 33 knots and/or sea conditions dangerous to small craft are forecast.

**Gale Warning:** Two red pennants displayed by day and a white light above a red light at night to indicate that winds ranging from 34 to 47 knots are forecast for the area.

**Storm Warning:** A single square red flag with a black center displayed during daytime and two red lights at night to indicate that winds above 48 knots are forecast for the area.

**Hurricane Warning:** Two square red flags with black centers displayed by day and a white light between two red lights at night to indicate that winds 64 knots and above are forecast for the area.

# Speed of Winds in the United States

Miles per hour—Average thru 1967. High thru 1967.
**Source:** Weather Bureau. Wind velocities in true values

| Stations | Avg. | High | Stations | Avg. | High | Stations | Avg. | High |
|----------|------|------|----------|------|------|----------|------|------|
| Albany, N. Y. | 8.8 | 71 | Helena, Mont. | 7.9 | 73 | Pensacola, Fla. | 7.9 | (b) 91 |
| Albuquerque, N. M. | 8.9 | 90 | Jacksonville, Fla. | 8.9 | 82 | Philadelphia, Pa. | 9.5 | 73 |
| Atlanta, Ga. | 9.2 | 70 | Key West, Fla. | 11.5 | 122 | Pittsburgh, Pa. | 9.4 | 58 |
| Bismarck, N. D. | 10.8 | 72 | Knoxville, Tenn. | 7.5 | 73 | Portland, Ore. | 7.7 | 88 |
| Boston, Mass. | 13.0 | 65 | Little Rock, Ark. | 8.2 | 65 | Rochester, N. Y. | 9.7 | 73 |
| Buffalo, N. Y. | 12.6 | 91 | Louisville, Ky. | 8.3 | 61 | St. Louis, Mo. | 9.4 | (b) 91 |
| Cape Hatteras, N. C. | 11.5 | (b) 110 | Memphis, Tenn. | 9.3 | 56 | Salt Lake City, Utah | 8.7 | 71 |
| Chattanooga, Tenn. | 6.3 | 82 | Miami, Fla. | 9.0 | (a) 80 | San Diego, Calif. | 6.5 | 51 |
| Chicago, Ill. | 10.2 | 60 | Minneapolis, Minn. | 10.7 | 92 | San Francisco, Calif. | 10.4 | 62 |
| Cincinnati, Ohio | 7.1 | 49 | Mobile, Ala. | 9.7 | (b) 98 | Savannah, Ga. | 8.4 | 66 |
| Cleveland, Ohio | 11.0 | 74 | Montgomery, Ala. | 6.9 | 60 | Spokane, Wash. | 8.3 | 56 |
| Denver, Colo. | 9.3 | 56 | Nashville, Tenn. | 7.7 | 73 | Toledo, Ohio | 9.5 | 72 |
| Detroit, Mich. | 10.1 | 77 | New Orleans, La. | 8.5 | (b) 98 | Washington, D. C. | 9.5 | 78 |
| Fort Smith, Ark. | 7.7 | 58 | New York, N. Y. (c) | 9.6 | | Mt. Wash'ton, N. H. | 35.6 | 231 |
| Galveston, Texas | 11.0 | (d) 100 | Omaha, Nebr. | 11.1 | 73 | | | |

(a) Highest velocity ever recorded in Miami area was 132 mph., at former station in Miami Beach in September, 1926. (b) Previous location. (c) Data for Central Park. Battery Place data through 1960, avg. 14.5, high 113. (d) Recorded before anemometer blew away. Estimated high 120.

## WINDS, THEIR FORCE AND OFFICIAL DESIGNATIONS

| Designation | Miles per hour | Designation | Miles per hour | Designation | Miles per hour | Designation | Miles per hour |
|-------------|----------------|-------------|----------------|-------------|----------------|-------------|----------------|
| Calm | Less than 1 | Moderate breeze | 13 to 18 | Near gale | 32 to 38 | Storm | 55 to 63 |
| Light air | 1 to 3 | Fresh breeze | 19 to 24 | Gale | 39 to 46 | Violent storm | 64 to 73 |
| Light breeze | 4 to 7 | Strong breeze | 25 to 31 | Strong gale | 47 to 54 | Hurricane | 74 and above |
| Gentle breeze | 8 to 12 | | | | | | |

# Explanation of Normal Temperatures

Normal temperatures listed in the tables on pages 291 and 292 are based on records of the Weather Bureau for the 30-year period from 1931 to 1960 inclusive.

To obtain the average maximum temperature for any month, the daily maximum temperatures are added; the total is then divided by the number of days in that month. The average minimum temperature for the month is obtained by adding the daily minimum temperatures during that month and dividing by the number of days in that month.

The normal maximum temperature for January, for example, is obtained by adding the average maximums for January, 1931, January 1932, etc., through January, 1960. The total is then divided by 30. The normal minimum temperature is obtained in a similar manner by adding the average minimums for each January in the 30-year period and dividing by 30. The normal temperature for January is one-half of the sum of the normal maximum and minimum temperatures for that month.

The mean temperature for any one day is one-half the total of the maximum and minimum temperatures for that day.

# Annual Climatological Data

Source: Environmental Science Services Administration, National Weather Records Center

| Station 1967 | Temperature Elevation (ft.) | Highest | Date | Lowest | Date | Precipitation Total (in.) | Greatest in 24 hrs. | Date¹ | Snow or Sleet Total (in.) | Greatest in 24 hrs. | Date¹ | Wind Fastest MPH | Date | No. of days Clear* | Cloudy* | Precip. .01 inch or more | Snow, sleet 1 inch or more |
|---|---|---|---|---|---|---|---|---|---|---|---|---|---|---|---|---|---|
| Albany, N. Y. | 275 | 96 | 6/16 | -14 | 2/8 | 33.28 | 1.76 | 10/25 | 78.3 | 12.2 | 12/28 | 45 | 4/23 | 50 | 216 | 139 | 20 |
| Albuquerque, N. M. | 5311 | 99 | 7/1 | 1 | 1/8 | 8.04 | 1.22 | 8/11 | 6.1 | 1.4 | 12/15 | 57 | 12/13 | 157 | 85 | 58 | 5 |
| Anchorage, Alaska | 114 | 78 | 7/11 | -18 | 2/14 | 19.16 | 0.79 | 9/5 | 79.6 | 8.3 | 12/7 | 44 | 1/28 | 79 | 226 | 131 | 21 |
| Asheville, N. C. | 2140 | 88 | 4/6 | -2 | 2/25 | 52.11 | 4.12 | 8/22 | 7.6 | 2.2 | 2/9 | 40 | 5/30 | 95 | 156 | 118 | 4 |
| Atlanta, Ga. | 1010 | 90 | 7/25 | 9 | 2/25 | 54.84 | 3.50 | 8/23 | 2.0 | 2.0 | 2/9 | 38 | 7/26 | 106 | 155 | 125 | 1 |
| Baltimore, Md. | 148 | 96 | 6/16 | -1 | 2/8 | 36.93 | 2.91 | 7/2 | 36.0 | 10.6 | 2/6 | 49 | 2/16 | 100 | 153 | 105 | 9 |
| Barrow, Alaska | 31 | 61 | 8/17 | -38 | 1/3 | 4.70 | 0.35 | 7/14 | 37.6 | 2.6 | 12/30 | 43 | 3/12 | 46 | 212 | 108 | 6 |
| Birmingham, Ala. | 620 | 94 | 6/20 | 12 | 2/25 | 66.84 | 4.64 | 12/14 | 0.8 | 0.8 | 2/9 | 41 | 3/6 | 108 | 178 | 119 | 0 |
| Bismarck, N. D. | 1647 | 102 | 7/31 | -43 | 12/31 | 13.54 | 1.22 | 5/30 | 69.4 | 11.0 | 5/30 | 52 | 5/7 | 82 | 171 | 93 | 27 |
| Boise, Idaho | 2838 | 107 | 7/12 | 2 | 12/16 | 7.68 | 0.62 | 4/19 | 17.8 | 6.0 | 4/19 | 34 | 6/21 | 130 | 161 | 85 | 6 |
| Boston, Mass. | 15 | 94 | 6/16 | -3 | 2/13 | 47.60 | 3.64 | 5/25 | 67.1 | 10.8 | 3/6 | 50 | 5/25 | 95 | 178 | 135 | 14 |
| Buffalo, N. Y. | 705 | 91 | 6/21 | -7 | 2/8 | 34.60 | 3.63 | 9/27 | 74.1 | 8.3 | 11/6 | 62 | 2/16 | 47 | 223 | 179 | 27 |
| Burlington, Vt. | 332 | 91 | 6/4 | -25 | 2/13 | 32.22 | 2.05 | 7/21 | 73.9 | 11.4 | 12/28 | 40 | 10/19 | 51 | 222 | 155 | 24 |
| Charleston, S. C. | 40 | 97 | 8/7 | 14 | 2/26 | 43.65 | 6.23 | 5/22 | T | T | 2/13 | 60 | 5/31 | 95 | 144 | 105 | 0 |
| Charleston, W. Va. | 939 | 93 | 6/23 | 0 | 2/8 | 41.68 | 2.86 | 3/6 | 43.2 | 11.2 | 12/28 | 37 | 2/16 | 61 | 177 | 144 | 10 |
| Chicago, Ill. | 607 | 93 | 5/26 | -10 | 12/31 | 41.10 | 2.95 | 6/10 | 68.5 | 19.8 | 1/26 | 51 | 2/15 | 73 | 175 | 133 | 16 |
| Cincinnati, Ohio | 761 | 94 | 7/25 | -3 | 2/25 | 32.48 | 1.90 | 5/6 | 18.6 | 9.0 | 3/6 | 47 | 2/15 | | | 130 | 6 |
| Cleveland, Ohio | 777 | 93 | 6/17 | -7 | 2/8 | 26.79 | 1.10 | 5/7 | 39.9 | 4.3 | 2/5 | 53 | 2/16 | 61 | 208 | 156 | 13 |
| Columbus, Ohio | 812 | 92 | 6/15 | -2 | 3/1¹ | 33.96 | 1.59 | 9/27 | 41.5 | 6.6 | 3/6 | 54 | 2/16 | 62 | 187 | 137 | 12 |
| Concord, N. H. | 342 | 92 | 6/16 | -23 | 2/13 | 34.19 | 2.16 | 7/4 | 96.5 | 10.4 | 3/7 | 36 | 4/10 | 87 | 175 | 127 | 24 |
| Dallas, Texas | 481 | 105 | 7/31 | 23 | 1/8 | 27.76 | 2.27 | 4/20 | T | T | 12/27 | 53 | 6/11 | 123 | 139 | 81 | 0 |
| Denver, Colo. | 5283 | 93 | 8/24 | -12 | 12/31 | 23.31 | 3.25 | 4/13 | 51.7 | 6.2 | 11/2 | 42 | 12/6 | 104 | 134 | 107 | 18 |
| Des Moines, Iowa | 938 | 98 | 5/25 | -13 | 1/18 | 21.82 | 2.20 | 6/9 | 13.4 | 2.4 | 10/26 | 50 | 4/17 | 91 | 173 | 96 | 4 |
| Detroit, Mich. | 633 | 93 | 6/16 | -5 | 12/31 | 33.53 | 2.17 | 12/21 | 29.8 | 4.0 | 1/26 | 52 | 2/16 | 76 | 190 | 133 | 10 |
| Dodge City, Kan. | 2582 | 102 | 5/24 | -1 | 12/31 | 21.30 | 2.14 | 8/31 | 8.7 | 2.2 | 1/25 | 54 | 6/28 | 125 | 139 | 86 | 2 |
| Duluth, Minn. | 1428 | 87 | 7/21 | -30 | 1/18 | 21.43 | 1.57 | 6/13 | 58.5 | 13.0 | 1/6 | 63 | 4/30 | 80 | 187 | 128 | 13 |
| Fairbanks, Alaska | 436 | 91 | 6/18 | -44 | 1/29 | 17.33 | 3.42 | 8/12 | 94.7 | 7.6 | 3/30 | 36 | 3/12 | 60 | 236 | 140 | 39 |
| Fort Worth, Texas | 537 | 104 | 7/31 | 20 | 2/7 | 27.30 | 2.47 | 4/20 | T | T | 12/27 | 39 | 4/13 | 130 | 143 | 81 | 0 |
| Fresno, Calif. | 328 | 108 | 8/15 | 21 | 12/14 | 12.98 | 1.22 | 4/18 | T | T | 12/12 | 29 | 5/31 | 175 | 106 | 50 | 0 |
| Galveston, Texas | 7 | 93 | 8/10 | 34 | 2/8 | 35.24 | 2.90 | 7/23 | .0 | .0 | | 47 | 10/30 | | | 81 | 0 |
| Grand Rapids, Mich. | 784 | 91 | 7/22 | -16 | 2/12 | 40.75 | 2.53 | 6/7 | 86.6 | 12.6 | 1/26 | 54 | 4/16 | 62 | 209 | 160 | 31 |
| Helena, Mont. | 3828 | 99 | 7/5 | -26 | 12/21 | 14.40 | 1.11 | 5/10 | 91.5 | 12.5 | 5/10 | 54 | 1/15 | 100 | 178 | 111 | 21 |
| Honolulu, Hawaii | 7 | 92 | 10/3 | 59 | 12/28 | 34.34 | 4.33 | 12/17 | .0 | .0 | | 34 | 1/10 | 81 | 124 | 138 | 0 |
| Houston, Texas | 50 | 99 | 6/26 | 26 | 1/4 | 36.45 | 3.12 | 9/4 | T | T | 1/9 | 35 | 12/2 | 86 | 150 | 92 | 0 |
| Huron, S. D. | 1282 | 101 | 7/31 | -25 | 12/31 | 15.17 | 5.48 | 6/17 | 32.7 | 6.7 | 2/14 | 57 | 1/16 | 102 | 169 | 96 | 10 |
| Indianapolis, Ind. | 792 | 93 | 7/11 | -9 | 12/31 | 34.75 | 1.96 | 10/16 | 23.3 | 4.1 | 2/27 | 49 | 2/15 | 73 | 186 | 126 | 9 |
| Jackson, Miss. | 310 | 96 | 6/19 | 17 | 2/8 | 45.71 | 3.26 | 5/21 | T | T | 12/28 | 40 | 5/31 | 113 | 159 | 93 | 0 |
| Jacksonville, Fla. | 20 | 100 | 5/13 | 22 | 2/26 | 49.68 | 3.67 | 8/21 | .0 | .0 | | 76 | 6/30 | 102 | 128 | 102 | 0 |
| Juneau, Alaska | 12 | 80 | 6/17 | -4 | 3/26 | 50.07 | 1.92 | 9/17 | 110.4 | 9.0 | 2/24 | 48 | 9/18 | 50 | 272 | 218 | 37 |
| Kansas City, Mo. | 742 | 99 | 7/24 | 1 | 12/31 | 48.69 | 3.32 | 9/13 | 16.8 | 7.5 | 1/25 | 41 | 6/7 | 100 | 165 | 92 | 5 |
| Lander, Wyo. | 5563 | 90 | 7/22 | -15 | 12/21 | 18.98 | 1.22 | 4/29 | 154.6 | 21.9 | 4/29 | 73 | 1/22 | 80 | 158 | 107 | 32 |
| Little Rock, Ark. | 257 | 95 | 8/9 | 11 | 1/18 | 50.75 | 4.05 | 9/7 | 2.7 | 1.6 | 1/17 | 36 | 2/15 | 101 | 155 | 105 | 2 |
| Los Angeles, Calif. | 97 | 97 | 10/15 | 38 | 12/21 | 15.90 | 5.60 | 11/21 | .0 | .0 | | 38 | 4/11 | 139 | 95 | 37 | 0 |
| Louisville, Ky. | 477 | 93 | 7/25 | 0 | 2/25 | 43.92 | 2.40 | 8/9 | 20.2 | 9.3 | 3/6 | 61 | 2/15 | 87 | 165 | 132 | 5 |
| Marquette, Mich. | 677 | 92 | 7/21 | -12 | 2/12 | 27.13 | 1.48 | 10/24 | 99.6 | 8.7 | 1/6 | 41 | 3/30 | 74 | 199 | 163 | 32 |
| Memphis, Tenn. | 258 | 94 | 6/21 | 13 | 1/18 | 46.44 | 2.92 | 12/2 | .0 | .0 | 1/17 | 42 | 8/3 | 98 | 184 | 99 | 0 |
| Miami, Fla. | 7 | 94 | 6/22 | 36 | 12/12 | 66.22 | 4.74 | 6/12 | .0 | .0 | | 38 | 12/23 | 57 | 137 | 132 | 0 |
| Milford, Utah | 5028 | 100 | 7/28 | -16 | 12/30 | 11.67 | 1.24 | 7/22 | 57.9 | 9.1 | 1/23 | | | 135 | 119 | 73 | 15 |
| Milwaukee, Wisc. | 672 | 91 | 7/22 | -16 | 1/18 | 28.85 | 2.02 | 6/10 | 50.0 | 10.3 | 2/5 | 45 | 7/23 | 90 | 178 | 131 | 14 |
| Minneapolis, Minn. | 834 | 91 | 7/22 | -31 | 1/18 | 25.44 | 1.45 | 4/1 | 65.6 | 8.5 | 2/15 | 63 | 8/6 | 95 | 171 | 108 | 19 |
| Mobile, Ala. | 211 | 100 | 6/26 | 25 | 2/26 | 61.34 | 6.58 | 9/6 | T | T | 2/9 | 28 | 10/30 | 100 | 141 | 110 | 0 |
| Moline, Ill. | 582 | 94 | 5/25 | -17 | 12/31 | 42.36 | 5.02 | 6/6 | 41.0 | 11.7 | 1/26 | 50 | 5/18 | 90 | 179 | 120 | 10 |
| Nashville, Tenn. | 590 | 95 | 6/16 | 5 | 2/25 | 45.22 | 3.65 | 3/6 | 9.6 | 4.9 | 12/31 | 36 | 2/15 | 85 | 162 | 114 | 4 |
| New Haven, Conn. | 6 | 86 | 7/12 | -3 | 2/13 | 40.63 | 2.24 | 3/6 | 63.9 | 10.1 | 2/7 | 41 | 2/16 | 87 | 173 | 133 | 18 |
| New Orleans, La. | 3 | 78 | 6/27 | 30 | 12/24 | 53.43 | 5.58 | 2/5 | .0 | .0 | | 30 | 12/18 | 124 | 126 | 100 | 0 |
| New York, N. Y. | 132 | 96 | 6/16 | 4 | 2/13 | 49.12 | 3.18 | 6/18 | 51.1 | 12.5 | 2/7 | 42 | 4/27 | | | 126 | 13 |
| Nome, Alaska | 13 | 79 | 8/7 | -33 | 2/13 | 12.59 | 1.40 | 8/11 | 41.3 | 4.4 | 4/4 | 54 | 1/4 | 68 | 229 | 134 | 13 |
| Norfolk, Va. | 22 | 94 | 7/12 | 16 | 2/25 | 45.21 | 4.14 | 8/23 | 11.3 | 5.1 | 2/9 | 42 | 3/7 | 109 | 168 | 109 | 3 |
| North Platte, Nebr. | 2775 | 98 | 7/22 | -25 | 12/31 | 17.45 | 2.10 | 7/7 | 25.2 | 4.3 | 1/6 | 51 | 6/14 | 106 | 141 | 69 | 8 |
| Okla. City, Okla. | 1285 | 103 | 8/2 | 9 | 3/8 | 25.81 | 3.11 | 4/12 | 2.9 | 1.2 | 11/2 | 45 | 12/2 | 115 | 152 | 80 | 1 |
| Omaha, Nebr. | 977 | 97 | 5/25 | -11 | 12/31 | 30.48 | 2.20 | 6/4 | 17.2 | 4.5 | 12/26 | 56 | 7/9 | 108 | 146 | 102 | 7 |
| Philadelphia, Pa. | 5 | 93 | 7/24 | 4 | 2/13 | 44.82 | 2.53 | 6/22 | 36.0 | 9.8 | 2/7 | 40 | 7/31 | 84 | 187 | 116 | 9 |
| Phoenix, Ariz. | 1117 | 110 | 8/26 | 21 | 1/7 | 8.34 | 1.89 | 12/14 | T | T | 12/13 | 47 | 12/19 | 199 | 85 | 36 | 0 |
| Pittsburgh, Pa. | 1137 | 93 | 6/17 | -6 | 2/8 | 36.38 | 1.57 | 3/5 | 64.7 | 13.6 | 3/6 | 58 | 2/16 | 46 | 226 | 143 | 18 |
| Portland, Me. | 47 | 92 | 6/16 | -22 | 2/13 | 44.16 | 5.58 | 6/20 | 114.0 | 17.1 | 2/23 | 41 | 2/16 | 91 | 187 | 127 | 31 |
| Portland, Ore. | 21 | 102 | 8/28 | 13 | 12/20 | 29.24 | 1.48 | 1/7 | 5.7 | 3.3 | 12/21 | 70 | 10/2 | 76 | 208 | 142 | 2 |
| Providence, R. I. | 51 | 93 | 6/16 | -5 | 2/13 | 46.75 | 3.76 | 5/25 | 70.7 | 10.5 | 3/15 | 46 | 2/16 | 103 | 179 | 134 | 16 |
| Raleigh, N. C. | 434 | 93 | 7/11 | 8 | 2/25 | 32.58 | 3.44 | 6/7 | 11.0 | 9.1 | 2/9 | 44 | 3/15 | 115 | 148 | 105 | 2 |
| Rapid City, S. D. | 3162 | 100 | 8/24 | -19 | 12/31 | 22.59 | 2.06 | 4/30 | 47.4 | 13.6 | 4/30 | 65 | 1/22 | 111 | 145 | 117 | 13 |
| Reno, Nev. | 4404 | 101 | 7/2 | 0 | 12/15 | 9.47 | 0.86 | 1/21 | 38.2 | 11.2 | 1/24 | 70 | 1/20 | 143 | 133 | 63 | 10 |
| Richmond, Va. | 164 | 94 | 8/19 | 3 | 1/20 | 37.64 | 2.39 | 8/23 | 29.0 | 6.4 | 2/9 | 38 | 7/20 | 96 | 165 | 100 | 7 |
| Rochester, N. Y. | 543 | 91 | 6/16 | -7 | 2/13 | 29.84 | 1.76 | 9/27 | 73.5 | 7.3 | 2/25 | 57 | 2/16 | 56 | 205 | 152 | 24 |
| St. Louis, Mo. | 535 | 95 | 7/23 | -5 | 12/31 | 41.30 | 2.16 | 1/25 | 9.3 | 1.7 | 12/2 | 48 | 10/24 | 84 | 159 | 114 | 5 |
| Salt Lake City, Utah | 4220 | 101 | 7/21 | 2 | 1/11 | 16.52 | 0.97 | 7/16 | 90.4 | 9.0 | 1/6 | 47 | 4/5 | 88 | 160 | 99 | 24 |
| San Antonio, Tex. | 788 | 102 | 7/31 | 21 | 1/4 | 29.26 | 2.71 | 9/20 | T | T | 2/6 | 40 | 5/20 | 95 | 147 | 74 | 0 |
| San Diego, Calif. | 13 | 91 | 10/16 | 38 | 12/14 | 11.21 | 1.57 | 1/22 | T | T | 12/13 | 32 | 12/18 | 157 | 99 | 45 | 0 |
| San Francisco, Calif. | 8 | 92 | 9/20 | 31 | 12/15 | 27.27 | 4.58 | 1/29 | .0 | .0 | | 49 | 12/13 | 163 | 110 | 70 | 0 |
| San Juan, P.R. | 13 | 94 | 9/14 | 64 | 12/25 | 42.55 | 2.17 | 12/9 | .0 | .0 | | 35 | 4/2 | 52 | 68 | 204 | 0 |
| Sault Ste. Marie, Mi. | 721 | 86 | 6/3 | -26 | 2/12 | 32.43 | 1.77 | 8/7 | 117.7 | 9.7 | 2/15 | 31 | 1/17 | 77 | 201 | 171 | 42 |
| Savannah, Ga. | 46 | 98 | 5/14 | 16 | 2/26 | 41.27 | 2.80 | 1/1 | .0 | .0 | | 31 | 11/27 | 108 | 146 | 112 | 0 |
| Seattle, Wash. | 400 | 98 | 8/16 | 25 | 12/14 | 35.58 | 2.14 | 1/18 | 9.5 | 5.9 | 1/4 | 40 | 3/23 | 70 | 221 | 146 | 3 |
| Sioux City, Iowa | 1095 | 102 | 5/25 | -19 | 1/18 | 22.43 | 2.09 | 5/29 | 10.4 | 2.8 | 1/6 | 66 | 7/9 | 99 | 157 | 97 | 3 |
| Spokane, Wash. | 2356 | 103 | 7/12 | 5 | 12/14 | 13.89 | 0.70 | 6/1 | 37.8 | 5.3 | 12/21 | 44 | 1/15 | 109 | 170 | 95 | 16 |
| Springfield, Mo. | 1268 | 96 | 8/29 | 3 | 1/18 | 43.74 | 3.41 | 10/29 | 9.7 | 2.4 | 12/30 | 47 | 4/23 | 110 | 159 | 110 | 4 |
| Syracuse, N. Y. | 410 | 88 | 6/16 | -22 | 2/13 | 36.02 | 2.09 | 11/2 | 78.8 | 5.7 | 2/24 | 62 | 2/16 | 64 | 202 | 159 | 29 |
| Tampa, Fla. | 19 | 96 | 6/1 | 27 | 2/26 | 39.36 | 5.10 | 8/12 | | | | 29 | 6/15 | 109 | 119 | 80 | 0 |
| Trenton, N. J. | 56 | 93 | 6/16 | 6 | 2/13 | 46.27 | 2.34 | 7/21 | 49.8 | 12.7 | 2/7 | 42 | 2/16 | 91 | 154 | 122 | 15 |
| Washington, D. C. | 14 | 95 | 6/13 | 11 | 2/25 | 38.15 | 3.63 | 8/24 | 34.2 | 10.3 | 2/6 | 42 | 3/16 | 93 | 179 | 98 | 9 |
| Williston, N. D. | 1899 | 100 | 7/29 | -34 | 1/17 | 12.68 | 2.04 | 4/20 | 58.5 | 5.6 | 4/29 | 52 | 3/31 | 104 | 149 | 99 | 21 |
| Wilmington, N. C. | 78 | 92 | 6/16 | 1 | 2/9 | 44.65 | 3.08 | 8/9 | 32.8 | 9.0 | 2/6 | 42 | 2/16 | 86 | 176 | 120 | 7 |

*To get partly cloudy days deduct the total of Clear and Cloudy days from 365 (one year). T-trace.
¹Date shown is the starting date of the storm (in some cases it lasted more than one day).

# Monthly Normal Temperature and Precipitation

**Source:** Weather Bureau, United States Department of Commerce

These normals are based on records for the thirty-year period 1931 to 1960 inclusive. See explanation on page 289. For stations that did not have continuous records from the same instrument site for the entire 30 years, the means have been adjusted to the record at the present site.

AP indicates airport station; those not so marked are city office stations.

T, Temperature in Fahrenheit; P, precipitation in inches; L, less than .05 inch.

| Stations | Jan. | | Feb. | | Mar. | | Apr. | | May | | June | | July | | Aug. | | Sept. | | Oct. | | Nov. | | Dec. | |
|---|---|---|---|---|---|---|---|---|---|---|---|---|---|---|---|---|---|---|---|---|---|---|---|---|
| | T. | P. | T. | P. | T. | P. | T. | P. | T. | P. | T. | P. | T. | P. | T. | P. | T. | P. | T. | P. | T. | P. | T. | P. |
| Albany, N.Y. (AP) | 23 | 2.5 | 24 | 2.2 | 33 | 2.7 | 46 | 2.8 | 58 | 3.5 | 67 | 3.3 | 72 | 3.5 | 70 | 3.1 | 62 | 3.6 | 51 | 2.8 | 39 | 2.7 | 27 | 2.8 |
| Albuquerque, N.M (AP) | 35 | .4 | 40 | .4 | 46 | .5 | 56 | .5 | 65 | .8 | 75 | .6 | 79 | 1.2 | 76 | 1.3 | 70 | 1.0 | 58 | .8 | 44 | 4 | 37 | .6 |
| Anchorage, Alaska (AP) | 12 | .8 | 19 | .7 | 25 | .5 | 37 | .4 | 47 | .5 | 56 | 1.0 | 58 | 1.9 | 56 | 2.6 | 48 | 2.5 | 36 | 1.9 | 22 | 1.0 | 14 | .9 |
| Asheville, N. C. (AP) | 38 | 4.2 | 39 | 4.0 | 45 | 4.8 | 55 | 4.0 | 63 | 3.7 | 70 | 3.5 | 72 | 5.9 | 72 | 4.9 | 66 | 3.6 | 56 | 3.1 | 45 | 2.8 | 38 | 3.6 |
| Atlanta, Ga. (AP) | 45 | 4.4 | 46 | 4.5 | 51 | 5.4 | 60 | 4.5 | 69 | 3.2 | 77 | 3.8 | 79 | 4.7 | 78 | 3.6 | 73 | 3.3 | 62 | 2.4 | 51 | 3.0 | 45 | 4.4 |
| Baltimore, Md. (AP) | 35 | 3.4 | 36 | 2.9 | 43 | 3.8 | 54 | 3.6 | 64 | 4.0 | 73 | 3.3 | 77 | 4.2 | 75 | 5.2 | 68 | 3.3 | 57 | 3.2 | 46 | 3.1 | 36 | 3.0 |
| Barrow, Alaska (AP) | -16 | .2 | -18 | .2 | -15 | .1 | 0 | .1 | 18 | .1 | 33 | .4 | 39 | .8 | 38 | .9 | 31 | .6 | 17 | .5 | -1 | .2 | -11 | .2 |
| Birmingham, Ala. (AP) | 47 | 5.0 | 49 | 5.3 | 55 | 6.0 | 63 | 4.5 | 72 | 3.4 | 79 | 4.0 | 82 | 5.2 | 81 | 4.9 | 76 | 3.3 | 66 | 3.0 | 53 | 3.5 | 47 | 5.0 |
| Bismarck, N. D. (AP) | 10 | .4 | 14 | .4 | 26 | .8 | 44 | 1.2 | 56 | 2.0 | 65 | 3.4 | 72 | 2.2 | 69 | 1.7 | 59 | 1.2 | 47 | .9 | 29 | .6 | 18 | .4 |
| Boise, Idaho (AP) | 29 | 1.3 | 34 | 1.3 | 41 | 1.3 | 50 | 1.2 | 58 | 1.3 | 65 | .9 | 75 | .2 | 72 | .2 | 63 | .4 | 53 | .8 | 39 | 1.2 | 32 | 1.3 |
| Boston, Mass. (AP) | 30 | 3.9 | 30 | 3.3 | 38 | 4.2 | 48 | 3.8 | 59 | 3.3 | 68 | 3.5 | 74 | 2.9 | 72 | 3.7 | 65 | 3.5 | 55 | 3.1 | 45 | 3.9 | 33 | 3.6 |
| Buffalo, N. Y. (AP) | 25 | 2.8 | 24 | 2.7 | 32 | 3.2 | 44 | 3.0 | 55 | 3.0 | 65 | 2.5 | 70 | 2.6 | 68 | 3.1 | 61 | 3.1 | 51 | 3.0 | 39 | 3.6 | 28 | 3.0 |
| Burlington, Vt. (AP) | 16 | 2.0 | 17 | 1.8 | 27 | 2.1 | 41 | 2.6 | 54 | 3.0 | 64 | 3.5 | 69 | 3.9 | 67 | 3.4 | 58 | 3.3 | 48 | 3.0 | 35 | 2.6 | 22 | 2.1 |
| Caribou, Maine (AP) | 11 | 2.1 | 13 | 2.2 | 23 | 2.4 | 36 | 2.6 | 50 | 3.0 | 59 | 4.1 | 65 | 4.0 | 63 | 3.7 | 54 | 3.5 | 43 | 3.4 | 30 | 3.0 | 16 | 2.4 |
| Charleston, S. C. (AP) | 50 | 2.5 | 52 | 3.3 | 57 | 3.9 | 65 | 2.9 | 73 | 3.6 | 79 | 5.0 | 81 | 7.7 | 80 | 6.6 | 76 | 5.8 | 66 | 2.8 | 56 | 2.1 | 50 | 2.9 |
| Chicago, Ill. (AP) | 26 | 1.9 | 28 | 1.6 | 36 | 2.7 | 49 | 3.0 | 60 | 3.7 | 71 | 4.1 | 76 | 3.4 | 74 | 3.2 | 66 | 2.7 | 55 | 2.8 | 40 | 2.2 | 29 | 1.9 |
| Cincinnati, Ohio | 36 | 3.7 | 37 | 2.9 | 44 | 3.9 | 56 | 3.5 | 66 | 3.8 | 75 | 4.2 | 79 | 3.5 | 77 | 3.0 | 71 | 2.6 | 60 | 2.2 | 46 | 2.9 | 37 | 2.7 |
| Cleveland, Ohio (AP) | 28 | 2.7 | 29 | 2.3 | 35 | 3.1 | 47 | 3.4 | 58 | 3.5 | 68 | 3.4 | 72 | 3.3 | 70 | 3.3 | 64 | 2.9 | 53 | 2.4 | 41 | 2.6 | 31 | 2.3 |
| Columbus, Ohio (AP) | 32 | 3.2 | 33 | 2.3 | 41 | 3.2 | 52 | 3.5 | 63 | 4.0 | 73 | 4.2 | 76 | 3.9 | 75 | 2.9 | 68 | 2.7 | 57 | 2.1 | 43 | 2.5 | 34 | 2.3 |
| Dallas, Texas (AP) | 46 | 2.3 | 50 | 2.6 | 56 | 2.9 | 65 | 4.0 | 73 | 4.8 | 81 | 3.2 | 85 | 1.9 | 85 | 1.9 | 78 | 2.8 | 68 | 2.7 | 55 | 2.7 | 48 | 2.7 |
| Denver, Colo. (AP) | 29 | .6 | 32 | .7 | 36 | 1.2 | 46 | 2.1 | 56 | 2.7 | 67 | 1.4 | 73 | 1.5 | 72 | 1.3 | 63 | 1.1 | 51 | 1.0 | 38 | .7 | 32 | .5 |
| Des Moines, Iowa (AP) | 20 | 1.3 | 23 | 1.1 | 34 | 2.1 | 49 | 2.5 | 61 | 4.1 | 71 | 4.7 | 76 | 3.1 | 74 | 3.7 | 65 | 2.9 | 54 | 2.1 | 37 | 1.8 | 25 | 1.1 |
| Detroit, Mich. (AP) | 26 | 1.9 | 27 | 2.0 | 34 | 2.4 | 47 | 3.1 | 58 | 3.5 | 68 | 3.3 | 72 | 2.7 | 71 | 2.8 | 63 | 2.3 | 52 | 2.6 | 39 | 2.3 | 29 | 1.9 |
| Dodge City, Kansas(AP) | 31 | .6 | 35 | .7 | 42 | 1.2 | 54 | 1.8 | 64 | 3.2 | 74 | 3.0 | 80 | 2.3 | 79 | 2.4 | 70 | 1.5 | 58 | 1.4 | 43 | .6 | 35 | .5 |
| Duluth, Minn. (AP) | 9 | 1.2 | 11 | 1.0 | 21 | 1.6 | 37 | 2.4 | 49 | 3.3 | 59 | 4.3 | 66 | 3.5 | 64 | 3.8 | 54 | 2.9 | 45 | 2.2 | 27 | 1.8 | 14 | 1.2 |
| Eureka, Calif. | 47 | 6.7 | 48 | 5.5 | 49 | 5.3 | 50 | 2.7 | 53 | 2.2 | 56 | .7 | 56 | .1 | 57 | 1 | 56 | .6 | 54 | 3.2 | 51 | 4.6 | 49 | 6.7 |
| Fairbanks, Alaska (AP) | -11 | .9 | -3 | .5 | 9 | .4 | 29 | .3 | 47 | .7 | 58 | 1.4 | 60 | 1.8 | 54 | 2.2 | 44 | 1.1 | 26 | .9 | 4 | .6 | -8 | .5 |
| Ft. Worth, Tex. (AP) | 46 | 2.0 | 49 | 2.2 | 56 | 2.5 | 65 | 3.6 | 73 | 4.6 | 82 | 3.0 | 85 | 1.8 | 85 | 1.7 | 78 | 2.5 | 68 | 2.6 | 55 | 2.5 | 48 | 2.4 |
| Fresno, Calif. (AP) | 46 | 2.0 | 51 | 2.2 | 55 | 2.0 | 61 | 1.1 | 68 | .3 | 75 | .1 | 81 | L | 79 | L | 74 | .1 | 65 | .4 | 54 | 1.0 | 47 | 2.0 |
| Galveston, Texas | 55 | 3.5 | 57 | 2.9 | 61 | 2.9 | 69 | 2.6 | 76 | 2.8 | 82 | 2.7 | 83 | 4.8 | 83 | 4.4 | 80 | 5.1 | 74 | 2.9 | 63 | 3.6 | 57 | 3.9 |
| Grand Junct., Colo.(AP) | 26 | .6 | 33 | .7 | 42 | .8 | 52 | .8 | 62 | .6 | 71 | .4 | 78 | .6 | 76 | 1.1 | 68 | .9 | 55 | .7 | 39 | .6 | 29 | .6 |
| Gr. Rapids, Mich. (AP) | 24 | 1.9 | 24 | 1.8 | 33 | 2.3 | 46 | 2.9 | 57 | 3.5 | 68 | 3.3 | 72 | 2.7 | 70 | 2.7 | 62 | 3.0 | 51 | 2.6 | 37 | 2.5 | 27 | 2.0 |
| Helena, Mont. (AP) | 19 | .5 | 23 | .4 | 31 | .7 | 43 | .8 | 53 | 1.6 | 60 | 2.2 | 68 | 1.0 | 66 | .9 | 56 | 1.0 | 46 | .7 | 32 | .6 | 24 | .5 |
| Honolulu, Hawaii (AP) | 73 | 3.8 | 72 | 3.3 | 73 | 2.9 | 74 | 1.3 | 76 | 1.0 | 78 | .3 | 79 | .4 | 79 | .9 | 79 | 1.0 | 78 | 1.8 | 76 | 2.2 | 74 | 3.0 |
| Houston, Tex. (AP) | 54 | 3.8 | 56 | 3.4 | 61 | 2.7 | 69 | 3.2 | 76 | 4.3 | 82 | 3.7 | 83 | 4.3 | 83 | 4.3 | 79 | 4.3 | 71 | 3.8 | 61 | 3.9 | 56 | 4.4 |
| Huron, S. D. (AP) | 13 | .5 | 17 | .6 | 29 | 1.1 | 45 | 1.8 | 58 | 2.4 | 68 | 3.1 | 75 | 1.8 | 73 | 2.1 | 62 | 1.5 | 49 | 1.2 | 31 | .7 | 19 | .6 |
| Indianapolis, Ind. (AP) | 29 | 3.1 | 31 | 2.3 | 39 | 3.4 | 51 | 3.7 | 61 | 4.0 | 71 | 4.6 | 75 | 3.5 | 74 | 3.0 | 67 | 3.2 | 55 | 2.6 | 41 | 3.1 | 31 | 2.7 |
| Jacksonville, Fla. (AP) | 56 | 2.5 | 58 | 2.9 | 62 | 3.5 | 69 | 3.6 | 76 | 3.5 | 81 | 6.3 | 83 | 7.7 | 82 | 6.9 | 79 | 7.6 | 71 | 5.2 | 62 | 1.7 | 56 | 2.2 |
| Juneau, Alaska (AP) | 25 | 4.0 | 27 | 3.1 | 30 | 3.3 | 38 | 2.9 | 46 | 3.2 | 52 | 3.4 | 55 | 4.5 | 54 | 5.0 | 49 | 6.7 | 42 | 8.3 | 34 | 6.1 | 28 | 4.2 |
| Kansas City, Mo. (AP) | 32 | 1.4 | 36 | 1.2 | 43 | 2.5 | 56 | 3.6 | 66 | 4.4 | 76 | 4.6 | 82 | 3.2 | 80 | 3.8 | 71 | 3.3 | 60 | 2.9 | 45 | 1.8 | 36 | 1.5 |
| Knoxville, Tenn. (AP) | 41 | 4.9 | 43 | 4.8 | 50 | 4.7 | 59 | 3.7 | 68 | 3.5 | 76 | 3.3 | 78 | 4.8 | 77 | 3.5 | 72 | 2.5 | 61 | 2.6 | 49 | 3.2 | 42 | 4.2 |
| Lander, Wyo. (AP) | 19 | .5 | 24 | .7 | 32 | 1.2 | 43 | 2.5 | 53 | 2.7 | 62 | 1.4 | 71 | .8 | 69 | .5 | 59 | 1.0 | 47 | 1.2 | 31 | .9 | 23 | .4 |
| Little Rock, Ark. (AP) | 41 | 5.2 | 44 | 4.3 | 52 | 4.8 | 62 | 4.9 | 71 | 5.3 | 79 | 3.6 | 82 | 3.3 | 81 | 2.8 | 74 | 3.2 | 63 | 2.9 | 50 | 4.1 | 42 | 4.1 |
| Los Angeles, Calif. | 56 | 3.1 | 57 | 3.3 | 59 | 2.3 | 62 | 1.2 | 65 | .2 | 68 | .1 | 73 | L | 73 | L | 72 | .2 | 67 | .4 | 63 | 1.1 | 58 | 2.9 |
| Louisville, Ky. (AP) | 35 | 4.1 | 36 | 3.3 | 43 | 4.6 | 55 | 3.8 | 64 | 3.9 | 73 | 4.0 | 78 | 3.4 | 76 | 3.0 | 70 | 2.6 | 58 | 2.3 | 45 | 3.2 | 36 | 3.2 |
| Marquette, Mich. | 20 | 1.9 | 20 | 1.7 | 27 | 1.9 | 39 | 2.7 | 50 | 3.0 | 60 | 3.5 | 67 | 3.2 | 66 | 3.0 | 58 | 3.3 | 48 | 2.3 | 34 | 3.3 | 24 | 1.9 |
| Memphis, Tenn. (AP) | 42 | 6.1 | 44 | 4.7 | 51 | 5.1 | 61 | 4.6 | 70 | 4.2 | 79 | 3.7 | 81 | 3.5 | 81 | 3.0 | 74 | 2.8 | 63 | 2.7 | 50 | 4.4 | 43 | 4.9 |
| Miami, Fla. (AP) | 67 | 2.0 | 68 | 1.9 | 71 | 2.3 | 74 | 3.9 | 78 | 6.4 | 81 | 7.4 | 82 | 6.8 | 82 | 7.0 | 81 | 9.5 | 78 | 8.2 | 72 | 2.8 | 68 | 1.7 |
| Milford, Utah (AP) | 25 | .6 | 30 | .7 | 39 | 1.0 | 48 | .7 | 57 | .7 | 65 | .4 | 74 | .7 | 72 | .7 | 63 | .4 | 51 | .8 | 36 | .5 | 28 | .7 |
| Milwaukee, Wisc. (AP) | 21 | 1.8 | 22 | 1.4 | 31 | 2.3 | 44 | 2.5 | 53 | 3.2 | 63 | 3.6 | 69 | 3.0 | 68 | 3.1 | 60 | 2.7 | 50 | 2.1 | 36 | 2.2 | 25 | 1.6 |
| Minneapolis, Minn.(AP) | 12 | .7 | 16 | .8 | 27 | 1.5 | 44 | 1.9 | 57 | 3.2 | 67 | 4.0 | 72 | 3.3 | 70 | 3.2 | 60 | 2.4 | 49 | 1.6 | 31 | 1.4 | 18 | .9 |
| Mobile, Ala. (AP) | 53 | 4.6 | 55 | 4.6 | 60 | 7.2 | 68 | 6.4 | 76 | 4.9 | 82 | 6.2 | 83 | 9.7 | 82 | 6.4 | 78 | 6.3 | 70 | 3.0 | 59 | 3.4 | 54 | 5.5 |
| Moline, Ill. (AP) | 23 | 1.6 | 26 | 1.4 | 35 | 2.4 | 50 | 3.2 | 61 | 3.8 | 71 | 4.4 | 76 | 3.3 | 74 | 3.5 | 65 | 3.3 | 55 | 2.5 | 39 | 2.0 | 27 | 1.7 |
| Nashville, Tenn. (AP) | 40 | 5.5 | 42 | 4.5 | 49 | 5.2 | 60 | 3.7 | 69 | 3.7 | 77 | 3.3 | 80 | 3.7 | 79 | 2.9 | 73 | 2.9 | 62 | 2.3 | 49 | 3.3 | 41 | 4.2 |
| Newark, N. J. (AP) | 32 | 3.3 | 33 | 2.8 | 41 | 4.1 | 51 | 3.5 | 62 | 3.7 | 71 | 3.4 | 76 | 3.7 | 74 | 4.4 | 67 | 3.8 | 57 | 3.1 | 45 | 3.4 | 35 | 3.2 |
| New Haven, Conn. (AP) | 30 | 4.0 | 30 | 3.2 | 37 | 4.6 | 47 | 3.9 | 57 | 3.7 | 66 | 3.5 | 72 | 3.4 | 71 | 4.2 | 64 | 3.9 | 54 | 3.5 | 43 | 4.1 | 32 | 4.0 |
| New Orleans, La. (AP) | 55 | 3.8 | 57 | 4.0 | 61 | 5.3 | 68 | 4.6 | 74 | 4.4 | 80 | 4.4 | 82 | 6.7 | 82 | 5.3 | 78 | 5.0 | 70 | 2.8 | 60 | 3.3 | 55 | 4.1 |
| New York City, N. Y. | 33 | 3.3 | 33 | 2.8 | 41 | 4.0 | 51 | 3.4 | 62 | 3.7 | 71 | 3.3 | 77 | 3.7 | 75 | 4.4 | 69 | 3.9 | 58 | 3.1 | 47 | 3.4 | 36 | 3.3 |
| Nome, Alaska (AP) | 4 | 1.0 | 6 | .9 | 8 | .9 | 21 | .8 | 35 | .7 | 46 | .9 | 50 | 2.3 | 49 | 3.8 | 42 | 2.7 | 30 | 1.7 | 17 | 1.2 | 6 | 1.0 |
| Norfolk, Va. (AP) | 41 | 3.3 | 42 | 3.2 | 48 | 3.5 | 58 | 3.2 | 68 | 3.4 | 76 | 3.6 | 79 | 5.9 | 78 | 6.0 | 73 | 4.2 | 62 | 2.9 | 51 | 3.1 | 43 | 2.7 |
| Okla. City, Okla. (AP) | 37 | 1.3 | 41 | 1.4 | 49 | 2.0 | 60 | 3.1 | 68 | 5.2 | 78 | 4.5 | 83 | 2.4 | 83 | 2.5 | 74 | 3.0 | 63 | 2.5 | 48 | 1.6 | 40 | 1.4 |
| Omaha, Nebr. (AP) | 21 | .8 | 25 | 1.0 | 35 | 1.5 | 50 | 2.6 | 61 | 3.5 | 71 | 4.5 | 77 | 3.4 | 74 | 4.0 | 66 | 2.6 | 54 | 1.7 | 37 | 1.3 | 27 | .8 |
| Parkersburg, W. Va. | 35 | 3.3 | 36 | 2.8 | 43 | 3.5 | 54 | 3.3 | 64 | 3.7 | 73 | 4.3 | 76 | 4.1 | 74 | 3.8 | 68 | 2.7 | 57 | 2.1 | 45 | 2.4 | 36 | 2.8 |
| Philadelphia, Pa. (AP) | 32 | 3.3 | 33 | 2.8 | 41 | 3.8 | 52 | 3.4 | 63 | 3.7 | 71 | 4.1 | 76 | 4.2 | 74 | 4.6 | 67 | 3.5 | 56 | 2.8 | 44 | 3.4 | 34 | 2.9 |
| Phoenix, Ariz. (AP) | 50 | .7 | 54 | .9 | 59 | .7 | 67 | .3 | 75 | .1 | 84 | .1 | 90 | .8 | 88 | 1.1 | 83 | .7 | 71 | .5 | 58 | .5 | 52 | .9 |
| Pittsburgh, Pa. (AP) | 29 | 3.0 | 29 | 2.2 | 37 | 3.3 | 49 | 3.1 | 60 | 3.9 | 68 | 3.8 | 72 | 3.9 | 71 | 3.3 | 64 | 2.5 | 53 | 2.5 | 41 | 2.2 | 31 | 2.4 |
| Portland, Me. (AP) | 22 | 4.4 | 23 | 3.8 | 31 | 4.3 | 43 | 3.7 | 53 | 3.4 | 62 | 3.2 | 68 | 2.9 | 67 | 2.4 | 59 | 3.5 | 49 | 3.2 | 38 | 4.2 | 26 | 3.9 |
| Portland, Ore. (AP) | 38 | 5.4 | 42 | 4.2 | 46 | 3.9 | 52 | 2.1 | 57 | 2.0 | 62 | 1.7 | 67 | .4 | 67 | .7 | 64 | 1.6 | 52 | 3.6 | 45 | 5.3 | 41 | 6.4 |
| Providence, R.I. (AP) | 29 | 3.8 | 30 | 3.1 | 37 | 4.1 | 47 | 3.8 | 58 | 3.4 | 66 | 2.8 | 72 | 2.9 | 71 | 4.0 | 63 | 3.5 | 53 | 3.1 | 43 | 4.1 | 32 | 3.6 |
| Raleigh, N. C. (AP) | 42 | 3.2 | 43 | 3.2 | 50 | 3.4 | 59 | 3.5 | 68 | 3.5 | 75 | 3.7 | 78 | 5.5 | 77 | 5.2 | 71 | 3.9 | 61 | 2.7 | 50 | 2.8 | 42 | 3.0 |
| Rapid City, S. D. (AP) | 22 | .4 | 24 | .5 | 31 | 1.0 | 45 | 1.7 | 56 | 2.7 | 65 | 3.1 | 74 | 1.8 | 72 | 1.2 | 62 | 1.0 | 50 | .8 | 35 | .4 | 27 | .3 |
| Reno, Nevada (AP) | 30 | 1.2 | 36 | 1.0 | 42 | .7 | 48 | .5 | 54 | .5 | 60 | .4 | 68 | .3 | 66 | .2 | 59 | .2 | 49 | .5 | 38 | .6 | 32 | 1.1 |
| Richmond, Va. (AP) | 39 | 3.5 | 40 | 2.9 | 48 | 3.4 | 58 | 3.2 | 67 | 3.7 | 75 | 3.8 | 78 | 5.6 | 76 | 5.5 | 70 | 3.7 | 59 | 3.0 | 49 | 3.0 | 40 | 3.0 |
| Roseburg, Ore. (AP) | 40 | 5.5 | 43 | 4.2 | 47 | 3.4 | 52 | 1.9 | 57 | 1.9 | 62 | 1.5 | 68 | .2 | 68 | .3 | 63 | 1.0 | 54 | 3.0 | 46 | 4.5 | 42 | 5.7 |
| St. Louis, Mo. (AP) | 32 | 2.0 | 35 | 2.0 | 43 | 3.1 | 55 | 3.7 | 64 | 3.7 | 74 | 4.3 | 78 | 3.3 | 77 | 3.0 | 70 | 2.8 | 58 | 2.9 | 44 | 2.6 | 35 | 2.0 |
| Salt Lake City, Utah (AP) | 27 | 1.4 | 33 | 1.2 | 40 | 1.6 | 50 | 1.8 | 59 | 1.4 | 67 | 1.0 | 77 | .6 | 75 | .9 | 64 | .5 | 52 | 1.2 | 37 | 1.3 | 30 | 1.2 |
| San Antonio, Tex.(AP) | 52 | 1.7 | 55 | 1.7 | 61 | 1.7 | 68 | 2.8 | 75 | 3.5 | 82 | 3.0 | 84 | 2.1 | 84 | 2.4 | 79 | 3.5 | 71 | 2.5 | 60 | 1.4 | 54 | 1.8 |
| San Diego, Calif. (AP) | 55 | 2.0 | 56 | 2.2 | 59 | 1.6 | 62 | .8 | 64 | .2 | 66 | L | 70 | L | 72 | .8 | 70 | .2 | 66 | .5 | 62 | .9 | 57 | 2.1 |
| San Francisco, Calif. (AP) | 49 | 4.0 | 51 | 3.5 | 53 | 2.7 | 56 | 1.3 | 58 | .5 | 61 | .1 | 63 | L | 63 | L | 64 | .2 | 61 | .7 | 55 | 1.6 | 50 | 4.1 |
| San Juan, P. R. (AP) | 74 | 4.7 | 74 | 2.9 | 75 | 2.2 | 77 | 3.7 | 79 | 7.1 | 80 | 5.7 | 80 | 6.3 | 81 | 7.1 | 81 | 6.8 | 80 | 5.8 | 78 | 6.5 | 76 | 5.5 |
| Sault Ste. Marie, Mich. | 16 | 2.1 | 16 | 1.5 | 24 | 1.8 | 38 | 2.2 | 50 | 2.8 | 59 | 3.3 | 65 | 2.5 | 64 | 2.9 | 56 | 3.8 | 46 | 2.8 | 33 | 3.3 | 21 | 2.3 |
| Savannah, Ga. (AP) | 52 | 2.8 | 53 | 3.7 | 58 | 4.0 | 66 | 3.7 | 73 | 3.8 | 80 | 5.1 | 81 | 6.6 | 81 | 6.6 | 77 | 5.3 | 67 | 2.6 | 57 | 2.1 | 51 | 2.8 |
| Sea.-Tac., Wash. (AP) | 38 | 5.7 | 41 | 4.2 | 44 | 3.8 | 49 | 2.4 | 56 | 1.7 | 60 | 1.6 | 65 | .8 | 64 | 1.0 | 60 | 2.1 | 52 | 4.0 | 44 | 5.4 | 41 | 6.3 |
| Spokane, Wash. (AP) | 25 | 2.4 | 30 | 1.9 | 38 | 1.5 | 47 | .9 | 56 | 1.2 | 62 | 1.5 | 71 | .4 | 68 | .4 | 61 | .8 | 49 | 1.6 | 36 | 2.2 | 30 | 2.4 |
| Springfield, Mo. (AP) | 34 | 2.0 | 37 | 2.1 | 44 | 2.8 | 56 | 4.1 | 65 | 5.3 | 74 | 5.0 | 79 | 3.9 | 78 | 3.3 | 70 | 3.9 | 60 | 3.8 | 45 | 2.8 | 37 | 2.2 |
| Syracuse, N. Y. (AP) | 24 | 3.2 | 24 | 3.1 | 33 | 3.6 | 46 | 3.1 | 58 | 3.3 | 67 | 3.0 | 72 | 3.1 | 70 | 3.3 | 62 | 2.8 | 52 | 3.2 | 40 | 2.9 | 28 | 3.2 |
| Tampa, Fla. (AP) | 61 | 2.1 | 63 | 2.8 | 66 | 3.8 | 71 | 2.8 | 77 | 2.9 | 81 | 7.3 | 82 | 8.6 | 82 | 8.2 | 81 | 7.0 | 75 | 2.8 | 67 | 1.5 | 62 | 1.9 |
| Trenton, N. J. | 33 | 3.1 | 33 | 2.6 | 41 | 3.8 | 52 | 3.2 | 62 | 3.6 | 71 | 3.6 | 76 | 4.2 | 74 | 4.8 | 67 | 3.5 | 57 | 2.8 | 46 | 3.2 | 35 | 2.9 |
| Vicksburg, Miss. | 49 | 5.1 | 52 | 5.3 | 58 | 5.7 | 66 | 4.9 | 73 | 4.1 | 80 | 3.5 | 82 | 3.9 | 82 | 3.0 | 77 | 2.5 | 68 | 2.0 | 56 | 4.4 | 50 | 4.9 |
| Washington, D. C. (AP) | 37 | 3.0 | 38 | 2.5 | 45 | 3.2 | 56 | 3.2 | 66 | 4.1 | 74 | 3.2 | 78 | 4.2 | 77 | 4.9 | 70 | 3.8 | 59 | 3.1 | 48 | 2.8 | 38 | 2.8 |
| Williston, N. D. | 8 | .6 | 12 | .5 | 24 | .7 | 42 | .9 | 55 | 1.4 | 63 | 3.3 | 71 | 1.9 | 68 | 1.5 | 57 | 1.1 | 46 | .7 | 28 | 6 | 16 | .5 |
| Wilmington, Del. (AP) | 33 | 3.4 | 34 | 3.0 | 41 | 4.0 | 52 | 3.3 | 63 | 3.5 | 71 | 4.1 | 76 | 4.3 | 74 | 5.6 | 68 | 4.0 | 57 | 2.9 | 45 | 3.5 | 35 | 3.0 |
| Wilmington, N. C. (AP) | 48 | 2.9 | 49 | 3.4 | 54 | 4.0 | 63 | 2.9 | 71 | 3.5 | 78 | 4.3 | 80 | 7.7 | 79 | 6.9 | 75 | 6.3 | 65 | 3.0 | 55 | 3.1 | 48 | 3.4 |

# Normal Temperatures, Highs, Lows; Precipitation

Source: National Weather Records, ESSA, Dept. of Commerce

These normals are based on records for the thirty-year period 1931 to 1960 inclusive. See explanation on page 289.

Extreme temperatures are based on records for the present and prior locations thru 1967. If the station is now at an airport, one or both extremes may have occurred at other than the airport location.

AP indicates airport station; those not so marked are city office stations.

The minus (—) sign indicates temperatures below zero. Fahrenheit thermometer registration.

| State | Station | Normal temperature | | | | Extreme temperature | | Normal annual precipitation (inches) |
|---|---|---|---|---|---|---|---|---|
| | | January | | July | | High-est | Lowest | |
| | | Max. | Min. | Max. | Min. | | | |
| Alabama....... | Mobile (AP)............ | 62 | 44 | 92 | 73 | 104 | −1 | 68.13 |
| Alabama....... | Montgomery (AP) ...... | 59 | 38 | 92 | 72 | 107 | −5 | 50.69 |
| Alaska........ | Juneau (AP)............ | 30 | 20 | 63 | 48 | 89 | −21 | 54.62 |
| Arizona....... | Phoenix (AP)........... | 64 | 35 | 105 | 75 | 118 | 16 | 7.20 |
| Arkansas...... | Little Rock (AP)........ | 51 | 31 | 93 | 71 | 110 | −13 | 48.66 |
| California..... | Los Angeles........... | 65 | 47 | 83 | 63 | 110 | 28 | 14.68 |
| California..... | San Francisco (AP)..... | 55 | 42 | 72 | 54 | 106 | 20 | 18.69 |
| Colorado...... | Denver (AP)........... | 42 | 15 | 88 | 57 | 105 | −30 | 14.81 |
| Connecticut... | New Haven (AP)....... | 37 | 22 | 81 | 63 | 101 | −15 | 46.02 |
| Delaware..... | Wilmington (AP)....... | 41 | 26 | 86 | 66 | 107 | −15 | 44.56 |
| Dist. of Col.... | Washington (AP)....... | 44 | 30 | 87 | 69 | 106 | −15 | 40.78 |
| Florida........ | Jacksonville (AP)....... | 67 | 45 | 92 | 73 | 105 | 10 | 53.36 |
| Florida........ | Key West (AP)......... | 74 | 65 | 87 | 79 | 100 | 41 | 39.99 |
| Florida........ | Miami (AP)............ | 76 | 58 | 89 | 75 | 100 | 28 | 59.76 |
| Georgia....... | Atlanta (AP).......... | 52 | 37 | 87 | 71 | 103 | −9 | 47.14 |
| Hawaii........ | Honolulu (AP)......... | 79 | 66 | 85 | 73 | 93 | 54 | 21.89 |
| Idaho......... | Boise (AP)............ | 36 | 22 | 91 | 59 | 112 | −28 | 11.43 |
| Illinois........ | Chicago (AP).......... | 33 | 19 | 84 | 67 | 105 | −23 | 33.18 |
| Indiana........ | Indianapolis (AP)...... | 37 | 21 | 86 | 64 | 107 | −25 | 39.25 |
| Iowa.......... | Des Moines (AP)....... | 29 | 11 | 87 | 65 | 110 | −30 | 30.37 |
| Iowa.......... | Dubuque (AP)......... | 27 | 11 | 84 | 62 | 110 | −32 | 35.71 |
| Kansas........ | Wichita (AP).......... | 42 | 22 | 92 | 69 | 114 | −22 | 28.41 |
| Kentucky...... | Louisville (AP) ........ | 44 | 27 | 89 | 67 | 107 | −20 | 41.32 |
| Louisiana...... | New Orleans (AP)...... | 64 | 45 | 91 | 73 | 102 | 7 | 62.96 |
| Maine......... | Portland (AP)......... | 32 | 12 | 80 | 57 | 103 | −39 | 42.85 |
| Maryland...... | Baltimore (AP)........ | 44 | 25 | 87 | 66 | 107 | −7 | 43.05 |
| Massachusetts... | Boston (AP).......... | 37 | 23 | 82 | 65 | 104 | −18 | 42.77 |
| Michigan...... | Detroit, City (AP)...... | 33 | 21 | 84 | 65 | 105 | −24 | 30.95 |
| Michigan...... | Sault Ste. Marie....... | 23 | 8 | 76 | 54 | 98 | −37 | 31.22 |
| Minnesota..... | Minn.-St. Paul (AP).... | 22 | 2 | 84 | 61 | 108 | −34 | 24.78 |
| Mississippi.... | Vicksburg............. | 57 | 40 | 90 | 73 | 104 | −1 | 49.50 |
| Missouri...... | St. Louis (AP)......... | 40 | 24 | 89 | 67 | 115 | −23 | 35.31 |
| Montana...... | Helena (AP).......... | 29 | 8 | 84 | 52 | 103 | −42 | 10.85 |
| Nebraska...... | Omaha (AP).......... | 32 | 13 | 90 | 67 | 114 | −32 | 27.56 |
| Nevada....... | Winnemucca (AP)...... | 40 | 15 | 92 | 50 | 108 | −36 | 8.63 |
| New Hampshire.. | Concord (AP)........ | 32 | 11 | 83 | 56 | 102 | −37 | 38.80 |
| New Jersey..... | Atlantic City (AP)...... | 43 | 27 | 84 | 66 | 104 | −9 | 42.36 |
| New Mexico.... | Albuquerque (AP)...... | 46 | 24 | 91 | 66 | 104 | −16 | 8.13 |
| New Mexico.... | Roswell (AP).......... | 55 | 21 | 95 | 62 | 110 | −29 | 11.62 |
| New York...... | Albany (AP).......... | 31 | 14 | 84 | 61 | 104 | −26 | 35.08 |
| New York...... | New York............ | 40 | 27 | 85 | 68 | 106 | −15 | 42.37 |
| No. Carolina... | Charlotte (AP)........ | 51 | 34 | 89 | 70 | 104 | −5 | 43.38 |
| No. Carolina... | Raleigh (AP).......... | 52 | 31 | 88 | 68 | 105 | −2 | 43.58 |
| No. Dakota.... | Bismarck (AP)......... | 20 | 0 | 86 | 58 | 114 | −45 | 15.15 |
| Ohio.......... | Cincinnati............ | 41 | 26 | 88 | 66 | 109 | −17 | 39.51 |
| Ohio.......... | Cleveland (AP)........ | 35 | 20 | 83 | 60 | 103 | −19 | 35.35 |
| Oklahoma...... | Oklahoma City (AP).... | 46 | 28 | 93 | 72 | 113 | −17 | 30.82 |
| Oregon....... | Portland............. | 44 | 35 | 79 | 56 | 107 | −3 | 42.87 |
| Pennsylvania... | Harrisburg (AP)....... | 39 | 24 | 87 | 65 | 107 | −14 | 37.65 |
| Pennsylvania... | Philadelphia (AP)...... | 40 | 24 | 86 | 66 | 106 | −11 | 42.48 |
| Rhode Island.... | Block Island (AP)...... | 38 | 26 | 76 | 63 | 91 | −4 | 40.45 |
| So. Carolina... | Charleston (AP)........ | 61 | 38 | 89 | 72 | 104 | 7 | 49.16 |
| So. Dakota..... | Huron (AP)........... | 23 | 2 | 90 | 60 | 112 | −43 | 17.33 |
| So. Dakota..... | Rapid City (AP)....... | 34 | 10 | 88 | 60 | 109 | −33 | 14.71 |
| Tennessee...... | Nashville (AP)........ | 49 | 31 | 91 | 70 | 107 | −15 | 45.14 |
| Texas......... | Amarillo (AP)......... | 50 | 24 | 94 | 67 | 108 | −16 | 19.67 |
| Texas......... | Galveston............ | 61 | 49 | 87 | 79 | 101 | 8 | 41.81 |
| Texas......... | Houston (AP)......... | 64 | 44 | 92 | 74 | 108 | 5 | 45.26 |
| Utah.......... | Salt Lake City (AP).... | 37 | 18 | 94 | 60 | 107 | −30 | 13.90 |
| Vermont...... | Burlington (AP)....... | 25 | 7 | 82 | 56 | 101 | −30 | 33.21 |
| Virginia....... | Norfolk (AP).......... | 50 | 32 | 88 | 70 | 105 | 2 | 44.94 |
| Washington.... | Seattle-Tacoma (AP).... | 44 | 33 | 76 | 54 | 99 | 0 | 38.94 |
| Washington.... | Spokane (AP)......... | 31 | 19 | 86 | 55 | 108 | −30 | 17.19 |
| West Virginia... | Parkersburg.......... | 43 | 26 | 86 | 65 | 106 | −27 | 38.77 |
| Wisconsin..... | Madison (AP)......... | 26 | 9 | 82 | 60 | 107 | −37 | 30.16 |
| Wisconsin..... | Milwaukee (AP)....... | 28 | 13 | 79 | 58 | 105 | −25 | 29.51 |
| Wyoming...... | Cheyenne (AP)........ | 37 | 14 | 85 | 55 | 100 | −38 | 15.06 |
| Puerto Rico.... | San Juan (AP)........ | 81 | 67 | 87 | 74 | 94 | 60 | 64.21 |

**Mean Annual Snowfall** (inches) based on record thru 1967—Denver, Colo. (AP) 58.3; Boston, Mass. (AP) 42.0; Sault Ste. Marie, Mich. (AP) 103.6; Minn.-St. Paul, Minn. (AP) 43.3; Albany, N. Y. (AP) 63.3; Rochester, N. Y. (AP) 81.9; Cleveland, Ohio (AP) 50.5; Burlington, Vt. (AP) 70.9; Cheyenne, Wyo. (AP) 52.6; Juneau, Alaska (AP) 103.0.

**Wettest Spot:** Mount Waialeale, Hawaii, on the island of Kauai, is the rainiest place in the world, according to the National Geographic Society, with an average annual rainfall of 471.68 inches.

**Highest Temperature:** A temperature of 136° F. observed at Azizia, Tripolitania in Northern Africa on Sept. 13, 1922 is generally accepted as the world's highest temperature recorded under standard conditions.
The record high in the United States was 134° in Death Valley, Calif., July 10, 1913.

**Lowest Temperature:** A record low temperature of —126.9°F (—88.3°C.) was recorded at the Soviet Antarctic station Vostok on Aug. 24, 1960.
The record low in the United States was —76° at Tanana, Alaska, Jan. 1886.
The lowest official temperature on the North American continent was recorded at 81 degrees below zero in February, 1947, at a lonely airport in the Yukon called Snag.
These are the meteorological champions—the official temperature extremes—but there are plenty of other claimants to thermometer fame. However, sun readings are unofficial records, since meteorological data to qualify officially must be taken on instruments in sheltered and ventilated location.

# Low and High Temperature Records of U. S. Weather Bureau

Data through 1967

| State | Temperature °F Lowest | Highest | Latest Date | Station (*) Approximate elevation | Elevation Feet |
|---|---|---|---|---|---|
| Alabama | −24 | | Jan. 30, 1966 | Russellville 2 | 880 |
| | | 112 | Sept. 5, 1925 | Centerville | 345 |
| Alaska | −76 | | Jan. 1886 | Tanana | *242 |
| | | 100 | June 27, 1915 | Fort Yukon | *419 |
| Arizona | −37 | | Jan. 13, 1963 | Maverick | 7,800 |
| | | 127 | July 7, 1905 | Parker | 345 |
| Arkansas | −29 | | Feb. 13, 1905 | Pond | 1,250 |
| | | 120 | Aug. 10, 1936 | Ozark | 396 |
| California | −45 | | Jan. 20, 1937 | Boca | 5,532 |
| | | 134 | July 10, 1913 | Greenland Ranch | −178 |
| Colorado | −60 | | Feb. 1, 1951 | Taylor Park | 9,206 |
| | | 118 | July 11, 1888 | Bennett | 5,484 |
| Connecticut | −32 | | Jan. 22, 1961 | Coventry | 480 |
| | | 105 | July 22, 1926 | Waterbury | 409 |
| Delaware | −17 | | Jan. 17, 1893 | Millsboro | 535 |
| | | 110 | July 21, 1930 | Millsboro | 20 |
| Dist. of Col | −15 | | Feb. 11, 1899 | Washington | 112 |
| | | 106 | July 20, 1930 | Washington | 112 |
| Florida | −2 | | Feb. 13, 1899 | Tallahassee | 193 |
| | | 109 | June 29, 1931 | Monticello | 207 |
| Georgia | −17 | | Jan. 27, 1940 | CCC Camp F-16 | 1,000 |
| | | 112 | July 24, 1952 | Louisville | 337 |
| Hawaii | 18 | | Feb. 20, 1962 | Mauna Loa Slope Obs | 11,146 |
| | | 100 | Apr. 27, 1931 | Pahala | 850 |
| Idaho | −60 | | Jan. 18, 1943 | Island Park Dam | 6,285 |
| | | 118 | July 28, 1934 | Orofino | 1,027 |
| Illinois | −35 | | Jan. 22, 1930 | Mount Carroll | 817 |
| | | 117 | July 14, 1954 | E. St. Louis | 410 |
| Indiana | −35 | | Feb. 2, 1951 | Greensburg | 954 |
| | | 116 | July 14, 1936 | Collegeville | 672 |
| Iowa | −47 | | Jan. 12, 1912 | Washta | 1,157 |
| | | 118 | July 20, 1934 | Keokuk | 614 |
| Kansas | −40 | | Feb. 13, 1905 | Lebanon | 1,812 |
| | | 121 | July 24, 1936 | Alton (near) | 1,651 |
| Kentucky | −34 | | Jan. 24, 1963 | Bonnieville 4, N. | 474 |
| | −34 | | Jan. 28, 1963 | Cynthiana 2 | 895 |
| | | 114 | July 28, 1930 | Greensburg | 581 |
| Louisiana | −16 | | Feb. 13, 1899 | Minden | 194 |
| | | 114 | Aug. 10, 1936 | Plain Dealing | 268 |
| Maine | −48 | | Jan. 19, 1925 | Van Buren | 510 |
| | | 105 | July 10, 1911 | North Bridgton | 450 |
| Maryland | −40 | | Jan. 13, 1912 | Oakland | 2,461 |
| | | 109 | July 10, 1936 | Cumberland and Frederick | 623-325 |
| Massachusetts | −34 | | Jan. 18, 1957 | Birch Hill Dam | 840 |
| | | 106 | July 4, 1911 | Lawrence | 51 |
| Michigan | −51 | | Feb. 9, 1934 | Vanderbilt | 785 |
| | | 112 | July 13, 1936 | Mio | 963 |
| Minnesota | −59 | | Feb. 16, 1903 | Pokegama Dam | 1,280 |
| | | 114 | July 6, 1936 | Moorhead | 940 |
| Mississippi | −19 | | Jan. 30, 1966 | Corinth 4 SW | 420 |
| | | 115 | July 29, 1930 | Holly Springs | 600 |
| Missouri | −40 | | Feb. 13, 1905 | Warsaw | 700 |
| | | 118 | July 14, 1954 | Warsaw | 687 |
| Montana | −70 | | Jan. 20, 1954 | Rogers Pass | 5,470 |
| | | 117 | July 5, 1937 | Medicine Lake | 1,950 |
| Nebraska | −47 | | Feb. 12, 1899 | Camp Clarke | 3,700 |
| | | 118 | July 24, 1936 | Minden | 2,169 |
| Nevada | −50 | | Jan. 8, 1937 | San Jacinto | 5,200 |
| | | 122 | June 23, 1954 | Overton | 1,240 |
| New Hampshire | −46 | | Jan. 28, 1925 | Pittsburg | 1,575 |
| | | 106 | July 4, 1911 | Nashua | 125 |
| New Jersey | −34 | | Jan. 5, 1904 | River Vale | 70 |
| | | 110 | July 10, 1936 | Runyon | 18 |
| New Mexico | −50 | | Feb. 1, 1951 | Gavilan | 7,350 |
| | | 116 | July 14, 1934 | Orogrande | 4,171 |
| New York | −52 | | Feb. 9, 1934 | Stillwater Reservoir | 1,670 |
| | | 108 | July 22, 1926 | Troy | 35 |
| North Carolina | −26 | | Jan. 30, 1966 | Grandfather Mtn | 5,300 |
| | | 109 | Sept. 7, 1954 | Weldon | 81 |
| North Dakota | −60 | | Feb. 15, 1936 | Parshall | 1,929 |
| | | 121 | July 6, 1936 | Steele | 1,857 |
| Ohio | −39 | | Feb. 10, 1899 | Milligan | 800 |
| | | 113 | July 21, 1934 | Gallipolis (near) | 673 |
| Oklahoma | −27 | | Jan. 18, 1930 | Watts | 958 |
| | | 120 | July 26, 1943 | Tishmoningo | 670 |
| Oregon | −54 | | Feb. 10, 1933 | Seneca | 4,700 |
| | | 119 | Aug. 10, 1898 | Pendleton | 1,074 |
| Pennsylvania | −42 | | Jan. 5, 1904 | Smethport | *1,500 |
| | | 111 | July 10, 1936 | Phoenixville | 100 |
| Rhode Island | −23 | | Jan. 11, 1942 | Kingston | 100 |
| | | 102 | July 30, 1949 | Greenville | 420 |
| South Carolina | −13 | | Jan. 26, 1940 | Longcreek (near) | 1,631 |
| | | 111 | June 28, 1954 | Camden | 170 |
| South Dakota | −58 | | Feb. 17, 1936 | McIntosh | 2,277 |
| | | 120 | July 5, 1936 | Gannvalley | 1,750 |
| Tennessee | −32 | | Dec. 30, 1917 | Mountain City | 2,471 |
| | | 113 | Aug. 9, 1930 | Perryville | 377 |
| Texas | −24 | | Feb. 19, 1963 | Orange Gulf States Utilities | 10 |
| | | 120 | Aug. 12, 1936 | Seymour | 1,291 |
| Utah | −50 | | Jan. 5, 1913 | Strawberry Tunnel | 7,650 |
| | | 116 | June 28, 1892 | Saint George | 2,880 |
| Vermont | −50 | | Dec. 30, 1933 | Bloomfield | 915 |
| | | 105 | July 4, 1911 | Vernon | 310 |
| Virginia | −29 | | Feb. 10, 1899 | Monterey | *3,008 |
| | | 110 | July 15, 1954 | Balcony Falls | 725 |
| Washington | −42 | | Jan. 20, 1937 | Deer Park (near) | 2,090 |
| | | 118 | Aug. 5, 1961 | Ice Harbor Dam | 475 |
| West Virginia | −37 | | Dec. 30, 1917 | Lewisburg | 2,200 |
| | | 112 | July 10, 1936 | Martinsburg | 435 |
| Wisconsin | −54 | | Jan. 24, 1922 | Danbury | 908 |
| | | 114 | July 13, 1936 | Wisconsin Dells | 900 |
| Wyoming | −63 | | Feb. 9, 1933 | Moran | 6,770 |
| | | 114 | July 12, 1900 | Basin | 3,500 |

# Tides and Their Causes

**Source:** U. S. Coast and Geodetic Survey, ESSA
*See index for tide tables*

The tides are a natural phenomenon involving the alternating rise and fall in the large fluid bodies of the earth caused by the combined gravitational attraction of the sun and moon. The combination of these two variable force influences, as modified by certain factors such as depth of the water, configuration of the shoreline, and geographic location, produce the complex recurrent cycle of the tides. Tides may occur in both oceans and seas, to a limited extent in large lakes, the atmosphere, and, to a very minute degree, in the earth itself. The period between succeeding tides varies as the result of many factors and force influences.

The tide-generating force represents the difference between (1) the centrifugal force produced by the revolution of the earth around the common center-of-gravity of the earth-moon system and (2) the gravitational attraction of the moon acting upon the earth's overlying waters. Similar tide-producing forces exist in the earth-sun system. Since, on the average, the moon is only 238,857 miles from the earth compared with the sun's much greater distance of 93,000,000 miles, this closer distance outranks the much smaller mass of the moon compared with that of the sun, and the moon's tide-raising force is, accordingly, $2\frac{1}{5}$ times that of the sun.

The effect of the tide-generating forces of the moon and sun acting tangentially to the earth's surface (the so-called "tractive force"), tends to cause a maximum accumulation of the waters of the oceans at two diametrically opposite positions on the surface of the earth and to withdraw compensating amounts of water from all points 90° removed from the positions of these tidal bulges. The presence of the continents, as well as other factors, prevent the total free movement of water. However, as the earth rotates beneath the maxima and minima of these tide-generating forces, a sequence of two high tides, separated by two low tides, ideally is produced each day.

Twice in each lunar month, when the sun, moon, and earth are directly aligned, with the moon between the earth and the sun (at new moon) or on the opposite side of the earth from the sun (at full moon), the sun and the moon exert their gravitational force in a mutual or additive fashion. Higher high tides and lower low tides are produced. These are called *spring* tides. At two positions 90° in between, the gravitational forces of moon and sun—imposed at right angles—tend to counteract each other to the greatest extent, and the range between high and low tides is reduced. These are called *neap* tides. This semimonthly variation between the spring and neap tides is called the *phase inequality.*

The inclination of the moon's orbit to the equator also produces a difference in the height of succeeding high tides and in the extent of depression of succeeding low tides which is known as the *diurnal inequality.* In extreme cases, this phenomenon can result in only one high tide and one low tide each day. The changing distance of the moon from the earth in each lunar month due to the elliptical orbit of the moon, produces a difference in the height of the tides known as the *lunar parallactic inequality.* The changing distance of the earth from the sun during the earth's annual revolution around the sun similarly introduces the *solar parallactic inequality.*

The actual amount of uplift of the waters in the deep ocean may amount to only one or two feet. However, as this tide approaches shoal waters and its effects are augmented, the tidal range may be greatly increased. In Nova Scotia, along the narrow channel of the Bay of Fundy, the range of tides, or difference between high and low waters, may reach $43\frac{1}{2}$ feet or more (under spring tide conditions) due to resonant amplification.

At New Orleans, the periodic rise and fall of the tide varies with the stage of the Mississippi River, being about 10 inches at low river stage and zero at high river stage. The Canadian Tide Tables for 1968 give a maximum range of nearly 50 feet at Leaf Basin, Ungava Bay, Canada. The mean range at Calais, Maine, is 20 feet but a range in excess of 23 feet can be expected each month.

# U. S. Weather Satellite System Views Entire Globe Daily

**Source:** Environmental Science Services Administration

Since the successful launching of ESSA 1 and ESSA 2 (Environmental Survey Satellites) in Feb. 1966, the United States has had an operational weather satellite system providing both global and local cloud-cover pictures at least once every day. The TOS (TIROS Operational Satellite) system is composed of two ESSA spacecraft, one with automatic-picture-transmission capability and one with picture-storage capability. These satellites are similar to the earlier TIROS spacecraft, but are redesigned so that all pictures are taken when the camera is looking directly at the earth. They view the entire earth at least once every 24 hours.

Additional spacecraft are launched as needed to maintain the operational capability of the system. Picture-storage satellites ESSA 1 (Feb. 1, 1966), ESSA 3 (Oct. 2, 1966), and ESSA 5 (Apr. 20, 1967) record photographs for transmission to a major command and data acquisition station. These global pictures are used in preparing charts for transmission by facsimile, teletypewriter, and radio to weather stations in the United States and other nations. Automatic-picture-transmission (APT) spacecraft ESSA 2 (Feb. 28, 1966), ESSA 4 (Jan. 26, 1967) and ESSA 6 (Nov. 10, 1967) carry special cameras which send pictures within seconds after they are taken directly to simple receiving stations on the ground. More than 400 APT ground stations are in operation around the world. The TOS system is managed and operated by the National Environmental Satellite Center of the Environmental Science Service Admin. The space-craft are launched by National Aeronautics & Space Admin.

The era of weather observation by satellite was inaugurated on April 1, 1960, with the successful launching and operation of the 270-lb. TIROS I. This satellite, equipped with two television cameras, obtained many thousand pictures of the cloud cover over large portions of the earth, including oceans and sparsely settled land regions where there are few fixed observation stations. TIROS I was followed by nine more equally successful satellites: TIROS II launched in November 1960, TIROS III in July 1961; IV in February 1962, V in June 1962, VI in September 1962, VII in June 1963, VIII in December 1963, IX in January 1965, and X in July 1965. Larger and more complex meteorological satellites, Nimbus I and Nimbus II, were launched by NASA on August 28, 1964 and May 15, 1966, respectively, as research and development experiments.

The Applications Technology Satellites, ATS I and III, launched respectively by NASA on Dec. 6, 1966, and November 5, 1967, carried experimental cloud cameras that can photograph a circular area of the earth 3600 nautical miles in radius. These cameras can take a picture once every 24 minutes from their geostationary location 22,300 miles above a point on the equator. These pictures, received on the ground by a television system, can be made into time-lapse motion pictures from which cloud motions and wind information can be extracted.

## Hurricanes' Names in 1969-70

The Weather Bureau has used girls' names to identify hurricanes in the Atlantic, Caribbean and Gulf of Mexico since 1953. A semi-permanent list of 4 sets of names in alphabetical order was established in 1960. Hurricane season begins June 1.

Names assigned to potential hurricanes: 1969—Anna, Blanche, Carol, Debbie, Eve, Francelia, Gerda, Holly, Inga, Jenny, Kara, Laurie, Martha, Netty, Orva, Peggy, Rhoda, Sadie, Tanya, Virgy, Wenda. 1970—Alma, Becky, Celia, Dorothy, Ella, Felice, Greta, Hallie, Inez, Judith, Kendra, Lois, Marsha, Noreen, Orpha, Patty, Rena, Sherry, Thora, Vicky and Wilna.

Hurricanes and typhoons in the Eastern North Pacific (U. S. West Coast) are also identified by girls' names. Names assigned are: 1969—Ava, Bernice, Claudia, Doreen, Emily, Florence, Glenda, Hazel, Irah, Jennifer, Katherine, Lillian, Mona, Natalie, Odessa, Prudence, Roslyn, Sylvia, Tillie, Victoria, Wallie. 1970—Adele, Blanca, Connie, Dolores, Eileen, Francesca, Gretchen, Helga, Ione, Joyce, Kirsten, Lorraine, Maggie, Norma, Orlene, Patricia, Rosalie, Selma, Toni, Vivian and Winona.

# MEMORABLE DATES

Consult also Chronology, Aviation Records, Polar Explorations, Fast Ocean Passages, Train Records, Marine Disasters, Political Assassinations, Earthquakes, Tornadoes, Amendments to the Constitution, Noted Personalities, Astronomical Data, Sporting Records and other classifications.

## B. C.

### 3000
**Indus Valley Civilization**, sites at Mohenjo-Daro and Harappa in West Pakistan. Civilization had complex form of government, elaborate irrigation and drainage system, writing, well laid out streets, and houses of several stories. End came about 1500 B.C.

**Pyramids begun** by kings of Egypt at Sakkara. Cheops built great pyramid at Giza; Chephren second largest. Sphinx built about 2900 B.C.

### c. 1792-1750
**Hammurabi ruled** west Semitic kingdom of Babylon; wrote great code of laws. Ruled Canaan in days of Abraham.

### 1450
**Moses led the Israelites** out of Egypt (approx.).

### 1360
**Ikhnaton** introduced monotheistic worship of Aten, or sun, in Egypt. A successor, Tutankhamen revived polytheistic orthodox, 1350 B.C. Tutankhamen buried at Thebes, 1344 B.C., tomb opened by Howard Carter and Lord Carnarvon, 1923-24 A.D.

### 1184
**Troy fell to Greeks** after 10-year siege, according to Homer. While poem is legendary, numerous battles were waged on site at northwest corner of Asia Minor, three miles from Hellespont (Dardanelles). Later town of Ilium was visited by Xerxes and exploited by Alexander the Great. Romans, glorifying their legendary descent from Aeneas, who escaped from Troy, built up Ilium.

In 1871 A.D. Henry Schliemann, German archaeologist, excavated site of Troy on hill of Hissarlik and found deposits of seven cities. Dorpfeld found two more. Schliemann identified second city with Homer's Troy, but objects found in sixth city correspond better with Greek remains of 1200 to 1100 B.C. found at Agamemnon's Mycenae.

### 1000
On death of King Saul, c. 1000 B.C., **David** became king of Israel but for 7½ years ruled only the southern kingdom of Judah. Thereafter he ruled all Israel, made Jerusalem capital. Solomon, son of David and Bathsheba, ruled c. 973-933 B.C.

### 753
**Romulus founded Rome**, according to legend. Hills occupied for centuries by Indo-Europeans and Sabines, sheep herders.

### 612
**Babylonians destroyed Nineveh**, Assyrian capital. Nebuchadnezzar's Babylonians defeated Egyptians at Carchemish 605 B.C. Built hanging gardens. Destroyed Solomon's temple. 589 B.C.

### 563
**Gautama (Sakyamuni) Buddha**, "the Enlightened," born near Himalayas; died 483 B.C., aged 80. Taught that painful life is caused by desire. End desire to end pain in life.

### 551
**Confucius** (Latinized form of K'ung-fu-tze) Chinese social philosopher, born; died 478 B.C. Taught: "Do not do to others what you do not wish done to you."

### 490
**King Darius'** Persian army landed at Marathon to march on Athens. Athenian infantry numbering 10,000 routed 30,000 Persians.

### 484-480
**Persian King Xerxes** assembled a great host at Sardis to invade Greece. His Phoenicians and Egyptians built two ship bridges across Hellespont from Abydos (Nagara) to Sestos, 2,000 yards long. One bridge of planks and dirt rested on 360 ships; the other on 314. Herodotus says army crossed for seven days and seven nights.

At Thermopylae, 480 B. C., Leonidas and 300 Spartans, supported by 700 Thespians and 400 Thebans, held off Persians in pass until overcome. Persians took Athens and Attica. Athenians under Themistocles destroyed Persian fleet at Salamis under eyes of Xerxes, won land battle. Rallying about 70,000 from Greek states, they routed Persians at Platea 479 B. C.

### 438
**Parthenon completed** at Athens, 101'4" by 228'2". Doric columns 33' tall, roof height 60'. Ictinus and Callicrates, designers; Phidias, chief sculptor.

### 431
**Peloponnesian War** began between Athens and Sparta. War ended 404 B.C. with Sparta victorious.

### 399
**Socrates, Greek philosopher**, condemned by Athenian state, drank hemlock (dropwort). Plato, his disciple, recorded 35 dialogues, great philosophical work. Dialogues recommended: Gorgias, Apology, Crito, Phaedo, Republic, Phaedrus, Banquet. Xenophon, another disciple, recorded memorabilia.

### 356
**Alexander "the Great" of Macedon**, born. Ruthless and energetic military leader, defeated Persians at Granicus, Issus, Arbela; conquered Asia Minor and Egypt, burned Persian capital, Persepolis, carried war to the Punjab. Founder of Alexandria. Died of fever at Babylon, 323 B. C.

### 322
**Aristotle**, Greek philosopher with scientific mind, disciple of Plato, died, 62. Demosthenes, Greek statesman, died.

### 300
**Invention of Mayan calendar** in Yucatan—approximate date—giving solar year 365.24 days and lunar month 29.52 days. Considered more exact than older calendars of Babylon, Assyria, Egypt, Greece.

### 264
**Rome began first Punic war** against Carthage, rich commercial seaport on Bay of Tunis. In 241 B.C., Carthage ceded Sicily and Lipari islands; in 239 B.C., Rome annexed Sardinia and Corsica.

### 218-146
**Hannibal, young Carthaginian**, started a campaign against Rome during the Second Punic War. Crossed from Spain to Italy via Mount Geneve in Alps with 20,000 infantry, 6,000 cavalry, and elephants. Defeated Romans at Lake Trasimene, 217 B.C., and Cannae, 216 B.C. Victories nullified by Fabius, "the delayer," hence "Fabian retreat." War closed with defeat of Carthage in Africa by Publius Scipio 202 B.C. Hannibal, after career in Asia Minor, committed suicide in Bithynia upon betrayal to Romans, c. 183 B.C.

**Third Punic war**, 149-146 B. C., ended with total destruction of Carthage. Later Roman colony built there; city eventually destroyed by Saracens, 698 A. D.

### 60-27
**Julius Caesar** formed first triumvirate with Pompey and Crassus 60 B. C.; defeated Helvetii, Belgae, 58-57 B. C.; entered Britain 55 and 54 B. C. Crossed river Rubicon to fight Pompey, defeated him at Pharsalus 48 B. C. Defeated Pharnaces at Zela, Asia Minor, 47 B. C., sent "veni, vidi, vici" message: "I came, I saw, I conquered," to Roman Senate. Lived with Cleopatra, queen of Egypt, in Rome 46-44 B. C. Was dictator but refused crown.

**Caesar assassinated** in Roman Senate by group led by Cassius and Brutus, 44 B. C. Caesar's will made his grand-nephew, Gaius Octavius, successor; he formed new triumvirate, Octavius ruling West, Mark Antony East and Lepidus Africa. At Philippi, 42 B. C., Antony defeated Cassius and Brutus; both committed suicide. Antony joined Cleopatra in Alexandria; they had 3 sons. Octavius defeated their fleet at Actium, 31 B. C.; they committed suicide. Octavius received title of Augustus (venerated) 27 B. C., called first Roman emperor. Pax Romana began. Romans victorious until 9 A.D., when Germans under Arminius defeated Varus. Augustus died 14 A.D.

### 4
**Birth of Jesus Christ** in Bethlehem.

### 1 B. C. and 1 A. D.
*The year 1 B. C. is the first year before the beginning of the Christian era. The year 1 A. D. is the first year of the Christian Era. Jan. 1, 1 B. C. is just one year before Jan. 1, 1 A. D. The elapsed number of years between a date B. C. and the same date A. D. is one less than the sum of the years. The Christian era was calculated by the monk Dionysius Exiguus in the 6th century after Christ. He placed Jesus' birth on Dec. 25 in the year 753 of Rome, and decided 754 should be the first year of the Christian era. Biblical scholars find his calculations in error and place the birth of Jesus at 4 B. C. or earlier.*

## A. D.

### THE CHRISTIAN ERA

### 29
**Crucifixion of Jesus** in reign of Roman emperor, Tiberius; Pontius Pilate procurator in Judea. The Roman Catholic church gives the date of the crucifixion as **April 7, 30 A. D.**

### 43
**Roman Emperor Claudius** subdued Britons; occupation of 300 years begun.

### 64
**Persecution of Christians** by Nero; burning of Rome. Apostles Paul and Peter martyred, c. 67.

### 70
**Jerusalem destroyed** by Titus, Christians persecuted, worship in catacombs of Rome.

### 79
**Pompeii, Herculaneum, Stabii**, destroyed by eruption of Mt. Vesuvius.

**180**

**Death of Marcus Aurelius:** onset of Roman decline.

**311**

**Emperor Galerius,** on deathbed, agreed to tolerance of Christians, Emperor Constantine, **313** promulgated Edict of Milan, made Christianity legal.

**325**

**Council of Nicaea** called by Constantine in Bithynia, Asia Minor, to get churchmen to define orthodox Christian belief. Divinity of Christ and Holy Trinity endorsed; minority view of Arius rejected.

**330**

**Constantine dedicated Byzantium** capital of Eastern Empire, henceforth called Constantinople, now Istanbul. Baptized a Christian on his deathbed by Eusebius, **337 A.D.**

**380**

**Theodosius,** Roman emperor, made Christianity based on Nicene creed official religion, banned pagan gods.

**410**

**Rome sacked by Alaric,** the Goth; by Genseric, the Vandal, **455.**

**432**

**Bishop Patrick,** native of Severn valley, sent as missionary to Ireland; labored 30 years, converting natives to Christianity. In 563 Columba founded church on Iona. In 597 Augustine arrived, founded church at Canterbury. All three were canonized.

**449**

**Anglo-Saxon migrations** from continent to Britain begin at Dover.

**483**

**Justinian I,** Byzantine emperor, born; died 565. During reign had Tribonian prepare Justinian Code (Corpus Juris Civilis) which became basic Roman law used later as a model by many medieval European states. Santa Sophia built.

**570**

**Mohammed, born in Mecca;** Hegira, flight from Mecca, 622. Year 1 of Moslem calendar. Saracens crossed to Spain 711, established Moorish kingdom, lasted until 1492.

**731**

**Great period of Mayan empire** began, closed **987.**

**732**

**Charles Martel,** Frankish ruler, defeated 90,000 Moors at Tours, France; highwater mark of Moslem invasion of Western Europe.

**800**

**Charlemagne, king of Franks,** proclaimed Holy Roman Emperor by Pope Leo III on Christmas Day in St. Peter's. Charlemagne fought Saxons, Lombards, Saracens 30 years to Christianize them; extended empire from Atlantic to eastern boundaries of Hungary. Died 814, aged 72, was buried in his cathedral at Aix. His empire broke apart.

**1000**

**Leif Ericsson's Norsemen** reach Vinland, land of grape vines. Variously identified as Labrador, New England coast and Martha's Vineyard.

**1014**

**Brian Boru,** Irish king, defeated Danes at Clontarf.

**1027**

**New empire of Mayas** extended north to Mexico. Disintegration accelerated by pestilence, 1480. Destruction of Tayasal, Guatemala, Itza capital, by Spanish governor of Yucatan, 1697, ended Mayan millennium.

**1054**

**Final break between Eastern** (Orthodox) and Western (Roman) church came when Pope Leo IX excommunicated Michael Cerularius and his followers. Eastern Orthodox Church became established religion of Russia under the Czars. Russian patriarchate formed 1589.

**1066**

**William of Normandy conquered England** at Hastings, **Oct. 14;** Harold II, last Saxon king of England, slain.

**1096**

**First crusade,** preached by Peter of Amiens, supported by Pope Urban II, raised 100,000 men. Captured Jerusalem, 1099, Acre, 1104. Second, 1146, lost Jerusalem to Saladin. Third, 1189, Richard I of England took Jaffa. Fourth, 1200, besieged Constantinople, 1204. Fifth, 1216, achieved 10-year truce. Sixth, 1238, lost ground. Seventh, 1245, led by Louis IX (St. Louis) of France, who was captured, 1250. Eighth, 1270, led by Louis, who died near Tunis, 1270. Children's crusade, 1212, 50,000 children (est.) disbanded in Italy or lost.

**1162**

**Genghis Khan,** Mongol chief, born; died 1227. Captured Peking, 1215, defeated Russians, 1223, conquered most of Central Asia, and massacred population of Herat, Afghanistan. By 1241, Mongols under Batu had burned Moscow and Kiev and invaded Poland, Hungary, and the Danube Valley.

**1215**

**Magna Carta,** the great charter of England, signed by King John at Runnymede at insistence of 2,000 English barons who refused to fight on foreign

soil and demanded end of illegal levies by king. Charter guaranteed privileges of nobility, church free from secular interference, right of freemen to legal protection. Freemen were privileged class; common people were villein farmers, practically serfs. But 400 years later Edward Coke and Puritans demanded protection for the common people under these rights of freemen. Also invoked Clause 39, out of which trial by jury developed. It reads:

*No freeman shall be taken or imprisoned, or dispossessed, or outlawed, or banished, or in any way destroyed, nor will we go upon him, nor send upon him, except by the legal judgment of his peers or by the law of the land.*

**1271**

**Marco Polo** started with father and uncle for Cathay (China), Mongol kingdom of Kublai Khan. Served under Khan, returned to Venice 1295. Wrote Travels.

**1272**

**Thomas Aquinas,** greatest scholastic philosopher, died.

**1300**

**Dante and Giotto** flourished: Dawn of Renaissance.

**1309**

**Clement V, French pope,** made Avignon seat of church; Urban V returned to Rome, 1367, abandoned it; Gregory XI finally reentered St. Peter's, 1377. During the Great Schism, 1378-1417, French and Italian factions chose popes for Avignon and Rome; breach healed by Martin V, 1417.

**1346**

**Battle of Crecy** (Dept. of Somme, France) **Aug.** 26, Edward III of England defeated Philip VI of France. Possibly first use of cannon.

**1348**

**Black Death** (bubonic plague) hit Venice, rapidly spreading to rest of Europe by 1349. An estimated one-fourth of European population killed.

**1382**

**John Wycliffe,** Oxford forerunner of Reformation, (1320-1384) directed translation of Vulgate Bible into English vernacular. Supported bill in parliament declaring it sinful for clergy to hold property. By elevating Scriptures above church authority he anticipated Lutheran doctrine by 150 years.

**1415**

**John Huss,** Bohemian preacher, follower of Wycliffe, agitator of ecclesiastic reforms, burned at stake in Constance **July 6** for heresy after German Emperor Sigismund revoked his safe-conduct.

**1429**

**Joan of Arc,** maid of Domremy, France, obeying voices of her saints, rallied French against English, raised siege of Orleans, effected coronation of Charles VII at Reims. Through carelessness or treachery she was captured by Burgundians **May** 24, 1430, and sold to English for 10,000 livres. Placed on trial before Bishop of Beauvais at Rouen for (1) magic, (2) disobeying parents, (3) wearing male attire, and (4) heresy, she admitted all after 114 days to escape persecution, was given life imprisonment. Tricked to resume male attire, she was condemned to death and burned at Rouen by English **May 30, 1431.** Sentence revoked 25 years later. Joan has been canonized as saint.

**1453**

Constantinople captured by Ottoman Turks. **End of 100-years' war** between England and France, begun 1338. England lost all except Calais, which French captured 1558.

**1456**

**Johann Gutenberg** (Gansfleisch) completed first Bible printed from movable type; 2 vols., folio, 42 lines 2 columns to page. Printing took five years. Date established by note in Mazarin copy.

**1457**

**Johann Fust and Peter Schoeffler** produced first book printed in colors, and having printers' name, date and place, a Psalter.

**1475**

**William Caxton** printed first book in English, translation of a French history of Troy, at Bruges, Belgium. He moved to Westminster, London, printed first book in England, 1477.

**1492**

**Christopher Columbus,** Genoese navigator, after years of agitation in Spain gained support of Queen Isabella for westward voyage. Left Palos **Aug. 3** with Santa Maria, 100 tons, 52 men; Pinta, 50 tons, 18 men; Nina, 40 tons, 18 men. On Oct. 12 at 2 a.m., Rodrigo de Triana on Pinta discovered land. Columbus landed on Guanahani, Bahamas, called it San Salvador. Discovered Cuba and Hispaniola (Haiti or San Domingo); built first fort, La Navidad, there. Made Admiral of the Ocean Sea. *For later voyages see Index.*

**1497**

**John Cabot,** Venetian employed by English, reached Canada. His son Sebastian joined second voyage, 1498. English claim to Canada based on their discoveries.

**Amerigo Vespucci,** Italian-born Spanish navigator, asserted he reached American mainland (New World) year before Columbus. Martin Waldsee-

muller of St. Die in book, **1507,** asked land be called America "because Americus discovered it."
**1498**
**Savonarola,** preacher against luxury and power of clergy, burned as heretic in Florence, May 23.
**Vasco da Gama,** Portuguese navigator, reached India, discovered all sea route from W. Europe.
**1506**
Pope Julius II (della Rovere) started new St. Peter's; employed Michelangelo, Bramante, Raphael.
**1509**
**Henry VIII** became king of England. Defeated Scots at Flodden Field, 1513. Named defender of the Faith by Pope Leo X for attacking Luther, **1521.** When pope refused to annul his marriage to Catherine of Aragon for lack of male issue, Henry divorced Catherine, married Anne Boleyn, 1533. Act of Supremacy abrogated pope's authority, made king head of church in England, 1534. He ordered monasteries closed, 1536.
Queen Anne Boleyn was tried for adultery on order of Henry VIII in 1536 and beheaded. Henry married Jane Seymour, who died 1537, after giving birth to son who became Edward VI. Henry married Anne of Cleves, divorced her 1540. Next Catherine Howard, beheaded 1542. Next, Catherine Parr, 1543, who survived him.
**1513**
**Juan Ponce de Leon,** veteran of one Columbus voyage, searched for Bimini, found and named Florida. Died in Cuba, 1521.
**Vasco Nunez de Balboa** left Spanish town of Santa Maria la Antigua del Darien on Isthmus of Panama, discovered South Sea, later called Pacific by Magellan.
**1517**
**Martin Luther,** Augustinian monk, preaching faith over works, attacked abuse of selling papal indulgences by posting 95 theses (propositions) on Wittenberg church-door, Oct. 31. Diet of Worms, under Charles V, January, 1521, ordered recantation. Luther, backed by German princes, refused; put Scriptures above papal authority. Defended stand in Rome. Translated Greek New Testament into German, 1522. Became head of German evangelical movement, broke with Rome, married. Augsburg Confession, basic Lutheran creed, presented to Diet there by Melanchthon, 1530.
**1519**
**Hernando Cortes** began conquest of Mexico.
**1520**
**Fernando Magellan** discovered Strait of Magellan, Tierra del Fuego, Ladrones, and Philippines, 1521, for Spain.
**1524**
**Giovanni da Verrazano,** Italian employed by French, explored New England coast, probably New York bay.
**1526**
**William Tyndale** produced in Cologne first printed version of New Testament in English, suppressed in England. Tyndale executed for heresy, Oct. 6, 1536, at Vilvorde, near Brussels, Belgium.
**1529**
**Turks** failed in siege of Vienna: Apex of Ottoman European expansion.
**1531-35**
**Francisco Pizarro** conquered Peru for Spain.
**1534**
**John Calvin,** French-born religious reformer, published his Institutes of the Christian Religion, influential Protestant doctrine. Rejected Lutheran doctrine of consubstantiation; believed in religious base of citizenship, original sin, infant damnation. Influence extended to Scotch Presbyterians, English Puritans and Puritan New England.
**Jacques Cartier,** sent by Francis I of France, in two voyages (1534-36) discovered St. Lawrence, reached site of Montreal. Third voyage 1541. Basis of French claims to Canada.
**1535**
**Miles Coverdale** published first complete Bible in English. Also worked on first authorized Bible, "the Great Bible," completed 1539. Other editions: Whittingham's New Testament, with Calvin's introduction, 1557; Geneva Bible, 1560; Bishops' Bible, 1568.
**1540**
**Francisco Coronado,** searching for gold and "Seven cities of Cibola," explored Southwest north of Rio Grande with 70 horse, 30 foot soldiers. Hernando de Alarcon discovered Colorado river. Don Garcia Lopez de Cardenas discovered Grand Canyon.
**1541**
**Hernando de Soto** discovered Mississippi River.
**1545**
**Council of Trent,** in Austrian Tyrol, urged on Pope Paul III by Emperor Charles V, to define Catholic dogma and remedy ecclesiastical abuses, opened Dec. 13; continued intermittently until 1563; reiterated supreme papal authority, outlined faith.
**1555**
Bishops Ridley and Latimer burned at Oxford, Oct. 16; Archbishop Cranmer of Canterbury burned Mar. 21, 1556; 277 other religious leaders

burned in attempt of Queen Mary Tudor to restore Catholic authority. Elizabeth became queen. 1558, made Anglican communion official church.
**1560**
**1200 Huguenots** hanged at Amboise. Catherine de Medici, Regent of France for son, Charles IX, by Edict of January, 1562, granted Huguenots right to worship outside walled towns. Infraction of edict led to massacre of Huguenots at Vassy, Mar. 1, 1562, beginning of eight wars of religion. Massacre of St. Bartholomew, Aug. 24, 1572, encouraged by Charles IX on marriage of sister, Marguerite de Valois to Henry of Navarre (non-Catholic). Henry III caused assassination of Catholic leaders, Duc de Guise and Cardinal of Lorraine, was himself murdered Aug. 1, 1589. Henry IV (of Navarre) first Bourbon king, promulgated Edict of Nantes, April 13, 1598, giving Huguenots and Catholics equality before law. Henry converted to Catholicism, assassinated, May 14, 1609. Revocation of edict by Louis XIV, Oct. 23, 1685, led to large Huguenot emigration to England and America.
**1564**
**William Shakespeare** born; traditional date. Apr. 23; baptismal record, Apr. 26.
**1565**
**St. Augustine, Florida,** founded by Menendez. Spaniard. Attacked by Sir Francis Drake, 1586.
**1566**
**Duke of Alva** persecuted Protestants in Netherlands.
**1568**
**Ivan the Terrible** of Russia executed hundreds accused of plot to kill crown prince.
**1579**
**Sir Francis Drake** claimed west coast (California) for Queen Elizabeth. Left metal plate, found in Marin county, 1936.
**1582**
First Catholic New Testament in English issued at Reims; Old Testament translated at Douai, 1609.
**1587**
**Mary, Queen of Scots,** executed for treason; actually, threat to throne of Queen Elizabeth.
**Virginia Dare,** first child born of English parents in the New World, on Roanoke Isl., N. C., Aug. 18, 7 days after Sir Walter Raleigh's second expedition with 117 persons, landed. (First, 1585 returned to England 1586.) By 1590 all trace of settlement had vanished except for a tree inscribed enigmatically "Croatoan."
**1588**
**Spanish Armada,** 132 ships, 33,000 soldiers and crews, sent by Philip II of Spain against England, destroyed by Drake's attacks and storms. July 21-29. Only 50 ships returned to Spain. Fading of Spanish power; flourishing of Elizabethan England.
**1590**
**Edmund Spenser** began The Faerie Queen. First Shakespeare poem, Venus and Adonis, registered 1593. First play to appear in quarto, Titus Andronicus, registered 1594. Romeo and Juliet performed, 1597.
**1600**
**Shakespeare's most productive** decade opened. Included Henry V, Midsummmer Night's Dream, Twelfth Night, Merry Wives of Windsor, Hamlet, Othello, Macbeth, King Lear, Tempest, etc. Shakespeare retired to Stratford 1610; died Apr.23, 1616, the same date that Cervantes died. First folio of 36 plays published 1623; second, 1632; third, 1663; fourth, 1675.
**1602**
**Capt. Bartholomew Gosnold,** English navigator, landed on Cape Cod, to which he gave the name it still bears.
**1605**
**Gunpowder Plot of Guy Fawkes** to blow up King James I and parliament foiled when 36 barrels of gunpowder were found in cellar under Parliament, Nov. 4.
**1607**
**Capt. John Smith** and 105 cavaliers in 3 ships landed at Virginia and started first permanent English settlement in New World at Jamestown, May 13. Virginia was first of the 13 colonies.
**1609**
**Henry Hudson,** English explorer of Northwest Passage, employed by Dutch East India Co.; sailed sloop Half Moon into New York harbor, Sept., and up river to Albany. In 1610, in English ship Discovery, 55 tons, explored Hudson Bay. On return, 1611, was put into open boat with his son and 8 others by mutinous sailors. All were lost.
Spaniards settled Santa Fe, erected presidio.
**1611**
**King James version** (authorized version) of English Bible published; ordered by James I in 1604, it reconciled earlier versions and became basic Protestant Bible.
**1618**
**Thirty Years' War** opened in Bohemia between Catholic and Protestant armies; ended 1648 with Peace of Westphalia. Alsace given to France.

Holland and Switzerland received independence.

**Sir Walter Raleigh,** convicted of conspiring in 1603 to remove James I; beheaded **Oct. 29.**

**1619**

**House of Burgesses,** first representative legislature, elected by popular vote at Jamestown, established principle of self-government for royal colony.

**First Negro** slaves in English N. American colonies, landed by Dutch at Jamestown, **August.**

**1620**

**Plymouth Pilgrims,** Puritan separatists from Church of England, some living in Leyden, Holland, since 1609, left Plymouth, England, **Sept. 16,** in Mayflower, 101 passengers, 48 crew. Original destination Virginia, they reached Cape Cod **Nov. 9-19,** explored coast, landed **Dec. 21** (Dec. 11, Old Style) at Plymouth, so named for Plymouth Co. on map made 1614 by Capt. John Smith. Mayflower Compact, signed on shipboard, was agreement to form a local government and abide by its laws. Started first common house, **Dec. 25.** Half of colony perished during hard winter.

Gov. Bradford's comment, "They knew they were pilgrims" (on religious journey), later led them to be called Pilgrims, as distinct from Puritans of Massachusetts Bay Colony (1630).

**1624**

Dutch landed eight men from ship, New Netherland, on Manhattan, May. Proceeded to Albany.

**1626**

**Peter Minuit** bought Manhattan from Indians May 6 for trinkets worth $24.

**1636**

**Harvard College** founded **Oct. 28.**

**1637**

Colonials destroyed Pequot fort at Mystic, Conn., killed 600 Indians, **June 5.**

**1638**

**Peter Minuit** landed two shiploads of Swedes and Finns at site of Wilmington, Del.

**1642**

**King Charles I** of England started war against Puritan parliament at York, **Aug. 22.** His tax exactions and attempts to force Anglican ceremonials on Scotch and Puritain clergy had wrecked his regime. Called first parliament in 11 years, 1640.

**Oliver Cromwell** led army of Roundheads for parliament, defeated Charles' Cavaliers at Marston Moor, 1644, and Naseby, 1645. Charles was delivered to parliament by the Scots, 1648.

**Galileo** died, **Newton** was born, **100** years after

**Copernicus** published heliocentric theory. Galileo defended theory: "Holy Spirit intended to teach us in the Bible how to go to Heaven, not how the heavens go." But in 1616 the Inquisition at Rome declared the assertion of earth's motion to be heretical and placed works of Copernicus, Kepler and Galileo on the Index until 1822.

**1648**

**Taj Mahal** outside Agra, India, completed by Mogul Emperor Shah Jahan for his wife. 20,000 workers used in construction.

**1649**

**Charles I** condemned by House of Commons, sitting as High Court; beheaded **Jan. 30.**

**Commonwealth** ruled by Commons and **Council of State** (John Milton, Latin secretary) with Cromwell at head. Cromwell annihilated Scots at Worcester, 1651. Cromwell made protector for life, actually dictator, 1653. Admiral Blake took Jamaica from Spain, 1655.

**Cromwell** died 1658. His son, Richard, resigned rule. Puritan government collapsed and parliament called Charles II.

**1656**

**Anne Hibbins** hanged as witch in Salem, Mass.

**1660**

**John Bunyan,** a tinker, imprisoned at Bedford, England, Nov., for unlawful preaching, released 1672, after writing part of Pilgrim's Progress.

**Restoration under Charles II,** "Merry Monarch." Charles' Cavalier parliament restored Anglican church and refused freedom of worship to dissenters, promised by King in Declaration of Breda.

**1664**

**King Charles II** ordered Col. Nicolls and 300 men to seize New Netherland (Manhattan and environs) from Dutch, granted territory to his brother James, Duke of York. Petrus Stuyvesant, Dutch Director General, yielded peacefully; province of New Netherland and city of New Amsterdam became New York. The Dutch recaptured both Aug. 9, 1673; ceded all by treaty to Britain Nov. 10, 1674.

**1665**

**Great Plague** in London killed 68,000. In 1666 great fire destroyed 13,200 houses. 89 churches.

**1676**

**Nathaniel Bacon** led planters, oppressed by taxes, against Gov. Berkeley at Jamestown; burned town, bacon died suddenly; 23 followers executed.

Bloody Indian war in New England ended **Aug. 12.** King Philip, Wampanoag chief, and many Narragansett Indians killed.

---

## American Revolution and War of Independence;

Great Britain, after acquiring Canada from France in 1763, tightened up colonial administration in North America. The Thirteen Colonies, used to self-government, resented duties on commerce and objected to paying for troops now quartered on them. **The Sugar Act,** 1764, placed duties on lumber, foodstuffs, molasses and rum. **The Stamp Act,** 1765, required revenue stamps to help defray cost of royal troops. The colonists formed Sons of Liberty groups and rejected British goods. Nine colonies, led by New York and Massachusetts at Stamp Act Congress in New York Oct. 7-25, 1765, adopted Declaration of Rights, opposing taxation without representation in parliament and trial without jury by admiralty courts. In the Virginia House of Burgesses Patrick Henry warned King George III of consequences, with "If this be treason make the most of it." Parliament repealed Stamp Act Mar. 17, 1766.

**Townshend Acts,** 1767, levied taxes on glass, painter's lead, paper and tea imports. In 1770 all duties except tax on tea were repealed, but principle of right to tax was maintained. British troops fired into a mob Mar. 5, 1770, killed 5 including Crispus Attucks, reportedly a Negro leader of the group; it was called the Boston Massacre. Tea ships of East India Co. turned back at Boston, New York, Philadelphia, May, 1773. Cargo ship burned at Annapolis, Oct. 14. Cargo thrown overboard at **Boston Tea Party,** Dec. 16. Parliament ordered port closed until tea was paid for, sent 4 regiments to Boston, suppressed town meetings and elective representation in Massachusetts.

**Samuel Adams,** Boston, began uniting patriot leaders by Committees of Correspondence, Virginia called for first **Continental Congress,** Philadelphia, Sept. 5-Oct. 26, 1774. On Mar. 23, 1775, **Patrick Henry** addressed revolutionary convention, Richmond, Va., with famous speech: "Give me liberty or give me death!"

### BATTLES OF 1775

**Paul Revere and Wm. Dawes,** on night of Apr. 18 on horseback aroused Sam Adams and John Hancock at Lexington and others that 700 British were on way to **Concord** to destroy arms. At **Lexington,** Apr. 19. Minutemen lost 8 killed, 10 wounded. On return from Concord the harassed British lost 273.

Col. Ethan Allen (joined by Col. Benedict

Arnold) captured Ft. Ticonderoga, May 10; also Crown Point. Colonials headed for Bunker Hill, fortified Breed's Hill, Charlestown, repulsed British under Gen. Wm. Howe twice before retreating June 17; British casualties 1,000; called Battle of **Bunker Hill.** Continental Congress June 15 named Geo. Washington commander-in-chief; he took command in Cambridge July 3. Maj. Gen. Richard Montgomery led troops against Canada via New York, Col. Arnold marched via Maine wilderness; captured **Montreal** Nov. 13, attacked **Quebec** Dec. 30-31; Montgomery killed. Colonials returned to New York state June, 1776.

Mecklenburg Declaration of Independence adopted at Charlotte, Mecklenburg County, N.C., **May 20** (a disputed tradition).

### DECLARATION OF INDEPENDENCE

Virginia voted for independence May 15. In Continental Congress June 7, 1776, Richard Henry Lee (Va.) moved "that these united colonies are and of right ought to be free and independent states." Resolutions adopted July 2. **Declaration of Independence** July 4. *See article.*

Col. Moultrie's batteries at Charleston, S. C. repulsed British sea attack June 28. Washington, with 10,000 lost **Battle of Long Island** to Howe and Gen. Sir Henry Clinton with 15,000 Aug. 27, evacuated New York.

**Nathan Hale,** executed as spy by British Sept. 22, said: "I regret that I have but one life to lose for my country."

Washington repulsed Howe at **Harlem Heights** Sept. 16, retreated to White Plains, N. Y. Brig. Gen. Arnold's Lake Champlain fleet was defeated at Valcour Oct. 11, but British returned to Canada. Howe failed to destroy Washington's army at **White Plains** Oct. 28. Hessians captured Ft. Washington, Manhattan, and 3,000 Nov. 16; Ft. Lee, N. J., Nov. 18.

Washington in New Jersey recrossed Delaware River Dec. 25-26, defeated 1,400 Hessians at **Trenton** N. J., Dec. 26.

### BRANDYWINE AND SARATOGA, 1777

Washington defeated Lord Cornwallis at Princeton Jan. 3. Continental Congress adopted Stars and Stripes June 14. *See article on Flag.* Maj. Gen. John Burgoyne with 8,000 from Canada captured Ft. Ticonderoga June 27. Brig. Gen. Nicholas Herkimer, to raise St. Leger's siege of Ft.

## 1682

**Robert Cavelier, Sieur de la Salle,** took lower Mississippi river country for Louis XIV. called it Louisiana, Apr. 9. Had built French outposts in Illinois. Established fort at Lavaca, **Texas, 1684,** with 400 men. Was killed by his own men on Trinity river, Texas **Mar. 19. 1687.**

## 1683

**William Penn** signed treaty with Indians.

## 1689

King William's War, British in America vs. French and Indians. Ended 1697.

## 1692

**Witchcraft** delusion at Salem, Mass., inspired by preaching; 19 persons hanged, 1 man crushed to death. Executions in Europe of women for witchcraft between 1484 and 1782 believed to have reached 300,000. Last in England 1716; in Scotland, 1722.

## 1696

**Capt. William Kidd,** American, hired by British king and nobles to fight pirates and take booty, became pirate. Returned to New York with treasure, 1698, buried it on Gardiner's Island. Arrested by Earl of Bellamont, governor of province, and sent to England for trial, he was hanged, 1701, for killing sailor. Treasure of gold and gems given Bellamont by Lord of Gardiner's island.

## 1704

**Indians** attacked Deerfield, Mass., **Feb. 28-29,** killed 40, carried off 100.
**Gibraltar** taken by England from Spain, **July 24;** formally ceded by Treaty of Utrecht, 1713.
**Boston News Letter,** first regular newspaper, started by John Campbell, postmaster. (Publick Occurrences, 1690, was suppressed after one issue.)

## 1709

**British-Colonial** troops captured French fort, Port Royal, Nova Scotia, in Queen Anne's War (1701-1713). France yielded Nova Scotia by treaty, 1713.

## 1712

**Slaves** revolted in New York **April 6. Six** committed suicide. 21 were executed. Second rising, 1741; 13 slaves hanged, 13 burned, 71 transported.

## 1720

**"Mississippi Bubble."** John Law, Scot, comptroller of finance in France, issued paper currency without security to back trading scheme. Shares reached **$4,000** before collapse. Many ruined; France assumed debt of **$340,000,000.**

## 1728

**Pennsylvania Gazette,** founded by Samuel Keimer, Philadelphia, Benj. Franklin bought interest. 1729.

## 1735

**Freedom of the press** recognized in New York by acquittal of **John Peter Zenger,** editor Weekly Journal, on charge of libelling British governor, Cosby, by criticizing conduct in office.

## 1740-1741

**Capt. Vitus Bering,** Dane employed by Russians, discovered Alaska.

## 1743

**King George's War.** British and American colonials vs. French. Siege of Louisbourg, Cape Breton Isl. led by Gov. Wm. Shirley of Mass. Surrendered to British **June 17, 1745.** Returned to France by Treaty of Aix la Chapelle 1748.

## 1746

**English** defeated Scots at Culloden, **April 16,** routing Stuart pretender, Prince Charles.

## 1751

**Publication** of the Encyclopédie began in France, great popularizer of the Enlightenment.

## 1752

**Benjamin Franklin,** flying kite in thunderstorm, proved lightning is electricity **June 15.**
**Gregorian calendar** adopted by Great Britain and American colonies, dropping 11 days after Sept. 2; next day Sept. 14.

## 1754

**French and Indian War** started after French occupied uncompleted British post, called it Ft. Duquesne (site of Pittsburgh). Col. Geo. Washington with Virginia troops clashed with French at Great Meadows, dug in at Ft. Necessity; capitulated and withdrew **July 3, 1754.** Boston's 3,000 provincial troops took Nova Scotia French forts **June 16, 1755.** French and Indians ambushed Gen. Wm. Braddock's expedition 10 mi. from Ft. Duquesne (now Braddock, Pa.) **July 9;** Washington helped retreat; Braddock fatally wounded, 714 killed. Gen. Sir Wm. Johnson defeated French and Indians under Baron Dieskau at Lake George **Sept. 8.** British moved Acadian French out of Canada. **Nov.** Britain formally declared war **May 18, 1756.** Surrendered Ft. Wm. Henry (Lake George) to Montcalm; Indians massacred many unarmed British, **Jan. 1, 1757.** Montcalm at Ft. Ticonderoga repulsed 17,000 British **July 8.** French gave up Louisburg, Ft. Frontenac, Ft. Duquesne, 1758; Niagara,

# Origins, Battles, Results, 1763-1783

Stanwix, routed Indians at Oriskany, N. Y. Aug. 6. Burgoyne's Hessians defeated by Brig. Gen. John Stark and the Green Mountain Boys at Bennington, Vt., Aug. 16. Arnold raised siege of Ft. Stanwix.
Howe defeated Washington at Chad's Ford on the Brandywine (Pa.) Sept. 11 and occupied Philadelphia. Congress moved to Lancaster, Pa. Inconclusive battle of Germantown, Pa., Oct 4. Washington's army wintered at Valley Forge.
Americans massed at Bemis Heights on Hudson under Maj. Gen. Horatio Gates, attacked by Burgoyne Sept. 19. At Freeman's Farm, Gen. Arnold and Col. Daniel Morgan's riflemen repulsed British, inflicting great loss. Gen. Clinton took Fts. Clinton and Montgomery below West Point Oct. 6, but did not support Burgoyne. Americans beat back Burgoyne at Bemis Heights Oct. 7 and cut off British escape route. Burgoyne surrendered 5,000 at Saratoga Oct. 17.
Marquis de la Fayette (Lafayette), aged 20, made major general.
Articles of Confederation and Perpetual Union adopted by Continental Congress Nov. 15.

### HELP FROM FRANCE

France recognized independence of 13 Colonies, signed treaty of aid with Benj. Franklin, Silas Deane, Arthur Lee, Feb. 6, 1778. Sent fleet under Adm. d'Estaing. British evacuated Philadelphia in consequence, June 18. Washington harassed British at Monmouth, N. J., June 28. Indian massacre at Wyoming, Pa., July 3. British overran Georgia, December.
George Rogers Clark, with foot Cahokia and Kaskaskia, (Ill.) 1778, took Vincennes Feb., 1779. Maj. Gen. Anthony Wayne, July 15, stormed Stony Point, on Hudson, but withdrew after victory.
John Paul Jones in Bonhomme Richard defeated Serapis on the Atlantic Sept. 23, 1779. French fleet and Maj. Gen. Benj. Lincoln's men were repulsed at Savannah Oct. 9.

### BENEDICT ARNOLD'S TREASON

Three Continental soldiers, Paulding, Williams and Van Wart, captured Major John Andre, adjutant general of the British army, in disguise at Tarrytown, N. Y., Sept. 23, 1780, finding papers betraying West Point, signed by Gen. Arnold, in his socks. He had lost way after rendezvous with Arnold at Haverstraw, N. Y. Arnold, informed of

Andre's capture, escaped from headquarters in Highlands, near present Garrison, N. Y., by barge to British sloop Vulture off Verplanck's Point.
Andre was found guilty by board of American officers at Tappan, N. Y., hanged as spy Oct. 2. Washington refused to intercede. Arnold made brigadier general in British army. Burned New London, Conn., 1781. His wife, Peggy Shippen of Philadelphia adjudged innocent by Washington, since proved implicated. Arnold died in London. Andre's body removed to Westminster Abbey, 1821.

### ROAD TO YORKTOWN

Charleston fell to the British May 12, 1780, but a segment of Lord Cornwallis' forces led by Maj. Patrick Ferguson was defeated near Kings Mountain, N. C. Oct. 7 by militiamen commanded by Cols. John Sevier, Isaac Shelby, Wm. Campbell and Benj. Cleveland. Operations in South under Cornwallis and Col. B. Tarleton in 1781 were checked by Maj. Gen. Nathanael Greene and Brig. Gen. Daniel Morgan. Cowpens, S. C., Jan. 17, was a victory, but Guilford Court House, N.C., Mar. 15 was a British gain. Greene's harassments caused Cornwallis to retire to Wilmington, N. C., and thence to Yorktown, Va.
While Lafayette waited near Yorktown, Adm. De Grasse landed 3,000 French and stopped Adm. Thos. Graves' British fleet in Hampton Roads. Adm. Barras joined De Grasse. Washington and Rochambeau joined forces and leaving 2,000 to mislead Sir Henry Clinton in New York, marched to Annapolis and took boats to James River near Williamsburg, arriving Sept. 26. When siege of Cornwallis began Oct. 6, British had 6,000, Americans 8,846, French 7,800. Clinton decided too late to relieve Cornwallis. Graves sailed from New York with 7,000 Oct. 17, too late to reach Cornwallis, who surrendered Oct. 19, 1781.

### INDEPENDENCE, 1782

A new British cabinet agreed to recognize independence, March, 1782. Preliminary agreement signed in Paris Nov. 30; treaty Sept. 3, 1783. (Congress ratified it Jan. 14, 1784.) Washington ordered army disbanded Nov. 3, 1783. British evacuated New York Nov. 25. Washington bade farewell to his officers at Fraunce's Tavern, New York, Dec. 4; resigned Dec. 23, retired to Mount Vernon, Va. *For casualties see index.*

Ticonderoga, Crown Point, 1759. British captured Quebec, Sept. 18, 1759, in battles in which Montcalm and Gen. Jas. Wolfe (Br.) died. Peace signed Feb. 10, 1763 (hence "Seven Years' War"). French lost Canada and American Midwest.

**1755**

Great earthquake, **Nov. 1.** In Lisbon, Portugal, 60,000 died; 12,000 in Fez, Morocco; half of Madeira levelled; 2,000 houses lost in Mitylene; Oporto, Braga, Malaga damaged.

Samuel Johnson issued English Dictionary.

**1756**

**Black Hole of Calcutta.** Nawab of Bengal, attacking British East India Co., threw 146 British prisoners into room less than 20 ft. square, **June 20:** only 23 survived overnight. Lord Robert Clive with 3,000 British troops defeated the Nawab's force of 50,000, June, 1757.

**1769**

**Napoleon Bonaparte** born **Aug. 15**, Ajaccio, Corsica; died at Longwood, St. Helena, **May 5, 1821.**

**1772**

**First Partition of Poland** by Austria, Prussia, and Russia. Second and third partitions of 1793 and 1795 erased Poland from map of Europe, not to re-emerge until after World War I.

**1781**

Bank of North America incorporated in Philadelphia, **May 26.** First chartered bank, Bank of Pennsylvania **(Mar. 1, 1780)** operated 1782-1784.

**1783**

**Massachusetts Supreme Court outlawed slavery** because of the words in the State Bill of Rights, "all men are born free and equal."

**First balloon** sent up **June 5** by Joseph and Jacques Montgolfier. J. A. C. Charles and the Robert brothers sent up first hydrogen-filled balloon, **Aug. 27.** J. F. Pilatre de Rozier made first human ascent in captive balloon, **Oct. 15.** De Rozier and Marquis d'Arlandes made first voyage in free Montgolfier hydrogen gas balloon, Paris, **Nov. 21.**

**1784**

Peter Carnes, Baltimore, using de Rozier model, sent up captive balloon with 13-year-old Edward Warren in it, **June 23.**

**First successful daily newspaper,** Pennsylvania Packet & General Advertiser, formed from triweekly, **Sept. 21.**

**1785**

**First steamboat experiment** by John Fitch. New Jersey granted him rights to rivers, 1786. Fitch demonstrated steamboat with 12 mechanical oars on Delaware river, 3 miles an hour, **Aug. 22, 1787.** Pennsylvania, Delaware, Virginia, New York gave him river rights, 1787. He operated steamboat between Trenton and Philadelphia, 1790. Allegedly ran boat on Collect Pond, now Foley Sq., New York, 1796. Died 1798.

**1786**

Delegates from 5 states at Annapolis asked Congress to call convention in Philadelphia to write practical constitution for the 13 states.

**1787**

**Shays' rebellion** in Massachusetts, led by Capt. Daniel Shays; the attempt to seize U. S. Arsenal in Springfield failed **Jan. 25.**

**Northwest Ordinance,** adopted **July 13** by Continental Congress, made effective Ordinance of 1784, drafted by Jefferson. Determined government of **Northwest Territory,** north of Ohio river, west of New York: 5,000 male voters could establish legislature; 60,000 inhabitants could get statehood. Guaranteed freedom of religion, support for schools, no slavery.

**James Rumsey,** encouraged by Washington, ran steamboat with power pump on Potomac **Dec. 3** and **11.** Patented 1791. He died 1792.

**Constitutional convention** opened at Philadelphia **May 14,** George Washington presiding; Constitution adopted by delegates **Sept. 17;** Ratification by 9th state, New Hampshire, **June 21, 1788,** meant adoption. *See Constitution of U. S.*

**1788**

**Warren Hastings,** Gov. Gen. of India, tried for treason in London; acquitted 1795.

First British settlement in Australia, a penal colony at Port Jackson, now Sydney.

**1789**

**George Washington chosen President** by all electors voting (73 eligible, 69 voting, 4 absent); John Adams Vice President, 34 votes, Feb.; First U. S. Congress called **Mar. 4,** Federal Hall, New York; regular sessions began **Apr. 6.** Washington inaugurated there **Apr. 30.** Supreme Court created by Federal Judiciary Act, **Sept. 24.**

**The French Revolution** began **June 20,** when the delegates to the Third Estate (Commons) met in the tennis court and took an oath not to disband until the King had granted France a constitution; Bastile stormed, **July 14,** and prisoners of state released. France was declared a limited monarchy, under Louis XVI; Mirabeau died **April 2, 1791;** the King and family arrested **June 21, 1791;** Revolutionary Tribunal set up on **Aug. 19, 1792.** National Convention opened **Sept. 17, 1792,** and a republic

was established on **Sept. 22.** King Louis was beheaded **Jan. 21, 1793;** the Reign of Terror began **May 31, 1793;** Charlotte Corday stabbed Marat **July 13, 1793;** the Queen was beheaded **Oct. 16, 1793.** Danton on **April 5, 1794,** Robispierre on **July 28, 1794.** Revolutionary Tribunal abolished **Dec. 15, 1794;** Louis XVII died in prison, **June 8, 1795,** peace was made with Prussia, the great revolution ended. Napoleon was declared First Consul **Dec. 24, 1799,** and was made Consul for life **Aug., 1802.**

**Mutiny on the British ship Bounty, April 28;** Capt. William Bligh and 18 sailors set adrift in a launch. They rowed 3,618 miles to Timor, near Java. The Bounty, in command of Fletcher Christian, rebel mate, sailed to Tahiti, where some of crew and 18 Polynesians of whom 12 were women, went to Pitcairn Island, arriving there 1790. They burned the vessel after landing the food and tools.

**1791**

Continued attacks on settlements north of Ohio River by Indians armed by British, led Washington to send Gen. Arthur St. Clair and Gen. Wilkinson to area with 1,400. St. Clair was surprised near Wabash River in Ohio **Nov 4,** lost 630 killed.

**1792-94**

**Gen. Anthony Wayne** made commander, took 2 years to train American Legion. Established Ft. Washington (Cincinnati), Ft. Recovery, O., 1793; Ft. Greeneville, Ft. Deposit, Ft. Defiance, 1794. Routed Indians (Ottawas, Shawnees, Miamis, Iroquois) with bayonet at Fallen Timbers on Maumee River **Aug. 20, 1794,** checkmated British at Ft. Miamis.

**Whiskey Rebellion,** west Pennsylvania protesting whiskey tax, suppressed by U. S. **Sept. 1794.**

**1795**

Gen. Wayne built Ft. Wayne; signed peace with Indians at Fort Greeneville.

**Triple Alliance** formed by Great Britain, Russia, and Austria, **Sept. 28.**

**U. S. bought peace from Algiers and Tunis** by paying $800,000, supplying a frigate and annual tribute of $25,000, **Nov. 28.**

**1796**

**Washington's Farewell Address** as President delivered **Sept. 19.** Gave strong warnings against permanent alliance with foreign powers, partiality toward favorite nation, big public debt, large military establishment and devices of "small artful, enterprising minority" to control or change government; praised reciprocal checks of Constitution; stressed need for enlightened public opinion; declared "religion and morality lead to political prosperity."

**Vaccination** discovered by Edward Jenner **May 14,** announced 1798.

**1797**

**U. S. frigate United States** launched at Philadelphia, **July 10; Constellation** at Baltimore, **Sept. 7; Constitution (Old Ironsides)** at Boston, **Sept. 20.**

France ordered capture of all neutral ships carrying British cargoes.

**1798**

**War with France** threatened over French raids on U. S. shipping and rejection of U. S. diplomats. Congress voided all treaties with France, ordered Navy to capture French armed ships. Navy (45 ships) and 365 privateers captured 84 French. U. S. Constellation took Fr. warship Insurgente, 1799. Napoleon, becoming First Consul, stopped French raids.

**1801**

**Tripoli declared war, June 10,** against U. S., which refused added tribute to commerce-raiding corsairs. U.S. frigate Philadelphia captured in Tripoli harbor **Oct.,** 1803, burned by Stephen Decatur **Feb. 16, 1804.** Expedition under William Eaton forced Tripoli to conclude peace **June 4, 1805.**

**1803**

**Robert Emmet** convicted of treason by British in Ireland; executed in Dublin, **Sept. 19.**

**Louisiana Purchase.** President Jefferson sent James Monroe to Paris to join Robert R. Livingston, American minister, in offering up to $10,000,-000 for the isle of Orleans (New Orleans) and West Florida. Napoleon, who had recovered Louisiana from Spain by secret treaty, offered all of Louisiana for $11,250,000 in bonds, plus $3,750,000 indemnities to American citizens with claims against France. U. S. took title **Dec. 20.**

**Robert Fulton** operated experimental steamboat unsuccessfully on Seine, Paris, France.

**1804**

**Lewis and Clark Expedition** ordered by Pres. Jefferson to explore what is now northwest U. S. Started from St. Louis **May 14;** ended **Sept. 23, 1806.**

**Alexander Hamilton** (ex-Secretary of the Treasury) and Vice President **Aaron Burr** (former U. S. Senator from N. Y. State but a native of Newark, N. J.), fought a duel, **July 11,** on the Hudson Palisades, Weehawken, N. J. Hamilton, who had fired in the air, was fatally shot.

**Code Napoleon** systematized French law under the auspices of Napoleon Bonaparte. It became a model for many countries.

John Stevens, Hoboken, operated experimental steamboat with twin-screw propellers, 9 mi.

### 1805

**Napoleon**, emperor since **May 18, 1804,** defeated Austrians at Ulm, Oct. 17; Russo-Austrians at Austerlitz ("masterpiece of battles") Dec. 2. Dissolved Holy Roman Empire. Made brothers Joseph, king of Naples, Louis, king of Holland.

**Lord Nelson defeated French-Spanish** fleet at Cape Trafalgar, Oct. 21; lost his own life.

### 1806

**Napoleon defeated Prussians** at Jena, Oct. 14. In 1807 he defeated Russians at Eylau; signed peace of Tilsit with Czar Alexander I. Made brother Jerome king of Westphalia; allotted Finland to Russia.

### 1807

**Robert Fulton** made first practical steamboat trip on Clermont (open boat, 140 by 13 ft., 7 ft. draft, side paddle wheels). Left New York Aug. 17, reached Albany, 150 mi., in 32 hrs.

**Aaron Burr was arrested** in Mississippi on a federal charge of treason and was put on trial in Richmond, Va., **May 22,** and was acquitted, **Sept. 1.** He was charged with having organized an expedition of 100 men, who embarked in flatboats on the Ohio River, and made their way to New Orleans, to establish an empire that was to comprise the Louisiana Territory, a large section of the Western States and Mexico.

### 1808–09

**French occupied Madrid,** March; Rome, April; Napoleon made brother Joseph king of Spain. French defeated in Spain and Portugal; Peninsular war begun by British. Napoleon defeated Austrians at Wagram, July 6, 1809. Annexed Papal States.

**Phoenix,** world's first ocean-going steamboat, built by John Stevens, left New York for Philadelphia, **June 8, 1809.**

### 1810

**Napoleon annulled marriage** with the Empress Josephine, who retired to Malmaison. **Married** Austrian Archduchess Maria Louisa. March. Son born Mar. 20, 1811, called King of Rome. As Duke of Reichstadt, he died in Vienna **July 22, 1832.** Called L'Aiglon (the Eaglet) by French, **he** inspired Edmond Rostand's drama.

### 1811

**William Henry Harrison,** gov. of Indiana territory, defeated Indians under the Prophet, brother of Tecumseh in battle of Tippecanoe, Nov. 7.

### 1812

**Napoleon invaded Russia,** with conscript army of 500,000; defeated Russians at Borodino. **Sept. 7;** took Moscow, **Sept. 14.** Russians burned 30,800 houses in Moscow. Napoleon ordered retreat Oct. 19, meeting huge losses from cold and guerrillas.

### 1813

**Napoleon with 180,000 French** decisively defeated at Leipzig by 200,000 allied Prussians, Austrians, Russians, under Austrian Gen. Schwartzenberg in Battle of the Nations, Oct. 16-19.

### 1814

**Allies entered Paris, March 21;** Napoleon abdicated, **April 11;** Louis XVIII restored to throne, May 3; Congress of Vienna opened, **Nov. 3.** Napoleon exiled to Elba.

### 1815

**Napoleon re-entered France** Mar. 1, assumed command, ruled 100 days, **Mar. 20-June 22.** Defeated at Waterloo, Belgium, **June 18,** by Duke of Wellington (British), Count von Blucher (Prussian) and allies. Deported to St. Helena Isl., died there **May 5, 1821.**

**Holy Alliance,** formed by Russia, Austria and Prussia; signed in Paris, **Sept. 26;** promulgated in Frankfort, **Feb. 2, 1816,** and acceded to **1818** by the rulers of Great Britain and France.

## War of 1812 between United States and Great Britain

The War of 1812 coming only 30 years after end of the Revolution, had 3 major causes: (1) Britain, blockading France, seized American ships trading with France; (2) Britain, refusing to recognize naturalized American sailors, seized 4,000 by 1810 and impressed two-thirds into British service; (3) British armed Indians who raided western border. H.M.S. Leopard attacked U. S. Chesapeake, 1807, killed 3 Americans, seized 4. Under President Jefferson U. S., 1807 and 1809, stopped trade with Europe, which ruined American shippers. Under President Madison, 1810, trade with Britain only was stopped.

War might have been averted. The British raised the blockade for American ships June 16, 1812, but the news did not reach U. S. by June 18, when Congress by a small majority voted a declaration of war. Congress voted to raise Army from 11,744 to 44,500 and to use militia. The Navy had 20 major ships of 500 guns. The West favored war; New England opposed it. The British were handicapped by war with France.

### WAR ON LAND

This was full of blunders caused by inefficient leaders and refusal of regulars to work with militia. U. S. lost Ft. Michilimackinac (Mich.) and Ft. Dearborn (Ill.). Brig. Gen. Wm. Hull surrendered Detroit Aug. 16, 1812, to Maj. Gen. Isaac Brock. Maj. Gen. Stephen van Rensselaer with 2,300 took Queenston Heights, Canada, Oct. 13, but retired when regulars did not support. Brig. Gen. Wm. H. Harrison had 1,000 casualties near Ft. Malden. Brig. Gen. Zebulon M. Pike (disc. Pike's Peak) took York, (Toronto), Apr. 27, 1813, killed in explosion. Brig. Gen. Jacob Brown May 27 repulsed Sir Geo. Prevost, Canadian Governor General. Gen. Henry Dearborn May 27 took Ft. George and Queenston Heights aided by amphibious assault led by Col. Winfield Scott and Comm. Oliver Hazard Perry. British defeated 2,000 Americans a few days later.

**Battle of the Thames,** Ontario, Can., Oct. 5, 1813. Harrison with 3,500 took Ft. Malden, pursued British 85 mi. Cavalry charge by Kentucky riflemen routed British and Indians, killing Shawnee chief, Tecumseh. Detroit frontier was safe for U. S. In the fall both Brig. Gen. Wade Hampton with 4,000 and Maj. Gen. Jas. Wilkinson, with 6,000 mismanaged attempts to invade Canada; Wilkinson was defeated at Ogdensburg. British recaptured Fts. George and Niagara, burned Buffalo; Americans burned Newark and Queenston.

**Battle of Lundy's Lane.** Brig. Gen. Winfield Scott (promoted) led fighting of Brown's army at Lundy's Lane, on road to Burlington, July 25, 1814; result a draw with heavy losses. Scott was wounded.

**Burning of Washington.** In August British landed 4,000 under Adm. Sir Geo. Cockburn and Maj. Gen. Robt. Ross. At Bladensburg Aug. 24, 1814, Ross routed 5,000 ill-assorted U. S. troops, then burned Capitol and White House. Maryland militia stopped British Sept. 12 from reaching Baltimore; Ross was killed.

**Battle of New Orleans.** Maj. Gen. Andrew Jackson, who had defeated the Creek Indians at Horseshoe Bend on the Tallapoosa Mar. 29, 1814, and captured British base at Pensacola, Fla., Nov., on Dec. 23 engaged 2,000 British east of New Orleans, then retired to earthworks built with cotton bales. On Jan. 8, 1815, 5,300 British under Maj. Gen. Sir Edward Pakenham attacked American entrenchments at Chalmette. Jackson had 3,500, a reserve of 1,000, 20 guns and an armed schooner. British had over 2,000 casualties. Pakenham was killed; Americans lost 71. British routed an American battery on the West bank, but withdrew and left by sea Jan. 18. On Feb. 8 they took Mobile. Word came Feb. 14 that a treaty of peace had been signed at Ghent Dec. 24, 1814. U.S. ratified it Feb. 17, 1815.

### WAR AT SEA

Brilliant American gunnery brought naval victories. US Essex captured Alert Aug. 13, 1812. US Constitution, 44 guns, Capt. Isaac Hull, destroyed Guerriere Aug. 19; thereafter nicknamed Old Ironsides. US Wasp took Frolic Oct. 18. US United States, Capt. Stephen Decatur, defeated Macedonian off Azores Oct. 25. Constitution took Java Dec. 29, 1812. US Chesapeake captured by Shannon June 1, 1813; Capt. Jas. Lawrence, dying, called out: "Don't give up the ship!" US Enterprise took Boxer Sept. 5.

**Battle of Lake Erie.** Commodore Perry, using Lawrence's words as slogan defeated British fleet near Put-in-Bay Sept. 10, 1813. Perry, transferred from disabled flagship Lawrence to Niagara during battle, sent message to Harrison: "We have met the enemy and they are ours: 2 ships, 2 brigs, 1 schooner, 1 sloop."

Essex, Capt. David Porter, first US warship to sail around South America, was defeated off Valparaiso, Chile, Mar. 28, 1814.

**Bombardment of Ft. McHenry,** Baltimore, for 25 hours, Sept. 13-14, 1814, by British fleet failed. Francis Scott Key, on board ship, wrote words for Star Spangled Banner. *See article.*

**Battle of Lake Champlain.** Commodore Thos. Macdonough defeated fleet of Sir Geo. Prevost near Plattsburg, Sept. 11, 1814, while Brig. Gen. Thos. Macomb held 4,500 ready to oppose 11,000. British withdrew to Canada.

U. S. frigate President was captured Jan., 1815. Constitution captured Cyane and Levant, Feb. 20, 1815. Hornet captured Penguin, Mar. 23.

The War of 1812 was costly, but inspired national unity, gave recognition to men of the western border, made Andrew Jackson political power.

## 1817

**Rush-Bagot treaty** signed, **April 28-29,** limiting naval armaments of the United States and Canada on the Great Lakes.

First poems by John Keats.

## 1820

**Henry Clay's Missouri Compromise** bill passed by Congress, **March 3.** Slavery was allowed in Missouri, but not elsewhere west of the Mississippi river north of 36° 30′ Latitude (the southern line of Missouri). Repealed 1854.

## 1822

**Revolution in Portugal.** Separation of Brazil which proclaimed independence **Sept. 7;** Dom Pedro was crowned emperor **Dec. 1;** he abdicated 1831; succeeded by his son; a republic proclaimed **1888.**

**Mexico separates from Spain,** makes Iturbide emperor, **May;** forms republic, **Oct., 1823.**

## 1823

**Monroe Doctrine** declared, **Dec. 2.**

**Mississippi River first ascended** by steamboat, the Virginia, as far as Fort Snelling, Minn., **April 21-May 10,** 729 miles.

Gas vacuum (internal combustion) engine operated successfully by Samuel Brown, London.

## 1824

**Marquis de Lafayette,** 67, visited each of the 24 states as guest of U.S.

**Simon Bolivar,** ruler of Venezuela, Colombia, Ecuador, Peru; broke Spanish power in South America (Died 1830).

## 1825

Trade unions allowed in Great Britain.

**First railroad to use steam locomotive** (on level grade only) Stockton & Darlington Ry., opened in Eng., **Sept. 27,** with Stephenson's engine "Locomotion." First public railroad to use steam exclusively for passenger and freight traffic, Liverpool & Manchester, opened **Sept. 15, 1830.**

**Erie Canal opened,** first boat left Buffalo, **Oct. 26,** and reached New York City, **Nov. 4.**

**First iron steamboat** built in America, the Codorus, at York, Pa., by John Elgar.

## 1827

**Slavery in New York State abolished July 4.**

**Steamship Curacao,** first European built oceanic vessel to use steam power alone, crossed the Atlantic **April** from Antwerp to Paramaribo, Dutch Guiana. The Royal William, launched in Montreal, **April 29, 1831,** left there **Aug. 18, 1833,** crossed to Europe in 25 days, using only steam.

## 1828

**First passenger railroad in U. S.,** Baltimore & Ohio, was begun **July 4,** first 14 miles opened to horse-drawn, railcar traffic **May 24, 1830.**

## 1830

**Mormon church** organized by Joseph Smith, in Fayette, Seneca County, N. Y., **Apr. 6.**

**Revolution in France.** Charles X abdicated, **Aug. 2,** and was succeeded by the Duke of Orleans as Louis Philippe I. There were revolts in Brunswick, Saxony and Belgium. Belgium became independent kingdom.

**First regularly scheduled passenger** train service in U. S. using steam power opened at Charleston on South Carolina Railroad **Dec. 25** with 3½-ton U. S.-built locomotive, Best Friend of Charleston.

## 1831

**Nat Turner,** a Negro slave from Virginia, led a band of men in a wild escapade, killed 57 whites, **Aug.** Army called in, Turner caught and hanged.

## 1832

**Black Hawk War** (Ill.-Wis.) **April-Sept.,** pushed Sac & Fox Indians across Mississippi.

**Ordinance of nullification** of the tariff passed by South Carolina convention **Nov.,** 1832, declaring that if the Federal government attempted to enforce the law the state would consider itself no longer a member of the Union. Congress, **Feb.** 1833, passed a compromise tariff act, whereupon South Carolina repealed act.

First British Reform Bill: Middle class enfranchised; step toward political democracy.

## 1833

**Slavery in British Empire** outlawed **Aug. 28** as of **Aug. 1, 1834.** About 700,000 were liberated at a cost of £20,000,000. Slavery was abolished in Britain **June 22,** 1772. Slave trade was suppressed 1807.

**Oberlin College,** first in U. S. to adopt co-education. 1835, Oberlin refused to bar students on account of race.

## 1835

**Texas proclaimed independence of Mexico** in convention **Nov. 1.** Provisional govt. formed. Stephen Austin and Sam Houston leaders.

**Fire in New York City, Dec. 16-17,** destroyed 674 buildings.

Gold discovered on Cherokee land in Georgia; Indians forced to cede lands for $5,000,000 **Dec. 20,** and to cross Mississippi.

## 1836

**Texans besieged in Alamo** (San Antonio) by Mexicans under Santa Anna **Feb. 23-Mar. 6,** garrison massacred, including W. B. Travis and David Crockett. At Goliad **Mar. 27** Capt. Fannin and 371 Texans who had surrendered were massacred by Mexicans. At San Jacinto **Apr. 21** Sam Houston and 800 Texans defeated 3,000 Mexicans. Santa Anna signed treaties ending hostilities, promised to recognize Texan independence, but Mexican congress repudiated treaties.

**Marcus Whitman,** H. H. Spaulding and wives reached Fort Walla Walla on Columbia River, Oregon. First white women to cross plains.

**Seminole Indians in Florida** under Oceola attacked whites **Nov. 1** in protest against removal. After massacres and battles, war ended **Aug. 14, 1842,** with Indian defeat.

## 1837

**Victoria,** 18, niece of William IV, became queen of England. Married her first cousin. German Prince Albert of Saxe-Coburg, **1840.** He died **1861.**

## 1838

**The Great Western,** a steamship, 236 ft. long, 450 horsepower, 1340 gross tons, left Bristol, England, **Apr. 8,** and arrived in New York City, **Apr. 23.** The Sirius, 178 ft. long, 703 tons, left Liverpool **Mar. 28,** and Queenstown, **Apr. 4,** and reached N. Y. C. **Apr. 22,** using only steam power.

## 1839

**Belgium and the Kingdom of the Netherlands** were separated by treaties signed by those two countries and by Great Britain, France, Austria, Prussia, and Russia, at London, **April 19.** To the treaties was annexed a document declaring Belgium independent and perpetually neutral.

**Opium War** broke out between China and Britain. China tried to prohibit opium trade in Canton. British resist and take Canton. War ended with Treaty of Nanking, **Aug. 1842.**

## 1840

**Antarctic Continent found** by Comdr. Charles Wilkes of First U. S. Exploring Expedition; named Wilkes Land, **Jan.-Feb.**

## 1841

First emigrant train for California, 47 persons, left Independence, Mo. **May 1,** reached Stanislaus River **Nov. 4.**

First passenger train on Erie R.R. **June 30.**

**First use of anaesthetic** (sulphuric ether gas) by Dr. Crawford W. Long, Jefferson, Ga. Dr. Wm. T. G. Morton, dentist, used ether for painless extraction of tooth, **Sept. 30, 1846;** administered ether in tumor operation, **Oct. 16, 1846,** at Mass. General Hospital, Boston.

## 1844

**First message over first telegraph line** (authorized 1843) sent from U. S. Supreme Court room in Capitol, **May 24,** to Baltimore by inventor S. F. B. **Morse:** "What hath God wrought!"

Jos. Smith, Mormon leader, and brother Hyrum killed in Carthage, Ill., jail by mob **June 27.**

## 1845

**Texas voted for annexation to U. S. July 4.** Congress admitted Texas as 28th state **Dec. 29.**

## 1846

**Mexican War.** President James K. Polk ordered **Gen. Zachary Taylor** to seize disputed Texan land settled by Mexicans. After border clash U. S. declared war, **May 13;** Mexico **May 23.**

**Bear flag of republic of California** raised by American settlers at Sonoma **June 14.** Gen. J. C. Fremont took charge **July 5.** Commodore J. S. Sloat took Monterey **July 7,** declared California annexed to U. S. Commodore Robt. F. Stockton succeeded Sloat, was ordered to recognize Gen. Kearny as governor and commander in chief in California. Kearny was defeated by Mexicans **Dec. 6,** retreated to San Diego.

**Gen. Taylor defeated Mexicans** at Buena Vista, **Feb. 23, 1847.** Gen. Winfield Scott with 12,000 troops (est.) took Vera Cruz **Mar. 27;** Mexico City, **Sept. 17,** captured Dictator Santa Anna. Serving during war were Col. Jefferson Davis, Capt. Robert E. Lee, Capt. Geo. B. McClellan, Lieut. U. S. Grant. By treaty, **Feb., 1848,** Mexico ceded claims to Texas, California, Arizona, New Mexico, Nevada, Utah, part of Colorado. U. S. assumed $3,-000,000 American claims, paid Mexico $15,000,000.

**Treaty with Great Britain, June 15,** set boundary in Oregon at 49th parallel (extension of existing line). Water boundary settled 1873. Expansionists in U.S., seeking boundary farther north, used slogan "54° 40′ or fight!"

**Mormons,** after violent clashes with settlers over polygamy, left Nauvoo, Ill., for West under Brigham Young. Settled, **July 1847,** at Salt Lake City, Utah.

## 1847

**First adhesive U. S. postage stamps** on sale **July 1;** Benjamin Franklin 5¢, Washington 10¢.

**Great period of Victorian writing** opened. Jane Eyre (C. Bronte); Wuthering Heights (E. Bronte); Vanity Fair (Thackeray). 1848: Pendennis (Thackeray). 1849: David Copperfield (Dickens); Seven Lamps of Architecture (Ruskin). 1850: Sonnets (Rossetti); In Memoriam (Tennyson). 1851: Laven-

gro (Borrow). 1852: Bleak House (Dickens); Henry Esmond (Thackeray). 1853: The Newcomes (Thackeray). 1854: Hard Times (Dickens). 1855: Little Dorrit (Dickens). 1856: History of England (Macaulay).

### 1848

**Gold discovered** Jan. 24 by James W. Marshall, who was erecting sawmill in partnership with Capt. John A. Sutter on American River, branch of the Sacramento, near Coloma, Calif. Small finds of gold were reported 45 mi. nw of Los Angeles, 1841-44.

**Louis Philippe dethroned** in France; Second Republic set up, Feb. 26.

In Austria, Ferdinand I abdicated, **Dec. 2,** in favor of his nephew, Franz Josef; in Hungary, freedom was declared under Kossuth; revolts in Ireland, Lombardy, Venice, Denmark, and Schleswig-Holstein.

**Communist Manifesto** written by Karl Marx (1818-1883) and Friedrich Engels (1820-1895). Work is still a basic doctrine of the Communist world.

### 1849

**Astor Place riots** in New York City against Macready, English actor, 34 killed, **May 10.** The outbreak was in retaliation for the treatment of Edwin Forrest, American actor, in London, **1845.**

### 1850

**Senator Henry Clay's Compromise of 1850** passed; admitted California as 31st state. Sept. 9, slavery forbidden; made Utah and New Mexico territories, without decision on slavery; amended Fugitive Slave Law punishing those who aided fugitive and abolished jury trial for fugitive and the slave trade in District of Columbia.

**President Zachary Taylor died** July 9, 65; Millard Fillmore 13th president, July 10. John C. Calhoun died Mar. 31, 68.

**Jenny Lind's first concert,** Castle Garden, New York, Sept. 11, P. T. Barnum manager.

**Taiping Rebellion,** led by Hung Hsiu-ch'uan, began in Kwangsi province, China. One of the largest civil wars in history, it resulted in the death of an estimated 20 to 40 million, devastated entire provinces, and nearly toppled the Manchu dynasty. The Taiping movement, pseudo-Christian in nature, was finally suppressed, **1864,** by Tseng Kuo-fan with the help of the "Ever Victorious Army" of Gen. Charles G. ("Chinese") Gordon.

### 1851

Gold found in Australia.

Cornerstones of wings of U. S. Capitol laid. New York & Hudson River R. R., New York to Albany, opened Oct.

Panic in Public School 26, New York City, **Nov. 20** caused deaths of 45 pupils, 60 injured.

### 1852

Louis Napoleon crowned emperor of the French. Uncle Tom's Cabin, by Harriet Beecher Stowe, published.

### 1853

**Commodore Matthew C. Perry, U.S.N.,** received by Lord of Toda, Japan, **July 14;** negotiated treaty to open Japan to U. S. ships. Ratified **Mar. 8, 1854.**

**Crimean War.** A dispute between Greek orthodox and Roman monks over holy shrines held by Turkey led Russian Czar Nicholas I to extend protection to Greeks. Turkey declared war Oct. 4, 1853. Britain and France, fearing expansion of Russia, declared war May 28, 1854. Russia occupied Moldavia and Wallachia. Fighting concentrated in the Crimea and included famous Charge of the Light Brigade at Balaklava, Oct. 25, 1854, 400 out of 607 killed; Russian defeat at Inkerman, Nov. 5, 1854; fall of Sebastopol, Sept. 11, 1855. Sardinia sent 15,000 troops to Allies; Prussia and Sweden cooperated. Florence Nightingale established first dressing stations. By treaty of Paris, Mar. 30, 1856, Russia ceded part of Bessarabia to Moldavia, freed Danube for navigation. Black Sea closed to warships (repudiated, 1870).

**James Gadsden** negotiated purchase of 29,640 sq. mi. of land down to Rio Grande from Mexico, **Dec. 30,** for $10,000,000.

### 1854

**Republican party** started at Ripon, Wis., **Feb. 28;** first state organization, Jackson, Mich., **July 6.** Opposed Kansas-Nebraska Act (became law May 30) which left issue of slavery in Kansas and Nebraska to vote of settlers.

Henry D. Thoreau wrote Walden.

### 1855

**Walt Whitman** issued Leaves of Grass; Henry W. Longfellow wrote Song of Hiawatha.

First cable, Nova Scotia to Newfoundland, laid by Cyrus W. Field.

### 1856

First railroad train crossed Mississippi at Rock Island, Ill.—Davenport, Ia., **April 21.**

**Republican party's first nominee** for President, John C. Fremont, **June-Nov.,** defeated by James Buchanan. Lincoln made 50 speeches for Fremont.

Lawrence, Kan., sacked **May 21** by slavery party; **Abolitionist John Brown** led anti-slavery men against Missourians at Osawatomie; Federal troops ousted Missourians.

### 1857

**Dred Scott decision** of U. S. Supreme Court, 6-3, Roger B. Taney ch. jus., that Negro slave did not become free when taken into free state and had no rights as citizen. Abraham Lincoln denounced decision. Minnesota outlawed slavery.

**Great Mutiny in India (Sepoy Rebellion)** began in Meerut, **May 10,** when Indian soldiers revolted against British officers. First major Indian rebellion against English rule, crushed 1858. British East India Company abolished and India placed under crown rule as a result of mutiny.

**John D. Lee,** a Mormon, led raid against wagon train at Mountain Meadows **Sept. 11,** killed 120, spared only 17 children under 7. U. S. Army supplies burned. Govt. sent 6,000 troops to suppress "rebellion." Mormon Church unjustly accused.

### 1858

**First Atlantic cable** completed by Cyrus W. Field **Aug. 5.** Queen Victoria and President Buchanan exchanged greetings but cable failed **Sept. 1.** Field tried again in 1865, succeeded in 1866.

**Lincoln-Douglas debates,** Ill., **Aug. 21-Oct. 15.**

### 1859

**Dixie composed** by Dan D. Emmett (1815-1904) minstrel.

**First commercially productive oil well,** 69½ ft., drilled near Titusville, Pa., by Edwin L. Drake, **Aug. 27,** started boom.

**John Brown,** abolitionist, with 21 men seized U. S. Armory at Harpers Ferry (then Va.) **Oct. 16.** U. S. Marines under Lt. Col. R. E. Lee captured raiders, killing 11. Five civilians, one Marine also killed. Brown was hanged for treason by Virginia, **Dec. 2,** as were 5 of his band, at Charlestown (now Charles Town, West Va.).

**Darwin's Origin of Species** published. His theory of evolution caused revolution in scientific, intellectual and religious thinking.

### 1860

**Abraham Lincoln,** Republican, elected president by 1,866,452 popular and 180 electoral votes; Stephen A. Douglas had 1,375,157 and 12; John C. Breckinridge, 847,953 and 72; John Bell 590,631 and 39. Lincoln took office **Mar. 4, 1861;** Breckinridge and Bell supported secession.

**First Pony Express** between Sacramento, Calif., and St. Joseph, Mo., 1,980 miles apart, started from each place at 5 p.m., **Apr. 3;** 80 men each rode 75 miles on 429 horses changed every 10 miles. There were 190 relay stations. The service ended **Oct. 24, 1861,** when first transcontinental telegraph line was completed.

**Giuseppe Garibaldi** led 1,000 volunteers to Sicily, **May,** to unify Italy by force; deposed Francis II of Naples; hailed Victor Emmanuel of Sardinia as King of Italy.

### 1861-65—Civil War. See Article Pages 304-305

### 1861

**Emancipation of Russian serfs** by Czar Alexander II. Paved the way for later reforms by Alexander.

### 1863

**Draft riots in N. Y. City** killed an estimated 1,000 including Negroes who were hung by mobs, July 13-16. More than 50 buildings were burned.

### 1866

**Ku Klux Klan** formed secretly in South to terrorize Negroes who voted. Disbanded, 1869. Not to be confused with Ku Klux Klan, Inc., organized 1915.

**First post of the Grand Army of the Republic** formed at Decatur, Ill. **April 6.** First national encampment met **Nov. 2** in Indianapolis, Ind. For years this Union veterans organization was a political force in the nation. Last encampment held **Aug. 31, 1949,** in Indianapolis; 6 of the 16 surviving veterans attended.

### 1867

**Alaska sold** to U. S. by Russia for $7,200,000 ($.02 an acre) **Mar. 30,** through efforts of Sec. of State Wm. H. Seward and Sen. Charles Sumner.

**Emperor Maximilian of Mexico** executed by Juarez party, **June 19.** He was an Austrian archduke, placed on throne **Apr. 10, 1864,** by French.

**Dominion of Canada** established **July 1.**

**Abolition of the Shogunate** and restoration of the Mikado marked beginning of Meiji Japan that industrialized and modernized Japan; feudalism abolished, **1871;** Constitution promulgated, 1889.

### 1868

**The World Almanac,** a publication of the New York World newspaper, appeared for the first time.

**Thomas D'Arcy McGee,** a "Father of Confederation," shot in only Canadian political assassination.

**President Andrew Johnson,** blocked by Senate in attempt to remove Edwin M. Stanton, secretary of war for opposing his policies, was impeached for violation of tenure of office act by radical Senators, tried and acquitted. March-May, Stanton resigned.

**Memorial Day first observed** officially May 30 on order by Gen. John A. Logan, Commander G.A.R.

### 1869

**Financial "Black Friday"** in New York, Sept. 24; caused by gold corner.

**Transcontinental railroad** completed; golden spike driven at Promontory, Utah, May 10, marking the junction of Central Pacific and Union Parcific.

**Woman's suffrage law** passed in territory of Wyoming, Dec. 10.

### 1870

**Franco-Prussian War.** Napoleon III, French emperor, tricked into declaring war on Prussia by Bismarck, Prussian chancellor, over Spanish succession issue, surrendered with large army at Sedan, Sept. 4. Nationalists declared republic, **Sept. 4.**

Leon Gambetta, bitter-ender, escaped from Paris in balloon Oct. 7 to carry on war.

The troops of Victor Emmanuel II, under Gen. Cadorna, took possession of Rome, **Sept. 20,** in the name of the Kingdom of Italy. Rome and the rest of the Papal States then were annexed by a plebiscite, taken Oct. 2.

### 1871

**Court of Arbitration** awarded United States damages of $15,500,000 gold against Britain because British equipped Alabama and 12 other Confederate raiders. After sinking 65 U. S. ships Alabama was destroyed by Kearsarge off Cherbourg, 1864.

**William I of Hohenzollern,** proclaimed German emperor at Versailles, **Jan. 18.** Paris "red republicans," supporting internationale, organized commune, **Mar. 18-May 29;** burned Hotel de Ville.

---

## Major Events of Civil War, 1861-1865;

*For origins of the Civil War see Confederate States and Secession.*

South Carolina, Georgia, Alabama, Mississippi, Louisiana and Florida formed the Confederate States of America Feb. 8, chose Jefferson Davis provisional president; were joined later by Texas, North Carolina, Arkansas and Virginia.

### FIRST YEAR OF WAR—1861

South Carolina, through Gen. Beauregard demanded surrender of Ft. Sumter in Charleston harbor Apr. 11, Major Robert Anderson, USA, refused. Bombardment started at 4:30 a.m. April 12. Anderson surrendered Apr. 14.

President Lincoln called for 75,000 militia from states by quotas, April 15. New York state voted to enlist 30,000 militia for 2 years and $3,000,000 for defense.

U. S. troops evacuated **Harpers Ferry** Apr. 18. On Apr. 19 the 6th Mass. Infantry en route to Washington was attacked in the streets of **Baltimore;** 4 soldiers were killed.

Col. Robert E. Lee resigned from the U. S. Army April 20, became commander of Virginia troops April 23, brigadier general May 14, full general of the Confederacy June 14.

Brig. Gen. Geo. B. McClellan, Dept. of the Ohio, made major general May 14, cleared western Virginia of Confederates. Made general in chief, USA, Nov. 1, on retirement of Gen. Winfield Scott.

In Missouri Brig. Gen. Nathaniel Lyon drove Confederates under Gen. Sterling Price out of Jefferson City and Boonville, June 17. Col. Franz Sigel was forced back at **Carthage** July 5. At **Wilson's Creek** Lyon was killed in losing battle with Price Aug. 10.

**Battle of Bull Run or Manassas.** Brig. General Irvin McDowell attacked Beauregard's forces on the Warrenton Road, July 21, pushed them back to Henry House hill, Confederates were based on Manassas Junction, Va. Gen. Jos. E. Johnston's army from Winchester, including forces commanded by Col. Thomas J. Jackson and Gen. E. Kirby Smith reinforced Confederates, and with help of Gen. Jubal Early's brigade routed Federals. Brig. Gen. B. E. Bee, CSA, said: "Look, there is Jackson standing like a stone wall!" McDowell had 28,455 troops, 18,500 engaged, 2,708 casualties; Confederates had 32,072 available, 18,000 engaged, 1,967 casualties. Congress July 22 authorized 500,-000 for army.

### EVENTS OF 1862

**Forts Henry and Donelson**—Maj. Gen. Henry W. Halleck, Western Dept., sent Brig. Gen. U. S. Grant with 17,000 on river craft of Flag Officer Andrew H. Foote vs. **Ft. Henry** on Tennessee River; it fell Feb. 6. Grant rushed troops across 10 mi. of bogs to **Ft. Donelson** on the Cumberland, sent his "unconditional surrender" message to Brig. Gen. Simon B. Buckner, CSA, who gave up with 11,500 Feb. 16. **At Pea Ridge,** Ark., **Mar. 6-8** Gen. Saml. R. Curtis, USA, defeated Gens. Van Dorn and Price. Casualties: USA, 1,351; CSA, 1,300.

New Madrid, Mo., captured Mar. 14, by Gen. John Pope. Island No. 10 surrendered to Pope and Foote with 7,000 men Apr. 7.

Gen. Albert Sidney Johnston, CSA, 40,000 from Corinth, Miss., surprised Grant at **Shiloh Church** near **Pittsburg Landing,** Tenn. Apr. 6; Johnston was killed. Gen. Beauregard retreated Apr. 7 after Brig. Gen. Don Carlos Buell reinforced Grant with about 20,000. U. S. had 44,895 engaged, with 1,734 killed out of 13,047 casualties; CSA, 1,728 killed out of 10,699 casualties.

Fighting ships and gunboats under Flag Officer David G. Farragut, Comm. D. D. Porter, in Mississippi silenced Chalmette batteries; with Gen. Benj. F. Butler took forts; **New Orleans** surrendered Apr. 25 to Farragut who turned it over to Butler May 1.

Farragut made rear admiral, July.

**Monitor and Merrimack**—Confederates rebuilt scuttled US frigate Merrimack into ironclad Virginia. Sank Cumberland, USN, destroyed Congress, USN, at Hampton Roads, Va., Mar. 8. Three other US ships ran aground, including Minnesota, Monitor, flat-decked ironclad, 900 tons, 172 ft. long, with revolving turret and 2 11-in. guns, built by John Ericsson at $275,000 cost; Lt. John L. Worden commander, crew of 58, badly damaged Virginia, Mar. 9, which withdrew. Monitor did not resume fighting. After Federals took Virginia's base Confederates scuttled ship May 11.

**Peninsular Campaign**—McClellan moved Army of the Potomac by sea to Fort Monroe, Va., 70 mi. from Richmond. Confederates sent Stonewall Jackson up Shenandoah Valley to divert Federals; Jackson lost at Kernstown, Va., but routed Federals at McDowell, Front Royal, Winchester, Cross Keys, Port Republic, Mar. 23-June 9. McClellan's advance troops clashed with Maj. Gen. James Longstreet at Williamsburg May 5. On May 25 2 US corps crossed to south side of Chickahominy leaving 3 on north side. Gen. Jos. E. Johnston attacked south side May 30, Battle of Fair Oaks or Seven Pines, was repulsed. Johnston was wounded and Lee took over Army of Northern Virginia. Gen. J. E. B. Stuart, CSA, June 13-15, led his cavalry on scout around McClellan.

Gen. Lee started Seven Days' Battles at Mechanicsville June 26. McClellan withdrew to Gaines Mill (1st Cold Harbor) where Lee with 57,000 assaulted Brig. Gen. Fitz John Porter's 34,000 June 27. McClellan held off Lee at Savage Station June 29, Frayser's Farm or Glendale June 30; stopped Stonewall Jackson at White Oak Swamp June 30. At Malvern Hill July 1 Confederates had 5,000 casualties from U. S. guns. Despite this success McClellan withdrew army to Harrison's Landing. With over 115,000 available against Confederates' 95,000, McClellan from June 25-July 1 had 1,734 killed, 8,062 wounded, 6,053 missing; CSA had 3,478 killed, 16,261 wounded, 875 missing. In July Halleck became general in chief. McClellan was succeeded by Maj. Gen. John Pope.

**Second Bull Run (Manassas).** Stonewall Jackson and Maj. Gen. A. P. Hill, CSA, attacked Maj. Gen. Nath. P. Banks (part of Maj. Gen. John Pope's Army of Virginia) at Cedar Mountain, Va., Aug. 9. Jackson destroyed Pope's supplies at Manassas Aug. 26. Major battle was fought Aug. 30. Pope, checked by Jackson and Longstreet, withdrew; was relieved.

**Antietam (Sharpsburg).** Lee with 50,000 crossed Potomac Sept. 4 to Frederick, Md., moved across South Mountain to Hagerstown, Md. McClellan, after finding Lee's orders fought Longstreet and D. H. Hill at South Mountain, Sept. 14, Lee dropped back to Antietam creek near Sharpsburg, Md., Sept. 15; Jackson took Harpers Ferry, where only 1,300 cavalry of 12,000 USA escaped. McClellan attacked Sept. 17; stopped Lee, but failed to use reserve and let Lee withdraw across Potomac. USA had 70,000 engaged, 13,000 casualties; CSA had 50,000 engaged, 13,000 cas. Maj. Gen. Stuart, CSA cavalry raided Chambersburg, Pa., Oct. 10.

**Fredericksburg, Va.** Lincoln relieved McClellan, gave Army of the Potomac to Maj. Gen. Ambrose E. Burnside. Burnside crossed Rappahannock, made frontal attacks on Marye's Heights above Fredericksburg Dec. 13. Lee, Longstreet and Jackson with 75,000 repulsed him. USA lost 12,653; CSA 5,377.

In Tennessee Maj. Gen. Wm. S. Rosecrans, USA, pushed back Gen. Braxton Bragg at battle of Stones River-Murfreesboro Dec. 31-Jan. 3. US 12,000 casualties; CSA 11,000.

Preliminary proclamation, Sept. 22, by President Lincoln announced that Jan. 1, 1863, slaves would be declared free in territory then in rebellion.

Tuileries palace, executed 67 hostages. Communards overcome by French army; deaths est. 20,000.

Treaty of Frankfort, **May 23**, ended Franco-Prussian War. France ceded Alsace, most of Lorraine, paid 5 billion francs indemnity.

The **Law of Guarantees**, passed by the Italian Parliament **May 13**, granted the Pope and his successors possession of the Vatican, the Lateran and the villa of Castel Gandolfo and a yearly allowance of 3,225,000 lire, or about $645,000. The money was not claimed.

**Great fire destroyed heart of Chicago, Oct. 8-11**; loss est. $196,000,000. Started in Mrs. O'Leary's barn, 558 De Koven St. by cow kicking over lantern, according to legend.

**Henry M. Stanley**, sent by James Gordon Bennett, owner of New York Herald, to find David

Livingstone, missionary, greeted him **Nov. 10** at Ujiji, in Central Africa, now Tanzania, with "Dr. Livingstone, I presume?"

First U. S. postal card issued, **May 1**.

**1872**

**Col. James Fisk, Jr.**, shot in New York City by Edward S. Stokes, **Jan. 6**; he died two days later; Stokes got four years in prison.

**1873**

**Panic in New York City** began with bank failures, **Sept. 20**.

**1874**

**Charley Ross**, 4, kidnapped in Germantown, Pa., **July 1**, caused national sensation.

"**Boss**" W. M. **Tweed** in New York City, convicted of fraud, **Nov. 19**, and sentenced to 12 years

## Emancipation and Lincoln's Assassination

### EVENTS OF 1863

**Lincoln's Emancipation Proclamation, Jan. 1**, declared free forever the slaves in Arkansas, Texas, Louisiana (certain parishes already occupied except); Mississippi, Alabama, Florida, Georgia, South Carolina, North Carolina, and Virginia (West Virginia and other portions excepted). About 3,000,000 slaves were thus declared free.

**Chancellorsville, Va.**—Maj. Gen. Jos. E. Hooker succeeded Burnside and with 90,000 available, attempted to envelop Lee May 2. Jackson led 32,000 around US Army, drove in right of Maj. Gen. O. O. Howard. Jackson wounded by own troops May 2, died May 10; succeeded by Maj. Gen. J. E. B. Stuart. Shell stunned Hooker May 3. Maj. Gen. John Sedgwick forced Confederates out of Marye's Heights; was pushed back May 4. Against consensus Hooker withdrew across Rappahannock. US casualties 17,197; CSA 13,000. Lincoln called for 100,000 for 6 mos. June 15.

**Gettysburg**—Lee with 76,224 and 272 guns, invaded Penn. Army of the Potomac had 115,256, about 90,000 effective, 362 guns. Maj. Gen. Jubal A. Early, CSA, levied on York, Pa., for $100,000 supplies June 27. Lincoln gave Maj. Gen. Geo. G. Meade top command June 28. 1st US Cavalry (Buford) pushed back at Gettysburg by Lt. Gen. A. P. Hill, CSA, July 1. Lt. Gen. Richard S. Ewell, CSA, forced US back to Cemetery Hill; Maj. Gen. Reynolds, USA, killed. US took Culp's Hill, extended line to Round Top, with Maj. Gens. Hancock, Sickles, Sedgwick, Howard, Slocum and Pleasonton (cavalry). Lee's attacks checked July 2. On July 3 Maj. Gen. Geo. E. Pickett, Maj. Gen. Isaac Trimble and Brig. Gen. Jas. J. Pettigrew with 12,400 made assault on foot from Seminary Ridge vs. US center (Hancock); were repulsed with 4,500 casualties. Lee retreated into Virginia; Meade did not pursue. Losses: US, 3,155 killed, 14,529 wounded, 5,365 missing; CSA, 3,903 killed, 12,709 wounded, 5,425 missing. Many of the missing were prisoners. Total casualties estimated at 23,049 USA, 20,451 CSA, or over 43,000.

**Vicksburg**—Gen. Wm. T. Sherman took **Jackson**, Miss., **May 14**, held back Jos. E. Johnston, CSA. Lt. Gen. John C. Pemberton, CSA, commanding 30,000, was defeated at **Champion's Hill and Black River Bridge**, shut up in Vicksburg. He surrendered July 4; Grant paroled prisoners. Gen. Banks with 15,000 captured **Port Hudson** July 8, giving US control of Mississippi River.

**Tennessee**—Maj. Gen. Wm. S. Rosecrans took **Chattanooga** Sept. 9. Braxton Bragg, CSA, drove him back to **Chickamauga**, but Maj. Gen. Geo. H. Thomas checked Bragg, Sept. 18-20; was called "Rock of Chickamauga." Grant made commander of all armies there: Sherman of Grant's Army of the Tennessee; Thomas replaced Rosecrans. Longstreet reinforced Bragg; Hooker supported Thomas. Hooker took **Lookout Mt.**, fought Battle Above the Clouds, Nov. 24. Sherman and Thomas dislodged Bragg at **Missionary Ridge**, Nov. 25. Bragg retreated to Georgia.

**Brig. Gen. John H. Morgan**, CSA, raided Indiana and Ohio; captured at New Lisbon, O., escaped from prison at Columbus, Nov. 27. Killed at Greeneville, Tenn., Sept. 4, 1864.

### EVENTS OF 1864

Grant made lieut. general Mar. 1, gen. in chief Mar. 12. Sherman succeeded him in West. Halleck made chief of staff. Draft for 500,000 to serve 3 yrs. or duration begun Mar. 10; 200,000 more Mar. 14.

Rear Adm. David G. Farragut won naval battle, **Mobile Bay**, Aug. 5.

**Wilderness; Spotsylvania**—Bloody battles followed when Grant crossed the Rapidan and was attacked by Lee at Wilderness, May 5. Longstreet was wounded by his own men. Grant attacked Lee at **Spotsylvania Court House** May 10 (2nd Wil-

derness). Maj. Gen. Franklin G. Barlow took Spotsylvania salient, including Bloody Angle, May 12 (3rd Wilderness). Maj. Gen. Sedgwick killed. US killed and wounded May 5-12 est. 26,813; missing 4,183. Maj. Gen. Sheridan's cavalry defeated Maj. Gen. J. E. B. Stuart at **Yellow Tavern**, Va., May 11; Stuart was fatally wounded, died May 12 in Richmond.

**Cold Harbor**—Lee took strong position near the Chicahominy. Grant made frontal attacks June 3, lost 7,000 casualties in 30 minutes, 11,000 June 1-3.

**USS Kearsarge**, Capt. John A. Winslow, defeated CSS Alabama, Capt. Rafel Semmes, off Cherbourg, France, June 19; Alabama surrendered and sank.

**Siege of Petersburg**—Grant assaulted Confederate positions June 15-18 with 7,881 casualties. Exploded a mine under Confederate works July 30; during fight in crater US lost 898 killed, 4,060 wounded, 3,110 missing; CSA 400 killed, 600 wounded, 200 missing.

**Early vs. Sheridan**—Lee sent Maj. Gen. Jubal A. Early to hold Shenandoah Valley. Early went through Maryland to outskirts of Fort Stevens near Washington, July 11. Sheridan defeated Early at **Winchester** Sept. 19, **Fisher's Hill**, Sept. 22. Early surprised Wright at **Cedar Creek** Oct. 19; Sheridan's famous ride from Winchester rallied troops, brought victory.

**Sherman's Campaign for Atlanta**—Sherman defeated Johnston at Resaca, Ga., May 14-15. Hooker repulsed at **New Hope Church**, Ga., May 25. Johnston repulsed Sherman at **Kenesaw Mtn.**, June 27 (US casualties 3,000, CSA 600), evacuated post, was superseded by Gen. J. B. Hood, CSA, July 17. Lt. Gen. Wm. J. Hardee, CSA, defeated at **Peach Tree Creek**, July 20. Hardee defeated in battle of Atlanta, July 22, by Gen. J. B. McPherson, who was killed. Sherman occupied Atlanta Sept. 2, burned it Nov. 15, started March to the Sea, reached Savannah Dec. 21. Thomas defeated Hood at Nashville, Tenn.

Gen. Nathan B. Forrest, CSA, captured Fort Pillow, Tenn., Apr. 12, inflicting heavy loss on U. S. Negro troops.

### EVENTS OF 1865

Confederates evacuated **Columbia**, S. C., and **Charleston**, S. C., Feb. 17. Cape Fear River forts captured Feb. 20-21. Brig. Gen. Geo. A. Custer defeated Early at **Waynesboro**, Va., Mar. 2. Confederates evacuated **Petersburg** and **Richmond** Apr. 2-3. Lee surrendered 27,805 to Grant at **Appomattox Court House**, Va., Apr. 9. Johnston surrendered 31,243 to Sherman at **Durham Sta.**, N.C., Apr. 18.

### MURDER OF LINCOLN

Lincoln was shot by John Wilkes Booth, an actor, in Ford's Theatre, in Washington, April 14, died, April 15; Booth was shot to death in the pursuit, April 26, at a burning barn, on a farm near Port Royal, Va. Those hanged for complicity were Mrs. Mary E. Surratt, David E. Herold, George A. Azerodt and Lewis Payne (Powell), July 7. Also convicted of conspiracy were Dr. Samuel A. Mudd, who set Booth's broken ankle, Samuel Arnold, Michael O'Laughlin, and Edward Spangler. All were sentenced to life imprisonment except Spangler, who received a 6-year sentence. They were sent to Dry Tortugas Prison, off Key West, where O'Laughlin died during an 1867 outbreak of yellow fever. Dr. Mudd's unselfish services as a physician during the outbreak won him a pardon; Arnold and Spangler were freed with Dr. Mudd in 1869. John H. Surratt, son of Mary E., fled to Europe, was brought back, tried and freed. Booth's body was buried under the stone floor of a naval prison in Washington, later reburied in the Booth family plot in Baltimore.

Slavery was abolished by adoption of the 13th amendment to the Constitution, Dec. 18.

in prison; the court released him from Blackwells Island prison **June, 1875,** on a technicality; he was committed to Ludlow St. jail in a civil suit; escaped, **Dec. 4, 1875,** and went to Cuba, then to Spain, brought back to New York City, **Nov. 1876;** he died in Ludlow St. jail, **April 12, 1878.**

### 1876
**Samuel J. Tilden,** Democrat, received majority of 250,000 popular votes for President over Rutherford B. Hayes, Republican, and had 184 electoral votes against 163, with returns from South Carolina, Florida, Louisiana and Oregon, 22 electoral votes, in dispute. Bitter contest for delegates with charges of corruption, left issue to Congress, which appointed electoral commission, 8 Republicans, 7 Democrats. Hayes given Presidency by strict party vote.

**Gen. George A. Custer** and 264 soldiers of the Seventh Cavalry killed **June 25** in Battle of the Little Big Horn, Mont., in Sioux Indian war; massacred by Indian tribes united by Sitting Bull, prophet; fighting led by Chiefs Gall and Crazy Horse.

**James Butler (Wild Bill) Hickok,** shot dead from behind by Jack McCall, a desperado, in Deadwood, S. D., **Aug. 2.** A vigilance committee acquitted McCall but the United States Court in Yankton, S. D., found him guilty and he was hanged.

### 1877
Russia declared war on Turkey, **April 24; peace** treaty signed, **March, 1878.**

**Molly Maguires,** Irish terrorist secret society in Pennsylvania, broken up by hanging of 11 leaders for murders.

### 1878
**First commercial telephone exchange** opened, New Haven, Conn., **Jan. 28, 1878.** First private exchange, used by physicians, reported in use July, 1877, Hartford, Conn.

### 1879
**F. W. Woolworth** opened his first five-and-ten store, Utica, N. Y., **Feb. 22.**

**Henry George** published Progress & Poverty, advocating single tax on land.

### 1881
**President James A. Garfield shot** in Washington **July 2;** died in Elberon, N. J., **Sept. 19.**

**Federation of Organized Trades and Labor Unions** formed, **Aug. 2,** at Terre Haute, Ind. The organization later joined with 25 independent unions to form the American Federation of Labor at Columbus, Ohio, **Dec., 1886.**

### 1882
**Prof. Robert Koch** announced, in Berlin, discovery of the tuberculosis germ. **March 24.**

**Triple Alliance** of Germany, Austria and Italy formed. Denounced by Italy, **1914.**

### 1883
**Brooklyn Bridge opened, May 24;** panic on it, **May 30;** twelve trampled to death.

### 1884
**Panic in New York, May 5–7.** U. S. Grant ruined by failure of Grant & Ward. To gain nest-egg for family he wrote his "Personal Memoirs," while ill of cancer. Marketed after his death **(July 23,** 1885) by Mark Twain's firm, book yielded $450,000.

### 1885
**Gen. Charles G. ("Chinese") Gordon,** British governor of the Sudan was slain, **Jan. 26,** by a Mohammedan soldier, who stuck the head on a spear, at Khartoum. Several thousand whites were massacred by the Mahdi's troops. Gen. Kitchener defeated the Mahdi's army **Sept. 2, 1898.**

**First electric street railway** in United States, in Baltimore, opened by Leo Daft, **Aug. 10.**

Canadian rebel Louis Riel hanged for treason at Regina, following crushing of Northwest Rebellion.

### 1886
**Haymarket riot,** evening of **May 4,** followed bitter labor battles for 8-hour day in Chicago, attacks on strike-breakers, police violence and attempts of anarchists to incite workers. A bomb killed seven police and wounded 66. Eight anarchists found guilty; August Spies, Adolph Fischer, George Engel and Albert R. Parsons were hanged; Louis Lingg committed suicide. Samuel Fielden, Michael Schwab, Oscar Neebe, sent to prison, were pardoned seven years later by Gov. John P. Altgeld who denounced trial as unfair. Bomb believed thrown by Rudolph Schnaubelt, who disappeared.

**Geronimo, Apache Indian,** surrendered **Mar. 27** to U. S. Gen. George Crook in Sonora, Mex., but fled the next day and finally surrendered **Sept. 4** to U. S. Gen. Nelson A. Miles in Arizona.

**Dr. A. Conan Doyle** invented famous detective Sherlock Holmes, in story, A Study in Scarlet. Published in Beeton's Christmas Annual, **1887.**

### 1887
**Flood in Hwang-ho River, China;** 900,000 persons perished.

Opera Comique, Paris, burned **May 25;** 200 lives lost.

Last spike driven in Canadian Pacific Railway at Craigellachie, B. C., giving Canada transcontinental railway system.

### 1888
**Great blizzard in eastern U. S. Mar. 11–14.** Roscoe Conkling, victim of exposure, died **April 18.**

### 1889
**Crown Prince Rudolf** of Austria and Baroness Maria Vetsera found slain in his hunting lodge, Mayerling, near Vienna, **Jan. 29.**

**Johnstown, Pa., flood, May 31;** 2,200 lives lost.

**Universal Exhibition in Paris, May 6** through **Nov. 6.** Eiffel Tower (984.25 ft.) opened. (Height with TV antenna 1,052 ft.) First automobile exhibited, a Benz.

**Dom Pedro II,** emperor of Brazil, forced off throne by planters after he freed slaves. Died in Paris, 1891, last emperor on American soil.

### 1890
**First execution by electrocution;** Wm. Kemmler, **Aug. 6** at Auburn prison, Auburn, N. Y., for murder.

**Castle Garden** closed as immigration depot and Ellis Island opened **Dec. 31** (Closed 1954).

### 1891
**Park Place disaster,** New York City, 64 killed, **Aug. 22,** by the collapse of upper floor.

### 1892
**Homestead, Pa., strike** at Carnegie steel mills, near Pittsburgh; conflict between 300 Pinkerton guards and strikers; seven guards and 11 strikers and spectators shot to death, many wounded **July 6.** Henry C. Frick, ch., wounded in Pittsburgh, **July 23,** by Alexander Berkman, anarchist.

### 1893
**Ford's Theater** building, Washington, where Lincoln was shot, used by Pension Bureau, collapsed **June 9,** killing 22.

### 1894
**Chinese-Japanese War** began, **July 25.** Battle of Yalu, **Sept. 17,** treaty of Shimonoseki, **April 17,** 1895, gave Japan Liaotung Peninsula, Formosa and the Pescadores.

**Jacob S. Coxey** led 20,000 unemployed from the Mid-West into Washington, **April 29.** Coxey died **May 18, 1951,** aged 97.

**Strike of employees** of Pullman Co., South Chicago, Ill., June, led Eugene V. Debs to call sympathetic strike of American Railway Union. President Cleveland called out Federal troops over protest of Gov. Altgeld (Illinois). Debs and 3 others were imprisoned 6 mos. for contempt of court. Strike called off **Aug. 7.**

**Thomas A. Edison's Kinetoscope** given first public showing at 1155 Broadway, New York, **April 14.** Was patented 1891 for U. S. only.

**Capt. Alfred Dreyfus** found guilty of betraying French army secrets **Dec. 22,** in sensational frameup; real culprit, Major Esterhazy, acquitted; Dreyfus condemned to Devil's Island, off French Guiana. Recalled for second trial by efforts of Emile Zola and Clemenceau, again condemned **Sept. 9,** 1899. Public clamor led to pardon, **Sept. 19.** Further proofs of innocence led to complete rehabilitation, 1906, with rank of major. He served as lieut. colonel in World War I.

### 1895
**Cuban Revolution** resumed **Feb. 20;** Gen. Antonio Maceo, leader of the insurrection, was killed in action, **Dec. 7, 1896.**

**X-rays discovered** by Wilhelm Konrad Roentgen, a German physicist; Nobel prize winner, **1901.**

### 1896
**President Cleveland** intervened in boundary dispute between Venezuela and British Guiana on basis of Monroe Doctrine; appointed arbitration commission, which settled it **Feb. 2, 1897.**

**Guglielmo Marconi** received first wireless patent from Britain **June 2.**

**William Jennings Bryan** delivered "Cross of Gold" speech at Democratic National Convention in Chicago, **July 8.** Bryan nominated for president but defeated by Republican Wm. McKinley.

### 1897
**Eugene V. Debs** formed Social Democratic party.

### 1898
**Radium discovered** by Pierre Curie, Mme. Curie and G. Bemont, Paris.

---

**1898—Spanish-American War.**

See Article Page 307

---

### 1899
**South African (Boer) war** began **Oct. 11;** Ladysmith relieved, **Feb. 28, 1900;** Pretoria fell **June 5,** 1900; war ended, **May 31, 1902,** with loss of independence of Boer republics, Transvaal and Orange Free State, now in Union of South Africa. British losses: 5,773 killed; 16,171 died of wounds or disease; 22,829 wounded. Boers engaged est. 65,000, losses unknown.

**Filipino insurgents** (est. 12,000 under arms) unable to get recognition of independence from

U. S. A., started guerrilla war, **Feb. 4.** Crushed with capture, **Mar. 23, 1901,** of leader, Emilio Aguinaldo, by Brig. Gen. Frederick Funston.

**Open Door Policy** of U. S. Secy. of State John Hay, supported by 6 nations. Policy was to make China an open market for international commerce and to preserve its integrity as a nation.

**Boxer** anti-foreign uprising started in China; missionaries and Christian Chinese murdered.

### 1900

**Carry Nation,** Kansas anti-saloon agitator, began raiding with hatchet. Died June 9, 1911.

**Boxers in China** killed German minister **June 20.** Foreigners besieged in Peking legations. Relief expedition of 18,000 American, British, French, Japanese and Russian troops took Tientsin **July 13;** Peking **Aug. 14.** U.S. had 2,500 under Maj. Gen. A. R. Chaffee, including two infantry regts., one troop of cavalry, one light battery, two batts. of Marines. Germans arrived and Field Marshal Count Alfred von Waldersee led army of occupation. Russia refused to yield parts of Manchuria. Dowager Empress of China accepted allied terms **Sept., 1901.** All except U.S. exacted large concessions and indemnity of $333,000,000, payable in 39 years. U.S. accepted $25,000,000, returned half in 1908 to provide student exchange fund.

**Campaign begun, June 26,** by Drs. Walter Reed, Aristides Agramonte, Jesse Lazear and James Carroll to wipe out yellow fever in Cuba.

**Galveston hurricane and tidal wave,** Sept. 8; 5,000 lives estimated lost.

### 1901

**President Wm. McKinley was shot** at the Pan-American Exposition in Buffalo, N. Y., **Sept. 6,** by Leon Czolgosz, anarchist; died Sept. 14. Theodore Roosevelt, vice pres., became 26th President. Czolgosz was executed. McKinley tomb in Canton, Ohio.

**Marconi signalled letter** "S" across Atlantic from Cornwall, Eng., to Newfoundland, **Dec. 12.**

### 1902

**Anglo-Japanese alliance formed Jan. 30** to protect Japan against encroaching Russians.

**Cuban Republic** inaugurated. American occupation under Gen. Leonard Wood, ended May 20.

**First International Arbitration Court** opened in The Hague, Holland, October.

### 1903

First automobile trip across U.S., San Francisco to New York, May 23-Aug. 1.

**Henry Ford,** having withdrawn from the Detroit Automobile Co. in 1901, organized Ford Motor Co.

**Treaty** between U. S. and Colombia to have U. S. dig Panama Canal signed **Jan. 22, 1903,** rejected by Colombia. Panama declared independence **Nov. 3,** recognized by President Theodore Roosevelt **Nov. 6.** *See Canal Zone and Panama.*

**First successful flight** in heavier-than-air mechanically propelled airplane, by **Orville Wright (1871-1948)** on **Dec. 17, 1903,** rising from base of Kill Devil hill, four miles south of Kitty Hawk, N. C., 120 ft. in 12 secs., in 27 mph wind. Fourth

flight, same day by **Wilbur Wright (1867-1912)** 852 ft., in 59 secs. Plane patented May 22, 1906.

**Fire killed 602 in Iroquois Theater,** Chicago, **Dec. 30.** Many were trampled to death.

### 1904

**Russo-Japanese War** began, **Feb. 6.** Port Arthur surrendered to Japanese, **Jan. 2, 1905.** Peace treaty signed in U. S. Navy Yard, Portsmouth, N.H., **Sept. 5, 1905.** *See Marine Disasters.*

New York subway opened, Oct. 27.

**Steamer Gen. Slocum** burned, Hell Gate, N. Y., June 15; 1,030 dead.

### 1905

**Russian Revolution crushed** by Czar Nicholas II. Resulted in creation of Duma (parliament) to placate liberals. First meeting of Duma, May 10; dissolved July.

Norway dissolved union with Sweden.

### 1906

**San Francisco earthquake and fire, April 18-19.** Dead: 452. Loss: $350,000,000.

**Harry K. Thaw,** Pittsburgh millionaire, shot and killed Stanford White, famous architect, on the roof of Madison Square Garden (26th and Madison, N. Y.) **June 25,** on ground of avenging honor of wife, Evelyn Nesbit. Prosecuted by Wm. Travers Jerome, D. A., he was committed to Matteawan State hospital, 1907. Escaped 1913. Declared sane and freed, he was indicted, 1917, for kidnapping; pronounced insane; declared sane, 1924. Died, Miami, Feb. 22, 1947.

### 1907

**Financial panic** in the United States.

**Standard Oil of Indiana** fined $29,240,000 by Judge K. M. Landis in U. S. Court, Chicago, for accepting freight rebates **Apr. 3.** Set aside July 22, 1908. Railroads found guilty of giving rebates.

**First round-world cruise** of U. S. Fleet; 16 battleships, Adm. Robley D. Evans, 12,000 men.

### 1908

**In fire and panic** at Collinwood, Ohio, 174 children and two teachers in Lake View School lost their lives **Mar. 4.**

**Chelsea (Mass.) destroyed** by fire; loss more than $6,000,000, **April 12.**

### 1909

**Admiral Robert E. Peary** reached North Pole **April 6** on sixth attempt, accompanied by Matthew Henson, Negro, and 4 Eskimos.

**Louis Bleriot** flew across the English Channel, Calais to Dover, 31 mi. in 37 min., **July 25.**

**Budget in Britain:** "Soak the Rich" taxation financed social security measures.

### 1910

**Boy Scouts of America** incorporated **Feb. 8** following visit to England by Wm. D. Boyce, Chicago publisher; while there he met Sir Robert Baden-Powell, founder of the Scouting movement, and was inspired to take the lead in transplanting the idea to the United States.

**Glenn H. Curtiss won $10,000** offered by the World, N. Y., for first continuous flight, Albany to

## Spanish-American War of 1898; United States Becomes Naval Power

Spanish misrule in Cuba led to repeated attempts by Cuban patriots to gain rights of citizenship, abolition of slavery, and finally independence. When South America broke from Europe in the 1820s pro-slavery influence in the U. S. blocked movements to free Cuba and Puerto Rico. But in 1852 President Fillmore refused to join Great Britain and France in guaranteeing Spanish authority in Cuba. In 1854 the Ostend Manifesto written largely by Jas. Buchanan, urged the U. S. to buy Cuba or seize it to abolish oppression. Grant's administration offered to buy Cuba, but Spain refused.

In Cuba revolts led by Marciso Lopez and Joaquin de Aguero, 1848-1851, were suppressed and the leaders executed. In 1868 a major revolt led by Carlos de Cespedes and Manuel de Quesada lasted 10 years. In 1873 the Virginius expedition, flying the American flag, was seized by the Spaniards and Americans and Cubans aboard were shot. This did not stop supplying of arms from the U. S. In 1895 the insurrection had spread so widely under Generals Calixto Garcia, Maximo Gomez and Antonio Macea that Spain landed 150,000 troops, but by 1896 over half of the island was in the hands of the patriots. The U. S. offered to mediate but was repulsed. The country was laid waste by Spanish troops and the accounts of suffering increased sentiment in the U. S. in favor of Free Cuba.

**The battleship Maine,** Capt. Chas. E. Sigsbee, sent to Havana in January on goodwill tour, was blown up **Feb. 15, 1898;** 264 men, 2 officers killed. U. S. inquiry, Capt. Wm. T. Sampson ch., blamed external explosion **Mar. 21.** Spanish inquiry **Mar. 28** blamed internal explosion. Congress **Mar. 9** voted $50,000,000 for defense. President McKinley **Mar. 27** demanded Spain grant armistice for negotiation with Cuba via U. S., end reconcentration. Spain **Mar. 31** offered to arbitrate Maine, end reconcentration, but wanted Cubans to ask for armistice. After appeal by foreign ministers Spain

granted armistice **Apr. 9.** President **Apr. 11** asked Congress for authority to intervene in Cuba. Congress **Apr. 20-25** debated joint resolution recognizing independence of Cuba, asked Spain to withdraw and empowered President to enforce it; adopted it with statement war existed since **Apr. 21.** Spain had declared war **Apr. 24.**

**Commodore Geo. Dewey,** with 6 warships, 1 revenue cutter, destroyed the Spanish fleet (10 ships) in Manila Bay **May 1,** occupied Cavite, Spain, 167 dead; U. S., 7 wounded. Spanish Admiral Cervera with 4 cruisers, 3 torpedo boats reached Santiago without interference **May 19.** Battleship Oregon made 16,000 mi. trip around Cape Horn, joined squadron of Acting Rear Adm. Sampson **May 26.** Collier Merrimac ineffectively sunk at mouth of Santiago harbor by Lieut. Richmond Pearson Hobson **June 3.** Marines landed at Guantanamo **May 11.** Maj. Gen. Wm. R. Shafter landed 10,000 men at Daiquiri and Siboney, including 1st U. S. Volunteer Cavalry (Rough Riders) recruited by Lt. Col. Theodore Roosevelt, commanded by Col. Leonard Wood. Brig. Gen. H. W. Lawton, Brig. Gen. Adna R. Chaffee with 6,654 men attacked El Caney, defended by 500 Spaniards, **July 1.** Maj. Gen. Jos. Wheeler, Brig. Gen. J. F. Kent carried San Juan hill with 8,336, same day.

**Admiral Cervera's fleet** left Santiago harbor **July 3,** was destroyed by ships of Acting Rear Adm. Sampson and Commodore Winfield S. Schley; 353 Spaniards killed, 151 wounded; 1 American killed. Santiago surrendered **July 17.** Maj. Gen. Nelson A. Miles took Puerto Rico **July 25-28.** Armistice signed, **Aug. 12.** Peace treaty signed in Paris **Dec. 10,** eliminated Spain from lands discovered by Columbus. U. S. acquired Puerto Rico, Guam and Philippines, paying $20,000,000 for all Spanish claims in latter; guaranteed Cuban independence. (Ratified **Feb. 6, 1899.**) U.S. had treaty rights in Cuba until 1934; granted Philippine independence **July 4, 1946.**

New York, 137 mi., 152 min., **May 29.**

**Dynamite explosion at Los Angeles Times Oct. 1** caused fire killing 21. Building contractors, in labor strife with structural iron workers, hired William J. Burns to find perpetrators. In sensational trial J. B. and J. J. McNamara pleaded guilty through Clarence Darrow, defense attorney, and were sentenced to San Quentin. Darrow tried twice for suborning juror, juries disagreed. Lincoln Steffens, "muckraking" journalist, conciliator.

**1911**

Italian-Turkish War began, **Sept. 29.**

**First transcontinental airplane flight** (interrupted by landings) by C. P. Rodgers, New York to Pasadena, **Sept. 17-Nov. 5**; time in air 82 hrs., 4 mins.

**Capt. Roald Amundsen,** Norwegian explorer, reached South Pole, **Dec. 14.**

**Mexican Revolution.** Porfirio Diaz, president of Mexico since 1877 (except 1880-1884), resigned **May 25,** after successful revolt by Francisco I. Madero, who succeeded him. People living in poverty wanted restoration of communal lands (ejidos), better conditions. In 1912 Madero, supported by Gen. Huerta, put down revolts by Gens. Orozco, Reyes and Felix Diaz. In Feb., 1913, Reyes was killed; Huerta helped depose Madero. Madero, his brother and Vice President Suarez were murdered. President Wilson refused recognition to Huerta and "government by assassination." Venustiano Carranza, rallying Maderos, was opposed by Gen. Francisco (Pancho) Villa in north. When American sailors were arrested at Tampico, **April 9, 1914,** U. S. sent Atlantic fleet to Vera Cruz. Marines landed and snipers killed 19. Brig. Gen. Frederick Funston was sent **Apr. 27.** Huerta resigned **July 14, 1914,** Carranza occupied Mexico City **Aug. 20.** Villa, supported by Zapata, forced Carranza to leave for Vera Cruz. U. S. recognized Carranza, **Oct. 19, 1915,** placed embargo on arms to other generals. Villa raided Santa Isabel, **Jan. 10,** killing 18; Columbus, N. M., **Mar. 9, 1916,** killed 17. Gen. John J. Pershing with 12,000 sent into Mexico **Mar. 15.** Fight at Parral, Durango, **April 12.** Carranza's troops attacked **June 21.** U. S. troops withdrawn **Feb. 4, 1917.** Carranza called constitutional convention. **Feb. 15,** 1917, became legal president **May 1, 1917.** He restored some of the land, nationalized coal and oil, expropriated some foreign holdings. Discontent caused new rising and he was ambushed and killed. Obregon became president **Dec. 1. 1920.** Villa was killed in ambush at Parral, **July 18, 1923.**

**Chinese Revolution** led by Sun Yat-sen overthrew Manchu dynasty. Republic formed **Feb. 12,** 1912; Yuan shih-K'ai elected president, **Feb. 15.**

**Parliament Act of 1911** reduced the power of British House of Lords to a suspensory veto, to delay but not deny bills.

**1912**

**Capt. Robert F. Scott** and 4 companions reached South Pole **Jan. 17;** died on return journey.

**White Star liner Titanic** wrecked on maiden trip, from Southampton to New York, by iceberg off Newfoundland. **April 14-15;** U. S. reported 1,517 lost; British Board of Trade reported 1,503 lost. Passengers and crew were 2,207. The ship was 882½ ft. long, and cost $7,500,000.

**Herman Rosenthal,** gambler, killed in New York. Four thugs convicted, executed at Sing Sing **Apr. 13, 1914.** Police Lieut. Chas. Becker, convicted of complicity, executed **July 30, 1915.**

**War in Balkans,** against Turkey by Montenegro, Bulgaria, Serbia and Greece, **Oct. 8-Dec. 3.**

**1913**

**Sixteenth Amendment** proclaimed in effect **Feb. 25,** empowering Congress to levy and collect income taxes.

**Act creating Federal Reserve** System became law **Dec. 23.**

**1914**

**Ford Motor Co.** raised basic wage rates from $2.40 for 9-hr. day to $5 for 8-hr. day, **Jan. 5.**

**First ship passed through Panama Canal, Aug. 15.**

**Second International; Brussels** meeting of International Socialist Bureau, **July.** Members included five men later heads of governments: Lenin (Russia); Ebert (German Republic); Stauning (Denmark); Branting (Sweden); MacDonald (Britain).

## Principal Events of World War 1, 1914-1918;

**ORIGINS.** Since the defeat of France by Prussia in 1870-71 major powers of Europe had kept peace by diplomatic negotiations and a balance of power. Triple Alliance, of Germany, Austria and Italy was defensive, with reservations; Triple Entente was an understanding between Britain, France and Russia. Nationalist aspirations in the Balkans had resulted in several wasteful wars and Italy had fought with Turkey and Ethiopia. Austria annexed Bosnia, Herzegovina, former Turkish Balkan provinces, 1908. Russia backed Serbia's efforts to get a port on the Adriatic. Germany's industrial expansion led to building of powerful navy, which Britain matched two for one for its own security. Germany's universal military service led France to adopt three-year training.

On **June 28, 1914,** Archduke Francis Ferdinand, heir to Austrian throne, was assassinated, with his wife, by Gavrillo Prinzip, Bosnian Serb terrorist, in Sarajevo, Bosnia. Austria-Hungary, through Count Berchthold, Austrian foreign minister, made 10 demands on Serbia for suppression of anti-Austrian agitation. Serbia conceded all but two, which called for Austrian enforcement police inside Serbia. It asked reference to The Hague peace tribunal. Austria demanded all or nothing.

Russia warned Austrian action was aimed at Russia, supported Serbia. Germany, allied with Austria, backed Austria. Britain, France, Italy proposed mediation. Sir Edward Grey, Br. foreign minister, **July 26** proposed conference of four major powers; Germany refused to join.

Austria declared war on Serbia **July 28.** Germany, citing Russian mobilization, declared war on Russia **Aug. 1;** on France, **Aug. 3.** Germans entered Belgium in violation of treaty, of which Britain was cosigner. Britain asked Germany to guarantee neutrality of Belgium by midnight **Aug. 4;** Germany refused; British declared war **Aug. 4.** Italy, declaring German aggression made Triple Alliance inoperative, proclaimed neutrality. Japan declared war on Germany **Aug. 23** because of Anglo-Japanese treaty on Far East. Turkey joined Central Powers **Nov. 23.**

Lord Kitchener became British secy. for war. Belgian forts at Liege stopped Germans until **Aug. 7,** delayed Ger. schedule. Germans entered Brussels **Aug. 20;** pushed back British Expeditionary Force (Sir John French) at Mons **Aug. 23-24;** burned most of Louvain **Aug. 25.** Von Hindenburg and Ludendorff defeated Russians at Tannenberg, East Prussia, **Aug. 26-31;** at Masurian Lakes **Sept. 5-10.**

In first Battle of the Marne, **Sept. 5-10,** French under Joffre, Foch and Gallieni, stopped German advance of Von Kluck and Von Bülow, toward Paris, forced them back to Aisne, where trench warfare began. British repulsed Germans at Ypres, **Oct. 16-Nov. 24.** Belgians lost Antwerp **Oct. 9.** Russians forced Austrians back in Galicia. Austrians took and lost Belgrade **Dec. 2-15.**

British bombarded Dardanelles forts **Nov. 3;** declared war on Turkey, annexed Cyprus **Nov. 5.** Japan took Tsingtau **Nov. 6.**

*Of many warships and merchantmen sunk, only major events are listed here. For others see Marine Disasters.*

**1915—SUBMARINE WAR BEGINS**

In 1915 the war became a desperate battle of attrition on land and sea. British sank Ger. cruiser Bluecher **Jan. 24.** Germany ordered submarine blockade of Britain to start **Feb. 18.** U. S. held Germany to "strict accountability" for American losses. Germans used liquid fire in Vosges **Mar. 3.** Roving cruiser Dresden sunk in Pacific **Mar. 15.** Three Br.-Fr. battleships sunk at Dardanelles **Mar. 18.** Ger. sank Falaba **Mar. 28,** 1 American lost. Turks sank Br. battleship Lord Nelson **Apr. 6.** Ger. introduced poison gas at Ypres, **Apr. 22,** Canadians saved the line. Allies landed at Gallipoli, **Apr. 25.** Ger. torpedoed Gulflight, U. S. tanker, **Apr. 30,** 2 Americans lost.

German sub sank Cunard liner Lusitania off Old Head of Kinsale, Ireland, **May 7;** of 1,959 aboard, including 702 crew, 1,198, including 124 Americans, died. This started a series of protests by U. S. to Germany. W. J. Bryan, secy. of state, resigned **June 8;** considered Wilson's Lusitania note too severe. After sinking Arabic **Aug. 19** Ger. agreed not to sink liners without warning, but U. S. considered promises inadequate. U. S. dismissed Austrian ambassador Dumba and Germans Boy-Ed and Von Papen for illegal activities.

South Africans under Gen. Botha captured German S. W. Africa. Italy declared war on Austria-Hungary **May 23,** on Turkey **Aug. 20,** on Germany **Aug. 27.** Bulgaria declared war on Serbia **Oct. 14;** Allies against Bulgaria **Oct. 15-19.** Germans occupied Russian Baltic ports, took Vilna, with Austrians occupied Serbia. Allies landed at Salonika **Oct. 5.** Edith Cavell, Br. nurse, executed by Germans in Brussels **Oct. 12** for aiding escapes. Sir John French replaced by Sir Douglas Haig on British front **Dec. 15.** Allies began evacuation of Gallipoli (Dardanelles) **Dec. 19.**

**1916—GREAT BATTLES**

Germany announced **Feb. 10** that armed merchant ships would be considered warships and

## 1915

**First telephone talk,** New York to San Francisco, **Jan. 25,** by Alexander Graham Bell and Thomas A. Watson.

**First successful** wireless from moving Lackawanna train to station. **Feb. 7.**

**Twenty-one Demands** presented by Japan to China. Demands asked for almost complete control of China.

## 1916

**Gregory Rasputin,** confessor to Czarina, killed in Petrograd (Leningrad) **December.**

**Bomb exploded during** San Francisco Preparedness Day Parade, **July 22,** killing 10, wounding 40. Thomas J. Mooney, 33, labor organizer; Mrs. Mooney, Warren K. Billings, shoe worker; Israel Weinberg and Edward D. Nolan were charged with murder. Mooney was sentenced to death, Billings to life imprisonment; others went free. President Wilson interceded for Mooney, who got life, 1918. Mooney was pardoned by Gov. C. L. Olson, **Jan. 7,** 1939, Billings freed Oct. 16, 1939.

**Black Tom explosion** at munitions docks, Jersey City, N. J., **July 30;** 2 killed, $40,000,000 damages. Traced to German saboteurs.

## 1917

**The 18th (Prohibition) Amendment** to the Constitution was submitted to the States by Congress, **Dec. 18.** The first State (Mississippi) ratified it **Jan. 8, 1918,** and Jan. 16, 1919, the 36th State (Nebraska) ratified it, whereupon, by proclamation of the Secretary of State, **Jan. 29, 1919,** it became effective one year from that date, **Jan. 16, 1920.** By **Feb. 25, 1919,** the Legislatures of 43 States had ratified it; the 46th State, New Jersey ratified it **March 9,** 1922. It was not ratified by Connecticut and Rhode Island. The **Volstead (Prohibition Enforcement) Act** was passed by Congress **Oct.,** 1919, vetoed by President Wilson, passed over his veto, in effect **Jan. 17, 1920.** New York, Montana and Wisconsin cancelled their enforcement acts by 1929. Franklin D. Roosevelt, presidential candidate, 1932, endorsed repeal; 21st amendment, repealing 18th, but guaranteeing dry states against liquor importation, became law. **Dec. 5, 1933.**

**Balfour Declaration,** Nov. 2, favored establishment of a national homeland in Palestine for Jewish people.

## 1918

**Romanovs killed.** Czar Nicholas of Russia, the Empress Alexandra; the daughters, Olga, Tatiana, Marie, Anastasia; the son, Alexis; Prince Dolgorolkoff, Dr. Botkin, a lady-in-waiting and a nurse were shot by Bolshevist orders in Ekaterinburg, **July 16;** in Perm, also, **July 12,** the Bolshevists assassinated the Czar's brother, Grand Duke Michael, and in Alapalievsky north of Ekaterinburg, they killed the Grand Dukes Sergius Mikhalilovitch, Igor Constantinovich and Ivan Constantinovich.

**Influenza epidemic** killed estimated 20,000,000 throughout world, 548,000 in U. S. and American armed forces.

**Malbone St.,** Tunnel subway wreck (Brighton line, Brooklyn): 97 killed, 100 hurt. **Nov. 2.**

## 1919

**Rosa Luxemburg and Karl Liebknecht,** leading German Communists and founders of the Spartacus Party, shot and killed **Jan.,** by soldiers who were taken to prison.

**Peace** conference opened in Paris, **Jan. 18;** treaty signed in palace at Versailles **June 28;** between German representatives and Allied powers and U. S. President Wilson submitted treaty to Senate **July 10.** Ratified by Germany **July 10,** Britain, **July 26,** Italy, **Oct. 7,** France, **Oct. 13,** Japan, **Oct. 27.** Not signed by China. Rejected by U. S. Senate, **Nov. 19,** which considered American sovereignty not properly safeguarded in League of Nations. Never ratified by U. S.

**In Amritsar, India,** Gen. Dyer led a group of Gurkha soldiers to the entrance of a walled-in garden where a crowd was listening to anti-British speeches. Dyer had soldiers fire into crowd, killing 379 and wounding 1,208.

**Three U. S. Navy** seaplanes left Trepassy, Newfoundland, **May 16;** one, the N-C 4, reached

---

# Why United States Intervened

sunk without warning. U. S. retorted **Feb. 15** international law permitted self-defense of commercial ships. Ger. made huge effort vs. Verdun **Feb. 21,** took Ft. Douaumont **Feb. 25.** Ger. declared war on Portugal **Mar. 8.** Russians invaded Persia, **Mar. 10.** Channel str. Sussex torpedoed, 80 casualties, **Mar. 24.** Wilson threatened **Apr. 18-19** to break relations unless Germany revised sub warfare; Ger. met most of U. S. demands.

**Rising in Ireland Apr. 24-May 1.** Patrick Pearse et al, executed; Sir Roger Casement hanged **Aug. 3.** Br. adopted conscription **May 24.** Jutland naval battle, **May 31-June 1.** Admirals Jellicoe and Beatty, Br., lost 5 major cruisers, 8 destroyers, 6,091 men; Admirals Scheer and von Hipper, Ger., lost 2 major ships, also cruisers & destroyers, 2,545 men, 3rd battle of Ypres, **June 2.** Lord Kitchener drowned when Hampshire sunk off Orkneys **June 5.** Battle of the Somme, **July 1-10;** second battle, **July 1l-Aug. 3.** Rumania joined Allies **Aug. 16,** was defeated by January, 1917. U. S. **Nov. 29** protested deportation of Belgian workers into Germany.

On **Dec. 12,** 1916, Germany and its allies called for peace negotiations, to halt bloodshed. Germany told the Vatican it was fighting for the integrity of its frontiers and development in peaceful competition. On **Dec. 18,** 1916, President Wilson asked the belligerents to state their aims and terms; in order to end rival leagues he asked formation of a league of nations and protection of "weak peoples." The Allies called the German offer "empty and insincere." They also told President Wilson they wanted "restorations, reparations, indemnities."

## 1917—U. S. ENTERS WAR

When Germany began unrestricted submarine war United States **Feb. 3** broke relations, refused negotiations until order was rescinded. Wilson **Feb. 26** asked Congress to order arming of merchant ships; when Senate refused Wilson armed them by executive order **Mar. 12.** Intercepted note of Ger. foreign secy. Zimmerman to Ger. minister in Mexico suggested Mexico be asked to enter war to recover U. S. Southwest, **Feb. 28.** U. S. declared war on Germany **Apr. 6,** adopted selective conscription **May 18,** registered men aged 21-30 **June 5.** First of American Expeditionary Force (AEF) landed in France **June 26;** Gen. John J. Pershing, c.-in-c., Adm. Wm. S. Sims, chief Naval operations, Europe. U. S. declared war on Austria-Hungary **Dec. 7.**

**Collapse of Russian Empire.** When Navy and Army revolted **Mar. 11-15** Czar Nicholas II abdicated. Provisional govt. made Kerensky premier **July 20.** Offensive in Galicia failed. **Aug.** Germans moved Lenin and associates from Switzerland to Russia via Sweden to disrupt war. Bolshevists overthrew Kerensky **Nov. 7,** formed socialist republic of workers and peasants with Lenin president of Council of Commissars. Armistice **Dec. 15,** made peace with Germany, Austria-Hungary, Bulgaria and Turkey at Brest-Litovsk **Mar. 3, 1918,** withdrawing from Lithuania, Estonia, Latvia, Ukraine, Poland, Finland, Aland Isls., Erivan, Kars, Batum.

**Other Fronts.** Huge losses by Allies at Vimy, Arras, Cambrai, Passchendaele, Verdun. Petain succeeded Nivelle as French c.-in-c. British took Jaffa, Baghdad, Jerusalem. Germans forced back Italians to Piave, Brenta; sank many ships.

**1918—VICTORY FOR U. S. & ALLIES**

German submarine war, **Feb. 1, 1917-Feb. 1,** 1918, cost U. S. 69 ships (171,061 tons); U. S. seized 686,494 German-Austrian tonnage. British lost 1,169 ships. Allies & neutrals lost 6,617,000 tons.

President Wilson presented his 14 points for peace to Congress **Jan. 8.** Asked open diplomacy; freedom of seas; restoration of Alsace-Lorraine to France; independence for Poland and Austrian minorities; "a general association of nations" to guarantee political and economic independence.

Collapse of Russian front released German troops for powerful thrusts on West front. Battle of the Somme, **Mar. 21-Apr. 6.** Gen. Ferdinand Foch made supreme commander **Mar. 26.** Battle of the Aisne, **May 27-June 5;** AEF took Cantigny, **May 28.** Germans reached Marne, AEF fought at Chateau Thierry, Belleau Woods. Ger. retreat began **July 19.** AEF took St. Mihiel salient, **Sept. 12-20,** fought at Meuse-Argonne, **Sept. 20-Nov. 11.** British broke Hindenburg line **Sept. 27.**

Bulgaria gave up **Sept. 30,** Czar Ferdinand abdicated. Turkish armistice, **Oct. 30.** Italians defeated Austrians at Vittorio Veneto; Austria and Hungary formed separate republics **Nov. 1,** Austria surrendered **Nov. 4.**

Germans accepted President Wilson's terms and recalled submarines, **Oct. 20;** United States troops reached Sedan, **Nov. 7;** revolution in Kiel and Hamburg, **Nov. 7;** Bavaria proclaimed a republic, **Nov. 8;** Kaiser abdicated, **Nov. 9,** fled to Holland. Armistice signed in Marshal Foch's railway coach, near Compiegne, France, **Nov. 11;** bugles sounded "cease firing" at 11 a.m. German fleet surrendered to British, **Nov. 21;** AEF entered Mainz, **Dec. 6;** crossed Rhine, **Dec. 13.**

*See Casualties, World War I.*

the Azores, **May 17**; Lisbon, **May 27**; Plymouth, England, **May 31**; Harry G. Hawker and McKenzie Grieve fell in mid-ocean on an attempted flight, **May 18**, from Newfoundland to Ireland, but were rescued; **John Alcock and A. W. Brown** made, **June 14-15**, a non-stop air flight from New-foundland to Ireland; a British dirigible balloon, R-34, left Scotland, **July 2**, and descended in Mineola, N. Y., **July 6**. It left for England, **July 10**, and arrived there **July 13**. A round-trip trans-continental air race, New York to San Francisco, was won by Lt. **W. B. Maynard** and Lt. **Alex Pearson**, Oct. 8-18.

### 1920

**League of Nations began** at Geneva, Switzerland, **Jan. 10**; dissolved **Jan. 10**, 1946.

**Nicola Sacco**, 29, shoe factory employee and philosophical anarchist and **Bartolomeo Vanzetti**, 32, fish peddler and radical agitator, accused of killing two men in payroll holdup at Braintree, Mass., **Apr. 15**. Found guilty 1921, they became objects of six-year campaign for release on grounds of want or conclusive evidence and prejudice of court. Sensational appeals failing, they were exe-cuted at Charlestown, Mass., prison **Aug. 22, 1927**. Trial sharply criticized by Wickersham Com-mission on law procedure.

**Wall St., New York City, bomb** explosion, killed 30; injured 100; did $2,000,000 damage. **Sept. 16**.

### 1921

**Joint Congressional resolution declaring peace** with Germany and Austria signed **July 2** by Presi-dent Harding. Treaty signed **Aug. 25** in Berlin, ratified by Senate **Oct. 18**.

**Limitation of Armaments Conference** met in Washington, **Nov. 12, 1921-Feb. 6, 1922**. U. S., Britain, France, Italy, Japan agreed to curtail naval construction. Nine powers outlawed poison gas and restricted submarine attack on merchant-men. U. S., Britain, France, Japan agreed on in-tegrity of China. Ratified **Aug. 5, 1925**.

### 1922

**Roof of Knickerbocker (movie) Theatre** col-lapsed in Washington, D. C., **Jan. 28**; 98 dead.

**Violence during coal-mine strike** at Herrin, Ill., **June 22-23** cost 36 lives, 21 non-union miners.

**Fascist march** on Rome, **Oct. 30**: Mussolini's power in Italy began.

### 1923

**Occupation of Ruhr** by French and Belgian troops to enforce reparations began **Jan. 11**.

**First sound-on-film talking pictures** (vaudeville shorts) shown by Lee de Forest at Rivoli Theatre, New York, N. Y. beginning April.

**Beer Hall Putsch in Munich**, led by Gen. Luden-dorff and Adolf Hitler, **Nov. 8-9**. Several support-ers killed in street clashes. Ludendorff was ar-rested and paroled; Hitler was wounded. He was arrested **Nov. 12** and imprisoned at Landsberg, where he wrote Mein Kampf.

### 1924

**Dawes Reparation Plan** accepted by Allies and Germany, in Agreement of London, **Aug. 16**: Owen D. Young put in charge. French troops began evacuation of the Ruhr **Aug. 18**.

**Nellie Tayloe Ross** elected Governor of Wyo-ming **Nov. 9** after death of her husband **Oct. 2**; installed **Jan. 5, 1925**; first woman so honored. Miriam (Ma) Ferguson elected Governor of Texas **Nov. 9**; installed **Jan. 20, 1925**.

### 1925

**Floyd Collins** unable to extricate himself from Sand Cave, near Cave City, Ky., which he dis-covered, died within 300 ft. of entrance, **Feb.**

**John T. Scopes**, in court in Dayton, Tenn., was found guilty of having taught evolution in the local high school and was fined $100 and costs, **July 24**. William Jennings Bryan, chief counsel for the prosecution, died in Dayton **July 26**. Clarence Darrow, chief defense counsel, died **March 13, 1938**.

**Pickwick Club**, Boston night club, collapsed **July 4**, killing 44.

**By treaty of Locarno**, **Oct. 16**, Germany agreed to demilitarization of Rhineland and security of Franco-German and Belgo-German frontiers.

### 1926

**Dr. Robert H. Goddard** demonstrated the prac-ticality of rockets **Mar. 16** at Auburn, Mass., with the first liquid fuel rocket flight; the rocket trav-eled 184 feet in 2.5 seconds.

**General strike paralyzed Britain May 3** to 12. Parliament passed act making general strike crim-inal conspiracy against nation.

**Germany admitted to the League of Nations Sept. 8**. Locarno treaties with Germany (1925) went into effect, **Sept. 14**.

### 1927

**600 U. S. Marines sent to Nicaragua**, **Jan. 6**, to protect U. S. interests. Withdrawn 1933.

**1,000 U. S. Marines landed in China**, **Mar. 5**, to protect property in civil war. U. S. and British consulates looted by Nationalists **Mar. 24**.

**Albert Snyder**, art editor, killed **Mar. 20**, by his wife, Ruth Brown Snyder, and Henry Judd Gray, corset salesmen. Both confessed and were ex-ecuted at Sing Sing, **Jan. 12, 1928**.

**Capt. Chas. A. Lindbergh**, U. S. air mail pilot, left Roosevelt Field, L. I., N. Y., at **7:52 A.M. May 20** alone in monoplane, Spirit of St. Louis, competing for Raymond Orteig's offer of $25,000 for first New York-Paris non-stop flight. Reached Le Bourget air field, Paris, **5:21 P.M. (10:21 P.M. Paris time) May 21**; 3610 miles in 33 hrs 29 mins., 30 secs. Returned on cruiser Memphis, U.S.N., with plane; welcomed by President Cool-idge in Washington, **June 11**, with rank of colonel. Tremendous demonstration, New York, **June 13**.

**The Jazz Singer**, with Al Jolson, demonstrated part-talking pictures in New York City **Oct. 6**.

### 1928

**The St. Francis water-supply dam**, 40 miles north of Los Angeles, Calif., collapsed; 450 lives lost. 700 houses swept away, **March 13**.

**First all-talking picture**, Lights of New York, presented at Strand, New York City, **July 6**.

**Times Square subway wreck**, New York City (IRT line) **Aug. 24**, killed 18, injured 97.

**Kellogg-Briand Peace Pact** signed, **Aug. 27**, by 62 nations. Condemned the use of war as an instrument of national policy.

**Dirigible Graf Zeppelin**, Capt. Hugo Eckner, with 20 passengers and 38 crew, flew from Fried-richshafen, Germany to Lakehurst, N. J., **Oct. 11-15**; returned **Oct. 29-31**. Made round the world trip from Friedrichshafen with 20 passengers, **Aug. 14-Sept. 4**, 1929, via Tokyo, Los Angeles, Lake-hurst, N. J.

**Arnold Rothstein**, N. Y. gambler, died of gun shots **Nov. 6**; killer never found.

**Stalin** issued **first 5 year plan**: Rapid, ruthless industrialization of Russian economy.

### 1929

**"St. Valentine's Day massacre"** in Chicago **Feb. 14**, when gangsters killed 7 rivals.

**The Papal State**, extinct since 1870, revived as State of Vatican City, at Rome **June 7**.

**Albert B. Fall**, former Secretary of the Interior, was convicted of accepting a bribe of $100,000 from Edward L. Doheny in the leasing of the Elks Hills (**Teapot Dome**) naval oil reserve. He was sentenced **Nov. 1**, to $100,000 fine and a year in prison. He died **Nov. 30**, 1944.

**Stock Market crash Oct. 29** marked end of post-war prosperity when 16,000,000 shares changed hands, including unrestricted short selling. Decline in value estimated at $15,000,000,000 by end of 1929; stock losses, 1929-1931, estimated at $50,000,-000,000. Worst American depression began.

### 1930

**London Naval Reduction Treaty** signed by U. S., Britain, Italy, France and Japan, **April 22**; in effect **Jan. 1**, 1931. Provided for the propor-tional reduction of the navies of each country. Its terms expired **Dec. 31**, 1936.

**Joseph F. Crater**, a justice of the State Supreme Court in New York City, vanished **Aug. 6**.

### 1931

**British Parliament enacted Statute of Westmin-ster**, giving legal status to declaration of Imperial Conference of 1926 proclaiming Britain and the dominions, including Canada, completely equal "in no way subordinate one to another."

**Knute Rockne**, Notre Dame football coach was killed in plane crash near Bazaar, Kans., **March 31**.

**Mukden Incident** occurred, **Sept. 18**, when Japanese troops attacked Mukden garrison and then overran Manchuria. China protested to League of Nations.

### 1932

**Japanese Buddhist priest slain in Shanghai**, **Jan. 15**. Japan used incident to land marines, **Jan. 27**.

**Manchuria became Manchukuo** (Japanese pup-pet State). **Feb. 18**; Henry Pu Yi, Manchu emperor who abdicated in 1912, installed as ruler, **Mar. 9**, at Changchun, called Hsingching.

**Charles A. Lindbergh, Jr., kidnaped** for ransom **Mar. 1**.

**Bonus March** on Washington, **May 29**, by World War I veterans demanding Congress pay their bonus in full. Army disbanded the marchers on President Hoover's orders.

**James J. Walker** resigned **Sept. 1** as mayor of New York City, thus ending inquiry into cor-ruption in conduct of his office before Gov. F. D. Roosevelt by a state legislative committee under Samuel Seabury. Walker died **Nov. 18**, 1946, 66.

### 1933

**Adolf Hitler**, German Chancellor **Jan. 30**.

**Gov. W. A. Comstock of Michigan Feb. 14** or-dered all banks in that state closed for eight days. All banks in the United States were ordered closed by President Roosevelt **March 6**.

**First "fireside chat"** broadcast by President Franklin D. Roosevelt, **March 12**.

**German Reichstag building**, Berlin, destroyed **Feb. 27** by fire believed set by Nazis. Marinus van der Lubbe, Dutch Communist, found guilty; be-headed **Jan. 10**, 1934, in Leipzig.

**Spain**, by Parliamentary edict, **May 17**, disestab-lished the Church.

**Germany**, **Oct. 14**, quit the League of Nations

and withdrew from the disarmament conference. **President Roosevelt** accorded diplomatic recognition to the Soviet Union, **Nov. 16**.

**Prohibition** ended in the United States as Utah, 36th State, ratified 21st Amendment to Constitution, **Dec. 5**, repealing 18th (prohibition).

### 1934

Bank robbers **John Dillinger, Charles Makley, Russell Clark and Harry Pierpont** captured in Tucson, Ariz., **Jan. 25** with $36,000. Dillinger was jailed at Crown Point, Ind., and the others at Lima, O. Dillinger and Herbert Youngblood escaped **Mar. 3**, Dillinger was shot to death **July 22**, outside a movie house in Chicago by FBI agents, Youngblood in Port Huron, Mich.

The **Dionne sisters**, first quintuplets to survive beyond infancy, were born **May 28** in Callender, Ont., Canada, to Mr. and Mrs. Oliva Dionne.

**Engelbert Dollfuss**, 41, chancellor of Austria, was shot to death by Nazi conspirators **July 25**.

President **von Hindenburg** of Germany died **Aug. 2**. **Adolf Hitler** consolidated offices of president and chancellor, became **Fuehrer**.

**Long March by Chinese Communists** started **Oct.** Mao Tse-tung led 100,000 in 6,000-mile trek from south to north China; only 20,000 completed journey and reached Yenan, **Oct., 1935**.

**Italy** refused to arbitrate disputes on Italian Somaliland border between Italian and Ethiopian troops, demanded reparations, apology. **Dec. 19**.

### 1935

**Hitler rejected Versailles Treaty**, ordered conscription in Germany **Mar. 10**.

**Will Rogers**, 56, comedian, and **Wiley Post**, 36, aviator, were killed **Aug. 15** when Post's airplane crashed in a fog near Point Barrow, Alaska.

**Social Security Act** passed by Congress, **Aug. 14**.

**Ethiopia appealed** to League of Nations against Italy. Italy invaded Ethiopia **Oct. 2-4**.

Economic sanctions against Italy went into effect **Nov. 18**, supported by 52 nation-members of the League of Nations, and by one non-member, Egypt. The sanctions ended **July 15, 1936**.

### 1936

**King George V**, 70, died, **Jan. 20** on his estate at Sandringham, England, and was succeeded by his eldest son, Prince of Wales, 42, who took the title of **King Edward VIII**. He abdicated **Dec. 11, 1936**, and was succeeded by his brother, the Duke of York, who became **King George VI**. The ex-ruler was created Duke of Windsor with the title of His Royal Highness which was not extended to his wife. He gave up the throne, he said, because he could not marry "the woman I love," Mrs. Wallis Warfield of Baltimore, Md., who, **Oct. 27**, obtained a divorce in Ipswich, Eng., from Ernest A. Simpson, an insurance agent. The decree became absolute **May 3, 1937**. The couple was married **June 3, 1937**, in Monts, France.

**Reoccupation of demilitarized Rhineland** zone, in violation of the Locarno pact, begun by German troops **Mar. 7**.

**Emperor Haile Selassie** of Ethiopia escaped Italian advance by boarding British cruiser for Palestine, **May 1**. Premier Mussolini of Italy announced end of war **May 5**, proclaimed annexation of Ethiopia with King Victor Emmanuel Emperor.

**Adolf Hitler** signed treaty with Austria **July 11** guaranteeing Austrian frontier.

**Revolt against Spain's Republican Government** began **July 17** in Morocco and spread to Spain, included much of the Army and Air Force and half of the Navy; Jose Giral became Loyalist premier; **July 18**, Loyalists defeated Insurgents in Madrid and **July 19** Insurgents gained control in Cadiz, Huelva, Seville, Cordoba and Granada; Insurgents set up own government **July 24**; Insurgents took Badajoj **Aug. 16**; began aerial bombing of Madrid **Aug. 24**; captured Irun **Sept. 4**; took San Sebastian and Toledo, **Sept. 12**; Gen. Francisco Franco proclaimed head of the Nationalist (Insurgent) government, **Oct. 1**; siege of Madrid begun by Insurgents, **Oct. 21**; Loyalist Government moved from Madrid to Valencia, **Nov. 6**.

**Japan and Germany** signed an anti-Comintern pact **Nov. 25**. Italy joined **Nov. 6. 1937**.

### 1937

**Spanish insurgents** took Malaga **Feb. 8**. Warships of Great Britain, France, Italy and Germany, **March 13**, began to police the coasts of Spain under the 27-nation neutrality agreement. Gen. Franco, **Apr. 19**, set up a one-party state, dissolving the Fascist and Carlist organizations. New Loyalist Government formed **May 17** under Premier Juan Negrin; Loyalists shifted government to Barcelona, **Oct. 28**; Insurgents proclaimed blockade of all Loyalist ports **Nov. 23**.

The **Army-supported Japanese Cabinet** of Hayashi resigned **May**. Fighting in China, west of Peiping, was renewed by Japanese, **July**; Tungchow was attacked **July 27**; the Japanese **July 29**, bombed Tientsin, destroying Nankai University; **Aug. 9**, they took formal possession of Peiping; **Aug. 11**, they landed marines at Shanghai and shelled Nankow. Nanking, Canton, and many other places in the eastern provinces of China were

attacked by Japanese planes. **Oct. 23**, Suiyuan Province declared independence from China. The Chinese abandoned Shanghai and the Japanese took control **Nov. 8**. Premier **Chiang Kai-shek** moved to Hankow **Dec. 12**.

**Japanese shells** sank the U. S. gunboat Panay, **Dec. 12**, with loss of two lives; and several American oil carriers (the captain of one died) on the Yangtze river above Nanking. Several British craft were hit by the shells. Several lives were lost. The Japanese apologized and paid.

**Hitler** repudiated war guilt clause of Versailles Treaty, **Jan. 30**. Treaty blamed Germany for World War I. Hitler stated that from this time onward Germany was free from obligations imposed upon her by the Treaty.

**Amelia Earhart Putnam**, aviator, and co-pilot, lost **July 2** near Howland Isl. in the Pacific.

**Italy** gave notice **Dec. 11** of withdrawal from the League of Nations.

### 1938

**Spanish insurgent planes** from Majorca began daily bombing of Barcelona **Jan. 16**. Insurgent cruiser, Baleares, sunk off Cartagena **March 6** by Loyalist forces; air raids killed 1,000 in Barcelona **March 7**; insurgents took Lerida; they reached the sea at Lerida cutting Loyalist Spain in two, **April 15**. Italy began token withdrawal of 10,000 troops, **Oct. 10**; Insurgents began final campaign **Dec. 23** against Barcelona, which fell **Jan. 10, 1939**.

**Hitler** invaded Austria **March 11**. After resignation of Chancellor Kurt von Schuschnigg and President Wilhelm Miklas, **March 13**, the new Chancellor, Arthur Seyss-Inquart, proclaimed the political and geographic union of Germany and Austria. This was ratified by a popular vote, excluding Jews, in Austria. **April 10**. The Italian Grand Council, headed by Premier Benito Mussolini, voted approval.

**Mexico** nationalized oil industry, **Mar. 18**.

**Douglas G. Corrigan** of Los Angeles flew from Brooklyn to Dublin, **July 17-18**. Having no permit or passport, he jokingly said he flew the "wrong way."

At a conference in **Munich**, Bavaria; Britain and France yielded **Sept. 30** to Nazi demands for the cession of the Sudetenland to Germany by Czechoslovakia, thus ending a 15-day international crisis during which British Prime Minister Neville Chamberlain made two flying visits to Chancellor Adolf Hitler. Premier Mussolini of Italy backed Hitler's territorial demands. Hitler signed a "Peace Declaration" with Britain, **Sept. 30**, occupied Sudetenland **Oct. 1-10**. President Roosevelt asked Hitler to preserve the peace. Eduard Benes, president of Czechoslovakia, resigned **Oct. 5**.

About 4,000 sq. mi. of Czech land was awarded to Hungary **Nov. 2** by German-Italian arbitrators (For. Mins. Joachim von Ribbentrop and Galeazzo Ciano) meeting in Vienna. The area was populated by Hungarians and contained 860,000 persons. With the new cessions to Poland agreed on between Prague and Warsaw, the partition of Czechoslovakia was completed.

### 1939

**Uranium atom split** in U. S. at Columbia Univ., **Jan. 22**. Later, 1940, Uranium 235, a rare isotope, proved to be prime fissionable form of uranium.

The **Loyalist Spanish government** surrendered Barcelona to the Insurgents, **Jan. 26**. Madrid surrendered, **Mar. 24**; war ended **Mar. 29** with Franco victor.

The **Republic of Czechoslovakia** was dissolved, **March 14**; Hungarian troops seized Carpatho-Ukraine, **March 14**; Nazis occupied Bohemia and Moravia, which became a German protectorate, **March 16**. Hitler annexed Memel **March 22**.

**Germany and Italy** announced military and political alliance, **May 7**; signed 10-year military pact in Berlin **May 22**.

**Japanese troops** in Manchukuo and Soviet and Mongol troops near Lake Bor opened 6-month border fight **May 11**; 20,000 killed.

**Nazi Germany and Soviet Union** signed a 10-yr. non-aggression treaty **Aug. 24**, following a trade agreement of **Aug. 19**.

**N. Y. World's Fair** opened, **Apr. 30**, closed, **Oct. 31**; reopened **May 11, 1940**, and finally closed **Oct. 21**.

**President Roosevelt** proclaimed a limited national emergency, **Sept. 8**, an unlimited emergency **May 27, 1941**. Both ended by President Truman, **Apr. 28, 1952**.

---

**1939-1945 World War II**
**See Article Pages 312-313**

---

### 1940

**Finnish-Russian peace** signed in Moscow **Mar. 12**. **Estonia, Latvia and Lithuania** annexed by Union of Soviet Socialist Republics **July 14**.

### 1941

The **Four Freedoms** termed essential by Pres. Franklin D. Roosevelt in a speech to Congress **Jan. 6** were freedom of speech and expression, freedom

of worship, freedom from want and freedom from fear.

**United States Marines occupied Iceland, July 7,** on invitation from that country.

**The Atlantic Charter,** an 8-point joint U.S.-British declaration of principles, was signed by President Roosevelt and Prime Minister Winston Churchill **Aug. 14** aboard the British battleship Prince of Wales, off Newfoundland.

President Roosevelt and Secretary of State Hull **Nov. 17** received special Japanese envoys, Saburo Kurusu and Admiral Nomura, for conference on the Far Eastern situation.

**Japan attacked U. S. fleet at Pearl Harbor Dec. 7,** as first act of war. *See World War II.*

**Hitler ordered policy of genocide** as the "final solution" to the Jewish "problem." By end of war an estimated 4,500,000 to 6,000,000 Jews had been exterminated in Nazi concentration camps. Many other groups also suffered with the Jews.

**1942**

**Fire swept through Cocoanut Grove,** a Boston night club, **Nov. 28,** killing 491 and injuring scores.

**First nuclear chain reaction** (fission of uranium isotope, U-235) at Univ. of Chicago, under physicists Arthur Compton, Enrico Fermi, et al., **Dec. 2.**

**1943**

**President Roosevelt signed June 10** the pay-as-you-go income tax bill. Starting **July 1,** wage and salary earners were subject to a 20% withholding tax, including 3% Victory tax.

**Race riot in Detroit, June 21;** 34 dead, 700 injured. Riot in Harlem section of New York; **6** Negroes killed.

**1944**

**Deadly coal fumes** from locomotive in Italian railway tunnel near Balvana, killed 521, **Mar. 2.**

**Ringling Brothers and Barnum & Bailey Circus** fire in Hartford, Conn., caused a stampede in the main tent; 168 killed, 487 injured, **July 6.**

## Principal Events of World War II, 1939-1945;

**Major Belligerents—Germany** (Adolf Hitler, Fuehrer) invaded Poland Sept. 1, 1939; Norway and Denmark, April 9, 1940; the Netherlands, Belgium and Luxemburg, May 10, 1940. King Leopold of Belgium surrendered 500,000 May 28. Occupied France (Vichy) signed an armistice with Germany June 22, 1940. Germany invaded Russia June 22, 1941, unoccupied France and Italy Nov. 11, 1942, surrendered unconditionally to Great Britain, the United States and the USSR at Reims, France, May 7, 1945 (May 6 EST). War with Germany formally declared ended by Britain, France, Australia, New Zealand, July 9, 1951; by U. S. Oct. 19, 1951.

**Great Britain declared war on Germany** Sept. 3, 1939, as did Australia and New Zealand. Union of South Africa declared war Sept. 6; Canada, Sept. 10, 1939. Britain declared war on Italy June 11, 1940; on Finland, Hungary and Rumania, Dec. 7, 1941; on Japan, Dec. 8, 1941; on Bulgaria, Dec. 13, 1941; on Thailand, Jan. 25, 1942.

**France declared war on Germany** Sept. 3, 1939; on Italy June 11, 1940. Free French (De Gaulle) declared war on Japan Dec. 8, 1941.

**Italy** (Benito Mussolini, Duce) declared war on Great Britain and France June 10, 1940; on the U. S., Dec. 11, 1941. Surrendered unconditionally Sept. 8, 1943. Declared war against Germany Oct. 13, 1943, against Japan July 14, 1945. Signed treaty of peace, Feb. 10, 1947, in Paris, with Britain, France, U. S. and USSR.

**Japan attacked French Indo-China** Sept. 22, 1940; attacked Pearl Harbor naval station and the Philippines by air Dec. 7, 1941 and declared war on the United States, Great Britain, Australia, Canada, New Zealand and the Union of South Africa, Dec. 7, 1941; on the Netherlands, Jan. 11, 1942. Japan accepted the Allied terms unconditionally Aug. 14, 1945; signed surrender terms Sept. 1, 1945 (Sept. 2, Tokyo time) on board U. S. S. Missouri; signed treaty of peace with all big powers except USSR and a total of 49 nations at San Francisco, Sept. 8, 1951.

**Union of Socialist Soviet Republics** (Russia) signed non-aggression pact with Germany, Aug., 1939; invaded Poland, Sept. 17, 1939, and Finland, Nov. 30, 1939. Signed peace with Finland Mar. 12, 1940. Finland declared war on Russia June 25, 1941. Russia was invaded by Germany and Rumania, June 22, 1941. Signed armistice with Finland, Sept. 19, 1944, peace treaty, Feb. 10, 1947. Signed peace treaty with Poland July 30, 1941. Declared war on Japan Aug. 8, 1945, effective Aug. 9. Signed treaties of peace with Italy, Hungary, Rumania, Bulgaria and Finland Feb. 10, 1947. Did not sign treaty of peace with Japan.

**U. S. declared war on Japan** Dec. 8, 1941. Germany and Italy declared war on U.S. Dec. 11, 1941. A few hours later U.S. declared war on Germany and Italy. Also Bulgaria, Hungary and Rumania, June 5, 1942; signed peace treaties with Italy, Bulgaria, Hungary and Rumania Feb. 10, 1947; with Japan Sept. 8, 1951. War against the U.S. also declared by Albania, the Japanese puppet states of Burma, Manchukuo, and Nanking; Croatia, Slovakia and Thailand. Britain and France ended war with Germany July 9, 1951; U.S. ended it Oct. 19, 1951.

**Retreat from Dunkirk** by British Expeditionary Force took place May 26-June 4, 1940, when 900 vessels took 338,226 troops across the English Channel, 26,175 of them French.

**Nazi bombing of Britain** began July 10, 1940 and reached its height Sept. 7, Oct. 15 and Dec. 29. Coventry was damaged Nov. 14; Birmingham Nov. 19-22. Many London churches were burned Dec. 29. Desperate attacks on German aircraft by RAF stopped threat of invasion. The U.S. defense Prime Minister Churchill said: "Never

in the field of human conflict was so much owed by so many to so few."

**Pearl Harbor**—Over 100 Japanese planes and a number of midget submarines attacked U.S. Pacific fleet (86 ships) at anchor at Pearl Harbor, Hawaii, Dec. 7, 1941. (7:55 A. M., Hawaiian time; 1:25 P.M. EST.) Totally lost, Battleship Arizona. Severely damaged, Battleships Oklahoma, Nevada, California, West Virginia, 3 destroyers, 1 target ship, 1 minelayer. Damaged and repaired: Battleships Pennsylvania, Maryland, Tennessee; cruisers, Helena, Honolulu, Raleigh; 1 seaplane tender, 1 repair vessel, 1 drydock. Airplanes lost, Navy 80; Army 97. Japan lost 28 planes to the Navy, 20 to the Army and 3 submarines of 45 tons each. Casualties: Navy, 2,117 officers and men killed, 960 missing, 876 wounded; Army, 226 officers and men killed, 396 wounded.

**Planes Over Tokyo**—Lt. Col. James H. Doolittle, with 16 B-25s and 79 pilots and crewmen, took off Apr. 18, 1942 from Carrier Hornet, 688 mi. from Tokyo by sea; 13 planes dropped 500-lb. bombs on Tokyo, 2 on Nagoya, 1 on Kobe. Eight airmen were captured off China coast; 3 were shot, others imprisoned. Total dead, 9. One plane landed near Vladivostok and was interned by Russians; the crew escaped to Iran, but plane was never returned.

**Loss and Recapture of Philippines**—Japanese aircraft bombed Manila and environs Dec. 8, 1941, Far Eastern Time, destroyed 12 B-17s and damaged 5 at Clark Field. Gen. Douglas MacArthur had 15,000 U. S. troops, 40,000 in Philippine Army and 100,000 Filipino reservists. Manila and Cavite were taken by Japan (Homma) Jan. 2, 1942. Maj. Gen. Jonathan M. Wainwright commanded at Bataan, which was attacked by 200,000 Japanese Jan. 10. U. S. shot down 168 Japanese planes by Feb. 18; U. S. Army Air Force sank 3 troopships in Subic Bay, Mar. 4. Gen. MacArthur, ordered to Australia, reached Darwin Mar. 17, vowed, "I shall return." Wainwright defended Bataan until Apr. 8, 1942, sent 3,500 to Corregidor. Japan took 35,000 U. S. and Filipino troops prisoner, including 5,000 Marines, forced them into prison via the "Death March" of Bataan. Wainwright surrendered Corregidor May 6 with 11,574 troops. Gen. MacArthur returned to the Philippines near Palo on Leyte, with President Osmena, Oct. 20, 1944. Land, naval, and air action by 738 ships, 193,841 troops defeated Japan. U. S. entered Luzon via Lingayen gulf Jan. 9, 1945. Manila was taken Feb. 3; Corregidor reoccupied Feb. 16-Mar. 1.

**Germany attacked the Soviet Union** June 22, 1941; took Minsk, Smolensk, Kiev, Kharkov, Orel; besieged Leningrad, fought a terrible battle in the ruins of Stalingrad August, 1942, and extended the Nazi lines to the Black Sea. Tide turned in Nov., 1942; the Russians encircled Stalingrad and the Nazi army there surrendered Jan. 31, 1943. As Russian power increased and the Nazis weakened the Germans were pushed back until the Russians reached the Oder Feb., 1945.

**North African coast** fighting began Aug. 6, 1941, when Marshal Graziani led the Italians against the British with some success. The first counteroffensive in December relieved Tobruk, where Britain had held out 8 mos. The British pushed the Nazis under Rommel back to El Agheila, but Rommel regained the lost ground. He captured Tobruk with its garrison of 25,000 British June 21, 1942, and pushed the British back to within 70 mi. of Alexandria. On Oct. 23, the British, heavily reinforced and under Lt. Gen. Bernard L. Montgomery, attacked Rommel at El Alamein and defeated the Nazi-Italians with heavy losses all the way to Tunisia.

**North African expedition** by U. S. and Britain landed 150,000 American and 140,000 British

**1945**

Yalta Conference met in the Crimea, Feb. 3-11. Pres. Roosevelt, Churchill, and Stalin arranged to get Russia into war against Japan.

President Roosevelt, 63, died of cerebral hemorrhage in Warm Springs, Ga., Apr. 12. Vice President Harry S. Truman became President. Roosevelt buried in Hyde Park, N. Y.

Mussolini caught by Partisans near Dongo on Lake Como while trying to get to Switzerland, executed Apr. 28.

Hitler committed suicide in ruined chancellery, Berlin, Apr. 30. Body burned. Goebbels and wife poisoned children, committed suicide.

United Nations Conference on International Organization of 46 nations, San Francisco, opened Apr. 25; closed June 26 with address by Truman and adoption of U.N. charter.

Potsdam, Germany, conference of President Truman, Stalin and Churchill July 17-Aug. 2.

After July 25 Attlee replaced Churchill.

First atomic bomb, produced at Los Alamos, N. M., exploded at Alamogordo, N. M., July 16. Bomb dropped on Hiroshima, Japan, by B-29, Aug. 6; on Nagasaki, Aug. 9.

United States forces entered Korea south of 38° parallel to displace Japanese, Sept. 8.

Gen. Douglas MacArthur took over supervision of Japan Sept. 9.

Vidkun Quisling, pro-Nazi premier of Norway, executed by a firing squad in Oslo, Oct. 23.

Nationalization of the Bank of France and four other major banks ordered by French, Dec. 2.

**1946**

The first World War II peace treaty was signed between Britain and Siam. Jan. 1.

William Joyce, "Lord Haw Haw," broadcaster for Nazis, hanged in London for treason Jan. 3.

Poland nationalized basic industries, Jan. 6.

The first General Assembly of the United Nations opened in London, Jan. 10.

## Summary of Aerial, Naval and Military Actions

troops on French North Africa Nov. 8, 1942 (Nov. 7 EST), with Lt. Gen. Dwight D. Eisenhower, C. in C. French resisted briefly at Oran, Algiers and Casablanca and Vichy govt. broke relations with U. S. The Allies began campaign against Italy by seizing Pantelleria Island June 11, 1943. U. S. 7th Army under Maj. Gen. Geo. S. Patton, Jr., and British-Canadian 8th Army landed on Sicily July 10. Mussolini was forced to resign July 25 and escaped to German lines Sept. 12. The Italian mainland was invaded and Italy surrendered Sept. 8, 1943, but heavy fighting with Nazis followed and they were not dislodged until spring of 1945.

Battle of the Coral Sea, May, 1942, took heavy toll of ships and planes on both sides, was first battle fought by naval planes from ships that had neither sight nor range of enemy. U. S. lost 66 planes, 543 men; Japan lost 80 planes, 900 men. Battle of Midway, June 3-6, 1942, U. S. lost 1 carrier (Yorktown), 1 destroyer, 150 planes, 307 men; Japan lost 4 carriers, 253 planes, 3,500 men.

Guadalcanal, in the southern Solomon Islands, site of a Japanese air base that threatened the Allied position in the southwest Pacific, was assaulted by U. S. Marines Aug. 7, 1942. In one of the most costly Allied Pacific campaigns, several major naval engagements, dozens of air battles and much bitter ground fighting followed before the island was finally won by the Allies in January, 1943. Two Marine divisions, two Army divisions and an additional Army regiment were committed to the fight by the United States before the issue was decided.

Battle for Leyte Gulf, biggest naval action ever fought, occurred Oct. 22-27, 1944, in three engagements destroying Japanese naval power. Battles were fought in Surigao strait, off Samar and off Cape Engano. Ships engaged, U. S. 166, Japanese 65. Airplanes, U. S. 1,280; Japanese 716. Losses for Philippine campaign—Japan: 3 large carriers, 3 light carriers, 1 escort carrier, 4 battleships, 14 cruisers, 32 destroyers, 11 submarines, total 68. U. S.: 1 light carrier, 3 escort carriers, 6 destroyers, 3 destroyer escorts, 1 high-speed transport, 7 submarines, total 21. U. S. lost 1 ship to a kamikaze (suicide) plane at Leyte and 5 in subsequent actions. Total airplane losses for Philippine campaign, October, 1944 through January, 1945: Japan (est.) 7,000, including 722 kamikaze; U. S. 967.

D-Day: Invasion of France—Invasion of France by Allies, June 6, 1944. 1,000 planes and gliders dropped paratroopers on Contentin peninsula, Normandy, 5 a.m. London time. 1,000 R.A.F., 1,400 U. S. bombers attacked installations. First assault troops landed 6:30 a.m. on beaches along line Carentan-Bayeux-Caen; U. S. on West, British-Canadians on East. Total Allied strength available 2,876,439, including 17 British divisions of which 3 Canadian; 20 U. S. divisions, 1 French, 1 Polish. Also available 5,049 fighter planes, 3,467 heavy bombers, 1,645 light and medium bombers, 2,316 transport aircraft, 2,591 gliders, 698 others; 835 L.C.T., 233 L.S.T. Beachhead 60 mi. long, 10 mi. deep.

Gen. Dwight D. Eisenhower was Supreme Commander of Allied Expeditionary Forces; Gen. Sir Bernard L. Montgomery commander of Allied assault troops; Sir Bertram Ramsay of Allied naval units (4,000 ships of all kinds); Air Marshal Trafford Leigh-Mallory of Air Forces; Lt. Gen. Omar N. Bradley of U. S. troops in field. Germans had available 65 divisions, including reserves extending back to Germany. Marshal Gunther von Kluge was German commander in France.

British took Bayeux June 7; Carentan fell June 13; U. S. took Cherbourg June 27; British-Canadians took Caen July 9 after desperate fighting. Lt. Gen. George S. Patton Jr. with 3rd U. S. Army attacked south and west of St. Lo Aug. 1. Canadians took Falaise Aug. 17. The Argentan gap was closed by the 3rd Army in terrible fighting. Germans lost 12 to 14 divisions in the Falaise pocket, many taken prisoner.

Aug. 14-15, 1944, Allies invaded France east of the mouth of the Rhone with 1,000 ships (641 U. S., 316 British). On Aug. 25 the 2nd French armored division and token force of U. S. Army entered Paris.

The Ardennes Bulge was a violent counter-attack by 15 German divisions under Gen. von Modell (Gen. von Rundstedt C. in C.) launched Dec. 16, 1944. By Dec. 19 the 1st U. S. Army was pushed out of Germany and the Germans penetrated 60 mi. west of Celles. Lt. Gen. Patton's 3rd U. S. Army rescued besieged Americans at Bastogne Dec. 21 and Nazi drive was stopped by Dec. 25. Allies wiped out the Bulge by Jan. 31, 1945. Near Malmedy Germans cut down captured American soldiers with machine guns and left them dead on the field. U. S. losses estimated at 40,000; Germans lost 220,000 in dead and prisoners.

Rhine Crossing—On Mar. 7, 1945, the 9th Armored Div., 3rd Corps, First Army, found Ludendorff bridge at Remagen on the Rhine intact; Gen. Eisenhower ordered Gen. Omar N. Bradley to put 5 divisions across; on 5th day Army ceased using bridge, used Treadway floating bridge, built in 10 hrs., 11 min.; Remagen bridge collapsed Mar. 17.

Iwo Jima was invaded by U. S. joint expeditionary force Feb. 19, 1945, with land action by U. S. Marines; invasion used 495 ships, including 17 aircraft carriers and 1,170 planes. U. S. troops engaged, 111,308, of which 75,144 were assault troops. Island was conquered by Mar. 16. U. S. lost 4,590 killed; Japanese deaths est. over 20,000.

Okinawa, principal Japanese base in the Ryukyu group, was invaded Apr. 1, 1945 in the final naval campaign of the war. The troops needed 1,300 vessels, including airplane carriers. After 83 days of fighting the end was signalized by the formal suicide of the two Japanese generals. U. S. men engaged up to June 30, 1945 reached 176,491 army, 88,500 Navy. Japanese strength at start was 77,199. U. S. losses were 49,151, of which 12,520 were killed or missing, 36,631 wounded. The Japanese lost 110,071 and 7,400 taken prisoner. U. S. lost 763 aircraft; Japan lost 7,830 of which 1,020 were destroyed on the ground. U. S. had 36 ships sunk, 369 damaged; Japan had 16 sunk, including the Yamato, world's largest battleship, full load displacement 72,809 tons, 861 ft. long, 9 18-in. guns, 3,333 personnel. Hit by over 10 aerial torpedoes at Kyushu; 300 survived.

V-E Day—German armies began surrendering May 4, 1945. Unconditional surrender was signed May 7 at 2:41 a.m. in Rheims Hq. (May 6, 8:41 p.m., EWT), designating cessation of operations May 9 at 12:01 a.m. (May 8, 6:01 p.m.). Surrender also signed in Berlin.

Atomic Bombs—First atomic bomb ever used in war was dropped by U. S. plane Aug. 6, 1945, on Hiroshima, Japan (pop. 343,969). Second U. S. bomb dropped on Nagasaki (pop. 252,630) Aug. 9, 1945. Estimates of dead from bombs and radiation exposure vary: Hiroshima, 80,000 to over 200,000; Nagasaki, 39,000 to 74,000. Japan surrendered Aug. 14. Formal surrender aboard U.S.S. Missouri Sept. 2, 1945, Far Eastern Time, celebrated as V-J Day.

*Consult Index for additional listings under World War II.*

**Radar beam reached** the moon **Jan. 10,** U. S. Army announced **Jan. 24.**

**League of Nations,** Geneva, Switzerland, closed its work, gave physical assets to the United Nations, **April 18.**

**Gen. Draja Mikhailovitch,** leader of the Chetniks, was executed by a firing squad in Belgrade, Yugoslavia, **July 17,** for alleged treason.

**Philippine independence** granted by U. S., **July 4.** Manuel Roxas elected first president of new Republic.

**Twenty-two Nazi leaders convicted** of war crimes **Sept. 30** by International Tribunal in Nuremberg. Eleven Nazis were sentenced to death by hanging, **Oct. 1.** No. 2 Nazi Hermann Goering committed suicide by poison in Nuremberg Prison, two hours before he was scheduled to be hanged, **Oct. 15.** The 10 other top Nazis were hanged individually. They were: Hans Frank, Wilhelm Frick, Col. Gen. Alfred Jodl, Gestapo Chief Ernst Kaltenbrunner, Field Marshal Wilhelm Keitel, Alfred Rosenberg, Fritz Sauckel, Arthur Seyss-Inquart, Julius Streicher and Foreign Minister Joachim von Ribbentrop.

**Others sentenced** for war crimes: Gen. Anton Dostler, Nazi, hanged in Rome, **Dec. 1,** 1945, for shooting 15 U. S. soldiers without trial; Jos. Kramer, "Beast of Belsen" and 10 others hanged **Dec. 14,** 1945, by British for atrocities at Belsen and Oswiecin concentration camps; Gen. T. Yamashita, Japanese commander in Philippines, hanged **Feb. 23,** 1946; Lt. Gen. Homma who ordered Bataan death march, shot near Manila, **Apr. 3,** 1946; Marshal Ion Antonescu, dictator of Rumania, hanged **June 1,** 1946; Karl Hermann Frank, Nazi ruler in Czechoslovakia, hanged in Prague May 22 for ordering massacre of Lidice; 43 Nazi officers and guards hanged by the U. S. Army at Landsberg, Germany, May, 1947, for mass murders at Mauthausen camp.

**Archbishop Aloysius Stepinac,** Roman Catholic Primate of Yugoslavia, was sentenced to 16 years at hard labor for alleged collaboration with Nazis, **Oct. 11.** He was released, **Dec.,** 1951; made a Cardinal, **Jan. 12,** 1952; died **Feb. 10,** 1960.

**John L. Lewis called out** 400,000 soft coal miners in strike against the U. S. government, **Nov. 20,** ignoring strike cancellation order by Federal Judge T. Alan Goldsborough in Washington. Found guilty of contempt of court, Lewis was fined $10,000, the United Mine Workers $3,500,000. Supreme Court, **Mar. 6,** 1947, affirmed Lewis' fine, reduced union's fine to $700,000 provided it cancelled strike notice. Strike **Mar. 15,** 1948 to **Apr. 22,** 1948, for guaranteed $100-a-month pension for retired mine workers resulted in Lewis being fined $20,000 and the union $1,400,000, **Apr. 20,** 1948.

**Peace treaties for Hitler's** European satellites, imposing $1.33 billion in reparations, drafted at a 5-week meeting of Big Four Foreign Ministers that ended in New York City **Dec. 12.** The treaties were signed, **Feb. 10,** 1947.

**President Truman proclaimed** the cessation of hostilities of World War II, **Dec. 31.**

### 1947

**British Labor government** took possession of coal mines, cables and wireless communications, **Jan. 1.**

**Truman Doctrine.** President Truman asked Congress to appropriate $400,000,000 for economic and military aid to Greece and Turkey to combat communism, **Mar. 12.** Approved, **May 15.**

**The United Nations** Security Council voted unanimously to place under U. S. trusteeship the Pacific Islands formerly mandated to Japan **April 2.**

**The Senate approved** the **Taft-Hartley Labor Act,** 68 to 24, **May 13.** The house concurred, **June 4,** by a vote of 320 to 79. The measure was vetoed by President Truman, **June 20,** but the House overrode the veto, 331 to 83, on the same day. The Senate overrode the veto, 68-25. **June 23.**

**Proposals known later as the Marshall Plan,** under which the U. S. would extend financial aid to any European countries "willing to assist in the task of recovery," were made by Secy. of State George C. Marshall in a speech **June 5** at Harvard University. Congress authorized the spending in the next 3½ years of some $12 billion on Marshall Plan aid, which was credited with restoring economic health to free Europe and halting the march of Communism in those countries cooperating in the plan. The Marshall proposals set the pattern for the vast U. S. post-war program of foreign aid.

**Hindu India and Moslem Pakistan,** formerly part of India, gained independence from England, **Aug. 15.** Lord Louis Mountbatten was the last British Viceroy of India.

### 1948

**British Labor govt.** nationalized railways, **Jan. 1.**

**Mohandas K. Gandhi,** Hindu spiritual leader and champion of freedom for India, was shot and killed by a Hindu fanatic in New Delhi, **Jan. 30.** Communal rioting took the lives of nearly 100 leaders and members of the Mahasabba, politico-religious group to which Gandhi's assassin belonged. **Jan. 30-Feb. 2.**

**Czechoslovakia joined the Communist** bloc in Eastern Europe after President Benes yielded **Feb. 25** to a Communist ultimatum to install a pro-

**Soviet Cabinet.** He resigned, **June 7,** and was succeeded by Klement Gottwald, Communist. Benes died **Sept. 3.** Communists reported Jan Masaryk, Foreign Minister, committed suicide **Mar. 10.**

**A land blockade of Berlin's Allied sectors** was started **Apr. 1** by the Soviet Military Govt., which refused to permit U. S. and British supply trains to pass through the Soviet zone of Germany. This blockade and a Western counter-blockade were lifted Sept. 30, 1949, after British and U. S. planes had airlifted 2,343,315 tons of food and coal into West Berlin.

**Charter of the Organization of American States** signed **Apr. 30** at 9th International Conference of American States at Bogota, Colombia. The conference had been interrupted for a week by rioting following the assassination of Jorge Eliecer Gaitan.

**The Free State of Israel** was proclaimed in Tel Aviv, **May 14,** as the British evacuated Palestine. First de facto recognition came from the United States, **May 14,** and Soviet Russia, **May 17.** Chaim Weizmann was elected first president by the Constituent Assembly, **Feb. 14,** 1949.

**The Cominform** (Communist Information Bureau), at a Prague meeting **June 28,** denounced Marshal Tito and other leaders of the Yugoslav Communist party as deserters from the Marxist-Leninist doctrine.

**Alger Hiss,** former State Department official, was indicted in New York City, **Dec. 15,** on two perjury charges after he had denied passing secret documents to Whittaker Chambers, a former magazine editor, for transmission to a Communist spy ring. A jury failed to reach an agreement, **July 8,** 1949. His second trial, Nov. 17, 1949-Jan. 21, 1950, ended with conviction on 2 counts and a sentence of 5 years in a Federal prison. Appeals to higher courts were rejected, and Hiss began his sentence **Mar. 22.** 1951. He denied all charges. He petitioned Federal Court, New York, for retrial on basis of new evidence of "forgery by typewriter," **Jan. 24,** 1952. Judge H. W. Goddard denied it, July 22, 1952, Supreme Court on Apr. 27, 1953. He was released **Nov. 27,** 1954.

**Former Premier Hideki Tojo** and six other Japanese war leaders were hanged in Tokyo, **Dec. 23,** as war criminals.

**Joseph Cardinal Mindszenty,** Roman Catholic primate of Hungary, arrested by Communist government in Budapest on charges of treason, espionage and black market dealings, **Dec. 27.** Convicted, given life imprisonment, **Feb. 8,** 1949. All persons taking part in the Cardinal's prosecution were excommunicated by Pope Pius XII. Mindszenty freed **Oct. 31,** 1956.

### 1949

**Mildred E. (Axis Sally) Gillars** was convicted by a Federal jury in New York City **Mar. 10** of treason in broadcasting Nazi propaganda during war. She received 10 to 30 years in prison. Freed 1961.

**North Atlantic Treaty** adopted **Mar. 18** by U. S. Canada and 10 Western European nations, agreeing that "an armed attack against one or more of them in Europe and North America shall be considered an attack against all." Signed **April 4,** ratified by Senate, **July 21.**

**Ireland** severed last ties with Britain by leaving Commonwealth, **April 18.**

**End of U. S. A-bomb monopoly** signalized by President Truman's announcement **Sept. 23** that an atomic explosion had occurred in the USSR.

**Mrs. I. Toguri D'Aquino,** Tokyo Rose of Japanese wartime broadcasts, was sentenced in San Francisco **Oct. 7** to 10 years in prison for treason. Paroled **Jan. 28,** 1956.

**Eleven leaders of U. S. Communist** party convicted **Oct. 14,** after 9-month trial in New York City of advocating violent overthrow of U. S. Government. Federal Judge Harold R. Medina, **Oct. 21,** sentenced 10 defendants to five years in prison each and the 11th, a war veteran, to 3 years. U. S. Court of Appeals upheld conviction **Aug. 1,** 1950. Supreme Court upheld the convictions **June 4,** 1951. Seven surrendered **July 2,** 1951; of the other 4, hunted as fugitives, one, Gus Hall, was captured **Oct. 8,** 1951, and given 3 additional years. Robert G. Thompson was captured **Aug. 27,** 1953. Five defense lawyers, cited for contempt during the trial, received sentences ranging from 1 to 6 months. **Apr. 24,** 1952, Supreme Court upheld sentences **Mar. 10,** 1952.

**Angus Ward,** U. S. Consul General in Mukden, Manchuria, and four consulate employees were arrested by Communists, **Oct. 24,** on charge of having beaten Chinese employee. Ward and others were sentenced to jail terms of five to six months, **Nov. 22,** but were released, **Nov. 25,** ordered to leave country after U. S. had appealed to 30 other nations to join in a protest.

**Nationalist China's government** fled to Formosa **Dec. 7.** Chinese Communists took Yunnan and Kunming as Nationalists deserted.

### 1950

**Protesting arrest of Robert A. Vogeler,** U. S. businessman, on charge of spying, U. S. **Jan. 2** ordered Hungary to close its consulates in N. Y. and Cleveland. Hungary released Vogeler **Apr. 28,**

1951 when U. S. agreed to let consulates reopen.

**Great Britain recognized Communist China Jan. 6**, one day after breaking diplomatic relations with Chiang Kai-shek's Nationalist Chinese regime.

**U. S. Jan. 14** recalled all consular officials from Communist China after the latter seized the American consulate general in Peiping.

**Masked bandits robbed Brink's**, Inc., Boston express office, **Jan. 17** of $2,775,395.12, of which $1,218,211.29 was in cash. Solution announced 1956 by FBI; 8 men sentenced to life.

President Truman **Jan. 31** authorized AEC to produce the hydrogen bomb (H-bomb).

**Dr. Klaus J. E. Fuchs**, German-born atomic research physicist at Harwell, Eng., pleaded guilty **Mar. 1** to violating the Official Secrets Act and received 14 years in prison. He had communicated valuable atomic information to Russian agents since 1942. At one time he worked at Los Alamos, N. M. Released **June 23, 1959**, went to East Germany, became citizen.

**Judith Coplon**, 28, former political analyst in Dept. of Justice, Washington, D. C., and Valentin A. Gubichev, 33, Russian engineer employed by United Nations, were found guilty of espionage **Mar. 7** in New York and sentenced to 15 years. Gubichev's sentence was suspended when he agreed to leave the country. Miss Coplon also had been sentenced to 40 months to 10 years after 1949 Washington trial for stealing secret documents. The New York convictions were reversed by the U. S. Circuit Court of Appeals, N. Y., **Dec. 5** because the FBI made the arrests without a warrant and the Government failed to show that its evidence was not obtained through wire-tapping. The indictment stood. U. S. Court of Appeals, D. C., upheld the Washington conviction **June 1, 1951**, but ruled the case should be retried because the Government used illegal wire-tap evidence. Miss Coplon won the right to a new trial **Jan. 28, 1952**, when the Supreme Court refused to review decisions on 3 appeals from lower court rulings. New trial never held. All charges dropped **Jan. 6, 1967.**

**The Army seized all railroads Aug. 27**, on orders of President Truman, to prevent a general strike after unions had rejected terms of an 18c an hour raise for yardmen but none for trainmen. Roads returned to owners **May 23, 1952**, after signing of new labor contract.

**In an attempt to kill President Truman**, two Puerto Rican fanatics, members of a nationalist movement, tried to shoot their way into the President's house, Washington, **Nov. 1**. Guards killed Griselio Torresola, New York; wounded Oscar Collazo, 36, New York pocketbook frame polisher, Pvt. Leslie Coffelt, a guard, was fatally shot; 2 other guards were seriously injured. Collazo was convicted of murder **Mar. 7, 1951**, and sentenced to death. President Truman commuted sentence to life imprisonment, **July 24, 1952.**

**U. S. Dec. 8 banned shipments** to Communist China and to Asiatic ports trading with it.

**Supreme Court ruled Dec. 11**, that under the 5th amendment no one could be forced to testify against himself.

**1951**

**Ilse Koch was sentenced** to life imprisonment by a German court in Frankfort **Jan. 15**, for inciting the murder of a Buchenwald prisoner.

**William W. Remington**, Commerce Dept. employe, was convicted of perjury in New York **Feb. 7**, and sentenced to 5 years and fined $2,000. U.S. Court of Appeals reversed decision **Aug. 22**, sent case back for retrial. Remington was convicted **Jan. 27, 1953** on 2 counts of a new 5-count perjury indictment, and sentenced **Feb. 4, 1953** to 3 years. Conviction upheld by Court of Appeals. He died in prison **Nov. 24, 1954**, after a beating by 2 convicts.

**With Sen. Estes Kefauver (D.-Tenn.)** as chairman, the Senate Committee to Investigate Organized Crime in Interstate Commerce, exposed nation-wide criminal organizations that reaped huge illegal profits, used these funds to enter legitimate businesses, influenced politicians and bought protection. Preliminary report, **Feb. 28**, said gambling took over $20 billion a year.

**Julius Rosenberg**, his wife, Ethel, and Morton Sobell, all U. S. citizens, were found guilty **Mar. 29**, of conspiracy to commit wartime sabotage. Rosenbergs sentenced to death. Sobell to 30 years. Appeals denied. David Greenglass, brother of Mrs. Rosenberg and a state witness, received 15 years in prison, Rosenbergs executed at Sing Sing prison, Ossining, N.Y., **June 19, 1953.**

**President Truman relieved Gen. Douglas Mac-Arthur** of his command in the Far East **Apr. 11**. *See Korean War.*

**William N. Oatis**, Associated Press correspondent in Prague, was arrested **April 26** as spy by Czechoslovakia, tried and sentenced **July 4** to 10 years in prison. U. S. denounced "mock trial," defended legitimate news gathering, enacted economic reprisals. Oatis was freed **May 16, 1953.**

**European Coal and Steel Plan** proposed by French Foreign Minister Robert Schuman, **May 9**. British Labor Government rejected plan but six other nations, France, West Germany, Italy, Belgium, Netherlands, and Luxembourg, agreed to

## Korean War and United States Intervention

**Republic of Korea was invaded** June 25, 1950 (June 24, EST) by over 60,000 North Korean troops spear-headed by over 100 Russian-built tanks. U. N. Security Council demanded cessation of hostilities and withdrawal to 38th parallel. On June 27 it asked U. N. members to help carry out its demand. President Truman, June 27, ordered Gen. of the Army Douglas MacArthur to aid South Korea and the 7th U. S. fleet to protect Formosa against possible aggression and keep the Chinese Nationalist forces from attacking the mainland. Requested by the UN to name a commander, the President designated Gen. MacArthur July 8, 1950.

North Korean forces took Seoul, South Korean capital, June 29, U. S. ground forces entered the conflict June 30. The President termed the intervention a "police action."

The war had three phases: (1) The North Korean drive was checked by U. S. and associated troops, with help of a brilliant landing by U. S. Marines at Inchon Sept. 15. Pyongyang, North Korean capital was taken Oct. 20. U. S. 7th Division reached Manchurian border Nov. 20.

(2) Counter-attack by 200,000 Chinese Communist "volunteers," who crossed Yalu river Nov. 26, forced evacuation of 105,000 UN troops and 91,000 Korean civilians at Hungnam Dec. 24. The Chinese pushed across 38th parallel, drove 70 mi. into South Korea. The UN General Assembly, Feb. 1, named Communist China the aggressor in Korea. UN troops pushed Chinese back across parallel Apr. 3, stopped offensive by 600,000 Chinese Apr. 22-30.

(3) Removal of Gen. MacArthur from command Apr. 11, 1951 and start of negotiations for truce along 38th parallel July 10. 1951.

**President Truman removed Gen. MacArthur** from all Far East commands and replaced him with Gen. Matthew B. Ridgway, commander of 8th Army. MacArthur had wished to pursue Chinese across Yalu to their air depots in Manchuria and on Mar. 25 had threatened Communist China with air and naval attack. He had been warned to clear all announcements of policy through Washington. The President opposed his views. A Senate inquiry May 3-June 27, 1951, found that MacArthur was not charged with insubordination, but had disregarded the President's order to clear policy statements through the Defense Dept.

**Cease fire and Armistice** talks began July 1951 and dragged on with numerous break-downs until July 27, 1953 (July 26, EST) when armistice was signed; fighting ended 12 hrs. later. A military armistice commission supervised truce; 10 joint UN-Communist teams policed demilitarized zone; Neutral Nations Supervisory Commission watched military movements in ports; voluntary repatriation of prisoners was provided and Communists had privilege of interviewing prisoners refusing repatriation. India furnished 6,000 troops as guards.

**Prisoner repatriation** began Aug. 6, 1953, at Panmunjom, ended Sept. 6, 1953. UN turned over 75,799 prisoners (70,159 North Koreans and 5,640 Chinese). Communists released 12,760, including 7,850 South Koreans, 3,597 Americans, 945 Britons and 228 Turks. Maj. Gen. Dean was released Sept. 4.

The troops from India departed in February, 1954. The Supervisory Commission, made up of members from Czechoslovakia, Poland, Sweden and Switzerland, was reduced one-half in Sept., 1955, on repeated complaints that the Communist members were spying in South Korea. Repeated reports indicated that the North Koreans had violated many terms of the armistice, built numerous airfields and received naval vessels. The UN Command expelled the commission from South Korea in June, 1956, on grounds that its Czech and Polish members and the North Korean government had frustrated the operation of the armistice agreement. The UN Command announced in June, 1957, that it could no longer be bound by armistice provisions controlling importation of military equipment into Korea, but would modernize UN forces "to restore the relative balance of military strength that the armistice was intended to preserve."

conference. Treaty ratified, June 16, 1952.

**U.N. General Assembly** voted arms embargo against Communist China May 18.

**Tariff concessions** by the U. S. to the Soviet Union, Communist China and all Communist-dominated lands were suspended Aug. 1.

**Transcontinental television** inaugurated Sept. 4, with President Truman's address at the Japanese Peace Treaty Conference in San Francisco.

**Japanese Peace Treaty** signed in San Francisco Sept. 8, by U.S. and 48 other nations.

**War between Germany** and the U.S. formally ended Oct. 19. Great Britain and France ended war with Germany July 9.

### 1952

**Queen Elizabeth II of Britain** proclaimed Queen of Canada Feb. 6, marking first time monarch was specifically enthroned in name of Canada.

**U. S. seizure of nation's steel mills** was ordered by President Truman **Apr. 8** to avert a strike by 600,000 CIO United Steelworkers. Seizure was ruled illegal by the Supreme Court **June 2**; strike followed **June 3**, was settled **July 24**.

**First jetliner passenger service** opened **May 2**, British DeHavilland Comet, London to Johannesburg, South Africa, 6,724 mi. in less than 24 hrs.

**Peace contract** between West Germany, U. S., Great Britain and France was signed in Bonn, May 26. Allied high commissions abolished.

**Puerto Rico became an "associated free state"** or commonwealth of the U. S., July 25, after Pres. Truman gave approval to a new constitution.

**West Germany** agreed Sept. 10, to pay Israel $822,000,000 over 12 to 14 years as indemnity for Nazi and anti-Semitic acts.

**Britain** successfully completed its first atomic test off northwest Australia Oct. 3, detonating a bomb aboard a naval vessel.

**First hydrogen device explosion** Nov. 1 at AEC Eniwetok proving grounds in Pacific reported by witnesses but not officially confirmed for more than a year. President Eisenhower told Congress Feb. 2, 1954, that the 1952 test was "the first full-scale thermonuclear explosion in history . . . the first step in the hydrogen weapon program of the United States."

**Vladimir Clementis, Rudolf Slansky** and 9 other purged Communists were hanged in Prague Dec. 3 for espionage and treason.

**Alan Nunn May**, British scientist who gave atom secrets to the U.S.S.R., was released from prison Dec. 29, after serving 6 yrs. 8 mos. of his 10-yr. term.

### 1953

**Joseph Stalin** died, March 5. By 1955, Nikita S. Khrushchev emerged as dominant political leader of Soviet Union.

**Mau Mau** or "Hidden Ones" of Kenya's Kikuyu tribe, formed to force whites from Kenya and to regain ancestral lands from gov't, climaxed sporadic violence **Mar. 26**, by murdering 71 and wounding 100 fellow Kikuyus who remained loyal to colonial gov't. 500 arrests made, 17 sentenced to death. Jomo Kenyatta, tribal leader, found guilty **Apr. 8** of organizing Mau Mau, sentenced to 7 years. **Dec. 12**, 1963 Kenya became independent and Jomo Kenyatta became Prime Minister; and on Dec. 12, 1964, President.

**Mount Everest was conquered** May 29, by Edmund P. Hillary of New Zealand and Tensing Norkay, Nepalese living in India. Expedition was under Col. Henry C. J. Hunt, Briton.

**Demonstration by workers in East Berlin** against increased work quotas **June 16**, erupted into an anti-Communist riot by 20,000 to 50,000 people **June 17**, and became a general strike involving 200,000 in East Germany. Soviet troops quelled disturbances killing 16.

**Lavrenti P. Beria**, chief of Soviet secret police, was dismissed July 10, as an enemy of the people. He was executed Dec. 23, along with 6 of his aides. Purge extended to Georgia, the Ukraine, Byelorussia and other Soviet states.

**First USSR announcement of H-bomb explosion** Aug. 20, AEC reported explosion occurred in USSR Aug. 12.

### 1954

**Nautilus, first atomic-powered submarine**, was launched at Groton, Conn., Jan. 21.

**Five members of Congress were wounded** in the House of Representatives, **Mar. 1**, by 4 Puerto Ricans, one a woman, who fired pistols at random from a spectators' gallery, shouting for Puerto Rican independence. Representatives recovered. Attackers were sentenced to prison.

**Dien Bien Phu**, French military outpost in northwest Vietnam, fell to the Vietminh army of Ho Chi Minh, **May**.

**Geneva Conference on Far Eastern Affairs**, Apr. 26–July 21, by foreign ministers of 19 nations, including Communist China. Free elections in Korea foundered on Communist objections to U. N. supervision. Armistice, effective **Aug. 11**, ended 7½ years of war in Indo-China, with French withdrawal, Vietminh won 62,000 sq. mi. and 13,000,000 pop. in North Vietnam. Cambodia and Laos became independent countries.

**Racial segregation in public schools** was ruled

unconstitutional in a unanimous decision of the Supreme Court, **May 17**.

**Southeast Asia Treaty Organization** (SEATO), formed by collective defense pact signed in Manila, Sept. 8 by the U. S., Britain, France, Australia, New Zealand, Philippines, Pakistan and Thailand.

**Agreement signed in Paris**, Oct. 23, provided for West German sovereignty, rearmament, and entrance into NATO and the Western European Union.

**Condemnation of Sen. Jos. R. McCarthy** (R.-Wis.) voted by Senate, 67–22, **Dec. 2** for contempt of a Senate elections subcommittee, for abuse of its members and for insults to the Senate during investigation, Apr. 22–June 17, of charges brought by the Dept. of the Army vs. Sen. McCarthy, growing out of the Senator's investigation of alleged subversive activities.

### 1955

**Afro-Asian conference** of 29 nations met in Bandung, Indonesia, **April**. Conference gave expression to new nationalism of developing nations.

**Federal Republic of West Germany** became a sovereign state **May 5** when ratifications were deposited in Bonn. U.S. completed ratification **Apr. 21**. President Eisenhower signed an order ending U. S. occupation but troops remained on a contractual basis.

**The Warsaw Pact**, a 20-yr. mutual defense treaty, was signed at Warsaw **May 14** by USSR, Albania, Bulgaria, Czechoslovakia, Hungary, Poland, Rumania and East Germany.

**The U. S. Supreme Court May 31 reaffirmed** the principle of public education without racial discrimination and said all provisions of Federal, state and local law must honor this principle. It gave local authorities the task of integrating schools.

**A meeting of heads of state "at the summit"** proposed by U.S., Great Britain and France, to the USSR, took place **July 18–23** in Geneva, Switzerland, with President Eisenhower top negotiator for the U.S. It was followed by a meeting of the Foreign Ministers, Oct. 27–Nov. 16, with Secy. of State Dulles acting for U. S.

**Juan D. Peron**, president and dictator of Argentina, was deposed **Sept. 19** after a military revolt begun **June 16** by naval and marine corps units. Maj. Gen. Eduardo Lonardi became provisional pres. **Sept. 23**, was displaced **Nov. 13** by a military junta, which chose Maj. Gen. Pedro Aramburu prov. pres.

**Merger of America's two largest labor organizations** was effected **Dec. 5**, under the name American Federation of Labor and Congress of Industrial Organizations. Geo. Meany became pres., Walter Reuther became vice pres. in charge of the industrial dept. The merged AFL-CIO had a membership estimated at 15,000,000.

### 1956

**At 20th Congress of Soviet Communist party** in Moscow, Feb. 14–25, party chief Nikita S. Khrushchev and other leaders denounced Joseph Stalin, repudiated cruelties of Stalinism, and proclaimed a policy of peaceful co-existence with the West. New party line helped to alienate Chinese communists and hasten Sino-Soviet split. U. S. State Dept. June 4 published text of Khrushchev's 7-hr. secret speech.

**Dr. Jesus de Galindez**, Columbia U. lecturer, disappeared in New York City **Mar. 12**. Dominican officials denied he had been murdered by agents of Trujillo regime which he opposed.

**Six U.S. Marine recruits drowned Apr. 8** in march through stream at Parris Island, S. C.

**Workers in Poznan, Poland, revolted June 28** against Communist rule; uprising crushed with 44 killed, hundreds wounded.

**Principles of Organization of American States** outlined in Panama Declaration signed in Panama City **July 22** by President Eisenhower and heads of 18 other Western Hemisphere states.

**Egypt seized Suez Canal July 26** under nationalization decree after Pres. Gamal Abdel Nasser denounced Western withdrawal of proposed Aswan dam financing.

**Army H21 helicopter** landed in Washington D.C., **Aug. 24** after first non-stop transcontinental helicopter flight—2,610 mi. in 37 hrs.

**First trans-Atlantic telephone cable system** went into use Sept. 25 between Clarenville, Newfoundland, and Oban, Scotland.

**Polish Communist leaders Oct. 19–21** defied Kremlin leadership and elected Wladyslaw Gomulka to head more independent government.

**Hungarian revolt** against Soviet-dominated regime began Oct. 23, was crushed **Nov. 4** by Soviet armed forces.

**Israel invaded Egypt's Sinai** peninsula **Oct. 29**. When Egypt rejected demand for cease-fire made by France and Britain, the two nations bombed Egypt by air Oct. 31, landed forces **Nov. 5–6**. U. S. condemned attack, supported cease-fire demand by UN. Egypt and Israel accepted cease-fire. Britain and France followed, fighting stopped **Nov. 7**.

**UN Nov. 5 established first international police** force to supervise truce in Middle East.

## 1957

**Britain set off its first hydrogen bomb** in Pacific test May 15.

**Soviet Union** announced **Aug. 26** that it had successfully tested an intercontinental ballistic missile.

**Sen. Strom Thurmond (D.-S.C.)** held Senate floor for 24 hrs. 18 mins. Aug. 28-29, eclipsing record filibuster of 22 hrs. 26 mins. set by Sen. Wayne Morse (D.-Ore.) in 1953.

**First underground nuclear explosion** set off by Atomic Energy Commission in Nevada Sept. 19.

**A Federal-state controversy** over admission of Negroes to the previously all-white Central High School in Little Rock, Ark., reached a showdown **Sept. 4** when National Guardsmen ordered out by Gov. Orval Faubus (D.) barred 9 Negro students from entering the school. A conference between Faubus and President Eisenhower brought no tangible result but Faubus complied **Sept. 21** with a Federal Court order to remove the National Guardsmen. The Negroes entered school **Sept. 23** but were ordered to withdraw by local authorities because of fear of mob violence. President Eisenhower sent Federal troops to Little Rock **Sept. 24** to enforce the Federal Court's order and the school began operation on an integrated basis.

**First man-made satellite, Sputnik I,** was launched by Soviet scientists Oct. 4. The 184-lb. sphere circled the earth about every 1½ hours in an elliptical orbit at altitudes ranging from some 140 miles to 560 miles above the earth. The Russians **Nov. 3** launched Sputnik II, weighing 1,120 lbs., carrying a live dog, Laika, as the world's first space passenger and orbiting the earth about every 103.7 minutes at altitudes ranging from some 160 miles to about 1,062 miles. Soviet authorities announced the dog's death **Nov. 10.** Sputnik I disintegrated **Jan. 4, 1958,** and Sputnik II **Apr. 14, 1958.**

## 1958

**First U. S. earth satellite** to go into orbit, Explorer I, launched by Army Jan. 31, Cape Canaveral, Fla.

**Gen. Charles de Gaulle** became French Premier **June 1,** averting threatened civil war; De Gaulle constitution, increasing power of executive, overwhelmingly adopted **Sept. 28.** De Gaulle elected **Dec. 21** as first president of 5th Republic.

**Arab nationalist rebels seized Iraqi** government **July 14,** killed King Faisal II and Premier Nuri as-Said, proclaimed republic. President Eisenhower sent U. S. Marines to Lebanon **July 15,** at Lebanese government's request, to forestall alleged effort by Soviet Union and United Arab Republic to engineer overthrow of Lebanon regime. Withdrawal of U. S. troops began **Aug. 12** after calm was restored.

**Jet airliner passenger service** across Atlantic was opened **Oct. 4** by British Overseas Airways Corp.

**First domestic jet airline passenger service** in U.S. opened by National Airlines **Dec. 10** between New York and Miami.

## 1959

**Fidel Castro assumed power** in Cuba following collapse of Fulgencio Batista's government Jan. 1.

**Lunik I** was launched by Soviet scientists Jan. 4, went into orbit around the sun as first man-made planet.

**St. Lawrence Seaway** opened **Apr. 25;** was dedicated **June 26** by President Eisenhower and Queen Elizabeth II.

**George Washington,** first U.S. ballistic-missile submarine, launched at Groton, Conn., **June 9.**

**N.S. Savannah,** world's first atomic-powered merchant ship, launched **July 21** at Camden, N. J.

**Lunik II hit the moon Sept. 13,** about 35 hours after launching by Soviet scientists.

**Soviet Premier Khrushchev** paid unprecedented visit to U.S. **Sept. 15-27,** made transcontinental tour, conferred with President Eisenhower.

**Lunik III launched Oct. 4** by Soviet scientists, circled moon and radioed to earth photographs of moon's other side.

## 1960

**First French** nuclear test explosion occurred **Feb. 13** in Sahara Desert.

**Caryl Chessman,** who had won 8 stays of execution since his 1948 conviction on robbery, kidnaping and attempted rape charges, was put to death **May 2** in the gas chamber at San Quentin Prison, near San Francisco.

**A U-2 reconnaissance plane** of the U. S., piloted by Francis Gary Powers, was shot down in the Soviet Union **May 1.** Soviet Premier Khrushchev refused to participate in the Paris summit conference scheduled for **May 16** unless President Eisenhower apologized for U-2 flights over the USSR; the Big Four leaders went to Paris but the conference did not take place. Powers was convicted of espionage in Moscow **Aug. 19** and sentenced to a 10-year term. Freed **Feb. 10, 1962,** in exchange for convicted Soviet spy Rudolf Abel, who was serving a 30-yr. term imposed by U. S. in 1957.

**Adolf Eichmann's capture** in Argentina by Israeli agents announced **May 22;** former Nazi SS general, accused of playing a major role in killing of mil-

lions of Jews. After 4-month trial in Jerusalem, sentenced by Israeli court **Dec. 15, 1961,** hanged for crimes against humanity **May 31, 1962.**

## 1961

**The United States** severed diplomatic and consular relations with Cuba Jan. 3.

**Patrice Lumumba,** ousted Premier of the Republic of the Congo, was murdered in the Congo's secessionist province of Katanga Jan. 17.

**Maj. Yuri Gagarin** of the Soviet Union became **Apr. 12** the first human space traveler; he was launched into orbit from Siberia in a spacecraft called Vostok I and returned to earth safely after one circuit of the globe. A second Soviet astronaut, **Maj. Gherman S. Titov,** made 17 orbits of the earth **Aug. 6-7** in spacecraft Vostok II and landed safely.

**An invasion of Cuba Apr. 17** by Cuban exiles attempting to overthrow the regime of Premier Fidel Castro was crushed.

**Commander Alan B. Shepard, Jr.,** was rocketed from Cape Canaveral, Fla., 116.5 miles above the earth in a Mercury capsule **May 5** in the first U. S. manned sub-orbital space flight; he landed safely in the Atlantic 302 miles away. **Capt. Virgil I. (Gus) Grissom** made a similar flight from Cape Canaveral **July 21;** he landed safely but his Mercury capsule sank and was lost after a hatch opened prematurely.

**East Germany closed** the border between East and West Berlin **Aug. 12-13** to stop the exodus of East Germans to the West; the East Germans built a wall dividing the city.

**Dag Hammarskjold,** Secy. Gen. of the United Nations, was killed in a plane crash near Ndola, Northern Rhodesia, **Sept. 18** while on a mission seeking a cease-fire between UN and Katanga forces in the Congo; U Thant of Burma was elected Acting Secy. Gen. **Nov. 3.**

**Nuclear blasts** of 25 megatons and over 50 megatons, largest man-made explosions to date, were set off by the Soviet Union Oct. 23 and Oct. 30, respectively, despite world protests.

## 1962

**Lt. Col. John H. Glenn, Jr.,** became the first American in orbit **Feb. 20** when he circled the earth 3 times in the Mercury capsule Friendship 7. **Lt. Comdr. M. Scott Carpenter** made a 3-orbit flight **May 24** in the Mercury capsule Aurora 7. **Comdr. Walter M. Schirra, Jr.,** orbited the earth 6 times **Oct. 3** in the Mercury capsule Sigma 7.

**A truce agreement Mar. 18** ended the 7-yr. Moslem revolt against French rule in Algeria, Algerians cast an overwhelming vote for independence in a referendum **July 1** and French President Charles de Gaulle declared the country independent **July 3.**

**The U. S. Supreme Court** ruled in a 6-1 decision **June 25** that the reciting of an official prayer in the public schools of New York State was unconstitutional.

**The third Soviet astronaut** was sent into orbit **Aug. 11** and the fourth followed him into a nearly identical orbit **Aug. 12,** both descending to earth safely **Aug. 15.** They were **Maj. Andrian G. Nikolayev,** who made a record 64 orbits of the earth, and **Lt. Col. Pavel R. Popovich,** who made 48 orbits. They said they were close enough at times to see each other.

**The largest cash robbery** to date in U. S. history occurred **Aug. 14** when a gang held up a U. S. mail truck near Plymouth, Mass., and stole $1,551,277.

**A Soviet offensive buildup** in Cuba was revealed to the American people **Oct. 22** by President Kennedy, who ordered a naval and air quarantine on shipment of offensive military equipment to the island. President Kennedy and Soviet Premier Khrushchev reached agreement **Oct. 28** on a formula to end the crisis, and the President said **Nov. 2** that Soviet missile bases in Cuba were being dismantled.

## 1963

**U. S. Air Force Maj. Leroy Gordon Cooper** orbited the earth 22 times **May 15-16** in the final and longest flight of Project Mercury. Because of failure of automatic equipment, Cooper had to control the craft manually in the closing minutes of the flight.

**Lt. Col. Valery F. Bykovsky** was launched into orbit in Vostok V **June 14,** the 5th Soviet astronaut to enter space. While Bykovsky was still circling the earth, the first woman space traveler, Soviet Jr. Lt. **Valentina V. Tereshkova,** was launched into orbit in Vostok VI **June 16.** Both landed safely by parachute **June 19,** the man after 81 orbits and the woman after 48.

**The U. S. Supreme Court** ruled, 8-1, **June 17** that state and local regulations requiring recitation of the Lord's Prayer or Bible verses in public schools were unconstitutional.

**A limited nuclear test-ban treaty** was agreed upon **July 25** by the United States, the Soviet Union and Britain, barring all nuclear tests except those conducted underground. It became formally effective **Oct. 10.**

**Dr. Stephen Ward**, British osteopath, was convicted in London **July 31** of living off the earnings of prostitution by **Christine Keeler** and **Marilyn Rice-Davies**. The case grew out of the scandal involving **John Profumo**, former Secy. of State for War, which had rocked the government of British Prime Minister Harold Macmillan. A few hours before the verdict, Ward was found in a coma from an overdose of drugs. His death **Aug. 3** was ruled a suicide.

**The biggest robbery to date** occurred **Aug. 8** when an armed holdup gang stole more than $7,000,000 (£2,500,000) in currency from a mail train near Cheddington, England. Some of the money was recovered and a dozen men were sentenced to long prison terms.

**Washington demonstration** by 200,000 persons **Aug. 28** in support of Negro demands for equal rights. Highlight was speech in which Dr. Martin Luther King said: "I have a dream that this nation will rise up and live out the true meaning of its creed, 'We hold these truths to be self evident: that all men are created equal.'"

**Quintuplets, all boys**, were born **Sept. 7** to **Mr. and Mrs. Efren Lubin Prieto** in Maracaibo, Venezuela. Quintuplets, 4 girls and a boy, were born **Sept. 14** to **Mr. and Mrs. Andrew Fischer** in Aberdeen, S. D. Only two sets of quintuplets born previously in the Western Hemisphere had survived infancy—the Dionnes, born in Canada in 1934, and the Diligentis, born in Argentina in 1943.

**The South Vietnamese** government of President Ngo Dinh Diem was overthrown **Nov. 1-2** in a coup by the armed forces. Diem and his brother, secret police chief Ngo Dinh Nhu, were captured and killed.

**John F. Kennedy**, 35th President of the United States, was shot and fatally wounded by an assassin **Nov. 22** as he rode in a motorcade through downtown Dallas, Tex. **Texas Gov. John B. Connally, Jr.**, riding in the same car, was also shot but not fatally injured. Vice President Lyndon B. Johnson was inaugurated President shortly afterward in Dallas. Lee Harvey Oswald, 24, was arrested and charged with the murder of the President. Oswald was shot and fatally wounded **Nov. 24** by **Jack Ruby**, 52, a Dallas night club owner, who was convicted of murder **Mar. 14, 1964**, and was sentenced to death. The murder conviction was reversed by the Texas Court of Criminal appeals. Ruby died of natural causes **Jan. 3, 1967**, while awaiting re-trial.

### 1964

**Pope Paul VI** toured the Holy Land **Jan. 4-6**, the first pope to visit there since the birth of Christianity, the first pope to travel by air, and the first to leave Italy in over 150 years.

**Three civil rights** workers were reported missing in Mississippi **June 22**. The bodies of Michael Schwerner, Andrew Goodman and James E. Chaney were found buried near Philadelphia, Miss., **Aug. 4**. Twenty-one white men were arrested. On **Oct. 20, 1967**, an all-white Federal jury convicted 7 who took part in the Ku Klux Klan conspiracy to murder the 3 young men.

**U. S. spacecraft Ranger 7** relayed thousands of close-up pictures of the moon back to earth **July 31** before crashing on the lunar surface.

**U. S. planes bombed** North Vietnamese bases and sank or damaged 25 North Vietnamese patrol boats **Aug. 4** in retaliation against North Vietnamese attacks on U. S. destroyers in the Gulf of Tonkin.

**The Warren Commission** released **Sept. 27** a report containing the conclusion that **Lee Harvey Oswald** was solely responsible for the killing of President Kennedy.

**A spacecraft** carrying 3 men was launched by the Soviet Union **Oct. 12**, the first spacecraft occupied by more than one person. The Voskhod (Sunrise) returned to earth safely **Oct. 13** after 16 orbits of the earth. Its passengers were Col. V. M. Komarov, a cosmonaut; Dr. B. B. Yegerov, a space physician; and K. P. Feoktistov, a scientist.

**Soviet Premier Khrushchev** was ousted as premier and Soviet Communist party chief **Oct. 14-15**. Aleksei N. Kosygin replaced him as premier and Leonid I. Brezhnev took over the party leadership.

**Communist China** conducted a successful test explosion of its first atomic bomb **Oct. 16**.

### 1965

**U. S. bombed North Vietnam, Feb. 7**, after Vietcong guerrillas attacked American installations at Pleiku, **Feb. 6**.

**Lt. Col. Aleksei A. Leonov**, stepping out of Soviet spaceship Voskhod 2, became the first man to "walk in space," **March 18**. **Maj. Edward H. White**, in U. S. spaceship Gemini 4, repeated the Russian feat and remained outside the ship for 20 minutes, **June 3**. On **Dec. 4**, Air Force Lt. Col. Frank Borman and Navy Comdr. James A. Lovell Jr., orbited in Gemini 7, stayed aloft 14 days and participated in first manned space rendezvous **Dec. 15** when Gemini 6, with Navy Capt. Walter M. Schirra, Jr., and Air Force Maj. Thomas P. Stafford, came within 10 ft. of Gemini 7.

**A Selma to Montgomery, Ala.**, civil rights march was led by Dr. Martin Luther King, **March 21-25**. The marchers, starting with 3,200 and swelling to 25,000, were guarded along the way by 4,000 troops dispatched by President Johnson.

**U. S. armed forces** sent to Dominican Republic to protect U. S. citizens and prevent a Communist revolution, **Apr. 28**. Later, **May 23**, the Organization of American States set up a peace-keeping force to maintain order.

**Los Angeles riot by discontented Negroes** living in the Watts area resulted in the death of 35 persons and property damage estimated at $200,000,000, **Aug. 11-16**.

**Pope Paul VI** visited N. Y. City **Oct. 4** and delivered a personal appeal for peace to the UN. It was the first time a Pope had come to America.

**Massive electric power failure** blacked out most of Northeastern U. S. plus parts of 2 Canadian provinces the night of **Nov. 9-10**. Approximately 80,000 sq. miles with a population of 30,000,000 were affected. In N. Y. City, over 800,000 were trapped in the subways for hours.

**Independence proclaimed in Rhodesia** by minority white regime, **Nov. 11**. Britain promptly declared the action illegal and announced the application of economic sanctions.

### 1966

**First soft landing on surface of moon** by an unmanned spacecraft **Feb. 3**, USSR Luna 9. U. S. achieved similar feat **June 2** with Surveyor 1.

**Kwame Nkrumah**, president of Ghana since independence in 1957, was overthrown **Feb. 24**.

**France** withdrew all its armed forces from the integrated NATO military alliance **July 1**.

**Medicare**, government program to pay part of the medical expenses of citizens over 65, went into effect **July 1**.

**Eight student nurses** were slain in a Chicago apartment building **July 14**. Richard Speck, 24, was convicted of the killings **Apr. 15, 1967**.

**A sniper atop** the University of Texas tower in Austin, Tex., shot 44 persons **Aug. 1**, killing 14 of them including an unborn child. Shot to death by police, the sniper was identified as Charles J. Whitman, 25, an honor student at the university. Police later found the bodies of his wife and his mother, whom he apparently had slain the night before.

**U. S. spacecraft Gemini 11** docked with a 26-foot Agena-D target vehicle **Sept. 12**.

**President Johnson** met with the leaders of 6 U. S. allies at the Manila Conference, Philippines, **Oct. 24-25** to discuss the war in Vietnam.

**Edward Brooke** (R., Mass.) elected **Nov. 8** as first Negro U. S. Senator in 85 years.

### 1967

**Fire aboard spacecraft Apollo I** on the ground at Cape Kennedy, Fla., **Jan. 27** killed Virgil I. Grissom, 40, one of first 7 Mercury astronauts; Edward H. White, 2d, 36, first American to "walk" in space; and Roger B. Chaffee, 31. First U. S. astronauts killed in space tests.

**Nat'l Student Assn.** disclosed **Feb. 13** it had secretly received over $3,000,000 from Central Intelligence Agency, 1952-1966, for use in exchange and other overseas programs. State Dept. admitted **Feb. 14** CIA support for NSA designed to counter Communist student activities.

**Rep. Adam Clayton Powell** (D., N. Y.) was denied **Mar. 1** his seat in 90th Congress because House of Representatives charged him with misuse of Govt. funds and nepotism. He won **Apr. 11** special election to fill vacancy despite not campaigning in Harlem, where he faced possible arrest in a civil suit, but did not take seat.

**In 6-day Israeli-Arab war June 5-10**, Israel smashed armed forces of United Arab Republic, Syria and Jordan; Israel conquered territory 4 times its own size.

**Sen. Thomas J. Dodd** (D., Conn.) censured by Senate **June 23** by 92-5 vote for using campaign and testimonial funds "for his personal benefit."

**President Johnson and Soviet Premier Aleksei N. Kosygin** met **June 23** and **25** for 10 hrs. of talks at Glassboro State College in N. J. Although neither changed opposing positions on Israeli-Arab crisis, Vietnam or nuclear weapons, both agreed not to let any crisis push them into nuclear war.

**Racial riots** in Newark, N. J., **July 12-17** killed some 26, injured 1,500, over 1,000 arrested. In Detroit, Mich., **July 23-30** at least 40 died, 2,000 injured and 5,000 left homeless by rioting, looting and burning in city's Negro ghetto. Quelled by 4,700 Federal paratroopers and 8,000 National Guardsmen.

**Thurgood Marshall** sworn in **Oct. 2**; first Negro U. S. Supreme Court justice. **Nov. 7: Carl B. Stokes** (D., Cleveland) and **Richard G. Hatcher** (D., Gary, Ind.) elected first Negro mayors of major U. S. cities. **Robert G. Clark** first Negro elected to Mississippi Legislature since Reconstruction.

**Vietnam war** protested **Oct. 21-22** by some 35,000 in Washington, D. C., peace march. At least 647 arrested, most when attempting to enter Pentagon.

*For Events of 1968 see Chronology*

# EDUCATION
## AMERICAN COLLEGES AND UNIVERSITIES

STUDENT AND FACULTY FIGURES FOR SPRING TERM, 1968

Source: World Almanac questionnaires and U. S. Office of Education

*See Page 345 for typical tuition fees*

All coeducational unless name followed by: (M) for men only, or (W) for women only. Even though marked (M) or (W), some are coeducational at graduate level and in evening and summer divisions. (Med) nas medical school; (T) has teachers' college or education department. Asterisk (*) denotes land-grant college.

Governing official is president unless otherwise designated. Year is that of founding. The word college is part of the name listed unless another designation is given.

Control: C-county; D-religious denomination; Di-district; F-federal; I-interdenominational; Mu-municipal; P-private; Pr-proprietary; S-state; T-territorial govt.; Y-YMCA.

Each institution listed has an enrollment of at least 100 students of college grade. Number of teachers is the total number of individuals on teaching staff. Enrollment and faculty figures in italics include all branches and campuses.

## Senior Colleges

| Name | Location | Yr. | Governing Official and Control | | Students | Teachers |
|------|----------|-----|-------------------------------|---|----------|----------|
| Abilene Christian | Abilene, Tex. | 1906 | Don H. Morris | P | 2,936 | 172 |
| Adams State (T) | Alamosa, Colo. | 1921 | John A. Marvel | S | 2,500 | 125 |
| Adelphi Univ. | Garden City, N. Y. | 1896 | R. G. Olmsted (Act.) | P | 8,668 | 275 |
| Adrian | Adrian, Mich. | 1859 | John H. Dawson | D | 1,442 | 108 |
| Agnes Scott (W) | Decatur, Ga. | 1889 | Wallace M. Alston | P | 750 | 95 |
| Air Force Inst. of Tech. (M) | Wright-Patters, AFB, Ohio. | 1919 | Maj. Gen. E. Pinson | F | 713 | 202 |
| Akron, Univ. of (T) | Akron, Ohio | 1870 | Norman P. Auburn | Mu | 12,878 | 702 |
| Alabama A. & M. | Normal, Ala. | 1875 | Richard D. Morrison | S | 2,400 | 116 |
| Alabama College | Montevallo, Ala. | 1896 | Kermit A. Johnson | S | 2,200 | 115 |
| Alabama State (T) | Montgomery, Ala. | 1874 | Levi Watkins | S | 1,862 | 87 |
| Alabama, Univ. of (T) (Med.) | University, Ala. | 1831 | Frank A. Rose | S | 18,870 | 1,596 |
| Alaska, Methodist Univ. (T) | Anchorage, Alaska | 1960 | Fred P. McGinnis | D | 656 | 55 |
| Alaska, Univ. of* | College, Alaska. | 1917 | William R. Wood | S | 1,828 | 399 |
| Albany State (T) | Albany, Ga. | 1903 | Thomas M. Jenkins | S | 1,375 | 82 |
| Albertus Magnus (W) | New Haven, Conn. | 1925 | Sister Marie Louise | D | 687 | 61 |
| Albion | Albion, Mich. | 1835 | Louis W. Norris | D | 1,654 | 130 |
| Albright | Reading, Pa. | 1856 | Arthur Schultz | D | 1,358 | 111 |
| Albuquerque, Univ. of | Albuquerque, N. M. | 1940 | Sis. M. Marilyn Doiron | D | 1,390 | 97 |
| Alcorn A. & M.* (T) | Lorman, Miss. | 1871 | John D. Boyd | S | 2,290 | 91 |
| Alderson-Broaddus (T) | Philippi, W. Va. | 1871 | Richard E. Shearer | D | 809 | 46 |
| Alfred Univ. | Alfred, N. Y. | 1836 | Leland Miles | S, P | 1,598 | 151 |
| Allegheny | Meadville, Pa. | 1815 | Lawrence L. Pelletier | P | 1,520 | 115 |
| Allen Univ. | Columbia, S. C. | 1870 | J. W. Hairston (Act.) | D | 957 | 57 |
| Alliance | Cambridge Spgs., Pa. | 1912 | Henry J. Parcinski | P | 602 | 44 |
| Alma | Alma, Mich. | 1886 | Robert D. Swanson | D | 1,078 | 70 |
| Alvernia (W) | Reading, Pa. | 1958 | Sis. M. Zygmunta | P | 236 | 22 |
| Alverno (T) (W) | Milwaukee, Wis. | 1936 | Sister M. Augustine | D | 1,391 | 106 |
| American Conservatory of Music. | Chicago, Ill. | 1886 | John R. Hattstaedt | P | 436 | 97 |
| Amer. Inst. for Foreign Trade.. | Phoenix, Ariz. | 1946 | Arthur L. Peterson | P | 515 | 60 |
| American International (T) | Springfield, Mass. | 1885 | R. Adm. John F. Hines. | P | 2,744 | 114 |
| American Univ. (T) | Washington, D. C. | 1893 | George H. Williams | P | 14,779 | 728 |
| Amherst (M) | Amherst, Mass. | 1821 | Calvin H. Plimpton | P | 1,204 | 137 |
| Anderson | Anderson, Ind. | 1917 | Robert H. Reardon | D | 1,447 | 85 |
| Andrews Univ. | Berrien Spgs., Mich. | 1874 | Richard Hammill | D | 1,480 | 125 |
| Angelo State (T) | San Angelo, Texas | 1928 | Lloyd Vincent | Mu | 2,493 | 106 |
| Anna Maria (T) (W) | Paxton, Mass. | 1946 | Sister Irene Marie | D | 635 | 55 |
| Annhurst (T) (W) | Woodstock, Conn. | 1941 | Sister Cecile | D | 398 | 40 |
| Antioch | Yellow Spgs., Ohio. | 1852 | James P. Dixon, Jr. | P | 1,845 | 145 |
| Appalachian St. Teachers (T) | Boone, N. C. | 1903 | William H. Plemmons. | S | 3,947 | 218 |
| Aquinas (T) | Grand Rapids, Mich. | 1922 | Msgr. A. F. Bukowski. | S | 1,500 | 105 |
| Arizona State Univ. (T) | Tempe, Ariz. | 1885 | G. Homer Durham | S | 21,037 | 1,432 |
| Arizona, Univ. of* (T) (Med.) | Tucson, Ariz. | 1885 | Richard A. Harvill | S | 21,284 | 1,831 |
| Arkansas A. & M. | College Hghts., Ark. | 1909 | Claude H. Babin | S | 1,664 | 83 |
| Ark. Agric., Mech. & Normal*. | Pine Bluff, Ark. | 1873 | Lawrence A. Davis | S | 2,785 | 152 |
| Arkansas College | Batesville, Ark. | 1872 | Paul M. McCain | D | 285 | 27 |
| Arkansas Polytechnic (T) | Russellville, Ark. | 1910 | George Pratt | S | 2,293 | 103 |
| Arkansas State Univ. (T) | State Univ., Ark. | 1909 | Carl R. Reng | S | 6,118 | 252 |
| Arkansas, State Coll. of (T) | Conway, Ark. | 1907 | Silas D. Snow | S | 3,556 | 127 |
| Arkansas, Univ. of* (T) (Med.) | Fayetteville, Ark. | 1871 | David W. Mullins | S | 9,823 | 547 |
| Armstrong | Berkeley, Calif. | 1918 | John E. Armstrong | Pr | 400 | 30 |
| Armstrong State (T) | Savannah, Ga. | 1935 | Henry L. Ashmore | S | 1,500 | 83 |
| Aroostook State (T) | Presque Isle, Me. | 1903 | Clifford Wieden | S | 450 | 28 |
| Art Center Coll. of Design | Los Angeles, Calif. | 1930 | Edward A. Adams | P | 1,030 | 93 |
| Art Institute of Chicago | Chicago, Ill. | 1866 | Vacant. | P | 685 | 83 |
| Asbury | Wilmore, Ky. | 1890 | C. R. Hager (Act.) | P | 1,039 | 67 |
| Asheville Biltmore | Asheville, No. Car. | 1927 | William E. Highsmith. | S | 671 | 54 |
| Ashland (T) | Ashland, Ohio. | 1878 | Glenn L. Clayton | D | 2,397 | 184 |
| Athenaeum of Ohio (M) | Norwood, Ohio. | 1829 | Msgr. R. H. Tensing. | D | 482 | 54 |
| Atlanta Univ. | Atlanta, Ga. | 1865 | Vacant. | P | 1,010 | 105 |
| Atlantic Christian (T) | Wilson, N. C. | 1902 | Arthur D. Wenger | D | 1,040 | 93 |
| Atlantic Union | So. Lancaster, Mass. | 1882 | H. E. Douglass | D | 889 | 79 |
| Auburn Univ.* (T) | Auburn, Ala. | 1856 | Harry Philpott | S | 12,250 | 830 |
| Augsburg (T) | Minneapolis, Minn. | 1869 | Oscar A. Anderson | D | 1,676 | 110 |
| Augusta | Augusta, Ga. | 1910 | Gerald B. Robins | S | 2,285 | 128 |
| Augustana (T) | Rock Island, Ill. | 1860 | C. W. Sorensen | D | 1,833 | 124 |
| Augustana | Sioux Falls, S. Dak. | 1860 | Charles L. Balcer | D | 1,888 | 135 |
| Aurora (T) | Aurora, Ill. | 1893 | James E. Crimi | D | 1,204 | 88 |
| Austin | Sherman, Tex. | 1849 | John D. Moseley | D | 972 | 96 |
| Austin Peay State Univ. (T) | Clarksville, Tenn. | 1929 | Joe Morgan | S | 2,779 | 131 |
| Austin Presby. Theol. Sem. | Austin, Tex. | 1902 | David L. Stitt | D | 127 | 14 |
| Avila (W) | Kansas City, Mo. | 1916 | Sis. Olive Louise | D | 390 | 41 |
| Azusa Pacific | Azusa, Calif. | 1899 | Cornelius Haggard | D | 790 | 57 |
| Babson Inst. (M) | Babson Park, Mass. | 1919 | Henry A. Kriebel | P | 1,004 | 50 |
| Baker Univ. | Baldwin City, Kan. | 1858 | James E. Doty | D | 1,046 | 71 |
| Baldwin-Wallace | Berea, Ohio. | 1845 | Alfred B. Bonds, Jr. | D | 2,668 | 174 |
| Ball State Univ. (T) | Muncie, Ind. | 1918 | John Emens | S | 13,687 | 615 |
| Baltimore Coll. of Commerce | Baltimore, Md. | 1909 | William Donahoo | Y | 950 | 57 |

319

| Name | Location | Yr. | Governing Official and Control | | Students | Teachers |
|------|----------|-----|-------------------------------|---|----------|----------|
| Baptist Bible Sem............ | Johnson City, N. Y.... | 1932 | G. Arthur Woolsey..... | D | 513 | 24 |
| Barat Coll. of the Sacred Heart (W) | Lake Forest, Ill...... | 1918 | Mother Margaret Burke | D | 652 | 52 |
| Bard........................ | Annandale, N. Y...... | 1860 | Reamer Kline......... | P | 557 | 59 |
| Barnard (a)................. | New York, N. Y...... | 1889 | Martha E. Peterson.... | P | 1,847 | 167 |
| Barrington................. | Barrington, R. I...... | 1900 | Charles Hummel....... | P | 631 | 42 |
| Barry..................(W) | Miami, Fla.......... | 1940 | Sister M. Dorothy..... | D | 1,122 | 102 |
| Bates...................... | Lewiston, Me........ | 1864 | Thomas H. Reynolds... | P | 975 | 67 |
| Baylor Univ........ (T) (Med.) | Waco, Tex.......... | 1845 | Abner V. McCall...... | D | 6,258 | 360 |
| Beaver..................(W) | Glenside, Pa........ | 1853 | Edward D. Gates...... | P | 807 | 81 |
| Belhaven................... | Jackson, Miss....... | 1883 | Howard J. Cleland..... | D | 552 | 50 |
| Belknap.................... | Center Harbor, N. H. | 1963 | Royal M. Frye........ | P | 440 | 41 |
| Bellarmine-Ursuline......... | Louisville, Ky...... | 1950 | Rt. Rev. A. F. Horrigan | D | *2,064* | *159* |
| Belmont Abbey...........(T) | Belmont, N. C...... | 1876 | V. Rev. Jude Cleary... | D | 852 | 67 |
| Belmont.................(T) | Nashville, Tenn..... | 1951 | Herbert C. Gabhart... | P | 1,060 | 62 |
| Beloit..................... | Beloit, Wis......... | 1846 | Miller Upton......... | P | 1,482 | 122 |
| Bemidji State.............. | Bemidji, Minn....... | 1918 | John Glas (Act.)...... | S | 3,800 | 230 |
| Benedict................... | Columbia, S. C...... | 1870 | Benjamin F. Payton... | D | 1,181 | 68 |
| Benjamin Franklin Univ..... | Washington, D. C.... | 1925 | C. A. Kennedy....... | Pr | 1,200 | 50 |
| Bennett................(T) (W) | Greensboro, N. C.... | 1873 | Isaac H. Miller....... | D | 662 | 67 |
| Bennington................ | Bennington, Vt...... | 1932 | Edward J. Bloustein... | P | 420 | 60 |
| Bentley................... | Boston, Mass........ | 1917 | T. L. Morison........ | P | 1,995 | 114 |
| Berea..................(T) | Berea, Ky.......... | 1855 | W. D. Weatherford, Jr. | P | 1,364 | 121 |
| Berry..................... | Mount Berry, Ga.... | 1902 | John R. Bertrand..... | D | 1,074 | 69 |
| Bethany Bible............. | Santa Cruz, Calif.... | 1919 | Cordas C. Burnett.... | D | 458 | 32 |
| Bethany College.......(T) | Lindsborg, Kan...... | 1881 | Alvin Hahn.......... | D | 503 | 41 |
| Bethany College.......... | Bethany, W. Va..... | 1840 | Perry E. Gresham..... | P | 1,091 | 70 |
| Bethany Nazarene......... | Bethany, Okla...... | 1899 | Roy H. Cantrell...... | D | 2,080 | 83 |
| Bethel.................(T) | Mishawaka, Ind..... | 1947 | Rev. R. P. Pannabecker. | P | 480 | 50 |
| Bethel................... | North Newton, Kan.. | 1887 | Orville L. Voth...... | D | 535 | 51 |
| Bethel.................(T) | McKenzie, Tenn..... | 1842 | Roy N. Baker........ | D | 804 | 54 |
| Bethel.................(T) | St. Paul, Minn...... | 1871 | Carl Lundquist....... | D | 976 | 88 |
| Bethune-Cookman......... | Daytona Beach, Fla.. | 1923 | Richard V. Moore..... | P | 987 | 57 |
| Biola.................(T) | La Mirada, Calif.... | 1907 | Samuel H. Sutherland.. | D | 1,235 | 87 |
| Birmingham-Southern...... | Birmingham, Ala.... | 1856 | *Vacant*............. | P | 1,005 | 82 |
| Bishop.................(T) | Dallas, Tex........ | 1881 | Milton K. Curry...... | D | 1,340 | 88 |
| Black Hills State........ | Spearfish, S. Dak... | 1883 | M. M. Freeman...... | S | *2,527* | *128* |
| Blackburn................ | Carlinville, Ill..... | 1857 | Glenn L. McConagha.. | P | 485 | 33 |
| Bliss.................... | Columbus, Ohio..... | 1899 | Gerald J. Wickham... | Pr | 550 | 40 |
| Bloomfield............... | Bloomfield, N. J.... | 1868 | Theodore A. Rath.... | D | 1,376 | 73 |
| Bloomsburg State......... | Bloomsburg, Pa..... | 1839 | Harvey A. Andruss.... | S | 3,531 | 210 |
| Blue Mountain........(W) | Blue Mountain, Miss. | 1873 | E. Harold Fisher..... | D | 349 | 32 |
| Bluefield State.......... | Bluefield, W. Va.... | 1895 | Wendell G. Hardway... | S | 2,876 | 61 |
| Bluffton................ | Bluffton, Ohio..... | 1900 | Robert S. Kreider.... | D | 733 | 60 |
| Bob Jones Univ.......... | Greenville, S. C.... | 1927 | Bob Jones, Jr........ | P | 3,264 | 216 |
| Boise................... | Boise, Idaho....... | 1932 | John Barnes......... | D1 | 4,903 | 252 |
| Borromeo Seminary....(M) | Wickliffe, Ohio..... | 1954 | Rt. Rev. R. C. Wolff.. | D | 198 | 17 |
| Boston.................. | Chestnut Hill, Mass. | 1863 | Rev. W. Seavey Joyce.. | D | *9,729* | *959* |
| Boston Conserv. of Music.. | Boston, Mass........ | 1867 | George Brambilla..... | P | 400 | 75 |
| Boston Univ.......(T) (Med) | Boston, Mass........ | 1869 | Arland F. Christ-Janer | P | 21,873 | 2,300 |
| Bowdoin...............(M) | Brunswick, Me...... | 1794 | A. P. Daggett (Act.).. | P | 900 | 99 |
| Bowie State............. | Bowie, Md......... | 1867 | Samuel L. Myers..... | S | 1,091 | 56 |
| Bowling Green State Univ.. (T) | Bowling Green, Ohio. | 1910 | William T. Jerome.... | S | *12,634* | *525* |
| Bradley Univ...........(T) | Peoria, Ill......... | 1897 | T. W. Van Arsdale.... | P | 5,649 | 425 |
| Brandeis Univ........... | Waltham, Mass...... | 1948 | Morris B. Abram..... | P | 1,921 | 374 |
| Brenau................(W) | Gainesville, Ga..... | 1878 | Josiah Crudup....... | P | 575 | 52 |
| Brescia...............(T) | Owensboro, Ky..... | 1925 | Sister J. Marie Lechner. | D | 1,075 | 89 |
| Briar Cliff............(W) | Sioux City, Iowa.... | 1930 | Sister Mary Jordan... | D | 1,02 | 87 |
| Briarcliff............(W) | Briarcliff Manor, N. Y. | 1903 | Charles Adkins...... | P | 640 | 60 |
| Bridgeport Eng. Inst...... | Bridgeport, Conn.... | 1924 | Arthur E. Keating.... | P | 555 | 91 |
| Bridgeport, Univ. of...... | Bridgeport, Conn.... | 1927 | H. W. I. Littlefield... | P | 7,800 | 485 |
| Bridgewater............. | Bridgewater, Va.... | 1880 | Wayne F. Geisert..... | D | 863 | 67 |
| Brigham Young Univ....(T) | Provo, Utah....... | 1875 | Ernest L. Wilkinson.. | D | 21,378 | 950 |
| Brooklyn Law Sch........ | Brooklyn, N. Y..... | 1901 | Leonard P. Moore.... | P | 1,153 | 28 |
| Brown Univ............. | Providence, R. I.... | 1764 | Ray L. Heffner...... | P | 2,587 | 1,114 |
| Pembroke............(W) | Providence, R. I.... | 1891 | Rosemary Pierrel (Dn.) | P | 967 | (b) |
| Bryan.................(T) | Dayton, Tenn...... | 1930 | Theodore C. Mercer... | P | 304 | 25 |
| Bryant.................(T) | Providence, R. I.... | 1863 | E. Gardner Jacobs.... | P | 2,500 | 102 |
| Bryn Mawr............(W) | Bryn Mawr, Pa..... | 1885 | Katherine E. McBride. | P | 1,252 | 174 |
| Bucknell Univ........... | Lewisburg, Pa...... | 1846 | C. H. Watts......... | P | 2,692 | 220 |
| Buena Vista............(T) | Storm Lake, Iowa... | 1891 | Wendell Q. Halverson. | D | 993 | 59 |
| Butler Univ...........(T) | Indianapolis, Ind.... | 1855 | Alexander E. Jones... | D | 4,350 | 250 |
| Caldwell Coll. for Women (T) (W) | Caldwell, N. J..... | 1939 | Sister Marguerite.... | D | 650 | 59 |
| California Baptist........ | Riverside, Calif..... | 1950 | Loyed R. Simmons.... | D | 583 | 45 |
| Calif. Coll. of Arts and Crafts... | Oakland, Calif...... | 1907 | Harry Xavier Ford... | P | 1,021 | 77 |
| California College of Medicine... | Los Angeles, Calif... | 1914 | W. Ballentine Henley.. | P | 315 | 584 |
| Calif. Coll. of Podiatric Medicine | San Francisco, Calif.. | 1914 | Pierce Nelson........ | P | 181 | 25 |
| Calif. Inst. of Tech......(M) | Pasadena, Calif..... | 1891 | Lee DuBridge....... | P | 1,457 | 600 |
| Calif. Maritime Academy..(M) | Vallejo, Calif...... | 1929 | R. Adm. F. T. Williamson (Supt.)...... | S | 248 | 25 |
| California State........... | California, Pa...... | 1852 | Michael Duda....... | S | 4,420 | 300 |
| Calif. State...........(T) | Dominguez Hills, Cal. | 1960 | Leo F. Cain......... | S | 545 | 55 |
| Calif. State...........(T) | Fullerton, Calif..... | 1959 | William B. Langsdorf.. | P | 9,177 | 542 |
| Calif. State...........(T) | Hayward, Calif..... | 1959 | Fred Harcleroad..... | S | 6,400 | 400 |
| Calif. State...........(T) | Long Beach, Calif... | 1949 | Carl W. McIntosh.... | S | 24,243 | 1,297 |
| Calif. State...........(T) | Los Angeles, Calif... | 1947 | J. A. Greenlee...... | S | 20,000 | 1,000 |
| Calif. State............. | San Bernardino, Calif. | 1962 | John Pfau.......... | S | 850 | 70 |
| Calif. State Polytechnic.... | San Luis Obispo, Calif. | 1901 | Robert Kennedy..... | S | 8,079 | 470 |
| California, Univ. of*...... | Berkeley, Calif..... | 1868 | Charles J. Hitch..... | S | *94,241* | *8,302* |
| Berkeley Campus......(T) | Berkeley, Calif..... | 1868 | Roger W. Heyns (Chan.) | S | 27,749 | 1,764 |
| Davis Campus......(Med) | Davis, Calif........ | 1908 | Emil M. Mrak (Chan.) | S | 9,800 | 1,770 |
| Irvine Campus.......(Med.) | Irvine, Calif....... | 1965 | D. G. Aldrich (Chan.). | S | 2,600 | 252 |
| L. Angeles Campus .(T) (Med.) | Los Angeles, Calif... | 1919 | *Vacant*............ | S | 28,000 | 1,370 |
| Riverside Campus....... | Riverside, Calif..... | 1954 | Ivan Hinderaker (Chan.) | S | 8,000 | 602 |
| San Diego Campus....(Med) | La Jolla, Calif..... | 1912 | J. S. Galbraith (Chan.) | S | 2,083 | 255 |
| San Francisco Campus..(Med) | San Francisco, Calif.. | 1864 | W. C. Fleming (Chan.) | S | 2,184 | 1,089 |
| Santa Barbara Campus...(T) | Santa Barbara, Calif. | 1891 | Vernon Cheadle (Chan.) | S | 12,000 | 1,050 |
| Santa Cruz Campus...... | Santa Cruz, Calif.... | 1965 | D. E. McHenry...... | S | 1,825 | 150 |
| California Western Univ.... | San Diego, Calif.... | 1952 | William C. Rust..... | D | 1,714 | 105 |
| Calvary Bible............ | Kansas City, Mo.... | 1932 | Roger J. Andrus..... | P | 367 | 19 |
| Calvin.................(T) | Grand Rapids, Mich. | 1876 | William Spoelhof..... | D | *3,269* | *173* |
| Cameron State Agricultural.. | Lawton, Okla...... | 1909 | Richard Birch....... | S | 2,676 | 112 |
| Campbell..............(T) | Buies Creek, N. C... | 1887 | Norman A. Wiggins... | D | 2,212 | 116 |

(a) Affiliated with Columbia Univ.    (b) Faculty of Brown Univ. teaches at Pembroke.

| Name | Location | Yr. | Governing Official and Control | | Stu dents | Teach ers |
|---|---|---|---|---|---|---|
| Campbellsville............(T) | Campbellsville, Ky... | 1906 | J. K. Powell.......... | D | 957 | 59 |
| Canisius.................... | Buffalo, N. Y........ | 1870 | V. Rev. James Demske. | D | 3,418 | 220 |
| Capital Univ............... | Columbus, Ohio...... | 1850 | Harold L. Yochum.... | D | 1,866 | 128 |
| Cardinal Cushing.......(W) | Brookline, Mass...... | 1952 | Sister M. Madonna.... | D | 350 | 46 |
| Cardinal Glennon.......(M) | St. Louis, Mo........ | 1900 | V. Rev. F. A. Gaydos.. | D | 196 | 29 |
| Cardinal Stritch .......(T) (W) | Milwaukee, Wis..... | 1937 | Sister Mary Aquin.... | D | 600 | 63 |
| Carleton................... | Northfield, Minn..... | 1866 | John W. Nason........ | P | 1,364 | 145 |
| Carnegie-Mellon Univ..... | Pittsburgh, Pa....... | 1900 | H. Guyford Stever..... | P | 5,100 | 520 |
| Carroll.................... | Helena, Mont........ | 1909 | Msgr. A. M. Brown... | D | 985 | 65 |
| Carroll................(T) | Waukesha, Wis...... | 1846 | John T. Middaugh..... | D | 1,018 | 83 |
| Carson-Newman........(T) | Jefferson City, Tenn. | 1851 | D. Harley Fite........ | D | 1,677 | 115 |
| Carthage.................. | Kenosha, Wis........ | 1847 | Harold H. Lentz...... | D | 1,925 | 94 |
| Case W. Reserve U... (Med.) (T) | Cleveland, Ohio..... | 1826 | Robert W. Morse..... | P | 10,130 | 1,200 |
| Castleton State............ | Castleton, Vt........ | 1867 | Richard J. Dundas.... | S | 983 | 82 |
| Catawba................... | Salisbury, N. C...... | 1851 | M. L. Shotzberger .... | D | 1,031 | 81 |
| Cathedral Coll. of the Immaculate Conception.............(M) | Brooklyn, N. Y...... | 1914 | Msgr. J. J. Fleming .. | D | 244 | 27 |
| Catherine Spalding.....(W) | Louisville, Ky....... | 1920 | Sis. M. C. Fowler..... | D | 1,766 | 116 |
| Catholic Univ. of America. | Washington, D. C.... | 1887 | Rev. Whalen (Act.)... | D | 6,185 | 825 |
| Catholic Univ. of Puerto Rico (T) | Ponce, Puerto Rico... | 1948 | Rev. T. E. McCarrick.. | D | 6,056 | 382 |
| Cedar Crest............(W) | Allentown, Pa........ | 1867 | Pauline Tompkins .... | D | 636 | 50 |
| Cedarville.............(T) | Cedarville, Ohio..... | 1887 | James Jeremiah ...... | D | 822 | 50 |
| Centenary Coll. of Louisiana. (T) | S'hreveport, La...... | 1825 | Jack S. Wilkes....... | D | 1,465 | 104 |
| Central College............ | P'lla, Iowa.......... | 1853 | Arend D. Lubbers..... | D | 968 | 73 |
| Central Connecticut State...(T) | N'w Britain, Conn... | 1849 | E. Don James........ | S | 4,775 | 558 |
| Central Methodist.......(T) | F'yette, Mo......... | 1854 | Ralph L. Woodward... | D | 934 | 65 |
| Central Michigan Univ..... | Mt. Pleasant, Mich.. | 1892 | Judson W. Foust...... | S | 9,076 | 387 |
| Central Missouri State.....(T) | Warrensburg, Mo.... | 1871 | Warren C. Lovinger... | S | 11,080 | 522 |
| Central State Univ........ | Wilberforce, Ohio... | 1887 | Harry E. Groves...... | S | 2,048 | 110 |
| Central State............(T) | Edmond, Okla....... | 1891 | Garland Godfrey...... | S | 8,808 | 280 |
| Central Washington State...(T) | Ellensburg, Wash.... | 1891 | James E. Brooks...... | S | 4,756 | 330 |
| Central Wesleyan........(T) | Central, S. C........ | 1906 | R. C. Mullinax....... | D | 239 | 18 |
| Centre Coll. of Kentucky... | Danville, Ky........ | 1819 | Thomas A. Spragens... | D | 697 | 62 |
| Chadron State............. | Chadron, Nebr...... | 1911 | Edwin Nelson........ | S | 1,788 | 93 |
| Chaminade Coll. of Honolulu.... | Honolulu, Hawaii.... | 1955 | V. Rev. W. R. Ferree.. | D | 714 | 65 |
| Chapman.................. | Orange, Calif........ | 1861 | John L. Davis........ | D | 3,500 | 269 |
| Charleston, Coll. of........ | Charleston, S. C..... | 1770 | Walter Coppedge ..... | P | 442 | 34 |
| Chase (Salmon P.)......... | Cincinnati, Ohio..... | 1893 | C. N. Revelos (Act.) .. | Y | 198 | 16 |
| Chatham................(W) | Pittsburgh, Pa....... | 1869 | Edward D. Eddy...... | P | 669 | 70 |
| Chattanooga, Univ. of..... | Chattanooga, Tenn... | 1886 | William H. Masterson.. | P | 2,638 | 160 |
| Chestnut Hill...........(W) | Philadelphia, Pa..... | 1876 | Sister C. Frances..... | D | 640 | 78 |
| Cheyney State............. | Cheyney, Pa......... | 1837 | LeRoy B. Allen....... | S | 1,773 | 128 |
| Chicago Coll. of Osteopathy.... | Chicago, Ill......... | 1913 | Thaddeus Kawalek .... | P | 278 | 75 |
| Chicago Conservatory...... | Chicago, Ill......... | 1857 | Francois D'Albert..... | P | 192 | 71 |
| Chicago-Kent Coll. of Law..... | Chicago, Ill......... | 1887 | E. Douglas Schwantes. | P | 512 | 22 |
| Chicago State............. | Chicago, Ill......... | 1869 | Milton B. Byrd....... | S | 4,678 | 309 |
| Chicago, Univ. of..... (T) (Med) | Chicago, Ill......... | 1891 | Edward H. Levi...... | P | 9,846 | 1,080 |
| Chico State.............(T) | Chico, Calif......... | 1887 | Robert E. Hill....... | S | 7,528 | 505 |
| Christian Brothers.......(M) | Memphis, Tenn...... | 1871 | Brother L. M. Grande.. | D | 1,095 | 78 |
| Christian Theol. Seminary... | Indianapolis, Ind.... | 1924 | Beauford A. Norris.... | D | 233 | 25 |
| Church Coll. of Hawaii..... | Lale, Hawaii........ | 1955 | Owen Cook.......... | D | 1,014 | 66 |
| Cincinnati Bible Seminary... | Cincinnati, Ohio..... | 1924 | Woodrow W. Perry.... | D | 601 | 34 |
| Cincinnati, Univ. of... (T) (Med) | Cincinnati, Ohio..... | 1819 | Walter Langsam...... | Mu | 25,071 | 2,400 |
| Citadel, The (Military)....(M) | Charleston, S. C..... | 1842 | Gen. Hugh P. Harris.. | S | 2,300 | 140 |
| Claflin.................(T) | Orangeburg, S. C.... | 1869 | Hubert V. Manning... | D | 779 | 51 |
| Claremont Graduate Sch..... | Claremont, Calif..... | 1925 | Louis T. Benezet..... | P | 1,017 | 287 |
| Claremont Men's.........(M) | Claremont, Calif..... | 1946 | George Benson....... | P | 737 | 95 |
| Clarion State............. | Clarion, Pa.......... | 1867 | James Gemmell....... | S | 3,425 | 246 |
| Clark.................... | Atlanta, Ga......... | 1869 | Vivian Henderson..... | D | 1,040 | 84 |
| Clark, Univ............... | Worcester, Mass..... | 1887 | Frederick H. Jackson.. | P | 2,733 | 227 |
| Clarke.............. (T) (W) | Dubuque, Iowa...... | 1843 | Sister Mary Benedict.. | D | 1,106 | 93 |
| Clarkson Coll. of Tech..... | Potsdam, N. Y...... | 1896 | John W. Graham, Jr... | P | 2,472 | 168 |
| Cleary................... | Ypsilanti, Mich...... | 1883 | Donald Silkworth..... | P | 770 | 44 |
| Clemson Univ...........(T) | Clemson, S. C....... | 1893 | Robert C. Edwards.... | S | 6,057 | 713 |
| Cleveland Inst. of Art..... | Cleveland, Ohio..... | 1882 | Joseph McCullough ... | P | 1,300 | 56 |
| Cleveland Inst. of Music... | Cleveland, Ohio..... | 1920 | Victor Rabin (Dir.) ... | P | 200 | 125 |
| Cleveland-Marshall Law School.. | Cleveland, Ohio..... | 1897 | H. J. Oleck (Dn.) .... | P | 720 | 30 |
| Cleveland State Univ...... | Cleveland, Ohio..... | 1965 | Harold L. Enarson.... | S | 8,715 | 470 |
| Coe...................... | Cedar Rapids, Iowa.. | 1851 | Joseph E. McCabe..... | P | 1,300 | 88 |
| Coker Coll. for Women....(W) | Hartsville, S. C...... | 1908 | Fenton Keyes ....... | P | 350 | 32 |
| Colby.................... | Waterville, Me....... | 1813 | Robert E. L. Strider... | P | 1,479 | 134 |
| Colgate Rochester Div. School. | Rochester, N. Y...... | 1817 | Gene E. Bartlett...... | D | 182 | 23 |
| Colgate Univ............(M) | Hamilton, N. Y...... | 1819 | Vincent M. Barnett... | P | 1,923 | 169 |
| Colorado.................. | Colo. Spgs., Colo.... | 1874 | Lloyd E. Worner..... | P | 1,584 | 149 |
| Colorado Sch. of Mines..... | Golden, Colo........ | 1874 | Orlo E. Childs....... | S | 1,504 | 150 |
| Colorado State..........(T) | Greeley, Colo........ | 1890 | Darrell Holmes....... | S | 7,268 | 550 |
| Colorado State Univ.*...... | Fort Collins, Colo.... | 1870 | William E. Morgan.... | S | 13,100 | 950 |
| Colorado, Univ. of... (T) (Med) | Boulder, Colo....... | 1876 | J. R. Smiley......... | S | 26,252 | 2,324 |
| Denver Center........(T) | Denver, Colo........ | 1964 | J. R. Smiley......... | S | 7,007 | 334 |
| Colorado Springs Center . (T) | Colo. Springs, Colo... | 1964 | J. R. Smiley......... | S | 2,318 | 99 |
| Columbia College.......(W) | Columbia, S. C...... | 1854 | R. Wright Spears..... | D | 840 | 67 |
| Columbia Union........... | Takoma Park, Md.... | 1904 | Winton H. Beaven.... | D | 944 | 110 |
| Columbia Univ.......(T) (Med) | New York, N. Y..... | 1754 | Grayson Kirk........ | P | 16,275 | 4,183 |
| Teachers College (a)....... | New York, N. Y..... | 1888 | John H. Fischer...... | P | 5,199 | 403 |
| Concord................(T) | Athens, W. Va....... | 1872 | Joseph F. Marsh, Jr... | S | 1,622 | 101 |
| Concordia................. | Moorhead, Minn..... | 1891 | Joseph Knutson...... | D | 2,117 | 162 |
| Concordia.............(T) | St. Paul, Minn...... | 1893 | W. A. Poehler....... | D | 674 | 49 |
| Concordia Seminary....... | St. Louis, Mo....... | 1839 | Alfred Fuerbringer... | D | 699 | 53 |
| Concordia Senior........(M) | Fort Wayne, Ind..... | 1957 | Martin J. Neeb....... | D | 461 | 44 |
| Concordia Teachers......(T) | River Forest, Ill..... | 1864 | Martin L. Koehneke... | D | 1,316 | 100 |
| Concordia Teachers......(T) | Seward, Nebr........ | 1894 | W. Theophil Janzow... | D | 1,386 | 101 |
| Connecticut............... | New London, Conn... | 1911 | Charles Shain ....... | P | 1,533 | 169 |
| Connecticut, Univ. of*.... (Med) | Storrs, Conn........ | 1881 | Homer D. Babbidge, Jr. | S | 15,321 | 1,022 |
| Converse................. | Spartanburg, S. C.... | 1889 | Robert T. Coleman, Jr. | P | 750 | 75 |
| Cooper Union............. | New York, N. Y..... | 1859 | Richard F. Humphreys. | P | 1,248 | 164 |
| Coppin State............(T) | Baltimore, Md....... | 1900 | Parlett L. Moore..... | S | 720 | 43 |
| Cornell................... | Mt. Vernon, Iowa... | 1853 | Samuel Stumpf ...... | P | 925 | 110 |
| Cornell Univ.*........... (Med) | Ithaca, N. Y........ | 1865 | James A. Perkins.... | S, P | 14,259 | 3,809 |
| Corpus Christi, Univ. of.. (T) | Corpus Christi, Tex.. | 1947 | K. A. Maroney (Act.) .. | D | 648 | 38 |
| Cranbrook Academy of Art.... | Bloomfield Hills, Mich. | 1927 | Glen Paulsen........ | P | 123 | 12 |
| Creighton Univ.......... (Med) | Omaha, Nebr........ | 1878 | V. Rev. H. W. Linn... | D | 3,952 | 606 |
| Culver-Stockton........(T) | Canton, Mo......... | 1853 | Fred Helsabeck...... | D | 811 | 51 |

(a) Affiliated with Columbia University.

| Name | Location | Yr. | Governing Official and Control | | Students | Teachers |
|------|----------|-----|-------------------------------|---|----------|----------|
| Cumberland | Williamsburg, Ky. | 1889 | J. M. Boswell | D | 1,625 | 96 |
| Curry (T) | Milton, Mass. | 1879 | John S. Hafer | P | 699 | 52 |
| Curtis Institute of Music | Philadelphia, Pa. | 1924 | Mary C. Zimbalist | P | 113 | 35 |
| Dakota Wesleyan Univ. | Mitchell, S. Dak. | 1885 | Jack J. Early | D | 763 | 51 |
| Dallas, Univ. of | Dallas, Tex. | 1956 | Donald A. Cowan | D | 1,107 | 88 |
| Dana (T) | Blair, Nebr. | 1884 | C. Clifford Madsen | D | 901 | 52 |
| Dartmouth (M, Med) | Hanover, N. H. | 1760 | John S. Dickey | P | 3,101 | 329 |
| David Lipscomb | Nashville, Tenn. | 1891 | Athens C. Pullias | P | 1,905 | 96 |
| Davidson (M) | Davidson, N. C. | 1837 | *Vacant* | D | 1,000 | 83 |
| Davis and Elkins | Elkins, W. Va. | 1904 | Rev. G. E. Hermanson | D | 740 | 58 |
| Dayton, Univ. of | Dayton, Ohio | 1850 | V. Rev. R. A. Roesch | D | *9,623* | *528* |
| Defiance | Defiance, Ohio | 1850 | W. Noel Johnston | D | 1,091 | 68 |
| Delaware State* | Dover, Del. | 1891 | Luna I. Mishoe | S | 937 | 71 |
| Delaware, Univ. of* | Newark, Del. | 1833 | John Shirley (Act.) | S | 11,055 | 595 |
| Del. Valley Coll. of S. & A. (M) | Doylestown, Pa. | 1896 | James Work | D | 1,013 | 68 |
| Delta State | Cleveland, Miss. | 1924 | James M. Ewing | S | 2,321 | 109 |
| Denison Univ. (T) | Granville, Ohio | 1831 | *Vacant* | D | 1,824 | 147 |
| Denver, Univ. of | Denver, Colo. | 1864 | Maurice B. Mitchell | D | *8,000* | *590* |
| DePaul Univ. (T) | Chicago, Ill. | 1898 | V. Rev. J. R. Cortelyou | D | *7,564* | *487* |
| DePauw Univ. | Greencastle, Ind. | 1837 | William E. Kerstetter | D | 2,340 | 197 |
| Detroit Bible | Detroit, Mich. | 1945 | W. A. Bevier (Act.) | P | 323 | 22 |
| Detroit Coll. of Business | Detroit, Mich. | 1962 | Frank Paone (Dn.) | Pr. | 1,000 | 43 |
| Detroit Coll. of Law | Detroit, Mich. | 1891 | John J. Danhof | P | 675 | 21 |
| Detroit Inst. of Technology | Detroit, Mich. | 1891 | Dewey F. Barich | P | 1,566 | 89 |
| Detroit, Univ. of | Detroit, Mich. | 1877 | V. Rev. M. Carron | D | *8,804* | *542* |
| Dickinson | Carlisle, Pa. | 1773 | Howard L. Rubendall | P | 1,510 | 110 |
| Dickinson Sch. of Law | Carlisle, Pa. | 1834 | Dale F. Shughart | P | 270 | 20 |
| Dickinson State (T) | Dickinson, N. Dak. | 1918 | O. A. DeLong | S | 1,170 | 72 |
| Dillard Univ. | New Orleans, La. | 1930 | Albert W. Dent | P | 944 | 67 |
| Doane | Crete, Nebr. | 1872 | Philip C. Heckman | D | 682 | 47 |
| Dominican | Racine, Wis. | 1946 | Sister Rosita Uhen | P | 598 | 55 |
| Dominican Coll. of Blauvelt (T) | Blauvelt, N. Y. | 1952 | Sis. M. Natalie | D | 450 | 30 |
| Dominican Coll. of S. Rafael (W) | San Rafael, Calif. | 1890 | Sister M. Patrick | D | 774 | 80 |
| Don Bosco (M) | Newton, N. J. | 1928 | Rev. J. S. Bajorek | D | 152 | 17 |
| Dordt | Sioux Center, Iowa | 1955 | Bernard Haan | D | 700 | 35 |
| Drake Univ. | Des Moines, Iowa | 1881 | Paul F. Sharp | P | 7,028 | 371 |
| Drew Univ. | Madison, N. J. | 1866 | Robert F. Oxnam | D | 1,459 | 153 |
| Drexel Inst. of Technology | Philadelphia, Pa. | 1891 | William W. Hagerty | P | 11,058 | 600 |
| Dropsie Coll. for Hebrew & Cognate Learning | Philadelphia, Pa. | 1907 | Abraham I. Katsh | D | 155 | 24 |
| Drury | Springfield, Mo. | 1873 | Alfred O. Canon | D | 2,580 | 148 |
| Dubuque, Univ. of | Dubuque, Iowa | 1852 | William G. Chalmers | D | 907 | 54 |
| Duchesne Coll. of the S. H. (W) | Omaha, Nebr. | 1881 | Sis. Jeannette Kimball | P | 336 | 40 |
| Duke Univ. (Med) | Durham, N. C. | 1838 | Douglas M. Knight | P | 7,581 | 1,084 |
| Dunbarton College of Holy Cross (W) | Washington, D. C. | 1935 | Walter Hess | D | 512 | 56 |
| Duquesne Univ. (T) | Pittsburgh, Pa. | 1878 | V. Rev. H. J. McAnulty | D | 6,700 | 425 |
| Dyke | Cleveland, Ohio | 1848 | Jay R. Gates | P | 1,178 | 57 |
| D'Youville (T)(W) | Buffalo, N. Y. | 1908 | Sis. Francis Xavier | D | 1,300 | 108 |
| Earlham | Richmond, Ind. | 1847 | Landrum Bolling | D | 1,081 | 117 |
| East Carolina Univ. | Greenville, N. C. | 1907 | Leo W. Jenkins | S | 10,758 | 647 |
| East Central State (T) | Ada, Okla. | 1909 | Charles F. Spencer | S | 2,719 | 101 |
| East Stroudsburg, State (T) | E. Stroudsburg, Pa. | 1893 | LeRoy J. Koehler | S | 2,318 | 164 |
| East Tennessee State Univ. (T) | Johnson City, Tenn. | 1909 | Delos Culp | S | *8,307* | *445* |
| East Texas Baptist | Marshall, Texas | 1912 | Howard C. Bennett | D | 629 | 38 |
| East Texas State Univ. (T) | Commerce, Texas | 1889 | Daniel W. Halladay | S | 7,971 | 457 |
| Eastern Baptist | St. Davids, Pa. | 1932 | Thomas B. McDormand | D | 513 | 47 |
| Eastern Coll. | Baltimore, Md. | 1928 | A. Risley Ensor | P | 1,120 | 65 |
| Eastern Illinois Univ. (T) | Charleston, Ill. | 1899 | Quincy Doudna | S | 6,000 | 509 |
| Eastern Kentucky Univ. (T) | Richmond, Ky. | 1906 | Robert R. Martin | S | 8,500 | 450 |
| Eastern Mennonite (T) | Harrisonburg, Va. | 1917 | Myron S. Augsburger | D | 844 | 85 |
| Eastern Michigan Univ. (T) | Ypsilanti, Mich. | 1849 | Harold E. Sponberg | S | 14,694 | 1,008 |
| Eastern Montana (T) | Billings, Mont. | 1927 | Stanley Heywood | S | 2,650 | 146 |
| Eastern Nazarene | Quincy, Mass. | 1918 | Edward S. Mann | D | 825 | 62 |
| Eastern New Mexico Univ. (T) | Portales, N. Mex. | 1934 | Charles Meister | S | *3,597* | *296* |
| Eastern Oregon (T) | La Grande, Ore. | 1929 | Averno M. Rempel | S | 1,310 | 100 |
| Eastern Pilgrim | Allentown, Pa. | 1921 | Charles Felsburg (Act.) | P | 148 | 12 |
| Eastern Washington State (T) | Cheney, Wash. | 1890 | Emerson C. Shuck | S | 4,450 | 267 |
| Edgewood | Madison, Wis. | 1927 | Sister Mary Cecilia | D | 688 | 65 |
| Edinboro State (T) | Edinboro, Pa. | 1857 | Chester T. McNerney | S | *5,200* | *296* |
| Edwards Waters | Jacksonville, Fla. | 1867 | William B. Stewart | D | 957 | 60 |
| Elizabeth City State (T) | Elizabeth, N. C. | 1891 | Walter N. Ridley | S | 940 | 76 |
| Elizabethtown | Elizabethtown, Pa. | 1899 | Morley J. Mays | D | 1,739 | 99 |
| Elmhurst | Elmhurst, Ill. | 1871 | Donald Kleckner | D | 2,517 | 120 |
| Elmira (W) | Elmira, N. Y. | 1855 | J. Ralph Murray | P | 2,457 | 101 |
| Elon (T) | Elon College, N. C. | 1889 | J. E. Danieley | D | 1,407 | 84 |
| Embry-Riddle Aeron. Inst. | Daytona Beach, Fla. | 1926 | Jack R. Hunt | P | 1,050 | 103 |
| Emerson (T) | Boston, Mass. | 1880 | Richard Chapin | P | 1,258 | 110 |
| Emmanuel (T)(W) | Boston, Mass. | 1919 | Sister Ann Bartholomew | D | 1,453 | 130 |
| Emory and Henry | Emory, Va. | 1836 | William C. Finch | D | 837 | 65 |
| Emory Univ. (T)(Med) | Atlanta, Ga. | 1836 | S. S. Atwood | D | *5,273* | *1,581* |
| Emporia, Coll. of | Emporia, Kan. | 1882 | Joseph R. Laughlin | D | 908 | 52 |
| Episcopal Theol. Sch. | Cambridge, Mass. | 1867 | Rev. J. B. Coburn (Dean) | D | 137 | 17 |
| Erskine | Due West, S. C. | 1839 | Joseph Wightman | D | 715 | 55 |
| Eureka | Eureka, Ill. | 1855 | Ira W. Langston | D | 500 | 37 |
| Evangel | Springfield, Mo. | 1955 | J. Robert Ashcroft | D | 755 | 60 |
| Evansville, Univ. of (T) | Evansville, Ind. | 1854 | Wallace B. Graves | P | 4,300 | 225 |
| Fairfield Univ. (M) | Fairfield, Conn. | 1947 | Rev. William C. McInnes | D | 1,661 | 119 |
| Fairleigh Dickinson Univ. (T) | Rutherford, N. J. | 1941 | P. Sammartino (Chan.) | P | *19,042* | *1,100* |
| Fairmont State | Fairmont, W. Va. | 1867 | Eston K. Feaster | S | 2,755 | 140 |
| Farmington State (T) | Farmington, Me. | 1864 | Melvin G. Scarlett | S | 1,055 | 60 |
| Fayetteville State (T) | Fayetteville, N. C. | 1877 | Rudolph Jones | S | 1,207 | 75 |
| Ferris State (T) | Big Rapids, Mich. | 1884 | Victor F. Spathelf | S | 6,881 | 341 |
| Finch (W) | New York, N. Y. | 1900 | Roland De Marco | P | 393 | 45 |
| Findlay | Findlay, Ohio | 1882 | Ivan E. Frick | D | 1,339 | 92 |
| Fisk Univ. | Nashville, Tenn. | 1866 | J. R. Lawson (Act.) | P | 1,070 | 57 |
| Florence State (T) | Florence, Ala. | 1872 | E. B. Norton | S | 2,687 | 140 |
| Florida Atlantic Univ. (T) | Boca Raton, Fla. | 1961 | K. R. Williams | S | 3,751 | 265 |
| Florida A. & M. Univ.* | Tallahassee, Fla. | 1887 | George W. Gore, Jr. | S | 3,500 | 207 |
| Florida Inst. of Tech. | Melbourne, Fla. | 1958 | Jerome P. Keuper | P | 1,644 | 150 |
| Florida Memorial | St. Augustine, Fla. | 1892 | R. W. Puryear | P | 588 | 35 |
| Florida Presbyterian | St. Petersburg, Fla. | 1958 | William H. Kadel | D | 853 | 65 |
| Florida Southern | Lakeland, Fla. | 1885 | Charles T. Thrift, Jr. | D | 1,545 | 100 |
| Florida State Univ. (T) | Tallahassee, Fla. | 1857 | John E. Champion | S | 14,629 | 947 |

| Name | Location | Yr. | Governing Official and Control | | Stu- dents | Teach- ers |
|---|---|---|---|---|---|---|
| Florida, Univ. of*......(T) (Med) | Gainesville, Fla..... | 1853 | Stephen O'Connell | S | 17,000 | 1,930 |
| Fontbonne............(T) (W) | St. Louis, Mo...... | 1917 | Sister E. M. Schmidt.. | D | 931 | 95 |
| Fordham Univ.............. | Bronx, N. Y........ | 1841 | Rev. L. McLaughlin... | S | 7,000 | 539 |
| Ft. Hays Kansas State.....(T) | Hays, Kan......... | 1902 | M. C. Cunningham.... | S | 5,013 | 258 |
| Ft. Kent State............. | Ft. Kent, Me....... | 1878 | Joseph M. Fox....... | S | 271 | 28 |
| Ft. Lewis............(T) | Durango, Colo...... | 1962 | John F. Reed........ | S | 1,450 | 75 |
| Fort Valley State*......... | Fort Valley, Ga..... | 1895 | W. W. E. Blanchet.... | S | 1,858 | 94 |
| Ft. Wayne Art Inst........ | Fort Wayne, Ind.... | 1922 | Russell Oettel....... | P | 351 | 16 |
| Fort Wayne Bible.......... | Fort Wayne, Ind.... | 1904 | Jared F. Greig....... | P | 560 | 36 |
| Ft. Wright............(T) | Spokane, Wash..... | 1907 | Sister B. Carlson..... | D | 450 | 57 |
| Francis T. Nicholls State... | Thibodaux, La...... | 1948 | Vernon Galliano..... | S | 3,836 | 146 |
| Franklin.................. | Franklin, Ind...... | 1834 | Wesley N. Haines.... | D | 689 | 51 |
| Franklin and Marshall......(M) | Lancaster, Pa...... | 1787 | Keith Spalding...... | P | 2,266 | 154 |
| Franklin Pierce........... | Rindge, N. H...... | 1962 | Frank S. DiPietro.... | P | 800 | 47 |
| Franklin Univ............. | Columbus, Ohio.... | 1902 | Joseph Frasch....... | P | 2,225 | 95 |
| Frederick............(T) | Portsmouth, Va.... | 1958 | Ernest R. Wood...... | P | 731 | 49 |
| Free Will Baptist Bible..... | Nashville, Tenn.... | 1942 | L. C. Johnson....... | D | 353 | 21 |
| Fresno State..........(T) | Fresno, Calif....... | 1911 | Frederic W. Ness.... | S | 10,190 | 647 |
| Friends Univ.............. | Wichita, Kan...... | 1898 | Roy F. Ray......... | D | 915 | 49 |
| Frostburg State.........(T) | Frostburg, Md..... | 1898 | John H. Morey...... | D | 2,315 | 115 |
| Fuller Theol. Seminary..... | Pasadena, Calif..... | 1947 | David A. Hubbard.... | P | 301 | 24 |
| Furman Univ.............. | Greenville, S. C.... | 1826 | Gordon W. Blackwell.. | P | 1,947 | 115 |
| Gallaudet................ | Washington, D. C... | 1864 | Leonard Eistad...... | P | 675 | 108 |
| Gannon...............(M) | Erie, Pa.......... | 1944 | Rev. W. J. Nash..... | D | 3,185 | 153 |
| Garrett Theol. Sem........ | Evanston, Ill...... | 1855 | Orville H. McKay.... | D | 300 | 30 |
| Gen. Beadle State........(T) | Madison, S. Dak.... | 1881 | Harry Bowes........ | S | 1,299 | 51 |
| General Motors Institute.... | Flint, Mich........ | 1919 | Harold P. Rodes..... | P | 2,624 | 235 |
| General Theol. Sem........(M) | New York, N. Y.... | 1817 | V. Rev. S. J. Wylie (Dn.) | D | 181 | 30 |
| Geneva................... | Beaver Falls, Pa.... | 1848 | Edwin C. Clarke..... | D | 1,731 | 116 |
| George Fox............... | Newberg, Ore...... | 1891 | Milo C. Ross........ | D | 375 | 42 |
| George Peabody Coll. for Teachers | Nashville, Tenn.... | 1875 | John Claunch....... | P | 1,810 | 125 |
| Geo. Washington Un. (T) (Med) | Washington, D. C... | 1821 | Lloyd H. Elliott..... | P | 12,545 | 1,300 |
| George Williams.......(T) | Downers Grove, Ill. | 1890 | Richard E. Hamlin.... | P | 782 | 56 |
| Georgetown............... | Georgetown, Ky.... | 1829 | Robert L. Mills...... | D | 1,409 | 100 |
| Georgetown Univ.......(Med) | Washington, D. C... | 1789 | V. Rev. G. J. Campbell. | D | 7,480 | 1,585 |
| Georgia Coll. at Milledgeville.. | Milledgeville, Ga... | 1889 | J. Whitney Bunting.. | S | 1,400 | 77 |
| Georgia Inst. of Technology... | Atlanta, Ga....... | 1888 | Edwin D. Harrison... | S | 7,800 | 458 |
| Georgia, Medical Coll. of...... | Augusta, Ga....... | 1828 | Harry B. O'Rear..... | S | 697 | 250 |
| Georgia Southern.......... | Statesboro, Ga..... | 1908 | Zach S. Henderson... | S | 3,925 | 258 |
| Georgia Southwestern.....(T) | Americus, Ga...... | 1908 | William B. King..... | S | 1,700 | 93 |
| Georgia State.........(T) | Atlanta, Ga....... | 1913 | Noah N. Langdale.... | S | 9,379 | 528 |
| Georgia, Univ. of*.......(T) | Athens, Ga........ | 1785 | Fred C. Davison..... | S | 20,400 | 1,700 |
| Georgian Court..........(W) | Lakewood, N. J.... | 1908 | Sis. Mary Pierre..... | D | 528 | 50 |
| Gettysburg................ | Gettysburg, Pa.... | 1832 | Carl Arnold Hanson.. | D | 1,840 | 161 |
| Glassboro State..........(T) | Glassboro, N. J.... | 1923 | Thos. E. Robinson... | S | 8,450 | 315 |
| Glenville State.........(T) | Glenville, W. Va.... | 1872 | D. Banks Wilburn.... | S | 1,416 | 78 |
| Goddard.................. | Plainfield, Vt...... | 1938 | Royce S. Pitkin..... | P | 700 | 75 |
| Golden Gate Bapt. Theol. Sem.. | Mill Valley, Calif... | 1944 | Harold K. Graves.... | D | 350 | 23 |
| Golden Gate.............. | San Francisco, Calif. | 1901 | Russell T. Sharpe.... | P | 2,560 | 125 |
| Gonzaga Univ............. | Spokane, Wash..... | 1887 | V. Rev. J. P. Leary.... | D | 2,573 | 239 |
| Good Counsel..........(W) | White Plains, N. Y. | 1923 | Mother M. Dolores... | D | 501 | 60 |
| Gordon.................. | Wenham, Mass..... | 1889 | James Forrester..... | D | 1,089 | 37 |
| Gorham State..........(T) | Gorham, Me....... | 1878 | Kenneth T. H. Brooks. | S | 1,750 | 87 |
| Goshen.................. | Goshen, Ind....... | 1903 | Paul Mininger...... | D | 1,183 | 89 |
| Goucher.............(T) (W) | Towson, Md....... | 1885 | Marvin B. Perry, Jr... | P | 1,048 | 118 |
| Grace Bible Institute....... | Omaha, Nebr...... | 1943 | Waldo Harder....... | P | 424 | 24 |
| Grace................... | Winona Lake, Ind... | 1948 | Herman A. Hoyt..... | D | 490 | 40 |
| Graceland................ | Lamoni, Iowa...... | 1895 | William Higdon..... | D | 1,111 | 67 |
| Grambling...........(T) | Grambling, La..... | 1901 | Ralph W. E. Jones... | S | 3,410 | 248 |
| Grand Canyon............ | Phoenix, Ariz...... | 1949 | Arthur K. Tyson..... | D | 544 | 37 |
| Grand Rapids Bapt. Bible Coll. & Sem. | Grand Rapids, Mich. | 1941 | W. Wilbert Welch.... | D | 443 | 23 |
| Grand Valley State.......(T) | Allendale, Mich.... | 1960 | James H. Zumberge... | S | 1,604 | 85 |
| Great Falls, Coll of.....(T) | Great Falls, Mont... | 1932 | Sister Rita......... | D | 1,128 | 58 |
| Greensboro............... | Greensboro, N. C... | 1838 | J. Ralph Jolly...... | D | 608 | 51 |
| Greenville............... | Greenville, Ill..... | 1892 | Glenn A. Richardson.. | D | 748 | 52 |
| Grinnell................. | Grinnell, Ia....... | 1846 | Glenn H. Leggett.... | P | 1,139 | 119 |
| Grove City............(T) | Grove City, Pa..... | 1876 | John S. Harker..... | P | 1,921 | 100 |
| Guam, Coll. of........... | Agana, Guam...... | 1952 | A. C. Yamashito.... | T | 1,700 | 80 |
| Guilford................. | Greensboro, N. C... | 1837 | Grimsley T. Hobbs... | D | 1,499 | 139 |
| Gustavus Adolphus.....(T) | St. Peter Minn..... | 1862 | Edgar M. Carlson.... | D | 1,701 | 131 |
| Gwynedd-Mercy.........(W) | Gwynedd Valley, Pa. | 1948 | Sis. M. Gregory..... | D | 1,025 | 90 |
| Hahnemann Medical....... | Philadelphia, Pa.... | 1848 | Charles S. Cameron... | P | 400 | 500 |
| Hamilton.............(M) | Clinton, N. Y...... | 1812 | R. W. Couper (Act.)... | P | 807 | 85 |
| Hamline Univ............. | St. Paul, Minn..... | 1854 | Richard Bailey...... | D | 1,244 | 75 |
| Hampden-Sydney........(M) | Hampden-Sydney, Va. | 1776 | W. Taylor Reveley... | D | 559 | 45 |
| Hampton Institute.......(T) | Hampton, Va...... | 1868 | Jerome H. Holland... | P | 2,584 | 201 |
| Hanover................. | Hanover, Ind...... | 1827 | John E. Horner..... | D | 983 | 72 |
| Hardin-Simmons Univ....(T) | Abilene, Tex....... | 1891 | Elwin L. Skiles..... | D | 1,664 | 112 |
| Harding................. | Searcy, Ark....... | 1924 | Clifton L. Ganus, Jr... | D | 1,760 | 95 |
| Harris Teachers.......... | St. Louis, Mo...... | 1857 | Richard Stumpe...... | Mu | 937 | 78 |
| Hartford, Univ. of......(T) | W. Hartford, Conn.. | 1957 | A. M. Woodruff (Chan.) | P | 7,458 | 500 |
| Hartwick................ | Oneonta, N. Y..... | 1928 | Frederick M. Binder.. | D | 1,497 | 100 |
| Harvard, Univ. (a)......(Med) | Cambridge, Mass... | 1636 | Nathan M. Pusey.... | P | 15,215 | 7,330 |
| Harvey Mudd............ | Claremont, Calif.... | 1955 | Joseph B. Platt..... | P | 292 | 60 |
| Hastings................. | Hastings, Nebr..... | 1882 | Theron B. Maxson... | D | 805 | 58 |
| Haverford............(M) | Haverford, Pa..... | 1833 | John R. Coleman.... | P | 563 | 79 |
| Hawaii, Univ. of*........(T) | Honolulu, Hawaii... | 1907 | Thomas H. Hamilton.. | S | 21,256 | 1,917 |
| Hebrew Union Coll.—Jewish Inst. of Religion...........(M) | Cincinnati, Ohio.... | 1875 | Nelson Glueck....... | D | 268 | 34 |
| Heidelberg............... | Tiffin, Ohio....... | 1850 | Terry Wickham..... | D | 1,161 | 89 |
| Henderson State.......(T) | Arkadelphia, Ark... | 1890 | M. H. Russell...... | S | 3,000 | 125 |
| Hendrix................. | Conway, Ark...... | 1884 | Marshall T. Steel.... | D | 833 | 48 |
| Herron Sch. of Art........ | Indianapolis, Ind... | 1902 | Donald Mattison (Dir.) | P | 318 | 33 |
| High Point............... | High Point, N. C... | 1924 | Wendell M. Patton... | D | 1,070 | 68 |
| Hillsdale................. | Hillsdale, Mich..... | 1844 | J. Donald Phillips.... | P | 1,160 | 85 |
| Hiram................... | Hiram, Ohio....... | 1850 | Elmer Jagow....... | D | 1,076 | 95 |
| Hobart & Wm. Smith Colleges.. | Geneva, N. Y...... | 1822 | Rev. A. E. Holland... | P | 1,411 | 114 |
| Hofstra Univ.............. | Hempstead, N. Y... | 1935 | Clifford L. Lord..... | P | 11,870 | 692 |
| Hollins...............(W) | Hollins, Coll., Va... | 1842 | John A. Logan, Jr.... | P | 951 | 97 |
| Holy Cross, Coll. of the...(M) | Worcester, Mass.... | 1843 | V. Rev. R. J. Swords.. | D | 2,353 | 173 |
| Holy Family...........(W) | Philadelphia, Pa.... | 1954 | Sis. M. Aloysius..... | D | 628 | 51 |

(a) Oldest college in the United States.

| Name | Location | Yr. | Governing Official and Control | | Students | Teachers |
|---|---|---|---|---|---|---|
| Holy Family............(W) | Manitowoc, Wis... | 1935 | Sister M. Brideen...... | P | 562 | 45 |
| Holy Names, Coll. of the...(W) | Oakland, Calif...... | 1880 | Sister Mary Ambrose... | D | 960 | 105 |
| Hood................(W) | Frederick, Md...... | 1893 | Randle Elliott....... | P | 750 | 76 |
| Hope................. | Holland, Mich..... | 1866 | C. Vander Werf...... | D | 1,788 | 159 |
| Houghton.............(T) | Houghton, N. Y... | 1883 | Stephen W. Paine..... | D | 1,128 | 90 |
| Houston, Univ. of.....(T) | Houston, Tex...... | 1934 | Philip G. Hoffman.... | S | 21,170 | 1,093 |
| Howard Payne......... | Brownwood, Tex.. | 1889 | Guy D. Newman..... | D | 1,200 | 78 |
| Howard Univ......(Med) | Washington, D. C.. | 1867 | James Nabrit, Jr..... | F, P | 8,153 | 1,014 |
| Humboldt State........ | Arcata, Calif...... | 1913 | Cornelius Siemens.... | S | 3,850 | 325 |
| Huntingdon........... | Montgomery, Ala.. | 1854 | Allen Jackson ...... | D | 882 | 67 |
| Huntington............ | Huntington, Ind... | 1897 | E. DeWitt Baker..... | D | 432 | 35 |
| Huron................(T) | Huron, S. Dak.... | 1883 | Richard H. Timmins.. | D | 690 | 45 |
| Husson...............(T) | Bangor, Me....... | 1898 | Chesley H. Husson... | Pr | 1,200 | 56 |
| Huston-Tillotson...... | Austin, Tex....... | 1876 | John T. King....... | P | 771 | 59 |
| Idaho, Coll. of........(T) | Caldwell, Idaho... | 1891 | Warren B. Knox..... | D | 1,057 | 81 |
| Idaho State Univ...(Med.)(T) | Pocatello, Idaho... | 1901 | William E. Davis..... | S | 4,906 | 300 |
| Idaho, Univ. of*......(T) | Moscow, Idaho.... | 1889 | Ernest W. Hartung... | S | 5,914 | 433 |
| Iliff School of Theology... | Denver, Colo...... | 1892 | Lowell B. Swan..... | D | 120 | 14 |
| Illinois............... | Jacksonville, Ill... | 1829 | I. Vernon Calme..... | D | 800 | 51 |
| Illinois Coll. of Optometry... | Chicago, Ill....... | 1872 | Eugene W. Strawn... | P | 260 | 26 |
| Illinois Inst. of Technology... | Chicago, Ill....... | 1892 | John T. Rettaliata... | P | 7,585 | 683 |
| Illinois St. Univ......... | Normal, Ill....... | 1857 | Samuel E. Braden... | S | 11,072 | 850 |
| Illinois, Univ. of*.....(T)(Med) | Urbana & Chicago, Ill. | 1868 | David D. Henry..... | S | 30,748 | 8,613 |
| Illinois Wesleyan Univ....(T) | Bloomington, Ill... | 1850 | Robert C. Eckley.... | D | 1,550 | 120 |
| Immaculata............(W) | Immaculata, Pa.... | 1920 | Sis. Mary of Lourdes.. | D | 1,602 | 136 |
| Immaculate Conception Sem. (M) | Conception, Mo... | 1882 | V. Rev. C. Falk..... | D | 320 | 30 |
| Immaculate Heart.....(W) | Los Angeles, Calif.. | 1916 | Sister M. William... | D | 1,098 | 98 |
| Incarnate Word........(W) | San Antonio, Tex.. | 1881 | S. T. Greenburg.... | D | 1,396 | 101 |
| Indiana Central........(T) | Indianapolis, Ind... | 1902 | I. Lynd Esch....... | D | 2,271 | 113 |
| Indiana Inst. of Tech..... | Ft. Wayne, Ind... | 1930 | Edward Dugan, Jr... | P | 1,036 | 59 |
| Indiana State Univ......(T) | Terre Haute, Ind... | 1870 | Alan Rankin....... | S | 12,056 | 650 |
| Indiana Univ. of Penn....(T) | Indiana, Pa....... | 1875 | Willis E. Pratt..... | S | 8,500 | 450 |
| Indiana Univ......(T)(Med) | Bloomington, Ind.. | 1820 | Elvis J. Stahr...... | S | 47,000 | 2,970 |
| Institute for Adv. Study (a).. | Princeton, N. J.... | 1930 | Carl Kaysen (Dir.).... | | 114 | 22 |
| Insurance, Coll. of....... | New York, N. Y... | 1962 | A. Leslie Leonard... | P | 2,299 | 154 |
| Iona.................(T) | New Rochelle, N. Y.. | 1940 | Rev. Bro. McKenna... | D | 3,016 | 210 |
| Iowa State Univ.*....... | Ames, Iowa...... | 1858 | W. Robert Parks.... | S | 15,541 | 1,279 |
| Iowa, Univ. of.......(Med) | Iowa City, Iowa... | 1847 | Howard R. Bowen... | S | 17,707 | 1,062 |
| Iowa Wesleyan......... | Mt. Pleasant, Iowa.. | 1842 | Franklin Littell..... | D | 1,033 | 66 |
| Ithaca............... | Ithaca, N. Y...... | 1892 | Howard I. Dillingham.. | P | 3,327 | 267 |
| Jackson State.........(T) | Jackson, Miss..... | 1877 | John A. Peoples.... | S | 2,990 | 128 |
| Jacksonville State Univ....(T) | Jacksonville, Ala... | 1883 | Houston Cole...... | S | 4,479 | 192 |
| Jacksonville Univ......(T) | Jacksonville, Fla... | 1934 | Robert H. Spiro..... | P | 2,517 | 120 |
| Jamestown............(T) | Jamestown, N. Dak. | 1884 | Dan J. Sillers...... | D | 578 | 52 |
| Jarvis Christian........ | Hawkins, Tex..... | 1912 | J. O. Perpener...... | D | 497 | 44 |
| Jefferson Medical....... | Philadelphia, Pa... | 1824 | Peter A. Herbut..... | P, S | 731 | 756 |
| Jersey City State....... | Jersey City, N. J... | 1929 | W. A. Liggitt (Act.) ... | S | 6,400 | 250 |
| Jewish Studies, Coll. of...(T) | Chicago, Ill....... | 1925 | D. Weinstein....... | D | 300 | 22 |
| JewishTheol.Sem.ofAmerica (M) | New York, N. Y.... | 1886 | L. Finkelstein (Chan.).. | D | 2,059 | 186 |
| John Brown Univ........ | Siloam Springs, Ark.. | 1919 | John E. Brown, Jr ... | P | 681 | 48 |
| John Carroll Univ......(T) | Cleveland, Ohio... | 1886 | Rev. Joseph Schell... | D | 4,700 | 180 |
| Johns Hopkins Univ....(Med) | Baltimore, Md..... | 1876 | Lincoln Gordon..... | P | 9,684 | 2,073 |
| Johnson C. Smith Univ.... | Charlotte, N. C... | 1867 | Rufus P. Perry..... | D | 1,031 | 86 |
| Johnson State.........(T) | Johnson, Vt...... | 1867 | Arthur J. Dibden.... | S | 547 | 42 |
| Jones................ | Jacksonville, Fla... | 1918 | Jack H. Jones...... | P | 616 | 35 |
| Judson...........(T)(W) | Marion, Ala...... | 1838 | James H. Edmondson.. | D | 434 | 39 |
| Juilliard Sch. of Music.... | New York, N. Y... | 1906 | Peter Mennin...... | P | 1,000 | 140 |
| Juniata..............(T) | Huntingdon, Pa... | 1876 | John Stauffer...... | D | 1,100 | 93 |
| Kalamazoo............ | Kalamazoo, Mich... | 1833 | Weimer K. Hicks.... | D | 1,230 | 70 |
| Kans. City Art Inst....... | Kansas City, Mo... | 1885 | Andrew W. Morgan... | P | 767 | 50 |
| Kan. City Coll. of Osteop. & Sur. | Kansas City, Mo... | 1916 | Eugene Powers..... | P | 425 | 75 |
| Kansas St. Coll......... | Pittsburg, Kan.... | 1903 | George F. Budd..... | S | 5,393 | 341 |
| Kansas State Teachers....(T) | Emporia, Kan..... | 1863 | John E. Visser..... | S | 6,558 | 286 |
| Kansas State Univ......(T) | Manhattan, Kan... | 1863 | James A. McCain.... | S | 11,200 | 1,240 |
| Kansas, Univ. of....(T)(Med) | Lawrence, Kan.... | 1866 | W. C. Wescoe (Chan.).. | S | 14,891 | 925 |
| Kansas Wesleyan Univ..... | Salina, Kan...... | 1886 | D. Arthur Zook..... | D | 716 | 43 |
| Kearney State.........(T) | Kearney, Nebr.... | 1905 | Milton J. Hassel.... | S | 4,660 | 238 |
| Keene State...........(T) | Keene, N. Hamp... | 1909 | Roman J. Zorn..... | S | 1,652 | 84 |
| Kent State Univ........(T) | Kent, Ohio....... | 1910 | Robert White...... | S | 22,795 | 836 |
| Kentucky Southern...... | Louisville, Ky.... | 1960 | Rollin Burhans..... | D | 640 | 42 |
| Kentucky State*........ | Frankfort, Ky.... | 1886 | Carl M. Hill....... | S | 1,535 | 105 |
| Kentucky, Univ. of*...(T)(Med) | Lexington, Ky.... | 1865 | Vacant............ | S | 13,762 | 1,150 |
| Kentucky Wesleyan...... | Owensboro, Ky.... | 1858 | Harold P. Hamilton... | D | 1,161 | 67 |
| Kenyon...............(M) | Gambier, Ohio.... | 1824 | F. Edward Lund.... | P | 790 | 76 |
| Keuka................(W) | Keuka Park, N. Y.. | 1890 | G. Wayne Glick.... | P | 800 | 70 |
| King................. | Bristol, Tenn..... | 1867 | Robert Liston...... | D | 316 | 38 |
| King's................ | Briarcliff Manor, N. Y. | 1938 | Robert A. Cook..... | P | 659 | 64 |
| King's................(M) | Wilkes-Barre, Pa... | 1946 | Rev. L. D. Kilburn... | D | 1,895 | 122 |
| Kirksville Coll. of Ost. & Surg. | Kirksville, Mo.... | 1892 | Morris Thompson.... | P | 393 | 168 |
| Knox................ | Galesburg, Ill..... | 1837 | Sharvy G. Umbeck... | P | 1,221 | 98 |
| Knoxville............. | Knoxville, Tenn... | 1875 | Robert Owens...... | D | 922 | 79 |
| Kutztown State........(T) | Kutztown, Pa..... | 1866 | Cyrus E. Beekey.... | S | 3,863 | 216 |
| Ladycliff.............(W) | Highland Falls, N. Y. | 1933 | Sister M. Jane Thomas.. | P | 596 | 51 |
| Lafayette.............(M) | Easton, Pa....... | 1826 | K. R. Bergethon..... | D | 1,941 | 166 |
| LaGrange............. | LaGrange, Ga..... | 1831 | Waights Henry, Jr... | D | 550 | 45 |
| Lake Erie............. | Painesville, Ohio... | 1856 | Paul Weaver...... | D | 989 | 88 |
| Lake Forest........... | Lake Forest, Ill... | 1857 | William G. Cole.... | D | 1,218 | 101 |
| Lakeland............. | Sheboygan, Wis... | 1862 | John B. Morland.... | D | 643 | 42 |
| Lamar State Coll. of Tech...(T) | Beaumont, Tex... | 1923 | R. W. Setzer...... | Di | 9,989 | 371 |
| Lambuth.............. | Jackson, Tenn.... | 1843 | James S. Wilder.... | D | 805 | 62 |
| Lancaster Theol. Sem..... | Lancaster, Pa..... | 1825 | Robert V. Moss, Jr... | D | 110 | 11 |
| Lander............... | Greenwood, S. C... | 1872 | E. Don Herd, Jr.... | P | 548 | 43 |
| Lane................. | Jackson, Tenn.... | 1882 | Chester Kirkendoll... | D | 981 | 46 |
| Langston Univ.*.......(T) | Langston, Okla.... | 1897 | William H. Hale.... | S | 1,106 | 82 |
| La Roche.............(W) | Allison Pk., Pa.... | 1963 | Sister M. Annunciata .. | D | 355 | 26 |
| La Salle.............. | Philadelphia, Pa... | 1863 | Bro. Daniel Bernian... | D | 6,200 | 330 |
| La Verne.............(T) | La Verne, Calif... | 1891 | Harold Fasnacht.... | D | 730 | 51 |
| Lawrence Univ......... | Appleton, Wis.... | 1847 | Curtis W. Tarr..... | D | 1,213 | 120 |
| Lawrence Inst. of Tech.... | Southfield, Mich... | 1932 | W. H. Buell....... | P | 3,929 | 110 |
| Layton Sch. of Art...... | Milwaukee, Wis... | 1920 | E.D.Lewandowski(Dir.) | P | 590 | 45 |
| Lebanon Valley........ | Annville, Pa...... | 1866 | Frederick Sample... | D | 1,257 | 78 |
| Lee.................. | Cleveland, Tenn... | 1918 | James A. Cross..... | D | 1,162 | 60 |

(a) Post-doctoral research.

| Name | Location | Yr. | Governing Official and Control | | Students | Teachers |
|---|---|---|---|---|---|---|
| Lehigh Univ.............(M) | Bethlehem, Pa...... | 1865 | W. Deming Lewis...... | P | 4,843 | 484 |
| Le Moyne................... | Syracuse, N. Y...... | 1946 | Rev. William L. Reilly.. | D | 1,536 | 103 |
| Le Moyne-Owen............. | Memphis, Tenn...... | 1870 | Hollis F. Price......... | D | 614 | 47 |
| Lenoir Rhyne.............. | Hickory, N. C....... | 1891 | Raymond Bost........ | D | 1,264 | 94 |
| Lesley............(W) (T) | Cambridge, Mass.... | 1909 | Don A. Orton......... | P | 611 | 48 |
| LeTourneau................ | Longview, Tex...... | 1946 | R. H. LeTourneau..... | P | 615 | 50 |
| Lewis................(T) | Lockport, Ill........ | 1930 | Brother Paul French... | D | 1,630 | 92 |
| Lincoln Christian.......... | Lincoln, Ill......... | 1944 | Earl C. Hargrove...... | D | 675 | 32 |
| Lincoln Memorial Univ.....(T) | Harrogate, Tenn..... | 1897 | H. Y. Livesay ........ | P | 675 | 42 |
| Lincoln Univ.............. | Lincoln Un., Pa..... | 1854 | Marvin Wachnan...... | P | 780 | 75 |
| Lincoln Univ.........(T) | Jefferson City, Mo.... | 1866 | Earl Edgar Dawson ... | S | 2,014 | 123 |
| Lindenwood......(T) (W) | St. Charles, Mo...... | 1827 | John A. Brown........ | D | 648 | 69 |
| Linfield................... | McMinnville, Ore.... | 1849 | Harry L. Dillin....... | D | 1,072 | 78 |
| Little Rock Univ.......... | Little Rock, Ark..... | 1927 | Carey V. Stabler...... | D | 3,099 | 140 |
| Livingston State......(T) | Livingston, Ala...... | 1840 | John Deloney......... | S | 1,300 | 75 |
| Livingstone............... | Salisbury, N. C...... | 1879 | Samuel E. Duncan.... | D | 866 | 52 |
| Lock Haven State.......(T) | Lock Haven, Pa...... | 1870 | Richard T. Parsons.... | S | 2,001 | 136 |
| Loma Linda Univ......(Med) | Loma Linda, Calif.... | 1905 | David J. Bieber....... | D | *2,936* | *1,223* |
| Long Island Univ.......... | Greenvale, N. Y..... | 1926 | R. Gordon Hoxie (Chan.) | P | 18,000 | 1,000 |
| Longwood.........(T) (W) | Farmville, Va....... | 1839 | Henri I. Willett, Jr.... | S | 1,702 | 122 |
| Loras.................(M) | Dubuque, Iowa...... | 1839 | Rt. Rev. J. A. Driscoll.. | D | 1,600 | 125 |
| Loretto Heights.......(T) (W) | Denver, Colo........ | 1918 | Sister Patricia Jean.... | D | 895 | 97 |
| Louisiana................. | Pineville, La........ | 1906 | G. Earl Guinn........ | D | 1,079 | 61 |
| Louisiana Polytechnic Inst....(T) | Ruston, La.......... | 1894 | F. J. Taylor.......... | S | 6,489 | 369 |
| Louisiana St. Univ.*......(Med) | Baton Rouge, La.... | 1860 | John A. Hunter....... | S | *25,079* | *1,468* |
| Main Campus............ | Baton Rouge, La.... | 1860 | C. G. Taylor (Chan.)... | S | 16,000 | 950 |
| Medical Center.......... | New Orleans, La..... | 1931 | William W. Frye (Chan.) | S | 650 | 185 |
| New Orleans Campus..... | New Orleans, La..... | 1958 | Homer L. Hitt (Chan.).. | S | 6,807 | 245 |
| Louisville Presbyt. Sem....... | Louisville, Ky....... | 1853 | Albert C. Winn....... | D | 122 | 14 |
| Louisville, Univ. of....(T) (Med) | Louisville, Ky....... | 1798 | Woodrow Strickler..... | Mu | *7,787* | *959* |
| Lowell Technological Inst. | Lowell, Mass........ | 1895 | Martin J. Lydon...... | S | 5,600 | 459 |
| Loyola.................... | Baltimore, Md....... | 1852 | V. Rev. J. A. Sellinger.. | D | 2,778 | 191 |
| Loyola Univ.......(T) (Med) | Chicago, Ill......... | 1869 | V. Rev. J. F. Maguire.. | D | 12,651 | 1,100 |
| Loyola Univ............... | New Orleans, La..... | 1849 | V. Rev. H. R. Jolley... | D | 4,334 | 364 |
| Loyola Univ. of L. A....... | Los Angeles, Calif... | 1911 | V. Rev. C. S. Casassa.. | D | *2,372* | *154* |
| Luther................(T) | Decorah, Iowa...... | 1861 | Elwin D. Farwell..... | D | 1,950 | 124 |
| Luther Theol. Sem........(M) | St. Paul, Minn...... | 1869 | Alvin N. Rogness..... | D | 530 | 43 |
| Lutheran Sch. of Theology..... | Chicago, Ill......... | 1860 | Stewart W. Herman... | D | 340 | 32 |
| Lutheran Theol. Sem....... | Philadelphia, Pa.... | 1864 | Rev. D. R. Heiges...... | D | 237 | 26 |
| Lycoming................. | Williamsport, Pa.... | 1812 | D. Frederick Wertz... | D | 1,569 | 102 |
| Lynchburg................ | Lynchburg, Va...... | 1903 | Carey Brewer........ | D | 1,592 | 97 |
| Lyndon State........(T) | Lyndonville, Vt..... | 1911 | Robert E. Long....... | S | 374 | 36 |
| Macalester................ | St. Paul, Minn...... | 1874 | Harvey M. Rice....... | P | 1,769 | 148 |
| MacMurray............(W) | Jacksonville, Ill..... | 1846 | Gordon E. Michalson.. | D | 1,064 | 70 |
| Madison.................. | Harrisonburg, Va.... | 1908 | G. Tyler Miller....... | S | 3,000 | 199 |
| Madonna........(T) (W) | Livonia, Mich....... | 1947 | Sister Mary Danatha.. | D | 700 | 44 |
| Maine Maritime Academy...(M) | Castine, Me........ | 1941 | E. A. Rodgers (Supt.).. | S | 510 | 39 |
| Maine, Univ. of........... | Orono, Me......... | 1865 | Edwin Young........ | S | *13,732* | *748* |
| Malone................... | Canton, Ohio....... | 1892 | Everett L. Cattell..... | D | 1,129 | 59 |
| Manchester............... | No. Manchester, Ind.. | 1889 | Alfred B. Helman..... | D | 1,483 | 71 |
| Manhattan................ | Bronx, N. Y........ | 1853 | Brother Gregory...... | D | 4,598 | 335 |
| Manhattan Sch. of Music..... | New York, N. Y..... | 1917 | John Brownlee....... | P | 680 | 175 |
| Manhattanville............ | Purchase, N. Y...... | 1841 | Mo. E. J. McCormack.. | D | 1,402 | 135 |
| Mankato State.........(T) | Mankato, Minn...... | 1867 | James F. Nickerson... | S | *11,304* | *473* |
| Mansfield State.........(T) | Mansfield, Pa....... | 1857 | Fred E. Bryan....... | S | 2,600 | 195 |
| Marian................... | Indianapolis, Ind.... | 1937 | D. J. Guzzetta....... | D | 1,061 | 77 |
| Marian Coll. of Fon du Lac (T)(W) | Fon du Lac, Wis..... | 1936 | Sister Mary Sheila.... | D | 472 | 47 |
| Marietta.................. | Marietta, Ohio...... | 1835 | Frank E. Duddy...... | P | 2,075 | 125 |
| Marillac.............(T)(W) | St. Louis, Mo....... | 1955 | Sister Rose Collins.... | D | 407 | 55 |
| Marion................(T) | Marion, Ind........ | 1920 | Woodrow Goodman... | D | 680 | 43 |
| Marist................(T) | Poughkeepsie, N. Y.. | 1929 | Bro. Linus Richard Foy.. | D | 1,860 | 98 |
| Marlboro................. | Marlboro, Vt....... | 1946 | Thomas B. Ragle..... | P | 175 | 28 |
| Marquette Univ........... | Milwaukee, Wis..... | 1881 | V. Rev. J. P. Raynor... | D | 11,611 | 730 |
| Mars Hill............(T) | Mars Hill, N. C..... | 1856 | Fred Blake Bentley.... | D | 1,403 | 90 |
| Marshall Univ............ | Huntington, W. Va.. | 1837 | Roland H. Nelson Jr... | S | *8,200* | *330* |
| Martin Luther............ | New Ulm, Minn..... | 1884 | Conrad Frey......... | D | 617 | 45 |
| Mary Baldwin.........(W) | Staunton, Va....... | 1842 | Samuel R. Spencer, Jr.. | D | 701 | 51 |
| Mary Hardin Baylor......(T) | Belton, Tex......... | 1845 | Leonard L. Holloway... | D | 955 | 62 |
| Mary Manse......(T) (W) | Toledo, Ohio....... | 1922 | Sis. Mary Lawrence... | D | 1,284 | 80 |
| Marycrest........(T) (W) | Davenport, Iowa.... | 1939 | Sister Mary Ellen..... | D | 1,091 | 67 |
| Marygrove............(W) | Detroit, Mich....... | 1910 | Sis. Jane Mary (Act.).. | D | *1,369* | *109* |
| Maryknoll............(M) | Glen Ellyn, Ill...... | 1949 | Rev. Charles Kenney.. | D | 368 | 41 |
| Maryland Inst............ | Baltimore, Md....... | 1826 | Eugene W. Leake..... | P | 1,850 | 70 |
| Maryland, Univ. of*...(T) (Med) | College Park, Md.... | 1812 | Wilson H. Elkins..... | S | *40,347* | *3,178* |
| Marylhurst..........(T)(W) | Marylhurst, Ore..... | 1893 | Sister Anselm Mary... | D | 616 | 73 |
| Marymount...........(W) | Los Angeles, Calif.... | 1932 | Sister M. Raymunde. McKay........... | D | *415* | *44* |
| Marymount...........(T) (W) | Salina, Kan........ | 1922 | Sister Etta L. Knaup... | D | 555 | 75 |
| Marymount...........(W) | Tarrytown, N. Y..... | 1907 | Sister Brendan....... | D | 1,042 | 92 |
| Marymount Manhattan..(T) (W) | New York, N. Y..... | 1948 | Sis. Colette Mahoney.. | D | 525 | 63 |
| Maryville................. | Maryville, Tenn..... | 1819 | Joseph J. Copeland.... | D | 829 | 69 |
| Maryville............(W) (T) | St. Louis, Mo....... | 1872 | Mary Grey McNally... | D | 575 | 67 |
| Mary Washington (a)...(T) (W) | Fredericksburg, Va.. | 1908 | G. C. Simpson (Chan.).. | S | 2,091 | 163 |
| Marywood............(W) | Scranton, Pa....... | 1915 | Sister M. St. Mary.... | D | 1,900 | 120 |
| Massachusetts Coll. of Art...... | Boston, Mass....... | 1873 | Robert L. Bertolli..... | S | 631 | 40 |
| Mass. Coll. of Pharmacy...... | Boston, Mass....... | 1823 | Leonard F. Tibbetts... | P | 633 | 45 |
| Mass. Institute of Tech.*...... | Cambridge, Mass.... | 1865 | Howard Johnson...... | P | 7,293 | 774 |
| Mass. Maritime Academy...(M) | Buzzards Bay, Mass.. | 1891 | A. Sanford Limouze... | S | 218 | 23 |
| Massachusetts State Colleges: | | | | | | |
| State Coll. at Boston.....(T) | Boston, Mass....... | 1852 | William F. Looney.... | S | 6,532 | 320 |
| State Coll. at Bridgewater..(T) | Bridgewater, Mass... | 1840 | Adrian Rondileau.... | S | 5,000 | 225 |
| State Coll. at Fitchburg..(T) | Fitchburg, Mass..... | 1894 | James J. Hammond... | S | 3,232 | 216 |
| St. Coll. at Framingham....(T) | Framingham, Mass.. | 1839 | D. Justin McCarthy... | S | 2,700 | 149 |
| State Coll. at Lowell......(T) | Lowell, Mass....... | 1894 | Daniel H. O'Leary.... | S | 1,761 | 140 |
| State Coll. at No. Adams..(T) | N. Adams, Mass..... | 1894 | Andrew S. Flagg..... | S | 1,200 | 61 |
| State Coll. at Salem......(T) | Salem, Mass........ | 1854 | Frederick A. Meler.... | S | 5,439 | 221 |
| State Coll. at Westfield....(T) | Westfield, Mass..... | 1839 | Leonard J. Savignano.. | S | 2,838 | 107 |
| State Coll. at Worcester...(T) | Worcester, Mass..... | 1871 | Eugene A. Sullivan.... | S | 1,614 | 100 |
| Massachusetts,Univ. of*(T)(Med) | Amherst, Mass...... | 1863 | John W. Lederle...... | S | *17,351* | *1,036* |
| Boston Campus.......... | Boston, Mass....... | 1964 | John W. Ryan (Chan.).. | S | 1,244 | 73 |
| Maryville State.........(T) | Maryville, N. Dak... | 1889 | T. S. Jenkins........ | S | 750 | 48 |
| McKendree...........(T) | Lebanon, Ill........ | 1828 | E. E. Voigt.......... | D | 499 | 37 |

(a) Affiliated with Univ. of Virginia.

| Name | Location | Yr. | Governing Official and Control | | Students | Teachers |
|---|---|---|---|---|---|---|
| McMurry | Abilene, Tex. | 1923 | Gordon Bennett | D | 1,522 | 85 |
| McNeese State (T) | Lake Charles, La. | 1939 | W. N. Cusic | S | 4,366 | 214 |
| McPherson | McPherson, Kan. | 1887 | J. Jack Melhorn | D | 753 | 41 |
| Medaille (T) | Buffalo, N. Y. | 1937 | Sis. Mary Lawrence | D | 457 | 51 |
| Meharry Medical | Nashville, Tenn. | 1876 | Lloyd C. Elam | P | 392 | 252 |
| Memphis Academy of Arts | Memphis, Tenn. | 1936 | Edwin C. Rust (Dir.) | P | 519 | 37 |
| Memphis State Univ. (T) | Memphis, Tenn. | 1912 | Cecil C. Humphreys | S | 14,300 | 650 |
| Menlo (M) | Menlo Park, Calif. | 1915 | William Kratt | P | 520 | 42 |
| Mercer Univ. | Macon, Ga. | 1833 | Rufus C. Harris | D | 1,868 | 100 |
| Mercy (W) | Dobbs Ferry, N. Y. | 1950 | Sis. M. E. Christie | D | 640 | 69 |
| Mercy Coll. of Detroit (W) | Detroit, Mich. | 1941 | Sis. Mary Karl George | D | 1,132 | 110 |
| Mercyhurst (T) (W) | Erie, Pa. | 1926 | Sis. Mary Carolyn | D | 673 | 55 |
| Meredith (W) | Raleigh, N. C. | 1891 | E. Bruce Hellman | D | 856 | 69 |
| Merrimack | No. Andover, Mass. | 1947 | Rev. V. A. McQuade | D | 2,413 | 150 |
| Messiah | Grantham, Pa. | 1909 | D. Ray Hostetter | D | 447 | 35 |
| Methodist | Fayetteville, N. C. | 1956 | L. S. Weaver | P | 994 | 56 |
| Miami Univ. (T) | Oxford, Ohio | 1809 | Phillip R. Shriver | S | 13,451 | 697 |
| Miami, Univ. of (T) | Coral Gables, Fla. | 1925 | Henry K. Stanford | P | 16,195 | 1,400 |
| Michigan State Univ.* (T) (Med) | East Lansing, Mich. | 1855 | John A. Hannah | S | 45,949 | 3,051 |
| Oakland Univ. (T) | Rochester, Mich. | 1957 | Durward B. Varner | S | 4,000 | 185 |
| Michigan Technological Univ. | Houghton, Mich. | 1885 | Raymond L. Smith | S | 4,950 | 358 |
| Michigan, Univ. of (T) (Med) | Ann Arbor, Mich. | 1817 | Robbin W. Fleming | S | 37,283 | 4,081 |
| Middle Tennessee State Univ. (T) | Murfreesboro, Tenn. | 1911 | Quill W. Cope | S | 6,041 | 300 |
| Middlebury | Middlebury, Vt. | 1800 | James I. Armstrong | P | 1,357 | 136 |
| Midland Lutheran | Fremont, Nebr. | 1883 | L. Dale Lund | D | 954 | 57 |
| Midwestern Baptist Theol. Sem. | Kansas City, Mo. | 1957 | Millard J. Berquist | D | 206 | 19 |
| Midwestern Univ. (T) | Wichita Falls, Tex. | 1922 | Travis A. White | Mu | 3,391 | 138 |
| Miles | Birmingham, Ala. | 1907 | Lucius H. Pitts | D | 963 | 63 |
| Millersville State (T) | Millersville, Pa. | 1854 | Robert Christie | S | 4,253 | 272 |
| Milligan | Milligan Coll., Tenn. | 1881 | Dean E. Walker (Chan.) | P | 795 | 62 |
| Millikin Univ. | Decatur, Ill. | 1901 | Paul L. McKay | P | 1,797 | 125 |
| Mills (W) | Oakland, Calif. | 1852 | Robert J. Wert | P | 711 | 87 |
| Mills Coll. of Education (T) (W) | New York, N. Y. | 1909 | Margaret Devine (Act.) | P | 495 | 42 |
| Millsaps | Jackson, Miss. | 1890 | Benjamin B. Graves | D | 940 | 79 |
| Milton (T) | Milton, Wis. | 1844 | C. W. Banta | P | 645 | 52 |
| Milwaukee Sch. of Eng. | Milwaukee, Wis. | 1903 | Karl O. Werwath | P | 2,753 | 152 |
| Minneapolis Sch. of Art | Minneapolis, Minn. | 1886 | A. Herstand (Dir.) | P | 553 | 43 |
| Minnesota Bible | Minneapolis, Minn. | 1913 | Galen E. Skinner | P | 130 | 11 |
| Minnesota, Univ. of* (T) (Med) | Minneapolis, Minn. | 1851 | Malcolm C. Moos | S | 66,000 | 2,450 |
| Duluth Campus (T) | Duluth, Minn. | 1947 | R. W. Darland (Prov.) | S | 4,917 | 250 |
| Morris Campus (T) | Morris, Minn. | 1960 | Rodney A. Briggs (Dn.) | S | 1,100 | 80 |
| Minot State (T) | Minot, N. Dak. | 1913 | Gorden B. Olsen | S | 2,059 | 120 |
| Misericordia (T) (W) | Dallas, Pa. | 1924 | Sister Miriam Teresa | D | 1,134 | 98 |
| Mississippi | Clinton, Miss. | 1826 | Richard A. McLemore | D | 2,113 | 99 |
| Mississippi Industrial | Holly Springs, Miss. | 1905 | E. E. Rankin | D | 350 | 21 |
| Miss. St. Coll. for Women (W) | Columbus, Miss. | 1884 | Charles P. Hogarth | S | 2,419 | 169 |
| Mississippi State Univ.* | State Coll., Miss. | 1878 | William L. Giles | S | 8,633 | 650 |
| Mississippi, Univ. of (T) (Med) | University, Miss. | 1844 | P.E.Fortune,Jr.(Chan.) | S | 7,468 | 700 |
| Mississippi Valley State (T) | Ita Bena, Miss. | 1946 | J. H. White | S | 2,468 | 118 |
| Missouri, Univ. of* (T) (Med) | Columbia, Mo. | 1839 | John C. Weaver | S | 40,000 | 2,200 |
| At Kansas City (T) | Kansas City, Mo. | 1933 | *Vacant* | S | 8,025 | 879 |
| At Rolla (T) | Rolla, Mo. | 1870 | Merl Baker (Chan.) | S | 4,563 | 293 |
| At St. Louis (T) | St. Louis, Mo. | 1963 | J. L. Bugg (Chan.) | S | 6,110 | 227 |
| Missouri Valley (T) | Marshall, Mo. | 1889 | M. Earle Collins | D | 833 | 48 |
| Mobile | Mobile, Ala. | 1961 | William H. Weaver, Jr. | D | 343 | 30 |
| Molloy Cath. Coll. for Women (W) | Rockville Ctre., N. Y. | 1955 | Mother M. Celeste | D | 912 | 77 |
| Monmouth | Monmouth, Ill. | 1853 | G. Duncan Wimpress | P | 1,296 | 94 |
| Monmouth (T) | W. Long Branch, N. J. | 1933 | William G. Van Note | P | 4,742 | 263 |
| Montana Coll. of Mineral Science and Technology | Butte, Mont. | 1893 | Edwin G. Koch | S | 552 | 41 |
| Montana State Univ. (T) | Bozeman, Mont. | 1893 | Leon H. Johnson | S | 6,301 | 477 |
| Montana, Univ. of (T) | Missoula, Mont. | 1893 | Robert Pantzen | S | 5,700 | 340 |
| Montclair State (T) | Upper Montclair, N. J. | 1908 | T. H. Richardson | S | 7,100 | 320 |
| Moore Coll. of Art (W) | Philadelphia, Pa. | 1844 | Mayo Bryce | P | 514 | 71 |
| Moorhead State (T) | Moorhead, Minn. | 1885 | John J. Neumaier | S | 4,100 | 275 |
| Moravian | Bethlehem, Pa. | 1807 | Raymond S. Haupert | P | 1,563 | 111 |
| Morehead State Univ. (T) | Morehead, Ky. | 1923 | Adron Doran | S | 5,779 | 279 |
| Morehouse (M) | Atlanta, Ga. | 1867 | Hugh Gloster | P | 989 | 80 |
| Morgan State (T) | Baltimore, Md. | 1867 | Martin D. Jenkins | S | 3,643 | 267 |
| Morningside | Sioux City, Iowa | 1894 | J. Richard Palmer | D | 1,387 | 105 |
| Morris Brown (M) | Atlanta, Ga. | 1881 | John A. Middleton | D | 1,065 | 80 |
| Morris Harvey | Charleston, W. Va. | 1888 | Marshall Buckalew | D | 2,900 | 150 |
| Mt. Angel (T) | Mt. Angel, Ore. | 1887 | Bro. LaSalle Woelfel | D | 960 | 53 |
| Mt. Holyoke (W) | So. Hadley, Mass. | 1837 | Richard G. Gettell | P | 1,749 | 180 |
| Mt. Marty (T) (W) | Yankton, S. D. | 1936 | Sister Evangeline | D | 509 | 64 |
| Mt. Mary (T) (W) | Yankton, S. Dak. | 1936 | Sister M. Evangeline | D | 491 | 56 |
| Mt. Mary (T) (W) | Milwaukee, Wis. | 1913 | Sister Mary Francis | D | 1,103 | 113 |
| Mt. Mercy (T) (W) | Cedar Rapids, Iowa | 1957 | Sister Mary Agnes | D | 650 | 40 |
| Mt. Mercy (W) | Pittsburgh, Pa. | 1929 | Sister M. C. Scully | P | 885 | 70 |
| Mt. St. Agnes (T) (W) | Baltimore, Md. | 1890 | Sister Mary Cleophas | D | 450 | 55 |
| Mt. St. Joseph-on-the-Ohio (W) | Mt. St. Joseph, Ohio | 1854 | Sister Adele | D | 988 | 93 |
| Mt. St. Mary (T) | Hooksett, N. Hamp. | 1934 | Sister Mary Vianney | D | 303 | 45 |
| Mt. St. Mary (T) | Newburgh, N. Y. | 1959 | Mo. M. F. McDonald | D | 471 | 65 |
| Mt. St. Mary's (W) | Los Angeles, Calif. | 1925 | Sister Cecilia Louise | D | 1,299 | 117 |
| Mt. St. Mary's (M) | Emmitsburg, Md. | 1808 | Rev. Hugh Phillips | D | 850 | 67 |
| Mt. St. Paul | Waukesha, Wis. | 1962 | V. Rev. G. Stapleton | D | 196 | 37 |
| Mt. St. Scholastica (T) | Atchinson, Kans. | 1924 | Sis. Mary Noel (Act.) | D | 823 | 60 |
| Mt. St. Vincent, Coll. of (W) | Bronx, N. Y. | 1847 | Sister Mary David | D | 990 | 85 |
| Mt. Senario (T) | Ladysmith, Wis. | 1962 | Sis. Mary Hyacinth | D | 183 | 27 |
| Mt. Union (T) | Alliance, Ohio | 1846 | Ronald Weber (Act.) | D | 1,200 | 84 |
| Muhlenberg | Allentown, Pa. | 1848 | Erling N. Jensen | D | 1,732 | 103 |
| Multnomah Sch. of the Bible | Portland, Ore. | 1936 | Willard M. Aldrich | D | 447 | 27 |
| Mundelein (W) | Chicago, Ill. | 1929 | Sister Mary Ann Ida | D | 1,112 | 100 |
| Murray State Univ. (T) | Murray, Ky. | 1922 | Harry Sparks | S | 6,637 | 376 |
| Muskingum | New Concord, Ohio | 1837 | Harry S. Manley | D | 1,322 | 103 |
| Nasson | Springvale, Me. | 1912 | Roger C. Gay | P | 877 | 60 |
| Nathaniel Hawthorne | Antrim, N. H. | 1962 | Kenneth McLaughlin | P | 580 | 35 |
| Nazareth (W) | Kalamazoo, Mich. | 1924 | Sis. Mary L. Bader | D | 450 | 60 |
| Nazareth Coll. of Rochester (W) | Rochester, N. Y. | 1924 | Sister Helen Daniel | D | 1,381 | 115 |
| Nazareth (T) | Nazareth, Ky. | 1914 | Charles Karcher | D | 443 | 59 |
| Nebraska, Univ. of* (T) (Med) | Lincoln, Nebr. | 1869 | Clifford Hardin (Chan.) | S | 18,802 | 937 |
| At Omaha | Omaha, Nebr. | 1908 | Kirk Naylor | S | 8,288 | 350 |
| Nebraska Wesleyan Univ. | Lincoln, Nebr. | 1897 | Vance D. Rogers | D | 1,278 | 103 |

| Name | Location | Yr. | Governing Official and Control | | Students | Teachers |
|---|---|---|---|---|---|---|
| Ner Israel Rabbinical...(T) (M) | Baltimore, Md...... | 1933 | Rabbi J. I. Ruderman.. | D | 242 | 20 |
| Nevada, Univ. of*..........(T) | Reno, Nev......... | 1864 | N. O. Humphrey(Chan.) | S | 9,481 | 442 |
| New .................... | Sarasota, Fla...... | 1960 | John Elmendorf....... | P | 2 0 | 43 |
| New England .........(T) | Henniker, N. H ..... | 1946 | H. Raymond Danforth.. | P | 765 | 73 |
| New England Conservatory.... | Boston, Mass...... | 1867 | Gunther Schuller ..... | P | 524 | 97 |
| N. H. Coll. of Acct. & Comm. .. | Manchester, N. H. ... | 1932 | Gertrude Shapiro ..... | Pr. | 1,521 | 55 |
| New Haven............. | New Haven, Conn. .. | 1926 | John W. McConnell .... | S | 8,815 | 723 |
| New Haven............. | New Haven, Conn. .. | 1926 | Marvin K. Petersen.... | Y | 3,156 | 265 |
| N. J. Coll. of Med. & Dent. .... | Jersey City, N. J.... | 1965 | Robert Cadmus ....... | S | 490 | 217 |
| New Mexico Highlands Univ. (T) | Las Vegas, N. Mex. | 1893 | Thomas Donnelly ..... | S | 2,022 | 103 |
| N. Mex. Inst. of Min. & Tech... | Socorro, N. Mex..... | 1889 | Stirling A. Colgate..... | S | 588 | 56 |
| New Mexico State Univ.*....... | Las Cruces, N. Mex. | 1888 | Roger B. Corbett....... | S | 6,305 | 434 |
| New Mexico, Univ. of (T) (Med) | Albuquerque, N. Mex. | 1889 | Ferrel Heady ........ | S | 13,024 | 747 |
| New Orleans Bapt. Theol. Sem. . | New Orleans, La. .. | 1917 | H. Leo Eddleman...... | D | 825 | 52 |
| New Rochelle, Coll. of...(T) (W) | New Rochelle, N. Y.. | 1904 | Mother M. R. Falls.... | D | 940 | 88 |
| New Sch. for Social Research.... | New York, N. Y. .. | 1919 | John R. Everett....... | P | 11,175 | 383 |
| New York City Un. of........ | | 1961 | A. H. Bowker (Chan.).. | Mu | 90,900 | 5,620 |
| Brooklyn.............(T) | Brooklyn, N. Y. ... | 1930 | Harold C. Syrett...... | Mu | 19,631 | 1,453 |
| City.................(T) | New York, N. Y. ... | 1847 | Buell G. Gallagher .... | Mu | 28,862 | 1,700 |
| Hunter...............(T) | New York, N. Y. ... | 1870 | Robert D. Cross....... | Mu | 18,000 | 1,000 |
| Queens...............(T) | Flushing, N. Y. .... | 1937 | Joseph P. McMurray... | Mu | 24,397 | 1,467 |
| New York Coll. of Music ...... | New York, N. Y. .. | 1878 | Jerrold Ross.......... | P | [315 | 106 |
| N. Y. Inst. of Technology...... | New York, N. Y. .. | 1910 | Alexander Schure ..... | P | 4,494 | 390 |
| New York Law School........ | New York, N. Y. .. | 1891 | Sylvester C. Smith, Jr. . | P | 500 | 20 |
| New York Medical........... | New York, N. Y. .. | 1860 | David Denker......... | P | 608 | 1,160 |
| New York, State Univ. of...... | Albany, N. Y. ..... | 1948 | Samuel B. Gould...... | S | 91,188 | 6,407 |
| State Univ. ............ | Albany, N. Y. ..... | 1844 | Evan R. Collins ...... | S | 9,089 | 560 |
| "      "      ...........(Med) | Buffalo, N. Y. ..... | 1846 | Martin Meyerson ..... | S | 19,113 | 1,170 |
| "      "      .......... | Binghamton, N. Y. . | 1946 | G. Bruce Dearing ..... | S | 4,028 | 268 |
| "      "      .......... | Stony Brook, N. Y. . | 1957 | John Toll........... | S | 5,199 | 400 |
| State Univ. College ......(T) | Brockport, N. Y. ... | 1867 | Albert W. Brown...... | S | 4,574 | 243 |
| "      "      "       (T) | Buffalo, N. Y. ..... | 1867 | Elbert K. Fretwell..... | S | 7,561 | 468 |
| "      "      "       (T) | Cortland, N. Y. .... | 1868 | Kenneth E. Young..... | S | 4,127 | 242 |
| "      "      "       (T) | Fredonia, N. Y. .... | 1867 | Oscar F. Lanford ..... | S | 3,112 | 196 |
| "      "      "       (T) | Geneseo, N. Y ..... | 1871 | R. W. MacVittle...... | S | 3,562 | 223 |
| "      "      "       (T) | New Paltz, N. Y. ... | 1885 | John J. Neumaier ..... | S | 4,519 | 335 |
| "      "      "       (T) | Oneonta, N. Y. .... | 1887 | Royal F. Netzer ...... | S | 4,251 | 287 |
| "      "      "       (T) | Oswego, N. Y. ..... | 1861 | James E. Perdue...... | S | 5,029 | 346 |
| "      "      "       (T) | Plattsburgh, N. Y... | 1889 | George W. Angell...... | S | 3,496 | 215 |
| "      "      "       (T) | Potsdam, N. Y. .... | 1867 | H. Austin Peck ...... | S | 3,009 | 214 |
| College of Agriculture....... | Ithaca, N. Y. ..... | 1904 | Chas. E. Palm (Dean).. | S | 2,989 | 134 |
| Buffalo Health Science Center. | Buffalo, N. Y. ..... | 1846 | P. F. Regan........ | S | 1,682 | (a) |
| College of Ceramics......... | Alfred, N. Y. ..... | 1900 | Edward E. Mueller..... | S | 541 | 56 |
| College of Forestry.......(M) | Syracuse, N. Y. .... | 1911 | E. C. Jahn (Act.)...... | S | 1,349 | 107 |
| College of Home Econ.....(W) | Ithaca, N. Y. ..... | 1925 | H. G. Canoyer (Dean). | S | 993 | 65 |
| Downstate Health Science Cen. | Brooklyn, N. Y. .... | 1858 | Joseph K. Hill........ | S | 884 | 584 |
| Maritime College.........(M) | Ft. Schuyler, N. Y... | 1874 | Edward J. O'Donnell... | S | 716 | 50 |
| Sch. of Ind. & Labor Rel ...... | Ithaca, N. Y. ..... | 1944 | David C. J. Moore (Dn.). | S | 484 | 32 |
| Upstate Health Science Center. | Syracuse, N. Y. .... | 1834 | W. W. Westerfeld (Act.) | S | 575 | 176 |
| Veterinary College.......... | Ithaca, N. Y. ..... | 1894 | G. C. Poppensieck (Dn.) | S | 306 | 46 |
| New York Univ. ....(T) (Med) | New York, N. Y. .. | 1831 | James M. Hester...... | P | 42,184 | 5,320 |
| Newark Coll. of Engineering ... | Newark, N. J. ..... | 1881 | Robert W. Van Houten. | SMu | 3,654 | 280 |
| Newark State...........(T) | Union, N. J. ...... | 1855 | Eugene G. Wilkins .... | S | 3,189 | 300 |
| Newberry.................. | Newberry, S. C..... | 1856 | A. G. D. Wiles........ | D | 760 | 55 |
| Newton Coll. of Sacred Heart (W) | Newton, Mass...... | 1946 | Mother Gabrielle Husson | D | 819 | 85 |
| Niagara Univ. ............ | Niagara Un., N. Y... | 1856 | Rev. K. F. Slattery..... | D | 2,663 | 169 |
| Nichols Coll. of Bus. Admin. (M) | Dudley, Mass...... | 1815 | Gordon B. Cross...... | P | 670 | 42 |
| No. Carolina A. & T. State U. ... | Greensboro, N. C. .. | 1891 | Lewis Dowdy ........ | S | 3,940 | 230 |
| North Carolina Coll.at Durham(T) | Durham, N. C. .... | 1909 | Albert N. Whiting..... | S | 3,086 | 230 |
| North Carolina, Univ. of....... | Chapel Hill, N. C. . | 1795 | William Friday ...... | S | 32,393 | 2,300 |
| at Raleigh............(T) | Raleigh, N. C. ..... | 1887 | J. T. Caldwell (Chan.).. | S | 10,392 | 764 |
| at Chapel Hill......(T) (Med) | Chapel Hill, N. C. .. | 1789 | J. C. Sitterson (Chan.).. | S | 15,110 | 1,100 |
| at Greensboro.......... | Greensboro, N. C. .. | 1891 | J. S. Ferguson (Act.)... | S | 5,364 | 334 |
| at Charlotte............ | Charlotte, N. C. .... | 1946 | D. W. Colvard (Chan.). | S | 1,527 | 101 |
| North Carolina Wesleyan...(T) | Rocky Mount, N. C. | 1956 | Thomas A. Collins .... | D | 643 | 51 |
| North Central Bible......... | Minneapolis, Minn.. | 1930 | G. Raymond Carlson... | D | 363 | 20 |
| North Central............(T) | Naperville, Ill...... | 1861 | Arlo L. Schilling ..... | D | 1,080 | 87 |
| North Dakota State Univ. ...(T) | Fargo, N. Dak...... | 1890 | L. D. Loftsgard (Act.) . | S | 5,800 | 300 |
| No. Dak., Univ. of... (T) (Med) | Grand Forks, N. Dak. | 1883 | George W. Starcher.... | S | 6,686 | 380 |
| North Georgia............(T) | Dahlonega, Ga..... | 1873 | Merritt E. Hoag....... | S | 1,044 | 60 |
| North Park............... | Chicago, Ill........ | 1891 | Karl A. Olsson ...... | D | 1,704 | 112 |
| North Texas State Univ. ....(T) | Denton, Tex........ | 1890 | J. C. Matthews....... | S | 13,356 | 552 |
| Northeast La. State.......(T) | Monroe, La........ | 1931 | George T. Walker ..... | S | 6,328 | 315 |
| Northeast Mo. St..........(T) | Kirksville, Mo...... | 1867 | F. Clark Elkins....... | S | 5,319 | 240 |
| Northeastern State........(T) | Tahlequah, Okla.... | 1919 | Harrell E. Garrison..... | S | 5,398 | 185 |
| Northeastern Univ..........(T) | Boston, Mass...... | 1898 | Asa S. Knowles....... | P | 31,432 | 897 |
| Northern Arizona Univ.....(T) | Flagstaff, Ariz...... | 1899 | J. Lawrence Walkup... | S | 7,250 | 345 |
| Northern Ill. Univ..........(T) | DeKalb, Ill........ | 1895 | Rhoten A. Smith ..... | S | 17,251 | 1,048 |
| Northern Iowa, Univ. of...... | Cedar Falls, Iowa .. | 1876 | James W. Maucker..... | S | 6,930 | 405 |
| Northern Michigan Univ. ...(T) | Marquette, Mich..... | 1899 | John X. Jamrich ...... | S | 6,585 | 380 |
| Northern Montana.........(T) | Harve, Mont....... | 1929 | Joseph R. Crowley .... | S | 1,195 | 86 |
| Northern St.............(T) | Aberdeen, S. Dak... | 1902 | J. Howard Kramer..... | S | 3,000 | 130 |
| Northland................ | Ashland, Wis....... | 1892 | Robert Cramer ...... | P | 698 | 55 |
| Northrop Inst. of Tech....... | Inglewood, Calif..... | 1942 | Homer H. Grant ..... | P | 1,830 | 93 |
| Northwest Christian......... | Eugene, Ore....... | 1895 | Barton A. Dowdy...... | D | 394 | 23 |
| Northwest................ | Kirkland, Wash..... | 1934 | Rev. D. V. Hurst...... | D | 406 | 24 |
| Northwest Missouri State....(T) | Maryville, Mo...... | 1905 | Robert P. Foster...... | S | 3,936 | 215 |
| Northwestern............. | Orange City, Iowa .. | 1882 | Lars Granberg........ | D | 727 | 51 |
| Northwestern State........(T) | Natchitoches, La. .. | 1884 | Arnold R. Kilpatrick... | S | 5,487 | 303 |
| Northwestern State........(T) | Alva, Okla........ | 1897 | Jesse W. Martin...... | S | 2,303 | 83 |
| Northwestern Univ. ...(T) (Med) | Evanston, Ill....... | 1851 | J. Roscoe Miller ..... | P | 16,766 | 2,297 |
| Norwich Univ. ...........(M) | Northfield, Vt....... | 1819 | Gen. Barksdale Hamlett | P | 1,195 | 102 |
| Notre Dame, Coll. of........ | Belmont, Calif...... | 1868 | Sister Catharine Julie... | D | 1,647 | 129 |
| Notre Dame............(W) | St. Louis, Mo....... | 1954 | Mother M. Francis..... | D | 338 | 36 |
| Notre Dame.............(T) | Cleveland, Ohio..... | 1922 | Sister Jeannette....... | D | 375 | 33 |
| Notre Dame..............(W) | Cleveland, Ohio..... | 1922 | Sister Mary Luke ..... | D | 573 | 65 |
| Notre Dame.of Maryland (W)(T) | Baltimore, Md...... | 1873 | Sister M. Mary....... | D | 1,232 | 82 |
| Notre Dame Coll. of S. I. ...(W) | Staten Island, N. Y.. | 1931 | Sister Rita Donahue.... | D | 499 | 37 |
| Notre Dame Seminary....... | New Orleans, La. .. | 1923 | Rev. Albert Ernst ..... | D | 133 | 20 |
| Notre Dame, Univ. of......(M) | Notre Dame, Ind. .. | 1846 | Rev. T. M. Hesburgh... | D | 7,500 | 600 |
| Nyack Missionary.........(T) | Nyack, N. Y. ..... | 1882 | Harold W. Boon...... | D | 560 | 52 |
| Oakland City.............(T) | Oakland City, Ind... | 1885 | Carl E. Shepard...... | D | 600 | 37 |

(a) Included with staff of Univ. of Buffalo.

| Name | Location | Yr. | Governing Official and Control | | Students | Teachers |
|---|---|---|---|---|---|---|
| Oberlin | Oberlin, Ohio | 1833 | Robert K. Carr | P | 2,492 | 245 |
| Occidental | Los Angeles, Calif | 1887 | Richard C. Gilman | P | 1,714 | 117 |
| Oglethorpe (T) | Atlanta, Ga. | 1835 | Paul K. Vonk | P | 898 | 53 |
| Ohio Dominican (T) | Columbus, Ohio | 1911 | Sister M. Suzanne | D | 997 | 77 |
| Ohio Coll. of Podiatry | Cleveland, Ohio | 1916 | M. M. Pomerantz | P | 289 | 65 |
| Ohio Northern Univ (T) | Ada, Ohio | 1871 | Samuel L. Meyer | D | 2,650 | 165 |
| Ohio State Univ.* (T) (Med) | Columbus, Ohio | 1870 | Novice G. Fawcett | S | 38,300 | 3,971 |
| Ohio Univ (T) | Athens, Ohio | 1804 | Vernon R. Alden | S | 19,681 | 1,159 |
| Ohio Wesleyan Univ | Delaware, Ohio | 1842 | *Vacant* | D | 2,450 | 160 |
| Oklahoma Baptist Univ (T) | Shawnee, Okla | 1910 | Grady C. Cothen | D | 1,325 | 96 |
| Oklahoma Christian | Oklahoma City, Okla | 1950 | James O. Baird | P | 905 | 45 |
| Oklahoma City Univ (T) | Oklahoma City, Okla | 1904 | John F. Olson | D | 2,458 | 110 |
| Okla. Coll. of Liberal Arts(T)(W) | Chickasha, Okla. | 1908 | Robert Martin | S | 910 | 61 |
| Oklahoma State Univ.* (T) | Stillwater, Okla. | 1890 | Robert B. Kamm | S | 18,282 | 918 |
| Oklahoma, Univ. of (T) (Med) | Norman, Okla. | 1890 | George L. Cross | S | 17,737 | 515 |
| Old Dominion (T) | Norfolk, Va. | 1930 | Lewis W. Webb, Jr. | S | 8,266 | 439 |
| Olivet (T) | Olivet, Mich. | 1844 | Gorton Riethmiller | P | 730 | 52 |
| Olivet Nazarene (T) | Kankakee, Ill. | 1907 | Harold W. Reed | D | 1,803 | 95 |
| Oregon State Univ.* (T) | Corvallis, Ore. | 1868 | James H. Jensen | S | 12,150 | 950 |
| Oregon Technical | Klamath Falls, Ore. | 1947 | W. D. Purvine | S | 1,050 | 105 |
| Oregon, Univ. of (Med) | Eugene, Ore. | 1872 | Arthur S. Flemming | S | 12,800 | 1,400 |
| Osteop. Med. & Surg., Coll. of | Des Moines, Iowa | 1898 | T. F. Vigorito (Dn.) | P | 307 | 31 |
| Otis Art Institute of L. A. County | Los Angeles, Calif | 1918 | A. S. Andersen (Dir.) | C | 303 | 26 |
| Ottawa Univ (T) | Ottawa, Kan. | 1865 | Peter H. Armacost | D | 974 | 60 |
| Otterbein | Westerville, Ohio | 1847 | Lynn W. Turner | D | 1,416 | 104 |
| Ouachita Baptist Univ (T) | Arkadelphia, Ark. | 1885 | Ralph Phelps, Jr. | D | 1,561 | 106 |
| Our Lady of Cincinnati (W) | Cincinnati, Ohio | 1935 | Sis. M. Honora Kroger | D | 1,062 | 75 |
| Our Lady of the Elms, Coll. of (W) | Chicopee, Mass. | 1928 | V. Rev. T. F. Devine | D | 636 | 53 |
| Our Lady of the Lake (T) (W) | San Antonio, Tex. | 1911 | John L. McMahon | D | 1,421 | 110 |
| Ozark Bible | Joplin, Mo. | 1942 | Don E. Boatman | D | 591 | 42 |
| Ozarks, Coll. of the (T) | Clarksville, Ark | 1834 | Don Davis | D | 587 | 40 |
| Ozarks, School of the (T) | Pt. Lookout, Mo. | 1906 | M. Graham Clark | D | 752 | 40 |
| Pace | New York, N. Y. | 1906 | Edward J. Mortola | P | 8,700 | 474 |
| Pacific | Fresno, Calif. | 1944 | Arthur J. Wiebe | D | 343 | 31 |
| Pacific Christian | Long Beach, Calif | 1928 | Kenneth A. Stewart | D | 150 | 19 |
| Pacific Lutheran Univ (T) | Tacoma, Wash. | 1890 | Robert Mortvedt | D | 2,739 | 139 |
| Pacific School of Religion | Berkeley, Calif. | 1866 | Stuart L. Anderson | I | 170 | 17 |
| Pacific Union (T) | Angwin, Calif. | 1882 | F. O. Rittenhouse | D | 1,467 | 126 |
| Pacific Univ (T) | Forest Grove, Ore. | 1849 | Miller A. F. Richie | D | 1,035 | 74 |
| Pacific, Univ. of the (T) | Stockton, Calif. | 1851 | Robert E. Burns | P | 3,770 | 339 |
| Paine | Augusta, Ga. | 1883 | E. Clayton Calhoun | D | 653 | 40 |
| Pan American | Edinburg, Tex. | 1927 | Ralph Schilling | C | 3,717 | 134 |
| Panhandle State | Goodwell, Okla. | 1909 | J. Freeman McKee | S | 1,267 | 65 |
| Park (T) | Parkville, Mo. | 1875 | Donald MacKenzie | D | 553 | 65 |
| Parsons | Fairfield, Iowa | 1875 | W. E. Stamper (Act.) | P | 2,110 | 97 |
| Parsons Sch. of Design | New York, N. Y. | 1909 | Francis A. Ruzicka | P | 580 | 102 |
| Pasadena (T) | Pasadena, Calif. | 1902 | W. S. Brown | D | 1,200 | 60 |
| Pasadena Playhouse Coll. of Theatre Arts | Pasadena, Calif. | 1926 | Winston O'Keefe | D | 175 | 25 |
| Paterson State (T) | Wayne, N. J. | 1855 | James J. Forcina | S | 6,149 | 282 |
| Paul Quinn (T) | Waco, Tex. | 1872 | L. H. McCloney | D | 540 | 40 |
| Peabody Cons. of Music | Baltimore, Md. | 1868 | John M. Nelson | P | 471 | 77 |
| Pembroke State (T) | Pembroke, N. C. | 1887 | English E. Jones | S | 1,418 | 97 |
| PMC Colleges | Chester, Pa. | 1821 | Clarence R. Moll | P | 1,550 | 203 |
| Penna. Coll. of Optometry | Philadelphia, Pa. | 1919 | Lawrence Fitch | P | 348 | 46 |
| Penna. St. Univ.* (T) (Med) | University Park, Pa. | 1855 | Eric A. Walker | S, P | 41,508 | 2,700 |
| Penna., Univ. of (T) (Med) | Philadelphia, Pa. | 1740 | Gaylord P. Harnwell | P | 18,173 | 4,223 |
| Pepperdine | Los Angeles, Calif | 1937 | M. Norvel Young | D | 1,521 | 250 |
| Peru State | Peru, Nebr. | 1867 | Neal S. Gomon | S | 1,076 | 55 |
| Pestalozzi-Froebel Teachers | Chicago, Ill. | 1896 | Daniel D. Howard | P | 380 | 25 |
| Pfeiffer (T) | Misenheimer, N. C. | 1885 | J. Lem Stokes, 2nd | D | 906 | 80 |
| Phila. Coll. of Art | Philadelphia, Pa. | 1876 | George D. Culler | P | 1,396 | 189 |
| Phila. Coll. of Bible | Philadelphia, Pa. | 1913 | D. B. MacCorkle | P | 994 | 58 |
| Phila. Coll. of Osteopathy | Philadelphia, Pa. | 1899 | Frederick H. Barth | P | 379 | 165 |
| Phila. Coll. of Pharm. & Science | Philadelphia, Pa. | 1821 | Arthur Osol | P | 872 | 92 |
| Phila. Coll. of Textiles & Sc | Philadelphia, Pa. | 1884 | Bertrand W. Hayward | P | 1,678 | 155 |
| Philander Smith | Little Rock, Ark | 1877 | Ernest T. Dixon, Jr | D | 663 | 47 |
| Phillips Univ (T) | Enid, Okla. | 1906 | Hallie G. Gantz | D | 1,404 | 105 |
| Piedmont Bible | Winston-Salem, N. C. | 1945 | Charles H. Stevens | P | 528 | 17 |
| Piedmont | Demorest, Ga. | 1897 | James E. Walter | D | 448 | 27 |
| Pikeville (T) | Pikeville, Ky. | 1889 | Thomas Johns | D | 1,183 | 45 |
| Pittsburgh Theological Sem | Pittsburgh, Pa. | 1794 | Donald G. Miller | D | 288 | 31 |
| Pittsburgh, Un. of (T) (Med) | Pittsburgh, Pa. | 1787 | Wesley W. Posvar | P | 23,168 | 1,601 |
| Pitzer | Claremont, Calif. | 1963 | John W. Atherton | P | 515 | 62 |
| Plymouth State (T) | Plymouth, N. H. | 1871 | Harold E. Hyde | S | 1,869 | 103 |
| Point Park (T) | Pittsburgh, Pa. | 1960 | Arthur M. Blum | P | 3,018 | 157 |
| Polytechnic Inst. of Brooklyn | Brooklyn, N. Y. | 1854 | Ernst Weber | P | 5,003 | 387 |
| Pomona | Claremont, Calif. | 1887 | Elijah Wilson Lyon | P | 1,273 | 117 |
| Portland State (T) | Portland, Ore. | 1955 | Branford P. Millar | S | 8,304 | 564 |
| Portland, Univ. of (T) | Portland, Ore. | 1901 | Rev. P. E. Waldschmidt | D | 1,870 | 130 |
| Pratt Institute | Brooklyn, N. Y. | 1887 | James B. Donovan | P | 4,445 | 475 |
| Presbyterian | Clinton, S. C. | 1880 | Marc C. Weersing | D | 648 | 49 |
| Princeton Theol. Sem | Princeton, N. J. | 1812 | James I. McCord | D | 552 | 47 |
| Princeton Univ (M) | Princeton, N. J. | 1746 | Robert F. Goheen | P | 4,675 | 854 |
| Principia (T) | Elsah, Ill. | 1898 | David K. Andrews | P | 662 | 64 |
| Providence College | Providence, R. I. | 1917 | V. Rev. W. P. Haas | D | 3,357 | 192 |
| Puerto Rico, Univ. of* (T) (Med) | Rio Piedras, P. R. | 1903 | Jaime Benitez | (a) | 28,230 | 2,225 |
| Puerto Rico, Inter. Am. Univ. of | San German, P. R. | 1912 | Raymond B. Hoxeng | P | 7,523 | 271 |
| Puget Sound, Univ. of (T) | Tacoma, Wash. | 1888 | R. Franklin Thompson | P | 2,371 | 159 |
| Purdue Univ.* | Lafayette, Ind | 1869 | Frederick L. Hovde | S | 34,263 | 2,173 |
| Queens (W) | Charlotte, N. C. | 1857 | John Smylie | D | 779 | 78 |
| Quincy (T) | Quincy, Ill. | 1859 | Rev. G. Brinkman | D | 1,567 | 97 |
| Quinnipiac | Hamden, Conn. | 1929 | Nils G. Sahlin | P | 2,116 | 147 |
| Rabb. Coll. of Telshe (T) (M) | Wickliffe, Ohio | 1875 | Rabbi M. Gifter | P | 232 | 7 |
| Radcliffe (W) | Cambridge, Mass. | 1879 | Mary I. Bunting | P | 1,200 | (b) |
| Radford (W) | Radford, Va. | 1910 | Charles K. Martin | S | 3,600 | 202 |
| Randolph-Macon (M) | Ashland, Va. | 1830 | Luther W. White | D | 845 | 62 |
| Randolph-Macon Woman's (W) | Lynchburg, Va. | 1891 | William F. Quillian, Jr. | D | 893 | 54 |
| Redlands, Univ. of (T) | Redlands, Calif. | 1909 | George H. Armacost | P | 1,716 | 131 |
| Reed | Portland, Ore. | 1909 | Richard H. Sullivan | P | 1,063 | 118 |
| Regis | Denver, Colo | 1877 | Rev. L. G. Mattione | D | 973 | 78 |
| Regis (W) | Weston, Mass. | 1927 | Sister M. Jeanne D'Arc. | D | 1,189 | 100 |

(a) Controlled by Puerto Rican Govt. (b) Faculty at Harvard Univ. furnishes instruction.

| Name | Location | Yr. | Governing Official and Control | | Students | Teachers |
|---|---|---|---|---|---|---|
| Rensselaer Poly. Inst. | Troy, N. Y. | 1824 | Richard G. Folsom | P | *5,496* | *617* |
| Rhode Island (T) | Providence, R. I. | 1854 | Joseph Kauffman | S | 4,400 | 220 |
| R. I. School of Design | Providence, R. I. | 1877 | Albert Bush-Brown | P | 1,004 | 108 |
| Rhode Island, Univ. of | Kingston, R. I. | 1892 | Werner Baum | S | *5,618* | *500* |
| Rice Univ. | Houston, Tex. | 1912 | Kenneth S. Pitzer | P | 2,767 | 342 |
| Richmond Prof. Inst. (T) | Richmond, Va. | 1917 | Vacant | S | 9,233 | 570 |
| Richmond, Univ. of | Richmond, Va. | 1830 | George M. Modlin | D | 4,104 | 290 |
| Ricker (T) | Houlton, Me. | 1848 | C. Worth Howard | D | 553 | 38 |
| Rider (T) | Trenton, N. J. | 1865 | Franklin F. Moore | P | 5,184 | 269 |
| Rio Grande (T) | Rio Grande, Ohio | 1876 | Alphus R. Christensen | I | 774 | 42 |
| Ripon | Ripon, Wis. | 1851 | Bernard S. Adams | P | 930 | 91 |
| Rivier (W) | Nashua, N. H. | 1933 | Sister Clarice Dion | D | 830 | 58 |
| Roanoke | Salem, Va. | 1842 | Perry F. Kendig | P | 1,233 | 84 |
| Roberts Wesleyan | North Chili, N. Y. | 1866 | Ellwood A. Voller | D | 674 | 57 |
| Rochester Inst. of Technology | Rochester, N. Y. | 1829 | Mark Ellingson | P | 8,528 | 691 |
| Rochester, Univ. of... (T) (Med) | Rochester, N. Y. | 1850 | W. Allen Wallis | P | *8,400* | *1,678* |
| Rockefeller Univ. | New York, N. Y. | 1901 | Frederick Seitz | P | 138 | 255 |
| Rockford | Rockford, Ill. | 1847 | John A. Howard | P | 1,137 | 93 |
| Rockhurst (T) | Kansas City, Mo. | 1910 | Rev. M. E. Van Ackeren | D | 2,117 | 137 |
| Rocky Mountain | Billings, Mont. | 1883 | Lawrence F. Small | D | 445 | 16 |
| Rollins | Winter Park, Fla. | 1885 | Hugh F. McKean | P | 1,050 | 95 |
| Roosevelt Univ. | Chicago, Ill. | 1945 | Rolf A. Weil | P | 6,292 | 332 |
| Rosary (W) | River Forest, Ill. | 1901 | Sister Candida Lund | D | 1,253 | 109 |
| Rosary Hill (W) | Buffalo, N. Y. | 1948 | Sister M. Angela | D | *1,345* | *112* |
| Rose Polytechnic Inst. (M) | Terre Haute, Ind. | 1884 | John A. Logan | P | 809 | 60 |
| Rosemont (W) | Rosemont, Pa. | 1921 | Sister Mary George | D | 690 | 82 |
| Russell Sage (T) (W) | Troy, N. Y. | 1916 | Lewis A. Froman | P | *3,500* | *88* |
| Rust | Holly Spgs., Miss. | 1866 | W. A. McMillan | D | 506 | 31 |
| Rutgers, Univ.* (T) (Med) | New Brunswick, N. J. | 1766 | Mason W. Gross | S | *25,852* | *2,009* |
| Sacramento State | Sacramento, Calif. | 1947 | Robert Johns | S | 12,000 | 600 |
| Sacred Heart (W) | Wichita, Kan. | 1933 | Sister M. Sylvia | D | 728 | 51 |
| Sacred Heart, Coll. of the... (W) | Santurce, P. R. | 1935 | Sis. E. M. O'Byrne (Act.) | D | 518 | 53 |
| Sacred Heart Dominican (W) | Houston, Tex. | 1945 | Toney P. Brown | D | 338 | 60 |
| Sacred Heart Seminary (M) | Detroit, Mich. | 1919 | Rt. Rev. F. X. Canfield | D | 200 | 26 |
| Sacred Heart Univ. (T) | Bridgeport, Conn. | 1963 | William H. Conley | D | 1,900 | 120 |
| St. Ambrose (T) | Davenport, Iowa | 1882 | Rev. S. G. Menke | D | 1,458 | 88 |
| St Andrews Presbyterian | Laurinburg, N. C. | 1858 | Ansley C. Moore | D | 906 | 79 |
| St. Anselm's | Manchester, N. H. | 1889 | Gerald F. McCarthy | D | 1,395 | 105 |
| St. Benedict (T) | Ferdinand, Ind. | 1914 | Sis. M. D. Wilson | D | 287 | 26 |
| St. Benedict, Coll. of... (T) (W) | St. Joseph, Minn. | 1913 | Sister M. Grell | D | 571 | 55 |
| St. Benedict's (M) | Atchison, Kan. | 1858 | Rev. T. Hartmann (Chan.) | D | 1,008 | 63 |
| St. Bernard | St. Bernard, Ala. | 1892 | Rev. Gregory Roettger | D | 735 | 55 |
| St. Bonaventure Univ. (T) | St. Bonaventure, N. Y. | 1856 | V. Rev. R. A. Redlon | D | 2,439 | 215 |
| St. Catherine, Coll. of (W) | St. Paul, Minn. | 1905 | Sister Fides Huber | D | 1,316 | 128 |
| St. Cloud State (T) | St. Cloud, Minn. | 1869 | Robert H. Wick | S | 8,140 | 421 |
| St. Dominic (T) | St. Charles, Mo. | 1963 | Sister Marie Carolyn | D | 192 | 38 |
| St. Edward's Univ. | Austin, Tex. | 1885 | Bro. Raymond Fleck | D | 865 | 70 |
| St. Elizabeth, Coll. of (W) | Convent Station, N. J. | 1899 | Sis. H. M. Mahoney | D | 979 | 101 |
| St. Francis (M) | Fort Wayne, Ind. | 1890 | Sister M. Rosanna | D | 1,805 | 97 |
| St. Francis (T) (M) | Brooklyn, N. Y. | 1884 | Bro. Urban Gonnoud | D | 2,221 | 106 |
| St. Francis (M) | Loretto, Pa. | 1847 | Rev. V. R. Negherbon | D | 1,680 | 107 |
| St. Francis (W) | Joliet, Ill. | 1930 | Sister Anita Marie | D | 994 | 85 |
| St. Francis Seminary | Milwaukee, Wis. | 1856 | Rt. Rev. W. N. Schult. | D | 252 | 25 |
| St. John Coll. of Cleveland (T) (W) | Cleveland, Ohio | 1928 | Rt. Rev. L. P. Cahill | D | 1,082 | 94 |
| St. John Fisher (M) | Rochester, N. Y. | 1951 | V. Rev. C. J. Lavery | D | 1,177 | 83 |
| St. John's | Annapolis, Md. | 1784 | Richard D. Weigle | P | *463* | *75* |
| St. John's Prov. Seminary (M) | Plymouth, Mich. | 1949 | V. Rev. E. Van Antwerp | D | 162 | 15 |
| St. John's Univ. (M) | Collegeville, Minn. | 1856 | Rt. Rev. B. Dwarchak. | D | 1,481 | 125 |
| St. John's Univ. (T) | Jamaica, N. Y. | 1870 | V. Rev. Joseph T. Cahill | D | *11,419* | *620* |
| St. Joseph (W) | W. Hartford, Conn. | 1932 | Sister M. Theodore | D | 901 | 90 |
| St. Joseph (W) | Emmitsburg, Md. | 1809 | Sister Margaret | D | 645 | 75 |
| St. Joseph's (T) | Rensselaer, Ind. | 1889 | Rev. Charles Banet | D | *2,400* | *150* |
| St. Joseph's (W) | North Windham, Me. | 1915 | Sis. Mary De La Salle | D | 216 | 30 |
| St. Joseph's | Philadelphia, Pa. | 1851 | V. Rev. W. F. Maloney | D | 6,377 | 299 |
| St. Joseph's Coll. of Orange (W) | Orange, Calif. | 1959 | Mother M. Felix | D | 195 | 21 |
| St. Joseph's Coll. for Women (W) | Brooklyn, N. Y. | 1916 | Sister Vincent Therese | D | 709 | 76 |
| St. Lawrence Univ. | Canton, N. Y. | 1856 | Foster S. Brown | P | 1,987 | 145 |
| St. Leo (T) | St. Leo, Fla. | 1963 | Rev. Stephen Herrmann | D | 1,200 | 90 |
| St. Louis Coll. of Pharmacy | St. Louis, Mo. | 1864 | Charles C. Rabe | P | 393 | 23 |
| St. Louis Inst. of Music | St. Louis, Mo. | 1924 | John P. Blake, Jr. | P | 850 | 65 |
| St. Louis Univ. (Med) | St. Louis, Mo. | 1818 | V. Rev. Paul Reinert | D | *10,951* | *1,649* |
| Parks Coll. | E. St. Louis, Ill. | 1927 | L. F. Seltzer (Dn.) | D | 650 | 47 |
| St. Martin's (T) | Olympia, Wash. | 1895 | Rt. Rev. Michael Feeney | D | 652 | 69 |
| St. Mary, Coll. of (W) | Omaha, Nebr. | 1923 | Sister Mary Patricia | D | 657 | 63 |
| St. Mary (W) | Xavier, Kan. | 1923 | Sister Mary Janet | D | 604 | 51 |
| St. Mary of the Plains (T) | Dodge City, Kan. | 1952 | Sister M. Cecilia Bush. | D | 756 | 59 |
| St. Mary-of-the-Woods. (T) (W) | St. Mary-of-the-Woods, Ind. | 1840 | Sister Mary Perpetua | D | 631 | 74 |
| St. Mary's (T) | Notre Dame, Ind. | 1844 | Rev. John McGrath | D | 1,395 | 127 |
| St. Mary's (M) | Winona, Minn. | 1912 | Brother Gregory | D | 1,100 | 92 |
| St. Mary's Coll. of Calif. (T) (M) | St. Mary's Coll., Calif. | 1863 | Bro. Michael Quinn | D | 900 | 88 |
| St. Mary's Dominican (T) (W) | New Orleans, La. | 1910 | Sister Mary Ursula | D | 560 | 52 |
| St. Mary's Semin. & Univ. (M) | Baltimore, Md. | 1791 | Rev. Paul Purta | D | *725* | *57* |
| St. Mary's Univ. | San Antonio, Tex. | 1852 | Rev. L. J. Blume | D | 3,742 | 140 |
| St. Meinrad's (M) | St. Meinrad, Ind. | 1861 | V. Rev. H. Ottensmeyer | D | 274 | 34 |
| St. Michael's (M) | Winooski, Vt. | 1903 | V. Rev. G. E. Dupont. | D | 1,453 | 92 |
| St. Norbert | West De Pere, Wis. | 1898 | V. Rev. D. M. Burke. | D | 1,528 | 120 |
| St. Olaf. (T) | Northfield, Minn. | 1874 | Sidney A. Rand | D | 2,536 | 180 |
| St. Patrick's (M) | Menlo Park, Calif. | 1898 | Rev. A. C. Giaquinto | D | 163 | 32 |
| St. Paul Bible | St. Paul, Minn. | 1916 | Rev. Harry T. Hardwick | D | 394 | 30 |
| St. Paul Schl. of Theol.-Meth. | Kansas City, Mo. | 1958 | Don W. Holter | D | 163 | 20 |
| St. Paul's (T) | Lawrenceville, Va. | 1888 | Earl H McClenney | D | 520 | 43 |
| St. Peter's | Jersey City, N. J. | 1872 | V. Rev. V. R. Yanitelli | D | 3,959 | 298 |
| St. Procopius (T) | Lisle, Ill. | 1887 | Rev. R. S. Gallardo | D | 751 | 72 |
| St. Rose, Coll. of (T) (W) | Albany, N. Y. | 1920 | Sister Clarence Paul | D | 1,318 | 100 |
| St. Scholastica, Coll. of. (T) (W) | Duluth, Minn. | 1912 | Sister Mary Richard. | D | 583 | 70 |
| St. Teresa, Coll. of (W) | Winona, Minn. | 1907 | Sister M. Camille Bowe. | D | 1,341 | 132 |
| St. Thomas, Coll. of (M) | St. Paul, Minn. | 1885 | Msgr. Terrence Murphy. | D | 2,144 | 129 |
| St. Thomas Theolog. Semin. (M) | Denver, Colo. | 1906 | Rev. H. B. Persich. | D | 209 | 36 |
| St. Thomas, Univ. of | Houston, Tex. | 1947 | Rev. William Young. | D | 899 | 75 |
| St. Vincent (M) | Latrobe, Pa. | 1846 | Rev. M. J. Brennan. | D | 1,031 | 88 |
| St. Xavier (T) (W) | Chicago, Ill. | 1847 | Sister Mary Olivia. | D | 984 | 111 |
| Salem (W) | Winston-Salem, N. C. | 1772 | Dale H. Gramley. | D | 574 | 69 |

| Name | Location | Yr. | Governing Official and Control | | Students | Teachers |
|------|----------|-----|-------------------------------|---|----------|----------|
| Salem................................(T) | Salem, W. Va..... | 1888 | K. Duane Hurley..... | D | 1,549 | 87 |
| Salisbury State...................(T) | Salisbury, Md..... | 1925 | Wilbur Devilbiss..... | S | 821 | 52 |
| Salve Regina.....................(W) | Newport, R. I..... | 1947 | Sister Mary Emily..... | D | 836 | 81 |
| Sam Houston State..............(T) | Huntsville, Tex..... | 1879 | A. B. Templeton..... | S | 6,795 | 354 |
| Samford Univ..................... | Birmingham, Ala..... | 1842 | Leslie S. Wright..... | D | 2,669 | 162 |
| San Diego College for Women.......................(T) | San Diego, Calif..... | 1949 | Mother Nancy Morris. | D | 630 | 62 |
| San Diego State..................(T) | San Diego, Calif..... | 1897 | Malcolm A. Love..... | S | 20,037 | 1,400 |
| San Diego, Univ. of..............(T) | San Diego, Calif..... | 1949 | V. Rev. J. E. Baer..... | D | 575 | 83 |
| San Fernando Valley St..........(T) | Northridge, Calif..... | 1948 | Ralph Prator..... | S | 15,995 | 650 |
| San Fran. Coll. for Women(T)(W) | San Francisco, Calif.. | 1921 | Sister Gertrude Patch. | D | 676 | 67 |
| San Francisco State..............(T) | San Francisco, Calif.. | 1899 | Robert R. Smith..... | S | 18,500 | 1,400 |
| San Francisco Theol. Sem....... | San Anselmo, Calif... | 1871 | Rev. A. B. Come..... | D | 230 | 29 |
| San Francisco, Univ. of..........(T) | San Francisco, Calif.. | 1855 | Rev. C. W. Dullea..... | D | 6,259 | 382 |
| San Jose State...................(T) | San Jose, Calif..... | 1857 | Robert D. Clark..... | S | 22,364 | 1,400 |
| Santa Clara, Univ. of............ | Santa Clara, Calif.. | 1851 | Rev. Thomas Terry.... | D | 5,114 | 296 |
| Santa Fe, Coll. of................ | Santa Fe, N. M..... | 1947 | Bro. Cyprian Luke.... | D | 1,226 | 65 |
| Sarah Lawrence.................(W) | Bronxville, N. Y..... | 1928 | Esther Raushenbush.... | P | 572 | 104 |
| Savannah State................... | Savannah, Ga..... | 1890 | Howard Jordan, Jr.... | S | 1,652 | 85 |
| Scarritt Coll. for Christian Workers........................ | Nashville, Tenn..... | 1892 | D. Dillon Holt..... | D | 149 | 18 |
| Scranton, Univ. of...............(T) | Scranton, Pa..... | 1888 | V. Rev. A. C. Galvin.. | D | 2,188 | 129 |
| Scripps..........................(W) | Claremont, Calif..... | 1926 | Mark H. Curtis..... | P | 465 | 56 |
| Seattle Pacific...................(T) | Seattle, Wash..... | 1891 | David L. McKenna.... | D | 1,919 | 120 |
| Seattle Univ.....................(T) | Seattle, Wash..... | 1891 | Rev. John A. Fitterer... | D | 3,400 | 302 |
| Seneca (see Hobart & Wm. Smith) | | | | | | |
| Seton Hall Univ..................(T) | So. Orange, N. J..... | 1856 | M. Rev. J. J. Dougherty | D | 8,800 | 509 |
| Seton Hill....................(T)(W) | Greensburg, Pa..... | 1883 | Rev. William G. Ryan.. | P | 934 | 70 |
| Shaw Univ....................... | Raleigh, N. C..... | 1865 | James E. Creek..... | D | 1,056 | 70 |
| Shenandoah Cong. of Music..... | Winchester, Va..... | 1875 | Forrest S. Racey..... | D | ¹516 | 54 |
| Shepherd.......................(T) | Shepherdstown, W.Va. | 1871 | Oliver S. Ikenberry.... | S | 1,396 | 80 |
| Shimer.......................... | Mt. Carroll, Ill..... | 1853 | F. Joseph Mullin..... | P | 467 | 47 |
| Shippensburg State..............(T) | Shippensburg, Pa..... | 1871 | Ralph E. Heiges..... | S | 3,965 | 225 |
| Shorter.......................... | Rome, Ga..... | 1873 | Randall H. Minor..... | D | 750 | 55 |
| Siena........................... | Loudonville, N. Y.... | 1937 | Rev. Brian Duffy..... | D | 1,843 | 121 |
| Siena.......................(T)(W) | Memphis, Tenn..... | 1922 | Sister Agatha Dutton.. | P | 310 | 34 |
| Siena Heights.................(W) | Adrian, Mich..... | 1919 | Sister M. Petronilla.... | D | 889 | 68 |
| Simmons...................(T)(W) | Boston, Mass..... | 1899 | William E. Park..... | P | 2,147 | 268 |
| Simpson Bible.................... | San Francisco, Calif.. | 1921 | Rev. J. C. Wenninger.. | D | 210 | 23 |
| Simpson......................... | Indianola, Iowa..... | 1860 | Ralph C. John..... | D | 904 | 73 |
| Sioux Falls......................(T) | Sioux Falls, S. Dak.. | 1883 | Reuben P. Jeschke.... | D | 1,052 | 52 |
| Skidmore......................(W) | Saratoga Spgs., N. Y. | 1911 | Joseph C. Palamountain | P | 1,568 | 163 |
| Slippery Rock State.............(T) | Slippery Rock, Pa.... | 1889 | Robert S. Carter..... | S | 4,100 | 280 |
| Smith.........................(W) | Northampton, Mass... | 1871 | Thomas C. Mendenhall. | P | 2,627 | 240 |
| Sonoma State...................(T) | Rohnert Pk., Calif.... | 1960 | Ambrose R. Nichols... | S | 2,122 | 120 |
| South Alabama, Univ. of........(T) | Mobile, Ala..... | 1964 | Frederick P. Whiddon.. | S | 3,092 | 213 |
| So. Carolina, Med. Coll. of...... | Charleston, S. C..... | 1823 | William M. McCord... | S | 867 | 349 |
| South Carolina St.*..............(T) | Orangeburg, S. C.... | 1896 | M. M. Nance..... | S | 1,452 | 113 |
| South Carolina, Univ. of......... | Columbia, S. C..... | 1801 | Thomas F. Jones..... | S | 13,023 | 600 |
| S. Dak. Sch. of Mines & Tech.... | Rapid City, S. Dak... | 1885 | Harvey R. Fraser..... | S | 1,380 | 120 |
| S. Dak. St. Univ.*...............(T) | Brookings, S. Dak... | 1889 | H. M. Briggs..... | S | 5,213 | 317 |
| South Dakota, Univ. of(T)(Med) | Vermillion, S. Dak... | 1882 | Edward Q. Moulton.. | S | 4,600 | 310 |
| South-Eastern Bible............. | Lakeland, Fla..... | 1935 | Arthur Graves..... | D | 515 | 19 |
| South Florida, Univ. of..........(T) | Tampa, Fla..... | 1956 | John S. Allen..... | S | 10,848 | 530 |
| South, Univ. of the.............. | Sewanee, Tenn..... | 1858 | Edward McCrady..... | D | 800 | 68 |
| Southeast Missouri State.....(T) | Cape Girardeau, Mo.. | 1873 | Mark Scully..... | S | 5,800 | 288 |
| Southeastern Bapt. Theol. Sem... | Wake Forest, N. C.... | 1951 | O. T. Binkley..... | D | ¹446 | 27 |
| Southeastern Louisiana.......... | Hammond, La..... | 1925 | Clea E. Parker..... | S | 4,992 | 327 |
| Southeastern Mass. Tech. Inst... | No. Dartmouth, Mass. | 1895 | Joseph L. Driscoll.... | S | 3,300 | 264 |
| Southeastern State.............. | Durant, Okla..... | 1909 | Leon Hibbs..... | S | 1,985 | 105 |
| Southern California............. | Costa Mesa, Calif.... | 1920 | O. Cope Budge..... | D | 478 | 33 |
| Southern Calif., Univ. Of (T) (Med) | Los Angeles, Calif.... | 1880 | Norman Topping..... | P | 17,500 | 1,900 |
| Southern Coll. of Optometry..... | Memphis, Tenn..... | 1932 | Spurgeon B. Eure..... | P | 592 | 30 |
| Southern Colorado St...........(T) | Pueblo, Colo..... | 1933 | J. Victor Hopper..... | S | 5,200 | ²225 |
| Southern Conn. State...........(T) | New Haven, Conn.... | 1893 | Hilton C. Buley..... | S | 8,976 | ¹435 |
| Southern Illinois Univ..........(T) | Carbondale, Ill..... | 1869 | Delyte W. Morris..... | S | 26,661 | 2,829 |
| Southern Methodist Univ........ | Dallas, Tex..... | 1911 | Willis M. Tate..... | D | 8,010 | 450 |
| Southern Missionary............(T) | Collegedale, Tenn.... | 1892 | W. M. Schneider..... | D | 1,100 | 110 |
| Southern Mississippi, Univ. of (T) | Hattiesburg, Miss.... | 1910 | William D. McCain.... | S | 7,000 | 350 |
| Southern Oregon................ | Ashland, Ore..... | 1926 | Elmo N. Stevenson.... | S | 3,500 | 220 |
| Southern State.................. | Magnolia, Ark..... | 1909 | Imon E. Bruce..... | S | 2,273 | 109 |
| Southern State.................(T) | Springfield, S. Dak... | 1897 | Allen Millar..... | S | 923 | 74 |
| Southern Univ. & A. M. Coll.*.. | Baton Rouge, La..... | 1880 | Felton G. Clark..... | S | 7,250 | 399 |
| Southern Utah, Coll. of......... | Cedar City, Utah.... | 1897 | R. C. Braithwalte.... | S | 1,660 | 95 |
| Southwest Baptist.............. | Bolivar, Mo..... | 1878 | Courts Redford..... | D | 1,167 | 64 |
| Southwest, Coll. of the......... | Hobbs, N. M..... | 1956 | J. L. Burke, Jr..... | P | 124 | 22 |
| Southwest Missouri State......(T) | Springfield, Mo..... | 1906 | Arthur Mallory..... | S | 6,200 | 300 |
| Southwest Texas State.........(T) | San Marcos, Tex..... | 1899 | James H. McCrocklin.. | S | 7,075 | 440 |
| Southwestern College...........(T) | Winfield, Kan..... | 1885 | C. Orville Strohl..... | D | 644 | 58 |
| Southwestern La., Univ. of.....(T) | Lafayette, La..... | 1901 | Clyde Rougeou..... | S | 8,409 | 490 |
| Southwestern at Memphis...... | Memphis, Tenn..... | 1848 | John D. Alexander.... | D | 1,010 | 115 |
| Southwestern State.............(T) | Weatherford, Okla... | 1901 | Al Harris..... | S | 4,500 | 180 |
| Southwestern Univ............. | Los Angeles, Calif.... | 1913 | Miriam Schumacher.... | P | 1,152 | 49 |
| Southwestern Univ............. | Georgetown, Tex..... | 1840 | Durwood Fleming..... | D | 781 | 69 |
| Spelman.......................(W) | Atlanta, Ga..... | 1881 | Albert E. Manley..... | D | 821 | 90 |
| Spring Arbor...................(T) | Spring Arbor, Mich... | 1873 | David McKenna..... | D | 580 | 45 |
| Spring Hill.....................(T) | Mobile, Ala..... | 1830 | V. Rev. W. J. Rimes... | D | 1,100 | 110 |
| Springfield.....................(T) | Springfield, Mass.... | 1885 | Wilbert Locklin..... | P | 2,079 | 151 |
| Stanford Univ...............(T)(Med) | Stanford, Calif..... | 1891 | J. E. Wallace Sterling.. | P | 10,922 | 1,232 |
| Stanislaus State................(T) | Turlock, Calif..... | 1957 | Alexander Capurso.... | S | 1,064 | 88 |
| Stephen F. Austin State.......(T) | Nacogdoches, Tex.... | 1923 | Ralph W. Steen..... | S | 7,458 | 360 |
| Stephens......................(W) | Columbia, Mo..... | 1833 | Seymour Smith..... | P | 1,808 | 225 |
| Stetson Univ.................... | De Land, Fla..... | 1883 | Paul Green..... | D | 2,172 | 155 |
| Steubenville, Coll. of........... | Steubenville, Ohio.... | 1946 | Rev. C. J. Devlin..... | P | 1,135 | 85 |
| Stevens Inst. of Tech..........(M) | Hoboken, N. J..... | 1870 | Jess H. Davis..... | P | 2,703 | 190 |
| Stillman........................ | Tuscaloosa, Ala..... | 1876 | Harold N. Stinson.... | D | 612 | 58 |
| Stirling......................... | Stirling, Kansas..... | 1887 | William McCreery.... | D | 592 | 36 |
| Stonehill....................... | No. Easton, Mass.... | 1948 | Rev. John T. Corr..... | P | 1,214 | 74 |
| Stout State Univ...............(T) | Menomonie, Wis..... | 1893 | William J. Micheels... | S | 3,954 | 295 |
| Suffolk Univ.................... | Boston, Mass..... | 1906 | John E. Fenton..... | P | 3,571 | 141 |
| Sul Ross State..................(T) | Alpine, Tex..... | 1919 | Norman L. McNeil.... | S | 1,971 | 119 |
| Susquehanna Univ.............. | Selinsgrove, Pa..... | 1858 | Gustave W. Weber.... | D | 1,180 | 99 |
| Swarthmore.................... | Swarthmore, Pa..... | 1864 | Courtney C. Smith.... | P | 998 | 137 |
| Sweet Briar...................(W) | Sweet Briar, Va..... | 1901 | Anne G. Pannell..... | P | 718 | 75 |

| Name | Location | Yr. | Governing Official and Control | | Stu- dents | Teach ers |
|---|---|---|---|---|---|---|
| Syracuse Univ..............(T) | Syracuse, N. Y..... | 1870 | William Tolley (Chan.).. | P | 22,866 | 1,298 |
| Tabor.................... | Hillsboro, Kan..... | 1908 | Roy Just............. | D | 381 | 40 |
| Talladega................ | Talladega, Ala...... | 1867 | Herman H. Long...... | P | 493 | 48 |
| Tampa, Univ. of......... | Tampa, Fla........ | 1931 | David M. Delo....... | P | 2,149 | 91 |
| Tarkio................(T) | Tarkio, Mo........ | 1883 | William H. Schechter.. | D | 687 | 47 |
| Taylor Univ.............. | Upland, Ind....... | 1846 | Milo Rediger........ | P | 1,217 | 77 |
| Temple Univ....(T)(Med) | Philadelphia, Pa.... | 1884 | Paul R. Anderson.... | P | 31,018 | 1,679 |
| Temple Buell............ | Denver, Colo...... | 1888 | Eugene E. Dawson.... | D | 1,100 | 91 |
| Tenn. Ag. & Inst. St. Univ.*..(T) | Nashville, Tenn.... | 1912 | Walter S. Davis..... | S | 4,750 | 285 |
| Tennessee Tech. Univ......(T) | Cookeville, Tenn.... | 1915 | Everett Derryberry... | S | 5,700 | 320 |
| Tennessee Temple.......(T) | Chattanooga, Tenn.. | 1946 | Lee Roberson....... | D | 884 | 49 |
| Tennessee, Univ. of*......(Med) | Knoxville, Tenn.... | 1794 | Andrew D. Holt..... | S | 29,088 | 2,689 |
| Tennessee Wesleyan......(T) | Athens, Tenn...... | 1857 | Charles Turner...... | D | 850 | 45 |
| Tex. A. & M. Univ........ | College Station, Tex.. | 1876 | Earl Rudder........ | S | 10,918 | 875 |
| Prairie View A. & M....(T) | Prairie View, Tex... | 1876 | Alvin Thomas....... | S | 3,948 | 187 |
| Tarleton State.......... | Stephenville, Tex... | 1899 | William O. Trogden... | S | 2,079 | 109 |
| Texas Christian Univ......(T) | Fort Worth, Tex.... | 1873 | J. M. Moudy (Chan.).. | D | 6,078 | 564 |
| Texas.................(T) | Tyler, Tex........ | 1894 | Allen C. Hancock.... | D | 458 | 30 |
| Texas A & I Univ........ | Kingsville, Tex.... | 1925 | James. C. Jernigan... | S | 5,332 | 265 |
| Texas Lutheran......... | Seguin, Tex....... | 1891 | Martin L. Cole...... | D | 780 | 53 |
| Texas Southern Univ......(T) | Houston, Tex...... | 1947 | *Vacant*........... | S | 4,076 | 225 |
| Texas, Univ. of......... | Austin, Tex....... | 1883 | Harry R. Ransom (Ch.) | S | 52,681 | 5,292 |
| At Arlington.......... | Arlington, Tex..... | 1895 | J. R. Woolf....... | S | 11,873 | 450 |
| At Austin............. | Austin, Tex....... | 1883 | Norman Hackerman... | S | 29,841 | 2,183 |
| At Houston........... | Houston, Tex...... | 1905 | J. V. Olson (Dean)... | S | 517 | 234 |
| Medical Branch....... | Galveston, Tex..... | 1891 | Truman G. Blocker, Jr. | S | 865 | 424 |
| Southwestern Medical Sch. | Dallas, Tex....... | 1943 | C. C. Sprague (Dean).. | S | 469 | 1,229 |
| At El Paso........... | El Paso, Tex...... | 1913 | *Vacant*.......... | S | 9,029 | 357 |
| Texas Technological......(T) | Lubbock, Tex..... | 1923 | Grover Murray...... | S | 18,080 | 1,213 |
| Texas Wesleyan.......... | Fort Worth, Tex.... | 1891 | William Pearce..... | D | 1,999 | 87 |
| Texas Woman's Univ......(W) | Denton, Tex....... | 1902 | John A. Guinn...... | S | 4,949 | 332 |
| Thiel..................(T) | Greenville, Pa..... | 1866 | Chauncey G. Bly.... | D | 1,300 | 92 |
| Thomas................(T) | Waterville, Maine.. | 1894 | John L. Thomas, Jr... | P | 360 | 28 |
| Thomas More.........(T) | Ft. Mitchell, Ky... | 1921 | Msgr. John Murphy... | D | 1,732 | 114 |
| Tift...................(W) | Forsyth, Ga....... | 1849 | Carey T. Vinzant.... | D | 574 | 33 |
| Toledo, Univ. of......... | Toledo, Ohio...... | 1872 | William S. Carlson... | Mu | 11,350 | 691 |
| Tougaloo................ | Tougaloo, Miss.... | 1869 | George A. Owens.... | D | 627 | 51 |
| Towson State..........(T) | Baltimore, Md..... | 1866 | Earle T. Hawkins.... | S | 6,671 | 309 |
| Transylvania............ | Lexington, Ky..... | 1780 | Irvin E. Lunger..... | P | 824 | 68 |
| Trenton State..........(T) | Trenton, N. J..... | 1855 | Robert Heussler..... | S | 8,691 | 459 |
| Trevecca Nazarene.......(T) | Nashville, Tenn.... | 1901 | W. M. Greathouse... | D | 601 | 39 |
| Trinity................(M) | Hartford, Conn.... | 1823 | Theodore Lockwood... | P | 1,465 | 145 |
| Trinity................(W) | Burlington, Vt..... | 1925 | Sister Mary Patrick.. | D | 470 | 45 |
| Trinity................. | Deerfield, Ill..... | 1897 | Harry Evans....... | D | 583 | 51 |
| Trinity Univ............ | San Antonio, Tex... | 1869 | James W. Laurie.... | D | 2,376 | 149 |
| Trinity................(W) | Washington, D. C... | 1897 | Sis. Margaret...... | D | 995 | 111 |
| Tri-State............... | Angola, Ind...... | 1884 | Richard Bateman.... | P | 1,522 | 95 |
| Troy State.............(T) | Troy, Ala........ | 1887 | Ralph W. Adams.... | S | 2,541 | 120 |
| Tufts Univ............(Med) | Medford, Mass.... | 1852 | Burton Hallowell.... | P | 5,022 | 688 |
| Tulane Univ........(T)(Med) | New Orleans, La.... | 1834 | H. E. Longenecker... | P | 8,325 | 2,045 |
| Newcomb............(W) | New Orleans, La.... | 1886 | C. D. Hounshell (Dn.).. | P | 1,161 | 118 |
| Tulsa, Univ. of......... | Tulsa, Okla....... | 1894 | Eugene L. Swearingen.. | P | 6,262 | 262 |
| Tusculum............... | Greenville, Tenn... | 1794 | Rev. D. G. Trout.... | P | 558 | 45 |
| Tuskegee Institute......(T) | Tuskegee Inst., Ala.. | 1881 | Luther H. Foster.... | P | 2,980 | 342 |
| Union................(T) | Barbourville, Ky... | 1879 | Mahlon A. Miller.... | D | 872 | 63 |
| Union.................. | Lincoln, Nebr..... | 1891 | Ray W. Fowler...... | D | 1,208 | 108 |
| Union.................. | Schenectady, N. Y... | 1795 | Harold C. Martin.... | P | 2,617 | 212 |
| Union Theol. Sem........ | New York, N. Y.... | 1836 | Rev. J. C. Bennett... | I | 662 | 94 |
| Union Univ............. | Jackson, Tenn..... | 1825 | Robert E. Craig..... | D | 780 | 60 |
| U. S. Air Force Academy..(M) | Colo. Springs, Colo.. | 1955 | Gen. T. S. Moorman (Supt.).......... | F | 3,028 | 466 |
| U. S. Coast Guard Academy (M) | New London, Conn... | 1876 | R. Adm. A. B. Engel.. | F | 700 | 86 |
| U. S. Dept. of Agric. Grad. Sch.. | Washington, D. C.... | 1921 | John B. Holden (Dir.).. | F | 6,800 | 300 |
| U. S. Merchant Marine Acad.(M) | Kings Point, N. Y... | 1938 | R. Adm. G. McLintock.. | F | 707 | 92 |
| U. S. Military Academy..(M) | West Point, N. Y... | 1802 | Maj. Gen. S. W. Koster (Supt.).......... | F | 3,285 | 538 |
| U. S. Naval Academy......(M) | Annapolis, Md..... | 1845 | R. Adm. James Calvert (Supt.).......... | F | 4,091 | 547 |
| U. S. Naval Postgraduate Sch... | Monterey, Calif.... | 1909 | R. Adm. R. W. McNitt. | F | 1,171 | 225 |
| United Theol. Sem........ | Dayton, Ohio..... | 1871 | John Knecht........ | D | 186 | 19 |
| Upper Iowa.............(T) | Fayette, Iowa..... | 1857 | Eugene E. Garbee.... | D | 1,018 | 84 |
| Upsala.................. | E. Orange, N. J.... | 1893 | Carl J. Fjellman..... | D | 1,809 | 109 |
| Ursinus................. | Collegeville, Pa.... | 1869 | Donald L. Helfferich.. | P | 1,814 | 124 |
| Ursuline Coll. for Women..(W) | Cleveland, Ohio.... | 1874 | Sis. Rose Angela.... | D | 468 | 43 |
| Utah State Univ.*........ | Logan, Utah...... | 1888 | Glen L. Taggart..... | S | 7,293 | 530 |
| Utah, Univ. of......(T)(Med) | Salt Lake City, Utah.. | 1850 | James C. Fletcher.... | S | 17,488 | 2,100 |
| Valdosta State.........(T) | Valdosta, Ga...... | 1906 | S. Walter Martin.... | S | 2,322 | 127 |
| Valley City State........ | Valley City, N. D... | 1890 | Roscoe L. Lokken.... | S | 1,064 | 65 |
| Valparaiso Univ.......... | Valparaiso, Ind.... | 1859 | Otto P. Kretzmann... | D | 4,173 | 282 |
| Vanderbilt Univ........(Med) | Nashville, Tenn.... | 1873 | Alexander Heard (Ch.).. | P | 5,362 | 1,070 |
| Vassar................(W) | Poughkeepsie, N. Y... | 1861 | Alan Simpson...... | P | 1,570 | 205 |
| Vermont, Univ. of*...(T)(Med) | Burlington, Vt..... | 1791 | Lyman S. Rowell.... | S | 6,292 | 689 |
| Villa Maria............(W) | Erie, Pa......... | 1925 | Sis. M. L. Antoun... | D | 746 | 67 |
| Villanova Univ.......... | Villanova, Pa..... | 1842 | Rev. R. J. Welsh.... | D | 6,182 | 440 |
| Virgin Islands, Coll. of...(T) | St. Thomas, V. I... | 1962 | L. C. Wanlass...... | T | 609 | 109 |
| Virginia, Medical Coll. of.. | Richmond, Va..... | 1838 | R. Blackwell Smith, Jr... | S | 1,600 | 900 |
| Virginia Military Institute..(M) | Lexington, Va..... | 1839 | Gen. George R. E. Shell.. | S | 1,141 | 111 |
| Virginia Poly. Inst.*...... | Blacksburg, Va.... | 1872 | T. Marshall Hahn, Jr.. | S | 8,510 | 843 |
| Virginia Southern........ | Roanoke, Va..... | 1933 | A. R. Kennett...... | Pr | 200 | 15 |
| Virginia State*.......... | Petersburg, Va.... | 1882 | Robert P. Daniel.... | S | 1,960 | 231 |
| Virginia Union, Univ...... | Richmond, Va..... | 1865 | Thomas H. Henderson.. | D | 1,280 | 95 |
| Virginia, Univ. of....(T)(Med) | Charlottesville, Va... | 1819 | Edgar F. Shannon, Jr... | S | 8,457 | 867 |
| Viterbo................(W) | La Crosse, Wis.... | 1931 | Sister M. Justille.... | D | 600 | 56 |
| Voorhees................ | Denmark, So. Car... | 1897 | John F. Potts....... | D | 510 | 34 |
| Wabash..........(T) (M) | Crawfordsville, Ind... | 1832 | Paul W. Cook, Jr.... | P | 860 | 87 |
| Wagner................. | Staten Island, N. Y... | 1883 | Arthur O. Davidson... | D | 2,674 | 175 |
| Wake Forest Univ....(T) (Med) | Winston-Salem, N. C... | 1834 | James R. Scales..... | D | 3,070 | 447 |
| Walla Walla............. | College Place, Wash.. | 1892 | Robert Reynolds..... | D | 1,355 | 100 |
| Walsh.................. | Canton, Ohio..... | 1960 | Br. T. S. Farrell.... | D | 836 | 52 |
| Warner Pacific.......... | Portland, Ore..... | 1937 | E. J. Gilliam (Act.)... | D | 309 | 33 |
| Warren Wilson.........(T) | Swannanoa, No. Car.. | 1894 | Arthur M. Bannerman.. | D | 306 | 33 |
| Wartburg..............(T) | Waverly, Iowa.... | 1852 | John W. Bachman.... | D | 1,235 | 88 |
| Washburn, Univ.........(T) | Topeka, Kan..... | 1865 | John W. Henderson... | Mu | 4,076 | 123 |
| Washington............(T) | Chestertown, Md.... | 1782 | Daniel Z. Gibson.... | P | 600 | 54 |

| Name | Location | Yr. | Governing Official and Control | | Stu-dents | Teach-ers |
|---|---|---|---|---|---|---|
| Washington and Jefferson... (M) | Washington, Pa... | 1781 | Boyd C. Patterson... | P | 821 | 82 |
| Washington and Lee Univ... (M) | Lexington, Va... | 1749 | Robert Huntley... | P | 1,472 | 133 |
| Washington School of Psychiatry | Washington, D. C... | 1936 | Seymour S. Mintz... | P | 200 | 15 |
| Washington State... (T) | Machias, Me... | 1909 | Lincoln Sennett... | S | 357 | 30 |
| Washington State Univ.*... (T) | Pullman, Wash... | 1890 | W. Glenn Terrell, Jr... | S | 11,162 | 1,273 |
| Washington, Univ. of... (Med) | St. Louis, Mo... | 1853 | T. H. Eliot (Chan.)... | P | 10,968 | 2,944 |
| Washington, Univ. of... (T) (Med) | Seattle, Wash... | 1861 | Charles E. Odegaard... | S | 28,505 | 3,492 |
| Wayland Baptist... (T) | Plainview, Tex... | 1908 | Roy C. McClung... | D | 667 | 51 |
| Wayne State... (T) | Wayne, Nebr... | 1910 | W. A. Brandenburg... | S | 2,578 | 126 |
| Wayne State Univ... (T) (Med) | Detroit, Mich... | 1868 | William R. Keast... | S | 32,370 | 1,215 |
| Waynesburg... | Waynesburg, Pa... | 1850 | B. M. Rich... | D | 1,033 | 74 |
| Weber State... (T) | Ogden, Utah... | 1889 | William P. Miller... | S | 8,200 | 349 |
| Webster... | Webster Groves, Mo... | 1915 | Sis. J. Grennan... | D | 1,050 | 100 |
| Wellesley... (W) | Wellesley, Mass... | 1870 | Ruth M. Adams... | P | 1,729 | 171 |
| Wells... | Aurora, N. Y... | 1868 | Louis J. Long... | P | 615 | 67 |
| Wesleyan... (W) | Macon, Ga... | 1836 | W. Earl Strickland... | D | 651 | 61 |
| Wesleyan Univ... (T) | Middletown, Conn... | 1831 | Edwin D. Etherington... | P | 1,594 | 236 |
| West Chester State... (T) | West Chester, Pa... | 1812 | Earl F. Sykes... | S | 5,293 | 365 |
| West Coast Univ... | Los Angeles, Calif... | 1909 | Victor Elconin... | P | 1,550 | 62 |
| West Georgia... | Carrollton, Ga... | 1933 | James E. Boyd... | S | 2,536 | 130 |
| West Liberty State... (T) | West Liberty, W. Va... | 1837 | Paul N. Elbin... | S | 3,299 | 175 |
| West Texas State Univ... (T) | Canyon, Tex... | 1910 | James Cornette... | S | 6,118 | 298 |
| W. Va. Inst. of Technology... (T) | Montgomery, W. Va... | 1895 | Leonard C. Nelson... | S | 2,064 | 142 |
| West Virginia State*... | Institute, W. Va... | 1891 | William J. L. Wallace... | S | 2,811 | 136 |
| West Virginia Univ.*... (T) (Med) | Morgantown, W. Va... | 1867 | James G. Harlow... | S | 12,008 | 1,185 |
| W. Va. Wesleyan... (T) | Buckhannon, W. Va... | 1890 | Stanley H. Martin... | D | 1,619 | 110 |
| Western Bapt. Bible... | El Cerrito, Calif... | 1936 | F. R. Brock... | P | 327 | 22 |
| Western Carolina... (T) | Cullowhee, N. C... | 1889 | Paul A. Reid... | S | 3,399 | 183 |
| Western Coll. for Women... (W) | Oxford, Ohio... | 1853 | Herrick B. Young... | P | 620 | 64 |
| Western Conn. State... | Danbury, Conn... | 1903 | Ruth A. Haas... | S | 2,782 | 154 |
| Western Illinois Univ... (T) | Macomb, Ill... | 1899 | Arthur L. Knoblauch... | S | 8,119 | 595 |
| Western Kentucky Univ... (T) | Bowling Green, Ky... | 1906 | Kelly Thompson... | S | 9,339 | 423 |
| Western Maryland... (T) | Westminster, Md... | 1867 | Lowell S. Ensor... | D | 1,170 | 120 |
| Western Mich. Univ... (T) | Kalamazoo, Mich... | 1903 | James W. Miller... | S | 17,325 | 771 |
| Western Montana... (T) | Dillon, Mont... | 1897 | James E. Short... | S | 860 | 44 |
| Western New England... | Springfield, Mass... | 1919 | Beaumont A. Herman... | P | 2,127 | 120 |
| Western New Mexico Univ... (T) | Silver City, N. M... | 1893 | John Snedeker... | S | 1,247 | 72 |
| Western State... (T) | Gunnison, Colo... | 1901 | Harlan Bryant... | S | 2,577 | 116 |
| Western Washington State... (T) | Bellingham, Wash... | 1893 | Charles Flora (Act.)... | S | 5,600 | 370 |
| Westmar... | Le Mars, Iowa... | 1890 | Harry H. Kalas... | D | 1,240 | 71 |
| Westminster Choir... | Princeton, N. J... | 1926 | Lee H. Bristol, Jr... | P | 341 | 55 |
| Westminster College... (M) | Fulton, Mo... | 1851 | Robert L. D. Davidson... | D | 663 | 71 |
| Westminster College... | New Wilmington, Pa... | 1852 | Earland I. Carlson... | P | 1,921 | 103 |
| Westminster College... (T) | Salt Lake City, Utah... | 1875 | Manfred A. Shaw... | I | 794 | 40 |
| Westminster Theol. Sem... (M) | Philadelphia, Pa... | 1929 | Edmund Clowney... | P | 135 | 16 |
| Westmont... | Santa Barbara, Calif... | 1940 | Roger J. Voskuyl... | P | 650 | 53 |
| Wheaton... | Wheaton, Ill... | 1860 | Hudson T. Armerding... | P | 1,846 | 146 |
| Wheaton... (W) | Norton, Mass... | 1834 | William C. H. Prentice... | P | 1,096 | 97 |
| Wheeling... | Wheeling, W. Va... | 1954 | V. Rev. F. R. Haig... | D | 775 | 63 |
| Wheelock... (W, T) | Boston, Mass... | 1888 | Margaret H. Merry... | P | 617 | 52 |
| Whitman... | Walla Walla, Wash... | 1859 | Vacant... | P | 1,010 | 88 |
| Whittier... | Whittier, Calif... | 1901 | Paul S. Smith... | P | 2,078 | 125 |
| Whitworth... | Spokane, Wash... | 1890 | M. E. Koehler... | D | 1,722 | 99 |
| Wichita State Univ... (T) | Wichita, Kan... | 1895 | Emory Lindquist... | Mu | 10,535 | 476 |
| Wilberforce Univ... (T) | Wilberforce, Ohio... | 1856 | Rembert E. Stokes... | D | 835 | 55 |
| Wiley... (T) | Marshall, Tex... | 1873 | Thomas W. Cole... | D | 703 | 56 |
| Wilkes... | Wilkes-Barre, Pa... | 1933 | Eugene S. Farley... | P | 2,800 | 175 |
| Willamette Univ... | Salem, Ore... | 1842 | G. Herbert Smith... | D | 1,435 | 123 |
| William Carey... | Hattiesburg, Miss... | 1906 | J. Ralph Noonkester... | D | 831 | 58 |
| William Jewell... | Liberty, Mo... | 1849 | H. Guy Moore... | D | 997 | 86 |
| William and Mary, College of. (T) | Williamsburg, Va... | 1693 | Davis Y. Paschall... | S | 4,526 | 371 |
| William Penn... | Oskaloosa, Iowa... | 1873 | Duane Moon... | D | 947 | 57 |
| William Woods... (W) | Fulton, Mo... | 1870 | Randall B. Cutlip... | D | 702 | 61 |
| Williams... (M) | Williamstown, Mass... | 1793 | John E. Sawyer... | P | 1,215 | 151 |
| Willimantic State... | Willimantic, Conn... | 1889 | Searle F. Charles... | S | 860 | 128 |
| Wilmington... | Wilmington, N. C... | 1947 | William Wagoner... | C | 1,080 | 83 |
| Wilmington... | Wilmington, Ohio... | 1870 | James M. Read... | D | 875 | 67 |
| Wilson... (W) | Chambersburg, Pa... | 1869 | Paul S. Havens... | P | 709 | 75 |
| Windham... | Putney, Vt... | 1951 | Eugene C. Winslow... | P | 504 | 59 |
| Winona State... (T) | Winona, Minn... | 1858 | Robt. DuFresne... | S | 3,591 | 175 |
| Winston-Salem State... (T) | Winston-Salem, N. C... | 1892 | Kenneth R. Williams... | S | 1,270 | 108 |
| Winthrop... (W, T) | Rock Hill, S. C... | 1886 | Charles S. Davis... | S | 2,986 | 158 |
| Wisconsin State Univ... (T) | Eau Claire, Wis... | 1916 | Leonard Haas... | S | 5,883 | 392 |
| Wisconsin State Univ... (T) | La Crosse, Wis... | 1908 | Sam G. Gates... | S | 4,773 | 320 |
| Wisconsin State Univ... (T) | Oshkosh, Wis... | 1871 | Roger E. Gulles... | S | 8,230 | 504 |
| Wisconsin State Univ... (T) | River Falls, Wis... | 1874 | Richard Delorit... | S | 3,500 | 246 |
| Wisconsin State Univ... (T) | Stevens Point, Wis... | 1894 | Lee Sherman Dreyfus... | S | 6,050 | 380 |
| Wisconsin State Univ... (T) | Superior, Wis... | 1896 | K. W. Meyer... | S | 3,300 | 207 |
| Wisconsin State Univ... (T) | Whitewater, Wis... | 1868 | William L. Carter... | S | 8,064 | 526 |
| Wisconsin State Univ... (T) | Platteville, Wis... | 1866 | Bjarne R. Ullsvik... | S | 5,000 | 330 |
| Wisconsin, Univ. of*... (T) (Med) | Madison, Wis... | 1848 | Fred Harrington... | S | 31,226 | 3,800 |
| Milwaukee Campus... | Milwaukee, Wis... | 1956 | J. M. Klotsche (Chan.)... | S | 14,128 | 950 |
| Wittenberg Univ... | Springfield, Ohio... | 1845 | John N. Stauffer... | D | 2,684 | 285 |
| Wofford... (M) | Spartanburg, S. C... | 1854 | Charles F. Marsh... | D | 968 | 66 |
| Woman's Med. Coll. of Pa... (W) | Philadelphia, Pa... | 1850 | G. R. Leymaster... | P | 208 | 246 |
| Woodbury... (T) | Los Angeles, Calif... | 1884 | D. E. Kirby... | Pr | 1,726 | 73 |
| Woodstock... (M) | Woodstock, Md... | 1869 | Rev. F. F. Cardegna... | D | 200 | 20 |
| Wooster, Coll. of... | Wooster, Ohio... | 1866 | J. G. Drushal (Act.)... | D | 1,533 | 151 |
| Worcester Polytechnic Inst... | Worcester, Mass... | 1865 | Harry P. Storke... | P | 1,655 | 239 |
| Wyoming, Univ. of*... (T) | Laramie, Wyo... | 1886 | William Carlson... | S | 6,883 | 474 |
| Xavier Univ. of Louisiana... (T) | New Orleans, La... | 1915 | Norman C. Francis... | D | 1,207 | 103 |
| Xavier Univ... | Cincinnati, Ohio... | 1831 | V. Rev. P. L. O'Connor... | D | 5,809 | 286 |
| Yale Univ... (M, Med) | New Haven, Conn... | 1701 | Kingman Brewster, Jr... | P | 8,666 | 2,487 |
| Yankton... | Yankton, S. Dak... | 1881 | Donald B. Ward... | P | 701 | 58 |
| Yeshiva Univ... (T) (Med) | New York, N. Y... | 1886 | Samuel Belkin... | P | 7,580 | 2,200 |
| Youngstown Univ... (T) | Youngstown, Ohio... | 1908 | Albert L. Pugsley... | P | 12,600 | 695 |

## Many Words Rarely Used

Despite the fact that English is the richest language in the world with some 800,000 words, the speaking vocabulary of well-educated Americans is about 5,000 words. Experts doubt if any one person has an active vocabulary of 60,000 words—a mere 7½% of the entire English language.

# Junior Colleges

See explanatory notes on page 319

| Name | Location | Yr. | Governing Official and Control | Students | Teachers |
|---|---|---|---|---|---|
| Abraham Baldwin Agricultural. | Tifton, Ga. | 1933 | J. Clyde Driggers | S | 1,105 | 63 |
| Adirondacks Community | Hudson Falls, N. Y. | 1960 | Charles R. Eisenhart | C | 1,315 | 53 |
| Aeronautics, Academy of. | Flushing, N. Y. | 1932 | Walter M. Hartung | Pr | 1,447 | 63 |
| Albany, Jr. Coll. of (b) | Albany, N. Y. | 1957 | Lewis Froman | P | 620 | 41 |
| Albermarle, Coll. of. | Elizabeth City, N. C. | 1960 | B. A. Barringer | S, C | 491 | 35 |
| Alice Lloyd | Pippa Passes, Ky. | 1923 | Will Hayes | P | 267 | 17 |
| Allan Hancock | Santa Maria, Calif. | 1920 | Walter E. Conrad | Dl | 3,324 | 125 |
| Allen County Comm. Jr. | Iola, Kan. | 1923 | Paul Parker | Mu | 426 | 23 |
| Allegany Community | Cumberland, Md. | 1961 | W. Ardell Haines | C | 516 | 31 |
| Alpena Community | Alpena, Mich. | 1952 | S. E. Van Lare (Dn.) | Mu | 806 | 51 |
| Altus Junior. | Altus, Okla. | 1926 | Clifford Peterson | Dl | 458 | 28 |
| Alvin Junior. | Alvin, Tex. | 1949 | D. P. O'Quinn. | Dl | 1,388 | 75 |
| Amarillo. | Amarillo, Tex. | 1929 | Albert B. Martin | Mu | 3,006 | 117 |
| American River. | Sacramento, Calif. | 1955 | Kenneth Boettcher | Dl | 10,042 | 451 |
| Anderson. | Anderson, S. C. | 1911 | John E. Rouse. | D | 778 | 46 |
| Andrew. | Cuthbert, Ga. | 1854 | George W. Gambill. | D | 385 | 25 |
| Anne Arundel Community | Arnold, Md. | 1961 | Andrew G. Truxal | C | 1,346 | 80 |
| Anoka-Ramsey St. Jr. | Coon Rapids, Minn. | 1965 | Emil Wilken. | S | 1,320 | 65 |
| Antelope Valley. | Lancaster, Calif. | 1929 | William Kepley, Jr. | Mu | 2,524 | 119 |
| Apprentice School. (M) | Newport News, Va. | 1919 | John Pirkle (Supt.) | Pr | 700 | 53 |
| Arizona Western. | Yuma, Ariz. | 1963 | George H. Hall. | C | 1,580 | 82 |
| Atlantic Comm. | Mays Landing, N. J. | 1964 | Luther G. Shaw. | C | 1,150 | 51 |
| Auburn Community | Auburn, N. Y. | 1953 | Albert T. Skinner. | Mu | 2,732 | 63 |
| Austin State Junior. | Austin, Minn | 1940 | R. I. Meland (Dean) | Dl | 757 | 41 |
| Averett. (W) | Danville, Va. | 1859 | Conwell Anderson. | D | 573 | 38 |
| Bacone. | Bacone, Okla. | 1880 | Garold D. Holstine. | D | 606 | 31 |
| Bakersfield. | Bakersfield, Calif. | 1913 | Edward Simonsen. | Dl | 3,710 | 350 |
| Baltimore Junior. | Baltimore, Md. | 1947 | Harry Bard | Mu | 2,918 | 42 |
| Barstow. | Barstow, Calif. | 1960 | Donald White. | Dl | 1,279 | 42 |
| Bay de Noc Comm. | Escanaba, Mich. | 1962 | R. L. Rinehart. | C | 650 | 35 |
| Bay Path Junior. | Longmeadow, Mass. | 1949 | Thomas G. Carr. | P | 500 | 27 |
| Becker Junior. | Worcester, Mass. | 1887 | T. F. Fleming (Chan.) | P | 613 | 28 |
| Beckley. | Beckley, W. Va. | 1933 | D. K. Shroyer. | P | 1,422 | 33 |
| Belleville Junior. | Belleville, Ill. | 1946 | H.J. Haberaecker. | Dl | 2,784 | 225 |
| Bennett. (W) | Millbrook, N. Y. | 1891 | Donald A. Eldridge. | P | 330 | 47 |
| Berkshire Community. | Pittsfield, Mass. | 1960 | T. E. O'Connell. | S | 1,069 | 85 |
| Big Bend Community | Moses Lake, Wash. | 1962 | Don A. Morgan. | Dl | 1,050 | 132 |
| Bismarck Junior. | Bismarck, N. Dak. | 1939 | Ralph Werner. | Dl | 1,151 | 52 |
| Black Hawk. | Moline, Ill. | 1946 | Alban E. Reid. | Dl | 1,988 | 163 |
| Blinn. | Brenham, Tex. | 1883 | James H. Atkinson. | Dl | 1,318 | 69 |
| Bloom Community | Chicago Heights, Ill | 1958 | Richard Sherman. | Dl | 1,426 | 89 |
| Bluefield. | Bluefield, Va. | 1922 | Charles Harman. | D | 375 | 28 |
| Blue Mountain Community | Pendleton, Ore. | 1962 | Wallace C. McCrae. | Dl | 650 | 62 |
| Boone Junior. | Boone, Iowa. | 1927 | Clair E. Abbott (Dn.) | Dl | 408 | 25 |
| Borough of Manhattan Comm.(a) | New York, N. Y. | 1963 | Murray H. Block. | S | 4,747 | 230 |
| Bradford Junior. | Bradford, Mass. | 1803 | Robert Vogel. | P | 425 | 44 |
| Brainerd State Junior. (W) | Brainerd, Minn. | 1938 | J. E. Chalberg. | Dl | 475 | 24 |
| Brevard. | Brevard, N. C. | 1853 | Emmett K. McLarty, Jr. | D | 585 | 44 |
| Brevard Junior. | Cocoa, Fla. | 1960 | Leo C. Muller. | C | 5,978 | 200 |
| Brewton Parker. | Mt. Vernon, Ga. | 1904 | J. Theodore Phillips. | D | 500 | 33 |
| Bronx Community (b) | Bronx, N. Y. | 1958 | James A. Colston. | Mu | 7,337 | 275 |
| Broome Tech. Community | Binghamton, N. Y. | 1946 | Cecil C. Tyrrell. | C | 3,371 | 131 |
| Broward Co., Jr. Coll. of | Ft. Lauderdale, Fla. | 1960 | Hugh Adams. | C | 4,461 | 168 |
| Bryant & Stratton Bus. Inst | Buffalo, N. Y. | 1865 | Llewellyn White. | Pr | 2,000 | 70 |
| Burdett. | Boston, Mass. | 1879 | C. Fred Burdett. | Pr | 916 | 48 |
| Burlington Community | Burlington, Iowa. | 1920 | R. Burkheimer (Supt.). | Mu | 822 | 40 |
| Butler County Comm. Jr. | El Dorado, Kansas. | 1927 | Edwin J. Walbourn. | Mu | 1,957 | 70 |
| Cabrillo. | Aptos, Calif. | 1959 | Robert E. Swenson. | Dl | 3,325 | 77 |
| Canal Zone | Balboa, C. Z. | 1933 | D. W. Skinner (Dean) | F | 1,401 | 77 |
| Canton Community | Canton, Ill. | 1959 | Philip S. Osborn. | Dl | 1,129 | 48 |
| Cape Cod Comm. | Hyannis, Mass. | 1961 | E. Carleton Nickerson. | S | 825 | 47 |
| Casper. | Casper, Wyo. | 1945 | Tilghman R. Aley. | C | 2,340 | 123 |
| Catonsville Community | Baltimore, Md. | 1958 | James Newpher. | C | 1,837 | 111 |
| Cazenovia. (W) | Cazenovia, N. Y. | 1824 | Rhea M. Eckel. | P | 568 | 51 |
| Centenary Coll. for Women. (W) | Hackettstown, N. J. | 1867 | Edward W. Seay. | P | 662 | 68 |
| Centerville Community | Centerville, Iowa. | 1930 | Lyle Hellyer (Dn.). | Dl | 800 | 43 |
| Central. | McPherson, Kan. | 1914 | Bruce L. Kline. | D | 172 | 19 |
| Central Florida Junior. | Ocala, Fla. | 1958 | Henry E. Goodlett. | C | 1,250 | 64 |
| Central Oregon Community | Bend, Oregon. | 1949 | Frederick Boyle. | Dl | 1,000 | 55 |
| Central Piedmont Comm. | Charlotte, N. C. | 1963 | Richard H. Hagemeyer. | Dl | 2,891 | 150 |
| Central Pilgrim College. | Bartlesville, Okla. | 1959 | Norman N. Bonner. | D | 180 | 15 |
| Central Tech. Institute. | Kansas City, Mo. | 1931 | C. L. Foster. | Pr | 478 | 23 |
| Central YMCA Comm. | Chicago, Ill. | 1961 | Donald A. Canar. | P | 3,607 | 180 |
| Centralia. | Centralia, Wash. | 1925 | Nels W. Hanson. | Dl | 1,400 | 79 |
| Cerritos. | Norwalk, Calif. | 1955 | Jack W. Mears. | Dl | 9,877 | 246 |
| Chabot. | Hayward, Calif. | 1961 | Reed L. Buffington. | Dl | 7,239 | 260 |
| Chaffey. | Alta Loma, Calif. | 1922 | Harry Wiser. | Dl | 6,740 | 227 |
| Champlain. | Burlington, Vt. | 1878 | C. Bader Brouilette. | P | 720 | 44 |
| Charles Co. Community. | La Plata, Md. | 1958 | J. N. Carsey. | C | 547 | 30 |
| Chicago City. | Chicago, Ill. | 1911 | Oscar Shabat. | Mu | 30,980 | 885 |
| Chipola Junior. | Marianna, Fla. | 1947 | Ned L. Haven. | S, C | 1,083 | 75 |
| Chowan. | Murfreesboro, N. C. | 1848 | Bruce E. Whitaker. | D | 1,155 | 71 |
| Christian. (W) | Columbia, Mo. | 1851 | W. Merle Hill. | D | 522 | 40 |
| Christian Coll. of the Southwest | Dallas, Tex. | 1962 | W. E. Kirk. | D | 304 | 30 |
| Christopher Coll. of. Corpus Christi | Corpus Christi, Tex. | 1958 | Sis. Jeanne Francis. Minner | D | 178 | 23 |
| Cisco Junior. | Cisco, Texas. | 1940 | Leland Willis. | Mu | 813 | 48 |
| Citrus. | Azusa, Calif. | 1915 | Robt. D. Haugh. | Dl | 5,483 | 104 |
| Clarendon. | Clarendon, Tex. | 1898 | Kenneth D. Vaughan. | Dl | 231 | 15 |
| Clark. | Vancouver, Wash. | 1933 | Dwight C. Baird. | Dl | 2,829 | 159 |
| Clarke Memorial. | Newton, Miss. | 1908 | W. L. Compere. | D | 239 | 18 |
| Clatsop Community | Astoria, Ore. | 1962 | Stewart F. McCollom. | Dl | 790 | 87 |
| Cloud County Comm. Junior. | Concordia, Kansas. | 1965 | Arley Bryant, (Dean). | C | 299 | 25 |
| Coahoma Junior. | Clarksdale, Miss. | 1949 | James Earl Miller. | S | 882 | 38 |
| Coalinga. | Coalinga, Calif. | 1941 | Robert Annand. | Dl | 1,165 | 100 |
| Cochise. | Douglas, Ariz. | 1964 | Jack R. Netcher. | S | 1,186 | 65 |
| Coffeyville Community Junior. | Coffeyville, Kan. | 1923 | Russell Graham. | Mu | 577 | 30 |
| Colby Comm. Junior. | Colby, Kansas. | 1964 | Richard Mosier. | C | 394 | 21 |
| Colby Junior. (W) | New London, N. H. | 1837 | Everett M. Woodman. | P | 570 | 57 |

| Name | Location | Yr. | Governing Official and Control | Stu-dents | Teach-ers |
|---|---|---|---|---|---|
| Columbia Basin | Pasco, Wash. | 1955 | Fred L. Esvelt | Dt | 2,114 | 123 |
| Compton | Compton, Calif. | 1927 | Foster Davidoff | Dt | 4,802 | 172 |
| Concordia | Portland, Ore. | 1950 | Erhardt P. Weber | D | 148 | 18 |
| Concordia | Milwaukee, Wis. | 1881 | Walter W. Stuenkel | D | 299 | 23 |
| Concordia Junior | Bronxville, N. Y. | 1881 | Albert E. Meyer | D | 421 | 49 |
| Concordia Lutheran | Austin, Tex. | 1926 | Walter C. Rubke | D | 169 | 19 |
| Concordia Lutheran Jr. | Ann Arbor, Mich. | 1962 | P. A. Zimmermann | D | 479 | 59 |
| Contra Costa | San Pablo, Calif. | 1948 | Raymond Dondero | Dt | 5,290 | 195 |
| Cooke County Jr. | Gainsville, Tex. | 1924 | John H. Parker | C | 1,030 | 60 |
| Coplah-Lincoln Junior | Wesson, Miss. | 1928 | Billy Thames | C | 625 | 54 |
| Corning Community | Corning, N. Y. | 1956 | Robt. W. Frederick, Jr. | Mu | 2,699 | 84 |
| Cottey............(W) | Nevada, Mo. | 1884 | Ted McCarrel | P | 337 | 33 |
| Cowley County Comm. Jr. | Arkansas City, Kans. | 1922 | Paul M. Johnson | M | 1,079 | 45 |
| Crowder | Neosho, Mo. | 1963 | Donald D. Shook | Dt | 515 | 24 |
| Cuesta | San Luis Obispo, Calif. | 1963 | Merlin Eisenbise | Dt | 2,800 | 93 |
| Cumberland Coll. of Tenn. | Lebanon, Tenn. | 1842 | Ernest L. Stockton | P | 291 | 21 |
| Cuyahoga Community | Cleveland, O. | 1963 | Charles E. Chapman | Dt | 12,637 | 533 |
| Danville Junior | Danville, Ill. | 1949 | Mary Miller | Mu | 1,298 | 100 |
| Davenport Coll. of Business | Grand Rapids, Mich. | 1866 | Robert W. Sneden | P | 925 | 44 |
| Dawson Junior | Glendive, Mont. | 1940 | Richard Starr (Dn.) | Dt | 400 | 27 |
| Daytona Beach Junior | Daytona Beach, Fla. | 1958 | Roy F. Bergengren | C | 8,696 | 371 |
| Dean Junior | Franklin, Mass. | 1865 | William Garner | P | 987 | 78 |
| DeKalb | Clarkston, Ga. | 1964 | James Hinson, Jr. | C | 2,917 | 118 |
| Del Mar | Corpus Christi, Tex. | 1935 | Jean Richardson | Mu | 3,658 | 172 |
| Delta | University Ctr., Mich. | 1957 | Donald Carlyon | Dt | 3,738 | 209 |
| DeVry Inst. of Tech. | Chicago, Ill. | 1931 | Orville Thompson | Pr | 3,100 | 169 |
| Desert, Coll. of the | Palm Desert, Calif. | 1958 | Roy C. McCall | Dt | 3,642 | 169 |
| Diablo Valley | Pleasant Hill, Calif. | 1948 | William P. Niland | Dt | 8,467 | 345 |
| Dixie Junior | St. George, Utah | 1913 | Ferron C. Losee | S | 1,000 | 50 |
| Dodge City Community Jr. | Dodge City, Kan. | 1935 | Chas. M. Barnes | Dt | 774 | 39 |
| Donnelly | Kansas City, Kan. | 1949 | Sister Richard | D | 866 | 42 |
| Du Page, Coll. of | Naperville, Ill. | 1967 | Rodney W. Berg | C | 2,500 | 227 |
| Dutchess Community | Poughkeepsie, N. Y. | 1958 | James F. Hall | C | 3,538 | 115 |
| East Central Junior | Decatur, Miss. | 1928 | Charles V. Wright | Dt | 759 | 45 |
| East Los Angeles | Los Angeles, Calif. | 1945 | John K. Wells | Dt | 13,109 | 585 |
| Eastern Arizona | Thatcher, Ariz. | 1888 | Dean Curtis | Dt | 1,032 | 51 |
| Eastern Iowa Comm. | Muscatine, Iowa | 1929 | R. W. Johnson (Supt.) | C | 626 | 37 |
| Eastern Okla. State | Wilburton, Okla. | 1909 | J. N. Baker | S | 958 | 42 |
| Eastern Wyoming | Torrington, Wyo. | 1948 | Albert C. Conger | Dt | 377 | 19 |
| Edison Junior | Ft. Myers, Fla. | 1962 | David G. Robinson | C | 1,200 | 60 |
| El Camino | Torrance, Calif. | 1946 | Stuart E. Marsee | Dt | 14,500 | 435 |
| El Reno Junior | El Reno, Okla. | 1938 | Leslie F. Roblyer | Dt | 266 | 19 |
| Elgin Community | Elgin, Ill. | 1949 | Gilbert Renner | Dt | 1,904 | 146 |
| Elizabeth Seton........(W) | Yonkers, N. Y. | 1960 | Sis. Dolores Mary | D | 430 | 45 |
| Ellsworth | Iowa Falls, Iowa | 1890 | G. P. Warford (Dn.) | Mu | 981 | 49 |
| Emmanuel | Franklin Spgs., Ga. | 1919 | Woodward G. Drum | D | 265 | 29 |
| Endicott Junior........(W) | Beverly, Mass. | 1939 | George Bierkoe | P | 859 | 59 |
| Erie County Tech. Inst. | Buffalo, N. Y. | 1946 | James Shenton | Dt | 4,158 | 138 |
| Essex Community | Essex, Md. | 1957 | M. S. Koch, Jr. | C | 1,269 | 87 |
| Everett Junior | Everett, Wash. | 1941 | Paul McCurley | Dt | 3,100 | 192 |
| Fairbury Junior | Fairbury, Nebr. | 1941 | Ivan R. Simpson | Mu | 423 | 23 |
| Fashion Inst. of Technology | New York, N. Y. | 1944 | Lawrence L. Jarvie | S,Mu | 5,220 | 122 |
| Fergus Falls State Jr. | Fergus Falls, Minn. | 1960 | W. A. Waage | Dt | 531 | 30 |
| Ferrum Junior | Ferrum, Va. | 1913 | C. Ralph Arthur | D | 993 | 57 |
| Fisher Junior........(W) | Boston, Mass. | 1903 | Sanford L. Fisher | P | 500 | 30 |
| Flint Community Junior | Flint, Mich. | 1923 | Chas. Donnelly | Mu | 6,073 | 172 |
| Florida | Temple Terrace, Fla. | 1946 | James R. Cope | P | 365 | 28 |
| Foothill | Los Altos Hills, Calif. | 1958 | H. H. Semans | Dt | 7,992 | 255 |
| Fort Scott Community Junior | Fort Scott, Kan. | 1919 | Leon Foster | Mu | 439 | 18 |
| Ft. Worth Christian | Ft. Worth, Tex. | 1959 | Cursti Ramey | P | 200 | 15 |
| Frank Phillips | Borger, Tex. | 1948 | James W. Dillard | Dt | 700 | 43 |
| Franklin Inst. of Boston | Boston, Mass. | 1908 | L. J. Dunham Jr. (Dir.) | P | 1,091 | 73 |
| Frederick Community | Frederick, Md. | 1957 | Lewis W. Stephens | C | 719 | 47 |
| Freed-Hardeman | Henderson, Tenn. | 1908 | Hubert A. Dixon | D | 661 | 46 |
| Fresno City | Fresno, Calif. | 1910 | Clyde C. McNally | Dt | 7,802 | 356 |
| Friendship Junior | Rock Hill, S. C. | 1891 | James H. Goudlock | D | 375 | 18 |
| Fullerton Junior | Fullerton, Calif. | 1913 | H. Lynn Sheller | Dt | 11,297 | 354 |
| Fulton-Montgomery Community | Johnstown, N. Y. | 1963 | William L. Gregg | S | 1,150 | 47 |
| Garden City Community Junior | Garden City, Kan. | 1919 | L. C. Crouch | Mu | 414 | 30 |
| Gardner-Webb Junior | Boiling Springs, N. C. | 1905 | E. Eugene Poston | D | 1,134 | 67 |
| Garland Junior........(W) | Boston, Mass. | 1952 | Frederic B. Viaux | P | 370 | 43 |
| Gaston | Gastonia, N. C. | 1964 | W. B. Sugg | C | 1,691 | 73 |
| Gavilan | Gilroy, Calif. | 1919 | Ralph Schroder | Dt | 1,340 | 76 |
| Genesee Community | Batavia, N. Y. | 1965 | Alfred C. O'Connell | S | 625 | 16 |
| Georgia Military........(M) | Milledgeville, Ga. | 1879 | R. A. Thorne | Mu | 242 | 20 |
| Glendale | Glendale, Calif. | 1927 | John T. Mc Cuen | Dt | 4,988 | 163 |
| Gogebic Community | Ironwood, Mich. | 1932 | James Perry | Mu | 515 | 24 |
| Goldey Beacon Junior | Wilmington, Del. | 1886 | Jay W. Miller | Pr | 1,466 | 60 |
| Gordon Military | Barnesville, Ga. | 1852 | Woodrow Light | P | 600 | 70 |
| Grahm Junior | Boston, Mass. | 1950 | Milton Grahm | Pr | 1,300 | 75 |
| Grand Rapids Junior | Grand Rapids, Mich. | 1914 | Francis McCarthy (Dn.) | Mu | 4,428 | 209 |
| Grand View | Des Moines, Iowa | 1896 | Ernest D. Nielsen | D | 1,420 | 77 |
| Grays Harbor | Aberdeen, Wash. | 1930 | Edward P. Smith | Dt | 1,794 | 101 |
| Greenbrier | Lewisburg, W. Va. | 1812 | John F. Montgomery | Pr | 204 | 18 |
| Greenfield Comm. | Greenfield, Mass. | 1962 | Lewis O. Turner | S | 915 | 63 |
| Green Mountain........(W) | Poultney, Vt. | 1834 | Raymond A. Withey | D | 647 | 44 |
| Grossmont | El Cajon, Calif. | 1961 | Harold Hughes | Dt | 5,444 | 150 |
| Gulf Coast Junior | Panama City, Fla. | 1957 | Richard E. Morley | S, Dt | 2,000 | 70 |
| Gulf Park........(W) | Long Beach, Miss. | 1919 | William T. Sadler | P | 283 | 32 |
| Hagerstown Junior | Hagerstown, Md. | 1946 | Atlee Kepler | D | 898 | 63 |
| Harcum Junior........(W) | Bryn Mawr, Pa. | 1915 | Michael A. Duzy | P | 975 | 52 |
| Hartford Jr. | Bel Air, Md. | 1957 | Joseph N. Hankin | C | 1,193 | 72 |
| Harrisburg Area Community | Harrisburg, Pa. | 1964 | Clyde E. Blocker | Dt | 2,153 | 110 |
| Hartford Coll. for Women | Hartford, Conn. | 1939 | Laura A. Johnson | P | 187 | 40 |
| Hartnell | Salinas, Calif. | 1920 | William Harwood | Dt | 3,150 | 112 |
| Henderson County Junior | Athens, Tex. | 1946 | Orval Pirtle | C | 1,174 | 67 |
| Henry Ford Community | Dearborn, Mich. | 1936 | James O. McCann | Mu | 11,245 | 605 |
| Herkimer County Comm. | Ilion, N. Y. | 1966 | Robert McLaughlin | S | 305 | 10 |
| Hesston | Hesston, Kan. | 1909 | Leban Peachey | D | 425 | 33 |
| Hibbing State Junior | Hibbing, Minn. | 1916 | Ove. C. Nordvold (Dn.) | Dt | 795 | 36 |
| Highland Comm. | Freeport, Ill. | 1962 | Kenneth E. Borland | C | 902 | 105 |
| Highland Community Junior | Highland, Kan. | 1858 | T. E. Woodrum | Dt | 349 | 18 |
| Highland Park | Highland Park, Mich. | 1918 | Paul H. Jones (Dean) | Mu | 3,750 | 195 |
| Highline Comm. | Midway, Wash. | 1961 | M. A. Allan | Dt | 3,600 | 271 |

| Name | Location | Yr. | Governing Official and Control | | Students | Teachers |
|---|---|---|---|---|---|---|
| Hill Junior | Hillsboro, Texas | 1962 | Oran Bailey | D1 | 700 | 41 |
| Hinds Junior | Raymond, Miss | 1917 | Robert Mayo | D1 | 2,412 | 125 |
| Hiwassee | Madisonville, Tenn. | 1849 | Horace N. Barker | D | 650 | 36 |
| Holmes Junior | Goodman, Miss | 1928 | Frank B. Branch | D1 | 852 | 43 |
| Holyoke Community | Holyoke, Mass. | 1946 | George E. Frost | Mu | 1,945 | 136 |
| Howard County Junior | Big Springs, Tex. | 1945 | William A. Hunt | C | 980 | 56 |
| Hudson Valley Community | Troy, N. Y. | 1953 | James J. Fitzgibbons | C | 4,955 | 227 |
| Humphreys | Stockton, Calif. | 1896 | John R. Humphreys | P | 440 | 22 |
| Hutchinson Community Junior | Hutchinson, Kan. | 1928 | A. H. Elland | Mu | 1,464 | 80 |
| Illinois Valley Comm. | La Salle, Ill. | 1924 | Kenneth H. Freeman | Mu | 1,721 | 87 |
| Imperial Valley | Imperial, Calif. | 1960 | Terrel Spencer | D1 | 1,640 | 70 |
| Independence Community Jr. | Independence, Kan. | 1925 | Neil Edds | Mu | 479 | 40 |
| Indian River Junior | Ft. Pierce, Fla. | 1960 | Maxwell C. King | C | 960 | 46 |
| Iowa Central Comm. | Ft. Dodge, Iowa | 1967 | Edwin Barbour | C | 1,530 | 137 |
| Iowa Lakes Comm. | Esterville, Iowa | 1924 | Arvil Parks | D1 | 627 | 44 |
| Iowa Western Comm. | Clarinda, Iowa | 1923 | Orin C. Mann (Dn.) | C | 602 | 34 |
| Itasca State Junior | Grand Rapids, Minn. | 1922 | H. E. Wilson | D1 | 540 | 32 |
| Itawamba Junior | Fulton, Miss. | 1948 | J. S. Crubaugh | D1 | 880 | 60 |
| Jackson Community | Jackson, Mich. | 1928 | Wm. N. Atkinson | C | 2,900 | 110 |
| Jamestown Community | Jamestown, N. Y. | 1950 | Albert W. Baisler | S,Mu | 1,357 | 55 |
| Jefferson | Hillsboro, Mo. | 1963 | Charles J. McClain | D1 | 943 | 34 |
| Jefferson Community | Watertown, N. Y. | 1963 | James E. McVean | C | 1,042 | 67 |
| Johnson & Wales Jr. Coll. of Bus. | Providence, R. I. | 1914 | Edward P. Triangolo | Pr | 1,600 | 60 |
| Joliet Junior | Joliet, Ill. | 1901 | Elmer Rowley | Mu | 3,100 | 136 |
| Jones County Junior | Ellisville, Miss | 1927 | James B. Young | Di, S | 2,260 | 96 |
| Kan. City Kan. Comm. Junior | Kansas City, Kan | 1923 | Jack M. Flint | Mu | 1,367 | 61 |
| Kaskaskia | Centralia, Ill. | 1940 | Eugene McClintock | D1 | 1,130 | 56 |
| Kellogg Community | Battle Creek, Mich. | 1956 | Dr. Whitmore (Dir.) | D1 | 2,700 | 110 |
| Kemper Military School | Boonville, Mo. | 1844 | James Kelly | P | 260 | 41 |
| Kendall | Evanston, Ill. | 1934 | Wesley M. Westerberg | D | 709 | 64 |
| Keokuk Community | Keokuk, Iowa | 1953 | R. O. Birkhimer | D1 | 687 | 27 |
| Keystone Junior | La Plume, Pa. | 1868 | Harry K. Miller, Jr. | P | 683 | 43 |
| Kilgore | Kilgore, Tex. | 1935 | Randolph C. Watson | D1 | 2,216 | 101 |
| King's | Charlotte, N. C. | 1901 | Milo O. Kirkpatrick | Pr | 878 | 37 |
| Kingsborough Community (a) | Brooklyn, N. Y. | 1963 | Jacob I. Hartstein | S | 2,935 | 200 |
| Kittrell | Kittrell, N. C. | 1886 | Larnie G. Horton | D | 276 | 17 |
| Labette Community Jr. | Parsons, Kans. | 1923 | Charles E. Thiebaud | Mu | 397 | 29 |
| Lackawanna Junior | Scranton, Pa. | 1894 | H. G. Seeley | P | 310 | 12 |
| Lake City Jr. Coll. & Forest Ranger School | Lake City, Fla. | 1962 | Herbert E. Phillips | C | 858 | 39 |
| Lake Michigan | Benton Harbor, Mich. | 1946 | Robert H. Plummer | Mu | 2,250 | 67 |
| Lake Region Jr. | Devils Lake, N. Dak. | 1941 | Merril Berg (Dn.) | D1 | 450 | 38 |
| Lake-Sumter Jr. | Leesburg, Fla. | 1962 | Paul P. Williams | C | 909 | 42 |
| Lamar Community | Lamar, Colo. | 1937 | Carl Gerber | D1 | 550 | 45 |
| Lansing Community | Lansing, Mich | 1957 | Phillip Gannon | Mu | 4,621 | 183 |
| Laredo Junior | Laredo, Tex. | 1947 | Ray A. Laird | Mu | 1,300 | 47 |
| Lasell Junior (W) | Auburndale, Mass. | 1851 | Vincent DeBaun | P | 905 | 91 |
| Lassen | Susanville, Calif. | 1925 | Robert Theiler | D1 | 885 | 35 |
| Lee | Baytown, Tex. | 1934 | Richard Strahan | Mu | 2,000 | 90 |
| Lees Junior | Jackson, Ky | 1891 | Troy R. Eslinger | D | 319 | 18 |
| Lees-McRae | Banner Elk, N. C. | 1929 | H. C. Evans, Jr. | D | 600 | 39 |
| Leicester Junior (M) | Leicester, Mass. | 1784 | Henry Borger | P | 228 | 15 |
| Limestone | Gaffney, S. C. | 1840 | J. C. McCollister | P | 645 | 53 |
| Lindsey Wilson | Columbia, Ky. | 1903 | John B. Horton | D | 547 | 25 |
| Lon Morris | Jacksonville, Tex. | 1873 | Cecil E. Peeples | D | 376 | 24 |
| Long Beach City | Long Beach, Calif. | 1927 | Wiley Garner | Mu | 22,496 | 480 |
| Lorain County Comm. | Elyria, Ohio | 1964 | Max Lerner | C | 2,624 | 97 |
| Los Angeles City | Los Angeles, Calif. | 1929 | Glenn Gooder | Mu | 18,000 | 600 |
| Los Angeles Harbor | Wilmington, Calif. | 1949 | Wendell C. Black | D1 | 6,927 | 334 |
| Los Angeles Pierce | Woodland Hills, Calif. | 1947 | Marie Martin | Mu | 13,732 | 435 |
| L. A. Trade Technical | Los Angeles, Calif. | 1949 | F. Parker Wilber | Mu | 13,359 | 665 |
| Los Angeles Valley | Van Nuys, Calif. | 1949 | Wm. J. McNells | Mu | 16,200 | 400 |
| Louisburg | Louisburg, N. C. | 1787 | Cecil W. Robbins | D | 691 | 46 |
| Lower Columbia | Longview, Wash. | 1934 | Harold A. Lang | D1 | 2,200 | 61 |
| Macomb County Community | Warren, Mich. | 1959 | J. R. Dimitry (Act.) | D1 | 10,300 | 459 |
| Madison Business | Madison, Wis. | 1856 | Otto J. Madland | Pr | 455 | 25 |
| Manatee Junior | Bradenton, Fla. | 1957 | Samuel R. Neel, Jr. | C | 2,800 | 113 |
| Manchester Comm. | Manchester, Conn. | 1963 | F. W. Lowe | Mu | 1,491 | 100 |
| Manor Junior (W) | Jenkintown, Pa. | 1959 | Mo. M. Jerome | P | 124 | 25 |
| Marla Regina | Syracuse, N. Y. | 1961 | Sis. M. Rosalie | P | 533 | 33 |
| Marin, Coll. of | Kentfield, Calif. | 1926 | William Ramstad | D1 | 4,674 | 123 |
| Marion Institute (M) | Marion, Ala. | 1842 | Paul B. Robinson | P | 647 | 48 |
| Marjorie Webster Junior | Washington, D. C. | 1920 | Sherwood Webster | Pr | 500 | 50 |
| Marshalltown Community | Marshalltown, Iowa | 1927 | Robert Horstall | D1 | 1,060 | 60 |
| Mary Holmes Jr. | West Point, Miss. | 1892 | Donovan Smucker | D | 367 | 30 |
| Marymount, Coll. of Virginia (W) | Arlington, Va. | 1950 | Mother M. M. Berg | D | 730 | 50 |
| Marymount | Boca Raton, Fla. | 1963 | Sis. de la Croix | D | 340 | 22 |
| Massachusetts Bay Comm. | Watertown, Mass. | 1961 | J. F. McKenzie | S | 1,655 | 109 |
| Maunaelu | Pala Maui, Hawaii | 1861 | Cummins Speakman | D | 155 | 17 |
| McCook | McCook, Nebr. | 1926 | A. W. Kuper | Mu | 457 | 29 |
| MacCormac Junior | Chicago, Ill. | 1904 | Gorpon Borchardt | P | 250 | 12 |
| Merced | Merced, Calif. | 1963 | Lowell Barker | D1 | 3,150 | 57 |
| Mercer County Comm. | Trenton, N. J. | 1966 | Richard Greenfield | S | 2,507 | 137 |
| Meridian Junior | Meridian, Miss | 1937 | William Scaggs | Mu | 1,245 | 65 |
| Mesa | Gd. Junction, Colo | 1925 | William A. Medesy | Mu | 2,314 | 135 |
| Mesabi State Jr. | Virginia, Minn. | 1921 | Gilbert Staupe | S | 619 | 29 |
| Metropolitan Jr. Coll—Kansas City | Kansas City, Mo. | 1915 | H. N. Monnett (Act.) | D1 | 5,140 | 123 |
| Miami-Dade Jr. | Miami, Fla. | 1960 | Peter Masiko, Jr. | C | 23,341 | 827 |
| Miami-Jacobs Jr. Coll. of Business | Dayton, Ohio | 1860 | Charles P. Harbottle | Pr | 791 | 35 |
| Michigan Christian Jr. | Rochester, Mich. | 1959 | E. Lucien Palmer | P | 220 | 10 |
| Middle Georgia | Cochran, Ga. | 1887 | Louis C. Alderman, Jr. | S | 1,503 | 82 |
| Midway Junior (W) | Midway, Ky. | 1849 | Albert N. Cox | P | 147 | 24 |
| Miles Comm. | Miles City, Mont. | 1939 | K. O. Smith (Dn.) | Mu | 350 | 20 |
| Miltonvale Wesleyan | Miltonvale, Kansas | 1909 | Wesley Knapp | D | 177 | 14 |
| Milwaukee Technical | Milwaukee, Wis. | 1951 | George Parkinson (Dir.) | Mu | 7,615 | 365 |
| Mineral Area | Flat River, Mo. | 1922 | Richard Caster | D1 | 780 | 53 |
| Mira Costa | Oceanside, Calif. | 1934 | John MacDonald | D1 | 1,936 | 75 |
| Mississippi Delta Jr. | Moorhead, Miss. | 1926 | J. T. Hall | D1 | 795 | 40 |
| Missouri Baptist | Hannibal, Mo. | 1858 | L. A. Foster | D | 458 | 34 |
| Missouri Southern | Joplin, Mo. | 1937 | Leon C. Billingsley | D1 | 2,399 | 74 |
| Missouri Western Junior | St. Joseph, Mo. | 1915 | M. O. Looney | Mu | 985 | 42 |
| Mitchell | Statesville, N. C. | 1856 | John Montgomery | D | 499 | 33 |
| Modesto Junior | Modesto, Calif. | 1921 | Roy Mikalson | D1 | 9,111 | 452 |

| Name | Location | Yr. | Governing Official and Control | | Students | Teachers |
|---|---|---|---|---|---|---|
| Mohawk Valley Community.... | Utica, N. Y......... | 1946 | R. D. Larsson (Act.).... | C | 3.387 | 86 |
| Monroe Community............ | Rochester, N. Y...... | 1962 | LeRoy V. Good........ | C | 4,838 | 150 |
| Monterey Peninsula.......... | Monterey, Calif...... | 1947 | George J. Faul........ | D1 | 4,800 | 142 |
| Montgomery Junior........... | Takoma Park, Md.... | 1946 | William Strasser...... | C | 4,685 | 279 |
| Monticello...............(W) | Godfrey, Ill......... | 1835 | Gail E. Myers........ | P | 365 | 41 |
| Montreat-Anderson........... | Montreat, N. C...... | 1916 | C. Grier Davis........ | D | 418 | 33 |
| Morristown.................. | Morristown, Tenn.... | 1881 | Elmer P. Gibson...... | D | 280 | 15 |
| Morse....................... | Hartford, Conn...... | 1860 | Vacant.............. | Pr | 200 | 12 |
| Morton Junior............... | Cicero, Ill.......... | 1924 | J. Philip Dalby....... | Mu | 2,429 | 146 |
| Mt. Aloysius Junior....(W) | Cresson, Pa.......... | 1939 | Sis. Mary Ursula..... | D | 450 | 47 |
| Mt. Ida Junior.........(W) | Newton Ctr., Mass... | 1899 | F. Roy Carlson....... | P | 600 | 51 |
| Mt. Olive Junior............ | Mt. Olive, N. C..... | 1951 | William B. Raper...... | D1 | 340 | 30 |
| Mt. St. Clare..........(W) | Clinton, Iowa....... | 1928 | Sister Mary Phelan.... | D | 280 | 33 |
| Mt. San Antonio............. | Walnut, Calif....... | 1946 | Oscar H. Edinger, Jr... | D1 | 12,202 | 431 |
| Mt. San Jacinto............. | Gilman Hot Spgs,Calif. | 1963 | Milo P. Johnson...... | C | 1,010 | 62 |
| Mt. Vernon Community........ | Mt. Vernon, Ill..... | 1956 | Eltis Henson ........ | D1 | 589 | 38 |
| Mt. Vernon Junior......(W) | Washington, D. C.... | 1875 | Peter D. Pelham...... | P | 276 | 32 |
| Mt. Wachusett Comm.......... | Gardner, Mass....... | 1963 | Arthur F. Haley...... | S | 1,032 | 49 |
| Multnomah................... | Portland, Ore....... | 1897 | John S. Griffith...... | P | 899 | 79 |
| Murray State................ | Tishomingo, Okla.... | 1908 | Clyde Kindell........ | S | 656 | 34 |
| Muskegon County Community.. | Muskegon, Mich..... | 1926 | Ralph A. Austermiller.. | Mu | 3,475 | 169 |
| Muskegon Business........... | Muskegon, Mich..... | 1885 | Robert Jewell........ | Pr | 360 | 15 |
| Napa Junior................. | Napa, Calif......... | 1942 | George Clark........ | D1 | 2,800 | 72 |
| Nassau Community............ | Garden City, N. Y... | 1959 | George F. Chambers.... | C | 9,941 | 254 |
| Natchez Junior.............. | Natchez, Miss....... | 1885 | Rev. LeVander Kinds.. | D | 245 | 10 |
| National Business........... | Roanoke, Va........ | 1886 | Murray K. Coulter.... | Pr | 435 | 21 |
| Navarro Junior.............. | Corsicana, Tex...... | 1946 | Ben W. Jones........ | C | 1,203 | 60 |
| Neosho County Comm. Jr...... | Chanute, Kans...... | 1936 | Buford E. Fisher..... | D1 | 310 | 31 |
| New Hampshire Voc. Inst..... | Manchester, N. H.... | 1946 | George C. Knox (Dir.).. | S | 358 | 24 |
| New Hampshire Voc. Inst..... | Portsmouth, N. H.... | 1945 | E. A. McCourt (Prin.).. | S | 200 | 17 |
| New Mexico Military Inst...(M) | Roswell, N. M....... | 1891 | Maj. Gen Sam W. Agee. | S | 950 | 54 |
| N. Y. City Community Coll. (a) | Brooklyn, N. Y...... | 1946 | Milton G. Bassin...... | Mu | 11,518 | 397 |
| New York, State Univ. of.... | Albany, N. Y....... | 1948 | Samuel B. Gould...... | S | 181,293 | 4,712 |
|   Agric. & Tech. Inst...... | Alfred, N. Y........ | 1908 | David H. Huntington.. | S | 2,751 | 173 |
|     ''    ''    ''    (Act.) | Canton, N. Y........ | 1906 | G. E. Wright (Act.).... | S | 1,264 | 87 |
|     ''    ''    ''    ''...... | Cobleskill, N. Y..... | 1911 | Walton A. Brown..... | S | 1,619 | 92 |
|     ''    ''    ''    ''...... | Delhi, N. Y......... | 1913 | William R. Kunsela... | S | 1,398 | 89 |
|     ''    ''    ''    ''...... | Farmingdale, N. Y... | 1912 | Chas. W. Laflin...... | S | 9,041 | 256 |
|     ''    ''    ''    ''...... | Morrisville, N. Y.... | 1908 | Royson N. Whipple.... | S | 1,566 | 103 |
| Newton Junior............... | Newtonville, Mass... | 1946 | Charles W. Dudley.... | Mu | 650 | 55 |
| Niagara County Community.... | Niagara Falls, N. Y.. | 1963 | Ernest Notar......... | C | 2,776 | 95 |
| Norfolk Junior.............. | Norfolk, Nebr....... | 1942 | F. Don Maclay....... | D | 600 | 31 |
| Norman...................... | Norman Park, Ga.... | 1900 | Guy Atkinson........ | D | 264 | 17 |
| North Central Michigan...... | Petoskey, Mich...... | 1958 | A. D. Shankland...... | D1 | 553 | 27 |
| N. Dak. Sch. of Forestry.... | Bottineau, N. Dak... | 1906 | C. N. Nelson........ | S | 300 | 22 |
| N. Dak. St. Sch. of Science.. | Wahpeton, N. Dak... | 1903 | Clair T. Blikre....... | S | 2,100 | 144 |
| North Florida Junior........ | Madison, Fla....... | 1958 | Marshall Hamilton.... | C | 1,159 | 73 |
| North Greenville Junior..... | Tigerville, S. C..... | 1892 | Thomas L. Neely..... | D | 430 | 39 |
| North Idaho Junior.......... | Coeur d'Alene, Idaho | 1939 | P. A. Christianson.... | D1 | 930 | 54 |
| North Iowa Area Comm........ | Mason City, Iowa.... | 1918 | C. H. Beem (Dn.)..... | Mu | 1,797 | 130 |
| North Shore Community....... | Beverly, Mass....... | 1965 | Harold Shively....... | S | 1,684 | 120 |
| Northampton Commercial...... | Northampton, Mass.. | 1896 | Richard D. Pickett.... | Pr | 553 | 28 |
| Northeast Miss. Junior...... | Booneville, Miss.... | 1948 | Harold White........ | D1 | 920 | 54 |
| Northeastern Junior......... | Sterling, Colo...... | 1941 | Ervin S. French...... | C | 1,705 | 92 |
| Northeastern Okla. A. & M... | Miami, Okla........ | 1919 | Bruce G. Carter...... | S | 1,806 | 72 |
| Northern Essex Comm......... | Haverhill, Mass..... | 1960 | Harold Bentley...... | D1 | 1,447 | 71 |
| Northern Okla.............. | Tonkawa, Okla...... | 1901 | Edwin Vineyard...... | S | 1,025 | 51 |
| Northwest Community......... | Powell, Wyo........ | 1946 | Sinclair Orendorff.... | D1 | 505 | 38 |
| Northwest Miss. Junior...... | Senatobia, Miss..... | 1927 | R. D. McLendon...... | D1 | 1,500 | 80 |
| Northwestern Michigan....... | Traverse City, Mich.. | 1951 | P. N. Tanis (Dir.)..... | D1 | 1,285 | 78 |
| Northwood Institute......... | Midland, Mich...... | 1959 | Arthur Turner....... | P | 950 | 47 |
| Norwalk Community........... | Norwalk, Conn...... | 1961 | E. I. L. Baker....... | Mu | 1,951 | 79 |
| Norwalk State Tech.......... | Norwalk, Conn...... | 1961 | Frank Juszli......... | S | 1,525 | 77 |
| Odessa...................... | Odessa, Tex........ | 1946 | Jack Rodgers........ | D1 | 2,828 | 160 |
| Ohio Coll. of Applied Science.... | Cincinnati, Ohio.... | 1828 | William W. Culp...... | P | 2,534 | 161 |
| Okaloosa-Walton Jr.......... | Valparaiso, Fla..... | 1963 | J. E. McCracken..... | C | 2,552 | 124 |
| Oklahoma Military Academy... | Claremore, Okla.... | 1918 | John F. Smoller...... | S | 325 | 38 |
| Oklahoma Sch. of Business Accountancy, Law & Finance. | Tulsa, Okla........ | 1919 | H. Everett Pope...... | Pr | 734 | 28 |
| Olney Comm................. | Olney, Ill.......... | 1963 | Leslie E. Purdy...... | D1 | 455 | 18 |
| Olympic..................... | Bremerton, Wash.... | 1946 | James D. Park....... | D1 | 3,550 | 105 |
| Onondaga Community.......... | Syracuse, N. Y...... | 1962 | Marvin Rapp........ | C | 3,175 | 81 |
| Orange Coast................ | Costa Mesa, Calif.... | 1947 | Robert Moore........ | D1 | 14,828 | 509 |
| Orange County Community..... | Middletown, N. Y.... | 1950 | Robert T. Novak..... | C | 3,578 | 115 |
| Orlando Junior.............. | Orlando, Fla........ | 1941 | Morris S. Hale, Jr.... | P | 1,672 | 75 |
| Otero Jr.................... | La Junta, Colo...... | 1941 | William L. McDivitt... | D1 | 1,046 | 45 |
| Ottumwa Heights............ | Ottumwa, Iowa..... | 1925 | Sister M. Hogan...... | D | 435 | 35 |
| Owen........................ | Memphis, Tenn..... | 1954 | Charles L. Dinkins... | D | 437 | 35 |
| Oxford Coll. of Emory Univ.. | Oxford, Ga........ | 1836 | S. S. Atwood........ | D1 | 367 | 28 |
| Paducah Junior.............. | Paducah, Ky....... | 1932 | R. G. Matheson...... | Mu | 1,153 | 62 |
| Palm Beach Junior.......... | Lake Worth, Fla..... | 1933 | Harold C. Manor..... | C | 4,001 | 180 |
| Palmer...................... | Charleston, S. C.... | 1954 | Charles E. Palmer.... | P | 918 | 44 |
| Palomar..................... | San Marcos, Calif.... | 1945 | Frederick R. Huber.... | D1 | 5,123 | 154 |
| Palo Verde.................. | Blythe, Calif....... | 1947 | Stuart M. Bundy..... | D1 | 550 | 30 |
| Panola...................... | Carthage, Tex...... | 1947 | Q. M. Martin........ | C | 638 | 35 |
| Paris Junior................ | Paris, Tex.......... | 1924 | Louis B. Williams.... | Mu | 504 | 29 |
| Pasadena City............... | Pasadena, Calif..... | 1924 | Armen Sarafian...... | D1 | 13,119 | 565 |
| Paul Smiths................. | Paul Smiths, N. Y... | 1946 | Chester L. Buxton.... | P | 934 | 52 |
| Peace...................(W) | Raleigh, N. C....... | 1857 | S. David Frazier..... | D | 435 | 28 |
| Pearl River Junior......... | Poplarville, Miss.... | 1926 | M. R. White......... | D1 | 858 | 70 |
| Peirce Junior............... | Philadelphia, Pa..... | 1865 | Thomas M. Peirce.... | Pr | 1,889 | 82 |
| Peninsula................... | Port Angeles, Wash.. | 1961 | E. John Maier....... | S | 997 | 50 |
| Pensacola Jr................ | Pensacola, Fla...... | 1948 | T. Felton Harrison.... | D1 | 3,943 | 226 |
| Peralta Jr. Coll. Dist...... | Oakland, Calif...... | 1953 | John W. Dunn (Supt.).. | Mu | 16,490 | 829 |
|   Laney.................... | Oakland, Calif...... | 1953 | Wallace T. Honitz.... | D1 | 8,025 | 379 |
|   Merritt.................. | Oakland, Calif...... | 1920 | Edward H. Redford.... | D1 | 8,465 | 450 |
| Phoenix..................... | Phoenix, Ariz....... | 1920 | J. Lee Thompson..... | D1 | 9,787 | 499 |
| Pine Manor Junior......(W) | Chestnut Hill, Mass.. | 1911 | Frederick C. Ferry, Jr.. | P | 395 | 37 |
| Polk Junior................. | Winter Haven, Fla... | 1964 | Frederick T. Lenfestey.. | D1 | 3,275 | 137 |
| Port Huron Junior.......... | Port Huron, Mich... | 1923 | J. C. Browning (Dean).. | Mu | 4,126 | 110 |
| Porterville................. | Porterville, Calif.... | 1927 | O. H. Shires......... | D1 | 1,044 | 47 |
| Post Junior................. | Waterbury, Conn.... | 1890 | Harold B. Post...... | Pr | 500 | 41 |
| Poteau Community............ | Poteau, Okla....... | 1933 | Orville Johnson...... | Mu | 295 | 16 |
| Potomac St. Coll............ | Keyser, W. Va...... | 1901 | Todd H. Bullard..... | S | 841 | 44 |

| Name | Location | Yr. | Governing Official and Control | | Students | Teachers |
|---|---|---|---|---|---|---|
| Pratt Community Jr. | Pratt, Kan. | 1938 | Jess V. Cooper | Di | 343 | 25 |
| Prentiss Institute | Prentiss, Miss. | 1931 | Mrs. J. E. Johnson | P | 437 | 21 |
| Presentation | Aberdeen, S. D. | 1951 | Sister F. M. Dunn | D | 285 | 35 |
| Prince George's Community | Largo, Md. | 1958 | Watson F. Pindell | C | 3,023 | 143 |
| Queensborough Community (a) | Bayside, N. Y. | 1958 | Kurt R. Schmeller | Mu | 6,460 | 257 |
| Quincy Junior | Quincy, Mass. | 1958 | Kenneth P. White | Mu | 977 | 57 |
| Racine-Kenosha Co. Teachers | Union Grove, Wisc. | 1916 | W. D. Thompson | C | 192 | 9 |
| RCA Institutes | New York, N. Y. | 1909 | A. L. Baker | Pr | 4,000 | 150 |
| Ranger Junior | Ranger, Tex. | 1926 | E. W. Mince | Mu | 335 | 24 |
| Reedley | Reedley, Calif. | 1926 | Clifford M. Boyer | Di | 1,896 | 86 |
| Reinhardt | Waleska, Ga. | 1883 | James Burgess, Jr. | D | 300 | 25 |
| Rhode Island Jr. | Providence, R. I. | 1964 | William F. Flanagan | S | 2,166 | 140 |
| Ricks | Rexburg, Idaho | 1888 | John L. Clarke | D | 3,384 | 160 |
| Rio Hondo Jr. | Whittier, Calif. | 1963 | Walter Garcia | Di | 5,600 | 450 |
| Riverside City | Riverside, Calif. | 1916 | R. H. Bradshaw | Di | 7,390 | 267 |
| Robert Morris | Carthage, Ill. | 1965 | Lawrence Sherman | P | 609 | 35 |
| Robert Morris Junior | Pittsburgh, Pa. | 1921 | Charles L. Sewall | Pr | 3,090 | 109 |
| Rochester State Junior | Rochester, Minn. | 1915 | Charles Hill | Mu | 1,700 | 80 |
| Rockland Community | Suffern, N. Y. | 1960 | Seymour Eskow | C | 3,266 | 84 |
| Roger Williams Junior | Providence, R. I. | 1948 | Ralph E. Gauvey | P | 1,116 | 72 |
| Sacramento City | Sacramento, Calif. | 1916 | Oliver Durand | Di | 9,395 | 388 |
| Sacred Heart............(W) | Cullman, Ala. | 1940 | Sister M. L. Michel | D | 181 | 32 |
| St. Catharine | St. Catharine, Ky. | 1931 | Sister M. M. Hofstetter | D | 222 | 22 |
| St. Gregory's | Shawnee, Okla. | 1875 | Richard Sneed | D | 582 | 47 |
| St. John's | Winfield, Kan. | 1893 | Rev. Reuben C. Beisel | D | 288 | 40 |
| St. John's River Junior | Palatka, Fla. | 1958 | Charles W. La Pradd | C | 1,441 | 94 |
| St. Louis, Jr. Coll. Dist. of | St. Louis, Mo. | 1962 | Joseph Cosand | Di | 9,000 | 500 |
| St. Mary's Jr. | Minneapolis, Minn. | 1964 | Sis. Anne Joachim | Di | 494 | 61 |
| St. Mary's Junior.........(W) | Raleigh, N. C. | 1842 | Richard G. Stone | D | 354 | 37 |
| St. Paul's | Concordia, Mo. | 1883 | Lambert J. Mehl | D | 307 | 30 |
| St. Petersburg Junior | St. Petersburg, Fla. | 1927 | Michael Bennett | C | 8,527 | 369 |
| San Antonio | San Antonio, Tex. | 1925 | Wayland P. Moody | Di | 10,800 | 465 |
| San Bernardino Valley | San Bernardino, Calif. | 1927 | Arthur Jensen | Di | 11,317 | 467 |
| San Diego Junior | San Diego, Calif. | 1914 | Charles W. Patrick | Mu | 16,059 | 731 |
| San Francisco, City Coll of | San Francisco, Calif. | 1935 | Louis G. Conlan | Mu | 11,000 | 358 |
| San Jacinto | Pasadena, Texas | 1960 | Thomas M. Spencer | Di | 4,857 | 161 |
| San Joaquin Delta | Stockton, Calif. | 1935 | Burke W. Bradley | Mu | 6,635 | 328 |
| San Jose City | San Jose, Calif. | 1921 | Otto Roemmich | Di | 10,722 | 384 |
| San Mateo, Coll. of | San Mateo, Calif. | 1922 | Julio L. Bortolazzo | Di, C | 20,500 | 598 |
| Santa Ana | Santa Ana, Calif. | 1915 | John E. Johnson | Di | 6,468 | 116 |
| Santa Barbara City | Santa Barbara, Calif. | 1946 | Robert C. Rockwell | Di | 3,861 | 179 |
| Santa Monica City | Santa Monica, Calif. | 1929 | Wade Thomas | Mu | 12,479 | 300 |
| Santa Rosa Junior | Santa Rosa, Calif. | 1918 | Randolph Newman | Di | 6,165 | 250 |
| Sayre Junior | Sayre, Okla. | 1938 | Harry Patterson | Di | 196 | 11 |
| Schreiner Institute | Kerrville, Tex. | 1923 | Andrew Edington | D | 407 | 35 |
| Scottsbluff | Scottsbluff, Nebr. | 1932 | William Ptacek | Mu | 507 | 26 |
| Schoolcraft | Livonia, Mich. | 1961 | Eric Bradner | Di | 3,779 | 150 |
| Sequoias, Coll. of the | Visalia, Calif. | 1925 | Ivan Crookshanks | Di | 4,134 | 157 |
| Shasta | Redding, Calif. | 1950 | Gilbert Collyer | Di | 4,980 | 211 |
| Sheldon Jackson Jr. | Sitka, Alaska | 1878 | Orin Stratton | D | 159 | 23 |
| Sheridan | Sheridan, Wyo. | 1948 | Jefferson Haney | Di | 384 | 29 |
| Shoreline Community | Seattle, Wash. | 1964 | Richard S. White | Di | 3,112 | 173 |
| Shorter | No. Little Rock, Ark. | 1885 | H. Solomon Hill | D | 219 | 18 |
| Sierra | Rocklin, Calif. | 1936 | Harold M. Weaver | Di | 2,500 | 91 |
| Silvermine Coll. of Art | New Canaan, Conn. | 1960 | R. H. Grey (Dn.) | P | 150 | 20 |
| Sinclair Community | Dayton, Ohio | 1887 | Marvin Knudson | Y | 2,587 | 125 |
| Siskiyous, Coll. of the | Weed, Calif. | 1959 | W. E. Roberts | Di | 2,000 | 77 |
| Skagit Valley | Mt. Vernon, Wash. | 1926 | Norwood Cole | Di | 2,659 | 140 |
| Snead State Junior | Boaz, Ala. | 1935 | Virgil McCain | D | 393 | 27 |
| Snow | Ephraim, Utah | 1888 | Floyd S. Holm | S | 967 | 34 |
| Solano | Vallejo, Calif. | 1945 | M. Dallas Evans | Di | 4,267 | 145 |
| South Georgia | Douglas, Ga. | 1927 | Pope A. Duncan | S | 805 | 49 |
| South Plains | Levelland, Tex. | 1957 | Marvin L. Baker | C | 1,359 | 66 |
| South Texas Junior | Houston, Tex. | 1948 | William Dykes | Y | 4,602 | 121 |
| Southeastern | Harrisburg, Ill. | 1960 | John Murphy (Dn.) | Di | 649 | 27 |
| Southern Baptist | Walnut Ridge, Ark. | 1941 | H. E. Williams | P | 593 | 32 |
| Southern Sem. & Junior...(W) | Buena Vista, Va. | 1867 | Sidney Sandridge | P | 325 | 36 |
| Southern Tech. Institute | Marietta, Ga. | 1948 | Hoyt L. McClure (Dir.) | S | 1,049 | 60 |
| Southwest Mississippi Junior | Summit, Miss. | 1918 | H. T. Huddleston | Di | 508 | 33 |
| Southwest Texas Junior | Uvalde, Tex. | 1946 | Wayne Matthews | Di | 905 | 41 |
| Southwestern Comm | Creston, Iowa | 1966 | W. R. Pierce, Jr. (Supt.) | Mu | 670 | 41 |
| Southwestern Oregon Comm | Coos Bay, Ore. | 1961 | Jack E. Brookins | Di | 1,800 | 101 |
| Spartanburg Junior | Spartanburg, S. C. | 1911 | H. Lester Kingman | D | 646 | 34 |
| Spring Garden Institute | Philadelphia, Pa. | 1850 | Robert Thompson | P | 337 | 38 |
| Spokane Comm | Spokane, Wash. | 1963 | Walter S. Johnson | Di | 4,972 | 363 |
| Springfield Junior | Springfield, Ill. | 1929 | Mo. M. Borgia | D | 782 | 51 |
| Staten Island Community (a) | Staten Island, N. Y. | 1955 | Walter L. Willig | Mu | 3,579 | 170 |
| Stevens Henager | Salt Lake City, Utah | 1907 | Leroy Stevens | Pr | 904 | 43 |
| Strayer Jr. | Washington, D. C. | 1904 | M. T. Donoho, III | Pr | 1,595 | 118 |
| Sue Bennett | London, Ky. | 1896 | Earl F. Hays | D | 386 | 21 |
| Suffolk County Community | Selden, N. Y. | 1959 | Albert M. Ammerman | C | 6,789 | 192 |
| Sullins..................(W) | Bristol, Va. | 1870 | William Martin | P | 350 | 35 |
| Sullivan County Community | So. Fallsburg, N. Y. | 1963 | Richard F. Grego | C | 1,057 | 54 |
| Suomi | Hancock, Mich. | 1896 | Ralph J. Jalkanen | D | 320 | 25 |
| Tacoma Comm | Tacoma, Wash. | 1965 | Thornton Ford | C | 2,100 | 120 |
| Taft | Taft, Calif. | 1922 | Garlyn A. Basham | Di | 1,241 | 43 |
| Temple Junior | Temple, Tex. | 1926 | H. M. Dawson | Mu | 1,021 | 57 |
| Texarkana | Texarkana, Tex. | 1927 | J. W. Cady | Mu | 1,612 | 77 |
| Texas Southmost | Brownsville, Tex. | 1926 | C. J. Garland | Mu | 1,296 | 54 |
| Thames Valley St. Tech. Inst. | Norwich, Conn. | 1963 | Donald Welter | S | 697 | 42 |
| Thornton Junior | Harvey, Ill. | 1929 | J. D. Logsdon | Mu | 3,580 | 124 |
| Treasure Valley Comm. | Ontario, Ore. | 1962 | E. J. Skinner | Di | 2,000 | 120 |
| Trinidad State Junior | Trinidad, Colo. | 1925 | Guy C. Davis | Mu | 1,372 | 57 |
| Truett McConnell | Cleveland, Ga. | 1946 | Warner Fusselle | D | 446 | 17 |
| Tyler Junior | Tyler, Tex. | 1926 | Harry E. Jenkins | Mu | 2,900 | 146 |
| Ulster County Community | Stone Ridge, N. Y. | 1963 | George B. Erbstein | C | 1,495 | 47 |
| Umpqua Comm | Roseburg, Ore. | 1964 | Harry Jacoby | Di | 608 | 73 |
| Union | Cranford, N. J. | 1933 | Kenneth MacKay | P | 1,450 | 78 |
| Utica Junior | Utica, Miss. | 1954 | Walter Washington | C | 591 | 38 |
| Valley Forge Military Junior (M) | Wayne, Pa. | 1928 | Lt. Gen. M. G. Baker | P | 250 | 25 |
| Ventura | Ventura, Calif. | 1929 | Ray E. Loehr | Di | 9,507 | 367 |
| Vermont.................(W) | Montpelier, Vt. | 1834 | William L. Irvine | | 492 | 45 |
| Vermont Technical | Randolph Center, Vt. | 1957 | Hare Iffer | | 348 | 35 |

| Name | Location | Yr. | Governing Official and Control | | Students | Teachers |
|------|----------|-----|-------------------------------|--|----------|----------|
| Victor Valley | Victorville, Calif | 1961 | Fred F. Berger, Jr | Di | 1,400 | 44 |
| Victoria | Victoria, Tex | 1925 | J. D. Moore | Mu | 1,387 | 60 |
| Villa Julie | Stevenson, Md | 1952 | Sis. Mary Stephen | D | 210 | 38 |
| Vincennes Univ | Vincennes, Ind | 1801 | Isaac K. Beckes | Mu | 1,946 | 106 |
| Virginia Intermont (W) | Bristol, Va | 1884 | Floyd V. Turner | D | 550 | 38 |
| Virginia Southern | Roanoke, Va | 1933 | A. R. Kennett | Pr | 175 | 8 |
| Voorhees | Denmark, S. C | 1897 | John F. Potts | D | 704 | 35 |
| Voorhees Technical Inst | New York, N. Y | 1881 | Edwin H. Miner | P | 482 | 61 |
| Wabash Valley | Mt. Carmel, Ill | 1960 | Robert W. Bowen | Di | 700 | 52 |
| Waldorf | Forest City, Iowa | 1903 | Rev. Sigvald D. Fauske | D | 600 | 38 |
| Walker | Jasper, Ala | 1938 | David J. Rowland | P | 750 | 45 |
| Weatherford | Weatherford, Tex | 1869 | J. C. Nichols | Di | 976 | 45 |
| Wenatchee Valley Community | Wenatchee, Wash | 1939 | William Stewart | Di | 1,440 | 99 |
| Wentworth Institute (M) | Boston, Mass | 1904 | H. Russell Beatty | P | 1,955 | 151 |
| Wentworth Military Acad | Lexington, Mo | 1880 | Col. L. B. Wikoff | P | 304 | 30 |
| Wesley | Dover, Del | 1873 | Robert H. Parker | D | 884 | 57 |
| Westbrook Junior (W) | Portland, Me | 1831 | Edward Y. Blewett | P | 460 | 40 |
| Westchester Community | Valhalla, N. Y | 1946 | Philip C. Martin | C | 4,809 | 87 |
| Wharton County Junior | Wharton, Tex | 1946 | Theodore Nicksick, Jr | C | 1,868 | 86 |
| Willmar State Junior | Willmar, Minn | 1961 | Dale A. Lorenz | S | 448 | 33 |
| Wingate | Wingate, N. C | 1896 | Budd E. Smith | D | 1,560 | 88 |
| Wood Junior | Mathiston, Miss | 1885 | Felix Sutphin | Di | 175 | 14 |
| Worcester Junior | Worcester, Mass | 1905 | Clifton W. Emery, Jr | Y | 2,250 | 114 |
| Worthington State Junior | Worthington, Minn | 1936 | W. Donald Olsen (Dn.) | Di | 600 | 35 |
| Yakima Valley | Yakima, Wash | 1928 | Omar Scheidt | Di | 2,715 | 127 |
| York | York, Nebr | 1890 | Dale Larsen | P | 350 | 23 |
| York Junior | York, Pa | 1941 | Ray A. Miller | P | 1,800 | 87 |
| Young Harris | Young Harris, Ga | 1886 | Douglas R. Sasser | D | 414 | 29 |
| Yuba Junior | Marysville, Calif | 1927 | James M. Starr | C | 4,507 | 195 |

(a) Division of the City Univ. of New York. (b) Division of Russell Sage College.

# Selected Colleges with Major Endowment Funds

Table shows the latest available figures. They represent book values (italics indicate market value), excluding federal, state or municipal appropriations, value of plant or of contributed services.

| Institution | Location | Amount | Institution | Location | Amount |
|-------------|----------|--------|-------------|----------|--------|
| Agnes Scott | Decatur, Ga | 12,300,000 | Minnesota, Univ. of | Minneapolis, Minn. | 78,320,382 |
| Alabama, Univ. of | University, Ala | 13,054,910 | Missouri, Univ. of | Columbia, Mo | 10,080,876 |
| Amherst College | Amherst, Mass | 55,542,444 | Mt. Holyoke College | So. Hadley, Mass. | 31,314,000 |
| Atlanta Univ | Atlanta, Ga | 11,100,721 | Northeastern Univ | Boston, Mass | 20,182,619 |
| Barnard College | New York, N. Y. | 14,249,783 | Northwestern Univ | Evanston, Ill. | 155,305,447 |
| Baylor Univ | Waco, Tex | 25,766,870 | Notre Dame, U. of | Notre Dame, Ind. | 65,000,000 |
| Berea College | Berea, Ky | 40,000,000 | Oberlin College | Oberlin, Ohio | 66,666,540 |
| Berry College | Mt. Berry, Ga | 10,794,103 | Occidental | Los Angeles, Calif. | 15,735,482 |
| Boston Univ | Boston, Mass | 26,000,000 | Ohio State Univ | Columbus, Ohio | 381,800,000 |
| Bowdoin College | Brunswick, Me | 27,170,000 | Penna. Univ. of | Philadelphia, Pa. | 158,000,000 |
| Brandeis Univ | Waltham, Mass | 19,500,000 | Pittsburgh, Univ. of | Pittsburgh, Pa. | 76,934,652 |
| Brown Univ | Providence, R. I. | 63,655,584 | Pomona College | Claremont, Calif. | 17,624,325 |
| Bryn Mawr College | Bryn Mawr, Pa | 30,213,994 | Pratt Institute | Brooklyn, N. Y. | 15,700,000 |
| Bucknell Univ | Lewisburg, Pa | 17,878,223 | Princeton Univ | Princeton, N. J. | 316,497,854 |
| Calif. Inst. of Tech. | Pasadena, Calif. | 110,217,000 | Queens Univ | Kingston, Ont. | 16,020,000 |
| Calif., Univ. of | Berkeley, Calif. | 250,000,000 | Radcliffe College | Cambridge, Mass. | 20,554,146 |
| Carleton College | Northfield, Minn. | 20,425,000 | Redlands, Univ. of | Redlands, Calif. | 11,596,312 |
| Carnegie-Mellon | Pittsburgh, Pa. | 125,000,000 | Rensselaer Poly. | Troy, N. Y. | 54,196,862 |
| Case W. Reserve | Cleveland, O. | 126,055,000 | Rice Univ | Houston, Tex. | 96,144,630 |
| Chatham | Pittsburgh, Pa. | 10,370,895 | Richmond, Univ. of | Richmond, Va. | 13,377,867 |
| Chicago, Univ. of | Chicago, Ill | *286,000,000* | Rochester I. of T. | Rochester, N. Y. | 21,649,369 |
| Cincinnati, Univ. of | Cincinnati, Ohio | 36,493,721 | Rochester, Univ. of | Rochester, N. Y. | 138,176,936 |
| Claremont Graduate | | | Rockefeller Univ. | New York, N. Y. | *198,447,798* |
| School | Claremont, Calif. | 18,000,000 | Rutgers, the St. U. | New Bruns., N. J. | 25,766,049 |
| Colby College | Waterville, Maine | 12,250,000 | St. John's Univ | Jamaica, N. Y. | 11,000,000 |
| Colgate Univ | Hamilton, N. Y. | 18,877,000 | St. Lawrence Univ. | Canton, N. Y. | 10,367,724 |
| Columbia Univ | New York, N. Y. | *405,600,000* | St. Louis Univ | St. Louis, Mo. | 20,847,026 |
| Cooper Union | New York, N. Y. | 38,084,754 | Santa Clara, U. of | Santa Clara, Calif. | 10,821,195 |
| Cornell Univ | Ithaca, N. Y. | 181,536,308 | Smith College | N'hampton, Mass. | 48,686,285 |
| Dalhousie Univ | Halifax, N. S. | 31,624,403 | South, Univ. of the | Sawanee, Tenn. | 16,908,334 |
| Dartmouth College | Hanover, N. H. | 110,700,000 | So. Methodist Univ | Dallas, Tex. | 23,525,000 |
| Delaware, Univ. of | Newark, Del. | 49,568,687 | Stanford Univ | Stanford, Calif. | 216,224,503 |
| Denison Univ | Granville, O. | 12,821,193 | Stevens Inst. of | | |
| Denver, Univ. of | Denver, Colo. | 12,000,000 | Tech. | Hoboken, N. J. | 36,000,000 |
| DePauw Univ | Greencastle, Ind. | 13,993,227 | Swarthmore Coll. | Swarthmore, Pa. | 24,555,589 |
| Drew Univ | Madison, N. J. | 13,965,649 | Syracuse Univ | Syracuse, N. Y. | 38,879,000 |
| Duke Univ | Durham, N. C. | 60,301,844 | Texas Christ'n U. | Fort Worth, Tex. | 27,000,000 |
| Emory Univ | Atlanta, Ga. | 64,000,000 | Texas Univ. of | Austin, Tex. | 544,372,593 |
| Fairleigh Dickinson | | | Toronto, Univ. of | Toronto, Ont. | 24,588,154 |
| Univ. | Rutherford, N. J. | 11,000,000 | Trinity | Hartford, Conn. | 15,000,000 |
| Fordham Univ | Bronx, N. Y. | 10,610,000 | Tufts Univ | Medford, Mass. | 21,285,756 |
| George Peabody | | | Tulane Univ | New Orleans, La. | 40,296,627 |
| Coll. for Teachers | Nashville, Tenn. | 12,509,000 | Tuskegee Inst. | Alabama | 17,744,552 |
| George Wash. U. | Washington, D. C. | 10,000,000 | Union Coll. | Schenectady, N. Y. | 20,946,966 |
| Georgetown Univ | Washington, D. C. | 12,000,000 | Union Theol. Sem. | New York, N. Y. | 24,949,533 |
| Grinnell College | Grinnell, Iowa | 11,064,389 | Vanderbilt Univ | Nashville, Tenn. | 76,406,110 |
| Gustavus Adolphus | St. Peter, Minn. | 14,157,624 | Vassar College | Poughkeepsie, N.Y. | 48,572,902 |
| Hampton Inst. | Hampton, Va. | 37,000,000 | Vermont, Univ. of | Burlington, Vt. | 11,996,386 |
| Harding | Searcy, Ark. | 13,000,000 | Virginia, Univ. of | Charlottesville, Va. | 48,220,341 |
| Harvard Univ | Cambridge, Mass. | 621,795,041 | Wabash Coll. | Crawfordsville, Ind. | 15,000,000 |
| Idaho, Univ. of | Moscow, Idaho | 14,700,000 | Wake Forest Coll. | Winston-Sa., N. C. | 17,739,100 |
| Illinois, Univ. of | Urbana, Ill. | 13,647,154 | Washington State | Pullman, Wash. | 41,794,076 |
| Johns Hopkins Univ. | Baltimore, Md. | 150,200,000 | Washington Univ. | St. Louis, Mo. | 75,100,868 |
| Kalamazoo | Kalamazoo, Mich. | 11,000,000 | Washington, U. of | Seattle, Wash. | 52,331,911 |
| Kansas, Univ. of | Lawrence, Kans. | 22,000,000 | Washington & Lee. | Lexington, Va. | 12,943,372 |
| Lafayette College | Easton, Pa. | 25,000,000 | Wellesley College. | Wellesley, Mass. | 72,651,285 |
| Lawrence Univ. | Appleton, Wis. | 20,946,225 | Wesleyan Univ | Middleton, Conn. | 109,000,000 |
| Lehigh Univ. | Bethlehem, Pa. | 31,267,441 | Whitman College | Walla Walla, Wash | 12,642,236 |
| Mary Washington | Fredericksburg, Va. | 12,977,775 | Williams College | Williamst'n Mass. | 43,067,000 |
| Mass. Inst. of Tech. | Cambridge, Mass. | 120,877,000 | Wisconsin, Univ. of | Milwaukee, Wisc. | 15,568,088 |
| McGill Univ | Montreal, Can. | 76,623,018 | Wittenberg Coll. | Springfield, O. | 10,990,260 |
| Miami, Univ. of | Coral Gables, Fla. | 17,698,827 | Wooster, Coll. of | Wooster, Ohio | 11,502,000 |
| Michigan, Univ. of | Ann Arbor, Mich. | 49,883,733 | Worcester Poly. Inst. | Worcester, Mass. | 21,628,000 |
| Middlebury College. | Middlebury, Vt. | 16,749,676 | Wyoming, Univ. of. | Laramie, Wyo. | 12,846,287 |
| | | | Yale Univ. | New Haven, Conn. | 457,951,886 |

# American College Fraternities, Sororities and Societies

### Source: World Almanac Questionnaire

American college fraternal organizations include the fraternities and sororities that organize the social life of their members, and the honor and recognition societies that elect members primarily for their achievement in some field of education. Among the fraternities and sororities, there is a distinction between the so-called social college fraternities that draw their membership mainly from the undergraduate student body, and the professional fraternities that confine their membership to a specific field of professional education.

The oldest American college Greek letter fraternity is Phi Beta Kappa, organized Dec. 5, 1776 at William and Mary College, Williamsburg, Va. It was not continuously active. Originally founded as a secret fraternity, Phi Beta Kappa was reorganized in 1883 as an honor society and students with the highest standing on graduation are nominated for membership by college authorities. Kappa Alpha Society, founded Nov. 26, 1825 at Union College, Schenectady, N. Y., is the oldest of all Greek letter fraternities to have maintained a continuous existence.

## NATIONAL INTERFRATERNITY ORGANIZATIONS

National Interfraternity Conference: 271 Madison Ave., New York, N. Y. 10016.
Professional Intrafraternity Conference: Sec., W. E. Koch, Jr., 29 N. Gore Ave., Webster Groves, Mo.
Assn. of College Honor Societies: Sec.-Treas., Donald Hoffman, 2812 Livingston St., Allentown, Pa.
National Panhellenic Conference: Mrs. Karl Miller, 8747 Greenwood Ave., Chicago, Ill.
Professional Panhellenic Association: Sec., Mrs. Sybil A. Lambert, 1323 Manget Way, Atlanta, Ga.

## Social College Fraternities and Sororities

### FRATERNITIES

| Name | Year Found. | Active Chapt. | Members | National Headquarters |
|---|---|---|---|---|
| Acacia | 1904 | 52 | 25,977 | 1611 Chicago Ave., Evanston, Ill. 60201 |
| Alpha Chi Rho | 1895 | 28 | 12,010 | 1 Maiden Lane, New York, N. Y. 10038 |
| Alpha Delta Gamma | 1924 | 14 | 746 | 6332 No. Kenmore, Chicago, Ill. 60626 |
| Alpha Delta Phi | 1832 | 30 | 31,314 | 125 E. 50th St., New York, N. Y. 10022 |
| Alpha Epsilon Pi | 1913 | 92 | 31,000 | 7730 Carondelet Ave., St. Louis, Mo. 63105 |
| Alpha Kappa Lambda | 1914 | 40 | 9,140 | 4700 S. College Ave., Ft. Collins, Colo. |
| Alpha Phi Alpha | 1906 | 337 | 30,842 | 4432 South Pkwy., Chicago, Ill. 60653 |
| Alpha Phi Delta | 1914 | 20 | 7,500 | P.O. Box 8474, Pittsburgh, Pa. 15220 |
| Alpha Phi Omega (A) | 1925 | 420 | 107,000 | 1100 Waltower Bldg., Kansas City, Mo. 64106 |
| Alpha Sigma Phi | 1845 | 60 | 35,406 | 24 W. William St., Delaware, Ohio 43015 |
| Alpha Tau Omega | 1865 | 130 | 96,400 | 107 E. Green St., Champaign, Ill. 61820 |
| Beta Sigma Psi | 1925 | 14 | 2,550 | 60 Progress Pkwy., Maryland Hts., Mo. 63042 |
| Beta Sigma Rho | 1910 | 10 | 5,200 | 250 Broadway, New York, N. Y. 10007 |
| Beta Theta Pi | 1839 | 103 | 73,500 | 208 E. High St., Oxford, Ohio 45056 |
| Chi Phi | 1824 | 36 | 20,370 | 3330 Peachtree Rd., N.E. Atlanta, Ga. 30326 |
| Chi Psi | 1841 | 27 | 16,500 | 1705 Washtenaw Ave., Ann Arbor, Mich. 48104 |
| Delta Chi | 1890 | 54 | 25,000 | 16 So. Clinton St., Iowa City, Ia., 52240 |
| Delta Kappa Epsilon | 1844 | 42 | 25,000 | 50 Vanderbilt Ave., New York, N. Y. 10017 |
| Delta Phi | 1827 | 15 | 7,500 | 331 Madison Ave., New York, 10017 |
| Delta Psi | 1847 | 9 | 4,763 | 16 East 64th St., New York, N. Y. 10021 |
| Delta Sigma Phi | 1899 | 117 | 46,299 | 1445 Steele St., Denver, Colo. 80206 |
| Delta Tau Delta | 1858 | 97 | 73,796 | 3665 Washington Blvd., Indianapolis 46205 |
| Delta Upsilon | 1834 | 80 | 60,000 | 271 Madison Ave., New York, N. Y. 10016 |
| Farmhouse | 1905 | 22 | 8,600 | 424 So. Sixth Ave., La Grange, Ill. 60525 |
| Kappa Alpha Order | 1865 | 88 | 61,000 | 1252 W. Peachtree St., N.W., Atlanta, Ga. |
| Kappa Alpha Psi | 1911 | 277 | 38,000 | 2320 No. Broad St., Philadelphia, Pa. 19132 |
| Kappa Alpha Society | 1825 | 9 | 3,850 | 1 Elk St., Albany, N. Y. 12207 |
| Kappa Delta Rho | 1905 | 20 | 10,000 | 481 No. Dean St., Englewood, N. J. 07631 |
| Kappa Sigma | 1869 | 155 | 107,500 | P.O. Box 5066, Charlottesville, Va. |
| Kappa Sigma Kappa | 1867 | 12 | 14,339 | P.O. Box 609, Fairmont, W. Va. 26554 |
| Lambda Chi Alpha | 1909 | 170 | 103,000 | 3434 Washington Blvd., Indianapolis, Ind. 46205 |
| Omega Psi Phi | 1911 | 300 | 37,000 | 2714 Georgia Ave., Washington, D. C. 20001 |
| Phi Beta Sigma | 1914 | 215 | 23,501 | none |
| Phi Delta Theta | 1848 | 131 | 115,800 | 2 So. Campus Ave., Oxford, Ohio 45056 |
| Phi Epsilon Pi | 1904 | 55 | 28,500 | 225 S. 15th St., Philadelphia, Pa. 19102 |
| Phi Gamma Delta | 1848 | 100 | 80,000 | 1757 B. St., N.W., Washington, D. C. 20036 |
| Phi Kappa Psi | 1852 | 73 | 56,600 | 1940 East 6th St., Cleveland, Ohio 44114 |
| Phi Kappa Sigma | 1850 | 45 | 31,614 | 335 So. 16 St., Philadelphia, Pa. 19102 |
| Phi Kappa Tau | 1906 | 85 | 37,000 | 15 No. Campus Ave., Oxford, Ohio 45056 |
| Phi Kappa Theta | 1889 | 63 | 27,000 | 544 Main, Worcester, Mass. 01608 |
| Phi Lamba Chi | 1924 | 6 | 3,050 | Box 521,College Hills Branch,Monticello, Ark. |
| Phi Mu Delta | 1918 | 14 | 8,750 | 450 Murray Hill Dr., Lancaster, Pa. 17601 |
| Phi Sigma Delta | 1909 | 49 | 19,950 | 120 East 34th St., New York, N. Y. 10016 |
| Phi Sigma Epsilon | 1910 | 45 | 19,500 | 2829 No. Pennsylvania, Indianapolis, Ind. 46205 |
| Phi Sigma Kappa | 1873 | 87 | 38,500 | 2528 Garrett Road, Drexel Hill, Pa. |
| Pi Kappa Alpha | 1868 | 142 | 79,000 | 577 University Blvd., Memphis, Tenn. 38112 |
| Pi Kappa Phi | 1904 | 60 | 25,900 | 229 Vail Ave., Charlotte, N. C. 28204 |
| Pi Lambda Phi | 1895 | 46 | 20,782 | 125 West 43d St., New York, N. Y. 10036 |
| Psi Upsilon | 1833 | 27 | 16,500 | 4 West 43d St., New York, N. Y. 10036 |
| Sigma Alpha Epsilon | 1856 | 161 | 114,600 | 1856 Sheridan Rd., Evanston, Ill. 60201 |
| Sigma Alpha Mu | 1909 | 64 | 24,500 | 250 West 57th St., New York, N. Y. 10019 |
| Sigma Chi | 1855 | 144 | 115,000 | 1714 Hinman Ave., Evanston, Ill. |
| Sigma Nu | 1869 | 141 | 85,932 | P.O. Box 1869, Lexington, Va. 24450 |
| Sigma Phi | 1827 | 10 | 4,390 | 25 Broadway, New York, N. Y. 10004 |
| Sigma Phi Epsilon | 1901 | 174 | 85,184 | 5800 Chamberlayne Rd., Richmond, Va. |
| Sigma Pi | 1897 | 80 | 26,730 | County Highway 225, Vincennes, Ind. |
| Sigma Tau Gamma | 1920 | 67 | 30,857 | 23 No. Gore Ave., St. Louis, Mo. 63119 |
| Tau Delta Phi | 1910 | 33 | 13,791 | 171 Madison Ave., New York, N. Y. 10016 |
| Tau Epsilon Phi | 1910 | 80 | 24,000 | 250 Fifth Ave., New York, N. Y. 10001 |
| Tau Kappa Epsilon | 1899 | 248 | 77,000 | 3755 Washington Blvd., Indianapolis, Ind. 46205 |
| Theta Chi | 1856 | 141 | 65,234 | 436 Broad St., Bk. Bldg., Trenton, N. J. 08608 |
| Theta Delta Chi | 1857 | 32 | 17,000 | Hotel Biltmore, New York, N. Y. 10017 |
| Theta Xi | 1864 | 71 | 33,161 | 9974 Old Olive St., St. Louis, Mo. 63141 |
| Triangle | 1907 | 28 | 12,000 | P.O. Box 1336, Evanston, Ill. 60204 |
| Zeta Beta Tau | 1898 | 75 | 35,600 | Statler Hilton Hotel, New York, N. Y. 10001 |
| Zeta Psi | 1847 | 37 | 20,100 | 125 East 50th St., New York, N. Y. 10022 |

(A) A service society.

## SOCIAL COLLEGE SORORITIES

| Name | Year Found. | Active Chapt. | Members | National Headquarters |
|------|-------------|---------------|---------|----------------------|
| Alpha Chi Omega | 1885 | 109 | 65,553 | 3445 N. Washington Blvd., Indianapolis Ind., 46205 |
| Alpha Delta Pi | 1851 | 122 | 68,797 | 1386 Ponce de Leon Ave., N.E., Atlanta, Ga. |
| Alpha Epsilon Phi | 1909 | 59 | 24,500 | 3600 Forbes Sts., Pittsburgh, Pa. 15213 |
| Alpha Gamma Delta | 1904 | 87 | 45,000 | 3444 Washington Blvd., Indianapolis, Ind. 46205 |
| Alpha Kappa Alpha | 1908 | 320 | 45,000 | 5211 So. Greenwood Ave., Chicago, Ill. 60615 |
| Alpha Omicron Pi | 1897 | 88 | 42,038 | 300 Meadows Pkwy. Court, Indianapolis, Ind. |
| Alpha Phi | 1872 | 90 | 46,000 | 634 Foster St., Evanston, Ill. 60201 |
| Alpha Sigma Alpha | 1901 | 50 | 25,000 | 1201 E. Walnut, Springfield, Mo. 65802 |
| Alpha Sigma Tau | 1899 | 34 | 14,000 | 6200 Hoffman Ave., St. Louis, Mo. 63139 |
| Alpha Xi Delta | 1893 | 115 | 49,500 | 3447 N. Washington Blvd., Indianapolis, Ind. 46205 |
| Chi Omega | 1895 | 150 | 96,281 | 2245 Grandin Rd., Cincinnati, Ohio 45208 |
| Delta Delta Delta | 1888 | 109 | 85,000 | 6 No. Michigan Ave., Chicago, Ill. 60602 |
| Delta Gamma | 1873 | 93 | 64,000 | 3250 Riverside Dr., Columbus, Ohio 43221 |
| Delta Phi Epsilon | 1917 | 37 | 15,000 | 41-25 Kissena Blvd., Flushing, N. Y. 11355 |
| Delta Zeta | 1902 | 173 | 62,560 | 3561 N. Pennsylvania St., Indianapolis, Ind. 46205 |
| Gamma Phi Beta | 1874 | 87 | 49,000 | 630 Green Bay Rd., Kenilworth, Ill. 60043 |
| Iota Alpha Pi | 1903 | 11 | 7,000 | 81 E. Beverly Pkwy., Valley Stream, N. Y. 11580 |
| Kappa Alpha Theta | 1870 | 93 | 74,500 | Suite 342, 1589 Sherman Ave., Evanston, Ill. 60201 |
| Kappa Delta | 1897 | 104 | 63,257 | 900 Landers Bldg., Springfield, Mo. 65806 |
| Kappa Kappa Gamma | 1870 | 94 | 82,276 | 530 E. Town St., Columbus, Ohio 43216 |
| Phi Mu | 1852 | 96 | 48,000 | 22 No. Front St., Memphis, Tenn. 38103 |
| Phi Sigma Sigma | 1913 | 33 | 13,569 | 161 Madeira Ave., Coral Gables, Fla. 33134 |
| Pi Beta Phi | 1867 | 112 | 88,000 | 112 S. Hanley Rd., St. Louis, Mo. 63105 |
| Sigma Delta Tau | 1917 | 50 | 17,000 | 630 Green Bay Rd., Kenilworth, Ill. 60043 |
| Sigma Gamma Rho | 1922 | 130 | 7,212 | 1254 West 25th St., Indianapolis, Ind. |
| Sigma Kappa | 1874 | 106 | 50,000 | 3433 Washington Bldg., Indianapolis, Ind. 46205 |
| Sigma Sigma Sigma | 1898 | 65 | 31,000 | 225 N. Muhlenberg, Woodstock, Va. |
| Theta Phi Alpha | 1912 | 17 | 8,800 | 3738 Clifton Ave., Cincinnati, Ohio 45220 |
| Zeta Phi Beta | 1920 | 250 | 20,000 | 1734 New Hampshire Ave., Wash., D. C. 20009 |
| Zeta Tau Alpha | 1898 | 111 | 52,094 | 708 Church St., Evanston, Ill. 60201 |

## Professional Fraternities and Sororities
## Honor and Recognition Societies

**Abbreviations:** (H.) honor society; (R.) recognition society. All others are professional fraternities and sororities. Organizations marked with (*) asterisk admit both men and women.

### FRATERNITIES AND SOCIETIES

| **Accounting** | | | | |
|------|------|------|------|------|
| Beta Alpha Psi* | 1919 | 77 | 34,000 | Bowling Green St. Univ., Ohio |
| **Advertising** | | | | |
| Alpha Delta Sigma | 1913 | 46 | 21,563 | Southern Ill. Univ., Carbondale, Ill. 62901 |
| **Agricultural** | | | | |
| Alpha Gamma Rho | 1904 | 43 | 25,500 | 323 Cornell Ave., Des Plaines, Ill., 60016 |
| Alpha Tau Alpha (Agric. Educ.) | 1921 | 30 | 10,000 | Kansas St. Univ., Manhattan, Kans. |
| Alpha Zeta (H.) | 1897 | 57 | 53,000 | 1010 Vermont Ave., Wash., D. C. 20005 |
| Gamma Sigma Delta* (H.) | 1905 | 30 | 25,000 | Auburn Univ., Ala. 36830 |
| **Architecture** | | | | |
| Alpha Rho Chi | 1914 | 8 | 4,000 | 4256 N. High St., Columbus, Ohio 43214 |
| Scarab | 1909 | 7 | 5,115 | Calif. St. Poly. Coll., San Luis Obispo, Calif. |
| Tau Sigma Delta* (H.) | 1913 | 23 | 5,014 | Kansas State Univ., Manhattan, Kan. 66502 |
| **Arts** | | | | |
| Delta Phi Delta* (H.) | 1909 | 40 | 14,500 | P.O. Box 635, De Kalb, Ill. |
| Kappa Pi* (R.) | 1911 | 127 | 48,950 | 209 N. Adams St., Mt. Pleasant, Iowa |
| **Athletic** | | | | |
| Sigma Delta Psi (H.) | 1912 | 146 | 3,655 | Univ. of Arizona, Tucson, Ariz. 85721 |
| **Aviation** | | | | |
| Alpha Eta Rho* | 1929 | 18 | 2,000 | Parks College, Cahokia, Ill. 62201 |
| **Band** | | | | |
| Kappa Kappa Psi (R.) | 1919 | 128 | 37,568 | Okla. State Univ., Stillwater, Okla. 74074 |
| **Biology** | | | | |
| Beta Beta Beta* | 1922 | 200 | 3,000 | Drew Univ., Madison, N. J. |
| Phi Sigma Society* (H.) | 1915 | 40 | 32,600 | 1305 Hillcrest Dr., Blacksburg, Va. 24060 |
| **Broadcasting** | | | | |
| Alpha Epsilon Rho* | 1943 | 35 | 6,200 | St. Coll. at Los Angeles, Calif. 90032 |
| **Business** | | | | |
| Alpha Kappa Psi | 1904 | 172 | 72,386 | 111 E. 38th St., Indianapolis, Ind. 46205 |
| Beta Gamma Sigma* (H.) | 1913 | 118 | 45,000 | 101 No. Skinker Blvd., St. Louis, Mo. 63130 |
| Delta Sigma Pi | 1907 | 139 | 66,365 | 330 S. Campus Ave., Oxford, Ohio 45056 |
| **Business Education** | | | | |
| Delta Pi Epsilon* | 1936 | 45 | 10,574 | Gustavus Adolphus Coll. St. Peter, Minn. |
| Pi Omega Pi* (H.) | 1923 | 109 | 31,000 | Bowling Green St. Univ., Bowling Green, Ky. |
| **Ceramic Engineering** | | | | |
| Keramos* | 1902 | 12 | 3,289 | Univ. of Washington, Seattle, Wash. 98105 |
| **Chemistry** | | | | |
| Alpha Chi Sigma | 1902 | 45 | 34,420 | 5503 E. Wash. St., Indianapolis, Ind. 46220 |
| Gamma Sigma Epsilon* (R.) | 1919 | 16 | 6,000 | W. A. Powell, Univ. of Richmond |
| Phi Lambda Upsilon (H.) | 1899 | 50 | 37,175 | Ohio Northern Univ., Ada, Ohio |
| **Classics** | | | | |
| Eta Sigma Phi* (H.) | 1914 | 74 | 1,200 | Birmingham-Southern Coll., Ala. 35204 |
| **Dentistry** | | | | |
| Alpha Omega | 1907 | 100 | 15,000 | None |
| Delta Sigma Delta | 1882 | 91 | 20,857 | 2204 Constitution Ave., Colo. Spgs., Colo. 80909 |
| Omicron Kappa Upsilon* (H.) | 1914 | 51 | 13,427 | P.O. Box 64, Esparto, Calif. 95627 |
| Psi Omega | 1892 | 35 | 25,000 | 1030 Lincoln Ave., Prospect Pk., Pa. 19076 |
| Xi Psi Phi | 1889 | 28 | 26,000 | 23 No. Gore, Webster Groves, Mo. 63119 |
| **Drama** | | | | |
| Alpha Psi Omega & Delta Psi Omega* (H.) | 1925 | 639 | 55,000 | New York Univ., N. Y. |
| Natl. Collegiate Players* (H.) | 1922 | 67 | 10,000 | 4645 E. Granada Rd., Phoenix, Ariz. 85008 |
| Theta Alpha Phi* (H.) | 1919 | 52 | 22,000 | Brigham Young Univ., Provo, Utah 84601 |
| **Earth Sciences** | | | | |
| Sigma Gamma Epsilon* (H.) | 1915 | 62 | 18,000 | Univ. of Oklahoma, Norman, Okla. 73069 |

## FRATERNITIES AND SOCIETIES (continued)

| Name | Year Found. | Active Chapt. | Members | National Headquarters |
|---|---|---|---|---|
| **Economics** | | | | |
| Lambda Alpha* (H.) (Land Econ.) | 1930 | 7 | 450 | None |
| Omicron Delta Epsilon* (H.)... | 1963 | 150 | 28,300 | Univ. of So. Calif., Los Angeles, Calif. 90007 |
| **Education** | | | | |
| Iota Lambda Sigma (Voc.).... | 1927 | 27 | 7,500 | 3002 Woodside Pl., Cincinnati, Ohio |
| Kappa Delta Pi* (H.) | 1911 | 298 | 239,505 | Box A, W. Lafayette, Ind. 47906 |
| Kappa Phi Kappa | 1922 | 36 | 24,000 | Miami Univ., Oxford, Ohio |
| Phi Delta Kappa | 1906 | 320 | 74,000 | Eighth St. & Union Ave., Bloomington, Ind. 47401 |
| **Engineering** | | | | |
| Alpha Pi Mu (Industrial)* (H.) | 1949 | 34 | 5,700 | Box 2589, San Juan, P. R. |
| Chi Epsilon (Civil)* (H.) | 1922 | 65 | 22,708 | Univ. of Texas, Austin, Tex. 78712 |
| Eta Kappa Nu (Electrical)* (H.) | 1904 | 113 | 65,000 | Univ. of Ill., Urbana |
| Kappa Eta Kappa (Electrical) | 1923 | 4 | 80 | 1221 N. Milwaukee St., Milwaukee, Wisc. |
| Pi Tau Sigma (Mechanical)* (H.) | 1915 | 84 | 40,000 | Univ. of Illinois, Urbana, Ill. |
| Sigma Gamma Tau (Aerospace)* (H.) | 1953 | 20 | 5,736 | Univ. of Kansas, Lawrence |
| Sigma Phi Delta | 1924 | 12 | 5,200 | 828 Hawthorn Dr., Naperville, Ill. 60540 |
| Sigma Tau* (H.) | 1904 | 33 | 37,000 | Miller Freeman Publications, 500 Howard St. San Francisco |
| Tau Beta Pi (H.) | 1885 | 128 | 145,000 | Univ. of Tenn., Knoxville, Tenn. 37916 |
| Theta Tau | 1904 | 29 | 19,037 | 13 Sona Lane, St. Louis, Mo. 63141 |
| **Forensic** | | | | |
| Delta Sigma Rho & Tau Kappa Alpha* (H.) | 1963 | 192 | 20,000 | Butler Univ., Indianapolis, Ind. 46207 |
| Pi Kappa Delta* (R.) | 1913 | 240 | 41,400 | Bradley Univ., Peoria, Ill. 61606 |
| **Forestry** | | | | |
| Xi Sigma Pi* (H.) | 1908 | 28 | 8,300 | Univ. of Missouri, Columbia, Mo. 65201 |
| **Geography** | | | | |
| Gamma Theta Upsilon* | 1931 | 128 | 17,350 | Clarion State Coll., Clarion, Pa. |
| **History** | | | | |
| Phi Alpha Theta* (H.) | 1921 | 350 | 50,781 | 2812 Livingston St., Allentown, Pa. 18104 |
| **Journalism** | | | | |
| Alpha Phi Gamma* (R.) | 1919 | 62 | 8,817 | Ohio Univ., Athens, Ohio 45701 |
| Kappa Tau Alpha* (H.) | 1910 | 47 | 8,000 | Univ. of Missouri, Columbia, Mo. 65201 |
| Pi Delta Epsilon* (R.) | 1909 | 130 | 31,657 | 5738 Howe St., Pittsburgh, Pa. 15232 |
| Sigma Delta Chi | 1909 | 198 | 19,000 | 35 E. Wacker Dr., Chicago, Ill. 60601 |
| **Languages** | | | | |
| Delta Phi Alpha (German)* (H.) | 1929 | 112 | 24,703 | Univ. of Hawaii, Honolulu, Hawaii 96822. |
| Phi Sigma Iota (Romance)* (H.) | 1922 | 60 | 15,600 | 416 Woodside Ave., Ripon, Wis. 54971 |
| Pi Delta Phi (French)* (H.) | 1906 | 137 | 26,500 | 6039 N. Kedvale Ave., Chicago, Ill. 60646 |
| Sigma Delta Pi (Spanish)* (H.) | 1919 | 160 | 27,000 | Kent St. Univ., Kent, Ohio |
| Sigma Tau Delta (English)* .. | 1924 | 125 | 15,000 | 698 Brookfield Dr., Largo, Fla. 33540 |
| **Law** | | | | |
| Delta Theta Phi | 1900 | 70 | 52,000 | 1020 Commerce Bldg., Kansas City, Mo. 64106 |
| Order of the Coif* (H.) | 1902 | 50 | 15,000 | Univ. of Texas, Austin, Tex. 78705 |
| Phi Alpha Delta | 1902 | 112 | 53,500 | 10722 White Oak Ave., Granda Hills, Calif. |
| Phi Beta Gamma | 1922 | 15 | 2,500 | 425 St. Paul Place, Baltimore, Md. |
| Phi Delta Phi | 1869 | 85 | 76,259 | 9601 Wilshire Blvd., Beverly Hills, Calif. |
| Sigma Delta Kappa | 1914 | 27 | 18,290 | 2009 N. 14th St., Arlington, Va. 22201 |
| Sigma Nu Phi | 1903 | 4 | 4,901 | 2026 P St., N.W., Washington D. C. 20036 |
| Tau Epsilon Rho | 1926 | 22 | 6,000 | Washington & Rugby, Philadelphia, Pa. 19138 |
| **Leadership and Activities** | | | | |
| Blue Key (H.) | 1924 | 135 | 61,000 | P.O. Box 4010, New Orleans, La. 70118 |
| Omicron Delta Kappa (H.)... | 1914 | 117 | 49,050 | Univ. of Kentucky, Lexington, Ky. 40506 |
| **Library Science** | | | | |
| Alpha Beta Alpha* | 1950 | 28 | 1,200 | Millersville St. Coll., Pa. 17551 |
| **Mathematics** | | | | |
| Kappa Mu Epsilon* (H.) | 1931 | 77 | 23,886 | Washburn Univ., Topeka, Kan. 66621 |
| Pi Mu Epsilon* (H.) | 1914 | 125 | 30,000 | Univ. of Okla., Norman, Okla. 73069 |
| **Medicine** | | | | |
| Alpha Kappa Kappa | 1888 | 24 | 12,000 | 703-A, S.E. 1st St., Evansville, Ind. 47713 |
| Alpha Omega Alpha* (H.) | 1902 | 88 | 40,500 | Box 47, Slaterville Springs, N. Y. 14881 |
| Chi Delta Mu (Med., Dent. and Pharm.) | 1913 | 20 | 1,700 | 1336 Oak St., Washington, D. C. 20010 |
| Delta Sigma Theta (Med., Dent. and Pharm.) | 1913 | 20 | 3,000 | 1814 M. St., Wash., D. C. 20036 |
| Nu Sigma Nu | 1882 | 30 | 26,000 | 123 Keller Ave., N. Amery, Wis. 54001 |
| Phi Beta Pi & Theta Kappa Psi | 1891 | 30 | 25,000 | 3800 Woodward Ave., Detroit, Mich. 48210 |
| Phi Chi | 1889 | 43 | 52,880 | P.O. Box 2035, Valdosta, Ga. 31601 |
| Phi Delta Epsilon | 1904 | 83 | 20,000 | 145 East 52nd St., New York, N. Y. 10022 |
| Phi Lambda Kappa | 1907 | 12 | 3,500 | 1205 Spruce St., Philadelphia 7, Pa. |
| Phi Rho Sigma | 1890 | 23 | 27,057 | P.O. Box 10886, Pittsburgh, Pa. 15236 |
| **Military** | | | | |
| Pershing Rifles (H.) | 1894 | 165 | 8,500 | Univ. of Nebraska, Lincoln, Nebr. |
| Scabbard and Blade (H.) | 1905 | 157 | 109,482 | P.O. Box 1021, Stillwater, Okla. 74074 |
| **Music** | | | | |
| Mu Beta Psi* (R.) | 1925 | 3 | 1,100 | Box 27534, Atlanta, Ga. 30327 |
| Phi Mu Alpha (Sinfonia) | 1898 | 275 | 50,000 | Southern Securities Bldg, Evansville, Ind. |
| Pi Kappa Lambda* (H.) | 1918 | 64 | 12,000 | P.O. Box 2886, University, Ala. 35486 |
| **Nursing** | | | | |
| Sigma Theta Tau* (H.) | 1922 | 43 | 9,000 | 20 Hillside Circle, Storrs, Conn. |
| **Optometric** | | | | |
| Omega Delta | 1917 | 5 | 2,800 | 100 N. Main St., Memphis, Tenn. |
| Omega Epsilon Phi* | 1919 | 7 | 3,900 | 1022 Hamilton St., Allentown, Pa. |
| **Osteopathic** | | | | |
| Atlas Club | 1898 | 5 | 3,500 | 1010 E. 5th So., Salt Lake City, Utah 84102 |
| Iota Tau Sigma | 1902 | 5 | 2,200 | P.O. Box 792, Kirksville, Mo. 63501 |
| Lambda Omicron Gamma | 1924 | 4 | 750 | 300 Spruce St., Philadelphia, Pa. 19106 |
| Phi Sigma Gamma | 1915 | 3 | 2,600 | 1601 Belmont Ave., Kan. City, Mo. 64126 |
| Psi Sigma Alpha* (H.) | 1924 | 3 | 820 | P.O. Box 654, East Liverpool, Ohio 43920 |
| Sigma Sigma Phi (R.) | 1921 | 4 | 953 | 25 E. Washington St., Chicago, Ill. |
| **Pharmacy** | | | | |
| Alpha Zeta Omega | 1919 | 42 | 5,693 | 2456 Elmdale Rd., University Heights, Ohio |
| Delta Sigma Theta (R.) | 1913 | 316 | 40,000 | None |
| Kappa Psi | 1873 | 82 | 29,707 | 275 Union Blvd., St. Louis, Mo. |
| Phi Delta Chi | 1883 | 46 | 20,000 | 2070 E. 54 th St., Indianapolis, Ind. |
| Rho Chi* (H.) | 1922 | 68 | 16,126 | 500 W. 12th St., Columbus, Ohio |
| Rho Pi Phi | 1919 | 38 | 10,000 | 32 City Terrace North, Newburgh, N. Y. |

## FRATERNITIES AND SOCIETIES (continued)

| Name | Year Found. | Active Chapt. | Members | National Headquarters |
|---|---|---|---|---|
| **Philosophy** | | | | |
| Phi Sigma Tau* (H.)......... | 1930 | 35 | 7,111 | Baldwin-Wallace Coll., Berea, Ohio 44017 |
| **Physical Education** | | | | |
| Phi Epsilon Kappa........... | 1913 | 58 | 19,575 | 4000 Meadows Dr., Indianapolis, Ind. 46205 |
| **Physics** | | | | |
| Lambda Delta Lambda* (H.).. | 1925 | 7 | 3,000 | Kansas St. Teachers Coll., Emporia, Kan. |
| Sigma Pi Sigma* (H.)........ | 1921 | 135 | 30,000 | Osmond Laboratory, Univ. Park, Pa. 16802 |
| **Political Science** | | | | |
| Pi Sigma Alpha* (H.)........ | 1920 | 125 | 27,500 | Univ. of Maryland, College Park, Md. 20742 |
| **Premedical** | | | | |
| Alpha Epsilon Delta* (H.)..... | 1926 | 89 | 31,500 | 7 Brookside Circle, Bronxville, N. Y. 10708 |
| **Psychology** | | | | |
| Psi Chi* (H.)............... | 1929 | 225 | 46,000 | 1200 17th St., N.W., Washington, D. C. 20016 |
| **Real Estate** | | | | |
| Rho Epsilon* (R.).......... | 1947 | 13 | 1,554 | Univ. of Nebr. at Omaha |
| **Scholarship (General)** | | | | |
| Alpha Chi* (H.)............ | 1922 | 75 | 34,000 | Southwest Tex. St. Coll., San Marcos, Tex. |
| Alpha Kappa Mu* (H.)....... | 1937 | 71 | 10,593 | Florida A. & M. Univ., Tallahassee, Fla. |
| Delta Epsilon Sigma* (H.).... | 1939 | 93 | 17,000 | Loras College, Dubuque, Iowa 52001 |
| Phi Beta Kappa* (H.)........ | 1776 | 184 | 195,000 | 1811 Q St. N.W., Wash., D. C. 20009 |
| Phi Eta Sigma (Freshman) (H.) | 1923 | 153 | 104,248 | 304 Martin Hall, Auburn Univ., Auburn, Ala. |
| Phi Kappa Phi* (H.)......... | 1897 | 101 | 181,000 | 3839 Wilshire Blvd., Los Angeles, Calif. 90005 |
| Phi Theta Kappa* (H.)....... | 1918 | 341 | 12,000 | Box 230, Canton, Miss. 39046 |
| **Science** | | | | |
| Chi Beta Phi* (H.).......... | 1916 | 25 | 8,500 | Randolph-Macon Coll., Ashland, Va. |
| Gamma Alpha (graduate) (R.). | 1899 | 11 | 11,056 | Cornell Univ., Ithaca, N. Y. |
| Sigma Xi* (H.)............. | 1886 | 166 | 110,000 | 155 Whitney Ave., New Haven, Conn. 06510 |
| Sigma Zeta* (undergrad.) (H.) | 1925 | 21 | 7,333 | Anderson Coll., Anderson, Ind. |
| **Social Science** | | | | |
| Alpha Kappa Delta* (H.)..... | 1920 | 110 | 20,000 | Iowa State Univ., Ames, Iowa |
| Pi Gamma Mu* (H.)......... | 1924 | 142 | 86,559 | 1719 Ames St., Winfield, Kan. |
| **Veterinary** | | | | |
| Alpha Psi................. | 1907 | 8 | 8,600 | Mich. St. Univ., E. Lansing, Mich. 48823 |
| Omega Tau Sigma............ | 1906 | 9 | 5,652 | Univ. of Illinois, Urbana, Ill. |

## SORORITIES AND SOCIETIES

| Name | Year Found. | Active Chapt. | Members | National Headquarters |
|---|---|---|---|---|
| **Advertising** | | | | |
| Gamma Alpha Chi.......... | 1920 | 27 | 8,500 | 917 Cruce St., Norman, Okla. 73069 |
| **Architecture** | | | | |
| Alpha Alpha Gamma......... | 1922 | 20 | 1,145 | P.O. Box 1, Clayton, Mo. 63105 |
| **Band** | | | | |
| Tau Beta Sigma (R.)........ | 1946 | 93 | 23,158 | Okla. State Univ., Stillwater, Okla. 74074 |
| **Chemistry** | | | | |
| Iota Sigma Pi (H.).......... | 1912 | 26 | 1,500 | None |
| **Commerce and Business** | | | | |
| Alpha Iota (H.)............. | 1925 | 170 | 57,000 | 1002 Grand Ave., Des Moines, Iowa 50309 |
| Epsilon Eta Phi............. | 1927 | 5 | 2,000 | 5348 N. Meade Ave., Chicago, Ill. |
| Phi Chi Theta.............. | 1924 | 75 | 14,500 | 718 Judah St., San Francisco, Calif. 94122 |
| Phi Gamma Nu............. | 1924 | 43 | 7,500 | 275 Roosevelt Pl., Grosse Pointe, Mich. 48230 |
| **Education** | | | | |
| Alpha Delta Kappa (H.)..... | 1947 | 1,191 | 34,660 | 1615 W. 92nd St., Kansas City, Mo. 64114 |
| Kappa Delta Epsilon........ | 1933 | 40 | 15,585 | 608 Superior Ave., Decatur, Ga. 30033 |
| Pi Lambda Theta (H.)....... | 1917 | 90 | 14,500 | 815 17th St. N.W., Washington, D. C. 20006 |
| **Dentistry** | | | | |
| Upsilon Alpha.............. | 1918 | 7 | 350 | 832 Marquette Bank Bldg., Minneapolis |
| **Fine Arts** | | | | |
| Phi Mu Gamma (R.)......... | 1898 | 10 | 5,628 | Box 363, East Bank, W. Va. |
| **Home Economics** | | | | |
| Kappa Omicron Phi (H.)...... | 1922 | 42 | 9,200 | R.R. 1, P.O. Box 268A, Williamsburg, Pa. |
| Omicron Nu* (H.).......... | 1912 | 46 | 26,000 | Mich. State Univ., East Lansing, Mich. 48823 |
| Phi Upsilon Omicron (H.)..... | 1909 | 56 | 32,774 | Box 5471, State U. Sta., Fargo, N. D. |
| **Journalism** | | | | |
| Theta Sigma Phi............ | 1909 | 114 | 4,500 | 1018 W. 11th St., Austin, Tex. 78703 |
| **Law** | | | | |
| Iota Tau Tau............... | 1925 | 37 | 1,050 | 1367 S.E. Sycamore Ave., Santa Ana, Calif. |
| Kappa Beta Pi............. | 1908 | 88 | 4,700 | 570 Neff Road, Grosse Pointe, Mich. |
| Phi Delta Delta............. | 1911 | 55 | 5,000 | 860 5th Ave., New York, N. Y. 10021 |
| **Literature** | | | | |
| Chi Delta Phi* (H.)......... | 1919 | 10 | 170 | 51 Westwood Ave., Columbus, Ohio 43212 |
| **Medicine** | | | | |
| Alpha Delta Theta (Medical technology)............... | 1944 | 27 | 1,750 | P.O. Box 7241, Milwaukee, Wis. 53213 |
| **Music** | | | | |
| Delta Omicron............. | 1909 | 75 | 13,000 | 18518 Cherrylawn, Detroit, Mich. 48221 |
| Mu Phi Epsilon............. | 1903 | 196 | 30,000 | 1139 N. Ridgewood, Wichita, Kan. 67208 |
| Phi Beta (Music and Speech).. | 1912 | 60 | 15,198 | 4950 W. Walton St., Chicago, Ill. 60651 |
| Sigma Alpha Iota........... | 1903 | 155 | 45,000 | 4119 Rollins Ave., Des Moines, Iowa |
| **Nursing** | | | | |
| Alpha Tau Delta........... | 1921 | 20 | 1,800 | 13301 El Dorado Dr., Seal Beach, Calif. 90740 |
| **Osteopathic** | | | | |
| Delta Omega.............. | 1904 | 5 | 300 | Dr. Worley, 226 W. 39th St., Kansas City, Mo. |
| **Pharmacy** | | | | |
| Kappa Epsilon............. | 1921 | 32 | 4,600 | 514 29th Ave., Fargo, N. D. 58102 |
| Lambda Kappa Sigma........ | 1913 | 50 | 6,050 | 4509 Regent, Philadelphia, Pa. 19143 |
| **Physical Education** | | | | |
| Delta Psi Kappa............ | 1916 | 40 | 7,364 | None |
| Phi Delta Pi............... | 1916 | 11 | 3,200 | 4595 E. 4th Ave., Hialeah, Fla. 33012 |
| **Scholastic** | | | | |
| Alpha Lambda Delta (H.)..... | 1924 | 150 | 84,385 | P.O. Box 866, So. Miami, Fla. 33143 |
| Cardinal Key (R.).......... | 1932 | 33 | 1,750 | Northern Arizona Univ., Flagstaff, Ariz. |
| Cwens (Sophomore) (H.)..... | 1932 | 22 | 9,000 | 1177 Woodland Ave., Atlanta, Ga. |
| Kappa Gamma Pi (H.)....... | 1926 | 41 | 13,500 | 3821 Kirkwood Rd., Cleveland, Ohio 44118 |
| Mortar Board (H.).......... | 1918 | 117 | 42,838 | 6150 W. 76 St., Los Angeles, Calif. |
| National Spurs (R.)......... | 1922 | 51 | 1,500 | Univ. of Idaho, Moscow, Idaho |
| Phi Delta Gamma........... | 1923 | 19 | 4,700 | 2752 N. Lefeber Ave., Wauwatosa, Wisc. |
| Sigma Epsilon Sigma (H.)..... | 1927 | 7 | 420 | 433 N. Murray St., Madison, Wis. |
| **Science** | | | | |
| Sigma Delta Epsilon......... | 1921 | 17 | 1,400 | 316 Kingston Ave., Barrington, N. J. |
| **Speech Arts** | | | | |
| Zeta Phi Eta............... | 1893 | 50 | 11,094 | P.O. Box 1236, Seattle, Wash. 98111 |

# Degrees Conferred by Higher Educational Institutions
## UNITED STATES AND OUTLYING AREAS, 1965-66
### Source: United States Office of Education
Major sub-classifications do not necessarily add to totals.

| Field of study | Bachelor's & first professional[1] Men | Women | Master's Men | Women | Doctor's (Ph.D. Ed. D., etc.) Men | Women |
|---|---|---|---|---|---|---|
| **Agriculture**[2] | 5,578 | 152 | 1,295 | 68 | 530 | 7 |
| Agronomy, field crops | 626 | 4 | 235 | 5 | 107 | 1 |
| Animal Science | 1,376 | 64 | 283 | 10 | 119 | 1 |
| **Architecture**[2] | 2,496 | 103 | 365 | 16 | 8 | 1 |
| **Biological Sciences**[2] | 19,428 | 7,620 | 3,087 | 1,148 | 1,792 | 305 |
| Pre-medical, dental and veterinary | 2,948 | 273 | 10 | 1 | 1 | |
| Biology, general | 11,373 | 5,493 | 1,105 | 441 | 181 | 45 |
| Zoology, general | 3,198 | 921 | 485 | 175 | 246 | 47 |
| **Business and Commerce**[2] | 58,074 | 5,426 | 12,656 | 332 | 370 | 17 |
| Accounting | 14,203 | 898 | 834 | 28 | 31 | 3 |
| Secretarial studies | 50 | 1,396 | | | | |
| Computer Science and Systems Analysis | 76 | 13 | 221 | 17 | 19 | |
| **Education**[2] | 29,267 | 89,154 | 25,837 | 24,641 | 2,461 | 602 |
| *Specialized teaching fields* | | | | | | |
| Physical education | 8,294 | 4,721 | 2,093 | 672 | 86 | 42 |
| Agriculture | 885 | 1 | 419 | 11 | 30 | |
| Art | 1,086 | 2,620 | 267 | 347 | 10 | 4 |
| Business and commercial | 1,731 | 4,437 | 490 | 680 | 37 | 6 |
| Home economics | 3 | 4,504 | | 450 | | 18 |
| Industrial arts | 3,445 | 20 | 955 | 8 | 31 | |
| Music education | 2,347 | 3,151 | 862 | 530 | 41 | 7 |
| *General teaching fields* | | | | | | |
| Early childhood | 12 | 3,522 | 1 | 159 | | |
| Elementary education | 6,780 | 58,274 | 1,772 | 6,941 | 86 | 54 |
| Secondary education | 1,338 | 1,318 | 2,360 | 1,564 | 93 | 21 |
| *Non teaching fields* | | | | | | |
| Counseling and guidance | 9 | 2 | 3,125 | 2,756 | 232 | 54 |
| Education general | 129 | 469 | 4,225 | 3,900 | 589 | 129 |
| **Engineering** | 35,669 | 146 | 13,602 | 76 | 2,295 | 9 |
| **English and Journalism** | 15,154 | 27,169 | 3,249 | 3,539 | 552 | 162 |
| English and literature | 13,244 | 25,948 | 2,854 | 3,411 | 540 | 150 |
| Journalism | 1,910 | 1,221 | 395 | 128 | 12 | 3 |
| **Fine and Applied arts**[2] | 7,940 | 10,765 | 2,760 | 2,259 | 396 | 80 |
| Art, general | 1,782 | 3,462 | 495 | 445 | 22 | 3 |
| Music | 1,554 | 2,011 | 974 | 721 | 145 | 19 |
| Speech & dramatic arts | 2,266 | 3,003 | 780 | 755 | 201 | 39 |
| **Foreign Languages and literature**[2] | 4,553 | 10,974 | 1,579 | 2,052 | 361 | 151 |
| Latin and/or Greek | 634 | 611 | 187 | 174 | 51 | 12 |
| French | 1,045 | 4,543 | 313 | 741 | 46 | 34 |
| German | 837 | 1,224 | 260 | 254 | 69 | 24 |
| Russian | 253 | 284 | 83 | 59 | 6 | 3 |
| Spanish | 1,377 | 3,662 | 387 | 480 | 55 | 27 |
| **Forestry** | 1,464 | 2 | 299 | 4 | 51 | |
| **Geography** | 1,529 | 405 | 309 | 61 | 52 | 6 |
| **Health professions**[2] | 16,042 | 12,265 | 1,610 | 1,257 | 225 | 26 |
| Dentistry, D.D.S. and D.M.D. only | 3,229 | 35 | in | in | in | in |
| Medicine, M. D. only | 7,204 | 516 | in | in | in | in |
| Nursing and/or public health nursing | 96 | 7,735 | 17 | 846 | | 1 |
| Pharmacy | 3,227 | 536 | 159 | 28 | 73 | 5 |
| **Home economics**[2] | 145 | 5,579 | 29 | 711 | 12 | 42 |
| Child developments, family relations | 16 | 628 | 13 | 109 | 11 | 12 |
| Clothing and textiles | 2 | 592 | | 94 | | 3 |
| Foods and nutrition | 10 | 650 | 2 | 116 | | 14 |
| **Law** | 13,169 | 518 | 743 | 37 | 27 | 2 |
| **Library science** | 53 | 589 | 1,002 | 2,914 | 14 | 5 |
| **Mathematical subjects** | 13,404 | 6,689 | 3,771 | 1,001 | 725 | 57 |
| **Merchant marine—deck officer** | 181 | | in | in | in | in |
| **Military, naval or airforce science** | 1,798 | | | | | |
| **Philosophy** | 4,306 | 730 | 504 | 109 | 181 | 22 |
| **Physical sciences**[2] | 14,853 | 2,333 | 4,464 | 528 | 2,914 | 131 |
| Chemistry | 7,934 | 1,801 | 1,472 | 350 | 1,442 | 91 |
| Physics | 4,385 | 224 | 1,869 | 80 | 952 | 21 |
| Geology | 1,181 | 126 | 445 | 33 | 259 | 9 |
| **Psychology** | 10,041 | 6,981 | 1,680 | 850 | 826 | 220 |
| **Religion**[2] | 7,004 | 1,475 | 1,475 | 471 | 314 | 19 |
| Religious education and bible | 1,691 | 938 | 336 | 261 | 39 | 10 |
| Theology | 4,490 | 112 | 965 | 150 | 171 | 5 |
| **Social sciences**[2] | 60,876 | 32,793 | 11,369 | 5,091 | 1,919 | 239 |
| *Basic* | | | | | | |
| General | 8,212 | 6,073 | 988 | 411 | 30 | 3 |
| Economics | 10,447 | 1,138 | 1,359 | 169 | 436 | 22 |
| History | 18,829 | 9,941 | 2,800 | 1,083 | 527 | 72 |
| Political science or government | 11,994 | 3,381 | 1,152 | 277 | 307 | 29 |
| Sociology | 6,139 | 9,064 | 680 | 301 | 208 | 36 |
| *Applied* | | | | | | |
| Agricultural economics | 683 | 6 | 363 | 10 | 126 | 2 |
| Industrial relations | 860 | 58 | 178 | 5 | 15 | |
| Public administration | 348 | 30 | 691 | 48 | 27 | 2 |
| Social work, social administration | 476 | 1,188 | 1,588 | 2,324 | 34 | 30 |
| **Trade and industrial training** | 2,334 | 23 | 42 | 2 | 11 | |
| **All other** | 5,688 | 2,587 | 1,236 | 404 | 66 | 15 |
| **Total** | 331,122 | 224,491 | 93,184 | 47,588 | 16,121 | 2,118 |
| **Grand total** | 555,613 | | 140,772 | | 18,239 | |

**Number of degrees conferred—men 440,427; women 274,197; total 714,624**

1—Includes bachelor of arts, bachelor of science, and such first professional degrees as M.D., LL.B., D.D.S., and B.D.    2—Includes fields of study not listed. (Note—in = inapplicable.)

# Fall Enrollment in Higher Educational Institutions

| Year | Total | In all institutions Men | Women | Public | Private |
|---|---|---|---|---|---|
| **All students[1]** | | | | | |
| Fall 1967 | 6,963,687 | 4,158,557 | 2,805,130 | 4,850,330 | 2,113,357 |
| Fall 1966 | 6,438,477 | 3,880,557 | 2,557,920 | 4,381,086 | 2,057,391 |
| Fall 1965 | 5,967,411 | 3,652,675 | 2,314,736 | 3,999,940 | 1,967,471 |
| Fall 1964 | 5,320,294 | 3,268,188 | 2,052,106 | 3,494,489 | 1,825,805 |
| **First-time students** | | | | | |
| Fall 1967 | 1,652,317 | 936,406 | 715,911 | 1,212,846 | 439,471 |

| Level of institution 1967 | Full-time resident Men | Women | Part-time resident Men | Women | Total | First time[2] Men | Women |
|---|---|---|---|---|---|---|---|
| **Public:** | | | | | | | |
| All institutions | 1,995,618 | 1,285,613 | 865,582 | 703,517 | 4,850,330 | 693,550 | 519,296 |
| 4-year institutions | 1,537,190 | 1,038,516 | 485,475 | 414,479 | 3,475,660 | 355,417 | 295,458 |
| Universities | 915,350 | 521,698 | 268,243 | 198,074 | 1,903,365 | 193,674 | 141,276 |
| All other 4-year | 621,840 | 516,818 | 217,232 | 216,405 | 1,572,295 | 161,743 | 154,182 |
| 2-year institutions | 458,428 | 247,097 | 380,107 | 289,038 | 1,374,670 | 338,133 | 223,838 |
| **Private:** | | | | | | | |
| All institutions | 945,370 | 600,390 | 351,987 | 215,610 | 2,113,357 | 242,856 | 196,615 |
| 4-year institutions | 881,440 | 546,484 | 337,187 | 204,837 | 1,969,948 | 208,051 | 163,187 |
| Universities | 325,657 | 142,973 | 157,316 | 89,786 | 715,732 | 59,497 | 33,825 |
| All other 4-year | 555,783 | 403,511 | 179,871 | 115,051 | 1,254,216 | 148,554 | 129,362 |
| 2-year institutions | 63,930 | 53,906 | 14,800 | 10,773 | 143,409 | 34,805 | 33,428 |

[1]Includes students whose programs of work consist wholly or chiefly of work normally creditable toward a bachelor's or higher degree and students in 1-, 2-, or 3-year undergraduate programs which are not chiefly creditable toward a bachelor's degree but which are designed to prepare for immediate employment or to provide general education.

[2]Included in other columns.

**All Institutions:** 1967—2,382; 1966—2,337. Universities 1967—157; 1966—157. All other 4-year institutions 1967—1,436; 1966—1,425. 2-year institutions 1967—789; 1966—755.

# Federal Funds for Education

Source: Office of Education, Dept. of Health, Education and Welfare.
(*In millions of dollars.* Includes grants, loans, and directly administered services.)

| Type of support, level and program | 1967 | Type of support, level and program | 1967 |
|---|---|---|---|
| **Supporting ed. in educational insts.[1]** | **8,326.3** | Loans | 743.1 |
| Grants | 7,583.2 | Elementary-secondary education | 1.5 |
| Elementary-secondary education | 3,084.1 | Higher education | 741.3 |
| Assistance for ed. deprived children | 1,057.4 | Student loan programs[8] | 237.7 |
| School asst.—federally affected areas | 469.1 | Loans for facilities[9] | 503.6 |
| Assistance for special groups[2] | 721.3 | Vocational education insured loan fund | .3 |
| National Defense Education Act | 107.7 | **Other federal funds[10]** | **3,871.9** |
| Supporting services[3] | 273.6 | Applied research and development | 1,064.7 |
| Public lands revenue for schools | 50.2 | Related school services | 448.0 |
| Dependents schools abroad | 87.5 | Training of federal personnel | 1,537.4 |
| Vocational education | 194.6 | Professional and tech. training (mil.) | 1,443.0 |
| School assistance in special areas[4] | 57.0 | Training in nongovernment facilities | 94.4 |
| Teacher Corps | 11.3 | Library services | 141.4 |
| Veterans education | 49.3 | Grants to public libraries | 76.0 |
| Other | 5.1 | National library services | 65.4 |
| Higher education | 3,590.7 | International education | 326.5 |
| Basic research | 1,036.5 | Educational Exchange Program | 44.7 |
| Research facilities | 203.0 | AID education projects and training | 203.3 |
| Training grants | 363.6 | Peace Corps | 41.9 |
| Fellowships and traineeships | 350.2 | Other int'l education and training | 36.6 |
| Institutional support—facilities[5] | 822.2 | Other | 353.9 |
| Institutional support—other[6] | 170.0 | Extension services | 92.9 |
| Other student assistance[7] | 590.6 | Educational television facilities | 3.3 |
| Other support | 54.6 | Education in Federal correctional institutions | 6.3 |
| Adult vocational-tech. and continuing ed. | 908.4 | Other education and training | 15.2 |
| Vocational-technical education | 470.8 | Surplus property transferred[11] | 236.2 |
| Assistance for special groups[2] | 345.8 | | |
| Veterans education | 11.3 | **Total** | **12,198.2** |
| General continuing education | 29.2 | | |
| Training state and local personnel | 28.6 | | |
| Other | 22.7 | | |

[1]Excludes payments for services rendered to the Federal Government. [2]Includes Indian education and Economic Opportunity Act programs. [3]Includes Titles III (part) and X of NDEA and Titles II, III, and V of ESEA. [4]Includes District of Columbia, Canal Zone, national parks and territories, Cuban refugee education, etc. [5]Includes construction at Howard University and Gallaudet College, Washington, D.C., Higher Education Facilities Act, AEC and NSF grants. [6]Includes AEC, NSF, and PHS grants, language and area centers, land-grant colleges, and support of Howard University, Gallaudet College, East-West Center for Cultural and Technical Interchange, and State merchant marine schools. [7]Includes Veterans education and work-study programs. [8]Includes college, health professions, nursing and Cuban refugee programs. [9]Includes college housing and Higher Education Facilities Act programs. [10]Includes payments for services rendered to the Federal Government and education and related activities excluded above. [11]Estimated actual value of surplus real and personal property at time of transfer for education use.

## Science Service Popularizes Science

Science Service, Inc., 1719 N St., N.W., Washington, D. C., Edward G. Sherburne, Jr., director, the institution for the popularization of science, was organized as a non-profit corporation, with trustees nominated by the National Academy of Sciences, the National Research Council, the American Association for the Advancement of Science, the journalistic profession and the Edward W. Scripps Trust.

Through its services to newspapers, Science Service has been since 1921 telling the public about science and technology. It covers the broad fields of science—physics, chemistry, medicine, biology, astronomy, anthropology, archaeology, psychology, mathematics, atomics, electronics, etc.—by a specialized science writing staff. It publishes the weekly SCIENCE NEWS and produces monthly the unique THINGS of science experimental kits.

More than a million boys and girls participate annually in Science Service's International Science Youth Program, doing projects and making exhibits shown in science fairs. Some 25,000 science teachers and other science youth leaders, mostly in secondary schools, upon request are sent without charge "know-how" literature and material for inspiring and instructing science students. The International Science Youth Program consists of Science Clubs of America, International Science Fair and the Science Talent Search for the Westinghouse Science Scholarships and awards.

# Average Tuition Fee at Selected Colleges and Universities

Source: World Almanac Questionnaire

Fees for tuition charged per year by colleges and universities for courses, use of libraries, laboratories and other facilities, are a major part of student expenses. Tuition varies considerably, depending on the type of institution, its control and location. The lowest tuition fees are those of state-controlled or other public-controlled institutions for residents of their state, city, etc. Students from other states or areas have to pay more. In the following list, such state or other public institutions are shown with two figures. The lower one is the tuition fee for residents, the higher one the tuition fee for students from other states or areas.

It should be noted that the tuition fee does not cover room, board, and other personal expenses.

*For location of College or University see pages 319-338*

| School | Tuition | School | Tuition | School | Tuition |
|---|---|---|---|---|---|
| Abilene Christian.... | 944 | Fairleigh Dickinson.. | 1,250 | Oberlin............ | 2,000 |
| Adelphi............ | 1,500 | Florida State....... | 375-975 | Oglethorpe........ | 1,100 |
| Akron, Univ. of..... | 495-1,095 | Florida, Univ. of.... | 375-975 | Ohio Univ......... | 525-1,050 |
| Alabama, Univ. of... | 350-700 | Franklin & Marshall. | 2,200 | Oklahoma State.... | 360-900 |
| Alaska, Univ. of.... | 100-250 | Fresno State....... | 128-848 | Oklahoma, Univ. of. | 360-900 |
| Albuquerque, Univ. of | 900 | Furman Univ....... | 1,100 | Oregon State Univ.. | 369-999 |
| Amherst........... | 2,125 | George Washington U. | 1,700 | Oregon, Univ. of.... | 369-999 |
| Antioch............ | 2,200 | Georgetown U...... | 1,500 | Pan American...... | 100-400 |
| Arizona State Univ... | 286-815 | Georgia............ | 333-753 | Pennsylvania...... | 2,150 |
| Arizona, Univ. of.... | 289-1,104 | Grambling.......... | 100-500 | Pennsylvania St.... | 450-1,050 |
| Arkansas, Univ. of... | 250-650 | Grinnell........... | 2,125 | Pittsburgh, Univ. of. | 450-1,400 |
| Athenaeum of Ohio.. | 600 | Hamline Univ....... | 1,500 | Princeton.......... | 2,150 |
| Auburn............ | 360-720 | Hampton Inst...... | 800 | Purdue............ | 200-600 |
| Baldwin-Wallace ... | 1,700 | Hartford, Univ. of .. | 1,500 | Radcliffe.......... | 2,000 |
| Barrington......... | 1,400 | Harvard........... | 2,000 | Rensselaer Poly. Inst. | 2,050 |
| Baylor............. | 900 | Hawaii, Univ. of.... | 206 | Rice............... | 1,800 |
| Boston Coll........ | 1,600 | Holy Cross........ | 1,700 | Rutgers........... | 400-636 |
| Boston Univ........ | 1,875 | Houston, Univ. of... | 210-510 | St. Bonaventure.... | 1,400 |
| Bowdoin........... | 2,150 | Howard Univ....... | 500 | St. John's Univ..... | 1,500 |
| Bowling Green State. | 540-1,140 | Idaho, Univ. of..... | 275-775 | St. Lawrence Univ... | 2,025 |
| Bradley Univ....... | 1,300 | Illinois State Univ... | 120-600 | St. Peter's......... | 1,425 |
| Brandeis Univ...... | 2,100 | Illinois, Univ. of.... | 270-550 | San Diego, Univ. of.. | 1,200 |
| Bridgeport, Univ. of. | 1,200 | Indiana State Univ... | 360-720 | Santa Fe.......... | 860 |
| Brigham Young (a).. | 430 | Indiana Univ....... | 360-990 | Sarah Lawrence.... | 2,600 |
| Brown............. | 2,150 | Iowa State Univ..... | 375-1,005 | Smith............. | 2,050 |
| Bryn Mawr........ | 1,850 | Iowa, Univ. of...... | 370-1,000 | So. Carolina....... | 460-1,010 |
| Bucknell.......... | 1,900 | Jacksonville Univ. (c) | 1,050 | So. Dakota State Un. | 423-850 |
| Butler Univ........ | 1,450 | John Carroll Univ... | 1,190 | So. Dakota, Univ. of. | 304-800 |
| California......... | 219-1,200 | Kansas, Univ. of.... | 338-798 | South, Univ. of the.. | 1,550 |
| Carnegie-Mellon U.. | 1,950 | Kansas State....... | 332-792 | So. Ill. Univ....... | 241-631 |
| Case Western Reserve | | Kent State......... | 510-960 | So. Methodist...... | 1,200 |
| Univ............. | 1,900 | La Salle........... | 1,400 | Stanford........... | 1,920 |
| Chattanooga, Univ. of | 1,000 | Lawrence Univ..... | 1,870 | Swarthmore....... | 2,260 |
| Chicago, Univ. of... | 2,100 | Lehigh............ | 2,000 | Syracuse Univ..... | 2,100 |
| Cincinnati (b)...... | 750-1,215 | Loma Linda Univ... | 1,350 | Tampa, Univ. of.... | 1,200 |
| Clemson........... | 496-996 | Long Island Univ... | 1,676 | Temple........... | 450-1,350 |
| Colgate............ | 2,250 | Louisville, Univ. of.. | 1,200-1,800 | Tennessee......... | 315-885 |
| Colorado State Univ. | 402-1,284 | Maine, Univ. of..... | 400-1,000 | Texas Christian Univ. | 1,200 |
| Colorado, Univ. of... | 378-1,226 | Marquette......... | 1,450 | Texas, Univ. of.... | 100-400 |
| Columbia.......... | 1,700 | Marshall Univ...... | 242-992 | Toledo, Univ. of.... | 556-1,086 |
| Connecticut, Univ. of | 290-640 | Maryland, Univ. of.. | 300-525 | Tufts Univ......... | 2,300 |
| Cooper Union...... | None | Mass., Univ. of..... | 200-600 | Tulane............ | 1,900 |
| Cornell............ | 2,200 | Miami............. | 1,650 | Tulsa Univ......... | 750 |
| Corpus Christi, Un. of | 660-760 | Mich. State........ | 505-1,204 | Utah State Univ.... | 327-801 |
| Creighton Univ..... | 1,230 | Michigan.......... | 420-1,300 | Valparaiso Univ.... | 1,300 |
| Dallas, Univ. of.... | 475 | Midwestern........ | 100-400 | Vanderbilt Univ.... | 1,760 |
| Dana.............. | 930 | Minnesota......... | 385-931 | Vassar............ | 2,100 |
| Dartmouth......... | 2,075 | Mississippi........ | 356-956 | Vermont, Univ. of... | 600-1,800 |
| Davidson.......... | 1,150 | Mississippi State.... | 342-942 | Wake Forest Univ... | 1,200 |
| Davis & Elkins..... | 1,500 | Missouri, Univ. of... | 350-500 | Washington & Lee... | 1,800 |
| Dayton, Univ. of.... | 1,200 | Montana St. U...... | 375-983 | Washington, Univ. of | 345-825 |
| Defiance........... | 1,500 | Montana........... | 359-966 | Wayne State Univ... | 411-1,050 |
| Delaware.......... | 315-750 | Nebraska.......... | 433-933 | Wesleyan Univ..... | *3,100 |
| Denison Univ...... | 1,650 | Nevada............ | None-600 | West Virginia Univ.. | 230-710 |
| Denver............ | 1,680 | New Hampshire.... | 630-1,375 | Western Kentucky... | 240-740 |
| Depauw........... | 1,900 | New Mexico State... | 414-1,044 | Wichita State Univ.. | 317-775 |
| Dickinson.......... | 1,850 | New Mexico, U. of.. | 420-1,500 | Wilberforce........ | 930 |
| Dordt............. | 1,000 | New York State..... | 425-625 | Willamette Univ.... | 1,600 |
| Drake............. | 1,400 | New York Univ..... | 2,100 | William & Mary.... | 438-560 |
| Dubuque.......... | 1,260 | Niagara........... | 1,400 | Worcester Poly. Inst. | 2,100 |
| Duke.............. | 1,800 | North Carolina..... | 175-700 | Wyoming.......... | 347-963 |
| Duquesne.......... | 1,400 | North Dakota State.. | 360-864 | Yale.............. | 2,150 |
| Eastern Ill. U...... | 267-747 | North Dakota Un. of | 360-864 | Yeshiva Univ...... | 1,500 |
| Eastern Kentucky U. | 240-740 | Notre Dame, Univ. of | 1,800 | Youngstown State U. | 450-525 |

*Includes room and board. (a) Additional fee for non-members of the Church of Jesus Christ of Latter-Day Saints. (b) Residents of Cincinnati—$480. (c) Residents of Duval County—$900.

## Public School Attendance, Teachers, Expenditures

Source: U. S. Office of Education; Salaries cover supervisors, principals, and teachers

| School year ended in | Pop. 5 to 17 yrs. | Pupils | | Teachers[1] | | | Av. salary[2] per member | Total Expend. |
|---|---|---|---|---|---|---|---|---|
| | | Enrolled | Av. daily attend. | Male | Female | Total | | |
| 1900..... | 21,404,322 | 15,503,110 | 10,632,772 | 126,588 | 296,474 | 423,062 | $325 | $214,964,618 |
| 1910..... | 24,239,948 | 17,813,852 | 12,827,307 | 110,481 | 412,729 | 523,210 | 485 | 426,250,434 |
| 1920..... | 27,728,788 | 21,578,316 | 16,150,035 | 95,654 | 583,648 | 679,302 | 871 | 1,036,151,209 |
| 1930..... | 31,571,322 | 25,678,015 | 21,264,886 | 141,771 | 712,492 | 854,263 | 1,420 | 2,316,790,384 |
| 1940..... | 29,805,259 | 25,433,542 | 22,042,151 | 194,725 | 680,752 | 875,477 | 1,441 | 2,344,048,927 |
| 1950..... | 30,788,000 | 25,111,427 | 22,283,845 | 194,968 | 718,703 | 913,671 | 3,010 | 5,837,643,000 |
| 1960..... | 43,881,000 | 36,086,771 | 32,477,440 | 392,700 | 962,300 | 1,355,000 | 5,174 | 15,613,255,000 |
| 1964..... | 49,536,000 | 41,025,000 | 37,405,000 | 487,967 | 1,080,007 | 1,567,974 | 6,240 | 21,482,425,000 |
| 1966..... | 49,993,000 | 42,849,900 | 39,159,000 | 526,800 | 1,166,100 | 1,692,900 | 6,907 | 26,195,500,000 |
| 1967(Fall) | 51,584,000 | 43,886,805 | 40,708,000 | 577,200 | 1,277,500 | 1,854,700 | 7,630 | 31,511,051,000 |

[1]Prior to 1954 includes other nonsupervisory instructional staff (librarians and guidance and psychological personnel) [2]Average annual salary per member of instruction staff.

## Degree Granting Canadian Colleges and Universities
### Excluding those granting degrees in theology only.
See explanatory notes on page 319

| Name | Location | Year | Governing Official | Students | Teachers |
|------|----------|------|--------------------|----------|----------|
| Acadia Univ............. (T) | Wolfville, Nova Scotia | 1838 | James Beveridge....... | 1,836 | 108 |
| Alberta, Univ. of...... (T) (Med) | Edmonton, Calgary, Al. | 1908 | Walter H. Johns....... | 15,725 | 965 |
| Bishop's Univ............(T) | Lennoxville, Que..... | 1843 | C. L. O. Glass ....... | 1,010 | 77 |
| Brit. Columbia, Univ. of (T) (Med) | Vancouver, B. C..... | 1912 | F. Kenneth Hare...... | 19,994 | 1,267 |
| Brock Univ............... | St. Catharines, Ont... | 1964 | James A. Gibson...... | 1,378 | 89 |
| Carleton Univ........... | Ottawa, Ont......... | 1942 | A. Davidson Dunton.... | 8,781 | 320 |
| College De Bathurst......... | Bathurst, N. B...... | 1899 | Rev. Leopold Lanteigne. | 1,053 | 60 |
| Dalhousie Univ........ (T) (Med) | Halifax, Nova Scotia.. | 1818 | Henry D. Hicks........ | 4,010 | 651 |
| King's Coll., Univ. of......... | Halifax, Nova Scotia . | 1789 | H. D. Smith......... | 210 | 16 |
| Laurentian Univ............(T) | Sudbury, Ont...... | 1960 | Stanley G. Mullins..... | 2,625 | 200 |
| Laval, Universite..... (T) (Med) | Quebec, Que........ | 1852 | Msgr. L. A. Vachon.... | 25,952 | 2,320 |
| Loyola.................. | Montreal, Que....... | 1899 | V. Rev. P. G. Malone.... | 5,258 | 250 |
| Manitoba, Univ. of.... (T) (Med) | Winnipeg, Man...... | 1877 | Hugh H. Saunderson.... | 12,550 | 800 |
| McGill Univ............ (T) (Med) | Montreal, Que....... | 1821 | H. R. Robertson (Prin.), | 15,141 | 1,910 |
| McMaster Univ............... | Hamilton, Ont...... | 1887 | H. G. Thode........ | 8,951 | 440 |
| Moncton, Universite de ......(T) | Moncton, N. B...... | 1963 | Adelard Savoie........ | 1,961 | 160 |
| Montreal, Universite de (T) (Med) | Montreal, Que....... | 1919 | R. Gaudry............ | 13,014 | 904 |
| Mt. Allison Univ............. | Sackville, N. B...... | 1840 | Laurence H. Cragg..... | 1,320 | 109 |
| Mt. St. Vincent Univ..... (T) (W) | Halifax, Nova Scotia.. | 1925 | Sister Alice Michael.... | 757 | 79 |
| New Brunswick, Univ. of....(T) | Fredericton, N. B.... | 1785 | M. A. Bart (Chan.)..... | 5,472 | 380 |
| Newfoundland, Mem. Univ. of (T) | St. John's Newfdld.... | 1949 | Lord Taylor of Harlow.. | 5,600 | 300 |
| Notre Dame Univ. of Nelson..(T) | Nelson, B. C....... | 1950 | Rev. Aquinas Thomas.. | 541 | 48 |
| Nova Scotia Technical......... | Halifax, Nova Scotia.. | 1907 | George W. Holbrook.... | 470 | 71 |
| Osgoode Hall Law School....... | Toronto, Ont....... | 1881 | Dean Le Dain ..... | 575 | 39 |
| Ottawa, Univ. of...........(Med) | Ottawa, Ont......... | 1848 | V.Rev.R.Guindon(Rect.) | 8,032 | 900 |
| Queen's Univ..........(T) (Med) | Kingston, Ont........ | 1841 | J. B. Stirling (Chan.)... | 6,174 | 603 |
| Royal Military Coll. of Canada (M) | Kingston, Ont....... | 1876 | Hon. L. A. Cadieux..... | 549 | 115 |
| St. Anne's............... | Church Pt., N. S.... | 1890 | Rev. Raymond Le Blanc | 163 | 24 |
| St. Dunstan's Univ.........(T) | Charlottetown, P.E.I... | 1855 | V. Rev. G. MacDonald.. | 1,015 | 70 |
| St. Francis Xavier Univ......(T) | Antigonish, N. S...... | 1853 | Rt. Rev. M. A. MacLellan | 2,507 | 125 |
| St. Louis.................. | Edmundston, N. B.... | 1946 | Rev. Louis Cyr....... | 678 | 45 |
| St. Mary's Univ............. | Halifax, Nova Scotia.. | 1841 | V. Rev. C.J. Fischer.... | 1,603 | 110 |
| St. Thomas Univ............. | Fredericton, N. B..... | 1910 | V. Rev. D. C. Duffie.... | 600 | 36 |
| Saskatchewan, Un. of.. (T) (Med) | Saskatoon, Sask...... | 1907 | J. W. T. Spinks........ | 15,455 | 900 |
| Sherbrooke, Univ. de.. (T) (Med) | Sherbrooke, Que...... | 1954 | Msgr. R. Maltais....... | 7,846 | 396 |
| Simon Fraser Univ...........(T) | Burnaby, B. C....... | 1965 | Patrick McTaggart..... | 5,185 | 726 |
| Sir George Williams Univ...... | Montreal, Que....... | 1926 | Fraser F. Fulton (Chan.) | 16,296 | 467 |
| Toronto, Univ. of..... (T) (Med) | Toronto, Ont....... | 1827 | Claude T. Bissell..... | 26,305 | 4,215 |
| Trent Univ............... | Peterborough, Ont.... | 1963 | T. H. Symons....... | 800 | 78 |
| Victoria, Univ. of........... | Victoria, B. C....... | 1903 | Vacant.............. | 4,075 | 274 |
| Waterloo Lutheran Univ........ | Waterloo, Ont...... | 1911 | W.R.MacDonald(Chan.) | 5,154 | 113 |
| Waterloo, Univ. of............ | Waterloo, Ont...... | 1957 | J. Gerald Hagey..... | 9,500 | 590 |
| West'n Ontario Un. of (Med) (T) | London, Ont....... | 1878 | D. C. Williams........ | 8,500 | 1,200 |
| Windsor, Univ. of.............. | Windsor, Ont........ | 1857 | John F. Leddy........ | 5,424 | 260 |
| York Univ................ | Toronto, Ont........ | 1960 | Murray G. Ross........ | 4,000 | 400 |

# American Field Service (AFS) International Scholarship Program

The American Field Service is a privately-sponsored, non-profit, non-sectarian, non-political organization which operates the world's largest international scholarship program for high school students.

The AFS was founded in 1914 as a volunteer ambulance service with the French Armies. Between the two World Wars, it sponsored a "Fellowships for French Universities" program, and in 1939, reorganized its ambulance corps with the Allied Armies. In 1946 it established its present international scholarship programs on the teenage level when it brought 52 students from 10 countries to the United States.

During 1967, AFS brought more than 3,000 high school students (ages 16-18) to the U.S.A. from 60 countries to participate wholeheartedly in the life of an American community where they attend a secondary school and live in carefully selected homes as members of their host families. During the same period more than 1,300 American students were sent overseas to 44 countries for a similar experience. Since 1947, some 42,712 students in 78 countries have participated in the AFS Scholarship programs.

A grass-roots organization, AFS is operated principally by volunteers worldwide, including 4,300 host families and 20,000 bus stop families who open their homes to students during the cross country trip at the end of the year. In each of the participating countries, there is a far-flung structure involving in-toto thousands of volunteers.

Many organizations as well as individuals contribute to the AFS scholarship programs. Schools have waived non-resident tuition, and other fees and host families welcome students without pay. Local chapters contribute approximately 50% of the funds to administer the AFS. Approximately 32% of the budget comes from the natural families whose payments are adjusted according to their financial resources. The balance of AFS support is dependent upon general fund raising in the United States and abroad.

Arthur Howe, Jr., is president of AFS, which has its international headquarters at 313 East 43rd Street, New York, N. Y. 10017.

---

## Government Publications and How to Get Them

The United States Government, through the Government Printing Office, issues a vast number of pamphlets, books and reports of studies and research conducted by departments and agencies. It has 335 periodicals or subscription services, with more than 1,231,000 subscribers. It sells about 72,000,000 publications annually and distributes many more to libraries and offices. Receipts are more than $16,000,000 and more than $7,000,000 is turned over annually to the U. S. Treasury.

Catalogues and price lists are available to the public. Pamphlets dealing with every conceivable subject related to human living—the farm, the home, child care, education, business, fiscal matters—are published regularly. A list of selected publications, issued biweekly, can be had free on request. In addition to free price lists, the Monthly Catalogue of Publications is sold by subscription, $6, foreign $7. Address the Supt. of Documents, Government Printing Office, Washington, D. C. 20402.

# Scholarships, Fellowships, and Other Financial Aid

Rising costs of higher tuition of colleges and universities have led more and more students to finance their education by summer jobs, part-time work on and off campus, loans, scholarships and fellowships.

Scholarships are usually outright grants to undergraduates, while fellowships are awarded to graduate students. Scholarships which may range from as little as $10 to as much as $3,000 annually are usually given to students of proven talent and need. Scholarship donors as a rule require applicants to answer questionnaires and to take talent tests.

To help assure that the available scholarships will go to those who deserve and need them, the College Scholarship Service was created 15 years ago as an agency of the College Entrance Examination Board. More than 1,450 of the nation's colleges and universities are served by this agency. The College Scholarship Service, Box 592, Princeton, N. J., and for residents of the Western states Box 1025, Berkeley, Calif. 94701, requires parents to answer a confidential questionnaire on finances.

**National Defense Student Loan Program**—is a program of long-term low-interest student loans, administered by the participating colleges. The Federal Government contributes 90% of the total amount of each institutional loan fund. Eligibility is based upon the financial needs of the student although preference is given to students with superior academic backgrounds. The amount of the loan cannot exceed $1,000 for any one undergraduate academic year (up to $5,000), or $2,500 for any graduate academic year (up to $10,000). Repayment of the loan must begin 9 months after the borrower is graduated or leaves the school, and may be extended over a 10-year period, except that the institution may require a repayment of no less than $15 a month. An interest charge of 3% is in effect during the repaying period. No repayment is required during those periods when the borrower is serving in the Armed Forces, the Peace Corps, or as a Volunteer in Service to America (VISTA), providing such periods do not exceed 3 years. If a borrower should become a full-time teacher, as much as half of the loan may be forgiven at the rate of 10% for each year of teaching service. Borrowers who elect to teach in certain eligible schools located in areas of primarily low-income families or who teach handicapped children may qualify for cancellation of their entire obligation at the rate of 15% per year. A student should address his inquiry concerning the program to the appropriate official (usually the Director of Admissions) of the institution in which he expects to enroll.

**The Guaranteed Student Loan Programs**—Banks, savings and loan associations, insurance companies, credit unions and similar supervised lending institutions may be lenders under this program. The program may vary from state to state but generally the maximum amount borrowed will range from $1,000 to $1,500. The Federal Government pays the lender the total interest while the student is in school, and 3 percent on the unpaid balance during the repayment period after the student has withdrawn or graduated. The program is designed to make it possible for students to borrow money for educational expenses in college or in nursing, business, trade, technical or other vocational schools. The loans are guaranteed by State or private nonprofit agencies, or in some states by the Federal government. Students should contact the financial aid officer at their schools for further details.

**The College Work-Study Program**—is designed to help students, particularly those from low income families, who need jobs to meet college expenses. Students may work up to 15 hours weekly while attending classes full time and 40 hours weekly during summer and vacation periods. Work may be for the institution or for an approved off-campus agency. To be eligible, a student must be enrolled and be in good standing, or be accepted for enrollment as a full-time student, at a college which participates in the program.

**The Educational Opportunity Grants Program** —Colleges participating in this program select the recipients of this program and also determine the amount of the grant. Grants range from $200 to $800 for each year of undergraduate study, but can be no more than one-half of the total assistance given the student. As an academic incentive to students, an additional award of $200 may be given to those students who were in the upper half of their college class during the preceding academic year.

**National Merit Scholarship Program**—The Natl. Merit Scholarship Corp., estab. in 1955 with grants from the Ford Foundation and the Carnegie Corp. of N. Y., awards over 2,400 scholarships annually to students who demonstrate extraordinary ability to benefit from a college education. Students may participate in the Natl. Merit Scholarship Program through their high schools. They become eligible by taking the Qualifying Test. Top scorers take a second examination, the Scholastic Aptitude Test of the College Entrance Examination Board and have to submit biographical and financial information. Scholarships range from $100 to $1,500 a year, depending on needs.

**General Motors Scholarship Plan**—Another contributor of a large number of scholarships is the General Motors Corp. Under the General Motors Scholarship plan, about 300 4-year undergraduate scholarships for any field of study are awarded annually to entering freshmen by over 200 participating institutions throughout the nation. Scholarships range from $200 to $2,000 per year depending upon need. Applications are made through the directors of admission of participating colleges.

**Fulbright-Hays Scholarships**—As part of an international educational exchange program, the U. S. Government, under the Fulbright-Hays Act provides scholarships for graduate study, research, lecturing and teaching abroad. There are full grants that cover transportation, tuition, books, living expenses and other costs, and there are grants which cover travel costs, with tuition and other expenses fully or partly paid by foreign governments, universities, and other institutions.

Detailed information on these exchange grants may be obtained from the Fulbright Program Adviser at college and university campuses. Persons not currently enrolled at an institution of higher learning should contact one of the following agencies:

a) For graduate study and pre-doctoral research —Institute of International Education, 809 United Nations Plaza, New York, N. Y. 10017.

b) For teaching in elementary and secondary schools—U. S. Office of Education, Bureau of International Education, Dept. of Health, Education & Welfare, Washington, D. C. 20202.

c) For university lecturing and post-doctoral research—Conference Board of Associated Research Councils, Committee on Intl. Exchange of Persons, 2101 Constitution Ave., Washington D. C. 20418.

**Rhodes Scholarships for Study at Oxford**—Thirty-two qualified American students, regardless of race or religion, are chosen every year to receive Rhodes Scholarships for a minimum of two years of study at Oxford University. Rhodes Scholarships, estab. under the will of Cecil John Rhodes, carry a stipend of approximately £1,500 a year. At Oxford work may be done in any field of study for which the university awards a degree. Applicants must be male, unmarried U. S. citizens, 18 to 24 years of age at the time of application, and with at least junior standing at a recognized degree-granting college or university at time of application. Information may be obtained from President Courtney Smith, American Secretary of the Rhodes Scholarships, Swarthmore College, Swarthmore, Pa. 19081.

**American Academy in Rome Prize Fellowships**—The American Academy in Rome, estab. 1894, chartered 1905 by Act of Congress, offers a limited number of fellowships to young American artists and scholars capable of doing independent creative work or research in architecture, landscape architecture, musical composition, painting, sculpture, history of art and classical studies. Fellowships are awarded for one year with a possibility of renewal. A fellowship consists of a grant of $3,650 a year, studio or study, and residence at the Academy. Information may be obtained from the American Academy in Rome, 101 Park Avenue, New York, N. Y. 10017.

# Public Libraries in Selected American Cities

Source: United States Office of Education

| City | No. of volumes | Circulation | Cost of operation | City | No. of volumes | Circulation | Cost of operation |
|---|---|---|---|---|---|---|---|
| Akron, Ohio | 602,781 | 2,067,608 | $1,387,554 | Mobile, Ala. | 201,970 | 668,341 | $ 393,540 |
| Albany, N.Y. | 521,543 | 1,307,118 | 740,083 | Montgomery, Ala. | 122,773 | 426,644 | 113,926 |
| Albuquerque, N.M. | 247,364 | 953,107 | 347,948 | Nashville, Tenn. | 244,624 | 827,079 | 648,320 |
| Allentown, Pa. | 125,608 | 383,029 | 228,675 | Newark, N.J. | 914,684 | 2,226,108 | 2,256,190 |
| Anaheim, Calif. | 148,799 | 824,379 | 593,460 | New Bedford, Mass. | 296,481 | 591,135 | 285,412 |
| Atlanta, Ga. | 700,051 | 2,282,278 | 1,011,903 | New Haven, Conn. | 396,216 | 580,031 | 533,175 |
| Austin, Texas | 210,507 | 1,278,121 | 499,820 | New Orleans, La. | 500,933 | 997,390 | 999,987 |
| Baltimore, Md. | 1,761,023 | 4,559,195 | 3,954,881 | New York, N.Y. | | | |
| Baton Rouge, La. | 179,161 | 709,618 | 312,276 | Public Library | | | |
| Berkeley, Calif. | 279,575 | 892,058 | 501,272 | Circulation | 17,490,650 | 12,644,518 | 15,631,396 |
| Birmingham, Ala. | 696,673 | 3,342,750 | 785,140 | Reference | | | |
| Boston, Mass. | 2,306,711 | 3,104,217 | 4,050,400 | Brooklyn | 2,604,112 | 10,147,116 | 8,217,236 |
| Bridgeport, Conn. | 444,911 | 980,713 | 550,449 | Queens | 2,084,997 | 8,721,818 | 7,484,741 |
| Buffalo, N.Y. | 2,120,020 | 6,800,210 | 4,413,900 | Norfolk, Va. | 265,876 | 838,328 | 592,144 |
| Cambridge, Mass. | 232,851 | 630,061 | 359,510 | Oakland, Calif. | 659,205 | 1,676,863 | 1,804,161 |
| Camden, N.J. | 105,728 | 169,434 | 215,787 | Oklahoma City | 268,218 | 1,003,588 | 573,225 |
| Canton, Ohio | 399,583 | 1,847,569 | 578,477 | Omaha, Nebr. | 369,950 | 1,468,944 | 613,562 |
| Charlotte, N.C. | 398,555 | 1,230,401 | 608,720 | Pasadena, Calif. | 362,172 | 1,168,911 | 848,023 |
| Chattanooga, Tenn. | 174,888 | 469,562 | 265,430 | Paterson, N.J. | 240,778 | 496,217 | 318,216 |
| Chicago, Ill. | 3,124,686 | 10,342,771 | 7,585,030 | Peoria, Ill. | 331,886 | 745,792 | 495,304 |
| Cincinnati, Ohio | 2,344,166 | 5,719,402 | 3,197,689 | Philadelphia, Pa. | 2,408,341 | 6,664,745 | 6,212,870 |
| Cleveland, Ohio | 3,305,759 | 7,450,466 | 5,624,924 | Phoenix, Ariz. | 815,590 | 1,791,395 | 949,748 |
| Columbus, Ohio | 785,299 | 2,795,962 | 2,033,140 | Pittsburgh, Pa. | 1,900,014 | 4,340,201 | 3,243,349 |
| Corpus Christi, Tex. | 154,662 | 694,998 | 233,754 | Portland, Ore. | 896,917 | 3,504,963 | 1,849,660 |
| Dallas, Texas | 821,377 | 3,465,402 | 2,284,651 | Portsmouth, Va. | 46,479 | 222,835 | 133,451 |
| Dayton, Ohio | 957,492 | 3,606,321 | 1,501,323 | Providence, R.I. | 536,256 | 902,771 | 993,605 |
| Dearborn, Mich. | 218,005 | 744,010 | 483,051 | Richmond, Va. | 364,925 | 1,115,985 | 511,612 |
| Denver, Colo. | 965,754 | 3,057,244 | 1,827,677 | Rockford, Ill. | 213,826 | 1,008,568 | 571,022 |
| Des Moines, Iowa | 336,084 | 1,294,796 | 697,841 | Sacramento, Calif. | 455,273 | 1,105,950 | 669,158 |
| Detroit, Mich. | 2,057,905 | 4,653,065 | 5,572,347 | St. Louis, Mo. | 1,235,213 | 3,164,859 | 2,459,108 |
| Duluth, Minn. | 171,873 | 601,033 | 277,528 | St. Paul, Minn. | 659,349 | 2,277,368 | 1,198,765 |
| Elizabeth, N.J. | 248,932 | 458,583 | 488,111 | St. Petersburg, Fla. | 199,500 | 1,058,160 | 399,900 |
| Erie, Pa. | 263,014 | 633,145 | 226,206 | Salt Lake City | 380,832 | 886,400 | 590,849 |
| Evansville, Ind. | 359,781 | 1,264,217 | 499,452 | San Antonio, Tex. | 484,184 | 1,852,686 | 816,645 |
| Flint, Mich. | 292,062 | 1,337,703 | 855,612 | San Diego, Calif. | 753,838 | 3,174,329 | 1,531,909 |
| Fort Wayne, Ind. | 1,120,884 | 2,692,751 | 1,319,482 | San Francisco, Calif. | 1,008,935 | 3,400,476 | 2,909,046 |
| Fort Worth, Tex. | 459,011 | 1,080,222 | 620,000 | San Jose, Calif. | 286,570 | 2,195,820 | 723,126 |
| Gary, Ind. | 332,630 | 805,822 | 720,357 | Santa Ana, Calif. | 175,290 | 861,194 | 351,931 |
| Glendale, Calif. | 254,112 | 922,419 | 573,951 | Scranton, Pa. | 158,967 | 522,540 | 205,056 |
| Grand Rapids, Mich. | 502,909 | 985,731 | 508,282 | Seattle, Wash. | 1,243,891 | 3,904,684 | 2,425,145 |
| Hammond, Ind. | 230,153 | 1,109,758 | 340,855 | Shreveport, La. | 208,484 | 992,676 | 279,422 |
| Hartford, Conn. | 404,901 | 728,471 | 742,241 | South Bend, Ind. | 248,455 | 993,232 | 726,777 |
| Houston, Texas | 788,964 | 2,476,178 | 1,098,181 | Spokane, Wash. | 335,206 | 1,087,942 | 605,647 |
| Indianapolis, Ind. | 836,831 | 2,195,633 | 1,672,075 | Springfield, Mass. | 568,162 | 1,113,000 | 906,833 |
| Jacksonville, Fla. | 459,782 | 583,665 | 551,496 | Tacoma, Wash. | 442,660 | 1,135,691 | 685,016 |
| Jersey City, N.J. | 456,653 | 797,539 | 1,011,799 | Tampa, Fla. | 237,782 | 1,132,510 | 450,322 |
| Kansas City, Kans. | 108,222 | 305,242 | 220,539 | Toledo, Ohio | 865,472 | 2,351,326 | 1,341,561 |
| Kansas City, Mo. | 1,068,804 | 3,023,225 | 1,621,381 | Topeka, Kans. | 189,539 | 631,214 | 351,401 |
| Knoxville, Tenn. | 259,766 | 933,566 | 516,136 | Trenton, N.J. | 214,775 | 333,904 | 332,017 |
| Little Rock, Ark. | 157,619 | 356,427 | 188,165 | Tucson, Ariz. | 233,942 | 1,053,476 | 583,370 |
| Long Beach, Calif. | 449,447 | 2,146,306 | 1,262,778 | Tulsa, Okla. | 449,657 | 1,932,693 | 997,408 |
| Los Angeles, Calif. | 3,189,122 | 14,022,126 | 8,195,646 | Washington, D.C. | 1,552,280 | 2,858,583 | 4,060,500 |
| Louisville, Ky. | 774,328 | 1,848,919 | 1,395,110 | Waterbury, Conn. | 168,283 | 328,959 | 285,676 |
| Lubbock, Texas | 87,920 | 441,278 | 85,748 | Wichita, Kans. | 240,027 | 1,006,108 | 462,142 |
| Madison, Wis. | 200,300 | 943,849 | 607,179 | Wichita Falls, Tex. | 74,219 | 156,951 | 77,527 |
| Memphis, Tenn. | 607,946 | 3,245,666 | 1,151,364 | Wilmington, Del. | 345,223 | 965,999 | 484,051 |
| Miami, Fla. | 429,269 | 1,284,619 | 1,396,201 | Worcester, Mass. | 569,503 | 894,083 | 1,261,529 |
| Milwaukee, Wis. | 1,754,359 | 4,258,216 | 3,040,260 | Youngstown, Ohio | 518,183 | 1,473,085 | 945,160 |
| Minneapolis, Minn. | 1,029,698 | 2,410,526 | 2,250,826 | | | | |

# 50 Leading U. S. Academic Libraries

Source: U. S. Office of Education

Data for 1965-1966

| Name | Total Volumes | Volumes Added | Expenditures | Name | Total Volumes | Volumes Added | Expenditures |
|---|---|---|---|---|---|---|---|
| Harvard U. | 7,600,357 | 208,534 | $6,728,455 | U. of Iowa | 1,284,836 | 63,762 | $1,587,514 |
| Yale U. | 4,826,148 | 128,281 | 4,153,155 | U. of Va. | 1,288,634 | 67,837 | 1,145,956 |
| U. of Ill. | 4,083,634 | 197,190 | 4,209,478 | Rutgers U. | 1,289,554 | 85,993 | 1,539,362 |
| Columbia U. | 3,675,920 | 121,894 | 3,434,419 | U. of Mo. | 1,656,935 | 94,950 | 1,735,998 |
| U. of Mich. | 3,516,355 | 142,859 | 4,528,331 | Mich. State U. | 1,224,528 | 80,840 | 1,661,925 |
| U. of Calif. (Berkeley) | 3,179,633 | 155,175 | 4,588,759 | Wayne State U. | 992,242 | 64,798 | 1,866,213 |
| Cornell U. | 2,892,539 | 171,012 | 3,412,034 | U. of So. Calif. | 1,192,040 | 57,331 | 1,284,699 |
| Stanford U. | 2,764,211 | 177,684 | 4,413,683 | U. of Kan. | 1,122,158 | 54,417 | 1,230,833 |
| U. of Chicago | 2,437,717 | 120,489 | 2,468,913 | Brown U. | 1,150,052 | 40,310 | 1,212,534 |
| U. of Minn. | 2,480,097 | 109,758 | 2,534,361 | U. of Fla. | 1,117,711 | 62,592 | 1,493,375 |
| U. of Calif. (L. A.) | 2,333,442 | 142,002 | 4,132,807 | U. of Ky. | 1,131,070 | 63,115 | 1,234,484 |
| U. of Pa. | 1,958,602 | 72,954 | 1,736,979 | U. of Ore. | 1,112,743 | 58,710 | 1,069,332 |
| Ind. U. | 1,943,256 | 171,356 | 2,515,462 | U. of Okla. | 1,012,093 | 36,706 | 736,318 |
| Princeton U. | 1,846,776 | 78,473 | 892,571 | M. I. T. | 900,468 | 79,723 | 1,430,108 |
| Ohio State U. | 1,845,069 | 99,926 | 2,058,193 | Joint U. Lib. (Nashville) | 995,839 | 50,340 | 995,912 |
| U. of Texas | 1,838,645 | 115,836 | 2,237,895 | U. of Colo. | 1,011,533 | 68,198 | 1,451,715 |
| Duke U. | 1,783,803 | 71,706 | 1,565,067 | U. of Pittsburgh | 997,896 | 71,316 | 1,106,984 |
| Northwestern U. | 1,771,899 | 65,605 | 1,723,632 | Tulane U. | 950,710 | 33,291 | 902,311 |
| U. of Wis. | 2,147,885 | 187,612 | 4,138,761 | Dartmouth Coll. | 924,396 | 24,022 | 732,445 |
| New York U. | 1,387,885 | 81,427 | 1,992,424 | U. of Cincinnati | 905,047 | 19,582 | 652,476 |
| Johns Hopkins U. | 1,500,510 | 100,998 | 1,014,123 | U. of Rochester | 906,410 | 51,484 | 1,244,339 |
| U. of Wash. (Seattle) | 1,466,906 | 78,522 | 3,112,009 | Wash. U. (St. L.) | 936,754 | 83,131 | 1,707,209 |
| U. of N. C. | 1,385,234 | 70,962 | 1,558,236 | U. of Utah | 924,381 | 75,906 | 898,472 |
| La. State U. & A & M Col. | 1,410,760 | 84,423 | 1,817,945 | Wash. State U. | 879,094 | 29,094 | 1,024,544 |
| | | | | West. Reserve U. | 864,885 | 26,309 | 691,019 |
| | | | | U. of Ariz. | 858,067 | 64,643 | 943,700 |

# Fall Enrollment and Teachers in Full Time Day Schools

### PUBLIC ELEMENTARY AND SECONDARY DAY SCHOOLS 1967
#### Source: United States Office of Education

| Region and state | Pupils enrolled | | Teachers[1] | |
|---|---|---|---|---|
| | Elementary | Secondary | Elementary | Secondary |
| **Total United States**............... | **43,886,805** | | **1,854,700** | |
| **(50 states and D. C.)**............... | **27,381,259** | **16,505,546** | **1,040,160** | **814,540** |
| **North Atlantic**................... | **6,122,697** | **4,243,863** | **253,431** | **221,589** |
| Connecticut....................... | 400,228 | 214,280 | 16,920 | 12,019 |
| Delaware......................... | 66,354 | 51,124 | 2,608 | 2,566 |
| Maine............................ | 168,876 | 59,950 | 7,186 | 3,688 |
| Maryland......................... | 479,730 | 346,162 | 19,388 | 16,701 |
| Baltimore...................... | 120,149 | 72,396 | 4,926 | 3,968 |
| Massachusetts.................... | 614,660 | 465,137 | 25,551 | 21,914 |
| Boston......................... | 57,022 | 36,314 | 2,272 | 1,606 |
| New Hampshire................... | 84,433 | 54,064 | 3,635 | 2,758 |
| New Jersey....................... | 905,084 | 472,560 | 36,614 | 25,880 |
| New York......................... | 1,903,900 | 1,417,200 | 83,200 | 78,700 |
| New York City.................. | 626,200 | 468,600 | 27,900 | 25,800 |
| Pennsylvania..................... | 1,241,800 | 1,014,200 | 48,436 | 49,056 |
| Philadelphia................... | 171,860 | 120,497 | 6,248 | 5,457 |
| Rhode Island..................... | 95,424 | 71,751 | 3,643 | 3,642 |
| Vermont.......................... | 66,481 | 24,012 | 2,500 | 2,000 |
| District of Columbia............. | 95,727 | 53,423 | 3,750 | 2,665 |
| **Great Lakes and Plains**........... | **7,961,590** | **4,429,466** | **299,999** | **231,984** |
| Illinois.......................... | 1,442,494 | 772,834 | 59,103 | 39,839 |
| Chicago....................... | 420,610 | 132,728 | 15,504 | 6,603 |
| Indiana.......................... | 720,778 | 460,662 | 26,643 | 21,724 |
| Iowa............................. | 359,479 | 284,479 | 17,303 | 13,800 |
| Kansas........................... | 371,130 | 149,626 | 14,046 | 10,671 |
| Michigan......................... | 1,188,000 | 854,000 | 42,200 | 40,000 |
| Detroit[2]....................... | 183,771 | 114,256 | 6,037 | 4,362 |
| Minnesota........................ | 476,267 | 387,168 | 18,679 | 19,558 |
| Missouri......................... | 741,662 | 260,877 | 26,450 | 13,774 |
| St. Louis...................... | 92,417 | 24,378 | 3,089 | 1,069 |
| Nebraska......................... | 194,542 | 131,827 | 8,882 | 7,175 |
| North Dakota..................... | 94,181 | 53,663 | 4,334 | 3,154 |
| Ohio............................. | 1,706,540 | 652,360 | 53,560 | 38,600 |
| Cleveland[2].................... | 93,127 | 59,805 | 3,169 | 2,248 |
| South Dakota..................... | 117,850 | 49,606 | 6,143 | 3,214 |
| Wisconsin........................ | 548,668 | 372,364 | 22,656 | 20,475 |
| Milwaukee...................... | 78,309 | 50,099 | 2,502 | 2,276 |
| **Southeast**....................... | **6,105,962** | **3,826,222** | **226,599** | **166,257** |
| Alabama.......................... | 456,469 | 374,416 | 16,300 | 15,700 |
| Arkansas......................... | 249,760 | 201,722 | 9,870 | 9,184 |
| Florida.......................... | 721,039 | 575,915 | 28,025 | 24,886 |
| Georgia.......................... | 709,079 | 377,802 | 25,587 | 16,062 |
| Kentucky......................... | 447,544 | 339,807 | 17,282 | 10,892 |
| Louisiana........................ | 511,250 | 329,064 | 19,827 | 14,663 |
| New Orleans.................... | 67,312 | 42,372 | 2,324 | 1,948 |
| Mississippi...................... | 346,447 | 236,141 | 11,660 | 9,370 |
| North Carolina................... | 852,841 | 340,426 | 32,515 | 15,440 |
| South Carolina................... | 386,110 | 260,797 | 13,785 | 11,541 |
| Tennessee........................ | 563,816 | 310,517 | 19,620 | 12,630 |
| Virginia......................... | 628,674 | 393,620 | 23,550 | 18,889 |
| West Virginia.................... | 232,933 | 182,995 | 8,578 | 7,000 |
| **West and Southwest**.............. | **7,191,009** | **4,005,995** | **260,131** | **194,710** |
| Alaska........................... | 47,050 | 18,701 | 1,886 | 1,184 |
| Arizona.......................... | 289,500 | 109,950 | 12,049 | 4,132 |
| California....................... | 2,849,275 | 1,616,991 | 101,540 | 70,560 |
| Los Angeles.................... | 372,148 | 272,911 | 13,190 | 10,989 |
| San Francisco.................. | 52,387 | 42,147 | 1,817 | 1,950 |
| Colorado......................... | 295,523 | 214,801 | 12,282 | 11,023 |
| Hawaii........................... | 97,696 | 71,734 | 3,980 | 2,690 |
| Idaho............................ | 91,709 | 84,395 | 3,656 | 3,987 |
| Montana.......................... | 110,005 | 61,801 | 5,354 | 2,790 |
| Nevada........................... | 69,279 | 42,474 | 2,800 | 1,965 |
| New Mexico....................... | 151,875 | 119,470 | 6,119 | 5,218 |
| Oklahoma......................... | 338,884 | 254,233 | 13,467 | 12,519 |
| Oregon........................... | 276,777 | 186,151 | 12,596 | 9,806 |
| Texas............................ | 1,917,555 | 716,030 | 59,500 | 47,500 |
| Dallas......................... | 93,289 | 64,549 | 3,218 | 2,485 |
| Houston........................ | 149,139 | 91,634 | 5,302 | 3,827 |
| Utah............................. | 170,434 | 127,280 | 5,840 | 5,170 |
| Washington....................... | 436,958 | 344,907 | 16,800 | 14,250 |
| Wyoming.......................... | 48,489 | 37,077 | 2,262 | 2,116 |
| **Outlying areas:** | | | | |
| American Samoa................... | 6,115 | 1,884 | 262 | 88 |
| Canal Zone....................... | 8,169 | 5,697 | 335 | 250 |
| Guam............................. | 11,612 | 7,572 | 429 | 346 |
| Puerto Rico...................... | 427,448 | 227,314 | 12,614 | 9,296 |
| Virgin Islands................... | 7,586 | 3,859 | 267 | 236 |
| Trust territory of the Pacific islands.. | 22,597 | 3,054 | 895 | 140 |

[1]Full-time and Part-time Classroom Teachers.  [2]Data for fall 1966.

## Air Force Library Service

The Air Force library program is designed to support all the missions of the Air Force. This includes not only providing opportunity for the constructive use of leisure time, but also support for education and training programs and scientific and technical research requirements. Library service is worldwide. There are 224 main libraries and service centers. A total of 667 service units, including main libraries, branches and field collections are required to serve all Air Force personnel, whether on large Air Force bases or at small, remote or isolated sites. Over 6,095,568 volumes are in Air Force library collections. Annual book circulation is over 16,203,545. Reader services for 933,682 reference and bibliographic requests are provided each year. An annual library publicity contest is conducted.

## Cobwebs and Spider Webs

There is a popular but erroneous belief that cobwebs are merely dust. The fact is that cobweb means spider web, cob being an old English word for spider. Most cobwebs are the work of a little house spider whose handiwork usually goes unnoticed until it becomes covered with dust.

# The Principal Languages of the World

Total number of speakers of languages spoken by at least one million persons (Midyear 1968)
Parenthesized numbers after names of languages refer to notes below table
Source: Sidney S. Culbert, Assoc. Professor of Psychology, University of Washington

| Language | Millions |
|---|---|
| Afrikaans (S. Africa) | 4 |
| Albanian | 3 |
| Amharic (Ethiopia) | 8 |
| Arabic | 98 |
| Armenian | 4 |
| Assamese (1) (India) | 10 |
| Azerbaijani (USSR; Iran) | 7 |
| Bahasa Indonesia (see Malay-Indonesian) | |
| Balinese | |
| Baluchi (Pakistan; Iran) | 2 |
| Bashkir (USSR) | 1 |
| Batak (Indonesia) | 1 |
| Bengali (1) (India; Pakistan) | 98 |
| Berber (2) (N. Africa) | |
| Bhili (India) | 4 |
| Bihari (India) | 18 |
| Bikol (Philippines) | 2 |
| Bisaya (see Cebuano, Panay-Hiligaynon, and Samar-Leyte) | |
| Bugi (Indonesia) | 1 |
| Bulgarian | 8 |
| Burmese | 19 |
| Byelorussian (mainly USSR) | 10 |
| Cambodian (Cambodia, Asia) | 4 |
| Cantonese (China) | 45 |
| Catalan (Spain; France; Andorra) | 5 |
| Cebuano (Philippines) | 8 |
| Chinese (3) | |
| Chuvash (USSR) | 1 |
| Czech | 10 |
| Danish | 5 |
| Dayak (Borneo) | 1 |
| Dutch (see Netherlandish) | |
| Efik | 1 |
| English | 314 |
| Esperanto | 1 |
| Estonian | 1 |
| Ewe (W. Africa) | 1 |
| Fang-Bulu (W. Africa) | 1 |
| Finnish | 5 |
| Flemish (see Netherlandish) | |
| French | 75 |
| Fula (W. Africa) | 6 |
| Galician (Spain) | 2 |
| Galla (Ethiopia) | 5 |
| Ganda (or Luganda) (Africa) | 3 |
| Georgian (USSR) | 3 |
| German | 120 |
| Gondi (India) | 2 |
| Greek | 10 |
| Guarani (mainly Paraguay) | 2 |
| Gujarati (1) (India) | 25 |
| Hakka (China) | 20 |
| Hausa (W. and Central Africa) | 14 |
| Hebrew | 3 |
| Hindi (1) (4) | 181 |
| Hindustani (4) | |
| Hungarian (or Magyar) | 13 |
| Ibibio (see Efik) | |
| Ibo (or Igbo) (W. Africa) | 6 |
| Ilocano (Philippines) | 4 |
| Italian | 58 |
| Japanese | 102 |
| Javanese | 42 |
| Kanarese (see Kannada) | |
| Kannada (1) (India) | 24 |
| Kanuri (W. and Cent. Africa) | 1 |
| Kashmiri (1) | 3 |
| Kazakh (USSR) | 5 |
| Khalkha (Mongolia) | 1 |
| Kikongo (see Kongo) | |
| Kikuyu (Kenya, Africa) | 1 |
| Kimbundu (Angola, Africa) | 1 |
| Kirghiz (USSR) | 2 |
| Kituba (Congo) | 1 |
| Kongo (Congo) | 1 |
| Konkani (India) | 2 |
| Korean | 43 |
| Kumauni (India) | 1 |
| Kurdish (S. W. of Caspian Sea) | 6 |
| Kurukh (or Oraon) (India) | 1 |
| Lao (Laos, Asia) | 2 |
| Latvian (or Lettish) | 2 |
| Lingala (see Ngala) | |
| Lithuanian | 3 |
| Luba-Lulua (Dem. Rep. Congo) | 6 |
| Luganda (see Ganda) | |
| Macedonian (Yugoslavia) | 1 |
| Madurese (Indonesia) | 7 |
| Makua (S. E. Africa) | 6 |
| Malagasy (Madagascar) | 6 |
| Malay-Indonesian | 80 |
| Malayalam (1) (India) | 20 |
| Malinke-Bambara-Diula (Africa) | 6 |
| Mandarin (China) | 567 |
| Marathi (1) India) | 43 |
| Min (China) | 37 |
| Mordvin (USSR) | 1 |
| Mossi (W. Africa) | 4 |
| Nepali (Nepal; India) | 10 |
| Netherlandish (Dutch and Flemish) | 19 |
| Ngala (or Lingala) (Africa) | 2 |
| Norwegian | 4 |
| Nyanja (S.-E. Africa) | 4 |
| Oraon (see Kurukh) | |
| Oriya (1) (India) | 20 |
| Panay-Hiligaynon (Philippines) | 4 |
| Panjabi (see Punjabi) | |
| Pashto (see Pushtu) | |
| Persian | 22 |
| Polish | 33 |
| Portuguese | 97 |
| Provençal (Southern France) | 7 |
| Punjabi (1) (India; Pakistan) | 41 |
| Pushtu (mainly Afghanistan) | 13 |
| Quechua (S. American) | 5 |
| Rajasthani (India) | 17 |
| Romanian | 20 |
| Rundi (S.-Central Africa) | 2 |
| Russian (Great Russian only) | 188 |
| Rwanda (S.-Central Africa) | 6 |
| Samar-Leyte (Philippines) | 1 |
| Santali (India) | 4 |
| Serbo-Croatian (Yugoslavia) | 17 |
| Shona (S.E. Africa) | 1 |
| Siamese (see Thai) | |
| Sindhi (India; Pakistan) | 8 |
| Sinhalese (Ceylon) | 9 |
| Slovak | 4 |
| Slovene (Yugoslavia) | 2 |
| Somali (E. Africa) | 3 |
| Sotho, Northern (S. Africa) | 2 |
| Sotho, Southern (S. Africa) | 2 |
| Spanish | 179 |
| Sundanese (Indonesia) | 13 |
| Swahili (E. Africa) | 12 |
| Swedish | 9 |
| Tagalog (Philippines) | 17 |
| Tajiki (USSR) | 2 |
| Tamil (1) (India; Ceylon) | 45 |
| Tatar (or Kazan-Turkic) (USSR) | 5 |
| Telugu (1) (India) | 48 |
| Thai | 26 |
| Tibetan | 7 |
| Tswana (S. Africa) | 1 |
| Tulu (India) | 1 |
| Turkish | 36 |
| Turkoman (USSR) | 2 |
| Twi-Fante (or Akan) (W. Africa) | 4 |
| Uighur (Sinkiang, China) | 4 |
| Ukrainian (mainly USSR) | 41 |
| Umbundu (Angola, Africa) | 2 |
| Urdu (1) (Pakistan; India) | 55 |
| Uzbek (USSR) | 7 |
| Vietnamese | 32 |
| Visayan (see Cebuano, Panay-Hilligaynon, and Samar-Leyte) | |
| White Russian (see Byelorussian) | |
| Wu (China) | 40 |
| Xhosa (S. Africa) | 4 |
| Yiddish (5) | |
| Yoruba (W. Africa) | 5 |
| Zulu (S. Africa) | 4 |

(1) One of the fourteen languages of the Constitution of India. (2) Here considered a group of dialects. (3) See Mandarin, Cantonese, Wu, Min, and Hakka. The "national language" (kuo-yü) is a standardized form of Mandarin as spoken in the area of Peking. (4) Hindi and Urdu are essentially the same language, Hindustani. As the official language of India it is written in the Devanagari script and called Hindi. As one of the two official languages of Pakistan (the other is Bengali), it is written in a modified Arabic script and called Urdu. (5) Yiddish is usually considered a variant of German, though it has its own standard grammar, dictionaries, a highly developed literature, and is written in Hebrew characters. Speakers number about 3,000,000.

## National Spelling Bee Champions

The National Spelling Bee, conducted by Scripps-Howard Newspapers and other newspapers since 1939, was instituted by the Louisville (Ky.) Courier-Journal in 1925. Children under 16 years of age sponsored by participating newspapers are eligible to compete for the cash prizes and prize trips. Recent winners are:

1966—1, Robert A. Wake, 13, Houston, Tex. (Houston Chronicle); 2, Beth Sherrill, 14, Millington, Tenn. (Memphis Press-Scimitar); 3, Sonya Gilliam, 13, Lubbock, Tex. (Lubbock Avalanche-Journal).

1967—1, Jennifer Reinke, 14, Deshler, Neb. (The Omaha World-Herald). 2, Anne Clark, 14, Huntington, W. Va. (The Herald-Dispatch). 3, Milene Henley, 14, Houston, Tex. (The Houston Chronicle).

1968—1, Robert L. Walters, 14, Russell, Kan. (Topeka Daily Capital). 2, Ann Johnson, 13, Richfield, Minn. (Minneapolis Tribune). 3, Stephen Bacher, 14, Middle Village, Queens, N. Y. (N. Y. Daily News).

## How to Obtain Birth, Marriage, Death Records

The United States Government has published a series of inexpensive booklets entitled Where to Write for Birth & Death Records; Where to Write for Marriage Records; Where to Write for Divorce Records; Where to Write for Birth and Death Records of U. S. Citizens who were born or died outside of the U. S. and birth certifications for alien children adopted by U. S. citizens; How to obtain death certificates in each state; How to obtain birth certificates, table showing where to apply for birth certificates in each State; Marriage and divorce registration; You May Save Time Proving Your Age and Other Birth Facts. They tell where to write to get a certified copy of or original vital record. Supt. of Documents, Government Printing Office, Washington, D. C. 20402.

# Forms of Address for Persons of Rank and Public Office

In these examples John Smith is used as a representative American name. The salutation Dear Sir is always permissible when addressing a person not known to the writer.

## PRESIDENT OF THE UNITED STATES

Address: The President, The White House, Washington, D. C. Also, The President and Mrs. —. Salutation: Dear Sir or Mr. President or Dear Mr. President. More intimately: My dear Mr. President. Also: Dear Mr. President and Mrs. The Vice President takes the same forms as President.

## CABINET OFFICERS

Address: Mr. John Smith, Secretary of State, Washington, D. C., or The Hon. John Smith. Similar addresses for other members of the Cabinet. Also: Secretary and Mrs. John Smith. Salutation: Dear Sir, or Dear Mr. Secretary. Also: Dear Mr. and Mrs. Smith.

## THE BENCH

Address: The Hon. John Smith, Chief Justice of the United States. The Hon. John Smith, Associate Justice of the Supreme Court of the United States. The Hon. John Smith, Associate Judge, U. S. District Court. Salutations: Dear Sir or Dear Mr. Chief Justice. Dear Mr. Justice. Dear Judge Smith.

## MEMBERS OF CONGRESS

Address: The Hon. John Smith, United States Senate, Washington, D. C. Or Sen. John Smith, etc. Also The Hon. John Smith, House of Representatives, Washington, D. C. Or Rep. John Smith, etc. Salutation: Dear Mr. Senator, Dear Mr. Representative, or more generally, Dear Mr. Smith. A Representative is sometimes addressed colloquially as Congressman.

## OFFICERS OF ARMY AND NAVY

Address: Careful attention should be given to the precise rank, thus: General of the Army Douglas MacArthur; Fleet Admiral Chester W. Nimitz. Also Brigadier General John Smith, United States Army, or abbreviated, Brig. General John Smith, USA, or Captain (Capt.) John Smith, USN. If he is retired, Rtd. is added.

Salutation: Dear Sir, or Dear General. All general officers, whatever rank, are entitled to be addressed as generals. Likewise a lieutenant colonel is addressed as colonel and first and second lieutenants are addressed as lieutenant.

Warrant officers and flight officers are addressed as Mister. Chaplains are addressed as Father. A Catholic chaplain may be addressed as Father. Cadets of the United States Military Academy and Air Force Academy are addressed as Cadet. Noncommissioned officers are addressed by their titles. In the U. S. Navy all men from midshipman at Annapolis up to and including Lieut. Commander are addressed as Mister.

## AMBASSADOR, GOVERNOR, MAYOR

Address: The Hon. John Smith, followed by his title. He can be addressed either at his embassy, or at the Department of State, Washington, D. C. A foreign ambassador is His Excellency. Salutation: Dear Mr. Ambassador. A foreign ambassador is Your Excellency.

Governors and Mayors are often addressed as The Hon. John Smith, Governor of ———, or The Hon. John Smith, Mayor of ———; also Governor John Smith, State House, Albany, N. Y., or Mayor John Smith, City Hall, Erie, Pa.

## THE CLERGY

Address: His Holiness, the Pope, or His Holiness Pope (name), State of Vatican City, Italy. Salutation: Your Holiness or Most Holy Father. Also: His Eminence, John, Cardinal Smith; salutation: Your Eminence. An archbishop or a bishop is addressed The Most Reverend, and the salutation is Your Excellency. A monsignor who is a papal chamberlain is The Very Reverend Monsignor and saluted as Very Reverend Monsignor; a monsignor who is a domestic prelate is The Right Reverend Monsignor and salutation is Right Reverend Monsignor. A priest is addressed Reverend John Smith, and saluted as Reverend Father, or Dear Reverend Father. A Brother of an order is addressed Brother ———, and saluted Dear Brother ———. A Sister takes the same form.

A bishop of the Protestant Episcopal Church is The Right Reverend John Smith; salutation is Right Reverend Sir, or Dear Bishop Smith. If a clergyman is a Doctor of Divinity, he is addressed: The Reverend John Smith, D. D., and the salutation is Reverend Sir, or Dear Dr. Smith. When a clergyman does not have the degree the salutation is Dear Mr. Smith.

A bishop of the Methodist Church is addressed Bishop John Smith with titles following, and saluted as Dear Bishop Smith.

## ROYALTY AND NOBILITY

An Emperor is to be addressed in a letter as Sir, or Your Imperial Majesty.

A King or Queen is addressed as His Majesty (Name), King of (Name), or Her Majesty (Name), Queen of (Name). Salutation: Sir, or Madam, or May it please Your Majesty.

Princes and Princesses and other persons of royal blood are addressed as His (or Her) Royal Highness, and saluted with May it please Your Royal Highness.

A Duke or Marquis is My Lord Duke (or Marquis), a Duke is His (or Your) Grace.

Wives of any peer may be addressed as Madam, with the further alternative of Your Ladyship, or Your Grace, if she is of high rank.

# Vocational Education

Source: United States Office of Education

All Federal funds expended for vocational education are matched by state and local funds. This does not include expenditures for plant and equipment for vocational schools, for which Federal funds cannot be used.

## ENROLLMENT IN FEDERALLY AIDED VOCATIONAL CLASSES

| Year | Total* | Agri. | Trade | Econ. | Year | Total* | Agri. | Trade | Econ. |
|---|---|---|---|---|---|---|---|---|---|
| 1935 | 1,178,896 | 325,685 | 503,865 | 349,346 | 1960 | 3,768,149 | 796,237 | 938,490 | 1,588,109 |
| 1940 | 2,290,741 | 584,133 | 758,409 | 818,766 | 1964 | 4,566,399 | 860,605 | 1,069,274 | 2,022,138 |
| 1945 | 2,012,931 | 446,953 | 522,733 * 890,464 | | 1965 | 5,430,611 | 887,529 | 1,087,807 | 2,098,520 |
| 1950 | 3,364,613 | 764,975 | 804,602 | 1,430,366 | 1966 | 6,070,059 | 907,354 | 1,269,051 | 1,897,670 |
| 1955 | 3,314,255 | 776,138 | 870,954 | 1,431,808 | 1967 (prel.) | 7,002,598 | 951,972 | 1,439,046 | 2,179,356 |

*Total figures since 1957 include enrollment for health occupations—(1966) 83,677; (1967 prel.) 114,652. Total figures since 1965 include enrollment for office occupations—(1966) 1,238,043; (1967 prel.) 1,568,197.

Total figures since 1959 include enrollment for technical education—(1967 prel.) 268,174.

## ENROLLMENT IN FEDERALLY AIDED VOCATIONAL CLASSES BY STATES

Fiscal Year 1967 Provisional figures

| State | Enroll. | State | Enroll. | State | Enroll. | State | Enroll. |
|---|---|---|---|---|---|---|---|
| Alabama | 126,574 | Indiana | 81,711 | Nevada | 17,939 | Tennessee | 124,688 |
| Alaska | 6,103 | Iowa | 80,394 | N. Hampshire. | 10,879 | Texas | 363,558 |
| Arizona | 50,739 | Kansas | 57,032 | New Jersey | 175,171 | Utah | 62,995 |
| Arkansas | 91,519 | Kentucky | 94,903 | New Mexico | 22,390 | Vermont | 9,774 |
| California | 951,862 | Louisiana | 121,915 | New York | 595,980 | Virginia | 197,363 |
| Colorado | 78,025 | Maine | 21,582 | N. Carolina | 271,098 | Washington | 210,067 |
| Connecticut | 90,593 | Maryland | 157,991 | N. Dakota | 20,656 | West Virginia. | 49,834 |
| Delaware | 17,323 | Massachusetts. | 135,564 | Ohio | 243,818 | Wisconsin | 150,141 |
| Dist. of Col. | 10,521 | Michigan | 263,844 | Oklahoma | 91,193 | Wyoming | 9,650 |
| Florida | 302,732 | Minnesota | 138,887 | Oregon | 58,709 | Guam | 639 |
| Georgia | 268,815 | Mississippi | 106,263 | Pennsylvania | 219,156 | Puerto Rico. | 104,579 |
| Hawaii | 17,215 | Missouri | 100,934 | Rhode Island | 9,007 | Virgin Islands. | 1,418 |
| Idaho | 23,293 | Montana | 14,654 | S. Carolina | 128,977 | | |
| Illinois | 180,696 | Nebraska | 43,825 | S. Dakota | 17,410 | Total | 7,002,598 |

# Circulation of Leading U. S. Magazines

**General and farm magazines, exclusive of groups and comics,** of the Audit Bureau of Circulations. Statistics based on average circulation per issue during the 6 months prior to Jan. 1, 1968. **Source:** Magazine Advertising Bureau of Magazine Publishers Assn., Inc.

| Magazine | Circulation | Magazine | Circulation |
|---|---|---|---|
| Reader's Digest | 17,336,168 | Presbyterian Life | 1,026,517 |
| TV Guide | 12,718,141 | Ebony | 1,012,381 |
| McCall's | 8,545,839 | American Girl | 1,006,861 |
| Look | 7,756,351 | National Enquirer | 994,447 |
| Family Circle | 7,386,700 | Co-Ed | 982,394 |
| Life | 7,354,615 | House Beautiful | 974,744 |
| Better Homes & Gardens | 7,274,726 | Cosmopolitan | 961,508 |
| Woman's Day | 7,225,073 | Sunset | 838,570 |
| Saturday Evening Post | 6,811,418 | Nation's Business | 838,520 |
| Ladies' Home Journal | 6,779,059 | TV Radio Mirror | 834,896 |
| Good Housekeeping | 5,618,738 | Modern Screen | 831,594 |
| National Geographic | 5,607,457 | Ingenue | 810,210 |
| Playboy | 4,708,261 | Modern Romances | 784,985 |
| Redbook | 4,465,991 | 'Teen | 752,291 |
| Time | 3,710,134 | Our Sunday Visitor | 749,497 |
| American Home | 3,536,638 | Hot Rod Magazine | 744,207 |
| Farm Journal | 3,045,913 | Mademoiselle | 697,870 |
| American Legion | 2,523,356 | Simplicity Fashion Magazine | 650,425 |
| Boys' Life | 2,425,927 | Flower & Garden Magazine | 625,401 |
| True | 2,420,572 | Lion | 609,613 |
| True Story | 2,286,653 | Catholic Digest | 582,490 |
| Newsweek | 2,128,032 | Together | 569,382 |
| Parents' | 2,037,182 | True Confessions | 558,204 |
| Senior Scholastic Unit | 1,937,486 | Lutheran, The | 556,483 |
| Popular Mechanics | 1,662,961 | Business Week | 555,139 |
| Junior Scholastic Unit | 1,631,719 | Young Catholic Messenger | 543,769 |
| U.S. News & World Report | 1,584,073 | Saturday Review | 521,074 |
| Popular Science | 1,545,841 | Motion Picture | 515,241 |
| Outdoor Life | 1,503,318 | Motor Trend | 504,395 |
| Workbasket | 1,496,991 | Forbes | 500,191 |
| Seventeen | 1,457,348 | Pageant | 489,515 |
| Elks | 1,438,662 | McCall's Patterns & Home Decorating | 485,133 |
| Field & Stream | 1,425,931 | National Observer | 480,309 |
| Mechanix Illustrated | 1,390,713 | Family Handyman | 478,980 |
| Scouting | 1,384,709 | New Yorker | 475,029 |
| Glamour | 1,381,324 | Fortune | 465,363 |
| Argosy | 1,370,073 | Capper's Weekly | 455,422 |
| Sports Illustrated | 1,361,543 | Hairdo | 454,247 |
| Sports Afield | 1,361,156 | Vogue | 449,722 |
| V.F.W. Magazine | 1,345,698 | Westways | 442,622 |
| Successful Farming | 1,330,831 | Harper's Bazaar | 437,752 |
| Progressive Farmer | 1,254,928 | Popular Photography | 432,813 |
| House & Garden | 1,211,068 | Car & Driver | 424,304 |
| Grit | 1,134,137 | Rotarian | 423,156 |
| Holiday | 1,110,745 | Scientific American | 420,748 |
| Photoplay | 1,103,213 | Movie Mirror | 420,494 |
| Esquire | 1,081,110 | Farmer-Stockman | 417,585 |
| Sport | 1,046,576 | Home Garden | 414,044 |
| Columbia | 1,040,189 | Southern Living | 411,408 |
| 1,001 Decorating Ideas | 1,035,093 | Christian Herald | 398,501 |

# Breaking the Sound Barrier; Speed of Sound

The prefix Mach is used to describe supersonic speed. It derives from Ernst Mach, a Czech-born German physicist, who contributed to the study of sound. When a plane moves at the speed of sound it is Mach 1. When twice the speed of sound it is Mach 2. When it is near but below the speed of sound its speed can be designated at less than Mach 1, for example, Mach .10. Mach is defined as "in jet propulsion, the ratio of the velocity of a rocket or a jet to the velocity of sound in the medium being considered."

When a plane passes the sound barrier—flying faster than sound travels—listeners in the area hear thunderclaps, but pilots do not hear them.

Sound is produced by vibrations of an object and is transmitted by alternate increase and decrease in pressures that radiate outward through a material media of molecules—somewhat like waves spreading out on a pond after a rock has been tossed.

The frequency of sound is determined by the number of times the vibrating waves undulate per second, and is measured in cycles per second. The slower the cycle of waves, the lower the sound. As the frequencies increase, the sound rises higher.

Sound is audible to human beings only if the frequency falls within a certain range. The human ear is usually not sensitive to frequencies of less than 20 vibrations per second, or more than about 20,000 vibrations per second—although this range varies among individuals. Anything at a pitch higher than the human ear can hear is termed ultrasonic.

Intensity or loudness is the strength of the pressure of these radiating waves, and is measured in decibels. The human ear responds to intensity in a range from zero to 120 decibels. Any sound with pressure over 120 decibels is painful.

The speed of sound is generally placed at 1088 ft. per second at sea level at 32° F. It varies in other temperatures and in different media. Sound travels faster in water than in air, and even faster in iron and steel. If in air it travels a mile in 5 seconds, it does a mile under water in 1 second, and through iron in ⅓ of a second. It travels through ice-cold vapor at approximately 4,708 ft. per sec., ice-cold water, 4,938; granite, 12,960; hard wood, 12,620; brick, 11,960; glass, 16,410 to 19,690; silver, 8,658; gold, 5,717.

# Colors of the Spectrum

Color, an electromagnetic wave phenomenon, is a sensation produced through the excitation of the retina of the eye by rays of light. The colors of the spectrum may be produced by viewing a light beam refracted by passage through a prism, which breaks the light into its wave lengths.

Customarily, the primary colors of the spectrum are thought of as those six monochromatic colors which occupy relatively large areas of the spectrum: red, orange, yellow, green, blue and violet. However, Sir Isaac Newton named a seventh, indigo, situated between blue and violet on the spectrum. Aubert estimated (1865) the solar spectrum to contain approximately 1,000 distinguishable hues of which according to Rood (1881) 2,000,000 tints and shades can be distinguished; Luckiesh stated (1915) that 55 distinctly different hues have been seen in a single spectrum.

By many physicists only three primary colors are recognized: red, yellow and blue (Mayer, 1775); red, green and violet (Thomas Young, 1801); red, green and blue (Clerk Maxwell, 1860).

The color sensation of black is due to complete lack of stimulation of the retina, that of white to complete stimulation. The infra-red and ultra-violet rays, below the red (long) end of the spectrum and the violet end (short end) respectively, are invisible. Heat is the principal effect of the infra-red rays and chemical action that of the ultra-violet rays.

# U. S. Daily Newspapers of Large Circulation

**Source:** Publishers' statements to Audit Bureau of Circulations of total average paid circulation for 6 months ending Sept. 30, 1967.

As of Feb. 1, 1968 there were 1,749 English language daily newspapers in the U.S. (311 morning; 1,422 evening; 16 "all day") with a combined circulation of 61,560,952. Sunday newspapers numbered 573 with a total circulation of 49,224,125.

(m) Morning; (e) Evening; *Based on Monday to Friday average. Brackets indicate joint publication.

| Newspaper | Daily | Sunday |
|---|---|---|
| Akron Beacon Journal (e) | *175,179 | 199,950 |
| Atlanta Constitution (m) | 200,682 | |
| Atlanta Journal (e) & Sunday Journal Constitution | 252,688 | 525,519 |
| Baltimore News American (e) | *219,795 | 315,418 |
| Baltimore Sun (m & e) | *398,508 | 345,601 |
| Birmingham News (e) | 181,098 | 220,993 |
| Birmingham Post-Herald (m) | 83,006 | |
| Boston Globe (m & e) | *438,635 | 555,905 |
| Boston Herald (e) | *230,817 | 302,436 |
| Boston Traveler (e) | *136,971 | |
| Boston Record American (m) & Sunday Advertiser | 455,873 | 431,430 |
| Buffalo Courier-Express (m) | 158,973 | 306,989 |
| Buffalo News (e) | *284,568 | |
| Charlotte News (e) | 63,396 | |
| Charlotte Observer (m) | 175,076 | 202,016 |
| Chicago's American (e) | *446,945 | 586,643 |
| Chicago News (e) | *462,946 | |
| Chicago Sun-Times (m) | *552,155 | 717,814 |
| Chicago Tribune (m) | 805,851 | 1,124,946 |
| Christian Science Monitor (e) | 202,155 | |
| Cincinnati Enquirer (m) | 190,169 | 302,042 |
| Cincinnati Post & Times-Star (e) | 243,165 | |
| Cleveland Plain Dealer (m) | 388,261 | 532,193 |
| Cleveland Press (e) | 389,695 | |
| Columbus Citizen-Journal (m) | 115,215 | |
| Columbus Dispatch (e) | 220,105 | 310,335 |
| Dallas News (m) | 226,804 | 264,344 |
| Dallas Times Herald (e) | *209,449 | 243,379 |
| Dayton Journal Herald (m) | 109,502 | |
| Dayton News (e) | 159,529 | 211,696 |
| Denver Post (e) | *253,280 | 341,595 |
| Denver: Rocky Mountain News (m) | 194,933 | 209,571 |
| Des Moines Register (m) | 242,371 | 512,401 |
| Des Moines Tribune (e) | 116,120 | |
| Detroit Free Press (m) | 590,546 | 631,175 |
| Detroit News (e) | 700,321 | 947,155 |
| Flint Journal (e) | 111,376 | 110,756 |
| Fort Worth Star-Telegram (m & e) | *237,043 | 212,194 |
| Fresno Bee (e) | 116,418 | 146,481 |
| Grand Rapids Press (e) | 129,946 | 123,788 |
| Hackensack Record (e) | 145,566 | |
| Harrisburg News (e) | 74,460 | |
| Harrisburg Patriot (m) & Sunday Patriot News | 44,959 | 160,588 |
| Hartford Courant (m) | 147,068 | 193,944 |
| Hartford Times (e) | 135,474 | |
| Honolulu Advertiser (m) | 67,550 | |
| Honolulu Star-Bulletin (e) & Sunday Star-Bulletin & Advertiser | 112,182 | 160,147 |
| Houston Chronicle (e) | *280,472 | 327,121 |
| Houston Post (m) | *274,248 | 304,238 |
| Indianapolis News (e) | 197,305 | |
| Indianapolis Star (m) | 230,685 | 377,027 |
| Jacksonville: Florida Journal (e) | 54,982 | |
| Jacksonville: Florida Times Union (m) | 149,440 | 174,721 |
| Jersey City: Jersey Journal (e) | *91,883 | |
| Kansas City Star (e) | 327,623 | 396,260 |
| Kansas City Times (m) | 334,746 | |
| Knoxville Journal (m) | 66,696 | |
| Knoxville News-Sentinel (e) | 105,207 | 153,109 |
| Little Rock: Arkansas Democrat (e) | *81,467 | 96,515 |
| Little Rock: Arkansas Gazette (m) | *105,363 | 120,830 |
| Long Beach Independent (m) & Sunday Independent-Press-Telegram | 46,281 | 144,531 |
| Long Beach Press-Telegram (e) | 107,737 | |
| Los Angeles Herald Examiner (e) | *731,473 | 726,127 |
| Los Angeles Times (m) | 856,621 | 1,145,695 |
| Louisville Courier-Journal (m) | 230,434 | 343,823 |
| Louisville Times (e) | 171,477 | |
| Memphis Commercial Appeal (m) | 220,370 | 270,397 |
| Memphis Press-Scimitar (e) | 135,256 | |
| Miami Herald (m) | 343,456 | 433,187 |
| Miami News (e) | *90,248 | |
| Milwaukee Journal (e) | 368,520 | 561,851 |
| Milwaukee Sentinel (m) | 170,264 | |
| Minneapolis Star (e) | 282,219 | |
| Minneapolis Tribune (m) | 238,776 | 668,941 |
| Nashville Banner (e) | 96,629 | |
| Nashville Tennessean (m) | 141,709 | 231,784 |

| Newspaper | Daily | Sunday |
|---|---|---|
| New Orleans Times-Picayune (m) | 194,454 | 310,889 |
| New Orleans States & Item (e) | *138,462 | |
| New York: Long Island Press (e) | 350,885 | 419,563 |
| New York: Long Island Star-Journal (e) (1) | 95,689 | |
| New York: Newsday (e) | 421,356 | |
| New York News (m) | *2,112,244 | 3,104,076 |
| New York Post (e) | *628,146 | 354,497 |
| New York Times (m) | *840,495 | 1,494,704 |
| Newark News (e) | *278,235 | 423,157 |
| Newark Star-Ledger (m) | *249,729 | 403,863 |
| Norfolk Ledger-Star (e) | 104,580 | |
| Norfolk Virginian-Pilot (m) | 125,503 | 170,122 |
| Oakland Tribune (e) | *218,393 | 248,433 |
| Oklahoma City Oklahoman (m) | 176,235 | 270,975 |
| Oklahoma City Times (e) | 116,437 | |
| Omaha World-Herald (m & e) | 251,831 | 271,998 |
| Orlando Sentinel (m) | 112,715 | 145,553 |
| Orlando Star (e) | 33,683 | |
| Philadelphia Bulletin (e) | *671,525 | 728,276 |
| Philadelphia Inquirer (m) | *516,640 | 936,135 |
| Philadelphia News (e) | *238,837 | |
| Phoenix Republic (m) | 155,995 | 231,269 |
| Phoenix Gazette (e) | 91,779 | |
| Pittsburgh Post Gazette (m) | *247,007 | |
| Pittsburgh Press (e) | *344,575 | 740,523 |
| Portland: Oregonian (m) | 240,566 | 401,946 |
| Portland: Oregon Journal (e) | *142,517 | 135,513 |
| Providence Bulletin (e) | 148,039 | |
| Providence Journal (m) | 65,731 | 206,985 |
| Raleigh News & Observer (m) | 130,088 | 146,216 |
| Raleigh Times (e) | 23,979 | |
| Richmond News Leader (e) | 124,545 | |
| Richmond Times-Dispatch (m) | 148,673 | 199,297 |
| Rochester Democrat & Chronicle (m) | 142,794 | 218,586 |
| Rochester Times-Union (e) | 143,855 | |
| Sacramento Bee (e) | 177,100 | 202,617 |
| St. Louis Globe-Democrat (m) | *327,594 | 356,929 |
| St. Louis Post-Dispatch (e) | *366,906 | 580,238 |
| St. Paul Dispatch (e) | 128,459 | |
| St. Paul Pioneer Press (m) | 103,543 | 217,372 |
| St. Petersburg Independent (e) | 23,627 | |
| St. Petersburg Times (m) | 137,265 | 151,087 |
| Salt Lake City Tribune (m) | 108,566 | 188,217 |
| Salt Lake City Deseret News (e) | 85,735 | |
| San Antonio Express (m) & Sat.-Sun. Express-News | *81,165 | 111,657 |
| San Antonio News (e) | *62,797 | |
| San Antonio Light (e) | *118,807 | 141,175 |
| San Diego Union (m) | 131,091 | 237,289 |
| San Diego Tribune (e) | 118,445 | |
| San Francisco Examiner (e) | *220,610 | |
| San Francisco Chronicle (m) & Sunday Examiner Chronicle | *493,020 | 691,510 |
| San Jose Mercury (m) & Sunday Mercury-News | 122,703 | 182,497 |
| San Jose News (e) | 72,322 | |
| Seattle Post-Intelligencer (m) | *205,859 | 256,930 |
| Seattle Times (e) | *242,807 | 298,298 |
| South Bend Tribune (e) | 120,408 | 125,468 |
| Spokane Chronicle (e) | 70,955 | |
| Spokane Spokesman-Review (m) | 86,673 | 128,778 |
| Syracuse Herald-Journal (e) & Sunday Herald-American | 137,093 | 260,836 |
| Syracuse Post-Standard (m) | *101,520 | 94,883 |
| Tampa Tribune (m) | 160,570 | 180,637 |
| Tampa Times (e) | 37,953 | |
| Toledo Blade (e) | 172,008 | 183,093 |
| Toledo Times (m) | 29,554 | |
| Tulsa Tribune (e) | 80,089 | |
| Tulsa World (m) | 109,496 | 175,416 |
| Wall St. Journal (m) (total) | 1,079,616 | |
| Washington (D. C.) News (e) | *225,874 | |
| Washington Post (m) | *467,505 | 600,357 |
| Washington Star (e) | *309,245 | 358,738 |
| Wichita Eagle (m) & Sunday Eagle-Beacon | 127,612 | 166,145 |
| Wichita Beacon (e) | 66,843 | |
| Winston-Salem Journal (m) & Sunday Journal Sentinel | 76,244 | 90,701 |
| Winston-Salem Sentinel (e) | 44,049 | |
| Worcester Gazette (e) | 94,543 | |
| Worcester Telegram (m) | 62,682 | 107,892 |
| Youngstown Vindicator (e) | 99,776 | 154,761 |

(1) N. Y. Long Island Star-Journal suspended publication March 16, 1968.

# STATES OF THE UNION
## Their Resources, Histories, Industries, Agricultural and Mineral Products, Tourist Attractions, Nicknames, State Symbols

Areas of the states are total land and water areas reported by the Geography Division, Bureau of the Census; agricultural figures are based on reports of the Dept. of Agriculture and state agencies; mineral statistics are those reported by the Bureau of Mines.

*For maps and for descriptive articles on great cities, see Index.*

## Alabama
### *Heart of Dixie, Cotton State*

**CAPITAL:** Montgomery. **AREA:** 51,609 sq. mi., rank, 29th. **POPULATION:** (1960 Census), 3,266,-740, rank, 19th. **MOTTO:** We Dare Defend Our Rights. **FLOWER:** Camellia. **BIRD:** Yellowhammer. **FISH:** Tarpon. **TREE:** Southern (Longleaf) Pine. **SONG:** Alabama. **ADMISSION:** 22nd.

Alabama lies in the cotton belt of the Old South but introduction of new and diversified industries has given the state a more balanced economy. Natural wealth includes coal, which underlies about 7,000 sq. mi. in the northern Appalachian region, iron, bauxite and timber.

Cheaha Mtn., 2,407 ft., is the state's highest point. Est. pop. July 1, 1967, was 3,540,000.

Abundant water for hydroelectric power and river shipping has contributed to the growth of Alabama's economy. Three Tennessee Valley Authority dams are in the northern part of the state. Historic sites, fishing and hunting are among its attractions.

Agriculture remains a vital part of the economy despite the growth of manufacturing. Cotton, long king among Alabama's crops, dropped to 3rd place behind corn and soybeans in 1967, mainly because of poor growing weather. Among the states, Alabama was 4th in production of pecans and 5th in peanuts. Also important are potatoes, watermelons, tobacco and sugarcane.

Livestock, especially poultry, has grown in importance; Alabama moved up to 6th place in number of chickens in 1968. Farm receipts for livestock and livestock products totaled $435,410,000 in 1967; for crops, the total was $167,014,000.

Alabama ranks 2nd in the nation in pulpwood production; lumber and furniture are important; the output of wood products is valued at over $550,000,000 a year, providing 100,000 jobs.

Industrial growth in 1966 saw $320,289,000 invested in 330 new or expanded plants, providing 24,441 additional jobs; the rate of growth was not quite up to previous records. Largest industries in terms of value added by manufacture are iron and steel, chemicals, textiles, food processing, paper, clothing, fabricated metals, transportation equipment (including aircraft). Birmingham, center of the steel industry, is known as "the Pittsburgh of the South." Value added by manufacture totals over $2.3 billion a year.

Alabama ranks 2nd behind Arkansas in production of bauxite and is the 3rd largest producer of asphalt, mica and pyrites. But bituminous coal accounts for 40% of the value of its total mineral production, which in 1967 reached a record $249,-828,000. Also important are cement, stone and petroleum.

At Huntsville is the George C. Marshall Space Flight Center of NASA.

Total employment in the state showed gains in both 1966 and 1967.

Educational institutions include the Univ. of Alabama, Univ. of South Alabama, Auburn Univ., Alabama College and Tuskegee Institute.

Alabama, first explored by De Narvaez, Spanish, 1528, is rich in historical markers and sites. Andrew Jackson defeated the Creek Indians at Talledega and Horseshoe Bend. The Confederate States were organized at Montgomery, Feb. 4, 1861, and Jefferson Davis took oath as president at State Capitol there Feb. 18. Davis' "first White House" now is a state shrine; others include the house in Tuscumbia where Helen Keller was born June 27, 1880; statue of Vulcan near Birmingham.

The state was organized as a Territory Mar. 3, 1817, and became a state Dec. 14, 1819.

Mobile, colonized by French, 1699, ceded to Spain, 1799, but not turned over till 1813, is the state's principal seaport; shipments to foreign countries are valued at $328,000,000 a year. Mobile's carnival dates from 1704. Azalea Trail (February-March) and tarpon fishing are tourist attractions.

At Russell Cave National Monument, near Bridgeport, may be seen a detailed record of occupancy by humans from about 7000 B.C. to 1650 A.D., including tools, weapons and pottery. The exhibit is free.

The George Washington Carver Museum at Tuskegee Institute, Tuskegee, contains records of the famous scientist's contributions to agronomy and dioramas of achievements by Negroes.

The University of Alabama Museum of Natural History, in University, displays Alabama fossils, shells and aboriginal materials and collections of native and foreign beetles, birds, batrachians and reptiles. Mound State Monument, Moundville, an adjunct of the museum, shows aboriginal burials.

*(See also Index for Birmingham.)*

## Alaska
### *No official nickname*

**CAPITAL:** Juneau. **AREA:** 586,412 sq. mi., rank, 1st. **POPULATION** (1960 Census), 226,167, rank 50th. **FLOWER:** Forget-me-not. **BIRD:** Willow Ptarmigan. **TREE:** Sitka Spruce. **SONG:** Alaska's Flag. **FISH:** King Salmon. **ADMISSION:** 49th.

Alaska became the 49th state Jan. 3, 1959. Largest political division of the U. S., it is two and one-fifth times the size of Texas. Alaska occupies the NW part of North America, separated from the rest of the continental U. S. by Canada's British Columbia. Alaska's general coastline runs 6,640 mi.; including all its islands, 33,904 mi. It has mountain ranges, volcanoes, fjords and glaciers; 98% of the total land is owned by the Federal Government.

Est. pop. July 1, 1967, was 273,000. About one-sixth of the pop. are Eskimos and Indians.

Pt. Barrow in Arctic Alaska is the northernmost point of the state. The Yukon River flows E to W 1,200 mi. through Central Alaska, from the Canadian border to the Bering Sea. In South Central Alaska stands Mt. McKinley, 20,320 ft., highest point in North America; also in McKinley National Park is Mt. Wrangell, 14,163 ft., a steaming volcano.

In West Central Alaska, off the tip of the Seward Peninsula, lies Little Diomede Is., only 2.4 mi. from Big Diomede Is., owned by the USSR. The Alaska Peninsula and the Aleutian Islands, into which it tapers, extend SW and W for 1,200 mi., with numerous volcanoes; at the SE base of the peninsula is Katmai National Monument, containing the Valley of 10,000 Smokes, scene of a 1912 eruption.

Alaska's Panhandle stretches SE; it is a narrow strip of mainland and islands, with fjords and Glacier Bay National Monument (containing the Muir Glacier, 2 mi. wide and 250 ft. high), facing the Pacific W of British Columbia.

**History.** Vitus Bering, a Dane employed by Russia, discovered Bering Strait, separating Asia and North America, in 1728, but may not have found Alaska until his second voyage, in 1741, when he explored Alaska's coast. Other early visits were made by Spanish explorers (1775, 1788); by the British Cook (1776), Vancouver (1791-94) and Mackenzie (1793); by the French La Perouse (1786); and by the U. S. Capts. Robert Gray and John Kendrick (1788). Alexander Baranov, first Russian governor of Alaska, set up headquarters at New Archangel, near present Sitka, 1799.

William H. Seward, as Secy. of State under President Andrew Johnson, bought Alaska from Czarist Russia for $7,200,000, a transaction some labeled at the time "Seward's Folly." The treaty was signed Mar. 30, 1867, the transfer of territory took place Oct. 18, 1867. Alaska was a District until Aug. 24, 1912, and an Organized Territory until becoming a state in 1959.

The "Gold Rush" began when gold was discovered near the Klondike River in Canada, Aug. 16, 1896. Out of 100,000 prospectors, 1897-1899, many died of exposure, others took up trading and farming. On the south coast of Seward Peninsula

354

lies **Nome**, where gold-bearing sands were worked by placer mining.

**Resources and Industries.** The Good Friday, Mar. 27, 1964, earthquake, the most powerful ever recorded in North America, caused a temporary setback to the economic development of Southwestern Alaska, but reconstruction was speedily completed. Anchorage, Seward, Valdez and Kodiak benefited with new facilities.

Principal income is from fisheries, minerals (esp. oil), timber and wood products, and furs. Salmon, halibut, herring, cod and shellfish are frozen or canned; Alaska is the top state in value of its commercial catch, $80,677,000 in 1966.

Processing of fish and other foods is the largest manufacturing industry, followed by lumber and wood products. Total value added by manufacture in 1963 was an est. $89,311,000.

Spruce, yellow cedar and hemlock are plentiful; there also are red cedar and birch. Commercial timberland of Alaska's vast forest totals 28,000,-000 acres. The forest products industry in SE is expanding as pulp mills increase. There are also hardwood forests in the interior.

Furs produced are those of the seal, sable, ermine, wolverine, land otter, muskrat, beaver, mink, red fox, blue fox, lynx, marten. The black fox and white fox are less frequent. Wild life includes the gray wolf, moose, caribou, and 5 kinds of bear: black, grizzly, Polar, Kodiak and glacier. There are plenty of sea fowl, but whales, walrus, sea lion and sea otter have diminished.

The seal herd on the Pribilof islands is owned by the Government and protected by the U. S. Fish & Wildlife Service. Reindeer herds are multiplying and their meat is marketed.

Oil and natural gas have long since taken over from gold as the mainstay of mineral production.

Oil production, boosted by new offshore fields in Cook Inlet, almost doubled in value in 1967, reaching $84,644,000 compared to $44,007,000 in 1966, and accounting for some 65% of the value of the total mineral output, est. at $129,897,000. New oil discoveries were made along the Arctic coast.

Gold production was valued at $910,000 in 1967, continuing an annual decline. Alaska remained the leading platinum-producing state and was 2nd to Colorado in tin. It also has considerable copper, coal, mercury and uranium.

Principal ports are in the Panhandle where Juneau, the capital, is on the mainland shore; N of it is Skagway, historic entry to Klondike gold fields via Chilkoot Pass and White Pass. Sitka, Wrangell and Ketchikan (center of salmon industry), are on islands of the Alexander group.

At the head of Cook Inlet, in S Central Alaska, is the state's largest city, Anchorage. Seward, S of Anchorage, is terminus for the govt.-owned Alaska Railroad, which runs N to Fairbanks.

Twelve domestic airlines serve Alaska. International lines flying via Arctic routes make stops.

Ships transport 90% of the goods and foods to and from Alaska with the Alaska Steamship Co. linking some 50 Alaskan ports with Seattle, etc.

An est. 100,000 tourists visit Alaska annually, spending over $25,000,000.

There are now two motor routes to Alaska. The newer is by way of Marine Highway, a 450-mile ferry route from Prince Rupert, B. C., to Haines, Alaska. Motorists leaving one of the three ferries at Haines have 785 mi. of paved highway to Anchorage, 662 mi. to Fairbanks. The older route is Alaska Highway, which starts at Dawson Creek, B. C., and ends via Richardson Highway in Fairbanks, 1,523 mi. away. The system also links Anchorage, Homer, Kodiak, Valdez and Cordova. Fairbanks, largest city in Central Alaska, has the northernmost airport on the continent. Nearby are Fort Wainwright and Eielson AFB

Higher education is provided by Univ. of Alaska, near Fairbanks, with 5 junior colleges in other cities; Alaska Methodist Univ., Anchorage; Sheldon Jackson Junior College, Sitka.

The Alaska State Museum in Juneau features Eskimo and Indian exhibits, mounted wildlife specimens, rocks and minerals and historical exhibits.

The University of Alaska Museum, in College, near Fairbanks, maintains cultural and natural history collections for research and for the public.

# Arizona
*Grand Canyon State*

**CAPITAL: Phoenix. AREA: 113,909 sq. mi., rank, 6th. POPULATION: (1960 Census), 1,302,161, rank, 35th. MOTTO: Ditat Deus, God Enriches. FLOWER: Giant Cactus or Saguaro. BIRD: Cactus Wren. TREE: Paloverde. SONG: Arizona. ADMISSION: 48th.**

Arizona leads the nation in copper production with 55% of the total U. S. output, but ranks high among cotton-growing states, but its rapidly-growing manufacturing industries, such as machinery, aerospace and electronics, form the largest source of income. Mining, agriculture and tourism follow in that order.

Loads of sunshine and a wealth of scenic attractions give Arizona a steadily mounting tourist business est. at $450,000,000 for 1966. Est. pop. July 1, 1967, was 1,635,000.

The climate is dry in southern regions and the northern plateau, but high mountains and forests in central areas have heavy snows in winter. Highest point is Humphreys Peak, 12,633 ft. Over 44% of the land is Federally owned.

The only point in the U. S. at which 4 states meet is the juncture of Arizona, Utah, Colorado and New Mexico.

Arizona is noted for the Grand Canyon of the Colorado, an immense, vari-colored fissure 217 mi. long, 4 to 18 mi. wide at brim, 4,000 to 5,500 ft. deep. It also has one of man's greatest water barriers, Hoover Dam (formerly Boulder) in Black Canyon of the Colorado, 726 ft. high, 660 ft. wide at base, 1,244 ft. long at top, creating Lake Mead.

Nature has given Arizona the Painted Desert, extending for 30 mi. along U. S. 66; the Petrified Forest; Canyon Diablo, 225 ft. deep, 500 ft. wide, and Meteor Crater, 4,150 ft. across, 570 ft. deep, made by a prehistoric meteor, near U. S. 66. The state has 15 national monuments, 2 national parks. Rodeos and historic sites of Indian and Spanish eras are other attractions.

Manufacturing production rose 7% in 1967.

Copper is king among Arizona's many minerals, and Arizona normally produces 51% of the nation's copper output. A prolonged copper strike in 1967 trimmed the value of the yield to $380,369,000 which was 81% of the state's total mineral production, valued at $465,449,000. Arizona also ranks 1st in pumice, 3rd in silver, molybdenum and asphalt, and 4th in gold. Also important are uranium, helium, mercury and vanadium.

Cotton is the major crop; Arizona's harvest ranks 5th among the states although it fell off from 515,000 bales in 1966 to 460,000 in 1967. Receipts for all crops rose slightly in 1967, reaching $272,820,-000, as did receipts for livestock and livestock products, $233,882,000. The state ranks 14th in number of sheep. Important produce includes lettuce, alfalfa, melons, oranges, grapefruit, lemons and tangerines.

Federal spending on defense contracts, construction projects, air bases, etc., is an important factor in Arizona's economy.

Schools include the Univ. of Arizona at Tucson, Arizona State Univ. at Tempe and Northern Arizona Univ. at Flagstaff. The new observatory of the National Science Foundation is located on Kitt Peak near Tucson. Taliesin West is the Frank Lloyd Wright architectural school near Phoenix.

Originally part of the Territory of New Mexico, which was ceded in 1848 by Mexico with the Gadsden Purchase added in 1853, Arizona became a Territory itself in 1863 and a state Feb. 14, 1912.

Museums include Arizona State Museum, Tucson, which stresses the archeology and ethnology of the Southwest with exhibits on Hohakam prehistory, early elephant hunters, tree-ring dating of prehistoric cultures and Pima and Apache ethnology. The Museum of Northern Arizona, 3 mi. N of Flagstaff, has exhibits illustrating the geology and paleontology of the area, and the culture of prehistoric and modern Indians, with a Navajo rug display and a Hopi kiva.

The Southwestern Arboretum, on U. S. 60 and 70 near Superior, has over 6,000 plants and trees from arid regions of the world, from lowly cactus to lofty boojum tree.

The Arizona-Sonora Desert Museum, near Tucson, displays animals and plants of the desert.

England's historic London Bridge, purchased in 1968 for $2,460,000, was to be re-erected as a tourist attraction at Lake Havasu City, 150 mi. NW of Tucson.

*(See also Phoenix in Index.)*

# Arkansas
*Land of Opportunity*

**CAPITAL: Little Rock. AREA: 53,104 sq. mi.,** rank, 27th. **POPULATION** (1960 Census), 1,786,272, rank, 31st. **MOTTO:** Regnat Populus. Let the People Rule. **FLOWER:** Apple Blossom. **BIRD:** Mockingbird. **TREE:** Pine. **SONG:** Arkansas. **ADMISSION:** 25th.

Arkansas is an important agricultural state with growing industries, has large oil production, valuable thermal springs and is popular with sportsmen. Highest point is Magazine Mtn., 2,753 ft.

Arkansas became a state June 15, 1836; it seceded in 1861 and was readmitted to the Union in 1868. Est. pop. July 1, 1967, was 1,969,000.

Manufacturing is growing in importance with an 86% increase in employees from 1955 to 1968. Per capita income in Arkansas increased 2.5 times between 1950 and 1967. Lumber, bauxite and cotton are major products.

The $1.2 billion Arkansas River program, involving navigation, flood control and power developments and construction of 17 dams and locks in Arkansas and Oklahoma, is scheduled for completion in 1970. It is expected to provide a great boost to the area's economy.

The state has 20,052,000 acres of oak, hickory, gum, cypress and pine, and mechanization has increased output of lumber products. Cotton accounts for 48% of farm income and Arkansas ranked 4th in cotton production in the U. S. in 1967 with 520,000 bales. It is 3rd in rice. It was 3rd in number of chickens as of Jan. 1, 1968.

Arkansas accounts for 96% of the bauxite (aluminum ore) produced in the U. S. It also has the only diamond field in the U. S., near Murfreesboro, where visitors may keep any diamond they find up to 5 carats.

Oil is the state's main mineral product; 1967 output was valued at $57,262,000, that of bauxite was $18,200,000. Total value of mineral production was $182,131,000.

Arkansas has 23 institutions of higher learning —13 colleges and universities, one professional school, two teachers' colleges and a number of junior colleges. It has 11 vocational-technical schools, and a technical institute.

Fresh-water fishing, duck-hunting in southeast lowlands, and recreation areas in 14 state parks and two national forests attract visitors. There are several reservoir-recreation areas, as at Norfolk, Bull Shoals, Nimrod and Dardanelle, and others are being created. There are 47 hot springs in government-owned and operated Hot Springs National Park, which entirely surrounds the city of Hot Springs, about 50 mi. SW of Little Rock. Spring water ranges from 95° to 147° F. and is piped in insulated conduits for baths and drinking. The state has 83 airports.

Little Rock is served by 3 major railroads, 5 airlines and 31 motor carriers. Hot Springs has 2 main railroads, 3 airlines and 10 truck lines.

Historic attractions in Little Rock include the Territorial Capital Restoration, a block of 13 original frame and brick buildings, furnished as in 1820-36, including the governor's home and the first print shop of the Arkansas Gazette, oldest newspaper west of the Mississippi. The Old State House in Little Rock was the state capitol 1836-1912; it houses many historical exhibits and a library of 100,000 vols.

The Arkansas Museum of Natural History and Antiquities in Little Rock occupies the building where Gen. Douglas MacArthur was born; also in MacArthur Park is the Arkansas Museum of Fine Arts.

# California
*Golden State*

**CAPITAL:** Sacramento. **AREA:** 158,693 sq. mi., rank, 3rd. **POPULATION:** (1960 Census), 15,717,-204, rank 2nd (see text below). **MOTTO:** Eureka, I Have Found It. **FLOWER:** California Poppy. **BIRD:** Valley Quail. **TREE:** Redwood. **SONG:** I Love You, California. **ADMISSION:** 31st.

California is the leading agricultural state and is 2nd only to New York in manufacturing.

Third largest in area, California also has, within only 85 mi. of each other, the highest and lowest points in the conterminous 48 states, Mt. Whitney, 14,494 ft., and Death Valley, 282 ft. below sea level. The U. S. Bureau of the Census estimated Cali-

fornia's population, as of July 1, 1964, at 18,084,000 and New York's at 17,915,000, giving California 1st place; New York had been in 1st place from 1820 through the Census of 1960. (See N. Y. article for further figures.) Est. pop. July 1, 1967, was 19,163,000. It also has the most dogs and cats—an est. 50,000,000.

Among scenic regions are the Yosemite Valley, Lassen and Sequoia-Kings Canyon national parks, Lake Tahoe, the Mohave and Colorado deserts, San Francisco Bay and Monterey Peninsula. National forests cover one-fifth of the state.

Oldest living things on earth are believed to be a stand of bristlecone pine in the Inyo National Forest, est. to be 4,500 years old.

The world's tallest tree, the Howard Libbey redwood, 367.6 ft. with a girth of 44 ft., stands on Redwood Creek, Humboldt County.

California's huge fruit and vegetable production is fed by large irrigation systems. Receipts from crops in 1967 totaled $2.4 billion (tops in U. S.); from livestock, $1.5 billion (2nd to Iowa); total receipts were $3.9 billion (most in U. S.).

The state ranked 1st in numbers of chickens and turkeys, 3rd in sheep, 5th in cattle, as of Jan. 1, 1968.

California produces the most apricots, avocados, grapes and raisins, peaches, persimmons, pomegranates, plums, prunes, lemons, nectarines, olives, dates, almonds, walnuts and sugarbeets. Its total vegetable crop is the largest; it ranks 2nd to Florida in oranges and 3rd in potatoes.

It is 2nd to Alaska in commercial fishing, with a catch valued at $55,446,000 in 1966.

The state's giant aerospace industries employ a third of all its manufacturing employees, est. at 1,565,000 in 1966. Value added by manufacture was $18.9 billion in 1965: transportation equipment, esp. aircraft and missiles, led; food products, particularly frozen and canned foods, were 2nd; electrical machinery, including electronic components, was 3rd, followed by other machinery, metal products.

California received $6.16 billions in defense and aerospace prime contracts in 1966, or 17.2% of the national total.

Gold, discovered at Sutter's sawmill Jan. 24, 1848, set off the historic Gold Rush and gave initial impetus to California's development, but petroleum is the leading mineral product today.

Oil output in 1967 was valued at $845,387,000, almost half the state's total mineral production value, $1.7 billion (3rd highest in the U. S.). Ranking 3rd among the states in oil production, California leads in output of asbestos, boron, cement, diatomite, mercury, rare-earth metals, sand and gravel, sodium sulfate, sulphur ore and tungsten.

The Oroville Dam, main unit in the world's largest water project—the $2.8 billion Feather River Project—was dedicated May 4, 1968, N of Sacramento; electric power and water for irrigation were flowing even before completion.

Some 7,229,000 out-of-state visitors spent $1.33 billion in California in 1965.

There were, in 1965, 252 institutions of higher learning in California, 77 public junior colleges, 20 state colleges, 8 campuses of the Univ. of California, and 147 independent colleges and universities. During the 1964-65 school year, 39,711 baccalaureate degrees, 10,859 masters degrees, and 2,992 doctorates were conferred.

Three of the world's largest observatories are located on Palomar Mtn., Mt. Hamilton and Mt. Wilson.

The Tournament of Roses and the Rose Bowl football game at Pasadena are held annually, Jan. 1. Winter sports are featured in many mountain areas.

Vandenberg AFB, 170 mi. NW of Los Angeles, is center of an interservice missile range extending from San Nicholas Island to Point Sur.

California, named by Spanish explorers, was Alta (Upper) California under Spain. Mexico took over, 1822, ceded it 1848. California Republic (Bear Flag) at Sonoma, June 14, 1846, was led by Gen. William B. Ide. Commander John D. Sloat raised U. S. flag at Monterey July 7, 1846. The state was admitted to the Union Sept. 9, 1850.

Among museums the Pasadena Art Museum has collections of modern German painting, American painting, Oriental art and prints. The Santa Barbara Museum of Art has exhibits of Greek and Roman sculpture, Oriental art, old master and modern paintings, primitive arts, American paintings and old and modern European drawings. The

Santa Barbara Historical Society Museum displays and interprets objects of state and local history, owns several historic houses and operates the Gledhill Library for historical research. In Sacramento, the Crocker Art Gallery has collections of paintings, drawings, prints, sculpture and crafts representing all European schools from early Renaissance, American glass and a cross section of pottery from 5th Century B.C. to contemporary American.

**SPANISH MISSIONS.** Twenty-one churches built by Franciscans of the Roman Catholic Church, 1769-1823, have been restored, rebuilt or are in ruins. They are located on or near El Camino Real, the Royal Highway, U. S. 101. Father Junipero Serra led a missionary expedition from Mexico City and founded 9 churches between 1769 and his death, 1784. The missions converted Indians and raised livestock and grain. Mexico secularized and sold the missions in the 1830s. After the Mexican War the U. S. returned the missions to the church. The buildings suffered from fire, earthquake, military and secular use; some have been entirely rebuilt.

**San Diego de Alcala**, near San Diego. Restored.
**San Luis Rey de Francia**, near Oceanside. Seminary for priests.
**San Juan Capistrano**, 30 mi. from San Luis Rey. Famous for tradition that swallows arrive on St. Joseph's Day, Mar. 19, depart on St. John's Day, Oct. 23.
**San Buenaventura**, Ventura. Restored.
**Santa Barbara**, Los Olivos St., Santa Barbara. Enlarged, restored since 1925 earthquake.
**San Gabriel Arcangel**, near Los Angeles.
**San Fernando Rey de Espana**, San Fernando. Oblate fathers. A museum.
**Santa Ines**, Solvang. Parish church.
**La Purisima Concepcion**, near Lompoc. State monument, rebuilt by CCC, 1935.
**San Luis Obispo de Tolosa**, San Luis Obispo.
**San Miguel Arcangel**, San Miguel.
**San Antonio de Padua**, 20 mi. SW of King City. Restored and rebuilt.
**Nuestra Senora de la Soledad**, Soledad. In course of restoration.
**San Carlos de Borromeo de Carmelo**, near Carmel. Tomb of Father Junipero Serra.
**San Juan Bautista**, 18 mi. N of Salinas.
**Santa Cruz**, Santa Cruz. New church, 1858.
**Santa Clara**, Santa Clara. On campus of Univ.
**San Jose**, 15 mi. N of San Jose. Original destroyed; wooden church since 1891.
**Mission Dolores** (San Francisco de Asis) 16th and Dolores Sts., San Francisco. Restored chapel.
**San Rafael Arcangel**, A and Fifth Sts., San Rafael. New church, 1917.
**San Francisco de Solano**, Sonoma. Owned by state; chapel museum. Stands on plaza where Bear Flag was raised June 14, 1846.

Not one of the original 21 missions is **San Antonio de Pala**, originally a dependency of San Luis Rey de Francia, erected 1810, abandoned 1846, restored 1959.

(See also Index for Los Angeles, Oakland, Sacramento, San Diego, San Francisco, San Jose.)

# Colorado
*Centennial State*

**CAPITAL:** Denver. **AREA:** 104,247 sq. mi., rank, 8th. **POPULATION:** (1960 Census), 1,753,947, rank 33rd. **MOTTO:** Nil Sine Numine. Nothing Without Deity. **FLOWER:** Columbine. **BIRD:** Lark Bunting. **TREE:** Colorado Blue Spruce. **ANIMAL:** Big Horn Sheep. **SONG:** Where the Columbines Grow. **ADMISSION:** 38th.

Once primarily a mining and grazing state, Colorado now draws the largest segment of its income from manufacturing, with livestock and crops 2nd, mining 3rd. Its snow-capped peaks, ski centers, ghost towns and health spas make it a popular vacation-recreation area.

Colorado was organized as a Territory Feb. 28, 1861, and was admitted to the Union Aug. 1, 1876, 100 years after the Declaration of Independence; hence its nickname, the Centennial State. Est. pop. July 1, 1967, was 1,975,000.

Total of value added by Colorado's varied manufacturing industries is over $1.2 billion yearly. Processing of meat, dairy and other food products ranks 1st, followed by stone-clay-glass products, chemicals and electrical machinery.

Farm receipts in 1967 totaled $807,524,000, 75% from livestock products. Colorado was 4th among the states in number of sheep, 1,384,000 in 1968; 12th in cattle, 3,021,000. Its sugarbeet crop is 3rd

in the U. S.; other large crops are wheat, corn, barley, alfalfa, potatoes, apples, peaches, pears. Large areas are irrigated.

Gold was found on the Platte, 1858, and at Leadville, 1860. Climax, near Leadville, now produces 72% of the world's molybdenum; 1967 output was valued at $76,408,000. Colorado is also 1st among the states in production of tin and vanadium, 2nd in tungsten and carbon dioxide, 3rd in uranium, 4th in lead, zinc and pyrites. Total 1967 mineral output was valued at $352,347,000, with petroleum the biggest money-producer at $99,-445,000.

With Utah and Wyoming, Colorado shares the world's richest oil shale deposits, still to be developed.

Colorado is the highest state in the Union, with an average altitude of 6,800 ft. It has 52 of the nation's highest mountains and 1,500 peaks over 10,000 ft. Pikes Peak, 14,110 ft., was found by Lt. Zebulon M. Pike, 1806. Highest is Mt. Elbert, 14,433. Frozen Lake, altitude 12,940 ft., is the highest lake in the 48 conterminous states.

The Continental Divide, which forms the crest of the continent and separates watersheds of the Pacific Ocean and the Gulf of Mexico, runs through the west-central part in a general N-S direction.

Six major rivers—the Colorado, Rio Grande, Arkansas, North Platte, South Platte and Republican—rise in Colorado, supply water to 19 states. The western rivers have cut great canyons: the Black Canyon of the Gunnison and the Royal Gorge of the Arkansas, 1,000 to 1,500 ft. deep. One of the world's highest bridges crosses the Arkansas 1,053 ft. above the river at Royal Gorge.

The Federal government owns 36.4% of the land, including two National Parks, 6 Monuments, one Recreation Area, 12 Forests, one Indian reservation, 7 major military reservations.

Colorado has 9 state colleges and universities, 12 junior colleges and 5 private colleges.

Colorado was the 1st of several states which in 1966 liberalized their abortion laws.

Tourist attractions include Rocky Mountain National Park, Garden of the Gods, Great Sand Dunes and Dinosaur National Monuments, Pikes Peak and Mt. Evans Highways, Mesa Verde National Park (pre-historic cliff dwellings). The Grand Mesa tableland comprises Grand Mesa Forest, 659,584 acres, with 200 lakes stocked with trout. Other attractions include the U. S. Air Force Academy near Colorado Springs, Denver Western Stock Show, Colorado State Fair, horse, dog and auto races, rodeos and pioneer celebrations. Twenty ski areas operate from November to May.

Aspen and Central City, old mining towns, are also cultural centers.

Big game include deer, bear, elk, mountain lion, gray wolf, coyote. There are thousands of miles of trout streams and 2,000 fishing lakes.

Museums include the Colorado Springs Fine Arts Center which has paintings, prints and drawings by contemporary artists, exhibits of the cultural history of the SW and Latin America, and the John F. Huckel collection of 112 Navajo sand painting reproductions. The University of Colorado Museum, in Boulder, has more than a million objects in its exhibits of rocks, plants and early peoples as well as in its art gallery.

(See also Index for Denver.)

# Connecticut
*Nutmeg State, Constitution State*

**CAPITAL:** Hartford. **AREA:** 5,009 sq. mi., rank, 48th. **POPULATION:** (1960 Census), 2,535,234, rank, 25th. **MOTTO:** Qui Transtulit, Sustinet. He Who Transplanted, Sustains. **FLOWER:** Mountain Laurel. **BIRD:** American Robin. **TREE:** White Oak. Fifth of the Original 13 States to ratify Constitution.

Connecticut's heavily industrialized cities are in sharp contrast to its picturesque New England villages and scenic countryside. Despite its small size, the state has large and diverse manufacturing industries, mainly of high-value specialty products. Est. pop. July 1, 1967, was 2,925,000.

It is a leading maker of jet engines, helicopters, nuclear subs, pins and needles, silverware, hardware, clocks, typewriters, cutlery, and ball bearings. Ranking 48th in area, it is 13th in value added by manufacturing, a total of over $4.8 billion annually. Its factories employ 43% of the working force. Hartford is headquarters for many of the nation's largest insurance companies.

Poultry and dairy products account for the larg-

est part of farm receipts, which totaled $159,722,-000 in 1967. Much of the soil is stony, but tobacco, potatoes, fruits and vegetables are grown.

The vacation-recreation industry is important. Attractions include historic sites, charming villages, the American Shakespeare Festival in Stratford, Mystic Seaport and Marine Museum, trolley museums, skiing, boating on Long Island Sound. There are 83 state parks, recreation areas and historic sites, covering 22,237 acres.

Tourism brings Connecticut over $200,000,000 a year from out-of-state vacationers.

Mineral production is mostly of sand, stone and gravel, feldspar and clays. Total value for 1967 output was est. at $20,725,000.

Adriaen Block, Dutch, explored the Connecticut R., 1614. English from Massachusetts settled in 1630s. First practical constitution was the Fundamental Orders, adopted by Wethersfield, Windsor and Hartford, 1639; gave superior powers to legislature. The royal charter of 1662 was exceptionally liberal; when Gov. Edmund Andros tried to seize it, 1687, it was hidden in the Hartford Oak, commemorated in Charter Oak Place.

Free public schools were established in New Haven, 1642, Hartford, 1643. Compulsory education in elementary and Latin grammar schools was established in 1650.

Of 33 major colleges and universities, Yale Univ. (estab. 1701, named 1718) is the largest privately endowed. The public education system is topped by 4 state colleges and the Univ. of Connecticut. Trinity (Hartford), Wesleyan (Middletown), and Univ. of Hartford are well known; Connecticut College, for women, and U. S. Coast Guard Academy are at New London. Preparatory schools include Taft (Watertown), Choate (Wallingford), Hotchkiss (Lakeville), Kent (Kent) and Loomis (Windsor).

Museums include the P. T. Barnum Museum, Bridgeport; American Clock and Watch Museum, Bristol; Trolley Museums, East Haven and Warehouse Point; Hill-Stead Museum, a country house with paintings by famous Impressionists, Farmington; Museum of American Art, New Britain; Old Lighthouse, Stonington; Lyman Allyn Museum, New London; Bruce Museum, Greenwich.

In New Haven museums include the Winchester Gun Museum, with 5,000 items from the 15th Century to present. The Yale University Art Gallery's collections illustrate the ancient civilizations of Greece, Rome, Egypt, Mesopotamia; far east and Italian Renaissance art; European and American painting and sculpture, African and pre-Columbian arts. The Peabody Museum at Yale has collections in paleontology, mineralogy, zoology, archeology and a leading collection of dinosaurs.

Mystic Seaport, Mystic, is a recreated 19th Century village, including smithy, chapel and schoolhouse. At the docks lie the wooden whaleship Charles W. Morgan, the squarerigger Joseph Conrad; the Gloucester fishing schooner L. A. Dunton.

*(See also Index for Hartford.)*

# Delaware

### First State, Diamond State

CAPITAL: Dover. AREA: 2,057 sq. mi., rank, 49th. POPULATION: (1960 Census), 446,292, rank, 46th. MOTTO: Liberty and Independence. FLOWER: Peach Blossom. BIRD: Blue Hen Chicken. TREE: American Holly. SONG: Our Delaware. First of Original 13 States to ratify Constitution.

Delaware occupies part of the Delmarva Peninsula, so-called because Delaware and parts of Maryland and Virginia share the peninsula separating Delaware and Chesapeake Bays. Delaware is 96 mi. long and from 9 to 35 mi. wide. The land slopes from rolling hills (442 ft. highest elevation) in the N to a near sea-level plain.

Second smallest of the states in area, Delaware has a high level of income, with large chemical and other industries, the hqs. of many large corporations, prosperous farms and important shellfish production. A special Federal Census, Sept. 1967, showed the pop. at 526,414.

Chemicals are by far the largest industry, accounting for $181,965,000 of the total est. value added by manufacture, $666,245,000 in 1963. Frozen and canned foods, dairy and poultry products and grain milling were 2nd, $56,143,000. Also important are apparel, rubber and plastics, metal products, leather, textiles.

Broiler chickens are the largest item of farm income; farm receipts for 1966 were $132,676,000. Fruit and vegetables are the most important crops. Mineral production is mainly sand, gravel, stone, clays, gem stones, valued at $1,937,000 for 1966. Delaware ranks 6th among the states in value of its commercial fishing catch.

The state has several famed beaches, racing at Delaware Park, numerous historic sites. The Atlantic terminal of the Air Transport Command is at Dover Air Force Base. Wilmington is the largest city.

Delaware Bay was reported in 1609 by Henry Hudson, under Dutch commission, and in 1610 by Samuel Argall, in Virginia service. The latter called the estuary after his Governor, Thomas West, Lord de la Warr, a name soon extended to the river and its lower western shore, and later adopted by the state.

An attempted Dutch settlement at Zwaanendael (Lewes) in 1631, failed. Swedish colonization began at Fort Christina (Wilmington) in 1638. New Sweden fell to Dutch forces in 1655. English conquered the area in 1664 under the Duke of York, who in 1682 transferred the Counties on Delaware to William Penn. Though in his proprietorship to 1776, they were separately governed from 1704 and fought during the Revolution as a state. On Dec. 7, 1787, Delaware became the first state to ratify the Federal Constitution.

Fort Christina Monument marks the site of founding of New Sweden in 1638. Holy Trinity (Old Swedes) Church erected 1698 is the oldest Protestant Church in the U. S. still in use. Center New Castle comprises a unique survival of a colonial capital nearly in its late 18th century form. The home of John Dickinson, "Penman of the Revolution," and drafter of the Articles of Confederation, has been restored near Dover.

Museums include the Delaware Art Center in Wilmington which has collections of Pre-Raphaelite English paintings, American paintings and manuscripts and drawings. The Henry Francis du Pont Winterthur Museum, at Winterthur near Wilmington, has 100 American period rooms from 17th to early 19th Centuries (reservations required to visit some of them). The Hagley Museum at Wilmington includes many of the old du Pont powder mills and other exhibits illustrating the development of American industry.

The Delaware State Museum at Dover includes a collection of early "talking machines."

## WILMINGTON

Wilmington had 85,690 pop. (1967 Special Census); and 366,298 in the standard metropolitan area. Laid out near Fort Christina, 1730-1736, by Thomas Willing and others, it was chartered in 1739 as Wilmington. Early a milling, shipping and manufacturing center, its business has remained varied. Notable current industries include vulcanized fibre, glazed kid and morocco leather, the largest braided hose plant, and the largest single cotton dyeing and finishing works. It is a world chemical center, with the home office and central laboratories of the Atlas, du Pont and Hercules companies.

The E. I. du Pont de Nemours Co., makers of over 1,400 products including many synthetics, maintains its executive department and a number of its research laboratories in Wilmington. In 1802, Eleuthère Irenée du Pont established a powder works on the Brandywine, the forerunner of the present corporation. Its original nylon plant is at Seaford, Del.

# Florida

### Sunshine State

CAPITAL: Tallahassee. AREA: 58,560 sq. mi., rank, 22nd. POPULATION: (1960 Census), 4,951,-560, rank, 10th. MOTTO: In God We Trust. FLOWER: Orange Blossom. BIRD: Mockingbird. TREE: Sabal Palm. SONG: The Swanee River. ADMISSION: 27th.

Florida's many miles of beaches and other resort areas offer fun in the sun to millions of vacationers, and its semi-tropical climate provides a pleasant retirement haven for thousands of oldsters. But the state also has a tremendous agricultural output, producing 80% of the nation's citrus fruits and ranking 2nd only to California in production of vegetables. And, its growing and diversified manufacturing industries provide even more income than its agriculture.

The Florida peninsula juts southward 500 mi. between the Atlantic and the Gulf of Mexico; Cuba

is only 90 mi. from its southern tip. It has some 30,000 lakes; Okeechobee, covering 700 sq. mi., is the 4th largest natural lake inside the U. S. Highest elevation in the state is 345 ft., in the NW.

Florida was discovered by Ponce de Leon 1513; acquired from Spain 1819 by treaty ratified 1821. It was organized as a Territory Mar. 30, 1822, and admitted to the Union Mar. 3, 1845. It seceded 1861 and was readmitted 1868.

Tourism is a major industry; about 18,000,000 visitors spend some $4.3 billion annually in Florida. It offers a wide variety of tourist attractions in addition to climate, resorts and water sports.

Many of the tourists become permanent residents. The state's population has boomed from 4,951,560 in the 1960 Census to 5,996,000 in the official July 1, 1967, est.

Major tourist objectives are metropolitan Miami, with the nation's greatest concentration of luxury hotels at Miami Beach; Palm Beach; St. Augustine, founded 1565 and oldest city in U. S.; Daytona Beach, Fort Lauderdale, all on the E coast; Sarasota, Tampa, Key West, St. Petersburg on the W; Panama City on N Gulf Coast.

Everglades National Park, 1,258,670 acres of land and water, preserves the beauty of the vast Everglades swamp. Castillo de San Marcos (St. Augustine), Fort Mantanzas, Fort Jefferson (Dry Tortugas), De Soto National Memorial (Bradenton), and Fort Caroline (Jacksonville) are national monuments.

The USAF Missile Test Center is at Cape Kennedy, formerly Canaveral. From it the nation's first earth satellite was launched Jan. 31, 1958, first U. S. manned space flight, May 5, 1961, and the first manned orbital flight, Feb. 20, 1962, by Col. John H. Glenn.

Key West became the 1st U. S. city to get its fresh water from the sea when a desalting plant, capable of producing 2,620,000 gallons a day, was opened in 1967.

Florida produces most of the nation's oranges and grapefruit; 1967 output was 4,428,000 tons of oranges (almost 5 times California output) and 1,381,000 tons of grapefruit (almost 10 times California's). It is also 1st in watermelons and is 2nd to California in fresh vegetables. It also produces limes, tangerines, sugarcane, peanuts, cotton, tobacco. Citrus fruits are the most valuable, followed by livestock and vegetables.

The cattle industry is important; on Jan. 1, 1968, Florida had 1,788,000 hd. Farm receipts for 1967 were $1.03 billion.

Manufacturing has made great gains and accounts for twice as much total personal income as agriculture. Leading industries, in terms of value added by manufacturing, are food processing, chemicals, paper and products, printing and publishing, stone-clay-glass, transportation, in that order.

Florida leads the U. S. in production of phosphate rock, is 2nd to New York in titanium and 3rd in rare-earth metals. Total mineral production in 1967 was valued at a record high of $299,624,000.

The commercial catch of fish and shellfish is worth over $34,000,000 a year, ranking 6th among the states. It includes a large portion of the nation's mullet, shrimp and blue crab.

Florida has 21 airports with scheduled service, 36 scheduled airlines and 7 major railroads. There are 14 deepwater ports which handle domestic and foreign trade valued at $1.24 billion a year.

Construction of the Cross-Florida Barge Canal, linking the Atlantic just N of Jacksonville with the Gulf of Mexico at Yankeetown, 90 mi. N of Tampa, is to be completed in 1972. The canal will be open to pleasure and fishing craft, as well as commercial traffic.

There are 28 4-year colleges and 32 junior colleges, including Univ. of Florida (Gainesville); Univ. of Miami (Coral Gables); Univ. of Tampa (Tampa); John B. Stetson Univ. (Deland); Rollins College (Winter Park); Florida State Univ. (Tallahassee); Univ. of South Florida (Tampa); New College (Sarasota); Univ. of West Florida (Pensacola) and Florida Tech Univ. (Orlando).

Florida has no state income tax and no bonded debt. Its excise taxes (beverage, tobacco, parimutuel), sales and other taxes account for 69% of total state revenue.

Museums include the Florida State Museum in Gainesville, which does field work in natural and social sciences in the southeast U.S. and Caribbean area, displays exhibits in archeology, ethnology, paleontology, ornithology, history and industry. Castillo de San Marcos in St. Augustine is a well-

preserved Spanish fort built 1672-1696 which is now a national monument. Marineland of Florida, 18 mi. S of St. Augustine, has some 2,500 marine specimens ranging from sharks and porpoises to tiny tropical fish living in oceanarium tanks; visitors may view and photograph them through portholes; trained porpoises and pilot whales perform in shows. Miami's Seaquarium has similar shows.

At Pensacola is the Naval Aviation Museum with exhibits tracing flight development into the space age; also several forts, including Fort Pickens, built 1829, where Geronimo was imprisoned; the T. T. Wentworth Museum, with exhibits of local historical interest; the Pensacola Historical Museum and Spanish Village Museum.

In Sarasota, the John and Mable Ringling Museum of Art, willed to the state, contains works by Rembrandt, Rubens, Hals, Tiepolo, Velasquez, Murillo, Gainsborough, Reynolds and other masters. The Ringling Museum of the Circus includes elaborately decorated wagons, costumes and printed bills showing performers at fairs and circuses from the 16th to 20th centuries; the Asolo Theater presents plays and operas.

Also in Sarasota, the Circus Hall of Fame gives circus acts and puppet shows, displays mementos such as a coach given Tom Thumb by Queen Victoria, a sleigh P. T. Barnum gave Jenny Lind, costumes, rigging and circus equipment.

*(See also Index for Miami, Orlando, St. Petersburg, Tampa.)*

# Georgia
*Empire State of the South, Peach State*

**CAPITAL: Atlanta. AREA: 58,876 sq. mi., rank, 21st. POPULATION: (1960 Census), 3,943,116, rank, 16th. MOTTO: Wisdom, Justice, Moderation. FLOWER: Cherokee Rose. BIRD: Brown Thrasher. TREE: Live Oak. SONG: Georgia. Fourth of the Original 13 States to ratify Constitution.**

Largest in area of the states east of the Mississippi, Georgia is rich in a number of natural resources and in its growing, diversified industries.

There are large deposits of marble in the mountainous N, along with fertile plains and industry centers in the NW. The Central Georgia Piedmont plateau boasts rich farmlands and a flourishing textile industry. The SE Coastal Plain produces pecans and peanuts and its forests yield a wealth of pulpwood and turpentine. Off its 100-mi. Atlantic coast lie its famed Sea Islands. The state also has large deposits of clay, limestone and bauxite, bases for important industries.

Okefenokee in the SE is one of the largest swamps in the U. S., a wetland wilderness and peat bog covering 660 sq. mi. A large part of it is a National Wildlife Refuge, a home for wild birds, alligators, bear, deer, otter, etc.

Highest point in the state is Brasstown Bald in the NE, 4,784 ft.; Stone Mtn., near Atlanta, is 1,686 ft. Est. pop. July 1, 1967, was 4,511,000.

Manufacturing production in Georgia has increased about 9 times in value since the start of World War II, a rate twice the national average. The textile industry is Georgia's oldest and largest.

Georgia is by far the nation's largest producer of peanuts, harvesting 487,560 tons in 1967, almost 3 times as many as the next largest producer, North Carolina. It is 2nd in pecans and in chickens, and 4th among the states in tobacco. Total farm receipts for 1967 were $1.03 billion, up from 1966; the increase in crop receipts more than offset a decline in livestock income.

Georgia ranks high in lumber production and its output of pulpwood is tops in the U. S. The state produces more than half the world's turpentine.

It is 1st in the U. S. in production of china clays; 2nd in zirconium; 3rd in bauxite, barite and kyanite. Value of total mineral production in 1967 was $145,633,000, a drop of 2% from the record 1966 figure.

Leading manufacturing industries in 1965, in order of importance, were textiles, transportation equipment, food products, paper products, apparel, chemicals. The largest private employer is Lockheed-Georgia, producing large transport planes, etc.

There are 49 institutions of higher learning, including the Univ. of Georgia. The state is served by 5 major railroads and 9 airlines. Savannah and Brunswick are its main ports.

About 28,000,000 vacation travelers spent an est. $429,900,000 in Georgia in 1966.

Notable among attractions are Warm Springs Memorial and Little White House where President Franklin D. Roosevelt died April 12, 1945, the

Roosevelt Museum and nearby Ida Cason Callaway Gardens and Roosevelt State Park; Stone Mtn. and Jekyll Island State Park.

Andersonville Prison Park and National Cemetery are on the site of the Confederate prison camp in which a total of 50,000 Union soldiers were confined, Feb. 1864 to Apr. 1865, in conditions so infamous that over 900 died in each of the 13 months the camp existed. Park and cemetery are administered by the U. S. Army Department.

Georgia was visited by DeSoto, 1540. It was a part of land granted to the lords proprietors of Carolina, 1663 and 1685; became an independent colony by charter of 1732 with first permanent settlement under James Oglethorpe, 1733. Georgia ratified the Confederate constitution, Mar. 1861, was readmitted to the Union, July, 1870.

*(See also Index for Atlanta.)*

# Hawaii
## *Aloha State*

**CAPITAL:** Honolulu. **AREA:** 6,450 sq. mi., rank, 47th. **POPULATION:** (1960 Census), 632,772, rank, 43rd. **MOTTO:** The Life of the Land is Perpetuated in Righteousness. **FLOWER:** Hibiscus. **BIRD:** Nene (Hawaiian Goose). **TREE:** Kukui (Candlenut). **OFFICIAL SONG:** Hawaii Ponoi. **ADMISSION:** 50th.

Hawaii, prosperous paradise of the Pacific, became the 50th state Aug. 21, 1959, and the 50-star U. S. flag became official the following July 4.

The Hawaiian Islands lie in the North Pacific, 2,395 mi. from San Francisco (5 hrs. by commercial jet). They consist of 8 major islands (7 inhabited) and 114 minor islands (4 inhabited). The principal islands are Hawaii (4,021 sq. mi.); Oahu (595 sq. mi.), on which are Honolulu and Pearl Harbor; Lanai, Maui, Molokai, Kauai, Niihau and Kahoolawe (uninhabited).

The islands are volcanic. Highest point is Mauna Kea, on Hawaii, an extinct volcano 13,796 ft. above sea level. Its twin is Mauna Loa, 13,680 ft., largest active volcano in the world. Average annual rainfall is 22 inches at Honolulu Airport, 140 inches in Hilo, and 472 inches atop Waialeale, a mountain on Kauai. Honolulu is subtropical (alltime range, 56° to 88°) but Mauna Kea is often snow capped.

Lake Waiau, at 13,020 ft. near the summit of Mauna Kea, is the highest lake in the U. S.

Ka Lae, or South Cape, on the island of Hawaii, is the southernmost point in the 50 states.

The islands were settled by Polynesians, probably about 700-750 A.D. These Polynesians sailed to Hawaii from Tahiti, over 2,000 mi. to the south, in large outrigger canoes.

Hawaii was visited 1778 by British Capt. James Cook who called the group the Sandwich Islands. It was a kingdom until Jan. 17, 1893, when Queen Liliuokalani was deposed and annexation to the United States asked. President Cleveland blocked this on the ground of American collusion. Hawaii organized a republic, 1894, with Sanford B. Dole as president. Congress voted annexation July 7, 1898 under President McKinley. The Territory was established June 14, 1900.

Hawaii, among the states, has the most heterogeneous of populations, with Americans of Polynesian, Asian, European and African extraction living together with a notable lack of racial tensions.

Many of the Polynesians intermarried with the other racial groups, which arrived mainly in the 19th Century.

The 1960 Census gave as racial origins: Japanese 32.2%, Caucasian 32%, part-Hawaiian 14.5%, Filipino 10.8%, Chinese 6%, Hawaiian 1.7%, Negro 0.8%, American Indian 0.1%. It has since been unofficially est. that the Caucasian-descent category slightly outnumbered those of Japanese descent. Total est. pop., July 1, 1967, was 741,000.

Tourism is Hawaii's 2nd largest industry, next to national defense and ahead of sugar, 3rd, and pineapples, 4th. Total visitors in 1966 were est. at 710,000, with an average of 21,866 present daily.

In 1966 gross state product was $2.7 billion, construction completed was $392,400,000 and bank assets (Jan. 1, 1967) totaled $1.2 billion, all up.

Most mineral output is for local consumption; continued heavy demand for construction materials, such as cement and stone, kept total mineral production, 1966, above $20,000,000 for the 2nd consecutive year. Volcanic cinder is used in roads, salt is obtained from sea water by evaporation, scuba divers get black coral for gems off Maui,

lime is used to clarify cane juice and cut acidity in pineapple juice, basalt and limestone are used for building.

More than 1,800 ships put into Honolulu each year. Honolulu International Airport has an average of 790 arrivals and departures daily.

*(See also Index for Honolulu.)*

# Idaho
## *Gem State*

**CAPITAL:** Boise. **AREA:** 83,557 sq. mi. rank, 13th. **POPULATION:** (1960 Census), 667,191, rank, 42nd. **MOTTO:** Esto Perpetua. Exist Forever. **FLOWER:** Lewis Mock Orange (Syringa). **BIRD:** Mountain Bluebird. **TREE:** Western White Pine. **SONG:** Here We Have Idaho. **GEM:** Star Garnet. **ADMISSION:** 43rd.

A land of rugged grandeur, Idaho nevertheless ranks high in agricultural production.

Exploration of Idaho began with the visits of the Lewis & Clark Expedition, 1805-6. Fur traders and missionaries followed and the area became part of Oregon Territory, 1848; Idaho Territory, Mar. 3, 1863, and a state July 3, 1890.

Est. pop. July 1, 1967, was 699,000.

Idaho was chiefly a farming, grazing, timber and mineral state for many years, but manufacturing has recently become second in importance to agriculture. There are rugged mountains, beautiful valleys, plateau regions, and extensive lava fields. Mt. Borah, in the Sawtooth Mts., is the highest peak, 12,662 ft. The Snake River runs through Hells Canyon, which averages 5,510 ft. in depth for 40 mi., at one point 7,900 ft., exceeding Grand Canyon, and is 10 mi. from rim to rim at widest point. The Snake has several noted waterfalls, among them Shoshone, Twin and American.

Idaho is the nation's leading potato producer, with 63,900,000 cwt. in 1967, far ahead of the next state, Maine. It is 2nd in sugarbeets and 5th in barley, and has crops of wheat, hay and apples. It ranks high in wool production and was 9th in number of sheep in 1968 with 834,000, more than one per person. Total farm receipts in 1967 were $537,224,000, more from crops than from livestock.

Manufacturing's gains were mainly in processing of potatoes and other foods, phosphates, paper, etc. Total value added by manufacturing was an est. $520,000,000 in 1967.

Discovery of silver in 1884 at Coeur d'Alene caused a stampede, and Idaho still leads the nation in production of that metal.

It also ranks 1st among the states in antimony, 2nd in lead, cobalt, garnet, phosphate rock and vanadium, 3rd in zinc and mercury. Total mineral production in 1967 was valued at $106,187,000.

With 39% of its area in forests, Idaho produces much lumber, with the world's largest white pine lumber mill at Lewiston. Yellow pine, Douglas fir, white spruce, larch, hemlock abound; the Roosevelt Grove has cedars 1,000 years old. Total value of forest products in 1967 was $190,000,000.

Hells Canyon, Brownlee and Oxbow Dams, 3 recent hydroelectric projects on the Snake River, are in operation. The National Reactor Testing Station of the AEC on Upper Snake River Plains has 21 reactors in operation, more building.

Tourism brought in an est. $202,000,000 from 6,100,000 visitors in 1967, ranking it 3rd to agriculture and manufacturing, and ahead of forest products and mining.

The state offers excellent hunting and fishing and Lake Pend Oreille, which has a 500-mile shoreline, is home of the world's largest trout, Kamloop rainbow.

Craters of the Moon National Monument, 18 mi. W of Arco, is a jagged landscape. Lava covers the land and subterranean explosions have created multitudes of caves.

The State Historical Museum in Boise has displays of early Idaho Indians, the fur trade, mining, farm and household gear of the pioneers.

# Illinois
## *Prairie State*

**CAPITAL:** Springfield. **AREA:** 56,400 sq. mi., rank, 24th. **POPULATION:** (1960 Census), 10,081,-158, rank 4th. **MOTTO:** State Sovereignty, National Union. **FLOWER:** Native Violet. **BIRD:** Cardinal. **TREE:** Bur Oak. **SONG:** Illinois. **SLOGAN:** Land of Lincoln. **ADMISSION:** 21st.

Illinois ranks high among the states as both an

agricultural and industrial empire. It is rich in coal and oil reserves and boasts highly developed rail, water and air transportation facilities.

The soil is rich and level, with the high point, Charles Mound near the Wisconsin line, only 1,235 ft.

Est. pop. July 1, 1967, was 10,894,000.

In 1967 Illinois ranked 2nd among the states in income from crops, 4th for livestock products and 3rd in total agricultural receipts, $2.6 billion. It was the nation's largest producer of corn and soybeans, 6th in winter wheat, 7th in oats. It was 2nd to Iowa in number of hogs, 6,772,000, and 11th in cattle.

Manufacturing employment in 1964 averaged 1,233,800, with payrolls est. at over $8 billion. Non-agricultural employment was 4,132,900, a new high. Major manufacturing lines are food products (especially grain, beverages, candy, meat) and machinery (particularly construction and farm), each accounting for about $2 billion annually in value added by manufacturing. Electrical machinery, primary metals (mainly iron and steel), printing-publishing, chemicals and fabricated metals each account for over $1 billion in value added. Rockford is the nation's 2nd largest machine-tool center; Peoria is a distilling center.

Illinois has the largest coal reserves, an est. 137 billion tons, in the U. S.

In 1967 coal output was 65,500,000 tons, 4th highest in the nation and up 3% over 1966. Large oil deposits underlie much of the state; petroleum production in 1967 was valued at $181,255,000. Illinois ranks 1st in fluorspar and tripoli, 2nd in stone, 3rd in peat. Total 1967 mineral production was valued at $638,098,000.

A major research and development installation of the Atomic Energy Commission is the Argonne National Laboratory, Lemont, Ill., directed by the Univ. of Chicago, which also operates the Argonne Cancer Research Hospital in Chicago. Dresden Nuclear Power Station, using a boiling water type of reactor, has been built for Commonwealth Edison Co. and the seven other companies in Nuclear Power Group, Inc., near Joliet, Ill. It has a capacity of 180,000 kilowatts.

Illinois has 130 public and private colleges and universities, including Univ. of Illinois with campuses in Champaign-Urbana and Chicago and an enrollment of 37,164 in 1966. It has medical facilities in Chicago as do Northwestern Univ. and the Univ. of Chicago.

The Illinois State Fair is held annually in August in Springfield. A total of 35,000 entries compete for more than $1,000,000 in cash awards. Annual attendance is about 1,000,000.

State forests, parks and conservation areas cover 100,000 acres. Some are associated with the history of the Middle West, including Lincoln's home and tomb in Springfield; the restored Fort de Chartres, seat of French 18th Century authority; old settlements, such as Kaskaskia. Illinois was part of the territory taken from the British by George Rogers Clark. It became a state 1818.

The Illinois State Museum in Springfield has large collections of local art and archeology; art and architecture of the ancient Near East, and antique clocks, glass, china and furniture.

Located in Springfield is a state memorial including Abraham Lincoln's tomb and the Lincoln home which the family occupied for 17 years beginning in 1844.

New Salem State Park, 20 mi. NW of Springfield, contains the restored pioneer village of New Salem where Lincoln lived as storekeeper, surveyor and postmaster, 1831-37. Annual performances are staged of Robert Sherwood's Abe Lincoln in Illinois.

*(See also Index for Chicago.)*

# Indiana
*Hoosier State*

**CAPITAL: Indianapolis. AREA: 36,291 sq. mi., rank, 38th. POPULATION: (1960 Census), 4,662,-498, rank, 11th. MOTTO: Cross-roads of America. FLOWER: Peony. BIRD: Cardinal. TREE: Tulip (Yellow Poplar). SONG: On the Banks of the Wabash. ADMISSION: 19th.**

Indiana is heavily industrialized, yet also ranks high as an agricultural state. It is 3rd among the states in output of both steel and corn; it quarries most of the building limestone used in the U. S. and also ranks high in coal production.

It was explored by LaSalle, 1679; French trading posts grew during the 18th Century. Vincennes,

the 1st permanent settlement, was taken over by the British, 1763, and its capture by George Rogers Clark in 1779 led to the opening of the old Northwest Territories to the U. S. Indiana became a Territory July 4, 1800, and a state Dec. 11, 1816.

Est. pop. July 1, 1967, was 4,999,000.

There are sand dunes and lakes in the N, a level plain through most of the central area, and hills in the S. Highest point is 1,257 ft. in Wayne Co., in the east central area.

The Calumet region in the state's NW corner, including Gary, Hammond, East Chicago and Whiting, has one of the world's greatest concentrations of heavy industry, especially steel, cement and oil refining plants. Gary was a sand dune in 1905 when U. S. Steel located mills there, in 1960 it had a pop. of 177,913. Inland Steel and Youngstown have large plants in East Chicago. Another vast steel complex is rising further E on Lake Michigan where a $92,000,000 port is being planned at Burns Harbor in the famed Dunes area; Midland Steel Div. of the National Steel Corp. has erected a plant nearby and Bethlehem Steel Corp. is building a $250,000,000 group of facilities.

While steel and other metal industries are responsible for $1.4 billion of the $7.6 billion in value added annually by manufacturing, electrical machinery, including television sets and household appliances, is a close 2nd with $1.14 billion. Auto parts, aircraft and other transportation equipment is next, with $1.1 billion, followed by industrial, farm and other machinery, 4th; chemicals, 5th; farm products, 6th.

Corn is the principal crop (447,804,000 bu. in 1967) and much of it goes to fatten the hogs (4,111,000 on farms Jan. 1, 1968). Indiana ranks 1st in popcorn, 3rd in grain corn, 4th in hogs and soybeans, 8th in chickens. Total farm receipts in 1967 were $1.4 billion.

Coal accounted for a quarter of the total value of mineral production, est. at $241,196,000 in 1967; petroleum output was about a seventh of the total. Cement, limestone, clay and gypsum are also important.

Indiana limestone, from vast quarries in the southern part of the state, sheaths tens of thousands of buildings, including the Empire State, Rockefeller Center, the United Nations, the Pentagon, the National Cathedral, many Federal buildings and many state capitols.

Indiana has 21 state parks and recreation areas, including Dunes State Park on Lake Michigan and prehistoric Indian mounds at Mounds State Park; over 1,000 lakes; French Lick and other mineral spas; Wyandotte Cave, 3rd largest in the U. S., and other caverns, and the famous postoffice, Santa Claus.

Lincoln's boyhood home in Spencer County and the grave of his mother, Nancy Hanks Lincoln, are part of the Lincoln Boyhood National Memorial. State memorials commemorate the capture of Vincennes by George Rogers Clark in the Revolution, the defeat of Tecumseh's Indians at Tippecanoe, and the Rappite and Robert Owen communities at New Harmony.

Spring Mill Village, 3 mi. E of Mitchell, is a restored pioneer settlement, with grist mill, general store, apothecary's shop, tavern, distillery and sawmill.

The Evansville Museum of Arts and Science has collections including paintings, sculpture, textiles, ceramics, period rooms and anthropology.

Among 38 institutions of higher education are Indiana Univ., Purdue Univ., Ball State Univ., Indiana State Univ., Notre Dame Univ., Indiana Central College, Valparaiso Univ., De Pauw Univ., Wabash College.

*(See also Index for Indianapolis.)*

# Iowa
*Hawkeye State*

**CAPITAL: Des Moines. AREA: 56,290 sq. mi., rank, 25th. POPULATION: (1960 Census), 2,757,-537, rank, 24th. MOTTO: Our Liberties We Prize and Our Rights We Will Maintain. FLOWER: Wild Rose. BIRD: Eastern Goldfinch. TREE: Oak. SONG: Iowa. ADMISSION: 29th.**

Iowa, the heart of the rich Midwest farm belt, is one of the nation's leading agricultural states, but its industrial buildup has been so great that in 1967 the value of its manufacturing output passed $10.2 billion while the market value of its agricultural products was $3.4 billion.

Many industries process farm products or produce farm implements. However, the fast-growing industrial economy includes a wide variety of manufacturing plants, with electronics items, washing machines, tires, railway equipment, furnaces, automobile accessories, chemicals and fertilizers, vending machines, office furniture, and gypsum wallboard among the diversified products. Iowa developed the pearl button industry from Mississippi River clamshells.

Iowa's broad plains contain much of the finest soil in the world. Its huge harvests support the nation's largest livestock industry. Iowa has by far the most hogs, 13,740,000 on Jan. 1, 1968, more than twice the number in Illinois, the next largest raiser. In cattle, with 7,183,000, Iowa was 2nd only to Texas.

Receipts for livestock and livestock products in 1967 totaled $2.5 billion, $1 billion more than Texas, the next-ranking state. Iowa stood 4th in receipts for crops, $897,481,000. Its total farm receipts were $3.4 billion, 2nd only to California.

In field crops, Iowa ranked 1st in popcorn, 2nd in soybeans and grain corn, 4th in oats and alfalfa.

Mineral production was valued at $114,775,000 for 1967. Products, in order of value, were cement, limestone, sand and gravel, gypsum and coal.

Highest point in the state is Ocheyedan Mound, 1,675 ft., in the NW.

Est. pop. July 1, 1967, was 2,753,000. More than 12,000,000 travelers from other states visit Iowa annually, adding nearly $250,000,000 to the state's economy.

Tourist attractions include the Herbert Hoover birthplace and library near West Branch, tulip festivals at Pella and Orange City in May, Iowa State Fair at Des Moines in August, several rodeos. The Little Brown Church in the Vale, near Nashua, inspired a well-known hymn and draws about 100,000 visitors annually. There are 90 state parks and other recreation areas. Effigy Mounds National Monument at Marquette is a prehistoric Indian burial site.

The Davenport Municipal Art Gallery has a collection of paintings and memorabilia of the Iowa painter Grant Wood, as well as other American, Mexican and European paintings. Old masters include Breughel, Constable, Reynolds. The Davenport Public Museum displays the history of the area from pre-historic Indians to the steamboat and modern eras; archeology and ethnology of Egypt, Greece, Rome, Europe, South America and Asia; extensive collections of birds, mammals, insects, fossils, minerals and a herbarium of 20,000 plants.

In Decorah, the Norwegian-American Museum preserves homes, household utensils, etc., of pioneers who came from Norway.

Waterloo's Museum of History and Science has exhibits on Iowa history, pioneer life, Indian lore and earth sciences and a planetarium.

Iowa's institutions of higher learning include 27 colleges, 24 junior colleges and 3 state universities. Best known are the Univ. of Iowa, Iowa City; Iowa State University, Ames; Univ. of Northern Iowa, Cedar Falls; Coe College, Cedar Rapids; Drake Univ., Des Moines; Grinnell College, Grinnell.

The first Europeans to visit the Iowa area were the French explorers, Father Jacques Marquette and Louis Jolliet, in 1673. It formed part of the Louisiana Purchase in 1803 and became a state Dec. 28, 1846.

(See also Index for Des Moines.)

# Kansas

*Sunflower State*

**CAPITAL:** Topeka. **AREA:** 82,264 sq. mi., rank, 14th. **POPULATION:** (1960 Census), 2,178,611, rank, 28th. **MOTTO:** Ad Astra per Aspera. To the Stars Through Difficulties. **FLOWER:** Sunflower. **BIRD:** Western Meadow Lark. **TREE:** Cottonwood. **ANIMAL:** Buffalo. **SONG:** Home on the Range. **ADMISSION:** 34th.

Rolling fields of wheat, clusters of oil well derricks, great herds of cattle and towering grain storage elevators feature the landscape of Kansas, the geographical center of the 48 conterminous states. The land rises from broad plains in the E, 680 ft. above sea level, to Mt. Sunflower, 4,039 ft., in the W.

Manufacturing, farming and mining (especially petroleum and natural gas) are major factors in Kansas' economy. Growing industries include food products, paper, printing, chemicals, fabricated metals, machinery and transportation equipment.

Farms cover 50,000,000 acres, 95% of the land area. They produce a sixth of the nation's wheat crop. The 1967 Kansas output was 221,620,000 bu. of winter wheat, almost twice that of Washington, next largest producer. Total farm income was $1.5 billion in 1967, ranking 7th. It was 4th in number of cattle, 5,564,000 on Jan. 1, 1968.

Kansas City, Kan., borders on Kansas City, Mo., but is a separate city. It has huge stockyards and packing plants.

Wichita is the nation's 3rd largest aircraft center in employment; ranks 1st in production of personal aircraft. Major producers are Boeing, Beech, Cessna, Lear.

Kansas ranks high in petroleum production and has large reserves of natural gas and helium. The world's largest helium production plant was opened in Otis, Kan., in 1966. Kansas ranks 1st among the states in helium production.

Oil output in 1967 was valued at $305,244,000, more than half the total mineral production value, $579,964,000.

Est. pop. July 1, 1967, was 2,275,000.

Coronado in 1541 headed a Spanish troop in a vain search for wealth in the area. France claimed all territory drained by the Mississippi through LaSalle's explorations, 1682. France ceded the vast area to Spain, 1763, and received it back, 1800. In 1803 the U. S. obtained the land through the Louisiana Purchase. The Kansas part of it became a Territory May 30, 1854; a state Jan. 29, 1861.

During the fight over statehood Kansas was rent between free-state and pro-slavery forces. Kansas furnished one-fifth of her men for Union armies in the Civil War. Frontier posts were at Fort Leavenworth, now site of the U. S. Army Command and General Staff College; Fort Riley, Fort Scott, Fort Larned, Fort Hays, and other sites.

The boyhood home of President Eisenhower in Abilene is now a shrine and adjoins the Eisenhower Museum and the Eisenhower Presidential Library. Pioneer days are reproduced in Old Abilene Town.

The Agricultural Hall of Fame and National Center, 14 mi. W of Kansas City, Kan., displays farm equipment of the past such as a wooden-wheeled corn planter, anvils, wheat drills, etc.

The Wichita Art Museum has works by Bellows, Eakins, Copley, Sargent, Cassatt, Hopper, Ryder, Grosz, Marin, Andrew Wyeth, Stuart Davis, Lachaise, De Creeft, Zorach. The Kansas State Historical Society in Topeka has displays and period rooms of Midwest history and a library with newspaper and manuscript collections.

In Lawrence, the Univ. of Kansas has a Museum of Natural History which presents a panorama of North American mammals from the Arctic to the tropics; a Museum of Art, with European and American painting and sculpture and European and Oriental decorative arts; and the Snow Entomological Museum, with over 2,000,000 insects.

There are 6 state colleges, 1 municipal university and many private colleges.

Kansas has developed an extensive system of recreation around its federal reservoirs, lakes and roadside parks. The Interstate System and Kansas Turnpike are part of a large highway system.

(See also Index for Kansas City.)

# Kentucky

*Blue Grass State*

**CAPITAL:** Frankfort. **AREA:** 40,395 sq. mi., rank, 37th. **POPULATION:** (1960 Census), 3,038,-156, rank, 22nd. **MOTTO:** United We Stand, Divided We Fall. **FLOWER:** Goldenrod. **BIRD:** Cardinal. **SONG:** My Old Kentucky Home. **TREE:** Tuliptree. **ADMISSION:** 15th.

Kentucky was the first area W of the Allegheny Mtns. settled by American pioneers, and one of the first of them to arrive was Daniel Boone, 1769. The first permanent settlement was that of James Harrod at Harrodsburg in 1774; the following year Boone blazed the Wilderness Trail and founded Boonesboro. Originally part of Fincastle Co., Va., the area became Kentucky Co., Va., in 1776, and an independent state in 1792.

Kentucky rises from an elevation of less than 260 ft., at the Mississippi, to over 4,000 ft. in the Cumberland and Pine mountains. Over 45% of the state is forested, and lumbering, particularly of hardwoods, is an important industry.

Agriculture is Kentucky's largest single industry. Tobacco is the principal crop; with 418,959,000 lbs. in 1967, the output was 2nd to North Carolina's.

Corn, soybeans, wheat, fruit, cattle and hogs are also important. Farm receipts in 1967 totaled $385,662,000 from crops, $377,804,000 from livestock.

Kentucky ranked 3rd among the states in 1967 in production of coal, with 99,500,000 tons, up 7% from the record year, 1966. It ranked 2nd in the U. S. in fluorspar. Also important are petroleum, natural gas and clay. Total mineral production was valued at $517,876,000 for 1967, up 4% from 1966.

Manufacturing is gaining, mainly of food and tobacco products, apparel, machinery, metals, wood products and furniture, chemicals. Value added by manufacture is over $2.62 billion per yr.

Tourists bring in an est. $425,000,000 a year. There are 40 state and national parks and shrines.

In 1966 Kentucky enacted a law requiring surface and strip miners of coal to restore and regrade earth removed by their operations.

Also adopted were a broad civil rights law and legislation to develop water resources and regulate water and air pollution.

Est. pop. July 1, 1967, was 3,191,000.

Two of the largest man-made lakes in the world, Kentucky Lake and Lake Barkley, parallel each other in Western Kentucky, creating a 170,-000-acre isthmus called the Land Between the Lakes National Recreation Area, being developed by the Tennessee Valley Authority. Two major vacation resort parks, Kentucky Dam Village and Kenlake, are on the west shore of Kentucky Lake. Approximately 4,000,000 people visited this area in 1965. TVA estimates that this will increase to 10,000,000 yearly by 1970.

Lexington, heart of the Bluegrass country, is seat of Univ. of Kentucky and Transylvania, oldest college west of Alleghenies (1780), has a large tobacco market and holds annual trotting and running races and a horse show. Near Lexington are farms famous for blooded horses, including the Calumet, Castleton, Spendthrift, Walnut Hall, Greentree. It is also a manufacturing center.

Fort Knox, repository of the nation's gold reserve, also contains the George S. Patton, Jr., Military Museum of World War II equipment.

Mammoth Cave, 40 mi. from Bowling Green, is in a national park. Discovered 1799, it has 150 mi. of passageways, rooms with 200-ft. ceilings, gypsum flowers, blind fish and an Echo River 360 ft. below ground.

Old Fort Harrod State Park, Harrodsburg, contains the reconstructed fort with stockade, blockhouses and cabins; the log cabin in which Thomas Lincoln and Nancy Hanks, Abraham Lincoln's parents, were married, and a museum with relics of Shakertown, Ky.

Abraham Lincoln Birthplace National Historic Site, 3 mi. from Hodgenville, contains the original Thomas Lincoln farm and the traditional Lincoln Birthplace cabin.

My Old Kentucky Home, 1 mi. E of Bardstown, was the home of John Rowan, senator and state chief justice. Stephen Foster, a relative, visited the Rowan family in 1852 and is said to have written My Old Kentucky Home on a desk preserved in the house.

*(See also Index for Louisville.)*

# Louisiana

*Pelican State*

**CAPITAL: Baton Rouge. AREA: 48,523 sq. mi., rank, 31st. POPULATION: (1960 Census), 3,257,-022, rank, 20th. MOTTO: Union, Justice, Confidence. FLOWER: Southern Magnolia. BIRD: Eastern Brown Pelican. SONG: Song of Louisiana. TREE: Bald Cypress. ADMISSION: 18th.**

Louisiana blends a wealth of historic charm, rich natural resources and giant modern industries. Fertile soil, huge mineral deposits and over 7,000 mi. of navigable waterways linking the nation's heart with deepsea ports are factors basic to the state's wealth.

Mardi Gras and other festivals, the beat of Dixieland jazz in the land of its origin, and the nostalgic relics of the days of French and Spanish rule and the prosperous pre-Civil War era are among the attractions which bring Louisiana an est. $1 billion a year in tourist revenues.

In total value of its 1967 mineral output, $3.4 billion, Louisiana was 2nd only to Texas among the 50 states. It was 1st in value of its sulphur and salt production, and 2nd to Texas in petroleum and natural gas output. Much of the oil and sulphur is from offshore deposits.

The lush Louisiana land produces the nation's largest crop of sweet potatoes; the state is also 1st in output of sugarcane syrup. It is 2nd to Texas in rice. Also important are perique tobacco, cotton and corn.

Farm receipts for 1967 totaled $602,182,000, up about 9% from 1966.

Total value added by manufacture is over $2.22 billion annually.

Leading industry is chemicals and allied products, with nearly a half-billion dollars in value added annually by manufacturing. Other products, in order of value added, are food, petroleum and coal products, paper, transportation equipment, stone-clay-glass, metals.

With 7,409 sq. mi. under water, Louisiana marshes supply most of the nation's muskrat fur; nutria has become the state's leading fur; there are also opossum, raccoon, mink, otter, and large numbers of game birds. The annual catch of fresh and salt water fish, shrimp and oyster is valued at over $39,000,000. Lake Pontchartrain covers 630 sq. mi., is the 5th largest wholly within the U. S.

Much of the land is a rich alluvial plain; there are also rolling hills, bluffs on the Mississippi and coastal marshes. The elevation ranges from 5 ft. below sea level, protected by vast levees, to 535 above.

Louisiana is rich in historical relics and traditions, with Spanish-French backgrounds, pirate lore, fashionable French society in the 18th Century, picturesque customs today. Early explorers were Pineda, 1519, de Vaca, 1528, De Soto, 1541, LaSalle, 1682. New Orleans was founded 1718. Louisiana became a French crown colony under Louis XV, 1731; was ceded to Spain, 1763, returned to France, 1801; sold by Napoleon to U. S. Dec. 20, 1803 (with large territory to N and NW). It became a U. S. Territory Mar. 26, 1804, effective Oct. 1. State was admitted to the Union, Apr. 30, 1812; seceded Jan. 26, 1861, and joined Confederacy; readmitted June 25, 1868.

The Louisiana State Exhibit Museum in Shreveport features dioramas depicting the state's agricultural and mineral resources; there are also art shows, and exhibits of antique china, ceramics and Indian relics.

Louisiana Creoles are descendants of early French and/or Spanish settlers. About 4,000 Acadians, French settlers in Nova Scotia, Canada, were forcibly transported by the British to Louisiana in 1755 (an event commemorated in Longfellow's Evangeline) and settled near Bayou Teche; their descendants became known as Cajuns. Another group, the Islenos, are descendants of Canary Islanders brought to Louisiana by a Spanish governor in 1770. Traces of Spanish and French survive in local dialects.

Est. pop. July 1, 1967, was 3,660,000.

*(See also Index for New Orleans.)*

# Maine

*Pine Tree State*

**CAPITAL: Augusta. AREA: 33,215 sq. mi., rank, 39th. POPULATION: (1960 Census), 969,265, rank, 36th. MOTTO: Dirigo, I Direct. FLOWER: Pine Cone and Tassel. BIRD: Chickadee. TREE: Eastern White Pine. SONG: State of Maine Song. ADMISSION: 23rd.**

Maine is noted for its scenic and vacation attractions, lobsters, potatoes, poultry and forest products, fishing and hunting.

Largest of the 6 New England states, it is the farthest NE and borders on only one other state, New Hampshire. Its rugged coast, because of deep indentations, measures 3,478 mi. Tides are often high; in Passamaquoddy Bay they average 20 ft.

Mt. Cadillac, on Mt. Desert Is., 1,532 ft., is the highest Atlantic seacoast point N of Brazil; West Quoddy Head, Long. 66° 57', W, is the farthest east point on the U. S. Atlantic coast. Lubec is the most easterly town on the U. S. mainland.

John Cabot and his son, Sebastian, are believed to have visited the Maine coast in 1498. Long governed as a part of Massachusetts, Maine became a state in 1820.

Est. pop. July 1, 1967, was 973,000.

Maine's coastal waters produce an annual 20,-000,000 lbs. of lobsters, 75% of the nation's total, and 30% of its soft shell clams. The state packs over 120,000,000 cans of sardines a year. The fish and shellfish catch is valued at over $24,000,000 annually.

Maine grows about 8% of the nation's potatoes, second to Idaho, and is the leading supplier of

potato seed. It produces 90% of the nation's low bush blueberries and cans a third of this crop. Also grown are apples, sweet corn, peas, beans. Farm income totals about $250,000,000 a year, with poultry and eggs the largest item.

With 87% of its area forested, Maine turns out wood products from boats to toothpicks, paper, lumber and Christmas trees. Over 98% of forest land is privately owned. The wood products industry is the largest in the state, employing 26% of all wage-earners. Spruce, white pine and birch are the most important species. Est. value of finished products is $697,000,000 a year. Processed food, shoes and textiles rank next in factory products. It ranks 4th in shoe production.

Granite, cement and feldspar account for much of the total value of mineral products, est. at $16,785,000 in 1967.

Maine's scenic seacoast, beaches, lakes, mountains and resorts make it a popular vacationland; tourism is a $348,000,000-a-year industry. There are 20 state parks, including Baxter, where Mt. Katahdin, tallest of the state's 10 mountains over 4,000 ft., rises 5,268 ft. Maine has over 2,500 lakes, 1,300 wooded islands and 5,000 streams. Moosehead Lake is 40 mi. long and 2 to 10 mi. wide. Deer, grouse, black bear abound; game fish include salmon, bluefish, tuna, trout, bass. There are over 65 public skiing facilities. Acadia National Park and the famed resort of Bar Harbor are on Mt. Desert Island.

Museums include the Bowdoin College Museum of Fine Arts, Brunswick, which has portraits by Gilbert Stuart, Smibert, Feke, Blackburn, Copley, Winslow Homer, Cassatt, etc.; also Assyrian, Greek and Roman sculpture.

The Colby College Art Museum, Waterville, has paintings by classic and contemporary Europeans and by Americans—Hassam, Homer, Denn, Inness, Moran, Poor, Sterne, Andrew Wyeth.

The Farnsworth Library and Museum, Rockland, has 19th and 20th Century American paintings, drawings, prints and sculpture.

The Portland Museum of Art comprises the Sweat Museum of American art and the Sweat Mansion, a Federal-style house built in 1800. Other historic homes in Portland are the Tate House, 1755, and the Victoria Mansion, 1859.

Colleges and universities include the Univ. of Maine, Bowdoin (1794), Colby and Bates.

Maine has no state individual property, state income, corporate income or corporate excise taxes.

## Maryland

*Old Line State, Free State*

CAPITAL: Annapolis. AREA: 10,577 sq. mi., rank, 42nd. POPULATION: 3,100,689 (1960 Census), rank, 21st. MOTTO: Fatti Maschii, Parole Femine, Manly Deeds, Womanly Words; and Scuto Bonae Voluntatis Tuae Coronasti Nos, With the Shield of Thy Good-will Thou Hast Covered Us. FLOWER: Black-eyed Susan. BIRD: Baltimore Oriole. TREE: White Oak. SONG: Maryland, My Maryland. Seventh of the Original 13 States to ratify Constitution.

Maryland stretches from the Atlantic Ocean to the Allegheny Mountains with 2 major interruptions, Chesapeake Bay and the District of Columbia. Both contribute importantly to the state's economy.

The bay cuts off the low coastal plain of the Eastern Shore from the rest of the state, provides both commercial and sports fishing and leads to the port of Baltimore, which handles some $1.6 billion in imports and exports a year. The 7.11-mi. Chesapeake Bay Highway Bridge spans the bay near Annapolis, S of Baltimore.

The national Capital area provides a market for much of Maryland's produce as well as adding to the crowds which enjoy the state's many recreational facilities.

Backbone Mtn. in the far W part of the state is its highest point, 3,360 ft.

First settled was St. Clements Island, Mar. 25, 1634, by Leonard Calvert, brother of Cecilius Calvert, who moved to St. Mary's on mainland and formally established the colony. Settlement was Catholic, but Maryland in 1649 guaranteed religious tolerance to all.

Est. pop. July 1, 1967, was 3,685,000.

Gross state product in 1965 was $12.4 billion, up 5.1%; unemployment was 3.4%, below national average. Industries are diversified, producing primary metals, food products and beverages, transportation equipment, chemicals, missiles, nuclear equipment, scientific instruments, electric tools

Total value added by manufacture is over $2.9 billion annually.

Almost half of the land area is covered with forests. About 50% of timber cut is softwood. Cement is the leading mineral product; there is some coal mining and coke production.

Seafood is an important industry. In a typical year fish and shellfish will reach 83,000,000 lbs. and be worth over $14,000,000 to the fisherman. Striped bass is the chief contributor to fin fish revenues, oysters lead shellfish, but soft-shell clams have been gaining. Frozen, canned and cured fish have been increasing in production, but the industry is subject to variations.

Maryland has a large tomato crop and also produces tobacco, sweet potatoes, melons and vegetables. Commercial broilers are the largest agricultural revenue producer.

The 1st U. S. steam locomotive, Peter Cooper's Tom Thumb, was built in Baltimore and made its 1st run on the tracks of the Baltimore & Ohio R.R., 1830.

The University of Maryland (1807) has the Glenn L. Martin Institute of Technology. Other educational institutions: Johns Hopkins Univ. (estab. 1876), St. John's (1696), Goucher College (1885), U. S. Naval Academy (1845).

Famous racing events include Preakness, at Pimlico track, Baltimore; Grand National Steeplechase at Butler; the International at Laurel Race Course, and John B. Cambell Handicap at Bowie. Gibson Island is a center for yacht races.

Famous historic sites include Fort McHenry, Baltimore, restored, where in 1814 waved the flag that inspired Francis Scott Key to write the Star-Spangled Banner; Antietam Battlefield near Hagerstown (1862); South Mountain (1862); Edgar Allan Poe house, Baltimore. The State House, Annapolis (1772), is the oldest in the U. S.

The Chesapeake Bay Maritime Museum in St. Michael's exhibits typical bay boats, including the last surviving oyster sloop, a cottage-type lighthouse and models of Baltimore clippers, log canoes, bugeyes and skipjacks.

(See also Index for Baltimore, Washington, D. C.)

## Massachusetts

*Bay State, Old Colony*

CAPITAL: Boston. AREA: 8,257 sq. mi., rank 45th. POPULATION: (1960 Census), 5,149,834, rank, 9th. MOTTO: Ense Petit Placidam Sub Libertate Quietem. By the Sword We Seek Peace, but Peace Only Under Liberty. FLOWER: Mayflower. BIRD: Chickadee. TREE: American Elm. SONG: (unofficial) Massachusetts. Sixth of the Original 13 States to ratify Constitution.

Massachusetts has played important roles in the political, intellectual and economic development of the U. S. Here the Pilgrims, seeking religious freedom, founded Plymouth Colony in 1620.

As Massachusetts grew, it became a leader in resisting British oppression. Its citizens staged the Boston Tea Party in 1773 to protest unjust taxation. The Minutemen battled British troops at Lexington and Concord, Apr. 19, 1775, launching the American Revolution.

The state became the home of great universities such as Harvard and Massachusetts Institute of Technology. In the 19th Century its authors were giants among the nation's men of letters. The state was also a hotbed of abolitionism.

In Massachusetts ports a great shipping industry, including the famed China trade, developed, along with vast whaling and fishing interests. Abundant waterpower helped create a variety of manufacturing industries.

While the Puritans demanded religious freedom for themselves, their leaders denied it to others; but some among them protested this, and the loudest protesters, Roger Williams, Anne Hutchinson and others were banished and settled Rhode Island in the 1630s as a haven for religious liberty. Meanwhile, in Massachusetts, Quakers and Baptists were persecuted and in Salem the infamous witchcraft trials and hangings were staged in 1692.

Eventually, religious freedom was achieved. In 1867, Mary Baker Eddy founded Christian Science in Lynn. Heavy immigration of Irish, Italians, Poles, Czechs and French Canadians brought many Catholics to the state.

Est. pop. July 1, 1967, was 5,421,000.

In addition to Harvard (founded 1636) and M.I.T., other respected institutes of higher learning include Amherst, Andover Theological, Boston

Teachers, Holy Cross, Lowell Technological, Mt. Holyoke, Northeastern, Radcliffe, Simmons, Smith, Tufts, Univ. of Mass., Wellesley, Williams and Worcester Polytechnic.

The state had the first tax to support free schools and its first school at Dedham, 1649, and a uniform system in 1840.

Commercial fishing, in the rich waters off Massachusetts and the Grand Banks off Newfoundland, was one of the area's earliest industries. Whalers sailed the oceans around the world. Modern trawlers with huge nets help bring in a catch valued at over $49,000,000 a year, ranking 3rd behind Alaska and California.

Massachusetts pioneered in shoes, textiles and tools for them. The Bay State is 2nd to Pennsylvania in shoe production. Haverhill, Boston, Brockton, Lawrence, Lowell and Lynn are shoe centers. Francis Cabot Lowell perfected a power loom, 1822, started cotton manufacture at Lowell. Electrical machinery, including electronics and communications equipment, has become the state's leading product. Total value added by manufacture is over $7.3 billion per yr. About 42% of all workers are employed in manufacturing.

Massachusetts' cranberry crop is the nation's largest, 560,000 bbl. in 1967. Also important are dairy and poultry products, cigar wrapper tobacco, apples, peaches, maple syrup. Farm receipts totaled $159,157,000 in 1967. Mineral production for that year was valued at a record $39,111,000, mostly stone, gravel and lime.

Cape Cod has summer theaters, sports and an artists' colony at Provincetown. Tanglewood, in the Berkshires, has the summer concerts of Boston Symphony Orchestra, and Jacobs' Pillow is a ballet center.

In New Bedford the Old Dartmouth Historical Society and Whaling Museum has a large and unique collection of whaling implements, scrimshaw and log-books as well as furniture, costumes, firearms, etc.

In Old Deerfield are Deerfield Memorial Hall (1799), Hall Tavern (1765), Parson Ashley House (1732) and other old buildings.

In Pittsfield, the Berkshire Athenaeum has memorabilia of Herman Melville, who lived there while writing Moby Dick, a scrimshaw and whaling collection and a large library. The Berkshire Museum, Pittsfield, has paintings by Rubens, Van Dyck, Reynolds, Murillo, the Hudson River artists, etc.; mineral and animal rooms; one of the sledges with which Robert E. Peary reached the North Pole.

In Plymouth, Pilgrim Hall contains relics of the Mayflower Pilgrims, including swords of Myles Standish, Bibles of Gov. William Bradford and John Alden, and the cradle of Peregrine White, first child born in the colony.

Old Sturbridge Village, in Sturbridge, is a recreated early New England village of 35 authentic homes and shops, shown functioning.

The Sterling and Francine Clark Art Institute, Williamstown, displays 14th-17th Century European paintings, a large collection of Impressionists, sculpture, silver and drawings.

The Worcester Art Museum presents a survey of art through 50 centuries, stressing early American painting, pre-Columbian and contemporary arts. Also in Worcester, the John W. Higgins Armory displays medieval armor, and the American Antiquarian Society has a collection of early printing, including newspapers and almanacs.

*(See also Index for Boston.)*

# Michigan

*Wolverine State*

**CAPITAL:** Lansing. **AREA:** 58,216 sq. mi., rank, 23rd. **POPULATION:** 7,823,194 (1960 Census), rank 7th. **MOTTO:** Si Quaeris Peninsulam Amoenam Circumspice. If You Seek a Pleasant Peninsula, Look About You. **FLOWER:** Apple Blossom. **BIRD:** Robin. **TREE:** White Pine. **SONG:** (unofficial) Michigan, My Michigan. **ADMISSION:** 26th.

Bordering on 4 of the 5 Great Lakes, Michigan is divided into an Upper and Lower Peninsula by the Straits of Mackinac, which link Lakes Michigan and Huron. The 2 parts of the state are connected by the Mackinac Bridge, which has the 3rd largest suspension span in the U. S. To the N, separating Michigan from Canada, is the Sault Ste. Marie (Soo) Ship Canal, one of the world's most heavily used waterways.

Michigan is the world's largest auto producer;

grow huge fruit crops; the Upper Peninsula produces important amounts of iron and copper, and the state's lakes and forests make it a highly popular vacationland. Highest point is Mt. Curwood, 1,980 ft., in the Upper Peninsula.

Est. pop. July 1, 1967, was 8,584,000.

It ranks 1st in the world in production of motor vehicles and parts, cereal preparations, machine tools, hardware, steel springs, public office furniture, padding and upholstering, industrial patterns, nonferrous castings, industrial leather belts, paperboard mills and gray iron foundries. It ranks 2nd in U. S. in average weekly earnings of production workers. Value added by manufacturing is over $13 billion annually; $4.9 billion of it in motor vehicles and equipment. Also important are paper, chemicals, lumber.

Tourist attractions are many and spending by tourists was est. at over $1 billion for 1967. The state has 36,000 mi. of streams, over 11,000 lakes and the longest freshwater shoreline (facing 4 of the Great Lakes). Water sports, music festivals, skiing, winter carnivals, trout fishing and deer hunting are among attractions. Isle Royale in Lake Superior is a national park with 539,339 acres. There are 5 national forests, 73 state parks and recreational areas and numerous canoe trails.

Farm receipts in 1967 totaled $882,144,000, more than half from livestock products. Among the states, it ranks 1st in tart cherries and dried beans, 3rd in sweet cherries and apples, 4th in pears, 5th in grapes. Fruit output totals over 850,000 tons a year.

Iron ore production, source of a quarter of Michigan's income from minerals, continued to increase in 1967, thanks to greater output of taconite pellets from low-grade ores.

Total mineral production for the year was valued at $599,384,000. Michigan was 2nd only to Minnesota in value of iron ore output, $159,000,000. It ranked 1st among the states in gypsum, peat, iodine, bromine and magnesium compounds; 2nd in lime and gravel; 4th in cement.

There are some 88 institutions of higher learning, headed by Michigan State Univ., East Lansing, and Univ. of Michigan, Ann Arbor. Also important are Univ. of Detroit and Wayne, Western Michigan, Eastern Michigan, Central Michigan and Michigan Technological Univs.

The Grand Rapids Art Museum, in addition to its permanent collections, holds special monthly and traveling exhibits and art classes conducted for adults by the Univ. of Michigan.

The state was originally explored by the French and many names (Detroit, Sault Ste. Marie) are of French origin. Etienne Brulé (1618), Jean Nicolet (1634), Père Allouez (1666), Père Marquette (1668) and Louis Jolliet (1669) were early visitors. France was ousted by Britain, 1763. Under the Ordinance of 1787 Michigan Terr. embraced parts of other western states. It was organized as a separate territory 1805, admitted to the Union Jan. 26, 1837.

*(See also Index for Detroit.)*

# Minnesota

*North Star State, Gopher State*

**CAPITAL:** St. Paul. **AREA:** 84,068 sq. mi., rank, 12th. **POPULATION:** (1960 Census), 3,413,864, rank, 18th. **MOTTO:** L'Etoile du Nord, Star of the North. **FLOWER:** Showy Lady's-slipper. **BIRD:** Loon. **TREE:** Red (Norway) Pine. **SONG:** Hail! Minnesota. **ADMISSION:** 32nd.

Minnesota is a land rich in natural resources. Its fertile prairies support large crops and an important dairy industry, its mines yield most of the iron ore produced in the U. S., its forests produce mountains of pulpwood, its manufacturing is varied and vigorous, its thousands of lakes and other attractions lure millions of sportsmen and vacationers.

The headwaters of 3 great water systems lie within Minnesota; the Mississippi, leading to the Gulf of Mexico, with its source at Lake Itasca; the Red River of the North, which flows into Canada's Lake Winnipeg, draining into Hudson Bay; the St. Louis and other rivers draining into Lake Superior and thence through the Great Lakes and the St. Lawrence to the Atlantic.

Known as the "land of 10,000 lakes," Minnesota actually has 15,291 larger than 10 acres. Two-thirds of the state is rolling prairie. Highest point is Eagle Mt. in the NE, 2,301 ft. Fishing, hunting

tioners who spend over a half billion dollars annually.

The multiplicity of lakes has resulted in 99 being named Long, 91 Mud, 76 Rice, 43 Bass, 40 Twin, 39 Round, 36 Clear, 32 Sandy.

Est. pop. July 1, 1967, was 3,582,000.

Minnesota produces 60% of the iron ore mined in the U. S., despite depletion of the high-grade ore in the famed Mesabi and other ranges in the NE part of the state. Lost production from the huge open pit and underground mines is being replaced by high-grade pellets refined from low-grade taconite iron ore. Total iron ore production in 1967 was valued at $467,000,000. Total mineral production was valued at $518,794,000. Shipments of taconite pellets comprised 48% of total iron ore tonnage, up from 39% the previous year.

Manufacturing has shown steady growth and value added by manufacture in 1968 was est. at $4.5 billion. Top industry is food processing, followed by machinery.

Much of the land is richly fertile. With $1.8 billion in farm receipts for 1967, Minnesota ranked 5th among the states. Two-thirds of that income was from livestock products, the rest from crops. Minnesota was 1st among the states in butter, 2nd to Wisconsin in milk cows, 2nd to California in turkeys, 5th in hogs.

Minnesota's farms grew the most oats and sweet corn, were 3rd in rye, 4th in barley, 5th in soybeans, 6th in potatoes.

Forest products have a yearly est. value of over $328,000,000, most of it in pulpwood.

Nationally known is the Mayo Clinic at Rochester, founded by Drs. Wm. J. and Charles H. Mayo.

There are 27 private colleges, 6 state colleges, the Univ. of Minnesota and 14 junior colleges.

The Minneapolis Symphony Orchestra, Tyrone Guthrie Theater in Minneapolis and St. Olaf college choir in Northfield are highly regarded.

There are 85 state parks and many recreational facilities; Minnehaha Falls (54 ft.), in Minneapolis, was celebrated by Longfellow.

French traders and missionaries first penetrated Minnesota. Father Hennepin, 1680, named St. Anthony Falls, a 50-ft drop in the Mississippi in present-day Minneapolis. France ceded the land E of the Mississippi to Great Britain, 1763; Britain to U.S., 1783. It became part of Northwest Terr. The land W of the Mississippi was part of Louisiana Purchase, 1803. Henry R. Schoolcraft found source of Mississippi in Lake Itasca, July 13, 1832. Organized as a Territory in 1849, it became a state May 11, 1858.

*(See also Index for Minneapolis, St. Paul.)*

# Mississippi
*Magnolia State*

**CAPITAL: Jackson. AREA: 47,716 sq. mi., rank, 32nd. POPULATION: (1960 Census), 2,178,141, rank, 29th. MOTTO: Virtute et Armis. By Valor and Arms. FLOWER: Magnolia. TREE: Magnolia. BIRD: Mockingbird. SONG: Go, Mississippi! ADMISSION: 20th.**

Cotton is king in Mississippi and the state is 2nd only to Texas in the amount produced, but other crops, livestock, forest products, petroleum and expanding factories are increasingly important.

The land slopes from the NE hills, where the high point is Woodall Mt. (806 ft.), to the Delta, a cotton-producing alluvial plain in the W and NW lying between the Yazoo River and the Mississippi, which flows along the state's western border.

The land also slopes to the S where the sandy beaches on the Gulf of Mexico have created a popular vacationland.

Indian tribes, including the Chickasaw, Choctaw and Natchez, inhabited the Mississippi area when the 1st Europeans, under Spain's Hernando de Soto, passed through in 1540. The first permanent settlement by Europeans was by a French group under Pierre le Moyne, Sieur d'Iberville, in 1699, at Fort Maurepas near present-day Biloxi.

Great Britain took over the area in 1763 after the French and Indian War, ceding it to the U. S. in 1783 after the Revolution. Spain also claimed the land and did not relinquish it until 1798.

The population grew steadily and Mississippi became a state Dec. 10, 1817. It was the 2nd state to join the Confederacy, 1861, and was readmitted to the Union in 1870.

Est. pop. July 1, 1967, was 2,348,000.

Cotton has long been the mainstay of Mississippi agriculture; production in 1967 was 1,100,000 bales. But the state ranks 4th in the U. S. in sweet po-

tatoes and sugarcane syrup, 5th in rice, 6th in pecans and 7th in soybeans.

Biloxi has a large seafood canning industry, operating deep-sea trawlers for shrimp and oysters. Value of the commercial catch in 1966 was $9,-502,000.

With 70% of the land classified as forest, timber products yield more than $500,000,000 annually.

The state produces the most hardwood pulp wood, much hardwood lumber and slashpine products, including fibre board, kraft paper, newsprint.

Petroleum, natural gas and natural gas products represented 85% of the total value of mineral production, $213,740,000 in 1967.

Industrial expansion in 1967 provided 12,237 new jobs, with new capital investment totaling $218,-148,000, much of it for food processing and chemical plants. Factory employment reached 167,000.

A $250,000,000 center for static testing of space rockets was put in operation by the National Aeronautics and Space Administration in 1967 in Hancock County.

Mississippi became the last state to abandon prohibition, adopting a local-option liquor law May 21, 1966. The state had adopted prohibition in 1908.

Tourism is of growing economic importance. About 17,600,000 out-of-state tourists spent an est. $160,000,000 in Mississippi in 1967.

Gulfport holds an annual yacht regatta and a mackerel rodeo in July, Biloxi has a Mardi Gras in February, and Pass Christian, a tarpon rodeo. Natchez is famous for its formal antebellum houses, open in March and April. The mile-long Iberville Memorial bridge at Biloxi Bay and Vicksburg National Military park are of interest to tourists.

The Old Court House Museum in Vicksburg, built in 1858 by slave labor, has a museum with relics of the siege of Vicksburg, including flags, documents, newspapers printed on the back of wallpaper, guns, swords, etc., and exhibits of the ante-bellum South.

The Lauren Rogers Library and Museum of Art in Laurel contains works of 19th and early 20th Century Americans and Europeans, local artifacts and an unusual basket collection (about half of them Indian).

# Missouri
*Show Me State*

**CAPITAL: Jefferson City. AREA: 69,686 sq. mi., rank, 19th. POPULATION: (1960 Census), 4,319,-813, rank, 13th. MOTTO: Salus Populi Suprema Lex Esto, The Welfare of the People Shall Be the Supreme Law. FLOWER: Hawthorn. BIRD: Eastern Bluebird. TREE: Dogwood. SONG: Missouri Waltz. ADMISSION: 24th.**

The gateway through which the pioneers passed on their way West, Missouri today is a leading manufacturing state, with aerospace and a wide variety of other industries; it is the nation's largest producer of lead; it ranks 10th among the states in agricultural products; its areas of scenic and historic interest attract some 20,000,000 vacationers each year.

Gently rolling hills in the N and W produce large crops and support cattle, sheep and hogs. The Ozark highlands in the S are famed for fishing, hunting and rugged scenery, including numerous caves and springs. The "delta" area in the SE produces long staple cotton and melons.

The Mississippi forms the state's boundary on the E; the Missouri forms part of the boundary in the W, then flows across the state to join the Mississippi above St. Louis. Highest point in the state is Taum Sauk Mt., 1,772 ft., in the E central area.

Missouri has endeared itself to generations of Americans with its river lore, folk tales and especially the writings of Mark Twain (Samuel L. Clemens). Statues of two of his creations, Tom Sawyer and Huckleberry Finn, stand in Hannibal, his boyhood home. His birthplace near Florida, Mo., has been enshrined in Mark Twain State Park.

The farm birthplace of notorious bandit Jesse James (1847–1882) is near Excelsior Springs. A log cabin built by U. S. Grant is near St. Louis. The farm where George Washington Carver, agricultural scientist, was born near Diamond is now a National Monument. The Harry S. Truman Library, near Independence, contains Presidential papers and memorabilia.

Est. pop. July 1, 1967, was 4,605,000.

Manufacturing, paced by the state's large aero-

space industries, is the top income producer and employs more persons than any other segment of the economy. Value added by manufacture is over $4.4 billion yearly. Transportation equipment, including space capsules, rocket engines, aircraft and auto assemblies, ranks 1st, followed by food processing, esp. meat packing, grain milling, beer and other beverages. Also important are chemicals, printing, metal products, machinery, shoes. Corn-cob pipes are a well-known product.

Agriculture ranks 2nd among income producers. Farm receipts in 1967 totaled $1.4 billion, two-thirds from livestock products. Missouri ranks 3rd among the states in hogs, 5th in turkeys, 6th in cattle. It is 4th in soybeans, 7th in corn. Other crops are winter wheat, tobacco, apples, peaches, alfalfa, popcorn, rye.

Tourism, the 3rd largest industry, produced $721,700,000 in 1966. Some 20,033,500 out-of-state auto tourists visited Missouri that year; 11,606,021 persons visited its 37 state parks, which cover 77,326 acres. There is a wide variety of vacation facilities; large resort areas include Lake of the Ozarks, Lake Taneycomo and Table Rock Lake.

Missouri is rich in minerals. Its output of lead, largest in the U. S., was valued at $41,941,000 for 1967; total mineral production was worth a record $234,642,000. It was also 1st in barite and 4th in lime. Other products are coal, iron ore, cement, asphalt, copper, zinc.

There are 59 institutions of higher learning. The Univ. of Missouri has campuses at Columbia, Rolla, Kansas City and St. Louis. The Univ. of Missouri at Rolla was formerly the Missouri School of Mines & Metallurgy. The Univ. of Missouri at Columbia has the country's first School of Journalism, founded 1908 by Walter Williams.

De Soto visited the Missouri area in 1541. French fur traders founded Ste. Genevieve about 1735, St. Louis 1764. It was part of the Louisiana Territory purchased by U. S. from France in 1803. Missouri was organized as a separate territory, 1812; admitted to the Union, Aug. 10, 1821.

The St. Joseph Museum in St. Joseph stresses the natural history and wildlife of the region and has exhibits on Indian tribes from Alaska to Florida. Also in St. Joseph is the Pony Express Museum.

*(See also Index for Kansas City and St. Louis.)*

## Montana
*Treasure State*

CAPITAL: Helena. AREA: 147,138 sq. mi., rank, 4th. POPULATION: (1960 Census), 674,767, rank, 41st. MOTTO: Oro y Plata. Gold and Silver. FLOWER: Bitterroot. TREE: Ponderosa Pine. BIRD: Western Meadow Lark. SONG: Montana. ADMISSION: 41st.

The Rocky Mountains, with snow-capped peaks, forested slopes, broad valleys and many lakes, cover the western 40% of Montana; the rest is High Plains country devoted to grazing and farming. Montana is rich in minerals, hydroelectric power and impressive scenery. Highest mountain is Granite Peak, 12,799 ft. Est. pop. July 1, 1967, was 701,000.

Agriculture is the largest contributor to Montana's economy, followed by manufacturing, mining, and tourism and recreation.

Oceans of grain cover much of Montana's plains; it ranks 3rd among the states in wheat and barley output. Also grown are rye, oats, flaxseed, sugarbeets and potatoes. Montana ranks 5th in sheep and 13th in cattle. Farm receipts totaled just over a half billion dollars in 1967, more than half from livestock.

Manufacturing plays a growing role in the state's economy. Value added by manufacture reached $284,809,000 in 1965. Processing of forest products is most important, followed by primary metal industries and food products. Wood products account for $100,000,000 annually and include pulp, plywood and lumber. The state ships more than 3,000,000 Christmas trees annually.

Copper is normally king among Montana's minerals, but a nationwide strike cut production in 1967. Montana ranked 3rd among the states in copper and fluorspar, 1st in manganese and vermiculite. Petroleum produced the most income in 1967, $83,960,000. Total mineral production, including zinc, gold, silver, coal, natural gas and others, was valued at $186,182,000.

The tourist industry was valued at $127,000,000 annually.

Tourist attractions include hunting, fishing, skiing, dude ranching. Montana has the nation's first luge course; luge is a sport similar to bobsledding.

Hunters annually take about 100,000 deer, 18,000 antelope, 10,000 elk, 1,100 black bear, 500 moose, 350 mountain goats.

Glacier National Park, on the Continental Divide, is a scenic and recreational wonderland, with 60 glaciers, 200 lakes and many streams with good trout fishing.

Flathead Lake, in the NW, covers 189 sq. mi. and is the largest natural body of fresh water within a single state W of the Mississippi in conterminous U. S. Fort Peck Reservoir, in the NE, covers 382.8 sq. mi., is 2nd largest (after North Dakota's Garrison Reservoir) man-made lake in U. S.

Important historical site is Custer Battlefield National Cemetery, in Big Horn County (near Hardin), site of defeat of Custer by Sioux, June 25, 1876. First visited by the French Verendryes, father and sons, 1743; Lewis and Clark, 1805. It became a Territory, 1864, and a state Nov. 8, 1889.

There are 7 Indian reservations, covering over 5,000,000 acres; tribes are Blackfeet, Crow, Confederated Salish & Kootenai, Assiniboine, Gros Ventre, Sioux, Northern Cheyenne, Chippewa, Cree. Population approx. 25,500.

The Museum of the Plains Indian, on the Blackfeet Res. near Browning, features exhibits of historic and contemporary arts and crafts of the Northern Plains Indians and an Indian craft shop; the museum is administered by the U. S. Interior Dept.

The Historical Society of Montana, in Helena, has paintings, dioramas and other exhibits of Montana's Indian and buffalo days, mining camps, frontier settlements, cattle roundups. Outstanding is the collection of nearly 100 Charles M. Russell paintings.

There are nine colleges and universities and two junior colleges. Great Falls is the largest city, with population (1960) 55,357.

## Nebraska
*Beef State, Cornhusker State*

CAPITAL: Lincoln. AREA: 77,227 sq. mi., rank, 15th. POPULATION: (1960 Census), 1,411,330, rank, 34th. MOTTO: Equality Before the Law. FLOWER: Goldenrod. TREE: American Elm. BIRD: Western Meadow Lark. ADMISSION: 37th.

Fields of corn, rye and sorghum cover the Nebraska plain, sloping gently toward the Missouri River, the eastern border of the state; vast herds of cattle roam the grassy sandhills which rise to the W, ending in the broken table lands which mark the foothills of the Rockies. Highest point, 5,426 ft., is in the far SW corner.

With 22,000,000 acres under cultivation, Nebraska is an important grain and livestock producer; agriculture is the primary source of income and provides the most jobs. Oil and natural gas are also important products.

New chemical fertilizer, meatpacking and food processing plants have contributed to the growth of manufacturing in recent years. Est. pop. July 1, 1967, was 1,435,000.

Nebraska ranked 6th among the states in farm receipts in 1967, $1.7 billion, two-thirds of it from livestock products. Its cattle herds ranked 3rd in size behind those of Texas and Iowa, 6,475,000 in 1968, a 2% increase over 1967. It was 6th in hogs, 2,738,000. Its crop yield ranked it 3rd in sorghum, 4th in winter wheat and rye, 5th in corn and alfalfa.

Mineral production continued declining in 1967, totaling $75,846,000, a decline of $2,700,000 from 1966, mainly because of depletion of older oil and natural gas fields. Oil was still the main product, valued at $36,520,000. Also important are cement, pumice, sand and gravel.

Manufacturing has shown steady growth. During 1967, 53 industries announced new plants and 84 announced plant expansions; these were expected to create 4,800 new jobs.

Nebraska has a unicameral or one-house legislature with 49 members elected on a nonpartisan ballot. All electric power facilities are state or municipally owned.

The state university has campuses at Lincoln and Omaha; there are two sectarian universities and numerous colleges.

Arbor Lodge State Park at Nebraska City is a memorial to J. Sterling Morton, founder of Arbor

Day, which is observed as a legal holiday on his birthday, Apr. 22. Boys Town is 11 mi. W. of Omaha.

The Sheldon Memorial Art Gallery at the Univ. of Nebraska, Lincoln, housed in a building designed by Philip Johnson, has works by Bellows, Stuart Davis, Eakins, Gauguin, Homer, Hopper, Miro, O'Keeffe, Picasso, Ryder, Calder, Lachaise, Henry Moore, Rodin, Zorach, etc.

The Joslyn Art Museum, Omaha, has works by Titian, El Greco, Rembrandt, Goya, Renoir, etc.; exhibits of furniture, the early West, fur trade, Indian art, etc.

Pioneer Village, Minden, has some 30,000 items of Americana displayed in a rural schoolhouse, depot, general store, fort, fire house, sod house, Pony Express station, etc., plus old locomotives, tractors, a steam-powered merry-go-round.

The House of Yesterday, Hastings, has exhibits of pioneer days and natural science and the J. M. McDonald Planetarium.

French fur traders visited the Nebraska area about 1700. It was part of the Louisiana Purchase, 1803, and was visited by Lewis & Clark, 1804-06. The Union Pacific began its transcontinental railroad at Omaha in 1865 (completed 1869). The Territory of Nebraska was created by the Kansas-Nebraska Act. 1854; it became a state Mar. 1, 1867.

## OMAHA

**Omaha**, incorporated 1857, lies on the W bank of the Missouri River. It had more than 300,000 people in 1960 and an estimated 375,000 in 1967. It is the nation's largest livestock and meatpacking center. About 55% of its industry is food processing; it distributes more than $1 billion worth of foodstuffs annually including frozen dinners.

Omaha has 4 colleges and universities. It is the site of the Strategic Air Command at Offutt AFB, and hq of the Naval Reserve Training Command. It is served by 9 trunk railroads and 5 airlines.

# Nevada
*Sagebrush State, Silver State*

CAPITAL: Carson City. AREA: 110,540 sq. mi., rank, 7th. POPULATION: (1960 Census), 285,278, rank, 49th. MOTTO: All for Our Country. FLOWER: Sagebrush. BIRD: Mountain Bluebird. TREE: Single-leaf Piñon. SONG: Home Means Nevada. ADMISSION: 36th.

Nevada lies mostly in the Great Basin, a rugged plateau region broken by mountain chains running N-S. It is enclosed on the E by the Rockies and the Wasatch Range in Utah, and on the W by California's Sierra Nevada and Cascade Ranges which rob the clouds of moisture, making Nevada's climate extremely dry. Boundary Peak, near the SW border with California, is the state's highest point, 13,140 ft.

One of the smallest states in population, Nevada has attracted large numbers of outsiders, starting with the famed rush to the Comstock Lode (discovered 1859) and other fabulous gold and silver mines. Today, the attractions are legalized gambling, highly-developed entertainment and recreation facilities, and lenient divorce laws requiring only 6-weeks residence. Est. pop. July 1, 1967, was 444,000.

Spending by visitors is the biggest factor in Nevada's economy. Over 20,000,000 visitors (about 45 times the state's population) spent some $713,-647,000 in Nevada in 1967.

Tourist-connected industries—hotels, casinos, amusement and recreation facilities—make up the largest employment category.

State taxes and fees from casino entertainment were $22,108,640 in 1966-67, up $4,859,961 from the previous fiscal year and providing 35% of the state's revenue. Gross gambling revenues were $358,000,000 for 1966-67.

There are big resort areas, with nearby skiing as well as sunbathing, near Lake Tahoe, Reno, Las Vegas and elsewhere. Ghost towns, rodeos, trout fishing and deer hunting are other attractions. There are 9 state parks, and recreation areas include those at Pyramid Lake, wholly within the state; Lake Tahoe, partly in California; Lake Mead, formed by Hoover Dam, and Lake Mohave, by Davis Dam, both in Lake Mead National Recreation Area, shared with Arizona.

Income from mineral production fell off during 1967, mainly because of a nationwide copper strike which also affected Nevada's normal output of lead and zinc. Of the total 1967 mineral production value, $85,876,000, copper still accounted for $35,-

394,000. The state ranked 2nd in the U. S. in mercury, antimony and lithium, 3rd in gold and barite.

Nevada is the largest manufacturer of gaming devices. Also important are electronic devices, chemicals, forest products, suntan lotion, stone-clay-glass products. About $112,000,000 is the est. value added annually by growing manufacturing industries.

Farm receipts totaled $63,864,000 in 1967, 82% of that from livestock; the dry climate makes much of the state more suitable for grazing than for crops, although large-scale irrigation has expanded growing areas.

The Nevada Test Site, NW of Las Vegas, is a proving ground for various atomic devices.

The Univ. of Nevada is at Reno and Nevada Southern Univ. at Las Vegas.

Trappers and traders entered the Nevada area in the 1820s, including Jedediah Smith and Peter Skene Ogden. It became U. S. territory at the end of the Mexican War. It became a state Oct. 31, 1864.

The Nevada State Museum, Carson City, occupies a former U. S. Mint, and exhibits coins, habitat groups of mammals and birds of the Great Basin area, Indian baskets, full-scale replicas of underground mining operations and thousands of arrowheads.

## LAS VEGAS

**Las Vegas** (The Meadows), in southern Nevada, is the state's largest city and seat of Clark County; 1966 pop. was 144,000 and total in county 253,000. Over 13,000,000 visitors in 1965 spent $350,-000,000 in this resort and gambling mecca. Gross gaming revenues totaled $166,111,179. The city has 16 major resort hotels, 280 motels, 35 other hotels, with a total of 25,000 rooms. It is served by 7 airlines which brought 1,700,000 passengers to McCarran Field in 1964, and the Union Pacific. There is a convention hall seating 8,500. Nearby are Valley of Fire Park, Lakes Mead and Mohave; Nellis and Indian Springs Air Force Bases, Las Vegas Air Force Station; Mt. Charleston Recreation Area.

# New Hampshire
*Granite State*

CAPITAL: Concord. AREA: 9,304 sq. mi., rank, 44th. POPULATION: (1960 Census), 606,921, rank, 45th. MOTTO: Live Free or Die. FLOWER: Common Lilac. BIRD: Purple Finch. TREE: Paper (White) Birch. SONG: Old New Hampshire. Ninth of the Original 13 States to ratify Constitution.

One of the 6 New England states, New Hampshire is a land of impressive mountains, picturesque lakes, swift rivers and thick forests. Mountain slopes provide excellent ski trails. Numerous lakes and streams afford fishing for trout, bass, pickerel, perch, whitefish.

Abundant water power early turned New Hampshire into an industrial state, with manufacturing the principal source of income. Soil and climate have curtailed agricultural growth, but scenic and recreation resources have been developed and the tourist-vacation business, over $200,000,000 a year, ranks 2nd in its contribution to the state's economy.

Est. pop. July 1, 1967, was 685,000.

In 1964, to raise funds to support education, the state ran the 1st legal sweepstakes lottery in the U. S. since 1894 (in that year, a lottery in Louisiana was outlawed). Profits from the state lottery are turned over to local school districts.

Most important industrial products are shoes and boots, followed by electrical and other machinery, wool and other textiles, and paper. Most factories are concentrated along the Merrimack River which furnishes hydroelectric power. More than 85,000 are employed in manufacturing. Value added by manufacture is over $650,000,000 a year.

Farm receipts for 1967 totaled $54,895,000, four-fifths from dairy and poultry products. Crops include apples, peaches, maple sugar and syrup, hay.

Mineral products, mainly sand and gravel, stone, clay, feldspar and gem stones, were valued at $7,922,000 for 1967.

Recreation and vacation attractions include Lake Winnipesaukee, largest of 1,300 lakes and ponds; the White Mountains, with skiing and scenic beauty; beaches on the Atlantic Coast and numerous historic sites.

One-third of the state is over 2,000 ft. above sea level. Highest land in Northeast U. S. is the Presidential range of the White Mountains, with Mt. Washington, 6,288 ft. (First cog ry. in world opened 1869); Mt. Jefferson, 5,717 ft.; Mt. Adams, 5,789 ft. National forests cover 677,559 acres; 142

state forests and parks, 63,805 acres. State-owned are Crawford Notch, Dixville Notch and Franconia Notch the last near Profile, or Cannon Mtn., 4,077 ft. (with Hawthorne's Great Stone Face); Whiteface, 3,985 ft.

Portsmouth is the state's only port. Manchester is the largest city; pop. (1960 Census) 88,262.

New Hampshire was visited by Samuel Champlain in 1605. Under an English land grant, Capt. John Mason in 1623 sent two groups to establish a fishing colony at the mouth of the Piscataqua River. One group settled Little Harbor of Pannaway (now town of Rye); the other set up fishing stages at Northam, later named Dover. The colony was called after Hampshire, 1629. It declared its independence Jan. 5, 1776, and contributed to the victories at Bennington and Saratoga, entering the Union June 21, 1788.

New Hampshire shared the educational pioneering of Massachusetts Bay from 1642; established first free public library at Dublin, 1822. It has Univ. of N. H., Durham; Dartmouth (1769), Phillips Exeter (1781), St. Paul's, Colby Junior College and others. The MacDowell Colony at Peterborough, estab. 1908 in honor of Edward MacDowell, is a summer haven for writers.

The Currier Gallery of Art, Manchester, exhibits silver by Paul Revere and others, textiles, hooked rugs, pewter and glass and a rich collection of works by Tintoretto, Ruisdael, Monet, Corot, Constable, Picasso, Roualt, Copley, Stuart, Trumbull, Sargent, Homer, Wyeth, Marin, etc.

The New Hampshire Historical Society, Concord, has a museum displaying New Hampshire furniture, silver, pewter, glass, china, quilts, costumes, weapons, kitchen woodenware, etc.

# New Jersey
*Garden State*

CAPITAL: Trenton. AREA: 7,836 sq. mi., rank, 46th. POPULATION: (1960 Census), 6,066,782, rank, 8th. MOTTO: Liberty and Prosperity. FLOWER: Purple Violet. BIRD: Eastern Goldfinch. TREE: Red Oak. Third of the Original 13 States to ratify Constitution.

Smallest of the Middle Atlantic states, New Jersey was settled by the Dutch early in the 17th Century and was the scene of much action during the American Revolution. Today it has the heaviest pop. per sq. mi. of the 50 states, ranks near the top in manufacturing, is rich in poultry and vegetable production, and has a flourishing resort industry.

There are vast shipping facilities and New Jersey divides authority over airports, harbors, tunnels and bridges with the Port of New York Authority and the states of Delaware and Pennsylvania.

Much of the tonnage total of the Port of New York is loaded or unloaded at piers on the New Jersey side of the harbor.

About 71% of the state's land area is in farms and forests. Highest point is High Point, Sussex County, 1,803 ft.

Small in area, New Jersey has a heavy concentration of factories, highways, railroads and farms, and is a leader in many fields. It also has the greatest pop. density (based on the July 1, 1965, Census est. pop. of 6,774,000), reaching 891.1 per sq. mi. and passing Rhode Island's corresponding figure, 869.1. Est. pop. July 1, 1967, was 7,004,000.

The state stands 7th in the U. S. in value added by manufacture. It ranks 1st in value of chemical products; 3rd in apparel; 4th in instruments, rubber and plastic products, petroleum and coal products; 5th in electrical machinery; 6th in food products, stone-clay-glass products; 7th in printing-publishing, fabricated metals; 8th in textiles; 9th in paper, leather, machinery, transportation equipment; 10th in primary metals. It has a heavy concentration of pharmaceutical plants and research installations.

New Jersey is 1st in gross income per farm acre. Chief crops are tomatoes, corn, asparagus, apples, cranberries, peaches, spinach. It holds high rank in poultry, dairying and processing of vegetables, especially tomatoes. The first dairy cattle artificial insemination project was launched in Hunterdon County; also the common-carrier shipment of day-old baby chicks.

Total farm receipts for 1967 were $253,267,000.

Mineral production dropped 3% in 1967, a decline mainly attributable to the cessation of iron mining, an important industry since colonial days. Of the total value, $73,482,000, gravel and stone (including traprock, granite and marble) accounted for the largest part. Zinc is also important.

Seven refineries, processing oil from out of state, have a total crude capacity of 529,950 bbl. a day.

Among New Jersey's institutions of higher learning are Princeton and Rutgers (the state university); the Institute for Advanced Study; 3 other universities; 18 colleges, 11 junior colleges, 7 professional and technological colleges.

Atlantic City, Ocean City, Cape May, Asbury Park, Ocean Grove, Wildwood are among more than 100 resorts. The resort industry generates over $2 billion in business annually. There are 36 state parks with 37,150 acres. The 11 state forests comprise 166,435 acres. There are many historic sites, mainly Revolutionary.

In Camden, the Walt Whitman House, home of the poet from 1884 until his death, Mar. 26, 1892, contains books, mementos and furnishings used by Whitman. The U. S. Army Signal Corps Museum, Fort Monmouth, contains communications equipment from the earliest visual methods to modern satellites.

The Montclair Art Museum exhibits art of many periods and lands, emphasizing the American. The Newark Museum is a museum of art, science and industry, including American paintings and sculpture; Chinese, Japanese and Tibetan art; collections of economic botany, birds, insects, minerals, shells, glass, ceramics and jewelry. The New Jersey Historical Society Museum, Newark, has old New Jersey rooms and collections of New Jersey furniture, paintings, china, silver, glass, costumes, etc.

The Garden State Arts Center, an amphitheater for concerts and stage shows, was opened at Telegraph Hill Park in 1968.

The Johnston Historical Museum, adjacent to the national hq. of the Boy Scouts of America, New Brunswick, depicts Scouting history, has a registered weather station, a ham radio station (K2BFW) and a 22-acre Outdoor Museum of Nature and Conservation.

The Edison National Historic Site, West Orange, displays in buildings set up by Thomas Alva Edison his chemical laboratory, machine shop and library; a reproduction of the "Black Maria," Edison's 1st movie studio; originals or replicas of his phonograph, incandescent lamp and movie camera. In South Orange, the New Jersey Fire Museum displays 19th Century hand-pumpers, hose carts, helmets, etc.

In Trenton, the New Jersey State Museum displays the state's achievements in the arts, sciences, history, technology and industry, and has a planetarium.

Extensive research projects in 1966 were aimed at eliminating pollution of shellfish areas and protecting beaches from erosion. To combat the prolonged northeast U. S. drought, construction was completed on Round Valley Reservoir (expected to reach full capacity of 55 billion gal. in 1968); Spruce Run Reservoir, also in Hunterdon Co., reached full level of 11 billion gal.

The state's network of modern highways gives New Jersey more miles of roads per sq. mi. of area than any other state. A new ferry between Cape May and Lewes, Del., opened in 1964. The Port of N. Y. Authority says its Newark Union Truck Terminal is the world's largest.

There are 13 airlines and 19 railroads. New Jersey has the most concentrated trackage per sq. mi. in the U. S.

# New Mexico
*Land of Enchantment*

CAPITAL: Santa Fe. AREA: 121,666 sq. mi., rank, 5th. POPULATION: (1960 Census), 951,023, rank, 37th. MOTTO: Crescit Eundo, It Grows as It Goes. FLOWER: Yucca. BIRD: Road Runner. TREE: Piñon (Nut Pine). SONG: O, Fair New Mexico. ADMISSION: 47th.

New Mexico is a land of contrasts, presenting remnants of old Indian and Spanish cultures along with nuclear and space research centers; mountains over 13,000 ft. and a cavern 829 ft. below ground; ski slopes and desert resorts.

Vast areas are made fertile by irrigation via dams and reservoirs on the Rio Grande, San Juan, Pecos, Canadian, Cimarron, Gila, San Francisco Rivers. Wheeler Peak, 13,161 ft., is highest point. Est. pop. July 1, 1967, was 1,003,000.

The climate is dry and invigorating; annual rainfall is 7" to 16"; mean temperature is 50°, reaching 100° on plains in summer.

National forests cover 13,281 sq. mi. Douglas fir, Ponderosa pine and spruce are cut for timber. Over 34% of the land is Federally owned.

Minerals are New Mexico's richest natural re-

source and the state leads the U. S. in uranium output and produces 90% of the nation's potash.

Mineral production reached a record value of $867,194,000 in 1967. Petroleum output was at a new high, valued at $363,234,000, and natural gas brought $139,149,000, also up. Also important are copper, helium, manganese, zinc, lead, gold, silver, molybdenum, gypsum, coal. New Mexico ranks 1st among the states in uranium, carbon dioxide and perlite production.

Farm receipts brought in $286,989,000 in 1967, two-thirds of it from livestock products. Cotton, hay and sorghum account for 80% of the value of field crops. Also grown are corn, pecans, peanuts, beans, onions and lettuce.

Manufacturing production gained about 10.6% in 1966 and employment was up 8.1%. Principal lines are food products, chemicals, ordnance and transportation equipment, lumber, electrical machinery, stone-clay-glass products. Value added by manufacturing is over $170,000,000 annually.

Federal government activities, especially nuclear and space research and testing, have played a large role in New Mexico's economic growth. Nuclear and space centers are at Los Alamos, White Sands, Holloman, Kirtland and Sandia.

New Mexico's most awe-inspiring natural wonder, Carlsbad Caverns, has more than a half-million visitors annually. A national park, the caverns are on 3 levels and have the largest natural cave "room" in the world, 1,500 by 300 ft., 300 ft. high.

There are 4 large Indian reservations and 18 inhabited pueblos, including Acoma, the "sky city," built atop a 357-ft. mesa. There are numerous pueblo ruins from 1000 A.D. in Chaco Canyon.

Skiing, hunting, fishing, ghost towns and dude ranches help tourism show steady gains. Visitors spent about $108,000,000 in the state in 1967.

Spaniards seeking gold explored New Mexico in the early 16th Century; the area was labeled New Mexico on a 1583 map. It was colonized 1598, with the 1st church at San Juan pueblo. The land remained under Spain until 1821, then under Mexico till U. S. troops occupied it in 1846.

It was formally ceded by Mexico to the U. S. in 1848, was made a Territory in 1850, was separated in 1863 from the part which was to become Arizona. New Mexico became a state in 1912.

There are 9 universities and 4-year colleges. Santa Fe (1610) is the 2nd oldest city in the U. S. It and Taos have large artist colonies. Albuquerque (1706) is the state's largest city, pop. 331,684 (1967).

The Museum of Navaho Ceremonial Art, Santa Fe, housed in a modernized version of a ceremonial hogan, contains over 600 sandpaintings, recordings of some 2,000 Navaho chants, books, manuscripts, baskets, blankets, silver, etc.

The Museum of New Mexico, Santa Fe, maintains the oldest public building in the U. S., the Palace of the Governors (built 1610), a hall of modern Indian culture, collected works of artists of the SW, international folk art exhibits.

The Roswell Museum and Art Center, Roswell, has 19th and 20th Century art collections, archeology and geology exhibits, the Robert H. Goddard rocket collection.

# New York
*Empire State*

**CAPITAL:** Albany. **AREA:** 49,576 sq. mi., rank, 30th. **POPULATION:** (1960 Census), 16,782,304, rank, 1st (see text below). **MOTTO:** Excelsior, Ever Upward. **FLOWER:** Rose. **BIRD:** Bluebird (unofficial). **TREE:** Sugar Maple. Eleventh of the Original 13 States to ratify Constitution.

New York is the nation's leading manufacturing state and within its borders are the financial capital of the nation, the largest city and port, the United Nations hq., the head offices of many of the greatest national corporations and insurance companies and a variety of industries.

New York's manufacturing industries outrank those of all other states in number, employees, payrolls and value added by manufacture ($22.7 billion annually). Value added by manufacture in New York exceeded that of every other state in apparel ($2.6 billion), printing and publishing ($2.9 billion), instruments ($1.6 billion), paper and paper products ($700,000,000), and in the miscellaneous group, which includes jewelry, silverware, toys and sporting goods, office supplies, musical instruments, pens and pencils, etc. ($800,000,000), according to the 1965 Survey of Manufactures.

The state produces 69% by value of the nation's photographic equipment, 54% of the periodicals, 50% of leather gloves, 39% of books and 31% of apparel.

Average employment for 1967 was 7,715,000. Over $42 billion in wages and salaries were paid in 1966.

The bi-state Port of New York (New York and New Jersey) handled 27.8% of the nation's foreign trade by value in 1967; 28.8% in 1966, by U. S. Commerce Dept. figures. The 3 customs districts (New York, Buffalo and Ogdensburg) handled 35.6% of U. S. exports and imports by value in 1967.

One of every 4 domestic air passengers in the U. S. lands or takes off from Port of New York Authority airports; Kennedy International Airport in N. Y. City handles about 54% of the nation's overseas air travel and is the world's largest air cargo center, handling 64% of export-import tonnage by value.

The State Barge Canal System is 800 mi. long. There are 36 railroads and 384 landing fields, including 27 seaplane bases and 28 heliports. The Verrazano-Narrows Bridge is the world's longest suspension bridge.

The Dewey Thruway runs from N. Y. City to the Pennsylvania border on Lake Erie, 559 mi.; most of the state's 1,226-mi. portion of the Interstate Highway System was completed in 1967. The Northway, which links the Thruway with the Canadian border, was completed in 1967.

Tourism and business travel provide $3.2 billion a year to businesses in the state. Major vacation areas include the Adirondack and Catskill Mtns., Finger Lakes, Great Lakes, Thousand Islands, Long Island, N. Y. City and Niagara Falls.

Rich, rolling farmlands support a large agricultural output. It ranks 1st among the states in clover and timothy, buckwheat, maple syrup and ice cream; is 2nd to Washington in apples, 2nd to California in grapes (it has large wine and grape juice industries), 2nd to Wisconsin in milk production; 2nd to Michigan in tart cherries; 5th in vegetables and melons, sweet cherries, pears, potatoes. Also important are corn, oats, wheat, peaches, peas, beans, beets, cabbages. Farm production also supports a large food-canning, freezing and processing industry.

Farm receipts for 1967 totaled $1.01 billion, up over 1% from 1966, more than two-thirds of the total from livestock and dairy products.

The state also has a rich mineral industry, ranking 1st in the U. S. in talc, titanium, emery, abrasive garnet and wollastonite; 2nd in zinc; 4th in salt, iron, sand and gravel. Other products include lead, petroleum, silver, gypsum. Total value for 1967 was $299,871,000.

Highest point in the state is Mt. Marcy in the Adirondacks, 5,344 ft. The 88 state parks are visited annually by over 35,000,000 persons.

There are 207 institutions of higher learning, providing instruction to 645,000 students.

In 1967, a state lottery, with proceeds to be used for education, went into operation. In Nov. 1967, New York State voters approved a $2.5-billion transportation bond issue to modernize the state's transportation system to meet the needs of an estimated 20,000,000 citizens in 1975.

New York was the nation's most populous state from 1820 through 1964. As of July 1, 1964, the U. S. Census Bureau estimated California's pop. reached 18,084,000, New York's 17,915,000 (including Armed Forces stationed in the 2 states; without them, New York still led 17,870,000 to 17,749,000). By July 1, 1965, the Bureau est. California led in both categories. Total New York pop. July 1, 1967, was est. at 18,335,000; total California, 19,163,000.

Giovanni da Verrazano, Italian-born navigator sailing for France, probably saw what is now New York Bay in 1524. Henry Hudson, an Englishman sailing for the Dutch, reached the bay in 1609.

Sunnyside, the home of Washington Irving, "as full of angles and corners as an old cocked hat," is in Tarrytown. The Dutch Church of Sleepy Hollow (1697), North Tarrytown, overlooks a bridge commemorating Irving's story of the "headless horseman"; Irving is buried close by in Sleepy Hollow Cemetery. Also in Tarrytown is Lyndhurst, 19th Century mansion of Jay Gould, maintained by the National Trust for Historic Preservation.

The Franklin D. Roosevelt National Historic Site, in Hyde Park, includes the graves of President and Mrs. Roosevelt, the home occupied by the Roosevelt family since 1867, greenhouse, etc. The Roosevelt Library has historic papers, trophies

and ship models.

Philipsburg Manor, in North Tarrytown, a trading center of the early 1700s, includes the restored Frederick Philipse home, a dam and grist mill. Van Cortlandt Manor, Croton-on-Hudson, has the restored Van Cortlandt home and ferry house.

In Kingston, the Senate House, seat of the 1st Senate of the state, exhibits early historical objects; its Museum has works by John Vanderlyn, local historical painter. In Newburgh, Washington's Hq., the Jonathan Hasbrouck House, has Revolutionary relics.

The Suffolk Museum and Carriage House, Stony Brook, L. I., has early American paintings and furniture, apothecary shop, tavern, Wells Fargo stage, Conestoga and gypsy wagons, etc.

In Cooperstown are the National Baseball Hall of Fame and Museum with a wide collection of mementos of the national game; nearby is Abner Doubleday Field, said to be where baseball originated in 1839. Near Cooperstown are Fenimore House, hq. of the State Historical Society, with collections including James Fenimore Cooper memorabilia and an art gallery; the Farmer's Museum, with craft demonstrations, and the Village Crossroads, with blacksmith shop, country store, etc.; the Carriage and Harness Museum preserves the stables and vehicles of the early 20th Century.

The restored Fort Ticonderoga, overlooking the waters connecting Lakes George and Champlain, has a museum of relics of the French and Indian War and the Revolution, in which the fort played important roles.

The New York State Museum in Albany has exhibits of natural resources, Indian life, Louis Agassiz Fuertes' paintings of birds, colonial houseware, etc.

The Corning Glass Center, Corning, has a museum and the Steuben factory, where visitors may see crystal glass formed and engraved. Also in the Finger Lakes area are the Curtiss Museum of aviation and the Wine Museum at Hammondsport and several wineries which offer tours to visitors. In Binghamton, the Roberson Center for the Arts and Sciences has art and historical collections.

In Utica, the Munson-Williams-Proctor Institute has a museum of 19th and 20th Century art and Fountain Elms, a restored mid-19th Century home.

The Remington Art Memorial Museum, Ogdensburg, has paintings and bronzes by Frederic Remington (1861-1909), who was born in nearby Canton.

*(See also Index for N. Y. City, Buffalo, Rochester, Syracuse.)*

# North Carolina
*Tar Heel State, Old North State*

**CAPITAL: Raleigh. AREA: 52,586 sq. mi., rank, 28th. POPULATION: (1960 Census), 4,556,155, rank, 12th. MOTTO: Esse Quam Videri, To Be, Rather Than To Seem. FLOWER: Dogwood. BIRD: Cardinal. TREE: Pine. SONG: The Old North State. Twelfth of the Original 13 States to ratify Constitution.**

From a low coastal plain, with Capes Hatteras, Lookout and Fear jutting into the Atlantic, North Carolina rises to a central Piedmont plateau region and, in the W, to the scenic Blue Ridge and Great Smoky Mountains. Mt. Mitchell, 6,684 ft., is the highest peak E of the Mississippi.

Modernization of production methods has brought North Carolina increasing prosperity from its factories, farms and mines in recent years.

The state leads the U. S. in production of textiles, brick, and household furniture, and in both tobacco grown and cigarettes made. Tourism is an important industry. Est. pop. July 1, 1967, was 5,027,000.

In 1967, 130 new industrial plants opened and 338 expanded their facilities, creating 24,774 new jobs through an added investment of $661,957,000.

About 665,000 are employed in factories. The textile industry is the state's largest with production valued at over $3 billion annually.

North Carolina ranks 1st in tobacco production; in 1967 it totaled 842,530,000 lbs. It was 2nd to Louisiana in sweet potatoes and 2nd to Georgia in peanuts. Other large crops are cotton, corn and soybeans; also grown are wheat, oats, barley, peaches, apples. In field crop receipts the state ranked 5th in 1967 with $845,069,000; livestock product receipts totaled $454,134,000.

There is a large commercial broiler business; the state ranked 4th in chickens in 1968. It was also 4th in turkeys and 12th in hogs.

Mineral production was up 5% to a record high value of $75,294,000 in 1967. North Carolina ranked 1st in mica, feldspar and lithium; 3rd in talc, 4th in asbestos.

Tourism is a large industry; in 1967 travelers spent $647,000,000 in the state. There are 635,000 acres of game refuges, with bear, deer, opossum, raccoon, quail and rabbit, as well as wild ducks and geese.

Among attractions are the Great Smoky Mtns. (half in Tennessee), the Blue Ridge Parkway (partly in Virginia) and the Cape Hatteras and Cape Lookout National Seashores.

Other attractions include the restored Fort Raleigh National Historic Site, Roanoke Is., where Virginia Dare, 1st child of English parents in the New World, was born Aug. 18, 1587; Wright Brothers National Memorial, near Kitty Hawk, has aviation exhibits and a reproduction of the plane in which Wilbur and Orville Wright made their 1st flights, 1903; Guilford Court House and Moore's Creek parks, sites of Revolutionary battles. The Battleship North Carolina, a war memorial, is berthed at Wilmington.

In Asheville is one of the world's largest rayon plants as well as Biltmore Industries, native craft plants set up by Mrs. George W. Vanderbilt in 1901 to continue handweaving traditions of the area. Just S of Asheville is the 19th Century Biltmore mansion of the Vanderbilts, which has a large collection of paintings, antiques and Ming china. Also in Asheville, the Thomas Wolfe Memorial was the home of the author.

Bennett Place, 6 mi. NW of Durham, is the site where Gen. Joseph E. Johnston surrendered the last Confederate army to Gen. William Tecumseh Sherman.

The Mint Museum of Art, Charlotte, has collections of painting, sculpture and ceramics. The North Carolina Museum of Art, Raleigh, exhibits American and European paintings, sculpture and decorative art. Tryon Palace, New Bern, is the reconstructed colonial capital of 1770-1794, furnished with antiques.

Old Salem, in Winston-Salem, includes buildings erected by the Moravians from 1766 on. The R. J. Reynolds Tobacco Co. welcomes visitors at its plant and warehouses.

More than 120,000 students are enrolled in 70 senior and junior colleges and universities, 28 of them state-supported with enrollment of over 73,000; among them are Duke, Univ. of N. C., Wake Forest, N. C. State Univ., and Campbell College.

Verrazano, 1524, touched the coast. DeSoto went into the Great Smoky Mts. in 1540. Sir Walter Raleigh sent an expedition to Roanoke Is., 1584; colony was settled 1585, 1587; this, the Lost Colony, disappeared. Albemarle was the first permanent settlement, 1660. Revolutionary battles were fought in the state. North Carolina seceded from the Union May 20, 1861; revoked secession, 1865; was readmitted 1868.

# North Dakota
*Sioux State, Flickertail State*

**CAPITAL: Bismarck. AREA: 70,665 sq. mi., rank, 17th. POPULATION: (1960 Census), 632,446, rank, 44th. MOTTO: Liberty and Union, Now and Forever, One and Inseparable. FLOWER: Wild Prairie Rose. BIRD: Western Meadow Lark. TREE: American Elm. SONG: North Dakota Hymn. ADMISSION: 39th or 40th, with South Dakota.**

The eastern plains of North Dakota are rich in vast fields of grain and support large numbers of livestock, in sharp contrast to the rough, colorful Badlands in the W which have elements of scenic beauty and include Theodore Roosevelt National Memorial Park. Highest point is White Butte, 3,506 ft., in the SW.

North Dakota's economy is based on agriculture and mining; manufacturing, especially food processing, is gaining. Agriculture is the principal industry, with 93% of the land in farms or ranches. Est. pop. July 1, 1967, was 639,000.

North Dakota led the nation in production of spring and durum wheat, rye, barley and flaxseed; it was 5th in oats. Farm receipts for 1967 totaled $727,034,000, more than half from its huge grain crops. In 1968 there were 2,132,000 cattle on farms.

Mineral production in 1967 was valued at $97,-729,000, a drop of 4%, mainly caused by a 6% drop in the value of oil produced, $64,902,000; petroleum, natural gas and natural gas liquids account for 80% of the value of all minerals produced. Others include coal (lignite), uranium, vanadium, clays.

Tourism provided an est. $60,000,000 in 1967.

There are 66 state parks and historic sites. The International Peace Garden, on a 2,200-acre tract extending across the border into Manitoba, commemorates the friendly relations between the U. S. and Canada. The state is known for its waterfowl, grouse and deer hunting, and bass, trout and northern pike fishing. Lake Sakakawea, formed by the Garrison Dam across the Missouri River, is 609 sq. mi. in area.

A museum with exhibits of pioneer life, the Northern Plains Indians and natural history of the area, is maintained by the State Historical Society on the State Capitol grounds, Bismarck.

Explorations in what is now North Dakota were made as early as 1738-1740 by French-Canadians. The Lewis and Clark expedition (1804-1806) passed through the territory and established Fort Mandan. With South Dakota and parts of Montana and Wyoming it comprised Dakota Territory, organized Mar. 2, 1861. It became a separate state Nov. 2, 1889.

Fort Abraham Lincoln, now a state park near Mandan, was the base from which Col. George Custer set out in 1876 on the campaign which ended in the deaths of Custer and 5 companies of the 7th Cavalry at the hands of Sioux Indians at the Little Big Horn in Montana.

# Ohio
*Buckeye State*

**CAPITAL: Columbus. AREA: 41,222 sq. mi., rank, 35th. POPULATION: (1960 Census), 9,706,-397, rank, 5th. MOTTO: With God, All Things Are Possible. FLOWER: Scarlet Carnation. BIRD: Cardinal. TREE: Ohio Buckeye. ADMISSION: 17th.**

Ohio is the nation's 3rd greatest industrial state; it ranks among the wealthier states in livestock and crop receipts, and is a leader in output of lime, coal and coke.

It leads the U. S. in a variety of products: tires, machine tools, playing cards, business machines, glassware, printing inks, clay and metal products. Industrial expansion continues at a rapid pace; in 1967 new capital invested in manufacturing totaled $2.3 billion, a record for the state.

Total value added by manufacturing was $18.4 billion in the 1965 Survey of Manufactures. Of this, autos, aircraft, boats and parts accounted for $2.9 billion; iron, steel and other metals, $2.7 billion; machinery, esp. industrial, $2.6 billion; electrical machinery, esp. household appliances, $1.7 billion. Also important are hardware, dairy and meat products, tires and other rubber and plastic products, chemicals.

Farm products were valued at over $1.2 billion in 1967, more than two-thirds from livestock products. Ohio is the nation's largest producer of hot-house tomatoes and ranks high in milk, corn, grapes, clover, hogs, oats, soybeans and others.

Mineral production for 1967 was valued at a record $495,118,000, with the largest part coming from bituminous coal. Ohio was the top state in lime production, 2nd in clays, 3rd in salt, sand and gravel. Among other products are cement, natural gas and gypsum.

Tourism produced an est. $2.8 billion in 1967. Est. pop. July 1, 1967, was 10,462,000.

There are 71 state parks, over 275 roadside parks, and many historic memorials including Fallen Timbers Battlefield, prehistoric Indian mounds and the restored first settlement, Schoenbrunn (1772). The American Trapshooting Tournament is held annually at Vandalia. The state is served by 10 major railroads, 13 airlines and busy ports on Lake Erie and the Ohio River.

There are 100 institutions of higher learning, including Miami (Ohio), Oberlin, Ohio State, Antioch, Kenyon, Ohio Wesleyan, Wittenberg, Ohio Univ., Heidelberg, Case Institute, Western Reserve.

George Rogers Clark defeated the Indians at Piqua, 1780; thereafter Ohio had British-Indian raids and battles; Gen. Anthony Wayne defeated Indians at Fallen Timbers Aug. 20, 1794, imposed Treaty of Greenville, 1795. Oliver Hazard Perry defeated British on Lake Erie near Put-in-Bay, Sept. 10, 1813. As governor of Northwest Territory, Gen. Arthur St. Clair sat at Marietta (1789) and Cincinnati (1791). Ohio became a state in 1803. Columbus became seat of government in 1816.

**Toledo,** on Lake Erie, 4th largest Ohio city, is a major port, handling more than 38,000,000 tons annually. It is a center for bituminous coal shipments. Its glass industry has net sales of over $1 billion a year. Its oil refineries handle up to 8,000,-

000 bbls. of crude. It is the home of the Kaiser Jeep Corp. It is the largest manufacturing center for motor car accessories. Est. pop. 1967, was 392,733.

The **Toledo** Museum of Art has paintings by El Greco, Velasquez, Goya, Holbein, Rembrandt, Cezanne, Gauguin, Van Gogh, Picasso, Samuel F. B. Morse, Gilbert Stuart, Benjamin West, etc.; ancient and modern sculpture, mummies and extensive glass collections. The Toledo Zoo has about a million visitors a year.

In **Canton,** the Pro Football Hall of Fame has a museum, library and daily movies; the Stark County Historical Society has science, industry and historical museums.

*(See also Index for Akron, Cincinnati, Cleveland, Columbus, Dayton.)*

# Oklahoma
*Sooner State*

**CAPITAL: Oklahoma City. AREA: 69,919 sq. mi., rank, 18th. POPULATION: (1960 Census), 2,328,284, rank, 27th. MOTTO: Labor Omnia Vincit —Labor Conquers All Things. FLOWER: Mistletoe. BIRD: Scissortailed Flycatcher. TREE: Redbud. SONG: Oklahoma. ADMISSION: 46th.**

Most of Oklahoma is a great, rolling plain sloping S and E with a mean altitude of 1,300 ft. The Ozarks, in the NE, the Boston Mtns. in the E and the Ouachita Mtns. in the SE are heavily wooded. In the western Panhandle the land rises toward the Rockies with Black Mesa, 4,973 ft., the highest point.

Oil, wheat and cattle are the main ingredients of Oklahoma's economy, and oil is by far the richest.

The state's output of oil was valued at $694,-710,000 in 1967, up 6% from the previous year, accounting for 70% of the total value of the state's mineral production, and ranking it 4th highest in the U. S.

Natural gas was another large income producer, providing $203,203,000, or 20% of the total mineral value. Other minerals include helium, in which the state ranks 3rd, zinc, gypsum, cement, lead, coal.

Oklahoma's rich plains produced the nation's 3rd largest winter wheat crop in 1967 and the state ranked 5th in sorghum. Its cattle herd was the nation's 7th largest. Total income from farms was $825,011,000, more than half from livestock products.

Much of the manufacturing industry is based on processing of the state's own wheat, meat and oil, but diversification is increasing. Value added by manufacturing totals over $1 billion annually. Important lines, in order of value added, are food products (especially meat and flour), petroleum and coal products, machinery (especially construction and oil tools), metal products.

Est. pop. July 1, 1967, was 2,496,000.

There are 20 colleges and universities and 15 junior colleges. The state is served by 7 major railroads and 5 airlines. Attractions include 21 state parks, large lakes and reservoirs such as Eufaula (104,000 acres), Lake Texoma (93,080 acres); Ouachita National Forest (176,000 acres), the Will Rogers Memorial, rodeos, bass fishing and quail hunting.

The Will Rogers Memorial, Claremore, has collections of the great humorist's saddles and ropes, as well as trophies; his tomb is also here. In Anadarko, the Southern Plains Indian Museum and Crafts Center exhibits Indian arts and has a crafts sales shop. The Woolaroc Museum near Bartlesville has 55,000 exhibits in a panorama of New World history, and a collection of paintings of the West.

The restored Fort Gibson Stockade, with many of the original buildings, near Muskogee, was erected 1824 and was the army's largest outpost in the Indian lands.

The Philbrook Art Center, Tulsa, has paintings by European and American masters, collections of Indian and Spanish cultures, and conducts an annual national competition for artists of Indian or Eskimo extraction, exhibited each May and June.

Also in Tulsa, the Thomas Gilcrease Institute has paintings by Remington, Catlin, Russell, Bierstadt, Moran, Copley, Sully, Homer, Eakins, etc., sculpture and Indian artifacts.

The 1st permanent white settlement in the area was made in 1796 by Maj. Jean Pierre Chouteau on the site of present-day Salina.

Part of the Louisiana Purchase, 1803, Oklahoma was known as Indian Territory (but was not given territorial government) after it became the home of the Five Civilized Tribes—Cherokee, Choctaw, Chickasaw, Creek and Seminole—1828-1846. The land was also used by Comanche, Osage and other plains Indians. As white settlers pressed west, land was opened for homesteading by runs and lottery, a run being a race for a claim at a specific time. The first run took place Apr. 22, 1889, the most famous was the run to the Cherokee Outlet, 1893. The portion thus opened was organized as a Territory; this and Indian Territory were joined by Congress in the State of Oklahoma, admitted to the Union Nov. 16, 1907. Oklahoma's Indian population (1960 Census) was 64,689, 2nd to Arizona.

*(See also Index for Oklahoma City.)*

# Oregon
*Beaver State*

**CAPITAL: Salem. AREA: 96,981 sq. mi., rank, 10th. POPULATION: 1,768,687 (1960 Census), rank 32nd. MOTTO: The Union. FLOWER: Oregon Grape. BIRD: Western Meadow Lark. COLORS: Navy blue and gold. FISH: Chinook salmon. TREE: Douglas Fir. SONG: Oregon, My Oregon. ADMISSION: 33rd.**

Oregon is rich in timber, fish and wildlife, water power and scenic beauty, with lofty mountain ranges, deep river gorges and broad, fertile valleys.

Half of Oregon, or about 30,000,000 acres, is thickly forested and the state leads the nation in value of forest products, over $1.5 billion a year. Production of lumber, paper and other forest products provides full-time jobs for about 85,000 workers and accounts for over 50% of the state's economy.

Also important are food products, fabricated metals and machinery. Value added by manufacture is over $1.8 billion a year.

Agriculture is a large industry; the average number of agricultural workers was 60,200 in 1967. Farm receipts for the year totaled $530,133,000, 56% from crops, the rest from livestock. Oregon is 1st among the states in pears and sweet cherries, 2nd in hops, 7th in turkeys, 12th in sheep.

Stone, nickel, cement, lime and pumice are important in mineral production, which was valued at $77,259,000 in 1967.

The commercial fish catch, including salmon, tuna, halibut, sole, cod and shellfish, is worth over $11,000,000 a year.

Tourism is also an important industry, est. at over $258,000,000 annually. There are 210 state parks and both state and national forests. Crater Lake, a national park, is a body of sapphire blue water in a former volcano, 6 mi. in diameter and 1,932 ft. deep—deepest lake in the U. S. Fort Clatsop National Memorial includes a replica of the fort in which the Lewis and Clark expedition spent the winter of 1805-06. Oregon Caves National Monument contains stone waterfalls. Skiing and the annual Pendleton Round-Up are other attractions. By 1972, Oregon will spend $730,000,000 on highway expansion. Mt. Hood, 11,235 ft., is the highest point in the state.

The Columbia River brings ocean shipping to Portland, 100 miles inland but one of the Pacific Coast's principal ports, and to other river ports. The Bonneville Power Administration, a federal agency, delivers electric power from 21 federal dams in the Pacific Northwest to 141 public and private utilities and industries. Seven more dams, under construction, will have a capacity of 3,605,000 kw.

Oregon has 39 colleges and universities and is served by 5 major railroads and 13 airlines.

The Univ. of Oregon in Eugene has a Museum of Art with Oriental, Pacific Northwest and other art collections. It also has a Museum of Natural History.

Est. pop. July 1, 1967, was 1,999,000.

Capt. Robert Grey, in the Columbia, discovered the river named after his ship May 11, 1792, and claimed the area for the U. S. President Jefferson sent the Lewis & Clark Expedition to the area, 1804-06. John Jacob Astor's fur depot, Astoria, was founded in 1811.

A provisional government was established in Champoeg, May 2, 1843, and U. S. title was established in 1846 in a settlement of U. S. and British claims to the area. Oregon became a state Feb. 14, 1859.

*(See also Index for Portland.)*

# Pennsylvania
*Keystone State*

**CAPITAL: Harrisburg. AREA: 45,333 sq. mi., rank, 33rd. POPULATION: (1960 Census), 11,319,-366, rank, 3rd. MOTTO: Virtue, Liberty and Independence. FLOWER: Mountain Laurel. BIRD: Ruffed Grouse. TREE: Eastern Hemlock. Second of Original 13 States to ratify Constitution.**

Pennsylvania has extensive mineral resources and fertile farmlands, is a leader in manufacturing and boasts a wealth of historic landmarks and scenic attractions. Est. pop. July 1, 1967, was 11,626,000.

Roughly rectangular in shape, Pennsylvania has prosperous farmlands in the SE and the W; through the center, running NE-SW, are parallel mountain ridges with valleys between. Highest point is Mt. Davis in the SW, 3,213 ft.

A third of the nation's steel plants are in Pennsylvania. It ranks 1st in iron and steel production with 24.4% of the U. S. total. Mill and factory products are many and varied; value added by manufacturing was est. at $17 billion for 1965. Metals, $3.1 billion, led, followed by dairy, beverage, candy and other food products, $1.4 billion; electrical machinery, $1.4 billion; machinery, $1.3 billion, chemicals, metal products, transportation equipment, clothing.

The state ranked 1st in manufacturing of shoes in 1966 with 90,590,000 pairs.

Pennsylvania produces almost all of the nation's anthracite coal; it ranked 2nd in bituminous coal in 1967. Also important are stone, cement, natural gas, petroleum, clays, zinc, iron, gold, cobalt. Total mineral production value for 1967 was $909,682,000.

Prosperous farms, such as those in the Pennsylvania Dutch country in the SE, increased total livestock and crops receipts in 1967 to $913,447,000, much of it from dairy and poultry products.

The state ranks 1st in sausage products, scrapple, pretzels, cigar-filler tobacco, plantation-grown Christmas trees; 2nd in ice cream, 4th in grapes, 5th in milk and apples, 6th in peaches, 7th in chickens. Forest products are worth over $1 billion annually.

The Commonwealth is rich in historic areas, including Valley Forge and the Gettysburg Battlefield, both national shrines. The Articles of Confederation, the Declaration of Independence and the Constitution were all adopted in Philadelphia.

There are more than 150 state and federal parks, recreation areas and historic sites. Scenic attractions include the Delaware Water Gap in the east and the 1,000-ft. deep Pine Creek Gorge in the north. Dutch folk festivals, county fairs, and fall foliage in the Poconos draw many visitors.

Valley Forge State Park, 22 mi. NW of Philadelphia, preserves the site of Washington's encampment during the winter of 1777-78; of 11,098 soldiers, close to 3,000, ill-equipped, died during the bitter weather; there is a museum, restored buildings, etc.

Longwood Gardens, near Kennett Square, include conservatories and rock, heather, flower and water gardens; arboretum, illuminated fountains, open-air theater; open every day of the year.

Lancaster County and nearby areas in the southeast are known as Pennsylvania Dutch Country. Descendants of early German (Deutsch) and Swiss settlers still maintain many of the early customs and "old world" culture which make their farms, festivals and market places attractive to tourists.

The William Penn Memorial Museum, Harrisburg, has collections of folk art, ironwork, glass, pewter, china, textiles, stage coaches, sleighs; replicas of artisans' shops, period rooms; fine arts exhibits and a planetarium.

There are 131 institutions of higher learning including Univ. of Pennsylvania (founded 1740), Univ. of Pittsburgh, Carnegie-Mellon-Univ., Bryn Mawr, Swarthmore, Lehigh, Lafayette, Dickinson, Drexel Institute, Temple, Villanova, Bucknell, Penn State, Duquesne.

First permanent settlement was in 1643 on Tinicum Is., near Chester, as part of New Sweden. In 1655, the Dutch took over; in 1664, the English. In 1681, Charles II granted land to Wm. Penn as payment for debts owed Penn's father. Penn made a treaty with the Indians, 1682, and called the land Pennsylvania (Penn's Woods) in honor of his father

*(See also Index for Philadelphia, Pittsburgh.)*

# Rhode Island

*Little Rhody*

**CAPITAL: Providence. AREA: 1,214 sq. mi., rank, 50th. POPULATION: (1960 Census), 859,488, rank, 39th. MOTTO: Hope. FLOWER: Violet. BIRD: Rhode Island Red. TREE: Red Maple. SONG: Rhode Island. Thirteenth of Original 13 States to ratify Constitution.**

Rhode Island is the smallest of the 50 states but has the longest official name: State of Rhode Island and Providence Plantations. It is not an island, although its Naragansett Bay, extending from the Atlantic 28 mi. inland, contains many islands, the largest of which is named Rhode Is. Highest point, Jerimoth Hill in Providence, is 812 ft.

Tiny Rhode Island is densely populated and highly industrialized. Population per sq. mi. of land (1960 Census) averaged 812.4, highest of the 50 states. But, by the July 1, 1965, Census pop. est. (920,000), Rhode Island pop. per sq. mi. was 869.6, 2nd to New Jersey which had 891.1.

Est. pop. July 1, 1967, was 901,000.

Industries show more than $1.1 billion in value added annually by manufacturing, with textiles accounting for about 17% of that figure. Until 1940, textile mills, dating back to Samuel Slater's 1790 cotton mill, employed more workers than all other Rhode Island industries put together. Employment in the mills has fallen off sharply in recent years, but jobs in other areas have increased. The state also pioneered in jewelry and silverware manufacture and these are still 2nd to textiles in value added by manufacture followed by metals, machinery and rubber and plastics.

Rhode Island's recent economic gains, replacing with other industries the decline in its textile mills, have been dramatic; from 1947 to 1958, unemployment had been almost double the national average; by 1966, the state's unemployment rate fell below the nation's—3.7% for Rhode Island, 3.8% for the U. S.

Only 1% of the labor force is engaged in farming, and farm receipts in 1967 totaled $20,353,000. Dairy and poultry (notably Rhode Island reds) are the most important lines; potatoes and apples are principal crops. The fish and shellfish catch is valued at over $5,300,000 annually.

There are 16 colleges and universities, including Brown Univ. (1764), and 3 junior colleges. The Naval War College and Hq. of the Atlantic Cruiser-Destroyer Force are at Newport. A major Naval Air Station is at Quonset Point. Tourism produces about $35,000,000 annually.

Rhode Island is distinguished historically for its battle for freedom of conscience and action, begun by Roger Williams, founder of Providence, exiled for religious dissent from Mass. Bay Colony, 1636. Wm. Coddington, John Clark, other religious exiles founded Pocasset, now Portsmouth, 1638, and Newport, 1639. First Baptist church in U. S. at Providence, 1638. Rhode Island gave protection to Quakers, 1657; to Jews from Holland, 1658.

Battle for individual rights brought resistance to British impressment of seamen, 1764, and to unjust taxation by burning of revenue vessel Gaspee, 1772. Rhode Island denounced allegiance to British King, May 4, 1776, before the Declaration of Independence. Ratified Constitution, May 29, 1790, 13th of original 13. Rhode Island had prohibition of liquor in 19th century, repealed it 1889, and refused to ratify the 18th amendment.

**Providence** is a major manufacturing and educational center and a port handling over 9,000,000 tons of cargo per year.

The Rhode Island Historical Society in Providence occupies the historic John Brown House, with rooms containing furniture by 18th Century cabinet makers and other items of local origin. Also in Providence, the Rhode Island School of Design has a museum with collections of classic art, 18th Century American furniture, 19th Century paintings, etc.

**Newport** became famous as the summer capital of society in the mid-19th Century, when industrial magnates built showy mansions. Easton's Beach and Bailey's Beach are noted resorts and Ocean Drive and Bellevue Avenue are showplaces. Touro Synagogue (1763) is the oldest in the U. S. and is a national historic site. Music festivals and water sports are among attractions.

The Newport Historical Society has a marine museum; extensive exhibits of silver, furniture, china, etc.; a grist mill, several forts, a Seventh Day Baptist meeting house built 1729.

In Pawtucket, the Old Slater Mill Museum is a restored 1793 cotton mill, considered the 1st to spin yarn successfully in this country; it has demonstrations of hand spinning and weaving.

# South Carolina

*Palmetto State*

**CAPITAL: Columbia. AREA: 31,055 sq. mi., rank, 40th. POPULATION: (1960 Census), 2,382,594, rank, 26th. MOTTO: Dum Spiro, Spero—While I Breathe, I Hope, and Animis Opibusque Parati—Prepared in Spirit and Resources. FLOWER: Carolina (Yellow) Jessamine. BIRD: Carolina Wren. SONG: Carolina. TREE: Cabbage Palm. Eighth of the Original 13 States to ratify Constitution.**

In South Carolina the land slopes from the Blue Ridge Mtns. in the NW, through thick pine forests and fertile farmlands with great fields of tobacco and cotton, to semi-tropic beaches and busy ports on the Atlantic. Deep-sea and inland fishing, hunting, the charm of ante-bellum houses, public gardens and famed shore resorts are among the state's attractions. Highest point is Sassafras Mtn. in NW, 3,560 ft.

Est. pop. July 1, 1967, was 2,603,000.

Efforts to diversify industry and expand foreign trade and tourism have been highly successful. Manufacturing is by far the major source of income; value added by manufacturing is about $2.8 billion annually. The textile industry is still the most important, comprising 45% of the value of all manufactured products and employing the most workers. South Carolina's mills rank first in the nation in cotton consumption and in output of yard goods. They are also a major producer of synthetic and woolen goods. Other important lines, in order of value, are chemicals, apparel, paper, food products, machinery and stone-clay-glass products.

In 1967, new industrial investment was valued at $305,797,000, providing an est. 11,176 new jobs.

Farms have become fewer but larger in recent years. South Carolina grows more peaches than any other state except California; it ranks 3rd in tobacco. Also grown are cotton, peanuts, sweet potatoes, pecans, etc. Poultry and eggs are important revenue producers; the state has large sales of chickens and turkeys. Total farm receipts for 1967 were $414,792,000, two-thirds from crops, one-third from livestock.

The state's mineral production, mostly non-metallic, was up slightly in 1967 to a record $46,029,000. It ranked 2nd among the states in vermiculite, used in insulation, and in kyanite, used in ceramics, and 4th in mica. Stone, including Winnsboro blue granite, accounts for 25% of income from the minerals industry.

Lumber for pulp and saw-timber is a major resource, especially the loblolly pine. Pulpwood production is over 2,800,000 cords annually.

Travel business was up 8% in 1967, travelers spending an est. $307,000,000 in the state, $189,-000,000 of it by tourists from other states. Attractions include 28 state parks, famed gardens, historic sites, coastal islands and shore resorts such as Myrtle Beach, fishing and quail hunting. There are many historic churches and white-pillared houses in Charleston, Columbia and Beaufort. Gardens near Charleston include Middleton Place, Magnolia and Cypress; Brookgreen, south of Myrtle Beach, has 340 outdoor statues; other gardens are Edisto, at Orangeburg, Glencairn, at Rock Hill, Swan Lake, at Sumter.

Fort Sumter National Monument in Charleston harbor is the place where the Civil War began with bombardment of the fort by Confederate batteries, Apr. 12-13, 1861.

Charleston Museum, estab. 1773, has exhibits of interior paneling, furniture, arts, crafts and utensils from early South Carolina days.

The state has 32 institutions of higher learning, including the Univ. of South Carolina, Clemson and The Citadel. Columbia is the largest city, 97,433 (1960 Census).

South Carolina played an important part in American beginnings. First settled by Spaniards, 1526 and 1566, it was given by England's Charles I to Robert Heath as Carolina, 1629; had first royal governor, 1730. Charles Pinckney helped frame the Constitution of the U. S., 1787. The state was 1st to secede, Dec. 20, 1860; readmitted in 1868.

## South Dakota

*Coyote State, Sunshine State*

CAPITAL: Pierre. AREA: 77,047 sq. mi.; rank, 16th. POPULATION: (1960 Census) 680,514, rank, 40th. MOTTO: Under God, the People Rule. FLOWER: American Pasque. BIRD: Ringnecked Pheasant. SONG: Hail South Dakota. TREE: Black Hills Spruce. ADMISSION: 39th or 40th with North Dakota.

South Dakota is a rectangle split down the middle by the Missouri and a chain of huge lakes formed behind dams on the river. In the E are rich farmlands which produce large crops of rye, oats and other grains. In the W are rolling grasslands which support millions of cattle and sheep, as well as vast acreages of wheat. In the far W are the Black Hills with Harney Peak, 7,242 ft., the highest point in the nation E of the Rockies.

With 55,000 farms occupying 93% of the land, agriculture is South Dakota's leading industry, and livestock produces over 80% of farm income. Mining and lumbering rank next in natural resource industries. Est. pop. July 1, 1967, was 674,000.

South Dakota led the nation in gold production in 1967 for the 19th consecutive year; the Homestake Mine in Lawrence Co. is the largest in the U. S. Gold accounted for $21,000,000 of the state's total mineral production value, $51,043,000 in 1967. The state also ranked 1st in beryllium and was 3rd in feldspar and 4th in lithium. Other products include petroleum, uranium, tin, vanadium.

The state ranked 1st in the U. S. in size of its rye crop, was 2nd to North Dakota in spring wheat, 2nd to Minnesota in oats, 3rd in durum wheat. The land supports twice as many sheep as people; in 1968 it had 1,382,000 sheep, ranking 5th among the states. It stood 8th in cattle and hogs.

With 130,000 acres under irrigation, plans were underway in 1966 to supply 300,000 acres in central South Dakota from the large Oahe Reservoir and to use Missouri River projects to provide for municipal water supplies.

Value added by manufacture is over $157,000,000 a year; leading industries are food processing, electronics products, printing and publishing, stone-clay-glass products, in that order.

South Dakota has 8,400 sq. mi. of Indian Reservations. Indians, est. 28,000, are largely Sioux.

South Dakota has 17 institutions of higher learning—including seven state colleges and universities. There are 11 state parks and over 100 other state recreation areas totaling 90,000 acres. Pheasant, duck and geese are abundant. There are large herds of white-tail and mule deer and elk and about 3,800 bison in state and private herds.

Mount Rushmore in the Black Hills has an altitude of 6,200 ft. Sculptured on its granite face are the heads of Washington, Jefferson, Lincoln and Theodore Roosevelt. These busts by Gutzon Borglum are proportionate to men 465 ft. tall. Rushmore is visited by over 1,500,000 persons annually.

Other tourist attractions include Custer State Park, nation's largest state-owned park with the world's largest herd of bison; the Black Hills Passion Play, staged from June to Sept. in an amphitheater at Spearfish; the "Great Lakes of South Dakota." 4 reservoirs behind Oahe, Big Bend, Fort Randall and Gavins Point Dams on the Missouri with total water surface area of 571,000 acres. Out-of-state tourists spent an est. $118,000,000 in South Dakota in 1965.

Fort Sisseton State Park, 18 mi. SE of Britton, is a restored Army frontier post of 1864. The Sioux Indian Museum in Rapid City features historic and contemporary arts of the Sioux and an Indian craft sales shop.

Discovery of this area dates back to 1743 when the first white men, the Verendrye brothers, Frenchmen, came in search of a route to the Pacific. South Dakota was admitted to the Union Nov. 2, 1889, together with its twin state, North Dakota, after 28 years as a part of Dakota Territory. South Dakota Historical Society asserts both states can be 39th or 40th state, since President Harrison intentionally shuffled the proclamations before signing.

## Tennessee

*Volunteer State*

CAPITAL: Nashville. AREA: 42,244 sq. mi., rank, 34th. POPULATION: (1960 Census), 3,567-089, rank, 17th. MOTTO: America At Its Best. FLOWER: Iris. BIRD: Mockingbird. TREE: Tulip Poplar. SONG: Tennessee Waltz. ADMISSION: 16th.

Eastern Tennessee is rugged country with the Great Valley separating the Great Smoky Mtns., on the state's E border, from the Cumberland Mtns.; the Central Basin is a plateau area containing the famed Bluegrass country; from there the state slopes W to the bottomlands on the Mississippi River. Clingman's Dome, in the Great Smokies, is the highest point, 6,643 ft.

Est. pop. July 1, 1967, was 3,888,000.

Manufacturing has taken the top place in Tennessee's economy, with factory payrolls now twice farm income. Principal industries, in order of value, are chemicals, food products, apparel, textiles, paper, stone-clay-glass products, electrical machinery. Also important are furniture and other wood products.

There are 24 research centers including Oak Ridge, TVA and Arnold Engineering Development Center for airplane research. Value added by manufacture is over $3.3 billion annually.

Farm income in 1967 included $343,128,000 from livestock products and $242,295,000 from crops. Tennessee ranked 6th among the states in tobacco production.

Lumbering is also important, providing full-time jobs to 40,000 persons. Wood products are valued at over $500,000,000 annually and the state is known as the U. S. hardwood flooring center.

Tennessee produces a wide range of minerals and leads the other states in zinc and pyrites. Other products include silver, cement, copper, coal and phosphate rock. Total mineral production was valued at $182,745,000 in 1967.

Tourism is of increasing importance; visitors spend about $327,000,000 annually in Tennessee.

With six other states, Tennessee shares in Federal reservoir developments on the Tennessee and Cumberland River systems. About 41,000 sq. mi. are drawn on by Tennessee Valley Authority, which built Norris Dam on the Clinch River and operates a number of other dams in the state. Their reservoirs cover 756,321 acres.

Tennessee has a number of natural wonders—Reelfoot Lake, the reservoir basin of the Mississippi River formed by an earthquake (1811); Lookout Mountain a rock-faced promontory carved by the currents of the Tennessee River and overlooking Moccasin Bend, at Chattanooga; Fall Creek Falls, 256 ft. high; and the west half of Great Smoky Mountains National Park.

The American Museum of Atomic Energy in Oak Ridge has displays, models, lectures. The Hermitage, 13 mi. E of Nashville, home of Andrew Jackson, contains furniture and personal effects of the President. The Ancestral Home of James K. Polk, in Columbia, has portraits, furniture and various articles used by President Polk in the White House. The Parthenon, in Centennial Park, Nashville, is a full-size replica of the Parthenon of Athens, contains paintings and casts of the Elgin marbles.

There are 47 colleges and universities among them Univ. of Tennessee in Knoxville; Vanderbilt and Fisk in Nashville.

Tennessee is believed to have been reached by De Soto, 1541. La Salle built a fort 1682. It was part of the Carolina grant of Charles II and home of Cherokee tribes. During 1784-1788 settlers formed the "state" of Franklin, North Carolina ceded it to the Federal govt. 1790; it was part of the Territory South of the Ohio until it became a state in 1796. It seceded 1861, was the site of Civil War battles and was readmitted 1866.

(*See also Index for Knoxville, Memphis, Nashville.*)

## Texas

*Lone Star State*

CAPITAL: Austin. AREA: 267,339 sq. mi., including 4,999 water, rank 2nd. POPULATION: (1960 Census), 9,579,677, rank 6th. MOTTO: Friendship. (Carrying out meaning of Indian word, Tejas—friends, from which Texas derives name). FLOWER: Bluebonnet. TREE: Pecan. BIRD: Mockingbird. SONG: Texas, Our Texas. ADMISSION: 28th.

Texas leads all other states in many categories, among them oil, cattle, sheep, cotton and rice. While these are basic to the Texas economy, manufacturing, as measured in terms of value added, makes an even greater contribution than either mineral output or farm receipts.

It is 2nd only to Alaska in area. Est. pop. July 1, 1967, was 10,873,000, ranking 5th among the states.

Texas oil fields produce 35% of the nation's petroleum; the state's 1967 output, 1.1 billion bbl., was valued at over $3.3 billion. It is also the No. 1 producer of natural gas, asphalt, granite, natural gas liquids and magnesium chloride; it ranks 2nd in sulphur, salt, sodium sulphate, helium and bromine, and 3rd in cement and clays.

The total value of the state's mineral production is by far the greatest of any state, $5.4 billion in 1967, up 8% from 1966 for a new record.

Texas stood 4th among the states in value of agricultural receipts, $2.5 billion for 1967, 52% from livestock products, the rest from crops.

It led all states in number of cattle, 10,972,000 (about the same number as people) in 1968, and in sheep, 4,206,000; it ranked 3rd in turkeys and 5th in chickens. It grew the largest crops of cotton, rice and sorghum and was 3rd in peanuts, pecans and vegetables and melons. Also important are grapefruit, oranges, peaches, roses. Irrigation has reclaimed large arid areas in the W.

The Southwest Exposition & Fat Stock Show is held annually in Fort Worth; the nation's largest state fair in October in Dallas; the largest cattle auction in Amarillo.

Value added by manufacture was est. at $12.4 billion for 1968, about 25% of it in chemicals, the largest industry—particularly petro-chemicals. Total manufacturing employment was 709,200 workers; largest employer is the transportation equipment industry with 95,400.

Texas is 4th among the states in commercial fishing with the annual catch valued at over $42,000,000.

Tourists spend over a half billion dollars annually in Texas. There are 64 state parks, recreation areas and historic sites, including the Alamo, mountainous Big Bend National Park, Fort Davis National Historic Site and 4 national forests. Some 90 peaks reach altitudes of a mile or more; there are 640 miles of beaches on the Gulf of Mexico; there are numerous deep canyons and caverns.

The Texas Memorial Museum of the Univ. of Texas, Austin, has dioramas of oilfields, the Odessa, Tex., meteor crater, Texas mammals, Indian tribes; exhibits of fossils, minerals, guns, pioneers' tools; large relief maps illustrating the changing face of Texas through 250,000,000 years.

Texas has 56 colleges and universities and 47 junior colleges; enrollment 1964-65 was 223,000. Important schools include Univ. of Texas, Baylor, Rice, Southern Methodist, Texas Western, Texas A. & M., Texas Christian, Texas Technological, Univ. of Houston.

Texas is the only state that was an independent republic, recognized by the U. S., before annexation. Over it have flown the flags of Spain, France, Mexico, the Lone Star Flag of the Republic, the Confederate States and the United States.

The first Europeans to arrive in the area were Spaniards. Alonso de Pineda, in 1519, and Cabeza de Vaca, 1536, explored coastal areas; Francisco de Coronado crossed inland in 1541. The first missions were founded in 1659, 1690. Texas became a Spanish province in 1691 and a Mexican state in 1821.

American settlers revolted in 1835; after defeat at the Alamo, Mar. 6, 1836, they defeated the Mexicans at San Jacinto, Apr. 21, 1836. They formed the Republic of Texas and, in 1845, voted for annexation to the U. S. Texas was admitted as a state Dec. 29, 1845. It seceded and joined the Confederacy Feb. 1, 1861. It freed all slaves June 19, 1865, and was readmitted to the Union Mar. 30, 1870.

(See also Index for Dallas, Houston, San Antonio.)

# Utah
## Beehive State

CAPITAL: Salt Lake City. AREA: 84,916 sq. mi., rank, 11th. POPULATION: (1960 Census) 890,627, rank, 38th. MOTTO: Industry. FLOWER: Sego Lily. BIRD: California Gull. TREE: Blue Spruce. EMBLEM: Beehive. SONG: Utah We Love Thee. ADMISSION: 45th.

Wrested from the wilderness by Mormon settlers in the mid-19th Century, Utah is for the most part a mountainous area, broken by fertile irrigated valleys, several deserts and two large lakes, Great Salt Lake in the N and Lake Powell in the S.

Great Salt Lake is 4,200 ft. above sea level, but has no known outlet. Its salt density varies from 20 to 25%, 2nd only to that of the Dead Sea; it covers more than 1,500 sq. mi.; it is crossed by a 13-mi., rock-fill, railroad causeway. Lake Powell, created by construction of the Glen Canyon Dam on the Colorado River just over the border in Arizona, is 186 mi. long, most of it in Utah. Highest point in Utah is Kings Peak in the NE, 13,528 ft.

Est. pop., July 1, 1967, was 1,022,000.

Manufacturing has become the state's major industry, well ahead of mining, agriculture and tourism. Value added by manufacture in 1967 was $720,000,000 with primary metals accounting for $212,000,000 and transportation equipment $145,000,000.

Utah is an important center for research and production of intercontinental missiles, rocket engines, solid fuel propellants, supersonic engines, navigational systems for long-range, high-speed aircraft and electronic components for military computers. It has divisions of Thiokol, Hercules Inc., Boeing, Marquardt, Litton, Sperry.

Utah is a storehouse of many minerals. It ranks 2nd among the states in production of gold, silver, copper, asphalt, molybdenum and magnesium chloride; 3rd in lead, carbon dioxide, vanadium and potassium salts; 4th in uranium. Value of all minerals produced in 1967 totaled $360,017,000, a decrease from the previous year, mainly because of a nationwide copper strike.

The nation's largest open-pit copper mine at Bingham Canyon normally hires about 7,100 men and produces about 20% of newly-mined copper in the U. S. Operations are being expanded in a 4-year program. Two great copper smelters are operated by Kennecott and International. An electrolytic refinery produces copper 99.96% pure and has a capacity of 384,000,000 lbs. annually. Geneva Works of U. S. Steel has a capacity of 2,300,000 ingot tons of steel a year.

The state ranked 6th in number of sheep in 1968, 1,074,000. Crops include barley, sugarbeets, alfalfa, winter wheat, potatoes. Farm receipts in 1967 included $145,182,000 from livestock products, $43,550,000 from crops.

Over 67% of the land is owned by the Federal government.

More than 5,000,000 visitors annually spend about $183,000,000 in the state.

Utah is a great recreational area, with 11,000 mi. of fishing streams and 147,000 acres of lakes and reservoirs, numerous winter sports areas and camp grounds. Natural wonders may be seen at Zion and Bryce Canyon National Parks and Dinosaur, Rainbow Bridge and Natural Bridges National Monuments. A new national park, Canyonlands, the Lake Powell Recreation Area and Flaming Gorge Dam are other attractions.

Works by Utah artists and archeological, botanical, mineral and fossil collections may be seen at the Brigham Young Univ. Collections in Provo.

The Latter-day Saints number 72% of the population of the state (1960 census). The Mormons reached Utah July 24, 1847.

Utah was organized as a Territory Sept. 9, 1850; admitted to the Union Jan. 4, 1896.

(See also Index for Salt Lake City.)

# Vermont
## Green Mountain State

CAPITAL: Montpelier. AREA: 9,609 sq. mi., rank, 43rd. POPULATION: (1960 Census) 389,881, rank, 47th. MOTTO: Freedom and Unity. FLOWER: Red Clover. TREE: Sugar Maple. BIRD: Hermit Thrush. ANIMAL: Morgan Horse. SONG: Hail, Vermont. ADMISSION: 14th.

Vermont, 1st state to join the Union after the original 13, was the home of the Green Mountain Boys who played heroic roles in several victories of the American Revolution. They took their name from the Green Mountains which form the N-S backbone of the state. There are rich marble quarries in the western part of the state and large granite beds in the E. The Connecticut River runs along the E boundary, Lake Champlain forms much of the W line; among the many lakes is Memphremagog which lies partly in Canada to the N. Seven peaks rise over 4,000 ft. with Mt. Mansfield, 4,393 ft., the highest.

Est. pop. July 1, 1967, was 416,000.

Vermont has long been known for its stoneworking, forest and dairy industries, but manufacturing and the recreation-tourist business have expanded greatly.

Improved highways and truck facilities are credited with aiding the industrial growth. Principal manufactured goods are machinery (including business machines), stone and clay products, lumber, furniture and paper. Value added by manufacturing in 1967 was an est. $449,000,000.

Recreation is a $164,000,000-a-year business. Skiing accounted for most of the growth, with spending by skiers jumping from $14,000,000 in 1958 to $70,000,000 in 1966-67. There are over 60 miles of ski lifts in the state and 46 ski areas including Stowe, Killington, Mt. Snow, Stratton, Bromley, Jay Peak and Sugarbush.

Vermont has 68 state parks and forests covering nearly 100,000 acres. The Long Trail is popular for hiking and camping. There is fishing for trout, salmon, bass, muskellunge, and hunting for deer and game birds.

Vermont produced 310,000 gallons of maple syrup in 1967, the largest amount of any state. Large milk and butter production accounted for 80% of the total value of farm receipts in 1967, $139,629,000.

The state ranks high in output of marble, granite, limestone; it ranks 2nd in asbestos and 4th in talc. Total mineral production value for 1967 was $26,542,000.

The Shelburne Museum, 7 mi. S of Burlington, preserves 35 early American buildings, including furnished homes, doctor's and dentist's offices, stagecoach inn; covered bridge, sidewheeler, old trains, folk art, etc.; Webb gallery of paintings by Rembrandt, Goya, Corot, Manet, Cassatt.

The Bennington Museum displays early American glass, furniture, pottery and what is said to be the oldest Stars and Stripes flag in existence

The Vermont area was visited by Samuel de Champlain, 1609, and had its first permanent settlement at Fort Dummer near Brattleboro, 1724.

Jurisdiction over the area was disputed by New Hampshire and New York. During the Revolution, the Green Mountain Boys under Ethan Allen took Fort Ticonderoga and under Seth Warner captured Crown Point; later they helped defeat the British in the Battle of Bennington and at Saratoga.

In 1777 the colonists declared their independence, adopted a constitution, the first giving universal manhood suffrage without property qualifications, elected a governor. They chose the name Vermont, suggested by Dr. Thos. Young, Philadelphia, from Vert Mont (Green Mountain). Vermont ratified U. S. Constitution Jan. 1791, entered Union Mar. 4, 1791. Vermonters were intense anti-slavery men and supported Lincoln over their native son Stephen Douglas.

Vermont has 19 institutions of higher learning, including Univ. of Vermont at Burlington, Middlebury College and Norwich Univ.

# Virginia

### *Old Dominion*

**CAPITAL:** Richmond. **AREA:** 40,817 sq. mi., rank, 36th. **POPULATION:** (1960 Census), 3,966,-949, rank, 14th. **MOTTO:** Sic Semper Tyrannis. Thus Always to Tyrants. **FLOWER:** Flowering Dogwood. **BIRD:** Cardinal. **TREE:** Flowering Dogwood (Unofficial). **SONG:** Carry Me Back to Old Virginia. Tenth of the Original 13 States to ratify Constitution.

The Commonwealth of Virginia is famed for its colonial heritage, for the statesmen it produced, its historic homes and estates, and the great battlefields on which the fate of the nation was decided in both the 18th and 19th Centuries.

It was first settled, 1607, at Jamestown by English colonists and named for Elizabeth I, called the Virgin Queen. It had the New World's 1st representative legislature, the House of Burgesses, 1619; this assembly was elected by male suffrage. Virginia was active in resistance to the British Stamp Act and it provided much of the leadership that led to American independence and the writing of the Constitution.

Virginia's coastal plain, the Tidewater, consists mostly of 4 peninsulas formed by Chesapeake Bay and the Potomac, Rappahannock, York and James Rivers. The central Piedmont plateau rises, toward the W, to the Blue Ridge Mts. Beyond the Blue Ridge and between it and the Alleghenies on the W border lies the Shenandoah Valley, a rich farming region. Highest point is Mt. Rogers in the SW, 5,729 ft.

Est. pop. July 1, 1967, was 4,533,000.

Manufacturing has grown steadily and is diversified; it provides jobs for 320,186 while agriculture employs 91,100. Total value added by manufacturing is est. at over $3.5 billion annually with payrolls totaling $1.8 billion. Wood products, including furniture, paper and lumber, provided jobs for 58,300 in 1965; finished wood output was valued at $700,000,000. Other leading products are chemicals, processed foods, textiles, clothing, cigarettes, machinery and ships. Hampton Roads is the major port, a leader in bulk export tonnage.

Agriculture remains a vital factor in the economy. In 1967 Virginia ranked 3rd among the states in sweet potatoes, 4th in apples, 5th in tobacco. Other important crops are peanuts, peaches, corn. It ranks 8th in turkeys; its Smithfield hams, from peanut-fed hogs, are famous. Farm receipts for 1967 totaled $519,916,000.

Coal provides most of Virginia's mineral wealth. Record-breaking production of the fuel accounted for more than half the value of the state's total mineral output for 1967, $290,738,000. Also important are lime, zinc, stone, natural gas, cement.

The commercial fishing catch is valued at over $20,000,000 annually.

With its wealth of historical attractions and recreational facilities such as Shenandoah National Park in the Blue Ridge Mts. and Virginia Beach, the state has a large tourist business, est. at over $800,000,000 a year. Tourism is 2nd to manufacturing and ahead of agriculture as a source of income.

Virginia was the birthplace of 8 Presidents: Washington, Jefferson, Monroe, Madison, Tyler, William H. Harrison, Taylor and Wilson—the last 3 elected from other states. It has many historic shrines, including Washington's birthplace, Wakefield; his home and grave at Mount Vernon; Jefferson's Monticello, near Charlottesville and the Univ. of Virginia he designed; Robert E. Lee's birthplace, Stratford Hall, and grave at Lexington.

Colonial Williamsburg is a restoration of the 18th Century buildings and living conditions in what was the capital of Virginia when Washington, Jefferson, Patrick Henry and George Mason were young men. There are more than 500 buildings, many of them the originals.

At Jamestown, 1st permanent English settlement, are foundations and ruins of early buildings, relics, statues and monuments and a nearby exhibit of early glassblowing.

At Yorktown, where the surrender of British Gen. Cornwallis to American and French forces, Oct. 19, 1781, virtually ended the American Revolution, may be seen Colonial buildings, the restored house in which terms of surrender were drawn up, earthworks and Revolutionary cannons.

In Fredricksburg, the James Monroe Law Office and Museum is the original building in which President Monroe practiced law in the 1780s; among other possessions is the desk at which he signed the Monroe Doctrine.

Appomattox Court House National Monument includes the rebuilt Wilmer McLean house in which Gen. Lee surrendered the Confederate Army of Northern Virginia to Lt. Gen. Ulysses S. Grant, Apr. 9, 1865.

Fort Monroe Casement Museum has relics of the imprisonment in the fort of Jefferson Davis and Chief Black Hawk and of the battle between the Monitor and Merrimac. The Quartermaster Museum, Fort Lee, exhibits clothing, saddles, etc., of American soldiers from the Revolution on. The War Memorial Museum of Virginia, in Newport News, displays World War I and II weapons and equipment of many nations.

In Lexington are Washington and Lee Univ. and Virginia Military Institute, both closely linked with leaders and action in the Civil War. Also in Lexington is the George C. Marshall Research Library and Museum with displays of the life of the famed World War II general and statesman.

At Staunton is the Woodrow Wilson Birthplace, with memorabilia of his family. The Gen. Douglas MacArthur Memorial in Norfolk contains the general's sarcophagus, flags of 30 units he commanded, documents and murals of important events in his life.

Virginia seceded from the Union Apr. 17, 1861, and Richmond became the capital of the Confederate States. Virginia was readmitted Jan. 26, 1870.

There are 53 institutions of higher learning, including 31 colleges and universities, 7 professional schools and 15 junior colleges.

(*See also Index for Norfolk, Richmond.*)

# Washington

*Evergreen State*

CAPITAL: Olympia. AREA: 68,192 sq. mi., rank 20th. POPULATION: (1960 Census), 2,853,214, rank, 23rd. MOTTO: Al-Ki, By and By. FLOWER: Coast Rhododendron. TREE: Western Hemlock. BIRD: American Goldfinch. SONG: Washington, My Home. ADMISSION: 42nd.

The state of Washington in the Pacific Northwest is a leader in many ways—in lumber, in fruit and other crops, and in aircraft production; its ports on Puget Sound are gateways to Alaska and the Far East; the great dams on the Columbia River provide power for production of aluminum and irrigation for the rich Columbia Basin.

The lofty Cascade Range splits the state N-S. To the W, the Puget Sound lowlands support dairy, poultry and truck-farming; in the extreme W, the Olympic Peninsula is studded with the peaks of the Olympic Mtns. and the Coast Ranges. On the E slopes of the Cascades are the state's great fruit orchards; further E, plateau country provides sheep and cattle lands and a rich wheat belt. Highest peak is Mt. Rainier in the Cascades, 14,410 ft.

The Columbia River cuts a zig-zag course across Washington from the NE, then flows W along the Oregon border to the Pacific.

Puget Sound has many deep harbors beside which Seattle, Tacoma, Everett and other great cities have grown.

Est. pop. July 1, 1967, was 3,089,000.

Manufacturing industries in Washington employ a quarter of a million workers with payrolls totaling $2 billion and value added by manufacture est. at nearly $3.5 billion a year. Transportation equipment, mostly aircraft but including ships and trucks, is itself a billion dollar industry. Other products, in order of value, are lumber, processed food, paper, chemicals and metals. The Atomic Energy Commission plant at Hanford produces nuclear fuels and electricity.

Washington's huge fruit and berry production and other crops place it 1st among the states in apples, hops, late summer potatoes, raspberries, blueberries, currants; 2nd in pears, sweet cherries, apricots, winter wheat, asparagus; 3rd in grapes, 4th in cranberries, 6th in peaches. Farm receipts for 1967 totaled $767,531,000.

The commercial fishing catch is valued at over $20,000,000 a year. Salmon accounts for half the total, followed by halibut and bottomfish.

Mineral production in 1967 was worth an est. $68,577,000. Zinc, cement, uranium, gold, lead and silver were important.

Large aluminum reduction plants, using refined ore from out-of-state and low-cost electric power, expanded operations in 1967. Primary aluminum output was valued at $378,728,833, compared to $294,115,000 in 1966.

A series of great dams on the Columbia, including the massive Grand Coulee in the NE and Bonneville on the Oregon border, provide low-cost electric power

More than half the state is in forests; one-sixth of the nation's standing sawtimber is in Washington. Towering Douglas firs and Ponderosa pines, western hemlocks and red cedars are among commercially important trees.

There are 37 institutions of higher education—15 colleges and universities, with Univ. of Washington, Washington State Univ. and Seattle Univ. the largest.

First visited by explorers in the late 18th Century, Washington was organized as a territory Mar. 2, 1853; admitted to the Union Nov. 11, 1889.

The state has two national parks, Mt. Rainier and Olympic National Park. Its state parks and national forests of nearly 10,000,000 acres have large hunting, fishing and recreation areas.

The Washington State Historical Society, Tacoma, has exhibits of the fur trade, Indian and Eskimo arts, and pioneer cabins, schoolhouse and covered wagon.

Tourism in 1967, it was est., would bring 8,600,000 visitors to the state, spending approx. $300,000,000.

*(See also Index for Seattle.)*

# West Virginia

*Mountain State*

CAPITAL: Charleston. AREA: 24,181 sq. mi., rank 41st. POPULATION: (1960 Census), 1,860,421, rank, 30th. MOTTO: Montani Semper Liberi. Mountaineers Always Free. FLOWER: Rosebay Rhododendron Maximum. BIRD: Cardinal. TREE: Sugar Maple. ANIMAL: Black Bear. SONGS: The West Virginia Hills. This Is My West Virginia, and West Virginia, My Home, Sweet Home. ADMISSION: 35th.

West Virginia's fortunes have long been based on those of the bituminous coal industry; the state leads all others in coal production with about 30% of the U. S. total. Increased output of coal and natural gas, plus growth in the chemical, steel, glass and tourist industries, have aided the economy. Highway development is underway.

The terrain is mountanious with Alleghenies running NE-SW in the eastern half of the state; the western half is a plateau sloping down to the Ohio River which forms most of the boundary on the W. Highest point is Spruce Knob in the NE, 4,862 ft.

Est. pop. July 1, 1967, was 1,798,000.

West Virginia was part of Virginia until that state seceded in 1861; delegates of 40 western counties adopted a state government at Wheeling, Nov. 27, 1861; West Virginia was admitted to the Union June 20, 1863.

Coal accounts for 80% of the state's total income from minerals and a substantial increase in coal output in 1967 set the pace for a 5% rise in total mineral income which reached $936,093,000.

West Virginia produces and markets more natural gas than any other state east of the Mississippi. Also important are petroleum, salt, stone, cement, lime and clays.

Production of a wide variety of chemicals, based in the state's resources of salt brine, gas, oil and coal, and including synthetic fibers and plastics, dominates the manufacturing field, accounting for 43% of the $1.8 billion in value added annually by manufacturing. Large plants are in the Ohio and Kanawha valleys, where electric power is abundant. The state is also a major producer of steel and iron, glass and pottery.

Investment in new plants and plant expansion reached a record $487,000,000 in 1967, providing an est. 7,000 additional jobs.

Farm receipts totaled $104,198,000 in 1967; the hilly terrain is not conducive to large-scale agriculture. Poultry, dairy products, cattle and sheep accounted for most of the receipts. Apples and peaches are profitable crops. About 65% of the state is in forests, including valuable hardwoods.

Tourism is being promoted and the influx of visitors grows at about 8% yearly. More than a million acres have been set aside for recreation in 20 state parks, 9 state forests, Monongahela National Forest and large reservoir recreation areas. Attractions include Harpers Ferry National Historical Park, mineral water resorts at White Sulphur and Berkeley Springs, trout fishing, turkey, deer and bear hunting.

Part of the town of Harpers Ferry is being restored to its condition in 1859, when John Brown seized the U. S. Armory. Still standing is the fire-engine house in which Brown and a score of followers were beseiged and captured by a force of U. S. Marines under Robert E. Lee, then a U. S. colonel.

The State Museum in Charleston displays local relics and artifacts from prehistoric cultures (as early as 8,000 B.C.), Indians and pioneers, and the life of the area's people, past and present.

The Huntington Galleries, Huntington, has collections of 19th and 20th Century European and American paintings, furniture and decorative arts. The Oglebay Mansion-Museum displays Colonial furniture and 19th Centry glassware.

There are 21 institutions of higher learning.

# Wisconsin

*Badger State*

CAPITAL: Madison. AREA: 56,154 sq. mi., rank 26th. POPULATION: (1960 Census), 3,951,777, rank, 15th. MOTTO: Forward. FLOWER: Butterfly Violet. BIRD: Robin. TREE: Sugar Maple. ANIMAL: Badger. FISH: Muskellunge. WILDLIFE ANIMAL: White-tailed deer. SONG: On, Wisconsin! ADMISSION: 30th.

Known as America's Dairyland, Wisconsin pro-

duces more milk and cheese than any other state and agriculture is a vital part of the state's economy. However, manufacturing, including processing of foods, has become the state's largest employer and biggest income producer.

Mining has declined with the near-cessation in 1965 of iron mining, but output of zinc and other minerals has increased. Reforestation has kept the paper and wood product industries important. There are 14 ports on Lakes Michigan and Superior with access to the St. Lawrence Seaway.

The state has an abundance of recreation resources; water and winter sports, hunting and fishing are among its attractions.

Est. pop. July 1, 1967, was 4,188,000. Highest point is Timms Hill in the N, 1,952 ft.

Wisconsin's rolling pasturelands and large crops support the nation's largest herd of milk cows, 2,147,000 in 1968; 80% of its farms are dairy farms. The state produces the most milk, cheese, malted milk, hay, alfalfa, peas; it ranks 2nd in butter, 3rd in oats, 6th in turkeys, 8th in corn, 9th in hogs.

Farm receipts for 1967 totaled $1.4 billion, 8th highest in the U. S.

About 40% of income produced in Wisconsin comes from manufacturing and, with 493,000 factory employees, the state ranks among the top 12. Value added by manufacturing is over $6.1 billion a year. Most important products, in order of value added, are: machinery, especially engines, turbines and construction; food products, including dairy, meat and beer; transportation equipment, particularly motor vehicles.

Mineral production for 1967 was valued at $76,522,000, up 1%. Zinc, lime, cement and stone are important. Plans were underway to revitalize the iron ore industry through proposed production of pelletized low-grade ore.

Most of Wisconsin's timber production goes into pulp and paper, but the state is also a leading producer of hardwood, plywood and veneer.

Wisconsin has over 8,500 lakes, of which Winnebago is the largest, and fronts on both Lakes Michigan and Superior. Water sports, ice-boating, and fishing for trout, bass and muskellunge are popular as are skiing and hunting for deer, bear and wildfowl. Public parks and forests take up one-seventh of the land area; there are 32 state parks, 9 state forests, two national forests. Other attractions include small towns which preserve Swiss, Scandinavian, German and other European cultures, visits to breweries and cheese factories, Indian festivals and the Dells (scenic gorges) of the Wisconsin River.

There are more than 40 institutions of higher learning, among them the Univ. of Wisconsin, Wisconsin State Univ., Marquette and Lawrence Univs.; Beloit, Ripon and Carroll Colleges.

The 1st Euorpean to visit the Wisconsin area was Jean Nicolet in 1634; he was followed by French explorers and missionaries and the land became part of New France. The French surrendered it to the British in 1763; the British ceded it to the U. S. in 1783, but were not completely dislodged until 1815. Wisconsin became a state May 29, 1848.

The Circus World Museum in Baraboo has over 100 circus wagons and other displays, and presents circus shows daily, early May-early Sept.

*(See also Index for Milwaukee.)*

# Wyoming
*Equality State*

**CAPITAL:** Cheyenne. **AREA:** 97,914 sq. mi., rank, 9th. **POPULATION:** (1960 Census), 330,066, rank, 48th. **MOTTO:** Equal Rights. **FLOWER:** Wyoming Paint Brush. **BIRD:** Western Meadow Lark. **TREE:** Plains Cottonwood (Balsam Poplar). **SONG:** Wyoming State Song. **ADMISSION:** 44th.

Wyoming's towering mountains and rolling plains provide spectacular scenery, grazing ranges for sheep and cattle, and a wealth of mineral resources. Most important industry is mining, including oil and gas; agriculture, including livestock, is 2nd; tourism is 3rd and manufacturing 4th. Est. pop. July 1, 1967, was 315,000.

Ranges of the Rockies cover the western two-thirds of the state; the eastern third is Great Plains country. Highest point is Gannett Peak in the W, 13,785 ft. The spectacular Teton Mtns. lie S of Yellowstone National Park, which is mostly carved out of Wyoming's NW corner.

Wyoming has large reserves of coal (deposits underlie 41% of the land), oil (it has 5% of the nation's proven reserves), natural gas (ranking 6th in the U. S.) and uranium (2nd in the U. S.).

Oil output for 1967 was valued at $349,796,000, 66% of the total mineral production value for the year, $530,792,000. The state ranked 1st in sodium carbonate production, 2nd in uranium, 3rd in sodium sulphate, 4th in vanadium. Also important are coal, clays and natural gas.

Wyoming is 2nd in the U. S. in wool production and in 1968 its sheep numbered 1,857,000, exceeded only by Texas; it also had 1,420,000 cattle. Principal crops include wheat, oats, sugarbeets, corn, potatoes, barley, hay, alfalfa. Livestock receipts for 1967 totaled $166,794,000; crop receipts $36,233,-000.

Manufacturing includes petroleum and coal products, food products, soda ash, steel and iron, pumps and plumbing supplies. Value added by manufacturing is about $94,000,000 annually.

Wyoming is a main source for 3 important river systems, the Missouri, Colorado and Columbia. Both power and irrigation are provided by a growing number of dams and reservoirs. Tourism produces an est. annual $100,000,000.

Wyoming was organized as a Territory July 25, 1868; admitted to the Union July 10, 1890. Women were given the right to vote, for the first time in the U. S., by the Territorial Legislature in 1869.

Grand Teton National Park, with mountains 13,000 ft. high, comprises 299,326 acres; the National Elk Refuge covers 25,000 acres. Devils Tower, a cluster of rock columns 865 ft. high, became the first National Monument in the U. S. in 1906. Fort Laramie, partly preserved, partly restored, is a National Historic Site. The annual Cheyenne Frontier Days Celebration, last full week in July, is the state's largest rodeo. Hunting, fishing and skiing are other attractions.

The Buffalo Bill Historical Center in Cody has a museum with personal effects of William F. Cody (Buffalo Bill) and the Whitney Gallery of Modern Art with Indian art and paintings by Frederick Remington, Charles M. Russell, George Catlin, etc.

The Bradford Brinton Memorial Ranch, near Big Horn, has collections of western painting and sculpture, antiques, Indian arts, hunting trophies and firearms; open May 15-Sept. 15.

The University of Wyoming is in Laramie and there are six state community colleges.

*(See Index for Yellowstone National Park).*

# District of Columbia

**AREA:** 67 sq. mi. **POPULATION:** (1960 Census), 763,956. **MOTTO:** Justitia Omnibus. Justice for All. **FLOWER:** American Beauty Rose. **TREE:** Scarlet Oak. **BIRD:** Wood Thrush. The City of Washington is co-extensive with the District of Columbia.

The District of Columbia is the seat of the Federal Government of the United States. It lies on the west central edge of Maryland on the Potomac, opposite Virginia. Its area was originally 100 sq. mi. taken from the sovereignty of Maryland and Virginia. Virginia's portion S of the Potomac was given back to that state in 1846.

The 23rd Amendment, ratified in 1961, granted residents of the District the right to vote for President and Vice President for the first time and gave it three members in the Electoral College. Residents cast the first such votes in Nov. 1964.

Congress governed the District 1878-1967 through 3 Commissioners appointed by the President. The Reorganization Plan of 1967 substituted a single Commissioner and assistant and a 9-member City Council, all likewise appointed by the President; budgetary funds are still appropriated by Congress; residents have no vote in local government (except for recently granted right to elect school board members) and no representative in Congress.

Est. pop. July 1, 1967, was 809,000.

Proposals for a "federal town" for the deliberations of the Continental Congress were made in 1783, four years before the adoption of the Constitution that gave the Confederation a national government. Rivalry between northern and southern delegates over the site appeared in the First Congress, meeting in New York in 1789. John Adams, presiding officer of the Senate, cast the

deciding vote of that body for Germantown, Pa. In 1790 Congress compromised by making Philadelphia the temporary capital for ten years. The Virginia members of the House wanted a capital on the eastern bank of the Potomac; they were defeated by the Northerners, while the Southerners defeated the Northern attempt to have the nation assume the war debts of the 13 original states, the Assumption bill fathered by Alexander Hamilton. Hamilton and Jefferson arranged a compromise; the Virginia men voted for the Assumption bill, and the Northerners conceded the capital to the Potomac. President Washington chose the site in October, 1790, and persuaded landowners to sell their holdings to the government at £25, then about $66, an acre. The capital was named Washington.

Washington appointed Pierre Charles L'Enfant, a French engineer who had come over with Lafayette, to plan the capital on an area not over 10 miles square. The L'Enfant plan was considered grandiose, for streets 100 to 110 feet wide and one avenue 400 feet wide and a mile long on the Potomac pastures seemed foolhardy. But Washington endorsed his plans. When L'Enfant ordered a wealthy landowner to remove his new manor house because it obstructed his vista, and demolished it when the owner refused, Washington had to step in and dismiss L'Enfant.

On Sept. 18, 1793, the cornerstone of the north wing of the Capitol was laid by President Washington. The occasion was expected to drum up sales of city lots, but there were few purchasers. Washington bought several lots. In the next few years Robert Morris and others invested. By 1799 the Senate wing of the Capitol had been roofed, the walls of the President's house were up and the Treasury building was ordered. On June 3, 1800, President John Adams moved to Washington and on June 10, Philadelphia ceased to be the temporary capital. The City of Washington was incorporated in 1802; the District of Columbia was created as a municipal corporation in 1871, embracing Washington, Georgetown and County of Washington.

*(See also Washington, D. C.)*

# OUTLYING U. S. AREAS

## Commonwealth of Puerto Rico

*Estado Libre Asociado de Puerto Rico*

**CAPITAL:** San Juan. **AREA:** 3,435 sq. mi. **POPULATION:** 1960 Census, 2,349,544. **FLAG: Three red, two white horiz. stripes; white star in blue triangle at staff. SONG: La Borinquena.**

Puerto Rico is a hilly, tropical island lying between the Atlantic to the N and the Caribbean to the S; it is the easternmost of the West Indies group called the Greater Antilles, of which Cuba, Hispaniola and Jamaica are the larger units. It lies about 1,600 mi. SE of New York, 500 mi. N of Venezuela. It is roughly rectangular, 105 mi. long by 35 mi. wide. Numerous small islands include Vieques, Culebra and Mona.

The soil of the coastal plain is fertile and there are many lush valleys, but there are dry areas in the S which need irrigation and an extensive system has been constructed by the government. The climate is mild, with a mean temperature of 76°; the mean maximum is 82° and the mean minimum 73°. Highest point is Cerro de Punta, 4,389 ft., near the island's center.

President Truman, on Aug. 5, 1947, signed an act giving Puerto Rico the right to choose its chief executive by popular vote. An act of 1950, affirmed by special election, June 4, 1951, permitted Puerto Rico to draft its own constitution. One similar to that of the United States was approved in a convention Feb. 4, 1952, and ratified by a popular vote March 3, 1952. President Truman signed, July 3, 1952, a Congressional resolution approving the new constitution, elevating Puerto Rico to the status of a free commonwealth associated with the United States, effective July 25, 1952. In 1961 Pres. Kennedy appointed two Puerto Ricans to important posts in his administration.

In a July 23, 1967, referendum, Puerto Ricans strongly favored continuation of commonwealth status. The vote was: commonwealth, 425,081; statehood, 273,315; independence, 4,205.

The Legislative Assembly consists of a Senate and House of Representatives, whose members are elected by direct vote every 4 years. Eight senatorial districts elect two Senators each, and 40 representative districts one member each; also 11 Senators and 11 Representatives at large. Its Resident Commissioner in the U.S. Congress does not have a vote. Puerto Ricans were granted American citizenship under the Organic (or Jones) Act of 1917. They do not vote for President, unless they move to the U. S., where they come under local laws.

Executive power is vested in a governor elected by direct vote. There are 9 executive departments each headed by a secretary: State, Justice, Education, Health, Treasury, Labor, Agriculture, Commerce, and Public Works. The governor is Roberto Sanchez Vilella, elected Nov., 1964. The judiciary is vested in a Supreme Court and lower courts.

The Commonwealth's "Operation Bootstrap" program for economic development has radically raised the standard of living; per capita income for 1967 was $1,047, up $279 from 1963.

Puerto Rico derives its largest income from manufacturing, $678,200,000 in 1967 (up $66,000,000 from 1966). Products include textiles and apparel, electrical and electronic equipment, plastics and chemicals. The chemical products include pharmaceuticals, cosmetics, ammoniated super-phosphate, ethylene glycol and potassium sulphate.

Agriculture is a large but declining source of income, valued at $182,200,000 for 1967, down 1%. Income from dairy and livestock products has surpassed that from sugar. Also important are tobacco, coffee, pineapples, coconuts, fruits and garden truck. Sugar derivatives include rum and molasses.

Mineral production was valued at $56,862,000 for 1967, up 12%. Cement accounted for almost half the total value.

Gross capital investment in 1966 reached $754,000,000; gross product, 1967, $3.4 billion, both up.

Off-island trade is chiefly with the United States.

| | Imports | Exports |
|---|---|---|
| 1966 | $1,659,400,000 | $1,154,000,000 |
| 1967 | $1,799,000,000 | $1,321,000,000 |

While migration to the U. S. mainland after 1945 varied from 28,000 to 45,000 annually, flow was reversed in 1963 when Puerto Ricans returning to the island exceeded those leaving by 5,479; in 1967 the flow to the mainland was greater by 26,553. These changes are mainly caused by employment conditions, mainland and Puerto Rican. Unemployment rate on the island is usually over 11%. Est. pop. July 1, 1967, was 2,697,000. About 765,000 of Puerto Rican origin live in N. Y. City.

San Juan, with its international airport and many resort hotels, is the center of the ever-growing tourist industry which, in 1967, attracted 819,000 visitors who spent some $163,000,000.

Spanish is the official language but most persons also speak English. Public school education is free and compulsory at the elementary school level; English is taught as a language and is compulsory in all 8 grades. Chief religion is Roman Catholicism.

Puerto Rico (or Borinquen, after the original Indian name Boriquen) was discovered by Columbus, Nov. 19, 1493. Ponce de Leon conquered it for Spain, 1509, and established the first settlement at Caparra, across the bay from San Juan. Ruled by Spain until 1898, it was occupied by Maj. Gen. Nelson A. Miles in the Spanish-American war and ceded to the U. S. by the Treaty of Paris, Dec. 10, 1898.

## Canal Zone and Panama Canal

*For Panama Canal cargo traffic see Index.*

The Canal Zone has been, in effect, a U. S. Government reservation. It is a strip of land extending 5 mi. on each side of the axis of the Panama Canal, under jurisdiction of the U. S. by treaty with the Republic of Panama.

In 1967 Panama and the U. S. jointly announced that agreement had been reached on 3 new treaties. The treaties, in part, would provide for the U. S. to relinquish its sovereignty over the Canal Zone, for operation of the Canal by a binational authority, for increased payments to Panama to come from tolls revenue, and for political integration of the Zone with Panama.

Another major treaty provision would give the U. S. an option to build a new, larger, sea-level canal in Panama. A U. S. commission is studying the feasibility of a route to the east of the present canal and alternate routes through northern Colombia and along the Nicaragua-Costa Rica border. The proposed new treaties were awaiting finalization.

Negotiations for the new treaties were launched

by U. S. President Johnson and Panama President Robles after Panamanian riots protesting the 1903 and 1955 treaties caused the deaths of 21 Panamanians and 3 U. S. soldiers, Jan. 9, 1964. *(See Panama in Index for further developments.)*

The canal connects the Caribbean with the Bay of Panama on the Pacific. Because of the geographic loop made by the Isthmus of Panama, the Caribbean end of the canal, which could be called the eastern end, is actually further west than the Pacific end.

The Zone has an area of 553 sq. mi. of which 371 are land: Est. pop., 1967, was 55,600.

The Canal Zone Government and the Panama Canal Co. are the two operating agencies, both headed by an individual who acts as Governor of the Canal Zone and President of the Company. The governor is appointed by the President of the U. S. As governor he reports directly to the Secy. of the Army. As president of the company he reports to the board of directors, appointed by the Secy. of the Army. The Canal Zone Government maintains civil government. The Company operates the Canal, the Panama Railroad and a ship between New Orleans and the Canal Zone.

A French syndicate under Ferdinand de Lesseps failed to complete a canal, 1880-89, and a second French company failed in 1899. The U. S. bought their rights and offered Colombia compensation for a canal zone, but Colombia failed to ratify the treaty Oct. 1903. Panama declared itself independent of Colombia Nov. 3, 1903, and was recognized by President Theodore Roosevelt Nov. 6. American naval forces discouraged action by Colombia. On Nov. 18 Panama granted the Canal strip to the U. S. by treaty, ratified Feb. 26, 1904, compensation $10,000,000, with annual payments of $250,000 after 9 years, and a guarantee of Panama independence.

Under terms of the 1903 treaty, Panama granted the U. S. perpetual sovereignty over the Canal Zone "to the entire exclusion of the exercise by the Republic of Panama of any such sovereign rights, power or authority."

The canal was opened to traffic Aug. 15, 1914. In 1922 Colombia accepted $25,000,000 from the U. S. plus special land transportation privileges, and agreed to recognize Panama. The U. S. increased its annual payment to Panama to $430,000 and withdrew its guarantee of independence, and agreed to bar all commercial enterprise with the Zone except that directly concerned with shipping.

A further treaty regulating relations between the U. S. and Panama was signed Jan. 25, 1955, increasing the annuity paid Panama to $1,930,000. In addition, the U. S. gave Panama about $28,000,-000 worth of real estate and buildings no longer needed by the Canal Zone administration. U. S. citizen and non-citizen employees were guaranteed equality of pay and opportunity. In addition, the U. S. agreed to build the high level bridge over the Pacific entrance to the Canal, opened Oct. 12, 1962, as a link in the Inter-American Highway.

### THE PANAMA CANAL

The Panama Canal is a lock and lake canal, crossing the Isthmus of Panama from the Caribbean Sea in a southeasterly direction to the Bay of Panama of the Pacific Ocean. It is 50 mi. long from deep water to deep water, at least 300 ft. wide at the bottom of excavated channels, 110 ft. wide in lock chambers, which have a usable length of 1,000 ft. Depth varies, but is not less than 41 ft. Average transit time is 8 hours.

Gatun Dam blocks the Chagres river near its Atlantic mouth, creating Gatun lake, 23¾ mi. long, 85 ft. above sea level, about 45 ft. deep. Ships ascend to the lake by locks and then pass through Gaillard (formerly Culebra) Cut, 8 mi.

## Virgin Islands

**CAPITAL:** Charlotte Amalie, on St. Thomas Is. **AREA:** 133 sq. mi. **POPULATION:** (1960 Census), 31,904; (1968 est.) 60,000. **FLOWER:** Yellow Cedar.

The Virgin Islands of the United States, an unincorporated territory administered by the Interior Dept., lie to the E of Puerto Rico at the western end of the Lesser Antilles, 1,629 mi. SE of New York. There are about 100 islands in the Virgins, of which the western 65 belong to the U. S.; the remainder are the British Virgin Islands.

The three largest and most populous of the U. S. islands are St. Croix, St. Thomas and St. John. Formerly the Danish West Indies, the 65

islands were purchased by the U. S. from Denmark for $25,000,000 (effective Mar. 31, 1917) for defense purposes. The islands were discovered by Columbus in 1493. About 80% of the population is of Negro descent.

Mean winter temperature is 78°; summer, 82°. Virgin Islands National Park occupies about three-fourths of St. John, smallest of the three principal islands.

The inhabitants have been citizens of the U. S. since 1927, but do not vote in U. S. elections. Legislation originates in a unicameral house of 15 senators, elected for 2 years. The Governor is appointed by the President of the U. S.

Tourism is the largest industry and is growing. Principal exports are watch movements, jewelry, rum, wool textile products, thermometers, bay rum.

## Minor Caribbean Islands

The **Swan Islands** lie 97 mi. NE of Honduras; **Great Swan** is 2 mi. by ½ mi. with pop. of 28 (1960 Census), chiefly employees of the U. S. Weather Bureau, which operates an upper-air observing station, and the Federal Aviation Administration, serving air navigation and communications functions; **Little Swan**, 1½ by ½ mi., is uninhabited. They are classified as unincorporated territory of the U. S.; they have also been claimed by Honduras.

The **Corn Islands**, consisting of **Great Corn** and **Little Corn**, lie 30 mi. off the SE coast of Nicaragua, have a pop. of 1,872 (1960 Census), were leased by the U. S. in 1914 from Nicaragua for 99 years.

**Quita Sueno Bank, Roncador Cay, Serrana Bank** and **Seranilla Bank** lie in the Caribbean between Nicaragua and Jamaica. They are uninhabited. Colombia also claims sovereignty over them, and Honduras claims ownership of Quita Sueno and Roncador.

**Navassa** lies between Jamaica and Haiti, covers about 2 sq. mi., is reserved by the U. S. for a lighthouse.

## American Samoa

**CAPITAL:** Pago Pago. Island of Tutuila. **AREA:** 76 sq. mi. **POPULATION:** (1960 Census): 20,051; (1968 est.) 26,000.

Blessed with spectacular scenery and delightful South Seas climate, American Samoa is the most southerly of all lands under U. S. ownership. It is an unincorporated territory consisting of 6 small islands of the Samoan group: Tutuila (where Pago Pago, the capital, lies by a crescent bay beneath tall mountains), Aunuu, the Manua Islands (Tau, Olosega and Ofu), and Rose. Also administered as part of American Samoa is Swain's Is., 210 mi. to the NW, acquired by the U. S. in 1925. The islands are 2,300 mi. SW of Hawaii.

American Samoa became U. S. territory by a treaty with the United Kingdom and Germany in 1899, confirmed by local chiefs in 1900 and 1904. Pago Pago had been a U. S. Navy coaling station under an 1872 commercial treaty.

Western Samoa, comprising the larger islands of the Samoan group, was a New Zealand mandate and UN Trusteeship until it became an independent nation Jan. 1, 1962. *(See Index.)*

Tutuila has an area of 52 sq. mi. Tau has an area of 17 sq. mi., and the islets of Ofu and Olosega 5 sq. mi., with a population of a few thousand. Swain's Island has nearly 2 sq. mi. and about 100 population. Highest peak is Lata, on Tau Is., 3,056 ft.

About 70% of the land is forest. Chief products and exports are fish products, copra and handicrafts. Taro, bread-fruit, yams, coconuts, pineapples, oranges and bananas also are produced.

Formerly under jurisdiction of the Navy, since July 1, 1951, it has been administered by the Interior Dept. which appoints a Governor and a Secretary. It has a bicameral legislature.

The American Samoans are of Polynesian origin. They are nationals of the U. S.

Educational television was started in Sept. 1964, and serves as the core of education in Samoa's public schools.

## Wake, Midway, Other Islands

**Wake Island**, and its sister islands, **Wilkes** and **Peale**, lie in the Pacific Ocean on the direct route from Hawaii to Hong Kong, about 2,000 mi. W of Hawaii and 1,290 mi. E of Guam. The group is 4½ mi. long, 1½ mi. wide and totals about 3 sq. mi.

The United States flag was hoisted over Wake Island, July 4, 1898, by Gen. F. V. Greene, commanding Second Detachment, Philippine Expedition. Formal possession was taken Jan. 17, 1899; Wake is administered by the Federal Aviation Administration which provides civil and military air traffic control.

The **Midway Islands**, acquired in 1867, are a group of two, **Sand** and **Eastern**, in the North Pacific, 1,150 mi. NW of Hawaii, with area of about 2 sq. mi., administered by the Navy Dept.

**Johnston Island**, SW of Hawaii, and **Kingman Reef**, S of Hawaii, are under Navy control.

**Howland, Jarvis** and **Baker Islands**, south of the Hawaiian group, uninhabited since World War II, are under the Interior Dept.

**Palmyra** is an atoll SW of Hawaii, 4 sq. mi. until 1959 administered by Honolulu.

Certain islands taken from Japan in World War II were retained by the U. S. as possible military bases with the understanding they would eventually be returned to Japan.

On June 26, 1968, these islands were returned to Japanese control and administration. They included: the **Bonin Islands**, with an area of about 40 sq. mi., S of Japan; the **Volcano Islands**, S of the Bonins, including **Iwo Jima** (about 8 sq. mi.), scene of the famous World War II battle; **Marcus Island**, about 1 sq. mi., E of the Volcanoes.

The 1968 agreement provided that the U. S. would continue the use of Loran navigational stations on Iwo Jima and Marcus.

## Ryukyu Islands (Okinawa)

The Ryukyu Islands, 73 in number, lie in an arc stretching SW from Japan toward Taiwan (Formosa), between the North Pacific and the East China Sea. They have an area of 848 sq. mi. and pop. (1967) of 952,000.

**Okinawa**, largest of the group, has an area of 454 sq. mi. and population of 746,742 (1966). Independent for centuries, they paid tribute to both China and Japan until they were annexed in 1874 by Japan.

Okinawa was taken by U. S. troops during World War II, June 21, 1945. Administration of the islands was vested in the U. S. by the Japanese peace treaty (1951), effective Apr. 28, 1952. The Ryukyus are an important American base. The nearby **Daito Islands**, also formerly Japanese, are included in the administrative area.

Naha, Okinawa, is the seat of the U. S. civil administration and of the local Ryukyuan government. Administration is carried out by a High Commissioner, responsible to the U. S. Secretary of Defense. The local Ryukyuan government has a popularly elected legislature, a chief executive elected since Nov. 1968 by popular vote (previously chosen by the legislature) and an independent judiciary.

High Commissioner: Lt. Gen. F. T. Unger; Civil Administrator: Stanley W. Carpenter; Chief Executive: Seiho Matsuoka.

Statements by U. S. officials have indicated that the islands eventually may revert to Japanese jurisdiction. Some of the islands, the Amami group, were returned to Japan in 1953.

Sugar, pineapples, vegetables, and marine products are the main exports.

## Guam

**CAPITAL: Agana. AREA: 209 sq. mi. POPULATION: (1960 Census) 67,044; (1968 est.) 101,000.**

Guam, the largest of the Mariana Islands, now an unincorporated territory, was ceded to the U. S. by Spain in the Treaty of Paris, Dec. 10, 1898. It is 30 mi. long and 4 to 8½ mi. wide. Distance from Manila, 1,499 mi.; from San Francisco, 5,053 mi. Mean annual temp. is 81°, average annual rainfall, July to September, 70 in. The island is volcanic and mountains rise 700 to 1,329 ft. Highest peak is Mt. Lamlam.

In March, 1967, President Johnson visited the island for talks with Vietnam advisers.

Magellan discovered the group of islands, Mar. 6, 1521, and called them the Ladrones (thieves). They were colonized in 1668 by Spanish missionaries who renamed them the Mariana Islands in honor of Maria Anna, queen of Spain.

When Spain ceded Guam to the U. S. it sold the other Marianas to Germany. Japan obtained a League of Nations mandate over the German islands in 1919; in Dec. 1941 it seized Guam; the island was retaken by the U. S. in July 1944. Guam is a base for both the Navy and Air Force.

Guam is under the jurisdiction of the Dept. of the Interior. It is administered under the Organic Act of 1950, which provides for a governor, named for 4 years by the President of the U. S., a 21-member unicameral legislature, elected biennially by the residents, who are American citizens but do not vote for President. Guamanians are of primarily Chamorro (Micronesian) stock.

School attendance is compulsory. There are a Territorial College and a vocational school. English is the official language. Chief religion is Roman Catholicism.

Principal products are fruits and vegetables; virtually all other commodities are imported. Except for metal scrap, there are virtually no exports.

## Islands Under Trusteeship

### CAROLINES, MARIANAS, MARSHALLS

The U. S. Trust Territory of the Pacific Islands includes 3 major archipelagoes: the **Caroline Islands, Marshall Islands** and **Mariana Islands** (*except Guam: See above*). There are 2,141 islands, 98 of them inhabited; land area total 687 sq. mi. but the islands are scattered over 3,000,000 sq. mi. of Micronesia in the western Pacific, N of the Equator and E of the Philippines. Total pop. (1967 est.) was 91,448.

In 1885, many of the islands were claimed by Germany. Others, held by Spain, were sold to Germany at the time of the Spanish-American War, 1898. After the outbreak of World War I, Japan took over the islands and, after the war, League of Nations mandates over them were awarded to Japan.

After World War II, the United Nations assigned them (1967) as a Trust Territory to be administered by the U. S. They are under administration of the U. S. Interior Dept.

Among the noted islands are: **Saipan** and **Tinian** in the Marianas, scene of a bitter engagement when they were taken by the U. S. from Japan in World War II; the former Japanese strongholds of **Palau, Peleliu, Truk** and **Yap** in the Carolines; **Bikini** and **Eniwetok**, where U. S. nuclear tests were staged, and **Kwajalein**, another World War II battle scene, all in the Marshalls.

Most of the islands are volcanic and picturesque, with luxuriant vegetation, but only a few are self-sustaining. Principal exports are copra, trochus shells, fish products, handicrafts and vegetables.

In 1967 U. S. President Johnson proposed that a plebiscite might be held in 1972 to allow the Micronesians to decide their future government. Opinion on the islands was divided on whether to seek independence or affiliation with the U. S. Islanders complained that some projects, such as schools, hospitals and roads, had been delayed or postponed by Federal economy measures.

## Disputed Pacific Islands

In the central Pacific, S and SW of Hawaii, lie 25 islands and atolls claimed by the U. S.; 18 of them are also claimed by the United Kingdom, and 7 by New Zealand. All are S of the Equator with the exception of Christmas Island.

Those claimed by the U. K. are:

The **Line Islands**, S of Hawaii, including Christmas, Flint, Malden, Starbuck and Vostok Islands and Caroline Atoll; only Christmas is inhabited. All are administered by the U. K.

Also, the **Phoenix Islands**, SW of Hawaii, including Canton and Enderbury Islands and Birnie, Gardner, Hull, McKean, Sydney and Phoenix Atolls. All are inhabited and administered by the U. K. except for Canton and Enderbury which are uninhabited and are under joint U. S. and U. K. administration. A U. S. missile tracking station on Canton was discontinued in Dec. 1967.

Also, the **Ellice Islands**, further to the SW, including Funafuti, Nukufetau and Nukulailai Atolls and Nurakita; all inhabited and all administered by the U. K.

Those claimed by New Zealand are:

The **Union (Tokelau) Islands**, S of the Phoenix group, including Nukunono, Atafu and Fafaofu Atolls. All are inhabited and administered by New Zealand.

Also, the **Northern Cook Islands**, E of the Unions, including Danger, Manahiki, Rakahanga and Penrhyn (Tongareva) Atolls. All are inhabited and administered by New Zealand.

# Origin of the Names of U. S. States

Source: State officials, and a study by John P. Harrington, Bureau of American Ethnology,
Smithsonian Institution, Washington, D. C.

**Alabama**—Indian for tribal town, later tribe, of the Creek confederacy.

**Alaska**—Russian version of Aleutian (Eskimo) word for Alaska Peninsula.

**Arizona**—Spanish version of Pima Indian word for "little spring place," identified as in Arizona Creek.

**Arkansas**—French variant of Kansas, a Sioux Indian name for south wind people.

**California**—Bestowed by the Spanish Conquistadores, being the name of an imaginary island, near the earthly paradise, in "Las Serges de Esplandian," a romance of chivalry written by Montalvo, 1510. Baja California (Lower California, Mexico) was first penetrated 1533. The state later was Alta (Upper) California.

**Colorado**—Spanish, red, first applied to Colorado River.

**Connecticut**—From Mohican and other Algonquian words meaning "long river place."

**Delaware**—Lord De La Warre, first governor of Virginia Company, entered bay, 1610. Name first applied to river, then to Indian tribe and state.

**District of Columbia**—For Columbus, 1791.

**Florida**—Named by Ponce de Leon on Pascua Florida, feast of flowers, Easter Sunday, 1513.

**Georgia**—For King George II of England by James E. Oglethorpe, colonial administrator, 1732.

**Hawaii**—Possibly derived from native word for homeland.

**Idaho**—Shoshone derivation. State calls it "light on the mountains."

**Illinois**—French for Illini or land of Illini, Algonquian word meaning men or warriors.

**Indiana**—Named because Indians lived there.

**Iowa**—A Sioux word, meaning "one who puts to sleep."

**Kansas**—Sioux word for south wind people.

**Kentucky**—Wyandot word for plain, originally applied to Kentucky Plains, Clark County.

**Louisiana**—Part of territory called Louisiana by LaSalle for French King Louis XIV.

**Maine**—From Maine, ancient French province.

**Maryland**—For Queen Henrietta Maria, wife of Charles I of England.

**Massachusetts**—From Indian tribe named after "large hill place" identified by Capt. John Smith as near Milton, Mass.

**Michigan**—Alouet, 1672, makes it designate a clearing, but later writers mentioned Chippewa micigama, large water.

**Minnesota**—From Dakota Sioux word meaning "clouded or milky" water of Minnesota River.

**Mississippi**—Probably Chippewa: mici, large; zibi, river. Tonti wrote it Michi Sepe.

**Missouri**—Algonquian word, "canoe haver," applied to tribe on river which received their name.

**Montana**—Latin for mountainous.

**Nebraska**—From Omaha Indian name for Platte River, both meaning flat.

**Nevada**—Spanish, meaning snow-clad.

**New Hampshire**—Named 1629 by Capt. John Mason of Plymouth Council for county in England.

**New Jersey**—The Duke of York, 1664, gave a patent to Lord John Berkeley and Sir Geo. Carteret to be called Nova Caesaria, or New Jersey.

**New Mexico**—Spaniards in Mexico applied term to land north and west of Rio Grande.

**New York**—For Duke of York and Albany who received patent to New Netherland from his brother Charles II and sent an expedition to capture it, 1664.

**North Carolina**—In 1629 Charles I gave a large patent to Sir Robt. Heath to be called Province of Carolana, from Carolus, Latin name for Charles. A new patent was granted by Charles II to Earl of Clarendon and others. Divided into North and South Carolina, 1710.

**North Dakota**—Dakota is Sioux for friend or ally.

**Ohio**—Indian, great, applied to river.

**Oklahoma**—Choctaw coined word meaning red man, proposed by Rev. Allen Wright, Choctaw-speaking Indian.

**Oregon**—In 1765 Maj. Robert Rogers proposed to George III to seek Northwest Passage by travel from Great Lakes to "a river called by the Indians Ouragon." In 1772 he spelled it Ourigan. In 1778 his associate, Jonathan Carver, wrote of "River Oregon or River of the West." In 1817 William Cullen Bryant wrote "where rolls the Oregon." In 1822 Rep. John Floyd (Va.) proposed creation of Oregon Terr. Wauregan is Algonquian for beautiful water. Presumably Rogers and Carver meant the Columbia.

**Pennsylvania**—William Penn, the Quaker, who was made full proprietor by King Charles II in 1681, suggested Sylvania, or woodland, for his tract. The king's government owed Penn's father, Admiral William Penn, £16,000, and the land being granted in part settlement, the king added the name Penn to Sylvania, against the desires of the modest proprietor, in honor of the admiral.

**Puerto Rico**—Spanish for Rich Port.

**Rhode Island**—Red island, first named by Adrian Block because of its red clay. Roger Williams suggested Island of Rhodes. His settlement, Providence Plantations, was also used.

**South Carolina**—See North Carolina.

**South Dakota**—See North Dakota.

**Tennessee**—From 1784 to 1788 this was the State of Franklin, or Frankland. Tanasi was the name of Cherokee villages on the Little Tennessee river.

**Texas**—Variant of word used by Caddo and other Indians meaning friends or allies, and applied to them by the Spanish in eastern Texas. Also written texias, tejas, teysas.

**Utah**—From a Navajo word meaning upper, or higher up, as applied to a Shoshone tribe called Utes. Spanish form is Yutta, English Uta or Utah. Proposed name Deseret, "land of honeybees," from Book of Mormon, was rejected by Congress.

**Vermont**—From French words Vert, green, and Mont, mountain. The Green Mountains were said to have been named by Samuel de Champlain. The Green Mountain Boys were Gen. Stark's men in the Revolution. When the state was formed, 1777, Dr. Thos. Young suggested combining vert and mont into Vermont.

**Virginia**—Named by Sir Walter Raleigh, who fitted out the expedition of 1584, in honor of Queen Elizabeth, the Virgin Queen of England.

**Washington**—Named after George Washington. When the bill creating the Territory of Columbia was introduced in the 32nd Congress, the name was changed to Washington because of the existence of the District of Columbia.

**West Virginia**—So named when western counties of Virginia rejected secession, 1863.

**Wisconsin**—An Indian name, spelled Ouiscousin and Misconsing by early chroniclers. Means "grassy place" in Chippewa. Congress made it Wisconsin.

**Wyoming**—The word was taken from Wyoming Valley, Pa., which was the site of an Indian massacre and became widely known by Campbell's poem, Gertrude of Wyoming. In Algonquin it means "large prairie place."

## ACCESSION OF TERRITORY BY THE UNITED STATES

Source: Statistical Abstract of the United States

| Division | Yr. | Sq. mi.[1] | Division | Yr. | Sq. mi.[1] | Division | Yr. | Sq. mi.[1] |
|---|---|---|---|---|---|---|---|---|
| Total (1960).... | | 3,628,150 | Texas............ | 1845 | 390,144 | American Samoa.. | 1900 | 76 |
| | | | Oregon........... | 1846 | 285,580 | Canal Zone[4]...... | 1904 | 553 |
| United States.... | | 3,615,211 | Mexican cession... | 1848 | 529,017 | Corn Islands[5]..... | 1914 | 4 |
| Territory of 1790[2].. | .... | 888,811 | Gadsden Purchase. | 1853 | 29,640 | Virgin Islands..... | 1917 | 133 |
| Louisiana Purchase. | 1803 | 827,192 | Alaska........... | 1867 | 586,400 | Trust Territory of | | |
| By treaty with | | | Hawaii........... | 1898 | 6,424 | the Pacific Isl.... | 1947 | 8,484 |
| Spain | | | *The Philippines*[3]. | 1898 | 115,600 | All other[6]........ | .... | 42 |
| Florida......... | 1819 | 58,560 | Puerto Rico....... | 1899 | 3,435 | | | |
| Other areas..... | 1819 | 13,443 | Guam............ | 1899 | 212 | | | |

[1]Gross area (land and water). [2]Includes drainage basin of Red River on the North, south of 49th parallel, sometimes considered a part of the Louisiana Purchase. [3]Area not included in totals; became Republic of the Philippines July 4, 1946. [4]Under U. S. jurisdiction by treaty with Panama. [5]Leased from Nicaragua. [6]See index for Outlying Areas, U. S.

## States: Capitals, Settled, Entry into Union, Area, Rank

**The Original Thirteen States**—The 13 colonies that seceded from Great Britain and fought the War of Independence (American Revolution) became the 13 original states. They were Massachusetts, Rhode Island, Connecticut, New Hampshire, New York, New Jersey, Pennsylvania, Delaware, Maryland, Virginia, North Carolina, South Carolina and Georgia.

| State | Capital | Settled* | Entered Union | Extent in Miles — Long | Wide | Area in square miles — Land† | Inland water† | Total† | Rank In Area |
|---|---|---|---|---|---|---|---|---|---|
| Ala...... | Montgomery.... | 1702 | 1819, Dec. 14 | 330 | 200 | 50,851 | 758 | 51,609 | 29 |
| Alaska.. | Juneau........ | 1784 | 1959, Jan. 3 | (a) 900 | 800 | 566,432 | 19,980 | 586,412 | 1 |
| Ariz.... | Phoenix....... | 1848 | 1912, Feb. 14 | 390 | 335 | 113,563 | 346 | 113,909 | 6 |
| Ark..... | Little Rock.... | 1785 | 1836, June 15 | 275 | 240 | 52,175 | 929 | 53,104 | 27 |
| Cal..... | Sacramento.... | 1769 | 1850, Sept. 9 | 770 | 375 | 156,537 | 2,156 | 158,693 | 3 |
| Colo.... | Denver........ | 1858 | 1876, Aug. 1 | 390 | 270 | 103,797 | 450 | 104,247 | 8 |
| Conn.... | Hartford...... | 1635 | 1788, Jan. 9 | 90 | 75 | 4,870 | 139 | 5,009 | 48 |
| Del..... | Dover......... | 1638 | 1787, Dec. 7 | 110 | 35 | 1,983 | 74 | 2,057 | 49 |
| Dist. Col. | Washington.... | ..... | ..... | .... | .... | 61 | 6 | 67 | 51 |
| Fla..... | Tallahassee.... | 1565 | 1845, Mar. 3 | 460 | 400 | 54,136 | 4,424 | 58,560 | 22 |
| Ga...... | Atlanta....... | 1733 | 1788, Jan. 2 | 315 | 250 | 58,197 | 679 | 58,876 | 21 |
| Hawaii.. | Honolulu..... | ..... | 1959, Aug.21 | .... | .... | 6,425 | 25 | 6,450 | 47 |
| Idaho... | Boise........ | 1842 | 1890, July 3 | 490 | 305 | 82,677 | 880 | 83,557 | 13 |
| Ill..... | Springfield... | 1720 | 1818, Dec. 3 | 380 | 205 | 55,877 | 523 | 56,400 | 24 |
| Ind..... | Indianapolis... | 1733 | 1816, Dec. 11 | 265 | 160 | 36,189 | 102 | 36,291 | 38 |
| Iowa.... | Des Moines.... | 1788 | 1846, Dec. 28 | 300 | 210 | 56,043 | 247 | 56,290 | 25 |
| Kan..... | Topeka........ | 1727 | 1861, Jan. 29 | 400 | 200 | 82,056 | 208 | 82,264 | 14 |
| Ky...... | Frankfort..... | 1774 | 1792, June 1 | 350 | 175 | 39,851 | 544 | 40,395 | 37 |
| La...... | Baton Rouge.... | 1699 | 1812, Apr. 30 | 280 | 275 | 45,155 | 3,368 | 48,523 | 31 |
| Me...... | Augusta....... | 1624 | 1820, Mar. 15 | 235 | 205 | 30,933 | 2,282 | 33,215 | 39 |
| Md...... | Annapolis..... | 1634 | 1788, Apr. 28 | 200 | 120 | 9,888 | 689 | 10,577 | 42 |
| Mass.... | Boston........ | 1620 | 1788, Feb. 6 | 190 | 110 | 7,833 | 424 | 8,257 | 45 |
| Mich.... | Lansing....... | 1668 | 1837, Jan. 26 | 400 | 310 | 56,818 | 1,398 | 58,216 | 23 |
| Minn.... | St. Paul...... | 1805 | 1858, May 11 | 400 | 350 | 79,278 | 4,790 | 84,068 | 12 |
| Miss.... | Jackson....... | 1699 | 1817, Dec. 10 | 340 | 180 | 47,358 | 358 | 47,716 | 32 |
| Mo...... | Jefferson City.. | 1764 | 1821, Aug. 10 | 300 | 280 | 69,046 | 640 | 69,686 | 19 |
| Mont.... | Helena........ | 1809 | 1889, Nov. 8 | 580 | 315 | 145,603 | 1,535 | 147,138 | 4 |
| Nebr.... | Lincoln....... | 1847 | 1867, Mar. 1 | 415 | 205 | 76,522 | 705 | 77,227 | 15 |
| Nev..... | Carson City... | 1850 | 1864, Oct. 31 | 485 | 315 | 109,889 | 651 | 110,540 | 7 |
| N. H.... | Concord....... | 1623 | 1788, June 21 | 185 | 90 | 9,033 | 271 | 9,304 | 44 |
| N. J.... | Trenton....... | 1664 | 1787, Dec. 18 | 160 | 70 | 7,532 | 304 | 7,836 | 46 |
| N. M.... | Santa Fe...... | 1605 | 1912, Jan. 6 | 390 | 350 | 121,445 | 221 | 121,666 | 5 |
| N. Y.... | Albany........ | 1614 | 1788, July 26 | 320 | 310 | 47,869 | 1,707 | 49,576 | 30 |
| N. C.... | Raleigh....... | 1650 | 1789, Nov. 21 | 520 | 210 | 48,880 | 3,706 | 52,586 | 28 |
| N. D.... | Bismarck...... | 1766 | 1889, Nov. 2 | 360 | 210 | 69,280 | 1,385 | 70,665 | 17 |
| Ohio.... | Columbus..... | 1788 | 1803, Mar. 1 | 230 | 205 | 41,108 | 204 | 41,222 | 35 |
| Okla.... | Oklahoma City. | 1889 | 1907, Nov. 16 | 585 | 210 | 68,984 | 935 | 69,919 | 18 |
| Ore..... | Salem........ | 1811 | 1859, Feb. 14 | 375 | 290 | 96,209 | 772 | 96,981 | 10 |
| Pa...... | Harrisburg.... | 1682 | 1787, Dec. 12 | 300 | 180 | 45,025 | 308 | 45,333 | 33 |
| R. I.... | Providence.... | 1636 | 1790, May 29 | 50 | 35 | 1,049 | 165 | 1,214 | 50 |
| S. C.... | Columbia...... | 1670 | 1788, May 23 | 285 | 215 | 30,280 | 775 | 31,055 | 40 |
| S. D.... | Pierre........ | 1856 | 1889, Nov. 2 | 380 | 245 | 75,956 | 1,091 | 77,047 | 16 |
| Tenn.... | Nashville..... | 1757 | 1796, June 1 | 430 | 120 | 41,267 | 977 | 42,244 | 34 |
| Texas... | Austin........ | 1691 | 1845, Dec. 29 | 760 | 620 | 262,970 | 4,369 | 267,339 | 2 |
| Utah.... | Salt Lake City. | 1847 | 1896, Jan. 4 | 345 | 275 | 82,381 | 2,535 | 84,916 | 11 |
| Vt...... | Montpelier.... | 1724 | 1791, Mar. 4 | 155 | 90 | 9,274 | 335 | 9,609 | 43 |
| Va...... | Richmond...... | 1607 | 1788, June 26 | 425 | 205 | 39,841 | 976 | 40,817 | 36 |
| Wash.... | Olympia....... | 1811 | 1889, Nov. 11 | 340 | 230 | 66,663 | 1,529 | 68,192 | 20 |
| W. Va... | Charleston.... | 1727 | 1863, June 20 | 225 | 200 | 24,084 | 97 | 24,181 | 41 |
| Wis..... | Madison....... | 1766 | 1848, May 29 | 300 | 290 | 54,464 | 1,690 | 56,154 | 26 |
| Wyo..... | Cheyenne...... | 1834 | 1890, July 10 | 365 | 275 | 97,281 | 633 | 97,914 | 9 |

*First permanent settlement. †Revised 1967 by Geography Division, Bureau of the Census. (a) Aleutian Islands and Alexander Archipelago are not considered in these lengths.

## Chronological List of Territories

| Name of Territory | Date of Organic Act | Organic Act Effective | Admission as State | Yrs. Terr. |
|---|---|---|---|---|
| Northwest territory (a)........... | July 13, 1787 | No fixed date...... | .......... | .... |
| Territory south of Ohio River..... | May 26, 1790 | No fixed date...... | June 1, 1796b | 6 |
| Mississippi...................... | Apr. 7, 1798 | When President acted...... | Dec. 10, 1817 | 19 |
| Indiana.......................... | May 7, 1800 | July 4, 1800...... | Dec. 11, 1816 | 16 |
| Territory northwest of Ohio River.. | May 7, 1800 | July 4, 1800...... | Mar. 1, 1803c | 2 |
| Orleans.......................... | Mar. 26, 1804 | Oct. 1, 1804...... | Apr. 8, 1812d | 7 |
| Michigan......................... | Jan. 11, 1805 | June 30, 1805...... | Jan. 26, 1837 | 31 |
| Louisiana-Missouri (e)........... | Mar. 3, 1805 | July 4, 1805...... | Aug. 10, 1821 | 16 |
| Illinois......................... | Feb. 3, 1809 | Mar. 1, 1809...... | Dec. 3, 1818 | 9 |
| Alabama.......................... | Mar. 3, 1817 | When Miss. became a State.. | Dec. 14, 1819 | 2 |
| Arkansas......................... | Mar. 2, 1819 | July 4, 1819...... | June 15, 1836 | 17 |
| Florida.......................... | Mar. 30, 1822 | No fixed date...... | Mar. 3, 1845 | 23 |
| Indian (organized 1834)*......... | ..... | ..... | ..... | .... |
| Wisconsin........................ | Apr. 20, 1836 | July 3, 1836...... | May 29, 1848 | 12 |
| Iowa............................. | June 12, 1838 | July 3, 1838...... | Dec. 28, 1846 | 7 |
| Oregon........................... | Aug. 14, 1848 | Date of act...... | Feb. 14, 1859 | 10 |
| Minnesota........................ | Mar. 3, 1849 | Date of act...... | May 11, 1858 | 9 |
| New Mexico....................... | Sept. 9, 1850 | On President's Proclamation. | Jan. 6, 1912 | 61 |
| Utah............................. | Sept. 9, 1850 | Date of act...... | Jan. 4, 1896 | 44 |
| Washington....................... | Mar. 2, 1853 | Date of act...... | Nov. 11, 1889 | 36 |
| Nebraska......................... | May 30, 1854 | Date of act...... | Mar. 1, 1867 | 12 |
| Kansas........................... | May 30, 1854 | Date of act...... | Jan. 29, 1861 | 6 |
| Colorado......................... | Feb. 28, 1861 | Date of act...... | Aug. 1, 1876 | 15 |
| Nevada........................... | Mar. 2, 1861 | Date of act...... | Oct. 31, 1864 | 3 |
| Dakota........................... | Mar. 2, 1861 | Date of act...... | Nov. 2, 1889 | 28 |
| Arizona.......................... | Feb. 24, 1863 | Date of act...... | Feb. 14, 1912 | 49 |
| Idaho............................ | Mar. 3, 1863 | Date of act...... | July 3, 1890 | 27 |
| Montana.......................... | May 26, 1864 | Date of act...... | Nov. 8, 1889 | 25 |
| Wyoming.......................... | July 25, 1868 | When officers were qualified.. | July 10, 1890 | 22 |
| Oklahoma......................... | May 2, 1890 | Date of act...... | Nov. 16, 1907 | 17 |
| Hawaii........................... | Apr. 30, 1900 | June 14, 1900...... | Aug. 21, 1959 | 59 |
| Alaska........................... | Aug. 24, 1912 | Nov. 5, 1912...... | Jan. 3, 1959 | 47 |

(a) Included present Ohio, Indiana, Illinois, Michigan, Wisconsin, eastern Minnesota; (b) as the State of Tennessee; (c) as the State of Ohio; (d) as the State of Louisiana; (e) organic act for Missouri Territory of June 4, 1812, became effective Dec. 7, 1812.

*Indian Territory was set aside in 1834 for the 5 civilized Indian tribes—Cherokee, Choctaw, Chickasaw, Creek and Seminole. In 1889 part of it was included in the Territory of Oklahoma. In 1906 Indian Territory and the Territory of Oklahoma were merged to form the state of Oklahoma.

# American Territorial Expansion

When the War of the Revolution ended the 13 original states—Massachusetts, Rhode Island, Connecticut, New Hampshire, New York, New Jersey, Pennsylvania, Delaware, Maryland, Virginia, North Carolina, South Carolina and Georgia had a land and water area of 892,135 sq. mi., comprising New England, all land from Canada to Florida and from the Atlantic to the Mississippi. At the request of Congress (acting under the Articles of Confederation) the states gave their unorganized land to the Congress, which passed the Northwest Ordinance of 1787, and formed Northwest Terr., north of the Ohio river and another territory south of it.

France originally occupied and fortified a large area from Canada to the Gulf via the Great Lakes and the Mississippi, which it lost to Britain by the Treaty of 1763 after the French and Indian War, Britain yielded this territory to the U. S. by the Treaty of Paris, 1783. After fighting Indians and British in border campaigns, the U. S. took possession July 11, 1796.

## LOUISIANA PURCHASE

The first accession to the United States was the Louisiana Purchase, 827,192 sq. mi. west of the Mississippi. This was held by Spain until ceded to France in 1800, with the proviso that it go back to Spain if France gave it up. In order to free navigation on the Mississippi President Jefferson sent James Monroe and Robert R. Livingston to Paris to buy the isle of Orleans (New Orleans) and West Florida, for which Congress voted $2,-000,000. Napoleon, defeated in San Domingo, offered the vast Louisiana area. The treaty was signed Apr. 30, 1803; Congress ratified it in October; the U. S. took possession at New Orleans Dec. 20, 1803. The U. S. paid $11,250,000 (60,000,000 francs), assumed claims of Americans against France, $3,750,000. Total cost $15,000,000.

Nobody knew the exact boundaries. After Mar. 10, 1804, the U. S. divided the Purchase into the Territory of Orleans, later the state of Louisiana, and the Territory of Louisiana. Included in the Purchase were the present state of Louisiana west to the Sabine River plus the port of New Orleans; the present areas of Arkansas, Missouri, Nebraska, Iowa and South Dakota; North Dakota except the northeast corner, held by Britain until the treaty of 1819; Minnesota west of the Mississippi; Kansas except a small part in the southwest; Oklahoma except the Panhandle no-man's-land; parts of Colorado and Montana. Sometimes Wyoming was claimed and the territory was thought to have run as far as the Pacific coast, but U. S., Britain, Spain and Russia had conflicting claims and settled them by treaty.

## SPAIN GIVES UP FLORIDA

Spain, which still claimed East Florida and West Florida as far as Mobile, Ala., ceded all rights to the U. S. by treaty Feb. 22, 1819, ratified by Spain 1821. The U. S. gave up claims to an undetermined border in Texas and on the Rio Grande and assumed $5,000,000 worth of Spanish obligations to Americans; total cost, $6,674,057.

Spain, Britain, France and the Americans had fought in this territory. Spain's title was recognized in 1783. In 1810 the U. S. took possession of large areas along the Gulf, except Mobile, and West Florida declared itself independent and asked annexation. In 1814 Gen. Andrew Jackson took Pensacola from the British.

## OREGON TERRITORY ORGANIZED

Organization of the Territory of Oregon in 1848 was not called an accession because the U. S. claimed title by (1) discovery and occupation; (2) a free interpretation of the Louisiana Purchase; (3) treaties with Spain, 1819, Great Britain, 1818, Russia, 1824. The northern boundary was settled by treaty with Britain in 1846.

The Territory extended from the crest of the Rockies to the Pacific coast, north of 42° N. Lat. and included the present states of Oregon. Washington, Idaho and parts of Montana and Wyoming.

## ADMISSION OF TEXAS AS STATE

The third accession came when the Republic of Texas was admitted to the Union as a state, Dec. 29, 1845. This was part of a Mexican state settled by many U. S. citizens. Texas declared its independence in 1836, was recognized by the U. S. and applied for admission into the Union. It was bounded by the Rio Grande on the Southwest, and the Sabine, Red and Arkansas Rivers on the North and Northeast, and roughly comprised parts of present New Mexico, Colorado, Wyoming and a bit of Kansas as well as Texas of today, 390,144 sq. mi. Today the state has 267,-339 sq. mi. Texas had declared for slavery and its admission was opposed by anti-slavery men. Since a two-thirds majority of the Senate could not be attained it was admitted, Mar. 1, 1845, by a joint resolution of Congress, requiring only a majority of both houses. Texas ratified the agreement July 4, 1845.

Texas formally became a state Dec. 29, 1845. Congress gave Texas the right to divide itself into as many as five states "of convenient size" and sufficient population, at its own discretion. The Lone Star flag of the republic has been retained as the state flag of Texas. It can be flown by the side of the Stars and Stripes, but not above it.

## TERRITORY FROM MEXICO

At the end of the Mexican War the U. S. and Mexico signed the treaty of Guadelupe-Hidalgo, Feb. 2, 1848, which gave the fourth large accession of territory. This included the present states of Arizona, New Mexico, California, Nevada, Utah, and Colorado west of the Rockies. The Gila river was a boundary line. The U. S. paid $15,000,000 to Mexico and assumed claims of U. S. citizens against Mexico. The claim of Texas to part of New Mexico territory was settled in 1850 by paying Texas $10,000,000. Interest increased both totals.

Inexact boundaries and agitation by railroad men for the Gila river valley to build the Southern Pacific led President Franklin Pierce to send James Gadsden as ambassador to Mexico to negotiate concessions of land. Gadsden got the Mexican dictator, Santa Anna, to yield 29,640 sq. mi. for $10,-000,000 in 1853. This made the Rio Grande the boundary line on the South and the Colorado river on the West.

## ALASKA FROM RUSSIA

Russia, which operated Alaska as a fur and fishing station at a loss, first offered to sell it during President Pierce's administration, about 1856. President Buchanan wanted to pay $5,-000 for it in 1860. Secy. Seward, an expansionist, signed a treaty with Baron Stoeckl, Russian minister, Mar. 30, 1867, to buy it for $7,200,000. Senate ratified it Apr. 9, 1867, and it was transferred to U. S. at Sitka Oct. 18, 1867, before it had been paid for. The House, by 113 to 43, appropriated the money July 14, 1868. The legend that the U. S. bought Alaska to repay Russia for checkmating Britain during the Civil War is without foundation.

## ACQUISITION OF HAWAII

A British naval officer seized the kingdom of Hawaii, 1843, but was disavowed. Britain and France recognized its independent status 1843. France seized it, 1849, but restored it at once. In 1851 the King offered it to the U. S.; Danl. Webster, Secy. of State, refused it. Annexation was urged, 1854, but rejected. A reciprocity treaty with U. S., 1875, increased trade; it was renewed 1884 to include lease of Pearl Harbor as naval base. Jas. G. Blaine, Secy. of State, in 1881 had practically extended Monroe Doctrine to Hawaii. After revolution, 1893 (with American connivance) the republic, 1894, asked annexation. U.S. voted this July 7, 1898, effective Aug. 12, 1898, and assumed a national debt of $4,000,000.

## ISLANDS FROM SPAIN

After the 1898 war with Spain, Spain by treaty of Dec. 10, 1898, ceded Puerto Rico, Guam and the Philippine islands for $20,000,000. An additional $100,000 was paid later for islands of the Philippines not in the original treaty. Puerto Rico is a free commonwealth electing its own executives. Guam is administered by the Dept. of the Interior. The Philippine Islands received their independence July 4, 1946, as the Republic of the Philippines.

## PACIFIC AND CARIBBEAN

American Samoa in the Pacific. Port of Pago Pago was ceded 1872. Tutuila and other islands ceded to U.S. by convention with Great Britain and Germany, Dec. 2, 1899. Swain's Isl. annexed 1925. Dept. of the Interior.

Wake annexed Jan. 17, 1899, from Spain.

Midway Islands (Sand Isl., Eastern Isl.) occupied Sept. 30, 1867. Under Navy Dept.

Baker Island, discovered 1832, U. S. since 1857. Also Jarvis, and Howland. Under Interior Dept.

Virgin Islands in the Caribbean, the former Danish West Indies, comprising St. Croix, St. Thomas, St. John and islets, bought from Denmark Jan. 25, 1917, for $25,000,000.

Panama Canal Zone, acquired from the Republic of Panama.

# Public Lands of the United States

Source: Bureau of Land Management, U. S. Dept. of the Interior

### Acquisition of the Public Domain 1781-1867

| Acquisition | Area* (In acres) | Land | Water | Total | Cost[1] |
|---|---|---|---|---|---|
| State Cessions (1781-1802) | | 233,415,680 | 3,409,920 | 236,825,600 | [2]$6,200,000 |
| Louisiana Purchase (1803)[3] | | 523,446,400 | 6,465,280 | 529,911,680 | 23,213,568 |
| Red River Basin[4] | | 29,066,880 | 535,040 | 29,601,920 | |
| Cession from Spain (1819) | | 43,342,720 | 2,801,920 | 46,144,640 | 6,674,057 |
| Oregon Compromise (1846) | | 180,644,480 | 2,741,760 | 183,386,240 | |
| Mexican Cession (1848) | | 334,479,360 | 4,201,600 | 338,680,960 | 16,295,149 |
| Purchase from Texas (1850) | | 78,842,880 | 83,840 | 78,926,720 | 15,496,448 |
| Gadsden Purchase (1853) | | 18,961,920 | 26,880 | 18,988,800 | 10,000,000 |
| Alaska Purchase (1867) | | 365,481,600 | 9,814,400 | 375,296,000 | 7,200,000 |
| **Total** | | **1,807,681,920** | **30,080,640** | **1,837,762,560** | **$85,079,222** |

*All areas except Alaska were computed in 1912, and have not been adjusted for the recomputation of the area of the United States which was made for the 1950 Decennial Census.

[1]Cost data for all except "State Cessions" obtained from U. S. Geological Survey.
[2]Paid by Federal Government for Georgia Cession, 1802 (56,689,920 acres).
[3]Excludes areas eliminated by Treaty of 1819 with Spain.
[4]Basin of the Red River of the North, south of the 49th parallel.

### Disposition of Public Lands 1781 to 1967 (In acres)

| Disposition by methods not elsewhere classified[1] | | Granted to States for: | |
|---|---|---|---|
| Granted or sold to homesteaders | 301,800,000 | Support of common schools | 77,600,000 |
| Granted to railroad corporations | 287,300,000 | Reclamation of swampland | 64,900,000 |
| Granted to veterans as military | 94,300,000 | Construction of railroads | 37,100,000 |
| bounties | 61,000,000 | Support of misc. institutions[6] | 21,500,000 |
| Confirmed as private land claims[2] | 34,000,000 | Purposes not elsewhere classified[7] | 18,700,000 |
| Sold under timber and stone law[3] | 13,900,000 | Canals and rivers | 6,100,000 |
| Granted or sold under timber culture | | Construction of wagon roads | 3,400,000 |
| law[4] | 10,900,000 | **Total granted to States** | **229,300,000** |
| Sold under desert land law[5] | 10,600,000 | **Grand Total** | **1,041,400,000** |

[1]Chiefly public, private, and preemption sales, but includes mineral entries, script locations, sales of townsites and townlots.
[2]The Government has confirmed title to lands claimed under valid grants made by foreign governments prior to the acquisition of the public domain by the United States.
[3]The law provided for the sale of lands valuable for timber or stone and unfit for cultivation.
[4]The law provided for the granting of public lands to settlers on condition that they plant and cultivate trees on the lands granted. Payments for the lands was permitted under certain conditions.
[5]The law provided for the sale of arid agricultural public lands to settlers who irrigate them and bring them under cultivation.
[6]Universities, hospitals, asylums, etc.
[7]For construction of various public improvements (individual items not specified in the granting act), reclamation of desert lands, construction of water reservoirs, etc.

### Land Owned by Federal Government (In acres)

| Agency (June 30, 1966) | Public Domain | Acquired | Total |
|---|---|---|---|
| U.S. Park Service | 18,275,875.8 | 4,653,686.1 | 22,929,561.9 |
| Bureau of Land Management | 477,587,634.8 | 2,425,291.5 | 480,012,926.3 |
| Forest Service | 160,209,839.1 | 26,261,681.3 | 186,471,520.4 |
| Fish & Wildlife | 23,935,589.7 | 3,178,682.9 | 27,114,272.6 |
| Bureau of Indian Affairs | 4,204,692.7 | 730,552.7 | 4,935,245.4 |
| Bureau of Reclamation | 7,283,435.5 | 1,733,579.4 | 9,017,014.9 |
| Atomic Energy Commission | 1,432,167.6 | 719,977.4 | 2,152,145.0 |
| Army | 7,270,675.0 | 4,181,804.0 | 11,452,479.0 |
| Air Force | 6,958,174.0 | 1,669,893.0 | 8,628,067.0 |
| Navy | 2,289,597.5 | 1,367,467.5 | 3,657,065.0 |
| Corps of Engineers | 866,697.5 | 5,868,246.9 | 6,734,944.4 |
| Other Agencies | 506,910.7 | 1,149,975.9 | 1,656,886.6 |
| **Total** | **710,821,289.9** | **53,940,838.6** | **764,762,128.5** |

## The Homestead Act; Sale of Public Land

The Homestead Act became effective Jan. 1, 1863, the same day that President Lincoln issued his Emancipation Proclamation. Its purpose was to open the vacant lands of America's vast public domain to agricultural settlement.

To qualify for a homestead a person had to be a citizen of the United States or express his intention of becoming one, be over 21 years of age or the head of a household, and own less than 160 acres of land.

To acquire title to 160 acres of public land the homesteader had to establish residence on the land and bring a portion under cultivation. After 6 months residence he could purchase the land for $1.25 per acre, or after 5 years residence he could acquire title for a $15 filing fee.

Originally passed by Congress on May 20, 1862, the Homestead Act was later amended to increase acreage limitations under certain conditions. Under the Homestead Act and its several amendments, more than a million families received title to over 248,000,000 acres of public land across the plains, prairies and mountains of western United States. But as subsequent waves of settlers moved onto vacant land the supply of arable land dwindled; by the late 1930s some homesteaders had settled on submarginal lands that would not support a farm family. In 1937 Congress passed the Bankhead-Jones Act authorizing the Government to repurchase bankrupt farms to relieve the plight of such families. Under this program about 2,000,000 acres of homestead land was returned to Federal ownership.

Alaska is the last frontier for the homesteader, but with statehood most of that State's potential farm land has been acquired by the State under terms of the Alaskan Homestead Act.

By the time of its 100th anniversary the Homestead Act had accomplished its purpose—the transformation of a wilderness into productive farmland. Now outdated, the Homestead Act will always be a part of the American heritage.

### PUBLIC LAND SALE

From time to time the Bureau of Land Management sells public land to private individuals. Public land is always sold for its fair market value as determined by public auction. The Federal Government offers no free land. Persons wishing to purchase public land should contact the Bureau of Land Management, Washington, D. C. 20240, or one of the Bureau's Land Offices in the public land states.

The Bureau stresses that it is the only authoritative source of information on the sale of land under its jurisdiction. No person or firm outside of Government is authorized to dispense information regarding public land sales.

# Confederate States and Secession, 1861-1865

The American Civil War, 1861-1865, grew out of sectional disputes over the employment of slavery in the South and the contention of southern legislators that the states retained many sovereign rights, including the right to secede from the Union.

The principal product of the South was cotton, harvested by slave labor. For 50 years Northern leaders had been trying to curtail slavery, but were checkmated in Congress by Southern legislators. Extreme partisans in the North, who demanded the immediate end of slavery for moral reasons, were called Abolitionists.

The Southern states argued that the U. S. Constitution was a contract between sovereign states, which could withdraw (secede) when state rights were violated. This has led Southern historians to call the Civil War the War Between the States. Actually the war was not fought by state against state but by one federal regime against another, the Confederate government in Richmond assuming control over the economic, political and military life of the South, under protest from Georgia and South Carolina.

The Census of 1860 gave the United States a population of 31,443,321. This included 487,690 free Negroes and 3,953,780 Negro slaves.

Earlier acts against slavery included the **Missouri Compromise of 1820** which admitted Missouri as a slave state but prohibited slavery in the Louisiana Terr. N of Arkansas; the **Compromise of 1850,** which admitted California as a free state, omitted action on slavery in organizing Utah and New Mexico as territories, ended slave trade in Dist. of Columbia, amended Fugitive Slave Act to punish any who aided a fugitive and abolished trial by jury for fugitive; **Kansas-Nebraska Act, 1854,** which left choice of slavery in Kansas and Nebraska to residents there. (Squatter sovereignty)

Harriet Beecher Stowe's *Uncle Tom's Cabin,* 1851-52, intensified feeling against slavery.

Tension increased when the Supreme Court ruled Mar. 6, 1857, that Dred Scott, a Negro, did not become free when taken to a free state and did not have rights as a citizen; also that the Missouri compromise on slavery was unconstitutional.

John Brown's attempt to arm slaves at Harpers Ferry, Oct. 16-18, 1859, inflamed partisans.

Abraham Lincoln's stand for free soil (no slavery) in new states and territories, and his general condemnation of slavery, caused Southern fanatics to threaten secession if he were elected. When Sen. Stephen A. Douglas split the Democratic party by his stand against secession, Lincoln's election was assured. Even before inauguration Lincoln had Sen. Wm. H. Seward (N. Y.) offer a resolution that the Constitution never be altered to interfere with slavery where established, that the Fugitive Slave Law be amended to include trial by jury, that all states repeal laws contrary to the Constitution.

## SECESSION OF STATES

South Carolina voted an ordinance of secession from the Union, repealing its 1788 ratification of the U. S. Constitution, Dec. 20, 1860, proclaimed in effect Dec. 24. Other states seceding in 1861 and their votes in convention were:

Mississippi, Jan. 9, 1861 by 84 to 15
Florida, Jan. 10, 1861, by 62 to 7
Alabama, Jan. 11, 1861, by 61 to 39
Georgia, Jan. 19, 1861, by 208 to 89
Louisiana, Jan. 26, 1861, by 113 to 17
Texas, Feb. 1, 1861, by 166 to 7, ratified by popular vote Feb. 23, 1861; for secession, 34,794; against 11,235.

Virginia had delayed action, but when President Lincoln called for troops after Sumter fell it voted for secession April 17, 1861, by 88 to 55, ratified by popular vote May 23, 1861; for secession, 128,884; against, 32,134.

Arkansas, May 6, 1861, by 69 to 1.
North Carolina, May 21, 1861, voted secession but refused by two-thirds vote to submit it to people for ratification.

Tennessee, May 7, 1861, entered a military league with the Confederacy; popular vote, June 8, for secession, 104,019; against 47,238.

Missouri Unionists stopped secession in the convention at Jefferson City Feb. 28 and at the second session in St. Louis Mar. 9. The legislature condemned secession Mar. 7. Under the protection of Confederate troops secessionist members of the legislature adopted a resolution of secession at Neosho, Oct. 31, 1861. The Confederate Congress seated representatives.

Kentucky did not secede and its government remained Unionist. In a part occupied by Confederate troops Kentuckians passed an act of secession and the Confederate Congress admitted representatives.

Maryland legislature voted against secession Apr. 27, 53 to 13. Delaware did not secede. Western Virginia held conventions at Wheeling, named a pro-Union governor June 11, 1861; admitted to Union as West Virginia June 20, 1863; its constitution provided for gradual abolition of slavery.

## CONFEDERATE GOVERNMENT

Forty-two delegates from South Carolina, Georgia, Alabama, Mississippi, Louisiana and Florida met in convention at Montgomery, Ala., Feb. 4, 1861. Howell Cobb of Georgia was chosen to preside. On Feb. 6 delegates from North Carolina arrived to plead in vain for conciliation. The first delegate from Texas came Feb. 13. The congress adopted a provisional constitution of the Confederate States of America Feb. 8, 1861, and on the next day elected Jefferson Davis (Miss.), provisional president, and Alexander H. Stephens (Ga.), provisional vice president. Davis was inducted into office at Montgomery, Feb. 18, 1861.

A permanent constitution was adopted Mar. 11, 1861. It provided that the president should be elected for a single term of 6 years and abolished the African slave trade. The congress moved to Richmond, Va., July 20, 1861. Jefferson Davis was elected president, October, 1861, inaugurated Feb. 22, 1862.

Jefferson Davis (1808-1889) was a West Point graduate, 1828; served in Black Hawk and Mexican wars; Senator from Mississippi, 1847-1851; Secretary of War, 1853-1857; Senator, 1857-1861.

The congress adopted a flag, consisting of a red field with a white stripe in the middle third, and a blue jack with a circle of white stars, going two-thirds of the way down the flag. This flag was unfurled in Montgomery Mar. 4, 1861. Later the more popular flag was the red field with blue diagonal cross bars that held 13 white stars, designed by Gen. P. G. T. Beauregard.

# Nicknames of the States

Aloha State—Hawaii
Badger State—Wisc.
Bay State—Mass.*
Beaver State—Ore.
Beef State—Nebr.*
Beehive State—Utah
Blue Grass State—Ky.
Buckeye State—Ohio
Centennial State—Colo.
Constitution State—Conn.*
Cornhusker State—Nebr.*
Cotton State—Ala.*
Coyote State—S.D.*
Diamond State—Del.*
Empire State—N.Y.
Empire State of the South—Ga.*
Equality State—Wyoming
Evergreen State—Wash.
First State—Del.*
Flickertail State—N.D.*
Free State—Md.*

Garden State—N.J.
Gem State—Idaho
Golden State—Calif.
Gopher State—Minn.*
Grand Canyon—Ariz.
Granite State—N.H.
Green Mountain State—Vt.
Hawkeye State—Iowa
Heart of Dixie—Ala.*
Hoosier State—Ind.
Keystone State—Pa.
Land of Enchantment—N.M.
Land of Opportunity—Ark.
Little Rhody—R.I.
Lone Star State—Texas
Magnolia State—Miss
Mountain State—W.Va.
North Star State—Minn.*
Nutmeg State—Conn.*
Old Colony—Mass.*
Old Dominion—Va.

Old Line State—Md.*
Old North State—N.C.*
Palmetto State—S.C.
Peach State—Ga.*
Pelican State—La.
Pine Tree State—Me.
Prairie State—Ill.
Sagebrush State—Nev.*
Show Me State—Mo.
Silver State—Nev.*
Sioux State—N.D.*
Sooner State—Okla.
Sunflower State—Kans.
Sunshine State—Fla.
Sunshine State—S.D.*
Tar Heel State—N.C.*
Treasure State—Mont.
Volunteer State—Tenn.
Wolverine State—Mich.
Yellowhammer State—Ala.*

*States with more than one nickname.

# National Parks and Other Units of the National Park System

Source: National Park Service

The year is that of creation of the park; figures in parentheses show Federal land acres.

## NATIONAL PARKS

**Acadia**, 1919, Maine (32,264)—The group of granite mountains upon Mount Desert Island, also Schoodic Point on mainland.

**Big Bend**, 1944, Texas (706,538) on Rio Grande.

**Bryce Canyon**, 1928, Southwestern Utah (36,010) —Box canyon filled with countless array of fantastically eroded pinnacles of vivid coloring.

**Canyonlands**, 1964, Southeastern Utah (257,640) —at junction of the Colorado and Green rivers.

**Carlsbad Caverns**, 1930, Southeastern New Mexico (46,433)—Stupendous caverns not yet wholly explored, limestone decorations.

**Crater Lake**, 1902, Southwestern Oregon (160,- 290)—Lake of extraordinary blue in crater of extinct volcano. Sides 500 to 2,000 feet high.

**Everglades**, 1947, Southern Florida (1,325,895)— Portion of only subtropical area in the United States; extensive watercourses; abundant bird life.

**Glacier**, 1910, Northwestern Montana (1,010,936) —Rugged mountain region of great beauty; more than 200 glacier-fed lakes, 60 small glaciers. Precipices thousands of feet deep.

**Grand Canyon**, 1919, North Central Arizona (673,203)—A vast and picturesque example of erosion with spectacular color effects.

**Grand Teton**, 1928, Northwestern Wyoming (303,174)—Includes most spectacular portion of Teton Mountains, an uplift of unusual grandeur.

**Great Smoky Mountains**, 1930, North Carolina and Tennessee (512,655)—Massive mountain uplift; magnificent forests.

**Guadalupe Mountains**, 1966, Texas (19,640).

**Haleakala**, 1961 Hawaii (17,130)—Huge dormant volcano on the island of Maui.

**Hawaii Volcanoes**, 1916, Hawaii (201,007)—Interesting volcanic areas—Kilauea and Mauna Loa, active volcanoes on the island of Hawaii.

**Hot Springs**, 1921, Middle Arkansas (1,035)— Hot Springs said to have therapeutic value. Bathhouses under Government supervision.

**Isle Royale**, 1940, Michigan (539,341)—Largest island in Lake Superior; rugged forested wilderness.

**Kings Canyon**, 1940, Middle Eastern California (459,468)—Sierra wilderness with numerous peaks 13,000 to 14,000 feet high; park also contains groves of giant sequoias.

**Lassen Volcanic**, 1916, Northern California (106,- 277)—Only recently active volcano in United States proper. Lassen Peak, 10,453 feet; Cinder Cone. 6,913 feet; hot springs; mud geysers.

**Mammoth Cave**, 1936, Southwestern Kentucky (51,351)—Series of caverns including spectacular onyx cave formation. Became nationally known in the war of 1812 when saltpeter from the cave was used in making gunpowder.

**Mesa Verde**, 1906. Southwestern Colorado (51,- 525)—Most notable and best preserved prehistoric cliff dwellings in the United States.

**Mount McKinley**, 1917, South Central Alaska (1,939,493)—Highest mountain in North America; caribou, Dall sheep, and other unusual wildlife.

**Mount Rainier**, 1899, West Central Washington (241,781)—Greatest single-peak glacial system in the United States, radiating from the summit and slopes of an ancient volcano; dense forests.

**Olympic**, 1938, Northwest Washington (888,927) —Notable as finest remnant of the Pacific Northwest forests, including the famous "rain forests." and for its numerous glaciers; also as the summer feeding ground for the rare Roosevelt Elk.

**Petrified Forest**, 1962, Arizona (94,189).

**Platt**, 1906, Southern Oklahoma (912)—Numerous cold mineral springs.

**Rocky Mountain**, 1915. North Middle Colorado (260,591)—Heart of the Rockies, snowy range, peaks 11,000 to 14,255 feet altitude. Remarkable records of glacial period.

**Sequoia**, 1890, Middle Eastern California (385- 413)—Great groves of giant sequoias, world's largest and probably oldest living things; magnificent High Sierra scenery, including Mount Whitney, highest mountain in United States proper.

**Shenandoah**, 1935, in Northern Virginia (193,- 080)—Outstanding scenic section of the Blue Ridge Mts.

**Virgin Islands**, 1956, V. I. (11,055).

**Wind Cave**, 1903, Southwestern South Dakota (28,059). Limestone caverns having galleries containing peculiar formations. Buffalo herd.

**Yellowstone**, 1872. Northwestern Wyoming, Southwestern Montana, and Northeastern Idaho (2,213,207)—More geysers than in all rest of world together. Boiling springs; mud volcanoes; petrified forests. Grand Canyon of the Yellowstone, remarkable for gorgeous coloring. Large lakes; many large streams and waterfalls. Wild animal herds.

**Yosemite**, 1890. Middle Eastern California (759,- 080)—Mountainous region of unusual beauty; Yo-semite and other inspiring gorges; many waterfalls

**Zion**, 1919, Southwestern Utah (136,271)—Magnificent gorge (Zion Canyon), depth from 1,500 to 2,500 feet, with precipitous walls.

## NATIONAL HISTORICAL PARKS

**Appomattox Court House**, 1954, Virginia (937), **Chalmette**, 1939, Louisiana (141)—Site of Battle of New Orleans, Jan. 8, 1815.

**City of Refuge**, 1961, Hawaii (181)—Until 1819, vanquished Hawaiian warriors, noncombatants, and taboo breakers found sanctuary here.

**Colonial**, 1936, Virginia (7,205)—Includes most of Jamestown Isl., the first permanent English settlement in America; historic Yorktown; the parkway connecting these and other Colonial sites with Colonial Williamsburg and Cape Henry Memorial.

**Cumberland Gap**, 1955, Ky., Tenn., Va. (20,- 169)—Wilderness Road Crossing, used by pioneers.

**George Rogers Clark**, 1966, Indiana (17) Commemorates the winning of the northwest.

**Harpers Ferry**, 1963, West Virginia-Maryland (1,280). Site of important events of Colonial times and of the famous John Brown raid.

**Independence**, 1956, Philadelphia, Pa. (16)— Scene of adoption of the Declaration of Independence, meeting place of the Continental Congress and of the Constitutional Convention of 1787; Federal Capital, 1790 to 1800.

**Minute Man**, 1959, Massachusetts (435)—Tract of natural setting where, on April 19, 1775, British troops retreating from Battles of Lexington and Concord were fired on by Colonial Minute Men.

**Morristown**, 1933, New Jersey (1,215)—Sites of important military encampments during the Revolution; Washington's Headquarters, 1779-80.

**Nez Perce**, 1965, Idaho (83), a group of 22 sites.

**San Juan Island**, 1966, Wash., 1859 Canadian agreement.

**Saratoga**, 1948, New York (2,432)—Scene of the American victory over the British General Burgoyne, 1777; turning point of the Revolution.

## NATIONAL MILITARY PARKS

**Chickamauga-Chattanooga** (8,190) Ga., Tenn.

**Fort Donelson** (197) Dover, Tenn.

**Fredericksburg & Spotsylvania Co., Battlefields Memorial Va.**, (2,546) Va.

**Gettysburg** (3,277) Pa.

**Guilford Courthouse** (221) Greensboro, N. C.

**Horseshoe Bend** (2,040) Tallapoosa County, Ala.

**Kings Mountain** (3,850) S. C.

**Moores Creek** (42) Currie, N. C.

**Pea Ridge** (4,276) Arkansas.

**Shiloh** (3,511) Pittsburg Landing, Tenn.

**Vicksburg** (1,543) Miss.

## NATIONAL BATTLEFIELDS

**Big Hole** (536) Montana. **Fort Necessity** (352) SE of Uniontown, Pa. **Petersburg** (1,523) Virginia. **Stones River** (331) Murfreesboro, Tenn. **Tupelo** (1) Miss.

## NATIONAL BATTLEFIELD SITES

**Antietam** (781), Sharpsburg, Md. **Brices Cross Roads** (1), Bethany, Miss. **Cowpens** (1), near Gaffney, S. C.

## NATIONAL BATTLEFIELD PARKS

**Kennesaw Mountain**, 1947, Georgia, (2,883)— Commemorates the Battle of Kennesaw Mountain, a major battle of Sherman's flanking movement during the Atlanta Campaign.

**Manassas**, 1946, Virginia (2,541). Site of Bull Run and Manassas battles.

**Richmond**, 1944, Virginia (747)—Scene of battles in defense of Richmond during Civil War.

**Wilson's Creek**, 1965, Missouri (1,008) Site of early battles in Civil War to determine control of Missouri.

## NATIONAL RECREATIONAL AREAS

**Amistad**, Texas (43,559); **Arbuckle**, Okla. (5,646); **Bighorn** (57,810) Wyo.-Mont.; **Coulee Dam**, Wash. (98,500); **Curecanti**, Colo. (41,103); **Delaware Water Gap**, Pa.-N. J. (4,801); **Flaming Gorge**, Utah-Wyo. (84,412); **Glen Canyon**, Ariz.-Utah (1,174,- 970); **Lake Mead**, Ariz.-Nev. (1,910,319); **Sanford**, Tex. (41,097); **Shadow Mountain**, Colo. (15,540); **Whiskeytown-Shasta-Trinity**, Calif. (18,194).

## NATIONAL SEASHORE

**Assateague Island** (1,063) Md.-Va.; **Cape Cod** (16,645) Mass.; **Cape Hatteras** (28,500) N. C.; **Cape Lookout**, N. C.; **Fire Island** (2,158) N. Y.; **Padre Island** (133,840) Texas; and **Point Reyes** (32,217) Calif.

## NATIONAL PARKWAYS

**Baltimore-Washington**, Md.-D. C. (2,490) 39 mi.

**Blue Ridge**, Va., N. C. (70,173) follows Blue Ridge Mountains. Length when completed 469 miles.

**George Washington Memorial** (6,119) along Maryland and Virginia shores of the Potomac River. Length, when completed, 49 miles.

**Natchez Trace** (36,720) follows old Indian trail between Nashville, Tenn., and Natchez, Miss. Length when completed 450 miles.

## NATIONAL MONUMENTS

| Name | State | Area in acres | Name | State | Area in acres |
|---|---|---:|---|---|---:|
| Agate Fossil Beds(nr.Scottsbluff) | Nebr. | 1,970 | Glacier Bay | Alaska | 2,803,522 |
| Alibates Flint Quarries | Texas | 500 | Grand Canyon | Ariz. | 193,019 |
| Arches | Utah | 34,010 | Grand Portage | Minn. | 594 |
| Aztec Ruins | N. M. | 27 | Gran Quivira | N. M. | 611 |
| Badlands | S. D. | 104,355 | Great Sand Dunes | Colo. | 35,530 |
| Bandelier | N. M. | 29,661 | Homestead | Nebr. | 153 |
| Black Canyon of the Gunnison | Colo. | 13,150 | Hovenweep | Utah-Colo. | 505 |
| Booker T. Washington | Va. | 218 | Jewel Cave | S. D. | 1,275 |
| Buck Island Reef | Virgin Isl. | 850 | Joshua Tree | Calif. | 511,580 |
| Cabrillo | Calif. | 81 | Katmai | Alaska | 2,697,590 |
| Canyon de Chelly | Ariz. | 83,840 | Lava Beds | Calif. | 46,239 |
| Capitol Reef | Utah | 37,906 | Lehman Caves | Nev. | 640 |
| Capulin Mountain | N. M. | 680 | Montezuma Castle | Ariz. | 783 |
| Casa Grande Ruins | Ariz. | 473 | Mound City Group | Ohio. | 68 |
| Castillo de San Marcos | Fla. | 20 | Muir Woods | Calif. | 484 |
| Castle Clinton | N. Y. | | Natural Bridges | Utah. | 7,126 |
| Cedar Breaks | Utah. | 6,155 | Navajo | Ariz. | 360 |
| Chaco Canyon | N. M. | 20,989 | Ocmulgee | Ga. | 683 |
| Channel Islands | Calif. | 18,167 | Oregon Caves | Oreg. | 480 |
| Chesapeake and Ohio Canal | Md.-W.Va. | 4,477 | Organ Pipe Cactus | Ariz. | 328,691 |
| Chiricahua | Ariz. | 10,561 | Pecos | N. M. | 341 |
| Colorado | Colo. | 17,311 | Perry's Victory Memorial | Ohio. | 21 |
| Craters of the Moon | Idaho. | 53,545 | Pinnacles | Calif. | 13,618 |
| Custer Battlefield | Mont. | 765 | Pipe Spring | Ariz. | 40 |
| Death Valley | Calif.-Nev. | 1,882,999 | Pipestone | Minn. | 276 |
| Devils Postpile | Calif. | 798 | Rainbow Bridge | Utah. | 160 |
| Devils Tower | Wyo. | 1,267 | Russell Cave | Alabama. | 310 |
| Dinosaur | Utah-Colo. | 197,265 | Saguaro | Ariz. | 76,188 |
| Effigy Mounds | Iowa. | 1,374 | Saint Croix | Maine. | 4 |
| El Morro | N. M. | 960 | Scotts Bluff | Nebr. | 2,208 |
| Fort Frederica | Ga. | 210 | Sitka | Alaska. | 54 |
| Fort Jefferson | Fla. | 47,125 | Statue of Liberty | N. Y. | 58 |
| Fort Matanzas | Fla. | 299 | Sunset Crater | Ariz. | 3,040 |
| Fort McHenry | Md. | 43 | Timpanogos Cave | Utah. | 250 |
| Fort Pulaski | Ga. | 5,364 | Tonto | Ariz. | 1,120 |
| Fort Stanwix | N. Y. | 18 | Tumacacori | Ariz. | 10 |
| Fort Sumter | S. C. | 34 | Tuzigoot | Ariz. | 43 |
| Fort Union | N. M. | 721 | Walnut Canyon | Ariz. | 1,642 |
| George Washington Birthplace | Va. | 394 | White Sands | N. M. | 140,247 |
| George Washington Carver | Mo. | 210 | Wupatki | Ariz. | 35,233 |
| Gila Cliff Dwellings | N. M. | 533 | Yucca House | Colo. | 10 |

## NATIONAL HISTORIC SITES AND MEMORIALS
(Acres in parentheses)

### HISTORIC SITES

**Abraham Lincoln Birthplace**, Hodgenville, Ky. (117).

**Adams House**, Quincy, Mass. (5). Home of Presidents John and John Quincy Adams.

**Allegheny Portage RR**, (Penn. Canal) Pa. (838).

**Andrew Johnson**, Greenville, Tenn. (17).

**Ansley Wilcox House**, Buffalo, N. Y. (1) Teddy Roosevelt took oath 1901.

**Bent's Old Fort** near La Junta, Colo., (178).

**Christiansted Virgin Islands** (27). Commemorates colonial development of the Virgin Islands.

**Edison Home**, West Orange, N. J. (20).

**Eisenhower Home**, Gettysburg, Pa. (230).

**Fort Bowie**, Ariz. (900).

**Fort Davis**, Texas (447).

**Fort Laramie**, Wyo. (563).

**Fort Larned**, Kan. (403).

**Fort Raleigh**, N. C. (140). First attempted English settlement.

**Fort Smith**, Ark. (13).

**Fort Union Trading Post**, N. D.-Mont. (49).

**Fort Vancouver**, Wash. (89).

**Franklin D. Roosevelt Home**, Hyde Park, N. Y. (188). The library is administered by the Archivist of the United States.

**Golden Spike**, (Utah) (908) linking of railroad tracks joining east and west about 31 miles NE of Brigham City.

**Hampton**, Md., Georgian mansion, 1783 (45).

**Herbert Hoover**, West Branch, Iowa (12).

**Hopewell Village**, Pa. (848). Early iron-making.

**Hubbell Trading Post**, Ariz. (156).

**Jefferson Memorial**, Mo. (85). Commemorates national expansion.

**John F. Kennedy birthplace**, Brookline, Mass. (.09).

**John Muir**, Martinez, Calif. (9).

**Pennsylvania Avenue**, Washington, D. C.

**Sagamore Hill**, Oyster Bay, Long Island, N. Y. (85). Home of Theodore Roosevelt.

**St. Gaudens**, Cornish, N. H. (83) home of sculptor Augustus St. Gaudens.

**St. Thomas**, Virgin Islands (2). Includes Port Christian, oldest standing structure in the Virgin Islands.

**Salem Maritime**, Mass. (9).

**San Juan**, Puerto Rico (38). Ancient Spanish fortifications.

**Theodore Roosevelt Birthplace**, (.11) 28 E. 20 St., New York City.

**Vanderbilt Mansion**, near Hyde Park, N. Y. (212). With arboretum.

**Whitman Mission**, Washington (98).

### NATIONAL MEMORIAL PARK
**Theodore Roosevelt**, 1947, North Dakota (69,351) —Badlands along Little Missouri River; part of

### MEMORIALS

**Arkansas Post**, Ark. (221) First white settlement in lower Mississippi Valley.

**Chamizal**, Tex. (55) Twin memorials, Mexico and Texas.

**Coronado**, Ariz. (2,834). Route of Spaniards. 16th century.

**Custis-Lee Mansion**, Arlington, Va. (3) Antebellum home of Robert E. Lee.

**De Soto**, Fla. (25). Commemorates 16th-century explorer.

**Federal Hall**, Nassau and Wall Sts., New York City (.45). First seat of U.S. Government.

**Fort Caroline**, Fla. (120). French settlement in Florida, 1564, destroyed by Spaniards, 1565.

**Fort Clatsop**, Oregon (125).

**Frederick Douglass home**, Wash., D. C. (8).

**General Grant** (Grant's Tomb) New York City. (.76).

**Hamilton Grange**, New York City (.71).

**House where President Lincoln died**, Washington, D. C. (.05).

**Johnstown Flood**, Pa. (55).

**Lincoln Boyhood in Indiana** (128).

**Lincoln Memorial**, Washington, D. C. (164). Classical monument with statue.

**Lincoln Museum**, Washington, D. C. (.18). Ford theatre where Lincoln was shot.

**Mount Rushmore**, S. D. (1,246). Colossal profiles of 4 Presidents.

**Roger Williams**, R. I. (5).

**Thomas Jefferson Memorial**, Washington, D. C. (18). Classical circular colonnade.

**Washington Monument**, Washington, D. C. (106). Obelisk commemorates first President.

**Wright Brothers**, N. C. (330). Site of first motor-propelled airplane's flight.

#### Not Owned by Federal Government
Chicago Portage, Ill. (91).
Chimney Rock, Nebr. (83).
Dorchester Hgts., Mass. (5).
Fort Scott, Kansas (21).
Jamestown, Va. (21).
McLoughlin House, Ore. (1).
St. Paul's Church, N. Y. C. (6).
San Jose Mission, Tex. (4).
Touro Synagogue, R. I. (.23).

### NATIONAL LAKESHORES
Indiana Dunes, near Mich. City, Indiana (94).
Pictured Rocks, Munising, Mich.

### NATIONAL CAPITAL PARKS
**National Capital Parks** total 7,978 acres—comprises 727 units in the District of Columbia and

# GREAT CITIES OF NORTH AMERICA

### Their History, Business and Industry, Educational Facilities, Cultural Advantages, Tourist Attractions and Transportation

## Akron, Ohio

The World Almanac is sponsored in the Akron area by the Akron Beacon Journal, 44 E. Exchange St., Akron, Ohio 44309; telephone (216) 253-1111; founded 1809 by Hiram Bowen; circulation daily 176,656, Sunday 202,221; president & editor, John S. Knight; executive editor & publisher, Ben Maidenburg; general manager, Sam McKeel.

Akron, "The Rubber Capital of the World," is on the Ohio Canal and Big and Little Cuyahoga Rivers 30 miles south of Lake Erie in northeastern Ohio, and covers 56 sq. mi. within the 413-sq. mi. metropolitan Akron area of Summit County.

Founder was Gen. Simon Perkins, who served in the area during the War of 1812. He returned after the war and began to acquire vast areas of the wilderness.

In 1825 the Legislature authorized construction of the Ohio Canal from Lake Erie to Portsmouth on the Ohio River, with 17 locks to be built in a two-mile stretch all owned by Gen. Perkins. Workers and tradesmen poured in and Gen. Perkins started a town; the plat was recorded Dec. 1825.

The name, Akron, comes from the classical Greek and means "High Point"; 395 ft. above Lake Erie, it is the highest point on the Ohio Canal. Incorporated as a city Jan. 21, 1865, it is Ohio's 5th largest, est. population 299,341. It has a mayor-manager charter government.

Growth of the rubber industry in Akron can be traced to Nov., 1870, when an eastern physician, Dr. Benjamin Franklin Goodrich, enticed by a booster pamphlet, arrived in town. With $16,000 pledged by local townspeople, he opened a small, two-story building on the site of the present B. F. Goodrich complex and started making fire hoses and beer tubing.

Many earlier firms have passed out of existence, but home offices and plants of 4 of the world's 5 largest rubber firms—Goodrich, Goodyear, Firestone and General—employ 45,000 Akronites.

With 113 motor freight carriers and 58 contract carriers located here, Akron is the largest trucking center in the nation, as well as home of the Quaker Oats Co., one of the world's largest cereal manufacturing firms. Other Akron-produced products include automobile bodies and wheel rims, fishing tackle, matches, salt,

clay products, rubber toys, batteries, synthetic rubber, road-building machinery and missile components.

Two airports, Akron Municipal and Akron-Canton, handle more than 60 jet and propeller plane flights daily through four airlines, and six railroads serve the city through two passenger stations. Greyhound bus lines averages 73 daily arrivals and departures through the city. Akron Municipal Airport is the site of the Goodyear Zeppelin Dock, one of the largest buildings without interior supports.

Also in the Akron Airport vicinity are Derby Downs, home of the All-American Soap Box Derby, and a 36,000-seat municipal stadium, "The Rubber Bowl," home of the University of Akron Zips.

Another well-known sports center in Akron is the Firestone Country Club, home of the American Golf Classic, World Series of Golf, and twice since 1960 site of the PGA championship.

One of the nation's top cultural attractions is Akron's Stan Hywet, the former baronial mansion of F. A. Seiberling, founder of the Goodyear and Seiberling Rubber Cos.

The city is the seat of the University of Akron. Other points of interest include the Akron Art Institute, the Goodyear Rubber Exhibit in Goodyear Hall, and the Akron Children's Zoo.

Urban renewal and downtown revitalization are the theme of multi-million dollar construction projects now under way. There are plans for $13,000,000 private construction in the business district.

Specialized information may be obtained from the Area Development Committee, First National Tower, Akron, Ohio 44308, and the Akron Area Chamber of Commerce, Delaware Building, Akron, Ohio 44308.

## Atlanta, Georgia

Atlanta is the capital of Georgia, largest state in area east of the Mississippi, and is the center of the first metropolitan statistical area in the Southeast to reach 1,000,000 population (1966 U. S. Census). The U. S. Census estimates rank Metropolitan Atlanta, with 1,258,000, as the 21st such area in population in the nation. Atlanta is the county seat of Fulton. The metro area includes Fulton, Clayton, Cobb, DeKalb and Gwinnett Counties.

Financial, manufacturing, industrial and communications center of the region, Atlanta also is a transportation hub. It has the nation's fourth busiest airport, 7 airlines, 7 bus lines and 13 rail lines. Six legs of 3 Federal Interstate Highways converge at an interchange behind the State Capitol, itself a symbol of the Midas-touched economy. The Capitol dome is covered with gold leaf beaten from nuggets donated by citizens of Dahlonega, in northern Georgia, once the site of a U. S. mint and where gold may still be panned.

Diversity of manufacturing keeps the economy stable. Over 1,650 manufacturers produce more than 3,500 commodities, in-

cluding automobiles, aircraft, textiles, chemicals, furniture, food, iron and steel. Annual retail sales exceed $2.3 billion.

Atlanta's first official marker was the Zero Mile Post of 1850, marking the Southeastern terminus of the Western and Atlantic Railroad. Not far away, the original 1837 surveyor's stake had been pounded to connect the Western and Atlantic with the Georgia Railroad and the Central of Georgia. There grew a settlement appropriately called Terminus. Incorporated in 1843 and named Marthasville after Gov. Wilson Lumpkin's youngest daughter, the city's name was changed to Atlanta Dec. 26, 1845. One theory is that the word Atlanta was the feminine of Atlantic.

At the time of its incorporation, the city's limits extended one mile in all directions from the area of the Zero Mile Post. In almost the same spot today towers the First National Bank Building at Five Points, still the center of the city. A block away begins famous Peachtree Street.

Situated on the Piedmont Plateau of the Blue Ridge Mountains' foothills, Atlanta has an altitude of 1,050 feet with a

390

7-month casual living season stretching from April through October.

Nearby Stone Mountain, looming 630 feet above a surrounding memorial park, is the largest piece of exposed granite in the world. On one side are carved likenesses of 3 colossal figures of the Confederacy—Robert E. Lee, Stonewall Jackson and Jefferson Davis. At the park is the detailed diorama and map of Georgia depicting Union Gen. William Tecumseh Sherman's sweep through Georgia.

As a U. S. Army lieutenant, Sherman was stationed near Atlanta for 6 weeks in 1844, when he had an opportunity to study the area's terrain. Twenty years later, as Gen. Sherman, he came back to capture Atlanta in September, 1864. He burned most of it to the ground before his March to the Sea.

For the same reasons Sherman militarily had to destroy this key point of the Confederacy — transportation, communications, commerce—Atlanta grew again. In New York City in 1866 Henry Woodfin Grady, editor of the Atlanta Constitution, made his famous New South speech, which urged the putting aside of hate and slavery and predicted the glowing future to come. In his audience was Sherman.

Symbolically Atlanta's official seal, adopted in 1877, is the phoenix, fabled bird that rose from the ashes to begin a new life. The city government is administered by a mayor and aldermen.

With the world's largest Bell System toll-free dialing area, one of the world's largest telegraph installations, one of the nation's 5 TV-radio control centers and the South's largest Sunday newspaper in circulation, Atlanta is a vital communications center.

Atlanta has extensive hospital, medical research and educational facilities. It is national headquarters of the Communicable Disease Center of the U. S. Public Health Service.

Recreational and cultural facilities include a regional amusement park, Six Flags Over Georgia; the multimillion dollar Atlanta Sports Stadium, home of the baseball Braves (National League), Falcons (National Football League), and Chiefs (North American Soccer Assn.). Also in Atlanta are the Hawks (National Basketball Assn.).

The Memorial Arts Center encompasses the Atlanta Symphony Orchestra, Atlanta Ballet, Opera Company and Repertory Theatre, and the High Museum of Art, where some of the famous Kress collection of Renaissance paintings hang. Another point of interest is the Cyclorama, huge circular painting of the Battle of Atlanta. The $10,000,000 Civic Center, auditorium-exhibition hall complex, offers 70,000 sq. ft. of exhibit space.

Among institutions of higher learning are the Georgia Institute of Technology, Georgia State College, Emory University, Agnes Scott College, Oglethorpe College and the Atlanta University Complex.

## Baltimore, Maryland

The World Almanac is sponsored in the Baltimore area by the Baltimore News-American, 301 E. Lombard St., Baltimore, Md. 21203; telephone 752-1212; founded Aug. 20, 1773, as The Maryland Journal and Baltimore Advertiser, merged with Baltimore News founded Nov. 2, 1872, adopted present name Jan. 13, 1964; circulation daily 219,580, Sunday 318,425; publisher, Mark F. Collins; executive editor, Sterling Noel; managing editor, Thomas J. White; business manager, W. Melvin Street; winner American Medical Association award and Albert Lasker Medical award; sponsors I Am an American Day parade, Teen-Age Fair, Old Newsboys' Day, Hole-in-one golf tournament.

Baltimore City is the core of a metropolitan area extending into 4 adjacent counties (Baltimore, Anne Arundel, Harford and Howard) which covers 2,259 square miles and has 2,035,700 inhabitants. The city itself has a population of 912,500 (June, 1968, estimate) and includes 92 sq. mi., 13 of which are water-covered.

Important to the city's development has been that it is a seaport 50 to 200 miles nearer the Midwest than other North Atlantic ports. Alone among Atlantic ports, it has two routes to the sea: by way of Chesapeake Bay, and through the Chesapeake and Delaware Canal.

The port has 45 miles of waterfront, a 42-foot channel, and handles some 45,000,-000 tons of freight per year. Leading imports are ores, steel and bananas, Baltimore is the leading receiver of foreign autos. It has 3 trunk line railroads and over 150 certified truck transport lines. Truck and auto tourist traffic are aided by a twin-tube tunnel through the city under the Patapsco River. Friendship International Airport, used by 11 major airlines, is 15 minutes from downtown Baltimore.

Industries are highly diversified, with none dominating the city's economy. Among the most important are shipbuilding and repairing, steel fabricating, manufacture of electrical equipment and food containers, processing of foods, sugar, petroleum, chemicals and copper. Research and development activities, chiefly in the fields of aerospace, bioscience, oceanography, chemistry, metallurgy and electronics are carried on by 122 firms employing 90,700 persons.

Sixteen colleges offering 4-year courses and 6 junior colleges are in the Baltimore area. Johns Hopkins University and the University of Maryland each has two campuses, including a large hospital, at Baltimore. Among other educational institutions are Goucher, Morgan State, Loyola, Towson State, Mt. St. Agnes and Western Maryland colleges, the University of Baltimore and the Maryland Institute. Other cultural facilities include the Baltimore Art Museum, Walters Art Gallery, Baltimore Symphony Orchestra, Baltimore Civic Opera, Center Stage Theater and the Enoch Pratt Free Library.

A downtown renewal project, begun in 1958, cleared 32 acres of the central business section and erected on the site a Civic Center, office buildings, a hotel and the Morris A. Mechanic Theater. Another project, to include a World Trade Building, office buildings, apartment houses and a marina is now under way.

In sports, Baltimore is the home of the Orioles (baseball), the Colts (football), the Bullets (basketball), the Bays (soccer), and the Clippers (ice hockey). Pimlico race track, where the famous Preakness race is held annually, is within the city limits. Two other mile tracks and two half-mile tracks are nearby, including Laurel where the Inter. Race is held.

An outstanding tourist attraction is Fort McHenry, which withstood 25 hours of bombardment from British ships during the War of 1812, during which Francis

Scott Key, a Maryland lawyer who was held captive on a British ship, wrote "The Star-Spangled Banner." His original manuscript is at the Maryland Historical Society building in Baltimore and the fort is a National Shrine and Historic Museum.

Among other places of historic interest are the first architectural monument erected to George Washington, the U. S. frigate Constellation, the Baltimore and Ohio Railroad Museum at Mt. Clare, first passenger railroad station in the country, and the Peale Museum building. The grave of Edgar Allan Poe is in Westminster Church yard, and the city in 1968 purchased as a memorial the house in which baseball star Babe Ruth was born.

Baltimore was founded in 1729 by an act of the Provincial Assembly of the Maryland colony which was establihed by members of the Calvert family, Barons of Baltimore. Its early economy was based largely on trans-Atlantic and coastal shipment of tobacco, grain and flour and on shipbuilding. By the time of the Revolution it was an important port which sent privateers that harassed British shipping. In the War of 1812, similar activities caused the British to term Baltimore a "nest of pirates" and to try to capture the city by land and sea attacks. Both were repulsed.

After this war, Baltimore's economic growth was threatened by New York's completion of the Erie Canal and the city's business leaders countered by building the nation's first railroad, the Baltimore and Ohio. During the Civil War the sympathies of Baltimoreans were sharply divided, and the war's first blood was shed when a mob attacked Union troops who were marching from one railroad station to another en route to protect Washington. Though Maryland did not secede, Federal troops occupied Baltimore for 5 years.

Much of downtown Baltimore was destroyed by fire in 1904. No lives were lost and the rebuilding resulted in improvements to the area which, though great, have been far surpassed by the accomplishments of the last 10 years.

# Birmingham, Alabama

The World Almanac is sponsored in the Birmingham area by the Birmingham Post-Herald, 2200 Fourth Ave., North, Birmingham, Alabama 35202; telephone (205) 323-5381; Post founded Jan. 21, 1921, by Scripps-Howard Newspapers; Herald founded 1887 by W. P. Pinckard, Rufus N. Rhodes and Frank P. O'Brien; circulation 82,230; editor, Duard Le Grand; vice president W. H. Metz; managing editor, George Cook; major public service projects include Goodfellow Christmas Fund and Alabama Favorite Teacher Selection.

Birmingham, situated in the north central portion of Alabama, is the state's largest city and one of the world's youngest major cities. It is located in Jones Valley, named for the family that settled the area in the early 1800s. Between its incorporation on December 19, 1871, and the turn of the century, Birmingham acquired the name "Magic City" for its rapid growth rate.

Overlooking Birmingham from nearby Red Mountain is Vulcan, the mythical god of the forge, in a cast iron statue that is second only to the Statue of Liberty in size. Vulcan symbolizes the reason for Birmingham's rapid growth into a metropolis, the iron and steel industry, which expanded quickly because of the availability of the three basic elements of iron making—ore, coal and lime—in the area. The related mining industry also grew rapidly, but has now declined because of the relatively low grade of ore and the scarcity of new coal seams. Most ore used locally is now imported from rich fields in South America.

The city is still a heavy manufacturing center. U. S. Steel Corporation has its southern headquarters in Fairfield, a suburb, and a large Republic Steel Corporation mill is in Birmingham. Dozens of other plants manufacture steel and iron products.

For the past two decades, however, Birmingham has been involved in a switch from blue to white collar workers. A focal point of the change is the sprawling University of Alabama Medical Center a few blocks south of the downtown business area. At the end of a current expansion, the Medical Center will encompass 60 square blocks with nearly a dozen hospitals, research facilities, related businesses and the University of Alabama in Birmingham's College of General Studies. The Medical Center is now the second largest employer in the Birmingham area, ranking behind U. S. Steel.

Birmingham has a population of 340,887 (1960 census), and a 3-county metropolitan area of almost a million. It is surrounded by 35 municipalities within Jefferson County.

Birmingham has been the scene of major civil rights incidents, starting with the Mother's Day "freedom riders" disturbance of 1961 and mostly ending by the time 16th Street Baptist Church was bombed, killing 4 Negro girls on Sept. 15, 1963. There has been little racial trouble since that time, largely because of policies established by a new mayor and 9-member city council voted in to replace the old 3-man city commission. The new government took office in 1963, has been more moderate on the racial issue, and is leading the city in its biggest building boom in 40 years. Birmingham's skyline, with only about 4 new, large buildings added since 1925, is now undergoing a major change, with 3 new skyscrapers under construction. Among them is the multi-million dollar headquarters for South Central Bell Telephone Company, formed in 1968 from the Southern Bell area.

Now in the planning stages is a civic center, already funded by new taxes, which will cost more than $25,000,000 and will include a coliseum, theater, music hall and exhibit hall. The complex is due to be finished by the beginning of the city's centennial year, December, 1971.

In addition to the University of Alabama complex, Birmingham has 6 colleges and universities—Samford University, Birmingham-Southern College, Miles College, Daniel Payne College and Wenonah and Jefferson State Junior Colleges.

The city's Municipal Airport, served by 4 major airlines, is due to undergo expansion in the near future. A recent $12,500,000 bond issue was approved to expand the modern terminal, completed in 1961, and the runway system. Birmingham is also served by 13 railroads, and the two interstate highways due to serve the city are under construction, I-59 and I-65.

Specialized information may be obtained from the Birmingham Area Chamber of Commerce, 1914 Sixth Avenue North.

# Boston, Massachusetts

The World Almanac is sponsored in the Boston area by the Boston Herald-Traveler, 300 Harrison Ave., Boston, Mass. 02106; telephone (617) 426-3000; Traveler founded 1825, Herald 1846, consolidated July 10, 1967; daily circulation, 216,000, Sunday, 301,000; chairman of the board, George E. Akerson; president and publisher, Harold E. Clancy; executive editor, Eugene J. Moriarty; editor, John R. Herbert; major awards include four Pulitzer Prizes for editorial writing (to Herald staff members), two for photography (to Traveler staff members); sponsors Herald Traveler Charity Fund, Repertory of Classical Drama and Festival of Music.

Boston, founded in 1630 by a company of Puritans under the leadership of John Winthrop and incorporated as a city Feb. 23, 1822, has been known variously as The Hub and the Athens of America; more recently, as a result of broad programs of urban renewal and a quickening of civic interest, commercial and cultural, as The New Boston.

It is the capital city of the Commonwealth of Massachusetts, with the Governor's Office and the Senate and House of the Legislature (officially the Great and General Court) meeting in the historic Bulfinch State House with its striking gold-sheathed dome.

Boston itself is governed by a Mayor and 9-man City Council, elected at large in non-partisan elections, the Mayor for a 4-yr. term, councilmen for two-yr. terms. A 5-member school committee directs the public school system, with an enrollment of 90,000, the members also elected at large on a non-partisan basis for two-yr. terms.

The city has a population of 616,326 (1965 state census), its standard metropolitan area a population of 2,605,452. Recent years have seen a steady drop in the population of the city proper, a corresponding rise in the residential suburbs.

City planners hope to arrest that trend with construction of high and middle income apartment complexes, such as Charles River Park, overlooking the river and Cambridge, and along the historic waterfront.

The city's unhappy experience with massive low-income housing has brought a change of thinking in that field, with new emphasis on smaller projections and rehabilitation of existing properties.

Beacon Hill, so evocative of London, had been declared a historical district to preserve it from drastic or startling change.

Renewal has had its biggest impact downtown, where a new glass-and-concrete government center now stands in what was the old honky tonk area of Scollay Square.

In the Back Bay, there is the Prudential Center, with its 52-story tower rising from a complex of low-rise buildings which includes a new War Memorial Auditorium.

A terminus for three major railroads, the New York, New Haven & Hartford, the Penn Central (Boston & Albany) and the Boston & Maine, the city in recent years has become a center of experiments in mass transportation.

The Massachusetts Bay Transportation Authority was established by the Legislature to take over operation of the deficit-plagued municipal transportation network of subways and surface lines and to extend service to a total of 78 cities and towns.

To keep the railroad commuter lines in operation, the MBTA is paying the deficits incurred in operations of the B&M and the New Haven which service more than 20,000 riders from the suburbs daily.

The city is also served by Logan International Airport, on 2,200 acres of "made" land in Boston Harbor, and by 18 major airlines.

In 1967, the field handled 178,446 domestic and international flights, carrying a total of 6,691,246 passengers. With completion of new terminals now under construction or in design in 1972, the field expects to handle 22,000,000 to 25,000,000 passengers annually, with parking for 12,000 cars.

Boston is the world's leading wholesale wool market, has a thriving shoe manufacturing industry and lands annually a fish catch valued at more than $10,000,000.

Major corporations based in or near the city include Raytheon, General Electric, Gillette Co., Prudential Insurance Co. of North America and John Hancock Mutual Life Insurance Co.

Boston is a major medical center, with such institutions as Massachusetts General Hospital, Children's Hospital Medical Center and Peter Bent Brigham Hospital, and Harvard, Boston University and Tufts Medical Schools. It ranks third in the country in the number of persons employed in the field of medicine.

Today, there are 52 colleges and universities in the immediate area of the city, among them Harvard, Massachusetts Institute of Technology, Tufts, Boston College, Boston University, Northeastern University, Radcliffe, Wellesley, Jackson, Simmons, Emmanuel, Regis, Brandeis, Wentworth Institute, Emerson College and a new campus of the University of Massachusetts.

The city's museums and cultural activities reflect the broad range of intellectual interest which runs back to Emerson, Thoreau, Hawthorne and Parkman.

They include the Boston Museum of Fine Arts, the Museum of Science, a new aquarium on the waterfront, the Isabella Stewart Gardner Museum, the Museum of Contemporary Art.

Cultural activities include the Boston Symphony, the Pops Concerts in the spring, those on the Esplanade in early summer, a Winterfest and a Christmas Festival which sees thousands of lights sparkling on Boston Common.

Places of historical interest include Paul Revere's House, Park Street Church at "Brimstone Corner" on the Common, Old Granary Burying Ground, King's Chapel, Old South Meeting House, the Old State House, the Old North Church of Paul Revere fame, Copps Hill Burying Ground.

Among the famous churches are Trinity in Copley Square, the Mother Church of Christian Science in the Back Bay, Holy Cross Cathedral in the South End. The Boston Public Library in Copley Square is considered one of the finest examples of Italian Renaissance architecture.

Professional sports is represented by the Red Sox, 1967 American League baseball champions; the Celtics (National Basketball Association); the Bruins (National Hockey League); the Patriots (American Football League); and by the Beacons (North American Soccer League).

The city is served by 6 television stations, four VHF and two UHF, and a number of radio stations.

# Buffalo, New York

The World Almanac is sponsored in the Buffalo area by the Courier-Express, 785 Main St., Buffalo, N. Y. 14240; telephone (716) 852-5353; founded June 14, 1926, as a merger of the Courier and the Express by William J. Conners, Sr. circulation morning 154,165, Sunday 311,112; publisher, William J. Conners, III; asst. to publisher, Howard W. Clother; gen. mgr., A. Gordon Bennett; business mgr., Richard C. Lyons, Jr.; sponsors hole-in-one tournament, learn to swim program, ski school, Goodfellows.

Buffalo, the hub of the "Niagara Frontier," is located in Western New York at the end of Lake Erie and the beginning of the Niagara River. The first white settlers came to the area then called New Amsterdam in 1784. The British and hostile Indians burned the settlement of 1,500 in 1813. It was rebuilt and incorporated as the Village of Buffalo in 1816. With the opening of the Erie Canal in 1825, Buffalo's growth began as the village became the transfer point of immigration and commerce for the movement to the west. Buffalo was chartered as a city in 1832 when the population reached 10,000.

The city now operates under the mayoral form of government with the mayor being elected every four years. The Buffalo Metropolitan area, referred to as the Niagara Frontier, consists of Erie and Niagara counties and ranks 16th in metropolitan population in the nation (1965 Census Bureau estimate). The City of Buffalo itself, according to a special 1966 U. S. Census, has a population of 481,453 with Erie County, in which the city is located, having 1,087,183. The Niagara county portion of the metropolitan area including the City of Niagara Falls, has a population of 234,477 (1967 special census).

The Niagara Frontier trade market has 1,300,000 population with an annual income of $3.5 billion. Some 55% of the U. S. population and two-thirds of the Canadian population live within a 500-mile radius.

With ample hydro-electric power from Niagara Falls augmented by the Niagara Power Project, industry on the Niagara Frontier has flourished. The area has over 2,000 manufacturing firms representing 99% of all major categories listed by the Census Bureau. Corporations with headquarters in the area include National Gypsum, Carborundum, Hooker Chemical, Trico Products and Houdaille Industries.

The Niagara Frontier is a research center of growing importance with 115 research operations. It is the home of Textron's Bell Aerosystems Co., Cornell Aeronautical Laboratory, the Western New York Nuclear Research Center on the campus of the State Univ. at Buffalo.

The city's flour milling and grain distribution facilities are among the world's largest, with 27 grain elevators having a total storage capacity of 51,915,000 bushels. In 1967, Buffalo had retail sales estimated at $2.1 billion for the metropolitan area and $700,422,000 for the city itself.

Buffalo became a world port with the opening in 1959 of the St. Lawrence Seaway. The port handled more than 15,000,-000 tons of cargo from both the Great Lakes and ocean-going shipping in 1966. During the year 67 ocean-going vessels with 103,901 tons of cargo visited Buffalo.

The Greater Buffalo International Airport is serviced by 6 airlines. The airport handled 147,842 scheduled and non-scheduled flights with a total of 2,010,000 passengers. It is being expanded.

Buffalo also is one of the largest railroad centers in the U. S., with 15 freight terminals scheduling 25,000 trains annually. It is serviced by 8 major railroads. Approximately 150 motor carriers serve industries on the Niagara Frontier, while cross-country bus lines operate in and out.

The city currently is in the midst of a major redevelopment program highlighted by a privately-financed renewal of a large section of the downtown area. Already completed is a $16,000,000 (22 stories) bank and office building for the Manufacturers & Traders Trust Co. and completed in 1968 a $20,000,000 shopping mall and 26-story building for the Erie County Savings bank. Government-sponsored projects also are underway.

A progressing cultural city, Buffalo is proud of its Albright-Knox Art Gallery and Kleinhans Hall, the home of the Buffalo Philharmonic orchestra. A full-time professional theater, Studio Arena, was founded in Buffalo in 1965. Also here are the Buffalo Museum of Science, Historical Museum and Zoological Gardens.

Metropolitan area universities and colleges include the State University at Buffalo, which is about to build a new $130,000,000 campus in suburban Amherst; State College at Buffalo, Canisius College, D'Youville College, Rosary Hill College, Niagara University, Medaille College, Villa Maria College, Trocaire College, Erie County Technical Institute, Niagara Community College.

In the world of sports, Buffalo is noted for the Buffalo Bills, twice champions of the American Football League. The city also has the Buffalo Bison baseball team in the International League and the Buffalo Bisons in the American Hockey League.

Information about Buffalo can be obtained from the Chamber of Commerce or the Boost Buffalo Committee, both at 238 Main St., Buffalo, N. Y. 14202.

## *Calgary, Canada* (see *Edmonton-Calgary*)

# Chicago, Illinois

The World Almanac is sponsored in the Chicago area by the Chicago Tribune, 435 N. Michigan Ave., Chicago, Ill. 60611; telephone (312) 222-3232; founded June 10, 1847, by Joseph Medill; circulation daily 831,257, Sunday 1,166,904; publisher, J. Howard Wood; president and general manager, Harold F. Grumhaus; editor, W. D. Maxwell; executive editor, Clayton Kirkpatrick; major awards include 3 Pulitzer Prizes won by staff members; sponsors college-pro all-star football game, Miracle of Books Fair, Good Fellows program, annual presentation of Nutcracker ballet.

Chicago, Illinois, is located just north and east of the center of population of the United States. Geography has helped in making Chicago the nation's center of industrial distribution and transportation.

Indians named the area Checagou for its strong-smelling wild onions. Wagon trains set up camp south of Fort Dearborn

in the 1830s on what was to become Michigan Avenue. On Mar. 4, 1837, Chicago was incorporated by 4,170 pioneers on the lower western shores of Lake Michigan.

At the time of the great Chicago fire in 1871 it had 300,000 residents. Now, as the nation's second largest city, Chicago proper has 3,538,000 people, according to Sales

Management. The same source shows Metropolitan Chicago, defined as the Illinois counties of Cook, Lake, McHenry, Du Page, Kane and Will, and the Indiana counties of Lake and Porter, with 7,492,400 people. The city, seat of Cook County, has 1,721,400 households; the 8-county area has 2,281,200. Some 64,000,000 people live within a 500-mile radius of the city. Chicago Tribune Research Dept. estimates project Metropolitan Chicago population to 8,012,000 in 1970, and 9,520,000 in 1980.

Chicagoans earn an average of $12,650 per household, 26.3% higher than the national average. Per capita income is $3,039, 28.2% more than the national average. Approximately 3,455,000 persons are employed in the area. Metropolitan Chicago, with 3.8% of the population of the U. S., accounts for 6.2% of the national output.

Voters elect the mayor, the city council of 50 aldermen, a city treasurer, city clerk, municipal court clerk, bailiff, judges.

Chicago leads all U. S. metropolitan areas in the production of steel, telephone equipment, radios, television sets, confectionery products, household appliances, metal wares, electrical machinery, non-electrical machinery, plastic products, diesel engines, sports and athletic goods, mirrors, picture frames, gloves and mittens, soaps, perfumes, cosmetics, window screens, blinds, shades, tin cans, snuff.

Chicago's biggest industry is primary metals, $5.5 billion. Next is food and kindred products at $5.2 billion; then electrical machinery, non-electrical machinery, chemical products, fabricated metal products, printing and publishing.

In the 8-county area, 14,384 manufacturers have sales of $35.6 billion compared to $22.5 billion only 5 years ago. More than 54,000 retail businesses in the area have combined sales of $13.8 billion, up from $8.5 billion 10 years ago. An $11.4 billion climb in sales from 1958 was achieved by the area's 12,700 wholesalers. Service establishments have doubled annual sales in 10 years, reaching $2.9 billion. The area's share of the gross national product is $40.3 billion.

Chicago's Midwest Stock Exchange provides a market for more than 478 different kinds of stocks and bonds, and has 415 members with more than 3,000 offices. The city is headquarters for the nation's Seventh Federal Reserve District Bank, home to world's leading grain futures market, the Chicago Board of Trade, the world's biggest farm produce market, and the Chicago Mercantile Exchange.

More than 1,200 industrial laboratories are spending more than $2 billion annually for private research and development. Argonne National Laboratory will soon be joined by the Atomic Energy Commission's 200 billion electron volt particle accelerator in nearby Weston.

Chicago hosts more than 900 trade shows and conventions annually; nearly 1,300,000 persons attend.

Chicago has more than a dozen major highways, tollways and expressways. Twenty trunk line railroads operate on half the nation's total railway mileage. Chicago's 3 principal airports handle more than 26,000,000 persons annually. Chicago combines lake, ocean and river shipping, serving as the link between the Mississippi River and the St. Lawrence Seaway.

Chicago's railroads handle more than 34,000 freight cars daily in the switching districts. Chicago is the terminal for western and eastern railroads.

The Port of Chicago handles 28.2% of all overseas cargo entering or leaving the Great Lakes, and is served by more than 100 steamship lines.

Twenty-six scheduled commercial airlines serve the city. The city originates 15.3% of the nation's air cargo. O'Hare Field is the world's largest and busiest commercial airport and handles as many as 2,000 aircraft movements a day. One of every 5 foreign visitors to the U. S. passes through customs at O'Hare Field.

Chicago's industrial complex has grown by more than 2,000 factories in the past 15 years. More than $900,000,000 in private and public funds have been scheduled for port and waterway developments. Announcements of new commercial construction since 1960 total $1.6 billion.

Higher education is provided by 83 colleges and universities including the University of Chicago, Illinois Tech, Roosevelt University, the new Chicago Circle Campus of the University of Illinois, Loyola, De Paul, and Northwestern. The city has 5 medical schools, 3 dental colleges, a pharmacy college, and a college of osteopathy. There are 154 hospitals in metropolitan Chicago.

Chicago's Art Institute is famous for its French impressionists and oriental collections. The Museum of Science and Industry displays wonders of space technology, electronics and industry. The Field Museum of Natural History has exhibits on anthropology, botany, zoology, and geology. The Shedd aquarium is the first and largest of its kind in the world. The Adler planetarium has a dome-shaped central chamber to show images of the heavens. Lincoln Park zoo and Brookfield zoo are popular year-round attractions.

The city's professional sports teams include the Chicago Bears, National Football League; Chicago White Sox, American (Baseball) League; Chicago Cubs, National (Baseball) League; Chicago Black Hawks, National Hockey League; Chicago Bulls, National Basketball Association; Chicago Spurs, National (Soccer) League; Chicago Mustangs, United (Soccer) Assn.

Information on the city may be obtained from the Visitors Bureau and Information Center of The Chicago Association of Commerce and Industry at 30 W. Monroe, Chicago 60603.

# Cincinnati, Ohio

The World Almanac is sponsored in the Cincinnati area by the Cincinnati Post & Times-Star, 800 Broadway, Cincinnati, Ohio 45202; telephone (513) 721-1111; founded Jan. 3, 1881, by Alfred and Walter Wellman; circulation 243,618; editor, Dick Thornburg; business manager, Arnold L. Royer; sponsors annual Zoo Food and Home Show, co-sponsors annual Post-Firemen's Mile of Dimes; major awards received include 1967 Scripps-Howard Roy Howard Award.

Cincinnati, with a population of 498,400 (Census estimate, 1968) is the hub of a 7-county metropolitan area of 1,393,200 (Ohio Development Dept. 1967 estimate) on the Ohio River in southwest Ohio.

The compact downtown, on a flat plain facing the river, is surrounded on 3 sides by steep, green hills. The metropolitan area spreads in a 30-mile circle over the hills and up industrialized valleys between, and encompasses parts of Kentucky and Indiana.

The first settlement was founded Nov. 11, 1788, by 23 settlers under Benjamin Stites. They flatboated down the Ohio. Their settlement, Columbia, is now a sub-

urb. On Dec. 28, 1788, another group came by flatboat and founded Losantiville 6 miles downstream. Losantiville's name was changed to Cincinnati. It was where today's downtown river front is.

The river was responsible for the city's early growth. Surplus crops were sent to markets down river by boat. Cincinnati already had established itself as a river port when the steamboat came along about 1816 and let the city capitalize on its reputation.

Cincinnati is governed by a 9-member council, elected in odd years and a city manager appointed by the council. The council elects a mayor from its ranks. Cincinnati's 1968 budget is $73,981,550.

No one industry dominates the city. Cincinnati is the home of Procter & Gamble, world's largest soap manufacturer (1967 sales $2.4 billion); the Kroger Co., world's third largest retail food chain (1967 sales $2.8 billion); the world's largest department store chain, Federated Department Stores, Inc. (1967 sales $1.7 billion), and the world's largest maker of playing cards, the U. S. Playing Card Co. (1967 sales $30,000,000).

The Cincinnati Milling Machine Co. (1967 sales $273,000,000) is the largest of several companies that make Cincinnati the world's leading producer of machine tools.

Cincinnati is a world leader in the production of jet engines, shoes, leather goods, pianos, cosmetics, chemicals, and in printing and publishing.

Total retail sales in the 7-county metropolitan area in 1967 were $1.950 billion (Sales Management Magazine estimate).

Cincinnati is a transport hub linking the South, the Great Lakes states, and the trans-Appalachian East. Seven railroads serve the city—Pennsylvania, New York Central, Chesapeake & Ohio, Baltimore & Ohio, Norfolk & Western, and Southern. The city owns the Southern's right-of-way to Chattanooga.

Six trunk airlines (TWA, American, Delta, Eastern, Piedmont, Lake Central) made 146,975 scheduled flights in 1967 into

and out of Greater Cincinnati Airport. The city-owned Lunken Airport handled 192,355 flights, mostly business and private craft.

River shipping on the Ohio in 1967 exceeded 110,000,000 tons and 24 billion ton-miles.

Cincinnati is in the midst of a $100,000,000 urban renewal program in which all or part of 12 downtown blocks will be razed and rebuilt. The city has a new $11,000,000 Convention-Exposition Center, and is getting 3 new high-rise downtown motels, garages for 2,500 cars downtown, and 4 new office buildings.

Downtown renewal includes a system of second-story-level "skywalks" linking major blocks by footbridges, covered arcades, second-story sidewalks, and corridors within buildings, all connected to street level by escalators and stairways.

A new $32,000,000 stadium planned for the downtown river front will be the new home of the Cincinnati Reds National League baseball team and of the city's new entry in the American Football League. The Cincinnati Royals of the National Basketball Assn. play in the 14,000-seat Cincinnati Gardens.

The urban renewal program also includes a $24,000,000 effort to rehabilitate and upgrade two older suburban neighborhoods. It also includes a now completed 296-acre industrial-commercial development adjacent to downtown, where the squalid West End slums once stood.

Cincinnati is the home of the University of Cincinnati, founded in 1819, one of the oldest municipally controlled universities. It has one of the nation's leading medical centers, where Dr. Albert Sabin, developer of the oral polio vaccine, works.

The Cincinnati Art Museum is famous for the quality of its permanent collections, reviewing the world's major civilizations of the past 5,000 years. The Taft Museum contains a famous art collection.

The Cincinnati Symphony Orchestra under director Max Rudolf, plays in Cincinnati Music Hall, also the home of the annual Cincinnati May Music Festival.

# Cleveland, Ohio

The World Almanac is sponsored in the Cleveland area by the Cleveland Press, 901 Lakeside Ave., Cleveland, Ohio 44114; telephone (216) 623-1111; founded Nov. 2, 1878, by E. W. Scripps; circulation 400,000; editor, Thomas L. Boardman; managing editor, Harding Christ; business manager, George E. Carter; major awards received, Pulitzer Prize, Lasker Award; sponsors Helping Hand Charity Fund, Cleveland Open Golf Tournament, NFL Pro Football doubleheader.

Visitors to "The Best Location in the Nation," as Cleveland calls itself, are greeted by a big sign as they leave the city's Hopkins International Airport. Within 500 miles, it tells them, are 53% of the U. S. population, 54% of the nation's retail sales, 59% of the nation's industries and 67% of the billion-dollar markets.

Location is a big part of the Cleveland story. It was here—where the twisting Cuyahoga River flows into Lake Erie—that Gen. Moses Cleaveland and his hardy band of pioneer-surveyors established the first settlement in the summer of 1796. The group had been sent here by the Connecticut Land Co. to found a "capital" town for the Western Reserve, a tract of western land reserved by the new state of Connecticut.

The new settlement was given the name of its founder, but spellings in early official documents omitted the "a," and the community became known from its first years as "Cleveland." Its strategic location along the waterways—the river, the Great Lakes and, in 1827, the Ohio Canal which penetrated the state's heartland—spurred

its growth. In 1836, it became a city.

This largest city in Ohio, 8th largest in the United States, lies along the south shore of Lake Erie east and west of the Cuyahoga River along whose winding valley lies the wealth of its heavy industries. The Public Square, commercial hub of the city, is marked by the 52-story Terminal Tower, one of the tallest U. S. buildings outside New York. From the Square radiate the main streets of the city like spokes on a wheel to the east and west and south.

Many of the people who live here are descendants of immigrants from more than 60 nations around the world. They live within the city's corporate limits of some 76 square miles or within city and suburbs (included within Cuyahoga County or Greater Cleveland) which embrace some 458 square miles. Population of the City of Cleveland (according to the 1965 special census) is 810,858. For Greater Cleveland the count is 1,738,797 (according to estimate by Real Property Inventory in 1965). City government is by mayor and council.

No single industry dominates Cleveland's economy, but the making of steel and the manufacturing of metal products are mainstays. Again the city's location is a factor, for it is in Cleveland that iron from the upper Great Lakes meets the coal from the lower Great Lakes. The city is basically a "hard-goods town," its manufacturing complex occupied essentially with the creation of capital goods—machine tools (Cleveland is second only to Cincinnati), steel (its flat-roll stock used heavily by automakers), automotive products, primary metals, fabricated metal products.

Important Cleveland industries include such diversified enterprises as the manufacture of electric motors, petroleum products, chemicals, paints, rubber products, wearing apparel, measuring instruments, electronic components. Value of Cleveland's products totals almost $7 billion a year. Greater Cleveland's retail sales come to $2.5 billion.

Eighteen Cleveland industrial firms are included in the 1967 Fortune Magazine listing of the nation's top 500 giants. These are Republic Steel Corp., TRW Inc., Eaton, Yale & Towne, Inc.; White Motor Co., Standard Oil Co. of Ohio; Sherwin-Williams Co., Midland-Ross Corp., Addressograph-Multigraph Corp., Diamond Alkali Co., Automatic Sprinkler Corp., Hupp Corp., Reliance Electric Co., Harris-Intertype Corp., White Consolidated Industries, Clevite Corp., Hanna Mining Co., Warner & Swasey Co., and Parker-Hannifin Corp.

Cleveland is a transportation crossroads and one of the city's most important facilities is its port. Cleveland is the largest city on Lake Erie, the third largest city on the Great Lakes, a competitor with Chicago in overseas tonnage, handling some 22,000,000 tons of bulk cargo and some 531,209 tons of general cargo. Forty steamship lines offer service to more than 140 ports in 70 countries.

Four major railroads serve the Cleveland area—the Baltimore and Ohio, Erie Lackawanna, Penn. Central and the Norfolk and Western. Some 4,000,000 passengers arrive at and leave from Cleveland Hopkins Airport each year. Another 170,-000 or so each year use the city's Burke Lakefront Airport, just 5 minutes from the center of Cleveland and capable of handling intermediate jets.

Cleveland's giant downtown rebuilding plan has seen the completion of a 40-story office building and plaza, and a nearby 32-story Federal Bldg. A number of other high-rise apartment and office buildings are under construction downtown.

The city's new Convention Center is the largest city-owned convention facility in the country. And Cleveland's cultural treasures are manifold.

There are the Cleveland Orchestra, world famous; the Cleveland Play House, the nation's oldest and largest resident professional theater; the Cleveland Museum of Art, with its internationally known collections housed in one of the most beautiful museum buildings in America; Karamu House, nationally acclaimed for its interracial artistic accomplishments; the Western Reserve Historical Society, and the Cleveland Health Museum. And there are the lovely Cultural Gardens, the Cleveland Zoo, the Natural Science Museum and an expansive system of metropolitan parks which has helped earn for Cleveland the title of "Forest City."

Cleveland is a sports-minded city, home of the Browns of the National Football League, the Indians of the American (baseball) League, the Barons of the American Hockey League. Professional soccer has become a part of the sports scene, too, and area fans have their calendars full the year around with such attractions as horse racing, stock car racing, basketball, even curling and judo.

Colleges and universities include Case Western Reserve University, Baldwin-Wallace College, Cleveland State University, Cuyahoga Community College, John Carroll University, Notre Dame College, St. John College and Ursuline College.

Companies or persons seeking information on Cleveland business and living conditions may write to the Greater Cleveland Growth Assn., Union Commerce Bldg., Cleveland, Ohio 44114.

## Columbus, Ohio

The World Almanac is sponsored in the Columbus area by the Columbus Citizen-Journal, 34 S. Third St., Columbus, Ohio 43216; telephone (614) 461-5000; The Citizen founded in 1899, The Ohio State Journal in 1811; circulation 117,940 six mornings of the week; owned by the E. W. Scripps Co.; editor, Charles Egger; business manager, Paul W. Ream; sponsors Citizen-Journal Spelling Bee, Adopt-A-Family, Sweepstakes Night at Scioto Downs, Outstanding Women's Tea, Broadway Theater Party; co-sponsors of Golden Age Hobby Show, Charity Newsies.

The capital city of Ohio, Columbus has an estimated population of 581,883 (1968) and is the state's largest city in area, the second largest in population.

Columbus is in the heart of Ohio, on rolling plains 777 feet above sea level at the confluence of the Scioto and Olentangy Rivers (both Indian names), and ever since its founding in 1812 has been a crossroads and mecca.

The central location led to its creation as the capital, the original streets being laid out in a forest in the gridiron pattern set by Philadelphia, Pa. Today the gridiron is surrounded by the Innerbelt, the Outerbelt, suburbs with winding streets, industrial parks and greenbelts.

Minerals and clay of the Hocking Valley coal field southeast of Columbus balanced agricultural areas north and west, leading to spectacular growth in wholesaling, which still supplies a vast sector of Ohio and two states to the south. Investment in Hocking Valley enterprises contributed greatly to the city's wealth.

Columbus has more than 900 manufacturing plants. The city produces jet planes, refrigerators, telephones, mining machinery, wheel assemblies for railroad cars, auto parts, electrical machinery, shoes, paint, food, packaging, plastics, wall coverings, bearings, grave vaults, tools, glassware, printing, cement mixers, heating and air-conditioning units. Columbus manufacturers employed 74,556 persons in 1967 with annual payroll of $485,405,577.

The city government has a council. Its members and the mayor are chosen in nonpartisan elections. The 1968 budget included $32,750,000 for general-fund operating expenses and $62,500,000 for capital improvements.

Ohio State University is largest among Columbus' colleges, other major ones including Capital University, Franklin University, Ohio Dominican College (formerly St. Mary of the Springs) and St. Charles Seminary. The horseshoe-shaped 84,000-seat Ohio Stadium has become a symbol

of the city, the OSU home football games attracting capacity crowds. Professional teams include Columbus Jets (baseball), Checkers (hockey) and Comets (basketball). Tracks are Beulah Park (thoroughbreds) and Scioto Downs (harness horses).

Worldwide in its research assistance to industry and government is Battelle Memorial Institute. Global also is Chemical Abstracts. Situated between them is the OSU Medical Center.

The Armed Forces has the world's largest materiel depot in Columbus. Thirty-six insurance firms have their home offices in Columbus, which is the seat of Franklin County that has a projected 1970 population of 942,386. Columbus retail sales were an estimated $1,462,318,976 in 1967, an increase of 61.7% over 1960. The city has 4 railroads; there are 9 airlines, most of them using Port Columbus International Airport. Yearly import-export business of Columbus firms is over $60,000,000.

The Ohio State Fair is held in late summer at the in-city Ohio Expositions Center, where the Ohio Historical Society has

built a spectacular museum. Tentative discussions have been held on a 1992 World's Fair inasmuch as the city is the largest in the world named for Christopher Columbus.

Downtown developments include a marina, a convention center and a sports arena. Two slum areas have been replaced by new, bright buildings. Tallest tower in the city is the LeVeque-Lincoln Tower, matching the 555 feet of the Washington Monument. High-rise apartments and dormitories overlook valleys.

Other attractions include the Park of Roses (world's largest), Columbus Symphony Orchestra, Ohio Railway Museum and German Village, an urban restoration. German immigrants were a major factor in the city's growth, and each year an Oktoberfest is held. The Columbus Gallery of Fine Arts has an outstanding collection of oils by George Bellows, artist born in Columbus.

Those wanting more information on Columbus can write or phone the Columbus Area Chamber of Commerce, 30 E. Broad St., Columbus, Ohio 43216.

# Dallas, Texas

The World Almanac is sponsored in the Dallas area by the Dallas Morning News, Communications Center, Dallas, Tex. 75222; telephone (214) RI 7-4611; founded in 1842 by Samuel Bangs; circulation 236,273 daily, 275,699 Sunday; president, Joseph M. Dealey; executive editor, Jack B. Krueger; managing editor, Thomas J. Simmons; major awards received include Pulitzer Prize and National Headliner Award; sponsors Dallas Beautification award, Teenage Citizenship Tributes, Fly-the-Flag campaign, etc.

The second largest city in Texas, Dallas is the financial, transportation, trade and cultural capital of its region.

According to Chamber of Commerce estimates based on employment figures, metropolitan Dallas with an estimated population of 1,430,500 in June 1968, had experienced since 1960 the fastest growth rate of the 20 leading U. S. standard metropolitan areas. Dallas County's population was estimated at 1,229,600, a gain of about 278,000 since the 1960 census. The incorporated area's population was estimated at 840,900.

The city sits astride the Trinity River in North Texas, about 75 miles south of the Oklahoma border, at an elevation ranging from 450 to 750 feet in an area of plains.

Lacking any significant natural advantage as a city site, Dallas was built largely through aggressive personal efforts of numerous commercial and civic leaders who promoted the city's interests. It is still noted for a "booster" spirit exemplified by its nickname "Big D."

The first settler was a frontiersman from Tennessee, John Neely Bryan, who chose a natural fording place on the Trinity, near the Three Forks of that stream, as the site for a trading post for the Caddo and Cherokee Indians of the vicinity. White settlers soon drove the Indians westward, however. Neely operated a ferry, and plotted the townsite in 1844. The log cabin he built in 1843, the first home in Dallas, still stands on the Old Courthouse grounds in downtown Dallas near its original site. Dallas County was created in 1846, named for Vice President George Mifflin Dallas, and the city was incorporated in 1856 with about 300 inhabitants.

Since 1931 the city has had a council-manager form of government. Although the fertile "Blackland" that made Dallas County productive of wheat and cotton in earlier years is rapidly being converted to industrial and residential use, the city remains the agribusiness capital of the Southwest, with a large trade in farm equipment, feeds, fertilizers and cotton

gin machinery.

Its spectacular population growth began with the post-World War II move of aircraft manufacturers to the Dallas suburban area, augmenting an economy that had been built first on cotton, then on oil, banking and insurance. The East Texas oil boom of the 1930s brought oil company offices and oilfield suppliers to Dallas.

Diversified economic expansion, marked by notable increases in aviation, aerospace and electronics manufacturing, has fed the growth of the 1960s.

Dallas ranks fourth among U. S. cities in the number of million-dollar-net-worth companies' headquarters. Four leading science-oriented industries (Texas Instruments, Ling-Temco-Vought, Dresser Industries and Collins Radio) together recorded sales over $1.8 billion in 1966.

Retail sales in the metropolitan area totaled $1.809 billion in 1963 and were estimated at $2.353 billion in 1966, while effective buying income per household in 1966 was estimated at $9,508.

Dallas is an important wholesale apparel center, with several seasonal market showings, and a regional retail trade center. Neiman-Marcus specialty store has built an international reputation for fashion leadership and merchandising.

In the past three years, more than 30 new first-class office buildings have been constructed, including the city's tallest skyscrapers, the First National Bank and the Republic National Bank Tower. A new county government center was completed in 1966. Major construction scheduled, newly completed or under way includes a $26,000,000 Federal center; a $30,000,000 post office; a $23,900,000 downtown municipal center; the Army and Air Force Post Exchange Service headquarters; a $65,-000,000 shopping center in the southwest section of the city, to be the largest such facility in the South; One Main Place, a downtown "superblock" of shops and offices to rise 34 stories at a cost of about $41,000,000.

The city is served by 8 airlines, 9 railroads, two transcontinental bus lines and

37 motor freight lines. They move an estimated 20,000 tons of freight into Dallas daily and carry more than 15,000 passengers a day. The city has 6 outlets on the interstate highway system. A long-sought canalization of the Trinity River for barge traffic awaits Federal appropriations.

Love Field is the nation's 7th busiest airport. In fiscal 1967, 3,807,760 passengers enplaned there. Dallas and its neighbor city of Fort Worth, 30 miles to the west, are building a new regional airport midway between the cities by the early 1970s.

Higher education is served by Southern Methodist University, the University of Dallas, Bishop College, Dallas Baptist College, Christian College of the Southwest, Dallas County Junior College, the Southwestern Medical School of the University of Texas and the Baylor University College of Dentistry.

Dallas is the site of the Texas State Fair for 16 days each October, the largest such exposition in the nation in attendance. Within Fair Park, open the year round, are the Hall of State historical museum, Dallas Museum of Fine Arts, Aquarium,

Museum of Natural History, Health and Science Museum, Dallas Garden Center, State Fair Music Hall, Cotton Bowl.

Also of interest to visitors are the Marsalis Park Zoo, Dallas Theater Center (designed by Frank Lloyd Wright), and SMU's Owens Fine Arts Center with a collection of paintings and sculpture. Leading musical events are the Dallas Symphony and Dallas Civic Opera seasons, an annual spring tour of the Metropolitan Opera and professional Summer Musicals at Fair Park.

The Cotton Bowl is the site of an annual New Year's Day football game as well as home games of the professional Dallas Cowboys (National Football League). Other sports are represented by the Dallas-Fort Worth Spurs (Texas League baseball) the pro basketball Chaparrals (American Basketball Assn.), the Black Hawks hockey team and the Dallas Tornado soccer team.

Information about Dallas business and living conditions may be obtained from the Chamber of Commerce, Fidelity Union Tower Building, Dallas, Tex. 75201.

# Dayton, Ohio

The World Almanac is sponsored in the Dayton area by The Journal Herald, 37 South Ludlow Street, Dayton, Ohio 45401; telephone (513) 223-1111; founded Sept. 18, 1808, as Dayton Repertory by William McClure and George Smith; circulation 111,062 daily (six months ending March 31, 1968); editor, Glenn Thompson; managing editor, Charles T. Alexander; editor, editorial page, Theodore Bingham; community projects include Neighborhood Beautification Awards, Senior Citizens' Tours, Fishing Clinic, Father-Son Sports Night, National Industrial Bowling Tournament, Learn-To-Swim, Cincinnati Reds' Baseball Clinic, Area Football and Basketball All-Stars Banquet and TV Program.

Dayton, the "Birthplace of Aviation," is one of the nation's major industrial and research centers, located in the rolling hills of west central Ohio where the Miami, Stillwater and Mad Rivers join.

Dayton is the fastest growing metropolitan area in Ohio and the center of the 10th largest local service market in the nation. Retail sales in the city totaled $539,606,000 in 1966 and $1,248,499,000 in the Dayton metropolitan area.

Dayton was the first major metropolitan city to install the commission-manager form of municipal government (1913); and the first area to have a comprehensive flood control project, the Miami Conservancy District, which was financed entirely by local funds (started in 1913). Dayton was also the first Ohio city to enact an income tax by popular election after the courts declared a council-enacted income tax unconstitutional (1950).

Dayton was settled by a score of men, women and children in 1796 when a group headed by Samuel Thompson left Cincinnati by boat for Dayton. The city was incorporated in 1805 and chartered as a city in 1841. It is the 4th largest standard metropolitan statistical area in the state.

The city of Dayton has a population of 272,000, while the metropolitan area is 851,100. Projections are for a population of 300,000 in the city and 1,081,800 in the metropolitan area by 1975.

From almost 1,000 industrial plants in the Dayton area come a variety of widely-known products. It is the home of the world's largest cash register manufacturing plant (National Cash Register Company), the world's largest magazine production facility (McCall Corporation); and the third largest concentration of General Motors Corporation operations (Delco Moraine, Delco Products, Frigidaire, Inland Mfg. and AC Electronics).

Dayton is the home of Wright-Patterson Air Force Base, which stands on land where the Wright Brothers did much of their early flying.

WPAFB is the worldwide headquarters

for the Air Force Logistics Command and headquarters for the Aeronautical Systems Division which conducts research and development and manages procurement of all aircraft used by the Air Force.

Other organizations at the base include the Foreign Technology Division, Aerospace Medical Research Laboratories, four other major laboratories (Avionics, Materials, Flight Dynamics, and Aero Propulsion), the Air Force Institute of Technology, the Air Force Museum (which draws an estimated one million visitors a year) and the 17th Bombardment Wing of the Strategic Air Command.

A second major defense installation is the Defense Electronics Supply Center which handles procurement of more than 500,000 electronic components for all branches of the military service.

Dayton is a growing city and has plans for an extensive new county government complex downtown as well as a redeveloped downtown section known as Center City West. In 1967, 264 commercial building permits were issued in Dayton, valued at $20,590,207. In the same year, 482 permits were issued in the metropolitan area, with a value of $37,465,906. Through April, 1968, 77 commercial building permits were issued in the city, valued at $11,726,757, and 141 in the metropolitan area for a value of $15,046,337.

Under construction in 1968 were a 22-story office building, an 11-story hotel and large buildings for Ohio Bell Telephone, Price Bros. Construction Company (64,000 square feet), a 3-story Senior Citizens Center (25,000 square feet), and a new Post Office (213,000 sq. ft.). Planned is a 30-story bank and office building.

Located in the center of a business center containing 7 metropolitan areas with a population of 3,700,000, Dayton is served by five airlines and 3 trunk line rail systems. Seven motor bus lines offer local and national service and a trolley system operates within the city.

Dayton is the home of the 118-year-old Catholic University of Dayton and Wright

State University, which accepted its first students in 1964 as a branch of two other state universities. It is now an independent state university. There are also two junior colleges, Sinclair with programs in business, liberal arts and engineering and Miami-Jacobs, an accredited junior college of business. The city is also home for the School of the Dayton Art Institute and United Theological Seminary.

College football and basketball are provided by the University of Dayton teams. UD's basketball team was the National Invitational Tournament champion in 1968. Other spectator sports include a professional hockey team, the Dayton Gems, and two stock-car raceways.

Dayton's Philharmonic Orchestra, a Civic Music Association and the Dayton Opera Association all present annual program series. Outdoor summer concerts are offered at the Diehl Memorial Shell and Deeds Carillon. Dayton Art Institute houses both permanent and special exhibits throughout the year. Four amateur theatrical groups perform in winter, two professional companies in summer.

Points of interest include the Amateur Trapshoot Association headquarters in suburban Vandalia, where the annual Grand American Trapshoot is held in August; Carillon Park, containing Deeds Carillon and historical exhibits pertinent to Dayton history; Paul Lawrence Dunbar homestead, home of the famed Negro poet now maintained as a national shrine; Wright Brothers Memorial; and the national Aviation Hall of Fame.

# Denver, Colorado

The World Almanac is sponsored in the Denver area by the Rocky Mountain News, 400 W. Colfax Ave., Denver, Colo. 80201; telephone (303) 892-5000; founded Apr. 23, 1859, by William N. Byers; circulation daily 195,448, Sunday 212,872; editor, Jack Foster; business manager, Edward W. Estlow; sponsors Colorado-Wyoming spelling bee, Golden Wedding party, Huck Finn Day, Ski School.

Denver, Colorado's capital, is exactly one mile above sea level at the far western edge of the Great Plains, near the foothills of the Rocky Mountains, lending it the dual designation of "Mile High City" and "Queen City of the Plains."

Largest city between Chicago, St. Louis and West Coast, its government is nonpartisan with mayor and nine councilmen.

Founded in 1858 with discovery of placer gold at the junction of South Platte River and Cherry Creek, now in geographical center of city, Denver rapidly became the supply center for mining camps in nearby mountains. It remains the largest distribution center in the region extending from Canada to Mexico and embracing one-third of the U. S. geographical area.

Since World War II, Denver has become center for "smokeless industries" with 1,400 manufacturing companies. A tourist mecca, Denver is a gateway to vast recreational areas, including more than 20 major winter sports resorts and more mountains than Switzerland.

The 1960 U. S. census gave Denver a population of 493,887. Today, population of its standard metropolitan area is estimated at 1,201,800, total effective buying power of $3.2 billion. Total retail sales in 1967 were $3.476 billion.

Denver-headquartered companies include the Gates Rubber Co., world's largest producer of V-belts and hose, sixth largest U. S. rubber company with plants in 8 U. S. cities and 5 foreign countries. It is family-owned, widely diversified.

Samsonite Corp., world's largest luggage manufacturer, also produces folding furniture and toys. It has 11 plants in U. S. and foreign cities.

Other large Denver-based firms include: Great Western Sugar, Ideal Cement, American Crystal Sugar, Colorado Milling & Elevator, and CF&I Steel.

Adults in Metro Denver have average of 12.2 years of formal education, second among major U. S. cities to Washington, D. C. Leading higher education institutions are: University of Colorado; University of Colorado Medical School; University of Denver; Iliff School of Theology; Colorado School of Mines; Regis College; Loretto Heights College; Temple Buell College (formerly Colorado Woman's College), and Metropolitan State College

Denver is served by six Class I railroads; 68 major interstate and 42 intrastate motor carriers; two transcontinental and two intrastate bus lines, and 10 commercial airlines.

Stapleton International Airport in 1967 handled average daily arrivals and departures of 420 commercial flights daily, or a total of 153,515 for the year. Passengers in and out, 1967, totaled 5,078,502. In addition, general aviation aircraft in and out averaged 791 planes daily for a yearly total of 288,735, making the airport the eighth busiest U. S. Airport. Air Freight in 1967 totaled 94,242,966 pounds, air express 8,679,403 pounds and air mail 43,320,359 pounds.

An airport improvement plan of $25,-000,000 has been completed. A new $50,-000,000 million expansion is under way.

Until recently, buildings were limited to 12 stories. In the last 15 years, 16 buildings, up to 32 stories, were built in the downtown area. Tallest building, a 42-story apartment, office and shop complex, is completed. More than 35 high-rise apartments have been built.

Military establishments include Lowry Air Force Base; Air Force Accounting and Finance Center; Army's Rocky Mountain Arsenal (fire bombs, nerve gas, etc.); Fitzsimons General Hospital.

Denver has the largest number of U. S. Government offices of any city outside of Washington, D. C. Also, site of Atomic Energy Commission's Rocky Flats plant and U. S. Mint.

A $25,000,000 urban renewal project was recently completed. A new, $250,000,000 project is under way, including an $11,-800,000, 3-square-block convention center.

Although in a semi-arid region with annual precipitation averaging less than 15 inches, Denver is known for its beautiful lawns and trees, thanks to the far-sighted municipal water department which has spent $120,000,000 to provide 520,000 acre feet of water storage.

Denver has more than 100 named parks and a 20,000-acre mountain park system.

Other points of interest include; Colorado Capitol Bldg., with its dome covered by 250 ounces of 28 karat Colorado gold leaf; world-renowned Colorado Museum of Natural History; City Park Zoo; Denver Art Museum; Denver Botanic Gardens; Metro Denver's 28 private and public golf courses (where golf is played 324 out of 365 days a year); and the 12,000-seat Red Rocks open-air theater.

Denver offers 4 professional sports teams—Denver Bears of the Triple-A Pacific Coast Baseball League; Denver Broncos of American Football League; Denver Rockets of the American Basketball Assn.; and Denver Spurs of the Western Hockey League.

# Des Moines, Iowa

The World Almanac is sponsored in the Des Moines area by the Des Moines Register & Tribune, 715 Locust St., Des Moines, Iowa 50304; telephone (515) 284-8000; founded July 26, 1849, by Barlow Granger; circulation Morning Register 255,474, Evening Tribune 116,722, Sunday Register 526,033; president, Gardner Cowles; board chairman, John Cowles; editor & publisher, Kenneth MacDonald; general manager, David Kruidenier; writers and photographers have won 11 Pulitzer Prizes; sponsors Tribune Community Service Award, Drake University-Register summer workshop.

Des Moines, Iowa's capital city, is located at the junction of the Des Moines and Raccoon rivers in south central Iowa. Its rolling hills and wooded areas make it a city of beautiful parks and residential sections.

A military post was established at this site in 1843 to protect Indian rights. In 1845 the surrounding land was thrown open to settlers. Des Moines was incorporated in 1851 and became the capital in 1857. The fort was disbanded in 1847, but a new Fort Des Moines was built in 1902 as a cavalry post. During World War Two it was the headquarters for the Women's Army Corps (WAC). Today military reserve forces use the remaining buildings.

The Greater Des Moines Chamber of Commerce estimates the present metropolitan area population to be 272,000. The city has had a council-city manager form of government since 1950.

Des Moines is an important retail center with annual sales of $662,000,000. Manufacturing plants produce more than 500 products valued at more than $1 billion annually. There are more than 700 wholesaling and jobbing firms.

Among the manufacturing plants are the North American headquarters of Massey-Ferguson, Inc., John Deere and Ford Motor Implement, manufacturers of farm implements. Firestone Tire and Rubber Co. and Armstrong Rubber Co. have large Des Moines plants.

Des Moines is a major publishing center. Located there are The Des Moines Register and Tribune, circulation offices of Look Magazine; Meredith Publishing Co. which publishes Better Homes and Gardens and Successful Farming; and Wallace Homestead Co., publisher of Wallaces Farmer Magazine. There are 11 radio and four television stations.

Des Moines contains home offices of 56 insurance companies. The Equitable Life Insurance Co. of Iowa, founded in 1867, is the oldest life insurance company west of the Mississippi River. Bankers Life Insurance Co. of Des Moines is the largest west of the Mississippi.

The city is served by 3 commercial air-lines, 7 railroads, 46 truck lines and two major bus lines. The municipal airport recorded 664,968 arriving and departing passengers in 1967. Two major interstate highways intersect at Des Moines.

New buildings recently completed or under construction include a 10-story Federal Office Building, regional post office, and a 300-unit, $3,800,000 low rent housing project by the Des Moines Area Council of Churches. Recently built homes and buildings have been designed by such renowned architects as Mies van der Rohe, Eliel Saarinen, Richard Neutra and Skidmore, Owings and Merrill. An older area just north of the downtown area is being revitalized by a large urban renewal project.

Other major buildings include the gold-domed State Capitol, built in the late 1800s atop a majestic hill; the Saarinen-designed Des Moines Art Center with an addition designed by I. M. Pei; Veterans Memorial Auditorium, a 15,000-seat convention and sports center; and civic buildings and a beautiful YMCA along the Des Moines River front. Construction began in 1968 on a new YWCA.

KRNT Theater seats 4,200 and is one of the largest legitimate theaters in the world. The Des Moines Community Playhouse, with 8,000 members, stages conventional theater and is supplemented by a theater-in-the-round called the Drama Workshop. The Iowa State Fair, one of the largest agricultural expositions in the world, is held in August. A Children's Zoo was opened in 1966. Des Moines has a professional hockey team and is the site of both the boys' and girls' state high school basketball tournaments.

Drake University is the home of the Drake Relays, an important annual track meet. Also in Des Moines are Grand View College, a two-year school, and the College of Osteopathic Medicine and Surgery. Iowa State University is located 25 miles north of Des Moines in Ames.

The Greater Des Moines Chamber of Commerce, Eighth and High streets, provides information on business and living conditions.

# Detroit, Michigan

The World Almanac is sponsored in the Detroit area by the Detroit News, 615 W. Lafayette Blvd., Detroit, Mich. 48231; telephone (313) 222-2000; founded 1873 by James E. Scripps; circulation daily 702,591, Sunday 953,929; board chairman, Warren S. Booth; president & pub., Peter B. Clark; executive v.p. & gen. mgr., Edwin K. Wheeler; editor, Martin S. Hayden; major awards won include University of Missouri Award, Pulitzer Prize; community projects include Policeman and Fire Fighter of Month awards, NCAA Championship Indoor Track Meet, Detroit Soap Box Derby, Science Fair, Scholastic Writing and Art Awards, Spelling Bee, Michigan Industrial Education Awards, and Green Pennant Safety Awards.

Detroit, "The Motor City," is the nation's fifth largest, with a 1967 population of 1,620,000 and a 3-county metropolitan area population of 4,214,000, by estimate of the regional planning commission. The city covers 139.6 square miles on the Detroit River, a Great Lakes connecting link and the world's busiest inland waterway.

The city government is headed by a mayor and 9 councilmen elected at large on a nonpartisan ballot, under a "strong mayor" city charter.

Detroit was founded in 1701 by the Frenchman Cadillac as a strategic frontier fort and trading post, ceded to the British in 1763 and turned over to the U. S. in 1796, a village of 2,500. Destroyed by fire in 1805 and rebuilt, it was reoccupied by British for a year in the War of 1812.

Completion of the Erie Canal in 1825 opened a cheap water transport route from New York to the Northwest and made Detroit an important commercial center. Rail service reached Chicago in 1852, New York in 1854.

Population in 1860 was 45,619. Detroit was an important terminus of the Underground Railroad by which fugitive slaves reached freedom.

By 1880 Detroit was a major industrial

city, with 116,000 people and 825 factories. Tobacco and metal products were leading industries, especially stoves and railroad cars. Pharmaceuticals and industrial chemicals (based on vast underlying strata of salt and brines) grew in importance by 1900, but metalworking industries led. Its thriving machine and foundry industries, carriage and wagon shops laid the foundation for Detroit's emergence as the nation's auto capital, along with the fact that several pioneer auto experimenters lived in the city.

Among them were R. E. Olds, who built Detroit's first auto factory in 1899, and Henry Ford, who hand-built his first car in 1896, formed his first company in 1899 and the present Ford Motor Co. in 1903.

Auto production, the World War I boom and the Roaring Twenties pushed Detroit's population from 285,000 in 1900 to 993,000 in 1920 (fourth largest in the U. S.) and 1,568,000 in 1930. The area's industries made it the "Arsenal of Democracy" in World War II.

Despite postwar decentralization, Detroit remains the capital of the auto industry. Area plants produce 25% of the nation's cars and trucks, employing 225,-000. Transportation equipment accounted for 42% of the total $6.6 billion value added by area manufacturers in 1963. But the area's business is highly diversified, with only 16% of its labor force in the auto industry. Nonautomotive manufacturing employs 354,000; 835,000 are in nonmanufacturing employment. Other leading products are machine tools, gray iron products, metal stampings, hardware, industrial chemicals, drugs, paints, wire products and office machinery.

In addition to the major auto firms, leading companies headquartered in Detroit include Parke, Davis & Co., drugs; Burroughs Corp., business machines; Ex-Cello-O Corp., milk carton machinery; R. P. Scherer, gelatin capsules.

Total metropolitan area personal income in 1967 was $14.25 billion, $11,804 per household. Area retail sales were $7.2 billion.

Detroit is served by 9 railroads, 200 truck lines, 15 airlines and 3 air freight carriers and 50 ship lines. Air passengers totaled 5,760,000 in 1967; rail freight tonnage was 26,750,000 in 1967. Port of Detroit cargo tonnage was 33,300,000 in 1966, of which 1,423,604 was overseas traffic. More than 7,500,000 vehicles a year cross the international border between Detroit and Canada.

Hub of the downtown business district

is the 75-acre, $100,000,000 Civic Center, including Cobo Hall and Convention Arena with its 400,000 square feet of exhibit space, which replaced a district of rundown riverfront warehouses. Other major urban rebuilding projects include 660 acres in the Lafayette and Elmwood downtown residential developments, valued at $284,000,000 when completed, a 235-acre, $151,000,000 midtown medical center and a 182-acre expansion of the Wayne State University campus.

Detroit's city-owned water system, now supplying 3,503,800 people in 70 communities, is in a $475,000,000 expansion program to serve 6,500,000 by 1985. Nearby Lake Huron affords an unlimited water supply. Expenditure of $36,000,000 was scheduled for 1968 in an area pollution control program to cost $922,000,000 by the year 2000.

Points of interest to visitors include Chrysler, Ford and General Motors auto plants, Henry Ford Museum and Greenfield Village historical displays, Cranbrook Institute (science museum and arts), Belle Isle (1,000-acre island park), Zoological Park (natural animal settings), Institute of Arts, Public Library, Historical Museum, and Fort Wayne Military Museum. There are 1,000 inland lakes within an hour's drive.

Cultural institutions and events include the Detroit Symphony Orchestra, International Institute, Meadow Brook music and drama programs and the annual Freedom Festival, celebrating Canada's Dominion Day, July 1, and the U. S. Independence Day, July 4.

Eleven colleges and universities are located in the metropolitan area, including Wayne State University, among the nation's leading urban universities, Univ. of Detroit, and branches of the Univ. of Michigan and Michigan State Univ.

Detroit is represented in professional sports by the Detroit Tigers baseball club (American League), Detroit Lions (National Football League), Detroit Red Wings (National Hockey League), Detroit Pistons (National Basketball Assn.) and Detroit Cougars (United Soccer Assn.).

Among Detroit-area "firsts" are the world's first mile of concrete highway, 1909; first scheduled radio broadcast station, WWJ-The Detroit News, 1920; first U. S. pouring of Bessemer steel, 1864.

Information about Detroit is available from the Greater Detroit Board of Commerce, 150 Michigan Ave., Detroit, Mich. 48226, and Mayor's Committee for Industrial and Economic Development, 322 Veterans Memorial Building, Detroit 48226.

## Edmonton-Calgary, Canada

Fort Edmonton, built in 1795, was related to the fur trade but today's Edmonton, a supply center for Canada's northland and of a mixed farming area, is expanding on a solid industrial base.

The economy of the region was transformed by the discovery of oil at Leduc (20 miles south) in 1947, and now agriculture and livestock-producing are balanced by refining and manufacturing operations. Edmonton is the originating terminus of 5 pipelines transporting Alberta crude oil and natural gas to eastern Canada and the U. S. The city is located on a transcontinental railroad, a new trans-Canada highway through the all-weather Yellowhead Pass, and is linked north and south via the Alaska Highway.

The city's population doubled in the decade 1950-1960. Now, with a population of 420,000, its 5-year growth rate is the fastest in Canada. Twenty-story towers

have become commonplace and current construction is highlighted by an office structure reaching to 40 stories.

Edmonton boasts a 2,700-seat auditorium, new $2,000,000 art gallery, new provincial Museum and Archives, new $5,000,000 Centennial Library, its own symphony orchestra and many live stage production groups.

Points of interest include the Alberta Game Farm, Storyland Valley Zoo, Canada's first public planetarium, and the University of Alberta.

In July the city relives the 1898 Yukon gold rush during "Klondike Days" as the 89-year-old Edmonton Exhibition is now known. Edmonton's amateur athletic teams have established an enviable record dating from the international champion Grads, a girls' basketball team that won 502 games and lost 20 between 1915 and 1940. The Superiors (1933) and the Mer-

cury (1950) hockey teams won world titles and the Mercury team (1952) won an Olympic title.

The Eskimos of the Canadian Football League are the sole professional sports organization, but Canada's largest motor sports complex is Edmonton's Speedway Park, site of many international races.

Specialized information about Edmonton is obtainable through Leo LeClerc, Industrial Development Coordinator, City Hall, Edmonton, Alberta.

## Calgary, Canada

The World Almanac is sponsored in the Calgary and southern Alberta area by The Calgary Albertan, 830 Tenth Ave., S.W., Calgary 3, Alberta; telephone (403) 263-7730; founded April 10, 1902; circulation 34,472; publisher, G. Max Bell; general manager, Frank McCool; managing editor, David Humphries; business manager, Al Vogt.

Calgary, one of Canada's highest cities (elevation: 3,440 feet) lies at the foothills of the Rocky Mountains, 180 miles south of Edmonton and 150 miles north of the Montana-Alberta border. The city began as a Mounted Police outpost and as early as 1885, when the railway arrived, it had a population of 1,800. The city now encompasses an area of 155.8 square miles with a population of 360,000. Its growth rate of 4.8% is the fastest in Canada in the latest 12-month census period.

Calgary became the trading center for southern Alberta in the early days and continues to hold a wholesale and manufacturing function. Oil was discovered in 1914 at Turner Valley, just south of the city and 400 firms directly connected with the oil industry have headquarters in Calgary. Although ninth in population, the city is fifth in bank clearings. Its industry includes oil refineries, chemical, fertilizer and supply industries and the older agricultural industries. Shipment of goods reaches $375,000,000 annually. Calgary is served by 5 airlines and two railroads.

The city's location close to the mountains (resulting in "chinook" winds that can provide pleasant spring-like interludes in the middle of a prairie winter) and its connection through history to the old west attract tourists from all parts of the continent. The civic symbol, the white cowboy hat, is an outgrowth of the Calgary Stampede, held each July. The city's motto is "Onward."

Calgary has a 2,700-seat auditorium, a gift of the province during Alberta's Jubilee year; the provincial government Glenbow Museum, Allied Arts Center, a Centennial Planetarium, symphony orchestra and live theatre. Attractions to visitors center on the western theme. Heritage Park reconstructs the early days; at the Horseman's Hall of Fame lifelike figures recall western historical events; and at the Calgary Zoo and Natural History Park life-size dinosaurs do battle. Happy Valley, a 460-acre park, is Canada's largest man-made recreation area. The 626-ft. rotating Husky Tower provides a panoramic view of the city with room for 200 for dining and 300 in its observation area. The University of Calgary has 6,000 students.

Every active sport is displayed in the city and newly-constructed facilities for hockey, football and curling rank with the finest in the nation. The professional Stampeders of the Canadian Football League often draw capacity crowds.

Assistance in locating industrial information is provided by Ken Ford, Industrial Coordination, City Hall, Calgary, Alberta.

## Hartford, Connecticut

The World Almanac is sponsored in the Hartford area by the Hartford Times, 10 Prospect St., Hartford, Conn. 06101; telephone (203) 249-8211; founded 1817 by Frederick D. Bolles and John M. Niles; circulation 145,000; general manager, Robert R. Eckert; editor, Stuart A. Dunham; Pulitzer Citation as one of Gannett Newspapers, Pulitzer Prize to staff member; major community projects included series on education, housing, urban renewal.

Hartford, capital and most populated city (165,000 residents) of Connecticut—core city of the Capitol Region (Greater Hartford) of 28 surrounding towns—is located generally in the center of the state midway between New York City and Boston via highway, rail or air, at the head of navigation on the Connecticut River 50 miles inland from Long Island Sound. Population of Capitol Region: 647,000.

First settlers were the Dutch, who erected a fort (1633) at the present site of Hartford, and in 1636 the Rev. Thomas Hooker and a company of settlers journeyed overland from Newtown (Cambridge), Mass., founded the city. Hooker and other leaders adopted the "Fundamental Orders" (1638-1639) which historian John Fiske called "the first written constitution known to history that created a government. . . ."

Hartford has a council-manager form of government, adopted by the voters and approved by the General Assembly (1947).

Hartford, the center of the insurance industry, is known as "The Insurance City" with 15 insurance companies headquartered in and around the city, and employing 26,000 locally. Combined assets of all the insurance firms: over $25 billion. Well-known companies include The Travelers Insurance Companies, Connecticut General, Aetna Life & Casualty and the Hartford Insurance Group.

Greater Hartford's second major industry is aircraft engines: East Hartford is home office of United Aircraft Corp., one of world's largest aircraft firms.

Rail passenger and freight service is provided by the New York, New Haven and Hartford Railroad, with direct service to New York and connections at Springfield to Boston or the West. High-speed service is expected soon.

The Hartford area, and many sections of the state, are serviced by Bradley International Airport in Windsor Locks, 20 minutes by car from Hartford on Interstate 91. The airport is served by 7 scheduled passenger and cargo carriers and one all-cargo carrier. Direct airline service is available from Bradley to 50 major cities in the U. S. International service is available, with passenger service direct to London; other cities for export cargo. Expansion of the airport is presently underway.

Hartford is the hub of a trunk-line highway network. And more than 3,000,000 tons of cargo, mainly fuels, are now carried annually by barge or tanker via the 15-foot-deep channel of the Connecticut River to Hartford and Wethersfield.

Hartford is now being redeveloped in what Architectural Forum has called, "one of the best-rounded renewal examples yet attempted in the United States." An example is the multi-million dollar Constitution Plaza, a 15-acre tract in the

center of the city which once contained deteriorated residential and commercial properties. The entire renewal package is expected to total $165,000,000 over 20 years. In 1968, several insurance and other companies planned new buildings in the Trumbull St. Redevelopment area, where a civic center with an arena is to be developed.

Educational and cultural institutions include Trinity College, the University of Hartford, Rensselaer Polytechnic Institute, St. Joseph College and, at nearby Middletown, Wesleyan University; the Wadsworth Atheneum is the oldest and one of the best-known public art museums in America. Mark Twain's House, where Samuel Clemens wrote "Tom Sawyer," "Huckleberry Finn" and "A Connecticut Yankee" is now a museum. The city also is the home of the Hartford Symphony Orchestra, the Connecticut Opera Association and the Hartford Stage Company, a resident professional theater.

Information on the city and its surrounding towns may be obtained from the Greater Hartford Chamber of Commerce, 250 Constitution Plaza, Hartford, Conn. 06103 or from the Mayor or City Manager, City Hall, Hartford, Conn. 06101.

# Honolulu, Hawaii

The World Almanac is sponsored in Honolulu by The Honolulu Advertiser, P. O. Box 3110, Honolulu, Hawaii 96802; telephone 52-977; founded July 2, 1856, as the Pacific Commercial Advertiser by Henry M. Whitney; circulation 66,499 mornings, 156,123 Sunday; president and publisher, Thurston Twigg-Smith; editor George Chaplin; managing editor, Buck Buchwach; major awards received from Alicia Patterson Fund, American Medical Association, Overseas Press Club of America, National Headliners Club and J. C. Penney-University of Missouri.

Honolulu (Hawaiian for "sheltered bay") was a small native Hawaiian village called Waikiki when first visited by two British ships in 1786, eight years after Capt. James Cook discovered the Hawaiian Islands. Today, with nearly 400,000 inhabitants, it is the capital of Hawaii.

The City and County of Honolulu has a total population of about 650,000 and covers all 595 square miles of Oahu, an island traversed by two rugged parallel mountain ranges. The city itself occupies 20 miles of Oahu's southeast coast—from Pearl Harbor to Koko Head—and its residential subdivisions reach back through lush fingerlike valleys and climb the ridges of the Koolau Range at its back. The combined city-county has a strong-mayor form of government, with an elected 9-member city council.

In the early 19th century, Honolulu became a favored port for whaling ships in the Pacific. Shortly after 1900 the U. S. Navy built its famous base at Pearl Harbor, now headquarters of the U. S. Pacific Fleet. Honolulu is the only American city to have been bombarded in modern times —when Japan launched its surprise attack on Pearl Harbor Dec. 7, 1941.

Tourism is rapidly becoming the dominant industry in Honolulu; the city greeted more than 1,000,000 visitors in 1967. The other big industries are sugar and pineapple (there are two large pineapple canneries in the city). The military is also big business in Honolulu, with facilities for all branches of the service, the largest being Pearl Harbor Naval Base and Hickam Air Force Base.

The city has become a business and financial center for the Pacific Basin; one of its major corporations does international construction work, another operates a large steamship line. Smaller industries include manufacturing of wooden bowls, serving trays and furniture from locally grown monkeypod and koa woods, and sewing of brightly colored Hawaiian-print shirts and dresses.

The University of Hawaii enrolls over 17,000 students and is especially noted for its departments in marine biology and tropical agriculture. Students from half-way around the world attend the East-West Center, an institution of higher learning co-sponsored by the university and the U. S. State Department. Other 4-year colleges are Chaminade College, operated by the Catholic Church, and the Church College of Hawaii, run by the Church of Jesus Christ of Latter-day Saints (Mormon).

The Bernice Pauahi Bishop Museum houses artifacts from throughout the Pacific and is a center of archaeological study of Hawaii. Art objects from all over the world are on display at the Honolulu Academy of Arts. The city has a 70-member symphony orchestra, a spring opera festival and several community theater groups. Other cultural institutions include Sea Life Park and the Waikiki Aquarium, displaying local marine life; Hawaiian Paradise Park, a bird sanctuary; and the Polynesian Cultural Center and Ulu Mau Village, both live re-creations of ancient Polynesian and Hawaiian culture.

The usual "outside" image of Honolulu is of Waikiki Beach and its famous view of Diamond Head. Waikiki, of course, is the hub of the tourist and convention industry; its high-rise hotels are mushrooming so fast the City Council has had to set limits to prevent them from blotting out Diamond Head altogether. But Honolulu's main attraction is a combination of its Polynesian heritage, cloud-topped majestic mountains, palm-fringed beaches along the deep-blue Pacific, and the most enjoyable sunny weather anywhere. Daytime temperatures average in the high 80s in summer, low 80s in winter; nighttime temperatures usually range 10 to 15 degrees lower. There is year-round surfing, swimming and fishing.

Three major U. S. airlines serve Honolulu from the West Coast, and two additional ones have been recommended. Foreign airlines connect Hawaii directly with most countries around the Pacific. Two steamship lines provide regular passenger service from the West Coast.

Most of Honolulu's incoming and outgoing cargo travels by ship, but airlines are winning an increasing share of the business. The airlines' share is expected to jump tremendously when "jumbo jets" begin flying in 1970.

There is bus service to most parts of the city, but outlying suburbs and small towns on Oahu have no public transportation. Studies are underway for a possible subway or other fixed-rail mass-transit system to relieve Honolulu's growing traffic congestion. New freeways connect the city with its suburbs, and tunnels carry two four-lane highways through the Koolau Range to the communities of Windward Oahu.

# Houston, Texas

The World Almanac is sponsored in the Houston area by The Houston Post, 2410 Polk Ave., Houston, Texas 77001, telephone (713) CA3-3131. Founded originally in 1836, the first edition was published with The Houston Post masthead on Feb. 1, 1880. Circulation: morning—280,268, Sunday—318,984. Chairman of the board and editor, Oveta Culp Hobby; president and executive editor, William P. Hobby, Jr.; executive vice president, John C. Stetson. Major awards include Pulitzer Prize. Sponsors Houston Post Charities, Inc.

Industrial giant of the Southwest, Houston is the nation's sixth largest and fastest growing major city. Located on the upper Gulf Coast prairies, connected to the Galveston Bay by a 50-mile ship canal, it enjoys an average temperature of 68.6°.

The fine weather helps to draw more than 3,000,000 visitors and tourists each year to see such points of interest as the new growing complex of concert music halls, theaters, art centers and museums which encircle the million dollar Jones Hall for the performing arts, in downtown Houston. Houston's Alley Theatre is considered to be one of the nation's foremost repertory theaters and represented the U. S. at the Brussels World's Fair. The Houston Music Theatre is one of the most successful theaters "in the round." Houston has two wide-screen cineramas, 66 movie theaters, and a symphony of 90 musicians conducted by Andre Previn.

The world famous Texas Medical Center represents an investment of more than $125,000,000 in 10 major hospitals and clinics, 3 medical schools, and 3 research institutes where many notable heart and organ transplants have been reported. The Astrodome, one of America's largest enclosed sports stadiums, is the home of the National League Astros baseball team, the American Football League Houston Oilers, Houston Stars soccer team, and the University of Houston football team, the Cougars, making Houston a sports center.

The Museum of Fine Arts houses a permanent collection valued at $6,000,000 plus 23 major art institutes. Twenty-two mi. from the downtown area is the Manned Spacecraft Center, controller of space orbit communications, which gives Houston its nickname, "Space City, U.S.A." A $250,000,000 complex, the installation is the center of astronaut training, equipment testing and flight control for the Project Apollo moon landings.

The San Jacinto Monument and Museum are on the San Jacinto Battleground. This 460-acre state park, 22 mi. east of Houston, honors the 910 Americans led by Gen. Sam Houston who routed Mexican forces of more than 1,200 under Gen. Santa Anna, April 21, 1836. The museum depicts the region's history from the early Indian civilization to Texas, a State in the Union.

Houston ranks first in the nation as a refinery center, housing 9 refineries which convert 830,000 bbl. of crude oil daily into gasoline and other products; first in the manufacture and distribution of petroleum equipment, and first in pipeline transmission with 14 major companies operating 83,000 mi. of natural gas pipelines.

Houston has the third largest seaport in the country, two major airports, the William P. Hobby Airport and the International Airport, and ranks third in the number of private aircraft. Other major industries are chemicals and petrochemicals, food products, primary and fabricated metals, lumber and wood products, synthetic rubber and plastics, electronic instruments, printing, and publishing. Nearly 60% of total U. S. sulphur is produced within 250 mi. of Houston.

To transport Houston's goods there are 23 airlines, 131 steamship lines, 6 major rail systems, 34 truck lines and 6 bus lines. In 1968, Houston's new International Airport handled 200 arrivals and departures daily. An elaborate 245-mi. inner and outer loop freeway system expedites traffic.

Population of the city of Houston is estimated at 1,187,000—up 26% from the 1960 Census. The metropolitan area (1,839,-000) is up 30% and is one of the fastest growing major metropolitan areas. Its average growth is 1,000 a week.

In 1966, retail sales for the metropolitan area increased 46% over 1960 to $2.8 billion, while wholesale sales have increased 25% to $5.3 billion. It is estimated that the annual manufacturing payroll for Houston is $1 billion. Through industrial expansion and diversification, Houston has become the largest industrial and manufacturing center in the South and Southwest.

The University of Houston has the largest of Houston's 14 college campuses. Houston is also the seat of the widely known Rice University.

The Houston metropolitan area is also an important agricultural center. The 13-county region, with less than 5% of the state's land area, receives approximately 7% of the state's farm cash income. Rice, grain, sorghum, and cattle are highly important in the farm picture of the area. The region produces about 86% of the state's rice, nearly 30% of the nation's total production, and contains the top cattle producing county in Texas. More than 50% of the export tonnage of the Port of Houston is agricultural.

The Houston region has extraordinary supplies of oil, gas, sulphur, salt, lime, timber, industrial soil, sea water, and fresh water. The value of annual mineral production in the Houston area is approximately $457,000,000.

Houston has a mayor-council form of government with the mayor and 8 councilmen serving as the legislative body. These 9 officials and the city controller are elected for 2-year concurrent terms.

# Indianapolis, Indiana

The World Almanac is sponsored in the Indianapolis area by the Indianapolis Star and the Indianapolis News, 307 N. Pennsylvania St., Indianapolis, Ind. 46206; telephone (317) 633-1240; News founded 1869 by John H. Holliday, Star 1903 by George F. McCulloch; circulation Star daily 229,954, Sunday 378,817, News 197,111; president & publisher, Eugene C. Pulliam; asst. publisher, Eugene S. Pulliam; Star editor, Jameson G. Campaigne; News editor, M. Stanton Evans; major awards include Pulitzer Prize to News, National Headliners first prize to Star; Star sponsors annual Indiana-Kentucky all-star basketball game, News sponsors Women's Anti-Crime Crusade, Junior Olympics.

Indianapolis, capital and largest city in Indiana, is located near the center of the state at the junction of White River and Fall Creek. Most early settlers came from Connersville 60 miles to the southeast, including George Pogue, who arrived first in 1819, and others who formed the first settlement in 1820. It was selected as the state capital in 1821 because of its central location and was named Indianapolis.

The city was laid out by Alexander Ralston, who earlier had assisted Major L'Enfant in laying out Washington, D. C. Because it was not on a navigable waterway, growth of Indianapolis was slow until the arrival of the first railroad in 1847 started its development as a major rail center. Today the city has a population of 519,400, with 1,049,000 in its metropolitan statistical area (estimated by Sales Management). It is governed by a mayor and city council.

Indianapolis is an industrial and trade center with more than 1,100 diversified plants turning out products valued at $1.362 billion annually (1963 Bureau of Census). Its leading industries are transportation equipment ($374,392,000 annually), chemicals and allied products ($200,-154,000) and electrical machinery ($162,-560,000). Major firms with headquarters in Indianapolis include Allison Division of General Motors Corp., Eli Lilly & Co., P. R. Mallory & Co., Inc., and the Home Instruments Division of Radio Corporation of America. Western Electric Co. makes most of the nation's telephones in its Indianapolis plant. The U. S. Army Finance Center at Ft. Benjamin Harrison employs 5,600 and handles the payroll for the entire Army. Retail sales in Indianapolis total $1.361 billion annually and $1.755 billion in the metropolitan statistical area.

The city is served by 5 railroads, 6 major airlines and 3 commuter airlines, 4 interstate bus lines and more than 100 truck lines. There are 144 scheduled airline arrivals and departures daily, and the city is the hub of four interstate highways.

Indianapolis is in an era of great progress. Major downtown projects underway include a 37-story Indiana National Bank Building which will be the tallest in the state and a 20-story Hilton Hotel, both to be completed in 1969. Preliminary work has begun on a new $10,000,000 Federal Building and an $18,000,000 convention-exposition center. A multi-million-dollar expansion of the Indiana University regional complex will make it a four-year campus, and Purdue University also plans to expand its regional center. On the north side of the city a new $10,000,000 art center is under construction.

Passenger facilities at Weir Cook Municipal Airport have been doubled in the last year by a $6,500,000 expansion program, and construction is now underway on a six-story administration building and other facilities. Some 3,200 housing units for low income and elderly persons are being completed, and more are planned. Most of the city's traffic problems will be solved with the completion of an inner loop and outer loop of expressways.

Monument Circle in the center of downtown has as its apex the Soldiers & Sailors Monument, 284½ feet tall, built in 1901. Five-block-long Memorial Plaza on the northern edge of downtown includes the World War Memorial and American Legion National Headquarters.

Indianapolis is the home of Butler University, on the campus of which was completed in 1963 a new center for the performing arts, Clowes Memorial Hall. This is headquarters for the Indianapolis Symphony Orchestra. The city also is the home of Indiana Central College, Marian College and Indiana University Medical Center.

The Indianapolis Indians baseball team plays in the Pacific Coast League, and the Indiana Pacers are in the American Basketball Association. The "500" Festival is an annual series of events in conjunction with the Indianapolis 500-Mile Race on Memorial Day.

# Kansas City, Missouri

The World Almanac is sponsored in the Kansas City area by the Kansas City Star, 1729 Grand Ave., Kansas City, Mo. 64108; telephone (816) HA1-1200; founded 1880 by William Rockhill Nelson; circulation evening 332,364, morning 340,013, Sunday 404,547; president, Richard B. Fowler; executive v.p., Paul V. Miner; gen. mgr., Frank McKinney; editor, W. W. Baker; executive editor, Cruise Palmer.

Its location at the confluence of the Missouri and Kansas Rivers amid the agricultural lands of the Middle West was important in the founding and development of Kansas City, which had a population of 599,100 in July, 1968 (City Plan Commission estimate). Its area of 316.3 sq. mi. is one of the nation's largest.

The beginnings of Kansas City can be traced to the establishment by French trappers of a trading post at the merging of the rivers about 1826. It became an important trade and transportation center as the overland routes of the Oregon and Santa Fe Trails spread westward. As agricultural production boomed, it became an important market and distribution center for crops from throughout the Middle West. Presently Kansas City is a leading hard wheat center, stocker and feeder market, and is among the top 5 cities in flour production, grain elevator capacity and meat packing. Its stockyards are among the nation's busiest.

Growing steadily as a market, Kansas City became important in transportation. It remains one of the busiest rail centers. Twelve railroad trunk lines had 108 arriving and 103 departing freight trains and 74 passenger trains daily in 1966.

The city's air facilities in 1966 handled nearly 3,400,000 persons with 8 airlines and 320 scheduled daily flights. Approval of $150,000,000 in revenue bonds in December, 1966, for construction of the Kansas City International Airport is expected to place the city among world leaders as an airline center with capacity for supersonic jumbo jets. More than 9,300 trucks from 197 truck lines serve the city over a growing network of interstate roadways. Four barge companies continue barge operation on the rivers.

Kansas City has emerged as an industrial, as well as an agricultural leader. Second in nation in car and truck assembly with large Ford and General Motors plants, the city is first in production of vending machines and sixth in production of wearing apparel. National firms with headquarters in Kansas City include Hallmark Cards, Interstate Bakeries, Farmland Industries, Panhandle Eastern Pipeline company, H. D. Lee company, Western Auto and Nelly Don. Trans World Airlines has maintenance and training headquarters, with plans for a multi-million dollar training center announced in July, 1967. Top employers include the U. S. Government, General Motors, TWA, Bendix, Western Electric, and Ford. A newly-constructed Federal office building houses 20,000 workers. A new state office building is now open. Plans are being studied for a civic plaza in the area of City Hall, County Courthouse, and Federal Buildings, including new facilities for police and municipal courts.

Total retail sales in 1967 were $311,550,-889. In January, 1967, Hallmark announced

plans to convert 85 acres just south of the downtown district into a model urban community. Several other plans have emerged for revitalization of the downtown district. Country Club Plaza was one of the first shopping centers.

More than 100 parks cover 5,345 acres, including Swope Park, second largest in the nation. Swope Park houses one of the few remaining free zoos in the country. Kansas City's boulevard and parkway system is a subject of pride.

Cultural activities include the Starlight Theater, the country's second largest outdoor theater; Kansas City Philharmonic; Lyric Theater; the William Rockhill Nelson Gallery of Art and Mary Atkins Museum of Fine Arts, among 6 top American museums with furnishings and displays valued at more than $25,000,000 including third largest Oriental collection outside China; and the Performing Arts Foundation, a group formed in 1965 to present festival events of all arts.

The American Royal Livestock and Horse Show each fall attracts entries from throughout the country. Kansas City is the home of the Chiefs of the American Football League, Royals of American Baseball League, Blues of Central Hockey League and K. C. Spurs of North American Soccer League.

Kansas City's government is manager-council form. The 29-story city hall was, when built, highest in the world.

A distinguished citizen of the area is Harry S. Truman, 33rd President of the United States, who was born in Lamar, Mo., and lives in Independence, a suburb.

The University of Missouri at Kansas City, Rockhurst College, Kansas City Institute of Art, and the University of Kansas Medical Center are in the metropolitan area. Within commuting distance are the University of Kansas, Park College, William Jewell College, and Central Missouri State College. Linda Hall Library of Science and Technology on the U. M. K. C. campus is one of the largest privately endowed technical reference libraries with more than 375,000 volumes and 11,500 current scientific journals. The Truman Library in Independence contains primary research material from the Truman Administration.

# Knoxville, Tennessee

The World Almanac is sponsored in the Knoxville area by The Knoxville News-Sentinel, 204-208 West Church Avenue, Knoxville, Tenn. 37901; telephone (615) 523-3131; Sentinel founded in 1886 by John T. Hearn, News in 1921 by Scripps-Howard Newspapers, Sentinel purchased by Scripps-Howard in 1926 and combined with News; circulation 107,390 daily and 157,342 Sunday; editor, Ralph L. Millett Jr.; managing editor, C. W. Orcutt; public service projects include Empty Stocking Fund, General Knox Mercy Fund, Southern Appalachian Spelling Bee and Science Fair.

Knoxville is an important commercial and manufacturing center in an area noted for its scenic beauty. Its first settler was James White, who came to the site in 1786, built a small fort and planted a turnip patch in the area of what now is the First Presbyterian Church Cemetery.

It became a city in 1791 and was designated capital of the Territory South of the Ohio River in 1792. Blount Mansion, home of the territorial governor, William Blount, still stands and is preserved as a national monument. It is the city's major historic visitor attraction and is believed to be the first frame house built west of the Allegheny Mountains. When Tennessee became a state in 1796, Knoxville was its first capital.

The city has an estimated population of 185,000 and it is the center of a 3-county metropolitan area of about 400,000.

The Holston and French Broad Rivers join immediately east of the city to form the Tennessee, which has a 9-foot channel linking Knoxville with the Ohio and Mississippi Rivers and the Inland Waterway System.

The administrative headquarters of the Tennessee Valley Authority is at Knoxville, and the city is situated on TVA's Fort Loudoun Lake, impounded by a TVA dam 53 river miles downstream. The city is within less than an hour's drive of 5 other major TVA lakes.

Situated near the lakes and between two mountain ranges of exceptional beauty, Knoxville and some of the smaller cities in the area thrive on tourist business. Great Smoky Mountains National Park, with 600 miles of hiking trails and nearly that many miles of productive trout streams, along with an exceptional variety of plant life, is 40 miles southeast of Knoxville. About 40 miles westward are the Cumberland Mountains, increasing in popularity with visitors.

Knoxville is in the heart of the Southern Appalachian dogwood region, and is the scene each April of the Dogwood Arts Festival, a 10-day event featuring about 45 miles of Dogwood Trails of outstanding beauty, along with hundreds of cultural and sports events.

The major manufacturing industry in Knoxville proper is clothing. Standard Knitting Mills, established in 1900, is the leader in the field. It employs about 3,000 persons and is the largest manufacturer of knitted clothing under one roof in the nation. Levi Strauss & Co., Palm Beach Co. and Apparel Corp. of America also have Knoxville clothing plants. Dempster Brothers, one of the nation's leaders in manufacturing of garbage collection equipment, was established in Knoxville in 1933. It employs about 775.

By far the biggest employer in the Knoxville area is Union Carbide Corp.'s Nuclear Division, at Oak Ridge, about 20 miles west of Knoxville. Carbide, which operates the Atomic Energy Commission's nuclear plants at Oak Ridge, employs more than 12,800. All told, nearly 15,000 are employed in AEC-related work at Oak Ridge.

Many Oak Ridge workers are Knoxville residents. The same is true of many workers at Aluminum Co. of America's plant at Alcoa, about 15 miles south of Knoxville. ALCOA, with about 6,800 employees, is the second largest employer.

Two rail lines, 5 airlines, two bus lines and 23 motor freight carriers serve Knoxville. Interstate Highways I-40 and I-75 intersect in the heart of the city; I-40 and I-81 intersect several mi. east of the city.

The Downtown Knoxville Association was formed in 1957 to rejuvenate the city's business district. One of its outstanding projects was the Market Mall, completed in 1961. The Mall, which replaced an old market house, has trees, flowers and fountains; it is flanked by stores with modernistic masonry sidewalk roofs which run the length of the Mall. At the north end is a covered area where vendors sell home-grown flowers and vegetables. The Mall was a joint project of the Association and the city.

One of the cultural and entertainment centers of the city is the James White Memorial Auditorium-Coliseum, opened in 1961. The six-story structure covers two and a half acres. The auditorium seats 2,536 and the coliseum 7,250. A Holiday on Ice troupe puts together a new show each year on the coliseum ice.

Knoxville in 1968 became the first of Tennessee's 4 major cities to provide both primary and secondary treatment for its sewage. Three treatment plants remove from 85 to 98% of suspended solids and biochemical oxygen demand from the sewage before the effluent is discharged into Fort Loudoun Lake.

# Los Angeles, California

The World Almanac is sponsored in the Los Angeles area by the Los Angeles Herald-Examiner, 1111 S. Broadway, Los Angeles, Calif. 90054; telephone (213) 748-4141; founded Mar. 27, 1871; circulation daily 623,474; Sunday 650,991; publisher, George R. Hearst, Jr.; managing editor, Donald Goodenow; general manager, George W. Sjostrom; sponsors annually American History Awards, Youth Forum, Bill of Rights Essay Contest, Carrierboy Scholarship Award, Junior Diplomat Program, etc.

When Juan Rodriguez Cabrillo, the Spanish explorer, anchored his caravel in Los Angeles Harbor in 1542, he wasn't too impressed. Looking over the broad mud flats, he saw the smoke of many primitive Indian fires drifting over the steep slopes and wide bay. He named the harbor the Bay of Smokes and Fires and sailed on.

Things hadn't changed much when on Sept. 4, 1781, Father Junipero Serra and Don Felipe de Neve, Spanish governor of California, founded a pueblo alongside the Indian village of Yang-na. They named it El Pueblo de Nuestra Senora la Reina de Los Angeles de Porciuncula (the City of Our Lady the Queen of the Angels of Porciuncula). The name was actually bigger than the city as 44 settlers built small adobe houses around a plaza by the Porciuncula River.

Until 1817, Los Angeles alternated with Monterey as the capital of the Mexican territory of Alta California. On Mar. 9, 1842, the first gold discovery in California was made at Placerita Canyon, in the northern part of Los Angeles County, 6 years before the famous strike was made at Sutter's Mill.

In 1846, the city was captured in a bloodless battle by U. S. Navy Commodore R. F. Stockton.

Today, the City of Los Angeles has an estimated population of nearly 3,000,000 and covers 458.2 square miles. It is the seat of Los Angeles County, which has a population of 7,087,667 and extends for 4,071 sq. mi., according to Chamber of Commerce surveys.

The City of Los Angeles was incorporated Apr. 4, 1850, and today is governed by a Mayor, 15-member Council, and commissions as provided for by a charter effective July 1, 1925. The Mayor, Council, City Controller and City Attorney are elected every 4 years. Members of commissions are appointed by the Mayor, subject to City Council approval.

As the city grew, its name was shortened to Los Angeles. Its growth came about for many reasons: the driving of the golden spike at Southern Pacific's Lang Station in Soledad Canyon Sept. 5, 1876, connecting Los Angeles by rail with the energetic East; the beginning of the greatest man-made harbor in the world at San Pedro Bay in 1899; the first complete motion picture in the city manufactured in 1908 in a rented house at Eighth and Olive Streets; only dry subtropical climate in North America with mild, sunny winter days and rainless summer days with cool nights; the annual average rainfall of 14.68 inches and the average mean temperature of 64.4 degrees, and proximity to the ocean, mountains and desert.

The smoky harbor dismissed with a shrug 426 years ago at San Pedro is today known as "The Cargo Capital of the West." General cargo for the 1965-66 fiscal year exceeded the 7,300,000-ton mark and total tonnage handled was a record 26,-293,560 tons. Ships of 30 nations, along with U. S. flagships, made 3,964 port calls with steel mill products, molasses, pipes, tubing, bananas, frozen fish and copra.

In the next 20 years, the new harbor headquarters on Terminal Island will oversee the development of 850 acres of land for 75 new deep-water berths for the Port of Los Angeles. The future Los Angeles World Trade Center also will be located on Terminal Island.

The economy of Los Angeles is diversified, composed of a variety of enterprises in agriculture, manufacturing, trade, fishing, mining, entertaining and other services. Los Angeles has a higher proportion of small business than any other large metropolitan area yet is the most popular location west of Chicago for branch plants as well as management headquarters for nationally-recognized companies. Major growth industries are electrical machinery and electronics, ordnance, instruments, rubber, petroleum refining, printing and publishing, furniture and chemicals.

The Greater Los Angeles area has more savings and loan holding companies than any other area of the United States. It is an important insurance center, housing 90 companies with home offices.

Sales of $3.4 billion were recorded in 1963 for the more than 600 electronics firms in the area. Los Angeles is the sportswear center of the nation and the second largest garment manufacturing center in the world. It ranks as one of the nation's leading fishing ports in both volume and value.

The Los Angeles Metropolitan Area ranks third in the nation as a banking center with a total of 860 banks and branches with deposits of over $13 billion. Retail sales currently total over $12 billion for the area and by 1970, the Chamber of Commerce estimates that retail sales should exceed $13,250,000,000.

Los Angeles is a city on wheels. There are over 3,400,000 automobiles registered in the Los Angeles Metropolitan Area, a car for every 2.2 persons, a higher ratio than any other major city in the world.

The area has 3 transcontinental railway systems; 22 certificated air carriers, carrying 18,000,000 passengers a year; 111 steamship lines and agencies with 5,290 ships carrying more than 37,000,000 tons of cargo annually, and 6 major passenger bus lines. Los Angeles ranks as the West's largest trucking center.

Each day 1,800 planes arrive and depart at the Los Angeles International Airport. Since the first movie made in Los Angeles in 1908, Los Angeles has become the film capital of the world. Hollywood was annexed to the city in 1910 and a recent report showed 617 firms engaged in the production, distribution and service of motion pictures, including those made for television. Many of the nation's top television shows originate from Hollywood studios.

Los Angeles leads the nation in the

manufacture of aircraft and parts. Since Galbraith Rodgers, completing the first transcontinental flight, landed at nearby Pasadena on Nov. 5, 1911, and the first round-the-world flight started from Santa Monica on Mar. 17, 1924, the area has been an aviation center.

Added to the natural recreational advantages of ocean, desert and mountains within an hour's drive, Los Angeles residents enjoy such man-made facilities as the Hollywood Bowl, the Huntington Library and Art Museum, the new Music Center, Griffith Park Planetarium, the Los Angeles Museum of History, Science and Art; Mt. Wilson Observatory, Pasadena's Rose Bowl, Marineland, Disneyland, Knott's Berry Farm, the new zoo in Griffith Park, and Pacific Ocean Park.

The Los Angeles Dodgers and Los Angeles Lakers keep baseball and basketball fans busy, while the Los Angeles Rams football team attracts capacity crowds.

Los Angeles County has such leading higher schools of learning as the California Institute of Technology, Loyola University, Occidental College, Pomona College, the University of California at Los Angeles, the University of Southern California, Whittier College, and 27 others.

Los Angeles has 154 parks totaling 9,875 acres, and 129 recreation centers.

The County of Los Angeles was established Feb. 18, 1850, and was one of California's original 27 counties. The county has a governing body consisting of a 5-member Board of Supervisors, each elected for a 4-year term. With a population in excess of 7,000,000, greater than that of any other county in the nation and exceeded by only 7 states, Los Angeles County is 800 square miles larger than the combined areas of the States of Delaware and Rhode Island.

## Louisville, Kentucky

Though Louisville is steeped in the leisurely traditions of the South, its location on the Ohio River makes it a major industrial and distributing center and a key city in the accelerating industrialization of the Southern states. The city was founded by the explorer George Rogers Clark, who in 1779 established a small community which would later be a base of supply for his exploration of the Northwest. In 1780, the city was given its name by the Virginia Legislature, which formally established the town, naming it after King Louis XVI of France.

The opening of the Louisville and Portland Canal in 1830 to allow river boats to circumvent the 25-ft. falls in the Ohio River, led to a rapid growth of the city. Today, Louisville is Kentucky's largest city with an estimated metropolitan area population of 775,000 in 1966.

Louisville is probably most famous as the site of the Kentucky Derby, which is held the first Saturday in May at Churchill Downs. The "Run for the Roses," as the race is often called, is traditionally preceded by the playing of "My Old Kentucky Home" and the winner is draped in a blanket of roses. The race has been held annually since 1875.

The city is one of the largest tobacco manufacturing centers in the world, and the counties of Louisville and Jefferson produce about 25% of all the liquor distilled in the country.

One of the largest manufacturing plants in Louisville is General Electric's Appliance Park, with 4,000,000 sq. ft. of space located on a 1,000-acre site.

The "Louisville Slugger," long a favorite bat with American youngsters and professional baseball players, is manufactured here by Hillerich & Bradsby Co., which has a Museum of Bats open to the public. The American Printing House for the Blind, the largest publishing company in the world producing Braille books and magazines as well as talking books, is also open to the public.

In addition to places of historic interest, such as the site of Ft. Nelson and the grave of George Rogers Clark in Cave Hill Cemetery, the visitor to Louisville will find many other attractions.

There are many municipal parks, Shawnee, Seneca, Cherokee and Iroquois being the largest. The J. B. Speed Art Museum houses outstanding collections of 19th century sculpture, paintings, tapestries and other art objects as well as paintings of American Indians by Kentucky artists. The University of Louisville, founded in 1798 and one of America's oldest municipal universities, has on its campus the Rauch Memorial Planetarium, which is open to the public at a nominal charge.

The Kentucky Fair and Exhibition Center, covering 357 acres, has a stadium which can seat some 20,000 people and is the site of the Kentucky State Fair and Horse Show usually held the last week in August.

## Memphis, Tennessee

The World Almanac is sponsored in the Memphis area by the Memphis Press-Scimitar, 495 Union Ave., Memphis, Tenn. 38101; telephone (901) 526-2141; Scimitar founded 1880 by G. P. M. Turner, Press 1906 by Scripps-McRae League, predecessor of Scripps-Howard Newspapers; circulation 133,644; editor, Charles H. Schneider; managing editor, Ed. Ray; associate editor, J. Z. Howard; major public service projects include Goodfellows Christmas Fund and Cynthia Milk Fund.

Memphis is on a bluff on the east bank of the Mississippi River, in the southwest corner of Tennessee. The city occupies 179 sq. mi. and is the center of a metropolitan area that includes large parts of Shelby County, Tenn., DeSoto County, Miss., and Crittenden County, Ark. There are 3 bridges across the Mississippi at Memphis —one highway bridge and two railroad bridges. A new 6-lane highway bridge is under construction and will be part of the Federal Interstate highway network.

The site of Memphis is a point where DeSoto stopped in 1541 when he discovered the Mississippi River. In 1797 a U. S. military post, Fort Adams, was established at the site of Memphis. In 1801 Fort Pickering was built, and a section of the city where the fort stood near the river now bears that name. In 1818 the U. S. purchased West Tennessee, including the Memphis site, from the Chickasaw Indians, and settlement of the area began. The town of Memphis was laid out in 1819 by owners of land grants, and incorporated in 1826. The following year Marcus B. Winchester was elected the first mayor.

A major yellow fever epidemic struck in 1878 and the city was nearly depopulated. The following year it surrendered its charter and became a taxing district. But by 1890 population was up to 64,589 and by 1900 to 102,320.

Latest population count for the city is 536,585, according to a special census by the U. S. Bureau of Census made in 1967. Population of Shelby County, which includes Memphis, is estimated at 772,200

and for the metropolitan area at 829,000, both by the Memphis Area Chamber of Commerce.

Memphis has a mayor-council form of government.

The city is the center of an important trade area ranging over much of Tennessee, Arkansas, and Mississippi and parts of Missouri and Alabama.

Memphis is the world's largest hardwood lumber center, and consequently has manufacturing of furniture and hardwood flooring. The city is the site of the world's largest inland spot cotton market, centered along picturesque Front St., overlooking the Mississippi River. The city is the nation's 10th largest distribution center, supplying dry goods, hardware, etc., for a large area of the South. It is headquarters for Plough, Inc., world-wide drug concern founded in Memphis by Abe Plough in 1908, and also for Holiday Inns of America, Inc., the world's largest motel chain, founded in Memphis in 1952 by Kemmons Wilson.

The city is served by 9 airlines with a total of 114 arrivals and 114 departures a day at Memphis Metropolitan Airport. The city is served by 8 trunk line railroads, 89 motor freight lines and 5 barge lines. Memphis is one of the nation's largest inland river ports, having handled 8,400,000 tons of freight in 1966.

On Presidents Island, once an island in the Mississippi River but now part of the city and joined to the mainland by a causeway, a 963-acre industrial park is now 83% filled with industries. Just across the harbor from that area, the city will soon open the 6,800-acre Frank C. Pidgeon Industrial Park.

Memphis is the home of the Cotton Carnival each May. The city's picturesque Beale Street, at the south end of downtown is famous in the world of blues music; it is where W. C. Handy, the composer, lived.

Colleges and universities include Southwestern at Memphis, Memphis State University, Christian Brothers College, Siena College, LeMoyne-Owen College, University of Tennessee Medical Units, Mid-South Bible College, Southern College of Optometry, and the State Technical Institute at Memphis.

Memphis Memorial Stadium is the home of the annual Liberty Bowl football game plus Memphis State's home games. The Mid-South Coliseum, adjacent to the stadium, is the site of Memphis State's basketball games and is home of the Memphis South Stars, which is a farm team of the Minnesota North Stars and plays in the Central Hockey League.

Also adjacent are the Fairgrounds, site of the annual Mid-South Fair, and Blues Stadium, home of the Memphis Blues baseball team, which is a farm club of the New York Mets and plays in the AA Texas League.

The annual Memphis Open Golf Tournament, on the PGA tour, is held at Colonial Country Club.

The Municipal Auditorium has annual performances of New York's Metropolitan Opera, as well as regular performances of the Memphis Symphony Orchestra and many other traveling cultural attractions.

Inquiries should be addressed to Dan Dale, director of industrial development, Memphis Light, Gas and Water Division, Madison and Third Sts., or to James Pirtle, manager of Industrial Department, Memphis Area Chamber of Commerce, Memphis, Tenn. 38101.

## Mexico City, Mexico

Mexico City (Ciudad de Mexico) is the oldest and one of the largest and most beautiful cities of North America.

Set in the lofty Valley of Mexico at an altitude of 7,349 ft., nearly a mile and a half above sea level, the city is the capital of Mexico and is the political, economic, cultural and transportation hub of the nation. Population of Mexico City (1968 est.) was 3,118,059. Including the suburbs, which make up the Federal District, the population was 6,815,800.

The art and architecture of the city present a striking exhibit of the three great cultures embodied in Mexican history: that of the Aztec Indians who founded the city on islands in Lake Texcoco in 1325; that of Europe imported by the Spaniards who conquered the Aztecs in 1519, and that created by the Mexicans of today in distinctive, ultra-modern design.

Here are the remains of grim pyramids from the days when Tenochtitlan, as the Aztecs called their capital, was a city of 300,000 or more.

Here, too, are the huge, ultra-baroque Metropolitan Cathedral, the arcaded buildings and the broad avenues, studded with a profusion of monuments, which were created by the Spaniards and the descendants of both races under the influence of European styles.

Finally, here are the daring forms of modern Mexican architecture, ranging from a glass-sided, skyscraper pyramid to the towering block of a university library whose exterior walls are entirely covered by colorful mosaic murals.

Places of particular interest include: Xochimilco and its "floating gardens" and flower-decked gondolas; the National University (founded 1551) which has 90,-000 students; the National Palace with its famed Diego Rivera murals, on the site where stood the palace of Moctezuma II, last of the Aztec emperors; the Palace of Fine Arts and its much-acclaimed Ballet Folklorico; the National Museum of Anthropology and the 22-ton, remarkably accurate Aztec Calendar Stone; Chapultepec Castle, where the ill-fated Maximilian and Carlota lived briefly as the French-supported Emperor and Empress of Mexico, 1864-67.

Mexico City has large low-cost housing developments, fine residential areas created by its new and affluent middle class, and large new apartment houses erected to house, during their visits, the athletes of the 1968 Olympics. In dramatic background to the city stands a ring of mountains, including the perpetually snow-capped volcanoes, Popocatepetl (17,887 ft.) and Iztaccihuatl (17,343 ft.).

The altitude and tropical latitude combine to give the city a perpetually spring-like climate.

In shops and markets visitors will find the distinctive artistic and craft products of Mexico: silver, tin and copperwork, jewelry, leather goods and textiles. The city is a sports center, from bullfights and jai alai to baseball and golf.

There are 23 international airlines serving the city and a network of modern highways. The city is 5 hrs. by jetliner from New York, 3 hrs. from Los Angeles.

The city is governed, as part of the

Federal District (Distrito Federal), by a Governor appointed by the President, and a council.

The tempo of business and industry, which show steady growth, is that of any great city. The traditional siesta is no longer observed in Mexico City.

For more information, write Mexican National Tourist Council, Mariano y Escobedo 726, Mexico, D.F.; or 677 5th Ave., N.Y. 10022; or 9445 Wilshire Blvd., Beverly Hills 90212.

# Miami, Florida

The World Almanac is sponsored in the Miami area by the Miami Herald, 1 Herald Plaza, Miami, Fla. 33101; telephone (305) 350-2111; founded Dec. 1, 1910, by Frank B. Shutts; circulation 369,609 daily, 463,782 Sunday; publisher, John S. Knight; president, James L. Knight; general manager, Alvah H. Chapman, Jr.; editor, Don Shoemaker; major awards include 1968 Pulitzer Prize to Publisher Knight for editorial writing, previous Pulitzer Prize to paper and one to staff member, Headliners Awards, and a Sigma Delta Chi 1st prize; sponsors annual Silver Knight Awards to high school seniors, fishing tournament, Science Fair, Dolphin Charity Football Game, program to send underprivileged children to summer camp.

Miami (Seminole for "Sweet Water") is wedded to the sea. Located at the southern tip of the Florida peninsula and brushed by the warm Gulf Stream, this sub-tropical city is surrounded by the Atlantic Ocean, Biscayne Bay and the "River of Grass," Everglades National Park.

It is America's newest big city. In 1895 there were only 3 houses and a handful of residents living in what was then called Fort Dallas, site of a military outpost used during the Seminole Indian wars in the 1830s. In that year, a hard freeze destroyed the Florida citrus crop upstate and a Miami widow, Julia Tuttle, convinced millionaire Henry Flagler to extend his railroad from West Palm Beach to Miami by sending him a green sprig, undamaged by frost, cut from her backyard orange tree. Flagler's trains began arriving in Miami the following year, bringing people and the migration south hasn't stopped yet. Except for a few months following the disastrous 1926 hurricane, Miami and its population have grown rapidly.

Incorporated in 1896, the year the first trains arrived, the City of Miami now has 343,500 year-round residents. But the metropolitan Miami area, which includes the cities of Miami, Miami Beach and 25 other municipalities, now has a permanent population of an estimated 1,200,000.

Dade County's 2,352 sq. mi. (more than half is under water and cannot be developed) are administered by a government in which 8 county commissioners and a mayor establish policy and the routine of administration is headed by a professional county manager. The City of Miami turned over many of its municipal functions to the county to avoid duplication as urban residents followed a national trend and moved to the suburbs. The city is governed by a 5-man commission, including a mayor, with a city manager.

Miami takes pride in calling itself "The Gateway to Latin America." It is increasingly the center of U. S.-Latin American trade with 4,000 small manufacturing plants serving virtually all of the Caribbean islands, Central and South America.

Tourism is still king although it is no longer the only industry in Miami. More than 20,000,000 visitors a year flock to Florida, producing a $5 billion annual tourist economy. Most head for Miami—"The Magic City"—and Miami Beach, which offers the world's largest concentration of luxury hotels. There are 45,000 first class hotel and motel rooms and 100,-000 rental apartments in Miami Beach.

While its reputation as an international playground is unchallenged, Miami is also on the road to becoming a center of business and commerce and science. It is the home base for Eastern Airlines, National Airlines and Family Finance Service, Inc. It also serves as international headquarters for Minnesota Mining and Manufac-

turing Co., Dow Chemical, Eastman Kodak, International Petroleum, Owens-Corning Fiber Glass Corp., and Pan American World Airways.

Miami, with the anticipated opening in the early 1970s of the Environmental Science Services Administration's Oceanographic Laboratory, will lead the world in undersea study. It is already the home for the University of Miami's famed Institute of Marine Science and the U. S. Bureau of Commercial Fisheries' Tropical Atlantic Laboratory.

Total retail sales in Miami in 1967 hit $2.6 billion.

Miami International Airport, as hub of air traffic between North and South America, is one of the world's busiest air terminals, served by all the major certified domestic and foreign airlines, 92 in all. An average of 47 commercial flights arrive or take off at Miami every hour—a total 446,-867 flight movements in 1967, carrying 8,722,032 passengers. Two railroads serve the city, the Florida East Coast and Seaboard Coast Line.

Dodge Island Seaport, currently in the middle of an expansion program, was visited by 2,200 ships in 1966 and 865,000 tons of cargo were handled. The port is home for cruise ships making regular runs to the Bahamas and Jamaica and some 260,-000 passengers passed through the seaport's terminal in 1966.

The Greyhound and Trailways bus systems provide service to all major U. S. cities with 62 departures daily.

Fifteen major inter-intrastate motor common carriers service Miami.

Since the 1959 takeover by Castro in Cuba, Miami has become the refugee center for fleeing exiles. Some 125,000 Cubans now make Miami their home.

Urban renewal plans and a comprehensive revitalization program submitted by city planner Constantinos Doxiadis are now under examination as the city prepares massive rehabilitation of the downtown business and financial district.

Completion of the $200,000,000 expressway system connecting the quadrants of the city is expected by early 1969.

The Orange Bowl is the home stadium for the University of Miami Hurricanes football team and the Miami Dolphins of the American Football League. It also hosts the traditional New Year's game between two of the nation's top-ranked teams and, in 1969, will again provide the setting for the Super Bowl game and the National Football League Playoff Game.

The University of Miami is the largest independent institution of higher learning in the Southeast, and Miami-Dade Junior College, which opened in 1960, is already the nation's largest junior college.

For information write: Dade County Development Department, 330 Biscayne Blvd., Miami, Fla. 33132.

# Milwaukee, Wisconsin

The World Almanac is sponsored in the Milwaukee area by the Milwaukee Journal, Journal Square, Milwaukee, Wis. 53201; telephone (414) 271-6000; founded 1882 by Lucius W. Nieman; circulation 374,623 daily, 570,342 Sunday; chairman of the board, Irwin Maier; president and publisher, Donald B. Abert; executive vice president and general manager, Robert K. Drew; business manager, Francis D. Kelly; editor, Richard H. Leonard; major awards include two Pulitzer Prizes to newspaper and two to staff members; sponsors various sports events, major home shows and cultural events annually.

Milwaukee, the largest city in Wisconsin and an important manufacturing center, was founded by Solomon Juneau, one of the many French explorers, traders and trappers who visited the Midwest in the early 1800s. Marquette, Joliet and La Salle had visited the site during their earlier explorations.

The name of Milwaukee was originally "Mahnawaukee-Seepe," or "gathering place by the rivers," referring to the level of land at the confluence of the Milwaukee, Menomonee and Kinnickinnic Rivers, all entering the Bay of Milwaukee on Lake Michigan.

Incorporated in 1846, the city now covers 96.5 sq. mi. and has an estimated population of 774,000. Its standard metropolitan statistical area, including Milwaukee, Waukesha, Ozaukee and Washington Counties, covers 1,458 sq. mi., with an estimated population of slightly over 1,400,000, and with 427,100 households.

Milwaukee has a mayor-council government, with aldermen elected for 4-year terms.

A leading brewing center, Milwaukee also is a major grain market. Its leading manufactured products include electrical machinery, outboard motors, motorcycles, chemicals and textiles. The metropolitan area is second in the U. S. in percentage of the labor force in manufacturing. Ten Milwaukee manufacturers are in Fortune magazine's list of the 500 top U.S. corporations in sales volume.

Total retail sales in the Milwaukee metropolitan area in 1967 were estimated at $2.4 billion, ranking 17th in the U. S. The metropolitan area ranked 7th in retail sales per household.

Milwaukee's General Mitchell Field, with facilities for the largest jet transports, is served by 5 major airlines; the field's passenger volume in 1967 was 1,378,-400. Five important rail systems serve the area; car ferry lines also operate out of Milwaukee's harbor. Railroad freight tonnage is over 10,000,000 annually. The area is served by 62 truck lines and there are 4 intercity bus lines.

A leading Great Lakes port, Milwaukee is an important export and import gateway between mid-America and overseas points. The municipally-owned port serves the lake vessels, barges, and ocean-going vessels of 48 lines.

An intensive program of building construction involving private, city, state and Federal enterprise has been under way in Milwaukee for the past 8 years.

The University of Wisconsin at Milwaukee and Marquette University are notable among the area's 18 universities and colleges, which have a total estimated enrollment of almost 43,000.

Notable buildings include the Greek Orthodox Annunciation Church, designed by Frank Lloyd Wright, and the Eero Saarinen-designed War Memorial Center on the lakeshore, housing the Milwaukee Art Center. By the end of 1969 Milwaukee will have a $9,500,000 Center for the Performing Arts and a Music Hall Theater, mostly financed by public subscriptions.

Milwaukee County has 12,630 acres of parks in 108 locations. The new Horticultural Conservatory in Mitchell Park consists of 3 glass conoidal domes duplicating climate and plant life found throughout the world.

Milwaukee's annual Fourth of July parade has been changed to a large exhibit of circus animals and reconstructed circus wagons from the Circus Museum in Baraboo, Wis.

Cultural enterprises include a permanent Milwaukee Repertory Theater and the Milwaukee Symphony Orchestra.

The Green Bay Packers of the National Football League play 4 regular league games a year in Milwaukee's County Stadium. The Chicago White Sox played 10 of their regular season games in Milwaukee in 1968.

Detailed information on the area can be obtained from the Milwaukee Journal's marketing research department and the Metropolitan Milwaukee Association of Commerce.

# Minneapolis, Minnesota

St. Anthony's Falls in the Mississippi River provided the geographical nucleus for Minneapolis—a city that would use the power of the 50-foot falls to become a flour-milling and lumber center and the urban heart of a vast agricultural region. The site of the city was first visited by Father Louis Hennepin in the 1680s. French fur traders next used it as a base of operations, and in 1805-06 the Sioux Indians gave up all rights to the land in a treaty concluded by Lt. Zebulon Pike. The city was incorporated in 1871.

Today, Minneapolis, along with its Twin City sister, St. Paul, is a manufacturing, wholesaling, retailing, financial and educational center with a combined population of 1,629,000, according to a provisional estimate of the Census Bureau.

Minneapolis has 25 industrial parks and such corporate giants as Honeywell Inc., General Mills, Pillsbury Co., National Biscuit Co., and Control Data, call the city home. In a move that is expected to attract more industry to the area, the city

is constructing Upper Harbor, a 12-acre river terminal that will handle the shipping and storage of grain, fertilizer, petroleum products, sand, gravel, salt and coal.

Massive freeway and urban renewal programs have been undertaken by both cities, with Minneapolis' $286,000,000 Gateway Center, already underway, transforming a 17-block area in the heart of the city into a modern building complex.

The Twin Cities are served by the Minneapolis-St. Paul International Airport which in 1966 handled more than 3,000,000 passengers and 50,000,000 pounds of cargo.

Minneapolis is an enthusiastic sports town featuring the Minnesota Twins of baseball's American League and the Minnesota Vikings of the National Football League, both of whom play their home games in Metropolitan Stadium at nearby Bloomington.

The Minneapolis Symphony Orchestra and the Tyrone Guthrie Theater are the two brightest lights in the city's cultural sky. The city plays host all year long to

national touring companies of ballet, opera and local performing arts groups.

The Minneapolis Institute of Arts is one of the foremost museums in the country with outstanding collections highlighted by masterpieces of El Greco, Van Gogh, Rembrandt, Gauguin, Matisse and other prominent artists. The Walker Art Center, primarily devoted to current trends in painting, sculpture, drawing and print

making, is connected to the Tyrone Guthrie Theater by a sculpture court.

There are 153 parks in the city comprising 5,906 acres with 22 lakes offering sailboating, fishing and various other summer and winter activities. The Minneapolis Aquatennial is held in July.

The University of Minnesota, Northwestern College, Augsburg College and Seminary are among the institutes of higher learning located in Minneapolis.

## Montreal, Canada

The World Almanac is sponsored in the Montreal area by The Gazette, 1000 St. Antoine Street, Montreal, Quebec, Canada; telephone (514) 861-1111; founded 1778 by Fleury Mesplet; circulation 283,613 daily; president, Charles H. Peters; general manager, H. J. Larkin; editor, Edgar Andrew Collard; managing editor, John A. Meyer; major prizes include four National Newspaper Awards to staff members; sponsors annual Christmas Fund for needy famlies; participates in various community service projects.

There is something for everybody in Montreal—after Paris, the second-largest French-speaking city in the world, and one of North America's most cosmopolitan centers.

The island city in the St. Lawrence River is Canada's largest urban center, ranks 9th on the continent with a metropolitan area population of 2,321,000 (with 1,400,000 in the city itself) and is the nation's financial, commercial and industrial hub. Two-thirds of its people are of French origin and 20% have an Anglo-Saxon heritage.

An international flavor is reflected in Montreal's theaters, shops, boutiques, its 4,000 restaurants which make it a gourmet's delight, and its celebrated night life —it has been called "the Paris of North America."

Located in the St. Lawrence where the Ottawa and Richelieu Rivers flow into it and at the head of the St. Lawrence Seaway, Montreal has become a great transportation center. The Seaway is a $1 billion Canadian-American waterway and power project which runs 1,300 miles to the Great Lakes in the heart of North America. It has helped Montreal, 1,000 miles from the sea, become the world's second greatest inland port, after only Rotterdam. Its harbor limits extend for 42 miles and its port annually produces revenues of more than $240,000,000, handles more than 2,000,000 tons of cargo and sees 125,000 passengers pass through it.

Montreal also is known as the air capital of the world, with the headquarters of both the International Civil Aviation Organization and the International Air Transport Association—the two global regulatory bodies—located in the city and 17 airlines serving its huge international airport. It also is Canada's railroad hub, and a leading truck and bus center.

The city is a leader—it has been called "the only 20th Century city in the world" —in terms of the redevelopment of its core and its underground, weather-proof facilities. Its most spectacular development is the $125,000,000 Place Ville Marie, a cruciform-shaped building of 42 stories which has more office space than any other complex in the world except Rockefeller Center in New York. The underground city covers 40 acres, connecting office skyscrapers, railroad stations, hotels; Place Bonaventure, the world's second largest trade and convention center, the Montreal and Canadian Stock Exchanges, cinemas and theaters, restaurants, hundreds of shops and boutiques; and the Metro, the city's two-year-old, $225,000,000, 16-mile subway system.

Montreal is a major cultural center. Facilities include the Place des Arts, which has a fine 3,000-seat concert hall and two theaters. It serves as the home of the Montreal Symphony Orchestra and at-

tracts the finest in drama, opera, ballet and music. The city has excellent art galleries, including the Montreal Museum of Fine Arts and the modern Musee de l'Art Contemporain. Its many specialized museums run the gamut.

Montreal also boasts some of the continent's most beautiful churches, including the Roman Catholic Mary Queen of the World Basilica, a half-size replica of St. Peter's in Rome, and it is the home of two of Canada's most famous universities, McGill and l'Universite de Montreal.

The city has more than 100 playgrounds covering more than 5,000 acres including one centered about the 764-foot-high Mount Royal, its most dominant physical characteristic. The parks include an outdoor art galley, a children's zoo, theater and concerts, excellent sports facilities of all kinds and the Botanical Garden, one of the world's largest and most beautiful.

The city has remembered its history, too. Old Montreal, some 1,000 acres in all, is the largest such area undergoing restoration in North America and retains unchanged the general atmosphere of the 18th Century.

Finally, among its many attractions, there is Man and His World, the largest permanent exhibition anywhere and the successor to the fabulously-successful Expo 67 on two man-made islands in the St. Lawrence. The 1968 version had participation by 45 nations, exhibiting both artistic treasures and commercial goods in their own pavilions, and a 135-acre amusement and entertainment area called La Ronde, which has been compared favorably with such places as the Tivoli Gardens in Copenhagen and California's Disneyland. The 1969 exhibition promises to be even bigger and better.

Montreal has a mayor-council form of government with elections each four years, and the major project now underway is a massive urban renewal scheme. The city is the home of two professional sports teams—the world champion Canadiens of the National Hockey League and the Alouettes of the Canadian Football League. Major league baseball is due to come to Montreal in 1969, with a National League franchise.

Montreal was first visited by Jacques Cartier in 1535 and was founded under the name of Ville Marie in 1642. Today, it shares the island with 29 other autonomous municipalities—its suburbs—and occupies 18 sq. mi. of the island's 60.

Its major industries include oil refining, petro-chemicals and chemicals, aircraft manufacturing, textiles, sugar refining, flour milling, meat packing, brewing and construction products. It boasts more head offices of major Canadian companies than any other city.

# Nashville, Tennessee

The World Almanac is sponsored in the Nashville area by The Nashville Tennessean, 1100 Broadway, Nashville, Tenn. 37202; telephone (615) 255-1221; founded as The Tennessean, May 12, 1907 by Col. Luke Lea; but other incorporated publications date to 1812; circulation daily 146,000, Sunday 240,000; publisher, Amon C. Evans; editor, John Seigenthaler; associate editor, Lloyd Armour; major public service projects include continuing efforts to further economic development of the Tennessee Valley region; a series of free concerts annually; an Outdoor Show to aid Girl Scouts; and annual publication of tabloids with proceeds going to local charities.

Nashville sits 500 feet above sea level on the banks of the Cumberland River in north central Tennessee. The state's capital city, it was settled in 1780 as a fort built by James Robertson and a group of settlers in what was then North Carolina. In 1783, the land around Fort Nashborough became a county under an act of the North Carolina legislature and was called Davidson County after Gen. William Davidson of Mechlenburg, N. C.

A year later Fort Nashborough was incorporated under the name Nashville; it had the first written constitutional government west of the Alleghenies. In 1778 a transient horseman named Andrew Jackson made Nashville his home and later put it on the map as the state's first congressman and the first of its three U. S. Presidents. His home, the famous Hermitage, still stands as a major Nashville landmark.

Federal troops occupied the city during the Civil War, and it was there that Gen. Thomas Hood's Confederate army suffered a disastrous defeat in 1864.

More than a century later, Nashville has grown into a major cultural, educational and commercial complex and the heart of a great regional trading area. It is served by nine major airlines, providing 83 flights daily, and is served by six routes of the Interstate Highway System.

Education has been a traditional trademark since the first public school system in the South opened its doors on a Nashville street Feb. 26, 1855.

Now 13 universities and colleges, 141 public schools and more than 40 commercial and vocational schools dot its landscape. Among the institutions of higher learning are Vanderbilt University, Fisk University, Tennessee A & I State University, a branch of the University of Tennessee, George Peabody College, Belmont College, David Lipscomb College and Meharry Medical College.

Rich in schools, it is even richer in churches and church-related industries, including several large publishing houses that have helped to make printing the city's largest single industry. Among them are the National Baptist Publishing Board, The Methodist Publishing House and the National Baptist Sunday School Publishing Board.

But printing is only a small part of Nashville's diversified economy, which boasts more than 500 individual manufacturers employing more than 28,000

workers and more than 40,000 individual business concerns.

It is also a banking and investment center and ranks second to Hartford, Conn., in the number of major insurance company offices. Two of the industry's largest, National Life and Accident Ins. Co. and Life and Casualty Ins. Co., have skyscraper headquarters in Nashville.

Other major employers include E.I. du Pont de Nemours Co., Ford Motor Co., Genesco Inc., Avco Corp. and Gates Rubber Co.

In 1925 radio station WSM, a National Life operation, went on the air and in November of that year presented a program of folk music known as the Grand Ole Opry. That program, still on the air, snowballed into a multi-million dollar music industry.

The music business now pumps an estimated $60,000,000 annually into the Nashville economy and the famous "Nashville sound" has made the city second only to New York as a recording center.

Recording studios and music publishing houses occupy a burgeoning section of the city, with an entire street now named "Music Row."

On it stands the "Country Music Hall of Fame," a relatively new building which must be numbered along with the Hermitage and a replica of the Greek Parthenon among Nashville's top attractions.

The city has a symphony orchestra and art showings are continuous at the Parthenon and at Cheekwood Botanical Gardens, a fine arts center.

On April 1, 1963, the local governments of Nashville and Davidson County were consolidated in a unique form of Metropolitan Government which encompasses all the county's 533 square miles.

The consolidation boosted Nashville's population to more than 465,000, second largest in the state. Nashville is ruled by a mayor-council form of government and constitutes the 5th Congressional District.

The city lies in the heart of a fertile valley served by the Tennessee Valley Authority, the source of electrical power and flood control for millions.

TVA dams in the area have surrounded Davidson County with major lakes and all the recreational facilities which accompany them.

Additional information on Nashville can be obtained from the Nashville Area Chamber of Commerce, 310 Union St., Nashville, Tenn. 37201.

# New Orleans, Louisiana

The World Almanac is sponsored in the New Orleans area by the New Orleans States-Item, 3800 Howard Ave., New Orleans, La. 70140; telephone (504) 821-1411; founded Jan. 3, 1880, by Maj. Henry J. Hearsey; circulation 140,201; executive editor, George W. Healy, Jr.; managing editor, Walter G. Cowan; general manager, Robert E. Gough; major awards received, Pulitzer Prize and two Sigma Delta Chi awards; sponsors Visual Education Program for High School Students, slum clearance campaigns and Football Fund for Underprivileged Children.

New Orleans, having completed its 250th anniversary year in 1968, combines Old World charm with New World progress and industry as the nation's second port, based on value of imports and exports.

Named after the Duke of Orleans, the city was founded on the edge of a swamp

within a crescent of the Mississippi River 100 miles upstream from the Gulf of Mexico by Jean Baptiste le Moyne, Sieur de Bienville.

The new settlement struggled for existence until 1722, when Bienville persuaded the French to make it the capital

of the Louisiana Territory. In that year Adrien de Pauger laid out the city, with a square on the bank of the river around which important public buildings stand. The area occupied by the original city is known as the Vieux Carre or French Quarter, which attracts millions of tourists to its museums, shops, restaurants, markets, jazz centers and residential patios.

Above Canal street, modern New Orleans is the banking and business center of the Deep South. For many years the city relied almost solely on shipping for economic support. Then agriculture—principally sugar, rice and cotton—manufacturing, trapping, fishing, production of petroleum and tourism became vital parts of its economy. Lands surrounding the city, including offshore areas, are the most productive sources of oil in the United States. The city produces Saturn rockets for the space program.

The port, served by the river, the Gulf Tidewater Channel, Inner Harbor Navigation canal, Intracoastal canal and Lake Pontchartrain, moved cargo valued at $2.34 billion in 1967.

The city proper, covering 363.5 square miles, of which 199.4 are land, is governed by a mayor and city council. The population of the metropolitan area was estimated at more than 1,076,600 in 1967.

Three airports, for scheduled airlines, commercial and private aviation and military use, serve the city. The Union Passenger Terminal, opened in 1954 in the center of the city, consolidated passenger services of six railroad stations.

Among New Orleans' educational institutions are Tulane University, Louisiana State University in New Orleans, the LSU Medical College, Loyola University and 4 other institutions of higher learning. Museums include the Louisiana State Museum, Isaac Delgado Museum of Art, the Middle American Research Institute of Tulane and many small galleries.

Ideally placed geographically for handling foreign and domestic commerce, the city had to conquer threats of yellow fever, of river floods and of hurricanes to achieve eminence as a world trade center.

Through its vicissitudes it has remained a play capital of America—home of North America's most lavish Mardi Gras celebrations and birthplace of jazz.

# New York, N. Y.

The World Almanac is sponsored in the greater New York City metropolitan area by the Daily News and Sunday News, 220 E. 42nd St., New York, N. Y. 10017, which this year celebrates its 50th Anniversary of publication; telephone (212) MU 2-1234; News Syndicate Co., Inc., founded June 26, 1919, by Joseph Medill Patterson; circulation daily 2,080,906, Sunday 3,221,849; president and publisher, F. M. Flynn; executive vice president, W. H. James; executive editor, W. A. Casselman; associate editor, Floyd Barger; treasurer, J. J. Lynch; business manager, V. E. Palmer; major awards include Pulitzer Prizes (news photography, international reporting, cartoon, editorial writing); sponsors Golden Gloves, Harvest Moon Ball, New York Relays, Ike Golf Championship and many community and school activities.

New York is the nation's largest city, its richest port and its leader in business, manufacturing, service industries, communications, fashion, art, music and literature, as well as the world's chief financial center and, as host to the headquarters of the United Nations, the "capital" of the world.

The city credits Giovanni da Verrazano with discovering its magnificent harbor in 1524. Henry Hudson explored Manhattan Island (now the seat of central government for the city's five boroughs) in 1609. Settlement by the Dutch soon followed, with the first houses built by Adriaen Block in lower Manhattan in 1613.

In 1626 Peter Minuit, first director general of the Dutch province of New Netherland, bought the island from the Manhattan Indians "for the value of 60 guilders," or about $24, probably in goods and trinkets. The settlement at the lower end of Manhattan was named New Amsterdam; Fort Amsterdam was built where the U. S. Customs House now stands.

The Dutch erected a church in 1633; in 1642 they built a public meeting house on the site of 73 Pearl St.; in 1653, to protect the settlement, they erected a wall from which Wall St. takes its name. On Feb. 2, 1653, when New Amsterdam reached 800 in population, it was incorporated as a city.

On Sept. 8, 1664, British troops occupied New Amsterdam without resistance, took over the government from the Dutch director general Peter Stuyvesant and named the city New York to honor the Duke of York, brother of King Charles II of England. Without notice to the Dutch, Charles had conferred on the Duke title to all Dutch land in North America, including much of the present states of New York, New Jersey and Connecticut.

Thomas Willett was named the first English mayor in June 1665. The Treaty of Breda, 1667, confirmed British ownership, giving the Dutch in exchange the former British colony of Surinam in South America. On Aug. 9, 1673, the Dutch recaptured New York and renamed it New Orange in honor of the Prince of Orange. In Nov. 1674 it was restored to the British and again named New York.

The British made easy terms for the Dutch and many prominent Dutch merchants and landowners became loyal subjects. The city was divided into 6 wards Dec. 8, 1683, with an alderman for each. The first charter was granted Apr. 27, 1686. The first printing press arrived Apr. 12, 1693, and the first newspaper was issued Oct. 16, 1725.

In 1700 the city built a city hall at the northeast corner of Broad and Wall Sts. A library was founded 1754. A stage service to Philadelphia was opened 1756. Streets were first lighted at public expense, 1762. Trinity Church, first of the Anglican communion, was first erected 1698.

New York was a focal point for both Continentals and British during the American Revolution. Washington had his headquarters for a time in the Kennedy house, which stood at present No. 1 Broadway and later became British headquarters. The Declaration of Independence was read to the American troops July 9, 1776, in the presence of Washington near the present City Hall. The Americans lost the Battle of Long Island Aug. 27, 1776, and the British occupied New York Sept. 15, 1776. Over 500 houses were destroyed by fire Sept. 21, 1776. The Americans entrenched on Harlem Heights, where they fought several actions; on Nov. 16, 1776, they lost Fort Washington, in upper Manhattan, to the British and left the island.

Washington reentered New York on Evacuation Day, Nov. 25, 1783. On Apr. 30, 1789, Washington took the oath of office as first President on the balcony of Federal Hall, Broad and Wall Sts., where a bronze

statue by J. Q. A. Ward now stands. New York was the national capital until 1790, when it had a population of 33,131. Until 1797 it was the capital of the state.

A new city hall was built 1803-12 in City Hall Park, bounded by Broadway, Park Row and Chambers St. It is still in use.

By act of the state legislature, Kingsbridge, West Farms and Morrisania, NE of Manhattan, were joined to the city Jan. 1, 1874. In 1894 adjacent towns voted on annexation. Eastchester and Pelham Manor voted favorably; Mount Vernon and Westchester (town) unfavorably, the latter by one vote. The legislature overrode Westchester and joined it to the city with Eastchester and Pelham Manor, total over 39 sq. mi., or 26,017 acres.

On Jan. 1, 1898, Manhattan and large areas to the NE, E and S were consolidated into one City of New York, a metropolis with 5 boroughs (which also are counties of the state). Manhattan became the Borough of Manhattan. The areas to the N became the Borough of the Bronx; originally parts of Westchester County, they had become part of New York County along with Manhattan; later they became Bronx County, and New York County was limited to Manhattan. The City of Brooklyn (Kings County) became the Borough of Brooklyn. Staten Island (Richmond County) became the Borough of Richmond. Areas on Long Island which are now Queens County became the Borough of Queens *(see also pages 436-438).*

### Population of New York City by Boroughs

| Year | | Manhattan | Bronx | Brooklyn | Queens | Richmond | Totals |
|---|---|---|---|---|---|---|---|
| 1790 | (U. S. Census) | 33,131 | 1,781 | 4,495 | 6,159 | 3,835 | 49,401 |
| 1850 | | 515,547 | 8,032 | 138,882 | 18,593 | 15,061 | 696,115 |
| 1900 | " " | 1,850,093 | 200,507 | 1,166,582 | 152,999 | 67,021 | 3,437,202 |
| 1910 | " " | 2,331,542 | 430,980 | 1,634,351 | 284,041 | 85,969 | 4,766,883 |
| 1920 | " " | 2,284,103 | 732,016 | 2,018,356 | 469,042 | 116,531 | 5,620,048 |
| 1930 | " " | 1,867,312 | 1,265,258 | 2,560,401 | 1,079,129 | 158,346 | 6,930,446 |
| 1940 | " " | 1,889,924 | 1,394,711 | 2,698,285 | 1,297,634 | 174,441 | 7,454,995 |
| 1950 | " " | 1,960,101 | 1,451,277 | 2,738,175 | 1,550,849 | 191,555 | 7,891,957 |
| 1960 | " " | 1,698,281 | 1,424,815 | 2,627,319 | 1,809,578 | 221,991 | 7,781,984 |
| 1967 | (estimated) | 1,750,000 | 1,470,000 | 2,650,000 | 1,985,000 | 270,000 | 8,125,000 |

# Norfolk, Virginia

The World Almanac is sponsored in the Norfolk Metropolitan Area by The Virginian-Pilot and Ledger-Star, 150 W. Brambleton Ave., Norfolk, Va. 23501; telephone (703) 625-1431; Virginian founded 1865 by G. A. Sykes & Co., Ledger founded 1876 by J. Richard Lewellen & Co.; circulation: L-S daily 105,470, V-P daily 126,393, Sunday 172,241; chairman of the board and publisher, Frank Batten; president, Paul S. Huber, Jr.; senior vice pres. and assistant publisher, Harold G. Sugg; V-P editor, Robert H. Mason; L-S editor, William H. Fitzpatrick. Major awards include two Pulitzer Prizes for The Virginian-Pilot. Both newspapers sponsor area-wide Christmas Joy Fund, founded 34 years ago; a scholastic achievement award program for high school students; other community relations projects.

Norfolk is the financial hub of the South Hampton Roads Metropolitan Area which encompasses the four contiguous cities of Norfolk, Portsmouth, Chesapeake and Virginia Beach. The metropolitan area covers 667 square miles; there are no counties. Its 88% urban population attests to its close knit nature. Estimated population for the four-city area is 690,360. It is Virginia's top-ranking area in population, income, and retail sales.

The cities of Norfolk and Portsmouth date back to the 17th Century. Chesapeake, the largest city in land area, and Virginia Beach were recently formed in annexation with surrounding counties. The town of Norfolk was established in 1682 on the site of an Indian village. Sold by its owner, Nicholas Wise, to the colonial government in Williamsburg for $400 worth of tobacco, it was chartered as a borough in 1736. Lt. Gov. Robert Dinwiddie, honorary citizen of Norfolk, presented the borough with a seal and silver mace, the city's official symbol still in ceremonial use. During the Revolutionary War Norfolk was destroyed by fire. Old St. Paul's Church, built in 1738, was the only major building to survive; an English cannonball remains embedded in its wall. The Norfolk Naval Shipyard, founded in Portsmouth in 1738, was also destroyed. By 1831, however, the rebuilt shipyard housed the oldest drydock in the western hemisphere. Here the engines for the Powhatan, Commodore Perry's ship, were built and installed. The world's first armored warship was built here on the scuttled hulk of the man-of-war, the Merrimack.

World War I saw the building of the first aircraft carrier, the U. S. S. Langley. But full recognition of the port's value came only with the founding of the Norfolk Naval Base on Independence Day in 1917.

From this beginning, the area has grown to house the greatest concentration of naval installations in the world. Among the 38 major commands in Norfolk alone are the Atlantic Fleet, the Second Fleet, NATO's Supreme Allied Command Atlantic (SACLANT), the Armed Forces Staff College and the Commandant 5th Naval District. Naval facilities have mushroomed to include a 1967 payroll for the Navy and Civil Service of more than $400,-000,000, with nearly $26,000,000 in other new construction for Norfolk's naval installations. An additional $364,000,000 is paid to fleet personnel, most of whom have families residing in the area.

As a port Hampton Roads has the world's finest natural harbor. Close to 6,000 ships from over 350 world ports navigate its deep, ice-free channels each year. Its temperate climate is ideal for the handling of all types of cargo. Among Atlantic ports, Norfolk holds first place in export tonnage. Both Portsmouth and Norfolk have new berths for containerized cargo. Norfolk International Terminals has projected a $50,000,000 investment in its port development.

Eight railroads, with Norfolk-Portsmouth as the terminus of a 7,400-mi. rail system, reach directly into the manufacturing heart of the nation. Over 50 common and contract motor carriers offer flexible service. The Chesapeake Bay Bridge Tunnel provides a direct North-South highway system from New York to Florida. Four airlines provide direct flights to major cities in the nation.

Educational institutions in Norfolk include 3 4-year liberal arts colleges. Old Dominion College has an engineering school and technical institute. Two-year colleges are located in Portsmouth and Chesapeake.

Norfolk has 7 hospitals; Portsmouth

has 3, including the nation's oldest naval medical center recently enlarged by a $17,000,000 addition. Virginia Beach has complete facilities in its new hospital.

Civic, social and recreational activities abound in the South Hampton Roads area. Norfolk has an excellent symphony orchestra, chamber group and civic chorus, a Little Theater and civic ballet. Norfolk has just begun construction of a $24,000,-000 cultural and convention center. Numerous dinner theaters operate in the area. The city's arts and sciences museum recently more than doubled its facilities. The Norfolk Tour includes the MacArthur Memorial, final resting place of Gen. Douglas MacArthur; the Adam Thoroughgood House, built in 1636 and the oldest brick home in the nation, and Norfolk's

Botanical Gardens which include 175 acres of azaleas to furnish a background for the annual NATO Azalea Festival.

Portsmouth is known for its Old Towne District and harbor tours. Much of the world famous Dismal Swamp is located in Chesapeake, with its vast rural area, woodlands, wild rivers and dense forests. The famed resort city of Virginia Beach offers 174 hotels, motels and tourist homes. Its 38 miles of beach provides excellent swimming, fishing and surfing area. Camping facilities are available at Seashore State Park. Each year Virginia Beach sponsors a Boardwalk Arts Festival where over 200 artists display their works.

The South Hampton Roads area is served by 11 AM, 9 FM and 5 television stations.

# Oklahoma City, Oklahoma

The World Almanac is sponsored in the Oklahoma City area by The Daily Oklahoman and Oklahoma City Times, Oklahoma City, Okla. 73125; telephone (405) 232-3311; The Oklahoman founded in 1894, Times in 1888; Oklahoma Publishing Co. acquired The Oklahoman 1903 and the Times 1916; circulation (March 31, 1968) Oklahoman, 185,306; Times, 115,541 and 274,785 Sunday; editor and publisher, E.K. Gaylord; managing editor, Charles L. Bennett.

Oklahoma City, capital and most populous city in Oklahoma, is located near the center of the state on the North Canadian River. Its population in 1968 was 405,000, with 635,000 in its metropolitan statistical area. The city is about 300 miles south of the exact center of the continental United States.

Oklahoma City exploded into being Apr. 22, 1889. In the morning, its site was a peaceful and quiet Indian Territory railroad stop. Twelve hours and the Run of '89 later, it boasted 10,000 residents, a tent city that spread over 3 townsites.

In the center of a rich agricultural area, the city is a manufacturing and distributing center of farm products.

Livestock plays a major role in the economic life of the area, with dairying and broiler growing increasing.

Oklahoma City lies in the heart of a rich oil producing area. Heaviest production in the state lies within 60 miles of the city, with approximately 1,800 producing wells in the metropolitan area. The original Oklahoma City field has produced more than 750,000,000 barrels of oil and the city is the gateway to heavy development taking place in western Oklahoma. In 1968 an estimated 39,500 Oklahoma Cityans were earning their living from the oil industry.

Oklahoma City, an aviation pioneer, is a major aeronautical center. Located here is Tinker Air Force Base, headquarters of the Oklahoma City Air Materiel Area, world's largest air depot. The $100,000,000 installation employs more than 26,000 civilians and 4,000 military personnel. The Federal Aviation Administration operates major facilities in the city, worth over $222,000,000, including the FAA Aeronautical Center and the Civil Aeromedical Institute. Some 38,000 city residents were employed in aviation occupations in 1968, with an estimated annual payroll of $287,-500,000.

Manufactured products include aircraft, telephone exchange equipment, space electronic components, auto bodies and parts, iron and steel products, oil field and refinery equipment and supplies, oil and greases, aviation gasoline, building materials, flour, feed, meat, cottonseed products, and paper products.

The city is a growing regional, national and international marketing center, and the Bureau of Customs opened an office in 1967 to expedite exports and imports.

Effective buying income in the city for 1967 was reported as $1.015 billion. In the Oklahoma City trade area, effective buying income was $2.863 billion. Consumer sales in 1967 totaled $1.052 billion.

Oklahoma City is served by 5 passenger airlines, American, Braniff, Trans World, Continental and Frontier. Four primary federal highways and 3 major state highways traverse the city; two Federal Interstate Highways (I-40 and I-35) pass through the city and I-44 terminates here. The city boasts a fully-planned urban expressway system, major bus lines and through railway service.

Points of interest include the National Cowboy Hall of Fame and Western Heritage Center, $5,000,000 center with exhibits of art, sculpture and relics and dance performances by authentic Plains Indians; Mummers Theater; the State Historical Society Building and Museum; State Capitol building; Oklahoma City Symphony and Junior Symphony; Oklahoma Art Center, and Oklahoma City Zoo.

In addition, Oklahoma City is one of the nation's leading convention centers. Some 350 conventions in 1967 attracted 160,000 delegates. Other attractions bring an additional 1,000,000 visitors annually.

Among universities and colleges in the metropolitan area are Oklahoma City University, the University of Oklahoma (18 miles to the south at Norman), Central State College, Oklahoma Christian College, Bethany Nazarene College, Southwestern Bible College and Midwest Christian College. Also in the city is the U. of Oklahoma School of Medicine.

Oklahoma City is one of the Southwest's leading medical centers. The city has fine hospitals and medical clinics and is currently expanding a research and treatment center.

The city is among the nation's largest in area, with a total of 647.5 sq. mi. The metropolitan statistical area includes 2,141 sq. mi.

Oklahoma City is in the midst of 3 major Urban Renewal renovation projects with an estimated total cost of $77,000,000.

Big Eight Conference sports are at the University of Oklahoma, 18 miles south, and at Oklahoma State University, 60 miles away. The city boasts the nation's oldest college basketball tournament classic, the All College Tournament, hosted by Oklahoma City University.

Professional sports teams include the Oklahoma City baseball 89ers (Pacific Coast League) and the Blazers (Central Hockey League), performing in the city's spacious new State Fair Arena, which seats more than 10,000.

# Orlando, Florida

The World Almanac is sponsored in the Orlando area by the Orlando Sentinel and Orlando Evening Star, 633 N. Orange Ave., Orlando, Fla. 32802; telephone (305) 423-4411; The Sentinel and Evening Star, published as dailies since 1913, were merged in 1931 under Publisher Martin Andersen; acquired by Tribune Company of Chicago in 1965; circulation 149,398 daily; 148,646 Sunday; Editor Publisher William G. Conomos; public service projects include Shoes for the Shoeless Fund and Florida Symphony $1 Charity Concert; sponsors annual Shad Fishing Derby, Cooking School, Spelling Bee in nine county area and Easter Parade Contest.

Orlando, "The City Beautiful," has been praised as one of the 14 most pleasant communities in the United States. In Orange County in east-central Florida, Orlando encompasses 30.55 sq. mi. of rolling countryside dotted with over 50 lakes.

Orlando had its beginning in 1842 at the end of the Seminole Indian War when Aaron Jernigan settled on land which is now a part of the city and gave his name to the small community. In 1857, Jernigan was changed to Orlando in memory of Orlando Reeves, a soldier killed in a skirmish with the Indians.

Incorporated in 1857 with a one-sq.-mi. area and only 75 citizens, Orlando now has more than 109,238 residents.

Current estimated population of metropolitan Orlando, consisting of Orange and Seminole Counties, is 406,100. But according to present-day estimates, the impact of almost unmatched industrial, commercial and recreational expansion will cause the population to reach 813,860 by 1982.

The $600,000,000 Florida Disney World, developing on a 27,400-acre tract 14 mi. southwest of downtown Orlando, is scheduled to open in 1971. Expected to attract 6,000,000 visitors during the first year, Disney World will include an amusement area, an unusual group of hotels surrounding the park, a jet airport and an Experimental Prototype Community of Tomorrow (EPCOT) planned for 20,000 permanent residents.

Another feature will be an industrial park covering approximately 1,000 acres of the Disney tract where some 10,000 employees will work.

The new Orlando Naval Training Center, officially commissioned July 1, 1968, is one of the Navy's largest recruit training centers. It will have a capacity to train 8,000 recruits at a time and accommodate 6,500 military personnel and 2,000 civilian workers when completed.

Florida Technological University, with an opening class of 1,500 students, Sept. 1968, will have a student body of more than 15,000 by 1978. Valencia Junior College, a public junior college, opened in 1967 and joined Orlando Junior College and Rollins College in the field.

Orlando is the home of the Martin-Marietta Co. plant, largest single industrial employer in Florida with some 9,000 persons on its payroll.

Orlando has become the most important insurance center in Florida with 7 home offices and 7 regional home offices. By the fall of 1970, an $8,500,000, 19-story building in downtown Orlando will be completed by Continental Casualty Co.

With new companies arriving on the average of two a week, Orlando has become more than the citrus capital of the past. There are 12 beautiful and well planned industrial parks and districts. Among already established industries in larger parks are: Xerox Corp., du Pont, National Biscuit Co., Sealtest Co. and Sealy Mattress Co. Industries with more than 200 employees include: American Bakeries, General Dynamics' Dynatronics, Frito-Lay, Minute Maid Co. and the Sentinel Star Co., publisher of Orlando's two daily newspapers, the Sentinel and the Evening Star.

Rapidly becoming a convention city, Orlando has a total of 143 hotels and motels with over 5,000 modern rooms.

One of the prime reasons for the concentration of new industry is the available transportation. Orlando is less than 4 hours from every major Florida market. In the geographic center of the state, it is the natural hub of Florida's network of modern highways and expressways.

National, Eastern and Delta airlines serve Orlando with 51 flights daily. Orlando is also served by Shawnee Airlines, Seaboard Coast Line Railroad, Greyhound and Trailways bus systems, 21 common carrier truck lines and 8 freight forwarding companies.

The City of Orlando operates under the Mayor-Council form of government.

Orlando's Tinker Field is the site of spring training and exhibition games of the major league Minnesota Twins. The local Orlando Twins are members of the Florida State League. The Orlando Panthers belong to the Continental Football League. In December the city has two nationally recognized post-season bowl games, the Tangerine Bowl and the Missile Bowl.

Orlando is also the home of the $115,000 Florida Citrus Open Golf Tournament held in March of each year at Rio Pinar Country Club.

City-owned Ben White Raceway gives Orlando the distinction of being the world's largest winter training headquarters for trotters and pacers.

The Orlando-based Florida Symphony Orchestra, the only all-professional symphony in Florida, gives 8 subscription concerts each season with renowned guest artists and conductors.

# Ottawa, Canada

The World Almanac is sponsored in the Ottawa area by the Ottawa Journal, 237 Queen St., Ottawa, Ontario; telephone (613) 236-7511; founded 1885 by A. S. Woodburn; circulation daily 78,220, Saturday 88,210; president and editor, I. Norman Smith; vice president and general manager, Lucien A. Lalonde; managing editor, W. H. Metcalfe; affiliation, FP Publications; Head Office, Winnipeg; sponsors annual Cup of Milk Fund, Unitarian Church; bicycle safe driving contest; Regional Water Safety Program.

Ottawa, Canada's national capital, is the country's 5th largest city.

Founded as Bytown in 1827, it was renamed Ottawa and incorporated as a city in 1855. Two years later, the progressive young community was chosen as capital of the United Province of Canada, which became the Dominion of Canada in 1867.

Now spread over 30,481 acres of land, of which 3,256 acres are covered with water,

the city itself has a population just shy of 300,000.

The capital is located on the provincial border of Ontario and Quebec at a point where the Ottawa River tumbles over the Chaudiere Falls. A short distance downstream, the Gatineau and Rideau Rivers flow in from the north and south.

The sprawling urban area surrounding Ottawa on the Ontario side was combined in mid-1968 to form the first regional government area of its kind in the province. The new regional municipality of Ottawa-Carleton covers an area of 1,100 sq. mi. with a population of 420,000. It includes the cities of Ottawa and Eastview and 14 other neighboring villages and townships.

The infant area-wide administration is headed by regional Chairman Denis Coolican, who receives an annual salary of $30,000. Mayor Don Reid is the city's chief administrator.

Just across the Ottawa River to the north in the Province of Quebec, the city of Hull and environs provide homes for another 116,000 people.

Ottawa is the Anglicized form of Outaouac or Outaouais, the name of a tribe of Indians from Lake Huron who were prominent in trade with the French in the 17th Century. They carried their furs along the Ottawa River in canoes.

The Parliament buildings—housing the nation's House of Commons and Senate—provide the city's main tourist attraction. Designed in the Gothic style and situated on Parliament Hill overlooking the city's main downtown business district, the seat of government occupies 3 main buildings. The Peace Tower, a famous landmark and memorial to Canada's war dead, towers above the main center block.

Not including the 22-mile Gatineau Parkway in a mountainous, lake-dotted district just north of the city in Quebec Province, there are 23 miles of parkways

and driveways in and around Ottawa. All have been designed and maintained by the Federally-operated National Capital Commission.

The Federal Government's continuing drive to develop the capital area has resulted in construction of a $45,000,000 National Arts Center in the heart of the city. The center, to be opened some time in 1969, will feature an opera house-concert hall, a theater, and an experimental studio.

Every summer, the Central Canada Exhibition, which runs for 10 days, provides the full variety entertainment of a fair including midway, grandstand performances, horse shows, and varied exhibits. The exhibition takes place at Lansdowne Park, where the new $9,000,000 Civic Center multi-purpose arena-stadium provides homes for the Canadian Football League Ottawa Rough Riders and the Ottawa 67's, a junior hockey team. The Ottawa Winter Fair takes over the Lansdowne facilities for a week every fall.

The Civil Service provides the bulk of employment for residents of the Greater Ottawa area, but in recent years the city has stepped up its drive to attract industry. However, the E. B. Eddy Co., producer of paper products and one of the area's oldest industries, is still the largest private employer.

Ottawa International Airport, 5th busiest in the nation, handles 60 scheduled flights daily for Air Canada and Eastern Airlines. It also serves as an alternate for Montreal's giant International Air Terminal, 120 miles away. Charter flights from almost all the world's major airlines make Ottawa stops.

Ottawa is served by both the Canadian Pacific and Canadian National Railways.

For further information contact Ottawa Tourist and Convention Bureau, 70 Besserer Street, Ottawa 2, Ontario, Canada.

## *Oakland, California* (See San Francisco-Oakland)

## Philadelphia, Pennsylvania

The World Almanac is sponsored in the Philadelphia area by The Philadelphia Inquirer, 400 N. Broad St., Philadelphia, Pa. 19101; telephone (215) LO 3-1600; traces its lineage to The Pennsylvania Packet, founded 1771; circulation 504,669 daily, 935,458 Sunday; editor and publisher, Walter H. Annenberg; editorial page director, Harold J. Wiegand; managing editor, John S. Gillen; sponsors Delaware Valley Science Fair, Old Newsboys' Day, Book and Author luncheons, awards scholarships and grants-in-aid to newsboys.

Birthplace of the nation, Philadelphia today is a major center of commerce, finance and culture, rich in both history and renewal, with a population of 4,690,-000 in the metropolitan area.

The English Quaker, William Penn, founded the city in 1682, giving it a name that means "city of brotherly love." His grid pattern of streets and public squares dictated the modern shape of the center city area from the broad Delaware River to the smaller Schuylkill.

The original two sq. mi. of Penn's "greene Country Towne" has grown to 129, and the early population, 400, to more than 2,000,000. But the Quaker influence remains strong in the fields of finance and private education.

Philadelphia was the largest and wealthiest of American cities in Colonial days. It held a pre-eminent position through the Revolution as the seat of the Continental Congress and for 10 years afterward during which it was the national capital.

The city abounds in relics of those days. The restored mansions of merchant princes dot the 4,000-acre Fairmont Park and there are buildings which still bear

the scars of the Battle of Germantown.

The Betsy Ross House in which the seamstress is said to have fashioned the Stars and Stripes still stands on Arch St., around the corner from Old Christ Church where George Washington worshipped.

The major historical shrines are clustered in Independence National Historical Park, focal point of which is Independence Hall where the Declaration of Independence was signed and the Constitution was framed. The Liberty Bell, symbol of freedom, occupies a place of honor in the building. (*See Index for Independence Hall, Liberty Bell and American Revolution.*)

Other buildings of outstanding interest in the park include Carpenters' Hall, meeting place of the First Continental Congress in 1774; Philosophical Hall, home of the American Philosophical Society founded in 1743 by Benjamin Franklin; the First Bank of the United States, erected in 1795 and probably the oldest bank building in the U. S., and the Bishop White House, home of the Rt. Rev. William White, "Father of the American Protestant Episcopal Church."

A new U. S. Mint is located on Independence Mall, and in the Delaware River a few blocks away is berthed the U.S.S. Olympia, Admiral Dewey's flagship in the Spanish-American War.

Adjoining the national park in what has been described as "America's most historic square mile" is Society Hill whose town houses of the Colonial and Federal periods have been restored amid modern apartment towers as part of Philadelphia's $600 million urban renewal program.

This program has spurred the development of a "new city" in the Penn Center complex of transportation terminals, office buildings and apartment houses. It has given Philadelphia a modern Food Distribution Center and has created on open land a community called Eastwick, the nation's largest renewal project.

One of the principal modernization projects of the 1960s has been the construction of a $16,000,000 exhibition hall addition to the Philadelphia Civic Center, which includes the 12,000-seat Convention Hall and a museum devoted primarily to the subject of trade.

Philadelphia's industrial base is widely diversified, embracing 87% of all the classifications listed by the U. S. Department of Labor. It is the largest petroleum refining center on the East Coast and the second largest in the nation.

In terms of employment, the building trades rank first among the city's industries, followed in order by machinery manufacturing, primary metals and metal fabrication, textile and clothing manufacturing, electrical machinery, food processing, chemicals, printing and publishing, paper manufacturing and instrument making.

Philadelphia has the largest fresh water port in the world with 50 miles of waterfront. Total foreign tonnage in 1967 was 49,175,803 tons, second highest in the nation. The vessels of more than 100 shipping lines link the city to 273 ports in 75 countries.

Serving the growing transportation needs of the Delaware Valley region is Philadelphia International Airport, which accommodated more than 5,000,000 passengers in 1967.

Philadelphia is corporate headquarters for the Penn-Central Railroad and has pioneered in subsidizing rail commuter service on an extensive network of lines of the Penn-Central and Reading Railroads through the Southeastern Pennsyl-

vania Transportation Authority.

The financial base of the city's economy is in 11 commercial banks and four mutual savings funds which have combined resources of more than $6.5 billion. Philadelphia is third in the nation in bank clearings. A number of nationwide insurance companies are headquartered in the city.

Philadelphia has a cultural tradition with its roots in Colonial times. The Philadelphia Orchestra of international renown makes its home in the Academy of Music, built in 1856 with an auditorium modeled after the La Scala opera house in Milan, Italy. The academy also plays host to the Pennsylvania Ballet Co. and to the Lyric Opera Co. and the Grand Opera Co.

The Philadelphia Museum of Art contains more than 100,000 works. It houses the Johnson Collection of Western art from the 14th through the 19th Centuries and the Arensburg Collection of modern masterpieces. The Rodin Museum is devoted to the works of the French sculptor, Auguste Rodin.

The Franklin Institute, dedicated to scientific research and education, provides visitors to its science teaching museum with the opportunity to operate exhibits illustrating basic scientific principles and to study the heavens as projected on the dome of the Fels Planetarium.

The Academy of Natural Sciences, founded in 1812, is the oldest scientific institution of its kind in the U. S. Exhibits feature lifelike animal groups in natural settings.

There are 17 colleges and universities in Philadelphia, the largest among them being the University of Pennsylvania and Temple University. Nearby are Villanova University and Bryn Mawr, Swarthmore and Haverford colleges.

The Philadelphia Phillies are the National League baseball team. Professional football is represented by the Philadelphia Eagles. The Philadelphia Flyers hockey club and the Philadelphia 76ers professional basketball team play in the 15,000-seat Spectrum, which opened in 1967. Crowds of more than 100,000 annually watch the traditional Army-Navy football game in John F. Kennedy Stadium.

Further information may be obtained from the Office of the City Representative and Department of Commerce, 1660 Municipal Services Building, Philadelphia, Pa. 19107, and from the Greater Philadelphia Chamber of Commerce, 121 South Broad Street, Philadelphia, Pa. 19107.

# Phoenix, Arizona

The World Almanac is sponsored in the Phoenix area by the Phoenix Gazette, 120 E. Van Buren St., Phoenix, Ariz. 85004; telephone (602) 271-8000; founded Oct. 28, 1880 as Arizona Gazette by Charles H. McNeil; circulation 95,952; publisher, Eugene C. Pulliam; managing editor, S. Lowell Parker; sponsors Golden Gloves, Science Fair, nutrition and medical forums, Music Memory programs and nine other events each year.

Phoenix is the capital and largest city of Arizona, with 1968 population estimated as 530,000. Metropolitan Phoenix covers 250 sq. mi. and includes satellite communities of Glendale, Scottsdale, Paradise Valley, Tempe, Mesa, Chandler, Buckeye and the remainder of Maricopa County, with 940,000 residents.

The first white settlement, a hay camp, was established in 1866 by John Y. T. Smith. He held a Government contract to supply mounted troops from Fort McDowell, 30 miles to the northeast.

In the winter of 1867 the John Swilling Co. began clearing out prehistoric canals to carry water from Salt River to the fertile lands of the valley.

Like the prehistoric people who lived here in 200 B.C., the white man found the

Valley of the Sun blessed by a mild climate with plentiful water. Cotton, citrus and cattle accounted for more than $260,-000,000 of farm income in 1967.

Phoenix, in south-central Arizona, was incorporated Feb. 11, 1881, and is governed by the mayor-council form of government with a city manager as executive officer.

It is a major Southwestern trading center and haven for winter tourists. Light manufacturing continues increasingly important to the city's economy.

The tourist business and conventions contributed $240,000,000 in 1967 and is projected to reach $260,000,000 in 1968.

Veterans Memorial Coliseum, a $6,000,-000 convention and sports facility opened in 1965 at the state fairground. With 10,294 permanent seats, it can accommodate

15,000 for many events.

Phoenix Civic Plaza, a $19,000,000 convention and cultural complex in the heart of Phoenix, will be completed in 1970.

Manufacturing is the area's major source of income, contributing $1.3 billion in 1967 and a predicted $1.5 billion in 1968.

Major employers are Western Electric, Cudahy, Swift and Company, Motorola, Reynolds, E. L. Gruber, Sperry Phoenix, General Electric, AiResearch, Goodyear Aerospace and Dickson Electronics. Both Motorola and Dickson Electronics are undergoing extensive plant expansions.

Transportation facilities include 9 airlines, two railroads, two transcontinental bus lines, 30 interstate and 39 intrastate truck lines.

Over 2,500,000 arrivals and departures are expected at Sky Harbor airport during 1968.

There are 111 shopping centers in the Metropolitan Phoenix area. Retail sales for 1967 were $1.62 billion while 1968 estimates are $1.75 billion.

A new $5,000,000 Post Office was dedicated in May, 1968. Pepsi-Cola Management Institute also opened during the year. In September of 1967 Arizona State University opened its new Law School on the campus at Tempe, Arizona.

Phoenix boasts a symphony orchestra, an art museum, Indian museum, zoo, musical theater, community theaters, and botanical garden. Nearby is Taliesen-West. Home of the late Frank Lloyd Wright, now an architectural school directed by Mrs. Wright.

A legitimate theater, running for 35 weeks, opened in October of 1968.

Sports events include horse, dog and auto racing, the Phoenix Open Golf Tournament, spring baseball with the San Francisco Giants, Chicago Cubs, Oakland Athletics and Seattle Pilots, Phoenix Suns, new member of the National Basketball Association, Phoenix Giants of the Pacific Coast Baseball League, and the Phoenix Roadrunners of the Western Hockey League.

Higher educational institutions include Arizona State University, Phoenix College, Grand Canyon College, the American Institute for Foreign Trade, a two-year community college at Mesa and Glendale, Southwestern College and Arizona Bible College.

Additional information on Phoenix may be obtained from the Arizona Development Board, Chamber of Commerce, Convention Bureau, and the Research Department of The Phoenix Gazette.

# Pittsburgh, Pennsylvania

The World Almanac is sponsored in the Pittsburgh area by the Pittsburgh Press, 34 Boulevard of the Allies, Pittsburgh, Pa. 15222; telephone (412) 263-1100; founded June 23, 1884, as Evening Press by Thomas J. Keenan; circulation 350,000 daily, 760,000 Sunday; editor, John Troan; business manager, Barney G. Cameron; major awards received include Edward J. Meeman Conservation Award; public service projects include campaigns for legislative action against ravages of strip mining, campaign to push mass immunization against polio.

Pittsburgh, one of the nation's top steel-making and coal mining areas, is a city of many hills and valleys through which run 3 major rivers as the Allegheny and Monongahela join to form the mighty Ohio, America's Gateway to the West for more than 200 years.

The first hunters and trappers came through here around 1714; the city itself dates from Nov. 25, 1759, when English forces under Brig. General John Forbes occupied the ruins of Fort Duquesne which French soldiers had burned and abandoned, and built a new and bigger fortress called Fort Pitt.

Protected by the fort and endowed by nature with fabulous riches, the area's first residents prospered as farmers and manufacturers. And the city grew steadily.

By the time it was incorporated as a city in 1816, it had already gained a reputation as a "Smoky City" because of the factories and coal-burning homes. It took 130 years to get rid of this grime.

Today, led by Mayor Joseph M. Barr and a nine-man council, Pittsburgh is one of 129 municipalities in Allegheny County. It has a population of 604,332 (1960 census) and is the center of a 4-county metropolitan area with 2,368,100 residents.

Pittsburgh is one of the country's top headquarters cities. It ranks second only to New York City in the amount of capital invested by its home-based firms, and ranks third—behind New York and Chicago—in the number of headquarter operations, as compiled in Fortune Magazine's Top 500 listing.

Concentrated in its metropolitan area is one-fifth of the nation's steelmaking capacity, and western Pennsylvania coal mines produce 40,000,000 tons of bituminous coal annually. Although steel and coal works dominate the area, around 6,000 different products are made here and 260,000 workers split an annual pay-roll of $1.8 billion. And there are 9 nuclear facilities hereabouts.

Although thought of as an inland city, Pittsburgh exports nearly $225,000,000 worth of goods annually, and its river ports handle 54,000,000 tons of freight annually; that's more than any other inland river area.

Retail sales total about $3.8 billion a year; wholesale, about $4.6 billion a year.

Pittsburgh is a vital transportation center. Besides its river traffic, it is served by 3 passenger rail carriers; 6 rail freight carriers; more than 350 common and contract motor carriers; 5 domestic air trunk-lines and 3 local service airlines.

Locally, the Port Authority of Allegheny County has welded some 30 independent bus lines and the Pittsburgh Railways Co. into an integrated transit system. A major plan for rapid and mass transit facilities is in preparation.

Pittsburgh is the home of the world's first full-scale nuclear power plant, the first industry-owned nuclear testing reactor; the first atomic engines were built here.

It's the home of the world's largest manufacturers of aluminum, steel rolls, rolling mill machinery, air brakes, plate and window glass, and safety equipment.

Here, too, are the largest American producers of bolts, nuts, and rivets; wrought iron pipe and bituminous coal.

There are around 125 industrial research and testing laboratories in the Pittsburgh area, along with facilities for basic and applied research in educational institutions.

Pittsburgh is a city of progress; this is where the guidebook on urban renewal was written in the 1940s. Pittsburgh's own war on poverty, through neighborhood programs carried out by ACTION-Housing, Inc., and others, predates the Great Society by several years.

More than $3 billion has been spent on urban renewal here since 1947 with 35 major buildings going up, and at least 5 more are planned, including a 64-story U. S. Steel headquarters that will tower above the city's skyline. Since World War II, more than $2.5 billion has gone into industrial expansion, and major smoke and flood control projects have cleared the skies and rivers. Still to come: a 50,-000-seat major league sports stadium; a downtown home for the famous Pittsburgh Symphony Orchestra, and the Pennsylvania Railroad has unveiled plans for a 147-acre downtown development that will increase the Golden Triangle by over one-third.

Among its schools are the University of Pittsburgh, Duquesne University, Point Park College, Chatham College, Mt. Mercy College, and Robert Morris Junior College. Mellon Institute and Carnegie Institute of Technology have merged to form Carnegie-Mellon University.

Its Health Center in Oakland, where Dr. Jonas Salk perfected his polio vaccine, is one of the best in the nation. In all, there are 62 hospitals scattered throughout the metropolitan area.

In Oakland, too—the area is considered the City's cultural center—is WQED, one of the nation's pioneer educational television stations. It went on the air April 1, 1954, and is considered the country's first. There are 18 Carnegie public libraries,

3 bookmobiles and dozens of community libraries. Theaters include the Civic Light Opera and 4 other summer showplaces, 3 community legitimate theaters and two commercial legitimate theaters. The Pittsburgh Symphony and the Pittsburgh Opera Company are widely known.

Points of interest include Buhl Planetarium, the Aviary with its rare birds, Phipps Conservatory, the Carnegie Museum and its Art Gallery, Highland Zoo, an aquarium, the Children's Zoo, the Underground Zoo, and the Allegheny Observatory for stargazers.

Notable buildings include the County Courthouse and Jail designed by H. H. Richardson, Mellon Institute; and the University of Pittsburgh's 42-story Cathedral of Learning, with its Gothic campus companions, the Stephen Foster Memorial and Heinz Chapel.

Historic sites includes the reconstructions of the walls of Fort Pitt in the downtown area and the Blockhouse, which stood outside the fort's ramparts and which is the only building still standing from the early days.

In sports, Pittsburgh has the Pittsburgh Pirates (baseball) in the National League, the Steelers in the National Football League and the Penguins in the National Hockey League.

Additional information on Pittsburgh can be obtained from The Chamber of Commerce of Greater Pittsburgh, 411 Seventh Ave., Pittsburgh, Pa. 15222.

## Portland, Oregon

The World Almanac is sponsored in the Portland area by the Oregon Journal, 1320 SW Broadway, Portland, Ore. 97201; telephone (503) 222-5511; founded April, 1902; circulation 141,242; publisher, Wm. W. Knight; editor, Arden X. Pangborn; executive news editor, Harry Leeding; editorial page editor, Donald J. Sterling, Jr.

Portland, Oregon's largest city, covers 80 sq. mi. at the junction of the Columbia and Willamette rivers in the northwest portion of the state. It was chartered in 1851 with a population of 821 and was named for Portland, Me., rather than for Boston, Mass., when two of its early citizens from those two New England cities flipped a penny to decide its name. Today's population is an estimated 385,500.

An important seaport, Portland grew as a commercial and industrial center of Oregon because of its strategic location, draining much of the Pacific Northwest's agricultural and forestry output down the Willamette and Columbia river valleys. Much of Oregon's produce in the mid-19th Century was shipped south by water from Portland to feed gold miners who rushed to California after 1849.

The Greater Portland Metropolitan area has an estimated 933,159 population.

Agricultural products and shipping were the city's original economic base, developing later to forest products processing and shipping. Today metal working, mostly aluminum, has become Portland area's biggest resource, plus some steel work, clothing, paper, electronics. It ranks first as manufacturer of huge, specialized equipment for the logging-lumbering industry. The city's economic base is varied and broad. It is the home of Georgia-Pacific Corporation (forest products, lumber, paper); Crown Zellerbach (forest products, paper); Tektronix and Electronics Specialty companies (sophisticated electronics testing equipment); Omark Industries (chain saws); Hyster Corporation (lifts, hoisting equipment, lumber handling devices); and White Stag, Jantzen and Pendleton (sports clothes).

Total retail sales for Greater Portland area (1967) were set at $1,595,773,000 and for the state of Oregon at $3,394,525,000.

Portland is served by 5 railroads, 10 airlines and two major bus lines. Since World War II it has become increasingly a warehousing center, and is served by many major truck lines.

Mild year-around weather makes Portland a pleasant living place, also makes it a rose-growing center and site of the annual June "Rose Festival," 50-yr.-old pageant and rose show.

Among its famous buildings is the Pittock Mansion, elaborate turn-of-century home which has become a unit of the Portland Public Parks system.

Portland's zoo has gained fame in past years as "outstanding producer of baby elephants in the Western Hemisphere" with herd sire Thonglaw having produced six offspring. The city has an outstanding public parks system, headed by Washington Park which houses International Rose Test Garden and outdoor summer theater; and which is adjacent to the Portland Zoo and the Oregon Museum of Science and Industry; and by Hoyt Arboretum, largest forested area inside a U. S. city's limits.

Memorial Coliseum is the home of the Portland Buckaroos, of the Western Hockey League. The city floated a bond issue for purchase of Multnomah Stadium and has renamed it Portland Civic Stadium, home of the Portland Beavers in the Pacific Coast Baseball League.

In or on the fringes of the city are Portland State College, University of Portland, Lewis & Clark College, Reed College, Marylhurst College, Multnomah College, Cascade College, and Concordia College.

Specialized information may be obtained from the Portland Development Commission, City Hall, Portland, and the Portland Chamber of Commerce, 824 SW 5th Ave., Portland.

# Regina, Canada

The World Almanac is sponsored in southern Saskatchewan by The Leader-Post, 1964 Park St., Regina, Sask.; telephone (306) 527-8511; founded 1885 by Nicholas Flood Davin; circulation, 64,911; president, Michael Sifton, Toronto; executive vice president, William Thomson; editor, Thomas Melville; managing editor, C. E. W. Bell; advertising manager, William Duffus; awards: MacLaren Trophy for editorial page excellence of reproduction; 4 awards by Canadian Circulation Managers' Assn., for newspaper sales promotion and carrier training; sponsors a variety of fund-raising campaigns for worthy causes.

Founded on the site of a pile of buffalo bones, Regina, Saskatchewan's capital, has overcome a lack of natural advantages to grow into a beautifully-treed urban community known as the Queen City of the Plains.

The community was founded in 1882 when the Canadian Government and Canadian Pacific Railway chose the site for the capital of the Northwest Territories. Indians had piled the bones of countless slaughtered buffalo on the banks of a creek in the vicinity. The settlement was called variously Pile O'Bones, Manybones, and Bone Creek. Later it became Wascana, a corruption of the Cree Indian word "oskana," meaning bones. The more dignified name of Regina was chosen by Princess Louise in honor of her mother, Queen Victoria. Incorporated as a city in 1903, Regina was named provincial capital two years later when Saskatchewan was formed.

Regina has survived cyclone, riot, drought and depression to become a prosperous city of some 140,000, riding a boom that has more than doubled the value of its taxable property—from $75,000,000 to $190,000,000—in the past 10 years. Regina is one of Western Canada's leading industrial centers. It is the service center for a prolific oil and grain producing area, and its industries include meat packing, steel, pipe, oil refining, paper box, paint manufacturing, cement and fertilizer, agricultural machinery and an industrial gas plant.

The rapid development of potash mining in the province has had a tremendous economic effect on Regina, where much of the activity is centered.

It was in Regina, in the depths of the depression in 1933, that the Co-operative Commonwealth Federation (CCF) was founded. The CCF formed the Saskatchewan Provincial Government in 1944, first Socialist government in North America, which remained in power for 20 years.

The head office of the Saskatchewan Wheat Pool is located in the city. Founded in 1924 because of farmer resentment of the railway and elevator monopoly, it is world's largest primary grain-handling organization with over 100,000 members.

Regina's modern steel and concrete high-rise buildings contrast with the portable wooden buildings shipped here in 1882 to accommodate the new headquarters of the North West Mounted Police. The city remains Western headquarters of the NWMP's successors, the Royal Canadian Mounted Police, and the Mounties' museum and chapel are tourist musts.

The impressive Saskatchewan Legislative Building stands on the south bank of Wanasca Lake. The lake is the focal point of a 100-yr. project called Wanasca Centre. The plan, financed by the province, city and University of Saskatchewan, is a multimillion-dollar development of public buildings, parks and recreation areas on a 1,600-acre site in the heart of the city.

Points of interest in Regina include the Natural History Museum, the Norman MacKenzie Art Gallery, and the 13-story Saskatchewan Power Building, an award-winning $10,000,000 S-shaped structure.

Educational institutions include the Regina Campus of the University of Saskatchewan.

In Regina are the Saskatchewan Roughriders, who in 1966 won their first Grey Cup as national professional football champions.

# Richmond, Virginia

The World Almanac is sponsored in the Richmond area by the Richmond Times-Dispatch and The Richmond News Leader, 333 East Grace St., Richmond, Va. 23213; telephone (703) 649-6000; Times-Dispatch founded 1850 by James A. Cowardin; circulation 148,413 daily, 200,389 Sunday; News Leader founded 1896 by Joseph Bryan; circulation 123,636; publisher, D. Tennant Bryan; president, Alan S. Donnahoe; managing editor, Times-Dispatch, John E. Leard; managing editor, News Leader, Charles H. Hamilton; sponsor Christmas Mother Fund, editorial campaigns for traffic safety, Beadle Bumble Fund for victims of injustice; major awards include Pulitzer Prize won by Virginius Dabney for Times-Dispatch editorials.

Richmond, a blend of the old and the new South, is on the James River 65 miles inland from the Chesapeake Bay.

In 1607, Captains John Smith, Christopher Newport and party explored the James River to the falls and there put a cross; the first settlement was in 1609.

The name was suggested by William Byrd II, who had frequently visited the English borough of the same name during his stay in London. In 1737 Byrd founded and Major William Mayo laid out the town, to be called Richmond because "its situation was like that of Richmond-on-the-Thames in England."

Richmond was incorporated as a town in 1742 and was made the Virginia capital in 1780. It was incorporated as a city in 1842 and was Confederate capital (1861-65).

The 1968 city population is 216,500 with 526,200 in the Standard Metropolitan Statistical Area that includes the counties of Henrico, Chesterfield and Hanover.

Richmond has survived a terrible flood in 1771, burning by Benedict Arnold in 1781, and the evacuation fire of 1865 when stores of cotton and tobacco were burned to prevent their use by Federal troops.

With corporate land area of 39.9 square miles, the city has under way a court action to annex 50 square miles and 75,000 residents of the County of Chesterfield.

Completely separate and independent from any county, the city operates with a nine-member council-city manager form of government. Financial bond rating services accord Richmond bonds the highest possible rating, AAA, and citizen activity has twice won the All-America City Award.

A headquarters city, Richmond serves as a distribution center with almost 50% of the total employment in white collar jobs. Manufacturing accounts for one-fourth of all employment.

The labor force expands at the rate of 6,000 workers per year. Special training is offered and productivity is 27% higher than the average of 72 major industrial areas.

Richmond is on the shortest and most economical highway route between New York and Florida. It is served by 3 interstate routes, 6 U. S. highway routes, 9 state highway routes, 4 railroads, 4 commercial airlines, two commuter airlines, 5 intercity bus lines and 50 fixed route motor truck lines.

The modern deepwater terminal and navigable James River with 25-foot channel help make Richmond a trade center of the South Atlantic with 860 wholesale distributors and more than $1.9 billion in annual sales. Nine institutions of higher learning offer education in the arts, business, science, medicine, law, humanities and theology.

"Tobacco Capital of the World," Richmond produces enough cigarettes each year to encircle the earth 200 times. The Richmond area has the largest nylon plant in the world and is a center for packaging with aluminum, cellophane and paper products. The city is one of the major financial centers in the United States.

The Richmond Braves play at Parker Field and represent Richmond in the (AAA) International League.

One of the nation's most interesting cities, Richmond has a bus tour sponsored by Richmond Jaycees that shows such points as St. John's Church, where Patrick Henry delivered his immortal "Give me liberty or give me death" speech; the Virginia Capitol designed by Thomas Jefferson, meeting place for the Virginia General Assembly, the oldest legislative body in the western hemisphere; Hollywood Cemetery with the graves of 18,000 Confederate soldiers, Confederate President Jefferson Davis, Gen. J. E. B. Stuart, and U. S. Presidents Tyler and Monroe. The Lee House, Confederate Museum, John Marshall House, Valentine Museum, Poe Museum, Battle Abbey and Virginia Museum of Fine Arts are attractions.

Preserving the splendor of old Richmond is Monument Ave. with its monuments of Gen. J. E. B. Stuart, Gen. Robert E. Lee, Jefferson Davis, Gen. Thomas J. "Stonewall" Jackson and Commodore Matthew Fontaine Maury.

Richmond has under construction a $23,000,000 coliseum-convention center seating 12,000, a new 17-story City Hall costing $17,000,000, and a 13-mile system of new expressways costing $95,000,000 to serve the heart of the city.

Additional information available from the Richmond Chamber of Commerce, 616 East Franklin St., Richmond, Va. 23219.

# Rochester, New York

The World Almanac is sponsored in the Rochester area by the Democrat & Chronicle and the Times-Union, 55 Exchange St., Rochester, N. Y. 14614; telephones, Democrat & Chronicle (716) 232-5300; Times-Union (716) 232-7100; Democrat & Chronicle founded as Morning Advertiser 1833 by Sidney Smith, Times-Union founded as Advertiser 1826 by Henry C. Sleight; circulation Democrat & Chronicle 142,794 (morning), 218,586 (Sunday), Times-Union 143,855 (evening); publisher, Paul Miller, president, Gannett Co., Inc.; general manager, Allen H. Neuharth; director of operations, Duane R. Jacobs; director of sales, Al F. Mahar; director of news, John Quinn; director of public service, Vince Spezzano; both papers shared in 1964 Pulitzer Prize awarded to Gannett Newspapers; public service projects include Lend-A-Hand Fund, Newspaper-In-The-Classroom, Harvest Queen.

Rochester, third largest city in New York State, is a world leader in the manufacture of precision goods and a major eastern U. S. cultural center. Located on Lake Ontario, it leads the world in the manufacture of photographic film and cameras, optical goods, dental equipment, and thermometers.

Settled in 1789 by Ebenezer Allen, who built a grist mill in a swamp on the Genesee River shore, it was established as a village in 1812, incorporated as Rochesterville in 1817, and became Rochester in 1822.

The Erie Canal boom in the 1820s established Rochester as a trade center. It became a city in 1834 and its many flour mills gained it the nickname "Flour City."

Rochester had 301,829 people in 1965, and an estimated 298,500 in 1967. Estimated metropolitan area population in 1968 was 832,200. It is governed by a city manager and a 9-member council.

Largest employers are Eastman Kodak Co. (46,000), Xerox (12,000), and Bausch & Lomb (5,300); all were founded in Rochester and have headquarters there.

Estimated retail sales for the metropolitan area in 1967 were $1.309 billion.

Rochester is served by 5 railroads and 3 airlines. Rochester-Monroe County Airport serviced 1,188,460 passengers in 1967, and was over the million mark in passengers serviced for the first time in history. There were 26,573 scheduled flights by commercial airlines, an increase of 2320 over 1966. The Port of Rochester docked 73 cargo-bearing ships, loading and unloading 65,016 tons.

Among major development programs are Xerox Square, a $20,000,000 downtown project dominated by a 30-story tower;

Genesee Crossroads Redevelopment project, a joint civic and business project expected to cost $70,000,000; and a $39,000,000 Civic Center and Plaza, a $70,000,000 Clinton Square redevelopment project, to be dominated by a 26-story $11,000,000 Lincoln-Rochester Bank and a 21-story Marine Midland bank-office building.

Rochester is now known as the "Flower City," because of its outstanding public and private floral and horticultural attractions. Its mid-May "Lilac Festival" is a major international attraction. The Monroe County Parks system includes 14 parks in and around the city, including Seneca Park Zoo and the lilac gardens at Highland Park. Community War Memorial auditorium is home of Rochester Americans of the American Hockey League. The International (baseball) League Red Wings play at Red Wing Stadium.

Eastman Theater is part of the home of the Eastman School of Music of the U. of Rochester and home auditorium of the Rochester Philharmonic, Eastman Philharmonia, and Eastman Wind Ensemble. Memorial Art Gallery has one of the country's largest gallery memberships. Other museums include Rochester Museum of Arts and Sciences; George Eastman House of Photography, and Ward's Natural Science Establishment. Colleges include University of Rochester, Rochester Institute of Technology, Roberts Wesleyan, Nazareth and St. John Fisher Colleges; State U. College at Brockport; Colgate Rochester Divinity School; Monroe Community College.

Information about Rochester is available from the Chamber of Commerce, 55 St. Paul St., Rochester, N. Y. 14604.

## Sacramento, California

The World Almanac is sponsored in the Sacramento area by The Sacramento Bee, 21st & Q. Sacramento, Calif. 95816; telephone (916) 442-5011. The Bee was founded Feb. 3, 1857, and developed into the Capitol City's leading newspaper under the direction of its pioneer editor, James McClatchy, and, later under his son, C. K. McClatchy. They served the Pulitzer Prize-winning Bee for almost 80 years. Daily circulation is 175,000; Sunday circulation, 203,000. Eleanor McClatchy is president of McClatchy Newspapers, which include The Modesto Bee and The Fresno Bee.

Sacramento, capital of California, is located in the Sacramento Valley, 85 mi. northeast of San Francisco and 385 mi. north of Los Angeles. It is the 13th fastest growing metropolitan area in the U. S.

The City of Sacramento, has an estimated population of 275,000 and covers 93 sq. mi. It is the seat of Sacramento County, estimated population 630,000, area 997 sq. mi. Sacramento also is the heart of a 19-county market area which includes the Sacramento Valley and the surrounding mountain counties. Within this large area are over 50 cities and towns with populations of 1,000 or more. The area possesses much natural wealth: lumber, minerals, petroleum and water, and is blessed with a mild climate and fertile land. Retail sales for the 19-county market exceed $2.077 billion annually.

Sacramento grew out of the founding by John Augustus Sutter of his famous fort near the confluence of the Sacramento and American Rivers in 1839. His adobe fort was civilization's lone outpost in the California interior. On Jan. 24, 1848, James Wilson Marshall discovered gold at Sutter's mill on the American River in Coloma, 35 mi. northeast of Sacramento.

In a short time Sacramento, gateway to the Mother Lode country, became the goal of a great migration. Approximately 100,000 gold seekers came to California by wagon-train and ship, most of them headed for Sacramento and Stockton.

Early Sacramento also saw the Pony Express and the Central Pacific Railroad which crossed the Sierra Nevada.

Levees built during this early period helped development of one of the world's most productive agricultural areas. There now are more than 15,500 farms in the 19-county area, producing 2,000 different crops annually worth over $462,000,000.

Water for irrigation and industry comes from the Sierra country where California's $1.75 billion Feather River water project and system of dams assures a year-round water supply. The Oroville Dam is the key unit in the project.

There are 367 manufacturing plants in Sacramento. Included are such names as Campbell Soup, Procter and Gamble, Libby, McNeil and Libby, California Almond Growers Exchange, Aerojet-General and McDonnell Douglas Astronautics.

The state employs over 26,000 in the Sacramento area and McClellan Air Force Base has 20,000 civilian employees.

Transportation and distribution facilities are highlighted by the new $55,000,000 Port of Sacramento which provides a deep water channel to the Pacific. Interstate and other major highways intersect within Sacramento city limits. Sacramento has a new, jet age Metropolitan Airport, a Municipal Airport and 14 smaller airfields. The city is served by the transcontinental lines of the Southern Pacific and Western Pacific railroads. It also has the freight facilities of the Central California Traction Co. and the Sacramento Northern.

Sacramento has a city manager form of government. The manager is selected by the City Council. The Councilmen are elected by the city at large for two-year terms.

Sacramento County has 12 general hospitals with a bed capacity of 1,907. There are two junior colleges, Sacramento State College and the University of Pacific's McGeorge Law School. Nearby at Davis is the University of California with an enrollment of nearly 10,000.

Twelve publicly-sponsored cultural organizations provide theatrical, ballet, symphony and art gallery programs. Recreational facilities include 95 public parks, a zoo, 74 playgrounds, 44 theaters, 6 18-hole and 6 9-hole public golf courses and 4 private golf clubs. Fishing, swimming, boating and camping facilities are found along the American and Sacramento Rivers. Nearby are the High Sierras with lake and stream fishing, hunting, boating and some of the nation's best skiing.

Historical points of interest include the State Capitol, John Sutter's Fort, Gov. Leland Stanford home, Pony Express Terminal, Crocker Art Gallery and the Governor's Mansion.

## St. Louis, Missouri

The World Almanac is sponsored in the St. Louis area by the St. Louis Post-Dispatch, 1133 Franklin Ave., St. Louis, Mo. 63101; telephone (314) MA 1-1111; founded Dec. 12, 1878, by Joseph Pulitzer; circulation 387,180 daily, 610,016 Sunday; editor and publisher, Joseph Pulitzer, Jr.; managing editor, Arthur R. Bertelson; general manager, Charles J. Hentschell; business manager, Alex T. Primm; director of public affairs and promotion, Frank Leeming; major awards include 5 Pulitzer Prizes to newspaper, 9 to staff members; community projects include high school scholar-athlete program, straight A baseball tickets, science fair and Silver Skates.

St. Louis, Mo., "Gateway to the West," is crowned at its downtown riverfront by the 630-foot-high Gateway Arch, a stainless steel, catenary arch designed by Eero Saarinen. The nation's tallest monument, it stands in an 85-acre park that once was filled with riverfront warehouses. It commemorates Jefferson's Louisiana Purchase, the westward expansion of America and the role of St. Louis as the gateway city for vast numbers of settlers who left the Mississippi River there and headed west. The arch has capsule cars for rides to the top; the park and underground museum are not yet finished.

The Arch stands near the place chosen by Pierre Laclede Ligueste, French fur trader, in 1763 as an ideal spot for a camp and village. The landing he chose was about 14 miles down the Mississippi from the mouth of the Missouri river. In 1764 Laclede sent his lieutenant, Auguste Chouteau, back to establish the post. Laclede named it St. Louis after Louis XV. St. Louis was governed by a succession of Spanish viceroys until 1804 and later was selected as a settlement center by generations of Germans; it attained early distinction as an American melting pot.

In 1876 the proud city fathers declared St. Louis a "free" city and legally separated it from St. Louis County. At the

time that was thought to be an advance in municipal government, but the strictly set boundaries have become a straitjacket, the city has been boundary-bound to 65 square miles, locked in by the Mississippi on the east and unable to expand west.

The city proper has declined in population to an estimated 693,000, the county has grown to 942,000 in 95 municipalities, the metropolitan area to an estimated 2,395,000. Negroes make up a third of the population of the city proper.

St. Louis is experiencing a renaissance. The spectacular World's Fair of 1904 gave impetus to growth that filled the city's boundaries; there was a surge of pride when Lindbergh flew the Atlantic in the "Spirit of St. Louis" in 1927, but by 1950 it seemed that the city had become a dowager and had gone to sleep. The Post-Dispatch ran a series of articles pointing out what had happened under the title, "Progress or Decay? St. Louis Must Choose." Businessmen and city government got together to shake the city awake.

Today, near the soaring Arch, the new 50,000-seat, $24,000,000 Busch Memorial Stadium provides a beautiful home for professional baseball, football and soccer; Mansion House Center, with apartment towers and business buildings, is a modern riverfront residence; new office buildings, motels and apartments stand where blight had spread. The Mississippi was spanned anew in 1967 by a $30,000,000 bridge downtown to connect interstate highways and trafficways to be completed by 1970.

Major industrial and commercial projects under construction, awarded or planned totaled $2.700 billion in 1967 for the metropolitan area. Still, while gleaming new buildings went up at some places, blight, decay and population loss attacked others. Although urban renewal has been extensive, vast areas remain to be rebuilt.

In the steamboat era, St. Louis grew into a city as a riverboat port. The Mississippi below St. Louis is the most heavily traveled river in the world and St. Louis remains the busiest port on the river except for the deep-water ports of New Orleans and Baton Rouge. St. Louis harbor cargo runs 9,500,000 tons a year.

St. Louis is second only to Detroit in automobile assembly. It is the home of the McDonnell Douglas Corp., aerospace manufacturers, who did pioneering work in space travel in making space capsules for the Mercury and Gemini projects. Lambert-St. Louis Field is served by 8 airlines with more than 400 jet flights to and from St. Louis each day. In 1967 more than 2,226,000 passengers arrived by air and a slightly smaller number departed. St. Louis is served by 16 trunk line railroads and 5 switching roads and there were more than 1,000,000 revenue car switchings by the terminal railroad in 1967. St. Louis is recognized as the second largest trucking center in the nation. More than 200 common carriers provide service to the U. S. and Canada. The city is served by 16 bus lines.

"First in shoes and first in booze" was an old St. Louis slogan. It has the headquarters of the two largest shoe manufacturers, Interco, Inc., and Brown Shoe Co., the biggest brewery, Anheuser-Busch, and a large competitor, Falstaff Brewing Corp. Monsanto Co., among the largest American industrial corporations, has headquarters and plants in St. Louis. The food industry is represented by Ralston-Purina Co. and Pet, Inc. Peabody Coal Co. is a leader and Granite City Steel Co. is a major producer. Emerson Electric Co. represents the electrical field. Retail sales for the year ended Apr. 30, 1968, were estimated at $3.976 billion.

St. Louis has wide manufacturing capabilities with firms operating in 431 of the standard industrial classifications. It is at the heart of the only such area in the country producing 6 basic metals: iron, lead, zinc, copper, magnesium and aluminum. It is the metropolitan area closest to the center of U. S. population.

The new downtown stadium and an excellent new planetarium in Forest Park have added to public attractions such as the Zoo, Missouri Botanical Gardens, City Art Museum and Symphony. The Spanish Pavilion from the New York World's Fair is being constructed downtown. Architectural attractions include the Eads Bridge, Old Courthouse and Old Cathedral on the riverfront, the Victorian Union Station, Old Post Office, Gen. Grant's cabin, Gen. Sherman's home and several restored historic houses. Professional sports teams are the 1967 World Champion St. Louis Cardinals of the National League, the Cardinals of the National Football League, Stars of the National Professional Soccer League, Blues of the National Hockey League.

Both Washington University and St. Louis University are engaged in building campaigns and a new campus of the University of Missouri has grown to more than 7,000 students in 5 years.

Specialized information may be obtained from the Chamber of Commerce of Metropolitan St. Louis, 224 North Broadway, or the Regional Industrial Development Corp., 7701 Forsyth Blvd.

# St. Paul, Minnesota

The World Almanac is sponsored in the St. Paul area by the St. Paul Dispatch and Pioneer Press, 55 E. 4th St., St. Paul, Minn. 55101; telephone (612) 222-5011; Dispatch founded 1868, Pioneer Press founded as Minnesota Pioneer 1849 by James Goodhue; circulation, Pioneer Press 104,088 (morning), 220,896 (Sunday), Dispatch 130,535 (evening); Bernard H. Ridder, chairman of the board; Bernard H. Ridder, Jr., president and publisher; Fred S. Heaberlin, executive editor; Willam G. Sumner, editor.

St. Paul is the capital city of Minnesota. It has an estimated (1967) population of 317,287 and is the second largest city in Minnesota, exceeded only by Minneapolis. St. Paul and Minneapolis are Minnesota's Twin Cities. They and their suburbs form a metropolitan area of nearly 2,000,000 people.

St. Paul is located on hilly banks of the Mississippi River in eastern Minnesota. It is close to vacation areas of both Minnesota and Wisconsin and is noted as a manufacturing, transportation, retail and education center.

The site of the city was Sioux (Dakota) Indian country when Father Louis Hennepin, Catholic missionary and explorer, visited it in 1680. Land near the confluence of the Minnesota and Mississippi Rivers, just southwest of the present city, was acquired for the U. S. in 1805. Fort Snelling was built there and after many years of service is now a Minnesota State Park. The old fort is being reconstructed.

St. Paul's first settler (1838) was a trader, Pierre Parrant, nicknamed "Pig's Eye." Parrant was one of the Fort Snelling squatters who in 1840 were removed from the military reservation and settled in what is now the heart of St. Paul. In 1841 Father Lucian Galtier, missionary at St. Peter's (Mendota) on the south side

of the river, built a chapel to serve the squatter community. He dedicated it to St. Paul and soon the settlement became known as St. Paul or St. Paul's rather than Pig's Eye. St. Paul was incorporated as a town in 1849 and as a city in 1854.

The first steamboat reached Fort Snelling in 1823 and St. Paul became the upstream terminus of regular shipping in 1847. The city remains a major river port, served by 7 barge lines. In 1967, receipts and shipments at the Port of St. Paul totaled 5,039,178 tons.

In the latter 1800s, St. Paul prospered as a rail and lumber center. It continues as the headquarters of the Great Northern Railway and the Northern Pacific Railway. The city is served by 62 railroads, including eight Class I lines.

More than 4,000,000 passengers were handled by 7 airlines at St. Paul-Minneapolis International Airport in 1967. There were 270,911 flight arrivals and departures. St. Paul Downtown Airport (Holman Field), which caters to business uses, saw 177,666 arrivals and departures. International Airport is home base for two major airlines, Northwest Orient and North Central.

There are three interstate bus lines and four transit lines operating in St. Paul, and the city forms the nation's third largest trucking center.

The Twin Cities area is now the fourth largest electronics center in the nation. St. Paul is fourth largest in publishing and printing, fifth in the production of cosmetics in the nation and the largest producer of refined petroleum products in the Midwest.

In 1888 St. Paul Union Stockyards were founded and now are second only to Omaha in the U. S., with a 1967 volume of 4,897,180 head of livestock.

Higher education facilities in St. Paul include the University of Minnesota Institute of Agriculture, Hamline University, Bethel College and Seminary, College of St. Thomas, College of St. Catherine, Concordia College, Macalester College, William Mitchell College of Law, Luther Theological Seminary, Northwestern Luther Theological Seminary, St. Paul Bible College, St. Paul Seminary and United Theological Seminary of the Twin Cities.

Attractions include the St. Paul Winter Carnival; the Minnesota State Fair, billed as the nation's largest; Como Park Zoo and Conservatory; the onyx statue of the Indian God of Peace by sculptor Carl Milles in the City Hall and Court House Building, the State Capitol, the St. Paul Arts and Science Center and the Minnesota Historical Society museums.

St. Paul is undergoing a vast downtown redevelopment program including a 12-block Capital Centre project that will feature year-round, temperature-controlled elevated sidewalks connecting new and existing buildings. About $90,000,000 in urban renewal land clearance and redevelopment is now underway.

St. Paul in 1967 issued $41,318,000 in non-residential and $11,026,000 in residential building permits. Its retail sales totalled $580,833,000.

The city has a commission-mayor form of government and also is the seat of Ramsey County government.

In suburban Bloomington are the American League Minnesota Twins baseball team, the National Football League's Minnesota Vikings, and the National Hockey League's Minnesota North Stars.

Specialized information is available from the Chamber of Commerce, Osborn Building, St. Paul, Minn. 55101.

# St. Petersburg, Florida

The World Almanac is sponsored in the St. Petersburg area by The St. Petersburg Times and Evening Independent, 490 First Avenue South, St. Petersburg, Fla. 33731; telephone (813) 894-1111; The Times founded 1884, The Independent 1906; circulation Times, morning, 151,615 daily, 166,711 Sunday; Independent, evening, 25,163 daily; papers produced by The Times Publishing Co., Nelson Poynter, editor and president; Donald K. Baldwin, executive editor; John B. Lake, general manager; major awards include Pulitzer Gold Medal for public service, National Headliners Award, University of Missouri Award; sponsors Most Valuable Legislators awards for Florida legislature, science fair, spelling bee, boat show, Christmas parade.

The story of St. Petersburg begins with the Caloosa Indians who lived hundreds of years on the rich game in the forest and succulent fish from the waters of the Gulf of Mexico. These first Floridians greeted Hernando De Soto and Ponce De Leon when they sailed on their historic voyages early in the 16th Century.

It was not until 1835 that Dr. ʿOdet Philippe, former surgeon in the armies of Napoleon, sailed into Old Tampa Bay and became the first permanent white settler. Hardy pioneers followed to conquer a wilderness and create one of America's leading resort areas.

St. Petersburg covers 58 square miles on the southern tip of Pinellas county, a peninsula separating the Gulf of Mexico and Tampa Bay, half way up Florida's west coast. Incorporated in 1892, the city now has a population estimated at 216,000, while Pinellas County's population has grown to 452,000.

The American Medical Association Journal in 1885 described the St. Petersburg area as the world's healthiest place to live because of its climate. The delightful year-round climate, coupled with tropic beauty, soon established St. Petersburg as a tourist mecca.

The Evening Independent's offer of a free paper on days when the sun fails to

shine—paid off on an average of 4 times a year since 1910—helped establish St. Petersburg as the Sunshine City.

Today, nearly 2,300,000 visitors come to St. Petersburg and Pinellas County each year, spending $600,000,000 to swim, fish, sail, ski and enjoy the attractions for which the area is famous.

St. Petersburg experienced rapid growth during the land boom of the 1920s when Gandy Bridge was built, linking peninsula Pinellas with the Florida mainland. Another expansion followed World War II, when thousands of servicemen who had trained in the area returned to make it their permanent home.

Space industry came to Pinellas County in the 1950s, bringing with it thousands of young engineers and technicians and their families. Honeywell, General Electric, Sperry Rand and Electronics Communications Inc. are among firms providing a stable, smokeless, industrial economy.

Effective buying income in the Pinellas metropolitan area in 1967 was estimated at $1.1 billion, second only to Miami-Dade County in Florida. Retail sales were set at $815,000,000, fourth highest in Florida.

Since 1950, bank deposits in Pinellas have risen from nearly $150,000,000 to over $810,000,000. Savings and loan deposits are up from $50,000,000 to $700,000,000.

More than 88,000 students attend school in the St. Petersburg metropolitan area, including St. Petersburg Junior College, Florida Presbyterian College, Bay Campus of the University of South Florida and Stetson University College of Law.

Among recent major city projects are the $5,000,000 Bayfront Center auditorium and arena, $1,000,000 art museum, $1,000,000 library, $5,000,000 Federal building, $1,000,000 municipal marina and development of recreation facilities along the downtown waterfront.

St. Petersburg is operated under a council-manager form of government.

It is a city of more than 230 churches, third in the nation in per capita church attendance for major metropolitan areas.

During February and March, the St. Louis Cardinals and New York Mets hold spring training at Al Lang Field, playing against other major league teams.

In the immediate area are greyhound racing, horse racing and jai alai, in addition to excellent golf, tennis, bowling, shuffleboard and water sports facilities.

St. Petersburg's downtown Albert Whitted Airport provides services for private planes, while commercial air transportation is available at nearby Tampa International Airport. The city also is served by Seaboard Coastline Railroad and Greyhound and Trailway Bus Lines.

Detailed information can be obtained from The St. Petersburg Times Public Service Department and the Greater St. Petersburg Chamber of Commerce.

## Salt Lake City, Utah

The World Almanac is sponsored in the Salt Lake City area by the Salt Lake Tribune, 143 S. Main St., Salt Lake City, Utah 84110; telephone (801) 524-4545; founded Apr. 15, 1871; circulation 110,146 daily, 190,790 Sunday; publisher, John W. Gallivan; executive editor, Arthur C. Deck; editorial page editor, Theodore W. Long; major awards received included 1957 Pulitzer Prize; civic projects include statewide civic beautification awards, Sub for Santa program, Community Christmas Tree.

Salt Lake City, capital of Utah and largest city in the state, with an estimated 1968 population of 210,000, is best known for being headquarters of the Church of Jesus Christ of Latter-day Saints (Mormon). Founded July 24, 1847, by Brigham Young and a contingent of ·pioneers, the settlement first was known as Great Salt Lake City, a name which continued for many decades.

Nestled between the Wasatch and Oquirrh mountains, Salt Lake City was the parent colony of nearly all early Western communities. From it were sent emigrant parties to all parts of Utah and to areas that were to become Idaho, Nevada, Wyoming, Arizona, New Mexico, Colorado, California, Mexico and Canada. Because of its location the city became the crossroads of Western travel and today is the geographical center of the 11 Western states. It is the mining, smelting and refining center of the West, and is the only city of metropolitan proportions between Denver and the Pacific Coast.

Situated near the southeast shore of the Great Salt Lake at an elevation of 4,327.27 feet (measured at the Mormon Temple Block, natural center of the community), Salt Lake City's most famous landmarks are the LDS Temple and Tabernacle. Other well-known buildings and places of interest include Brigham Young's Lion House and Beehive House, the Eagle Gate, and Kennecott Copper Corp.'s Bingham Mine—the world's first open pit copper mine and the world's largest man-made excavation—on the western outskirts.

Operating under a mayor-city commission form of government, Salt Lake City is completing a $17,000,000, 14,000 seat civic auditorium complex (Salt Palace). Grand opening is scheduled for April, 1969.

Salt Lake City is served by 4 air lines (in July, 1968, it seemed certain at least two others would receive CAB certification), and two railroads. During 1967 853,368 passengers deplaned and 852,905 enplaned at the Salt Lake City's International Airport. The city is a hub of the central Transcontinental Highway System, and is served by all of the major Western truck lines, plus bus lines operating in all directions.

Home of the world-famed Mormon Tabernacle Choir, it also is headquarters for the National Woolgrowers Assn., site of the 1967 World Championship Judo matches and was U. S. representative in bidding for the 1972 Winter Olympics.

The University of Utah and Westminster College are in the city.

Major employers are Hill Air Force Base 30 miles to the north, local defense industries and Kennecott Copper Corp.

Additional information is available from the Salt Lake Chamber of Commerce, 146 S. Main St., or the Utah Travel Council, Council Hall, Capitol Hill, Salt Lake City, Utah.

## San Antonio, Texas

The World Almanac is sponsored in the San Antonio area by San Antonio Express and San Antonio News, Ave. E at Third St., San Antonio, Texas 78205; telephone (512) CA 5-7411; morning Express founded Sept. 27, 1865, evening News founded Sept. 4, 1918; circulation Express 83,212, News 64,117, Sundays 119,721; publisher, Conway G. Craig; president, Houston H. Harte; executive editor, Charles O. Kilpatrick; the Express and News have won many journalistic awards, being consistent leader in South Texas in this respect.

San Antonio, one of the most historic and colorful of America's cities, stands at a meeting place of plains and hills in South Central Texas, within easy reach of the Gulf Coast and the Mexican border.

The city's best-known landmark is the Alamo, a symbol of man's fight for freedom since its stalwart defense against overwhelming odds in 1836. Today the old mission-fortress occupies a place of honor downtown in the modern city which has grown up around it, further symbolizing the easy blend of old and new which is part of the city's character.

The modern city lives with other signs of its past, notably the Missions San Jose, Concepcion, Capistrano and Espada. San Jose, called "Queen of Missions," is a National Historic Site.

The city's past has left it a rich heritage of diverse cultural influences. Founded in 1718 and made capital of the province of Texas, it was under Spanish rule until 1821, when revolt raised the flag of Mexico. In 1836, with battles at the Alamo and elsewhere, the Republic of Texas came into being, governing until Texas joined the union in 1845.

San Antonio in 1968 celebrated its 250th anniversary with the holding of Hemis-

Fair, a world's fair which built a glamorous spectacle of entertainment and education on a practical base of urban renewal.

The fair's benefits are expected to be felt for years to come, in intangible ways as well as in the permanent structures on the downtown fair site, including the city-built $14,000,000 convention center complex, and the 622-foot Tower of the Americas with its revolving restaurant.

Now in a new surge of growth, the city has expanded from population of 408,442 in 1950, to 587,718 in 1960, to present estimates of over three-quarters of a million. Population is 51.2% Anglo-American, 41.4% Latin American and 7.1% Negro.

San Antonio, which has council-manager government, covers an area of 182.73 square miles in Bexar County.

For the period of 1950-1966, San Antonio Chamber of Commerce estimates that Bexar County has grown 60.6% in population, 109.6% in effective buying income, and 113.2% in retail sales.

Long a commercial and financial center for a large ranching and farming region, San Antonio serves a 50-county retail trade area with 1966 population of 2,344,700, and retail sales of $2,829,085,000.

San Antonio's role as a military center is of prime economic importance. It is home of Kelly Air Force Base; of Brooks AFB, headquarters of the Air Force Aerospace Medical Division; of Lackland AFB and Randolph AFB with their training programs; and of historic Fort Sam Houston, headquarters of the Fourth Army and site of Brooke Army Medical Center.

In addition to economic influence of military and other governmental employment, San Antonio has other significant sources of income in trade and service industries, in tourism, and in area livestock production and truck crops. The city also has diverse manufacturing.

Of growing importance are the city's position as a medical center, based on military and civilian hospitals and the new University of Texas Medical School, and its science-related activities in which the Air Force's famed School of Aerospace Medicine, the fast-growing Southwest Research Institute and the biomedical Southwest Foundation for Research and Education are prominent.

Six scheduled airlines, 3 trunk railroads and many truck lines serve San Antonio.

San Antonio has 4 colleges and universities and two junior colleges, museums, a notable symphony orchestra, a fine expressway system, a reputation for cleanliness and well-lighted streets, and a calendar of cultural and other events in which the week-long gaiety of the spring Fiesta San Antonio is a highlight.

Detailed information may be obtained from San Antonio Chamber of Commerce, P.O. Box 1628, San Antonio, Texas 78206.

## San Diego, California

The World Almanac is sponsored in the San Diego area by The San Diego Union and Evening Tribune, 940 Third Ave., San Diego, Calif. 92112; telephone (714) 234-7111; Union founded 1868, Evening Tribune or predecessors 1881; circulation morning Union 137,014, Sunday Union 244,518, Evening Tribune 121,177; publisher, James S. Copley; president & general manager, Alex De Bakcsy; vice president, E. Robert Anderson; Evening Tribune editor, Eugene F. Williams; Union day managing editor Edward Thomas, night managing editor Fred Kinne.

San Diego, which observes the 200th anniversary of its founding in 1969, is the name of both a city and a county which are great not only in terms of area, population, industry and agriculture, but in human advantages as well. Sharing these are an estimated 680,500 residents of San Diego proper; the overall county population exceeds 1,314,000. City and county are among the nation's fastest growing areas; there are manager-type governments for both.

San Diego is the southwesternmost city in the U. S. The Pacific forms its western boundary, Mexico its southern. It has been under 4 flags since its discovery by Cabrillo in 1542 and its founding by Junipero Serrá, a Franciscan missionary, almost 200 years ago in 1769—Spanish, Mexican, Californian, and U. S. Within San Diego city, besides much oceanfront, are two famous bays, San Diego and Mission. Alive with sailing and other craft, the latter is home of Sea World, a marine entertainment park. San Diego Bay, one of the world's fine natural harbors, is home of great Navy shore and fleet establishments, which with shipbuilding and research help create in San Diego a "Maritime Pacific" complex.

A famous civic asset is Balboa Park and its great Zoo, with the world's largest wild animal exhibit. Close proximity to Mexico is another San Diego tourist feature. Tourism's growth has been spectacular, the city possessing more hotel accommodations than all of Hawaii, as well as fine restaurants. A complete convention center is part of a theater-government-visitor community concourse.

Sunny skies and beneficent temperatures, winter and summer, have been factors in San Diego's growth, as have Colorado River water resources, recruitment of "name" employers and the air transportation boom. San Diego has a fine freeway network, a new airport terminal and splendid sports facilities, including the 50,000-seat San Diego Stadium, soon to be a big league baseball park.

San Diego is an aerospace center—home of the Atlas missile—a leader in electronics and is staking its claim as an oceanography center. Industry location is assisted by Economic Development Corp. of San Diego County, 530 B St., San Diego 92101.

San Diego has collections of Old Masters, a noted Shakespeare Festival, and is scheduled to erect a repertory theater directed by the noted Michael Langham. Campuses include California Western University, a unit of United States International University, University of California at San Diego, San Diego State College, and the University of San Diego.

The city is a center for sportsfishing and, uniquely, whale-watching. In winter whales parade close to the coast en route to Mexico's "lying-in" lagoons. Horse racing, at nearby Del Mar and in Caliente in Mexico, is a tourist attraction.

San Diego ranks among the top 20 counties in the U. S. in agricultural production, with 685,000 of 2,700,000 county acres in cultivation. Tomatoes, oranges, avocados and eggs are important revenue sources. Neighboring Imperial County is the nation's wealthy winter "hothouse" for fresh fruits and vegetables.

Taxable retail sales in 1967 were $1.740 billion in San Diego county.

# San Francisco-Oakland, California

The World Almanac is sponsored in the San Francisco-Oakland area by the San Francisco Examiner, P. O. Box 3100, Rincon Annex, San Francisco, Calif. 94103; telephone (415) 781-2424; founded June 12, 1865, purchased in 1880 by Sen. George Hearst, who turned it over in 1887 to his son William Randolph Hearst; circulation Daily Examiner 213,649, Sunday Examiner & Chronicle 680,426; publisher, Charles Gould; editor, Edmund J. Dooley; executive editor, Thomas Eastham; managing editor, Rene Cazenave; advertising director, Bob Ward; major awards include Pulitzer Prize, Freedoms Foundation Award; sponsors Golden Gloves, Bridal Forum, Bay to Breakers Race, Hearst Regatta.

San Francisco, chief port and financial center of the Pacific Coast, is centrally located on the California shoreline at the entrance to one of the world's finest landlocked harbors. Famed for its hills, the city covers 44.6 sq. mi. on the northern tip of a peninsula.

San Francisco Bay was discovered in 1769 by a Spanish scouting expedition headed by Sgt. Jose Ortega, and the Presidio and Mission Dolores, both within present city limits, were founded in 1776 by Col. Juan Bautista de Anza. The pueblo of Yerba Buena was established on the site in 1834, and was renamed San Francisco on Jan. 3, 1847. Its population was 800. When gold was discovered at Sutter's Mill on the American River in 1848, the area grew rapidly. The spreading tent settlement was established as a county and incorporated as a city in April, 1850. Gold production declined after 1855, but the fine port made San Francisco the main Pacific Coast point of entry, and maritime trade helped the bay region prosper.

Estimated population of San Francisco on July 1, 1968, was 747,500. The city is second only to Manhattan Island in population density. Its combined county-city government gives legislative powers to an elected 11-member board of supervisors. Certain officials, including the mayor, are elected; others are appointed by the mayor and have permanent tenure.

The city and the surrounding counties of Alameda, Contra Costa, Marin and San Mateo comprise the San Francisco-Oakland Metropolitan Area. San Francisco is the financial center of the west, home of the Pacific Coast Stock Exchange, many banks and savings and loan associations.

The Port of San Francisco handled 4,-890,246 tons of cargo in 1967. Leading exports were dried fruit and fruit in airtight containers, non-electric machinery and appliances, and rice. Chief imports were green coffee, telecommunications apparatus, and nonmilitary road vehicles. Passenger liners make more than 100 calls at San Francisco each year.

Retail and wholesale trade account for the greatest number of jobs in the metropolitan San Francisco area, 282,700, and services are second, 275,000. Manufacturing employs 196,600, about 30% of the 5-county total, with food and kindred products; printing, publishing and allied arts,

and fabricated metal products as the leading industries. More than 65 industrial parks lie within a 50-mile radius of downtown San Francisco. The city has 8,577 retail establishments which reported taxable sales of $1.27 billion in 1967.

San Francisco International Airport is served by 19 trunk and regional airlines. In fiscal 1967, it processed 12,723,811 passengers, ranking fourth in the nation. A total of 481,168,609 lbs. of cargo, and 217,-791,000 lbs. of mail were also moved.

Three major transcontinental railroads and one regional railroad link San Francisco to all sections of the nation, Canada and Mexico. The transcontinental routes are connected to the San Francisco waterfront by rail ferry service.

A $1 billion Bay Area Rapid Transit System is under construction, scheduled for completion in 1969-70 to serve San Francisco and Alameda and Contra Costa counties. An office building boom has changed the city's skyline rapidly.

San Francisco is famous for its cable cars and Fisherman's Wharf, and for such varied structures as the Ferry Building, the new $45,000,000 Federal Office Building, the historic Fairmont, Mark Hopkins, and Sheraton-Palace hotels; the California Palace of the Legion of Honor, the newly renovated Palace of Fine Arts, and Grace Cathedral. The Cow Palace, home of political conventions, sports and livestock exhibitions, lies just across the boundary line in San Mateo County. The San Francisco Zoo and 1,013-acre Golden Gate Park, containing California Academy of Sciences, De Young Museum, lakes, deer and buffalo, are attractions.

Candlestick Park is the home of the San Francisco Giants, National Baseball League; Kezar Stadium, that of the San Francisco 49ers, National Football League. Other professional teams include the San Francisco Warriors of the National Basketball Assn., and the Golden Gate Gales of the United Soccer Assn.

The University of California maintains its medical school and extension classes in San Francisco, which is also known for San Francisco State College, the U. of San Francisco, City College of San Francisco, and San Francisco College for Women.

Detailed information may be obtained from the Greater San Francisco Chamber of Commerce, 420 Montgomery St., San Francisco, Calif. 94104.

## Oakland, California

The city of Oakland covers 53.4 sq. mi. of land and 25.7 of water on the east side of San Francisco Bay in California. Linked to San Francisco by the 8¼-mile Bay Bridge, it is the county seat of Alameda County. The area was first explored in 1772, and was settled in 1850 when it attracted the overflow from the Gold Rush. Oakland was incorporated as a town in 1852 and as a city in 1864. Fifteen years later, the first westbound transcontinental train brought commerce and steady growth. Population in July, 1968, was estimated at 386,000. The city has a council-manager government.

For the county, manufacturing with 85,000 workers and services with 73,100 workers are the major areas of employment. Other important job fields are retail trade,\62,600; wholesale trade 22,800; transportation, communications and utilities, 33,200; finance, insurance and real estate 16,700; and construction 23,200. Processed foods and fabricated metal products, including passenger cars and trucks, head the manufacturing output for Alameda County. The city's retail sales in 1967 were $822,531,000, the county's, $1,868,374,000.

Three transcontinental railroads serve metropolitan Oakland and 245,945 carloads

of freight were moved in 1967. The Port of Oakland handled 831 ocean-going vessels in 1967 and moved 3,070,007 tons of cargo. Metropolitan Oakland International Airport is served by 7 leading trunk and regional airlines and is headquarters for 3 chartered lines.

Oakland has an urban renewal program affecting 70 of 100 square blocks in the downtown area. Older neighborhoods are undergoing massive redevelopment. Oakland operates a Manpower Training Act job-training center.

Lake Merritt, a 160-acre body of salt water, provides a park-like setting in the heart of Oakland. The new $8,000,000 Oakland Museum and fabled Jack London square are major tourist attractions. Some 16,000 acres of East Bay Regional Parks offer nearby camping and recreation.

Knowland State Arboretum and Park is the home of the Oakland Zoo. The recently completed $25,500,000 multi-purpose Oakland Coliseum has a maximum capacity of over 50,000. Professional teams include the Oakland Raiders, American Football League; Oakland Oaks, American Basketball Assn.; California Seals, National Hockey League; and Oakland Clippers, National Professional Soccer League.

The University of California's Berkeley campus is only minutes from Oakland, and the city houses Mills College for Women, College of Holy Names, Peralta Junior College, and the California College of Arts and Crafts.

Detailed information may be obtained from the Oakland Chamber of Commerce, 1320 Webster St., Oakland, Calif. 94612.

## San Jose, California

The World Almanac is sponsored in the San Jose area by the San Jose Mercury and News, 750 Ridder Park Dr., San Jose, Calif. 95131; telephone (408) 289-5000; Mercury (California's second oldest daily newspaper) founded June 20, 1851, by J. C. Emerson, A. Jones, Jr., J. F. Damon, News founded July 23, 1883, by Hugh A. DeLacy; circulation morning Mercury 130,491, evening News 77,068, Sunday Mercury-News 192,230; publisher, Joseph B. Ridder; general manager, Anton F. Peterson; executive editor, Kenneth S. Conn; advertising director, Louis E. Heindel; new facility won Factory magazine's "Plants of the Year" award in 1968; since 1946 newspapers have won 44 first and 21 second place awards in national and state competition; co-sponsor International Invitational Swimming & Diving Championships.

San Jose is located in the Santa Clara Valley region of northern California at the southern end of San Francisco Bay. A city of 204,196 according to the 1960 Census, it has an estimated population of 412,700 as of Apr. 1, 1968. San Jose is the central city of one of the nation's 10 fastest growing metropolitan areas and the county seat of Santa Clara County. The county and official metropolitan area are coextensive and have a population presently estimated at 1,008,000.

San Jose can aptly be called California's "first city," as it lays claim to the following: 1st civilian settlement (November, 1777); 1st State Capitol (December, 1849) and home of its first governor; site of the first public school in California (1795) and first state institution of higher learning (San Jose State College, 1857); home of the first radio broadcasting station in America (1909). San Jose is the urban center of one of the largest aerospace industrial/research complexes.

Agriculture, which until the late 40's was the main "industry" in the area,

remains a factor in the local economy. Industrial growth since World War II has made the metropolitan area the state's 2nd county in value of manufactures, 3rd in number of manufacturing employees. It has a council-manager government.

San Jose is served by two major railroads, over 60 interstate truck lines, Greyhound passenger and parcel terminals, United Airlines, Air West and major intrastate airlines. Numerous daily helicopter flights connect to interstate and overseas flights. Several extensive urban renewal projects are transforming the face of the city's core into the cultural, commercial and educational center of the region.

The metropolitan area, home of San Jose State College, Stanford University and the University of Santa Clara, is one of the West's major seats of learning and research. An estimated 77,500 students will attend these and other local institutions during the fall (1968) term.

The nearby city of Santa Clara boasts the famous Santa Clara Swim Club.

## Saskatoon, Canada

The World Almanac is sponsored in the northern Saskatchewan area by the Saskatoon Star-Phoenix, 204 Fifth Ave. North, Saskatoon, Sask., Canada; telephone (306) 652-9200; founded 1902; circulation daily 51,480; publisher, Michael C. Sifton; general manager, Norman G. Paterson; editor, M. D. Macdonald.

About 85 years ago, temperance colonists camped on a high bank of the South Saskatchewan River in the center of the Canadian prairies. Their camp has grown into a city of 35 square miles, 123,000 people and 1,800 businesses. Its name, Saskatoon, is a derivative of a Cree Indian label for a berry found there.

It is the second fastest-growing city in Canada and the second largest city in a province of 251,700 square miles. Wide streets, spacious residential areas and 1,300 acres of parks add to its esthetic quality. Its university is internationally known in agricultural science, and its university hospital is the home of some of the most advanced medical work.

Saskatoon stands over the world's richest and largest known body of potash. Six mines will, by 1970, tap that bed.

In the best hard spring wheat area in the world, Saskatoon provides grain storage capacity for 6,000,000 bushels. The livelihood of many of the 425,000 people

in the 70,000-square-mile trading area is based on agriculture. The 1,200 retail stores, 240 wholesalers and 344 manufacturing plants report an annual volume of $452,000,000.

Unlimited power and water come from the fourth largest dam in the world, 70 miles from the city. Within or adjacent to Saskatoon are the head office of Intercontinental Packers (a meat-processing company), two chemical plants, a cement plant, machine and clothing manufacturers and several iron foundries.

Saskatoon is served by two railroads and 3 airlines, is a truck traffic hub, with 7 major highway approaches.

It features a museum containing machinery used by man since his earliest days in the West, and is the jumping-off point for some of the finest fishing and hunting in North America.

Additional information may be obtained from the Board of Trade, Bessborough Hotel, Saskatoon, Sask.

## Seattle, Washington

The World Almanac is sponsored in the Seattle area by the Seattle Times, Fairview Ave. N. & John St., Seattle, Wash. 98109; telephone (206) MA 2-0300; founded 1896 by Alden J. Blethen; circulation 251,617 daily, 310,040 Sunday; publisher, John A. Blethen; president, W. J. Pennington; general manager, Harry H. Cahill; sponsors 4-yr. scholarship annually to journalism student, two seasonal sports contests for boys, girls' track and field event.

Seattle, settled in 1851, derives its name from an Indian chief, Sealth, who befriended the early settlers. Seattle was incorporated in 1865. By 1884 the residents had built a rail connecton with the outside. In 1889, downtown Seattle burned but was rebuilt better than before.

The Gold Rush to Alaska in 1897 and 1898 gave Seattle, as the closest major port to Alaska, an impetus it never lost. Besides being an outfitter for Alaska, Seattle developed trade with the Orient, thereby gaining its name of "The American Gateway to Alaska and the Orient." Seattle is closer to Japan than any other major American city.

The estimated population (Apr. 1, 1968) was 587,000. Seattle's metropolitan area had 1,200,000. The city has only 91.6 sq. mi., on an isthmus between Puget Sound and Lake Washington. Seattle is noted for its mild climate and spectacular views of water and mountains. The city has a nonpartisan, mayor-council government.

Seattle is the home of the giant Boeing Co., world's largest producer of commercial jet passenger planes; more than 50% of the world's commercial jets were made by Boeing. Boeing employs almost 100,000 persons in the Seattle area.

Seattle also is noted for shipbuilding and forest-products industries, as a retail-trade and regional office center, for insurance headquarters and for tourism.

The city is served by 4 intercontinental railroads and 12 scheduled air lines, three of which began service June, 1967. The airlines served more than 3,800,000 passengers last year through the Seattle-Tacoma Internat'l Airport and Boeing Field.

The Seattle-Tacoma Airport is operated by the Port of Seattle, a $126,000,000 public agency, which also operates 9 miles of port facilities and serves more than 55 ocean and coastal lines.

Seattle-King County is in midst of a capital-improvements-priority program called Forward Thrust, which will attempt to budget some $1 billion of spending for the next 15 to 20 years. In Feb., 1968, voters approved seven of 12 proposed bond issues for a total expenditure of $321,900,-000 for major capital improvements, including a $40,000,000 domed multipurpose stadium. Other projects which failed to pass will be resubmitted in 1969.

The city has a $40,000,000, 74-acre legacy from the 1962 Century 21 World's Fair known as the Seattle Center. The Center features a 3,100-seat Opera House, a 5,200-seat Arena, an 800-seat Playhouse, two huge exhibit halls, an 18,000-seat Coliseum, the world-famous 605-foot Space Needle and the Pacific Science Center in the U. S. Science Pavilion for the fair.

The Seattle Center buildings are used by the noted Seattle Symphony Orchestra directed by Milton Katims; the Seattle Opera Association; the Seattle Repertory, a professional theater; the Totems hockey team, and the Seattle SuperSonics pro basketball team of the National Basketball Assn.

Seattle has the Woodland Park Zoo and University of Washington Arboretum, a botanical laboratory featuring a Japanese tea house. Seafair, a citywide annual festival, is held in Aug., climaxed by unlimited hydroplane racing before crowds estimated up to 250,000 on Lake Washington.

In other sports, Seattle in 1968 had the Pacific Coast League Angels, baseball, but will begin play in 1969 in the American League with a new expansion franchise, the Pilots; the Rangers, Continental Football League; SuperSonics, National Basketball Ass'n; and Totems, Western Hockey League.

There are two major universities, University of Washington and Seattle University; Seattle Pacific College, and a number of community colleges.

Cultural institutions include Seattle Art Museum, Frye Art Museum, Henry Art Gallery, Burke Memorial Museum, Museum of History and Industry and Pacific Science Center.

Metropolitan Seattle department store sales totaled $314,929,000 for April, 1967 through March, 1968, on revised basis; $271,140,000 for 1966.

For specialized information, contact the Seattle Chamber of Commerce, the Seattle Area Industrial Council, or the Seattle Visitors Bureau, all of 215 Columbia St., or the Central Assn. of Seattle, Joseph Vance Building, Third Ave. and Union St.

## Syracuse, New York

The World Almanac is sponsored in the Syracuse area by the Herald-Journal, 220 Herald Pl., Syracuse, N. Y. 13202; telephone (315) HA 2-0211; founded Jan. 15, 1877, by Arthur Jenkins; circulation 134,879 daily, 258,532 Sunday Herald-American/Post-Standard; publisher, Stephen Rogers; editor, William D. Cotter; business manager, Clarence H. Rinne; sponsors college scholarship fund for police, sponsors teacher at Newspaper in Classroom course, awards medals to fire and police heroes.

Syracuse, 4th largest city in New York State, is at the virtual geographic center of the state. The East-West Governor Thomas E. Dewey Thruway (Interstate Route 90) has 5 interchanges in the Syracuse area. The North-South Interstate Route 81 crosses the Thruway at Syracuse.

With an area of 25.82 sq. mi., Syracuse had an estimated 1968 population of 213,-500. The city is in the heart of a Standard Metropolitan Statistical Area composed of Onondaga County (in which the city is located), Oswego and Madison Counties. Population of the area in 1968 was estimated at 628,000.

Historically, Syracuse always has been a "crossroads," even before it became a city. The Iroquois Trail passed through the area from east to west, with tributary trails north and south. With the advent of the white man the trails became rough roads used for travel to the opening West.

The area first was explored in 1615 by the French under Samuel de Champlain. In 1654, Father Simon Le Moyne, a Jesuit missionary, visited the area. It was then that large quantities of salt were discovered in the water in the area. This salt was to play an important part in the early development of Syracuse, and even today Syracuse is known as "The Salt City."

The first white settler was Ephraim

Webster, who established a trading post in 1786. In 1825 the village was incorporated and in 1847 Syracuse annexed the village of Salina to the north and was chartered as a city.

Although the salt industry gave Syracuse its early impetus, the city's growth over the years is attributed to its strategic location. With the opening of the Erie Canal in 1825—it ran through the heart of the city—Syracuse became a key water link between Buffalo and New York City.

After the canal came the railroads which gave Syracuse added stature as a transportation hub. And today, the crisscrossing super-highways have enhanced Syracuse's position in the transportation and service industries.

Syracuse has a mayor/common council form of government.

Major products of some 500 manufacturing plants in the Syracuse area are soda ash and by-products, candles, air conditioning, china and pottery, electrical goods, agricultural implements, quality shoes, auto accessories, special steel and pharmaceuticals. Largest employers are General Electric, Carrier Corp., Crucible Steel Co. and Crouse-Hinds Co.

Retail sales for the city for 1967 were estimated at $369,000,000 and for Onondaga County at $732,000,000.

Syracuse is served by two railroads, some 140 truck lines and 3 airlines. The Barge Canal system provides commercial and recreational water transportation.

City-operated Hancock Airport handled 1,138,826 passengers in 1967, the first time it had gone over the million mark. Air traffic has doubled since 1961.

Recent improvements include a massive highway interchange that carries Interstate Route 81 non-stop through the city. Underway is a multi-million-dollar downtown Clinton Square Redevelopment Program to include a newspaper plant, department store, bank and other facilities. In partial operation is a new $45,-000,000 project carrying water 30 miles from Lake Ontario to Syracuse and Onondaga County.

The Everson Museum of Art boasts a new museum building, designed by I. M. Pei. Other attractions include an authentic restoration of a 17th Century French fort, the Salt Museum, Onondaga Historical Assn., Canal Museum, Burnet Park Zoo and the State Fairgrounds.

Syracuse is the home of Syracuse University, Le Moyne College, Maria Regina College, and Onondaga Community College. Sports arenas include War Memorial, Archbold Stadium, and MacArthur Stadium, home of the Syracuse Chiefs of the International League (baseball).

Specialized information is available from the Greater Syracuse Chamber of Commerce, One Mony Plaza, and Metropolitan Development Assn., State Tower Bldg., both Syracuse, N.Y. 13202.

# Tampa, Florida

The World Almanac is sponsored in the Tampa Bay area by The Tampa Tribune and The Tampa Times, 507 E. Kennedy Blvd., Tampa, Fla. 33601, telephone (813) 229-7777; Times founded in 1893 by S. A. Smith, Tribune in 1895 by W. F. Stovall; combined circulation 205,201; Alan S. Donnahoe, president; J. C. Council, chairman of editorial board; R. F. Pittman, Jr., business manager; major awards: Pulitzer Prize, Freedom Foundations Award, National Sigma Delta Chi awards, National Headliners Club Award, Heywood Broun Award, Green Eyeshade Award; sponsors Florida State Science Fair, Book Fair, Times honor student scholarships, all-city academic football team, and Tribune open (AAU) Basketball Tournament.

Industrial and commercial hub of Florida, Tampa is located on Tampa Bay about midway between the north edge of the Gulf of Mexico and the tip of the Florida peninsula.

Third most populous city in Florida, 316,673, Tampa is the principal marketing center of a population area estimated at 907,000.

Gasparilla, in early February, features the pirate invasion of the old port city. Jose Gasper's buccaneers seize the streets in an atmosphere of carnival. The event is coordinated with the Florida State Fair and a series of other events designed for the entertainment of residents and tourists.

Ybor City, Tampa's quaint Latin Quarter, is a site of historical interest and the location of some of the nation's leading Spanish restaurants.

Tampa's history dates back to 1545 when a Spanish caravel, in the gold trade, was shipwrecked in the bay.

Survivors told of the broad bay and safe anchorage they had almost found before their ship was lost. In subsequent years there were a number of attempts made to establish a permanent settlement, but Spain's retreat from empire left the area open for Anglo-Saxon settlement. During the Seminole Wars, Fort Brooke was established as a garrison near the mouth of the Hillsborough River and became the seed from which modern Tampa grew.

In the Civil War period Tampa was an attractive port for blockade runners, and in the 1880s railroad baron Henry Plant began developing the area as a railroad port and tourist center. During the Spanish-American War Tampa was a major port of embarkation for U. S. troops.

Continued growth of Tampa as a center of transportation and industry has made the community's economy contrast sharply with the tourist and retirement oriented economies of most other Florida metropolitan areas.

Tampa's port is currently undergoing a major redevelopment, with more than $7,000,000 in public funds being used to create new port lands, and public and private investment of more than $30,000,-000 anticipated in the future for creation of terminals and waterfront industry.

As a port, Tampa is the largest between Norfolk and New Orleans, handling more than 25,000,000 tons of cargo annually. Principal export cargo is phosphate, used for fertilizer material and industrial purposes. Rich phosphate mines, located only 40 miles from the port, have made Tampa the world's leading producer of this commodity.

Tampa International Airport, serving more than 2,500,000 air travelers a year, is in the process of building a $60,000,000 "terminal city" of unique and radical design. The airport is served by 9 major airlines, with domestic and foreign service.

One major urban renewal project, near downtown Tampa, is nearing completion, and two others are in progress.

Within the past 10 years the central business district of Tampa has been the scene of vast change as high-rise office buildings and new hotels have replaced obsolescent structures.

Downtown Tampa is immediately adjacent to the junction of Interstate-75 and Interstate-4. A crosstown expressway is

also projected on the fringe of the business district.

Tampa's mayor and seven-member city council are elected in a non-partisan campaign.

The University of South Florida, started less than 10 years ago, has more than 12,000 students. The University of Tampa, a private 4-year college, has an enrollment of more than 2,000 students.

A $1,700,000 library has recently been completed in downtown Tampa and holds 300,000 volumes. Eight branches serve neighborhoods throughout the city.

Tampa serves as spring training camp for the Cincinnati Reds, and is home of the Tampa Tarpons baseball team. A new football stadium has recently been completed. Major professional and collegiate football games are scheduled here.

Information on the city may be obtained from the Greater Tampa Chamber of Commerce, 801 E. Kennedy Blvd., Tampa, Fla., 33601.

# Toronto, Ontario

The World Almanac is sponsored in the Toronto area by the Toronto Telegram, 440 Front St. West, Toronto, Ont., Canada; telephone (416) 367-4500; founded 1876; circulation daily 227,700, Saturday 307,208; publisher, John W. Bassett; editor-in-chief, J. D. MacFarlane; executive editor, A. H. Agnew; managing editor, A. W. MacFarlane; major awards received include Sigma Delta Chi prize to staff member; sponsors Telegram-Maple Leaf Indoor Games, Telegram Trophy Race, Christmas Fairyland.

Metropolitan Toronto sprawls over 240 sq. mi. along the north shore of Lake Ontario. Although clusters of high-rise apartment buildings pierce the skyline, in the suburbs as well as the downtown core, Toronto is still known as a city of homes.

The city had its beginnings in 1793 when Gov. John Graves Simcoe established a frontier community known as the town of York. Forty-one years later, "muddy York" achieved the status of a city and was renamed Toronto, "a meeting place," as it was known to the Indians. At that time the city had a population of 9,000— today it has 2,200,000.

Its government is unique and the system has been studied by other cities around the world. The city proper, which includes the business and commercial hub, comes under the jurisdiction of Mayor William Dennison. Then, the city joins with five boroughs to form the Metropolitan Council, with William R. Allen as chairman.

Toronto's importance to the Canadian economy is underlined by the fact that one-third of the nation's economic activity gravitates within a 50-mile radius of the city. Toronto is unusual in that no one industry or service dominates its economic life, giving it great stability in times of slumps or labor stoppages in certain segments.

Some 70% of the country's automobile production comes from Oshawa and Oakville, cities about 20 miles east and west respectively from the heart of Toronto.

The city is the eastern terminus of the Interprovincial Pipe Line, which brings western Canadian crude oil to Toronto refineries. Trans-Canada Pipe Lines performs the same function with natural gas.

Hydro power is supplied from two coal-burning plants on the lakeshore, while a nuclear-powered station is being erected at Pickering, just east of the city.

Basically, Toronto is the financial capital of Canada. Three of the country's 5 major chartered banks have head offices here. The Toronto-Dominion has just opened a new 56-story building, tallest in Canada. In addition, the city is headquarters for many of the country's finance, trust and loan companies.

Sixty-five of the 140 life insurance companies doing business in Canada have Toronto head offices. Imperial Oil Ltd., a Standard of New Jersey subsidiary, has its head office on St. Clair Ave. The company holds almost a third of the country's refined products market.

Not only is Toronto the hub of the Canadian business scene, but a number of Toronto-based companies are leaders on a world-wide basis. Massey-Ferguson, for instance, operates 30 plants in 9 countries and sells its diverse line of farm and industrial machinery in 161 countries. A leader in the business-forms industry, Moore Corp., has its head office on University Ave. although it does 85% of its business in the U. S. Brazilian Light & Power, with offices on King St., controls much of Brazil's hydro capacity.

The Toronto Stock Exchange ranks right behind the New York and American exchanges in number of transactions and value of trading. The TSE handles some 70% of the brokerage business in all of Canada.

In addition to its network of superhighways and expressways, Toronto is well served by 3 major railroads—the privately-owned Canadian Pacific, which itself is a world wide complex of hotels, real estate, shipping, mining enterprises; the Federal Government's Canadian National, and the Provincial Government's Ontario Northland.

Toronto International Airport serves some half dozen major airlines and handles 3,000,000 passengers annually. The Island airport, just across the bay from the foot of Bay St., handles private aircraft, and is one of the busiest.

In addition, numerous truck and bus lines radiate from the city.

Since completion of the St. Lawrence Seaway, Toronto has also become an international port with tonnage handled growing every year.

Toronto's downtown is scheduled for a large injection of new life. The Toronto-Dominion Center and the New City Hall are destined to be part of a huge redevelopment which will stretch right to the water's edge. The whole complex will eventually be connected by underground malls, shops and walkways.

Toronto participates actively in just about every major sport, including hockey, curling and football.

In the field of entertainment, both private and publicly-owned television networks are headquartered in Toronto. The legitimate theatre is served well by the O'Keefe Center, the Royal Alexander Theatre, and Massey Hall.

Every summer, The Canadian National Exhibition, the continent's biggest annual fair, draws some 3,000,000 visitors to Toronto.

Additional information may be obtained from the Board of Trade of Metropolitan Toronto, 11 Adelaide St. W., Toronto.

# Vancouver, Canada

The World Almanac is sponsored in the Vancouver area by The Vancouver Sun, 2250 Granville Street, Vancouver, British Columbia, Canada; telephone (604) 732-2111; founded 1886; Canada's second largest daily newspaper; circulation 252,000; publisher, Stuart Keate; editorial director, Bruce Hutchison; managing editor, William T. Galt; sponsors world's largest free Salmon Derby; free Swim Classes (enrol. 10,000 annually); Christmas Fairyland, and many other community services.

Canada's third largest city, Vancouver lies in a setting of natural beauty, at the foot of soaring mountains, fringed by beaches and evergreen forests.

The Spaniards saw the site first, tucked between the fjord of Howe Sound and the Olympic Peninsula, "at the mouth of a copious river," said Don Jose Maria Narvaez, who mapped the area in 1791. But the following year Spain surrendered its claim to Britain, and Capt. George Vancouver, sailing HMS Discovery in quest of the Northwest Passage, took possession. The Hudson's Bay Co. established trading posts and a company of Royal Engineers arrived in 1859 to set up civic administration. The city was incorporated in Vancouver's name in April, 1886, and burned to the ground within two months. But its population of 2,000, enchanted with the site, rebuilt.

Vancouver today is a city of 44 sq. mi. with an estimated population of 450,000. Surrounding suburbs, climbing the North Shore mountains and reaching into the rich agricultural valley of the Fraser—that "copious river"—boost the Greater Vancouver population to some 930,000, almost half that of the province of British Columbia, of which Vancouver is the economic capital.

The fine natural harbor has 98 miles of waterfront stretching up Burrard Inlet, is the largest cargo port on the Pacific and Canada's second busiest. Tonnage in 1968 was estimated at 25,000,000. Preliminary work has begun on a joint federal-provincial venture to build a superport linking Vancouver harbor with a site at Roberts Bank, 20 miles south, at an initial investment of $50,000,000. Major cargo is grain, lumber and forest products, coal, mineral ore, chemicals and manufactured goods. The port is Canada's gateway to the Orient and the major importer of goods for Western Canada.

While service industries predominate in its economy, Vancouver has major wood product plants, a diversified secondary industry, fisheries and a major tourist trade which in 1967 brought 3,500,000 visitors and $165,000,000. Retail sales in 1968 were estimated at $1.25 billion.

Vancouver is the terminus of two trans-continental railways, is linked by a third major line to the U. S. Northwest, and headquarters of the provincially owned Pacific Great Eastern Railway. The freeway to the U. S. border 20 miles south at Blaine, Wash., runs due south to Los Angeles. Vancouver International airport handles 2,000,000 passengers a year and a new terminal was opened in fall, 1968.

Government and private ferry services link Vancouver with Seattle and Vancouver Island and cruise ships ply the northern coast to Alaska.

Vancouver's downtown core is currently undergoing a dramatic transformation with preliminary work under way on 3 major developments—the $300,000,000 Project 200, the $80,000,000 Pacific Centre, both shopping-office complexes, and a provincial government skyscraper which will house headquarters of the recently chartered Bank of British Columbia.

Center of education and the arts in B.C., Vancouver has two universities, the University of B.C. and Simon Fraser University, plus two two-year community colleges. Major arts center is the Queen Elizabeth Theatre complex and a new city museum and planetarium was opened in September, 1968. Year-round entertainment is provided by a symphony orchestra, opera company and professional theatre groups. There are 3 major summer features, the Sea Festival in July, the International Festival of the Arts in late July and August, and the Pacific National Exhibition in August.

Vancouver's natural beauty and temperate climate—a year-round mean of 50 degrees—encourage a strong accent on leisure and recreation, predominantly boating in summer and skiing in winter on mountains only minutes from downtown. A strong bid is being made for the 1976 Winter Olympics. There are 128 parks, the outstanding one being Stanley Park, 1,000 acres, much of it virgin forest, with a zoo and aquarium which features a performing killer whale.

Professional sports flourish year-round: football, soccer, baseball, horseracing, ice hockey (in the new Pacific Coliseum opened early in 1968 and expected to house a National Hockey League team by 1970)—there's even cricket, too.

# Washington, D. C.

The World Almanac is sponsored in the Washington, D. C., area by the Washington Daily News, 1013 13th St. N.W., Washington, D. C. 20005; telephone (202) 347-7777; founded Nov. 8, 1921, by Scripps-Howard Newspapers; circulation 226,000; editor, Richard Hollander; business manager, Ray F. Mack; associate editor, Nicholas Blatchford; managing editor, David Stolberg; major awards received by the newspaper and staff members include two Pulitzer Prizes, two Ernie Pyle Awards, two Heywood Broun Awards.

Although Washington, D. C., is best known as the capital of the United States and as one of the leading tourist meccas of this country, it is also an important business and financial center in its own right.

Its standard metropolitan statistical area, which includes suburban Maryland and Virginia, is one of the fastest growing of the nation's 20 largest. Its population increased by 35.9% between 1950 and 1960, and by an estimated 30.9% between 1960 and 1967. The 1960 census gave the population at 2,064,090, and the Census Bureau estimated it at 2,615,000 in 1966. The National Capital Regional Planning Council forecasts a population of 3,741,456 in 1980. Currently it is the 8th largest standard metropolitan statistical area in the U. S.

The Washington Metropolitan Transit Authority approved Mar. 1, 1968, a $2.5 billion project to build a 97.2-mile urban rapid transit system for Washington and its suburbs over a 12-year period. The authority previously had been authorized by Congress and the District of Columbia to build 38.4 miles of subway and surface rail lines inside the city at a cost of $188,000,000. The Federal share of the total cost was set at $1.1 billion, with the re-

mainder to be provided by local jurisdiction, chiefly through bond issues, and from receipts of the system. Construction of the center-city tunnels was scheduled to start late in 1968, and it was hoped that trains on the first line would be running by 1972.

With millions of Americans converging on Washington annually, transportation to and from the city are of major importance. There are 3 airports—Washington National, Friendship, and Dulles In-

ternational. Highways radiate from the city in all directions. The 65-mile Capital Beltway rings the metropolis. There is frequent train and bus service at all hours of day and night.

Specialized information is available from the Metropolitan Washington Board of Trade, 1616 K St. N.W., Washington, D.C. 20006.

*See also District of Columbia and other index listings under Washington, D. C.*

# Winnipeg, Canada

The World Almanac is sponsored in the Winnipeg area by the Winnipeg Free Press, 300 Carlton St., Winnipeg, Man., Canada; telephone (204) 943-9331; founded 1872; circulation daily 131,695; publisher and editor-in-chief, R. S. Malone; executive editor, Peter McLintock; managing editor, Albert Boothe; business manager, R. H. Shelford; the newspaper and its staff have received numerous awards for outstanding journalism.

Greater Winnipeg, Canada's fourth largest metropolitan area with an estimated population of 505,774, is located at the junction of the historic Red and Assiniboine Rivers near the geographical center of North America. The metropolitan area, covering 166.6 sq. mi., embraces 7 cities and 5 towns.

Winnipeg proper, heart of the metro area with an estimated population of 251,-995, is the capital city of the Province of Manitoba. Winnipeg is named after Lake Winnipeg, 40 miles to the north, the 13th largest lake in the world. It is a Cree Indian name meaning muddy water.

The area attracted its first settlers, the Lord Selkirk colonists, in 1812. A fur-trading post, Winnipeg was incorporated as a city in 1812. It had a population of 1,869.

A metropolitan government was established in 1960 to look after inter-municipal services in the area. The metro government is responsible for public transportation including the major bridges and thoroughfares, the water supply, sewage collection and disposal, area planning and zoning, and the major parks.

Manufacturing is one of the important factors in the area's economy and the largest single source of employment and income. Greater Winnipeg is the 6th largest manufacturing employment area in Canada, with 37,000 persons earning $150,-000,000 and producing $825,000,000 in manufactured goods a year. One of Canada's largest investment dealers has headquarters in Winnipeg, along with one of the largest insurance companies. The Canadian Wheat Board, charged with the responsibility of selling Canada's large wheat crop, also has headquarters in Winnipeg.

Construction of new buildings in the area totals about $100,000,000 a year. An urban renewal scheme to redevelop the downtown area is under way.

Utility services, except natural gas for heating, are government or municipally owned. The Provincial Government owns the hydro and telephone systems in the area while the City of Winnipeg owns the hydro distribution system in the city proper.

Winnipeg is western headquarters of Canadian Pacific Railway and Canadian National Railways, Canada's two transcontinental rail systems, with connecting lines to the United States.

Winnipeg International Airport handles about 600,000 passengers and 25,000,000 pounds of freight and express annually. A modern $12,000,000 terminal was opened in 1963 to service the 4 major airlines that have daily service to Canadian and U. S. points. In addition, 3 airlines use the airport for refueling and servicing planes on polar flights.

An amateur sports center, Winnipeg is the home of the Canadian national amateur hockey team. The 1967 Pan-American Games were held in Winnipeg, which will be host to 15 games of the 1970 World Amateur Hockey Championship. A professional team, the Winnipeg Blue Bombers, plays in the Canadian Football League.

Winnipeg's cultural life is highlighted by the Royal Winnipeg Ballet and the Winnipeg Symphony. A fine concert hall was opened in 1968 and a 6-story museum is being built.

Additional information is available from the Winnipeg Chamber of Commerce, 177 Lombard Avenue, Winnipeg, Man., Canada.

# New York City Museums, Libraries, Centers of Interest

**THE NEW YORK AQUARIUM,** in Coney Island, exhibits marine life from all climes, with over 2,500 live specimens including whales, sharks, seals, sea lions, fish, penguins, etc.

**THE NEW YORK BOTANICAL GARDENS,** founded in 1891, occupies 230 acres of Bronx Park adjacent to Pelham Parkway. An 11-greenhouse Main Conservatory features seasonal shows and permanent exhibits of palms, jungle and desert plants, ferns and orchids.

**THE FRICK COLLECTION,** 1 E. 70th St., was founded by Henry Clay Frick (1849-1919). The principal part of the Collection consists of 14th-19th Century paintings as well as sculpture.

**THE GALLERY OF MODERN ART** including the Huntington Hartford Collection is at Columbus Circle. The building, designed by Edward Durrell Stone, was opened in 1964. It houses mainly 19th and 20th-Century representational art.

**THE SOLOMON R. GUGGENHEIM MUSEUM,** Fifth Ave. and 89th St.; permanent collection contains over 3,000 paintings, drawings, sculptures

and graphic works by 19th and 20th Century artists. The Museum's unique circular building was designed by Frank Lloyd Wright.

**THE HAYDEN PLANETARIUM,** facing 81st St., near Central Park W., presents dramatic reproductions of the night skies inside a large hemispheric dome with a Zeiss planetarium projector and other instruments; about 9,000 stars are shown. There are weather, time, space exhibits.

**THE HISPANIC SOCIETY OF AMERICA** is a free public museum and reference library devoted to the art and literature of Spain and Portugal. It occupies two buildings on Audubon Terrace, between 155th and 156th Sts., west of Broadway. Paintings run from primitive to modern.

**THE JEWISH MUSEUM,** Fifth Ave. at 92nd St., offers exhibitions of Jewish ceremonial objects, as well as contemporary art and architecture. The permanent collection of Judaica is considered the most comprehensive in the world. There are lectures, gallery talks and a gift shop.

**THE METROPOLITAN MUSEUM OF ART,** Fifth Ave. at 82nd St., was founded in 1870. With more than 365,000 works of art, the Museum's collection is the largest of its kind in the Western Hemisphere.

Great masters of all the ages of art are included in the collections: Egyptian, Greek and Roman, Ancient Near Eastern, Islamic, Far Eastern, Medieval, Arms and Armor, European, Pre-Columbian, American, Musical Instruments, Costume Institute and Junior Museum.

The Cloisters, in Manhattan's Fort Tryon Park, is a branch of the Metropolitan devoted to Medieval art and architecture in 5 cloisters and other early European structures.

**THE MUSEUM OF THE AMERICAN INDIAN,** Heye Foundation, Broadway at 155th St., maintains the world's largest collection of American Indian materials, extensive archeological and ethnological displays and pre-Columbian arts, as well as study and photographic facilities.

**THE MUSEUM OF MODERN ART,** 11 W. 53rd St., est. 1929, presents 20th Century painting, sculpture, drawings, prints, architectural and industrial design, photography and film.

The library contains about 25,000 vols. and a reference collection of more than 100,000 photographs. The Film Dept. has more than 12,000,000 ft. of film. Bookstore, restaurant and gift shop.

**THE AMERICAN MUSEUM OF NATURAL HISTORY** occupies a group of buildings at Central Park West between 77th and 81st Sts. Here are large exhibits of man and beast from the most primitive times to the present, with extensive reconstruction of fossilized remains, dioramas of men and animals in their natural settings, dinosaurs, birds, Indians, Eskimos and glass models of protozoa, rotifers and coelenterates.

Noteworthy are the collections of minerals and gems, fossil fishes and marine life.

**THE MUSEUM OF THE CITY OF NEW YORK** on Fifth Ave. at 104th St., illustrates the history and life of the city. Its collections include dioramas, paintings, prints, maps, photographs, portraits, miniatures, vehicles, ship models, costumes, silver, furniture, theatrical and musical memorabilia, rare books and manuscripts.

**THE NEW-YORK HISTORICAL SOCIETY** (founded 1804) is at 170 Central Park W. between 76th and 77th Sts. The society maintains a library, museum and gallery of art. The library contains 400,000 volumes and large collections of pamphlets, newspapers, prints, cartoons, broadsides, maps and mss. of American and New York history.

The Gallery of Art has more than 2,000 paintings, including American portraits and the original water color drawings made by John James Audubon for his *Birds of America*.

**THE AMERICAN NUMISMATIC SOCIETY,** founded 1858, maintains a museum of coins and other currency, ancient and modern medals and decorations at Broadway and 156th St.

**THE PIERPONT MORGAN LIBRARY,** 29 E. 36th St., is a research-library museum based on collections formed by J. Pierpont Morgan (1837-1913). Main collections comprise medieval and renaissance illuminated and textual mss., incunabula, letters and documents, autograph mss., bookbindings, master drawings and Rembrandt etchings.

**THE NEW YORK PUBLIC LIBRARY:** In Jan. 1968, its resources were placed at approximately 30,000,000 items of which 8,250,000 were books, about 9,425,000 manuscripts, 6,800,000 pictures, 3,500,000 posters, photographs and broadsides, 6,000,000 pamphlets, scrapbooks and clippings. Of this total, 3,500,000 books and the pictures are in the collections of the Branch Libraries which are maintained by the City of New York and which operate 80 branch libraries in Manhattan, the Bronx, and Staten Island and 4 bookmobiles. The Research Libraries, based at Fifth Ave. and 42nd St., comprise one of the great research libraries in the world.

The Library & Museum of the Performing Arts at Lincoln Center has books, scores, recordings and exhibits of the performing arts.

**SEAMEN'S CHURCH INSTITUTE,** facing Manhattan's Battery Park, has dining room, cafeteria, collections of sailing ship models, ships' bells, marine paintings, tattoo designs, gym, sauna, showers, all open to public.

**THE STATEN ISLAND INSTITUTE OF ARTS AND SCIENCES,** founded 1881, has a museum of art, natural science, archeology, conservation and Indian life at 75 Stuyvesant Pl., St. George, S. I., and a library at 51 Stuyvesant Pl. It offers lectures, concerts and classes for children and adults.

**WHITNEY MUSEUM OF AMERICAN ART,** Madison Ave. at 75th St., holds exhibitions of group and individual artists, historical and contemporary. Its 1966 building was designed by Marcel Breuer.

## Brooklyn Centers

**BROOKLYN BOTANIC GARDEN,** Eastern Parkway, Washington and Flatbush Aves., has 50 acres of gardens, including rose, herb, wild flower and Japanese, and a fragrance garden for the blind.

**THE BROOKLYN MUSEUM,** Eastern Parkway and Washington Ave., estab. 1897, has comprehensive exhibitions in all major fields of art. An Outdoor Sculpture Garden contains ornaments from razed N. Y. area buildings.

**BROOKLYN ACADEMY OF MUSIC,** 30 Lafayette Ave., is the Brooklyn Center for the Performing Arts. It presents concerts, operas, etc., and has a program of films, lectures and workshops.

**THE BROOKLYN PUBLIC LIBRARY** occupies the Ingersoll Building, Grand Army Plaza, and 53 branches. It operates two bookmobiles. The Ingersoll Building has administrative offices and 5 major-subject divisions, a Young Teens division, Children's Room, Browsing Room, Student's Room and Micromaterials Room.

## Churches

**ARMENIAN CATHEDRAL** (Armenian Church of America), 2nd Ave. and 35th St. Steel arches support a gilded, conic, Armenian-style dome.

**JOHN ST. METHODIST CHURCH,** 44 John St., erected 1841, on site of Wesley Chapel of 1768, "first Methodist preaching-house in America," houses oldest Methodist Society, formed 1766. Has noontime services for office workers.

**PLYMOUTH CHURCH OF THE PILGRIMS** (Congregational), Orange St., Brooklyn, is a Nat'l Historic Landmark, built 1847, present structure 1849. Has windows illustrating Puritan influence on America and pew where Lincoln sat to hear Henry Ward Beecher, the first minister. In 1860 Beecher raised funds at an auction here to purchase the freedom of a slave girl, Pinky.

**RIVERSIDE CHURCH** (Interdenominational—American Baptist and United Church of Christ), Riverside Drive and W. 122nd St. The chief donor was John D. Rockefeller, Jr. The tower, reminiscent of Chartres, is 100 ft. square, rises 392 ft.

**CATHEDRAL OF ST. JOHN THE DIVINE** on Morningside Heights, Amsterdam Ave. and W. 112th St. (Protestant Episcopal), was begun 1892 as a Romanesque building; the design was changed to Gothic. The church is 601 ft. long, 146 wide at nave and will be 330 ft. wide at transept. Two front towers will rise to over 250 ft.

**ST. MARK'S-IN-THE-BOUWERIE** (Protestant Episcopal), 2nd Ave. and E. 10th St., originally a chapel built on the farm of Director General Peter Stuyvesant in 1660, rebuilt in 1799. A statue of Stuyvesant in the churchyard was presented by Queen Wilhelmina of the Netherlands in 1915.

**ST. PAUL'S CHAPEL OF TRINITY PARISH** (Protestant Episcopal), Broadway and Vesey St., is the oldest colonial church edifice in New York. It was opened Oct. 30, 1766. Much of the interior decoration was by L'Enfant, who laid the plans for Washington, D. C. There is a unique collection of 14 Waterford Irish cut glass chandeliers.

**ST. PATRICK'S CATHEDRAL** (Roman Catholic) occupies a block facing Fifth Ave., between E. 50th and E. 51st Sts., opposite Rockefeller Center. It was begun in 1858 in granite and marble in a Gothic revival style designed by James Renwick. It was opened in part in 1877 and dedicated May 25, 1879. It has two spires, 330 ft. tall, and a 26-ft. rose window. St. Patrick's is the cathedral church of the Archdiocese of N. Y.

**ST. PETER'S CHURCH** (Roman Catholic), Barclay and Church Sts., has the form of a Greek temple with large porch, wide steps and granite pillars, erected 1835 to replace the original church of 1785 of the first Catholic parish of New York.

**TEMPLE EMANU-EL**, Fifth Ave. and 65th St., was erected 1929 by Congregation Emanu-El (Reform), which dates from 1845. It was built of limestone in early Romanesque style, its auditorium 77 ft. wide by 150 ft. long and 103 ft. high, the largest temple in the country. Noteworthy are the high arch at the entrance, the rose window and 3 bronze doors. Open to visitors 10 a.m.-5 p.m.

**TRINITY CHURCH** (Protestant Episcopal) faces Broadway at the head of Wall St. It was built 1841-46 of brown sandstone in perpendicular Gothic, designed by Richard Upjohn, is 78 ft. wide by 202 ft. long and has an octagonal brownstone spire 280 ft. high. The first church was opened in 1698. In the churchyard are buried Alexander Hamilton, Robert Fulton, Capt. James Lawrence and Revolutionary soldiers who died in British prisons.

## Historic Sites

**EDGAR ALLAN POE COTTAGE**, Grand Concourse and Kingsbridge Road, Bronx, is a restored cottage, built 1812, in which Poe lived 1846-49, and in which his wife, Virginia Clem, died, 1847.

**FEDERAL HALL NATIONAL MEMORIAL**, Wall and Nassau Sts., is a Greek Revival structure of 1842, originally the Custom House, later the U. S. Sub-Treasury. On the site stood the Colonial City Hall and later Federal Hall, where the Stamp Act, Continental and U. S. Congresses met and George Washington took the oath of office as President.

**FRAUNCES TAVERN**, Broad and Pearl Sts., was erected 1719 as the DeLancey mansion, acquired 1762 by Samuel Fraunces and operated as the Queen's Head Tavern. The Long Room was the scene of Washington's farewell to his officers, Dec. 4, 1783. It was restored by the Sons of the Revolution in the State of New York and is their headquarters. It contains a Revolutionary War museum and art gallery, free to the public.

**GOVERNORS ISLAND**, in New York harbor south of the Battery, contains 173.35 acres. The picturesque old fort, Castle Williams, was built 1807-1811 by Col. Jonathan Williams, nephew of Benj. Franklin. It is 200 ft. in diameter, was used as a prison for Confederates during the Civil War. Fort Jay built 1794-1806, marks the site of Revolutionary fortifications.

For many years the headquarters of the First U. S. Army, Governors Island was turned over to the U. S. Coast Guard July 1, 1966. The island is now the Coast Guard's largest base.

**GENERAL GRANT NATIONAL MEMORIAL** (**GRANT'S TOMB**), Riverside Dr. and W. 122nd St., is a formal Roman-style mausoleum in which Gen. U. S. Grant, 18th President, and Mrs. Grant are buried. The tomb is 165 ft. tall.

**THE ROGER MORRIS-JUMEL MANSION**, W. 160th St. and Edgecombe Ave., is a 3-story colonial mansion with 4-pillared portico built in 1765 by Col. Roger Morris of the British Army. From Sept. 15-Oct. 19, 1776, it was the headquarters of Gen. George Washington.

In 1810 Stephen Jumel bought 63 acres of the property. In 1833, the widowed Mrs. Jumel married Aaron Burr. He lived there briefly.

**WASHINGTON SQUARE**, at the foot of Fifth Ave., is the best known landmark of **Greenwich Village**, distinguished for homes of artists, writers, and attractive small shops. Facing Fifth Ave. is the marble **Washington Arch**, designed by Stanford White to commemorate the centenary of the first inauguration and completed in 1895. At the east are buildings of **New York University**, which also owns many of the old redbrick houses of Federal design on the north side.

## Important Buildings

**THE CITY HALL**, headquarters of the Mayor, the City Council and the Board of Estimate of the City of New York, is in City Hall Park (the original Common), bounded by Broadway, Park Row and Chambers St. Erected 1803-1812, it is an adaptation of French Renaissance with a clock cupola surmounted by a figure of Justice.

Other public buildings in the vicinity are **Hall of Records**, north of Chambers St., and **Municipal Bldg.**, 40 stories arched over Chambers St. North of these bldgs. is Foley Square, the site of Collect Pond of colonial days. It is boxed by public buildings: **United States Court House**, built 1936, designed by Cass Gilbert, 32 stories; the hexagonal **State Supreme Court Bldg.**; the **State Office Bldg.**; the **Health Dept. Bldg.** and the new **Federal Bldg.**, 46 stories. North on Centre St. are the **Civil Court, Criminal Court** and **City Prison**.

**THE COLISEUM**, facing Columbus Circle betw. W. 58th and W. 60th Sts., is New York's principal center for national and international exhibitions. Opened Apr. 28, 1956, it cost about $35,000,000.

The Coliseum has over 9 acres of floor space. Its main halls can accommodate 8,000 people.

**COOPER UNION FOR THE ADVANCEMENT OF SCIENCE AND ART**, at Cooper Square, 7th St. and 4th Ave., was founded 1859 by Peter Cooper, ironmaster and public benefactor. Its college-level School of Engineering and Science and School of Art and Architecture are tuition-free to undergraduate students selected by competitive examination. Graduate courses in engineering are also tuition-free. Cooper Union is noted for the free Forum lectures and performances held from Oct. to Mar., on Mon., Wed. and Fri. evenings in the Great Hall where Abraham Lincoln made his famous Cooper Union address Feb. 27, 1860.

**EMPIRE STATE BUILDING**, Fifth Ave., between W. 33rd and 34th Sts., is the tallest building in the world, 1,472 ft. high including a 222-ft. television and FM radio transmitting tower. The building was completed May 1, 1931. More than 1,500,000 persons annually visit the 86th and 102nd floor Observatories. On a clear day viewers can see a distance of 80 mi.

**LINCOLN CENTER FOR THE PERFORMING ARTS** was opened Sept. 23, 1962, with a concert in Philharmonic Hall. The Center is located between W. 62nd and 65th Sts., Amsterdam and Columbus Aves. It is a private, nonprofit tax-exempt corporation of 7 constituent organizations. The New York State Theater, facing Philharmonic Hall, opened in 1964. The Vivian Beaumont Theater, for repertory, capacity 1,140, and the Library-Museum of the Performing Arts opened in 1965. The Metropolitan Opera House opened in 1966. The Juilliard School of Music is to open in 1969.

**MADISON SQUARE GARDEN CENTER**, Pennsylvania Plaza (7th-8th Aves., 31st-33rd Sts.), opened in the 1967-68 season. The huge development, above the modernized underground Pennsylvania RR station, includes a 29-story office building and the Sports and Entertainment Center which has an arena seating over 20,000, the 5,000-seat Felt Forum, 48 bowling lanes, the Garden Hall of Fame, the National Art Museum of Sport, an Exposition Rotunda for trade and walk-around shows, and a 500-seat Cinema.

**PAN AM BUILDING**, north of Grand Central Terminal Bldg., is the world's largest commercial office building. It has 59 floors rising 808 ft., with a rooftop heliport, and was erected over the tracks of the Grand Central Station. It covers a ground area of 3½ acres; est. office population is 17,000.

**ROCKEFELLER CENTER**, the largest privately owned business and entertainment center in America was started Sept. 1931. Its area includes the three blocks from 48th to 51st Sts. between Fifth Ave. and the Ave. of the Americas, a large portion of the 51st-52nd St. block and two blockfronts on the west side of the Ave. of the Americas between 48th and 51st Sts. There are 18 buildings with two more under construction. It has 160,000 daily visitors; 48,500 work there.

The surface area of Rockefeller Center covers 17 acres, most of which are leased for a long period from Columbia University. Rockefeller Center pays Columbia an annual rental of $3,800,000. The lease with options for renewal runs until 2069.

The part of Rockefeller Center comprising theaters and radio and television studios is often referred to as Radio City. Studios of the National Broadcasting Co. are located in the 70-story RCA building (850 ft. tall). There is an Observation Roof on the 70th floor.

**RADIO CITY MUSIC HALL**, Ave. of the Americas and W. 50th St., largest indoor theater in the world, seats 6,200 people. Its stage, 144 ft. wide by 67 ft. deep, has a proscenium arch 60 ft. high and 100 ft. wide. Has first-run films and stage spectacles featuring the Rockettes, Ballet Company, Symphony Orchestra and guest artists.

**UNITED NATIONS HEADQUARTERS** occupies 18 acres between 1st Ave. and F.D.R. (East River) Drive, E. 42nd and E. 48th Sts. Most unusual is the **Secretariat Bldg.**, 550 ft. tall, 289 ft. long and only 72 ft. wide. The 2 sides have 5,400 windows; the end walls are of 2,000 tons of Vermont marble. **General Assembly Bldg.** has a hall 165 ft. long, 115 ft. wide. **Conference Bldg.** houses 3 Council chambers, etc. There are guided tours daily.

**NEW YORK STOCK EXCHANGE**, 20 Broad St., has visitors' gallery, films, guided tours, Monday through Friday, 10 a.m. to 3:30 p.m.

# Washington, Capital of the United States

## The Capitol

**The Capitol** (building) since 1961 has presented an entirely new East Central front, the central portion having been reconstructed and extended. It was moved forward 32½ ft. The former facade of Virginia sandstone was reproduced in Georgia marble, the original wall becoming an interior wall. The new section added 78 offices and other important facilities. The cost of the extension project was $11,400,000; improved illumination and other work brought the total to $24,000,000.

The Capitol stands 88 ft. above the level of the Potomac River and covers approximately 4 acres. Its length, from north to south, is 751 ft. 4 in.; its width, including approaches, is 350 ft., and its height above the base line on the east front to the top of the statue of Freedom is 287 ft., 5½ ins.

The original plan for the Capitol was drawn by Dr. William Thornton, of Tortola, West Indies, and accepted April 5, 1793. It had a central section, nearly square, a low dome and rectangular buildings north and south, 126 by 120 ft. The southeast cornerstone of the north section was laid by President Washington with Masonic ceremonies Sept. 18, 1793. Sandstone from Aquia Creek, Va., was used. The northern wing was completed first. The Congress occupied it in Nov. 1800. The Supreme Court met in Feb. 1801, and other local courts also used the Capitol. In charge of early construction were architects Stephen H. Hallet, Geo. Hadfield, and James Hoban who was architect of the White House. Benjamin H. Latrobe was architect of the South or House wing which was occupied in 1807, but not completed until 1811. All the interiors were burned by the British in 1814. Latrobe had charge of the rebuilding until 1818 when Charles Bulfinch became the Architect for 11 years or until 1829. Congress reoccupied the Capitol in 1819 and the central rotunda area was finished in 1829.

The present Senate and House wings were designed and constructed under the architect Thomas U. Walter in 1851-1863. The wing extensions are white marble from Lee, Mass., and the columns are from Maryland. Daniel Webster spoke at the laying of the cornerstone.

The Senate Chamber is 113 ft. 3 in. long and 80 ft. 3 in. wide. The Hall of Representatives (House) is 139 ft. long and 92 ft. wide.

The House moved in Dec. 16, 1857; the Senate Jan. 4, 1859. In 1860 the Supreme Court moved into the former Senate Chamber, and in 1864 the old Hall of the House was designated Statuary Hall. The Court moved into its own building in 1935.

The original dome of the Capitol, wood covered with copper, was replaced, 1856, by the present dome of cast iron, completed 1865. Its greatest exterior diameter is 135 ft. 5 in. The rotunda is 96 ft. diameter, height from floor to base of lantern, 180 ft. 3 in. The dome has 108 windows and there are 365 steps from the Architect's Office to the top of the dome. In the "eye" of the dome is a fresco by Constantino Brumidi, the "Apotheosis of Washington." Below the dome runs a 300-ft. frieze in fresco, portraying history from Columbus, 1492, to Kitty Hawk, 1903. Brumidi painted part of it by 1880. Costaggini added panels by 1888. Allyn Cox completed the frieze in 1953 and it was dedicated in 1954.

The Statue of Freedom on the dome, 19½ ft. tall, is of bronze and weighs 14,985 pounds. At its base are the words "E Pluribus Unum" (Out of Many One). It was modeled in plaster by Thomas Crawford in Rome and cast in bronze. It cost $23,796 exclusive of erection.

Inaugurations of Presidents and Vice Presidents take place Jan. 20 following a national election. They are usually held on a platform erected over the great steps on the East front. The oath of office of the President is usually given by the Chief Justice of the United States.

### PRAYER ROOM

A nondenominational room for meditation and prayer is located off the rotunda. Decorated in blue, it has a white oak altar with an open Bible, and candelabra, 10 seats and 2 kneeling benches. A stained-glass window depicts Washington at prayer, while panels show the obverse and reverse of the Great Seal. Also depicted are a candle and an open book, and a sentence from the 119th Psalm: "Thy word is a lamp unto my feet and a light unto my path." The 13 original states have stars; other states appear in a laurel border.

### NATIONAL STATUARY HALL

Statuary Hall was created in 1864 to occupy the former Hall of the House of Representatives. States were invited to contribute not more than two statues of distinguished persons judged worthy of national commemoration by the States. In 1933 the number of statues in Statuary Hall was limited to one statue from each state, others to be placed in other parts of the Capitol. To date 88 statues have been contributed by 48 states. A plaque in the floor marks the spot where John Quincy Adams was fatally stricken Feb. 21, 1848. The statues in Statuary Hall:

**Alabama** — Gen. Jos. Wheeler, USA, CSA.

**Arkansas** — Uriah M. Rose, jurist.

**Arizona** — John C. Greenway, U. S. A.

**California** — Junipero Serra, mission founder.

**Colorado**—Dr.Florence Rena Sabin, scientist.

**Connecticut** — Roger Sherman, statesman.

**Delaware**—Caesar Rodney, statesman.

**Florida**—Dr. John Gorrie, inventor.

**Georgia** — Alex. H. Stephens, statesman.

**Idaho**—Geo. L. Shoup, first governor.

**Illinois** — Frances E. Willard, WCTU head.

**Indiana**—Lew Wallace, USA, author.

**Iowa**—Saml. J. Kirkwood, governor.

**Kansas**—John J. Ingalls, senator.

**Kentucky**—Henry Clay, statesman.

**Louisiana** — Huey P. Long, senator.

**Maine** — Hannibal Hamlin, vice president.

**Maryland** — Charles Carroll, signer, D. of I.

**Massachusetts**—Samuel Adams, statesman.

**Michigan**—Lewis Cass, statesman.

**Minnesota**—Henry M. Rice, senator.

**Mississippi** — Jefferson Davis, statesman.

**Missouri** — Thos. H. Benton, senator.

**Montana** — Charles Marion Russell, artist.

**Nebraska**—Wm. Jennings Bryan, statesman.

**Nevada**—Patrick A. McCarran, senator.

**New Hampshire**—Daniel Webster, statesman.

**New Jersey** — Richard Stockton, statesman.

**New York** — Robt. R. Livingston, statesman.

**North Carolina**—Zebulon B. Vance, governor.

**North Dakota**—John Burke, U. S. Treasurer.

**Ohio**—William Allen, senator, governor.

**Oklahoma** — Sequoya, Cherokee leader.

**Oregon** — Rev. Jason Lee, pioneer.

**Pennsylvania**—Robert Fulton, inventor.

**Rhode Island**—Roger Williams, founder.

**South Carolina**—John C. Calhoun, statesman.

**South Dakota** — Gen. W. H. H. Beadle, educator.

**Tennessee**—John Sevier, first governor.

**Texas**—Sam Houston, pioneer leader.

**Utah** — Brigham Young, Mormon leader.

**Vermont**—Ethan Allen, Revolutionary leader.

**Virginia** — Robt. E. Lee, USA, CSA.

**Washington**—Dr. Marcus Whitman, pioneer.

**West Virginia**—Francis H. Pierpont, statesman.

**Wisconsin**—Robt. M. LaFollette Jr., statesman.

**Wyoming**—Esther Hobart Morris, suffragette.

Under the dome in the **Great Rotunda** are statues and busts of Washington, Lincoln, Jefferson, Hamilton, Jackson, Lafayette, Grant, Garfield and Baker.

Adjoining it, the **South Small Rotunda** has statues of George Clinton (N. Y.), Stephen F. Austin (Tex.) and John Peter Muhlenberg (Pa.). The corridor leading from Statuary Hall to the House has statues of Jonathan Trumbull (Conn.), Wm. King (Me.), Father Jacques Marquette (Wis.), Wade Hampton (S. C.), Will Rogers (Okla.), and Dr. John McLoughlin (Ore.). At the foot of the grand East and West stairways on the House side are a statue of Jefferson (by Hiram Powers) and the bronze bust of Beeshekee, Chippewa chief.

In the foyer of the former Senate and Supreme Court Chamber are statues of John Stark (N. H.) and Nathanael Greene (R. I.). In the corridor leading to the Senate wing are statues of Dr. Ephraim McDowell, (Ky.) and Dr. Crawford W. Long (Ga.), first to use ether as anaesthetic; John Hanson (Md.), 9th president of the Continental Congress, and John M. Clayton (Del.), Secy. of State; Wm. E. Borah (Idaho), Edward D. White (La.) and Maria L. Sanford (Minn.). In the east corridor of the Senate wing is Benjamin Franklin by Hiram Powers. Other statues and busts in the Senate wing are of John Hancock, signer of the Declaration; Thos. Crawford, sculptor; Chas. Sumner, senator; Abraham Lincoln, Zachary Taylor, James Bryce and John Paul Jones with Kosciuszko, Pulaski and Garibaldi on the first floor, east side.

In the **Hall of Columns** on the first floor, House wing are statues of E. Kirby Smith (Fla.), Zachariah Chandler (Mich.), Jas. Harlan (Ia.), Francis P. Blair, Jr. (Mo.), Gen. Philip Kearny (N. J.), Gen. Jas. Shields (Ill.), John Winthrop (Mass.),

Oliver P. Morton (Ind.), J. Sterling Morton (Neb.), Rev. Thos. Starr King (Calif.), J. L. M. Curry (Ala.), J. P. Clarke (Ark.), Geo. W. Glick (Kan.), Jas. Z. George (Miss.), Chas. B. Aycock (N. C.), Jacob Collamer (Vt.), John E. Kenna (W. Va.), Joseph Ward (S. D.), and Eusebio F. Kino, S.J. (Ariz.). A statue of Dennis Chavez, U. S. Senator (New Mexico) was unveiled Mar. 31, 1966.

### OFFICE BUILDINGS FOR MEMBERS

Members of Congress meet constituents and transact other business in five office buildings on Capitol Hill, two for the Senate and three for the House.

The original Senate building was completed in 1909, enlarged in 1933; the second Senate building was completed in 1958. Both are connected with the Capitol by subway.

The original House building (1908) was named for former Speaker Joseph G. Cannon (R.-Ill.), the second (1933) for former Speaker Nicholas Longworth (R.-Ohio), and the third (1964) for former Speaker Sam Rayburn (D.-Tex.). The Rayburn Building has underground transportation to the Capitol.

Also on Capitol Hill is the bell tower and statue memorial to Sen. Robert A. Taft of Ohio (1889-1953). It was erected by popular subscription and dedicated Apr. 14, 1959 by President Eisenhower.

### HOURS FOR VISITING

The Capitol is normally open from 9 a.m. to 4:30 p.m. daily, but from Easter to Labor Day it stays open until 6 p.m. The Rotunda, Crypt and Statuary Hall sections remain open to the public until 10 p.m. The only exceptions are Christmas, New Year's Day and Thanksgiving Day. Should either the House or the Senate remain in session beyond closing time, the wing of the Capitol in use will stay open until the session closes.

Tours, through the Capitol, including the House and Senate Galleries, are conducted from 9 a.m. to 3:45 p.m. for a nominal charge. During the extended summer hours tours are accepted until 5:15 p.m.

It is not necessary to take a tour to see the Capitol. Visitors desiring to hear debate in either chamber for a longer period than the tour allows must obtain a visitor's card from their Senator or Representative.

## The White House

The **White House**, the President's residence, stands in tree-shaded grounds (18 acres) on the south side of Pennsylvania Avenue, between the Treasury and the Executive Office Building. The main building, 170 by 85 ft., has 6 floors, with the East Terrace, 135 by 35 ft., leading to the East Wing, a 3-story building, 139 by 82 ft., used for offices and as an entrance for official functions. The West Terrace, 174 by 35 ft., contains offices and a swimming pool, and leads to the Executive Office, 3 stories high, 148 by 98 ft., erected in 1902 and enlarged several times since.

The White House was designed by James Hoban, an Irish-born architect, in a competition that paid $500. The main facade resembles the Duke of Leinster's house in Dublin. He based it on plans for Georgian country houses popular in the 18th century. President Washington chose the site, which was included on the plan of the Federal City prepared by the French engineer, Major Pierre L'Enfant. The cornerstone was laid Oct. 13, 1792. President Washington never lived in the house. President John Adams entered in November, 1800, and Mrs. Adams hung her washing in uncompleted East Room.

The walls are of sandstone, quarried at Aquia Creek, Va. The exterior walls were painted during the course of construction, causing the building to be termed the "White House." For many years, however, it was generally referred to as the "President's House" or the "President's Palace." Thos. Jefferson developed the east and west terraces and built one-story offices, woodsheds and a wine cellar. On Aug. 24, 1814, during Madison's administration, the house was burned by the British. James Hoban completed rebuilding by Dec., 1817, and President Monroe moved in.

The south portico was added in 1824 and the north colonnade and porch in 1829 by Benjamin Latrobe, Surveyor of Public Buildings, based on sketches by Hoban, approved by Jefferson. In 1948 President Truman had a second-floor balcony built into the south portico. In 1948 he had Congress authorize complete rebuilding because the White House was unsafe. During its reconstruction he lived in Blair House, 1651 Pennsylvania Ave.

Reconstruction cost $5,761,000. The interior was completely removed, new underpinning 24 ft. deep was placed under the outside walls and a steel frame was built to support the interior. All original trim and metal work were preserved.

The **Green Room**, used for informal receptions, is in American Federal style, with green silk moire on the walls, a white marble fireplace and white enamel wainscoting and door trim. Over the fireplace hangs a portrait of Benjamin Franklin, painted in 1767. A pair of rare American settees and two armchairs are in front of the fireplace. There is also a sofa once owned by Daniel Webster.

The **Blue Room**, an oval drawing room, is the main reception room. The parquet floor is exposed; the walls are hung in white satin and blue taffeta. There are portraits of the first seven Presidents, and original chairs, a pier table, a French clock and candlesticks of gilt bronze, from James Monroe's 1817 furnishings.

The **Red Room**, used as a parlor, is furnished in the Empire period, hung in cerise silk with gold scroll borders. There are a Savonnerie carpet of the period, a marble-topped gueridon labeled by Charles Honore Lannuier, and a bronze inkstand used by Thomas Jefferson. There are portraits of Presidents Pierce, Van Buren, Truman, Theo. Roosevelt, Wilson and F. D. Roosevelt; also of Hamilton and John Marshall.

The **State Dining Room** has a large chief table and smaller tables capable of seating 140 at formal dinners. Centerpiece of the main table is a French bronze-doré plateau purchased by Monroe in 1817. China in use was ordered during the Lyndon B. Johnson Administration. Chairs are in Queen Anne style. The room is paneled in oak with Corinthian pilasters, painted white.

The **Family Dining Room** is used for breakfasts and luncheons. It has the Healy portrait of President Tyler. The **President's Dining Room** is on the second floor. It has scenic wallpaper and is furnished with American Federal furniture, an 18th Century chandelier and blue silk window hangings. There is a mahogany sideboard once owned by Daniel Webster.

The **Diplomatic Reception Room**, an oval room on the ground floor, is used as the entrance to the mansion at state functions. It has scenic wallpaper based on 1820 engravings and an Aubusson style rug with the seals of 50 states presented during the Eisenhower administration.

The **Library**, on the ground floor, has the painted decor of an early American room. On August, 1963, 2,780 titles were selected to be placed in the library. All but a few are by American authors. They were chosen by a committee headed by James T. Babb, librarian emeritus of Yale University.

The **Lincoln Bedroom**, which contains an ornately carved bed and furniture of his period, is at the east end of the second floor. It served as Lincoln's cabinet room and in it he signed the Emancipation Proclamation of Jan. 1, 1863. A portrait of Jackson, admired by Lincoln, hangs there today. Seven pieces of furniture have Lincoln associations. The bed was used in the State Bedroom during the Lincoln administration. In the room is a copy of the **Gettysburg Address**, written out by Lincoln and donated to the White House by the will of Oscar B. Cintas, one-time Cuban ambassador, who died in 1957.

The **Treaty Room**, one door removed from Lincoln's cabinet room was used by Andrew Johnson as his cabinet room, and so used until 1902, when it became a sitting room. Here in 1899 was signed the peace protocol treaty, a forerunner to the final treaty of peace with Spain. It is now a waiting or meeting room for the President and contains some of the original Victorian furniture. There are portraits of Presidents A. Johnson, Grant and Taylor and paintings of McKinley observing the signing of the treaty and of Lincoln and Grant in conference.

The **Queen's Bedroom** is assigned to distinguished women guests, and has sheltered five queens— Queen Mother Elizabeth, and Queen Elizabeth II of Britain, Wilhelmina and Juliana of the Netherlands, Queen Mother Frederika of Greece. The English overmantel mirror was presented by Princess Elizabeth in 1951.

The **Yellow Oval Room**, directly above the Blue Room, is used as a private sitting room by the President and Mrs. Johnson.

The **Empire Guest Room** has a "sleigh bed" probably owned by John Quincy Adams. Walls and upholstery are in red-and-white printed cotton showing scenes from the life of Franklin.

The President's Office in the West Wing, looks

out on the rose garden. Theodore Roosevelt built the West Wing in 1902. Previously the President's office had been on the second floor of the White House. The West Wing also contains the Conference Room and the Cabinet Room.

### VISITING HOURS

The White House is open from 10 a.m. to 12 noon, Tuesday through Friday, except on holidays. Also Saturdays, 10 a.m. to 2 p.m. Apr. 1 through Labor Day, and 10 a.m. to noon Labor Day through Mar. 31. Only the public rooms in the basement and the first floor rooms, may be visited. No permit is required.

*References: The White House: An Historic Guide, with forewords by Jacqueline Kennedy, Lady Bird Johnson and John Walker. The White House and its 34 Families by Amy Follette Jensen.*

### PRESIDENT'S GUEST HOUSE

**Blair House, the President's Guest House,** fronts on Pennsylvania Ave., nw of the White House grounds. It is supervised by the Dept. of State and is the official residence of heads of state who visit Washington. Built 1824, it was the home of Francis Preston Blair (1791-1876), political leader and Lincoln advisor. President Truman lived there 1948-1952 during rebuilding of the White House, and two Puerto Rican fanatics tried to shoot their way in Nov. 1, 1950, killing one guard and wounding two others.

Restoration and refurnishing began in 1963 and the house was reopened Jan. 14, 1964, on the occasion of the visit of President Antonio Segni of the Italian Republic. The Blair House Fine Arts Committee is continuing providing for the house.

## Arlington National Cemetery

**Arlington National Cemetery,** on the former Custis-Lee estate in Virginia, is the site of the **Tomb of the Unknown Soldier** and the final resting place of John Fitzgerald Kennedy, President of the United States, who was buried there Nov. 25, 1963. A torch burns day and night over his grave. The remains of his brother Sen. Robert F. Kennedy (N. Y.) were interred on June 8, 1968 in an area adjacent. Many other famous Americans also are buried at Arlington, as well as American soldiers from every major war.

Arlington National Cemetery, administered by the Department of the Army, was established June 15, 1864, on land originally the estate of George Washington Parke Custis. The land was a part of the District of Columbia, 1791 until 1847, when Arlington County was returned to Virginia.

The Unknown Soldier of World War I was entombed on the East front of the Arlington Memorial Amphitheater Nov. 11, 1921, in the presence of President Warren G. Harding. The tomb is inscribed: *Here rests in honored glory an American soldier known but to God.* The body had been chosen at Chalons-sur-Marne from unidentified dead in Europe. On Memorial Day, May 30, 1958, two unidentified servicemen, one of whom died in World War II and one in the Korean War, were placed in crypts beside the first, in ceremonies led by President Eisenhower and Vice President Nixon. The President placed the Medal of Honor on each of the two coffins.

As of Mar. 31, 1968, a total of 146,467 interments had been made in Arlington National Cemetery. Among the unknown dead are 2,111 who died on the battlefields of Virginia in the Civil War and 167 who lost their lives when the battleship Maine was blown up in Havana Harbor Feb. 15, 1898. The total of unknown dead interred in Arlington National Cemetery is 4,724.

Large memorial structures include the monument of the Unknown Dead of the Civil War, the Canadian Memorial, gift of Canada in honor of Americans who served with Canadian forces in World War I; a monument to the Confederate Dead, given by the United Daughters of the Confederacy, 1914; the Spanish-American War Memorial, a granite pillar surmounted by an eagle; the Coast Guard Memorial, and the USS Maine Memorial, with the mast of the Maine set in a granite base.

### CUSTIS-LEE MANSION

On the hilltop stands Arlington House, the former home of Robert E. Lee, which was officially designated the Custis-Lee Mansion by an act of Congress in 1955. The house has a portico 60 ft. wide, with 8 Doric columns and faces the Potomac. With its two wings the house extends 140 ft. It was built by George Washington Parke Custis, grandson of Martha Washington and father of Mary Ann Randolph Custis, who married Lee in this house

in 1831. Here Lee wrote his resignation from the U. S. Army, Apr. 20, 1861. The house became a military hq, and was confiscated by the Government. The U. S. Supreme Court restored it to the legal heir, grandson of the builder, and he sold it to the Government in 1883 for $150,000.

The mansion and grounds, administered by the National Park Service of the Dept. of the Interior, are reached by **Arlington Memorial Bridge,** a wide roadway over the Potomac.

## Library of Congress

Established by and for Congress in 1800, the services of the Library of Congress have been extended over the years to other Government agencies and other libraries, to scholars, and to the general public, and it now serves as the national library. Two buildings, an ornate Italian Renaissance structure (1897) and a modern annex (1939), cover 6 acres of the 15⅔-acre Library site, contain 35 acres of floor space, and have 270 miles of book shelves. In October, 1965, Congress passed a law authorizing construction of a third Library building, the James Madison Memorial Building.

L. Quincy Mumford, the 11th Librarian of Congress, took office September 1, 1954.

The Library had over 3,000 volumes when it was destroyed in the burning of the Capitol, August 24-25, 1814. In January 1815, Congress bought Thomas Jefferson's library of some 6,000 volumes. In 1851 fire destroyed about half the collections. In 1866 the science library of the Smithsonian Institution was transferred to the Library, and in 1870 the Library became the repository for materials deposited for copyright.

Many treasures of the Library are usually on exhibit, including the Gutenberg Bible, the first and second drafts of the Gettysburg Address, and Jefferson's so-called "rough draft" of the Declaration of Independence.

Some important recent additions to the Library's collections are the libretto of Handel's Messiah; some 185,000 separate plates or sheets of Sanborn fire insurance maps to supplement Sanborn materials acquired earlier; also papers of J. Robert Oppenheimer, Alan T. Waterman, John Glenn, Shirley Jackson, Truman Capote, John Toland, and Representative Emanuel Celler; works of the 19th Century French lithographer Charlet; and several rare volumes with Jeffersonian associations. Placed on deposit were the autograph manuscripts of Stravinsky's Petrouchka and Prokofiev's Classical Symphony, and the papers of Edna St. Vincent Millay.

In addition to its own world-wide acquisitions programs, the Library acquires nearly 2,000,000 publications a year from 8 foreign countries for some 300 American libraries through U. S.-owned foreign currencies under Public Law 480 as amended. Under the Higher Education Act of 1965, the Library also launched the National Program for Acquisitions and Cataloging (NPAC) in 1966 to solve a national cataloging problem in research libraries by obtaining all foreign books of value to scholarship and cataloging them promptly for all libraries needing such catalog data.

By fiscal 1968, the Library was obtaining foreign cataloging information from 20 countries for use in publishing the Library's famous 3 x 5 printed catalog cards. As part of its automation program, the Library also is distributing machine-readable cataloging (MARC) on magnetic tapes to libraries subscribing to this service.

Tours in the Library of Congress begin at the office of the Captain of the Guard, Main Building, Monday through Friday.

## Thomas Jefferson Memorial

**The Thomas Jefferson Memorial** stands on the south shore of the Tidal Basin in West Potomac park. It is a circular stone structure, with Vermont marble on the exterior and Georgia white marble inside and combines architectural elements of the dome of the Pantheon in Rome and the rotunda designed by Jefferson for the University of Virginia. The central circular chamber, 86.3 ft. in diameter, is dominated by a full-length figure of Thomas Jefferson 19 ft. tall, by the American sculptor Rudulph Evans. The architects were John Russell Pope and his associates Otto R. Eggers and Daniel P. Higgins. The Memorial was dedicated by President F. D. Roosevelt Apr. 13, 1943, the 200th anniversary of Jefferson's birth.

The exterior is surrounded by a peristyle of 26 Ionic columns, each 41 ft. tall, and 5 ft. 3 in. in diameter. Exterior of the dome is 95 ft. 8 in. from the floor. The interior columns are each 5 ft. in diameter and 39 ft. 2 in. tall. The Me-

morial stands on a circular stylobate of steps and terraces 183 ft. 10 in. in diameter.

On the pediment over the portico is a sculptured group by Adolph A. Weinman showing Jefferson standing before the committee appointed by the Continental Congress to draft the Declaration of Independence. On the interior walls are four panels with inscriptions from Jefferson's writings: (1) sentences from the Declaration; (2) the right of man to a free mind and liberty of religious opinion; (3) the duty of the state to bring bodily freedom and education to the common man; (4) the need of changes in laws and institutions to keep step with progress of the human mind and new circumstances. On the frieze of the main entablature are Jefferson's lines: "I have sworn upon the altar of God eternal hostility against every form of tyranny over the mind of man."

The Memorial is open daily from 8 a.m. to midnight, except Christmas Day.

## John F. Kennedy Center

**John F. Kennedy Center for the Performing Arts,** under construction on an 18-acre site on the Potomac River, is the sole official memorial to Pres. Kennedy in the capital and is expected to open in 1970. Financed by both Government and private funds, the marble building designed by Edward Durell Stone will house a 2,200-seat opera hall, a 2,700-seat concert hall, a 1,100-seat theater, a 500-seat studio playhouse, and other facilities. The building will be 630 ft. long, 300 ft. wide, 100 ft. high.

## Lincoln Memorial

**The Lincoln Memorial** in West Potomac Park, on the axis of the Capitol and the Washington Monument, consists of a large marble hall enclosing a heroic larger-than-life statue of Abraham Lincoln sitting as if in meditation on a large armchair. It was dedicated on Memorial Day, May 30, 1922. The Memorial was designed by Henry Bacon. The statue was made by Daniel Chester French. Murals and ornamentation on the bronze ceiling beams are by Jules Guerin.

The Memorial built on bedrock, is of white Colorado-Yule marble. It is 79 ft. 10 in. tall and is approached by a flight of steps 80 ft., 3 in. wide. The east and west walls are 155 ft., 6 in. long, and the north and south walls are 85 ft., 8 in. wide. The walls are enclosed by a continuous colonnade, 188 ft., 4 in. long and 118 ft., 6 in. wide. There are two Doric columns at the entrance and 36 others in the colonnade, each 44 ft. tall, 7 ft. 4 in. in diameter at the base, and the frieze above 36 columns bears the names of the 36 states existing at the time of Lincoln's death. On the attic parapet are recorded names of the 48 states existing in 1922.

Inside are three memorials to Lincoln. The seated figure of Lincoln is 19 ft. from head to foot and the classic armchair is 12½ ft. tall. Over the back of the chair a flag is draped in marble. The statue was fashioned out of 28 blocks of Georgia white marble.

On the north wall is inscribed the Second Inaugural Address. On the south wall is the Gettysburg Address.

Greek Ionic columns 50 ft. high and 5 ft. 6 in. in diameter at the base divide the interior of the Memorial into three chambers. The walls of the interior are Indiana limestone, and the ceiling, 60 feet above the floor, is designed with bronze girders ornamented with laurel and oak leaves. The panels between the girders are of Alabama marble saturated with melted beeswax to produce translucency. The interior floor and the wall base are of pink Tennessee marble. The central chamber, containing the statue, is 58 ft. wide and 74 ft. deep. The cost of the Memorial was $2,957,000 and of the statue $88,400.

The Memorial is open daily from 8 a.m. to midnight, except Christmas Day.

## Mount Vernon

**Mount Vernon** on the south bank of the Potomac, 16 miles below Washington, D. C., is part of a large tract of land in Northern Virginia which was originally included in a royal grant made to Lord Culpepper, who in 1674 granted 5,000 acres to Nicholas Spencer and John Washington. The division between Spencer and Washington put John Washington's son Lawrence in possession of the Washington half in 1690. Later it became the property of Lawrence Washington's son Augustine, the father of George Washington.

The present house is an enlargement of one apparently built on the site of an earlier one by Augustine Washington, who lived there 1735-1738. His son Lawrence came there in 1743, when he re-

named the plantation Mount Vernon in honor of Admiral Vernon under whom he had served in the West Indies. Lawrence Washington died in 1752 and was succeeded as proprietor of Mount Vernon by his half-brother, George Washington.

To Mount Vernon in 1759 Washington brought his wife, Martha Dandridge Custis, having previously enlarged the house from 1½ to 2½ stories. Here he cultivated a farm and employed a shoemaker, a tailor, a dozen textile workers and other help. Just before the Revolution he planned additions, and when he was called away to war his kinsman Lund Washington supervised the work, which was completed after Washington returned in 1783. During the Revolution Washington visited Mount Vernon only twice, on the way to and from Yorktown in 1781. His wife often stayed with him at headquarters. He returned to the house on Christmas Eve, 1783. In 1789 he left to become President and lived in New York and Philadelphia, with brief visits to the plantation. He came back in 1797 and died in Mount Vernon Dec. 14, 1799. He was buried in the old family vault. He had made plans for a new burial vault and this was built in 1831. Both his remains and those of Martha, who died in 1802, were transferred there.

Mount Vernon was left to Washington's nephew, U. S. Supreme Court Justice Bushrod Washington, and by him to his nephew, John Augustine Washington, whose son, John A. Washington, Jr., was the last private owner. In 1853, when the place was run down, Miss Ann Pamela Cunningham of South Carolina organized the Mount Vernon Ladies' Assn., which bought the mansion and 200 acres, since extended to 487 acres. The Association reassembled original Washington furniture and repaired the buildings. It restored the kitchen garden, flower garden and experimental botanical garden, reconstructed the greenhouse and built a museum. Several trees planted by Washington still exist, and the boxwood dates from 1798.

The Association preserves house and tomb with the visitor's fee. The Regent of the Mount Vernon Ladies' Association is Mrs. Francis F. Beirne. About 30 states are represented by vice regents. The Resident Director is Chas. C. Wall; the assistant to the Director is Walter C. Densmore.

## National Archives

The Declaration of Independence, the Constitution of the United States and the Bill of Rights are now enshrined in the National Archives Exhibition Hall. They are sealed in glass-and-bronze cases filled with inert helium gas. They can be lowered at a moment's notice into a large shockproof and fireproof safe.

Readable facsimiles of the three documents are available in an inexpensive 16-page publication. Charters of Freedom, and other historical documents are also available. Certain records of research value are available on microfilm.

The National Archives and Records Service is a part of the General Services Administration. It consists of the Offices of the National Archives, Administration and Technical Services, Federal Records Centers, Records Management, the Federal Register, and Presidential Libraries. The last-mentioned Office administers the Franklin D. Roosevelt Library at Hyde Park, N. Y., the Harry S. Truman Library at Independence, Mo., the Dwight D. Eisenhower Library at Abilene, Kan., and the Herbert Hoover Library at West Branch, Iowa. The John Fitzgerald Kennedy Library in Boston, Mass., and the Lyndon Baines Johnson Library in Austin, Tex., also will be administered by the National Archives and Records Service when they have been completed.

The National Archives is headed by Dr. James B. Rhoads, Archivist of the United States.

## National Gallery of Art

**The National Gallery of Art,** situated on the area bounded by Seventh Street, Constitution Avenue, Fourth Street, and Madison Drive on the Mall in Washington, D. C., was established by Joint Resolution of Congress Mar. 24, 1937 and opened Mar. 17, 1941. Attendance during fiscal 1967 was 1,577,108.

The building, costing about $15,000,000, was erected with funds given by the late Andrew W. Mellon. It was completed under the direction of Paul Mellon, Donald D. Shepard, and David K. E. Bruce, trustees of the A. W. Mellon Educational and Charitable Trust. The architects were John Russell Pope and associates, Otto R. Eggers and Daniel Paul Higgins. The building is of rose-white Tennessee marble, 785 feet long.

The central architectural feature of the Gallery

is the rotunda, covered with a coffered dome supported by 24 columns of dark green marble. The diameter of the rotunda and the height of the dome from the marble floor both measure 100 feet. Flanking the rotunda on either side are two long galleries for larger pieces of sculpture. At the end of each of these galleries is a garden court, with a colonnade of 16 monoliths of Indiana limestone. In the center of each court has been installed a 17th Century fountain from the park of Versailles. Across from the Gallery on Constitution Ave. is the Andrew W. Mellon Memorial Fountain, designed by Eggers and Higgins, dedicated 1952.

In addition to providing the building, Andrew Mellon also gave his collection, consisting of 126 paintings and 26 pieces of sculpture, the latter largely from the Dreyfus Collection. The paintings cover the various European schools from the 13th Century to the 19th, and include such masterpieces as Raphael's Alba Madonna, the Niccolini-Cowper Madonna, and St. George and the Dragon; Van Eyck's Annunciation; Botticelli's Adoration of the Magi; nine Rembrandts, and three Vermeers. Twenty-one paintings came from the Hermitage in Leningrad. Also in this collection are the Vaughan Washington, by Gilbert Stuart, and the Washington Family, by Edward Savage.

The Samuel H. Kress Collection of paintings in the National Gallery at its opening in 1941 included Giorgione's Adoration of the Shepherds, Raphael's portrait of Bindo Altoviti, Madonna by Giotto, and 9 paintings by Giovanni Bellini. Later additions include the great tondo of the Adoration of the Magi by Fra Angelico and Fra Filippo Lippi, the Laocoön and the early Christ Cleansing the Temple by El Greco, and fine examples by Giorgione, Titian, Grünewald, Dürer, Memling, Bosch, Pieter Bruegel the Elder, Juan de Flandes, Francois Clouet, Poussin, Watteau, Chardin, Boucher, Fragonard, David and Ingres. Also included are a number of masterpieces of sculpture, especially of the Italian and French schools.

The Jos. E. Widener Collection of over 100 paintings includes 14 Rembrandts, 8 Van Dycks, 2 Vermeers and examples of Italian masters; also Renaissance and French sculpture and examples of the decorative arts.

The Chester Dale Collection includes masterpieces by El Greco, Zurbarán, Boucher, Manet, Cezanne, Renoir, Monet, Modigliani, Pissarro, Degas, van Gogh, Gauguin, Toulouse-Lautrec, Matisse, Picasso, Braque, and a group of American paintings, sculpture, prints and drawings.

Many other masterpieces have been donated by foundations and individuals, and the names of Booth, Bliss, Carstairs, Frelinghuysen, Havemeyer, Hutton, Lewisohn, Timken, Whitney and Garbisch are prominent in the lists. Lessing J. Rosenwald has given over 20,000 prints and drawings.

Acquisition announcements for recent times by all museums were overshadowed by the disclosure on Feb. 20, 1967 of the purchase of America's first painting by Leonardo da Vinci. No other generally acknowledged painting by Leonardo is known to exist outside Europe. The famous picture of the Florentine woman Ginevra de'Benci was purchased from the ruling house of Liechtenstein by the National Gallery for an undisclosed sum that is believed to be the highest in the history of art. (Reportedly over $5,000,000.) After being reframed, the two-sided wooden panel painting was placed on view Mar. 17.

The Index of American Design, at the National Gallery of Art, is a collection of about 17,500 water color renderings and photographs of American crafts and folk arts. The Library has about 36,000 books and pamphlets.

The Gallery's Extension Service lends slide lectures, exhibits and other materials without charge to schools and groups throughout the nation.

Open every day except Christmas and New Years. Hours 10 a.m. to 5 p.m. weekdays, 2 p.m. to 10 p.m. Sundays. Summer hours: April 1 through Labor Day, 10 a.m. to 9 p.m. weekdays, 12 noon to 10 p.m. Sundays.

## National Geographic Society

The National Geographic Society, founded in 1888 "for the increase and diffusion of geographic knowledge," is the world's largest nonprofit scientific and educational institution. The Society produces the illustrated monthly *National Geographic*, books, maps, globes, atlases, other educational materials, and television programs. Its worldwide activities are supported by the dues of more than 6,100,000 members.

The Society's new 10-story headquarters building in Washington, D. C., dedicated by President Johnson in 1964, has attracted more than 2,000,000

visitors. Explorers Hall offers exhibits, artifacts, and mementoes depicting the research and exploration activities of the Society around the world.

In 1967, construction was started on the Society's new Membership Center Building on a 100-acre tract near Gaithersburg, Md. The five-story building, expected to be occupied in late 1968, will accommodate 1,100 employees charged with handling membership files, correspondence, changes of address, receipt of dues, and other clerical operations. Each floor will be more than 7 times the size of an average city lot.

Executive officers are: Melville Bell Grosvenor, editor-in-chief and chairman of the Board of Trustees; Thomas W. McKnew, advisory chairman of the Board; Melvin M. Payne, president of the Society; Hilleary F. Hoskinson, treasurer; Frederick G. Vosburgh, vice president and editor; Leonard Carmichael, vice president for research and exploration; Robert E. Doyle, vice president and secretary; Thomas M. Beers, vice president and associate secretary; Gilbert M. Grosvenor, vice president and associate editor.

## The Pentagon

The Pentagon is the world's largest office building. It is situated on the Virginia side of the Potomac River, and covers 34 acres, including a 5-acre center court. It houses personnel of the Dept. of Defense, which includes the Depts. of the Army, Navy and Air Force. The Secretary of Defense, the Secretaries of the three departments and the military Chiefs of Staff have offices here. The building does not accommodate all the personnel of the Dept. of Defense.

The Pentagon was completed Jan. 15, 1943, at a cost of about $83,000,000. It covers 34 acres and has 204 acres of lawns and terraces. It is 5 stories high and consists of 5 rings of buildings connected by 10 corridors, with a 5-acre pentagonal court in the center. Each of the outermost sides of the building is 921 ft. long and the perimeter is seven-eighths of a mile. Total length of corridors is $17\frac{1}{2}$ miles. There is a mezzanine below the first floor and a partial basement below that.

Population is 27,000, 60% civilians. Parking space, 67 acres, can hold 10,000 cars.

Many facilities for daily use, such as bank, drug store, medical and dental clinics, ticket agency, are located in the Pentagon. It has a switchboard console with approx. 175,000 calls a day over 30,000 phones. It has 4,200 clocks, 685 water fountains, 1,900 toilets and 280 rest rooms and 672 hose cabinets for fire protection.

Some of the workers eat 2 or 3 meals in the building. A staff of over 600 prepares and serves meals from 3 kitchens to 2 dining rooms, 6 cafeterias, 9 beverage bars and an outside snack bar. During an average day Pentagon personnel consume about 30,000 cups of coffee, 2,255 quarts of milk and milk products and 5,000 soft drinks.

## Smithsonian Institution

Smithsonian Institution is one of the world's great historical, scientific and cultural establishments. It comprises numerous facilities, mostly in the metropolitan Washington area. It was founded by an Act of Congress in 1846, pursuant to a bequest of James Smithson, a British scholar-scientist, to the United States to found at Washington "an establishment for the increase and diffusion of knowledge among men." The Smithsonian, ever since its founding, has been a center for basic scientific research; it is also the largest museum-gallery complex in the world. More than 18,000,000 persons visited its halls in fiscal 1967. S. Dillon Ripley became the 8th secretary of the Smithsonian Feb. 1, 1964.

The Museum of History and Technology. On Jan. 22, 1964, President Lyndon B. Johnson dedicated this museum. More than 5,000,000 visitors stream into the museum annually to enjoy the permanent, special and visiting exhibits illustrating the cultural and technological development of the United States. The museum consists of 3 floors of exhibitions, and convenient food facilities for its visitors in the basement. In the rotunda the visitor will find the original Star-Spangled Banner. The Growth of the United States exhibit portrays American civilization from its inception to modern times and includes such items as an early 18th-Century printing press used by Benjamin Franklin, a portion of a 17th-Century house from Ipswich, Mass., Eli Whitney's model of the cotton gin, the locomotive John Bull, a uniform worn by Gen. George Washington and the writing desk on which Thomas Jefferson drafted the Declaration of Independence. Large exhibits in-

clude Petroleum Hall, the history of transportation, machine and hand tools, American political and military history, numismatics, philately, ceramics and glass, heavy machinery, timekeeping, physical and medical sciences, graphic arts and electricity.

**The Museum of Natural History** abounds in the fields of natural history—zoology, botany, geology, paleontology and anthropology. **The Hall of Asia, Africa and the Pacific** contains exhibits illustrating aspects of the life and cultures of Southeastern Asia, India, Australia, New Zealand, the Pacific Islands and Africa. Exhibits include fossil plants and invertebrate animals, fishes, amphibians, dinosaurs, primitive reptiles, mammals in North America. Here also are animals collected by Theodore Roosevelt on his 1910 African safari, the Hall of Birds, the Fenykovi Elephant and the Hall of Gems and Minerals, including the 44½ carat blue Hope diamond.

**The National Collection of Fine Arts,** in its first permanent home in 122 years, opened its doors in 1968 in the renovated Old Patent Office Building, noted for its classical Greek architecture. In addition to its Two-Century Survey of American Art, there are special and loan exhibits of American sculpture and painting. The museum also sends the work of American artists abroad and exhibits the art of other countries.

**The National Portrait Gallery,** a new museum, traces America's history through the portraits of its people, in paintings, sculpture and photographs.

**The Renwick Gallery,** in process of restoration to be completed by early 1969, will house American arts, crafts and design.

**The Joseph H. Hirshhorn Museum and Sculpture Garden,** still in the planning stage, will house works in the Hirshhorn collections donated to the Smithsonian in 1966.

**The National Zoological Park** is noted for its outstanding collection of small mammals and for its six pigmy hippopotamuses, which are on the endangered list. It also has the only white tiger in the Western hemisphere, and the only Komodo dragon, the largest species of lizard.

**The Astrophysical Observatory** in Cambridge, Mass., performs research in 9 principal areas: radio astronomy; gamma-ray astronomy; meteorites and cosmic dust; theoretical astrophysics; optical observatory and observation; flight experiments; planetary and lunar science; meteors and comets; historical astronomy.

**The Smithsonian Institution Press** publishes books and scholarly papers in natural science, anthropology, history, astrophysics, geology, art.

**The Freer Gallery of Art,** the gift of Detroit industrialist Charles Lang Freer, is an outstanding center for research in the art of the Far and Near East. Major new accessions are added annually. The gallery also houses the Whistler Peacock Room and his etchings and paintings.

**The Science Information Exchange** was established to aid in closing the information gap between the time when a research project is started and when its results are published in scientific journals. Information on the scientist, his organization, and the subject on which he is working can be rapidly retrieved from the Exchange's computer system.

**The Smithsonian Institution Traveling Exhibition Service (SITES)** aids museums, libraries, universities, and other educational institutions in the development of their exhibition programs. In 1967, 108 exhibitions were sponsored.

**The National Air and Space Museum.** Pending new construction, the Arts and Industries building and the temporary Air and Space building house the historic Wright Brothers' airplanes, Charles A. Lindbergh's "Spirit of St. Louis," space satellites and missiles.

**Cooper-Hewitt Museum of Design,** in New York City, was formerly the Cooper Union Museum for the Arts of Decoration. It officially became a component of the Smithsonian on July 1, 1968.

## Washington National Monument

**The Washington National Monument** is a tapering shaft or obelisk of white marble, 555 feet, 5⅛ inches in height and 55 feet, 1½ inches square at the base. Eight small windows, two on each side, are located at the 500 foot level, where Washington points of interest are indicated.

The erection of the monument by the Washington National Monument society with funds obtained by popular subscription was authorized by Congress in 1848. The cornerstone was laid July 4

of the same year. Work progressed slowly until 1854 when $300,000 had been subscribed and 156 feet of the shaft erected. In that year the enterprise became controversial and contributions ceased. Work was resumed in 1880 at Government expense by the Corps of Engineers.

The capstone weighs 3,300 lbs. and was placed Dec. 6, 1884. The monument was dedicated Feb. 21, 1885, and opened Oct. 9, 1888. It weighs 81,120 tons. It is dressed with white Maryland marble in 2-ft. courses. The first 150 ft. are backed by rubble masonry. From that point to 452 ft. Maine granite was used as backing, and above 452 ft. marble was used. The face of the monument is marble, the first 5 courses from Sheffield, Mass., the rest from Maryland. Set into the interior wall are 190 memorial stones from states, foreign countries and organizations. An iron stairway has 50 landings and 898 steps. A modern elevator takes sightseers to the 500-foot level in one minute, compared with 12 "precarious minutes" in 1888.

The Monument is open 8 a.m. to 11 p.m. from March 20 to Labor Day, and 9 a.m. to 5 p.m. the rest of the year. It is closed Christmas Day.

## Famous Churches

**The National Shrine of the Immaculate Conception,** at Fourth St. and Michigan Ave., NE, Washington, D. C., is the largest Catholic Church in the United States and the 7th largest in the world. Built by all the Bishops and Catholics of the U. S., it honors the Blessed Virgin Mary as Patroness of the United States. The Shrine is impressive not only in size but also in beauty, its blue and gold dome and soaring bell-tower having become Washington landmarks. Open daily from 7 a.m. to 8 p.m., Sunday masses, 7, 8, 9, 10, 11 a.m. and noon, 1:15 and 4:30 p.m. Free guided tours are on the half-hour 9 a.m. to 5 p.m., daily —Sunday tours 2 p.m. to 4 p.m. Carillon concerts Sat. and Sun. 3:30 p.m. (except May through Aug. at 6:30 p.m.). Organ recitals every Sun. at 7:30 p.m. (May through Aug.).

**Washington National Cathedral,** Massachusetts and Wisconsin Aves., NW, is atop Mt. Saint Alban, the highest point in Washington, D. C. It is the seat of the Presiding Bishop of the Episcopal Church and of the Bishop of Washington. Started in 1907, it is only three-quarters complete, and when finished in 1985 is expected to be the 6th largest church in the world. Notables buried in the Cathedral include Woodrow Wilson, Adm. George Dewey, Cordell Hull and Frank B. Kellogg. The Cathedral is considered one of the finest examples of Gothic architecture in the country. On its 57 acres are the Bishop's Garden and Herb Cottage and five educational institutions.

Several Protestant churches commemorate the association of Presidents with their congregations. **St. John's Episcopal Church,** across Lafayette Sq. from the White House, designed by Benj. Latrobe in 1815, was regularly attended by Madison and F. D. Roosevelt and at times by other Presidents. **New York Ave. Presbyterian Church,** 1313 New York Ave., NW, preserves the pew in which Lincoln sat, also an original manuscript of the first draft of his first proposal to abolish slavery. Church rebuilt on same site in 1950-51.

President Eisenhower became a member of the National Presbyterian Church Feb. 1, 1953. The Church buildings were located then at Connecticut Ave. at N St., NW. The cornerstone for the new National Presbyterian Church and Center was laid by former President Eisenhower on his 77th birthday, Oct. 14, 1967. The main Chapel will be known as "The Chapel of the Presidents" in tribute to Dwight D. Eisenhower. The Chapel will contain the pew occupied by Pres. and Mrs. Eisenhower, and 15 or 16 other pews occupied by, or assigned to, former Presidents. It is under construction on a 12½-acre tract at Nebraska Ave. and Van Ness St., NW, and will incorporate all of the historical elements from the preceding buildings. This church was founded on two historic congregations, the First Presbyterian Church, which originated in a carpenter shop on the White House grounds in 1795, and the Church of the Covenant, formed in 1883. The old President's pew, brought from the First Church, was occupied by Presidents Jackson, Polk, Pierce, Buchanan, and Cleveland. Other pews were used by Presidents Grant and Benjamin Harrison.

**The Islamic Center,** 2551 Massachusetts Ave., NW. A magnificent monument of Islamic culture and outstanding landmark for visitors, a Mosque for worship, and an Institute for higher study of Islamic culture.

# Notable Tall Buildings in United States Cities

Height from sidewalk to roof, including penthouse and tower if enclosed as integral part of structure: actual number of stories beginning at street level. Asterisks (*) denote buildings still under construction Jan., 1969.

| City | Height Ft. | Stories No. |
|---|---|---|
| **NEW YORK CITY, MANHATTAN** | | |
| Empire State, 34th St., 5th Ave... | 1,250 | 102 |
| TV tower, 222 ft., makes total... | 1,472 | ..... |
| Chrysler, Lexington Ave. & 42d St. | 1,046 | 77 |
| 60 Wall Tower, 70 Pine St... | 950 | 67 |
| Bank of Manhattan, 40 Wall St... | 900 | 71 |
| RCA, Rockefeller Center... | 850 | 70 |
| Chase Manhattan Bldg. | 813 | 60 |
| Pan Am Bldg., 200 Park Ave... | 808 | 59 |
| Woolworth, 233 Broadway | 792 | 60 |
| *U.S. Steel, 165 Broadway... | 743 | 54 |
| City Bk. Farmers Trust, 20 Ex. Pl. | 741 | 57 |
| *One Astor Plaza | 730 | 54 |
| Marine Midland Bldg., 140 Bway.. | 724 | 52 |
| Union Carbide Bldg., 270 Park Ave. | 707 | 52 |
| General Motors Bldg. | 705 | 50 |
| Metropolitan Life, 1 Madison Ave.. | 700 | 50 |
| 500 Fifth Avenue | 697 | 60 |
| Chem. Bank N. Y. Trust Bldg.... | 687 | 50 |
| Chanin, Lexington Ave. and 42d St. | 680 | 56 |
| Lincoln, 60 E. 42d Street | 673 | 53 |
| *Gulf & Western Bldg., 15 Columbus Circle | 679 | 44 |
| American Tobacco, 245 Park Ave... | 656 | 47 |
| Irving Trust, 1 Wall Street... | 654 | 50 |
| 345 Park Ave... | 634 | 44 |
| Home Insurance Co. Bldg... | 630 | 44 |
| Waldorf-Astoria, 301 Park Ave... | 625 | 47 |
| 10 East 40th Street... | 620 | 48 |
| General Electric, Lexington Ave... | 616 | 50 |
| New York Life, 51 Madison Ave... | 615 | 40 |
| Penney Bldg., 1301 6th Ave... | 609 | 46 |
| U. S. Court House, 505 Pearl St... | 590 | 37 |
| Federal Bldg., Foley Square... | 587 | 41 |
| Time & Life, 1271 Ave. of the Am.. | 587 | 47 |
| Municipal, Park Row & Centre St.. | 580 | 34 |
| Westvaco Bldg., 299 Park ave... | 574 | 42 |
| Socony Mobil Bldg., East 42nd St... | 572 | 45 |
| Sperry Rand Bldg., 1290 Ave. of Am. | 570 | 43 |
| N. Y. General, 230 Park Ave... | 565 | 35 |
| 90 Broad Street... | 562 | 48 |
| Sherry-Neth'land, 5th Ave., 59th St. | 560 | 40 |
| Continental Can, 633 Third Ave... | 557 | 39 |
| Sperry & Hutchinson, 330 Madison Ave... | 555 | 39 |
| Interchem Bldg., 1133 Ave. of the Am. | 552 | 45 |
| United Nations, 405 E. 42 St...... | 550 | 39 |
| Burroughs Bldg., 605 3rd Ave... | 550 | 44 |
| Bankers Trust, 33 E. 48 St... | 547 | 41 |
| Transportation, Bldg., 225 Bway.. | 546 | 45 |
| Equitable Life, 1285 Ave. of the Am. | 540 | 42 |
| Ritz Tower, Park Ave. & 57th St... | 540 | 41 |
| Bankers Trust, 6 Wall Street... | 540 | 39 |
| Equitable, 120 Broadway... | 538 | 42 |
| 1700 Broadway | 533 | 41 |
| Downtown Athl. Club, 19 West St... | 530 | 45 |
| Nelson Towers, 7th Ave. & 34th St. | 525 | 45 |
| Hotel Pierre, Fifth Ave. & 61st St... | 525 | 44 |
| House of Seagram, 375 Park Ave... | 525 | 38 |
| Du Mont Bldg., 515 Madison Ave.. | 520 | 42 |
| 26 Broadway | 520 | 41 |
| Newsweek Bldg., 444 Madison Ave. | 518 | 43 |
| Sterling Drug Bldg., 90 Park Ave. | 515 | 41 |
| First Nat'l City Bank... | 515 | 41 |
| Bank of New York, 48 Wall Street.. | 513 | 32 |
| Navarre, 512 Seventh Avenue... | 513 | 43 |
| Williamsburgh Savings Bank, Bkln. | 512 | 42 |
| ITT—American, 437 Madison Ave.. | 512 | 40 |
| International, Rockefeller Center... | 512 | 41 |
| 1407 Broadway Realty Corp.... | 512 | 44 |
| 22 East 40th Street... | 503 | 43 |
| 60 Broad St... | 503 | 39 |
| Americana Hotel... | 501 | 51 |
| N. Y. Telephone, 140 West St... | 498 | 33 |
| 80 Pine Street... | 497 | 40 |
| A. B. C. Bldg... | 496 | 41 |
| Chemical Bank, 20 Pine St... | 494 | 38 |
| Fuller Bldg., 45 E. 57th St... | 492 | 40 |
| C.B.S. Bldg., 51 W. 52nd St... | 491 | 38 |
| Gen. Dynamics, 9 Rockefeller Plaza | 490 | 36 |
| N. Y. Hilton, Rockefeller Ctr... | 487 | 46 |
| Tishman Bldg., 666 Fifth Avenue.. | 483 | 40 |
| 2nd Ave. & 57th St... | 482 | 47 |
| Morgan Guarantee, 15 Broad St... | 480 | 40 |
| Con. Edison, 14th St. & Irving Pl.. | 474 | 34 |
| U.S. Plywood Bldg., 777 Third Ave. | 472 | 38 |
| New Yorker Hotel | 470 | 42 |
| Hampshire House, Central Park So. | 470 | 40 |
| McGraw-Hill, 333 West 42nd St... | 464 | 33 |
| Essex House, Central Park South.. | 460 | 44 |
| Barbizon-Plaza Hotel, Centr. Pk. So. | 456 | 41 |
| Lefcourt Bldg... | 454 | 40 |
| 111 West 40th Street... | 451 | 34 |
| Metropolitan Life, 25 E. 24th St... | 451 | 31 |
| **ALBANY, N. Y.** | | |
| *Office Tower, So. Mall... | 589 | 44 |
| University Towers... | 480 | 40 |
| State Office Building... | 388 | 34 |

| City | Height Ft. | Stories No. |
|---|---|---|
| **ALBANY, N. Y. cont.** | | |
| *Agency (four bldgs.), So. Mall.... | 310 | 23 |
| Home Savings Bank... | 250 | 21 |
| **AKRON, OHIO** | | |
| First Nat'l Tower Bldg... | 330 | 28 |
| *Cascade, 10 W. Bowery... | 316 | 24 |
| **ATLANTA, GA.** | | |
| First Natl. Bank, 2 Peachtree St... | 589 | 48 |
| Equitable Bldg., 100 Peachtree St. | 453 | 34 |
| Natl. Bank of Ga., 34 Peachtree... | 439 | 32 |
| Trust Co. of Ga., 36 Edgewood... | 377 | 28 |
| Peachtree Ctr. Bldg., 230 Peachtree | 374 | 31 |
| Life of Ga. Bldg., 600 W. Peachtree | 371 | 29 |
| *225 Peachtree Bldg., 225 Peachtree | 332 | 27 |
| Atlanta Gas Towers, 235 Peachtree | 331 | 27 |
| Regency-Hyatt House Polaris... | 330 | 23 |
| Ga. Power Co., 270 Peachtree... | 318 | 22 |
| *100 Colony Square, 1173 P'tree... | 316 | 25 |
| Merchandise Mart, 240 Peachtree. | 300 | 22 |
| Fulton Natl. Bank, 55 Marietta St. | 295 | 22 |
| Grady Hospital, 80 Butler St... | 277 | 22 |
| Peachtree Towers Apt... | 270 | 24 |
| C & S Bank North, 17 North Ave... | 266 | 20 |
| Southern Bell Telephone, 51 Ivy... | 256 | 17 |
| Lenox Towers East... | 251 | 17 |
| Lenox Towers West... | 251 | 17 |
| Rhodes Haverty Bldg... | 250 | 22 |
| **AUSTIN, TEXAS** | | |
| State Capitol... | 311 | ..... |
| Univ. of Texas Admin. Bldg... | 302 | 29 |
| Westgate Bldg... | 261 | 24 |
| **BALTIMORE, MD.** | | |
| Maryland Natl. Bank Bldg... | 495 | 33 |
| No. 2 Charles Center... | 383 | 39 |
| Blaustein Bldg... | 355 | 29 |
| Hearst Tower... | 330 | 16 |
| 222 St. Paul... | 328 | 39 |
| Emerson Tower... | 306 | 15 |
| First Natl. Bank... | 305 | 21 |
| Federal Bldg., 31 Hopkins Plaza... | 293 | 17 |
| Lord Baltimore Hotel... | 289 | 19 |
| Baltimore Gas and Electric Co.... | 289 | 21 |
| Consolidated Gas Bldg... | 280 | 21 |
| Mercy Hospital... | 277 | 20 |
| 1 Charles Center... | 270 | 23 |
| Commercial Credit Bldg... | 259 | 20 |
| **BATON ROUGE, LA.** | | |
| State Capitol... | 460 | 34 |
| La. Natl. Bank Bldg... | 277 | 21 |
| **BIRMINGHAM, ALA.** | | |
| Comer Bldg... | 325 | 27 |
| Thomas Jefferson Hotel... | 287 | 21 |
| Bank for Savings & Trust... | 264 | 19 |
| First Natl. Bank Bldg... | 256 | 21 |
| **BOSTON, MASS.** | | |
| Prudential Tower... | 750 | 52 |
| New England Merch. Bank Bldg... | 500 | 40 |
| U. S. Custom House... | 496 | 32 |
| John Hancock Bldg... | 495 | 26 |
| State St. Bank Bldg... | 477 | 34 |
| State Office Bldg... | 350 | 22 |
| Federal Bldg. & Post Office... | 345 | 22 |
| Suffolk County Courthouse... | 330 | 19 |
| Sheraton-Boston Hotel... | 310 | 29 |
| State Service Center... | 300 | 23 |
| United Shoe Mach. Bldg... | 298 | 24 |
| New England Tel. & Tel... | 298 | 20 |
| Travellers Insurance Bldg... | 253 | 16 |
| **BUFFALO, N. Y.** | | |
| City Hall... | 378 | 32 |
| Rand Bldg., not incl. 40-ft beacon. | 351 | 29 |
| Liberty Bank... | 345 | 23 |
| Erie County Savings Bank... | 340 | 26 |
| Manuf. & Traders Trust Co... | 315 | 21 |
| Electric Bldg... | 283 | 18 |
| 10 Lafayette Square... | 263 | 23 |
| N. Y. Telephone Bldg... | 258 | 16 |
| Marine Trust... | 250 | 16 |
| Statler Hilton... | 250 | 18 |
| **CHARLOTTE, N. C.** | | |
| *So. Tower St... | 420 | 32 |
| N. C. Natl. Bank Bldg... | 289 | 18 |
| Baugh Bldg... | 260 | 20 |
| Wachovia Bank Bldg... | 250 | 17 |
| **CHICAGO, ILL.** | | |
| John Hancock Center... | 1,107 | 100 |
| First Natl. Bank... | 850 | 60 |
| Civic Center (City Hall)... | 662 | 31 |
| Lake Point Towers... | 645 | 70 |
| Board of Trade, incl. 81 ft. statue. | 605 | 44 |
| Prudential Bldg., 130 E. Randolph | 601 | 41 |
| Antenna tower, 311 ft., makes total | 912 | ..... |
| 1000 Lake Shore Plaza Apts... | 590 | 55 |
| Marina City Apts., 2 buildings... | 588 | 61 |

| | Hgt.Ft. | Stories |
|---|---|---|
| Pittsfield, 55 E. Washington St..... | 557 | 38 |
| Kemper Insurance Bldg........... | 555 | 45 |
| Field Bldg., 135 S. LaSalle St...... | 535 | 42 |
| One LaSalle Street.............. | 530 | 49 |
| Pure Oil, 35 E. Wacker Drive...... | 523 | 40 |
| United Ins. Bldg., 1 E. Wacker Dr... | 522 | 41 |
| Lincoln Tower, 75 W. Wacker Dr.... | 519 | 42 |
| Carbide & Carbon, 230 N. Mich..... | 503 | 37 |
| LaSalle-Wacker, 221 N. LaSalle St.. | 491 | 41 |
| Amer. Nat'l Bank, 33 N. LaSalle St. | 479 | 40 |
| Bankers, 105 W. Adams St......... | 476 | 41 |
| Brunswick Bldg................. | 475 | 37 |
| Continental Companies........... | 475 | 32 |
| American Furniture Mart......... | 474 | 24 |
| Sheraton Hotel, 505 N. Mich. Ave. | 471 | 42 |
| Palmolive, 919 N. Mich. Ave...... | 468 | 37 |
| 188 Randolph Tower............. | 465 | 45 |
| Tribune Tower, 435 N. Mich. Ave... | 462 | 36 |
| Equitable Life, 401 N. Michigan... | 457 | 35 |
| Roanoke, 11 S. LaSalle St........ | 452 | 37 |
| Willoughby Tower, 8 S. Mich. Ave. | 438 | 38 |
| 1300 Lake Shore Apts........... | 404 | 40 |
| 777 N. Michigan Apts........... | 400 | 39 |
| Illinois Bell Telephone Bldg...... | 400 | 30 |
| Chicago Temple not incl. cross..... | 400 | 21 |
| Wrigley, 400 N. Mich. Ave ...... | 398 | 32 |
| Federal Bldgs., D'born & Jackson Sts. | 396 | 30 |
| 333 N. Michigan Ave............ | 394 | 34 |
| Executive House, 71 E. Wacker Dr. | 385 | 40 |
| Outer Drive East.............. | 378 | 40 |
| Allerton Hotel, 701 N. Mich. Ave... | 360 | 24 |
| The Brittany, 150 N. Wacker..... | 350 | 37 |
| 1550 Lake Shore Dr. Apts........ | 350 | 34 |
| Drake Towers, 179 E. Lake Shore Dr. | 347 | 32 |
| Builders, 228 N. LaSalle St....... | 342 | 32 |

### CINCINNATI, OHIO

| | | |
|---|---|---|
| Carew Tower................. | 574 | 48 |
| Central Trust Tower............ | 495 | 34 |
| *Cincinnati Center, 5th & Walnut. | 430 | 32 |
| Kroger Bldg.................. | 345 | 25 |
| Terrace Hilton Hotel........... | 273 | 19 |
| Cincinnati Gas & Electric Co...... | 268 | 18 |
| Provident Tower.............. | 267 | 20 |
| City Hall, clock tower.......... | 250 | ...... |

### CLEVELAND, OHIO

| | | |
|---|---|---|
| Terminal Tower............... | 708 | 52 |
| Federal Bldg................. | 419 | 32 |
| Erieview Plaza Tower........... | 418 | 40 |
| Ohio-Bell Telephone........... | 360 | 22 |
| CEI Bldg.................... | 300 | 22 |
| Union Commerce Bldg.......... | 289 | 21 |
| Standard Bldg................ | 282 | 21 |
| B. F. Keith Bldg.............. | 267 | 21 |
| Cleveland State Univ........... | 265 | 21 |
| NBC Bldg., 815 Superior Ave..... | 265 | 21 |
| Winton Place................ | 264 | 30 |

### COLUMBUS, OHIO

| | | |
|---|---|---|
| Lincoln-Le Veque Tower........ | 555 | 47 |
| Columbus Center.............. | 323 | 25 |
| State Office Bldg.............. | 317 | 14 |
| Columbus-Sheraton Motor Hotel.. | 275 | 22 |
| 88 E. Broad St............... | 253 | 20 |

### CORPUS CHRISTI, TEX.

| | | |
|---|---|---|
| Wilson Tower................ | 273 | 20 |
| 600 Broadway................ | 251 | 22 |

### DALLAS, TEXAS

| | | |
|---|---|---|
| First National Bank........... | 614 | 51 |
| Republic Bank Tower.......... | 594 | 53 |
| Southland Life Tower.......... | 550 | 42 |
| One Main Place.............. | 457 | 33 |
| Republic Bank Bldg., not incl. 150- ft. ornamental tower........ | 452 | 36 |
| Ling-Tempco-Vought Tower...... | 434 | 31 |
| Mercantile Natl. Bank Bldg., not incl. 115-ft weather beacon..... | 430 | 31 |
| Mobil Bldg.................. | 430 | 31 |
| Fidelity Union Tower.......... | 400 | 33 |
| Fairmont Hotel.............. | 395 | 24 |
| *Court House & Fed. Office Bldg.. | 362 | 16 |
| Mercantile Dallas Bldg......... | 360 | 22 |
| Sheraton Hotel.............. | 352 | 28 |
| Adolphus Tower.............. | 327 | 27 |
| Bell Telephone Bldg........... | 326 | 23 |
| Davis Bldg.................. | 323 | 21 |
| Tower Petroleum Bldg.......... | 315 | 23 |
| Adolphus Hotel.............. | 312 | 25 |
| Baptist Annuity Center......... | 303 | 17 |
| Life Bldg................... | 302 | 22 |
| Santa Fe Bldg. (1st unit)....... | 300 | 20 |

### DAYTON, OHIO

| | | |
|---|---|---|
| Hulman Bldg................ | 276 | 23 |
| *Grant-Deneau Bldg........... | 265 | 22 |
| Knott Bldg.................. | 261 | 21 |

### DENVER, COLO.

| | | |
|---|---|---|
| Brooks Towers, 1020 15th St...... | 420 | 42 |
| Security Life Bldg............. | 384 | 30 |
| First National Bank........... | 365 | 28 |
| Western Fed. Savings Bldg...... | 354 | 24 |
| Tower Merchandise Mart........ | 330 | 20 |
| Hilton Hotel................ | 299 | 21 |
| Denver U.S. Natl. Bldg......... | 293 | 25 |
| Denver Club Bldg............. | 277 | 23 |
| Brown Palace Hotel, West....... | 269 | 22 |

| | Hgt.Ft. | Stories |
|---|---|---|
| Farmers Union Bldg............ | 263 | 12 |
| Federal Office Bldg............ | 261 | 18 |
| Mountain States Tele. & Tele..... | 250 | 17 |
| State Capitol................ | 250 | 4 |

### DES MOINES, IOWA

| | | |
|---|---|---|
| Equitable Bldg............... | 318 | 19 |
| State Capitol................ | 275 | 4 |

### DETROIT, MICH.

| | | |
|---|---|---|
| Penobscot, 637 Griswold. ....... | 557 | 47 |
| Guardian, 500 Griswold......... | 482 | 40 |
| Book Tower, 1227 Wash. Blvd..... | 472 | 35 |
| Cadillac Tower, 51 Cadillac Sq.... | 437 | 40 |
| David Stott, 1150 Griswold....... | 436 | 38 |
| Mich. Cons. Gas Co. Bldg........ | 430 | 32 |
| Fisher, W. Grand Blvd. & 2d St.... | 420 | 28 |
| Detroit Bank & Trust Co. Bldg.... | 370 | 28 |
| David Broderick Tower......... | 358 | 34 |
| Buhl, 535 Griswold............ | 350 | 26 |
| Michigan Bell Telephone........ | 340 | 19 |
| 1st Federal Savings & Loan Assn.. | 338 | 23 |
| Pontchartrain Motor Hotel....... | 336 | 23 |
| 1300 Lafayette East........... | 325 | 30 |
| National Bank............... | 319 | 25 |
| Sheraton Cadillac Hotel........ | 310 | 28 |
| The Jeffersonian............. | 305 | 29 |

### FORT WAYNE, IND.

| | | |
|---|---|---|
| Lincoln Natl. Bank Bldg........ | 312 | 23 |
| Ft. Wayne Natl. Bank.......... | 280 | 26 |

### FORT WORTH, TEXAS

| | | |
|---|---|---|
| Continental Natl. Bank Bldg...... | 380 | 30 |
| Continental Life Ins. Bldg....... | 282 | 23 |
| First Natl. Bank............. | 272 | 22 |
| W. T. Waggoner Bldg.......... | 270 | 22 |
| Service Life Center........... | 270 | 19 |
| Federal Center.............. | 250 | 13 |

### HARRISBURG, PA.

| | | |
|---|---|---|
| State Capitol................ | 272 | 6 |
| Hotel Harrisburger........... | 257 | 19 |

### HARTFORD, CONN.

| | | |
|---|---|---|
| Travelers Ins. Co. Bldg......... | 527 | 34 |
| Hartford Bldg............... | 400 | 22 |
| Hartford Natl. Bank & Trust..... | 360 | 26 |
| *Bushnell Plaza.............. | 263 | 27 |
| Conn. Bank & Trust Co. Bldg..... | 257 | 20 |
| St. Joseph's Cathedral......... | 250 | ...... |

### HONOLULU, HAWAII

| | | |
|---|---|---|
| *Ala Moana Hotel............. | 390 | 38 |
| 1350 Ala Moana.............. | 309 | 33 |
| Ala Moana Bldg.............. | 300 | 23 |
| Financial Plaza of the Pacific..... | 269 | 21 |
| Ilikai Apartments............ | 260 | 26 |
| First Natl. Bank Bldg.......... | 254 | 19 |
| Foster Tower................ | 250 | 25 |

### HOUSTON, TEXAS

| | | |
|---|---|---|
| One Shell Plaza.............. | 700 | 50 |
| Humble Oil Bldg............. | 606 | 44 |
| Tenn. Bldg.................. | 497 | 33 |
| Gulf Bldg.................. | 428 | 37 |
| First City Natl. Bank.......... | 410 | 32 |
| Neils Eperson Bldg........... | 409 | 31 |
| Houston Lighting & Power...... | 410 | 27 |
| Houston Natural Gas Bldg....... | 386 | 28 |
| Bank of the Southwest......... | 369 | 24 |
| Sheraton-Lincoln Hotel........ | 352 | 28 |
| American General Life......... | 337 | 25 |
| Shell Bldg.................. | 325 | 22 |
| Capitol Natl. Bank........... | 320 | 21 |
| 500 Jefferson Bldg............ | 316 | 21 |
| Sterling Bldg................ | 312 | 22 |
| Southwest Tower............. | 310 | 20 |
| Melrose Bldg................ | 308 | 21 |
| Chamber of Commerce Bldg..... | 306 | 22 |
| South Coast Life Bldg......... | 302 | 22 |
| Prudential Bldg.............. | 300 | 21 |

### INDIANAPOLIS, IND.

| | | |
|---|---|---|
| *Indiana Natl. Bank Tower...... | 504 | 37 |
| City-County Bldg............. | 377 | 26 |
| Indiana Bell Telephone........ | 320 | 20 |
| JWR Center, Crown Tower Apts. 2 buildings............... | 294 | 30 |

### JACKSON, MISS.

| | | |
|---|---|---|
| First Natl. Bank Bldg......... | 259 | 14 |
| Deposit Guaranty Bank Bldg..... | 254 | 18 |
| Standard Life Bldg........... | 250 | 22 |

### JACKSONVILLE, FLA.

| | | |
|---|---|---|
| Gulf Life Ins. Co. Bldg......... | 430 | 27 |
| Prudential Ins. Co. of Amer...... | 295 | 22 |
| Universal Marion Bldg......... | 268 | 21 |
| Independent Life & Accident Ins.. | 258 | 18 |

### JERSEY CITY, N. J.

| | | |
|---|---|---|
| Medical Center, Tuberculosis..... | 320 | 24 |
| Medical Center, 4 other bldgs..... | 294 | 22 |

### KANSAS CITY, MO.

| | | |
|---|---|---|
| Kansas City Light and Power Bldg. | 503 | 36 |
| Federal Office Bldg........... | 434 | 33 |
| City Hall.................. | 417 | 30 |
| Commerce Tower............. | 402 | 32 |
| Telephone Bldg.............. | 382 | 28 |
| Continental Bldg............. | 365 | 30 |
| A. T. & T. Long Line Bldg....... | 331 | 20 |

| | Hgt.Ft. | Stories |
|---|---|---|
| Bryant Bldg...................... | 319 | 26 |
| Federal Reserve Bldg............. | 311 | 21 |
| **LOS ANGELES, CALIF.** | | |
| Crocker-Citizen Plaza........... | 602 | 43 |
| Union Bank Square............... | 516 | 41 |
| City Hall........................ | 454 | 28 |
| Occidental Life Bldg............ | 452 | 32 |
| *Equitable Life.................. | 430 | 32 |
| *1900 Ave. of Stars............. | 398 | 27 |
| 1 Wilshire Bldg.................. | 395 | 28 |
| Calif. Fed. Savings & Loan Bldg.. | 363 | 28 |
| *Bunker Hill Towers.............. | 349 | 32 |
| City Natl. Bank Bldg............ | 344 | 24 |
| Luxury Towers................... | 316 | 27 |
| Getty Realty Bldg............... | 312 | 22 |
| Water & Power Bldg.............. | 310 | 20 |
| Los Angeles Fed. Savings Bldg... | 306 | 22 |
| Barrington Plaza Bldg........... | 300 | 22 |
| Travelers Insurance............. | 294 | 22 |
| Grad Towers..................... | 290 | 23 |
| Crown Towers.................... | 278 | 22 |
| 1901 Ave. of the Stars.......... | 272 | 19 |
| Wilshire Flower Bldg............ | 269 | 21 |
| Spring Street Realty Bldg....... | 267 | 19 |
| Lee Towers Bldg................. | 261 | 21 |
| U. S. Post Office & Court House. | 257 | 18 |
| Tishman 615 Bldg................ | 250 | 22 |
| Wilshire-Ardmore Bldg........... | 250 | 23 |
| Wilshire-Comstock Bldg.......... | 250 | 20 |
| **LOUISVILLE, KY.** | | |
| Eighthundred Apt. Bldg.......... | 290 | 29 |
| Commonwealth Bldg............... | 255 | 21 |
| Heyburn Bldg.................... | 250 | 17 |
| **MEMPHIS, TENN.** | | |
| 100 N. Main Bldg................ | 430 | 38 |
| Sterick Bldg.................... | 365 | 31 |
| First Natl. Bank Bldg........... | 318 | 25 |
| Lowenstein's Dept. Store........ | 296 | 25 |
| Clark Towers.................... | 273 | 24 |
| Columbian Mutual Life Tower..... | 265 | 22 |
| Exchange Bldg................... | 264 | 22 |
| **MIAMI, FLA.** | | |
| Ponce Products.................. | 350 | 30 |
| Dade County Court House......... | 325 | 27 |
| Du Pont Bldg.................... | 285 | 16 |
| Brickell Town House............. | 283 | 21 |
| Freedom Tower Bldg.............. | 256 | 17 |
| Fed. Office Bldg................ | 256 | 18 |
| **MILWAUKEE, WIS.** | | |
| City Hall....................... | 350 | 9 |
| Wisconsin Telephone Co.......... | 313 | 19 |
| Marine Plaza Bldg............... | 288 | 22 |
| Marshall & Ilsley Bank.......... | 277 | 21 |
| Juneau Village Apts............. | 265 | 28 |
| Schroeder Hotel................. | 265 | 24 |
| Clark Bldg...................... | 252 | 20 |
| Wisconsin Gas Co................ | 250 | 20 |
| Wisconsin Tower................. | 250 | 21 |
| Pfister Hotel................... | 250 | 21 |
| **MINNEAPOLIS, MINN.** | | |
| Foshay Tower, not including 163-ft. antenna tower................ | 447 | 32 |
| First Natl. Bank Bldg........... | 366 | 28 |
| Municipal Building.............. | 355 | 14 |
| North Western Bell Telephone.... | 350 | 26 |
| Rand Tower...................... | 311 | 26 |
| Midwest Federal Savings & Loan.. | 276 | 20 |
| River Towers Apts............... | 260 | 27 |
| **NASHVILLE, TENN.** | | |
| *Natl. Life & Acc. Ins. Co...... | 452 | 31 |
| Nashville Life & Casualty Tower.. | 409 | 30 |
| Third Natl. Bank Bldg........... | 292 | 20 |
| **NEWARK, N. J.** | | |
| National Newark & Essex Bank.... | 465 | 36 |
| Raymond-Commerce............... | 448 | 36 |
| Prudential Corporate Bldg....... | 369 | 27 |
| American Insurance Company...... | 326 | 21 |
| Prudential Insurance Company.... | 301 | 21 |
| N. J. Bell Telephone Co......... | 275 | 21 |
| Mutual Benefit Life Ins. Co..... | 271 | 18 |
| **NEW HAVEN, CONN.** | | |
| Knights of Columbus Hqs......... | 320 | 24 |
| Harkness Memorial Quadrangle.... | 257 | ...... |
| Kline Biology Tower............. | 250 | 13 |
| **NEW ORLEANS, LA.** | | |
| Plaza Tower..................... | 516 | 45 |
| Int'l Trade Mart Bldg........... | 407 | 33 |
| 225 Baronne St.................. | 362 | 28 |
| Hibernia Bank Bldg.............. | 355 | 23 |
| American Bank Bldg.............. | 330 | 23 |
| Charity Hospital of Louisiana... | 279 | 19 |
| **OAKLAND, CALIF.** | | |
| Kaiser Bldg..................... | 390 | 28 |
| City Hall....................... | 319 | 15 |
| Tribune Tower................... | 305 | 21 |
| First Western Bank Bldg......... | 297 | 18 |
| Telephone Bldg.................. | 289 | 15 |
| 565 Bellevue Apts............... | 270 | 25 |
| St. Paul Towers................. | 267 | 22 |
| **OKLAHOMA CITY, OKLA.** | | |
| First National Bank............. | 447 | 33 |
| Liberty National Bank........... | 440 | 33 |
| Oklahoma Continental Apts....... | 288 | 25 |
| United Founders Life Bldg....... | 264 | 20 |

| | Hgt.Ft. | Stories |
|---|---|---|
| **OMAHA, NEBR.** | | |
| Woodmen Tower................... | 453 | 30 |
| Masonic Manor................... | 320 | 22 |
| **PHILADELPHIA, PA.** | | |
| City Hall Tower incl. 35-ft. statue of Wm. Penn.. | 548 | 9 |
| Phila. Saving Fund Society...... | 491 | 39 |
| *5 Penn Center.................. | 488 | 36 |
| Philadelphia National Bank...... | 473 | 25 |
| Girard Trust, Broad & Chestnut.. | 450 | 30 |
| Industrial Valley Bank Bldg..... | 431 | 32 |
| Lewis Tower, 15th & Locust...... | 400 | 33 |
| Fidelity-Philadelphia Trust..... | 377 | 30 |
| Penn Mutual Life................ | 375 | 20 |
| The Drake, 15th & Spruce........ | 365 | 30 |
| Medical Tower, 255 So. 17th..... | 364 | 33 |
| State Bldg., 1400 Spring Garden.. | 351 | 18 |
| Hopkinson House................. | 350 | 35 |
| 1 East Penn Square.............. | 349 | 24 |
| Packard, 15th & Chestnut........ | 340 | 25 |
| Inquirer Building............... | 340 | 18 |
| Land Title, Broad & Chestnut.... | 331 | 22 |
| Edison, 9th & Sansom............ | 325 | 23 |
| Penn Towers..................... | 320 | 31 |
| Architects, 17th & Sansom....... | 316 | 24 |
| Sheraton Hotel.................. | 315 | 22 |
| Rittenhouse Towers.............. | 312 | 28 |
| 1500 Walnut Street.............. | 310 | 23 |
| Society Hill Towers............. | 308 | 32 |
| 1616 Walnut Street.............. | 303 | 25 |
| Chateau Crillon, 19th & Locust.. | 303 | 27 |
| Dorchester Apts................. | 300 | 32 |
| **PHOENIX, ARIZ.** | | |
| First Federal Savings Bldg...... | 341 | 27 |
| Mayer Central Plaza............. | 315 | 25 |
| Regency Apts.................... | 297 | 21 |
| Rosenzweig Center No. 2......... | 280 | 22 |
| Rosenzweig Center No. 1......... | 271 | 25 |
| **PITTSBURGH, PA.** | | |
| *U.S. Steel Bldg................ | 841 | 64 |
| Gulf, 7th Ave. and Grant St..... | 582 | 44 |
| University of Pittsburgh........ | 535 | 42 |
| 525 Wm. Penn Place (U. S. Steel). | 520 | 41 |
| Grant, Grant St. at 3d Ave...... | 485 | 40 |
| Koppers, 7th Ave. and Grant..... | 475 | 34 |
| Alcoa Bldg., 425 Sixth Ave...... | 410 | 30 |
| First National Bank, 511 Wood St. | 387 | 26 |
| Oliver, 535 Smithfield St....... | 347 | 25 |
| Gateway Bldg No. 3.............. | 344 | 24 |
| Federal Bldg., 1000 Liberty Ave.. | 340 | 23 |
| Bell Telephone, 416 7th Ave..... | 339 | 21 |
| Hilton Hotel, 1000 Liberty Ave.. | 333 | 22 |
| Frick, 437 Grant St............. | 330 | 20 |
| Rockwell-Standard Bldg.......... | 322 | 24 |
| Washington Plaza Apts., 1420 Centre Ave. .................. | 300 | 23 |
| Commonwealth, 316 Fourth Ave... | 300 | 24 |
| **RICHMOND, VA.** | | |
| Central National Bank Bldg...... | 282 | 24 |
| First National Bank Bldg........ | 262 | 19 |
| Fidelity Bankers Life........... | 261 | 23 |
| **ROCHESTER, N. Y.** | | |
| Xerox Tower..................... | 443 | 30 |
| Eastman Kodak Bldg.............. | 360 | 19 |
| Lincoln Rochester Trust Bldg.... | 261 | 17 |
| Times Square Bldg............... | 256 | 10 |
| Midtown Office & Hotel Bldg..... | 251 | 18 |
| **ST. LOUIS, MO.** | | |
| Gateway Arch.................... | 630 | ...... |
| Laclede Gas Bldg., 8th & Olive... | 400 | 34 |
| S. W. Bell Tele. Bldg........... | 398 | 31 |
| Civil Courts.................... | 387 | 13 |
| Queeny Tower.................... | 321 | 19 |
| Park Plaza Hotel................ | 310 | 30 |
| Riverfront Inn, 3rd St.......... | 301 | 30 |
| Mansion House................... | 285 | 28 |
| Continental Bldg................ | 277 | 23 |
| Railroad Exchange Bldg.......... | 277 | 24 |
| Pierre Laclede Plaza Bldg....... | 276 | 23 |
| Ben Franklin Motor Hotel........ | 270 | 25 |
| Park Tower Apts................. | 264 | 24 |
| Missouri Pacific Bldg........... | 264 | 23 |
| Gateway Towers, 1 Mem. Drive.... | 261 | 20 |
| Executive Office Bldg........... | 250 | 20 |
| Colony Motor Hotel.............. | 250 | 19 |
| Gateway Hotel................... | 250 | 21 |
| Southwestern Bell Telephone Microwave Bldg. .............. | 250 | 16 |
| **ST. PAUL, MINN.** | | |
| First Natl. Bank Bldg., not incl. 100-ft. sign. ............... | 402 | 32 |
| Osborn Bldg..................... | 368 | 20 |
| Northwestern Bell Telephone Bldg. | 340 | 15 |
| St. Paul Cathedral.............. | 307 | ...... |
| U. S. Post Office Bldg.......... | 274 | 12 |
| St. Paul Hilton Hotel........... | 273 | 24 |
| City Hall & Court House......... | 261 | 18 |
| Montgomery Ward & Co. Bldg...... | 257 | 9 |
| **SALT LAKE CITY, UTAH** | | |
| City & County Bldg.............. | 290 | ...... |
| State Capitol................... | 285 | ...... |
| Univ. Club Bldg................. | 277 | 24 |
| Kennecott Bldg.................. | 267 | 18 |
| Walker Bank Bldg................ | 262 | 19 |

| SAN ANTONIO, TEXAS | Hgt.Ft. | Stories | | Hgt.Ft. | Stories |
|---|---|---|---|---|---|
| Tower of the Americas | 622 | ...... | Federal Office Bldg | 312 | 20 |
| Tower Life | 550 | 30 | Bank of Calif | 311 | 21 |
| Nix Professional Bldg | 375 | 23 | 100 McAllister Bldg | 310 | 28 |
| Natl. Bank of Commerce | 310 | 24 | 111 Sutter Bldg | 309 | 24 |
| Alamo National Bldg | 288 | 23 | Mark Hopkins Hotel | 306 | 19 |
| Milam Bldg | 280 | 20 | Mills Tower | 302 | 22 |
| Southwestern Bell Telephone Co. | | | City Hall | 301 | 5 |
| Bldg | 260 | 16 | 1200 California Apts | 300 | 27 |
| **SAN DIEGO, CALIF.** | | | **SEATTLE, WASH.** | | |
| So. Calif. First Natl. Bank Bldg | 388 | 25 | *Seattle-1st Natl. Bank Bldg | 609 | 52 |
| U.S. Natl. Bank Bldg | 340 | 25 | Space Needle | 605 | ...... |
| *Union Bank | 320 | 22 | L. C. Smith Bldg | 500 | 42 |
| *Westgate Plaza Hotel | 317 | 20 | *Washington Plaza Hotel | 490 | 40 |
| Electric Bldg | 293 | 21 | *Federal Office Bldg | 465 | 37 |
| Electronics Capital Bldg | 281 | 23 | IBM Bldg | 425 | 20 |
| Home Tower | 278 | 18 | Northern Life Tower | 314 | 27 |
| | | | Norton Bldg | 298 | 18 |
| **SAN FRANCISCO, CALIF.** | | | Washington Bldg | 289 | 21 |
| Bank of America | 778 | 52 | United Exchange Bldg | 275 | 23 |
| Wells Fargo Bldg | 561 | 43 | | | |
| *Embarcadero Center #1 | 569 | 45 | **SYRACUSE, N. Y.** | | |
| Crocker, Market & Post | 529 | 38 | State Tower | 315 | 22 |
| *Pacific Gas & Electric | 470 | 32 | Mony Office Bldg | 307 | 20 |
| Hartford Bldg | 465 | 33 | | | |
| Mutual Benefit Life | 438 | 32 | **TOLEDO, OHIO** | | |
| Russ Bldg | 435 | 31 | *Owens-Corning Fiberglas Tower | 400 | 30 |
| Telephone Bldg | 435 | 30 | Owens Illinois Bldg | 368 | 27 |
| Alcoa Bldg | 398 | 27 | Toledo Trust Bldg | 288 | 21 |
| Shell Bldg | 386 | 29 | | | |
| First Savings | 359 | 26 | **TULSA, OKLA.** | | |
| Equitable Life Bldg | 355 | 25 | 4th Natl. Bank of Tulsa | 412 | 32 |
| Fox Plaza | 354 | 29 | National Bank of Tulsa | 400 | 24 |
| International Bldg | 350 | 22 | Univ. Club Towers | 377 | 32 |
| 450 Sutter Street | 343 | 26 | Philtower | 343 | 23 |
| Cathedral Apartments | 340 | 21 | Liberty Towers | 254 | 24 |
| Royal Towers | 330 | 24 | Skelly Bldg | 253 | 17 |
| Fairmont Hotel | 330 | 30 | First Natl. Bank | 250 | 20 |
| Bechtel Bldg | 327 | 22 | | | |
| Standard Oil Bldg | 327 | 22 | **WILMINGTON, DEL.** | | |
| Crown Zellerbach Bldg | 320 | 20 | Hercules Tower | 287 | 23 |
| 555 Market St | 317 | 22 | American Life Ins. Co. Bldg | 282 | 21 |
| Sir Francis Drake Hotel | 315 | 22 | Farmers Bank Bldg | 253 | 20 |
| Eichler Summit | 314 | 29 | **WINSTON-SALEM, N. C.** | | |
| | | | Wachovia Bldg | 410 | 30 |
| | | | Reynolds Bldg | 315 | 21 |

## TALL BUILDINGS IN SMALLER UNITED STATES CITIES

Figures denote number of stories. Height in feet is in parentheses.
Cape Kennedy, Fla., Vehicle Assembly Bldg., 40 (552); Allentown, Pa., Penna. Power & Light Bldg., 23 (322); Greenville, S. C., Daniel Bldg., 22 (305); Lansing, Mich., Michigan Nat'l Tower, 25 (300, not including antenna tower); Las Vegas, Nev., Mint Hotel, 26 (268); Lincoln, Neb., State Capitol (432 incl. 32-ft. bronze statue); Portland, Ore., Georgia-Pacific Bldg., 29 (356); Providence, R. I., Industrial Trust Co. Bldg., 26 (420); Shreveport, La., Beck Bldg., 20 (266); Tampa, Fla., Exchange Nat'l Bldg., 22 (280); Waco, Tex., Amicable Life Bldg., 21 (282, incl. observation tower).

## Tallest Television Towers

| Station | Location | Ht. Ft. | Station | Location | Ht. Ft. |
|---|---|---|---|---|---|
| KTHI-TV | Fargo, N. D. | 2063 | KVII-TV | Amarillo, Tex. | 1922 |
| KATV | Little Rock, Ark. | 2000 | KTUL-TV | Tulsa, Okla. | 1909 |
| WEAU-TV | Eau Claire, Wisc. | 2000 | | | |
| KTIV-TV | Sioux City, Iowa | 2000 | | **Self-Supporting** | |
| KVTV-TV | Sioux City, Iowa | 2000 | WITI-TV | Milwaukee, Wis. | 1079 |
| KCRG-TV | Cedar Rapids, Iowa | 2000 | WNAC-TV | Boston, Mass. | 1069 |
| WLBT-TV | Jackson, Miss. | 1998 | KJRJ-TV | Atlanta, Ga. | 1049 |
| KNOE-TV | Monroe, La. | 1986 | KCMO-TV | Kansas City, Mo. | 1042 |
| KELO-TV | Sioux Falls, S. D. | 1984 | WKRC-TV | Cincinnati, Ohio | 971 |
| KSOO-TV | Sioux Falls, S. D. | 1984 | WCPO-TV | Cincinnati, Ohio | 909 |

# Few Know Why Famous Mason-Dixon Line Was Drawn

The Mason-Dixon Line, drawn over 200 years ago, is probably America's most famous boundary —yet few know why it was established.

In popular belief, the boundary separated Confederate States from the Union during the Civil War. It remains the symbolic division between South and North.

The line was drawn earlier, however, to end a bitter colonial land dispute, the National Geographic Society says. Completed in 1767, the line extends from east to west between Pennsylvania and Maryland, with a shorter branch reaching southward then east between Maryland and Delaware. All three states were on the Union side.

The English surveyor-astronomers Charles Mason and Jeremiah Dixon wound up four years of arduous work in the summer and fall of 1767. Working westward through wilderness, they reached the "top of the Great dividing Ridge of the Alleganey Mountains" in July.

The Englishmen and their assistants and guides, all fearful of Shawnee and Delaware Indians, reached the so-called War Path on Oct. 9. The Indians with them refused to go any farther. Thus a point 230 miles 18 chains and 21 links from the beginning of the line formed its western terminus.

The boundary controversy flared in the mid-1600s when the Dutch Government and the Calverts of Maryland both claimed the big fertile peninsula between the Delaware and Chesapeake Bays.

After the Dutch were pushed out of the region,

William Penn inherited the dispute. The bickering, kindled by conflicting interpretations of the Penn and Calvert charters, continued for generations.

At last the case came before England's Court of Chancery. A compromise decision gave Maryland the bulk of the peninsula. Pennsylvania retained the northeast portion that later attained independence as Delaware State.

The American disputants signed the agreement in 1760, and work was begun by local surveyors. They made so little progress that Mason and Dixon were invited to the Colonies to "mark, run out, settle, fix, and determine" the line. Mason, 35, was assistant astronomer at England's Greenwich Observatory. He recently had been abroad with Dixon, 30, a quiet-mannered Quaker, to observe a transit of Venus.

Mason and Dixon arrived in Philadelphia in 1763. They set to work checking and correcting the peninsula lines, then took the westward trail with a large party of assistants, axmen and guides.

Handsome boundary stones, inscribed with the arms of Penn and Calvert on opposite sides, were set at five-mile intervals. Simpler intermediary stones bore the letters P and M.

The 4-year project cost $75,000. When Mason and Dixon sailed back to England, they left behind them the largest engineering-surveying achievement of 18th-century America. The job they did in trackless wilderness with crude instruments was astonishingly accurate. Modern surveyors have found a difference in latitude of only 2.3 seconds (232 feet) from the Mason-Dixon figure.

# ASSOCIATIONS AND SOCIETIES, U. S.

Source: World Almanac Questionnaire
Arranged according to key words in titles. Figures indicate membership.

—A—

**Aaron Burr Association** (1946), N. Inca Rd., Linden, Va. 22642; 100; Sec. Gen., Col. Henry d'Arcy.

**Accountants, American Institute of Certified Public** (1887), 666 Fifth Ave., New York, N. Y. 10019; 63,766; Exec. Dir., John L. Carey.

**Accountants, National Assn. of** (1919), 505 Park Ave., New York, N. Y. 10022; 62,484; Exec. Dir., Rawn Brinkley.

**Accountants, Natl. Society of Public** (1945), 1717 Pennsylvania Ave., N.W., Washington, D. C. 20006; 12,000; Exec. Dir., Stanley H. Stearman.

**Acoustical Society of America** (1929), 335 E. 45 St., New York, N. Y. 10017; 4,200; Sec., Wallace Waterfall.

**Actors Equity Assn.** (1913), 165 W. 46 St., New York, N. Y. 10036; 15,000; Pres., Frederick O'Neal.

**Actors' Fund of America** (1882), 1619 Broadway, New York, N. Y. 10019; 2,967; Sec., Warren P. Munsell.

**Actuaries, Society of** (1949), 208 S. La Salle St., Chicago, Ill. 60604; 3,193; Pres., Morton D. Miller.

**Adirondack Mountain Club** (1923), Gabriels, N. Y. 12939; 3,805; Sec., P. F. Loope.

**Administrative Management Society** (1919), Maryland Rd., Willow Grove, Pa. 19090; 15,000; Exec. Dir., Robert C. Walter.

**Adult Education Assn. of the U. S. A.** (1951), 1225 19th St., N.W., Wash., D. C. 20036; 4,200; Exec. Dir., Dr. Eugene I. Johnson.

**Advancement of Management, Soc. for** (1912), 1472 Broadway, New York, N. Y. 10036; 16,000; Sec., William Mumpower.

**Adventurers Club of N. Y.** (1912), 54 West 40th St., New York, N. Y. 10018; 270; Pres., Herman W. Kitchen.

**Advertisers, Assn. of National** (1910), 155 East 44th St., New York, N. Y. 10017; 525 companies; Pres., Peter W. Allport.

**Advertising Agencies, American Assn. of** (1917), 200 Park Ave., New York, N. Y. 10017; 355 agencies; Pres., John Crichton.

**Advertising Club of New York** (1906), 23 Park Ave., New York, N. Y. 10016; 2,100; Sec., Arthur V. Schmitt.

**Advertising Federation, American** (1905), 655 Madison Ave., N. Y., N. Y. 10021; 40,000; Pres., Howard H. Bell.

**Aeronautical Historical Assn., Connecticut** (1959), Box 44, Hebron, Conn. 06248; 400; Pres., Harvey H. Lippincott.

**Aeronautic Assn., Natl.** (1905), 806 15th St., N.W., Washington, D. C. 20005; 7,000; Pres. James F. Nields.

**Aeronautics and Astronautics, American Inst. of** (1963), 1290 Ave. of the Americans, New York, N. Y. 10019; 33,000; Sec., James J. Harford.

**Aerospace Industries Assn. of America** (1919), 1725 DeSales St., N.W., Washington, D. C. 20036; 88; Sec., Samuel L. Wright.

**Aerospace Medical Association,** (1929), Washington National Airport, Washington, D. C. 20001; 4,920; Sec., Merrill H. Goodwin.

**Agricultural Economics Assn., American** (1967), Warren Hall, Cornell Univ., Ithaca, N. Y. 14850; 4,200; Sec., C. D. Kearl.

**Agricultural Engineers, American Society of** (1907), P. O. Box 229, 420 Main St., St. Joseph, Mich. 49085; 6,209; Exec. Sec., J. L. Butt.

**Agricultural History Society** (1919), Exec. Sec., Wayne D. Rasmussen, c/o Economic Research Services, U. S. Dept. of Agriculture, Washington, D. C. 20250.

**Agronomy, American Soc. of** (1907), 677 So. Segoe Rd., Madison, Wis. 53711; 6,509; Sec., Dr. Mathias Stelly.

**Ahepa, Order of** (1922), 1422 K St., N.W., Washington, D. C. 20005; 26,500; Exec. Sec., George J. Leber.

**Air Force Aid Society** (1942), Washington, D. C. 20333; 22,000; Sec., Carl H. McClure III.

**Air Force Association** (1946), 1750 Pennsylvania Ave., N.W., Washington, D. C. 20006; 92,000; Sec., Glenn D. Mishler.

**Air Force Sergeants Association** (1961), 1501 Pennsylvania Ave., S.E., Washington D. C. 20003; 18,000; Exec. Dir., Joseph F. Brosnan.

**Air Line Pilots Assn.** (1931), 55th St., & Cicero Ave., Chicago, Ill. 60638; 31,000; Pres., Charles H. Ruby.

**Air Pollution Control Assn.** (1907), 4400 Fifth Ave., Pittsburgh, Pa. 15213; 4,700; Sec., Arnold Arch.

**Air Transport Assn. of America** (1936), 1000 Connecticut Ave., N.W., Washington, D. C. 20036; 36 airlines; Sec., Frederick Davis.

**Aircraft Owners and Pilots Assn.** (1939), 4650 East-West Highway, Bethesda, Md. 20014; 150,000; Pres., J. B. Hartranft, Jr.

**Alcoholics Anonymous** (1935); 305 E. 45th St., New York, N. Y. 10017; 400,000; address communications to secretary.

**Alcohol Problems, American Council on** (successor to National Temperance League) (1895), 119 Constitution Ave. N. E., Washington, D. C. 20002; Exec. Dir., Rev. Billy E. McCormack.

**Allergy, American Academy of** (1943). 756 N. Milwaukee St., Milwaukee, Wis. 53202; 1,803; Exec. Sec., James O. Kelley.

**Allied Youth** (1931), Rosslyn Building, 1901 Ft. Myer Drive, Arlington, Va. 22209; 15,000; Deputy Dir., Rubye Kelley.

**Alpine Club, American** (1902), 113 East 90th St., New York, N. Y. 10028; 800; Sec., J. P. McCarthy.

**Altrusa International** (1917), 332 So. Michigan Ave., Chicago, Ill. 60604; 18,850; Dir. Pub., Lucille Hecht.

**Aluminum Assn.** (1933), 420 Lexington Ave., New York, N. Y. 10017; 74 companies; Exec. Sec., Richard A. Lillquist.

**Alumni Council, American** (1913), 1707 N St., N.W., Washington, D. C. 20036; 1,450; Sec., George Cooke, Jr.

**American Citizens of German Descent, Federation of** (1946), 59-17 Palmetto St.. Ridgewood, N. Y. 11227; 2,300; Sec., Edmund Eckhardt.

**American Federation of Labor and Congress of Industrial Organizations (AFL-CIO)** (Dec. 5, 1955, by merging American Federation of Labor, estab. 1881 and Congress of Industrial Organizations, estab. 1935). 815-16th St., N.W., Washington D. C. 20006; 14,300,000; Pres., George Meany; Sec.-Treas., William F. Schnitzler.

**American Field Service** (1914), 313 E. 43rd St., New York, N. Y. 10017; Pres., Arthur Howe, Jr.

**American Latvian Association** (1951), Suite 913 Shoreham Bldg., 806 15th St. N.W., Washington, D. C. 20005; 10,000; Sec. Gen., Bruno Albats.

**American Legion, The** (Mar. 15, 1919). 700 No. Pennsylvania St., Indianapolis, Ind. 46204; 2,381,-339; Natl. Comdr., William C. Doyle; Natl. Adjt., William F. Hauck.

**American Legion Auxiliary** (Nov. 10, 1919). 777 No. Meridian St., Indianapolis, Ind. 46204; 910,204; Natl. Sec., Miss Doris Anderson.

**American Medical Association,** (1847), 535 North Dearborn, Chicago, Ill. 60610; 215,807; Exec. V.P., Dr. F. J. L. Blasingame.

**American-Scandinavian Foundation,** (1910), 127 East 83rd St., New York, N. Y. 10021; 5,400; Pres., Corrin P. Strong.

**American Society for Prevention of Cruelty to Animals** (1866), 441 East 92nd St., New York, N. Y. 10028; Sec., John W. Ream.

**American Swedish Historical Foundation** (1926), 1900 Pattison Ave., Philadelphia, Pa. 19145; 1,200; Pres., Dr. Walter G. Nord.

**American Training Corps** (1961), 107-12 Jamaica Ave., Richmond Hill, N. Y. 11418; 600; Commandant, P. E. Kendall.

**American Veterans of World War II and Korea (AMVETS)** (1944), 1710 Rhode Island Ave., N.W., Washington, D. C. 20036; 200,000; Natl. Exec. Dir., Ralph E. Hall. AMVETS Natl. Auxiliary (1946), 3607 Maplegrove Dr., Grove City, Ohio 43123; 15,000; Sec., Kathleen Hengely.

**Amputation Foundation, National,** (1919), 12-45 150th St., Whitestone, L. I. N. Y. 11357; 2,500; Sec., Sol Kaminsky.

**Antarctic Association, American** (1944) 6323 Wiscassett Rd., N.W., Washington, D. C. 20016; Pres., Capt. Finn Ronne, USNR (Ret.)

**Anthropological Assn., American** (1902), 3700 Mass. Ave., N.W., Washington, D. C. 20016; 5,200; Pres., Dr. Irving Rouse.

**Antiquarian Society, American** (1812), 185 Salisbury St., Worcester, Mass. 01609; 225; Dir., M. A. McCorison.

**Antique Automobile Club of America** (1935), West Derry Rd., Hershey, Pa. 17033; 20,578; Pres., John Lambert, Jr.

**Appalachian Mountain Club** (1876), 5 Joy St., Boston, Mass. 02108; 12,000; Exec. Dir., C. Francis Belcher.

**Appraisers, American Soc. of** (1955), 1101 17th St., N.W., Washington, D. C. 20036; 2,910; Exec. Dir., Richard Eppstein.

**Arbitration Association, American** (1926), 140 W. 51st St., New York, N. Y. 10020; Sec., Edwin W. Dippold.

**Archaeological Institute of America** (1879), 100 Washington Square East, New York, N. Y. 10003; 5,500; Sec., Claireve Grandjouan.

**Architects, American Institute of** (1857), 1735 New York Ave., N.W., Washington, D. C. 20007; 22,200, Exec. Dir., William H. Scheick.

**Architects, New York Society of,** (1911), 101 Park Ave., New York, N. Y.; 650; Pres., Fred L. Liebmann.

449

**Archivists, Society of American** (1936), Wayne State Univ., Detroit, Mich. 48202; 2,100; Sec., Dr. Philip P. Mason.

**Armed Forces Communications and Electronics Association** (1946), 1725 Eye Street N.W., Washington, D. C. 20006; 13,000; Gen. Mgr., Col. W. J. Baird, USA, Ret.

**Army and Navy Union of USA** (1886), 1391 Main St., Lakemore, Ohio 44250; 50,000; Natl. Adjt., Joseph P. Burger.

**Art Society of N. Y., Municipal** (1898), 41 E. 65th St., New York, N. Y. 10021; 1,300; Exec. Sec., Frederick Williams.

**Art Students League of N. Y.** (1875), 215 West 57th St., New York, N. Y. 10019; 4,500; Pres., Walker G. Everett.

**Artists of America, Allied** (1914), 1083 Fifth Ave., New York, N. Y. 10028; 349; Sec., Frank Liljegren.

**Arts, American Federation of** (1909), 41 E. 65th St., New York, N. Y. 10021; 3,500; Sec., Hudson Walker.

**Arts and Letters, American Academy of** (1904), 633 West 155th St., New York, N. Y. 10032; 48; Sec., John Hersey.

**Arts and Letters, National Institute of** (1898 as Amer. Social Science Assn.), 633 West 155th St., New York, N. Y. 10032; 244; Sec., William Maxwell.

**Arts and Sciences, American Academy of** (1780), 280 Newton St., Brookline, Mass. 02138; 2,000; Pres., Talcott Parsons.

**Arts, Associated Councils of the** (1965), 1564 Broadway, N. Y., N. Y. 10036; 550; Exec. Dir., Ralph Burgard.

**Arts Federation of New York, Fine** (1895), 115 E. 40th St., N. Y., N. Y. 10016; 5,434; Pres., William Ballard.

**Assistance League, National** (1935), 5538 Fernwood Ave., Hollywood, Calif. 90028; 10,000; Pres., Mrs. Burton Collins.

**Associated Press, The** (1848), 50 Rockefeller Plaza, New York, N. Y. 10020; Sec., Harry T. Montgomery.

**Astronautical Society, American** (1952), 1629 K St., N.W., Washington, D. C. 20006; 1,700; Sec., Mrs. Sandra Steinberg.

**Astronomical Society, American** (1899), Univ. of Illinois Observatory, Urbana, Ill. 61801; 2,300; Sec., G. C. McVittie.

**Atheism, American Assn. for the Advancement of** (1925), P. O. Box 2832, San Diego, Calif. 92112; 75; Pres., James Johnson.

**Athletes of America, Intercollegiate Assn. of Amateur** (1876), Hotel Manhattan, 8th Ave. at 44th St., New York, N. Y. 10036; 77 colleges; Sec., Asa S. Bushnell.

**Athletic Associations, Natl. Federation of State High School** (May 14, 1920), 7 So. Dearborn St., Chicago, Ill. 60603; 50 State Assns.; Sec., Clifford B. Fagan.

**Athletic Conference, Eastern College** (1938), Hotel Manhattan, 8th Ave. at 44th St., New York, N. Y. 10036; 161 colleges; Sec., Asa S. Bushnell.

**Athletic Union of the U. S., Amateur** (1888), 231 West 58th St., New York, N. Y. 10019; Pres., David A. Marlin.

**Attorneys General, National Assn. of** (1907), 1313 East 60th St., Chicago, Ill. 60637; 54; Pres., Frank Kelley.

**Audit Bureau of Circulations** (1914), 123 N. Wacker Dr., Chicago, Ill. 60606; 4,100; Pres., Alan Wolcott.

**Audubon Society, National** (1905), 1130 Fifth Ave., New York, N. Y. 10028; 65,069; Exec. V. P., Charles H. Callison.

**Authors and Composers, American Guild of** (1931), 50 W. 57th St., New York, N. Y. 10019; 2,089; Exec. Dir., Miriam Stern.

**Authors League of America** (1912), 234 W. 44th St., N. Y., N. Y. 10033; 4,700; Exec. Sec., Mills Ten Eyck, Jr.

**Automobile Association, American** (1902), 1712 G St., N.W., Washington, D. C. 20006; 10,900,000; Pres., George M. Frauenheim.

**Automobile Club, National** (1924), 65 Battery St., San Francisco, Calif. 94111; 355,000; Sec., Bert Stewart.

**Automobile Dealers Assn., National** (1917), 2000 K St., N.W., Washington, D. C., 20006; 22,000; Sec., Archie Pozzi, Jr.

**Automobile Manufacturers Association** (1913), 320 New Center Bldg., Detroit, Mich. 48202; 11 companies; Pres., Thomas Mann.

**Automobile Touring Alliance, American** (1932), 220 So. Broad St., Philadelphia, Pa. 19102; 560,000; Sec., William Berry.

**Automotive Engineers, Society of** (1905); 2 Pennsylvania Plaza, New York, N. Y. 10001; 26,544; Sec., Joseph Gilbert.

**Automotive Old Timers** (1939), P. O. Box 62, Warrenton, Va. 22186; 2,350; Sec., Miss Dorothy Ross.

**Aztec Club of 1847** (1847), 5225 Westpath Way, Washington, D. C. 20036; 134; Sec., J. Conway Hunt.

## —B—

**Babysitter Registries, National Association of** (1957), 2145 West Wilshire Dr., Phoenix, Ariz. 85009; 20-26 registries; Sec., Virginia Pearson.

**Ball Players of America, Assn. of Professional** (Oct. 9, 1924), 650 So. Spring St., Room 1026, Los Angeles, Calif. 90014; Sec., Charles Stevens.

**Bankers Association, American** (1875), 90 Park Ave., New York, N. Y. 10016; 18,365 banks incl. branches; Exec. Mgr., Charls E. Walker.

**Bankers Assn., Independent** (1930), 1168 S. Main St., Sauk Centre, Minn. 56378; 6,543 banks; Exec. Dir., Howard F. Bell.

**Bar Association, American** (1878), 1155 East 60th St., Chicago, Ill. 60637; 129,000; Sec., William Reece Smith, Jr.

**Bar Assn., Federal** (1920), 1815 H Street, N.W., Washington, D. C. 20006; 13,200; Exec. Sec., Miss Betty Baker.

**Barber Shop Quartet Singing in America, Society for the Preservation and Encouragement of** (1938), 6315 Third Ave., Kenosha, Wis. 53141; 31,000; Exec. Dir., Barrie Best.

**Barbers and Beauticians of Amer., Associated Master** (1924), 219 Greenwich Rd., P. O. Box 17782, Charlotte, N. C. 28211; 12,000; Pres., Paul B. Sparaco.

**Baseball Congress, National** (1931), Box 1420 Wichita, Kan. 67201; 4,000 teams; Sec., Larry Davis.

**Baseball Leagues, Natl. Assn. of Professional** (1901), 720 E. Broad St., Columbus, Ohio 43215; 21 leagues,; Pres., Phillip Piton.

**Battleship Assn., American** (1964), P. O. Box 11247, San Diego, Calif. 92111; 2,500; Sec., Margaret Graham.

**Belgian American Educational Foundation** (1920), 420 Lexington Ave., New York, N. Y. 10017; Sec., Miss Margaret Fennessy.

**Better Business Bureaus, Assn. of** (1921), 405 Lexington Ave., New York, N. Y. 10017; 135 bureaus; Pres., Victor H. Nyborg.

**Bible Society, American** (1816), 1865 Broadway, N. Y., N. Y. 10023; 977,185; Gen. Sec., Rev. Robert T. Taylor.

**Biblical Literature, Society of** (1880), Vanderbilt Divinity School, Nashville, Tenn. 37203; 2,488 Exec. Sec., Robert Funk.

**Bibliographical Society of America** (1904), P. O. Box 397, Grand Central Sta., New York, N. Y. 10017; 1,484; Sec., Dr. James Heslin.

**Bicycle Institute of America** (1919), 122 East 42nd St., New York, N. Y. 10017; 250 companies; Exec. Sec., John Auerbach.

**Bicycle League of America, Amateur** (1920), 4233 205th St., Bayside, L. I., N. Y. 11361; 5,000; Sec., Frank Small.

**Big Brothers of America** (1947), 341 Suburban Station Bldg., Philadelphia, Pa. 19103; 128 agencies; Sec., Margaret M. Hanley.

**Bill of Rights Day Assn., American** (1941), 39 Highlawn Ave., Brooklyn, N. Y. 11223; 1,000; Natl. Dir., Vincent Rossini.

**Billiard Congress of America** (1948), 20 No. Wacker Dr., Chicago, Ill. 60606; 300; Sec. Don L. Neer.

**Biological Chemists, American Society of** (1906), 9650 Rockville Pike, Bethesda, Md. 20014; 2,500; Exec. Officer, R. A. Harte.

**Blind, American Foundation for the** (1921), 15 W. 16th St., New York, N. Y. 10011; Exec. Dir., M. Robert Barnett.

**Blind, N. Y. Assn. for the** (1905), 111 East 59th St., New York, N. Y. 10022; Sec., John L. McCormick.

**Blinded Veterans Association** (1945), 2430 Pennsylvania Ave., N.W., Washington, D. C. 20037; 1,200; Admin. Dir., Jack H. Street.

**Blindness, Natl. Society for the Prevention of** (1908), 79 Madison Ave., N. Y., N. Y. 10016; 131,-576; Sec., Charles C. MacLean, Jr.

**Blindness, Research to Prevent** (1960), 598 Madison Ave., N. Y., N. Y. 10022; Exec. Dir., David F. Weeks.

**Blizzard Men and Ladies of 1888** (Mar. 12, 1929), 6384 Fitchett St., Forest Hills, L. I., N. Y. 11374; 200; Sec., Fred Schneider.

**Blood Banks, American Assn. of** (1947), 30 North Michigan Ave., Chicago, Ill. 60602; 4,200; Sec., Wm. G. Battaile, M.D.

**B'nai B'rith** (Oct. 13, 1843), 1640 Rhode Island Ave., N.W., Washington, D. C. 20036; 500,000; Exec. V. P., Rabbi Jay Kaufman. Component units include: B'nai B'rith Hillel Foundations (1923), Natl. Dir., Rabbi Benjamin M. Kahn; B'nai B'rith Youth Organization (1924), Natl. Dir., Dr. Max F. Baer. Other units: B'nai B'rith Women, Anti-Defamation League of B'nai B'rith, and B'nai B'rith Vocational Service.

**Board of Trade of the City of Chicago** (1848), 141 West Jackson Blvd., Chicago, Ill. 60604; 1,402; Sec., Warren W. Lebeck.

**Board of Trade, New York** (1873), 642 Fifth Ave., New York, N.Y. 10019; 1,400; Exec. V. P., Neil H. Anderson.

**Boating Law Administrators, Natl. Assn. of State** (1962), State Office Bldg., Annapolis, Md. 21404; 100; Pres., William Matthews, Jr.

**Book Manufacturers' Institute** (1933), 161 E. 42nd St., N. Y., N. Y. 10017; 122 companies; Exec. Dir., Robert M. Peck.

**Booksellers Association, American** (1900), 175 Fifth Ave., New York, N. Y. 10010; 2,700; Exec. Dir., Joseph A. Duffy.

**Botanical Society of America** (1906), Dept. of Botany, Indiana Univ., Bloomington, Ind. 47401; 3,200; Sec., Richard C. Starr.

**Bowling Congress, American** (Sept. 9, 1895), 1572 E. Capitol Dr., Milwaukee, Wis. 53211; 4,500,000; Exec. Sec., Frank K. Baker.

**Bowling Congress, Woman's International** (1916), 1225 Dublin Rd., Columbus, O. 43212; 2,896,693; Pres., Alberta E. Crowe.

**Bowls Assn., American Lawn** (1915), 10337 Cheryl Dr., Sun City, Ariz. 85351; 10,500; Sec., John W. Deist.

**Boy Scouts of America, National Council** (Feb. 8, 1910), New Brunswick, N. J., 08903; 6,058,508; Chief Scout Exec., Alden G. Barber.

**Boy Scouts of America, Greater N. Y. Councils** (1922), 25 W. 43rd St., N. Y., N. Y. 10036; 87,160 boys, 30,000 adults, Scout Exec., Dan O. Henry.

**Boys' Brigades of America, United** (Nov. 4, 1893), 512 Overbrook Rd., Baltimore, Md. 21212; Maj. Gen., Walter A. Koerber.

**Boys' Clubs of America** (1906), 771 First Ave., New York, N. Y. 10017; 1,000,000; Sec., Grant B. Simmons.

**Brewers Assn., U. S.** (1862), 535 Fifth Ave., New York, N. Y. 10017; Pres., Henry B. King.

**Brith Abraham** (1887), 37 East 7th St., New York, N. Y. 10003; 10,000; Sec., Louis Clark.

**Brith Sholom** (1905), 121 S. Broad St., Philadelphia, Pa. 19107; 20,000; Exec. Dir., Albert Liss.

**Broadcasters, Natl. Assn. of** (1922), 1812 K St., N.W., Washington, D. C. 20006; 4,128; Sec., Everett E. Revercomb.

**Burroughs Bibliophiles** (1960), 454 Elaine Dr., Pittsburgh, Pa. 15236; 825; Pres., Clarence B. Hyde.

**Business Clubs, Natl. Assn. of American** (1922), P.O. Box 5127, High Point, N. C. 27262; 4,500; Sec., H. C. Pearson.

**Business Education Association, National** (1892), 1201 16th St., N.W., Washington, D. C. 20036; 13,920; Exec. Dir., Hollis Guy.

**Business Law Association, American** (1923), Dept. of Business Law., Bowling Green State Univ., Bowling Green, Ohio 43402; 450; Pres., Mr. Russell Decker.

**Business Press Editors, American Society of** 1012 14th St., N.W., Washington, D. C. 20005; 300; Exec. V. P., Calvin K. Snyder.

**Business Communication Association, American** (1935), 317b David Kinley Hall, Urbana, Ill. 61801; 1,000; Exec. Dir., Francis W. Weeks.

**Button Society of America, Natl.**, (1938); 353 Stockton St., Hightstown, N. J. 08520; 2,342, Pres. Mrs. Edith A. Rodway.

—C—

**Camp Fire Girls** (1910), 65 Worth St., New York, N. Y. 10013; 580,351; Pres., Mrs. Alann P. Bedford.

**Camping Assn., American** (1910), Bradford Woods, Martinsville, Ind., 46151; 7,200; Exec. Dir., Ernest F. Schmidt.

**Cancer Society, American** (1913), 219 E. 42nd St., New York, N. Y. 10017; 182; Sec., Joseph S. Silber.

**Canners Assn., National** (1907), 1133 20th St., N.W., Washington, D. C. 20036; 560; Exec. V. P. Milan D. Smith.

**Capital Punishment, American League to Abolish** (1927), 14 Irving St., Brookline, Mass. 02147; 2,000; Exec. Dir., Mrs. Herbert B. Ehrmann.

**Captive European Nations, Assembly of** (1954), 29 West 57th St., New York, N. Y. 10019; Sec., Feliks Gadomski.

**CARE** (Cooperative For American Relief Everywhere) (1945), 660 First Ave., New York, N. Y. 10016; Exec. Dir., Frank L. Goffio.

**Carl Schurz Assn., Natl.**, (1930), 339 Walnut St., Philadelphia, Pa.; 3,916; Exec. Dir., Alice H. Finckh.

**Cartoonists Society, Natl.** (1946), 130 W. 44th St., New York, N. Y. 10018; 450; Pres., Jerry Robinson.

**Catholic Assn. for International Peace** (1927), 1312 Massachusetts Ave., N.W., Washington, D. C. 20005; Pres., Dr. William V. O'Brien.

**Catholic Charities, Natl. Conference of** (1910), 1346 Connecticut Ave., N.W., Washington, D. C. 20036; 6,000; Sec. Very Rev. Msgr. Lawrence J. Corcoran.

**Catholic Church Extension Society** (1905), 1307 S. Wabash Ave., Chicago, Ill. 60605; Gen. Sec., Rev. Joseph A. Cusack.

**Catholic Civics Clubs of America** (1940), Commission on American Citizenship, Catholic Univ. of America, Washington, D. C. 20017; 200,000; Exec. Head, W. Wingate Snell.

**Catholic Daughters of America** (1903), 10 West 71st St., New York, N. Y. 10023; 205,000; Supr. Sec., Mrs. Manila J. Caprine.

**Catholic Hospital Assn.** (1915), 1438 So. Grand Blvd., St. Louis, Mo. 63104; 899 hospitals; Exec. Dir., Rev. Thomas Casey, S.J.

**Catholic Office for Motion Pictures, Natl.**, (1934), 453 Madison Ave., N. Y., N. Y. 10022; Exec. Sec., Rev. Patrick J. Sullivan.

**Catholic Press Assn.** (1911), 432 Park Ave., So., New York, N. Y. 10016; 520; Exec. Sec., James A. Doyle.

**Catholic Rural Life Conference, National** (1923), 3801 Grand Ave., Des Moines, Iowa 50312; 4,000; Sec., Rev. John George Weber.

**Catholic War Veterans of U. S. A.** (1935), 2 Massachusetts Ave., N.W., Washington, D. C. 20001; 50,000; Natl. Comm., Martin G. Riley.

**Catholic Welfare Conference, National** (1919), 1312 Massachusetts Ave., N.W., Wash., D. C. 20005.

**Ceramic Society, American** (1899), 4055 No. High St., Columbus, O. 43214; 7,210; Gen. Sec., Frank P. Reid.

**Cerebral Palsy Association, United** (1949), 66 East 34th St., New York, N. Y.; Pres., Palmer Turnheim

**Chamber of Commerce of the U. S.** (1912), 1615 H St., N.W., Washington, D. C. 20006; Exec. V. P., Arch N. Booth

**Charge Account Bankers Assn.** (1952), 375 Jackson Ave., St. Louis, Mo. 63130; 126; Sec., Arthur H. Hert.

**Charities Aid Assn., State** (May 11, 1872), 105 East 22d St., New York, N. Y. 10010; 250; Exec. Dir., Gordon E. Brown.

**Chartered Life Underwriters, American Society of** (1946), 270 Bryn Mawr Ave., Bryn Mawr, Pa. 19010; 14,000; Exec. V. P., Paul S. Mills.

**Chautauqua Institution** (1876), Chautauqua N. Y. 14722; 598; Pres., Curtis W. Haug.

**Chemical Engineers, American Inst. of** (1908), 345 East 47th St., New York, N. Y. 10017; 33,973; Sec., F. J. van Antwerpen.

**Chemical Society, American** (1876), 1155 16th St., N.W., Washington, D. C. 20036; 109,700; Exec. Sec., Dr. B. R. Stanerson.

**Chemists, Amer. Inst. of** (1923), 60 East 42d St., New York, N. Y. 10017; 3,500; Sec. John Kotrady.

**Chicago Crime Commission** (1919), 79 W. Monroe St., Chicago, Ill. 60603; 235; Admin. Asst., Nat Cosnow.

**Chief Warrant and Warrant Officers Assn., USCG** (1929), P. O. Box 574, Benajmin Franklin Sta., Washington, D. C. 20044; 2,300; Pres., John A. Keller.

**Child Study Assn. of America** (1888), 9 East 89th St., New York, N. Y. 10028; 3,500; Pres., Mrs. Herbert W. Haldenstein.

**Child Welfare League of America** (1920), 44 East 23rd St., New York, N. Y. 10010; 369 member agencies; Exec. Dir., Joseph H. Reid.

**Children of the American Revolution, Natl. Society** (1895), 1776 D St., N.W., Washington, D. C. 20006; 17,000; Exec. Sec., Mrs. David D. Porter.

**Children's Aid Society** (1853), 105 East 22nd St., New York, N. Y. 10010; Pres., John S. Griswold.

**Children's Book Council** (1945), 175 Fifth Ave., New York, N. Y. 10010; 82; Sec., John Donovan.

**Chinese Women's Association** (1932), 5432 152nd St., Flushing, N. Y. 11355; 358; Sec., Katharine E. Lee.

**Chiropractic Association, American**, (1937), 2200 Grand Ave., Des Moines, Ia. 50306; 7,300; Pres., Dr. S. C. Birdsley.

**Chiropractors Association, International** (1926) 741 Brady St., Davenport, Iowa 52808; 4,500; Pres., Dr. L. W. Rutherford.

**Choral Conductors Guild** (1952), P.O. Box 714, Mt. Vernon, N. Y. 10551; 2,800; Pres., Roy Anderson.

**Cincinnati, Society of the** (1783), 2118 Massachusetts Ave., N.W., Washington, D. C. 20008; 2,440; Sec. Gen., Irving C. Hanners.

**Circus Fans Assn. of America** (1926), P.O. Box 605 Aurora, Ill. 60507; 1,700; Sec., Herman J. Linden.

**Circus Saints & Sinners Club of Amer., Dexter Fellows Tent of the** (1935), 441 Lexington Ave., New York, N. Y. 10017; 900; Exec. Sec., Herbert Walmsley.

**Cities, Natl. League of** (1924), City Bldg., 1612 K St., N.W., Rm. 600, Washington, D. C. 20006; 14,400 municipalities; Exec. Dir., Patrick Healy.

**City Club of N. Y.** (1892), 6 West 48th St., New York, N. Y. 10036; 500; Pres. Stanley Turkel.

**City Managers' Association, International** (1914), 1313 East 60th St., Chicago, Ill. 60637; 4,128; Exec. Dir., Orin F. Nolting.

**Civil Engineers, American Society of** (1852), 345 East 47th St., New York, N. Y. 10017; 60,421; Exec. Sec., William H. Wisely.

**Civil Liberties Union, Amer.** (1920), 156 Fifth Ave., New York, N. Y. 10010; 110,000; Exec. Dir., John de J. Pemberton, Jr.

**Civil Service League, Natl.** (1881), 1346 Connecticut Ave., N. W., Washington, D. C. 20036; 2,000;

Pres., Mortimer M. Caplin.

**Civil War Round Table of N. Y.** (1950), 289 New Hyde Park Rd., Garden City, N. Y. 11530; 450; Sec., Arnold Gates.

**Civitan International** (April 15, 1920), 115 North 21st St., Birmingham, Ala. 35203; 45,000; Exec. Sec., Rudolph T. Hubbard.

**Clay Products Institute, Structural** (1934), 1750 Old Meadow Rd., McLean, Va., 22101; 78 companies; Sec. Charles N. Farley.

**Clinical Pathologists, American Society of,** (1922), 445 N. Lake Shore Dr., Chicago, Ill. 60611; 5,500; Sec., William D. Dolan, M.D.

**Coal Association, National** (1917), Coal Bldg., 1130 17th St., N. W., Washington, D. C. 20036; 250; Pres., Stephen F. Dunn.

**Coast Guard League** (1944), U. S. Coast Guard, Washington, D. C. 20226; 3,500; Exec. Dir., Commander A. J. Caliendo.

**Cocoa Exchange, New York** (1925), 92 Beaver St., New York, N. Y. 10005; 183; Pres., Julian Hemphill.

**Coffee and Sugar Exchange, New York,** (1882), 79 Pine St., New York, N. Y. 10005; 337; Exec. Dir., E. B. Dexter.

**Collectors Association, American** (1939), 5011 Ewing Ave. South Minneapolis, Minn. 55410; 2,600; Exec. V. P., John W. Johnson.

**College Entrance Examination Board** (1900). 475 Riverside Dr., New York, N. Y. 10027; 782 colleges and universities, 237 secondary schools; Sec., Miss Anne Speirs.

**College Physical Education Assn. for Men, National** (1897), 203 Cooke Hall, Univ. of Minnesota, Minneapolis, Minn. 55455; 1,150; Sec., C. E. Mueller.

**College Placement Council** (1956), 35 E. Elizabeth Ave., Bethlehem, Pa. 18018; 8 regional assns.; Exec. Dir., Robert F. Herrick.

**College Public Relations Assn. Amer.** (1917), 1785 Massachusetts Ave., N.W., Washington, D. C. 20036; 1,130 colleges and universities; Exec. V. P., John W. Leslie.

**College of Medical Technologists** (1942), 406 West Andrews Ave., Wildwood, N. J.; 600; Sec., Clinton J. Newman.

**College of Physicians, American** (1915), 4200 Pine St., Philadelphia, Pa. 19104; 13,429; Exec. Dir., Edward C. Rosenow, Jr., M.D.

**College of Surgeons, American,** (1913), 55 E. Erie St., Chicago, Ill. 60611; 29,000 in 88 countries; Sec., Dr. Samuel P. Harbison.

**College of Surgeons, International,** (1935), 1516 N. Lake Shore Dr., Chicago, Ill. 60610; 12,000; Sec., Dr. Aldo Parentela.

**Colleges, Assn. of American** (1915), 1818 R St., N.W., Washington, D. C. 20009; 892 institutions; Chairman, Calvert N. Ellis.

**Collegiate Athletic Assn., National** (1906), 1221 Baltimore, Kansas City, Mo. 64105; 694; Pres., Marcus L. Plant.

**Collegiate Schools of Business, American Assn. of** (1916), 101 N. Skinker Blvd., St. Louis, Mo. 631; 127 schools; Exec. Sec., Dir., Cyril C. Ling.

**Colonial Dames of America** (1890), 421 East 61 St., New York, N. Y. 10021; 2,000; Exec. Sec., Mrs. C. R. Botsford.

**Colonial Dames XVII Century, National Society,** (1915), 2009 N St., Washington, D. C. 20036; 5,619; Sec., Mrs. Richard O'Bannon.

**Colonial Wars, Society of** (1892), 342 Madison Ave., N. Y., N. Y. 10017; 4,165; Gov. Gen., Nathaniel C. Hale.

**Columbia University Club** (1901), 4 West 43rd St., New York, N. Y. 10036; 1,380; Pres., Herbert G. MacIntosh.

**Commerce and Industry Association of New York** (1917), 99 Church St., N. Y., N. Y. 10007; 3,500; Sec., Arnold Witte.

**Commercial Law League of America** (1895), 222 West Adams St., Chicago, Ill. 60606; 4,700; Sec., Leo E. Smith.

**Commercial Travelers of America, Order of** United (Jan. 16, 1888), 632 No. Park St., Columbus, Ohio 43215; 247,000; Sup. Sec., L. B. Hart.

**Community Councils of the City of N. Y.** (1917). 201 West 80th St., New York, N. Y. 10024; 68,000; Sec., Edward T. Russell.

**Community Service Society of N. Y.** (1939 by merger of Assn. for Improving Condition of the Poor, 1843, and Charity Organization Soc. of N. Y., 1882); 105 22d St., New York, N. Y. 10010; 186; Pres., Clifton W. Phelen.

**Companions of the Forest of America** (June 1, 1835), 250 West 57th St., New York, N. Y. 10019; 250,000; Sec., Mrs. Alma Claire Clark.

**Compensation Insurance Rating Board, New York** (1914), 200 East 42nd St., New York, N. Y. 10017; 181; Gen. Mgr., Henry W. Menzel.

**Composers, Authors and Publishers, American Society of (ASCAP)** (1914), 575 Madison Ave., N. Y., N. Y. 10022; 11,100; Dir. Pub. Rels., Richard F. Froelich.

**Computing Machinery, Assn. for** (1947), 211 East 43rd St., New York, N. Y. 10017; 23,000; Exec. Sec., Mrs. Irene Hollister.

**Concrete Institute, American** (1904), 22400 W. 7 Mile Rd., Detroit, Mich. 48219; 14,000; Sec., William A. Maples.

**Congress of Racial Equality** (1941), 200 West 135th St., New York, N. Y. 10030; 3,000; Natl. Dir., Roy Innis.

**Consulting Chemists and Chemical Engineers, Association of** (1928), 50 E. 41st St., New York, N. Y. 10017; 110; Exec. Sec., Mrs. Agnes Peterson.

**Consulting Engineers, American Institute of** (1910), 345 East 47th St., New York, N. Y. 10017; 407; Sec., T. T. McCrosky.

**Consulting Management Engineers, Assn. of** (1929), 347 Madison Ave., New York, N. Y. 10017; 45 firms; Exec. Dir., Philip W. Shay.

**Consumer Credit Assn., International** (1912). 375 Jackson Ave., St. Louis, Mo. 63130; 58,500; Sec., Arthur H. Hert.

**Contract Bridge League, Amer.** (1927), 125 Greenwich Ave., Greenwich, Conn. 06830; 180,000; Exec. Sec., Easley Blackwood.

**Cooperative College Projects, Council on** (1956), Kentucky State College, Frankfort, Ky.; Pres., Dr. C. M. Hill.

**Cooperative League of the U. S. A.** (1916), 59 East Van Buren St., Chicago, Ill. 60605; Pres., Stanley Dreyer.

**Cornell Club of N. Y.** (1889), 155 East 50th St., New York, N. Y. 10022; 2,000; Pres., Joseph D. Tooker, Jr.

**Correctional Association, American** (1870), Woodridge Sta., P.O. Box 10176, Washington, D.C. 20018; 8,600; Gen. Sec., Dr. E. Preston Sharp.

**Correctional Assn. of New York** (1844), 135 East 15th St., New York, N. Y. 10003; 500; Gen. Sec, Donald H. Goff.

**Cosmopolitan International** (1919). P. O. Box 12186, Ft. Worth, Tex. 76116; 4,202; Exec. Sec., Paul Bryant.

**Cotton Council of America, Natl.** (Nov. 22, 1938), 1918 North Parkway, Memphis, Tenn. 38112; Exec. V. P., Wm. Rhea Blake.

**Cotton Exchange, New York,** (1870), 37 Wall St., St., New York, N. Y. 10005; 355; Sec., J. William Donaghy.

**Counter Intelligence Corps Association, National,** (1948), P. O. Box 762, Baltimore, Md. 21203; 8,000; Sec., Richard L. Goodbar.

**Country Music Assn.** (1958), 700 16th Ave. South, Nashville, Tenn. 37203; 2,000; Pres., Hubert Long.

**Credit Management, National Assn. of** (1896), 44 East 23rd St., New York, N. Y. 10010; 35,865; Exec. V. P., Robert L. Roper.

**Crime and Delinquency, Natl. Council on** (1907). 44 East 23rd St., New York, N. Y. 10010; 60,000; Dir., Milton G. Rector.

**Criminology, American Assn. of** (1953), Box 3014, Univ. Station, Eugene Ore. 97403; 2,500; Sec., W. A. Forester.

**Crippled Children and Adults, Natl. Soc. for** (1921), 2023 West Ogden Ave., Chicago, Ill. 60612; Exec. Dir., Sumner Whittier.

**Crop Science Soc. of America** (1954), 677 S. Segoe Rd., Madison, Wis. 53711; 2,576; Exec. Sec., Matthias Stelly.

**Cryptogram Assn., American** (1929), 405 William St., S.W., Decatur, Ala. 35601; 500; Treas., Frederic Flindt.

**CUNA International** (1934), 1617 Sherman Ave., Box 431, Madison, Wis. 53701; 52,147 credit unions; Pres., A. R. Glen.

**Customs Brokers & Forwarders Assn. of America, National** (1897), 26 Beaver St., N. Y., N. Y. 10004; 525; Exec. Sec., John F. Budd.

**—D—**

**Dairy Council, Natl.** (1915), 111 No. Canal St., Chicago, Ill. 60606; 3,000; Pres., Ralph Charbeneau.

**Dairy and Food Industries Supply Assn.** (1912), 1145 19th St., N.W., Washington, D. C. 20036; 425 companies; Exec. V. P., Joseph S. Cunningham.

**Dairy Science Assn., Amer.** (1906), 903 Fairview Ave., Urbana, Ill. 61801; 2,400; Exec. Sec., Claude Cruse.

**Dairymen's League Cooperative Assn.** (1907), 100 Park Ave., New York, N. Y. 10017; 13,000; Pres., Lester W. Martin.

**Dartmouth College Club** (1925), 109 East 42nd St., N. Y., N. Y. 10017; 800; Sec., C. J. Schaefer.

**Daughters of the American Revolution, Natl. Society** (1890), 1776 D St., N.W., Washington, D. C. 20006; 186,926; Sec., Mrs. George J. Walz.

**Daughters of the Cincinnati** (1894), Sec., Mrs. Bronson Trevor, 122 E. 58th St., N. Y., N. Y.; 369.

**Daughters of the Confederacy, United** (1894), 328 North Blvd., Richmond, Va. 23220; 35,000; Exec. Sec., Mrs. Kermit F. Crippen.

**Daughters of 1812, U. S. Natl. Society** (Jan. 8, 1892, 1461 Rhode Island Ave., N.W. Washington, D. C. 20005; 3,700; Pres., Mrs. Cecil T. Hays.

**Daughters of Isabella,** (1897), 375 Whitney Ave., New Haven, Conn. 06511; 118,000; Supreme Sec., Miss Mary A. Barron.

**Daughters of the Revolution, Natl. Society** (1891), 132 Nassau St., New York, N. Y. 10038; 700; Pres., Mrs. Henry J. Castles.

**Deaf, Alexander Graham Bell Assn. for the** (1890), 1537 35th St., N.W., Washington, D. C. 20007; 7,000; Exec. Dir., George W. Fellendorf.

**Deaf, Conference of Executives of American Schools for the** (1868), 5115 MacArthur Blvd., Washington, D. C. 20016; 250; Pres., E. W. Tillinghast.

**Deaf, National Assn. of the** (1880), 2025 Eye St. N.W., Suite 311, Washington, D. C. 20006; 25,000; Exec. Sec., Frederick C. Schreiber.

**Defenders of Bataan and Corregidor, American** (1945), 5002 Columbia Pike, Arlington, Va. 22204; 2,700; Sec., J. Walter Foy.

**Delta Kappa Gamma Society** (1929), P. O. Box 1589, 416 West 12th St., Austin, Tex. 78767; 100,000; Exec. Sec., Miss Catherine Rathman.

**DeMolay, Order of** (Mar. 18, 1919), 201 East Armour Blvd., Kansas City, Mo. 64111; 163,800; Exec. Dir., Richard E. Harkins.

**Dental Association, American,** (1859), 211 E. Chicago Ave., Chicago, Ill. 60611; 110,000; Sec., Dr. Harold Hillenbrand.

**Descendants of the Colonial Clergy, Society of the** (1933), 44 Day St. South, West Granby, Conn. 06090; 554; Gov. Gen., Harold E. Mayo.

**Descendants of the Signers of the Declaration of Independence** (1907), 1300 Locust St., Philadelphia, Pa. 19107; 515; Pres., R. Adm. Schuyler N. Pyne.

**Desert Protective Council** (1954), Box 33, Banning, Calif. 92220; 560; Exec. Dir., Robert G. Bear.

**Dialect Society, American** (1889), Box 95, Prince Station, N. Y., N. Y 10012; 525; Sec., Sumner Ives.

**Dietetic Assn., American** (1917), 620 No. Michigan Ave., Chicago, Ill. 60611; 20,000; Exec. Dir., Ruth M. Yakel.

**Directors Guild of America** (1936), 7950 Sunset Blvd., Los Angeles, Calif. 90046; 3,448; Exec. Sec., Joseph Youngerman.

**Disabled American Veterans** (1921), 3725 Alexandria Pike, Cold Spring, Ky. 424,500; Natl. Adj. Denvel D. Adams.

**Disaster Mobilization, Natl. Inst. for** (1942), P. O. Drawer U, Lake Charles, La. 70601; 475; Exec. Dir., S. A. Anthony, Jr.

**Divorce Reform, United States** (1961), P. O. Box 243, Kenwood, Calif. 95452; 6,000; Exec. Dir., George Partis.

**Drum Corps Publicists Assn.** (1963), 34 Metropolitan Oval, Bronx, N. Y. 10462; 2,050; Pres., Harvey N. Berish.

**Ducks Unlimited** (1937), 30 Rockefeller Plaza, New York, N. Y. 10020; 35,000; Sec., Henry E. Coe, III.

**Duodecimal Society of America** (1944), 20 Carlton Pl., Staten Island, N. Y. 10304; 155; Sec., Tom Linton.

—E—

**Eagles, Fraternal Order of** (1898), 2401 W. Wisconsin Ave., Milwaukee, Wis. 53233; 850,000; Gr. Sec., Robert H. Maxson.

**Eastern Star, Order of the, General Grand Chapter** (1876), 1618 New Hampshire Ave., N.W. Washington, D. C. 20009; 3,000,000; Grand Sec., Mrs. Mamie Lander.

**Econometric Society** (1930), Box 1264 Yale Station, New Haven, Conn. 06520; 2,500; Pres., Frank Hahn.

**Economic Assn., American** (1885), Northwestern Un., 629 Noyes St., Evanston, Ill. 60201; 16,675; Sec., Dr. Harold F. Williamson.

**Economic Development, Committee for** (1942), 711 Fifth Ave., New York, N. Y. 10022; 200 trustees; Sec., S. Charles Bleich.

**Edison Electric Institute** (1933), 750 Third Ave., New York, N. Y. 10017; Sec., John Thornborrow.

**Editors, Internatl. Council of Industrial** (1941), 2108 Braewick Circle, Akron, Ohio 44313; 3,000; Exec. Sec., Mrs. Geraldine Keating.

**Education, American Council on** (1918), 1785 Massachusetts Ave., N.W., Washington, D. C. 20036; Pres., Logan Wilson.

**Education, Council for Basic** (1956), 725 15th St., N.W., Washington, D. C. 20005; 3,200; Exec. Dir., Mortimer Smith.

**Education Assn. of the U. S., Natl.** (1857), 1201 16th St., N.W., Washington, D. C. 20036; 1,081,660; Exec. Sec., Sam M. Lambert.

**Education, Society for the Advancement of** (1939), 1860 Broadway, New York, N. Y. 10023; 905; Sec., Dr. William W. Brickman.

**Education, Natl. Society for the Study of** (1901) 5835 Kimbark Ave., Chicago, Ill. 60637; 5,500; Sec., Herman G. Richney.

**Education of Young Children, Natl. Assn. for the** (1931), 1629 21st St., N.W., Washington, D. C. 20009; 13,000; Pres., Eveline Omwake.

**Education Society; Comparative,** (1957), College of Education, Univ. of Illinois, Urbana, Ill. 61801; 1,026; Sec. Dr. B. A. Yates.

**Educational Broadcasters, Natl. Assn. of** (1925), 1346 Connecticut Ave., N.W., Washington, D. C. 20036; 3,500; Sec., James A. Fellows.

**Educational Publishing Institute, American** (1942), 432 Park Ave., New York, N. Y. 10016;

110; Exec. Dir., Dr. Austin McCaffrey.

**Educational Theatre Association, American,** (1936), 726 Jackson Pl., N.W., Washington, D. C. 20566; 6,600; Sec. Dr. H. Beresford Managh.

**Educational Research Assn., American** (1915), 1126 16th St., N.W., Washington, D. C. 20036; 7,494; Exec. Officer, Richard A. Dershimer.

**80th Division Veterans Association** (1919), 1085 Hillview Ave., Latrobe, Pa. 15650; 2,000; Sec., Robert E. Cook.

**82nd Division Association,** (1918), 28 East 39th St., New York, N. Y. 10016; 800; Sec., Ira L. Greenhut.

**87th Infantry Division Assn.** (1945), 52 Broadway, New York, N. Y. 10004; 900; Sec., Isidore Beerman.

**Electric Railroaders Assn.** (1934), 145 Greenwich St., New York, N. Y. 10006; 3,139; Sec., Herman Rinke.

**Electrical and Electronics Engineers, Inst. of** (1884), 345 East 47th St., New York, N. Y. 10017; 160,000; Gen. Mgr., Donald G. Fink.

**Electrical Manufacturers Assn., Natl.** (1926), 155 East 44th St., New York, N. Y. 10017; 450 companies; Man. Dir., Joseph F. Miller.

**Electrochemical Society** (1902), 30 East 42nd St., New York, N. Y. 10017; 4,100; Exec. Sec., Ernest G. Enck.

**Electronics Industries Assn.,** (1924), 2001 Eye St., N.W., Washington, D. C. 20006; 300 corporations; Sec., James D. Secrest.

**Electroplaters' Society, American** (1909), 56 Melmore Gardens, E. Orange, N. J. 07117; 8,400; Sec. Rodney Leeds.

**Elks, Benevolent and Protective Order of** (Feb. 16, 1868), 2750 Lake View Ave., Chicago, Ill. 60614; 1,417,435; Gr. Ruler, Robert E. Boney.

**Elks, Grand Temple Daughters of the Improved, Benevolent, Protective Order of** (1902), 1023 Maltby Ave., Norfolk, Va. 23504; 50,000; Gr. Ruler, Mrs. Nettie Smith.

**Elks, Improved, Benevolent, Protective Order of** (1898), 1522 N. 16th St., Philadelphia, Pa. 19121; 450,000; Gr. Ruler, Hobson R. Reynolds.

**Emblem Club, Supreme Order of the U. S. A.** (1926), 109 Henry St., Manchester, Conn. 06040; 35,000; Pres., Mrs. George Graziadio.

**Emerson Society, The** (1955), P. O. Box 1080, Hartford, Conn. 06101; 425; Chmn., Dr. K. W. Cameron.

**Engine and Boat Manufacturers, Natl. Assn. of** (1904), 420 Lexington Ave., New York, N. Y. 10017; 425; Sec., Peter M. Wilson.

**Engineering Education, Amer. Society for** (1893), 2100 Pennsylvania Ave., N.W., Washington, D. C. 20037; 12,000; Exec. Sec., W. Leighton Collins.

**Engineering, National Academy of** (1964), 2101 Constitution Ave., N.W. Washington, D. C. 20418; 237; Exec. Sec., Harold Work.

**Engineering Society, German** (1958), 735 Geary St., San Francisco, Calif. 94109; 50,000; Pres., Dr. W. J. Sivel.

**Engineering Trustees, United** (1904), 345 East 47th St., New York, N. Y. 10017; Sec., John A. Zecca.

**Engineers, Amer. Assn of** (1914), 8 So. Michigan Ave., Chicago, Ill. 60603; 4,300; Sec., M. E. McIver.

**Engineers Joint Council** (1945), 345 East 47th St., New York, N. Y. 10017; 40 societies; Sec., Carl Frey.

**Engineers, Natl. Soc. of Professional** (1934), 2029 K St., N.W., Washington, D. C. 20006; 66,000; Exec. Dir., Paul H. Robbins.

**Engineers, Western Society of** (1869), 314 S. Federal St., Chicago, Ill. 60604; 2,000; Sec., F. R. Bruce.

**English Association, College** (1939), California State College, Fullerton, Calif. 92631; 3,000; Exec. Dr., Donald Sears.

**English-Speaking Union of the U. S.** (1920), 16 East 69th St., New York, N. Y. 10021; 36,000; Sec., William G. Gridley.

**Epilepsy Foundation of American** (Jan. 1968, merger of Epilepsy Foundation and Epilepsy Assn. of America), 1419 H St., N.W., Washington, D. C. 20005; Sec., Mrs. Edward McSweeney.

**Esperanto Assn., of No. Amer.** (1905), 1837 N.E. 49th Ave., Portland, Ore. 97213; 621; Gen. Sec., George Alan Connor.

**Esperanto Assn., Internatl. Catholic** (1910), 38 Marcy Place, Bronx, N. Y. 10452; 1,600; U. S. Rep., Mrs. Berthold Schmidt.

**Esperanto League for No. America** (1952), Calvin St., R.F.D. #1, Meadeville, Pa. 16335; 500; Sec., Conrad Fisher.

**Esperanto Society, American Catholic** (1967), 38 Marcy Pl., Bronx, N. Y. 10452; 105; Sec., Mrs. Berthold Schmidt.

**Eugenics Society, American** (1926), 245 Park Ave., New York, N. Y. 10017; 375; Sec., Frederick Osborn.

**Evangelicals, Natl. Assn. of** (1942), Main St. at Gunderson Dr., Wheaton, Ill. 60187; 2,500,000; Sec., Dr. Cordas C. Burnett.

**Evangelism Crusades, International** (1959), 7970

Woodman Ave., Van Nuys, Calif. 91402; 5,079; Sec., Rev. Bernice Stranges.

**Exchange Club, National** (Mar. 27, 1911), 3050 Central Ave., Toledo, Ohio 43606; 45,000; Exec. Sec., Lee Wells.

**Eye-Bank Assn. of America** (1961), 3195 Maplewood Ave., Winston-Salem, N. C. 27103; 54 eye banks; Pres., Dr. Morris Kaplan.

**Eye-Bank for Sight Restoration,** (1944) 210 E. 64th St., New York, N. Y. 10021; Exec. Dir., Mrs. Cornelius P. Rhoads.

## —F—

**Faculty Representatives, Intercollegiate Conference of,** (1895), 505 N. Michigan Ave., Chicago, Ill. 60611; 10 Univ.; Chairman, Frank J. Remington.

**Fairs & Expositions, International Assn.** (1920), 777 Arbor Rd., Winston-Salem, N. C. 27106; 541; Sec., Frank H. Kingman.

**Family Protection League of USA, Inc.,** (1932), Box 221, Huntington Pk., Calif.; 400; Pres., Ted Bridgewater.

**Family Service Assn. of America** (1911), 44 East 23rd St., New York, N. Y. 10010; 337 agencies; Gen. Dir., Clark W. Blackburn.

**Farm Bureau Federation, Amer.,** (1919), 1000 Merchandise Mart, Chicago, Ill. 60654; 1,753,532 families; Pres., Charles B. Shuman.

**Farmer Cooperatives, Natl. Council of** (1929), 1200 17th St., N.W., Washington, D. C. 20036; Exec. V. P., Kenneth D. Naden.

**Farmers' Educational and Co-Operative Union of America (National Farmers Union)** (1902), 1575 Sherman St., Denver, Colo. 80201; 250,000 farm families; Pres., Tony T. Dechant.

**Federal Employees, Natl. Federation of** (1917), 1737 H St., N. W., Washington, D. C. 20006; 101,-000; Sec., Miss Florence I. Broadwell.

**Feline Society, American** (1938), 41 Union Square West, New York, N. Y. 10003; Sec., Mrs. Helen Alexander.

**Fellowship of Reconciliation** (1915), Box 271, Nyack, N. Y. 10960; 15,300; Chmn., Robert W. Moon.

**Fencers League of America, Amateur** (1891), 33 62nd St., West New York, N. J. 07093; 4,000; Corr. Sec., Mrs. W. J. Latzko.

**Financial Analysts Federation** (1947), 477 Madison Ave., New York, N. Y. 10022; 12,000; Exec. Sec., George M. Hansen.

**Financial Executives Institute** (1931), 50 West 44th St., New York, N. Y. 10036; 6,600; Man. Dir., Paul Haase.

**Fire Chiefs, International Assn. of** (1873), 232 Madison Ave., New York, N. Y. 10016; 6,622; Gen. Mgr., Donald M. O'Brien.

**Fire Fighters, International Assn. of** (1918), 905 16th St., N.W., Washington, D. C. 20006; 130,000; Sec., Albert E. Albertoni.

**Fire Marshals Assn. of No. America** (1906), 60 Batterymarch St., Boston, Mass. 02110; 600; Sec., Robert W. Grant.

**Fire Protection Assn., Natl.** (1896), 60 Batterymarch St., Boston, Mass. 02110; 22,000; Pres., Elmer F. Reske.

**Fire Protection Engineers, Society of** (1950), 60 Batterymarch St., Boston, Mass. 02110; 1,408; Sec., Richard E. Stevens.

**First Cavalry Division Assn.** (1944), P. O. Box 11201, Albuquerque, N. M. 87112; 9,470; Sec., Col. Alfred E. Stevens, USA (Ret.).

**First Division, Society of the** (1919), 5 Montgomery Ave., Philadelphia, Pa. 19118; 19,000; Exec. Sec., Arthur L. Chaitt.

**Fisheries Society, American** (1870), 1040 Washington Bldg., 14th & New York Ave., N.W., Washington, D. C. 20005; 5,000; Sec., Dr. Robert F. Hutton.

**Fishing Institute, Sport** (1949), 719 13th St., N.W., Washington, D. C. 20005; 300; Exec. Sec., Philip A. Douglas.

**Flag Day Assn., American** (1888), P. O. Box 1121, Denver, Colo. 80201; Natl. Sec., Verne Bentley.

**Flag Foundation, U. S.,** (1942), 115 East 86th St., New York, N. Y. 10028; Pres., Lawrence P. Tower.

**Fleet Reserve Assn.** (1924), 1303 New Hampshire Ave., N.W., Washington, D. C. 20036; 68,000; Sec., Robert W. Nolan.

**Florists, Society of American** (1884), Sheraton-Park Hotel, Washington, D. C. 20008; 5,000; Exec. Dir., John H. Walker.

**Folklore Society, American** (1888), Box 5, Bennett Hall, Univ. of Pa., Philadelphia, Pa. 19104; 1,800; Sec.-Treas., Dr. Kenneth Goldstein.

**Footwear Manufacturers Assn., Natl.** (1905), 342 Madison Ave., N. Y., N. Y. 10017; 500 firms, Sec., Harold R. Giblin.

**Foreign Policy Assn.** (1918), 345 E. 46th St., New York, N. Y. 10017; Pres., Samuel P. Hayes.

**Foreign Press Assn.** (1918), 340 East 46th St., New York, N. Y. 10017; 400; Sec. Gen., George Venizalos.

**Foreign Trade Council, Natl.** (1914), 10 Rocke-

feller Plaza, New York, N. Y. 10020; 600 companies; Sec., Helene Bienzle.

**Forensic League, Natl.** (1925), Ripon College, Ripon, Wis. 54971; 270,000; Sec., Bruno E. Jacob.

**Forest Products Assn., Natl.** (1902), 1619 Massachusetts Ave. N.W., Washington, D. C. 20036; 17 regional assns.; Sec., Ralph H. Gloss.

**Forest Products Industries, American** (1941), 1835 K St., N.W., Washington, D. C. 20006; 500; Man. Dir., Charles A. Gillett.

**Forest Products Research Society** (1947), 2801 Marshall Ct., Madison, Wis. 53705; 4,200; Exec. Sec., Kenneth E. Huddleston.

**Foresters, Society of American** (1900), Suite 300, 1010 16th St., N.W., Washington, D. C. 20036; 16,000; Sec., Hardin R. Glascock.

**Forestry Assn., American** (1875), 919 17th St., N.W., Washington, D. C. 20006; 57,000; Pres., William E. Towell.

**Forty and Eight, The** (1920), 777 No. Meridian St., Indianapolis, Ind. 46204; 73,000; Sec., Joel A. Bunch.

**Founders and Patriots of America, Order of the** (1896), Federal Hall Memorial, 15 Pine St., N. Y., N. Y. 10005; 955; Gov. Gen., Grahame Smallwood, Jr.

**Foundrymen's Society, American** (1896), Golf & Wolf Roads, Des Plains, Ill. 60016; 14,000; Exec. V. P., Ashley B. Sinnett.

**4-H Clubs** (betw. 1901-05), Federal Extension Service, U. S. Dept. of Agric., Washington, D. C. 20250; 3,000,000; Dir., Dr. E. Dean Vaughan. (Pledge of the Clubs: I pledge—My Head to clear thinking. My Heart to great loyalty. My Hands to larger service. My Health to better living. For my club, my community, and my country.)

**Free Sons of Israel** (1849), 257 West 93rd St., New York, N. Y. 10025; 9,500; Grand Secy., Herman S. Kaplan.

**Free Trade Unions, International Confederation of** (1949), International headquarters: 37-41 rue Montagne aux Herbes Potagères, Brussels 1, Belgium. Regional office for U. S. and Canada: 20 West 40th St., New York, N. Y. 10018; 60,000,000; Gen. Sec., Bruno Storti.

**French Institute** (1911), 22 East 60th St., New York, N. Y. 10022; 4,563; Pres., Robert G. Goelet.

**French Legion of Honor, American Society of the** (1922), 22 East 60th St., New York, N. Y. 10022; Sec., Mrs. Sylviane Glad.

**Friendly Sons of St. Patrick, Society of the** (1784), 80 Wall St., N. Y., N. Y. 10005; 1,400; Corres. Sec., Philip J. Curry.

**Friends Service Committee, American** (1917), 160 No. 15th St., Philadelphia, Pa. 19102; Exec. Sec., Stephen G. Cary.

**Future Farmers of America** (1928), c/o U.S. Office of Education, Dept. of Health, Ed. & Welfare, Washington, D. C. 20202; 438,429; Exec. Sec., William Paul Gray.

**Future Homemakers of America** (1945), c/o U.S. Office of Education, Washington, D. C. 20202; 602,-000; Natl. Adviser, Mildred Reel.

## —G—

**Game Fish Assn., International** (1939), 2190 S.E. 17th St., Ft. Lauderdale, Fla. 33316; 600 clubs; Pres., William K. Carpenter.

**Garden Club of America** (1913), 598 Madison Ave., New York, N. Y. 10022; 12,500; Sec., Mrs. Frederick N. Blodgett.

**Garden Clubs of America, Men's** (1932), P. O. Box 160, Johnston, Iowa 50131; 10,000; Exec. Sec., Guy D. Dichester.

**Garden Clubs, Natl. Council of State** (1929), 4401 Magnolia Ave., St. Louis, Mo. 63110; 400,000; Exec. Sec., Mrs. Earl H. Hath.

**Gas Appliance Manufacturers Assn.** (1935), 60 East 42nd St., New York, N. Y. 10017; 670 companies; Man. Dir., Harold Massey.

**Gas Assn., American** (1918), 605 Third Ave., New York, N. Y. 10016; 5,500; Sec., Vaughan O'Brien.

**Genealogical and Biographical Society, N. Y.** (Feb. 27, 1869), 122 East 58th St., New York, N. Y. 10022; 730; Exec. Sec., Marie F. Berry.

**General Contractors of America, Associated** (1921), 1957 E St., N.W., Washington, D. C. 20006; 8,458; Pres., Fred W. Mast.

**General Practice, American Academy** (1947), Volker Blvd. at Brookside, Kansas City, Mo. 64112; 30,670; Exec. Dir., Mac F. Cahal, J.D.

**Genetic Assn., American** (1903), 1507 M St. N.W., Washington, D. C. 20005; 1,447; Sec., Robert C. Carter.

**Geographers, Assn. of American** (1904), 1146 16th St., N.W., Washington, D. C. 20036; 5,250; Pres., Clyde F. Kohn.

**Geographic Education, Natl. Council for** (1914), Room 1532, 111 West Washington St., Chicago, Ill. 60602; 6,900; Exec. Sec., Dr. Elizabeth Eiselen.

**Geographic Society, National** (1888), 17th & M Sts., N.W., Washington, D. C. 20036; 6,100,000; Pres., Melville B. Grosvenor; Sec., Robert E. Doyle.

**Geographical Society, American** (1852), Broadway at 156th St., New York, N. Y. 10032; 3,250;

Pres., Dr. Serge A. Korff.

**Geological Institute, American** (1948), 1444 N St., N.W., Washington, D. C. 20005; 32,000; Exec. Dir., Dr. Linn Hoover.

**Geological Society of America** (1888), Box 1719, Colorado Bldg., Boulder, Colo. 80302; 7,621; Sec., Raymond C. Becker.

**Geophysical Union, American** (1919), 2100 Pennsylvania Ave., N.W., Washington, D. C. 20037; 9,000; Exec. Dir., Waldo E. Smith.

**Geriatrics Society, American** (1942), 10 Columbus Circle, New York, N. Y. 10019; 8,500; Exec. Dir., Edward Henderson, M.D.

**Gideons International** (July 1, 1899), 2900 Lebanon Rd., Nashville, Tenn. 37214; 25,000; Pres., Clarence H. Gilkey, Jr.

**Gifted Children, American Assn. for** (1946), 15 Gramercy Park, New York, N. Y. 10003; 100; Sec., Pauline Williamson.

**Gifted Children, Natl. Assn. for** (1954), 8080 Springvalley Dr., Cincinnati, Ohio 45236; 3,000; Exec. Dir., Ann F. Isaacs.

**Girl Scouts of the U. S. A.** (Mar. 12, 1912), 830 Third Ave., New York, N. Y. 10022; 3,652,000; Pres., Mrs. Holton R. Price, Jr.

**Girls Clubs of America** (1945), 133 East 62nd St., New York, N. Y. 10021; 100,000; Pres., Mrs. J. Robert Eubanks.

**Gladiolus Council, North American** (1943), 30 Highland, Peru, Ind. 46970; 2,000; Sec., Bob Dorsam.

**Gold Star Mothers, American** (1928); 2128 Leroy Pl., N.W., Washington, D. C. 20008; 17,000; Sec., Mrs. Elva P. Newman.

**Golf Association, U. S.** (Dec. 22, 1894), 40 East 38th St., New York, N. Y. 10016; 3,654 clubs; Exec. Dir., Joseph C. Dey, Jr.

**Good Templars, Internatl. Organization of** (1851), 2815 W. 71st St., Minneapolis, Minn. 55423; 300,000 world wide; Pres., Mrs. Carl A. Crusell.

**Governmental Research Assn.** (1914), 4 Washington Sq. No., New York, N. Y. 10003; 450; Sec., Troy R. Westmeyer.

**Grandmother Clubs of America, Natl. Federation of** (1938), 203 No. Wabash Ave., Chicago, Ill. 60601; 20,000; Pres., Hallie Bridges.

**Grand Street Boy's Association** (1920), 131-135 West 56th St., N. Y., N. Y. 10019; 5,500; Pres., Louis Tauscher.

**Grange, The National** (1867), 1616 H St., N.W., Washington, D. C. 20006; 800,000; Natl. Master, Herschel D. Newsom.

**Graphic Artists, Society of American** (1916), 1083 Fifth Ave., New York, N. Y. 10028; 250; Pres., David Shapiro.

**Green Mountain Club** (1910), 45 Park St., Rutland, Vt. 05701; 1,500; Corr. Sec., H. Minerva Hinchey.

**Grocery Manufacturers of America** (1908), 205 East 42nd St., New York, N. Y. 10017; 300 companies; Pres., George W. Koch.

**Group Health Assn. of America** (1959), 1321 14th St., N.W., Washington, D. C. 20005; 5,000,000; Sec., Jerry Voorhis.

**Gyro International** (1912), 1096 Mentor Ave., P. O. Box 489, Painesville, Ohio 44077; 5,500; Sec., C. W. St. Clair.

## —H—

**Hadassah (Women's Zionist Organization of America)** (1912), 65 East 52nd St., New York, N. Y. 10022; 318,000; Exec. Dir., Hannah L. Goldberg.

**Handicapped, Federation of the** (1935), 211 West 14th St., New York, N. Y. 10011; 1,000; Exec. Dir., Milton Cohen.

**Harvard Club of N. Y. City** (Nov. 3, 1865), 27 West 44th St., New York, N. Y. 10036; 7,591; Sec., Peter S. Heller.

**Hay Fever Prevention Society** (1935), 2300 Sedgwick, Rosewell Gardens, Bronx., N. Y. 10468; 450; Exec. Dir., Louis V. Fucci.

**Hay Fever Relief Assn., Natl.** (1923), 401 Broadway, New York, N. Y. 10013; 1,000; Sec., Sarah Masor.

**Health Council, Natl.** (1921), 1740 Broadway, New York, N. Y. 10019; Exec. Dir., Peter G. Meek.

**Health Foundations, United** (1961), 820 Second Ave., New York, N. Y. 10017; 125; Exec. Sec., Bertram Loeb.

**Health Insurance Assn. of America** (1956), 1701 K St., N.W., Washington, D. C. 20006; 324 insurance companies; Gen. Mgr., Leslie P. Hemry.

**Health Insurance Institute** (1956), 277 Park Ave., New York, N. Y. 10017; 300 insurance companies; Sec., R. Wilfred Kelsey.

**Health, Physical Education & Recreation, American Assn. for** (1885), 1201 16th St., N.W., Washington, D. C. 20036; 50,000; Exec. Sec., Carl Troester, Jr.

**Hearing and Speech Agencies, Natl. Assn. of,** (formerly American Hearing Society) (1919), 919 18th Street, N.W., Washington, D. C. 20006; 12,000; Pres., Edward Dexter.

**Heart Association, American** (1924), 44 E. 23rd St., New York, N. Y. 10010; 70,000; Pres., Dr.

Walter B. Frommeyer, Jr.

**Heating, Refrigerating and Air Conditioning Engineers, Amer. Soc. of** (1894), 345 East 47th St., New York, N. Y. 10017; 21,000; Sec., Andrew T. Boggs III.

**Helicopter Society, Amer.** (1943), 141 East 44th St., New York, N. Y. 10017; 4,600; Exec. Sec., H. M. Lounsbury.

**Hias Service, United** (1884), 200 Park Ave. South, N.Y., N. Y. 10003; 40,000; Exec. Dir., Gaynor I. Jacobson.

**Hibernians in America and Ladies Auxiliary, Ancient Order of** (1836), 248 East 31st St., Brooklyn, N. Y. 11226; 194,000; Natl. Sec., John F. Goeghan.

**Historians, Organization of American** (1907), (Formerly the Mississippi Valley Historical Association, name changed April, 1965), Univ. of Utah, Salt Lake City, Utah 84112; 9,200; Sec., W. D. Aeschbacher.

**Historians, Society of American** (1939), Fayerweather Hall, Columbia Univ., New York, N. Y. 10027; 400; Sec., Dr. Eric F. Goldman.

**Historic Preservation, National Trust for in the United States** (1949) 748, Jackson Place N.W., Washington, D. C. 20006; 14,686; Pres., James Bibble.

**Historical Assn., American** (1884), 400 A St., S.E., Washington, D. C. 20003; 16,500; Exec. Sec., Paul L. Ward.

**Historical Assn. of N. Y. State** (1899), Fenimore House, Cooperstown, N. Y. 13326; 2,500; Exec. Dir., Dr. Louis C. Jones.

**Historical Society, East Tennessee** (1925), Lawson McGhee Library, 217 Market St., Knoxville, Tenn. 37902; 900; Sec., Pollyanna Creekmore.

**Historical Society, Illinois State** (1899), Old State Capitol, Springfield, Ill. 62706; 4,036; Exec. Dir., William K. Alderfer.

**Historical Society of Iowa, State** (1857), Centennial Bldg., Iowa City, Ia. 52240; 10,500; Supt., Wm. J. Petersen.

**Historical Society of Missouri, State** (1898), Univ. Library Bldg., Hitt & Lowry Sts., Columbia, Mo. 65201; 15,472; Sec., Dr. Richard S. Brownlee.

**Historical Society, New York** (1804), 170 Central Park West, N. Y., N. Y. 10024; 1,500; Dir., James J. Heslin.

**Historical Society, Ohio.** (1885), State Museum, Columbus, O. 43210; 4,800; Dir., Daniel R. Porter.

**Historical Society, Okla.** (1893), Historical Bldg., Lincoln Blvd. at NE 19th St., Okla. City, Okla. 73105; 2,700; Adm. Sec., Elmer L. Fraker.

**Historical Society of Pennsylvania** (1824), 1300 Locust St., Philadelphia, Pa.; 2,400; Dir., Nicholas B. Wainwright.

**Historical Society, Presbyterian** (1852), 425 Lombard St., Philadelphia, Pa. 19147; 1,100; Sec. William B. Miller.

**Holland Society of N. Y.** (1885), 122 East 58th St., New York, N.Y. 10022; 1,002; Pres., Walter E. Hopper Jr.

**Home Economics Assn., American** (1909), 1600 20th St., N.W., Washington, D.C. 20009; 56,000; Pres., Louise Gauthier.

**Homeopathy, American Institute of,** (1884), 2726 Quebec St., N.W., Washington, D.C. 20008; 115; Sec., William A. Weaver, M.D.

**Hoo Hoo, Intl.** (1892), 161 W. Wisconsin Ave., Milwaukee, Wis. 53203; 8,500; Exec. Sec., B. F. Springer.

**Horatio Alger Society** (1961), 1325 Burlington Rd., Mendota, Ill. 61342; 135; Pres., Carl T. Hartmann.

**Horse Show Assn., Natl.** (1883, Empire Hotel—Suite 101, Broadway & 63rd St., N.Y., N.Y. 10023; Exec. Sec., Dr. Henry A. Chase.

**Horseshoe Pitchers Assn. of America, Natl.** (1914). 341 Polk St., Gary, Ind. 46402; 4,400; Sec., Robert G. Pence.

**Horticultural Society, American** (1922), 2401 Calvert St., N.W., Washington, D. C. 20008; 4,500; Exec. Dir., Mrs. Glenn Eastburn.

**Horticultural Society of New York** (1902), 160 Central Pk. So., New York, N.Y. 10019; 4,200; Exec. Sec., Alexander W. Allport.

**Hospital Fund of N. Y., United** (1879), 3 East 54th St., New York, N. Y. 10022; 78 hospitals; Sec., Frederick E. Donaldson.

**Hospital Public Relations Directors, American Soc. for,** (1965), 840 N. Lake Shore Dr., Chicago, Ill.. 60611; 600; Sec., Barbara Carner.

**Hotel & Motel Assn., American** (1910), 221 West 57th St., New York, N.Y. 10019; 6,500; Exec. V. P. Lawson A. Odde.

**Hudson Valley Art Assn.** (1928), 243 So. Broadway, Hastings-on-Hudson, N. Y. 10706; 250; Pres., Mrs. Georgie R. Barton.

**Humane Assn., American** (1877) P.O. Box 1266, Denver, Colo. 80201; Sec., Rutherford T. Phillips.

**Humane Society of the U.S.** (1954), 1145 19th St., N.W., Washington, D. C. 20036; 60,000; Pres., Mel L. Morse.

**Humanics Foundation, American** (1948), 912 Baltimore Ave., Kansas City, Missouri 64105; 1,000;

Pres., Dwight J. Thomson.

**Humanist Associaton, American** (1943), 125 El Camino del Mar, San Francisco, Calif. 94121; 6,000; Pres., Robert W. McCoy.

**Hundred Year Assn. of New York** (1927), 99 Church St., New York, N. Y. 10007; 350; Sec., Ralph C. Gross.

## —I—

**Iceland Veterans** (1947), 2101 Walnut St., Philadelphia, Pa. 19103; 1,470; Dir., Dave Zinkoff.

**Identification, International Assn. for** (1915), P. O. Box 139, Utica, New York 13503; 1,650; Pres., Albert W. Somerford.

**Illuminating Engineering Society** (1906), 345 East 47th St., New York, N. Y. 10017; 11,000; Man. Dir., Paul C. Ringgold.

**Illustrators, Society of** (1901), 128 E. 63rd St., New York, N.Y. 10021; 550; Mgr. Dir., Ernest Button.

**Immigration and Nationality Lawyers, Assn. of** (1946), 50 Court St., Brooklyn, N. Y. 11201; 450 Pres., Elmer Fried.

**Imperial Order of the Dragon** (1900, in Temple of Agric., Peking, China; commemorating China Relief Expedition), P. O. Box 1707, San Francisco Calif. 94101; Sec., Enoch Jones, Sr.

**Indian Rights Assn.** (1882), 1505 Race St., Philadelphia, Pa. 19102; 1,200; Gen. Sec., Armin L. Saeger, Jr.

**Indoor Sports' Club** (1930), 3445 Trumbull St., San Diego, Calif. 92106; 3,000; Exec. Sec., Mrs. Dorothy J. Mason.

**Industrial Advertisers, Assn. of** (1922), 41 East 42nd St., N. Y., N. Y. 10017; 4,500; Man. Dir., Robert T. Griffiths.

**Industrial Conference Board, Natl.** (1916), 845 Third Ave., New York, N. Y. 10022; 4,265; Sec., Herbert S. Briggs.

**Industrial Democracy, League for** (1905), 112 East 19th St., New York, N. Y. 10003; 2,000; Exec. Sec., Tom Kahn. **Students for Democratic Society** (student dept. of the League), Pres., Paul Potter.

**Industrial Designers Society of America** (Jan. 1965), 60 W. 55th St., N. Y., N. Y. 10019; 588; Exec. Sec., Mrs. Ramah R. Larisch.

**Industrial Diamond Assn. of America** (1946), 2017 Walnut St., Philadelphia, Pa. 19103; 120; Donald A. Trescott.

**Industrial Editors, American Assn. of** (1938), 802 Kenmore Ave., Buffalo, N. Y. 14216; 1,200; Exec. Sec., Donald W. Boyd, Jr.

**Industrial Editors, International Council of** (1941), 2108 Braewick Circle, Akron, Ohio 44313; 3,500; Pres., Fredric J. Felton.

**Industrial Engineers, American Institute of** (1948), 345 East 47th St., New York, N. Y. 10017; 19,000; Sec., J. F. Jericho.

**Industrial Hygiene Foundation of America** (1935), Mellon Institute, 4400 Fifth Ave., Pittsburgh, Pa. 15213; 400; Man. Dir., Dr. R. T. P. de Treville.

**Industrial Management Society** (1934), 330 South Wells, Chicago, Ill. 60606; 1,000; Exec. Mgr., Robert J. Mayer.

**Instrument Society of America** (1945), 530 William Penn Pl., Pittsburgh, Pa. 15219; 18,000; Pres., Dr. T. J. Williams.

**Insurance Society of N. Y.** (1901), 150 Williams St., New York, N. Y. 10038; 1,300; Sec., Donald Rindell.

**Insured Savings Associations, Natl. League of** (1943), 1200 17th St., N.W., Suite 700, Washington, D. C. 20036; 370 associations; Man. Dir., Kenneth G. Heisler.

**Intercollegiate (Big Ten) Conference** (1895), Suite 1600; Sheraton-Chicago Hotel, Chicago, Ill. 60611; Commissioner, William R. Reed.

**Intercollegiate Lacrosse Assn., U. S.** (1883), 276 Recreation Bldg., Penn State Univ., Univ. Park, Pa. 16802; 76 colleges; Sec., Glenn N. Thiel.

**Interfraternity Conference, National** (1909), 271 Madison Ave., New York, N. Y. 10016; 2,250,000; Admin. Sec., Paul K. Addams.

**International Law, American Society of** (1906), 2223 Massachusetts Ave., N.W., Washington, D. C. 20008; 4,000; Pres., Oscar Schachter.

**Investment Bankers Assn. of America** (1912), 425 13th St., N.W., Washington, D. C.; 670 organizations; Sec., John A. Falrey.

**Investment Clubs, Natl. Assn. of** (1951), 1300 Washington Blvd. Building, Detroit, Mich., 48226; 160,082; Chairman, Thomas E. O'Hara.

**Investment Company Institute** (1940), 61 Broadway, New York, N. Y. 10006; 300 Mutual Fund Groups; Exec. V. P., Bruce B. Robe.

**Iron Founders Society, Gray and Ductile,** (1928), 930 National City-E 6th Bldg., Cleveland, Ohio 44114; 260 companies; Exec. V. P., Donald H. Workman.

**Iron and Steel Engineers, Assn. of** (1907), 1010 Empire Bldg., Pittsburgh, Pa. 15222; 11,002; Man. Dir., T. J. Ess.

**Iron and Steel Institute, American** (1908), 150

East 42nd St., New York, N. Y. 10017; 2,833; Pres., John P. Roche.

**Italian Historical Society of America** (1949), 111 Columbia Heights, Brooklyn, N. Y. 11201; 973; Dir., John N. La Corte.

**Italy-America Chamber of Commerce,** (1887), 350 Fifth Ave., N. Y., N. Y. 10001; 550; Exec. Sec., Arthur De Santis.

**Izaak Walton League of America** (1922), 1326 Waukegan Rd., Glenview, Ill. 60025; 54,000; Exec. Dir., William A. Riaski.

## —J—

**Jamestowne Society** (1936), 4313 N. Ashlawn Dr., Richmond, Va.; 1,400; Sec., Mrs. James R. Lindsay.

**Jaycees, United States** (1920), P.O. Box 7, Tulsa, Okla. 74102; 275,000; Exec. V. P., C. Robert Cronk.

**Jewish Agricultural Society** (1900), 386 Park Ave. So., New York, N. Y. 10016; Sec., Rachel Silberstein.

**Jewish Braille Institute** (1931), 48 East 74th St., New York, N. Y. 10021; 14,000; Exec. Dir., Dr. Jacob Freid.

**Jewish Committee, American** (1906), 165 East 56th St., New York, N. Y. 10021; 30,000; Pres., Morris B. Abram.

**Jewish Congress, Amer.** (1918), 15 East 84th St., New York, N. Y. 10028; 50,000; Exec. Dir., Will Maslow.

**Jewish Federations and Welfare Funds, Council of** (1932), 315 Park Ave. South, N. Y., N. Y. 10010; 222 agencies; Pres., Louis J. Fox.

**Jewish Historical Society, Amer.** (1892), 2 Thornton Rd., Waltham, Mass. 02154; 3,100; Dir., Bernard Wax.

**Jewish Labor Committee** (1935), 25 East 78th St., New York, N. Y. 10021; 500,000; Natl. Dir., Emanuel Muravchik.

**Jewish Philanthropies of N. Y., Federation of** (1917), 130 East 59th St., New York, N. Y. 11358; 120,000; Publicity Dir., Robert I. Smith.

**Jewish Publication Society of America** (1888), 222 No. 15th St., Philadelphia, Pa. 19102; 13,850; Exec. Dir., Lesser Zussman.

**Jewish Teachers Assn.** (1928), 1182 Broadway, New York, N. Y. 10001; 26,000; Sec., Israel Rosenblum.

**Jewish War Veterans of the U. S. A.** (1896), 1712 New Hampshire Ave., N.W., Washington, D. C. 20009; Natl. Exec. Dir., Monroe R. Sheinberg.

**Jewish Welfare Board, National** (1917), 15 East 26th St., New York, N. Y. 10010; 447 community centers; Exec. V. P., Sanford Solender.

**Jewish Women, National Council of** (1893), 1 West 47th St., New York, N. Y. 10024; 100,000; Exec. Dir., Hannah Stein.

**Jockey Club** (1894), 300 Park Ave., New York, N. Y. 10022; 72; Exec. Sec., John F. Kennedy.

**John Birch Society, The** (1958), 395 Concord Ave., Belmont, Mass. 02178; between 60,000 and 100,000; Pres., Robert Welch.

**Judaism, American Council for** (1943), 201 East 57th St., New York, N. Y. 10022; 20,000; Exec. Dir., Jerome Frankle.

**Judicature Society, American** (1913). 1155 East 60th St., Chicago, Ill. 60637; 34,000; Pres., Herbert Brownell.

**Junior Achievement** (1919), 51 West 51st St., New York, N. Y. 10019; 140,000 teenagers, 21,364 adults; P. R. Dir., James F. Barrett.

**Junior Colleges, American Assn. of** (1920), 1315 16th St., N.W., Washington, D. C. 20036; 759 institutions; Exec. Dir., Edmund J. Gleazer, Jr.

**Junior League of the City of N. Y.** (1902), 130 East 80th St., New York, N. Y. 10021; 1,900; Exec. Sec., Mrs. Henry Blodget.

**Junior Leagues of America, Assn. of the** (1921) Waldorf-Astoria Hotel, 301 Park Ave., New York, N. Y. 10022; 98,000; Exec. Dir., Lucile G. Mason.

## —K—

**Kennel Club, American** (1884), 51 Madison Ave., New York, N. Y. 10010; 369 Clubs; Sec., Roy H. Carlberg.

**Key Club International** (1925), Kiwanis International Bldg., 101 E. Erie St., Chicago, Ill. 60611; 87,000; Dir., Robert F. Lucas.

**Kindergarten Assn., National** (1909), 8 West 40th St., New York, N. Y. 10018; Exec. Dir., Mrs. Creighton Peet.

**Kiwanis International** (1915), 101 East Erie St., Chicago, Ill. 60611; 275,000; Sec., R. P. Merridew. **Circle K International** (1947), 732 colleges; Dir., Donald R. Teasley.

**Knights of Columbus** (Mar. 29, 1882; merged with Supreme Council Catholic Benevolent Legion, Jan. 1, 1968), 71 Meadow St., New Haven, Conn. 06507; 1,200,000; Sec., Virgil C. Dechant.

**Knights of Pythias** (1864), 1212 Dodds Ave., Chattanooga, Tenn. 37404; 190,000; Pres., Joseph B. Hacker.

**Knights Templar of the U.S.A., Grand Encampment of** (1816), 14 East Jackson Blvd., Suite 1733,

Chicago, Ill. 60604; 387,500; Grand Recorder, Paul C. Rodenhauser.

**Kosciuszko Foundation** (1925), 15 East 65th St., New York, N. Y. 10021; 2,100; Pres., Stephen Mizwa.

**—L—**

**Lambs, The** (1874), 130 West 44th St., New York, N. Y. 10036; 1,200; Pres., Harry Hershfield.

**Landscape Architects, American Society of** (1899), 2013 Eye St., N.W., Washington, D. C. 20006; 3,200; Pres., Theodore Osmundson.

**Language Teachers Associations, Natl. Federation of Modern,** (1916), 760 Elm Spring Rd., Pittsburgh, Pa. 15243; Sec., J. Alan Pfeffer.

**Latin, Assn. for Promotion of Study of** (1929), P. O. Box 501, Elizabeth, N. J. 07207; 16,400; Sec., Dr. Albert E. Warsley.

**Law Institute, American,** (1923), 101 N. 33rd St., Philadelphia, Pa. 19104; 1,500; Sec., Paul A. Wolkin.

**Law Libraries, American Assn. of** (1906), 53 W. Jackson Blvd., Chicago, Ill. 60604; 1,350; Pres., William D. Murphy.

**Learned Societies, American Council of** (1919), 345 East 46th St., New York, N. Y. 10017; 33 societies; Pres., Frederick Burkhardt.

**Legal Aid and Defender Assn., National** (1911), 1155 East 60th St., Chicago, Ill. 60637; 1,700; Exec. Dir., Junius L. Allison.

**Legal Aid Society** (1876), 1155 East 60th St., Chicago, Ill. 60637.

**Legal Secretaries, Natl. Assn. of** (1950), 29 S. LaSalle St., Chicago, Ill. 60603; 14,000; Pres., Mrs. Haru K. Hains.

**Legion of Soldier's Friends** (1966), P.O. Box 4506, Washington, D. C. 20017; 11,014; Pres., John L. Gamble.

**Legion of Valor of the U. S. A.** (1890), 621 S. Taylor St., Arlington, Va. 22204; 1,200; Sec., Col. Robert M. Gaynor.

**Leprosy, Leonard Wood Memorial for the Eradication of (American Leprosy Foundation)** (1928), 79 Madison Ave., New York, N. Y. 10016; Sec., Robert W. Watt.

**Leprosy Missions, American** (1906), 297 Park Ave. So., New York, N. Y. 10010; 48,228; Pres., Oliver W. Hasselblad, M.D.

**Letter Carriers, National Association of** (1889), 100 Indiana Ave., N.W., Washington, D. C. 20001; 210,000; Sec., J. S. Lewis.

**Leukemia Society** (1949), 211 E. 43 St., N. Y., N. Y. 10017; Pres., John J. Kenny, M.D.

**Librarians, American Assn. of Medical Record** (1928), 211 East Chicago Ave., Chicago, Ill. 60611; 7,000; Exec. Dir., Mrs. Mary Waterstraat.

**Libraries Association, Special** (1909), 235 Park Ave. South, New York, N. Y. 10003; 7,000; Exec. Dir., George Ginader.

**Library Association, American** (Oct. 6, 1876), 50 East Huron St., Chicago, Ill. 60611; 38,000; Exec. Dir., David H. Clift.

**Library Assn., Home and School** (1938), 144 No. Limestone St., Lexington, Ky. 40507; Exec. Sec., Paul J. Hines.

**Library Assn., Medical** (1898), 919 No. Michigan Ave., Chicago, Ill. 60611; 728 institutions; Exec. Sec., Mrs. Helen Brown Schmidt.

**Life Convention, American** (1906), 211 East Chicago Ave., Chicago, Ill. 60611; 342 insurance companies; Sec., Ida Weber.

**Life Insurance Assn. of America** (1906), 277 Park Ave., New York, N. Y. 10017; 118 insurance companies; Sec., James Andrews, Jr.

**Life Insurance, Institute of** (1939), 277 Park Ave., New York, N. Y. 10017; Pres., B. T. Newton, Jr.

**Life Underwriters Assn. of the City of N. Y.** (1886), 500 Fifth Ave., N. Y., N. Y. 10036; 3,000; Man. Dir., Joseph M. Fenton, Jr.

**Life Underwriters, National Assn. of** (1890), 1922 F St., N.W., Washington, D. C. 20006; 105,000; Pres., Francis G. Bray.

**Lions International (Intl. Assn. of Lions Clubs)** (1917), 209 No. Michigan Ave., Chicago, Ill. 60601; 851,988; Sec., John Vogt.

**Log Rolling Assn., International** (1926), 5855 N. Sheridan Rd., Apt. 5-J, Chicago, Ill. 60626; 65; Exec. Sec., George Mathison.

**Long Island Assn. of Commerce and Industry** (1926), 131 Jericho Turnpike, Jericho, L. I., N. Y. 11753; 1,000 firms; Sec., J. F. Dutra.

**Lubrication Engineers, American Society of** (1944), 838 Busse Highway, Pk. Ridge, Ill. 60068; 3,200; Exec. Sec., Donald B. Sandberg.

**Lumbermen's Assn., Middle Atlantic** (1892), 7 E. Lancaster Ave., Ardmore, Pa. 19003; 350; Exec. V. P., Robert A. Jones.

**Lutheran Education Assn.** (1942), 7400 Augusta St., River Forest, Ill. 60305; 2,944; Sec., Lyle Saeger.

**—M—**

**Magazine Photographers, American Soc. of** (1944), 60 E. 42nd St., New York, N. Y. 10017; 700; Exec. Dir., Miss Regina Benedict.

**Magazine Writers, Society of** (1948), c/o Overseas Press Club, 54 West 40th St., New York, N. Y. 10018; 230; Pres., William Surface.

**Magicians Guild of America** (1944), 37 5th Ave., Bay Shore, L. I., N. Y.; 100; Sec., Georgia Kondos.

**Mammalogists, American Society of** (1919), Department of Zoology, Oklahoma State Univ., Stillwater, Okla. 74074; 3,000; Sec., Bryan P. Glass.

**Management, American Institute of** (1948), 125 East 38th St., New York, N. Y. 10016; 10,000; Sec., Edward L. Dobson.

**Management Assn., National** (1925), 333 West 1st St., Dayton, O. 45402; 88,000; Exec. V. P., Marion N. Kershner.

**Manufacturers' Agents National Assn.** (1947), 626 No. Garfield Ave., Alhambra, Calif. 91802; 2,800; Exec. Sec., A. X. Schilling.

**Manufacturers, Natl. Assn. of** (1895), 277 Park Ave., New York, N. Y. 10017; 14,000; Sec., John McGraw.

**Manufacturing Chemists Assn.** (1872), 1825 Connecticut Ave., N.W., Washington, D. C. 20009; 199 corporations; Sec.-Treas., James R. Carnes.

**Manuscript Society** (1948), Morris Library, Southern Illinois University, Carbondale, Ill. 62901; 1,021; Exec. Sec., Kenneth W. Duckett.

**Marathon Swimming Federation, World Professional** (1963), 10102 Pierce Dr., Silver Spring, Md. 20901; 220; Sec., Joe Grossman.

**Marine Corps League** (1923), 939 N. Kenmore St., Arlington, Va. 22201; 12,000; Natl. Comm., Claude H. Downing.

**Marine Society of the City of N. Y.** (1770), 80 Broad St., New York, N. Y. 10004; 325; Sec., Capt. Aime J. Gerber.

**Marine Technology Society** (1963), 1030 15th St., N.W., Washington, D. C. 20005; 4,000; Sec., RAdm. M. H. Simons, Jr., USN Ret.

**Maritime Assn. of the Port of N. Y.** (Feb. 5, 1873), 80 Broad St., New York, N. Y. 10004; 1,500; Gen. Mgr., William F. Giesen.

**Maritime History, Society for** (1966), Box 3014, University Station, Eugene, Ore. 97403; Pres., John D. Allan.

**Marketing Assn., American** (1915), 230 North Michigan Ave., Chicago, Ill. 60601; 14,429; Exec. Dir., Earl G. Johnson.

**Masonic Service Assn. of the U. S.** (1919), 700 10th St., N.W., Washington, D. C. 20001; 43 Lodges; Exec. Sec., Conrad Hahn.

**Masons, Ancient Accepted Scottish Rite, Northern Masonic Jurisdiction, Supreme Council 33°** (Aug. 5, 1813), 1117 Statler Bldg., Boston, Mass. 02116; 506,635; Grand Sec. Gen., Laurence E. Eaton.

**Masons, Ancient and Accepted Scottish Rite, Southern Jurisdiction, Supreme Council** (1801), 1733 16th St., N.W., Washington, D. C. 20009; 540,000; Sovereign Grand Commander, Luther A. Smith, 32°.

**Masons of the State of N. Y., Grand Lodge of Free & Accepted** (Sept. 5, 1781), 71 West 23rd St., New York, N. Y. 10010; 262,000; Sec., Wendell K. Walker.

**Masons, Royal Arch, General Grand Chapter** (1797), 1084 New Circle Rd., N.E., Lexington, Ky. 40505; 563,775; Gen. Gr. Sec., Charles K. A. McGaughey.

**Mathematical Assn. of America** (1915), State Univ. at Buffalo, Buffalo, N. Y. 14214; 18,000; Exec. Dir., Prof. Harry M. Gehman.

**Mathematical Society, American** (1888), 321 S. Main St., P. O. Box 6248, Providence, R. I. 02904; 13,000; Sec., Everett Pitcher.

**Mathematical Statistics, Institute of** (1935), Dept. of Statistics, Michigan State Univ., East Lansing, Mich. 48823; 2,730; Sec., Leo Katz.

**Mayflower Descendants, Gen. Soc. of** (1897), P. O. Box 297, Plymouth, Mass. 02360; 13,256; Sec. Gen., Mrs. Robert M. Sherman.

**Mayors, U. S. Conference of** (1933), 1707 H St., N.W., Washington, D. C. 20006; Exec. Dir., John J. Gunther.

**Mechanical Engineers, American Society of** (1880), 345 East 47th St., New York, N. Y. 10017; 54,183; Sec., O. B. Schier.

**Mediaeval Academy of America** (1925), 1430 Massachusetts Ave., Cambridge, Mass. 02138; 2,500; Sec., Van Courtlandt Elliott.

**Medical Association, National** (1895), 520 W. St., N.W., Washington, D. C. 20001; 5,500; Admin. Sec., Samuel C. Smith.

**Medical Colleges, Assn. of American** (1876), 2530 Ridge Ave., Evanston, Ill. 60201; 3,754; Sec., Dr. Robert B. Howard.

**Medical Technologists, American** (1939), 710 Higgins Rd., Park Ridge, Ill. 60068; 10,239; Exec. Sec., Chester B. Dziekonski.

**Medical Vocabulary, Natl. Assn. on Standard** (1958), 934 Monroe St., Charlestown, Ind. 47111; 4,200; Chairman, Dr. J. E. Schmidt.

**Medical Women's Association, American** (1915), 1740 Broadway, N. Y., N. Y. 10019; 5,000; Exec. Dir., Mrs. G. F. Conroy.

**Medicine, New York Academy of** (1847), 2 E. 103

St., New York, N. Y. 10029; 2,500; Dir., James E. McCormack, M.D.

**Mensa** (1945), 50 East 42nd St., N. Y., N. Y. 10017; 12,000; Chairman, Herbert Ahreud.

**Mental Health, Natl. Assn. for** (1950), 10 Columbus Circle, N. Y., N. Y. 10019; 939 chapters; Pres., Earl Warren, Jr.

**Merchant Marine Library Assn., American** (1921), 45 Broadway, New York, N. Y. 10006; 3,079; Exec. Sec., William P. Bollman.

**Metal Finishers, National Association of** (1955), 248 Lorraine Ave., Upper Montclair, N. J. 07043; 700 companies; Sec., P. Peter Kovatis.

**Metals, American Society for** (1913), Metals Park, O. 44073; 39,025; Man. Sec., Dr. Thomas E. Leontis.

**Meteorological Society, American** (1919), 45 Beacon St., Boston, Mass. 02108; 8,500; Sec., Kenneth C. Spengler.

**Microbiology, American Society for** (1899), 115 Huron View Blvd., Ann Arbor, Mich. 48103; 12,000; Exec. Sec., R. W. Sarber.

**Military Chaplains Assn. of The U.S.A.** (1925), 1710 16th St., N.W., Washington, D. C. 20009; 2,900; Exec. Dir., Dr. Karl B. Justus.

**Military Engineers, Society of American** (1920), Fleming Building, 800 17th St., N.W., Washington, D. C. 20006; 27,000; Sec., Brig. Gen. William C. Hall.

**Military Order of the Carabao** (Nov., 1900, in Manila, P. I.), 1632 K St., N.W., Washington, D. C. 20006; 1,300; Sec., Capt. William J. G. Davis, AUS.

**Military Order of the Loyal Legion of the U. S.** (1865), 1805 Pine St., Philadelphia, Pa. 19103; 2,000; Sec., H. Durston Saylor II.

**Military Order of the Purple Heart** (Aug. 7, 1782, by Gen. George Washington; reactivated Feb. 22, 1932, by President Herbert Hoover and Chief of Staff Douglas MacArthur). P. O. Box 5727, Daytona Beach, Fla. 32020; 15,200; Exec. Sec., Victor F. Kubly.

**Military Order of the World Wars** (1919), 910 17th St., N. W., Washington, D. C. 20006; 11,300; W. K. Schwerdtfeger, USN (ret.).

**Military Surgeons of the U. S., Assn. of** (1891), 1500 Massachusetts Ave., N.W., Washington, D. C 20005; 5,563; Exec. Dir., Brig. Gen. Frank E. Wilson.

**Mining, Metallurgical and Petroleum Engineers, American Institute of** (1871), 345 East 47th St., New York, N. Y. 10017; 44,166; Sec. Gen., R. William Taylor.

**Mining and Metallurgical Society of America** (1908), 11 Broadway, New York, N. Y. 10004; 420; Sec., Lendall P. Warrner.

**Ministerial Assn., American** (1929), P. O. Box 1252, York, Pa. 17405; 5,308; Sec., Dr. Wilbur Lyons.

**Minute Men of America** (April 6, 1917), 834 Riverside Dr., Stuart, Fla. 33494; Dir. Gen., Francis A. Adams.

**Missouri Valley Conference** (1907). President Hotel, Kansas City, Mo. 64105; 9 member schools; Exec. Sec., Norwall Neve.

**Modern Language Assn. of America** (1883), 62 Fifth Ave., N. Y., N. Y. 10011; 26,000; Exec. Sec., Prof. John H. Fisher.

**Moose, Loyal Order of** (1888), Mooseheart, Ill. 60539; 1,078,521; Dir. Gen., Paul P. Schmitz.

**Mothers Committee, American** (1935), Waldorf-Astoria, 301 Park Ave., New York, N. Y. 10022; 3,000; Pres., Mrs. Dorothy Lewis.

**Motion Picture Arts and Sciences, Academy of** (May 4, 1927), 9038 Melrose Ave., Los Angeles, Calif. 90069; 3,200; Exec. Dir., Mrs. Margaret Herrick.

**Motion Picture Assn. of America** (1922), 522 Fifth Ave., New York, N. Y. 10036; Sec., Sidney Schreiber.

**Motion Picture and Television Engineers, Society of** (1916), 9 East 41st St., New York, N. Y. 10017; 7,000; Exec., G. Carleton Hunt.

**Motion Pictures, Natl. Board of Review of** (1909), 31 Union Square, New York, N. Y. 10003; 225; Exec. Dir., Henry Hart.

**Motor Bus Owners, Natl. Assn. of** (1926) 839 17th St., N.W., Washington, D. C. 20006; 391; Sec., Stanley Hamilton.

**Motor Vehicle Administrators, American Assn. of** (1933), 1155 15th St., N.W., Washington, D. C. 20005; 125; Exec. Dir., Louis P. Spitz.

**Motorcycle Assn., American** (1927), P. O. Box 231, Worthington, Ohio 43085; 100,000; Exec. Dir., Wm. T. Berry, Jr.

**Multiple Sclerosis Society, National** (1946), 257 Park Ave. South, New York, N. Y. 10010; 140,000; Pres., Nathan Mobley.

**Municipal Finance Officers Assn. of the U. S. and Canada** (1906), 1313 East 60th St., Chicago, Ill. 60637; 4,242; Exec. Dir., Joseph F. Clark.

**Municipal League, National** (1894), 47 East 68th St., New York, N. Y. 10021; 6,300; Exec. Dir., Alfred Willoughby.

**Mural Painters, Natl. Society of** (1895), 41 E. 65th St., N. Y., N. Y. 10021; 150; Pres., Helen Treadwell.

**Muscular Dystrophy Associations of America,** (1950), 1790 Broadway, New York, N. Y. 10019; 15,000; Pres., Paul Cohen.

**Museums, American Assn. of** (1906), 2306 Massachusetts Ave., N.W., Washington, D. C. 20008; 954 museums; Pres., Charles Parkhurst.

**Music Center, American** (1940), 2109 Broadway, N.Y., N. Y. 10023; 800; Pres., Hugo Weisgall.

**Music Conference, American** (1947), 332 S. Michigan Ave., Chicago, Ill. 60604; Exec. V. P., James L. Bixby.

**Music Clubs, Natl. Federation of** (1898), Suite 1215, 600 So. Michigan Ave., Chicago, Ill. 60605; 600,000; Admin. Dir., Miss Lois Winterberg.

**Music Council, National** (1940), 2109 Broadway, New York, N. Y. 10023; Exec. Sec., James Browning.

**Music Educators National Conference** (1907), 1201 16th St., N.W., Washington, D. C. 20036; 54,-000; Exec. Sec., Miss Vanett Lawler.

**Music Players, Amateur Chamber** (1947), 15 W. 67th St., N. Y., N. Y. 10023; 5,000; Sec., Helen Rice.

**Music Publishers, National Assn.** (1917), 460 Park Ave., New York, N .Y. 10022; 62; Exec. Dir., Leonard Feist.

**Music Teachers Natl. Assn.** (1876), 2209 Carew Tower, Cincinnati, Ohio 45202; 12,000; Exec. Sec., G. William Fahrer, Jr.

**Musicians, American Fed. of** (1896), 641 Lexington Ave., N. Y., N. Y. 10022; 285,000; Sec., Stanley Ballard.

**Mutual Savings Banks, National Assn. of** (1920), 200 Park Ave., New York, N. Y. 10017; 503 banks; Exec. V. P., Grover W. Ensley.

## —N—

**Name Society, American** (1951), State University College, Potsdam, N. Y. 13676; 950; Pres., E. C. Ehrensperger.

**National Assn. for the Advancement of Colored People (NAACP)** (Feb. 12, 1909), 1790 Broadway, New York, N. Y. 10019; 450,000; Exec. Dir., Roy Wilkins.

**National Conference of Christians and Jews** (1928), 43 West 57th St., New York, N. Y. 10019; 250,000; Sec., Oscar M. Lazrus.

**Nationalities Service, American Council for** (1958), 20 West 40th St., New York, N. Y. 10018; Exec. Dir., Read Lewis.

**Nature Conservancy** (1952), 1522 K St., N.W., Washington, D. C. 20005; 15,000; Sec., Elting Arnold.

**Naval Architects and Marine Engineers, Society of** (1893), 74 Trinity Pl., New York, N. Y. 10006; 8,700; Sec., Capt. M. H. Gluntz, USN, Ret.

**Naval Cadets of America, Junior** (1958), P. O. Box 725, Groton, Conn. 06340; 2,500; Nat. Comm., Capt. John McCaffery.

**Naval Engineers, American Soc. of** (1888), Suite 507, 1012 14th St., N.W., Washington, D. C. 20005; 3,687; Sec., Capt. J. E. Hamilton, USN, Ret.

**Naval Inst., U. S.** (1873), U. S. Naval Academy, Annapolis, Md. 21402; 57,424; Sec., Cmdr. R. T. E. Bowler, Jr.

**Naval Reserve Assn.** (1954), 1913 Eye St., N.W., Washington, D. C. 20006; 8,400; Exec. Dir., RAdm. John S. Lewis, USN, Ret.

**Navigation, Institute of** (1945), Rm. 700, 711 14th St., N.W., Washington, D. C. 20005; 2,250; Exec. Sec., Capt. Ross E. Freeman, USN, Ret.

**Navy Club of the U. S. A.** (1940), 320 Riverside Blvd., Loves Park, Ill. 61111; 2,000; Sec., LeRoy H. Hahn. **Navy Club of the U. S. A. Auxiliary, Natl.**, Commandant, Mrs. Stanley Pazera, 2508 Drexel Ave., Fort Wayne, Ind. 46806.

**Navy League of the U. S.** (1902), 818—18th St. N.W., Washington, D. C. 20006; 41,000; Exec. Sec., Evelyn M. Collins.

**Navy Mother's Clubs of America** (1930), P. O. Drawer E, Fremont, Neb. 68025; 25,000; Sec., Mrs. Leona Jacobs.

**Near East College Association** (1926). 548 Fifth Ave., New York, N. Y. 10036; 6 colleges; Sec., William H. Fox.

**Needlework Guild of America** (1885), 124 So. 12th St., Philadelphia, Pa. 19107; 6,399; Exec. Dir., Mildred N. Michener.

**Negro Life and History, Assn. for the Study of** (1915), 1538 Ninth St., N.W., Washington, D. C. 20001; 25,000; Sec., Charles H. Thomas.

**New England Historic Genealogical Society** (Mar. 18, 1845), 101 Newberry St., Boston, Mass. 02116; 3,400; Dir., Edgar P. Dean.

**New England Women, National Society of** (1895), Box 114, Rogers Lake, Old Lyme, Conn. 06371; 2,530; Sec., Lillian P. DuCharme.

**New York Chamber of Commerce** (1768), 65 Liberty St., New York, N. Y. 10005; 1,520; Sec., John T. Gwynne.

**New York Clearing House** (1853), 100 Broad St., N. Y., N. Y. 10004; Sec., John F. Lee.

**New York-New Jersey Trail Conference** (1920), P. O. Box 2250; New York, N. Y. 10001; 15,000; Sec., Mrs. Mary Coen.

**Newspaper Editors, American Society of** (1922), 750 Third Ave., New York, N. Y. 10017; 700; Exec. Sec., Gene Giancarlo.

**Newspaper Enterprise Association** (1902), Editorial, 230 Park Ave., N. Y. C. 10017; Business and Production: 1200 W. 3rd St., Cleveland, O. 44113; Services over 800 newspapers; Pres. and Ed., Boyd Lewis; V. P. and Gen. Mgr., Meade Monroe.

**Newspaper Guild, American, AFL-CIO** (1933), 1126 16th St., N.W., Washington, D. C. 20036; 32,500; in U. S. & Canada; Exec. V. P., William J. Farson.

**Newspaper Promotion Assn., International** (1930), 750 Third Ave., New York, N. Y. 10017; 900; Sec., Gerald J. Rock.

**Newspaper Promotion Assn., National** (1938), 75 Fountain St., Providence, R. I.; 769; Sec., Clifford A. Shaw.

**Newspaper Publishers Assn., American** (1887), 750 Third Ave., New York, N. Y. 10017; 1,018 dailies; Gen. Mgr., Stanford Smith.

**Newspaper Reporters Assn. of NYC** (1948), Hotel New Yorker, 34th and 8th Ave., N. Y., N. Y. 10001; 800; Pres., Tom Poster.

**Newspaper Women's Club of N. Y.** (1924), 54 West 40th St., New York, N. Y. 10018; 200; Pres., Aileen Snoddy.

**Ninety-Fifth Infantry Division Assn.** (1950). P. O. Box 1274; Chicago, Ill. 60690; 2,500; Sec., Theodore S. Nelson.

**Ninety-Nines** (1929), P.O. Box 59964, Will Rogers World Airport, Oklahoma City, Okla. 73159; 3,300; Sec., Mrs. Cornelius Hagan.

**Ninety-ninth Infantry Division Association** (1948), 926 Clark Lane, Des Plaines, Ill. 60016; 650; Pres. Frank Gran.

**Ninety-Sixth Infantry Division Association** (1958), 929 S. Myrtle, Kankakee, Ill. 60901; 7,250; Sec., Richard Klassen.

**Non-Commissioned Officers Assn. of U. S. A.** (1960), 802 Brooklyn, San Antonio, Tex. 78206; 30,000; Sec., Peter F. Butlin.

**Norway, Sons of** (1895), 1455 West Lake St., Minneapolis, Minn. 55408; 45,000; Gen. Mgr., Magne Smedvig.

**Notaries, American Society of** (1965), 1629 K St., N.W., Washington, D. C. 20006; 845; Chmn., Arthur C. Barton, Jr.

**Nuclear Society, American** (1954), 244 East Ogden Ave., Hinsdale, Ill. 60521; 8,000; Exec. Sec., Octave J. Du Temple.

**Numismatic Assn., American** (1891), 818 N. Cascade St., Colorado Springs, Colo. 80901; 27,000; Exec. Dir., Eward Rochette.

**Numismatic Society, American** (1858), Broadway at 155th St., New York, N. Y. 10032; 1,626; Sec., George C. Mills.

**Nurse Education and Service, Natl. Assn. for Practical** (1941), 535 Fifth Ave., N. Y., N. Y. 10017; 30,000; Pres., Rose G. Martin, R.N.

**Nurses' Assn., American** (1896), 10 Columbus Circle, New York, N. Y. 10019; 212,000; Exec. Dir., Mrs. Judith G. Whitaker.

**Nurses, Assn. of Operating Room** (1949), 575 Madison Ave., N. Y., N. Y. 10022; 9,000; Pres., Audrey N. Bell, R.N.

**Nurses, Natl. Fed. of Licensed Practical** (1949), 250 West 57th St., New York, N. Y. 10019; 30,000; Exec. Dir., Etta B. Schmidt.

**Nursing, Natl. League for** (1952), 10 Columbus Circle, New York, N. Y. 10019; 25,000; Sec., Inez Haynes.

**Nut Growers Assn., Northern** (1910), 4518 Holston Hills Rd., Knoxville, Tenn. 37914; 1,059; Sec., Spencer Chase.

—O—

**Occupational Therapy Assn., American** (1917), 251 Park Ave. South, N. Y., N. Y. 10010; 10,000; Exec. Dir., Mrs. Harriet Tiebel.

**Odd Fellows, Ind. Order of** (1819), 16 W. Chase St. Baltimore, Md. 21201; 1,250,000; Gr. Sec., A. Ford Winters.

**Old Guard of City of New York** (1826), 307 W. 91st St., New York, N. Y. 10024; 63; Pres., LTC. Matthew G. Cusack.

**Olympic Committee, U. S.** (1921), 57 Park Ave., N. Y., N. Y. 10016; 219 organizations; Exec. Dir., Arthur G. Lentz.

**Optical Society of America** (1916), 2100 Pennsylvania Ave., N.W., Washington, D. C. 20037; 5,404; Sec., Dr. Mary E. Warga.

**Optimist International** (1919), 4494 Lindell Blvd., St. Louis, Mo. 63108; 100,000; Exec. Sec., Hugh H. Cranford.

**Optometric Assn., American** (1898), 7000 Chippewa St., St. Louis, Mo. 63119; 14,600; Adm. Dir., J. Harold Bailey.

**Oral Surgery, American Society of** (1918), 211 E. Chicago Ave., Chicago, Ill. 60611; 1,745; Exec. Sec., Bernard J. Degen, II.

**Order of Does of the U. S. A. Benevolent, Patriotic** (1921), Omaha, Neb.; 17,650; Supreme Sec., Ellen Erickson.

**Ordnance Assn., American** (1919), 616 Transportation Bldg., Washington, D. C. 20006; 46,000; Sec., Maj. Gen. W. K. Ghormley, Ret.

**Organ, American Academy of** (1949), P. O. Box 714 Mt. Vernon, N. Y. 10551; 1,826; Sec., Roy Anderson.

**Organists, American Guild of** (1896), 630 Fifth Ave., New York, N. Y. 10020; 17,500; Exec. Dir., James E. Bryan.

**Organization of American States** (1890), Pan American Union, 17th & Constitution Ave., N.W., Washington, D. C. 20006; Sec. Gen., Galo Plaza Lasso.

**Oriental Research, Amer. Schools of** (1900), 126 Inman St., Cambridge, Mass. 02139; 2,000; Dr. G. Ernest Wright.

**Oriental Society, American** (1842), 329 Sterling Memorial Library, New Haven, Conn. 06520; 1,669; Sec., Ferris J. Stephens.

**ORT Federation, American (Organization for Rehabilitation through Training)** (1922), 222 Park Ave. South, New York, N. Y. 10003; 80,000; Sec., Charles Kreindler.

**Osteopathic Association, American,** (1897), 212 E. Ohio St., Chicago, Ill. 60611; 10,053; Sec., True B. Everleth.

**Overseas Press Club of America** (1939), 54 West 40th St., New York, N. Y. 10018; 3,400; Pres., Hal Lehrman.

—P—

**Paleontological Research Institution** (1932), 109 Dearnborn Pl., Ithaca, N. Y. 14850; 300; Dir., Kenneth Caster.

**Pan American Society of the U. S.,** (1912), Suite 362, 630 Fifth Ave., New York, N. Y. 10020; 1,000; Sec., Harold E. Montanat.

**Panhellenic Conference, National** (1902), 4261 Palm Lane, Bay Point, Miami, Fla. 33137; 1,350,-000; Chmn., Mrs. George K. Roller.

**Paper Institute, American** (1964), 260 Madison Ave., New York, N. Y. 10016; Pres., Edwin A. Locke, Jr.

**Paper Stationery & Tablet Manufacturers Assn.** (1934), 444 Madison Ave., New York, N. Y. 10022; 40 companies; Exec. Sec., Frank Cowan, Jr.

**Parasitologists, American Society of** (1924), Dept. of Microbiology, U. of Texas Southwestern Medical School, Dallas, Tex. 75235; 1,500; Sec., Dr. Donald V. Moore.

**Parents and Teachers, Natl. Congress of** (Feb. 17, 1897), 700 No. Rush St., Chicago, Ill. 60611; 11,029,396; Sec., Mrs. William C. Baisinger.

**Parking Assn., Natl.** (1951), 1101 17th St., N.W., Washington, D. C. 20036; 1,200; Pres., John Lyon.

**Parkinson's Disease Foundation** (1957), Wm. Black Medical Research Center, 640 W. 168th St., N. Y., N. Y. 10032; Pres., H. Huston Merritt, M.D.

**Parks Association, National** (1919), 1901 18th St., N.W., Washington, D. C. 20009; 38,200; Pres., Anthony W. Smith.

**Pennsylvania Society** (1899), Suite 594, Waldorf-Astoria Hotel, 301 Park Ave., New York, N. Y. 10022; 2,300; Exec. Sec., William P. Doyle.

**P.E.O. Sisterhood** (Jan. 21, 1869), 3700 Grand Ave., Des Moines, Ia. 50312; 162,000; Exec. Sec., Miss Margaret L. Mohler.

**Poetry Day Committee, National** (1949), 1110 North Venetian Dr., Miami Beach, Fla. 33139; 5,000; Natl. Dir., Frances C. Handler.

**Personnel and Guidance Assn., American** (1952), 1607 New Hampshire Ave., N.W., Washington, D. C. 20009; 28,000; Sec., Dr. Willis E. Dugan.

**Petroleum Geologists, American Assn. of** (1917), 1444 So. Boulder, Tulsa, Okla. 74101; 15,088; Pres., J. Ben Carsey.

**Petroleum Institute, American** (1919), 1271 Ave. of the Americas, New York, N. Y. 10020; 7,800; Sec., Willard M. Wilson.

**Pharmaceutical Assn., American** (1852), 2215 Constitution Ave., N.W., Washington, D. C. 20037; 48,000; Exec. Dir., Dr. William S. Apple.

**Pharmaceutical Manufacturers Assn.** (1958), 1155 15th St., N.W., Washington, D. C. 20005; 136 companies; Pres., C. Joseph Stetler.

**Philatelic Americans, Society of** (1894), Box 266, Cincinnati, O. 45201; 5,923; Exec. Sec., Stewart T. Bailey.

**Philatelic Society, American** (Sept. 14, 1886), P. O. Box 800, State College, Pa. 16801; 18,500; Exec. Sec., Col. James T. DeVoss.

**Philharmonic-Symphony Society of New York** (1928 by merger of Philharmonic Soc. of N. Y., estab. 1842, and Symphony Soc. of N. Y., estab. 1787), Philharmonic Hall, Lincoln Center, New York, N. Y. 10023; Man. Dir., Carlos Moseley.

**Philological Assn., American** (1869), Herbert H. Lehman College, 224 Shuster Hall, Bronx, N. Y. 10468; 2,200; Sec., Wm. W. Minton.

**Philological Association of the Pacific Coast,** (1899), Dept. of For. Lgs., San Fernando Valley State College, Northridge, Calif. 91324; 1,057; Sec., R. S. Meyerstein.

**Philosophical Assn., American** (1900), Philosophy Dept., Ohio State Univ., 216 North Oval Dr., Columbus, O. 43210; 2,800; Sec., Robert G. Turnbull.

**Philosophical Society, American** (1743), 104 So. 5th St., Philadelphia, Pa. 19106; 491; Exec. Officer, Dr. George W. Corner.

**Photographers of America, Professional** (1880), 1090 Executive Way, Oak Leaf Commons, Des Plains, Ill. 60018; 11,500; Exec. V. P., Frederick Quellmalz.

**Photographic Society of America** (1935), 2005 Walnut St., Philadelphia, Pa. 19103; 10,800; Exec. Sec., Frederic B. Shaw.

**Physical Therapy Association, American** (1921), 1740 Broadway, N. Y., N. Y. 10019; 12,186; Exec. Dir., Lucy Blair.

**Physics, American Institute of** (1931), 335 East 45th St., New York, N. Y. 10017; 42,000; Sec., Wallace Waterfall.

**Physiological Society, American,** (1887), 9650 Rockville Pike, Bethesda, Md. 20014; 3,067; Exec. Sec., Ray G. Daggs.

**Pilgrim Society** (1820), Pilgrim Hall, 219 Court St., Plymouth, Mass. 02360; 550; Sec., John J. Magee.

**Pilgrims of the United States** (1903), 74 Trinity Pl., New York, N. Y. 10006; 1,000; Sec., Walter S. Marvin.

**Pilot Club International,** (Oct. 18, 1921), Pilot P. O. Box 4844, Macon, Ga. 31208; 14,000; Exec. Dir., Miss Wilda Richardson.

**Planned Parenthood Federation of America** (1921 as Amer. Birth Control League; 1939, Birth Control Fed. of Amer.; renamed 1942), 515 Madison Ave., New York, N. Y. 10022; Chmn., George Lindsay.

**Plastics Engineers, Society of** (1942), 65 Prospect St., Stamford, Conn. 06902; 14,200; Exec. Sec., Colin C. Campbell.

**Plastics Industry, Society of the** (1937), 250 Park Ave., New York, N. Y. 10017; 1,425 companies; Dir., Public Relations, Langdon P. Williams.

**Plattsburg, Society of,** (1935), c/o James N. MacLean, Exec. Dir., 14 Farmstead Lane, Brookville, Long Island, N. Y. 11545.

**Podiatry Association, American,** (1912), 3301 16th St., N.W., Washington, D. C. 20010; 5,000; Exec. Dir., S. P. Nyman, D.S.C.

**Poetry Day Committee, Natl.** (1965), 1110 N. Venetian Dr., Miami Beach, Fla. 33139; 5,000; Natl. Dir., Frances C. Handler.

**Poetry Society, Florida State** (1965), 1110 N. Venetian Dr., Miami Beach, Fla. 33139; 3,000; Sec.-Treas., Frances C. Handler.

**Poetry Society of America,** (1910), 142 E. 35th St., N. Y., N. Y. 10016; 750; Sec., Charles A. Wagner.

**Poets, Academy of American** (1934), 1078 Madison Ave., N. Y., N. Y. 10028; 1,000; Pres., Mrs. Hugh Bullock.

**Polar Society, American** (1934), 98-20 62nd Dr., Apt. 7H, Rego Park, N. Y. 11374; 2,057; Sec., August Howard.

**Police, International Assn. of Chiefs of** (1893), 1319 18th St., N.W., Washington, D. C. 20036; 7,000; Exec. Dir., Quinn Tamm.

**Police Officers Association of America, National,** (1955), 1890 South Tamiami Trail, Venice, Fla. 33595; 17,000; Exec. Dir., Frank J. Schira.

**Polish Army Veterans Assn. of America** (1921), 17 Irving Pl., New York, N. Y. 10003; 12,000; Adj. Gen., Zbigniew A. Konikowski.

**Political Science, Academy of** (1880), Columbia Univ., 413 Fayerweather Hall, New York, N. Y. 10027; 10,000; Sec., Philip E. Mosely.

**Political Science Assn., American** (1903), 1527 New Hampshire Ave., N.W., Washington, D. C. 20036; 15,000; Pres., Dr. Merle Fainsod.

**Political and Social Science, American Academy of** (Dec. 14, 1889), 3937 Chestnut St., Philadelphia, Pa. 19104; 24,000; Pres., Dr. James C. Charlesworth.

**Polo Association, U. S.** (1890), Exec. Plaza, Suite 706, 1301 W. 22nd St., Oak Brook, Ill. 60521; 90 clubs; Sec., Ruthe Pursley.

**Population Assn. of America** (1932), Box 14182, Benjamin Franklin Sta., Washington, D. C. 20044; 1,500; Sec.-Treas., Dr. Anders S. Lunde.

**Portuguese Continental Union of the U. S. A.** (1925), 899 Boyston St., Boston, Mass. 02115; 9,411; Sup. Sec., Anibal S. Branco.

**Postal Clerks, United Federation of** (1906), 817 14th St., N.W., Washington, D. C.; 155,000; Sec., Owen H. Schoon.

**Postmasters of the U. S., National League of,** (1904), 927 Munsey Bldg., Washington, D. C. 20004; 19,500; Pres., Henry H. Womack.

**Poultry Science Assn.** (1908), Dept. of Poultry Science, Texas A & M College, College Station,

Tex. 77843; 1,650; Sec.-Treas., Prof. C. B. Ryan.

**Power Boat Assn., American** (1903), The Whittier, 415 Burns Dr., Detroit, Mich. 48214; 6,164; Exec. Sec., Harry Smith, Jr.

**Power Conference, American** (1938), Illinois Inst. of Technology, 10 W. 32nd St., Chicago, Ill. 60616; Dir., R. A. Budenholzer.

**Power Engineers, National Assn. of** (1882), Suite 1411, 176 W. Adams St., Chicago, Ill. 60603; 12,500; Pres., Edward J. Schuetz.

**Power Squadron, U. S.** (1914), 96 West St., Englewood, N. J. 07631; 70,000; Chief Cmdr., Emery E. Ellis.

**Press Photographers Assn., N. Y.** (1915), 54 W. 40th St., N. Y., N. Y. 10018; 274; Sec., Jack Balletti.

**Press and Radio Club** (1948), P. O. Box 7023, Montgomery, Ala. 36107; 669; Exec. Sec., Charlie Casmus.

**Press Women, National Fed. of** (1934), 206 Ellis St., Kewaunee, Wis. 54216; 2,278; Pres., Ulrich Troubetzkoy.

**Princeton Club of N. Y.** (1899), 15 West 43rd St., New York, N. Y. 10036; 5,350; Sec., R. Leigh Duemler.

**Produce Exchange, New York,** (1862), 2 Broadway, New York, N. Y. 10004; 327; Man. Dir., C. R. Berg.

**Production and Inventory Control Society, American** (1957), Suite 504, Watergate Bldg., 2600 Virginia Ave., N.W., Washington, D. C. 20037; 7,000; Exec. Sec., Robert D. Tapleit.

**Propeller Club of the U. S.** (Nov. 9, 1927), 17 Battery Pl., New York, N. Y. 10004; 12,500; Pres., Floyd H. Blaske.

**Psychiatric Association, American,** (1844), 1700 18th St., N.W., Washington, D. C. 20009; 16,000; Pres., Lawrence C. Kolb, M.D.

**Psychological Assn., American,** (1892), 1200 17th St., N.W., Washington, D. C. 20036; 27,250; Exec. Officer, Arthur H. Brayfield.

**Psychological Assn. for Psychoanalysis, Natl.** (1948), 29 E. 10th St., New York, N. Y. 10003; 120; Sec., Anne Wexler.

**Psychological Minorities, Soc. for the Aid of** (1961), 310 Lexington Ave., New York, N. Y. 10016; 25; Pres., Mrs. Marie Dedouch.

**Psychotherapy Assn., American Group** (1942), 1790 Broadway, Rm. 702; N. Y., N. Y. 10019; 1,984; Admin. Sec., Mrs. Marilyn Schiff.

**Public Education Assn.** (1895), 20 West 40th St., New York, N. Y. 10018; 2,000; Sec., Clarence H. Tompkins.

**Public Health Assn., American** (1872), 1740 Broadway, N. Y., N. Y. 10019; 19,800; Exec. Dir., Dr. Berwyn F. Mattison.

**Public Relations Society of America** (1947), 845 Third Ave., New York, N. Y. 10022; 6,000; Pres., Eward P. Vonder Haar.

**Public Welfare Assn., American** (1930), 1313 E. 60th St., Chicago, Ill. 60637; 1,667 agencies and 8,019 indiv.; Dir., Guy R. Justis.

**Pulp and Paper Industry, Technical Assn. of the** (1915), 360 Lexington Ave., New York, N. Y. 10017; 12,975; Exec. Sec., Philip E. Nethercut.

# —Q & R—

**Racing Assns., Thoroughbred** (1942), 220 East 42nd St., New York, N. Y. 10017.

**Racing Commissioners, National Assn. of State** (1934), P. O. Box 4216, Lexington, Ky. 40504; 175; Sec., Mrs. A. E. Smith.

**Radiological Society of North America** (1915), 713 E. Genesee St., Syracuse, New York 13210; 4,720; Sec., Maurice D. Frazer, M.D.

**Radio Liberty Committee** (1951), 30 East 42nd St., New York, N. Y. 10017; Pres., Howland H. Sargeant.

**Radio Relay League, American** (1914), 225 Main St., Newington, Conn. 06111; 100,000; Sec. John Huntoon.

**Radio and Television Society, International,** (1939), 420 Lexington Ave., N. Y., N. Y. 10017; 1,350; Exec. Dir., Lawrence W. Bruff.

**Radio Union, International Amateur** (1925), 225 Main St., Newington, Conn. 06111; 77; Sec., John Huntoon.

**Railroads, Assn. of American** (1934), Transportation Bldg., 815 17th St., N.W., Washington, D. C. 20006; Sec.-Treas., R. E. Keefer.

**Railway Engineering Assn., American** (July 14, 1899), 59 E. Van Buren St., Chicago, Ill. 60605; 3,500; Sec., E. W. Hodgkins.

**Rainbow Division Veterans, National** **'Assn.** (1919), P. O. Box 342, Roanoke, Va. 24003; 5,535; Sec., R. Allen Gibbons.

**Real Estate Boards, Natl. Assn. of** (1908), 155 E. Superior St., Chicago, Ill. 60611; 85,000; Exec. V. P., Eugene P. Conser.

**Real Estate Investment Funds, Natl. Assn. of** (1960), P. O. Drawer 1227, Darien, Conn. 06820; 104; Exec. Dir., Robert M. Burr.

**Record Industry Assn. of America** (1952), 1 East

57th St., New York, N. Y. 10022; 43 firms; Exec. Sec., Henry Brief.

**Recreation and Park Assn., Natl.** (1906), 1700 Pennsylvania Ave., N.W., Washington, D. C. 20006; 14,000; Sec., Dr. Sal J. Prezioso.

**Red Cross, American National** (May 21, 1881), 17th & D Sts., N.W., Washington, D. C. 20006; 30,463,700; Pres., James F. Collins.

**Red Men, Improved Order of, Greater Council of U. S.** (1847), 1525 West Ave., Waco, Tex. 76703; 77,790; Sec., Carl R. Lemke.

**Regional Plan Assn.** (1922), 230 West 41st St., New York, N. Y. 10036; 1,250; Pres., C. McKim Norton.

**Rehabilitation Assn., Natl.** (1925), 1522 K St., N.W., Washington, D. C. 20005; 28,000; Exec. Dir., E. B. Whitten.

**Religion, American Academy of** (1909), Wilson Coll., Chambersburg, Pa. 17201; 2,509; Sec., Dr. Milo Milanovich.

**Renaissance Society of America** (1954), 1161 Amsterdam Ave., New York, N. Y. 10027; 3,200; Exec. Dir., William Nelson.

**Reserve Officers Assn. of the U. S.** (1922), 1 Constitution Ave., N.E., Washington, D. C. 20002; 56,000; Exec. Dir., Col. John T. Carlton, USAR.

**Resources Council of America, Natural** (1947), Office of the Secretary, 709 Wire Bldg., Washington, D. C. 20005; 30 societies; Sec., Daniel A. Poole.

**Restaurant Assn., Natl.** (1919), 1530 Lake Shore Dr., Chicago, Ill. 60610; 13,000; Sec., Donald Grant.

**Retail Druggists, National Assn. of** (1898), 1 East Wacker Dr., Chicago, Ill. 60601; 36,000; Exec. Sec., Willard R. Simmons.

**Retail Grocers, National Association of** (1893), 360 North Michigan Ave., Chicago, Ill. 60601; 44,000; Exec. Dir., Frank D. Register.

**Retail Merchants Assn., National** (1911), 100 West 31st St., New York, N. Y. 10001; 14,000 retail stores; Exec. V. P., James J. Bliss.

**Retarded Children, Natl. Assn. for,** (1950), 420 Lexington Ave., N. Y., N. Y. 10017; 122,000; Pres., Mrs. Philip Elkin.

**Retired Officers Assn.,** (1929), 1625 Eye St., N.W., Washington, D. C. 20006; 94,000; Sec., RAdm. Howard L. Collins.

**Retired Persons, American Assn. of** (1958), The Andrus Bldg., 215 Long Beach Blvd., Long Beach, Calif. 90802; 1,250,000; Pres., George W. Schluderberg.

**Retired Teachers Assn., Natl.** (1947), Andrus Bldg., 215 Long Beach Blvd., Long Beach, Calif. 90802; 215,000; Pres., Cecelia O'Neil.

**Retreads** (1947), 40–07 154th St., Flushing, N. Y. 11354; 1,200; Natl. Adjt., Elmer H. Braun.

**Revolver Assn., U. S.** (1900), 59 Alvin St., Springfield, Mass. 01104; 1,500; Exec. Sec., Stanley A. Sprague.

**Rhodes Scholars, Assn. of American** (1907), 1100 Phila. Natl. Bank Bldg., Philadelphia, Pa. 19107; 1,500; Sec., Jack B. Justice.

**Rifle Assn. of America, Natl.** (1871), 1600 Rhode Island Ave., N.W., Washington, D. C. 20036.

**Road Builders Assn., American** (1902), 525 School St., S.W., Washington, D. C. 20024; 5,400; Pres., Robert S. Holmes.

**Rodeo Cowboys Assn.** (1936), 2929 W. 19th Ave., Denver, Colo. 80204; 11,000; Sec., Gene Pruett.

**Roller Skating Rink Operators Assn. of America** (1937), 20600 Woodward, Detroit, Mich. 48203; 600 rinks; Sec., Charles E. Cahill.

**Rose Society, American** (1899), 4048 Roselea Pl., Columbus, O. 43214; 17,500; Exec. Sec., O. Keister Evans, Jr.

**Rosicrucian Fraternity** (1614 in Germany, 1859 in U. S.), Beverly Hall, Quakertown, Pa. 18951; Pres., Emerson M. Clymer.

**Rosicrucian Order, AMORC** (1915), Rosicrucian Park, San Jose, Calif. 95114; 120,000; Sec., A. C. Piepenbrink.

**Rosicrucians, Society of** (1909), 321 West 101st St., New York, N. Y. 10025; Pres., Mrs. G. E. S. DeWitow.

**Rotary International** (1905), 1600 Ridge Ave., Evanston, Ill. 60201; 631,633; Gen. Sec., G. R. Means.

**Round Table International** (1922), 279 Bayview Ave., San Jose, Calif. 95127; 1,000; Exec. Dir., Eugene A. Silva.

**Rowing Assn., Intercollegiate** (1895), Hotel Manhattan, 8th Ave. at 44th St., New York, N. Y. 10036; Sec., Asa S. Bushnell.

**Royal Arcanum, Supreme Council of the** (June 23, 1877), 61 Batterymarch St., Boston, Mass. 02110; 34,036; Supr. Regent, J. Paul Masse.

**Rubber Manufacturers Assn.,** (1915), 444 Madison Ave., New York, N. Y. 10022; 172 firms; Sec., Charles C. Miller.

**Ruritan National** (1928), Box 487, Dublin, Va. 24084; 32,210; Exec. Sec., Russell Burgess.

**Russian Orthodox Clubs, Federated** (1927), 84 East Market St., Wilkes Barre, Pa. 18701; 4,887; Sec., Helen R. Russin.

## —S—

**Safety Council, National** (Oct. 13, 1913), 425 No. Michigan Ave., Chicago, Ill. 60611; 10,000 companies, organizations and individuals; Sec. H. W. Champlin.

**Safety Engineers, American Society of** (1911), 850 Busse Highway, Park Ridge, Ill. 60068; 9,000; Sec., A. C. Blackman.

**St. Andrew's Society of the State of N. Y.** (1756), 281 Park Ave. South, New York, N. Y. 10010; 1,137; Rec. Sec., Walter P. Marshall.

**St. David's Society of the State of N. Y.** (1835), 71 West 23rd St., New York, N. Y. 10010; 275; Sec., W. C. W. James.

**St. George's Society of N. Y.** (1770), 15 East 26th St., New York, N. Y. 10010; 900; Exec. Sec., H. J. Mitchell.

**St. Paul, National Guilds of** (1937), 601 Hill N' Dale, Lexington, Ky. 40503; 12,960; Dir., Rt. Rev. Msgr. Leonard B. Nienaber.

**Sales Executives Club of N. Y.** (1932), Hotel Roosevelt, Madison Ave. at 45th St., New York N. Y. 10017; 3,500; Sec., Harry R. White.

**Save-the-Redwoods League** (1918), 114 Sansome St., San Francisco, Calif. 94104; 40,000; Sec., Newton B. Drury.

**Savings and Loan League, U. S.** (1892), 221 No. LaSalle St., Chicago, Ill. 60601; 5,058; Exec. V. P., Norman Strunk.

**School Administrators, American Assn. of** (1865), 1201 16th St., N.W., Washington, D. C. 20036; 17,000; Exec. Sec., Dr. Forrest E. Conner.

**School Boards Assn., Natl.** (1940), 1233 Central St., Evanston, Ill. 60201; 85,000; Sec., Kenneth E. Buhrmaster.

**School, College and University Staffing, Assn. for** (1934), Box G, Hershey, Pa. 17033; Sec., Dr. Aubrey L. Berry.

**School Garden Assn. of New York** (1908), 70 Mulberry St., New York, N. Y. 10013; 8,000; Sec., Antoinette E. Fusco.

**School Principals, Natl. Assn. of Secondary** (1916), 1201 16th St., N.W., Washington, D. C. 20036; 35,292; Exec. Sec., Ellsworth Tompkins.

**Schools and Colleges, American Council on** (1927), P. O. Box 1252, York, Pa. 17405; 93 schools; Sec., Dr. Wilbur Lyons.

**Schools & Colleges Association, American** (1910), Suite 2007, One Rockefeller Plaza, New York, N. Y. 10020; Pres., Kenneth Beebe.

**Schools of Music, Natl. Assn. of** (1924), 1424 16th St., N. W., Washington, D. C. 20036; 320 schools; Exec. Sec., Dr. David A. Ledet.

**Science, American Assn. for the Advancement of** (1848), 1515 Massachusetts Ave., N.W., Washington, D. C. 20005; 125,000; Exec. Off., Dael Wolfle.

**Science Clubs of America** (1941), 1719 N St., N.W., Washington, D. C. 20036; 28,000 groups; Exec. Sec., Lloyd Ulmer.

**Science Service** (1941), 1719 N. St., N.W., Washington, D. C. 20036; 25,000 in affiliated groups; Dir., E. G. Sherburne.

**Science Teachers Assn., Natl.** (1944), 1201 16th St., N. W., Washington, D. C. 20036; 22,000; Exec. Sec., Robert H. Carleton.

**Science Writers, Natl. Assn. of** (1934), 75 Bayview Ave., Port Washington, N. Y. 11050; 830; Sec., Mrs. Howard W. Blakeslee.

**Sciences, Maryland Academy of,** (1797), 7 West Mulberry St., Baltimore, Md. 21201; 1,800; Dir., Nigel O'C. Wolff.

**Sciences, National Academy of—National Research Council** (1863), 2101 Constitution Ave., N.W., Washington, D. C. 20418; 745; Pres., Dr. Frederick Seitz.

**Sciences, New York Academy of** (1817), 2 East 63rd St., New York, N. Y. 10021; 24,417; Exec. Dir., Edwin S. Schanze.

**Scientific Apparatus Makers Association** (1918), 1140 Connecticut Ave., N.W., Washington, D. C. 20036; 230 companies; Pres., Herbert J. Mossien.

**Scottish Clans, Order of, Royal Clan** (Nov. 30, 1878), 38 Chauncey St., Boston, Mass. 02111; 12,840; Royal Sec., William Slater.

**Sculpture Society, Natl.** (1893), 250 E. 51st St., New York, N. Y. 10022; 350; Pres., Frank Eliscu.

**Seamen's Service, United** (1942), 17 Battery Place, N. Y., N. Y. 10004; Exec. Dir., Edward J. Sette.

**Secretaries Assn., National** (1942), 1103 Grand Ave., Suite 410, Kansas City, Mo. 64118; 26,000; Exec. Sec., Mrs. Lillian C. Martino.

**Security Industrial Assn., National** (Sept., 1944), 1030 15th St., N.W., Washington, D. C. 20005; 410 corporations; Pres., V. Adm. Joseph M. Lyle.

**Seeing Eye, The** (Jan. 29, 1929), Morristown, N. J. 07960; 18,000; Exec. V. P., George Werntz, Jr.

**Sertoma International** (1912), 3200 Broadway, Kansas City, Mo. 64111; 24,500; Man. Dir., George B. Williams.

**Settlements and Neighborhood Centers, Natl.**

**Federation of,** (1911), 232 Madison Ave., N. Y., N. Y. 10016; 411 agencies; Exec. Sec., Frederick B. Taylor.

**77th Division Assn.** (1921), 28 East 39th St., New York, N. Y. 10016; 25,000; Sec., Charles Rist.

**Sheriffs Assn., Natl.** (1940), Suite 209, 1250 Connecticut Ave., N.W., Washington, D. C. 20036; 23,500; Exec. Dir., Ferris E. Lucas.

**Shipbuilders Council of America** (1921), 1730 K St., N.W., Washington, D. C. 20006; 40; Sec., E. P. Ruddy.

**Shoe Retailers Assn., Natl.** (1912), 200 Madison Ave., New York, N. Y. 10016; 3,000 store units; Exec. V. P., Edward J. McDonald.

**Showmen's Assn., National** (1938), 123 West 56th St., New York, N. Y. 10019; 600; Exec. Sec., Ethel Weinberg.

**Showmen's League of America** (1913); 300 West Randolph St., Chicago, Ill. 60606; 1,500; Sec., Henry N. Shelby.

**Shrine, Imperial Council of the A. A. Order of Nobles of the Mystic** (1876), 323 No. Michigan Ave., Chicago, Ill. 60601.

**Sierra Club** (1892), 1050 Mills Tower, 220 Bush St., San Francisco, Calif. 94104; 62,000; Sec., George Marshall.

**Silurians, Society of the** (1924), 405 Lexington Ave., New York, N. Y. 10017; 700; Exec. Sec., Charles Speaks.

**Simpler Spelling Assn.** (1876), Lake Placid Club, N. Y. 12946; 100; Sec., Godfrey Dewey.

**Skate-Sailing Assn. of America** (1922), 548 Herrick Dr., Dover, N. J. 07801; 100; Sec., Basil Kamener.

**Skeet Shooting Assn., National** (1946), 212 Linwood Bldg., 2608 Inwood Rd., Dallas, Texas 75235; 15,325; Pres., Edward Docherty.

**Ski Assn., United States,** (1904), The Broadmoor Hotel, Colorado Springs, Colo. 80906; 100,243; Exec. Sec., Gloria C. Chadwick.

**Small Business Assn.** (1937), 1225 19th St., N.W., Washington, D. C. 20036; 30,000; Pres., Carl A. Beck.

**Soaring Society of America** (1932), P.O. Box 66071, Los Angeles, Calif. 90066; Exec. Dir., Lloyd M. Licher.

**Social Health Assn., American** (1914), 1740 Broadway, New York, N. Y. 10019; 1,700; Sec., Joyce Yerwood.

**Social Science Research Council** (1923), 230 Park Ave., New York, N. Y. 10017; 30; Vice Pres., Paul Webbink.

**Social Sciences, Natl. Institute of** (1865), P. O. Box 251, Lenox Hill Station, N. Y., N. Y. 10021; 650; Sec., Mary C. Flynn.

**Social Welfare, Internatl. Council on** (1928), 345 E. 46th St., New York, N. Y. 10017; Exec. Dir., Kate Katzki.

**Social Welfare, Natl. Conference on** (1874), 22 West Gay St., Columbus, Ohio 43215; 8,500; Exec. Sec., Joe R. Hoffer.

**Social Work Education, Council on** (1952), 345 East 46th St., New York, N. Y. 10017; 4,300; Exec. Dir., Harry N. Sachs.

**Social Workers, National Assn. of** (1955), 2 Park Ave., New York, N. Y. 10016; 50,000; Exec. Dir., Joseph P. Anderson.

**Sociological Assn., American** (1905), 1001 Connecticut Ave., N.W., Washington, D. C. 20036; 12,300; Pres., Philip M. Hauser.

**Softball Assn., Amateur** (1934), 1351 Skirvin Tower, Oklahoma City, Okla. 73102; 6,500,000; Exec. Sec., D. E. Porter.

**Soft Drink Assn., National** (1919), 1128 16th St., N.W., Washington, D. C. 20036; 2,400; Exec. V. P., Thomas F. Baker.

**Soil Conservation Soc. of America** (1946), 7515 N.E. Ankeny Rd., Ankeny, Iowa 50021; 12,056; Exec. Sec., H. Wayne Pritchard.

**Soil Science Soc. of America** (1936), 677 S. Segoe Rd., Madison, Wis. 53711; 3,581; Exec. Sec., Matthias Stelly.

**Sojourners, National** (1919), 711 14th St., N.W., Washington, D. C. 20005; 11,000; Sec., CWO Melvin W. Byers.

**Soldier, Sailors and Airmen's Club** (1919), 283 Lexington Ave., N. Y., N. Y. 10016; Sec., Mrs. DeSales Harrison Jr.

**Sons of the American Legion** (1932), The American Legion, P. O. Box 1055, Indianapolis, Ind. 46206; 20,000; Coordinator, C. L. Johnson.

**Sons of the American Revolution, National Society** (Apr. 30, 1889), 2412 Massachusetts Ave., N.W., Washington, D. C. 20008; 19,986; Exec. Sec., Warren S. Woodward.

**Sons of Poland, Assn. of the** (1903), 665 Newark Ave., Jersey City, N. J. 07306; 16,000; Sec., Alexander Sudnik.

**Sons of the Revolution in the State of N. Y.** (1876), Fraunces Tavern, 54 Pearl St., New York, N. Y. 10004; 1,500; Pres., George E. Doty.

**Sons of Sherman's March to the Sea** (1966), 1725 Farmer Ave., Tempe, Arizona 85281; 30; Natl. Dir., Stan Schirmacher.

**Sons of Union Veterans of the Civil War** (1881), P. O. Box 24, Federal Bldg., Gettysburg, Pa. 17325; 3,300; Sec., Chester S. Shriver.

**Soroptimist Federation of the Americas** (1921), 1616 Walnut St., Philadelphia, Pa. 19036; 26,000; Pres., Ethel F. Lord.

**Southern Christian Leadership Conference** (1957), Atlanta, Ga. 30304; 300 affiliate organizations; Pres., Rev. Ralph D. Abernathy.

**Southern Regional Council** (1944), 5 Forsyth St., N.W., Atlanta, Ga. 30303; 100; Exec. Dir., Paul Anthony.

**Southern Society, N. Y.** (1886), Plaza Hotel, Fifth Ave. at 59th St., New York, N. Y. 10019; 900; Exec. Sec., Harvey L. Clinkscales.

**Spanish War Veterans, United** (1898), 810 Vermont Ave., Washington, D. C. 20013; 3,541; Adj. Gen., James H. McElroy.

**Speech Assn. of America** (1914), Statler Hilton Hotel, New York, N. Y. 10001; 7,000; Exec. Sec., William Work.

**Speech and Hearing Assn., American** (1925), 9030 Old Georgetown Rd., Washington, D. C. 20014; 13,000; Exec. Sec., Kenneth O. Johnson.

**Speleological Society, Natl.** (1941), 2318 No. Kenmore St., Arlington, Va. 22201; 3,500; Pres., John A. Stellmack.

**Sports Fans of America, Professional** (1962), 22880 Chardon Rd., Cleveland, Ohio 44117; 84; Sec., E. Allan Anderson.

**Stamp Dealers' Association, American** (1914), 116 Nassau St., New York, N. Y. 10038; 1,100; Pres., Phillip Robbins.

**Standards Institute, U. S. of America** (1918), 10 East 40th St., New York, N. Y. 10016; Sec., Donald L. Peyton.

**State & Local History, American Assn. of** (1940), 132 9th Ave., No., Nashville, Tenn 37203; 3,208; Dir., William T. Alderson Jr.

**State Budget Officers, Natl. Assn. of** (1944), c/o Council of State Governments, 1313 East 60th St., Chicago, Ill. 60637; Sec., George A. Bell.

**State Communities Aid Assn.** (1872), 105 E. 22nd St., New York, N. Y. 10010; 255; Exec. Dir., Gordon E. Brown.

**State Governments, Council of** (1933), 1313 East 60th St., Chicago, Ill. 60637; Exec. Dir., Brevard Crihfield.

**State Parks, Natl. Conference on** (1921), 1700 Pennsylvania Ave., N.W., Washington, D. C. 20005; 500; Exec. Sec., Ben H. Thompson.

**State Universities and Land-Grant Colleges, National Assn. of** (1887), 1785 Massachusetts Ave., N.W., Washington, D. C. 20036; 99 institutions; Exec. Sec., Russell I. Thackrey.

**Statistical Assn., American** (1839), 810 18th St., N.W., Washington, D. C. 20006; 10,000; Exec. Dir., John W. Lehman.

**Steamship Historical Society of America** (1935), 4 Broad St., Staten Island, N. Y. 10304; 1,269; Sec., Mrs. Alice S. Wilson.

**Steel Construction, American Institute of** (1921), 101 Park Ave., New York, N. Y. 10017; 300; Sec., M. Harvey Smedley.

**Steel Founders Society of America** (1902), 21010 Center Ridge Road, Rocky River, Ohio 44116; 127 foundries; Sec., T. E. Barlow.

**Steeplechase and Hunt Assn., Natl.** (1895), Box 308, Elmont, N. Y. 11003; 101; Exec. Sec., John E. Cooper.

**Sterilization, Association for Voluntary** (1937), 14 W. 40th St., N. Y., N. Y. 10018; Pres., H. W. Stinson, M.D.

**Steuben Society of America** (1919), 369 Lexington Ave., New York, N. Y. 10017; Exec. Sec., Edward J. Sussman.

**Stock Exchange, American** (1849), 86 Trinity Pl., New York, N. Y. 10006.

**Stock Exchange, Midwest** (1882), 120 So. LaSalle St., Chicago, Ill. 60603; 423; Sec., John G. Weithers.

**Stock Exchange, N. Y.** (May 17, 1792), 11 Wall St., New York, N. Y. 10005; 1,366; Sec., John J. Mulcahy.

**Stock Exchange, Pacific Coast** (Jan. 2, 1957 by amalgamation of San Francisco Stock Exch., estab. 1882 and Los Angeles Stock Exch., estab. 1899), 301 Pine St., San Francisco 4, Calif.

**Stock Exchange, Philadelphia-Baltimore-Washington** (1790), 17th St. and Stock Exchange Pl., Philadelphia, Pa. 19103; 216; Sec., Charles L. Wilson.

**Student Assn., U. S. National** (1947). 2115 S St., N.W., Washington, D. C. 20008; 340 schools; Pres., Edward A. Schwartz.

**Student Councils, National Assn. of** (1931), 1201 16th St., N.W., Washington, D. C. 20036; 9,800 high schools; Sec., Dr. Ellsworth Tompkins.

**Sugar Brokers Assn., National** (1903), 79 Wall St., Room 205, N. Y., N. Y. 10005; 340; Exec. Sec., Mrs. Josephine R. Koop.

**Sunbathing Assn., American** (1936), 6 East Main St., Mays Landing, N. J. 08330; 15,000; Exec. Dir.,

Rose Holroyd.

**Sunday League** (1932), 279 Highland Ave., Newark, N. J. 07104; 25,000; Gen. Sec., R. S. Womer.

**Sunday School Union, American** (1817), 1816 Chestnut St., Philadelphia, Pa. 19103; 1,586 Sunday Schools; Dir. Pub. Rel., Paul E. Almquist.

**Surveying and Mapping, American Congress on** (1941), 430 Woodward Bldg., 733 15th St., N.W., Washington, D. C. 20005; 6,000; Exec. Sec., Walter S. Dix.

**Symphony Orchestra League, American** (1942), P. O. Box 66, Vienna, Va. 22180; 2,105; Exec. V. P., Helen M. Thompson.

**Systems & Procedures Assn.** (1947), 24587 Bagley Rd., Cleveland, Ohio 44138; 7,500; Exec. Dir., Richard L. Irwin.

## —T—

**Table Tennis Assn., United States** (1933), Box 8587, Kensington Sta., Detroit, Mich. 48224; 10,000; Pres., Graham B. Steenhoven.

**Tax Accountants, Natl. Assn. of Enrolled Federal** (1930), 162 N. Clinton St., Chicago, Ill. 60606; Exec. Sec., Seymour Rish.

**Tax Administrators, Natl. Assn. of** (1937), 1313 East 60th St., Chicago, Ill. 60637; Exec. Dir., Charles F. Conlon.

**Tax Assn., National** (1907), 100 East Broad St., Columbus, Ohio 43215; 2,000; Exec. Dir., Stanley J. Bowers.

**Tax Inst. of America** (1932), 457 Nassau St., Princeton, N. J. 08540; 1,000; Sec., Mabel Walker.

**Tea Assn. of the U. S. A.** (1899), 10 E. 56th St., N. Y., N. Y. 10022; 115; Sec., Teresa K. Kulka.

**Teachers Agencies, Natl. Assn. of** (1915), 64 E. Jackson Blvd., Rm. 400, Chicago, Ill. 60604; 53 agencies; Sec., Charles A. Lutton.

**Teachers, American Federation of** (1916), 1012 14th St., N.W., Washington, D. C. 20005; 150,000; Sec., Robert G. Porter.

**Teachers of English, Natl. Council of** (1911), 508 So. 6th St., Champagne, Ill. 61820; 131,602; Exec. Sec., Robert F. Hogan.

**Teachers of French, Amer. Assn. of** (1927), Eastern Michigan Univ., Ypsilanti, Mich. 48197; 11,000; Sec. J. Henry Owens.

**Teachers of Spanish and Portuguese, Assn. of** (1917), Wichita State Univ., Wichita, Kansas 67208; 13,000; Sec., Eugene Savaiano.

**Technical Writers and Publishers, Society of** (1958), 1010 Vermont Ave., N.W., Suite 421, Washington, D. C. 20005; 4,000; Pres., Joseph Godfrey.

**Television Arts and Sciences, National Academy of** (1957), 54 West 40th St., New York, N. Y. 10018; and 7188 Sunset Blvd., Hollywood, Calif. 90046; 6,000; Exec. Sec., Peter Cott.

**Telluride Assn.** (1911), 217 West Ave., Ithaca, N. Y. 14850; 89; Exec. Sec., Beatrice MacLeod.

**Tennis Assn., U. S. Lawn** (May 21, 1881), 51 E. 42nd St., New York, N. Y. 10017; 2,500 clubs; Exec. Sec., Robert S. Platt.

**Testing and Materials, American Society for** (1898), 1916 Race St., Philadelphia, Pa. 19103; 15,500; Exec. Sec., T. A. Marshall, Jr.

**Textile Association, Northern** (1854), 211 Congress St., Boston, Mass. 02110; 300; Sec., Daniel D. Gordon.

**Textile Manufacturers Institute, American** (1949), 1501 Johnston Bldg., Charlotte, N. C. 28202; Sec., F. S. Love.

**Theatre and Academy, American National** (1935), 245 West 52nd St., New York, N. Y. 10019; 3,500; Pres., Walter Abel.

**Theodore Roosevelt Assn.** (1920), 28 East 20th St., New York, N. Y. 10003; Pres., Elisha Dyer.

**Theological Library Assn., Amer.** (1947), Fisher Library-Asbury Theological Seminary, Wilmore, Ky. 40390; Exec. Sec., Susan A. Schultz.

**Theological Schools, Amer. Assn. of** (1918), 534 Third National Bldg., Dayton, Ohio 45402; 156 schools; Exec. Dir., Jesse H. Ziegler.

**Theosophical Society in America** (1886), 1926 North Main St., Wheaton, Ill. 60187; 4,000; Natl. Sec., Mrs. Ann Wylie.

**37th Division Veterans Assn.** (1920), 21 W. Broad St., Columbus, Ohio 43215; 5,000; Exec. Sec., Jack C. Wander.

**Thoreau Society** (1941), State Univ. College, Geneseo, N. Y. 14454; 900; Sec., Walter Harding.

**Thoroughbred Racing Assn.** (1942), 220 E. 42nd St., New York, N. Y. 10017; 54 race tracks; Exec. V. Pres., Wathen Knebelkamp.

**Toastmasters International** (1932), 2200 North Grand Ave., Santa Ana, Calif. 92711; 73,600; Mgr. of World Hdqt., Robert T. Engle.

**Tool and Manufacturing Engineers, American Soc. of,** (1932), 20501 Ford Rd., Dearborn, Michigan 48128; 40,031; Pres., Robert M. Johnson.

**Topical Assn., American** (1949), 3306 North 50th St., Milwaukee, Wis. 53216; 8,000; Exec. Sec., Jerome Husak.

**Torch Clubs, International Assn. of** (1924), 508 Dougherty Hall, Univ. of Tenn., Knoxville, Tenn. 37916; 6,000; Sec., Robert H. Nagel.

**Toy Manufacturers of the U. S. A.** (1916), 200 Fifth Ave., New York, N. Y. 10010; 320 firms; Pres., William R. McLain.

**Trade Relations Council** (1885), 1001 Connecticut Ave., N.W., Washington, D.C. 20036; 100; Sec., J. Joseph Whelan.

**Traffic and Transportation, American Society of** (1946), 22 West Madison St., Chicago, Ill. 60602; 2,100; Pres., Dr. L. L. Waters.

**Traffic Engineers, Institute of** (1930), 2029 K St., N.W., Washington, D. C. 20006; 3,500; Pres., David M. Baldwin.

**Training Corps, American** (1961), 107-12 Jamaica Ave., Richmond Hill, N. Y. 11418; 600; Comdt., Capt. Paul E. Kendall.

**Training & Development, American Society of** (1943), P. O. Box 5307, 313 Price Pl., Madison, Wis. 53706; 8,000; Exec. Dir., Gordon M. Bliss.

**Transit Assn., Amer.** (1882), 815 Connecticut Ave., N.W., Washington, D. C. 20006; 422; Gen. Sec. Robert Sloan.

**Transportation Assn. of America,** (1935), 1101 17th St., N.W., Washington, D. C. 20036; 1,600; Sec., Robert E. Redding.

**Trapshooting Assn. of America, Amateur** (1924), P. O. Box 246, 601 W. National Rd., Vandalia, Ohio 45377; 50,000; Sec., Clayton Bond.

**Travel Agents, American Society of** (1931), 360 Lexington Ave., New York, N. Y. 10017; 7,887; Pres., Gordon R. Girvan.

**Travel Organizations, Natl. Assn. of** (1941), 1100 Connecticut Ave., N.W., Washington, D. C. 20036; 800 firms; Exec. Dir., James C. Gross.

**Travelers Aid Assn. of America** (1917), 44 East 23rd St., New York, N. Y. 10010; 87 societies; Gen. Dir., Paul W. Guyler.

**Travelers Aid Society of N. Y.** (1905), 204 East 39th St., New York, N. Y. 10016; 4,583; Sec., Mrs. A. Perry Osborn.

**Travelers International** (1943), P. O. Box 2, Delanson, N. Y. 12053; 10,688; Pres., Roy A. Carson.

**Trial Lawyers, American College of,** (1950), 10889 Wilshire Blvd., Los Angeles, Calif. 90024; 1,803; Pres., Joseph A. Ball.

**Trotting Assn., U. S.** (1939), 750 Michigan Ave., Columbus, Ohio 43215; 26,774; Pub. Rel. Dir., Larry Evans.

**Trucking Assns., American** (1933), 1616 P St., N.W., Washington, D. C. 20005; 50 state associations; Pres., J. David Brothers.

**True Sisters, United Order of** (April 21, 1846), 150 West 85th St., New York, N. Y. 10024; 13,500; Natl. Sec., Rosalle Donahue.

**Tuberculosis and Respiratory Disease Assn., Natl.** (1904), 1740 Broadway, N. Y., N. Y. 10019; Man. Dir., Dr. James E. Perkins.

**Turf and Field Club** (1895), 300 Park Ave., New York, N. Y. 10022; 600; Sec., Miss W. Helen Eden.

**Turners, American** (1848), 1550 Clinton Ave., No. Rochester, N. Y. 14621; 17,927; Sec., Dr. E. A. Eklund.

## —U—

**Unbiased Women, League of** (1956), Box 1043, Nevada City, Calif. 95959; 4,893; Pres., Lizzie Glotzmier.

**Unidentified Flying Objects, Natl. Investigations Comm.** (1967), 7970 Woodman Ave., Van Nuys, Calif. 91402; 701; Pres., Dr. Frank E. Stranges.

**United Nations Association of the U. S. A.,** (1923 as League of Nations Assn.; renamed 1945), 345 East 46th St., New York, N. Y. 10017; 62,000; Sec., Miss Anna Lord Strauss.

**United Press International** (1907, formerly United Press Assns.; renamed 1958 after merger with International News Service), 220 East 42d St., New York, N. Y. 10017.

**United Service Organizations** (Feb. 4, 1941), 237 East 42nd St., New York, N. Y. 10022; Sec., Mrs. Frances T. Christy.

**United States Army, Assn. of the** (1892), 1529 18th St., N.W., Washington, D. C. 20036; 105,000; Sec., Col. Arthur Symons, USAR (Ret.).

**Universities, Assn. of American** (1900), 1785 Massachusetts Ave., N.W., Washington, D. C. 20036; 44 universities; Exec. Sec., Charles P. McCurdy, Jr.

**University Club** (1865), 1 West 54th St., New York, N. Y. 10019; 4,281; Sec., A. Fairfield Dana.

**University Professors, American Assn. of** (1915), 1785 Massachusetts Ave., N.W., Washington, D. C. 20036; 92,000; Gen. Sec., Dr. Bertram H. Davis.

**University Women, American Assn. of** (1882), 2401 Virginia Ave., N.W., Washington, D. C. 20037; 177,000; Pres., Dr. Anne G. Pannell.

**Urban League, National** (1910), 55 East 52nd St., New York, N. Y. 10022; Exec. Dir., Whitney M. Young, Jr.

**Urological Association, American** (1902), 1120 N. Charles St., Baltimore, Md. 21201; 2,230; Exec. Dir., Dr. Wyland F. Leadbetter.

—V—

**Vegetable Growers Assn. of America,** (1908), Suite 226, Transportation Bldg., 815 17th St., N.W., Washington, D. C. 20006; 841; Sec., A. E. Mercker.

**Veteran Corps of Artillery, S.N.Y., Constituting the Military Soc. of the War of 1812** (1790), 7th Regiment Armory, 643 Park Ave., N. Y., N. Y. 10021; 180; Adj., Capt. George Brower.

**Veteran Motor Car Club of America** (1938), 15 Newton St., Brookline, Mass. 02146; 3,500; Sec., J. Byron Hull.

**Veterans Committee, American** (1943), 1830 Jefferson Pl., N.W., Washington, D. C. 20036; 25,000; Exec Dir., June A. Willenz.

**Veterans of Foreign Wars of the U. S.** (1899), V.F.W. Bldg., Broadway at 34th St., Kansas City Mo. 64111; 1,800,000; Adjt. Gen., Julian Dickenson.

**Ladies Auxiliary to the VFW,** (1914), 406 W. 34th St., Kansas City, Mo. 64111; 400,000; Sec., Mrs. Hazel Miller.

**Veterans of World War I of the U. S. A.** (1949), 40 G St., N.E., Washington, D. C. 20002; 228,551; Natl. Adjt., W. Ed. Hudson.

**Veterinary Medical Assn., American** (1863), 600 So. Michigan Ave., Chicago, Ill. 60605; 19,000; Exec. Sec., M. R. Clarkson.

**Victorian Society in America** (1966), 44 West 9th St., Rm. 20, New York, N. Y. 10011; 612; Sec., Margot Gayle.

**Village Neighborhood Committee** (1959), 44 W. 9th St., Rm. 20, New York, N. Y. 10011; 50; Chmn., Margot Gayle.

**Vocational Assn., American** (1921), 1025 15th St., N.W., Washington, D. C. 20005; 50,000; Exec. Dir., Lowell A. Burkett.

**Volleyball Assn., U. S.** (1923), 224 East 47th St., New York, N. Y. 10017; 500; Sec. W. H. Peck.

**Volunteer Civic Association** (1963), P. O. Box 323; Babelay Rd., Knoxville, Tenn. 37014; 300; Exec. Dir., V. Campbell Smith.

—W—

**Walther League** (1893). 875 No. Dearborn St., Chicago, Ill. 60610; 100,000; Exec. Sec., Dean C. Kell.

**War Dads Auxiliary, American** (1945), 304 Scarritt Arcade Bldg., Kansas City, Mo. 64106; 2,345; Pres., Mrs. Franklin Wirges.

**War Mothers, American** (1917), 2615 Woodley Pl. N.W., Washington, D. C. 20008; 15,650; Pres., Mrs. Ethel Beck.

**War of 1812, General Society of the** (Sept. 14. 1814), 3311 Columbia Pike, Lancaster, Pa. 17603; 1,104; Sec., Gen. John Ward Willson Loose.

**Watch and Clock Collectors, Natl. Assn. of** (1943), P. O. Box 33, Columbia, Pa. 17512; 10,500; Man. Dir., Earl T. Strickler.

**Water Pollution Control Federation** (1928), 3900 Wisconsin Ave., N.W., Washington, D. C. 20016; 15,000; Exec. Sec., Dr. Ralph E. Fuhrman.

**Water Works Assn., Amer.** (1881), 2 Park Ave., New York, N. Y. 10016; 20,000; Exec. Sec., Eric F. Johnson.

**Welding Society, American** (1919). 345 East 47th St., New York, N. Y. 10017; 20,000; Exec. Dir., Fred L. Plummer.

**Wesleyan Service Guild** (1940), 475 Riverside Dr., Rm. 1414; New York, N. Y. 10027; 126,000; Exec. Dir., Lillian A. Johnson.

**Western Forestry and Conservation Assn.** (1909), 1326 American Bank Bldg., Portland, Ore. 97205; 600; Pres., Arthur M. Roberts.

**Wilderness Society** (1935), 729 15th St., N.W., Washington, D. C. 20005; 40,000; Exec. Dir., Stewart M. Brandborg.

**Wildlife, Defenders of** (1925), 731 Dupont Circle Bldg., 1346 Connecticut Ave., N.W., Washington, D. C. 20036; 15,000; Exec. Sec., Mary H. Harris.

**Wildlife Federation, Natl.** (1936), 1412 16th St., N.W., Washington, D. C. 20036; 2,500,000; Exec. Dir., Thomas L. Kimball.

**Wildlife Management Institute** (1946), 709 Wire Bldg., Washington, D. C. 20005; 900; Pres., Ira N. Gabrielson.

**Williams Club** (1913), 24-26 East 39th St., New York, N. Y. 10016; 1,500; Sec., Frederick B. Paton.

**Woman Geographers, Society of** (1925), 1619 New Hampshire Ave., N.W., Washington, D. C. 20009; 425; Exec. Sec., Mrs. Benita S. Harris.

**Woman's Christian Temperance Union, National** (Nov. 18, 1874), 1730 Chicago Ave., Evanston, Ill. 60201; 250,000; Pres., Mrs. Fred J. Tooze.

**Woman's National Farm and Garden Assn.** (1914), 230 Park Ave., New York, N. Y. 10017; 9,000; Pres., Mrs. Nelson B. Sackett.

**Woman's Press Club of N. Y. City** (1889), Hotel Statler Hilton, 7th Ave. at 33rd St., New York,

N. Y. 10001; 325; Pres., Miss Jessie B. Chamberlin.

**Women Artists, National Assn. of** (1889), 156 Fifth Ave., New York, N. Y. 10010; 700; Exec. Sec., Beverly Boxer.

**Women Engineers, Society of** (1952), 345 E. 47th St., New York, N. Y. 10017; 1,000; Pres., Mrs. Alice M. Martin.

**Women Voters of the U. S., League of** (1920), 1200 17th St., N.W., Washington, D. C. 20036; 150,000; Exec. Dir., Miss Dixie Drake.

**Women World War Veterans** (1930), 237 Madison Ave., Rm. 204, New York, N. Y. 10016; 200,000; Sec., Ruth Manning.

**Women's Army Corps Veterans Assn.** (1946), 1080-83 N. Fairoaks Ave., Sunnyvale, Calif. 94086; 2,000; Sec., Evelyn Siems.

**Women's City Club of N. Y.** (1915), 6 West 48th St., New York, N. Y. 10036; 1,103; Exec. Sec., Mrs. Edward Weinberger.

**Women's Clubs, General Federation of** (1890). 1734 N St., N.W., Washington, D. C. 20036; 11,-000,000; Exec. Dir., Mrs. William O'Brien.

**Women's Clubs, Natl. Federation of Business and Professional** (1919). 2012 Massachusetts Ave., N.W., Washington, D. C. 20036; 180,000; Exec. Dir., Miss E. C. Hermans.

**Women's Educational and Industrial Union** (1877), 264 Boylston St., Boston, Mass. 02116; 2,519; Exec. Dir., Mrs. Ruth L. Bean.

**Women's International League for Peace and Freedom** (1915), U.S. Section—2006 Walnut St., Philadelphia, Pa. 19103; 10,000; Exec. Dir., Mrs. M. Hanson.

**Women's National Republican Club** (1921), 3 West 51st St., New York, N. Y. 10019; 3,000; Pres., Mrs. John Whelchel Finger.

**Women's Overseas Service League** (1921), 2026 Eye St., N.W., Washington, D. C. 20006; 1,846; Sec., Mrs. Harry L. Perry.

**Woodmen of America, Modern** (1883), 1701 1st Ave., Rock Island, Ill. 61201; 420,000; Sec. Alfred S. Edler.

**Woodmen of the World** (1890), 1450 Speer Blvd., Denver, Colo. 80204; 36,209; Sec.-Treas., E. N. Olson.

**Wool Growers Assn., National** (1865), 600 Crandall Bldg., Salt Lake City, Utah 84101; 12,000; Exec. Sec., Edwin E. Marsh.

**Wool Manufacturers. National Assn. of** (1864), 1200 17th St., N.W., Washington, D. C. 20036; 150 companies; Sec., Gordon Graham.

**Workmen's Circle** (1900), 175 East Broadway, New York, N. Y. 10002; 60,000; Exec. Sec., Benjamin A. Gebiner.

**World Health, American Association For** (1953), 777 United Nations Plaza, New York, N. Y. 10017; 93 organizations; Exec. V. Pres., Philip E. Nelbach.

**Writers Assn. of America, Outdoor** (1928). 205 Outdoors Bldg., Columbia, Mo. 65201; 1,400; Exec. Dir., Don G. Cullimore.

—Y & Z—

**Yale Club of N. Y. City** (1897), 50 Vanderbilt Ave., New York, N. Y. 10017; 6,330; Pres., Edgar M. Church, Jr.

**Yeomen F, National** (1926), 924 Stokes Ave., Collingwood, N. J. 08108; 1,287; Pres., Marguerite Geiger.

**YMHAs and Jewish Community Centers, World Federation of** (1946), 15 East 26th St., New York, N. Y. 10010; Adm. Sec., Louis Kraft.

**YM-YWHAs of Greater New York, Associated** (1957), 33 West 60th St., New York, N. Y. 10023; 52,000; Exec. V. P., Irving Brodsky.

**Young Men's Christian Assns., Natl. Council of** (1844 in London, 1851 in U.S.A.), 291 Broadway, New York, N. Y. 10007; 5,200,000; Gen. Sec., James F. Bunting.

**Young Republican National Federation** (1935), 1625 Eye St., N.W., Washington. 417 D. C. 20006; Exec. Dir., Ted Cormaney.

**Young Women's Christian Assn. of the U.S.A.** (1855 in England; 1858 in U.S.A). 600 Lexington Ave., New York, N. Y. 10022; 2,200,000 in the U.S.A.; Gen. Sec., Miss Edith M. Lerrigo.

**Youth Hostels, Amer.** (1934). 20 West 17th St., N. Y., N. Y. 10011; 35,000; Sec., Edmund J. Nagle.

**Zionist Organization of America** (1897). 145 East 32nd St., New York, N. Y. 10016; 100,000; Natl. Sec., Leon Ilutovich.

**Zonta International** (Nov. 8, 1919), 59 E. Van Buren St., Chicago, Ill. 60605; 20,000; Exec. Dir., Mrs. Pauline C. Fyler.

**Zoological Society, N. Y.** (1895), 630 Fifth Ave., New York, N. Y. 10020; 6,700; Pres., Dr. Fairfield Osborn.

**Zoologists, American Society of** (1913), Department of Zoology, Michigan State Univ., East Lansing, Mich. 48823; 4,500; Sec., John R. Shaver.

# WORLD FLAGS & MAPS

See Final Flag Page for Newest Nations

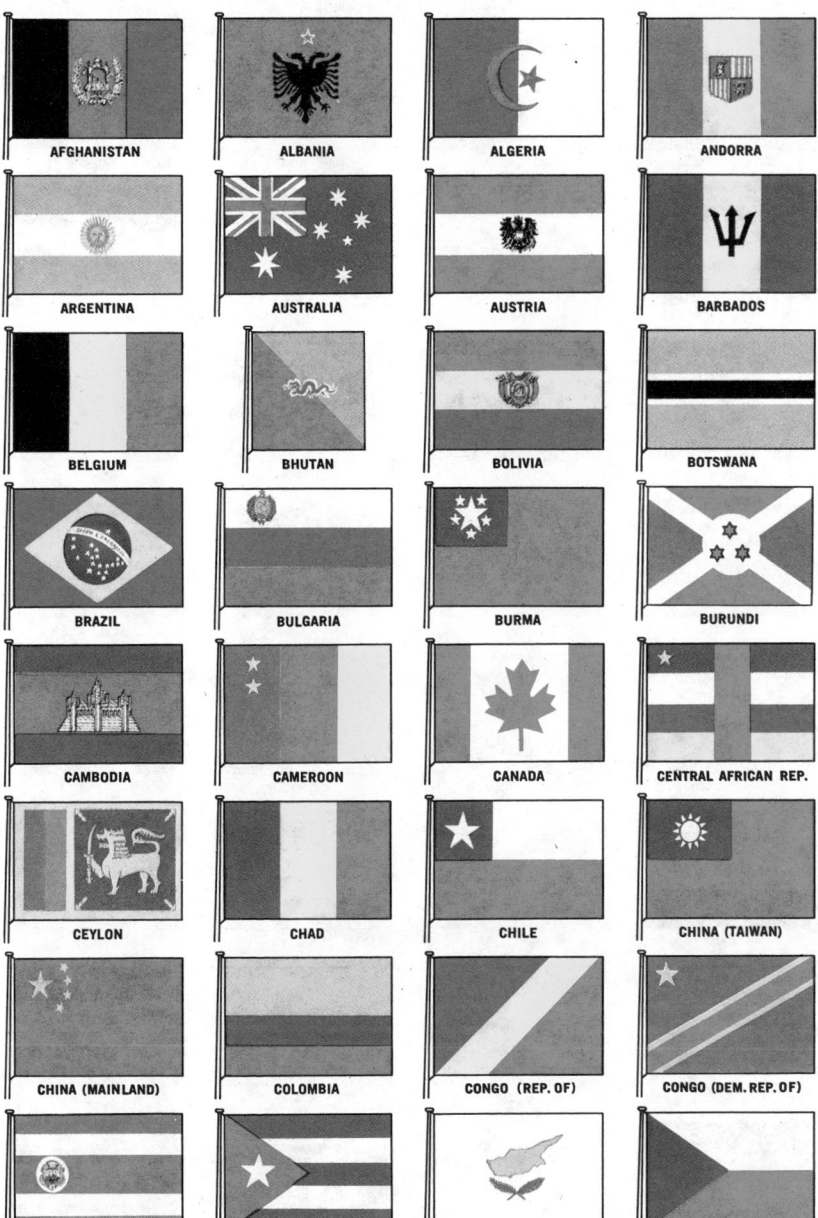

| | | | |
|---|---|---|---|
| AFGHANISTAN | ALBANIA | ALGERIA | ANDORRA |
| ARGENTINA | AUSTRALIA | AUSTRIA | BARBADOS |
| BELGIUM | BHUTAN | BOLIVIA | BOTSWANA |
| BRAZIL | BULGARIA | BURMA | BURUNDI |
| CAMBODIA | CAMEROON | CANADA | CENTRAL AFRICAN REP. |
| CEYLON | CHAD | CHILE | CHINA (TAIWAN) |
| CHINA (MAINLAND) | COLOMBIA | CONGO (REP. OF) | CONGO (DEM. REP. OF) |
| COSTA RICA | CUBA | CYPRUS | CZECHOSLOVAKIA |

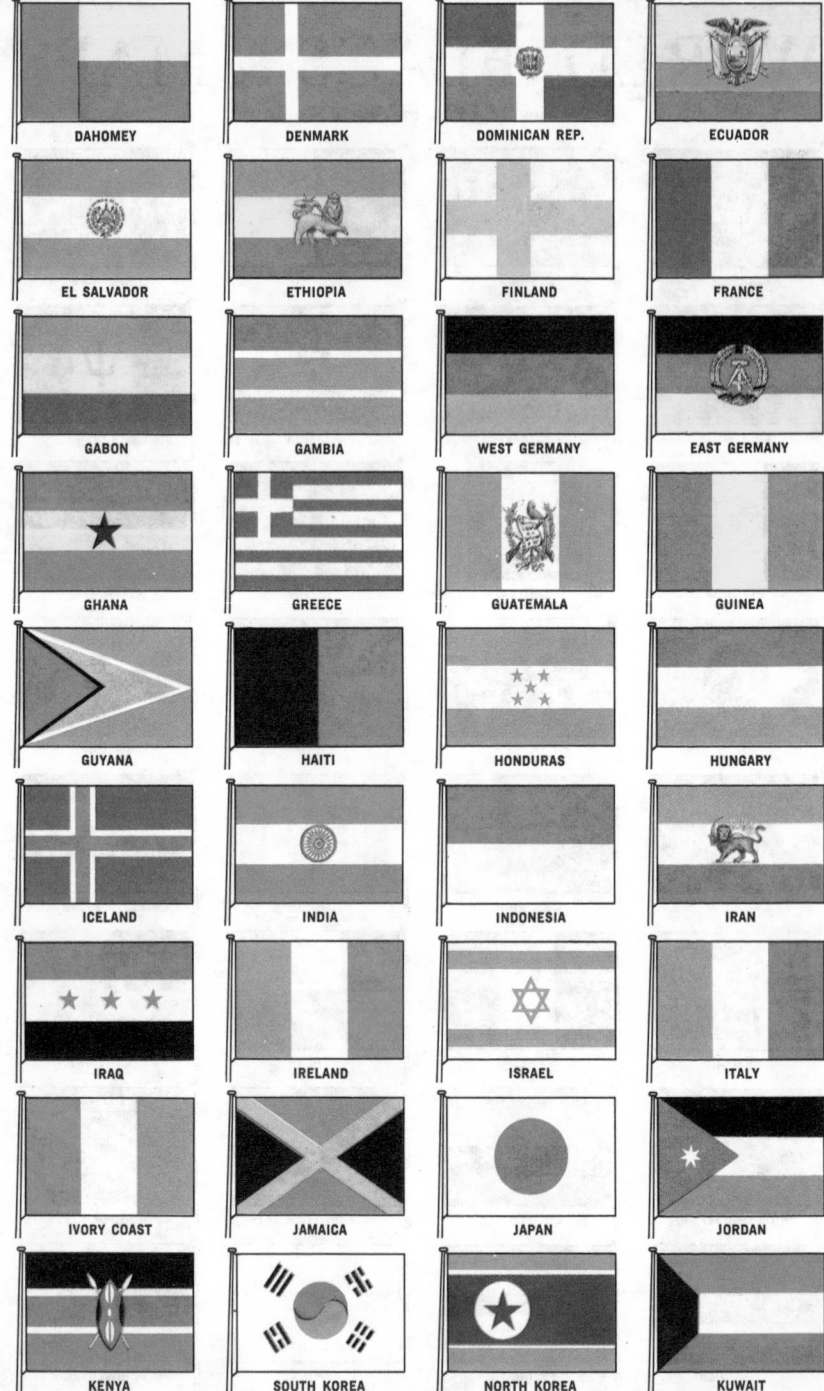

| | | | |
|---|---|---|---|
| DAHOMEY | DENMARK | DOMINICAN REP. | ECUADOR |
| EL SALVADOR | ETHIOPIA | FINLAND | FRANCE |
| GABON | GAMBIA | WEST GERMANY | EAST GERMANY |
| GHANA | GREECE | GUATEMALA | GUINEA |
| GUYANA | HAITI | HONDURAS | HUNGARY |
| ICELAND | INDIA | INDONESIA | IRAN |
| IRAQ | IRELAND | ISRAEL | ITALY |
| IVORY COAST | JAMAICA | JAPAN | JORDAN |
| KENYA | SOUTH KOREA | NORTH KOREA | KUWAIT |

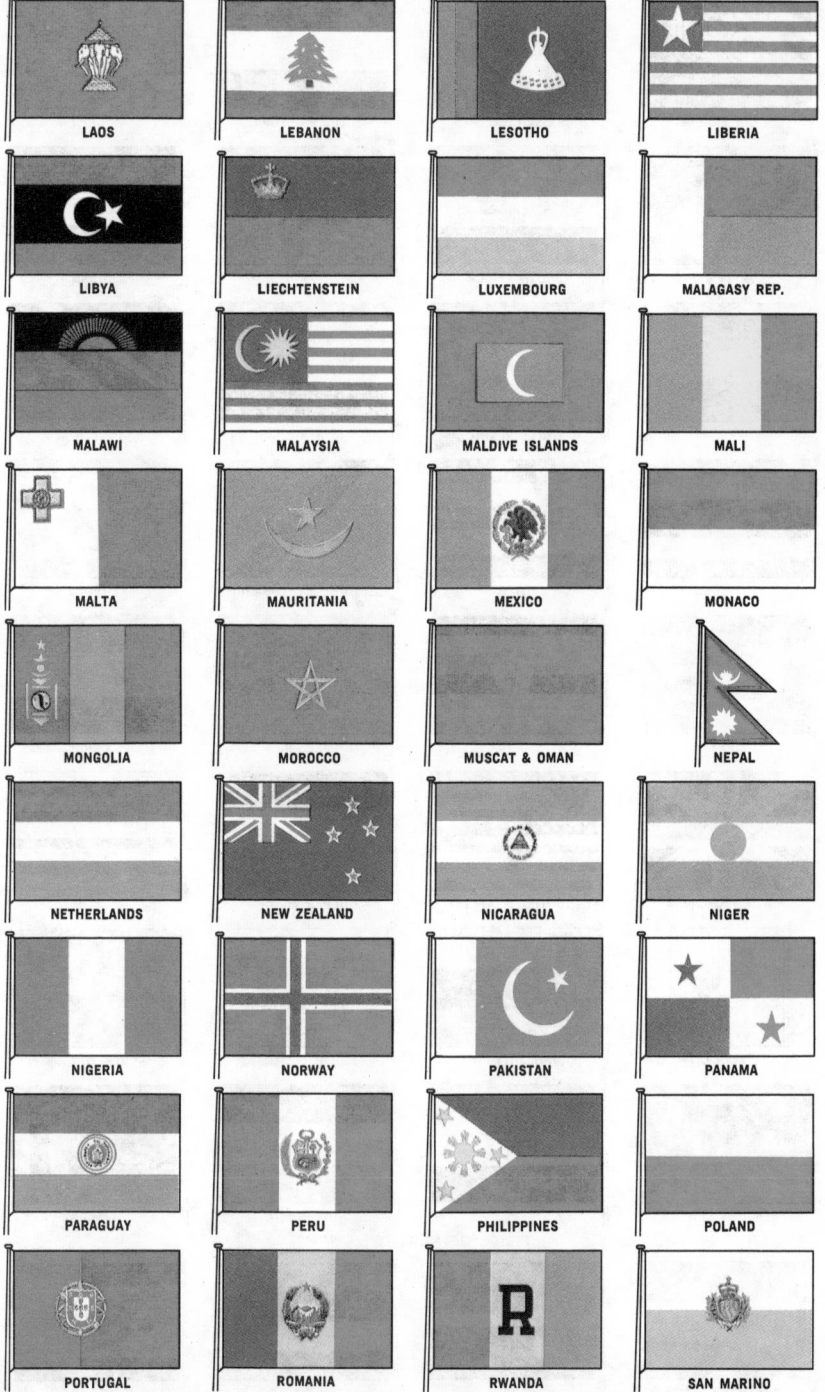

467

| | | | |
|---|---|---|---|
| LAOS | LEBANON | LESOTHO | LIBERIA |
| LIBYA | LIECHTENSTEIN | LUXEMBOURG | MALAGASY REP. |
| MALAWI | MALAYSIA | MALDIVE ISLANDS | MALI |
| MALTA | MAURITANIA | MEXICO | MONACO |
| MONGOLIA | MOROCCO | MUSCAT & OMAN | NEPAL |
| NETHERLANDS | NEW ZEALAND | NICARAGUA | NIGER |
| NIGERIA | NORWAY | PAKISTAN | PANAMA |
| PARAGUAY | PERU | PHILIPPINES | POLAND |
| PORTUGAL | ROMANIA | RWANDA | SAN MARINO |

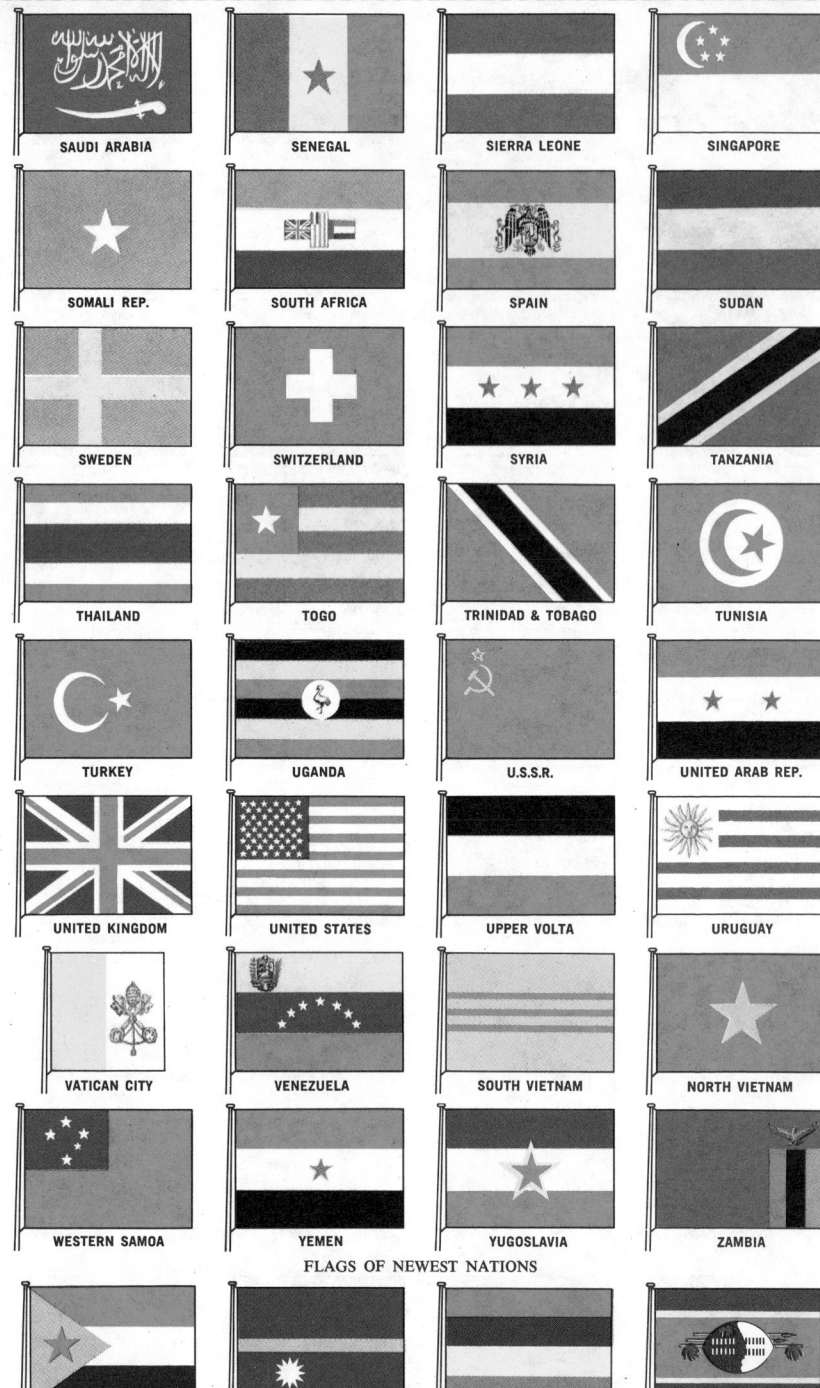

468

| | | | |
|---|---|---|---|
| SAUDI ARABIA | SENEGAL | SIERRA LEONE | SINGAPORE |
| SOMALI REP. | SOUTH AFRICA | SPAIN | SUDAN |
| SWEDEN | SWITZERLAND | SYRIA | TANZANIA |
| THAILAND | TOGO | TRINIDAD & TOBAGO | TUNISIA |
| TURKEY | UGANDA | U.S.S.R. | UNITED ARAB REP. |
| UNITED KINGDOM | UNITED STATES | UPPER VOLTA | URUGUAY |
| VATICAN CITY | VENEZUELA | SOUTH VIETNAM | NORTH VIETNAM |
| WESTERN SAMOA | YEMEN | YUGOSLAVIA | ZAMBIA |

FLAGS OF NEWEST NATIONS

| | | | |
|---|---|---|---|
| SOUTHERN YEMEN | NAURU | MAURITIUS | SWAZILAND |

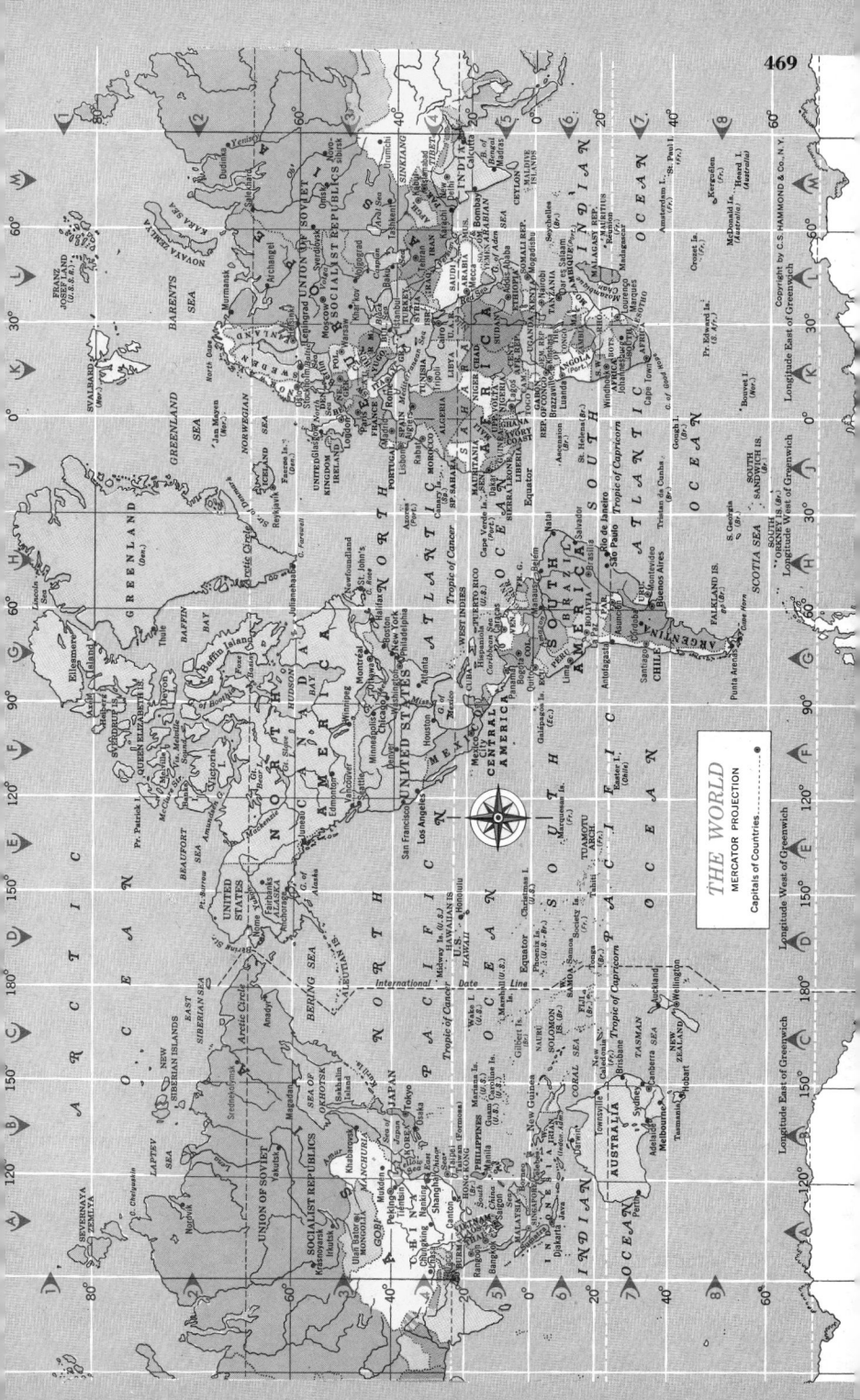

# CANADA

CONIC PROJECTION

SCALE OF MILES
0 100 200 300 400 500

SCALE OF KILOMETRES
0 100 200 300 400 500

Capitals of Countries ⊛
Provincial & Territorial Capitals ⊛
Canals

Copyright by C.S. Hammond & Co., N.Y.

GREENLAND

ATLANTIC OCEAN

BAFFIN BAY

DAVIS STRAIT

BAFFIN ISLAND

FRANKLIN

BASIN

NORTHWEST TERRITORIES

DISTRICT OF KEEWATIN

DISTRICT OF MACKENZIE

HUDSON BAY

BEAUFORT SEA

YUKON

ALASKA

UNITED STATES

ROCKY MTS

BRITISH COLUMBIA

COAST MTS

ALBERTA

SASKATCHEWAN

MANITOBA

ONTARIO

QUEBEC

NEWFOUNDLAND

NEW BRUNSWICK

NOVA SCOTIA

MAINE

UNITED STATES

MINN.

IOWA

NEBR.

S. DAK.

N. DAK.

MICH.

WASH.

Winnipeg
Regina
Edmonton
Calgary
Saskatoon
Vancouver
Victoria
Toronto
Ottawa
Montreal
Quebec
Halifax
Fredericton
Detroit
Buffalo
Cleveland
Chicago
Milwaukee
Minneapolis
St. Paul
Duluth
Fargo
Bismarck
Seattle
Portland

UNITED STATES
POLYCONIC PROJECTION
SCALE OF MILES
0    100   200   300   400
SCALE OF KILOMETRES
0   100  200  300  400  500

Capitals of Countries........ ⊛
International Boundaries ........
State Capitals ........ ⊛
State Boundaries ........
Copyright by C. S. HAMMOND & Co., N. Y.

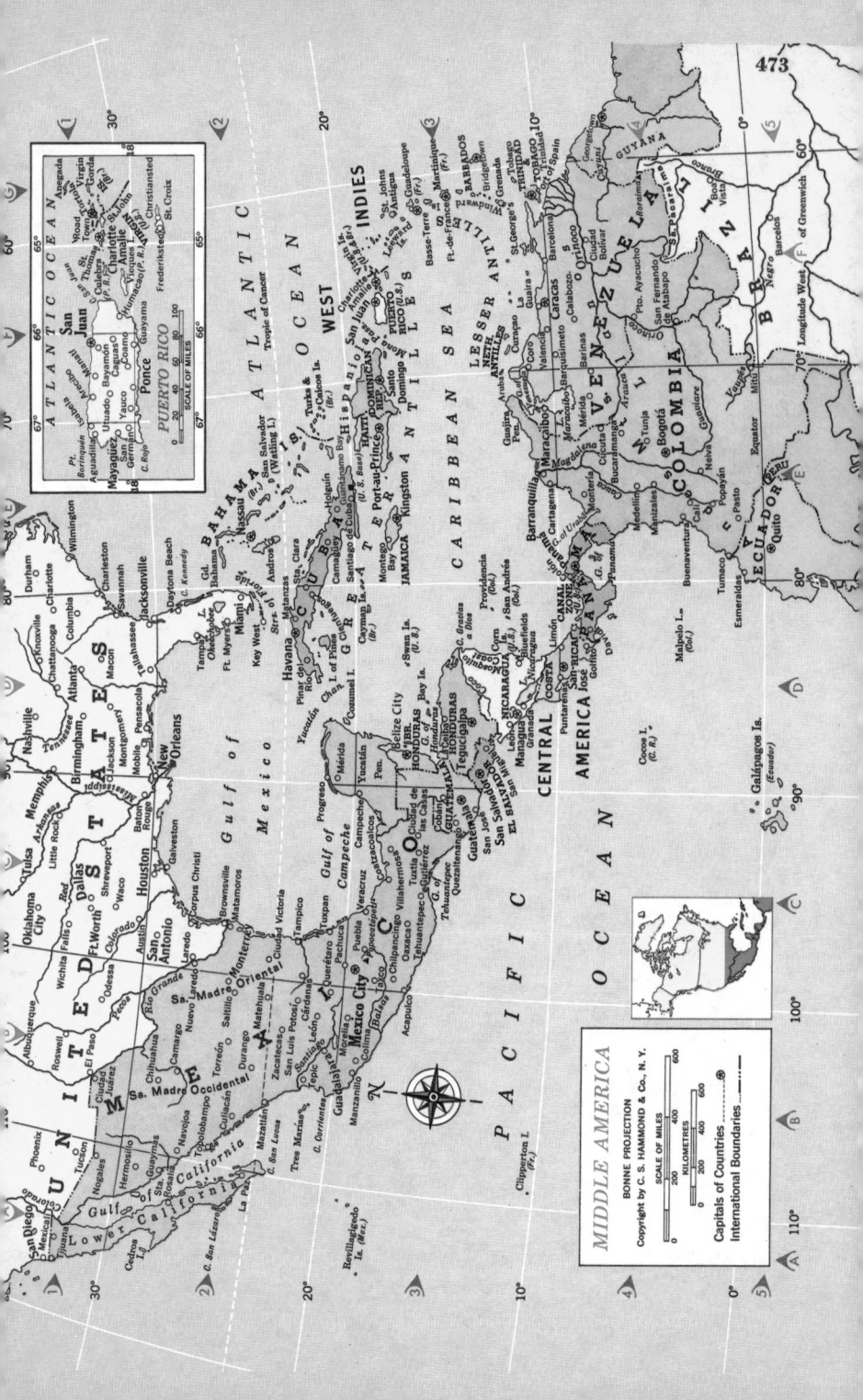

473

## MIDDLE AMERICA

BONNE PROJECTION

Copyright by C. S. HAMMOND & Co., N. Y.

SCALE OF MILES

| 0 | 200 | 400 | 600 |

KILOMETRES

| 0 | 200 | 400 | 600 |

Capitals of Countries ⊛
International Boundaries

### PUERTO RICO

ATLANTIC OCEAN

San Juan

Ponce

SCALE OF MILES

| 0 | 20 | 40 | 60 | 80 | 100 |

### WEST INDIES

ATLANTIC OCEAN

BAHAMA IS.

CUBA

Havana

JAMAICA

HISPANIOLA

HAITI

DOMINICAN REP.

PUERTO RICO (U.S.)

CARIBBEAN SEA

LESSER ANTILLES

NETH. ANTILLES

### UNITED STATES

Gulf of Mexico

### MEXICO

Mexico City ⊛

### CENTRAL AMERICA

GUATEMALA
BR. HONDURAS
HONDURAS
EL SALVADOR
NICARAGUA
COSTA RICA
PANAMA
CANAL ZONE

### VENEZUELA

Caracas ⊛

### COLOMBIA

Bogotá ⊛

### ECUADOR

Quito ⊛

### BRAZIL

GUYANA

PACIFIC OCEAN

Galápagos Is. (Ecuador)

Equator

ASIA
LAMBERT AZIMUTHAL
EQUAL-AREA PROJECTION

SCALE OF MILES
300    600    900    1200

SCALE OF KILOMETRES
300    600    900    1200

Capitals of Countries .............. ●
International Boundaries .............. — — —
Canals .............. — — — — —

Longitude 80° East of Greenwich 100°    120°

477

THE NEAR AND
MIDDLE EAST
CONIC PROJECTION
SCALE OF MILES
0    100   200   300   400
KILOMETRES
0  100 200 300 400
Capitals of Countries .......... ⊛
Other Capitals ....................... ⊛
International Boundaries
Other Boundaries .................

Areas occupied
by Israel

Copyright by C. S. HAMMOND & Co., N. Y.

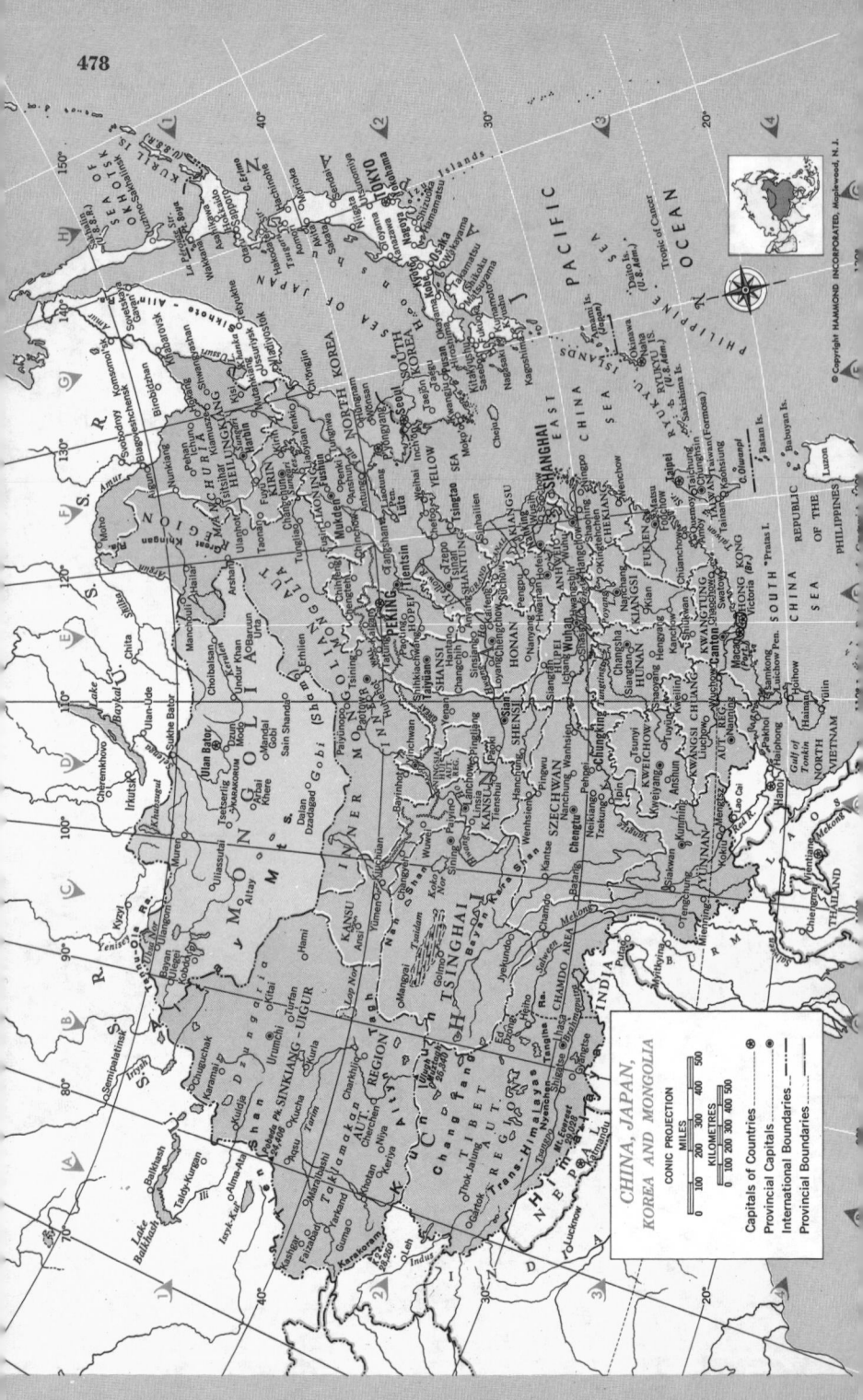

CHINA, JAPAN,
KOREA AND MONGOLIA
CONIC PROJECTION

MILES
0 100 200 300 400 500

KILOMETRES
0 100 200 300 400 500

Capitals of Countries ............
Provincial Capitals ...............
International Boundaries ––––––
Provincial Boundaries ————

© Copyright HAMMOND INCORPORATED, Maplewood, N.J.

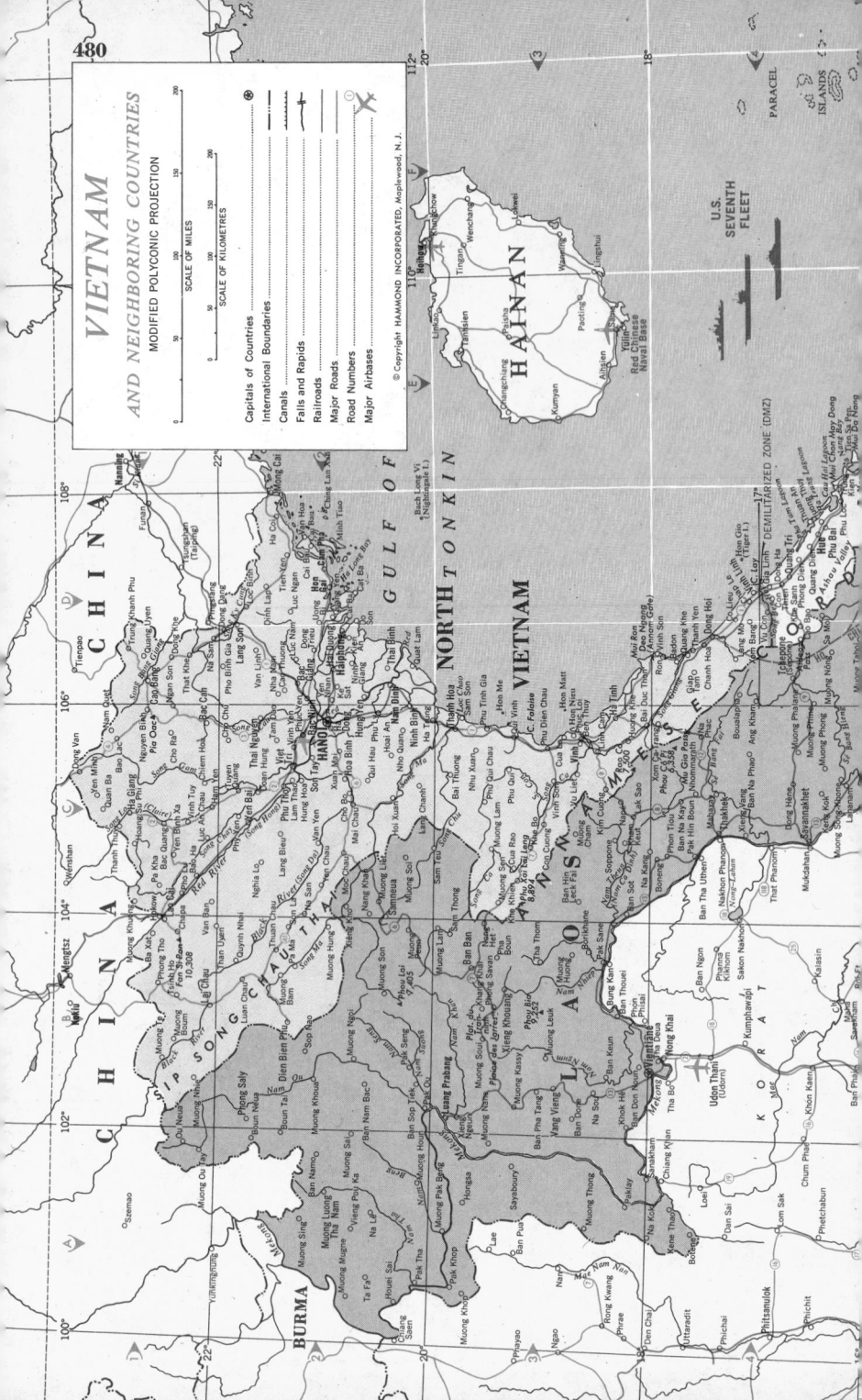

# VIETNAM
## AND NEIGHBORING COUNTRIES
MODIFIED POLYCONIC PROJECTION

SCALE OF MILES

SCALE OF KILOMETRES

Capitals of Countries

International Boundaries

Canals

Falls and Rapids

Railroads

Major Roads

Road Numbers

Major Airbases

© Copyright HAMMOND INCORPORATED, Maplewood, N.J.

CHINA

HAINAN

U.S. SEVENTH FLEET

PARACEL ISLANDS

Red Chinese Naval Base

GULF OF TONKIN

NORTH VIETNAM

HANOI

Haiphong

DEMILITARIZED ZONE (DMZ)

LAOS

THAILAND

BURMA

Vientiane

Luang Prabang

Mekong

C A M B O D I A

K O R A T

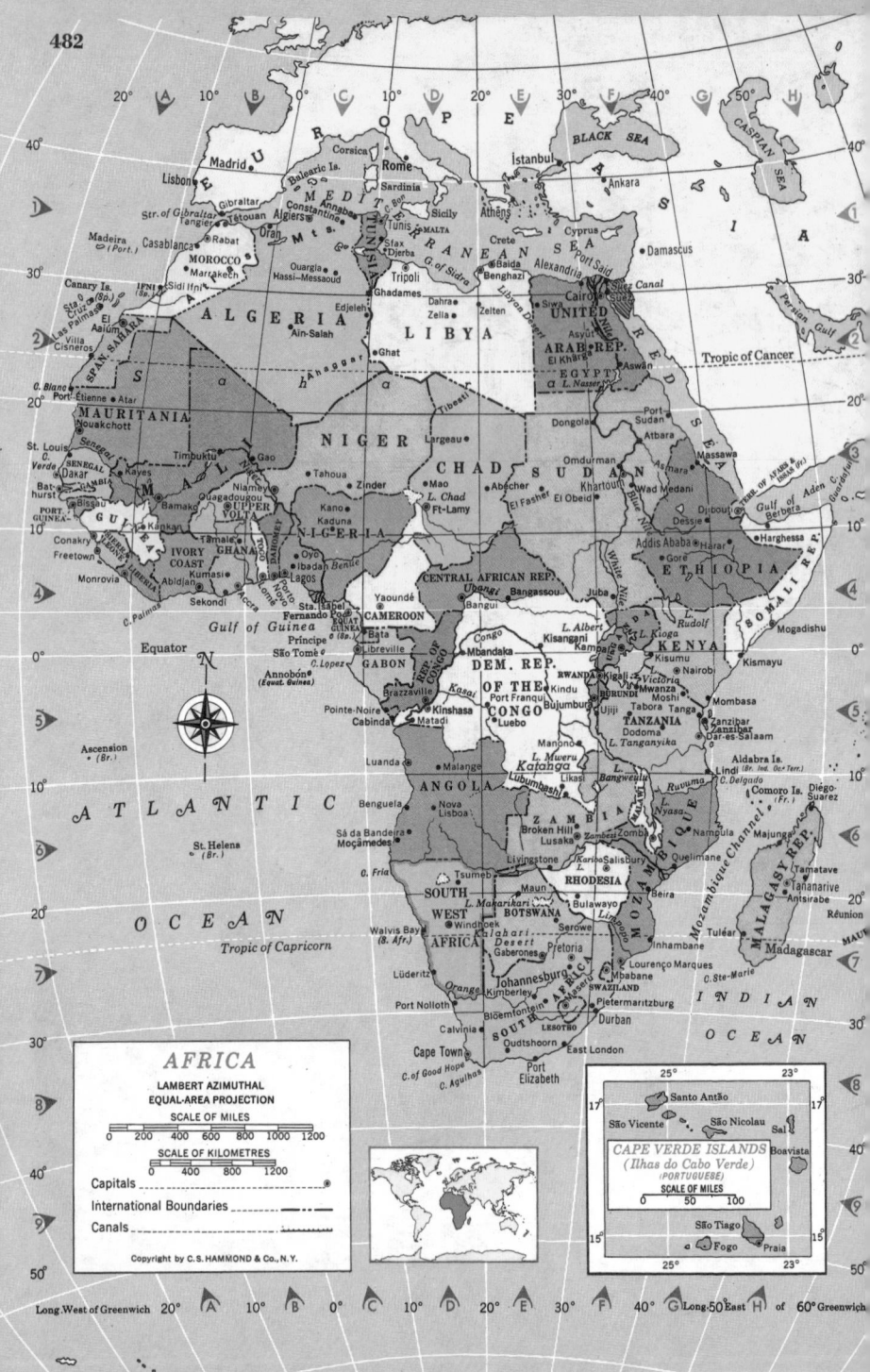

AFRICA

LAMBERT AZIMUTHAL
EQUAL-AREA PROJECTION

SCALE OF MILES

0 200 400 600 800 1000 1200

SCALE OF KILOMETRES

0 400 800 1200

Capitals

International Boundaries

Canals

Copyright by C.S. HAMMOND & Co., N.Y.

CAPE VERDE ISLANDS
(Ilhas do Cabo Verde)
(PORTUGUESE)

SCALE OF MILES

0 50 100

Santo Antão
São Vicente
São Nicolau
Sal
Boavista
São Tiago
Fogo
Praia

Long. West of Greenwich 20° 10° 0° 10° 20° 30° 40° Long. 50° East of 60° Greenwich

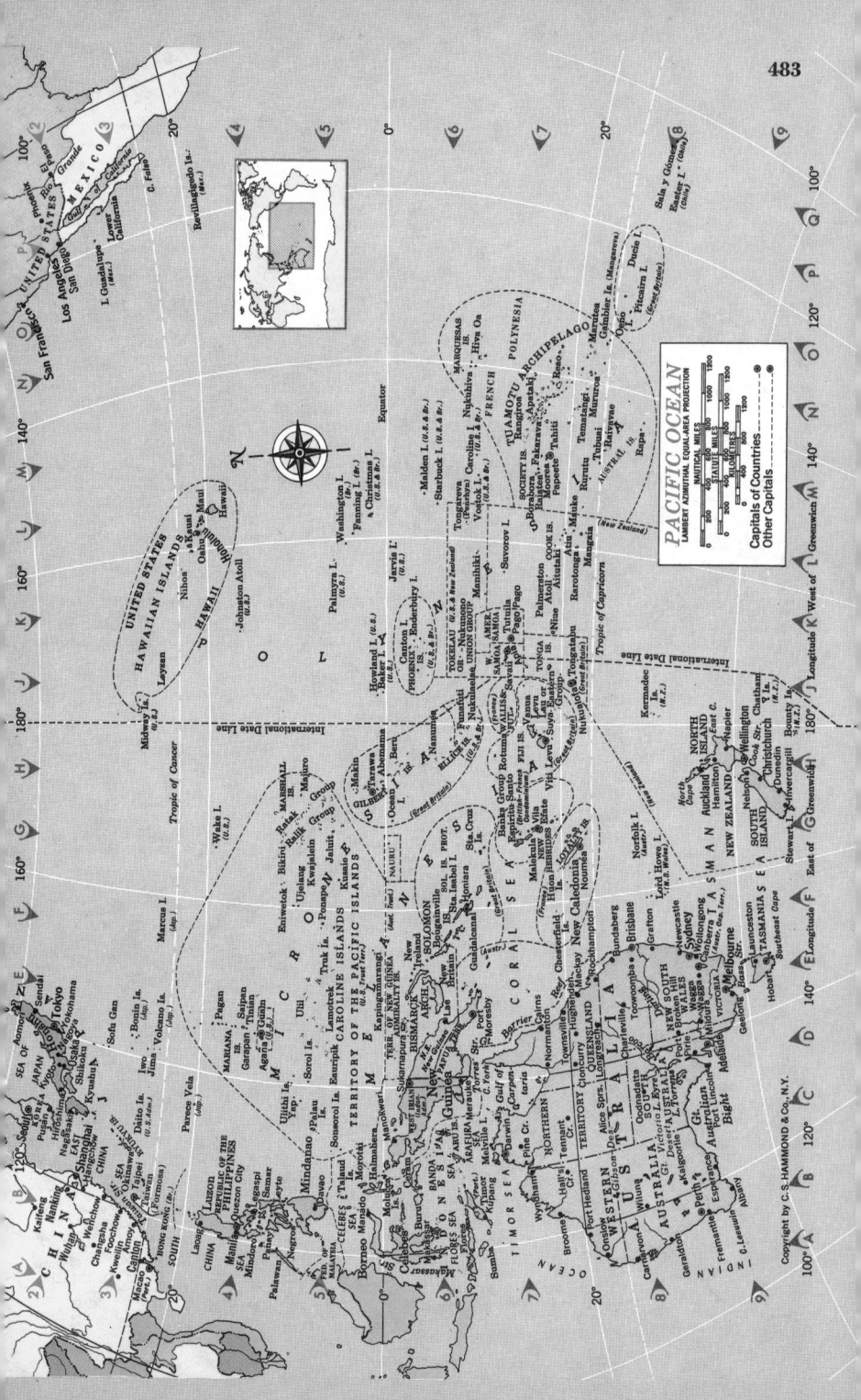

483

20° Longitude West 18 of Greenwich 0° Longitude East 1 of Greenwich 20°

17

A T L A N T I C   O C E A N

E

40°

50°

D

Limit of Drift Ice

Bouvet I.
(Nor.)

ANTARCTICA
AZIMUTHAL EQUIDISTANT PROJECTION

SCALE OF MILES
0   200   400   600   800

SCALE OF KILOMETRES
0  200 400 600 800 1000

© C. S. HAMMOND & Co., N. Y.

Prince Edward Is.°°
(S. Afr.)

16

FALKLAND ISLANDS DEPENDENCIES
(Br.)

Grytviken
South
Georgia I.

South
Sandwich
Is.

60°

N O R W E G I A N   S E C T O R

C

Antarctic Circle

S C O T I A   S E A

A R G E N T I N E   S E C T O R

Norway Sta. 70°
C. Norwegia

PRINCESS
MARTHA
COAST

PRINCESS
ASTRID
COAST

New Schwabenland

PRINCESS RAGNHILD
COAST

Riiser-Larsen Pen.

Lützow-Holm Bay

Amundsen Bay

C. Batterbee

60

15

Stanley
Falkland Is.
(Br.)

Elephant I.

King George I.

South Shetland
Is.

Joinville I.

James Ross I.

C. Horn

SOUTH
AMERICA

Hope
Bay

Palmer
Arch.

Biscoe Is.

Adelaide I.

Marguerite
Bay

Larsen
Ice Shelf

Hearst I.

Hilton Inlet

Pen. PALMER LAND

Alexander I.

Berkner I.

Q u e e n   M a u d   L a n d

CAIRD
COAST

LUITPOLD
COAST

Filchner

PRINCE
OLAV COAST

Enderby
Land

KEMP
COAST

Edward VIII Bay

Mawson

C. Daly

MAC-ROBERTSON
COAST

C. Darnley

MacKenzie Bay

American
Highland

Amery Ice
Shelf

Prydz
Bay

WEDDELL

SEA

80°

Charcot
I.

Ronne
Entr.

ENGLISH
COAST

Edith Ronne
Ice Shelf

80°

14

Drake Passage

Vinson Massif

Ellsworth Mts.

South Polar Plateau
SOUTH POLE
Amundsen-Scott Sta.

AREA OF
POLE OF
INACCESSIBILITY

WILHELM II
COAST

West Ice
Shelf

Gaussberg

QUEEN MARY COAST

Davis
Sea

Peter I.
I. (Nor.)

BELLINGSHAUSEN
SEA

Thurston

Pine Island Bay

EIGHTS
COAST

Amundsen Dec. 14, 1911
Scott Jan. 17, 1912
Byrd Nov. 29, 1929 (airplane)
Fuchs Jan. 20, 1958

Mirnyy

Mt. Barr Smith

Farr Bay

Shackleton
Ice
Shelf

100°

Amundsen

WALGREEN
COAST

HOLLICK-
KENYON
PLATEAU

Byrd

Byrd Sta.

Beardmore Glacier

Mt. Kirkpatrick

Mt. Markham

KNOX
COAST

BUDD
COAST

SABRINA
COAST

Vincennes
Bay

100°

13

C. Dart

Getz Ice Shelf

Mt. Siple

Executive
Comm. Ra.

Mt. Sidley

HOBBS
COAST

Edward VII Land

Ford
Ranges

Roosevelt I.

Ross Ice Shelf

Little America

Kainan Bay

Mt.
Lister

Mt.
Scott
Ross I.
McMurdo

V i c t o r i a   L a n d

W i l k e s   L a n d

BANZARE
COAST

C. Goodenough

6

120°

Colbeck Bay

R o s s   S e a

Mt.
Sabine

Adare

Lillie
Glacier
Tongue

70°

Scott I.

Balleny Is.

SOUTH MAGNETIC
POLAR AREA
GEORGE V.
COAST
Port-Martin

Adélie
Land

Ninnis
Glacier
Tongue

Mertz
Glacier
Tongue

C. Keltie

FRENCH
SECTOR

12

Antarctic Circle

R O S S   D E P E N D E N C Y   (N. Z.)

60°

AUSTRALIAN
ANTARCTIC TERR.

Limit of Drift Ice

7

P A C I F I C   O C E A N

Macquarie I.
(Australia)

14

Campbell I.
(N. Z.)

Auckland Is.
(N. Z.)

Hobart
Tasmania

King

140°

Antipodes Is.
(N. Z.)

Bounty Is.
(N. Z.)

Stewart I.

Dunedin

NEW
ZEALAND

T a s m a n

S e a

Furneaux
Gr.

Melbourne
AUSTRALIA

160° Longitude West 10 of Greenwich 180° Longitude East 9 of Greenwich 160°

11

40°

Antarctic Circle

South
Orkney Is.
Coronation I.

# From the Prime Minister of Canada:

The World Almanac has been in publication for just a year less than Canada has been a nation. In 1868 it was a slim volume indeed, but the facts and figures of the 20th Century have built it into a robust tool of reference.

For Canadians, the 1969 edition of the World Almanac will be particularly significant. A special section on Canada has been added, and the city section now includes material from 9 major Canadian cities.

In thus serving as a Canadian as well as an American reference work, the World Almanac takes on a truly North American character and is another reflection of the intimate relationship which exists between our two countries.

We welcome the 1969 edition of the World Almanac to the Canadian scene.

Pierre Elliott Trudeau
Prime Minister of Canada

---

# Canada—A Nation Come of Age

*See Index for Calgary, Edmonton, Montreal, Ottawa, Regina, Saskatoon, Toronto, Vancouver, Winnipeg.*

Capital: Ottawa. Area: 3,851,809 sq. mi. Population (Govt. est. July 19, 1968): 20,789,390. Monetary unit: Dollar (1.0781 per U. S. $1).

Canada stood, at the threshold of 1969, as one of the world's leading industrial and political states. Its people felt a new pride and purpose as the country's social and cultural achievements began to catch up with its potential and its promise.

At the beginning of this century, the famed Canadian Prime Minister, Sir Wilfrid Laurier, proclaimed that "the 20th Century belongs to Canada." He was undoubtedly thinking that while Canada had been forged into a nation by the 1867 act of Confederation which united 4 of the British colonies of North America, the land was still sparsely settled and only modestly productive. The neighboring United States had survived a great Civil War and had emerged stronger than ever, pushing its borders to the Pacific Coast. Canada at the beginning of the 20th Century also had become a continental state extending from Atlantic to Pacific; now the challenge was to fill in the immense emptiness of its heartland.

World War I, while it began an industrial expansion which goes on to this day, drained off much of the best young blood of the nation; its young men either did not come back at all from the battlefields of Europe, or came back tired and shell-shocked, in no condition mentally or physically to conquer new frontiers. The brief prosperity of the 1920s faded quickly in the dust bowls of the '30s, a decade which virtually depopulated much of the prairie provinces and which was followed by an even greater World War.

But the second war let loose new creative energies at home; returning soldiers vowed that the Canada they had fought for would this time be rebuilt, that time would not again drag endlessly on with little achievement or accomplishment.

World War II had fired the furnaces of Canadian industry, had seen a million men and women take up arms in the nation's defense, and had shown Canadians that their country was no insignificant British colony lost in the mainstream of North American development.

A vast natural resources boom echoed through the empty forests and mountain ranges in the 1950s. On the Pacific Coast, a great chain of rivers and lakes was reversed to flow backwards through the mountains and so power electric generators for the vast aluminum smelters of Kitimat. Oil wells sprouted like some new crop on the prairies; in Alberta oil gushed and gurgled out of wheat fields and poured so much wealth into the province's treasury that it became one of the few (if not only) debt-free governments in North America, and which to this day doesn't have a sales tax.

Canada shared with the U. S. the construction of the St. Lawrence Seaway and after years of stops and starts finally completed the 4,860-mile Trans-Canada Highway, longest in the world.

Immense iron ore developments in Labrador paved the way for the harnessing of Churchill Falls, a mighty cataract whose energy will soon help light the electric bulbs of New York City. Uranium deposits which rank among the world's largest were developed in Ontario. More secondary industry was added to the picture in the 1960s so that the Canadian living standard today rivals that of Sweden and the U. S. and in some respects, exceeds all the rest of the world.

Population, through natural growth and encouragement of immigration, passed the 20,000,-000 mark for Canada's 1967 Centennial and stood, according to official government estimate, at 20,-789,390 on July 19, 1968, the day the Bureau of Statistics unveiled in Ottawa a "pop clock"—an electric clock ticking off the population changes minute by minute.

The 1967 Centennial was immensely successful, featuring such special events as Expo '67 in Montreal, and the results left it clear to Canadians that their nation had come of age.

Canadians recognized that while the country faced many problems, not the least of them a resolution of its political and economic ties with the U. S., their land was nevertheless favored by history and geography as perhaps no other country on earth.

**CANADA: THE OUTLINES.** Second largest nation in the world, Canada extends north from the U. S.-Canadian boundary to the North Pole. It includes all the islands of the Arctic even near Greenland to near the Alaska border. Its seacoast, one of the longest in the world, comprises 17,860 mi. of mainland and 41,810 mi. of islands. The 3,986-mi. border between Canada and the U. S. has been unfortified for more than a century. Canada's southernmost point, Point Pelee in Lake Erie, is further south than is the California-Oregon border.

Canada's continental climate, while generally temperate, includes extremely cold winter weather through the prairie provinces and much of Ontario and Quebec. British Columbia and the Atlantic provinces, where the weather is moderated by the oceans, are milder.

Beginning on the West Coast, the Pacific region is a mountainous area which includes the Rockies. The prairie region extends from there to the Great Lakes. Ontario and Quebec are areas of forest and farmland, while the Atlantic coast region has gently rolling valleys and hills. A great sweep of the nation, stretching through northern Quebec and Ontario and glancing off Lake Superior to run out across the plains and into the northern territories, is known as the Canadian Shield, where past ice ages scraped most soil and vegetation off the land.

This is the world's oldest surface rock, and it is among these outcroppings that most Canadian mining discoveries have been made, including gold, uranium, lead, silver, zinc and iron ore.

**A NATION'S STORY.** French explorer Jacques Cartier is generally regarded as the founder of Canada, although his 1534 voyage up the St. Lawrence followed by 37 years the 1497 sighting of Newfoundland by Italian navigator John Cabot, sailing for the English king. Even further back, as increasing evidence being unearthed today shows, the Vikings sailing from Scandinavia or the northern islands had reached Newfoundland and Canada's Atlantic Coast.

The French pioneered Canadian settlement, with the result that today about one-third of the nation remains of French descent. Quebec was

*For Population and Area of Canada by Provinces see index.*

settled in 1608, Montreal in 1642 and New France became a colony in 1663.

Britain and France clashed over the Canadian colony as a result of European rivalries and British expansion from the original American colonies. Britain obtained Acadia (later Nova Scotia) in 1713 and the Acadian expulsion followed in 1755.

Britain obtained control of the rest of New France in 1763 by the settlement of the Seven Years' War in Europe, the North American phase of which saw French and Indian tribes (except some Iroquois) fighting the British and American colonists.

However, by terms of the peace the French were guaranteed their language, religion and civil rights. This is regarded as one of the main reasons why French Canadian settlers did not join American colonists farther to the south in the War of Independence in 1776.

Following the American War of Independence, many settlers loyal to Britain moved north to the Canadian territories; the chief influx became known as United Empire Loyalists.

Years of relative peace, highlighted by transcontinental exploration, followed. Alexander Mackenzie scrawled on a rock washed by the Pacific "From Canada, by land, 1793." An elected legislative assembly was permitted in 1791. The peace, however, was interrupted by the War of 1812. The war ended in stalemate, but not before heavy battles had been fought in Upper Canada—the last military action ever to occur on Canadian soil.

Political agitation for more democratic government culminated in ill-fated rebellions led by William Lyon Mackenzie in Upper Canada (Ontario) and Louis Joseph Papineau (Lower Canada) in 1837. It was not until complete democratic freedom was won in 1867 with the passage by the British Parliament of the British North America Act, that a start was made in uniting the various British colonies into a self-governing Canadian Confederation.

Since then, Canada has remained a self-government nation in what was the British Empire and is now the Commonwealth.

**CANADA: ITS HOW AND WHY:** Essentially, the Queen reigns but does not rule over her Canadian domain. The Queen's representative in Canada and Head of State is the Governor-General, chosen by the Federal Cabinet.

Under Canada's parliamentary system, modeled on the British system, the party securing the largest number of seats in elections to fill the House of Commons forms the government. The party leader, who becomes Prime Minister, chooses his Cabinet from members of the House of Commons (and sometimes from the Senate, to which the Prime Minister holds exclusive rights to make appointments).

The system ensures that at no time will the Cabinet be of a different party than that which controls Parliament. No regular date is set for elections, as the government can call an election any time it chooses. Normally, however, elections are held every 4 years, or more often when no party has a clear majority in the House.

Because Canada is technically a monarchy, and yet also a North American democracy in which the trappings of monarchy are seldom seen, the country has been referred to as a "crowned republic."

Sentiment toward the ideas of a republic have been growing in Canada and arise partly from the split between English-speaking and French-speaking Canadians. As might be expected, more French-speaking Canadians appear inclined toward the idea of making Canada a republic than do English-speaking Canadians. The proposal has been advanced that Canada could abolish its monarchial constitution and yet retain its parliamentary forms. Under such a scheme, the Governor General might remain Head of State.

Public opinion polls have shown in past years that as much as one-third of the electorate favored Canada joining the U. S. This element has declined sharply in recent years, however.

Under the British North America Act, which created the Canadian Confederation and remains as the country's constitution, certain rights were given over to the provincial governments with all remaining jurisdictions going to the Federal authorities.

The Federal Government is responsible for all matters of national concern, including defense and foreign affairs, banking and the money system, criminal law, transportation, and trade and commerce. Provinces are responsible for civil rights, education, direct taxation, hospitals, welfare and municipal institutions. Education is compulsory to age 16.

Government conferences have been held on proposals to effect constitutional change and it is expected that the British North America Act will ultimately be replaced or substantially modified by a Canadian-written constitution.

The Federal Government proposed that a "Charter of Human Rights" be written into the BNA Act as a constitutional guarantee of certain individual freedoms which now are protected only by common law and could be suppressed by legislation. Not all provinces were agreeable to this, however, and as civil rights are a provincial responsibility, little change could be effected under the present Act.

The greatest political problem facing Canada is the future role of French-speaking Quebec in Confederation. Beginning in the late 1950s, a "quiet revolution" transformed Quebec from a classical, semi-industrial society to a modern, progressive province in which the French majority has been securing greater control over the economy and tax structure. While most Quebec leaders based their appeal on remaining within Confederation, extremists such as former Quebec cabinet minister Rene Levesque demand complete independence. Levesque led a group of separatists to form a party dedicated to the secession of Quebec from Canada under some type of economic "common market."

The search for harmony between French and English-speaking Canadians was not limited to Quebec, however. French-speaking Canadians insisted on educational rights wherever in Canada they were in sufficient numbers to warrant such facilities. They also insisted on the right to deal with the Federal Government in their own language. All political parties have endorsed these proposals and a government royal commission on bilingualism and biculturalism has recommended further recognition of French culture across Canada. Canada is officially bilingual.

From 1962 to 1968, Canada had a series of minority federal governments as neither the Conservatives, led until 1968 by former Prime Minister John Diefenbaker, nor the Liberals, were

## Canadian Winners Of The Victoria Cross

The Victoria Cross is Britain's highest military honor. It has been accorded to 94 Canadians since its inception in 1856. The cross was originally cast from metal of a Russian cannon captured during the Crimean War. Canadian winners in World War II:

| Name | Unit | Theater of War & Date |
|---|---|---|
| Sgt. Mjr. J. R. Osborn | Winnipeg Grenadiers | Hong Kong, Dec. 19, 1941 |
| Lt. Col. C. C. Merritt | S. Sask. Regiment | Dieppe, Aug. 19, 1942 |
| Capt. J. W. Foote | Royal Hamilton Light Infantry | Dieppe, Aug. 19, 1942 |
| Capt. F. T. Peters | Royal Navy | Oran, North Africa, Nov. 8, 1942 |
| Capt. Paul Triquet | Royal 22nd Regiment | Casa Berardi, Dec. 14, 1943 |
| Maj. C. F. Hoey | Lincolnshire Regiment | Burma, Feb. 16, 1944 |
| Maj. John K. Mahoney | Westminster Regiment | Melfa River, May 24, 1944 |
| P. O. A. C. Mynarski | RCAF | Cambria, France, June 12, 1944 |
| Flt. Lieut. D. E. Hornell | RCAF | "Northern waters" June 25, 1944 |
| Sqd. Ldr. Ian Bazalgette | RAF | Trossy St. Maximin, Aug. 4, 1944 |
| Maj. D. V. Currie | South Alberta Regiment | Normandy, Aug. 20, 1944 |
| Pvt. E. A. Smith | Seaforth Highlanders | Savio River, Italy, Oct. 22, 1944 |
| Sgt. Aubrey Cosens | Queen's Own Rifles | Holland, Feb. 26, 1945 |
| Maj. F. A. Tilston | Essex Scottish | Hochwald Forest, March 1, 1945 |
| Cpl. F. G. Topham | 1st Canadian Parachute Battalion | Germany, March 24, 1945 |
| Lt. R. H. Gray | Royal Canadian Navy | Pacific, Aug. 9, 1945 |

able to gain a majority. The Liberals replaced the Conservatives in 1963 with Lester B. Pearson as Prime Minister.

Majority government returned in 1968 with the election of a Liberal government under Prime Minister Pierre Elliott Trudeau, 48-year-old "new look" politician.

Trudeau, whose personality captivated much of the nation, is of French-Canadian stock but is fluently bilingual and opposes any special status for his native Quebec Province.

**The Undefended Border.** The biggest fact in Canadian life is the U. S. The two countries are each other's best trading partners. With closely related historic and racial backgrounds, they are also probably the world's closest allies.

However, many Canadians have become increasingly uneasy over the control by U. S. industry of large segments of the Canadian economy. This ranges from a bare majority in some fields up to nearly 100% in such important fields as auto manufacturing and the oil industry. Canadian governments have rejected policies which would discriminate against U. S. investment in Canada, recognizing the contribution such investment makes toward the nation's high living standards. But Canadians may well be encouraged to invest more themselves in their own industries to ensure that economic partnership does not turn into political partnership.

Tourists do not require visas or passports to visit back and forth between the two countries. U. S. immigration laws have been tightened in recent years, however, which is expected to reduce the number of Canadians emigrating to the U. S. There is now considerable movement the other way.

**Canada and the World.** Canadian foreign policy appears aimed primarily at supporting the Western alliance between Britain and the U. S., while developing increasing contacts with Communist countries. Substantial trade, especially in the sale of Canadian grain, is carried on with Communist China and the Soviet Union. There is also a steady trade with Cuba.

Canada was one of the original signatories to the UN and NATO but she has resisted invitations to join the Organization of American States. Foreign affairs are carried on by the Department of External Affairs, which in 1968 began a study of Canada's future role in NATO and of whether the country should recognize Communist China.

Canada also participates in NORAD (North American Air Defense agreement) in which the U. S. and Canada maintain joint air defenses involving the U. S. Air Force and the air branch of the Canadian Armed Services.

Defense is directed by the Department of National Defense, which in 1964 united the separate army, navy and air force into the Canadian Armed Forces. Army ranks were adopted for both naval and air branches. Combined strength in mid-1968 was about 110,000.

**A MIXED ECONOMY.** The Canadian economy features a blend of private ownership, public co-operatives, and government ownership. Electric utilities are owned by both provinces and municipalities in many areas, as are some telephone com-

panies. In Saskatchewan, automobile insurance is government-operated.

Air Canada, which operates throughout North America and in Europe, is government-owned while the competing Canadian Pacific Airlines, operating chiefly in the Pacific and Latin America, are privately-owned. The Canadian National Railway System is government-owned and the Canadian Pacific Railway Co. is privately owned.

In broadcasting, the chief radio-TV network, Canadian Broadcasting Corp., is government-owned. But many private stations carry its broadcasts, while an independent network, Canadian Television Network, also links other privately-owned stations.

**SOCIAL WELFARE.** There is a complex apparatus of social welfare in Canada. Most provinces and municipalities provide for welfare, or assistance payments for unemployed and others without income, including mothers' allowances. A program of contributory unemployment insurance provides benefits for most workers who become jobless. Allowances are paid to blind and disabled persons and workmen injured by accident receive compensation.

Two universal programs are the federally-sponsored Family Allowances, and Old Age Security. Under the former, monthly allowances of from $6 to $10 per month are paid to mothers for each child. Under the latter, minimum old age pensions of up to $105 per month are paid to persons over 66; this will be lowered to 65 in 1970.

A contributory pension program, the Canada Pension Plan, was established in 1966, with workers paying in 2% of their earnings between $600 and $5000. Pensions are paid at age 65.

Two Canadian provinces, with others expected to join later, inaugurated universal medical insurance programs July 1, 1968. Government-sponsored hospital insurance programs have operated throughout Canada for many years.

**AN ETHNIC DIVERSITY.** Canadian citizenship policies have never been aimed at producing a "melting pot" or assimilating all immigrants. Rather, individual national ethnic groups are encouraged to maintain their identity while giving loyalty to an over-all Canadian unity.

There are about 80,000 persons of Negro descent, most of whom originated either in the U. S. or the West Indies or are descendants of immigrants from those areas. There are no immigration quotas, but prospective immigrants must meet educational and job standards to enter the country.

Canada has some 225,000 native Indians and some 13,000 Eskimos. The Eskimos, inhabiting the Arctic or sub-Arctic, seldom come in contact with large Canadian communities. Most Indians live on reserves where their lands are held in trust. However, the Federal Government has been charged with being sharply neglectful of the conditions and opportunities affecting these peoples and it is certain that increased efforts will be made to win for them a better role in Canadian life.

Canadian health standards are extremely high and public service and facilities are among the most advanced in the world. Air and water pollution is a growing problem, however.

## Canadian Population By Origin

1961 Census

### Country of Birth

| | | | | | | |
|---|---|---|---|---|---|---|
| Canada | 15,393,984 | 84.4% | Scotland | 244,052 | 1.3% |
| England | 638,855 | 3.5% | Germany | 189,131 | 1.0% |
| United States | 283,908 | 1.5% | USSR | 186,653 | 1.0% |
| Italy | 258,908 | 1.4% | Other | 1,043,593 | 5.9% |

### By Ethnic Origin

| | | | | | |
|---|---|---|---|---|---|
| British Isles | 7,996,669 | Italian | 450,351 | Native Indian, Eskimo | 220,121 |
| French | 5,540,346 | Netherlands | 429,679 | Jewish | 173,344 |
| German | 1,049,337 | Scandinavian | 386,534 | Hungarian | 126,200 |
| Ukrainian | 473,337 | Polish | 323,517 | Russian | 119,534 |

## Canadian Cities With Metropolitan Populations Over 100,000

Source: 1966 Census. *Metropolitan Census Area

| | Population Metropolitan Area* | City | | | Population Metropolitan Area* | City |
|---|---|---|---|---|---|---|
| 1 Montreal | 2,436,817 | 1,222,255 | 12 Halifax | 198,193 | 86,792 |
| 2 Toronto | 2,158,496 | 664,584 | 13 Kitchener | 192,275 | 93,255 |
| 3 Vancouver | 892,286 | 410,375 | 14 Victoria | 173,455 | 57,453 |
| 4 Winnipeg | 508,759 | 257,005 | 15 Regina | 131,127 | 131,127 |
| 5 Ottawa | 494,535 | 290,741 | 16 Sudbury | 117,075 | 84,888 |
| 6 Hamilton | 449,116 | 298,121 | 17 Saskatoon | 115,892 | 115,892 |
| 7 Quebec | 413,397 | 166,984 | 18 St. Catharines | 109,418 | 97,101 |
| 8 Edmonton | 401,299 | 376,925 | 19 Saint John | 101,192 | 51,567 |
| 9 Calgary | 330,575 | 330,575 | 20 St. John's | 101,161 | 79,884 |
| 10 Windsor | 211,697 | 192,544 | 21 Oshawa | 100,255 | 78,082 |
| 11 London | 207,396 | 194,416 | | | |

# The Government of Canada

Canada is a federal state and a constitutional monarchy whose Head of State is Queen Elizabeth, proclaimed Queen of Canada in 1952 as well as of the United Kingdom and her other realms. The Queen is represented in Canada, a self-governing member of the Commonwealth of Nations, by a resident Governor-General appointed by Her Majesty on the advice of the Canadian federal cabinet. The cabinet is drawn from members of the party holding the largest number of seats in the Canadian House of Commons and the Senate. The cabinet, together with the Governor-General, comprises the executive branch of the government with a Prime Minister as head of the government. Ottawa is the federal capital.

## Head of State

**Queen Elizabeth**—Succeeded to throne 1952.
**Governor-General**—Rt. Hon. Roland Michener, appointed 1967.

## The Cabinet

Sworn in July 6, 1968:

**Prime Minister**—Pierre Elliott Trudeau.
**Government leader in the Senate**—Sen. Paul Martin.
**Minister of Transport, Acting Prime Minister**—Paul Hellyer.
**Secretary of State for External Affairs**—Mitchell Sharp.
**President of the Privy Council**—Donald Macdonald.
**Solicitor-General**—George McIlraith.
**Minister of Public Works**—Arthur Laing.
**Minister of Manpower and Immigration**—Allan MacEachen.
**President of the Treasury Board**—Charles Drury.
**Minister of Finance and Receiver-General**—Edgar J. Benson.
**Minister of National Defense**—Leo Cadieux.
**Minister of Industry, Trade and Commerce**—Jean-Luc Pepin.
**Minister of Forestry and Rural Development**—Jean Marchand.
**Minister of Energy, Mines and Resources**—J. J. Greene.
**Minister of National Revenue**—Jean-Pierre Cote.
**Minister of Justice and Attorney-General**—John Turner.
**Minister of Indian Affairs and Northern Development**—Jean Chretien.
**Minister of Labor**—Bryce Mackasey.
**Minister of National Health and Welfare**—John Munro.
**Secretary of State**—Gerard Pelletier.
**Minister of Fisheries**—Jack Davis.
**Minister of Agriculture**—Horace Olson.
**Minister for Veterans Affairs**—Jean-Eudes Dube.
**Minister of Consumer and Corporate Affairs**—Ron Basford.
**Postmaster-General, Minister of Communications**—Eric Kierans.
**Minister of Supply and Services**—Donald Jamieson.
**Minister without portfolio**—Robert K. Andras.
**Minister without portfolio**—James Richardson.
**Minister without portfolio**—Otto Lang.

## House of Commons

The House of Commons is the lower but more important body in Canada's bi-cameral parliament. Members are elected to the 264 seats at federal elections held at least every five years; four years is the traditional term. The government of the day (the party with the most seats in the House) chooses the date of the election, with voting by universal suffrage over the age of 21.

The House of Commons is controlled by the government party through the cabinet. The business of the House, however, is directed by an impartial Speaker who until 1968 had always been a member of the governing party. In that year, by agreement between the two largest parties, the former Speaker, Lucien Lamoureux, successfully stood for election as an Independent and on resumption of Parliament, became the first non-party speaker.

Legislation becomes law by receiving three "readings" in the House of Commons, passing the Senate, or upper chamber, for approval, and obtaining Royal Assent from the Governor-General. Only in the House of Commons can legislation be introduced requiring the spending of public monies.

Hon. Robert L. Stanfield, leader of the Progressive Conservative party, is Leader of the Official Opposition in the House of Commons. Other opposition party leaders are T. C. Douglas of the New Democratic party (who failed to win a seat in the 1968 election) and Real Caouette of the Creditiste party.

### 1968 FEDERAL ELECTION

| Party | Seats | % of Vote |
|---|---|---|
| Liberal | 155 | 45.7% |
| Progressive Conservative | 72 | 31.4% |
| New Democratic | 22 | 17.2% |
| *Creditiste | 14 | 4.4% |
| Independents | 1 | 1.3% |
| TOTAL | 264 | 100.0% |

*French-Canadian splinter of Social Credit party, which failed to elect any members outside Quebec.

## Seats Won in Federal Elections by Provinces, 1968

| Party | B.C. | Alta. | Sask. | Man. | Ont. | Que. | P.E.I. | N.B. | N.S. | Nfld. |
|---|---|---|---|---|---|---|---|---|---|---|
| Liberal | 16 | 4 | 2 | 5 | 88 | 74 | — | 5 | 1 | 1 |
| Prog. Cons. | — | 15 | 5 | 5 | 17 | 4 | 4 | 5 | 10 | 6 |
| N.D.P. | 7 | — | 6 | 3 | 6 | — | — | — | — | — |
| Creditiste | — | — | — | — | — | 14 | — | — | — | — |

Note: Liberals won Northwest Territory seat; Progressive Conservatives Yukon Territory seat. One independent elected in Ontario.

## The Senate

The Senate comprises 102 members appointed by the Prime Minister for life, but with automatic retirement at age 75. The British North America Act requires that membership be divided 24 to Quebec, 24 to Ontario, 30 to the Atlantic provinces, and 24 to the Western provinces.

Hon. Paul Martin is government leader in the Senate. Sen. Jacques Flynn, Prog. Cons., is leader of the Opposition in the Senate.

### GOVERNORS-GENERAL

Since 1952, the Governors-General of Canada have been native-born, replacing the former practice of appointing distinguished Britons. Canadian-born appointees have been:

Rt. Hon. Vincent Massey ........1952-1959
Gen. Rt. Hon. Georges Vanier ...1959-1967
Rt. Hon. Roland Michener ......1967-

## Mayors of Canada's Largest Cities

| | | | | | |
|---|---|---|---|---|---|
| Montreal | Jean Drapeau | Winnipeg | Stephen Juba | Quebec | Gilles Lamontagne |
| Toronto | William Dennison | Ottawa | Donald Reid | Edmonton | Vincent M. Dantzer |
| Vancouver | Tom Campbell | Hamilton | Victor Copps | Calgary | J. C. Leslie |

# Supreme Court of Canada

Canada's chief judicial bodies are the Supreme Court of Canada, which sits in Ottawa and hears civil and criminal appeals from lower courts, and the Exchequer Court of Canada which hears claims made by or against the Crown and also serves as a Court of Admiralty. The nine members of the Supreme Court and the five members of the Exchequer Court are appointed by the federal cabinet.

As the Supreme Court does not interpret legislation in respect to constitutional statutes (except to determine whether an act falls within the jurisdiction of a provincial or the federal government), it does not figure nearly as prominently in national life as does the Supreme Court in the United States. The Chief Justice of the Supreme Court of Canada is Hon. J. R. Cartwright.

# Prime Ministers Since Confederation

| Name | Party | Term | Name | Party | Term |
|------|-------|------|------|-------|------|
| Sir John A. Macdonald | Conserv. | 1867-1873, 1878-1891 | Arthur Meighen | Conserv. Unionist | 1920-1921, 1926 |
| Alexander Mackenzie | Liberal | 1873-1878 | W. L. M. King | Liberal | 1921-1926, 1926-1930, 1935-1948 |
| Sir John J. C. Abbott | Conserv. | 1891-1892 | | | |
| Sir John S. D. Thompson | Conserv. | 1892-1894 | | | |
| Sir Mackenzie Bowell | Conserv. | 1894-1896 | R. B. Bennett | Conserv. | 1930-1935 |
| Sir Charles Tupper | Conserv. | 1896 | Louis St. Laurent | Liberal | 1948-1957 |
| Sir Wilfrid Laurier | Liberal | 1896-1911 | John G. Diefenbaker | Prog. Conserv. | 1957-1963 |
| Sir Robert L. Borden | Conserv. Unionist | 1911-1920 | Lester B. Pearson | Liberal | 1963-1968 |
| | | | Pierre Elliott Trudeau | Liberal | 1968- |

# Canada's Provincial Governments

Each Canadian province except one maintains a single legislative assembly, the exception being Quebec which also has an appointive Consultative Council. The parliamentary system applies in each province, the head of the government bearing the title of Premier (or Prime Minister in Quebec and Ontario). The Queen's representative in each province is a Lieutenant-Governor, appointed by the federal cabinet.

| Province | Premier | Party Affiliation | Party in Power Since |
|----------|---------|-------------------|----------------------|
| Newfoundland | Joseph E. Smallwood | Liberal | 1949 |
| Prince Edward Island | Alexander Campbell | Liberal | 1966 |
| Nova Scotia | G. I. Smith | Prog. Cons. | 1956 |
| New Brunswick | Louis J. Robichaud | Liberal | 1960 |
| Quebec | Daniel Johnson | Union Nationale | 1966 |
| Ontario | John Robarts | Prog. Cons. | 1943 |
| Manitoba | Walter Weir | Prog. Cons. | 1958 |
| Saskatchewan | Ross Thatcher | Liberal | 1964 |
| Alberta | E. C. Manning | Social Credit | 1935 |
| British Columbia | W. A. C. Bennett | Social Credit | 1952 |

# Canadian Taxation Structure

The Government of Canada levies corporate and personal income taxes; old age security tax; excise (import) taxes; and a federal sales tax. Provincial governments levy personal income taxes and sales taxes. Municipalities levy commercial and private property taxes. Some rates:

## Personal Income Tax

In all provinces except Quebec, taxpayers receive an abatement of their federal personal income tax equal to the amount of their provincial income tax. Quebec levies and collects its own income tax in addition to the federal levy. For a Canadian resident in most provinces, married, with two children, his basic tax rate will be as follows (slightly higher in Saskatchewan, Manitoba and Quebec):

| Weekly Earning | Income Tax |
|----------------|------------|
| $ 75.00 | $ 3.55 |
| 100.00 | 8.45 |
| 125.00 | 13.95 |
| 150.00 | 20.80 |
| 175.00 | 27.20 |
| 200.00 | 34.20 |

## Corporate Income Tax

The federal corporate income tax rate in Canada is 18 per cent on taxable income up to $35,000 annually, and 47 per cent on any amount in excess of $35,000. There is a federal abatement of 10 per cent on these taxes, but provincial corporate income taxes range from 10 to 12 per cent. In addition, there is a federal old age security tax of 3 per cent. These taxes provide a total corporate income tax, in Ontario as an example, of 23 per cent under $35,000 and 52 per cent over $35,000.

## Sales Taxes

The federal sales tax of 12 per cent is applied at the wholesale level. Provincial sales taxes, mostly 5 per cent, are applied at the retail level. Alberta is the only province without a retail sales tax.

# Canadian Postal Information

The Canada Post Office, reorganized in 1968 as part of the newly-created Department of Communications, employs more than 40,000 and operates more than 11,000 Post Offices.

## Postal Rates

### First Class

Five cents for the first ounce, 3¢ each additional ounce. Local delivery, 4¢ first ounce, 2¢ each additional ounce. Postcards, 4¢ to Canadian destinations.

### Air Mail

All first class mail up to 8 oz. goes automatically by air at the standard rates where such will speed delivery. Air mail exceeding 8 oz. is 7¢ for the first oz. and 5¢ for each oz. after.

### Printed Matter

Books, newspapers, magazines, etc. mailed by the public, including unsealed Christmas, Easter and other such greeting cards, 3¢ first two oz., 2¢ each additional 2 oz. up to 1 lb., 1¢ each additional 2 oz. over 1 lb.

### International

**Surface:** To Great Britain and northern Ireland and other places in the Commonwealth, Republic of Ireland, France, Spain, United States and rest of North, Central and South America—Letters, 5¢ for first oz. and 3¢ each oz. after. Postcards, 4¢. All other countries—4¢ first two oz., 2¢ each two oz. after.

**Air Mail:** To United States and all of North, Central and South America—Letters, 8¢ first oz., 6¢ each oz. after. Postcards, 10¢. All other countries—Letters, 25¢ each half oz. Postcards, 10¢. Aerogrammes to all countries, 10¢.

### Registration Fees

To Canada and U. S.—50¢ for $50.00 indemnity; 75¢, $100.00 indemnity. All other countries, 50¢, $8.83 indemnity. Acknowledgement of receipt, 15¢.

### Special Delivery

Additional fee of 40¢ on first class mail, 50¢ on parcels, to Canada, Australia, France, Germany, Great Britain, Netherlands, Switzerland, United States only.

# Canadian Agriculture—Income And Employment

Source: 1966 Census

Although some 70% of Canadians live in urban centers, agriculture remains the nation's largest single industry. According to the 1966 census, Canada had a total of 430,522 farms, providing direct employment to some 600,000 persons.

However, according to a 1958 survey, one-third of total farm family income is obtained from off-the-farm work.

Ontario accounts for more total farm production than any other province but Saskatchewan, noted for its wheat, is Canada's greatest grain producing province.

Most Canadian farms are large—50.1% over 200 acres, 24.2% from 100 to 200 acres, and 25.7% under 100 acres. Only 4.5% are less than 10 acres.

## Value of Agricultural Products Sold Annually

| | | | |
|---|---|---|---|
| Field crops | $8,24,150,150 | Livestock | 753,114,440 |
| Vegetables, fruits, greenhouse | | Dairy products | 402,944,560 |
| and nursery products | 123,684,700 | Other (includes wool) | 46,891,430 |
| Poultry and eggs | 195,905,950 | **Total agricultural products sold** | **$2,346,691,230** |

## Livestock and Poultry

| | | | |
|---|---|---|---|
| Cattle | 11,941,184 | Hens and chickens | 69,612,229 |
| Pigs | 5,332,736 | Turkeys | 7,670,479 |
| Sheep | 1,563,534 | Ducks | 397,964 |
| Horses | 512,021 | Geese | 314,800 |

## Crop Acreage in Canada

| | | | |
|---|---|---|---|
| Wheat | 25,315,964 | Other fodder crops | 368,875 |
| Oats | 10,515,367 | Flaxseed | 2,083,218 |
| Barley | 5,528,424 | Rapeseed | 711,054 |
| Mixed grains | 1,564,707 | Mustard seed | 120,812 |
| Rye | 561,834 | Soybeans | 212,776 |
| Field peas | 66,658 | Potatoes | 305,727 |
| Field beans | 68,387 | Sugar beets | 93,127 |
| Corn | 407,174 | Tobacco | 139,638 |
| Tame hay | 12,238,263 | Vegetables | 216,993 |
| Oats cut for fodder | 1,222,946 | Tree fruits | 148,159 |
| Corn cut for fodder | 366,358 | Small fruits | 54,539 |

# Labor Unions In Canada

Canadian industry is highly unionized, in most cases through Canadian branches of international unions having their headquarters in the United States. Most of these unions, with a total membership of about 1,200,000, are affiliated in the Canadian Labor Congress. A Quebec-based labor body, the Confederation of National Trade Unions, has about 150,000 members. Two smaller groupings of independent Canadian unions are the 11,000-member National Council of Canadian Labor and the 20,000-member Council of Canadian Unions.

# Canada's Chartered Banks

The Canadian banking system is built around nationwide banking chains, chartered by acts of Parliament. Local banks are thus branches and are not locally owned. The government-owned Bank of Canada has been the sole authority to issue paper money since 1945. It does not operate as a commercial bank, but sets fiscal policy and controls the money supply through the chartered banks.

In addition to the chartered banks, the Post Office operates a savings bank as do the provincial governments in Ontario and Alberta. There are also two independent savings banks in Quebec.

Trust companies have assumed an increasingly active role in public savings in the recent years. Thousands of credit unions also provide savings and loan facilities to their members. As of April 30, 1968, the chartered banks held 14,497,017 savings accounts.

Assets of chartered banks:

| Bank | Assets (1967) |
|---|---|
| Royal Bank | $7,779,659,283 |
| Canadian Imperial Bank of Commerce | 7,481,582,256 |
| Bank of Montreal | 6,132,452,838 |
| Bank of Nova Scotia | 4,138,719,179 |
| Toronto-Dominion Bank | 3,458,300,753 |
| Banque Canadienne Nationale | 1,235,077,693 |
| Banque Provinciale du Canada | 642,455,289 |
| Mercantile Bank | 222,838,454 |
| Bank of British Columbia | Not available |
| | (opened July 18, 1968.) |

# Education and Religion

Canada is officially bilingual, employing English and French. Educational institutions include provincially controlled schools, private schools, universities and colleges, and Dominion Indian schools.

### COMMUNICANTS, 1961 CENSUS

| | | | |
|---|---|---|---|
| Roman Catholic | 8,342,826 | Jewish | 254,368 |
| United Church of Canada | 3,664,008 | Greek Orthodox | 239,766 |
| Anglican Church of Canada | 2,409,068 | Ukrainian (Greek) Catholic | 189,653 |
| Presbyterian | 818,558 | Mennonite | 152,452 |
| Lutheran | 662,744 | Others and not stated | 911,251 |
| Baptist | 593,553 | | |

# Canadian Consumer Price Index

(1958=100%)

| Year | Level | % Increase | Year | Level | % Increase |
|---|---|---|---|---|---|
| 1959 | 101.1 | 1.1 | 1964 | 108.2 | 1.8 |
| 1960 | 102.3 | 1.2 | 1965 | 110.9 | 2.5 |
| 1961 | 103.3 | 1.0 | 1966 | 115.0 | 3.7 |
| 1962 | 104.5 | 1.2 | 1967 | 119.1 | 3.6 |
| 1963 | 106.3 | 1.7 | 1968 (Jan.-May) | 122.4 | 4.3 |

## Canada's Population Clock Hits 20,800,000

The new population clock at the Dominion Bureau of Statistics in Ottawa hit the unprecedented mark of 20,800,000 on July 29, 1968. At the current rate, one new Canadian is added to the estimated population when the clock's illuminated figures change every 82 seconds. The totals reflect the bureau's calculations of births, immigration, deaths and emigration.

## Canadian Government Revenue and Expenditures (in Canadian Dollars)

Source: Department of Finance (p-preliminary)

### CHIEF SOURCES OF REVENUE AND GRAND TOTAL ($1,000 omitted)

| Fiscal Year ending | Income tax | Sales tax | Other excise taxes | Excise duties | Customs duties | Estate taxes | Other taxes | Post office | Other non-tax rev. | Total budge-tary rev. |
|---|---|---|---|---|---|---|---|---|---|---|
| 1964.. | 3,248,531 | 946,055 | 273,415 | 393,326 | 581,441 | 90,671 | 92 | 200,717 | 518,955 | 6,253,204 |
| 1965.. | 3,770,814 | 1,204,610 | 269,082 | 411,402 | 622,102 | 88,626 | 140 | 230,436 | 583,098 | 7,180,310 |
| 1966.. | 3,919,095 | 1,395,129 | 296,178 | 445,885 | 685,519 | 108,352 | 161 | 237,482 | 665,181 | 8,358,178 |
| 1967.. | 4,270,666 | 1,513,566 | 315,581 | 460,980 | 777,586 | 101,106 | 170 | 253,342 | 683,185 | 8,376,182 |
| 1968p.. | 4,738,000 | 1,600,000 | 337,000 | 489,000 | 746,000 | 102,000 | — | 280,000 | 763,000 | 9,055,000 |

### CHIEF AND TOTAL EXPENDITURES ($1,000 omitted)

| Fiscal year ending | Defense expend-iture | Inter-est on public debt | Pay-ments to prov-inces[1] | Health and welfare services | Post office | Public works | Trans-porta-tion serv-ices | Vet-erans affair | Total budge-tary expen-ditures[2] |
|---|---|---|---|---|---|---|---|---|---|
| 1964......... | 1,730,032 | 954,544 | 254,330 | 1,167,826 | 206,895 | 167,001 | 423,258 | 333,740 | 6,872,402 |
| 1965......... | 1,585,644 | 1,012,097 | 358,357 | 1,261,513 | 210,459 | 234,412 | 470,813 | 352,098 | 7,218,275 |
| 1966......... | 1,594,981 | 1,077,296 | 465,993 | 1,129,749 | 240,206 | 275,147 | 532,499 | 369,337 | 7,734,796 |
| 1967......... | 1,695,872 | 1,190,523 | 515,523 | 1,315,943 | 268,494 | 294,373 | 568,178 | 390,821 | 8,779,681 |
| 1968p........ | 1,811,000 | 1,295,000 | 737,500 | 1,489,200 | 304,800 | 301,600 | 612,600 | 403,821 | 9,863,000 |

[1]Fiscal, tax-sharing, subsidy and other payments.
[2]Total includes other unenumerated items.

### ASSETS, DEBT, PER CAPITA TAX REVENUE, IN DOLLARS[1]

| Fiscal year ending | Gross debt | Net assets | Net debt | Per capita net debt[2] | Inter. paid on debt | Per capita tax revenue[2] |
|---|---|---|---|---|---|---|
| 1964........ | 25,923,732,116 | 10,853,582,664 | 15,070,149,452 | 785.97 | 954,543,790 | 288.60 |
| 1965........ | 26,573,425,709 | 11,068,953,165 | 15,504,472,544 | 794.44 | 1,012,097,143 | 326.23 |
| 1966........ | 27,482,940,350 | 11,939,492,485 | 15,543,447,865 | 782.69 | 1,077,295,513 | 344.95 |
| 1967........ | 30,340,137,314 | 14,375,186,836 | 15,964,950,478 | 785.14 | 1,190,523,000 | 365.87 |
| 1968p....... | 32,925,300,000 | 16,152,300,000 | 16,773,000,000 | 810.29 | 1,295,000,000 | 387.05 |

[1]Figures apply to Government of Canada only.
[2]Based on population as of Apr. 1 of the same year.

### EXTERNAL TRADE OF CANADA (Excluding Gold), In Thousands of Dollars

| Year | Imports | | | Exports | | |
|---|---|---|---|---|---|---|
| | Dutiable | Free | Total | Domestic | Re-exports | Total |
| 1960............. | 3,048,583 | 2,434,112 | 5,284,695 | 5,255,575 | 131,217 | 5,386,792 |
| 1961............. | 3,115,408 | 2,653,170 | 5,768,578 | 5,754,986 | 140,229 | 5,895,215 |
| 1962............. | 3,480,282 | 2,777,494 | 6,257,776 | 6,178,523 | 169,190 | 6,347,713 |
| 1963............. | 3,542,601 | 3,015,607 | 6,558,208 | 6,798,529 | 181,613 | 6,980,142 |
| 1964............. | 4,034,903 | 3,452,804 | 7,487,707 | 8,094,219 | 209,186 | 8,303,546 |
| 1965............. | 4,266,300 | 4,366,848 | 8,633,148 | 8,525,078 | 241,599 | 8,766,677 |
| 1966............. | 4,831,709 | 5,034,730 | 9,866,439 | 10,070,627 | 254,693 | 10,325,320 |
| 1967............. | 5,096,920 | 5,984,233 | 11,081,153 | 11,111,804 | 299,284 | 11,411,088 |

### TRADE OF CANADA WITH U. S. AND BRITAIN (In Thousands of Dollars)

| Year | United States | | | | Britain | |
|---|---|---|---|---|---|---|
| | Imports | Domestic Exports | Re-exports | Total Exports | Imports | Domestic Exports |
| 1961............. | 3,863,542 | 3,107,176 | 107,342 | 3,214,518 | 618,221 | 909,344 |
| 1962............. | 4,299,539 | 3,608,439 | 136,226 | 3,744,665 | 563,062 | 909,041 |
| 1963............. | 4,444,556 | 3,766,380 | 146,972 | 3,913,352 | 526,800 | 1,006,838 |
| 1964............. | 5,164,285 | 4,271,059 | 165,899 | 4,436,958 | 573,995 | 1,199,779 |
| 1965............. | 7,135,611 | 4,840,456 | 206,756 | 6,234,478 | 619,058 | 1,174,309 |
| 1966............. | 7,135,860 | 6,027,722 | 207,137 | 6,234,859 | 644,741 | 1,122,574 |
| 1967............. | 8,021,771 | 7,079,296 | 243,747 | 7,323,143 | 673,050 | 1,169,052 |

## Public Days in Canada, 1969

New Year's Day, Jan. 1; Good Friday, April 4; Easter Monday, April 7; Sovereign's Birthday, May 19 (always first Monday preceding May 25); Dominion Day, July 1; Labour Day, Sept. 1; Thanksgiving Day, Oct. 13 (the second Monday of October); Remembrance Day, Nov. 11; Christmas Day, Dec. 25.

When the statutory holidays fall on Sunday, the following day is observed. Although the general observation of holidays on Mondays, in order to give people long weekends, has been a matter of discussion, no legislation has yet been passed on this regard, with the exception for Victoria Day.

Civic Holiday is not a statutory holiday, but any city, town or municipality may appoint any day as such by resolution of the Council or the statutory body. However, the first Monday in August is generally observed throughout Canada as Civic Holiday (August 4, in 1969).

# NATIONS OF THE WORLD

The nations of the world are listed in alphabetical order, except for Canada and the United States, about which separate articles and other information and statistical tables appear in other sections of the Almanac (see Index for listings).

The article on Rhodesia, whose independence has been an unsettled question, will be found under United Kingdom among other states not completely independent. These also include Bahrain, Qatar, the Trucial States and Brunei, all British Protected States. Sikkim, an Indian Protected State, is described under India.

Some international groups, of which various nations are members, are referred to, in the following articles, by initials (such as NATO). Articles on these groups may be found through the Index.

**See special color section for maps and flags of all nations.**

*Note—Exchange rate of foreign currencies in terms of U. S. dollars is latest available, but in some cases is subject to frequent fluctuation.*

## Afghanistan

### DOULAT I PADSHAHI YE AFGHANISTAN

**Capital: Kabul. Area: 253,861 sq. mi. Population (UN est. 1967): 15,751,000. Monetary unit: Afghan (45 per U. S. $1, official rate).**

Afghanistan is a landlocked constitutional monarchy occupying a mountainous area much of which is 4,000 ft. and more above sea level. It is slightly smaller than Texas. Its neighbors are Iran, Pakistan, India and the USSR. The northeast tip of the country just touches China's Sinkiang Province.

The Hindu Kush mountains tower 16,000 ft. above the capital of Kabul and reach a height of more than 25,000 ft. some 200 miles to the east of the capital. Trade with India flows through the 35-mile long Khyber Pass from Kabul to Peshawar. The climate is dry, with extreme temperatures.

Ninety percent of the country's exports are agricultural products. Chief items are cotton, wool, karakul pelts, hides, casings, oil seed and fresh and dried fruit. Handwoven carpets are the only manufactured goods exported. Some 4,000,000 head of broad-tail Karakul sheep are raised, as well as goats and camels. The sheep provide the principal meat item in the Afghan's diet and the tightly curled, glossy black coats of the newborn lambs are a valuable fur. Minerals include copper, lead, zinc, iron, silver, asbestos and oil. The country has received considerable economic aid from the U. S., USSR and Communist China.

**History and Government.** Afghanistan was so named in about the middle of the 18th Century. In ancient times it was known as Aryana, in the Middle Ages as Khorasan. Pukhtuns (Pashtuns) comprise 53.5% of the population; Tajiks 36.7%; Uzbeks 6%; Hazaras 3%.

On Sept. 19, 1964 a Grand Assembly approved a new constitution providing for an elected Lower House, partly-elected Upper House, an independent judiciary, a prime minister chosen by the King and barring relatives of the King from important posts—reforms the King had sought. Under the old government, legislative power was vested in a parliament consisting of the King, a Senate appointed by the King for life, and a National Assembly. The reigning King is Mohammed Zahir Shah, born Oct. 15, 1914, who ascended the throne Nov. 8, 1933, on the assassination of his father, Mohammed Nadir Shah. Afghanistan is a member of the UN.

Bordering on both Russia and China, Afghanistan has been traditionally neutral. Student riots in 1965 were followed by appointment of a new Prime Minister, Mahammed Hasim Maiwandal, who appointed at least 4 Afghans educated in the U. S. to his Cabinet, along with the first woman Cabinet minister. In 1966 the government refused to condemn U. S. policy in Vietnam as urged by visiting Communist Chinese leaders.

**Education and Religion.** Education is free and, where facilities are available, compulsory. The University of Kabul was established in 1932. Principal languages are Pushtu and Persian. English is taught. Islam is the predominant religion.

**Defense.** There is compulsory military service for a two-year period.

## Albania

### SHQIPERIA
### REPUBLIKA POPULLORE E SHQIPERISE

**Capital: Tirana. Area: 11,100 sq. mi. Population (1968 Govt. est.): 2,000,000. Monetary unit: Lek (5 per U. S. $1, basic rate).**

Albania, a Balkan communist republic, is a narrow mountainous land, slightly larger than Maryland, extending for 225 mi. along the E coast of the Adriatic. Yugoslavia and Greece are its neighbors. Off the E coast in the Strait of Otranto is the island of Saseno. The Buna is the principal navigable river. Mt. Korab, 9,066 ft. is the tallest peak.

**Resources and Industries.** There are important forest resources and some mineral wealth, the latter not fully developed. Chief products of the country are tobacco, timber, wool, hides, furs, cheese, and dairy products, fish, olive oil, corn and cattle. Industrial output in 1964 increased 7%. Minerals, including chromite, petroleum, iron and copper, account for over half the value of exports. Durazzo is the main seaport.

**History and Government.** Albania has been overrun by warring armies for over 2,000 years. It declared its independence from the Turks in 1912; this was backed by a conference of European powers which placed Prince William of Wied on the throne in 1914. He fled within months because of uprisings. During World War I armies of several nations occupied the land by turns. In 1920, a republic was set up. In 1925, Ahmed Zogu seized the presidency; in 1928 he proclaimed himself King, assuming the title Zog I.

King Zog fled in 1939 when Italy invaded and annexed Albania. When Italy surrendered to the Allies in 1943, German troops took over; they left in 1944 and Communist partisans seized power. Gen. Enver Hoxha was named provisional president; a Communist front won a 1945 election; in 1946 a new constitution, modeled on that of the USSR, was adopted under Hoxha's leadership.

Albania requested U. S. recognition early in 1945, and a U. S. mission was sent to the country to make arrangements. Albania did not agree to one condition, that it recognize pre-war treaties between the U. S. and Albania. The U. S. mission was withdrawn in Nov. 1946.

Britain recognized Albania in 1945 but broke off relations in 1946. The U. S. and Britain voted against Albanian admission to the UN in 1946; it finally won admission in 1955 with Britain voting "yes" and the U. S. abstaining. In 1955 it was admitted to the Warsaw Pact. Its policies have been strongly pro-Stalinist, anti-Khrushchev, pro-Communist China and hostile to Tito's Yugoslav regime. The USSR broke relations with Albania in Dec. 1961 and blocked its participation in the Jan. 1962 meeting of the Warsaw Pact nations in Prague.

Ties with Communist China were strengthened in 1966 as the Premiers of the two countries exchanged visits, and Albania, like China, abolished the insignia of rank in its armed forces.

**Education and Religion.** There is no state religion. The largest segment of the population is Moslem, followed by Orthodox Christians (Church of Albania), and Roman Catholics. Primary education nominally is compulsory and free under the constitution.

492

Racially the Albanians are mainly Ghegs in the north and Tosks in the south.

**Defense:** Service is compulsory between 19 and 35. The Army numbers about 25,000. The Navy has 3,000 men and the Air Force, under the command of the army, has 7,000 men.

# Algeria
## ALGERIE
### REPUBLIC OF ALGERIA

**Capital:** Algiers. **Area:** 919,591 sq. mi. **Population** (UN est. 1967): 12,540,000. **Monetary unit:** Dinar (4.937 per U. S. $1).

Algeria, an independent republic more than 3 times the size of Texas, is located in northern Africa extending for 640 mi. along the Mediterranean Sea between Tunisia and Morocco. The southern Saharan Departments extend into the Sahara Desert and border on Niger, Mali and Mauritania. The Tell, located on the coast, comprises fertile plains from 50 to 100 mi. wide. Several chains of the Atlas Mtns., running roughly E-W and reaching altitudes of 7,000 ft., separate the coast regions from inland plateaus and the Sahara. Algiers, the capital, is the largest city.

**Resources and Industries.** Agricultural products include wheat, barley, oats, corn, potatoes, artichokes, flax and tobacco. Wine and olive oil are produced. Dates, pomegranates and figs grow abundantly. Cattle raising is paramount. There are large deposits of iron, zinc, lead, mercury, copper and antimony.

Exports consists chiefly of wines, cereals, skins, fruits, iron and zinc ores, phosphate rock, cork, esparto grass, manufactured tobacco products, vegetables and petroleum. Production of the latter is valued at over $470,000,000 a year. Trade is mainly with France.

Exploitation of the Sahara's vast oil and gas deposits and its tourist potentiality is being pressed.

On Aug. 30, 1967 the government nationalized 5 U. S.-owned oil companies which had been seized June 6, at the outbreak of the Israeli-Arab war. In 1968, several British and French industries were nationalized. Foreign observers reported unemployment had risen to 50%.

**History and Government.** The fertile Tell plains have attracted a succession of conquerors to Algeria from before the time of Christ. Once ruled over by Carthage, the country after 146 B.C. came under control of the Roman Empire and it was not until the incursions by the Vandals, 430-31 A.D., that the Roman hold was fully broken. The Byzantines regained part of Roman Africa in 534, but it was the Arabs, who arrived in the 7th Century who were to have the most lasting influence on the country, forging it into the Moorish Empire. But local control was lax and local potentates rose and fell, and in 1518 Algiers and the coastal area came under Turkish domination. The country did not become a political entity until France took control in 1830, annexed it in 1842 and began to develop the land.

From 1954-62 growing Arab nationalism led to outright warfare between the French and the Algerians. The political impasse was not broken until French President Charles de Gaulle negotiated with the Front de Liberatione Nationale (FLN). Algeria in a referendum July, 1962, voted overwhelmingly for independence; De Gaulle proclaimed it independent July 3.

Internal strife continued, however, between opposing Algerian factions, and Ahmed Ben Bella, with Army support, assumed control in Aug. 1962. A constitution was approved Sept. 8, 1963, and Premier Ben Bella, sole candidate, was elected President for a 5-year term Sept. 15. Nationalization of lands and industries proceeded rapidly. Algeria received a $100,000,000 long-term industrial loan from the USSR in Sept. 1963, and continues to receive French aid.

President Ben Bella was arrested and deposed June 19, 1965, in a bloodless, army-backed coup d'etat led by Col. Houari Boumedienne (born Mohammed Boukharouba), Defense Minister and Vice President. Col. Boumedienne assumed leadership of a new 26-man Revolutionary Council and, on July 11, announced a new Cabinet with himself as President and Defense Minister and including 9 members of the former Cabinet. U. S. Government aid, which had tapered off as Ben Bella's alignment with the Communist world grew, was stepped up after his ouster.

Algeria is a member of the UN and Arab League.

**Education and Religion.** The population before independence included approx. 1,000,000 Europeans, 80% of them Algerian-born, since reduced to about one-tenth of that total. The natives are Arabs and Berbers, of Moslem faith. There is a university at Algiers. French and Moslem primary schools have been amalgamated.

**Defense.** The Army and Air Force are being expanded and modernized with aid from USSR and UAR.

# Andorra
## PRINCIPAT D'ANDORRA

**Capital:** Andorra la Vella. **Area:** 179 sq. mi. **Population** (est. 1968): 17,216. **Monetary units:** Franc, Peseta (4.9371 and 69.76 per U. S. $1).

Andorra is a tiny principality of valleys and mountains set high in the Pyrenees on the border of France and Spain. It has two Co-Princes, the President of France and the Spanish Catholic Bishop of Urgel, whose representatives are charged with the administration of justice, but the country has enjoyed practical sovereignty since 1278. It pays an annual tribute of 960 francs to France and 460 pesetas to the Bishop of Urgel.

Actual government is in the hands of a Council-General of 24 elected members (suffrage is for men only) who enact laws and elect a Syndic General, the top administrator.

The main industry is tourism (150 hotels), followed by sheep-raising. Andorra has considerable iron, lead, alum, stone and timber. Skiing, trout fishing and chamois hunting are among tourist attractions.

The official language is Catalan; principal religion is Roman Catholicism.

# Argentina
## REPUBLICA ARGENTINA

**Capital:** Buenos Aires. **Area:** 1,072,068 sq. mi. **Population** (UN est. 1967): 23,031,000. **Monetary unit:** Peso (350 per U. S. $1, free rate).

Argentina, 4 times the size of Texas, extends from Bolivia 2,300 miles to Tierre del Fuego and from the Andes to the South Atlantic, and is the 2nd largest and 2nd most populous country in South America, next to Brazil.

The mountains are grouped into 4 isolated systems: the Andean, Central, Misiones and Southern. Aconcagua is the highest peak in the Western Hemisphere, altitude 22,834 ft. (Official Arg. figure.) The southern Andes have lakes, trout and salmon streams.

East of the Andes are great plains, heavily wooded and called the Gran Chaco in the north, and the fertile, treeless Pampas, given over to wheat and cattle raising, in the central region. Patagonia, in the south, is bleak and arid; petroleum and sheep are its main products.

**Rio de la Plata** is the estuary of one of the world's great drainage systems. It is a wide gulf of mostly fresh water, 170 mi. long, 140 mi. wide at its mouth. On its banks are 3 important cities, Buenos Aires and La Plata in Argentina and Montevideo in Uruguay. Emptying into it are the Parana River, 2,500 mi. long, and the Uruguay, 1,000, both starting far to the north in Brazil. Further south, other large rivers flow from the Andes, in the west, to the Atlantic, including the Colorado, Negro and Chubut.

**Buenos Aires,** the capital, is one of the largest cities in South America.

**Resources and Industries.** The mountains of Argentina contain deposits of coal, lead, zinc, iron, sulphur, silver, copper and gold. Petroleum is produced by the government and by private companies; production in 1967 was 18,200,000 metric tons.

Cotton, wheat, barley, rye, linseed, oats, alfalfa are important. Sugar, wine, cotton, and fruit industries are large. Sunflower seeds, tobacco and peanuts are cultivated. Sheep, cattle, horses, goats and pigs form the chief wealth of the ranches. In 1968, there were 55,000,000 cattle, 5th highest in the world, and 51,000,000 sheep. Meat processing is the chief industry. Flour milling is 2nd.

Railroads and one domestic airline are state-owned. Three other domestic airlines are privately owned.

Foreign trade (in U. S. dollars):

|      | Imports         | Exports         |
|------|-----------------|-----------------|
| 1966 | $1,124,000,000  | $1,593,200,000  |
| 1967 | $1,096,000,000  | $1,464,000,000  |

**History and Government.** Discovered 1515-16 by

Spanish explorers headed by Juan Diaz de Solis, Argentina remained under Spanish domination until the provinces, in a successful revolt May 25, 1810, established an independent republic. In 1853 a liberal constitution was adopted.

The present constitution, proclaimed May 1, 1956, is essentially that of 1853.

There are 22 provinces which elect their own governors and legislatures, and a Federal District, Buenos Aires (area 72 sq. mi.), whose Mayor is appointed by the President.

The President and Vice President must be Roman Catholic and Argentine by birth. They are elected for six-year terms by direct popular vote. Congress consists of a Senate of 46 and a House of Deputies. Voting is compulsory for both men and women.

Beginning in 1944, and after the election of Juan D. Peron, an army officer, as President in 1946, Argentine democracy was replaced by a dictatorship. By concessions to labor Peron built a following; he then suppressed freedom of speech and of the press, religious schools and ran the country deeply into debt. Civilians, clericals and part of the armed forces unseated Peron Sept. 16, 1955, and he went into exile. A provisional government was replaced November, 1955, by a military junta, which chose Maj. Gen. Pedro Aramburu provisional President. He restored civil liberties, dissolved the Peronist party and returned expropriated property.

In the first free elections in 12 years, Feb. 22, 1958, Dr. Arturo Frondizi was elected President. Dissension among military leaders, democratic parties and the Peronist unions which had supported Dr. Frondizi resulted in a bloodless military coup Mar. 29, 1962. He was succeeded by Jose Maria Guido, head of the Senate. Elections were ordered and Dr. Arturo Illia was elected President, July 7, 1963, taking office Oct. 12, 1963.

Early in 1966 Peronists won several provincial elections. On May 30 inflation brought the 7th devaluation of the peso within two years.

On June 28, 1966, a 3-man military junta ousted Dr. Illia and named retired Lt. Gen. Juan Carlos Ongania President; the junta dissolved Congress and all political parties and temporarily closed national universities in a move against leftist activities. Gen. Ongania had accused the Illia government of allowing Peronists and Communists too much freedom.

In March, 1967, the peso was devalued from 255 to 350 per U. S. $1. And in June, Argentina announced a new oil law inviting private companies to return after a 3½-year absence.

Argentina is a member of the UN and OAS.

**Education and Religion.** The population is about 90% Roman Catholic, the constitutional religion since 1810. Primary education is free, secular, and compulsory. There are national universities in Cordoba (founded in 1613), Buenos Aires, Mendoza, La Plata, Tucuman, Santa Fe, Bahia Blanca and Cuyo. Private universities have been founded in Buenos Aires, Cordoba, Mar del Plata, Mendoza and San Juan. The language is Spanish. The people are of Spanish and Italian descent, with Basques, Swiss, Germans and British represented.

**Defense.** Service in the Army is compulsory from 20 years to 45. In addition to the Army of about 85,000, there is a trained reserve of 300,000 of whom 250,000 are members of the National Guard and 50,000 the Territorial Guard.

The Navy includes an aircraft carrier, several cruisers, destroyers and submarines and other craft; total personnel is about 20,000. The Air Force includes fighter, fighter-bomber and transport groups.

# Australia
## COMMONWEALTH OF AUSTRALIA

**Capital:** Canberra. **Area:** 2,967,902 sq. mi. **Population** (Govt. est. 1967): 11,928,889. **Monetary unit:** Australian dollar (.8962 per U. S. $1).

The continent of Australia, a huge island 5 times the size of Alaska, is situated SE of Asia proper and below the islands of Indonesia. The Indian Ocean is W and S, the Pacific E and their waters meet N of Australia in the Timor and Arafura Seas. The Great Barrier Reef extends along the NE coast. About 150 mi. S of the state of Victoria lies the island state, Tasmania. Branches of the Pacific are the Coral Sea, NE, and the Tasman Sea, SE.

The Tropic of Capricorn bisects Australia. The Great Dividing Range along the E coast has Mt.

Kosciusko, 7,316 ft., in New South Wales. The W plateau rises to 2,000 ft., with arid areas in the Great Sandy and Great Victoria Deserts. The NW part of Western Australia and Northern Territory are arid and torrid; Arnhem Land, in the latter, is a rugged wooded area reserved for aborigines. The NE has heavy rainfall and Cape York Peninsula has jungles. The Murray River rises in New South Wales, flows 1,600 mi. into the Indian Ocean and supplies hydroelectric plants.

States and territories of the Commonwealth with their areas in sq. mi. and populations, Dec. 1967, were:

|  | Area | Population |
|---|---|---|
| New South Wales | 309,433 | 4,347,309 |
| Victoria | 87,884 | 3,303,631 |
| Queensland | 667,000 | 1,718,266 |
| South Australia | 380,070 | 1,118,477 |
| Western Australia | 975,920 | 892,763 |
| Tasmania | 26,383 | 379,628 |
| Northern Territory | 520,280 | 60,639 |
| Australian Capital Territory | 939 | 108,176 |
| Totals | 2,967,909 | 11,928,889 |

The capitals are: New South Wales, Sydney; Victoria, Melbourne; Queensland, Brisbane; South Australia, Adelaide; Western Australia, Perth; Tasmania, Hobart; Northern Terr., Darwin; Capital Territory, Canberra.

Home of the kangaroo, Australia also is the habitat of other strange flora and fauna: the koala, or living teddy bear; the platypus, wombat, dingo, Tasmanian devil, a blind mole, and barking and frilled lizards.

By 1968, Australia had added more than 2,-150,000 population from immigration since World War II. About one-half was British. Australia's aborigines in the tribal state are primitive and nomadic, but most now are detribalized. Programs are directed toward their ultimate assimilation.

The Melbourne Cup horse race is the biggest annual sports event; cricket, tennis and football also are played extensively. Excellent beaches are numerous and surf riding is popular.

**Resources and Industries.** Almost from earliest days of settlement a primary producing country, Australia has become highly industrialized. More than 25% of the total labor force of approx. 4,750,-000 work in factories; about 15% are engaged in rural occupations.

Wool is Australia's greatest industry. With an annual clip of more than 1.7 billion lbs., Australia produces 30% of the world's wool, 50% of its merino wool. The continent also is one of the world's largest wheat producers, reaching 290,000,-000 bu. annually. About one-half is exported. Other important products are sugar, wine, fruit, vegetables, meat, grains, minerals, including uranium, gold, coal, copper, iron, silver, lead, bauxite, rutile and petroleum products.

Discovery of vast iron ore deposits in Western Australia brought a mining boom to desolate areas in the northwest in 1965. New oil and gas fields were discovered 1965-1968, including a major oil field on Barrow Is., off the NW coast.

Principal manufactures include iron and steel, textiles, electrical and radio equipment, drugs, chemicals, paints, machinery, metal work, clothing, motor cars and engines, aircraft and ships. Unemployment in 1967 was est. at 1% of the work force. Gross national product in 1967 was est. at $22.7 billion, up 5%; per capita income was $1,600, 38% above 1958.

In recent years exports of industrial products have increased considerably. Main imports: Metals, textiles, machinery, paper and drugs (United Kingdom); metals, machinery, paper and timber (Canada); machinery, tobacco, drugs, optical and surgical instruments, paper (United States); tea, rubber, silk, cotton, linen, burlap (Asia).

Australia changed its currency from pounds-shillings-pence to dollars and cents Feb. 14, 1966, with its dollar worth $1.12 U. S., or half the old Australian pound.

Foreign trade, in thousands of U. S. dollars:

|  | Imports | Exports |
|---|---|---|
| 1966 | $3,246,000 | $3,157,000 |
| 1967 | $3,410,000 | $3,386,000 |

Tourism is a rapidly expanding industry. In 1967 Australia had 255,221 overseas visitors, more than double the number 5 years earlier.

**History and Government.** Australia has been settled since 1788. The Commonwealth, proclaimed Jan. 1, 1901, is a self-governing federation of six

states and two territories. Parliament consists of the Crown (represented by the Governor-General), the Senate and House of Representatives.

In 1966 elections, the Liberal-Country party coalition increased its majority in the House of Representatives from 71 seats to 81, while the Labor party (which favored withdrawal of Australian forces from Vietnam) dropped from 51 seats to 41.

Prime Minister Harold E. Holt was lost at sea while swimming Dec. 17, 1967, and presumed drowned. John McEwen served briefly in his place until Jan. 10, 1968, when John G. Gorton became Prime Minister.

Australia is a member of the UN, Commonwealth and SEATO; and has had a Mutual Defense Assistance Agreement with the U. S. since 1951.

Pension acts provide for payments of war, old age and invalid pensions; also cover the blind, the unemployed, victims of tuberculosis and, in some cases, dependents of former soldiers. The National Health Scheme provides free drugs and subsidizes hospital and medical expenses.

A maternity act provides for the payment of a maternity allowance for every child born in Australia. Social security for children includes child endowment payments for children under 16.

**Education and Religion.** Education is free and compulsory. There are 10 universities and two university colleges. The Church of England claims 37.7% of the population, the remainder being Roman Catholic, 23.3%; Presbyterian, 9.7%; Methodist, 10.8%, and others.

**Defense.** Australia has expanded its small Army, Navy and Air Force, adopting its first peacetime draft in 1966. By 1967 the armed forces totaled over 79,000 plus 35,000 in volunteer Citizens Forces. Troops fighting alongside the U. S. in Vietnam were increased from 1,350 in 1965 to 4,500 in 1966 and to 8,500 in 1967-68.

## AUSTRALIAN TERRITORIES

The jointly administered **Territory of Papua and New Guinea**, originally two separate territories, is governed by a 1949 Act placing New Guinea under the UN Trusteeship system, but retaining the status of Papua as a Crown territory. Combined pop. of the two was est. in 1967 at 2,200,000.

**New Guinea,** once German New Guinea, later a League of Nations mandate and UN Trust Territory of Australia, occupies the NE quarter of the island of New Guinea, N of Australia, and includes nearby island groups: **New Britain, New Ireland** and the **Admiralty Islands** of the Bismarck Archipelago; **Bougainville,** 3,880 sq. mi.; **Buka,** 220 sq. mi., and smaller islands of the Solomons. Total area of the territory is about 93,000 sq. mi., with a population est. in 1966 at 1,576,000.

**Papua** is the southeastern part of the island. Area, 90,540 sq. mi.; population est. 1965, 573,000.

Papua-New Guinea is governed by an Administrator, a cabinet and a legislative House of Assembly, popularly elected for the first time in 1964; native members outnumbered whites, 38-26. Its acts are subject to veto by Australian authorities.

Principal products are copra, cacao, rubber and coffee.

**Norfolk Island** was taken over by Australia, 1914. It has an area of 13.5 sq. mi. and a population (est. 1966) of 1,152. The soil is very fertile and is suitable for the cultivation of citrus fruits, bananas and coffee. Many of the inhabitants are descendants of the Bounty mutineers; some descendants moved to Norfolk in 1856 from Pitcairn Is.; some stayed, some returned to Pitcairn.

**Territory of Ashmore and Cartier Islands** in the Indian Ocean came under the authority of Australia May, 1934 and are administered as part of Northern Territory. **Heard and McDonald Islands** are governed by Capital Territory.

**Cocos-Keeling Islands,** 27 small coral islands in the Indian Ocean 1,300 miles NW of Australia, formerly administered from Singapore, are important for aviation use. Pop. (est. 1966): 684.

**Christmas Island,** 64 sq. mi., pop. est. 1966, 3,381, 230 mi. S of Java, was taken over from Singapore in 1958. It has phosphate deposits.

**Australian Antarctic Territory** came under the authority of Australia in 1933. It claims 2,472,000 sq. mi. of territory S of 60th parallel S. Lat. and between 160th-45th meridians E. Long. except for French-claimed Adelie Land.

(*Nauru, former UN trust territory, became independent Jan. 31, 1968. See separate article, Nauru.*)

# Austria
## REPUBLIK OESTERREICH

**Capital: Vienna. Area: 32,374 sq. mi. Population (UN est. 1967): 7,323,000. Monetary unit: Schilling (25.90 per U. S. $1).**

Austria is a republic in the mountainous region of central Europe, 360 mi. long, 160 mi. wide—slightly smaller than Maine. It is bounded by Switzerland with the Rhaetian Alps, Liechtenstein, Italy's South Tyrol, Carnic Alps and Dolomite Mts., Yugoslavia and the Karawanken Mts., Czechoslovakia with the Little Carpathians, Bavaria (Federal Republic of Germany) and Hungary.

Near Switzerland are the Oetztal Alps, with Wildspitze, 12,309 ft. tall. The Hohe Tauern range has Gross Glockner, 12,457 ft., and a 6-mile glacier. Mountain passes cross frontiers; the Brenner, below the Stubai Alps, has been a major route to Italy since ancient times. Austria has many forests, rich in conifers; the Wiener Wald is a forest belt near Vienna.

Principal river, the Danube, flows from Bavaria in NW to Czechoslovakia, E. Others are the Enns, Inn, Drau, Ill, Mur and Salzach, some furnishing hydroelectric power. There are numerous lakes and popular spas, such as Bad Gastein and Bad Ischl.

**Resources and Industries.** Austria produces iron ore, oil, timber, magnesite, aluminum, coal, lignite, cement and copper. It is an important source of high-grade graphite. Hydroelectric power, with high potential, is under extensive development. It manufactures steel, machinery, vehicles, electrical and optical instruments, glassware, sporting goods, paper, yarns, textiles, fertilizers, chemicals and artistic leather goods.

Although farmland is limited, Austria produces about 90% of its foodstuffs. It grows wheat, rye, barley, oats, corn, potatoes, sugar beets. Vineyards flourish in Lower Austria and in Burgenland. Principal livestock: cattle, sheep, pigs, horses, goats.

Tourism, largest source of foreign funds, earns about $400,000,000 annually. The annual Mozart festival at Salzburg and the Vienna State Opera are internationally famous.

Principal exports are iron, steel, paper, textiles, machinery, chemicals, metal products, vehicles, aluminum, electric power. Trade is heavy with West Germany, Italy and United States.

Foreign trade in thousands of U. S. dollars:

|      | Imports | Exports |
|------|---------|---------|
| 1966 | $2,328,000 | $1,684,000 |
| 1967 | $2,309,000 | $1,809,000 |

**History and Government.** Austria, the East Mark (Ost Mark) of Charlemagne (788 A. D.) came under the Hapsburgs in 1278. Tyrol was added 1363, Bohemia (Czech) and Hungary, 1526. The Turks were twice turned back at Vienna, 1529 and 1683. Austrian dominance of German lands was challenged in the 18th century and Empress Maria Theresa (ruled 1740-1780) lost Silesia to Frederick II (the Great) of Prussia. Austria took slices of Poland in the partitions of 1772, 1793 and 1795. Austria was the scene of major Napoleonic battles and helped defeat him. The Congress of Vienna, 1815, awarded it Istria, Illyria, and the Italian provinces of Lombardy and Venetia. Austria lost Lombardy to Italy 1859 and Venetia 1866, after Prussia defeated Austria in the Seven Weeks' War.

Under the Dual Monarchy of Austria-Hungary, estab. 1867, to recognize the aspirations of the Magyars, Francis Joseph was Emperor of Austria and King of Hungary. The country had an area of 261,259 sq. mi., population c. 51,000,000. It contained Austria, Hungary, Bohemia, Transylvania, Polish Galicia, Trentino, Slavonia, Croatia, Bosnia, Herzegovina, Banat. After Archduke Francis Ferdinand, heir to the Austrian throne, and his consort were assassinated in Sarajevo, Bosnia, June 28, 1914, Austria declared war on Serbia, which helped precipitate World War I. It was dismembered after that war; became a republic comprised of nine states in 1918.

Between the two world wars Austria had a turbulent political history. Socialists introduced some socio-economic changes. These were checked by Chancellor Engelbert Dollfuss, 1934. Dollfuss was murdered by Nazi conspirators July 25, 1934. Adolf Hitler, German Fuehrer, occupied Austria Mar. 13, 1938, and proclaimed its union with Germany. It was re-established as a republic in 1945, consisting of the states of Burgenland, Lower Austria, Upper Austria, Salzburg, Styria, Carinthia, Tyrol, Vorarlberg, and the city of Vienna.

Dr. Karl Renner was elected President of the provisional government after liberation by the

Allies, 1945 (died 1950). After 17 years of occupation, delayed by tactics of the Soviet Union, a treaty of May 15, 1955 restored the frontiers existing Jan. 1, 1938, prohibited economic or political union with Germany, required support of democratic institutions. With final ratification July 27, 1955, Austria formally regained sovereignty.

Austria was relieved of reparations payments to the Soviet Union under the treaty of 1955 on Feb. 20, 1964. It had delivered 10,000,000 tons of crude oil and goods valued at $150,000,000 to buy back its wells, refineries, factories and Danube shipping.

The President is elected by secret ballot for a 6-year term. He appoints the Chancellor and approves the ministers.

Parliamentary elections Mar. 6, 1966, gave the conservative People's party of Chancellor Josef Klaus a majority of 85 of the 165 seats; the Socialists won 74, the right-wing Freedom party 6. Dr. Klaus formed a conservative cabinet, ending 21 years of conservative-Socialist coalition governments. The Communists had lost their last 3 seats in 1959.

Austria is a member of the UN and EFTA.

**Education and Religion.** The predominant religion is Roman Catholicism. Elementary education is free and compulsory between the ages of 6 and 14. There are universities in Vienna, Graz, Innsbruck and Salzburg. The language is almost entirely German.

**Defense.** Under agreements after World War II, Austria may not possess atomic or other major offensive weapons. The armed forces presently comprise an Army and Air Force totaling about 60,000 men. By a law of Oct. 26, 1955, Austria declared its permanent neutrality.

# Barbados

**Capital: Bridgetown. Area: 166 sq. mi. Population (UN est. 1967): 246,000. Monetary unit: West Indies Dollar (2 per U. S. $1).**

Barbados achieved full independence from Great Britain Nov. 30, 1966. It became a member of the UN Dec. 9, 1966. Furthest east of the West Indies, the island is about 2½ times the size of the District of Columbia; it lies alone in the Atlantic almost completely surrounded by coral reefs. Its highest point is Mt. Hillaby, 1,115 ft. The name Barbados (bearded) was believed given it by Portuguese or Spanish sailors, referring to bearded fig trees.

An English ship visited the island in 1605; English settlers arrived in 1627. Slaves were imported, but freed in 1834. Most of the islanders are Negroes, the language is English and the religion of most is Anglican.

A charter of 1652 provided for a governor-general, council and assembly. Self-rule was achieved gradually; universal suffrage was granted in 1950, cabinet government in 1958, full internal self-government in 1961.

Sugar, molasses, rum, cotton and building lime are the main products; there is a lively flying fish industry and, thanks mainly to the attractions of excellent beaches, the tourist business is booming.

With about 1,506 persons per sq. mi., the population density is one of the world's highest. Barbados also has one of the world's lowest illiteracy rates—less than 1%.

# Belgium
### ROYAUME DE BELGIQUE—
### KONINKRIJK BELGIE

**Capital: Brussels. Area: 11,781 sq. mi. Population (UN est. 1967): 9,581,000. Monetary unit: Franc (49.63 per U. S. $1).**

Belgium's seacoast of 40 mi. borders on the North Sea at the Strait of Dover. Slightly larger than Maryland, the country shares borders with the Netherlands, Germany, Luxembourg and France. The Meuse (Maas) River crosses the country from France to the Netherlands. The Scheldt (Escaut Schelde) makes Antwerp an ocean port via the Netherlands. Annual mean temperature in the capital, Brussels, is 49°: summer 65°, winter 37°.

Brussels, Bruges, Ghent and Antwerp are noted for art and architecture; Liege and Charleroi are important industrially. Antwerp is the world's 4th largest port. Total net tonnage entering the harbor in 1965 was 55,383,000 tons.

**Resources and Industries.** Coal is the nation's only important mineral. Although Belgium is essentially a manufacturing country, agriculture and forestry are profitable industries. The principal crops are oats, rye, wheat, potatoes, barley and sugar beets.

Important industries are mining, steel manufacture, glassware, diamond cutting, food and beverages, fishing, textiles and chemicals. Beurs voor Diamant in Antwerp is the world's largest diamond trading center.

Belgium lives by its foreign trade; about 40% of its entire production is sold abroad (75% of steel and glass). The Belgium-Luxembourg Economic Union is the world's foremost exporter of steel.

The gross national product rose from $17.9 billion in 1965 to $19.7 billion in 1966 (U. S. dollars).

Foreign trade in thousands of U. S. dollars:

| | Imports | Exports |
|---|---|---|
| 1966 | $7,054,000 | $6,811,000 |
| 1967 | $7,118,000 | $7,037,000 |

**History and Government.** Belgium, land of the Belgae conquered by Julius Caesar, has a 2,000-year history during which it was ruled by the Romans, Merovingian Franks, Burgundy, Spain, Austria and France. After the fall of Napoleon, 1815, Belgium was made a part of the Netherlands. Its citizens demanded separation from the Dutch in 1830. Belgium became an independent constitutional monarchy in 1830 and chose Prince Leopold of Saxe-Coburg King, as Leopold I.

By the treaty of London, Apr. 19, 1839, Austria, France, Great Britain, Netherlands, Prussia and Russia guaranteed the inviolability of Belgium; this was the "scrap of paper" repudiated by Germany when its troops entered Belgium, Aug. 2, 1914. After World War I the Treaty of Versailles gave Belgium the cantons Eupen, Malmedy and Moresnet, 382 sq. mi., 64,250 population, added to the province of Liège in 1925.

Leopold II, son of Leopold I, was King 1865-1909, succeeded by his nephew, Albert I. Albert was killed while mountain climbing, Feb. 17, 1934; Leopold III, his son, succeeded.

During World War II, Leopold surrendered to Germany, May 28, 1940, to avoid further bloodshed. His cabinet maintained a government-in-exile in London. Nevertheless, Belgium suffered heavily. Ancient churches, houses and records were ruined at Nivelles, Mons, Tournai, Liège, Louvain; the University Library at Louvain, burned in 1914, restored with American aid, was again burned with 900,000 vols. About 50,000 Belgians died, some in Nazi prison camps.

**Bastogne,** in the Ardennes, became famous as the site of the heroic defense by the 101st U. S. Airborne troops, Dec. 20-26, 1944, during the Battle of the Bulge. Called upon to surrender Maj. Gen. McAuliffe replied: "Nuts." The defenders were rescued.

In 1950 Belgians voted 57% in favor of recalling Leopold III (who had been in Switzerland since being freed from German internment), but Socialist opposition was so vehement that the King abdicated and his son became King Baudouin I July 17, 1951. Born Sept. 7, 1930, he is the son of Leopold's first wife, Princess Astrid of Sweden. Baudouin married (Dec. 15, 1960) Dona Fabiola de Mora y Aragon of Spain.

Universal suffrage is in force and those who fail to vote are fined. Women have voted since 1949.

Parliament consists of a Senate with members elected for four years, partly directly and partly indirectly; the number elected directly is equal to half the number of members of the House of Representatives. The members of Parliament are directly elected, for four years, by proportional representation (one for every 40,000 population).

Flemish, a form of Dutch, is the language of northern Belgium and French is the language in the south. The language difference has been a perennial source of controversy, particularly as it affects education, with Flemish parents unwilling to have their children taught in French.

Disagreement between the two groups became embittered in Mar. 31, 1968, elections in which minority extremist parties increased their strength. Dr. Gaston Eyskens, named Premier June 12, 1968, headed a center-left coalition and sought to end the crisis by naming a Cabinet of 14 Flemings and 14 Walloons.

Belgium is a member of the UN, NATO, EEC and the Benelux economic union.

On June 30, 1960, Belgium granted full independence to its colony, Belgian Congo. See *Democratic Republic of Congo*. In 1962 Ruanda and Urundi, former Belgian UN trusteeships, became independent nations. See *Index for Rwanda and Burundi, their new names.*

**Education and Religion.** The population is divided into two well defined groups, the Flemings and the Walloons. Roman Catholicism is the

religion of the great majority. Part of the income of the ministers of the Catholic, Jewish, Church of England and Protestant Evangelical religions is paid by the government. There are universities in Ghent, Liege, Brussels and Louvain and agricultural, technical, art and music schools.

**Defense.** Universal military training has been in force since World War I. Conscript service term was reduced from 18 to 12 mos. in 1957 except for officers on reserve. The Navy comprises small warcraft.

## Bhutan
### DRUK-YUL

**Capital: Thimbu. Area: 18,147 sq. mi. Population (est. 1966): 750,000. Monetary unit: Indian rupee (7.539 per U. S. $1).**

The tiny kingdom of Bhutan is a semi-independent state in the eastern Himalayas, adjoining Tibet, Sikkim and the Indian provinces of West Bengal and Assam. It is 190 mi. long from east to west and 90 mi. across at its widest point. Punakha, winter residence of the king, is a great natural fortress. The inhabitants are Mongolians and adhere to a form of Buddhism.

Agriculture is the chief industry. The principal products are rice, corn, yak butter, lac, wax, cloth, musk, elephants, ponies and chowries.

The ruler of the kingdom is the Dragon King, Jigme Dorji Wangchuk (born 1929), who ascended the throne Oct. 27, 1952. The 130-member Tsongdu (Assembly) is an advisory body. By a treaty signed with India, Aug. 8, 1949, Bhutan receives an annual cash subsidy of 500,000 rupees and transportation rights through India, the state's only avenue to the outside. India controls its external relations.

Modernization has begun, including the country's first road network usable by automobiles, linking central Bhutan and India.

## Bolivia
### REPUBLICA DE BOLIVIA

**Capital: Sucre. Seat of gov't: La Paz. Area: 424,163 sq. mi. Population (UN est. 1967): 3,801,-000. Monetary unit: Peso (11.88 per U. S. $1).**

Bolivia is a landlocked nation, over 8 times the size of N.Y. State. It lies across the Andes, and its chief topographical feature is the great central plateau at an attitude of 12,000 ft., over 500 mi. long, lying between two great cordilleras having three of the highest peaks in America. More than 50% of the population are Indians; 13% are white, and 25% are mixed.

Lake Titicaca, on the Peruvian-Bolivian border, is the highest lake in the world on which steamboats ply (12,506 ft.), and is the 2nd largest lake in South America (est. 3,200 sq. mi.).

The legal capital is Sucre, but La Paz, a city more accessible, is the actual seat of government. La Paz lies in the heart of a gigantic canyon about 3 mi. wide, 10 mi. long and 1,500 ft. deep, at an altitude of about 11,800 ft., and framed with high Andean peaks. Its huge cathedral seating 12,000, begun 1835, was dedicated 1933.

**Resources and Industries.** Agriculture claims 70% of the population. Products include potatoes, cacao, sugar, coffee, barley, cocoa, highland rice, corn, bananas, citrus, rubber and cinchona bark. Much rubber is exported and some raw sugar.

The most important industry is mining. There are large deposits of tin, silver, copper, lead, zinc, petroleum, antimony, bismuth, wolfram, gold, iron, cadmium, borate of lime and natural gas. More than 15% of the world's output of tin is produced in Bolivia, running to 25,000 tons or more annually. The three largest tin producers—Patino, Hochschild and Aramayo companies—were nationalized Oct. 31, 1952. The country ranks high in the mining of antimony and tungsten. Oil and natural gas are growing industries. In 1966 a pipeline was constructed to carry oil 360 mi. from Santa Cruz in the eastern lowlands across the Andes, nearly 2½ mi. high, to join another pipeline carrying it 210 mi. to the Chilean port of Arica on the Pacific.

Bolivia receives economic aid from the U. S. and the Inter-American Development Bank, the World Bank and the International Monetary Fund. It is a member of the UN and OAS.

**History and Government.** Once part of the ancient Inca empire, Bolivia was under Spanish domination for centuries before it gained independence Aug. 6, 1825, naming itself after Simon Bolivar, famed liberator.

Bolivia's 16th constitution, adopted in 1967, provides for strong executive power, nationalization

of mines, and agrarian reform. The President is elected for 4 years by direct popular vote. Congress is composed of a Senate of 27 members elected for 6 years, one-third renewable every 2 years, and a Chamber of Deputies of 102 elected for 4 years, one-half renewable every 2 years.

Dr. Victor Paz Estenssoro, elected to a 3rd term as President May 31, 1964, was ousted Nov. 4 and the government was taken over by a military junta headed by Gen. Rene Barrientos Ortuno. On July 3, 1966, Gen. Barrientos was elected President in a constitutional election and was inaugurated Aug. 6.

Communist guerillas, led by Ernesto Che Guevara, once Cuban Premier Fidel Castro's righthand man, began operating in Bolivia in March 1967. Guevara was captured and executed by the Bolivian Army Oct. 9, 1967.

Bolivian tin-miners' attempts to negotiate better working conditions with the Government-owned Bolivian Mining Corp. were led during 1967-68 by a group of Roman Catholic priests. An agreement was reached in March 1968 in which the corporation agreed to permit union activities and provide better working conditions and more housing and hospitals for the 23,000 workers.

**Education and Religion.** Primary education is free and compulsory. Adult illiteracy, estimated at 58%, is being lowered. There are 7 universities. Roman Catholicism is the predominant religion. Spanish is the official language.

**Defense.** There is compulsory military service beginning at 19 years of age.

## Botswana
### (FORMER BECHUANALAND)

**Capital: Gaberones. Area: 275,000 sq. mi. Population (UN est. 1967): 593,000. Monetary unit: South African rand (.7143 per U. S. $1).**

This former British protectorate received full independence Sept. 30, 1966 and joined the UN Oct. 17, 1966.

In the center of southern Africa and populated predominantly by Negroes, Botswana shares borders with the Republic of South Africa, South-West Africa (administered by South Africa) and Rhodesia. It is slightly larger than Texas.

The Kalahari Desert, supporting only nomadic Bushmen and a few wild animals, spreads over the southwestern areas of Botswana; there are swamplands and farming areas in the north, and rolling plains in the east where livestock are grazed.

Cattle raising is the largest industry but in 1966-67 it was suffering the effects of a 5-year drought. Large copper and nickel deposits were discovered in 1967. Corn, sorghum, beans and peanuts are raised in the north. Tourism is flourishing; black-maned lions and swamp antelopes are hunted by safaris.

Many Bechuanas work as migrant labor in South Africa and much of the country's chief export, meat, goes to that country. British grants also provide much of the country's income.

In 1885, Bechuanaland was made a British protectorate after local chiefs appealed to Great Britain for aid to halt encroachment on their territories by Boers of South Africa's Transvaal. In March, 1965, the British granted Bechuanaland internal self-rule as a step toward independence.

Its new constitution forbids any form of racial discrimination.

## Brazil
### BRASIL

**Capital: Brasilia. Area: 3,286,473 sq. mi. Population (UN estimate 1967): 85,655,000. Monetary unit: Cruzeiro (3.22 free market rate per U. S. $1).**

Brazil is the largest nation in South America in area and population. Larger in area than the 48 states in conterminous U. S., it is smaller than the 50 states. It has a coastline on the Atlantic Ocean of 4,603 mi., and extends approximately 2,689 from N to S and 2,684 from E to W. The northern part is the great, heavily-wooded basin of the Amazon (1,465,637 sq. mi. in Brazil) which rises in the Peruvian Andes and empties into the Atlantic at the Equator.

The Amazon basin has a network of rivers which are navigable for 15,814 mi. The Amazon River by itself is navigable for 2,093 mi., the extent of its course in Brazilian territory. In all its rivers, Brazil possesses 27,318 mi. of navigable waterways. The majestic falls of the Iguazu, 230 ft. high but extremely wide, are on the Brazil-Argentina

border; Glass Falls, in Bahia west of Salvador, are 1,325 ft. high. Tallest mountain is Pico da Neblina, 10,046 ft., on the Venezuela border.

The south central region, favored by climate, resources and communications, has 45% of population and produces 75% of agricultural goods and 80% of industrial output.

**Brasilia**, the capital city, was inaugurated Apr. 21, 1960, superseding Rio de Janeiro.

**Resources and Industries:** Brazil has vast mineral wealth and exploitation is being spurred. It leads the world in output of quartz crystal and beryl; is 2nd in sheet mica; 3rd in manganese, columbium and tantalum; 8th in iron ore. It has large deposits of iron (one-third of the world's reserves) and monazite, a source of thorium, alternate to uranium as a supplier of fissionable material. Gold output is about 142,000 troy oz. annually. Also important are oil, nickel, chrome, diamonds, coal, tungsten, bauxite, various gem stones.

Hydroelectric power potential is est. at more than 80,000,000 kw (4th in the world).

Cotton weaving is the most important manufacturing industry, occupying 25% of workers. Brazil produces more than 3,000,000 tons of steel annually, about 40% in the Volta Redonda national mills. Automotive, aluminum, petrochemical, cement, pharmaceutical, plastics, food and beverage, electrical appliances, shipbuilding, ceramics, glass and heavy machinery industries are growing.

Brazil, world's greatest coffee grower, supplies about 30% of coffee consumed in the U. S. Paranagua, Santos, Rio and Vitoria are the largest coffee ports. Brazil has become a world leader in sugar. There also are large crops of bananas, cotton, oranges, pineapples, rice, cotton and corn.

Brahman (zebu) cattle of India thrive in Brazil, which is among world leaders with 91,000,000 cattle, 63,000,000 hogs and 22,000,000 sheep.

Rice, cocoa, pinewood, castor beans, cotton, sugar, coffee, tobacco, hides and oiticica oil are important agricultural exports. The country is the only producer of Carnauba wax.

Foreign trade in thousands of U. S. dollars:

|  | Imports | Exports |
|---|---|---|
| 1966 | $1,496,000 | $1,742,000 |
| 1967 | $1,668,000 | $1,654,000 |

**History and Government.** Pedro Alvares Cabral, a Portuguese navigator is generally credited as the first European to reach Brazil, 1500.

Brazil was developed as a colony of Portugal until the royal house of Braganca, fleeing from Lisbon before Napoleon's army in 1807, transferred the seat of government to Rio de Janeiro, March, 1808. Brazil thereupon became a kingdom under Dom Joao VI. After his return to Portugal, his son Pedro I, proclaimed the independence of the country, Sept. 7, 1822, and was acclaimed emperor, Oct. 12, 1822. The second emperor, Dom Pedro II, was driven from the throne Nov. 15, 1889, by a revolution which established a republic, the United States of Brazil, which was the country's official name until Jan. 1967 when a new constitution shortened it to Brazil.

There are 22 states, with limited autonomy, a federal district and four territories: Roraima (formerly Rio Branco), Rondonia (formerly Guapore), Amapa, and Fernando de Noronha Island.

Brazil took part in World Wars I and II on the Allied side. It is associated with the U. S. in the Mutual Security Agreement for Hemisphere Defense (1953) and the Inter-American Treaty of Reciprocal Assistance (1947).

It is a member of the UN and OAS.

Since 1930, when a military junta took control, Brazil has fought depression, inflation and economic crises. Getulio D. Vargas (Labor party) became provisional President until 1933, when he was elected President under a new constitution. Out in 1945, he was reelected in 1950, but in 1954 the army forced him to retire; he immediately committed suicide.

President Janio Quadros, elected in Oct. 1960, became President Feb. 1 1961, resigned Aug. 25, 1961, blaming "reactionary forces." In Sept. 1961, a constitutional amendment gave Brazil a parliamentary government and Vice President Joao Goulart succeeded to the presidency with reduced powers. The amendment was repealed Jan. 6, 1963, and Brazil returned to the presidential form of government.

Pres. Goulart, whose regime was criticized as leftist, was ousted Apr. 1, 1964, and Gen. Humberto Castelo Branco was elected Pres. Apr. 11. In 1966 his government decreed that elections of national, state and municipal executives would be indirect, by legislative bodies, rather than by direct popular vote as provided in the 1946 constitution.

Under this decree, Arthur Costa e Silva, an anti-Communist and former Army marshal, was elected Pres. by Congress Oct. 3, 1966 and inaugurated Mar. 15, 1967.

A new constitution adopted in 1967, strengthened the powers of the presidency, reducing those of Congress.

**Education and Religion.** Roman Catholicism is the predominant religion.

There are 32 official universities including the Univ. of Brazil, established in 1920; in addition, there are 3 Catholic universities and 486 others of high rank. Primary education is free and compulsory. The language is Portuguese.

**Defense.** All males between the ages of 18 and 45 are subject to military duty under a selective service system. There is one year of service in the first line and five years in the reserve. The Air Force, largest in South America, is equipped with American-built planes.

# Bulgaria
## BULGARIYA
### NARODNA REPUBLIKA BULGARIA

**Capital:** Sofia. **Area:** 42,729 sq. mi. **Population** (UN est. 1967): 8,309,000. **Monetary unit:** Lev (1.17 official rate per U. S. $1).

Bulgaria, fronting on the Black Sea, is about the size of Ohio. It is bounded by Romania, Turkey, Greece and Yugoslavia. The Balkan Mts. stretch across the center of the country with the Danubian Plain in the north and the Rhodope Mts. and Thracian Plain in the south.

**Resources and Industries.** The principal crops are wheat, rye, barley, oats, corn, potatoes and tobacco. Fruit is exported. Agriculture claims a large percentage of the population, but the country is being industrialized under a nationalized planned economy which emphasizes electric power, chemicals, coal, machinery, metals, textiles, building materials, fur, leather goods and oil. A socialized economy embraces 98% of industry, 95% of agriculture and 99% of retail trade. Rich oil and gas fields were discovered near Pleven in 1964.

New economic reforms were launched Jan. 1, 1966, to decentralize planning and management. Industrial output rose 12.2% in 1966, 13.2% in 1967. Exports were also up. About 1,000,000 tourists now visit Bulgaria each year.

About 80% of trade is with nations of the Communist bloc. Exports include maize, wheat, vegetables, chemicals, silver, textiles, hides, tobacco, rose attar, lead, zinc, cement, machinery.

Foreign trade in thousands of U. S. dollars:

|  | Imports | Exports |
|---|---|---|
| 1966 | $1,478,000 | $1,305,000 |
| 1967 | $1,572,000 | $1,458,000 |

**History and Government.** The Bulgars, a Slavic people, settled Bulgaria in the 7th Century and became Christians in 865 A.D. The Turks conquered Bulgaria in 1393. It revolted in 1875 and in 1878 was made a principality. In 1908 it became an independent kingdom and Ferdinand of Saxe-Coburg-Gotha became Czar Ferdinand I of Bulgaria. It expanded after the first Balkan war but lost its Aegean coastline in World War I, when it sided with Germany.

Under the influence of King Boris III, Bulgaria joined the Axis in World War II, occupying considerable Balkan territory. King Boris died 1943 and a regency ruled for Simeon II, born 1937. In 1944 Bulgaria withdrew from the war, but the USSR refused to recognize its neutrality, declared war Sept. 5. Bulgaria asked for an armistice and declared war on Germany Sept. 7. In a one-ticket plebiscite Sept. 8, 1946, the monarchy was abolished and a republic voted, which was established one week later. Georgi Dimitrov, Communist party leader, became premier.

Present premier is Todor Zhivkov who is also first secretary of the Communist party.

The constitution of Dec. 4, 1947, modeled after that of the USSR, provides that the unicameral National Assembly shall be the supreme organ of government. The National Assembly is elected for a four-year term and chooses the Presidium and Premier.

It was admitted to the UN in 1955 and is a member of the Warsaw Pact.

**Education and Religion.** Bulgarian is a Slavonic language. Elementary education is obligatory from seven to 14 years of age. There are 21 universities

and colleges, including the University of Sofia. The main religion is Eastern Orthodox. The National Church is disestablished and may not have schools or hospitals. There are over 750,000 Moslems.

**Defense.** Army service is compulsory between the ages of 17 and 65 and usually is for two years.

# Burma
### PYEE-DAUNG-SU MYANMA NAINGGAN-DAW UNION OF BURMA

**Capital:** Rangoon. **Area:** 261,789 sq. mi. **Population** (UN est. 1967): 25,811,000. **Monetary unit:** Kyat (4.778 per U. S. $1).

The Union of Burma, slightly smaller than Texas, is a republic in the western part of the former Indo-Chinese peninsula. It is bounded by China, Laos, Thailand, India, Pakistan and the Bay of Bengal. Rivers flowing from the rugged mountains in the north provide habitable valleys down the peninsula. The largest is the Irrawaddy River which is navigable for 900 mi. A tributary, the Chindwin, is navigable for 300 mi.

The **Burma Road,** extending from Lashio to Kunming in Yunnan province, China, was the principal military supply line from Burma into China 1938-1942. It winds for 700 mi. over an airline distance of 260 mi. It was completed by American help and protected by Gen. Claire Chennault's Flying Tigers. The **Ledo Road** was used when the Japanese closed the Burma Road.

Rangoon, on the Gulf of Martaban is the chief port; Mandalay is on the Irrawaddy River. Mingaladon airport, near Rangoon, handles international traffic.

**Resources and Industries.** Mineral wealth is great; included are petroleum, lead, silver, tin, tungsten, zinc, and gem stones. The rubies, sapphires and jade are of highest quality. The principal products are rice, cotton, maize, teakwood, tobacco, tin, silver and petroleum. In value of exports, rice accounts for 70%.

Large expenditures are being made on agriculture, water resources, mining, power, transport, and communications. The country has an unfavorable balance of trade. Both exports and imports fell off in 1965, 1966 and 1967.

**History and Government.** Burma was a Buddhist monarchy in the Middle Ages and came under the influence of the East India Co. (British) about 1612. Britain gained control of Lower Burma in 1824 and of Upper Burma in 1884 and administered them as part of India until 1937, when Burma became a self-governing unit of the British Commonwealth. It was overrun by the Japanese in World War II. Burma became an independent nation outside the Commonwealth by treaty effective Jan. 4, 1948 and a member of the UN 1948.

Constituent units of the Union, resulting from amalgamations of a number of smaller states, are Shan State, Karen, Kachin, Kayah (former Karenni states), Special Division of the Chins (Chin Hills District and Arakan Hill Tracts).

A constitution, adopted 1947, guarantees private property but forbids monopolies and provides for nationalization of certain enterprises. The Union Parliament, elected for four-year terms, consists of the Chamber of Deputies, comprising about 250 members, and a Chamber of Nationalities of 125 members. The President is elected by Parliament for a five-year term and may be reelected once.

The government of Premier U Nu, elected in 1960, was overthrown Mar. 2, 1962, by a military coup by Gen. Ne Win, Chief of Staff, who formed a junta. Parliamentary rule was dissolved and a new constitution promised. Gen. Ne Win had previously ruled, Oct. 28, 1958, to Feb. 6, 1960.

The Ne Win government pursues a socialistic program and has nationalized many industries. It holds to a neutralist foreign policy.

In June, 1967 Rangoon was placed under martial law for a month to control riots against local Chinese who had provoked the attacks by holding pro-Communist China rallies. Communist China discontinued its aid program in Burma in July as the Sino-Burmese friendship became a casualty of Mao Tse-Tung's "cultural revolution."

**Education and Religion.** The indigenous races of Burma are of Mongoloid stock, allied to the Thais, Tibetans, Malays, Chinese and others of eastern Asia. Burmese or one of its variants is spoken by nearly three-fourths of the population. Higher education is provided at the Universities of Rangoon, Mandalay and constituent colleges. A

state-controlled and homogeneous system of schools was introduced after 1948. The Burmese language is preferred, with English second.

The chief religion is Buddhism (about 90%), adopted as the state religion Aug. 18, 1961.

**Defense.** Compulsory military service was voted 1959 for men between 18 and 46, and women between 18 and 36; technical specialists 18-56.

# Burundi

**Capital:** Bujumbura. **Area:** 10,747 sq. mi. **Population** (UN est. 1967): 3,340,000. **Monetary unit:** Franc (87.5 per U.S. $1).

Burundi, a country the size of Maryland in east central Africa, became independent July 1, 1962. Formerly part of the Belgian UN Trusteeship of Ruanda-Urundi, it is bordered by Rwanda, Tanganyika, Lake Tanganyika and the Democratic Republic of Congo. Much of the country is grasslands and mountains.

For 3 centuries in the present Burundi and Rwanda area, the Batutsi, a minority tribe, were overlords and political masters of the Bahutu. (The Batutsi are an extremely tall race; the Bahutu, the vast majority, are of average height; a 3rd tribe, the Batwa, are pygmies.) Under German control in the late 19th Century, the area was taken over by Belgium in World War I; the League of Nations in 1923 gave the king of Belgium a mandate over the combined Ruanda-Urundi territory; Belgium received a UN Trusteeship in 1946.

Burundi became an independent constitutional monarchy in 1962 with Mwami Mwambutsa IV as King; there are a premier and cabinet, an Assembly elected by universal suffrage and a Senate. The government was mainly supported by the Uprena party, a coalition of moderate Batutsi and Bahutu. Two premiers were slain by extremists and in Oct. 1965 a 3rd, Leopold Biha, was severely wounded. Bahutu extremists opposed the power of the minority Batutsi in the government; Batutsi extremists, accused of receiving Chinese Communist aid, opposed the government as too moderate.

In July 1966 the King's son, Prince Charles, 19, deposed him and ousted Premier Biha, appointing Michael Micombero Premier. Extremist Batutsi returned to power; on Sept. 1 Prince Charles was proclaimed King Mwami Ntare V. But in a coup d'etat Nov. 28, King Ntare was overthrown by Col. Micombero, who declared himself president. Micombero reportedly had the backing of the Communist Chinese, whose embassy and staff had been ousted from Burundi in 1966.

The economy is agricultural, with 90% of the people farmers or livestock raisers. Coffee is the main crop and export. Much of the land is overgrazed and eroded. The nation receives aid from Belgium and the UN. It is a member of the UN and OAU.

About half the population is Christian, mostly Roman Catholic. Many others believe in a supreme deity, Imana, called the Principle of Good. Kirundi, a Bantu tongue, and French are the official languages; Swahili is also widely used. (*See also Rwanda.*)

# Cambodia
### PREAH REACH ANA CHAK KAMPUCHEA

**Capital:** Phnom Penh. **Area:** 69,898 sq. mi. **Population** (UN est. 1967): 6,415,000. **Monetary unit:** Riel (35 per U. S. $1).

Cambodia is a constitutional monarchy in southern Asia which, with Vietnam and Laos, comprised the former associated states of French Indo-China. It is slightly larger than Utah. It is bordered by Laos, Thailand, the Gulf of Siam and Vietnam. About three-fourths is forested; the central part is level, forming a huge basin for the Mekong River. The climate is tropical. Sihanoukville is the principal seaport.

**Resources and Industries.** The country is largely undeveloped; 50% of the land is virgin forest. Main industries are forestry, fishing, and agriculture, rice occupying about 80% of the land usage. Other products are rubber, maize, pepper, kapok, palm-sugar, tobacco, cotton, silk, oil seeds, beans. Cattle flourish; the forests have valuable hardwoods. Some iron, copper, manganese and gold exist. Industry is developing, featuring textiles, paper, plywood.

**History and Government.** Early kingdoms dating from that of Founan in the 1st Century A.D. culminated in the great Khmer civilization which flourished from the 9th Century to the 14th. The

Khmer "God-Kings" built a series of monumental cities, distinguished for their temple tower architecture and striking wall sculptures. Abandoned and overgrown by jungles, the cities remained lost until one of the greatest, Angkor Wat, was found by French explorer Henri Mouhot, 1860.

Cambodia came under French protection in 1863. A national constitution promulgated May 6, 1947, replaced the former absolutism. It became an associated state within the French Union by a treaty of Nov. 8, 1949, but declared its independence from France, Nov. 9, 1953. It is a UN member.

Prince Norodom Sihanouk was King, 1941-55; he abdicated in favor of his father, Norodom Suramarit, who died Apr. 3, 1960. On June 13, 1960, Sihanouk, refusing to become King again, was named Chief of State with wide powers.

The legislature consists of a National Assembly of 77 members elected for 4-year terms and a Council of the Kingdom (upper house) of 24.

Cambodia severed its economic and military ties with the United States Nov. 20, 1963, charging U.S. intervention in its affairs, and in March, 1964, sent military missions to Communist China and the USSR to purchase arms. Because of an attack by South Vietnam planes on Cambodian villages, Sihanouk broke off diplomatic relations with U.S. in May 1965. Cambodia has also accused the U.S. and Thailand of border violations; South Vietnam and the U.S. have charged that Vietcong forces attacked their troops from Cambodian soil.

In 1967 and 1968 Sihanouk charged that Vietnamese and Thailand Communists were supplying arms to Cambodian insurgents who were terrorizing remote villages. He also charged that Communist China was "behind" these troubles. Further, he invited the U. S. to send a special envoy to discuss problems of "hot pursuit" of Communist forces from Vietnam into Cambodia.

In Jan. 1968, Chester Bowles, U. S. Ambassador to India, met with Sihanouk in Phnom Penh. The two announced agreement on proposals to strengthen the 1954 Geneva International Control Commission so it might investigate any foreign infiltration into Cambodia.

**Education and Religion.** The national language is Cambodian, or Khmer; French is widely spoken and English is taught. In 1965 there were over 4,000 schools and 37 faculties of higher learning. Buddhism is the state religion.

## Cameroon

### REPUBLIQUE FEDERALE DU CAMEROUN
### FEDERAL REPUBLIC OF CAMEROON

**Capital: Yaoundé. Area: 183,581 sq. mi. Population (UN est. 1967): 5,470,000. Monetary unit: CFA franc (246.85 per U. S. $1).**

Cameroon, which became a republic in 1960, lies on the western coast of Africa, bounded N and NW by Nigeria, NE by Chad, E by Central African Republic, S by Congo (Brazzaville), Gabon and Rio Muni, W by Gulf of Guinea. It is larger than California.

Cameroon is comprised of two states: East Cameroon, formerly Republic of Cameroon, previously a French mandate and trusteeship; and West Cameroon, formerly British Southern Cameroons. Douala is the principal seaport and one of nine airports.

The population comprises some 200 tribes, including Bantus, Semitic and Sudanese peoples, Kirdi Animists, Foulbes and Bamilekes. There are about 600,000 Christians and 600,000 Moslems.

**Resources and Industries.** Mainly agricultural. Cameroon exports cocoa, coffee, palm products, leather, timber, rubber, peanut oil, tea, bananas, ginned cotton. Livestock includes cattle, horses, donkeys, pigs, sheep and goats.

Aluminum processing is the most important manufacturing industry. Trade is heavy with France and United Kingdom. Import and export totals are each over $135,000,000 annually.

To combat a rural exodus, a program of resettlement of unemployed persons on farms was under way in 1968, along with modernization of agriculture.

**History and Government.** Cameroon embraces the larger part of the former German colony of Kamerun which was occupied by France and Britain in 1916, and placed under trusteeship, 1919. France passed a statute Dec. 31, 1958, conferring internal autonomy on the French trusteeship as a step toward complete independence which took effect Jan. 1, 1960.

Following a referendum by the UN in former British Cameroons, the southern section joined the Republic to form the Federal Republic of Cameroon, Oct. 1, 1961. The republic, composed of two federated states, is a member of the UN. (The northern section of British Cameroons voted to become part of Nigeria.)

The 50-member Federal Assembly is elected by direct universal suffrage, 40 from the eastern zone and 10 from the western portion. President: Ahmadou Ahidjo, elected May 5, 1960, reelected March 20, 1965.

## Canada

*See Index and special article preceding this section.*

## Central African Republic

**Capital: Bangui. Area: 236,293 sq. mi. Population (UN est. 1967): 1,459,000. Monetary unit: CFA franc (246.85 per U. S. $1).**

The former French Overseas Territory of Ubangi-Shari in Equatorial Africa is 350 mi. NE of the Gulf of Guinea and is bounded by Chad, Sudan, the two Congos and Cameroon. Slightly N of the Equator, it is mostly rolling plateau, average alt. about 2,000 ft. with rivers draining S to the Congo and N to Lake Chad. Landlocked, it is slightly smaller than Texas.

It achieved partial self-government in 1958. Complete independence was proclaimed Aug. 13, 1960, and the Republic became a UN member Sept. 20. It is a member of the French Community.

A few months after his election in 1960, Pres. David Dacko dissolved all political parties. He was re-elected Jan. 1965, running as the sole candidate. The country became a center for Chinese Communist activities.

On Jan. 1, 1966, the Army Chief of Staff, Col. Jean Bedel Bokassa, deposed Pres. Dacko; a few days later Pres. Bokassa broke off diplomatic relations with Peking.

Diamonds are the main export, amounting to over $15,000,000 or half the total outgoing trade in 1967. Cotton, coffee and peanuts are also important. Some 90% of the pop. earns its living from farming. There are thick forests and lumber exports are increasing. Manufacturing showed a 20% gain in 1967 and a large textile mill was under construction in Bangui in 1968.

In 1968, the nation joined Chad and the Democratic Republic of Congo in a common market plan, the Union of Central African States.

French is the official language; Sangho is a lingua franca of the 4 ethnic groups: Banda, M'Baka, Zande, Mandjia-Baya.

## Ceylon
### SRI LANKA

**Capital: Colombo. Area: 25,332 sq. mi. Population (UN est. 1967): 11,741,000. Monetary unit: Rupee (5.928 per U. S. $1).**

Ceylon, an independent nation within the Commonwealth, is an island in the Indian Ocean 31 mi. off the southern tip of India at its closest point. Its greatest length from N to S is 270 mi., and its greatest width, 140 mi. The coastal area of the island is flat, but the central part is mountainous with the highest peak, Pidurutalagala, 8,281 ft. The climate is hot, with high relative humidity. There are many mountain streams, which are navigable only by small river craft. Colombo is served by world airlines.

**Resources and Industries.** Minerals and metals include graphite, limestone, iron, precious and semi-precious stones, ilmenite, monazite, zircon, quartz. Manufactures include plywood, paper, glassware, ceramics, cement, chemicals, textiles, fertilizers and vegetable oil products.

Principal agricultural products are tea, rubber, coconuts, rice, cacao, cinnamon, citronella, tobacco. Ceylon produces over 500,000,000 lbs. of tea annually, equal to about 60% of India's production. But Ceylon exports more tea than India or any other country.

A major source of precious stones, the island produces about 20 varieties including sapphires, star sapphires, rubies, alexandrites, topaz, tourmalines and cat's-eyes. Most are mined at pits in Ratnapura.

**History and Government.** Ceylon was known to the ancient Romans as Taprobane (copper-colored). It was first settled by colonists from the valley of the Ganges in India who immigrated about 543 B.C. and whose descendants, the Sinhalese, still form three-fourths of the population.

Descendants of Tamil immigrants from Southern India account for one-tenth of the population. Parts of the maritime areas were occupied in turn by the Portuguese in 1505 and by the Dutch in 1658. The British annexed the island to the presidency of Madras, India, in 1796 and it became a Crown colony in 1802. Universal suffrage was granted in 1931 and a new constitution on the British model in 1946.

Ceylon became an independent member of the Commonwealth in 1948. It is a member of the UN.

The constitution provides for a parliament composed of a Senate, with 30 members, and a House of Representatives currently with 151 members. The administration of the island is in the hands of the Cabinet of Ministers, headed by the Prime Minister and responsible to the legislature.

Prime Minister W. R. D. Bandaranaike, appointed Apr. 12, 1956, was assassinated Sept. 25, 1959. After two short-lived regimes, new elections were held in which the Sri Lanka Freedom party was victorious. Its leader, Mrs. Sirimavo Bandaranaike, widow of the former Prime Minister, was sworn in to the office.

The regime pledged itself to a neutralist policy and nationalized a number of industries. In April, 1962, the government expropriated service and terminal facilities of one British and two U. S. oil companies and announced contracts to purchase oil from the USSR and the UAR. In March 1965 elections the conservative, pro-Western United National party won the largest number of seats and its leader, Dudley Senanayake, became Prime Minister.

In Dec. 1965, the new government agreed to pay compensation for the seized oil companies. The U. S., in Feb. 1966, agreed to resume economic aid, which had been cut off when the oil companies were expropriated.

In 1966, with financial aid from a group of Western nations, the government launched a 5-year plan to expand the tea, rubber and coconut industries which together account for 98% of Ceylon's export income.

Private industry has been growing, with gains in 1967 in food processing and confectioneries, chemicals and machinery.

On Jan. 1, 1966, Parliament abolished Sunday as a legal holiday, substituting "poya" days—which mark the 4 phases of the moon in the Buddhist lunar calendar.

**Education and Religion.** All education is free in government schools from kindergarten to university. The majority of the population, Sinhalese, numbering over 6,000,000 belongs to the Buddhist faith. The Tamils, mostly Hindu, are est. at about 1,000,000. Sinhalese became the official language in 1961 but in Jan. 1966 Parliament amended the law to permit the Tamil minority to transact business in its own language.

**Defense.** Organized in Oct., 1949, Ceylon's armed forces comprise a regular force, a reserve, a volunteer force and volunteer reserves, a small Navy and an Air Force.

# Republic of Chad
## LA REPUBLIQUE DU TCHAD

**Capital: Fort-Lamy. Area: 495,753 sq. mi. Population (Govt. est. 1967): 3,500,000. Monetary unit: CFA franc (246.85 per U. S. $1).**

A former French Overseas Territory in Equatorial Africa, 500 mi. NE of the Gulf of Guinea, 550 mi. S of the Mediteranean, Chad is bounded N by Libya, E by Sudan, S by Central African Republic, W by Cameroon, Nigeria, Niger. It is four-fifths the size of Alaska.

Moslem groups predominate in the north, and Negro Animists and others in the south. The country is completely rural, its geographic zones including a southern wooded savannah, a steppe and a desert region, part of the Sahara, in the north. On the west is Lake Chad, the dwindling remains of what was once a large inland sea. There is a wide variety of wild animals, particularly in the southeast.

Chad proclaimed complete independence Aug. 11, 1960, and joined the UN Sept. 20. President: Francois Tombalbaye, appointed Aug. 12, 1960. It is a member of the French Community, OAU and UN. French is the official language.

Cotton is the main export; others are cattle, meat, hides, fish and natron (sodium carbonate), the country's only mineral product.

With UN aid, land is being reclaimed from Lake Chad, 17th largest lake in the world, for wheat growing. Dikes are being built across the shallow lake: water is then pumped out of the enclosed polder. In 1966, the 4,900 acres in the first polder produced 1,800 tons of wheat.

The UNESCO Chad Basin Commission was hoping in 1968 to tap a large, natural reservoir beneath the lake for irrigation of neighboring areas.

# Chile
## REPUBLICA DE CHILE

**Capital: Santiago. Area: 286,396 sq. mi. Population (UN est. 1967): 8,935,000. Monetary unit: Escudo (official rate 6.53 per U.S. $1).**

The Republic of Chile lies along the southern half of the west coast of South America, a narrow strip of land 2,620 mi. long between the towering Andes and the South Pacific.

Most of Chile lies in the temperate zone, but the Atacama Desert in the north is one of the world's driest regions, with little or no rainfall. Chile itself is slightly larger than Texas; it also claims sovereignty over a large area of the Antarctic Continent, some 500,000 sq. mi.

The Andes have many lofty peaks, notably Aconcagua in Argentina near the Chilean border, the highest peak in the Americas (23,081 ft. acc. to Chile, 22,834 acc. to Argentina); Ojos Del Salado (Argentina-Chile, 22,539 ft.); Tupungato (Argentina-Chile, 22,310 ft.).

The Christ of the Andes, a heroic-size statue in Uspallata Pass, symbolizes peace between Chile and Argentina.

**Tierra del Fuego** is the largest (18,800 sq. mi.) island in the archipelago of the same name at the southern tip of South America, an area of majestic mountains, tortuous channels and high winds. It was discovered 1520 by Magellan, who sailed through the strait (named after him) which separates the main island from the mainland; he named the island Land of Fire because of its many Indian bonfires. Two-thirds of the island are in Chile, the eastern third in Argentina. Punta Arenas, on a mainland peninsula in Chile, is a center of sheep-raising and the world's southernmost city (pop. over 44,500); Puerto Williams, pop. 350, at a Chilean naval base on Navarino Is., is the southernmost settlement. Beagle Channel, between Navarino and the main island, and Mt. Darwin were named after Chas. Darwin's visit to the area aboard the ship Beagle. The area's tallest mt. is Sarmiento, 7,546 ft. Cape Horn, about 1,400 ft., is a tiny island, named Hoorn by Dutch explorers after a town in the Netherlands.

Possessions in Pacific: **Sala y Gomez** and **Easter Is. (Rapa Nui),** with its huge stone statues, both over 2,000 mi. west; **San Ambrosio** and **San Felix,** 600 mi. west, and **Juan Fernandez Islands** (2 large, 1 small), center of lobster fishing and place where Alexander Selkirk, whose life reputedly was the inspiration for Defoe's Robinson Crusoe, lived 4 years.

**Resources and Industries.** The arid deserts of northern Chile contain incalculable mineral wealth. Mining industries account for approx. 65% of Chile's exports. Nitrate production is about 100,000 metric tons a month. About 47% of the world's supply of iodine is a by-product of Chilean nitrate works. Chile is the world's 3rd largest copper producer, behind the U. S. and Canada; estimated annual output is 780,000 tons.

The provinces of Atacama and Coquimbo have enormous iron deposits estimated at a billion tons. Coal reserves are estimated at 2 billion tons. Oil wells, mostly in Tierra del Fuego, supply Chile's needs and offer an export potential. Other minerals are gold, silver, molybdenum, cobalt, zinc, manganese, borate, mica, mercury, iodine, salt, sulphur, marble, onyx. Chile has abundant water-power. Patagonia, the sparsely-populated southern third of the nation, is undergoing extensive industrial development.

Agriculture is an important industry. There are many large dairy farms. Wheat, rice, barley, oats, beans, lentils, apples, melons, peaches, plums, nectarines, peas and potatoes are grown in abundance. Sugar beet, automotive, aviation and textile industries are being developed. Vineyards cover 250,000 acres and much wine is exported. Forests have large reserves of hard and soft woods. Coastal waters have shellfish, lobster, tuna, swordfish, sardines.

Manufacturing industries have developed greatly. With the creation of the Corporacion de Fomento de la Produccion (Chilean Development Corporation) with a capital of $40,000,000, agricul-

tural and factory production has vastly increased. Huachipato, steel plant near Concepcion, is second only to Brazil's Volta Redonda plant in Latin America.

Besides minerals the exports are mainly fishmeal, barley, oats, wine, lentils, fruits, fish, sea-food, cellulose, newsprint, wood.

Chile has many airports and is served by 11 international airlines. About 85% of Chile's 6,700 mi. of railroads is state owned.

Since 1965 under an agrarian reform program more than 2,000,000 acres have been expropriated, with due compensation to the owners, to be distributed among rural workers. A new Agrarian Reform Law passed in 1967 will give 60,000 rural families land within the next 3 years.

In Santiago the Jesuit House of Christ housing program has provided, 1960-66, some 40,000 small homes, at low or no cost. Thousands of low-cost houses have been built by the government to meet an estimated shortage of 500,000 houses.

The government in 1966 set out to abolish the traditional two- or three-hour siesta, first for government workers, then for private businesses.

In 1968 Chile was struck by the worst drought in its history. More than 150,000 cattle died from lack of feed; lack of hydroelectric power caused industrial cutbacks.

**History and Government.** Diego de Almagro entered Chile for Pizarro 1536 and Valdivia completed Spanish conquest 1540. Sir Francis Drake raided the coast. A Captain General appointed by Spain ruled Chile until 1778, when it was made a separate colonial division under a governor.

Independence was gained, 1810-18, under Jose de San Martin and Bernardo O'Higgins; the latter as supreme director, 1817-1823, sought social and economic reforms until deposed. Chile defeated Peru-Bolivia in 1836-39 and 1879-84, taking Tacna and Arica provinces from Peru, returned Tacna, 1929. Arica (town) and Antofagasta are free ports for landlocked Bolivia.

Valparaiso, chief seaport, was founded in 1536; Santiago, the capital, in 1541.

Under the constitution the President is elected for 6 years, the 45 senators for 8 and deputies (1 for each 45,000 pop.) for 4. all by direct popular vote. President: Eduardo Frei Montalva, Christian Democrat, elected Sept. 4, 1964. Suffrage is universal for literate persons over 21. Chile is a member of the UN and OAS.

About two-thirds of the Chileans are of mixed Spanish and Indian descent; about one-fourth of Spanish only; a small percentage are Indian only; there are some of German and other European descent.

**Education and Religion.** Education is free and compulsory between 7 and 15. A National Library, the Univ. of Chile, State Technical Univ. and a Catholic Univ. are in Santiago. There are universities in Concepcion, Valparaiso, Antofagasta and Valdivia. A Council of Rectors of the 8 principal universities fosters research and teaching progress. The Roman Catholic religion is dominant though not state-supported. The language is Spanish.

**Defense.** All able-bodied citizens from 18 years to 45 are liable for army service. Service in the reserve of active Army is for 12 years and with the second reserve to the end of the 45th year. The Navy consists of two cruisers, 8 destroyers, 3 frigates, 3 corvettes, 2 submarines and auxiliary vessels. There is an Air Force of about 8,000 personnel, with modern equipment.

# China

The ancient land of China is split into two hostile parts, with the Republic of China limited to Taiwan (Formosa) and the mainland controlled by a Communist regime called the People's Republic of China.

China, with about one-fourth of the world's population, occupies a territory in the eastern part of Asia about one-third larger than continental United States.

The mainland is of rolling topography, rising to high elevations in the N in the Khinghan Mtns., separating Manchuria and Mongolia; the Tarabagata Mtns. in Sinkiang; the Himalayan and Kunlun Mtns. in the SW in Tibet. Its length from N to S is 1,860 mi. and its breadth from E to W more than 2,000 mi.

The eastern half of China is one of the best-watered lands in the world. Three great river systems, the Yangtze, the Hwang (Yellow) and the Si (Si Kiang) provide water for vast farmlands.

**Resources and Industry.** Until Communism prevailed, China was chiefly agricultural. Wheat, barley, corn, koaliang, and millet and other cereals, peas and soy beans are produced in the north; rice, sugar and indigo in the south. Rice is the staple food of the Chinese. Fruit is grown in abundance. Fiber crops are important and include abutilon, hemp, jute, ramie and flax. Cotton is produced mostly in the Yangtze and Yellow River valleys. Tea is cultivated principally in the west and south. One of the most important industries of prewar China was silk culture which has flourished 4,000 years. Livestock is raised in large numbers. In years before World War II flour and rice milling had become extensive, together with tanning, cement and glass manufacture.

China is one of the foremost coal countries in the world. Other minerals are iron ore, tin, antimony, petroleum, tungsten, molybdenum, salt.

**Education and Religion.** Buddhism had the largest following. Confucianism, which reveres God but stresses ethical and philosophical principles rather than divine revelation, had wide acceptance. Taoism (after Lao-Tze, b. 604 B. C.) is more metaphysical and looks to immortality. Islam, at one time, had 50,000,000; there were 3,280,000 Roman Catholics and 700,000 Protestants. On the mainland foreign missionaries and church schools are no longer tolerated.

## Republic of China
### CHUNG-HUA MIN-KUO

**Provisional Capital: Taipei, Taiwan. Area under control, 13,886 sq. mi. Population (UN est. 1967): 13,142,000. Monetary unit: Taiwan dollar (40.10 per U. S. $1).**

**History and Government.** One of the oldest of monarchies, with a history reaching back to 2205 B.C., China became a republic Jan. 1, 1912, following the Wuchang Uprising inspired by Dr. Sun Yat-sen, begun Oct. 10, 1911.

For a period of 50 years after the Sino-Japanese War, 1894-95, China was involved in conflicts with Japan. On Sept. 18, 1931, Japan seized the Northeastern Provinces (Manchuria) and set up a puppet state called Manchukuo. The border province of Jehol was cut off as a buffer state in 1933. Japan invaded China in the vicinity of Peiping (now Peking), July 7, 1937, precipitating war. After its defeat in World War II Japan returned all seized land.

After more than seven years of war with Japan ending Aug. 5, 1945, internal disturbances arose involving the Kuomintang, Communists and other factions. Manchuria was lost by the Chiang regime Oct. 30, 1948, and China proper came under domination of Chinese Communist armies during 1949-1950. The Nationalist government moved to Taipei, Taiwan (Formosa), 90 mi. off the mainland Dec. 8, 1949.

China concluded a treaty of friendship and alliance with the USSR, Aug. 14, 1945. After the Chinese Communists overran the mainland in 1949, the Soviet Union repudiated the treaty, withdrew its recognition of the Nationalist government, and signed a new treaty with the Communist regime, Feb. 15, 1950.

A new constitution became effective Dec. 25, 1947. The National Assembly is the supreme organ of the people. Members are elected on the basis of territorial and professional representation. They serve for a six-year term, subject to recall. The Assembly elects the President and Vice President, who likewise serve six-year terms; it also has the power to amend the constitution. A Yuan (Council), elected on the basis of regional and vocational representation, serves as the legislature. The cabinet, appointed by the President, is responsible to the Legislative Yuan.

Generalissimo Chiang Kai-shek, except for a period of semi-retirement, has been virtual ruler since 1927. He was elected President for a six-year term in April, 1948; reelected in 1954, 1960 and 1966. C.K. Yen was elected Vice President in April, 1966. The Nationalist government is a founding member of the UN.

**Defense.** Nationalist China has compulsory universal service. The regular Army requires service for 6 years. The armed forces had an estimated strength of about 600,000 on Taiwan and adjacent islands in 1966, including a Navy and an Air Force, largely equipped by the U. S. The U. S. Navy maintains a peace patrol in Taiwan waters.

The Nationalist government signed a mutual defense treaty with the U. S., in force Mar. 3, 1955. It provides for consultation on threats of

attack and promises that if China is subject to unprovoked attack the U. S. will act according to its constitutional procedures.

The government broke off diplomatic relations with France Feb. 10, 1964, after the latter recognized the People's Republic.

## TAIWAN (FORMOSA)

**Taiwan** is an island 110 mi. E of the mainland, but the term Taiwan is used by the Nationalist government to include 14 other islands nearby and 64 others comprising the Penghu group. Principal harbors are Keelung, Kaohsiung and Hualien.

Taiwan was ceded by China to Japan in 1895, after the Sino-Japanese War and was returned to China as a province, 1945, after the surrender of Japan. Japan renounced all claims to Taiwan and the Penghus in the Treaty of Peace, Sept. 8, 1951. China did not take part in the treaty, signing a separate treaty with Japan Apr. 27, 1952.

A range of mountains forms the backbone of the island. The eastern half is exceedingly steep and craggy but the western slope is flat, fertile and well cultivated, yielding two rice crops a year. The principal crops, besides rice, are tea, sugar, sweet potatoes, ramie, jute, turmeric and camphor. Minerals include gold, silver, copper and coal. A joint U. S.-Chinese commission aids agriculture, rural health, forestry, irrigation and food.

Taiwan's economic growth rate in recent years has been 8-10% annually. Index of industrial production in 1967 (1963=100) was 171. Industries include flour-milling, tobacco, oil, lumber products, textiles, machinery, glass and other manufactures.

Foreign trade has shown steady gains.

U. S. economic aid, begun in 1951 and totaling $1.5 billion, terminated June 30, 1965 (with exception of some funds previously committed through 1967). Military aid, which totaled $2.5 billion, continued, but at a reduced scale of about $90,000,000 a year. During the 15 years, industrial production went up 300%, agricultural 70%; exports nearly tripled. Switching roles, the republic has begun extending technical assistance to some 30 countries in Asia, Africa and Latin America.

**The Penghus** (Pescadores), 50 sq. mi., pop. (1964) 108,800, lie between Taiwan and the coast of China, by which they were ceded to Japan in 1895. The islands remained under Japanese rule until restored to China, 1945.

The islands of **Quemoy** and **Matsu**, near the mainland, have been under Communist artillery fire at intervals since 1958.

## People's Republic of China
### CHUNG-HUA JEN-MIN KUNG-HO KUO

**Capital: Peking. Area under control; 3,746,453 sq. mi. Population (U. S. est. 1966): 760,300,000. Monetary unit: Yuan (basic rate 2 per U. S. $1).**

The People's Republic of China was proclaimed in Peking (Peiping) Sept. 21, 1949, by the Chinese People's Political Consultative Conference under Mao Tse-tung, Communist leader. Chou En-lai was named premier and foreign minister Oct. 1, 1949. With defeat of the Nationalist armies, the Chinese mainland, the islands of Hainan and Chusan and the principal cities fell to the Communists.

Under the Communist regime, China comprises 22 provinces, including Taiwan, which it claims; 5 autonomous regions (Inner Mongolia, Sinkiang-Uighur, Kwangsi-Chuang, Ningsia-Hui, Tibet-Chamdo) and two municipalities—Peking and Shanghai. Government estimate of population in 1964 approached 750,000,000. The government pressed birth control programs; without them experts said, China's population would reach 1 billion by 1980.

Communist party chairman: Mao Tse-tung, Chief of State or President: Liu Shao-chi, elected Apr. 27, 1959. re-elected 1965. Premier: Chou En-lai, app. 1949, reapp. 1965.

The Communist regime and the USSR signed a 30-year treaty of "friendship, alliance and mutual assistance," Feb. 15, 1950, repudiating the 1945 treaty between the Soviet Union and Nationalist China authorized by the Yalta Agreement. Great Britain recognized the People's Republic Jan. 1, 1950; the two countries have embassies in each other's capitals headed only by charge d'affaires. Recognition has been granted by about 20 nations.

**United States Policies.** The U. S. refused recognition, and after its consular officers met with abuse, withdrew them. On Nov. 26, 1950, when U.S. military forces and those of certain other UN members had the North Korean Communist rebels virtually defeated, the People's Republic sent armies of "volunteers" into Korea and, with the help of limitations on U. S. offensive action, forced a stalemate.

The U. S. has led opposition to the entry of Communist China in the UN as representative of all China and, in concert with its major allies, restricts trading with Communist China, but Great Britain and Canada resumed trade. In 1966, U. S. President Johnson, Vice Pres. Humphrey and Secy. of State Rusk all suggested in speeches that the U. S. and Communist China might eventually be reconciled. The suggestions were rebuffed.

France recognized the Peking regime in Jan. 1964 and Nationalist China broke off relations with France Feb. 10, 1964.

**Peking Foreign and Domestic Policies.** On Feb. 27, 1957, Mao Tse-tung, then Chief of State, condemned the Stalinist terror but admitted an est. 800,000 anti-Communist Chinese were executed 1949-54. Leniency for political criticism, proposed by Mao Tse-tung, led to anti-Communist disturbances among students and a quick return to repressive measures. In 1958 the regime announced all "rightists" in govt. service had been removed. It endorsed the Soviet attack on Hungary, condemned Yugoslavia's independence. It pursued a more rigid Communist ideology than the USSR and, with Albania, has maintained a continuous propaganda campaign against the USSR. The regime called on the international Communist movement Mar. 31, 1964, to repudiate Khrushchev's leadership.

It hailed Khrushchev's ouster, Oct. 14-15, 1964, as a victory for its own policies but soon attacked the new Soviet leaders for continuing a policy of "peaceful coexistence" with the West. A visit by Chou En-lai to Moscow in Nov. 1964 failed to heal the bitter rift between the two Communist powers. Vituperative Chinese attacks on Russian "revisionism" grew during 1966.

Early in 1966 a long, widespread purge of "anti-party intellectuals" was launched; it was viewed as a possible symptom of a struggle for power and the succession to the aging Mao. Premier Chou En-lai called the purge a "cultural revolution." Ousted from office and denounced were the Chief of the Army's General Staff, Minister of Culture, the party propaganda chief, 3 university presidents, newspaper editors and writers, opera producers, youth officials, economists, Peking's Mayor, atom experts and others.

In August, 1966 Defense Minister Lin Piao emerged as top deputy and heir apparent to Mao.

In the same month the "cultural revolution" took a new turn as thousands of Peking teen-agers, calling themselves the Red Guards and acting with official blessing, took over the city, ordering everyone to rid themselves of "western ways." Women took the curls out of their hair, streets were renamed, shopkeepers were ordered to remove foreign names from goods, the few churches in the city were defaced, bloodshed and beatings of old people were reported and the reign of terror spread to other cities.

The "cultural revolution" continued unabated in 1967 with reports of fighting in many provinces between pro and anti-Maoists.

In 1968 student unrest and the official press continued attacking President Liu Shao-chi, calling him an agent of Nationalist Pres. Chiang Kai-shek.

On Oct. 16, 1964, Communist China exploded a low-yield atomic bomb in Sinkiang Province, becoming the 5th nation to possess such power, and announced May 14, 1965, it had exploded a 2nd bomb. A 3rd was exploded May 9, 1966. An explosion of a hydrogen bomb was announced June 17, 1967.

Internationally, Communist China has sought to promote revolutionary movements in Africa, Asia and South America. The program suffered serious setbacks, 1965-66. An abortive Communist coup in Indonesia, Sept. 30, 1965, was followed by destruction of the party there and attacks on Red Chinese representatives. Three friends and a lot of influence were lost in the ouster of Algeria's Ahmed Ben Bella, June 19, 1965; in a squabble with Cuba's Fidel Castro over a cut in rice exports to Cuba; and in the overthrow of Ghana's Kwame Nkrumah, Feb. 24, 1966. Dahomey and the Central African Republic broke off relations with China in Jan. 1966 and the Ivory Coast

accused it of plotting a rebellion in that country.

Application of radical theories to industry and agriculture have resulted in erratic economic development. Serious food shortages have existed since 1959 after more than 148,000,000 acres of farm land were damaged by storms, floods, drought and mismanagement. The regime has been forced to obtain grain from Tibet, Argentina, Mexico, Canada and Australia. Light industries dependent on agriculture for their raw materials also were affected—cotton textiles, knitted goods, vegetable oils, sugar and cigarets. The "people's commune" system of agriculture, in effect since 1958 and which had disrupted family life, was drastically modified in 1960-61 to increase individual incentives to stimulate production, but the collectivization drive was renewed in 1963-1964. Many thousands fled to overcrowded Hong Kong.

Vast hydroelectric and irrigation projects are under construction or in partial operation. Largest of 11 major water projects is the Sanmen Gorge project on the Yellow River in Honan, expected to store 84.6 billion cu. yds. of water, with power stations to have capacity of 1,100,000 kw. The nation plans a new canal system with four trunk routes spanning China from south to north, to connect the Yangtze with the Yellow River. Industrial progress was hampered, 1960-1964 by the withdrawal by the USSR of technicians and equipment. Steel production in 1963 was est. 9-10,000,000 metric tons, 50% below that of 1960.

Institutes of higher education include 15 universities, 48 engineering colleges and 31 agricultural colleges. English and Russian are required in high schools.

The regular Army is estimated at approx. 2,600,-000, formed into 160 divisions—3 armored, one air-borne, a number of cavalry and the remaining in infantry divisions. Air Force equipment and training were originally furnished by the USSR. The Air Force has an est. 3,000 planes of Soviet design. The Navy, with est. 135,000 personnel, has 2 light cruisers, 5 destroyers, 24 submarines, 32 frigates and smaller craft.

**Manchuria,** 404,428 sq. mi., is administered as part of Communist China. Seized by Japan in 1931, it was renamed Manchukuo, a puppet "independent" nation, Mar. 1, 1932. In 1945 it was returned to China.

**Kwantung** is the southern part of the Liaotung peninsula, the southernmost portion of Manchuria. Russia in 1898 forced China to lease it Kwantung and constructed the strongly fortified city of Port Arthur and the nearby commercial ice-free port of Dairen (Talien).

Japan seized Port Arthur in 1905, and at the close of the Russo-Japanese War took over the lease in the Treaty of Portsmouth. It was restored to the USSR by the Yalta Agreement, Feb. 11, 1945, which also internationalized Dairen. Following the 1950 Soviet-Chinese treaty the USSR returned the Changchun railroad, Port Arthur and Dairen to Communist China

### INNER MONGOLIA

**Inner Mongolia** was organized by the People's Republic as an Autonomous Region in May 12, 1947. Its boundaries have undergone frequent changes. In 1950 it comprised northern Chahar and parts of former Manchuria. Suiyan province was incorporated June 1954, and parts of Jehol in Aug. 1955. Population is about 6,200,000 of which less than 20% are Mongol. Capital: Huhehot (Kweisui).

**Outer Mongolia:** *For People's Republic of Mongolia, see Mongolia in Index.*

### SINKIANG

**Sinkiang** (New Dominion), in Central Asia, comprising Chinese Turkestan, Kulia and Kashgaria, is 633,802 sq. mi.; pop. (est. 1958), is 6,000,000, of whom 75% are Uighurs, a Turkic Moslem group, with a heavy Chinese increase in recent years. Tihwa (Urumchi), the capital, and Kuldja are the chief cities.

Sinkiang is considered China's richest region in strategic materials, including tungsten, wolfram, molybdenum, copper, zinc, coal, uranium and oil. The province was declared autonomous in 1953.

### TIBET (PÖ)

**Tibet,** 470,000 sq. mi., is a thinly populated region of high plateaus and massive mountains, almost twice the size of Texas. The Himalayas ring it on the S, the Kunluns on the N. Lofty passes link it with India and Nepal to the S; roads and a railroad lead into China proper. The capital is Lhasa. The average altitude is 15,000 ft.

Gartok, 15,100 ft., is believed to be the highest inhabited town on earth. Agricultural methods are primitive. Cereals are the main crops. The religion is Lamaism, a form of Buddhism. Pop. (1964 est.) 1,300,000.

With only token resistance, Tibet accepted suzerainty of the Chinese Communist regime under a pact signed May 23, 1951. A communist Tibetan Autonomous Government was announced Dec. 20, 1953, revising the quasi-religious administration of the Dalai and Panchen Lamas.

A revolt against the Communists occurred in 1959, when the latter attempted to arrest the Dalai Lama. The Tibetan cabinet denounced the 1951 treaty. The Communists crushed the revolt and placed the Panchen Lama on the Tibetan throne. The Dalai Lama fled to India. The Panchen Lama was demoted Dec. 1964. A new ruler was sponsored by Peking Sept. 9, 1965, when it announced election of Ngapo Ngawang Jigme as chairman of the newly-established Tibet Autonomous Region. Revolts continued in 1965 and 1966.

A reform program, including land redistribution and abolition of serfdom (assertedly practiced in some monasteries) was announced July 3, 1959.

The International Commission of Jurists at Geneva in 1961 charged the Communist regime with genocide in Tibet. About 20,000 Tibetans have fled to India since the Chinese takeover.

# Colombia
### LA REPUBLICA DE COLOMBIA

**Capital:** Bogota. **Area** (UN est.): 455,335 sq. mi. **Population** (Govt. est. 1968): 19,300,000. **Monetary unit:** Peso (16.30 per U. S. $1).

The Republic of Colombia, situated in the extreme northwest of South America, extends up the Isthmus of Panama to the Republic of Panama. It has a coast line of 913 mi. on the Pacific Ocean, and 1,094 mi. on the Caribbean Sea. It has as neighbors Venezuela and Brazil on the E, and Ecuador and Peru on the S. It is 4 times the size of Arizona.

Three great ranges of the Andes, the Western, Central and Eastern Cordilleras, run through the country from N to S. The eastern range consists mostly of high table lands, cool and healthful, and densely populated. The Magdalena River, in the NE, rises in the high Andes and flows N into the Caribbean Sea near Barranquilla. It is navigable over 800 mi. The Magdalena Valley is a plain of rich alluvial land.

Snow-crested mountains standing almost directly over the Equator are one of many examples of scenic splendor in Colombia. Tourists are also attracted by the famous Tequendama Falls, a natural wonder near Bogota, 427 ft. high.

The Salt Cathedral of Zipaquira, 32 mi. N of Bogota, is an actual church carved with Gothic arches 1,300 ft. underground in a salt mine. It can accommodate 10,000 worshipers.

Bogota, the capital founded in 1538, is in the Andes, 8,660 ft. alt.

**Resources and Industries.** Colombia is second to Brazil in exports of coffee, annually shipping approx. 6,600,000 bags of 132 lbs. each, accounting for 70% of export trade. Rice, tobacco and cotton are cultivated, besides cocoa, sugar, tagua, wheat and bananas. Dyewoods, rubber, balsam and copaiba trees are important.

The country is rich in minerals. It has become a heavy producer of petroleum, with more than 72,670,000 bbl. in 1965. Seventy-five miles from Bogota are the Muzo emerald mines which have been in operation for four centuries. Colombia produces 95% of the world's gem emeralds. Other minerals are gold, silver, copper, lead, mercury, cinnabar, manganese, platinum, coal, iron, limestone, salt. Colombia is accelerating expansion of its hydro-electric power which has est. potential of 40,000,000 kw. Food processing leads industry; other products are textiles, rubber goods, steel, and chemicals. Colombia has received loans from the Inter-American Development and World Banks.

An Atlantic railroad, completed in 1961, running from Santa Marta on the Caribbean Sea to Salgar, opened the Magdalena Valley to cultivation and improved travel between the coast and industrial cities of the interior. Aviation has done much to unify the country. An oil pipeline from the new Orito field in the SE, across the Andes to the Pacific port of Tumaco, was to be finished in late 1968.

**History and Government.** The country, conquered and ruled by Spain for 300 years, won its freedom

in the revolt of the Spanish-American colonies 1810-1824, the liberator, Simon Bolivar, establishing the Republic of Greater Colombia in 1819 from which Venezuela and Ecuador withdrew in 1829-1830. From the remainder of the confederation evolved New Granada, Confederation Granadina, and finally the Republic of Colombia under a constitution dated Aug. 5, 1886. Panama withdrew, Nov. 3, 1903, becoming a separate republic.

The Congress consists of a Senate of 106 members, elected for a term of four years, and a House of Representatives (one to every 90,000 pop.), elected directly by the people every two years. The President is elected by direct vote for four years and is ineligible for the following term.

Dr. Carlos Lleras Restrepo, a Liberal, was inaugurated Colombia's 110th President Aug. 7, 1966. He was the candidate of the National Front coalition (started in 1958 to run to 1974) under which Liberals and Conservatives agreed to alternate the Presidency and share other government posts equally.

The government has sought to reduce vast landholdings and increase the size of small farms. From 1961 to 1968 the Institute for Land Reform acquired or developed 6,000,000 acres; more than 60,000 families were given title to farm plots.

**Education and Religion.** Most of the people are of mixed Indian and white descent; the next largest group is white; the smallest groups are Indians and Negroes. Education is free but not compulsory. The National Univ., founded 1572, is in Bogota. Roman Catholicism is the prevailing religion, but others are tolerated. Spanish is the language.

**Defense.** Military service is compulsory between the ages of 21 and 30 with actual service for one year. The Navy consists of 4 destroyers, 3 frigates, gunboats and others. The Air Force is equipped with American and Canadian fighters, fighter-bombers, transports and a number of helicopters. Member: UN, OAS.

## Republic of Congo—Brazzaville
### (FORMER FRENCH CONGO)

**Capital: Brazzaville. Area: 132,046 sq. mi. Population (UN est. 1967): 860,000. Monetary unit: CFA franc (246.85 per U. S. $1).**

Formerly the French Middle Congo Overseas Territory, the Republic of Congo (Brazzaville) straddles the Equator. It is bounded on the E and S by the Democratic Republic of Congo; on the W by Cabinda (Port.), the Atlantic and Gabon; on the N by Cameroon and Central African Republic. It is twice the size of Missouri.

Complete independence was proclaimed Aug. 15, 1960, and the Republic joined the UN Sept. 20. Fulbert Youlou was elected President Nov. 21, 1959, and resigned in Aug. 1963 in a coup sparked by trade unions. In March 1965 he escaped house arrest and fled the country. Under his successor, Pres. Alphonse Massamba-Debat, the country moved into the Red Chinese sphere of influence and announced a "scientific Socialist state" with one-party control.

In Aug. 1965 the U. S. withdrew its embassy staff, a step short of breaking off relations, charging harassment of American officials.

A member of the French Community, the nation receives aid from France and Communist China.

Forests are a prime resource, covering 54,000,000 acres, and wood products form a major export. Chief commercial agricultural products are palm oil and kernels, cacao, bananas, and peanuts. Industrialization has progressed and its output now accounts for 11% of the total national product. Petroleum reserves are extensive. Brazzaville and Pointe-Noire have modern airports.

## Democratic Republic of Congo
### REPUBLIQUE DEMOCRATIQUE DU CONGO
### (FORMER BELGIAN CONGO)

**Capital: Kinshasa (former Leopoldville). Area (estimated): 905,563 sq. mi. Population (UN est. 1967): 16,353,000. Monetary unit: Zaire (.5 per U. S. $1).**

Until June 30, 1960, the Congo was a colony of Belgium in Equatorial Africa, entirely inland except for 25 mi. on the Atlantic Ocean, N of the mouth of the Congo River. It is larger than Texas and Alaska combined.

Along the eastern border lie several of Africa's Great Lakes: Albert, Edward, Kivu, Tanganyika and Mweru. North of the Equator on the Uganda border, stand the Ruwenzori Mtns., believed to be the "Mountains of the Moon" of ancient legend. Mt. Margherita is 16,763 ft.

The Congo River, one of the world's longest, rises near the Zambian border in the SE and flows 2,718 mi. N, then W and finally SW, emptying into the South Atlantic.

Wildlife is abundant and includes most of the species Africa is famous for: elephant, lion, gorilla, hippopotamus, crocodile, python, etc.

**Resources and Industry.** There are extensive mineral deposits in the Katanga, Ituri and Kivu highlands. The Congo normally produces 6% of the world's copper and over 50% of its cobalt and industrial diamonds. Also produced are cadmium, gold, silver, tin, germanium, zinc, iron, tungsten, manganese, uranium and radium.

Tropical rain forests cover much of the land; trees often are 150 to 200 ft. tall. They include mahogany, ebony, teak, copal, palms, cedars and gum and resin trees. Some livestock is raised in insect-free areas. Bananas, coffee, rubber, mangoes, plantain, coconuts are grown. Chief agricultural exports normally are fats and oils, timber, coffee, cotton, rubber and bananas.

**History and Government.** Leopold II, King of the Belgians, formed an international group to exploit the Congo in 1876. In 1877 Henry M. Stanley explored the Congo and in 1878 the King's group sent him back to organize the region and win over the native chiefs. Claims having been advanced by Portugal and others, the Conference of Berlin, 1884-85, organized the Congo Free State with Leopold as King and chief owner. Exploitation of native laborers on the rubber plantations caused international criticism and led to granting of a colonial charter, Oct. 18, 1908, whereby the state became a Belgian colony.

Belgian and Congolese leaders agreed Jan. 27, 1960, that the Congo would become independent June 30. In the first general elections, May 31, the National Congolese movement of Patrice Lumumba won 35 of 137 seats in the National Assembly, lower House of Parliament. He was appointed Premier June 21, and formed a coalition cabinet. Belgium's King Baudouin formally proclaimed the territory's independence at Leopoldville (now Kinshasa) June 30, 1960.

Widespread violence in which mutinous Congolese troops took part caused Europeans and others to flee the country. Pres. Moise Tshombe of Katanga seceded from the republic July 11, but ended the secession Jan. 15, 1963. Katanga was the seat of the copper-mining operations of the Union Miniére, which paid taxes formerly sufficient to defray one-half of the costs of the government. The UN Security Council Aug. 9, 1960, called on Belgium to withdraw its troops and sent a UN contingent to guard against civil war. Pres. Kasavubu removed Lumumba as premier and Lumumba fought for control with the backing of Ghana, Guinea and India. On Feb. 12, 1961, Lumumba was murdered by tribesmen in Katanga and Antoine Gizenga, vice premier, attempted to succeed him.

The last UN troops left the Congo June 30, 1964, and Cyrille Abdoula, Premier since Aug. 1, 1961, resigned, succeeded by Tshombe.

On Sept. 7, 1964, leftist rebels set up a "Peoples Republic" in Stanleyville with Christopher Gbenye as president. Premier Tshombe hired foreign mercenaries and sought to rebuild the Congolese Army. In Nov. and Dec. 1964 rebels slew scores of white hostages and thousands of Congolese; Belgian paratroops, dropped from U. S. transport planes, rescued hundreds. By July 1965 the rebels, though supplied with smuggled arms, had lost their effectiveness.

Growing rivalry between Pres. Kasavubu and Premier Tshombe ended when the former ousted the latter from office Oct. 13, 1965. Evariste Kimba became Premier but both he and Pres. Kasavubu were ousted Nov. 25 by Gen. Joseph D. Mobutu who named himself President. Tshombe went into exile.

In March 1966 Pres. Mobutu took over from Parliament all of its legislative powers. On July 1 he renamed Leopoldville Kinshasa; Stanleyville, Kisangani; and Elisabethville, Lubumbashi.

On June 2 ex-Premier Kimba and 3 former Cabinet ministers were hanged on charges of plotting to kill Pres. Mobutu.

In 1967 Tshombe was kidnaped in a private plane over the Mediterranean and flown to Algeria, where attempts were made to extradite him to the Congo where he faced execution. Shortly afterward, a revolt, led by Belgian and French mercenaries, broke out in the eastern Congo.

This revolt died and most of the mercenaries fled the country; the government was aided by 3 large U. S. transport planes sent to the Congo to help transport government troops and supplies.

**Education and Religion.** The population is principally Bantu. More than 200 tribes are represented. Swahili, Lingala, Tshiluba and Kikongo are most widely spoken languages. There are an estimated 5,000,000 African Christians, predominantly Roman Catholic. Most schools are operated by church missions.

# Costa Rica

## REPUBLICA DE COSTA RICA

**Capital:** San Jose. **Area:** 19,575 sq. mi. **Population** (UN est. 1967): 1,594,000. **Monetary unit:** Colon (6.62 per U. S. $1).

Costa Rica, in Central America, has Nicaragua for its neighbor on the N and Panama on the S. The lowlands by the Caribbean have a tropical climate. The interior plateau, with an altitude of about 4,000 ft., is temperate.

San Jose, the capital, situated inland—103 mi. by rail from Puerto Limon on the Atlantic; 93 by rail from Puntarenas on the Pacific —is the country's industrial and cultural center. Limon and Puntarenas are the principal ports. The crater atop Poas Volcano is the largest in the world. Puerto Limon occupies one of the sites where Columbus landed on his fourth and last visit to America.

**Resources and Industries.** A 1962 law giving new industries a tax holiday of up to 10 years has brought a wide variety of factories. The Irazu volcano near San Jose erupted from March 1963 to Dec. 1964, dropping millions of tons of ash which severely damaged coffee, vegetable and dairy crops, but higher world coffee prices aided the economy. Coffee of a high quality is the chief crop and export, followed by bananas, cocoa, cattle, cotton, fish and hemp.

New industries include fiberglass products, aluminum, fertilizer, roofing and cement.

The forests are extensive, and the lumber industry is important. Gold and silver are mined on the Pacific slope. Other minerals are quartz, alabaster, granite, oil, alum, slate, onyx, mercury, sulphur, copper.

Chief imports are flour, textiles, industrial machinery, gasoline, leather, hardware and tools. Three-fourths of foreign trade is with U. S. The balance of trade is adverse although increasing light industry and membership in the Central American Common Market have improved the situation.

Costa Rica was one of the Central American nations visited and promised aid in July 1968 by U. S. President Johnson.

The nation has a comparatively high standard of living and of social services.

**History and Government.** Although once a part of the Confederation of Central America, 1824-1829, Costa Rica has been independent since 1821.

An unusual Constitution was adopted Nov. 8, 1949. It abolishes the Army as a permanent institution. The legislative power is vested in a Chamber of Deputies, 57 in number, with four-year terms, under universal suffrage. The President, elected for four years, appoints a Cabinet of nine. Deputies may not serve successive terms but may be reelected after an intervening 4 years. A President may not be reelected until two succeeding terms have elapsed. There is a fine for not voting.

**Religion and Education.** Primary education is compulsory. Higher education is free; its institutions include the University of Costa Rica in San Jose; Inter-American Institute of Agriculture Sciences in Turrialba. The language of the country is Spanish. English is taught in the public schools. Roman Catholicism is the predominant religion, but the nation has religious liberty.

**Defense.** Order within the country is kept by a Civil Guard force of about 3,500. Costa Rica is a member of the UN and OAS.

# Cuba

## REPUBLICA DE CUBA

**Capital:** Havana. **Area:** 44,218 sq. mi. **Population** (UN est. 1967): 8,033,000. **Monetary unit:** Peso (1 per U. S. $1).

Cuba, the Pearl of the Antilles, is both an island, the largest in the West Indies, and, including its offshore islands, a nation which is about the area of Pennsylvania. The Straits of Florida lie to the

N, the Gulf of Mexico to the W, the Caribbean to the S.

Key West, Fla., is about 90 mi. N. The Windward Passage, 50 mi. wide, separates Cuba from Haiti to the E, and Jamaica lies 90 mi. to the S. Cuba's length is 730 mi.; its breadth averages 50 mi. The coastline, including the larger keys, is about 2,500 mi. It has numerous harbors, notably that of Havana, one of the finest in the world. **The Isle of Pines** (Isla de Pinos) is 1,180 sq. mi. in area.

Mountains rise in Pinar del Rio Province in the W, and in Oriente in the E where they reach a general elevation of about 3,000 ft., with Pico Turquino, 6,467 ft., the highest.

**Havana** (La Habana), pop. over 1,000,000, is the busiest port. Santiago de Cuba, on the SE coast, is next largest port.

**Resources and Industries.** Chief barometer of the nation's economy is the sugar industry which represents about 85% of exports. U. S. sugar mills, seized by the revolutionary regime in 1960, represented an investment of approx. $275,000,000, producing about 40% of Cuba's output.

In 1968 the government indicated sugar production would fall short of the 1967 total.

Tobacco raising and the manufacturing of cigars and cigarettes rank second. Other products are molasses, coffee, pineapples, bananas, citrus fruit and coconuts. Textiles, cabinet woods (mahogany and cedar), dyewoods, fibers, gums, resins and oils are important. Iron, copper, manganese, nickel and salt are some of the minerals. Industries include rayon, cement, naphtha and gasoline, chemicals.

Cuba was discovered by Christopher Columbus, Oct. 28, 1492. Its name derives from the Indian Cubanacan. Except for British occupation of Havana, 1762-63, Cuba remained Spanish until 1898.

Under Spanish governors Cubans were denied citizenship, slavery was retained until 1886, and patriots who revolted were executed. On Oct. 10, 1868, Carlos Manuel de Cespedes led Cubans in a proclamation of independence. Their ten-years' war ended in 1878 with guarantees of rights by Spain, which Spain failed to carry out. A full-scale movement for independence began Feb. 24, 1895, under Jose Marti, with the military under the command of Maximo Gomez, Antonio Maceo and Calixto Garcia. By 1897 over half the island was in Cuban hands. The Spanish governor, Valeriano Weyler, destroyed sugar plantations, banned export of tobacco and held patriots in "reconcentration camps." A U. S. offer to mediate was rejected by Spain.

The movement to help Cuba gain its independence was speeded up by the sinking of the U.S.S. Maine in Havana harbor. The U. S. declared war on Spain Apr. 25, 1898, and defeated it in the short Spanish-American War. In the Treaty of Paris, Dec. 10, 1898, Spain gave up all claims to Cuba. The U. S. formally withdrew May 20, 1902, when Tomas Estrada Palma was inaugurated first president of the republic.

Under 1903 and 1934 agreements, the U. S. leases a site for its naval base at Guantanamo Bay, on the SE coast.

In 1952 Fulgencio Batista seized control of the government and imposed a dictatorship.

Opposition to the corrupt Batista regime became vigorous in 1956 under leadership of Fidel Castro, born 1927, lawyer and former leader of student opposition. Known as the 26th of July Movement, the revolutionists in 1958 carried on intensified guerrilla warfare. Batista resigned Jan. 1, 1959, and fled to Lisbon.

Castro proclaimed Dr. Manuel Urrutia Lleo Provisional President and Urrutia dissolved the Cuban Congress, Jan. 6. Castro became Premier Feb. 16.

Pres. Urrutia resigned after accusing Communists of plotting treason. Dr. Osvaldo Dorticos Torrado was made Provisional President July 17, 1959.

The government, quickly dominated by left-wing extremists, began a program of sweeping economic and social changes, led by an agrarian reform law approved May 18, 1959. It executed hundreds of dissidents, and ousted moderates.

The National Institute of Agrarian Reform, principal agent for economic control, nationalized cattle and tobacco lands and instituted a system of cooperatives. All private enterprise was brought under control by a Central Planning Board created Feb. 20, 1960. By the end of 1960 all Cuban banks and industrial companies had been nationalized, including an est. $1 billion worth of U. S. owned properties.

Soviet, Communist Chinese and Czechoslovakian

economic penetration was extended by trade and credit agreements, including sugar purchases and a USSR credit equiv. to $100,000,000 for construction of factories and other installations.

Citing the open hostility of the regime, the U. S. cut back Cuba's remaining 1960 sugar quota by 700,000 tons. The U. S., Oct. 19, imposed an extensive embargo on exports to Cuba and, Feb. 4, 1962, Pres. Kennedy ordered a total embargo. Another U. S. order, July 8, 1963, halted virtually all financial transactions.

The OAS nations voted July 26, 1964, 15-4, resolution for mandatory sanctions against Cuba and for strengthening defenses against Cuban subversion efforts.

In 1962-1964 deficiency in the sugar crop and food shortages resulted in collectivization of farming and stringent labor controls, As the economic crisis deepened, food, shoes, clothing, gasoline were rationed.

In 1968, restrictions similar to rationing were in effect for eggs, bread, sugar, milk, etc.

**Bay of Pigs Raid.** In April, 1961, Jose Miro Cardona, pres., Cuban National Revolutionary Council, called on Cubans to unite to overthrow the Castro regime. On Apr. 17 about 1,400 Cuban patriots, who had trained in the U. S. and Guatemala, landed in the Bahia de Cochinos (Bay of Pigs) on Cuba's southern coast. They were overwhelmed by Castro forces and killed or imprisoned. The attempt created severe criticism in Congress of activities of the U. S. Central Intelligence Agency. Pres. Kennedy previously had declared there would be no intervention by the U. S. On Dec. 21, 1962, Castro agreed with James B. Donovan, representing welfare agencies, to release 1,113 prisoners in exchange for medical supplies worth a reputed $53,000,000. American drug concerns and religious groups raised the supply. Eventually Donovan was able to effect the transfer of nearly 10,000 Cubans, including families of exiles.

**Kennedy vs. Soviet Missiles.** In the fall, 1962, the U. S. ascertained that the Soviet Union was delivering nuclear missiles and other weapons to Cuba and building bases. On Oct. 22 Pres. Kennedy warned that any missile launched from Cuba would be regarded as an attack by the Soviet Union and would call for full retaliation. He asked Premier Khrushchev to halt this "clandestine, reckless and provocative threat to world peace." Khrushchev removed the missiles.

Cuba complained of numerous raids by infiltrators, 1964-66. The U. S. said a Guantanamo Base sentry fired on an armed Cuban soldier who infiltrated base territory, May 21, 1966, Castro charged the Cuban was killed on Cuban soil.

In Feb. 1966, Castro denounced Communist China for "blackmail and extortion" for slashing rice exports to Cuba.

In 1968, Anibal Escalante, leader of a pro-Soviet party clique, was sentenced to 15 years and 34 followers drew lesser terms.

Cuba is a member of the UN.

**Education and Religion.** Education is compulsory between the ages of 6 and 14. Among the institutions of higher learning is the University of Havana, founded in 1721. The Roman Catholic religion is dominant. The language is Spanish with English widely understood.

Education was nationalized June 7, 1961, and many Catholic schools were seized. Many Catholic priests of Spanish origin were ordered deported.

**Defense.** Compulsory military service was established Jan. 5, 1942. A large defense force, including women, has been trained by the Castro regime and arms have been supplied by Communist countries.

# Cyprus

## KYPRIAKE DIMOKRATIA
## KIBRIS CUMHURIYETI

**Capital:** Nicosia. **Area:** 3,572 sq. mi. **Population** (UN est. 1967): 614,000. **Monetary unit:** Pound (.4167 per U. S. $1).)

Cyprus, former British Crown Colony, became a republic Aug. 16, 1960, and joined the Commonwealth, UN and Council of Europe. It is the third largest island in the Mediterranean Sea, 40 mi. S of Turkey, 60 mi. W of Syria, and 350 mi. E of Crete. Two mountain ranges run E-W, separated by a wide, fertile plain. It is smaller than Connecticut.

Four-fifths of the inhabitants are Greek Orthodox Christians, nearly all the rest are Turkish Moslems. Greek and Turkish are official languages; English is widely spoken.

Chief ports are Limassol, Larnaca and Famagusta.

**Resources and Industries.** Cyprus is mainly agricultural, with cereals, grapes, wine, carobs, citrus fruits, potatoes and olives as principal crops. Agricultural products account for about 50% of the island's exports, but minerals are the mainstay—cupreous and iron pyrites, asbestos, gypsum, chrome and umber—making up 36% of total exports. Manufacturing is limited mainly to light industries. Cement and oil refining industries are under development.

The nation suffers an unfavorable balance of trade. Value of imports (in U. S. dollars) rose from $159,000,000 in 1966 to $167,000,000 in 1967. Exports in 1966 totaled $82,000,000; in 1967, $83,-000,000.

**History and Government.** Cyprus was inhabited as early as the New Stone Age in the 4th millennium B.C. Achaeans from Greece traded with the early Cypriots from 1600 B.C., set up colonies after the end of the Trojan War (c. 1184 B.C.). From the middle of the 8th Century B.C., Cyprus was dominated successively by Phoenicians, Assyrians, Egyptians, Persians, Alexander and the Ptolemies, Romans, Byzantines, Moslems, Crusaders, Venetians and Turks. Great Britain took over administration in 1878 under an agreement with Turkey, annexed the island in 1914, made it a Crown Colony in 1925.

Agitation for enosis (union) with Greece resulted in the British abolishing the legislative council in 1931. Demands for enosis were renewed after World War II; the Turkish minority, about 100,000, was opposed. Widespread violence in 1955-56, led by EOKA, an underground organization, brought harsh disciplinary measures, including the temporary exiling of Archbishop Makarios III, patriarch of the Orthodox Church in Cyprus and leader of the enosis movement.

In 1959, conflict was brought to a temporary halt by an agreement signed by British, Greek, Turkish and Cypriot leaders; under which Cyprus would become a republic, with a President elected from and by the ethnic Greek community, and a Vice President from and by the corresponding Turkish community. A 70-30% proportion of the Greek and Turkish communities was to be represented in the House of Representatives. Britain retained 2 military enclaves, Akrotiri and Dekelia, approx. 99 sq. mi.

Separate Greek and Turkish Communal Chambers dealt with religious, educational and other communal affairs.

Archbishop Makarios was elected President for a 5-year term and Dr. Fazil Kutchuk Vice President, Dec. 14, 1959. The constitution was approved April 6, 1960; independence became final Aug. 16, 1960, and Pres. Makarios took office.

Communal strife again broke out in December, 1963, following proposals by Pres. Makarios to make changes in the constitution which the Turkish minority felt would reduce their rights.

The UN Security Council approved Mar. 4, 1964, a resolution providing for an international peacekeeping force and UN troops began action Mar. 27.

Tension worsened after Turkey charged that Turkish Cypriots had been massacred in a Greek push against the northwest coast and bombed and strafed Greek positions Aug. 7-10, 1964. Both sides accepted a UN appeal for a cease-fire Aug. 10.

During a 1965 crisis, the UN Security Council urged all parties to avoid increasing tensions.

Another crisis ended in Aug. 1966 when Pres. Makarios, on an appeal from UN Sec. Gen. U Thant, lifted a blockade imposed on Turkish Cypriots which had led to a threat of "countermeasures" by Turkey.

War between Greece and Turkey over Cyprus appeared imminent in Nov. 1967 but was averted mainly because of mediation work by Cyrus R. Vance, special envoy of U. S. President Johnson.

Archbishop Makarios, whose term as Pres. had been twice extended by Parliament, was reelected Feb. 25, 1968, by an overwhelming popular vote. Vice Pres. Kutchuk was returned to office unopposed.

# Czechoslovakia

## CZECHOSLOVAK SOCIALIST REPUBLIC

**Capital:** Prague (Praha). **Area:** 49,370 sq. mi. **Population** (UN est. 1967): 14,305,000. **Monetary unit:** Koruna (7.2 official rate per U. S. $1).

Czechoslovakia is a central European socialist republic about 600 mi. long and 50 to 100 mi. wide —about the size of New York State. It is bounded

by West Germany (Bavaria), East Germany (Saxony), Poland, the Soviet Union; Austria and Hungary.

The Vltava (Moldau) and Labe (Elbe) flow from Bohemia to Germany; the Danube separates Slovakia from Hungary. The Carpathian Mts. are in the E and NE; tallest are the Tatras, with Gerlachovka peak 8,737 ft. The Ore Mts. (Ger. Erzgebirge) are on the Saxon border. The Great Bohemian Forest, rich in game and timber, lies on the Bavarian border.

**Resources and Industries.** Czechoslovakia has considerable natural resources, developed by farming, mining and industry. About one-third is agricultural, with about 60% in grain. Sugar beets and hops are grown and beer is exported from Plzen (Pilsen).

Coal is mined in the Ostrava-Karvina basin and at Plzen and Brno. Much iron is found in the Beroun basin and Slovakia. Oil, imported mainly from the USSR via the "Friendship Pipeline," is refined at Bratislava on the Danube. Jachymov (Joachimstal), has Europe's richest deposits of pitchblende (for radium) and uranium, extensively mined by the USSR under contract. Czechoslovakia is a major exporter of arms and machinery. Ostrava and Kosice are important steel centers.

Glass crystals and kaolin support a large glass and china industry; other products include light aircraft, wood pulp, textiles, shoes.

The nation bettered its balance of trade in 1967. Imports in 1967 were worth $2.68 billion ($2.736 billion in 1966). Exports in 1967 were worth $3.013 billion ($2.745 billion in 1966).

**History and Government.** Since February, 1948, Czechoslovakia has been a unitary socialist republic composed of two Slav nations—the Czechs and the Slovaks—with a socialist constitution, nationalized industry and one-slate elections. The Czechs number over 8,000,000 and Slovaks about 4,000,000. In addition, there are some 450,000 Hungarians, 200,000 Germans, 200,000 gypsies, 100,000 Ruthenian-Ukrainians and 100,000 Poles. Large numbers of Hungarians were moved out of Slovakia and many Slovaks were moved from Hungary to Slovakia in 1945-46. An estimated 3,000,000 Sudeten Germans were transferred to Germany under the Potsdam Agreement.

Bohemia, Moravia and Slovakia were part of the Great Moravian Empire when overrun by the Magyars 906 A.D. Bohemia and Moravia later became part of the Holy Roman Empire. Under the kings of Bohemia Prague in the 14th Century was the cultural center of Central Europe. The Hussite religious wars were fought here, 1420-36. In 1526 Ferdinand, brother of Emperor Charles V, became king of Bohemia and Hungary and began Germanization of the Slavs, never fully successful. In 1618 the Thirty Years' War opened in Prague.

In 1914-1918 Thomas G. Masaryk and Eduard Benes formed a provisional government with the support of Slovak leaders, of whom Milan Stefanik organized freedom fighters in foreign countries. When Austria fell, Oct. 28, 1918, they proclaimed the republic of Czechoslovakia Oct. 30. Masaryk became President, Benes Foreign Minister and Stefanik Minister of War. Benes succeeded Masaryk in 1935.

By 1938 Adolf Hitler of Nazi Germany had worked up disaffection among German-speaking citizens in Sudetenland and demanded its cession. To avoid war Prime Minister Neville Chamberlain of Great Britain, with the acquiescence of France, signed an agreement with Hitler at Munich, Sept. 30, 1938, agreeing to the cession, with a guaranty of peace by Hitler and Mussolini. Nazi Germany occupied Sudetenland Oct. 1-2. President Benes resigned Oct. 5, Germany and Italy agreed Nov. 2 to convey 4,000 sq. mi. of Czechoslovakia to Hungary. Other parts of the nation were sliced off to benefit Poland.

Hitler on Mar. 15, 1939, dissolved Czechoslovakia, made protectorates of Bohemia and Moravia, and supported the autonomy of Slovakia, which was proclaimed independent Mar. 14, 1939, with Jozef Tiso as President.

In May, 1942, the German governor, Reinhard Heydrich, was assassinated near Prague; Hitler in reprisal leveled the village of Lidice, shot the men, interned the women and sent the children to Germany.

Soviet troops with some Czechoslovak contingents entered eastern Czechoslovakia in 1944 and reached Prague in May 1945; Benes returned as President. In May 1946 elections, the Communists won 38% of the votes, largest for a single party,

and Benes accepted Klement Gottwald, a Communist, as Prime Minister. Tiso was executed in 1947.

In Feb. 1948 a crisis resulted in the resignation of 12 anti-Communist ministers and Benes accepted a new Gottwald Cabinet Feb. 25. Jan Masaryk, son of Thomas Masaryk, had not resigned as Foreign Minister. He was found dead March 10, apparently a suicide but there was widespread speculation he was murdered.

In May 1948 a new constitution was approved by the constituent assembly; Benes refused to sign it. On May 30 the voters were offered a one-slate ballot and the Communists won full control. Benes resigned June 7, Gottwald became President and Benes died Sept. 3.

The present constitution, announced in July, 1960, reorganized the nation into a highly centralized state. It has a National Assembly of 300 and a Slovak National Council, the latter limited to regional matters.

In Jan. 1968 a liberalization movement spread explosively through Czechoslovakia. Antonin Novotny, long the Communist boss of the nation, was deposed as party leader and succeeded by Alexander Dubcek, a Slovak, who declared he intended to make Communism democratic. On Mar. 22 Novotny resigned as President and was succeeded by Gen. Ludvik Svoboda. On Apr. 6, Premier Joseph Lenart resigned and was succeeded by Oldrich Cernik, whose new cabinet was pledged to carry out democratization and economic reforms.

In July 1968 the USSR and 4 hard-core Warsaw Pact nations demanded an end to liberalization. At summit meetings held in Czechoslovakia, it was apparently agreed the nation could continue these policies. But on Aug. 20, Russian, Polish, East German, Hungarian and Bulgarian military forces invaded Czechoslovakia. (*See Index for further details.*)

**Education and Religion.** An estimated 75% of the population is Roman Catholic, the rest are Protestant (Hussite), Greek Orthodox, etc.

Institutions of higher learning are the Czech University in Prague, founded in 1348; the Universities of Brno, Bratislava, Kosice, Hradec, Kralove, Plzen; also technical universities. Czech and Slovak are official languages.

**Defense.** Universal military service for all between 20 and 50 was re-established in 1945, with service for two years. Since 1950 the Army has been trained by Soviet advisers. Its strength is est. at 185.000, with an additional 45,000 men in security forces and frontier guards. The Air Force is believed to have 25,000 personnel and about 1,500 Soviet-type jet planes.

# Dahomey
## REPUBLIC OF DAHOMEY

**Capital:** Porto-Novo. **Area:** 43,483 sq. mi. **Population** (UN est. 1967): **2,505,000. Monetary unit:** CFA franc (246.85 per U. S. $1).

The Republic of Dahomey, former Overseas Territory in French West Africa, is a narrow strip 415 mi. long and 77 mi. wide, bounded by the Republics of the Niger and Upper Volta, Nigeria, Gulf of Guinea and the Republic of Togo. It is about as large as Tennessee.

In accordance with the 1958 French constitution, Dahomey became fully independent Aug. 1, 1960, and became a member of the UN Sept. 20. It is a member of an economic alliance known as the Council of the Entente, formed May 29, 1959, the other members being Ivory Coast, Niger and Upper Volta. Dahomey signed agreements Apr. 24, 1961, providing for close ties with France outside of the French Community proper.

Under the constitution the President and National Assembly are elected for five-year terms. Pres. Hubert Maga, elected Dec. 11, 1960, was deposed Oct. 28, 1963, and replaced by a provisional government headed by Gen. Christophe Soglo. The constitution of the second republic was adopted Dec. 19, 1963. Sourou Migan Apithy was elected Pres. Jan. 24, 1964; he was deposed by Soglo Nov. 27, 1965; Tahiro Congacou was named Provisional Pres.; he was ousted by Soglo Dec. 22 and Soglo took over the Presidency.

**Principal products:** palm oil, kernels and nuts; peanuts, cotton, kapok, coffee, tobacco.

Gen. Soglo was ousted Dec. 17, 1967, by a military group. Lt. Col. Alphonse Alley became head of state. A constitution providing for a one-party state for 5 years was approved Mar. 31, 1968. An

election for President in May was boycotted by most voters and was declared void.

The military leaders installed Emile Derlin Zinsou, a civilian, as President June 27, 1968.

Small industries were under construction in 1968, including a bicycle plant, cotton mill and peanut-oil plant.

# Denmark
## KONGERIGET DANMARK

**Capital: Copenhagen. Area: 16,619 sq. mi. Population including Faeroe Islands and Greenland (UN est. 1967): 4,839,000. Monetary unit: Krone (7.466 per U. S. $1).**

Denmark, a kingdom, occupies the peninsula of Jutland, thrusting out to the North from Germany, which is its only land neighbor, between the North Sea and the Baltic Sea, and adjacent islands. The Skagerrak separates it from Norway; the Kattegat and Oresund from Sweden. The country consists of low undulating plains. It is about the size of New Hampshire and Massachusetts combined.

The **Faeroe Islands** in the North Atlantic, about 300 mi. NE of the Shetlands, and 850 mi. from Denmark proper, 18 inhabited, have an area of 540 sq. mi. and pop. (est. 1967) of 37,000. They are part of the kingdom as is Greenland, described below.

**Resources and Industries.** About 25% of the population lives by agriculture on more than 70% of the usable land. Denmark normally exports more butter and produces more bacon than any other country except the U. S. Fisheries are valuable. Tourist trade accounts for 5% of foreign exchange. Denmark exports machinery, ships, textiles, furniture, iron and steel goods. Most raw materials and fuels have to be imported, but manufactures have increased; industrial exports jumped 228%, 1956-66, surpassing agricultural exports. Danish furniture has a large sale in the U. S.

The first cooperative consumers' society was established 1866; the system currently has about 1950 affiliated societies and includes 517,000 households, about 45% of the whole population.

More than 1,000,000 tourists visited Denmark in 1966. Many tourists leave their children in Danish camps while visiting other countries.

Denmark's merchant fleet comprises an est. 335 vessels over 1,500 gross tons aggregating more than 2,250,000 gross tons.

Foreign trade in thousands of U. S. dollars:

| | Imports | Exports |
|---|---|---|
| 1966 | $3,002,000 | $2,454,000 |
| 1967 | $3,152,000 | $2,537,000 |

**History and Government.** The origin of Copenhagen dates back to ancient times, when the fishing and trading place named Havn (port) grew up on a cluster of islets in the Sound, but Bishop Absalon (1128-1201) is regarded as the actual founder of the city. On one of the islets he built a stronghold against the pirating Wends and the remnants of this still exist underground in front of Christiansborg. Elsinore (Helsingör) contains the reputed grave of Hamlet, the Danish prince immortalized by Shakespeare.

The King and Parliament jointly hold legislative power. A new constitution, signed June 5, 1953, made women eligible to succeed to the throne, substituted a unicameral Parliament (the Folketing) of 179 members for the former two-chamber Rigsdag, made Greenland a full member of the Danish Realm with representatives in Parliament.

The King of Denmark is Frederick IX (born March 11, 1899) who succeeded to the throne on the death of his father, King Christian X, April 20, 1947. He married Princess Ingrid of Sweden and they have three daughters: Princess Margrethe, heir (born Apr. 16, 1940), Princess Benedikte (born Apr. 29, 1944, married Feb. 3, 1968, to Prince Richard-Casimir of Sayn-Wittgenstein) and Princess Anne-Marie (born Aug. 30, 1946, Queen of Greece). The King has one brother, Prince Knud (born July 27, 1900).

On Sept. 18, 1964, Princess Anne-Marie married King Constantine of Greece. On July 10, 1965, their 1st child, a daughter, Alexia, was born. A son, Paul, was born May 20, 1967.

Princess Margrethe was wed June 10, 1967, to Count Henri Marie Jean Andre de Laborde de Monpezat of France, now Prince Henrik of Denmark. A son, Frederik Andre Henrik Christian, was born May 26, 1968. He is 2nd in line to the throne.

Denmark has public assistance, health insurance, disability and old-age pensions, workmen's compensation and unemployment insurance. If a worker refuses to take an offered job, aid ceases. A pension is paid to men aged 67, widows and single women aged 62.

Denmark is a member of the UN, NATO and EFTA.

**Education and Religion.** The Evangelical Lutheran is the established religion, but there is complete religious tolerance. Education is compulsory and includes vocational courses. Leading institutions are the Univ. of Copenhagen (1479), the Univ. of Arhus (1934), the Technical Univ. (1824), and the Univ. of Odense. Apprenticeship training and occupational training of unskilled workers are provided by law. State grants aid the nation's 1,460 libraries. Royal Library has more than 1,650,000 vols.

**Defense:** The Army has compulsory training ages 19-25. The Navy comprises fleet and coast defense forces. Mobilized strengths are: Army, 98,000; Navy, 12,000; Air Force, 7 fighter and fighter-bomber squadrons totaling 16,000, and a home guard of 71,000 men and women. Seven airfields come under the NATO program.

### GREENLAND

Greenland, a huge island between the North Atlantic and the Polar Sea, is separated from the North American continent by Davis Strait and Baffin Bay. Its total area is 840,000 sq. mi., 705,234 of which are ice-capped. Most of the island is a lofty plateau 9,000 to 10,000 ft. in altitude. The average thickness of the ice cap is 1,000 ft. The population (est. 1965) is 39,615. The capital is Godthaab. Under the 1953 Danish constitution the colony became an integral part of the realm.

The deposits of cryolite are the largest in the world. Fish and fur are exported.

Denmark has built six Loran towers up to 1,345 ft. tall on Greenland and the Faeroe Islands to provide navigational aid to ships and planes.

# Dominican Republic
## REPUBLICA DOMINICANA

**Capital: Santo Domingo. Area: 18,816 sq. mi. Population (UN est. 1967): 3,889,000. Monetary unit: Peso (1 per U. S. $1).**

The Dominican Republic occupies the eastern two-thirds of the Island of Hispaniola (discovered by Columbus in 1492), second largest of the Greater Antilles, lying between Cuba on the W and Puerto Rico on the E. The boundary between it and the Republic of Haiti, which occupies the western part of the island, is 241 mi. long. It has a coastline of 979 mi. It is twice the size of New Hampshire. Climate is generally sub-tropical.

The city of Santo Domingo, founded 1496, is the oldest settlement by Europeans in the hemisphere and has the supposed ashes of Columbus in an elaborate tomb in its ancient cathedral.

**Resources and Industries.** The land is fertile. Chief products are sugar, cocoa, coffee, tobacco, corn, peanuts, bananas and livestock products.

The country has gold, copper, iron, salt, chalk, bauxite, marble, amber, kaolin.

Chief manufactures are sugar, molasses, rum, alcohol, cement, peanut oil, chocolate, tobacco products, cordage, textiles, apparel, lumber, furniture. The U. S. buys more than 50% of its exports, mostly sugar, cocoa and coffee, and supplies about 50% of imports.

In 1968 a group of U. S., European and Japanese companies joined the Dominican government in a consortium designed to press industrial development and technical training.

**History and Government.** Spain ceded Santo Domingo to France, 1795. Toussaint L'Ouverture, Haitian leader, seized it, 1801. Spain returned intermittently 1803-1821, and several native republics came and went. From 1822 to 1844 Haiti governed it. The republic was formed 1844. Spain occupied it 1861-63.

The country was occupied by American Marines from 1916 until 1924, when a constitutionally elected government was installed.

In 1930, Gen. Rafael Leonidas Trujillo Molina was elected President. Trujillo remained in power, ruling the nation with an iron hand (though turning the Presidency over to his brother, Hector, in 1952 and to Joaquin Balaguer in 1960) until his assassination May 27, 1961.

Pres. Balaguer resigned under pressure Jan. 17, 1962. Pending general elections, the country was governed by a 7-member Council of State headed by Rafael F. Bonnelly who was named President

Jan. 18, 1962. He was succeeded by Juan Bosch, elected President Dec. 20, 1962, in first free elections in 38 years. Pres. Bosch was overthrown Sept. 25, 1963, and his regime replaced by an army-backed civilian triumvirate led by Donald Reid Cabral.

On April 24, 1965, a revolt was launched by followers of Bosch and others, including Communists, and led by Col. Francisco Caamano Deno. The Reid Cabral government was ousted, but the rebel regime was replaced Apr. 28 by a 3-man counter-revolutionary junta led by Gen. Elias Wessin y Wessin; on May 7 it was succeeded by a 5-man regime headed by Gen. Antonio Imbert Barreras, another anti-Bosch leader; fighting continued in Santo Domingo.

A force of 405 U. S. Marines landed by helicopter April 28, primarily, according to U. S. Pres. Johnson, to save American and other lives; U. S. forces were expanded to a high of 24,000 as the U. S. sought to restore order and prevent a Communist take-over.

At U. S. urging, the Organization of American States sent an Inter-American Peace Force to Santo Domingo starting May 23, under a Brazilian commander with the head of the U. S. forces as deputy commander. Some U. S. forces were withdrawn and the Inter-American Force consisted of 11,200 men, including 9,400 U. S. troops, 1,100 Brazilians, and units from Honduras, Nicaragua, Paraguay and Costa Rica.

On Sept. 3, Hector Garcia-Godoy became provisional President under sponsorship of the OAS with agreement by all major local groups. The junta and Col. Caamano announced their resignations as heads of their rival governments.

An election was held June 1, 1966; former Pres. Balaguer defeated former Pres. Bosch, 754,409 votes to 517,783. The Balaguer Reformist party won control of both houses of Congress. The new President was inaugurated July 1. The Inter-American Peace Force began moving troops out and completed their departure Sept. 20.

Thousands of Dominicans had lost their lives in the communal strife; U. S. forces suffered 26 dead, 155 wounded.

**Education and Religion.** The population is mostly mixed white and Negro, plus about 15% white and a slightly larger number of Negro. The people are mostly Roman Catholics. Education is free and compulsory. The language is Spanish, but English is widely spoken. The University of Santo Domingo was established 1538 by Dominican fathers.

**Defense.** Active armed forces comprise approximately 25,000 officers and men. The Navy has modern units—2 destroyers, 4 frigates, 5 corvettes, patrol vessels and coast guards. The Air Force has fighters, light bombers, transport and rescue squadrons. The republic is a member of the UN and OAS.

phur are known to exist. Modern farm methods have speeded agricultural growth and made Ecuador the world's largest exporter of bananas. Other agricultural products are rice, cereals, potatoes, fruits, cocoa, coffee, kapok, rubber, mangrove bark.

Industry now contributes 20% to the national income, with large production increases in cement, edible oils, textiles, sugar, chemicals. The U. S. is Ecuador's principal customer.

The so-called Panama hats, made of Toquilla straw, are hand-woven in Ecuador. It is also the chief source of extremely light but strong balsa wood. Ecuador was the original home of the Cinchona tree, source of quinine.

**History and Government.** Spain conquered the region, which was the northern Inca empire, in the 16th Century. Liberation forces defeated the Spanish May 24, 1822, near Quito. Ecuador became part of the Republic of Colombia but seceded, May 13, 1830, and became a republic. It has had a history of numerous coups and military rule.

Under the republic's constitution of 1967 the President is elected directly by the people for a 4-year term and is eligible for re-election after a 4-year interval. Congress consists of a Senate and a Chamber of Representatives.

A military junta seeking reforms ousted and exiled Pres. Carlos J. Arosemena Monroy July 11, 1963, and outlawed the Communist party. Anti-government demonstrations in July 1965 brought appointment of a new coalition Cabinet by the junta. More demonstrations brought ouster of the junta, Mar. 29, 1966, by military leaders and agreement by major political parties to name Clemente Yerovi Indaburu Provisional President. Yerovi convened a National Constitutional Assembly and elections were held Oct. 1966. The Assembly met Nov. 18, 1966 and elected Dr. Otto Arosemena Gomez Interim President.

In June 1968 elections, Dr. Jose Maria Velasco Ibarra, who had been elected Pres. 4 times but had been ousted 3 times by coups, was again chosen by the voters.

Ecuador's 17th Constitution was adopted May 25, 1967. It is a UN and OAS member.

**Education and Religion.** Roman Catholicism is the chief religion. Primary education is compulsory. The language is Spanish. The population is over one-third Indian and one-third mixed; whites are in the minority but American, British, Italian and Spanish immigrants are encouraged.

**Defense.** Military service is compulsory. The U. S. has a military assistance advisory agreement with Ecuador.

### EGYPT
*See Index for United Arab Republic*

# Ecuador
### REPUBLICA DEL ECUADOR

**Capital: Quito. Area (govt. est.): 116,270 sq. mi. Population (UN est. 1967): 5,508,000. Monetary unit: Sucre (18.18 official rate per U. S. $1).**

On the northwestern coast of South America, Ecuador (Sp. for Equator) straddles the world's midsection, extending 100 mi. into the Northern Hemisphere, 400 into the Southern. It is bounded by Colombia, Peru and the Pacific. Two ranges of the Andes run N and S, splitting the country into 3 zones—hot, humid lowlands on the coast; temperate highlands between the ranges, and rainy, tropical lowlands to the E. There are 22 peaks over 14,000 ft.; highest is Chimborazo, 20,561 ft.; many are snowcapped; some volcanoes have erupted in recent years. It is larger than Arizona.

The Galapagos Islands, 600 mi. to the W, are the home of huge tortoises and other unusual animals. Charles Darwin visited the islands aboard the Beagle in 1835; his studies of wildlife there provided most of the facts for his theory of evolution.

Ecuador has claimed an est. 100,000 sq. mi. of Amazon valley land awarded to Peru in a 1942 treaty.

Guayaquil, Ecuador's largest city, is the chief seaport and, together with Quito, is served by major airlines. Rail lines link Quito with Guayaquil and San Lorenzo on the coast. Quito is famed for its 17th Century churches.

**Resources and Industries.** The country is rich in undeveloped minerals. Silver ore is found at Pillzhum in Cañar. Petroleum output is increasing. Large deposits of copper, iron, lead, coal and sul-

# El Salvador
### REPUBLICA de EL SALVADOR

**Capital: San Salvador. Area: 8,260 sq. mi. Population (UN est. 1967): 3,151,000. Monetary unit: Colon (2.5 per U. S. $1).**

El Salvador, smallest of the six Central American or Middle American republics and the only one without an Atlantic seacoast, is bounded by Guatemala, Honduras, the Gulf of Fonesca and a Pacific coastline of about 160 mi. A country of mountains, including many volcanoes, and upland plains, it is entirely within the tropics, but tropic heat is modified by the elevation. It is about the size of Massachusetts.

La Libertad, Acajutla and La Union (Cutuco) are the principal seaports.

The three racial types are white, 10%; mixed white and Indian descent, 85%; Indian, 5%.

**Resources and Industries.** Mountain slope plantations make El Salvador the world's 7th largest producer and 4th largest exporter of coffee. Cotton production has made large strides; coffee represents 52% of the value of exports, cotton 21%. Primarily agricultural, the country is becoming industrialized; it produces cement, refined sugar and textiles.

In July 1968 U. S. President Johnson visited El Salvador and announced new financial aid to the 5 members of the Central American Common Market: El Salvador, Costa Rica, Honduras, Guatemala and Nicaragua.

**History and Government.** El Salvador became independent of Spain in 1821; member of the Central American Federation until 1839. The consti-

tution provides for a unicameral legislative system, the National Assembly of Deputies, elected by popular vote. Voting is compulsory for all over 18 years of age. Executive power is vested in the President who is elected for a 5-year term by direct, popular vote and is ineligible for immediate reelection. The President is assisted by a Council of Ministers who are named by him.

**Education and Religion.** Education is free and compulsory, but illiteracy rate is 50%. The language is Spanish. The dominant religion is Roman Catholicism.

**Defense.** There is military instruction between the ages of 18 and 40. The Army is organized in five divisions. There is one aviation corps, one marine corps, and a national guard. El Salvador is a member of the UN and OAS.

## ESTONIA
*See Index for Estonian SSR*

## Ethiopia
### YE ITIOPIA NEGUSE NEGUEST MENGUIST
(Abyssinia)

**Capital: Addis Ababa. Area: 398,350 sq. mi., including Eritrea. Population (UN est. 1967): 23,-457,000. Monetary unit: Ethiopian dollar (2.5 per U. S. $1).**

Ethiopia is a ruggedly mountainous, independent empire in NE Africa. It faces on the Red Sea, but its main rivers are important tributaries of the Nile; the Abbai or Blue Nile, one of the two main branches of that mighty river, has its source in Ethiopia's Lake Tana. The country is as large as Texas and New Mexico combined.

**Resources and Industries.** Economy is some 70% agricultural but industrial resources are potentially great, including vast hydroelectric power, surveys of which are under way with aid of the International Bank. Modern industrial enterprises are conducted by American and other firms.

Fertile soil and abundant rainfall produce two crops annually. Coffee, wheat, barley, millet, tobacco, and sugar are principal crops. Coffee of extremely high quality from Kaffa, in SW Ethiopia, reputed birthplace of the coffee plant, accounts for half of the country's foreign exchange. Over 1,600,000 bags were produced in 1965.

An unfavorable balance of trade continued in 1967. Exports declined from $112,000,000 to $102,-000,000. Imports dropped from $163,000,000 to $144,000,000.

Cattle, sheep, mules and goats are raised, cattle numbering an est. 25,325,000. Hides and skins, oilseeds and pulses also are exported. Mineral resources include platinum, gold, silver, manganese, tin, copper, asbestos, potash, sulphur, mica, cement and salt. There are known deposits of coal and iron; tests are in progress for petroleum.

Ethiopia has used large credits from the World Bank and International Development Assn. for road building (it now has 3,200 mi. of all-weather roads). Aid and investment funds are received from the U. S. and other western nations and from Communist countries. Ethiopia is a member of the UN and Addis Ababa is hq. for the Organization of African Unity.

**History and Government.** Ethiopia is a constitutional monarchy derived from a number of earlier kingdoms, descendants of ancient Hamite and Semite tribes. Italy invaded the country in 1880 and acquired a sphere of influence and later organized its colony of Eritrea. In 1936 Italy invaded Ethiopia without declaring war. Emperor Haile Selassie fought until forced to withdraw. The League of Nations applied sanctions against Italy, which proved ineffective. Mussolini added Ethiopia to Italy with Victor Emmanuel III emperor. British forces freed Ethiopia 1941.

In 1964, armed clashes featured a border dispute with Somalia. A truce was arranged by the Org. of African Unity and foreign ministers of the two nations met in Khartoum, Sudan, and agreed to withdraw troops from the border. In 1965 Ethiopia set up camps for 70,000 refugees who crossed the border from former British Somaliland with 250,000 cattle, saying the Somali Government was discriminating against them.

The present Emperor, Haile Selassie I, 225th consecutive Solomonic ruler, was born July 23, 1892, crowned Nov. 2, 1930. He voluntarily established a parliament and judiciary system, 1931, and promulgated a new constitution 1955, incorporating a liberal bill of rights, and granting the franchise to all over 21. The Senate (Upper

House) of 105 is appointed for 6-year terms; Chamber of Deputies, approx. 250, is elected for 4 years. In April 1966, the Emperor made further moves toward democracy, including empowering the Premier to appoint his own Cabinet, a power formerly reserved by the Emperor.

**Education and Religion.** Ethiopian culture has been influenced by Greece and Egypt. Christianity is the predominant religion, embraced in 330 A.D.; the Coptic, Monophysite branch is practiced. Until 1952 the Egyptian Coptic Patriarch was the head of the Church, but the Emperor now appoints the Ethiopian Archbishop. The population is largely composed of a mixture of Hamites, Semites and Negroes. The largest number are Coptic Christians; next are Moslems; others practice tribal religions.

There are two universities and a number of colleges. The official language is Amharic; English is widely taught.

Eritrea, which had been an Italian colony since 1890, was administered after World War II by Great Britain; the UN General Assembly voted to return it to Ethiopia and the action became effective Sept. 11, 1952.

## Finland
### SUOMEN TASAVALTA—REPUBLIKEN FINLAND

**Capital: Helsinki. Area: 130,119 sq. mi. Population (Govt. est. 1967): 4,678,000. Monetary unit: Mark (4.2 per U. S. $1).**

Finland is a republic in northern Europe, with Sweden, Norway and the USSR for neighbors. South and central Finland are mostly flat areas with low hills; there are mountainous areas, 3,000-4,000 ft., in the N. It is half the size of Texas.

About 70% of the land is forested. Lakes and canal waterways are navigable for 3,000 mi. Rail and air transport is well developed.

**Aland Islands,** constituting the autonomous department of Aland, is a group of small islands, 572 sq. mi., in the Gulf of Bothnia, 25 mi. from Sweden, 15 mi. from Finland. They are demilitarized. Mariehamn is the principal port.

**Resources and Industries.** Rapid industrialization has taken place, especially since World War II, but agriculture is still a vital factor. Principal crops are oats, barley, wheat, rye, potatoes, hay. Woodworking and paper and pulp products account for about 60% of total exports. Expansion is expected to increase pulp production to 5,430,000 metric tons annually. Other chief industries are shipbuilding, metals, machinery, food and beverages, textiles, leather, chemicals.

In 1967, 1,100,000 tourists visited Finland.

The merchant marine, Feb. 29, 1968, comprised 522 vessels totaling 1,099,919 gross tons.

The cooperative system is carried on in Finland with marked success.

Foreign trade (in thousands of U. S. dollars):

| | Imports | Exports |
|---|---|---|
| 1966 | $1,726,000 | $1,506,000 |
| 1967 | $1,694,000 | $1,531,000 |

**History and Government.** The original Finns lived thousands of years ago, probably in the Ural area, and were part of a larger Finno-Ugrian (Hungarians etc.), group of peoples. The Finns migrated in a northerly direction, first to the Baltic area and then, at about the beginning of the Christian era, to what is today Finland. Swedish settlers brought the country into the kingdom of Sweden, 1154 to 1809, when Finland became an autonomous grand duchy of the Russian Empire. Russian exactions created a strong national spirit; on Dec. 6, 1917, Finland declared its independence and on July 17, 1919, became a republic. On Nov. 30, 1939, the Soviet Union invaded Finland, and although the Finns took heavy toll, they surrendered after 3 mos. and in March, 1940, were forced to cede 16,173 sq. mi., including the Karelian isthmus, Viipuri, and an area on Lake Lagoda. When Germany attacked the USSR June 22, 1941, Finland went to war to take back its lands. An armistice was signed Sept. 19, 1944, and the USSR exacted the former cessions, plus Petsamo in the North and a lease for 50 years on Porkkala, near Helsinki, for a military base. The treaty of Feb. 10, 1947, also exacted $300,000,000 in goods in term payments. In April, 1948, Finland signed a 10-year treaty of mutual assistance and friendship with USSR, extended in 1956 until 1975, after the USSR agreed to return Porkkala, which it did Jan. 26, 1956.

The President is chosen for a term of six years by an Electoral College of 300 named by direct

vote: he appoints the Cabinet. The President is Dr. Urho Kekkonen, elected Feb. 15, 1956; re-elected 1962, 1968.

There is a single legislative chamber, the Eduskunta, numbering 200, elected to 4-year terms. The voting system is designed for proportional representation. In general elections Mar. 21-22, 1966, the Social Democrats, a moderate Socialist party, displaced the Center party as the largest single party. Seats won: Social Democrats 55, Center party 50, Communists 41, Conservatives 26, Swedish National 12, Liberals 8, Social Dem. Unionists 7, Small Farmers' party 1. A coalition Cabinet, headed by Dr. Mauno Koivisto, Social Democrat, took office Mar. 22, 1968.

**Education and Religion.** The Evangelical Lutheran Church is the leading religion, but there is freedom of worship. The nation is considered completely free from illiteracy. The Finnish language belongs to the Finno-Ugrian group, which also includes Magyar and Estonian. Swedish is the 2nd national language. There are 6 major universities (the oldest founded 1640) and six colleges of university level.

**Defense.** Universal military service prevails from 17 years to 60. Males reaching 19 are called up for training. There are an Air Force and a naval force. Finland's effective force is limited by its World War II peace treaty to 41,900.

Finland is a member of the UN and the Nordic Council, and an associate member of EFTA.

# France
## LA REPUBLIQUE FRANCAISE

**Capital: Paris. Area: 212,918 sq. mi. Population (Govt. est., Jan. 1, 1968): 50,662,000. Monetary unit: Franc (U. S. 20.2¢).**

France has coastlines on the Atlantic and Mediterranean and is about four-fifths the size of Texas. It shares borders with Belgium, Luxembourg, Germany, Switzerland, Italy, Andorra and Spain. It is separated from England by the English Channel and the Strait of Dover. The Rhine River is on the German boundary, the Jura Mts. form the Swiss boundary and the Pyrenees Mts. rise along the borders of Andorra and Spain.

Mont Blanc, on the Franco-Italian border, is the tallest mtn. W of the Caucasus, 15,771 ft. The world's longest highway tunnel, 7.25 mi. under Mont Blanc, was opened July 16, 1965, linking France and Italy.

The island of Corsica, which lies in the Mediterranean W of Italy and N of Sardinia, forms an integral part of France. It has an area of 3,367 sq. mi. and a population of about 280,000. The capital is Ajaccio, birthplace of Napoleon.

There are four important rivers, the Seine, the Loire, the Garonne and the Rhône. France controls the left bank of the Rhine from Basel, Switzerland, to Lauterbourg, France. There are some 4,750 mi. of navigable rivers and canals. Major riverports are Bordeaux, Lyons, Paris, Rouen and Strasbourg.

**Resources and Industries.** Agriculturally, France is a country of small diversified farms occupying 45,800,000 acres and 18% of the employed, making France the biggest food producer in Western Europe. Agricultural exports are valued at more than $1.7 billion annually. Leading crops are wheat, barley, corn, oats, rice, and a wide variety of fruits and vegetables. Cattle, poultry, forestry and fishing are large-scale. France is the world's 4th ranking producer of beef. Approx. 1,500,000 farmers belong to cooperative unions, including farm machinery and marketing cooperatives.

The country is rich in minerals, and the basins of Pas de Calais and Lorraine are noted for their huge coal deposits, iron ore, bauxite, pyrites, mineral oils, auriferous ore, asphalt, rock salt and potash salts. The iron ore deposits in eastern France and the bauxite deposits in central France are among the richest in the world. Power stations produced about 114 billion kwh in 1967.

Southwest France became an important oil area with the discovery of the Lacq and Parentis fields. The Lacq gas field in Aquitaine has large reserves of natural gas and sulphur. Parentis field, near Bordeaux, yields approx. 1,374,000 metric tons of petroleum annually and the Sahara fields in Africa supply an est. 33,860,000 metric tons. In 1965, France and Algeria agreed on joint exploitation of oil and gas fields in the Sahara.

Some of the basic principles of atomic energy were discovered by French scientists. France is the foremost uranium producer in Western Europe, with output about 1,500 metric tons per year. Since

February, 1960, France has exploded 5 atomic devices in the Sahara, 4 above ground and one underground. On July 2, 1966, France exploded a small A-bomb over Mururoa, a tiny atoll 750 mi. SE of Tahiti; it was the 1st in a series of 6 explosions. In June 1967 and July 1968 new series of tests were started at Mururoa. France was not a signatory to the 1963 treaty banning such tests.

**Manufacturers** stress chemicals, silk and cotton textiles, perfumes, automobiles, aircraft, ships, instruments, electronic equipment. Index of industrial production (1963=100) was 120 in 1967.

France is the most important vinery in the world and its wines, of which it produces about 1.6 billion gallons a year, are of high value for export. Names of French provinces and regions, such as Bordeaux, Champagne, Burgundy, identify wines highly esteemed.

Foreign trade in thousands of U. S. dollars:

|      | Imports       | Exports       |
|------|---------------|---------------|
| 1966 | $11,843,000   | $10,889,000   |
| 1967 | $12,352,000   | $11,377,000   |

**History and Government.** The monarchial system was overthrown by the French Revolution 1789-1793) and succeeded by the First Republic; thereafter successively followed by the First Empire under Napoleon (1804-1814), a monarchy (1814-1848), the Second Republic (1848-1852), the Second Empire (1852-1870), the Third Republic (1871-1946), the Fourth Republic (1946-1958), Fifth Republic and French Community (1958). *For list of rulers consult Index.*

France suffered severe losses in manpower and wealth in the first World War, 1914-1918, when it was invaded by the German Empire. With Britain and the U. S. as its principal allies it threw back the Germans and by the Treaty of Versailles exacted return of Alsace and Lorraine, French provinces seized by Germany in 1871. As Allied controls on Germany were reduced Adolf Hitler and the Nazi party gained power, Germany invaded France in May, 1940, occupied Paris June 14, 1940, and signed an armistice with a government that made its hq. in Vichy, in unoccupied France. Marshal Phillippe Petain became chief of state, but underground forces (Resistance) operated as guerrillas while Gen. Charles de Gaulle formed an army in Africa. After France was liberated by the Allies Sept., 1944, Gen. De Gaulle became Premier of the provisional government, serving from Nov. 1944 to Jan. 1946.

Gen. De Gaulle again became Premier June 1, 1958. His proposed constitution for the Fifth Republic and new French Community was approved by the voters by an overwhelming margin, Sept. 28, 1958, with the exception of the West African territory of Guinea which voted for immediate independence outside the Community, becoming a republic Oct. 2, 1958.

Gen. De Gaulle was elected first President of the Fifth Republic Dec. 21, 1958; inaugurated Jan. 8, 1959.

Pres. De Gaulle ran for reelection Dec. 5, 1965; he failed to win a majority of the votes, getting about 44% compared to 32% for Francois Mitterand, left wing candidate. In a runoff election Dec. 19, Pres. De Gaulle won with about 55%; Mr. Mitterand got 45%.

The constitution provides for a strong executive branch headed by the President, a legislature composed of a National Assembly and a Senate.

A constitutional amendment adopted by referendum Oct. 28, 1962, provided that future Presidents be elected by popular vote rather than by an electoral college. The President, elected for 7 years, appoints the Premier (formerly invested by the Assembly), and may dissolve the Assembly and call for new elections; he may call for referendums on specific issues and may assume full powers in a national emergency. An absolute majority vote of the Assembly is required to overthrow a government. The President is assisted by an Executive Council comprising the Premier, heads of states and certain Cabinet members.

Women, who had less than equal rights under provisions of the 1804 Code Napoleon, won the right to take jobs, open checking accounts and own their own businesses by a 1966 law.

In May 1968 rebellious students at the Sorbonne and elsewhere rioted, battled police and were joined by some 10,000,000 workers who launched nationwide strikes and took over many factories. The nation was almost completely paralyzed. On May 22 the Gaullist government narrowly defeated a censure motion in the National Assembly. The government awarded 35% minimum pay increases

to the strikers May 26; on May 30 Pres. De Gaulle dissolved the Assembly. A threat of civil war was eased as Army tank units, loyal to the government, maneuvered in Paris outskirts, and Pres. De Gaulle warned of a Communist dictatorship threat. By early June, normalcy was returned.

In elections June 23 and 30, 1968, Pres. De Gaulle's regime won its greatest victory; 291 Gaullists and 64 allied Independent Republicans were elected to the 487-seat Assembly; the Communists won 33 seats, a loss of 40 from their previous holding.

**Education and Religion.** Primary, secondary and higher education are free and instruction is compulsory between the ages of 6 and 16. There are 23 universities.

The country is predominantly Roman Catholic, only about 800,000 being Protestants. The state recognizes no religion and tolerates all.

Both employers and employees contribute to the old-age pension fund. There is provision for family allowances and compulsory social insurance for illness, maternity, disability and death. A profit-sharing agreement was signed Jan. 7, 1959.

**Defense.** Compulsory service for 20-year-olds was reduced from 24 to 18 months May 1, 1963. Compulsory military training has existed since 1798. The armed forces in 1966 numbered approx. 578,000 including 338,000 Army, 111,000 Air Force, 68,000 Navy, 61,000 Gendarmery. Gradual reduction of the forces was planned for 1965-1970, with emphasis on nuclear devices.

France is a member of the UN, NATO, SEATO, EEC and French Community.

Pres. De Gaulle announced Mar. 9, 1966, France would withdraw all its troops from the integrated military command of NATO and that NATO hq. and bases would have to be removed from France. But he said France would still be a member of the Atlantic Alliance.

**The French Community** (*See Index*). As provided in the 1958 Constitution and later amendments, the Community includes the French Republic and:

Six of 12 African republics which won complete independence in 1960: Central African Rep., Chad, Congo (Brazzaville), Gabon, Malagasy (Madagascar), Senegal. (*See Index for individual articles.*)

Four Overseas Departments, seven Overseas Territories and one Condominium (New Hebrides). (*See descriptions below.*)

Not members of the Community are former French possessions or trust territories such as Cambodia, Laos and Vietnam (former parts of French Indo-China), Tunisia, Algeria; also 9 African republics which won independence and decided to remain outside the Community but to retain certain economic and cultural ties with France—Cameroon, Dahomey, Guinea, Ivory Coast, Mali, Mauritania, Niger, Togo, Upper Volta. (*See Index for individual articles.*)

### AFARS & ISSAS TERRITORY (Formerly French Somaliland)

The French Territory of the Afars and the Issas lies between Ethiopia and Somalia and is separated by the Straits of Bab-el-Mandeb from South Arabia.

The area is 8,880 sq. mi. and population (est. 1963): 86,000; the capital is Djibouti. France took control of the area in gradual steps, beginning in 1839.

The Territory has few industries, except fishing and livestock. Salt is its most valuable product. Half of Ethiopia's foreign commerce passes along the rail line from Addis Ababa and through the port of Djibouti.

In a referendum Mar. 19, 1967, the Territory elected to remain French and by a decree signed by the High Commissioner French Somaliland changed its name to the French Territory of the Afars and the Issas. It sends a Deputy and a Senator to the French Parliament.

### COMORO ISLANDS

**Comoro Islands,** an Overseas Territory, is an archipelago of small islands off SE Africa in Mozambique Channel NW of Madagascar. Chief islands are Grande Comore, Anjouan, Mayotte, Moheli. Total area, about 863 sq. mi.; population (est. 1964): 207,000. Capital: Moroni. Chief products are vanilla, coconuts and essential oils. It elects two Deputies, one Senator to the French Parliament.

### REUNION

**Reunion,** Overseas Department is an island in the Indian Ocean, about 420 miles east of Madagascar, and has belonged to France since 1643. The area is 969 sq. mi.; the population (est. 1964), 382,000 is 30% of French extraction. Capital: Saint-Denis. The chief products are sugar, rum, corn, perfume essences, vanilla and spices. It elects 3 Deputies, two Senators to the French Parliament.

### GUADELOUPE

**Guadeloupe.** Overseas Department in the West Indies' Leeward Islands, consists of two large islands, Basse-Terre and Grande-Terre, separated by the Salt River, plus Marie Galante and the Saintes group to the S and, to the N, Desirade, Bathelemy and almost half of St. Martin (the Netherlands portion is St. Maarten). A French possession since 1634, the department is represented in the French Parliament by two Senators and 3 Deputies; administration consists of a Prefect (governor) and an elected General Council.

Area of the islands is 687 sq. mi.; pop. over 306,000 mainly descendants of slaves; capital is Basse-Terre on Basse-Terre Is. The land is fertile; sugar, rum and bananas are exported; tourism is an important industry.

### MARTINIQUE

**Martinique,** one of the Windward Islands, in the West Indies, has been a possession since 1635, and a Department since March, 1946. It is represented in the French Parliament by two Senators and three Deputies. In Martinique is located the famous volcano, Mt. Pelee which erupted on May 8, 1902, destroyed the city of St. Pierre with more than 30,000 inhabitants. The island is the birthplace of the Empress Josephine.

Martinique has an area of 425 sq. mi. and a population of over 303,000 mostly descendants of slaves. The capital is Fort-de-France. It is a popular tourist stop.

The chief exports are sugar, rum, bananas, pineapples and cacao beans. Trade is mainly with France and the United States.

### ST. PIERRE AND MIQUELON

**St. Pierre** and **Miquelon,** an Overseas Territory, are two groups of rocky barren islands close to the southwestern coast of Newfoundland, inhabited by fishermen. An administrator, assisted by a Council rules the islands. The exports are chiefly cod, dried and fresh, and other fish products. Imports consist of textiles, salt, wines, foodstuffs and meat. A regular boat service is maintained with North Sydney and Halifax. A telegraph cable connects St. Pierre with Europe and the American continent.

The St. Pierre group has an area of 10 sq. mi.; Miquelon, 83 sq. mi. Total pop. (est. 1963), 5,025. The capital is St. Pierre. A Deputy and a Senator are elected to the French Parliament.

### FRENCH GUIANA

**French Guiana,** an Overseas Department, is on the NE coast of South America with Surinam (Netherlands Guinea) on the W and Brazil on the E and S. Its area is 35,135 sq. mi.; population (est. 1966) is 37,000. Guiana sends one Senator and one Deputy to the French Parliament. Guiana has a Prefect and a Council General of 16 elected members; capital is Cayenne.

In 1944 France closed the famous penal colony, Devil's Island, and repatriated 2,800 inmates.

Immense forests of rich timber cover 90% of the land. Very little of the land is cultivated. The principal crops are rice, corn, manioc, cacao, bananas, and sugar cane. Placer gold mining is the most important industry. Exports comprise cacao, bananas, various woods, gold, fish glue, rum, rosewood essence, lumber and hides.

### FRENCH POLYNESIA

**French Polynesia,** Overseas Territory, comprises 130 islands widely scattered among 5 archipelagos in the South Pacific; administered by a Governor, Territorial Assembly and a Council with headquarters at Papeete, **Tahiti,** one of the **Society Islands.** A Deputy and a Senator are elected to the French Parliament.

Other groups are the **Marquesas Islands,** the **Tuamotu Archipelago,** the **Gambier Islands,** and the **Austral Islands.**

Total area of the islands administered from Tahiti is 1,544 sq. mi.; pop. (est. 1966) 90,000, more than half on Tahiti. Tahiti is picturesque and mountainous with a productive coastline bearing coconut, bananas and orange trees, sugar cane and vanilla.

Tahiti was visited by Capt. James Cook in 1769 and by Capt. Bligh in the Bounty, 1788-89. The beauty of its women and the landscape impressed Herman Melville, Paul Gaugin, Charles Darwin

and Robert Louis Stevenson who called Tahitians "God's sweetest works."

## NEW CALEDONIA

**New Caledonia** and its dependencies, an Overseas Territory, are a group of islands in the Pacific Ocean about 1,115 mi. E of Australia and approx. the same distance NW of New Zealand. Dependencies are the **Loyalty Islands**, the **Isle of Pines, Huon Islands**, and the **Chesterfield Islands.**

New Caledonia, the largest, has 6,530 sq. mi. Total area of the Territory is 7,335 sq. mi.; population (est. 1966) 86,500. The group was acquired by France in 1854. A penal colony was maintained on Nou Island until 1896.

The Territory is administered by a Commissioner and government council. There is a popularly elected Territorial Assembly. A Deputy and a Senator are elected to the French Parliament. Capital: Noumea.

Mining is the chief industry. New Caledonia has the world's largest deposits of nickel. Other minerals found are chrome, cobalt, manganese, antimony, mercury, cinnebar, silver, gold, lead and copper. Agricultural products include coffee, copra, cotton, manioc (cassava), corn, tobacco, bananas and pineapples.

## WALLIS AND FUTUNA ISLANDS

**Wallis and Futuna Islands**, two archipelagos raised to status of Overseas Territory July 29, 1961, are situated in the SW Pacific south of the Equator between Fiji and Samoa. The islands have a total area of 106 sq. mi. and population (est. 1963) of 11,000. **Alofi**, attached to Futuna, is uninhabited. Capital: Mata-Utu. Chief products are copra, yams, taro roots, bananas.

## FRENCH ANTARCTICA

**French Antarctica and Southern Lands**, Overseas Terr., comprises **Adelie Land**, on Antarctica, and 4 island groups in the Indian Ocean. Adelie, discov. 1840, has 2 research bases, a coastline of 185 mi. and tapers 1,240 mi. inland to the South Pole. Heights rise to 8,200 ft. There are two huge glaciers, Ninnis, 22 mi. wide, 99 mi. long, and Mentz, 11 mi. wide, 140 mi. long. Climate varies from −36° F. to 40° F.

**Kerguelen Archipelago**, discov. 1772, has 300 islands. The chief is 87 mi. long, 74 mi. wide, and has Mt. Ross, 6,429 ft. tall. Principal research station is Port-aux-Francais. Seals often weigh 2 tons; there are blue whales, coal, peat, semiprecious stones. **Crozet Archipelago** (discov. 1772), covers 125 sq. mi. Eastern Island rises to 6,560 ft. **Saint Paul**, in southern Indian Ocean, has warm springs and tropical climate, with earth at places heating to 120° to 390° F. **New Amsterdam**, nearby, has temperate climate, produces cod and rock lobster.

## NEW HEBRIDES

**New Hebrides**, a condominium administered since 1906 by France and Great Britain, is a group of 11 main islands and about 69 islets 250 mi. northeast of New Caledonia and 500 mi. west of Fiji. It has an est. 5,700 sq. mi. and population (est. 1963) of 70,000, mostly Melanesian. It has two administrations—French and British. Chief products are copra, cotton, cacao and coffee.

## Gabon Republic
### LA REPUBLIQUE GABONAISE

**Capital:** Libreville. **Area:** 102,089 sq. mi. **Population** (UN est. 1967): 473,000. **Monetary unit:** CFA franc (246.85 per U. S. $1).

A former French Overseas Territory, Gabon is on the west coast of Equatorial Africa, straddling the Equator and bounded by Cameroon and Continental Guinea (Sp.), the Republic of Congo-Brazzaville, and the Atlantic. Heavily forested, the country consists of coastal lowlands, plateaus in N, E and S, mountains in N, SE and center. It is about the size of Colorado.

Gabon's economy is thriving, with exports exceeding imports by about 30%. Forest products—timber, plywood and veneers, chiefly Okoume wood—were the chief export until 1965 when exports of manganese, valued at $35,000,000, equaled the forestry exports. There are large iron ore and uranium deposits and oil production is increasing.

Agriculture, roads, port facilities and hydroelectric power are being extensively developed. Main crops are cocoa, coffee, rice, peanuts, palm products, cassava, bananas.

Gabon proclaimed complete independence Aug. 17, 1960, and has been a UN member since Sept. 20, 1960. President: Leon M'Ba, elected Feb. 12, 1961. In Feb. 1964 French troops, airlifted into the country, restored Pres. M'Ba after an attempted coup. In April backers of Pres. M'Ba won 27 of the 47 seats in the National Assembly. Gabon is a member of the French Community.

Dr. Albert Schweitzer, Nobel Peace Prize winner, physician, philosopher, musicologist and theologian, founded a hospital for lepers and others in 1913 at Lambaréné. He died Sept. 4, 1965, at the age of 90 and was buried at the hospital.

## The Gambia

**Capital:** Bathurst. **Area:** 4,005 sq. mi. **Population** (UN est. 1967): 343,000. **Monetary unit:** Pound (.4167 per U. S. $1).

Gambia, Africa's smallest country in both size and population, is a former British Colony and Protectorate in western Africa. It includes the island of St. Mary at the mouth of the Gambia River and a 10-mile wide strip of territory on each side of the river. Except for its Atlantic coastline, Gambia is surrounded by Senegal.

Gambia attained internal self-government Oct. 4, 1963. Its legislature comprises a speaker and 32 elected members. Britain agreed, July 30, 1964, to grant complete independence to the colony, which became effective Feb. 18, 1965. Gambia is a member of the Commonwealth and became a UN member Sept. 21, 1965.

In May 1966 Prime Minister Sir Dawda K. Jawara's People's Progressive party won 24 of the 32 legislature seats in the first general election since independence.

Peanuts are the main crop, along with rice and palm kernels. Gambia is receiving over $1,000,000 annually in subsidies from Britain.

In 1968 Gambia joined 8 neighboring nations in forming the West African Regional Group, to promote mutual economic betterment.

## Germany
### DEUTSCHLAND

**Area:** 137,596 sq. mi. **Population** (UN est. 1967): **76,954,000. Now comprises two units: Federal Republic of Germany (West Germany), German Democratic Republic (East Germany). A large area of the former empire, east of the Oder-Neisse line 43,900 sq. mi., is occupied by Poland and USSR.**

Germany is a central European nation composed of numerous states which had a common language and traditions but which did not become unified in one country until 1871; since World War II it has been split in two parts, West and East.

The climate and terrain are varied. West Germany includes large parts of the Rhine basin, with hilly sections adjoining both banks of the Rhine river filling center of the country. North of Bonn are the plains of the lower Rhine and lowlands of Cologne. East Germany is composed largely of the region of the Elbe river and its tributaries and part of the Oder basin. Most of the territory is level, except for the hilly Erzgebirge and Riesengebirge. Its climate is cooler than that of West Germany with long, cold winters and short summers.

**Resources and Industries.** Some of more important crops are wheat, rye, barley, oats, potatoes, sugar beets and hay. Other commercial plants are fruit, tobacco, hops, nuts.

Principal minerals are coal, lignite, iron, zinc, lead, copper, salt, potash and petroleum. Bulk of mining is in North Rhine-Westphalia, Upper Silesia, Central Germany, the Harz, and Westerwald. Oil comes chiefly from Emsland near Netherlands border, and Lower Saxony. Iron and steel production is greatest in the Ruhr and Saar.

**History and Government.** Germanic tribes were defeated by Julius Caesar, 55 and 53 B. C. but Roman expansion north of the Rhine was stopped with the wiping out of 3 legions under Varus in 9 A.D. Charlemagne, ruler of the Franks, consolidated Saxon, Bavarian, Rhenish, Frankish and other lands; after him the eastern part became the German Empire. *Consult Rulers of Middle Europe.* The Thirty Years' War, 1618-1648, split Germany into small principalities and kingdoms. After Napoleon, Austria contended with Prussia for dominance, but lost the Seven Weeks' War to Prussia, 1866. Otto von Bismarck, Prussian chancellor, formed the North German Confederation, 1867.

In 1870 Bismarck maneuvered Napoleon III into declaring war. After the quick defeat of France Bismarck formed the **German Empire (Deutsches Reich)** and on Jan. 18, 1871, in Versailles, proclaimed King Wilhelm I of Prussia German Emperor (Deutscher **Kaiser**).

The German Empire reached its peak before World War I in 1914. At that time the homeland comprised 208,780 sq. mi., plus a colonial empire. After that war Germany ceded Alsace-Lorraine to France; Eupen and Malmedy to Belgium; parts of Silesia to Poland and Czechoslovakia; part of Schleswig to Denmark; lost all of its colonies as well as the ports of Memel and Dansig. *Consult World War I.*

**Republic of Germany,** 1919-1933, adopted the Weimar constitution, met reparation payments and elected Frederick Ebert and Gen. Paul von Hindenburg presidents.

**Third Reich,** 1933-1945. Adolf Hitler, born in Braunau, Austria, 1889, led the National Socialist German Workers' (Nazi) party after World War I. In 1923 with the help of Gen. Erich Ludendorff he attempted to unseat the Bavarian government in the "Beer Hall putsch," and was imprisoned. He wrote Mein Kampf while in prison. President von Hindenburg named Hitler chancellor Jan. 30, 1933; on Aug. 3, 1934, the day after Hindenburg's death, the cabinet joined the offices of President and Chancellor and made Hitler Fuehrer (Leader). Hitler abolished freedom of speech and assembly, and began a long series of persecutions climaxed by the mass extermination of Jews and opponents.

Hitler repudiated the Versailles treaty and reparations agreements. He remilitarized the Rhineland 1936 and annexed Austria (Anschluss, 1938). At Munich he made an agreement with Neville Chamberlain, British Prime Minister, enabling him to annex Czechoslovakia's Sudetenland. He signed a non-aggression treaty with the Soviet Union, 1939. He declared war on Poland Sept. 1, 1939, precipitating World War II.

With total defeat near, Hitler committed suicide in Berlin Apr. 29, 1945. The victorious Allies voided all acts and annexations of Hitler's Reich.

**Postwar Changes**—The zones of occupation administered by the Allied Powers and later relinquished gave the Soviet Union Saxony, Saxony-Anhalt, Thuringia, and Mecklenburg, and the former Prussian provinces of Saxony and Brandenburg. The United States administered territory bounded on the East by the Russian zone and Czechoslovakia, on the North by the British zone, on the West by the French zone, and on the South by Austria, including Bavaria (except Lindau district), Wurttemberg (northern), Baden (northern), most of Hesse and Hesse-Nassau, and the city state of Bremen.

The territory east of the Oder-Neisse line within 1937 boundaries comprising the provinces of Silesia, Pomerania, West Prussia and the southern part of East Prussia, totaling about 41,220 square miles, population (1939) 9,600,000, is under Polish administration; northern East Prussia is under Soviet domination. The United States has not recognized these changes nor the East German regime. The Western Allies ended the state of war with Germany in 1951. The USSR did so in 1955.

There was also created the area of Greater Berlin, within but not part of the Soviet zone, administered by the four occupying powers under the Allied Command. In 1948 the Soviet Union withdrew and established its single command in East Berlin. The Communists cut off supplies, whereupon the Allies utilized a gigantic airlift to bring food to West Berlin during 1948-1949. In Aug. 1961 the East Germans built a wall dividing Berlin.

In June 1968 East Germany imposed restrictions on travel from West Germany to West Berlin, including transit visas and fees, and transport taxes on trucks, buses and barges. The U. S., Britain and France denounced the action and, with approval of their NATO partners, imposed a ban on travel by East German political figures and journalists to NATO countries and a $5 tax on other East German travelers. West Germany barred a group of 700 East Germans from visiting Munich.

# West Germany
## BUNDESREPUBLIK DEUTSCHLAND
### FEDERAL REPUBLIC OF GERMANY

**Capital: Bonn. Area (including West Berlin):** 95,937 sq. mi. **Population** (UN est. 1967): 59,872,000. **Monetary unit: Deutsche Mark (3.988 per U. S. $1).**

The Federal Republic of Germany was proclaimed May 23, 1949 (effective Sept. 1, 1949), in Bonn, after a constitution had been drawn up by a consultative assembly formed by representatives of the 11 Laender (states) in the French, British and American zones. Later reorganized into 9 units, the Laender number 10 with the addition of the Saar Jan. 1, 1957: Schleswig-Holstein, Hamburg, Lower Saxony, Bremen, North Rhine-Westphalia, Hesse, Rhineland-Palatinate, Baden-Wuerttemberg, Bavaria, Saarland. Berlin also was granted Land (state) status, but the 1945 occupation agreements render it inoperative.

The occupying powers, the United States, Britain and France, restored the civil status, Sept. 21, 1949. The U. S. resumed diplomatic relations July 2, 1951. The powers lifted controls and the republic became fully independent May 5, 1955.

Parliament has two chambers, serving 4-yr. terms. The Bundestag, lower house, is elected. It has 496 voting members from the republic and 22 non-voting observers from West Berlin. The Bundesrat, upper house, represents the states; it has 41 delegates from the Laender and 4 nonvoting members from West Berlin. The Bundesrat President serves one year and acts as deputy to the federal President.

The federal President is elected for a 5-yr. term by the Federal Assembly, convened for this purpose only and made up of deputies of the Bundestag and an equal number of delegates from the Land parliaments. Re-election is possible only once. The President concludes treaties with foreign states, and signs laws, which must be countersigned by the Chancellor and the minister in charge. On proposal of the President the Chancellor is elected by majority vote of the Bundestag. Ministers are named by the President at the instance of the Chancellor. The President appoints and dismisses judges, civil servants and officers and non-com. officers of the armed forces and exercises power of pardon.

Theodor Heuss, Free Democrat, was chosen first President Sept. 12, 1949, re-elected July 17, 1954. Succeeded by Heinrich Luebke, elected July 1, 1959, reelected July 1, 1964.

Dr. Konrad Adenauer, Christian Democrat, was made Chancellor Sept. 15, 1949, reelected 1953, 1957, 1961. Dr. Ludwig Erhard, Christian Democrat, was elected 1963, 1965. Kurt Georg Kiesinger was elected Chancellor Dec. 1, 1966, heading a coalition government of Christian Democrats and Social Democrats.

West Germany is a member of NATO, EEC, European Coal and Steel Community and Council of Europe. It also has been admitted to UNESCO, International Monetary Fund, and EURATOM.

The Western Allies have sought unification of Germany by free elections. The USSR has blocked action, demanding direct negotiation between East and West Germany, which would imply recognition of the East German puppet state and troop withdrawal.

**Resources and Industries.** West Germany has experienced tremendous economic growth since 1950. Gross national product rose from $23.1 billion in 1950 to $120 billion in 1967. The index of industrial production (1963=100) was 114 in 1967.

West Germany leads Western Europe as a steel producer. Shipyards annually produce more than 1,000,000 gross registered tons of shipping, more than half of it for export. The oil industry has a refining capacity of more than 10,500,000 tons annually.

Germany lost most of its merchant marine during World War II. However, the merchant fleet recovered rapidly and on Jan. 1, 1964 comprised 2,626 vessels aggregating 5,500,000 gross tons.

The total foreign debt on Jan. 1, 1968, was $125,000,000, reduced from $3.05 billion of prewar and postwar liabilities determined by the London Agreement of 1953.

Frankfurt Rhine-Main airport, 3rd largest in Europe, handles annually 4,850,000 passengers and is 2nd largest in freight shipments.

Foreign trade (in thousands of U. S. dollars):

| | Imports | Exports |
|---|---|---|
| 1966 | $18,023,000 | $20,135,000 |
| 1967 | $17,352,000 | $21,737,000 |

**Education and Religion.** The Federal Republic and West Berlin have 22 universities 9 technical universities and 91 musical, theological and other institutions of higher education. School attendance is compulsory, ages 6 to 14.

Complete religious freedom is guaranteed by the constitution. The country is 51% Protestant, 45% Roman Catholic. The Evangelical Church in Ger-

many (EKD) was formed by the Lutheran, United and Reformed churches after World War II, supplanting an earlier group.

**Defense.** The German Armed Forces (Bundeswehr) are civilian-controlled. Conscription of 18-year-olds for 12-month terms began in Jan. 1957; raised to 18-month terms in 1962. Volunteers are enlisted for 3 or more years. Most Air Force and Navy personnel are volunteers. Strength of the Bundeswehr in 1968 was 460,000 including 317,000 Army, 97,000 Air Force, 33,000 Navy, plus Territorial Defense Forces.

The Army has 12 Divisions—7 infantry, 3 armored, one airborne, one mountain. It has U. S. Honest John and Sergeant ground-to-ground rockets.

The Air Force (Luftwaffe) has 20 squadrons of F-104-G jet Starfighters and other craft, ground-to-air Nike and Hawk rockets and Pershing missiles.

The Navy has 10 destroyers, 11 submarines, 6 frigates, 45 torpedo boats and other craft. The naval air arm has Starfighters, anti-submarine planes and helicopters.

**Helgoland,** an island of 130 acres in the North Sea, was taken from Denmark by a British Naval Force in 1807 and later ceded to Germany to become a part of Schleswig-Holstein province in return for rights in East Africa. The heavily fortified island was surrendered to Great Britain, May 23, 1945, demilitarized in 1947 and returned to West Germany, Mar. 1, 1952. It is a free port.

**The Saar** (Fr. Sarre), 10th Land (state) of the Federal Republic, is an industrial and mining area north of Lorraine, originally 738 sq. mi., now extended to about 991 and population (est. 1967) )of 1,132,800, mostly German. Capital: Saarbrucken. It was separated from Germany after World War I and administered by the League of Nations through a commission. The Saar was returned to the Reich by the League of Nations, Mar. 1, 1935.

After World War II, the Saar came under French administration and following an election, Oct. 5, 1947, was attached economically to France. It had semi-autonomy from Jan. 3, 1948, until West Germany and France signed the Luxembourg Agreement, June 4, 1956, providing that the Saar should be united politically with the Federal Republic Jan. 1, 1957, and economically Jan. 1, 1960.

## East Germany
### GERMAN DEMOCRATIC REPUBLIC
#### Deutsche Demokratische Republik

**Capital: East Berlin (Soviet Sector). Area: 41,-659 sq. mi. Population (UN est. 1967): 17,082,000. Monetary unit: Ostmark (2.22 official rate per U. S. $1).**

The German Democratic Republic was proclaimed in the Soviet sector of Berlin Oct. 7, 1949. Wilhelm Pieck was named President, reelected Oct. 7, 1953, and Oct. 7, 1957 (died Sept. 7, 1960); Willi Stoph, Minister-President, or prime minister; Walter Ulbricht, Communist party secretary; deputy prime minister. A ministry of state security, the SSD, and a militarized People's Police were organized.

The Soviet Union proclaimed East Germany a sovereign republic Mar. 26, 1954, but kept Soviet troops on grounds of security and the four-power Potsdam agreement.

Parliament approved a constitutional amendment Sept. 12, 1960, that abolished the Presidency, replacing it with a new Council of State designated as East Germany's highest governing body, with Walter Ulbricht as Chairman.

Ulbricht negotiated a treaty with Poland placing Poland's boundary at the line formed by the Oder and Neisse Rivers. The United States registered its disapproval, declaring that it violated the Potsdam agreement and that no boundaries could be settled "unilaterally or bilaterally" outside a peace treaty. The Republic also ratified an agreement with Czechoslovakia, accepting the expulsion of over 2,000,000 Germans from Sudetenland as "permanent and just." Its industry was integrated with that of the Soviet Union.

Parliament abolished, 1952, the five traditional provinces of East Germany as administrative units in favor of 14 districts of 217 counties. Brandenburg, Mecklenburg, Saxony and Thuringia were divided into three districts each, Saxony-Anhalt into two.

Coincident with the entrance of the Federal Republic into the European Defense Community, May 27, 1952, the East German Government decreed a

prohibited zone three miles deep along its 600-mile border with West Germany, separated Berlin's telephone system into two sections and cut many of its lines to the West. Berlin was further divided, 1953-1961, by reduction of crossing points and erection of a fortified wall, but the exodus of refugees from East Germany into Western sectors continued though on a much smaller scale.

In elections to the Volkskammer, 1965, the single list of National Front candidates received 99.89% of the eligible vote.

The regime signed a 20-year treaty of friendship and cooperation with the USSR June 12, 1964. The treaty stated that it did not constitute a formal peace treaty.

East Germany suffered severe economic problems until the mid-1960s. A "new economic system" was introduced, easing the former central planning controls and allowing factories to make "profits" provided they were reinvested in operations or distributed to workers as bonuses. By 1967, East German figures showed the gross national product had risen to $52 billion from $35 billion in 1960. But living standards were still far below those of West Germany.

On Apr. 8, 1968, a new constitution, announced as approved by 94.49% of voters, went into effect. It reaffirmed Communist one-party rule and close ties with the USSR and declared German reunification could "take place only on the basis of Socialism."

In East Germany the school system has been reorganized on a Communist basis, with centralized control over education. Religious instruction no longer is part of the public school curriculum, but is imparted by the churches.

Creation of a National People's Army was authorized by Parliament, Jan. 18, 1956. Service is compulsory. Armed strength of the People's Army reached 195,000 in 1965, organized in two corps and equipped with Soviet tanks, jet planes and artillery. Another 320,000 militiamen are organized in combat groups. Navy and Air Force have about 10,000 each and there is a police force numbering 42,500.

An est. 20 Soviet divisions totaling approx. 400,-000 also are stationed in East Germany.

The Navy includes 5 destroyers, 5 frigates, 6 corvettes and numerous minesweepers, patrol vessels and other craft.

## Ghana
### FORMER GOLD COAST STATE

**Capital: Accra (Ghana). Area: 91,843 sq. mi. Population (UN est. 1967): 8,143,000. Monetary unit: New Cedi (1.0204 per U. S. $1).**

The Republic of Ghana, a member of the UN and the Commonwealth, is composed of the former British Gold Coast colony with its territories of Ashanti and Northern Territories, and British Togoland, former UN trusteeship. Slightly smaller than Oregon, it faces on the Gulf of Guinea in Western Africa, bounded N by Republic of Upper Volta, E by Togo Republic and W by the Ivory Coast Republic.

**Resources and Industries.** Ghana is rich in mineral wealth. Ghana ranks 5th in the world in production of diamonds (mostly industrial type), 7th in manganese, 6th in gold, 18th in bauxite.

Ghana is the world's leading cocoa producer; it exports over 400,000 tons annually, about 40% of world output. Timber is 2nd in value, including mahogany and rare woods.

The huge Akosombo hydroelectric project on the Volta River, partly financed by U. S., was completed in 1965 and began serving Ghana's 1st giant industry, an aluminum reduction plant near the port of Tema, built and owned by U. S. companies. The dam was to create the world's largest artificial lake, covering 3,275 sq. mi.

**History and Government.** Named after an earlier African state along the Niger River, 800-1076 A.D., Ghana has long been settled by the Adansi, Akwamu, Ga and other tribes, and was ruled by Great Britain for 113 years. Its independence was gained by rapid steps after 1951 when Britain granted the colony a new constitution and its chief spokesman, Kwame Nkrumah, was elected Prime Minister. The UN General Asembly on Dec. 13, 1956, approved termination of the British Togoland trusteeship and merger of the territory with the new state following a 1956 plebiscite.

Full independence within the Commonwealth, with a British Governor-General, was effective Mar. 6, 1957. It became a republic, July 1, 1960, but remained within the Commonwealth. Kwame

Nkrumah became Pres.

In May 1961 Pres. Nkrumah announced he had taken "absolute control" of his Convention Peoples party. On Sept. 7, 1962, Parliament voted to make him Pres. for life. In Jan. 1964 the government announced the result of a nationwide vote to give him dictatorial powers and make Ghana a one-party Socialist state was 99.9% "yes."

Pres. Nkrumah built hospitals and schools, raised the literacy rate, created a state-owned airline and ship line, but ran the country into debt, jailed hundreds of political dissenters and was accused of corruption.

On Feb. 24, 1966, a National Liberation Council of Army and police officers took over the government, freed over 400 political prisoners and jailed many Nkrumah regime officials. Lt. Gen. Joseph Ankrah, Council chairman, promised elections and a popularly approved Constitution within 18 mos. The Council expelled Communist Chinese and East German teachers and technicians. It promised a "balanced neutrality" and slashed expenditures. Ex-Pres. Nkrumah, on a trip to North Vietnam and Peking at the time of the coup, found asylum in Guinea.

In 1967 and 1968, civilians were added to the Cabinet, outnumbering the military and police members.

**Defense:** The army, navy and air force have undergone large-scale expansion since 1961.

# Greece
## VASILEION TIS ELLADOS— KINGDOM OF HELLAS

**Capital: Athens. Area: 50,944 sq. mi. Population (UN est. 1967): 8,716,000. Monetary unit: Drachma (30 per U. S. $1).**

Greece occupies the southern part of the Balkan peninsula, reaching into the Mediterranean Sea with the Ionian Sea on the W and the Aegean Sea on the E. Its neighbors are Albania, Yugoslavia, Bulgaria and Turkey. The Pindus Mtns. run through the country N to S. Total length of the heavily indented coastline is 9,385 mi. Hundreds of islands account for 8,918 sq. mi. of the total land area, which is approx. that of Alabama; 166 islands are inhabited, among them Crete, Rhodes, Milos, Kerkira (Corfu), Chios, Lesbos, Samos. Principal seaport is Piraeus, near Athens.

**Resources and Industries.** Greece proper is chiefly agricultural. Only one-fourth of the total area is arable; 13,350,000 of the total of 16,074,000 acres are covered by mountains, lakes and rivers. Four-fifths of the forests are state-owned. Chief agricultural products are wheat, rye, barley, oats, corn, rice, cotton, tobacco, olives, citrus fruits, raisins and figs. Sheep are the most important livestock.

Heavily damaged in World War II, Greece's industrial and agricultural output has far surpassed pre-war levels thanks to economic development programs helped in part by U. S. aid. Hydroelectric development is remedying the lack of coal. Principal industries are textiles, food-processing, wine, cement, chemicals.

Greek-owned merchant marine tonnage totals 19,250,000 tons, actually third in the world, but most of it is registered under other flags.

Exports are mainly agricultural—tobacco, cotton, citrus fruits, raisins, vegetables. Ores, esp. bauxite, are also important. Aiding the economy is the tourist industry, with 1,000,000 visitors spending $100,000,000 yearly.

Foreign trade, in thousands of U. S. dollars:

| | Imports | Exports |
| --- | --- | --- |
| 1966 | $1,223,000 | $406,000 |
| 1967 | $1,186,000 | $495,000 |

**History and Government.** The achievements of Ancient Greece in art, architecture, science, mathematics, philosophy, drama, literature and democracy became legacies for succeeding ages. Greece reached the height of its glory and power, particularly in the Athenian city-state, in the 5th Century B.C.

Greece fell under Roman domination in the 2nd and 1st Centuries B. C. In the 4th Century A. D. it became part of the Eastern Byzantine Empire and, after the fall of Constantinople to the Turks in 1453, part of the Ottoman Empire.

Greece won its war of independence from Turkey 1821-1829, and became a kingdom under guarantee of Britain, France and Russia, 1830. A republic was established 1925; the monarchy was restored, 1935, and George II, King of the Hellenes, resumed the throne. In Oct., 1940, Greece rejected an ultimatum from Italy and when attacked Greece drove the Italians back into Albania. Nazi support resulted in the defeat and occupation of Greece by Germans, Italians and Bulgarians. By the end of 1944 the invaders withdrew. Armed Communists attempted to seize the country but were thwarted by British liberation troops.

A plebiscite recalled King George II. He died Apr. 1, 1947, and was succeeded by his brother, Paul I. King Paul died Mar. 6, 1964, succeeded by his son, Crown Prince Constantine, born June 2, 1940. The King married Princes Anne-Marie of Denmark Sept. 18, 1964. A daughter, Princess Alexia, was born July 10, 1965, and is heir to the throne.

Communists waged guerrilla war 1947-49 against the government but were defeated with the aid of the U. S. (acting under the Truman Doctrine). Communists kidnaped thousands of Greek children to neighboring Communist countries; after Yugoslavia broke with Moscow some were repatriated.

Greece is governed under a constitution effective Jan. 1, 1952. Women were granted suffrage, 1952.

In Feb. 16, 1964, elections the coalition Center Union led by George Papandreou won 174 of 300 seats in the Chamber of Deputies. A prolonged government crisis was precipitated July 15, 1965, when Premier Papandreou resigned; at issue was a Papandreou plan to purge the Army of right-wing officers. King Constantine opposed the purge saying it would expose the armed forces to Communist influence. Leftists and backers of Papandreou staged riots in Athens as the King sought a new Premier who could win a Parliamentary majority over the opposition of the Papandreou bloc and the extreme leftists. He finally won with Stephanos Stephanopoulos, who was sworn in Sept. 17, 1965.

Continuing political crises ended in a pre-election coup d'etat Apr. 21, 1967, by rightist Army officers under Col. George Papadopoulos. They jailed hundreds of monarchists, Communists and political leaders. King Constantine on Dec. 13 sought to oust the junta but failed to rally military support and flew with his family to exile in Rome, Dec. 14. Papadopoulos was named Premier and a general was appointed "viceroy." In 1968 the Papadopoulos government freed some political prisoners but tightened its hold, replacing many officials including judges. It also ordered curbs on teenagers' clothes and conduct and banned the sale of records by Melina Mercouri, a critic of the regime.

**Education and Religion.** Greek Orthodox is the official church. Nine years of education is compulsory. There are 6 schools of university rank in Athens, and others in Thessaloniki, Patras and Ioannina.

The rocky promontory of Mount Athos (121 sq. mi.) is occupied by 20 monasteries of the Greek Orthodox Church, forming an almost completely self-governing community of about 3,000 monks. No females may enter the territory.

**Defense.** Military service is compulsory between the ages of 21 and 50. There is an Air Force and a Navy of light craft.

Greece is a member of the UN and NATO and an associate member of EEC.

## DODECANESE AND CRETE

The **Dodecanese** are a group of 13 islands in the southeastern Aegean Sea. They were occupied by Italy during the Balkan War of 1912 with Turkey and though claimed by Greece were retained by Italy. Rhodes is the capital.

After World War II the islands were ceded to Greece at the Paris Conference of Foreign Ministers, June 27, 1946, and annexed Mar. 7, 1948.

**Crete,** largest Greek island and 4th largest in Mediterranean, original site of Minoan civilization, lies south of the Peloponnesos peninsula and is 160 mi. long, 35 mi. wide, with area of 3,324 sq. mi. and 482,021 population. Principal towns: Heraklion (Candia) and Khania (Canea).

# Guatemala
## REPUBLICA DE GUATEMALA

**Capital: Guatemala City. Area: 42,042 sq. mi. Population (UN est. 1967): 4,717,000. Monetary unit: Quetzal (1 per U. S. $1).**

Guatemala is the most northerly country of Central America and about the size of Ohio. It faces on both the Caribbean and the Pacific. There are numerous volcanoes in the south, more than a half dozen over 11,000 ft.

More than 50% of the population is pure Indian

and most of the remainder is of mixed Spanish and Indian descent.

There are famous Mayan ruins in Uaxatcun and Tikal, in Petén, northern Guatemala. Other Mayan ruins of temples and monoliths are at Zaculeu in the west and at Quirigua, about 140 mi. from Guatemala City.

Puerto Barrios, main port on the Atlantic, is connected by railroad with Guatemala City in the highlands and ports on the Pacific.

**Resources and Industries.** Agriculture is the most important industry, the Guatemalan soil being exceedingly fertile. Coffee accounts for bulk of the exports. Other important export crops are bananas, cotton, chicle gum. Sugar, maize, rice are domestic crops. Rare woods and cattle are important. Silver, gold, copper, iron, lead, zinc, and chrome are found. A search for oil is being pressed in the north, where natural gas has been found.

**History and Government.** The old Mayan Indian empire flourished in what is today Guatemala during the first 1,000 years of the Christian era.

Guatemala was a Spanish colony 1524-1821; briefly a part of Mexico and then of the U. S. of Central America; the republic was established in 1839.

Since 1945 when a labor government was elected to replace the long-term dictatorship of Jorge Ubico, the country has seen a swing toward Communism, an allegedly U. S.-sponsored revolt, renewed attempts at social reform and a military coup. Communist-led guerrillas have terrorized parts of the nation and kidnaped officials.

Col. Enrique Peralta Azurdia, who became Pres. in the 1963 coup, sponsored free elections in March 1966. Prof. Julio Cesar Mendez Montenegro, a left-of-center reformist, won and was inaugurated Pres. July 1. He launched agrarian reforms.

Two U. S. Embassy military attaches were shot to death Jan. 16, 1968 in what was called a leftist terrorist raid. In the same week, rightist terrorists slew a lawyer and Miss Guatemala of 1950, accused of leftist leanings. A state of siege was declared after the Archbishop of Guatemala was kidnaped by right-wingers Mar. 16 (he was freed). The emergency ended June 20 after terrorism eased.

**Education and Religion.** Roman Catholicism is the dominant religion. Education is compulsory. The University of Guatemala is in Guatemala City, with divisions in Quetzaltenango. The language is Spanish.

**Defense.** Military service is compulsory between the ages of 18 and 50. The strength of the Army is approximately 7,000 plus a 3,000-man police force and a small Air Force. Guatemala is a member of the UN and OAS.

# Guinea
### REPUBLIC OF GUINEA

**Capital:** Conakry. **Area** 94,925 sq. mi. **Population** (UN est. 1967): 3,702,000. **Monetary unit:** Guinea franc (246.85 per U. S. $1).

Guinea, a former French Overseas Territory, is in western Africa with the Atlantic on the W; Portuguese Guinea, Senegal and Mali on the N, Ivory Coast on the E and Liberia and Sierra Leone on the S. Chief tribes are the Fullah, Malinké and Soussou. Guinea is about the size of Oregon.

Guinea has a variety of climates, from the humid coastal tropics (Conakry, the capital has an average annual rainfall of 169") to cooler plateaus and uplands. Wildlife is varied and abundant, including elephant, hippopotamus, buffalo, antelope, lion, leopard, chimpanzee.

**Resources and Industries.** Although Guinea is still primarily an agricultural country, the importance of minerals to its economy is growing. Bauxite, iron and diamonds (both gem and industrial) are the principal minerals. Harvey Aluminum, Inc., of the U. S., and the Guinean Government are engaged in a joint $200,000,000 exploitation of one of the world's richest bauxite deposits, at Boke.

Guinea's second economic plan (1964-1971) is being aided by large grants from both Communist and non-Communist countries. Acceleration of agricultural output is a Government goal. Chief agricultural exports are bananas (to France, West Germany and the USSR), and pineapples. Production of rice, the staple food of the population, has been expanded. Other crops include corn, palm nuts, coffee and honey.

**History and Government.** Under provisions of the 1958 constitution of the Fifth Republic of France, Guinea voted Sept. 28, 1958, to secede from the French Community and proclaimed itself

an independent republic Oct. 2. Premier Sekou Touré became first President. The nation's first constitution was adopted Nov. 12, 1958. It provided for rule by a President with a term of 7 years and a National Assembly elected by universal suffrage. The Political Bureau of the single legal party, the Parti Democratique de Guinee, exercises great power in making governmental decisions. Guinea is a member of the UN.

It has agreements with Czechoslovakia, East Germany, Poland, USSR and Communist China, and criticized U. S. "colonial" attitudes in Africa, but continues to avow a neutral course.

Kwame Nkrumah, deposed President of Ghana, was given asylum in Guinea, Mar. 2, 1966.

Guinea signed an agreement with France, May 22, 1963, providing for French technical assistance and development of cultural relations. It also receives U. S. aid. French is the official language.

On Apr. 24, 1968, Guinea and 8 other nations formed the West African Regional Group to promote economic cooperation.

# Guyana
### (FORMER BRITISH GUIANA)

**Capital:** Georgetown. **Area:** 83,000 sq. mi. **Population** (UN est. 1967): 680,000. **Monetary unit:** Guyana Dollar (2 per U. S. $1).

A British colony for 152 years, Guyana became independent May 26, 1966, the first South American country to do so since Venezuela in 1830.

Fronting on the Atlantic in NE South America, Guyana borders on Venezuela, Brazil and Dutch Guiana. The nation is about the size of Kansas. The population is about 50% of East Indian (from India) descent, 31.5% of African descent, 12% of mixed descent, 4.6% American Indian descent, and small numbers of Chinese or European descent.

Dense tropical forests cover much of the land, although a flat coastal area about 50 mi. wide, where 90% of the population lives, provides space for agriculture.

The country is basically agricultural but only about 6.5% of the land is cultivated. Sugar and rice are the main cash crops and account for about half of the total exports. Other products are: coconuts, coffee, cocoa, citrus fruits, timber and livestock.

The main industry is the mining of bauxite ore; Guyana is the 4th largest producer of the mineral, supplying about one-tenth of the world's needs. Also exported are manganese, gold and diamonds. Deposits of a wide range of other minerals have been found but not yet exploited.

Manufacturing has shown an average 5% annual growth, products include cigarettes, rum, clothing, furniture, drugs and insecticides.

Guyana was discovered in 1499 by Spanish sailors. The country became a British possession in 1814. African slaves and indentured servants from India were brought in to work on plantations. The Indians soon outnumbered the Negro population and still do today. Racial tension is a major problem for the nation.

Guyana is a parliamentary democracy, with universal adult suffrage, a Governor General representing the British Queen, a Prime Minister and Cabinet. Guyana is a member of the UN and Commonwealth.

# Haiti
### REPUBLIQUE D'HAITI

**Capital:** Port-au-Prince. **Area:** 10,714 sq. mi. **Population** (UN est. 1967): 4,581,000. **Monetary unit:** Gourde (5 per U. S. $1).

Haiti, only French-speaking republic in the Americas, occupies the western third of the island known as Hispaniola, the second largest of the Greater Antilles, lying between Cuba on the W and Puerto Rico on the E. The boundary which separates Haiti from the Dominican Republic to the E is 241 mi. long. Haiti is a little larger in area than Maryland.

Negroes form the majority of the population, the remainder being mulattoes descended from former French settlers and slaves.

**Resources and Industries.** Major mineral exports are bauxite (to U. S.) and copper (to Japan). Other minerals, largely undeveloped, are gold, silver and cement.

Coffee is the chief product, along with sisal, cotton, raw sugar, bananas, cocoa, tobacco and rice. Molasses and rum are produced; valuable woods are exported.

Haiti encourages tourism and is served by several major airlines, with an international jet airport at Port-au-Prince. However, tourist spending and private foreign investment in Haiti have dwindled under the regime of Pres. François Duvalier.

**History and Government.** Haiti, discovered by Columbus, 1492, and a French colony from 1677, attained its independence, 1804, following the rebellion begun by Toussaint L'Ouverture and has been a republic since 1820. Following a period of political violence, 1910-1915, the United States occupied the country and restored order. The occupation terminated Aug. 14, 1934.

Five regimes failed between 1950-1957. On Sept. 22, 1957, Dr. Duvalier was elected President for a 6-year term.

During widespread Haitian opposition to Duvalier's repressive regime in 1963, Haitian police broke into the Dominican Republic Embassy in Port-au-Prince and seized 22 Haitian political refugees there. Dominican armed reprisals were threatened: Haiti withdrew its police and released the refugees. Haiti severed diplomatic relations with the Dominican Republic. They were not resumed until July 22, 1966.

A new constitution, making Dr. Duvalier President for life, was approved by referendum June 14, 1964. Haiti is a member of the UN and OAS.

A reported invasion attempt May 20, 1968, resulted in the arrest of 10 Haitians by the Duvalier government.

**Education and Religion.** Roman Catholicism is the main religion and the clergy are largely French and Canadian. Education is compulsory, but illiteracy rate is high. French is the official language of the country, but French Creole, a dialect, is spoken by the majority. The teaching of English in the schools is obligatory.

## Honduras

### REPUBLICA DE HONDURAS

**Capital: Tegucigalpa. Area (Govt. est.): 43,277 sq. mi. Population (UN est. 1967): 2,445,000. Monetary unit: Lempira (2 per U. S. $1).**

Honduras is a republic in Central or Middle America, bounded on the N by the Caribbean; E and S by Nicaragua; S by Pacific Ocean and El Salvador; W by Guatemala. It is about the size of Pennsylvania.

The coast line on the Caribbean is 500 mi. long. On the Pacific side it has a coast line of 40 mi. on the Gulf of Fonseca. There are ports on both coasts. The country is mountainous, very fertile, though mostly uncultivated, and covered with rich forests. The inhabitants are of Spanish and Indian extraction.

At Copan, near the western border, are the imposing remains of a large Mayan city which flourished from the 4th Century A.D.; there are numerous statues, stelae, pyramids, temples, etc.; the city had a pop. of about 150,000; it had declined by the time of its discovery by Spaniards in 1576.

**Resources and Industries.** Mineral resources are abundant but undeveloped, and include gold, silver, copper, lead, zinc, iron, antimony and coal. The chief export (65%) is bananas, grown on the Caribbean coast. Coffee, timber, cotton, maize, tobacco and cattle raising are important. The mountainous terrain has hindered development but membership in the Central American Common Market has boosted foreign trade considerably.

Honduras was one of the Central American nations visited and promised additional aid in July 1968 by U. S. President Johnson.

**History and Government.** Honduras became independent after freeing itself from Spain, Sept. 15, 1821, and from the Federation of Central America, 1838. The country is divided into 18 departments containing 31 districts.

Pres. Ramon Villeda Morales, elected Nov. 15, 1957, was overthrown in a military coup Oct. 3, 1963, and replaced by a regime headed by Col. Oswaldo Lopez Arellano.

The country returned to constitutional government and Lopez Arellano was inaugurated President June 6, 1965, after elections for a new Constituent Assembly.

Municipal elections Mar. 31, 1968, resulted in overwhelming approval of candidates of the President's National party and charges of fraud were made by the Liberal party.

Honduras is a member of the UN and OAS.

**Education and Religion.** Education is compulsory, secular and free. National University is located in Tegucigalpa. Roman Catholicism is the prevailing religion. The language is Spanish.

## Hungary

### MAGYAR NEPKOZTARSASAG
### HUNGARIAN PEOPLE'S REPUBLIC

**Capitol: Budapest. Area: 35,918 sq. mi. Population (UN est. 1967): 10,212,000. Monetary unit: Forint (11.73 official rate per U. S. $1).**

Hungary, a Communist republic in Central Europe, is bounded by Czechoslovakia, the USSR, Romania, Yugoslavia and Austria. It is about the size of Indiana.

The Danube forms the Czech border in the NW, then swings S to bisect the country. The eastern half of Hungary is mainly a great fertile plain, the Alfold; the west and north are hilly.

**Resources and Industries.** Before World War II, Hungary was primarily agricultural, but industry is becoming increasingly important. Its share in national income rose to 66% in 1966 compared to 49.9% in 1949.

Major economic reforms were launched early in 1968, switching from a central planning system to one where market forces and a profit principle control much of production. The change boosted farm incomes 20% and industrial wages 6% by mid-1968.

About 64% of foreign trade is with Eastern bloc countries. Value of imports rose from $1.6 billion in 1966 to $1.8 billion in 1967. Exports rose from $1.6 billion to $1.7 billion.

In addition to a wide range of grains and vegetable crops, fruit production has been expanded. Near Tokay, in the northeast, the most famous Hungarian wines are vinted.

Hungary's bauxite deposits are very large. About three-quarters of its oil comes from the southwest corner. Industries include iron and steel, machines, machine tools, chemicals, vehicles, railways and communications equipment, milling and distilling. Hungary has become an important supplier of industrial products to Communist-bloc countries.

**History and Government.** Earliest settlers, chiefly Slav and Germanic, were overrun by Huns and Magyars from the east. Stephen I (997-1038) was made King by Pope Silvester II in 1001 A.D. The country suffered repeated Turkish invasions in the 15th-17th centuries. After the defeats of the Turks, 1686-1697, Austria dominated, but Hungary obtained concessions until it regained full independence in 1867, with the Emperor of Austria as King of Hungary in a dual monarchy with a single diplomatic service. Defeated with the Central Powers in 1918, Hungary lost Transylvania to Romania, Croatia and Bacska to Yugoslavia, Slovakia and Carpatho-Ruthenia to Czechoslovakia. A republic under Michael Karoly and a bolshevist revolt under Bela Kun were followed by a vote for a monarchy in 1920 with Admiral Nicholas Horthy as regent.

Hungary joined Germany in World War II; Horthy was removed and Nazi supporters put in power, 1944. Russian troops captured most of the country, 1945. By terms of an armistice with the Allied powers Hungary agreed to give up territory acquired by the 1938 dismemberment of Czechoslovakia and to return to its borders of 1937.

Hungary declared for a republic Feb. 1, 1946, and elected Zoltan Tildy President. In 1947 the Communists forced Tildy out.

A Soviet-type constitution was adopted Aug. 18, 1949, which vests power in Parliament and a Presidium. Parliament since 1953 consists of a group of deputies numbering one to every 32,000 population, elected for 4-year terms. Hungary is a member of the UN and Warsaw Pact.

Since Communism gained control, all industries have been nationalized and an intensive campaign has been conducted to establish cooperatives, and increase farm production. Since 1962 the regime has encouraged privately owned farm plots which produce 63% of total farm production as essential to the country's well-being.

Premier Imre Nagy, in office since mid-1953, was ousted for his moderate policy of favoring agriculture and consumer production, April 18, 1955; succeeded by Andras Hegedus.

In 1956, popular demands for the ousting of Erno Gero, Hungarian Communist party secretary, and for formation of a new government by Imre Nagy, resulted in the latter's appointment Oct. 23, but demonstrations against Communist rule in Buda-

pest developed into open revolt when the security police fired on the people. Gero called in Soviet armed forces to crush the rioting as Revolutionary Councils spread through the country. The insurrection appeared halted by Oct. 28 when Premier Nagy announced the Soviet Union had agreed to withdraw its troops from Hungary. However, by Nov. 1 Soviet forces again surrounded Budapest and, despite Nagy's protests to the USSR and the UN, launched a massive surprise attack against the city Nov. 4 with an estimated 200,000 troops, 2,500 tanks and armored cars.

The bid for free government was crushed. Estimates of casualties varied from 6,500 to 32,000 dead. Many rebels were reported executed and thousands deported. Between 170,000 and 196,000 persons fled the country. The U. S. received 38,248 under a refugee emergency program. In the spring of 1963 the regime freed many anti-Communists and captives from the revolution in a sweeping amnesty.

Premier Nagy was removed in November, 1956, and Janos Kadar installed as the Soviet-sponsored Premier. Kadar also became first secretary of the Patriotic People's Front (Communist party) in 1957. He stepped out of the Premier's post in June 1965 and was succeeded by Deputy Premier Gyula Kallai but remained party leader. In April 1967 Kallai became Pres. of Parliament and Jeno Fock became Prime Minister.

**Education and Religion.** There is no state religion and all are tolerated, but under the Communist regime the church has been restricted. A law effective April 6, 1959, requires government approval of direct Papal appointments. About two-thirds of the population are Roman Catholics; most of the remainder are Calvinists.

Public school education is compulsory and free for 8 years. Church schools were nationalized in 1948. There are 91 institutes of higher learning. The language, Hungarian (Magyar), is one of the Finno-Ugrian group.

**Defense.** Since 1963 all males at age 18 are liable for military service.

# Iceland
## LYDVELDID ISLAND

**Capital: Reykjavik. Area: 39,768 sq. mi. Population (Govt. est. 1968): 200,000. Monetary unit: Krona (57 per U. S. $1).**

The Republic of Iceland is an island of volcanic origin, close to the Arctic Circle in the North Atlantic. There are geysers and hot springs and the climate is modified by the Gulf Stream. Iceland is about the size of Virginia.

Natural hot water from many of Iceland's volcanic springs is piped into towns and provides heat for office buildings, homes and hot houses. Keflavik is an important airport.

**Resources and Industries.** Agriculture engages about 13.5% of the population; industry and services 70%; fishing 10%. About six-sevenths of the land is unproductive and only about 65,000 acres are under cultivation, producing potatoes, turnips and hay. The fishing industry is most important and has led Iceland to extend its exclusive fishery limits to 12 mi. The catch, of which herring comprises about 50%, also includes cod and haddock. Fish products, in salted, smoked, canned or frozen form, account for 95% of exports.

Iceland's largest industrial plants include an ammonium nitrate factory and a cement factory.

**History and Government.** Iceland was an independent republic, 930-1262; then it joined with Norway. The two came under Danish rule in 1380. When Norway separated from Denmark, 1814, Iceland remained under Denmark. Denmark acknowledged Iceland as a sovereign state, 1918, united with Denmark only in that the Danish King Christian X, was also King of Iceland. In 1941 the Althing (Parliament) voted to dissolve all ties with Denmark, elect a regent and adopt the constitution of a republic. This was endorsed by popular vote, and the republic proclaimed June 17, 1944.

Iceland celebrated the 1,000th anniversary of the Althing, the oldest parliamentary assembly in the world, June 23-28, 1930. Under a constitutional amendment of 1959, the Althing increased from 52 to 60 members. The Prime Minister and his cabinet are responsible to the Althing. There is universal suffrage for men and women over 21.

On May 26, 1968 the country switched to driving on the right side of the road.

**Education and Religion.** The Icelandic language has maintained its purity, as in Eddas and Sagas, for 1,000 years. Danish and English also are taught. Eight years of elementary education is compulsory. There is no illiteracy. There are 3 colleges and a university. The national church is Evangelical Lutheran, but there is complete religious freedom.

**Defense:** Iceland has no Army, Navy, Air Force or forts. It is a charter member of NATO which maintains an air-radar base in Keflavik. It is also a member of the UN, Council of Europe and Nordic Council.

# India
## BHARAT

**Capital: New Delhi. Area: 1,261,597 sq. mi. Population (UN est. 1967): 511,115,000. Monetary unit: Rupee (7.579 per U. S. $1).**

India, an independent republic since 1950 and a member of the Commonwealth, occupies the larger part of the subcontinent of India. It is one-third the size of the U. S.

India's climate varies from tropical heat in the south to the nearly Arctic cold of the Himalayas. Approximately 22.3% of the area is forested.

Main communities, 1961 census, are: Hindus, 366,162,693; Moslems, 46,911,731; Christians, 10,-498,077; Sikhs, 7,846,074. Of the population 82.2% is rural and 17.8% urban. The annual rate of increase of 2½% continued to harass economic planners with food and housing shortages.

A severe 2-year drought in Bihar and other northern areas threatened mass starvation and brought large shipments of grain from the U. S.; in July, 1967, plentiful rains gave promise of better harvests. In 1968 there was a bumper wheat crop.

Also in 1967 the Government supplemented its birth control programs with monetary inducements to men to volunteer for sterilization. In 1968 the government reported 3,500,000 persons had undergone sterilization operations.

**Sikkim,** Indian state bordered by Tibet, Bhutan, Nepal and India, formerly British protected, became a protectorate of India in 1950. Area, 2,744 sq. mi.; population 1967, of 179,700. The ruler is Chogyal (Maharaja) Palden Thondup Namgyal; in 1963, while Crown Prince, he married Hope Cooke, a New York debutante. He became ruler in 1964 but was not coronated until April 4, 1965, a date chosen as auspicious by court astrologers. Capital, Gangtok. Buddhism is the state religion.

**Kashmir,** a predominantly Moslem region in the northwest, has been in dispute between India and Pakistan since 1947 when British rule was ending and Indian and Pakistani troops entered the area. A cease-fire was negotiated by the UN, effective Jan. 1, 1949; it gave Pakistan control of one-third of the area, in the west and northwest, and India the remaining two-thirds, the Indian state of Jammu and Kashmir. In late Aug. 1965, clashes broke out along the line and soon involved the armed forces of the two nations in a spreading war. Pakistan later claimed its forces killed 7,000 Indian troops. India said its troops killed 5,000 Pakistani soldiers. Several hundred civilian deaths were also reported.

On Sept. 20, 1965, the UN Security Council demanded a cease-fire and both sides agreed Sept. 22, to stop the fighting, but did not comply with a call for them to withdraw their forces across the old cease-fire line.

USSR Premier Aleksei N. Kosygin invited Indian Prime Minister Lal Bahadur Shastri and Pakistan Pres. Ayub Khan to a conference at Tashkent, USSR, and on Jan. 10, 1966, the two signed the "Tashkent Declaration," pledging to withdraw their armed forces in Kashmir to behind the cease-fire line by Feb. 28.

Prime Minister Shastri died of a heart attack in Tashkent a few hours after signing the agreement.

The U. S. announced it would resume both economic and "nonlethal" military aid, suspended when the war broke out, to both India and Pakistan.

There were also clashes in April 1965 along the Assam-East Pakistan border and in the Rann (swamp) of Cutch area along the West Pakistan-Gujarat border near the Arabian Sea.

An international arbitration commission on Feb. 19, 1968, awarded 90% of the Rann to India, 10% to Pakistan.

France, 1952-54, peacefully yielded to India its 5 colonies on the Bay of Bengal, former French India, comprising Pondicherry, Kirkal, Mahe, Yanaon and Chandernagor, totalling 196 sq. mi. and 346,000 pop.

Goa, 1,426 sq. mi., pop., 1962, 626,978, which had been administered by Portugal as a colony since 1505 A.D., was taken by India by military action Dec. 18, 1961, together with two other Portuguese enclaves, Damao and Diu, located about 250 mi. S of Bombay. The World Court, Apr. 12, 1960, had rejected Portugal's claim to sovereignty by a 1779 treaty over Dadra and Nagar Haveli, subsidiaries of Damao. India's Parliament, Mar. 14, 1962, incorporated Goa, Damao and Diu in the Indian Union. Following elections for an assembly Dec. 9, 1963, Goa became internally self-governing.

India is a union of 16 federated states and 8 centrally administered union territories:

| State | Capital | Sq. mi. | Pop. 1960 |
|---|---|---|---|
| Andhra Pradesh. | Hyderabad.... | 106,052 | 39,602,400 |
| Assam.......... | Shillong..... | 84,899 | 14,076,500 |
| Bihar.......... | Patna........ | 67,198 | 52,063,500 |
| Gujarat........ | Ahmedabad... | 72,226 | 23,618,700 |
| Jammu-Kashmir. | Srinagar..... | 86,024 | 3,815,700 |
| Kerala......... | Trivandrum... | 15,005 | 19,136,800 |
| Madhya Pradesh | Bhopal....... | 171,210 | 36,623,800 |
| Madras......... | Madras City.. | 50,132 | 36,640,100 |
| Maharashtra... | Bombay...... | 118,741 | 44,931,300 |
| Mysore......... | Bangalore.... | 74,191 | 26,463,400 |
| Nagaland....... | Kohima...... | 6,366 | 401,300 |
| Orissa......... | Bhubaneswar | 60,162 | 19,586,900 |
| Punjab........ | Chandigarh... | 47,084 | 23,646,800 |
| Rajasthan..... | Jaipur....... | 132,150 | 23,257,000 |
| Uttar Pradesh. | Lucknow..... | 113,454 | 82,364,100 |
| West Bengal.... | Calcutta..... | 33,928 | 39,945,000 |
| **Territories** | | | |
| Andaman and Nicobar...... | Port Blair.... | 3,215 | 77,900 |
| Dadra & Nagar Haveli....... | Dadra....... | 160 | 65,400 |
| Delhi.......... | Delhi City... | 9,573 | 3,407,700 |
| Goa............ | Panjim...... | 1,426 | 659,300 |
| Himachal Pradesh | Simla....... | 10,879 | 1,517,600 |
| Laccadive and Amindivi..... | Kozhikode.... | 11 | 25,900 |
| Manipur........ | Imphal...... | 8,628 | 940,900 |
| Pondicherry.... | Pondicherry.. | 186 | 408,900 |
| Tripura........ | Agartala..... | 4,036 | 1,325,800 |

**Resources and Industries.** Agriculture occupies 70% of the people and is being helped by government planning to reach eventual self-sufficiency. Cooperative farms societies have been formed with state support, as well as a committee to supervise development and marketing of rice. The government is supporting the cooperative cotton, silk and woolen handloom industry with appropriations to the states for providing capital, supplies and housing for weavers, and sales depots.

Principal food products are rice, corn, millet, wheat, barley, coffee, sugar cane, spices, tea, cashew nuts. Other important products include cotton, copra, coir, jute, linseed, rubber, lumber. India's 4th 5-year plan, launched Apr. 1, 1966, was to spur agriculture and industry toward self-sufficiency.

Chief industries are textiles, with a wide variety of woolen, cotton and silk products; steel and cement. The Tata Iron & Steel works in Jamshedpur is the largest in Asia, with capacity of 800,000 tons a year and expanding.

Also manufactured were rayon yarn, plywood, ammonium sulphate, soda ash, caustic soda, sheet glass, ball bearings, transformers, sewing machines, bicycles.

The 1967 index of industrial production (1963= 100) was 118.

Industrial production, distribution and prices are regulated by law. Practically all utilities are state-owned, including railroads and airlines.

India is a leading producer of iron ore, mica and manganese; also important are salt, coal, bauxite and gypsum.

Exports include tea, sugar, raw and processed jute, cotton fabrics and other textiles, tanned hides and skins, manganese ore, pepper, tobacco. Imports: mineral oils, machinery, millwork, food grains, raw cotton, metals. Largest trade is with the U. S., which purchases tea, spices, burlap, wool, psyllium seed, gum, nuts, and hides.

Foreign trade, in thousands of U. S. dollars:

| | Imports | Exports |
|---|---|---|
| 1966 | $2,730,000 | $1,577,000 |
| 1967 | $2,718,000 | $1,614,000 |

**History and Government.** India has one of the oldest civilizations in the world. Excavations trace the Indus Valley civilization back for at least 5,000 years. Beautiful paintings in the mountain caves of Ajanta in South India, richly carved temples, the Taj Mahal in Agra, and the Kutab Minar in Delhi are among relics of the glorious past.

Vasco da Gama established Portuguese trading posts 1498-99, 1502-03. The Dutch followed. The English East India Co. sent Capt. Wm. Hawkins, 1609, to get concessions from the Mogul emperor for spices and textiles. The English founded Madras and Calcutta and acquired Bombay from Portugal. Operating as the East India Company the British gained control of all of India. Warren Hastings, first Governor-General (1774-1785), set up civil government, later India Civil Service. The British Parliament assumed political direction. Under Lord Bentinck, 1828-35, misrule by rajahs was abolished, infanticide stopped, suttee—suicide of a widow on her husband's funeral pyre—made illegal.

Liberal policies were set back when the Sepoy troops mutinied, 1857-58. Thereafter the British supported the native rulers. During the Boer War India supplied an ambulance corps. During World War I India provided 800,000 troops; 24,000 were killed, 70,000 wounded. The National Congress of India refused to support the Allies in World War II, but about 2,000,000 men served in the Indian Army, chiefly against Japanese in Burma.

Indian nationalism grew rapidly after World War I. The National Congress and the Moslem League demanded constitutional reform. A leader emerged in Mohandas K. Gandhi (called Mahatma, or Great Soul), born Oct. 2, 1869, assassinated Jan. 30, 1948. A Hindu, trained in law in England, he first championed rights of Indians in South Africa. In 1919 in India he began advocating self-rule, non-violence, pursuit of native handicrafts, removal of untouchability (which forced millions of poor to remain menials by heredity). In 1930 he launched "civil disobedience," including boycott of British goods and rejection of taxes without representation. Gandhi and about 60,000 were jailed.

In 1935 Britain gave India a constitution providing a bicameral federal congress, with a council of states and an assembly. Suffrage was granted about 30,000,000 in separate electorates. The Moslems objected that Hindu dominance injured their culture and freedom. Mohammed Ali Jinnah, head of the Moslem League, sought creation of a Moslem nation, Pakistan.

Following more than 40 years' active struggle for freedom by both Hindus and Moslems, the British government announced Feb. 20, 1947, its intention to partition India into two dominions and set June, 1948, for British withdrawal from India. Aug. 15, 1947, was designated Indian Independence Day. India became a self-governing member of the Commonwealth and assumed charter membership British India had held in the UN. The dominion became a sovereign democratic republic under a constitution adopted Nov. 26, 1949, effective Jan. 26, 1950, but elected to remain a member of the Commonwealth. (*See Pakistan.*)

It has been estimated that more than 11,000,000 refugees (Hindus and Moslems) crossed the India-Pakistan borders in a mass transferral of some of the two peoples during 1947.

The constitution provides for a President, elected for a five-year term by an electoral college consisting of members of both houses of Parliament (Council of States and House of the People), and elected members of the lower houses of the federating states. A Vice President elected by members of both houses presides over the Council of States. A Council of Ministers (cabinet), headed by a Prime Minister, aids and advises the President. The federating states have governors, appointed by the President, at the head of state organizations similar to the federal system.

The Council of States is a permanent body, not subject to dissolution, but one-third of its members retire at the end of every second year. The House of the People may be dissolved by the President and new elections called.

The Congress party has been in power since India's first general election, 1951-52. In general elections Feb., 1967, for the lower house (Lok Sabah), the Congress party won 278 seats; opposition parties won 234.

Prime Minister Mrs. Indira Gandhi, named Jan. 19, 1966, succeeded Lal Bahadur Shastri, who on June 2, 1964, succeeded India's first Prime Minister, Jawaharlal Nehru. Shastri died Jan. 11, 1966, hours after signing the "Tashkent Declaration" on Kashmir. Mrs. Gandhi, Nehru's daughter, was no relation to Mahatma Gandhi. Nehru, Prime Minister from the beginning of India's independence in 1947, died May 24, 1964.

President Dr. Zakir Husain, a Moslem, was elected May 9, 1967.

**Education and Religion.** The constitution pro-

vides for free, compulsory education through age
14. There are now 62 universities, 1,946 colleges,
and 27 research institutes.

There are 14 main languages, 12 originating from
Sanskrit, with several hundred varied dialects.
Hindi is spoken by nearly 50%, with Urdu, the
principal Moslem language, spoken by 10%. Hindi
became the official language in Jan. 1965 with
English the associate official language. Much
official government work and instruction at universities continues to be done in English.

The religion of more than 85% of the people is
Hinduism. The constitution guarantees freedom
of worship. Moslems are the largest minority, est.
at 50,000,000 in 1965; there are about 10,000,000
Christians, 8,000,000 Sikhs, 100,000 Parsis (chiefly
around Bombay) and 30,000 Jews.

Defense. All recruitment for India's armed forces
is voluntary. Army, navy and air force are headed
by chiefs of staff under the Defense Minister.
The navy consists of one aircraft carrier, 2 cruisers, 3 destroyers, 5 anti-submarine frigates, 3
anti-aircraft frigates, 7 frigates, 12 minesweepers
and other vessels.

# Indonesia

### REPUBLIK INDONESIA
### (Former Netherlands Indies)

Capital: Jakarta (Djakarta). Area: 735,865 sq.
mi. Population (UN est. 1967): 110,100,000. Monetary unit: Rupiah (10 per U. S. $1 official rate,
open market rate 340 per $1).

Indonesia, world's largest archipelago, formerly
the Netherlands East Indies, lies along the
Equator SE of Asia, N and NW of Australia.
Indonesia comprises about 3,000 islands, the 5
largest being Java (one of the most densely
populated areas in the world with 1,000 persons to
the sq. mi.), Sumatra, Kalimantan (most of Borneo), Sulawesi (Celebes) and West Irian (west
half of New Guinea). Among others are Bangka,
Billiton, Madura, Bali, Lombok, Sumbawa, part
of Timor. The land area is 6 times that of New
Mexico.

Many races are included, the principal ones being Achinese, Bataks, Menangkabaus, Javanese,
Sundanese, Madurese, Balinese, Sasaks, Menadon-
ese, Buginese, Dayaks, and Papuans.

Areas and population of the principal divisions:

|                          | Sq. mi. | Pop. 1962 |
|--------------------------|---------|-----------|
| Kalimantan (West Borneo) | 208,286 | 4,101,475 |
| Sumatra                  | 182,859 | 15,739,363 |
| Java and Madura          | 51,032  | 63,059,575 |
| Sulawesi (Celebes)       | 72,986  | 7,079,349 |
| Bali and Nusa Tenggara   | 35,000  | 5,557,656 |
| Moluccas and West Irian  | 182,308 | 1,547,930 |

The capital, called Batavia by the Dutch, is
Jakarta (Djakarta), on the island of Java.

Indonesia's national airways system covers 17,000
mi., linking 30 cities plus international service.

Resources and Industries. Indonesia is one of the
richest countries in natural resources. There are
vast supplies of tin, oil and coal, and sizable deposits of bauxite, manganese, copper, nickel, gold
and silver.

Agriculture occupies 80% of the population.
Products include rice, maize, casava, ground nuts,
soya beans, tobacco, coffee, rubber, cinchona, pepper, kapok, coconuts, palm oil, tea, sugar and
indigo.

Inflation and the cost of living spiraled during
the Suharto regime. High prices continued to
plague the new government in 1968.

History and Government. Until March, 1942, Indonesia was a Netherlands overseas territory. Following Japanese military occupation, 1942-1945,
Nationalists, led by Dr. Sukarno and Dr. Hatta,
proclaimed a republic Aug. 17, 1945. Four years
of intermittent warfare between Netherlands and
Indonesian forces ended with agreements signed
Nov. 2, 1949, transferring sovereignty over all
Indonesia, except Netherlands New Guinea (Irian)
to a new interim government effective Dec. 27,
1949. Dr. Sukarno was elected President, Dec. 16,
1949. On July 20, 1950, the member states agreed
to form a strongly centralized government; a unitarian state with an amended constitution was
proclaimed Aug. 15 and its name formally changed
to Republic of Indonesia. It joined the UN 1950.

After the UN, Nov. 29, 1957, rejected a proposal
for new negotiations over West New Guinea, Indonesia's government stepped up the seizure of Dutch
plantations, shipping, banks, railways, electrical

facilities and mercantile concerns. A U. S. mediator's plan was adopted in 1962, providing that
West Irian be turned over temporarily to the UN,
then to Indonesia. Under the agreement Indonesia
pledged to hold a plebiscite by the end of 1969
allowing the people of West Irian the choice of
staying with Indonesia or separating from it. The
UN turned the area over to Indonesia May 1,
1963. In April 1965 Pres. Sukarno announced no
plebiscite would be held.

Pres. Sukarno suspended the original elected 257-
member Parliament Mar. 5, 1960, and announced a
new 261-member appointed group, Mar. 27, and
swept aside anti-Leftist criticism. He was named
President for life May 18, 1963.

The USSR announced June 25, 1964, plans to
step up its already large contributions of modern
arms to Indonesia to aid in attempting to "crush"
the new nation, Malaysia, formation of which
Indonesia opposed. In 1964 and 1965 Indonesia
staged numerous guerrilla raids into Malaysia.

Indonesia withdrew from the UN in Jan. 1965
and from the World Bank in Aug. Many anti-
American demonstrations were staged at U. S.
consulates, including stonings, during the year.
In Aug. Pres. Sukarno announced plans for an
Indonesian-Red Chinese axis aimed at driving
the U. S. and Britain out of southwest Asia.

Indonesia's large, pro-Peking Communist party
tried to seize complete control Sept. 30, 1965, taking strategic points and murdering 6 high generals. The army smashed the coup and later
intimated that Pres. Sukarno had played a role in
it. Following the abortive putsch, anti-Communist
rioters set fire to Communist hq. and a Red Chinese university and ransacked the Peking embassy in Jakarta. In Central and East Java, Reds
seized control of several districts and fighting continued. It was later estimated that up to 400,000
Communists were executed.

Gen. Suharto was named head of the Army; on
Mar. 12, 1966, Pres. Sukarno turned over all government powers to him but continued as Pres.,
apparently in name only. In 1967 Sukarno was reportedly stripped of all titles. Gen. Suharto was
officially named President for a 5-year term by
the Consultative Assembly Mar. 27, 1968.

On Aug. 11, 1966, Indonesia and Malaysia signed
an agreement ending the Sukarno policy of hostility to Malaysia. On Sept. 28 Indonesia resumed
membership in the UN. The U. S. resumed economic aid.

Under Sukarno, Indonesia in April 1965 announced seizure of control of all foreign-owned
enterprises in the country. In Oct. 1967 the Suharto
government returned a seized rubber plantation to
the Goodyear Tire & Rubber Co.

Education and Religion. 90% of the inhabitants
are Moslems, the remainder Christians, Hindus and
Buddhists. There is compulsory primary education
for children 6 to 12, plus optional secondary training and higher education. Major institutions
of higher education are Univ. of Indonesia (Jakarta and Bandung), Gadjah Mada Univ., National
Academy, Islam Univ., Pantja-sila Univ. Many
languages are spoken; official language is Bahasa
Indonesia, derived from Malay. Dutch and English
are taught.

# Iran

### KESHVARE SHAHANSHAHIYE IRAN
### (Persia)

Capital: Tehran. Area: 636,293 sq. mi. Population (UN est. 1967): 26,284,000. Monetary unit:
Rial (75.75 per U. S. $1).

The Kingdom of Iran is a mountainous land,
much of it a high plateau region, in southwestern
Asia. Slightly larger than Alaska, it has coastlines
on the Caspian Sea, Persian Gulf and Gulf of
Oman. For neighbors it has the USSR, Afghanistan, Pakistan, Iraq and Turkey. Large salt deserts comprise 25% of the land but there are many
beautiful oases.

Tehran, Isfahan, Shiraz and Abadan have jet
airports. Important ports are Bandar Shahpur,
Bandar Pahlavi, Khurramshahr and Bandar Shah.
Shiraz is noted for ancient ruins of Persepolis.

Resources and Industries. Iran is the world's 4th
largest oil producer; petroleum provides most of
its foreign exchange and government income. A
$92,000,000 oil loading terminal was opened in 1966
at Kharg Island in the Persian Gulf.

Other mineral wealth includes chromite, copper,
iron, lead, manganese, zinc, barite, sulphur and
coal. Also mined are emeralds and turquoise.

The first Iranian steel mill is planned near Isfahan, to be built by the Soviet Union and paid for by natural gas piped to the USSR. Iran has contracted with the French for development of a petrochemical industry.

Agriculture is a prime industry, wheat, barley, corn, rice, fruits, gums, wool, tobacco, raw silk, sugar beets and cotton being the chief products. Some wines are famous. Persian carpets, all made on hand looms, are produced in Kerman, Qum, Tabriz, Arak, Meshed, Isfahan and Kashan. Sturgeon fishing in Caspian Sea is important, especially for caviar. Three new major dams provide hydroelectric power and aid irrigation—Karadj (1961), in Tehran; Sefidrud (1962), north of Tehran; and Dez (1963), in Khuzestan.

Under Shah Mohammed Riza Pahlevi's leadership, Iran has undergone an economic and social revolution to become a vigorous modern state. His improvements included major land reform, introduction of industry to towns, the spread of literacy and drastic gains in women's rights.

On Nov. 29, 1967, the U. S. and Iran celebrated the end of American economic aid, begun in 1951; it had totaled $605,000,000 plus other aid. Both countries agreed it was no longer necessary in view of Iran's growing prosperity.

**History and Government.** Iran, derived from Aryan, is the correct name of the country long referred to as Persia. The Iranians, who came from the East during the 2nd millenium B.C., were Aryans, an Indo-European people related to the Aryans of India, and included Medes, Persians and other groups. Use of the name Iran became widespread in the 1920s and 1930s.

In 549 B.C. Cyrus the Great united the Medes and Persians in the Persian Empire, conquered Babylonia, 538 B.C.; restored Jerusalem to the Jews.

Darius I began the invasion of Greece; crossed the Hellespont (Bosphorus), was defeated at Marathon, 490 B.C. Xerxes I crossed the Hellespont, fought Spartans at Thermopylae, was defeated at Salamis, 480 B.C. and Plataea, 479 B.C. Alexander of Macedon (the Great) invaded Persia, defeated Darius III at Issus, 333 B.C.

Subsequently Persia was ruled by the Seleucids; the Parthians beginning c. 250 B.C.; the Sassanians, c. 226 A.D.

Arabs brought Islam to Persia in the 7th Century and for over 600 years the religious-political Caliphate ruled the land. Omar Khayyam (c. 1050-c. 1123) wrote his famous Rubaiyat and created a calendar renowned for its accuracy.

Mongols invaded the country in 1250 and again under Tamerlane c. 1370. After the downfall of the Mongols in 1502 Persia became a monarchy under a Shah.

In 1906 a constitution was enacted. It provides for an executive with power vested in a cabinet and government officials who act in the name of the Shah. The legislature has a national assembly (Majlis) elected for 4 years and a senate of 60, 30 elected and 30 nominated by the Shah. Laws require the Shah's signature and he may dissolve the legislature. Women voted and were elected to the legislative for the first time in 1963.

The Shah is Mohammed Reza Pahlavi (born Oct. 26, 1919), ascended in 1941. He married Princess Fawzia, eldest sister of Farouk I of Egypt, March 15, 1939; divorced Nov. 19, 1948. A daughter, Princess Shahnaz, was born in 1940. The Shah married his 2nd wife, Soraya Esfandiary, Feb. 12, 1951, divorced Mar. 14, 1958. Both wives had failed to produce a male heir. The Shah married Farah Diba Dec. 21, 1959; Crown Prince Reza Pahlavi was born Oct. 31, 1960.

A two-year observance of Iran's 2,500th birthday culminated in October, 1967, with the coronation of the Shah. (No Shah can be crowned until a male succession is assured.)

British and Russian forces entered Iran Aug. 25, 1941, withdrawing later. Britain and the USSR signed an agreement Jan. 29, 1942, to respect Iran integrity and give economic aid. In 1946 a Soviet attempt to take over the Azerbaijan region in northeast Iran was defeated when a puppet regime was ousted by force.

In March, 1951, radicals in the Majlis voted nationalization of the oil industry. This led to closing of the Abadan refinery of the Anglo-Iranian Oil Co., a diplomatic break with Britain and wide unemployment. After a brief uprising, Aug. 1953, the royalists regained control and Dr. Mohammed Mossadegh, appointed Premier Apr. 29, was given 3 years in prison for treason. The oil dispute was settled Aug. 8, 1954, by the signing of a contract with a consortium of British, American, Dutch and French companies for 25 years, plus 15 optional, to produce, refine and market Iran's oil, with 50% of the earnings going to Iran.

An increase in direct taxation on hitherto privileged landholders and people of high incomes is being developed to insure mass welfare. A Pahlavi Estates distribution program has operated since 1949. A new land reform law, passed Jan. 15, 1962, further increased opportunities for landless peasants to become owners, enhanced by the Shah's distribution of land from his own estates.

**Education and Religion.** The Shiah branch of Islam predominates. Education is nominally compulsory. Higher education is available at the Universities of Tehran, Shiraz, Isfahan, Tabriz, Meshed, National Univ., and Ahwaz. A Literacy Corps is composed of high school and college graduates who teach in rural areas in lieu of military service. A Health Corps of graduate doctors and other graduates is patterned after the Literacy Corps. The language is Farsi (Persian), written in Arabic script.

**Defense.** Two years' service is compulsory. Iran is a member of the UN and CENTO.

# Iraq
## AL JAMHOURIYAH AL IRAQUIA (MESOPOTAMIA)

**Capital: Baghdad. Area: 173,259 sq. mi. Population (UN est. 1967): 8,440,000. Monetary unit: Dinar (.3571 per U. S. $1).**

Iraq is the modern name for Mesopotamia, the area around the Euphrates and Tigris Rivers, about twice the size of Utah. It is bounded by Turkey, Iran, the Persian (also called Arabian) Gulf, Kuwait, Saudi Arabia, Jordan and Syria.

The country is mostly alluvial plain. The temperature varies widely: 120°F in the shade is common, contrasted with severe frosts in the winter.

The soil is of extraordinary fertility, but since destruction of an intricate system of canals during invasions, 700-1258, the Tigris and Euphrates have caused recurring damage. Modern irrigation systems are under construction.

Baghdad and Basra have jet airports.

**Resources and Industries.** Wheat, barley, rice, millet and cotton are the chief crops, with tobacco in the Kurdish hills. Dates are grown in the tidal stretches of the Shatt el Arab and beyond. Large flocks of sheep are raised in the north and wool and skins are exported.

Iraq is one of the leading oil-producing countries of the world. Native companies, and American and other interests comprising the Iraq Petroleum Co. operating the rich Kirkuk field, produced 400,000,000 bbl. in 1967, a drop of 100,000,000 bbl. from 1966. Iraq charged that the Western-controlled company had sabotaged one of its own pipelines in Dec. 1967. In the same month Iraq announced signing of an agreement with the USSR to develop rich new fields in southern Iraq; the step was regarded as an important breakthrough for the USSR in obtaining Middle East oil.

**History and Government.** The Tigris-Euphrates valley was the site of the ancient cities of Eridu, Ur, Nineveh and Babylon. The Sumerian culture of 3000 B.C. influenced Crete, Egypt and Greece.

Iraq, then known as Mesopotamia, was taken from Turkey in World War I. The League of Nations gave a mandate to Britain, which ended 1932 when Iraq was recognized as a sovereign state and member of the League of Nations.

Emir Faisal, then King of the Hejaz, was chosen ruler by a referendum in 1921. A constitutional monarchy was created in 1924. On his death, Sept. 1933, he was succeeded by his son, Ghazi Ibn Faisal. King Ghazi was killed in an automobile accident April 4, 1939, and was succeeded by his son, King Faisal II (born May 2, 1935).

King Faisal was assassinated July 14, 1958, when the Free Officers, led by Brig. Gen. Abdul Karim Kassem revolted and proclaimed Iraq "part of the Arab nation." Gen. Kassem became premier of a republic which would follow the policies of the United Arab Republic but honor its international obligations. The United States recognized the government Aug. 2 and Kassem's representatives took the seat of Iraq in the UN Security Council. Iraq received Soviet arms aid. It withdrew from the Baghdad pact and 3 U. S. arms agreements.

Premier Kassem was deposed Feb. 8, 1963, by

military elements supporting UAR pan-Arab policies and executed Feb. 9.

A provisional constitution, announced May 3, 1964, provided for a 3-year transition period and strong ties with the UAR. Dr. Abdul Rahman al-Bazzaz became premier Sept. 21, 1965, after his predecessor, Brig. Arif Abdel Razzak, had fled Iraq following an abortive coup. Bazzaz announced June 29, 1966, settlement of the 5-yr. guerrilla war with Kurdish rebels, who were to be granted local autonomy. Bazzaz resigned Aug. 6 and was succeeded by Naji Taleb.

Lt. Gen. Abdel Rahman Arif was sworn in as President and Premier May 10, 1967.

On June 7, 1967, Iraq broke diplomatic relations with the U.S. following UAR charges that America was aiding Israel in the 6-day, 1967 war.

On July 17, 1968, Pres. Arif was ousted in a military coup by a group headed by Maj. Gen. Ahmed Hassan al-Bakr. He was a member of the right wing of the international Baath Socialist party, the leftist wing of which controlled Syria.

**Education and Religion.** Elementary and secondary education is free and compulsory. Arabic is the language of the majority. The people are preponderantly Moslems, divided between the Sunni and Shiah sects. Christians number 150,000.

**Defense.** Military service is compulsory between the ages of 18 and 25. The Iraq Army comprises 3 infantry divisions, an armored division and special troops, organized along modern lines. There is a small Air Force and a river flotilla.

# Ireland

## EIRE
## POBLACHT NA H'EIREANN

**Capital:** Dublin. **Area** 27,136 sq. mi. **Population (UN est. 1967):** 2,899,000. **Monetary unit:** Irish pound (.4195 per U. S. $1).

Ireland, an island in the Atlantic near the European mainland, is a sovereign democratic republic about the size of W. Va. It is separated from Great Britain on the E by the Irish Sea and the North Channel and on the SE by St. George's Channel.

Ireland, the Emerald Isle, consists mainly of a central plateau surrounded by isolated groups of hills and mountains. Ireland's coastline is much indented by the sea, affording many inlets and coves. The mean annual temperature ranges from 48°F, in the N to 52°F, in the S. Dublin has an average temperature of 39 in the coldest month and 60 in the warmest. There are numerous lakes (called loughs); the best known are those of Killarney. The most important river is the Shannon, about 250 mi. long. Tallest mountains are in SW; Carrantuohill, 3,414 ft., and Mangerton, 2,756 ft., are in Kerry; Brandon Hill on the coast, 3,127 ft.; Boggeragh, in County Cork, 2,118 ft.

Wildlife is scarce, and snakes are considered non-existent.

The famous Blarney stone is located in an old castle in the village of Blarney, 4 mi. NW of Cork. A legend says it confers oratorical powers on those who kiss it.

Emigration had been high and for years the population steadily declined. Since 1961, however, it has annually increased.

**Resources and Industries.** More than a third of the population works on farms. The nearness of the Gulf Stream causes considerable rainfall; lush pastures support valuable horse and cattle industries. Important crops are potatoes, wheat, oats, barley, rye, turnips, sugar beets, cabbage and flax.

A land rehabilitation project has reclaimed 1,410,000 acres in recent years. A Peat Board supervises drainage of bogs to recover peat and increase acreage. An Agricultural Institute was established in 1958 to coordinate and promote research.

Major industries are tobacco, food processing, vehicle assembly, metals, textiles, chemicals and brewing. Marked gains have been recorded in electrical and non-electrical machinery, fertilizers and metals.

A mining boom, following discovery of zinc, lead and silver deposits, brought new strength to the economy in the mid-1960s. The index numbers of industrial production (1963=100) showed that the mining index jumped from 105 in 1965 to 206 in 1967. The index for general industrial production rose to 129 in 1967.

Tourism, growing annually, provided Ireland

with earnings of $232,000,000 in 1966.

Foreign trade, in thousands of U. S. dollars:

|  | Imports | Exports |
|---|---|---|
| 1966 | $1,046,000 | $683,000 |
| 1967 | $1,081,000 | $785,000 |

A switch to the decimal coinage system is planned for 1971.

**History and Government.** Celtic tribes invaded the islands about the 4th Century B.C.; their Gaelic culture and literature flourished and spread to Scotland and elsewhere in the 5th Century A.D., the same century in which St. Patrick converted the Irish to Christianity. Invasions by Norsemen began in the 8th Century, but were ended by defeat of the Danes by the Irish King Brian Boru in 1014. English invasions started in the 12th Century; for over 700 years the Anglo-Irish struggle continued with bitter rebellions and savage repressions.

The Easter Monday Rebellion (1916) failed but was followed by guerrilla warfare and harsh reprisals by British troops, the "Black and Tans." The Dail Eireann, or Irish parliament in Dublin, reaffirmed independence in Jan., 1919. The British offered dominion status to Ulster (6 counties) and southern Ireland (26 counties), Dec., 1921, which Northern Ireland accepted. The constitution of the Irish Free State, a British dominion, was adopted Dec. 11, 1922. By treaty with Great Britain Northern Ireland could vote itself out, which it did, Dec. 12, 1922.

A new constitution adopted by plebiscite came into operation Dec. 29, 1937. It declared the name of the state Eire in the Irish language and Ireland in the English and declared in a sovereign democratic state.

On Dec. 21, 1948, an Irish law declared the country a republic rather than a dominion and withdrew it from the Commonwealth. In 1949 the British Parliament recognized both actions, but re-asserted its claim to incorporate the six northeastern counties (Antrim, Armagh, Derry, Down, Fermanagh and Tyrone) in the United Kingdom. This claim has not been recognized by Ireland. *See United Kingdom—Northern Ireland.*

William T. Cosgrave was chosen President of the Executive Council, Dec. 1922. He was in office until Mar., 1932, when Eamon de Valera became President of the Executive Council and Minister for External Affairs, holding both offices until 1938. Leaders since 1938 have been:

**Presidents:** (7-year terms): Douglas Hyde, 1938-1945. Sean T. O'Kelly, first term, 1945-1952: re-elected 1952-1959. Eamon de Valera, 1959-1966; re-elected 1966.

**Prime Ministers:** Eamon de Valera, 1938-1948; John A. Costello, 1948-1951; Eamon de Valera, 1951-1954; John A. Costello, 1954-1957; Eamon de Valera, 1957-1959; Sean Lemass, 1959-66; John M. Lynch, chosen Nov. 10, 1966.

The parliament is composed of a house, Dail Eireann, of 144 elected members, and a senate, Seanad Eireann, of 60, 11 of them nominated by the prime minister, 6 by the universities and the rest elected from 5 panels of candidates representing public interests. The president, on nomination of the Dail, appoints the prime minister and on nomination of the latter with Dail approval names the other ministers.

Following the general election, April 7, 1965, seats were distributed as follows, compared with the previous Parliament:

|  | 1965 | 1961 |
|---|---|---|
| Fianna Fáil | 72 | 70 |
| Fianna Gael | 47 | 47 |
| Labor | 22 | 16 |
| Clann na Publachta | 1 | 1 |
| Independents | 2 | 6 |
| Nat'l Progressive Dem. | 0 | 2 |
| Clann na Talmhan | 0 | 2 |

**Education and Religion.** Roman Catholicism is the prevailing religion, claiming more than 90% of the population.

Elementary education is free and compulsory, and the Irish language is a required study in all national schools. Institutions of higher learning include the National University, founded 1908, comprising the Constituent Colleges of Dublin, Cork, Galway and St. Patrick's, Maynooth; Trinity College, Dublin, founded 1591; the Dublin Institute for Advanced Studies; the Royal Irish Academy.

**Defense.** Recruitment is voluntary. Permanent force of the Army, Navy, and Air Force is set at 13,000; first and second line reserves number 25,000. The Navy consists of small vessels.

It is a member of the UN and Council of Europe.

# Israel

## MEDINAT ISRAEL
## STATE OF ISRAEL

**Capital:** Jerusalem. **Area:** 7,993 sq. mi. **Population** (UN est. 1967): 2,669,000. **Monetary unit:** Israeli pound (3.5 per U. S. $1).

The nation of Israel was reestablished, as a republic, in 1948. It occupies part of the ancient land first called Canaan, then Israel, then Palestine. About the size of New Jersey, it faces the Mediterranean to the W, Lebanon to the N, Syria and Jordan to the E, and the United Arab Republic to the SE.

The coastal plain on the W is 120 mi. long, 15 wide, fertile and well watered. In the center is the plateau of Judea. A triangular-shaped semidesert region, the Negev, extends from south of Beersheba to an apex at the head of the Gulf of Aqaba. The eastern border drops sharply into the depressed valley of the River Jordan and the Dead Sea, 46 mi. long, with an average width of 8 mi., 1,296 ft. below sea level, lowest point on the earth's surface.

Israel's area, as defined by armistices with the Arab nations, includes all the land assigned to it under the 1947 partition resolution of the UN General Assembly, as well as Western Galilee and a corridor to Jerusalem. By the terms of the armistice with Syria, July 20, 1949, last of the Arab states to end military action after the creation of modern Israel, demilitarized zones were set up on the eastern edge of Lake Huleh and the southeastern shore of the Sea of Galilee, site of Israel's Ein Gev settlement.

After the Israeli-Arab war of June 1967 in which Israel occupied the Sinai Peninsula, the west bank of the Jordan and a small area of Syria, Israel indicated it would not consider returning these areas unless the Arab states negotiated peace treaties directly with Israel and unless the U.A.R. agreed Israel would have the same shipping rights as other nations in the Suez Canal.

Non-Jewish population: Moslem, 220,000; Christion, 59,000; Druse, 31,000.

The chief ports of Israel are Haifa, Tel Aviv-Jaffa, and Elath (on Red Sea). A new port, Ashdod, was constructed S of Tel Aviv and opened 1965.

**Resources and Industries.** Citrus fruit is the most valuable agricultural product. Other principal crops include wheat, barley, durra, olives, melons, grapes, figs, tomatoes, bananas, cotton. Since 1955 total cultivated area has been increased from 412,500 to more than 1,000,000 acres, of which 380,000 acres are under irrigation. Wine making is an extensive industry.

Israel has abundant deposits of some minerals including limestone, sandstone, gypsum, copper, iron, phosphates, magnesium, manganese, ceramic clays. The valley of Jordan and the Dead Sea yield rock salt, sulphur and potash.

Israel's over-all economy has grown rapidly since 1954 and industrialization is proceeding. Foreign investment rose from $105,000,000 in 1960 to $180,700,000 in 1965. Its economy has been aided by German reparations payments. U. S. aid, international loans and contributions. West Germany completed payment of $860,000,000 in reparations (cash and goods) in 1965. The two countries also set up full diplomatic relations.

Gross national product in 1966 was $3.9 billion compared with $2.8 billion in 1964.

The Negev region in the South is Israel's primary development area, receiving nearly half of the immigrants. It has huge phosphate deposits, copper, oil, natural gas and potash.

A 150-mi. pipeline, major link in Israel's national water plan, was completed in June, 1964 and began carrying water from Lake Kinneret (Sea of Galilee) to the Negev. The project was opposed by neighboring Arab nations. Other water resources being explored include various desalination processes.

The Dead Sea gas pipeline, opened 1961, carries methane from the fields of Rosh Zohar and Kodod to the potash and bromine works on the shores of the sea.

In 1968 Israel began construction of a 160-mi., 42-inch, oil pipeline from Elath on the Gulf of Aqaba to Ascalon on the Mediterranean. Scheduled for completion in July 1969, it would provide an alternative to the Suez Canal.

Israel's first atomic reactor at Nahal Rubin began operations in July, 1960. The nation launched its first successful solid-fuel rocket 50 mi. into the atmosphere July 5, 1961, for meteorological study.

Israel's main exports are citrus fruits, polished diamonds, autos, textiles and fashion goods, building materials, tires and pharmaceutical products.

Tourism is second only to citrus products in earnings.

Foreign trade in thousands of U. S. dollars:

|  | Imports | Exports |
|---|---|---|
| 1966 | $812,000 | $477,000 |
| 1967 | $734,000 | $522,000 |

**History and Government.** The Jewish people lived in Israel from about 1200 B.C.; many were driven from the land by some of its various conquerors. The Judaic moral and ethical code and the Bible originated here. The modern Zionist movement for a homeland in Palestine, led by Dr. Chaim Weizmann (born in Motele, Russia, Nov. 27, 1874) caused the cabinet of Great Britain to give its support in the Balfour Declaration, Nov. 2, 1917. Under the Palestine Mandate, about four-fifths of historic Palestine was detached in 1922 to form Trans-Jordan, now the Kingdom of Jordan. When the Nazi persecutions began in Germany great numbers of Jews set out for Palestine. The UN General Assembly voted Nov. 29, 1947, to partition Palestine into two independent states by Oct. 1, 1948. The Arab state would have 4,500 sq. mi. A separate enclave of Jerusalem, area 289 sq. mi., was to be administered by a governor appointed by the UN. British troops were to be withdrawn and separate governments elected. Great Britain gave up its mandate May 15, 1948.

A new Zionist state, the Republic of Israel, was proclaimed May 14-15, 1948. Israel took charge of the New City in Jerusalem and Jordan held the Old City. The UN adopted a resolution to internationalize Jerusalem, but was unable to get support from the two states. Israel was elected to the UN May 11, 1949.

The Arab League opposed the creation of modern Israel and May 15, 1948, a few hours after Israel proclaimed its independence, the armies of Egypt, Jordan, Syria, Lebanon and Iraq, with Saudi Arabian contingents, crossed its frontiers at several points.

Separate armistices with the Arab nations were signed in 1949, but no general peace settlement was obtained. The Arab nations continued policies of economic boycott, blockade in the Suez Canal, political warfare and local incitement.

Most of the territory designated for the proposed Arab state was annexed by Egypt and Jordan and the future home of more than 1,000,000 displaced and nomadic Arabs remains uncertain. They receive UN aid.

An uneasy truce between Israel and the Arab countries, supervised by a United Nations Emergency Force, prevailed until May 19, 1967, when the UN force withdrew at the demand of Egypt's President Gamal Abdel Nasser. Egyptian forces rapidly reoccupied the Gaza Strip and closed the Gulf of Aqaba to Israeli shipping. In a full-scale 6-day war that started June 5, the Israelis took the Gaza Strip, occupied the Sinai Peninsula to the Suez Canal, and captured Old Jerusalem and other Jordanian and Syrian territory. The fighting was halted June 10 by UN-arranged cease-fire agreements.

Following the war, Arab guerillas from Jordan continued raids into Israel and shooting incidents occurred repeatedly across the Jordan border and the Suez Canal. A reprisal raid by Israelis into Jordan brought a UN Security Council resolution condemning Israel and deploring all violence whether by Arabs or Israelis.

A UN mission, headed by Dr. Gunnar V. Jarring of Sweden, sought to get both sides to agree to a peace formula during 1968. The USSR and the Communist bloc, with the exception of Romania, supported the Arabs. In July 1968 UAR. Pres. Nasser and Soviet Union leaders held talks and announced they had agreed on "further joint steps" in the Middle East.

Israel is a parliamentary democracy. The first constituent assembly (Knesset), was formed Feb. 14, 1949, with 120 members, including eight Arabs. The assembly elected Dr. Chaim Weizmann, who had been provisional President from the start, first President of Israel Feb. 17, 1949. His successor was Izhak Ben-Zvi, President from 1952 until his death April 24, 1963. President: Shneour Zalman Shazar, elected by Parliament May 21, 1963.

The Knesset (Parliament) members are elected by universal suffrage for 4-year terms by all citizens over 18, under proportional representation.

In general elections Aug. 15, 1961, Premier David Ben-Gurion's Mapai party was returned to power. He resigned June 16, 1963, and was succeeded by Levi Eshkol whose coalition was kept in power by elections Nov. 2, 1965.

Israel maintains formal diplomatic relations with 90 nations. About 800 specialists in many fields share their knowledge with those in less developed nations in Africa and elsewhere.

**Education.** Israel has compulsory education from ages 5 to 14, 1 year of kindergarten and 8 of elementary school, with high schools mostly private. Institutes of higher education are Hebrew, Tel Aviv and Bar-Ilan Univs. Elementary enrollment increased from 100,000 in 1948 to 650,000 in 1963. In 1963, 98% of Jewish children and 90% of Arab boys were in school. After elementary school, vocational training is provided. In 1961-62 about 10,000 boys and girls were studying carpentry, tool & die making, electronics, home economics, dress making, secretarial work. Agricultural training is given and 15,000 pupils are transported every week to work on farms. There is an apprenticeship program for 10 trades. In 1960-61, 6,100 were enrolled in 10 government teachers' colleges, including one for Arabs in Jaffa. Engineers, technicians and architects study at Technion (Israel Inst. of Technology, Haifa), staff 488, regular students, 3,317, extension courses 5,000. About 5,000 adults take vocational training annually; popular adult education reaches 50,000. The general labor federation, Histadrut, trains Arab apprentices. Israel has 296 schools for Arabs, with 1,615 teachers and 40,768 pupils; also 29 private schools, some Christian, with 10,830 pupils. Construction of new schools is continuing. The official languages are Hebrew and Arabic.

**Defense.** There is compulsory 26-month service for men 18 to 26 and 20 months for unmarried women 18 to 26. The Navy includes destroyers, frigates, submarines, minesweepers and others. The Air Force uses modern military aircraft, mainly of French types.

# Italy
## REPUBBLICA ITALIANA

**Capital:** Rome. **Area:** 116,303 sq. mi. **Population (Govt. est. 1968):** 53,648,000. **Monetary unit:** Lira, pl. lire (623.30 per U. S. $1).

The Republic of Italy occupies a long peninsula shaped like a boot, extending SE from the Alps into the Mediterranean, with the island of Sicily separated from the mainland by the 2-mi. Strait of Messina at the toe of the boot. The country is about 760 mi. long and not over 220 mi. wide. Its area is about the same as Arizona's. Lying directly W of mid-Italy is the major island of Sardinia, slightly smaller than Sicily.

**Sicily,** 9,927 sq. mi., pop (1965), 4,721,000, is a triangular island 180 by 120 mi., seat of a Region that embraces the island of **Pantelleria,** 32 sq. mi., and the **Lipari** group, 44 sq. mi., pop. 14,000, including two with active volcanoes: **Vulcano,** 1,637 ft. and **Stromboli,** 3,038 ft. From prehistoric times Sicily has been settled by Mediterranean peoples; a strong Greek state had its capital at Syracuse, on Ortygia Is., off Catania, where Dionysius "the Tyrant" ruled Rome took Sicily from Carthage 215 B.C.

Mt. Etna, 10,705 ft. active volcano, is tallest peak. Sicily leads in citrus fruits, also produces wheat, grapes, wine, sulphur, salt, olives. Cattle, sheep, hogs and mules are raised.

**Sardinia,** 9,283 sq. mi., pop. (1965), 1,419,362, lies in the Mediterranean, 115 mi. W of Italy and 7½ mi. S of Corsica. Like Sicily, it is under a regional administration. It is 160 mi. long, 68 mi. wide, mountainous, with mining of coal, zinc, lead, copper; it raises grapes, olives, tobacco, also cattle and sheep. In 1720 Sardinia was added to the possessions of the Dukes of Savoy in Piedmont and Savoy to form the Kingdom of Sardinia. They fought in the Crimean War and the House of Savoy gave Italy its kings, 1861-1946. Giuseppe Garibaldi is buried on the nearby isle of Caprera. Capital: Cagliari.

**Elba,** 87 sq. mi., pop. 30,000, 6 mi. west of Tuscany. Industries include fishing, iron mining, wine making. Napoleon I lived here in exile, 1814-1815.

**Capri,** 4 sq. mi., pop. c. 9,000, 20 mi. SW of Naples, is famous for its beauty and equable climate.

Italy's largest seaports are Genoa, Naples, Venice, Trieste, Ancona, Bari, Brindisi and Palermo.

The allure of historical monuments, great museums of painting and sculpture, imposing churches, as well as good living, brought 27,500,000 tourists in 1967. Florence, with its galleries; Rome with its religious associations and ancient relics, Venice, and the resorts of the Riviera are the principal objectives.

The 3.4-mi. Great St. Bernard tunnel, between Italy and Switzerland, first auto tunnel in the Alps, was opened Mar. 19, 1964. The longest highway tunnel in the world, the Mont Blanc tunnel, 7.25 mi., linking Italy and France, was opened July 16, 1965.

**Resources and Industries.** Chief farm crops are wheat, sugar beets, potatoes, corn, grapes and tomatoes.

Italy is adapting production of fruits, vegetables and other garden products to the needs of the European Common Market. Grapes lead but olives, oranges, lemons, apples, pears are produced in large quantities. Rice is grown in Piedmont and Lombardy. Cattle constitute the largest livestock item, followed by sheep, horses, mules and goats.

The wines of Italy have great variety. Chianti from Tuscany is popular, as are Asti Spumante, Orvieto, Capri.

White marble is quarried at Carrara, Volterra and Pisa; colored marble at Verona, Siena, Vicenza and Genoa. Alabaster comes chiefly from Volterra.

Natural gas is found in the valley of the Po, the Marches, Abruzzi, Apulia, Basilicata and Sicily. In Sicily oil is carried by pipeline to the port of Augusta on the Gulf of Catania. In 1966 crude oil production was 1,812,000 metric tons.

In 1966 Italy had more than 2,300 hydroelectric and 750 thermoelectric stations which produced a total of 87.4 billion kwh. High-tension cables distribute electrical energy from the Alps to Sicily, crossing the Straits of Messina on overhead cables. In 1964 Italy had two nuclear power plants completed and a third under construction. The electrical industry was nationalized in 1962.

Steel production was 16,300,000 metric tons in 1967, up 13%. Italy is a heavy producer of industrial and electrical machinery, automobiles, steel products, typewriters, shoes, textiles, synthetic fabrics, machine tools. Its chemical industry is expanding.

There are state monopolies in tobacco, salt and quinine. Tobacco returns the largest income with cigarettes about 85% of the total. Salt is produced from sea water.

Italy's merchant marine ranks high. On Dec. 31, 1965, it had 632 ships over 1,000 gross tons totaling 5,395,000 gross tons.

Tourism is important, bringing a record $1.5 billion in 1966. The U. S. takes 5.9% of Italy's exports.

**Foreign trade, in thousands of U. S. dollars:**

| | Imports | Exports |
|---|---|---|
| 1966 | $8,571,000 | $8,031,000 |
| 1967 | $9,696,000 | $8,702,000 |

**History and Government.** Divided and dismembered for centuries, modern Italy began to develop after the war of 1859 when Lombardy came under the crown of King Victor Emmanuel II of Sardinia of the house of Savoy. By plebiscite in 1860, Parma, Modena, Romagna and Tuscany joined, followed by Sicily and Naples, and by the Marches and Umbria. The first Italian Parliament declared Victor Emmanuel King of Italy Mar. 17, 1861. Mantua and Venetia were added in 1866 as an outcome of the Austro-Prussian war. The Papal States were taken by Italian troops, Sept. 20, 1870, with the withdrawal of the French garrison after Napoleon III surrendered Sept. 2, 1870. The states were annexed to the kingdom by plebiscite. The King entered Rome July 2, 1871. Italy recognized the State of Vatican City as independent Feb. 11, 1929.

Fascism appeared in Italy Mar. 23, 1919 when the original Fascisti organized an association against Communism and Socialism under the guidance of Benito Mussolini. They took over the government at the invitation of the King Oct. 28, 1922. Mussolini acquired dictatorial powers and was called Duce (Leader). He made war on Ethiopia and proclaimed Victor Emmanuel III emperor; defied the sanctions of the League of Nations; joined the Berlin-Tokyo axis; sent troops to fight for Franco against the Republic of Spain; joined Germany in World War II with defeat of France. After Fascism was overthrown in 1943, Italy declared war on Germany and Japan and

contributed to the Allied victory. It surrendered conquered lands and lost colonies. Part of Venezia Giulia went to Yugoslavia and Trieste was made a free territory. Mussolini was put to death by a firing squad of Partisans near the village of Dongo on Lake Como, Apr. 28, 1945.

King Victor Emmanuel III abdicated May 9, 1946; his son, Humbert II, was king until June 10, when Italy became a republic after a referendum, June 2-3, in which the people voted 12,718,641 for a republic, 10,718,502 for a monarchy. King Humbert departed and Premier Alcide de Gaspari became head of the government. Victor Emmanuel went to Egypt where he died Dec. 28, 1947.

The Constituent Assembly elected Enrico de Nicola provisional Head of State. He was succeeded by Luigi Einaudi, first President of the Republic, 1948-1955.

The Senate has one member for each 160,000 pop. (currently 315), elected for 5-year terms, excepting 5 whom the President may appoint for life. Ex-Presidents are eligible for life membership. The Chamber of Deputies has one deputy for each 80,000 (currently 630), elected for 5 years. Titles of nobility are no longer recognized. Reorganization of the Fascist party is forbidden.

In May 1968 elections, the dominant, church-supported Christian Democratic party increased its seats in the Chamber of Deputies from 260 to 266. The Communist party also increased its seats from 166 to 177. The United Socialist party, which normally joins the Christian Democrats in coalition governments, lost 3 of its 94 seats. Other losers were several right-wing parties.

**Trieste,** part of which is now claimed as an Italian Department bounded E and S by Yugoslavia, was organized as a Free Territory by the Big Four in the peace treaty with Italy, Feb. 10, 1947, placed under jurisdiction of the UN Security Council, garrisoned by troops of the United States and Great Britain in the northern section (Zone A), and by Yugoslavia in the south (Zone B). It had about 320 sq. mi. Following prolonged negotiations an agreement was signed Oct. 5, 1954, by Italy and Yugoslavia which gave Italy provisional administration over the northern section and the seaport of Trieste, with 90 sq. mi. and about 300,000 pop., and Yugoslavia the Istrian peninsula it had occupied, 200 sq. mi. and 73,500 pop., and provision for emergency access to the port. The two areas are treated as parts of Italy and Yugoslavia.

Italy is a member of NATO, EEC and Council of Europe; admitted to the UN Dec. 14, 1955.

**Education and Religion.** Roman Catholicism is the state religion.

Italy has 29 state universities, including Bologna (founded 1088): Genoa (1243); Naples (1224); Padua (1222); Pisa (1338); Rome (1303), and Turin (1404). Education is compulsory between 6 and 14.

**Defense.** The Allied nations have largely rescinded the restriction placed on Italy's military establishment by the World War II peace treaty.

The Army has built an efficient training organization and constituted modern units, a large proportion of which is committed to NATO. The army has 2 armored divisions, 5 infantry divisions, 5 Alpine brigades, 5 infantry brigades, 1 paratroop brigade, 1 lagoon special force, 1 cavalry brigade and 1 missile brigade.

The Italian Navy cooperates with defense plans of NATO and pursues a long-term program of construction including 3 heavy missile cruisers, 2 light missile cruisers, 4 large missile carrier destroyers, 18 modern anti-submarine frigates, 6 submarines and other vessels; much of this program was completed in 1967.

The Air Force has been extensively built up in recent years. New air fields have been built and existing ones adapted for use of jets. It also has air defense squadrons with missiles of the Nike type.

# Ivory Coast
## COTE D'IVOIRE

**Capital:** Abidjan. **Area:** 127,520 sq. mi. **Population** (UN est. 1967): 4,010,000. **Monetary unit:** CFA franc (246.85 per U. S. $1).

The Republic of the Ivory Coast, a former French Overseas Territory in West Africa, is located on the northern coast of the Gulf of Guinea. Roughly square in shape and about the size of New Mexico, it is bounded by Liberia, Guinea, Mali, Upper Volta and Ghana. It has 340 mi. of coastline on the Atlantic. Abidjan, the capital, is the chief port.

In accordance with provisions of the 1958 French constitution, Ivory Coast became fully independent Aug. 7, 1960; it became a member of the UN Sept. 20. Its present constitution was adopted Oct. 31, 1960. It elected to remain outside the French Community proper, but signed a bilateral agreement Apr. 24, 1961, retaining close ties with France. Ivory Coast is a member of a regional alliance called the Council of the Entente formed May 29, 1959, other members of which are Dahomey, Niger, Togo and Upper Volta.

Agriculture, forestry, stock raising and fishing occupy 90% of the population. Chief export crops are coffee, cocoa, tropical woods and bananas; cotton, rice, oil palms also are raised. Electric power, lumbering and industrialization are being promoted.

The Ivory Coast has been the most prosperous of West African nations. Exports in 1967 were valued at $325,000,000, compared to $310,000,000 in 1966. With imports valued at $258,000,000 in 1967 and slightly less in 1966, the nation had a favorable balance of trade.

About 18% of the people are Catholics or Protestants; 20% are Moslems and the rest animists.

# Jamaica

**Capital:** Kingston. **Area:** 4,411 sq. mi. **Population** (UN est. 1967): 1,876,000. **Monetary unit:** Pound (.4167 per U. S. $1).

Jamaica is a mountainous island in the Caribbean Sea, 90 mi. south of Cuba. Its area is 12% less than that of Connecticut.

Temperatures range from 80 to 86 on the coast and down to 40 in the Blue Mtns. Montego Bay and Ocho Rios are among popular resort areas; most of 345,000 annual tourists are American.

Jamaica was discovered by Columbus, 1494, and ruled by Spanish (under whom native Arawak Indians died out) until captured by the English, 1655. The island figures largely in the history of the buccaneers of the West Indies before and during the time of Sir Henry Morgan, once its governor. Port Royal, old haunt of the pirate, at the entrance to Kingston harbor, was largely destroyed by earthquake, 1692.

Jamaica became independent within the Commonwealth Aug. 6, 1962, and joined the UN. Prime Min. is Hugh Lawson Shearer; Gov. Gen., Sir Clifford Campbell, representing Queen Elizabeth II; legislature is bicameral.

Principal exports are bauxite (world's largest production) and alumina. A $175,000,000 plant to be built by 3 U. S. companies will double alumina production (792,000 long tons in 1966). Other products include sugar cane, coffee, bananas, rum, coconuts, ginger, cocoa, pimento, citrus fruits and cigars. Gross national product, 1966, was $945,-840,000.

Imports in 1967 (in U. S. dollars) totaled $347,-000,000, compared to $321,000,000 in 1966. Exports in 1967 were valued at $222,000,000; in 1966, $229,-000,000.

# Japan

## NIPPON—LAND OF THE RISING SUN

**Capital:** Tokyo. **Area:** 142,726 sq. mi. **Population** (Govt. est. 1967): 100,000,000. **Monetary unit:** Yen (362 per U. S. $1).

Japan consists of four main islands: Honshu ("mainland"), 88,952 sq. mi.; Hokkaido, 30,304; Kyushu, 16,191; and Shikoku, 7,240. Total area is about twice that of Missouri. The islands lie in the North Pacific separated from the Soviet Union and Korea by the Sea of Japan and from China by the East China Sea.

By the terms ending World War II, Japan was forced to surrender captured lands, including Manchuria (Manchukuo), the southern half of Sakhalin Is., the Kurils, Korea, Taiwan, and the mandated islands in the Pacific, the Marshalls, the Carolines and the Marianas. (See Index for these; also for Okinawa and the Ryukyu Islands.)

The Japanese coast is deeply indented, measuring 16,654 mi. The northern islands are a continuation of the Sakhalin mountain chain running through Hokkaido and the main island. The continuation of the Kunlun mountain range of China appears in the southern islands, the ranges meeting in the Japanese Alps. In the vast transverse fissure crossing the main island from the Sea of Japan to the Pacific rises a group of volcanoes, mostly extinct or dormant, with Fuji-

San (Fujiyama), 60 mi. SW of Tokyo, lifting its white cone 12,388 ft.

Most important ports are Yokohama, Kobe, Nagoya, and Osaka. **Tokyo,** the capital, is one of the three largest cities of the world. It has a modern business section centering about the Ginza, a major avenue. The Imperial Palace, surrounded by a moat on a 250-acre site and the white-marble Diet building, erected in 1936, are also in Tokyo. Its International Airport is Asia's busiest.

Tokyo Tower is a 1,089-ft. steel structure built for radio-TV broadcasting and sightseeing.

At Kamakura, 30 mi. SW of Tokyo is the Great Buddha or Daibutsu, a bronze figure 42 ft. 6 in. tall with base, cast in 1252. The Hakone hot spring area is noted for the reflection in Lake Hakone of Fuji-San. Also famous is the Toshogu Shrine at Nikko, where a national park of 347,000 acres preserves the natural beauty of Japanese flora. Kyoto, for 1,000 years a capital city, with massive temples and colorful shrines, is a cultural center. The 2.34-mi. Kanmon undersea highway tunnel connecting Shimonoseki, Honshu, and Moji, Kyushu, is the world's first double-deck tunnel, with one level for vehicles and one for pedestrians. Other projects to link the islands are under study.

**Resources and Industries.** More than half the arable land is used for growing rice, the chief food. Wheat, barley, sweet and white potatoes, tobacco, tea, beans, peaches, pears, apples, grapes, persimmons and mandarins are also produced. Minerals include gold, silver, copper, lead, zinc, chromite, white arsenic, coal, sulphur, salt and petroleum.

The principal industries are iron and steel products, transportation equipment, machinery, electronics, shipbuilding, precision instruments, chemicals, fertilizers, textiles (cotton, wool, silks, synthetics), ceramics, wood products, fisheries.

Japan has become the world's 2nd largest auto producer; 285,000 were exported in 1967.

The index of industrial production (1963=100) zoomed to 162 by 1967.

Japan's shipyards lead the world, especially in construction of super tankers and bulk carriers of over 300,000 tons. The yards can deliver more than 2,380,000 gross tons annually. Japan's own merchant fleet included over 1,400 ships of 1,000 or more gross tons, totaling over 13,400,000 gross tons.

Electric power capacity is est. at 154 billion kwh and annual consumption at 114.5 billion kwh, about half from hydroelectric plants. An atomic power station at Tokai, near Tokyo, began commercial distribution of electricity July 27, 1966.

Major exports are steel and related products, clothing, chemicals, motor vehicles, optical goods, ships, radio receivers, toys.

Tourism is an increasingly important source of foreign exchange—in 1967 476,753 visitors spent about $100,000,000. A World's Fair will be held 1970 in Osaka.

The U. S. is Japan's biggest customer, taking 26-30% of all its exports.

Foreign trade in thousands of U. S. dollars:

| | Imports | Exports |
|---|---|---|
| 1966 | $ 9,524,000 | $ 9,777,000 |
| 1967 | $11,663,000 | $10,442,000 |

**History and Government.** According to Japanese legend, the empire was founded by Emperor Jimmu 660 B.C. Temporal power was exercised by successive families of Shoguns (military dictators), 1192-1867, until recovered by the Emperor Meiji in 1868. The Portuguese and Dutch had minor trade with Japan in the 16th and 17th Centuries. Commodore Matthew C. Perry, USN, opened it to U. S. trade in a treaty ratified 1854. Japan acquired a constitution in 1889. It fought China, 1894-95, gaining Formosa. In war with Russia, 1904-05, both nations lost heavily at Mukden; Russia's fleet was wiped out at Tsushima; Russia ceded S half of Sakhalin and gave concessions in China. Japan annexed Korea, 1910. In first World War Japan ousted Germany from Shantung, took over German Pacific islands as mandates from the League of Nations. Japan took Manchuria, 1931, started war with China 1932, taking Peiping and Shanghai and bombing Nanking, Canton, Tientsin. Japan, frustrated in efforts to have a free hand in the East, started a war against the U. S. by attack on Pearl Harbor, Dec. 7, 1941. Japan surrendered Aug. 14, 1945, and Gen. Douglas MacArthur headed occupation of Japan as Supreme Commander for the Allied Powers.

In a new constitution adopted May 3, 1947, the Japanese people renounced the right to wage war; the Emperor was acknowledged as hereditary symbol of the nation, but gave up claims to divinity; the Diet became the sole law-making authority. The House of Councilors has 250 members elected for 6 yr. terms and the House of Representatives 486 members, elected for 4 yrs., both by popular vote. The constitution separates church and state. Japan has granted suffrage to women, lowered the voting age to 20.

The Emperor is Hirohito, the 124th of his line, born April 29, 1901, succeeded to the throne Dec. 25, 1926; married Jan. 26, 1924, to Princess Nagako Kuni. The Crown Prince is Akihito Tsugu No Miya, born Dec. 23, 1933; married, Apr. 10, 1959, Michiko Shoda. (Issue: Prince Naruhito Hironomiya, born Feb. 23, 1960.) Other children are Princess Shigeko, born Dec. 6, 1925, died July 23, 1961; Princess Kazuko, born Sept. 30, 1929; Princess Atsuko, born Mar. 7, 1931; Prince Masahito, born Nov. 28, 1935; Princess Takako, born Mar. 2, 1939.

Japan was elected 80th member of the UN Dec. 19, 1956. It is a member of UNESCO, World Court, Econ. Comm. for Asia and the Far East, Colombo Plan, International Monetary Fund and GATT.

The United States and 48 other non-Communist nations signed a peace treaty and the U. S. a bilateral defense agreement with Japan, in San Francisco, Sept. 8, 1951; ratified by the Senate, March 20; signed by President Truman, April 15, restoring Japan's sovereignty April 28, 1952. The Senate, in approving the treaty, Feb. 5, advised repudiation of the section of the Yalta agreement that gave to the USSR South Sakhalin, the Kuril Islands and Habomai and Shikotan Islands. Under the treaty, Japan was reduced territorially to the four main islands, but it was to have an opportunity eventually to regain the Ryukyus and Bonin Islands. Japan signed separate treaties with Nationalist China, April 27, 1952; India, June 9, 1952; a declaration with USSR ending a technical state of war, Oct. 19, 1956; in Dec. 1965 Japan and South Korea agreed to resume diplomatic relations.

On June 26, 1968, the U. S returned to Japanese control the Bonin Islands, the Volcano Islands (including Iwo Jima) and Marcus Island. It was agreed the U. S. would continue using Loran navigational stations on Iwo Jima and Marcus.

The Diet, following elections to the House of Councilors July 7, 1968, and to the House of Representatives, Jan. 29, 1967, comprised:

| | Representatives | Councilors |
|---|---|---|
| Liberal-Democrats | 277 | 137 |
| Socialists | 140 | 65 |
| Democratic Socialists | 30 | 10 |
| Communists | 5 | 7 |
| Komei Party | 25 | 24 |
| Independents | 9 | 7 |

Eisaku Sato became Premier Nov. 9, 1964.

**Education and Religion.** The principal forms of religion are Buddhism, with 12 sects, and Shintoism with 13. There are more than 100,000 Shinto shrines, 106,634 Buddhist temples and several thousand Christian churches. Roman Catholics have an archbishop and 3 suffragan bishops.

Nine years of education is compulsory, consisting of six years of elementary and three years of lower secondary education. There were 317 colleges and universities, including the seven main national universities, and 369 junior colleges in 1965. English is the language of commerce and required study in the high schools.

**Defense.** Legislation effective July 1, 1954, established a new national army, navy and air force.

The Ground Self-Defense Force has an authorized strength of 171,500 uniformed personnel and 24,000 reserves. It is divided into 5 armies with 13 divisions. The GSDF has 276 aircraft including 136 helicopters.

The Maritime Self-Defense Force has one fleet, 5 regional districts, a training squadron and an air training command. It has 35,941 uniformed personnel; 214 vessels including destroyers, escorts, subs, torpedo vessels and minesweepers; 194 antisub patrol aircraft and 46 helicopters.

The Air Self-Defense Force has 40,703 uniformed personnel and 1,104 aircraft, two-thirds of which are jets, including Lockheed F-104J Super Starfighters; the remaining third are transports and helicopters.

A mutual assistance pact with the U. S. was signed Mar. 8, 1954. A revised mutual security treaty signed Jan. 19, 1960, and ratified by Japan June 19 was designed to develop close cooperation for defense within the framework of the two nations' respective constitutions.

# Jordan
## AL-MAMLAKAH
## AL URDINIYAH AL HASHIMIYAH
## HASHEMITE KINGDOM OF JORDAN

**Capitals: Amman, Jerusalem. Area: 34,820 sq. mi. Population (UN est. 1967): 2,145,000. Monetary unit: Dinar (.3571 per U. S. $1).**

Jordan is a constitutional monarchy in southwest Asia, formerly under the Palestine Mandate. The country's former name, Transjordan, was dropped Apr. 26, 1949, in favor of the constitutional name, Hashemite Kingdom of Jordan. Hashemite is a family name and honors the loyalty of the original holder, disciple of Mohammed and the Guardian of Mecca.

Two areas comprise the country: Western Jordan, fairly fertile; and Eastern Jordan (Amirate), part fertile, part arid steppe. In the extreme south is its only port, Aqaba, on the Gulf of Aqaba. It shares the Dead Sea (1,296 ft. below sea level) with Israel. Jordan is slightly larger than Indiana.

In 1961 there were 630,725 registered Arab Palestinian refugees.

**Resources and Industries.** The country is largely desert, but the fertile western portion has a high agricultural potential. Principal crops are tomatoes, vegetables, wheat, barley, olives, grapes, citrus fruits and bananas.

Construction was started May 1966 on the Mokheiba Dam on the Yarmuk River, a tributary of the Jordan, to provide electric power and irrigation for 18,000 acres.

Industries include tobacco, flour milling, distilling, building materials, olive oil, soap, mother-of-pearl, textiles, plastics, cement, steel, batteries, leather. Airlines include Royal Jordan (ALYA).

Potash from the Dead Sea and phosphate rock are the main minerals. Phosphate is 30% of value of exports.

**History and Government.** Jordan was part of the Ottoman Empire from the 16th Century until World War I. It was set up within the Palestine Mandate Sept. 1, 1922, and gained its independence in 1946. Abdullah Ibn Al Hussein, born 1882, was proclaimed King, May 25, 1946; he was assassinated by an Arab extremist July 20, 1951. His eldest son was proclaimed King Talal I, Sept. 5, 1951.

Parliament removed King Talal on medical advice, installing his son King Hussein I (born Nov. 14, 1935), May 11, 1952. His first marriage to Sherifa Deena (a daughter, Princess Alya, was born 1956) was dissolved 1958. He married (May 25, 1961) Antoinette Avril Gardiner, of England, entitled Princess Muna. They have two sons, Prince Abdullah, b. 1962, Prince Feisal, b. 1964, and twin daughters, Zein and Aisha, born 1968, but in 1965 King Hussein designated one of his younger brothers, Hassan, to be Crown Prince and heir to the throne.

Legislature comprises a Senate of 30 nominated by the King and a lower house of 60 elected by manhood suffrage. Wasfi El-Tall became Prime Minister Feb. 13, 1965. Jordan is a member of the UN and Arab League.

A decision of the UN to partition former Palestine resulted in guerrilla warfare between Arabs and Jews. After May 15, 1948, Jordan and other members of the Arab League joined in military operations against Israel. Under the truce agreement with Israel, Jordan controlled the old city of Jerusalem.

During 1958 pro-Nasser and Communist groups attempted to undermine Hussein's authority. After King Faisal was killed in the Iraq revolt July 14, King Hussein called on Great Britain for help and British paratroopers were landed, coincident with the landing of United States Marines in Lebanon.

In the 6-day Israeli-Arab war in June 1967 Israel took control of the old city of Jerusalem and Jordanian territory west of the Jordan River.

Arab guerrillas based in Jordan continued raids on Israel during late 1967 and 1968. In Feb. 1968 King Hussein condemned the guerrillas for using Jordan as a base. In March, Israeli Army units attacked a terrorist base in Jordan. This brought a UN Security Council condemnation of Israel and a statement from King Hussein indicating he would not seek to restrain the guerrillas. In April the King ousted two officials who had opposed use of Jordan by terrorist raiders.

The U. S. gave Patton tanks to Jordan in 1965; in Feb. 1968 the U. S. announced resumption of arms shipments to Jordan.

**Education and Religion.** The population is chiefly Arab, of whom the majority are Arab Moslems, 180,000 Arab Christians, and 10,000 Moslem Circassians. The language is Arabic. Public school education is growing, with English and Arabic taught. The Jordanian Univ. was established in 1962 and offers 4-yr. courses in arts and sciences.

# Kenya

**Capital: Nairobi. Area: 224,960 sq. mi. Population (UN est. 1967): 9,948,000. Monetary unit, E. African shilling (7.143 per U. S. $1).**

Kenya, former British Colony and Protectorate which became independent in 1963, extends from its Indian Ocean coast NE to Somalia, N to Ethiopia, W to Uganda, and S to Tanzania. It has twice the area of New Mexico.

The northern three-fifths is arid. Most economic production is centered in the south, a low coastal area and a plateau varying from 3,000 to 10,000 ft. The main products are coffee, tea, cereals, cotton, sisal, dairy products, hides and skins, bark extract, timber and minerals. Kenya is the largest producer of tea in Africa.

In 1953 Kenya became the scene of terroristic activities of the Mau Mau, an oath-bound unit of some of the Kikuyu, Meru, Embu and other tribes which killed Africans and whites during an 8-year rebellion. More than 60,000 Africans were jailed during the rebellion.

Kenya won independence as a dominion within the Commonwealth Dec. 12, 1963, and joined the UN Dec. 16. Jomo Kenyatta, once imprisoned as a Mau Mau leader, became its first Prime Minister. It became a republic within the Commonwealth Dec. 12, 1964, and Kenyatta became its first Pres.

Since independence, Kenya's economy has continued to grow, including both agricultural and manufacturing. Tourism has boomed. Schools and health centers have increased.

On Dec. 1, 1967, Kenya, Uganda and Tanzania set up a 3-nation bloc as a move toward a common market. In Jan. 1968 Kenya and Somalia resumed diplomatic relations as efforts were made to end 4 years of skirmishes caused by "invasions" of nomadic Somali herders seeking grass and water.

In 1968, thousands of Indians, losing their jobs to Africans, emigrated from Kenya to Great Britain.

# Republic of Korea
## DAEHAN-MINKUK

**Capital: Seoul. Area (South Korea): 38,004 sq. mi. Population (UN est. 1967): 29,784,000. Monetary unit: Won (274 per U. S. $1).**

Korea, Land of the Morning Calm, occupies a mountainous peninsula in northeast Asia separating the Yellow Sea from the Sea of Japan. South Korea is about the size of Indiana.

**Resources and Industries.** Chiefly an agricultural country, South Korea has a cultivated area of about 5,095,655 acres. The main crops are rice, barley, wheat, tobacco and beans, but the mountainous terrain, poor soil and cold winters limit agricultural potential.

Division of Korea in 1945 left the South with only light industry and about 10% of the power generating capacity. Large infusions of foreign aid have since helped to build an industrial base especially in mining of tungsten (supplies 13% of world's needs), coal, iron ore, bismuth, fluorspar, graphite and cement. Gold, silver, copper, zinc and petroleum are also present. The fishing, timber, rubber, glass, shipbuilding, electronics and silk industries are expanding rapidly.

The former UN Korean Reconstruction Agency helped develop textiles, steel, straw pulp, rayon, wire, dyes, and automotive equipment.

U. S. support in South Korea has been military, financial, technical and educational. Since 1954 it has totaled more than $2.2 billion. Index of industrial production (1963=100) was 181 for 1967.

Foreign trade in U. S. dollars:

|  | Imports | Exports |
|---|---|---|
| 1966 | $716,000,000 | $250,000,000 |
| 1967 | $999,000,000 | $320,000,000 |

**History and Government.** Korea, formerly the Hermit Kingdom, has a recorded history since the 1st Century B.C. and was united in a kingdom under the Silla Dynasty, 668 A.D. It was at times

associated with the Chinese empire and the treaty that concluded the Sino-Japanese war of 1894-95 recognized Korea's complete independence. After Russia obtained a lease-hold on Port Arthur and developed its big port in Vladivostok, conflicting interests helped bring on the Russo-Japanese war of 1904-1905. Japan occupied Korea; Russia recognized Japan's paramount interest there. In 1910 Japan forcibly annexed Korea as Chosun (Chosen).

At the Cairo conference, Nov. 1943, it was agreed that Korea should be "free and independent." At the Potsdam conference, July, 1945, the 38th parallel was designated as the line dividing the Soviet and the American occupation. Russian troops entered Korea Aug. 10, 1945, U. S. troops entered Sept. 8, 1945. The Soviet military organized Socialists and Communists and blocked efforts to let the Koreans unite their country. Although the Soviet Union, at a foreign ministers' conference in Moscow, Dec., 1945, agreed to a joint trusteeship for Korea, it thwarted efforts to put this into effect. A commission appointed by the UN to supervise elections in Korea in 1948 was denied admission to North Korea. (*See Index for Korean War.*)

The South Koreans formed the **Republic of Korea** in May, 1948, with Seoul as the capital. Dr. Syngman Rhee was chosen President July 20 and the republic was formally proclaimed Aug. 15, 1948. By June 29, 1949, the U. S. had withdrawn its troops, leaving behind a Korean constabulary. President Rhee was reelected to a third term May 15, 1956 and reelected for a fourth term, Mar. 15, 1960, when 85 years old. A national movement spearheaded by college students forced his resignation, Apr. 19, amid charges of corruption in his government and fraudulent elections. Huh Chung, Foreign Minister, became Acting Premier. Dr. Rhee died July 19, 1965, in exile in Hawaii.

A constitutional amendment passed June 15, 1960, replaced an autocratic presidential system with a cabinet system modeled on that of Britain.

In stormy elections, July 29, 1960, the former regime's opposition, Dr. John M. Chang's Democratic party, won control of the National Assembly and House of Councilors.

Unrest stemming from failure of Premier Chang's government to oust corruption and stabilize the economy led to an army coup which seized control May 16, 1961. Premier Chang resigned. Gen. Chung Hee Park became chairman of the ruling junta and later acting President. He was formally elected President Oct. 15, 1963 and re-elected May 1967. A 175-seat National Assembly was elected June 4, 1967 and the fourth republic was inaugurated July 1, 1967.

In 1968, North Korean troops repeatedly staged raids into South Korea, attacking both U. S. and South Korean troops.

South Korea has sent about 50,000 troops to fight alongside the U. S. in South Vietnam.

**Education and Religion.** Christianity, Confucianism, Buddhism and Chondogyo are the principal religions. Christian missionaries established seminaries and institutions of higher learning.

Primary education is compulsory. Many new schools have been built since 1945. In 1965 there were 5,125 primary schools, 1,208 junior high schools, 701 high schools, 131 universities and colleges including 61 junior colleges.

Korea's 24-letter alphabet, a hybrid comprised of ancient Chinese with Tibetan consonants of Sanskrit derivation, is a practical phonetic system.

**Defense.** The South Korea Army numbers about 600,000, and it has a small Navy and Air Force. The U.S. Eighth Army has two combat divisions in Korea with 11,500 men in each. Its commander also is commander of the UN forces there.

# North Korea
## PEOPLE'S DEMOCRATIC REPUBLIC OF KOREA
### CHOSON MINCHU-JUUI INMIN KONGHWA-GUK

**Capital:** Pyongyang. **Area:** 46,540 sq. mi. **Population** (UN est. 1967): 12,700,000. **Monetary unit:** Won (1.2 per U. S. $1).

The People's Democratic Republic of Korea was formed May 1, 1948. The U. S. did not recognize it.

North Korea has good mineral resources that are fairly well developed. The country ranks among the first 5 in the world in the output of tungsten, graphite and magnesite. Other products of significance include lead, zinc, pyrite, cement, iron ore, copper, gold, phosphate, salt and fluorspar. A well developed hydroelectric system and sizeable

reserves of coal provide power needs for industry. Mineral output was valued at $440,000,000 in 1964.

North Korea is slightly larger than N. Y. State.

The import and export trade is largely with Communist countries, particularly China and Russia.

The USSR signed a 10-year military aid treaty with North Korea July 6, 1961, pledging defense protection and financial help. A similar treaty was signed with Communist China. (*See Index for Korean War.*)

Soviet prestige declined in the early 1960s as North Korea sided with the Chinese in the Sino-Soviet dispute. In 1966 Pyongyang showed signs of trying to disengage from the dispute and maintain a more independent stand.

In March, 1967, North Korea and the Soviet Union signed a new defense agreement which was viewed as a further move to isolate the Chinese Communists.

North Korean patrol boats seized the U. S. Navy intelligence ship Pueblo on Jan. 23, 1968, charged it had entered North Korean territorial waters and held its crew captive. (*See Pueblo in Index.*)

# Kuwait
## AL-KUWAIT

**Capital:** Kuwait City. **Area:** 6,178 sq. mi. **Population** (1965 Census): 467,789. **Monetary unit:** Kuwaiti Dinar (.3571 per U. S. $1).

Kuwait, a small Arab state formerly under British protection, became fully independent June 19, 1961. It extends along the northwest coast of the Persian (also called Arabian) Gulf; bordered by Iraq, Saudi Arabia and a Kuwaiti-Saudi neutral zone. Kuwait City is a principal Gulf port. In area it is slightly larger than Connecticut.

**Resources and Industries.** Petroleum, discovered in 1938 and first exported in 1946, is Kuwait's economic mainstay and the nation now is the world's 2nd largest exporter and 5th largest producer of crude oil. Reserves are estimated at more than 70 billion bbls., one-fourth of the free world's total. Crude oil production in 1967 was 824,000,000 bbls. Annual payments to the Kuwait government in royalties and taxes exceed $560,-000,000, some 98% of its income. Per capita income is estimated at over $3,000, probably the world's highest.

Revenues from oil from the Kuwaiti-Saudi neutral zone are split 50-50 with Saudi Arabia.

**History and Government.** Kuwait traditionally is governed by members of the Al-Sabah dynasty founded in 1756. Under a treaty of 1899 Great Britain administered its foreign relations and guaranteed its territorial integrity until it became fully independent June 19, 1961, by mutual agreement. It joined the Arab League 1961, the UN 1963. The nation's first constitution was proclaimed in January, 1963, and the first general elections for a 50-member National Assembly were held.

The Emir Sabah Al-Salim Al-Sabah became ruler Nov. 27, 1965, after the death of his older brother, the Emir Abdulla Al-Salim Al-Sabah. Jaber Al-Ahmed became the new prime minister and crown prince.

**Education and Religion.** The government has utilized its enormous national income from petroleum to create a welfare state that guarantees free medical care, education and social security for all. A 200,000,000 dinar fund aids other Arab nations. There are no taxes except customs duties. Educational facilities are being rapidly expanded. There were, in 1966, 176 schools of all types, with 91,788 students and 5,036 teachers. The University of Kuwait was opened in Oct. 1966. Islam is the official religion, about three-fourths Sunni, the remainder Shia.

**Defense:** Kuwait's Army numbers approx. 2,400.

# Laos

**Capitals:** Vientiane, Luang Prabang. **Area:** 91,-429 sq. mi. **Population** (UN est. 1967): 2,770,000. **Monetary unit:** Kip (240 per U. S. $1).

Laos is a constitutional monarchy of Thai origin in southeast Asia, one of the three former French Indo-Chinese states. It is bounded by Communist China, North and South Vietnam, Cambodia, Thailand and Burma. It is landlocked, smaller than Oregon, largely rugged jungle and mountains, with no railroads and only 3,540 mi. of roads.

Laos became a French protectorate in 1893 and a member of the Indo-Chinese Union in 1899. As in

Vietnam and Cambodia, nationalism aims grew in the 1940s, and the King promulgated a constitution May 11, 1947, providing for a constitutional monarchy under the Luang Prabang dynasty, and a parliamentary government.

Laos became an independent sovereign state by a treaty with France, July 19, 1949. The regime was recognized by the Communist forces in Indo-China in the cease-fire agreements with France, signed in Geneva, July 21, 1954, and by the U. S. and most members of the UN. It joined UN December, 1955.

The King is Sri Savang Vatthana, acceded Oct. 30, 1959, on the death of his father, King Sisavang Vong.

The National Assembly, elected for 5 years, may be dissolved by the King.

Conflicts among neutralist, Communist and anti-Communist factions created a chaotic political situation despite 1954 agreements. Although Laos was intended to be neutral, rivalry between the Communist Pathet Lao movement in the northern third of the country, led by Prince Souphanouvong, and right-wing and neutralist factions prevented integration of the Pathet Lao into the royalist army and government. Armed conflict has increased since 1960 with the arrival of Soviet arms and North Vietnamese technicians and troops. Western and neutral big power proposals have been rebuffed by the Communist bloc which threatened direct intervention.

The 3 Princes heading the 3 factions formed a coalition government in June 1962, with neutralist Prince Souvanna Phouma as Premier. The 14-nation conference that had begun in Geneva May 15, 1961, signed agreements July 23, 1962, guaranteeing neutrality and independence of Laos.

Cease-fire orders were issued several times between May, 1961, and mid-1963, but fighting between the Pathet Lao and neutralist forces intensified during 1963-66.

Early in 1965 there was an unsuccessful rightist coup. Both Laos and U. S. planes bombed Pathet Lao positions along the Ho Chi Minh trail, supply line from North Vietnam to Communist forces in north Laos and South Vietnam, with increasing frequency, 1965-67. A branch of the trail, crossing Laos from Cambodia and called the Sihandur Trail, was also under attack.

Chief products are tin, rice, maize, tobacco, cotton, opium, citrus fruits, benzoin, shellac, teak-wood and coffee. The population comprises peoples of Thai-Indonesian and Chinese origin, mostly Buddhist. French and English are the most important languages. Buddhism is the state religion.

## LATVIA

*See Index for Latvian SSR*

# Lebanon

### AL-JUMHOURIYA AL-LUBNANIYA

**Capital: Beirut. Area: 4,015 sq. mi. Population (UN est. 1967): 2,520,000. Monetary unit: Lebanese pound (3.16 per U. S. $1).**

The Republic of Lebanon, in southwest Asia, occupies a strip along the Mediterranean coast about 120 mi. long and 30 to 35 mi. wide, extending from the Israeli frontier on the S to Syria on the E and N. It is smaller than Connecticut. There is a narrow coastal strip and two main mountain ranges running N and S with fertile land between. Beirut, with one-third of the country's population, is the chief seaport and has a jet airport.

**Resources and Industries.** Trade provides two-thirds of national income, agriculture 15%, industry 12%. Agriculture employs half the workers; chief crops are apples, citrus fruit, olives, tobacco, vegetables, cereals. Manufacturing is growing rapidly; important are food products, textiles, leather goods, cement, oil refining. Tripoli and Sidon are terminals of oil pipelines from Iraq and Saudi Arabia. Large hydroelectric and irrigation projects are being developed.

Lebanon has a free enterprise economy and banking secrecy laws. Fugitive capital from Arab Socialist states has poured into the country. Tourism is also a source of wealth. In 1966 many government officials were replaced in an "efficiency shakeup" aimed at spurring the nation's 5-year development program.

Principal exports are apples, citrus fruits, cereals, textiles, cement.

**History and Government.** Lebanon was formed from the five former Turkish Empire Sanjaks (districts) of North Lebanon, Mount Lebanon, South Lebanon, Beirut and Bekaa, and became, with

Syria, an independent state Sept. 1, 1920, administered under French Mandate 1920-1941. In 1944 France yielded its powers to the Syrian and Lebanese governments. Foreign troops were withdrawn in 1946.

Attempts by several factions to undermine the pro-western administration of Lebanon led to open revolt in May, 1958. Lebanon became the center of international controversy when the United States sent Marines in reply to President Chamoun's call for help and Great Britain supported the American position. The revolt dwindled and American forces were withdrawn in Oct., 1958.

The republic's constitution instituted a democratic parliamentary regime. There is a unicameral legislature (Chamber of Deputies) of 99, elected every four years.

The President normally is elected for a six-year term. The President must be a Christian, the Premier a Moslem. Lebanon is a member of the UN and Arab League.

**Education and Religion.** Christians number about half the population, Moslems of various sects most of the remainder. There are 8 universities and institutions of higher learning in Beirut: American, French, Lebanese, and the private Academy of Arts. Arabic is the official language.

# Lesotho

### (FORMER BRITISH BASUTOLAND)

**Capital: Maseru. Area: 11,716 sq. mi. Population (UN est. 1967): 885,000. Monetary unit: South African Rand (.7143 per U. S. $1).**

The former British dependency, Basutoland, became independent as Lesotho Oct. 4, 1966. An African state without white settlers or landowners, it is about the size of Maryland and completely surrounded by the Republic of South Africa. It was admitted to the UN Oct. 17, 1966.

The land is arid and mountainous, altitudes ranging from 5,000 to 11,000 ft. One railroad connects the capital with South Africa; virtually no paved roads exist. Heavy erosion has hindered agriculture although maize, sorghum, barley, beans and peas are grown. The main industry is livestock raising which produces wool and mohair, the chief exports. The country suffered a severe drought in the early 1960s. About 40% of the men work in South Africa, many in the mines, earning about $2,800,000 a year.

In 1868, Lesotho became a British protectorate upon the request of Moshesh, the Paramount Chieftain, who sought protection against the Boers of South Africa. The British granted a constitution for the area in 1959 providing for a universally elected Legislative Council. The government is headed by a King. There is also a Parliament of 60 elected members, a Cabinet and a Prime Minister.

# Liberia

**Capital: Monrovia. Area: 43,000 sq. mi. Population (UN est. 1967): 1,110,000. Monetary unit: U. S. dollar; also Liberian silver and copper coinage.**

The independent Republic of Liberia lies on the southern side of the west African bulge adjacent to Sierra Leone, Guinea and the Ivory Coast and has an Atlantic coastline of about 350 mi. Much of the country is forest with valuable timber and mineral resources. It is slightly larger than Ohio.

Liberia has no natural harbors. The Free Port of Monrovia, built 1945-48 with U. S. funds, was turned over to the Liberian Government in 1964, with payments to be concluded by 1999. The country is served by several international airlines.

**Resources and Industries.** Iron ore and rubber are the main products; ore production boomed 1964-66.

Lower prices for exported iron ore and rubber, plus increasingly high payments on debts incurred during boom years, depressed the economy in 1967-68; an austerity program was launched.

With U. S. aid and investment by U. S., Sweden, Canada, West Germany, iron and rubber production increased in 1966. Monrovia got the country's first telephone system in 1965. A U. S. loan financed the 30,000-kw Mt. Coffee hydroelectric plant, completed in 1966.

Diamonds and gold are also mined; other products are fibers, palm kernels, rice, cassava, coffee, cocoa and sugar. U. S. aid is promoting schools, hospitals, and food production.

**History and Government.** The population is entirely of African descent. Liberia was founded in 1822 when a settlement was made at Monrovia by Negro freedmen from the U. S. with the assistance of American colonization societies. It was declared a republic July 26, 1847. Its constitution is modeled on that of the U. S. Only persons of African descent may acquire citizenship and only citizens may own real estate.

There is a President elected for one 8-year term (thereafter for 4-year terms); a Senate of 10 elected for 6 years and a House of Representatives of 39, elected for 4 years. The President is William V. S. Tubman, elected for 8 years, May 4, 1943, reelected to 4-year terms, May 1951, 1955, 1959, 1963. Liberia is a charter member of UN.

**Education and Religion.** Christianity predominates. There are nearly 4,000 schools, one university and two colleges. English is the official language.

**Defense.** All citizens between the ages of 16 and 45 are liable for service.

## Libya
### AL MAMLAKA AL LIBIYYA

**Capital: Tripoli and Benghazi. Area: 679,358 sq. mi. Population (UN est. 1967): 1,738,000. Monetary unit: Libyan pound, 100 piastres (.3571 per U. S. $1).**

Libya, first country to receive independence fully under United Nations auspices, is a constitutional monarchy comprising 10 provinces in the former states of Tripolitania, Cyrenaica and Fezzan. Larger than Alaska, it is on the north African coast, bounded by the Mediterranean, UAR, Sudan, Chad, Niger, Algeria and Tunisia.

**Resources and Industries.** Discovery of major oil fields in the northern part of the country beginning in 1957 brought prosperity and an improved standard of living to the country.

Government revenues from taxes on oil companies were increased in 1967. It was estimated that in 1968 the country would be exporting 2,500,000 bbl. a day.

During 1964-66, several hundred schools were built, boosting enrollment from 40,000 to over 250,000. Homes, hospitals, roads and power stations were constructed. Per capita income rose from $40 in 1951 to $425 in 1965. Education and health services are provided free.

Libya is basically agricultural, producing dates, olives, lemons, almonds, figs, grapes and tobacco.

Carpets, leather goods and embroidered fabrics are also produced.

The Government planned in 1966 to construct 100,000 homes in the next 5 years.

**History and Government.** Libya's strategic position has caused it to come under the domination successively of Carthage, Rome, the Vandals, the Ottoman Empire and Italy. After World War II Tripoli and Cyrenaica were placed under British administration, the Fezzan under French.

Emir Mohammed Idris El Senussi (born 1890), spiritual and temporal ruler of the Senussi tribesmen, was recognized by Great Britain as Emir of Cyrenaica, June, 1949. He promulgated a constitution and set up an interim government over internal affairs, Sept. 18, 1949. Libya, as a sovereign state, was approved by the UN, 1949, effective Jan. 2, 1952. A pre-independence constituent assembly chose the constitutional monarchy form of government and named the Emir as King of Libya, Dec. 3, 1950. A hereditary monarchy was proclaimed by King Idris I in Bengazi, Dec. 24, 1951.

Parliament consists of a senate of 42 members with 8-year terms, appointed by the King; and a House of 91, elected for 4-year terms.

Libya is a UN and Arab League member.

**Education and Religion.** Libya's population is mostly Arab Moslems; minority groups include Italians, Jews and others. About 40% are literate. There are public elementary and secondary schools, and private Koranic, Greek, Italian and Jewish schools. There are two universities.

**Defense.** Status quo agreements with Britain and the United States allow each to maintain military forces in Libya, including a large U. S. Air Force base at Wheelus, near Tripoli, but both plan to withdraw. In 1968 Libya launched an extensive renovation of its defense forces.

## Liechtenstein
### FURSTENTUM LIECHTENSTEIN

**Capital: Vaduz. Area: 62 sq. mi. Population (Govt. est. 1966): 19,917. Monetary unit: Swiss franc (4.296 per U. S. $1).**

Liechtenstein is a principality on the Upper Rhine between Austria and Switzerland. It is slightly smaller than the District of Columbia. It received nominal independence in 1866 when the German Confederation dissolved but became practically a dependency of Austria until the Diet declared its complete independence, Nov. 7, 1918. By treaty with Switzerland (1920-23) that country administers its posts and telegraphs, customs and foreign interests. There is no army, only a police force of 26 with 24 auxiliaries.

**Resources and Industries.** The country is highly industrialized. Chief industries are machines and tools, cotton spinning and weaving, false teeth, ceramics and canned food. Finely engraved postage stamps are sold to philatelists around the world. Forty factories exported $35,000,000 in goods in 1965. Thousands of foreign workers are employed in Liechtenstein and constitute about 30% of the resident population.

**History and Government.** Liechtenstein is an hereditary monarchy. Under the constitution, granted in 1921, legislative powers rest in a Diet of 15 members, elected for four years by direct vote, on a basis of male suffrage and proportional representation. The reigning prince is Franz Joseph II. He succeeded his uncle, Prince Franz I, on the latter's abdication March 30, 1938. The Head of Government is Gerald Batliner. Taxes are very low and consequently many international corporations have made their headquarters there.

It is a member of EFTA and the International Court of Justice.

**Education and Religion.** The country is predominantly Catholic. German is the language.

### LITHUANIA
*See Index for Lithuanian SSR*

## Luxembourg
### GRAND-DUCHE DE LUXEMBOURG

**Capital: Luxembourg. Area: 999 sq. mi. Population (UN est. 1967): 335,000. Monetary unit: Luxembourg franc (49.82 per U. S. $1).**

Luxembourg is a European Grand Duchy, bounded by Germany, Belgium and France. It measures only 55 mi. long by 34 mi. wide, smaller than R. I.

**Resources and Industries.** About 9,500 farmers cultivate 336,000 acres. The principal crops are oats, wheat, rye, barley and potatoes.

Luxembourg's iron ore deposits, in the south, are the basis for an important steel industry, using imported coke. It employs more than half the labor force, and accounts for 70% of total industrial production, 90% of value of exports. The country also produces chemicals, beer, tires, tobacco and metal products, cement, roses and dairy products.

**History and Government.** Luxembourg, founded about 963, passed under the domination of Burgundy, Spain, Austria and France from 1443 to 1815; regained autonomy under the Treaty of Vienna, 1815. It left the Germanic Confederation in 1866, its integrity and neutrality guaranteed by the Treaty of London, May 1, 1867. Overrun by Germany in two World Wars, Luxembourg abolished its unarmed neutrality in 1948. Customs union with Netherlands and Belgium was adopted Jan. 1, 1948, expanded to the Benelux Economic Union, Feb. 3, 1958. Luxembourg is a member of the UN, NATO, OECD, Council of Europe, European Coal & Steel Community, Western European Union, and in 1957 signed agreements establishing Euratom and European Common Market.

As a Grand Duchy, Luxembourg is a constitutional monarchy, governed under the Constitution of 1868, with modifications. Legislative power rests with a Council of State of 21, chosen for life, and a Chamber of Deputies, 56 in number, elected by universal suffrage with executive power delegated to a Minister of State and a Cabinet of at least 10 Ministers. The country is headed by Grand Duke Jean (b. Jan. 5, 1921) who became Chief of State Nov. 12, 1964, when his mother, Grand Duchess Charlotte, abdicated in his favor after a 45-year reign. On April 9, 1953, he married Princess Josephine-Charlotte of Belgium. They have 3 sons and 2 daughters; Prince Henri (b. April 16, 1955) is hereditary Grand Duke.

The population is almost entirely Roman Catholic. Education is compulsory. Official languages are French and German; national language is Letzeburgesch.

## Malagasy Republic
### REPOBLIKA MALAGASY
### MADAGASCAR

**Capital: Tananarive. Area: 228,000 sq. mi. Population (Govt. est. 1967): 6,350,000. Monetary unit: Malagasy franc (246.85 per U. S. $1).**

Formerly the French Overseas Territory of Madagascar, the Malagasy Republic is a large island off the SE coast of Africa, from which it is separated by the 240-mi. wide Mozambique Channel. It is about 980 mi. long and 360 mi. wide at its greatest breadth. It is a little smaller than Texas. There is a humid coastal strip on the E, fertile valleys in the mountainous center plateau region, and a wider coastal strip on the W.

The nation is officially called either Madagascar or the Malagasy Republic.

The population consists of many ethnic groups from succeeding waves of immigration, including peoples of SE Asian, Arab and African descent. They speak a language of Malayan origin. About 3,000,000 are animists; 2,000,000 are Christians, about equally divided between Catholics and Protestants.

Madagascar came under a French protectorate, 1885, and was declared a French colony in 1896. It proclaimed itself an autonomous republic Oct. 14, 1958, and was granted full sovereignty effective June 26, 1960. It is a member of the UN and French Community.

About 90% of the population is engaged in agriculture; the chief crops being vanilla (it produces half the world's supply), rice, manioc, beans, maize, sweet potatoes, corn, coffee, cloves, tobacco, sugar cane and cocoa.

The forests are rich in cabinet wood and tanning bark, raffia, resins, gums and beeswax. Water power is abundant. Minerals found include graphite, mica, precious and industrial stones, coal, nickel ore, phosphate, gold, bauxite, uranium and thorium. There are 10,000,000 head of cattle, most of them the humped Zebu type.

In 1966, the U. S. loaned Madagascar $2,700,000 for the improvement of railroad service. In 1966-67 the government's "belly policy" improved agricultural production and thereby cut imports of rice.

## Malawi
### (FORMER NYASALAND)

**Capital: Zomba. Area: 36,100 sq. mi. Population (UN est. 1967): 4,130,000. Monetary unit: Malawi pound (.4167 per U. S. $1).**

Malawi stretches more than 500 mi. north and south along the western and southern shores of Lake Nyasa (Lake Malawi) in southwest Africa. High mountains, dense forests and broad plains make it a scenic though landlocked country. It is about the size of N. Y. State.

Visited by Dr. David Livingstone in 1859, it became a British Protectorate in 1891. From 1953 to 1963 it was a member of the Federation of Rhodesia and Nyasaland. On Feb. 1, 1963, it became internally self-governing and, on July 6, 1964, achieved full independence from Britain. It became a republic within the Commonwealth July 6, 1966. It is a member of the UN. The President is Dr. H. Kamuzu Banda.

Malawi is almost entirely an agricultural country with only a few light industries. Four crops—tea, tobacco, peanuts and cotton—account for 90% of the exports. Other important products are sugar, rubber, soybeans and coffee. Farming improvements are being pressed in hopes of building exports. Illiteracy is high, but a program for universal primary education is underway; colleges are planned and the U. S. has promised $1,000,000 to help build a technical college.

In 1967-68, factories were built for textiles, shoes, sugar, farm implements, and other products formerly imported. The Republic of South Africa, in May 1968, provided loans to build a rail line into Mozambique and to help construct a new capital for Malawi at Lilongwe.

Population is mostly African; there are about 12,000 Indians and 8,000 of European descent.

## Malaysia
### FEDERATION OF MALAYSIA

**Capital: Kuala Lumpur, Selangor. Area: 128,430 sq. mi. Population (UN est. 1967): 10,071,000. Monetary unit: Malayan dollar (3.07 per U. S. $1).**

Occupying the southern part of the Malay Peninsula in SE Asia and the northern part of the island of Borneo, the Federation of Malaysia is the world's largest producer of rubber and tin. Total area is larger than Arizona.

The Federation was formed Sept. 16, 1963. It included the old Federation of Malaya (11 Malayan states which had become an independent constitutional monarchy and member of the Commonwealth Aug. 31, 1957), plus the formerly-British Singapore (an island and city off the southern tip of the Malay Peninsula), Sabah (former British North Borneo) and Sarawak (former British colony in NW Borneo). The British-protected Sultanate of Brunei in north Borneo did not join.

Indonesia harassed the new nation with guerrilla action 1963-65. After Indonesian Pres. Sukarno lost power, 1965-66, Malaysia and Indonesia agreed Aug. 11, 1966, to restore normal relations; full relations were restored Aug. 31, 1967.

On Aug. 9, 1965, the separation of Singapore from the Federation was announced under an agreement by Malaysia and Singapore officials that this was the best way to end tensions between the ethnic Chinese, largest group in Singapore and in the Federation as a whole, and the Malays, 2nd largest group, who were in control of the Federation government. (*See Index for Singapore.*)

Malaysia's population, before Singapore's separation, was composed of: Malays and closely related groups, 40%; Chinese, 42%; Indians and Pakistanis 10%; others, 8%. With Singapore's departure, the Malays became the numerical majority in Malaysia, with ethnic Chinese totaling over a third of the population.

The 11 Malay states and their capitals are: Johore (Johore Bahru), Kedah (Alor Star), Kelantan (Kota Bharu), Malacca (Malacca), Negri Sembilan (Seremban), Pahang (Kuantan), Penang (George Town), Perak (Ipoh), Perlis (Kangar), Selangor (Kuala Lumpur), Trengganu (Kuala Trengganu). Largest in area is Pahang, 13,820 sq. mi.; largest in population is Perak, 1,488,754 (1963).

With the exception of Malacca, Penang, Sabah and Sarawak, each of the states has a hereditary ruler; the above exceptions have governors, as did Singapore. Each state has its own flag, constitution and legislative assembly.

In 1966 the Government announced that Sabah and Sarawak would be known as East Malaysia and the 11 states as West Malaysia.

The monarch, known as the Yang di-Pertuan Agong (Paramount Ruler, ceremonial chief of state who has no political power) is elected by a council of hereditary rulers of the Malayan states.

**Resources and Industries.** Rubber, tin, iron ore, palm oil and copra are the main products. Rubber, much of it produced by new high-yield trees, accounts for 41% of exports; tin, of which Malaysia produces 33% of the world output, amounts to 13% of her exports.

Other agricultural products are rice, coconuts, tapioca, sugar, pepper, camphor. Rubber trees were originally introduced from Brazil. Small-scale industry includes rubber goods, pottery, cement, pewterware, furniture, bricks, tiles, soap.

A $17,300,000 jet airport was opened at Kuala Lumpur in Aug. 1965.

**Religion and Language.** The Malays and some others are Moslems; other religions are Buddhist, Christian and Hindu. Malay is the national language; Malay and English are official languages.

**Defense:** Malaya expanded its small Army, Navy and Air Force in 1963 in anticipation of the formation of the Federation of Malaysia and Britain agreed to extend its defense and mutual assistance treaty with the new nation. Malaysia also receives military aid from Australia. In 1966, after the peace agreement with Indonesia, it was announced British troops would leave Sabah and Sarawak.

### SABAH
#### (Former British North Borneo)

Sabah, formerly North Borneo, occupies the northern part of Borneo, third largest island in the world, 400 mi. east of Malaya in the Pacific Ocean. It has an area of 29,388 sq. mi. and a population (1963) of 498,031, including 80,000 Chinese and a few Europeans. Included is the island of Labuan, area 35 sq. mi., which was united with North Borneo, July 15, 1946. Exports are mainly rubber, copra, timber, tobacco, firewood, cutch, fish and hemp. Capital: Jesselton. The Philippines also claims title to Sabah.

### SARAWAK

Sarawak lies along the northwest coast of Borneo, between the mountains and the China

Sea. Its coast line is 450 mi. long and its area 48,250 sq. mi. Its population (1963) was 809,737. The capital is Kuching. The chief exports are sago, pepper, gold, plantation rubber. It refines petroleum from the Seria field in Brunei. Sarawak was freed from the Sultanate of Brunei in 1840 by James Brooke, an Englishman who was named Rajah in 1841. In 1946, after Japanese occupation, the 3rd Rajah ceded the country to Britain.

## Maldive Islands

**Capital: Malé. Area: 112 sq. mi. Population (1967 Census): 103,801. Monetary unit: Rupee (5.952 per U. S. $1).**

The Maldive Islands are a group of 19 atolls containing 1,087 islands, 210 of which are inhabited. Totaling about twice the area of the District of Columbia, they are in the Indian Ocean 300 mi. SW of the southern tip of India. The Maldives obtained full independence from Great Britain on July 26, 1965, in an agreement under which Britain retained its RAF base on Gan Is. in Addu Atoll in the southern Maldives. The Maldives became a member of the UN Sept. 21, 1965.

The islands had been a British-protected state since 1887. The country became a republic in 1953 but returned to the status of a Sultanate by decision of its Assembly, Feb. 22, 1954. The Assembly elected Al Amir Mohammed Farid Didi as Sultan; Ibrahim Nasir is Prime Minister. Until the 1965 agreement, Britain was responsible for the islands' defense and foreign relations.

The people are Moslems and seafarers. Coconuts, fruit and millet are grown; the chief occupation is fishing. Production of processed fish, to be marketed in Ceylon, is the main industry. Also exported is coir, a coconut fiber.

## Mali
### REPUBLIC OF MALI

**Capital: Bamako. Area: 464,000 sq. mi. Population (UN est. 1967): 4,745,000. Monetary unit: Franc (246.85 per U. S. $1).**

The Republic of Mali, formerly the Sudanese Republic (1959-60) and a one-time French Overseas Territory in West Africa, is a landlocked nation which is larger than Texas but smaller than Alaska.

Mali is mostly a vast plain in the upper basins of the Senegal and Niger Rivers, extending N into the Sahara.

From the 11th to 15th Centuries the area was part of the great Mali Empire which stretched from the western Sudan to the Atlantic; Timbuktu was a renowned center of Islamic learning.

Under provisions of the 1958 French constitution French Sudan became the Sudanese Republic, an autonomous republic within the French Community and formed with neighboring Senegal Jan. 17, 1959, the Mali Federation. Complete independence was proclaimed June 20, 1960. Senegal withdrew from the federation Aug. 20, 1960, and Sudan took the name of Republic of Mali Sept. 22. It became a UN member Sept. 28, 1960. Mali remained outside the French Community, but signed economic and cultural agreements with France. It joined Ghana and Guinea Apr. 29, 1961, in a Union of African States which did not become effective. On June 8, 1963, Mali and Senegal ended their differences with customs, trade and railway traffic agreements, and use of Senegalese harbors by Mali.

In 1968 Mali joined 8 other nations in forming the West African Regional Group, aimed at promoting joint economic benefits.

The President and ministers are responsible to the National Assembly, members of which are elected to five-year terms.

The country is mainly agricultural and pastoral. Millet, rice and peanuts are the chief crops. Cotton, rubber and river fishing are also important. Livestock raising is a major prop of the economy. Trade is primarily with neighboring countries.

## Malta

**Capital: Valletta. Area: 122 sq. mi. Population (1967 Census): 319,000,000. Monetary unit: Pound (.4167 per U. S. $1).**

Malta lies in the Mediterranean 58 mi. S of Sicily and 180 mi. from Africa. The island of Malta itself is 95 sq. mi.; the other two islands in the group are Gozo, 26 sq. mi., and Comino, one sq. mi. Total is twice the size of the District of Columbia.

For 35 centuries Malta was under successive rule by Phoenicians, Carthaginians, Romans, Arabs, Normans, the Knights of Malta, France and Britain (which annexed Malta in 1814). It achieved limited self-government in 1887; home rule on Oct. 24, 1961. On Sept. 21, 1964, it became independent, with the British monarch as head of state, represented by a governor general, and agreed to permit British forces to maintain a base for 10 years. It is a member of the Commonwealth, Council of Europe and UN. A House of Representatives with 50 members is elected by universal suffrage; the Prime Minister and Cabinet are chosen from members of the House.

Once a vital British stronghold, it withstood Axis air attacks for 3 years during World War II, but is now used only as a supply base for the British Navy, with consequent loss of employment for Maltese. Population density in 1965 was 2,578 per sq. mi.; there is continuous migration, much of it to Australia, the United Kingdom and Canada.

The protection of NATO was extended to Malta in 1965.

A 5-year development program, started in 1964, offers attractions to new industries and encourages tourism through building of modern hotels.

Leading industries are ship repairing, food and beverages, textiles and tourism. Gross national product rose from $142,500,000 in 1965 to $156,-500,000 in 1966. Visiting tourists rose from 23,000 in 1962 to 100,000 in 1967. Historic sites, a casino and village fetes are among the attractions.

## Mauritania
### ISLAMIC REPUBLIC OF MAURITANIA

**Capital: Nouakchott. Area: 419,231 sq. mi. Population (UN est. 1967): 1,100,000. Monetary unit: CFA franc (246.85 per U. S. $1).**

The Islamic Republic of Mauritania, former French Overseas Territory in West Africa, is bounded by the Atlantic Ocean, the Rio de Oro (Spanish), Algeria, Mali and Senegal. Population is largely Moorish. Mauritania is about four-fifths the size of Alaska.

The economy has been agricultural and pastoral. Products include dates, grain, tobacco, fish. There are large herds of cattle, camels, sheep and goats and large deposits of iron and copper.

But a large new iron mine was opened in 1968 to add to the nation's annual production of 8,000,000 tons of iron ore; fishing, which produced 200,000 tons of fish in 1967, was being expanded; a copper mine was under construction; a new cattle slaughterhouse and freezing plant was opened, also in 1968.

In accordance with the provisions of the 1958 French constitution, Mauritania became an autonomous state Nov. 28, 1958, and became fully independent Nov. 28, 1960. It elected to remain outside the framework of the French Community, but has expressed its desire to retain close ties with France. Prime Minister Mokhtar Ould Daddah, appointed June 26, 1959, became President by popular vote in August, 1962. It is a member of the UN.

During the Israeli-Arab war of June, 1967, Mauritania was one of 7 Arab countries that severed diplomatic relations with the U. S.

## Mauritius

**Capital: Port Louis. Area: 720 sq. mi. Population (UN est. 1967): 774,000. Monetary unit: Rupee (11.1 per U. S. $1).**

Mauritius, an island in the Indian Ocean 550 mi. E of Malagasy (Madagascar), became an independent nation within the Commonwealth on Mar. 12, 1968, after 158 years of British rule. The Hindu majority favored independence, whereas Moslems, Creoles and whites, fearing oppression by the Hindu majority and loss of close economic ties with Britain, opposed it. The country became the 124th member of the UN Apr. 24, 1968.

Mauritius has one of the world's most complex racial, religious and political mixtures as well as one of the world's highest population densities. The people belong to five main groups: About 380,000 Hindus; 210,000 Creoles, Christians of mixed European and African descent; 125,000 Moslems; 25,000 Chinese and 25,000 whites. Although the official language is English, French is spoken by most of the educated and the whites; Creole, a French patois, is the lingua franca. Chinese and the Indian languages Hindi, Tamil and Telegu are also spoken.

The country has a nearly one-crop economy, sugar. Population has boomed in recent years and

unemployment runs about 25%. Commonwealth subsidies support sugar prices and aid the economy.

Mauritius was uninhabited until 1638 when the Dutch settled there and gave the island its present name in honor of Prince Maurice of Nassau. The French took over in 1721 and introduced sugar cane and African slaves. The British, who seized the island in 1810, brought Hindus and Moslems from India to work the sugar plantations.

Mauritius was the home of the famed dodo, a heavy, flightless bird which became extinct in the 17th Century.

## Mexico

### ESTADOS UNIDOS MEXICANOS

**Capital: Mexico City. Area: 758,259 sq. mi. Population (Govt. est. 1967): 45,671,000. Monetary unit: Peso (12.49 per U. S. $1).**

Second most populous nation in Latin America and third largest in area, Mexico compiled an enviable record for orderly progress, social improvement and fiscal responsibility in the middle decades of the 20th Century.

With housing, health, farm and industrial programs, the nation has lifted itself and its people into the mainstream of the modern world; life expectancy, for example, has been raised from 39 years in 1940 to 67 years in 1968.

Ever-growing streams of foreign visitors (958,000 in 1962; 1,656,000 in 1967) find spectacular scenery, striking art and architecture, cosmopolitan and colonial cities and luxurious resorts. The mountainous topography provides a variety of climates, from temperate to tropical.

The Sierra Madre Occidental Mtns. run NW-SE near the west coast. The Sierra Madre Oriental Mtns., a continuation of the Rockies, run near the Gulf of Mexico coast nearly as far S as Veracruz.

Between the two ranges lies the central plateau of Mexico, altitude from 5,000 to 8,000 ft. with a delightful climate and with the vegetation and products of the temperate zone varying with the altitude. The lowlands along the coast are tropical, rising to subtropical in the foothills, with a heavy rainfall on the Gulf side. Along the Pacific slope and in the interior irrigation is needed. Mexico is nearly 3 times the size of Texas.

Tampico and Veracruz, on the Gulf, are the busiest of Mexico's 49 ocean ports.

Mexico's population is composed of descendants of the Toltecs, Aztecs, Mayas and the Spaniards who conquered and colonized the country. Archeological remains of the early Indian civilizations are important tourist attractions.

The Summer Olympic Games were held at Mexico City in Oct. 1968.

**Resources and Industries.** Mexico is rich in minerals and timber. It is the second largest producer of silver; also important are gold, copper, lead, zinc, antimony, mercury, arsenic, amorphous graphite, molybdenum, sulphur, coal and opal. Petroleum production is large, reaching 140,000,000 bbl. in 1966. The industry is nationalized. Natural gas is supplied by the U. S. Electric power generated in 1966 was 18.5 billion kwh.

Farming, stock raising and fishing are important. The land is rich, but the rugged topography and lack of sufficient rainfall are major obstacles. Crops and farm prices are controlled, as are export and import. Large estates have been expropriated; since 1915 the government has distributed over 135,000,000 acres to small farmers through landholding communities (ejidos). Major irrigation projects in Sonora and Sinaloa have increased production of cotton and wheat.

In 1966 the Lerma Plan, an attempt to improve production and living conditions among 8,000,000 people in western rural areas, was launched with the aid of a $150,000,000 Bank for Inter-American Development loan.

Principal export crops are cotton, coffee, cane sugar, tomatoes, cattle, fresh and frozen meats. Coffee is valued at more than $100,000,000 annually; other major crops are corn, rice, tobacco, garbanzos, cocoa, sisal, bananas. About 50% of the world supply of sisal comes from Yucatan, in the S.

Mexican industry is producing products formerly imported, especially in iron and steel, chemicals, electric goods. Other products are cotton, wool and synthetic textiles, flour, beverages, soap, cigarettes and cigars, rubber, paper, rubber products, cement, shoes, glass, furniture and tiles. Mexico is famous for industrial and native handicraft in silver, pottery, leather, wood, fibers and textiles. The U. S. buys a large portion of Mexico's exports.

Index of industrial production (1963=100) was 119 in 1965, 142 in 1967. The estimated gross na-

tional product (in U. S. dollars) was $21.7 billion for 1966, $24.7 billion (est.) for 1968.

Tourism is an important revenue source. Gross earnings in 1967 totaled $960,000,000.

Foreign trade, in thousands of U. S. dollars:

|      | Imports     | Exports     |
|------|-------------|-------------|
| 1966 | $1,605,000  | $1,229,000  |
| 1967 | $1,748,000  | $1,191,000  |

**History and Government.** Mexico was the site of advanced Indian civilizations before the Spanish conquest. The Mayas, an agricultural people, moved up from Yucatan and built immense stone pyramids and invented a calendar. The Toltecs were overcome by the Aztecs, who founded Tenochtitlan 1325 A.D., now Mexico City. Hernando Cortes, Spanish conquistador, destroyed the Aztec empire, 1519-1521.

After 3 centuries of misrule the people rose, under Fr. Miguel Hidalgo y Costilla (a priest), 1810, Fr. Morelos y Pavon (another priest), 1812, and Gen. Agustin Iturbide, who made independence effectual Sept. 27, 1821, but made himself emperor as Agustin I. A republic was chosen in 1823; Iturbide was executed 1824.

Mexican authority extended into the present American Southwest and California until Texas revolted and established a republic in 1836; the Mexican legislature refused recognition but was unable to enforce its authority there. After numerous clashes, the U.S.-Mexican War, 1846-48, resulted in the loss by Mexico of the lands north of the Rio Grande, about half its total area.

French arms supported an Austrian archduke on the throne of Mexico as Maximilian I, 1864-67, but pressure from the U. S. forced France to withdraw troops, and led to his defeat by Mexican patriots under Benito Juarez, and subsequent execution. A dictatorial rule by Porfirio Diaz, president 1877-80, 1884-1911, led to demands for economic amelioration and fighting by rival forces until the new constitution of Feb. 5, 1917, provided social reform. Since then Mexico has developed large-scale programs of social security, labor protection and school improvement. A constitutional provision requiring management to share profits with labor became effective Dec. 12, 1963.

Mexico is a federal democratic republic of 29 states, with President, legislature and judiciary elected by universal suffrage; two territories with governors appointed by the President, and a federal district containing Mexico City. The President is elected for 6 years and thereafter ineligible; 60 senators for 6 years and deputies for 3 years, ineligible for reelection until one term has intervened. The deputies are one to every 200,000 pop.

In 1967 congressional elections, the long-dominant Institutional Revolutionary party won 87% of the vote and all 178 contested seats in the Chamber of Deputies.

**Education and Religion.** Education is secular, with primary education free and compulsory up to 15 years of age. Vocational instruction particularly in agriculture is promoted and there are many technical schools. The National University of Mexico continues an educational foundation of 1551 A.D. Spanish is the language.

Most of the people are Roman Catholics. All church real estate is vested in the nation, but care of church buildings is the responsibility of the clergy.

**Defense.** Military training is compulsory; draftees serve one year, then form part of the reserves. The regular army is comprised of about 50 infantry battalions and other units. In addition Mexico has a conscript Army of approx. 250,000 organized into national service divisions, plus a small Navy and an Air Force. Mexico is a member of the UN and OAS.

## Monaco

### PRINCIPAUTE DE MONACO

**Capital: Monaco. Area: 370 acres. Population (Govt. est. 1961): 22,297. Monetary unit: French franc (U. S. 20.2¢).**

Monaco is a small principality on the Mediterranean surrounded on all but the sea side by France. It is noted for an exceptionally mild climate and magnificent scenery .

There is a local police force of 200.

**Resources and Industries.** Monaco's fame as a tourist resort and international conference city is widespread. Its revenues derive from indirect taxation, a tobacco monopoly, postage and the gambling tables of the Monte Carlo Casino.

About a dozen subsidiaries of large drug manufacturers were established in Monaco and their drugs entered France free of duty. In October, 1962, when the customs union with France ex-

pired, France put up customs barriers pending imposition of taxes and ended domestic mail rates. By a 1963 agreement the customs barriers were eliminated in April and domestic mail rates restored. French citizens living in Monaco less than 5 years must pay income taxes to France. Drug laboratories became subject to French controls; this applied also to their products sold in France.

Monaco endeavored to cover possible revenue losses by enacting a profits tax on Monaco companies that do 25% of their business outside Monaco. The company tax rate is now 35%.

**History and Government.** An independent principality for over 300 years. Monaco has belonged to the House of Grimaldi except during the French Revolution. It was placed under the protectorate of Sardinia in 1815 (Treaty of Vienna), and under that of France, 1861. The Prince of Monaco was an absolute ruler until a constitution was promulgated in 1911.

A new constitution, proclaimed Dec. 17, 1962, provided for female suffrage and abolition of capital punishment, and established a supreme tribunal to guarantee fundamental liberties. The legislature (National Council) consists of 18 members elected for 5 years.

The ruler of Monaco is Prince Rainier III who succeeded his grandfather, Prince Louis II, who died May 9, 1949. He married Grace Kelly, American motion picture actress, Apr. 18, 1956. A daughter, Princess Caroline Louise Marguerite, was born Jan. 23, 1957. The heir apparent, Prince Albert Alexander Louis Pierre, was born Mar. 14, 1958. Princess Stephanie Marie Elizabeth was born Feb. 1, 1965.

During 1965 a feud developed between Prince Rainier and Aristotle S. Onassis, shipping magnate who owned 52% of the Societe des Bains de Mer, which owns the Casino, several hotels and night clubs. The Prince pressed a development plan to attract more middle-class vacationers. Onassis opposed the plan.

In March, 1967, the government bought out Onassis' holdings for $8,000,000.

# Mongolia
**BUGHUT NAIRAMDAKH MONGOL ARAT ULUS**
**MONGOLIAN PEOPLE'S REPUBLIC**
**Capital:** Ulan Bator (Urga). **Area:** 592,664 sq. mi. **Population** (UN est. 1967): 1,170,000. **Monetary unit: Tughrik** (4 official rate per U. S. $1).

The Mongolian People's Republic comprises Outer Mongolia in northeastern Asia. It is bounded on the N by the Siberian provinces of USSR, and on 3 other sides by Communist China. It is larger than Alaska.

NW Mongolia is an elevated plateau, well watered by lakes and rivers; SE and S Mongolia include part of the Gobi Desert. Travel and communication and building methods are being modernized, but the population remains nomadic.

**Resources and Industries.** Livestock raising is the principal industry, including cattle, sheep, camels and oxen. Other activities under the planned economy include food processing, wool-cleaning, tanning, shoe-making, and production of building materials. Mongolia mines fluorspar, gold, coal, tungsten, marble, and some uranium. Oil has been found.

**History and Government.** One of the world's oldest countries, Mongolia reached the zenith of its power in the 13th Century when Genghis Khan and his successors conquered all of China and extended their influence as far W as Hungary and Poland. In later centuries, the empire dissolved and Mongolia came under the suzerainty of China.

With the advent of the 1911 Chinese revolution, Mongolia, with Russian backing, declared its independence. The Mongolian People's Republic was proclaimed Mar. 13, 1921. China, however, continued to claim the country until 1945 when recognition of independence was given.

A Constitution of 1940, since amended, vested power in the Great People's Khural from which is drawn a 7-member Presidium.

Mongolia has sided with the Russians in the Sino-Soviet dispute and has received large amounts of Soviet aid for the development of mines and industry. A Mongolian-Soviet mutual assistance pact was signed Jan. 15, 1966.

In 1963, Great Britain became the first Western country to extend diplomatic relations to Mongolia. Parts of Ulan Bator, the capital, were inundated by a severe flood July, 1966, causing loss of life and property. Mongolia is a UN member.

**Education and Religion.** There are primary, secondary and technical schools, and a university in Ulan Bator. An Academy of Sciences was founded in 1953. Buddhist Lamaism is the leading religion.

# Morocco
**AL-MAMLAKA AL-MAGHREBIA**
**Capital: Rabat. Area:** 172,834 sq. mi. **Population** (UN est. 1967): 14,140,000. **Monetary unit: Dirham** (5.06 per U. S. $1).

The monarchy of Morocco lies on the NW coast of Africa separated from Europe by the 8-mile-wide Strait of Gibraltar. It is bounded by Algeria, Spanish Sahara, the Mediterranean and the Atlantic. Until 1956 it was a protectorate of France and Spain.

It consists of 5 natural regions: A series of mountain ranges (Riff, facing Gibraltar; Middle Atlas, extending NW of Marrakesh; Upper Atlas, and Anti-Atlas); a series of rich plains in the W; the alluvial plains of Haouz in the SW; the "mesata," a well-cultivated series of plateaus in the center; a pre-Saharan zone extending from S to E.

The inhabitants largely are a mixture of Arabs and the original Berbers.

**Tangier,** a seaport with pop. 1965 of 164,232, and surrounding territory in extreme NW corner on the Atlantic, was internationalized during the French and Spanish protectorates. The Tangier Zone comprised 225 sq. mi. A provisional agreement in July 1956, provided for Tangier's incorporation into Morocco as a new province. International rule officially ended Oct. 29, 1956. Certain free zone provisions were restored in 1962.

**Ifni,** Spanish coastal enclave, comprises 740 sq. mi. and 49,889 population, mostly of the Ait Ba Amaron tribe, which demands return of the enclave to Morocco.

**Resources and Industries.** Morocco is primarily agricultural and pastoral. Cereals rank 1st among agricultural products, including barley, wheat and corn. Fruit and vineyards are abundant and dates a regular crop. Carpets, leather goods, fezzes, woolen and silk stuffs are among the manufactures.

Morocco ranks 2nd to U. S. in production of phosphate rock and is 1st in phosphate exports. It produces 10% of the world's cobalt and 2% of manganese ore. Other minerals are antimony, zinc, lead ore, oil and anthracite.

Wheat is normally one of Morocco's food exports, but droughts have forced the country to import it in some years; in 1967 the U. S. gave Morocco 140,000 tons. In 1967 and 1968 construction was started on two river dams for irrigation projects.

Modern industrialization has expanded a number of industries. Casablanca handles heavy annual tonnages. Its 11,480-ft. jetty shelters 2½ mi. of piers.

Tourism attracts 500,000 visitors annually to see Morocco's casbahs, Roman ruins, old fortresses and oases.

**History and Government.** Morocco is a remnant of the Shereefian Empire founded by the Arabs at the close of the 7th Century which encompassed all NW Africa and most of the Iberian Peninsula.

It came under French influence because of its proximity to Algeria. A general uprising of tribes in 1910 culminated in the dispatch of a French expeditionary force that occupied Fez in 1911. Frequent uprisings continued for two decades until the exile of Abd-el-Krim in 1926 and the surrender of Sidi Ali Hociene in 1933.

The French section encompassed the whole of Morocco except for the Spanish-controlled Ifni enclave, the Cape Juby area in the SW, and the international Tangier area.

France ended its protectorate over Morocco by a joint declaration and protocols between the two countries, Mar. 2, 1956 which recognized Morocco's independence and suspended the protectorate treaty (Treaty of Fez, 1912). Spain signed similar agreements, Apr. 7, 1956, recognizing Morocco's independence. Spain agreed to relinquish its Southern Morocco Protectorate effective Apr. 10, 1958. French forces completed their withdrawal in Sept. 1961. The U. S. built 3 large Air Force bases but evacuated them under a 1957 agreement, keeping only a Navy air transport base at Kenitra on the Atlantic.

Sidi Mohammed Ben Youssef, third son of Moulay Youssef (reigned 1912-1927), was proclaimed Nov. 18, 1927, as Mohammed V. His eldest son, Moulay Hassan, was invested as Crown Prince and heir apparent July 9, 1957. On Aug. 11, 1957, the ruler's title of King (Melek) was ordered used instead of Sultan.

Mohammed V died Feb. 26, 1961, and the Crown Prince ascended the throne as King Hassan II. Under a constitution approved by referendum Dec. 7, 1962, Morocco became a constitutional

monarchy. The first 144-seat Parliament was elected by universal vote May 17, 1963.

Morocco accepted U. S. and USSR military and economic aid on a basis of non-interference in its internal affairs. It has agreements with France on economic, technical and cultural cooperation. It is a member of the UN and Arab League.

**Education and Religion.** The native population is largely illiterate, but trade schools and agricultural training centers have been considerably developed. There are Koranic, Franco-Moslem and French schools. The most notable Islamic school is Kairoween University in Fez. Arabic is the official language. The population is Sunni Moslem.

**Defense.** Morocco's volunteer Army numbers approx. 40,000.

## Muscat and Oman
### SULTANAT MASQAT WA OMAN

**Capital:** Muscat. **Area:** 82,000 sq. mi. **Population (est. 1964):** 750,000. **Monetary unit:** Indian Rupee (7.579 per U. S. $1).

The Sultanate of Muscat and Oman is an independent, absolute monarchy occupying the E corner of the Arabian Peninsula and including the tip of a nearby peninsula, Ruus-al-Jebal, to the N. The Sultanate has a coastline of 1,000 mi. along the Gulf of Oman to the NE and the Arabian Sea to the SE. Climate is generally hot and dry.

There is a narrow coastal plain up to 10 mi. wide, a range of barren mountains with Jebal Akhbar, the highest, reaching c. 9,900 ft., and a wide, stony, mostly waterless plateau averaging 1,000 ft. altitude. The Sultanate is the size of Utah.

Exports are mainly dates and some dried fish, limes and pomegranates. Cultivated areas also produce bananas, grapes, wheat, vegetables, coconuts and frankincense.

Oil was discovered in 1964, giving promise of a boost to the sparse economy.

The people are predominantly Arab, but there are also Indians, Baluchi, Negroes and others. The language is Arabic, but Hindi, Urdu, Baluchi and others are also spoken. The religion is mainly the Ibadhi branch of the Moslem faith.

The area's history is a long one. Early Semitic tribes were conquered by the Persians about 550 B.C.; later conquerors were the Parthians, the Caliphs of Baghdad, Turks, Portuguese and Persians again. The present al-bu-Said dynasty threw off the last of Persian rule 1744.

The armed forces include two regiments, a small Air Force and other troops and a gendarmery regiment.

## Nauru

**Capital:** Nauru. **Area:** 8 sq. mi. **Population (UN est. 1966):** 6,056. **Monetary unit:** Australian dollar (.9010 per U. S. $1).

Nauru, one of the world's smallest nations, became independent Jan. 31, 1968, after 80 years of foreign rule. In the southwest Pacific about 30 mi. S of the Equator and 1,300 mi. NE of Australia, Nauru is comfortably affluent because of its highgrade phosphate deposits.

The native population of 3,100 (about 3,000 foreign residents work in the phosphate industry) receive about £1,700 (U. S. $4,000) per capita a year in royalties from sale of phosphates, and with independence royalties were expected to increase. However, this bright economic picture is not without flaws; the deposits are expected to become depleted around 1990.

The island was discovered in 1798 by the British but was formally annexed to the German Empire in 1888. After World War I, Nauru became a League of Nations mandate administered by Australia. During World War II the Japanese occupied the island and shipped 1,200 Nauruans to the fortress island of Truk as slave laborers, including the nation's present Head Chief Hammer De Roburt.

In 1947 Nauru was made a UN trust territory, administered by Australia on behalf of the three trust powers—Australia, Great Britain and New Zealand. Because of its small size Nauru has not sought membership in the UN.

## Nepal

**Capital:** Katmandu. **Area:** 54,362 sq. mi. **Population (UN est. 1967):** 10,500,000. **Monetary unit:** Nepalese rupee (10.125 per U. S. $1).

Nepal is a constitutional monarchy in the Himalayas, bounded on the N by China (Tibet) and E, S and W by India. It is about the size of Arkansas.

There are many fertile valleys lying in the slopes of the lofty mountains, including Mt. Everest, on the Tibet border. The capital is in the fertile val-

ley of Katmandu, 15 mi. long and 20 wide, which supports 450,000 inhabitants and is noted for its many, lavishly decorated shrines.

Virtually closed to the outside world for centuries, Nepal is now linked to India and Pakistan by modern roads and air service.

A northern section called Mustang, at a mean altitude of 15,000 ft. and bordered on 3 sides by Tibet, is actually a district of Nepal although it has its own Rajah and a measure of internal autonomy.

Nepal has established a 500 sq. mi. game preserve for elephants, tigers, rhinoceroses, leopards, boars, crocodiles and over 500 species of birds.

**Resources and Industries.** Nepal has rich forests and quartz deposits. The country exports jute, rice, grain, cattle, hides, wheat and drugs, and imports textiles, sugar, salt, hardware, etc.

U. S. technical aid has made possible settlement of the fertile but once inaccessible Rapti Valley with a 53-mi., $500,000 highway. Nepal also receives financial aid from India, Australia, Communist China and USSR. Its 2nd 5-year plan stresses hydroelectric power and roads

**History and Government.** Nepal was originally divided into petty principalities, the inhabitants of one of which—the Gurkhas—became dominant about 1769. Maharajadhiraja Tribhubana Bir Bikram (born June 30, 1906), member of the Shah family, returned from exile, ended the system of rule by hereditary premiers of the Ranas family, Hindu Rajputs, 1848-1951, who kept the Kings virtual prisoners. He established a popular government Feb. 18, 1951.

King Tribhubana died Mar. 13, 1955, and was succeeded by his son, Mahendra Bir Bikram Shah Deva, officially crowned May 2, 1956.

King Mahendra promulgated a new constitution, Dec. 16, 1962, providing for a four-tier governmental system culminating in a National Assembly (Panchayat) of 125 elected members. There are no political parties.

**Education and Religion.** There are more than 2,400 English schools in addition to Sanskrit and Nepali schools and other institutions of learning. Buddha was born at Lumbini in South-Central Nepal. Hinduism and Buddhism are the main religions. Polygamy, child marriage and the caste system were abolished in 1963.

**Defense.** The Army consists of about 25,000 regular infantrymen. Nepal is a UN member.

## Netherlands
### KONINKRIJK DER NEDERLANDEN

**Capital:** Amsterdam. **Area (land):** 15,800 sq. mi. **Population (UN est. 1967):** 12,597,000. **Monetary unit:** Guilder (3.615 per U. S. $1).

The Kingdom of the Netherlands, a constitutional monarchy in northwestern Europe, is bounded by Germany, Belgium, and the North Sea. Its surface is flat, with an average heigh above sea level of 37 ft., with much land below sea level, reclaimed and protected by dikes, of which there are 1,500 mi. The country is about the size of Vermont and Massachusetts combined.

Since the end of World War II the government has been draining the IJsselmeer, formerly Zuider Zee, and converting the reclaimed land into farms. The total will add over 550,000 acres. By 1968, 305,000 acres had been reclaimed.

The Hague is the seat of government, but Amsterdam is the sole capital of the kingdom and the inaugurations of sovereigns are held there.

**Rotterdam,** located along the principal mouth of the Rhine, handles the most cargo of any ocean port in the world. The heart of the city, destroyed by a Nazi air attack in 1940, has been completely restored. A subway line was opened in 1968.

A 3.125-mi. causeway bridge for autos, longest in Europe, was opened Dec. 15, 1965, in South Holland.

**Resources and Industries.** Forty percent of the land is given to pasture, farming takes 30%, forest 7%, horticulture 3%. Of the land 90% is in holdings of fewer than 50 acres and more than 50% of fewer than 10 acres. Cereals, potatoes, sugar beets and other crops are raised. Agriculture and fishing engage approx. 12% of the workers. Dairy products are an important industry; the cheese products are famous and the cattle high grade. Tulips and other flowering bulbs and roots are grown. The Dutch bulb is not indigenous to Holland but originated in Persia, whence it was taken to Holland several hundred years ago.

The most important industries are shipbuilding, the manufacture of machinery, textiles (including rayon), and chemical products; also brewing and distilling and flour milling. Amsterdam is famous

for diamond cutting; Delft for pottery. Eindhoven has electrical and radio factories. Coal, oil and salt are found. Natural gas reserves are large. Index of industrial production (1963=100) was 129 for 1967.

Canals, of which there are 4,203 mi., are important in transportation. The Rhine, Meuse and Schelde reach the sea through the Netherlands and carry enormous traffic.

Royal Dutch Airlines (KLM) is one of the world's largest international airlines, reaching 120 cities in 75 countries.

Foreign trade in thousands of U. S. dollars:

|      | Imports     | Exports     |
|------|-------------|-------------|
| 1966 | $8,018,000  | $6,750,000  |
| 1967 | $8,338,000  | $7,288,000  |

History and Government. After the empire of Charlemagne (d.814) fell apart, the Netherlands—Holland, Belgium, Flanders—split among counts, dukes and bishops, passed to Burgundy and thence to Charles V of Spain. His son, Philip II, sent the Duke of Alva as governor to check the Dutch drive toward political freedom and Protestantism (1568-1573). William the Silent, prince of Orange, led a confederation of the northern provinces, called Estates, in the Union of Utrecht, 1579. The Estates retained individual sovereignty, but were represented jointly in the States-General, a body that had control of foreign affairs and defense. In 1581 they repudiated allegiance to Spain. The rise of the Dutch republic to naval, economic and artistic eminence came in the 17th Century.

The United Dutch Republic ended 1795 when the French formed the Batavian Republic, ended 1798. Napoleon made his brother Louis King of Holland, 1806; Louis abdicated 1810 when Napoleon annexed Holland. In 1813 the French were expelled. In 1815 the Congress of Vienna formed a kingdom of the Netherlands, including Belgium, under William I, with Brussels and The Hague as alternative capitals. In August, 1830, the Belgians revolted and formed a separate kingdom, which was recognized by the European powers in November, 1831; later by Holland.

The constitution, promulgated 1814, and subsequently revised, assures a hereditary constitutional monarchy. Executive power rests exclusively in the Crown (the Queen and ministers). Legislative powers are exercised jointly by the Crown and Parliament (States-General) of two Chambers: First Chamber, 75 members, elected for six years (one half every third year) by the provincial legislatures, and the Second Chamber, 150 Deputies, elected for four years directly. Universal suffrage for citizens of both sexes over 23 years of age and proportional representation are in force. The sovereign exercises the executive authority through a Council of Ministers, the President thereof corresponding to a Prime Minister. There is a State Council named by the sovereign, of which she is president, to be consulted on all legislative and some executive matters.

The reigning sovereign is Queen Juliana Louise Emma Marie Wilhelmina, born April 30, 1909, only daughter of former Queen Wilhelmina. She succeeded to the throne, Sept. 6, 1948, on the abdication of her mother. Queen Juliana on Jan. 7, 1937, married Prince Bernhard of Lippe-Biesterfeld, born June 29, 1911, known as the Prince of the Netherlands since the accession of Juliana. They have 4 daughters, Princess Beatrix Wilhelmina Armgard, born Jan. 31, 1938, heir presumptive, married Claus von Amsberg, West German diplomat, Mar. 10, 1966; Princess Irene Emma Elizabeth, born Aug. 5, 1939, married Prince Carlos Hugo, Bourbon-Parma, Apr. 29, 1964; Princess Margriet Francisca, born Jan. 19, 1943, in Ottawa, Canada, married Pieter van Vollenhoven, Jan. 10, 1967, and Princess Maria-Christine, born Feb. 18, 1947.

On Apr. 27, 1967, Princess Beatrix gave birth to a son, Willem-Alexander, Prince of Orange, first male heir to the throne in three generations.

Education and Religion. There is complete liberty of worship. The royal family belongs to the Netherlands Reformed Church (Prot.). The population is 38% Protestant; 40% Roman Catholic; others, including non-church members, 22%.

Education is obligatory from ages 6 to 15. Instruction is free or subject to a small fee, in both public and denominational schools and teachers are paid by the state. There are universities in Amsterdam (two), Utrecht, Leyden, Delft (Engineering), Groningen, Wageningen (Agriculture), Rotterdam (Commerce), Nijmegen, Eindhoven (Engineering) and Tilburg.

Defense. Army service is compulsory between the ages of 20 and 40. The Navy consists of one carrier, two cruisers, 12 destroyers, 24 frigates, 6 submarines and minor miscellaneous craft. The Netherlands modern Air Force contributes to NATO's tactical air force.

The Netherlands is a member of the UN, NATO, EEC, Council of Europe and Benelux.

Sovereignty over the Netherlands East Indies was transferred to the Republic of Indonesia, excepting Netherlands New Guinea, Dec. 27, 1949. The latter was transferred to the UN, 1962, and then to Indonesia, 1963.

SURINAM AND NETHERLANDS ANTILLES

A revision of the Netherlands charter, promulgated Dec. 15, 1954, raised Surinam and the Netherlands Antilles to equality with the Netherlands homeland in the Kingdom of the Netherlands, with complete internal autonomy and a voice in government of the kingdom. The kingdom is represented in each by the governor who also is head of government for his respective county. Local governments comprise the governor, council, ministers, and representative bodies (Staten), the latter elected by universal suffrage.

Surinam, also known as Dutch Guiana, is on the N coast of South America, between French Guiana on the E and British Guiana on the W; forests and savannahs on the S stretch to the Tumuc Humac Mountains. The area is approximately 55,400 sq. mi. The population (est. 1964) is 325,000. Capital: Paramaribo.

The country is rich in minerals and hydroelectric power is being developed on a large scale. Oil was discovered, 1966. Exports include bauxite, alumina, lumber, sugar, rice, citrus, coffee, bananas and shrimp. The Surinam gulder (SFlorin) is 1.87 per U. S. $1.

The Dutch by the Treaty of Breda, 1667, ceded New Netherland (New York) to England in exchange for Surinam.

The Netherlands Antilles consist of two groups of islands in the West Indies: Curaçao, Aruba and Bonaire are near the South American coast; St. Eustatius, Saba and the southern part of St. Maarten are southeast of Puerto Rico. Northern two-thirds of St. Maarten belongs to French Guadeloupe; the French call the island St. Martin. Total area of the two groups is 393 sq. mi., including: Aruba 70, Bonaire 110, Curaçao 180, St. Eustatius 12, Saba 5, St. Maarten (Dutch part) 16.

Tourism in recent years has been increasing, especially to the islands of Curaçao and Aruba.

The Netherlands Antilles population (est. 1967) was 212,000. Willemstad is the capital. Chief products are corn, pulse, salt and phosphate; principal industry is the refining of oil. On Curaçao the Royal Dutch Shell and on Aruba the Standard Oil Co. of New Jersey have large oil refineries, receiving crude oil from Venezuela.

# New Zealand

Capital: Wellington. Area: 103,736 sq. mi. Population (UN est. 1967): 2,726,000. Monetary unit: New Zealand dollar (.8946 per U. S. $1).

The main islands of New Zealand lie in the South Pacific about 1,200 mi. E of Australia. The total area is about that of Colorado. Including remote islands to the N and the Ross Dependency to the S, the reach of New Zealand is from the tropics to Antarctica.

Snow-topped mountains, smoking volcanoes, deep fjords, boiling geysers, golden beaches and the glow-worm caves of Waitomo are among the scenic attractions.

New Zealand comprises North Island, 44,281 sq. mi.; South Island, 58,093 sq. mi.; Stewart Island, 670 sq. mi.; Chatham Islands, 372 sq. mi. Both the North and South Islands slightly exceed 500 mi. in length. Cook Strait, separating the two islands, is only 16 mi. wide at its narrowest.

Included within the administrative boundaries of New Zealand are Campbell Island, Solander Island, the Three Kings, Kermadec Islands, Auckland, Antipodes, Bounty and Snare Islands, a total area of 320 sq. mi. Annexed to New Zealand are Niue Island, and Tokelau Islands in the Pacific totaling 104 sq. mi., with a population of 7,018 (1965). In 1965, the Cook Islands (pop. 1965 20,519, area 93 sq. mi.) became self-governing although New Zealand retains responsibility for defense and foreign affairs.

Wellington and Auckland, on North Is., are the chief ports. South Is. has the picturesque Southern Alps and Tasman, Fox and Franz Josef Glaciers. There are 15 named peaks over 10,000 ft., the highest being Mt. Cook, 12,349 ft. Christchurch and Dunedin are the main cities of South Is.

Resources and Industries. New Zealand is largely dependent on agricultural products for export in-

come; wool, meat and dairy products account for 91% of the total.

Exports in 1966 totaled $1.08 billion (in U. S. dollars), in 1967 $.99 billion; imports in 1966 were $1.09 billion, in 1967 $.96 billion.

Agriculture engages 13.5% of the population, manufacturing industries 26%. Private enterprise is basic in the economy, but state ownership or regulation affects many industries. Railroads are largely state-owned and operated.

Food processing is the largest industry with value added amounting to over $200,000,000; forest products account for more than $162,000,000.

The pulp and paper industry on North Is. is partly powered by natural steam from volcanic areas. Construction of the first iron and steel plant started 1966. Natural gas was discovered at Kapuni, North Is., 1967, and was to be piped to several towns. A large hydroelectric plant was under construction at Lake Manapouri, South Is., to provide power for a proposed aluminum smelter.

About 100,000 tourists visit New Zealand annually, some 17,000 of them from the U. S.

New Zealand changed its currency from pounds to dollars July 10, 1967; the old currency was also to continue in use until late 1968.

**History and Government.** New Zealand was discovered in 1642 by Abel Janszoon Tasman, a Dutch navigator, and its coasts were explored by Capt. James Cook, 1769-1770. British sovereignty was proclaimed in 1840, with organized settlement commencing in the same year. Representative institutions were granted in 1853. The Colony became a Dominion in 1907 and an independent member of the Commonwealth in 1947.

The native Maoris are Polynesians. Early in the 19th Century they numbered an est. 200,000; violence and European diseases cut them to 40,000 by the end of the century. Recently they have increased at 4% annually, twice the rate of other New Zealanders, and totaled 206,054 in Dec. 1966.

Government consists of a governor general, representing the British Crown; a House of Representatives whose members are elected by universal suffrage for a 3-year term; a Prime Minister and Cabinet who are members of the House and accountable to it.

New Zealand is a member of the UN, Commonwealth, SEATO and Colombo Plan.

In national elections Nov. 26, 1966, the 80 seats in the House of Representatives were distributed: National party 44, Labor 35, Social Credit 1.

New Zealand's tax rates reach a maximum of 67½ cents per dollar at the $10,080 income level. "Cradle-to-grave" social security includes maternity, school, medical, hospital, medicine, pension and other benefits.

**Education and Religion.** Education is free and compulsory between the ages of 7 and 15. There are universities in Dunedin, Christchurch, Wellington, Auckland, Hamilton, and Palmerston North. The Anglican and Presbyterian Churches have the largest followings.

**Defense.** There are regular army, navy and air forces, supplemented by a Territorial Army and a Naval Reserve. A proportion of youths become eligible for military training at age 20. New Zealand had a force of 360 men in Vietnam in 1967.

**Ross Dependency,** administered by New Zealand since 1923, comprises Antarctic territory between the 160th meridian E. Long. and 150th W. Long. south of the 60th parallel of S. Lat., including Edward VII Land and portions of Victoria Land with total est. area of 160,000 sq. mi.

## Nicaragua
### REPUBLICA DE NICARAGUA

**Capital: Managua. Area: 53,938 sq. mi. Population (UN est. 1967): 1,783,000. Monetary unit: Cordoba (7.026 per U. S. $1).**

Nicaragua, largest of the Central or Middle American States, lies between the Caribbean and the Pacific with more than 200 mi. of coastline on each. The country is bordered by Honduras on the N and Costa Rica on the S. The Cordillera range of mountains, including many volcanic peaks, runs NW-SE through the middle of the country. Between this range and a range of volcanic peaks to the W lie Lake Managua, 38 mi. by 15, and Lake Nicaragua, 100 mi. by 45, of great importance to the transport system. The government-owned Pacific railroad, Corinto to Leon and Managua to Granada, 171 mi., is the principal rail line. There is daily air service to the U. S. and South America.

**Resources and Industries.** The nation has valuable forests, some gold is mined. It is essentially an agricultural country, but industrialization, including oil refining, is growing. On the broad tropical plains of the east coast, bananas, cotton, fruit and yucca are cultivated. Products of the western half include coffee, sugar cane, corn, beans, cocoa, rice, tobacco and wheat.

Foreign trade, 1967, was: exports $146,000,000, imports $204,000,000, both up from 1966.

**History and Government.** After gaining independence from Spain, 1821, Nicaragua was united for a short period with Mexico, then with the United Provinces of Central America, finally becoming an independent republic, 1838.

The constitution, revised in 1960, provides for a Congress of two chambers, a House of Deputies of 45 members and a Senate of 18 members, all elected by popular vote for 4 years. Ex-presidents also serve in the Senate and are appointed for life. The President is elected for 4 years and may not succeed himself.

Pres. Rene Schick Gutierrez, elected Feb. 3, 1963, died Aug. 3, 1966, and Congress elected Dr. Lorenzo Guerrero, a vice president, to fill out the unexpired term. Anastasio Somoza Debayle was elected president Feb. 5, 1967.

Nicaragua was one of the Central American nations visited in July 1968 by U. S. President Johnson and promised increased aid.

**Education and Religion.** Roman Catholicism is the prevailing religion.

A Central University of Nicaragua was established in 1941. The University of Leon, since 1947 called National University of Nicaragua, was founded in 1814. Spanish is the official language.

Nicaragua is a member of the UN and OAS.

## Niger
### REPUBLIC OF THE NIGER

**Capital: Niamey. Area: 489,189 sq. mi. Population (UN est. 1967): 3,546,000. Monetary unit: CFA franc (246.85 per U. S. $1).**

The Republic of the Niger, a former French Overseas Territory in the heart of West Africa, is bounded by Libya, the Algerian Saharan Department of Oases, Chad, Upper Volta, Dahomey, Federation of Nigeria, and Mali. Chief access to the country, a vast plateau, almost twice the size of Texas, is by air. The Niger River flows through the western corner.

Under provisions of the 1958 French constitution, Niger became fully independent Aug. 3, 1960, and joined the UN Sept. 20. It elected to remain outside the framework of the French Community proper, but signed a bilateral agreement Apr. 24, 1961, retaining close ties with France. It is a member of an economic alliance called the Council of the Entente formed May 29, 1959; other members are Dahomey, Ivory Coast, and Upper Volta.

Niger has limited resources and is an agricultural and pastoral land. Peanuts are the principal cash crop; livestock (cattle, sheep, camels, donkeys, goats) are second in importance. Cotton is being promoted.

In 1967 Niger signed an agreement with France for exploitation of large, high-grade uranium deposits in the north. Television is used to spread instruction to some village schools.

## Nigeria

**Capital: Lagos. Area: 356,669 sq. mi. Population (UN est. 1967): 61,450,000. Monetary unit: Pound (.3571 per U. S. $1).**

The Federation of Nigeria, Africa's most populous country, became independent in 1960. Larger than Texas and Oklahoma combined, it lies on the southern side of the West African bulge, between Dahomey and Cameroon, with Niger Republic to the N and Chad NE. It comprises nearly 250 tribal and linguistic groups, including the Hausas in the N, Ibos in the E, Yorubas in the W. Nigerians constitute almost one-fifth of the population of the African continent.

Nigeria was composed of four distinct autonomous regions each with its own administration: Northern, Western, Mid-Western and Eastern, plus the Federal Territory of Lagos. Included in Nigeria's territory is the northern portion of the former British Cameroons, a British UN trusteeship that ended in 1961.

Its rich natural resources include oil, coal, iron, limestone and natural gas. It produces 45% of the world's columbium ore (important in steel alloys).

Cocoa is the main crop. Production of oil has grown rapidly; in 1965 oil exports were valued at $190,000,000, doubling the 1964 total and, for the 1st time, exceeding the value of cocoa exports. Other exports are tobacco, tin, palm oil, palm

kernels, cotton lint, hides and skins, lumber, rubber and peanuts.

Nigeria became a sovereign country Oct. 1, 1960, and a republic within the British Commonwealth Oct. 1, 1963. It is a member of the UN. Nigeria's first federal constitution guaranteed personal liberties and regional autonomy, and provided for a Parliament comprised of a 312-member House, directly elected, and a Senate, indirectly elected.

In 1966 there were two military coups and periods of interracial strife ending a long period of coalition governments of the majority Northern Region and other regions. On Jan. 15, junior Army officers seized control; Gen. Johnson Aguyi-Ironsi, an easterner, made himself head of state, Prime Minister Abubakar Tafawa Balewa was assassinated. On Aug. 1, Col. Yakubu Gowon, a northerner, became head of state; Gen. Ironsi was assassinated.

On May 30, 1967 the Eastern Region seceded from Nigeria and proclaimed itself the Republic of Biafra. The move plunged the country into civil war.

The war went badly for the outnumbered 13,-000,000 Ibos of Biafra. By mid-1968 at least 100,000 including women and children were reported facing starvation as supplies were blockaded by the Nigerian Government forces. Attempts by international groups to bring in aid were stymied, despite an urgent appeal, July 11, by U. S. President Johnson that food be allowed to reach the starving.

Islam is the principal religion of Northern Nigeria and among the Yorubas. English is the official language.

# Norway
### KONGERIKET NORGE

**Capital:** Oslo. **Area:** 125,181 sq. mi. **Population (UN est. 1967):** 3,784,000. **Monetary unit: Krone, pl. kroner (7.15 per U. S. $1).**

Norway occupies the W part of the Scandinavian Peninsula in NW Europe. It shares borders with Sweden, Finland and the USSR. The rocky W coast is cut deep by fjords of scenic grandeur. Norway is about the size of New Mexico.

The country's greatest length is 1,100 mi.; its width varies from 270 to only 4 mi. at the narrowest point. The coastline, including the fjords and largest of the 150,000 islands, is 12,500 mi. long. The climate is mild and moist on the W coast, but fairly cold and dry in the E.

The midnight sun is a phenomenon of the North Cape area. The sun does not set from the middle of May until the end of July, nor does it rise above the horizon from approximately Nov. 20 to Jan. 24. The Northern Lights are visible in winter.

**Resources and Industries.** More than 72% of the land is unproductive and only 4,300 sq. mi. are cultivated; rivers and lakes occupy 5,000; forests 29,455.

Forests supply a sizable wood-processing industry. Huge quantities of cod, herring, mackerel and salmon are caught. Mining is an important industry and the country yields copper, pyrites, nickel, iron, zinc, lead, aluminum.

Lacking oil or sufficient coal (only 442,000 tons of coal were produced in Spitsbergen in 1964), Norway has harnessed its waterfalls to provide power. Manufacturing, mainly processing of forest, fishing and mining products, consumes 65% of the hydroelectric output, which is over 48 billion kwh per year. Norway has the highest per capita consumption of electricity in the world.

Farm products include oats, rye, potatoes, dairy products and fruits.

Norway's merchant marine now ranks 3rd in the world, with 2,835 ships totalling 17,000,000 gross tons Jan. 1, 1967.

Unemployment is virtually non-existent.

Foreign trade in thousands of U. S. dollars:

| | Imports | Exports |
|---|---|---|
| 1966 | $2,403,000 | $1,563,000 |
| 1967 | $2,746,000 | $1,736,000 |

**History and Government.** The first supreme ruler of Norway was Harald the Fairhaired who came to power in 872 A.D. Between 800 and 1000, the Vikings raided and occupied parts of Europe. Christianity was introduced 1030.

The country was united with Denmark 1381-1814, and with Sweden 1814-1905. The Swedish union was dissolved in 1905 and a Danish prince was named King Haakon VII of Norway. Nazi Germany attacked Norway Apr. 9, 1940 and held it until liberation May 8, 1945.

Norway is a constitutional monarchy.

The King of Norway is Olav V (born July 2,

(1903), son of Haakon VII. On the death of his father he became King Sept. 21, 1957. He married (Mar. 21, 1929) Princess Martha of Sweden (who died Apr. 5, 1954). The heir to the throne, Crown Prince Harald, was born Feb. 21, 1937. The King also has two daughters, Princess Ragnhild Alexandra (June 9, 1930) and Princess Astrid (Feb. 12, 1932). Both are married to commoners.

Legislative power is vested in the Storting, whose 150 members are elected for four years. The Labor party, dominant for 30 years, was swept from power by a coalition of non-Socialist parties Sept. 13-14, 1965.

**Education and Religion.** The Evangelical Lutheran religion is endowed by the state and its clergy are nominated by the King. All religions enjoy complete freedom of worship.

Since 1860, education has been free and compulsory from ages 7 to 14. The universities of Oslo (founded 1811) and Bergen are subsidized by the state, as are the Technological Institute (Trondheim) and the Agricultural College (Aas).

**Defense.** Military service is universal and compulsory. Conscripts are drafted at 20, serve 12-15 months. The Navy includes destroyers, frigates, submarines, etc. There is a small Air Force.

Norway is a member of UN, NATO, EFTA, Nordic Council and Council of Europe.

### SPITSBERGEN
#### (Svalbard)

Spitsbergen is a group of mountainous islands in the Arctic Ocean, c. 23,957 sq. mi., pop. varying seasonally from 1,500 to 3,000, incorporated in Norway as Svalbard. The largest, West Spitsbergen, c. 15,000 sq. mi., seat of governor, is about 370 mi. N of Norway. Named Svalbard by Norse who discovered it in 1194, it was visited by Barents 1596 and became locale of whaling until 19th Century. By a treaty signed in Paris, February, 1920, major European powers recognized the sovereignty of Norway, which incorporated it 1925. Sealing, fishing are followed; rich coal deposits are worked by Norwegians and Russians. Mt. Newton (West Spitsbergen) is 5,633 ft. tall.

### OTHER ISLAND POSSESSIONS

**Jan Mayen,** a desolate area of 147 sq. mi. in the Arctic Ocean between Greenland and Northern Norway used as a weather station.

**Bouvet Island,** area 22 sq. mi., is an uninhabited tract in the Southern Atlantic.

**Peter I Island,** with an area of 97 sq. mi., lies in the Antarctic and is uninhabited.

**Norwegian Antarctic Dependency** (Queen Maud Land), lying between the Falkland Islands dependency and the Australian Antarctic dependency, was placed under Norwegian sovereignty Jan. 14, 1939.

# Pakistan

**Capital:** Islamabad. **Area:** 365,529 sq. mi. **Population (UN est. 1967):** 107,258,000. **Monetary unit: Pakistan rupee (4.789 per U. S. $1).**

Pakistan became a sovereign nation Aug. 14, 1947, when what had been the British Empire of India achieved independence and was partitioned into two countries, Pakistan and India. At first a dominion, Pakistan declared itself a republic on Mar. 23, 1956. Its name means "Land of the Pure" in Urdu.

Pakistan is divided into two sections, West Pakistan and East Pakistan. The two areas lie nearly 1,000 mi. apart on opposite sides of India.

West Pakistan, larger than Texas, is 310,403 sq. mi. It adjoins Iran, Afghanistan, India and the Arabian Sea. To the NE lies the disputed Kashmir region.

East Pakistan, about the size of Arkansas, is 55,126 sq. mi. It is bordered by India, Burma and the Bay of Bengal.

West Pakistan is a land of rugged mountains and river valleys, where irrigation aids agriculture, the occupation of 80% of the people. The Indus flows for c. 1,000 mi. from the base of the Himalayas to the Arabian Sea and with its tributaries supplies reservoirs, canals and hydroelectric plants. In the W are the Hindu Kush Mts., with Tirich Mir 25,230 ft. In the N is Mt. K2 (Godwin Austen), 28,250 ft., 2nd highest in the world. The climate is mostly dry with little rainfall and summer temperatures up to 120° F.

East Pakistan has vast delta areas where the Ganges and the Brahmaputra-Jamuna reach the Bay of Bengal. It has a rainfall up to 100 in. in the monsoon season, July-September.

Islamabad, under construction for 6 years, became the official seat of government in 1967. Rawalpindi had been the interim capital since 1959 when it replaced Karachi as the capital. Ayub Nagar in East Pakistan serves as a 2nd capital.

Resources and Industries. Rice, wheat, cotton, oilseeds, tea, tobacco, sugar, flour, wool, jute and fish are important products. Minerals include sulphur, gypsum, salt, chromite, cement, petroleum, gas, coal, asbestos, antimony, magnesite and silica. Pakistan has the world's largest jute production, 5-6,000,000 bales annually, constituting its largest export.

West Pakistan manufactures cotton textiles (its largest industry), wool, silk, rayon, cement, card and paper board, sugar, chemicals, dyes, synthetic fertilizers. East Pakistan manufactures burlap and other jute products, paper, fertilizers, cotton textiles and produces tea.

The Indus Basin irrigation project which Pakistan shares with India, a $2 billion development aided by Western nations, is scheduled for completion in 1970. The multipurpose Karnafuli Dam, largest U. S. aid-financed project in East Pakistan, was inaugurated in 1962.

Foreign trade in thousands of U. S. dollars:

| | Imports | Exports |
|---|---|---|
| 1966 | $900,000 | $601,000 |
| 1967 | $1,101,000 | $604,000 |

History and Government. The land now called Pakistan shares the 5,000-year history of the India-Pakistan subcontinent. At the present day sites of Harappa and Mohenjo Daro, the Indus Valley Civilization, with large cities and elaborate irrigation systems, flourished c. 4000-2500 B.C.

Armies of Alexander the Great invaded regions which are now Pakistan c. 326 B.C.

A lasting influence on Pakistan was the arrival of Islam with the first Arab invasion of 711 A.D.

After World War I the Moslems of British India felt handicapped as a minority and began agitation for minority rights in elections and preservation of communal entities.

Mohammad Ali Jinnah (1876-1948) was the principal architect of the Pakistan state. A lawyer who studied in England, he was a leader of the Moslem League from 1916, and worked for constitutional reform and dominion status for India. Convinced Moslem-Hindu relations in government were irreconcilable, he first advocated a separate Moslem state in 1940.

When the British withdrew Aug. 14, 1947, the Islamic majority areas of India acquired self-government with dominion status in the Commonwealth and Jinnah became the first Governor General (1947-1948). He died in 1948.

After creation of a republic in 1956, President Iskander Mirza briefly took power with the aid of the army in Oct. 1958 but was supplanted that same month by Gen. Mohammad Ayub Khan.

A new 5-level political system was inaugurated June 13, 1959. As amended in 1967, it comprises a pyramidal series of councils called Basic Democracies. It puts Presidential elections in the hands of 120,000 representatives chosen by secret ballot in units of 700-800 voters each.

Gen. Ayub, who had become President in the 1958 coup, became the first elected President on Feb. 17, 1960, under the councils system.

Pakistan's 2nd constitution came into force June 8, 1962, providing for a stronger presidential government and a unicameral legislature, the National Assembly, comprised of 218 members including 8 reserved for women and 10 for "men of outstanding merit."

President Ayub was reelected Jan. 2, 1965. His sweeping land reform, started in 1959, abolished feudalism. Reforms in law and education were also launched.

(See article on India for disputes over Kashmir, Rann of Cutch, etc.)

Education and Religion. About 88% of the population are Moslem. Minorities include 10,000,000 Hindus, 700,000 Christians, and smaller groups of Parsees and Buddhists. Free and compulsory elementary education is a prime goal. There are 12 universities. Of the many languages spoken, Urdu and Bengali are national languages; English is official language.

Defense. Pakistan has an Army, Navy and Air Force, and civil defense units. Army service is voluntary.

Pakistan is a member of the UN, Commonwealth, SEATO and CENTO; has a regional defense agreement with Turkey (1954); mutual defense agreement with the U. S. (1954 and Mar. 5, 1959), and other agreements of trade, friendship, and cooperation with the U. S. By 1965, the U. S. had provided Pakistan with nearly $4 billion in economic and military aid. Following border warfare between India and Communist China in 1962 and increase in U. S. aid to India, Pakistan made commercial and aid agreements with Communist China

and Indonesia. U. S. aid to both Pakistan and India was suspended during the 1966 war over Kashmir but both economic aid and "nonlethal" military aid were resumed in 1966.

## PALESTINE
*See Index for Israel, Jordan, United Arab Rep.*

# Panama
## REPUBLICA DE PANAMA

Capital: Panama. Area: 29,208 sq. mi. Population (UN est. 1967): 1,329,000. Monetary unit: Balboa (1 per U. S. $1).

The Republic of Panama occupies the isthmus of Panama, connecting Central and South America. It is smaller than South Carolina. It has a shoreline of 477 mi. on the Caribbean and a shoreline of 767 mi. on the Pacific. Its width varies from about 37 to 110 mi. It is bounded by Colombia and Costa Rica, and is bisected by the U. S. Canal Zone.

Resources and Industries. Panama has extensive forests, and exports mahogany. Only about half of the rich arable land is cultivated. Sufficient cement, clay and salt are produced for domestic needs. Bananas are the main export, rivaled by products of a large petroleum refinery (which imports crude oil). Also exported are pineapples, cocoa, coconuts, sugar, shrimp.

Due to easy shipping regulations and strictures in the U. S., merchant tonnage registered in Panama since World War II ranks high in size. Registered tonnage of ships 1,000 or more tons Jan. 1, 1967, was 4,574,000 gross tons.

History and Government. The coast of Panama was discovered by Rodrigo de Bastidas, sailing with Columbus for Spain in 1501, and was visited by Columbus in 1502. Vasco Nunez de Balboa crossed the isthmus and "discovered" the Pacific Ocean Sept. 13, 1513. Spanish colonies were ravaged by Francis Drake, 1572-95, and Henry Morgan, 1668-71. Morgan destroyed the old city of Panama which had been founded in 1519. Freed from Spain, Panama joined Colombia in 1821. Separatist forces in Panama sought to gain independence from Colombia several times.

Panama declared its independence from Colombia Nov. 3, 1903, with U. S. recognition. U. S. Naval forces discouraged action by Colombia. On Nov. 18, 1903, Panama granted use, occupation and control of the Canal Zone to the U. S. by treaty, ratified Feb. 26, 1904. (See also Canal Zone and Panama Canal.)

Panama adopted universal suffrage in 1945 and its third constitution in 1946. The National Assembly (one for every 15,000 pop.) is elected for four years. Panama is a member of UN and OAS.

Rioting began Jan. 9, 1964, in a dispute over the flying of the U. S. and Panamanian flags and terms of the 1903 treaty. A joint declaration by the two governments Apr. 3, 1964, called for action to pave the way for peaceful negotiations. The International Commission of Jurists in Geneva absolved the U. S. of violating human rights in the rioting which killed at least 21 Panamanians and three U. S. soldiers.

U. S. President Johnson proposed on Dec. 18, 1964, that the two nations negotiate new treaties. Panama President Marco Aurelio Robles hailed the proposal. In 1967 new treaties were negotiated under which the U. S. would give up sovereignty over the canal to a U. S.-Panamanian authority, the U. S. would provide military defense for the canal, and construction of an additional canal might be undertaken. In 1968 the treaties still awaited ratification by the two governments.

In a bitter election, May 12, 1968, Dr. Arnulfo Arias was elected President, defeating a candidate backed by President Robles. Both sides charged widespread fraud and the election results were not announced until May 30.

Education and Religion. The Roman Catholic religion prevails but other faiths have representation. Education is compulsory for all children between 7 and 15. The National and Santa Maria de Antigua Universities are in Panama City. Spanish is the official language and its use is compulsory.

# Paraguay
## REPUBLICA DEL PARAGUAY

Capital: Asuncion. Area: 157,047 sq. mi. Population (UN est. 1967): 2,161,000. Monetary unit: Guarani (126 per U. S. $1).

Paraguay, one of the two landlocked countries of South America, is bounded by Bolivia, Brazil, and Argentina. The extensive plains are excellent

for pasturage and agriculture, and the mountain slopes are covered with luxuriant forests. It is about the size of California and is one of the best watered countries in the world. The Paraguay River, the Republic's most important waterway, is 1,800 mi. long.

**Resources and Industries.** Timber resources are large. Iron, manganese, copper are largely unexploited. Most of the population is agricultural and pastoral, with cattle breeding the principal industry. Most important agricultural crops are corn, mandioca (starch), cotton, beans, peanuts, tobacco and citrus fruits.

Chief exports are beef and other food products: cotton, quebracho (hardwood), hides, tobacco, yerba mate (tea), vegetable oils.

Completion of roads in the western Chaco cattle country (1964) and to the Brazilian port of Paranagua (1965) helped boost exports, which rose from $40,000,000 in 1963 to $57,000,000 in 1965. Imports rose from $33,000,000 in 1963 to $48,000,000 in 1967.

**History and Government.** Visited by Sebastian Cabot, 1527; settled as a Spanish possession in 1535, Paraguay gained its independence from Spain in 1811, was governed by a dictator from 1815-1840. After fighting Brazil, Argentina and Uruguay (War of the Triple Alliance 1865-1870) it adopted in 1870 a democratic constitution.

A new constitution, adopted in Aug. 1967, provided for a President and a bicameral legislature, a Senate of 30 members and a House of Representatives of 60 members. The party polling the largest number of votes in Congressional elections receives two-thirds of the seats in the Senate and the House, the rest to be divided proportionately among other contending parties. There is a 3-man Supreme Court and lower courts.

In elections held Feb. 11, 1968, Gen. Alfredo Stroessner, who had ruled Paraguay since 1954, was reelected President.

**Education and Religion.** The Roman Catholic religion is established, but others are tolerated. Primary education is compulsory between the ages of 7 and 14. Spanish is the official language and Guarani, an ancient Indian tongue, is the national language.

# Peru
## REPUBLICA DEL PERU

**Capital: Lima. Area: 496,222 sq. mi. Population (UN est. 1967): 12,385,000. Monetary unit: Sol (38.7 per U. S. $1).**

Peru, on the Pacific coast of South America, is bounded by Ecuador, Colombia, Brazil, Bolivia, Chile and the Pacific. It has a Pacific coastline of 1,410 mi. and an extreme width, from western coast to eastern jungle, of about 800 mi. It is about the size of Arizona, New Mexico and Texas combined.

Here the Andes reach 22,205 ft. (Mt. Huascaran); 7 peaks tower above 19,000 ft. The uplands of western slopes of the Andes are well watered as are the eastern slopes and lowlands reaching the Amazon basin, where the port of Iquitos loads ocean-going vessels for a 2,300 mi. trip down the Amazon through Peru and Brazil.

The coastal area on the west is almost rainless, but the soil is fertile and irrigation, using rivers pouring down from the Andes, has made the area highly productive.

Lima, the capital, is in the coastal region and is also the nation's commercial center. Callao, the chief seaport, is 7 mi. west of Lima.

Inca and earlier Chimu ruins make Peru a mecca for archeologists, notably at Cuzco, Chan Chan and the Andean city of Machu Picchu.

**Resources and Industries.** Agriculture and stock raising occupy 58% of the population and farm products comprise 47% of the value of exports.

The leading agricultural product is cotton. About 100,000 persons are engaged in the industry. Wool, hides, skins, sugar, coffee, rice, potatoes, beans, barley and tobacco also are produced. Corn, native to Peru, is a staple food among Indians, who also raise alfalfa. Peruvian bark is used for drugs.

Peru is the world's top fishing nation; of the 46,600,000 tons of fish caught by all nations in 1964, Peru took in 6,901,300 tons, mostly anchovies from the plankton-rich waters of the coastal Peru current. Most of the take is ground into fish meal for poultry and livestock feed. Guano, from birds which feed on offshore fish, is used for fertilizer.

The mountains are rich in minerals and many valuable mines, some dating back to the Incas, are being worked. The Toquepala copper mine

in the southern Andes, being worked by American companies, is one of the world's largest; another is at Cerro de Pasco. The steel industry is expanding. Petroleum production is growing; it reached over 23,000,000 bbl. in 1964.

Fishmeal is the largest export with copper 2nd. Other exports are cotton, sugar, iron ore, lead.

With its large fishing industry, Peru claims jurisdiction over Pacific waters 200 mi. offshore.

**History and Government.** The powerful Inca empire had its seat at Cuzco in the Andes (alt. 11,000 ft.) when Francisco Pizarro, Spanish conquistador, began raiding Peru for its wealth, 1532. In 1533 he had the ruling Inca, Atahualpa, fill a room with gold, then executed him and enslaved the natives. In 1535 he established Lima and in 1537 its port, Callao. War with Incas and rival Spaniards resulted in Pizarro's assassination, 1541, and the execution of his half-brother, Gonzalo, 1548.

Lima was the seat of Spanish viceroys until the Argentine liberator, Jose de San Martin, captured it in 1821; Spain was defeated by Simon Bolivar and Antonio J. de Sucre and recognized Peruvian independence, 1824. Chile defeated Peru and Bolivia, 1879-84, and took Tarapaca, Tacna and Arica; returned Tacna, 1929.

The constitution of 1933 provides for a president and two vice presidents, elected by direct suffrage for 6-yr. terms. Congress is composed of a chamber of deputies (members must be 25 or over) and a senate (members 35 or over), all native-born Peruvians, for 6-year terms.

**Education and Religion.** Religious liberty prevails but the Roman Catholic religion is protected. About 47% of the population is Indian; most of the remainder are of Spanish descent, or mestizos (mixed), with small percentages of Negroes, Chinese and Japanese.

Education is free and compulsory between 7 and 14. The University of San Marcos (founded 1551) is one of the oldest in the western hemisphere. There are 8 other universities.

Spanish is the official language, but many Indians speak Quecha or Aymara.

**Defense.** Military service is compulsory with two years in the active Army, 5 years in the first reserve, 5 in the second reserve and 20 years in the National Guard. Peru has a modern Navy and Air Force. It is a member of the UN and OAS.

# Philippines
## REPUBLIKA NG PILIPINAS

**Capital: Quezon City (Luzon). Area: 115,707 sq. mi. Population (UN est. 1967): 34,656,000. Monetary unit: Peso (3.92 per U. S. $1).**

The Republic of the Philippines occupies an archipelago in the western Pacific, 500 mi. from the SE coast of Asia, 7,000 mi. from San Francisco. About 7,100 islands extend 1,150 mi. N to S, 682 E to W.

Eleven of the islands comprise the bulk of the area. Only 462 islands have areas of more than 1 sq. mi. The country is about the size of Arizona.

The archipelago has a coastline of 14,407 mi. Manila Bay, with an area of 770 sq. mi., and a circumference of 120 mi., is the finest harbor in the Far East.

There are 10 more or less active volcanoes. Mount Apo, 9,690 ft., in Mindanao, and Mayon Volcano, 7,943 ft. in Albay, are the best known.

Quezon City, near Manila, is the official capital, but pending completion many government offices remain in Manila

**Resources and Industries.** Agriculture, livestock, mining, lumbering and fishing are the main activities. Forests, which cover 42% of the area, provide cabinet and construction lumber, also gums and resins, vegetable oils, rattan and bamboo, tan and dye barks, beeswax, charcoal, medicinal plants and orchids.

The islands are rich in mineral resources. Gold, silver, lead, zinc, nickel, copper, iron, coal, chromite, asbestos and manganese are mined, as well as clay, marble and salt.

The chief agricultural products are manila hemp from abaca, copra, sugar, rice, corn and tobacco.

Tourists numbered 116,000 in 1967.

In 1967 the nation scored significant growth in all fields, particularly in production of new "miracle" varieties of rice, achieving self-sufficiency in that staple for the first time in half a century.

**History and Government.** The archipelago was visited by Magellan 1521. The Spanish founded Manila 1571 and began their conquest. The islands, named for King Philip II of Spain, were ceded to

the U. S. by the Treaty of Paris (Dec. 10, 1898), following the Spanish-American War, the U. S. paying Spain $20,000,000 for the territory.

Japan attacked the Philippines Dec. 8, 1941 (Far Eastern time). Gen. Douglas MacArthur was put in command of the U. S.-Filipino forces (15,000 Americans, 40,000 in Filipino army, 100,000 Filipino reservists). Japan conquered the islands in May, 1942, and was ousted by Sept. 1945.

On July 4, 1946, independence was proclaimed in accordance with the Tydings-McDuffie Act passed by the U. S. Congress in 1934, providing for Philippine independence in 1946.

The government is republican in form, founded on democratic principles. The constitution provides for a Congress consisting of a Senate of 24 members, elected at large to 6-year terms, and a House of Representatives apportioned among the 56 provinces according to population, with a maximum membership of 120, elected to 4-year terms.

The terms of the President and Vice President are 4 years, and the President may be re-elected only once.

All natural resources of the Philippines belong to the state and their exploitation is limited to citizens of the Philippines or corporations and associations of which 60% of the capital is owned by citizens. In 1946 the right to develop natural resources and to own and operate public utilities until 1974 was extended to U. S. citizens.

President Ferdinand E. Marcos visited the U. S. Sept. 1966; concluded pact reducing U. S. base leases from 99 to 25 years and was promised increased military and technical aid.

The Philippines maintains a contingent of troops, mostly engineers, in Vietnam.

**Education and Religion.** Primary and secondary education is free, instruction is in English. Institutions of higher education include the University of the Philippines, Far Eastern Univ., Univ. of Santo Tomas (founded 1611), and Silliman Univ.

The official national language is Filipino (Pilipino), based on Tagalog, a Malayan dialect. English and Spanish, also official, are commonly used in government and commerce.

About 83% of the inhabitants are Roman Catholics and about 10% belong to the Philippine Independent Church, organized by a Filipino priest, Fr. Gregorio Aglipay. Other Christians, Moslems, Buddhists are among minorities.

**Defense.** The Philippines and U. S. have treaties for U. S. military and naval bases and a 1951 Mutual Defense Treaty, pledging joint action against external attack. The Republic is a member of the UN and SEATO.

# Poland
### POLSKA RZECZPOSPOLITA LUDOWA

**Capital: Warsaw. Area: 120,664 sq. mi. Population (UN est. 1967): 31,944,000. Monetary unit: Zloty (4 official rate per U. S. $1).**

Poland, Polish People's Republic, in Central Europe, is bounded by the Baltic Sea, USSR, Czechoslovakia and East Germany. It is about the size of New Mexico.

Its terrain consists largely of lowlands. Gdynia, Gdansk (once Danzig), Szczecin, Swinoujscie and Kolobrzeg are the principal ports.

**Resources and Industries.** In 1966, 35.5% of the population engaged in agriculture. Chief crops are rye, wheat, barley, oats, potatoes, sugar beets, tobacco, flax. Coal mining, shipbuilding, textiles chemicals, woodworking and metal industries are important. New industries include automobiles, tractors, heavy machinery, aircraft. Key industries are nationalized and operate under a planned economy. Rate of industrial growth is estimated at 8% annually in recent years.

Poland possesses great mineral wealth. It produces 5% of world coal and zinc output. Other minerals are sulphur, cement, salt, cadmium, iron, copper. Imported raw materials supply aluminum plants and oil refineries.

**History and Government.** Poland, whose history dates from 966, was a great power from the 14th to the 17th Centuries. In 3 partitions (1772, 1793, 1795) it was apportioned among Prussia, Russia and Austria, and in 1939 between Germany and the USSR. Overrun by the Austro-German armies in World War I, its independence, self-declared on Nov. 11, 1918, was recognized by the Treaty of Versailles, June 28, 1919, and the Treaty of Riga.

Nazi Germany and the Soviet Union invaded Poland Sept. 1-27, 1939, and divided the country. With Germany's defeat, a Polish government-in-exile in London was recognized by the U. S., but the Soviet Union pressed the claims of a Lublin group, the Polish Committee of National Liberation, to which a few members of the London committee were admitted. The U. S. and Britain opposed it but compromised with Stalin when he agreed to free elections in Poland. However, he rejected international supervision and the election of 1947 was completely dominated by the Communists.

Before World War II, Poland's population was 34,775,698 and its area 150,470 sq. mi. In compensation for 69,860 sq. mi. ceded to the USSR, 1945, Poland received aprox. 40,000 sq. mi. of German territory east of the Oder-Neisse line comprising Silesia, Pomerania, West Prussia and part of East Prussia. This has not been recognized by the West.

The 1952 constitution describes Poland as a people's republic with a Sejm (Parliament) elected for 4-year terms by direct ballot. The Sejm elects a Council of State and a Council of Ministers (cabinet). The office of president was abolished.

During 12 years of rule by Stalinist extremists large estates were abolished, industry was nationalized, schools secularized and some Roman Catholic prelates jailed. Farm production fell off. Harsh working conditions caused a riot by workmen in Poznan June 28-29, 1956, which was suppressed by troops with 44 dead, hundreds injured and 1,000 imprisoned.

A new Politburo, committed to development of Polish Communism independent of Russian control, was elected Oct. 1956, with Wladyslaw Gomulka as First Secretary of the Communist party.

Beginning in March 1968, following student unrest, a purge of many old-line party officials, including numerous Jews, was launched. It was believed led by a nationalist wing within the party. The "anti-Zionist" feature of the purge was denied; Gomulka sought to moderate the campaign.

**Education and Religion.** Education is free and compulsory. There are 74 institutions of higher learning. Leading universities are at Warsaw, Lodz, Torun, Poznan, Krakow, Lublin and Wroclaw (Breslau).

Roman Catholicism is the chief religion. A law promulgated Feb. 13, 1953, requires government consent to high church appointments. In October, 1956, Gomulka released Stefan Cardinal Wyszynski from prison and agreed to permit religion in the schools, religious liberty in public institutions and religious publications, provided the church kept out of politics. A large percentage of the people are said to attend services regularly.

In 1966 the Government celebrated 1,000 years of Polish nationhood and the Roman Catholic Church celebrated the 1,000th anniversary of the nation's conversion to Christianity. Cardinal Wyszynski led pilgrimages in several Polish cities, attended by hundreds of thousands of worshipers. The Government held rival demonstrations, also heavily attended. The Government staged a huge military review in Warsaw in July but barred a pilgrimage in the capital city in Aug. It also barred the Cardinal from visiting the Vatican, the U. S. and Canada.

**Defense.** Military age extends from 19 to 50. In 1950 the Army was reorganized along Soviet lines. Officers are required to learn Russian. Strength of the armed forces is estimated at 370,000. The Navy has one cruiser, 6 destroyers, 9 submarines and other craft. The Air Force has an est. 50,000 personnel and 1,000 aircraft.

Poland is a UN and Warsaw Pact member.

# Portugal
### REPUBLICA PORTUGUESA

**Capital: Lisbon. Area: 35,510 sq. mi. Population (UN est. 1967): 9,440,000. Monetary unit: Escudo (28.84 per U. S. $1).**

Portugal occupies the W part of the Iberian Peninsula in SW Europe, and is bounded by Spain and the Atlantic. It is about the size of Indiana. The Azores Islands, in the Atlantic 740 mi. W of Portugal, have an area of 888 sq. mi. and population (1960) of 336,393. The Madeira Islands, 360 mi. off the NW coast of Africa, have an area of 308 sq. mi. and a population (1960) of 282,678. Other overseas areas in Africa, Asia and Oceania (see below) are provinces, having equal status with provinces of continental Portugal.

Portugal is mountainous. About two-thirds of the land is cultivated.

**Resources and Industries.** Wheat corn, oats, barley, rye and rice are important crops. Wines, olive oil, sardines, anchovies, resins and fruits are major industries. Forests of pine, oak and chestnut cover 19% of the country, and the nation leads the world in cork production. Portugal

has lead, copper, tin, wolfram, kaolin, sulphur, iron, tungsten and cement. Textiles, pottery, chemical products, paper and glassware are principal manufactures.

The Salazar Bridge spanning the Tagus River in Lisbon, opened Aug. 5, 1966. The longest suspension bridge in Europe, it has a main span of 3,323 ft. and cost $75,000,000.

**History and Government.** Portugal, an independent state since the 12th Century, was a kingdom until a revolution in 1910 drove out King Manoel II and a republic was proclaimed.

A new constitution adopted by a plebiscite in 1933 and several times amended, provides some features of a corporative state. Two assemblies of 120 members each were created—the first, the National Assembly, to exercise legislative powers, by direct election by heads of families regardless of sex for 4 years; the second, the Corporative Chamber, chosen through a system of guild or syndical representation. The Corporative Chamber deals with economic and social matters, and advises the National Assembly. The Assembly may override a Presidential veto by a two-thirds vote.

The President is elected for 7 years, the method of selection since 1959 being by an electoral college composed of members of the Assembly and Chamber and representatives from the various districts.

The government's National Union party has been in power since 1934. Antonio de Oliveira Salazar has been Premier since 1932.

The President is Rear Admiral Americo Rodrigues Thomaz, elected June 9, 1958, reelected June 25, 1965.

**Education and Religion.** The dominant religion is Roman Catholicism; there is freedom of worship. Primary education is compulsory. There are 5 universities, 3 university schools, 4 colleges of music, 43 lyceums, a number of technical and art schools. Portugal went on year-long daylight saving time in 1966.

**Defense.** Military service is compulsory between the ages of 20 and 45. There is a small Navy, and an Air Force equipped with modern jet fighters. During World War II Portugal granted facilities in the Azores to U. S. and British Air Forces. A 1951 agreement gave the U. S. additional rights in the Azores for defense purposes and integrates the islands into the framework of NATO. Portugal is a member of NATO, UN and EFTA.

Faced with intermittent rebel attacks in its African provinces, Portugal has sought to convince Africans there that they enjoy greater economic progress than if independent, while developing school and health facilities.

The small Portuguese enclaves of Goa, Damao and Diu on the Indian sub-continent were seized by India Dec. 18, 1961.

## PORTUGUESE OVERSEAS PROVINCES

**Angola, Portuguese West Africa,** has a 1,000 mi. coast line stretching S from the mouth of the Congo. It is governed by a Governor General and an elected Legislative Council. The Portuguese have owned it since 1575. Its area is 481,351 sq. mi., population (UN est. 1965), 5,154,000, including about 250,000 Europeans. The capital is Luanda.

In 1968 a pipeline was being laid to tap huge supplies of oil discovered in Angola's northern coastal area, Cabinda.

Chief products are coffee, fishmeal, corn, sisal, fish, sugar, cotton, coconuts, oilseeds, ivory, cattle, tobacco, rubber. There are deposits of diamonds, copper, iron, manganese, petroleum, mica, salt. Gold has been discovered. Manufacturing of alcohol, cotton goods, fish products, paper, footwear, soap, sugar, tobacco is growing. Metropolitan Portugal supplies nearly 50% of the imports. Lobito, an Atlantic seaport, is western terminal of a railroad reaching Beira in Mozambique.

**Mozambique, Portuguese East Africa,** faces the Indian Ocean and Mozambique Channel in SW Africa. More than 400 sq. mi. of former German E. Africa, the Kionga Triangle, was transferred to Mozambique in 1919.

Mozambique has 297,731 sq. mi., and a population (UN est. 1965) of 6,956,000. The capital is Lourenco Marques. Chief products are cement, flour, sugar, coconuts, cotton, copra, sisal, and beeswax. Minerals include tantalum, columbian, coal, copper, gold, asbestos.

**The Cape Verde Islands** in the North Atlantic, 280 mi. W of Dakar, Africa, are 15 in number. The total area is 1,557 sq. mi. and the population (UN est. 1964), 218,00. Chief products are coffee, medicinal products, hides, fruits and grain.

**Portuguese Guinea,** on the W coast of Africa between Senegal and Guinea, has an area of 13,948 sq. mi. and a population, 1962, of 549,000. Chief exports are wax, oils, ivory and hides.

**The Islands of Sao Tome and Principe** are about 125 mi. off the W coast of Africa on the Gulf of Guinea. The islands have an area of 372 sq. mi.; population 1960, 63,676. Chief products are cocoa, coffee, coconut, copra, palm oil and cinchona.

**Macao,** with an area of 6 sq. mi., is an enclave, a peninsula and two small islands, at the mouth of the Canton River in China. Population (UN est. 1965): 280,000.

**Portuguese Timor** occupies the E part of an island of that name N of Australia in the Timor Sea. Indonesia owns the W part. The area is 7,330 sq. mi. and the population, 1967, 570,000. Exports are coffee, sandlewood, sandal root, copra and wax. Capital, Dili.

# Romania
## REPUBLICA SOCIALISTA ROMANIA

**Capital: Bucharest. Area:** 91,699 sq. mi. **Population (Census 1968):** 19,540,000. **Monetary unit:** Leu (pl. lei) (6, official rate, per U. S. $1).

Romania, a Balkan state in SE Europe, is almost the size of Oregon. It is bounded by the USSR, the Black Sea, Bulgaria, Yugoslavia and Hungary. The Danube flows along the southern border and through eastern Romania into the Black Sea. The Carpathian Mts. enclose the north-central Transylvanian plateau. There are wide plains S and E of the mountains.

**Resources and Industries.** Romania has become heavily industrialized, industry accounting for 51.3% of the total national product in 1967. Average annual growth of industrial output, 1951-1967, was 13.2%.

Main industries are iron-steel, other metallurgy, machinery, oil and chemicals, building materials, timber, textiles, footwear, food processing.

There is considerable mineral wealth: oil, natural gas, coal, salt, bauxite, manganese, lead, zinc, gold, silver. Annual production (1967) was 13,206,000 tons of crude oil, 15,019,000 tons of coal, 4,088,000 tons of steel.

Farm and forests contributed 29% of the national product, 1967. State farms and cooperatives own 96.4% of arable land. Romania is the world's 6th largest corn producer; also important are wheat, sugar beets, grapes and fruits.

In Jan. 1968 Romania had 14,300,000 sheep, 5,739,000 hogs and 5,331,000 cattle.

Exports in 1967 were valued at $1.4 billion, imports at $1.5 billion.

**History and Government.** Romania's earliest known people were merged with invading Proto-Thracians, preceding by centuries the Dacians. The Dacian kingdom was occupied by Rome 101 A.D.-271 A.D.; the people and language were Romanized. The principalities of Wallachia and Moldavia, dominated by Turkey, were united in 1859; became Romania in 1861. In 1866 the house of Hohenzollern-Sigmaringen placed a prince in control. In 1877 Romania proclaimed independence from Turkey, became an independent state by the Treaty of Berlin, 1870, and kingdom, 1881, under Carol I. In 1886 Romania became a constitutional monarchy with a bicameral legislature.

Romania's location on the border of warring states made it a frequent victim of strife. It helped Russia against Turkey, 1877-78. It was defeated by Germany and Austria-Hungary in World War I, 1914-15; later rejoined the Allies and won Bessarabia, Bukovina, Transylvania and Banat. In 1940 it ceded Bessarabia and Northern Bukovina to the USSR and part of Southern Dobrudja to Bulgaria.

King Carol II made himself dictator in 1938, abdicated 1940 (died 1953). Michael I (born Oct. 25, 1921) became king 1940.

Marshal Ion Antonescu, leader of militarist movement, came to power and forced Romania to join Germany against the USSR in World War II in 1941. In 1944 Antonescu was overthrown by King Michael with Soviet help and Romania joined the Allies.

With occupation by Soviet troops the National Democratic Front, headed by the Communist party, displaced the National Peasant party. A People's Republic was proclaimed, Dec. 30, 1947, and Michael was forced to abdicate. Land owners were dispossessed and practically all banks, factories and transportation units were nationalized. A new constitution on the Soviet model was voted Sept. 24, 1952. A modification,

March 1961, replaced the Presidium with the State Council, elected by the Grand National Assembly from its own membership. The Assembly, supreme organ of state power, has 465 Deputies, elected for 4-year terms from one-list slates.

On Aug. 22, 1965, a new Constitution proclaimed Romania a Socialist, rather than People's Republic. Since 1966, Romania has adopted an increasingly independent attitude toward the USSR and for greater control of their own armed forces within the Warsaw Pact.

**Education and Religion.** Education is compulsory for 10 years, all education is free. There are universities in Bucharest, Jassy, Cluj, Craiova and Timisoara.

The language has a Latin base, with traces of French, Greek, Slav and Turkish influences.

Romanian Orthodox clergy are paid by the state, other clergy receive subsidies but church and state are called separated. Roman Catholic orders have been abolished and the Greek Catholic Church has been absorbed by the Romanian Orthodox.

**Defense.** Military service is compulsory for 16 months. Romania has a small Navy and Air Force. It is a member of the UN and Warsaw Pact.

# Rwanda
## REPUBLIQUE RWANDAISE

**Capital: Kigali. Area: 10,166 sq. mi. Population (Govt. est. 1967): 3,306,000. Montary unit: Franc (100 per U. S. $1).**

The Republic of Rwanda, which became independent July 1, 1962, had been part of the former Belgian UN Trusteeship of Ruanda-Urundi. Rwanda lies in East Central Africa, bounded N by Uganda, E by Tanzania, W by the Democratic Republic of Congo and S by Burundi.

The source of the Nile River, long sought by explorers and geographers, has been located in the headwaters of the Kagera River, SW of Kigali; from there it is 4,145 mi. to where the Nile empties into the Mediterranean.

About the size of Maryland, Rwanda is the most densely populated country in Africa. The population includes the Bahutu (90% of population), the Batutsi (Watusi, 8%) and the Batwa (2%). For centuries the Batutsi (an extremely tall race) subjugated the Bahutu (average height) and the Batwa (pygmies). A civil war broke out in 1960 and Batutsi power was ended. *See Index for Burundi.*

A Legislative Council, organized in Oct. 1960, declared Rwanda a republic Jan. 28, 1961, and a referendum, Sept. 25, abolished the monarchic system. The new government was dominated by the Bahutu. President: Gregoire Kayibanda, elected Oct. 26, 1961. Rwanda is a member of the UN and OAU.

Coffee is the principal crop; cotton, tea, pyrethrum, tobacco, cattle and hides also are produced. Minerals include tin, gold, wolframite.

Kagera National Park, in the northeast, covers a tenth of the country; here the flora and fauna of East Central Africa are preserved intact. Lake Kivu, on the nation's western border with the Democratic Republic of Congo, is 4,788 ft. above sea level and considered one of Africa's most beautiful. Rwandans are noted for performances on massed drums, accompanied by singers and dancers.

# San Marino
## REPUBBLICA DI SAN MARINO

**Area: 23.5 sq. mi. Population (est. 1966): 17,000.**

San Marino, the world's smallest republic, lies on the slope of Mt. Titano in the Apennines near Rimini, in the heart of Italy. It is one-third the size of the District of Columbia.

Principal industries are printing postage stamps, tourism, woolen goods, paper, cement, industrial ceramics. There is no unemployment. Cradle-to-grave social security is provided. Italian and Vatican City money is used. A ceremonial army of 180 men is maintained.

**History and Government.** The Republic claims to be the oldest state in Europe and to have been founded in the 4th Century. It has had a treaty of friendship with Italy since 1862. It is a member of the International Court of Justice.

San Marino is governed by a Grand Council of 60 members elected by popular vote, two of whom are chosen to exercise executive power for a term of 6 months. Women were allowed to vote for the first time Sept. 13, 1964.

# Saudi Arabia
## AL-MAMLAKA AL-'ARABIYA AS-SA'UDIYA

**Capital: Riyadh. Area: 870,000 sq. mi. Population (Govt. est. 1963): 8,000,000. Monetary unit: Riyal (4.5 per U. S. $1).**

Saudi Arabia occupies four-fifths of the Arabian Peninsula, with the Red Sea on most of its W coast and the Persian Gulf (also called Arabian Gulf) on the E. The highlands of the W, up to 9,000 ft., slope as an arid, barren desert to the Persian Gulf. Its neighbors are Jordan, Iraq, Kuwait, Muscat and Oman, Southern Yemen and Yemen. It is more than three times the size of Texas.

Saudi Arabia comprises four provinces: the former sultanate of Nejd, the kingdom of Hejaz, Asir and El Hasa (now known as the Eastern Province).

The Hejaz contains the holy cities of Islam—Medina where the Mosque of the Prophet enshrines the tomb of Mohammed, who died in the city June 7, 632, and Mecca, his birthplace, containing a great mosque sheltering the sacred shrine, the Kaaba, which holds the black stone given by Gabriel to Abraham. More than 300,000 Moslems visit Mecca annually.

Two major airports, Dhahran and Jidda, handle the bulk of international traffic. Jidda, on the Red Sea, is the main seaport. A 357-mi. railroad runs from Dammam on the Persian Gulf to Riyadh.

**Resources and Industries.** Saudi Arabia possesses one of the great oil reservoirs of the world second only to that of Kuwait in the Middle East. Production centers along the Persian Gulf at Ghawar, Abqaiq, Safaniya, Dammam, Qatif and Khursaniyah. Refineries and piers for tankers are at Ras Tanura, and a pipeline runs from Abqaiq to Saida on the Lebanese coast. Operations are in the hands of the Arabian American Oil Co. (Aramco), owned by several American companies; Getty Oil Co., and Arabian Oil Co., Ltd. (Japan). Production is valued at over $1.1 billion a year and is about 7% of world output.

Income from oil royalties defrays many expenses of the state, the cost of internal improvements and free medical care for its citizens.

An agricultural country except for oil, and recently discovered gold, silver and rich iron ore, Saudi Arabia's products are dates, wheat, barley, fruit, hides, wool. Camels, horses, donkeys and sheep are raised. Some hides, wool and gum are exported. It receives UN technical assistance.

**History and Government.** Nejd, long an independent state and center of the Wahhabi sect, fell under Turkish rule in the 18th Century, but in 1913 Ibn Saud, founder of the Saudi dynasty, overthrew the Turks and captured the Turkish province of Hasa; took the Hejaz in 1925 and by 1926 most of Asir.

The form of government is a hereditary monarchy. King Saud ibn Abdul Aziz (born 1902) who succeeded his father Nov. 9, 1953, was stripped of his powers after a family council, Mar. 28, 1964, but was allowed to retain his title. Crown Prince Faisal, the King's half-brother, assumed the title of Viceroy; on Nov. 2, he was named King in place of Saud.

**Education and Religion.** Elementary, secondary and higher education are free, but not compulsory. Development of education is extensive, taking more than 10% of the government budget. The population is almost entirely Moslem.

**Defense.** Saudi Arabia's defense force consists of a regular Army and a military academy to train officers. It is a member of the UN and Arab League.

Saudi Arabia and the United Arab Republic opposed each other during 3 years of warfare in Yemen, with Saudi Arabia supplying arms and other aid to the royalists and Pres. Gamal Abdel Nasser providing troops to fight for the republicans. King Faisal and Pres. Nasser reached another in a series of cease-fire agreements Aug. 24, 1965, with negotiations continuing in 1966 and 1967. In 1968, King Faisal said he would resume aid to the royalists, charging Syria, Russia and Southern Yemen with intervention.

# Senegal

**Capital: Dakar. Area: 75,750 sq. mi. Population (UN est. 1967): 3,670,000. Monetary unit: CFA franc (246.85 per U. S. $1).**

A former French Overseas Territory on the Atlantic coast of western Africa, Senegal has for neighbors Mauritania, Mali, Guinea and Portuguese Guinea and it almost surrounds tiny Gambia on 3 sides. It is about as large as South Dakota.

Senegal became an autonomous state in 1958 and with the Sudanese Republic formed the Mali Federation Jan. 17 1959. The two members became completely independent June 20, 1960, but after political conflict arose Senegal withdrew from the federation Aug. 20, 1960. The Sudanese Republic assumed the name Mali. Senegal elected to remain within the French Community. It is a member of the UN.

About 85% of the population is engaged in agriculture and stock raising; peanuts are the mainstay of the economy. Dakar on Cape Verdi, is an important seaport, handling 4,000 ships annually. There are important deposits of aluminum phosphate. Developing industries include food processing, chemicals, cement.

Efforts were pressed, 1967-68, to increase production of rice, the staple food, most of which had to be imported. A team of experts from Nationalist China was aiding the effort. Other crops were also being promoted.

## Sierra Leone

**Capital: Freetown. Area: 27,699 sq. mi. Population (UN est. 1967): 2,439,000. Monetary unit: Leone (.8333 per U. S. $1).**

Sierra Leone, former British Colony and Protectorate which became an independent state within the Commonwealth Apr. 27, 1961, is in the SE corner of the West African bulge. The coast line on the Atlantic is about 210 mi.; the country extends inland about 180 mi., between Guinea and Liberia. It is a bit smaller than South Carolina. Its name, meaning Mountain of the Lion, was applied by an early Portuguese mariner because of thunderstorms around its coastal peaks.

Freetown, the capital, was founded in 1787 by the British government as a home for destitute freed slaves. Their descendants, known as Creoles, number more than 50,000. The city has one of the finest seaports in West Africa.

Principal exports are industrial diamonds, iron ore, bauxite, cocoa, coffee, palm kernels, kola nuts, ginger, piassava (palm fiber). More than 80% are employed in agriculture.

Successive steps toward independence followed introduction of the first constitution in 1951. The Sierra Leone People's party was dominant until a military coup d'etat Mar. 23, 1967.

The coup followed general elections in which the vote was almost equally divided between the People's party and the All People's Congress.

Col. A. T. Juxon-Smith, who led the coup, was himself ousted in another coup, Apr. 8, 1968, led by non-commissioned officers. The nation was returned to civilian rule with swearing-in of Siaka Stevens as Prime Minister, Apr. 26. Stevens, head of the All People's Congress party, had been Prime Minister for two hours at the time of the 1967 coup.

Sierre Leone is a member of the UN.

The Univ. College of Sierra Leone was founded in 1876 as Fourah Bay College. Njala Univ. was founded in 1964 with the aid of the Univ. of Illinois. English is the official language.

## Singapore
### MAJULAH SINGAPURA

**Capital: Singapore. Area: 225 sq. mi. Population (Govt. est. 1967): 1,955,600. Monetary unit: Singapore dollar (3.07 per U. S. $1).**

Singapore is an independent island republic 27 mi. wide and 14 mi. long at the southern tip of the Malay Peninsula in SE Asia. About 3 times the size of the District of Columbia, the main island is linked to the mainland by a three-quarter mile-long causeway. The narrow Strait of Singapore separates it from several of its islets to the south.

Singapore, the capital, is the world's 4th largest port and the largest in SE Asia.

Founded in 1819 by Sir Thomas Stamford Raffles, Singapore was a British colony until 1959 when it became an internally autonomous state within the Commonwealth. On Sept. 16, 1963, it joined with Malaya, Sarawak and Sabah to form the Federation of Malaysia. The new state vested control in the Malays, although with Singapore, the Chinese formed the largest ethnic group in Malaysia's population. Racial and political tensions developed and both Singapore and Malaysian officials agreed that separation was the only way to solve the problem. Prime Minister Lee Kuan Yew, Aug. 9, 1965, in announcing the separation, stated that Singapore would continue its cooperation with Britain in defense matters but would

seek new understandings with Indonesia and Communist nations. Britain maintains its largest military base in the Far East at Singapore.

Singapore's population is 75% Chinese, 12% Malay and 13% Indians, Pakistanis, Ceylonese, Eurasians, etc. Industries include ship building, tin smelting, and food, rubber, copra and lumber processing.

Tourism is an important source of income; 204,- 852 visitors in 1967 (59% above 1966) spent an est. $47,270,400 (U. S. dollars). Attractions include festivals, foods, Tiger Balm Gardens, some 500 Chinese temples, the harbor with its junks and sampans and Malay sea villages.

Primary education for 6 years is free but not compulsory. There are two main univs.: Singapore and Nanyang. A small army of 4 infantry battalions is maintained in addition to the police force of over 7,000. Singapore is a member of the Commonwealth and the UN.

## Somalia
### SOMALI REPUBLIC

**Capital: Mogadishu. Area: 246,201 sq. mi. Population (UN est. 1967): 2,660,000. Monetary unit: Somali shilling (7.143 per U. S. $1).**

The Somali Republic is comprised of the former protectorate of British Somaliland and the former Italian UN trusteeship of Somalia in eastern Africa. It is bordered by the Gulf of Aden, Indian Ocean, Kenya, Ethiopia and French Somaliland. It is about the size of Texas. Chief ports are Berbera, Mogadishu, and Kismayou.

**Resources and Industries.** Somalia has a weak economy of its own and depends on outside aid, part of which is being received from the United States, Italy, Great Britain and the USSR. Principal occupations are livestock raising and agriculture. Products include incense, sugar, bananas, durra (sorghum), corn, gum, hides, kapok.

Its mineral resources, largely undeveloped, include iron, tin, gypsum, sandstone, bauxite, meerschaum, titanium and others. In 1968 the Government announced discovery of large uranium deposits.

**History and Government.** Many of the Somali peoples are nomadic and include, in addition to those in French Somaliland, some 20,000 in Kenya and 1,500,000 in Ethiopia. The Italian UN Trusteeship of Somalia, 194,000 sq. mi., population (est.), 2,000,000, extended along the Indian Ocean from the Gulf of Aden to the Juba River. It was proclaimed a protectorate by Italy, 1889. The UN General Assembly, Nov. 21, 1949, approved creation of Somalia as a sovereign state and on April 1, 1950, Italy took over the trusteeship held by Great Britain during World War II.

Former **British Somaliland Protectorate**, with 68,000 sq. mi., and 640,000 population with Ethiopia to the S and W and Somalia to the E, was freed June 26, 1960, to enable it to unite with Somalia.

The Republic was proclaimed July 1, 1960. The National Assembly has 123 Deputies. The President must be a Moslem. Somalia is a member of the UN.

In 1965-66 tribesmen carried on sporadic strife on the Kenya and Ethiopia borders. A settlement of these disputes was reached in 1967-68.

## Republic of South Africa
### REPUBLIEK VAN SUID-AFRIKA

**Capitals: Pretoria and Cape Town. Area: 472,359 sq. mi. Population (UN est. 1967): 18,733,000. Monetary unit: Rand (.719 per U. S. $1).**

The Republic of South Africa occupies the southern portion of the continent and includes the former colonies of the Cape of Good Hope, Natal, the Transvaal and the Orange Free State. It is about the size of Texas, Oklahoma and New Mexico.

| Province | Sq. mi. | Pop., 1963 | Capital |
|---|---|---|---|
| Transvaal | 110,450 | 6,273,477 | Pretoria |
| C. of Good Hope | 278,465 | 5,362,853 | Cape Town |
| Orange Fr. State | 49,866 | 1,386,547 | Bloemfontein |
| Natal | 33,578 | 2,979,920 | Pietermaritz- [burg |

Population growth of government-designated racial groups, in terms of 1963 and 1967 estimates, was: Bantu, 11,007,000, 12,750,000; White, 3,106,000, 3,563,000; Colored (mixed) 1,522,000, 1,859,000; Asiatics, 487,000, 561,000.

Cape Town, seat of Parliament, is the legislative capital and Pretoria the administrative capital.

Largest cities are Johannesburg and Cape Town.

Kruger National Park, an 8,000-sq. mi. wild game preserve; Cape Peninsula, and the Drakensberg Mtns., are among numerous tourist attractions.

**Resources and Industries.** Corn, cotton, wool, wheat, tobacco, sugar cane, citrus fruits, butter and cheese are major agricultural products.

With vast mineral resources, South Africa leads the world in production of gold, gem diamonds, platinum and antimony; is 2nd in chrome, vanadium, vermiculite; third in uranium, manganese and asbestos. Coal and iron resources are unlimited. Annual production of more than 50 minerals is est. at $1.5 billion.

South Africa has enjoyed an industrial boom. Index numbers of industrial production (1963= 100) were 138 in 1967 for manufacturing and 117 for mining.

Air service is provided by 19 international lines. Railroads are state-controlled.

Foreign trade (in thousands of U. S. dollars):

| | Imports | Exports |
|---|---|---|
| 1966 | $2,300,000 | $1,688,000 |
| 1967 | $2,687,000 | $1,908,000 |

**History and Government.** The Union was formed by act of the British Parliament, effective May 31, 1910, 8 years after the British defeated the independent republics of the Transvaal and the Orange Free State in the Boer War (1899-1902). The nation was settled by emigrants from Cape Colony, mostly of Dutch extraction in the Great Trek of 1831 and later. After gold was discovered in 1886 the Boers faced repeated difficulties from the Uitlanders (Outlanders) and the wildcat Jameson raid against the gold-bearing ridge, the Witwatersrand, at Johannesburg in 1896 increased the tension. The Boer War made a national hero of Paul Kruger ("Oom Paul"), Pres. of the Transvaal, who died in exile, 1904.

With the election victory of Daniel Malan's Nationalist party in 1948, white supremacy became official policy in the form of *apartheid,* which calls for separate development of the non-white population groups—Indians, the mixed group called Coloreds, and the Bantu.

In 1959 the Nationalists passed the Bantu Self-Government act which recognized the principle of separate residential areas and social development. In white South Africa, Bantus may be employed but have no civil rights.

The Union became a Republic May 31, 1961. Prime Minister Hendrik F. Verwoerd had withdrawn his application for South Africa's readmission to the Commonwealth in March, in the face of opposition of the other Commonwealth heads of government to his country's apartheid policy. South Africa is a member of the UN.

Under the Republic's constitution, there is a State President, chosen by an electoral college composed of members of the Senate and Assembly for a 7-year term and not ordinarily eligible for reelection. The Senate of 54 members and Assembly of 160 are elected for 5-year terms. An elective Provincial Council meets in each of the four provinces.

**Education and Religion.** There are 16 universities, including 11 for white students, average enrollment exceeding 45,000 students. Primary education is free to all citizens and compulsory for white children over 7 years of age. There are 5 universities for non-whites.

Dutch Protestant churches predominate, with Anglicans and Methodists next among whites. English and Afrikaans are official languages.

**Defense.** The defense system makes every white citizen between 17 and 60 eligible for military duty in time of war. Those between 17 and 25 are obligated to undergo training in the Active Citizen Force with its Army, Air Force and Naval components, or as a Rifle Commando over a period of 4 years.

The Navy includes destroyers, frigates, minesweepers, anti-submarine frigates, and coastal defense ships. The Air Force is modern.

### SOUTH-WEST AFRICA
#### NAMIBIA

South-West Africa, a sparsely populated land twice the size of California, became the object of international dispute in 1966. Made a German protectorate in 1884, it was surrendered to South Africa in 1915 and was administered by that country under an old League of Nations mandate. South Africa refused to accept UN authority over the mandate as other nations did with their mandates.

Other African nations charged South Africa imposed apartheid, built military bases and exploited S-W Africa; Ethiopia and Liberia lost, on a technicality, a suit against South Africa in the International Court of Justice; 36 African states called on the UN to take over the mandate.

The UN General Assembly in May 1968 created an 11-nation council to take over administration of South-West Africa and lead it to independence. In April 1968 the council charged that South Africa had blocked its effort to visit South-West Africa.

On June 12, 1968, the UN General Assembly by 96 to 2 vote urgently called on the Security Council to secure the area's independence. The resolution also gave South-West Africa the name Namibia.

Most of S-W Africa is a plateau, 3,600 ft. high, with plains in the N, Kalahari Desert to the E, Orange River on the S, the Atlantic on the W. Area is 317,887 sq. mi.; population (UN est. 1967) 594,000, including over 75,000 of European descent; capital, Windhoek. There is a South African administrator; voters choose 18 members of a Legislative Assembly and send 6 members to the South African Assembly; 4 are appointed to the South Africa Senate.

Products include cattle, sheep, diamonds, lead, zinc, vanadium, fish. People include Namas (Hottentots), Ovambos (Bantus), Bushmen and others.

## Southern Yemen

**Capital: Medina as-Shaab. Area: 112,000 sq. mi. Population (Govt. est. 1967): 1,500,000. Monetary unit: Dinar (.4195 per U. S. $1).**

Southern Yemen became independent Nov. 30, 1967, after more than a century of British rule. It consists of the port city of Aden, 17 states of the former South Arabian Federation, 3 small sheikdoms, 3 larger sultanates, Quaiti, Kathiri and Mahri, which made up the Eastern Aden Protectorate, and Socotra, the largest island in the Arabian Sea.

One of the cities mentioned in the Bible, Aden has been a port for the trade in incense, spices and silk between the East and West for two millenia. British rule began in 1839 when the British East India Co. seized control to put an end to the piracy threatening trade with India. Aden provided Britain with a controlling position at the southern entrance to the Red Sea and became a strategic outpost of the Empire in the East.

With only 1% of the land fertile and few mineral deposits, the Port of Aden has been Southern Yemen's most valuable natural resource. The port is 10 mi. across, well-sheltered and deep. In 1966 more than 6,000 ships put in at Aden for refueling, servicing and transshipment of goods, bringing over 227,000 visitors and $22,000,000.

But, since the closing of the Suez Canal as a result of the Israeli-Arab War in June 1967, the port has been paralyzed and the economy depressed.

Loss of spending by the British military forces, which withdrew in 1967, amounted to $50,000,000 a year. Joblessness in Aden was est. at 35,000 in 1968.

Southern Yemen is a member of the UN.

The struggle for independence began in earnest in Dec. 1963, when two nationalist groups, the National Liberation Front (NLF) and the UAR-supported Front for the Liberation of Occupied South Yemen (FLOSY), waged a guerrilla war against the British and local dynastic rulers. The two groups vied with each other for political control. The NLF succeeded in naming the first President, Qahtan al-Shaabi.

## Spain
### ESTADO ESPANOL

**Capital: Madrid. Area: 194,883 sq. mi. Population (UN est. 1967): 32,140,000. Monetary unit: Peseta (69.8 per U. S. $1).**

Spain, a nominal monarchy, occupies the entire Iberian peninsula in Western Europe, except for Portugal. It is separated from France by the Pyrenees.

The interior is a high arid plateau traversed E and W by mountain ranges. Spain is twice the size of Wyoming.

The **Balearic Islands** in the western Mediterranean, 1,935 sq. mi., pop. (1961), 443,327, are a

province of Spain; they include **Majorca** (Mallorca), with the capital, Palma; **Minorca**, **Cabrera**, **Ibiza** and **Formentera**. The **Canary Islands**, 2,807 sq. mi., in the Atlantic W of Morocco, pop., (1961), 944,448, also are provinces and include the islands of **Tenerife, Gomera, Hierro, Grand Canary, Fuerteventura** and **Lanzarote** with Las Palmas and Santa Cruz thriving ports. **Ceuta,** in Africa opposite Gibraltar, and **Melilla,** on the Riff coast, are part of Metropolitan Spain.

**Resources and Industries.** Only about 40% of the land is cultivable, the remainder is arid or mountainous. Farm mechanization and irrigation are increasing.

The principal agricultural products are wheat, barley, oats, rye, olives, grapes, lemons, oranges and other fruit, onions, almonds, esparto, flax, hemp, pulse and cork. Tobacco, cotton, and rice are also grown. Wine-making is a large and ancient industry. Spain possesses an abundance of minerals, including lead, iron, copper, zinc, coal, cobalt, mercury, silver, sulphur and phosphates.

Manufacturing includes cotton and woolen goods, paper, automobiles, cork and cement. Sardines, tuna fish and cod are most important fish catches. Coal production is more than 15,000,000 tons annually.

The index of general industrial production showed a large rise from 100 in 1963 to 144 in 1967. Electric power output rose from 37.7 billion kwh in 1966 to 41 billion in 1967; steel production from 3,800,000 tons to 4,400,000 tons; motor vehicles from 257,910 units to 290,000.

More than 18,000,000 tourists spend $1.3 billion a year in Spain.

**History and Government.** Since Roman times Spain has had a major part in the political, religious and cultural fortunes of Europe. It was settled by Iberians, Basques and Celts, partly overrun by Carthaginian armies, conquered by Rome under Scipio Africanus c. 200 B.C. The Germanic Visigoths, in power by the 5th Century A.D., adopted Christianity but by 711 A.D. lost to the Islamic invasion from Africa. The Christian reconquest from the N led to a Spanish nationalist movement. Foremost Christian leader was the Cid Campeador (Lord Champion), d. 1099 A.D. In 1469 the kingdoms of Aragon and Castile were united by the marriage of Ferdinand II and Isabella I, and the last Moorish power broken by the fall of the kingdom of Granada, 1492. Spain became a bulwark of Roman Catholicism and the Inquisition, under which non-believers were slain, converted or exiled, came into power.

Spain obtained a great colonial empire with the discovery of America by Columbus, 1492, the conquest of Mexico by Cortes and Peru by Pizarro. It also controlled the Netherlands and parts of Italy and Germany. Charles I (Charles V, Holy Roman emperor), 1519-1556, attempted to halt Luther's Reformation and reestablish religious unity. Philip II, 1556-1598, tried to uproot heresy. The Spanish Armada failed to subdue England, 1588. Napoleon seized control of Portugal and Spain, 1808, made his brother Joseph King of Spain and precipitated the Peninsular War. Spain lost Mexico, Peru and other American colonies in the 1820s. It lost Cuba, the Philippines and Puerto Rico during the Spanish-American War, 1898. It gained concessions in Morocco by 1912, where it had to suppress a Moorish uprising led by Abd-el-Krim.

Primo de Rivera became dictator in 1923. King Alfonso XIII revoked the dictatorship, 1930, but was forced to leave the country Apr. 14, 1931. A republic was proclaimed which disestablished the church, curtailed its privileges and secularized education. A conservative reaction to these measures occurred 1933 but was followed by a Popular Front (1936-1939) composed of socialists, communists, republicans, and anarchists.

Army officers in Morocco headed a revolt against the government July 18, 1936, under Francisco Franco (b. Dec. 14, 1892). They established a provisional govt. at Burgos. In a destructive 3-yr. war, in which 1,000,000 are said to have died, Franco received help from Italy and Germany, while the Soviet Union, France and Mexico were active on behalf of the republic. About 600 Americans served in the Abraham Lincoln brigade for the republic. War ended when Madrid fell to Franco Mar. 28, 1939.

Franco was named caudillo, or leader of the nation, Chief of State, Commander in Chief, Prime Minister and head of the Falange party. The Cortes was reestablished July 1942, with elected, appointed and ex-officio members.

Spain was neutral in World War II but its relations with fascist countries and support for repressive measures caused its exclusion from UN in 1946. It was admitted in 1955.

Dec. 14, 1966, a new constitution, called the "Organic Law," was approved by the people in a plebiscite. The new law implied a liberalization of government policy in the areas of religion, the press, trade unions and other social and political aspects of Spanish life.

**Education and Religion.** Franco reestablished Catholicism as the state religion. The clergy are paid by the state. Primary education is compulsory and free. There are 13 universities. More than two-thirds speak Castilian; Basque is spoken in the N; Galician in the NW, and Catalan in the NE.

**Defense.** Service in the Army is compulsory for two years. Under a 10-year defense agreement with the U. S. signed Sept. 26, 1953, renewed 1963 for 5 years, Spain receives military and economic aid; in turn it permits use of air and naval bases on Spanish soil.

## SPANISH OVERSEAS PROVINCES

Aside from Ceuta and Melilla on the North African Coast, which are considered parts of the motherland and the Canary Islands, which are provinces, Spain has several provinces in Western Africa:

### EQUATORIAL GUINEA
#### (Spanish Guinea)

Equatorial Guinea was a Spanish province which was promised independence during 1968.

It is composed of the island of **Fernando Po** and smaller islands in the Gulf of Guinea, known as **Insular Guinea,** and **Rio Muni,** called **Continental Guinea,** a larger area on the nearby mainland coast.

Products include cocoa, gold, coffee, wood and wool. Capital: Santa Isabel (on Fernando Po). Area: 10,852 sq. mi. Population (est. 1963): 250,000.

**Spanish Sahara,** Africa, extending from Cape Blanco to a line south of Cape Ifni, includes the zones of **Rio de Oro, 73,362 sq. mi.,** and **Sekia el Hamra,** 33,047 sq. mi. Population (est.): 23,700.

**Ifni,** an enclave on Morocco's Atlantic coast, comprises 740 sq. mi. with pop. (est. 1960) of 49,889, claimed as a perpetual possession under an 1860 agreement.

# Sudan

### JAMHURYAT EL-SUDAN
### REPUBLIC OF THE SUDAN

**Capital: Khartoum. Area: 967,500 sq. mi. Population** (UN est. 1967): 14,355,000. **Monetary unit;** Sudanese pound (.3482 per U. S. $1).

Sudan, a former Anglo-Egyptian condominium in Africa, proclaimed itself a republic Jan. 1, 1956. It is bounded by the United Arab Republic, the Red Sea, Ethiopia, Uganda, Kenya, the Democratic Republic of the Congo, the Central African Republic, Chad and Libya. It is about the size of Texas, Alaska and New Mexico combined.

The northern zone consists of the Libyan Desert, on the W, and the mountainous Nubian Desert, extending to the Red Sea on the E, separated by the narrow valley of the Nile; the central zone contains large fertile areas, including the rainlands of Kassala and Tokar, the Gezira plain and the pastures and gum forests of Kordofan; and the southern equatorial belt where the soil is richest and watered by tropical rains.

The White Nile flows N through the center of the country; the Blue Nile, rising in the mountains of Ethiopia, joins the White at Khartoum; the combined river flows N in a huge S curve to enter the UAR north of Wadi Halfa.

**Resources and Industries.** The Sudan is the world's principal source of gum arabic. Chief grain crop is durra (sorghum), the country's staple food. Cotton is the principal export; American and extra-long staple cottons are grown in the fertile Gezira, between the White and Blue Niles. Other important products are sesame, senna peanuts, rice, coffee, sugar cane, tobacco, dates, hides, mahogany, beans, corn, mother of pearl, shea nuts, salt, ivory.

The Sudan has small scale production of gold, iron ore, gypsum, chromite, cement.

**History and Government.** In the 1820s Egypt took over the Sudan, defeating the last of earlier empires, including the Fung. In the 1880s a revolution was led by Mohammed Ahmed who called himself the Mahdi (leader of the faithful) and

his followers, the dervishes. British Gen. Charles Gordon (called Chinese Gordon for his exploits in China), who had earlier put down the slave trade in the Sudan, was sent by Egypt to evacuate its troops; he was beseiged and finally slain at Khartoum Jan. 26, 1885.

In 1898 Horatio Kitchener (later titled Lord Kitchener of Khartoum) led an Anglo-Egyptian force which crushed the successors of the Mahdi at Omdurman Sept. 2.

In October, 1951, the Egyptian Parliament abrogated its 1899 and 1936 treaties with Great Britain, and amended the constitution, Oct. 16, to provide for a separate Sudanese constitution.

Sudan voted for complete independence effective Jan. 1, 1956. A five-member Supreme Commission (Council of State) and a Cabinet were sworn in.

On Nov. 17, 1958, Gen. Ibrahim Abboud ousted Premier Abdullah Khalil of the Umma party, head of a coalition government. Abboud resigned under pressure Nov. 15, 1964; a new Constituent Assembly was elected April 21-May 8, 1965, and approved a coalition government headed by Premier Mohammed Ahmed Mahgoub. Only 5 northern provinces took part in the election; the 3 southern provinces did not. A large part of the southern provinces, a pagan and Christian Negro area, was swept by guerrilla warfare, 1963-68, against the forces of the predominantly Arab-Moslem north, which controls the government.

During the Israeli-Arab war of June, 1967, Sudan broke off diplomatic relations with the U. S. in response to charges that U. S. warplanes were assisting the Israelis.

Sudan is a member of the UN and Arab League.

**Education and Religion.** Sudanese inhabitants are Arabs, Negros and Nubians of mixed Arab and Negro blood; the Arabs and Nubians are Mohammedans. The educational system in the South, formerly largely administered by Christian missions, now also is in hands of the government. Higher education is available at Khartcum Univ. (formerly Gordon College). Arabic is the national language.

# Swaziland

**Capital: Mbabane. Area: 6,704 sq. mi. Population** (UN est. 1967): 385,000. **Monetary unit: Rand** (.7190 per U. S. $1).

Swaziland is in SE Africa, almost completely surrounded by the Republic of South Africa except for part of the E border which adjoins Mozambique (Portuguese East Africa). The Swazis came under British rule in the late 18th Century as a means of gaining protection from their traditional enemies, the warlike Zulus.

The example of neighboring former British territories Bechuanaland and Basutoland, which became the independent nations of Botswana and Lesotho in 1966, encouraged the drive for Swazi independence; Swaziland was economically the most healthy of the 3. On Apr. 25, 1967, it achieved full internal self-government under a constitution and on Sept. 6, 1968, it became completely independent and the 28th member of the Commonwealth, leaving rebel Rhodesia as Britain's last colonial "possession" in Africa.

The constitution provided for an elected Parliament, and the former Paramount Chief, Sobhuza II, became King Sobhuza, a constitutional head of state. The Royal house of Swaziland traces back 400 years, and remains one of Africa's last ruling dynasties. The King was reputed to have 90 wives, but to avoid dissension, none of them was named queen. Instead, an aged aunt was named the official Queen Mother Regent. To avoid a succession conflict among the many princes, the next king was to be chosen by a royal advisory body.

Polygamy has been the common marital status. Women have the right to vote. Many Swazi women dye their hair bright orange or soak it with soap and pile it up like a beehive.

About 97% of the residents are Swazi, a group that broke off from the Bantu tribe about 1750. South African whites constitute a small but powerful minority. English is the official language but Swazi is spoken by the vast majority of people.

The country is rich in mineral resources, including one of the world's 5 largest asbestos mines, the Havelock Mine, and iron ore resources estimated at some 47,000,000 tons in the Ngwenya Mines. In addition, there are gold, tin, silver, mica and other minerals.

In recent years Swaziland developed a multi-million-dollar timber and pulp industry, a railway link out of the landlocked country to ports in Mozambique, hydro-electric power and tarred roads. Exports rose from $16,800,000 in 1965 to over $45,000,000 by 1968. The first quarter of 1968 saw Swaziland's exports to Britain alone mount to more than the entire budget figure of Lesotho. The major export items are asbestos, iron ore, citrus fruits and sugar.

The land is fertile and has abundant water, producing such other crops as corn, cotton, rice, pineapples and cattle.

About 10,000 Swazis hold jobs in South Africa and the currency is the South African rand. Most of the population, however, is agricultural, living in grass huts and maintaining old tribal customs.

# Sweden

## KONUNGARIKET SVERIGE

**Capital: Stockholm. Area: 173,378 sq. mi.** **Population (Govt. est. 1967): 7,847,395. Monetary unit: Krona; pl. kronor (5.168 per U. S. $1).**

Sweden occupies the eastern and largest part of the Scandinavian peninsula in NW Europe. Its greatest N-S length is 977 mi.; greatest width 311 mi. The country is larger than Calif. but smaller than Texas. Sweden is separated from Norway on the W by the Kölen (or Kjölen) mountain range, and from Finland on the E by the Baltic Sea except in the N where the two meet along the Tornea River.

Stockholm and Goteborg are the largest ports.

**Resources and Industries.** Although the topography is mountainous, Sweden contains much productive land, well watered, on which the Swedes have attained high efficiency in agriculture. Of Sweden's total land area, 8% is cultivated, 2.5% pasture, and 55% forests. About one-third is unreclaimable. Chief agricultural products are cheese, butter, beef, pork, wheat, rye, potatoes, sugar beets and vegetable oils.

Many industries flourish in Sweden, whose main natural resources are forests, iron ore and water power. Coal and oil have to be imported; oil constitutes 10% of all imports. Industry employs 45% of the work-population, agriculture 8%. Swedish steel is of especial value for tool making. Other metals produced are: lead, copper, zinc, gold and silver. In 1966, 51 billion kwh. were produced. The Stornorrforsen hydroelectric plant on the Ume River is the largest in Western Europe.

Although over 95% of the economy is in private hands, the government holds a large interest in water power production and the railroads are operated by a public agency.

Consumer cooperatives are in extensive operation, with 1,250,000 members served by about 5,000 stores. Cooperatives also are important in agriculture and housing.

Shipping is privately operated and not subsidized. The merchant marine totaled approx. 4,470,-000 gross-tons on Dec. 31, 1966. Swedish shipbuilders account for about 10% of the world's output of commercial tonnage. In 1966 their shipyards launched 65 ships totaling 1,160,000 gross tons.

Sweden is one of the leading exporters of iron ore and cellulose. About one-fourth of the exports come from pulp, lumber, paper and other forestry products. Other important products are steel, automobiles, ships, airplanes, ball bearings, textiles, electrical goods, petrochemicals.

Foreign trade in thousands of U. S. dollars:

| | Imports | Exports |
|---|---|---|
| 1966 | $4,576,000 | $4,264,000 |
| 1967 | $4,705,000 | $4,534,000 |

**History and Government.** Sweden is a parliamentary democracy with a King as head of state and a prime minister as political chief executive. The Riksdag (Parliament) has two chambers, the first of 151 members elected for 8 years, and the second of 233 members, elected for 4. All over 20 are entitled to vote.

The first peaceful consolidation of Sweden with other Scandinavian countries was the union of Kalmar, 1397. Sweden revolted 1434-1523. Reformation was introduced 1527; Lutheranism dominated from about 1600.

The King is Gustav VI Adolf (born Nov. 11, 1882), who succeeded on the death of his father, Gustav V, Oct. 29, 1950 (reigned since Dec. 8, 1907). The King married (June 15, 1905) Princess Margaret (died May 1, 1920). He has three living sons, two of them commoners through marriage, and one daughter, Queen Ingrid of Denmark. One son, Gustaf Adolf, was killed in an airplane accident Jan. 26, 1947 and his son, Prince Carl Gustaf (born 1946), became heir apparent. The

King's second wife (married Nov. 3, 1923) was Lady Louise Mountbatten, who died Mar. 7, 1965.

About 14% of the national income is redistributed through the social welfare system which includes compulsory health insurance. Unemployment during 1966 was about 1%.

Sweden is a member with Denmark, Norway and Iceland of the Nordic Council, estab. Feb., 1953, and of the UN, EFTA and GATT.

**Education and Religion.** The population is very homogenous, being of the Scandinavian branch of the Germanic family, except about 30,000 Finns and 10,000 Lapps. Approx. 95% of the people are Lutheran, which is the state religion. Education is compulsory and illiteracy is non-existent. There are state universities at Uppsala (founded 1477), Lund, Stockholm, Goteborg and Umea.

**Defense.** Service in the Army is compulsory between 19 and 47. A first 10-month training period is followed by 5 refreshers of 25 days each. There is an Army of approximately 600,000, plus a voluntary Home Guard of 125,000. The Air Force has 15 wings of about 45 combat squadrons totaling 600 planes, mostly Swedish-built jets. The Navy has one cruiser, 8 destroyers, 8 frigates, 20 submarines, 38 motor torpedo boats and 35 minesweepers and other units.

The coast artillery is largely dug into atom-bomb-proof rock shelters along nearly 700 mi. of coastline.

# Switzerland
### SCHWEIZ—SUISSE—SVIZZERA

**Capital: Berne. Area: 15,941 sq. mi. Population (Govt. est. 1967): 6,071,000. Monetary unit: Franc (3.82 per U. S. $1).**

Switzerland, a federal republic in Central Europe, is bounded by France, Germany, Austria, Liechtenstein and Italy. It is twice the size of New Jersey.

Switzerland is the most mountainous of all European countries. The Alps cover 61% of land area, the Jura 12%; running between them, NE to SW, are the midlands, about 27%. Highest peak is Monte Rosa, 15,203 ft.; the Matterhorn is 14,690 ft.; more than 70 are over 10,000 ft. Lakes famous for their beauty include Maggiore, Lucerne, Geneva, Neuchatel, Constance, Thun, Brienz. The Rhine, Rhone and feeders of the Danube and Po originate in Switzerland.

**Resources and Industries.** Switzerland's abundant water power is exploited by 431 major hydroelectric plants. Salt is the principal mineral. Watches (50% of world's watch trade), machinery, and precision instruments are important manufactures; also silk, wool and cotton articles; iron and steel and electrical products; industrial chemicals, clothing, perfumes, and pharmaceuticals. Dairy products, especially cheese, lead agriculture, followed by cattle, pigs, fruit, poultry, tobacco, wheat, rye, oats, potatoes and wine. Machine making employs 26% of all factory workers and accounts for 28% of exports. Included are textile machinery, machine tools, dynamo-electric plants, transformers and diesels.

Switzerland is one of the world's greatest banking centers. Stability of its currency brings funds there from many quarters. Tourism is a vital part of the economy. Nearly 6,000,000 foreign tourists visited Switzerland in 1967.

**History and Government.** Switzerland, the Helvetia of ancient times, is a confederation of 22 cantons, three of which once (1291) were members of a defensive league and later were joined by other districts. In 1648 the Swiss Confederation obtained its independence from the Holy Roman Empire. The cantons were joined under a Federal Constitution in 1848, with large powers of local control retained by each canton. Legislative authority vests in a parliament of two chambers, a Ständerat or State Council to which each canton sends two members; and a lower house, Nationalrat or National Council, with 200 members.

Executive power is vested in the Bundesrat (Federal Council) of 7 members.

The President is selected from membership of the Federal Council, serves for one year and customarily is succeeded by the Vice President.

Switzerland enters into no military alliance and is not a member of UN or NATO. It is however a member of various international agencies of the UN, such as the International Labor Org., World Health Org., UNESCO, FAO and others. It also is a member of EFTA.

Geneva is the seat of a number of UN organiza-

tions, International Committee of the Red Cross, League of Red Cross Societies and Int'l Union for Telecommunications. The Universal Postal Union is in Berne.

**Education and Religion.** Primary education has been free and compulsory since 1874. There are 7 universities; the oldest is Basel, founded in 1460. Swiss German dialects are spoken by a majority of the people in 16 of the cantons; other languages are French, Italian, and Romansch.

There is complete freedom of worship. Of the population 52.7% are Reformed Protestant, 45.4% Roman Catholics.

**Defense.** Service in the national militia is compulsory; liability extends from 20 to 50 years. Its 12 easily mobilized divisions comprise more than 700,000 men.

# Syria
### SOURIYA
### SYRIAN ARAB REPUBLIC

**Capital: Damascus. Area: 72,234 sq. mi. Population (Govt. est. 1967): 5,761,349. Monetary unit: Syrian pound (4.2 per U. S. $1).**

A land of Middle East contrasts, the Syrian Arab Republic has a short coastline on the Mediterranean, then stretches east and south with fertile valleys and plains alternating with mountainous and desert areas. The main rivers are the Euphrates and Orontest. Chief seaport is Latakia. The nation is about the size of South Dakota.

**Resources and Industries.** Mineral wealth is small except for oil deposits. Actual oil production is limited, but the Iraq Petroleum Co. pays for oil pipelines transit and terminal rights. Agriculture and stock raising are chief occupations. Main crops are cotton, wheat, barley, tobacco, citrus fruits, olives, grapes and sorghum. Industries include flour, oils, soap, textiles, cement, tanning, tobacco, knitwear, glassware, sugar, hosiery, footwear and brassware. Raw cotton and textiles followed by tobacco are the principal exports.

Syria's gross national product rose from $935,-656,000 for 1963 to $1.04 billion for 1964. Receipts from tourism increased from $10,418,000 for 1965 to $13,080,000 for 1966.

**History and Government.** One of the world's ancient inhabited lands, the state (later republic) of Syria was formed from former Turkish Empire Sanjaks (districts). Syria was made a separate entity by the Treaty of Sevres, Aug. 10, 1920, and divided into the states of Syria and Greater Lebanon Sept. 1, 1920. Both were administered under a French mandate 1920-1941.

Syria was proclaimed a republic by the occupying French authorities Sept. 16, 1941, and exercised full power effective Jan. 1, 1944. French troops left by April 17, 1946.

Syria joined with Egypt in Feb. 1958 in the United Arab Republic but seceded Sept. 30, 1961. The Socialist Baath party and military leaders seized power in March 1963, led by Lt. Gen. Amin el-Hafez. The Baath, an international Arab organization, became the only legal party.

The Baath regime in 1965 nationalized most industries.

Over the years there had been intermittent border clashes with Israel and in the Israeli-Arab war of June, 1967, Israel occupied heights 12 mi. inside Syria from which Israeli border settlements in northern Galilee had been shelled for years.

Syria severed diplomatic relations with the U. S. as a result of the war. It is a member of the UN.

**Education and Religion.** The population is composed mainly of Sunni Moslems but there are many Christians, Arabic is the official language. Syria has universities in Damascus and Aleppo.

# Tanzania
### (Formerly Tanganyika and Zanzibar)

**Capital: Dar es Salaam. Area 363,708 sq. mi. Population (Govt. est. 1967): 12,231,342. Monetary unit: Tanzanian shilling (7.143 per U. S. $1).**

The republic of Tanganyika in E Africa and the republic of Zanzibar, a large island in the Indian Ocean off the coast of Tanganyika, joined in a single republic Apr. 26, 1964. The new central government at Dar es Salaam (Haven of Peace), an important port and capital of Tanganyika, was given jurisdiction over defense, foreign affairs and public services.

Julius K. Nyerere, Tanganyika's President, became President of the new nation; Abeid Amani Karume, Zanzibar's President, became Vice President.

At first the combined nation was called the United Republic of Tanganyika and Zanzibar. In Oct. 1964 the name was changed to Tanzania.

A member of the UN and the Commonwealth, Tanganyika has received aid from Communist China, the USSR, the U. S. and Canada.

In 1967 the government nationalized all banks, including some in which U. S. banks held a part interest, and many industries; some of the latter were taken over completely, in others the government took a part interest. The government also ordered that Swahili, not English, be used in all official business.

### TANGANYIKA

Tanganyika stretches from the Indian Ocean on the E to 3 of Africa's Great Lakes: Victoria, Tanganyika and Nyasa (now also called Malawi). Its area is 362,688 sq. mi., larger than Texas and Oklahoma combined; pop. (Govt. est. 1965) 10,-178,100. Most of the people are Bantus and speak Swahili.

Snow-capped Mt. Kilimanjaro, tallest in Africa, rises majestically in the N. Nearby are the famed Serengeti Plains, teeming with vast herds of wild animals, protected in one of Tanzania's several large national park game preserves. Safaris, sport fishing and mountain climbing are among attractions. In Olduvai Gorge, prehistoric man-like remains, over a million years old, were discovered by Dr. and Mrs. Louis Leakey.

Principal products are sisal, cotton, coffee, tea, tobacco and hides. Both gem and industrial diamonds are mined, as are gold, salt, tin and mica. Diamonds account for 77% of the mineral income, gold for 12%.

Arab colonization began in the 8th Century A.D.; Portuguese sailors explored the coast by about 1500. Other Europeans followed and it was under a mango tree at Ujiji on Lake Tanganyika that Henry M. Stanley found David Livingstone Nov. 10, 1871.

In 1885 Germany established German East Africa of which Tanganyika formed the bulk. After World War I it was taken and administered by Britain as a League of Nations mandate and since 1946 as a UN trust territory.

Constitutional changes gave it internal autonomy in Sept. 1960. It became fully independent Dec. 9, 1961, and was proclaimed a republic within the Commonwealth a year later.

### ZANZIBAR

Zanzibar, the Isle of Cloves. lies 23 mi. off the coast of Tanganyika; its area is 640 sq. mi. The island of Pemba, 25 mi. to the NW, area 380 sq. mi., is included in the administration. The population is chiefly Moslem. The total area of the two islands is about the size of Rhode Island; population (Govt. est. 1967): 354,360.

Attractions include numerous public gardens and ancient palaces.

Chief industry is the production of cloves and clove oil of which Zanzibar and Pemba produce the bulk of the world's supply. Coconuts and copra also are exported. Pottery, coir fiber, rope, soap, oil, jewelry and mats are manufactured.

Portugal ruled Zanzibar for two centuries until ousted by Arabs around 1700. Zanzibar became an independent Sultanate in 1856 and a British Protectorate in 1890 by agreement with Germany and France.

Independence within the Commonwealth was attained Dec. 10, 1963. Rebel forces overthrew Sultan Seyyid Jamshid bin Abdullah bin Khalifa Jan. 12, 1964. The revolutionary government ousted American and British diplomats and newsmen and nationalized farms. Union with Tanganyika followed, 1964.

## Thailand (Siam)

### PRADES THAI; MUANG-THAI

**Capital: Bangkok. Area: 200,148 sq. mi. Population (UN est. 1967): 32,680,000. Monetary unit: Baht (20.75 per U. S. $1).**

Thailand is a constitutional monarchy in SE Asia bordered by Burma, Laos, Cambodia, the Gulf of Thailand (or Siam) and Malaysia. It is a country of rolling hills, about twice the size of Colorado with large areas under irrigation.

Bangkok, the capital, is a modern city. Its Don Muang airfield is one of the largest and most modern in Southeast Asia, served by 24 international airlines. An important port, Bangkok is 25 mi. in from the sea in the Menam delta. There is an extensive inland waterway system and network of modern roads.

**Resources and Industries.** There are many large forests, teakwood being an important article of export. Agriculture occupies 91% of the population.

Thailand is the world's 3rd largest producer of tin ore; other minerals are coal, iron, manganese, tungsten, antimony and fluorspar.

The chief crop is rice, the staple food of the people and heavily exported, accounting for a third of foreign exchange earnings. Other important exports are tin, rubber, teak and tungsten. Coconuts, tobacco, pepper, tapioca flour, corn, peanuts, beans and cotton are produced in quantity.

Foreign investment in industry is encouraged—auto assembly plants, pharmaceuticals, textiles, electrical goods.

**History and Government.** Thailand, an ancient monarchy, noted for picturesque architecture and pageantry, is the only country in SE Asia never taken over by a colonial power, thanks to King Mongkut and his son King Chulalongkorn who ruled from 1851 to 1910, modernized the country and signed trade treaties with both Britain and France.

Thailand underwent a bloodless revolution in 1932. King Prajadhipok, a liberal, signed a new constitution, establishing a limited monarchy, but he refused to sign a measure abdicating the royal power of life and death and resigned. He was succeeded by his nephew, Prince Ananda, who was found dead of a bullet wound, June 9, 1946, and the legislature named his brother, Prince Phumiphol Aduldet (Bhumibol Adulyadej) (born 1927), to succeed him. King Phumiphol formally took the throne May 5, 1950, as Rama IX.

Since World War II there have been several military coups and changes in government. On June 21, 1968, a new constitution was promulgated, providing for an elected Assembly which would have limited powers.

There was sporadic Communist terrorism in the NE and far S in 1968 and earlier.

About 40,000 U. S. servicemen, two thirds of them Air Force, were stationed in Thailand in 1967. Air strikes against North Vietnam and the Ho Chi Minh trail in Laos were conducted from air bases constructed by the U. S. in Thailand. About 2,000 Thai combat troops served with South Vietnam in the latter country.

**Education and Religion.** Education is compulsory between 8 and 15. There are 7 universities, 31 training colleges and many vocational schools. The language is Thai, derived from Pali and Sanskrit. There is much official use of English. About 93% of the people are Buddhists; others are Moslems, Christians, etc.

**Defense.** Of Thailand's total armed forces of 85,000, the militarized police force comprises 40,-000; army about 30,000; air force 4,000. The Navy has five frigates and many small craft, with 18,000 personnel. Thailand is a member of the UN and SEATO.

## Togo

### REPUBLIQUE TOGOLAISE

**Capital Lomé. Area, 20,400 sq. mi. Population (UN est. 1967): 1,724,000. Monetary unit: CFA franc (246.85 per U. S. $1).**

The republic of Togo (Togoland) which became independent April 27, 1960, is comprised of part of the one-time German colony of Togoland, surrendered in 1914, and administered by France as a UN trusteeship, 1946-1960.

Togo is a thin sliver of land, about twice the size of Vermont, facing the Atlantic on the southern edge of the West African bulge. It is bounded by Upper Volta, Dahomey, the Atlantic and Ghana.

In 1958 France received UN approval to end its trusteeship and the republic was proclaimed Apr. 27, 1960. It chose to remain outside the French Community. It is a member of the UN.

A draft constitution on the U. S. model was published Mar. 20, 1961. It provided for a President and a 46-member unicameral Parliament. First President, Sylvanus Olympio, elected Apr. 9, 1961, was assassinated by a military junta Jan. 13, 1963. His successor was Nicolas Grunitzky,

elected May 5, 1963. Grunitzky resigned Jan. 13, 1967, and was replaced by Etienne Eyadema, head of the armed forces.

A friendship and commercial treaty with the U. S. was agreed on in 1966.

Principal products: coffee, cocoa, palm kernels, copra, cotton, kapok, manioc and peanuts.

# Trinidad and Tobago

**Capital:** Port of Spain. **Area:** 1,979 sq. mi. **Population (UN est. 1967):** 1,016,000. **Monetary unit:** Trinidad and Tobago Dollar (2 per U. S. $1).

Trinidad, area 1,864 sq. mi., is the most southerly of the West Indies lying off the NE coast of South America approx. 7 mi. from Venezuela. It was discovered by Columbus in 1498. **Tobago**, 116 sq. mi. lies 20 mi to the NE of Trinidad.

Second largest of the old British West Indies and a British possession since 1802, Trinidad and Tobago won independence Aug. 31, 1962. A Governor General represents the British Sovereign. Parliament consists of a 24-member Senate appointed by the Gov. Gen. and a 36-member House of Representatives elected by universal suffrage. The country is a member of the UN, the Commonwealth and the OAS.

Chaguaramas, a promontory near Port of Spain, was an important U. S. naval air base and a link in the anti-submarine defense of the Caribbean. The base was acquired by the U. S. under a lease at start of World War II, but June 9, 1967, was formally returned by the U. S., 73 years ahead of schedule.

Import trade is heaviest with England, export trade with the U. S. Exports are mostly petroleum, sugar, asphalt, rum, cocoa, coffee, citrus, bananas, cement, bitters. Pitch Lake, 114 acres, is world's largest supply of asphalt.

The economic picture in the nation, one of the most prosperous in the West Indies, improved during 1967. The total national product rose 4%; exports were increased and imports decreased sufficiently to give the country a favorable balance of trade; the Government's family planning program cut the birth rate from 3.1% to 2.4%; the unemployment rate, still high, was cut from 20% to 15%.

Trinidad claims to have originated the steel band (instrument fashioned from oil drums), calypso songs and the limbo dance. Tourism is an important source of revenue.

The population is mixed: Negro 44%, East Indian (descended from immigrants from India) 36%, Lebanese, Syrian, white and Chinese comprise the rest. Religions include Roman Catholic 36%, Protestant 34%, Hindu 23%, Moslem 6%.

Public primary and secondary education is free to age 18. Some units of Univ. of West Indies are in Trinidad, some in Jamaica. There are two technical institutes.

# Tunisia

### AL-JOUMHOURIA ATTUNUSIA

**Capital:** Tunis. **Area:** 58,000 sq. mi. **Population (UN est. 1967):** 4,560,000. **Monetary Unit:** Dinar (.525 per U. S. $1).

Tunisia is a former French protectorate which was proclaimed a republic in 1957. It is on the Mediterranean coast of Africa wedged between Algeria and Libya. It is about the size of Florida. The people are mostly Arabs and Berbers.

**Resources and Industries.** The chief industry is agriculture and the fertile soil produces an abundance of wheat, barley, oats, dates, olives, apricots, almonds, figs, peaches, vegetables, alfa grass. Livestock is extensively raised. Phosphates, iron, lead and zinc are leading minerals.

Industries include canning, fertilizers, carpets, blankets, shoes, and building materials. Principal exports are olive oil, wine, iron ore, lead, phosphates and grains. A 10-year economic development program was begun in 1962.

Oil was discovered in 1965 at El Borma in the S in sufficient quantity to meet domestic needs.

Tourism is growing and attractions include numerous well-preserved Roman ruins, excellent beaches, and resorts on Djerba Is., reputed home of the Lotus Eaters of the Odyssey.

The tourist industry earned $26,000,000 in 1967. Irrigation has aided agriculture. Fish and textile industries have boosted exports. Other new industries include steel and auto-assembly plants, a paper mill and sugar refinery.

**History and Government.** A former Barbary state under the suzerainty of Turkey, Tunisia became a protectorate of France under a treaty signed May 12, 1881, after France sent a military force to combat the raiding Khroumer tribes. After receiving increasing measures of self-government since 1947, a constituent assembly, elected Mar. 25, 1956, chose a government headed by Habib Bourguiba of the dominant Neo-Destour party, named Premier Apr. 10. The basic law, adopted by the assembly, Apr. 13, vested sovereignty in the people, ignoring the titular ruler, Mohammed el Amim, Bey of Tunis. The assembly unanimously voted, July 25, 1957, to end the monarchy. It deposed the Bey and proclaimed a republic, electing Premier Bourguiba interim President.

Under a U. S.-style constitution adopted June 1, 1959, the President is elected for 5 years, limited to 3 consecutive terms. The National Assembly of 90 also is elected for 5-year terms. In national elections Nov. 8, 1959, the National Front won all the seats. Women have equal rights, but in 1966 miniskirts were banned by the government.

President: Habib Bourguiba, elected 1959, 1964.

A law passed May 11, 1964, nationalized all farmland still owned by foreigners, providing for compensation in return. A system of cooperative farms was started.

Tunisia is a member of the UN and Arab League but in April 1965 Pres. Bourguiba proposed negotiations to reach settlement of the Arab-Israel dispute. He was denounced by other Arab League countries. In May he did not attend an Arab-League heads-of-state meeting and assailed UAR Pres. Nasser for trying to force Tunisia to take an anti-U. S. stand. On Oct. 3, 1966, he broke diplomatic relations with the UAR, which were not resumed until after the outbreak of the Israeli-Arab war June 5, 1967. In Aug. he urged Arab nations to end their state of belligerency with Israel.

**Education and Religion.** The majority of the population is Moslem. Europeans number about 120,000, Jews 65,000. Fifty percent are under age 20; estimated birth rate: 40 per 1,000; death rate, 15 per 1,000. Arabic is the national and official language. In 1966 Pres. Bourguiba said that in 10 years Tunisia had raised the number of primary school students from 200,000 to 734,000, secondary from 15,500 to 80,000 and higher education from 1,350 to 5,000. The former Moslem University of Zitouna and the Institute of Advanced Studies are incorporated in the new University of Tunis, due for completion in 1968.

**Defense.** A National Army was created in 1956; it consists of about 20,000 officers and men. Nuclei of a Navy and an Air Force have been formed.

# Turkey

### TURKIYE CUMHURIYETI

**Capital:** Ankara. **Area:** 296,500 sq. mi. **Population (UN est. 1967):** 32,710,000. **Monetary unit:** Lira (9.08 per U. S. $1).

About 90% of Turkey's population lives in the Asian portion of the country on the Anatolian Peninsula—an area of 287,500 sq. mi. The remainder live in the European part which is bordered by Bulgaria and Greece. A republic since 1923, Turkey is a little larger than Texas and has extensive coastlines on the Black Sea, the Mediterranean and the Aegean. Its Asian neighbors are the USSR, Syria, Iraq and Iran.

Central Turkey is a great plateau, with hot dry summers and cold winters with snow remaining until May. High mountains ring the plateau on all but the W side. More than 20 peaks top 10,000 ft.

Izmir (ancient Smyrna) is the principal export outlet.

**Resources and Industries.** Approx. 75% of the labor force is engaged in agriculture, the products including tobacco (more than 250,000,000 lbs. annually), cereal, cotton, olive oil, wool, silk, figs, nuts, fruits, sugar, opium for medicinal purposes, and gums. About 20,000,000 acres are in forests.

There are large deposits of antimony, borate, copper, and chrome (of which Turkey is the world's largest producer). Other minerals include manganese, lead, zinc, coal, iron, oil, silver, mercury, sulphur, molybdenum, magnesite and asbestos.

Turkey manufactures silk, cotton and woolen yarn and cloth, steel, foundry products, sugar, footwear, office furniture, cement, paper, glass-

ware and appliances. The country has the largest arms industry in the Middle East. About 23% of trade is with the U. S.

Foreign trade, in thousands of U.S. dollars:

| | Imports | Exports |
|---|---|---|
| 1966 | $725,000 | $491,000 |
| 1967 | $691,000 | $522,000 |

**History and Government.** Up to World War I, Turkey, or the Ottoman Empire, included European Turkey, Anatolia, Syria, Lebanon, Iraq, Jordan, Palestine, Arabia, Yemen and islands in the Aegean Sea.

Turkey joined Germany and Austria in World War I and its defeat resulted in loss of much territory and fall of the sultanate. A republic was declared Oct. 29, 1923, with Mustafa Kemal Ataturk first President. The Caliphate (spiritual leadership of Islam) was renounced 1924. Turkey was permitted (1936) to refortify the Dardanelles and Bosporus, to close them if threatened, but to permit free passage of merchant vessels in peace or war. The USSR has proposed joint control of the straits but Turkey has refused.

But in 1968 Turkey and the USSR agreed on a $200,000,000 loan from the Soviet to build factories in Turkey which would be paid for in Turkish products.

The present constitution, adopted July 9, 1961, provides for a civilian parliamentary government, protection of human rights, guards against abuses of executive power, and provides for a bicameral legislature composed of a Senate of 185 and a National Assembly of 450 deputies. The President is elected by Parliament to a 7-year term and is ineligible for reelection.

Turkey is a member of the UN, CENTO, NATO, Council of Europe. Communism is outlawed.

For years Turkey and Greece have been involved in a controversy over Cyprus (see Cyprus).

**Education and Religion.** Church and State are separated. About 98% of the Turkish population is Moslem.

Education is compulsory, free and secular between the ages of 7 and 12, and optional, but free, through the university. There are universities in Istanbul, Ankara, Izmir and Erzurum. Robert College, 1865, is oldest American college abroad.

**Defense.** Military service is compulsory. Turkey supplies a large ground force to NATO.

Turkey is a member, with Greece and Yugoslavia, of the Balkan defense group by a treaty signed in Ankara, Feb. 27, 1953, and a 20-year military aid pact, Aug. 9, 1954. It also concluded pacts with Pakistan in 1954, and has a defense pact with the U. S. signed Mar. 5, 1959.

## Uganda

**Capital: Kampala. Area: 91,134 sq. mi. Population (UN est. 1967): 7,934,000. Monetary unit: Uganda shilling (7.143 per U. S. $1).**

Uganda, a former British protectorate, is in central Africa with Kenya to the E, Lake Victoria and Tanzania to the S, Lakes Albert and Edward and Democratic Republic of Congo to the W, Sudan to the N. It is about the size of Minnesota.

Uganda is the largest coffee producer in the Commonwealth. Cotton, tea, maize, peanuts, sisal, oil seeds, tobacco, sugar, are also produced. Copper and tin are important mineral exports.

The nation has made steady economic progress.

In 1966-67 uninhabited areas in western Uganda which had been infested with tsetse flies, carriers of sleeping sickness, were transformed into cattle ranches, thanks to eradication of the tsetse with the aid of a U. S. loan.

Uganda became independent within the Commonwealth Oct. 9, 1962, a republic Oct. 9, 1963.

President is Milton Obote. Uganda is a member of the UN and the Commonwealth.

A long-standing political feud erupted Feb. 22, 1966, when Obote, then Prime Minister, seized full power and on Mar. 2 ousted President Edward Mutesa (who was also the Kabaka, or King, of Buganda). On May 24 army troops shelled and destroyed the king's palace but the king escaped the country.

Lake Victoria, 26,828 sq. mi., is Africa's largest lake. It is 3,720 ft. above sea level and over 200 mi. long. It was explored in 1875 by Henry M. Stanley.

It lies partly in Tanzania and Kenya and lake steamers connect their ports and Uganda. At Owen Falls on the Victoria Nile, outlet of Lake Victoria, a major dam and hydroelectric project has been constructed.

Further N on the Victoria Nile is Murchison Falls, 130 ft., in the heart of one of Uganda's national parks. On the W border with the Democratic Republic of the Congo, the Ruwenzori Range, identified with the legendary "Mountains of the Moon," rises over 16,000 ft. Pygmy tribes live in the nearby forests. In the SW there are several volcanoes over 11,000 ft. high; on their slopes is a gorilla sanctuary.

## Union of Soviet Socialist Republics

**SOYUZ SOVYETSKIKH SOTSIALISTICHESKIKH RESPUBLIK (Formerly Russian Empire)**

**Capital: Moscow. Area: 8,647,172 sq. mi. Population (Govt. est. 1968): 236,700,000. Monetary unit: Ruble (.90 official rate per U. S. $1).**

The Union of Soviet Socialist Republics—in area the largest country in the world—stretches across two continents from the North Pacific to the Baltic Sea. It occupies the northern part of Asia and the eastern half of Europe. Its western borders brush against Finland, the Baltic, Poland, Czechoslovakia, Hungary and Romania. On the S it is bounded by Romania, the Black Sea, Turkey, Iran, Afghanistan, China, Mongolian Peoples Republic and North Korea. In the far NE, Bering Strait separates it from Alaska.

The vast territory of the USSR, one-sixth of the earth's land surface, contains every phase of climate, except the distinctly tropical, and a varied topography. The European portion is a vast low plain with the Ural Mtns. on its eastern edge, the Caucasus Mtns. and others on the S. The Urals, separating the European from the Asiatic portions of the country, stretch N and S for 2,500 mi. The Asiatic portion also consists largely of an immense plain, with mountain ranges on its E and S.

There are some 150,000 rivers and 250,000 lakes. The larger European rivers include the Dnieper, flowing into the Black Sea, the Volga and the Ural into the Caspian Sea, the Don into the Sea of Azov, the Western Dvina into the Baltic and the Northern Dvina into the White Sea. The Asiatic section is drained by the Ob, the Yenisei and the Lena, each over 2,000 mi. long, which flow into the Arctic Ocean, and the Amur, which flows into the Pacific.

In the European section there is an 88,000-mi. inland waterway system in which canals link rivers (Moscow-Volga, 80 mi.; Dnieper-Bug, 58 mi.; Volga-Balt, 700 mi.; Volga-Don, 64 mi.), leading to 5 seas: Caspian, Azov, Black, Baltic and White.

The Caspian Sea, of which only the S end is in Iran, is the world's largest lake (143,550 sq. mi.). Other lakes are the Aral Sea (25,300 sq. mi.), Lake Baykal (11,780 sq. mi.), Lake Balkhash (6,720 sq. mi.), Lake Ladoga (6,835 sq. mi.).

In Moscow, the Kremlin, ancient citadel of the Czars, forms the nerve center of the federated republics. Leningrad (formerly St. Petersburg and Petrograd), in the delta of the Neva River, is the 2nd largest city, Kiev, the 1,000-year-old capital of the Ukrainian SSR, is the industrial center of the south. The Crimea and the eastern shore of the Black Sea, beneath the towering Caucasus Mtns., are a modern vacationland.

Beginning in 1939 the USSR by means of military action and negotiation overran contiguous territory and independent republics. Transfer of part of East Germany was approved at the Potsdam Conference. The Yalta Agreement conceded Soviet claims to Japanese territory in the Kurile islands and southern half of Sakhalin.

### POLITICAL ORGANIZATION

The USSR is a federation consisting of 15 Union Republics, within certain of which are further subdivisions, such as Autonomous Soviet Socialist Republics, Autonomous Regions and National Districts. Four of the Union Republics contain 20 Autonomous Soviet Socialist Republics and 8 Autonomous Regions; the largest Union Republic, the Russian Soviet Federal Socialist Republic,

has also 10 National Districts. The Union Republics are:

| Republic | Area sq. miles | Population (Est. 1968) |
|---|---|---|
| Russian SFSR......... | 6,593,391 | 127,911,000 |
| Ukrainian SSR......... | 232,046 | 46,381,000 |
| Kazakh SSR........... | 1,064,092 | 12,678,000 |
| Uzbek SSR........... | 158,069 | 11,266,000 |
| Byelorussian SSR...... | 80,154 | 8,820,000 |
| Azerbaijan SSR........ | 33,436 | 4,917,000 |
| Georgian SSR......... | 26,911 | 4,659,000 |
| Moldavian SSR........ | 13,012 | 3,484,000 |
| Lithuanian SSR........ | 26,173 | 3,064,000 |
| Kirghiz SSR.......... | 76,642 | 2,836,000 |
| Tadzhik SSR.......... | 54,019 | 2,736,000 |
| Armenian SSR......... | 11,306 | 2,306,000 |
| Latvian SSR.......... | 24,695 | 2,298,000 |
| Turkmen SSR......... | 188,417 | 2,029,000 |
| Estonian SSR......... | 17,413 | 1,304,000 |

The 1959 census, first since 1939, reported 208,-826,000 population, an increase of approx. 38,226,-000 over the census of 1939, or about 19.5%. Sex ratio in 1959 was 45% male, 55% female. Marriage rate per year per 1,000 pop. is 12. In 1965 urban population was est. 54%; rural, 46%. Births (1965), 18.4 per 1,000; deaths 7.3 per 1,000; natural increase (excess of births over deaths), 11.1 per 1,000.

**The Russian Soviet Federal Socialist Republic** (Soviet Russia proper), contains over 50% of the population of the Soviet Union and includes 76% of its territory. Its territories stretch from the Estonian, Latvian and Finnish borders and the Byelorussian and Ukrainian lines on the W, to the shores of the Pacific, and from the Arctic on the N to the Black and Caspian Seas and the borders of Kazakh SSR, Mongolia and Manchuria on the S. Siberia (Sibir), divided into a number of administrative units, encompasses a large part of the RSFSR area. Capital: Moscow.

In 1956 the USSR incorporated the **Karelo-Finnish Republic** as an autonomous republic within the RSFSR, reducing the federation by one to 15. It comprises territory ceded by Finland after World War II. The capital, Petrozavodsk, was founded in the 18th century by Peter the Great. Forests cover two-thirds of the area and the underground wealth includes non-ferrous metal and mineral deposits.

Eastern and Western Siberia of the RSFSR have been transformed by steel mills, huge dams, oil and gas industries, electric railroads and new highways.

**Ukrainian Soviet Socialist Republic** is the most densely populated of the constituent republics. It borders on the Black Sea, with Poland, Czechoslovakia, Hungary and Romania on the W and SW. The population is 80% Ukrainian. Capital: Kiev. Northern Bukovina was added to the Ukrainian SSR from Romania in 1940. The Crimea was transferred to the Ukraine, 1954.

The Ukraine contains the arable black soil belt, the chief wheat-producing section of the Soviet Union. Sugar beets and oil seeds are important crops and livestock breeding is rapidly advancing.

The Donets Basin has a huge storage of coal iron and other metals. Here are produced 34% of the coal mined in the country, 50% of the pig iron, 40% of the steel and 35% of the manganese. There are chemical and dye industries and salt mines.

**Byelorussian Soviet Socialist Republic** (White Russia), situated on the western border of the USSR, suffered greatly under the Czars from periodical pogroms and from inter-racial struggles. Between 1914 and 1920 it was a field for military operations. Minsk is the capital.

Chief industries include machinery, tools, appliances, tractors, clocks, cameras, steel, cement, textiles, paper, leather, glass. Main crops are grain, flax, potatoes.

**Azerbaijan SSR** boasts near Baku, the capital, oil fields which produced 9% of the national total in 1965. Its natural wealth includes deposits of iron ore, barite, fossil copal, zinc, silver, gold, copper, tin, vanadium and molybdenum. Irrigation has boosted cotton production. A high-yield winter wheat also is grown. It produces iron, steel, cement, fertilizers, synthetic rubber, electrical and chemical equipment.

**Georgian SSR**, which lies in the western part of Transcaucasia, contains the largest manganese mines in the world. There are rich timber resources. Large coal deposits have been discovered. Basic industries are food, textiles, iron, steel. Grain, tea, tobacco, grapes are grown. The capital is Tbilisi (Tiflis).

**Armenian SSR** is mountainous, sub-tropical,

extensively irrigated with a wide range of crops. Copper, iron, marble are mined. Capital is Erevan.

**Uzbek Soviet Socialist Republic,** most important economically of the Central Asia republics, produced in 1966 68% of USSR cotton, 50% of silk, 34% of astrakhan, 85% of hemp. Industries include iron, steel, cars, tractors, TV and radio sets, textiles, food. Mineral wealth includes coal, sulphur, copper and oil. Capital: Tashkent, shaken by more than 600 earthquakes in 1966.

**Turkmen SSR** in Central Asia, produces cotton, grain, carpets, Turkoman horses. Mineral wealth includes oil, coal, sulphur, barite, lime, gypsum. The Kara Kum desert occupies four-fifths of the territory. Capital: Ashkhabad.

**Tadzhik SSR (Tadzhikistan),** formed from the former regions of Bokhara and Turkestan, was admitted as a constituent republic on Dec. 5, 1929. Three-quarters of the population are Tadzhiks, mostly Sunnis, speaking an Iranian dialect. Chief occupations are farming and cattle breeding. Cotton, grain, rice and a variety of fruits are grown. Heavy industry, based on rich mineral deposits, coal and hydroelectric power, has replaced handicrafts. Dushanbe is the capital.

**Kazakh Soviet Socialist Republic** extends from the lower reaches of the Volga in Europe to the Altai Mtns. on the Chinese border. It has vast deposits of coal, oil, iron, tin, copper, etc., and large quantities of non-ferrous metals. Fish for its canning industry are caught in Lake Balkhash and the Caspian and Aral Seas. The capital, Alma-Ata, produces movies. Karaganda Temir-Tau, Tselinograd, Balkhash, Aktyubinsk, Pavlodar, Semipalatinsk and Chimkent are large new centers.

**Kirghiz Soviet Socialist Republic** is in the eastern part of Soviet Central Asia, on the frontier of Sinkiang (Western China). The people, once nomadic, breed cattle and horses and grow tobacco, cotton, rice, sugar beets. New industries include machine and instrument making, chemistry. Capital: Frunze.

**Moldavian Soviet Socialist Republic,** in the SW part of the USSR, is a fertile black earth plain bordering Romania, and includes Bessarabia. It is an agricultural region that grows grains, fruits, vegetables and tobacco. Textiles, wine, food and electrical equipment industries have been developed. Capital: Kishinev.

**Lithuanian Soviet Socialist Republic,** on the Baltic, produces cattle, hogs, electric motors and appliances. The capital is Vilnius (Vilna). **The Latvian Soviet Socialist Republic** on the Baltic and the Gulf of Riga, has timber and peat resources estimated at 3,000,000,000 tons. In addition to agricultural products it produces rubber goods, dyes, fertilizers, glassware, telephone apparatus, TV and radio sets, railroad cars. The capital is Riga, on the Western Dvina River. **The Estonian Soviet Socialist Republic,** also on the Baltic, has textiles, shipbuilding, road-making and mining equipment industries and its shale refining industry is large. Tallinn is the capital. The 3 Baltic states were provinces of imperial Russia before World War I, were independent nations between World Wars I and II, and became SSRs, within the USSR, in 1940. They were occupied by Germany 1941-44. The U. S. has never formally recognized the incorporation of Lithuania, Latvia and Estonia into the USSR.

## ECONOMICS AND PRODUCTION

The economic foundation of the USSR is the socialist ownership of the instruments and means of production. Socialist property exists in two forms: (1) State property; (2) Cooperative and collective farm property. State property includes the land, minerals, waters, forests, mills, factories, mines, rail, water and air transport, banks, communicators, large agricultural enterprises, municipal enterprises and the bulk of dwellings.

The common enterprises of collective farms and cooperative organizations, their output and common buildings constitute their socialized property. Members may use small plots of land attached to their dwellings.

"Backyard" farms, from which farmers may sell produce and keep the profit, swelled in size and number in the 1960s.

Cultivated land in 1965 was est. at 496,320,000 acres. There were 37,100 collective farms and 12,196 state farms. In 1968 there were 97,100,000 cattle, 51,000,000 hogs and 138,300,000 sheep, all up from a year earlier.

In 1963-5-6 the USSR was forced to make huge purchases of wheat in Canada and other countries,

but a record surplus harvest was produced in 1966.

The USSR is incalculably rich in natural resources. It claims to possess 57% of the world's coal deposits, 58% of its oil, 41% of iron ore, 88% of manganese, 54% of potassium salts, 30% of phosphates, and 25% of all timber land. Gold production is est. at from 12,000,000 to 15,000,000 fine oz. annually, about half exported.

The USSR produces about 25% of world iron ore output, 19.5% of steel, 20% of coal.

The index of industrial production (1963=100) was 139 for 1967.

A new 5-year plan, prepared in 1966, set goals of a 40% rise in national income, 50% in industrial output, 25% in farm production. Premier Kosygin urged continued emphasis on consumer goods, adjustment of wholesale prices (last revised in 1955) to permit all enterprises to operate profitably without subsidies, wage incentives, and reduced central controls to stimulate production. Early in 1966 many major factories were put on an incentive profit-sharing system. In mid-1966 a system of bonuses to farms and farm works (called "Socialist competition") was introduced to spur food production.

The industrial output rose by 10% in 1967. Poor weather hurt agriculture.

## ELECTRIC POWER

Electric power output under a 15-year plan is projected to reach 900-1,000 billion kwh by 1970.

Of many large hydroelectric developments, the world's largest is at Bratsk on the Angara River, capable of producing 22 billion kwh annually. Its dam rises 400 ft. above the river, forming a reservoir 350 mi. long containing 145,000,000 acre-ft. of water.

Atomic power stations have been built and others are under construction.

## FOREIGN TRADE

Exports include petroleum and its products, iron and steel, rolled non-ferrous metals, industrial plant equipment, lumber, cotton, asbestos, gold, manganese and others. Most of its trade is with Socialist nations, but trade with others is increasing. East Germany presently is the Soviet Union's biggest customer.

Foreign trade, in thousands of U. S. dollars:

|      | Imports      | Exports      |
|------|--------------|--------------|
| 1966 | $7,913,000   | $8,841,000   |
| 1967 | $8,536,000   | $9,649,000   |

In the USSR budget for 1968, as announced by the Soviet government, the defense budget was increased by $2.4 billion. Output of consumer goods was scheduled to rise by 8.6%, a greater rate than that for heavy industry, 7.9%.

(The defense budget for 1968 totaled $18.7 billion, but Western experts said it actually might have been twice that figure, with some military spending concealed in other items.)

## EARLY HISTORY

The first Russian state centered on Kiev in the 9th Century. In the 13th Century the Mongols overran the country. It recovered under the grand-dukes and princes of Muscovy, or Moscow, and by 1480 freed itself from the Mongols. Ivan IV, the Terrible, was the first to be formally proclaimed Czar (1547). Peter the Great (1682-1725), extended the domain and in 1721 founded the Russian empire.

## REVOLUTION OF 1917

The abortive Revolution of 1905 demonstrated the insecurity of the czarist regime and led to mild concessions. The 1917 Revolution began in March with a series of sporadic strikes for higher wages by factory workers. A provisional democratic government under Prince Georgi Lvov was established but was quickly followed in May by the second provisional government, led by Alexander Kerensky. The Kerensky government was overthrown in a Communist coup led by Vladimir Ilyich (Nikolai) Lenin Nov. 7.

Lenin's death Jan. 21, 1924, resulted in an internal power struggle from which Joseph Stalin eventually emerged the absolute ruler of Russia. Stalin secured his position at first by exiling opponents such as Leon Trotsky. But in the 1930s he resorted to a series of "purge" trials in which virtually all opposition was directly eliminated.

## RECENT EVENTS

After Premier Stalin died, Mar. 5, 1953, Nikita Khrushchev was elected First Secretary of the Central Committee for 5 years; reelected 1956, 1959, 1961. In 1956 he condemned Stalin and his tyrannical methods before the Soviet Communist Party Congress in Moscow, said Stalin cultivated a "cult of personality" and subverted Communist aims. Khrushchev lifted some restrictions, extended barter and trade policies. The names of Stalin, Molotov, Malenkov and other supporters of Stalin were eliminated from regions, cities and other sites in 1961-62 after Stalin's body was removed from the Lenin-Stalin tomb in Moscow.

Khrushchev was elected Premier by the Supreme Soviet, Mar. 27, 1958, succeeding Marshal Bulganin. He was reelected Apr. 24, 1962.

Under Khrushchev the open antagonism of Poland and Hungary against domination by Moscow was brutally suppressed in 1956. He advocated peaceful co-existence with the capitalist countries, but continued arming the USSR with nuclear weapons, promised aid to all "suppressed peoples" and so-called wars of liberation, delayed a final peace treaty with all Germany. He warned the Western nations against intervention in Laos and Vietnam and aided the Cuban revolution under Fidel Castro but withdrew Soviet missiles from Cuba during confrontation by U. S. President Kennedy, Sept.-Oct. 1962.

The USSR, the U. S. and Great Britain initialed a joint treaty July 25, 1963, which would ban all except underground nuclear tests.

The policy of co-existence alienated the leaders of Albania and Communist China. The latter continued to preach world revolution and denounced the Khrushchev methods as deviating from true Communism.

Khrushchev was suddenly deposed, Oct. 14-15, 1964, and replaced as party First Secretary by Leonid I. Brezhnev, 57, and as Premier by Aleksei N. Kosygin, 60. An editorial in Pravda, Communist party newspaper, indicated Khrushchev had been accused of "hare-brained scheming, bragging and phrase-mongering." (Brezhnev's title was changed in 1966 to General Secretary, and Khrushchev's de-Stalinization policy was relaxed.)

Communist China's Premier Chou En-lai visited the new USSR chiefs in Nov. 1964 but the visit failed to heal the growing rift between the two Communist powers. In 1965-67 the public squabble between the two increased with the questions of aid to North Vietnam and the anti-USSR activity of Communist China's Red Guards the major issues.

There were several significant developments on the international scene in 1967 as President Johnson in March signed a consular treaty which was the first bilateral treaty with the Russians since the 1917 Revolution.

Soviet Premier Aleksei N. Kosygin and President Johnson met for the first time in Glassboro, N. J., in June after the Russian leader came to the U. S. to attend a meeting of the UN which was dealing with the Israeli-Arab crisis.

In April Svetlana Alliluyeva, only daughter and last surviving child of the late Soviet dictator Joseph Stalin, arrived in New York after defecting from the Soviet Union.

In July 1968 the U. S. and the USSR agreed to open talks on cutting both offensive nuclear weapons and defensive anti-missile systems. They also joined 59 other nations in signing a treaty to bar spread of nuclear weapons.

## GOVERNMENT

The first Soviet constitution was adopted in 1918 for the RSFSR, The USSR was formed in Dec., 1922, and the first Union constitution adopted in 1923. The current constitution, adopted in 1936, provides for universal direct suffrage with secret ballot. It was modified, 1944, to give each of the constituent republics the right to have separate commissions for defense and foreign affairs. Voting age is 18; candidates for election must have reached 23. Each Union republic is organized similarly to the central govt.

The highest legislative authority is the Supreme Soviet consisting of two chambers, the Soviet of the Union and the Soviet of Nationalities. The first house is elected on the basis of one deputy for every 300,000 population; the second on the basis of 25 deputies from each Union republic, 11 from each autonomous republic, 5 from each autonomous region, and one from each national district. The Supreme Soviet normally meets twice a year, serves for a four-year term. It elects a 33-member Presidium which serves between sessions.

Titular chief of state, Chairman of the Presidium (President) of the Supreme Soviet, is Nikolai V. Podgorny, chosen Dec. 9, 1965, succeeding the aging Anastas I. Mikoyan.

In general elections June 12, 1966, the single slate of approved candidates for the Soviet of the Union and Soviet of Nationalities was elected by 99.8% of the voters. Of 144,000,000 registered voters, 99.94% cast ballots. Fewer than 5% availed themselves of the right to vote against a candidate by striking out his name—the only choice offered voters.

On Aug. 2, 1966, the new Supreme Soviet convened and unanimously re-elected Aleksei N. Kosygin Premier.

The highest judicial organ is the Supreme Court, whose members are elected by the Supreme Soviet for five-year terms. Other courts are elected within the constituent republics. Since Feb. 1957, the Supreme Court has been restricted to appellate functions.

The highest executive and administrative organ of state power is the Council of Ministers (Premier and deputies) appointed by and theoretically responsible to the Supreme Soviet.

The Communist party of the USSR is the only legal party. Its highest organ is the Party Congress of about 1,500 elected representatives which normally meets once every 4 years. It elects a Central Committee, the party's directive body, and other committees. The Central Committee elects from its number a Politburo (until 1966 was called Presidium) which makes party policy between Central Committee meetings; and a Secretariat, the party's chief executive body.

The Communist party Politburo normally consists of 12 full members and 6 alternates. In 1967 full members were: Party General Secretary Leonid Brezhnev, Premier Aleksei Kosygin, G. I. Voronov, A. P. Kirilenko, Arvio J. Pelshe, N. V. Podgorny, D. S. Polyansky, Mikhail A. Suslov, A. N. Shelepin, K. T. Mazurov, P. E. Shelest.

Membership in the Communist party in 1966 was reported at over 12,000,000.

## EDUCATION

Universal compulsory education was introduced in 1930; education is free. Under reforms introduced in 1959-60, the primary education of 7 years is being extended into an 8-year course that will embrace polytechnical training in industry or agriculture. Students may then go on to a 3-year secondary school to prepare for entrance to a technical institute, university or art school.

In 1966-67 there were 210,000 primary, secondary and technical schools with enrollment of 48,168,000, 3,969 technical colleges with 3,979,000 students; 23,893 schools providing a 10-year secondary education for 4,835,000 workers who already had begun to earn a living, and 767 universities and other places of higher learning with 4,123,-000 students. The USSR annually graduates more than 432,000 from higher education establishments, including an est. 239,700 engineers and other scientists. Illiteracy has been reduced to 1.5%.

## SOCIAL BENEFITS

All workers are entitled to free public health services, paid vacations, sickness insurance, pensions for men at 60 and women at 55 (extended to collective farm members 1965). There are lower pension requirements for those in hazardous or difficult occupations. State payments are made to mothers on the birth of the 3rd and successive children. Social benefits paid in 1966 totaled 40.5 billion rubles, up 6% from 1965.

## RELIGION

Separation of church and state was effected in 1918. Nine branches of Christianity are represented, led by the Orthodox Church, which in 1956 had 22,000 congregations. Islam has the second largest following. Jewish and Buddhist faiths are also present.

Marriages must be registered and divorce is discouraged.

## DEFENSE

In 1964 Western authorities believed Soviet forces to total approx. 3,300,000. The Army had 2,300,000 in about 150 firstline divisions, plus 40 (est.) artillery and anti-aircraft artillery divisions, comprising about 10,000 men apiece, and missile and specialized units. Approx. 100 divisions were stationed in Europe. Total manpower of the Communist bloc, including China, was est. at 7,500,000.

The Navy in 1964 was believed to include upward of 35 cruisers, 180 destroyers and escort vessels, 465 modern long-range submarines, 1,000 torpedo boats, and patrol vessels, minesweepers and auxiliaries. Navy personnel is estimated at 750,000.

In 1966 a squadron of nuclear-powered Soviet missile submarines made a 6-week round-the-world voyage.

The Air Force was est. to have 20,000 first-line planes, including a possible 200-300 heavy bombers and 500 medium bombers, in addition to another 20,000 second-line, cargo and training aircraft. The bomber force was equipped with Myasishchev 4-jet planes and Tupolev 4-turboprop and twin-jet bombers with intercontinental range. Other equipment includes several thousand Il-28 jet bombers, MIG jet fighters, Yak-25s, several new supersonic bombers and interceptors, and Sukhoi delta-wing and swept-wing fighters.

While the USSR was believed to possess only 270 intercontinental ballistic missiles in 1965, the U. S. Defense Dept. confirmed in 1968 that the Soviet was expected to catch up with the U. S. force of slightly over 1,000 ICBMs by mid-1969. Both nations were believed planning to produce missiles with multiple, separately aimable, warheads.

The USSR and the United States signed an agreement June 20, 1963, establishing an instantaneous teletype-and-radio communications system between Moscow and Washington, known as the "hot line," designed for emergency communications and as a safeguard against accidental war.

The USSR is a member of the UN and Warsaw Pact.

# United Arab Republic
## AL-JUMHURIA AL-ARABIA AL-MUTTAHIDA
### Egypt (Misr)

**Capital: Cairo. Area: 386,100 sq. mi. Population (UN est. 1967): 30,907,000. Monetary unit: Egyptian pound (.4348 official rate per U. S. $1).**

The United Arab Republic, a name adopted by Egypt and Syria during their brief union, Feb. 1, 1958, to Sept. 30, 1961, comprised only Egypt after Syria withdrew from the merger.

Egypt, itself a republic since 1953, occupies the NE corner of Africa on the Mediterranean. On the E lie Israel and 1,200 mi. of Red Sea separating Egypt from Saudi Arabia. Libya is to the W and Sudan to the S. Egypt's Sinai Peninsula extends into the Red Sea, with the Gulf of Aqaba on the E. The Gulf of Suez and the Suez Canal (connecting the Gulf with the Mediterranean) are in Egypt. Jurisdiction over a 28-mi. wide strip of Asia Minor west of Israel, including Gaza, was given Egypt by an armistice agreement, 1949, as a refuge for displaced Palestinian Arabs.

Alexandria, founded 332 B.C., is the chief port. Cairo, largest city, is rich in archeological treasures, cafes, bazaars. Tourist attractions include the pyramids, Sphinx, temple ruins at Karnak and Luxor, and other ancient monuments.

In 1966 removal of the Abu Simbel temples of Ramses II and his wife, Nefertari, from the path of rising waters behind the Aswan High Dam was completed. The U. S. gave over $12,000,000 toward removal costs.

In July 1968 the UAR shipped a smaller monument, the 2,000-year-old Temple of Dendur, to the U. S. as a gift in gratitude for American aid to the Abu Simbel project. The temple was dismantled and its 661 huge stones, weighing some 800 tons, were to be reassembled outside the Metropolitan Museum of Art in N. Y.

**Resources and Industries.** Productive acreage lies in the Valley of the Nile and in its delta, or Lower Egypt, north of Cairo. The Nile flows through 960 mi. in Egypt and covers 2,850 sq. mi. with waters and marshes. About 13,000 sq. mi. are cultivated for cereals, vegetables, cotton and sugar cane, and 1,900 sq. mi. have canals and fruit plantations. The Nile rises in June and reaches its peak by August, regulated by dams and networks of canals. Fruit is plentiful and includes grapes, dates, figs, pomegranates, peaches, apricots, oranges, lemons, bananas and olives. Egypt is one of the world's top producers of cotton.

The dams conserving Nile waters are among the largest in the world. Aswan, at the First Cataract, is 176 ft. high, creating a reservoir 230 mi. long. Gabel Awila dam is over 3 mi. long. The Aswan High Dam project in southern Egypt, begun in 1960, was to add 2,000,000 acres of arable land. Deep artesian wells, drilled in the Western Desert, reclaimed 43,000 acres for cultivation, 1960-66.

A variety of minerals is found in Egypt; petroleum is most important, providing 90% of total mineral production value. Others are phosphate rock, salt, coal (found in Sinai in 1963), iron, manganese, cement, gold, gypsum, kaolin, titanium.

A series of decrees in July, 1961, nationalized about 90% of industry and reduced land holdings from 200 to 100 acres.

Egypt has textile plants, yarn factories, cement and fertilizer factories, and a film industry supplying the Middle East, Africa and Asia.

Principal exports are cotton, rice, mineral products, textiles, refrigerators, tires, cement, electrical instruments.

**History and Government.** Archeological records of ancient empires in Egypt go back to 4000 B.C. A high civilization of rulers and priests dominated the lowly serfs. Assyrians, Persians, Greeks (Alexander of Macedon), Romans, Saracens, Turks, French (Napoleon) and British invaded Egypt. Under Turkish sultans the khedive as hereditary viceroy had wide authority but repeated insolvency led to regulation by European powers. Britain, which supervised the administration after 1882, made Egypt a protectorate 1914-1922. Britain then recognized Egypt as a sovereign state but reserved defense, security of British communications, and the Sudan.

The sultan became King Fouad I in 1922 and a constitution was adopted in 1923. King Fouad I died in 1936 and was succeeded by his son, Farouk I. Farouk abdicated in 1952 and left the country. His son was named nominal ruler under a regency council, Aug. 5, 1952, but the crown was abolished when Egypt was declared a republic, June 18, 1953.

In 1936 an Anglo-Egyptian treaty of alliance revised the conditions of association. Britain agreed to a condominium over the Sudan, with British and Egyptian troops cooperating, and obtained the right to retain 10,000 soldiers and 400 airmen to defend the Suez Canal for 20 years until Egypt would take over, and also held naval bases in Alexandria and Port Said.

Egypt became a charter member of the UN and in 1944 led in organizing the Arab League. In 1947 Egypt brought before the UN Security Council a demand for unification of Egypt and Sudan and evacuation of all British troops from the Suez. In Oct. 1951 Egypt abrogated its 1936 treaty with Britain. The Sudan, with UN support, became independent in 1956.

Delays in reforms, corruption in public office and royal extravagance led to an uprising July 23, 1952, led by the Society of Free Officers which named Maj. Gen. Mohammed Naguib commander in chief and forced Farouk to abdicate. Naguib became Premier Sept. 7, 1952. When the republic was proclaimed June 18, 1953, Naguib became its first President and Premier. Lt. Col. Gamal Abdel Nasser, the principal influence behind the revolt, removed Naguib and succeeded him as Premier on Apr. 18, 1954.

On June 23, 1956, voters elected Col. Nasser President (99.9% of total votes) and adopted a constitution providing for freedom of worship, press, speech, assembly and private ownership, and election of a national assembly. The constitution proclaimed Egypt to be an Arab state under a republican and democratic form of government.

In July, 1956, the United States, Great Britain and the International Bank withdrew support from loans to start the Aswan High Dam. President Nasser nationalized the Suez Canal and seized control of the assets of the Canal company. Later he obtained credits and technicians from the USSR, which began to build the dam. First stage was opened May 14, 1964.

When the state of Israel was proclaimed in 1948, Egypt joined other Arab nations invading Israel and was defeated. No peace treaties were made and Egypt later denied Israeli shipping the use of the Suez Canal.

Border hostilities with Israel heightened and on Oct. 29, 1956, Israeli forces invaded Egypt's Sinai Peninsula. Egypt rejected a cease-fire demand by Britain and France; on Oct. 31 the two nations dropped bombs and on Nov. 5-6 landed forces. Egypt and Israel accepted a UN cease-fire, followed by Britain and France; fighting ended Nov. 7.

A UN Emergency Force guarded the 117-mile long border between Egypt and Israel until May 19, 1967, when it was withdrawn at Nasser's demand. The Egyptians quickly reoccupied the Gaza Strip and the heights at Sharm el Sheikh and three days later closed the Strait of Tiran leading into the Gulf of Aqaba to all Israeli shipping. Full-scale war broke out June 5 and before it ended under a UN cease-fire five days later, Israel had captured Gaza and the Sinai Peninsula, controlled the east bank of the Suez Canal and reopened the gulf.

In 1962-65 the UAR supported a campaign to destroy royalist guerrilla forces in Yemen after the Imam's regime had been deposed in a military coup. Saudi Arabia had been supplying royalist supporters of the Imam. The latest in a number of cease-fire agreements was reached by Pres. Nasser and Saudi Arabia's King Faisal Aug. 31, 1967.

The UAR was accused in 1965-66 of inspiring guerrilla attacks from Yemen into Aden, which in 1967 became independent as Southern Yemen.

**Education and Religion.** Three distinct ethnic elements are represented: the Fellahin, basic Egyptian group; the Bedouin, nomadic Arabs; Nubians, a mixed group. Moslems form over 91% of the population and Christians about 7%.

Education is compulsory for all children beginning at age 7 and free through high school. There is a famous seat of Moslem learning in the University of Al-Azhar in Cairo, founded about 968 A.D. Four modern universities are Cairo, Alexandria, Ein-Shams and Assiut. Arabic is the official language. American schools, managed by Egyptians since 1956, include American University, Cairo; Cairo American College; American Mission, Heliopolis.

**Defense.** After the 1967 defeat by Israel, the UAR rapidly rebuilt its armed forces with equipment supplied by the USSR.

Cairo was the original site of the Arab League, formed in 1945 to foster the cause of the Arab nations.

## THE SUEZ CANAL

The Suez Canal, 103 mi. long, links the Mediterranean and the Red Sea. Its minimum width is 196 ft., 10 in., and maximum draft for vessels 38 ft. It was begun April 25, 1859, by a French corporation under Ferdinand de Lesseps and opened Nov. 17, 1869. Benj. Disraeli, British prime minister, obtained control for Britain Nov. 24, 1875, by buying 176,752 shares from the Khedive Ismail of Egypt for £3,976,582 (nearly $20,000,000). Prolonged agitation led to an agreement July 27, 1954, by which Britain agreed to withdraw all troops (est. 80,000) within 20 mos. after signing pact on Oct. 19, 1954. The 74-year British military occupation ended June 13, 1956. On July 26, Pres. Nasser proclaimed nationalization of the canal, seizing it from its French and British stockholders.

Egypt on Apr. 24, 1957, promised to abide by the Constantinople Convention of 1888, and to accept the jurisdiction of the International Court in differences arising from its interpretation. Citing Item 10 of the Convention, it has continued to bar Israeli shipping and cargoes destined for Israel. Item 10 provides that freedom of passage "shall not interfere with measures Egypt might find necessary to take to secure the defense of Egypt."

A final agreement between the UAR and the Universal Suez Canal Co., signed July 13, 1958, called for payments to stockholders of $64,400,000. Final payments were made Jan. 1, 1963.

Since nationalization, the UAR has widened and deepened the canal. In the year before the seizure, the canal handled 14,666 ships, max. draft 35 ft., max. loaded capacity 30,000 tons, gross revenue $75,000,000. For the year ended June 30, 1966, the figures were 20,285 ships, 38 ft., 60,000 tons, $197,000,000.

The canal was closed to all shipping by Cairo at the height of the Israeli-Arab War June 6, 1967. A year later the canal was still closed, with 14 ships still trapped in it by sunken vessels.

# The United Kingdom of Great Britain and Northern Ireland

**Capital: London. Area: 94,209 sq. mi. Population (Govt. est. 1967): 55,068,000. Monetary unit: Pound (U. S. 2.394).**

The United Kingdom of Great Britain and Northern Ireland comprises England, Wales, Scotland and Northern Ireland.

The term British Isles is applied to these divisions and to the separately-governed island dependencies, Isle of Man and the Channel Islands.

The Isle of Man lies in the Irish Sea and the Channel Islands lie off the coast of France. The whole British Isles lie off the NW corner of Europe, with the North Atlantic on the N and W; separating England from the mainland are the North Sea on the E, the Strait of Dover on the SE and the English Channel on the S. The Thames,

## BUDGETS OF GREAT BRITAIN
### Fiscal year ends March 31

| Year | Revenues 1,000 £ | Expendit's 1,000 £ | Year | Revenues 1,000 £ | Expendit's 1,000 £ | Year | Revenues 1,000 £ | Expendit's 1,000 £ |
|---|---|---|---|---|---|---|---|---|
| 1930..... | 814,970 | 829,493 | 1956..... | 4,893,000 | 4,496,000 | 1964..... | 6,890,000 | 6,817,000 |
| 1935..... | 804,629 | 797,067 | 1958..... | 5,343,009 | 4,920,000 | 1965..... | 8,157,000 | 7,712,900 |
| 1940..... | 1,025,192 | 1,032,217 | 1960..... | 5,630,529 | 5,222,996 | 1966..... | 9,145,000 | 8,456,000 |
| 1945..... | 3,098,000 | 6,062,904 | 1961..... | 5,934,000 | 5,787,000 | 1967..... | 10,279,000 | 9,541,000 |
| 1950..... | 3,924,031 | 3,356,569 | 1962..... | 6,645,000 | 6,235,000 | 1968..... | 11,177,000 | 10,878,000 |
| 1955..... | 4,738,000 | 4,305,000 | 1963..... | 6,794,000 | 6,441,000 | 1969 (est.) | 12,875,000 | 11,489,000 |

210 mi. from its source to the North Sea, is England's longest river.

England has an area of 50,331 sq. mi. and a population of 45,680,870; Wales, 8,016 sq. mi., 2,709,930; Scotland, 30,411 sq. mi., 5,187,000; Northern Ireland, 5,451 sq. mi., 1,491,000. (All populations by Govt. est., mid-1967.)

The climate of the British Isles is equable, mild and somewhat warmer than that of the continent because of the Gulf Stream modifying the temperature, which has a mean of 48°. Rainfall averages 41 inches annually, and fogs are frequent.

On Apr. 1, 1965, new boundaries and a new government system for Greater London went into effect. The boundaries cut the size from 692 to 620 sq. mi. and the population from 8,176,810 (est. 1963) to 7,880,762 (est. 1967). A new Greater London Council administers most citywide services; local councils for 32 boroughs, formed from 100 former areas, conduct local services; the old City of London (675 acres), financial capital of the Commonwealth, retains independent status plus powers as a new borough and continues to provide the Lord Mayor of London.

**QUEEN AND ROYAL FAMILY.** The ruling sovereign is Elizabeth II of the House of Windsor, the former Princess Elizabeth Alexandra Mary, born April 21, 1926, eldest daughter of King George VI and Queen Elizabeth. She succeeded to the throne Feb. 6, 1952, and was crowned June 2, 1953. Her title in the United Kingdom and the Colonies is: "Elizabeth II, by the Grace of God of the United Kingdom of Great Britain and Northern Ireland and of her other realms and territories, Queen, Head of the Commonwealth, Defender of the Faith." The title varies in other countries of the Commonwealth. The Queen is a great-great-granddaughter of Queen Victoria.

The Queen, as Princess Elizabeth, was married Nov. 20, 1947 to Lt. Philip Mountbatten, born June 10, 1921, former Prince of Greece. He was created Duke of Edinburgh Nov. 19, 1947. H.R.H. Prince Philip Nov. 20, 1947, and given the title Prince of the United Kingdom Feb. 22, 1957. He is a son of late Prince Andrew of Greece and Princess Alice, sister of Earl Mountbatten (former Governor-General of India); his grandfather, Prince Louis of Battenberg, became admiral in Royal Navy and changed the family name to Mountbatten; the Duke is great-grandson of Christian IX of Denmark and great-great-grandson of Queen Victoria.

They have four children: (1) Prince Charles Philip Arthur George, born Nov. 14, 1948, named Prince of Wales, July 26, 1958, (2) Princess Anne Elizabeth Alice Louise, born Aug. 15, 1950, (3) Prince Andrew Albert Christian Edward, born Feb. 19, 1960; (4) Prince Edward Antony Richard Louis, born Mar. 10, 1964, third in line for the throne. Prince Charles is the heir apparent.

The Queen has one sister, Princess Margaret Rose, born Aug. 21, 1930; married Antony Armstrong-Jones, a commoner, May 6, 1960. He received an Earldom as the Earl of Snowdon Oct. 3, 1961. Issue: David Albert Charles, Viscount Linley, born Nov. 3, 1961, sixth in line for the throne, and a daughter, Sarah Frances Elizabeth (known as Lady Sarah Armstrong-Jones), born May 1, 1964.

The late King George VI was born Dec. 14, 1895, son of King George V (died Jan. 20, 1936), and Queen Mary (died March 24, 1953). He succeeded to the throne on the abdication of his brother, Edward VIII, Dec. 11, 1936. As Prince Albert Duke of York, he married April 26, 1923, Lady Elizabeth Bowes-Lyon (born Aug. 4, 1900). He died Feb. 6, 1952.

His widow became Queen Mother Elizabeth. Two brothers and a sister also survived George VI.

They were H.R.H. Prince Edward Albert (born June 23, 1894) Prince of Wales; proclaimed King Edward VIII, acceded Jan. 20, 1936 but never crowned, abdicated Dec. 10, 1936; created Duke of Windsor (Dec. 12, 1936) married (June 3, 1937) Mrs. Wallis Warfield; appointed Governor

of the Bahamas July 9, 1940, resigned Mar. 15, 1945; H.R.H. Prince Henry William (born March 31, 1900), created Baron Culloden, Earl of Ulster and Duke of Gloucester (March 31, 1928), married (Nov. 6, 1935), Lady Alice Montagu-Douglas-Scott (born Dec. 25, 1901), daughter of the Duke and Duchess of Buccleuch and Queensbury—issue: William Henry Andrew Frederick (born Dec. 18, 1941), Richard Alexander Walter George (born Aug. 26, 1944); Princess (Victoria Alexandra Alice) Mary, Princess Royal (born April 25, 1897, died Mar. 28, 1965), married (Feb. 28, 1922) Viscount Lascelles, later Earl of Harewood (died May 24, 1947)—issue: George Henry Hubert, Earl of Harewood (born Feb. 7, 1923), Gerald David (born Aug. 21, 1924).

A third brother, the Duke of Kent, was killed in an airplane accident in Scotland (Aug. 25, 1942). He was H.R.H. Prince George (born Dec. 20, 1902), married (Nov. 29, 1934) Princess Marina of Greece (born Nov. 30, 1906)—issue: Edward George Nicholas Patrick, Duke of Kent (born Oct. 9, 1935), married (June 8, 1961) Katharine Worsley; Alexandra Helen Elizabeth Olga Christabel (born Dec. 25, 1936) married Hon. Angus Ogilvy (April 1963); Michael George Charles Franklin (born July 4, 1942).

Queen Elizabeth announced Feb. 8, 1960, that her descendants, except princes and princesses of the royal family, would bear the surname Mountbatten-Windsor.

The Queen receives from Parliament an annuity of £475,000 ($1,140,000), comprising her privy purse of £60,000 ($144,000), and the rest for her household salaries and expenses. The Civil List grants Prince Philip £40,000 ($96,000), Queen Mother Elizabeth £70,000 ($168,000); the Duke of Gloucester £35,000 ($84,000); Prince Charles £30,000 ($72,000), Princess Margaret £15,000 ($36,000).

**PARLIAMENT** is the legislative governing body for the United Kingdom, with certain powers over dependent units but none over the independent states. It consists of two Houses. The **House of Lords** is divided into (1) the Lords Temporal, consisting of hereditary peers and peeresses who have not disclaimed their titles, life peers created by the Crown, and Lords of Appeal; and (2) the Lords Spiritual who are the Archbishops of Canterbury and York and 24 diocesan bishops of the Church of England. Full membership of the House of Lords is over 1,000 but actual average voting strength is approx. 90-120.

Women became eligible to sit in the House of Lords for the first time, July 23, 1958. Previously, women had been eligible to sit only in Commons.

**The House of Commons** has 630 members, who are elected by direct ballot and divided as follows: England, 511; Wales and Monmouth, 36; Scotland 71; Northern Ireland, 12.

Clergymen of the Church of England, ministers of the Church in Scotland and Roman Catholic clergymen are disqualified from sitting as members, also certain government officers, and sheriffs. Women have had the right to vote since 1918.

Members of Parliament are paid £3,250 ($7,800). Most cabinet Ministers are paid £8,500 ($20,400). Ministers in the House of Commons draw an additional allowance of £1,250 ($3,000) from their pay as M.Ps.

The Labor party ended 13 years of Conservative party rule by winning a close verdict in general parliamentary elections Oct. 15, 1964. Labor party leader Harold Wilson became Prime Minister, succeeding Conservative Sir Alec Douglas-Home.

Elections Mar. 31, 1966, gave Labor an over-all majority of 97 seats. The popular vote was: Labor, 13,064,951 (47.9%); Conservatives, 11,418,433 (41.9%); Liberals, 2,327,533 (8.6%); others, 452,689 (1.6%).

As of May 1968 the parties had the following number of seats in Commons: Labor, 348; Conservatives and Associates, 260; Liberal, 12; others, 6, vacancies, 4.

The Labor Government, on July 27, 1965, announced a wide variety of austerity moves aimed to speed deflation and strengthen the pound. In 1966 it took further action, raising taxes, cutting expenditures and imposing a wage and price freeze. In 1967 the freeze was slightly relaxed. The unemployment rate had risen from 1.3% in July 1966 to 2.3% in July 1967.

By Feb. 15, 1971, Britain will have completed a changeover to a system of decimal currency, continuing the same pound but dividing it into 100 new pence. In 1968, two of the new coins, a 5 pence equal to an old shilling and a 10 pence equal to the old two-shilling piece, were introduced. All 4 coins were in circulation but the shillings (worth 20 to the pound) were due to be retired and would not be a part of the new system. New pence (p) would entirely replace old pence (d) by 1971.

Also in 1968, Parliament approved a bill adopting a new British Standard Time for year-round use, keeping its clocks, during a 3-year test, one hour ahead of Greenwich Mean Time. This would make British time 5 hours ahead of New York in summer and 6 hours ahead in winter.

**RESOURCES AND INDUSTRIES.** Great Britain's major occupations are manufacturing and trade. Metals and metal-using industries contribute more than 50% of the exports. Agriculture provides wheat, barley, oats, sugar beets, rye and garden truck. Of about 60,000,000 acres of land in England, Wales and Scotland, 49,000,000 are farmed, of which 18,000,000 are arable, the rest pastures.

The country is rich in mineral resources. There are huge deposits of coal, the annual output approximates $2 billion in value. Limestone, igneous rock and iron ore are valuable products. Other important minerals, in the order of their value, are gravel and sand, clay and shale, slate, sandstone, salt, China clay, fireclay, chalk, gypsum, oil shale, lead ore, tin ore and silica.

The railway systems, approx. 47,000 mi. of tracks, have been nationalized since 1948.

There are approx. 175 airports for civil use in Great Britain. There are two state-owned airlines, British European Airways and British Overseas Airways Corp.

Telephone service is a part of the postal system. Telephones number more than 11,400,000.

Broadcast receiving licenses in 1967 totaled 2,583,000 for radio only (including car radios) and 14,910,000 for both radio and TV.

The government, on July 28, 1967, took ownership of 14 steel companies which comprised 90% of the nation's steelmaking industry, paying shareholders in the companies more than $1.4 billion in government securities. The new British Steel Corp. became Britain's largest industrial enterprise.

Tourism ranks high in earnings. Visitors from abroad average more than 2,500,000 annually, of whom about 650,000 are from the U. S.

Index of industrial production (1963=100) has been: 1964, 108; 1965, 111; 1966, 112; 1967, 112. Industrial production:

| | 1964 | 1966 | 1967 |
|---|---|---|---|
| Coal (million tons) ........ | 185.4 | 174.6 | 172.2 |
| Crude steel (million tons) .. | 26.2 | 24.3 | 23.9 |
| Automobiles (thousands) .. | 1,867.6 | 1,603.7 | 1,552.0 |
| Trucks, etc. (thousands) .. | 467.8 | 438.7 | 385.2 |

The merchant marine totaled 21,530,264 gross registered tons on June 30, 1965, comprising about 13.3% of active world shipping. British shipyards have an estimated annual capacity of 1,300,000 tons.

The world's first power station using atomic energy to create electricity for civilian use began operation Oct. 17, 1956, at Calder Hall in Cumberland.

The largest aluminum rolling mill in Europe is the Alcan Industries' works at Rogerstone, Wales, with a capacity est. at 70,000 tons annually.

Britain's aid to less developed countries has more than doubled since 1956, totaling over $2.5 billion and amounting to $492,000,000 in 1967-68.

The United Kingdom is a member of the UN, Commonwealth, NATO, SEATO, CENTO, EFTA, Council of Europe. In 1967 the Government decided to reapply for membership in the European Common Market but France vetoed the application.

Britain imports all of its oil, cotton, rubber, sulphur, four-fifths of its wool, half of its food and iron ore, also certain amounts of paper, tobacco, chemicals. Manufactured goods made from these basic materials have been exported since the industrial age began.

Gross national product for 1967 was $81.4 billion. Main exports are machinery, chemicals, woolen and synthetic textiles, autos and trucks, iron and steel, locomotives, jet aircraft, farm machinery, drugs, radio, TV, radar and navigation equipment, whisky.

British imports and exports account for 8.1% of total world trade.

Britain devalued the pound in Nov. 1967, from a value of $2.80 to $2.40. In March 1968 it raised taxes by $2.2 billion a year, and took other measures designed to improve exports and cut imports.

Foreign trade in thousands of U. S. dollars:

| | Imports | Exports |
|---|---|---|
| 1966 | $16,107,000 | $14,132,000 |
| 1967 | $17,207,000 | $13,862,000 |

**RELIGION AND CHURCHES.** The Church of England is Protestant Episcopal. The Queen is supreme governor, with rights of appointment to archbishoprics, bishoprics and other offices. There are two provinces, Canterbury and York. The 100th Archbishop of **Canterbury** and Primate of All England is the Most Rev. Arthur Michael Ramsey (b. Nov. 14, 1904) whose seat is Lambeth Palace, London. Annual salary £7,500 ($18,000). Dean is the Very Rev. Ian White-Thomson. The 114th Bishop of London is the Rt. Rev. Robert W. Stopford, £5,500 ($13,200). The Dean of Westminster is the Very Rev. Eric Symes Abbott, £3,000 ($7,200).

The 93rd Archbishop of **York** and Primate of England is the Most Rev. Donald Coggan, Bishopthorpe, York; £6,000 ($14,400).

The Church of England has an est. 27,750,000 members. In 1967 there were some 14,400 parishes. Most famous church is Westminster Abbey (1050-1760), site of coronations; tombs of Elizabeth I, Mary of Scots, kings, poets and of the Unknown Warrior. St. Paul's Cathedral, London, 365 ft. to top of cross, has American War Memorial Chapel. Altogether, the Anglican Commission in the UK and overseas has over 40,000,000 members.

**The Roman Catholic Church**—Archbishop of Westminster, John Cardinal Heenan. Membership in England and Wales, 1965, 4,000,690. In Scotland, 809,000; in Northern Ireland, 498,000.

**The Methodist Church**—The Pres. of the Conference (governing body) is the Rev. Dr. I. Morgan (1967-68). There were 14,287 churches and 690,000 members in 1968.

**Others.** There are an est. 450,000 Jews in the British Isles, 80% orthodox, over half in the London area. There are over 290,000 Baptists and more than 198,000 Congregationalists. The Calvinistic Methodist (Presbyterian) Church of Wales has over 122,600 communicants. The Unitarians have 330 chapels. The Presbyterian Church of England has 318 congregations, 68,000 members. The Society of Friends has 433 meeting houses, an est. 21,000 members. The Church of Christ, Scientist, has 330 branches in Great Britain and Ireland. There are some 250,000 Moslems in Britain.

**The Church of Scotland** is Presbyterian. It is presided over by a Moderator, chosen annually. Churches, 2,016; members, 1,233,800.

**The Church of Ireland (Episcopalian)** was disestablished in 1869. The Primate is the Archbishop of Armagh, St. Patrick's Cathedral, Armagh.

**Education.** Primary and secondary education is free and compulsory from 5 to 15.

The most celebrated of British universities are Oxford and Cambridge, each with colleges founded in the 13th Century. There are 42 other universities in England, Scotland, Wales and Northern Ireland.

**SOCIAL WELFARE, TAXES.** Under the Ministry of Social Security, National Insurance provides for virtually universal compulsory insurance covering sickness, maternity, unemployment and industrial accidents, and death benefits and pensions for widows, orphans and the aged. The National Health Service provides free medical, dental and nursing care and makes minimum charges for certain appliances and prescriptions. Under the Family Allowance Act the government pays 8 shillings a week for each child of compulsory school age, after the first, and 10 shillings each for the third or more.

Supplementary Benefits provide for those not fully protected by National Insurance. Contributions are made by purchase of National Insurance stamps, the amounts varying according to sex and classification (employed, self-employed, non-employed). In the case of employed, the employer pays nearly one-half.

Standard income tax rate, 1967-68, was 41¼%, after allowances. Allowances, in addition to earned income credit: single persons, £220; married, £340,

plus £115 to £165 for each child according to age. Rate, including surtax, reaches 91¼% on largest incomes. A capital gains tax was instituted in 1962.

**DEFENSE:** In 1964, a new ministry headed by the Secretary of State for Defense was formed. It absorbed the Admiralty, War Office and Air Ministry, but the government said the separate identities of the three forces would be maintained.

The government announced in 1968 it would cut British forces abroad sharply; those in Singapore and Malaysia would be completely withdrawn by the end of 1971.

Total strength of the armed forces in 1968 was over 400,000, comprised of the Army, 190,600; Navy, 94,900; RAF, 120,900.

The Territorial Army corresponds to the National Guard in the United States, is voluntary, and serves only at home in peacetime. The women's services are integrated into the three branches of the armed forces.

In 1967-68 there were 167 ships in the operational fleet, including 2 aircraft carriers, 2 commando ships, 6 guided-missile destroyers, 11 other destroyers, 55 frigates, 33 subs, 57 minesweepers, etc. The Resolution, Britain's 1st Polaris-firing submarine, was launched in 1966.

Britain exploded its 1st atomic bomb in 1952 and has a stockpile of these weapons. The Air Force is equipped with Blue Steel air-to-surface nuclear missiles.

## WALES

The Principality of Wales and Monmouthshire in western Britain has an area of 8,016 sq. mi. and a population (est. 1967) of 2,709,930.

England and Wales are administered as a unit and Wales does not have a separate local government act, as has Scotland. Approximately 600,000 people, less than one-fourth of its total, speak both English and Welsh and under 50,000 speak Welsh solely. Welsh nationalism is advocated by a small segment.

Early Anglo-Saxon invaders drove certain Celtic peoples into the mountains of Wales, terming them Waelise (Welsh, or foreign). There they developed a distinct nationality and culture. Members of the ruling house of Gwynedd in the 13th Century fought England for sovereignty but were crushed, 1282-1283. Edward of Caernarvon, son of Edward I of England, was created Prince of Wales Feb. 7, 1301.

## SCOTLAND

Scotland, a kingdom now united with England and Wales in Great Britain, occupies the northern 37% of the main British island, and the Hebrides, Orkney, Shetland and smaller islands. The Atlantic lies N and W; the North Sea, E. Length, 275 mi.; breadth approx. 150 mi., area, 30,411 sq. mi., population (est. 1967) 5,187,000. Principal rivers are the Clyde, 106 mi.; the Tay, 117 mi., and the Tweed, 96 mi.

The Lowlands, a belt of land approximately 60 miles wide from the Firth of Clyde to the Firth of Forth, divide the farming region of the Southern Uplands from the granite Highlands of the north. Only one-tenth of the land area, the Lowlands contain three-quarters of the population and most of the industry. The Highlands, famous for hunting and fishing, have been opened to industry by many hydroelectric power stations.

**Edinburgh**, pop. (1967) 467,986, is the capital. It lies on the Firth of Forth in Midlothian County, 42 mi. from Glasgow, and has notable memorials of its royal and cultural history.

**Glasgow**, pop. (1967) 960,527, is the largest city, third largest in Britain, and Britain's greatest industrial center. It is a shipbuilding complex on the Clyde and an ocean port. Prestwick International Airport is a major transatlantic stop.

**Aberdeen**, pop. (1967) 182,117, 95 mi. NE of Edinburgh, is a major North Sea port, center of granite industry and fish processing.

**Dundee**, pop. (1967) 182,284, 40 mi. NE of Edinburgh, is an industrial and fish processing center on the Firth of Tay.

Scotland was called Caledonia by the Romans who battled early Picts and Scots and Celtic tribes and occupied southern areas from the 1st to the 4th Centuries. The Romans supposedly called one group Picti because they painted their bodies. The Scots were an Irish tribe from Scotia (an early name for Ireland). Missionaries from Britain introduced Christianity in the 4th Century; St. Columba, an Irish monk, converted most of Scotland to Christianity in the 6th Century.

The Kingdom of Scotland was established in the 11th Century. William Wallace, patriot leader, defeated an invading English army at Stirling Bridge, 1297, and Robert Bruce defeated another at Bannockburn, 1314.

In 1603 James VI of Scotland, son of Mary, Queen of Scots, succeeded Queen Elizabeth I on the throne of England as James I, and effected the Union of the Crowns. In 1707 Scotland received representation in the British Parliament, resulting from the union of former separate Parliaments. Its executive in the British cabinet is the Secretary of State for Scotland. John Knox led the Scottish church Reformation in the 16th Century. There is a small but growing Scottish Nationalist party which urges independence for Scotland.

There are 8 universities, at Aberdeen, Edinburgh, Glasgow, St. Andrews, Dundee and Stirling Education receives some support from trusts, founded by Andrew Carnegie. St. Andrews is the birthplace of golf.

Historic sites and literary associations, where memorials of Robert Burns, Sir Walter Scott, John Knox, Mary, Queen of Scots, are preserved, draw many tourists, as do the beauties of the Trossachs, Loch Katrine, Loch Lomond and abbey ruins that are now state property.

Engineering products are the most important industry, with growing emphasis on lighter products such as office machinery, autos, electronics and other consumer goods and less dependence on locomotives, boilers, pumps, valves and other industrial machinery. Scotland contributes over a third of all British shipbuilding.

Scotland produces fine woolens, worsteds, tweeds; silk textiles at Paisley and Glasgow; fine linens and jute. It is known for its Ayrshire, Aberdeen-Angus, Galloway, Belted Galloway, Highland and Scottish Shorthorn cattle. It raises Shetland, Highland and Cheviot sheep, Shetland ponies and Clydesdale draft horses. Fisheries have large hauls of herring, cod, whiting. Whisky remains the biggest export product.

Atomic projects to produce plutonium and electrical energy are at Dounreay, Dumfriesshire, Chapel Cross and Hunterston.

**The Hebrides** are a group of c. 500 islands, 100 inhabited, off the W coast. The Inner Hebrides include Skye, Mull and Iona, the last famous for the arrival of St. Columba, 563 A.D. The Outer Hebrides include St. Kilda and Harris. Industries include sheep raising and weaving (Harris tweeds).

**The Orkney Islands**, c. 90, are separated from Scotland by the Pentland Firth. The capital is Kirkwall, on Pomona Isl. Fish curing, sheep raising and weaving are occupations. Northeast of the Orkneys are the 200 **Shetland Islands**, 24 inhabited, home of the Shetland pony.

## NORTHERN IRELAND

**Descriptive.** Six of the 9 counties of Ulster, the NE corner of Ireland, constitute Northern Ireland, with the parliamentary boroughs of Belfast and Londonderry; they are Antrim, Armagh, Down, Londonderry, Fermanagh and Tyrone. The country has an area of 5,451 sq. mi. and a population (est. 1967) of 1,491,000. Belfast is the capital and chief industrial center.

The finest scenery in Northern Ireland is to be found on or close to the coast line. From Belfast northward the Antrim road takes the visitor to the famous **Giant's Causeway**, which consists of a perfect honeycomb of stone columns, 40,000 in all. Lough Erne, studded with islands, is one of the most famous of lakes, and Lough Neagh the largest in the British Isles.

**Resources and Industries.** Agriculture is the main industry; 66,000 small farms produce fat cattle, sheep, eggs, poultry, potatoes and milk. Much of the milk is shipped to England. Butter and cheese are produced, as well as many canned foods. Four-fifths of Northern Ireland's whisky is exported.

Annual estimated agricultural output is valued at $317,800,000. There are 466,000 cattle, 887,000 sheep, and 2,010,000 hogs.

Linen and ships are the chief manufacturing products. Belfast shipyards launch more than 100,000 tons annually and the city is Ireland's largest port, with 10 mi. of wharves. Ropes and twines, rayon, clothing, aircraft, engineering products, hosiery and underwear are also made.

**Government.** An act of the British parliament, 1920, divided Northern from Southern Ireland, each with a parliament and government. When Ireland became a dominion, 1921, and later a republic, Northern Ireland elected to remain a part of the United Kingdom.

Parliament consists of a Senate of 26, and House of Commons of 52, both elected with power to legislate in local matters except such as are reserved to the British Parliament; Northern Ireland elects 12 members of the British House of Commons.

The government has outlawed the Irish Republican Army and other extremists and in 1956 banned the Sinn Fein party.

**Education and Religion.** Northern Ireland is preponderantly Protestant. Elementary education is compulsory to age 15. Queens Univ. of Belfast (1908) had a 1968 enrollment of 5,527. The new Univ. of Ulster was opened in 1968.

Northern Ireland closely followed Britain in systems of social insurance, industrial accident and disability benefits, family allowances and pensions.

## Dependencies

### CHANNEL ISLANDS

The Channel Islands, area 75 sq. mi., pop., 1967 110,644, off the NW coast of France, the only parts of the one-time Dukedom of Normandy belonging to England, are Jersey, **Guernsey and the** dependencies of Guernsey—**Alderney, Brechou, Great Sark, Little Sark, Herm, Jethou and Lihou.** Jersey has a separate legal existence and a lt. gov. named by the Crown. The islands are not bound by acts of Parliament unless named in the legislation. The islands were the only British soil occupied by German troops in World War II.

### ISLE OF MAN

The Isle of Man, area 227 sq. mi., est. 1966 pop. 50,423, is in the Irish Sea, 20 mi. from Scotland, 30 mi. from Cumberland. It is rich in lead and iron. The island has its own laws and a lt. gov. who has wide constitutional powers, appointed by the Crown. The Tynwald (legislature) consists of the Legislative Council, partly elected, the House of Keys, elected. The island is not bound by acts of Parliament unless named in the legislation. Capital: Douglas.

Farming, tourism and fishing are chief occupations. The mild climate is popular with tourists. Ronaldsway Airport handles 250,000 passengers a year. Herring (kippers) and scallops top fishing trade. Man is famous for the Manx tailless cat.

## Mediterranean Possession

### GIBRALTAR

**Gibraltar,** a colony southeast of Spain, guards the entrance to the Mediterranean. The width of the strait dividing Europe from Africa varies from 7.75 mi. at the narrowest part to 23.75 at the widest. The Rock has been in British possession since 1713. There is a large harbor and as a naval base its position is of the greatest strategic importance. The Rock is 2¾ mi. long, ¾ of a mi. wide and 1,396 ft. in height; a narrow isthmus connects it with the mainland. The population, 1965 est., was 24,485.

In 1966 Spain called on Britain to give "substantial sovereignty" of Gibraltar to Spain and imposed a partial blockade of the isthmus. On Sept. 10, 1967, in a referendum sponsored by Britain despite Spain's objection, the residents voted 12,138 for remaining under British rule against 44 for returning to Spain.

## British West Indies and Other American Possessions

### WEST INDIES

Swinging in a vast arc from the coast of Venezuela northeast, then north and northwest toward Puerto Rico are the Windward and Leeward Islands, forming a coral and volcanic barrier sheltering the Caribbean from the open Atlantic. Most of the islands are British possessions which have internal self-government. Universal suffrage was instituted 1951-4; ministerial systems of government were set up 1956-1960.

Moving northward from the southern end of the arc lie the **Windward Islands**, starting with **Grenada** (1964 pop. est. 91,967, area 133 sq. mi., capital St. George's), **St. Vincent** (1965 pop. 88,451, area 150 sq. mi., capital Kingstown), **St. Lucia** (1966 pop. 110,142, area 238 sq. mi., capital Castries) and **Dominica** (1966 pop. 68,501, area 290 sq. mi., capital Roseau).

Further north, in the Leeward Islands, are **Montserrat** (1966 pop. 14,056, area 33 sq. mi., capital Plymouth), **Antigua** (1963 pop. 61,664, area 171 sq. mi., capital St. John's) and **St. Christopher-**

Nevis-Anguilla, three islands also referred to as St. Kitts (1965 pop. 59,476, area 138 sq. mi., capital Basseterre on St. Christopher). Nearby are the small **British Virgin Islands**.

Britain granted self-government to 5 of these islands and island groups in 1967; each became an Associated State, with Britian retaining responsibility for the foreign affairs and defense of each. These 5 were Antigua, Dominica, Grenada, St. Lucia and the St. Christopher-Nevis-Anguilla Federation. Similar status was offered St. Vincent, but action was delayed.

Anguilla, however, announced its independence from both the Federation and Britain June 16, 1967, and said it would like to become a U. S. Territory. On July 12, voters in Anguilla, which is a 35-sq.-mi. coral island with a pop. of 6,000, voted 1,813 to 4 in favor of independence and also approved a 15-man council of government. Anguilla rejoined the Federation on Dec. 22, 1967, after agreement for appointment of a British Administrator to be stationed on Anguilla and represent the island's interests. The islanders make a bare existence by exporting lobsters and salt.

Sugar is the major crop of Antigua and St. Kitts; bananas are the main product of the Windwards; Dominica and Grenada produce cocoa; Antigua, Montserrat, St. Kitts and St. Vincent have Sea Island cotton; St. Vincent and Grenada have arrowroot; Grenada grows spices, and Dominica citrus fruits. Many of these products are exported; imports include other foods, clothing, machinery. Tourism is of mounting importance.

The three **Cayman Islands**, a colony formerly under administration of Jamaica, lie S of Cuba, NW of Jamaica. Population is 9,374, most of it on Grand Cayman, about 1,000 on Cayman Brac, about two dozen on Little Cayman. It is a free port; inhabitants are exempt from British taxes. Fishing and tourism are the main industries. Total area: over 100 sq. mi. Capital: Georgetown.

The **Turks and Caicos Islands**, at the SE end of the Bahama Islands, are a separate British possession. There are about 30 islands, only 6 inhabited, 1964 pop. 6,770, area 166 sq. mi., capital Grand Turk. Salt, crayfish and conch shells are the main exports.

### BERMUDA

**Bermuda** (or the Bermuda Islands) is a British possession governed by a royal governor and a representative legislature, the oldest legislative body among British dependencies.

It is a group of 360 small islands of coral formation, 20 inhabited, comprising 21 sq. mi. in the western Atlantic, 677 mi. SE of New York, 580 mi. E of North Carolina. Population, est. 1966, was 49,448 (about 30,000 of African or mixed descent, the rest of European descent).

It was named for Juan de Bermudez, Spanish explorer, and settled by Virginia-bound British colonists under Sir George Somers who were wrecked in the islands, 1609. Its capital is Hamilton.

Bermuda's Parliament dates from 1620. In general elections May 22, 1968, the first on the basis of full universal adult suffrage without property qualifications, the predominantly white United Bermuda party won 30 of the 40 Assembly seats. The predominantly Negro Progressive Labor party won the other 10. Negroes make up about 63% of the population; many of them voted for the United Bermuda party.

The British-appointed governor controls foreign and defense affairs and internal security. The Assembly, its members elected for 5-year terms, controls all local affairs; a Prime Minister was chosen for the first time in 1968.

The United States maintains air and naval bases in the Bermudas, under long-term lease, and a NASA tracking station.

Bermuda levies no taxes on real estate, incomes or inheritance, but raises revenue by excise, postal, transportation, stamp taxes and duties. Cruise ships and airlines bring large numbers of tourists; there are many modern resort hotels.

Bermuda exports Easter lilies, drugs, essences, beauty preparations.

### BAHAMAS

The Bahamas comprise nearly 700 islands (30 inhabited) and over 2,000 rocks in the Atlantic, extending NW to SE from a point near Florida toward Haiti. Nassau, on the Island of New Providence, near the Florida coast, is the capital and popular tourist resort. The land area of the grou

is 4,404 sq. mi.; population, 1967 UN est., was 144,000 (84% Negro).

A new constitution, effective Jan. 7, 1964, replacing a 235-year-old charter, granted the islands internal self-government. In 1966 the government adopted a 7-shilling dollar, replacing the old 20-shilling pound, to facilitate business with the U. S. and tourists.

Elections in Jan. 1967 to the Assembly resulted in the selection of Lynden O. Pindling as the Bahamas' first Negro Prime Minister. Mr. Pindling launched an inquiry into alleged underworld control of gambling, one of the islands' many tourist attractions

Prime Minister Pindling's all-Negro Government won 29 of the 38 seats in the Assembly in elections Apr. 10, 1968. He indicated more independence would be sought, particularly control of the police forces, still held by the Governor.

Principal exports are salt, crayfish, pulpwood and cucumbers.

### BRITISH HONDURAS

**British Honduras** is in Middle America facing the Caribbean to the E, with Mexico on the N and Guatemala on the W. Population (UN est. 1966) 109,000, area 8,867 sq. mi., capital Belize.

Internal self-government was granted by Britain in 1964.

The country had long been claimed by Guatemala, but also was promised independence by Britain. In Apr. 1968, U. S. lawyer Bethuel Webster, serving as mediator, proposed that British Honduras be made independent by the end of 1970, but have close association with Guatemala, consulting with it on foreign affairs of mutual concern.

Main export is sugar, along with citrus fruits, mahogany and other hardwoods, chicle, lobsters and fish.

## British Antarctica

**Falkland Islands and Dependencies**, a Colony, lies 300 mi. E. of the Strait of Magellan at the southern end of South America.

The Falklands or Islas Malvinas include about 200 islands with an area of 4,618 sq. mi and pop., est. 1966, of 2,170. Sheep-grazing is the main industry; wool is the principal export. The islands are also claimed by Argentina. **South Georgia**, area 1,450 sq. mi., and pop. 439, and the uninhabited **South Sandwich Islands** are dependencies of the Falklands

Britain and Argentina discussed Argentine claims to the Falklands, but in Mar. 1968 officials of the islands declared their opposition to being ceded to Argentina.

**British Antarctic Territory**, south of 60° S lat., was made a separate Colony in 1962 and comprises mainly the **South Shetland Islands**, the **South Orkneys** and **Graham's Land**. A chain of meteorological stations is maintained.

Although Great Britain has held possession of the Islands since 1834, Argentina and Chile also claim ownership.

## Atlantic Ocean Possessions

**St. Helena**, an island 1,200 mi. off the W coast of Africa and 1,800 E of South America, has 47 sq. mi. and population 1965, of 4,702. Flax, lace and rope making are the chief industries. After Napoleon Bonaparte was defeated at Waterloo the British exiled him to St. Helena, where he lived from Oct. 16, 1815, to his death, May 5, 1821. He was buried there until 1840, when his remains were transferred to Paris.

**Tristan da Cunha** is the principal of a group of islands of volcanic origin, total area 40 sq. mi., half way between the Cape of Good Hope and South America, which form one of the loneliest places on the globe. The other islands are Inaccessible, Gough (or Diego Alvarez) and the 3 Nightingale Islands. An ancient volcanic peak 6,760 ft. high erupted in Oct. 1961, and ruined the settlement. The 262 inhabitants were removed to England for resettlement, but most returned in 1963. The islands are administered as dependencies of St. Helena.

**Ascension** is an island of volcanic origin, 34 sq. in area, 700 mi. NW of St. Helena, through h it is administered. It is lies midway between and South America and is an important nications relay center for Britain and has a satellite tracking center. Est. pop., 1965, was

1,217, about half of them communications workers. The island is noted for its sea turtles.

## Former African Possessions

*For various former British possessions in southern Africa which have recently become independent countries with changed names, see Index for Botswana (Bechuanaland), Malawi (Nyasaland), Lesotho (Basutoland), Zambia (Northern Rhodesia). See also Swaziland.*

### RHODESIA

**Rhodesia** is a self-governing country (formerly a British colony) which declared its independence Nov. 11, 1965, but to which Britain has refused to grant independence unless its white-dominated government broadens voting rights to include eventually its vast majority of native Africans.

Rhodesia (formerly Southern Rhodesia) lies in the east central part of southern Africa with the Zambesi River and Zambia (formerly Northern Rhodesia) to the N. Mozambique (Port. East Africa) to the E, Republic of South Africa to the S and Botswana to the W. Area, 150,333 sq. mi., almost the size of California; population, 1967 UN est., 4,530,000 including about 220,000 of European descent

Victoria Falls on the Zambezi, partly in Zambia, are a tremendous spectacle, 355 ft. high, 5,580 ft. wide, dropping into a deep, narrow gorge. The falls were discovered by Dr. David Livingstone in 1855.

The country is rich in mineral wealth and farming is profitable. Tobacco is the largest crop and is normally by far the leading export along with asbestos, sugar, copper, pig iron, chrome, coal, ferro-chrome and tin, in that order. Also important are corn, cobalt, lead, zinc and gold.

When Rhodesian Prime Minister Ian D. Smith announced his country's unilateral declaration of independence the British government termed the act illegal, and imposed sanctions, including embargoes on oil shipments to Rhodesia, which were backed by most nations, including the U. S. Some oil and gasoline reportedly reached the country by truck from South Africa and Mozambique. Some African nations denounced Britain for failing to use force against the Rhodesian government. U. S. President Johnson denounced Rhodesia's white supremacy policies.

In Mar. 1968, Rhodesia condemned 3 black Africans to death on murder charges. British Queen Elizabeth commuted their sentences to life imprisonment. Rhodesia defied the commutations and executed the 3.

In May 1968 the UN Security Council ordered a complete trade and travel blockade against Rhodesia, but provided no punishment for nations continuing to trade with it.

## British Asiatic States

*For Aden and South Arabia, see Index for Southern Yemen.*

### BAHRAIN, QATAR, TRUCIAL STATES

These are British Protected States on the Persian Gulf which have treaties giving Britain responsibility for their foreign relations.

Britain has announced plans to withdraw its military forces from the Persian Gulf area by 1971. In July 1968, the rulers of Bahrain, Qatar and the 7 Trucial Sheikdoms agreed on forming a federation which would have a common currency, postal system, flag and anthem, a High Council of sheiks and a Federal Council of notables to be named by the sheiks.

**Bahrain** is an Arab sheikdom consisting of the island of Bahrain, 250 sq. mi., and several smaller islands, halfway down the Persian Gulf 20 mi. off Arabia's NE coast, under British protection since 1861. Formerly known for pearl fishing, it is now being developed for oil found in the central plateau of Bahrain Is., mostly by American corporations. Population, UN est. 1967, 195,000, chiefly Moslem. Manama is the capital. It has international air service. Fruit raising, shrimp fishing, boat building, weaving and modern light industries are among occupations.

**Qatar**, also an Arab sheikdom, occupies the Qatar peninsula on the Persian Gulf on Arabia's NE coast. Area (est.), 8,000 sq. mi.; population est., 1965, 55,000. Capital: Doha. It is rich in oil.

The seven **Trucial Sheikdoms**, semi-independent, occupy approx. 32,300 sq. mi. along a 400-mile strip from Sha'am to Khor el Odeid at SE end of

Qatar peninsula. Population is est. 86,000. Dubai is the main port. Fishing and pearling are industries. The states are Abu Dhabi, Ajman, Dubai, Fujaira, Ras al Khaima, Sharja, Umm al Quaiwain.

## BRUNEI

Brunei has been since 1888 a protected sultanate on the north side of the Island of Borneo, between the Malaysian states of Sarawak and Sabah. Its area is about 2,226 sq. mi., the size of Delaware, with population (1967 UN est.) 107,000, two-thirds Malay and indigenous races, one-third of Chinese descent.

A 1959 constitution was amended, 1965, to provide for general elections to the Legislative Council, some members of which are appointed. There is a Sultan and a British High Commissioner.

Brunei's rich Seria oilfield provides tax revenues well in excess of government expenditures. Rubber is also exported. In recent years, some of the surplus has been spent on a growing program of school building and social services.

## HONG KONG

Hong Kong is a Crown Colony at the mouth of the Canton River in China, 90 mi. south of Canton. Its nucleus is Hong Kong Island, 35½ sq. mi., acquired from China 1841, on which is located Victoria, the colonial capital. Opposite is Kowloon peninsula, 3 sq. mi., and Stonecutters Island, ¼ sq. mi., added to the colony by convention of Peking, 1860. An additional 355 sq. mi. known as the New Territories, comprised of an adjacent mainland area and numerous islands, were leased from China, 1898, for 99 years. Total area of the colony is 391 sq. mi., with a population, est. in 1967, of 3,877,700, including many refugees from Communist China and fewer than 20,000 British. From 1949 to 1962 Hong Kong absorbed more than 1,000,000 refugees from the mainland.

Hong Kong harbor, one of the finest in the East, is an important British naval station and one of the world's greatest trans-shipment ports. It is served by many international airlines.

Principal industries are shipbuilding and textiles; also iron and steel, agriculture, fishing, cement, and small manufactures. American tourists spend an est. $29,000,000 annually.

Since 1945 Hong Kong industry has zoomed from a few hundred factories to over 5,000. Its spinning mills, among the best in the world, and low wages compete with textiles elsewhere and have resulted in protective measures in some countries. It also has a booming electronics industry. The U. S. is the largest market for Hong Kong products.

During 1967 Communist China launched a campaign against British authority in Hong Kong, including demonstrations, strikes, riots, bombings, border incidents and slowdowns in supplying food from the mainland, accompanied by charges the British were mistreating Chinese residents.

## Indian Ocean Possessions, Etc.

*For the former British possession, Mauritius, see Index.*

**Seychelles and Dependencies** are a group of islands N of Madagascar, area 69 sq. mi., population 1965 over 45,000. The capital is Victoria, on Mahe, a port with a coaling station. Coconuts are the chief product, followed by cinnamon, patchouli, mangrove bark, vanilla and tortoise shell. Copra is the chief export.

**British Indian Ocean Territory** was formed Nov. 1965, embracing islands formerly dependencies of Mauritius or Seychelles; the Chagos Archipelago (including Diego Garcia), Aldabra, Farquhar and Des Roches. Population 1966 was 1,500.

## British Pacific Islands
### FIJI ISLANDS

The Fiji Islands, a Colony, number 844 (106 inhabited), with an area of 7,055 sq. mi., in the South Pacific, E of Northern Australia. Population, UN est. 1966 was 478,000, including 228,000 of Indian descent and 11,000 of European descent.

The larger islands are mountainous; the highest peak, Mt. Victoria, is 4,341 ft. The southern islands contain dense forests with many valuable woods. The islands are very fertile and well watered. The climate is comparatively cool for the tropics, the temperature seldom rises above 90°.

The capital is Suva, on Viti Levu, largest of the islands (area 4,010 sq. mi.). Sugar is the principal export, accounting for 40% of total. Other

products are coconuts, gold, manganese, bananas. Britain holds 83% of the land in trust for the Fijis.

There is a British Governor and a Legislative Council with 36 of its 40 members elected by universal adult suffrage under a 1966 constitution.

## TONGA ISLANDS

The Tonga, or Friendly Islands, an internally self-governing Polynesian kingdom of some 150 small islands E of Fiji, is a British Protected State, with an area of 269 sq. mi. and a population, 1968, of 77,500. Main exports are copra and bananas. There is a British Commissioner; a native King, Taufaahau Tupou IV, and a partly-elected Legislative Assembly. The capital is Nukualofa on Tongatapu.

## PITCAIRN ISLAND

Pitcairn Island is in the Pacific, halfway between South America and Australia. The island was discovered in 1767 by Carteret but was not inhabited until 23 years later when the mutineers of the Bounty landed there. The area is less than two sq. mi. and population, 1967, was about 90. It is a British Colony and is administered by the British Governor of Fiji and a local Council. The uninhabited islands of **Henderson, Ducie** and **Oeno** are in the Pitcairn group.

*Principal island groups administered by the British High Commissioner for the Western Pacific Islands, seated at Honiara, Guadalcanal, include the British Solomon Islands and the Gilbert and Ellice Islands:*

## BRITISH SOLOMON ISLANDS

The British Solomon Islands, a Protectorate, number 10 large islands and four groups of small islands with a total area of 11,500 sq. mi. and population, est. 1967, of 139,730, mostly Melanesians. The Solomons lie E of New Guinea. The chief islands in the group are **Guadalcanal, Malaita, San Cristobal, New Georgia, Santa Ysabel, Choiseul, Shortland, Mono** or **Treasury, Vella Lavella, Ganongga, Gizo, Rendova, Russell, Florida** and **Rennell.** Among the groups of islands are the **Lord Howe, Santa Cruz, Tucopia, Mitre, Duff** or **Wilson,** and **Reef.** Some of the Solomons, including Bougainville, are an Australian UN Trusteeship.

Exports: copra, timber, nuts, and trochus shell.

## GILBERT AND ELLICE ISLANDS

Gilbert and Ellice Islands Colony. The group of islands in the Crown Colony was proclaimed a Protectorate in 1892 and, at the request of the native governments, was annexed Nov. 10, 1915, as the Gilbert and Ellice Islands Colony. The Colony includes the **Gilbert Islands** (16), **Ellice islands** (9), **Phoenix Islands, Ocean Island, Line Islands,** composed of Fanning, Washington and Christmas **Islands,** the last the largest atoll in the Pacific (also claimed by the United States). The total area is 375 sq. mi. and the population, 1966 est., 53,450. Exports: chiefly copra and phosphates.

## NEW HEBRIDES

New Hebrides, a Condominium jointly administered since 1906 by Great Britain and France, is a group of 11 main islands and about 69 islets lying 500 mi. W of Fiji, with an aggregate area of approx. 5,700 sq. mi. Population, est. 1964, over 65,000, mostly Melanesian. Chief products are copra, cotton, cocoa, fish and coffee.

British and French Resident Commissioners are joint heads of the administration.

Banks (309 sq. mi.) and Torres (40 sq. mi.) Islands, with pop. of 2,640, are attached to the New Hebrides for administration.

## United States
*(See Index for listings)*

## Upper Volta
### REPUBLIC OF THE UPPER VOLTA

**Capital:** Ouagadougou. **Area:** 105,869 sq. mi. **Population** (UN est. 1967): 5,054,000. Monetary unit: CFA franc (246.85 per U. S. $1).

The Republic of the Upper Volta, one-time French Overseas Territory, is an inland plateau region in west Africa, bounded by Mali, Niger, the Ivory Coast, Ghana, Togo and Dahomey. It is the size of Colorado.

More than 90% of the people are subsistence farmers. Greatest wealth is in livestock, mostly cattle and sheep, accounting for 55% of exports.

Principal market crops are cotton, rice, peanuts and karite. Climate is extremely dry but irrigation efforts, using water from the Black Volta, White Volta and pumped from underground, have been started with aid from the UN Special Fund.

In accordance with provisions of the 1958 French constitution, Upper Volta became an autonomous state Dec. 11, 1958. It became fully independent Aug. 5, 1960, and a member of the UN Sept. 20. It elected to remain outside the French Community proper, but signed a bilateral agreement Apr. 24, 1961, maintaining close ties with France.

The constitution, adopted Nov. 27, 1960, provides for a presidential form of government and a unicameral National Assembly. On Jan. 3, 1966, the army chief of staff, Lt. Col. Sangoule Lamizana, took control of the Presidency during demonstrations against austerity measures and at the request of the labor unions set up a provisional government of 7 officers and 5 civilians, promising elections.

# Uruguay
## REPUBLICA ORIENTAL DEL URUGUAY

**Capital: Montevideo. Area: 72,172 sq. mi. Population (Govt. fig. 1967): 2,845,734. Monetary unit: Peso (250 per U. S. $1).**

Uruguay is one of the smallest but most advanced republics in South America. Slightly larger than Missouri, it is a country of rich, rolling, grassy plains on the South Atlantic coast. Brazil and Argentina are its neighbors, with the Uruguay River forming the boundary line with Argentina. The Uruguay is navigable from the mouth of the Rio de la Plata, its estuary, to Salto, 200 mi. north.

**Resources and Industries.** Some 85% of Uruguay's area is devoted to stock raising; 9.6% to agriculture; 3.5% woods and forests; 1.8% is unproductive. The chief products are meat, wool, hides, corn, wheat, citrus fruits, rice, oats and linseed. The meat packing, metallurgical, textile and wine making industries are important.

More than one-third of the country's population lives in one city, Montevideo. More than one-third of the nation's workers are employed by the Government. The state owns the power, telephone, railroad, cement, oil-refining and other industries.

Uruguay's standard of living has been one of the highest in South America. Inflation, plus floods, drought and a cold wave in 1967 and a general strike in 1968 brought attempts by the Government to strengthen the economy through another in a series of devaluations of the peso, rationing of electricity and wage and price controls.

**History and Government.** Uruguay, once a part of the Spanish Viceroyalty of Rio de la Plata and later a province of Brazil, declared its independence, Aug. 25, 1825, which was confirmed by a treaty with Brazil and Argentina, Aug. 27, 1828. The first constitution was adopted July 18, 1830. The constitution provides for a Chamber of Deputies and a Senate elected for 4-year terms. Suffrage is universal, with proportional representation.

In late 1966 the nation approved a proposal to strengthen the powers of the President's office, permitting a President to serve 5 years.

Uruguay has one of the world's most extensive social welfare programs with old age pensions, child welfare, etc.

**Education and Religion.** Church and state are separate and there is complete religious tolerance. The preponderant religion is Roman Catholic. Education, including college is free; primary education is compulsory. Univ. of Montevideo was founded in 1849. The language is Spanish.

**Defense.** The Army is composed of hired volunteers between the ages of 18 and 45. Uruguay has a small Air Force and Navy. It is a member of the UN and OAS.

# State of Vatican City
## STATO DELLA CITTA DEL VATICANO

**Area: 108.7 acres. Population: over 1,000.**

The Popes for many centuries, with some slight interruptions, held temporal sovereignty over mid-Italy (the so-called Papal States), comprising an area of some 16,000 sq. mi., with a population in the 19th Century of more than 3,000,000. This territory in the reign of Pius IX, was incorporated in the Kingdom of Italy, the sovereignty of the Pope being confined to the palaces of the Vatican and the Lateran in Rome and the villa of Castel Gandolfo, by an Italian law, May 13, 1871. This law also guaranteed to the Pope and his successors in the chair of St. Peter a yearly indemnity of 3,225,000 lire ($622,425 at par of exchange), which allowance, however, remained unclaimed.

Final settlement of the Roman question came when the Treaty of Conciliation, the Concordat and a financial convention were signed in the Lateran Palace, Feb. 11, 1929, by Cardinal Gasparri and Premier Mussolini. The Treaty and Concordat established the independent state of Vatican City, and gave the Catholic religion special status in Italy. The treaty (Lateran Agreement) was duly ratified by the Pope and by the Italian Parliament, May 14 and 25, and signed by the King, May 27, and became effective June 7 by exchange of ratification at the Vatican.

The Lateran Agreement was made an integral part of the Constitution of Italy (Article 7) March 26, 1947.

Vatican City includes St. Peter's, the Vatican Palace and Museum covering more than 13 acres, the Vatican gardens, and neighboring buildings between Viale Vaticano and the Church. Thirteen buildings in Rome, although outside the boundaries, enjoy extra-territorial rights; these include buildings housing the congregations or officers necessary for the administration of the Holy See.

The legal system is based on the code of canon law, the apostolic constitutions and the laws especially promulgated for the Vatican City by the Sovereign Pontiff or those to whom he may delegate legislative power. In all cases not covered the Italian law of Rome applies. The Secretariat of State represents the Holy See in its diplomatic relations. By the Treaty of Conciliation the Pope is pledged to a perpetual neutrality unless his mediation is specifically requested by both parties in political disputes. This, however, does not prevent the defense of the Church whenever it is persecuted. A total of 56 nations maintain diplomatic representatives in Vatican City. The United States is not represented.

Police duties are carried out by the Pontifical Armed Corps comprised of the Noble Guards, the Swiss Guards, the Palatine Guards of Honor and the Pontifical Gendarmerie. The state has its own railway station, postal facilities, radio.

The present sovereign of the State of Vatican City is the Supreme Pontiff, Paul VI, Giovanni Battista Montini, born in Concesio, Italy, Sept. 26, 1897, elected Pope June 21, 1963, in succession to Angelo Giuseppe Roncalli, John XXIII, who died June 3, 1963.

# Venezuela
## REPUBLICA DE VENEZUELA

**Capital: Caracas. Area: 352,148 sq. mi. Population (Govt. est. 1967): 9,600,000. Monetary unit: Bolivar (4.5 per U. S. $1).**

Venezuela, a land of wide plains and lofty mountains, lies within the Torrid Zone in northern South America, with a 1,750-mi. coastline on the Caribbean and the Atlantic. Its neighbors are Guyana, Brazil and Colombia. It includes 72 islands totaling 14,650 sq. mi., the largest being Margarita, 40 mi. by 20, which is one of Venezuela's 20 states and an important pearl center. Venezuela is more than twice the size of California.

The Orinoco River with its tributaries, drains about four-fifths of the country. About 1,700 mi. in length and 13½ mi. across at its widest point, it is the 2nd largest river system in South America, and is navigable for about 700 mi. Its headwaters near the Parima Sierra and the Venezuelan-Brazilian border were located in 1951.

Angel Falls, said to be the tallest in the world, 3,212 ft. in all, with one drop of 2,648 ft., was found on the Churun, a branch of the Caroni River by Jimmy Angel, American aviator, in 1937.

Caracas, the capital, is 12 mi. inland from its port, La Guaira. It has an international airport and airlines reach cities in the interior. It is noted for its modern architecture and luxury hotels. In its Pantheon are enshrined the ashes of Simon Bolivar, South American liberator (1763-1830).

**Resources and Industries.** Mining, agriculture, fishing and stock raising are the chief industries. Venezuela in 1967 was the world's 3rd largest oil producer, behind U. S. and USSR, and largest oil exporter. Lake Maracaibo is the largest oil field in South America. In 1967, production was 3,511,300 bbls. per day, up 5% from 1966. Concessions are held by foreign interests, with 60% of the revenue going to the government. Other minerals are iron, gold, copper, coal, salt, tin, manganese, asbestos, diamonds and mica. Iron ore production is more than 15,000,000 tons annually and supplies

a high percentage of total U. S. iron imports. Coffee is the major agricultural product and is 2nd only to petroleum in export value. Exports also include fish, cocoa, rubber, sisal, balata and tonka beans. Industries include steel, petrochemicals, textiles, containers, tobacco products, paper and tires.

Tourists increased from 95,000 in 1965 to 152,515 in 1967. Attractions include resorts on Margarita Is.; Merida in the Andes with its cable car to snow-capped Mirror Peak, 15,000 ft.; beaches near Caracas.

Construction is booming, including a 30-story skyscraper in Caracas; a new, $3.8 billion city, Ciudad Guyana, 300 mi. SE of Caracas, and a 4,175-ft. suspension bridge across the Orinoco which was opened in 1967 and is South America's largest.

Oil profits help finance the extensive industrial development. The gross national product rose from $7.9 billion in 1966 to $8.3 billion in 1967.

Foreign trade, in thousands of U. S. dollars:

|      | Imports     | Exports     |
|------|-------------|-------------|
| 1966 | $1,188,000  | $2,713,000  |
| 1967 | $1,400,000  | $3,000,000  |

**History and Government.** Columbus first set foot on the South American continent on the peninsula of Paria, Aug. 1498; on the same voyage he found the mouth of the Orinoco. Alonso de Ojeda, 1499, found Lake Maracaibo, called the land Venezuela, or Little Venice, because natives had houses on stilts. Vespucci was in Ojeda's expedition. Venezuela was under Spanish domination until about 1821. The republic was formed after secession from the Colombian Federation in 1830.

The 1961 Constitution provided for a strong central government; a President, Senate and Chamber of Deputies elected for 5 years by direct universal vote, and a Supreme Court appointed by the Congress. Member: UN, OAS.

**Education and Religion.** The language is Spanish and Roman Catholic is the religion of the majority of the people, but religious freedom is guaranteed. All education, including college, is free. Primary education is compulsory.

**Defense.** Military service is obligatory for all men, 18 to 45. The Navy consists of 9 destroyers, 4 frigates, one submarine and other craft.

# Vietnam

**Total area: 127,241 sq. mi. Population (UN est. 1967): 37,073,000.** Vietnam is split between two hostile governments, the Republic of Vietnam, which controls the southern half, and the Communist regime of North Vietnam.

Vietnam, one of 3 former French Indo-Chinese Associated States, is in SE Asia, bounded on the N by China, on the E and S by the South China Sea, and on the W by Cambodia and Laos. It consists of the former French protectorates of Tonkin and Annam, and former colony of Cochin China. Principal cities are Saigon, Hanoi, Haiphong, Hue and Danang.

**Resources and Industries.** Chief products are rice, principal food staple; rubber; and coal. Peacetime exports included rubber, rice, fish, coal, lumber, pepper, cattle and hides, corn, zinc and tin. Tea, coffee and quinine are grown in the South. Rice and coal are chief products of the North; also coffee, tea, maize, sweet potatoes, tobacco, sugar cane and shellac.

**History and Government.** Vietnam's recorded history began in Tonkin before the Christian era; settled by the Viets who emigrated from central China. It was held by China, 111-939 A.D., and was a vassal state during many subsequent periods. Vietnam defeated the armies of Kublai Khan at Bach Dang Giang, 1288. The French and Portuguese came in the late 16th Century. Piecemeal conquest by France began in 1858 and ended in 1884 with acceptance of a French protectorate.

In 1940 Vietnam was occupied by Japan and used as a base for the invasion of Malaya. During the occupation nationalist aims gathered force. A number of groups formed the Vietminh (Independence) League, headed by Ho Chi Minh, Communist guerrilla leader. In August, 1945, the Vietminh forced out Bao Dai, former Emperor of Annam, head of a short-lived regime sponsored by Japan. France, seeking to reestablish colonial control, battled Communist and nationalist forces, 1946-1954, incurring huge losses and was finally defeated at Dienbienphu, May 8, 1954. Meanwhile, on July 1, 1949, Bao Dai had formed a State of Vietnam, with its capital at Saigon and himself

as Chief of State, with French approval. Communist China backed Ho Chi Minh.

A cease-fire accord signed in Geneva July 21, 1954, divided Vietnam along the Ben Hai River. It provided for a buffer zone, withdrawal of French troops from Northern Vietnam and elections to determine the country's future. Under the agreement the Communists gained control of the territory north of the 17 parallel, 22 provinces with an area of approx. 62,000 sq. mi. and 13,000,000 pop. (est.), with its capital at Hanoi, and Ho Chi Minh as President. South Vietnam was to comprise the 39 southern provinces with an area of 65,000 sq. mi. and pop. of 12,000,000 (est.). Approx. 800,000 North Vietnamese fled to South Vietnam. Neither South Vietnam nor the U. S. signed the agreement.

## Republic of Vietnam
### VIET NAM CONG HOA

**Capital: Saigon. Area: 65,948 sq. mi. Population (UN est. 1967): 16,973,000. Monetary unit: Piastre (117.5 per U. S. $1).**

On Oct. 26, 1955, Ngo Dinh Diem, Premier of the interim government of South Vietnam, proclaimed the Southern Zone a republic and became its first President under a provisional constitution act, following a referendum Oct. 23 which ousted Bao Dai as Chief of State. Pres. Diem was re-elected for a second 5-year term, Apr. 9, 1961.

Guerrilla fighting has persisted since 1956, with the Communist Vietcong, aided by North Vietnam, pressing a spreading war, and South Vietnam receiving increasing U. S. aid and, since June 1965, active U. S. combat participation.

A serious political conflict arose in 1963 when Buddhist groups charged the government with authoritarianism and brutality. This and government delays in reforms paved the way for a military coup Nov. 1-2, 1963, which overthrew the Diem regime and resulted in the deaths of Pres. Diem and his brother and political adviser, Ngo Dinh Nhu. A third brother, Ngo Dinh Can, was executed May 9, 1964.

A military triumvirate headed by Maj. Gen. Duong Van Minh formed the nucleus of a 23-member interim junta which was overthrown Jan. 30, 1964, in a bloodless coup led by Maj. Gen. Nguyen Khanh. Other governments followed; Air Force Commander Nguyen Cao Ky became Premier, on June 19, 1965, of the 9th regime since the fall of Pres. Ngo Dinh Diem.

On Sept. 11, 1966, South Vietnamese voters chose members of an assembly which was to draft a new constitution for a civilian government early in 1967. Despite anti-election Vietcong terrorism, 80% of eligible voters took part in the election.

In elections Sept. 3, 1967, Chief of State Nguyen Van Thieu was chosen Pres. and Premier Ky, Vice Pres. A 60-member Senate was also elected Sept. 3 and 137-member House on Oct. 22.

Despite U. S. aid, the Saigon regime failed to halt the growing Communist Vietcong guerrilla war. Following attacks on two U. S. destroyers by North Vietnamese PT boats in the Gulf of Tonkin Aug. 2-4, 1964, the U. S. retaliated with heavy air strikes against North Vietnamese torpedo bases and oil storage depots, and increased its fleet.

In 1965-67 the war accelerated as the U. S. stepped up bombing raids on the North and increased the number of Americans fighting in the country from 23,000 at the start of 1965 to a projected total of 525,000 by June 1968.

On Mar. 31, 1968, U. S. President Johnson announced the unilateral halting of bombing of North Vietnam, except for the southernmost area, and urged North Vietnam to join in peace talks. Hanoi agreed Apr. 3 to preliminary talks which began May 10 in Paris. Meanwhile, U. S. casualties continued rising to new weekly highs; as early as mid-March they had exceeded U. S. casualties in the Korean War in numbers of wounded and soon were approaching the earlier war's total of dead. In June 1968 South Vietnam ordered a general draft making males 18-38 eligible for military duty for the duration.

*(For details of war and of peace negotiations during 1968 see Vietnam in Index.)*

Most Vietnamese practice parts of several religions or mixtures of Confucianism, Taoism, Buddhism, ancestor worship and animism. About 20% practice Buddhism and about 12% Roman Catholic. New indigenous religions include Cao Dai (1919) and Hoa Hao (1939).

There is a National Univ. in Saigon, others at Hue, Dalat and Cantho.

## Democratic Republic of Vietnam
### VIET NAM DAN CHU CONG HOA

**Capital:** Hanoi. **Area:** 61,293 sq. mi. **Population** (UN est. 1967): 20,100,000. **Monetary unit: Dong** (2.94 per U. S. $1).

A Vietminh constitution, adopted Dec. 31, 1959, is based on Communist principles and calls for re-unification of all Vietnam. It provides for a Presi-dent elected by Parliament and a Prime Minister appointed by the President. President Ho Chi Minh, reelected July 15, 1960, by unanimous vote of the National Assembly, has held office since 1945. Prime Minister since 1955: Pham Van Dong.

United States and South Vietnamese forces began air attacks against military bases in North Viet-nam in February, 1965, in retaliation against what the White House called "provocations ordered and directed by the Hanoi regime," including infiltra-tion from North Vietnam into South Vietnam. North Vietnam maintained that the U. S. was waging an "aggressive war" in Vietnam.

## Western Samoa

**Capital:** Apia. **Area:** 1,130 sq. mi. **Population** (UN est. 1967): 135,000. **Monetary unit: Tala** (.7143 per U. S. $1).

Western Samoa, which became an independent nation Jan. 1, 1962, comprises 4 inhabited islands of a group in the South Pacific Ocean lying about 2,600 mi. SW of Hawaii. Largest of the islands are Savaii and Upolu. Eastern Samoa, the smaller portion of the group with its capital at Pago Pago, remains a dependency of the U. S.

Western Samoa was a German colony, 1899 to 1914, when New Zealand landed troops and took over. It became a New Zealand mandate under the League of Nations and, in 1945, a New Zealand UN Trusteeship.

An elected local government took office in Oct. 1959 and the country became fully independent in 1962. New Zealand has continued economic aid and educational assistance. Western Samoa changed from pounds to decimal currency July 10, 1967.

The population is composed almost solely of Polynesians. The islands are fertile and life is lei-surely. Chief products are fish, copra, cocoa, coco-nuts, bananas, taro, coffee, bark cloth (tapa) and mats.

Robert Louis Stevenson's grave is on a hill near Apia.

## Yemen

**Capital:** Sana. **Area:** 75,289 sq. mi. **Population** (Govt. est. 1967): 5,000,000. **Monetary unit:** Yemeni rial (official rate 1.071 per U. S. $1).

Yemen is an ancient, mountainous country, near the southern tip of the Arabian Peninsula on the Red Sea. Its neighbors are Southern Yemen (formerly Aden) and Saudi Arabia. It is about the size of Nebraska.

Hodeida, with its deep-water facilities at Ahmedi, is a major port on the Red Sea; others are Mocha and Loheiya. Marib and Sana are archeological sites.

**Resources and Industries.** On the plateau of El Jebel, the most fertile section of Arabia, coffee, barley and grain are grown. Mocha coffee, hides, dates, charcoal, sesame, herbs, fruits and precious stones are exported It has granted several oil con-cessions to American companies, with half the revenues to go to the government.

**History and Government.** Yemen's territory once was part of the ancient kingdom of Sheba, or Saba, a prosperous link in trade between Africa and India. A Biblical reference speaks of its gold, spices and precious stones as gifts borne by the Queen of Sheba to King Solomon.

Yemen was described as a democratic Islamic monarchy during the regime of the Imam Ahmed, who had ruled 1948-1962. The King was reported assassinated Sept. 26, 1962, and a revolution-ary group headed by Brig. Gen. Abdullah al-Salal declared the country a republic. He became Pres.

The Imam Ahmed's heir, the Imam Mohamad al-Badr, fled to the mountains where tribesmen joined royalist forces; internal warfare between them and the republican forces continued into 1967. UAR Pres. Nasser sent 70,000 troops to aid the republicans; Saudi Arabia supported the royal-ists with military aid.

A cease-fire was agreed on by Pres. Nasser and Saudi Arabia's King Faisal Aug. 24, 1965; the UAR was to pull out its troops and a plebiscite on the form of government was to be held, with a care-taker government set up temporarily. In 1967 the UAR was accused of dropping poison gas on vil-lages in royalist-held territory.

The agreement, like others before it, collapsed. During 1966 UAR planes from Yemen bombed towns in Saudi Arabia near the Yemen border.

In Oct. 1966 Premier Hassan al-Amri was ousted, one of his ministers and 7 other officials were shot, and several hundred persons were arrested by the pro-UAR government of Pres. al-Salal.

After the UAR defeat in the June 1967 Israeli-Arab war, the UAR announced it would withdraw its troops from Yemen; the last of them left Nov. 29, 1967, and Saudi Arabia said it would stop aiding the royalists.

Fighting continued between the Republican and royalist forces; troops from Southern Yemen aided those of the Republicans in 1968. Saudi Arabia announced in Feb. 1968 it was renewing its aid to the royalists, charging that both Soviet Russia and Syria, as well as Southern Yemen, were aiding the Republicans. Russian MIG planes had been delivered to the Republicans and a Russian pilot had been shot down by royalists.

Yemen is a member of the UN and Arab League.

## Yugoslavia
### SOCIJALISTICKA FEDERATIVNA REPUBLIKA JUGOSLAVIJA

**Capital:** Belgrade. **Area:** 98,766 sq. mi. **Popula-tion** (UN est. 1967): 19,958,000. **Monetary unit:** Dinar (official rate, 1966 dinar, 12.5 per U. S. $1).

The Socialist Federal Republic of Yugoslavia is a rugged mountainous land, densely forested, which rises from the eastern shore of the Adriatic Sea. Its neighbors are Italy, Austria, Hungary, Romania, Bulgaria, Greece and Albania. It is about the size of Wyoming.

The federation comprises 6 republics: Serbia, Croatia, Slovenia, Montenegro, Bosnia-Herzego-vina and Macedonia.

Rijeka, on the northern Adriatic, formerly Italian Fiume, is the largest port.

**Resources and Industries.** Chief crops are cereals, maize, wheat, barley, rye, tobacco, oats, hops and fruits. The principal minerals are coal, iron, cop-per, chrome ore, antimony, manganese, lead, mercury, salt and bauxite.

Because of its intensive program of industrial-ization the country is gradually losing its pre-dominantly agricultural character. Most industry is socialized and private enterprise is limited to small-scale production. Central planning guides the economy and the free play of the market is limited. Since 1952 workers are guaranteed a basic wage and a share in cooperative profits. Manage-ment of industrial enterprises is handled by some 220,000 members of workers' councils. The com-mune is the basic territorial and administrative unit, with autonomy in local government, workers' affairs and social management.

A 7-year development plan, 1964-1970, em-phasizes all branches of the economy and living standards.

The index for industrial production (1963=100) was 130 in 1967.

Foreign trade in thousands of U. S. dollars:

|  | Imports | Exports |
| --- | --- | --- |
| 1966 | $1,570,000 | $1,221,000 |
| 1967 | $1,707,000 | $1,252,000 |

**History and Government.** Serbia, which had since the Battle of Kosovo (1389), been a vassal principality of Turkey, was established as an inde-pendent kingdom by the Treaty of Berlin, 1878. After the Balkan wars its boundaries were enlarged by the annexation of Old Serbia and Macedonia, 1913. When the Austrian Archduke Francis Fer-dinand and wife were assassinated at Sarajevo June 28, 1914, the Austrian government forced war on Serbia, the onset of World War 1, 1914-1918.

When the Austro-Hungarian empire collapsed the Kingdom of the Serbs, Croats and Slovenes was formed from the former provinces of Croatia, Dal-matia, Bosnia, Herzegovina, Slovenia, Voyvodina and the independent state of Montenegro, with Peter I of Serbia as king. The name was later changed to Yugoslavia. Peter (d. 1921) was suc-ceeded by his son Alexander I (assassinated at Marseille Oct. 9, 1934), after which Prince Paul became regent. He was overthrown in Mar. 1941 and Crown Prince Peter, born Sept. 6, 1923, was proclaimed king. Germany invaded April, 1941, and King Peter II fled to London.

But many Yugoslav troops continued to fight the Nazis from their mountainous strongholds. Foremost among these were the chetniks led by Draja Mikhailovich. Mikhailovich became involved in open warfare with other partisan forces led by Josip Broz, known as Marshal Tito, for control of the resistance movement. Tito, backed by the USSR and Great Britain, won and by the time the Germans had been driven from Yugoslavia in 1944, was in control. Mikhailovich was captured and executed in Belgrade July 17, 1946, by the Tito regime.

The constituent assembly proclaimed Yugoslavia a republic Nov. 29, 1945. It became a federated republic Jan. 31, 1946, and Marshal Tito, a Communist, became head of the government. By terms of a treaty with Italy the greater part of Venezia-Giulia, Zara, Pelagosa and adjacent islands were ceded to Yugoslavia.

The Stalin policy of dictating the Communist line to all Communist nations was rejected by Marshal Tito. He accepted economic aid and military equipment from the U. S., and received aid in foreign trade also from France and Great Britain.

In 1968 Pres. Tito supported the liberalization government of Czechoslovakia.

Yugoslavia is governed by the President, a cabinet (Federal Executive Council), and a parliament (Federal Assembly), from which cabinet members are drawn. The Assembly is composed of five chambers which deal with economic, political, health and cultural matters.

A new constitution was approved by Parliament, Apr. 7, 1963, replacing that in force since 1946. It made the country's official name the Socialist Federal Republic of Yugoslavia, limited political parties to the Communists and the Communist-dominated Socialist Alliance of Working People, and provided that future presidents be elected by parliament and restricted to two consecutive 4-year terms. A new office of vice president was created. The ballot is secret and freedom of worship is guaranteed. Tito was reelected President for 4 more years in May, 1967.

In 1966, Pres. Tito ousted Vice Pres. Aleksandar Rankovic after a hidden microphone was found in Pres. Tito's home; Rankovic had been in charge of the secret police. Writer Mihajlo Mihajlov was sentenced to a year in prison for writings published abroad. In a reorganization of the Communist party, Pres. Tito, 74, added a new title Pres. of the League of Communists, in place of General Secretary.

**Education and Religion.** All education is free; elementary training is compulsory to age 14. There are universities in Belgrade, Zagreb, Ljubljana, Skopje and Sarajevo. Principal languages are Slovene, Macedonian, Serbo-Croat. All religions are recognized and enjoy equal rights. Serbia-Orthodox comprises 42%, Roman Catholic 32%, Moslem 12%. Complete free social security is in force, including unemployment, medical, maternity benefits.

**Defense.** Army service is compulsory for men over 18. The air force comprises two corps, equipped with more than 500 first-line planes. The navy comprises 3 destroyers, 4 escorts, 68 torpedo boats, 2 submarines, a minelayer, numerous sweepers, patrol vessels and others.

Yugoslavia is a member of the UN and, with Greece and Turkey, of a Balkan defense group under a treaty signed in Ankara, Turkey, Feb. 27, 1953, and a 20-year military aid pact, Aug. 9, 1954.

# Zambia

### REPUBLIC OF ZAMBIA
#### (Former Northern Rhodesia)

**Capital:** Lusaka. **Area:** 288,130 sq. mi. **Population** (UN est. 1967): 3,947,000. **Monetary unit:** Kwacha (.7143 per U. S. $1).

The Republic of Zambia is the former British Protectorate of Northern Rhodesia. It is a landlocked country located in South Central Africa. Bordering nations are the Democratic Republic of the Congo, Tanzania, Malawi, Mozambique, Rhodesia, Botswana, South-West Africa and Angola. It is slightly larger than Texas.

The terrain is mostly high plateau covered with thin forest and suitable for both farming and grazing. The country is rich in minerals, including copper, zinc, cobalt, gold, vanadium, manganese, and coal. Zambia's wealth is mainly its copper; it is the world's 3rd largest copper producer.

Victoria Falls on the Zambezi River, the border with Rhodesia, is 3 times the width and more than twice the height of Niagara. Further down the river, the Kariba Dam, completed 1961, created Lake Kariba, 175 mi. long.

As Northern Rhodesia, the country was under the administration of the South Africa Company, 1889 until 1924 when the office of governor was established, with an executive council and, subsequently, a legislature.

A new constitution, announced in 1963, granted internal self-government with a prime minister and cabinet, effective Jan. 22, 1964. The United National Independence party won the first elections Jan. 21 and its leader, Kenneth D. Kaunda, became the country's first Prime Minister. He was elected President and, on Oct. 24, 1964, Zambia became an independent republic within the Commonwealth. It has a National Assembly of 75 elected members and 5 nominated by the President. It is a member of the UN and the OAU.

After the white government of Rhodesia declared its independence from Britain Nov. 17, 1965, relations between Zambia and Rhodesia became increasingly strained and use of their jointly owned railroad was disputed.

Britain gave Zambia an extra $12,000,000 in 1966 after imposing an oil embargo on Rhodesia, and Zambia bought cargo planes from the Lockheed Aircraft Corp. of the U. S. to carry copper out from its mines and gasoline in. In Aug. 1968 a 1,958-mi. pipeline was completed, bringing oil from Dar es Salaam, Tanzania.

In Apr. 1968 Pres. Kaunda announced plans for nationalizing some major industries; he said studies of economies in both East and West countries had convinced him none were completely capitalist or completely state-controlled.

---

# The "Wealth" of Nations

Some of the world's peoples have, since time immemorial, measured their wealth in terms of how many cattle or other livestock they own. While this is not true of most nations in the 20th Century, nevertheless large numbers of livestock are still an important source of wealth for many countries.

Figures gathered by the U. S. Department of Agriculture show that in 1968 the total number of cattle in the world was 1.15 billion, up a little less than 1% from 1967.

The world's sheep totaled 1.008 billion, also up a little less than 1%. But hogs, totaling just over half a billion, had increased 2%.

The leading cattle raiser was the U. S., which had 108,813,000 head. The USSR was 2nd with 97,100,000; Brazil was 3rd with 91,093,000; Argentina ranked 4th although figures were not available for that country.

The No. 1 sheep-raising nation was Australia with 165,000,000. Soviet Russia ranked 2nd in sheep, as in cattle, with 138,300,000. Next came New Zealand, its sheep estimated at something over 60,000,000, followed by Argentina, about 48,-000,000. The U. S. ranked 5th with 22,122,000, Brazil 6th with 22,000,000, the United Kingdom 7th with 20,446,000.

Tops in hogs was Brazil, 63,000,000; the U. S. was 2nd with 54,263,000. Soviet Russia was 3rd with 51,000,000 and West Germany 4th with 19,-032,000.

Another measure of wealth could be a nation's mineral production. Among the more widely used metals, the U. S. and Canada are tops. While the U. S., according to the Bureau of Mines, ranked 1st in 1967 in coal, copper, magnesium, petroleum and uranium, Canada was the leader in asbestos, nickel, silver and zinc.

Other leaders were: Jamaica, bauxite; Democratic Republic of Congo, industrial diamonds; South Africa, gold; Spain, mercury; USSR, platinum; Malaysia, tin.

# Cost of Living in Various Cities of the World

This comparison of the cost of living in various cities in 1968 was drawn up by the UN Statistical Bureau, based on prices for goods, services and housing for international officials stationed in these cities. Figures show relative costs, based on about 120 items. New York City was assigned the index figure 100. Thus, while expenditure for these items might be $1,000 in New York, it would be $950 for them in Copenhagen and $1,040 in Caracas. Figures with an asterisk (*) omit cost of housing (rent, utilities and domestic service) in cities where they were furnished at nominal cost by governments.

| Index | City | Index | City |
|---|---|---|---|
| *113 | Abidjan, Ivory Coast | 83 | La Paz, Bolivia |
| *93 | Accra, Ghana | 77 | Lima, Peru |
| 94 | Addis Ababa, Ethiopia | *103 | Lome, Togo |
| 85 | Algiers, Algeria | 70 | London, United Kingdom |
| 84 | Amman, Jordan | 86 | Lusaka, Zambia |
| 81 | Ankara, Turkey | 93 | Managua, Nicaragua |
| 89 | Athens, Greece | 89 | Manila, Philippines |
| 82 | Baghdad, Iraq | 87 | Mexico City, Mexico |
| *86 | Bamako, Mali | 89 | Mogadishu, Somalia |
| 91 | Bangkok, Thailand | *109 | Monrovia, Liberia |
| 84 | Beirut, Lebanon | 52 | Montevideo, Uruguay |
| 73 | Bogota, Colombia | 87 | Montreal, Canada |
| 80 | Bonn, West Germany | 83 | Nairobi, Kenya |
| *114 | Brazzaville, Rep. of Congo | 79 | New Delhi, India |
| 86 | Bridgetown, Barbados | 100 | New York, U. S. |
| 74 | Buenos Aires, Argentina | *116 | Nouakchott, Mauritania |
| 105 | Bujumbura, Burundi | *108 | Ouagadougou, Upper Volta |
| 80 | Cairo, United Arab Rep. | 86 | Panama City, Panama |
| 104 | Caracas, Venezuela | 102 | Paris, France |
| 71 | Colombo, Ceylon | 74 | Port-of-Spain, Trinidad & Tobago |
| 95 | Copenhagen, Denmark | 79 | Quito, Ecuador |
| 72 | Damascus, Syria | 82 | Rabat, Morocco |
| 87 | Dar es Salaam, Tanzania | 94 | Rio de Janeiro, Brazil |
| 101 | Jakarta, Indonesia | 105 | Riyadh, Saudi Arabia |
| *113 | Fort-Lamy, Chad | 84 | Rome, Italy |
| 79 | Gaberones, Botswana | 84 | San Jose, Costa Rica |
| 89 | Geneva, Switzerland | 92 | San Salvador, El Salvador |
| 66 | Georgetown, Guyana | 78 | Santiago, Chile |
| 92 | Guatemala City, Guatemala | 84 | Seoul, South Korea |
| 86 | The Hague, Netherlands | 74 | Taipei, Republic of China |
| 95 | Havana, Cuba | 95 | Tananarive, Malagasy Republic |
| 72 | Kabul, Afghanistan | 88 | Tegucigalpa, Honduras |
| *95 | Kampala, Uganda | 86 | Tehran, Iran |
| 87 | Karachi, Pakistan | 101 | Tripoli, Libya |
| 88 | Katmandu, Nepal | 80 | Tunis, Tunisia |
| *99 | Khartoum, Sudan | 83 | Vienna, Austria |
| 75 | Kingston, Jamaica | 88 | Vientiane, Laos |
| *76 | Kinshasa, Dem. Rep. of Congo | 92 | Washington, D. C., U. S. |
| 87 | Kuala Lumpur, Malaysia | *111 | Yaounde, Cameroon |
| *103 | Lagos, Nigeria | 68 | Zomba, Malawi |

# The Monroe Doctrine; Its Origin and Meaning

President James Monroe, in his annual message to Congress on Dec. 2, 1823, made the statement of policy since known as the Monroe Doctrine. Its major assertion is that the United States would consider as dangerous to its peace and safety any attempt of the European powers to extend their political system to any portion of the western hemisphere.

Balancing this statement in the same message is Monroe's declaration that in regard to Europe it is the policy of the United States "not to interfere in the internal concerns of any of its powers, to consider the government *de facto* as the legitimate (one) for us . . ."

Statesmen besides Monroe associated in the development of the Doctrine were John Quincy Adams, Secretary of State; Richard Rush, American Minister in London, and George Canning, British Secretary for Foreign Affairs. Consulted were Thomas Jefferson, John C. Calhoun, Secretary of War, and William Wirt, Attorney General.

**History of Its Origin.** The message grew out of two complications. The first was the decree of Russia reserving exclusively to Russian subjects the whole of the northwest coast of North America, from the Bering Straits to 51° N. Lat. and from the Aleutians to Siberia, for commerce, whaling, fishery and other industries, and prohibiting any foreign ship from approaching within 100 miles, on penalty of seizure. Secretary Adams rejected this, and after negotiations Russia re-

versed itself. In the message President Monroe said the American continents, "by the free and independent condition which they have assumed and maintain, are henceforth not to be considered as subjects for colonization by any European power."

The other part originated in the threat of foreign encroachment on Latin-American states, the independence of which had been recognized by the United States. George Canning, British Foreign Secretary, on Aug. 20, 1823, suggested to Rush, the American Minister, that the British and American governments declare "in the face of the world" their attitude toward the Spanish-American countries. He believed the two governments entertained similar views, and cited that the British conceived the recovery of the colonies by Spain to be hopeless; thought recognition of them as independent states to be a matter "of time and circumstances"; would not interfere with amicable negotiation between them and their mother country (Spain); did not wish to possess any portion of them or see it go to any other power with indifference.

Canning thought such a declaration might forestall any military attempts to coerce Latin America. When the United States did not act by October he addressed a similar statement to the French ambassador in London, Prince de Polignac, and received the assurance that France did not intend to take any of the Spanish colonies in America.

Secretary Adams, writing to Minister Rush Nov. 29, 1823, endorsed Canning's views but urged as indispensable the recognition of the independence of the new governments by Britain. He thought a unilateral statement better, and the joint declaration was never issued.

# UNITED NATIONS

## History, Membership, Organization and Purpose

The 23rd regular session of the United Nations General Assembly opened Sept. 1968. *See Chronology for developments at UN sessions during 1968.*

The resumed twenty-second session of the General Assembly, which began on Apr. 24, 1968, adjourned on June 12 after adopting a resolution commending the Treaty on the Non-Proliferation of Nuclear Weapons and another resolution on Namibia, formerly called South West Africa, declaring that the situation in the territory was "a grave threat to international peace and security," and calling on all States to help the Namibian people in their struggle for independence and to assist the United Nations Council for Namibia in ending South Africa's illegal occupation of the territory.

The membership of the UN rose to 124 states during the 22nd regular session of the General Assembly. This resulted from the admission of 2 new nations—Southern Yemen and Mauritius.

Foundations of the United Nations were laid at the Dumbarton Oaks Conference in Washington between the United States, the United Kingdom and the Soviet Union, Aug. 21-Sept. 28, 1944, and between the United States, the United Kingdom and the Republic of China (Nationalist) Sept. 29-Oct. 7, 1944. Proposals to establish an organization of nations for maintenance of world peace led to the United Nations Conference on International Organization at San Francisco, Apr. 25-June 26, 1945, where the charter of the United Nations was drawn up. It was signed June 26 by 50 nations, and by Poland, one of the original 51, on Oct. 15, 1945. The charter came into effect Oct. 24, 1945, when the requisite ratification by the 5 permanent members of the Security Council, China, France, Soviet Union, United Kingdom and United States, and a majority of other signatories had been completed.

United Nations headquarters are located in New York, N. Y., between First Ave. and Roosevelt Drive and E. 42nd St. and E. 48th St. The General Assembly Bldg. (opened 1952), Secretariat, Conference and Library bldgs. are interconnected. The Dag Hammarskjold Library, built by a $6,200,000 grant from the Ford Foundation, was dedicated Nov. 16, 1961. It has room for 400,000 vols. To build the headquarters the U. S. Government advanced an interest-free loan of $65,000,000, payable in annual installments until 1982. John D. Rockefeller, Jr., contributed $8,000,000 for land and the City of New York contributed an est. $26,500,000 for adapting the site. United Nations has a post office originating its own stamps. *See Postal Information.*

### Roster of the United Nations
#### (As of August, 1968)

The 124 Members of the United Nations, with the dates on which they became Members.

| Member | Date | Member | Date | Member | Date |
|---|---|---|---|---|---|
| Afghanistan | Nov. 19, 1946 | Ghana | Mar. 8, 1957 | Niger | Sept. 20, 1960 |
| Albania | Dec. 14, 1955 | Greece | Oct. 25, 1945 | Nigeria | Oct. 7, 1960 |
| Algeria | Oct. 8, 1962 | Guatemala | Nov. 21, 1945 | Norway | Nov. 27, 1945 |
| Argentina | Oct. 24, 1945 | Guinea | Dec. 12, 1958 | Pakistan | Sept. 30, 1947 |
| Australia | Nov. 1, 1945 | Guyana | Sept. 20, 1966 | Panama | Nov. 13, 1945 |
| Austria | Dec. 14, 1955 | Haiti | Oct. 24, 1945 | Paraguay | Oct. 24, 1945 |
| Barbados | Dec. 9, 1966 | Honduras | Dec. 17, 1945 | Peru | Oct. 31, 1945 |
| Belgium | Dec. 27, 1945 | Hungary | Dec. 14, 1955 | Philippines | Oct. 24, 1945 |
| Bolivia | Nov. 14, 1945 | Iceland | Nov. 19, 1946 | Poland | Oct. 24, 1945 |
| Botswana | Oct. 17, 1966 | India | Oct. 30, 1945 | Portugal | Dec. 14, 1955 |
| Brazil | Oct. 24, 1945 | Indonesia | Sept. 28, 1950 | Romania | Dec. 14, 1955 |
| Bulgaria | Dec. 14, 1955 | Iran | Oct. 24, 1945 | Rwanda | Sept. 18, 1962 |
| Burma | Apr. 19, 1948 | Iraq | Dec. 21, 1945 | Saudi Arabia | Oct. 24, 1945 |
| Burundi | Sept. 18, 1962 | Ireland | Dec. 14, 1955 | Senegal | Sept. 28, 1960 |
| Byelorussian Soviet | | Israel | May 11, 1949 | Sierra Leone | Sept. 27, 1961 |
| Socialist Rep | Oct. 24, 1945 | Italy | Dec. 14, 1955 | Singapore | Sept. 21, 1965 |
| Cambodia | Dec. 14, 1955 | Ivory Coast | Sept. 20, 1960 | Somalia | Sept. 20, 1960 |
| Cameroon | Sept. 20, 1960 | Jamaica | Sept. 18, 1962 | South Africa | Nov. 7, 1945 |
| Canada | Nov. 9, 1945 | Japan | Dec. 18, 1956 | Southern Yemen | Dec. 14, 1967 |
| Central African | | Jordan | Dec. 14, 1955 | Spain | Dec. 14, 1955 |
| Republic | Sept. 20, 1960 | Kenya | Dec. 16, 1963 | Sudan | Nov. 12, 1956 |
| Ceylon | Dec. 14, 1955 | Kuwait | May 14, 1963 | Sweden | Nov. 19, 1946 |
| Chad | Sept. 20, 1960 | Laos | Dec. 14, 1955 | Syria² | Oct. 24, 1945 |
| Chile | Oct. 24, 1945 | Lebanon | Oct. 24, 1945 | Tanzania³ | Dec. 14, 1961 |
| China | Oct. 24, 1945 | Lesotho | Oct. 17, 1966 | Thailand | Dec. 16, 1946 |
| Colombia | Nov. 5, 1945 | Liberia | Nov. 2, 1945 | Togo | Sept. 20, 1960 |
| Congo—Brazzaville | Sept. 20, 1960 | Libya | Dec. 14, 1955 | Trinidad & Tobago | Sept. 18, 1962 |
| Congo, Dem. Rep. | Sept. 20, 1960 | Luxembourg | Oct. 24, 1945 | Tunisia | Nov. 12, 1956 |
| Costa Rica | Nov. 2, 1945 | Madagascar | Sept. 20, 1960 | Turkey | Oct. 24, 1945 |
| Cuba | Oct. 24, 1945 | Malawi | Dec. 1, 1964 | Uganda | Oct. 25, 1962 |
| Cyprus | Sept. 20, 1960 | Malaysia¹ | Sept. 17, 1957 | Ukrainian Soviet | |
| Czechoslovakia | Oct. 24, 1945 | Maldive Islands | Sept. 21, 1965 | Socialist Republic | Oct. 24, 1945 |
| Dahomey | Sept. 20, 1960 | Mali | Sept. 28, 1960 | Union of Soviet | |
| Denmark | Oct. 24, 1945 | Malta | Dec. 1, 1964 | Socialist Repub's. | Oct. 24, 1945 |
| Dominican Rep. | Oct. 24, 1945 | Mauritania | Oct. 27, 1961 | United Arab Rep.² | Oct. 24, 1945 |
| Ecuador | Dec. 21, 1945 | Mauritius | Apr. 24, 1968 | United Kingdom | Oct. 24, 1945 |
| El Salvador | Oct. 24, 1945 | Mexico | Nov. 7, 1945 | United States | Oct. 24, 1945 |
| Ethiopia | Nov. 13, 1945 | Mongolia | Oct. 27, 1961 | Upper Volta | Sept. 20, 1960 |
| Finland | Dec. 14, 1955 | Morocco | Nov. 12, 1956 | Uruguay | Dec. 18, 1945 |
| France | Oct. 24, 1945 | Nepal | Dec. 14, 1955 | Venezuela | Nov. 15, 1945 |
| Gabon | Sept. 20, 1960 | Netherlands | Dec. 10, 1945 | Yemen | Sept. 30, 1947 |
| Gambia | Sept. 21, 1965 | New Zealand | Oct. 24, 1945 | Yugoslavia | Oct. 24, 1945 |
| | | Nicaragua | Oct. 24, 1945 | Zambia | Dec. 1, 1964 |

[1] The Federation of Malaya joined the UN on Sept. 17, 1957. On Sept. 16, 1963, its name changed to Malaysia, following the admission to the new Federation of Singapore, Sabah (North Borneo) and Sarawak. Singapore became an independent State Aug. 9, 1965 and a Member of the UN Sept. 21.

[2] Egypt and Syria were original Members of the United Nations from Oct. 24, 1945. Following a plebiscite held on Feb. 21, 1958, the United Arab Republic was established by a union of Egypt and Syria and continued as a single Member of the United Nations. On Oct. 13, 1961, Syria, having resumed its status as an independent State, resumed its separate membership in the Organization.

[3] Tanganyika was a Member of the United Nations from Dec. 14, 1961 and Zanzibar was a Member from Dec. 16, 1963. Following the ratification, on Apr. 26, 1964, of Articles of Union between Tanganyika and Zanzibar, the United Republic of Tanganyika and Zanzibar continued as a single Member of the United Nations, later changing its name to United Republic of Tanzania.

# Operations of the United Nations Under Its Charter

*The following article describes both the powers of the United Nations and its present organization. It is based on the provisions of the charter of the United Nations, and on an official report furnished by the Secretariat. The text of the Charter may be obtained from the Office of Public Information, United Nations, N. Y.*

## GENERAL ASSEMBLY

**Officers and Committees 22nd (1967-68) Regular session:**

President—Corneliu Manescu, Romania.

Vice Presidents—Australia, China, Dahomey, Dominican Republic, Ecuador, France, Iceland, Jordan, Laos, Libya, Nepal, Nicaragua, Sudan, Union of Soviet Socialist Republics, United Kingdom, United Republic of Tanzania, United States.

**Committee Chairmen:** First Committee (Political and Security)—Ismail Fahmy, United Arab Republic. Special Political Committee—Humberto Lopez Villamil, Honduras. Second Committee (Economic and Financial)—Jorge Pablo Fernandini, Peru. Third Committee (Social, Humanitarian and Cultural)—Mrs. Mara Radié, Yugoslavia. Fourth Committee (Trust and Non-Self-Governing Territories)—George J. Tomeh, Syria. Fifth Committee (Administrative and Budgetary)—Harry L. Morris, Liberia. Sixth Committee (Legal)—Edvard Hambro, Norway.

The General Assembly is composed of representatives of all the member nations. Each nation may send not more than five representatives to each session. Each nation is entitled to one vote.

The General Assembly meets in regular annual sessions and in special session when necessary. Special sessions are convoked by the Secretary General at the request of the Security Council or of a majority of the members of the UN.

Any matter within the scope of the charter may be brought before the General Assembly, which may make recommendations on all except issues on the agenda of the Security Council. However, the General Assembly in November, 1950, decided that if the Security Council, because of lack of unanimity of the permanent members, fails to exercise its primary responsibility for the maintenance of international peace and security, in any case where there appears to be a threat to the peace, breach of the peace or act of aggression, the Assembly may consider it and recommend collective measures, including, in the case of a breach of the peace or act of aggression, the use of armed forces to maintain or restore peace. In such cases, the General Assembly may be convened within 24 hours in an emergency special session.

On important questions a two-thirds majority of members present and voting is required; on other questions a simple majority is sufficient. Questions that require a two-thirds majority include: recommendations on maintenance of international peace and security, election of non-permanent members of the Security Council, election of members of the Economic and Social Council, election of members of the UN that are to designate the members of the Trusteeship Council, admission of members to the UN, suspension and expulsion of members, trusteeship questions and budgetary matters.

The General Assembly must approve the budget and apportion expenses among members. A member in arrears will have no vote if the amount of arrears equals or exceeds the amount of the contributions due for the preceding two full years. The General Assembly may permit such a member to vote if it is satisfied that the failure is due to conditions beyond control.

A general or steering committee co-ordinates the proceedings of the Assembly and is composed of 26 members—the president of the Assembly, the 18 vice-presidents, and the chairmen of the seven main committees.

## SECURITY COUNCIL

The Security Council consists of 15 members, 5 with permanent seats. The remaining 10 are elected for 2-year terms by the General Assembly; they are not eligible for immediate re-election.

**Permanent members of the Council:** China, France, USSR, United Kingdom, United States.

**Non-permanent members** are Algeria, Brazil, Canada, Denmark, Ethiopia, Hungary, India, Pakistan, Paraguay, Senegal.

The Presidency of the Council is held monthly in turn by the member states in English alphabetical order.

The Security Council has the primary responsibility for maintaining international peace and security and members agree to carry out its de-

cisions. The Council may investigate any dispute that threatens international peace and security. When the Security Council is handling a dispute or situation the General Assembly makes no recommendation unless the Council requests it. The Secretary General notifies the General Assembly what matters are being dealt with, and if the G.A. is not in session he so notifies the members of the UN. The Security Council makes full reports to the G.A.

The Security Council functions continuously, each member being represented at all times. It may change its place of meeting. Any member of UN may participate in its discussions even if without a vote and a nation not a member of UN may appear if it is a party to a dispute.

Decisions on procedural questions are made by an affirmative vote of 9 members. On all other matters the affirmative vote of 9 members must include the concurring votes of all permanent members; it is this clause which gives rise to the so-called "veto." A party to a dispute must refrain from voting.

Reporting to the Security Council are: the Military Staff Committee, which advises the Council on military requirements for maintaining peace; and the Disarmament Commission which is concerned with the regulation and reduction of armaments and the control of nuclear weapons. The latter also reports to the General Assembly.

The Security Council may decide to enforce its decisions without the use of arms. Such measures include interruption of economic relations, break in transportation and communications, and severance of diplomatic relations. If such measures fail the Council may call on UN members to furnish armed forces, assistance and facilities, based on agreements made by the Council with the states and subject to ratification by the members of the UN "in accordance with their constitutional processes."

The right of individual or collective self-defense is not prohibited by membership in the UN, and if a member nation is attacked it may do what is necessary, reporting this to the Security Council, which may take independent action. However, the Council encourages regional arrangements or agencies by means of which local disputes can be settled without getting as far as the Council, after the Council has approved this method.

In the event of a conflict between the obligations of members to the UN and to other international bodies of which they may be members then obligations to the UN are paramount.

## ECONOMIC AND SOCIAL COUNCIL

The Economic and Social Council consists of 27 members elected by the General Assembly for 3-year terms of office. The council is responsible under the General Assembly for carrying out the functions of the United Nations with regard to international economic, social, cultural, educational, health and related matters. The council meets usually twice a year.

### Membership of the Council

**Until Dec. 31, 1968**—Czechoslovakia, Iran, Morocco, Panama, Philippines, Sweden, Union of Soviet Socialist Republics, United Kingdom, Venezuela.

**Until Dec. 31, 1969**—Belgium, France, Guatemala, Kuwait, Libya, Mexico, Sierra Leone, Turkey, Tanzania.

**Until Dec. 31, 1970**—Argentina, Bulgaria, Chad, Congo (Brazzaville), India, Ireland, Japan, United States, Upper Volta.

The President for 1968 was Manuel Perez Guerrero, Venezuela. The Economic and Social Council had the following commissions in 1967:

### Functional Commissions

Statistical; Population; Social; Narcotic Drugs; Human Rights (and its Sub-Commission on the Prevention of discrimination and the protection of minorities); Status of Women.

**Regional Economic Commissions**

Economic Commission for Europe.
Economic Commission for Asia and the Far East.
Economic Commission for Latin America.
Economic Commission for Africa.

Also reporting to the Economic and Social Council are the Permanent Central Opium Board and the Drug Supervisory Body, the United Nations Children's Fund (UNICEF), the Council of the United Nations Development Program (UNDP) and the United Nations Special Fund, established to assist the economy of less-developed countries.

The Economic & Social Council may make recommendations for the purpose of promoting respect for, and observance of, human rights and fundamental freedoms for all.

It may call international conferences on matters falling within its competence.

## TRUST AND NON-SELF GOVERNING TERRITORIES

The work of the United Nations in the field of dependent territories falls into two categories: (1) the duties and functions of the Trusteeship Council with respect to those territories placed under the International Trusteeship System; and (2) the responsibility of the Organization in connection with information on non-self-governing territories other than Trust territories. The objectives of trusteeship are to further international peace and security; promote the political, economic, social and educational advancement of the inhabitants and their progressive development toward self-government or independence. Also to encourage respect for human rights and fundamental freedoms without distinction as to race, sex, language or religion, and to encourage recognition of the interdependence of all peoples; to insure equal treatment in social, economic and commercial matters for all members of the United Nations and their nationals, and also equal treatment for the latter in the administration of justice.

## TRUSTEESHIP COUNCIL

The administration of Trust territories is subject to the supervision of the United Nations. Administering authorities are required to render an account of their stewardship to the Trusteeship Council. The Council may entertain petitions from private persons or organizations regarding conditions in the Trust territories and may dispatch missions to study conditions there.

The membership of the Council is made up of (1) countries which administer trust territories (Australia, the United Kingdom and the United States); (2) countries which are permanent members of the Security Council but which do not administer trust territories (China, France, USSR); and (3) as many other countries as may be necessary to ensure equal representation in the Council between administering and non-administering members. Those in the last named category are elected by the General Assembly for 3-year terms and are eligible for immediate reelection.

The Council usually meets once a year, in the spring. The President of the 35th session (1968) was Mrs. Eugenie M. Anderson, United States.

The trust territories and the members administering them are: New Guinea (Australia), Pacific Islands (United States). New Zealand is no longer a member of the Council. Its membership ceased as a result of the accession to independence of Nauru, in January 1968, which Australia had administered on behalf of herself, New Zealand and the United Kingdom. A former trust territory, Togoland (United Kingdom) became independent in 1957, joining the Gold Coast, formerly a British colony, to become the new State of Ghana. In April 1960 the former trust territories, Cameroons and Togoland (France), gained their independence and formed the Republics of Cameroon and Togo. In July 1960 the former trust territory of Somaliland (Italy) became together with British Somaliland, the Republic of Somalia. After plebiscites held in the Cameroons (United Kingdom) in 1961, the Northern section joined Nigeria, and the southern section joined the Republic of Cameroon. Tanganyika (United Kingdom), gained independence in December 1961, Western Samoa (New Zealand), became independent in January 1962, and Ruanda-Urundi (Belgium), in July 1962, separated into two independent countries, the Kingdom of Burundi and the Republic of Rwanda.

## NON-SELF-GOVERNING TERRITORIES

Members of the United Nations responsible for the administration of non-self-governing territories not under trusteeships recognize the principle that the interests of the inhabitants are paramount and promote their welfare. They are bound by the charter to transmit to the Secretary-General technical information concerning economic, social and educational conditions in the territories. This information is summarized, analyzed and classified by the Secretariat. Since 1961 a committee has been studying the implementation of the 1960 general assembly declaration on the granting of independence to colonial countries and peoples. This committee also receives the reports on non self-governing territories.

## INTERNATIONAL COURT OF JUSTICE

The International Court of Justice is the principal judicial organ of the United Nations. All members are *ipso facto* parties to the statute of the Court. Other states may become parties to the Court's statute on conditions determined in each case by the General Assembly on the recommendation of the Security Council.

The jurisdiction of the Court comprises cases which the parties submit to it and matters especially provided for in the charter or in treaties. The Court gives advisory opinions and renders judgments. Its decisions, which are final, are only binding between the parties concerned and in respect of a particular dispute. Of any party to a case fails to heed a judgment of the Court, the other party may have recourse to the Security Council, which may decide what is to be done.

The Court consists of 15 judges elected for 9-year terms by the General Assembly and the Security Council voting independently. No two of the judges may be nationals of the same state. Retiring judges are eligible for re-election. The Court remains permanently in session, except during the judicial vacations. A quorum of 9 judges suffices to constitute the Court. All questions are decided by majority. In the event of a tie, the President of the Court or the judge who acts in his place casts the deciding vote.

### Judges

**Nine-year term of office ending on Feb. 5, 1976:**
Sture Petren, Sweden
Cesar Bengzon, Philippines
Fouad Ammoun, Lebanon
Manfred Lachs, Poland
Charles D. Onyeama, Nigeria

**Nine-year term of office ending on Feb. 5, 1973:**
Sir Gerald Fitzmaurice, United Kingdom
Isaac Forster, Senegal
Andre Gros, France
Luis Padilla Nervo, Mexico
Muhammad Zafrulla Khan, Pakistan

**Nine-year term of office ending on Feb. 5, 1970:**
Jose Luis Bustamante y Rivero, Peru
Philip C. Jessup, United States
Vladimir M. Koretsky, USSR
Gaetano Morelli, Italy
Kotaro Tanaka, Japan

## AGENCIES RELATED TO THE UNITED NATIONS

Working in partnership with the United Nations in various economic, social, scientific and technical fields is a group of intergovernmental organizations related to the United Nations by special agreements. Among these agencies (with their headquarters) are:

**International Atomic Energy Agency (IAEA)** aims to promote the peaceful uses of atomic energy. (Vienna)

**International Labor Org. (ILO)** aims to promote social justice; improve labor conditions and living standards; and promote economic stability. (Geneva)

**Food & Agriculture Org. (FAO)** aims to raise nutrition levels and living standards; secure improvements in production and distribution of food and agricultural products. (Rome)

**United Nations Educational, Scientific & Cultural Org. (UNESCO)** aims to promote collabora-

tion among nations through education, science and culture in order to further human rights and freedoms without distinction of race, sex, language or religion. (Paris)

**World Health Org. (WHO)** aims to aid the attainment of the highest possible level of health. (Geneva)

**International Bank for Reconstruction & Development (World Bank)** aims to help in reconstruction and development of territories of members by facilitating investment of capital; promote foreign investment and supplement private investment by providing loans for productive purposes out of its capital, funds raised by it and its other resources; and to promote growth of international trade and equilibrum in balance of payments. (Washington, D. C.)

**International Development Assn. (IDA)** aims to further economic development of members by financing on terms bearing less heavily on balance of payments than those of conventional loans. (Washington, D. C.)

**International Finance Corp. (IFC)** aims to further economic development by encouraging productive private enterprise, particularly in less developed areas. It is empowered to invest in private enterprises in association with private investors, and without government guarantee of repayment in cases where sufficient private capital is not available on reasonable terms; and to bring together private capital and management. (Washington, D. C.)

**International Monetary Fund (Fund)** aims to promote international monetary co-operation and expansion of international trade; to promote exchange stability and avoid competitive exchange depreciations; to assist in the establishment of a multilateral system of payments between members and in the elimination of foreign restrictions. (Washington, D. C.)

**International Civil Aviation Org. (ICAO)** promotes international standards and regulations. (Montreal)

**Universal Postal Union (UPU)** aims to perfect postal services and promote development of international collaboration. To this end, member countries unite in a single postal territory for reciprocal exchange of mail. (Berne)

**International Telecommunication Union (ITU)** sets up international regulations for radio, telegraph and telephone services and studies means to lower costs on international services. (Geneva)

**World Meteorological Org. (WMO)** aims to co-ordinate, standardize and improve world meteorological work. (Geneva)

**Intergovernmental Maritime Consultative Org. (IMCO)** aims to promote co-operation in technical problems of international shipping and to encourage the removal of discriminatory action by governments and restrictive practices by shippers. (London)

**General Agreement on Tariffs and Trade (GATT)** was drafted in 1946. Its functions are to ease trade barriers and establish rules of fair trade. In recent years, GATT has made special efforts to develop international trade and also has given particular emphasis to increasing the export trade of developing countries. (Geneva)

**United Nation's Children's Fund (UNICEF)** helps requesting countries meet the urgent needs of their children. Supported entirely by voluntary contributions from governments and individuals, UNICEF is currently helping 112 countries, mainly in the developing areas of the world. It is governed by a thirty-nation executive board. (New York)

## SECRETARIAT

The Secretariat is composed of a Secretary-General appointed by the General Assembly upon the recommendation of the Security Council and such staff as the organization may require.

The Secretary General is the chief administrative officer of the UN. He may bring to the attention of the Security Council any matter that threatens international peace. He reports to the General Assembly.

**Secretary General—U Thant (Burma).**

An international staff assists the Secretary-General. Its members are recruited on a wide geographical basis and are appointed by him. The Secretary General and staff may not receive instructions from outside authorities or be influenced by the UN members.

The principal officers as of August 1, 1968 were: Officials of the rank of under-Secretary-General at Headquarters:

**Conference Services**—Jiri Nosek (Czech.).

**Economic and Social Affairs**—Philippe de Seynes (France).

**General Assembly Affairs and Chef de Cabinet**—C. V. Narasimhan (India).

**Political and Security Council Affairs**—Leonid N. Kutakov (USSR).

**Special Political Affairs**—José Rolz-Bennett (Guatemala), Ralph J. Bunche (U. S.).

**Trusteeship and Non-Self-Governing Territories**—Issoufou S. Djermakoye (Niger).

Officials of the rank of Assistant-Secretary-General at Headquarters:

**Controller**—Bruce Turner (New Zealand).

**General Services**—David Vaughn (U. S.).

**Legal Counsel**—Constantin A. Stavropoulos (Greece).

**Personnel**—William W. Cox (U. S.).

**Public Information**—Agha Abdul Hamid (Pakistan).

**Technical co-operation**—Victor Hoo (China).

**UN Children's Fund**—Henry R. Labouisse (U. S.).

**UN Development Program**—Paul G. Hoffman (U. S.), David Owen (U. K.), Roberto Heurtematte (Panama).

**UN Institute for Training and Research**—Chief S. O. Adebo (Nigeria).

### Offices Overseas

**Africa**—Robert K. A. Gardiner (Addis-Ababa).

**Asia and Far East**—U Nyun (Bangkok).

**Europe**—Janez Stanovnik (Geneva).

**Geneva**—Vittorio W. Guicciardi (Geneva).

**Latin America**—Carlos Quintana (Santiago).

**Industrial Development Organization**—Ibrahim Helmi Abdel-Rahman (Vienna).

**Conference on Trade and Development**—Raúl Prebish (Geneva).

In charge of Missions, or Special Assignments: **Chief of Staff, UNTSO**—General Odd Bull (Jerusalem).

**UN Relief and Works Agency for Palestine Refugees in the Near East**—Laurence V. Michelmore (Beirut).

**Refugees**—Prince Sadruddin Aga Khan (Geneva).

**Commander, UN Force in Cyprus**—General I. A. E. Martola (Nicosia).

**Special Representative of Secretary-General in Cyprus**—B. F. Osorio-Tafall (Nicosia).

**Chief Officer UN India-Pakistan Observation Mission**—Dr. P. Graham (New York).

## UNITED NATIONS BUDGET

The General Assembly voted a gross budget of $140,430,950 for 1968—$10,116,720 higher than the gross budget for 1967. It also approved estimates of income totalling $23,635,000, thus bringing the net budget for 1968 to $116,795,950.

## SOURCES OF INFORMATION

**Public Inquiries Unit, Office of Public Information,** United Nations, N. Y. Provides pamphlets, study guides, speakers, films; arranges group visits. Telephones—Information on UN activities: PL 4-1234, Ext. 2526. Inquiries on tickets to meetings: Ext. 711.

**UN Publications:** UN Bookshop, United Nations, N. Y.

**United Nations Assn. of the United States of America Inc.,** 345 E. 46th St., New York, N. Y. Tel. OX 7-3232. Publications Center, 78 Fifth Ave., New York, N. Y. Tel.: CH 3-1521.

# Major International Organizations
*(See also United Nations)*

**THE COMMONWEALTH,** originally called the British Commonwealth of Nations, is an association of nations and dependencies loosely joined by a common interest based on having been parts of the old British Empire. The British monarch is the symbolic head of the Commonwealth. By tacit agreement, the name British Commonwealth of Nations has been shortened to the Commonwealth.

There are 28 self-governing independent nations which are full members of the Commonwealth, plus some 50 colonies, protectorates and trust territories which are dependencies of the United Kingdom, Australia or New Zealand and which are thus part of the Commonwealth.

The 28 members, as of Aug. 1968 were the United Kingdom of Great Britain and Northern Ireland and 12 other nations recognizing the British monarch, represented by a governor-general, as their head of state: Australia, Barbados, Canada, Ceylon, Gambia, Guyana, Jamaica, Malta, Mauritius, Sierra Leone, Trinidad and Tobago, New Zealand; and 15 countries with their own heads of state: Botswana, Cyprus, Ghana, India, Kenya, Lesotho, Malawi, Malaysia, Nigeria, Pakistan, Singapore, Swaziland, Tanzania, Uganda, Zambia.

The Commonwealth is an evolving organization. Many of its members have obtained independence from Britain and became full members since 1945. Members may secede; Ireland left in 1949, the Republic of South Africa left in 1961. Nations which have won independence since 1945 and did not join the Commonwealth are Burma (1948), Sudan (1956), Somaliland (1960), Southern Cameroons (1961), Maldive Islands (1965), Southern Yemen (1967).

The Commonwealth facilitates consultation among member states through meetings of prime ministers and finance ministers; economic, scientific and educational standing committees provide information and other services. Population (est. 1966) was 737,300,000 in member nations and 12,000,000 in dependencies.

**THE FRENCH COMMUNITY** was created in the 1958 French Constitution and modified by later amendment. It is an association of France, its Overseas Departments and Territories, 6 African republics (former possessions) and one Condominium (New Hebrides). France aids members in construction of roads, railroads, etc., and in improvement of agricultural production, health and education. France and the 6 African republics have cultural, economic, financial and technical cooperation agreements. Nine other African republics have bilateral agreements of cooperation with France. There are also economic, customs and monetary unions to which various African states belong. *(See France for Community members.)*

**NORTH ATLANTIC TREATY ORG. (NATO)** was created April 4, 1949, in a treaty signed in Washington, effective Aug. 24, by Belgium, Canada, Denmark, France, Iceland, Italy, Luxembourg, the Netherlands, Norway, Portugal, the United Kingdom and the U. S. Greece, Turkey and West Germany have joined since. The members agreed to settle disputes by peaceful means; to develop their individual and collective capacity to resist armed attack; to regard an attack on one as an attack on all and to take necessary action to repel it under Art. 51 of the UN Charter.

NATO Council meetings may consist of heads of government, cabinet ministers, or permanent NATO representatives, who hold the rank of ambassadors. The Military Committee is composed of the Chiefs-of-Staff of the member countries and permanent representatives.

Armed forces of NATO members include forces assigned to NATO commands, forces earmarked for NATO commands and forces under national command. There is a Supreme Allied Commander Europe (SACEUR); a Supreme Allied Commander Atlantic (SACLANT); a Channel Committee and Allied Command Channel (covering the English Channel and southern North Sea); a Canada-U. S. Regional Planning Group.

Following announcement in 1966 of nearly total French withdrawal from the military affairs of NATO, the Council moved its hq. in 1967 from Paris to Evere, near Brussels, and SACEUR's hq. (SHAPE) to Casteau, Belgium; a subordinate command, Allied Forces Central Europe, was to go to Maastrict, Netherlands; the Military Committee's Standing Group (the U. K., U. S. and France) was abolished.

**EUROPEAN ECONOMIC COMMUNITY (EEC)** generally called the Common Market (or "Inner Six"), came into effect Jan. 1, 1958, after Belgium, France, Italy, Luxembourg, the Netherlands and West Germany signed a treaty in Rome in March, 1957, to work toward a customs union and free flow of goods and services. Britain's applications for admission were vetoed by France in 1963 and 1967. Other nations have become associate members.

**ORGANIZATION OF AMERICAN STATES (OAS)** grew out of the Pan American Union, which, with hq in Washington, is its general secretariat. OAS (formed at Bogota, Colombia, 1948) has a Council, to which each of the member nations sends a representative. The Council can call meetings of ministers of foreign affairs to make decisions under the **Inter-American Treaty of Reciprocal Assistance,** formed in Rio de Janeiro 1947, to which most countries of the western hemisphere belong. There are 23 members, each with one vote on the Council and other organizations: Argentina, Barbados, Bolivia, Brazil, Chile, Colombia, Costa Rica, Cuba, Dominican Republic, Ecuador, El Salvador, Guatemala, Haiti, Honduras, Mexico, Nicaragua, Panama, Paraguay, Peru, Trinidad-Tobago, U. S., Uruguay, Venezuela. In 1962, the OAS excluded Cuba "from participation in the inter-American system," a step motivated by Cuba's "alignment with the Communist bloc" and designed to exclude it from OAS activities but not to deprive it of OAS membership.

**CENTRAL TREATY ORG. OF THE MIDDLE EAST (CENTO)** was formed 1959 by Iran, Turkey, Pakistan and the United Kingdom to continue the mutual security and economic development objectives of the 1955 Baghdad Pact from which Iraq had withdrawn. The U. S. is represented on some of its committees and signed bilateral defense agreements with Iran, Turkey and Pakistan. Funds of the 4 members and the U. S. have been used in economic programs. Rail, road and radio links, harbors and schools are included.

**EUROPEAN FREE TRADE ASSOCIATION (EFTA),** consisting of Austria, Denmark, Norway, Portugal, Sweden, Switzerland and the United Kingdom (sometimes called the "Outer Seven"), was created by treaty Jan. 4, 1960, effective May 3, to gradually reduce customs duties and quantitative restrictions between members on industrial (but not agricultural) products. By Dec. 31, 1966, tariffs and restrictions had been eliminated. Finland became an associate member in 1961.

**WARSAW TREATY ORGANIZATION (WARSAW PACT)** was created May 14, 1955, as a 20-year mutual defense alliance by Albania, Bulgaria, Czechoslovakia, East Germany, Hungary, Poland, Romania and the USSR. However, Albania was excluded from the group's meetings in 1962. It provides for a unified military command with headquarters in Moscow; if one member is attacked, the others will aid it with all necessary steps including armed force; joint maneuvers are held; there is a Political Consultative Committee and economic cooperation is advanced.

**SOUTHEAST ASIA TREATY ORGANIZATION (SEATO)** was established Sept. 8, 1954, by Australia, France, New Zealand, Pakistan, the Philippines, Thailand, the United Kingdom and the U. S. to provide for collective defense and economic cooperation in SE Asia. France boycotted the 1967 annual ministers' meeting. Bangkok is hq.

**LEAGUE OF ARAB STATES (THE ARAB LEAGUE)** was created March 22, 1945, by Egypt (United Arab Republic), Iraq, Jordan, Lebanon, Saudi Arabia, Syria and Yemen. Joining later were Algeria, Kuwait, Libya, Morocco, Southern Yemen, Sudan and Tunisia. Cairo is headquarters for the Secretary-General. The League has created Arab Postal and Telecommunications Unions. The League has maintained a boycott of Israel.

**ORGANIZATION OF AFRICAN UNITY (OAU)** was formed May 25, 1963, by 30 African countries to coordinate cultural, political, scientific and economic policies; to end colonialism in Africa; to promote a common defense of members' independence. It holds conferences of heads of government, has a council of foreign ministers, a secretary-general and a mediation-arbitration commission. Hq. is in Addis Ababa, Ethiopia.

# International Bank for Reconstruction and Development

Robert S. McNamara, President
**Address, 1818 H St., N.W., Washington, D. C. 20433. European Office, Paris**

The Articles of Agreement of the International Bank for Reconstruction and Development, also known as the World Bank, were drawn up by representatives of 44 nations at the United Nations Monetary and Financial Conference, Bretton Woods, N. H., July 1-12, 1944. Its official existence dates from December 27, 1945, when the articles were signed by 28 nations in Washington. By June 30, 1968, 107 countries were members.

The purposes of the Bank are: to assist the economic development of member countries by facilitating investment of capital for productive purposes, and thereby promote growth of international trade and improvement of standards of living; to promote participation in loans and investments made by private investors, and to make loans for productive purposes when private capital is not easily available.

The Bank's chief sources of funds for loans are derived from paid-in capital subscriptions and from the sale of its own bonds and by other borrowing in the capital markets. By June 30, 1968, the subscribed capital was $22,941,900,000. Of this $2,294,190,000 was paid-in capital, the greater part of which has been made available for loans; $20,647,710,000 was on call and serves as a guarantee fund for the Bank's bonds and other obligations. The Bank's funded debt at that time amounted to $3,289,568,000 which included obligations in U. S. dollars, Canadian dollars, Belgian francs, Netherlands guilders, pounds sterling, Swedish kroner, Swiss francs, Deutsche marks and Italian lire. The Bank's funds for loans also are replenished through sales of parts of Bank loans to outside investors. Funds from this source amounted to $2,142,637,000.

By June 30, 1968, the Bank had made 552 loans totaling over $11,246,854,000 in 85 countries or territories. Where the government itself was not the borrower the government guaranteed the loan. Disbursements on loans approximated $8,820,919,000.

Net income for the fiscal year ended June 30, 1968, was $169,124,000. Loan commissions were $595,000. Commissions were added to the Special Reserve, raising it to $291,017,000. After the close of the fiscal year ended June 30, 1968, the Executive Directors of the Bank allocated $96,124,000 from net income for 1967-68 to Supplemental Reserve, increasing it to $963,108,000, and recommended to the Board of Governors that the balance of $75,000,000 of that year's net income be transferred to the International Development Association (IDA), an affiliate of the Bank, as a grant.

There was a further expansion in the Bank's technical assistance services. It assisted member countries in preparing development projects and programs of high priority. It also acted as executing agency for a number of pre-investment studies financed by the United Nations Development Programme. Members of the Bank's Development Advisory Service worked with several countries on planning and development policy.

**International Development Assn.** (IDA) provides finance on terms more flexible and bearing less heavily on the balance of payments of recipient countries than those of conventional loans. IDA's funds are kept separate from those of the Bank. Membership is open to the Bank's members. By June 30, 1968, 98 countries had become members with initial subscriptions amounting to $1,000,222,-000. Its supplementary resources amounted to $1,004,230,000, including $49,495,000 additional

contributions by Sweden and $210,000,000 transfers from the Bank. It has also borrowed $12,100,000 from the Swiss Confederation. $1,829,100,000 of usable funds had been available for commitment as of June 30, 1968. IDA had extended 127 development credits totaling $1,788,400,000 in 40 countries; 21 in Africa, 8 in Asia and the Middle East, 10 in the Western Hemisphere, and one in Europe.

These credits are on identical terms: each is for 50 years, free of interest. Repayment is due in foreign exchange; amortization is to begin after a ten-year period; thereafter, 1% of the principal is repayable annually for 10 years and 3% annually for the final 30 years. A service charge of ¾ of 1% per annum, payable on the amounts withdrawn and outstanding is made to meet IDA's costs.

## International Finance Corporation

The International Finance Corporation (IFC) was established by member governments in July 1956, as an affiliate of the International Bank for Reconstruction and Development (World Bank). Its objective is to assist less developed member countries by helping to promote the growth of productive private enterprise.

At June 30, 1968, IFC's share capital was $101,-368,000, subscribed by 86 countries. IFC is empowered to increase its lending resources by borrowing up to approximately $400,000,000 from the World Bank. The first use of this line of credit, a $100,-000,000 drawing, was approved in October 1966.

IFC provides risk capital for productive private enterprises, in association with private investors and management. It encourages the development of local capital markets and it seeks to stimulate the international flow of private capital. The Corporation makes investments in the form of share subscriptions and long-term loans. It carries out standby and underwriting arrangements and it provides financial and technical assistance to privately controlled development finance companies. It neither seeks nor accepts government guarantees.

IFC is responsible for the technical and financial appraisal and supervision of all industrial, mining and development finance company projects submitted to the World Bank Group (the World Bank, the International Development Assn. and IFC).

In the year ended June 30, 1968, IFC's commitments rose to a record annual level of $50,700,000 from $49,100,000 in the previous year. This brought the cumulative total of gross commitments to $271,800,000, representing 154 transactions in 39 countries.

IFC expanded its geographic scope in the 1967/68 fiscal year by making its first investment in Korea, Mauritania and Nicaragua. This brought to 39 the number of countries in which IFC has operated.

Net income of IFC in 1967/68 rose to $6,200,000 from $6,000,000 in the previous year. The reserve against losses increased to $41,000,000 from $34,-700,000. Sales of portions of IFC commitments to other investors came to $18,600,000. These items, together with subscriptions from three new members—Vietnam, Mauretania and Indonesia—and loan repayment, raised the cumulative total of funds available to the IFC to $340,000,000.

Robert S. McNamara, President of the World Bank, is Chairman and President of IFC. Martin M. Rosen is Executive Vice President. The address of IFC is 1818 H Street, N.W., Washington, D. C. 20433.

# International Monetary Fund

Pierre-Paul Schweitzer, Managing Director and Ch. of Executive Board
19th and H Sts., NW, Washington, D. C.

The International Monetary Fund, with over $21 billion in gold and national currencies, is the world's largest source of quickly available international credit. By April 30, 1968, the 107-nation Fund had provided $14.6 billion in short-term financial assistance to 64 of its member countries. Its activities reached a record level in 1961 when 22 members drew the equivalent of $2,478.5 million.

The Fund was established in terms of Articles of Agreement formulated at the Bretton Woods Conference, July, 1944, effective Dec. 27, 1945.

The purposes of the Fund are: (1) to promote international monetary cooperation through a permanent institution which provides machinery for consultation and collaboration on international

monetary problems, and, more specifically, (2) to promote exchange stability and avoid competitive exchange depreciation, (3) to assist in the establishment of a multilateral system of payments in respect of current transactions, which means the eventual elimination of restrictions on the making of payments and transfers for current international transactions and the avoidance of discriminatory currency arrangements or multiple currency practices, and (4) to permit members, under appropriate conditions, to draw upon the resources of the Fund with a view to shortening the duration and lessening the degree of any disequilibrium which may from time to time arise in their balances of payments.

The Fund obtains its resources from the payment by members of quotas, the size of which was agreed for original members at Bretton Woods. Each member pays in gold either 25% of its quota or 10% of its net official holdings of gold and convertible currency, as of a certain date, and the remainder in the member's own currency. The aggregate of members' quotas as of April 30, 1968 was equivalent to $21,119,400,000. The total subscriptions paid on that date amounted to the equivalent of $20,350,400,000, of which $4,908,200,-000 was received in gold.

Members are under an obligation, once the foreign exchange values of their currencies have been agreed with the Fund, to make no change in their exchange rates without consultation with the Fund. The Fund, however, is not entitled to object if the proposed change does not exceed 10% of the original par value. By the end of April 30, 1968, 76 countries had effective par value agreed with the Fund. From the commencement of operations on Mar. 1, 1947, through April 30, 1968, exchange drawings on the Fund amounted to the equivalent of U. S. $14,630,600,000. On that date repurchases amounted to $7,439,500,000 in gold and currencies. Sales of members' currencies and other items reduced the net amount due to $4,549,900,000.

## Inter-American Development Bank

### Felipe Herrera, President, 808 17th St., NW., Washington, D. C. 20577

The Inter-American Development Bank was created Dec. 30, 1959, to foster the individual and collective development of its member countries, which are:

| | | |
|---|---|---|
| Argentina | Ecuador | Paraguay |
| Bolivia | El Salvador | Peru |
| Brazil | Guatemala | Trinidad & |
| Chile | Haiti | Tobago |
| Colombia | Honduras | United States |
| Costa Rica | Mexico | Uruguay |
| Dominican | Nicaragua | Venezuela |
| Republic | Panama | |

The Bank was set up with two completely separate funds: the ordinary capital resources, currently authorized at $3.15 billion, and a Fund for Special Operations totaling $2,321,436,000.

The authorized ordinary resources include $475,-000,000 in "paid in" capital and $2,675,000,000 in "callable" capital. A total of $383,650,000 of the paid in portion has been subscribed by the member countries and another $91,350,000 is available for subscription by countries which might join the Bank in the future. Of the callable portion, $2,-356,710,000 has been subscribed and $318,290,000 is available for subscription by present or future members. The callable capital, in effect, constitutes a guarantee of the Bank's securities and thus enables the Bank to borrow funds in the world's capital markets. As of June 30, 1968, the Bank's outstanding borrowings amounted to $540 million.

With its ordinary resources, the Bank makes "hard" loans for development projects on conventional terms, including repayment in the currencies lent, and interest rates which reflect the cost to the Bank of borrowing funds in the world's capital markets.

The Fund for Special Operations is used to make "soft" loans, on terms and conditions which are more flexible than those applied to loans made from the ordinary capital resources, which are made primarily for economic or infrastructure projects.

In addition to its own resources, the Bank also administers other funds. Since 1961 it has been the Administrator of the Social Progress Trust Fund, which the United States Government established to promote social development in Latin America as part of the Alliance for Progress program. The U. S. has contributed $525,000,000 to this Fund.

It also administers resources totaling $52,000,-000 entrusted to it by Canada, Sweden and the United Kingdom for economic development projects in Latin America.

As of June 30, 1968, the Bank had authorized 466 loans totaling $2.5 billion in Latin America for projects whose total cost is estimated at $6.6 billion. Of this amount, 158 loans totaling $926 million were authorized from the ordinary capital resources, 177 loans totaling $1,046 million from the Fund for Special Operations, 117 loans totaling $501 million from the Social Progress Trust Fund and 14 loans totaling $27 million from the resources it administers for non-member countries.

The distribution of the loans by fields of investment was: Industry and mining $500 million; Agriculture $577 million; Water supply and Sewage systems $413 million; Transportation $256 million; Electric power $257 million; Housing $300 million; Advanced education $108 million; Pre-investment $60 million; and Credit to finance export of capital goods $29 million.

## The Voice of America and Other World-Wide Broadcasting

**VOICE OF AMERICA,** a division of the United States Information Agency (USIA), furnishes countries all over the globe with news of American events and policies, analyses of current issues and programs about life in the United States. It broadcasts some 800 hours weekly in 36 languages over 102 medium and shortwave transmitters, 61 overseas and 41 in the U. S. About 40% of these broadcasts are directed toward Communist countries. These had about 2,000 transmitters that in the past have tried to jam the American stations. In mid-1963 the USSR ceased jamming and some of the other communist countries did likewise, but a certain amount of jamming has continued.

It is estimated that 42,000,000 listeners hear the programs during an average week with many more in times of crisis. Estimate based on mail received (over 200,000 letters annually), surveys, etc.

USIA also has 213 posts in 101 countries (where they are known as the U. S. Information Service or USIS). The Motion Picture and Television Service of USIA annually produces films and television programs, illustrating various facets of American life. These are shipped in several language versions to USIS posts which arrange for commercial and private showings, as well as telecasts on foreign TV stations. The Press and Publications Service radioteletypes a daily 12,000-word compilation of major addresses and statements of general interest by American leaders to USIS posts for placement in foreign newspapers and periodicals. It also publishes magazines such as *America Illustrated*, which is distributed and sold in two editions in USSR and Poland. The cultural aspects of USIA's programs are carried out by the above services and information centers, libraries, reading rooms and binational centers in more than 80 countries. USIA director is Leonard H. Marks.

**RADIO FREE EUROPE** is the major division of Free Europe, Inc., 2 Park Ave., New York. William P. Durkee is president. Ralph E. Walter, director, is based at RFE headquarters in Munich, West Germany. RFE is a privately operated network of 5 radio stations that broadcasts to the 84,000,000 people of Communist-ruled Bulgaria, Czechoslovakia, Hungary, Poland and Romania in their native languages. It operates 32 transmitters, located in West Germany and Portugal, with a total power of 2,260,000 watts. RFE is on the air 536 hours a week, broadcasting news and information about the free world and the countries under Communist domination, as well as programs of music, political comment, entertainment, sports and religion beamed at all age groups. Surveys indicate RFE has a regular audience exceeding 25,000,000.

**RADIO LIBERTY** speaks to the peoples of the Soviet Union as the free voice of their fellow countrymen abroad. It is supported by the Radio Liberty Committee, Inc., a private, non-profit organization with headquarters at 30 East 42nd Street, New York, N. Y. Howland H. Sargeant, President. In its transmission to the Soviet Union, Radio Liberty uses 17 languages of that country. Radio Liberty broadcasts 24 hours a day, 7 days a week. Fourteen transmitters in Spain and Western Germany and 3 transmitters on Taiwan broadcast a total of 235-315 transmitter hours daily. Total transmitting power is 1,840,000 watts.

# Heads of States and Prime Ministers

Data to Aug. 15, 1968

| Country | Head of State, Title | Born | Acceded or Elected | Premier or Prime Minister |
|---|---|---|---|---|
| Afghanistan.... | Mohammad Zahir Shah, King.... | Oct. 15, 1914 | Nov. 8, 1933 | Noor Ahmad Etemadi |
| Albania......... | Maj.-Gen. Haxhi Lleshi, Pres..... | ............. | July 1953 | Maj.-Gen. Mehmet Shehu |
| Algeria......... | Col. Houari Boumedienne, Pres.. | 1925 | June 19, 1965 | |
| Andorra........ | Pres. of France & Spanish Bishop of Urgel......................... | ............. | ............. | ............. |
| Argentina...... | Lt. Gen. Juan Carlos Onganía, Pres......................... | May 17, 1914 | June 28, 1966 | ............. |
| Australia (C).... | Lord Richard G. Casey, Gov. Gen. (*)................ | Aug. 29, 1890 | Sept. 22, 1965 | John G. Gorton |
| Austria......... | Franz Jonas, Pres............... | Oct. 4, 1899 | June 9, 1965 | Josef Klaus |
| Barbados (C).... | Dr. A. W. Scott, Gov. Gen. (*) ... | Mar. 17, 1900 | May 18, 1967 | E. W. Barrow |
| Belgium......... | Baudouin I, King............... | Sept. 7, 1930 | July 17, 1951 | Gaston Eyskens |
| Bhutan......... | Maharajah Jigme Dorji Wangchuk............... | 1929 | Oct. 27, 1952 | Lhendnp Dorji |
| Bolivia......... | Gen. Rene Barrientos, Pres...... | May 30, 1918 | Aug. 6, 1966 | |
| Botswana (C)... | Sir Seretse Khama, Pres........ | 1921 | Oct. 1, 1966 | |
| Brazil.......... | Arthur da Costa e Silva, Pres... | Oct. 3, 1902 | Mar. 15, 1967 | |
| Bulgaria........ | Georgi Traikov, Pres............ | 1898 | Apr. 23, 1964 | Todor Zhivkov |
| Burma.......... | | | | Gen. Ne Win |
| Burundi........ | Michael Micombero, Pres........ | 1939 | Nov. 28, 1966 | |
| Cambodia....... | Prince Norodom Sihanouk, Chief of State................... | Oct. 31, 1932 | June 20, 1960 | Son Sann |
| Cameroon....... | Ahmadou Ahidjo, Pres........... | | 1960 | Charles Assale |
| Canada (C)..... | Roland Michener, Gov. Gen. (*).. | Apr. 19, 1900 | Apr. 5, 1967 | Pierre E. Trudeau |
| Central African Rep. (F)........ | Col. Jean Bedel Bokassa......... | ............. | Jan. 1, 1966 | |
| Ceylon (C)...... | William Gopallawa, Gov. Gen. (*) | 1898 | Mar. 2, 1962 | Dudley Senanayake |
| Chad Rep. (F)... | Francois Tombalbaye, Pres....... | 1918 | Aug. 11, 1960 | |
| Chile........... | Eduardo Frei Montalva, Pres..... | June 16, 1911 | Sept. 4, 1964 | |
| China, People's Republic...... | Liu Shao-chi................... | c. 1898 | Apr. 27, 1959 | Chou En-Lai |
| China (Taiwan) | Gen'lissimo. Chiang Kai-shek, President.................. | 1887 | Apr. 1948 | C. K. Yen |
| Colombia........ | Dr. Carlos Lleras Restrepo, Pres.. | Apr. 12, 1908 | Aug. 7, 1966 | |
| Congo—Brazzaville (F)....... | Alphonse Massamba—Debat, Pres.................... | ............. | Aug. 10, 1963 | Alphonse Massamba-Debat |
| Congo, Dem. Rep. | Lt. Gen. Joseph Mobutu, Pres... | Oct. 30, 1930 | Nov. 25, 1965 | Brig. Gen. Leonard Mulamba |
| Costa Rica...... | Jose Joaquin Trejos, Pres....... | Apr. 18, 1916 | May 8, 1966 | |
| Cuba........... | Dr. Osvaldo Dorticos Torrado, Pres..................... | 1919 | July 17, 1959 | Fidel Castro |
| Cyprus (C)...... | Archbishop Makarios, Pres...... | Aug. 13, 1913 | Dec. 14, 1959 | |
| Czechoslovakia.. | Ludvik Svoboda, Pres.......... | Nov. 25, 1895 | Mar. 30, 1968 | Oldrich Cernik |
| Dahomey Rep... | Emile Derlin Zinsou, Pres....... | 1918 | June 27, 1968 | |
| Denmark........ | Frederick IX, King............. | Mar. 11, 1899 | Apr. 20, 1947 | Hilmar Baunsgaard |
| Dominican Rep.. | Dr. Joaquin Balaguer.......... | 1907 | July 1, 1966 | |
| Ecuador........ | Jose Maria Velasco Ibarra, Pres.. | 1893 | June 3, 1968 | |
| El Salvador..... | Col. F. Sanchez Hernandez, Pres.. | 1918 | July 1, 1967 | |
| Ethiopia........ | Haile Selassie I, Emperor........ | July 23, 1892 | Nov. 2, 1930 | Aklilou Abde Wold |
| Finland......... | Dr. Urho Kekkonen, Pres........ | Mar. 9, 1900 | Feb. 15, 1956 | Mauno Koivisto |
| France (F)...... | Gen. Charles A. de Gaulle, Pres.. | Nov. 22, 1890 | Dec. 21, 1958 | Maurice Couve de Murville |
| Gabon Rep. (F).. | Albert Bernard Bongo, Pres...... | 1935 | Dec. 1, 1967 | |
| Gambia (C)..... | Sir Farimang Singhatch......... | 1912 | July 1966 | D. K. Jawara |
| Germany, Fed. Republic...... | Heinrich Luebke, Pres.......... | Oct. 14, 1894 | July 1, 1959 | Kurt G. Kiesinger |
| Germany, East.. | Walter Ulbricht, Chairman...... | June 30, 1893 | Sept. 12, 1960 | Willi Stoph |
| Ghana (C)....... | Lt. Gen. J. A. Ankrah.......... | 1917 | Feb. 24, 1966 | |
| Greece.......... | King Constantine XIII.......... | June 2, 1940 | Mar. 6, 1964 | George Papadopoulos |
| Guatemala...... | Julio Cesar Mendez Montenegro,. | Nov. 23, 1915 | July 1, 1966 | |
| Guinea, Rep..... | Sekou Toure, Pres.............. | Jan. 9, 1922 | Oct. 2, 1958 | Sekou Toure |
| Guyana (C)..... | Sir David Rose, Gov. Gen. (*)... | 1923 | Dec. 16, 1966 | Forbes Burnham |
| Haiti........... | Dr. Francois Duvalier, Pres...... | Apr. 14, 1909 | Oct. 22, 1957 | |
| Honduras....... | Col. Oswaldo Lopez Arellano, Pres. | June 30, 1921 | Oct. 3, 1963 | |
| Hungary........ | Pal Losonczy, Pres............. | 1919 | Apr. 14, 1967 | Jano Fock |
| Iceland......... | Kristian Eldjarn, Pres.......... | 1917 | July 1, 1968 | Bjarni Benediktsson |
| India (C)....... | Dr. Zakir Husain, Pres......... | Feb. 8, 1897 | May 13, 1967 | Indira Nehru Gandhi |
| Indonesia....... | Lt. Gen. Suharto, Pres......... | Feb. 28, 1921 | Mar. 11, 1967 | |
| Iran............ | Mohammed Reza Pahlavi, Shah.. | Oct. 26, 1919 | Sept. 18, 1941 | Amir Abass Hoveida |
| Iraq............ | Ahmed Hassan al-Bakr, Pres..... | 1912 | July 17, 1968 | Ahmed Hassan al-Bakr |
| Ireland......... | Eamon de Valera, Pres.......... | Oct. 14, 1882 | June 25, 1959 | John Mary Lynch |
| Israel.......... | Zalman Shazar, Pres........... | Oct. 6, 1889 | May 21, 1963 | Levi Eshkol |
| Italy........... | Giuseppe Saragat.............. | Sept. 19, 1898 | Dec. 28, 1964 | Giovanni Leone |
| Ivory Coast.... | Felix Houphouet-Boigny, Pres... | Oct. 18, 1905 | Nov. 27, 1960 | ............. |
| Jamaica (C).... | Sir Clifford Campbell, Gov. Gen. (*)............ | June 28, 1892 | Dec. 1, 1962 | Hugh Shearer |
| Japan.......... | Hirohito, Emperor............. | Apr. 29, 1901 | Dec. 25, 1926 | Eisaku Sato |
| Jordan......... | Hussein I, King................ | Nov. 14, 1935 | May 2, 1952 | Bahjot Telhouny |
| Kenya (C)...... | Jomo Kenyatta, Pres........... | 1890 | Dec. 12, 1964 | |
| Korea, Republic.. | Gen. Chung Hee Park, Pres..... | Sept. 30, 1917 | Nov. 26, 1963 | Chung Il Kwon |
| Korea, People's Dem. Rep.... | Kim Du-Bong, Pres............. | ............. | ............. | Marshall Kim Il-Sung |
| Kuwait......... | Sabah al-Salim al-Sabah, Emir................... | 1915 | Nov. 27, 1965 | Jaber al-Ahmed al-Jaber |
| Laos........... | Sri Savang Vatthana, King...... | Nov. 13, 1907 | Oct. 30, 1959 | Souvanna Phouma |
| Lebanon........ | Charles Helou, Pres............ | 1913 | Sept. 23, 1964 | Rashid Karame |
| Lesotho (C)..... | Motlotlehi Moshoeshoe II, King. | 1938 | Oct. 4, 1966 | Chief Leabua Jonathan |
| Liberia......... | William V. Tubman, Pres........ | Nov. 29, 1895 | May 6, 1943 | ............. |
| Libya.......... | Mohammed Idris el Senussi, King. | Mar. 13, 1890 | Dec. 24, 1951 | Abdulhamid el-Bakoush |

# Heads of States and Prime Ministers (continued)

| Country | Head of State, Title | Born | Acceded or Elected | Premier or Prime Minister |
|---|---|---|---|---|
| Liechtenstein.... | Prince Franz Joseph II, Ruler.... | July 16, 1906 | Mar. 30, 1938 | Gerald Batliner |
| Luxembourg..... | Grand Duke Jean............... | Jan. 5, 1921 | Nov. 12, 1964 | Pierre Werner |
| Malagasy Rep. (F) | Philibert Tsiranana, Pres....... | 1912 | May 1, 1959 | ................ |
| Malawi (C)..... | Dr. H. Kamuzu Banda, Pres..... | 1906 | July 6, 1966 | ................ |
| Malaysia (C).... | Sultan Ismail Nasiruddin Shah, Paramount Ruler............. | | Aug. 19, 1965 | Tunku Abdul Rahman |
| Maldive Islands.. | Sultan Mohammed Farid Didi I... | June 12, 1901 | Mar. 7, 1954 | Ibrahim Nasir |
| Mali.......... | Modibo Keita, Pres........... | June 4, 1915 | 1960 | Modibo Keita |
| Malta (C)...... | Sir Maurice Henry Dorman, Gov. Gen. (*)................... | Aug. 7, 1912 | Sept. 21, 1964 | Dr. G. Borg Olivier |
| Mauritania...... | Moktar O. Daddah, President.... | Apr. 25, 1925 | Nov. 1958 | ................ |
| Mauritius (C).... | Sir John Rennie, Gov. Gen. (*).. | ............ | Sept. 17, 1962 | Sir Seewoosagur Ramgoolam |
| Mexico......... | Gustavo Diaz Ordaz, Pres...... | Mar. 12, 1911 | Dec. 1, 1964 | ................ |
| Monaco......... | Rainier III, Prince........... | May 31, 1923 | May 9, 1949 | ................ |
| Mongolia....... | Yumzhagin Tsedenbal, Chairman of Presidium........... | | | Y. Tsedenbal |
| Morocco........ | Hassan II, King........... | July 11, 1929 | Mar. 3, 1961 | Mohamed Benhima |
| Muscat and Oman | Sultan Said bin Taimur........ | Aug. 13, 1910 | Feb. 10, 1932 | ................ |
| Nauru.......... | Chief Hammer De Roburt, Chmn., Coun. of State........ | Sept. 25, 1922 | Jan. 31, 1968 | ................ |
| Nepal.......... | Mahendra Bir Bikram, Shah..... | June 11, 1920 | Mar. 14, 1955 | Surya Bahadur Thapa |
| Netherlands..... | Juliana, Queen.............. | Apr. 30, 1909 | Sept. 4, 1948 | Petrus J. S. de Jong |
| New Zealand (C). | Sir Arthur Porritt, Gov. Gen. (*). | Aug. 10, 1900 | Nov. 1967 | Keith J. Holyoake |
| Nicaragua....... | Anastasio Somoza Debayle, Pres.. | Dec. 5, 1925 | Feb. 6, 1967 | ................ |
| Niger.......... | Hamani Diori, Pres........... | ............ | 1960 | ................ |
| Nigeria (C)..... | Maj. Gen. Yakubu Gowon, Head of Mil. Council............ | Oct. 19, 1934 | Aug. 1, 1966 | ................ |
| Norway........ | Olav V., King.............. | July 2, 1903 | Sept. 21, 1957 | Per Borten |
| Pakistan (C).... | Mohammad Ayub Khan, Pres... | May 14, 1907 | Oct. 27, 1958 | ................ |
| Panama........ | Dr. Arnulfo Arias, Pres........ | 1901 | May 30, 1968 | ................ |
| Paraguay....... | Gen. Alfredo Stroessner, Pres.... | Nov. 3, 1912 | Aug. 15, 1954 | ................ |
| Peru.......... | Fernando Belaunde Terry, Pres.. | Oct. 7, 1912 | June 9, 1963 | Oswaldo Hercelles |
| Philippines..... | Ferdinand Marcos, Pres....... | Sept. 11, 1917 | Dec. 30, 1965 | ................ |
| Poland........ | Marian Spychalski, Chmn, Council of State........ | Dec. 6, 1906 | Apr. 11, 1968 | Josef Cyrankiewicz |
| Portugal....... | Rear Admiral Americo R. Thomaz, Pres................ | Nov. 19, 1894 | July 22, 1958 | Antonio de Oliveira Salazar |
| Romania........ | Nicolae Ceausescu, Pres. of State. Council............... | Jan. 26, 1918 | Dec. 7, 1967 | Ion G. Maurer |
| Rwanda........ | Georgoire Kayibanda, Pres...... | May 1, 1924 | Oct. 26, 1961 | ................ |
| San Marino..... | Leonida Luzzi Valli and Stello Montironi, Co-Regents...... | ............ | | Federico Bigi |
| Saudi Arabia.... | Faisal Abdel Aziz al Saud, King.. | 1906 | Nov. 2, 1964 | ................ |
| Senegal Rep. (F) | Leopold S. Senghor, Pres....... | 1907 | Sept. 1960 | Lamine Gueye |
| Sierra Leone (C). | Henry J. L. Boston, Gov. Gen. (*) | ............ | 1962 | Siaka Stevens |
| Singapore (C).... | Inche Yusof bin Ishak, Pres... | Aug. 12, 1910 | Dec. 3, 1959 | Lee Kuan Yew |
| Somalia........ | Abdirashid Ali Shermarke, Pres.. | ............ | June 10, 1967 | Mohamed Ibrahim Egal |
| South Africa.... | Jacobus J. Fouché, Pres....... | June 6, 1898 | Apr. 10, 1968 | Balthazar, J. Vorster |
| Southern Yemen. | Qahtan al-Shaabi, Pres........ | ............ | Nov. 30, 1967 | ................ |
| Spain.......... | Gen. Francisco Franco Bahamonde, Chief of State.... | Dec. 4, 1892 | Aug. 9, 1939 | Gen. Francisco Franco |
| Sudan......... | Ismail al Azhari, Pres........ | ............ | Sept. 1965 | Mohammed Ahmed Mahgoub |
| Swaziland (C)... | Sobhuza II, King.............. | 1899 | Apr. 25, 1967 | Makhosini Dlamini |
| Sweden........ | Gustav VI Adolf, King.......... | Nov. 11, 1882 | Oct. 29, 1950 | Tage Erlander |
| Switzerland (1).. | Dr. Willy Spuhler, Pres......... | Jan. 31 1902 | Dec. 14, 1967 | ................ |
| Syria.......... | Nureddin al-Attassi, Chief of State | 1928 | Feb. 25, 1966 | Dr. Youssef Zayyin |
| Tanzania (C).... | Julius K. Nyerere, Pres........ | 1922 | Apr. 26, 1964 | ................ |
| Thailand....... | Phumiphol Aduldet, King....... | Dec. 5, 1927 | June 9, 1946 | Thanom Kittikachorn |
| Togo.......... | Gen. Etienne Eyadema......... | 1932 | Jan. 13, 1967 | ................ |
| Trinidad-Tobago (C) | Sir Solomon Hochoy, Gov. Gen. (*)....... | Apr. 20, 1905 | Aug. 31, 1962 | Dr. Eric E. Williams |
| Tunisia........ | Habib Bourguiba, Pres........ | Aug. 3, 1903 | July 25, 1957 | ................ |
| Turkey........ | Cevdet Sunay, Pres........... | 1900 | Mar. 28, 1966 | Suleyman Demirel |
| Uganda (C)..... | A. Milton Obote, Pres........ | 1924 | Apr. 15, 1966 | ................ |
| USSR......... | Nikolai V. Podgorny, Pres., Presidium............ | 1903 | Dec. 9, 1965 | Aleksei N. Kosygin |
| United Arab Rep. | Gamal Abdel Nasser, Pres....... | Jan. 18, 1918 | June 23, 1956 | Gamal Abdel Nasser |
| United Kingdom (C)... | Elizabeth, II, Queen.......... | Apr. 21, 1926 | Feb. 6, 1952 | Harold Wilson |
| United States.... | Lyndon B. Johnson, Pres........ | Aug. 27, 1908 | Nov. 22, 1963 | ................ |
| Upper Volta.... | Lt. Col. Sangoule Lamizana, Chief of State............ | 1921 | Jan. 3, 1966 | ................ |
| Uruguay........ | Jorge Pacheco Areco......... | Apr. 9, 1920 | Dec. 6, 1967 | ................ |
| Vatican City.... | Giovanni Battista Montini, Pope Paul VI............ | Sept. 26, 1897 | June 21, 1963 | ................ |
| Venezuela....... | Dr. Raul Leoni, Pres........... | Apr. 26, 1905 | Dec. 1, 1963 | ................ |
| Vietnam, Dem. Republic of... | Ho Chi Minh, Pres............ | 1880 | | Pham Van Dong |
| Vietnam, Rep. of. | Maj. Gen. Nguyen Van Thieu, Pres................. | Apr. 5, 1923 | June 12, 1965 | Tran Van Huong |
| Western Samoa.. | Malietoa Tanumafili II, Head of State............ | 1913 | Jan. 1, 1962 | Fiame Mata'afa Faumuina Mulinu'u II |
| Yemen......... | Abdul Rahman al-Iryani, Pres. of Republican Council.... | July 18, 1917 | | Hassan al-Amri |
| Yugoslavia...... | Marshal Tito (Joseph Broz), President................ | May 25, 1892 | Jan. 31, 1946 | Mika Spiljak |
| Zambia (C)..... | Kenneth Kaunda, Pres......... | 1925 | Oct. 24, 1964 | ................ |

(1) President serves one-year term, the Vice President customarily succeeds him.

(C) Member of the Commonwealth of Nations.

(F) Member of French Community.

(*) Gov. Gen. acts as representative of the British monarch, who is recognized as head of state.

# Population of Important World Cities

Source: Latest census reports and latest official estimates; *(asterisk) denotes capital;
Gr. denotes Greater, or metropolitan area

For U. S. Cities see Index

| City | Population |
|---|---|
| **Afghanistan** | |
| *Kabul...... | 292,294 |
| Kandahar.... | 121,152 |
| **Albania** | |
| Tirane...... | 180,000 |
| **Algeria** | |
| *Algiers...... | 943,142 |
| Constantine... | 253,649 |
| Oran......... | 328,257 |
| **Andorra** | |
| *Andorra La Vella....... | 6,972 |
| **Argentina** | |
| Avellaneda... | 329,626 |
| *Buenos Aires. | 2,966,816 |
| Cordoba..... | 589,153 |
| General San Martin.... | 279,213 |
| La Plata..... | 330,310 |
| Lanus....... | 244,473 |
| Mar del Plata. | 141,886 |
| Rosario...... | 671,852 |
| Santa Fe .... | 259,560 |
| Tucuman .... | 251,000 |
| **Australia** | |
| Adelaide...... | 726,930 |
| Brisbane .... | 719,140 |
| *Canberra.... | 100,938 |
| Hobart...... | 119,415 |
| Melbourne... | 2,228,511 |
| Newcastle ... | 233,967 |
| Perth ...... | 499,494 |
| Sydney...... | 444,735 |
| **Austria** | |
| Graz........ | 250,300 |
| Innsbruck.... | 110,209 |
| Linz........ | 203,983 |
| Salzburg..... | 115,720 |
| *Vienna..... | 1,640,106 |
| **Barbados** | |
| *Bridgetown.. | 94,000 |
| **Belgium** | |
| Antwerp..... | 661,697 |
| *Brussels.... | 1,074,586 |
| Charleroi.... | 282,444 |
| Ghent....... | 232,736 |
| Liege....... | 450,387 |
| **Bolivia** | |
| Cochabamba.. | 120,000 |
| La Paz...... | 360,329 |
| Santa Cruz .. | 139,000 |
| *Sucre ...... | 58,359 |
| **Botswana** | |
| *Gaberones... | 4,200 |
| **Brazil** | |
| Belem....... | 471,000 |
| Belo Horizonte | 929,000 |
| *Brasilia.... | 200,000 |
| Curitiba .... | 582,000 |
| Fortaleza ... | 486,000 |
| Niteroi ..... | 271,000 |
| Porto Alegre. | 822,000 |
| Recife...... | 1,010,000 |
| Rio de Janeiro | 3,909,000 |
| Salvador..... | 842,000 |
| Santos ..... | 307,000 |
| Sao Paulo ... | 4,098,000 |
| **Bulgaria** | |
| Plovdiv ..... | 220,600 |
| *Sofia...... | 793,300 |
| Varna ...... | 177,400 |
| **Burma** | |
| Mandalay ... | 195,348 |
| Moulmein ... | 108,020 |
| *Rangoon ... | 821,800 |
| **Burundi** | |
| *Bujumbura.. | 71,000 |
| **Cambodia** | |
| *Phnom-Penh. | 403,500 |
| **Cameroon** | |
| Douala ..... | 200,000 |
| *Yaounde ... | 101,000 |
| **Canada** | |
| Calgary, Gr.. | 330,575 |
| Edmonton ... | 376,925 |
| Edmonton, Gr. | 401,299 |
| Halifax...... | 86,792 |
| Hamilton.... | 298,121 |
| Hamilton, Gr. | 449,116 |
| Kitchener ... | 93,255 |
| Laval ...... | 196,088 |
| London ..... | 194,416 |
| London, Gr... | 207,396 |
| Montreal.... | 1,222,255 |
| Montreal, Gr. | 2,436,817 |
| *Ottawa..... | 290,741 |
| *Ottawa, Gr.. | 494,535 |
| Quebec...... | 166,984 |
| Quebec, Gr... | 413,397 |
| Regina...... | 131,127 |
| St. Catherines | 97,101 |
| St. John, Gr.. | 101,192 |
| St. John's, Gr. | 101,161 |
| Saskatoon ... | 115,892 |
| Sudbury..... | 84,888 |
| Toronto..... | 664,584 |
| Toronto, Gr.. | 2,158,496 |
| Vancouver... | 410,375 |
| Vancouver, Gr. | 892,286 |
| Windsor..... | 192,544 |
| Windsor, Gr.. | 211,697 |
| Winnipeg.... | 257,005 |
| Winnipeg, Gr. | 508,759 |
| **Central Africa Rep.** | |
| *Bangui..... | 111,266 |
| **Ceylon** | |
| *Colombo.... | 510,947 |
| Jaffna...... | 94,248 |
| Kandy ...... | 67,768 |
| **Chad** | |
| *Fort-Lamy... | 99,000 |
| **Chile** | |
| Concepcion... | 174,224 |
| *Santiago.... | 248,378 |
| Valparaiso... | 276,330 |
| **China** | |
| Amoy........ | 224,300 |
| Anshan...... | 805,000 |
| Canton..... | 1,840,000 |
| Changsha ... | 703,000 |
| Changteh.... | 300,000 |
| Chengtu..... | 1,107,000 |
| Chenteh (Jehol).... | 510,000 |
| Chungking... | 2,121,000 |
| Darien...... | 1,590,000 |
| Fatshan..... | 122,500 |
| Foochow .... | 616,000 |
| Hangchow ... | 784,000 |
| HongKong,Br. | 3,739,900 |
| Hsinking (Changchun) | 975,000 |
| Kowloon .... | 675,000 |
| Lanchow .... | 699,000 |
| Macao, Port. | 161,252 |
| Nanking .... | 1,419,000 |
| *Peking..... | 4,010,000 |
| Pin-chiang (Harbin).... | 1,552,000 |
| Shanghai.... | 6,900,000 |
| Shenyang (Mukden).. | 2,411,000 |
| Sian........ | 1,310,000 |
| Taiyuan..... | 1,020,000 |
| Tientsin..... | 3,220,000 |
| Tsinan...... | 862,000 |
| Tsingtao .... | 1,121,000 |
| Wenchow.... | 201,600 |
| Wuhan...... | 2,146,000 |
| **China (Taiwan)** | |
| Kaohsiung ... | 596,092 |
| Keelung..... | 278,320 |
| Taichung.... | 364,262 |
| Tainan...... | 369,820 |
| *Taipei..... | 1,135,500 |
| **Colombia** | |
| Barranquilla.. | 593,779 |
| *Bogota..... | 2,206,091 |
| Bucaramanga. | 285,499 |
| Cali........ | 815,294 |
| Cartagena... | 293,113 |
| Medellin .... | 976,010 |
| **Congo—Brazzaville** | |
| *Brazzaville.. | 136,200 |
| **Congo, Democratic Rep.** | |
| Lubumbashi.. | 233,145 |
| *Kinshasa.... | 507,868 |
| **Costa Rica** | |
| *San Jose.... | 177,969 |
| **Cuba** | |
| Camaguey... | 204,254 |
| *Havana, Gr.. | 1,517,700 |
| Holguin..... | 226,644 |
| Marianao.... | 229,576 |
| Santa Clara.. | 144,630 |
| Santiago de Cuba...... | 231,000 |
| **Cyprus** | |
| Famagusta.... | 39,200 |
| Limassol .... | 48,100 |
| *Nicosia..... | 105,600 |
| **Czecho-slovakia** | |
| Bratislava.... | 268,513 |
| Brno........ | 328,457 |
| Ostrava ..... | 262,064 |
| Pizen (Pilsen). | 140,181 |
| *Prague..... | 1,022,957 |
| **Dahomey** | |
| Cotonou..... | 109,328 |
| **Denmark** | |
| Aarhus...... | 187,342 |
| *Copenhagen. | 1,377,605 |
| Frederiksborg. | 112,211 |
| Odense...... | 132,978 |
| **Dominican Republic** | |
| *Santo Domingo... | 560,636 |
| **Ecuador** | |
| Guayaquil.... | 651,542 |
| *Quito...... | 401,811 |
| **El Salvador** | |
| *San Salvador. | 281,122 |
| Santa Ana ... | 72,839 |
| **Ethiopia** | |
| *Addis Ababa. | 560,000 |
| Asmara..... | 131,000 |
| **Finland** | |
| *Helsinki(Helsingfors)... | 528,000 |
| Tampere..... | 150,000 |
| Turku (Abo).. | 148,000 |
| **France** | |
| Bordeaux..... | 283,528 |
| Le Havre..... | 184,133 |
| Lille........ | 199,033 |
| Lyon........ | 543,519 |
| Marseille..... | 850,362 |
| Nantes...... | 246,248 |
| Nice........ | 294,976 |
| *Paris...... | 2,811,171 |
| *Paris, Gr... | 9,811,171 |
| St. Etienne ... | 203,633 |
| Strasbourg.... | 233,549 |
| Toulouse..... | 330,570 |
| **Gabon** | |
| *Libreville.... | 45,909 |
| **Gambia** | |
| *Bathurst .... | 27,809 |
| **Germany, West** | |
| Aachen...... | 177,900 |
| Augsburg.... | 212,200 |
| Berlin (West). | 2,190,600 |
| Bielefeld..... | 170,660 |
| Bochum ..... | 355,500 |
| *Bonn...... | 140,500 |
| Bremen ..... | 599,000 |
| Brunswick ... | 233,000 |
| Cologne..... | 861,000 |
| Dortmund.... | 657,100 |
| Duesseldorf... | 698,400 |
| Duisburg .... | 484,000 |
| Essen....... | 721,200 |
| Frankfurt.... | 684,800 |
| Gelsenkirchen. | 367,000 |
| Hamburg.... | 851,300 |
| Hannover .... | 547,800 |
| Heidelberg.... | 124,400 |
| Karlsruhe.... | 255,000 |
| Kassel...... | 214,100 |
| Kiel........ | 269,400 |
| Krefeld...... | 223,200 |
| Luebeck..... | 241,800 |
| Ludwigshafen. | 177,500 |
| Mannheim.... | 329,900 |
| Muelheim (Ruhr)..... | 191,200 |
| Munich..... | 1,231,500 |
| Nuremberg... | 472,300 |
| Oberhausen... | 257,900 |
| Stuttgart..... | 630,500 |
| Wiesbaden... | 261,100 |
| Wuppertal... | 422,900 |
| **Germany (East)** | |
| *Berlin (East). | 1,073,647 |
| Chemnitz Karl Marx Stadt)..... | 293,736 |
| Dresden..... | 504,910 |
| Erfurt........ | 190,620 |
| Halle........ | 274,904 |
| Leipzig...... | 594,661 |
| Magdeburg... | 265,968 |
| Rostock..... | 181,606 |
| **Ghana** | |
| *Accra...... | 521,900 |
| **Greece** | |
| *Athens (incl. Piraeus)... | 1,852,709 |
| Patras ...... | 95,364 |
| Thessaloniki (Salonika).. | 309,205 |
| **Guatemala** | |
| *Guatemala City...... | 577,120 |
| Quezaltenango | 56,921 |
| **Guinea** | |
| *Conakry..... | 175,000 |
| **Guyana** | |
| *Georgetown.. | 72,964 |
| **Haiti** | |
| Cap-Haitien .. | 30,000 |
| *Port-au-Prince...... | 240,000 |
| **Honduras** | |
| *Tegucigalpa. | 170,535 |
| San Pedro Sula | 95,890 |
| **Hungary** | |
| *Budapest.... | 1,928,000 |
| *Budapest, Gr. | 1,970,000 |
| Debrecen .... | 150,000 |
| Miskolc ..... | 170,000 |
| Pecs ....... | 140,000 |
| Szeged ..... | 120,000 |
| **Iceland** | |
| *Reykjavik... | 92,000 |
| **India** | |
| Agra........ | 530,548 |
| Ahmedabad .. | 1,316,723 |
| Allahabad ... | 465,128 |
| Amritsar .... | 403,255 |
| Bangalore ... | 972,419 |
| Benares ..... | 540,239 |
| Bombay .... | 4,784,136 |
| Calcutta .... | 3,049,316 |
| Calcutta (Met.)...... | 4,703,398 |
| *Delhi ..... | 2,440,473 |
| Howrah..... | 1,554,715 |
| Hyderabad ... | 1,261,085 |
| Kanpur ..... | 1,011,700 |
| Lucknow.... | 675,829 |
| Madras .... | 1,896,122 |
| Madurai..... | 458,426 |
| Nagpur ..... | 729,712 |
| Patna ...... | 406,484 |
| Poona...... | 793,016 |
| **Indonesia** | |
| Bandung .... | 972,566 |
| *Jakarta (Batavia)... | 2,906,533 |
| Jogjakarta.... | 312,698 |
| Makassar.... | 384,159 |
| Malang ..... | 341,452 |
| Medan...... | 479,098 |
| Palembang... | 474,971 |
| Semarang.... | 503,153 |
| Surabaya.... | 1,007,945 |
| Surakarta.... | 367,626 |
| **Iran** | |
| Abadan ..... | 302,189 |
| Hamedan.... | 114,610 |
| Isfahan..... | 339,909 |
| Meshed ..... | 312,186 |
| Shiraz...... | 229,761 |
| Tabriz...... | 387,803 |
| *Tehren..... | 2,317,116 |
| **Iraq** | |
| *Baghdad .... | 1,745,328 |
| Basrah ..... | 313,327 |
| Mosul...... | 243,311 |
| **Ireland** | |
| Cork....... | 77,980 |
| *Dublin..... | 537,448 |
| Drogheda.... | 17,085 |
| Galway...... | 22,028 |
| Kilkenny .... | 10,159 |
| Limerick .... | 50,786 |
| Waterford.... | 28,216 |

**Israel**
Haifa........ 207,000
*Jerusalem... 195,700
Ramat Gan... 105,000
Tel Aviv-Jaffa. 389,700

**Italy**
Bari........ 332,486
Bologna...... 481,527
Catania..... 391,709
Florence..... 454,858
Genoa........ 845,427
Messina...... 263,254
Milan........ 675,000
Naples....... 1,245,000
Palermo...... 640,000
*Rome....... 2,560,000
Trieste...... 281,000
Turin........ 1,108,000
Venice....... 365,000
Verona....... 236,700

**Ivory Coast**
*Abidjan.... 400,000

**Jamaica**
*Kingston... 493,619

**Japan**
Amagasaki... 500,990
Fukuoka..... 749,808
Hakodate.... 243,418
Hiroshima... 504,245
Kawasaki.... 854,866
Kita Kyushu.. 1,042,388
Kobe........ 1,216,666
Kyoto....... 1,365,007
Nagasaki.... 405,479
Nagoya...... 1,935,430
Osaka....... 3,156,222
Sapporo..... 794,908
Sendai...... 480,925
Shizuoka.... 367,705
*Tokyo, Gr...11,027,000
Yokohama.... 1,788,915

**Jordan**
*Amman..... 330,000

**Kenya**
*Nairobi.... 314,760

**Korea**
Inchon...... 485,511
Pusan....... 1,419,808
Pyongyang... 653,100
*Seoul...... 3,800,000
Taegu....... 811,406

**Kuwait**
*Kuwait..... 99,609

**Laos**
*Luang
  Prabang.... 45,000
*Vientiane... 138,000

**Lebanon**
*Beirut...... 700,000
Sidon....... 50,000
Tripoli...... 127,611

**Lesotho**
*Maseru..... 14,000

**Liberia**
*Monrovia... 80,992

**Libya**
*Bengazi.... 137,295
Misurata..... 63,000
*Tripoli..... 213,506

**Liechtenstein**
*Vaduz...... 3,966

**Luxembourg**
*Luxembourg. 77,055

**Malagasy Rep.**
*Tananarive.. 321,654

**Malawi**
Blantyre-
  Limbe...... 109,795

**Malaysia**
*Kuala
  Lumpur... 316,230
Penang..... 234,930

**Maldive Islands**
*Male....... 11,561

**Mali**
*Bamako.... 165,000

**Malta**
*Valletta..... 17,679
Sliema...... 21,000

**Mauritania**
*Nouakchott.. 35,000

**Mauritius**
*Port Louis... 129,700

**Mexico**
Chihuahua... 232,000
Guadalajara.. 1,138,000
Juarez...... 442,000
Leon........ 299,000
Mexicali..... 367,000
*Mexico..... 3,118,059
*Mexico, D.F.. 6,815,800
Monterrey.... 908,000
Puebla...... 369,000
San Luis Potosi 198,000
Torreon...... 233,000
Veracruz..... 200,000

**Mongolian Rep.**
*Ulan Bator.. 195,300

**Morocco**
Casablanca... 1,085,000
Fez......... 235,000
Marrakesh.... 255,000
Meknes...... 185,000
*Rabat...... 355,000
Tangier...... 110,000
Tetuan...... 101,352

**Muscat and Oman**
*Muscat..... 5,080
Matrah...... 14,000

**Nepal**
*Katmandu... 122,507

**Netherlands**
*Amsterdam.. 864,940
Arnhem...... 131,193
Eindhoven... 179,979
Enschede.... 134,907
Groningen.... 152,594
The Hague... 602,448
Haarlem..... 171,965
Rotterdam.... 731,315
Tilburg...... 145,591
Utrecht..... 268,583

**New Zealand**
Auckland.... 548,300
Christchurch.. 247,200
Dunedin..... 108,700
*Wellington
  (incl. Hutt). 282,500

**Nicaragua**
*Managua... 262,047

**Niger**
*Niamey..... 40,172

**Nigeria**
Ibadan...... 627,379
Kano....... 295,432
*Lagos...... 665,246
Ogbomosho... 343,279

**Norway**
Bergen...... 117,000
*Oslo....... 483,196
Stavanger.... 79,400
Trondheim... 118,000

**Pakistan**
Chittagong... 364,205
Dacca....... 556,712
*Islamabad... 50,000
Karachi..... 1,912,598
Lahore...... 1,296,477
Rawalpindi... 340,175

**Panama**
Colon....... 64,900
*Panama.... 373,200

**Paraguay**
*Asuncion.... 305,160
Concepcion... 33,886
Encarnacion... 35,186
Villarica..... 30,000

**Peru**
Arequipa..... 135,358
Callao...... 155,358
Cuzco...... 671,106
*Lima...... 1,436,231

**Philippines**
Cebu....... 299,700
Davao...... 269,300
Iloilo....... 180,900
Manila...... 1,356,000
Manila, Gr... 3,100,000
*Quezon City. 482,400
Zamboanga... 158,000

**Poland**
Bydgoszcz.... 254,500
Gdansk
  (Danzig) ... 324,300
Krakow...... 525,000
Lodz....... 745,400
Poznan..... 440,700
Szczecin
  (Stettin)... 314,700
*Warsaw.... 1,261,300
Wroclaw
  (Breslau) ... 477,300

**Portugal**
Funchal..... 99,645
*Lisbon..... 822,000
Porto....... 319,250

**Rhodesia**
*Salisbury... 324,800

**Romania**
Arad....... 115,468
Braila...... 122,410
*Bucharest... 1,246,878
Cluj....... 167,930
Ploesti...... 136,757
Timisoara.... 152,552

**Saudi Arabia**
Jedda....... 194,000
Mecca...... 185,000
*Riyadh..... 225,000

**Senegal**
*Dakar...... 374,700

**Sierra Leone**
*Freetown.... 148,000

**Singapore**
*Singapore... 1,955,600

**Somalia**
*Mogadishu... 170,000

**So. Africa**
Bloemfontein.. 145,273
*Cape Town.. 808,000
Durban...... 682,000
Johannesburg.. 1,244,000
*Pretoria.... 423,000

**Southern Yemen**
Aden....... 150,000

**Spain**
Barcelona.... 1,696,756
Bilbao...... 334,198
Cadiz...... 126,409
Cordoba..... 214,296
Granada..... 157,990
*Madrid..... 2,599,330
Malaga..... 312,018
Murcia..... 264,505
Palma...... 169,754
Seville...... 474,082
Valencia..... 501,795
Zaragoza.... 357,693

**Sudan**
*Khartoum... 135,000
Omdurman... 167,000

**Sweden**
Boras...... 69,443
Goteborg.... 443,292
Halsingborg... 79,460
Linkoping.... 77,365
Malmo...... 253,502
Norrkoping... 94,067
Orebro...... 86,003
*Stockholm... 777,115
*Stockholm
  Gr...... 1,262,402
Uppsala..... 94,587
Vasteras.... 107,048

**Switzerland**
Basel....... 212,100
*Berne...... 166,800
Geneva...... 170,500
Lausanne.... 136,600
Zurich...... 432,500

**Syria**
Aleppo...... 562,753
*Damascus... 599,669
Hama....... 135,523
Homs....... 189,898
Lattakia..... 85,993

**Tanzania**
*Dar es Salaam 272,515
Tanga...... 60,935

**Thailand**
*Bangkok.... 1,608,305
Thonburi.... 459,555

**Togo Rep.**
*Lome...... 86,400

**Trinidad and Tobago**
*Port of Spain. 93,954

**Tunisia**
Bizerte...... 46,681
*Tunis...... 662,000
Sfax....... 65,635
Sousse...... 48,172

**Turkey**
Adana...... 290,515
*Ankara..... 1,067,048
Bursa...... 212,518
Istanbul..... 1,750,642
Izmir....... 417,411

**Uganda**
*Kampala.... 46,736

**USSR**
Alma-Ata.... 668,000
Astrakhan.... 368,000
Baku....... 1,218,000
Barnaul..... 407,000
Cheliabinsk... 851,000
Dniepro-
  petrovsk.... 837,000
Donetsk..... 855,000
Erevan...... 687,000
Frunze..... 412,000
Gorky...... 1,140,000
Gorlovka.... 343,000
Irkutsk..... 420,000
Ivanovo..... 407,000
Izhevsk..... 376,000
Karaganda... 505,000
Kazan...... 838,000
Kemerovo.... 364,000
Kharabovsk... 435,000
Kharkov..... 1,148,000
Kiev....... 1,457,000
Krasnodar... 467,000
Krasnoyarsk.. 592,000
Krivoy Rog... 523,000
Kuibyshev.... 1,016,000

Leningrad.... 3,341,000
Lugansk..... 352,000
Lvov....... 524,000
Magnitogorsk.. 357,000
Makeyevka... 414,000
Minsk...... 805,000
*Moscow.... 6,422,000
*Moscow, Gr.. 6,507,000
Novokuz-
  netsk...... 493,000
Novosibirsk... 1,080,000
Odessa..... 797,000
Omsk...... 801,000
Perm....... 811,000
Riga....... 691,000
Rostov..... 774,000
Saratov..... 738,000
Sverdlovsk... 981,000
Tallin...... 346,000
Tashkent.... 1,295,000
Tbilisi...... 861,000
Tula....... 377,000
Ufa........ 724,000
Vladivostok... 397,000
Volgograd... 757,000
Voronezh.... 626,000
Yaroslavl.... 508,000
Zaporozhie... 616,000
Zhdanov.... 385,000

**United Arab Republic (Egypt)**
Alexandria... 1,800,951
Assiut...... 137,000
*Cairo...... 4,196,998
Gizeh...... 285,700
Port Said.... 282,876
Suez....... 264,025
Tanta...... 215,400

**United Kingdom**
ENGLAND
Birmingham... 1,101,990
Bradford..... 296,860
Bristol...... 429,020
Coventry.... 333,830
Kingston-upon
  -Hull...... 295,900
Leeds....... 507,780
Leicester.... 282,800
Liverpool.... 705,310
*London, GR.. 7,880,760
Manchester... 616,520
Newcastle... 251,650
Nottingham... 309,740
Oxford..... 109,350
Plymouth.... 247,400
Portsmouth... 219,110
Sheffield..... 534,100
Stoke-on-
Trent..... 275,730

WALES
Barry...... 42,430
Cardiff..... 289,320
Merthyr
Tydfil..... 57,200
Swansea.... 170,940

SCOTLAND
Aberdeen.... 182,117
Dundee..... 182,284
Edinburgh... 467,986
Glasgow.... 960,527

NORTHERN IRELAND
Belfast..... 406,800
Londonderry.. 56,300

**Upper Volta**
*Ouagadougou 59,126

**Uruguay**
*Montevideo.. 1,158,632

**Venezuela**
Barquisimeto.. 253,820
*Caracas.... 1,694,586
Maracaibo... 535,320
Valencia..... 207,942

**Vietnam**
Haiphong.... 369,248
*Hanoi...... 643,576
Hue....... 104,500
*Saigon..... 3,000,000
Da Nang.... 250,000
Vinh....... 150,000

**Western Samoa**
*Apia...... 25,000

**Yemen**
Hodeida..... 45,000
*Sana...... 70,000
*Taiz...... 40,000

**Yugoslavia**
*Belgrade.... 585,234
Ljubljana.... 134,169
Sarajevo.... 143,117
Skopje..... 165,529
Zagreb..... 430,802

**Zambia**
*Lusaka..... 138,000

# U. S. Aid to Foreign Countries

**Source: Office of Business Economics, U. S. Department of Commerce**

For security reasons data by country do not include the military aid furnished principally under the mutual security program. Data shown include credits which have been extended to private entities in the country specified.

Grants are largely outright gifts for which no payment is expected or which at most involve an obligation on the part of the receiver to extend aid to the United States or other countries to achieve a common objective.

Credits are loans or other agreements which give rise to specific obligations to repay, over a period of years, usually with interest.

Net grants and credits take into account all known returns to the U. S. Government, including reverse grants, returns of grants and payments of principal. A minus sign indicates that the total of these returns to the U. S. is greater than the total of grants or credits.

Other assistance represents the transfer of U. S. farm products in exchange for foreign currencies, less the Government's disbursement of the currencies as grants, credits, or for purchases. The net acquisitions of currencies represents net transfers of resources to foreign currencies, in addition to those classified as grants or credits.

Amounts do not include investments in international financial institutions as follows: Asian Development Bank (ADB) $10,000,000; Inter-American Development Bank (IDB), $65,000,000; International Development Association (IDA) $119,000,000.

(In millions of dollars or equivalent) (*Less than $500,000)

| Calendar Year 1967 | Total | Net grants | Net credits | Net other assist. | Calendar Year 1967 | Total | Net grants | Net credits | Net other assist. |
|---|---|---|---|---|---|---|---|---|---|
| Total............ | 4,865 | 2,766 | 2,377 | −278 | Trust Territory of | \$ | | | |
| Military grants..... | 974 | 974 | — | — | the Pacific Islands | 20 | 20 | — | — |
| Other grants, credits | | | | | Vietnam........... | 399 | 543 | −48 | −95 |
| & other assistance.. | 3,891 | 1,792 | 2,377 | −278 | Other & unspecified. | 13 | 11 | 3 | −* |
| Western Europe..... | 264 | 11 | 286 | −32 | Africa............. | 330 | 186 | 158 | −15 |
| Austria........... | −1 | — | −1 | — | Algeria........... | 11 | 12 | −1 | — |
| Belgium–Luxemb'g. | 11 | — | 11 | −* | Cameroon......... | 3 | 2 | 1 | — |
| Finland........... | −6 | — | −5 | −* | Congo (Kinshasa).. | 34 | 9 | 31 | −5 |
| France............ | −2 | (*) | −4 | 1 | Ethiopia.......... | 11 | 10 | 1 | −1 |
| Germany.......... | 13 | 1 | 13 | −1 | Ghana............ | 33 | 5 | 25 | 2 |
| Italy............. | 41 | (*) | 41 | −* | Guinea........... | 7 | 3 | 4 | −1 |
| Portugal.......... | −4 | 3 | −6 | — | Kenya............ | 2 | 5 | −3 | — |
| Spain............ | 69 | 3 | 65 | (*) | Liberia........... | 37 | 11 | 25 | — |
| United Kingdom... | 126 | −* | 126 | −1 | Morocco.......... | 32 | 14 | 19 | −1 |
| Yugoslavia........ | −12 | 4 | 17 | −32 | Nigeria........... | 35 | 27 | 9 | (*) |
| Other & unspecified | 29 | (*) | 28 | −* | Sierra Leone...... | 4 | 4 | −* | — |
| Eastern Europe..... | −23 | 6 | −14 | −14 | Somali Republic.... | 5 | 4 | 1 | — |
| Poland........... | −14 | 6 | −6 | −14 | South Africa...... | −2 | — | −2 | −* |
| Other............ | −8 | — | −8 | — | Sudan............ | 5 | 6 | (*) | −2 |
| Near East & S. Asia | 1,435 | 300 | 1,238 | −104 | Tanzania.......... | 9 | 7 | 2 | — |
| Afghanistan........ | 24 | 16 | 9 | −* | Tunisia........... | 45 | 9 | 43 | −6 |
| Ceylon............ | 14 | 4 | 10 | −1 | Other & unspecified. | 58 | 56 | 3 | −1 |
| Greece............ | 3 | 4 | 3 | −4 | Western Hemisphere | 619 | 219 | 414 | −13 |
| India............. | 835 | 107 | 824 | −96 | Argentina......... | −20 | 2 | −22 | (*) |
| Iran.............. | 18 | 6 | 17 | −5 | Bolivia........... | 25 | 9 | 19 | −3 |
| Iraq.............. | 2 | (*) | 1 | — | Brazil............ | 141 | 58 | 87 | −4 |
| Israel............ | 25 | 3 | 35 | −12 | Canada........... | 31 | — | 31 | — |
| Jordan............ | 19 | 20 | (*) | −2 | Chile............. | 50 | 12 | 42 | −4 |
| Nepal............ | 11 | 11 | (*) | (*) | Colombia......... | 86 | 18 | 68 | −* |
| Pakistan.......... | 321 | 66 | 235 | 20 | Costa Rica........ | 12 | 4 | 7 | — |
| Turkey........... | 101 | 16 | 90 | −4 | Dominican Republic | 60 | 14 | 46 | (*) |
| United Arab Rep... | 5 | 8 | −3 | (*) | Ecuador.......... | 27 | 8 | 19 | −* |
| Yemen............ | 1 | 1 | — | — | El Salvador....... | 11 | 5 | 6 | — |
| Other & unspecified. | 54 | 38 | 17 | −1 | Guatemala........ | 15 | 8 | 7 | −* |
| East Asia & Pacific. | 986 | 819 | 266 | −99 | Honduras......... | 6 | 4 | 3 | — |
| Australia......... | 153 | — | 153 | −* | Jamaica.......... | 10 | 3 | 7 | −* |
| China–Taiwan...... | 38 | 6 | 36 | −5 | Mexico........... | 50 | 1 | 49 | — |
| Indonesia......... | 40 | 4 | 37 | −* | Nicaragua........ | 9 | 4 | 6 | — |
| Japan............ | −9 | −* | −9 | −* | Panama.......... | 17 | 8 | 9 | — |
| Korea............ | 193 | 109 | 78 | 6 | Paraguay......... | 3 | 4 | (*) | −1 |
| Laos............. | 58 | 58 | — | — | Peru............. | 24 | 16 | 9 | −2 |
| New Zealand...... | −6 | — | −6 | — | Trinidad & Tobago. | 2 | 2 | −1 | — |
| Philippines........ | 36 | 23 | 18 | −4 | Venezuela......... | 48 | 7 | 41 | — |
| Ryukyu Islands.... | 12 | 11 | 1 | — | Other & unspecified | 45 | 31 | 14 | −* |
| Thailand.......... | 39 | 35 | 4 | — | International institutions & unspecified areas........ | 249 | 250 | −1 | — |

# Major U. S. Foreign Aid, by Type

**Source: Office of Business Economics, U. S. Department of Commerce**

Grants and credits are generally goods delivered or shipped by services rendered by, or funds disbursed by U. S. Government to or for account of a foreign government. Reverse grants and returns, and principal collections, are comprised of goods, services, and funds received by U. S. Government. Assistance through net accumulation of foreign currency claims represents transfer of U. S. farm products in exchange for foreign currencies, less U. S. disbursements of the currencies as grants, credits, or for purchases.

| Type—Post-war period (a) | 1945-1967 (In millions) | Type—Post-war period (a) | 1945-1967 (In millions) |
|---|---|---|---|
| Total, net.................... | \$111,874 | Gross grants................. | 51,924 |
| | | Less: Reverse grants and returns | 1,677 |
| Investment in 5 international financial institutions (b) | 1,384 | Net new credits (c)............. | 19,373 |
| Under assistance programs, net.... | 110,490 | New credits................. | 33,354 |
| Military grants (supplies and services), net.................. | 37,611 | Less: Principal collections..... | 13,981 |
| Gross grants................. | 38,095 | Other assistance (through net accumulation of foreign currency claims), net.................. | 3,259 |
| Less: Reverse grants and returns. | 484 | Farm products sales (claims acquired (d)................ | 14,115 |
| Other aid, net................ | 72,879 | Less: Currency disbursed....... | 10,855 |
| Net, new grants (c).......... | 50,247 | | |

(a) July 1, 1945, through Dec. 31, 1967; all lend-lease from V-J Day (Sept. 2, 1945) (b) Asian Development Bank, Inter-American Development Bank, International Bank for Reconstruction & Development, International Development Assn., and International Finance Corp. (c) Net new grants have not been adjusted for postwar relief and other grants under agreements. Net new credits exclude prior grants converted into credits, totaling $2,747 billion. Repayments on these settlements are included in net new credits. (d) Includes foreign currencies acquired through second stage operations under farm sales legislation, such as principal and interest amounted to $548,000,000.

# WEIGHTS AND MEASURES

**Source:** National Bureau of Standards, Department of Commerce

## Tables of United States Customary Weights and Measures

### LINEAR MEASURE

| | | |
|---|---|---|
| 12 inches (in.) | = 1 foot (ft) | |
| 3 feet | = 1 yard (yd) | |
| 5½ yards | = 1 rod (rd), pole, or perch (16½ ft) | |
| 40 rods | = 1 furlong (fur.) = 220 yards = 660 feet | |
| 8 furlongs | = 1 statute mile (mi) = 1,760 yards = 5,280 feet | |
| 3 miles | = 1 league = 5,280 yards = 15,840 feet | |
| 6,076.11549 feet | = 1 International Nautical Mile | |

### AREA MEASURE

Squares and cubes of units are sometimes abbreviated by using "superior" figures. For example, ft² means square foot, and ft³ means cube foot.

| | |
|---|---|
| 144 square inches | = 1 square foot (ft²) |
| 9 square feet | = 1 square yard (yd²) = 1,296 square inches |
| 30¼ square yards | = 1 square rod (rd²) = 272¼ square feet |
| 160 square rods | = 1 acre = 4,840 square yards = 43,560 square feet |
| 640 acres | = 1 square mile (mi²) |
| 1 mile square | = 1 section (of land) |
| 6 miles square | = 1 township = 36 sections = 36 square miles |

### CUBIC MEASURE

| | |
|---|---|
| 1,728 cubic inches (in³) | = 1 cubic foot (ft³) |
| 27 cubic feet | = 1 cubic yard (yd³) |

### GUNTER'S OR SURVEYORS' CHAIN MEASURE

| | |
|---|---|
| 7.92 inches (in.) | = 1 link |
| 100 links | = 1 chain (ch) = 4 rods = 66 feet |
| 80 chains | = 1 statute mile (mi) = 320 rods = 5,280 feet. |

### LIQUID MEASURE

When necessary to distinguish the liquid pint or quart from the dry pint or quart, the word "liquid" or the abbreviation "liq" should be used in combination with the name or abbreviation of the liquid unit.

| | |
|---|---|
| 4 gills | = 1 pint (pt) (= 28.875 cubic inches) |
| 2 pints | = 1 quart (qt) (=57.75 cubic inches) |
| 4 quarts | = 1 gallon (gal) (=231 cubic inches) = 8 pints = 32 gills |

### DRY MEASURE

When necessary to distinguish the dry pint or quart from the liquid pint or quart, the word "dry" should be used in combination with the name or abbreviation of the dry unit.

| | |
|---|---|
| 2 pints (pt) | = 1 quart (qt) (= 67.200 6 cubic inches) |
| 8 quarts | = 1 peck (pk) (= 537.605 cubic inches) = 16 pints |
| 4 pecks | = 1 bushel (bu) (= 2,150.42 cubic inches) = 32 quarts |

### AVOIRDUPOIS WEIGHT

When necessary to distinguish the avoirdupois ounce or pound from the troy ounce or pound, the word "avoirdupois" or the abbreviation "avdp" should be used in combination with the name or abbreviation of the avoirdupois unit.

(The "grain" is the same in avoirdupois and troy weight.)

| | |
|---|---|
| 27 11/32 grains | = 1 dram (dr) |
| 16 drams | = 1 ounce (oz) =437½ grains |
| 16 ounces | = 1 pound (lb) = 256 drams = 7,000 grains |
| 100 pounds | = 1 hundredweight (cwt)* |
| 20 hundredweights | = 1 ton = 2,000 pounds* |

In "gross" or "long" measure, the following values are recognized:

| | |
|---|---|
| 112 pounds | = 1 gross or long hundredweight* |
| 20 gross or long hundredweights | = 1 gross or long ton = 2,240 pounds* |

*When the terms "hundredweight" and "ton" are used unmodified, they are commonly understood to mean the 100-pound hundredweight and the 2,000-pound ton, respectively; these units may be designated "net" or "short" when necessary to distinguish them from the corresponding units in gross or long measure.

### TROY WEIGHT

| | |
|---|---|
| 24 grains | = 1 pennyweight (dwt) |
| 20 pennyweights | = 1 ounce troy (oz t) = 480 grains |
| 12 ounces troy | = 1 pound troy (lb t) = 240 pennyweights = 5,760 grains |

## Tables of Equivalents

When the name of a unit is enclosed in brackets thus, [1 hand], this indicates (1) that the unit is not in general current use in the United States, or (2) that the unit is believed to be based on "custom and usage" rather than on formal definition. *See above about superior figures in Area Measure.* Equivalents involving decimals are, in most instances, rounded off to the third decimal place except where they are exact, in which cases these exact equivalents are so designated.

### LENGTHS

| | |
|---|---|
| 1 Angstrom (A) | 0.1 nanometer (exactly)<br>0.000 1 micron (exactly)<br>0.000 000 1 millimeter (exactly)<br>0.000 000 004 inch |
| 1 cable's length | 120 fathoms<br>720 feet<br>219.456 meters (exactly) |
| 1 centimeter (cm) | 0.393 7 inch |
| 1 chain (ch) (Gunter's or surveyors) | 66 feet<br>20.1168 meters (exactly) |
| 1 chain (engineers) | 100 feet<br>30.48 meters (exactly) |
| 1 decimeter (dm) | 3.937 inches |
| 1 dekameter (dam) | 32.808 feet |
| 1 fathom | 6 feet<br>1.8288 meters (exactly) |
| 1 foot (ft) | 0.3048 meters (exactly) |
| 1 furlong (fur.) | 10 chains (surveyors)<br>660 feet<br>220 yards<br>⅛ statute mile<br>201.168 meters |
| [1 hand] | 4 inches |
| 1 inch (in.) | 2.54 centimeters (exactly) |
| 1 kilometer (km) | 0.621 mile<br>3,280.8 feet |
| 1 league (land) | 3 statute miles<br>4.828 kilometers |
| 1 link (Gunter's or surveyors) | 7.92 inches<br>0.201 meter |

| | |
|---|---|
| 1 link (engineers) | 1 foot<br>0.305 meter |
| 1 meter (m) | 39.37 inches<br>1.094 yards |
| 1 micron (μ [the Greek letter mu]) | 0.001 millimeter (exactly)<br>0.000 039 37 inch |
| 1 mil | 0.001 inch (exactly)<br>0.025 4 millimeter (exactly) |
| 1 mile (mi) (statute or land) | 5,280 feet<br>1.609 kilometers |
| 1 International Nautical Mile (INM) | 1.852 kilometers (exactly)<br>1.150779 statute miles<br>6,076.11549 feet |
| 1 millimeter (mm) | 0.039 37 inch |
| 1 nanometer (nm) | 0.001 micron (exactly)<br>0.000 000 039 37 inch (exactly) |
| 1 point (typography) | 0.013 837 inch (exactly)<br>0.351 millimeter |
| 1 rod (rd), pole, or perch | 16½ feet<br>5½ yards<br>5.029 meters |
| 1 yard (yd) | 0.9144 meter (exactly) |

### AREAS OR SURFACES

| | |
|---|---|
| 1 acre | 43,560 square feet<br>4,840 square yards<br>0.405 hectare |
| 1 are (a) | 119.599 square yards<br>0.025 acre |

**(Tables of Equivalents continued)**

1 hectare (ha)...........................2.471 acres
[1 square (building)]................100 square feet
1 square centimeter (cm²).......0.155 square inch
1 square decimeter (dm²)......15.500 square inches
1 square foot (ft²)........929.030 square centimeters
1 square inch (in.²).......6.452 square centimeters

1 square kilometer (km²).......$\begin{cases} 247.105 \text{ acres} \\ 0.386 \text{ square mile} \end{cases}$

1 square meter (m²)...........$\begin{cases} 1.196 \text{ square yards} \\ 10.764 \text{ square feet} \end{cases}$

1 square mile (mi²)................258.999 hectares
1 square millimeter (mm²)........0.002 square inch
1 square rod ( rd²), sq pole, or
  sq perch..................25.293 square meters
1 square yard (yd²)............0.836 square meter

## CAPACITIES OR VOLUMES

1 barrel (bbl)..................31 to 42 gallons*
*There are a variety of "barrels", established by law or usage. For example: Federal taxes on fermented liquors are based on a barrel of 31 gallons; many State laws fix the "barrel for liquids" as 31½ gallons; one State fixes a 36-gallon barrel for cistern measurement; Federal law recognizes a 40-gallon barrel for "proof spirits"; by custom, 42 gallons comprise a barrel of crude oil or petroleum products for statistical purposes, and this equivalent is recognized "for liquids" by four States.

1 barrel (bbl), standard, for fruits, vegetables, and other dry commodities except cranberries......$\begin{cases} 7,056 \text{ cubic inches} \\ 105 \text{ dry quarts} \\ 3.281 \text{ bushels, struck} \\ \text{measure} \end{cases}$

1 barrel (bbl), standard, cranberry.............$\begin{cases} 5,826 \text{ cubic inches} \\ 86 \text{ } 45/64 \text{ dry quarts} \\ 2.709 \text{ bushels, struck} \\ \text{measure} \end{cases}$

1 bushel (bu) (U. S.) (struck measure).......$\begin{cases} 2,150.42 \text{ cubic inches} \\ \text{(exactly)} \\ 35.238 \text{ liters} \end{cases}$

[1 bushel, heaped (U. S.) ]..$\begin{cases} 2,747.715 \text{ cubic inches} \\ 1.278 \text{ bushels, struck} \\ \text{measure*} \end{cases}$
*Frequently recognized as 1¼ bushels, struck measure.

[1 bushel (bu) (British Imperial) (struck measure) ].$\begin{cases} 1.032 \text{ U. S. bushels,} \\ \text{struck measure} \\ 2,219.36 \text{ cubic inches} \end{cases}$
1 cord (cd) (firewood)...............128 cubic feet
1 cubic centimeter (cm³).........0.061 cubic inch
1 cubic decimeter (dm³).........61.023 cubic inches
1 cubic foot (ft³)........$\begin{cases} 7.481 \text{ gallons} \\ 28.317 \text{ cubic decimeters} \end{cases}$
1 cubic inch ( in.³).....$\begin{cases} 0.554 \text{ fluid ounce} \\ 4.433 \text{ fluid drams} \\ 16.387 \text{ cubic centimeters} \end{cases}$
1 cubic meter (m³).............1.308 cubic yards
1 cubic yard (yd.³)........0.765 cubic meter
1 cup, measuring...............$\begin{cases} 8 \text{ fluid ounces} \\ \frac{1}{2} \text{ liquid pint} \end{cases}$
1 dram, fluid (fl dr) (British) ]...........$\begin{cases} 0.961 \text{ U. S. fluid dram} \\ 0.217 \text{ cubic inch} \\ 3.552 \text{ milliliters} \end{cases}$
1 dekaliter (dal).............$\begin{cases} 2.642 \text{ gallons} \\ 1.135 \text{ pecks} \end{cases}$
1 gallon (gal) (U. S.).......$\begin{cases} 231 \text{ cubic inches} \\ 3.785 \text{ liters} \\ 0.833 \text{ British gallon} \\ 128 \text{ U.S. fluid ounces} \end{cases}$
[1 gallon (gal) British Imperial ]...........$\begin{cases} 277.42 \text{ cubic inches} \\ 1.201 \text{ U. S. gallons} \\ 4.546 \text{ liters} \\ 160 \text{ British fluid ounces} \end{cases}$
1 gill........................$\begin{cases} 7.219 \text{ cubic inches} \\ 4 \text{ fluid ounces} \\ 0.118 \text{ liter} \end{cases}$
1 hectoliter (hl)...........$\begin{cases} 26.418 \text{ gallons} \\ 2,838 \text{ bushels} \end{cases}$
1 liter.....................$\begin{cases} 1.057 \text{ liquid quarts} \\ 0.908 \text{ dry quart} \\ 61.025 \text{ cubic inches} \end{cases}$
1 milliliter (ml)..........$\begin{cases} 0.271 \text{ fluid dram} \\ 16.231 \text{ minims} \\ 0.061 \text{ cubic inch} \end{cases}$
1 ounce, liquid (U. S.)............$\begin{cases} 1.805 \text{ cubic inches} \\ 29.573 \text{ milliliters} \\ 1.041 \text{ British fluid ounces} \end{cases}$

[1 ounce, fluid (fl oz) (British) ]...........$\begin{cases} 0.961 \text{ U. S. fluid ounce} \\ 1.734 \text{ cubic inches} \\ 28.412 \text{ milliliters} \end{cases}$
1 peck (pk).........................8.810 liters
1 pint (pt), dry............$\begin{cases} 33.600 \text{ cubic inches} \\ 0.551 \text{ liter} \end{cases}$
1 pint (pt), liquid...........$\begin{cases} 28.875 \text{ cubic inches} \\ \text{(exactly)} \\ 0.473 \text{ liter} \end{cases}$
1 quart (qt), dry (U. S.)...$\begin{cases} 67.201 \text{ cubic inches} \\ 1.101 \text{ liters} \\ 0.969 \text{ British quart} \end{cases}$
1 quart (qt), liquid.... (U.S.)........$\begin{cases} 57.75 \text{ cubic inches (exactly)} \\ 0.946 \text{ liter} \\ 0.833 \text{ British quart} \end{cases}$
[1 quart (qt) (British) ]..$\begin{cases} 69.354 \text{ cubic inches} \\ 1.032 \text{ U. S. dry quarts} \\ 1.201 \text{ U. S. liquid quarts} \end{cases}$
1 tablespoon.................$\begin{cases} 3 \text{ teaspoons*} \\ 4 \text{ fluid drams} \\ \frac{1}{2} \text{ fluid ounce} \end{cases}$
1 teaspoon...................$\begin{cases} \frac{1}{3} \text{ tablespoon*} \\ 1\frac{1}{3} \text{ fluid drams*} \end{cases}$
*The equivalent "1 teaspoon = 1⅓ fluid drams" has been found by the Bureau to correspond more closely with the actual capacities of "measuring" and silver teaspoons than the equivalent "1 teaspoon = 1 fluid dram" which is given by a number of dictionaries.

## WEIGHTS OR MASSES

1 assay ton** (AT)................29.167 grams
**Used in assaying. The assay ton bears the same relation to the milligram that a ton of 2000 pounds avoirdupois bears to the ounce troy; hence the weight in milligrams of precious metal obtained from one assay ton of ore gives directly the number of troy ounces to the net ton.

1 carat (c)..............$\begin{cases} 200 \text{ milligrams} \\ 3.086 \text{ grains} \end{cases}$
1 dram avoirdupois (dr avdp)........$\begin{cases} 27 \text{ } 11/32 \text{ (= 27.344) grains} \\ 1.772 \text{ grams} \end{cases}$
gamma, *see* microgram
1 grain..................64.799 milligrams
1 gram (g)................$\begin{cases} 15.432 \text{ grains} \\ 0.035 \text{ ounce, avoirdupois} \end{cases}$
1 hundredweight, gross or long*** (gross cwt).......$\begin{cases} 112 \text{ pounds} \\ 50.802 \text{ kilograms} \end{cases}$
***The gross or long ton and hundredweight are used commercially in the United States to only a limited extent, usually in restricted industrial fields. These units are the same as the British "ton" and "hundredweight."
1 hundredweight, net or short (cwt. or net cwt.)..........$\begin{cases} 100 \text{ pounds} \\ 45.359 \text{ kilograms} \end{cases}$
1 kilogram (kg)....................2,205 pounds
1 microgram (γ [the Greek letter gamma])...........0.000,001 gram (exactly)
1 milligram (mg.)................0.015 grain
1 ounce, avoirdupois (oz avdp)......$\begin{cases} 437.5 \text{ grains (exactly)} \\ 0.911 \text{ troy ounce} \\ 28.350 \text{ grams} \end{cases}$
1 ounce, troy (oz t)......$\begin{cases} 480 \text{ grains} \\ 1.097 \text{ avoirdupois ounces} \\ 31.103 \text{ grams} \end{cases}$
1 pennyweight (dwt).................1.555 grams
1 pound, avoirdupois (lb avdp)......$\begin{cases} 7,000 \text{ grains} \\ 1.215 \text{ troy pounds} \\ 453.592 \text{ 37 grams (exactly)} \end{cases}$
1 pound, troy (lb t)......$\begin{cases} 5,760 \text{ grains} \\ 0.823 \text{ avoirdupois pound} \\ 373.242 \text{ grams} \end{cases}$
1 ton, gross or long* (gross tn).............$\begin{cases} 2,240 \text{ pounds} \\ 1.12 \text{ net tons (exactly)} \\ 1.016 \text{ metric tons} \end{cases}$
*The gross or long ton and hundredweight are used commercially in the United States to only a limited extent, usually in restricted industrial fields. These units are the same as the British "ton" and "hundredweight."
1 ton, metric (t)...............$\begin{cases} 2,204.623 \text{ pounds} \\ 0.984 \text{ gross ton} \\ 1.102 \text{ net tons} \end{cases}$
1 ton, net or short (sh ton)......$\begin{cases} 2,000 \text{ pounds} \\ 0.893 \text{ gross ton} \\ 0.907 \text{ metric ton} \end{cases}$

## Roman and Arabic Numerals
### Source: Historical Records

| | | | | | |
|---|---|---|---|---|---|
| I.........1 | VI......6 | XI.......11 | XVI......16 | XXX....30 | LXXX...80 | CD....400 | CM....900 |
| II........2 | VII.....7 | XII......12 | XVII.....17 | XL.....40 | XC.....90 | D.....500 | M....1000 |
| III.......3 | VIII....8 | XIII.....13 | XVIII....18 | L......50 | C.....100 | DC....600 | MCM...1900 |
| IV.......4 | IX......9 | XIV......14 | XIX......19 | LX.....60 | CC....200 | DCC...700 | MM....2000 |
| V........5 | X.......10 | XV.......15 | XX.......20 | LXX....70 | CCC...300 | DCCC...800 | V̄....5000 |

NOTE—A dash line over a numeral multiplies the value by 1,000: thus, X̄=10,000; L̄=50,000; C̄=100,000; D̄=500,000; M̄=1,000,000; C̄L̄IX=159,000; D̄L̄IX=559,000.

Other general rules in Roman numerals are as follows: (1), repeating a letter repeats its value—XX=20; CCC=300; (2), a letter placed after one of greater value adds thereto—VI=6; DC=600; (3), a letter placed before one of greater value subtracts therefrom—IV=4.
Arabic numerals are those now commonly in use—0, 1, 2, 3, 4, 5, 6, 7, 8, 9.

## Tables of Interrelation of Units of Measurement

Bold face type indicates exact values

### UNITS OF LENGTH

| Units | Inches | Links | Feet | Yards | Rods | Chains | Miles | Cm. | Meters |
|---|---|---|---|---|---|---|---|---|---|
| 1 inch = | 1 | 0.126 263 | 0.083 333 | 0.027 778 | 0.005 051 | 0.001 263 | 0.000 016 | 2.54 | 0.025 4 |
| 1 link = | 7.92 | 1 | 0.66 | 0.22 | 0.04 | 0.01 | 0.000 125 | 20.117 | 0.201 168 |
| 1 foot = | 12 | 1.515 152 | 1 | 0.333 333 | 0.060 606 | 0.015 152 | 0.000 189 | 30.48 | 0.304 8 |
| 1 yard = | 36 | 4.545 45 | 3 | 1 | 0.181 818 | 0.045 455 | 0.000 568 | 91.44 | 0.914 4 |
| 1 rod = | 198 | 25 | 16.5 | 5.5 | 1 | 0.25 | 0.003 125 | 502.92 | 5.029 2 |
| 1 chain = | 792 | 100 | 66 | 22 | 4 | 1 | 0.012 5 | 2011.68 | 20.116 8 |
| 1 mile = | 63 360 | 8000 | 5280 | 1760 | 320 | 80 | 1 | 160 934.4 | 1609.344 |
| 1 cm = | 0.3937 | 0.049 710 | 0.032 808 | 0.010 936 | 0.001 988 | 0.000 497 | 0.000 006 | 1 | 0.01 |
| 1 meter = | 39.37 | 4.970 970 | 3.280 840 | 1.093 613 | 0.198 839 | 0.049 710 | 0.000 621 | 100 | 1 |

### UNITS OF AREA

| Units | Square inches | Square links | Square feet | Square yards | Square rods | Square chains |
|---|---|---|---|---|---|---|
| 1 sq. inch = | 1 | .015 942 3 | 0.006 944 | 0.000 771 605 | 0.000 025 5 | 0.000 001 594 |
| 1 sq. link = | 62.726 4 | 1 | 0.435 6 | 0.0484 | 0.0016 | 0.000 1 |
| 1 sq. foot = | 144 | 2.295 684 | 1 | 0.111 111 1 | 0.003 673 09 | 0.000 229 568 |
| 1 sq. yard = | 1296 | 20.661 16 | 9 | 1 | 0.033 057 85 | 0.002 066 12 |
| 1 sq. rod = | 39 204 | 625 | 272.25 | 30.25 | 1 | 0.062 5 |
| 1 sq. chain = | 627 264 | 10 000 | 4356 | 484 | 16 | 1 |
| 1 acre = | 6 272 640 | 100 000 | 43 560 | 4840 | 160 | 10 |
| 1 sq. mile = | 4 014 489 600 | 64 000 000 | 27 878 400 | 3 097 600 | 102 400 | 6400 |
| 1 sq. cm = | 0.155 000 3 | 0.002 471 05 | 0.001 076 | 0.000 119 599 | 0.000 003 954 | 0.000 000 247 |
| 1 sq. meter = | 1550.003 | 24.710 54 | 10.763 91 | 1.195 990 | 0.039 536 86 | 0.002 471 054 |
| 1 hectare = | 15 500 031 | 247,105 | 107 639.1 | 11 959.90 | 395.368 6 | 24,710,54 |

| Units | Acres | Square miles | Square centimeters | Square meters | Hectares |
|---|---|---|---|---|---|
| 1 sq. inch = | 0.000 000 159 423 | 0.000 000 000 249 10 | 6.451 6 | 0.000 645 16 | 0.000 000 065 |
| 1 sq. link = | 0.000 01 | 0.000 000 015 625 | 404.685 642 24 | 0.040 468 56 | 0.000 004 047 |
| 1 sq. foot = | 0.000 022 956 84 | 0.000 000 035 870 06 | 929.030 4 | 0.092 903 04 | 0.000 009 290 |
| 1 sq. yard = | 0.000 206 611 6 | 0.000 000 322 830 6 | 8 361.273 6 | 0.836 127 36 | 0.000 083 613 |
| 1 sq. rod = | 0.006 25 | 0.000 009 765 625 | 252 928.526 4 | 25.292 852 64 | 0.002 529 285 |
| 1 sq. chain = | 0.1 | 0.000 156 25 | 404.685 642 24 | 404.685 642 24 | 0.040 468 564 |
| 1 acre = | 1 | 0.001 562 5 | 40 468 564 | 4046.856 422 4 | 0.404 685 642 |
| 1 sq. mile = | 640 | 1 | 25 899 881 103 | 2 589 988.11 | 258.998 811 034 |
| 1 sq. centim'r = | 0.000 000 024 711 | 0.000 000 000 038 610 | 1 | 0.0001 | 0.000 000 01 |
| 1 sq. meter = | 0.000 247 105 4 | 0.000 000 386 102 2 | 10 000 | 1 | 0.0001 |
| 1 hectare = | 2.471 054 | 0.003 861 022 | 100 000 000 | 10 000 | 1 |

### UNITS OF MASS NOT GREATER THAN POUNDS AND KILOGRAMS

| Units | Grains | Pennyweights | Avoirdupois Drams | Avoirdupois Ounces |
|---|---|---|---|---|
| 1 grain = | 1 | 0.041 666 67 | 0.036 571 43 | 0.002 285 71 |
| 1 pennyweight = | 24 | 1 | 0.877 714 3 | 0.054 857 14 |
| 1 dram avdp. = | 27.343 75 | 1.139 323 | 1 | 0.062 5 |
| 1 ounce avdp. = | 437.5 | 18.229 17 | 16 | 1 |
| 1 ounce troy = | 480 | 20 | 17.554 29 | 1.097 143 |
| 1 pound troy = | 5760 | 240 | 210.651 4 | 13.165 71 |
| 1 pound avdp. = | 7000 | 291.666 7 | 256 | 16 |
| 1 milligram = | 0.015 432 | 0.000 643 015 | 0.000 564 383 | 0.000 035 274 |
| 1 gram = | 15.432 36 | 0.643 014 9 | 0.564 383 4 | 0.035 273 96 |
| 1 kilogram = | 15 432.36 | 643.014 9 | 564.383 4 | 35.273 96 |

| Units | Troy Ounces | Troy Pounds | Avoirdupois Pounds | Milligrams | Grams | Kilograms |
|---|---|---|---|---|---|---|
| 1 grain = | 0.002 083 33 | 0.000 173 611 | 0.000 142 857 | 64.798 91 | 0.064 798 91 | 0.000 064 799 |
| 1 pennyw't = | 0.05 | 0.004 166 667 | 0.003 428 571 | 1555.173 84 | 1.555 173 84 | 0.001 555 174 |
| 1 dram avdp. = | 0.056 966 15 | 0.004 747 179 | 0.003 906 25 | 1771.845 195 | 1.771 845 195 | 0.001 771 845 |
| 1 oz. avdp. = | 0.911 458 3 | 0.075 954 86 | 0.062 5 | 28 349.523 125 | 28.349 523 125 | 0.028 349 52 |
| 1 oz. troy = | 1 | 0.083 333 333 | 0.068 571 43 | 31 103.476 8 | 31.103 476 8 | 0.031 103 48 |
| 1 lb. troy = | 12 | 1 | 0.822 857 1 | 373 241.721 6 | 373.241 721 6 | 0.373 241 722 |
| 1 lb. avdp. = | 14.583 33 | 1.215 278 | 1 | 453 592.37 | 453.592 37 | 0.453 592 37 |
| 1 milligram = | 0.000 032 151 | 0.000 002 679 | 0.000 002 205 | 1 | 0.001 | 0.000 001 |
| 1 gram = | 0.032 150 75 | 0.002 679 229 | 0.002 204 623 | 1000 | 1 | 0.001 |
| 1 kilogram = | 32.150 75 | 2.679 229 | 2.204 623 | 1000 000 | 1000 | 1 |

### UNITS OF MASS NOT LESS THAN AVOIRDUPOIS OUNCES

| Units | Avdp. Ounces | Avdp. Pounds | Short Cwt. | Short Tons | Long Tons | Kilograms | Metric Tons |
|---|---|---|---|---|---|---|---|
| 1 oz av. = | 1 | 0.0625 | 0.000 625 | 0.000 031 25 | 0.000 027 902 | 0.028 349 523 | 0.000 028 350 |
| 1 lb av. = | 16 | 1 | 0.01 | 0.0005 | 0.000 446 429 | 0.453 592 37 | 0.000 453 592 |
| 1 sh cwt. = | 1 600 | 100 | 1 | 0.05 | 0.044 642 86 | 45.359 237 | 0.045 359 237 |
| 1 sh ton = | 32 000 | 2000 | 20 | 1 | 0.892 857 1 | 907.184 74 | 0.907 184 74 |
| 1 long ton = | 35 840 | 2240 | 22.4 | 1.12 | 1 | 1016.046 908 8 | 1.016,046 909 |
| 1 kg = | 35.273 96 | 2.204 623 | 0.022 046 23 | 0.001 102 311 | 0.000 094 207 | 1 | 0.001 |
| 1 metric ton = | 35 273.96 | 2204.623 | 22.046 23 | 1.102 311 | 0.984 206 5 | 1000 | 1 |

### UNITS OF VOLUME

| Units | Cubic inches | Cubic feet | Cubic yards | Cubic centimeters | Cubic decimeters | Cubic meters |
|---|---|---|---|---|---|---|
| 1 cubic inch = | 1 | 0.000 578 704 | 0.000 021 433 | 16.387 064 | 0.016 387 | 0.000 016 387 |
| 1 cubic foot = | 1728 | 1 | 0.037 037 04 | 28 316.846 592 | 28.316 847 | 0.028 316 847 |
| 1 cubic yard = | 46 656 | 27 | 1 | 764 554.857 984 | 764.554 858 | 0.764 554 858 |
| 1 cubic cm = | 0.061 023 74 | 0.000 035 315 | 0.000 001 308 | 1 | 0.001 | 0.000 000 1 |
| 1 cubic dm = | 61.023 74 | 0.035 314 67 | 0.001 307 951 | 1 000 | 1 | 0.001 |
| 1 cubic meter = | 61 023.74 | 35.314 67 | 1.307 951 | 1 000 000 | 1000 | 1 |

## UNITS OF CAPACITY (Liquid Measure)

| Units | Minims | Fluid drams | Fluid ounces | Gills | Liquid pt. |
|---|---|---|---|---|---|
| 1 minim = | 1 | 0.016 666 7 | 0.002 083 33 | 0.000 520 833 | 0.000 130 208 |
| 1 liquid dram = | 60 | 1 | 0.125 | 0.031 25 | 0.007 812 5 |
| 1 liquid ounce = | 480 | 8 | 1 | 0.25 | 0.062 5 |
| 1 gill = | 1920 | 32 | 4 | 1 | 0.25 |
| 1 liquid pint = | 7680 | 128 | 16 | 4 | 1 |
| 1 liquid quart = | 15 360 | 256 | 32 | 8 | 2 |
| 1 gallon = | 61 440 | 1024 | 128 | 32 | 8 |
| 1 cubic inch = | 265.974 | 4.432 900 | 0.554 112 6 | 0.138 528 1 | 0.034 632 03 |
| 1 cubic foot = | 459 603.1 | 7660.052 | 957.506 5 | 239.376 6 | 59.844 16 |
| 1 milliliter = | 16.230 73 | 0.270 512 18 | 0.033 814 02 | 0.008 453 506 | 2.002 113 376 |
| 1 liter = | 16 230.73 | 270.512 18 | 33.814 02 | 8.453 506 | 2113 376 |

| Units | Liquid quarts | Gallons | Cubic inches | Cubic feet | Liters |
|---|---|---|---|---|---|
| 1 minim = | 0.000 065 104 17 | 0.000 016 276 04 | 0.003 759 766 | 0.000 002 175 790 | 0.000 061 611 52 |
| 1 liq. dram = | 0.003 906 25 | 0.000 976 562 5 | 0.225 585 9 | 0.000 130 547 4 | 0.003 696 691 |
| 1 liquid oz.= | 0.031 25 | 0.007 812 5 | 1.804 687 5 | 0.001 044 379 | 0.029 573 53 |
| 1 gill = | 0.125 | 0.031 25 | 7.218 75 | 0.004 177 517 | 0.118 294 118 25 |
| 1 liquid pt.= | 0.5 | 0.125 | 28.875 | 0.016 710 07 | 0.473 176 473 |
| 1 liquid qt.= | 1 | 0.25 | 57.75 | 0.033 420 14 | 0.946 352 946 |
| 1 gallon = | 4 | 1 | 231 | 0.133 680 6 | 3.785 411 784 |
| 1 cubic in. = | 0.017 316 02 | 0.004 329 004 | 1 | 0.000 578 703 7 | 0.016 387 064 |
| 1 cubic foot= | 29.922 08 | 7.480 519 | 1728 | 1 | 28.316 846 592 |
| 1 liter = | 1.056 688 | 0.264 172 05 | 61.023 74 | 0.035 314 67 | 1 |

## UNITS OF CAPACITY (Dry Measure)

| Units | Dry pints | Dry quarts | Pecks | Bushels | Cubic inches | Liters |
|---|---|---|---|---|---|---|
| 1 dry pint = | 1 | 0.5 | 0.062 5 | 0.015 625 | 33.600 312 5 | 0.550 610 47 |
| 1 dry quart = | 2 | 1 | 0.125 | 0.031 25 | 67.200 625 | 1.101 220 9 |
| 1 peck = | 16 | 8 | 1 | 0.25 | 537.605 | 8.809 767 5 |
| 1 bushel = | 64 | 32 | 4 | 1 | 2150.42 | 35.239 07 |
| 1 cubic inch = | 0.029 761 6 | 0.014 880 8 | 0.001 860 10 | 0.000 465 025 | 1 | 0.016 387 064 |
| 1 liter = | 1.816 166 | 0.908 083 | 0.113 510 37 | 0.028 377 59 | 61.023 74 | 1 |

# Tables of Metric Weights and Measures

### LINEAR MEASURE

10 millimeters (mm) = 1 centimeter (cm)
10 centimeters = 1 decimeter (dm) = 100 millimeters
10 decimeters = 1 meter (m) = 1,000 millimeters
10 meters = 1 dekameter (dam)
10 dekameters = 1 hectometer (hm) = 100 meters
10 hectometers = 1 kilometer (km) = 1,000 meters

### AREA MEASURE

100 square millimeters (mm²) = 1 square centimeter (cm²)
10,000 square centimeters = 1 square meter (m²) = 1,000,000 square millimeters
100 square meters = 1 are (a)
100 ares = 1 hectare (ha) = 10,000 square meters
100 hectares = 1 square kilometer (km²) = 1,000,000 square meters

### VOLUME MEASURE

10 milliliters (ml) = 1 centiliter (cl)
10 centiliters = 1 deciliter (dl) = 100 milliliters

10 deciliters = 1 liter (l) = 1,000 milliliters
10 liters = 1 dekaliter (dal)
10 dekaliter3 = 1 hectoliter (hl) = 100 liters
10 hectolit3rs = 1 kiloliter (kl) = 1,000 liters

### CUBIC MEASURE

1,000 cubic millimeters (mm³) = 1 cubic centimeter (cm³)
1,000 cubic centimeters = 1 cubic decimeter (dm³) = 1,000,000 cubic millimeters
1,000 cubic decimeters = 1 cubic meter (m³) = 1 stere = 1,000,000 cubic centimeters = 1,000,000,000 cubic millimeters

### WEIGHT

10 milligrams (mg) = 1 centigram (cg)
10 centigrams = 1 decigram (dg) = 100 milligrams
10 decigrams = 1 gram (g) = 1,000 milligrams
10 grams = 1 dekagram (dag)
10 dekagrams = 1 hectogram (hg) = 100 grams
10 hectograms = 1 kilogram (kg) = 1,000 grams
1,000 kilograms = 1 metric ton (t)

## Special Terms Used in Metric System

In the metric system of weights and measures, designations of multiples and subdivisions of any unit may be arrived at by combining with the name of the unit the prefixes deka, hecto, kilo, mega, giga, and tera, meaning, respectively, 10, 100, 1,000, 1,000,000, 1,000,000,000, and 1,000,000,-000, and deci, centi, milli, micro, nana, pico, femto and atto, meaning, respectively, one-tenth, one-hundreth, one-thousandth, one-millionth, one-billionth, one-trillionth, one-quadrillionth and one-quintillionth. In some of the foregoing metric tables some such multiples and subdivisions have not been included for the reason that these have little, if any, currency.

A special case is found in the term "micron" (abbreviated as μ [the Greek letter mu], a coined word meaning one-millionth of a meter) equivalent to one-thousandth of a millimeter; a milli-micron (mμ) is a billionth of a meter and hence should always be designated as a nanometer, and a micromicron (abbreviated as μμ) which is a trillionth of a meter and hence should always be designated as a picometer.

In October, 1960, the Eleventh General (International) Conference on Weights and Measures redefined the meter as 1 650 763.73 wavelengths of the orange-red radiation in vacuum of krypton 86 corresponding to the unperturbed transition between the $2p_{10}$ and $5d_5$ levels. The platinum-iridium meter bars formerly used as standards will remain important because of the ease with which they can be used for certain types of measurements.

## Weight of Water

Source: National Bureau of Standards

| 1 | cubic inch | .0360 | pound | 1 | imperial gallon | 10.0 | pounds |
|---|---|---|---|---|---|---|---|
| 12 | cubic inches | .433 | pound | 11.2 | imperial gallons | 112.0 | pounds |
| 1 | cubic foot | 62.4 | pounds | 224 | imperial gallons | 2240.0 | pounds |
| 1 | cubic foot | 7.48052 | U. S. gals. | 1 | U. S. gallon | 8.33 | pounds |
| 1.8 | cubic feet | 112.0 | pounds | 13.45 | U. S. gallons | 112.0 | pounds |
| 35.96 | cubic feet | 2240.0 | pounds | 269.0 | U. S. gallons | 2240.0 | pounds |

# Squares, Square Roots, Cubes and Cube Roots of Nos. 1 to 100

| No. | Sq. | Cube | Sq. Root | Cube Root | No. | Sq. | Cube | Sq. Root | Cube Root | No. | Sq. | Cube | Sq. Root | Cube Root |
|---|---|---|---|---|---|---|---|---|---|---|---|---|---|---|
| 1 | 1.000 | 1.000 | 1.000 | 1.000 | 35 | 1225 | 42875 | 5.916 | 3.271 | 68 | 4624 | 314432 | 8.246 | 4.081 |
| 2 | 4 | 8 | 1.414 | 1.259 | 36 | 1296 | 46656 | 6.000 | 3.301 | 69 | 4761 | 328509 | 8.306 | 4.101 |
| 3 | 9 | 27 | 1.732 | 1.442 | 37 | 1369 | 50653 | 6.082 | 3.332 | 70 | 4900 | 343000 | 8.366 | 4.121 |
| 4 | 16 | 64 | 2.000 | 1.587 | 38 | 1444 | 54872 | 6.164 | 3.362 | 71 | 5041 | 357911 | 8.426 | 4.140 |
| 5 | 25 | 125 | 2.236 | 1.710 | 39 | 1521 | 59319 | 6.245 | 3.391 | 72 | 5184 | 373248 | 8.485 | 4.160 |
| 6 | 36 | 216 | 2.449 | 1.817 | 40 | 1600 | 64000 | 6.324 | 3.420 | 73 | 5329 | 389017 | 8.544 | 4.179 |
| 7 | 49 | 343 | 2.645 | 1.913 | 41 | 1681 | 68921 | 6.403 | 3.448 | 74 | 5476 | 405224 | 8.602 | 4.198 |
| 8 | 64 | 512 | 2.828 | 2.000 | 42 | 1764 | 74088 | 6.480 | 3.476 | 75 | 5625 | 421875 | 8.660 | 4.217 |
| 9 | 81 | 729 | 3.000 | 2.080 | 43 | 1849 | 79507 | 6.557 | 3.503 | 76 | 5776 | 438976 | 8.717 | 4.235 |
| 10 | 100 | 1000 | 3.162 | 2.154 | 44 | 1936 | 85184 | 6.633 | 3.530 | 77 | 5929 | 456533 | 8.775 | 4.254 |
| 11 | 121 | 1331 | 3.316 | 2.224 | 45 | 2025 | 91125 | 6.708 | 3.556 | 78 | 6084 | 474552 | 8.831 | 4.272 |
| 12 | 144 | 1728 | 3.464 | 2.289 | 46 | 2116 | 97336 | 6.782 | 3.583 | 79 | 6241 | 493039 | 8.888 | 4.290 |
| 13 | 169 | 2197 | 3.605 | 2.351 | 47 | 2209 | 103823 | 6.855 | 3.608 | 80 | 6400 | 512000 | 8.944 | 4.308 |
| 14 | 196 | 2744 | 3.741 | 2.410 | 48 | 2304 | 110592 | 6.928 | 3.634 | 81 | 6561 | 531441 | 9.000 | 4.326 |
| 15 | 225 | 3375 | 3.873 | 2.466 | 49 | 2401 | 117649 | 7.000 | 3.659 | 82 | 6724 | 551368 | 9.055 | 4.344 |
| 16 | 256 | 4096 | 4.000 | 2.519 | 50 | 2500 | 125000 | 7.071 | 3.684 | 83 | 6889 | 571787 | 9.110 | 4.362 |
| 17 | 289 | 4913 | 4.123 | 2.571 | 51 | 2601 | 132651 | 7.141 | 3.708 | 84 | 7056 | 592704 | 9.165 | 4.379 |
| 18 | 324 | 5832 | 4.242 | 2.620 | 52 | 2704 | 140608 | 7.211 | 3.732 | 85 | 7225 | 614125 | 9.219 | 4.396 |
| 19 | 361 | 6859 | 4.358 | 2.668 | 53 | 2809 | 148877 | 7.280 | 3.756 | 86 | 7396 | 636056 | 9.273 | 4.414 |
| 20 | 400 | 8000 | 4.472 | 2.714 | 54 | 2916 | 157464 | 7.348 | 3.779 | 87 | 7569 | 658503 | 9.327 | 4.431 |
| 21 | 441 | 9261 | 4.582 | 2.758 | 55 | 3025 | 166375 | 7.416 | 3.803 | 88 | 7744 | 681472 | 9.380 | 4.448 |
| 22 | 484 | 10648 | 4.690 | 2.802 | 56 | 3136 | 175616 | 7.483 | 3.825 | 89 | 7921 | 704969 | 9.434 | 4.464 |
| 23 | 529 | 12167 | 4.795 | 2.843 | 57 | 3249 | 185193 | 7.549 | 3.848 | 90 | 8100 | 729000 | 9.486 | 4.481 |
| 24 | 576 | 13824 | 4.899 | 2.884 | 58 | 3364 | 195112 | 7.615 | 3.870 | 91 | 8281 | 753571 | 9.539 | 4.497 |
| 25 | 625 | 15625 | 5.000 | 2.924 | 59 | 3481 | 205379 | 7.681 | 3.893 | 92 | 8464 | 778688 | 9.591 | 4.514 |
| 26 | 676 | 17576 | 5.099 | 2.962 | 60 | 3600 | 216000 | 7.746 | 3.914 | 93 | 8649 | 804357 | 9.643 | 4.530 |
| 27 | 729 | 19683 | 5.196 | 3.000 | 61 | 3721 | 226981 | 7.810 | 3.936 | 94 | 8836 | 830584 | 9.695 | 4.546 |
| 28 | 784 | 21952 | 5.291 | 3.036 | 62 | 3844 | 238328 | 7.874 | 3.957 | 95 | 9025 | 857375 | 9.746 | 4.562 |
| 29 | 841 | 24389 | 5.385 | 3.072 | 63 | 3969 | 250047 | 7.937 | 3.979 | 96 | 9216 | 884736 | 9.798 | 4.578 |
| 30 | 900 | 27000 | 5.477 | 3.107 | 64 | 4096 | 262144 | 8.000 | 4.000 | 97 | 9409 | 912673 | 9.848 | 4.594 |
| 31 | 961 | 29791 | 5.567 | 3.141 | 65 | 4225 | 274625 | 8.062 | 4.020 | 98 | 9604 | 941192 | 9.899 | 4.610 |
| 32 | 1024 | 32768 | 5.656 | 3.174 | 66 | 4356 | 287496 | 8.124 | 4.041 | 99 | 9801 | 970299 | 9.949 | 4.626 |
| 33 | 1089 | 35937 | 5.744 | 3.207 | 67 | 4489 | 300763 | 8.185 | 4.061 | 100 | 10000 | 1000000 | 10.000 | 4.641 |
| 34 | 1156 | 39304 | 5.831 | 3.239 | | | | | | | | | | |

# Square Roots and Cube Roots, 1000 to 2000

| No. | Square Root | Cube Root | No. | Square Root | Cube Root | No. | Square Root | Cube Root | No. | Square Root | Cube Root |
|---|---|---|---|---|---|---|---|---|---|---|---|
| 1000 | 31.62 | 10.00 | 1255 | 35.43 | 10.79 | 1510 | 38.86 | 11.47 | 1765 | 42.01 | 12.09 |
| 1005 | 31.70 | 10.02 | 1260 | 35.50 | 10.80 | 1515 | 38.92 | 11.49 | 1770 | 42.07 | 12.10 |
| 1010 | 31.78 | 10.03 | 1265 | 35.57 | 10.82 | 1520 | 38.99 | 11.50 | 1775 | 42.13 | 12.11 |
| 1015 | 31.94 | 10.07 | 1275 | 35.71 | 10.84 | 1530 | 39.12 | 11.52 | 1785 | 42.25 | 12.13 |
| 1025 | 32.02 | 10.08 | 1280 | 35.78 | 10.86 | 1535 | 39.18 | 11.54 | 1790 | 42.31 | 12.14 |
| 1030 | 32.09 | 10.10 | 1285 | 35.85 | 10.87 | 1545 | 39.31 | 11.56 | 1795 | 42.37 | 12.15 |
| 1035 | 32.17 | 10.12 | 1290 | 35.92 | 10.89 | 1555 | 39.43 | 11.59 | 1805 | 42.49 | 12.17 |
| 1045 | 32.33 | 10.15 | 1300 | 36.06 | 10.91 | 1560 | 39.50 | 11.60 | 1810 | 42.54 | 12.19 |
| 1050 | 32.40 | 10.16 | 1305 | 36.12 | 10.93 | 1570 | 39.62 | 11.62 | 1815 | 42.60 | 12.20 |
| 1060 | 32.56 | 10.20 | 1315 | 36.26 | 10.96 | 1575 | 39.69 | 11.63 | 1825 | 42.72 | 12.22 |
| 1065 | 32.63 | 10.21 | 1320 | 36.33 | 10.97 | 1585 | 39.81 | 11.66 | 1830 | 42.78 | 12.23 |
| 1075 | 32.79 | 10.24 | 1330 | 36.47 | 11.00 | 1590 | 39.87 | 11.67 | 1840 | 42.90 | 12.25 |
| 1080 | 32.86 | 10.26 | 1335 | 36.54 | 11.01 | 1595 | 39.94 | 11.68 | 1845 | 42.95 | 12.26 |
| 1085 | 32.94 | 10.28 | 1340 | 36.61 | 11.02 | 1600 | 40.00 | 11.70 | 1850 | 43.01 | 12.28 |
| 1090 | 33.02 | 10.29 | 1345 | 36.67 | 11.04 | 1605 | 40.06 | 11.71 | 1855 | 43.07 | 12.29 |
| 1095 | 33.09 | 10.31 | 1350 | 36.74 | 11.05 | 1610 | 40.12 | 11.72 | 1860 | 43.13 | 12.30 |
| 1100 | 33.17 | 10.32 | 1355 | 36.81 | 11.07 | 1615 | 40.19 | 11.73 | 1865 | 43.19 | 12.31 |
| 1105 | 33.24 | 10.34 | 1360 | 36.88 | 11.08 | 1620 | 40.25 | 11.74 | 1870 | 43.24 | 12.32 |
| 1110 | 33.32 | 10.35 | 1365 | 36.95 | 11.09 | 1625 | 40.31 | 11.76 | 1875 | 43.30 | 12.33 |
| 1115 | 33.39 | 10.37 | 1370 | 37.01 | 11.11 | 1630 | 40.37 | 11.77 | 1880 | 43.36 | 12.34 |
| 1120 | 33.47 | 10.38 | 1375 | 37.08 | 11.12 | 1635 | 40.44 | 11.78 | 1885 | 43.42 | 12.35 |
| 1125 | 33.54 | 10.40 | 1380 | 37.15 | 11.13 | 1640 | 40.50 | 11.79 | 1890 | 43.47 | 12.36 |
| 1130 | 33.62 | 10.42 | 1390 | 37.28 | 11.16 | 1645 | 40.56 | 11.81 | 1895 | 43.53 | 12.37 |
| 1135 | 33.69 | 10.43 | 1395 | 37.35 | 11.17 | 1650 | 40.62 | 11.82 | 1900 | 43.59 | 12.39 |
| 1140 | 33.76 | 10.45 | 1400 | 37.42 | 11.19 | 1655 | 40.68 | 11.83 | 1905 | 43.65 | 12.40 |
| 1145 | 33.84 | 10.46 | 1405 | 37.48 | 11.20 | 1660 | 40.74 | 11.84 | 1910 | 43.70 | 12.41 |
| 1150 | 33.91 | 10.48 | 1410 | 37.55 | 11.21 | 1665 | 40.80 | 11.85 | 1915 | 43.76 | 12.42 |
| 1155 | 33.99 | 10.49 | 1415 | 37.62 | 11.23 | 1670 | 40.87 | 11.86 | 1920 | 43.82 | 12.43 |
| 1160 | 34.06 | 10.51 | 1420 | 37.68 | 11.24 | 1675 | 40.93 | 11.88 | 1925 | 43.87 | 12.44 |
| 1165 | 34.13 | 10.52 | 1425 | 37.75 | 11.25 | 1680 | 40.99 | 11.89 | 1930 | 43.93 | 12.45 |
| 1170 | 34.21 | 10.54 | 1430 | 37.82 | 11.27 | 1685 | 41.05 | 11.90 | 1935 | 43.99 | 12.46 |
| 1175 | 34.28 | 10.55 | 1435 | 37.88 | 11.28 | 1690 | 41.11 | 11.91 | 1940 | 44.05 | 12.47 |
| 1180 | 34.35 | 10.57 | 1440 | 37.95 | 11.29 | 1695 | 41.17 | 11.92 | 1945 | 44.10 | 12.48 |
| 1185 | 34.42 | 10.58 | 1445 | 38.01 | 11.31 | 1700 | 41.23 | 11.93 | 1950 | 44.16 | 12.49 |
| 1190 | 34.50 | 10.60 | 1450 | 38.08 | 11.32 | 1705 | 41.29 | 11.95 | 1955 | 44.22 | 12.50 |
| 1195 | 34.57 | 10.61 | 1455 | 38.14 | 11.33 | 1710 | 41.35 | 11.96 | 1960 | 44.27 | 12.51 |
| 1200 | 34.64 | 10.63 | 1460 | 38.21 | 11.34 | 1715 | 41.41 | 11.97 | 1965 | 44.33 | 12.53 |
| 1205 | 34.71 | 10.64 | 1465 | 38.28 | 11.36 | 1720 | 41.47 | 11.98 | 1970 | 44.38 | 12.54 |
| 1210 | 34.79 | 10.66 | 1470 | 38.34 | 11.37 | 1725 | 41.53 | 11.99 | 1975 | 44.44 | 12.55 |
| 1215 | 34.86 | 10.67 | 1475 | 38.41 | 11.38 | 1730 | 41.59 | 12.00 | 1980 | 44.50 | 12.56 |
| 1220 | 34.93 | 10.69 | 1480 | 38.47 | 11.40 | 1735 | 41.65 | 12.02 | 1985 | 44.55 | 12.57 |
| 1225 | 35.00 | 10.70 | 1490 | 38.60 | 11.42 | 1740 | 41.71 | 12.03 | 1990 | 44.61 | 12.58 |
| 1235 | 35.14 | 10.73 | 1500 | 38.73 | 11.45 | 1745 | 41.77 | 12.04 | 1995 | 44.67 | 12.59 |
| 1245 | 35.28 | 10.76 | | | | 1755 | 41.89 | 12.06 | 2000 | 44.72 | 12.60 |

## Simple Interest Table

| Time | 4% | 5% | 6% | 7% | 8% | Time | 4% | 5% | 6% | 7% | 8% |
|---|---|---|---|---|---|---|---|---|---|---|---|
| $1.00 1 month | $.003 | $.004 | $.005 | $.005 | $.006 | $100.00 4 days | $.045 | $.053 | $.066 | $.077 | $.089 |
| "  2 months | .007 | .008 | .010 | .011 | .013 | "  5 " | .056 | .069 | .082 | .097 | .111 |
| "  3 " | .010 | .013 | .015 | .017 | .020 | "  6 " | .067 | .083 | .100 | .116 | .133 |
| "  6 " | .020 | .025 | .030 | .035 | .040 | "  1 month | .334 | .416 | .500 | .583 | .667 |
| "  12 " | .040 | .050 | .060 | .070 | .080 | "  2 months | .667 | .832 | 1.000 | 1.166 | 1.333 |
| $100.00 1 day | .011 | .013 | .016 | .019 | .022 | "  3 " | 1.000 | 1.250 | 1.500 | 1.750 | 2.000 |
| "  2 days | .022 | .027 | .032 | .038 | .044 | "  6 " | 2.000 | 2.500 | 3.000 | 3.500 | 4.000 |
| "  3 " | .034 | .041 | .050 | .058 | .067 | "  12 " | 4.000 | 5.000 | 6.000 | 7.000 | 8.000 |

# Mathematical Formulas

### To find the CIRCUMFERENCE of a:
Circle—Multiply the diameter by 3.14159265 (usually 3.1416).

### To find the AREA of a:
Circle—Multiply the square of the diameter by .785398 (usually .7854).
Rectangle—Multiply the length of the base by the height.
Sphere (surface)—Multiply the square of the radius by 3.1416 and multiply by 4.
Square—Square the length of one side.
Trapezoid—Add the two parallel sides, multiply by the height and divide by 2.
Triangle—Multiply the base by the height and divide by 2.

### To find the VOLUME of a:
Cone—Multiply the square of the radius of the base by 3.1416, multiply by the height, and divide by 3.
Cube—Cube the length of one edge.
Cylinder—Multiply the square of the radius of the base by 3.1416 and multiply by the height.
Pyramid—Multiply the area of the base by the height and divide by 3.
Rectangular Prism—Multiply the length by the width by the height.
Sphere—Multiply the cube of the radius by 3.1416, multiply by 4 and divide by 3.

# Common Fractions Reduced to Decimals

| 8ths | 16ths | 32ds | 64ths | Decimal |
|---|---|---|---|---|
| | | | 1 | .015625 |
| | | 1 | 2 | .03125 |
| | | | 3 | .046875 |
| | 1 | 2 | 4 | .0625 |
| | | | 5 | .078125 |
| | | 3 | 6 | .09375 |
| | | | 7 | .109375 |
| 1 | 2 | 4 | 8 | .125 |
| | | | 9 | .140625 |
| | | 5 | 10 | .15625 |
| | | | 11 | .171875 |
| | 3 | 6 | 12 | .1875 |
| | | | 13 | .203125 |
| | | 7 | 14 | .21875 |
| | | | 15 | .234375 |
| 2 | 4 | 8 | 16 | .25 |
| | | | 17 | .265625 |
| | | 9 | 18 | .28125 |
| | | | 19 | .296875 |
| | 5 | 10 | 20 | .3125 |
| | | | 21 | .328125 |
| | | 11 | 22 | .34375 |
| 3 | 6 | 12 | 23 | .359375 |
| | | | 24 | .375 |
| | | | 25 | .390625 |
| | | 13 | 26 | .40625 |
| | | | 27 | .421875 |
| | 7 | 14 | 28 | .4375 |
| | | | 29 | .453125 |
| | | 15 | 30 | .46875 |
| | | | 31 | .484375 |
| 4 | 8 | 16 | 32 | .5 |
| | | | 33 | .515625 |
| | | 17 | 34 | .53125 |
| | | | 35 | .546875 |
| | 9 | 18 | 36 | .5625 |
| | | | 37 | .578125 |
| | | 19 | 38 | .59375 |
| | | | 39 | .609375 |
| 5 | 10 | 20 | 40 | .625 |
| | | | 41 | .640625 |
| | | 21 | 42 | .65625 |
| | | | 43 | .671875 |
| | 11 | 22 | 44 | .6875 |
| 6 | 12 | 24 | 45 | .703125 |
| | | | 46 | .71875 |
| | | | 47 | .734375 |
| | | | 48 | .75 |
| | | 25 | 49 | .765625 |
| | | | 50 | .78125 |
| | | | 51 | .796875 |
| | 13 | 26 | 52 | .8125 |
| | | | 53 | .828125 |
| | | 27 | 54 | .84375 |
| | | | 55 | .859375 |
| 7 | 14 | 28 | 56 | .875 |
| | | | 57 | .890625 |
| | | 29 | 58 | .90625 |
| | | | 59 | .921875 |
| | 15 | 30 | 60 | .9375 |
| | | | 61 | .953125 |
| | | 31 | 62 | .96875 |
| | | | 63 | .984375 |
| 8 | 16 | 32 | 64 | 1. |

# Multiplication and Division Table

A number in the top line (19) multiplied by a number in the last column on the left (18) produces the number where the top line and the side line meet (342), and so on throughout the table.

A number in the table (342) divided by the number at the top of that column (19) results in the number (18) at the extreme left; also, a number in the table (342) divided by the number (18) at the extreme left gives the number (19) at the top of the column, and so on throughout the table.

| 1 | 2 | 3 | 4 | 5 | 6 | 7 | 8 | 9 | 10 | 11 | 12 | 13 | 14 | 15 | 16 | 17 | 18 | 19 | 20 | 21 | 22 | 23 | 24 | 25 | 1 |
|---|---|---|---|---|---|---|---|---|---|---|---|---|---|---|---|---|---|---|---|---|---|---|---|---|---|
| 2 | 4 | 6 | 8 | 10 | 12 | 14 | 16 | 18 | 20 | 22 | 24 | 26 | 28 | 30 | 32 | 34 | 36 | 38 | 40 | 42 | 44 | 46 | 48 | 50 | 2 |
| 3 | 6 | 9 | 12 | 15 | 18 | 21 | 24 | 27 | 30 | 33 | 36 | 39 | 42 | 45 | 48 | 51 | 54 | 57 | 60 | 63 | 66 | 69 | 72 | 75 | 3 |
| 4 | 8 | 12 | 16 | 20 | 24 | 28 | 32 | 36 | 40 | 44 | 48 | 52 | 56 | 60 | 64 | 68 | 72 | 76 | 80 | 84 | 88 | 92 | 96 | 100 | 4 |
| 5 | 10 | 15 | 20 | 25 | 30 | 35 | 40 | 45 | 50 | 55 | 60 | 65 | 70 | 75 | 80 | 85 | 90 | 95 | 100 | 105 | 110 | 115 | 120 | 125 | 5 |
| 6 | 12 | 18 | 24 | 30 | 36 | 42 | 48 | 54 | 60 | 66 | 72 | 78 | 84 | 90 | 96 | 102 | 108 | 114 | 120 | 126 | 132 | 138 | 144 | 150 | 6 |
| 7 | 14 | 21 | 28 | 35 | 42 | 49 | 56 | 63 | 70 | 77 | 84 | 91 | 98 | 105 | 112 | 119 | 126 | 133 | 140 | 147 | 154 | 161 | 168 | 175 | 7 |
| 8 | 16 | 24 | 32 | 40 | 48 | 56 | 64 | 72 | 80 | 88 | 96 | 104 | 112 | 120 | 128 | 136 | 144 | 152 | 160 | 168 | 176 | 184 | 192 | 200 | 8 |
| 9 | 18 | 27 | 36 | 45 | 54 | 63 | 72 | 81 | 90 | 99 | 108 | 117 | 126 | 135 | 144 | 153 | 162 | 171 | 180 | 189 | 198 | 207 | 216 | 225 | 9 |
| 10 | 20 | 30 | 40 | 50 | 60 | 70 | 80 | 90 | 100 | 110 | 120 | 130 | 140 | 150 | 160 | 170 | 180 | 190 | 200 | 210 | 220 | 230 | 240 | 250 | 10 |
| 11 | 22 | 33 | 44 | 55 | 66 | 77 | 88 | 99 | 110 | 121 | 132 | 143 | 154 | 165 | 176 | 187 | 198 | 209 | 220 | 231 | 242 | 253 | 264 | 275 | 11 |
| 12 | 24 | 36 | 48 | 60 | 72 | 84 | 96 | 108 | 120 | 132 | 144 | 156 | 168 | 180 | 192 | 204 | 216 | 228 | 240 | 252 | 264 | 276 | 288 | 300 | 12 |
| 13 | 26 | 39 | 52 | 65 | 78 | 91 | 104 | 117 | 130 | 143 | 156 | 169 | 182 | 195 | 208 | 221 | 234 | 247 | 260 | 273 | 286 | 299 | 312 | 325 | 13 |
| 14 | 28 | 42 | 56 | 70 | 84 | 98 | 112 | 126 | 140 | 154 | 168 | 182 | 196 | 210 | 224 | 238 | 252 | 266 | 280 | 294 | 308 | 322 | 336 | 350 | 14 |
| 15 | 30 | 45 | 60 | 75 | 90 | 105 | 120 | 135 | 150 | 165 | 180 | 195 | 210 | 225 | 240 | 255 | 270 | 285 | 300 | 315 | 330 | 345 | 360 | 375 | 15 |
| 16 | 32 | 48 | 64 | 80 | 96 | 112 | 128 | 144 | 160 | 176 | 192 | 208 | 224 | 240 | 256 | 272 | 288 | 304 | 320 | 336 | 352 | 368 | 384 | 400 | 16 |
| 17 | 34 | 51 | 68 | 85 | 102 | 119 | 136 | 153 | 170 | 187 | 204 | 221 | 238 | 255 | 272 | 289 | 306 | 323 | 340 | 357 | 374 | 391 | 408 | 425 | 17 |
| 18 | 36 | 54 | 72 | 90 | 108 | 126 | 144 | 162 | 180 | 198 | 216 | 234 | 252 | 270 | 288 | 306 | 324 | 342 | 360 | 378 | 396 | 414 | 432 | 450 | 18 |
| 19 | 38 | 57 | 76 | 95 | 114 | 133 | 152 | 171 | 190 | 209 | 228 | 247 | 266 | 285 | 304 | 323 | 342 | 361 | 380 | 399 | 418 | 437 | 456 | 475 | 19 |
| 20 | 40 | 60 | 80 | 100 | 120 | 140 | 160 | 180 | 200 | 220 | 240 | 260 | 280 | 300 | 320 | 340 | 360 | 380 | 400 | 420 | 440 | 460 | 480 | 500 | 20 |
| 21 | 42 | 63 | 84 | 105 | 126 | 147 | 168 | 189 | 210 | 231 | 252 | 273 | 294 | 315 | 336 | 357 | 378 | 399 | 420 | 441 | 462 | 483 | 504 | 525 | 21 |
| 22 | 44 | 66 | 88 | 110 | 132 | 154 | 176 | 198 | 220 | 242 | 264 | 286 | 308 | 330 | 352 | 374 | 396 | 418 | 440 | 462 | 484 | 506 | 528 | 550 | 22 |
| 23 | 46 | 69 | 92 | 115 | 138 | 161 | 184 | 207 | 230 | 253 | 276 | 299 | 322 | 345 | 368 | 391 | 414 | 437 | 460 | 483 | 506 | 529 | 552 | 575 | 23 |
| 24 | 48 | 72 | 96 | 120 | 144 | 168 | 192 | 216 | 240 | 264 | 288 | 312 | 336 | 360 | 384 | 408 | 432 | 456 | 480 | 504 | 528 | 552 | 576 | 600 | 24 |
| 25 | 50 | 75 | 100 | 125 | 150 | 175 | 200 | 225 | 250 | 275 | 300 | 325 | 350 | 375 | 400 | 425 | 450 | 475 | 500 | 525 | 550 | 575 | 600 | 625 | 25 |
| | 2 | 3 | 4 | 5 | 6 | 7 | 8 | 9 | 10 | 11 | 12 | 13 | 14 | 15 | 16 | 17 | 18 | 19 | 20 | 21 | 22 | 23 | 24 | 25 | |

# Electrical Units
### Source: National Bureau of Standards

The watt is the unit expressing electrical power as horsepower (hp) represents power in mechanics; it is equal to the product of the volts (pressure) times amperes—(rate of flow). Thus, 2 volts times 2 amperes would give in a direct current circuit 4 watts.

A kilovolt is equal to 1,000 volts. A kilowatt is equal to 1,000 watts. A megawatt is equal to 1,000,000 watts.

Electrical energy is sold at so much per watt hour or more generally at a given amount per kilowatt hour—which means 1,000 watt hours.

This may represent 1 watt for 1,000 hours or 1,000 watts for 1 hour. 746 watts are equal to one horsepower or inversely 1 kilowatt (kw) is equal to about 1⅓ horsepower.

The horsepower represents the power required to lift a weight of 33,000 pounds 1 foot in 1 minute or 550 pounds 1 foot in 1 second.

The ohm is the unit of electrical resistance and represents the physical property of a conductor which offers a resistance to the flow of electricity, permitting just 1 ampere to flow at 1 volt of pressure.

# Foreign Weights and Measures

Exclusive of the Metric System, which is used by many foreign countries, and for which see page 584
Source: National Bureau of Standards, Department of Commerce

| Denominations | Where Used | American Equivalents | Denominations | Where Used | American Equivalents |
|---|---|---|---|---|---|
| Almude...... | Portugal........ | 4.423 gal | Kwan........ | Japan........... | 8.2673 lb |
| Ardeb....... | Egypt......... | 5.6189 bu | Last........ | Belgium, Holland. | 85.134 bu |
| Arratel (Libra) | Portugal........ | 1.012 lb | " | England.......... | 82.56 bu |
| Arroba...... | Argentina....... | 25.32 lb | " | Germany.......... | 2 metric tons |
| " ....... | Brazil.......... | 32.38 lb | " | Prussia.......... | 112.29 bu |
| " ....... | Cuba........... | 25.36 lb | League (land). | Paraguay........ | 4.633 acres |
| " ....... | Paraguay........ | 25.32 lb | Li............ | China........... | 1890 ft |
| " ....... | Venezuela....... | 25.40 lb | " | China........... | 0.01260 in |
| " (liquid) | Cuba, Spain and |  | " |  | (1-1000 ch'ih |
| | Venezuela...... | 4.263 gal | Libra (lb)..... | Argentina....... | 1.0128 lb |
| Arshine..... | U.S.S.R......... | 28 in | " | Central America.. | 1.014 lb |
| " ..(sq.) | U.S.S.R......... | 6.44 sq ft | " | Chile........... | 1.014 lb |
| Artel....... | Morocco........ | 1.12 lb | " | Cuba........... | 1.0143 lb |
| Baril....... | Argentina....... | 20.077 gal | " | Mexico.......... | 1.01467 lb |
| | and Mexico.... | 20.0787 gal | " | Peru............ | 1.0143 lb |
| Barile (wine).. | Malta.......... | 11.2 gal | " | Uruguay......... | 1.0127 lb |
| Berkovets.... | U.S.S.R......... | 361.128 lb | " | Venezuela....... | 1.0143 lb |
| Bongkal...... | Fed. Malay States. | 832 grains | Load, timber.. | England.......... | 50 cu ft |
| Bouw....... | Sumatra........ | 7,096.5 sq meter | Manzana..... | Nicaragua....... | 1.742 acres |
| Bu......... | Japan.......... | 0.12 inch | " | Costa Rica....... | 1.727 acres |
| Bushel..... | British......... | 1.03205 U. S. bu | " | Salvador......... | 1.727 acres |
| Caballeria.... | Cuba........... | 33,162 acres | Marco........ | Bolivia.......... | 0.507 lb |
| Caban (cavan) | Philippines...... | { 2.13 bu / 19.8 gal } | Maund....... | Bengal.......... | 82. 2/7 lb |
| Caffiso...... | Malta.......... | 5.40 gal | Mil.......... | Denmark........ | 4.68 miles |
| Candy...... | Bombay........ | 560 lb | " (geographic) | Denmark........ | 4.6036 miles |
| " ...... | India (Madras).. | 500 lb | Milla........ | Nicaragua....... | 1.1594 miles |
| Cantaro..... | Malta.......... | 175 lb | " | Honduras........ | 1.1493 miles |
| Carat (metric) | World......... | 3.086 grains | Mina........ | Greece.......... | 0.95 lb |
| Catty....... | China.......... | 1.333⅓ lb | Morgen...... | Germany......... | 0.63 acre |
| " (see Kin) | Japan.......... |  | Oka (Oke).... | Greece.......... | 2.82 lb |
| " ....... | Java, Malacca... | 1.36 lb | Oke.......... | Egypt........... | 2.7514 lb |
| " ....... | Siam........... | 2⅔ lb | " | Turkey.......... | 2.826 lb |
| " (stand). | Siam........... | 1.32 lb | Pic.......... | Egypt........... | 22.83 inches |
| " ....... | Sumatra........ | 2.12 lb | Picul........ | Borneo—Celebes. | 135.64 lb |
| Centaro..... | Central America.. | 4.2631 gal | " | China........... | 133⅓ lb |
| Centner..... | Brunswick....... | 117.5 lb | " | Java............ | 136.16 lb |
| " ..... | Bremen......... | 127.5 lb | " | Philippines...... | 139.44 lb |
| " ..... | Denmark, Norway | 110.23 lb | Pie.......... | Argentina....... | 0.9471 ft |
| " ..... | Germany........ | 113.44 lb | " | Spain........... | 0.91416 ft |
| " ..... | Sweden......... | 93.7 lb | Pik.......... | Turkey.......... | 27.9 inches |
| Chetvert.... | U.S.S.R......... | 5.957 bu | Pood........ | Russia.......... | 36.113 lb |
| Ch'ih....... | China.......... | 12.60 in | Pund........ | Denmark........ | 1.102 lb |
| " (metric) | China.......... | 39.37 in.==1 meter | Quart....... | British.......... | 1.20094 liq qt |
| Cho........ | Japan.......... | 2.451 acres | " | " | 1.03205 dry qt |
| Coomb....... | England......... | 4.1282 bu | Quarter..... | " | 8.256 bu |
| Coyan....... | Siam........... | 2,645.5 lb | Quintal..... | Argentina....... | 101.3 lb |
| Cuadra...... | Argentina....... | 4.2 acres | " | Brazil.......... | 129.54 lb |
| " ...... | Paraguay........ | 94.71 yd | " | Castile, Peru.... | 101.43 lb |
| " (sq.). | Paraguay........ | 1.85 acres | " | Chile........... | 101.43 lb |
| " ...... | Uruguay........ | 1.82 acres | " | Mexico.......... | 101.47 lb |
| Cwt. (hund. |  |  | Rotl........ | Palestine........ | 6.35 lb |
| weight).... | British......... | 112 lb | Sagene...... | U.S.S.R......... | 7 feet |
| Dessiatine.... | U.S.S.R......... | 2.6997 acres | Salm........ | Malta.......... | 8.26 bu |
| Drachma.... | Greece.......... | 49.38 grains | Se.......... | Japan.......... | 0.02451 acre |
| Dunam...... | Palestine........ | 0.22239 acre | Seer........ | India........... | 2 2-35 lb |
| Fanega (dry). | Ecuador, Salvador. | 1.5745 bu | Shaku....... | Japan.......... | 11.9303 in |
| " (dry). | Chile.......... | 2.75268 bu | Sho......... | Japan.......... | 1.91 liq qt |
| " (dry). | Guatemala, Spain. | 1.57744 bu | Skalpund.... | Sweden......... | 0.937 lb |
| " ..... | Mexico......... | 2.57716 bu | Stone....... | British......... | 14 lb |
| " (dry). | Spain.......... | 1.57501 bu | Sun......... | Japan.......... | 1.193 inches |
| " (liquid) | Spain.......... | 16 gal | Tael (Kuping). | China........... | 575.64 grs (troy) |
| " (dry)... | Trinidad & Tobago | 110 lbs. | Tan......... | Japan.......... | 0.25 acre |
| " (double) | Uruguay........ | 7.776 bu | To.......... | Japan.......... | 2.05 pecks |
| " (single) | Uruguay........ | 3.888 bu | Tonde (cereal) | Denmark........ | 3.9480 bu |
| " ..... | Venezuela....... | 3.334 bu | Tonde (land). | Denmark........ | 1.36 acres |
| Feddan...... | Egypt.......... | 1.04 acres | Tonne....... | France.......... | 2204.62 lb |
| Frail (raisins). | Spain.......... | 50 lb | Tsubo....... | Japan.......... | 35.58 sq ft |
| Frasco...... | Argentina....... | 2.51 liq qt | Ts'un....... | China........... | 1.26 inches |
| Frasila...... | Zanzibar........ | 35 lb | Tunna (wheat) | Sweden......... | 4.16 bu |
| Fuder....... | Luxemburg...... | 264.18 gal | Tunnland.... | " | 1.22 acres |
| Funt........ | U.S.S.R......... | 0.9028 lb | Vara........ | Argentina....... | 34.0944 inches |
| Gallon...... | British......... | 1.20094 U. S. gal | " | Costa Rica....... | 32.913 inches |
| Garniec..... | Poland......... | 1.0567 gal | " | Salvador......... | 32.913 inches |
| Jerib....... | Iran........... | 2.471 acres | " | Guatemala....... | 32.909 inches |
| Joch........ | Austria......... | 1.422 acres | " | Honduras........ | 32.874 inches |
| " ........ | Hungary........ | 1.067 acres | " | Nicaragua....... | 33.057 inches |
| Kantar...... | Egypt.......... | 99.05 lb | " | Chile and Peru... | 32.913 inches |
| " ...... | Morocco........ | 112 lb | " | Cuba........... | 33.386 inches |
| " ...... | Turkey.......... | 124.45 lb | " | Mexico.......... | 32.992 inches |
| Ken........ | Japan.......... | 5.97 feet | Vedro....... | U.S.S.R......... | 3.249 gal |
| Kin......... | Japan.......... | 1.32 lb | Verst....... | " | 0.663 mile |
| Klafter..... | Austria......... | 2.074 yd | Vloka....... | Poland......... | 41.50 acres |
| Klafter..... | Germany........ | 1.90 yd | Wey......... | Scotland........ | 40 bu |
| Koku....... | Japan.......... | 5.119 bu | " | Ireland......... | 40 bu |

The metric carat of 200 milligrams is now very generally in use. The word carat also is used to denote the proportion of alloy in a metal. Thus, pure gold is 24 carats fine.

## Knots and Miles: Nautical Measures
Source: Coast and Geodetic Survey (ESSA)

A **Knot** is a measure of speed, one knot being a speed of one nautical mile an hour.

The **U. S. Statute Mile** is 5,280 feet. In Europe, the old miles, which varied in length from about 3,300 feet to over 36,000 feet, have been mostly replaced, officially at least, by the kilometer, which equals 0.6214 statute mile or of 3,280.8 feet.

The **International Nautical Mile** is 1,852 meters or 6076.1155 feet; this distance is equivalent to 1.150779 statute miles.

**To convert statute miles into international** nautical miles multiply statute miles by 0.868976; to convert international nautical miles into statute miles multiply nautical miles by 1.150779 or 1 1/7.

A **Nautical, Geographic, or Sea Mile** at any place is considered, for purposes of navigation, to be equal to the length of one minute of the meridian at that place.

A **fathom**—6 feet, chiefly water depth.

A **cable**—100 fathoms or 600 feet or approximately 0.1 nautical mile (In U.S. Navy, 120 fathoms or 720 feet).

## Chemical Elements, Discoverers, Atomic Weights

Atomic weights, based on the exact number 12 as the assigned atomic mass of the principal isotope of carbon, carbon 12, are provided through the courtesy of the International Union of Pure and Applied Chemistry and Butterworth Scientific Publications.

For the radioactive elements with the exception of uranium and thorium, the mass number of either the isotope of longest half-life (marked with a star) or the better known isotope (marked with two stars) is given.

| Chemical element | Symbol | Atomic number | Atomic weight | Year discov. | Discoverer |
|---|---|---|---|---|---|
| Actinium | Ac | 89 | 227* | 1899 | Debierne |
| Aluminum | Al | 13 | 26.9815 | 1825 | Oersted |
| Americium | Am | 95 | 243* | 1944 | Seaborg, et al |
| Antimony | Sb | 51 | 121.75 | 1450 | Valentine |
| Argon | Ar | 18 | 39.948 | 1894 | Rayleigh, Ramsay |
| Arsenic | As | 33 | 74.9216 | 13th C. | Magnus |
| Astatine | At | 85 | 210* | 1940 | Corson, et al. |
| Barium | Ba | 56 | 137.34 | 1808 | Davy |
| Berkelium | Bk | 97 | 247* | 1949 | Thompson, Ghiorso, Seaborg |
| Beryllium | Be | 4 | 9.0122 | 1798 | Vauquelin |
| Bismuth | Bi | 83 | 208.980 | 15th C. | Valentine |
| Boron | B | 5 | 10.811a | 1808 | Davy |
| Bromine | Br | 35 | 79.904b | 1826 | Balard |
| Cadmium | Cd | 48 | 112.40 | 1817 | Stromeyer |
| Calcium | Ca | 20 | 40.08 | 1808 | Davy |
| Californium | Cf | 98 | 249** | 1950 | Thompson, et al. |
| Carbon | C | 6 | 12.01115a | B. C. | |
| Cerium | Ce | 58 | 140.12 | 1803 | Klaproth |
| Cesium | Cs | 55 | 132.905 | 1861 | Bunsen, Kirchoff |
| Chlorine | Cl | 17 | 35.453b | 1774 | Scheele |
| Chromium | Cr | 24 | 51.996b | 1797 | Vauquelin |
| Cobalt | Co | 27 | 58.9332 | 1735 | Brandt |
| Copper | Cu | 29 | 63.546b | B. C. | |
| Curium | Cm | 96 | 247* | 1944 | Seaborg, et al. |
| Dysprosium | Dy | 66 | 162.50 | 1886 | Boisbaudran |
| Einsteinium | Es | 99 | 254* | 1952 | Ghiorso, et al. |
| Erbium | Er | 68 | 167.26 | 1843 | Mosander |
| Europium | Eu | 63 | 151.96 | 1901 | Demarcay |
| Fermium | Fm | 100 | 257* | 1953 | Ghiorso, et al. |
| Fluorine | F | 9 | 18.9984 | 1771 | Scheele |
| Francium | Fr | 87 | 223* | 1939 | Perey |
| Gadolinium | Gd | 64 | 157.25 | 1886 | Marignac |
| Gallium | Ga | 31 | 69.72 | 1875 | Boisbaudran |
| Germanium | Ge | 32 | 72.59 | 1886 | Winkler |
| Gold | Au | 79 | 196.967 | B. C. | |
| Hafnium | Hf | 72 | 178.49 | 1923 | Coster, Hevesy |
| Helium | He | 2 | 4.0026 | 1895 | Ramsay |
| Holmium | Ho | 67 | 164.930 | 1879 | Cleve |
| Hydrogen | H | 1 | 1.00797a | 1766 | Cavendish |
| Indium | In | 49 | 114.82 | 1863 | Reich, Richter |
| Iodine | I | 53 | 126.9044 | 1811 | Courtois |
| Iridium | Ir | 77 | 192.2 | 1804 | Tennant |
| Iron | Fe | 26 | 55.847b | B. C. | |
| Krypton | Kr | 36 | 83.80 | 1898 | Ramsay, Travers |
| Lanthanum | La | 57 | 138.91 | 1839 | Mosander |
| Lawrencium | Lw | 103 | 256* | 1961 | Ghiorso, T. Sikkeland, A. E. Larsh, and R. M. Latimer |
| Lead | Pb | 82 | 207.19 | B. C. | |
| Lithium | Li | 3 | 6.939 | 1817 | Arfvedson |
| Lutetium | Lu | 71 | 174.97 | 1907 | Welsbach, Urbain |
| Magnesium | Mg | 12 | 24.312 | 1830 | Liebig, Bussy |
| Manganese | Mn | 25 | 54.9380 | 1774 | Gahn |
| Mendelevium | Md | 101 | 256* | 1955 | Ghiorso, et al. |
| Mercury | Hg | 80 | 200.59 | B. C. | |
| Molybdenum | Mo | 42 | 95.94 | 1782 | Hjelm |
| Neodymium | Nd | 60 | 144.24 | 1885 | Welsbach |
| Neon | Ne | 10 | 20.183 | 1898 | Ramsay, Travers |
| Neptunium | Np | 93 | 237* | 1940 | McMillan and Abelson |
| Nickel | Ni | 28 | 58.71 | 1751 | Cronstedt |
| Niobium (Form. Columbium) | Nb | 41 | 92.906 | 1801 | Hatchett |
| Nitrogen | N | 7 | 14.0067 | 1772 | Rutherford |
| Nobelium | No | 102 | 255* | 1958 | Ghiorso, et al. |
| Osmium | Os | 76 | 190.2 | 1804 | Tennant |
| Oxygen | O | 8 | 15.9994a | 1774 | Priestly, Scheele |
| Palladium | Pd | 46 | 106.4 | 1803 | Wollaston |
| Phosphorus | P | 15 | 30.9738 | 1669 | Brandt |
| Platinum | Pt | 78 | 195.09 | 1735 | Ulloa |
| Plutonium | Pu | 94 | 242** | 1940 | Seaborg, et al. |
| Polonium | Po | 84 | 210** | 1898 | P. and M. Curie |
| Potassium | K | 19 | 39.102 | 1807 | Davy |
| Praseodymium | Pr | 59 | 140.907 | 1885 | Welsbach |
| Promethium | Pm | 61 | 147** | 1945 | Glendenin and Marinsky |
| Protactinium | Pa | 91 | 231* | 1917 | Hahn and Meitner |
| Radium | Ra | 88 | 226* | 1898 | P. & M. Curie, Bemont |
| Radon | Rn | 86 | 222* | 1900 | Dorn |
| Rhenium | Re | 75 | 186.2 | 1925 | Noddack and Tacke |
| Rhodium | Rh | 45 | 102.905 | 1803 | Wollaston |
| Rubidium | Rb | 37 | 85.47 | 1861 | Bunsen, Kirchoff |
| Ruthenium | Ru | 44 | 101.07 | 1845 | Claus |
| Samarium | Sm | 62 | 150.35 | 1879 | Boisbaudran |
| Scandium | Sc | 21 | 44.956 | 1879 | Nilson |
| Selenium | Se | 34 | 78.96 | 1817 | Berzelius |
| Silicon | Si | 14 | 28.086a | 1823 | Berzelius |
| Silver | Ag | 47 | 107.868b | B. C. | |
| Sodium | Na | 11 | 22.9898 | 1807 | Davy |
| Strontium | Sr | 38 | 87.62 | 1790 | Crawford |
| Sulfur | S | 16 | 32.064a | B. C. | |
| Tantalum | Ta | 73 | 180.948 | 1802 | Eckeberg |
| Technetium | Tc | 43 | 99** | 1937 | Perrier and Segre |
| Tellurium | Te | 52 | 127.60 | 1782 | Von Reichenstein |
| Terbium | Tb | 65 | 158.924 | 1843 | Mosander |
| Thallium | Tl | 81 | 204.37 | 1861 | Crookes |
| Thorium | Th | 90 | 232.038 | 1828 | Berzelius |
| Thulium | Tm | 69 | 168.934 | 1879 | Cleve |

| Chemical element (continued) | Symbol | Atomic number | Atomic weight | Year discov. | Discoverer |
|---|---|---|---|---|---|
| Tin................................ | Sn | 50 | 118.69 | B. C. | |
| Titanium........................ | Ti | 22 | 47.90 | 1789 | Gregor |
| Tungsten (Alternate Wolfram) | W | 74 | 183.85 | 1783 | d'Elhujar |
| Uranium........................ | U | 92 | 238.03 | 1789 | Klaproth |
| Vanadium....................... | V | 23 | 50.942 | 1830 | Sefstrom |
| Xenon........................... | Xe | 54 | 131.30 | 1898 | Ramsay, Travers |
| Ytterbium....................... | Yb | 70 | 173.04 | 1878 | Marignac |
| Yttrium......................... | Y | 39 | 88.905 | 1794 | Gadolin |
| Zinc............................ | Zn | 30 | 65.37 | B. C. | |
| Zirconium....................... | Zr | 40 | 91.22 | 1789 | Klaproth |

aAtomic weights so designated are known to be variable because of natural variations in isotopic composition. The observed ranges are: hydrogen $\pm$ 0.00001; boron $\pm$ 0.003; carbon $\pm$ 0.00005; oxygen $\pm$ 0.0001; silicon $\pm$ 0.001; sulfur $\pm$ 0.003.

bAtomic weights so designated are believed to have the following experimental uncertainties: chlorine $\pm$ 0.001; chromium $\pm$ 0.001; iron $\pm$ 0.003; bromine $\pm$ 0.001; silver $\pm$ 0.001; copper $\pm$ 0.001.

## Density of Gases and Vapors
Source: National Bureau of Standards (Grams per liter)

| Gas | Wt. | Gas | Wt. | Gas | Wt. |
|---|---|---|---|---|---|
| Acetylene.............. | 1.171 | Ethylene............... | 1.260 | Methyl fluoride........ | 1.545 |
| Air.................... | 1.293 | Fluorine............... | 1.696 | Mono methylamine....... | 1.38 |
| Ammonia............... | .759 | Helium................. | .178 | Neon.................. | .900 |
| Argon.................. | 1.784 | Hydrogen............... | .090 | Nitric oxide........... | 1.341 |
| Arsene................. | 3.48 | Hydrogen bromide....... | 3.50 | Nitrogen (chem.)...... | 1.250 |
| Butane-iso............. | 2.60 | Hydrogen chloride...... | 1.639 | Nitrosyl chloride...... | 2.99 |
| Butane-n............... | 2.519 | Hydrogen iodide........ | 5.724 | Nitrous oxide.......... | 1.997 |
| Carbon dioxide......... | 1.977 | Hydrogen selenide...... | 3.66 | Oxygen................ | 1.429 |
| Carbon monoxide........ | 1.250 | Hydrogen sulfide....... | 1.539 | Phosphine............. | 1.48 |
| Carbon oxysulfide...... | 2.72 | Krypton................ | 3.745 | Propane............... | 2.020 |
| Chlorine............... | 3.214 | Methane................ | .717 | Silicon tetrafluoride.. | 4.67 |
| Chlorine monoxide...... | 3.89 | Methyl chloride........ | 2.25 | Sulfur dioxide......... | 2.927 |
| Ethane................. | 1.356 | Methyl ether........... | 2.091 | Xenon................. | 5.897 |

## Temperature Conversion Table
Source: National Bureau of Standards, U. S. Department of Commerce

The numbers in **bold face type** refer to the temperature either in degrees Centigrade or Fahrenheit which are to be converted. If converting from degrees Fahrenheit to Centigrade, the equivalent will be found in the column on the left, while if converting from degrees Centigrade to Fahrenheit the answer will be found in the column on the right.

**For temperatures not shown.** To convert Fahrenheit to Centigrade subtract 32 degrees and multiply by 5, divide by 9: to convert Centigrade to Fahrenheit, multiply by 9, divide by 5 and add 32 degrees.

| Centigrade | Fahrenheit | Centigrade | | Fahrenheit | Centigrade | | Fahrenheit |
|---|---|---|---|---|---|---|---|
| −273.2 | −459.7 | .......... | −17.8 | **0** | 32 | 35.0 | **95** | 203 |
| −184 | −300 | .......... | −12.2 | **10** | 50 | 36.7 | **98** | 208.4 |
| −169 | −273 | −459.4 | −6.67 | **20** | 68 | 37.8 | **100** | 212 |
| −157 | −250 | −418 | −1.11 | **30** | 86 | 43 | **110** | 230 |
| −129 | −200 | −328 | 4.44 | **40** | 104 | 49 | **120** | 248 |
| −101 | −150 | −238 | 10.0 | **50** | 122 | 54 | **130** | 266 |
| −73.3 | −100 | −148 | 15.6 | **60** | 140 | 60 | **140** | 284 |
| −45.6 | −50 | −58 | 21.1 | **70** | 158 | 66 | **150** | 302 |
| −40.0 | −40 | −40 | 23.9 | **75** | 167 | 93 | **200** | 392 |
| −34.4 | −30 | −22 | 26.7 | **80** | 176 | 121 | **250** | 482 |
| −28.9 | −20 | −4 | 29.4 | **85** | 185 | 149 | **300** | 572 |
| −23.3 | −10 | 14 | 32.2 | **90** | 194 | | | |

Water boils at 212° Fahrenheit at sea level. For every 550 feet above sea level, boiling point of water is lower by about 1° Fahrenheit. Methyl alcohol boils at 148° Fahrenheit. Average human oral temperature, 98.6° Fahrenheit. Water freezes at 32° Fahrenheit. Although "Centigrade" is still frequently used, the International Committee on Weights and Measures and the National Bureau of Standards have recommended since 1948 that this scale be called "Celsius."

## Factors and Prime Numbers

Factors are such numbers as multiplied together will produce a required number.
A Prime Number is one that cannot be resolved into two or more factors; or, it is a number exactly divisible only by itself and unity. A Composite Number is one that can be resolved into factors.

### TABLE OF PRIME NUMBERS FROM 1 TO 1000

| | | | | | | | | | |
|---|---|---|---|---|---|---|---|---|---|
| (*) | 59 | 139 | 233 | 337 | 439 | 557 | 653 | 769 | 883 |
| 2 | 61 | 149 | 239 | 347 | 443 | 563 | 659 | 773 | 887 |
| 3 | 67 | 151 | 241 | 349 | 449 | 569 | 661 | 787 | 907 |
| 5 | 71 | 157 | 251 | 353 | 457 | 571 | 673 | 797 | 911 |
| 7 | 73 | 163 | 257 | 359 | 461 | 577 | 677 | 809 | 919 |
| 11 | 79 | 167 | 263 | 367 | 463 | 587 | 683 | 811 | 929 |
| 13 | 83 | 173 | 269 | 373 | 467 | 593 | 691 | 821 | 937 |
| 17 | 89 | 179 | 271 | 379 | 479 | 599 | 701 | 823 | 941 |
| 19 | 97 | 181 | 277 | 383 | 487 | 601 | 709 | 827 | 947 |
| 23 | 101 | 191 | 281 | 389 | 491 | 607 | 719 | 829 | 953 |
| 29 | 103 | 193 | 283 | 397 | 503 | 613 | 727 | 839 | 967 |
| 31 | 107 | 197 | 293 | 401 | 509 | 617 | 733 | 853 | 971 |
| 37 | 109 | 199 | 307 | 409 | 521 | 619 | 739 | 857 | 977 |
| 41 | 113 | 211 | 311 | 419 | 523 | 631 | 743 | 859 | 983 |
| 43 | 127 | 223 | 313 | 421 | 541 | 641 | 751 | 863 | 991 |
| 47 | 131 | 227 | 317 | 431 | 643 | 757 | 877 | 997 |
| 53 | 137 | 229 | 331 | 433 | 547 | 647 | 761 | 881 |

(*) The number 1 is usually excluded.

## Bell Time on Shipboard
Source: Maritime Administration

| Time, A.M. | Time, A.M. | Time, A.M. | Time, P.M. | Time, P.M. | Time, P.M. |
|---|---|---|---|---|---|
| 1 Bell....12:30 | 1 Bell.... 4:30 | 1 Bell.... 8:30 | 1 Bell....12:30 | 1 Bell.... 4:30 | 1 Bell.... 8:30 |
| 2 Bells.... 1:00 | 2 Bells.... 5:00 | 2 Bells.... 9:00 | 2 Bells.... 1:00 | 2 Bells.... 5:00 | 2 Bells.... 9:00 |
| 3 " .... 1:30 | 3 " .... 5:30 | 3 " .... 9:30 | 3 " .... 1:30 | 3 " .... 5:30 | 3 " .... 9:30 |
| 4 " .... 2:00 | 4 " .... 6:00 | 4 " ....10:00 | 4 " .... 2:00 | 4 " .... 6:00 | 4 " ....10:00 |
| 5 " .... 2:30 | 5 " .... 6:30 | 5 " ....10:30 | 5 " .... 2:30 | 5 " .... 6:30 | 5 " ....10:30 |
| 6 " .... 3:00 | 6 " .... 7:00 | 6 " ....11:00 | 6 " .... 3:00 | 6 " .... 7:00 | 6 " ....11:00 |
| 7 " .... 3:30 | 7 " .... 7:30 | 7 " ....11:30 | 7 " .... 3:30 | 7 " .... 7:30 | 7 " ....11:30 |
| 8 " .... 4:00 | 8 " .... 8:00 | 8 " ....Noon | 8 " .... 4:00 | 8 " .... 8:00 | 8 " ....Midnight |

# Legal or Public Holidays in the United States in 1969

NOTE—See Index under Holidays for new Federal legislation.

Federal "Legal Public Holidays" are New Year's, Washington's Birthday, Memorial or Decoration Day, Independence Day, Labor Day, Veterans Day, Thanksgiving, and Christmas. The President and Congress designate only for the District of Columbia and Federal employees throughout the nation. Each State has jurisdiction over the holidays it will observe. They are designated either by legislative enactment or executive proclamation. There are no national holidays in the United States.

Christmas is observed by Christians the world over.

New Year's Day is observed by Christians and many other religions.

In Episcopal countries, the only other church days which are regular legal holidays are Good Friday, Easter Monday, and Whit Monday.

In Roman Catholic countries, the church days other than Christmas which are usually legal holidays are Epiphany, Ascension, Assumption, All Saints', and Immaculate Conception. In Latin American countries, it is usual to observe Good Friday and Corpus Christi.

In Lutheran countries, Epiphany, Annunciation, Ash Wednesday, Good Friday, Easter Monday, Ascension Day, Whit Monday, and Corpus Christi are holidays.

---

## CHIEF LEGAL OR PUBLIC HOLIDAYS

When a holiday falls on a Sunday it is usually observed on the following Monday.

**Saturday**—In most of the states banks close at noon or are closed all day.

**Jan. 1 (Wednesday)—New Year's Day.** All the states and possessions.

**Feb. 12 (Wednesday)—Lincoln's Birthday.** All the states, Puerto Rico and Virgin Islands, with the following exceptions—Ala., Fla., Ga., Hawaii, Idaho, Me., Mass., Miss., Mo., Nev., N. H., N. C., Okla., R. I., S. C., Tex., Va., (In Ark. a memorial day.)

**Feb. 22 (Saturday)—Washington's Birthday.** All the states and possessions (except Nev. and Okla.). (Presidents' Day in Hawaii; in Massachusetts celebrated on third Monday of Feb.)

**April 4—Good Friday.** Observed in all the states and possessions. A legal holiday in Conn., Del., Fla., Hawaii, Ill., Ind., La., Minn., N. J., N. D., Penn., Tenn., Guam, Canal Zone, Puerto Rico, and Virgin Islands.

**May 30 (Friday)—Memorial or Decoration Day.** All the states and possessions with the following exceptions—Ala., Ga., Miss., S. C. (In Florida, Memorial Day for Veterans of all Wars. In Massachusetts celebrated on last Monday in May.)

**July 4 (Friday)—Independence Day.** All the states and possessions.

**Sept. 1—Labor Day.** (First Monday in September.) All the states and possessions.

**Oct. 12 (Sunday)—Columbus Day.** All the states and Puerto Rico with the following exceptions—Alaska, Hawaii, Idaho, Maine, Miss., N. M., Nev., N. C., Okla., Ore., S. C., S. D., Tenn., Va., Wyo. (Discovery Day in Indiana and North Dakota; Landing Day in Wisconsin. In Arkansas and Oregon, a memorial day. Observed on the Saturday nearest Oct. 12 in Michigan.)

**Nov. 4—General Election Day.** (First Tuesday after the first Monday in November.) All the states, Puerto Rico, Virgin Islands, with the following exceptions—Ala., Alaska, Conn., D. of C., Ga., Idaho, Ky., Mass., Minn., Miss., Neb., Nev., N. M., Utah; Vt., Ohio, a half-holiday after 12 noon. (Observed usually only when presidential or general elections are held. Primary election days are observed in some states; see list of Days Usually Observed.)

**Nov. 11 (Tuesday)—Veterans, or Armistice Day.** All the states and possessions.

**Nov. 27—Thanksgiving Day.** (Always the fourth Thursday in November) All states and possessions. (The day after Thanksgiving is a legal holiday in Fla.)

**Dec. 25 (Thursday)—Christmas Day.** All the states and possessions (South Carolina and the Virgin Islands also observe Second Christmas Day, Dec. 26.)

## OTHER LEGAL OR PUBLIC HOLIDAYS

**Jan. 6—Three Kings' Day (Epiphany).** In Puerto Rico and Virgin Islands.

**Jan. 8—Battle of New Orleans.** In Louisiana.

**Jan. 11—De Hostos' Birthday.** In Puerto Rico.

**Jan. 17—Arbor Day. In Florida** (always third Friday in January).

**Jan. 19—Robert E. Lee's Birthday.** Ala., Ark., Fla., Ga., Ky., La., Miss., N. C., S. C., Tenn., Tex.; Lee-Jackson Day in Virginia.

**Jan. 20—Inauguration Day.** The District of Columbia, observed every fourth year since 1937.

**Jan. 30—Franklin D. Roosevelt Day.** Kentucky and Virgin Islands.

**Feb. 14—Admission Day.** In Arizona.

**Feb. 18—Mardi Gras (Shrove Tuesday).** Alabama; Florida; Louisiana.

**March 2—Texas Independence Day.** In that state.

**March 11—Town Meeting Day.** In Vermont (always first Tuesday in March).

**March 15—Andrew Jackson's Birthday.** In Tennessee.

**March 17—Evacuation Day.** In Boston and Suffolk County, Mass.

**March 22—Emancipation Day.** In Puerto Rico.

**March 25—Maryland Day.** In that state.

**March 26—Kuhio Day.** In Hawaii.

**March 30—Seward's Day.** In Alaska.

**March 31—Transfer Day.** Virgin Islands.

**April 2—Pascua Florida Day.** In that state.

**April 3—Holy Thursday.** Virgin Islands.

**April 7—Easter Monday.** North Carolina and Virgin Islands.

**April 12—Halifax Day.** In North Carolina.

**April 13—Thomas Jefferson's Birthday.** Ala., Mo., Va.

**April 14—Pan American Day.** In Florida.

**April 16—De Diego's Birthday.** In Puerto Rico.

**April 19—Patriots' Day.** Maine.

**April 21—Patriots Day.** In Massachusetts (always third Monday in April).

**April 21—San Jacinto Day.** In Texas.

**April 22—Arbor Day.** In Nebraska; **Oklahoma Day,** in that state.

**April 22—Fast Day.** New Hampshire (always fourth Monday in April).

**April 25—Arbor Day,** in Utah (always last Friday in April).

**April 26—Confederate Memorial Day.** Alabama, Florida, Georgia, Mississippi.

**May 10—Confederate Memorial Day.** North Carolina and South Carolina.

**May 20—Mecklenburg Day.** In North Carolina.

**May 26—Whit Monday.** Virgin Islands.

**June 3—Birthday of Jefferson Davis or \*Confederate Memorial Day.** In Alabama, Georgia, \*Kentucky, \*Louisiana, Mississippi, South Carolina, \*Tennessee and Texas. (In Arkansas a memorial day.)

**June 11—Kamehameha Day.** In Hawaii.

**June 14—Flag Day.** In Pennsylvania.

**June 17—Bunker Hill Day.** In Boston and Suffolk County, Mass.

**June 20—West Virginia Day,** in that state.

**June 22—Organic Act Day.** Virgin Islands.

**July 13—Nathan Bedford Forrest's Birthday.** In Tennessee.

**July 17—Muñoz Rivera's Birthday.** Puerto Rico.

**July 21—Liberation Day.** In Guam.

**July 24—Pioneer Day.** In Utah.

**July 25—Constitution Day.** In Puerto Rico; Supplication Day (beginning of hurricane season), Virgin Islands.

**July 27—Barbosa's Birthday.** In Puerto Rico.

**Aug. 4—Colorado Day.** In that state. (Always first Monday in August).

**Aug. 14—Victory Day.** In Rhode Island. **World War II Memorial Day.** In Arkansas.

**Aug. 16—Bennington Battle Day.** In Vermont.

**Aug. 30—Huey P. Long's Birthday.** In Louisiana.

**Sept. 9—Admission Day.** In California.

**Sept. 12—Defenders' Day.** In Maryland.

**Oct. 18—Alaska Day.** In that state.

**Oct. 25—Thanksgiving Day** (end of hurricane season). Virgin Islands.

**Oct. 31—Nevada Day.** In that state.

**Nov. 1—All Saints' Day.** In Louisiana; **Liberty Day** in the Virgin Islands.

Nov. 3—**Panama Independence Day.** Canal Zone.
Nov. 19—**Discovery Day.** In Puerto Rico.
Nov. 28—**Day After Thanksgiving.** In Florida.
Dec. 10—**Wyoming Day.** In that state.

### DAYS USUALLY OBSERVED

Not legal or public holidays:
**Air Force Day** (see Armed Forces Day).
**American Indian Day** (Sept. 26 in 1969). Always fourth Friday in September.
**Arbor Day.** Tree-planting day. First observed April 10, 1872, in Nebraska. Over one million trees were set out. Now observed in every state in the Union (except Alaska) and Puerto Rico. A legal holiday in Utah (always last Friday in April), in Florida (always third Friday in January), in Nebraska (April 22) and in Wyoming. (Date to be proclamed by Governor.)
**Armed Forces Day** (May 17 in 1969) Always third Saturday in that month, by Presidential proclamation. Replaced Army, Navy and Air Force Days. (Air Force Day was the 2nd Saturday in September; Army Day April 6th; Navy Day October 27, the birthday of Theodore Roosevelt. October is also the month in which the American Navy was founded (1775) by the Continental Congress.)
**Bill of Rights Day, Dec. 15.** By Act of Congress. Bill of Rights took effect Dec. 15, 1791.
**Bird Day.** Often observed with Arbor Day. In Iowa, March 21.
**Child Health Day** (Oct. 6 in 1969). Always first Monday in October, by Presidential proclamation.
**Citizenship Day, Sept. 17.** President Truman, Feb. 29, 1952, signed bill designating Sept. 17 as annual Citizenship Day. It replaced I Am An American Day, formerly 3rd Sunday in May and Constitution Day formerly Sept. 17.
**Easter Sunday** (April 6 in 1969).
**Elizabeth Cady Stanton Day, Nov. 12.** Birthday of pioneer leader for equal rights for women.
**Father's Day** (June 15 in 1969). Always third Sunday in that month.
**Feast of the Immaculate Conception, Dec. 8.** A memorial day in Guam.
**Flag Day, June 14.** By Presidential proclamation. It is a legal holiday in Pennsylvania.
**Forefathers' Day, Dec. 21.** Landing on Plymouth Rock, in 1620. Is celebrated with dinners by New England societies, especially "Down East."
**Frances Willard Day, Sept. 28.** Observed in Minnesota.
**Four Chaplains Memorial Day, February 3.**
**Gen. Douglas MacArthur Day, Jan. 26.** A memorial day in Arkansas.
**Gen. Pulaski Memorial Day, Oct. 11.** Native of Poland and Revolutionary War hero; died (Oct. 11, 1779) from wounds received at the siege of Savannah, Ga.
**Gen. von Steuben Memorial Day, Sept. 17.** By Presidential proclamation.
**Groundhog Day, Feb. 2.** A popular belief is that if the groundhog sees his shadow this day he returns to his burrow and winter continues 6 weeks longer.
**Halloween, Oct. 31.** The evening before All Saints or All-Hallows Day. Informally observed in the United States with masquerading and pumpkin-decorations. Traditionally an occasion for children to play harmless pranks (trick or treat, ticktack).
**Independence Sunday (June 29 in 1969).** The Sunday preceding the Fourth of July. Observed in Iowa.
**Leif Ericsson Day, Oct. 9.** Observed in Minnesota.
**Loyalty Day, May 1.** By act of Congress.
**May Day.** Popularly given to May 1st.
**Minnesota Day, May 11.** In that state.
**Mother's Day (May 11 in 1969).** Always second Sunday in that month.
**National Aviation Day, Aug. 19.** By Presidential proclamation.
**National Day of Prayer.** By Presidential proclamation each year on a day other than a Sunday.
**National Freedom Day, February 1.** To commemorate the signing, by President Lincoln, of the document to abolish slavery, Feb. 1, 1865. By Presidential proclamation.
**National Maritime Day, May 22.** First proclaimed 1935 in commemoration of the departure of the SS Savannah, from Savannah, Ga., on May 22, 1819, on the first successful transatlantic voyage under steam propulsion. By Presidential proclamation.
**Pan American Day, April 14.** In 1890 the First International Conference of American States, meeting in Washington, was held on that date. A resolution was adopted which resulted in the creation of the organization known today as the Pan American Union. By Presidential proclamation. A legal holiday in Florida.
**Poetry Day, Oct. 15.**
**Primary Election Day.** A legal holiday in Ark., Cal., Ind., Me., Mo., Mont., N. D., Ore., S. D., Tenn., W. Va., and Wis. Observed usually only when presidential or general elections are held.
**Reformation Day, Oct. 31.** Observed by Protestant groups.
**Sadie Hawkins Day,** first Saturday after November 11.
**St. Patrick's Day, March 17.** Observed by Irish Societies with parades.
**St. Valentine's Day, Feb. 14.** Festival of a martyr beheaded at Rome under Emperor Claudius. Association of this day with lovers has no connection with the saint and probably had its origin in an old belief that on this day birds begin to choose their mates.
**Susan B. Anthony Day, Feb. 15.** Birthday of a pioneer crusader for equal rights for women. Observed in Minnesota.
**United Nations Day, Oct. 24.** By Presidential proclamation, to commemorate founding of United Nations.
**Verrazano Day, April 17.** Observed in New York State, to commemorate the probable discovery of New York harbor by Giovanni da Verrazano in April, 1524.
**Wright Brothers Day, Dec. 17.** By Presidential designation, to commemorate first successful flight by Orville and Wilbur Wright, Dec. 17, 1903.
**Youth Honor Day, Oct. 31.** A day of observance in Iowa.

### WEEKS AND MONTHS

*The following list contains special weeks and months designed to call to the attention of the public an event of importance. The dates usually change each year at the discretion of the sponsoring organization.* Among the Weeks observed each year are American Art Week, American Education Week, American Heart Month, American Red Cross Fund Drive, Boys and Girls Week, Boy Scout Week, Brotherhood Week, Camp Fire Girls Birthday Week, Cancer Control Month, Christmas Seal Sale (sponsored by National Tuberculosis Association), Constitution Week, Fire Prevention Week, Girl Scout Week, Human Rights Week, Jewish Youth Week, March of Dimes (sponsored by National Foundation), Mutual Insurance Week, National Allergy Month, National Bible Week, National Boys' Club Week (sponsored by Boys Clubs of America), National Crime Prevention Week, National Drum Corps Week, National Employ the Physically Handicapped Week, National Heart Month, National Farm Safety Week, National 4-H Club Week, National Garden Week, National Highway Week, National Hospital Week, National Letter Writing Week, National Library Week, National Safe Boating Week, National Salvation Army Week, National School Lunch Week, National Stamp Collecting Week, National Transportation Week, National Wildlife Week (sponsored by National Wildlife Federation), Poppy Week (sponsored by Veterans of Foreign Wars of the U. S.), Red Cross Month, Save Your Vision Week, United Nations Week, United States-Canada Good Will Week (sponsored by the Kiwanis International), World Trade Week, and Youth Week (sponsored by United Christian Youth Movement).

# Old English Holidays

**Jan. 6.** TWELFTH DAY, or Twelfth-tide, sometimes called Old Christmas Day, the same as Epiphany (Feast of the Three Kings). It is celebrated in Spain as Christmas and in Italy as Epiphany (Befana Day). The previous evening is Twelfth Night. Since 1900 the Russian Orthodox Church has observed Jan. 7 as Christmas, inasmuch as 13 days instead of 12 now mark the difference between the old and the new or Gregorian calendar.
**Feb. 2.** CANDLEMAS: Festival of the Purification of the Virgin. Consecration of the lighted candles to be used in the church during the year.
**Feb. 14.** OLD CANDLEMAS: St. Valentine's Day.
**Mar. 25.** LADY DAY: Annunciation of the Virgin.
**April 6** is OLD LADY DAY.
**June 24.** MIDSUMMER DAY: Feast of the Nativity of John the Baptist.

**July 6** is OLD MIDSUMMER DAY.
**July 15.** ST. SWITHIN'S DAY. An old superstition: if rain fell it would continue forty days.
**Aug. 1.** LAMMAS DAY. Originally in England the festival of the wheat harvest. In the church the festival of St. Peter's miraculous deliverance from prison. Old Lammas Day is August 13.
**Sept. 29.** MICHAELMAS—Feast of St. Michael the Archangel.
**Nov. 1.** HALLOWMAS. All-Hallows or All Saints Day. Previous evening is Hallowmas Eve.
**Nov. 2.** ALL SOULS' DAY. Day of prayer for the souls of the dead.
**Nov. 11.** MARTINMAS. Feast of St. Martin. Old Martinmas is Nov. 23.
**Dec. 28.** CHILDERMAS. Holy Innocents' Day.

# UNITED STATES POPULATION
## 1970 Census Will Be Taken by Mail in Major Metropolitan Areas
Source: U. S. Bureau of the Census

**Plans for the 1970 Census**—The Bureau of the Census in 1968 continued to perfect its plans to take the 1970 Census of Population and Housing principally by mail. In late March 1970, letter carriers will deliver census forms to all households. In major metropolitan areas, with 60% of the total population, households will be asked to fill out the questionnaires and return them by mail on Apr. 1. Census workers will visit only households failing to return forms or failing to answer all questions. Elsewhere in the nation, census workers will visit every household to pick up questionnaires.

In 1968, the Bureau conducted "rehearsal" censuses in Sumter and Chesterfield Counties, South Carolina; Dane County, Wisconsin; and Trenton, New Jersey.

The 1970 Census will provide up-to-date information concerning numbers of people, their education, income, housing and other important factors for the nation, each state, county, city, metropolitan area, and for small segments of each area. The new information will be used to determine representation in government and to guide many programs aimed at meeting the needs of the American people.

**Total Population**—The total population of the United States including members of the armed services overseas on Apr 1, 1968, reached 200,658,000, according to Census Bureau estimates. This figure represented an increase of 20,651,000 over the Apr. 1, 1960, census count.

**Elements of Change**—The estimated rate of population growth in the United States in calendar year 1967 was 1.01%, a rate lower than any year since 1940. It compared with 1.15% in 1966 and 1.23 in 1965, and the low of 0.92 in 1940. The 1967 rate represents a continuing decline in the annual population growth rate that began in 1957—influenced primarily by the lowering of the birth rate.

**Deaths** numbered about 1,860,000 in 1967, slightly less than in 1966. Since 1960, the death rate has remained virtually unchanged at about 9.5 deaths per thousand people. Since 1954, the death rate has fluctuated between 9.3 and 9.6 per thousand with no definite trend appearing in the 1954-1967 period.

**Net civilian immigration**, averaging about 390,000 annually since 1960, has contributed about 14.7% to population growth in that period. This represented an increase over the 300,000 annual average for the 1950s. The largest net gain from this source since 1950 was in 1966, when immigration added 456,000 persons to the population and in 1967, when net immigration amounted to 444,000. These recent increases probably reflect the effect of the Immigration Act of 1965 and the U. S.-Cuban agreement on the transfer of Cuban refugees to the U. S., both of which took effect in 1965.

**Educational Attainments and Projections**—About 55,100,000 persons 5 to 34 years old were enrolled in school or college in the United States in the fall of 1966. This represents 30% of the total population.

Of these, about 32,900,000 were enrolled in grades 1 to 8, 13,400,000 in grades 9 to 12, and 6,100,000 in college. There were an additional 2,700,000 children in kindergarten excluding those below age 5.

The increase of enrollment in the last 6 years has been 8,800,000 or 19% over the 46,300,000 enrolled in October 1960. The rate of increase varied considerably by level of school. During this 6-year period, there was a 70% gain in college enrollments, 30% in high schools (grades 9 to 12) and 8% in elementary (grades 1 to 8).

Increased enrollment in elementary and secondary schools was due primarily to increases in the population 5 to 17 years old rather than in changes in the percent of persons enrolled. College and professional enrollments, however, reflect both an increase in the percent enrolled among persons aged 18 to 34, and an increase in the total population at these ages.

In May, 1967, Census Bureau population specialists revised school enrollment projections for 1985 upward from those anticipated just a year earlier. College enrollment, according to the new projections, would rise to between 9,700,000 and 11,800,000 by 1985 from the October, 1966 total of 6,100,000 depending upon assumptions about the proportions of the population enrolled in colleges. A year earlier, specialists projected college enrollment to a 1985 range of between 9,000,000 and 11,600,000 students. High school enrollment by 1985 would rise to a range of 13,800,000 to 17,300,000, the revised projections indicate. A year earlier, the projections for high school were in the range of 13,300,000 and 17,000,000. The 1966 total was 13,400,000. New projections for elementary and kindergarten call for a range of 35,400,000 to 47,700,000 pupils by 1985. A year earlier, the range was 34,300,000 to 46,600,000 pupils, and the total for October, 1966, was 35,600,000.

**Farm Population Drop Continues**—An average of 10,817,000 persons lived on farms in rural areas of the United States in 1967. Of the total U. S. population, 5.5% or 1 in 18, lived on a farm. The 1967 estimate of farm residents is 778,000 less than 1966.

Since 1960, when there were 15,600,000 farm residents, the farm population has declined approximately 4.8 million persons, an average annual decline of 5.3%.

**Family Income Higher**—Median income for all families in 1966 was $7,400, more than double the median figure of $3,000 in 1947. Despite rises in consumer prices the gain in real income over 1947 is about 69%.

Over the past 19 years, median family income has increased at an average annual rate of 5% in current dollars and 3% in constant dollars. This increase in family income parallels the expansion of general economic activity in the U. S. for the same period during which time the Gross National Product increased at an annual rate of about 6% in current dollars and 4% in constant dollars.

Families receiving income under $3,000 (in current dollars) have decreased from 49% in 1947 to 14% in 1966, and those receiving $10,000 or more have increased from 3% in 1947 to about 30% in 1966.

## ESTIMATED POPULATION OF THE UNITED STATES

| Date | Inc. armed forces overseas | Resident population | Date | Inc. armed forces overseas | Resident population |
|---|---|---|---|---|---|
| 1960 Census | 180,007,000 | 179,323,175 | July 1, 1965.. | 194,592,000 | 193,815,000 |
| July 1, 1961.. | 183,756,000 | 183,057,000 | July 1, 1966.. | 196,920,000 | 195,936,000 |
| July 1, 1962.. | 186,656,000 | 185,890,000 | July 1, 1967.. | 199,118,000 | 197,836,000 |
| July 1, 1963.. | 189,417,000 | 188,658,000 | July 1, 1968.. | 201,087,000 | 199,809,000 |
| July 1, 1964.. | 192,120,000 | 191,372,000 | | | |

# POPULATION OF THE UNITED STATES, 1950-1960

## By States, Regions, Geographic Divisions, Urban, Rural and Rank
Source: Bureau of the Census. *See States of the Union section for latest official estimates.*

| Region, division and state | April 1, 1960 census | April 1, 1950 census | Pct. + or − | 1960 census Urban | 1960 census Rural | Per cent urban | Rank 1960 | Rank 1950 |
|---|---|---|---|---|---|---|---|---|
| UNITED STATES.... | 179,323,175 | 151,325,798 | 18.5 | 125,268,750 | 54,054,425 | 69.9 | ...... | ...... |
| **REGIONS** | | | | | | | | |
| Northeast............ | 44,677,819 | 39,477,986 | 13.2 | 35,840,140 | 8,837,679 | 80.2 | ...... | ...... |
| North Central........ | 51,619,139 | 44,460,762 | 16.1 | 35,481,254 | 16,137,885 | 68.7 | ...... | ...... |
| South................ | 54,973,113 | 47,197,088 | 16.5 | 32,160,250 | 22,812,863 | 58.5 | ...... | ...... |
| West................. | 28,053,104 | 20,189,962 | 38.9 | 21,787,106 | 6,265,998 | 77.7 | ...... | ...... |
| **DIVISIONS;** | | | | | | | | |
| New England........ | 10,509,367 | 9,314,453 | 12.8 | 8,031,795 | 2,477,572 | 76.4 | | |
| Middle Atlantic...... | 34,168,452 | 30,163,533 | 13.3 | 27,808,345 | 6,360,107 | 81.4 | | |
| E. No. Central...... | 36,225,024 | 30,399,368 | 19.2 | 26,434,937 | 9,790,087 | 73.0 | | |
| W. No. Central...... | 15,394,115 | 14,061,394 | 9.5 | 9,046,317 | 6,347,798 | 58.8 | | |
| So. Atlantic........ | 25,971,732 | 21,182,335 | 22.6 | 14,851,516 | 11,120,216 | 57.2 | | |
| E. So. Central...... | 12,050,126 | 11,477,181 | 5.0 | 5,830,569 | 6,219,557 | 48.4 | | |
| W. So. Central...... | 16,951,255 | 14,537,572 | 16.6 | 11,478,165 | 5,473,090 | 67.7 | | |
| Mountain............ | 6,855,060 | 5,074,998 | 35.1 | 4,600,852 | 2,254,208 | 67.1 | | |
| Pacific............. | 21,198,044 | 15,114,964 | 40.2 | 17,186,254 | 4,011,790 | 81.1 | | |
| **NEW ENGLAND** | | | | | | | | |
| Maine............... | 969,265 | 913,774 | 6.1 | 497,114 | 472,151 | 51.3 | 36 | 35 |
| New Hampshire...... | 606,921 | 533,242 | 13.8 | 353,766 | 253,155 | 58.3 | 45 | 44 |
| Vermont............ | 389,881 | 377,747 | 3.2 | 149,921 | 239,960 | 38.5 | 47 | 46 |
| Massachusetts...... | 5,148,578 | 4,690,514 | 9.8 | 4,302,530 | 846,048 | 83.6 | 9 | 9 |
| Rhode Island........ | 859,488 | 791,896 | 8.5 | 742,897 | 116,591 | 86.4 | 39 | 36 |
| Connecticut........ | 2,535,234 | 2,007,280 | 26.3 | 1,985,567 | 549,667 | 78.3 | 25 | 28 |
| **MID. ATLANTIC** | | | | | | | | |
| New York............ | 16,782,304 | 14,830,192 | 13.2 | 14,331,925 | 2,450,379 | 85.4 | 1 | 1 |
| New Jersey.......... | 6,066,782 | 4,835,329 | 25.5 | 5,374,369 | 692,413 | 88.6 | 8 | 8 |
| Pennsylvania........ | 11,319,366 | 10,498,012 | 7.8 | 8,102,051 | 3,217,315 | 71.6 | 3 | 3 |
| **E. NO. CENTRAL** | | | | | | | | |
| Ohio............... | 9,706,397 | 7,946,627 | 22.1 | 7,123,162 | 2,583,235 | 73.4 | 5 | 5 |
| Indiana............. | 4,662,498 | 3,934,224 | 18.5 | 2,910,149 | 1,752,349 | 62.4 | 11 | 12 |
| Illinois............. | 10,081,158 | 8,712,176 | 15.7 | 8,140,315 | 1,940,843 | 80.7 | 4 | 4 |
| Michigan............ | 7,823,194 | 6,371,766 | 22.8 | 5,739,132 | 2,084,062 | 73.4 | 7 | 7 |
| Wisconsin........... | 3,951,777 | 3,434,575 | 15.1 | 2,522,179 | 1,429,598 | 63.8 | 15 | 14 |
| **W. NO. CENTRAL** | | | | | | | | |
| Minnesota.......... | 3,413,864 | 2,928,483 | 14.5 | 2,122,566 | 1,291,298 | 62.2 | 18 | 18 |
| Iowa............... | 2,757,537 | 2,621,073 | 5.2 | 1,462,512 | 1,295,025 | 53.0 | 24 | 22 |
| Missouri........... | 4,319,813 | 3,954,653 | 9.2 | 2,876,557 | 1,443,256 | 66.6 | 13 | 11 |
| North Dakota....... | 632,446 | 619,636 | 2.1 | 222,708 | 409,738 | 35.2 | 44 | 41 |
| South Dakota....... | 680,514 | 652,740 | 4.3 | 267,180 | 413,334 | 39.3 | 40 | 40 |
| Nebraska........... | 1,411,330 | 1,325,510 | 6.5 | 766,053 | 645,277 | 54.3 | 34 | 33 |
| Kansas............. | 2,178,611 | 1,905,299 | 14.3 | 1,328,741 | 849,870 | 61.0 | 28 | 31 |
| **SO. ATLANTIC** | | | | | | | | |
| Delaware........... | 446,292 | 318,085 | 40.3 | 292,788 | 153,504 | 65.6 | 46 | 47 |
| Maryland........... | 3,100,689 | 2,343,001 | 32.3 | 2,253,832 | 846,857 | 72.7 | 21 | 24 |
| Dist. of Col....... | 763,956 | 802,178 | −4.8 | 763,956 | ........ | 100.0 | ...... | ...... |
| Virginia............ | 3,966,949 | 3,318,680 | 19.5 | 2,204,913 | 1,762,036 | 55.6 | 14 | 15 |
| West Virginia...... | 1,860,421 | 2,055,552 | −7.2 | 711,101 | 1,149,320 | 38.2 | 30 | 29 |
| North Carolina..... | 4,556,155 | 4,061,929 | 12.2 | 1,801,921 | 2,754,234 | 39.5 | 12 | 10 |
| South Carolina..... | 2,382,594 | 2,117,027 | 12.5 | 981,386 | 1,401,208 | 41.2 | 26 | 27 |
| Georgia............ | 3,943,116 | 3,444,578 | 14.5 | 2,180,236 | 1,762,880 | 55.3 | 16 | 13 |
| Florida............ | 4,951,560 | 2,771,305 | 78.7 | 3,661,383 | 1,290,177 | 73.9 | 10 | 20 |
| **E. SO. CENTRAL** | | | | | | | | |
| Kentucky........... | 3,038,156 | 2,944,806 | 3.2 | 1,353,215 | 1,684,941 | 44.5 | 22 | 19 |
| Tennessee.......... | 3,567,089 | 3,291,718 | 8.4 | 1,864,828 | 1,702,261 | 52.3 | 17 | 16 |
| Alabama............ | 3,266,740 | 3,061,743 | 6.7 | 1,791,721 | 1,475,019 | 54.8 | 19 | 17 |
| Mississippi........ | 2,178,141 | 2,178,914 | ...... | 820,805 | 1,357,336 | 37.7 | 29 | 26 |
| **W. SO. CENTRAL** | | | | | | | | |
| Arkansas........... | 1,786,272 | 1,909,511 | −6.5 | 765,303 | 1,020,969 | 42.8 | 31 | 30 |
| Louisiana.......... | 3,257,022 | 2,683,516 | 21.4 | 2,060,606 | 1,196,416 | 63.3 | 20 | 21 |
| Oklahoma........... | 2,328,284 | 2,233,351 | 4.3 | 1,464,786 | 863,498 | 62.9 | 27 | 25 |
| Texas.............. | 9,579,677 | 7,711,194 | 24.2 | 7,187,470 | 2,392,207 | 75.0 | 6 | 6 |
| **MOUNTAIN** | | | | | | | | |
| Montana............ | 674,767 | 591,024 | 14.2 | 338,457 | 336,310 | 50.2 | 41 | 42 |
| Idaho.............. | 667,191 | 588,637 | 13.3 | 317,097 | 350,094 | 47.5 | 42 | 43 |
| Wyoming............ | 330,066 | 290,529 | 13.6 | 187,551 | 142,515 | 56.8 | 48 | 48 |
| Colorado........... | 1,753,947 | 1,325,089 | 32.4 | 1,292,790 | 461,157 | 73.7 | 33 | 34 |
| New Mexico......... | 951,023 | 681,187 | 39.6 | 626,479 | 324,544 | 65.9 | 37 | 39 |
| Arizona............ | 1,302,161 | 749,587 | 73.7 | 970,616 | 331,545 | 74.5 | 35 | 37 |
| Utah............... | 890,627 | 688,862 | 29.3 | 667,158 | 223,469 | 74.9 | 38 | 38 |
| Nevada............. | 285,278 | 160,083 | 78.2 | 200,704 | 84,574 | 70.4 | 49 | 49 |
| **PACIFIC** | | | | | | | | |
| Washington......... | 2,853,214 | 2,378,963 | 19.9 | 1,943,249 | 909,965 | 68.1 | 23 | 23 |
| Oregon............. | 1,768,687 | 1,521,341 | 16.3 | 1,100,122 | 668,565 | 62.2 | 32 | 32 |
| California......... | 15,717,204 | 10,586,223 | 48.5 | 13,573,155 | 2,144,049 | 86.4 | 2 | 2 |
| Alaska............. | 226,167 | 128,643 | 75.8 | 85,767 | 140,400 | 37.9 | 50 | 50 |
| Hawaii............. | 632,772 | 499,794 | 26.6 | 483,961 | 148,811 | 76.5 | 43 | 45 |

## Households by Type, Color of Head and Residence
Source: Bureau of the Census (Numbers in thousands)

| Type of household March 1967 | Total No. | Total % | Color of head White No. | White % | Nonwhite No. | Nonwhite % | Residence Nonfarm No. | Nonfarm % | Farm No. | Farm % |
|---|---|---|---|---|---|---|---|---|---|---|
| All households... | 58,845 | 100.0 | 52,826 | 100.0 | 6,018 | 100.0 | 55,910 | 100.0 | 2,934 | 100.0 |
| Primary families... | 48,791 | 82.9 | 43,934 | 83.2 | 4,856 | 80.7 | 46,097 | 82.4 | 2,693 | 91.8 |
| Husband-wife.... | 42,489 | 72.2 | 38,963 | 73.8 | 3,526 | 58.6 | 40,022 | 71.6 | 2,467 | 84.1 |
| Other male head. | 1,185 | 2.0 | 992 | 1.9 | 192 | 3.2 | 1,100 | 2.0 | 84 | 2.9 |
| Female head.... | 5,117 | 8.7 | 3,979 | 7.5 | 1,138 | 18.9 | 4,975 | 8.9 | 142 | 4.8 |
| Primary individuals | 10,054 | 17.1 | 8,892 | 16.8 | 1,162 | 19.3 | 9,813 | 17.6 | 241 | 8.2 |
| Male........... | 3,408 | 5.8 | 2,890 | 5.5 | 518 | 8.6 | 3,292 | 5.9 | 116 | 4.0 |
| Female......... | 6,646 | 11.3 | 6,002 | 11.4 | 644 | 10.7 | 6,521 | 11.7 | 125 | 4.3 |

# United States Population (Official Census), 1790-1880
### Source: Bureau of the Census

| State | 1810 | 1820 | 1830¹ | 1840¹ | 1850 | 1860 | 1870 | 1880 |
|---|---|---|---|---|---|---|---|---|
| Alabama | 9,046 | 127,901 | 309,527 | 590,756 | 771,623 | 964,201 | 996,992 | 1,262,505 |
| Arizona | | | | | | | 9,658 | 40,440 |
| Arkansas | 1,062 | 14,273 | 30,388 | 97,574 | 209,897 | 435,450 | 484,471 | 802,525 |
| California | | | | | 92,597 | 379,994 | 560,247 | 864,694 |
| Colorado | | | | | | 34,277 | 39,864 | 194,327 |
| Connecticut | 261,942 | 275,248 | 297,675 | 309,978 | 370,792 | 460,147 | 537,454 | 622,700 |
| Delaware | 72,674 | 72,749 | 76,748 | 78,085 | 91,532 | 112,216 | 125,015 | 146,608 |
| Dist. of Col. | 24,023 | 33,039 | 39,834 | 43,712 | 51,687 | 75,080 | 131,700 | 177,624 |
| Florida | | | 34,730 | 54,477 | 87,445 | 140,424 | 187,748 | 269,493 |
| Georgia | 252,433 | 340,989 | 516,823 | 691,392 | 906,185 | 1,057,286 | 1,184,109 | 1,542,180 |
| Idaho | | | | | | | 14,999 | 32,610 |
| Illinois | 12,282 | 55,211 | 157,445 | 476,183 | 851,470 | 1,711,951 | 2,539,891 | 3,077,871 |
| Indiana | 24,520 | 147,178 | 343,031 | 685,866 | 988,416 | 1,350,428 | 1,680,637 | 1,978,301 |
| Iowa | | | | 43,112 | 192,214 | 674,913 | 1,194,020 | 1,624,615 |
| Kansas | | | | | | 107,206 | 364,399 | 996,096 |
| Kentucky | 406,511 | 564,317 | 687,917 | 779,828 | 982,405 | 1,155,684 | 1,321,011 | 1,648,690 |
| Louisiana | 76,556 | 153,407 | 215,739 | 352,411 | 517,762 | 708,002 | 726,915 | 939,946 |
| Maine | 228,705 | 298,335 | 399,455 | 501,793 | 583,169 | 628,279 | 626,915 | 648,936 |
| Maryland | 380,546 | 407,350 | 447,040 | 470,019 | 583,034 | 687,049 | 780,894 | 934,943 |
| Massachusetts | 472,040 | 523,287 | 610,408 | 737,699 | 994,514 | 1,231,066 | 1,457,351 | 1,783,085 |
| Michigan | 4,762 | 8,896 | 31,639 | 212,267 | 397,654 | 749,113 | 1,184,059 | 1,636,937 |
| Minnesota | | | | | 6,077 | 172,023 | 439,706 | 780,773 |
| Mississippi | 40,352 | 75,448 | 136,621 | 375,651 | 606,526 | 791,305 | 827,922 | 1,131,597 |
| Missouri | 19,783 | 66,586 | 140,455 | 383,702 | 682,044 | 1,182,012 | 1,721,295 | 2,168,380 |
| Montana | | | | | | | 20,595 | 39,159 |
| Nebraska | | | | | | 28,841 | 122,993 | 452,402 |
| Nevada | | | | | | 6,857 | 42,491 | 62,236 |
| New Hampshire | 214,460 | 244,161 | 269,328 | 284,574 | 317,976 | 326,073 | 318,300 | 346,991 |
| New Jersey | 245,562 | 277,575 | 320,823 | 373,306 | 489,555 | 672,035 | 906,096 | 1,131,116 |
| New Mexico | | | | | 61,547 | 93,516 | 91,874 | 119,565 |
| New York | 959,049 | 1,372,812 | 1,918,608 | 2,428,921 | 3,097,394 | 3,880,735 | 4,382,759 | 5,082,871 |
| North Carolina | 555,500 | 638,829 | 737,987 | 753,419 | 869,039 | 992,622 | 1,071,361 | 1,399,750 |
| North Dakota | | | | | | | *2,405 | 36,909 |
| Ohio | 230,760 | 581,434 | 937,903 | 1,519,467 | 1,980,329 | 2,339,511 | 2,665,260 | 3,198,062 |
| Oklahoma | | | | | | | | |
| Oregon | | | | | 13,294 | 52,465 | 90,923 | 174,768 |
| Pennsylvania | 810,091 | 1,049,458 | 1,348,233 | 1,724,033 | 2,311,786 | 2,906,215 | 3,521,951 | 4,282,891 |
| Rhode Island | 76,931 | 83,059 | 97,199 | 108,830 | 147,545 | 174,620 | 217,353 | 276,531 |
| South Carolina | 415,115 | 502,741 | 581,185 | 594,398 | 668,507 | 703,708 | 705,606 | 995,577 |
| South Dakota | | | | | | *4,837 | *11,776 | 98,268 |
| Tennessee | 261,727 | 422,823 | 681,904 | 829,210 | 1,002,717 | 1,109,801 | 1,258,520 | 1,542,359 |
| Texas | | | | | 212,592 | 604,215 | 818,579 | 1,591,749 |
| Utah | | | | | 11,380 | 40,273 | 86,786 | 143,963 |
| Vermont | 217,895 | 235,981 | 280,652 | 291,948 | 314,120 | 315,098 | 330,551 | 332,286 |
| Virginia | 974,600 | 1,065,366 | 1,211,405 | 1,239,797 | 1,421,661 | 1,596,318 | 1,225,163 | 1,512,565 |
| Washington | | | | | | 11,594 | 23,955 | 75,116 |
| West Virginia | | | | | | | 442,014 | 618,457 |
| Wisconsin | | | | 30,945 | 305,391 | 775,881 | 1,054,670 | 1,315,497 |
| Wyoming | | | | | | | 9,118 | 20,789 |
| **Total U. S.** | **7,239,881** | **9,638,453** | **12,866,020** | **17,069,453** | **23,191,876** | **31,443,321** | **38,558,371** | **50,189,209** |

*1860 figure is for Dakota Territory; 1870 figures are for parts of Dakota Territory.
¹U. S. total includes persons (5,318 in 1830 and 6,100 in 1840) on public ships in the service of the United States not credited to any region, division, or state.
1790—Connecticut 237,946; Delaware 59,096; Georgia 82,548; Kentucky 73,677; Maine 96,540; Maryland 319,728; Massachusetts 378,787; New Hampshire 141,885; New Jersey 184,139; New York 340,120; North Carolina 393,751; Pennsylvania 434,373; Rhode Island 68,825; South Carolina 249,073; Tennessee 35,691; Vermont 85,425; Virginia 747,610. Total 3,929,214.
1800—Connecticut 251,002; Delaware 64,273; Dist. of Col. 14,093; Georgia 162,686; Indiana 5,641; Kentucky 220,955; Maine 151,719; Maryland 341,548; Massachusetts 422,845; Mississippi 8,850; New Hampshire 183,858; New Jersey 211,149; New York 589,051; North Carolina 478,103; Ohio 45,365; Pennsylvania 602,365; Rhode Island 69,122; South Carolina 345,591; Tennessee 105,602; Vermont 154,465; Virginia 880,200. Total 5,308,483.

# United States Area and Population: 1790 to 1960
### Source: Bureau of the Census
Area figures represent area on indicated date including in some cases considerable areas not then organized or settled, and not covered by the census. Area figures have been adjusted to bring them into agreement with remeasurements made in 1940.

| Census date | Area (square miles) | | | Population | | | |
|---|---|---|---|---|---|---|---|
| | Gross | Land | Water | Number | Per sq. mile of land area | Increase over preceding census No. | % |
| **Conterminous U.S.¹** | | | | | | | |
| 1790 (Aug. 2) | 888,811 | 864,746 | 24,065 | 3,929,214 | 4.5 | (X) | (X) |
| 1800 (Aug. 4) | 888,811 | 864,746 | 24,065 | 5,308,483 | 6.1 | 1,379,269 | 35.1 |
| 1810 (Aug. 6) | 1,716,003 | 1,681,828 | 34,115 | 7,239,881 | 4.3 | 1,931,398 | 36.4 |
| 1820 (Aug. 7) | 1,788,006 | 1,749,462 | 38,544 | 9,638,453 | 5.5 | 2,398,572 | 33.1 |
| 1830 (June 1) | 1,788,006 | 1,749,462 | 38,544 | 12,866,020 | 7.4 | 3,227,567 | 33.5 |
| 1840 (June 1) | 1,788,006 | 1,749,462 | 38,544 | 17,069,453 | 9.8 | 4,203,433 | 32.7 |
| 1850 (June 1) | 2,992,747 | 2,940,042 | 52,705 | 23,191,876 | 7.9 | 6,122,423 | 35.9 |
| 1860 (June 1) | 3,022,387 | 2,969,640 | 52,747 | 31,443,321 | 10.6 | 8,251,445 | 35.6 |
| 1870 (June 1) | 3,022,387 | 2,969,640 | 52,747 | ²39,818,449 | ²13.4 | 8,375,128 | 26.6 |
| 1880 (June 1) | 3,022,387 | 2,969,640 | 52,747 | 50,155,783 | 16.9 | 10,337,334 | 26.0 |
| 1890 (June 1) | 3,022,387 | 2,969,640 | 52,747 | 62,947,714 | 21.2 | 12,791,931 | 25.5 |
| 1900 (June 1) | 3,022,387 | 2,969,834 | 52,553 | 75,994,575 | 25.6 | 13,046,861 | 20.7 |
| 1910 (Apr. 15) | 3,022,387 | 2,969,565 | 52,822 | 91,972,266 | 31.0 | 15,977,691 | 21.0 |
| 1920 (Jan. 1) | 3,022,387 | 2,969,451 | 52,936 | 105,710,620 | 35.6 | 13,738,354 | 14.9 |
| 1930 (Apr. 1) | 3,022,387 | 2,977,128 | 45,259 | 122,775,046 | 41.2 | 17,064,426 | 16.1 |
| 1940 (Apr. 1) | 3,022,387 | 2,977,128 | 45,259 | 131,669,275 | 44.2 | 8,894,229 | 7.2 |
| 1950 (Apr. 1) | 3,022,387 | 2,974,726 | 47,661 | 150,697,361 | 50.7 | 19,028,086 | 14.5 |
| 1960 (Apr. 1) | 3,022,387 | 2,971,494 | 50,893 | 178,464,236 | 60.1 | 27,766,875 | 18.4 |
| 1950 (Apr. 1)³ | 3,615,211 | 3,552,206 | 63,005 | 151,325,798 | 42.6 | 19,161,229 | 14.5 |
| 1960 (Apr. 1)³ | 3,615,211 | 3,548,974 | 66,237 | 179,323,175 | 50.5 | 27,997,377 | 18.5 |

X Not applicable. ¹Excludes Alaska and Hawaii. ²Revised to include adjustments for underenumeration in Southern States; unrevised number is 38,558,371. ³Includes Alaska and Hawaii.

# United States Population (Official Census), 1890-1960

Source: Bureau of the Census

| State | 1890 | 1900 | 1910 | 1920 | 1930 | 1940 | 1950 | 1960 |
|---|---|---|---|---|---|---|---|---|
| Alabama.... | 1,513,401 | 1,828,697 | 2,138,093 | 2,348,174 | 2,646,248 | 2,832,961 | 3,061,743 | 3,266,740 |
| Alaska..... | | | | | | | | 226,167 |
| Arizona.... | 88,243 | 122,931 | 204,354 | 334,162 | 435,573 | 499,261 | 749,587 | 1,302,161 |
| Arkansas... | 1,128,211 | 1,311,564 | 1,574,449 | 1,752,204 | 1,854,482 | 1,949,387 | 1,909,511 | 1,786,272 |
| California.. | 1,213,398 | 1,485,053 | 2,377,549 | 3,426,861 | 5,677,251 | 6,907,387 | 10,586,223 | 15,717,204 |
| Colorado... | 413,249 | 539,700 | 799,024 | 939,629 | 1,035,791 | 1,123,296 | 1,325,089 | 1,753,947 |
| Connecticut. | 746,258 | :908,420 | 1,114,756 | 1,380,631 | 1,606,903 | 1,709,242 | 2,007,280 | 2,535,234 |
| Delaware... | 168,493 | 184,735 | 202,322 | 223,003 | 238,380 | 266,505 | 318,085 | 446,292 |
| Dist. of Col.. | 230,392 | 278,718 | 331,069 | 437,571 | 486,869 | 663,091 | 802,178 | 763,956 |
| Florida..... | 391,422 | 528,542 | 752,619 | 968,470 | 1,468,211 | 1,897,414 | 2,771,305 | 4,951,560 |
| Georgia.... | 1,837,353 | 2,216,331 | 2,609,121 | 2,895,832 | 2,908,506 | 3,123,723 | 3,444,578 | 3,943,116 |
| Hawaii..... | | | | | | | | 632,772 |
| Idaho...... | 88,548 | 161,772 | 325,594 | 431,866 | 445,032 | 524,873 | 588,637 | 667,191 |
| Illinois.... | 3,826,352 | 4,821,550 | 5,638,591 | 6,485,280 | 7,630,654 | 7,897,241 | 8,712,176 | 10,081,158 |
| Indiana.... | 2,192,404 | 2,516,462 | 2,700,876 | 2,930,390 | 3,238,503 | 3,427,796 | 3,934,224 | 4,662,498 |
| Iowa...... | 1,912,297 | 2,231,853 | 2,224,771 | 2,404,021 | 2,470,939 | 2,538,268 | 2,621,073 | 2,757,537 |
| Kansas.... | 1,428,108 | 1,470,495 | 1,690,949 | 1,769,257 | 1,880,999 | 1,801,028 | 1,905,299 | 2,178,611 |
| Kentucky.. | 1,858,635 | 2,147,174 | 2,289,905 | 2,416,630 | 2,614,589 | 2,845,627 | 2,944,806 | 3,038,156 |
| Louisiana... | 1,118,588 | 1,381,625 | 1,656,388 | 1,798,509 | 2,101,593 | 2,363,880 | 2,683,516 | 3,257,022 |
| Maine..... | 661,086 | 694,466 | 742,371 | 768,014 | 797,423 | 847,226 | 913,774 | 969,265 |
| Maryland... | 1,042,390 | 1,188,044 | 1,295,346 | 1,449,661 | 1,631,526 | 1,821,244 | 2,343,001 | 3,100,689 |
| Massach'ts. | 2,238,947 | 2,805,346 | 3,366,416 | 3,852,356 | 4,249,614 | 4,316,721 | 4,690,514 | 5,148,578 |
| Michigan... | 2,093,890 | 2,420,982 | 2,810,173 | 3,668,412 | 4,842,325 | 5,256,106 | 6,371,766 | 7,823,194 |
| Minnesota.. | 1,310,283 | 1,751,394 | 2,075,708 | 2,387,125 | 2,563,953 | 2,792,300 | 2,982,483 | 3,413,864 |
| Mississippi.. | 1,289,600 | 1,551,270 | 1,797,114 | 1,790,618 | 2,009,821 | 2,183,796 | 2,178,914 | 2,178,141 |
| Missouri.... | 2,679,185 | 3,106,665 | 3,293,335 | 3,404,055 | 3,629,367 | 3,784,664 | 3,954,653 | 4,319,813 |
| Montana.... | 142,924 | 243,329 | 376,053 | 548,889 | 537,606 | 559,456 | 591,024 | 674,767 |
| Nebraska... | 1,062,656 | 1,066,300 | 1,192,214 | 1,296,372 | 1,377,963 | 1,315,834 | 1,325,510 | 1,411,330 |
| Nevada.... | 47,355 | 42,335 | 81,875 | 77,407 | 91,058 | 110,247 | 160,083 | 285,278 |
| N. Hamp... | 376,530 | 411,588 | 430,572 | 443,083 | 465,293 | 491,524 | 533,242 | 606,921 |
| New Jersey. | 1,444,933 | 1,883,669 | 2,537,167 | 3,155,900 | 4,041,334 | 4,160,165 | 4,835,329 | 6,066,782 |
| New Mexico | 160,282 | 195,310 | 327,301 | 360,350 | 423,317 | 531,818 | 681,187 | 951,023 |
| New York.. | 6,003,174 | 7,268,894 | 9,113,614 | 10,385,227 | 12,588,066 | 13,479,142 | 14,830,192 | 16,782,304 |
| No. Carolina | 1,617,949 | 1,893,810 | 2,206,287 | 2,559,123 | 3,170,276 | 3,571,623 | 4,061,929 | 4,556,155 |
| No. Dakota. | 190,983 | 319,146 | 577,056 | 646,872 | 680,845 | 641,935 | 619,636 | 632,446 |
| Ohio...... | 3,672,329 | 4,157,545 | 4,767,121 | 5,759,394 | 6,646,697 | 6,907,612 | 7,946,627 | 9,706,397 |
| Oklahoma... | 258,657 | 790,391 | 1,657,155 | 2,028,283 | 2,396,040 | 2,336,434 | 2,233,351 | 2,328,284 |
| Oregon..... | 317,704 | 413,536 | 672,765 | 783,389 | 953,786 | 1,089,684 | 1,521,341 | 1,768,687 |
| Penn..... | 5,258,113 | 6,302,115 | 7,665,111 | 8,720,017 | 9,631,350 | 9,900,180 | 10,498,012 | 11,319,366 |
| Rhode Is... | 345,506 | 428,556 | 542,610 | 604,397 | 687,497 | 713,346 | 791,896 | 859,488 |
| So. Carolina. | 1,151,149 | 1,340,316 | 1,515,400 | 1,683,724 | 1,738,765 | 1,899,804 | 2,117,027 | 2,382,594 |
| So. Dakota.. | 348,600 | 401,570 | 583,888 | 636,547 | 692,849 | 642,961 | 652,740 | 680,514 |
| Tennessee... | 1,767,518 | 2,020,616 | 2,184,789 | 2,337,885 | 2,616,556 | 2,915,841 | 3,291,718 | 3,567,089 |
| Texas...... | 2,235,527 | 3,048,710 | 3,896,542 | 4,663,228 | 5,824,715 | 6,414,824 | 7,711,194 | 9,579,677 |
| Utah...... | 210,779 | 276,749 | 373,351 | 449,396 | 507,847 | 550,310 | 688,862 | 890,627 |
| Vermont.... | 332,422 | 343,641 | 355,956 | 352,428 | 359,611 | 359,231 | 377,747 | 389,881 |
| Virginia.... | 1,655,980 | 1,854,184 | 2,061,612 | 2,309,187 | 2,421,851 | 2,677,773 | 3,318,680 | 3,966,949 |
| Washington. | 357,232 | 518,103 | 1,141,990 | 1,356,621 | 1,563,396 | 1,736,191 | 2,378,962 | 2,853,214 |
| W. Virginia. | 762,794 | 958,800 | 1,221,119 | 1,463,701 | 1,729,205 | 1,901,974 | 2,005,553 | 1,860,421 |
| Wisconsin.. | 1,693,330 | 2,069,042 | 2,333,860 | 2,632,067 | 2,939,006 | 3,137,587 | 3,434,575 | 3,951,777 |
| Wyoming... | 62,555 | 92,531 | 145,965 | 194,402 | 225,565 | 250,742 | 290,529 | 330,066 |
| **Tot. U. S...** | **62,947,714** | **75,994,575** | **91,972,266** | **105,710,620** | **122,775,046** | **131,669,275** | **150,697,361** | **179,323,175** |

## U. S. Center of Population, 1790 to 1960

Source: Bureau of the Census

**Center of population** is that point which may be considered as center of population gravity of the U. S. or that point upon which the U. S. would balance if it were a rigid plane without weight and the population distributed thereon with each individual being assumed to have equal weight and to exert an influence on a central point proportional to his distance from that point.

| Year | North latitude | West longitude | Approximate location |
|---|---|---|---|
| **CONTERMINOUS U.S.[1]** | | | |
| 1790............ | 39 16 30 | 76 11 12 | 23 miles east of Baltimore, Md. |
| 1800............ | 39 16 6 | 76 56 30 | 18 miles west of Baltimore, Md. |
| 1810............ | 39 11 30 | 77 37 12 | 40 miles northwest by west of Washington, D. C. (in Virginia). |
| 1820............ | 39 5 42 | 78 33 0 | 16 miles east of Moorefield, W. Va.[2] |
| 1830............ | 38 57 54 | 79 16 54 | 19 miles west-southwest of Moorefield, W. Va.[2] |
| 1840............ | 39 2 0 | 80 18 0 | 16 miles south of Clarksburg, W. Va.[2] |
| 1850............ | 38 59 0 | 81 19 0 | 23 miles southeast of Parkersburg, W. Va.[2] |
| 1860............ | 39 0 24 | 82 48 48 | 20 miles south by east of Chillicothe, Ohio. |
| 1870............ | 39 12 0 | 83 35 42 | 48 miles east by north of Cincinnati, Ohio. |
| 1880............ | 39 4 8 | 84 39 40 | 8 miles west by south of Cincinnati, Ohio (in Ky.) |
| 1890............ | 39 11 56 | 85 32 53 | 20 miles east of Columbus, Ind. |
| 1900............ | 39 9 36 | 85 48 54 | 6 miles southeast of Columbus, Ind. |
| 1910............ | 39 10 12 | 86 32 20 | In the city of Bloomington, Ind. |
| 1920............ | 39 10 21 | 86 43 15 | 8 miles south-southeast of Spencer, Owen County, Ind. |
| 1930............ | 39 3 45 | 87 8 6 | 3 miles northeast of Linton, Greene County, Ind. |
| 1940............ | 38 56 54 | 87 22 35 | 2 miles southeast by east of Carlisle, Haddon township, Sullivan County, Ind. |
| 1950............ | 38 50 21 | 88 9 33 | 8 miles north-northwest of Olney, Richland County, Ill. |
| 1960............ | 38 37 57 | 88 52 23 | 4 miles east of Salem in Marion County, Ill. |
| **UNITED STATES[3]** | | | |
| 1950............ | 38 48 15 | 88 22 8 | About 3 miles northeast of Louisville, in Clay County, Ill. |
| 1960............ | 38 35 58 | 89 12 35 | 6½ miles northwest of Centralia, Ill., and approximately 50 miles east of East St. Louis, Ill. |

[1]Excludes Alaska and Hawaii.
[2]West Virginia was set off from Virginia Dec. 31, 1862, and admitted as a State June 20, 1863.
[3]Includes Alaska and Hawaii.

## U. S. Population, White and Nonwhite, by States

Source: Bureau of the Census (Census of 1960)

| State | All classes | | White | | Nonwhite | |
|---|---|---|---|---|---|---|
| | Male | Female | Male | Female | Male | Female |
| Alabama | 1,591,709 | 1,675,031 | 1,124,061 | 1,159,548 | 467,648 | 515,483 |
| Alaska | 128,811 | 97,356 | 101,194 | 73,352 | 27,617 | 24,004 |
| Arizona | 654,928 | 647,233 | 587,872 | 581,645 | 67,056 | 65,588 |
| Arkansas | 878,987 | 907,285 | 690,762 | 704,941 | 188,225 | 202,344 |
| California | 7,836,707 | 7,880,497 | 7,193,094 | 7,262,136 | 643,613 | 618,361 |
| Colorado | 870,467 | 883,480 | 843,575 | 857,125 | 26,892 | 26,355 |
| Connecticut | 1,244,229 | 1,291,005 | 1,189,653 | 1,234,163 | 54,576 | 56,842 |
| Delaware | 221,136 | 225,156 | 190,186 | 194,141 | 30,950 | 31,015 |
| Dist. of Col | 358,171 | 405,785 | 158,124 | 187,139 | 200,047 | 218,646 |
| Florida | 2,436,783 | 2,514,777 | 2,000,593 | 2,063,288 | 436,190 | 451,489 |
| Georgia | 1,925,913 | 2,017,203 | 1,391,735 | 1,425,488 | 534,178 | 591,715 |
| Hawaii | 338,173 | 294,599 | 112,915 | 89,315 | 225,258 | 205,284 |
| Idaho | 338,421 | 328,770 | 333,298 | 324,085 | 5,123 | 4,685 |
| Illinois | 4,952,866 | 5,128,292 | 4,435,687 | 4,574,565 | 517,179 | 553,727 |
| Indiana | 2,298,738 | 2,363,760 | 2,165,509 | 2,223,045 | 133,229 | 140,715 |
| Iowa | 1,359,047 | 1,398,490 | 1,344,933 | 1,383,776 | 14,114 | 14,714 |
| Kansas | 1,081,377 | 1,097,234 | 1,031,409 | 1,047,257 | 49,968 | 49,977 |
| Kentucky | 1,508,448 | 1,529,708 | 1,401,904 | 1,418,179 | 106,544 | 111,529 |
| Louisiana | 1,592,254 | 1,664,768 | 1,090,306 | 1,121,409 | 501,948 | 543,359 |
| Maine | 479,054 | 490,211 | 475,682 | 487,609 | 3,372 | 2,602 |
| Maryland | 1,533,200 | 1,567,489 | 1,273,444 | 1,300,475 | 259,756 | 267,014 |
| Massachusetts | 2,486,235 | 2,662,343 | 2,423,947 | 2,599,197 | 62,288 | 63,146 |
| Michigan | 3,882,868 | 3,940,326 | 3,520,422 | 3,565,443 | 362,446 | 374,883 |
| Minnesota | 1,692,962 | 1,720,902 | 1,671,493 | 1,700,110 | 21,469 | 20,792 |
| Mississippi | 1,067,933 | 1,110,208 | 625,011 | 632,535 | 442,922 | 477,673 |
| Missouri | 2,108,279 | 2,211,534 | 1,918,378 | 2,004,589 | 189,901 | 206,945 |
| Montana | 343,743 | 331,024 | 331,374 | 319,364 | 12,369 | 11,660 |
| Nebraska | 700,026 | 711,304 | 681,603 | 693,161 | 18,423 | 18,143 |
| Nevada | 147,521 | 137,757 | 136,298 | 127,145 | 11,223 | 10,612 |
| New Hampshire | 298,107 | 308,814 | 296,662 | 307,672 | 1,445 | 1,142 |
| New Jersey | 2,971,991 | 3,094,791 | 2,717,512 | 2,821,491 | 254,479 | 273,300 |
| New Mexico | 479,770 | 471,253 | 442,352 | 433,411 | 37,418 | 37,842 |
| New York | 8,123,239 | 8,659,065 | 7,421,364 | 7,865,707 | 701,875 | 793,358 |
| North Carolina | 2,247,069 | 2,309,086 | 1,684,797 | 1,714,488 | 562,272 | 594,598 |
| North Dakota | 323,208 | 309,238 | 316,637 | 302,901 | 6,571 | 6,337 |
| Ohio | 4,764,225 | 4,942,169 | 4,376,126 | 4,533,572 | 388,102 | 408,597 |
| Oklahoma | 1,147,851 | 1,180,433 | 1,041,202 | 1,066,698 | 106,649 | 113,735 |
| Oregon | 879,951 | 888,736 | 861,040 | 870,997 | 18,911 | 17,739 |
| Pennsylvania | 5,509,851 | 5,809,515 | 5,093,879 | 5,360,125 | 415,972 | 449,390 |
| Rhode Island | 421,845 | 437,643 | 411,265 | 427,447 | 10,580 | 10,196 |
| South Carolina | 1,175,818 | 1,206,776 | 775,754 | 775,268 | 400,064 | 431,508 |
| South Dakota | 344,271 | 336,243 | 330,434 | 322,664 | 13,837 | 13,579 |
| Tennessee | 1,740,690 | 1,826,399 | 1,459,508 | 1,518,245 | 281,182 | 308,154 |
| Texas | 4,744,981 | 4,834,696 | 4,159,510 | 4,215,321 | 585,471 | 619,375 |
| Utah | 444,924 | 445,703 | 436,198 | 437,630 | 8,726 | 8,073 |
| Vermont | 191,743 | 198,138 | 191,321 | 197,771 | 422 | 367 |
| Virginia | 1,979,372 | 1,987,577 | 1,571,139 | 1,571,304 | 408,233 | 416,273 |
| Washington | 1,435,037 | 1,418,177 | 1,381,261 | 1,370,414 | 53,776 | 47,763 |
| West Virginia | 915,035 | 945,386 | 871,178 | 898,955 | 43,857 | 46,431 |
| Wisconsin | 1,964,512 | 1,987,265 | 1,918,199 | 1,940,704 | 46,313 | 46,568 |
| Wyoming | 169,015 | 161,051 | 165,349 | 157,573 | 3,666 | 3,471 |
| **Total** | **88,331,494** | **90,991,681** | **78,367,149** | **80,464,583** | **9,964,345** | **10,527,098** |

## Latest U. S. Population by Age, Color and Sex

Source: Bureau of Census

Estimates of the total population of the United States and Armed Forces Abroad, July, 1967

| Age | All classes | | | White | | Nonwhite | |
|---|---|---|---|---|---|---|---|
| | Total | Male | Female | Male | Female | Male | Female |
| **All ages** | 199,118,000 | 97,945,000 | 101,173,000 | 86,258,000 | 88,797,000 | 10,629,000 | 11,354,000 |
| Under 5 years | 19,191,000 | 9,795,000 | 9,397,000 | 8,196,000 | 7,822,000 | 1,463,000 | 1,443,000 |
| 5 to 9 years | 20,910,000 | 10,642,000 | 10,268,000 | 9,071,000 | 8,700,000 | 1,434,000 | 1,433,000 |
| 10 to 14 years | 19,885,000 | 10,101,000 | 9,784,000 | 8,696,000 | 8,378,000 | 1,292,000 | 1,298,000 |
| 15 to 19 years | 17,868,000 | 9,082,000 | 8,786,000 | 7,889,000 | 7,593,000 | 1,098,000 | 1,102,000 |
| 20 to 24 years | 15,197,000 | 7,665,000 | 7,531,000 | 6,769,000 | 6,617,000 | 823,000 | 840,000 |
| 25 to 29 years | 12,118,000 | 6,035,000 | 6,083,000 | 5,343,000 | 5,330,000 | 630,000 | 685,000 |
| 30 to 34 years | 10,975,000 | 5,437,000 | 5,538,000 | 4,823,000 | 4,839,000 | 552,000 | 626,000 |
| 35 to 39 years | 11,610,000 | 5,713,000 | 5,897,000 | 5,095,000 | 5,172,000 | 551,000 | 644,000 |
| 40 to 44 years | 12,374,000 | 6,034,000 | 6,341,000 | 5,416,000 | 5,627,000 | 554,000 | 645,000 |
| 45 to 49 years | 11,841,000 | 5,745,000 | 6,097,000 | 5,185,000 | 5,464,000 | 506,000 | 583,000 |
| 50 to 54 years | 10,780,000 | 5,224,000 | 5,556,000 | 4,729,000 | 5,001,000 | 450,000 | 518,000 |
| 55 to 59 years | 9,525,000 | 4,574,000 | 4,952,000 | 4,155,000 | 4,489,000 | 378,000 | 435,000 |
| 60 to 64 years | 8,048,000 | 3,798,000 | 4,250,000 | 3,452,000 | 3,875,000 | 305,000 | 346,000 |
| 65 to 69 years | 6,501,000 | 2,958,000 | 3,543,000 | 2,714,000 | 3,269,000 | 214,000 | 252,000 |
| 70 to 74 years | 5,177,000 | 2,236,000 | 2,941,000 | 2,067,000 | 2,726,000 | 154,000 | 202,000 |
| 75 to 79 years | 3,785,000 | 1,587,000 | 2,198,000 | 1,462,000 | 2,038,000 | 114,000 | 152,000 |
| 80 to 84 years | 2,160,000 | 874,000 | 1,286,000 | 800,000 | 1,195,000 | 66,000 | 87,000 |
| 85 years and over | 1,174,000 | 446,000 | 727,000 | 396,000 | 661,000 | 47,000 | 64,000 |
| 1 to 4 years | 15,652,000 | 7,988,000 | 7,664,000 | 6,695,000 | 6,390,000 | 1,183,000 | 1,167,000 |
| 5 to 13 years | 36,965,000 | 18,799,000 | 18,167,000 | 16,088,000 | 15,457,000 | 2,482,000 | 2,486,000 |
| 14 to 17 years | 14,625,000 | 7,434,000 | 7,191,000 | 6,432,000 | 6,190,000 | 922,000 | 926,000 |
| 18 to 21 years | 13,632,000 | 6,913,000 | 6,720,000 | 6,073,000 | 5,874,000 | 774,000 | 782,000 |
| 14 years and over | 142,961,000 | 69,351,000 | 73,609,000 | 61,975,000 | 65,518,000 | 6,684,000 | 7,425,000 |
| 18 years and over | 128,336,000 | 61,918,000 | 66,418,000 | 55,543,000 | 59,329,000 | 5,762,000 | 6,499,000 |
| 21 years and over | 117,503,000 | 56,418,000 | 61,085,000 | 50,710,000 | 54,663,000 | 5,147,000 | 5,880,000 |
| 62 years and over | 23,463,000 | 10,294,000 | 13,169,000 | 9,429,000 | 12,144,000 | 772,000 | 955,000 |
| 65 years and over | 18,796,000 | 8,101,000 | 10,695,000 | 7,438,000 | 9,889,000 | 594,000 | 755,000 |
| Median age, years | 27.7 | 26.4 | 29.0 | 27.4 | 30.1 | 20.2 | 22.4 |

# U. S. Population, Nonwhite, by States and Races

Source: Bureau of the Census (Census of 1950-1960.)

| State | Total | | Negro | | Indian | | Japanese | | Chinese | |
|---|---|---|---|---|---|---|---|---|---|---|
| | 1960 | 1950 | 1960 | 1950 | 1960 | 1950 | 1960 | 1950 | 1960 | 1950 |
| Alabama.... | 983,131 | 982,152 | 980,271 | 979,617 | 1,276 | 928 | 500 | 88 | 288 | 187 |
| Alaska...... | 51,621 | 35,835 | 6,771 | (1) | 14,444 | 14,089 | 818 | (1) | 137 | (1) |
| Ariz........ | 132,644 | 95,076 | 43,403 | 25,974 | 83,387 | 65,761 | 1,501 | 780 | 2,936 | 1,951 |
| Ark........ | 390,569 | 428,004 | 388,787 | 426,639 | 580 | 533 | 237 | 113 | 676 | 592 |
| Calif....... | 1,261,974 | 671,050 | 883,861 | 462,172 | 39,014 | 19,947 | 157,317 | 84,956 | 95,600 | 58,324 |
| Colo....... | 53,247 | 28,436 | 39,992 | 20,177 | 4,288 | 1,567 | 6,846 | 5,412 | 724 | 458 |
| Conn...... | 111,418 | 54,951 | 107,449 | 53,472 | 923 | 333 | 653 | 254 | 865 | 450 |
| Dist. of Col.. | 418,693 | 284,313 | 411,737 | 280,803 | 587 | 330 | 900 | 353 | 2,632 | 1,825 |
| Del........ | 61,965 | 44,207 | 60,688 | 43,598 | 597 | ..... | 152 | 14 | 191 | 85 |
| Fla........ | 887,679 | 605,254 | 880,186 | 603,101 | 2,504 | 1,011 | 1,315 | 238 | 1,023 | 429 |
| Ga......... | 1,125,893 | 1,064,001 | 1,122,596 | 1,062,762 | 749 | 333 | 885 | 128 | 686 | 511 |
| Hawaii..... | 430,542 | 385,001 | 4,943 | 2,651 | 472 | (1) | 203,455 | 184,611 | 38,197 | 32,376 |
| Idaho...... | 9,808 | 7,242 | 1,502 | 1,050 | 5,231 | 3,800 | 2,254 | 1,980 | 311 | 244 |
| Ill.......... | 1,070,906 | 666,118 | 1,037,470 | 645,980 | 4,704 | 1,443 | 14,074 | 11,646 | 7,047 | 4,207 |
| Ind........ | 273,944 | 175,712 | 269,275 | 174,168 | 948 | 438 | 1,093 | 318 | 952 | 496 |
| Ia......... | 28,828 | 21,527 | 25,354 | 19,692 | 1,708 | 1,084 | 599 | 310 | 423 | 310 |
| Kan....... | 99,945 | 76,338 | 91,445 | 73,158 | 5,069 | 2,381 | 1,362 | 116 | 537 | 315 |
| Kentucky... | 218,073 | 202,716 | 215,949 | 201,921 | 391 | 234 | 774 | 74 | 288 | 335 |
| La......... | 1,045,307 | 886,833 | 1,039,207 | 882,428 | 3,587 | 409 | 519 | 127 | 731 | 526 |
| Me......... | 5,974 | 2,928 | 3,318 | 1,221 | 1,879 | 1,522 | 343 | 30 | 123 | 77 |
| Md........ | 526,770 | 388,026 | 518,410 | 385,972 | 1,538 | 314 | 1,842 | 289 | 2,188 | 795 |
| Mass...... | 125,434 | 79,011 | 111,842 | 73,171 | 2,118 | 1,201 | 1,924 | 384 | 6,745 | 3,627 |
| Mich...... | 737,329 | 453,941 | 717,581 | 442,296 | 9,701 | 7,000 | 3,211 | 1,517 | 3,234 | 1,619 |
| Minn...... | 42,261 | 28,786 | 22,263 | 14,022 | 15,496 | 12,533 | 1,726 | 1,049 | 1,270 | 720 |
| Miss....... | 920,595 | 990,282 | 915,743 | 986,494 | 3,119 | 2,502 | 178 | 62 | 1,244 | 1,011 |
| Mo........ | 396,846 | 299,060 | 390,853 | 297,088 | 1,723 | 547 | 1,473 | 527 | 954 | 519 |
| Mont...... | 24,029 | 18,986 | 1,467 | 1,232 | 21,181 | 16,606 | 589 | 524 | 240 | 209 |
| Nebr...... | 36,566 | 24,182 | 29,262 | 19,234 | 5,545 | 3,954 | 905 | 619 | 290 | 202 |
| Nev....... | 21,835 | 10,175 | 13,484 | 4,302 | 6,681 | 5,025 | 544 | 382 | 572 | 281 |
| N. H...... | 2,587 | 967 | 1,903 | 731 | 135 | 74 | 207 | 25 | 152 | 93 |
| N. J...... | 527,779 | 323,744 | 514,875 | 318,565 | 1,699 | 621 | 3,514 | 1,784 | 3,813 | 1,818 |
| N. M...... | 75,260 | 50,976 | 17,063 | 8,408 | 56,255 | 41,901 | 930 | 251 | 362 | 166 |
| N. Y...... | 1,495,233 | 958,097 | 1,417,511 | 918,191 | 16,491 | 10,640 | 8,702 | 3,893 | 37,573 | 20,171 |
| N. C...... | 1,156,870 | 1,078,808 | 1,116,021 | 1,047,353 | 38,129 | 3,742 | 1,265 | 98 | 404 | 345 |
| N. D...... | 12,908 | 11,188 | 777 | 257 | 11,736 | 10,766 | 127 | 61 | 100 | 82 |
| Ohio...... | 796,699 | 518,405 | 786,097 | 513,072 | 1,910 | 1,146 | 3,135 | 1,986 | 2,507 | 1,542 |
| Okla...... | 220,384 | 200,825 | 153,084 | 145,503 | 64,689 | 53,769 | 749 | 137 | 398 | 397 |
| Ore....... | 36,650 | 24,213 | 18,133 | 11,529 | 8,026 | 5,820 | 5,016 | 3,660 | 2,995 | 2,102 |
| Pa........ | 865,362 | 644,164 | 852,750 | 638,485 | 2,122 | 1,141 | 2,348 | 1,029 | 3,741 | 2,258 |
| R. I....... | 20,776 | 14,881 | 18,332 | 13,903 | 932 | 385 | 192 | 25 | 574 | 403 |
| S. C...... | 831,572 | 823,622 | 829,291 | 822,077 | 1,098 | 554 | 460 | 34 | 158 | 101 |
| S. D...... | 27,416 | 24,236 | 1,114 | 727 | 25,794 | 23,344 | 188 | 56 | 89 | 44 |
| Tenn...... | 589,336 | 531,461 | 586,876 | 530,603 | 638 | 339 | 507 | 104 | 487 | 230 |
| Texas..... | 1,204,846 | 984,660 | 1,187,125 | 977,458 | 5,750 | 2,736 | 4,053 | 957 | 4,172 | 2,435 |
| Utah...... | 16,799 | 11,953 | 4,148 | 2,729 | 6,961 | 4,201 | 4,371 | 4,452 | 629 | 335 |
| Vt........ | 789 | 559 | 519 | 443 | 57 | 30 | 79 | 14 | 68 | 34 |
| Va........ | 824,506 | 737,125 | 816,258 | 734,211 | 2,155 | 1,056 | 1,733 | 193 | 1,135 | 565 |
| Wash...... | 101,539 | 62,467 | 48,738 | 30,691 | 21,076 | 13,816 | 16,652 | 9,694 | 5,491 | 3,408 |
| W. Va..... | 90,288 | 115,270 | 89,378 | 114,867 | 181 | 160 | 176 | 46 | 138 | 99 |
| Wis....... | 92,874 | 41,885 | 74,546 | 28,182 | 14,297 | 12,196 | 1,425 | 529 | 1,010 | 590 |
| Wyo....... | 7,144 | 6,520 | 2,183 | 2,557 | 4,020 | 3,237 | 514 | 450 | 192 | 106 |
| **Total....** | **20,491,443** | **16,176,169** | **18,871,831** | **15,044,937** | **523,591** | **357,499** | **464,332** | **326,379** | **237,292** | **150,005** |

| State | Filipino * | All other ** | State | Filipino * | All other ** | State | Filipino * | All other ** |
|---|---|---|---|---|---|---|---|---|
| | 1960 | 1960 | | 1960 | 1960 | | 1960 | 1960 |
| Ala......... | 127 | 669 | La......... | 754 | 509 | Okla....... | 267 | 1,197 |
| Alaska...... | 814 | 28,637 | Me......... | 131 | 180 | Ore........ | 1,109 | 1,371 |
| Ariz........ | 943 | 474 | Md......... | 1,670 | 1,122 | Pa......... | 1,640 | 2,761 |
| Ark........ | 83 | 206 | Mass...... | 809 | 1,996 | R. I....... | 424 | 322 |
| Calif....... | *65,459 | 20,723 | Mich...... | 1,134 | 2,468 | S. C....... | 328 | 237 |
| Colo....... | 605 | 792 | Minn...... | 646 | 860 | S. D....... | 59 | 172 |
| Conn...... | 726 | 802 | Miss...... | 59 | 252 | Tenn...... | 249 | 579 |
| D. of C..... | 1,158 | 1,679 | Mo........ | 719 | 1,124 | Texas..... | 1,623 | 2,123 |
| Del........ | 67 | 270 | Mont...... | 253 | 299 | Utah...... | 207 | 483 |
| Fla........ | 1,361 | 1,290 | Nebr...... | 123 | 441 | Vt........ | 25 | 41 |
| Ga......... | 433 | 544 | Nev....... | 286 | 268 | Va........ | 1,857 | 1,368 |
| Hawaii..... | *69,070 | 114,405 | N. H....... | 41 | 149 | Wash...... | *7,110 | 2,472 |
| Idaho...... | 193 | 317 | N. J....... | 1,451 | 2,427 | W. Va..... | 105 | 310 |
| Ill......... | 3,587 | 4,024 | N. M...... | 192 | 458 | Wis....... | 401 | 1,195 |
| Ind........ | 402 | 1,274 | N. Y...... | *5,403 | 9,553 | Wyo....... | 99 | 136 |
| Ia......... | 167 | 577 | N. C...... | 343 | 708 | | | |
| Kan........ | 372 | 1,160 | N. D...... | 47 | 121 | **Total.....** | **176,310** | **218,807** |
| Ky........ | 236 | 435 | Ohio...... | 943 | 2,107 | | | |

¹Not available.

*Filipino 1950—California 40,424; Hawaii 61,071; New York 3,719; Washington 4,274. All other states not available.

**All other total for 1950, 174,642.

# Foreign Born and 2nd Generation in U. S.: Countries of Origin

## BY NATIVITY, COLOR AND SEX

"Foreign stock," as used in this table, includes foreign born American residents, plus native born
American residents whose father, mother or both were immigrants

Source: Bureau of the Census (Census of 1960)

| Country of Origin | Total foreign stock | | | Foreign born[1] | | Native of foreign or mixed parentage[2] | |
|---|---|---|---|---|---|---|---|
| | Total | White | Non-white | White | Non-white | White | Non-white |
| Austria.............. | 1,098,630 | 1,097,581 | 1,049 | 304,192 | 315 | 793,389 | 734 |
| Belgium............. | 140,266 | 140,028 | 238 | 50,210 | 84 | 89,818 | 154 |
| Canada*............. | 3,181,051 | 3,153,514 | 27,537 | 941,906 | 10,594 | 2,211,608 | 16,943 |
| China............... | 208,455 | 32,543 | 175,912 | 12,858 | 86,877 | 19,685 | 89,035 |
| Cuba............... | 124,416 | 116,354 | 8,062 | 74,921 | 4,229 | 41,433 | 3,833 |
| Czechoslovakia...... | 917,830 | 917,172 | 658 | 227,467 | 151 | 689,705 | 507 |
| Denmark........... | 399,350 | 398,806 | 544 | 84,989 | 71 | 313,817 | 473 |
| Finland............ | 240,827 | 240,525 | 302 | 67,540 | 84 | 172,985 | 218 |
| France............. | 351,681 | 349,360 | 2,321 | 110,864 | 718 | 238,496 | 1,603 |
| Germany........... | 4,330,664 | 4,312,638 | 8,026 | 980,564 | 3,251 | 3,326,074 | 4,775 |
| Greece............. | 378,586 | 377,973 | 613 | 158,894 | 273 | 219,079 | 340 |
| Hungary........... | 701,637 | 700,899 | 738 | 244,945 | 307 | 455,954 | 431 |
| Ireland (Eire)...... | 1,773,312 | 1,771,070 | 2,242 | 338,350 | 372 | 1,432,720 | 1,870 |
| Italy.............. | 4,543,935 | 4,539,692 | 4,243 | 1,255,812 | 1,187 | 3,283,880 | 3,056 |
| Japan.............. | 322,090 | 30,169 | 291,921 | 11,686 | 97,489 | 18,483 | 194,432 |
| Lithuania.......... | 402,846 | 402,498 | 348 | 121,349 | 126 | 281,149 | 222 |
| Mexico............. | 1,735,992 | 1,724,838 | 11,154 | 572,564 | 3,338 | 1,152,274 | 7,816 |
| Netherlands........ | 398,658 | 398,151 | 507 | 118,160 | 255 | 279,991 | 252 |
| Norway............ | 774,754 | 774,081 | 673 | 152,644 | 54 | 621,437 | 619 |
| Philippines......... | 201,746 | 45,328 | 156,418 | 15,624 | 89,219 | 29,704 | 67,199 |
| Poland............. | 2,780,026 | 2,778,210 | 1,816 | 747,250 | 500 | 2,030,960 | 1,316 |
| Romania........... | 233,805 | 233,540 | 265 | 84,471 | 104 | 149,069 | 161 |
| Spain.............. | 126,163 | 125,167 | 996 | 44,815 | 184 | 80,352 | 812 |
| Sweden............ | 1,046,942 | 1,045,763 | 1,179 | 214,313 | 178 | 831,450 | 1,001 |
| Switzerland........ | 263,054 | 262,734 | 320 | 61,490 | 78 | 201,244 | 242 |
| Turkey............ | 106,225 | 105,790 | 435 | 51,887 | 341 | 53,903 | 94 |
| United Kingdom..... | | | | | | | |
| England........ | 1,826,825 | 1,820,740 | 6,085 | 526,157 | 2,048 | 1,294,583 | 4,037 |
| Scotland....... | 668,672 | 667,672 | 1,000 | 213,026 | 193 | 454,646 | 807 |
| Wales......... | 134,008 | 133,793 | 215 | 23,407 | 62 | 110,386 | 153 |
| Northern Ireland.... | 255,146 | 254,809 | 337 | 68,083 | 79 | 186,726 | 258 |
| USSR.............. | 2,290,267 | 2,286,986 | 3,281 | 689,462 | 1,136 | 1,597,524 | 2,145 |
| Yugoslavia.......... | 448,503 | 448,142 | 361 | 165,658 | 140 | 282,484 | 221 |
| **Total.........** | **32,396,362** | **31,686,566** | **709,796** | **8,741,558** | **304,037** | **22,945,008** | **405,759** |
| **Other Countries.....** | **1,653,992** | **1,391,773** | **262,219** | **552,434** | **140,062** | **839,339** | **122,157** |
| **Total all countries...** | **34,050,354** | **33,078,339** | **972,015** | **9,293,992** | **444,099** | **23,784,347** | **527,916** |

*Includes Newfoundland.

[1]Foreign born—White, Male 4,507,502, Female 4,786,490. Nonwhite, Male 252,930, Female 191,169.
[2]Native of foreign or mixed parentage—White, Male 11,568,891, Female 12,215,456. Nonwhite, Male 266,746, Female 261,170.

# Foreign Born in U. S. Standard Metropolitan Statistical Areas

See pages 652-654 for total population
Source: Bureau of the Census (Census of 1960)

| Country | Boston | Chicago | Cleveland | Detroit | Los Angeles-Long Beach | New York | Philadelphia | San Francisco Oakland |
|---|---|---|---|---|---|---|---|---|
| Austria.......... | 2,683 | 20,805 | 8,274 | 6,725 | 12,278 | 95,631 | 9,441 | 4,431 |
| Belgium......... | 777 | 3,451 | 298 | 6,840 | 2,855 | 6,413 | 760 | 979 |
| Canada[1]........ | 83,364 | 21,428 | 7,827 | 94,027 | 83,685 | 42,823 | 8,682 | 24,323 |
| China........... | 2,790 | 3,011 | 481 | 1,022 | 8,924 | 21,529 | 1,287 | 23,207 |
| Cuba........... | 385 | 1,736 | 212 | 400 | 2,194 | 30,018 | 788 | 416 |
| Czechoslovakia... | 573 | 28,156 | 16,985 | 5,024 | 6,656 | 33,756 | 4,005 | 1,861 |
| Denmark....... | 940 | 6,093 | 456 | 1,628 | 6,275 | 7,205 | 811 | 4,680 |
| Finland......... | 1,622 | 2,036 | 1,030 | 1,966 | 2,152 | 8,200 | 468 | 2,382 |
| France......... | 2,118 | 3,872 | 986 | 2,339 | 7,860 | 23,875 | 3,166 | 6,460 |
| Germany........ | 8,744 | 74,120 | 16,496 | 25,942 | 43,056 | 199,685 | 32,643 | 25,052 |
| Greece......... | 7,787 | 14,995 | 2,212 | 5,873 | 4,849 | 32,250 | 2,962 | 4,740 |
| Hungary........ | 1,189 | 13,645 | 18,249 | 10,790 | 13,340 | 52,305 | 8,549 | 2,737 |
| Ireland (Eire).... | 38,741 | 25,795 | 4,238 | 4,402 | 7,321 | 119,280 | 17,745 | 9,254 |
| Italy........... | 57,718 | 61,930 | 19,317 | 30,794 | 31,934 | 345,489 | 63,570 | 34,051 |
| Japan.......... | 532 | 2,882 | 237 | 638 | 17,186 | 4,413 | 1,285 | 6,823 |
| Lithuania....... | 6,416 | 24,802 | 3,755 | 4,479 | 3,760 | 13,531 | 4,728 | 523 |
| Mexico......... | 248 | 23,450 | 447 | 3,565 | 117,004 | 3,909 | 557 | 18,977 |
| Netherlands..... | 1,082 | 6,462 | 800 | 2,777 | 12,814 | 7,433 | 1,004 | 3,766 |
| Norway........ | 2,106 | 9,854 | 523 | 1,164 | 6,483 | 24,783 | 1,213 | 4,635 |
| Philippines...... | 488 | 2,358 | 191 | 673 | 9,323 | 4,399 | 936 | 16,476 |
| Poland......... | 12,323 | 90,199 | 19,437 | 49,993 | 23,371 | 188,492 | 24,741 | 4,450 |
| Romania....... | 760 | 6,893 | 3,540 | 5,219 | 5,433 | 27,085 | 4,258 | 1,063 |
| Spain.......... | 325 | 485 | 178 | 782 | 2,630 | 12,193 | 591 | 4,005 |
| Sweden........ | 6,526 | 26,316 | 1,425 | 2,875 | 11,709 | 17,011 | 1,632 | 6,902 |
| Switzerland..... | 597 | 2,112 | 467 | 913 | 4,168 | 8,636 | 1,043 | 4,304 |
| Turkey........ | 3,701 | 1,902 | 492 | 3,500 | 4,425 | 13,213 | 1,623 | 1,282 |
| United Kingdom.. | | | | | | | | |
| England....... | 14,728 | 18,530 | 7,613 | 23,479 | 47,250 | 58,259 | 18,441 | 16,966 |
| Scotland....... | 8,318 | 8,835 | 3,895 | 18,132 | 14,644 | 30,229 | 8,863 | 6,187 |
| Wales........ | 328 | 846 | 599 | 960 | 1,719 | 1,478 | 726 | 759 |
| North'n Ireland.. | 3,099 | 3,194 | 791 | 2,224 | 3,529 | 15,516 | 7,956 | 2,121 |
| USSR.......... | 28,863 | 43,700 | 11,487 | 19,435 | 43,544 | 222,854 | 46,038 | 12,399 |
| Yugoslavia...... | 306 | 21,574 | 15,505 | 8,570 | 9,656 | 13,954 | 2,738 | 3,475 |
| Other Countries.. | 20,151 | 25,633 | 6,691 | 17,425 | 44,646 | 172,991 | 13,979 | 40,550 |
| **Total........** | **320,328** | **601,010** | **175,134** | **364,575** | **616,673** | **1,858,898** | **297,229** | **300,241** |

[1]Includes Newfoundland.

## Country of Birth of Foreign Born
Source: Bureau of the Census (1960 Census)

| State | Total Foreign Born | Austria | Belgium | Canada[1] | China | Czechoslov. | Denmark | England[2] | Finland | France | Germany |
|---|---|---|---|---|---|---|---|---|---|---|---|
| Alabama..... | 14,955 | 357 | 78 | 1,171 | 124 | 223 | 114 | 2,350 | 39 | 465 | 3,196 |
| Alaska...... | 8,227 | 105 | 37 | 1,866 | 108 | 99 | 157 | 641 | 201 | 153 | 1,103 |
| Arizona..... | 70,318 | 1,061 | 268 | 6,234 | 1,053 | 643 | 430 | 4,101 | 219 | 624 | 4,273 |
| Arkansas.... | 7,457 | 250 | 69 | 687 | 251 | 175 | 63 | 1,128 | 21 | 143 | 1,457 |
| California.... | 1,343,686 | 21,269 | 5,012 | 149,351 | 40,796 | 10,847 | 17,503 | 121,442 | 6,809 | 20,585 | 95,279 |
| Colorado..... | 59,874 | 2,067 | 291 | 3,954 | 449 | 910 | 979 | 5,269 | 198 | 904 | 8,522 |
| Connecticut.. | 275,523 | 6,096 | 647 | 34,253 | 543 | 6,616 | 1,816 | 21,960 | 1,962 | 2,770 | 19,446 |
| Delaware.... | 14,650 | 330 | 87 | 912 | 60 | 201 | 64 | 1,982 | 41 | 150 | 1,726 |
| Dist. of Col.. | 38,971 | 862 | 164 | 1,902 | 1,411 | 523 | 242 | 3,406 | 146 | 1,280 | 3,166 |
| Florida...... | 272,161 | 7,830 | 1,378 | 31,905 | 631 | 4,217 | 2,752 | 32,324 | 2,710 | 4,022 | 24,757 |
| Georgia...... | 25,300 | 649 | 173 | 2,048 | 344 | 316 | 179 | 3,616 | 94 | 776 | 6,906 |
| Hawaii...... | 68,897 | 141 | 92 | 1,312 | 3,541 | 75 | 78 | 1,229 | 28 | 202 | 1,287 |
| Idaho....... | 15,542 | 336 | 70 | 2,500 | 140 | 208 | 588 | 1,731 | 216 | 245 | 1,685 |
| Illinois...... | 686,093 | 23,288 | 6,495 | 25,268 | 3,520 | 30,345 | 7,087 | 37,179 | 2,297 | 5,684 | 87,707 |
| Indiana...... | 93,202 | 2,579 | 1,645 | 6,533 | 596 | 3,773 | 411 | 8,465 | 187 | 1,215 | 13,474 |
| Iowa........ | 56,278 | 845 | 565 | 2,725 | 246 | 2,307 | 4,864 | 3,917 | 88 | 662 | 14,368 |
| Kansas...... | 33,268 | 1,242 | 401 | 2,038 | 291 | 786 | 454 | 3,067 | 64 | 765 | 7,049 |
| Kentucky.... | 16,830 | 463 | 117 | 1,161 | 155 | 168 | 85 | 2,091 | 4 | 511 | 5,015 |
| Louisiana.... | 30,557 | 365 | 165 | 1,611 | 331 | 182 | 199 | 2,622 | 67 | 1,357 | 3,091 |
| Maine....... | 60,403 | 150 | 28 | 44,075 | 107 | 225 | 285 | 3,939 | 653 | 309 | 1,378 |
| Maryland.... | 94,174 | 2,468 | 435 | 5,847 | 974 | 2,187 | 639 | 9,453 | 481 | 1,618 | 15,239 |
| Massachusetts. | 576,452 | 5,026 | 1,537 | 152,057 | 3,256 | 1,762 | 1,536 | 49,285 | 6,050 | 4,839 | 17,593 |
| Michigan..... | 529,624 | 10,649 | 9,034 | 126,095 | 1,628 | 10,005 | 3,009 | 57,217 | 9,111 | 3,526 | 43,655 |
| Minnesota.... | 143,874 | 3,753 | 881 | 13,722 | 760 | 3,592 | 4,717 | 5,936 | 8,717 | 635 | 18,129 |
| Mississippi... | 8,058 | 63 | 32 | 567 | 546 | 56 | 83 | 1,150 | 34 | 211 | 1,083 |
| Missouri..... | 77,756 | 3,926 | 546 | 3,563 | 432 | 1,803 | 588 | 5,515 | 41 | 1,041 | 15,728 |
| Montana..... | 30,646 | 1,058 | 259 | 5,619 | 98 | 425 | 1,010 | 3,349 | 727 | 256 | 2,568 |
| Nebraska.... | 40,238 | 871 | 247 | 1,562 | 108 | 3,819 | 2,888 | 2,333 | 37 | 257 | 8,743 |
| Nevada..... | 13,133 | 343 | 76 | 1,798 | 322 | 57 | 330 | 1,381 | 57 | 621 | 1,120 |
| N. Hampshire. | 44,772 | 423 | 298 | 26,301 | 81 | 109 | 118 | 3,630 | 542 | 333 | 1,639 |
| New Jersey... | 615,474 | 22,397 | 2,723 | 17,674 | 2,028 | 16,341 | 3,704 | 55,203 | 2,163 | 7,290 | 81,505 |
| New Mexico... | 21,408 | 320 | 108 | 1,123 | 211 | 149 | 84 | 1,810 | 23 | 395 | 1,949 |
| New York.... | 2,289,310 | 107,101 | 7,955 | 111,280 | 22,251 | 42,021 | 9,462 | 131,122 | 9,765 | 27,639 | 250,173 |
| North Carolina | 21,978 | 506 | 163 | 2,113 | 255 | 186 | 160 | 3,052 | 35 | 547 | 4,657 |
| North Dakota. | 29,907 | 562 | 105 | 3,749 | 75 | 418 | 764 | 730 | 182 | 103 | 2,794 |
| Ohio........ | 396,610 | 17,340 | 1,380 | 20,643 | 1,473 | 29,304 | 1,139 | 34,760 | 2,216 | 3,312 | 46,988 |
| Oklahoma.... | 20,003 | 503 | 103 | 1,674 | 184 | 681 | 169 | 2,342 | 11 | 468 | 4,234 |
| Oregon...... | 71,314 | 1,520 | 409 | 15,853 | 1,161 | 950 | 1,813 | 7,366 | 2,227 | 782 | 6,907 |
| Pennsylvania.. | 603,490 | 36,750 | 2,018 | 14,432 | 1,738 | 34,646 | 1,303 | 52,030 | 947 | 5,361 | 54,878 |
| Rhode Island.. | 85,974 | 830 | 524 | 18,072 | 393 | 197 | 123 | 12,321 | 414 | 1,320 | 2,535 |
| South Carolina | 11,140 | 242 | 61 | 1,039 | 122 | 112 | 44 | 2,022 | 31 | 446 | 2,266 |
| South Dakota. | 18,577 | 340 | 95 | 1,050 | 37 | 593 | 1,624 | 993 | 151 | 51 | 3,342 |
| Tennessee..... | 15,843 | 306 | 92 | 1,575 | 226 | 200 | 106 | 2,111 | 16 | 261 | 2,836 |
| Texas........ | 298,791 | 2,752 | 738 | 7,960 | 1,941 | 5,054 | 893 | 12,176 | 172 | 2,444 | 19,506 |
| Utah........ | 32,133 | 441 | 232 | 2,256 | 287 | 112 | 1,665 | 5,568 | 169 | 359 | 5,585 |
| Vermont..... | 23,336 | 133 | 27 | 15,092 | 59 | 107 | 98 | 1,997 | 269 | 179 | 746 |
| Virginia..... | 48,181 | 996 | 328 | 4,736 | 745 | 861 | 531 | 7,321 | 151 | 1,547 | 8,132 |
| Washington... | 178,658 | 2,868 | 706 | 44,423 | 2,925 | 1,266 | 3,336 | 18,552 | 4,703 | 1,501 | 14,483 |
| West Virginia. | 23,863 | 912 | 323 | 822 | 84 | 947 | 71 | 2,545 | 72 | 337 | 1,536 |
| Wisconsin..... | 171,519 | 8,411 | 1,020 | 7,505 | 547 | 6,679 | 4,400 | 7,519 | 1,946 | 899 | 43,554 |
| Wyoming..... | 9,663 | 412 | 57 | 774 | 91 | 140 | 303 | 1,535 | 120 | 182 | 827 |
| Totals....... | 9,738,091 | 304,507 | 50,294 | 952,500 | 99,735 | 227,618 | 85,060 | 764,893 | 67,624 | 111,582 | 989,815 |

[1]Includes Newfoundland. [2]Includes Scotland and Wales

| State | Greece | Hungary | Ireland (Eire) | Italy | State | Greece | Hungary | Ireland (Eire) | Italy |
|---|---|---|---|---|---|---|---|---|---|
| Alabama........ | 715 | 262 | 243 | 1,151 | Nebraska........ | 454 | 283 | 500 | 1,996 |
| Alaska.......... | 63 | 110 | 82 | 101 | Nevada......... | 383 | 171 | 202 | 1,665 |
| Arizona......... | 599 | 798 | 610 | 2,450 | N. Hampshire... | 2,006 | 121 | 1,221 | 1,138 |
| Arkansas........ | 229 | 130 | 108 | 525 | New Jersey...... | 7,396 | 27,389 | 22,386 | 137,356 |
| California....... | 14,491 | 19,799 | 21,340 | 102,366 | New Mexico..... | 321 | 99 | 188 | 809 |
| Colorado........ | 903 | 1,049 | 894 | 4,797 | New York....... | 36,579 | 60,382 | 131,764 | 440,063 |
| Connecticut..... | 3,459 | 7,954 | 12,262 | 65,233 | North Carolina... | 1,549 | 253 | 268 | 567 |
| Delaware....... | 374 | 259 | 606 | 2,914 | North Dakota.... | 106 | 515 | 221 | 73 |
| Dist. of Col..... | 1,774 | 639 | 1,005 | 3,086 | Ohio........... | 8,872 | 35,082 | 7,184 | 50,338 |
| Florida......... | 3,720 | 7,404 | 4,408 | 16,217 | Oklahoma...... | 387 | 256 | 203 | 710 |
| Georgia......... | 884 | 244 | 389 | 750 | Oregon......... | 897 | 866 | 1,378 | 3,024 |
| Hawaii......... | 48 | 117 | 115 | 249 | Pennsylvania.... | 8,816 | 23,823 | 22,534 | 131,149 |
| Idaho.......... | 209 | 147 | 172 | 420 | Rhode Island.... | 858 | 220 | 4,426 | 18,438 |
| Illinois......... | 16,660 | 15,652 | 26,880 | 72,139 | South Carolina... | 739 | 108 | 188 | 260 |
| Indiana......... | 3,517 | 5,816 | 1,673 | 4,756 | South Dakota.... | 183 | 79 | 161 | 174 |
| Iowa........... | 1,145 | 324 | 769 | 2,254 | Tennessee...... | 426 | 279 | 176 | 1,383 |
| Kansas......... | 431 | 274 | 496 | 1,024 | Texas.......... | 2,034 | 1,238 | 2,228 | 4,568 |
| Kentucky....... | 400 | 299 | 437 | 911 | Utah........... | 1,537 | 79 | 139 | 1,437 |
| Louisiana....... | 356 | 303 | 563 | 5,470 | Vermont........ | 141 | 104 | 327 | 1,208 |
| Maine.......... | 482 | 136 | 1,219 | 1,568 | Virginia........ | 1,709 | 811 | 945 | 2,468 |
| Maryland....... | 2,818 | 1,775 | 2,202 | 10,454 | Washington..... | 1,918 | 1,170 | 2,158 | 6,072 |
| Massachusetts... | 13,519 | 1,871 | 51,428 | 86,921 | West Virginia.... | 1,292 | 1,380 | 235 | 5,882 |
| Michigan....... | 7,782 | 14,996 | 5,582 | 36,879 | Wisconsin....... | 1,891 | 5,787 | 945 | 8,479 |
| Minnesota...... | 1,176 | 1,297 | 1,398 | 3,541 | Wyoming........ | 498 | 95 | 254 | 555 |
| Mississippi..... | 247 | 46 | 159 | 923 | | | | | |
| Missouri........ | 1,833 | 2,636 | 2,513 | 9,033 | Totals........ | 159,167 | 245,252 | 338,722 | 1,256,999 |
| Montana........ | 341 | 325 | 938 | 1,055 | | | | | |

(Continued on page 600)

## Country of Birth of Foreign Born

(Continued from page 599)    Source: Bureau of the Census (1960 Census)

| States | Japan | Lith-uania | Mexi-co | Neth-er-lands | North Ire-land | Nor-way | Phil-ip-pines | Po-land | Por-tugal | Ro-mania | Spain |
|---|---|---|---|---|---|---|---|---|---|---|---|
| Alabama........ | 329 | 136 | 141 | 144 | 68 | 128 | 113 | 415 | 12 | 56 | 44 |
| Alaska......... | 376 | 8 | 77 | 52 | 49 | 982 | 515 | 97 | 4 | 8 | 10 |
| Arizona........ | 538 | 339 | 35,834 | 529 | 202 | 434 | 554 | 1,489 | 59 | 278 | 291 |
| Arkansas...... | 137 | 74 | 209 | 44 | 29 | 58 | 63 | 198 | 4 | 82 | 38 |
| California...... | 38,332 | 5,068 | 248,542 | 23,513 | 7,258 | 15,723 | 44,635 | 31,877 | 13,921 | 7,718 | 10,897 |
| Colorado....... | 1,964 | 196 | 4,882 | 966 | 237 | 580 | 559 | 2,032 | 15 | 450 | 135 |
| Connecticut.... | 303 | 7,508 | 245 | 1,132 | 2,278 | 1,734 | 630 | 30,326 | 3,253 | 862 | 1,045 |
| Delaware...... | 133 | 79 | 51 | 250 | 242 | 110 | 34 | 1,599 | 35 | 61 | 32 |
| Dist. of Col..... | 642 | 385 | 330 | 308 | 122 | 227 | 877 | 1,943 | 117 | 187 | 390 |
| Florida........ | 945 | 2,126 | 1,312 | 3,132 | 1,690 | 2,744 | 1,307 | 11,770 | 443 | 2,519 | 3,475 |
| Georgia........ | 548 | 118 | 161 | 287 | 140 | 142 | 348 | 1,138 | 88 | 154 | 138 |
| Hawaii......... | 24,658 | 38 | 112 | 90 | 43 | 82 | 28,649 | 93 | 764 | 29 | 146 |
| Idaho......... | 497 | 20 | 1,010 | 383 | 96 | 725 | 64 | 134 | 4 | 48 | 961 |
| Illinois........ | 3,551 | 27,977 | 25,477 | 7,734 | 3,554 | 11,524 | 2,534 | 94,132 | 136 | 7,194 | 735 |
| Indiana........ | 601 | 1,410 | 5,058 | 1,729 | 499 | 440 | 283 | 9,600 | 25 | 1,587 | 382 |
| Iowa.......... | 258 | 427 | 1,038 | 4,335 | 395 | 3,159 | 130 | 1,133 | 10 | 180 | 23 |
| Kansas........ | 1,154 | 81 | 3,495 | 323 | 134 | 239 | 408 | 836 | 9 | 89 | 93 |
| Kentucky...... | 603 | 137 | 116 | 152 | 107 | 49 | 118 | 511 | 11 | 119 | 40 |
| Louisiana...... | 396 | 45 | 3,714 | 367 | 111 | 362 | 594 | 742 | 46 | 144 | 374 |
| Maine......... | 304 | 574 | 63 | 69 | 176 | 366 | 112 | 773 | 73 | 35 | 25 |
| Maryland...... | 1,299 | 2,602 | 478 | 912 | 526 | 730 | 1,280 | 7,825 | 94 | 801 | 340 |
| Massachusetts.. | 1,397 | 13,387 | 403 | 1,902 | 4,848 | 3,401 | 703 | 36,536 | 21,453 | 1,042 | 579 |
| Michigan...... | 1,324 | 7,143 | 6,292 | 20,395 | 3,014 | 2,868 | 919 | 63,378 | 117 | 6,037 | 893 |
| Minnesota..... | 533 | 785 | 846 | 2,649 | 358 | 20,009 | 511 | 6,295 | ...... | 902 | 32 |
| Mississippi.... | 160 | 50 | 232 | 88 | 30 | 87 | 96 | 134 | 8 | 31 | 51 |
| Missouri....... | 816 | 642 | 2,506 | 451 | 304 | 199 | 600 | 5,072 | 53 | 1,512 | 361 |
| Montana....... | 262 | 78 | 430 | 748 | 201 | 3,371 | 167 | 611 | ...... | 141 | 38 |
| Nebraska...... | 307 | 763 | 1,521 | 258 | 119 | 367 | 103 | 1,836 | 4 | 160 | 43 |
| Nevada........ | 257 | 24 | 920 | 130 | 71 | 159 | 240 | 188 | 63 | 56 | 620 |
| New Hampshire. | 165 | 607 | 28 | 115 | 191 | 303 | 104 | 1,907 | 91 | 33 | 52 |
| New Jersey.... | 1,832 | 6,667 | 769 | 10,928 | 6,672 | 6,432 | 1,115 | 63,689 | 4,027 | 4,030 | 3,626 |
| New Mexico.... | 467 | 57 | 10,725 | 226 | 56 | 103 | 181 | 182 | 4 | 33 | 110 |
| New York...... | 5,564 | 17,815 | 4,496 | 13,132 | 18,749 | 27,125 | 5,037 | 234,742 | 4,489 | 29,040 | 13,563 |
| North Carolina.. | 1,140 | 105 | 207 | 521 | 145 | 190 | 261 | 554 | 28 | 66 | 57 |
| North Dakota... | 152 | 42 | 72 | 241 | 49 | 7,274 | 28 | 545 | 7 | 267 | 4 |
| Ohio.......... | 1,256 | 5,473 | 2,639 | 2,233 | 1,835 | 1,079 | 652 | 34,597 | 226 | 9,134 | 1,075 |
| Oklahoma...... | 600 | 88 | 1,105 | 249 | 94 | 146 | 198 | 534 | 28 | 65 | 58 |
| Oregon........ | 1,297 | 261 | 1,000 | 1,178 | 376 | 3,908 | 728 | 1,110 | 98 | 335 | 221 |
| Pennsylvania... | 1,307 | 13,301 | 1,437 | 1,781 | 9,388 | 1,669 | 1,204 | 63,386 | 836 | 6,565 | 1,443 |
| Rhode Island.... | 174 | 455 | 47 | 144 | 790 | 263 | 354 | 4,002 | 6,664 | 209 | 102 |
| South Carolina.. | 383 | 45 | 52 | 126 | 81 | 79 | 235 | 430 | 12 | 45 | 36 |
| South Dakota... | 104 | 35 | 56 | 1,055 | 72 | 3,079 | 30 | 216 | 4 | 122 | 5 |
| Tennessee..... | 449 | 75 | 232 | 108 | 63 | 55 | 212 | 921 | 8 | 69 | 56 |
| Texas......... | 2,893 | 374 | 202,315 | 1,333 | 454 | 843 | 1,412 | 3,725 | 124 | 459 | 785 |
| Utah.......... | 1,049 | 7 | 1,153 | 3,905 | 95 | 967 | 197 | 151 | ...... | 21 | 134 |
| Vermont....... | 82 | 35 | 30 | 101 | 87 | 84 | 17 | 678 | 24 | 23 | 224 |
| Virginia....... | 1,273 | 480 | 270 | 716 | 476 | 571 | 1,386 | 1,398 | 101 | 190 | 260 |
| Washington.... | 5,625 | 485 | 3,407 | 3,495 | 1,039 | 18,522 | 3,999 | 2,458 | 46 | 442 | 228 |
| West Virginia... | 115 | 364 | 194 | 49 | 86 | 25 | 82 | 1,896 | 27 | 154 | 564 |
| Wisconsin...... | 477 | 2,471 | 1,880 | 3,678 | 414 | 8,693 | 229 | 17,695 | 25 | 768 | 106 |
| Wyoming...... | 147 | 13 | 770 | 29 | 49 | 289 | 36 | 221 | ...... | 23 | 59 |
| **Totals......** | **109,175** | **121,475** | **575,902** | **118,415** | **68,162** | **152,698** | **104,843** | **747,750** | **57,690** | **84,575** | **44,999** |

| State | Swe-den | Switz-erland | U.S. S.R. | Yugo-slavia | State | Swe-den | Switz-erland | U.S. S.R. | Yugo-slavia |
|---|---|---|---|---|---|---|---|---|---|
| Alabama......... | 160 | 112 | 477 | 104 | Nebraska......... | 2,892 | 334 | 4,826 | 577 |
| Alaska.......... | 442 | 74 | 155 | 139 | Nevada.......... | 267 | 254 | 325 | 225 |
| Arizona......... | 894 | 346 | 1,800 | 731 | New Hampshire.... | 716 | 109 | 927 | 82 |
| Arkansas........ | 171 | 132 | 260 | 112 | New Jersey...... | 6,287 | 4,832 | 46,268 | 5,490 |
| California........ | 26,553 | 15,157 | 68,677 | 18,210 | New Mexico...... | 136 | 102 | 202 | 236 |
| Colorado........ | 2,468 | 460 | 7,583 | 1,628 | New York........ | 23,516 | 10,926 | 245,068 | 17,488 |
| Connecticut...... | 7,668 | 1,545 | 16,542 | 1,159 | North Carolina.... | 222 | 162 | 554 | 106 |
| Delaware....... | 146 | 92 | 944 | 90 | North Dakota..... | 1,838 | 102 | 7,851 | 71 |
| Dist. of Col..... | 447 | 357 | 3,884 | 223 | Ohio........... | 3,368 | 2,513 | 20,530 | 28,870 |
| Florida......... | 6,323 | 1,596 | 18,183 | 1,520 | Oklahoma...... | 191 | 149 | 1,281 | 138 |
| Georgia......... | 204 | 108 | 1,280 | 98 | Oregon........ | 4,538 | 1,685 | 4,349 | 998 |
| Hawaii.......... | 78 | 58 | 183 | 20 | Pennsylvania..... | 4,603 | 2,331 | 59,894 | 18,450 |
| Idaho.......... | 1,035 | 304 | 736 | 204 | Rhode Island..... | 2,019 | 152 | 3,960 | 55 |
| Illinois......... | 34,606 | 2,940 | 45,522 | 24,570 | South Carolina.... | 65 | 55 | 347 | 56 |
| Indiana......... | 1,710 | 436 | 3,113 | 5,531 | South Dakota.... | 1,430 | 161 | 2,480 | 69 |
| Iowa........... | 3,813 | 522 | 1,777 | 867 | Tennessee..... | 177 | 168 | 986 | 68 |
| Kansas......... | 1,243 | 337 | 2,735 | 1,252 | Texas.......... | 1,625 | 743 | 3,472 | 627 |
| Kentucky....... | 128 | 253 | 699 | 148 | Utah.......... | 1,316 | 870 | 229 | 305 |
| Louisiana....... | 179 | 84 | 760 | 358 | Vermont....... | 345 | 118 | 364 | 41 |
| Maine.......... | 586 | 63 | 1,082 | 30 | Virginia....... | 387 | 332 | 1,859 | 251 |
| Maryland........ | 874 | 575 | 10,332 | 566 | Washington...... | 13,507 | 1,682 | 6,611 | 2,775 |
| Massachusetts..... | 13,607 | 954 | 38,604 | 625 | West Virginia.... | 56 | 132 | 774 | 1,017 |
| Michigan........ | 7,790 | 1,513 | 25,784 | 11,633 | Wisconsin...... | 5,519 | 3,633 | 9,145 | 9,364 |
| Minnesota....... | 25,323 | 673 | 6,676 | 4,328 | Wyoming....... | 451 | 126 | 822 | 428 |
| Mississippi...... | 84 | 16 | 233 | 145 | | | | | |
| Missouri........ | 947 | 88 | 6,837 | 2,578 | | | | | |
| Montana........ | 1,541 | 303 | 2,616 | 1,142 | **Totals........** | **214,491** | **61,568** | **690,598** | **165,798** |

# Population of Voting Age—Votes Cast for President 1964-1960

Source: Bureau of the Census
(Population includes armed forces stationed in each state. Percentages based on unrounded numbers.)

| State | 1964 Pop. of voting age | Votes cast Number (Rounded) | Per-cent | 1960 Pop. of voting age | Votes cast Number (Rounded) | Per-cent |
|---|---|---|---|---|---|---|
| Alabama | 1,915,000 | 690,000 | 36.0 | 1,834,000 | 570,000 | 31.1 |
| Alaska | 138,000 | 67,000 | 48.7 | 134,000 | 61,000 | 45.5 |
| Arizona | 879,000 | 481,000 | 54.7 | 732,000 | 398,000 | 54.5 |
| Arkansas | 1,124,000 | 560,000 | 49.8 | 1,043,000 | 429,000 | 41.1 |
| California | 10,916,000 | 7,058,000 | 64.7 | 9,660,000 | 6,507,000 | 67.4 |
| Colorado | 1,142,000 | 777,000 | 68.0 | 1,031,000 | 736,000 | 71.4 |
| Connecticut | 1,698,000 | 1,219,000 | 71.8 | 1,591,000 | 1,223,000 | 76.8 |
| Delaware | 283,000 | 201,000 | 71.0 | 267,000 | 197,000 | 73.6 |
| District of Columbia | 517,000 | 199,000 | 38.4 | 509,000 | ......... | .... |
| Florida | 3,516,000 | 1,854,000 | 52.8 | 3,088,000 | 1,544,000 | 50.0 |
| Georgia | 2,636,000 | 1,139,000 | 43.2 | 2,410,000 | 733,000 | 30.4 |
| Hawaii | 395,000 | 207,000 | 52.5 | 360,000 | 185,000 | 51.3 |
| Idaho | 386,000 | 292,000 | 75.8 | 372,000 | 300,000 | 80.7 |
| Illinois | 6,358,000 | 4,703,000 | 74.0 | 6,281,000 | 4,757,000 | 75.7 |
| Indiana | 2,826,000 | 2,092,000 | 74.0 | 2,778,000 | 2,135,000 | 76.9 |
| Iowa | 1,638,000 | 1,185,000 | 72.3 | 1,664,000 | 1,274,000 | 76.5 |
| Kansas | 1,323,000 | 858,000 | 64.8 | 1,322,000 | 929,000 | 70.3 |
| Kentucky | 1,976,000 | 1,046,000 | 52.9 | 1,898,000 | 1,124,000 | 59.2 |
| Louisiana | 1,893,000 | 896,000 | 47.3 | 1,804,000 | 808,000 | 44.8 |
| Maine | 581,000 | 381,000 | 65.6 | 581,000 | 422,000 | 72.6 |
| Maryland | 1,995,000 | 1,116,000 | 56.0 | 1,845,000 | 1,055,000 | 57.2 |
| Massachusetts | 3,290,000 | 2,345,000 | 71.3 | 3,245,000 | 2,469,000 | 76.1 |
| Michigan | 4,647,000 | 3,203,000 | 68.9 | 4,580,000 | 3,318,000 | 72.4 |
| Minnesota | 2,024,000 | 1,554,000 | 76.8 | 2,001,000 | 1,542,000 | 77.0 |
| Mississippi | 1,243,000 | 409,000 | 32.9 | 1,171,000 | 298,000 | 25.5 |
| Missouri | 2,696,000 | 1,818,000 | 67.4 | 2,696,000 | 1,934,000 | 71.8 |
| Montana | 399,000 | 279,000 | 69.9 | 389,000 | 278,000 | 71.4 |
| Nebraska | 877,000 | 584,000 | 66.6 | 858,000 | 613,000 | 71.4 |
| Nevada | 244,000 | 135,000 | 55.5 | 175,000 | 107,000 | 61.2 |
| New Hampshire | 396,000 | 288,000 | 72.3 | 373,000 | 296,000 | 79.4 |
| New Jersey | 4,147,000 | 2,847,000 | 68.6 | 3,861,000 | 2,773,000 | 71.8 |
| New Mexico | 514,000 | 328,000 | 63.7 | 501,000 | 311,000 | 62.1 |
| New York | 11,330,000 | 7,166,000 | 63.2 | 10,851,000 | 7,291,000 | 67.0 |
| North Carolina | 2,753,000 | 1,425,000 | 51.5 | 2,557,000 | 1,369,000 | 53.5 |
| North Dakota | 358,000 | 258,000 | 72.2 | 355,000 | 278,000 | 78.5 |
| Ohio | 5,960,000 | 3,969,000 | 66.6 | 5,839,000 | 4,162,000 | 71.3 |
| Oklahoma | 1,493,000 | 932,000 | 62.5 | 1,416,000 | 903,000 | 63.8 |
| Oregon | 1,130,000 | 786,000 | 69.6 | 1,073,000 | 776,000 | 72.3 |
| Pennsylvania | 7,080,000 | 4,823,000 | 68.1 | 7,100,000 | 5,007,000 | 70.5 |
| Rhode Island | 568,000 | 390,000 | 68.6 | 540,000 | 406,000 | 75.1 |
| South Carolina | 1,380,000 | 525,000 | 38.0 | 1,266,000 | 387,000 | 30.5 |
| South Dakota | 404,000 | 293,000 | 72.6 | 392,000 | 306,000 | 78.3 |
| Tennessee | 2,239,000 | 1,144,000 | 51.1 | 2,093,000 | 1,052,000 | 50.3 |
| Texas | 5,922,000 | 2,627,000 | 44.4 | 5,534,000 | 2,312,000 | 41.8 |
| Utah | 522,000 | 401,000 | 76.9 | 468,000 | 375,000 | 80.1 |
| Vermont | 240,000 | 163,000 | 67.9 | 231,000 | 167,000 | 72.5 |
| Virginia | 2,541,000 | 1,042,000 | 41.0 | 2,313,000 | 771,000 | 33.4 |
| Washington | 1,759,000 | 1,258,000 | 71.5 | 1,718,000 | 1,242,000 | 72.3 |
| West Virginia | 1,053,000 | 792,000 | 75.2 | 1,083,000 | 838,000 | 77.3 |
| Wisconsin | 2,391,000 | 1,692,000 | 70.8 | 2,354,000 | 1,729,000 | 73.4 |
| Wyoming | 195,000 | 143,000 | 73.2 | 190,000 | 141,000 | 74.0 |
| **Total** | **113,931,000** | **70,642,000** | **62.0** | **108,458,000** | **68,839,000** | **63.5** |

# U. S. Population, Urban and Rural, by Color: 1950 and 1960

Source: Bureau of the Census
Includes Alaska and Hawaii. An urbanized area comprises at least 1 city of 50,000 inhabitants (central city) plus contiguous, closely settled areas (urban fringe).

| Year and area | Total | White | Nonwhite | Percent distribution Total | White | Non. |
|---|---|---|---|---|---|---|
| **1950** | **151,326,000** | **135,150,000** | **16,176,000** | **100.0** | **100.0** | **100.0** |
| Urban | 96,847,000 | 86,864,000 | 9,983,000 | 64.0 | 64.3 | 61.7 |
| Urbanized areas | 69,249,000 | 61,925,000 | 7,324,000 | 45.8 | 45.8 | 45.3 |
| Central cities | 48,377,000 | 42,042,000 | 6,335,000 | 32.0 | 31.1 | 39.2 |
| Urban fringe | 20,872,000 | 19,883,000 | 989,000 | 13.8 | 14.7 | 6.1 |
| Other urban | 27,598,000 | 24,939,000 | 2,659,000 | 18.2 | 18.5 | 16.4 |
| Rural | 54,479,000 | 48,286,000 | 6,193,000 | 36.0 | 35.7 | 38.3 |
| **1960** | **179,323,000** | **158,832,000** | **20,491,000** | **100.0** | **100.0** | **100.0** |
| Urban | 125,269,000 | 110,428,000 | 14,840,000 | 69.9 | 69.5 | 72.4 |
| Urbanized areas | 95,848,000 | 83,770,000 | 12,079,000 | 53.5 | 52.7 | 58.9 |
| Central cities | 57,975,000 | 47,627,000 | 10,348,000 | 32.3 | 30.0 | 50.5 |
| Urban fringe | 37,873,000 | 36,143,000 | 1,731,000 | 21.1 | 22.8 | 8.4 |
| Other urban | 29,420,000 | 26,658,000 | 2,762,000 | 16.4 | 16.8 | 13.5 |
| Rural | 54,054,000 | 48,403,000 | 5,651,000 | 30.1 | 30.5 | 27.6 |

# U. S. Population Urban, Rural, White, Nonwhite

Source: Bureau of the Census (Census of 1960)

| Area | All classes Total | Male | Female | White Male | Female | Nonwhite Male | Female |
|---|---|---|---|---|---|---|---|
| Total | 179,323,175 | 88,331,494 | 90,991,681 | 78,367,149 | 80,464,583 | 9,964,345 | 10,527,098 |
| Urban | 125,268,750 | 60,733,005 | 64,535,745 | 53,631,145 | 56,797,187 | 7,101,860 | 7,738,558 |
| Urbanized areas | 95,848,487 | 46,494,210 | 49,354,277 | 40,706,094 | 43,063,841 | 5,788,116 | 6,290,436 |
| Central cities | 57,975,132 | 27,927,624 | 30,047,508 | 22,976,282 | 24,650,950 | 4,951,342 | 5,396,558 |
| Urban fringe | 37,873,355 | 18,566,586 | 19,306,769 | 17,729,812 | 18,412,891 | 836,774 | 893,878 |
| Other urban | 29,420,263 | 14,238,795 | 15,181,468 | 12,925,051 | 13,733,346 | 1,313,744 | 1,448,122 |
| Places of 10,000 or more | 16,172,839 | 7,838,676 | 8,334,163 | 7,070,615 | 7,490,599 | 768,061 | 843,564 |
| 2,500 to 10,000 | 13,247,424 | 6,400,119 | 6,847,305 | 5,854,436 | 6,242,747 | 545,683 | 604,558 |
| Rural | 54,054,425 | 27,598,489 | 26,455,936 | 24,736,004 | 23,667,396 | 2,862,485 | 2,788,540 |
| Places of 1,000 to 2,500 | 6,496,788 | 3,149,869 | 3,346,919 | 2,909,209 | 3,086,545 | 240,660 | 260,374 |
| Other rural | 47,557,637 | 24,448,620 | 23,109,017 | 21,826,795 | 20,580,851 | 2,621,825 | 2,528,166 |

## Jewish Population by Countries and Cities

Source: Jewish Statistical Bureau, Dr. H. S. Linfield, Exec. Secy. Figures are 1968 estimates

| | | | |
|---|---|---|---|
| North America | 5,995,000 | Australia and New Zealand | 74,000 |
| Central and South America | 745,350 | Africa | 238,650 |
| Europe | 4,020,950 | | |
| Asia(a) | 2,896,500 | **World total(a)** | **13,970,450** |

| Country | | Country | | Country | | Country | |
|---|---|---|---|---|---|---|---|
| **Europe** | | Switzerland | 20,000 | Honduras | 150 | Philippines | 500 |
| Albania | 300 | Turkey | 44,000 | Jamaica | 600 | Singapore | 600 |
| Austria | 12,000 | Yugoslavia | 7,000 | Mexico | 30,000 | Syria | 4,000 |
| Belgium | 41,000 | | | Nicaragua | 200 | Thailand | 100 |
| Bulgaria | 7,000 | **North America** | | Panama | 2,000 | Yemen | 2,000 |
| Czechoslovakia | 14,000 | Canada | 275,000 | Paraguay | 1,200 | | |
| Denmark | 6,000 | United States | 5,720,000 | Peru | 4,000 | **Africa** | |
| Finland | 1,500 | | | Trinidad | 400 | Abyssinia | 12,000 |
| France | 520,000 | **Central and** | | Uruguay | 50,000 | Algeria | 3,000 |
| Germany | 30,000 | **South America** | | Venezuela | 8,500 | Congo | 500 |
| Gibraltar | 650 | Argentina | 450,000 | | | Egypt | 2,500 |
| Great Britain | 450,000 | Barbados | 100 | **Asia** | | Kenya | 1,000 |
| Greece | 6,500 | Bolivia | 4,000 | Aden | 150 | Libya | 4,000 |
| Hungary | 80,000 | Brazil | 140,000 | Afghanistan | 800 | Morocco | 70,000 |
| Irish Free State | 5,500 | Chile | 30,000 | Burma | 50 | Rhodesia | 5,500 |
| Italy | 35,000 | Colombia | 10,000 | Cyprus | 50 | Sudan | 350 |
| Luxemburg | 1,000 | Costa Rica | 1,500 | China | 150 | Tunisia | 23,000 |
| Malta | 50 | Cuba | 2,000 | Hong Kong | 200 | Union of | |
| Netherlands | 30,000 | Curacao | 700 | India | 16,000 | South Africa | 116,000 |
| Norway | 750 | Dominican | | Indonesia | 100 | Zambia | 800 |
| Poland | 25,000 | Republic | 500 | Iran | 80,000 | | |
| Portugal | 700 | Dutch Guiana | 500 | Iraq | 4,000 | **Australia and** | |
| Romania | 120,000 | Ecuador | 2,000 | Israel(a) | 2,780,500 | **New Zealand** | |
| Soviet Union | 2,543,000 | El Salvador | 300 | Japan | 1,000 | Australia | 69,000 |
| Spain | 7,000 | Guatemala | 1,500 | Lebanon | 6,000 | New Zealand | 5,000 |
| Sweden | 13,000 | Haiti | 200 | Pakistan | 300 | | |

(a) Includes 392,500 Christians, Mohammedans and others; 65,000 in East Jerusalem and 327,000 in other cities and villages in State of Israel.

### ESTIMATED JEWISH POPULATION IN FOREIGN CITIES (Over 5,000)

| | | | | | | | |
|---|---|---|---|---|---|---|---|
| Amsterdam | 12,000 | Czernowitz | 70,000 | Manchester | 28,000 | Sao Paulo | 60,000 |
| Antwerp | 13,000 | Elat[1] | 10,500 | Marseilles | 60,000 | Santiago | 30,000 |
| Ascalon[1] | 37,000 | Glasgow | 13,500 | Melbourne | 35,000 | Stockholm | 7,000 |
| Ashdod[1] | 27,000 | Haifa[1] | 207,500 | Milan | 9,000 | Strasbourg | 14,000 |
| Beersheba[1] | 67,500 | Istanbul | 38,000 | Montreal | 105,000 | Sydney | 28,000 |
| Berlin | 6,000 | Jerusalem(a) | 261,500 | Moscow | 285,000 | Teheran | 30,000 |
| Bet Shean[1] | 12,500 | Johannesburg | 57,500 | Nazareth[1] | 30,000 | Tel Aviv- | |
| Birmingham | 6,300 | Kharkov | 80,000 | Nazareth | | Jaffa[1] | 389,500 |
| Bordeaux | 6,500 | Kiev | 220,000 | Illet[1] | 11,000 | Tiberias[1] | 23,500 |
| Brussels | 25,000 | Leeds | 18,000 | Nice | 20,000 | Toronto | 88,000 |
| Bucharest | 50,000 | Leningrad | 165,000 | Paris | 300,000 | Toulouse | 20,000 |
| Budapest | 65,000 | Liverpool | 7,500 | Petach Tikvah | 71,500 | Vienna | 9,000 |
| Buenos Aires | 360,000 | Lod (Lydda)[1] | 25,000 | Ramath Gan[1] | 105,000 | Warsaw | 5,000 |
| Casablanca | 52,000 | London (gr.) | 280,000 | Rio de Janeiro | 55,000 | Winnipeg | 21,000 |
| Copenhagen | 6,000 | Lyons | 25,000 | Rome | 13,000 | Zurich | 6,200 |

[1]Includes also Christians, Mohammedans and others.

### ESTIMATED JEWISH POPULATION IN LARGE U. S. CITIES (Over 10,000)

| | | | | | | | |
|---|---|---|---|---|---|---|---|
| Albany | 12,000 | Hollywood, Fla. | 13,500 | Brooklyn | 760,000 | Philadelphia* | 330,000 |
| Atlanta | 15,500 | Houston | 20,000 | Queens | 420,000 | Phoenix* | 13,500 |
| Atlantic City* | 10,000 | Jersey City | 13,000 | Richmond | 11,000 | Pittsburgh | 45,000 |
| Baltimore | 85,000 | Kansas City | 22,000 | N. Y. City environs: | | Prince George | |
| Bergen County | 80,000 | Long Beach Cal | 12,000 | Nassau Co. | 372,000 | County, Md | 19,000 |
| Boston* | 185,000 | Los Angeles* | 500,000 | Suffolk Co. | 42,000 | Providence | 20,000 |
| Bridgeport* | 14,500 | Lynn | 12,000 | Westchester | | Rochester | 21,500 |
| Buffalo | 25,000 | Miami | 100,000 | County | 131,000 | St. Louis | 57,000 |
| Camden | 15,000 | Milwaukee | 24,000 | Newark: | | St. Paul | 10,000 |
| Chicago* | 270,000 | Minneapolis | 20,000 | Essex Co. | 100,000 | San Diego | 10,000 |
| Cincinnati | 27,000 | Montg'y Co. | | Oakland: | | San Francisco* | 71,000 |
| Cleveland | 85,000 | Md. | 47,000 | Alemeda | | Seattle | 11,000 |
| Columbus | 10,000 | New Brunswick | 11,000 | and Contra | | Springfield, | |
| Dallas | 20,000 | New Haven | 20,000 | Costa | 18,000 | Mass. | 12,000 |
| Denver | 22,000 | New Orleans | 10,000 | Orange Co. | | Stamford | 10,000 |
| Detroit | 85,000 | New York City | 1,836,000 | Calif. | 14,000 | Syracuse | 11,000 |
| Elizabeth* | 16,500 | Manhattan | 250,000 | Passaic | 10,500 | Washington* | 90,000 |
| Hartford | 26,000 | Bronx | 395,000 | Paterson | 15,000 | Worcester | 10,000 |

*Indicates greater area.

## United States Foreign Stock by States
Source: Bureau of the Census. Census of 1960.

| State | Foreign born | Native of foreign or mixed parentage | State | Foreign born | Native of foreign or mixed parentage | State | Foreign born | Native of foreign or mixed parentage |
|---|---|---|---|---|---|---|---|---|
| Ala. | 14,955 | 39,839 | La. | 30,557 | 92,983 | Okla. | 20,003 | 69,151 |
| Alaska | 8,227 | 22,847 | Me. | 60,403 | 165,996 | Ore. | 71,314 | 229,734 |
| Ariz. | 70,318 | 165,308 | Md. | 94,178 | 277,379 | Pa. | 603,490 | 1,898,343 |
| Ark. | 7,457 | 26,328 | Mass. | 576,452 | 1,481,557 | R. I. | 85,974 | 253,745 |
| Calif. | 1,343,710 | 2,650,052 | Mich. | 529,624 | 1,368,903 | S. C. | 11,140 | 26,429 |
| Colo. | 59,881 | 201,355 | Minn. | 143,878 | 730,648 | S. D. | 18,577 | 123,268 |
| Conn. | 275,523 | 706,620 | Miss. | 8,058 | 20,657 | Tenn. | 15,843 | 43,106 |
| Dela. | 14,650 | 44,240 | Mo. | 77,756 | 289,490 | Texas | 298,791 | 783,677 |
| D. of C. | 38,971 | 57,557 | Mont. | 30,646 | 119,048 | Utah. | 32,133 | 107,269 |
| Fla. | 272,161 | 460,892 | Neb. | 40,238 | 217,921 | Vt. | 23,336 | 62,498 |
| Ga. | 25,300 | 53,090 | Nev. | 13,133 | 36,692 | Va. | 48,185 | 129,670 |
| Hawaii | 68,900 | 173,684 | N. H. | 44,772 | 132,348 | Wash. | 178,658 | 474,879 |
| Idaho | 15,542 | 67,217 | N. J. | 615,479 | 1,493,286 | W. Va. | 23,863 | 67,401 |
| Ill. | 686,098 | 1,763,000 | N. M. | 21,408 | 57,556 | Wisc. | 171,519 | 742,583 |
| Ind. | 93,202 | 283,895 | N. Y. | 2,289,314 | 4,198,130 | Wyo. | 9,663 | 38,753 |
| Iowa. | 56,278 | 331,864 | N. C. | 21,978 | 46,483 | | | |
| Kan. | 33,268 | 172,296 | N. D. | 29,907 | 159,711 | **Total.** | **9,738,155** | **24,312,287** |
| Ky. | 16,830 | 58,553 | Ohio. | 396,614 | 1,094,056 | **Total** | **34,050,442** | |

# Marital Status of United States Population by States
### Source: Bureau of the Census (1960 Census)

| States | Male 14 years old and over | | | | Female 14 years old and over | | | |
|---|---|---|---|---|---|---|---|---|
| | Total | Single | Married | Widowed or divorced | Total | Single | Married | Widowed or divorced |
| Alabama | 1,059,866 | 270,845 | 735,545 | 53,476 | 1,157,626 | 221,981 | 752,437 | 183,208 |
| Alaska | 89,132 | 30,756 | 52,958 | 5,418 | 59,626 | 9,236 | 45,821 | 4,569 |
| Arizona | 435,986 | 108,368 | 301,183 | 26,435 | 435,196 | 76,873 | 298,782 | 59,541 |
| Arkansas | 606,401 | 145,217 | 423,049 | 38,135 | 643,007 | 108,663 | 428,607 | 105,737 |
| California | 5,530,596 | 1,371,603 | 3,786,286 | 372,707 | 5,652,177 | 928,656 | 3,771,579 | 951,942 |
| Colorado | 594,842 | 144,886 | 414,228 | 35,728 | 616,527 | 109,310 | 415,785 | 91,432 |
| Connecticut | 881,494 | 221,220 | 613,984 | 46,290 | 942,847 | 197,177 | 616,690 | 128,980 |
| Delaware | 151,235 | 36,305 | 106,852 | 8,078 | 157,955 | 29,546 | 107,250 | 21,159 |
| Dist. of Col | 265,503 | 82,417 | 164,116 | 18,970 | 313,161 | 84,367 | 168,601 | 60,193 |
| Florida | 1,730,220 | 374,544 | 1,241,993 | 113,683 | 1,827,398 | 272,521 | 1,249,347 | 305,530 |
| Georgia | 1,290,444 | 335,377 | 891,632 | 63,435 | 1,397,751 | 261,801 | 909,546 | 226,404 |
| Hawaii | 232,805 | 84,965 | 134,421 | 13,419 | 193,684 | 44,376 | 128,526 | 20,780 |
| Idaho | 226,097 | 55,122 | 157,798 | 13,177 | 221,205 | 36,234 | 157,901 | 27,160 |
| Illinois | 3,498,909 | 862,301 | 2,421,448 | 215,160 | 3,719,766 | 705,236 | 2,439,625 | 574,905 |
| Indiana | 1,580,100 | 357,882 | 1,127,277 | 94,941 | 1,670,751 | 288,626 | 1,132,436 | 249,689 |
| Iowa | 941,937 | 225,414 | 663,565 | 52,958 | 999,250 | 186,617 | 665,925 | 146,708 |
| Kansas | 754,886 | 174,588 | 537,048 | 43,250 | 783,472 | 129,835 | 537,325 | 116,312 |
| Kentucky | 1,036,635 | 272,754 | 703,396 | 60,485 | 1,074,053 | 203,317 | 707,757 | 162,979 |
| Louisiana | 1,037,798 | 267,633 | 716,265 | 53,900 | 1,126,618 | 220,706 | 734,376 | 171,536 |
| Maine | 334,141 | 86,356 | 224,921 | 22,864 | 349,182 | 68,276 | 225,143 | 55,763 |
| Maryland | 1,054,302 | 267,338 | 733,011 | 53,953 | 1,100,932 | 210,392 | 740,061 | 150,498 |
| Massachusetts | 1,767,940 | 487,744 | 1,177,799 | 102,397 | 1,971,652 | 479,217 | 1,190,007 | 302,472 |
| Michigan | 2,622,801 | 626,942 | 1,845,155 | 150,704 | 2,725,768 | 500,994 | 1,856,372 | 368,428 |
| Minnesota | 1,148,286 | 313,625 | 775,743 | 58,918 | 1,196,196 | 257,360 | 778,308 | 160,551 |
| Mississippi | 693,456 | 190,286 | 465,811 | 37,359 | 746,017 | 147,842 | 478,764 | 119,429 |
| Missouri | 1,496,446 | 346,446 | 1,053,285 | 96,715 | 1,620,617 | 286,446 | 1,059,992 | 274,118 |
| Montana | 234,200 | 63,000 | 155,254 | 15,943 | 224,198 | 38,191 | 154,769 | 31,278 |
| Nebraska | 488,723 | 120,473 | 341,033 | 27,217 | 507,502 | 92,119 | 341,875 | 73,534 |
| Nevada | 105,363 | 24,827 | 71,084 | 9,452 | 96,690 | 13,167 | 69,509 | 14,004 |
| New Hampshire | 209,518 | 52,846 | 143,172 | 13,500 | 223,616 | 45,038 | 144,104 | 34,418 |
| New Jersey | 2,125,478 | 519,170 | 1,497,601 | 108,707 | 2,278,413 | 442,593 | 1,511,112 | 324,777 |
| New Mexico | 305,452 | 79,090 | 210,812 | 15,550 | 301,432 | 56,403 | 209,892 | 35,101 |
| New York | 5,888,946 | 1,537,321 | 4,035,908 | 315,717 | 6,498,895 | 1,407,437 | 4,109,697 | 981,738 |
| North Carolina | 1,518,107 | 421,557 | 1,036,364 | 60,186 | 1,600,462 | 332,546 | 1,054,388 | 213,562 |
| North Dakota | 217,868 | 69,007 | 139,140 | 9,721 | 208,074 | 44,814 | 139,138 | 24,128 |
| Ohio | 3,267,146 | 742,609 | 2,322,247 | 202,290 | 3,499,338 | 642,553 | 2,333,487 | 523,222 |
| Oklahoma | 812,235 | 184,934 | 574,424 | 52,877 | 856,059 | 130,662 | 576,185 | 149,291 |
| Oregon | 616,766 | 139,280 | 435,000 | 42,486 | 634,518 | 102,736 | 436,231 | 95,512 |
| Pennsylvania | 3,915,461 | 987,646 | 2,701,373 | 226,442 | 4,270,170 | 904,654 | 2,740,734 | 624,757 |
| Rhode Island | 303,887 | 84,312 | 202,075 | 17,500 | 323,812 | 72,513 | 203,042 | 48,286 |
| South Carolina | 768,653 | 233,698 | 505,151 | 29,804 | 810,626 | 177,777 | 516,583 | 116,253 |
| South Dakota | 233,532 | 66,168 | 155,237 | 12,127 | 229,543 | 44,426 | 155,464 | 29,667 |
| Tennessee | 1,199,101 | 298,535 | 836,525 | 64,041 | 1,300,251 | 245,625 | 850,469 | 204,153 |
| Texas | 3,212,658 | 769,443 | 2,261,537 | 181,678 | 3,349,072 | 562,011 | 2,269,898 | 517,158 |
| Utah | 281,896 | 70,980 | 198,330 | 12,586 | 289,631 | 56,529 | 198,914 | 34,168 |
| Vermont | 132,187 | 36,571 | 87,567 | 8,049 | 141,327 | 30,724 | 88,365 | 22,280 |
| Virginia | 1,368,706 | 379,473 | 923,830 | 65,403 | 1,393,767 | 272,930 | 925,637 | 195,239 |
| Washington | 1,003,704 | 247,500 | 687,435 | 68,769 | 1,001,924 | 162,947 | 687,228 | 151,705 |
| West Virginia | 627,445 | 162,916 | 427,931 | 36,598 | 667,970 | 133,557 | 435,018 | 99,343 |
| Wisconsin | 1,347,890 | 352,665 | 919,328 | 75,897 | 1,395,184 | 285,762 | 921,919 | 187,592 |
| Wyoming | 114,875 | 27,775 | 79,852 | 7,248 | 108,991 | 16,780 | 78,679 | 13,503 |
| **Total** | **61,362,055** | **15,412,733** | **42,416,979** | **3,532,343** | **64,913,989** | **12,380,049** | **42,749,302** | **9,784,638** |

## Density of Population by States
### BY SQUARE MILE, LAND AREA ONLY
### Source: Bureau of the Census

| State | 1920 | 1950 | 1960** | State | 1920 | 1950 | 1960** | State | 1920 | 1950 | 1960** |
|---|---|---|---|---|---|---|---|---|---|---|---|
| Ala | 45.8 | 59.9 | 64.2 | La | 39.6 | 59.4 | 72.1 | Okla | 29.2 | 32.4 | 33.8 |
| Alaska* | 0.1 | 0.2 | .59 | Maine | 25.7 | 29.4 | 31.3 | Oregon | 8.2 | 15.8 | 18.4 |
| Ariz | 2.9 | 6.6 | 11.5 | Md | 145.8 | 237.1 | 313.5 | Pa | 194.5 | 233.1 | 251.4 |
| Ark | 33.4 | 36.3 | 34.2 | Mass | 479.2 | 596.2 | 657.5 | R.I. | 566.4 | 748.5 | 819.3 |
| Calif | 22.0 | 67.5 | 100.4 | Mich | 63.8 | 111.7 | 137.6 | S.C. | 55.2 | 69.9 | 78.7 |
| Colo | 9.1 | 12.8 | 16.9 | Minn | 29.5 | 37.3 | 43.1P | S.D. | 8.3 | 8.5 | 9.0 |
| Conn | 286.4 | 409.7 | 520.6 | Miss | 38.6 | 46.1 | 46.0 | Tenn | 56.1 | 78.8 | 86.2 |
| Del | 113.5 | 160.8 | 225.2 | Mo | 49.5 | 57.1 | 62.6 | Texas | 17.8 | 29.3 | 36.4 |
| D.C. | 7,292.9 | 13,150.5 | 12,442.3 | Mont | 3.8 | 4.1 | 4.6 | Utah | 5.5 | 8.4 | 10.8 |
| Fla | 17.7 | 51.1 | 91.5 | Neb | 16.9 | 17.3 | 18.4 | Vt | 38.6 | 40.7 | 42.0 |
| Ga | 49.3 | 58.9 | 67.8 | Nev | .7 | 1.5 | 2.6 | Va | 57.4 | 83.2 | 99.3 |
| Hawaii | 39.9 | 78.0 | 98.4 | N.H. | 49.1 | 59.1 | 67.2 | Wash | 20.3 | 35.6 | 42.8 |
| Idaho | 5.2 | 7.1 | 8.1 | N.J. | 420.0 | 642.8 | 805.5 | W. Va. | 60.9 | 83.3 | 77.2 |
| Illinois | 115.7 | 155.8 | 180.4 | N.M. | 2.9 | 5.6 | 7.8 | Wis | 47.6 | 62.8 | 72.6 |
| Indiana | 81.3 | 108.7 | 128.8 | N.Y. | 217.9 | 309.3 | 350.8 | Wyo | 2.0 | 3.0 | 3.4 |
| Iowa | 43.2 | 46.8 | 49.2 | N.C. | 52.5 | 82.7 | 93.2 | | | | |
| Kan | 21.6 | 23.2 | 26.6 | Ohio | 141.4 | 193.8 | 236.6 | U.S. | *29.9 | *42.6 | 50.5 |
| Ky | 60.1 | 73.9 | 76.2 | | | | | | | | |

*For purposes of comparison, Alaska and Hawaii included in above tabulation for 1920 and 1950 even though not states then. **Revised 1967. P-Preliminary.
Number of inhabitants per sq. mi. of Land Area in U. S. (1790) 4.5; (1800) 6.1; (1810) 4.3; (1820) 5.5; (1830) 7.4; (1840) 9.8; (1850) 7.9; (1860) 10.6; (1870) 13.0; (1880) 16.9; (1890) 21.2; (1900) 25.6; (1910) 31.0; (1920) 35.5; (1930) 41.2; (1940) 44.2; (1950) 50.7; (1960) 50.5 (Alaska and Hawaii included only in 1960).

## Males per 100 Females in U. S.
### Source: Bureau of the Census
Ratio represents number of males per 100 females. Total population including Armed Forces overseas.

| Age | 1910 | 1920 | 1930 | 1940 | 1950 | 1960 | 1967[1] | | |
|---|---|---|---|---|---|---|---|---|---|
| | | | | | | | Total | White | Negro |
| All ages | [2]106.2 | [2]104.1 | [2]102.5 | 100.8 | 99.2 | 97.8 | 96.8 | 97.1 | 93.6 |
| Under 15 years | 102.2 | 102.1 | 102.6 | 103.0 | 103.8 | 103.8 | 103.7 | 104.3 | 100.3 |
| 15 to 24 years | 101.2 | 96.9 | 98.2 | 98.7 | 100.0 | 100.3 | 102.6 | 103.2 | 98.9 |
| 25 to 44 years | 110.5 | 105.3 | 101.0 | 98.7 | 97.2 | 97.2 | 97.3 | 98.6 | 88.0 |
| 45 to 64 years | 114.7 | 115.4 | 109.2 | 105.3 | 100.1 | 98.9 | 92.7 | 93.1 | 87.0 |
| 65 and over | 101.2 | 101.5 | 100.6 | 95.7 | 89.5 | 88.3 | 75.7 | 75.2 | 78.7 |

[1] Estimated as of July 1. [2] Includes figures for "age not reported."

# Population of U. S. Cities of 100,000 or more
## 1960 CENSUS OF POPULATION
### Source: Bureau of the Census

| City | 1960 | 1950 | City | 1960 | 1950 |
|---|---|---|---|---|---|
| 1—New York, N. Y. | 7,781,984 | 7,891,957 | 66—Worcester, Mass. | 186,587 | 203,486 |
| 2—Chicago, Ill. | 3,550,404 | 3,620,962 | 67—Austin, Texas | 186,545 | 132,459 |
| 3—Los Angeles, Calif. | 2,479,015 | 1,970,358 | 68—Spokane, Wash. | 181,608 | 161,721 |
| 4—Philadelphia, Pa. | 2,002,512 | 2,071,605 | 69—St. Petersburg, Fla. | 181,298 | 96,738 |
| 5—Detroit, Mich. | 1,670,144 | 1,849,568 | 70—Gary, Ind. | 178,320 | 133,911 |
| 6—Baltimore, Md. | 939,024 | 949,708 | 71—Grand Rapids, Mich. | 177,313 | 176,515 |
| 7—Houston, Texas | 938,219 | 596,163 | 72—Springfield, Mass. | 174,463 | 162,399 |
| 8—Cleveland, Ohio | 876,050 | 914,808 | 73—Nashville, Tenn. | 170,874 | 174,307 |
| 9—Washington, D. C. | 763,956 | 802,178 | 74—Corpus Christi, Texas | 167,670 | 108,287 |
| 10—St. Louis, Mo. | 750,026 | 856,796 | 75—Youngstown, Ohio | 166,689 | 168,330 |
| 11—Milwaukee, Wisc. | 741,324 | 637,392 | 76—Shreveport, La. | 164,372 | 127,206 |
| 12—San Francisco, Calif. | 740,316 | 775,357 | 77—Hartford, Conn. | 162,178 | 177,397 |
| 13—Boston, Mass. | 697,197 | 801,444 | 78—Fort Wayne, Ind. | 161,776 | 133,607 |
| 14—Dallas, Texas | 679,684 | 434,462 | 79—Bridgeport, Conn. | 156,748 | 158,709 |
| 15—New Orleans, La. | 627,525 | 570,445 | 80—Baton Rouge, La. | 152,419 | 125,629 |
| 16—Pittsburgh, Pa. | 604,332 | 676,806 | 81—New Haven, Conn. | 152,048 | 164,443 |
| 17—San Antonio, Texas | 587,718 | 408,442 | 82—Savannah, Ga. | 149,245 | 119,638 |
| 18—San Diego, Calif. | 573,224 | 334,387 | 83—Tacoma, Wash. | 147,979 | 143,673 |
| 19—Seattle, Wash. | 557,087 | 467,591 | 84—Jackson, Miss. | 144,422 | 98,271 |
| 20—Buffalo, N. Y. | 532,759 | 580,132 | 85—Paterson, N. J. | 143,663 | 139,336 |
| 21—Cincinnati, Ohio | 502,550 | 503,998 | 86—Evansville, Ind. | 141,543 | 128,636 |
| 22—Memphis, Tenn. | 497,524 | 396,000 | 87—Erie, Pa. | 138,440 | 130,803 |
| 23—Denver, Colo. | 493,887 | 415,786 | 88—Amarillo, Texas | 137,969 | 74,246 |
| 24—Atlanta, Ga. | 487,455 | 331,314 | 89—Montgomery, Ala. | 134,393 | 106,525 |
| 25—Minneapolis, Minn. | 482,872 | 521,718 | 90—Fresno, Calif. | 133,929 | 91,669 |
| 26—Indianapolis, Ind. | 476,258 | 427,173 | 91—South Bend, Ind. | 132,445 | 115,911 |
| 27—Kansas City, Mo. | 475,539 | 456,622 | 92—Chattanooga, Tenn. | 130,009 | 131,041 |
| 28—Columbus, Ohio | 471,316 | 375,901 | 93—Albany, N. Y. | 129,726 | 134,995 |
| 29—Phoenix, Ariz. | 439,170 | 106,818 | 94—Lubbock, Texas | 128,691 | 71,747 |
| 30—Newark, N. J. | 405,220 | 438,776 | 95—Lincoln, Nebr. | 128,521 | 98,884 |
| 31—Louisville, Ky. | 390,639 | 369,129 | 96—Madison, Wisc. | 126,706 | 96,056 |
| 32—Portland, Ore. | 372,676 | 373,628 | 97—Rockford, Ill. | 126,706 | 92,927 |
| 33—Oakland, Calif. | 367,548 | 384,575 | 98—Kansas City, Kans. | 121,901 | 129,553 |
| 34—Fort Worth, Texas | 356,268 | 278,778 | 99—Greensboro, N. C. | 119,574 | 74,389 |
| 35—Long Beach, Calif. | 344,168 | 250,767 | 100—Topeka, Kans. | 119,484 | 78,791 |
| 36—Birmingham, Ala. | 340,887 | 326,037 | 101—Glendale, Calif. | 119,442 | 95,702 |
| 37—Oklahoma City, Okla. | 324,253 | 243,504 | 102—Beaumont, Texas | 119,175 | 94,014 |
| 38—Rochester, N. Y. | 318,611 | 332,488 | 103—Camden, N. J. | 117,159 | 124,555 |
| 39—Toledo, Ohio | 318,003 | 303,616 | 104—Columbus, Ga. | 116,779 | 79,611 |
| 40—St. Paul, Minn. | 313,411 | 311,349 | 105—Pasadena, Calif. | 116,407 | 104,577 |
| 41—Norfolk, Va. | 304,869 | 213,513 | 106—Portsmouth, Va. | 114,773 | 80,039 |
| 42—Omaha, Nebr. | 301,598 | 251,117 | 107—Trenton, N. J. | 114,167 | 128,009 |
| 43—Honolulu, Hawaii | 294,194 | 248,034 | 108—Newport News, Va. | 113,662 | 42,358 |
| 44—Miami, Fla. | 291,688 | 249,276 | 109—Canton, Ohio | 113,631 | 116,912 |
| 45—Akron, Ohio | 290,351 | 274,605 | 110—Dearborn, Mich. | 112,007 | 94,994 |
| 46—El Paso, Texas | 276,687 | 130,485 | 111—Knoxville, Tenn. | 111,827 | 124,769 |
| 47—Jersey City, N. J. | 276,101 | 299,017 | 112—Hammond, Ind. | 111,698 | 87,594 |
| 48—Tampa, Fla. | 274,970 | 124,681 | 113—Scranton, Pa. | 111,443 | 125,536 |
| 49—Dayton, Ohio | 262,332 | 243,872 | 114—Berkeley, Calif. | 111,268 | 113,805 |
| 50—Tulsa, Okla. | 261,685 | 182,740 | 115—Winston-Salem, N. C. | 111,135 | 87,811 |
| 51—Wichita, Kans. | 254,698 | 168,279 | 116—Allentown, Pa. | 108,347 | 106,756 |
| 52—Richmond, Va. | 219,958 | 230,310 | 117—Little Rock, Ark. | 107,813 | 102,213 |
| 53—Syracuse, N. Y. | 216,038 | 220,583 | 118—Lansing, Mich. | 107,807 | 92,129 |
| 54—Tucson, Ariz. | 212,892 | 45,454 | 119—Cambridge, Mass. | 107,716 | 120,740 |
| 55—Des Moines, Iowa | 208,982 | 177,965 | 120—Elizabeth, N. J. | 107,698 | 112,817 |
| 56—Providence, R. I. | 207,498 | 248,674 | 121—Waterbury, Conn. | 107,130 | 104,477 |
| 57—San Jose, Calif. | 204,196 | 95,280 | 122—Duluth, Minn. | 106,884 | 104,511 |
| 58—Mobile, Ala. | 202,779 | 129,009 | 123—Anaheim, Calif. | 104,184 | 14,556 |
| 59—Charlotte, N. C. | 201,564 | 134,042 | 124—Peoria, Ill. | 103,162 | 111,856 |
| 60—Albuquerque, N. M. | 201,189 | 96,815 | 125—New Bedford, Mass. | 102,477 | 109,189 |
| 61—Jacksonville, Fla. | 201,030 | 204,517 | 126—Niagara Falls, N. Y. | 102,394 | 90,872 |
| 62—Flint, Mich. | 196,940 | 163,143 | 127—Wichita Falls, Texas | 101,724 | 68,042 |
| 63—Sacramento, Calif. | 191,667 | 137,572 | 128—Torrance, Calif. | 100,991 | 22,241 |
| 64—Yonkers, N. Y. | 190,634 | 152,798 | 129—Utica, N. Y. | 100,410 | 101,531 |
| 65—Salt Lake City, Utah | 189,454 | 182,121 | 130—Santa Ana, Calif. | 100,350 | 45,533 |
| | | | San Juan, P. R. | 432,377 | 224,767 |
| | | | Ponce, P. R. | 114,286 | 99,492 |

# Farm Population of the United States

| | Both sexes | | Male | | Female | |
|---|---|---|---|---|---|---|
| Age and color | 1967 | 1960 | 1967 | 1960 | 1967 | 1960 |
| Total | 10,817,000 | 15,669,000 | 5,587,000 | 8,184,000 | 5,230,000 | 7,485,000 |
| White | 9,534,000 | 13,092,000 | 4,933,000 | 6,871,000 | 4,601,000 | 6,221,000 |
| Nonwhite | 1,283,000 | 2,577,000 | 654,000 | 1,313,000 | 629,000 | 1,264,000 |
| Under 14 years | 3,001,000 | 4,995,000 | 1,548,000 | 2,586,000 | 1,453,000 | 2,409,000 |
| White | 2,485,000 | 3,851,000 | 1,291,000 | 1,995,000 | 1,194,000 | 1,856,000 |
| Nonwhite | 516,000 | 1,144,000 | 257,000 | 591,000 | 259,000 | 553,000 |
| 14 years and over | 7,816,000 | 10,674,000 | 4,039,000 | 5,598,000 | 3,777,000 | 5,076,000 |
| White | 7,049,000 | 9,241,000 | 3,642,000 | 4,876,000 | 3,407,000 | 4,365,000 |
| Nonwhite | 767,000 | 1,433,000 | 397,000 | 722,000 | 370,000 | 711,000 |

# Negro Population in 30 Largest Cities by Percentage (*Estimated)

| | 1950 | 1960 | 1965* | | 1950 | 1960 | 1965* | | 1950 | 1960 | 1965* |
|---|---|---|---|---|---|---|---|---|---|---|---|
| New York | 10 | 14 | 18 | Milwaukee | 3 | 8 | 11 | Cincinnati | 16 | 22 | 24 |
| Chicago | 14 | 23 | 28 | San Francisco | 6 | 10 | 12 | Memphis | 37 | 37 | 40 |
| Los Angeles | 9 | 14 | 17 | Boston | 5 | 9 | 13 | Denver | 4 | 6 | 9 |
| Philadelphia | 18 | 26 | 31 | Dallas | 13 | 19 | 21 | Atlanta | 37 | 38 | 44 |
| Detroit | 16 | 29 | 34 | New Orleans | 32 | 37 | 41 | Minneapolis | 1 | 2 | 4 |
| Baltimore | 24 | 35 | 38 | Pittsburgh | 12 | 17 | 20 | Indianapolis | 15 | 21 | 23 |
| Houston | 21 | 23 | 23 | San Antonio | 7 | 7 | 8 | Kansas City, Mo. | 12 | 18 | 22 |
| Cleveland | 16 | 29 | 34 | San Diego | 5 | 6 | 7 | Columbus | 12 | 16 | 18 |
| Washington, D. C. | 35 | 54 | 66 | Seattle | 3 | 5 | 7 | Phoenix | 5 | 5 | 6 |
| St. Louis | 18 | 29 | 36 | Buffalo | 6 | 13 | 17 | Newark, N. J. | 17 | 34 | 47 |

# U. S. Places of 2,500 or More Population—with ZIP Codes

Source: U. S. Bureau of the Census, U. S. Post Office Dept.

Below are the population figures and ZIP codes of all the urban places in the United States (all incorporated and unincorporated places of 2,500 inhabitants or more, and the towns, townships and counties classified by the Bureau of the Census as urban). Included are data from the 1960 census and from all special censuses conducted by the Bureau of the Census between April 1, 1960, and Jan. 1, 1968. Also listed, in italics, are the towns of 2,500 inhabitants or more in New England (Connecticut, Maine, Massachusetts, New Hampshire, Rhode Island and Vermont), where such minor civil divisions have greater significance than in most other states. It will be noted that some sizable unincorporated areas such as certain towns in New York State are not listed by the Bureau of the Census as urban places.

*ZIP Code numbers appear in left-hand column. If the place name is not the name of a post office, the ZIP Code number for the post office serving that place is listed where possible. If not possible, no ZIP code is listed.*

*CAUTION—Where an asterisk (*) appears before the ZIP Code number of a city, ask your local postmaster for the correct ZIP Code number for a specific address within that city.*

*A national directory showing all ZIP codes may be purchased for $7.00 from the Superintendent of Documents, Government Printing Office, Washington, D. C. 20402.*

Where special censuses were taken after April 1, 1960, the year taken appears after the name of the place. Places where population was changed by annexing areas after April 1, 1960, are indicated by (A). In many cases both annexation and a special census have taken place.

| ZIP Code | Place | 1960 | 1950 | ZIP Code | Place | 1960 | 1950 |
|---|---|---|---|---|---|---|---|
| | **ALABAMA** | | | | **ALABAMA—Continued** | | |
| 36310 | Abbeville | 2,524 | 2,162 | 35476 | Northport | 5,245 | 3,885 |
| 35950 | Albertville | 8,250 | 5,397 | 35121 | Oneonta | 4,136 | 2,802 |
| 35010 | Alexander City | 13,140 | 6,430 | 36801 | Opelika | 15,678 | 12,295 |
| 35442 | Aliceville | 3,194 | 3,170 | 36467 | Opp | 5,535 | 5,240 |
| 36420 | Andalusia | 10,263 | 9,162 | 36203 | Oxford | 3,603 | 1,697 |
| 36201 | Anniston | 33,657 | 31,066 | 36360 | Ozark, '65 | 10,368 | 5,238 |
| 35016 | Arab | 2,989 | 1,592 | 35125 | Pell City (A) '67 | 4,859 | 1,189 |
| 35611 | Athens, '64 | 13,652 | 6,309 | 36867 | Phenix City | 27,630 | 23,305 |
| 36502 | Atmore | 8,173 | 5,720 | 36272 | Piedmont | 4,794 | 4,498 |
| 35954 | Attalla | 8,257 | 7,537 | 35127 | Pleasant Grove '64 | 3,977 | 1,802 |
| 36830 | Auburn | 16,261 | 12,939 | 36067 | Prattville (A) '67 | 12,015 | 4,385 |
| 36507 | Bay Minette | 5,197 | 3,732 | 36612 | Prichard | 47,371 | 19,014 |
| 36509 | Bayou La Batre | 2,572 | ...... | 36274 | Roanoke | 5,288 | 5,392 |
| 35020 | Bessemer | 33,054 | 28,445 | 35653 | Russellville | 6,628 | 6,012 |
| *35203 | Birmingham | 340,887 | 326,037 | 36571 | Saraland (A) '67 | 6,922 | ...... |
| 35957 | Boaz | 4,654 | 3,078 | 35768 | Scottsboro, '66 | 8,452 | 4,731 |
| 36426 | Brewton | 6,309 | 5,146 | 36701 | Selma | 28,385 | 22,840 |
| 35740 | Bridgeport | 2,906 | 2,386 | 35660 | Sheffield | 13,491 | 10,767 |
| 35020 | Brighton | 2,884 | 1,689 | 35150 | Sylacauga | 12,857 | 9,606 |
| 36010 | Brundidge | 2,523 | 2,605 | 35160 | Talladega | 17,742 | 13,134 |
| 36611 | Chickasaw | 10,002 | 4,920 | 36078 | Tallassee | 4,934 | 4,225 |
| 35044 | Childersburg | 4,884 | 4,023 | 35217 | Tarrant City | 7,810 | 7,571 |
| 35045 | Clanton | 5,683 | 4,640 | 36784 | Thomasville | 3,182 | 2,425 |
| 35550 | Cordova | 3,184 | 3,156 | 36081 | Troy | 10,234 | 8,555 |
| 35055 | Cullman | 10,883 | 7,523 | 35173 | Trussville | 2,510 | 1,575 |
| 36853 | Dadeville | 2,940 | 2,354 | 35401 | Tuscaloosa | 63,370 | 46,396 |
| 36322 | Daleville, '64 | 2,510 | ...... | 35674 | Tuscumbia | 8,994 | 6,734 |
| 35601 | Decatur | 29,217 | 19,974 | 36083 | Tuskegee | 7,240 | 6,712 |
| 36732 | Demopolis | 7,377 | 5,004 | 36089 | Union Springs | 3,704 | 3,232 |
| 36301 | Dothan | 31,440 | 21,584 | 35216 | Vestavia Hills | 4,029 | ...... |
| 36426 | East Brewton | 2,511 | 2,173 | 36201 | West End Anniston | 5,485 | ...... |
| 36323 | Elba | 4,321 | 2,936 | 36092 | Wetumpka | 3,672 | 3,813 |
| 36330 | Enterprise | 11,410 | 7,288 | 35594 | Winfield | 2,907 | 2,108 |
| 36027 | Eufaula | 8,357 | 6,906 | 36925 | York | 2,932 | 1,774 |
| 35462 | Eutaw | 2,784 | 2,348 | | | | |
| 36401 | Evergreen | 3,703 | 3,454 | | **ALASKA** | | |
| 36854 | Fairfax | 3,107 | 2,717 | *99501 | Anchorage | 44,237 | 11,254 |
| 35064 | Fairfield | 15,816 | 13,177 | 99790 | Fairbanks | 13,311 | 5,771 |
| 36532 | Fairhope | 4,858 | 3,354 | 99801 | Juneau | 6,797 | 5,956 |
| 35555 | Fayette | 4,227 | 3,707 | 99901 | Ketchikan | 6,483 | 5,305 |
| 36442 | Florala | 3,012 | 2,713 | 99615 | Kodiak | 2,628 | 1,710 |
| 35630 | Florence | 31,649 | 23,879 | 99835 | Sitka | 3,237 | 1,985 |
| 36535 | Foley | 2,889 | 1,901 | 99503 | Spenard | 9,074 | 2,108 |
| 35967 | Fort Payne | 7,029 | 6,226 | | | | |
| 35068 | Fultondale, '62 | 2,820 | 1,304 | | **ARIZONA** | | |
| *35901 | Gadsden | 58,088 | 55,725 | 85321 | Ajo | 7,049 | 5,817 |
| 35071 | Gardendale, '67 | 6,207 | ...... | 85323 | Avondale | 6,581 | 2,505 |
| 36340 | Geneva | 3,840 | 3,579 | 85603 | Bisbee, '65 | 9,272 | 3,801 |
| 35905 | Glencoe | 2,592 | 1,466 | 85326 | Buckeye (A) | 2,518 | 1,932 |
| 35073 | Graysville | 2,870 | 879 | 85222 | Casa Grande, '65 | 8,485 | 4,181 |
| 36744 | Greensboro | 3,081 | 2,217 | 85224 | Chandler (A), '65 | 12,181 | 3,799 |
| 36037 | Greenville | 6,894 | 6,781 | 85532 | Claypool | 2,505 | ...... |
| 35976 | Guntersville | 6,592 | 5,253 | 85533 | Clifton | 4,191 | 3,466 |
| 35565 | Haleyville | 3,740 | 3,331 | 85228 | Coolidge, '65 | 5,012 | 4,306 |
| 35640 | Hartselle | 5,000 | 3,429 | 85607 | Douglas, '65 | 12,370 | 9,442 |
| 36345 | Headland | 2,650 | 2,091 | 85335 | El Mirage (A), '65 | 3,258 | ...... |
| 35209 | Homewood (A) | 20,641 | 12,866 | 85231 | Eloy | 4,899 | 3,580 |
| 35020 | Hueytown | 5,997 | ...... | 86001 | Flagstaff, '65 | 24,592 | 7,663 |
| *35801 | Huntsville, '64 | 123,519 | 16,437 | 85301 | Glendale (A), '65 | 30,760 | 8,179 |
| 35210 | Irondale | 3,501 | 1,876 | 85501 | Globe, '65 | 6,299 | 6,419 |
| 36545 | Jackson | 4,959 | 3,072 | 85025 | Holbrook, '65 | 4,481 | 2,336 |
| 36265 | Jacksonville | 5,678 | 4,751 | 86401 | Kingman, '65 | 6,021 | ...... |
| 35501 | Jasper | 10,799 | 8,589 | 85201 | Mesa, '65 | 50,529 | 16,790 |
| 36862 | Lafayette | 2,605 | 2,353 | 85539 | Miami | 3,350 | 4,329 |
| 36863 | Lanett | 7,674 | 7,434 | 85621 | Nogales | 7,286 | 6,153 |
| 36864 | Langdale | 2,528 | 2,721 | 86040 | Page | 2,960 | ...... |
| 35094 | Leeds | 6,162 | 3,306 | 85251 | Paradise Valley, '65 | 4,650 | ...... |
| 36748 | Linden | 2,516 | 1,363 | 85345 | Peoria (A), '65 | 3,802 | ...... |
| 35020 | Lipscomb | 2,811 | 2,550 | *85026 | Phoenix (A), '65 | 505,666 | 106,818 |
| 36756 | Marion | 3,807 | 2,822 | 86301 | Prescott, '65 | 13,823 | 6,764 |
| 35228 | Midfield (A) '67 | 4,771 | ...... | 85546 | Safford, '65 | 5,165 | 3,756 |
| 35150 | Mignon | 2,271 | 3,053 | 85631 | San Manuel | 4,524 | ...... |
| *36601 | Mobile | 202,779 | 129,009 | 85251 | Scottsdale (A), '65 | 54,504 | ...... |
| 36460 | Monroeville | 3,632 | 2,772 | 85635 | Sierra Vista, '65 | 4,635 | ...... |
| 35115 | Montevallo | 2,755 | 2,150 | 85713 | South Tucson | 7,004 | 2,364 |
| *36104 | Montgomery | 134,393 | 106,525 | 85273 | Superior | 4,875 | ...... |
| 35223 | Mountain Brook (A) '67 | 18,414 | 8,359 | 85281 | Tempe, '65 | 45,919 | 7,684 |
| 35660 | Muscle Shoals | 4,084 | 1,937 | 85353 | Tolleson | 3,886 | 3,042 |

| ZIP Code | Place | 1960 | 1950 |
|---|---|---|---|
| | **ARIZONA—Continued** | | |
| *85702 | Tucson, '65 | 236,877 | 45,454 |
| 85344 | West Yuma | 2,781 | 4,741 |
| 85643 | Willcox, '65 | 3,018 | 1,266 |
| 86046 | Williams | 3,559 | 2,152 |
| 86047 | Winslow | 8,862 | 6,518 |
| 85364 | Yuma, '65 | 28,005 | 9,145 |
| | **ARKANSAS** | | |
| 71923 | Arkadelphia, '65 | 10,108 | 6,819 |
| 71822 | Ashdown, '67 | 3,449 | 2,738 |
| 72006 | Augusta, '65 | 2,624 | 2,317 |
| 72501 | Batesville, '64 | 7,129 | 6,414 |
| 72015 | Benton (A), '64 | 15,018 | 6,277 |
| 72712 | Bentonville, '65 | 4,519 | 2,942 |
| 72315 | Blytheville, '62 | 25,883 | 16,234 |
| 72927 | Booneville | 2,690 | 2,433 |
| 72021 | Brinkley | 4,636 | 4,173 |
| 71701 | Camden, '66 | 14,604 | 11,372 |
| 72029 | Clarendon, '65 | 2,564 | 2,547 |
| 72830 | Clarksville (A), '67 | 4,388 | 4,343 |
| 72032 | Conway, '66 | 14,507 | 8,610 |
| 72422 | Corning, '62 | 2,565 | 2,045 |
| 71635 | Crossett, '64 | 5,548 | 4,619 |
| 72834 | Dardanelle (A), '67 | 2,605 | 2,098 |
| 71832 | De Queen, '65 | 3,889 | 3,015 |
| 71638 | Dermott | 3,665 | 3,611 |
| 72042 | De Witt, '65 | 3,900 | 2,843 |
| 71639 | Dumas, '65 | 4,213 | 2,512 |
| 72331 | Earle, '63 | 2,896 | |
| 71730 | El Dorado City | 25,292 | 23,076 |
| 72046 | England | 3,027 | 2,136 |
| 71640 | Eudora | 3,598 | 3,072 |
| 72701 | Fayetteville (A), '67 | 29,724 | 17,071 |
| 71742 | Fordyce, '66 | 4,579 | 3,754 |
| 72335 | Forrest City (A), '67 | 12,763 | 7,607 |
| 72901 | Fort Smith (A), '64 | 64,874 | 47,942 |
| 71646 | Hamburg | 2,904 | 2,655 |
| 72601 | Harrison, '64 | 7,015 | 5,542 |
| 72342 | Helena | 11,500 | 11,236 |
| 71801 | Hope | 8,399 | 8,605 |
| 71901 | Hot Springs (A), '65 | 37,286 | 29,307 |
| 72076 | Jacksonville, '65 | 18,078 | 2,474 |
| 72401 | Jonesboro, '63 | 23,944 | 16,310 |
| 71653 | Lake Village, '64 | 3,297 | 2,484 |
| *72201 | Little Rock (A) | 128,929 | 102,213 |
| 72086 | Lonoke, '64 | 2,856 | |
| 71654 | McGehee (A) | 5,101 | 3,854 |
| 71753 | Magnolia, '65 | 11,159 | 6,918 |
| 72104 | Malvern, '65 | 9,268 | 8,072 |
| 72360 | Marcanna, '64 | 5,653 | 4,530 |
| 72365 | Marked Tree | 3,216 | 2,878 |
| 71953 | Mena | 4,388 | 4,445 |
| 71655 | Monticello, '64 | 5,031 | 4,501 |
| 72110 | Morrilton (A), '67 | 6,955 | 5,483 |
| 72653 | Mountain Home, '66 | 3,258 | 2,217 |
| 71852 | Nashville, '64 | 4,109 | 3,548 |
| 72112 | Newport (A), '67 | 7,607 | 6,254 |
| *72114 | North Little Rk., '65 | 61,510 | 44,097 |
| 72949 | Ozark, '65 | 2,568 | 1,757 |
| 72370 | Osceola, '62 | 7,055 | 5,006 |
| 72450 | Paragould, '64 | 10,053 | 9,668 |
| 72855 | Paris, '67 | 3,597 | 3,731 |
| 72454 | Piggott, '66 | 2,842 | 2,558 |
| 71601 | Pine Bluff (A), '66 | 57,108 | 37,162 |
| 71601 | Pine Bluff SE | 2,679 | |
| 72455 | Pocahontas (A), '67 | 4,610 | 3,840 |
| 71857 | Prescott (A), '67 | 3,849 | 3,960 |
| 72756 | Rogers, '65 | 8,284 | 4,962 |
| 72801 | Russellville, '66 | 11,154 | 8,166 |
| 72143 | Searcy, '66 | 8,841 | 6,024 |
| 72761 | Siloam Springs (A), '67 | 5,553 | 3,270 |
| 72764 | Springdale, '65 | 14,044 | 5,835 |
| 71860 | Stamps | 2,591 | 2,552 |
| 72160 | Stuttgart, '65 | 10,252 | 7,276 |
| 75501 | Texarkana (A) | 21,652 | 15,875 |
| 72472 | Trumann, '63 | 5,013 | 3,741 |
| 72956 | Van Buren, '65 | 7,805 | 6,413 |
| 72476 | Walnut Ridge, '67 | 3,679 | 3,106 |
| 71671 | Warren | 6,752 | 2,615 |
| 72390 | West Helena, '65 | 9,482 | 6,107 |
| 72301 | West Memphis, '66 | 23,909 | 9,112 |
| 72396 | Wynne, '65 | 6,014 | 4,142 |
| | **CALIFORNIA** | | |
| 95350 | Airport (Stanislaus Co.) | 3,689 | |
| 94501 | Alameda | 63,855 | 64,430 |
| 94706 | Albany | 14,804 | 17,590 |
| 91801 | Alhambra | 54,807 | 51,359 |
| 93901 | Alisal | 16,473 | 16,714 |
| 91001 | Altadena | 40,568 | |
| 96101 | Alturas | 2,819 | 2,819 |
| 95116 | Alum Rock | 18,942 | |
| *92803 | Anaheim | 104,184 | 14,556 |
| 96007 | Anderson | 4,492 | |
| 94509 | Antioch (A), '67 | 23,431 | 11,051 |
| 91006 | Arcadia | 41,005 | 23,066 |
| 95521 | Arcata | 5,235 | 3,729 |
| 95825 | Arden-Arcade | 73,332 | |
| 93420 | Arroyo Grande | 3,291 | 1,723 |
| 90701 | Artesia | 9,993 | |
| 93203 | Arvin, '61 | 5,440 | 5,007 |
| 93422 | Atascadero | 5,983 | 3,443 |

| ZIP Code | Place | 1960 | 1950 |
|---|---|---|---|
| | **CALIFORNIA—Continued** | | |
| 94025 | Atherton | 7,717 | 3,630 |
| 95401 | Atwater, '63 | 11,105 | 2,856 |
| 95603 | Auburn | 5,586 | 4,653 |
| 93204 | Avenal | 3,147 | 3,982 |
| 91702 | Azusa | 20,497 | 11,042 |
| *93302 | Bakersfield | 56,848 | 34,784 |
| 91706 | Baldwin Park | 33,951 | |
| 92220 | Banning | 10,250 | 7,034 |
| 92311 | Barstow | 11,644 | 6,135 |
| 93501 | Bayview-Rosewood | 2,980 | |
| 92223 | Beaumont, '61 | 4,432 | 3,152 |
| 90201 | Bell | 19,450 | 15,430 |
| 90706 | Bellflower | 45,909 | |
| 90201 | Bell Gardens, '65 | 28,779 | |
| 94002 | Belmont | 15,996 | 5,567 |
| 94510 | Benicia | 6,070 | 7,284 |
| *94704 | Berkeley | 111,268 | 113,805 |
| *90210 | Beverly Hills | 30,817 | 29,032 |
| 93514 | Bishop, '65 | 2,955 | 2,891 |
| 92225 | Blythe | 6,023 | 4,089 |
| 90001 | Bonnyville | 4,686 | |
| 92227 | Brawley, '66 | 14,467 | 11,922 |
| 92621 | Brea | 8,487 | 3,208 |
| 90620 | Buena Park | 46,401 | |
| *91503 | Burbank | 90,155 | 78,577 |
| 94010 | Burlingame | 24,036 | 19,886 |
| | Burton | 4,635 | 2,381 |
| 92231 | Calexico, '66 | 9,850 | 6,433 |
| 92233 | Calipatria | 2,548 | 1,428 |
| 95008 | Campbell | 11,863 | |
| 92007 | Cardiff | 3,149 | |
| 92008 | Carlsbad | 9,253 | |
| 93921 | Carmel-by-the-Sea, '66 | 4,136 | 4,351 |
| 95608 | Carmichael | 20,455 | 4,499 |
| 93013 | Carpinteria | 4,998 | 2,864 |
| 90744 | Carson | 38,059 | |
| 94546 | Castro Valley | 37,120 | |
| 95012 | Castroville | 2,838 | 1,865 |
| 96019 | Central Valley | 2,854 | 2,202 |
| 95307 | Ceres, '66 | 5,573 | 2,351 |
| 95926 | Chico | 14,757 | 12,272 |
| 95926 | Chico Vecino | 4,688 | 3,607 |
| 91710 | Chino, '65 | 14,246 | 5,784 |
| 93610 | Chowchilla, '65 | 4,611 | 3,893 |
| | Chrisman | 3,923 | 4,211 |
| 92010 | Chula Vista | 42,034 | 15,927 |
| 91711 | Claremont | 12,633 | 6,327 |
| 95425 | Cloverdale, '65 | 3,201 | 1,292 |
| 93612 | Clovis, '66 | 11,461 | 2,766 |
| 92236 | Coachella (A), '67 | 7,502 | 2,755 |
| 93210 | Coalinga | 5,965 | 5,539 |
| 95350 | College Gardens | 4,132 | |
| 92324 | Colton, '66 | 19,470 | 14,465 |
| 95501 | Colusa | 3,518 | 3,031 |
| 90022 | Commerce | 9,555 | |
| 90220 | Compton | 71,812 | 47,991 |
| *94520 | Concord | 36,208 | 6,953 |
| 93212 | Corcoran | 4,976 | 3,150 |
| 96021 | Corning | 3,006 | 2,537 |
| 91720 | Corona | 13,336 | 10,223 |
| 92118 | Coronado | 18,039 | 12,700 |
| 94925 | Corte Madera | 5,962 | 1,933 |
| 92626 | Costa Mesa, '66 | 66,396 | |
| 91722 | Covina | 20,124 | 3,956 |
| 95531 | Crescent City | 2,958 | 1,706 |
| 95531 | Crescent City NW | 3,086 | |
| 95277 | Crowley | 3,950 | |
| 90230 | Culver City | 32,163 | 19,720 |
| 95014 | Cupertino | 3,664 | |
| 90630 | Cypress, '66 | 19,005 | |
| 90701 | Dairy Valley | 3,508 | |
| *94014 | Daly City | 44,791 | 15,191 |
| 94526 | Danville | 3,585 | |
| 95616 | Davis | 8,910 | 3,554 |
| 93215 | Delano | 11,913 | 8,717 |
| 92014 | Del Mar | 3,124 | |
| 95838 | Del Paso Heights-Robla | 11,495 | |
| 93618 | Dinuba | 6,103 | 4,971 |
| 95620 | Dixon | 2,970 | 1,714 |
| *90240 | Downey | 82,505 | |
| 91010 | Duarte | 13,962 | |
| 96025 | Dunsmuir | 2,873 | 2,256 |
| 93219 | Earlimart | 2,697 | 2,162 |
| 90022 | East Los Angeles | 104,270 | |
| 93257 | East Porterville | 3,538 | |
| 90603 | East Whittier | 19,884 | |
| 92020 | El Cajon | 37,618 | 5,600 |
| 92243 | El Centro, '66 | 19,280 | 12,590 |
| 94530 | El Cerrito | 25,437 | 18,011 |
| *91731 | El Monte City | 13,163 | 8,101 |
| 94520 | El Monte (uninc.) | 4,186 | 2,502 |
| 93446 | El Paso de Robles | 6,677 | 4,835 |
| 93030 | El Rio | 6,966 | 1,376 |
| 90245 | El Segundo | 14,219 | 8,011 |
| 94608 | Emeryville | 2,686 | 2,889 |
| 92024 | Encinitas | 2,786 | |
| 96001 | Enterprise | 4,946 | |
| 95501 | Escondido | 16,377 | 6,544 |
| 95501 | Eureka | 28,137 | 23,058 |
| 93221 | Exeter | 4,264 | 4,078 |
| 94930 | Fairfax | 5,813 | 4,078 |
| 94533 | Fairfield | 14,968 | 3,118 |
| 95350 | Fairview | 3,586 | |

## CALIFORNIA—Continued

| ZIP Code | Place | 1960 | 1950 |
|---|---|---|---|
| 92028 | Fallbrook | 4,814 | 1,735 |
| 93223 | Farmersville | 3,101 | |
| 93015 | Fillmore | 4,808 | 3,884 |
| 93622 | Firebaugh, '62 | 2,627 | 821 |
| 90001 | Florence-Graham | 38,164 | |
| 95630 | Folsom | 3,925 | 1,690 |
| 92335 | Fontana | 14,659 | |
| 93268 | Ford City | 3,926 | 4,347 |
| 95437 | Fort Bragg | 4,433 | 3,826 |
| 95540 | Fortuna | 3,523 | 1,762 |
| 92708 | Fountain Valley, '65 | 13,099 | |
| 95019 | Freedom | 4,206 | 2,765 |
| 94536 | Fremont | 43,790 | |
| *93721 | Fresno | 133,929 | 91,669 |
| *92631 | Fullerton | 56,180 | 13,958 |
| *90247 | Gardena | 35,943 | 14,405 |
| *92640 | Garden Grove | 84,238 | |
| 95020 | Gilroy | 7,348 | 4,951 |
| 92509 | Glen Avon Hts. | 3,416 | |
| *91209 | Glendale | 119,442 | 95,702 |
| 91740 | Glendora, '66 | 29,513 | 3,988 |
| 95945 | Grass Valley | 4,876 | 5,283 |
| 95948 | Gridley | 3,343 | 3,054 |
| 93433 | Grover City | 5,210 | |
| 93434 | Guadalupe | 2,614 | 2,429 |
| | Hagginwood | 11,469 | |
| 93230 | Hanford | 10,133 | 10,028 |
| 90701 | Hawaiian Gardens, '64 | 3,366 | |
| 90250 | Hawthorne | 33,035 | 16,316 |
| *94543 | Hayward | 72,700 | 14,272 |
| 95448 | Healdsburg, '65 | 5,132 | 3,258 |
| 92343 | Hemet, '64 | 7,943 | 3,386 |
| 90254 | Hermosa Beach | 16,115 | 11,826 |
| 91745 | Hillgrove | 14,669 | |
| 94010 | Hillsborough | 7,554 | 3,552 |
| 95023 | Hollister | 6,071 | 4,903 |
| 92250 | Holtville, '66 | 3,638 | 2,472 |
| 92646 | Huntington Beh, (A), '67 | 94,377 | 5,237 |
| 90255 | Huntington Pk | 29,920 | 29,450 |
| 92251 | Imperial, '66 | 3,271 | 1,759 |
| 92032 | Imperial Beach | 17,773 | |
| 92201 | Indio | 9,745 | 5,300 |
| *90306 | Inglewood | 63,390 | 46,185 |
| 93630 | Kerman, '64 | 2,545 | 1,563 |
| 93930 | King City, '66 | 3,060 | 2,347 |
| 93631 | Kingsburg | 3,093 | 2,310 |
| 91011 | La Canada-Flintridge | 18,338 | |
| 94549 | Lafayette | 7,114 | |
| 92651 | Laguna Beach | 9,288 | 6,661 |
| 90631 | La Habra, '64 | 35,253 | 4,961 |
| 92330 | Lakeland Village | 3,539 | |
| 90712 | Lakewood | 67,126 | |
| 92041 | La Mesa | 30,441 | 10,946 |
| 90638 | La Mirada | 22,444 | |
| 93241 | Lamont | 6,177 | 3,571 |
| 93534 | Lancaster | 26,012 | 3,594 |
| 90620 | La Palma (A) '67 | 4,661 | 622 |
| *91744 | La Puente | 24,723 | |
| 94939 | Larkspur | 5,710 | 2,905 |
| 91750 | La Verne | 6,516 | 4,198 |
| 90260 | Lawndale | 21,740 | |
| 92045 | Lemon Grove | 19,348 | |
| 93245 | Lemoore | 2,561 | 2,153 |
| 90304 | Lennox | 31,224 | |
| 92046 | Leucadia | 5,665 | |
| 95648 | Lincoln | 3,197 | 2,410 |
| | Linda | 6,129 | |
| 93247 | Lindsay | 5,397 | 5,060 |
| 95953 | Live Oak | 3,518 | |
| 94550 | Livermore | 16,058 | 4,364 |
| 95240 | Lodi, '66 | 27,018 | 13,798 |
| 90717 | Lomita | 14,983 | |
| 93436 | Lompoc | 14,415 | 5,520 |
| *90801 | Long Beach | 344,168 | 250,767 |
| 90720 | Los Alamitos, '65 | 8,197 | |
| 94022 | Los Altos | 19,696 | |
| 94022 | Los Altos Hills | 3,412 | |
| *90053 | Los Angeles | 2,479,015 | 1,970,358 |
| 93635 | Los Banos, '64 | 9,943 | 3,865 |
| 95030 | Los Gatos | 9,036 | 4,907 |
| 90262 | Lynwood | 31,614 | 25,823 |
| 93250 | McFarland | 3,686 | |
| 93637 | Madera | 14,430 | 10,497 |
| 90266 | Manhattan Beach, '62 | 34,513 | 17,330 |
| 95336 | Manteca | 8,242 | 3,804 |
| 93933 | Marina | 3,310 | |
| 94553 | Martinez | 9,604 | 8,268 |
| 94553 | Martinez East | 3,958 | |
| 95901 | Marysville | 9,553 | 7,826 |
| 90270 | Maywood | 14,588 | 13,292 |
| 93023 | Meiners Oaks | 3,513 | 2,446 |
| 93640 | Mendota, '61 | 3,086 | |
| 94025 | Menlo Park | 26,957 | 13,587 |
| 95340 | Merced | 20,068 | 15,278 |
| 94030 | Millbrae | 15,873 | 8,972 |
| 94941 | Mill Valley | 10,411 | 7,331 |
| 95035 | Milpitas | 6,572 | |
| 91752 | Mira Loma | 3,982 | 1,555 |
| *95350 | Modesto | 36,585 | 17,389 |
| 91016 | Monrovia | 27,079 | 20,186 |
| 91763 | Montclair | 13,546 | |
| 90640 | Montebello, '65 | 40,613 | 21,735 |
| 93940 | Monterey, '66 | 25,436 | 16,250 |
| 91754 | Monterey Park | 37,821 | 20,395 |
| 93021 | Moorpark | 2,902 | 1,146 |
| 95037 | Morgan Hill, '63 | 4,068 | 1,627 |
| 93442 | Morro Bay | 3,692 | 1,659 |
| 94040 | Mountain View | 30,889 | 6,563 |
| 95926 | Mulberry | 2,643 | 2,545 |
| 94558 | Napa | 22,170 | 13,579 |
| 92050 | National City | 32,771 | 21,199 |
| 92363 | Needles | 4,590 | 4,051 |
| 94560 | Newark | 9,884 | |
| 91321 | Newhall | 4,705 | 2,527 |
| 95360 | Newman, '64 | 2,558 | 1,815 |
| 92660 | Newport Beach | 26,564 | 12,120 |
| 91760 | Norco, '66 | 12,508 | 1,584 |
| 95660 | North Highlands | 21,211 | |
| 95815 | North Sacramento (A) | 16,346 | 6,029 |
| 95380 | North Turlock | 2,535 | 1,586 |
| 90650 | Norwalk | 88,739 | |
| 94947 | Novato | 17,881 | 3,496 |
| 95361 | Oakdale | 4,980 | 4,064 |
| *94615 | Oakland | 367,548 | 384,575 |
| 92054 | Oceanside, '66 | 31,824 | 12,881 |
| 93023 | Ojai | 4,495 | 2,519 |
| 95961 | Olivehurst | 4,835 | 3,588 |
| 91761 | Ontario | 46,617 | 22,872 |
| 95060 | Opal Cliffs | 3,825 | |
| *92666 | Orange, '65 | 67,206 | 10,027 |
| 93646 | Orange Cove | 2,885 | 2,395 |
| 94563 | Orinda | 4,712 | |
| 94563 | Orinda Village | 5,568 | |
| 95963 | Orland | 2,534 | 2,067 |
| 95965 | Oroville | 6,115 | 5,387 |
| 93030 | Oxnard, '64 | 58,269 | 21,567 |
| 94044 | Pacifica | 20,995 | |
| 93050 | Pacific Grove, '66 | 12,208 | 9,623 |
| 93550 | Palmdale | 11,529 | |
| 92262 | Palm Springs | 13,468 | 7,660 |
| *94301 | Palo Alto | 52,287 | 25,475 |
| 91274 | Palos Verdes Estates | 9,564 | 1,963 |
| 95969 | Paradise Butte | 8,268 | |
| 95350 | Paradise Stanislaus | 5,616 | 4,426 |
| 90723 | Paramount | 27,249 | |
| *91102 | Pasadena | 116,407 | 104,577 |
| 95363 | Patterson, '63 | 2,429 | |
| 92370 | Perris | 2,950 | 1,807 |
| 94952 | Petaluma | 14,035 | 10,315 |
| 90660 | Pico Rivera | 49,150 | |
| 94611 | Piedmont | 11,117 | 10,132 |
| 94564 | Pinole | 6,064 | 1,147 |
| 94565 | Pittsburg | 19,062 | 12,763 |
| 94565 | Pittsburg West | 5,188 | |
| 92670 | Placentia | 5,861 | 1,682 |
| 95667 | Placerville, '65 | 4,997 | 3,749 |
| 94523 | Pleasant Hill | 23,844 | 5,686 |
| 94566 | Pleasanton | 4,203 | 2,244 |
| *91766 | Pomona | 67,157 | 35,405 |
| 93257 | Porterville | 7,991 | 6,904 |
| 93041 | Port Hueneme | 11,067 | 3,024 |
| 93534 | Quartz Hill | 3,325 | |
| 95971 | Quincy-East Quincy | 2,723 | |
| 95670 | Rancho Cordova | 7,429 | |
| 96080 | Red Bluff | 7,202 | 4,905 |
| 96001 | Redding | 12,773 | 10,256 |
| 92373 | Redlands | 26,829 | 18,429 |
| 90277 | Redondo Beach | 46,986 | 25,226 |
| *94061 | Redwood City | 46,290 | 25,544 |
| 93654 | Reedley | 5,850 | 4,135 |
| 92376 | Rialto | 18,567 | 3,156 |
| *94802 | Richmond | 71,854 | 99,545 |
| 93555 | Ridgecrest | 5,099 | 2,028 |
| 95562 | Rio Dell | 3,222 | 1,862 |
| 94571 | Rio Vista | 2,616 | 1,831 |
| 95367 | Riverbank | 2,786 | 2,662 |
| *92502 | Riverside | 84,332 | 46,764 |
| 94928 | Rohnert Park | 4,343 | |
| 90274 | Rolling Hills Estates | 3,941 | |
| 95401 | Roseland | 4,510 | 1,552 |
| 91770 | Rosemead | 15,476 | |
| 95678 | Roseville | 13,421 | 8,723 |
| 94957 | Ross | 2,551 | 2,179 |
| | Ryans Slough | 3,634 | 1,727 |
| *95501 | Sacramento (A), '64 | 237,712 | 137,572 |
| 94574 | St. Helena | 2,722 | 2,297 |
| 93901 | Salinas | 28,957 | 13,917 |
| 94960 | San Anselmo | 11,584 | 9,188 |
| *92402 | San Bernardino | 91,922 | 63,058 |
| 94066 | San Bruno | 29,063 | 12,478 |
| | San Buenaventura (See Ventura) | | |
| 94070 | San Carlos | 21,370 | 14,371 |
| 92672 | San Clemente, '64 | 13,167 | 2,008 |
| 92101 | San Diego | 573,224 | 334,387 |
| 91773 | San Dimas, '65 | 11,520 | |
| 91340 | San Fernando | 16,093 | 12,992 |
| *94101 | San Francisco | 740,316 | 775,357 |
| 91775 | San Gabriel | 22,561 | 20,343 |
| 93657 | Sanger, '65 | 9,627 | 6,400 |
| 92383 | San Jacinto | 2,553 | 1,778 |
| *95113 | San Jose | 204,196 | 95,280 |
| 92675 | San Juan Capistrano (A) '67 | 2,551 | 1,120 |
| *94557 | San Leandro | 65,962 | 27,542 |
| 94580 | San Lorenzo | 23,773 | |
| 93401 | San Luis Obispo | 20,437 | 14,180 |

| ZIP Code | Place | 1960 | 1950 |
|---|---|---|---|
| | **CALIFORNIA—Continued** | | |
| 91108 | San Marino | 13,658 | 11,230 |
| *94401 | San Mateo | 69,870 | 41,782 |
| 94806 | San Pablo | 19,687 | 14,476 |
| 94901 | San Rafael | 20,460 | 13,848 |
| *92702 | Santa Ana | 100,350 | 45,533 |
| *93102 | Santa Barbara | 58,768 | 44,854 |
| *95050 | Santa Clara | 58,880 | 11,702 |
| 95060 | Santa Cruz | 25,596 | 21,970 |
| 90670 | Santa Fe Springs | 16,342 | .... |
| 93454 | Santa Maria | 20 027 | 10,440 |
| *90406 | Santa Monica | 83,249 | 71,595 |
| 93060 | Santa Paula | 13,279 | 11,049 |
| *95401 | Santa Rosa, '65 | 41,615 | 17,902 |
| ..... | Saranap | 6,450 | 2,362 |
| 95070 | Saratoga | 14 861 | .... |
| 94965 | Sausalito | 5,331 | 4 828 |
| 90740 | Seal Beach | 6,994 | 3 553 |
| 93955 | Seaside, '66 | 20,917 | .... |
| 95472 | Sebastopol | 2,694 | 2,601 |
| 93662 | Selma, '66 | 7,173 | 5,964 |
| 93263 | Shafter, '64 | 5,312 | 2,207 |
| 94565 | Shore Acres | 3,093 | .... |
| 91024 | Sierra Madre | 9,732 | 7,273 |
| 90806 | Signal Hill | 4,627 | 4,040 |
| 93960 | Soledad, '66 | 3,715 | 2,441 |
| 95476 | Sonoma, '65 | 3,351 | 2,015 |
| 95370 | Sonora | 2,725 | 2,448 |
| 91733 | South El Monte | 4,850 | .... |
| 90280 | South Gate | 53,831 | 51,116 |
| 95705 | South Lake Tahoe, '65 | 14,427 | .... |
| 95550 | South Modesto | 5,465 | .... |
| 95065 | South Oroville | 3,704 | .... |
| 95404 | South Park | 3,261 | 1,837 |
| 91030 | South Pasadena | 19,706 | 16,935 |
| ..... | South Sacramento-Fruitridge | 16,443 | .... |
| 94080 | South San Francisco | 39,418 | 19,351 |
| 91777 | South San Gabriel | 26,213 | .... |
| 95991 | South Yuba | 3,200 | .... |
| 90680 | Stanton | 11,163 | .... |
| *95202 | Stockton (A) '67 | 97,680 | 70,853 |
| 92388 | Sunnymead | 3,404 | .... |
| *94086 | Sunnyvale | 52,898 | 9,829 |
| 96130 | Susanville, '65 | 6,912 | 5,338 |
| 93268 | Taft | 3,822 | 3 707 |
| 93268 | Taft Heights | 2,661 | 2,176 |
| 93561 | Tehachapi, '65 | 3,838 | 1,685 |
| 91780 | Temple City | 31,838 | .... |
| 91360 | Thousand Oaks | 2,934 | 1,243 |
| *90507 | Torrance | 100,991 | 22,241 |
| 95376 | Tracy (A) '67 | 14,443 | 8,410 |
| 93274 | Tulare | 13,824 | 12 445 |
| 95380 | Turlock | 9,116 | 6,235 |
| 95482 | Ukiah | 9,900 | 6,120 |
| 94587 | Union City | 6,618 | .... |
| 91786 | Upland | 15,918 | 9,203 |
| 95688 | Vacaville | 10,898 | 3,109 |
| 94590 | Vallejo | 60,877 | 26,038 |
| 93001 | Ventura | 29,114 | 16,534 |
| 92392 | Victorville, '64 | 9,655 | .... |
| 93277 | Visalia | 15,791 | 11,749 |
| 92083 | Vista, '65 | 19,625 | 1,705 |
| 94598 | Walnut Creek, '65 | 23,328 | 2,420 |
| ..... | Walnut Heights | 5,080 | .... |
| 93280 | Wasco | 6,841 | 5,592 |
| 95076 | Watsonville | 13,293 | 11,572 |
| 96094 | Weed | 3,223 | 2,739 |
| 91790 | W. Covina '64 | 60,329 | 4,499 |
| ..... | West Hollywood | 28,870 | .... |
| 92683 | Westminster, '63 | 44,859 | .... |
| *90605 | Whittier | 33,663 | 23,433 |
| 95490 | Willits | 3,410 | 2,691 |
| 95988 | Willows | 4,139 | 3,019 |
| 93286 | Woodlake | 2,623 | 2,525 |
| 95695 | Woodland | 13,524 | 9,386 |
| 94061 | Woodside | 3,592 | .... |
| 96097 | Yreka City | 4,759 | 3,227 |
| 95991 | Yuba City | 11,507 | 7,861 |
| | **COLORADO** | | |
| 81101 | Alamosa | 6,205 | 5,354 |
| 80002 | Arvada | 19,242 | 2,359 |
| 80010 | Aurora | 48,548 | 11,241 |
| 80302 | Boulder | 37,718 | 19,999 |
| 80601 | Brighton | 7,055 | 4 336 |
| 80020 | Broomfield Hts | 4,535 | .... |
| 80723 | Brush | 3 621 | 2,431 |
| 81212 | Canon City | 8,973 | 6,345 |
| *80901 | Colorado Spgs | 70,194 | 45,472 |
| 80022 | Commerce City | 8,970 | .... |
| 81321 | Cortez | 6,764 | 2,680 |
| 81625 | Craig | 3,984 | 3,080 |
| 81416 | Delta | 3,832 | 4,097 |
| *80201 | Denver | 493,887 | 415,786 |
| 80022 | Derby (*Annexed to Commerce City in 1962*) | 10,124 | 2,840 |
| 81301 | Durango | 10,530 | 7,459 |
| 80214 | Edgewater | 4,314 | 2,580 |
| 80110 | Englewood | 33,398 | 16,869 |
| 81226 | Florence | 2,821 | 2,773 |
| 80521 | Fort Collins | 25,027 | 14,937 |
| 80701 | Fort Morgan | 7,379 | 5,315 |
| 81601 | Glenwood Spgs | 3,637 | 2,412 |
| 80401 | Golden | 7 118 | 5,238 |

| ZIP Code | Place | 1960 | 1950 |
|---|---|---|---|
| | **COLORADO—Continued** | | |
| 81501 | Grand Junction | 18,694 | 14,504 |
| 80631 | Greeley | 26,314 | 20,354 |
| 81230 | Gunnison | 3,477 | 2,770 |
| 80906 | Ivywild | 11,065 | 2,849 |
| 80026 | Lafayette | 2,612 | 2,090 |
| 81050 | La Junta | 8,026 | 7,712 |
| 80215 | Lakewood | 19,338 | .... |
| 81052 | Lamar | 7,397 | 6,829 |
| 81054 | Las Animas | 3,402 | 3,223 |
| 80461 | Leadville | 4,008 | 4,081 |
| 80120 | Littleton | 13 670 | 3,378 |
| 80501 | Longmont | 11,489 | 8,099 |
| 80537 | Loveland | 9,734 | 6,773 |
| 80829 | Manitou Spgs | 3,626 | 2,580 |
| 81144 | Monte Vista | 3,585 | 3,272 |
| 81401 | Montrose | 5,044 | 4 964 |
| 81501 | Orchard Mesa | 4,956 | .... |
| *81003 | Pueblo | 91,181 | 63,685 |
| 81067 | Rocky Ford | 4,929 | 4,087 |
| 81201 | Salida | 4,560 | 4,553 |
| 80911 | Security | 9,017 | .... |
| 80110 | Sheridan | 3,559 | 1,715 |
| 80751 | Sterling | 10,751 | 7,534 |
| 80229 | Thornton | 11,353 | .... |
| 81082 | Trinidad | 10 691 | 12,204 |
| 81089 | Walsenburg | 5,071 | 5,596 |
| 80030 | Westminster | 13,850 | 1,686 |
| 80033 | Wheat Ridge | 21,619 | .... |
| | **CONNECTICUT** | | |
| | *See Note on Page 605* | | |
| 06401 | Ansonia | 19,819 | 18,706 |
| 06001 | *Avon* | 5,273 | 3,171 |
| 06403 | *Beacon Falls* | 2,886 | 2,067 |
| 06801 | Bethel | 5,624 | 4,145 |
| | *Bethel (town)* | 8,200 | 5,104 |
| 06037 | *Berlin* | 11,250 | 7,470 |
| 06002 | *Bloomfield* | 13,613 | 5,746 |
| 06040 | *Bolton* | 2,933 | 1,279 |
| 06405 | *Branford* | 16,610 | 10,944 |
| *06602 | Bridgeport | 156,748 | 158,709 |
| 06010 | Bristol | 45,499 | 35,961 |
| 06804 | *Brookfield* | 3,405 | 1,688 |
| 06234 | *Brooklyn* | 3,312 | 2,652 |
| 06085 | *Burlington* | 2,790 | 1,846 |
| 06019 | *Canton* | 4,783 | 3,613 |
| 06410 | *Cheshire* | 4,072 | 1,826 |
| | *Cheshire (town)* | 13,383 | 6,295 |
| 06412 | *Chester* | 2,520 | 1,920 |
| 06413 | Clinton | 2,693 | .... |
| | *Clinton (town)* | 4,166 | 2,466 |
| 06415 | *Colchester* | 4,648 | 3,007 |
| 06340 | Conning Towers | 3,457 | .... |
| 06238 | *Coventry* | 6 356 | 4,043 |
| 06416 | Cromwell | 2,889 | 1,541 |
| | *Cromwell (town)* | 6,780 | 4,286 |
| 06810 | Danbury | 22,928 | 22,067 |
| | *Danbury (town)* | 39,382 | 30,337 |
| 06239 | Danielson | 4,642 | 4,554 |
| 06820 | *Darien* | 18,437 | 11,767 |
| 06417 | *Deep River* | 2,968 | 2,570 |
| 06418 | Derby | 12,132 | 10,259 |
| 06422 | *Durham* | 3,096 | 1,804 |
| 06423 | *East Haddam* | 3 637 | 2,554 |
| 06424 | *East Hampton* | 5,403 | 4,000 |
| 06108 | East Hartford | 43,977 | 29,933 |
| 06512 | East Haven | 21,388 | 12,212 |
| 06333 | *East Lyme* | 6,782 | 3,870 |
| 06425 | *Easton* | 3,407 | 2,165 |
| | *East Windsor* | 7,500 | 4,859 |
| 06029 | *Ellington* | 5,580 | 3,099 |
| 06030 | Enfield | 31,464 | 15,464 |
| 06426 | *Essex* | 4,057 | 3,491 |
| 06430 | *Fairfield* | 46,183 | 30,489 |
| 06032 | *Farmington* | 10,813 | 7,026 |
| 06810 | Germantown | 2,893 | 1,598 |
| 06033 | *Glostonbury* | 14,497 | 8,818 |
| 06035 | *Granby* | 4 968 | 2,693 |
| 06830 | Greenwich | 53,793 | 40,835 |
| | *Griswold* | 6,472 | 5,728 |
| 06340 | Groton | 10,111 | 7,036 |
| | *Groton (town)* | 29,937 | 21,896 |
| 06437 | *Guilford* | 7,913 | 5,092 |
| 06438 | *Haddam* | 3,466 | 2,636 |
| 06514 | Hamden | 41,056 | 29,715 |
| *06101 | Hartford | 162,178 | 177,397 |
| 06790 | *Harwinton* | 3,344 | 1,858 |
| 06351 | Jewett City | 3,608 | 3,702 |
| | *Killingly* | 11,298 | 10,015 |
| 06339 | *Ledyard* | 5,395 | 1 749 |
| 06759 | *Litchfield* | 6,264 | 4,964 |
| 06443 | *Madison* | 4,567 | 3,078 |
| 06040 | Manchester | 42,102 | 34,116 |
| 06250 | *Mansfield* | 14,638 | 10,008 |
| 06450 | Meriden | 51,850 | 44 088 |
| 06762 | *Middlebury* | 4,785 | 3,318 |
| 06455 | *Middlefield* | 3,255 | 1,983 |
| 06457 | Middletown | 33,250 | 29,711 |
| 06460 | *Milford* | 41,662 | 26,870 |
| 06468 | *Monroe* | 6,402 | 2,892 |
| 06353 | *Montville* | 7,759 | 4,766 |
| 06354 | Moosup | 2 760 | 2,909 |
| | Morningside Park | 3,181 | .... |
| 06355 | *Mystic* | 2,536 | 2,266 |

| ZIP Code | Place | 1960 | 1950 | ZIP Code | Place | 1960 | 1950 |
|---|---|---|---|---|---|---|---|
| | **CONNECTICUT—Continued** | | | | **FLORIDA—Continued** | | |
| 06770 | Naugatuck | 19,511 | 17,455 | 32233 | Atlantic Beach | 3,125 | 1,604 |
| *06051 | New Britain | 82,201 | 73,726 | 32823 | Auburndale | 5,595 | 3,763 |
| 06840 | New Canaan | 13,466 | 8,001 | 33825 | Avon Park | 6,073 | 4,612 |
| 06810 | New Fairfield | 3,355 | 1,236 | 33830 | Bartow | 12,849 | 8,694 |
| 06057 | New Hartford | 3,033 | 2,395 | | Bay Harbor Islands | 3,249 | 296 |
| *06510 | New Haven '67 | 141,752 | 164,443 | 33430 | Belle Glade | 11,273 | 7,219 |
| 06111 | Newington | 17,664 | 5,110 | 33152 | Biscayne Park | 2,911 | 2,009 |
| 06320 | New London | 34,182 | 30,551 | 33432 | Boca Raton | 6,961 | '992 |
| 06776 | New Milford | 3,023 | 2,673 | 33435 | Boynton Beach | 10,467 | 2,542 |
| | New Milford (town) | 3,318 | 5,799 | 33505 | Bradenton | 19,380 | 13,604 |
| 06470 | Newtown | 11,373 | 7,448 | 33505 | Bradenton South | 3,400 | .... |
| 06357 | Niantic | 2,788 | 1,746 | 33512 | Brooksville | 3,301 | 1,818 |
| 06471 | North Branford | 6,771 | 2,017 | 32505 | Brownsville | 38,417 | .... |
| | North Canaan | 2,836 | 2,647 | 33054 | Carol City | 21,749 | .... |
| 06473 | North Haven | 15,935 | 9,444 | 33505 | Cedar Hammock | 3,089 | 1,101 |
| 06854 | Norwalk | 67,775 | 49,460 | 32324 | Chattahoochee | 9,699 | 8,473 |
| 06360 | Norwich | 38,506 | 37,633 | 32428 | Chipley | 3,159 | 2,959 |
| 06371 | Old Lyme | 3,068 | 2,141 | *33515 | Clearwater | 34,653 | 15,581 |
| 06475 | Old Saybrook | 5,274 | 2,499 | 32711 | Clermont | 3,313 | 2,168 |
| 06477 | Orange | 8,547 | 3,032 | 33440 | Clewiston | 3,114 | 2,499 |
| 06483 | Oxford | 3,292 | 2,037 | 32922 | Cocoa | 12,294 | 4,245 |
| 02891 | Pawcatuck | 4,389 | 5,269 | 32931 | Cocoa Beach (A) '67 | 9,576 | 246 |
| 06374 | Plainfield | 8,884 | 8,071 | 32922 | Cocoa West | 3,975 | .... |
| 06062 | Plainville | 13,149 | 9,994 | 33801 | Combee Settlement | 2,697 | .... |
| 06479 | Plantsville | 2,793 | 1,536 | 33134 | Coral Gables | 34,793 | 19,837 |
| 06782 | Plymouth | 8,981 | 6,771 | 32536 | Crestview | 7,467 | 5,003 |
| 06480 | Portland | 5,587 | .... | 33157 | Cutler Ridge | 7,005 | .... |
| | Portland (town) | 7,496 | 5,186 | 33525 | Dade City | 4,759 | 3,806 |
| 06360 | Preston | 4,992 | 1,775 | 33004 | Dania | 7,065 | 4,540 |
| 06712 | Prospect | 4,367 | 1,896 | *32014 | Daytona Beach | 37,395 | 30,187 |
| 06260 | Putnam | 6,952 | 8,181 | 33441 | Deerfield Beach | 9,573 | 2,088 |
| | Putnam (town) | 8,412 | 9,304 | 32433 | De Funik Spgs | 5,282 | 3,077 |
| 06875 | Redding | 3,359 | 2,037 | 32720 | De Land | 10,775 | 8,652 |
| 06877 | Ridgefield | 2,954 | 2,347 | 33444 | Delray Beach | 12,230 | 6,312 |
| | Ridgefield (town) | 8,165 | 4,356 | 33528 | Dunedin | 8,444 | 3,202 |
| 06066 | Rockville | 9,478 | 8,016 | 32935 | Eau Gallie | 12,300 | 1,554 |
| 06067 | Rocky Hill | 7,404 | 5,108 | 33880 | Eloise | 3,256 | .... |
| 06068 | Salisbury | 3,309 | 3,132 | 33533 | Englewood | 2,877 | .... |
| 06483 | Seymour | 10,100 | 7,832 | 32726 | Eustis | 6,189 | 4,005 |
| 06484 | Shelton | 18,190 | 12,694 | 32034 | Fernandina Bch | 7,276 | 544 |
| 06070 | Simsbury | 2,745 | 1,771 | 32043 | Florida City | 4,114 | 1,547 |
| | Simsbury (town) | 10,138 | 4,822 | *33301 | Fort Lauderdale | 83,648 | 36,328 |
| 06071 | Somers | 3,702 | 2,631 | 33841 | Fort Meade | 4,014 | 2,803 |
| 06488 | Southbury | 5,186 | 3,828 | *33901 | Fort Myers | 22,523 | 13,195 |
| 06238 | South Coventry | 3,568 | 1,617 | 33450 | Fort Pierce | 25,256 | 13,502 |
| 06489 | Southington | 9,952 | 5,955 | 32548 | Fort Walton Bch | 12,147 | 2,463 |
| | Southington (town) | 22,797 | 13,061 | 33843 | Frostproof | 2,664 | 2,329 |
| 06074 | South Windsor | 9,460 | 4,066 | 32601 | Gainesville | 29,701 | 26,861 |
| 06075 | Sprague | 2,609 | 2,320 | 32601 | Gainesville North | 4,290 | .... |
| | Stafford | 7,476 | 6,471 | 32601 | Gainesville West | 2,725 | .... |
| 06076 | Stafford Springs | 3,332 | 3,396 | 32960 | Gifford | 3,509 | 1,459 |
| *06904 | Stamford | 92,713 | 74,293 | 33170 | Goulds | 5,121 | .... |
| 06378 | Stonington | 13,969 | 11,801 | 32043 | Green Cove Spgs | 4,233 | 3,291 |
| 06268 | Storrs | 6,054 | .... | 33737 | Gulfport | 9,730 | 3,702 |
| 06497 | Stratford | 45,012 | 33,428 | 33844 | Haines City | 9,135 | 5,630 |
| 06078 | Suffield | 6,779 | 4,895 | 33009 | Hallandale | 10,483 | 3,886 |
| 06786 | Terryville | 5,231 | .... | | Hayden | 5,471 | .... |
| 06787 | Thomaston | 3,579 | .... | *33010 | Hialeah | 66,972 | 19,676 |
| | Thomaston (town) | 5,850 | 4,896 | 32017 | Holly Hill | 4,182 | 3,232 |
| 06277 | Thompson | 6,217 | 5,585 | *33020 | Hollywood | 35,237 | 14,351 |
| 06084 | Tolland | 2,950 | 1,659 | 33030 | Homestead | 9,152 | 4,573 |
| 06790 | Torrington | 30,045 | 27,820 | 33934 | Immokalee | 3,224 | .... |
| 06611 | Trumbull | 20,379 | 8,641 | *32201 | Jacksonville | 201,030 | 204,517 |
| 06086 | Vernon | 16,961 | 10,115 | 32250 | Jacksonville Beach | 12,049 | 6,430 |
| 06492 | Wallingford | 29,920 | 16,976 | 33580 | Kensington Park | 2,969 | .... |
| 06793 | Washington | 2,603 | 2,227 | 33040 | Key West | 33,956 | 26,433 |
| *06701 | Waterbury | 107,130 | 104,477 | 32741 | Kissimmee | 6,845 | 4,310 |
| 06385 | Waterford | 15,391 | 9,100 | 32055 | Lake City | 9,465 | 7,571 |
| 06795 | Watertown | 14,837 | 10,699 | | Lake Holloway | 3,172 | .... |
| 06107 | West Hartford | 62,382 | 44,402 | *33801 | Lakeland | 41,350 | 30,851 |
| 06516 | West Haven | 43,002 | 32,010 | 33403 | Lake Park | 3,589 | 489 |
| 06388 | West Mystic | 3,268 | 2,962 | 33853 | Lake Wales | 8,346 | 6,821 |
| 06880 | Weston | 4,039 | 1,988 | 33460 | Lake Worth | 20,758 | 11,777 |
| 06880 | Westport | 20,955 | 11,667 | 33460 | Lantana | 5,021 | 773 |
| 06109 | Wethersfield | 20,561 | 12,533 | 33540 | Largo | 5,302 | 1,547 |
| 06226 | Willimantic | 13,881 | 13,586 | 32748 | Leesburg | 11,172 | 7,395 |
| 06897 | Wilton | 8,026 | 4,558 | 33030 | Leisure City | 3,001 | .... |
| 06094 | Winchester | 10,496 | 10,535 | 32060 | Live Oak | 6,544 | 4,064 |
| 06280 | Windham | 16,973 | 15,884 | 32444 | Lynn Haven | 3,078 | 1,787 |
| 06095 | Windsor | 19,467 | 11,833 | 32063 | Macclenny | 2,671 | 1,177 |
| 06096 | Windsor Locks | 11,411 | 5,221 | 33708 | Madeira Beach | 3,943 | 916 |
| 06098 | Winsted | 8,136 | 8,781 | 32340 | Madison | 3,239 | 3,150 |
| 06716 | Wolcott | 8,899 | 3,553 | 32751 | Maitland | 3,570 | 889 |
| 06525 | Woodbridge | 5,182 | 2,822 | 33063 | Margate | 2,646 | .... |
| 06281 | Woodstock | 3,177 | 2,271 | 32446 | Marianna | 7,152 | 5,845 |
| | | | | 32901 | Melbourne | 11,982 | 4,223 |
| | **DELAWARE** | | | | Memphis | 2,647 | .... |
| 19901 | Dover '67 | 14,814 | 6,223 | 32952 | Merritt Island | 3,554 | .... |
| 19805 | Elsmere | 7,319 | 5,314 | *33101 | Miami | 291,688 | 249,276 |
| 19956 | Laurel | 2,709 | 2,700 | 33139 | Miami Beach | 63,145 | 46,282 |
| 19958 | Lewes '67 | 2,661 | 2,904 | 33153 | Miami Shores | 8,865 | 5,086 |
| 19963 | Milford '67 | 5,702 | 5,179 | 33166 | Miami Springs | 11,229 | 5,108 |
| 19711 | Newark '67 | 19,398 | 6,731 | 32570 | Milton | 4,108 | 2,040 |
| 19720 | New Castle '67 | 4,682 | 5,396 | 33020 | Miramar | 5,485 | .... |
| 19973 | Seaford '67 | 4,799 | 3,087 | 32757 | Mount Dora | 3,756 | 3,028 |
| 19977 | Smyrna | 3,241 | 2,346 | 33860 | Mulberry | 2,922 | 2,024 |
| *19899 | Wilmington '67 | 85,690 | 110,356 | 33940 | Naples | 4,655 | 1,465 |
| | | | | 33031 | Naranja | 2,509 | .... |
| | **DISTRICT OF COLUMBIA** | | | 32250 | Neptune Beach | 2,868 | 1,767 |
| *20013 | Washington | 763,956 | 802,178 | 33552 | New Port Richey | 3,520 | 1,512 |
| | **FLORIDA** | | | 32069 | New Smyrna Beach | 8,781 | 5,775 |
| 32320 | Apalachicola | 3,099 | 3,222 | 32578 | Niceville | 4,517 | 2,497 |
| 32703 | Apopka | 3,578 | 2,254 | 33161 | North Miami | 28,708 | 10,734 |
| 33821 | Arcadia | 5,889 | 4,764 | | | | |

| ZIP Code | Place | 1960 | 1950 | ZIP Code | Place | 1960 | 1950 |
|---|---|---|---|---|---|---|---|
| | **FLORIDA—Continued** | | | | **GEORGIA—Continued** | | |
| 33160 | North Miami Beach.... | 21,405 | 2,129 | 30207 | Conyers.............. | 2,881 | 2,003 |
| 33403 | North Palm Beach..... | 2,684 | | 31015 | Cordele.............. | 10,609 | 9,462 |
| ..... | North Peninsula....... | 3,476 | | 30531 | Cornelia............. | 2,936 | 2,424 |
| 33307 | Oakland Park......... | 5,331 | 1,295 | 30209 | Covington............ | 8,167 | 5,192 |
| 32670 | Ocala............... | 13,598 | 11,741 | 31740 | Cuthbert............. | 4,300 | 4,025 |
| 32761 | Ocoee............... | 2,628 | 1,370 | 30533 | Dahlonega............ | 2,604 | 2,152 |
| 33472 | Okeechobee........... | 2,947 | 1,849 | 30720 | Dalton.............. | 17,865 | 15,968 |
| 33054 | Opa-Locka........... | 9,810 | 5,271 | 31742 | Dawson.............. | 5,062 | 4,411 |
| 32073 | Orange Park.......... | 2,624 | 1,502 | *30030 | Decatur............. | 22,026 | 21,635 |
| *32802 | Orlando.............. | 88,135 | 52,367 | 31520 | Dock Junction........ | 5,417 | 4,160 |
| 32074 | Ormond Beach (A) '67.. | 13,028 | 3,418 | 31745 | Donalsonville........ | 2,621 | 2,569 |
| 33476 | Pahokee............. | 4,709 | 4,472 | 30040 | Doraville............ | 4,437 | 472 |
| 32077 | Palatka............. | 11,028 | 9,176 | 31533 | Douglas............. | 8,736 | 7,428 |
| 32901 | Palm Bay............ | 2,808 | | 30134 | Douglasville......... | 4,462 | 3,400 |
| 33480 | Palm Beach.......... | 6,055 | 3,886 | 31095 | Dublin.............. | 13,814 | 10,232 |
| 33561 | Palmetto............ | 5,556 | 4,103 | 31023 | Eastman............. | 5,118 | 3,597 |
| 33460 | Palm Springs......... | 2,503 | | 30544 | East Point........... | 35,633 | 21,080 |
| 32401 | Panama City.......... | 33,275 | 25,814 | 31024 | Eatonton............ | 3,612 | 2,749 |
| 32401 | Parker.............. | 2,669 | | 30635 | Elberton............ | 7,107 | 6,772 |
| *32501 | Pensacola............ | 56,752 | 43,479 | 30060 | Fair Oaks........... | 7,969 | 3,131 |
| 33157 | Perrine............. | 6 424 | 2,859 | 31750 | Fitzgerald........... | 8,781 | 8,130 |
| 32347 | Perry............... | 8,030 | 2,797 | 30050 | Forrest Park......... | 14,201 | 2,653 |
| 33565 | Pinellas Park......... | 10,848 | 2,924 | 31029 | Forsyth............. | 3,697 | 3,125 |
| 33314 | Plantation........... | 4,772 | | 31030 | Fort Valley.......... | 8,310 | 6,820 |
| 33566 | Plant City........... | 15,711 | 9,230 | 30501 | Gainesville.......... | 16,523 | 11,936 |
| *33060 | Pompano Beach....... | 15,992 | 5,682 | 30415 | Garden City.......... | 5,451 | 1,557 |
| 33950 | Port Charlotte........ | 3,197 | | 30427 | Glennville........... | 2,791 | 2,327 |
| 32456 | Port St. Joe......... | 4,217 | 2,752 | 30642 | Greensboro........... | 2,773 | 2,688 |
| 33950 | Punta Gorda......... | 3,157 | 1,915 | 30223 | Griffin............. | 21,735 | 15,982 |
| 32351 | Quincy.............. | 8,874 | 6,505 | 30054 | Hapeville............ | 10,082 | 8,560 |
| 33158 | Richmond Heights...... | 4,311 | | 30643 | Hartwell............ | 4,599 | 2,964 |
| 33404 | Riviera Beach........ | 13,046 | 4,065 | 31036 | Hawkinsville......... | 3,967 | 3,342 |
| 32955 | Rockledge........... | 3,481 | 1,347 | 31539 | Hazlehurst........... | 3,699 | 2,687 |
| 33505 | Rosedale............ | 4,085 | | 31501 | Hebardville.......... | 2,758 | 1,113 |
| 32084 | St. Augustine........ | 14,734 | 13,555 | 31313 | Hinesville........... | 3,174 | 1,217 |
| 32769 | St. Cloud........... | 4,353 | 3,001 | 30230 | Hogansville.......... | 3,658 | 3,769 |
| *33739 | St. Petersburg....... | 181,298 | 96,738 | 31634 | Homerville........... | 2,634 | 1,787 |
| 33706 | St. Petersburg Beach... | 6,268 | 722 | 30233 | Jackson............. | 2,545 | 2,053 |
| 33508 | Samoset............. | 4,824 | 1,617 | 31545 | Jesup.............. | 7,304 | 4,605 |
| 32771 | Sanford............. | 19,175 | 11,935 | 30236 | Jonesboro........... | 3,014 | 1,741 |
| *33580 | Sarasota............ | 34,083 | 18,896 | 30728 | La Fayette.......... | 5,588 | 4,884 |
| 33870 | Sebring............. | 6,939 | 5,006 | 30240 | La Grange........... | 23,632 | 25,025 |
| 33143 | South Miami......... | 9,846 | 4,809 | 30245 | Lawrenceville........ | 3,804 | 2,932 |
| 32018 | South Peninsula....... | 3,741 | | 30147 | Lindale-Silver Creek.... | 2,800 | 3,234 |
| 32401 | Springfield........... | 4,628 | 1,084 | 30436 | Lyons.............. | 3,219 | 2,799 |
| 32091 | Starke.............. | 4,806 | 2,944 | 31055 | McRae.............. | 2,738 | 1,904 |
| 33494 | Stuart.............. | 4,791 | 2,912 | 30059 | Mableton............ | 7,127 | |
| ..... | Sunnyland........... | 4,761 | | *31202 | Macon (A).......... | 122,876 | 70,252 |
| 33154 | Surfside............ | 3,157 | 1,852 | 30650 | Madison............ | 2,680 | 2,489 |
| *32301 | Tallahassee (A)...... | 58,022 | 27,237 | 31816 | Manchester.......... | 4,115 | 4,036 |
| *33602 | Tampa.............. | 274,970 | 124,681 | 30060 | Marietta............ | 25,565 | 20,687 |
| 33589 | Tarpon Springs........ | 6,768 | 4,323 | 30060 | Marietta East........ | 4,535 | |
| 32778 | Tavares............. | 2,724 | 1,763 | 31034 | Midway-Hardwick...... | 16,909 | 14,774 |
| 33617 | Temple Terrace....... | 3,812 | 433 | 31061 | Milledgeville......... | 11,117 | 8,835 |
| 33905 | Tice............... | 4,377 | 1,133 | 30442 | Millen............. | 3,633 | 3,449 |
| 32780 | Titusville, '66....... | 27,998 | 2,604 | 30655 | Monroe............. | 6,826 | 4,542 |
| 33740 | Treasure Island....... | 3,506 | 75 | 31063 | Montezuma........... | 3,744 | 2,921 |
| 32580 | Valparaiso.......... | 5,975 | 1,047 | 31768 | Moultrie............ | 15,764 | 11,639 |
| 33595 | Venice............. | 3,444 | 727 | 31639 | Nashville........... | 4,070 | 3,414 |
| 32960 | Vero Beach.......... | 8,849 | 4,746 | 30263 | Newnan............. | 12,169 | 8,218 |
| 32507 | Warrington.......... | 16.752 | 13,570 | 30319 | North Atlanta........ | 12,661 | 5,930 |
| 33873 | Wauchula........... | 3,411 | 2,872 | 31774 | Ocilla............. | 3,217 | 2,697 |
| ..... | West End........... | 3,124 | 1,662 | 31779 | Pelham............. | 4,609 | 4,365 |
| ..... | West Miami......... | 5,296 | 4,043 | 31069 | Perry.............. | 6,032 | 3,849 |
| *33401 | West Palm Beach...... | 56,208 | 43,162 | 31407 | Port Wentworth....... | 3,705 | |
| 33880 | West Winter Haven.... | 5,050 | 2,326 | 31643 | Quitman............ | 5,071 | 4,769 |
| ..... | Westwood Lakes...... | 22,517 | | 30153 | Rockmart........... | 3,938 | 3,821 |
| 33305 | Wilton Manor........ | 8,257 | 883 | 30161 | Rome.............. | 32,226 | 29,615 |
| 33803 | Winston............ | 3,323 | 1,870 | 30741 | Rossville........... | 4,663 | 3,692 |
| 32787 | Winter Garden....... | 5,513 | 3,503 | 30075 | Roswell............ | 2,983 | 2,123 |
| 33880 | Winter Haven........ | 16,277 | 8,605 | 31558 | St. Marys........... | 3,272 | 1,348 |
| 32789 | Winter Park......... | 17,162 | 8,250 | 31522 | St. Simons.......... | 3,199 | |
| 33599 | Zephyrhills.......... | 2,887 | 1,826 | 31082 | Sandersville......... | 5,425 | 4,480 |
| | **GEORGIA** | | | 30080 | Smyrna............. | 10,157 | 2,005 |
| | | | | *31401 | Savannah........... | 149,245 | 119,638 |
| 31620 | Adel............... | 4,321 | 2,776 | 30458 | Statesboro.......... | 8,356 | 6,097 |
| *31701 | Albany............. | 55,890 | 31,155 | 30747 | Summerville......... | 4,706 | 3,973 |
| 31510 | Alma.............. | 3,515 | 2,588 | 30401 | Swainsboro......... | 5,943 | 4,300 |
| 30161 | Alto Park........... | 2,526 | 1,195 | 30467 | Sylvania............ | 3,469 | 2,939 |
| 31709 | Americus........... | 13,472 | 11,389 | 31791 | Sylvester........... | 3,610 | 2,623 |
| 31774 | Ashburn............ | 3,291 | 2,918 | 30176 | Tallapoosa.......... | 2,744 | 2,826 |
| 30601 | Athens, '63........ | 41,059 | 28,180 | 30286 | Thomaston.......... | 9,336 | 6,580 |
| *30304 | Atlanta............. | 487,455 | 331,314 | 31792 | Thomasville......... | 18,246 | 14,424 |
| *30901 | Augusta............ | 70,626 | 71,508 | 30824 | Thomson............ | 4,522 | 3,489 |
| 31717 | Bainbridge.......... | 12,714 | 7,562 | 31794 | Tifton............. | 9,903 | 6,831 |
| 30204 | Barnesville......... | 4,919 | 4,185 | 30577 | Toccoa............. | 7,303 | 6,781 |
| 31513 | Baxley............. | 4,268 | 3,409 | 31601 | Valdosta........... | 30,652 | 20,046 |
| 31723 | Blakely, '65....... | 5,190 | 3,234 | 30474 | Vidalia............ | 7,569 | 5,819 |
| ..... | Bloomfield Gardens... | 4,381 | | 30180 | Villa Rica.......... | 3,450 | 1,703 |
| 30110 | Bremen............ | 3,132 | 2,299 | 31093 | Warner Robins....... | 18,633 | 7,986 |
| 31520 | Brunswick.......... | 21,703 | 17,954 | 30673 | Washington.......... | 4,440 | 3,802 |
| 30518 | Buford............. | 4,168 | 3,812 | 31501 | Waycross........... | 20,944 | 18,899 |
| 31728 | Cairo.............. | 7,427 | 5,577 | 30830 | Waynesboro......... | 5,359 | 4,461 |
| 30701 | Calhoun............ | 3,587 | 3,231 | 31833 | West Point.......... | 4,610 | 4,079 |
| 31730 | Camilla............ | 4,753 | 3,745 | 30680 | Winder............ | 5,555 | 4,604 |
| 30117 | Carrollton.......... | 10,973 | 7,753 | | | | |
| 30120 | Cartersville........ | 8,668 | 7,270 | | **HAWAII** | | |
| 30125 | Cedartown.......... | 9,340 | 9,470 | 96701 | Aiea............... | 11,826 | 3,714 |
| 30005 | Chamblee........... | 6,635 | 3,445 | 96706 | Ewa............... | 3,257 | 3,429 |
| 30417 | Claxton............ | 2,672 | 1,699 | 96720 | Haleiwa............ | 2,504 | 2,142 |
| 31014 | Cochran............ | 4,714 | 3,357 | 96720 | Hilo............... | 25,966 | 27,198 |
| 33337 | College Park........ | 23,469 | 14,535 | *96813 | Honolulu............ | 294,194 | 248,034 |
| *31902 | Columbus........... | 116,779 | 79,611 | 96732 | Kahului............ | 4,223 | 6,306 |
| 30529 | Commerce.......... | 3,551 | 3,351 | 96734 | Kailua, Lanikai...... | 25,622 | 7,740 |

| ZIP Code | Place | 1960 | 1950 | ZIP Code | Place | 1960 | 1950 |
|---|---|---|---|---|---|---|---|
| | **Hawaii—Continued** | | | | **ILLINOIS—Continued** | | |
| 96744 | Kaneohe. | 14,414 | 3,208 | 61832 | Central Park. | 2,676 | 2,489 |
| 96746 | Kapaa. | 3,439 | 3,177 | 62206 | Centreville. | 12,769 | |
| 96761 | Lahaina. | 3,423 | 4,025 | 61820 | Champaign. | 49,583 | 39,563 |
| 96766 | Lihue. | 3,908 | 3,870 | 61920 | Charleston, '66. | 13,611 | 9,164 |
| 96792 | Lualualei-Maili. | 5,045 | 1,528 | 62233 | Chester, '65. | 5,300 | 5,389 |
| 96792 | Nanakuli. | 2,745 | 2,002 | *60607 | Chicago. | 3,550,404 | 3,620,962 |
| 96784 | Puunene. | 3,054 | | 60411 | Chicago Heights. | 34,331 | 24,551 |
| 96786 | Wahiawa. | 15,512 | 8,369 | 60415 | Chicago Ridge (A), '67. | 8,888 | 888 |
| 96791 | Waialua. | 2,689 | 2,602 | 61523 | Chillicothe. | 3,054 | 2,767 |
| 96792 | Waianae-Makaha. | 6,844 | 1,000 | 62822 | Christopher. | 2,854 | 3,545 |
| 96793 | Wailuku. | 6,969 | 7,424 | 60650 | Cicero. | 69,130 | 67,544 |
| 96795 | Waimanalo. | 3,011 | 868 | 60514 | Clarendon Hills. | 5,885 | 2,437 |
| | **IDAHO** | | | 61727 | Clinton. | 7,355 | 5,945 |
| 83201 | Alameda. | 10,660 | 4,694 | 60416 | Coal City. | 2,852 | 2,220 |
| 83211 | American Falls, '64. | 2,602 | 1,874 | 62234 | Collinsville. | 14,217 | 11,862 |
| 83221 | Blackfoot, '66. | 8,839 | 5,180 | 62236 | Columbia. | 3,174 | 2,179 |
| *83701 | Boise City (A), '66. | 72,090 | 34,393 | 62018 | Cottage Hills. | 3,976 | 3,357 |
| 83316 | Buhl. | 3,059 | 2,870 | 60478 | Country Club Hills, '66. | 5,838 | |
| 83313 | Burley, '66. | 8,262 | 5,924 | 60525 | Countryside, '64. | 2,626 | |
| 83605 | Caldwell (A). | 12,698 | 10,487 | 60435 | Crest Hill. | 5,887 | |
| 83814 | Coeur d'Alene. | 14,291 | 12,198 | 60445 | Crestwood, '63. | 3,918 | 739 |
| 83703 | Collister. | 5,436 | | 61610 | Creve Coeur, '67. | 6,742 | 5,499 |
| 83617 | Emmett. | 3,769 | 3,067 | 60014 | Crystal Lake (A), '67. | 12,493 | 4,823 |
| 83237 | Franklin. | 7,222 | | 61832 | Danville. | 41,856 | 37,864 |
| 83330 | Gooding. | 2,750 | 3,099 | *62521 | Decatur. | 78,004 | 66,266 |
| 83530 | Grangeville. | 3,642 | 2,544 | 60015 | Deerfield, '66. | 17,245 | 3,288 |
| 83401 | Idaho Falls, '66. | 35,711 | 19,218 | 60115 | De Kalb, '66. | 29,099 | 11,708 |
| 83338 | Jerome. | 4,761 | 4,523 | 60016 | Des Plaines, '65. | 50,739 | 14,994 |
| 83837 | Kellogg. | 5,061 | 4,913 | | Dixmoor. | 3,076 | 1,327 |
| 83501 | Lewiston. | 12,691 | 12,985 | 61021 | Dixon. | 19,565 | 11,523 |
| | Lewiston Orchards. | 9,680 | | 60419 | Dolton, '66. | 22,557 | 5,558 |
| 83254 | Montpelier. | 3,146 | 2,682 | 60515 | Downers Grove (A), '67. | 25,948 | 11,886 |
| 83843 | Moscow, '66. | 13,783 | 10,593 | 62239 | Dupo. | 2,937 | 2,239 |
| 83647 | Mountain Home, '62. | 10,075 | 1,887 | 62832 | Du Quoin. | 6,558 | 7,147 |
| 83704 | Mountain View. | 4,898 | 3,084 | 60420 | Dwight. | 3,086 | 2,843 |
| 83651 | Nampa. | 18,897 | 16,185 | 62024 | East Alton. | 7,630 | 7,290 |
| 83544 | Orofino '67. | 3,193 | 2,471 | 60411 | East Chicago Heights, '65 | 4,715 | 1,548 |
| 83661 | Payette. | 4,451 | 4,032 | 61244 | East Moline. | 16,732 | 13,913 |
| 83201 | Pocatello. | 28,534 | 26,131 | 61611 | East Peoria. | 12,310 | 8,698 |
| 83263 | Preston. | 3,640 | 4,045 | *62201 | East St. Louis. | 81,712 | 82,295 |
| 83440 | Rexburg, '66. | 7,025 | 4,253 | 62025 | Edwardsville (A), '67. | 10,750 | 8,776 |
| 83350 | Rupert. | 4,153 | 3,098 | 62401 | Effingham. | 8,172 | 6,892 |
| 83445 | St. Anthony. | 2,700 | 2,695 | 62930 | Eldorado. | 3,573 | 4,500 |
| 83467 | Salmon. | 2,944 | 2,648 | 60120 | Elgin. | 49,447 | 44,223 |
| 83864 | Sandpoint. | 4,355 | 4,265 | 60007 | Elk Grove Village (A), '67 | 16,905 | |
| 83274 | Shelley. | 2,612 | 1,856 | 60126 | Elmhurst, '63. | 40,329 | 21,273 |
| 83276 | Soda Springs (A), '67. | 3,456 | 2,424 | 60635 | Elmwood Park. | 23,866 | 18,801 |
| 83301 | Twin Falls, '66. | 20,893 | 17,600 | 61530 | Eureka. | 2,538 | 2,367 |
| 83672 | Weiser. | 4,208 | 3,961 | *60204 | Evanston. | 79,283 | 73,641 |
| 83705 | Whitney. | 13,603 | | 60642 | Evergreen Park, '67. | 26,552 | 10,531 |
| | **ILLINOIS** | | | 61739 | Fairbury. | 2,937 | 2,433 |
| 61410 | Abingdon. | 3,466 | 3,300 | 62837 | Fairfield. | 6,362 | 5,576 |
| 60101 | Addison (A), '67. | 20,232 | 813 | 62201 | Fairmont City. | 2,688 | 2,284 |
| 61231 | Aledo. | 3,080 | 2,919 | 61531 | Farmington. | 2,831 | 2,651 |
| 60102 | Algonquin, '63. | 2,692 | 1,223 | 62839 | Flora. | 5,331 | 5,255 |
| 62207 | Alorton. | 3,282 | 2,547 | 60422 | Flossmoor, '65. | 5,921 | 1,804 |
| 60658 | Alsip, '67. | 8,776 | 1,228 | 60130 | Forest Park. | 14,452 | 14,960 |
| 62002 | Alton. | 43,047 | 32,550 | 60020 | Fox Lake (A), '67. | 4,336 | 2,238 |
| 62906 | Anna. | 4,280 | 4,380 | 60131 | Franklin Park (A), '67. | 20,455 | 8,899 |
| 60002 | Antioch, '65. | 2,778 | 1,307 | 61032 | Freeport (A). | 26,802 | 22,467 |
| *60004 | Arlington Heights (A), '67 | 52,797 | 8,768 | 61252 | Fulton. | 3,387 | 2,706 |
| *60504 | Aurora. | 63,715 | 50,576 | 60030 | Gages Lake. | 3,395 | |
| 60010 | Barrington, '65. | 6,525 | 4,209 | 61036 | Galena. | 4,410 | 4,648 |
| 61609 | Bartonville. | 7,253 | 2,437 | 61401 | Galesburg. | 37,243 | 31,425 |
| 60510 | Batavia (A), '67. | 8,131 | 5,838 | 61434 | Galva. | 3,060 | 2,886 |
| 62618 | Beardstown. | 6,294 | 6,080 | 61254 | Geneseo (A), '67. | 5,761 | 4,325 |
| 62220 | Belleville (A), '67. | 40,680 | 32,721 | 60134 | Geneva, '66. | 8,573 | 5,139 |
| 60104 | Bellwood, '65. | 22,821 | 8,746 | 60135 | Genoa, '65. | 2,862 | 532 |
| 61008 | Belvidere (A), '67. | 13,049 | 9,422 | 61846 | Georgetown. | 3,544 | 3,294 |
| 60106 | Bensenville, '65. | 12,212 | 3,754 | 60936 | Gibson City. | 3,453 | 3,029 |
| 62812 | Benton. | 7,023 | 7,848 | 62033 | Gillespie. | 3,569 | 4,105 |
| 60162 | Berkeley, '64. | 6,326 | 1,882 | 60022 | Glencoe. | 10,472 | 6,980 |
| 60402 | Berwyn. | 54,224 | 51,280 | 60137 | Glendale Heights, '65. | 7,419 | |
| 62010 | Bethalto, '66. | 5,404 | 2,115 | 60137 | Glen Ellyn, '67. | 20,503 | 9,524 |
| 61701 | Bloomington, '65. | 37,791 | 34,163 | 60025 | Glenview, '66. | 23,521 | 6,142 |
| 60406 | Blue Island, '66. | 21,986 | 17,622 | 60425 | Glenwood (A), '67. | 4,894 | 762 |
| 60914 | Bourbonnais. | 3,336 | 1,598 | 62040 | Granite City (A), '67. | 39,850 | 29,465 |
| 60915 | Bradley, '65. | 9,381 | 5,699 | 60030 | Grayslake, '65. | 4,347 | 1,970 |
| 62230 | Breese, '66. | 2,810 | 2,181 | 61241 | Green Rock, '67. | 2,853 | |
| 60455 | Bridge View, '66. | 9,273 | 1,393 | 62246 | Greenville. | 4,569 | 4,069 |
| 60153 | Broadview, '63. | 9,638 | 5,196 | 62341 | Hamilton, '66. | 2,516 | 1,776 |
| 60513 | Brookfield. | 20,429 | 15,472 | 60103 | Hanover Park, '65. | 6,620 | |
| 60090 | Buffalo Grove, '63. | 3,429 | | 62947 | Harrisburg. | 9,171 | 10,999 |
| 61422 | Bushnell. | 3,710 | 3,317 | 60033 | Harvard, '65. | 5,019 | 3,464 |
| 62206 | Cahokia. | 15,829 | 794 | 60426 | Harvey, '65. | 33,230 | 20,683 |
| 62914 | Cairo. | 9,348 | 12,123 | | Harwood Heights, '65. | 8,808 | 655 |
| 60409 | Calumet City. '67. | 29,617 | 15,799 | 62644 | Havana. | 4,363 | 4,379 |
| 60643 | Calumet Park, '65. | 10,037 | 2,500 | 60429 | Hazel Crest, '64. | 8,907 | 2,129 |
| 61520 | Canton. | 13,588 | 11,297 | 62948 | Herrin. | 9,474 | 9,331 |
| 62901 | Carbondale, '64. | 18,531 | 10,921 | 60457 | Hickory Hills, '65. | 6,946 | |
| 62626 | Carlinville. | 5,440 | 5,116 | 62249 | Highland (A), '67. | 5,637 | 4,283 |
| 62231 | Carlyle, '66. | 3,193 | 2,669 | 60035 | Highland Park, '65. | 30,054 | 16,808 |
| 62821 | Carmi. | 6,152 | 5,574 | 60040 | Highwood. | 4,499 | 3,813 |
| 60187 | Carol Stream, '62. | 2,514 | | 62049 | Hillsboro. | 4,232 | 4,141 |
| 60110 | Carpentersville. | 17,424 | 1,523 | 60162 | Hillside, '64. | 9,404 | 2,131 |
| 62016 | Carrollton. | 2,558 | 2,437 | 60521 | Hinsdale (A), '65. | 14,738 | 8,676 |
| 62918 | Carterville. | 2,643 | 2,716 | 60172 | Hoffman Estates, '65. | 15,896 | |
| 62321 | Carthage. | 3,325 | 3,214 | 60456 | Hometown. | 7,479 | |
| 60013 | Cary, '66. | 3,839 | 943 | 60430 | Homewood, '66. | 17,399 | 5,887 |
| 62420 | Casey. | 2,890 | 2,734 | 60942 | Hoopeston. | 6,606 | 5,992 |
| 62232 | Caseyville, '65. | 2,856 | 1,209 | 60143 | Itasca (A), '67. | 4,339 | 1,274 |
| 62801 | Centralia. | 13,904 | 13,863 | 62650 | Jacksonville. | 21,690 | 20,387 |

| ZIP Code | Place | 1960 | 1950 | ZIP Code | Place | 1960 | 1950 |
|---|---|---|---|---|---|---|---|
| | **ILLINOIS—Continued** | | | | **ILLINOIS—Continued** | | |
| 62052 | Jerseyville............ | 7,420 | 5,792 | 60544 | Plainfield '67....... | 2,646 | 2,183 |
| 62951 | Johnson City......... | 3,891 | 4,479 | 60545 | Plano, '64.......... | 4,059 | 2,154 |
| *60431 | Joliet............... | 66,780 | 51,601 | 61064 | Polo............... | 2,551 | 2,242 |
| 60458 | Justice, '65......... | 5,252 | 854 | 61764 | Pontiac............ | 8,435 | 7,562 |
| 60901 | Kankakee............ | 27,666 | 25,856 | 60469 | Posen.............. | 4,517 | 1,795 |
| 60043 | Kenilworth.......... | 2,959 | 2,789 | 61356 | Princeton, '67...... | 6,771 | 5,765 |
| 61443 | Kewanee............ | 16,324 | 16,821 | 62301 | Quincy (A).......... | 43,693 | 41,450 |
| 61448 | Knoxville........... | 2,560 | 2,209 | 61866 | Rantoul, '66........ | 27,533 | 6,387 |
| 60525 | La Grange (A), '67.... | 16,177 | 12,002 | 60627 | Riverdale, '66...... | 15,517 | 5,840 |
| 60525 | La Grange Park, '63... | 15,430 | 6,176 | 60305 | River Forest........ | 12,695 | 10,823 |
| 60044 | Lake Bluff, '64...... | 4,345 | 2,000 | 60171 | River Grove, '66.... | 11,111 | 4,839 |
| 60045 | Lake Forest, '65..... | 13,345 | 7,819 | 60546 | Riverside.......... | 9,750 | 9,153 |
| 60102 | Lake In the Hills (A) '67. | 2,926 | 2,046 | 60472 | Robbins............ | 7,511 | 4,766 |
| 60047 | Lake Zurich, '66..... | 3,851 | 850 | 62454 | Robinson........... | 7,226 | 6,407 |
| 60438 | Lansing, '67........ | 23,143 | 8,682 | 61068 | Rochelle, '64....... | 7,554 | 5,449 |
| 61301 | La Salle............ | 11,897 | 12,088 | 61071 | Rock Falls (A), '67... | 10,439 | 7,983 |
| 62439 | Lawrenceville (A)..... | 6,136 | 6,328 | *61101 | Rockford, '64....... | 132,190 | 92,927 |
| 62254 | Lebanon (A), '67..... | 3,494 | 2,417 | 61201 | Rock Island........ | 51,863 | 48,710 |
| 60439 | Lemont, '64........ | 4,034 | 2,757 | 60008 | Rolling Meadows (A) '67 | 17,654 | ........ |
| 61542 | Lewistown.......... | 2,603 | 2,630 | 60441 | Romeoville, '63..... | 6,358 | 147 |
| 60048 | Libertyville, '65..... | 9,241 | 5,425 | 60172 | Roselle, '63........ | 4,827 | 1,038 |
| 62656 | Lincoln, '65........ | 17,364 | 14,362 | 60018 | Rosemont (A) '67.... | 3,457 | 978 |
| 60645 | Lincolnwood, '65..... | 13,546 | 3,072 | 62024 | Rosewood Heights.... | 4,572 | 1,836 |
| 60532 | Lisle, '64.......... | 5,037 | ..... | 60073 | Round Lake Beach.... | 5,011 | 1,892 |
| 62056 | Litchfield.......... | 7,330 | 7,208 | 60073 | Round Lake Park, '64... | 2,921 | 1,836 |
| 60441 | Lockport, '64....... | 8,785 | 4,955 | 62681 | Rushville.......... | 2,819 | 2,682 |
| 60148 | Lombard (A), '67.... | 31,314 | 9,817 | 60174 | St. Charles, '65..... | 11,158 | 6,709 |
| 60041 | Long Lake.......... | 2,502 | 2,637 | 62881 | Salem.............. | 6,165 | 6,157 |
| 61111 | Loves Park, '64...... | 10,891 | 5,366 | 60548 | Sandwich, '65...... | 4,500 | 3,029 |
| 60534 | Lyons, '64.......... | 10,891 | 6,120 | 60411 | Sauk, '61.......... | 5,774 | ..... |
| 60050 | McHenry (A), '67.... | 5,943 | 2,080 | 61074 | Savanna (A)......... | 5,190 | 5,058 |
| 62859 | McLeansboro........ | 2,951 | 3,008 | 60172 | Schaumburg, '66..... | 6,454 | ..... |
| 61455 | Macomb, '65........ | 16,094 | 10,592 | 60176 | Schiller Park, '64... | 8,610 | 1,384 |
| 62060 | Madison............ | 6,861 | 7,963 | 62565 | Shelbyville......... | 4,821 | 4,462 |
| 60152 | Marengo............ | 3,568 | 2,726 | 61282 | Silvis (A), '67...... | 5,052 | 3,055 |
| 62959 | Marion............. | 11,274 | 10,459 | 60076 | Skokie, '67......... | 70,178 | 14,832 |
| 60426 | Markham, '64....... | 14,595 | 2,753 | 61080 | South Beloit........ | 3,781 | 3,221 |
| 61554 | Marquette Heights..... | 2,517 | ..... | 60411 | South Chicago Heights.. | 4,043 | 2,912 |
| 61341 | Marseilles.......... | 4,347 | 4,514 | 60177 | South Elgin, '65..... | 3,589 | 1,220 |
| 62441 | Marshall........... | 3,270 | 2,960 | 60473 | South Holland, '66.... | 17,758 | 3,247 |
| 62258 | Mascoutah, '66...... | 4,664 | 3,009 | 62650 | South Jacksonville, '65.. | 2,654 | 797 |
| 60443 | Matteson, '65....... | 3,898 | 1,211 | 62286 | Sparta............. | 3,452 | 3,576 |
| 61938 | Mattoon............ | 19,088 | 17,547 | *62701 | Springfield......... | 83,271 | 81,628 |
| 60153 | Maywood, '65....... | 28,905 | 27,473 | 61362 | Spring Valley....... | 5,371 | 4,916 |
| *60160 | Melrose Park........ | 22,291 | 13,366 | 62088 | Staunton........... | 4,228 | 4,047 |
| 61342 | Mendota, '64........ | 6,714 | 5,129 | 60475 | Steger............. | 6,432 | 4,285 |
| 60655 | Merrionette Pk., '66... | 2,521 | 1,101 | 61081 | Sterling, 67........ | 16,432 | 12,817 |
| 62960 | Metropolis.......... | 7,339 | 6,093 | 60402 | Stickney........... | 6,239 | 3,317 |
| 60445 | Midlothian, '65...... | 11,789 | 3,216 | 60165 | Stone Park, '63..... | 4,242 | 1,414 |
| 61264 | Milan, '64.......... | 3,941 | 1,737 | 60103 | Streamwood, '65..... | 10,252 | ..... |
| 61265 | Moline............. | 42,705 | 37,397 | 61364 | Streator........... | 16,868 | 16,469 |
| 60954 | Momence........... | 2,949 | 2,644 | 61951 | Sullivan........... | 3,946 | 3,470 |
| 61462 | Monmouth.......... | 10,372 | 10,193 | 60501 | Summit............ | 10,374 | 8,957 |
| 60538 | Montgomery, '65..... | 2,744 | 773 | 62221 | Swansea........... | 3,018 | 1,816 |
| 61856 | Monticello, '65...... | 3,511 | 2,611 | 60178 | Sycamore.......... | 6,961 | 5,912 |
| 60450 | Morris............. | 7,935 | 6,926 | 62568 | Taylorville......... | 8,801 | 9,188 |
| 61270 | Morrison........... | 4,159 | 3,531 | 60476 | Thornton, '63....... | 3,667 | 1,217 |
| 61550 | Morton, '66......... | 8,248 | 3,693 | 61832 | Tilton............. | 2,598 | 1,638 |
| 60053 | Morton Grove (A), '67.. | 26,954 | 3,926 | 60477 | Tinley Park, '66..... | 8,750 | 2,326 |
| 62863 | Mount Carmel....... | 8,594 | 8,732 | 61953 | Tuscola........... | 3,875 | 2,960 |
| 61054 | Mount Morris....... | 3,075 | 2,709 | 61801 | Urbana............ | 27,294 | 22,834 |
| 60056 | Mt. Prospect, '66.... | 30,202 | 4,009 | 62471 | Vandalia........... | 5,537 | 5,471 |
| 62864 | Mount Vernon....... | 15,566 | 15,600 | 62090 | Venice............. | 5,380 | 6,226 |
| 60060 | Mundelein (A), '67... | 15,617 | 3,189 | 60181 | Villa Park, '65...... | 25,697 | 8,821 |
| 62966 | Murphysboro, '65..... | 9,393 | 9,241 | 62690 | Virden............ | 3,309 | 3,206 |
| 60540 | Naperville, '66...... | 18,734 | 7,013 | 60555 | Warrenville......... | 3,134 | 1,891 |
| 62263 | Nashville, '66....... | 2,805 | 2,432 | 61571 | Washington......... | 5,919 | 4,285 |
| 62448 | Newton............ | 2,901 | 2,780 | 62204 | Washington Park..... | 6,601 | 5,840 |
| 60648 | Niles (A), '67....... | 32,075 | 3,587 | 62204 | Waterloo........... | 3,739 | 2,821 |
| 61761 | Normal (A), '67..... | 23,213 | 9,772 | 60970 | Watseka........... | 5,219 | 4,235 |
| | Norridge, '65....... | 17,126 | 3,428 | 60084 | Wauconda, '66...... | 5,343 | 1,173 |
| 60542 | North Aurora, '66.... | 4,734 | 921 | 60085 | Waukegan.......... | 55,719 | 38,946 |
| 60062 | Northbrook (A), '67... | 19,169 | 3,348 | 60153 | Westchester........ | 18,092 | 4,308 |
| 60064 | North Chicago....... | 22,938 | 8,628 | 60185 | West Chicago, '66.... | 8,174 | 3,973 |
| 60093 | Northfield.......... | 4,005 | 1,426 | 60118 | West Dundee (A), '67... | 2,900 | 1,948 |
| 60164 | North Lake, '64..... | 14,115 | 4,361 | 60558 | Western Springs, '66... | 13,233 | 6,364 |
| 60547 | North Riverside, '62... | 8,401 | 3,230 | 62896 | West Frankfort...... | 9,027 | 11,384 |
| 60521 | Oak Brook, '66...... | 2,546 | ..... | 60901 | West Kankakee....... | 3,197 | 2,784 |
| 60452 | Oak Forest, '66...... | 11,107 | 1,856 | 60559 | Westmont (A), '67.... | 8,245 | 3,402 |
| 60453 | Oak Lawn (A), '67.... | 54,580 | 8,751 | 61883 | Westville.......... | 3,497 | 3,196 |
| *60302 | Oak Park, '66....... | 61,538 | 63,529 | 60187 | Wheaton, '66....... | 28,333 | 11,638 |
| 62269 | O'Fallon, '66........ | 5,796 | 3,022 | 60090 | Wheeling, '64....... | 11,756 | 916 |
| 61348 | Oglesby............ | 4,215 | 3,922 | 62092 | White Hall......... | 3,012 | 3,082 |
| 62450 | Olney............. | 8,780 | 8,612 | 60480 | Willow Springs, '66... | 3,158 | 1,314 |
| 60461 | Olympia Fields, '65... | 2,578 | 160 | 60091 | Wilmette, '65....... | 31,685 | 18,162 |
| 61061 | Oregon............ | 3,732 | 3,205 | 60481 | Wilmington, '67..... | 4,483 | 3,354 |
| 60462 | Orland Park, '64..... | 4,509 | 788 | 60190 | Winfield, '66....... | 3,265 | 714 |
| 61350 | Ottawa............ | 19,408 | 16,957 | 60093 | Winnetka........... | 13,368 | 12,105 |
| 60067 | Palatine, '65....... | 19,146 | 4,079 | 60096 | Winthrop Harbor, '66... | 4,427 | 1,762 |
| 60463 | Palos Heights....... | 3,775 | ..... | 60097 | Wonder Lake........ | 3,643 | 1,077 |
| 60465 | Palos Hills, '65..... | 5,303 | ..... | 60191 | Wood Dale (A), '67... | 7,872 | 1,850 |
| 62557 | Pana.............. | 6,432 | 6,178 | 60516 | Woodridge, '66...... | 5,263 | ..... |
| 61944 | Paris.............. | 9,823 | 9,460 | 62095 | Wood River......... | 11,694 | 10,195 |
| 60466 | Park Forest, '65..... | 31,324 | 8,138 | 60098 | Woodstock, '66...... | 9,910 | 7,192 |
| 60068 | Park Ridge (A), '67... | 40,125 | 16,602 | 60482 | Worth, '67......... | 11,702 | 1,472 |
| 60957 | Paxton............ | 4,370 | 3,795 | 60099 | Zion, '64.......... | 14,106 | 8,950 |
| 61554 | Pekin, '64.......... | 29,624 | 21,858 | | | | |
| *61601 | Peoria............. | 103,162 | 111,856 | | **INDIANA** | | |
| 61613 | Peoria Heights...... | 7,064 | 5,425 | 46001 | Alexandria......... | 5,582 | 5,147 |
| 61354 | Peru, '66.......... | 11,443 | 8,653 | *46011 | Anderson (A), '67.... | 70,020 | 46,820 |
| 60426 | Phoenix............ | 4,203 | 3,606 | 46012 | Anderson East Side.... | 3,778 | ..... |
| 62274 | Pinckneyville....... | 3,085 | 3,299 | 46703 | Angola, '66........ | 5,234 | 5,081 |
| 62363 | Pittsfield.......... | 4,089 | 3,564 | 47918 | Attica............. | 4,341 | 3,862 |

| ZIP Code | Place | 1960 | 1950 | ZIP Code | Place | 1960 | 1950 |
|---|---|---|---|---|---|---|---|
| | **INDIANA—Continued** | | | | **INDIANA—Continued** | | |
| 46706 | Auburn (A), '67 | 6,958 | 5,879 | 46563 | Plymouth | 7,558 | 6,704 |
| 47001 | Aurora, '62 | 4,756 | 4,780 | 46368 | Portage, '65 | 16,490 | ...... |
| 47102 | Austin | 3,838 | 2,906 | 46369 | Porter, '65 | 3,193 | 1,190 |
| 47006 | Batesville | 3,349 | 3,194 | 47371 | Portland | 6,999 | 7,064 |
| 47421 | Bedford (A), '67 | 13,479 | 12,562 | 47570 | Princeton | 7,906 | 7,673 |
| 46107 | Beech Grove, '64 | 12,632 | 5,685 | 47978 | Rensselaer | 4,740 | 4,072 |
| 46711 | Berne | 2,644 | 2,277 | 47374 | Richmond | 44,149 | 39,539 |
| 47512 | Bicknell | 3,878 | 4,572 | 46975 | Rochester | 4,883 | 4,673 |
| 47401 | Bloomington, '65 | 42,058 | 28,163 | 47872 | Rockville | 2,756 | 2,467 |
| 46714 | Bluffton (A) | 7,052 | 6,076 | 46173 | Rushville | 7,264 | 6,761 |
| 47601 | Boonville (A), '67 | 5,408 | 5,092 | 47167 | Salem | 4,546 | 3,271 |
| 47834 | Brazil | 8,853 | 8,434 | 46375 | Schererville, '67 | 3,347 | 1,457 |
| 46506 | Bremen | 3,062 | 2,664 | 47170 | Scottsburg, '66 | 4,506 | 2,953 |
| 47012 | Brookville, '63 | 2,603 | 2,538 | 47172 | Sellersburg, '64 | 3,007 | 1,664 |
| 46112 | Brownsburg, '66 | 5,121 | 1,578 | 47274 | Seymour | 11,629 | 9,629 |
| 47327 | Cambridge City | 2,569 | 2,559 | 46176 | Shelbyville, '66 | 14,744 | 11,734 |
| 46032 | Carmel, '66 | 3,023 | 1,009 | *46624 | South Bend | 132,445 | 115,911 |
| 46303 | Cedar Lake, '66 | 7,494 | 3,907 | 46224 | Speedway, '65 | 11,319 | 5,498 |
| 47111 | Charlestown, '64 | 5,571 | 4,785 | 47460 | Spencer | 2,557 | 2,394 |
| 46017 | Chesterfield | 2,588 | 1,086 | 47882 | Sullivan | 4,979 | 5,423 |
| 46304 | Chesterton, '66 | 5,058 | 3,175 | 47586 | Tell City, '65 | 7,715 | 5,735 |
| 47130 | Clarksville, '64 | 9,089 | 5,905 | *47808 | Terre Haute, '65 | 72,500 | 64,214 |
| 47842 | Clinton | 5,843 | 6,462 | 46072 | Tipton | 5,604 | 5,633 |
| 46725 | Columbia City | 4,803 | 4,745 | 47390 | Union City | 4,047 | 3,572 |
| 47201 | Columbus, '63 | 24,782 | 18,370 | 46383 | Valparaiso, '65 | 16,938 | 12,028 |
| 47331 | Connersville | 17,698 | 15,550 | 47591 | Vincennes, '65 | 20,061 | 18,831 |
| 47112 | Corydon | 2,701 | 1,944 | 46992 | Wabash, '66 | 13,448 | 10,621 |
| 47932 | Covington | 2,759 | 2,235 | 46580 | Warsaw | 7,234 | 6,625 |
| 47933 | Crawfordsville, '66 | 14,466 | 12,851 | 47501 | Washington (A), '67 | 11,230 | 10,987 |
| 46410 | Crown Point (A), '67 | 10,095 | 5,839 | 47906 | West Lafayette, '65 | 17,731 | 11,873 |
| 46122 | Danville | 3,287 | 2,802 | 47885 | West Terre Haute | 3,006 | 3,357 |
| 46733 | Decatur (A), '67 | 8,508 | 7,271 | 46394 | Whiting | 8,137 | 9,669 |
| 46923 | Delphi | 2,517 | 2,530 | 47394 | Winchester | 5,742 | 5,467 |
| 47336 | Dunkirk | 3,117 | 3,048 | | | | |
| 46311 | Dyer | 3,993 | 1,556 | | **IOWA** | | |
| 46312 | East Chicago | 57,669 | 54,263 | 52531 | Albia | 4,582 | 4,838 |
| 46405 | East Gary | 9,309 | 5,635 | 50511 | Algona, '66 | 5,977 | 5,415 |
| 46124 | Edinburg | 3,664 | 3,283 | 50010 | Ames, '65 | 34,826 | 22,898 |
| 46514 | Elkhart | 40,274 | 35,646 | 52205 | Anamosa | 4,616 | 3,919 |
| 46036 | Elwood | 11,793 | 11,362 | 50021 | Ankeny, '65 | 5,910 | 1,229 |
| *47708 | Evansville, '66 | 144,463 | 128,636 | 50022 | Atlantic | 6,890 | 6,480 |
| 46928 | Fairmount | 3,080 | 2,646 | 50025 | Audubon, '67 | 3,034 | 2,808 |
| *46802 | Fort Wayne (A), '67 | 172,594 | 133,607 | 52208 | Belle Plaine | 2,923 | 3,056 |
| 46041 | Frankfort | 15,302 | 15,028 | 50421 | Belmond | 2,506 | 2,169 |
| 46131 | Franklin, '66 | 11,292 | 7,316 | 52722 | Bettendorf, '65 | 17,264 | 5,132 |
| 46738 | Garrett, '66 | 4,725 | 4,291 | 52537 | Bloomfield | 2,771 | 2,688 |
| *46401 | Gary | 178,320 | 133,911 | 50036 | Boone | 12,468 | 12,164 |
| 46933 | Gas City (A), '67 | 5,249 | 3,787 | 52601 | Burlington, '65 | 33,285 | 30,613 |
| 46526 | Goshen | 13,718 | 13,003 | 52730 | Camanche, '65 | 3,055 | 814 |
| 46135 | Greencastle | 8,506 | 6,888 | 51401 | Carroll, '65 | 8,481 | 6,231 |
| 47025 | Greendale | 2,861 | 2,018 | 50613 | Cedar Falls, '65 | 26,016 | 14,334 |
| 46140 | Greenfield | 9,049 | 6,159 | *52401 | Cedar Rapids, '65 | 103,545 | 72,296 |
| 47240 | Greensburg | 7,492 | 6,619 | 52544 | Centerville | 6,629 | 7,625 |
| 46142 | Greenwood | 7,169 | 3,066 | 50049 | Chariton | 5,042 | 5,302 |
| 46319 | Griffith, '64 | 12,810 | 4,470 | 50616 | Charles City, '65 | 10,419 | 10,309 |
| *46325 | Hammond | 111,698 | 87,594 | 51012 | Cherokee | 7,724 | 7,705 |
| 47348 | Hartford City | 8,053 | 7,253 | 51632 | Clarinda, '66 | 5,714 | 5,086 |
| 46322 | Highland, '67 | 23,474 | 5,878 | 50525 | Clarion | 3,232 | 3,150 |
| 46342 | Hobart, '66 | 20,875 | 10,244 | 50428 | Clear Lake, '66 | 6,301 | 4,977 |
| 46952 | Home Corner | 2,636 | 3,950 | 52732 | Clinton, '65 | 33,331 | 30,379 |
| 47542 | Huntingburg | 4,146 | 4,056 | 52241 | Coralville, '65 | 3,390 | 977 |
| 46750 | Huntington | 16,185 | 15,079 | 51501 | Council Bluffs, '66 | 52,957 | 45,429 |
| *46206 | Indianapolis (A) | 491,360 | 427,173 | 52136 | Cresco, '65 | 3,878 | 3,638 |
| 47546 | Jasper, '63 | 7,910 | 5,215 | 50801 | Creston, '66 | 8,119 | 8,317 |
| 47130 | Jeffersonville, '66 | 20,060 | 14,685 | *52801 | Davenport, '66 | 95,796 | 74,549 |
| 46755 | Kendallville | 6,765 | 6,119 | 52742 | De Witt, '66 | 3,680 | 2,644 |
| 46534 | Knox | 3,458 | 3,034 | 52101 | Decorah, '66 | 7,054 | 6,060 |
| 46901 | Kokomo | 47,197 | 38,672 | 51442 | Denison, '66 | 6,780 | 4,554 |
| *47904 | Lafayette, '66 | 45,214 | 35,568 | *50318 | Des Moines, '66 | 206,739 | 177,965 |
| 46350 | La Porte, '66 | 21,917 | 20,414 | 52001 | Dubuque, '66 | 62,853 | 49,671 |
| 46226 | Lawrence | 10,103 | 1,951 | 52040 | Dyersville, '66 | 3,270 | 2,416 |
| 47025 | Lawrenceburg | 5,004 | 4,806 | 50533 | Eagle Grove | 4,381 | 4,176 |
| 46052 | Lebanon | 9,523 | 7,631 | 50627 | Eldora | 3,225 | 3,107 |
| 46767 | Ligonier | 2,595 | 2,375 | 50536 | Emmetsburg, '66 | 3,824 | 3,760 |
| 47441 | Linton | 5,736 | 5,973 | 51334 | Estherville, '66 | 8,092 | 6,719 |
| 46947 | Logansport | 21,106 | 21,031 | 50707 | Evansdale | 5,738 | 3,571 |
| 46542 | Loogootee | 2,858 | 2,424 | 52556 | Fairfield, '66 | 11,587 | 7,299 |
| 46356 | Lowell, '65 | 3,063 | 1,448 | 50436 | Forest City, '66 | 3,329 | 2,766 |
| 47250 | Madison (A), '67 | 11,857 | 7,506 | 50501 | Fort Dodge, '66 | 29,654 | 25,115 |
| 46952 | Marion | 37,854 | 30,081 | 52627 | Fort Madison | 15,247 | 14,954 |
| 46151 | Martinsville (A) | 8,476 | 5,991 | 51534 | Glenwood | 4,753 | 4,664 |
| 46360 | Michigan City | 36,653 | 28,395 | 50112 | Grinnell (A), '67 | 8,199 | 6,828 |
| 46544 | Mishawaka | 33,361 | 32,913 | 50441 | Hampton | 4,501 | 4,432 |
| 47446 | Mitchell | 3,552 | 3,245 | 51537 | Harlan, '66 | 4,775 | 3,915 |
| 47960 | Monticello | 4,035 | 3,467 | 51023 | Hawarden | 2,544 | 2,625 |
| 46158 | Mooresville | 3,856 | 2,264 | 50548 | Humboldt, '66 | 4,497 | 3,219 |
| 47620 | Mount Vernon, '67 | 6,201 | 6,150 | 50644 | Independence | 5,498 | 4,865 |
| *47302 | Muncie | 68,603 | 58,479 | 50125 | Indianola, '66 | 8,281 | 5,145 |
| 46321 | Munster, '67 | 14,612 | 4,753 | 52240 | Iowa City, '66 | 40,467 | 27,212 |
| 46550 | Nappanee | 3,895 | 3,393 | 50126 | Iowa Falls | 6,322 | 4,900 |
| 47150 | New Albany, '64 | 38,218 | 29,346 | 50129 | Jefferson | 4,570 | 4,326 |
| 47362 | New Castle | 20,349 | 18,271 | 52632 | Keokuk | 16,316 | 16,144 |
| 46774 | New Haven (A), '67 | 5,060 | 2,336 | 50138 | Knoxville, '66 | 8,521 | 7,625 |
| 46184 | New Whiteland | 3,488 | ...... | 51031 | Le Mars, '65 | 7,847 | 5,844 |
| 46060 | Noblesville | 7,664 | 6,567 | 52057 | Manchester, '66 | 4,611 | 3,987 |
| 46962 | North Manchester(A),'67 | 5,612 | 3,977 | 52060 | Maquoketa | 5,909 | 4,307 |
| 47265 | North Vernon | 4,307 | 3,488 | 52302 | Marion, '65 | 15,267 | 5,916 |
| 47560 | Oakland City | 3,016 | 3,539 | 50158 | Marshalltown | 22,521 | 19,821 |
| 47454 | Paoli | 2,754 | 2,575 | 50401 | Mason City, '66 | 30,711 | 27,980 |
| 46970 | Peru | 14,453 | 13,308 | 51555 | Missouri Valley | 3,567 | 3,546 |
| 47567 | Petersburg, '67 | 2,741 | 3,035 | 52310 | Monticello | 3,190 | 2,888 |
| 46168 | Plainfield | 5,460 | 2,585 | 52641 | Mount Pleasant | 7,339 | 5,843 |

| ZIP Code | Place | 1960 | 1950 | ZIP Code | Place | 1960 | 1950 |
|---|---|---|---|---|---|---|---|
| | **IOWA—Continued** | | | | **KANSAS—Continued** | | |
| 52314 | Mt. Vernon (A), '67.... | 3,030 | 2,320 | 67654 | Norton................. | 3,345 | 3,060 |
| 52761 | Muscatine, '66........ | 22,194 | 19,041 | 66061 | Olathe................. | 10,987 | 5,593 |
| 50201 | Nevada, '66.......... | 4,840 | 3,763 | 66064 | Osawatomie............ | 4,622 | 4,347 |
| 50659 | New Hampton, '66..... | 3,593 | 3,323 | 66067 | Ottawa................ | 10,673 | 10,081 |
| 50208 | Newton............... | 15,381 | 11,723 | 66204 | Overland Park......... | 21,110 | .... |
| 50662 | Oelwein.............. | 8,282 | 7,858 | 66071 | Paola................. | 4,784 | 3,972 |
| 51040 | Onawa................ | 3,176 | 3,498 | 67219 | Park City............. | 2,687 | .... |
| 51041 | Orange City, '67...... | 3,463 | 2,166 | 67357 | Parsons............... | 13,929 | 14,750 |
| 50461 | Osage................ | 3,753 | 3,436 | 67661 | Phillipsburg.......... | 3,233 | 2,589 |
| 50213 | Osceola.............. | 3,350 | 3,422 | 66762 | Pittsburg............. | 18,678 | 19,341 |
| 52577 | Oskaloosa, '66........ | 11,536 | 11,124 | 67663 | Plainville............ | 3,104 | 2,082 |
| 52501 | Ottumwa.............. | 33,871 | 33,634 | 66208 | Prairie Village....... | 25,356 | .... |
| 50219 | Pella, '66............ | 6,087 | 4,427 | 67124 | Pratt................. | 8,156 | 7,523 |
| 50220 | Perry................ | 6,442 | 6,174 | 66200 | Roeland Park.......... | 8,949 | .... |
| 51566 | Red Oak.............. | 6,421 | 6,526 | 67665 | Russell............... | 6,113 | 6,483 |
| 51246 | Rock Rapids, '66...... | 2,780 | 2,640 | 67401 | Salina................ | 43,202 | 26,176 |
| 50583 | Sac City............. | 3,354 | 3,170 | 67871 | Scott City............ | 3,555 | 3,204 |
| 51201 | Sheldon.............. | 4,251 | 4,001 | *66203 | Shawnee............... | 9,072 | 845 |
| 51601 | Shenandoah........... | 6,567 | 6,938 | *66601 | Topeka................ | 119,484 | 78,791 |
| 51249 | Sibley............... | 2,852 | 2,559 | 67880 | Ulysses............... | 3,157 | 2,243 |
| *51101 | Sioux City........... | 89,159 | 83,991 | 67147 | Valley Center......... | 2,570 | 854 |
| 51250 | Sioux Center, '66..... | 3,034 | 1,860 | 67672 | Wa Keeney............. | 2,808 | 2,446 |
| 51301 | Spencer (A), '67...... | 9,677 | 7,446 | 67152 | Wellington............ | 8,809 | 7,747 |
| 51360 | Spirit Lake, '67...... | 3,017 | 2,467 | *67202 | Wichita............... | 254,698 | 168,279 |
| 50588 | Storm Lake........... | 7,728 | 6,951 | 67156 | Winfield.............. | 11,117 | 10,264 |
| 52339 | Tama................. | 2,925 | 2,930 | | | | |
| 52772 | Tipton............... | 2,862 | 2,633 | | **KENTUCKY** | | |
| 50322 | Urbandale, '65........ | 10,310 | 1,777 | 41101 | Ashland............... | 31,283 | 31,131 |
| 52349 | Vinton, '66.......... | 4,899 | 4,307 | 40906 | Barbourville.......... | 3,211 | 2,926 |
| 52353 | Washington........... | 6,037 | 5,902 | 40004 | Bardstown............. | 4,798 | 4,154 |
| *50701 | Waterloo, '66........ | 74,023 | 65,198 | 41073 | Bellevue.............. | 9,336 | 9,040 |
| 52172 | Waukon............... | 3,639 | 3,158 | 42025 | Benton................ | 3,074 | 1,980 |
| 50677 | Waverly, '65......... | 6,822 | 5,124 | 40403 | Berea................. | 4,302 | 3,372 |
| 50595 | Webster City, '66..... | 8,671 | 7,611 | 42101 | Bowling Green......... | 28,338 | 18,347 |
| 52655 | West Burlington, '66... | 3,015 | 1,614 | 42718 | Campbellsville........ | 6,966 | 3,477 |
| 50265 | West Des Moines, '66... | 13,720 | 5,615 | 41008 | Carrollton............ | 3,218 | 3,226 |
| 52175 | West Union........... | 2,551 | 2,141 | 41129 | Catlettsburg.......... | 3,874 | 4,750 |
| 50311 | Windsor Heights, '65... | 6,409 | 1,414 | 42330 | Central City.......... | 3,694 | 4,110 |
| 50273 | Winterset............ | 3,639 | 3,570 | 40701 | Corbin................ | 7,119 | 7,744 |
| | | | | *41011 | Covington............. | 60,376 | 64,452 |
| | **KANSAS** | | | 40823 | Cumberland............ | 4,271 | 4,249 |
| 67410 | Abilene.............. | 6,746 | 5,775 | 41031 | Cynthiana............. | 5,641 | 4,847 |
| 67003 | Anthony.............. | 2,744 | 2,792 | 40422 | Danville.............. | 9,010 | 8,686 |
| 67005 | Arkansas City........ | 14,262 | 12,903 | 42408 | Dawson Springs........ | 3,002 | 2,374 |
| 66002 | Atchison............. | 12,529 | 12,792 | 41074 | Dayton................ | 9,050 | 8,977 |
| 67010 | Augusta.............. | 6,434 | 4,483 | 42410 | Earlington............ | 2,786 | 2,753 |
| 66713 | Baxter Springs....... | 4,498 | 4,647 | 42501 | East Somerset......... | 3,645 | .... |
| 66935 | Belleville........... | 2,940 | 2,858 | 42701 | Elizabethtown......... | 9,641 | 5,807 |
| 67420 | Beloit............... | 3,837 | 4,085 | 41018 | Elsmere............... | 4,607 | 3,483 |
| 66012 | Bonner Springs....... | 3,171 | 2,277 | 41018 | Erlanger.............. | 7,072 | 3,694 |
| 67333 | Caney................ | 2,682 | 2,876 | 41040 | Falmouth.............. | 2,568 | 2,186 |
| 66720 | Chanute.............. | 10,849 | 10,109 | 41139 | Flatwoods............. | 3,741 | .... |
| 67335 | Cherryvale........... | 2,783 | 2,952 | 41042 | Florence.............. | 5,837 | 1,325 |
| 67432 | Clay Center.......... | 4,613 | 4,528 | 41075 | Fort Thomas........... | 14,896 | 10,870 |
| 67337 | Coffeyville.......... | 17,382 | 17,113 | 40601 | Frankfort............. | 18,365 | 11,916 |
| 67701 | Colby................ | 4,210 | 3,859 | 42134 | Franklin.............. | 5,319 | 4,343 |
| 66725 | Columbus............. | 3,395 | 3,490 | 42041 | Fulton................ | 3,265 | 3,224 |
| 66901 | Concordia............ | 7,022 | 7,175 | 40324 | Georgetown............ | 6,986 | 5,516 |
| 66846 | Council Grove........ | 2,664 | 2,722 | 42141 | Glasgow............... | 10,069 | 7,025 |
| 67037 | Derby................ | 6,458 | 432 | 42345 | Greenville............ | 3,198 | 2,661 |
| 67801 | Dodge City........... | 13,520 | 11,262 | 40831 | Harlan................ | 4,177 | 4,786 |
| 67042 | El Dorado............ | 12,523 | 11,037 | 40330 | Harrodsburg........... | 6,061 | 5,262 |
| 67526 | Ellinwood............ | 2,729 | 2,569 | 41701 | Hazard................ | 5,958 | 6,985 |
| 66801 | Emporia.............. | 18,190 | 15,669 | 42420 | Henderson............. | 16,892 | 16,837 |
| 67045 | Eureka............... | 4,055 | 3,958 | 41076 | Highland Heights...... | 3,491 | 1,569 |
| 66205 | Fairway.............. | 5,398 | 1,816 | 42240 | Hopkinsville.......... | 19,465 | 12,526 |
| 66701 | Fort Scott........... | 9,410 | 10,335 | 40336 | Irvine................ | 2,955 | 3,259 |
| 66736 | Fredonia............. | 3,233 | 3,257 | 40029 | Jeffersontown, '64.... | 5,055 | 1,246 |
| 66739 | Galena............... | 3,827 | 4,029 | 41537 | Jenkins............... | 3,202 | 6,921 |
| 67846 | Garden City.......... | 11,811 | 10,905 | 40444 | Lancaster............. | 3,021 | 2,402 |
| 66032 | Garnett.............. | 3,034 | 2,693 | 40342 | Lawrenceburg.......... | 2,523 | 2,369 |
| 67735 | Goodland............. | 4,459 | 4,690 | 40033 | Lebanon............... | 4,813 | 4,640 |
| 67530 | Great Bend........... | 16,670 | 12,665 | 42754 | Leitchfield........... | 2,982 | 1,512 |
| 67601 | Hays................. | 11,947 | 8,625 | *40607 | Lexington............. | 62,810 | 55,534 |
| 67060 | Haysville............ | 5,836 | .... | 40741 | London................ | 4,035 | 3,426 |
| 67449 | Herington............ | 3,702 | 3,775 | *40201 | Louisville, '64....... | 389,044 | 369,129 |
| 66434 | Hiawatha............. | 3,391 | 3,294 | 41016 | Ludlow................ | 6,233 | 6,374 |
| 67544 | Hoisington........... | 4,248 | 4,012 | 40855 | Lynch................. | 3,810 | .... |
| 66436 | Holton............... | 3,028 | 2,705 | 42431 | Madisonville.......... | 13,110 | 11,132 |
| 67951 | Hugoton.............. | 2,912 | 2,781 | 42066 | Mayfield.............. | 10,762 | 8,990 |
| 67501 | Hutchinson........... | 37,574 | 33,575 | 41056 | Maysville............. | 8,484 | 8,632 |
| 67301 | Independence......... | 11,222 | 11,335 | 40965 | Middlesborough........ | 12,607 | 14,482 |
| 66749 | Iola................. | 6,885 | 7,094 | 40243 | Middletown............ | 2,764 | .... |
| 66441 | Junction City........ | 18,700 | 13,462 | 42633 | Monticello............ | 2,940 | 2,934 |
| *66110 | Kansas City.......... | 121,901 | 129,553 | 40351 | Morehead.............. | 4,170 | 3,102 |
| 67068 | Kingman.............. | 3,582 | 3,200 | 42437 | Morganfield........... | 3,741 | 3,257 |
| 67550 | Larned............... | 5,001 | 4,447 | 40353 | Mount Sterling........ | 5,370 | 5,294 |
| 66044 | Lawrence............. | 32,858 | 23,351 | 42071 | Murray................ | 9,303 | 6,035 |
| 66048 | Leavenworth.......... | 22,052 | 20,579 | *41071 | Newport............... | 30,070 | 31,044 |
| 66206 | Leawood.............. | 7,466 | 1,167 | 40356 | Nicholasville......... | 4,275 | 3,406 |
| 67901 | Liberal.............. | 13,813 | 7,134 | 42301 | Owensboro............. | 42,471 | 33,651 |
| 67456 | Lindsborg............ | 2,609 | 2,383 | 42001 | Paducah............... | 34,479 | 32,828 |
| 67554 | Lyons................ | 4,592 | 4,545 | 41240 | Paintsville........... | 4,025 | 4,309 |
| 67460 | McPherson............ | 9,996 | 8,689 | 40361 | Paris................. | 7,791 | 6,912 |
| 66502 | Manhattan............ | 22,993 | 19,056 | 41011 | Park Hills............ | 4,076 | 2,577 |
| 66505 | Marysville........... | 4,143 | 3,866 | 41501 | Pikeville............. | 4,754 | 5,154 |
| 67104 | Medicine Lodge....... | 3,072 | 2,288 | 40977 | Pineville............. | 3,181 | 3,890 |
| 66203 | Merriam.............. | 5,084 | .... | 40258 | Pleasure Ridge Park... | 10,612 | .... |
| 66222 | Mission.............. | 4,626 | .... | 41653 | Prestonsburg.......... | 3,133 | 3,585 |
| 66208 | Mission Hills........ | 3,621 | 1,275 | 42445 | Princeton............. | 5,618 | 5,388 |
| 67110 | Mulvane.............. | 2,981 | 1,387 | 42450 | Providence............ | 3,771 | 3,905 |
| 66757 | Neodesha............. | 3,594 | 3,723 | 40160 | Radcliff.............. | 3,384 | .... |
| 67114 | Newton............... | 14,877 | 11,590 | 40475 | Richmond.............. | 12,168 | 10,268 |

## KENTUCKY—Continued

| ZIP Code | Place | 1960 | 1950 |
|---|---|---|---|
| 42276 | Russellville | 5,861 | 4,529 |
| 40207 | St. Matthews, '64 | 10,796 | ...... |
| 42164 | Scottsville | 3,324 | 2,060 |
| 40065 | Shelbyville | 4,525 | 4,403 |
| 40216 | Shively, '64 | 18,180 | 2,401 |
| 42501 | Somerset | 7,112 | 7,097 |
| 41017 | South Fort Mitchell | 4,086 | 3,142 |
| 40172 | Valley Station | 10,555 | ...... |
| 40383 | Versailles | 4,060 | 2,760 |
| 40769 | Williamsburg | 3,478 | 3,348 |
| 40390 | Wilmore | 2,773 | 2,337 |
| 40391 | Winchester | 10,187 | 9,226 |

## LOUISIANA

| ZIP Code | Place | 1960 | 1950 |
|---|---|---|---|
| 70510 | Abbeville | 10,414 | 9,338 |
| 71301 | Alexandria | 40,279 | 34,913 |
| 71301 | Alexandria SW | 2,782 | ...... |
| 70422 | Amite City | 3,316 | 2,804 |
| 70788 | Anandale | 2,827 | ...... |
| 70001 | Arcadia | 2,547 | 2,241 |
| 70714 | Baker | 4,823 | 762 |
| 71220 | Bastrop | 15,193 | 12,769 |
| *70821 | Baton Rouge | 152,419 | 125,629 |
| 70360 | Bayou Cane | 3,173 | 2,212 |
| 70342 | Berwick | 2,880 | 2,619 |
| 70427 | Bogalusa | 21,423 | 17,798 |
| 71019 | Bossier City | 32,776 | 15,470 |
| 70517 | Breaux Bridge | 3,303 | 2,492 |
| 71322 | Bunkie | 5,188 | 4,666 |
| 70041 | Buras-Triumph | 4,908 | 1,799 |
| 70525 | Church Point | 3,606 | 2,897 |
| 70433 | Covington | 6,754 | 5,113 |
| 70526 | Crowley | 15,617 | 12,784 |
| 70360 | Daigleville | 5,906 | 4,809 |
| 71232 | Delhi | 2,514 | 1,861 |
| 70726 | Denham Springs | 5,991 | 2,053 |
| 70633 | De Quincy | 3,928 | 3,837 |
| 70634 | De Ridder | 7,188 | 5,799 |
| 70346 | Donaldsonville | 6,082 | 4,150 |
| 70535 | Eunice | 11,326 | 8,184 |
| 71241 | Farmerville | 2,727 | 2,173 |
| 71334 | Ferriday | 4,563 | 3,847 |
| 70538 | Franklin | 8,673 | 6,144 |
| 70438 | Franklinton | 3,141 | 2,342 |
| 70357 | Golden Meadow | 3,097 | ...... |
| 70737 | Gonzales | 3,252 | 1,642 |
| 70601 | Goosport | 16,778 | 8,318 |
| 71245 | Grambling | 3,144 | ...... |
| 70053 | Gretna | 21,967 | 13,813 |
| 70401 | Hammond | 10,563 | 8,010 |
| 70123 | Harahan | 9,275 | 3,394 |
| *71038 | Haynesville | 3,031 | 3,040 |
| 70360 | Houma (A) | 29,772 | 11,505 |
| 70360 | Houma | 29,772 | 11,505 |
| 70544 | Jeanerette | 5,568 | 4,692 |
| 70121 | Jefferson Heights | 19,353 | ...... |
| 70546 | Jennings | 11,887 | 9,663 |
| 71251 | Jonesboro | 3,848 | 3,097 |
| 70548 | Kaplan | 5,267 | 4,562 |
| 70062 | Kenner | 17,037 | 5,535 |
| 70444 | Kentwood | 2,607 | 2,417 |
| 70501 | Lafayette, '63 | 50,312 | 33,541 |
| 70501 | Lafayette SW | 6,682 | ...... |
| 70601 | Lake Arthur | 3,541 | 2,849 |
| 70601 | Lake Charles | 63,392 | 41,272 |
| 71254 | Lake Providence | 5,781 | 4,123 |
| 70065 | Laplace | 3,541 | 2,352 |
| 70373 | Larose | 2,796 | 1,286 |
| 71446 | Leesville | 4,689 | 4,670 |
| 70071 | Lutcher | 3,274 | 2,198 |
| 70554 | Mamou | 2,928 | 2,254 |
| 71052 | Mansfield | 5,839 | 4,440 |
| 71449 | Many | 3,164 | 1,681 |
| 71351 | Marksville | 4,257 | 3,635 |
| 71055 | Minden | 12,785 | 9,787 |
| 71201 | Monroe | 52,219 | 38,572 |
| 70380 | Morgan City | 13,540 | 9,759 |
| 71457 | Natchitoches | 13,924 | 9,914 |
| 70560 | New Iberia | 29,062 | 16,467 |
| *70113 | New Orleans | 627,525 | 570,445 |
| 70760 | New Roads | 3,965 | 2,818 |
| 70079 | Norco | 4,682 | ...... |
| 71101 | North Shreveport | 7,701 | ...... |
| 71463 | Oakdale | 6,618 | 5,598 |
| 70570 | Opelousas | 17,417 | 11,659 |
| 70392 | Patterson | 2,923 | 1,938 |
| 71360 | Pineville | 8,636 | 6,423 |
| 70764 | Plaquemine | 7,689 | 5,747 |
| 70454 | Ponchatoula | 4,727 | 4,090 |
| 70767 | Port Allen | 5,026 | 3,097 |
| 70083 | Port Sulphur | 2,868 | ...... |
| 70394 | Raceland | 3,666 | 2,025 |
| 70578 | Rayne | 8,634 | 6,485 |
| 71269 | Rayville | 4,052 | 3,138 |
| 70084 | Reserve | 5,297 | 4,465 |
| 71270 | Ruston | 13,991 | 10,372 |
| 70582 | St. Martinville | 6,468 | 4,614 |
| 71301 | Samtown | 4,008 | ...... |
| *71102 | Shreveport, '66 | 160,535 | 127,206 |
| 70458 | Slidell | 6,356 | 3,464 |
| 71075 | Springhill | 6,437 | 3,383 |
| 70663 | Sulphur | 11,429 | 5,996 |
| 71282 | Tallulah | 9,413 | 7,758 |

## LOUISIANA—Continued

| ZIP Code | Place | 1960 | 1950 |
|---|---|---|---|
| 70301 | Thibodaux | 13,403 | 7,730 |
| 71373 | Viadalia | 4,313 | 1,641 |
| 70586 | Ville Platte | 7,512 | 6,633 |
| 70668 | Vinton | 2,987 | 2,597 |
| 71082 | Vivian | 2,624 | 2,426 |
| 70591 | Welsh | 3,332 | 2,416 |
| 70669 | Westlake | 3,311 | 1,871 |
| 71291 | West Monroe | 15,215 | 10,302 |
| 70094 | Westwego | 9,815 | 8,328 |
| 71483 | Winnfield | 7,022 | 5,629 |
| 71295 | Winnsboro | 4,437 | 3,655 |
| 70791 | Zachary | 3,268 | 1,542 |

## MAINE

*See Note on Page 605*

| ZIP Code | Place | 1960 | 1950 |
|---|---|---|---|
| 04210 | Auburn | 24,449 | 23,134 |
| 04330 | Augusta | 21,680 | 20,913 |
| 04401 | Bangor | 38,912 | 31,558 |
| 04609 | Bar Harbor | 3,807 | 3,864 |
| 04530 | Bath | 10,717 | 10,644 |
| 04915 | Belfast | 6,140 | 5,960 |
| 03901 | *Berwick* | 2,738 | 2,166 |
| 04005 | Biddeford | 19,255 | 20,836 |
| 04412 | Brewer | 9,009 | 6,862 |
| 04009 | *Bridgton* | 2,707 | 2,950 |
| 04011 | Brunswick | 9,444 | 7,342 |
|  | *Brunswick (town)* | 15,797 | 10,996 |
| 04416 | *Bucksport* | 3,466 | 3,120 |
| 04619 | Calais | 4,223 | 4,589 |
| 04843 | Camden | 3,523 | 3,270 |
|  | *Camden (town)* | 3,988 | 3,676 |
| 04107 | *Cape Elizabeth* | 5,505 | 3,816 |
| 04736 | Caribou | 8,305 | 4,500 |
|  | *Caribou (town)* | 12,464 | 9,923 |
| 04021 | *Cumberland* | 2,765 | 2,030 |
| 04930 | Dexter | 2,720 | 2,809 |
|  | *Dexter (town)* | 3,951 | 4,126 |
| 04426 | *Dover-Foxcroft* | 4,173 | 4,218 |
| 04631 | Eastport | 2,537 | 3,123 |
| 03903 | *Eliot* | 3,133 | 2,509 |
| 04605 | Ellsworth | 4,444 | 3,936 |
| 04937 | Fairfield | 3,766 | 3,776 |
|  | *Fairfield (town)* | 5,829 | 5,811 |
| 04105 | *Falmouth* | 5,976 | 4,342 |
| 04938 | Farmington | 2,749 | ...... |
|  | *Farmington (town)* | 5,001 | 4,677 |
| 04742 | Fort Fairfield | 3,082 | 2,521 |
|  | *Fort Fairfield (town)* | 5,876 | 5,791 |
| 04743 | Fort Kent | 2,787 | 3,001 |
|  | *Fort Kent (town)* | 4,761 | 5,343 |
| 04032 | *Freeport* | 4,055 | 5,280 |
| 04345 | Gardiner | 6,897 | 6,649 |
| 04038 | *Gorham* | 5,767 | 4,742 |
| 04347 | Hallowell | 3,169 | 3,404 |
| 04444 | *Hampden* | 4,583 | 3,608 |
| 04730 | Houlton | 5,976 | 6,029 |
|  | *Houlton (town)* | 8,289 | 8,377 |
| 04239 | *Jay* | 3,247 | 3,102 |
| 04043 | Kennebunk | 2,804 | ...... |
|  | *Kennebunk (town)* | 4,551 | 4,273 |
| 03904 | Kittery | 8,051 | 6,692 |
|  | *Kittery (town)* | 10,689 | 8,380 |
| 04240 | Lewiston | 40,804 | 40,974 |
| 04750 | *Limestone* | 13,102 | 2,427 |
| 04457 | Lincoln | 3,616 | 2,548 |
|  | *Lincoln (town)* | 4,541 | 4,030 |
| 04252 | Lisbon Falls | 2,640 | 2,155 |
| 04254 | *Lisbon* | 5,042 | 4,318 |
|  | Livermore Falls | 2,882 | 3,015 |
|  | *Livermore Falls (town)* | 3,343 | 3,359 |
| 04652 | *Lubec* | 2,684 | 2,973 |
| 04654 | Machias | 2,614 | 2,063 |
| 04756 | Madawaska | 4,035 | 2,975 |
|  | *Madawaska (town)* | 5,507 | 4,900 |
| 04950 | Madison | 2,761 | 2,554 |
|  | *Madison (town)* | 3,935 | 3,639 |
| 04257 | Mexico | 3,951 | 3,821 |
|  | *Mexico (town)* | 5,043 | 4,762 |
| 04462 | Millinocket | 7,318 | 5,755 |
|  | *Millinocket (town)* | 7,453 | 5,890 |
| 04463 | *Milo* | 2,756 | 2,898 |
| 04260 | *New Gloucester* | 3,047 | 2,628 |
| 04268 | Norway | 2,654 | 2,687 |
|  | *Norway (town)* | 3,733 | 3,811 |
| 04963 | *Oakland* | 3,075 | 2,679 |
| 04064 | Old Orchard Beach | 4,431 | 4,593 |
|  | *Old Orchard Beach (town)* | 4,580 | 4,707 |
| 04468 | Old Town | 8,626 | 8,261 |
| 04473 | Orono | 3,234 | 3,634 |
|  | *Orono (town)* | 8,341 | 7,504 |
| 04474 | *Orrington* | 2,539 | 1,895 |
| 04271 | *Paris* | 3,601 | 4,358 |
| 04967 | Pittsfield | 3,232 | 3,012 |
|  | *Pittsfield (town)* | 4,010 | 3,909 |
| *04101 | Portland | 72,566 | 77,634 |
| 04769 | Presque Isle | 12,886 | 9,954 |
| 04841 | Rockland | 8,769 | 9,234 |
| 04276 | Rumford | 7,233 | 7,888 |
|  | *Rumford (town)* | 10,005 | 9,954 |
| 04072 | Saco | 10,515 | 10,324 |
| 04073 | Sanford | 10,936 | 11,094 |
|  | *Sanford (town)* | 14,962 | 15,177 |
| 04074 | Scarborough | 6,418 | 4,600 |

## MAINE—Continued

| ZIP Code | Place | 1960 | 1950 |
|---|---|---|---|
| 04976 | Skowhegan | 6,667 | 6,183 |
| | *Skowhegan (town)* | 7,661 | 7,422 |
| 03908 | *South Berwick* | 3,112 | 2,646 |
| 04106 | South Portland | 22,788 | 21,866 |
| 04861 | Thomaston | 2,780 | 2,810 |
| 04086 | Topsham | 3,818 | 2,626 |
| 04785 | Van Buren | 3,589 | 3,732 |
| | *Van Buren (town)* | 4,679 | 5,094 |
| 04572 | *Waldoboro* | 2,882 | 2,536 |
| 04901 | Waterville | 18,695 | 18,287 |
| 04473 | Webster | 4,747 | .... |
| 04090 | *Wells* | 3,528 | 2,321 |
| 04092 | Westbrook | 13,820 | 12,284 |
| 04294 | *Wilton* | 3,274 | 3,455 |
| | Windham | 4,498 | 3,434 |
| 04901 | Winslow | 3,640 | 2,916 |
| | *Winslow (town)* | 5,891 | 4,413 |
| 04364 | *Winthrop* | 3,537 | 3,026 |
| 04096 | Yarmouth | 2,913 | 2,189 |
| | *Yarmouth (town)* | 3,517 | 2,669 |
| 03909 | *York* | 4,663 | 3,256 |

## MARYLAND

| ZIP Code | Place | 1960 | 1950 |
|---|---|---|---|
| 21001 | Aberdeen | 9,679 | 2,944 |
| *21401 | Annapolis | 23,385 | 10,047 |
| 21227 | Arbutus-Halethorpe-Relay | 22,402 | .... |
| *21233 | Baltimore | 939,024 | 949,708 |
| 21014 | Bethesda | 56,527 | .... |
| 20710 | Bladensburg | 3,103 | 2,899 |
| 20722 | Brentwood | 3,693 | 3,523 |
| 21716 | Brunswick | 3,555 | 3,752 |
| 21613 | Cambridge | 12,239 | 10,351 |
| 20027 | Capitol Heights | 3,138 | 2,729 |
| 21025 | Carrollton | 3,385 | .... |
| 21228 | Catonsville | 37,372 | .... |
| 21620 | Chestertown | 3,602 | 3,143 |
| 20785 | Cheverly | 5,223 | 3,318 |
| 21030 | Cockeysville | 2,582 | .... |
| 20740 | College Park, '66 | 25,444 | 11,170 |
| 21817 | Crisfield | 3,540 | 3,688 |
| 21501 | Cumberland | 33,415 | 37,679 |
| 20028 | District Heights | 7,524 | 1,735 |
| 21222 | Dundalk | 82,428 | .... |
| 21601 | Easton | 6,337 | 4,836 |
| 21921 | Elkton | 5,089 | 5,245 |
| 21221 | Essex | 35,205 | .... |
| 20021 | Forest Heights | 3,524 | 1,125 |
| 21701 | Frederick | 21,744 | 18,142 |
| 21532 | Frostburg | 6,722 | 6,876 |
| 20760 | Gaithersburg | 3,847 | 1,755 |
| 21136 | Glyndon Reisterstown | 4,216 | .... |
| 20770 | Greenbelt | 7,479 | 7,074 |
| 21740 | Hagerstown | 36,660 | 36,260 |
| 21740 | Halfway | 4,256 | 2,153 |
| 21078 | Havre de Grace | 8,510 | 7,809 |
| 20031 | Hillcrest Heights | 15,205 | .... |
| *20781 | Hyattsville | 15,168 | 12,308 |
| 20787 | Langley Park | 11,510 | .... |
| 21227 | Lansdowne-Baltimore-Highlands | 13,134 | .... |
| 20810 | Laurel | 8,503 | 4,482 |
| 21502 | LaVale-Narrows Park | 4,031 | .... |
| 20653 | Lexington Park | 7,039 | .... |
| 21204 | Loch Raven | 23,278 | .... |
| 21220 | Middle River | 10,825 | .... |
| 20822 | Mount Rainier | 9,855 | 10,989 |
| 21206 | Overlea | 10,795 | .... |
| 21117 | Owings Mills | 3,810 | .... |
| 21234 | Parkville-Carney | 27,236 | .... |
| 21208 | Pikesville | 18,737 | .... |
| 21851 | Pocomoke City | 3,329 | 3,191 |
| 20840 | Riverdale | 4,389 | 5,530 |
| 21123 | Riviera Beach | 4,902 | 1,849 |
| *20850 | Rockville | 26,090 | 6,934 |
| 21801 | Salisbury | 16,302 | 15,141 |
| 20027 | Seat Pleasant | 5,365 | 2,255 |
| 21146 | Severna Park-Round Bay | 3,728 | 1,059 |
| *20907 | Silver Spring | 66,348 | .... |
| 21219 | Sparrows Point-Fort Howard-Edgemere | 11,775 | .... |
| 21207 | Stoneleigh-Rodgers Forge | 15,645 | .... |
| 20023 | Suitland-Silver Hills | 10,300 | .... |
| 20012 | Takoma Park | 16,799 | 13,341 |
| 21093 | Timonium-Lutherville | 12,265 | .... |
| 21204 | Towson | 19,090 | .... |
| 20752 | University Park | 3,098 | 2,205 |
| 21562 | Westernport | 3,559 | 3,431 |
| 21157 | Westminster | 6,123 | 6,140 |
| 20902 | Wheaton | 54,635 | .... |
| 21207 | Woodlawn-Rockdale-Milford Mills | 19,254 | .... |

## MASSACHUSETTS
See Note on Page 605

| ZIP Code | Place | 1960 | 1950 |
|---|---|---|---|
| 02351 | *Abington* | 10,607 | 7,152 |
| 01720 | *Acton* | 7,238 | 3,510 |
| 02743 | *Achusnet* | 5,755 | 4,401 |
| 01220 | *Adams (town)* | 12,391 | 12,034 |
| 01220 | Adams | 11,949 | .... |
| 01001 | *Agawam* | 15,718 | 10,166 |
| 01913 | Amesbury | 9,625 | 9,711 |

## MASSACHUSETTS—Continued

| ZIP Code | Place | 1960 | 1950 |
|---|---|---|---|
| | *Amesbury (town)* | 10,787 | 10,851 |
| 01002 | Amherst | 10,306 | 7,900 |
| | *Amherst (town)* | 13,718 | 10,856 |
| 01810 | *Andover* | 17,134 | 12,437 |
| 02174 | Arlington | 49,953 | 44,353 |
| 01430 | *Ashburnham* | 2,758 | 2,603 |
| 01721 | *Ashland* | 7,779 | 3,500 |
| 01331 | Athol | 10,161 | 9,708 |
| | *Athol (town)* | 11,637 | 11,554 |
| 02703 | Attleboro | 27,118 | 23,809 |
| 01501 | *Auburn* | 14,047 | 8,840 |
| 02322 | *Avon* | 4,301 | 2,666 |
| 01432 | Ayer | 3,323 | 3,107 |
| | *Ayer (town)* | 14,927 | 5,740 |
| 02630 | *Barnstable* | 13,465 | 10,480 |
| 01005 | *Barre* | 3,479 | 3,406 |
| 01730 | *Bedford* | 10,969 | 5,234 |
| 01007 | *Belchertown* | 5,186 | 4,487 |
| 02019 | *Bellingham* | 6,774 | 4,100 |
| 02175 | *Belmont* | 28,715 | 27,381 |
| 01915 | Beverly | 36,108 | 28,884 |
| 01821 | *Billerica* | 17,867 | 11,101 |
| 01504 | *Blackstone* | 5,130 | 4,968 |
| *02109 | Boston | 697,197 | 801,444 |
| 02532 | *Bourne* | 14,011 | 4,720 |
| 02184 | *Braintree* | 31,069 | 23,161 |
| 02324 | *Bridgewater* | 4,296 | 3,445 |
| | *Bridgewater (town)* | 10,276 | 9,512 |
| *02401 | *Brockton* | 72,813 | 62,860 |
| 02146 | *Brookline* | 54,044 | 57,589 |
| 02103 | *Burlington* | 12,852 | 3,250 |
| *02138 | *Cambridge* | 107,716 | 120,740 |
| 02021 | *Canton* | 12,771 | 7,465 |
| 01507 | *Charlton* | 3,685 | 3,136 |
| 02633 | *Chatham* | 3,273 | 2,457 |
| 01824 | *Chelmsford* | 15,130 | 9,407 |
| 02150 | *Chelsea* | 33,749 | 38,912 |
| 01013 | *Chicopee* | 61,553 | 49,211 |
| 01510 | *Clinton* | 12,848 | 12,287 |
| 02025 | *Cohasset* | 2,745 | 2,009 |
| | *Cohasset (town)* | 5,840 | 3,731 |
| 01742 | *Concord* | 3,188 | 2,299 |
| | *Concord (town)* | 12,517 | 8,623 |
| 01226 | *Dalton* | 6,436 | 4,772 |
| 01923 | *Danvers* | 21,926 | 15,720 |
| 02714 | *Dartmouth* | 14,607 | 11,115 |
| 02026 | *Dedham* | 23,869 | 18,487 |
| 01342 | *Deerfield* | 3,338 | 3,086 |
| 02638 | *Dennis* | 3,727 | 2,499 |
| 02715 | *Dighton* | 3,769 | 2,950 |
| 02030 | *Dover* | 2,846 | 1,722 |
| 01826 | *Dracut* | 13,674 | 8,666 |
| 01570 | *Dudley* | 6,510 | 5,261 |
| 02332 | *Duxbury* | 4,727 | 3,167 |
| 02333 | *East Bridgewater* | 6,139 | 4,412 |
| 01027 | *Easthampton* | 12,326 | 10,694 |
| 01028 | *East Longmeadow* | 10,294 | 4,881 |
| 02334 | *Easton* | 9,078 | 6,244 |
| 02149 | *Everett* | 43,544 | 45,982 |
| 02719 | *Fairhaven* | 14,339 | 12,764 |
| *02722 | *Fall River* | 99,942 | 111,963 |
| 02540 | *Falmouth* | 3,308 | 2,713 |
| | *Falmouth (town)* | 13,037 | 8,662 |
| 01420 | *Fitchburg* | 43,021 | 42,691 |
| 02035 | *Foxborough* | 3,169 | 2,774 |
| | *Foxborough (town)* | 10,136 | 7,030 |
| 01701 | *Framingham* | 44,526 | 28,086 |
| 02038 | *Franklin* | 6,391 | 5,348 |
| | *Franklin (town)* | 10,530 | 8,037 |
| | *Freetown* | 3,039 | 2,104 |
| 01440 | *Gardner* | 19,038 | 19,581 |
| 01830 | *Georgetown* | 3,755 | 2,411 |
| 01930 | *Gloucester* | 25,789 | 25,167 |
| 01519 | *Grafton* | 10,627 | 8,281 |
| 01033 | *Granby* | 4,221 | 1,861 |
| 01230 | *Great Barrington* | 2,943 | 3,913 |
| | *Great Barrington (town)* | 6,624 | 6,712 |
| 01301 | *Greenfield* | 14,389 | 15,075 |
| | *Greenfield (town)* | 17,690 | 17,349 |
| 01450 | *Groton* | 3,904 | 2,889 |
| 01830 | *Groveland* | 3,297 | 2,340 |
| 01035 | *Hadley* | 3,099 | 2,639 |
| 01982 | *Hamilton* | 5,488 | 2,764 |
| 02339 | *Hanover* | 5,923 | 3,389 |
| 02341 | *Hanson* | 4,370 | 3,264 |
| 01451 | *Harvard* | 2,563 | 3,983 |
| 02645 | *Harwich* | 3,747 | 2,649 |
| 01830 | *Haverhill* | 46,346 | 47,280 |
| 02043 | *Hingham* | 15,378 | 10,665 |
| 02343 | *Holbrook* | 10,104 | 4,004 |
| 01520 | *Holden* | 10,117 | 5,975 |
| 01746 | *Holliston* | 6,222 | 3,753 |
| 01040 | *Holyoke* | 52,689 | 54,661 |
| 01747 | *Hopedale* | 2,904 | 2,797 |
| | *Hopedale (town)* | 3,987 | 3,479 |
| 01748 | *Hopkinton* | 2,754 | 1,829 |
| | *Hopkinton (town)* | 4,932 | 3,486 |
| 01749 | *Hudson* | 7,897 | .... |
| | *Hudson (town)* | 9,666 | 8,211 |
| 02045 | *Hull* | 7,055 | 3,379 |
| 02601 | *Hyannis* | 5,139 | 4,235 |
| 01938 | *Ipswich* | 4,617 | 4,952 |
| | *Ipswich (town)* | 8,544 | 6,895 |

| ZIP Code | Place | 1960 | 1950 | ZIP Code | Place | 1960 | 1950 |
|---|---|---|---|---|---|---|---|
| | **MASSACHUSETTS—Continued** | | | | **MASSACHUSETTS—Continued** | | |
| 02360 | Kingston................ | 4,302 | 3,461 | | Scituate (town)........... | 11,214 | 5,993 |
| 02346 | Lakeville............... | 3,209 | 2,066 | 02771 | Seekonk................ | 8,399 | 6,104 |
| 01523 | Lancaster.............. | 3,958 | 3,601 | 02067 | Sharon................. | 5,888 | 2,815 |
| 01237 | Lanesborough........... | 2,933 | 2,069 | | Sharon (town)........... | 10,070 | 4,847 |
| 01840 | Lawrence............... | 70,933 | 80,536 | 01464 | Shirley................. | 5,202 | 4,271 |
| 01238 | Lee.................... | 3,078 | 2,847 | 01545 | Shrewsbury............. | 16,622 | 10,594 |
| | Lee (town)............. | 5,271 | 4,820 | 01876 | Silver Lake............. | 4,654 | 2,024 |
| 01524 | Leicester............... | 8,177 | 6,029 | 02725 | Somerset............... | 12,196 | 8,566 |
| 01240 | Lenox.................. | 4,253 | 3,627 | 02143 | Somerville.............. | 94,697 | 102,351 |
| 01453 | Leominster............. | 27,929 | 24,075 | 01772 | Southborough........... | 3,996 | 2,760 |
| 02173 | Lexington.............. | 27,691 | 17,335 | 01550 | Southbridge............ | 15,889 | 16,748 |
| 01773 | Lincoln................ | 5,613 | 2,427 | | Southbridge (town)...... | 16,523 | 17,519 |
| 01460 | Littleton............... | 5,109 | 2,349 | 01075 | South Hadley........... | 14,956 | 10,145 |
| 01106 | Longmeadow............ | 10,565 | 6,508 | 01077 | Southwick.............. | 5,139 | 2,855 |
| *01852 | Lowell................. | 92,107 | 97,249 | 01562 | Spencer................ | 5,593 | 5,259 |
| 01056 | Ludlow................. | 13,805 | 8,660 | | Spencer (town).......... | 7,838 | 7,027 |
| 01462 | Lunenburg............. | 6,334 | 3,906 | *01101 | Springfield............. | 174,463 | 162,399 |
| *01903 | Lynn.................. | 94,478 | 99,738 | 01564 | Sterling................ | 3,193 | 2,166 |
| 01940 | Lynnfield.............. | 5,398 | 3,927 | 02180 | Stoneham.............. | 17,821 | 13,229 |
| 02148 | Malden................ | 57,676 | 59,804 | 02072 | Stoughton.............. | 16,328 | 11,146 |
| 01944 | Manchester............. | 3,932 | 2,868 | 01775 | Stow.................. | 2,573 | 1,700 |
| 02048 | Mansfield.............. | 4,764 | 4,808 | 01566 | Sturbridge............. | 3,604 | 2,805 |
| | Mansfield (town)........ | 7,773 | 7,184 | 01776 | Sudbury................ | 7,447 | 2,596 |
| 01945 | Marblehead............ | 18,521 | 13,765 | | Sutton................. | 3,638 | 3,102 |
| 02738 | Marion................ | 2,881 | 2,250 | 01907 | Swampscott............ | 13,294 | 11,580 |
| 01752 | Marlborough............ | 18,819 | 15,756 | 02777 | Swansea............... | 9,916 | 6,121 |
| 02050 | Marshfield............. | 6,748 | 3,267 | 02780 | Taunton............... | 41,132 | 40,109 |
| 02739 | Mattapoisett........... | 3,117 | 2,265 | 01468 | Templeton............. | 5,371 | 4,757 |
| 01754 | Maynard............... | 7,695 | 6,978 | 01876 | Tewksbury............. | 15,902 | 7,505 |
| 02052 | Medfield............... | 6,021 | 4,549 | 01080 | Three Rivers........... | 3,082 | 2,359 |
| 02155 | Medford............... | 64,971 | 66,113 | 01983 | Topsfield.............. | 3,351 | 1,412 |
| 02053 | Medway................ | 5,168 | 3,744 | 01469 | Townsend.............. | 3,650 | 2,817 |
| 02176 | Melrose................ | 29,619 | 26,988 | 01376 | Turner Falls........... | 4,917 | 5,179 |
| 01570 | Merino Village......... | 3,099 | 3,118 | 01879 | Tyngsborough.......... | 3,302 | 2,059 |
| 01860 | Merrimac.............. | 3,261 | 2,394 | 01568 | Upton................. | 3,127 | 2,656 |
| 01844 | Methuen............... | 28,114 | 24,477 | 01569 | Uxbridge.............. | 3,377 | .... |
| 02346 | Middleborough......... | 6,003 | 5,889 | | Uxbridge (town)........ | 7,789 | 7,007 |
| | Middleborough (town)... | 11,005 | 10,164 | 01880 | Wakefield.............. | 24,295 | 19,633 |
| 01949 | Middleton.............. | 3,718 | 2,916 | 02081 | Walpole................ | 14,068 | 9,109 |
| 01757 | Milford................ | 13,722 | 14,396 | 02154 | Waltham............... | 55,413 | 47,187 |
| | Milford (town).......... | 15,749 | 15,442 | 01082 | Ware.................. | 6,650 | 6,217 |
| 01527 | Millbury............... | 9,623 | 8,347 | | Ware (town)............ | 7,517 | 7,517 |
| 02054 | Millis................. | 4,374 | 2,551 | 02571 | Wareham............... | 9,461 | 7,569 |
| | Millis-Clicquot......... | 2,588 | 1,419 | 01083 | Warren................ | 3,383 | 3,406 |
| 02186 | Milton................ | 26,375 | 22,395 | 02172 | Watertown............. | 39,092 | 37,329 |
| 01057 | Monson................ | 6,712 | 6,125 | 01778 | Wayland............... | 10,444 | 4,407 |
| 01351 | Montague.............. | 7,836 | 7,812 | 01570 | Webster............... | 12,072 | 12,160 |
| 01908 | Nahant................ | 3,960 | 2,679 | | Webster (town)......... | 13,680 | 13,194 |
| 02554 | Nantucket.............. | 2,804 | 2,901 | 02181 | Wellesley.............. | 26,071 | 20,549 |
| | Nantucket (town)....... | 3,559 | 3,484 | 01984 | Wenham................ | 2,798 | 1,644 |
| 01760 | Natick................. | 28,831 | 19,838 | 01581 | Westborough........... | 4,011 | 3,443 |
| 02192 | Needham............... | 25,793 | 16,313 | | Westborough (town)..... | 9,599 | 7,378 |
| *02740 | New Bedford........... | 102,477 | 109,189 | 01583 | West Boylston.......... | 5,526 | 2,570 |
| 01950 | Newbury............... | 2,519 | 1,994 | 02379 | West Bridgewater....... | 5,061 | 4,059 |
| 01950 | Newburyport........... | 14,004 | 14,111 | 01085 | Westfield.............. | 26,302 | 20,962 |
| 01246 | New Marlborough....... | 1,083 | 989 | 01886 | Westford.............. | 6,261 | 4,262 |
| 02158 | Newton................ | 92,384 | 81,994 | 01473 | Westminster........... | 4,022 | 2,768 |
| 02056 | Norfolk................ | 3,471 | 2,704 | 02193 | Weston................ | 8,261 | 5,026 |
| 01247 | North Adams........... | 19,905 | 21,567 | 02790 | Westport............... | 6,641 | 4,989 |
| 01060 | Northampton........... | 30 058 | 29,063 | 01089 | West Springfield....... | 24,924 | 20,438 |
| 01845 | North Andover......... | 10,908 | 8,435 | 02090 | Westwood.............. | 10,354 | 5,837 |
| 02760 | North Attleborough..... | 14,777 | 12,146 | 02188 | Weymouth.............. | 48,177 | 32,690 |
| 01532 | Northborough.......... | 2,516 | 1,442 | 01588 | Whitinsville........... | 5,102 | 5,662 |
| | Northboro (town)....... | 6,687 | 3,122 | 02382 | Whitman............... | 10,485 | 8,413 |
| 01534 | Northbridge............ | 10,800 | 10,476 | 01095 | Wilbraham............. | 7,387 | 4,003 |
| 01535 | North Brookfield....... | 2,615 | 2,599 | 01267 | Williamstown.......... | 5,428 | 5,015 |
| | North Brookfield (town).. | 3,616 | 3,444 | | Williamstown (town).... | 7,322 | 6,194 |
| 02360 | North Plymouth........ | 3,467 | .... | 01887 | Wilmington............ | 12,475 | 7,039 |
| 01864 | North Reading......... | 8,331 | 4,402 | 01475 | Winchendon............ | 3,839 | 4,019 |
| 02060 | North Scituate......... | 3,421 | .... | | Winchendon (town)..... | 6,237 | 6,585 |
| 02766 | Norton................ | 6,818 | 4,401 | 01890 | Winchester............ | 19,376 | 15,509 |
| 02061 | Norwell............... | 5,207 | 2,515 | 02152 | Winthrop.............. | 20,303 | 19,496 |
| 02062 | Norwood............... | 24,898 | 16,636 | 01801 | Woburn............... | 31,214 | 20,492 |
| 01364 | Orange................ | 3,689 | 4,048 | *01601 | Worcester.............. | 186,587 | 203,486 |
| | Orange (town).......... | 6,154 | 5,894 | 02093 | Wrentham.............. | 6,685 | 5,341 |
| 01540 | Oxford................ | 6,985 | 3,238 | 02675 | Yarmouth.............. | 5,504 | 3,297 |
| | Oxford (town).......... | 9,282 | 5,851 | | | | |
| 01069 | Palmer................ | 3,888 | 3,440 | | **MICHIGAN** | | |
| | Palmer (town).......... | 10,358 | 9,533 | 49221 | Adrian................ | 20,347 | 18,393 |
| 01960 | Peabody............... | 32,202 | 22,645 | 49224 | Albion................ | 12,749 | 10,406 |
| 02359 | Pembroke.............. | 4,919 | 2,579 | 48001 | Algonac............... | 3,190 | 2,639 |
| 01463 | Pepperell.............. | 4,336 | 3,460 | 49010 | Allegan............... | 4,822 | 4,501 |
| 01201 | Pittsfield.............. | 57,879 | 53,348 | 48101 | Allen Park............ | 37,494 | 12,329 |
| 02762 | Plainville.............. | 3,810 | 2,088 | 48801 | Alma.................. | 8,978 | 8,341 |
| 02360 | Plymouth.............. | 6,488 | 10,540 | 49707 | Alpena................ | 14,682 | 13,135 |
| | Plymouth (town)....... | 14,445 | 13,608 | *48103 | Ann Arbor............. | 67,340 | 48,251 |
| 02657 | Provincetown.......... | 3,346 | 3,745 | 48413 | Bad Axe............... | 2,998 | 2,973 |
| | Provincetown (town).... | 3,389 | 3,795 | *49015 | Battle Creek........... | 44,169 | 48,666 |
| 02169 | Quincy................ | 87,409 | 83,835 | 48706 | Bay City.............. | 53,604 | 52,523 |
| 02368 | Randolph.............. | 18,900 | 9,982 | 48809 | Belding............... | 4,887 | 4,436 |
| 02767 | Raynham.............. | 4,150 | 2,426 | 49022 | Benton Harbor......... | 19,136 | 18,769 |
| 01867 | Reading............... | 19,259 | 14,006 | | Benton Heights........ | 6,112 | 6,160 |
| 02769 | Rehoboth.............. | 4,953 | 3,700 | 48072 | Berkley............... | 23,275 | 17,931 |
| 02151 | Revere................ | 40,080 | 36,763 | 49911 | Bessemer.............. | 3,304 | 3,509 |
| 02370 | Rockland.............. | 13,119 | 8,960 | 48009 | Beverly Hills.......... | 8,633 | .... |
| 01966 | Rockport.............. | 3,511 | 2,911 | 49307 | Big Rapids............ | 8,686 | 6,736 |
| | Rockport (town)........ | 4,616 | 4,231 | *48010 | Birmingham............ | 25,525 | 15,467 |
| 01969 | Rowley................ | 2,783 | 1,768 | 49228 | Blissfield.............. | 2,653 | 2,365 |
| 01543 | Rutland............... | 3,253 | 3,056 | 49712 | Boyne................. | 2,797 | 3,028 |
| 01970 | Salem................. | 39,211 | 41,880 | 49017 | Brownlee Park......... | 5,307 | .... |
| 01950 | Salisbury.............. | 3,154 | 2,695 | 49107 | Buchanan.............. | 5,308 | 5,224 |
| 01906 | Saugus................ | 20,666 | 17,162 | 49601 | Cadillac............... | 10,112 | 10,425 |
| 02066 | Scituate............... | 3,229 | 1,457 | 48723 | Caro.................. | 3,534 | 3,464 |

| ZIP Code | Place | 1960 | 1950 |
|---|---|---|---|
| | **MICHIGAN—Continued** | | |
| 48015 | Center Line | 10,164 | 7,659 |
| 49720 | Charlevoix | 2,751 | 2,695 |
| 48813 | Charlotte | 7,657 | 6,606 |
| 49721 | Cheboygan | 5,859 | 5,687 |
| 48118 | Chelsea | 3,355 | 2,923 |
| 48616 | Chesaning | 2,770 | 2,264 |
| 48017 | Clawson | 14,795 | 5,196 |
| 49036 | Coldwater | 8,880 | 8,594 |
| 48817 | Corunna | 2,764 | 2,358 |
| 48423 | Davison | 3,761 | 1,745 |
| *48120 | Dearborn | 112,007 | 94,994 |
| *48233 | Detroit | 1,670,144 | 1,849,568 |
| 49047 | Dowagiac | 7,208 | 6,542 |
| 48429 | Durand | 3,312 | 3,194 |
| 48021 | East Detroit | 45,756 | 21,461 |
| 49506 | East Grand Rapids | 10,924 | 6,403 |
| 48823 | East Lansing | 30,198 | 20,325 |
| 48197 | Eastlawn | 17,652 | 4,127 |
| 48827 | Eaton Rapids | 4,052 | 3,509 |
| 48229 | Ecorse | 17,328 | 17,948 |
| 49829 | Escanaba | 15,391 | 15,170 |
| 48732 | Essexville | 4,590 | 3,167 |
| | Fair Plain | 7,998 | 4,134 |
| 48024 | Farmington | 6,881 | 2,325 |
| 48430 | Fenton | 6,142 | 4,226 |
| 48220 | Ferndale | 31,347 | 29,675 |
| 49409 | Ferrysburg | 2,590 | 1,454 |
| 48134 | Flat Rock | 4,696 | 1,931 |
| *48502 | Flint | 196,940 | 163,143 |
| *48433 | Flushing | 3,761 | 2,226 |
| 48026 | Fraser | 7,027 | 1,379 |
| 49412 | Fremont | 3,384 | 3,056 |
| 48135 | Garden City | 38,017 | 9,012 |
| 49735 | Gaylord | 2,568 | 2,271 |
| 49837 | Gladstone | 5,267 | 4,831 |
| 49417 | Grand Haven | 11,066 | 9,536 |
| 48837 | Grand Ledge | 5,165 | 4,506 |
| *49501 | Grand Rapids (A), '63 | 202,379 | 176,515 |
| 49418 | Grandville | 7,975 | 2,022 |
| 48838 | Greenville | 7,440 | 6,668 |
| 48236 | Grosse Pointe | 6,631 | 6,283 |
| 48236 | Grosse Pointe Farms | 12,172 | 9,410 |
| 48230 | Grosse Pointe Park | 15,457 | 13,075 |
| 48236 | Grosse Pointe Woods | 18,580 | 10,381 |
| 48212 | Hamtramck | 34,137 | 43,355 |
| 48230 | Hancock | 5,022 | 5,223 |
| 48236 | Harper Woods | 19,995 | |
| 49058 | Hastings | 6,375 | 6,096 |
| 48030 | Hazel Park | 25,631 | 17,770 |
| 48203 | Highland Park | 38,063 | 46,393 |
| 49242 | Hillsdale | 7,629 | 7,297 |
| 49423 | Holland | 24,777 | 15,858 |
| 48442 | Holly | 3,269 | 2,663 |
| 48842 | Holt | 4,818 | |
| 49931 | Houghton | 3,393 | 3,829 |
| 48843 | Howell | 4,861 | 4,353 |
| 49247 | Hudson | 2,546 | 2,773 |
| 49426 | Hudsonville | 2,649 | 1,101 |
| 48070 | Huntington Woods | 8,746 | 4,949 |
| 48141 | Inkster | 39,097 | 16,728 |
| 48846 | Ionia | 6,754 | 6,412 |
| 49801 | Iron Mountain | 9,299 | 9,679 |
| 49935 | Iron River | 3,754 | 4,048 |
| 49938 | Ironwood | 10,265 | 11,466 |
| 49849 | Ishpeming | 8,857 | 8,962 |
| 48847 | Ithaca | 2,611 | 2,377 |
| *49201 | Jackson | 50,720 | 51,088 |
| 49001 | Kalamazoo | 82,089 | 57,704 |
| 48043 | Keego Harbor | 2,761 | |
| 49801 | Kingsford | 5,084 | 5,038 |
| 48035 | Lake Orion | 2,698 | 2,385 |
| 48850 | Lakeview | 10,384 | |
| *48924 | Lansing (A) | 113,058 | 92,129 |
| 48446 | Lapeer | 6,160 | 6,143 |
| 48075 | Lathrup Village | 3,556 | |
| 49913 | Laurium | 3,058 | 3,211 |
| 49017 | Level Park-Oak Park | 3,017 | 1,364 |
| 48146 | Lincoln Park | 53,933 | 29,310 |
| *48150 | Livonia | 66,702 | 17,534 |
| 49331 | Lowell | 2,545 | 2,191 |
| 49431 | Ludington | 9,421 | 9,506 |
| 48071 | Madison Heights | 33,343 | |
| 49660 | Manistee | 8,324 | 8,642 |
| 49854 | Manistique | 4,875 | 5,086 |
| 48039 | Marine City | 4,404 | 4,270 |
| 49855 | Marquette | 19,824 | 17,202 |
| 49068 | Marshall | 6,736 | 5,777 |
| 48040 | Marysville | 4,065 | 2,534 |
| 48854 | Mason | 4,522 | 3,514 |
| 48122 | Melvindale | 13,089 | 9,483 |
| 49858 | Menominee | 11,289 | 11,151 |
| 49254 | Michigan Center | 4,611 | 3,012 |
| 48640 | Midland | 27,779 | 14,285 |
| 48160 | Milan | 3,616 | 2,768 |
| 48042 | Milford | 4,323 | 1,924 |
| 48161 | Monroe | 22,968 | 21,467 |
| 48043 | Mount Clemens | 21,016 | 17,027 |
| 48458 | Mount Morris | 3,484 | 2,890 |
| 48858 | Mount Pleasant | 14,875 | 11,393 |
| 49862 | Munising | 4,225 | 4,339 |
| 49443 | Muskegon | 46,485 | 48,429 |
| 49444 | Muskegon Heights | 19,552 | 18,828 |
| 49866 | Negaunee | 6,126 | 6,472 |
| | **MICHIGAN—Continued** | | |
| 48047 | New Baltimore | 3,159 | 2,043 |
| 49868 | Newberry | 2,612 | 2,802 |
| 49120 | Niles | 13,842 | 13,145 |
| 49445 | North Muskegon | 3,855 | 2,424 |
| 48167 | Northville | 3,967 | 3,240 |
| 49870 | Norway | 3,171 | 3,258 |
| 48050 | Novi | 6,390 | |
| 48237 | Oak Park | 36,632 | 5,267 |
| 49078 | Otsego | 4,142 | 3,990 |
| 48867 | Owosso | 17,006 | 15,948 |
| 49079 | Paw Paw | 2,970 | 2,382 |
| 49038 | Paw Paw Lake | 3,518 | 1,625 |
| 49770 | Petoskey | 6,138 | 6,468 |
| 49080 | Plainwell | 3,125 | 2,767 |
| 48069 | Pleasant Ridge | 3,807 | 3,594 |
| 48170 | Plymouth | 8,766 | 6,637 |
| *48056 | Pontiac | 82,233 | 73,681 |
| 48060 | Port Huron | 36,084 | 35,725 |
| 48875 | Portland | 3,330 | 2,807 |
| 48062 | Richmond | 2,667 | 2,025 |
| 48218 | River Rouge | 18,147 | 20,549 |
| 48192 | Riverview | 7,237 | 1,432 |
| 48063 | Rochester | 5,431 | 4,279 |
| 49779 | Rogers City | 4,722 | 3,873 |
| 48065 | Romeo | 3,327 | 2,985 |
| 49441 | Roosevelt Park | 2,578 | 1,254 |
| 48066 | Roseville | 50,195 | 15,816 |
| *48067 | Royal Oak | 80,612 | 46,898 |
| *48601 | Saginaw | 98,265 | 92,918 |
| 48079 | St. Clair | 4,538 | 4,098 |
| *48080 | St. Clair Shores | 76,657 | 19,823 |
| 49781 | St. Ignace | 3,334 | 2,946 |
| 48879 | St. Johns | 5,629 | 4,954 |
| 49085 | St. Joseph | 11,755 | 10,223 |
| 48880 | St. Louis | 3,808 | 3,347 |
| 49783 | Sault Ste. Marie | 18,722 | 17,912 |
| 48075 | Southfield | 31,501 | |
| 48192 | Southgate | 29,404 | |
| 49090 | South Haven | 6,149 | 5,629 |
| 48161 | South Monroe | 2,919 | 2,275 |
| 49345 | Sparta | 2,749 | 2,327 |
| 49015 | Springfield | 4,605 | |
| 49015 | Springfield Place | 5,136 | |
| 49091 | Sturgis | 8,915 | 7,786 |
| 48473 | Swartz Creek | 3,066 | |
| 49286 | Tecumseh | 7,045 | 4,020 |
| 49093 | Three Rivers | 7,092 | 6,785 |
| 49684 | Traverse City | 18,432 | 16,974 |
| 48183 | Trenton | 18,439 | 6,222 |
| 48084 | Troy | 19,058 | |
| 48768 | Vassar | 2,680 | 2,530 |
| 49968 | Wakefield | 3,231 | 3,344 |
| 48088 | Walled Lake | 3,550 | |
| *48089 | Warren | 89,246 | 727 |
| 48184 | Wayne (A) | 19,071 | 9,409 |
| 49461 | Whitehall | 2,590 | 1,819 |
| 48031 | White Lake-Seven Harbors | 2,748 | 1,385 |
| 49442 | Wolf Lake | 2,525 | 1,591 |
| 48192 | Wyandotte | 43,519 | 36,846 |
| 49509 | Wyoming (A) | 50,145 | |
| 48197 | Ypsilanti | 20,957 | 18,302 |
| 49464 | Zeeland | 3,702 | 3,075 |
| | **MINNESOTA** | | |
| 56007 | Albert Lea, '65 | 18,454 | 13,545 |
| 56308 | Alexandria | 6,713 | 6,319 |
| 55303 | Anoka, '65 | 11,529 | 7,396 |
| 55112 | Arden Hills, '65 | 4,436 | |
| 55705 | Aurora | 2,799 | 2,985 |
| 55912 | Austin | 27,908 | 23,100 |
| 55706 | Babbitt | 2,587 | |
| 55003 | Bayport | 3,205 | 2,502 |
| 56601 | Bemidji | 9,958 | 10,001 |
| 56215 | Benson | 3,678 | 3,398 |
| | Blaine | 15,544 | |
| 55420 | Bloomington, '65 | 66,542 | |
| 56013 | Blue Earth | 4,200 | 3,843 |
| 56401 | Brainerd | 12,898 | 12,637 |
| 56520 | Breckenridge | 4,335 | 3,623 |
| 55429 | Brooklyn Center, '65 | 30,108 | 4,284 |
| | Brooklyn Park, '65 | 14,785 | |
| 55378 | Burnsville, '65 | 10,721 | 583 |
| 55921 | Caledonia | 2,563 | 2,243 |
| 55008 | Cambridge, '65 | 2,728 | 1,790 |
| 55317 | Chanhassen (A) '67 | 4,112 | 244 |
| 55318 | Chaska, '65 | 3,268 | 2,008 |
| 55719 | Chisholm | 7,144 | 6,861 |
| 55014 | Circle Pines, '65 | 3,678 | |
| 55720 | Cloquet | 9,013 | 7,685 |
| 55421 | Columbia Heights, '65 | 23,285 | 8,175 |
| 55433 | Coon Rapids, '65 | 26,412 | |
| 56716 | Crookston | 8,546 | 7,352 |
| 56441 | Crosby | 2,629 | 2,777 |
| 55428 | Crystal, '65 | 29,089 | 5,713 |
| 55331 | Deephaven | 3,286 | 1,823 |
| 56501 | Detroit Lakes, '65 | 5,978 | 5,787 |
| *55601 | Duluth | 106,884 | 104,511 |
| 56721 | East Grand Forks, '65 | 7,898 | 5,049 |
| | Eden Prairie, '65 | 5,456 | 1,221 |
| 55424 | Edina, '65 | 35,302 | 9,744 |
| 55731 | Ely | 5,438 | 5,474 |

## MINNESOTA—Continued

| ZIP Code | Place | 1960 | 1950 |
|---|---|---|---|
| 55734 | Eveleth | 5,721 | 5,872 |
| 56031 | Fairmont | 9,745 | 8,193 |
| 55115 | Falcon Heights | 5,927 | 3,884 |
| 55021 | Faribault | 16,026 | 16,028 |
| 56537 | Fergus Falls | 13,733 | 12,917 |
| 55025 | Forest Lake, '65 | 2,809 | 1,120 |
| 55432 | Fridley, '65 | 24,789 | 3,796 |
| 55741 | Gilbert | 2,591 | 2,247 |
| 44336 | Glencoe | 3,216 | 2,801 |
| 56334 | Glenwood | 2,631 | 2,666 |
| 55427 | Golden Valley, '65 | 21,248 | 5,551 |
| 55744 | Grand Rapids | 7,265 | 6,019 |
| 56241 | Granite Falls, '65 | 3,171 | 2,511 |
| 55033 | Hastings, '65 | 10,588 | 6,560 |
| 55746 | Hibbing | 17,731 | 16,276 |
| 55343 | Hopkins, '65 | 12,187 | 7,595 |
| 55750 | Hoyt Lakes | 3,186 | |
| 55350 | Hutchinson | 6,207 | 4,690 |
| 56649 | International Falls | 6,778 | 6,269 |
| 56143 | Jackson | 3,370 | 3,313 |
| 55947 | La Crescent | 2,624 | 1,229 |
| 55041 | Lake City | 3,494 | 3,457 |
| 56058 | Le Sueur | 3,310 | 2,713 |
| ..... | Lino Lakes, '65 | 3,103 | |
| 55355 | Litchfield | 5,078 | 4,608 |
| 55117 | Little Canada | 3,512 | |
| 56345 | Little Falls | 7,551 | 6,717 |
| 56156 | Luverne | 4,249 | 3,650 |
| 56001 | Mankato, '65 | 28,454 | 18,809 |
| ..... | Maple Grove '65 | 3,653 | |
| 55109 | Maplewood, '65 | 21,438 | |
| 56258 | Marshall, '65 | 7,363 | 5,923 |
| 55118 | Mendota Heights, '65 | 5,778 | |
| *55401 | Minneapolis | 482,872 | 521,718 |
| 55343 | Minnetonka, '65 | 30,926 | |
| 56265 | Montevideo | 5,693 | 5,459 |
| 56560 | Moorhead, '65 | 26,964 | 14,870 |
| 56267 | Morris | 4,199 | 3,811 |
| 55364 | Mound, '65 | 5,992 | 2,061 |
| ..... | Mounds View | 6,416 | |
| 55112 | New Brighton, '65 | 10,890 | 2,218 |
| ..... | New Hope, '65 | 11,620 | |
| 56071 | New Prague | 2,533 | 1,915 |
| 56073 | New Ulm, '65 | 12,587 | 9,348 |
| 55057 | Northfield | 8,707 | 7,487 |
| 56001 | North Mankato, '65 | 6,618 | 4,788 |
| 55109 | North St. Paul, '65 | 10,531 | 4,248 |
| ..... | Orono | 5,643 | |
| 56278 | Ortonville | 2,674 | 2,577 |
| 55369 | Osseo, '65 | 2,726 | 738 |
| 55060 | Owatonna, '65 | 14,776 | 10,191 |
| 56470 | Park Rapids | 3,047 | 3,027 |
| 56164 | Pipestone | 5,324 | 5,296 |
| ..... | Plymouth, '65 | 13,064 | |
| 55810 | Proctor | 2,963 | 2,693 |
| 55066 | Red Wing | 10,528 | 10,645 |
| 56283 | Redwood Falls | 4,285 | 3,813 |
| 55423 | Richfield, '65 | 46,444 | 17,502 |
| 55422 | Robbinsdale | 16,381 | 11,289 |
| 55901 | Rochester, '65 | 47,797 | 29,855 |
| 55113 | Roseville, '65 | 29,581 | 6,437 |
| 55414 | St. Anthony, '65 | 7,170 | 1,406 |
| 56301 | St. Cloud, '65 | 37,746 | 28,410 |
| 56081 | St. James | 4,174 | 3,861 |
| 55416 | St. Louis Park, '65 | 48,021 | 22,644 |
| *55101 | St. Paul | 313,411 | 311,349 |
| 55071 | St. Paul Park, '65 | 5,111 | 2,438 |
| 56082 | St. Peter | 8,484 | 7,754 |
| 56375 | Sauk Centre | 3,573 | 3,140 |
| 55379 | Sauk Rapids, '65 | 4,570 | 3,410 |
| 55379 | Shakopee, '65 | 6,294 | 3,185 |
| 55112 | Shoreview, '65 | 8,450 | |
| 55331 | Shorewood | 3,197 | |
| 55614 | Silver Bay | 3,723 | |
| 56085 | Sleepy Eye | 3,492 | 3,278 |
| 55075 | South St. Paul, '65 | 24,429 | 15,909 |
| 56087 | Springfield | 2,701 | 2,574 |
| 55433 | Spring Lake Park, '65 | 5,148 | |
| 55975 | Spring Valley | 2,628 | 2,467 |
| 56479 | Staples | 2,706 | 2,782 |
| 55082 | Stillwater | 8,310 | 7,674 |
| 56701 | Thief River Falls | 7,151 | 6,926 |
| 56175 | Tracy | 2,862 | 3,020 |
| 55616 | Two Harbors | 4,695 | 4,400 |
| 55792 | Virginia | 14,034 | 12,486 |
| 55981 | Wabasha | 2,500 | 2,468 |
| 56482 | Wadena | 4,381 | 3,958 |
| 56093 | Waseca, '65 | 6,102 | 4,927 |
| 55391 | Wayzata | 3,219 | 1,791 |
| 56097 | Wells | 2,897 | 2,475 |
| 55118 | West St. Paul, '65 | 15,144 | 7,955 |
| 55110 | White Bear Lake, '65 | 19,410 | 3,646 |
| 56201 | Willmar | 10,417 | 9,410 |
| 56101 | Windom | 3,691 | 3,165 |
| 55987 | Winona, '65 | 26,771 | 25,031 |
| 56187 | Worthington | 9,015 | 7,923 |

## MISSISSIPPI

| ZIP Code | Place | 1960 | 1950 |
|---|---|---|---|
| 39730 | Aberdeen | 6,450 | 5,290 |
| 38821 | Amory | 6,474 | 4,990 |
| 38606 | Batesville | 3,284 | 2,463 |
| 39520 | Bay St. Louis | 5,073 | 4,621 |

## MISSISSIPPI—Continued

| ZIP Code | Place | 1960 | 1950 |
|---|---|---|---|
| 39038 | Belzoni | 4,142 | 4,071 |
| *39530 | Biloxi | 44,053 | 37,425 |
| 38829 | Booneville | 3,480 | 3,295 |
| 39601 | Brookhaven | 9,885 | 7,801 |
| 39046 | Canton | 9,707 | 7,840 |
| 38921 | Charleston | 2,528 | 2,629 |
| 38614 | Clarksdale | 21,105 | 16,539 |
| 38732 | Cleveland | 10,172 | 6,747 |
| 39056 | Clinton | 3,438 | 2,255 |
| 39429 | Columbia | 7,117 | 6,124 |
| 39701 | Columbus | 24,771 | 17,172 |
| 38834 | Corinth | 11,453 | 9,785 |
| 39059 | Crystal Springs | 4,496 | 3,676 |
| 39532 | D'Iberville | 3,005 | 1,429 |
| 39063 | Durant | 2,617 | 2,311 |
| ..... | East Side | 4,318 | 1,215 |
| 39437 | Ellisville | 4,592 | 3,579 |
| 39074 | Forest | 3,917 | 2,874 |
| 38701 | Greenville | 41,502 | 29,936 |
| 38701 | Greenville North | 2,516 | |
| 38930 | Greenwood | 20,436 | 18,061 |
| 39501 | Grenada | 7,914 | 7,388 |
| 39501 | Gulfport | 30,204 | 22,659 |
| 39401 | Hattiesburg | 34,989 | 29,474 |
| 39083 | Hazlehurst, '63 | 4,206 | 3,397 |
| 38748 | Hollandale | 2,646 | 2,346 |
| 38635 | Holly Springs | 5,621 | 3,276 |
| 38851 | Houston | 2,577 | 1,664 |
| 38751 | Indianola | 6,714 | 4,369 |
| *39205 | Jackson | 144,422 | 98,271 |
| 39090 | Kosciusko | 6,800 | 6,753 |
| 39440 | Laurel | 27,889 | 25,038 |
| 38756 | Leland | 6,295 | 4,736 |
| 39095 | Lexington | 2,839 | 3,198 |
| 39560 | Long Beach | 4,770 | 2,703 |
| 39339 | Louisville | 5,066 | 5,282 |
| 39648 | McComb | 12,020 | 10,401 |
| 39111 | Magee, '63 | 2,917 | |
| 39301 | Marks | 2,572 | 2,209 |
| 38646 | Meridian | 49,374 | 41,893 |
| 39562 | Mississippi City | 4,169 | |
| 39563 | Moss Point | 6,631 | 3,782 |
| 39120 | Natchez | 23,791 | 22,740 |
| 38652 | New Albany | 5,151 | 3,680 |
| 39345 | Newton | 3,175 | 2,912 |
| 39564 | Ocean Springs | 5,025 | 3,058 |
| 38860 | Okolona | 2,622 | 2,167 |
| 38655 | Oxford | 5,283 | 3,956 |
| 39567 | Pascagoula | 17,155 | 10,805 |
| 39571 | Pass Christian | 3,881 | 3,383 |
| 39208 | Pearl | 5,081 | |
| 39465 | Petal | 4,007 | 2,148 |
| 39350 | Philadelphia | 5,017 | 4,472 |
| 39466 | Picayune (A), '67 | 10,709 | 6,707 |
| 38863 | Pontotoc (A), '67 | 3,510 | 2,108 |
| 39150 | Port Gibson | 2,861 | 2,920 |
| 38663 | Ripley | 2,668 | 2,383 |
| 38668 | Senatobia | 3,259 | 2,108 |
| 39759 | Starkville | 9,041 | 7,107 |
| 38801 | Tupelo | 17,221 | 11,527 |
| 38677 | University | 3,597 | |
| 39180 | Vicksburg | 29,130 | 27,948 |
| 38965 | Water Valley | 3,206 | 3,213 |
| 39367 | Waynesboro | 3,892 | 3,442 |
| 39501 | West Gulfport | 3,323 | |
| 39773 | West Point | 8,550 | 6,432 |
| 38967 | Winona | 4,282 | 3,441 |
| 39194 | Yazoo City | 11,236 | 9,746 |

## MISSOURI

| ZIP Code | Place | 1960 | 1950 |
|---|---|---|---|
| 65605 | Aurora | 4,683 | 4,153 |
| 63011 | Ballwin | 5,710 | |
| 63137 | Bellefontaine Neighbors | 13,650 | |
| 63121 | Bel-Ridge | 4,395 | 1,116 |
| 64012 | Belton | 4,897 | 1,233 |
| 63134 | Berkeley | 18,676 | 5,268 |
| 64424 | Bethany | 2,771 | 2,714 |
| 64015 | Blue Springs | 2,555 | 1,068 |
| 65613 | Bolivar | 3,512 | 3,482 |
| 63628 | Bonne Terre | 3,219 | 3,533 |
| 65233 | Boonville | 7,090 | 6,886 |
| 63334 | Bowling Green | 2,650 | 2,396 |
| 63114 | Breckenridge Hills | 6,299 | 4,063 |
| 63144 | Brentwood | 12,250 | 7,504 |
| 63042 | Bridgeton | 7,820 | 202 |
| 64628 | Brookfield | 5,694 | 5,810 |
| 64730 | Butler | 3,791 | 3,333 |
| 65018 | California | 2,788 | 2,627 |
| 64720 | Cameron | 3,674 | 3,570 |
| 63435 | Canton | 2,562 | 2,490 |
| 63701 | Cape Girardeau | 24,947 | 21,578 |
| 64633 | Carrollton | 4,554 | 4,380 |
| 63330 | Carthage | 11,264 | 11,188 |
| 63830 | Caruthersville | 8,643 | 8,614 |
| 65240 | Centralia | 3,200 | 2,460 |
| 63740 | Chaffee | 2,862 | 3,134 |
| 63834 | Charleston | 5,911 | 5,501 |
| 64601 | Chillicothe | 9,236 | 8,694 |
| 63105 | Clayton | 15,245 | 16,035 |
| 64735 | Clinton | 6,925 | 6,075 |
| 65201 | Columbia | 36,650 | 31,974 |
| 63126 | Crestwood | 11,106 | 1,645 |
| 63141 | Creve Coeur | 5,122 | 2,040 |

| ZIP Code | Place | 1960 | 1950 | ZIP Code | Place | 1960 | 1950 |
|---|---|---|---|---|---|---|---|
| | **MISSOURI—Continued** | | | | **MISSOURI—Continued** | | |
| 63019 | Crystal City......... | 3,678 | 3,499 | 64093 | Warrensburg......... | 9,689 | 6,857 |
| 63135 | Dellwood............. | 4,720 | ...... | 63090 | Washington........... | 7,961 | 6,850 |
| 63020 | De Soto............. | 5,804 | 5,357 | 64870 | Webb City........... | 6,740 | 6,919 |
| 63131 | Des Peres............ | 4,362 | 1,172 | 63119 | Webster Groves...... | 28,990 | 23,390 |
| 63841 | Dexter.............. | 5,519 | 4,624 | 63112 | Wellston............ | 7,979 | 9,396 |
| 63845 | East Prairie......... | 3,449 | 3,033 | 63385 | Wentzville........... | 2,742 | 1,227 |
| 65026 | Eldon............... | 3,158 | 2,766 | 65775 | West Plains.......... | 5,836 | 4,918 |
| 64744 | Eldorado Springs..... | 2,864 | 2,618 | 65360 | Windsor............. | 2,714 | 2,429 |
| 63024 | Ellisville............ | 2,732 | 628 | 63134 | Woodson Terrace..... | 6,048 | 616 |
| 64024 | Excelsior Springs..... | 6,473 | 5,888 | | | | |
| 63640 | Farmington.......... | 5,618 | 4,490 | | **MONTANA** | | |
| 65248 | Fayette............. | 3,294 | 3,144 | 59711 | Anaconda........... | 12,054 | 11,254 |
| 63135 | Ferguson (A)........ | 22,952 | 11,573 | *59101 | Billings............. | 52,851 | 31,834 |
| 63028 | Festus.............. | 7,021 | 5,199 | 59715 | Bozeman............ | 13,361 | 11,325 |
| 63601 | Flat River........... | 4,515 | 5,308 | 59701 | Butte............... | 27,877 | 33,251 |
| 63031 | Florissant........... | 38,166 | 3,737 | 59701 | Centerville-Dublin Gulch | 3,398 | 1,825 |
| 63645 | Fredericktown........ | 3,484 | 3,696 | 59425 | Conrad.............. | 2,665 | 1,865 |
| 63131 | Frontenac........... | 3,089 | 1,099 | 59427 | Cut Bank........... | 4,539 | 3,721 |
| 65251 | Fulton.............. | 11,131 | 10,052 | 59722 | Deer Lodge.......... | 4,681 | 3,779 |
| 64118 | Gladstone........... | 14,502 | ...... | 59725 | Dillon.............. | 3,690 | 3,268 |
| 63122 | Glendale............ | 7,048 | 4,930 | 59701 | Floral Park.......... | 4,079 | ...... |
| 64030 | Grandview........... | 6,027 | 1,556 | 59230 | Glasgow............ | 6,398 | 3,821 |
| 63133 | Hanley Hills......... | 3,308 | 2,219 | 59330 | Glendive............ | 7,058 | 5,254 |
| 63401 | Hannibal............ | 20,028 | 20,444 | 59401 | Great Falls.......... | 55,244 | 39,214 |
| 64701 | Harrisonville........ | 3,510 | 2,530 | 59840 | Hamilton............ | 2,475 | 2,678 |
| 63851 | Hayti.............. | 3,737 | 3,302 | 59501 | Hardin............. | 2,789 | 2,306 |
| 63042 | Hazelwood........... | 6,045 | ...... | 59501 | Havre.............. | 10,740 | 8,086 |
| 65041 | Hermann............ | 2,536 | 2,523 | 59601 | Helena.............. | 20,227 | 17,581 |
| 64037 | Higginsville......... | 4,003 | 3,428 | 59901 | Kalispell............ | 10,151 | 9,737 |
| 63121 | Hillsdale............ | 2,788 | 2,902 | 59044 | Laurel.............. | 4,601 | 3,663 |
| *63050 | Independence (A)..... | 84,771 | 36,963 | 59457 | Lewistown........... | 7,408 | 6,573 |
| 63755 | Jackson (A).......... | 5,070 | 3,707 | 59923 | Libby............... | 2,828 | 2,401 |
| 65101 | Jefferson City........ | 28,228 | 25,099 | 59047 | Livingston........... | 8,229 | 7,683 |
| 63136 | Jennings............ | 19,965 | 15,282 | 59301 | Miles City........... | 9,665 | 9,243 |
| 64801 | Joplin.............. | 38,958 | 38,711 | 59801 | Missoula............ | 27,090 | 22,485 |
| *64108 | Kansas City......... | 475,539 | 456,622 | 59801 | Missoula S.W........ | 3,817 | ...... |
| 63857 | Kennett............. | 9,098 | 8,685 | 59072 | Roundup............ | 2,842 | 2,856 |
| 63140 | Kinloch............. | 6,501 | 5,957 | 59474 | Shelby.............. | 4,017 | 3,058 |
| 63501 | Kirksville........... | 13,123 | 11,110 | 59270 | Sidney.............. | 4,564 | 3,987 |
| 63122 | Kirkwood............ | 29,421 | 18,640 | 59701 | Silver Bow Park...... | 4,798 | ...... |
| 63124 | Ladue.............. | 9,466 | 5,386 | 59937 | Whitefish........... | 2,965 | 3,268 |
| 64759 | Lamar.............. | 3,608 | 3,233 | 59201 | Wolf Point.......... | 3,585 | 2,557 |
| 65536 | Lebanon............ | 8,220 | 6,808 | | | | |
| 64063 | Lees Summit......... | 8,267 | 2,554 | | **NEBRASKA** | | |
| 64067 | Lexington (A)........ | 5,140 | 5,074 | 69301 | Alliance............. | 7,845 | 7,891 |
| 64068 | Liberty............. | 8,909 | 4,709 | 68305 | Auburn............. | 3,229 | 3,422 |
| 63353 | Louisiana............ | 4,286 | 4,389 | 68818 | Aurora............. | 2,576 | 2,455 |
| 63552 | Macon.............. | 4,547 | 4,152 | 68310 | Beatrice............ | 12,132 | 11,813 |
| 63863 | Malden............. | 5,007 | 3,396 | 68005 | Bellevue, '66......... | 17,496 | 3,858 |
| 63143 | Maplewood.......... | 12,552 | 13,416 | 68008 | Blair............... | 4,931 | 3,815 |
| 64658 | Marceline........... | 2,872 | 3,172 | 68822 | Broken Bow......... | 3,482 | 3,396 |
| 65340 | Marshall (A)........ | 11,142 | 8,851 | 69337 | Chadron............ | 5,079 | 4,687 |
| 64468 | Maryville (A)........ | 7,946 | 6,834 | 68601 | Columbus........... | 12,476 | 8,884 |
| 65265 | Mexico............. | 12,889 | 11,623 | 69130 | Cozad.............. | 3,184 | 2,910 |
| 65270 | Moberly............ | 13,170 | 13,115 | 68333 | Crete............... | 3,546 | 3,692 |
| 63136 | Moline Acres (A)..... | 3,733 | 99 | 68352 | Fairbury............ | 5,572 | 6,395 |
| 63708 | Monett............. | 5,359 | 4,771 | 68355 | Falls City.......... | 5,598 | 6,203 |
| 65711 | Mountain Grove...... | 3,176 | 3,106 | 68025 | Fremont (A) '67...... | 22,317 | 14,762 |
| 64850 | Neosho............. | 7,452 | 5,790 | 69341 | Gering.............. | 4,585 | 3,842 |
| 64772 | Nevada (A).......... | 10,518 | 8,009 | 69138 | Gothenburg.......... | 3,050 | 2,977 |
| 63869 | New Madrid......... | 2,867 | 2,726 | 68801 | Grand Island........ | 25,742 | 22,682 |
| 63121 | Normandy........... | 4,452 | 2,306 | 68901 | Hastings............ | 21,412 | 20,211 |
| 64116 | North Kansas City.... | 5,657 | 3,886 | 68949 | Holdrege............ | 5,226 | 4,381 |
| 63121 | Northwoods.......... | 4,701 | 1,602 | 68847 | Kearney............ | 14,210 | 12,115 |
| 63366 | O'Fallon............ | 3,770 | 789 | 69145 | Kimball............. | 4,384 | 2,048 |
| 63132 | Olivette............ | 8,257 | 1,761 | 68128 | La Vista, '66........ | 3,507 | ...... |
| 63114 | Overland............ | 22,763 | 11,566 | *68501 | Lincoln............. | 128,521 | 98,884 |
| 63069 | Pacific............. | 2,795 | 1,985 | 69001 | McCook............ | 8,301 | 7,678 |
| 63133 | Pagedale............ | 5,106 | 3,866 | 68043 | Millard, '66......... | 5,270 | 391 |
| 63461 | Palmyra............ | 2,933 | 2,295 | 68410 | Nebraska City....... | 7,252 | 6,872 |
| 63775 | Perryville........... | 5,117 | 4,591 | 68701 | Norfolk............. | 13,640 | 11,335 |
| 63120 | Pine Lawn........... | 5,943 | 6,425 | 69101 | North Platte........ | 17,184 | 15,433 |
| 64090 | Pleasant Hill........ | 2,689 | 2,200 | 69153 | Ogallala............ | 4,250 | 3,456 |
| 63901 | Poplar Bluff......... | 15,926 | 15,064 | *68102 | Omaha............. | 301,598 | 251,117 |
| 63873 | Portageville......... | 2,505 | 2,662 | 68763 | O'Neill............. | 3,181 | 3,027 |
| 63664 | Potosi.............. | 2,805 | 2,359 | 64086 | Papillion, '66........ | 4,079 | 1,304 |
| 64133 | Raytown............ | 17,083 | ...... | 68048 | Plattsmouth......... | 6,244 | 4,874 |
| 64085 | Richmond........... | 4,604 | 4,299 | 68051 | Ralston............. | 2,977 | 1,500 |
| 63117 | Richmond Heights.... | 15,622 | 15,045 | 68661 | Schuyler............ | 3,096 | 2,883 |
| 63137 | Riverview........... | 3,706 | ...... | 69361 | Scottsbluff.......... | 13,377 | 12,858 |
| 63119 | Rock Hill........... | 6,523 | 3,847 | 68434 | Seward............. | 4,208 | 3,154 |
| 65401 | Rolla............... | 11,132 | 9,354 | 69162 | Sidney.............. | 8,004 | 4,912 |
| 63074 | St. Ann (A).......... | 15,654 | 4,557 | 68776 | South Sioux City..... | 7,200 | 5,557 |
| 63301 | St. Charles.......... | 21,189 | 14,314 | 68978 | Superior............ | 2,935 | 3,227 |
| 63077 | St. Clair........... | 2,711 | 1,779 | 69201 | Valentine........... | 2,875 | 2,700 |
| 63114 | St. John............ | 7,342 | 2,499 | 68066 | Wahoo............. | 3,610 | 3,128 |
| *64502 | St. Joseph.......... | 79,673 | 78,588 | 68787 | Wayne.............. | 4,217 | 3,595 |
| *63155 | St. Louis........... | 750,026 | 856,796 | 68788 | West Point.......... | 2,921 | 2,658 |
| 63670 | Ste. Genevieve....... | 4,443 | 3,992 | 68467 | York............... | 6,173 | 6,178 |
| 65560 | Salem.............. | 3,870 | 3,611 | | | | |
| 65301 | Sedalia............. | 23,874 | 20,354 | | **NEVADA** | | |
| 63119 | Shrewsbury.......... | 4,730 | 3,382 | 89005 | Boulder City........ | 4,059 | ...... |
| 63801 | Sikeston............ | 13,765 | 11,640 | 89701 | Carson City......... | 5,163 | 3,082 |
| 65349 | Slater............. | 2,767 | 2,836 | 89801 | Elko............... | 6,298 | 5,393 |
| *65801 | Springfield......... | 95,865 | 66,731 | 89301 | Ely................ | 4,018 | 3,558 |
| 64054 | Sugar Creek......... | 2,663 | 1,858 | 89406 | Fallon.............. | 2,734 | 2,400 |
| 63080 | Sullivan (A)......... | 4,368 | 3,019 | 89415 | Hawthorne.......... | 2,838 | ...... |
| 63127 | Sunset Hills......... | 3,525 | ...... | 89015 | Henderson.......... | 12,525 | ...... |
| 64683 | Trenton............ | 6,262 | 6,157 | *89101 | Las Vegas.......... | 64,405 | 24,625 |
| 63084 | Union.............. | 3,937 | 2,917 | 89030 | North Las Vegas..... | 18,422 | 3,875 |
| 63130 | University City....... | 51,249 | 39,892 | *89501 | Reno............... | 51,470 | 32,497 |
| 63088 | Valley Park......... | 3,452 | 2,956 | 89431 | Sparks............. | 16,618 | 8,203 |
| 63382 | Vandalia............ | 3,055 | 2,624 | 89445 | Winnemucca......... | 3,453 | 2,847 |

| ZIP Code | Place | 1960 | 1950 | ZIP Code | Place | 1960 | 1950 |
|---|---|---|---|---|---|---|---|
| | **NEW HAMPSHIRE** | | | | **NEW JERSEY**—Continued | | |
| | *See Note on Page 605* | | | *07011 | Clifton................ | 82,084 | 64,511 |
| 03102 | Bedford................ | 3,636 | 2,176 | 07624 | Closter................ | 7,767 | 3,376 |
| 03570 | Berlin................. | 17,821 | 16,615 | 08108 | Collingswood.......... | 17,370 | 15,800 |
| 03603 | Charlestown........... | 2,576 | 2,077 | 07016 | Cranford.............. | 26,424 | 18,602 |
| 03743 | Claremont............. | 13,563 | 12,811 | 07626 | Cresskill.............. | 7,290 | 3,534 |
| 03301 | Concord............... | 28,991 | 27,988 | 07627 | Demarest.............. | 4,231 | 1,786 |
| 03818 | Conway................ | 4,298 | 4,109 | 07801 | Dover................. | 13,034 | 11,174 |
| 03038 | Derry................. | 6,987 | 5,826 | 07628 | Dumont............... | 18,882 | 13,013 |
| 03820 | Dover................. | 19,131 | 15,874 | 08812 | Dunellen.............. | 6,840 | 6,291 |
| 03824 | Durham............... | 4,688 | 4,172 | 07017 | East Orange........... | 77,259 | 79,340 |
| | *Durham (town)*....... | 5,504 | 4,770 | 07407 | East Paterson......... | 19,344 | 15,386 |
| 03833 | Exeter................ | 5,896 | 4,977 | 07073 | East Rutherford....... | 7,769 | 7,438 |
| | *Exeter (town)*........ | 7,243 | 5,664 | 07724 | Eatontown............ | 10,334 | 3,044 |
| 03835 | Farmington............ | 3,287 | 3,454 | 07020 | Edgewater............ | 4,113 | 3,952 |
| 03235 | Franklin.............. | 6,742 | 6,552 | 08817 | Edison................ | 44,799 | 16,348 |
| 03045 | Goffstown............. | 7,230 | 5,638 | 08215 | Egg Harbor City...... | 4,416 | 3,838 |
| 03581 | Gorham................ | 3,039 | 2,639 | *07208 | Elizabeth............. | 107,698 | 112,817 |
| 03842 | Hampton.............. | 3,281 | 1,617 | 07630 | Emerson.............. | 6,849 | 1,744 |
| | *Hampton (town)*...... | 5,379 | 2,842 | 07631 | Englewood............ | 26,057 | 23,145 |
| 03755 | Hanover............... | 5,649 | 4,992 | 07632 | Englewood Cliffs...... | 2,913 | 966 |
| | *Hanover (town)*...... | 7,329 | 6,253 | ...... | Ewing................ | 26,628 | 16,840 |
| 03765 | Haverhill............. | 3,127 | 3,357 | 07701 | Fair Haven........... | 5,678 | 3,560 |
| 03106 | Hooksett.............. | 3,713 | 2,792 | 07410 | Fair Lawn............ | 36,421 | 23,885 |
| 03051 | Hudson................ | 3,651 | 2,382 | 07022 | Fairview.............. | 9,399 | 8,661 |
| | *Hudson (town)*....... | 5,876 | 4,183 | 07023 | Fanwood.............. | 7,963 | 3,228 |
| 03452 | Jaffrey............... | 3,154 | 2,911 | 08822 | Flemington............ | 3,232 | 3,058 |
| 03431 | Keene................. | 17,562 | 15,638 | 08518 | Florence.............. | 4,215 | ........ |
| 03246 | Laconia............... | 15,288 | 14,745 | 07932 | Florham Park......... | 7,222 | 2,385 |
| 03584 | Lancaster............. | 3,138 | 3,113 | 07024 | Fort Lee.............. | 21,815 | 11,648 |
| 03766 | Lebanon............... | 9,299 | 8,495 | 07416 | Franklin.............. | 3,624 | 3,864 |
| 03561 | Littleton............. | 3,355 | 3,819 | 07417 | Franklin Lakes........ | 3,316 | 2,021 |
| | *Littleton (town)*..... | 5,003 | 4,817 | 07728 | Freehold.............. | 9,140 | 7,550 |
| *03105 | Manchester............ | 88,282 | 82,732 | 07026 | Garfield.............. | 29,253 | 27,550 |
| 03054 | Merrimack............. | 2,989 | 1,908 | 07027 | Garwood.............. | 5,426 | 4,622 |
| 03055 | Milford............... | 3,916 | 3,269 | 08027 | Gibbstown............ | 2,820 | 2,546 |
| | *Milford (town)*...... | 4,863 | 4,159 | 08028 | Glassboro............ | 10,253 | 5,867 |
| 03060 | Nashua................ | 39,096 | 34,669 | 07028 | Glen Ridge........... | 8,322 | 7,620 |
| 03857 | Newmarket............ | 2,745 | 2,172 | 07452 | Glen Rock............ | 12,896 | 7,145 |
| | *Newmarket (town)*... | 3,153 | 2,709 | 08030 | Gloucester City....... | 15,511 | 14,357 |
| 03773 | Newport............... | 3,222 | 3,062 | 07093 | Guttenberg............ | 5,118 | 5,566 |
| | *Newport (town)*...... | 5,458 | 5,131 | *07601 | Hackensack........... | 30,521 | 29,219 |
| 05905 | Northumberland........ | 2,586 | 2,779 | 07840 | Hackettstown......... | 5,276 | 3,894 |
| 03076 | Pelham................ | 2,605 | 1,317 | 08108 | Haddon............... | 17,099 | 12,379 |
| | Pembroke.............. | 3,514 | 3,094 | 08033 | Haddonfield.......... | 13,201 | 10,495 |
| 03458 | Peterborough.......... | 2,963 | 2,556 | 08035 | Haddon Heights....... | 9,260 | 7,287 |
| 03865 | Plaistow.............. | 2,915 | 2,082 | 07508 | Haledon.............. | 6,461 | 6,204 |
| 03264 | Plymouth.............. | 3,210 | 3,039 | | Hamilton............. | 65,035 | 41,156 |
| 03801 | Portsmouth............ | 26,900 | 18,830 | 08037 | Hammonton........... | 9,854 | 8,411 |
| 03867 | Rochester............. | 15,927 | 13,776 | 07640 | Harrington Park...... | 3,581 | 1,634 |
| 03870 | Rye................... | 3,244 | 1,982 | 07029 | Harrison.............. | 11,743 | 13,490 |
| 03079 | Salem................. | 9,210 | 4,805 | 07604 | Hasbrouck Heights..... | 13,046 | 9,181 |
| 03079 | Salem Depot........... | 2,523 | 1,637 | 07641 | Haworth.............. | 3,215 | 1,612 |
| 03878 | Somersworth........... | 8,529 | 6,927 | 07506 | Hawthorne............ | 17,735 | 14,816 |
| | Swanzey............... | 3,626 | 2,806 | 08904 | Highland Park........ | 11,049 | 9,721 |
| 03608 | Walpole............... | 2,825 | 2,536 | 07732 | Highlands............ | 3,536 | 2,959 |
| 03038 | West Derry............ | 4,468 | ........ | 08520 | Hightstown........... | 4,317 | 3,712 |
| 03894 | Wolfeboro............. | 2,689 | 2,581 | 07642 | Hillsdale............. | 8,734 | 4,127 |
| | | | | 07205 | Hillside.............. | 22,304 | 21,007 |
| | **NEW JERSEY** | | | 07030 | Hoboken.............. | 48,441 | 50,676 |
| 08201 | Absecon............... | 4,320 | 2,355 | 07423 | Hohokus.............. | 3,988 | 2,254 |
| 07401 | Allendale............. | 4,092 | 2,409 | 07843 | Hopatcong............ | 3,391 | 1,173 |
| 07712 | Asbury Park........... | 17,366 | 17,094 | 07111 | Irvington............. | 59,739 | 59,201 |
| *08401 | Atlantic City......... | 59,544 | 61,657 | 08581 | Jamesburg............ | 2,853 | 2,307 |
| 07716 | Atlantic Highlands..... | 4,119 | 3,083 | *07303 | Jersey City........... | 276,101 | 299,017 |
| 08106 | Audubon............... | 10,440 | 9,531 | 07734 | Keansburg............ | 6,854 | 5,559 |
| 08007 | Barrington............ | 7,943 | 2,651 | 07032 | Kearny............... | 37,472 | 39,952 |
| 07002 | Bayonne............... | 74,215 | 77,203 | 07033 | Kenilworth........... | 8,379 | 4,922 |
| 08722 | Beachwood............ | 2,765 | 1,251 | 07735 | Keyport.............. | 6,440 | 5,888 |
| 07109 | Belleville............ | 35,005 | 32,019 | 07405 | Kinnelon............. | 4,431 | 1,350 |
| 08030 | Bellmawr............. | 11,853 | 5,213 | 08733 | Lakehurst............ | 2,780 | 1,518 |
| 07719 | Belmar................ | 5,190 | 4,636 | 07871 | Lake Mohawk......... | 4,647 | 1,873 |
| 07823 | Belvidere............. | 2,636 | 2,406 | 08701 | Lakewood............ | 13,004 | 9,970 |
| 07621 | Bergenfield........... | 27,203 | 17,647 | 08530 | Lambertville......... | 4,269 | 4,477 |
| 08009 | Berlin................ | 3,578 | 2,339 | 07605 | Leonia............... | 8,384 | 7,378 |
| 07924 | Bernardsville......... | 5,515 | 3,956 | ...... | Levittown  *(See Willingboro)* | | |
| 08010 | Beverly............... | 3,400 | 3,084 | 07035 | Lincoln Park.......... | 6,048 | 3,376 |
| 07003 | Bloomfield............ | 51,867 | 49,307 | 07036 | Linden............... | 39,931 | 30,644 |
| 07403 | Bloomingdale.......... | 5,293 | 3,251 | 08021 | Lindenwold........... | 7,335 | 3,479 |
| 07603 | Bogota................ | 7,965 | 7,662 | 08221 | Linwood.............. | 3,847 | 1,925 |
| 07005 | Boonton............... | 7,981 | 7,163 | 07424 | Little Falls........... | 9,730 | 6,405 |
| 08505 | Bordentown............ | 4,974 | 5,497 | 07643 | Little Ferry.......... | 6,175 | 4,955 |
| 08805 | Bound Brook.......... | 10,263 | 8,374 | 07739 | Little Silver......... | 5,202 | 2,595 |
| 07720 | Bradley Beach........ | 4,204 | 3,911 | 07039 | Livingston............ | 23,124 | 9,932 |
| 08302 | Bridgeton............. | 20,966 | 18,378 | 07644 | Lodi................. | 23,502 | 15,392 |
| 08730 | Brielle............... | 2,619 | 1,328 | 07740 | Long Branch.......... | 26,228 | 23,090 |
| 08203 | Brigantine............ | 4,201 | 1,267 | 07071 | Lyndhurst............ | 21,867 | 19,980 |
| 08030 | Brooklawn............ | 2,504 | 2,262 | 07940 | Madison.............. | 15,122 | 10,417 |
| 08310 | Buena................ | 3,243 | 2,640 | 08049 | Magnolia............. | 4,199 | 1,883 |
| 08016 | Burlington............ | 12,687 | 12,051 | 08736 | Manasquan........... | 4,022 | 3,178 |
| 07405 | Butler................ | 5,414 | 4,050 | 08835 | Manville............. | 10,995 | 8,597 |
| 07006 | Caldwell.............. | 6,942 | 6,270 | 08052 | Maple Shade.......... | 12,947 | 6,560 |
| *08101 | Camden............... | 117,159 | 124,555 | 07040 | Maplewood............ | 23,977 | 25,201 |
| 08204 | Cape May............. | 4,477 | 3,607 | 08402 | Margate City......... | 9,474 | 4,715 |
| 07072 | Carlstadt............. | 6,042 | 5,591 | 07747 | Matawan............. | 5,097 | 3,739 |
| 07008 | Carteret.............. | 20,502 | 13,030 | 07607 | Maywood............. | 11,460 | 8,667 |
| 07009 | Cedar Grove.......... | 14,603 | 8,022 | 08055 | Medford Lakes........ | 2,876 | 461 |
| 07928 | Chatham.............. | 9,517 | 7,391 | 08109 | Merchantville........ | 4,075 | 4,183 |
| 08034 | Cherry Hill *(formerly* | | | 08840 | Metuchen............. | 14,041 | 9,879 |
| | *Delaware)*.......... | 31,522 | 10,385 | 08846 | Middlesex............ | 10,520 | 5,943 |
| 07066 | Clark................. | 12,195 | 4,352 | 07748 | Middletown........... | 39,675 | 16,203 |
| 08312 | Clayton............... | 4,711 | 3,023 | 07432 | Midland Park......... | 7,543 | 5,164 |
| 08021 | Clementon............ | 3,766 | 3,191 | 07041 | Millburn............. | 18,799 | 14,506 |
| 07010 | Cliffside Park........ | 17,642 | 17,116 | 08850 | Millstown............ | 5,435 | 3,786 |

| ZIP Code | Place | 1960 | 1950 | ZIP Code | Place | 1960 | 1950 |
|---|---|---|---|---|---|---|---|
| | **NEW JERSEY—Continued** | | | | **NEW JERSEY—Continued** | | |
| 08332 | Millville................. | 19,096 | 16,041 | 07670 | Tenafly................. | 14,264 | 9,651 |
| *07042 | Montclair............... | 43,129 | 43,927 | 08753 | Toms River............. | 6,062 | 2,517 |
| 07645 | Montvale................ | 3,699 | 1,856 | 07512 | Totowa................. | 10,897 | 6,045 |
| 07074 | Moonachie.............. | 3,052 | 1,775 | *08609 | Trenton................. | 114,167 | 128,009 |
| 07950 | Morris Plains........... | 4,703 | 2,707 | 07083 | Union.................. | 51,499 | 38,004 |
| 07960 | Morristown............. | 17,712 | 17,124 | 07735 | Union Beach............ | 5,862 | 3,636 |
| 07046 | Mountain Lakes......... | 4,037 | 2,806 | 07087 | Union City............. | 52,180 | 55,537 |
| 07092 | Mountainside........... | 6,325 | 2,046 | 07458 | Upper Saddle River..... | 3,570 | 706 |
| 08059 | Mt. Ephraim............ | 5,447 | 4,449 | 08406 | Ventnor City........... | 8,688 | 8,158 |
| 08060 | Mt. Holly.............. | 13,271 | 8,206 | 07044 | Verona................. | 13,752 | 10,921 |
| 08063 | National Park.......... | 3,380 | 2,419 | 08360 | Vineland............... | 37,685 | 8,155 |
| 07753 | Neptune................ | 21,487 | 13,613 | 07463 | Waldwick............... | 10,495 | 3,963 |
| 07753 | Neptune City........... | 4,013 | 3,073 | 07463 | Wallington............. | 9,261 | 8,910 |
| 07857 | Netcong................ | 2,765 | 2,284 | 07712 | Wanamassa............. | 3,928 | 2,512 |
| *07102 | Newark................. | 405,220 | 438,776 | 07465 | Wanaque............... | 7,126 | 4,222 |
| *08901 | New Brunswick.......... | 40,139 | 38,811 | 07882 | Washington............. | 5,723 | 4,802 |
| | New Hanover............ | 28,528 | 18,168 | 07060 | Watchung.............. | 3,312 | 1,818 |
| 07646 | New Milford............ | 18,810 | 6,006 | 07470 | Wayne................. | 29,353 | 11,822 |
| 07974 | New Providence......... | 10,243 | 3,380 | 07087 | Weehawken............. | 13,504 | 14,830 |
| 07724 | New Shrewsbury........ | 7,313 | | 07719 | West Belmar............ | 2,511 | 2,058 |
| 07860 | Newton................ | 6,563 | 5,781 | 07006 | West Caldwell.......... | 8,314 | 4,666 |
| 07032 | North Arlington........ | 17,477 | 15,970 | 07090 | Westfield.............. | 31,447 | 21,243 |
| 07047 | North Bergen........... | 42,387 | 41,560 | 07764 | West Long Branch....... | 5,337 | 2,739 |
| 07006 | North Caldwell......... | 4,163 | 1,781 | 07093 | West New York......... | 35,547 | 37,683 |
| 08225 | Northfield.............. | 5,849 | 3,498 | 07052 | West Orange........... | 39,895 | 28,605 |
| 07508 | North Haledon.......... | 6,026 | 3,550 | 07424 | West Paterson.......... | 7,602 | 3,931 |
| 07060 | North Plainfield........ | 16,993 | 12,766 | 08093 | Westville............... | 4,951 | 4,731 |
| 08540 | North Princeton........ | 4,506 | 1,721 | 07675 | Westwood.............. | 9,046 | 6,766 |
| 07647 | Northvale.............. | 2,892 | 1,455 | 07885 | Wharton............... | 5,006 | 3,853 |
| 08260 | North Wildwood........ | 3,598 | 3,158 | 08260 | Wildwood.............. | 4,690 | 5,475 |
| 07648 | Norwood............... | 2,552 | 1,792 | 08260 | Wildwood Crest........ | 3,011 | 1,772 |
| 07110 | Nutley................. | 29,513 | 26,992 | 08094 | Williamstown.......... | 2,722 | 2,632 |
| 07755 | Oakhurst.............. | 4,374 | 2,388 | 08046 | Willingboro, '67....... | 33,656 | |
| 07436 | Oakland................ | 9,446 | 1,817 | 08270 | Woodbine.............. | 2,823 | 2,417 |
| 08107 | Oaklyn................. | 4,778 | 4,889 | 07095 | Woodbridge............ | 78,846 | 35,758 |
| 08226 | Ocean City............. | 7,618 | 6,040 | 08096 | Woodbury.............. | 12,455 | 10,931 |
| 07757 | Oceanport.............. | 4,937 | 7,588 | 07680 | Woodcliff Lake......... | 2,742 | 1,420 |
| 07649 | Oradell................ | 7,487 | 3,656 | 08107 | Wood-Lynne............ | 3,128 | 2,776 |
| *07050 | Orange................. | 35,789 | 38,037 | 07075 | Wood-Ridge............ | 7,964 | 6,283 |
| 07650 | Palisades Park.......... | 11,943 | 9,635 | 08098 | Woodstown............. | 2,942 | 2,345 |
| 08065 | Palmyra................ | 7,036 | 5,802 | 08562 | Wrightstown........... | 4,864 | 1,190 |
| 07652 | Paramus............... | 23,238 | 6,268 | 07481 | Wyckoff............... | 11,205 | 5,590 |
| 07656 | Park Ridge............. | 6,389 | 3,189 | | **NEW MEXICO** | | |
| 07054 | Parsippany-Troy Hills... | 25,557 | 15,290 | | | | |
| 07055 | Passaic................ | 53,963 | 57,702 | 88310 | Alamogordo............ | 21,723 | 6,783 |
| *07510 | Paterson............... | 143,663 | 139,336 | *87101 | Albuquerque............ | 201,189 | 96,815 |
| 08066 | Paulsboro.............. | 8,121 | 7,842 | 88210 | Artesia................ | 12,000 | 8,244 |
| 08110 | Pennsauken............ | 33,711 | 22,767 | 87410 | Aztec.................. | 4,137 | 885 |
| 08069 | Penns Grove............ | 6,176 | 6,669 | 87002 | Belen.................. | 5,031 | 4,495 |
| 08861 | Perth Amboy........... | 38,007 | 41,330 | 87004 | Bernalillo.............. | 2,574 | 1,922 |
| 08865 | Phillipsburg............ | 18,502 | 18,919 | 88220 | Carlsbad............... | 25,541 | 17,975 |
| 08021 | Pine Hill............... | 3,939 | 2,546 | 88415 | Clayton................ | 3,515 | 3,515 |
| 08071 | Pitman................. | 8,644 | 6,960 | 88101 | Clovis................. | 23,713 | 17,318 |
| *07060 | Plainfield.............. | 45,330 | 42,366 | 88030 | Deming................ | 6,764 | 5,672 |
| 08232 | Pleasantville........... | 15,172 | 11,938 | 88231 | Eunice................. | 3,531 | 2,352 |
| 08742 | Point Pleasant.......... | 10,182 | 4,009 | 87401 | Farmington............ | 23,786 | 3,637 |
| 08742 | Point Pleasant Beach.... | 3,873 | 2,900 | 87301 | Gallup................. | 14,089 | 9,133 |
| 07442 | Pompton Lakes......... | 9,445 | 4,654 | 87020 | Grants................. | 10,274 | 2,251 |
| 08540 | Princeton.............. | 11,890 | 12,230 | 88240 | Hobbs................. | 26,275 | 13,875 |
| | Prospect Park.......... | 5,201 | 5,242 | 88252 | Jal.................... | 3,051 | 2,047 |
| *07065 | Rahway................ | 27,699 | 21,290 | 88001 | Las Cruces............. | 29,367 | 12,325 |
| 07446 | Ramsey................ | 9,527 | 4,670 | 87701 | Las Vegas (city)....... | 7,790 | 7,494 |
| 08869 | Raritan (Somerset Co.). | 6,137 | 5,131 | 87701 | Las Vegas (town)....... | 6,028 | 6,269 |
| | Raritan (Monmouth Co.) | 15,334 | 2,763 | 88045 | Lordsburg............. | 3,436 | 3,525 |
| 07701 | Red Bank.............. | 12,482 | 12,743 | 87544 | Los Alamos............ | 12,584 | 9,934 |
| 07657 | Ridgefield.............. | 10,788 | 8,312 | 88260 | Lovington............. | 9,660 | 3,134 |
| 07660 | Ridgefield Park......... | 12,701 | 11,993 | 87020 | Milan.................. | 2,658 | ...... |
| *07450 | Ridgewood............. | 25,391 | 17,481 | 88130 | Portales............... | 9,695 | 8,112 |
| 07456 | Ringwood.............. | 4,182 | 1,752 | 87740 | Raton................. | 8,146 | 8,241 |
| 07457 | Riverdale.............. | 2,596 | 1,352 | 88201 | Roswell................ | 39,593 | 25,738 |
| 07661 | River Edge............. | 13,264 | 9,204 | 87501 | Santa Fe............... | 33,394 | 27,998 |
| 08075 | Riverside.............. | 8,474 | 7,199 | 88061 | Silver City............ | 6,972 | 7,022 |
| 08077 | Riverton............... | 3,324 | 2,761 | 87801 | Socorro................ | 5,271 | 4,334 |
| 07662 | Rochelle Park.......... | 6,119 | 4,483 | 88070 | State College )........ | 4,387 | ...... |
| 07866 | Rockaway.............. | 5,413 | 3,812 | 88047 | Mesilla Park }......... | | |
| 08554 | Roebling............... | 3,272 | ...... | 87901 | Truth or Consequences.. | 4,269 | 4,563 |
| 07068 | Roseland............... | 2,804 | 2,019 | 88401 | Tucumcari.............. | 8,143 | 8,419 |
| 07203 | Roselle................ | 21,032 | 17,681 | 88352 | Tularosa............... | 3,200 | 1,642 |
| 07204 | Roselle Park........... | 12,546 | 11,537 | 87327 | Zuni Pueblo............ | 3,585 | 2,563 |
| 07760 | Rumson................ | 6,405 | 4,044 | | **NEW YORK** | | |
| 08078 | Runnemede............ | 8,396 | 4,217 | | | | |
| *07070 | Rutherford............. | 20,473 | 17,411 | 14001 | Akron, '66............ | 2,786 | 2,481 |
| 07662 | Saddle Brook........... | 13,834 | 7,955 | *12201 | Albany................ | 129,726 | 134,990 |
| 08079 | Salem.................. | 8,941 | 9,050 | 14411 | Albion................ | 5,182 | 4,855 |
| 08872 | Sayreville.............. | 22,553 | 10,338 | 14004 | Alden, '66............ | 2,694 | 1,252 |
| 07076 | Scotch Plains.......... | 18,491 | 9,069 | 14802 | Alfred, '65............ | 3,303 | 2,053 |
| 07094 | Secaucus............... | 12,154 | 9,750 | 11701 | Amityville, '67........ | 8,675 | 6,164 |
| 07701 | Shrewsbury............ | 3,222 | 1,613 | 12010 | Amsterdam............ | 28,772 | 32,240 |
| 08083 | Somerdale.............. | 4,839 | 1,417 | 14006 | Angola, '66........... | 2,550 | 1,936 |
| 08244 | Somers Point........... | 4,504 | 2,480 | 10502 | Ardsley, '65........... | 4,486 | 1,744 |
| 08876 | Somerville............. | 12,458 | 11,571 | 12603 | Arlington.............. | 8,317 | 5,374 |
| 08879 | South Amboy........... | 8,422 | 8,422 | 14011 | Attica................. | 2,758 | 2,676 |
| 08880 | South Bound Brook..... | 3,626 | 2,905 | 13021 | Auburn................ | 35,249 | 36,722 |
| 07079 | South Orange.......... | 16,175 | 15,230 | 14410 | Avon.................. | 2,772 | 2,412 |
| 07080 | South Plainfield........ | 17,879 | 8,008 | 11702 | Babylon, '67.......... | 12,885 | 6,015 |
| 08882 | South River............ | 13,397 | 11,308 | 11510 | Baldwin............... | 30,204 | ...... |
| 08884 | Spotswood............. | 5,788 | 2,325 | 13027 | Baldwinsville, '65...... | 6,076 | 4,495 |
| 07081 | Springfield............. | 14,467 | 7,214 | 12020 | Ballston Spa, '66...... | 4,814 | 4,937 |
| 07762 | Spring Lake............ | 2,922 | 2,008 | 14020 | Batavia................ | 18,210 | 17,799 |
| 07762 | Spring Lake Heights.... | 3,309 | 1,798 | 14810 | Bath.................. | 6,166 | 5,416 |
| 08084 | Stratford.............. | 4,308 | 1,356 | 11709 | Bayville, '65.......... | 4,988 | 1,981 |
| 07901 | Summit................ | 23,677 | 17,929 | 12508 | Beacon................ | 13,922 | 14,012 |
| 07666 | Teaneck................ | 42,085 | 33,772 | 11710 | Bellmore.............. | 12,784 | ...... |

## NEW YORK—Continued

| ZIP Code | Place | 1960 | 1950 |
|---|---|---|---|
| 11713 | Bellport, '66 | 2,774 | ....... |
| 11714 | Bethpage-Old Bethpage. | 20,515 | ....... |
| *13901 | Binghamton, '66 | 69,435 | 80,674 |
| 14219 | Blasdell, '66 | 3,786 | 3,127 |
| 11715 | Blue Point, '64 | 2,676 | ....... |
| 11717 | Brentwood, '64 | 22,923 | 2,803 |
| 10510 | Briarcliff Manor, '65 | 3,735 | 2,494 |
| 11718 | Brightwaters, '64 | 3,389 | 2,336 |
| 14420 | Brockport, '64 | 6,058 | 4,748 |
| 10708 | Bronxville, '65 | 6,735 | 6,778 |
| 11545 | Brookville, '65 | 2,601 | 337 |
| *14205 | Buffalo, '66 | 481,453 | 580,132 |
| 13316 | Camden, '66 | 2,694 | 2,407 |
| 13317 | Canajoharie | 2,681 | 2,761 |
| 14424 | Canandaigua, '65 | 10,058 | 8,332 |
| 13032 | Canastota, '65 | 4,971 | 4,458 |
| 14823 | Canisteo | 2,731 | 2,625 |
| 13617 | Canton, '67 | 5,570 | 4,379 |
| 13619 | Carthage | 4,216 | 4,420 |
| 12414 | Catskill | 5,825 | 5,392 |
| 14850 | Cayuga Heights, '67 | 3,374 | 1,131 |
| 13035 | Cazenovia, '65 | 2,676 | 1,946 |
| 11516 | Cedarhurst, '65 | 6,824 | 6,051 |
| 11720 | Centereach, '64 | 10,921 | ....... |
| 11934 | Center Moriches, '64 | 3,010 | 1,761 |
| 11721 | Centerport | 3,628 | ....... |
| 14225 | Cheektowaga-Northwest. | 52,362 | ....... |
|  | Southwest. | 12,766 | ....... |
| 13037 | Chittenango, '65 | 3,479 | 1,307 |
| 14433 | Clyde, '66 | 2,735 | 2,492 |
| 12043 | Cobleskill, '67 | 4,000 | 3,208 |
| 12047 | Cohoes | 20,129 | 21,272 |
| ..... | Colonie, '66 | 8,453 | 2,068 |
| 11725 | Commack | 9,613 | ....... |
| 13326 | Cooperstown | 2,553 | 2,727 |
| 11726 | Copiague, '64 | 17,584 | ....... |
| 12822 | Corinth, '66 | 3,184 | 3,161 |
| 14830 | Corning | 17,085 | 17,684 |
| 12518 | Cornwall, '67 | 3,127 | 2,211 |
| 12518 | Cornwall SW | 2,824 | ....... |
| 13045 | Cortland | 19,181 | 18,152 |
| 12051 | Coxsackie | 2,849 | 2,722 |
| 10520 | Croton-on-Hudson, '66 | 7,039 | 4,837 |
| 12929 | Dannemora | 4,835 | 4,122 |
| 14437 | Dansville | 5,460 | 5,253 |
| 11729 | Deer Park, '64 | 24,700 | ....... |
| 13753 | Delhi, '65 | 2,664 | 1,841 |
| 14043 | Depew, '66 | 18,309 | 7,217 |
| 10522 | Dobbs Ferry, '65 | 10,076 | 6,268 |
| 13329 | Dolgeville | 3,058 | 3,204 |
| 14048 | Dunkirk | 18,205 | 18,007 |
| 14052 | East Aurora, '66 | 6,796 | 5,962 |
| 11576 | East Hills, '65 | 8,441 | 2,547 |
| 11758 | East Massapequa | 14,779 | ....... |
| 11554 | East Meadow | 46,036 | ....... |
| 11743 | East Neck | 3,789 | ....... |
| 11731 | East Northport | 8,381 | 3,842 |
| 11772 | East Patchogue, '64 | 6,883 | ....... |
| 14445 | East Rochester, '67 | 8,438 | 7,022 |
| 11518 | East Rockaway, '64 | 11,708 | 7,970 |
| 13057 | East Syracuse, '66 | 4,623 | 4,766 |
| 11596 | East Williston, '65 | 2,872 | 1,734 |
| 14226 | Eggertsville | 44,807 | ....... |
| 12428 | Ellenville | 5,003 | 4,225 |
| *14901 | Elmira | 46,517 | 49,716 |
| 14903 | Elmira Heights, '65 | 5,105 | 5,009 |
| 14904 | Elmira SE | 6,698 | ....... |
| 11003 | Elmont | 30,138 | ....... |
| 10523 | Elmsford, '65 | 4,031 | 3,147 |
| 13760 | Endicott, '66 | 17,473 | 20,050 |
| 13760 | Endicott, '64 | 17,704 | 20,050 |
| 14450 | Fairport, '67 | 5,993 | 5,267 |
| 12601 | Fairview | 8,626 | 1,721 |
| 14733 | Falconer | 3,343 | 3,292 |
| 11735 | Farmingdale, '65 | 7,637 | 4,492 |
| 11738 | Farmingville, '64 | 2,842 | ....... |
| 13066 | Fayette, '64 | 4,702 | 2,624 |
| *10001 | Floral Park, '65 | 17,762 | 14,558 |
| 11050 | Flower Hill, '65 | 4,706 | 1,948 |
| 12828 | Fort Edward | 3,737 | 3,797 |
| 13339 | Fort Plain | 2,809 | 2,935 |
| 13340 | Frankfort | 3,872 | 3,844 |
| 11010 | Franklin Square | 32,483 | ....... |
| 14063 | Fredonia, '65 | 9,388 | 7,095 |
| 11520 | Freeport, '65 | 38,429 | 24,680 |
| 13069 | Fulton | 14,261 | 13,922 |
| 11530 | Garden City, '65 | 24,661 | 14,486 |
| 11040 | Garden City Park- | | |
|  | Herricks | 15,364 | ....... |
| 14454 | Geneseo, '66 | 4,415 | 2,838 |
| 14456 | Geneva | 17,286 | 17,144 |
| 11542 | Glen Cove, '65 | 25,048 | 15,130 |
| 12801 | Glens Falls | 18,580 | 19,610 |
| 12078 | Gloversville | 21,741 | 23,634 |
| 10924 | Goshen, '67 | 4,133 | 3,311 |
| 13642 | Gouverneur | 4,946 | 4,916 |
| 14070 | Gowanda | 3,352 | 3,289 |
| 12832 | Granville | 2,715 | 2,826 |
| 11020 | Great Neck, '65 | 10,306 | 7,759 |
| 11021 | Great Neck Estates, '65 | 3,384 | 2,464 |
| 11021 | Great Neck Plaza, '65 | 5,456 | 4,246 |
| 12183 | Green Island | 3,533 | 4,016 |
| 11740 | Greenlawn | 5,422 | 1,000 |
| 11944 | Greenport | 2,608 | 3,028 |
| 11743 | Halesite | 2,857 | ....... |
| 14075 | Hamburg, '66 | 9,493 | 6,938 |
| 14075 | Hamburg-Lake Shore | 11,527 | ....... |
| 13346 | Hamilton, '66 | 3,499 | 3,507 |
| 14221 | Harris Hill | 3,944 | ....... |
| 10706 | Hastings-on-Hudson, '65 | 9,777 | 7,565 |
| 10927 | Haverstraw, '66 | 7,293 | 5,818 |
| *11550 | Hempstead, '65 | 37,192 | 29,135 |
| 14467 | Henrietta NE | 6,403 | ....... |
| 13350 | Herkimer | 9,396 | 9,400 |
| *11801 | Hicksville | 50,405 | ....... |
| 12528 | Highland | 2,931 | 3,035 |
| 10928 | Highland Falls, '67 | 4,600 | 3,930 |
| 11741 | Holbrook, '64 | 4,786 | ....... |
| 13077 | Homer | 3,622 | 3,244 |
| 12090 | Hoosick Falls | 4,023 | 4,297 |
| 14843 | Hornell | 13,907 | 15,049 |
| 14845 | Horseheads, '65 | 7,854 | 3,606 |
| 12534 | Hudson | 11,075 | 11,639 |
| 12839 | Hudson Falls | 7,752 | 7,236 |
| 11743 | Huntington | 11,255 | 9,324 |
| 11746 | Huntington Station | 23,438 | 9,924 |
| 13357 | Ilion | 10,199 | 9,363 |
| 11696 | Inwood | 10,362 | ....... |
| 10533 | Irvington, '65 | 5,686 | 3,657 |
| 11558 | Island Park, '65 | 4,713 | 2,031 |
| 14851 | Ithaca | 28,799 | 29,257 |
| 14701 | Jamestown | 41,818 | 43,354 |
| 11753 | Jericho | 10,795 | ....... |
| 13790 | Johnson City, '66 | 20,442 | 19,249 |
| 12095 | Johnstown | 10,390 | 10,923 |
| 14217 | Kenmore, '66 | 21,146 | 20,066 |
| 11754 | Kings Park, '64 | 5,673 | 10,960 |
| 11024 | Kings Point, '65 | 5,826 | 2,445 |
| 12401 | Kingston | 29,260 | 28,817 |
| 14218 | Lackawanna, '66 | 28,717 | 27,658 |
| 10512 | Lake Carmel | 2,735 | 1,055 |
| 12946 | Lake Placid | 2,998 | 2,999 |
| 11779 | Lake Ronkonkoma, '64 | 7,951 | ....... |
| 11040 | Lake Success, '65 | 3,176 | 1,264 |
| 14750 | Lakewood, '67 | 4,168 | 3,013 |
| 14086 | Lancaster, '66 | 13,408 | 8,665 |
| 10538 | Larchmont, '65 | 6,860 | 6,330 |
| 11559 | Lawrence, '65 | 5,813 | 4,681 |
| 14482 | Le Roy | 4,662 | 4,721 |
| 11756 | Levittown | 65,276 | ....... |
| 14092 | Lewiston, '67 | 3,337 | 1,626 |
| 12754 | Liberty | 4,704 | 4,658 |
| 14223 | Lincoln Park | 2,707 | 1,527 |
| 11757 | Lindenhurst, '67 | 25,790 | 8,644 |
| 13365 | Little Falls | 8,935 | 9,541 |
| 13088 | Liverpool, '65 | 3,308 | 2,933 |
| ..... | Lloyd Harbor, '67 | 3,124 | 945 |
| 14094 | Lockport, '67 | 25,616 | 25,133 |
| ..... | Locust Grove | 11,558 | ....... |
| 11561 | Long Beach, '64 | 28,490 | 15,586 |
| 13367 | Lowville | 3,616 | 3,671 |
| 11563 | Lynbrook, '65 | 20,784 | 17,314 |
| 14489 | Lyons, '66 | 4,397 | 4,217 |
| 12953 | Malone | 8,737 | 9,501 |
| 11565 | Malverne, '65 | 9,899 | 8,086 |
| 10543 | Mamaroneck, '65 | 19,074 | 15,016 |
| 13104 | Manlius, '64 | 2,781 | ....... |
| 11050 | Manorhaven, '65 | 4,738 | 1,819 |
| 11758 | Massapequa | 32,900 | ....... |
| 11762 | Massapequa Park, '65 | 21,886 | 2,334 |
| 13662 | Massena | 15,478 | 13,137 |
| 11951 | Mastic Beach, '64 | 3,607 | 1,079 |
| (X) | Mastic Shirley, '64 | 4,494 | ....... |
| 12118 | Mechanicville, '66 | 6,189 | 7,385 |
| 14103 | Medina | 6,681 | 6,179 |
| 12204 | Menands, '66 | 2,919 | ....... |
| 11566 | Merrick | 18,789 | ....... |
| 10940 | Middletown, '67 | 21,549 | 22,586 |
| 11501 | Mineola, '65 | 22,052 | 14,831 |
| 13407 | Mohawk | 3,533 | 3,196 |
| 10950 | Monroe, '67 | 3,885 | 1,753 |
| 12701 | Monticello | 5,222 | 4,223 |
| 10549 | Mount Kisco, '65 | 6,941 | 5,907 |
| 14510 | Mount Morris | 3,250 | 3,450 |
| *10550 | Mount Vernon, '65 | 72,918 | 71,899 |
| ..... | Munsey Park, '65 | 2,905 | 2,048 |
| 11767 | Nesconset, '64 | 2,628 | ....... |
| 14513 | Newark, '66 | 11,676 | 10,295 |
| 12550 | Newburgh, '65 | 27,171 | 31,956 |
| 11040 | New Hyde Park, '65 | 10,916 | 7,349 |
| 12561 | New Paltz, '65 | 4,161 | 2,285 |
| 10802 | New Rochelle, '65 | 75,206 | 59,725 |
| *12550 | New Windsor | 2,904 | 2,754 |
| *10001 | New York | 7,781,984 | 7,891,957 |
| *10451 | Bronx | 1,424,815 | 1,451,277 |
| *10001 | Brooklyn | 2,627,319 | 2,738,175 |
| *10001 | Manhattan | 1,698,281 | 1,960,101 |
| * (Q) | Queens | 1,809,578 | 1,550,849 |
| *10301 | Richmond | 221,991 | 191,555 |

(Q) There are 4 Zip Codes for Queens; 11101 for
L. I. City; 11691 for Far Rockaway; 11351 for
Flushing and 11431 for Jamaica.

(X) Mastic 11950; Shirley 11967.

| ZIP Code | Place | 1960 | 1950 |
|---|---|---|---|
| | **NEW YORK—Continued** | | |
| 13417 | New York Mills | 3,788 | 3,366 |
| *14302 | Niagara Falls, '67 | 88,286 | 90,872 |
| 11710 | North Bellmore | 19,639 | |
| 11566 | North Merrick | 12,976 | |
| 11040 | North New Hyde Park | 17,929 | |
| 10803 | North Pelham, '65 | 5,322 | 5,046 |
| 11768 | Northport, '67 | 6,848 | 3,859 |
| 13212 | North Syracuse, '67 | 8,395 | 3,356 |
| 10591 | North Tarrytown, '65 | 8,600 | 8,740 |
| 14120 | North Tonawanda, '67 | 35,994 | 24,731 |
| 11580 | North Valley Stream | 17,239 | |
| 13815 | Norwich | 9,175 | 8,816 |
| 10960 | Nyack, '66 | 5,400 | 5,889 |
| 11572 | Oceanside | 30,448 | |
| 13669 | Ogdensburg | 16,122 | 16,166 |
| 14760 | Olean | 21,868 | 22,884 |
| 13421 | Oneida | 11,677 | 11,325 |
| 13820 | Oneonta | 14,531 | 13,564 |
| 14127 | Orchard Park, '66 | 3,506 | 2,054 |
| 10562 | Ossining, '65 | 21,241 | 16,098 |
| 13126 | Oswego | 22,155 | 22,647 |
| 13827 | Owego, '66 | 5,439 | 5,350 |
| 14870 | Painted Post | 2,570 | 2,405 |
| 14522 | Palmyra, '66 | 3,486 | 3,034 |
| 11772 | Patchogue, '66 | 9,678 | 7,361 |
| 10566 | Peekskill, '65 | 18,504 | 17,731 |
| 10803 | Pelham Manor, '65 | 6,285 | 5,306 |
| 14527 | Penn Yan | 5,770 | 5,451 |
| 14530 | Perry | 4,629 | 4,533 |
| | Plainedge | 21,973 | |
| 11803 | Plainview | 27,710 | |
| 12901 | Plattsburgh, '64 | 21,090 | 17,738 |
| 10570 | Pleasantville, '65 | 6,361 | 4,861 |
| 10573 | Port Chester, '65 | 24,755 | 23,970 |
| 12466 | Port Ewen | 2,622 | 1,885 |
| 11777 | Port Jefferson, '66 | 4,440 | |
| 12771 | Port Jervis, '67 | 8,601 | 9,372 |
| 11050 | Port Washington | 15,657 | |
| 13676 | Potsdam, '65 | 8,673 | 7,491 |
| *12601 | Poughkeepsie | 38,330 | 41,023 |
| 12143 | Ravena, '65 | 2,718 | 2,006 |
| 12144 | Rensselaer | 10,506 | 10,856 |
| 11901 | Riverhead | 5,830 | 4,892 |
| *14603 | Rochester, '64 | 305,849 | 332,488 |
| *11570 | Rockville Centre, '65 | 26,413 | 22,362 |
| 11778 | Rocky Point, '64 | 2,848 | |
| 13440 | Rome, '67 | 46,171 | 41,682 |
| 11779 | Ronkonkoma | 4,220 | 1,334 |
| 11575 | Roosevelt | 12,883 | |
| 11576 | Roslyn, '65 | 2,515 | 1,612 |
| 12303 | Rotterdam | 16,871 | |
| 10580 | Rye, '65 | 15,232 | 11,721 |
| 11780 | St. James, '64 | 4,688 | 1,390 |
| 14779 | Salamanca | 8,480 | 8,861 |
| 11754 | San Remo | 11,996 | |
| 12983 | Saranac Lake | 6,421 | 6,913 |
| 12866 | Saratoga Springs, '66 | 17,288 | 15,473 |
| 12477 | Saugerties, '65 | 4,353 | 3,907 |
| 10583 | Scarsdale, '65 | 18,345 | 13,156 |
| *12305 | Schenectady | 81,682 | 91,785 |
| 12302 | Scotia | 7,625 | 7,812 |
| 11579 | Sea Cliff, '65 | 5,774 | 4,868 |
| 11783 | Seaford | 14,718 | |
| 13148 | Seneca Falls, '67 | 7,646 | 6,634 |
| 13461 | Sherrill | 2,922 | 2,236 |
| 13838 | Sidney | 5,157 | 4,815 |
| 14136 | Silver Creek | 3,310 | 3,068 |
| 13152 | Skaneateles | 2,921 | 2,331 |
| 14212 | Sloan, '66 | 5,493 | 4,698 |
| 10974 | Sloatsburg, '66 | 2,805 | 2,018 |
| 13209 | Solvay, '66 | 8,551 | 7,868 |
| 11968 | Southampton '66 | 4,833 | 4,042 |
| 11735 | South Farmingdale | 16,318 | |
| 12801 | South Glens Falls, '66 | 4,149 | 3,645 |
| | South Huntington | 7,084 | 1,274 |
| 10960 | South Nyack, '66 | 3,377 | 3,102 |
| 11590 | South Westbury | 11,977 | |
| 14559 | Spencerport, '64 | 2,676 | 1,595 |
| 10977 | Spring Valley, '66 | 12,892 | 4,500 |
| 14141 | Springville, '66 | 4,137 | 3,322 |
| 11530 | Stewart Manor, '65 | 2,514 | 1,879 |
| 11790 | Stony Brook | 3,548 | |
| 10980 | Stony Point | 3,330 | 1,438 |
| 10901 | Suffern, '66 | 6,121 | 4,010 |
| *13201 | Syracuse | 216,038 | 220,583 |
| 10591 | Tarrytown, '65 | 11,280 | 8,851 |
| 11021 | Thomaston, '66 | 3,150 | 2,045 |
| 12883 | Ticonderoga | 3,568 | 3,517 |
| 14150 | Tonawanda, '66 | 21,946 | 14,617 |
| 14150 | Tonawanda (uninc.) | 83,771 | |
| *12180 | Troy | 67,492 | 72,311 |
| 10707 | Tuckahoe, '65 | 6,237 | 5,991 |
| 12986 | Tupper Lake | 5,200 | 5,441 |
| 11553 | Uniondale | 20,041 | |
| *13503 | Utica | 100,410 | 101,531 |
| 11580 | Valley Stream, '65 | 38,591 | 26,854 |
| | Vernon Valley | 5,998 | |
| | Victory Heights | 2,528 | 1,857 |
| 12586 | Walden, '67 | 5,079 | 4,559 |
| 13856 | Walton | 3,855 | 3,947 |
| 11793 | Wantagh | 34,172 | |
| 12590 | Wappingers Falls, '65 | 4,816 | 3,490 |

| ZIP Code | Place | 1960 | 1950 |
|---|---|---|---|
| | **NEW YORK—Continued** | | |
| 14569 | Warsaw | 3,653 | 3,713 |
| 10990 | Warwick, '67 | 3,261 | 2,674 |
| 12188 | Waterford, '66 | 2,749 | 2,968 |
| 13165 | Waterloo | 5,098 | 4,438 |
| 13601 | Watertown | 33,306 | 34,350 |
| 12189 | Watervliet | 13,917 | 15,197 |
| 14891 | Watkins Glen | 2,813 | 3,052 |
| 14892 | Waverly | 5,950 | 6,037 |
| 14580 | Webster, '64 | 3,617 | 1,773 |
| 14895 | Wellsville | 5,967 | 6,402 |
| 11704 | West Babylon, '64 | 9,633 | |
| 11590 | Westbury, '65 | 14,618 | 7,112 |
| 14905 | West Elmira | 5,763 | 3,833 |
| 14787 | Westfield | 3,878 | 3,663 |
| 12801 | West Glens Falls | 2,725 | 1,665 |
| 10993 | West Haverstraw, '66 | 6,770 | 3,099 |
| 11552 | West Hampstead—Lakeview | 24,783 | |
| 14224 | West Seneca | 23,138 | |
| 12887 | Whitehall | 4,016 | 4,457 |
| *10602 | White Plains, '65 | 50,040 | 43,466 |
| 13492 | Whitesboro, '65 | 4,745 | 3,902 |
| 14221 | Williamsville, '66 | 6,659 | 4,649 |
| 11596 | Williston Park, '65 | 8,575 | 7,505 |
| 11598 | Woodmere | 14,011 | |
| 11798 | Wyandanch, '64 | 10,952 | |
| *10701 | Yonkers, '65 | 201,573 | 152,798 |
| 10598 | Yorktown | 3,576 | |
| 13495 | Yorkville, '65 | 3,581 | 3,528 |
| | **NORTH CAROLINA** | | |
| 27910 | Ahoskie | 4,583 | 3,579 |
| 28001 | Albemarle | 12,261 | 11,798 |
| 27203 | Asheboro | 9,449 | 7,701 |
| *28801 | Asheville | 60,192 | 53,000 |
| 28513 | Ayden | 3,108 | 2,282 |
| 28705 | Balfour | 3,805 | 1,939 |
| 28516 | Beaufort | 2,922 | 3,212 |
| 28012 | Belmont, '66 | 4,718 | 5,330 |
| 28016 | Bessemer City, '66 | 4,271 | 3,961 |
| 28303 | Bonnie Doone | 4,481 | |
| 28607 | Boone | 3,686 | 2,973 |
| 28712 | Brevard | 4,857 | 3,908 |
| 27315 | Burlington | 33,199 | 24,560 |
| 28716 | Canton | 5,068 | 4,906 |
| 27511 | Cary, '66 | 5,331 | 1,446 |
| 27514 | Chapel Hill | 12,573 | 9,177 |
| *28202 | Charlotte | 201,564 | 134,042 |
| 28021 | Cherryville, '66 | 4,056 | 3,492 |
| 27520 | Clayton, '66 | 2,965 | 2,229 |
| 28328 | Clinton | 7,461 | 4,414 |
| 28025 | Concord | 17,799 | 16,486 |
| 28032 | Cramerton | 3,123 | 3,211 |
| 28034 | Dallas, '66 | 3,591 | 2,454 |
| 28036 | Davidson | 2,573 | 2,423 |
| 27288 | Draper, '66 | 3,255 | 3,629 |
| 28334 | Dunn, '66 | 7,487 | 6,316 |
| *27701 | Durham | 78,302 | 71,311 |
| 28301 | East Fayetteville | 2,797 | |
| 28052 | East Gastonia | 3,326 | 3,733 |
| 28379 | East Rockingham | 3,211 | |
| 28401 | East Wilmington | 5,520 | 1,623 |
| 27932 | Edenton | 4,458 | 4,468 |
| 27909 | Elizabeth City | 14,062 | 12,685 |
| 28621 | Elkin | 2,868 | 2,842 |
| 27823 | Enfield | 2,978 | 2,361 |
| 28339 | Erwin | 3,183 | 3,344 |
| 28728 | Farmville | 3,997 | 2,942 |
| *28301 | Fayetteville, '64 | 51,022 | 34,715 |
| *28301 | Fayetteville North | 3,071 | |
| 28043 | Forest City | 6,556 | 4,971 |
| 27526 | Fuquay Springs, '66 | 3,420 | 1,992 |
| 27529 | Garner, '66 | 4,282 | 1,180 |
| 28052 | Gastonia, '66 | 45,429 | 23,069 |
| 27530 | Goldsboro | 28,873 | 21,454 |
| 27253 | Graham | 7,723 | 5,026 |
| 28630 | Granite Falls | 2,644 | 2,286 |
| *27401 | Greensboro, '66 | 131,711 | 74,389 |
| 27834 | Greenville | 22,860 | 16,724 |
| 28345 | Hamlet, '66 | 4,810 | 5,061 |
| 27536 | Henderson | 12,740 | 10,996 |
| 28739 | Hendersonville | 5,911 | 6,103 |
| 28601 | Hickory | 19,328 | 14,755 |
| 28601 | Hickory East | 3,274 | |
| *27260 | High Point, '66 | 61,396 | 39,973 |
| 28540 | Jacksonville | 13,491 | 3,960 |
| 28081 | Kannapolis | 34,647 | 28,448 |
| 27284 | Kernersville | 2,942 | 2,396 |
| 28086 | Kings Mountain, '66 | 8,256 | 7,206 |
| 28501 | Kinston | 24,819 | 18,336 |
| 28352 | Laurinburg | 8,242 | 7,134 |
| 27288 | Leaksville, '66 | 6,684 | 4,045 |
| 28645 | Lenoir | 10,257 | 7,865 |
| 27292 | Lexington | 16,093 | 13,571 |
| 28092 | Lincolnton | 5,699 | 5,423 |
| 28601 | Longview (A) | 3,290 | 2,291 |
| 27549 | Louisburg | 2,862 | 2,545 |
| 28098 | Lowell, '66 | 3,048 | 2,313 |
| 28358 | Lumberton | 15,305 | 9,186 |
| 28752 | Marion | 3,345 | 2,740 |
| 28544 | Midway Park | 4,164 | 3,703 |
| 28110 | Monroe, '66 | 10,913 | 10,140 |

| ZIP Code | Place | 1960 | 1950 |
|---|---|---|---|
| | **NORTH CAROLINA—Continued** | | |
| 28115 | Mooresville | 6,918 | 7,121 |
| 28557 | Morehead City | 5,583 | 5,144 |
| 28655 | Morganton | 9,186 | 8,311 |
| 27030 | Mount Airy | 7,055 | 7,192 |
| 28120 | Mount Holly, '66 | 5,120 | 2,241 |
| 28365 | Mount Olive | 4,673 | 3,732 |
| 27855 | Murfreesboro | 2,643 | 2,140 |
| 28560 | New Bern | 15,717 | 15,812 |
| 28658 | Newton | 6,658 | 6,039 |
| 28012 | North Belmont | 8,328 | 3,945 |
| 28659 | North Wilkesboro | 4,197 | 4,379 |
| *28301 | Owens | 5,207 | .... |
| 27565 | Oxford | 6,978 | 6,685 |
| 27962 | Plymouth | 4,666 | 4,486 |
| 28376 | Raeford | 3,058 | 2,030 |
| *27601 | Raleigh, '66 | 105,722 | 65,679 |
| 28377 | Red Springs | 2,767 | 2,245 |
| 27320 | Reidsville, '66 | 14,036 | 11,708 |
| ..... | Richmond Hill | 2,943 | 2,303 |
| 27870 | Roanoke Rapids | 13,320 | 8,156 |
| 28379 | Rockingham, '66 | 5,748 | 3,356 |
| 27801 | Rocky Mount | 32,147 | 27,697 |
| 27573 | Roxboro | 5,147 | 4,321 |
| 28139 | Rutherfordton | 3,392 | 3,146 |
| 28144 | Salisbury | 21,297 | 20,102 |
| 27330 | Sanford, '66 | 12,573 | 10,013 |
| 27874 | Scotland Neck | 2,974 | 2,733 |
| 27576 | Selma, '66 | 3,197 | 2,639 |
| 28150 | Shelby, '66 | 16,941 | 15,508 |
| 27344 | Siler City | 4,455 | 2,501 |
| 27577 | Smithfield, '66 | 6,315 | 5,574 |
| 28387 | Southern Pines | 3,198 | 4,272 |
| *28301 | South Fayetteville | 3,411 | 3,428 |
| 28052 | South Gastonia | 3,762 | 6,465 |
| 28144 | South Salisbury | 3,065 | .... |
| 28159 | Spencer | 2,904 | 3,242 |
| 28160 | Spindale | 4,082 | 3,891 |
| 27288 | Spray, '66 | 4,318 | .... |
| 28390 | Spring Lake | 4,110 | .... |
| 28777 | Spruce Pine | 2,504 | 2,280 |
| 28677 | Statesville | 19,844 | 16,901 |
| 27886 | Tarboro | 8,411 | 8,120 |
| 27360 | Thomasville | 15,190 | 11,154 |
| 28690 | Valdese | 2,941 | 2,730 |
| 28170 | Wadesboro | 3,744 | 3,408 |
| 27587 | Wake Forest, '66 | 2,681 | 3,704 |
| 27889 | Washington, '66 | 10,150 | 9,698 |
| 28786 | Waynesville | 6,159 | 5,295 |
| 28025 | West Concord | 5,510 | .... |
| 28472 | Whiteville | 4,683 | 4,238 |
| 27892 | Williamston | 6,924 | 4,975 |
| 28401 | Wilmington | 44,013 | 45,043 |
| 27893 | Wilson | 28,753 | 23,010 |
| *27101 | Winston-Salem | 111,135 | 87,811 |

| ZIP Code | Place | 1960 | 1950 |
|---|---|---|---|
| | **NORTH DAKOTA** | | |
| 58501 | Bismarck (A), '67 | 33,134 | 18,640 |
| 58318 | Bottineau (A), '67 | 2,767 | 2,268 |
| 58301 | Devils Lake, '65 | 6,670 | 6,427 |
| 58601 | Dickinson, '66 | 11,666 | 7,469 |
| 58102 | Fargo, '65 | 49,572 | 38,256 |
| 58237 | Grafton, '66 | 7,964 | 4,901 |
| 58201 | Grand Forks, '64 | 38,230 | 26,836 |
| 58401 | Jamestown, '66 | 15,580 | 10,697 |
| 58554 | Mandan | 10,525 | 7,298 |
| 58701 | Minot, '62 | 33,477 | 22,032 |
| 58368 | Rugby | 2,972 | 2,907 |
| | Southwest Fargo (*see West Fargo*) | | |
| 58072 | Valley City, 66 | 8,104 | 6,851 |
| 58075 | Wahpeton, '64 | 6,453 | 5,125 |
| 58078 | West Fargo (A) '67 | 4,340 | 1,032 |
| 58801 | Williston | 11,866 | 7,378 |

| ZIP Code | Place | 1960 | 1950 |
|---|---|---|---|
| | **OHIO** | | |
| 45810 | Ada | 3,918 | 3,640 |
| *44309 | Akron | 290,351 | 274,605 |
| 44601 | Alliance | 28,362 | 26,161 |
| ..... | Amberley | 2,951 | 885 |
| 44001 | Amherst | 6,750 | 3,542 |
| 44805 | Ashland | 17,419 | 14,287 |
| 44004 | Ashtabula (A) | 24,944 | 23,696 |
| 45701 | Athens | 16,470 | 11,660 |
| 44202 | Aurora | 4,049 | 571 |
| 44011 | Avon | 6,002 | 2,773 |
| 44012 | Avon Lake | 9,403 | 4,342 |
| 44203 | Barberton | 33,805 | 27,820 |
| 43713 | Barnesville | 4,425 | 4,665 |
| 44140 | Bay | 14,489 | 6,917 |
| 44122 | Beachwood | 6,089 | 1,073 |
| 44014 | Bedford | 15,223 | 9,105 |
| 44014 | Bedford Heights | 5,275 | .... |
| 43906 | Bellaire | 11,502 | 12,573 |
| 43311 | Bellefontaine | 11,424 | 10,232 |
| 44811 | Bellevue | 8,286 | 6,906 |
| 45714 | Belpre | 5,418 | 2,451 |
| 44017 | Berea | 16,592 | 12,051 |
| 43209 | Bexley | 14,319 | 12,378 |
| 45107 | Blanchester | 2,944 | 2,109 |
| ..... | Blue Ash | 8,341 | .... |

| ZIP Code | Place | 1960 | 1950 |
|---|---|---|---|
| | **OHIO—Continued** | | |
| 45817 | Bluffton | 2,591 | 2,423 |
| 43402 | Bowling Green | 13,574 | 12,005 |
| 44141 | Brecksville | 5,435 | 2,664 |
| 43912 | Bridgeport | 3,824 | 4,309 |
| 44141 | Broadview Heights | 6,209 | 2,276 |
| 44109 | Brooklyn | 10,733 | 6,317 |
| 44112 | Brook Park | 12,856 | 2,606 |
| 45309 | Brookville | 3,184 | 1,908 |
| 44212 | Brunswick | 11,725 | .... |
| 43506 | Bryan | 7,361 | 6,365 |
| 44820 | Bucyrus | 12,276 | 10,327 |
| 43907 | Cadiz | 3,259 | 3,020 |
| 43725 | Cambridge | 14,562 | 14,739 |
| 44405 | Campbell | 13,406 | 12,882 |
| 44406 | Canfield | 3,252 | 1,465 |
| *44701 | Canton | 113,631 | 116,912 |
| 43316 | Carey | 3,722 | 3,260 |
| 44615 | Carrollton | 2,786 | 2,658 |
| 45822 | Celina | 7,659 | 5,703 |
| 45459 | Centerville | 3,490 | 827 |
| 44022 | Chagrin Falls | 3,458 | 3,085 |
| 44024 | Chardon | 3,154 | 2,478 |
| 45211 | Cheviot | 10,701 | 9,944 |
| 45601 | Chillicothe | 24,957 | 20,133 |
| *45202 | Cincinnati | 502,550 | 503,998 |
| 43113 | Circleville | 11,059 | 8,743 |
| *44101 | Cleveland, '65 | 810,858 | 914,808 |
| 44118 | Cleveland Heights | 61,813 | 59,141 |
| 43410 | Clyde | 4,826 | 4,083 |
| 45638 | Coal Grove | 2,961 | 2,492 |
| 45828 | Coldwater | 2,766 | 2,217 |
| 44408 | Columbiana | 4,164 | 3,369 |
| *43216 | Columbus | 471,316 | 375,901 |
| 44030 | Conneaut | 10,557 | 10,230 |
| 43812 | Coshocton | 13,106 | 11,675 |
| 44827 | Crestline | 5,521 | 4,614 |
| 43731 | Crooksville | 2,958 | 2,960 |
| 44221 | Cuyahoga Falls | 47,922 | 29,195 |
| *45401 | Dayton | 262,332 | 243,872 |
| 45236 | Deer Park | 8,423 | 7,241 |
| 43512 | Defiance | 14,553 | 11,265 |
| 43015 | Delaware | 13,282 | 11,804 |
| 45833 | Delphos | 6,961 | 6,220 |
| 44621 | Dennison | 4,158 | 4,432 |
| 44622 | Dover | 11,300 | 9,852 |
| 44004 | East Ashtabula | 4,179 | 2,590 |
| 44112 | East Cleveland | 37,991 | 40,047 |
| 44094 | Eastlake | 12,467 | 7,486 |
| 43920 | East Liverpool | 22,306 | 24,217 |
| 44413 | East Palestine | 5,232 | 5,195 |
| 45320 | Eaton | 5,034 | 4,242 |
| 45216 | Elmwood Place | 3,813 | 4,113 |
| 44035 | Elyria | 43,782 | 30,307 |
| 44117 | Euclid | 62,998 | 41,396 |
| 45324 | Fairborn | 19,453 | 7,847 |
| 45014 | Fairfield | 9,734 | .... |
| 44077 | Fairport | 4,267 | 4,519 |
| 44126 | Fairview Park | 14,624 | 9,311 |
| 45840 | Findlay | 30,344 | 23,845 |
| 44830 | Fostoria | 15,732 | 14,351 |
| 45005 | Franklin | 7,917 | 5,388 |
| 43120 | Fremont | 17,573 | 16,537 |
| 43020 | Gahanna | 2,717 | 696 |
| 44833 | Galion | 12,650 | 9,925 |
| 45631 | Gallipolis | 8,775 | 7,871 |
| 44125 | Garfield Heights | 38,455 | 21,662 |
| 44041 | Geneva | 5,677 | 4,718 |
| 45121 | Georgetown | 2,674 | 2,200 |
| 45327 | Germantown | 3,399 | 2,478 |
| 43431 | Gibsonburg | 2,540 | 2,281 |
| 44420 | Girard | 12,997 | 10,113 |
| 45246 | Glendale | 2,823 | 2,402 |
| ..... | Golf Manor | 4,648 | 3,603 |
| 43212 | Grandview Heights | 8,270 | 7,659 |
| 43023 | Granville | 2,868 | 2,653 |
| 45123 | Greenfield | 5,422 | 4,862 |
| 45218 | Greenhills | 5,407 | 3,005 |
| 45331 | Greenville | 10,585 | 8,859 |
| 43123 | Grove City | 8,107 | 2,339 |
| *45011 | Hamilton | 72,354 | 57,951 |
| 45030 | Harrison | 3,878 | 1,943 |
| 43055 | Heath, '65 | 6,066 | .... |
| 43526 | Hicksville | 3,116 | 2,629 |
| 44124 | Highland Heights | 2,929 | 762 |
| 43026 | Hilliard | 5,633 | 610 |
| 45133 | Hillsboro | 5,474 | 5,126 |
| 44425 | Hubbard | 7,137 | 4,560 |
| 44839 | Huron | 5,197 | 2,515 |
| 44131 | Independence | 6,868 | 3,105 |
| ..... | Indian Hill | 4,526 | 2,090 |
| 45638 | Ironton | 15,745 | 16,333 |
| 45640 | Jackson | 6,980 | 6,504 |
| 44047 | Jefferson | 2,774 | 1,647 |
| 43031 | Johnstown | 2,881 | 1,220 |
| 44240 | Kent | 17,836 | 12,418 |
| 43326 | Kenton | 8,747 | 8,475 |
| 45429 | Kettering | 54,462 | .... |
| 44250 | Lakemore | 2,765 | 2,463 |
| 44638 | Lakeville | 4,181 | 3,432 |
| 44107 | Lakewood | 66,154 | 68,071 |
| 43130 | Lancaster | 29,916 | 24,180 |
| 45036 | Lebanon | 5,993 | 4,618 |
| 44431 | Leetonia | 2,543 | 2,565 |

| ZIP Code | Place | 1960 | 1950 | ZIP Code | Place | 1960 | 1950 |
|---|---|---|---|---|---|---|---|
| | **OHIO—Continued** | | | | **OHIO—Continued** | | |
| *45808 | Lima | 51,037 | 50,246 | 44131 | Seven Hills | 5,708 | 1,350 |
| ..... | Lincoln Heights (uninc.) | 8,004 | .... | 43947 | Shadyside | 5,028 | 4,433 |
| 45215 | Lincoln Heights | 7,798 | 5,531 | 44120 | Shaker Heights | 36,460 | 28,222 |
| 44432 | Lisbon | 3,579 | 3,293 | 45241 | Sharonville, '62 | 6,657 | 1,318 |
| 45215 | Lockland | 5,292 | 5,736 | 44438 | Sharon West | 3,865 | .... |
| 43138 | Logan | 6,417 | 5,972 | 44054 | Sheffield Lake | 6,884 | 2,381 |
| 43140 | London | 6,379 | 5,222 | 44875 | Shelby | 9,106 | 7,971 |
| 44052 | Lorain | 66,932 | 51,202 | 45365 | Sidney | 14,663 | 11,491 |
| 44842 | Loudonville | 2,611 | 2,523 | 44221 | Silver Lake | 2,655 | 1,040 |
| 44641 | Louisville | 5,116 | 3,801 | 45236 | Silverton | 6,682 | 4,827 |
| 45140 | Loveland | 5,008 | 2,149 | 44139 | Solon | 6,333 | 2,570 |
| 44124 | Lyndhurst | 16,805 | 7,359 | 44121 | South Euclid | 27,569 | 15,432 |
| 44437 | McDonald | 2,727 | 1,858 | 45065 | South Lebanon | 2,720 | 1,291 |
| 45243 | Madeira | 6,744 | 2,689 | 45246 | Springdale | 3,556 | .... |
| *44901 | Mansfield | 47,325 | 43,564 | *45501 | Springfield | 82,723 | 78,508 |
| 44901 | Mansfield SE | 2,961 | .... | 43952 | Steubenville | 32,495 | 35,872 |
| 44137 | Maple Heights | 31,667 | 15,586 | 44224 | Stow | 12,194 | .... |
| 45227 | Mariemont | 4,120 | 3,514 | 44136 | Strongsville | 8,504 | 3,504 |
| 45750 | Marietta | 16,847 | 16,006 | 44471 | Struthers | 15,631 | 11,941 |
| 43302 | Marion | 37,079 | 33,817 | 43560 | Sylvania | 5,187 | 2,433 |
| 43935 | Martins Ferry | 11,919 | 13,220 | 44278 | Tallmadge | 10,246 | 5,821 |
| 43040 | Marysville | 4,952 | 4,256 | 44883 | Tiffin | 21,478 | 18,952 |
| 45040 | Mason | 4,727 | 1,196 | 45371 | Tipp City | 4,267 | 3,304 |
| 44646 | Massillon | 31,236 | 29,594 | *43601 | Toledo | 318,003 | 303,616 |
| 44438 | Masury | 2,512 | 2,151 | 43964 | Toronto | 7,780 | 7,253 |
| 43537 | Maumee | 12,063 | 5,548 | 45067 | Trenton | 3,064 | 987 |
| 45042 | Mayfield | 2,747 | 1,926 | 45426 | Trotwood | 4,992 | 1,066 |
| 44124 | Mayfield Heights | 13,478 | 5,807 | 45373 | Troy | 13,685 | 10,661 |
| 44256 | Medina | 8,235 | 5,097 | 44087 | Twinsburg | 4,098 | .... |
| 44060 | Mentor | 4,354 | 2,383 | 44683 | Uhrichsville | 6,201 | 6,614 |
| 44060 | Mentor-on-the-Lake | 3,290 | 1,413 | 44118 | University Heights | 16,641 | 11,566 |
| 45342 | Miamisburg | 9,893 | 6,329 | 43221 | Upper Arlington | 28,486 | 9,024 |
| 44130 | Middleburg Heights | 7,282 | 2,299 | 43351 | Upper Sandusky | 4,941 | 4,397 |
| 45760 | Middleport | 3,373 | 3,446 | 43078 | Urbana | 10,461 | 9,335 |
| 45042 | Middletown | 42,115 | 33,695 | 45377 | Vandalia | 6,342 | 927 |
| 45150 | Milford | 4,131 | 2,448 | 45891 | Van Wert | 11,323 | 10,364 |
| 44654 | Millersburg | 3,101 | 2,398 | 44089 | Vermilion, '61 | 5,220 | 2,214 |
| 44657 | Minerva | 3,833 | 3,280 | 44281 | Wadsworth | 10,635 | 7,966 |
| 43938 | Mingo Junction | 4,987 | 4,464 | 45895 | Wapakoneta | 6,756 | 5,797 |
| 44260 | Mogadore | 3,851 | 1,818 | *44483 | Warren | 59,648 | 49,856 |
| 45342 | Montgomery | 3,075 | 579 | 44122 | Warrensville Heights | 10,609 | 4,126 |
| 43343 | Montpelier | 4,131 | 3,867 | 45787 | Washington | 12,388 | 10,560 |
| 45439 | Moraine, '65 | 5,455 | .... | 43567 | Wauseon | 4,311 | 3,494 |
| 43338 | Mount Gilead | 2,768 | 2,351 | 45690 | Waverly | 3,830 | 1,670 |
| 45231 | Mount Healthy | 6,553 | 5,533 | 44090 | Wellington | 3,599 | 2,992 |
| 45050 | Mount Vernon | 13,284 | 12,185 | 45692 | Wellston | 5,728 | 5,691 |
| 43545 | Napoleon | 6,739 | 5,335 | 43968 | Wellsville | 7,117 | 7,854 |
| 45764 | Nelsonville | 4,834 | 4,845 | 45449 | West Carrollton (A) '67 | 7,837 | 2,876 |
| 43055 | Newark | 41,790 | 34,275 | 43081 | Westerville | 7,011 | 4,112 |
| 45662 | New Boston | 3,984 | 4,754 | 44145 | Westlake | 12,906 | 4,912 |
| 44105 | Newburg Heights | 3,512 | 3,689 | 45383 | West Milton | 2,972 | 2,101 |
| 45344 | New Carlisle | 4,107 | 1,640 | 45662 | West Portsmouth | 3,100 | 2,613 |
| 43832 | Newcomerstown | 4,273 | 4,514 | 45694 | Wheelersburg | 2,682 | 1,013 |
| 43764 | New Lexington | 4,514 | 4,233 | 43213 | Whitehall | 20,818 | 4,877 |
| 44663 | New Philadelphia | 14,241 | 12,948 | 44092 | Wickliffe | 15,760 | 5,002 |
| 45157 | New Richmond | 2,834 | 1,960 | 44890 | Willard | 5,457 | 4,744 |
| 44444 | Newton Falls | 5,038 | 4,451 | 44094 | Willoughby | 15,058 | 5,602 |
| 44446 | Niles | 19,545 | 16,773 | 44094 | Willoughby Hills | 4,241 | .... |
| 45872 | North Baltimore | 3,011 | 2,771 | 44094 | Willowick | 18,749 | 3,677 |
| 44720 | North Canton | 7,727 | 4,032 | 45177 | Wilmington | 8,915 | 7,387 |
| 45239 | North College Hill | 12,035 | 7,921 | 44288 | Windham | 3,777 | 3,968 |
| 44070 | North Olmsted | 16,290 | 6,604 | 43952 | Wintersville | 3,597 | 1,950 |
| 44035 | North Ridgeville | 8,657 | .... | 45245 | Williamsville | 2,811 | .... |
| 44133 | North Royalton | 9,290 | 3,939 | 45215 | Woodlawn | 3,007 | 1,335 |
| 44857 | Norwalk | 12,900 | 9,775 | 43793 | Woodsfield | 2,956 | 2,410 |
| 45212 | Norwood | 34,580 | 35,001 | 44691 | Wooster | 17,046 | 14,005 |
| 43449 | Oak Harbor | 2,903 | 2,370 | 43085 | Worthington | 9,239 | 2,141 |
| 45419 | Oakwood City | 10,493 | 9,691 | 45215 | Wyoming | 7,736 | 5,582 |
| 44014 | Oakwood Village | 3,283 | .... | 45385 | Xenia | 20,445 | 12,877 |
| 44074 | Oberlin | 8,198 | 7,062 | 45387 | Yellow Springs | 4,167 | 2,896 |
| 45042 | Oneida-Rolling Mill Park | 6,504 | .... | *44501 | Youngstown | 166,689 | 168,330 |
| 44862 | Ontario | 3,049 | .... | 43701 | Zanesville | 39,077 | 40,517 |
| 43616 | Oregon | 13,319 | .... | | | | |
| 44667 | Orrville | 6,511 | 5,153 | | **OKLAHOMA** | | |
| 45875 | Ottawa | 3,245 | 2,962 | | | | |
| 43606 | Ottawa Hills | 3,870 | 2,333 | 74820 | Ada | 14,347 | 15,995 |
| 45056 | Oxford | 7,828 | 6,944 | 73521 | Altus | 21,225 | 9,735 |
| 44077 | Painesville | 16,116 | 14,432 | 73717 | Alva | 6,258 | 6,505 |
| 44129 | Parma | 82,845 | 28,897 | 73005 | Anadarko | 6,299 | 6,184 |
| 44130 | Parma Heights | 18,100 | 3,901 | 73401 | Ardmore | 20,184 | 17,890 |
| 45879 | Paulding | 2,936 | 2,352 | 74525 | Atoka | 2,877 | 2,653 |
| 44124 | Pepper Pike | 3,217 | 874 | 74003 | Bartlesville | 27,893 | 19,228 |
| 43351 | Perrysburg | 5,519 | 4,006 | 73008 | Bethany | 12,342 | 5,705 |
| 45356 | Piqua | 19,219 | 17,447 | 74631 | Blackwell | 9,588 | 9,199 |
| 44514 | Poland | 2,766 | 1,652 | 74010 | Bristow | 4,795 | 5,400 |
| 45769 | Pomeroy | 3,345 | 3,656 | 74012 | Broken Arrow | 5,928 | 3,262 |
| 43452 | Port Clinton | 6,870 | 5,541 | 74834 | Chandler | 2,524 | 2,724 |
| 45662 | Portsmouth | 33,637 | 36,798 | 74426 | Checotah | 2,614 | 2,638 |
| 44266 | Ravenna | 10,918 | 9,857 | 73018 | Chickasha | 14,866 | 15,842 |
| 45215 | Reading | 12,832 | 7,836 | 74017 | Claremore | 6,639 | 5,494 |
| 43068 | Reynoldsburg | 7,793 | 724 | 74020 | Cleveland | 2,519 | 2,464 |
| 44143 | Richmond Heights | 5,068 | 891 | 73601 | Clinton | 9,617 | 7,555 |
| 44270 | Rittman | 5,410 | 3,810 | 74021 | Collinsville | 2,526 | 2,011 |
| 44116 | Rocky River | 18,097 | 11,237 | 74023 | Cushing | 8,619 | 8,414 |
| ..... | Roseland | 8,204 | .... | 73115 | Del City | 12,934 | 2,504 |
| 43460 | Rossford | 4,406 | 3,963 | 74029 | Dewey | 3,994 | 2,513 |
| 45217 | Saint Bernard | 6,778 | 7,066 | 74030 | Drumright | 4,190 | 5,028 |
| 43950 | Saint Clairsville | 3,865 | 3,040 | 73533 | Duncan | 20,009 | 15,325 |
| 45885 | Saint Marys | 7,737 | 6,208 | 74701 | Durant | 10,467 | 10,541 |
| 44460 | Salem | 13,854 | 12,754 | 73034 | Edmond | 8,577 | 6,086 |
| 44870 | Sandusky | 31,989 | 29,375 | 73644 | Elk City | 8,196 | 7,962 |
| 44878 | Sandusky South | 4,724 | .... | 73036 | El Reno | 11,015 | 10,991 |
| 44672 | Sebring | 4,439 | 4,045 | 73701 | Enid | 38,859 | 36,017 |

| ZIP Code | Place | 1960 | 1950 |
|---|---|---|---|
| | **OKLAHOMA—Continued** | | |
| 73542 | Frederick | 5,879 | 5,467 |
| 73044 | Guthrie | 9,502 | 10,113 |
| 73942 | Guymon | 5,768 | 4,718 |
| 73438 | Healdton | 2,898 | 2,578 |
| 74437 | Henryetta | 6,551 | 7,987 |
| 73651 | Hobart | 5,132 | 5,380 |
| 74848 | Holdenville | 5,712 | 6,192 |
| 73550 | Hollis | 3,006 | 3,089 |
| 74035 | Hominy | 2,866 | 2,702 |
| 74743 | Hugo | 6,287 | 5,984 |
| 74745 | Idabel | 4,967 | 4,671 |
| 73750 | Kingfisher | 3,249 | 3,345 |
| 73501 | Lawton | 61,697 | 34,757 |
| 73052 | Lindsay | 4,258 | 3,021 |
| 74501 | McAlester | 17,419 | 17,878 |
| 73446 | Madill | 3,084 | 2,791 |
| 73554 | Mangum | 3,950 | 4,271 |
| 73055 | Marlow | 4,027 | 3,399 |
| 74354 | Miami | 12,869 | 11,801 |
| 73110 | Midwest City | 36,058 | 10,166 |
| 73060 | Moore (A) '67 | 16,649 | 1,783 |
| 74401 | Muskogee | 38,059 | 37,289 |
| 73632 | New Cordell | 3,589 | 2,920 |
| 73116 | Nichols Hills | 4,897 | 2,606 |
| 73069 | Norman | 33,412 | 27,006 |
| 74048 | Nowata | 4,163 | 3,965 |
| 74859 | Okemah | 2,836 | 3,454 |
| *73102 | Oklahoma City | 324,253 | 243,504 |
| 74447 | Okmulgee | 15,951 | 18,317 |
| 73075 | Pauls Valley | 6,856 | 6,896 |
| 74056 | Pawhuska | 5,414 | 5,331 |
| 73077 | Perry | 5,210 | 5,137 |
| 74360 | Picher | 2,553 | 3,951 |
| 74601 | Ponca City | 24,411 | 20,180 |
| 74953 | Poteau | 4,428 | 4,776 |
| 74063 | Prattville | 2,530 | |
| 74361 | Pryor Creek | 6,476 | 4,486 |
| 73080 | Purcell | 3,729 | 3,546 |
| 74955 | Sallisaw | 3,351 | 2,885 |
| 74063 | Sand Springs | 7,754 | 6,994 |
| 74066 | Sapulpa | 14,282 | 13,031 |
| 73662 | Sayre | 2,913 | 3,362 |
| 74868 | Seminole | 11,464 | 11,863 |
| 74801 | Shawnee | 24,326 | 22,948 |
| 74070 | Skiatook | 2,503 | 1,734 |
| 74074 | Stillwater | 23,969 | 20,238 |
| 73086 | Sulphur | 4,737 | 4,389 |
| 74464 | Tahlequah | 5,840 | 4,750 |
| 74873 | Tecumseh | 2,630 | 2,275 |
| 73120 | The Village | 12,118 | |
| 74653 | Tonkawa | 3,415 | 3,643 |
| *74101 | Tulsa | 261,685 | 182,740 |
| 74301 | Vinita | 6,027 | 5,518 |
| 74467 | Wagoner | 4,469 | 4,395 |
| 73572 | Walters | 2,825 | 2,743 |
| 73123 | Warr Acres | 7,135 | 2,378 |
| 73772 | Watonga | 3,252 | 3,249 |
| 73096 | Weatherford | 4,499 | 3,529 |
| 74884 | Wewoka | 5,954 | 6,747 |
| 73801 | Woodward | 7,747 | 5,915 |
| 73098 | Wynnewood | 2,509 | 2,423 |
| 73099 | Yukon | 3,076 | 1,990 |
| | **OREGON** | | |
| 97321 | Albany | 12,926 | 10,115 |
| 97601 | Altamont | 10,811 | 9,419 |
| 97520 | Ashland | 9,119 | 7,739 |
| 97103 | Astoria | 11,239 | 12,331 |
| 97814 | Baker | 9,986 | 9,471 |
| 97470 | Barnes | 5,076 | |
| 97005 | Beaverton | 5,937 | 2,512 |
| *97701 | Bend | 11,936 | 11,409 |
| 97415 | Brookings | 2,637 | |
| 97720 | Burns | 3,523 | 3,093 |
| 97420 | Coos Bay | 7,084 | 6,223 |
| 97423 | Coquille | 4,730 | 3,523 |
| 97330 | Corvallis | 20,669 | 16,207 |
| 97424 | Cottage Grove | 3,895 | 3,536 |
| 97338 | Dallas | 5,072 | 4,793 |
| 97058 | Dalles City | 10,493 | 7,676 |
| 97420 | Empire | 3,781 | 2,261 |
| *97401 | Eugene | 50,977 | 35,879 |
| 97116 | Forest Grove | 5,628 | 4,343 |
| 97301 | Four Corners | 4,743 | 1,284 |
| 97027 | Gladstone | 3,854 | 2,434 |
| 97526 | Grants Pass | 10,118 | 8,116 |
| 97030 | Gresham | 3,944 | 3,049 |
| 97303 | Hayesville | 4,565 | 2,697 |
| 97838 | Hermiston | 4,402 | 3,804 |
| 97123 | Hillsboro | 8,232 | 5,142 |
| 97031 | Hood River | 3,657 | 3,701 |
| 97303 | Keizer | 5,288 | |
| 97601 | Klamath Falls | 16,949 | 15,875 |
| 97850 | La Grande | 9,014 | 8,635 |
| 97630 | Lakeview | 3,260 | 2,831 |
| 97355 | Lebanon | 5,858 | 5,873 |
| 97128 | McMinnville | 7,656 | 6,635 |
| 97501 | Medford | 24,425 | 17,305 |
| 97862 | Milton-Freewater | 4,110 | |
| 97222 | Milwaukie | 9,099 | 5,253 |
| 97458 | Myrtle Point | 2,886 | 2,033 |
| 97132 | Newberg | 4,204 | 3,946 |
| 97365 | Newport | 5,344 | 3,241 |

| ZIP Code | Place | 1960 | 1950 |
|---|---|---|---|
| | **OREGON—Continued** | | |
| 97459 | North Bend | 7,512 | 6,099 |
| 97913 | Nyssa | 2,611 | 2,625 |
| 97914 | Ontario | 5,101 | 4,465 |
| 97045 | Oregon City | 7,996 | 7,682 |
| 97034 | Oswego | 8,906 | 3,316 |
| 97801 | Pendleton | 14,434 | 11,774 |
| *97208 | Portland | 372,676 | 373,628 |
| 97754 | Prineville | 3,263 | 3,233 |
| 97756 | Redmond | 3,340 | 2,956 |
| 97467 | Reedsport | 2,998 | 2,288 |
| 97470 | Roseburg | 11,467 | 8,390 |
| 97051 | Saint Helens | 5,022 | 4,711 |
| *97301 | Salem | 49,142 | 43,140 |
| 97302 | Salem Heights | 10,770 | 2,351 |
| 97138 | Seaside | 3,877 | 3,886 |
| 97381 | Silverton | 3,081 | 3,146 |
| 97477 | Springfield | 19,616 | 10,807 |
| 97386 | Sweet Home | 3,353 | 3,603 |
| | The Dalles (See Dalles City) | | |
| 97141 | Tillamook | 4,244 | 3,685 |
| 97391 | Toledo | 3,053 | 2,323 |
| 97068 | West Linn | 3,933 | 2,945 |
| 97071 | Woodburn | 3,120 | 2,395 |
| | **PENNSYLVANIA** | | |
| 19001 | Abington, '66 | 62,033 | 28,988 |
| 19018 | Aidan, '66 | 4,998 | 3,430 |
| 15001 | Aliquippa | 26,369 | 26,132 |
| *18101 | Allentown | 108,347 | 106,756 |
| 16601 | Altoona | 69,407 | 77,177 |
| 19002 | Ambler | 6,765 | 4,565 |
| 15003 | Ambridge | 13,865 | 16,429 |
| 17003 | Annville | 4,264 | 3,699 |
| 15613 | Apollo | 2,694 | 3,015 |
| 18403 | Archbald | 5,471 | 6,304 |
| 15068 | Arnold | 9,437 | 10,263 |
| 17921 | Ashland | 5,237 | 6,192 |
| 18706 | Ashley | 4,258 | 5,243 |
| 15215 | Aspinwall | 3,727 | 4,084 |
| 19014 | Aston, '66 | 12,783 | 5,576 |
| 18810 | Athens | 4,515 | 4,430 |
| 15202 | Avalon | 6,859 | 6,463 |
| 18641 | Avoca | 3,562 | 4,040 |
| 15005 | Baden | 6,109 | 3,732 |
| | Baldwin (borough) | 24,489 | |
| | Baldwin (township) | 3,004 | 10,743 |
| 18013 | Bangor | 5,766 | 6,050 |
| 15714 | Barnesboro | 3,035 | 3,442 |
| 15009 | Beaver | 6,160 | 6,360 |
| 15010 | Beaver Falls | 16,240 | 17,375 |
| 15522 | Bedford | 3,696 | 3,521 |
| 16823 | Bellefonte | 6,088 | 5,651 |
| 15202 | Bellevue | 11,412 | 11,604 |
| 15202 | Ben Avon | 2,553 | 2,465 |
| 18512 | Bentleyville | 3,160 | 3,295 |
| 18603 | Berwick | 13,353 | 14,010 |
| 19507 | Bethel | 23,650 | 11,324 |
| *18015 | Bethlehem | 75,408 | 66,340 |
| 19508 | Birdsboro | 3,025 | 3,158 |
| 15717 | Blairsville | 4,930 | 5,000 |
| 18447 | Blakely | 6,374 | 6,828 |
| 17815 | Bloomsburg | 10,655 | 10,633 |
| 15009 | Borough | 2,917 | 2,750 |
| 19512 | Boyertown | 4,067 | 4,074 |
| 15014 | Brackenridge | 5,697 | 6,178 |
| 15104 | Braddock | 12,337 | 16,488 |
| 16701 | Bradford | 15,061 | 17,354 |
| 15227 | Brentwood | 13,706 | 12,535 |
| 19405 | Bridgeport | 5,306 | 5,827 |
| 15017 | Bridgeville | 7,112 | 5,650 |
| 19007 | Bristol (borough) | 12,364 | 12,710 |
| | Bristol (township) | 59,298 | 12,184 |
| 15824 | Brockway | 2,563 | 2,650 |
| 19015 | Brookhaven | 5,280 | 1,042 |
| 15825 | Brookville | 4,620 | 4,274 |
| 15417 | Brownsville | 6,055 | 7,643 |
| 17009 | Burnham | 2,755 | 2,954 |
| 16001 | Butler | 20,975 | 23,482 |
| 15419 | California | 5,978 | 2,831 |
| 17011 | Camp Hill | 8,559 | 5,934 |
| 15317 | Canonsburg. (A) | 12,910 | 12,072 |
| 18407 | Carbondale | 13,595 | 16,296 |
| 17013 | Carlisle | 16,623 | 16,812 |
| 15106 | Carnegie | 11,887 | 12,105 |
| 15234 | Castle Shannon | 11,836 | 5,459 |
| 18032 | Catasauqua | 5,062 | 4,923 |
| 16404 | Centerville | 5,088 | 5,545 |
| 17201 | Chambersburg | 17,670 | 17,212 |
| 15022 | Charleroi | 8,148 | 9,872 |
| 19380 | Chatwood | 3,621 | 1,572 |
| 19012 | Cheltenham | 35,990 | 22,854 |
| 19013 | Chester (township) | 63,658 | 66,039 |
| 19013 | Chester (uninc.) | 3,602 | 3,547 |
| 15024 | Cheswick | 2,734 | 1,534 |
| | Churchill | 3,428 | 1,733 |
| 15025 | Clairton | 18,389 | 19,652 |
| 16214 | Clarion | 4,958 | 4,409 |
| 18411 | Clarks Summit | 3,693 | 2,940 |
| 16830 | Clearfield | 9,270 | 9,357 |
| 19018 | Clifton Heights | 8,005 | 7,549 |
| 18218 | Coaldale | 3,949 | 5,318 |
| 19320 | Coatesville | 12,971 | 13,826 |
| 19023 | Collingdale | 10,268 | 8,443 |

## PENNSYLVANIA—Continued

| ZIP Code | Place | 1960 | 1950 |
|---|---|---|---|
| 17512 | Columbia | 12,075 | 11,993 |
| 19023 | Colwyn | 3,074 | 2,143 |
| 15425 | Connellsville | 12,814 | 13,293 |
| 19428 | Conshohocken | 10,259 | 10,922 |
| 18037 | Coplay | 3,701 | 2,994 |
| 15108 | Coraopolis | 9,643 | 10,498 |
| 16407 | Corry | 7,744 | 7,911 |
| 16915 | Coudersport | 2,889 | 3,210 |
| 15205 | Crafton | 8,418 | 8,066 |
| 16630 | Cresson | 2,659 | 2,569 |
| 16833 | Curwensville | 3,231 | 3,332 |
| 15902 | Dale | 2,807 | 3,310 |
| 18612 | Dallas | 2,586 | 1,674 |
| 17313 | Dallastown | 3,615 | 3,304 |
| 17821 | Danville | 6,889 | 6,994 |
| 19023 | Darby | 14,059 | 13,154 |
| 19023 | Darby (township) '67 | 13,560 | 3,454 |
| 15627 | Derry | 3,426 | 3,752 |
| 18519 | Dickson City | 7,738 | 8,948 |
| 15033 | Donora | 11,131 | 12,186 |
| 15216 | Dormont | 13,098 | 13,405 |
| 19335 | Downingtown (boro.) '67 | 7,248 | 4,948 |
| 18901 | Doylestown | 5,917 | 5,262 |
| 15034 | Dravosburg | 3,668 | 3,786 |
| 15801 | Du Bois | 10,667 | 11,497 |
| 18512 | Dunmore | 18,917 | 20,305 |
| 18641 | Dupont | 3,669 | 4,107 |
| 15110 | Duquesne | 15,019 | 17,620 |
| 18642 | Duryea | 5,626 | 6,655 |
| 15909 | East Conemaugh | 3,334 | 4,101 |
| 15030 | East Deer | 2,865 | 3,185 |
| 17701 | East Faxon | 3,641 | |
| 19050 | East Lansdowne | 3,224 | 3,527 |
| 15137 | East McKeesport | 3,470 | 3,171 |
| 18042 | Easton | 31,955 | 35,632 |
| 15112 | East Pittsburgh | 4,122 | 5,259 |
| 18301 | East Stroudsburg | 7,674 | 7,274 |
| 15931 | Ebensburg | 4,111 | 4,086 |
| 15005 | Economy | 5,925 | |
| 19013 | Eddystone | 3,006 | 3,014 |
| 15218 | Edgewood (borough) | 5,124 | 5,292 |
| 17872 | Edgewood (uninc.) | 3,399 | |
| 18704 | Edwardsville | 5,711 | 6,686 |
| 15037 | Elizabeth | 2,597 | 2,615 |
| 17022 | Elizabethtown | 6,780 | 5,083 |
| 16117 | Ellwood City | 12,413 | 12,945 |
| 18049 | Emmaus | 10,262 | 7,780 |
| 15834 | Emporium | 3,397 | 3,646 |
| 15202 | Emsworth | 3,341 | 3,128 |
| 17522 | Ephrata | 7,688 | 7,027 |
| *16501 | Erie | 138,440 | 130,803 |
| 15223 | Etna | 5,519 | 6,750 |
| 18643 | Exeter | 4,747 | 5,130 |
| 15538 | Fairhope-Arnold City | 2,803 | |
| 17872 | Fairview-Ferndale (uninc.) | 4,067 | |
| 18615 | Falls | 29,082 | 3,540 |
| 16121 | Farrell | 13,793 | 13,644 |
| 15905 | Ferndale | 2,717 | 2,619 |
| 19522 | Fleetwood | 2,647 | 2,338 |
| 19032 | Folcroft. '64 | 9,008 | 1,909 |
| 16226 | Ford City | 5,440 | 5,352 |
| 18421 | Forest City | 2,651 | 3,122 |
| 15221 | Forest Hills | 8,796 | 6,301 |
| 18704 | Forty Fort | 6,431 | 6,173 |
| | Fountain Hill | 6,428 | 5,456 |
| 15215 | Fox Chapel | 3,302 | 1,721 |
| 17931 | Frackville | 5,654 | 6,541 |
| 16323 | Franklin | 9,586 | 10,006 |
| 15042 | Freedom | 2,895 | 3,000 |
| 18224 | Freeland | 5,068 | 5,909 |
| 16641 | Gallitzin | 2,783 | 3,102 |
| 15904 | Geistown | 3,186 | 2,148 |
| 17325 | Gettysburg | 7,960 | 7,046 |
| 17935 | Girardville | 2,958 | 3,864 |
| 15045 | Glassport | 8,418 | 8,707 |
| 18617 | Glen Lyon | 4,173 | 3,921 |
| 19036 | Glenolden (borough) '67 | 8,229 | 6,450 |
| 17225 | Greencastle | 2,988 | 2,661 |
| 15601 | Greensburg | 17,383 | 16,923 |
| 15220 | Green Tree | 5,226 | 2,818 |
| 16125 | Greenville | 8,765 | 9,210 |
| 16127 | Grove City | 8,368 | 7,411 |
| 19526 | Hamburg | 3,747 | 3,805 |
| 17331 | Hanover | 15,538 | 14,048 |
| 16037 | Harmony | 5,106 | 4,501 |
| *17105 | Harrisburg | 79,697 | 89,544 |
| 15065 | Harrison | 15,710 | 15,116 |
| 19040 | Hatboro | 7,315 | 4,788 |
| 19041 | Haverford | 54,019 | 39,641 |
| 18201 | Hazleton | 32,056 | 35,491 |
| 18055 | Hellertown | 6,716 | 5,435 |
| 15601 | Hempfield, '64 | 33,036 | 22,463 |
| 17033 | Hershey | 6,851 | |
| 17034 | Highspire | 2,999 | 2,799 |
| 15102 | Hillcrest | 3,541 | |
| 16648 | Hollidaysburg | 6,475 | 6,483 |
| 16001 | Homeacre | 3,508 | |
| 15120 | Homestead | 7,502 | 10,046 |
| 18431 | Honesdale | 5,669 | 5,662 |
| 17036 | Hummelstown | 4,474 | 3,789 |
| 16652 | Huntingdon | 7,234 | 7,330 |
| 15701 | Indiana | 13,005 | 11,743 |
| 15205 | Ingram | 4,730 | 4,236 |
| 15642 | Irwin | 4,270 | 4,228 |
| 15644 | Jeannette | 16,565 | 16,172 |
| 15344 | Jefferson | 8,280 | |
| 19046 | Jenkintown | 5,017 | 5,130 |
| 18433 | Jermyn | 2,568 | 2,535 |
| 17740 | Jersey Shore | 5,613 | 5,595 |
| 18229 | Jim Thorpe | 5,945 | |
| 15845 | Johnsonburg | 4,966 | 4,567 |
| *15901 | Johnstown | 53,949 | 63,232 |
| 16735 | Kane | 5,380 | 5,706 |
| | Kenhorst | 2,815 | 2,551 |
| 19348 | Kennett Square | 4,355 | 3,699 |
| 18704 | Kingston | 20,261 | 21,069 |
| 16201 | Kittanning | 6,793 | 7,731 |
| 17834 | Kulpmont | 4,288 | 5,199 |
| 19530 | Kutztown | 3,312 | 3,110 |
| *17601 | Lancaster (city) | 61,055 | 63,774 |
| 17601 | Lancaster (township) | 10,020 | 6,859 |
| 19446 | Lansdale | 12,612 | 9,762 |
| 19050 | Lansdowne | 12,601 | 12,169 |
| 18232 | Lansford | 5,959 | 7,487 |
| 15704 | Larksville | 4,390 | 6,360 |
| 18650 | Latrobe | 11,932 | 11,811 |
| 19605 | Laureldale | 4,051 | 3,585 |
| 16511 | Lawrence Park | 4,403 | 4,154 |
| 17042 | Lebanon | 30,045 | 28,156 |
| 15656 | Leechburg | 3,545 | 4,042 |
| 18235 | Lehighton | 6,318 | 6,565 |
| 17043 | Lemoyne | 4,662 | 4,605 |
| 17837 | Lewisburg | 5,523 | 5,268 |
| 17044 | Lewistown | 12,640 | 13,894 |
| 16930 | Liberty | 3,624 | 1,900 |
| 17543 | Lititz | 5,987 | 5,568 |
| 17340 | Littlestown | 2,756 | 2,635 |
| 17745 | Lock Haven | 11,748 | 11,381 |
| 15068 | Lower Burrell | 11,952 | |
| 19061 | Lower Chichester | 4,460 | 2,938 |
| | Lower Merion | 59,420 | 48,745 |
| 19047 | Lower Southampton | 12,619 | 3,562 |
| 18709 | Luzerne | 5,118 | 6,176 |
| 17045 | Lykens | 2,527 | 2,735 |
| 16045 | Lyndora | 3,232 | |
| 18237 | McAdoo | 3,560 | 4,260 |
| (Y) | McChesneytown-Loyalhanna | 3,138 | |
| 15057 | McDonald | 3,141 | 3,543 |
| 15130 | McKeesport | 45,489 | 51,502 |
| 15136 | McKees Rocks | 13,185 | 16,241 |
| 17344 | McSherrystown | 2,839 | 2,510 |
| 17948 | Mahanoy City | 8,536 | 10,934 |
| 17545 | Manheim | 4,790 | 4,246 |
| 16933 | Mansfield | 2,678 | 2,657 |
| 19061 | Marcus Hook | 3,299 | 3,843 |
| 19008 | Marple | 19,722 | 4,799 |
| 17053 | Marysville | 2,580 | 2,158 |
| 15461 | Masontown | 4,730 | 4,550 |
| 16335 | Meadville | 16,671 | 18,972 |
| 17055 | Mechanicsburg | 8,123 | 6,786 |
| *19063 | Media | 5,803 | 5,726 |
| 16137 | Mercer | 2,800 | 2,397 |
| 15552 | Meyersdale | 2,901 | 3,137 |
| 17057 | Middletown (borough) | 11,182 | 9,184 |
| 19047 | Middletown (township) | 26,936 | 4,987 |
| 15059 | Midland | 6,425 | 6,491 |
| 17060 | Millcreek, '66 | 32,081 | 17,037 |
| 17061 | Millersburg | 2,984 | 2,861 |
| 17551 | Millersville, '66 | 5,353 | 2,551 |
| 15209 | Millvale | 6,624 | 7,287 |
| 17847 | Milton | 7,972 | 8,578 |
| 17754 | Minersville | 6,606 | 7,783 |
| 15061 | Monaca | 8,394 | 7,415 |
| 15062 | Monessen | 18,424 | 17,896 |
| 15063 | Monongahela | 8,388 | 8,922 |
| 15146 | Monroeville | 22,446 | |
| 17754 | Montoursville | 5,211 | 3,293 |
| 18507 | Moosic | 4,243 | 3,965 |
| 19067 | Morrisville | 7,790 | 6,787 |
| 17851 | Mount Carmel | 10,760 | 14,222 |
| 17552 | Mount Joy | 3,292 | 3,006 |
| 15228 | Mount Lebanon | 35,361 | 26,604 |
| 15210 | Mount Oliver | 5,980 | 6,646 |
| 19606 | Mount Penn | 3,574 | 3,635 |
| 15666 | Mount Pleasant | 5,107 | 5,583 |
| 17066 | Mount Union | 4,091 | 4,690 |
| 17756 | Muncy | 2,830 | 2,756 |
| 15120 | Munhall | 17,312 | 16,437 |
| 17067 | Myerstown | 3,268 | 3,050 |
| 18634 | Nanticoke | 15,601 | 20,160 |
| 15943 | Nanty-Glo | 4,608 | 5,425 |
| 19072 | Narberth | 5,109 | 5,407 |
| 18064 | Nazareth | 6,209 | 5,830 |
| 18240 | Nesquehoning | 2,714 | |
| 19086 | Nether Providence | 10,380 | 6,173 |
| 15066 | New Brighton | 8,397 | 9,535 |
| 16101 | New Castle | 44,790 | 48,834 |
| 17070 | New Cumberland | 9,257 | 6,204 |
| 15067 | New Eagle | 2,670 | 2,316 |
| 17557 | New Holland | 3,425 | 2,602 |
| 15068 | New Kensington | 23,485 | 25,146 |
| *19401 | Norristown | 38,925 | 38,126 |
| 18067 | Northampton | 8,866 | 9,332 |

(Y)    McChesneytown 15650; Loyalhanna 15661.

| ZIP Code | Place | 1960 | 1950 | ZIP Code | Place | 1960 | 1950 |
|---|---|---|---|---|---|---|---|
| | **PENNSYLVANIA—Continued** | | | | **PENNSYLVANIA—Continued** | | |
| 15012 | North Belle Vernon.... | 3,148 | 3,147 | 19081 | Swarthmore.......... | 5,753 | 4,825 |
| 15104 | North Braddock....... | 13,204 | 14,724 | 15218 | Swissvale............ | 15,089 | 16,488 |
| 18032 | North Catasauqua..... | 2,805 | 2,629 | 18704 | Swoyersville......... | 6,751 | 7,795 |
| 16428 | North East........... | 4,217 | 4,247 | 18252 | Tamaqua............ | 10,173 | 11,508 |
| 17857 | Northumberland....... | 4,156 | 4,207 | 15084 | Tarentum............ | 8,232 | 9,540 |
| 15035 | North Versailles...... | 13,565 | 9,521 | 18517 | Taylor.............. | 6,148 | 7,176 |
| 19454 | North Wales.......... | 3,673 | 2,998 | 18969 | Telford............. | 2,763 | 2,042 |
| 9074 | Norwood............. | 6,729 | 5,246 | 16354 | Titusville........... | 8,356 | 8,923 |
| 15139 | Oakmont............. | 7,504 | 7,264 | 18848 | Towanda............ | 4,293 | 4,069 |
| 16101 | Oakwood............. | 3,303 | 2,267 | 15085 | Trafford............ | 4,330 | 3,965 |
| 16301 | Oil City............. | 17,692 | 19,581 | 17881 | Trevorton........... | 2,597 | 2,545 |
| 18518 | Old Forge............ | 8,928 | 9,749 | 15145 | Turtle Creek......... | 10,607 | 12,363 |
| 15472 | Oliver............... | 3,015 | 2,180 | 16686 | Tyrone.............. | 7,792 | 8,214 |
| 18447 | Olyphant............. | 5,684 | 7,047 | 16438 | Union City.......... | 3,819 | 3,911 |
| 19363 | Oxford.............. | 3,376 | 3,091 | 15401 | Uniontown........... | 17,942 | 20,471 |
| 18042 | Palmer Heights....... | 2,597 | ...... | 19015 | Upland............. | 4,343 | 4,081 |
| 18071 | Palmerton........... | 5,942 | 6,646 | 19082 | Upper Darby......... | 93,158 | 84,951 |
| 17078 | Palmyra............. | 6,999 | 5,910 | 19090 | Upper Moreland, '66.. | 23,857 | 8,936 |
| 19365 | Parkesburg.......... | 2,759 | 2,611 | 15690 | Vandergrift......... | 8,742 | 9,524 |
| 17331 | Parkville............ | 4,516 | 3,299 | 15147 | Verona............. | 4,032 | 4,325 |
| 16668 | Patton.............. | 2,880 | 3,148 | 18974 | Warminster.......... | 15,994 | 7,127 |
| 18072 | Pen Argyl............ | 3,693 | 3,878 | 16365 | Warren.............. | 14,505 | 14,849 |
| 17103 | Penbrook............ | 3,671 | 3,691 | 15301 | Washington.......... | 23,545 | 26,280 |
| 15235 | Penn Hills, '66....... | 59,317 | 25,280 | 15301 | Washington West...... | 3,951 | ...... |
| 18944 | Perkasie............. | 4,650 | 4,358 | 17268 | Waynesboro.......... | 10,427 | 10,334 |
| *19104 | Philadelphia.......... | 2,002,512 | 2,071,605 | 15370 | Waynesburg......... | 5,188 | 5,514 |
| 16866 | Philipsburg.......... | 3,872 | 3,988 | 18255 | Weatherly........... | 2,591 | 2,622 |
| 19460 | Phoenixville......... | 13,797 | 12,932 | 16901 | Wellsboro........... | 4,369 | 4,215 |
| 15140 | Pitcairn............ | 5,383 | 5,857 | 16510 | Wesleyville.......... | 3,534 | 3,411 |
| *15219 | Pittsburgh........... | 604,332 | 676,806 | 19380 | West Chester........ | 15,705 | 15,168 |
| *18640 | Pittston............. | 12,407 | 15,012 | 18201 | West Hazleton....... | 6,278 | 6,988 |
| 15236 | Pleasant Hills........ | 8,573 | 3,808 | 15120 | West Homestead...... | 4,155 | 3,257 |
| 15239 | Plum, '66............ | 17,910 | ...... | 15122 | West Mifflin......... | 27,289 | 17,985 |
| 18651 | Plymouth............ | 10,401 | 13,021 | 15905 | Westmont........... | 6,573 | 4,410 |
| 16342 | Polk................ | 3,574 | 4,004 | 15089 | West Newton......... | 3,982 | 3,619 |
| 15946 | Portage............. | 3,933 | 4,371 | 19401 | West Norriton........ | 8,342 | 4,879 |
| 16743 | Port Allegany........ | 2,742 | 2,519 | 18643 | West Pittston........ | 6,998 | 7,230 |
| 17965 | Port Carbon......... | 2,775 | 3,024 | 19602 | West Reading........ | 4,938 | 5,072 |
| 15133 | Port Vue............ | 6,635 | 4,756 | 15229 | West View........... | 8,079 | 7,581 |
| 19464 | Pottstown........... | 26,144 | 22,589 | 18644 | West Wyoming....... | 3,166 | 2,863 |
| 17901 | Pottsville........... | 21,659 | 23,640 | 17404 | West York........... | 5,526 | 5,756 |
| 19076 | Prospect Park, '67.... | 7,049 | 5,834 | 15236 | Whitehall........... | 16,075 | 7,342 |
| 15767 | Punxsutawney....... | 8,805 | 8,969 | 15131 | White Oak........... | 9,047 | 6,619 |
| 18951 | Quakertown......... | 6,305 | 5,673 | *18701 | Wilkes-Barre (city)... | 63,551 | 76,826 |
| 15087 | Radnor.............. | 21,697 | 14,709 | 18701 | Wilkes-Barre (Twnp.). | 4,319 | 5,267 |
| 15104 | Rankin.............. | 5,164 | 6,941 | 15145 | Wilkins............. | 8,272 | 4,261 |
| *19603 | Reading............. | 98,177 | 109,320 | 15221 | Wilkinsburg......... | 30,066 | 31,418 |
| 17356 | Red Lion............ | 5,594 | 5,119 | 17701 | Williamsport........ | 41,967 | 45,047 |
| 17764 | Renovo............. | 3,316 | 3,751 | 15148 | Wilmerding.......... | 4,349 | 5,325 |
| ...... | Reserve............. | 4,230 | 3,533 | 15025 | Wilson............. | 8,465 | 8,159 |
| 15851 | Reynoldsville........ | 3,158 | 3,569 | 15963 | Windber............ | 6,994 | 8,010 |
| 15853 | Ridgway............ | 6,387 | 6,244 | 18403 | Winton............. | 5,456 | 6,280 |
| ...... | Ridley.............. | 35,738 | 17,212 | 18644 | Wyoming............ | 4,127 | 4,511 |
| 19078 | Ridley Park.......... | 7,387 | 4,921 | 19610 | Wyomissing......... | 5,044 | 4,187 |
| 16673 | Roaring Spring....... | 2,937 | 2,771 | 19050 | Yeadon............. | 11,610 | 11,068 |
| 15074 | Rochester........... | 5,952 | 7,197 | *17405 | York............... | 54,504 | 59,953 |
| 19111 | Rockledge........... | 2,587 | 2,261 | 15697 | Youngwood......... | 2,813 | 2,720 |
| 16323 | Rocky Grove......... | 3,168 | 3,111 | 16063 | Zelienople........... | 3,284 | 2,981 |
| ...... | Ross................ | 25,952 | 15,744 | | | | |
| 19468 | Royersford.......... | 3,969 | 3,862 | | **RHODE ISLAND** | | |
| 17970 | St. Clair............ | 5,159 | 5,856 | | *See Note on Page 605* | | |
| 15857 | St. Marys........... | 8,065 | 7,846 | | | | |
| 18840 | Sayre.............. | 7,917 | 7,735 | | **Special census of state was taken Oct. 1, 1965.** | | |
| 17972 | Schuylkill Haven..... | 6,470 | 6,597 | | (New totals appear in 1960 column) | | |
| ...... | Scott............... | 19,094 | 8,686 | | | | |
| 15683 | Scottdale........... | 6,244 | 6,249 | 02806 | Barrington.......... | 16,390 | 8,246 |
| *18503 | Scranton............ | 111,443 | 125,536 | 02809 | Bristol.............. | 15,716 | 12,320 |
| 17870 | Selinsgrove.......... | 3,948 | 3,514 | | *Burrillville*......... | 9,682 | 8,774 |
| 15143 | Sewickley........... | 6,157 | 5,836 | 02863 | Central Falls........ | 18,677 | 23,550 |
| 15116 | Shaler.............. | 24,939 | 16,430 | 02813 | *Charlestown*........ | 2,586 | 1,598 |
| 17872 | Shamokin........... | 13,674 | 16,879 | 02816 | *Coventry*........... | 19,577 | 9,869 |
| 16146 | Sharon............. | 25,267 | 26,454 | 02910 | Cranston............ | 71,913 | 55,060 |
| 19079 | Sharon Hill '67...... | 7,464 | 5,464 | 02864 | *Cumberland*........ | 23,839 | 12,842 |
| 15215 | Sharpsburg......... | 6,096 | 7,296 | 02818 | *East Greenwich*..... | 8,228 | 4,923 |
| 16150 | Sharpsville......... | 6,061 | 5,414 | 02914 | East Providence..... | 44,828 | 35,871 |
| 17976 | Shenandoah......... | 11,073 | 15,704 | 02822 | *Exeter*............ | 2,987 | 1,870 |
| 19607 | Shillington.......... | 5,639 | 5,059 | | *Glocester*.......... | 4,142 | 2,686 |
| 17257 | Shippensburg....... | 6,138 | 5,722 | 02833 | *Hopkinton*......... | 4,674 | 3,672 |
| 18080 | Slatington.......... | 4,316 | 4,343 | 02835 | *Jamestown*........ | 2,567 | 2,068 |
| 16057 | Slippery Rock....... | 2,563 | 2,294 | 02919 | *Johnston*.......... | 19,547 | 12,725 |
| 15501 | Somerset............ | 6,347 | 5,936 | 02881 | *Kingston*.......... | 4,454 | 2,156 |
| 18964 | Souderton.......... | 5,381 | 4,521 | 02865 | *Lincoln*........... | 14,600 | 11,270 |
| 15601 | South Greensburg... | 3,058 | 2,980 | 02840 | *Middletown*........ | 19,562 | 7,382 |
| 15905 | Southmont.......... | 2,857 | 2,278 | 02882 | *Narragansett*...... | 5,043 | 2,288 |
| 15401 | South Uniontown.... | 3,603 | 3,425 | 02840 | Newport............ | 35,901 | 37,564 |
| 15601 | S.W. Greensburg.... | 3,264 | 3,144 | 02840 | Newport East....... | 2,891 | ...... |
| 17707 | S. Williamsport..... | 6,972 | 6,364 | 02852 | *North Kingstown*... | 23,013 | 14,810 |
| 15775 | Spangler............ | 2,658 | 3,013 | ...... | North Providence.... | 21,206 | 13,927 |
| 19475 | Spring City......... | 3,162 | 3,258 | | *North Smithfield*.... | 8,716 | 5,726 |
| 15144 | Springdale.......... | 5,602 | 4,939 | 02859 | *Pascoag*........... | 2,987 | ...... |
| 19064 | Springfield (Del. County) | 26,733 | 10,917 | *02860 | Pawtucket.......... | 77,538 | 81,436 |
| 19118 | Springfield (Montgomery County) | 20,652 | 11,403 | 02871 | *Portsmouth*........ | 10,664 | 6,578 |
| 17422 | Spring Garden........ | 11,387 | 8,333 | *02904 | Providence.......... | 187,061 | 248,674 |
| 16801 | State College, '64.... | 27,584 | 17,227 | | *Scituate*.......... | 6,180 | 3,905 |
| 17092 | Steelton............ | 11,266 | 12,574 | | *Smithfield*......... | 12,031 | 6,690 |
| 19464 | Stowe.............. | 11,730 | 12,210 | | *South Kingstown*... | 14,405 | 10,148 |
| 19465 | Stowe (uninc.)...... | 2,765 | 2,524 | 02878 | *Tiverton*.......... | 10,966 | 5,659 |
| 15363 | Strabane............ | 3,036 | 2,861 | 02879 | Wakefield-Peacedale. | 5,600 | 5,224 |
| 18360 | Stroudsburg......... | 6,070 | 6,361 | 02885 | *Warren*........... | 9,749 | 8,513 |
| 18250 | Summit Hill......... | 4,386 | 4,924 | 02886 | Warwick............ | 77,637 | 43,028 |
| 17801 | Sunbury............ | 13,687 | 15,570 | 02891 | Westerly............ | 10,050 | 8,415 |
| 18847 | Susquehanna Depot.... | 2,591 | 2,646 | | | | |

### RHODE ISLAND—Continued

| ZIP Code | Place | 1960 | 1950 |
|---|---|---|---|
| 02893 | *Westerly (town)* | 15,711 | 12,380 |
| 02893 | West Warwick | 21,915 | 19,096 |
| 02852 | Wickford | 3,074 | 2,437 |
| 02895 | Woonsocket | 46,678 | 50,211 |

### SOUTH CAROLINA

| ZIP Code | Place | 1960 | 1950 |
|---|---|---|---|
| 29620 | Abbeville | 5,436 | 5,395 |
| | Aiken | 11,243 | 7,083 |
| 29801 | Aiken South | 2,980 | ........ |
| | Aiken West | 2,602 | ........ |
| 29810 | Allendale | 3,114 | 2,474 |
| 29621 | Anderson | 41,316 | 19,770 |
| 29510 | Andrews | 2,995 | 2,702 |
| 29003 | Bamberg | 3,081 | 2,954 |
| 29812 | Barnwell | 4,568 | 2,005 |
| 29006 | Batesburg | 3,806 | 3,169 |
| 29902 | Beaufort | 6,298 | 5,081 |
| 29627 | Belton | 5,106 | 3,371 |
| 29512 | Bennettsville | 6,963 | 5,140 |
| 29010 | Bishopville | 3,586 | 3,076 |
| 29628 | Calhoun Falls | 2,525 | 2,396 |
| 29020 | Camden | 6,842 | 6,986 |
| 29033 | Cayce, '66 | 9,490 | 3,294 |
| *29401 | Charleston (A) | 75,940 | 70,174 |
| 29520 | Cheraw | 5,171 | 4,836 |
| 29706 | Chester | 6,906 | 6,893 |
| 29325 | Clinton | 7,937 | 7,168 |
| 29710 | Clover | 3,500 | 3,276 |
| *29201 | Columbia | 97,433 | 86,914 |
| 29526 | Conway | 8,563 | 6,073 |
| 29532 | Darlington | 6,710 | 6,619 |
| 29042 | Denmark | 3,221 | 2,814 |
| 29536 | Dillon | 6,173 | 5,171 |
| 29640 | Dasley | 8,283 | 6,316 |
| ........ | East Gaffney | 4,779 | 4,289 |
| 29824 | Edgefield | 2,876 | 2,518 |
| 29501 | Florence (A) | 27,208 | 22,513 |
| 29206 | Forest Acres (A) '67 | 5,894 | 3,240 |
| 29715 | Fort Mill | 3,315 | 3,204 |
| 29340 | Gaffney (A) | 11,448 | 8,123 |
| 29440 | Georgetown | 12,261 | 6,004 |
| 29055 | Great Falls | 3,030 | 3,533 |
| *29602 | Greenville | 66,188 | 58,161 |
| 29646 | Greenwood (A) | 19,861 | 13,806 |
| 29651 | Greer | 8,967 | 5,050 |
| 29550 | Hartsville (A) | 8,762 | 5,658 |
| 29654 | Honea Path | 3,453 | 2,840 |
| 29556 | Kingstree | 3,847 | 3,621 |
| 29560 | Lake City | 6,059 | 5,112 |
| 29720 | Lancaster | 7,999 | 7,159 |
| 29720 | Lancaster Mills | 3,274 | ........ |
| 29360 | Laurens | 9,598 | 8,658 |
| 29657 | Liberty | 2,657 | 2,291 |
| 29102 | Manning | 3,917 | 2,775 |
| 29571 | Marion | 7,174 | 6,834 |
| 29464 | Mount Pleasant | 5,116 | 1,857 |
| 29574 | Mullins | 6,229 | 4,916 |
| 29577 | Myrtle Beach | 7,834 | 3,345 |
| 29108 | Newberry (A) | 9,109 | 7,546 |
| 29841 | North Augusta | 10,348 | 3,659 |
| 29115 | Orangeburg | 13,852 | 15,322 |
| 29730 | Rock Hill | 29,404 | 24,502 |
| 29301 | Saxon | 3,917 | 3,088 |
| 29678 | Seneca | 5,227 | 3,649 |
| ........ | Shannontown | 7,064 | 5,828 |
| 29646 | South Greenwood | 2,520 | 3,712 |
| *29301 | Spartanburg | 44,352 | 36,795 |
| 29169 | Springdale | 2,981 | ........ |
| 29483 | Summerville | 3,633 | 3,312 |
| 29150 | Sumter | 23,062 | 20,185 |
| 29379 | Union | 10,191 | 9,730 |
| 29691 | Walhalla | 3,431 | 3,104 |
| 29488 | Walterboro | 5,417 | 4,616 |
| 29692 | Ware Shoals | 2,671 | 3,032 |
| 29169 | West Columbia | 6,410 | 1,543 |
| 29178 | Whitmire | 2,663 | 3,006 |
| 29303 | Whitney | 2,502 | 1,611 |
| 29697 | Williamston | 3,721 | 2,782 |
| 29853 | Williston | 2,722 | 896 |
| 29180 | Winnsboro | 3,479 | 3,267 |
| 29388 | Woodruff | 3,679 | 3,831 |
| 29745 | York | 4,758 | 4,181 |

### SOUTH DAKOTA

| ZIP Code | Place | 1960 | 1950 |
|---|---|---|---|
| 57401 | Aberdeen | 23,073 | 21,051 |
| 57717 | Belle Fourche | 4,087 | 3,540 |
| 57006 | Brookings | 10,558 | 7,764 |
| 57013 | Canton | 2,511 | 2,530 |
| 57325 | Chamberlain | 2,598 | 1,912 |
| 57732 | Deadwood | 3,045 | 3,288 |
| 57532 | Fort Pierre | 2,649 | 951 |
| 57747 | Hot Springs | 4,943 | 5,030 |
| 57350 | Huron | 14,180 | 12,788 |
| 57754 | Lead | 6,211 | 6,422 |
| 57042 | Madison | 5,420 | 5,153 |
| 57252 | Milbank | 3,500 | 2,982 |
| 57301 | Mitchell | 12,555 | 12,123 |
| 57601 | Mobridge | 4,391 | 3,753 |
| 57501 | Pierre | 10,088 | 5,715 |
| 57701 | Rapid City | 42,399 | 25,310 |
| 57469 | Redfield | 2,952 | 2,655 |

### SOUTH DAKOTA—Continued

| ZIP Code | Place | 1960 | 1950 |
|---|---|---|---|
| *57101 | Sioux Falls | 65,466 | 52,696 |
| 57262 | Sisseton | 3,218 | 2,871 |
| 57783 | Spearfish | 3,682 | 2,775 |
| 57785 | Sturgis | 4,639 | 3,471 |
| 57069 | Vermillion | 6,102 | 5,337 |
| 57201 | Watertown | 14,077 | 12,699 |
| 57580 | Winner | 3,705 | 3,252 |
| 57078 | Yankton | 9,279 | 7,709 |

### TENNESSEE

| ZIP Code | Place | 1960 | 1950 |
|---|---|---|---|
| 37701 | Alcoa | 6,395 | 6,355 |
| 37303 | Athens | 12,103 | 8,618 |
| 37205 | Belle Meade | 3,082 | 2,831 |
| 38314 | Bemis | 3,127 | 3,248 |
| 38008 | Bolivar | 3,338 | 2,429 |
| 37620 | Bristol | 17,582 | 16,771 |
| 38012 | Brownsville | 5,424 | 4,711 |
| 38320 | Camden | 2,774 | 2,029 |
| *37401 | Chattanooga | 130,009 | 131,041 |
| 37040 | Clarksville (A) '67 | 35,657 | 16,246 |
| 37311 | Cleveland | 16,196 | 12,605 |
| 37716 | Clinton | 4,943 | 3,712 |
| 37401 | Columbia | 17,624 | 10,911 |
| 38501 | Cookeville | 7,805 | 6,924 |
| 38019 | Covington | 5,298 | 4,379 |
| 38555 | Crossville | 4,668 | 2,291 |
| 37321 | Dayton | 3,500 | 3,191 |
| 37055 | Dickson | 5,028 | 3,348 |
| 37214 | Donelson | 17,195 | 1,765 |
| 38024 | Dyersburg | 12,499 | 10,885 |
| 37801 | Eagleton Village | 5,068 | ........ |
| 37412 | East Ridge '67 | 20,260 | 9,645 |
| 37311 | Elizabethton | 10,896 | 10,754 |
| 37650 | Erwin | 3,210 | 3,387 |
| 37331 | Etowah | 3,223 | 3,261 |
| 37334 | Fayetteville | 6,804 | 5,447 |
| 37918 | Fountain City | 10,365 | ........ |
| 37064 | Franklin | 6,977 | 5,475 |
| 37066 | Gallatin | 7,901 | 5,107 |
| 37072 | Goodlettsville | 3,163 | ........ |
| 37743 | Greeneville | 11,759 | 8,721 |
| 37748 | Harriman | 5,931 | 6,389 |
| 38340 | Henderson | 2,691 | 2,532 |
| 38343 | Humboldt | 8,482 | 7,426 |
| 37216 | Inglewood | 26,527 | ........ |
| 38301 | Jackson | 34,376 | 30,207 |
| 37760 | Jefferson City | 4,550 | 3,633 |
| 37601 | Johnson City | 31,187 | 27,864 |
| 37660 | Kingsport | 26,314 | 19,571 |
| *37901 | Knoxville | 111,827 | 124,769 |
| 37766 | La Follette | 6,204 | 5,797 |
| 38464 | Lawrenceburg | 8,042 | 5,442 |
| 37087 | Lebanon | 10,512 | 7,913 |
| 37771 | Lenoir City | 4,979 | 5,159 |
| 37091 | Lewisburg | 6,338 | 5,164 |
| 38351 | Lexington | 3,943 | 3,566 |
| 38570 | Livingston | 2,817 | 2,082 |
| 37774 | Loudon | 3,812 | 3,567 |
| 37665 | Lynn Gardens | 5,261 | ........ |
| 38201 | McKenzie | 3,780 | 3,774 |
| 37110 | McMinnville | 9,013 | 7,577 |
| 37115 | Madison | 13,583 | ........ |
| 37355 | Manchester, '66 | 4,342 | 2,341 |
| 38237 | Martin | 4,750 | 4,082 |
| 37801 | Maryville | 10,348 | 7,742 |
| *38101 | Memphis (A) '67 | 536,585 | 396,000 |
| 38358 | Milan | 5,208 | 4,938 |
| 38053 | Millington | 6,059 | 4,696 |
| 37814 | Morristown | 21,267 | 13,019 |
| 38474 | Mount Pleasant | 2,921 | 2,931 |
| 37130 | Murfreesboro | 18,991 | 13,052 |
| *37202 | Nashville | 170,874 | 174,307 |
| 37821 | Newport (A) '67 | 7,282 | 3,892 |
| 37040 | New Providence | 4,451 | 1,825 |
| 37204 | Oak Hill | 4,490 | ........ |
| 37830 | Oak Ridge, '64 | 29,696 | ........ |
| 38242 | Paris | 9,325 | 8,826 |
| 37211 | Providence | 3,830 | ........ |
| 38478 | Pulaski | 6,616 | 5,762 |
| 37415 | Red Bank-White Oak, '66 | 11,737 | ........ |
| 38063 | Ripley | 3,782 | 3,318 |
| 37854 | Rockwood | 5,345 | 4,272 |
| 37857 | Rogersville | 3,121 | 2,545 |
| 38372 | Savannah | 4,315 | 1,698 |
| 37862 | Sevierville | 2,890 | 1,620 |
| 37160 | Shelbyville | 10,466 | 9,456 |
| 37377 | Signal Mountain | 3,413 | 1,786 |
| 37167 | Smyrna | 3,612 | 1,544 |
| 38068 | South Fulton, '66 | 2,686 | 2,119 |
| 37748 | South Harriman | 2,884 | 2,761 |
| 37380 | South Pittsburg | 4,130 | 2,573 |
| 38583 | Sparta | 4,510 | 4,299 |
| 37172 | Springfield | 9,221 | 6,506 |
| 37874 | Sweetwater | 4,145 | 4,199 |
| 37419 | Tiftona | 3,520 | ........ |
| 38382 | Trenton | 4,225 | 3,868 |
| 38388 | Tullahoma, '65 | 13,657 | 7,562 |
| 38261 | Union City | 8,837 | 7,665 |
| 37185 | Waverly | 2,891 | 1,892 |
| 37665 | West View Park | 4,722 | ........ |
| 38116 | Whitehaven | 13,894 | 1,311 |
| 37398 | Winchester | 4,760 | 3,974 |

| ZIP Code | Place | 1960 | 1950 | ZIP Code | Place | 1960 | 1950 |
|---|---|---|---|---|---|---|---|
| | **TENNESSEE—Continued** | | | | **TEXAS—Continued** | | |
| 37211 | Woodbine-Radnor-Glencliff | 14,485 | .... | 78539 | Edinburg | 18,706 | 12,383 |
| (Z) | Woodmont-Green Hills-Glendale | 23,161 | .... | 77957 | Edna | 5,038 | 3,855 |
| | | | | 77437 | El Campo | 7,700 | 6,237 |
| | **TEXAS** | | | 76360 | Electra | 4,759 | 4,970 |
| | | | | 78621 | Elgin | 3,511 | 3,168 |
| *79604 | Abilene | 90,368 | 45,570 | *79910 | El Paso | 276,687 | 130,485 |
| 78516 | Alamo | 4,121 | 3,017 | 78543 | Elsa | 3,847 | 3,179 |
| 78209 | Alamo Heights | 7,552 | 8,000 | 75119 | Ennis | 9,347 | 7,815 |
| 78332 | Alice | 20,861 | 16,449 | 79838 | Fabens | 3,134 | 3,089 |
| 79830 | Alpine | 4,740 | 5,261 | 78355 | Falfurrias | 6,515 | 6,712 |
| 77511 | Alvin | 5,643 | 3,701 | 75234 | Farmers Branch | 13,441 | 915 |
| *79105 | Amarillo | 137,969 | 74,246 | 79235 | Floydada | 3,769 | 3,210 |
| 79714 | Andrews | 11,135 | 3,294 | 75703 | Forest Hill | 3,221 | 1,519 |
| 77515 | Angleton | 7,312 | 3,399 | 79735 | Fort Stockton | 6,373 | 4,444 |
| 79501 | Anson | 2,890 | 2,708 | *76101 | Fort Worth | 356,268 | 278,778 |
| 78336 | Aransas Pass | 6,956 | 5,396 | 78624 | Fredericksburg | 4,629 | 3,854 |
| 76010 | Arlington | 44,775 | 7,692 | 77541 | Freeport | 11,619 | 6,012 |
| 75751 | Athens | 7,086 | 5,194 | 78357 | Freer | 2,724 | 2,260 |
| 75551 | Atlanta | 4,076 | 3,782 | 76240 | Gainesville | 13,083 | 11,246 |
| *78710 | Austin | 186,545 | 132,459 | 77547 | Galena Park | 10,852 | 7,186 |
| 76020 | Azle | 2,969 | .... | 77550 | Galveston | 67,175 | 66,568 |
| 75149 | Balch Springs | 6,821 | .... | 75040 | Garland | 38,501 | 10,571 |
| 78821 | Ballinger | 5,043 | 5,302 | 76528 | Gatesville | 4,626 | 3,856 |
| 78602 | Bastrop | 3,001 | 3,176 | 78626 | Georgetown | 5,218 | 4,951 |
| 77414 | Bay City | 11,656 | 9,427 | 78942 | Giddings | 2,821 | 2,532 |
| 77520 | Baytown | 28,159 | 22,983 | 75644 | Gilmer | 4,312 | 4,096 |
| *77704 | Beaumont | 119,175 | 94,014 | 75647 | Gladewater | 5,742 | 5,305 |
| 76021 | Bedford | 2,706 | .... | 78629 | Gonzales | 5,829 | 5,659 |
| 78102 | Beeville | 13,811 | 9,348 | 76046 | Graham | 8,505 | 6,742 |
| 77401 | Bellaire | 19,872 | 10,173 | 75050 | Grand Prairie | 30,386 | 14,594 |
| 76705 | Bellmead | 5,127 | .... | 76051 | Grapevine | 2,821 | 1,824 |
| 76513 | Belton | 8,163 | 6,246 | 75401 | Greenville | 19,087 | 14,727 |
| 76126 | Benbrook | 3,254 | 617 | 77619 | Groves | 17,304 | .... |
| 76932 | Big Lake | 2,668 | 2,152 | 77964 | Hallettsville | 2,808 | 2,000 |
| 79720 | Big Spring | 31,230 | 17,286 | 76117 | Haltom City | 23,133 | 5,760 |
| 78343 | Bishop | 3,722 | 2,731 | 76531 | Hamilton | 3,106 | 3,077 |
| 75418 | Bonham | 7,357 | 7,049 | 79520 | Hamlin | 3,791 | 3,569 |
| 79007 | Borger | 20,911 | 18,059 | 78550 | Harlingen | 41,207 | 23,229 |
| 76230 | Bowie | 4,566 | 4,544 | 79521 | Haskell | 4,016 | 3,836 |
| 76825 | Brady | 5,338 | 5,944 | 77859 | Hearne | 5,072 | 4,872 |
| 76024 | Breckenridge | 6,273 | 6,610 | 78361 | Hebbronville | 3,987 | 4,302 |
| 77833 | Brenham | 7,740 | 6,941 | 75652 | Henderson | 9,666 | 6,833 |
| 77611 | Bridge City | 4,677 | .... | 76365 | Henrietta | 3,062 | 2,813 |
| 76026 | Bridgeport | 3,218 | 2,049 | 79045 | Hereford | 7,652 | 5,207 |
| 79316 | Brownfield | 10,286 | 6,161 | 75205 | Highland Park | 10,411 | 11,405 |
| 78520 | Brownsville | 48,040 | 36,066 | 77562 | Highlands | 4,336 | 2,723 |
| 76801 | Brownwood | 16,974 | 20,182 | 76645 | Hillsboro | 7,402 | 8,363 |
| 77801 | Bryan | 27,542 | 18,101 | 77563 | Hitchcock | 5,216 | .... |
| 76354 | Burkburnett | 7,621 | 4,555 | 78861 | Hondo | 4,992 | 4,188 |
| 76520 | Cameron | 5,640 | 5,052 | *77002 | Houston | 938,219 | 596,163 |
| 79015 | Canyon | 5,864 | 4,364 | 77340 | Huntsville | 11,999 | 9,820 |
| 78834 | Carrizo Springs | 5,699 | 4,316 | 76053 | Hurst | 10,165 | .... |
| 75006 | Carrollton | 4,242 | 1,610 | 78362 | Ingleside | 3,022 | .... |
| 75633 | Carthage | 5,262 | 4,750 | 76367 | Iowa Park | 3,295 | 2,110 |
| 78213 | Castle Hills | 2,622 | .... | 75060 | Irving | 45,985 | 2,621 |
| 75935 | Center | 4,510 | 4,323 | 77029 | Jacinto City | 9,547 | 6,856 |
| 79201 | Childress | 6,399 | 7,619 | 76056 | Jacksboro | 3,816 | 2,951 |
| 76437 | Cisco | 4,499 | 5,230 | 75766 | Jacksonville | 9,590 | 8,607 |
| 75426 | Clarksville | 3,851 | 4,353 | 75951 | Jasper | 4,889 | 4,403 |
| 76031 | Cleburne | 15,381 | 12,905 | 75657 | Jefferson | 3,082 | 3,164 |
| 77327 | Cleveland | 5,838 | 5,183 | 78118 | Karnes City | 2,693 | 2,588 |
| 77531 | Clute City | 4,501 | .... | 75142 | Kaufman | 3,087 | 2,714 |
| 75211 | Cockrell Hill | 3,104 | 2,207 | 78119 | Kenedy | 4,301 | 4,234 |
| 76834 | Coleman | 6,371 | 6,530 | 79745 | Kermit | 10,465 | 6,912 |
| 77840 | College Station | 11,396 | 7,925 | 78028 | Kerrville | 8,901 | 7,691 |
| 79512 | Colorado City | 6,457 | 6,774 | 75662 | Kilgore | 10,092 | 9,638 |
| 78934 | Columbus | 3,656 | 2,878 | 76544 | Killeen | 23,377 | 7,045 |
| 76442 | Comanche | 3,415 | 3,840 | 78363 | Kingsville | 25,297 | 16,898 |
| 75428 | Commerce | 5,789 | 5,889 | 77453 | Kleberg | 3,572 | .... |
| 77301 | Conroe | 9,192 | 7,298 | 78559 | La Feria | 3,047 | 2,952 |
| 76522 | Copperas Cove | 4,567 | 1,052 | 78945 | La Grange | 3,623 | 2,738 |
| *78403 | Corpus Christi | 167,690 | 108,287 | 77566 | Lake Jackson | 9,651 | 2,897 |
| 75110 | Corsicana | 20,344 | 19,211 | 79239 | Lakeview | 3,849 | 3,091 |
| 78014 | Cotulla | 3,960 | 4,418 | 76135 | Lake Worth Village | 3,833 | 2,351 |
| 79731 | Crane | 3,796 | 2,154 | 77568 | La Marque | 13,969 | .... |
| 75835 | Crockett | 5,356 | 5,932 | 79331 | Lamesa | 12,438 | 10,704 |
| 78839 | Crystal City | 9,101 | 7,198 | 76550 | Lampasas | 5,061 | 4,869 |
| 77954 | Cuero | 7,338 | 7,498 | 75146 | Lancaster | 7,501 | 2,632 |
| 75638 | Daingerfield | 3,133 | 1,668 | 77571 | La Porte | 4,512 | 1,429 |
| 79022 | Dalhart | 5,160 | 5,918 | 78040 | Laredo | 60,678 | 51,910 |
| *75221 | Dallas | 679,684 | 434,462 | 77573 | League City | 2,622 | 1,341 |
| 77535 | Dayton | 3,367 | 1,820 | 79336 | Levelland | 10,153 | 8,264 |
| 76234 | Decatur | 3,563 | 2,922 | 75067 | Lewisville | 3,956 | 1,516 |
| 77536 | Deer Park | 4,865 | 736 | 77575 | Liberty | 6,127 | 4,163 |
| 78840 | Del Rio | 18,612 | 14,211 | 79339 | Littlefield | 7,236 | 6,540 |
| 75020 | Denison | 22,748 | 17,504 | 77351 | Livingston | 3,398 | 2,865 |
| 76201 | Denton | 26,844 | 21,372 | 78643 | Llano | 2,656 | 2,954 |
| 79323 | Denver City | 4,302 | 1,855 | 78644 | Lockhart | 6,084 | 5,573 |
| 78016 | Devine | 2,522 | 1,672 | 75601 | Longview | 40,050 | 24,502 |
| 75941 | Diboll | 2,506 | 2,391 | *79408 | Lubbock | 128,691 | 71,747 |
| 77539 | Dickinson | 4,715 | 2,704 | 75901 | Lufkin | 17,641 | 15,135 |
| 79027 | Dimmitt | 2,935 | 1,461 | 78648 | Luling | 4,412 | 4,297 |
| 78537 | Donna | 7,522 | 7,171 | 78501 | McAllen, '66 | 35,411 | 20,067 |
| 77018 | Donnybrook Place | 2,537 | .... | 79752 | McCamey | 3,375 | 3,129 |
| 79029 | Dumas | 8,477 | 6,127 | 76657 | McGregor | 4,642 | 2,661 |
| 75116 | Duncanville | 3,774 | 841 | 75069 | McKinney | 13,763 | 10,560 |
| 77734 | Eagle Lake | 3,565 | 2,787 | 78843 | Marfa | 2,799 | 3,603 |
| 78852 | Eagle Pass | 12,094 | 7,276 | 76661 | Marlin | 6,918 | 7,099 |
| 76448 | Eastland | 3,292 | 3,626 | 75670 | Marshall | 23,846 | 22,327 |
| 78538 | Edcouch | 2,814 | 2,925 | 78368 | Mathis | 6,075 | 4,050 |
| | | | | 79245 | Memphis | 3,332 | 3,810 |
| | | | | 78570 | Mercedes | 10,943 | 10,081 |
| | | | | 75149 | Mesquite | 27,526 | 1,696 |

(Z) *Woodmont-Green Hills* 37215; *Glendale* 37204.

| ZIP Code | Place | 1960 | 1950 | ZIP Code | Place | 1960 | 1950 |
|---|---|---|---|---|---|---|---|
| | **TEXAS—Continued** | | | | **UTAH** | | |
| 76667 | Mexia | 6,121 | 6,627 | 76384 | Vernon | 12,141 | 12,651 |
| 79701 | Midland | 62,625 | 21,713 | 77901 | Victoria | 33,047 | 16,126 |
| 75773 | Mineola | 3,810 | 3,626 | 77662 | Vidor | 4,938 | 2,136 |
| 76067 | Mineral Wells | 11,053 | 7,801 | *76703 | Waco | 97,808 | 84,706 |
| 78572 | Mission | 14,081 | 10,765 | 75165 | Waxahachie | 12,749 | 11,204 |
| 79756 | Monahans | 8,567 | 6,311 | 76086 | Weatherford | 9,759 | 8,093 |
| 79346 | Morton | 2,731 | 2,274 | 79095 | Wellington | 3,137 | 3,676 |
| 75455 | Mount Pleasant | 8,027 | 6,342 | 78596 | Weslaco | 15,649 | 7,514 |
| 79347 | Muleshoe | 3,871 | 2,477 | 77486 | West Columbia | 2,947 | 2,100 |
| 75961 | Nacogdoches | 12,674 | 12,327 | 77630 | West Orange | 4,848 | |
| 77868 | Navasota | 4,937 | 5,188 | 77005 | West University Place | 14,628 | 17,074 |
| 77627 | Nederland | 12,036 | 3,805 | 76114 | Westworth | 3,321 | 529 |
| 75570 | New Boston | 2,773 | 2,688 | 77488 | Wharton | 5,734 | 4,450 |
| 78130 | New Braunfels | 15,631 | 12,210 | 76108 | White Settlement | 11,513 | 10,827 |
| 76255 | Nocona | 3,127 | 3,022 | *76307 | Wichita Falls | 101,724 | 68,042 |
| 76118 | North Richland Hills | 8,662 | | 75494 | Winnsboro | 2,675 | 2,512 |
| 79760 | Odessa | 80,338 | 29,495 | 79567 | Winters | 3,266 | 2,676 |
| 76374 | Olney | 3,872 | 3,765 | 77995 | Yoakum | 5,761 | 5,231 |
| 77630 | Orange | 25,605 | 21,174 | 78164 | Yorktown | 2,527 | 2,596 |
| 76943 | Ozona | 3,361 | 2,885 | 84003 | American Fork | 6,373 | 5,126 |
| 77465 | Palacios | 3,676 | 2,799 | 84010 | Bountiful | 17,039 | 6,004 |
| 75801 | Palestine | 13,974 | 12,503 | 84302 | Brigham City | 11,728 | 6,790 |
| 79065 | Pampa | 24,664 | 16,583 | 84720 | Cedar City | 7,543 | 6,106 |
| 75460 | Paris | 20,977 | 21,643 | 84015 | Clearfield | 8,833 | 4,723 |
| 77501 | Pasadena | 58,737 | 22,483 | 84520 | Dragerton | 2,959 | 3,453 |
| 77640 | Pear Ridge | 3,470 | 2,029 | 84032 | Heber | 2,936 | 2,936 |
| 78061 | Pearsall | 4,957 | 4,481 | 84037 | Kaysville | 3,608 | 1,898 |
| 79772 | Pecos | 12,728 | 5,054 | 84118 | Kearns | 17,172 | |
| 79070 | Perryton | 7,903 | 4,417 | 84041 | Layton | 9,027 | 3,456 |
| 78577 | Pharr, '66 | 15,279 | 8,690 | 84043 | Lehi | 4,377 | 3,627 |
| 79071 | Phillips | 3,605 | 4,105 | 84321 | Logan | 18,731 | 16,832 |
| 75686 | Pittsburg | 3,796 | 3,142 | 84044 | Magna | 6,442 | 3,502 |
| 79072 | Plainview | 18,735 | 14,044 | 84047 | Midvale | 5,802 | 3,996 |
| 75074 | Plano | 3,695 | 2,126 | 84532 | Moab | 4,682 | 1,274 |
| 78064 | Pleasanton | 3,467 | 2,913 | 84107 | Murray | 16,806 | 9,006 |
| 77640 | Port Arthur | 66,676 | 57,530 | 84648 | Nephi | 2,566 | 2,990 |
| 78578 | Port Isabel | 3,575 | 2,372 | 84404 | North Ogden | 2,621 | 1,105 |
| 78374 | Portland, '65 | 5,211 | 1,292 | *84401 | Ogden | 70,197 | 57,112 |
| 77779 | Port Lavaca | 8,864 | 5,599 | 84057 | Orem | 18,394 | 8,351 |
| 77651 | Port Neches | 8,696 | 5,448 | 84651 | Payson | 4,237 | 3,998 |
| 79356 | Post | 4,663 | 3,141 | 84062 | Pleasant Grove | 4,772 | 3,195 |
| 78065 | Poteet | 2,811 | 2,487 | 84501 | Price | 6,802 | 6,010 |
| 78375 | Premont | 3,049 | 2,619 | 84601 | Provo | 36,047 | 28,937 |
| 79252 | Quanah | 4,564 | 4,589 | 84701 | Richfield | 4,412 | 4,212 |
| 76470 | Ranger | 3,313 | 3,989 | 84067 | Roy | 9,239 | 3,723 |
| 78580 | Raymondville | 9,385 | 9,136 | 84770 | Saint George | 5,130 | 4,562 |
| 75377 | Refugio | 4,944 | 4,666 | *84101 | Salt Lake City | 189,454 | 182,121 |
| 75080 | Richardson | 16,810 | 1,289 | 84070 | Sandy City | 3,322 | 2,095 |
| 76118 | Richland Hills | 7,804 | | 84335 | Smithfield | 2,512 | 2,383 |
| 77469 | Richmond | 3,668 | 2,030 | 84403 | South Ogden | 7,405 | 3,763 |
| 78582 | Rio Grande City | 5,835 | 3,992 | 84115 | South Salt Lake | 9,520 | 7,704 |
| 77019 | River Oaks | 8,444 | 7,097 | 84660 | Spanish Fork City | 6,472 | 5,230 |
| 78380 | Robstown | 10,266 | 7,278 | 84663 | Springville | 7,913 | 6,475 |
| 76567 | Rockdale | 4,481 | 2,321 | 84015 | Sunset | 4,235 | 993 |
| 78382 | Rockport | 2,989 | 2,266 | 84074 | Tooele | 9,133 | 7,269 |
| 77471 | Rosenberg | 9,698 | 6,210 | 84078 | Vernal | 3,655 | 2,845 |
| 79546 | Rotan | 2,788 | 3,163 | 84403 | Washington Terrace | 6,441 | |
| 75785 | Rusk | 4,900 | 6,598 | 84084 | West Jordan | 3,009 | 2,107 |
| 76901 | San Angelo | 58,815 | 52,093 | | **VERMONT** | | |
| *78205 | San Antonio | 587,718 | 408,442 | | *See Note on Page 605* | | |
| 75972 | San Augustine | 2,584 | 2,510 | 05641 | Barre | 10,387 | 10,922 |
| 78586 | San Benito | 16,422 | 13,271 | | *Barre (town)* | 4,580 | 4,145 |
| 78384 | San Diego | 4,351 | 4,397 | 05822 | Barton | 3,066 | 3,298 |
| 78589 | San Juan | 4,371 | 3,413 | 05101 | Bellows Falls | 3,831 | 3,881 |
| 78666 | San Marcos | 12,713 | 9,980 | 05201 | Bennington | 8,023 | 8,002 |
| 78380 | San Pedro | 7,634 | 8,127 | | *Bennington (town)* | 13,002 | 12,411 |
| 76877 | San Saba | 2,728 | 3,400 | 05733 | Brandon | 3,329 | 3,304 |
| 78114 | Sansom Park Village | 4,175 | 1,611 | 05301 | Brattleboro | 9,315 | 9,606 |
| 75159 | Seagoville | 3,745 | 1,927 | | *Brattleboro (town)* | 11,734 | 11,522 |
| 78155 | Seguin | 14,299 | 9,733 | 05401 | Burlington | 35,531 | 33,155 |
| 79360 | Seminole | 5,737 | 3,479 | 05446 | Colchester | 4,718 | 3,897 |
| 76380 | Seymour | 3,789 | 3,779 | 05829 | Derby | 2,506 | 2,245 |
| 79079 | Shamrock | 3,113 | 3,322 | 05451 | Essex | 7,090 | 3,931 |
| 75090 | Sherman | 24,988 | 20,150 | 05452 | Essex Junction | 5,340 | 2,741 |
| 77656 | Silsbee | 6,277 | 3,179 | 05047 | Hartford | 6,355 | 5,827 |
| 78387 | Sinton | 6,008 | 4,254 | 05849 | Lyndon | 3,425 | 3,360 |
| 79364 | Slaton | 6,568 | 5,036 | 05753 | Middlebury | 3,688 | 3,614 |
| 78957 | Smithville | 2,933 | 3,379 | | *Middlebury (town)* | 5,305 | 4,778 |
| 79549 | Snyder | 13,850 | 12,010 | 05602 | Montpelier | 8,782 | 8,599 |
| 76950 | Sonora | 2,619 | 2,633 | 05661 | *Morristown* | 3,347 | 3,225 |
| 77587 | South Houston | 7,523 | 4,126 | 05855 | Newport | 5,019 | 5,217 |
| 79081 | Spearman | 3,555 | 1,852 | 05663 | *Northfield* | 4,511 | 4,314 |
| 77024 | Spring Valley | 3,004 | | 05764 | Poultney | 3,009 | 2,936 |
| 79553 | Stamford | 5,259 | 5,819 | 05060 | Randolph | 3,414 | 3,499 |
| 76401 | Stephenville | 7,359 | 7,155 | 05101 | Rockingham | 5,704 | 5,499 |
| 79083 | Stinnett | 2,695 | 1,170 | 05701 | Rutland | 18,325 | 17,659 |
| 77478 | Sugar Land | 2,802 | | 05478 | St. Albans | 8,806 | 8,552 |
| 75482 | Sulphur Springs | 9,160 | 8,991 | 05819 | St. Johnsbury | 6,809 | 7,370 |
| 77480 | Sweeny | 3,087 | 1,393 | | *St. Johnsbury (town)* | 8,869 | 9,292 |
| 79556 | Sweetwater | 13,914 | 13,619 | 05401 | South Burlington | 6,903 | 3,279 |
| 78390 | Taft | 3,463 | 2,978 | 05156 | Springfield | 6,600 | 4,940 |
| 79373 | Tahoka | 3,012 | 2,848 | | *Springfield (town)* | 9,934 | 9,190 |
| 76574 | Taylor | 9,434 | 9,071 | 05488 | Swanton | 3,946 | 3,710 |
| 75860 | Teague | 2,728 | 2,925 | 05676 | Waterbury | 2,984 | 3,153 |
| 76501 | Temple | 30,419 | 25,467 | | *Waterbury (town)* | 4,303 | 4,276 |
| 75160 | Terrell | 13,803 | 11,544 | 05001 | White River Junction | 2,546 | 2,365 |
| 78209 | Terrell Hills | 5,572 | 2,708 | 05495 | Williston Road Section | 3,259 | |
| 75501 | Texarkana | 30,218 | 24,753 | 05089 | Windsor | 3,256 | 3,467 |
| 77590 | Texas City | 32,065 | 16,620 | | *Windsor* | 4,468 | 4,402 |
| 79088 | Tulia | 4,410 | 3,222 | 05404 | Winooski | 7,420 | 6,734 |
| 75701 | Tyler | 51,230 | 38,968 | 05091 | Woodstock | 2,786 | 2,613 |
| 75205 | University Park | 23,202 | 24,275 | | | | |
| 78801 | Uvalde | 10,293 | 8,674 | | | | |

| ZIP Code | Place | 1960 | 1950 |
|---|---|---|---|
| | **VIRGINIA** | | |
| 24210 | Abingdon | 4,758 | 4,709 |
| *22313 | Alexandria | 91,023 | 61,787 |
| 24517 | Altavista | 3,299 | 3,332 |
| *22210 | Arlington Co. (uninc.) | 163,401 | 135,449 |
| 23005 | Ashland | 2,773 | 2,610 |
| 24055 | Bassetts | 3,148 | 3,421 |
| 24523 | Bedford | 5,921 | 4,061 |
| 24219 | Big Stone Gap | 4,688 | 5,173 |
| 24060 | Blacksburg | 7,070 | 3,358 |
| 23824 | Blackstone | 3,659 | 3,536 |
| 24605 | Bluefield | 4,235 | 4,212 |
| 24201 | Bristol | 17,144 | 15,954 |
| 24416 | Buena Vista | 6,300 | 5,214 |
| 22901 | Charlottesville | 29,427 | 25,969 |
| 23924 | Chase City | 3,207 | 2,519 |
| *23320 | Chesapeake (A) | 73,647 | .... |
| 24073 | Christiansburg | 3,653 | 2,967 |
| 24422 | Clifton Forge | 5,268 | 5,795 |
| 24078 | Collinsville | 3,586 | .... |
| 23834 | Colonial Heights | 9,587 | 6,077 |
| 24426 | Covington | 11,062 | 5,860 |
| 24541 | Danville | 46,577 | 35,066 |
| 23847 | Emporia | 5,535 | 5,664 |
| 23803 | Ettrick | 2,998 | 3,030 |
| 22030 | Fairfax | 13,585 | 1,946 |
| *22046 | Falls Church | 10,192 | 7,535 |
| 23901 | Farmville | 4,293 | 4,375 |
| 23851 | Franklin | 7,264 | 4,670 |
| 22401 | Fredericksburg | 13,639 | 12,158 |
| 22630 | Front Royal | 7,949 | 8,115 |
| 24333 | Galax | 5,254 | 5,248 |
| *23369 | Hampton | 89,258 | 5,966 |
| 22801 | Harrisonburg (A) | 12,842 | 10,810 |
| 23860 | Hopewell | 17,895 | 10,219 |
| 22075 | Leesburg | 2,869 | 1,703 |
| 24450 | Lexington | 7,557 | 5,976 |
| 22835 | Luray | 2,831 | 2,731 |
| *24504 | Lynchburg | 54,790 | 47,727 |
| 22110 | Manassas | 3,555 | 1,804 |
| 22110 | Manassas Park | 5,342 | .... |
| 24354 | Marion | 8,385 | 6,982 |
| 24112 | Martinsville | 18,798 | 17,251 |
| 24124 | Narrows | 2,508 | 2,520 |
| *23607 | Newport News | 113,662 | 42,358 |
| *23501 | Norfolk | 304,869 | 213,513 |
| 24273 | Norton | 5,013 | 4,315 |
| | N. Virginia Beach | 2,587 | 1,593 |
| 22960 | Orange | 2,955 | 2,571 |
| 23803 | Petersburg | 36,750 | 35,054 |
| 23434 | Pleasant Hills | 2,636 | .... |
| 23362 | Poquoson | 4,278 | .... |
| *23705 | Portsmouth | 144,773 | 80,039 |
| 24301 | Pulaski | 10,469 | 9,202 |
| 24141 | Radford | 9,371 | 9,026 |
| 24641 | Richlands | 4,963 | 4,648 |
| *23219 | Richmond | 219,958 | 230,310 |
| *24001 | Roanoke | 97,110 | 91,921 |
| 24153 | Salem | 16,058 | 6,823 |
| 24370 | Saltville | 2,844 | 2,678 |
| .... | Seatack | 3,120 | .... |
| 24592 | South Boston | 5,974 | 6,057 |
| 23970 | South Hill | 2,569 | 2,153 |
| 22150 | Springfield | 10,783 | .... |
| 24401 | Staunton | 22,232 | 19,927 |
| 23434 | Suffolk | 12,609 | 12,339 |
| 22651 | Tazewell | 3,000 | 1,347 |
| 22172 | Triangle | 2,948 | .... |
| 22180 | Vienna | 11,440 | 2,029 |
| 24179 | Vinton | 3,432 | 3,629 |
| *23458 | Virginia Beach (A) | 85,218 | 5,309 |
| 22186 | Warrenton | 3,522 | 1,797 |
| 22980 | Waynesboro | 15,694 | 12,357 |
| 23185 | Williamsburg | 6,832 | 6,735 |
| 22601 | Winchester | 15,110 | 13,841 |
| 24293 | Wise | 2,614 | 1,574 |
| 24382 | Wytheville | 5,634 | 5,513 |
| | **WASHINGTON** | | |
| 98520 | Aberdeen | 18,741 | 19,653 |
| 98221 | Anacortes | 8,414 | 6,919 |
| 98002 | Auburn | 11,933 | 6,497 |
| 98004 | Bellevue | 12,809 | .... |
| 98225 | Bellingham | 34,688 | 34,112 |
| 98310 | Bremerton | 28,922 | 27,678 |
| 98321 | Buckley | 3,538 | 2,705 |
| 98233 | Burlington | 2,968 | 2,350 |
| 98607 | Camas | 5,666 | 4,725 |
| 98531 | Centralia | 8,586 | 8,657 |
| 98532 | Chehalis | 5,199 | 5,639 |
| 99004 | Cheney | 3,173 | 2,797 |
| 99403 | Clarkston | 6,209 | 5,617 |
| 99111 | Colfax | 2,860 | 3,057 |
| 99324 | College Place | 4,031 | 3,174 |
| 99114 | Colville | 3,806 | 3,033 |
| 99328 | Dayton | 2,913 | 2,979 |
| 98020 | Edmonds | 8,016 | 2,057 |
| 98926 | Ellensburg | 8,625 | 8,430 |
| 98310 | Enetai | 2,539 | .... |
| 98022 | Enumclaw | 3,269 | 2,789 |
| 98823 | Ephrata | 6,548 | 4,582 |
| 98201 | Everett | 40,304 | 33,849 |
| 98901 | Fairview | 2,758 | 3,309 |

| ZIP Code | Place | 1960 | 1950 |
|---|---|---|---|
| | **WASHINGTON—Continued** | | |
| 98902 | Fircrest | 3,565 | 1,459 |
| 98902 | Fruitvale | 3,345 | 3,654 |
| 98620 | Goldendale | 2,536 | 1,907 |
| 98930 | Grandview | 3,366 | 2,503 |
| 98550 | Hoquiam | 10,762 | 11,123 |
| 98626 | Kelso | 8,379 | 7,345 |
| 99336 | Kennewick | 14,244 | 10,106 |
| 98031 | Kent | 9,017 | 3,278 |
| 98033 | Kirkland | 6,025 | 4,713 |
| 98501 | Lacey | 6,630 | .... |
| 98632 | Longview | 23,349 | 20,339 |
| 98264 | Lynden | 2,542 | 2,161 |
| 98036 | Lynnwood | 7,207 | .... |
| 98270 | Marysville | 3,117 | 2,259 |
| 99022 | Medical Lake | 4,765 | 4,488 |
| 98837 | Moses Lake | 11,299 | 2,679 |
| 98043 | Mountlake Terrace | 9,122 | .... |
| 98273 | Mount Vernon | 7,921 | 5,230 |
| 98310 | Navy Yard City | 3,341 | 3,030 |
| 98148 | Normandy Park | 3,224 | .... |
| 98277 | Oak Harbor (A) '67 | 4,812 | 1,193 |
| 98501 | Olympia | 18,273 | 15,819 |
| 98841 | Omak | 4,068 | 3,791 |
| 99214 | Opportunity | 12,465 | .... |
| 99344 | Othello | 2,669 | 526 |
| 99301 | Pasco | 14,522 | 10,228 |
| 99301 | Pasco West | 2,894 | .... |
| 98201 | Pinehurst | 3,989 | .... |
| 98362 | Port Angeles | 12,653 | 11,233 |
| 98366 | Port Orchard | 2,778 | 2,320 |
| 98368 | Port Townsend | 5,074 | 6,888 |
| 99350 | Prosser | 2,763 | 2,636 |
| 99163 | Pullman | 12,957 | 12,022 |
| 98371 | Puyallup | 12,063 | 10,010 |
| 98848 | Quincy | 3,269 | 804 |
| 99577 | Raymond | 3,301 | 4,110 |
| 98055 | Renton | 18,453 | 16,039 |
| 99352 | Richland | 23,548 | .... |
| 98310 | Rocky Point-Marine Drive | 2,733 | .... |
| *98101 | Seattle | 557,087 | 467,591 |
| 98284 | Sedro-Woolley | 3,705 | 3,299 |
| 98942 | Selah | 2,824 | 2,429 |
| 98584 | Shelton | 5,651 | 5,045 |
| 98270 | Shoultes | 3,159 | 1,973 |
| 98290 | Snohomish | 3,894 | 3,094 |
| 98902 | South Broadway | 3,661 | 3,229 |
| *99210 | Spokane | 181,608 | 161,721 |
| 98390 | Sumner | 3,156 | 2,816 |
| 98944 | Sunnyside | 6,208 | 4,194 |
| *98402 | Tacoma | 147,979 | 143,673 |
| 98948 | Toppenish | 5,667 | 5,265 |
| 98501 | Tumwater | 3,885 | 2,725 |
| 98660 | Vancouver | 32,464 | 41,664 |
| 99362 | Walla Walla | 24,536 | 24,102 |
| 99951 | Wapato | 3,137 | 3,185 |
| 98671 | Washougal | 2,672 | 1,577 |
| 98801 | Wenatchee | 16,726 | 13,072 |
| 99403 | West Clarkston-Highland | 2,851 | 1,920 |
| 98801 | West Wenatchee | 2,518 | 2,690 |
| 98901 | Yakima | 43,284 | 38,486 |
| | **WEST VIRGINIA** | | |
| 25801 | Beckley | 18,642 | 19,397 |
| 25015 | Belle | 2,559 | .... |
| 26031 | Benwood | 2,850 | 3,485 |
| 24701 | Bluefield | 19,256 | 21,506 |
| 26330 | Bridgeport | 4,199 | 2,414 |
| 26201 | Buckhannon | 6,386 | 6,016 |
| *25301 | Charleston | 85,796 | 73,501 |
| 25414 | Charles Town | 3,329 | 3,035 |
| 25315 | Chesapeake | 2,699 | 2,566 |
| 26034 | Chester | 3,787 | 3,758 |
| 26301 | Clarksburg | 28,112 | 32,014 |
| 25064 | Dunbar | 11,006 | 8,032 |
| 26241 | Elkins | 8,307 | 9,121 |
| 26554 | Fairmont | 27,477 | 29,346 |
| 26037 | Follansbee | 4,052 | 4,435 |
| 26354 | Grafton | 5,791 | 7,365 |
| 25951 | Hinton | 5,197 | 5,750 |
| *25701 | Huntington | 83,627 | 86,353 |
| 25530 | Kenova | 4,577 | 4,320 |
| 26726 | Keyser (A) | 7,041 | 6,347 |
| 26537 | Kingwood | 2,530 | 2,186 |
| 25601 | Logan | 4,185 | 5,079 |
| 26040 | McMechen | 2,599 | 3,518 |
| 26582 | Mannington | 2,996 | 3,241 |
| 25315 | Marmet | 2,500 | 2,515 |
| 25401 | Martinsburg | 15,179 | 15,621 |
| 25136 | Montgomery | 3,000 | 3,484 |
| 26505 | Morgantown | 22,487 | 25,525 |
| 26041 | Moundsville | 15,163 | 14,772 |
| 25637 | Mt. Gay | 3,386 | .... |
| 25882 | Mullens | 3,544 | 3,470 |
| 26155 | New Martinsville | 5,607 | 4,084 |
| 25143 | Nitro | 6,894 | 3,314 |
| 25901 | Oak Hill | 4,711 | 4,518 |
| 26159 | Paden City | 3,137 | 2,588 |
| 26101 | Parkersburg | 44,797 | 29,684 |
| 25550 | Point Pleasant | 5,785 | 4,596 |
| 24740 | Princeton | 8,393 | 8,279 |

| ZIP Code | Place | 1960 | 1950 |
|---|---|---|---|
| | **WEST VIRGINIA—Continued** | | |
| 26164 | Ravenswood | 3,410 | 1,175 |
| 26261 | Richwood | 4,110 | 5,321 |
| 25271 | Ripley | 2,756 | 1,813 |
| 25177 | Saint Albans | 15,103 | 9,870 |
| 26431 | Shinnston | 2,724 | 2,793 |
| 25303 | S. Charleston | 19,180 | 16,686 |
| 25276 | Spencer | 2,660 | 2,587 |
| 25926 | Sprague | 3,073 | 2,626 |
| 26101 | Vienna | 9,381 | 6,020 |
| 24892 | War | 3,006 | 3,992 |
| 26062 | Weirton | 28,201 | 24,005 |
| 24801 | Welch | 5,313 | 6,603 |
| 26070 | Wellsburg | 5,514 | 5,787 |
| 26452 | Weston | 8,754 | 8,945 |
| 26505 | Westover | 4,749 | 4,318 |
| 26003 | Wheeling | 53,400 | 58,891 |
| 24986 | White Sulphur Springs | 2,676 | 2,643 |
| 25661 | Williamson | 6,746 | 8,624 |
| 26187 | Williamstown | 2,632 | 2,001 |
| | **WISCONSIN** | | |
| 54201 | Algoma | 3,855 | 3,384 |
| 54409 | Antigo | 9,691 | 9,902 |
| 54911 | Appleton | 48,411 | 34,010 |
| 54806 | Ashland | 10,132 | 10,640 |
| 53913 | Baraboo | 7,660 | 7,264 |
| | Bayside | 3,181 | |
| 53916 | Beaver Dam | 13,118 | 11,867 |
| 53511 | Beloit, '62 | 35,199 | 29,590 |
| 54923 | Berlin | 4,838 | 4,693 |
| 54615 | Black River Falls | 3,195 | 2,824 |
| 54724 | Bloomer | 2,834 | 2,556 |
| 53805 | Boscobel | 2,608 | 2,347 |
| 53005 | Brookfield | 19,812 | |
| 53209 | Brown Deer | 11,280 | |
| 53105 | Burlington | 5,856 | 4,780 |
| 53012 | Cedarburg | 5,191 | 2,810 |
| 53014 | Chilton | 2,578 | 2,367 |
| 54729 | Chippewa Falls | 11,708 | 11,086 |
| 54929 | Clintonville | 4,775 | 4,657 |
| 53925 | Columbus | 3,467 | 3,250 |
| 53110 | Cudahy | 17,975 | 12,182 |
| 53115 | Delavan | 4,846 | 4,007 |
| 54115 | De Pere | 10,045 | 8,146 |
| 53533 | Dodgeville | 2,911 | 2,532 |
| 54701 | Eau Claire | 37,987 | 36,058 |
| 53534 | Edgerton | 4,000 | 3,507 |
| 53121 | Elkhorn | 3,586 | 2,935 |
| 53122 | Elm Grove | 4,994 | |
| 53536 | Evansville | 2,858 | 2,531 |
| 54935 | Fond du Lac, '66 | 34,180 | 29,936 |
| 53538 | Fort Atkinson | 7,908 | 6,280 |
| | Fox Point | 7,315 | 2,585 |
| 53132 | Franklin | 10,006 | |
| | Glendale, '61 | 10,432 | |
| 53024 | Grafton | 3,748 | 1,489 |
| *54301 | Green Bay | 62,888 | 52,735 |
| 53129 | Greendale | 6,843 | 2,752 |
| 53220 | Greenfield | 17,636 | |
| 53130 | Hales Corners | 5,549 | |
| 53027 | Hartford | 5,627 | 4,549 |
| 53032 | Horicon | 2,996 | 2,664 |
| | Howard | 3,485 | |
| 54016 | Hudson | 4,325 | 3,435 |
| 54534 | Hurley | 2,763 | 3,034 |
| 53545 | Janesville | 35,164 | 24,899 |
| 53549 | Jefferson | 4,548 | 3,625 |
| 54130 | Kaukauna | 10,096 | 8,337 |
| 53140 | Kenosha | 67,899 | 54,368 |
| 54216 | Kewaunee | 2,772 | 2,583 |
| 53042 | Kiel | 2,524 | 2,129 |
| 54136 | Kimberly | 5,322 | 3,179 |
| 54601 | La Crosse | 47,575 | 47,535 |
| 54848 | Ladysmith | 3,584 | 3,924 |
| 53147 | Lake Geneva | 4,929 | 4,300 |
| 53551 | Lake Mills | 2,951 | 2,516 |
| 53813 | Lancaster | 3,703 | 3,266 |
| 54140 | Little Chute | 5,099 | 4,152 |
| 53703 | Madison, '64 | 157,844 | 96,056 |
| 54220 | Manitowoc, '66 | 33,215 | 27,598 |
| 54143 | Marinette | 13,329 | 14,178 |
| 54449 | Marshfield | 14,153 | 12,394 |
| 53948 | Mauston | 3,531 | 3,171 |
| 53050 | Mayville | 3,607 | 3,010 |
| 54451 | Medford | 3,260 | 2,799 |
| 54952 | Menasha | 14,647 | 12,385 |
| 53051 | Menomonee Falls | 18,276 | 2,469 |

| ZIP Code | Place | 1960 | 1950 |
|---|---|---|---|
| | **WISCONSIN—Continued** | | |
| 54751 | Menomonie | 8,624 | 8,245 |
| 53092 | Mequon | 8,543 | |
| 54452 | Merrill | 9,451 | 8,951 |
| 53562 | Middleton | 4,410 | 2,110 |
| *53202 | Milwaukee | 741,324 | 637,392 |
| 53716 | Monona | 8,178 | |
| 53566 | Monroe | 8,050 | 7,037 |
| 53150 | Muskego, '64 | 10,947 | |
| 54956 | Neenah | 18,057 | 12,437 |
| 54456 | Neillsville | 2,728 | 2,663 |
| 54457 | Nekoosa | 2,515 | 2,352 |
| 53151 | New Berlin | 15,788 | |
| 54961 | New London | 5,288 | 4,922 |
| 54017 | New Richmond | 3,316 | 2,886 |
| 54935 | North Fond du Lac | 2,549 | 2,291 |
| 53154 | Oak Creek, '65 | 11,548 | |
| 53066 | Oconomowoc | 6,682 | 5,345 |
| 54153 | Oconto | 4,805 | 5,055 |
| 54650 | Onalaska | 3,161 | 2,561 |
| 54901 | Oshkosh | 45,110 | 41,084 |
| 54552 | Park Falls | 2,919 | 2,924 |
| 53511 | Perryo Place | 4,475 | 3,315 |
| 54157 | Peshtigo | 2,504 | 2,279 |
| 53818 | Platteville | 6,957 | 5,751 |
| 53073 | Plymouth | 5,128 | 4,543 |
| 53901 | Portage | 7,822 | 7,334 |
| 53074 | Port Washington | 5,984 | 4,755 |
| 53821 | Prairie du Chien | 5,649 | 5,392 |
| *53401 | Racine | 89,144 | 71,193 |
| 53959 | Reedsburg | 4,371 | 4,072 |
| 54501 | Rhinelander | 8,790 | 8,774 |
| 54868 | Rice Lake | 7,303 | 6,898 |
| 53581 | Richland Center | 4,746 | 4,608 |
| 54971 | Ripon | 6,163 | 5,619 |
| 54022 | River Falls | 4,857 | 3,877 |
| 54474 | Rothschild | 2,550 | 1,452 |
| 53207 | St. Francis | 10,065 | |
| 54476 | Schofield | 3,038 | 1,948 |
| 54166 | Shawano | 6,103 | 5,894 |
| 53081 | Sheboygan | 45,747 | 42,365 |
| 53085 | Sheboygan Falls | 4,061 | 3,599 |
| 53211 | Shorewood | 15,990 | 16,199 |
| 53172 | South Milwaukee | 20,307 | 12,855 |
| 54401 | S.W. Wausau | 4,105 | 2,677 |
| 54656 | Sparta | 6,080 | 5,893 |
| 54481 | Stevens Point | 17,837 | 16,564 |
| 53589 | Stoughton | 5,555 | 4,533 |
| 54235 | Sturgeon Bay | 7,352 | 7,054 |
| 53590 | Sun Prairie | 4,008 | 2,263 |
| 54880 | Superior City | 33,563 | 35,325 |
| 53092 | Thiensville | 2,507 | 897 |
| 54660 | Tomah | 5,321 | 4,760 |
| 54487 | Tomahawk | 3,348 | 3,534 |
| 54241 | Two Rivers | 12,393 | 10,243 |
| 54665 | Viroqua | 3,926 | 3,795 |
| 53094 | Watertown | 13,943 | 12,417 |
| 53186 | Waukesha, '66 | 36,339 | 21,233 |
| 54981 | Waupaca | 3,984 | 3,921 |
| 53963 | Waupun | 7,935 | 6,725 |
| 54401 | Wausau | 31,943 | 30,414 |
| 53213 | Wauwatosa | 56,923 | 33,324 |
| 53214 | West Allis | 68,157 | 42,959 |
| 53095 | West Bend | 9,969 | 6,849 |
| | West Milwaukee | 5,043 | 5,429 |
| 53217 | Whitefish Bay | 18,390 | 14,665 |
| 53190 | Whitewater, '65 | 10,353 | 5,101 |
| 54494 | Wisconsin Rapids | 15,042 | 13,496 |
| | **WYOMING** | | |
| 82834 | Buffalo | 2,907 | 2,674 |
| 82601 | Casper | 38,930 | 23,673 |
| 82001 | Cheyenne | 43,505 | 31,935 |
| 82414 | Cody | 4,838 | 3,872 |
| 82652 | Douglas | 2,822 | 2,544 |
| 82930 | Evanston | 4,901 | 3,863 |
| 82716 | Gillette | 3,580 | 2,191 |
| 82935 | Green River | 3,497 | 3,187 |
| 82520 | Lander | 4,182 | 3,349 |
| 82070 | Laramie | 17,520 | 15,581 |
| 82701 | Newcastle | 4,345 | 3,395 |
| 82435 | Powell | 4,740 | 3,804 |
| 82301 | Rawlins | 8,968 | 7,415 |
| 82501 | Riverton | 6,845 | 4,142 |
| 82901 | Rock Springs | 10,371 | 10,857 |
| 82801 | Sheridan | 11,651 | 11,500 |
| 82443 | Thermopolis | 3,955 | 2,870 |
| 82240 | Torrington | 4,188 | 3,247 |
| 82401 | Worland | 5,806 | 4,202 |

## Do You Need A Birth Certificate?

Although a birth certificate is of great value in situations requiring documentation of date and place of birth, such as qualifying for Social Security or Medicare benefits, in obtaining a passport or in qualifying for certain jobs, many Americans do not possess such a certificate and may not be able to obtain one because the birth was not recorded or because records are not available.

In most instances a transcript from early census records is acceptable as a substitute for a birth certificate. The Bureau of the Census maintains a special office and a staff of trained researchers especially to provide this service, and charges a fee to cover the cost.

You may obtain an application form at your local Social Security Office or from the Personal Census Service Branch. Bureau of the Census, Pittsburg, Kan. 66762. Your application form should be accompanied by a check or money order in the amount of $4 for a regular search, or $5 for an expedited search.

Transcripts from a regular search of census records usually are available within 4 to 6 weeks; from an expedited search about 2 weeks.

Applications should be made by the person himself or by a legally authorized representative.

# Population and Area of Counties, Census of 1960
## WITH NAMES OF COUNTY SEATS OR COURT HOUSES, LAND AREA IN SQUARE MILES
### Source: Bureau of the Census

There are 3,071 counties and parishes in the United States and 59 county equivalents making a total of 3,130. The county equivalents include 34 independent cities in Virginia, 1 in Maryland and 1 in Missouri; the District of Columbia; and the parts of Yellowstone National Park in each of 3 states—Idaho, Montana and Wyoming. Also included are 19 election districts in Alaska. It should be noted, however, that the 1950 and 1960 censuses list 24 election districts in Alaska; the number was reduced as of Dec. 7, 1961. Land areas revised in 1967.

*Where special censuses were taken after April 1, 1960, the year taken appears after the name of the county. The population total for the state does not reflect the change except in Rhode Island.*

| County | Land Area sq.mi | County Seats or Court Houses | County Pop. 1960 |
|---|---|---|---|
| **ALABAMA** | | | |
| *(67 counties, 50,851 sq. mi. land, pop., 3,266,740)* | | | |
| Autauga.... | 599 | Pratteville........ | 18,739 |
| Baldwin..... | 1,578 | Bay Minette...... | 49,088 |
| Barbour...... | 899 | Clayton......... | 24,700 |
| Bibb........ | 625 | Centreville..... | 14,357 |
| Blount...... | 640 | Oneonta......... | 25,449 |
| Bullock...... | 615 | Union Springs..... | 13,462 |
| Butler...... | 773 | Greenville...... | 24,560 |
| Calhoun.... | 611 | Anniston........ | 95,878 |
| Chambers.... | 599 | Lafayette........ | 37,828 |
| Cherokee.... | 600 | Centre.......... | 16,303 |
| Chilton.... | 699 | Clanton........ | 25,693 |
| Choctaw.... | 918 | Butler.......... | 17,870 |
| Clarke...... | 1,238 | Grove Hill...... | 25,738 |
| Clay........ | 603 | Ashland......... | 12,400 |
| Cleburne.... | 574 | Heflin.......... | 10,911 |
| Coffee...... | 677 | Elba........... | 30,583 |
| Colbert.... | 596 | Tuscumbia...... | 46,506 |
| Conecuh.... | 850 | Evergreen...... | 17,762 |
| Coosa...... | 650 | Rockford........ | 10,726 |
| Covington.... | 984 | Andalusia...... | 35,631 |
| Crenshaw.... | 611 | Luverne........ | 14,909 |
| Cullman.... | 743 | Cullman........ | 45,572 |
| Dale........ | 559 | Ozark.......... | 31,066 |
| Dallas...... | 976 | Selma.......... | 56,667 |
| De Kalb.... | 778 | Fort Payne..... | 41,417 |
| Elmore...... | 624 | Wetumpka...... | 30,524 |
| Escambia.... | 962 | Brewton........ | 33,511 |
| Etowah...... | 555 | Gadsden........ | 96,980 |
| Fayette.... | 627 | Fayette......... | 16,148 |
| Franklin.... | 644 | Russellville..... | 21,988 |
| Geneva...... | 577 | Geneva......... | 22,310 |
| Greene...... | 640 | Eutaw.......... | 13,600 |
| Hale........ | 662 | Greensboro...... | 19,537 |
| Henry...... | 565 | Abbeville....... | 15,286 |
| Houston.... | 577 | Dothan......... | 50,718 |
| Jackson.... | 1,079 | Scottsboro..... | 36,681 |
| Jefferson.... | 1,116 | Birmingham...... | 634,864 |
| Lamar...... | 605 | Vernon......... | 14,271 |
| Lauderdale.... | 662 | Florence........ | 61,622 |
| Lawrence.... | 685 | Moulton........ | 24,501 |
| Lee........ | 612 | Opelika........ | 49,754 |
| Limestone.... | 545 | Athens......... | 36,513 |
| Lowndes.... | 715 | Hayneville..... | 15,417 |
| Macon...... | 616 | Tuskegee....... | 26,717 |
| Madison, '64. | 803 | Huntsville..... | 173,285 |
| Marengo.... | 978 | Linden......... | 27,098 |
| Marion...... | 743 | Hamilton........ | 21,837 |
| Marshall.... | 571 | Guntersville..... | 48,018 |
| Mobile...... | 1,240 | Mobile......... | 314,301 |
| Monroe.... | 1,032 | Monroeville..... | 22,372 |
| Montgomery.. | 790 | Montgomery..... | 169,210 |
| Morgan...... | 075 | Decatur........ | 60,454 |
| Perry...... | 734 | Marion......... | 17,358 |
| Pickens.... | 887 | Carrollton...... | 21,882 |
| Pike........ | 673 | Troy........... | 25,987 |
| Randolph.... | 581 | Wedowee....... | 19,477 |
| Russell.... | 639 | Phenix City..... | 46,351 |
| St. Clair.... | 640 | Ashville & Pell City | 25,388 |
| Shelby.... | 798 | Columbiana..... | 32,132 |
| Sumter.... | 915 | Livingston..... | 20,041 |
| Talladega.... | 750 | Talladega...... | 65,495 |
| Tallapoosa.... | 705 | Dadeville..... | 35,007 |
| Tuscaloosa.... | 1,338 | Tuscaloosa...... | 109,047 |
| Walker.... | 808 | Jasper.......... | 54,211 |
| Washington.. | 1,066 | Chatom......... | 15,372 |
| Wilcox...... | 899 | Camden......... | 18,739 |
| Winston.... | 633 | Double Springs... | 14,858 |

### ALASKA
*24 Election Districts. (See top of page.)*
*(586,432 sq. mi. land; pop. 1960, 226,167)*

| District | Land Area Sq. Mi. | Pop. 1960 |
|---|---|---|
| Aleutian Islands............. | 14,583 | 6,011 |
| Anchorage................ | 2,225 | 82,833 |
| Barrow................... | 57,544 | 2,133 |
| Bethel................... | 19,642 | 5,537 |
| Bristol Bay............... | 36,196 | 4,024 |
| Cordova-McCarthy........ | 15,540 | 1,759 |
| Fairbanks................ | 23,253 | 43,412 |
| Juneau................... | 3,515 | 9,745 |
| Kenai-Cook Inlet.......... | 11,808 | 6,095 |
| Ketchikan................ | 5,269 | 10,070 |
| Kobuk................... | 42,978 | 3,560 |
| Kodiak................... | 7,467 | 7,174 |
| Kuskokwim................ | 56,976 | 2,301 |
| Lynn Canal-Icy Straits...... | 10,158 | 2,945 |
| Nome.................... | 24,968 | 6,091 |
| Palmer-Wasilla-Talkeetna..... | 23,545 | 5,188 |
| Prince of Wales.............. | 3,485 | 1,772 |
| Seward................... | 3,193 | 2,956 |
| Sitka.................... | 3,196 | 6,690 |
| Upper Yukon.............. | 84,138 | 1,619 |
| Valdez-Chitina-Whittier..... | 19,421 | 2,844 |
| Wade Hampton............ | 16,770 | 3,128 |
| Wrangell-Petersburg...... | 6,249 | 4,181 |
| Yukon-Koyukuk........... | 74,313 | 4,097 |

*Court Houses.* Anchorage, Fairbanks, Juneau and Nome.

| County | Land Area sq.mi | County Seats or Court Houses | County Pop. 1960 |
|---|---|---|---|
| **ARIZONA** | | | |
| *(14 counties, 113,563 sq. mi. land; pop., 1,302,161)* | | | |
| Apache...... | 11,171 | Saint Johns..... | 30,438 |
| Cochise, '66.. | 6,256 | Bisbee......... | 56,410 |
| Coconino.... | 18,562 | Flagstaff....... | 41,857 |
| Gila........ | 4,748 | Globe.......... | 25,745 |
| Graham.... | 4,618 | Safford........ | 14,045 |
| Greenlee.... | 1,879 | Clifton......... | 11,509 |
| Maricopa.... | 9,238 | Phoenix........ | 663,510 |
| Mohave.... | 13,227 | Kingman........ | 7,736 |
| Navajo.... | 9,910 | Holbrook........ | 37,994 |
| Pima...... | 9,240 | Tucson......... | 265,660 |
| Pinal, '65... | 5,386 | Florence....... | 62,805 |
| Santa Cruz.. | 1,246 | Nogales........ | 10,808 |
| Yavapai.... | 8,091 | Prescott........ | 28,912 |
| Yuma, '65... | 9,991 | Yuma.......... | 55,833 |
| **ARKANSAS** | | | |
| *(75 counties, 52,175 sq. mi. land; pop., 1,786,272)* | | | |
| Arkansas.... | 1,015 | DeWitt & Stuttgart | 23,355 |
| Ashley...... | 928 | Hamburg....... | 24,220 |
| Baxter...... | 537 | Mountain Home.. | 9,943 |
| Benton...... | 886 | Bentonville..... | 36,272 |
| Boone...... | 593 | Harrison........ | 16,116 |
| Bradley.... | 651 | Warren......... | 14,029 |
| Calhoun.... | 629 | Hampton........ | 5,991 |
| Carroll...... | 634 | Berryville and | |
| | | Eureka Spgs..... | 11,284 |
| Chicot...... | 642 | Lake Village..... | 18,990 |
| Clark...... | 878 | Arkadelphia..... | 20,950 |
| Clay........ | 639 | Corning & Piggott. | 21,258 |
| Cleburne.... | 554 | Heber Springs..... | 9,059 |
| Cleveland.... | 601 | Rison.......... | 6,944 |
| Columbia.... | 768 | Magnolia........ | 26,400 |
| Conway.... | 561 | Morrilton........ | 15,430 |
| Craighead.... | 716 | Jonesboro and | |
| | | Lake City...... | 47,303 |
| Crawford.... | 596 | Van Buren..... | 21,318 |
| Crittenden.... | 608 | Marion......... | 47,564 |
| Cross...... | 625 | Wynne......... | 19,551 |
| Dallas...... | 672 | Fordyce........ | 10,522 |
| Desha...... | 736 | Arkansas City... | 20,770 |
| Drew...... | 832 | Monticello..... | 15,213 |
| Faulkner.... | 641 | Conway........ | 24,303 |
| Franklin.... | 613 | Charleston and | |
| | | Ozark......... | 10,213 |
| Fulton...... | 608 | Salem.......... | 6,657 |
| Garland.... | 658 | HotSpgs.Nat'lPark | 46,697 |
| Grant...... | 631 | Sheridan....... | 8,294 |
| Greene...... | 579 | Paragould...... | 25,198 |
| Hempstead.. | 736 | Hope.......... | 19,661 |
| Hot Spring.. | 621 | Malvern........ | 21,893 |
| Howard.... | 600 | Nashville...... | 10,878 |
| Independence. | 752 | Batesville...... | 20,048 |
| Izard...... | 574 | Melbourne...... | 6,766 |
| Jackson.... | 629 | Newport........ | 22,843 |
| Jefferson.... | 873 | Pine Bluff...... | 81,373 |
| Johnson.... | 673 | Clarksville..... | 12,421 |
| Lafayette.... | 523 | Lewisville..... | 11,030 |
| Lawrence.... | 590 | Powhatan & | |
| | | Walnut Ridge... | 17,267 |
| Lee........ | 608 | Marianna...... | 21,001 |
| Lincoln.... | 563 | Star City...... | 14,447 |
| Little River.. | 541 | Ashdown....... | 9,211 |
| Logan...... | 718 | Booneville & Paris. | 15,957 |
| Lonoke...... | 796 | Lonoke......... | 24,551 |
| Madison.... | 832 | Huntsville...... | 9,068 |
| Marion...... | 584 | Yellville....... | 6,041 |
| Miller...... | 623 | Texarkana...... | 31,686 |
| Mississippi.. | 904 | Blytheville and | |
| | | Osceola........ | 70,174 |
| Monroe.... | 607 | Clarendon...... | 17,327 |
| Montgomery.. | 775 | Mount Ida..... | 5,370 |
| Nevada.... | 616 | Prescott........ | 10,700 |
| Newton.... | 822 | Jasper.......... | 5,963 |
| Ouachita.... | 736 | Camden........ | 31,641 |
| Perry...... | 551 | Perryville...... | 4,927 |
| Phillips.... | 686 | Helena........ | 43,997 |

| County | Land Area sq.mi | County Seats or Court Houses | County Pop. 1960 |
|---|---|---|---|
| **ARKANSAS—Continued** | | | |
| Pike | 600 | Murfreesboro | 7,864 |
| Poinsett | 760 | Harrisburg | 30,834 |
| Polk | 860 | Mena | 11,981 |
| Pope | 812 | Russellville | 21,177 |
| Prairie | 661 | Des Arc and De Valls Bluff | 10,515 |
| Pulaski | 765 | Little Rock | 242,980 |
| Randolph | 647 | Pocahontas | 12,520 |
| St. Francis | 635 | Forrest City | 33,303 |
| Saline | 724 | Benton | 28,956 |
| Scott | 898 | Waldron | 7,297 |
| Searcy | 664 | Marshall | 8,124 |
| Sebastian | 527 | Fort Smith and Greenwood | 66,685 |
| Sevier | 585 | De Queen | 10,156 |
| Sharp | 598 | Evening Shade & Hardy | 6,319 |
| Stone | 608 | Mountain View | 6,294 |
| Union | 1,050 | El Dorado | 49,518 |
| Van Buren | 699 | Clinton | 7,228 |
| Washington | 962 | Fayetteville | 55,797 |
| White | 1,041 | Searcy | 32,745 |
| Woodruff | 591 | Augusta | 13,954 |
| Yell | 929 | Danville and Dardanelle | 11,940 |

### CALIFORNIA
*(58 counties, 156,537 sq. mi. land; pop. 15,717,204)*

| County | Land Area sq.mi | County Seats or Court Houses | County Pop. 1960 |
|---|---|---|---|
| Alameda | 733 | Oakland | 908,209 |
| Alpine | 723 | Markleeville | 397 |
| Amador | 593 | Jackson | 9,990 |
| Butte | 1,668 | Oroville | 82,030 |
| Calaveras | 1,032 | San Andreas | 10,289 |
| Colusa | 1,152 | Colusa | 12,075 |
| Contra Costa | 733 | Martinez | 409,030 |
| Del Norte | 1,007 | Crescent City | 17,771 |
| El Dorado '65 | 1,726 | Placerville | 43,805 |
| Fresno | 5,968 | Fresno | 365,945 |
| Glenn | 1,319 | Willows | 17,245 |
| Humboldt | 3,586 | Eureka | 104,892 |
| Imperial | 4,241 | El Centro | 78,019 |
| Inyo | 10,130 | Independence | 11,684 |
| Kern | 8,152 | Bakersfield | 291,984 |
| Kings | 1,396 | Hanford | 49,954 |
| Lake | 1,261 | Lakeport | 13,786 |
| Lassen, '65 | 4,561 | Susanville | 17,053 |
| Los Angeles | 4,069 | Los Angeles | 6,038,771 |
| Madera | 2,145 | Madera | 40,468 |
| Marin | 520 | San Rafael | 146,820 |
| Mariposa | 1,453 | Mariposa | 5,064 |
| Mendocino | 3,511 | Ukiah | 51,059 |
| Merced | 1,981 | Merced | 90,446 |
| Modoc | 4,097 | Alturas | 8,308 |
| Mono | 3,027 | Bridgeport | 2,213 |
| Monterey, '6 | 3,324 | Salinas | 224,316 |
| Napa | 787 | Napa | 65,890 |
| Nevada | 975 | Nevada City | 20,911 |
| Orange | 782 | Santa Ana | 703,925 |
| Placer | 1,433 | Auburn | 56,998 |
| Plumas | 2,569 | Quincy | 11,620 |
| Riverside | 7,176 | Riverside | 306,191 |
| Sacramento | 975 | Sacramento | 502,778 |
| San Benito | 1,397 | Hollister | 15,396 |
| San Bernardino | 20,119 | San Bernardino | 503,591 |
| San Diego | 4,262 | San Diego | 1,033,011 |
| San Francisco | 45 | San Francisco | 740,316 |
| San Joaquin | 1,415 | Stockton | 249,989 |
| San Luis Obispo | 3,184 | San Luis Obispo | 81,044 |
| San Mateo | 447 | Redwood City | 444,387 |
| Santa Barbara | 2,738 | Santa Barbara | 168,962 |
| Santa Clara | 1,300 | San Jose | 642,315 |
| Santa Cruz | 440 | Santa Cruz | 84,219 |
| Shasta | 3,793 | Redding | 59,468 |
| Sierra | 958 | Downieville | 2,247 |
| Siskiyou | 6,264 | Yreka | 32,885 |
| Solano | 826 | Fairfield | 134,597 |
| Sonoma, '65 | 1,604 | Santa Rosa | 176,398 |
| Stanislaus | 1,511 | Modesto | 157,294 |
| Sutter | 603 | Yuba City | 33,380 |
| Tehama | 2,984 | Red Bluff | 25,305 |
| Trinity | 3,192 | Weaverville | 9,706 |
| Tulare | 4,844 | Visalia | 168,403 |
| Tuolumne | 2,279 | Sonora | 14,404 |
| Ventura | 1,863 | Ventura | 199,138 |
| Yolo | 1,028 | Woodland | 65,727 |
| Yuba | 640 | Marysville | 33,859 |

### COLORADO
*(63 counties, 103,797 sq. mi. land; pop., 1,753,947)*

| County | Land Area sq.mi | County Seats or Court Houses | County Pop. 1960 |
|---|---|---|---|
| Adams | 1,245 | Brighton | 120,296 |
| Alamosa | 719 | Alamosa | 10,000 |
| Arapahoe | 815 | Littleton | 113,426 |
| Archuleta | 1,364 | Pagosa Springs | 2,629 |
| Baca | 2,563 | Springfield | 6,310 |
| Bent | 1,519 | Las Animas | 7,419 |
| Boulder | 748 | Boulder | 74,254 |
| Chaffee | 1,038 | Salida | 8,298 |
| Cheyenne | 1,772 | Cheyenne Wells | 2,789 |
| Clear Creek | 394 | Georgetown | 2,793 |
| Conejos | 1,268 | Conejos | 8,428 |
| Costilla | 1,213 | San Luis | 4,219 |
| Crowley | 802 | Ordway | 3,978 |
| Custer | 737 | Westcliffe | 1,305 |

| County | Land Area sq.mi | County Seats or Court Houses | County Pop. 1960 |
|---|---|---|---|
| **COLORADO—Continued** | | | |
| Delta | 1,154 | Delta | 15,602 |
| Denver | 68 | Denver | 493,887 |
| Dolores | 1,026 | Dove Creek | 2,196 |
| Douglas | 843 | Castle Rock | 4,816 |
| Eagle | 1,682 | Eagle | 4,677 |
| Elbert | 1,864 | Kiowa | 3,708 |
| El Paso | 2,157 | Colorado Springs | 143,742 |
| Fremont | 1,561 | Canon City | 20,196 |
| Garfield | 2,997 | Glenwood Spgs. | 12,017 |
| Gilpin | 148 | Central City | 685 |
| Grand | 1,854 | Hot Sulphur Spgs. | 3,557 |
| Gunnison | 3,236 | Gunnison | 5,477 |
| Hinsdale | 1,054 | Lake City | 208 |
| Huerfano | 1,574 | Walsenburg | 7,867 |
| Jackson | 1,622 | Walden | 1,758 |
| Jefferson | 785 | Golden | 127,520 |
| Kiowa | 1,767 | Eads | 2,425 |
| Kit Carson | 2,171 | Burlington | 6,957 |
| Lake | 379 | Leadville | 7,101 |
| La Plata | 1,684 | Durango | 19,225 |
| Larimer | 2,611 | Fort Collins | 53,343 |
| Las Animas | 4,794 | Trinidad | 19,983 |
| Lincoln | 2,593 | Hugo | 5,310 |
| Logan | 1,822 | Sterling | 20,302 |
| Mesa | 3,303 | Grand Junction | 50,715 |
| Mineral | 921 | Creede | 424 |
| Moffat | 4,743 | Craig | 7,061 |
| Montezuma | 2,094 | Cortez | 14,024 |
| Montrose | 2,238 | Montrose | 18,286 |
| Morgan | 1,278 | Fort Morgan | 21,192 |
| Otero | 1,254 | LaJunta | 24,128 |
| Ouray | 540 | Ouray | 1,601 |
| Park | 2,002 | Fairplay | 1,822 |
| Phillips | 680 | Holyoke | 4,440 |
| Pitkin | 973 | Aspen | 2,381 |
| Prowers | 1,621 | Lamar | 13,296 |
| Pueblo | 2,405 | Pueblo | 118,707 |
| Rio Blanco | 3,263 | Meeker | 5,150 |
| Rio Grande | 915 | Del Norte | 11,160 |
| Routt | 2,330 | Steamboat Spgs. | 5,900 |
| Saguache | 3,144 | Saguache | 4,473 |
| San Juan | 391 | Silverton | 849 |
| San Miguel | 1,283 | Telluride | 2,944 |
| Sedgwick | 544 | Julesburg | 4,242 |
| Summit | 611 | Breckenridge | 2,073 |
| Teller | 553 | Cripple Creek | 2,495 |
| Washington | 2,526 | Akron | 6,625 |
| Weld | 4,002 | Greeley | 72,344 |
| Yuma | 2,379 | Wray | 8,912 |

### CONNECTICUT
*(8 counties, 4,870 sq. mi. land; pop., 2,535,234)*

| County | Land Area sq.mi | County Seats or Court Houses | County Pop. 1960 |
|---|---|---|---|
| Fairfield | 627 | Bridgeport | 653,589 |
| Hartford | 739 | Hartford | 689,555 |
| Litchfield | 930 | Litchfield | 119,856 |
| Middlesex | 372 | Middletown | 88,865 |
| New Haven | 605 | New Haven | 660,315 |
| New London | 667 | Norwich | 185,745 |
| Tolland | 416 | Rockville | 68,737 |
| Windham | 516 | Putnam | 68,572 |

### DELAWARE
*(3 counties, 1,982 sq. mi. land; pop., 446,292)*

| County | Land Area sq.mi | County Seats or Court Houses | County Pop. 1960 |
|---|---|---|---|
| Kent | 594 | Dover '67 | 81,530 |
| New Castle | 438 | Wilmington '67 | 366,298 |
| Sussex | 950 | Georgetown '67 | 78,586 |

### DISTRICT OF COLUMBIA
*(61 sq. mi. land; pop., 763,956)*

### FLORIDA
*(67 counties, 54,136 sq. mi. land; pop., 4,951,560)*

| County | Land Area sq.mi | County Seats or Court Houses | County Pop. 1960 |
|---|---|---|---|
| Alachua | 916 | Gainesville | 74,074 |
| Baker | 585 | Macclenny | 7,363 |
| Bay | 747 | Panama City | 67,131 |
| Bradford | 294 | Starke | 12,446 |
| Brevard | 1,011 | Titusville | 111,435 |
| Broward | 1,219 | Fort Lauderdale | 333,946 |
| Calhoun | 561 | Blountstown | 7,422 |
| Charlotte | 703 | Punta Gorda | 12,594 |
| Citrus | 560 | Inverness | 9,268 |
| Clay | 593 | Green Cove Spgs. | 19,535 |
| Collier | 2,006 | Naples | 15,753 |
| Columbia | 784 | Lake City | 20,077 |
| Dade | 2,042 | Miami | 935,047 |
| De Soto | 648 | Arcadia | 11,683 |
| Dixie | 692 | Cross City | 4,479 |
| Duval | 766 | Jacksonville | 455,411 |
| Escambia | 664 | Pensacola | 173,829 |
| Flagler | 487 | Bunnell | 4,566 |
| Franklin | 536 | Apalachicola | 6,576 |
| Gadsden | 512 | Quincy | 41,989 |
| Gilchrist | 346 | Trenton | 2,868 |
| Glades | 753 | Moore Haven | 2,950 |
| Gulf | 565 | Wewahitchka | 9,937 |
| Hamilton | 514 | Jasper | 7,705 |
| Hardee | 629 | Wauchula | 12,370 |
| Hendry | 1,187 | La Belle | 8,119 |
| Hernando | 484 | Brooksville | 11,205 |
| Highlands | 1,043 | Sebring | 21,338 |
| Hillsborough | 1,038 | Tampa | 397,788 |
| Holmes | 482 | Bonifay | 10,844 |
| Indian River | 507 | Vero Beach | 25,309 |
| Jackson | 905 | Marianna | 36,208 |
| Jefferson | 605 | Monticello | 9,543 |

## FLORIDA—Continued

| County | Land Area sq.mi | County Seats or Court Houses | County Pop. 1960 |
|---|---|---|---|
| Lafayette | 549 | Mayo | 2,889 |
| Lake | 961 | Tavares | 57,383 |
| Lee | 785 | Fort Myers | 54,539 |
| Leon | 670 | Tallahassee | 74,225 |
| Levy | 1,083 | Bronson | 10,364 |
| Liberty | 839 | Bristol | 3,138 |
| Madison | 703 | Madison | 14,154 |
| Manatee | 739 | Bradenton | 69,168 |
| Marion | 1,599 | Ocala | 51,616 |
| Martin | 556 | Stuart | 16,932 |
| Monroe | 1,034 | Key West | 47,921 |
| Nassau | 650 | Fernandina Beach | 17,189 |
| Okaloosa | 944 | Crestview | 61,175 |
| Okeechobee | 777 | Okeechobee | 6,424 |
| Orange | 910 | Orlando | 263,540 |
| Osceola | 1,310 | Kissimmee | 19,029 |
| Palm Beach | 2,023 | West Palm Beach | 228,106 |
| Pasco | 742 | Dade City | 36,785 |
| Pinellas | 265 | Clearwater | 374,665 |
| Polk | 1,861 | Bartow | 195,139 |
| Putnam | 779 | Palatka | 32,212 |
| St. Johns | 605 | Saint Augustine | 30,034 |
| St. Lucie | 584 | Fort Pierce | 39,294 |
| Santa Rosa | 1,032 | Milton | 29,547 |
| Sarasota | 587 | Sarasota | 76,895 |
| Seminole | 305 | Sanford | 54,947 |
| Sumter | 555 | Bushnell | 11,869 |
| Suwannee | 686 | Live Oak | 14,961 |
| Taylor | 1,051 | Perry | 13,168 |
| Union | 241 | Lake Butler | 6,043 |
| Volusia | 1,062 | De Land | 125,319 |
| Wakulla | 601 | Crawfordville | 5,257 |
| Walton | 1,053 | De Funiak Spgs. | 15,576 |
| Washington | 585 | Chipley | 11,249 |

## GEORGIA

*(159 counties, 58,197 sq. mi. land; pop., 3,943,116)*

| County | Land Area sq.mi | County Seats or Court Houses | County Pop. 1960 |
|---|---|---|---|
| Appling | 513 | Baxley | 13,246 |
| Atkinson | 318 | Pearson | 6,188 |
| Bacon | 293 | Alma | 8,359 |
| Baker | 355 | Newton | 4,543 |
| Baldwin | 255 | Milledgeville | 34,064 |
| Banks | 231 | Homer | 6,497 |
| Barrow | 171 | Winder | 14,485 |
| Bartow | 461 | Cartersville | 28,267 |
| Ben Hill | 255 | Fitzgerald | 13,633 |
| Berrien | 468 | Nashville | 12,038 |
| Bibb | 254 | Macon | 141,249 |
| Bleckley | 219 | Cochran | 9,642 |
| Brantley | 447 | Nahunta | 5,891 |
| Brooks | 490 | Quitman | 15,292 |
| Bryan | 443 | Pembroke | 6,226 |
| Bulloch | 685 | Statesboro | 24,263 |
| Burke | 831 | Waynesboro | 20,596 |
| Butts | 185 | Jackson | 8,976 |
| Calhoun | 289 | Morgan | 7,341 |
| Camden | 653 | Woodbine | 9,975 |
| Candler | 250 | Metter | 6,672 |
| Carroll | 495 | Carrollton | 36,451 |
| Catoosa | 167 | Ringgold | 21,101 |
| Charlton | 796 | Folkston | 5,313 |
| Chatham | 445 | Savannah | 188,299 |
| Chattahoochee | 253 | Cusseta | 13,011 |
| Chattooga | 317 | Summerville | 19,954 |
| Cherokee | 415 | Canton | 23,001 |
| Clarke | 125 | Athens | 45,363 |
| Clay | 224 | Fort Gaines | 4,551 |
| Clayton | 149 | Jonesboro | 46,365 |
| Clinch | 797 | Homerville | 6,545 |
| Cobb | 343 | Marietta | 114,174 |
| Coffee | 612 | Douglas | 21,953 |
| Colquitt | 563 | Moultrie | 34,048 |
| Columbia | 290 | Appling | 13,423 |
| Cook | 233 | Adel | 11,822 |
| Coweta | 442 | Newnan | 28,893 |
| Crawford | 315 | Knoxville | 5,816 |
| Crisp | 292 | Cordele | 17,768 |
| Dade | 168 | Trenton | 8,666 |
| Dawson | 211 | Dawsonville | 3,590 |
| Decatur | 575 | Bainbridge | 25,203 |
| De Kalb | 269 | Decatur | 256,782 |
| Dodge | 498 | Eastman | 16,483 |
| Dooly | 394 | Vienna | 11,474 |
| Dougherty | 324 | Albany | 75,680 |
| Douglas | 202 | Douglasville | 16,741 |
| Early | 525 | Blakely | 13,151 |
| Echols | 425 | Statenville | 1,876 |
| Effingham | 480 | Springfield | 10,144 |
| Elbert | 358 | Elberton | 17,835 |
| Emanuel | 686 | Swainsboro | 17,815 |
| Evans | 186 | Claxton | 6,952 |
| Fannin | 394 | Blue Ridge | 13,620 |
| Fayette | 199 | Fayetteville | 8,199 |
| Floyd | 514 | Rome | 69,130 |
| Forsyth | 218 | Cumming | 12,170 |
| Franklin | 269 | Carnesville | 13,274 |
| Fulton | 530 | Atlanta | 556,326 |
| Gilmer | 439 | Ellijay | 8,922 |
| Glascock | 143 | Gibson | 2,672 |
| Glynn | 412 | Brunswick | 41,954 |
| Gordon | 358 | Calhoun | 19,228 |
| Grady | 466 | Cairo | 18,015 |

## GEORGIA—Continued

| County | Land Area sq.mi | County Seats or Court Houses | County Pop. 1960 |
|---|---|---|---|
| Greene | 403 | Greensboro | 11,193 |
| Gwinnett | 437 | Lawrenceville | 43,541 |
| Habersham | 282 | Clarkesville | 18,116 |
| Hall | 378 | Gainesville | 49,739 |
| Hancock | 478 | Sparta | 9,979 |
| Haralson | 285 | Buchanan | 14,543 |
| Harris | 465 | Hamilton | 11,167 |
| Hart | 256 | Hartwell | 15,229 |
| Heard | 302 | Franklin | 5,333 |
| Henry | 331 | McDonough | 17,619 |
| Houston | 380 | Perry | 39,154 |
| Irwin | 372 | Ocilla | 9,211 |
| Jackson | 337 | Jefferson | 18,499 |
| Jasper | 373 | Monticello | 6,135 |
| Jeff Davis | 331 | Hazlehurst | 8,914 |
| Jefferson | 530 | Louisville | 17,468 |
| Jenkins | 351 | Millen | 9,148 |
| Johnson | 313 | Wrightsville | 8,048 |
| Jones | 402 | Gray | 8,468 |
| Lamar | 181 | Barnesville | 10,240 |
| Lanier | 177 | Lakeland | 5,097 |
| Laurens | 810 | Dublin | 32,313 |
| Lee | 355 | Leesburg | 6,204 |
| Liberty | 514 | Hinesville | 14,487 |
| Lincoln | 193 | Lincolnton | 5,906 |
| Long | 402 | Ludowici | 3,874 |
| Lowndes | 507 | Valdosta | 49,270 |
| Lumpkin | 292 | Dahlonega | 7,241 |
| McDuffie | 253 | Thomson | 12,627 |
| McIntosh | 426 | Darien | 6,364 |
| Macon | 403 | Oglethorpe | 13,170 |
| Madison | 281 | Danielsville | 11,246 |
| Marion | 365 | Buena Vista | 5,477 |
| Meriwether | 499 | Greenville | 19,756 |
| Miller | 287 | Colquitt | 6,908 |
| Mitchell | 509 | Camilla | 19,652 |
| Monroe | 398 | Forsyth | 10,495 |
| Montgomery | 237 | Mount Vernon | 6,284 |
| Morgan | 356 | Madison | 10,280 |
| Murray | 342 | Chatsworth | 10,447 |
| Muscogee | 220 | Columbus | 158,623 |
| Newton | 271 | Covington | 20,999 |
| Oconee | 186 | Watkinsville | 6,304 |
| Oglethorpe | 435 | Lexington | 7,926 |
| Paulding | 318 | Dallas | 13,101 |
| Peach | 115 | Fort Valley | 13,846 |
| Pickens | 225 | Jasper | 8,903 |
| Pierce | 342 | Blackshear | 9,678 |
| Pike | 230 | Zebulon | 7,138 |
| Polk | 312 | Cedartown | 28,015 |
| Pulaski | 353 | Hawkinsville | 8,204 |
| Putnam | 340 | Eatonton | 7,798 |
| Quitman | 171 | Georgetown | 2,432 |
| Rabun | 368 | Clayton | 7,456 |
| Randolph | 436 | Cuthbert | 11,078 |
| Richmond | 323 | Augusta | 135,601 |
| Rockdale | 128 | Conyers | 10,572 |
| Schley | 162 | Ellaville | 3,256 |
| Screven | 651 | Sylvania | 14,919 |
| Seminole | 246 | Donalsonville | 6,802 |
| Spalding | 201 | Griffin | 35,404 |
| Stephens | 180 | Toccoa | 18,391 |
| Stewart | 463 | Lumpkin | 7,371 |
| Sumter | 489 | Americus | 24,652 |
| Talbot | 390 | Talbotton | 7,127 |
| Taliaferro | 195 | Crawfordville | 3,370 |
| Tattnall | 490 | Reidsville | 15,837 |
| Taylor | 403 | Butler | 8,311 |
| Telfair | 440 | McRae | 11,715 |
| Terrell | 329 | Dawson | 12,742 |
| Thomas | 541 | Thomasville | 34,319 |
| Tift | 266 | Tifton | 23,487 |
| Toombs | 368 | Lyons | 16,837 |
| Towns | 166 | Hiawassee | 4,538 |
| Treutlen | 194 | Soperton | 5,874 |
| Troup | 446 | La Grange | 47,189 |
| Turner | 293 | Ashburn | 8,439 |
| Twiggs | 364 | Jeffersonville | 7,935 |
| Union | 309 | Blairsville | 6,510 |
| Upson | 334 | Thomaston | 23,800 |
| Walker | 445 | La Fayette | 45,264 |
| Walton | 326 | Monroe | 20,481 |
| Ware | 912 | Waycross | 34,219 |
| Warren | 284 | Warrenton | 7,360 |
| Washington | 674 | Sandersville | 18,903 |
| Wayne | 645 | Jesup | 17,921 |
| Webster | 195 | Preston | 3,247 |
| Wheeler | 306 | Alamo | 5,342 |
| White | 243 | Cleveland | 6,935 |
| Whitfield | 281 | Dalton | 42,109 |
| Wilcox | 383 | Abbeville | 7,905 |
| Wilkes | 468 | Washington | 10,961 |
| Wilkinson | 458 | Irwinton | 9,250 |
| Worth | 579 | Sylvester | 16,682 |

## HAWAII

*(5 counties, 6,425 sq. mi. land; pop., 632,772)*

| County | Land Area sq.mi | County Seats or Court Houses | County Pop. 1960 |
|---|---|---|---|
| Hawaii | 4,021 | Hilo | 61,332 |
| Honolulu | 598 | Honolulu | 500,409 |
| Kalawao | 14 | Kalaupapa | 279 |
| Kauai | 623 | Lihue | 28,176 |
| Maui | 1,159 | Wailuku | 42,576 |

| County | Land Area sq.mi | County Seats or Court Houses | County Pop. 1960 | County | Land Area sq.mi | County Seats or Court Houses | County Pop. 1960 |
|---|---|---|---|---|---|---|---|
| **IDAHO** | | | | **ILLINOIS—Continued** | | | |
| *(44 counties, 82,677 sq. mi. land; pop., 667,191)* | | | | Lee........ | 729 | Dixon.......... | 38,791 |
| Ada......... | 1,043 | Boise........... | 93,460 | Livingston.... | 1,043 | Pontiac........ | 40,344 |
| Adams..... | 1,371 | Council.......... | 2,978 | Logan....... | 622 | Lincoln........ | 33,656 |
| Bannock.... | 1,122 | Pocatello...... | 49,342 | McDonough... | 582 | Macomb........ | 28,928 |
| Bear Lake.... | 984 | Paris.......... | 7,148 | McHenry.... | 611 | Woodstock..... | 84,210 |
| Benewah...... | 788 | Saint Maries..... | 6,036 | McLean..... | 1,173 | Bloomington... | 83,877 |
| Bingham..... | 2,084 | Blackfoot...... | 28,218 | Macon..... | 576 | Decatur....... | 118,257 |
| Blaine....... | 2,647 | Hailey......... | 4,598 | Macoupin.... | 872 | Carlinville.... | 43,524 |
| Boise....... | 1,910 | Idaho City...... | 1,646 | Madison.... | 731 | Edwardsville.... | 224,689 |
| Bonner....... | 1,733 | Sandpoint...... | 15,587 | Marion..... | 580 | Salem........ | 39,349 |
| Bonneville..... | 1,836 | Idaho Falls..... | 46,906 | Marshall.... | 395 | Lacon........ | 13,334 |
| Boundary..... | 1,275 | Bonners Ferry... | 5,809 | Mason..... | 541 | Havana....... | 15,193 |
| Butte....... | 2,239 | Arco.......... | 3,498 | Massac.... | 246 | Metropolis..... | 14,341 |
| Camas...... | 1,054 | Fairfield........ | 917 | Menard..... | 312 | Petersburg.... | 9,248 |
| Canyon..... | 578 | Caldwell...... | 57,662 | Mercer..... | 556 | Aledo........ | 17,149 |
| Caribou..... | 1,746 | Soda Springs.... | 5,976 | Monroe.... | 380 | Waterloo...... | 15,507 |
| Cassia....... | 2,544 | Burley........ | 16,121 | Montgomery... | 706 | Hillsboro...... | 31,244 |
| Clark....... | 1,751 | Dubois........ | 915 | Morgan..... | 565 | Jacksonville.... | 36,571 |
| Clearwater.... | 2,521 | Orofino....... | 8,548 | Moultrie.... | 345 | Sullivan...... | 13,635 |
| Custer...... | 4,929 | Challis........ | 2,996 | Ogle....... | 757 | Oregon....... | 38,106 |
| Elmore...... | 3,048 | Mountain Home.. | 16,719 | Peoria..... | 624 | Peoria........ | 189,044 |
| Franklin..... | 664 | Preston........ | 8,457 | Perry..... | 443 | Pinckneyville... | 19,184 |
| Fremont..... | 1,806 | Saint Anthony... | 8,679 | Piatt..... | 437 | Monticello..... | 14,960 |
| Gem........ | 555 | Emmett....... | 9,127 | Pike...... | 829 | Pittsfield...... | 20,552 |
| Gooding..... | 720 | Gooding....... | 9,544 | Pope...... | 381 | Golconda..... | 4,061 |
| Idaho....... | 8,516 | Grangeville.... | 13,542 | Pulaski.... | 204 | Mound City.... | 10,490 |
| Jefferson..... | 1,096 | Rigby......... | 11,672 | Putnam.... | 166 | Hennepin..... | 4,570 |
| Jerome...... | 595 | Jerome........ | 11,712 | Randolph.... | 594 | Chester...... | 29,988 |
| Kootenai..... | 1,249 | Coeur d'Alene.... | 29,556 | Richland.... | 364 | Olney........ | 16,299 |
| Latah...... | 1,090 | Moscow....... | 21,170 | Rock Island... | 420 | Rock Island... | 150,991 |
| Lemhi...... | 4,580 | Salmon........ | 5,816 | St. Clair.... | 670 | Belleville..... | 262,509 |
| Lewis....... | 476 | Nezperce...... | 4,423 | Saline..... | 380 | Harrisburg.... | 26,227 |
| Lincoln..... | 1,203 | Shoshone...... | 3,686 | Sangamon.... | 880 | Springfield.... | 146,539 |
| Madison..... | 473 | Rexburg...... | 9,417 | Schuyler.... | 434 | Rushville..... | 8,746 |
| Minidoka.... | 750 | Rupert........ | 14,394 | Scott...... | 251 | Winchester.... | 6,377 |
| Nez Perce.... | 844 | Lewiston...... | 27,662 | Shelby..... | 772 | Shelbyville.... | 23,404 |
| Oneida...... | 1,191 | Malad City..... | 3,603 | Stark..... | 291 | Toulon...... | 8,152 |
| Owyhee..... | 7,641 | Murphy....... | 6,375 | Stephenson... | 568 | Freeport...... | 46,207 |
| Payette..... | 402 | Payette....... | 12,363 | Tazewell.... | 653 | Pekin........ | 99,789 |
| Power...... | 1,413 | American Falls... | 4,111 | Union..... | 414 | Jonesboro.... | 17,645 |
| Shoshone.... | 2,609 | Wallace....... | 20,876 | Vermilion.... | 898 | Danville...... | 96,176 |
| Teton...... | 457 | Driggs........ | 2,639 | Wabash.... | 221 | Mt. Carmel.... | 14,047 |
| Twin Falls.... | 1,947 | Twin Falls..... | 41,842 | Warren..... | 542 | Monmouth.... | 21,587 |
| Valley...... | 3,676 | Cascade....... | 3,663 | Washington... | 565 | Nashville..... | 13,569 |
| Washington... | 1,462 | Weiser........ | 8,378 | Wayne..... | 715 | Fairfield...... | 19,008 |
| Yel'stone Nat | | | | White..... | 501 | Carmi....... | 19,373 |
| Park (part).. | 58 | ............ | ....... | Whiteside.... | 690 | Morrison..... | 59,887 |
| | | | | Will....... | 845 | Joliet........ | 191,617 |
| **ILLINOIS** | | | | Williamson... | 427 | Marion....... | 46,117 |
| *(102 counties, 55,877 sq. mi. land; pop., 10,081,158)* | | | | Winnebago.... | 520 | Rockford..... | 209,765 |
| Adams....... | 866 | Quincy......... | 68,467 | Woodford.... | 537 | Eureka....... | 24,579 |
| Alexander.... | 224 | Cairo.......... | 16,061 | | | | |
| Bond....... | 383 | Greenville...... | 14,060 | **INDIANA** | | | |
| Boone...... | 283 | Belvidere...... | 20,326 | *(92 counties, 36,189 sq. mi. land; pop., 4,662,498)* | | | |
| Brown...... | 307 | Mount Sterling... | 6,210 | Adams....... | 345 | Decatur...... | 24,643 |
| Bureau..... | 868 | Princeton...... | 37,594 | Allen....... | 670 | Fort Wayne... | 232,196 |
| Calhoun..... | 259 | Hardin........ | 5,933 | Bartholomew... | 402 | Columbus..... | 48,198 |
| Carroll..... | 468 | Mount Carroll... | 19,507 | Benton..... | 409 | Fowler....... | 11,912 |
| Cass....... | 370 | Virginia....... | 14,539 | Blackford.... | 167 | Hartford City... | 14,792 |
| Champaign... | 1,000 | Urbana........ | 132,436 | Boone..... | 424 | Lebanon..... | 27,543 |
| Christian.... | 709 | Taylorville..... | 37,207 | Brown..... | 324 | Nashville..... | 7,024 |
| Clark....... | 505 | Marshall...... | 16,546 | Carroll.... | 374 | Delphi....... | 16,934 |
| Clay....... | 464 | Louisville...... | 15,815 | Cass..... | 415 | Logansport.... | 40,931 |
| Clinton..... | 498 | Carlyle........ | 24,029 | Clark..'64. | 384 | Jeffersonville... | 66,453 |
| Coles....... | 507 | Charleston..... | 42,860 | Clay..... | 364 | Brazil....... | 24,207 |
| Cook....... | 954 | Chicago........ | 5,129,725 | Clinton.... | 407 | Frankfort..... | 30,765 |
| Crawford.... | 442 | Robinson...... | 20,751 | Crawford.... | 312 | English...... | 8,379 |
| Cumberland... | 346 | Toledo........ | 9,936 | Daviess.... | 430 | Washington... | 26,636 |
| De Kalb..... | 636 | Sycamore...... | 51,714 | Dearborn.... | 306 | Lawrenceburg... | 28,674 |
| De Witt..... | 399 | Clinton....... | 17,253 | Decatur.... | 370 | Greensburg.... | 20,019 |
| Douglas..'64. | 420 | Tuscola....... | 19,281 | De Kalb.... | 366 | Auburn...... | 28,271 |
| Du Page..... | 331 | Wheaton...... | 313,459 | Delaware.... | 398 | Muncie...... | 110,938 |
| Edgar...... | 628 | Paris.......... | 22,550 | Dubois.... | 433 | Jasper....... | 27,463 |
| Edwards..... | 225 | Albion........ | 7,940 | Elkhart.... | 468 | Goshen...... | 106,790 |
| Effingham.... | 482 | Effingham...... | 23,107 | Fayette.... | 215 | Connersville... | 24,454 |
| Fayette..... | 718 | Vandalia....... | 21,946 | Floyd..'64. | 149 | New Albany.... | 53,008 |
| Ford....... | 488 | Paxton........ | 16,606 | Fountain.... | 397 | Covington.... | 18,706 |
| Franklin..... | 434 | Benton........ | 39,281 | Franklin.... | 394 | Brookville.... | 17,015 |
| Fulton..... | 874 | Lewistown..... | 41,954 | Fulton.... | 367 | Rochester..... | 16,957 |
| Gallatin..... | 328 | Shawneetown... | 7,638 | Gibson.... | 498 | Princeton..... | 29,949 |
| Greene...... | 543 | Carrollton..... | 17,460 | Grant..... | 421 | Marion....... | 75,741 |
| Grundy..... | 432 | Morris........ | 22,350 | Greene..... | 549 | Bloomfield.... | 26,327 |
| Hamilton.... | 435 | McLeansboro... | 10,010 | Hamilton.... | 401 | Noblesville.... | 40,132 |
| Hancock.... | 797 | Carthage...... | 24,574 | Hancock.... | 305 | Greenfield.... | 26,665 |
| Hardin..... | 183 | Elizabethtown... | 5,879 | Harrison.... | 479 | Corydon..... | 19,207 |
| Henderson.... | 381 | Oquawka...... | 8,237 | Hendricks.... | 417 | Danville...... | 40,896 |
| Henry...... | 826 | Cambridge..... | 49,317 | Henry..... | 400 | New Castle.... | 48,899 |
| Iroquois..... | 1,122 | Watseka...... | 33,562 | Howard.... | 293 | Kokomo..... | 69,509 |
| Jackson..... | 603 | Murphysboro... | 42,151 | Huntington... | 390 | Huntington.... | 33,814 |
| Jasper..... | 495 | Newton....... | 11,346 | Jackson.... | 520 | Brownstown... | 30,556 |
| Jefferson.... | 574 | Mount Vernon... | 32,315 | Jasper.... | 562 | Rensselaer.... | 18,842 |
| Jersey...... | 374 | Jerseyville..... | 17,023 | Jay...... | 386 | Portland...... | 22,572 |
| Jo Daviess... | 614 | Galena........ | 21,821 | Jefferson.... | 366 | Madison..... | 24,061 |
| Johnson..... | 345 | Vienna........ | 6,928 | Jennings.... | 377 | Vernon...... | 1,726 |
| Kane....... | 516 | Geneva........ | 208,246 | Johnson.... | 315 | Franklin...... | 43,704 |
| Kankakee.... | 680 | Kankakee...... | 92,063 | Knox..... | 516 | Vincennes.... | 41,561 |
| Kendall..... | 320 | Yorkville...... | 17,540 | Kosciusko.... | 540 | Warsaw...... | 40,373 |
| Knox....... | 728 | Galesburg..... | 61,280 | Lagrange.... | 381 | Lagrange..... | 17,380 |
| Lake....... | 457 | Waukegan..... | 293,656 | Lake..... | 513 | Crown Point... | 513,269 |
| La Salle..... | 1,153 | Ottawa....... | 110,800 | La Porte.... | 607 | La Porte..... | 95,111 |
| Lawrence.... | 374 | Lawrenceville.... | 18,540 | Lawrence.... | 459 | Bedford...... | 36,564 |
| | | | | Madison..... | 453 | Anderson..... | 125,819 |

| County | Land Area sq.mi | County Seats or Court Houses | County Pop. 1960 | County | Land Area sq.mi | County Seats or Court Houses | County Pop. 1960 |
|---|---|---|---|---|---|---|---|
| | | **INDIANA—Continued** | | | | **IOWA—Continued** | |
| Marion | 400 | Indianapolis | 697,567 | Lee | 527 | Fort Madison and Keokuk | 44,207 |
| Marshall | 443 | Plymouth | 32,443 | Linn | 717 | Cedar Rapids | 136,899 |
| Martin | 345 | Shoals | 10,608 | Louisa | 403 | Wapello | 10,290 |
| Miami | 380 | Peru | 38,000 | Lucas | 434 | Chariton | 10,923 |
| Monroe | 410 | Bloomington | 59,225 | Lyon | 588 | Rock Rapids | 14,468 |
| Montgomery | 507 | Crawfordsville | 32,089 | Madison | 564 | Winterset | 12,295 |
| Morgan | 406 | Martinsville | 33,875 | Mahaska | 572 | Oskaloosa | 23,602 |
| Newton | 413 | Kentland | 11,502 | Marion | 567 | Knoxville | 25,886 |
| Noble | 412 | Albion | 28,162 | Marshall | 574 | Marshalltown | 37,984 |
| Ohio | 87 | Rising Sun | 4,165 | Mills | 447 | Glenwood | 13,050 |
| Orange | 405 | Paoli | 16,877 | Mitchell | 467 | Osage | 14,043 |
| Owen | 390 | Spencer | 11,400 | Monona | 699 | Onawa | 13,916 |
| Parke | 451 | Rockville | 14,804 | Monroe | 435 | Albia | 10,463 |
| Perry | 384 | Cannelton | 17,232 | Montgomery | 422 | Red Oak | 14,467 |
| Pike | 335 | Petersburg | 12,797 | Muscatine | 443 | Muscatine | 33,840 |
| Porter | 425 | Valparaiso | 60,279 | O'Brien | 575 | Primghar | 18,840 |
| Posey '67 | 412 | Mount Vernon | 21,448 | Osceola | 398 | Sibley | 10,064 |
| Pulaski | 433 | Winamac | 12,837 | Page | 535 | Clarinda | 21,023 |
| Putnam | 490 | Greencastle | 24,927 | Palo Alto | 561 | Emmetsburg | 14,736 |
| Randolph | 457 | Winchester | 28,434 | Plymouth | 863 | Le Mars | 23,906 |
| Ripley | 442 | Versailles | 20,641 | Pocahontas | 581 | Pocahontas | 14,234 |
| Rush | 409 | Rushville | 20,393 | Polk | 594 | Des Moines | 266,315 |
| St. Joseph | 466 | South Bend | 238,614 | Pottawattamie | 963 | Council Bluffs | 83,102 |
| Scott | 193 | Scottsburg | 14,643 | Poweshiek | 589 | Montezuma | 19,300 |
| Shelby | 409 | Shelbyville | 34,093 | Ringgold | 538 | Mount Ayr | 7,910 |
| Spencer | 396 | Rockport | 16,074 | Sac | 578 | Sac City | 17,007 |
| Starke | 310 | Knox | 17,911 | Scott | 454 | Davenport | 119,067 |
| Steuben | 309 | Angola | 17,184 | Shelby | 587 | Harlan | 15,825 |
| Sullivan | 457 | Sullivan | 21,721 | Sioux | 766 | Orange City | 26,375 |
| Switzerland | 221 | Vevay | 7,092 | Story | 568 | Nevada | 49,327 |
| Tippecanoe | 500 | Lafayette | 89,122 | Tama | 720 | Toledo | 21,413 |
| Tipton | 261 | Tipton | 15,556 | Taylor | 528 | Bedford | 10,288 |
| Union | 168 | Liberty | 6,457 | Union | 425 | Creston | 13,712 |
| Vanderburgh | 241 | Evansville | 165,794 | Van Buren | 487 | Keosauqua | 9,778 |
| Vermillion | 263 | Newport | 17,683 | Wapello | 437 | Ottumwa | 46,126 |
| Vigo | 415 | Terre Haute | 108,458 | Warren | 572 | Indianola | 20,829 |
| Wabash | 421 | Wabash | 32,605 | Washington | 568 | Washington | 19,406 |
| Warren | 368 | Williamsport | 8,545 | Wayne | 532 | Corydon | 9,800 |
| Warrick | 391 | Boonville | 23,577 | Webster | 718 | Fort Dodge | 47,810 |
| Washington | 516 | Salem | 17,819 | Winnebago | 401 | Forest City | 13,099 |
| Wayne | 405 | Richmond | 74,039 | Winneshiek | 688 | Decorah | 21,651 |
| Wells | 368 | Bluffton | 21,220 | Woodbury | 871 | Sioux City | 107,849 |
| White | 497 | Monticello | 19,709 | Worth | 400 | Northwood | 10,259 |
| Whitley | 337 | Columbia City | 20,954 | Wright | 577 | Clarion | 19,447 |
| | | **IOWA** | | | | **KANSAS** | |
| *(99 counties; 56,043 sq. mi. land; pop.; 2,757,537)* | | | | *(105 counties, 82,056 sq. mi. land; pop.; 2,178,611)* | | | |
| Adair | 569 | Greenfield | 10,893 | Allen | 505 | Iola | 16,369 |
| Adams | 426 | Corning | 7,468 | Anderson | 577 | Garnett | 9,035 |
| Allamakee | 636 | Waukon | 15,982 | Atchison | 427 | Atchison | 20,898 |
| Appanoose | 523 | Centerville | 16,015 | Barber | 1,146 | Medicine Lodge | 8,713 |
| Audubon | 448 | Audubon | 10,919 | Barton | 894 | Great Bend | 32,368 |
| Benton | 718 | Vinton | 23,422 | Bourbon | 639 | Fort Scott | 16,090 |
| Black Hawk | 568 | Waterloo | 122,482 | Brown | 577 | Hiawatha | 13,229 |
| Boone | 573 | Boone | 28,037 | Butler | 1,442 | El Dorado | 38,395 |
| Bremer | 439 | Waverly | 21,108 | Chase | 774 | Cottonwood Falls | 3,921 |
| Buchanan | 568 | Independence | 22,293 | Chautauqua | 647 | Sedan | 5,956 |
| Buena Vista | 572 | Storm Lake | 21,189 | Cherokee | 586 | Columbus | 22,279 |
| Butler | 582 | Allison | 17,467 | Cheyenne | 1,027 | Saint Francis | 4,708 |
| Calhoun | 571 | Rockwell City | 15,923 | Clark | 983 | Ashland | 3,396 |
| Carroll | 574 | Carroll | 23,431 | Clay | 659 | Clay Center | 10,675 |
| Cass | 585 | Atlantic | 17,919 | Cloud | 711 | Concordia | 14,407 |
| Cedar | 585 | Tipton | 17,791 | Coffey | 656 | Burlington | 8,403 |
| Cerro Gordo | 575 | Mason City | 49,894 | Comanche | 800 | Coldwater | 3,271 |
| Cherokee | 573 | Cherokee | 18,598 | Cowley | 1,136 | Winfield | 37,861 |
| Chickasaw | 505 | New Hampton | 15,034 | Crawford | 598 | Girard | 37,032 |
| Clarke | 429 | Osceola | 8,222 | Decatur | 899 | Oberlin | 5,778 |
| Clay | 570 | Spencer | 18,504 | Dickinson | 855 | Abilene | 21,572 |
| Clayton | 779 | Elkader | 21,962 | Doniphan | 388 | Troy | 9,574 |
| Clinton | 693 | Clinton | 55,060 | Douglas | 571 | Lawrence | 43,720 |
| Crawford | 716 | Denison | 18,569 | Edwards | 617 | Kinsley | 5,118 |
| Dallas | 597 | Adel | 24,123 | Elk | 647 | Howard | 5,048 |
| Davis | 509 | Bloomfield | 9,199 | Ellis | 900 | Hays | 21,270 |
| Decatur | 530 | Leon | 10,539 | Ellsworth | 717 | Ellsworth | 7,677 |
| Delaware | 571 | Manchester | 18,483 | Finney | 1,301 | Garden City | 16,093 |
| Des Moines | 408 | Burlington | 44,605 | Ford | 1,091 | Dodge City | 20,938 |
| Dickinson | 380 | Spirit Lake | 12,574 | Franklin | 577 | Ottawa | 19,548 |
| Dubuque | 612 | Dubuque | 80,048 | Geary | 400 | Junction City | 28,779 |
| Emmet | 394 | Estherville | 14,871 | Gove | 1,070 | Gove | 4,107 |
| Fayette | 728 | West Union | 28,581 | Graham | 891 | Hill City | 5,586 |
| Floyd | 503 | Charles City | 21,102 | Grant | 571 | Ulysses | 5,269 |
| Franklin | 586 | Hampton | 15,472 | Gray | 872 | Cimarron | 4,380 |
| Fremont | 524 | Sidney | 10,282 | Greeley | 783 | Tribune | 2,087 |
| Greene | 569 | Jefferson | 14,379 | Greenwood | 1,142 | Eureka | 11 253 |
| Grundy | 501 | Grundy Center | 14,132 | Hamilton | 992 | Syracuse | 3,144 |
| Guthrie | 569 | Guthrie Center | 13,607 | Harper | 801 | Anthony | 9,541 |
| Hamilton | 577 | Webster City | 20,032 | Harvey | 540 | Newton | 25,865 |
| Hancock | 570 | Garner | 14,604 | Haskell | 580 | Sublette | 2,990 |
| Hardin | 573 | Eldora | 22,533 | Hodgeman | 860 | Jetmore | 3,115 |
| Harrison | 696 | Logan | 17,600 | Jackson | 656 | Holton | 10,309 |
| Henry | 440 | Mount Pleasant | 18,187 | Jefferson | 550 | Oskaloosa | 11,252 |
| Howard | 471 | Cresco | 12,734 | Jewell | 910 | Mankato | 7,217 |
| Humboldt | 435 | Dakota City | 13,156 | Johnson | 476 | Olathe | 143,792 |
| Ida | 431 | Ida Grove | 10,269 | Kearny | 855 | Lakin | 3,108 |
| Iowa | 584 | Marengo | 16,396 | Kingman | 865 | Kingman | 9,958 |
| Jackson | 644 | Maquoketa | 20,754 | Kiowa | 720 | Greensburg | 4,626 |
| Jasper | 734 | Newton | 35,282 | Labette | 654 | Oswego | 26,805 |
| Jefferson | 438 | Fairfield | 15,818 | Lane | 720 | Dighton | 3,060 |
| Johnson | 619 | Iowa City | 53,663 | Leavenworth | 466 | Leavenworth | 48,524 |
| Jones | 585 | Anamosa | 20,693 | Lincoln | 726 | Lincoln | 5,556 |
| Keokuk | 579 | Sigourney | 15,492 | Linn | 606 | Mound City | 8,274 |
| Kossuth | 979 | Algona | 25,314 | | | | |

| County | Land Area sq.mi | County Seats or Court Houses | County Pop. 1960 |
|---|---|---|---|

## KANSAS—Continued

| County | Land Area sq.mi | County Seats or Court Houses | County Pop. 1960 |
|---|---|---|---|
| Logan........ | 1,073 | Oakley............ | 4,036 |
| Lyon........ | 852 | Emporia.......... | 26,928 |
| McPherson.... | 896 | McPherson........ | 24,285 |
| Marion........ | 959 | Marion............ | 15,143 |
| Marshall........ | 883 | Marysville........ | 15,598 |
| Meade........ | 979 | Meade............ | 5,505 |
| Miami........ | 592 | Paola............ | 19,884 |
| Mitchell........ | 716 | Beloit............ | 8,866 |
| Montgomery.. | 649 | Independence...... | 45,007 |
| Morris........ | 706 | Council Grove...... | 7,392 |
| Morton........ | 728 | Elkhart.......... | 3,354 |
| Nemaha........ | 708 | Seneca............ | 12,897 |
| Neosho........ | 587 | Erie.............. | 19,455 |
| Ness........ | 1,081 | Ness City........ | 5,470 |
| Norton........ | 880 | Norton............ | 8,035 |
| Osage........ | 720 | Lyndon............ | 12,886 |
| Osborne........ | 898 | Osborne.......... | 7,506 |
| Ottawa........ | 723 | Minneapolis...... | 6,779 |
| Pawnee........ | 755 | Larned............ | 10,254 |
| Phillips........ | 897 | Phillipsburg...... | 8,709 |
| Pottawatomie.. | 820 | Westmoreland.... | 11,957 |
| Pratt........ | 729 | Pratt............ | 12,122 |
| Rawlins........ | 1,078 | Atwood............ | 5,279 |
| Reno........ | 1,262 | Hutchinson........ | 59,055 |
| Republic........ | 718 | Belleville........ | 9,768 |
| Rice........ | 725 | Lyons............ | 13,909 |
| Riley........ | 597 | Manhattan........ | 41,914 |
| Rooks........ | 886 | Stockton.......... | 9,734 |
| Rush........ | 724 | La Crosse........ | 6,160 |
| Russell........ | 897 | Russell.......... | 11,348 |
| Saline........ | 720 | Salina............ | 54,715 |
| Scott........ | 724 | Scott City........ | 5,228 |
| Sedgwick........ | 1,007 | Wichita.......... | 343,231 |
| Seward........ | 646 | Liberal.......... | 15,930 |
| Shawnee........ | 548 | Topeka............ | 141,286 |
| Sheridan........ | 893 | Hoxie............ | 4,267 |
| Sherman........ | 1,055 | Goodland.......... | 6,682 |
| Smith........ | 893 | Smith Center...... | 7,776 |
| Stafford........ | 795 | Saint John........ | 7,451 |
| Stanton........ | 676 | Johnson.......... | 2,108 |
| Stevens........ | 731 | Hugoton.......... | 4,400 |
| Sumner........ | 1,186 | Wellington........ | 25,316 |
| Thomas........ | 1,070 | Colby............ | 7,358 |
| Trego........ | 901 | Wakeeney.......... | 5,473 |
| Wabaunsee.... | 792 | Alma............ | 6,648 |
| Wallace........ | 911 | Sharon Springs.... | 2,069 |
| Washington.... | 891 | Washington........ | 10,739 |
| Wichita........ | 724 | Leoti............ | 2,765 |
| Wilson........ | 574 | Fredonia.......... | 13,077 |
| Woodson........ | 503 | Yates Center...... | 5,423 |
| Wyandotte.... | 152 | Kansas City...... | 185,495 |

## KENTUCKY

*(120 counties, 39,851 sq. mi. land; pop.; 3,038,156)*

| County | Land Area sq.mi | County Seats or Court Houses | County Pop. 1960 |
|---|---|---|---|
| Adair........ | 393 | Columbia.......... | 14,699 |
| Allen........ | 364 | Scottsville........ | 12,269 |
| Anderson........ | 206 | Lawrenceburg.... | 8,618 |
| Ballard........ | 259 | Wickliffe.......... | 8,291 |
| Barren........ | 486 | Glasgow.......... | 28,303 |
| Bath........ | 287 | Owingsville...... | 9,114 |
| Bell........ | 370 | Pineville.......... | 35,336 |
| Boone........ | 249 | Burlington........ | 21,940 |
| Bourbon........ | 300 | Paris............ | 18,178 |
| Boyd........ | 160 | Catlettsburg...... | 52,163 |
| Boyle........ | 183 | Danville.......... | 21,257 |
| Bracken........ | 204 | Brooksville........ | 7,422 |
| Breathitt........ | 494 | Jackson.......... | 15,490 |
| Breckinridge.. | 564 | Hardinsburg...... | 14,734 |
| Bullitt........ | 300 | Shepherdsville.... | 15,726 |
| Butler........ | 443 | Morgantown...... | 9,586 |
| Caldwell........ | 357 | Princeton.......... | 13,073 |
| Calloway........ | 384 | Murray............ | 20,972 |
| Campbell........ | 149 | Alexandria........ | 86,803 |
| Carlisle........ | 195 | Bardwell.......... | 5,608 |
| Carroll........ | 130 | Carrollton........ | 7,978 |
| Carter........ | 402 | Grayson.......... | 20,817 |
| Casey........ | 435 | Liberty............ | 14,327 |
| Christian........ | 725 | Hopkinsville...... | 56,904 |
| Clark,'64........ | 259 | Winchester........ | 21,075 |
| Clay........ | 474 | Manchester........ | 20,748 |
| Clinton........ | 190 | Albany............ | 8,886 |
| Crittenden.... | 365 | Marion............ | 8,648 |
| Cumberland.. | 310 | Burkesville........ | 7,835 |
| Daviess........ | 462 | Owensboro........ | 70,588 |
| Edmonson.... | 304 | Brownsville........ | 8,085 |
| Elliott........ | 240 | Sandy Hook........ | 6,330 |
| Estill........ | 260 | Irvine............ | 12,466 |
| Fayette........ | 280 | Lexington.......... | 131,906 |
| Fleming........ | 350 | Flemingsburg...... | 10,890 |
| Floyd........ | 399 | Prestonsburg...... | 41,642 |
| Franklin........ | 211 | Frankfort.......... | 29,421 |
| Fulton........ | 203 | Hickman.......... | 11,256 |
| Gallatin........ | 100 | Warsaw............ | 3,867 |
| Garrard........ | 236 | Lancaster.......... | 9,747 |
| Grant........ | 249 | Williamstown.... | 9,489 |
| Graves........ | 560 | Mayfield.......... | 30,021 |
| Grayson........ | 512 | Leitchfield........ | 15,834 |
| Green........ | 282 | Greensburg........ | 11,249 |
| Greenup........ | 351 | Greenup.......... | 29,238 |
| Hancock........ | 187 | Hawesville........ | 5,330 |
| Hardin........ | 616 | Elizabethtown.... | 67,789 |

## KENTUCKY—Continued

| County | Land Area sq.mi | County Seats or Court Houses | County Pop. 1960 |
|---|---|---|---|
| Harlan........ | 469 | Harlan............ | 51,107 |
| Harrison........ | 308 | Cynthiana........ | 13,704 |
| Hart........ | 425 | Munfordville...... | 14,119 |
| Henderson.... | 433 | Henderson........ | 33,519 |
| Henry........ | 289 | New Castle........ | 10,987 |
| Hickman........ | 246 | Clinton.......... | 6,747 |
| Hopkins........ | 553 | Madisonville...... | 38,458 |
| Jackson........ | 337 | McKee............ | 10,677 |
| Jefferson,'64. | 375 | Louisville........ | 649,455 |
| Jessamine.... | 177 | Nicholasville...... | 13,625 |
| Johnson........ | 264 | Paintsville........ | 19,748 |
| Kenton........ | 165 | Independence...... | 120,700 |
| Knott........ | 356 | Hindman.......... | 17,362 |
| Knox........ | 373 | Barbourville...... | 25,258 |
| Larue........ | 260 | Hodgenville........ | 10,346 |
| Laurel........ | 446 | London............ | 24,901 |
| Lawrence.... | 425 | Louisa............ | 12,134 |
| Lee........ | 210 | Beattyville........ | 7,420 |
| Leslie........ | 412 | Hyden............ | 10,941 |
| Letcher........ | 339 | Whitesburg........ | 30,102 |
| Lewis........ | 486 | Vanceburg........ | 13,115 |
| Lincoln........ | 340 | Stanford.......... | 16,503 |
| Livingston.... | 312 | Smithland........ | 7,029 |
| Logan........ | 563 | Russellville........ | 20,896 |
| Lyon........ | 253 | Eddyville.......... | 5,924 |
| McCracken.... | 250 | Paducah.......... | 57,306 |
| McCreary.... | 418 | Whitley City...... | 12,463 |
| McLean........ | 257 | Calhoun.......... | 9,355 |
| Madison........ | 446 | Richmond.......... | 33,482 |
| Magoffin........ | 303 | Salyersville........ | 11,156 |
| Marion........ | 343 | Lebanon.......... | 16,887 |
| Marshall........ | 303 | Benton............ | 16,736 |
| Martin........ | 231 | Inez.............. | 10,201 |
| Mason........ | 238 | Maysville.......... | 18,454 |
| Meade........ | 305 | Brandenburg...... | 18,938 |
| Menifee........ | 210 | Frenchburg........ | 4,276 |
| Mercer........ | 256 | Harrodsburg...... | 14,596 |
| Metcalfe........ | 296 | Edmonton.......... | 8,367 |
| Monroe........ | 334 | Thompkinsville.... | 11,799 |
| Montgomery.. | 204 | Mount Sterling.... | 13,461 |
| Morgan........ | 369 | West Liberty...... | 11,056 |
| Muhlenberg.. | 481 | Greenville........ | 27,791 |
| Nelson........ | 437 | Bardstown........ | 22,168 |
| Nicholas........ | 204 | Carlisle.......... | 6,677 |
| Ohio........ | 596 | Hartford.......... | 17,725 |
| Oldham........ | 184 | La Grange........ | 13,388 |
| Owen........ | 351 | Owenton.......... | 8,237 |
| Owsley........ | 197 | Booneville........ | 5,369 |
| Pendleton.... | 279 | Falmouth.......... | 9,968 |
| Perry........ | 343 | Hazard............ | 34,961 |
| Pike........ | 786 | Pikeville.......... | 68,264 |
| Powell........ | 173 | Stanton.......... | 6,674 |
| Pulaski........ | 654 | Somerset.......... | 34,403 |
| Robertson.... | 101 | Mount Olivet...... | 2,443 |
| Rockcastle.... | 311 | Mount Vernon.... | 12,334 |
| Rowan........ | 290 | Morehead.......... | 12,808 |
| Russell........ | 238 | Jamestown........ | 11,076 |
| Scott........ | 284 | Georgetown........ | 15,376 |
| Shelby........ | 383 | Shelbyville........ | 18,493 |
| Simpson........ | 239 | Franklin.......... | 11,548 |
| Spencer........ | 193 | Taylorsville........ | 5,680 |
| Taylor........ | 284 | Campbellsville.... | 16,285 |
| Todd........ | 376 | Elkton............ | 11,364 |
| Trigg........ | 459 | Cadiz............ | 8,870 |
| Trimble........ | 146 | Bedford.......... | 5,102 |
| Union........ | 340 | Morganfield........ | 14,537 |
| Warren........ | 546 | Bowling Green.... | 45,491 |
| Washington.... | 307 | Springfield........ | 11,168 |
| Wayne........ | 440 | Monticello........ | 14,700 |
| Webster........ | 333 | Dixon............ | 14,244 |
| Whitley........ | 459 | Williamsburg...... | 25,815 |
| Wolfe........ | 229 | Campton.......... | 6,534 |
| Woodford........ | 193 | Versailles.......... | 11,913 |

## LOUISIANA*

*(64 parishes, 45,155 sq. mi. land; pop. 3,257,022)*

| County | Land Area sq.mi | County Seats or Court Houses | County Pop. 1960 |
|---|---|---|---|
| Acadia........ | 663 | Crowley.......... | 49,931 |
| Allen........ | 774 | Oberlin............ | 19,867 |
| Ascension.... | 301 | Donaldsonville.... | 27,927 |
| Assumption.. | 356 | Napoleonville...... | 17,991 |
| Avoyelles.... | 832 | Marksville........ | 37,606 |
| Beauregard.. | 1,184 | De Ridder........ | 19,191 |
| Bienville........ | 832 | Arcadia.......... | 16,726 |
| Bossier........ | 848 | Benton............ | 57,622 |
| Caddo........ | 899 | Shreveport........ | 223,859 |
| Calcasieu.... | 1,105 | Lake Charles...... | 145,475 |
| Caldwell........ | 551 | Columbia.......... | 9,004 |
| Cameron........ | 1,441 | Cameron.......... | 6,909 |
| Catahoula.... | 742 | Harrisonburg...... | 11,421 |
| Claiborne.... | 763 | Homer............ | 19,407 |
| Concordia.... | 718 | Vidalia............ | 20,467 |
| De Soto........ | 904 | Mansfield.......... | 24,248 |
| East Baton Rouge........ | 459 | Baton Rouge...... | 230,058 |
| East Carroll... | 436 | Lake Providence.... | 14,433 |
| East Feliciana.... | 454 | Clinton............ | 20,198 |
| Evangeline.... | 669 | Ville Platte........ | 31,639 |
| Franklin........ | 648 | Winnsboro........ | 26,088 |
| Grant........ | 670 | Colfax............ | 15,330 |
| Iberia........ | 589 | New Iberia........ | 51,657 |
| Iberville........ | 627 | Plaquemine........ | 29,939 |
| Jackson........ | 582 | Jonesboro........ | 15,828 |

## LOUISIANA—Continued

| County | Land Area sq.mi | County Seats or Court Houses | County Pop. 1960 |
|---|---|---|---|
| Jefferson | 331 | Gretna | 208,769 |
| Jefferson Davis | 658 | Jennings | 29,825 |
| Lafayette | 283 | Lafayette | 84,656 |
| Lafourche | 1,111 | Thibodaux | 55,381 |
| La Salle | 643 | Jena | 13,011 |
| Lincoln | 469 | Ruston | 28,535 |
| Livingston | 654 | Livingston | 26,974 |
| Madison | 661 | Tallulah | 16,444 |
| Morehouse | 804 | Bastrop | 33,709 |
| Natchitoches | 1,295 | Natchitoches | 35,653 |
| Orleans | 205 | New Orleans | 627,525 |
| Ouachita | 638 | Monroe | 101,663 |
| Plaquemines | 1,030 | Pointe a la Hache | 22,545 |
| Pointe Coupee | 563 | New Roads | 22,488 |
| Rapides | 1,318 | Alexandria | 111,351 |
| Red River | 406 | Coushatta | 9,978 |
| Richland | 576 | Rayville | 23,824 |
| Sabine | 1,029 | Many | 18,564 |
| St. Bernard | 514 | Chalmette | 32,186 |
| St. Charles | 288 | Hahnville | 21,219 |
| St. Helena | 420 | Greensburg | 9,162 |
| St. James | 253 | Convent | 18,369 |
| St. John the Baptist | 250 | Edgard | 18,439 |
| St. Landry | 932 | Opelousas | 81,493 |
| St. Martin | 736 | Saint Martinville | 29,063 |
| St. Mary | 624 | Franklin | 48,833 |
| St. Tammany | 925 | Covington | 38,643 |
| Tangipahoa | 807 | Amite | 59,434 |
| Tensas | 626 | Saint Joseph | 11,796 |
| Terrebonne | 1,368 | Houma | 60,771 |
| Union | 906 | Farmerville | 17,624 |
| Vermillion | 1,205 | Abbeville | 38,855 |
| Vernon | 1,357 | Leesville | 18,301 |
| Washington | 665 | Franklinton | 44,015 |
| Webster | 615 | Minden | 39,701 |
| West Baton Rouge | 203 | Port Allen | 14,796 |
| West Carroll | 356 | Oak Grove | 14,177 |
| West Feliciana | 405 | Saint Francisville | 12,395 |
| Winn | 950 | Winnfield | 16,034 |

*Parishes and Parish Seats

## MAINE

*(16 counties, 30,933 sq. mi land; pop., 969,265)*

| County | Land Area sq.mi | County Seats or Court Houses | County Pop. 1960 |
|---|---|---|---|
| Androscoggin | 474 | Auburn | 86,312 |
| Aroostook | 6,821 | Houlton | 106,064 |
| Cumberland | 879 | Portland | 182,751 |
| Franklin | 1,709 | Farmington | 20,069 |
| Hancock | 1,537 | Ellsworth | 32,293 |
| Kennebec | 872 | Augusta | 89,150 |
| Knox | 369 | Rockland | 28,575 |
| Lincoln | 454 | Wiscasset | 18,497 |
| Oxford | 2,082 | South Paris | 44,345 |
| Penobscot | 3,390 | Bangor | 126,346 |
| Piscataquis | 3,903 | Dover-Foxcroft | 17,379 |
| Sagadahoc | 257 | Bath | 22,793 |
| Somerset | 3,894 | Skowhegan | 39,749 |
| Waldo | 737 | Belfast | 22,632 |
| Washington | 2,554 | Machias | 32,908 |
| York | 1,001 | Alfred | 99,402 |

## MARYLAND

*(23 cos. 1 ind. city, 9,891 sq. mi. land; pop., 3,100,689)*

| County | Land Area sq.mi | County Seats or Court Houses | County Pop. 1960 |
|---|---|---|---|
| Allegany | 428 | Cumberland | 84,169 |
| Anne Arundel | 423 | Annapolis | 206,634 |
| Baltimore | 598 | Towson | 492,428 |
| Calvert | 217 | Prince Frederick | 15,826 |
| Caroline | 321 | Denton | 19,462 |
| Carroll | 456 | Westminster | 52,785 |
| Cecil | 362 | Elkton | 48,408 |
| Charles | 459 | La Plata | 32,572 |
| Dorchester | 594 | Cambridge | 29,666 |
| Frederick | 665 | Frederick | 71,930 |
| Garrett | 659 | Oakland | 20,420 |
| Harford | 453 | Bel Air | 76,722 |
| Howard | 251 | Ellicott City | 36,152 |
| Kent | 281 | Chestertown | 15,481 |
| Montgomery | 496 | Rockville | 340,928 |
| Prince Georges | 484 | Upper Marlboro | 357,395 |
| Queen Annes | 375 | Centreville | 16,569 |
| St. Marys | 373 | Leonardtown | 38,915 |
| Somerset | 339 | Princess Anne | 19,623 |
| Talbot | 261 | Easton | 21,578 |
| Washington | 459 | Hagerstown | 91,219 |
| Wicomico | 381 | Salisbury | 49,050 |
| Worcester | 479 | Snow Hill | 23,733 |

### Independent City

| | | | |
|---|---|---|---|
| Baltimore | 78 | | 939,024 |

## MASSACHUSETTS

*(14 counties; 7,833 sq. mi. land; pop. 5,148,578)*

| County | Land Area sq.mi | County Seats or Court Houses | County Pop. 1960 |
|---|---|---|---|
| Barnstable | 393 | Barnstable | 70,286 |
| Berkshire | 941 | Pittsfield | 142,135 |
| Bristol | 554 | Taunton | 398,488 |
| Dukes | 104 | Edgartown | 5,829 |
| Essex | 494 | Salem | 568,831 |
| Franklin | 708 | Greenfield | 54,864 |
| Hampden | 622 | Springfield | 429,353 |
| Hampshire | 529 | Northhampton | 103,229 |
| Middlesex | 825 | Cambridge | 1,238,742 |
| Nantucket | 46 | Nantucket | 3,559 |

## MASSACHUSETTS—Continued

| County | Land Area sq.mi | County Seats or Court Houses | County Pop. 1960 |
|---|---|---|---|
| Norfolk | 394 | Dedham | 510,256 |
| Plymouth | 654 | Plymouth | 248,449 |
| Suffolk | 56 | Boston | 791,329 |
| Worcester | 1,513 | Worcester | 583,228 |

## MICHIGAN

*(83 counties; 56,818 sq. mi. land; pop., 7,823,194)*

| County | Land Area sq.mi | County Seats or Court Houses | County Pop. 1960 |
|---|---|---|---|
| Alcona | 678 | Harrisville | 6,352 |
| Alger | 905 | Munising | 9,250 |
| Allegan | 826 | Allegan | 57,729 |
| Alpena | 565 | Alpena | 28,556 |
| Antrim | 476 | Bellaire | 10,373 |
| Arenac | 367 | Standish | 9,860 |
| Baraga | 901 | L'Anse | 7,151 |
| Barry | 554 | Hastings | 31,738 |
| Bay | 447 | Bay City | 107,042 |
| Benzie | 316 | Beulah | 7,834 |
| Berrien | 580 | Saint Joseph | 149,865 |
| Branch | 506 | Coldwater | 34,903 |
| Calhoun | 709 | Marshall | 138,858 |
| Cass | 491 | Cassopolis | 36,932 |
| Charlevoix | 414 | Charlevoix | 13,421 |
| Cheboygan | 721 | Cheboygan | 14,550 |
| Chippewa | 1,590 | Sault Sainte Marie | 32,655 |
| Clare | 571 | Harrison | 11,647 |
| Clinton | 572 | Saint Johns | 37,969 |
| Crawford | 561 | Grayling | 4,971 |
| Delta | 1,177 | Escanaba | 34,298 |
| Dickinson | 757 | Iron Mountain | 23,917 |
| Eaton | 571 | Charlotte | 49,684 |
| Emmet | 461 | Petoskey | 15,904 |
| Genesee | 642 | Flint | 374,313 |
| Gladwin | 503 | Gladwin | 10,769 |
| Gogebic | 1,107 | Bessemer | 24,370 |
| Grand Traverse | 462 | Traverse City | 33,490 |
| Gratiot | 566 | Ithaca | 37,012 |
| Hillsdale | 600 | Hillsdale | 34,742 |
| Houghton | 1,017 | Houghton | 35,654 |
| Huron | 819 | Bad Axe | 34,006 |
| Ingham | 559 | Mason | 211,296 |
| Ionia | 575 | Ionia | 43,132 |
| Iosco | 544 | Tawas City | 16,505 |
| Iron | 1,171 | Crystal Falls | 17,184 |
| Isabella | 572 | Mount Pleasant | 35,348 |
| Jackson | 698 | Jackson | 131,994 |
| Kalamazoo | 562 | Kalamazoo | 169,712 |
| Kalkaska | 566 | Kalkaska | 4,382 |
| Kent | 857 | Grand Rapids | 363,187 |
| Keweenaw | 538 | Eagle River | 2,417 |
| Lake | 571 | Baldwin | 5,338 |
| Lapeer | 658 | Lapeer | 41,926 |
| Leelanau | 345 | Leland | 9,321 |
| Lenawee | 753 | Adrian | 77,789 |
| Livingston | 572 | Howell | 38,233 |
| Luce | 906 | Newberry | 7,827 |
| Mackinac | 1,014 | Saint Ignace | 10,853 |
| Macomb | 480 | Mount Clemens | 405,804 |
| Manistee | 553 | Manistee | 19,042 |
| Marquette | 1,829 | Marquette | 56,154 |
| Mason | 490 | Ludington | 21,929 |
| Mecosta | 560 | Big Rapids | 21,051 |
| Menominee | 1,038 | Menominee | 24,685 |
| Midland | 520 | Midland | 51,450 |
| Missaukee | 565 | Lake City | 6,784 |
| Monroe | 557 | Monroe | 101,120 |
| Montcalm | 712 | Stanton | 35,795 |
| Montmorency | 555 | Atlanta | 4,424 |
| Muskegon | 501 | Muskegon | 149,943 |
| Newaygo | 849 | White Cloud | 24,160 |
| Oakland | 867 | Pontiac | 690,259 |
| Oceana | 536 | Hart | 16,547 |
| Ogemaw | 571 | West Branch | 9,680 |
| Ontonagon | 1,316 | Ontonagon | 10,584 |
| Osceola | 581 | Reed City | 13,595 |
| Oscoda | 563 | Mio | 3,447 |
| Otsego | 527 | Gaylord | 7,545 |
| Ottawa | 563 | Grand Haven | 98,719 |
| Presque Isle | 648 | Rogers City | 13,117 |
| Roscommon | 521 | Roscommon | 7,200 |
| Saginaw | 814 | Saginaw | 190,752 |
| St. Clair | 734 | Port Huron | 107,201 |
| St. Joseph | 506 | Centreville | 42,332 |
| Sanilac | 961 | Sandusky | 32,314 |
| Schoolcraft | 1,181 | Manistique | 8,953 |
| Shiawassee | 540 | Corunna | 53,446 |
| Tuscola | 815 | Caro | 43,305 |
| Van Buren | 603 | Paw Paw | 48,395 |
| Washtenaw | 711 | Ann Arbor | 172,440 |
| Wayne | 605 | Detroit | 2,666,297 |
| Wexford | 559 | Cadillac | 18,466 |

## MINNESOTA

*(87 counties; 79,289 sq. mi. land; pop., 3,413,864)*

| County | Land Area sq.mi | County Seats or Court Houses | County Pop. 1960 |
|---|---|---|---|
| Aitkin | 1,828 | Aitkin | 12,162 |
| Anoka | 424 | Anoka | 85,916 |
| Becker | 1,297 | Detroit Lakes | 23,959 |
| Beltrami | 2,507 | Bemidji | 23,425 |
| Benton | 402 | Foley | 17,287 |
| Big Stone | 490 | Ortonville | 8,954 |
| Blue Earth | 737 | Mankato | 44,385 |
| Brown | 610 | New Ulm | 27,676 |

| County | Land Area sq.mi | County Seats or Court Houses | County Pop. 1960 |
|---|---|---|---|
| **MINNESOTA—Continued** | | | |
| Carlton | 862 | Carlton | 27,932 |
| Carver | 359 | Chaska | 21,358 |
| Cass | 1,998 | Walker | 16,720 |
| Chippewa | 582 | Montevideo | 16,320 |
| Chisago | 419 | Center City | 13,419 |
| Clay | 1,045 | Moorhead | 39,080 |
| Clearwater | 1,000 | Bagley | 8,864 |
| Cook | 1,346 | Grand Marais | 3,377 |
| Cottonwood | 636 | Windom | 16,166 |
| Crow Wing | 995 | Brainerd | 32,134 |
| Dakota | 576 | Hastings | 78,303 |
| Dodge | 435 | Mantorville | 13,259 |
| Douglas | 647 | Alexandria | 21,313 |
| Faribault | 711 | Blue Earth | 23,685 |
| Fillmore | 859 | Preston | 23,768 |
| Freeborn | 701 | Albert Lea | 37,891 |
| Goodhue | 753 | Red Wing | 33,035 |
| Grant | 546 | Elbow Lake | 8,870 |
| Hennepin | 567 | Minneapolis | 842,854 |
| Houston | 565 | Caledonia | 16,588 |
| Hubbard | 932 | Park Rapids | 9,962 |
| Isanti | 438 | Cambridge | 13,530 |
| Itasca | 2,633 | Grand Rapids | 38,006 |
| Jackson | 698 | Jackson | 15,501 |
| Kanabec | 524 | Mora | 9,007 |
| Kandiyohi | 783 | Willmar | 29,987 |
| Kittson | 1,123 | Hallock | 8,343 |
| Koochiching | 3,127 | International Falls | 18,190 |
| Lac qui Parle | 768 | Madison | 13,330 |
| Lake | 2,062 | Two Harbors | 13,702 |
| Lake of the Woods | 1,311 | Baudette | 4,304 |
| Le Sueur | 440 | Le Center | 19,906 |
| Lincoln | 531 | Ivanhoe | 9,651 |
| Lyon | 709 | Marshall | 22,655 |
| McLeod | 488 | Glencoe | 24,401 |
| Mahnomen | 563 | Mahnomen | 6,341 |
| Marshall | 1,789 | Warren | 14,262 |
| Martin | 703 | Fairmont | 26,986 |
| Meeker | 619 | Litchfield | 18,887 |
| Mille Lacs | 571 | Milaca | 14,560 |
| Morrison | 1,127 | Little Falls | 26,641 |
| Mower | 703 | Austin | 48,498 |
| Murray | 703 | Slayton | 14,743 |
| Nicollet | 432 | Saint Peter | 23,196 |
| Nobles | 712 | Worthington | 23,365 |
| Norman | 885 | Ada | 11,253 |
| Olmsted | 656 | Rochester | 65,532 |
| Otter Tail | 1,962 | Fergus Falls | 48,960 |
| Pennington | 622 | Thief River Falls | 12,468 |
| Pine | 1,414 | Pine City | 17,004 |
| Pipestone | 464 | Pipestone | 13,605 |
| Polk | 2,013 | Crookston | 36,182 |
| Pope | 669 | Glenwood | 11,914 |
| Ramsey | 155 | Saint Paul | 422,525 |
| Red Lake | 432 | Red Lake Falls | 5,830 |
| Redwood | 874 | Redwood Falls | 21,718 |
| Renville | 979 | Olivia | 23,249 |
| Rice | 496 | Faribault | 38,988 |
| Rock | 485 | Luverne | 11,864 |
| Roseau | 1,676 | Roseau | 12,154 |
| St. Louis | 6,092 | Duluth | 231,588 |
| Scott | 353 | Shakopee | 21,909 |
| Sherburne | 451 | Elk River | 12,861 |
| Sibley | 583 | Gaylord | 16,228 |
| Stearns | 1,342 | Saint Cloud | 80,345 |
| Steele | 425 | Owatonna | 25,029 |
| Stevens | 558 | Morris | 11,262 |
| Swift | 739 | Benson | 14,936 |
| Todd | 942 | Long Prairie | 23,119 |
| Traverse | 568 | Wheaton | 7,503 |
| Wabasha | 522 | Wabasha | 17,007 |
| Wadena | 536 | Wadena | 12,199 |
| Waseca | 415 | Waseca | 16,041 |
| Washington | 386 | Stillwater | 52,432 |
| Watonwan | 433 | Saint James | 14,460 |
| Wilkin | 752 | Breckenridge | 10,650 |
| Winona | 620 | Winona | 40,937 |
| Wright | 674 | Buffalo | 29,935 |
| Yellow Medicine | 753 | Granite Falls | 15,523 |
| **MISSISSIPPI** | | | |
| *(82 counties; 47,358 sq. mt. land; pop., 2,178,141)* | | | |
| Adams | 449 | Natchez | 37,730 |
| Alcorn | 405 | Corinth | 25,282 |
| Amite | 729 | Liberty | 15,573 |
| Attala | 724 | Kosciusko | 21,335 |
| Benton | 412 | Ashland | 7,723 |
| Bolivar | 923 | Cleveland and Rosedale | 54,464 |
| Calhoun | 575 | Pittsboro | 15,941 |
| Carroll | 637 | Carrollton & Vaiden | 11,177 |
| Chickasaw | 506 | Houston and Okolona | 16,891 |
| Choctaw | 417 | Ackerman | 8,423 |
| Claiborne | 489 | Port Gibson | 10,845 |
| Clarke | 697 | Quitman | 16,493 |
| Clay | 414 | West Point | 18,933 |
| Coahoma | 569 | Clarksdale | 46,212 |
| Copiah | 780 | Hazlehurst | 27,051 |
| Covington | 416 | Collins | 13,676 |

| County | Land Area sq.mi | County Seats or Court Houses | County Pop. 1960 |
|---|---|---|---|
| **MISSISSIPPI—Continued** | | | |
| De Soto | 476 | Hernando | 23,891 |
| Forrest | 468 | Hattiesburg | 52,722 |
| Franklin | 568 | Meadville | 9,286 |
| George | 481 | Lucedale | 11,098 |
| Greene | 728 | Leakesville | 8,366 |
| Grenada | 431 | Grenada | 18,409 |
| Hancock | 482 | Bay Saint Louis | 14,039 |
| Harrison | 585 | Gulfport | 119,489 |
| Hinds | 876 | Jackson and Raymond | 187,045 |
| Holmes | 769 | Lexington | 27,096 |
| Humphreys | 421 | Belzoni | 19,093 |
| Issaquena | 414 | Mayersville | 3,576 |
| Itawamba | 541 | Fulton | 15,080 |
| Jackson | 736 | Pascagoula | 55,522 |
| Jasper | 683 | Bay Springs and Paulding | 16,909 |
| Jefferson | 521 | Fayette | 10,142 |
| Jefferson Davis | 408 | Prentiss | 13,540 |
| Jones | 702 | Ellisville & Laurel | 59,542 |
| Kemper | 757 | De Kalb | 12,277 |
| Lafayette | 668 | Oxford | 21,355 |
| Lamar | 502 | Purvis | 13,675 |
| Lauderdale | 721 | Meridian | 67,119 |
| Lawrence | 433 | Monticello | 10,215 |
| Leake | 586 | Carthage | 18,660 |
| Lee | 455 | Tupelo | 40,589 |
| Leflore | 592 | Greenwood | 47,142 |
| Lincoln | 586 | Brookhaven | 26,759 |
| Lowndes | 508 | Columbus | 46,639 |
| Madison | 751 | Canton | 32,904 |
| Marion | 550 | Columbia | 23,293 |
| Marshall | 710 | Holly Springs | 24,503 |
| Monroe | 769 | Aberdeen | 33,953 |
| Montgomery | 403 | Winona | 13,320 |
| Neshoba | 568 | Philadelphia | 20,927 |
| Newton | 580 | Decatur | 19,517 |
| Noxubee | 695 | Macon | 16,826 |
| Oktibbeha | 454 | Starkville | 26,175 |
| Panola | 693 | Batesville & Sardis | 28,791 |
| Pearl River | 828 | Poplarville | 22,411 |
| Perry | 653 | New Augusta | 8,745 |
| Pike | 409 | Magnolia | 35,063 |
| Pontotoc | 501 | Pontotoc | 17,232 |
| Prentiss | 418 | Booneville | 17,949 |
| Quitman | 412 | Marks | 21,019 |
| Rankin | 780 | Brandon | 34,322 |
| Scott | 615 | Forest | 21,187 |
| Sharkey | 436 | Rolling Fork | 10,738 |
| Simpson | 587 | Mendenhall | 20,454 |
| Smith | 642 | Raleigh | 14,303 |
| Stone | 448 | Wiggins | 7,013 |
| Sunflower | 694 | Indianola | 45,750 |
| Tallahatchie | 644 | Charleston and Sumner | 24,081 |
| Tate | 405 | Senatobia | 18,138 |
| Tippah | 464 | Ripley | 15,093 |
| Tishomingo | 443 | Iuka | 13,889 |
| Tunica | 458 | Tunica | 16,826 |
| Union | 422 | New Albany | 18,904 |
| Walthall | 403 | Tylertown | 13,512 |
| Warren | 581 | Vicksburg | 42,206 |
| Washington | 734 | Greenville | 78,638 |
| Wayne | 827 | Waynesboro | 16,258 |
| Webster | 416 | Walthall | 10,580 |
| Wilkinson | 674 | Woodville | 13,235 |
| Winston | 606 | Louisville | 19,246 |
| Yalobusha | 488 | Coffeeville and Water Valley | 12,502 |
| Yazoo | 938 | Yazoo City | 31.653 |
| **MISSOURI** | | | |
| *(114 cos.; 1 Ind. city,69,046 sq.mt. land; pop.,4,319,813)* | | | |
| Adair | 574 | Kirksville | 20,105 |
| Andrew | 435 | Savannah | 11,062 |
| Atchison | 549 | Rockport | 9,213 |
| Audrain | 692 | Mexico | 26,079 |
| Barry | 789 | Cassville | 18,921 |
| Barton | 594 | Lamar | 11,113 |
| Bates | 841 | Butler | 15,905 |
| Benton | 742 | Warsaw | 8,737 |
| Bollinger | 618 | Marble Hill | 9,167 |
| Boone | 683 | Columbia | 55,202 |
| Buchanan | 404 | Saint Joseph | 90,581 |
| Butler | 714 | Poplar Bluff | 34,656 |
| Caldwell | 430 | Kingston | 8,830 |
| Callaway | 835 | Fulton | 23,858 |
| Camden | 655 | Camdenton | 9,116 |
| Cape Girardeau | 576 | Jackson | 42,020 |
| Carroll | 694 | Carrollton | 13,847 |
| Carter | 506 | Van Buren | 3,973 |
| Cass | 698 | Harrisonville | 29,702 |
| Cedar | 496 | Stockton | 9,185 |
| Chariton | 759 | Keytesville | 12,720 |
| Christian | 567 | Ozark | 12,359 |
| Clark | 509 | Kahoka | 8,725 |
| Clay | 413 | Liberty | 87,474 |
| Clinton | 420 | Plattsburg | 11,588 |
| Cole | 385 | Jefferson City | 40,761 |
| Cooper | 563 | Boonville | 15,448 |
| Crawford | 760 | Steelville | 12,647 |

| County | Land Area sq.mi | County Seats or Court Houses | County Pop. 1960 | County | Land Area sq.mi | County Seats or Court Houses | County Pop. 1960 |
|---|---|---|---|---|---|---|---|
| **MISSOURI—Continued** | | | | **MONTANA—Continued** | | | |
| Dade........ | 504 | Greenfield........ | 7,577 | Deer Lodge.... | 740 | Anaconda........ | 18,640 |
| Dallas....... | 537 | Buffalo.......... | 9,314 | Fallon...... | 1,633 | Baker.......... | 3,997 |
| Daviess...... | 563 | Gallatin........ | 9,502 | Fergus..... | 4,242 | Lewistown...... | 14,018 |
| De Kalb..... | 423 | Maysville...... | 7,226 | Flathead.... | 5,137 | Kalispell........ | 32,965 |
| Dent........ | 756 | Salem.......... | 10,445 | Gallatin.... | 2,517 | Bozeman........ | 26,045 |
| Douglas..... | 809 | Ava............ | 9,653 | Garfield.... | 4,455 | Jordan........ | 1,981 |
| Dunklin..... | 543 | Kennett........ | 39,139 | Glacier..... | 2,964 | Cut Bank...... | 11,565 |
| Franklin..... | 932 | Union.......... | 44,566 | Golden Valley.. | 1,176 | Ryegate........ | 1,203 |
| Gasconade... | 520 | Hermann........ | 12,195 | Granite..... | 1,733 | Philipsburg...... | 3,014 |
| Gentry...... | 488 | Albany.......... | 8,793 | Hill....... | 2,927 | Havre.......... | 18,653 |
| Greene...... | 677 | Springfield...... | 126,276 | Jefferson... | 1,652 | Boulder........ | 4,297 |
| Grundy...... | 435 | Trenton........ | 12,220 | Judith Basin... | 1,880 | Stanford........ | 3,085 |
| Harrison..... | 720 | Bethany........ | 11,603 | Lake...... | 1,494 | Polson.......... | 13,104 |
| Henry....... | 737 | Clinton........ | 19,226 | Lewis & Clark.. | 3,476 | Helena.......... | 28,006 |
| Hickory..... | 410 | Hermitage...... | 4,516 | Liberty.... | 1,439 | Chester........ | 2,624 |
| Holt........ | 464 | Oregon.......... | 7,885 | Lincoln.... | 3,714 | Libby.......... | 12,537 |
| Howard..... | 469 | Fayette........ | 10,859 | McCone.... | 2,607 | Circle.......... | 3,321 |
| Howell...... | 920 | West Plains...... | 22,027 | Madison... | 3,528 | Virginia City.... | 5,211 |
| Iron........ | 554 | Ironton........ | 8,041 | Meagher... | 2,354 | White Sulphur Springs... | 2,616 |
| Jackson..... | 603 | Independence.... | 622,732 | | | | |
| Jasper...... | 642 | Carthage........ | 78,863 | Mineral.... | 1,222 | Superior........ | 3,037 |
| Jefferson.... | 667 | Hillsboro...... | 66,377 | Missoula... | 2,612 | Missoula........ | 44,663 |
| Johnson..... | 826 | Warrensburg.... | 28,981 | Musselshell... | 1,887 | Roundup...... | 4,888 |
| Knox....... | 512 | Edina.......... | 6,558 | Park...... | 2,626 | Livingston...... | 13,168 |
| Laclede..... | 770 | Lebanon........ | 18,991 | Petroleum.. | 1,655 | Winnett........ | 894 |
| Lafayette.... | 634 | Lexington...... | 25,274 | Phillips.... | 5,213 | Malta.......... | 6,027 |
| Lawrence.... | 619 | Mount Vernon.... | 23,260 | Pondera... | 1,645 | Conrad........ | 7,653 |
| Lewis....... | 505 | Monticello...... | 10,984 | Powder River.. | 3,288 | Broadus........ | 2,485 |
| Lincoln..... | 629 | Troy............ | 14,783 | Powell.... | 2,336 | Deer Lodge...... | 7,002 |
| Linn........ | 624 | Linneus........ | 16,815 | Prairie.... | 1,730 | Terry.......... | 2,318 |
| Livingston... | 533 | Chillicothe...... | 15,771 | Ravalli.... | 2,382 | Hamilton........ | 12,341 |
| McDonald... | 540 | Pineville........ | 11,798 | Richland... | 2,079 | Sidney.......... | 10,504 |
| Macon...... | 814 | Macon.......... | 16,473 | Roosevelt.. | 2,385 | Wolf Point...... | 11,731 |
| Madison.... | 496 | Fredericktown.... | 9,366 | Rosebud... | 5,037 | Forsyth........ | 6,187 |
| Maries..... | 526 | Vienna.......... | 7,282 | Sanders... | 2,778 | Thompson Falls... | 6,880 |
| Marion..... | 440 | Palmyra........ | 29,522 | Sheridan... | 1,694 | Plentywood...... | 6,458 |
| Mercer..... | 456 | Princeton...... | 5,750 | Silver Bow.. | 715 | Butte.......... | 46,454 |
| Miller...... | 603 | Tuscumbia...... | 13,800 | Stillwater.. | 1,794 | Columbus...... | 5,526 |
| Mississippi.. | 411 | Charleston...... | 20,695 | Sweet Grass. | 1,840 | Big Timber...... | 3,290 |
| Moniteau... | 418 | California...... | 10,500 | Teton..... | 2,294 | Choteau........ | 7,295 |
| Monroe..... | 669 | Paris.......... | 10,688 | Toole..... | 1,950 | Shelby.......... | 7,904 |
| Montgomery.. | 533 | Montgomery City.. | 11,097 | Treasure... | 985 | Hysham........ | 1,345 |
| Morgan..... | 596 | Versailles...... | 9,476 | Valley.... | 4,974 | Glasgow........ | 17,080 |
| New Madrid.. | 679 | New Madrid...... | 31,350 | Wheatland.. | 1,420 | Harlowton...... | 3,026 |
| Newton..... | 629 | Neosho.......... | 30,093 | Wibaux.... | 890 | Wibaux........ | 1,698 |
| Nodaway... | 877 | Maryville...... | 22,215 | Yellowstone. | 2,642 | Billings........ | 79,016 |
| Oregon..... | 784 | Alton.......... | 9,845 | Yel'stone Nat. Park (part).. | 269 | ............ | 47 |
| Osage...... | 601 | Linn.......... | 10,867 | | | | |
| Ozark...... | 743 | Gainesville...... | 6,744 | **NEBRASKA** | | | |
| Pemiscot... | 488 | Caruthersville.... | 38,095 | _(93 counties, 76,522 sq. mi. land; pop., 1,411,330)_ | | | |
| Perry...... | 476 | Perryville...... | 14,642 | Adams..... | 562 | Hastings........ | 28,944 |
| Pettis..... | 679 | Sedalia........ | 35,120 | Antelope... | 853 | Neligh........ | 10,176 |
| Phelps..... | 677 | Rolla.......... | 25,396 | Arthur.... | 704 | Arthur........ | 680 |
| Pike....... | 681 | Bowling Green.... | 16,706 | Banner.... | 738 | Harrisburg...... | 1,269 |
| Platte..... | 420 | Platte City...... | 23,350 | Blaine.... | 710 | Brewster........ | 1,016 |
| Polk....... | 642 | Bolivar........ | 13,753 | Boone.... | 683 | Albion.......... | 9,134 |
| Pulaski.... | 551 | Waynesville.... | 46,567 | Box Butte.. | 1,065 | Alliance........ | 11,688 |
| Putnam.... | 518 | Unionville...... | 6,999 | Boyd..... | 538 | Butte.......... | 4,513 |
| Ralls...... | 478 | New London.... | 8,078 | Brown.... | 1,216 | Ainsworth...... | 4,436 |
| Randolph... | 484 | Huntsville...... | 22,014 | Buffalo... | 949 | Kearney........ | 26,236 |
| Ray....... | 574 | Richmond...... | 16,075 | Burt..... | 483 | Tekamah........ | 10,192 |
| Reynolds... | 819 | Centerville...... | 5,161 | Butler.... | 582 | David City...... | 10,312 |
| Ripley..... | 639 | Doniphan...... | 9,096 | Cass..... | 555 | Plattsmouth.... | 17,821 |
| St. Charles.. | 561 | St. Charles...... | 52,970 | Cedar.... | 742 | Hartington...... | 13,368 |
| St. Clair... | 699 | Osceola........ | 8,421 | Chase.... | 890 | Imperial........ | 4,317 |
| St. Francois. | 457 | Farmington...... | 36,516 | Cherry... | 5,971 | Valentine...... | 8,218 |
| St. Louis... | 497 | Clayton........ | 703,532 | Cheyenne.. | 1,186 | Sidney.......... | 14,828 |
| Ste. Genevieve. | 500 | Ste. Genevieve... | 12,116 | Clay..... | 570 | Clay Center.... | 8,717 |
| Saline..... | 759 | Marshall........ | 25,148 | Colfax... | 406 | Schuyler........ | 9,595 |
| Schuyler... | 306 | Lancaster...... | 5,052 | Cuming... | 571 | West Point...... | 12,435 |
| Scotland... | 441 | Memphis........ | 6,484 | Custer... | 2,558 | Broken Bow.... | 16,517 |
| Scott...... | 418 | Benton.......... | 32,748 | Dakota... | 255 | Dakota City.... | 12,168 |
| Shannon... | 999 | Eminence...... | 7,087 | Dawes... | 1,386 | Chadron........ | 9,536 |
| Shelby.... | 502 | Shelbyville...... | 9,063 | Dawson.. | 975 | Lexington...... | 19,405 |
| Stoddard... | 837 | Bloomfield...... | 29,490 | Deuel.... | 436 | Chappell........ | 3,125 |
| Stone..... | 463 | Galena.......... | 8,176 | Dixon... | 475 | Ponca.......... | 8,106 |
| Sullivan... | 654 | Milan.......... | 7,572 | Dodge... | 528 | Fremont........ | 32,471 |
| Taney..... | 626 | Forsyth........ | 10,238 | Douglas.. | 335 | Omaha.......... | 343,490 |
| Texas..... | 1,183 | Houston........ | 17,758 | Dundy... | 921 | Benkelman...... | 3,570 |
| Vernon.... | 838 | Nevada........ | 20,540 | Fillmore.. | 577 | Geneva........ | 9,425 |
| Warren.... | 428 | Warrenton...... | 8,750 | Franklin.. | 578 | Franklin........ | 5,449 |
| Washington.. | 760 | Potosi.......... | 14,346 | Frontier.. | 962 | Stockville...... | 4,311 |
| Wayne.... | 741 | Greenville...... | 8,638 | Furnas... | 722 | Beaver City.... | 7,711 |
| Webster... | 590 | Marshfield...... | 13,753 | Gage.... | 858 | Beatrice........ | 26,818 |
| Worth..... | 267 | Grant City...... | 3,936 | Garden... | 1,678 | Oshkosh........ | 3,472 |
| Wright.... | 684 | Hartville...... | 14,183 | Garfield.. | 569 | Burwell........ | 2,699 |
| **Independent City** | | | | Gosper... | 464 | Elwood........ | 2,489 |
| St. Louis.... | 61 | | 750,026 | Grant.... | 764 | Hyannis........ | 1,009 |
| | | | | Greeley... | 570 | Greeley........ | 4,595 |
| **MONTANA** | | | | Hall..... | 537 | Grand Island.... | 35,757 |
| _(56 counties, 145,603 sq. mi. land; pop., 674,767)_ | | | | Hamilton.. | 537 | Aurora........ | 8,714 |
| Beaverhead.. | 5,560 | Dillon.......... | 7,194 | Harlan... | 556 | Alma.......... | 5,081 |
| Big Horn.... | 5,028 | Hardin........ | 10,007 | Hayes.... | 711 | Hayes Center.... | 1,919 |
| Blaine...... | 4,275 | Chinook........ | 8,091 | Hitchcock.. | 712 | Trenton........ | 4,829 |
| Broadwater.. | 1,193 | Townsend...... | 2,804 | Holt.... | 2,405 | O'Neill........ | 13,722 |
| Carbon..... | 2,067 | Red Lodge...... | 8,317 | Hooker... | 722 | Mullen........ | 1,130 |
| Carter..... | 3,313 | Ekalaka........ | 2,493 | Howard.. | 564 | Saint Paul...... | 6,541 |
| Cascade.... | 2,661 | Great Falls...... | 73,418 | Jefferson.. | 577 | Fairbury........ | 11,620 |
| Chouteau... | 3,927 | Fort Benton.... | 7,348 | Johnson.. | 377 | Tecumseh...... | 6,281 |
| Custer..... | 3,756 | Miles City...... | 13,227 | Kearney.. | 512 | Minden........ | 6,580 |
| Daniels.... | 1,443 | Scobey........ | 3,755 | Keith.... | 1,032 | Ogallala........ | 7,958 |
| Dawson.... | 2,370 | Glendive........ | 12,314 | | | | |

| County | Land Area sq.mi | County Seats or Court Houses | County Pop. 1960 |
|---|---|---|---|

## NEBRASKA—Continued

| County | Land Area sq.mi | County Seats or Court Houses | County Pop. 1960 |
|---|---|---|---|
| Keya Paha | 768 | Springview | 1,672 |
| Kimball | 953 | Kimball | 7,975 |
| Knox | 1,107 | Center | 13,300 |
| Lancaster | 845 | Lincoln | 155,272 |
| Lincoln | 2,522 | North Platte | 28,491 |
| Logan | 570 | Stapleton | 1,108 |
| Loup | 574 | Taylor | 1,097 |
| McPherson | 856 | Tryon | 735 |
| Madison | 572 | Madison | 25,145 |
| Merrick | 480 | Central City | 8,363 |
| Morrill | 1,402 | Bridgeport | 7,057 |
| Nance | 439 | Fullerton | 5,635 |
| Nemaha | 400 | Auburn | 9,099 |
| Nuckolls | 579 | Nelson | 8,217 |
| Otoe | 619 | Nebraska City | 16,503 |
| Pawnee | 433 | Pawnee City | 5,356 |
| Perkins | 885 | Grant | 4,189 |
| Phelps | 544 | Holdrege | 9,800 |
| Pierce | 573 | Pierce | 8,722 |
| Platte | 667 | Columbus | 23,992 |
| Polk | 432 | Osceola | 7,210 |
| Red Willow | 716 | McCook | 12,940 |
| Richardson | 550 | Falls City | 13,903 |
| Rock | 1,009 | Bassett | 2,554 |
| Saline | 575 | Wilber | 12,542 |
| Sarpy | 239 | Papillion | 31,281 |
| Saunders | 759 | Wahoo | 17,270 |
| Scotts Bluff | 726 | Gering | 33,809 |
| Seward | 571 | Seward | 13,581 |
| Sheridan | 2,462 | Rushville | 9,049 |
| Sherman | 571 | Loup City | 5,382 |
| Sioux | 2,063 | Harrison | 2,575 |
| Stanton | 431 | Stanton | 5,783 |
| Thayer | 577 | Hebron | 9,118 |
| Thomas | 716 | Thedford | 1,078 |
| Thurston | 388 | Pender | 7,237 |
| Valley | 569 | Ord | 6,590 |
| Washington | 386 | Blair | 12,103 |
| Wayne | 443 | Wayne | 9,959 |
| Webster | 575 | Red Cloud | 6,224 |
| Wheeler | 576 | Bartlett | 1,297 |
| York | 577 | York | 13,724 |

## NEVADA

(17 counties, 109,889 sq. mi. land; pop., 285,278)

| County | Land Area sq.mi | County Seats or Court Houses | County Pop. 1960 |
|---|---|---|---|
| Churchill | 4,883 | Fallon | 8,452 |
| Clark | 7,874 | Las Vegas | 127,016 |
| Douglas | 723 | Minden | 3,481 |
| Elko | 17,162 | Elko | 12,011 |
| Esmeralda | 3,570 | Goldfield | 619 |
| Eureka | 4,182 | Eureka | 767 |
| Humboldt | 9,702 | Winnemucca | 5,708 |
| Lander | 5,621 | Austin | 1,566 |
| Lincoln | 10,649 | Pioche | 2,431 |
| Lyon | 2,010 | Yerington | 6,143 |
| Mineral | 3,765 | Hawthorne | 6,329 |
| Nye | 18,064 | Tonopah | 4,374 |
| Ormsby | 141 | Carson City | 8,063 |
| Pershing | 6,001 | Lovelock | 3,199 |
| Storey | 262 | Virginia City | 568 |
| Washoe | 6,375 | Reno | 84,743 |
| White Pine | 8,900 | Ely | 9,808 |

## NEW HAMPSHIRE

(10 counties, 9,033 sq. mi. land, pop., 606,921)

| County | Land Area sq.mi | County Seats or Court Houses | County Pop. 1960 |
|---|---|---|---|
| Belknap | 400 | Laconia | 28,912 |
| Carroll | 938 | Ossipee | 15,829 |
| Cheshire | 715 | Keene | 43,342 |
| Coös | 1,820 | Lancaster | 37,140 |
| Grafton | 1,732 | Woodsville | 48,857 |
| Hillsborough | 893 | Nashua | 178,161 |
| Merrimack | 930 | Concord | 67,785 |
| Rockingham | 691 | Exeter | 99,029 |
| Strafford | 376 | Dover | 59,799 |
| Sullivan | 539 | Newport | 28,067 |

## NEW JERSEY

(21 counties, 7,532 sq. mi. land; pop., 6,066,782)

| County | Land Area sq.mi | County Seats or Court Houses | County Pop. 1960 |
|---|---|---|---|
| Atlantic | 569 | Mays Landing | 160,880 |
| Bergen | 234 | Hackensack | 780,255 |
| Burlington | 819 | Mount Holly | 224,499 |
| Camden | 221 | Camden | 392,035 |
| Cape May | 267 | Cape May Court House | 48,555 |
| Cumberland | 500 | Bridgeton | 106,850 |
| Essex | 130 | Newark | 923,545 |
| Gloucester | 329 | Woodbury | 134,840 |
| Hudson | 47 | Jersey City | 610,734 |
| Hunterdon | 434 | Flemington | 54,107 |
| Mercer | 228 | Trenton | 266,392 |
| Middlesex | 312 | New Brunswick | 433,856 |
| Monmouth | 476 | Freehold | 334,401 |
| Morris | 468 | Morristown | 261,620 |
| Ocean | 642 | Toms River | 108,241 |
| Passaic | 193 | Paterson | 406,618 |
| Salem | 365 | Salem | 58,711 |
| Somerset | 307 | Somerville | 143,913 |
| Sussex | 527 | Newton | 49,255 |
| Union | 103 | Elizabeth | 504,255 |
| Warren | 362 | Belvidere | 63,220 |

## NEW MEXICO

(32 counties, 121,445 sq. mi. land; pop., 951,023)

| County | Land Area sq.mi | County Seats or Court Houses | County Pop. 1960 |
|---|---|---|---|
| Bernalillo | 1,169 | Albuquerque | 262,199 |
| Catron | 6,897 | Reserve | 2,773 |
| Chaves | 6,092 | Roswell | 57,649 |
| Colfax | 3,764 | Raton | 13,806 |
| Curry | 1,403 | Clovis | 32,691 |
| De Baca | 2,356 | Fort Sumner | 2,991 |
| Dona Ana | 3,804 | Las Cruces | 59,948 |
| Eddy | 4,167 | Carlsbad | 50,783 |
| Grant | 3,970 | Silver City | 18,700 |
| Guadalupe | 2,998 | Santa Rosa | 5,610 |
| Harding | 2,134 | Mosquero | 1,874 |
| Hidalgo | 3,447 | Lordsburg | 4,961 |
| Lea | 4,393 | Lovington | 53,429 |
| Lincoln | 4,858 | Carrizozo | 7,744 |
| Los Alamos | 108 | Los Alamos | 13,037 |
| Luna | 2,957 | Deming | 9,839 |
| McKinley | 5,453 | Gallup | 37,209 |
| Mora | 1,940 | Mora | 6,028 |
| Otero | 6,638 | Alamogordo | 36,976 |
| Quay | 2,882 | Tucumcari | 12,279 |
| Rio Arriba | 5,853 | Tierra Amarilla | 24,193 |
| Roosevelt | 2,454 | Portales | 16,198 |
| Sandoval | 3,714 | Bernalillo | 14,201 |
| San Juan | 5,506 | Aztec | 53,306 |
| San Miguel | 4,741 | Las Vegas | 23,468 |
| Santa Fe | 1,905 | Santa Fe | 44,970 |
| Sierra | 4,166 | Truth or Consequences | 6,409 |
| Socorro | 6,603 | Socorro | 10,168 |
| Taos | 2,256 | Taos | 15,934 |
| Torrance | 3,346 | Estancia | 6,497 |
| Union | 3,816 | Clayton | 6,068 |
| Valencia | 5,656 | Los Lunas | 39,085 |

## NEW YORK

(62 counties, 47,869 sq. mi. land; pop., 16,782,304)

| County | Land Area sq.mi | County Seats or Court Houses | County Pop. 1960 |
|---|---|---|---|
| Albany | 526 | Albany | 272,926 |
| Allegany | 1,047 | Belmont | 43,978 |
| Bronx | 41 | Bronx | 1,424,815 |
| Broome | 714 | Binghamton | 212,661 |
| Cattaraugus | 1,334 | Little Valley | 80,187 |
| Cayuga | 698 | Auburn | 73,942 |
| Chautauqua | 1,081 | Mayville | 145,377 |
| Chemung | 415 | Elmira | 98,706 |
| Chenango | 909 | Norwich | 43,243 |
| Clinton | 1,059 | Plattsburgh | 72,722 |
| Columbia | 645 | Hudson | 47,322 |
| Cortland | 502 | Cortland | 41,113 |
| Delaware | 1,458 | Delhi | 43,540 |
| Dutchess | 813 | Poughkeepsie | 176,008 |
| Erie | 1,058 | Buffalo | 1,064,688 |
| Essex | 1,823 | Elizabethtown | 35,300 |
| Franklin | 1,674 | Malone | 44,742 |
| Fulton | 499 | Johnstown | 51,304 |
| Genesee | 501 | Batavia | 53,994 |
| Greene | 653 | Catskill | 31,372 |
| Hamilton | 1,735 | Lake Pleasant | 4,267 |
| Herkimer | 1,435 | Herkimer | 66,370 |
| Jefferson | 1,293 | Watertown | 87,835 |
| Kings | 70 | Brooklyn | 2,627,319 |
| Lewis | 1,291 | Lowville | 23,249 |
| Livingston | 638 | Geneseo | 44,053 |
| Madison | 661 | Wampsville | 54,635 |
| Monroe '64 | 675 | Rochester | 625,128 |
| Montgomery | 408 | Fonda | 57,240 |
| Nassau | 289 | Mineola | 1,300,171 |
| New York | 23 | New York | 1,698,281 |
| Niagara '67 | 532 | Lockport | 234,477 |
| Oneida | 1,223 | Utica | 264,401 |
| Onondaga | 794 | Syracuse | 423,028 |
| Ontario | 651 | Canandaigua | 68,070 |
| Orange '67 | 833 | Goshen | 209,141 |
| Orleans | 396 | Albion | 34,159 |
| Oswego | 964 | Oswego | 86,118 |
| Otsego | 1,013 | Cooperstown | 51,942 |
| Putnam '65 | 231 | Carmel | 41,811 |
| Queens | 108 | Jamaica | 1,809,578 |
| Rensselaer | 665 | Troy | 142,585 |
| Richmond | 58 | Saint George | 221,991 |
| Rockland '66 | 176 | New City | 191,611 |
| St. Lawrence | 2,768 | Canton | 111,239 |
| Saratoga '65 | 818 | Ballston Spa | 101,345 |
| Schenectady | 207 | Schenectady | 152,896 |
| Schoharie | 624 | Schoharie | 22,616 |
| Schuyler | 330 | Watkins Glen | 15,044 |
| Seneca | 330 | Ovid & Waterloo | 31,984 |
| Steuben | 1,410 | Bath | 97,691 |
| Suffolk | 929 | Riverhead | 666,784 |
| Sullivan | 980 | Monticello | 45,272 |
| Tioga | 524 | Owego | 37,802 |
| Tompkins | 482 | Ithaca | 66,164 |
| Ulster | 1,141 | Kingston | 118,804 |
| Warren | 887 | Lake George | 44,002 |
| Washington | 835 | Hudson Falls | 48,476 |
| Wayne | 606 | Lyons | 67,989 |
| Westchester '65 | 443 | White Plains | 853,198 |
| Wyoming | 598 | Warsaw | 34,793 |
| Yates | 343 | Penn Yan | 18,614 |

## NORTH CAROLINA

(100 counties, 48,880 sq. mi. land; pop., 4,556,155)

## NORTH DAKOTA

(53 counties, 69,280 sq. mi. land; pop., 632,446)

| County | Land Area sq.mi | County Seats or Court Houses | County Pop. 1960 | County | Land Area sq.mi | County Seats or Court Houses | County Pop. 1960 |
|---|---|---|---|---|---|---|---|
| Alamance | 434 | Graham | 85,674 | Adams | 989 | Hettinger | 4,449 |
| Alexander | 255 | Taylorsville | 15,625 | Barnes | 1,479 | Valley City | 16,719 |
| Alleghany | 230 | Sparta | 7,734 | Benson | 1,403 | Minnewaukan | 9,435 |
| Anson | 533 | Wadesboro | 24,962 | Billings | 1,139 | Medora | 1,513 |
| Ashe | 427 | Jefferson | 19,768 | Bottineau | 1,677 | Bottineau | 11,315 |
| Avery | 247 | Newland | 12,009 | Bowman | 1,170 | Bowman | 4,154 |
| Beaufort, '66 | 831 | Washington | 36,143 | Burke | 1,119 | Bowbells | 5,886 |
| Bertie | 693 | Windsor | 24,350 | Burleigh | 1,625 | Bismarck | 34,016 |
| Bladen, '66 | 879 | Elizabethtown | 26,605 | Cass | 1,749 | Fargo | 66,947 |
| Brunswick | 873 | Southport | 20,278 | Cavalier | 1,512 | Langdon | 10,064 |
| Buncombe | 645 | Asheville | 130,074 | Dickey | 1,143 | Ellendale | 8,147 |
| Burke | 506 | Morganton | 52,701 | Divide | 1,300 | Crosby | 5,566 |
| Cabarrus | 360 | Concord | 68,137 | Dunn | 1,992 | Manning | 6,350 |
| Caldwell | 476 | Lenoir | 49,552 | Eddy | 635 | New Rockford | 4,936 |
| Camden, '66 | 239 | Camden | 5,407 | Emmons | 1,503 | Linton | 8,462 |
| Carteret | 532 | Beaufort | 30,940 | Foster | 645 | Carrington | 5,361 |
| Caswell | 435 | Yanceyville | 19,912 | Golden Valley | 1,014 | Beach | 3,100 |
| Catawba | 406 | Newton | 73,191 | Grand Forks | 1,438 | Grand Forks | 48,677 |
| Chatham | 707 | Pittsboro | 26,785 | Grant | 1,666 | Carson | 6,248 |
| Cherokee | 454 | Murphy | 16,335 | Griggs | 710 | Cooperstown | 5,023 |
| Chowan | 180 | Edenton | 11,729 | Hettinger | 1,134 | Mott | 6,317 |
| Clay | 213 | Hayesville | 5,526 | Kidder | 1,358 | Steele | 5,386 |
| Cleveland, '66 | 466 | Shelby | 69,372 | La Moure | 1,136 | La Moure | 8,705 |
| Columbus | 939 | Whiteville | 48,973 | Logan | 1,001 | Napoleon | 5,369 |
| Craven | 725 | New Bern | 58,773 | McHenry | 1,879 | Towner | 11,099 |
| Cumberland | 661 | Fayetteville | 148,418 | McIntosh | 992 | Ashley | 6,702 |
| Currituck | 273 | Currituck | 6,601 | McKenzie | 2,735 | Watford City | 7,296 |
| Dare | 388 | Manteo | 5,935 | McLean | 2,065 | Washburn | 14,030 |
| Davidson | 546 | Lexington | 79,493 | Mercer | 1,042 | Stanton | 6,805 |
| Davie | 264 | Mocksville | 16,728 | Morton | 1,920 | Mandan | 20,992 |
| Duplin, '65 | 822 | Kenansville | 37,959 | Mountrail | 1,819 | Stanley | 10,077 |
| Durham | 299 | Durham | 111,995 | Nelson | 995 | Lakota | 7,034 |
| Edgecombe | 511 | Tarboro | 54,226 | Oliver | 721 | Center | 2,610 |
| Forsyth | 424 | Winston-Salem | 189,428 | Pembina | 1,124 | Cavalier | 12,946 |
| Franklin | 494 | Louisburg | 28,755 | Pierce | 1,038 | Rugby | 7,394 |
| Gaston, '66 | 358 | Gastonia | 135,775 | Ramsey | 1,248 | Devils Lake | 13,443 |
| Gates | 343 | Gatesville | 9,254 | Ransom | 861 | Lisbon | 8,078 |
| Graham | 289 | Robbinsville | 6,432 | Renville | 886 | Mohall | 4,698 |
| Granville | 542 | Oxford | 33,110 | Richland | 1,449 | Wahpeton | 18,824 |
| Greene | 269 | Snow Hill | 16,741 | Rolette | 913 | Rolla | 10,641 |
| Guilford, '66 | 651 | Greensboro | 269,513 | Sargent | 853 | Forman | 6,856 |
| Halifax | 722 | Halifax | 58,956 | Sheridan | 989 | McClusky | 4,350 |
| Harnett, '66 | 606 | Lillington | 49,189 | Sioux | 1,103 | Fort Yates | 3,662 |
| Haywood | 543 | Waynesville | 39,711 | Slope | 1,225 | Amidon | 1,893 |
| Henderson | 382 | Hendersonville | 36,163 | Stark | 1,316 | Dickinson | 18,451 |
| Hertford | 356 | Winton | 22,718 | Steele | 710 | Finley | 4,719 |
| Hoke, '66 | 326 | Raeford | 16,356 | Stutsman | 2,264 | Jamestown | 25,137 |
| Hyde, '66 | 634 | Swanquarter | 5,456 | Towner | 1,042 | Cando | 5,624 |
| Iredell | 591 | Statesville | 62,526 | Traill | 861 | Hillsboro | 10,583 |
| Jackson | 495 | Sylva | 17,780 | Walsh | 1,286 | Grafton | 17,997 |
| Johnston, '66 | 795 | Smithfield | 60,939 | Ward | 2,044 | Minot | 47,072 |
| Jones, '65 | 467 | Trenton | 10,221 | Wells | 1,298 | Fessenden | 9,231 |
| Lee, '66 | 255 | Sanford | 29,197 | Williams | 2,064 | Williston | 22,057 |
| Lenoir | 391 | Kinston | 55,276 | **OHIO** | | | |
| Lincoln | 308 | Lincolnton | 28,814 | (88 counties, 41,018 sq. mi. land; pop., 9,706,397) | | | |
| McDowell | 442 | Marion | 26,742 | Adams | 588 | West Union | 19,982 |
| Macon | 517 | Franklin | 14,935 | Allen | 410 | Lima | 103,691 |
| Madison | 456 | Marshall | 17,217 | Ashland | 418 | Ashland | 38,771 |
| Martin, '66 | 481 | Williamston | 25,611 | Ashtabula | 706 | Jefferson | 93,067 |
| Mecklenburg | 542 | Charlotte | 272,111 | Athens | 504 | Athens | 46,998 |
| Mitchell | 220 | Bakersville | 13,906 | Auglaize | 400 | Wapakoneta | 36,147 |
| Montgomery | 488 | Troy | 18,408 | Belmont | 535 | Saint Clairsville | 83,864 |
| Moore | 760 | Carthage | 36,733 | Brown | 491 | Georgetown | 25,178 |
| Nash | 552 | Nashville | 61,002 | Butler | 471 | Hamilton | 199,076 |
| New Hanover | 194 | Wilmington | 71,742 | Carroll | 388 | Carrollton | 20,857 |
| Northampton | 539 | Jackson | 26,811 | Champaign | 433 | Urbana | 29,714 |
| Onslow | 756 | Jacksonville | 82,706 | Clark | 402 | Springfield | 131,440 |
| Orange | 398 | Hillsboro | 42,970 | Clermont | 458 | Batavia | 80,530 |
| Pamlico | 341 | Bayboro | 9,850 | Clinton | 411 | Wilmington | 30,004 |
| Pasquotank | 229 | Elizabeth City | 25,630 | Columbiana | 535 | Lisbon | 107,004 |
| Pender, '66 | 857 | Burgaw | 17,372 | Coshocton | 545 | Coshocton | 32,224 |
| Perquimans, '66 | 261 | Hertford | 8,675 | Crawford | 404 | Bucyrus | 46,775 |
| Person | 400 | Roxboro | 26,394 | Cuyahoga | 456 | Cleveland | 1,647,895 |
| Pitt | 656 | Greenville | 69,942 | Darke | 605 | Greenville | 45,612 |
| Polk | 234 | Columbus | 11,395 | Defiance | 410 | Defiance | 31,508 |
| Randolph | 801 | Asheboro | 61,497 | Delaware | 440 | Delaware | 36,107 |
| Richmond, '66 | 477 | Rockingham | 39,299 | Erie | 264 | Sandusky | 68,000 |
| Roveson, '66 | 944 | Lumberton | 89,102 | Fairfield | 505 | Lancaster | 63,912 |
| Rock'gham, '66 | 572 | Wentworth | 71,404 | Fayette | 406 | Washington C. H. | 24,775 |
| Rowan | 517 | Salisbury | 82,817 | Franklin | 537 | Columbus | 682,962 |
| Rutherford | 566 | Rutherfordton | 45,091 | Fulton | 407 | Wauseon | 29,301 |
| Sampson | 963 | Clinton | 48,013 | Gallia | 471 | Gallipolis | 26,120 |
| Sanly | 399 | Albemarle | 40,873 | Geauga | 407 | Chardon | 47,573 |
| Scotland | 317 | Laurinburg | 25,183 | Greene | 416 | Xenia | 94,642 |
| Stokes | 459 | Danbury | 22,314 | Guernsey | 519 | Cambridge | 38,579 |
| Surry | 537 | Dobson | 48,205 | Hamilton | 414 | Cincinnati | 864,121 |
| Swain | 530 | Bryson City | 8,387 | Hancock | 532 | Findlay | 53,686 |
| Transylvania | 379 | Brevard | 16,372 | Hardin | 467 | Kenton | 29,633 |
| Tyrrell | 399 | Columbia | 4,520 | Harrison | 403 | Cadiz | 17,995 |
| Union, '66 | 643 | Monroe | 48,389 | Henry | 416 | Napoleon | 25,392 |
| Vance | 249 | Henderson | 32,002 | Highland | 551 | Hillsboro | 29,716 |
| Wake, '66 | 864 | Raleigh | 197,617 | Hocking | 420 | Logan | 20,168 |
| Warren, '66 | 443 | Warrenton | 17,591 | Holmes | 423 | Millersburg | 21,591 |
| Washington, '65 | 336 | Plymouth | 13,937 | Huron | 497 | Norwalk | 47,326 |
| Watauge | 326 | Boone | 17,529 | Jackson | 420 | Jackson | 29,372 |
| Wayne | 555 | Goldsboro | 82,059 | Jefferson | 411 | Steubenville | 99,201 |
| Wilkes | 765 | Wilkesboro | 45,269 | Knox | 523 | Mount Vernon | 38,808 |
| Wilson | 373 | Wilson | 57,716 | Lake | 232 | Painesville | 148,700 |
| Yadkin | 335 | Yadkinville | 22,804 | Lawrence | 456 | Ironton | 55,438 |
| Yancey | 311 | Burnsville | 14,008 | Licking | 686 | Newark | 90,242 |

## OHIO—Continued

| County | Land Area sq.mi | County Seats or Court Houses | County Pop. 1960 |
|---|---|---|---|
| Logan | 461 | Bellefontaine | 34,803 |
| Lorain | 495 | Elyria | 217,500 |
| Lucas | 343 | Toledo | 456,931 |
| Madison | 464 | London | 26,454 |
| Mahoning | 419 | Youngstown | 300,480 |
| Marion | 405 | Marion | 60,221 |
| Medina | 424 | Medina | 65,315 |
| Meigs | 434 | Pomeroy | 22,159 |
| Mercer | 454 | Celina | 32,559 |
| Miami | 407 | Troy | 72,901 |
| Monroe | 455 | Woodsfield | 15,268 |
| Montgomery | 465 | Dayton | 527,080 |
| Morgan | 417 | McConnelsville | 12,747 |
| Morrow | 404 | Mount Gilead | 19,405 |
| Muskingum | 663 | Zanesville | 79,159 |
| Noble | 399 | Caldwell | 10,982 |
| Ottawa | 263 | Port Clinton | 35,323 |
| Paulding | 416 | Paulding | 16,792 |
| Perry | 409 | New Lexington | 27,864 |
| Pickaway | 507 | Circleville | 35,855 |
| Pike | 443 | Waverly | 19,380 |
| Portage | 504 | Ravenna | 91,798 |
| Preble | 427 | Eaton | 32,498 |
| Putnam | 484 | Ottawa | 28,331 |
| Richland | 497 | Mansfield | 117,761 |
| Ross | 687 | Chillicothe | 61,215 |
| Sandusky | 410 | Fremont | 56,486 |
| Scioto | 609 | Portsmouth | 84,216 |
| Seneca | 551 | Tiffin | 59,326 |
| Shelby | 409 | Sidney | 33,586 |
| Stark | 573 | Canton | 340,345 |
| Summit | 413 | Akron | 513,569 |
| Trumbull | 620 | Warren | 208,526 |
| Tuscarawas | 551 | New Philadelphia | 76,789 |
| Union | 434 | Marysville | 22,853 |
| Van Wert | 409 | Van Wert | 28,840 |
| Vinton | 411 | McArthur | 10,274 |
| Warren | 408 | Lebanon | 65,711 |
| Washington | 637 | Marietta | 51,689 |
| Wayne | 551 | Wooster | 75,497 |
| Williams | 421 | Bryan | 29,968 |
| Wood | 618 | Bowling Green | 72,596 |
| Wyandot | 406 | Upper Sandusky | 21,648 |

## OKLAHOMA

*(77 counties, 68,984 sq. mt. land; pop., 2,328,284)*

| County | Land Area sq.mi | County Seats or Court Houses | County Pop. 1960 |
|---|---|---|---|
| Adair | 570 | Stilwell | 13,112 |
| Alfalfa | 868 | Cherokee | 8,445 |
| Atoka | 991 | Atoka | 10,352 |
| Beaver | 1,790 | Beaver | 6,965 |
| Beckham | 907 | Sayre | 17,782 |
| Blaine | 917 | Watonga | 12,077 |
| Bryan | 889 | Durant | 24,252 |
| Caddo | 1,275 | Anadarko | 28,621 |
| Canadian | 897 | El Reno | 24,727 |
| Carter | 830 | Ardmore | 39,044 |
| Cherokee | 756 | Tahlequah | 17,762 |
| Choctaw | 781 | Hugo | 15,637 |
| Cimarron | 1,843 | Boise City | 4,496 |
| Cleveland | 541 | Norman | 47,600 |
| Coal | 526 | Colgate | 5,546 |
| Comanche | 1,087 | Lawton | 90,803 |
| Cotton | 651 | Walters | 8,031 |
| Craig | 764 | Vinita | 16,303 |
| Creek | 936 | Sapulpa | 40,495 |
| Custer | 1,001 | Arapaho | 21,040 |
| Delaware | 707 | Jay | 13,198 |
| Dewey | 1,018 | Taloga | 6,051 |
| Ellis | 1,242 | Arnett | 5,457 |
| Garfield | 1,054 | Enid | 52,975 |
| Garvin | 814 | Pauls Valley | 28,290 |
| Grady | 1,096 | Chickasha | 29,590 |
| Grant | 1,007 | Medford | 8,140 |
| Greer | 633 | Mangum | 8,877 |
| Harmon | 545 | Hollis | 5,852 |
| Harper | 1,041 | Buffalo | 5,956 |
| Haskell | 602 | Stigler | 9,121 |
| Hughes | 807 | Holdenville | 15,144 |
| Jackson | 810 | Altus | 29,736 |
| Jefferson | 780 | Waurika | 8,192 |
| Johnston | 638 | Tishomingo | 8,517 |
| Kay | 950 | Newkirk | 51,042 |
| Kingfisher | 904 | Kingfisher | 10,635 |
| Kiowa | 1,027 | Hobart | 14,825 |
| Latimer | 737 | Wilburton | 7,738 |
| Le Flore | 1,560 | Poteau | 29,106 |
| Lincoln | 973 | Chandler | 18,783 |
| Logan | 751 | Guthrie | 18,662 |
| Love | 513 | Marietta | 5,862 |
| McClain | 573 | Purcell | 12,740 |
| McCurtain | 1,849 | Idabel | 28,642 |
| McIntosh | 608 | Eufaula | 12,371 |
| Major | 963 | Fairview | 7,808 |
| Marshall | 366 | Madill | 7,263 |
| Mayes | 678 | Pryor | 20,073 |
| Murray | 428 | Sulphur | 10,622 |
| Muskogee | 818 | Muskogee | 61,866 |
| Noble | 743 | Perry | 10,376 |
| Nowata | 577 | Nowata | 10,848 |
| Okfuskee | 637 | Okemah | 11,706 |
| Oklahoma | 705 | Oklahoma City | 439,506 |
| Okmulgee | 700 | Okmulgee | 36,945 |

## OKLAHOMA—Continued

| County | Land Area sq.mi | County Seats or Court House | County Pop. 1960 |
|---|---|---|---|
| Osage | 2,272 | Pawhuska | 32,441 |
| Ottawa | 464 | Miami | 28,301 |
| Pawnee | 561 | Pawnee | 10,884 |
| Payne | 694 | Stillwater | 44,231 |
| Pittsburg | 1,241 | McAlester | 34,360 |
| Pontotoc | 714 | Ada | 28,089 |
| Pottawatomie | 794 | Shawnee | 41,486 |
| Pushmataha | 1,423 | Antlers | 9,088 |
| Roger Mills | 1,140 | Cheyenne | 5,090 |
| Rogers | 712 | Claremore | 20,614 |
| Seminole | 630 | Wewoka | 28,066 |
| Sequoyah | 696 | Sallisaw | 18,001 |
| Stephens | 891 | Duncan | 37,990 |
| Texas | 2,062 | Guymon | 14,162 |
| Tillman | 901 | Frederick | 14,654 |
| Tulsa | 573 | Tulsa | 346,038 |
| Wagoner | 563 | Wagoner | 15,673 |
| Washington | 424 | Bartlesville | 42,347 |
| Washita | 1,009 | Cordell | 18,121 |
| Woods | 1,298 | Alva | 11,932 |
| Woodward | 1,251 | Woodward | 13,902 |

## OREGON

*(36 counties, 96,209 sq. mi. land; pop., 1,768,687)*

| County | Land Area sq.mi | County Seats or Court House | County Pop. 1960 |
|---|---|---|---|
| Baker | 3,068 | Baker | 17,295 |
| Benton | 668 | Corvallis | 39,165 |
| Clackamas | 1,884 | Oregon City | 113,038 |
| Clatsop | 805 | Astoria | 27,380 |
| Columbia | 640 | Saint Helens | 22,379 |
| Coos | 1,604 | Coquille | 54,955 |
| Crook | 2,980 | Prineville | 9,430 |
| Curry | 1,627 | Gold Beach | 13,983 |
| Deschutes | 3,031 | Bend | 23,100 |
| Douglas | 5,063 | Roseburg | 68,458 |
| Gilliam | 1,208 | Condon | 3,069 |
| Grant | 4,531 | Canyon City | 7,726 |
| Harney | 10,166 | Burns | 6,744 |
| Hood River | 523 | Hood River | 13,395 |
| Jackson | 2,812 | Medford | 73,962 |
| Jefferson | 1,793 | Madras | 7,130 |
| Josephine | 1,625 | Grants Pass | 29,917 |
| Klamath | 5,970 | Klamath Falls | 47,475 |
| Lake | 8,231 | Lakeview | 7,158 |
| Lane | 4,562 | Eugene | 162,890 |
| Lincoln | 986 | Newport | 24,635 |
| Linn | 2,291 | Albany | 58,867 |
| Malheur | 9,861 | Vale | 22,764 |
| Marion | 1,166 | Salem | 120,888 |
| Morrow | 2,060 | Heppner | 4,871 |
| Multnomah | 423 | Portland | 522,813 |
| Polk | 736 | Dallas | 26,523 |
| Sherman | 830 | Moro | 2,446 |
| Tillamook | 1,115 | Tillamook | 18,955 |
| Umatilla | 3,227 | Pendleton | 44,352 |
| Union | 2,032 | La Grande | 18,180 |
| Wallowa | 3,178 | Enterprise | 7,102 |
| Wasco | 2,382 | The Dalles | 20,205 |
| Washington | 716 | Hillsboro | 92,237 |
| Wheeler | 1,707 | Fossil | 2,722 |
| Yamhill | 711 | McMinnville | 32,478 |

## PENNSYLVANIA

*(67 counties, 45,025 sq. mi. land; pop., 11,319,366)*

| County | Land Area sq.mi | County Seats or Court House | County Pop. 1960 |
|---|---|---|---|
| Adams | 526 | Gettysburg | 51,906 |
| Allegheny | 730 | Pittsburgh | 1,628,587 |
| Armstrong | 656 | Kittanning | 79,524 |
| Beaver | 441 | Beaver | 206,948 |
| Bedford | 1,016 | Bedford | 42,451 |
| Berks | 864 | Reading | 275,414 |
| Blair | 531 | Hollidaysburg | 137,270 |
| Bradford | 1,147 | Towanda | 54,925 |
| Bucks | 617 | Doylestown | 308,567 |
| Butler | 794 | Butler | 114,639 |
| Cambria | 695 | Ebensburg | 203,283 |
| Cameron | 399 | Emporium | 7,586 |
| Carbon | 405 | Jim Thorpe | 52,589 |
| Centre | 1,115 | Bellefonte | 78,580 |
| Chester | 760 | West Chester | 210,608 |
| Clarion | 599 | Clarion | 37,408 |
| Clearfield | 1,144 | Clearfield | 81,534 |
| Clinton | 902 | Lock Haven | 37,619 |
| Columbia | 484 | Bloomsburg | 53,489 |
| Crawford | 1,016 | Meadville | 77,956 |
| Cumberland | 555 | Carlisle | 124,816 |
| Dauphin | 520 | Harrisburg | 220,255 |
| Delaware | 185 | Media | 553,154 |
| Elk | 807 | Ridgway | 37,328 |
| Erie | 812 | Erie | 250,682 |
| Fayette | 794 | Uniontown | 169,340 |
| Forest | 416 | Tionesta | 4,485 |
| Franklin | 754 | Chambersburg | 88,172 |
| Fulton | 435 | McConnellsburg | 10,597 |
| Greene | 577 | Waynesburg | 39,424 |
| Huntingdon | 892 | Huntingdon | 39,457 |
| Indiana | 825 | Indiana | 75,366 |
| Jefferson | 652 | Brookville | 46,792 |
| Juniata | 387 | Mifflintown | 15,874 |
| Lackawanna | 454 | Scranton | 234,531 |
| Lancaster | 944 | Lancaster | 278,359 |
| Lawrence | 367 | New Castle | 112,965 |
| Lebanon | 363 | Lebanon | 90,853 |
| Lehigh | 347 | Allentown | 227,536 |

| County | Land Area sq.mi | County Seats or Court Houses | County Pop. 1960 | County | Land Area sq.mi | County Seats or Court Houses | County Pop. 1960 |
|---|---|---|---|---|---|---|---|
| **PENNSYLVANIA—Continued** | | | | **SOUTH DAKOTA—Continued** | | | |
| Luzerne....... | 891 | Wilkes-Barre..... | 346,972 | Corson........ | 2,470 | McIntosh........ | 5,798 |
| Lycoming..... | 1,214 | Williamsport..... | 109,367 | Custer........ | 1,557 | Custer.......... | 4,906 |
| McKean...... | 997 | Smethport....... | 54,517 | Davison....... | 432 | Mitchell........ | 16,681 |
| Mercer....... | 681 | Mercer......... | 127,519 | Day.......... | 1,030 | Webster........ | 10,516 |
| Mifflin....... | 431 | Lewistown...... | 44,348 | Deuel........ | 639 | Clear Lake..... | 6,782 |
| Monroe...... | 611 | Stroudsburg..... | 39,567 | Dewey........ | 2,351 | Timber Lake.... | 5,257 |
| Montgomery.. | 491 | Norristown...... | 516,682 | Douglas....... | 435 | Armour......... | 5,113 |
| Montour..... | 130 | Danville........ | 16,730 | Edmunds...... | 1,154 | Ipswich........ | 6,079 |
| Northampton.. | 374 | Easton......... | 201,412 | Fall River..... | 1,743 | Hot Springs.... | 10,688 |
| Northumb'land | 454 | Sunbury........ | 104,138 | Faulk........ | 996 | Faulkton....... | 4,397 |
| Perry........ | 550 | New Bloomfield.. | 26,582 | Grant......... | 681 | Milbank........ | 9,913 |
| Philadelphia... | 127 | Philadelphia.... | 2,002,512 | Gregory....... | 997 | Burke.......... | 7,399 |
| Pike......... | 545 | Milford........ | 9,158 | Haakon....... | 1,816 | Philip.......... | 3,303 |
| Potter....... | 1,090 | Coudersport.... | 16,483 | Hamlin....... | 511 | Hayti.......... | 6,303 |
| Schuylkill..... | 783 | Pottsville....... | 173,027 | Hand......... | 1,432 | Miller.......... | 6,712 |
| Snyder....... | 329 | Middleburg..... | 25,922 | Hanson....... | 430 | Alexandria..... | 4,584 |
| Somerset..... | 1,084 | Somerset....... | 77,450 | Harding....... | 2,682 | Buffalo........ | 2,371 |
| Sullivan...... | 478 | Laporte........ | 6,251 | Hughes....... | 748 | Pierre......... | 12,725 |
| Susquehanna... | 836 | Montrose...... | 33,137 | Hutchinson.... | 815 | Olivet......... | 11,085 |
| Tioga........ | 1,150 | Wellsboro..... | 36,614 | Hyde........ | 863 | Highmore...... | 2,602 |
| Union........ | 318 | Lewisburg..... | 25,646 | Jackson....... | 808 | Kadoka........ | 1,985 |
| Venango...... | 675 | Franklin....... | 65,295 | Jerauld....... | 527 | Wessington Spgs.. | 4,048 |
| Warren....... | 910 | Warren........ | 45,582 | Jones........ | 973 | Murdo......... | 2,066 |
| Washington.... | 857 | Washington..... | 217,271 | Kingsbury..... | 818 | De Smet....... | 9,227 |
| Wayne....... | 744 | Honesdale..... | 28,237 | Lake......... | 567 | Madison....... | 11,764 |
| Westmoreland.. | 1,023 | Greensburg.... | 352,629 | Lawrence...... | 800 | Deadwood..... | 17,075 |
| Wyoming..... | 396 | Tunkhannock.... | 16,813 | Lincoln....... | 576 | Canton........ | 12,371 |
| York......... | 911 | York.......... | 238,336 | Lyman........ | 1,683 | Kennebec...... | 4,428 |
| | | | | McCook...... | 575 | Salem......... | 8,268 |
| **RHODE ISLAND** | | | | McPherson..... | 1,147 | Leola.......... | 5,821 |
| *(5 counties, 1,049 sq. mi. land; pop., 892,709 '65)* | | | | Marshall...... | 848 | Britton........ | 6,663 |
| | | | | Meade....... | 3,465 | Sturgis........ | 12,044 |
| Bristol, '65.... | 25 | Bristol........ | 41,855 | Mellette...... | 1,306 | White River.... | 2,664 |
| Kent, '65.... | 173 | East Greenwich... | 128,856 | Miner........ | 570 | Howard........ | 5,398 |
| Newport, '65... | 115 | Newport....... | 81,700 | Minnehaha.... | 813 | Sioux Falls..... | 86,575 |
| Providence, '65. | 416 | Providence..... | 569,117 | Moody........ | 523 | Flandreau..... | 8,810 |
| Washington,'65 | 321 | West Kingston.... | 71,181 | Pennington.... | 2,779 | Rapid City.... | 58,195 |
| | | | | Perkins....... | 2,860 | Bison.......... | 5,977 |
| **SOUTH CAROLINA** | | | | Potter........ | 869 | Gettysburg..... | 4,926 |
| *(46 counties, 30,280 sq. mi. land; pop., 2,382,594)* | | | | Roberts....... | 1,108 | Sisseton....... | 13,190 |
| | | | | Sanborn...... | 570 | Woonsocket.... | 4,641 |
| Abbeville..... | 506 | Abbeville........ | 21,417 | Shannon...... | 2,100 | (Attached to Fall | |
| Aiken........ | 1,100 | Aiken.......... | 81,038 | | | River) | 6,000 |
| Allendale..... | 418 | Allendale...... | 11,362 | Spink........ | 1,505 | Redfield....... | 11,706 |
| Anderson..... | 775 | Anderson...... | 98,478 | Stanley....... | 1,414 | Fort Pierre.... | 4,085 |
| Bamberg..... | 395 | Bamberg....... | 16,274 | Sully......... | 1,004 | Onida......... | 2,607 |
| Barnwell..... | 553 | Barnwell....... | 17,659 | Todd........ | 1,388 | (Attached to Tripp) | 4,661 |
| Beaufort..... | 579 | Beaufort....... | 44,187 | Tripp........ | 1,620 | Winner........ | 8,761 |
| Berkeley..... | 1,110 | Moncks Corner.. | 38,196 | Turner....... | 612 | Parker......... | 11,159 |
| Calhoun...... | 377 | Saint Matthews.. | 12,256 | Union........ | 452 | Elk Point...... | 10,197 |
| Charleston.... | 939 | Charleston..... | 216,382 | Walworth..... | 718 | Selby......... | 8,097 |
| Cherokee..... | 394 | Gaffney....... | 35,205 | Washabaugh... | 1,061 | (Attached to | |
| Chester...... | 584 | Chester........ | 30,888 | | | Jackson) | 1,042 |
| Chesterfield... | 792 | Chesterfield.... | 33,717 | Yankton...... | 519 | Yankton....... | 17,551 |
| Clarendon.... | 599 | Manning....... | 29,490 | Ziebach...... | 1,981 | Dupree........ | 2,495 |
| Colleton...... | 1,049 | Walterboro..... | 27,816 | | | | |
| Darlington.... | 543 | Darlington..... | 52,928 | **TENNESSEE** | | | |
| Dillon....... | 407 | Dillon......... | 30,584 | *(95 counties, 41,366 sq. mi. land; pop., 3,567,089)* | | | |
| Dorchester.... | 569 | Saint George... | 24,383 | Anderson..... | 335 | Clinton........ | 60,032 |
| Edgefield..... | 481 | Edgefield...... | 15,735 | Bedford...... | 482 | Shelbyville..... | 23,150 |
| Fairfield...... | 696 | Winnsboro.... | 20,713 | Benton....... | 392 | Camden........ | 10,662 |
| Florence..... | 805 | Florence...... | 84,438 | Bledsoe...... | 404 | Pikeville....... | 7,811 |
| Georgetown... | 812 | Georgetown.... | 34,798 | Blount....... | 576 | Maryville...... | 57,525 |
| Greenville.... | 793 | Greenville..... | 209,776 | Bradley...... | 334 | Cleveland..... | 38,324 |
| Greenwood.... | 446 | Greenwood.... | 44,346 | Campbell..... | 451 | Jacksboro...... | 27,936 |
| Hampton..... | 562 | Hampton...... | 17,425 | Cannon...... | 271 | Woodbury..... | 8,537 |
| Horry....... | 1,154 | Conway....... | 68,247 | Carroll....... | 596 | Huntingdon.... | 23,476 |
| Jasper....... | 652 | Ridgeland..... | 12,237 | Carter....... | 348 | Elizabethton.... | 41,578 |
| Kershaw..... | 781 | Camden....... | 33,585 | Cheatham..... | 305 | Ashland City... | 9,428 |
| Lancaster..... | 502 | Lancaster...... | 39,352 | Chester...... | 285 | Henderson..... | 9,569 |
| Laurens...... | 711 | Laurens....... | 47,609 | Claiborne..... | 444 | Tazewell...... | 19,067 |
| Lee.......... | 409 | Bishopville..... | 21,832 | Clay......... | 232 | Celina......... | 7,289 |
| Lexington.... | 717 | Lexington...... | 60,726 | Cocke........ | 424 | Newport....... | 23,390 |
| McCormick... | 360 | McCormick.... | 8,629 | Coffee....... | 434 | Manchester.... | 28,603 |
| Marion...... | 488 | Marion........ | 32,014 | Crockett..... | 269 | Alamo........ | 14,594 |
| Marlboro..... | 483 | Bennettsville... | 28,529 | Cumberland... | 678 | Crossville..... | 19,135 |
| Newberry.... | 635 | Newberry..... | 29,416 | Davidson..... | 427 | Nashville...... | 399,743 |
| Oconee...... | 670 | Walhalla....... | 40,204 | Decatur...... | 337 | Decaturville.... | 8,324 |
| Orangeburg... | 1,106 | Orangeburg.... | 68,559 | De Kalb...... | 278 | Smithville..... | 10,774 |
| Pickens...... | 501 | Pickens........ | 46,030 | Dickson...... | 485 | Charlotte...... | 18,839 |
| Richland..... | 748 | Columbia...... | 200,102 | Dyer......... | 529 | Dyersburg..... | 29,537 |
| Saluda...... | 448 | Saluda........ | 14,554 | Fayette...... | 704 | Somerville..... | 24,577 |
| Spartanburg... | 831 | Spartanburg.... | 156,830 | Fentress..... | 498 | Jamestown.... | 13,288 |
| Sumter...... | 672 | Sumter........ | 74,941 | Franklin...... | 553 | Winchester.... | 25,528 |
| Union....... | 514 | Union......... | 30,015 | Gibson....... | 607 | Trenton....... | 44,699 |
| Williamsburg.. | 935 | Kingstree...... | 40,932 | Giles........ | 619 | Pulaski........ | 22,410 |
| York......... | 684 | York.......... | 78,760 | Grainger..... | 282 | Rutledge....... | 12,506 |
| | | | | Greene....... | 613 | Greeneville..... | 42,163 |
| **SOUTH DAKOTA** | | | | Grundy...... | 358 | Altamont...... | 11,512 |
| *(67 counties, 75,956 sq. mi. land; pop., 680,514)* | | | | Hamblen..... | 155 | Morristown.... | 33,092 |
| | | | | Hamilton..... | 550 | Chattanooga... | 237,905 |
| Aurora....... | 709 | Plankinton..... | 4,749 | Hancock..... | 230 | Sneedville..... | 7,757 |
| Beadle....... | 1,260 | Huron......... | 21,682 | Hardeman.... | 656 | Bolivar........ | 21,517 |
| Bennett...... | 1,181 | Martin........ | 3,053 | Hardin....... | 587 | Savannah..... | 17,397 |
| Bon Homme... | 560 | Tyndall........ | 9,229 | Hawkins..... | 480 | Rogersville.... | 30,468 |
| Brookings.... | 800 | Brookings..... | 20,046 | Haywood..... | 519 | Brownsville.... | 23,395 |
| Brown....... | 1,674 | Aberdeen..... | 34,106 | Henderson.... | 515 | Lexington..... | 16,115 |
| Brule........ | 818 | Chamberlain... | 6,319 | Henry....... | 567 | Paris.......... | 22,275 |
| Buffalo...... | 482 | Gannvalley.... | 1,547 | Hickman..... | 611 | Centerville.... | 11,862 |
| Butte........ | 2,250 | Belle Fourche... | 8,592 | Houston..... | 201 | Erin........... | 4,794 |
| Campbell.... | 732 | Mound City.... | 3,531 | Humphreys... | 530 | Waverly....... | 11,511 |
| Charles Mix... | 1,097 | Lake Andes.... | 11,785 | Jackson...... | 323 | Gainesboro.... | 9,233 |
| Clark........ | 964 | Clark.......... | 7,134 | | | | |
| Clay......... | 405 | Vermillion..... | 10,810 | | | | |
| Codington.... | 687 | Watertown.... | 20,220 | | | | |

## TENNESSEE—Continued

| County | Land Area sq.mi | County Seats or Court Houses | County Pop. 1960 |
|---|---|---|---|
| Jefferson | 274 | Dandridge | 21,493 |
| Johnson | 293 | Mountain City | 10,765 |
| Knox | 508 | Knoxville | 250,523 |
| Lake | 167 | Tiptonville | 9,572 |
| Lauderdale | 477 | Ripley | 21,844 |
| Lawrence | 634 | Lawrenceburg | 28,049 |
| Lewis | 285 | Hohenwald | 6,269 |
| Lincoln | 580 | Fayetteville | 23,829 |
| Loudon | 237 | Loudon | 23,757 |
| McMinn | 432 | Athens | 33,662 |
| McNairy | 569 | Selmer | 18,085 |
| Macon | 304 | Lafayette | 12,197 |
| Madison | 560 | Jackson | 60,655 |
| Marion | 506 | Jasper | 21,036 |
| Marshall | 377 | Lewisburg | 16,859 |
| Maury | 614 | Columbia | 41,699 |
| Meigs | 191 | Decatur | 5,160 |
| Monroe | 660 | Madisonville | 23,316 |
| Montgomery | 539 | Clarksville | 55,645 |
| Moore | 124 | Lynchburg | 3,454 |
| Morgan | 539 | Wartburg | 14,304 |
| Obion | 556 | Union City | 26,957 |
| Overton | 441 | Livingston | 14,661 |
| Perry | 411 | Linden | 5,273 |
| Pickett | 158 | Byrdstown | 4,431 |
| Polk | 435 | Benton | 12,160 |
| Putnam | 405 | Cookeville | 29,236 |
| Rhea | 312 | Dayton | 15,863 |
| Roane | 350 | Kingston | 39,133 |
| Robertson | 476 | Springfield | 27,335 |
| Rutherford | 630 | Murfreesboro | 52,368 |
| Scott | 544 | Huntsville | 15,413 |
| Sequatchie | 273 | Dunlap | 5,915 |
| Sevier | 597 | Sevierville | 24,251 |
| Shelby | 755 | Memphis | 627,019 |
| Smith | 323 | Carthage | 12,059 |
| Stewart | 470 | Dover | 7,851 |
| Sullivan | 413 | Blountville | 114,139 |
| Sumner | 534 | Gallatin | 36,217 |
| Tipton | 459 | Covington | 28,564 |
| Trousdale | 114 | Hartsville | 4,914 |
| Unicoi | 185 | Erwin | 15,082 |
| Union | 212 | Maynardville | 8,498 |
| Van Buren | 254 | Spencer | 3,671 |
| Warren | 439 | McMinnville | 23,102 |
| Washington | 324 | Jonesboro | 64,832 |
| Wayne | 739 | Waynesboro | 11,908 |
| Weakley | 576 | Dresden | 24,227 |
| White | 382 | Sparta | 15,577 |
| Williamson | 593 | Franklin | 25,267 |
| Wilson | 568 | Lebanon | 27,668 |

## TEXAS

*(254 counties, 262,970 sq. mi. land; pop., 9,579,677)*

| County | Land Area sq.mi | County Seats or Court Houses | County Pop. 1960 |
|---|---|---|---|
| Anderson | 1,072 | Palestine | 28,162 |
| Andrews | 1,504 | Andrews | 13,450 |
| Angelina | 804 | Lufkin | 39,814 |
| Aransas | 271 | Rockport | 7,006 |
| Archer | 913 | Archer City | 6,110 |
| Armstrong | 907 | Claude | 1,966 |
| Atascosa | 1,206 | Jourdanton | 18,828 |
| Austin | 663 | Bellville | 13,777 |
| Bailey | 835 | Muleshoe | 9,090 |
| Bandera | 763 | Bandera | 3,892 |
| Bastrop | 890 | Bastrop | 16,925 |
| Baylor | 875 | Seymour | 5,893 |
| Bee | 842 | Beeville | 23,755 |
| Bell | 1,066 | Belton | 94,097 |
| Bexar | 1,246 | San Antonio | 687,151 |
| Blanco | 719 | Johnson City | 3,657 |
| Borden | 907 | Gail | 1,076 |
| Bosque | 990 | Meridian | 10,809 |
| Bowie | 891 | Boston | 59,971 |
| Brazoria | 1,423 | Angleton | 76,204 |
| Brazos | 586 | Bryan | 44,895 |
| Brewster | 6,204 | Alpine | 6,434 |
| Briscoe | 874 | Silverton | 3,577 |
| Brooks | 904 | Falfurrias | 8,609 |
| Brown | 950 | Brownwood | 24,728 |
| Burleson | 683 | Caldwell | 11,177 |
| Burnet | 996 | Burnet | 9,265 |
| Caldwell | 544 | Lockhart | 17,222 |
| Calhoun | 527 | Port Lavaca | 16,592 |
| Callahan | 856 | Baird | 7,929 |
| Cameron | 896 | Brownsville | 151,098 |
| Camp | 192 | Pittsburg | 7,849 |
| Carson | 900 | Panhandle | 7,781 |
| Cass | 941 | Linden | 23,496 |
| Castro | 880 | Dimmitt | 8,923 |
| Chambers | 616 | Anahuac | 10,379 |
| Cherokee | 1,049 | Rusk | 33,120 |
| Childress | 699 | Childress | 8,421 |
| Clay | 1,102 | Henrietta | 8,351 |
| Cochran | 783 | Morton | 6,417 |
| Coke | 911 | Robert Lee | 3,589 |
| Coleman | 1,279 | Coleman | 12,458 |
| Collin | 867 | McKinney | 41,247 |
| Collingsworth | 894 | Wellington | 6,276 |
| Colorado | 949 | Columbus | 18,463 |
| Comal | 567 | New Braunfels | 19,844 |
| Comanche | 966 | Comanche | 11,865 |
| Concho | 1,004 | Paint Rock | 3,672 |

## TEXAS—Continued

| County | Land Area sq.mi | County Seats or Court Houses | County Pop. 1960 |
|---|---|---|---|
| Cooke | 905 | Gainesville | 22,560 |
| Coryell | 1,043 | Gatesville | 23,961 |
| Cottle | 900 | Paducah | 4,207 |
| Crane | 795 | Crane | 4,699 |
| Crockett | 2,794 | Ozona | 4,209 |
| Crosby | 911 | Crosbyton | 10,347 |
| Culberson | 3,851 | Van Horn | 2,794 |
| Dallam | 1,494 | Dalhart | 6,302 |
| Dallas | 875 | Dallas | 951,527 |
| Dawson | 902 | Lamesa | 19,185 |
| Deaf Smith | 1,510 | Hereford | 13,187 |
| Delta | 276 | Cooper | 5,860 |
| Denton | 911 | Denton | 47,432 |
| De Witt | 910 | Cuero | 20,683 |
| Dickens | 931 | Dickens | 4,963 |
| Dimmit | 1,344 | Carrizo Springs | 10,095 |
| Donley | 905 | Clarendon | 4,449 |
| Duval | 1,814 | San Diego | 13,398 |
| Eastland | 952 | Eastland | 19,526 |
| Ector | 907 | Odessa | 90,995 |
| Edwards | 2,076 | Rocksprings | 2,317 |
| Ellis | 950 | Waxahachie | 43,395 |
| El Paso | 1,058 | El Paso | 314,070 |
| Erath | 1,085 | Stephenville | 16,236 |
| Falls | 764 | Marlin | 21,263 |
| Fannin | 905 | Bonham | 23,880 |
| Fayette | 934 | La Grange | 20,384 |
| Fisher | 904 | Roby | 7,865 |
| Floyd | 993 | Floydada | 12,369 |
| Foard | 676 | Crowell | 3,125 |
| Fort Bend | 869 | Richmond | 40,527 |
| Franklin | 293 | Mount Vernon | 5,101 |
| Freestone | 865 | Fairfield | 12,525 |
| Frio | 1,116 | Pearsall | 10,112 |
| Gaines | 1,489 | Seminole | 12,267 |
| Galveston | 399 | Galveston | 140,364 |
| Garza | 914 | Post | 6,611 |
| Gillespie | 1,055 | Fredericksburg | 10,048 |
| Glasscock | 863 | Garden City | 1,118 |
| Goliad | 871 | Goliad | 5,429 |
| Gonzales | 1,056 | Gonzales | 17,845 |
| Gray | 934 | Pampa | 31,535 |
| Grayson | 940 | Sherman | 73,043 |
| Gregg | 282 | Longview | 69,436 |
| Grimes | 801 | Anderson | 12,709 |
| Guadalupe | 714 | Seguin | 29,017 |
| Hale | 979 | Plainview | 36,798 |
| Hall | 885 | Memphis | 7,322 |
| Hamilton | 844 | Hamilton | 8,488 |
| Hansford | 907 | Spearman | 6,208 |
| Hardeman | 687 | Quanah | 8,275 |
| Hardin | | Kountze | 24,629 |
| Harris | 1,723 | Houston | 1,243,158 |
| Harrison | 894 | Marshall | 45,594 |
| Hartley | 1,488 | Channing | 2,171 |
| Haskell | 877 | Haskell | 11,174 |
| Hays | 670 | San Marcos | 19,934 |
| Hemphill | 904 | Canadian | 3,185 |
| Henderson | 943 | Athens | 21,786 |
| Hidalgo | 1,543 | Edinburg | 180,904 |
| Hill | 1,012 | Hillsboro | 23,650 |
| Hockley | 908 | Levelland | 22,340 |
| Hood | 426 | Granbury | 5,443 |
| Hopkins | 793 | Sulphur Springs | 18,594 |
| Houston | 1,237 | Crockett | 19,376 |
| Howard | 911 | Big Spring | 40,139 |
| Hudspeth | 4,554 | Sierra Blanca | 3,343 |
| Hunt | 869 | Greenville | 39,399 |
| Hutchinson | 875 | Stinnett | 34,419 |
| Irion | 1,073 | Mertzon | 1,183 |
| Jack | 945 | Jacksboro | 7,418 |
| Jackson | 850 | Edna | 14,040 |
| Jasper | 927 | Jasper | 22,100 |
| Jeff Davis | 2,259 | Fort Davis | 1,582 |
| Jefferson | 951 | Beaumont | 245,659 |
| Jim Hogg | 1,143 | Hebbronville | 5,022 |
| Jim Wells | 845 | Alice | 34,548 |
| Johnson | 740 | Cleburne | 34,720 |
| Jones | 956 | Anson | 19,299 |
| Karnes | 758 | Karnes City | 14,995 |
| Kaufman | 815 | Kaufman | 29,931 |
| Kendall | 670 | Boerne | 5,889 |
| Kenedy | 1,394 | Sarita | 884 |
| Kent | 880 | Jayton | 1,727 |
| Kerr | 1,101 | Kerrville | 16,800 |
| Kimble | 1,274 | Junction | 3,943 |
| King | 944 | Guthrie | 640 |
| Kinney | 1,393 | Brackettville | 2,452 |
| Kleberg | 851 | Kingsville | 30,052 |
| Knox | 851 | Benjamin | 7,857 |
| Lamar | 906 | Paris | 34,234 |
| Lamb | 1,022 | Littlefield | 21,896 |
| Lampasas | 726 | Lampasas | 9,418 |
| La Salle | 1,500 | Cotulla | 5,972 |
| Lavaca | 975 | Halletsville | 20,174 |
| Lee | 644 | Giddings | 8,949 |
| Leon | 1,102 | Centerville | 9,951 |
| Liberty | 1,182 | Liberty | 31,595 |
| Limestone | 931 | Groesbeck | 20,413 |
| Lipscomb | 934 | Lipscomb | 3,406 |
| Live Oak | 1,055 | George West | 7,846 |
| Llano | 941 | Llano | 5,240 |

| County | Land Area sq.mi | County Seats or Court Houses | County Pop. 1960 |
|---|---|---|---|
| **TEXAS—Continued** | | | |
| Loving | 648 | Mentone | 226 |
| Lubbock | 893 | Lubbock | 156,271 |
| Lynn | 915 | Tahoka | 10,914 |
| McCulloch | 1,066 | Brady | 8,815 |
| McLennan | 1,030 | Waco | 150,091 |
| McMullen | 1,159 | Tilden | 1,116 |
| Madison | 480 | Madisonville | 6,749 |
| Marion | 380 | Jefferson | 8,049 |
| Martin | 911 | Stanton | 5,068 |
| Mason | 935 | Mason | 3,780 |
| Matagorda | 1,157 | Bay City | 25,744 |
| Maverick | 1,289 | Eagle Pass | 14,508 |
| Medina | 1,352 | Hondo | 18,904 |
| Menard | 914 | Menard | 2,964 |
| Midland | 939 | Midland | 67,717 |
| Milam | 1,028 | Cameron | 22,263 |
| Mills | 734 | Goldthwaite | 4,467 |
| Mitchell | 920 | Colorado City | 11,255 |
| Montague | 934 | Montague | 14,893 |
| Montgomery | 1,090 | Conroe | 26,839 |
| Moore | 909 | Dumas | 14,773 |
| Morris | 260 | Daingerfield | 12,576 |
| Motley | 980 | Matador | 2,870 |
| Nacogdoches | 943 | Nacogdoches | 28,046 |
| Navarro | 1,087 | Corsicana | 34,423 |
| Newton | 953 | Newton | 10,372 |
| Nolan | 922 | Sweetwater | 18,963 |
| Nueces | 845 | Corpus Christi | 221,573 |
| Ochiltree | 907 | Perryton | 9,380 |
| Oldham | 1,478 | Vega | 1,928 |
| Orange | 359 | Orange | 60,357 |
| Palo Pinto | 948 | Palo Pinto | 20,516 |
| Panola | 880 | Carthage | 16,870 |
| Parker | 903 | Weatherford | 22,880 |
| Parmer | 859 | Farwell | 9,583 |
| Pecos | 4,740 | Fort Stockton | 11,957 |
| Polk | 1,100 | Livingston | 13,861 |
| Potter | 898 | Amarillo | 115,580 |
| Presidio | 3,892 | Marfa | 5,460 |
| Rains | 219 | Emory | 2,993 |
| Randall | 914 | Canyon | 33,913 |
| Regan | 1,132 | Big Lake | 3,782 |
| Real | 622 | Leakey | 2,079 |
| Red River | 1,033 | Clarksville | 15,682 |
| Reeves | 2,608 | Pecos | 17,644 |
| Refugio | 774 | Refugio | 10,975 |
| Roberts | 899 | Miami | 1,075 |
| Robertson | 877 | Franklin | 16,157 |
| Rockwall | 147 | Rockwall | 5,878 |
| Runnels | 1,058 | Ballinger | 15,016 |
| Rusk | 939 | Henderson | 36,421 |
| Sabine | 562 | Hemphill | 7,302 |
| San Augustine | 545 | San Augustine | 7,722 |
| San Jacinto | 624 | Coldspring | 6,153 |
| San Patricio | 686 | Sinton | 45,021 |
| San Saba | 1,120 | San Saba | 6,381 |
| Schleicher | 1,331 | Eldorado | 2,791 |
| Scurry | 904 | Snyder | 20,369 |
| Shackelford | 887 | Albany | 3,990 |
| Shelby | 820 | Center | 20,479 |
| Sherman | 916 | Stratford | 2,605 |
| Smith | 934 | Tyler | 86,350 |
| Somervell | 197 | Glen Rose | 2,577 |
| Starr | 1,211 | Rio Grande City | 17,137 |
| Stephens | 923 | Breckenridge | 8,885 |
| Sterling | 914 | Sterling City | 1,177 |
| Stonewall | 926 | Aspermont | 3,017 |
| Sutton | 1,493 | Sonora | 3,738 |
| Swisher | 896 | Tulia | 10,607 |
| Tarrant | 868 | Fort Worth | 538,495 |
| Taylor | 913 | Abilene | 101,078 |
| Terrell | 2,391 | Sanderson | 2,600 |
| Terry | 899 | Brownfield | 16,286 |
| Throckmorton | 920 | Throckmorton | 2,767 |
| Titus | 418 | Mount Pleasant | 16,785 |
| Tom Green | 1,535 | San Angelo | 64,630 |
| Travis | 1,012 | Austin | 212,136 |
| Trinity | 707 | Groveton | 7,539 |
| Tyler | 919 | Woodville | 10,666 |
| Upshur | 584 | Gilmer | 19,793 |
| Upton | 1,312 | Rankin | 6,239 |
| Uvalde | 1,588 | Uvalde | 16,814 |
| Val Verde | 3,241 | Del Rio | 24,461 |
| Van Zandt | 851 | Canton | 19,091 |
| Victoria | 893 | Victoria | 46,475 |
| Walker | 790 | Huntsville | 21,475 |
| Waller | 508 | Hempstead | 12,071 |
| Ward | 827 | Monahans | 14,917 |
| Washington | 612 | Brenham | 19,145 |
| Webb | 3,306 | Laredo | 64,791 |
| Wharton | 1,076 | Wharton | 38,152 |
| Wheeler | 914 | Wheeler | 7,947 |
| Wichita | 611 | Wichita Falls | 123,528 |
| Wilbarger | 952 | Vernon | 17,748 |
| Willacy | 591 | Raymondville | 20,084 |
| Williamson | 1,126 | Georgetown | 35,044 |
| Wilson | 802 | Floresville | 13,267 |
| Winkler | 887 | Kermit | 13,652 |
| Wise | 922 | Decatur | 17,012 |
| Wood | 721 | Quitman | 17,653 |
| Yoakum | 830 | Plains | 8,032 |
| Young | 888 | Graham | 17,254 |

| County | Land Area sq.mi | County Seats or Court Houses | County Pop. 1960 |
|---|---|---|---|
| **TEXAS—Continued** | | | |
| Zapata | 1,025 | Zapata | 4,393 |
| Zavala | 1,291 | Crystal City | 12,696 |
| **UTAH** | | | |
| *(29 counties, 82,381 sq. mi. land; pop., 890,627)* | | | |
| Beaver | 2,584 | Beaver | 4,331 |
| Box Elder | 5,627 | Brigham City | 25,061 |
| Cache | 1,174 | Logan | 35,788 |
| Carbon | 1,476 | Price | 21,135 |
| Daggett | 706 | Manila | 1,164 |
| Davis | 297 | Farmington | 64,760 |
| Duchesne | 3,255 | Duchesne | 7,179 |
| Emery | 4,439 | Castle Dale | 5,546 |
| Garfield | 5,185 | Panguitch | 3,577 |
| Grand | 3,696 | Moab | 6,345 |
| Iron | 3,300 | Parowan | 10,795 |
| Juab | 3,411 | Nephi | 4,597 |
| Kane | 4,016 | Kanab | 2,667 |
| Millard | 6,793 | Fillmore | 7,866 |
| Morgan | 610 | Morgan | 2,837 |
| Piute | 754 | Junction | 1,436 |
| Rich | 1,023 | Randolph | 1,685 |
| Salt Lake | 764 | Salt Lake City | 383,035 |
| San Juan | 7,799 | Monticello | 9,040 |
| Sanpete | 1,597 | Manti | 11,053 |
| Sevier | 1,929 | Richfield | 10,565 |
| Summit | 1,848 | Coalville | 5,673 |
| Tooele | 6,923 | Tooele | 17,568 |
| Uintah | 4,472 | Vernal | 11,582 |
| Utah | 2,014 | Provo | 106,991 |
| Wasatch | 1,191 | Heber City | 5,308 |
| Washington | 2,427 | Saint George | 10,271 |
| Wayne | 2,486 | Loa | 1,728 |
| Weber | 581 | Ogden | 110,744 |
| **VERMONT** | | | |
| *(14 counties, 9,274 sq. mi. land; pop., 389,881)* | | | |
| Addison | 784 | Middlebury | 20,076 |
| Bennington | 672 | Bennington | 25,088 |
| Caledonia | 612 | Saint Johnsbury | 22,786 |
| Chittenden | 533 | Burlington | 74,425 |
| Essex | 663 | Guildhall | 6,083 |
| Franklin | 660 | Saint Albans | 29,474 |
| Grand Isle | 83 | North Hero | 2,927 |
| Lamoille | 474 | Hyde Park | 11,027 |
| Orange | 690 | Chelsea | 16,014 |
| Orleans | 715 | Newport | 20,143 |
| Rutland | 927 | Rutland | 46,719 |
| Washington | 707 | Montpelier | 42,860 |
| Windham | 787 | Newfane | 29,776 |
| Windsor | 965 | Woodstock | 42,483 |
| **VIRGINIA** | | | |
| *(96 cos., 34 ind. cities, 39,841 sq. mi.; pop., 3,966,949)* | | | |
| Accomack | 476 | Accomac | 30,635 |
| Albemarle | 745 | Charlottesville | 30,969 |
| Alleghany | 446 | Covington | 12,128 |
| Amelia | 366 | Amelia. C. H. | 7,815 |
| Amherst | 470 | Amherst | 22,953 |
| Appomattox | 345 | Appomattox | 9,148 |
| Arlington | 26 | Arlington | 163,401 |
| Augusta | 986 | Staunton | 37,363 |
| Bath | 540 | Warm Springs | 5,335 |
| Bedford | 756 | Bedford | 31,028 |
| Bland | 369 | Bland | 5,982 |
| Botetourt | 548 | Fincastle | 16,715 |
| Brunswick | 579 | Lawrenceville | 17,779 |
| Buchanan | 508 | Grundy | 36,724 |
| Buckingham | 582 | Buckingham | 10,877 |
| Campbell | 530 | Rustburg | 32,958 |
| Caroline | 545 | Bowling Green | 12,725 |
| Carroll | 496 | Hillsville | 23,178 |
| Charles City | 181 | Charles City | 5,492 |
| Charlotte | 470 | Charlotte Court House | 13,368 |
| Chesterfield | 465 | Chesterfield | 71,197 |
| Clarke | 174 | Berryville | 7,942 |
| Craig | 336 | New Castle | 3,356 |
| Culpeper | 389 | Culpeper | 15,088 |
| Cumberland | 291 | Cumberland | 6,360 |
| Dickenson | 335 | Clintwood | 20,211 |
| Dinwiddie | 507 | Dinwiddie | 22,183 |
| Essex | 250 | Tappahannock | 6,690 |
| Fairfax | 405 | Fairfax | 261,417 |
| Fauquier | 660 | Warrenton | 24,066 |
| Floyd | 383 | Floyd | 10,462 |
| Fluvanna | 288 | Palmyra | 7,227 |
| Franklin | 716 | Rocky Mount | 25,925 |
| Frederick | 433 | Winchester | 21,941 |
| Giles | 363 | Pearisburg | 17,219 |
| Gloucester | 228 | Gloucester | 11,919 |
| Goochland | 289 | Goochland | 9,206 |
| Grayson | 454 | Independence | 17,390 |
| Greene | 153 | Stanardsville | 4,715 |
| Greensville | 302 | Emporia | 16,155 |
| Halifax | 799 | Halifax | 33,637 |
| Hanover | 465 | Hanover | 27,550 |
| Henrico | 229 | Richmond | 117,339 |
| Henry | 382 | Martinsville | 40,335 |
| Highland | 416 | Monterey | 3,221 |
| Isle of Wight | 317 | Isle of Wight | 17,164 |
| James City | 153 | Williamsburg | 11,539 |

| County | Land Area sq.mi | County Seats or Court Houses | County Pop. 1960 |
|---|---|---|---|

## VIRGINIA—Continued

| County | Land Area sq.mi | County Seats or Court Houses | County Pop. 1960 |
|---|---|---|---|
| King & Queen. | 318 | King & Queen C. H. | 5,889 |
| King George... | 176 | King George. | 7,243 |
| King William... | 278 | King William. | 7,563 |
| Lancaster.... | 137 | Lancaster.... | 9,174 |
| Lee....... | 438 | Jonesville.... | 25,824 |
| Loudoun.... | 517 | Leesburg.... | 24,549 |
| Louisa.... | 517 | Louisa.... | 12,959 |
| Lunenburg.... | 442 | Lunenburg.... | 12,523 |
| Madison.... | 327 | Madison.... | 8,187 |
| Mathews.... | 89 | Mathews.... | 7,121 |
| Mecklenburg.. | 612 | Boydton.... | 31,428 |
| Middlesex.... | 130 | Saluda.... | 6,319 |
| Montgomery.. | 394 | Christiansburg.. | 32,923 |
| Nansemond... | 408 | Suffolk.... | 31,366 |
| Nelson.... | 471 | Lovingston.... | 12,752 |
| New Kent.... | 201 | New Kent.... | 4,504 |
| Northampton.. | 220 | Eastville.... | 16,966 |
| Northumberland.. | 190 | Heathsville.... | 10,185 |
| Nottoway.... | 308 | Nottoway.... | 15,141 |
| Orange.... | 355 | Orange.... | 12,900 |
| Page.... | 316 | Luray.... | 15,572 |
| Patrick.... | 464 | Stuart.... | 15,282 |
| Pittsylvania.... | 1,012 | Chatham.... | 58,296 |
| Powhatan.... | 269 | Powhatan.... | 6,747 |
| Prince Edward.. | 357 | Farmville.... | 14,121 |
| Prince George.. | 279 | Prince George.... | 20,270 |
| Prince William.. | 347 | Manassas.... | 50,164 |
| Pulaski.... | 328 | Pulaski.... | 27,258 |
| Rappahannock.. | 267 | Washington.... | 5,368 |
| Richmond.... | 190 | Warsaw.... | 6,375 |
| Roanoke.... | 277 | Salem.... | 61,693 |
| Rockbridge.... | 604 | Lexington.... | 24,039 |
| Rockingham.. | 868 | Harrisonburg.... | 40,485 |
| Russell.... | 483 | Lebanon.... | 26,290 |
| Scott.... | 539 | Gate City.... | 25,813 |
| Shenandoah.. | 507 | Woodstock.... | 21,825 |
| Smyth.... | 435 | Marion.... | 31,066 |
| Southampton.. | 606 | Courtland.... | 19,931 |
| Spotsylvania.. | 409 | Spotsylvania.... | 13,819 |
| Stafford.... | 270 | Stafford.... | 16,876 |
| Surry.... | 277 | Surry.... | 6,220 |
| Sussex.... | 494 | Sussex.... | 12,411 |
| Tazewell.... | 522 | Tazewell.... | 44,791 |
| Warren.... | 219 | Front Royal.... | 14,655 |
| Washington.... | 574 | Abingdon.... | 38,076 |
| Westmoreland.. | 229 | Montross.... | 11,042 |
| Wise.... | 412 | Wise.... | 43,579 |
| Wythe.... | 460 | Wytheville.... | 21,975 |
| York.... | 130 | Yorktown.... | 21,583 |

### Independent Cities

| County | Land Area sq.mi | | County Pop. 1960 |
|---|---|---|---|
| Alexandria.... | 15 | ............. | 91,023 |
| Bristol.... | 4 | ............. | 17,144 |
| Buena Vista... | 3 | ............. | 6,300 |
| Charlottesville.. | 6 | ............. | 29,427 |
| Chesapeake.... | 344 | ............. | 73,647 |
| Clifton Forge.. | 2 | ............. | 5,265 |
| Colonial Hghts. | 8 | ............. | 9,587 |
| Covington.... | 4 | ............. | 11,062 |
| Danville.... | 16 | ............. | 46,577 |
| Fairfax.... | 6 | ............. | 13,585 |
| Falls Church.. | 2 | ............. | 10,192 |
| Franklin.... | 4 | ............. | 7,264 |
| Fredericksburg. | 6 | ............. | 13,639 |
| Galax.... | 3 | ............. | 5,254 |
| Hampton.... | 55 | ............. | 89,258 |
| Harrisonburg.. | 3 | ............. | 11,916 |
| Hopewell.... | 7 | ............. | 17,895 |
| Lynchburg.... | 25 | ............. | 54,790 |
| Martinsville.. | 10 | ............. | 18,798 |
| Newport News.. | 69 | ............. | 113,662 |
| Norfolk.... | 52 | ............. | 304,869 |
| Norton.... | 3 | ............. | 5,013 |
| Petersburg.... | 8 | ............. | 36,750 |
| Portsmouth.... | 18 | ............. | 114,773 |
| Radford.... | 5 | ............. | 9,371 |
| Richmond.... | 38 | ............. | 219,958 |
| Roanoke.... | 26 | ............. | 97,110 |
| South Boston.. | 2 | ............. | 5,974 |
| Staunton.... | 9 | ............. | 22,035 |
| Suffolk.... | 2 | ............. | 12,609 |
| Virginia Beach. | 255 | ............. | 85,218 |
| Waynesboro... | 7 | ............. | 15,694 |
| Williamsburg.. | 3 | ............. | 6,832 |
| Winchester.... | 3 | ............. | 15,110 |

## WASHINGTON

(39 counties, 66,663 sq. mi. land; pop., 2,853,214)

| County | Land Area sq.mi | County Seats or Court Houses | County Pop. 1960 |
|---|---|---|---|
| Adams....... | 1,894 | Ritzville.... | 9,929 |
| Asotin....... | 633 | Asotin.... | 12,909 |
| Benton....... | 1,722 | Prosser.... | 62,070 |
| Chelan....... | 2,926 | Wenatchee.... | 40,744 |
| Clallam....... | 1,753 | Port Angeles.... | 30,022 |
| Clark....... | 627 | Vancouver.... | 93,809 |
| Columbia....... | 860 | Dayton.... | 4,569 |
| Cowlitz....... | 1,144 | Kelso.... | 57,801 |
| Douglas....... | 1,839 | Waterville.... | 14,890 |
| Ferry....... | 2,202 | Republic.... | 3,889 |
| Franklin....... | 1,260 | Pasco.... | 23,342 |
| Garfield....... | 713 | Pomeroy.... | 2,976 |

## WASHINGTON—Continued

| County | Land Area sq.mi | County Seats or Court Houses | County Pop. 1960 |
|---|---|---|---|
| Grant.... | 2,681 | Ephrata.... | 46,477 |
| Grays Harbor.. | 1,910 | Montesano.... | 54,465 |
| Island.... | 212 | Coupeville.... | 19,638 |
| Jefferson.... | 1,805 | Port Townsend.. | 9,639 |
| King.... | 2,131 | Seattle.... | 935,014 |
| Kitsap.... | 393 | Port Orchard.... | 84,176 |
| Kittitas.... | 2,320 | Ellensburg.... | 20,467 |
| Klickitat.... | 1,908 | Goldendale.... | 13,455 |
| Lewis.... | 2,449 | Chehalis.... | 41,858 |
| Lincoln.... | 2,306 | Davenport.... | 10,919 |
| Mason.... | 962 | Shelton.... | 16,251 |
| Okanogan.... | 5,301 | Okanogan.... | 25,520 |
| Pacific.... | 908 | South Bend.... | 14,674 |
| Pend Oreille.. | 1,402 | Newport.... | 6,914 |
| Pierce.... | 1,676 | Tacoma.... | 321,590 |
| San Juan.... | 179 | Friday Harbor.. | 2,872 |
| Skagit.... | 1,735 | Mount Vernon.. | 51,350 |
| Skamania.... | 1,672 | Stevenson.... | 5,207 |
| Snohomish.... | 2,098 | Everett.... | 172,199 |
| Spokane.... | 1,758 | Spokane.... | 278,333 |
| Stevens.... | 2,481 | Colville.... | 17,884 |
| Thurston.... | 714 | Olympia.... | 55,049 |
| Wahkiakum.... | 261 | Cathlamet.... | 3,426 |
| Walla Walla.. | 1,267 | Walla Walla.... | 42,195 |
| Whatcom.... | 2,126 | Bellingham.... | 70,317 |
| Whitman.... | 2,166 | Colfax.... | 31,263 |
| Yakima.... | 4,271 | Yakima.... | 145,112 |

## WEST VIRGINIA

(55 counties, 24,084 sq. mi. land; pop., 1,860,421)

| County | Land Area sq.mi | County Seats or Court Houses | County Pop. 1960 |
|---|---|---|---|
| Barbour.... | 341 | Philippi.... | 15,474 |
| Berkeley.... | 316 | Martinsburg.... | 33,791 |
| Boone.... | 501 | Madison.... | 28,764 |
| Braxton.... | 517 | Sutton.... | 15,152 |
| Brooke.... | 88 | Wellsburg.... | 28,940 |
| Cabell.... | 279 | Huntington.... | 108,202 |
| Calhoun.... | 281 | Grantsville.... | 7,948 |
| Clay.... | 343 | Clay.... | 11,942 |
| Doddridge.... | 319 | West Union.... | 6,970 |
| Fayette.... | 662 | Fayetteville.... | 61,731 |
| Gilmer.... | 339 | Glenville.... | 8,050 |
| Grant.... | 478 | Petersburg.... | 8,304 |
| Greenbrier.... | 1,026 | Lewisburg.... | 34,446 |
| Hampshire.... | 639 | Romney.... | 11,705 |
| Hancock.... | 83 | New Cumberland.. | 39,615 |
| Hardy.... | 585 | Moorefield.... | 9,308 |
| Harrison.... | 418 | Clarksburg.... | 77,856 |
| Jackson.... | 461 | Ripley.... | 18,541 |
| Jefferson.... | 211 | Charles Town.. | 18,665 |
| Kanawha.... | 907 | Charleston.... | 252,925 |
| Lewis.... | 392 | Weston.... | 19,711 |
| Lincoln.... | 438 | Hamlin.... | 20,267 |
| Logan.... | 456 | Logan.... | 61,570 |
| McDowell.... | 533 | Welch.... | 71,359 |
| Marion.... | 311 | Fairmont.... | 63,717 |
| Marshall.... | 304 | Moundsville.... | 38,041 |
| Mason.... | 433 | Point Pleasant.. | 24,459 |
| Mercer.... | 417 | Princeton.... | 68,206 |
| Mineral.... | 330 | Keyser.... | 22,354 |
| Mingo.... | 423 | Williamson.... | 39,742 |
| Monongalia.... | 365 | Morgantown.... | 55,617 |
| Monroe.... | 473 | Union.... | 11,584 |
| Morgan.... | 233 | Berkeley Springs.. | 8,376 |
| Nicholas.... | 650 | Summersville.... | 25,414 |
| Ohio.... | 106 | Wheeling.... | 68,437 |
| Pendleton.... | 695 | Franklin.... | 8,093 |
| Pleasants.... | 129 | St. Marys.... | 7,124 |
| Pocahontas.... | 943 | Marlinton.... | 10,136 |
| Preston.... | 645 | Kingwood.... | 27,233 |
| Putnam.... | 348 | Winfield.... | 23,561 |
| Raleigh.... | 605 | Beckley.... | 77,826 |
| Randolph.... | 1,036 | Elkins.... | 26,349 |
| Ritchie.... | 452 | Harrisville.... | 10,877 |
| Roane.... | 486 | Spencer.... | 15,720 |
| Summers.... | 350 | Hinton.... | 15,640 |
| Taylor.... | 174 | Grafton.... | 15,010 |
| Tucker.... | 421 | Parsons.... | 7,750 |
| Tyler.... | 256 | Middlebourne.... | 10,026 |
| Upshur.... | 352 | Buckhannon.... | 18,292 |
| Wayne.... | 513 | Wayne.... | 38,977 |
| Webster.... | 551 | Webster Springs.. | 13,719 |
| Wetzel.... | 363 | New Martinsville.. | 19,347 |
| Wirt.... | 235 | Elizabeth.... | 4,391 |
| Wood.... | 368 | Parkersburg.... | 78,331 |
| Wyoming.... | 504 | Pineville.... | 34,836 |

## WISCONSIN

(72 counties, 54,464 sq. mi. land; pop., 3,951,777)

| County | Land Area sq.mi | County Seats or Court Houses | County Pop. 1960 |
|---|---|---|---|
| Adams....... | 646 | Friendship.... | 7,566 |
| Ashland....... | 1,038 | Ashland.... | 17,375 |
| Barron....... | 864 | Barron.... | 34,270 |
| Bayfield....... | 1,460 | Washburn.... | 11,910 |
| Brown....... | 524 | Green Bay.... | 125,082 |
| Buffalo....... | 711 | Alma.... | 14,202 |
| Burnett....... | 840 | Grantsburg.... | 9,214 |
| Calumet....... | 322 | Chilton.... | 22,268 |
| Chippewa....... | 1,018 | Chippewa Falls.. | 45,096 |
| Clark....... | 1,221 | Neillsville.... | 31,527 |
| Columbia....... | 776 | Portage.... | 36,708 |
| Crawford....... | 568 | Prairie du Chien.. | 16,351 |
| Dane....... | 1,198 | Madison.... | 222,095 |
| Dodge....... | 889 | Juneau.... | 63,170 |

| County | Land Area sq.mi | County Seats or Court Houses | County Pop. 1960 | County | Land Area sq.mi | County Seats or Court Houses | County Pop. 1960 |
|---|---|---|---|---|---|---|---|
| **WISCONSIN—Continued** | | | | **WISCONSIN—Continued** | | | |
| Door........ | 492 | Sturgeon Bay.... | 20,685 | Sawyer........ | 1,259 | Hayward......... | 9,475 |
| Douglas...... | 1,305 | Superior....... | 45,008 | Shawano....... | 1,175 | Shawano......... | 32,006 |
| Dunn........ | 853 | Menomonie...... | 26,156 | Sheboygan..... | 505 | Sheboygan....... | 86,484 |
| Eau Claire.... | 647 | Eau Claire..... | 58,300 | Taylor........ | 975 | Medford........ | 17,843 |
| Florence..... | 487 | Florence....... | 3,437 | Trempealeau... | 735 | Whitehall....... | 23,377 |
| Fond du Lac.. | 725 | Fond du Lac.... | 75,085 | Vernon........ | 802 | Viroqua......... | 25,663 |
| Forest........ | 1,007 | Crandon....... | 7,542 | Vilas......... | 867 | Eagle River..... | 9,332 |
| Grant........ | 1,147 | Lancaster...... | 44,419 | Walworth..... | 557 | Elkhorn........ | 52,368 |
| Green........ | 585 | Monroe....... | 25,851 | Washburn..... | 817 | Shell Lake...... | 10,301 |
| Green Lake... | 354 | Green Lake..... | 15,418 | Washington.... | 429 | West Bend...... | 46,119 |
| Iowa......... | 762 | Dodgeville..... | 19,631 | Waukesha..... | 555 | Waukesha....... | 158,249 |
| Iron......... | 747 | Hurley........ | 7,830 | Waupaca...... | 751 | Waupaca........ | 35,340 |
| Jackson...... | 999 | Black River Falls. | 15,151 | Waushara..... | 627 | Wautoma........ | 13,497 |
| Jefferson..... | 564 | Jefferson...... | 50,094 | Winnebago.... | 448 | Oshkosh........ | 107,928 |
| Juneau....... | 774 | Mauston....... | 17,490 | Wood......... | 807 | Wisconsin Rapids.. | 59,105 |
| Kenosha...... | 272 | Kenosha....... | 100,615 | | | | |
| Kewaunee.... | 330 | Kewaunee...... | 18,282 | **WYOMING** | | | |
| La Crosse.... | 451 | La Crosse...... | 72,465 | *(23 counties; 97,281 sq. mi. land; pop., 330,066)* | | | |
| Lafayette.... | 643 | Darlington..... | 18,142 | Albany........ | 4,248 | Laramie........ | 21,290 |
| Langlade..... | 856 | Antigo........ | 19,916 | Big Horn...... | 3,177 | Basin.......... | 11,898 |
| Lincoln...... | 892 | Merrill........ | 22,338 | Campbell..... | 4,756 | Gillette........ | 5,861 |
| Manitowoc... | 590 | Manitowoc..... | 75,215 | Carbon........ | 7,905 | Rawlins........ | 14,937 |
| Marathon.... | 1,586 | Wausau....... | 88,874 | Converse..... | 4,281 | Douglas........ | 6,366 |
| Marinette.... | 1,378 | Marinette...... | 34,660 | Crook......... | 2,882 | Sundance....... | 4,691 |
| Marquette.... | 455 | Montello....... | 8,516 | Fremont...... | 9,196 | Lander......... | 26,168 |
| Menomonee... | 362 | Keshena....... | 2,606 | Goshen....... | 2,223 | Torrington..... | 11,941 |
| Milwaukee... | 237 | Milwaukee..... | 1,036,041 | Hot Springs... | 2,022 | Thermopolis.... | 6,365 |
| Monroe...... | 915 | Sparta........ | 31,241 | Johnson...... | 4,175 | Buffalo........ | 5,475 |
| Oconto...... | 1,104 | Oconto....... | 24,849 | Laramie...... | 2,703 | Cheyenne...... | 60,149 |
| Oneida...... | 1,112 | Rhinelander.... | 22,112 | Lincoln....... | 4,098 | Kemmerer...... | 9,018 |
| Outagamie... | 634 | Appleton....... | 101,794 | Natrona...... | 5,342 | Casper......... | 49,623 |
| Ozaukee..... | 236 | Port Washington.. | 38,441 | Niobrara..... | 2,614 | Lusk.......... | 3,750 |
| Pepin....... | 235 | Durand........ | 7,332 | Park......... | 5,209 | Cody.......... | 16,574 |
| Pierce....... | 590 | Ellsworth...... | 22,503 | Platte........ | 2,086 | Wheatland...... | 7,195 |
| Polk........ | 931 | Balsam Lake.... | 24,968 | Sheridan..... | 2,532 | Sheridan....... | 18,989 |
| Portage...... | 806 | Stevens Point... | 36,964 | Sublette...... | 4,851 | Pinedale....... | 3,778 |
| Price........ | 1,260 | Phillips........ | 14,370 | Sweetwater... | 10,473 | Green River..... | 17,920 |
| Racine....... | 337 | Racine........ | 141,781 | Teton........ | 2,805 | Jackson........ | 3,062 |
| Richland..... | 583 | Richland Center.. | 17,684 | Uinta........ | 2,806 | Evanston....... | 7,484 |
| Rock........ | 721 | Janesville...... | 113,913 | Washakie..... | 2,262 | Worland........ | 8,883 |
| Rusk........ | 906 | Ladysmith...... | 14,794 | Weston....... | 2,407 | Newcastle...... | 7,929 |
| St. Croix..... | 735 | Hudson........ | 29,164 | Yel'stone Nat. | | | |
| Sauk........ | 841 | Baraboo....... | 36,179 | Park (part).. | 2,944 | .............. | 420 |

## Population of World's Largest Urban Areas

City populations often cannot be used to compare urban areas because city limits may underbound or overbound the built-up or urban area. The problem of comparison is compounded by the difficulty in obtaining reliable population data for a common year. The ranking of urban areas below represents one attempt at comparing the world's largest urban areas, taking into account, where necessary and within the limits of available data, urban development extending outward from the principal city named in the table. Thus, the Tokyo area in 1965 included the cities of Tokyo and Yokohama plus neighboring smaller cities, towns and villages, and the New York urban area in 1960 included part or all the population of 8 New Jersey and 5 New York counties in addition to the 5 boroughs of New York city. On the other hand, the urban areas of Seoul and Madrid in 1965 did not run beyond the city limits.

| | | | |
|---|---|---|---|
| Tokyo, Japan (census 1965)........... | 14,770,727 | Djakarta, Indonesia (census 1961)...... | 2,906,533 |
| *New York, N. Y. (census 1960)...... | 14,114,927 | Delhi, India (est. 1966).............. | 2,793,131 |
| London, England (est. 1965).......... | 7,948,270 | Madrid, Spain (est. 1965)............ | 2,599,330 |
| Osaka, Japan (census 1965).......... | 7,781,000 | Sydney, Australia (est. 1966)........ | 2,540,000 |
| Paris, France (census 1962).......... | 7,369,387 | Rome, Italy (est. 1965).............. | 2,514,171 |
| Shanghai, China (est. 1958)......... | 6,977,000 | Manchester, England (est. 1965)...... | 2,437,349 |
| Buenos Aires, Argentina (census 1960).. | 6,762,629 | San Francisco, Calif. (census 1960)... | 2,430,663 |
| Moscow, U.S.S.R. (est. 1968)....... | 6,567,000 | Shenyang (Mukden), China (est. 1958).. | 2,423,000 |
| Los Angeles, Calif. (census 1960)...... | 6,488,791 | Boston, Mass. (census 1960)........ | 2,413,236 |
| Chicago, Ill. (census 1960)........... | 5,959,213 | Birmingham, England (est. 1965)...... | 2,392,610 |
| Sao Paulo, Brazil (est. 1966)......... | 5,383,000 | Montreal, Canada (est. 1965)........ | 2,321,000 |
| Bombay, India (est. 1966)........... | 4,784,136 | Teheran, Iran (est. 1963)............ | 2,317,116 |
| Calcutta, India (est. 1966)........... | 4,703,398 | Manila, Philippines (census 1960)..... | 2,256,471 |
| Mexico City, Mexico (census 1960)..... | 4,659,691 | Santiago, Chile (est. 1965).......... | 2,248,378 |
| Essen (Ruhr-Gebiet), W. Germany | | Melbourne, Australia (est. 1966)...... | 2,229,000 |
| (est. 1966).................... | 4,259,230 | Wuhan, China (est. 1958)........... | 2,226,000 |
| Cairo, United Arab Rep. (census 1966).. | 4,196,998 | Chungking, China (est. 1958)........ | 2,165,000 |
| Peking, China (est. 1958)............ | 4,148,000 | Bangkok, Thailand (est. 1963)....... | 2,106,881 |
| Rio de Janeiro, Brazil (est. 1967)...... | 4,076,000 | Toronto, Canada (est. 1965)......... | 2,066,000 |
| Seoul, Korea (census 1965)........... | 3,805,261 | Budapest, Hungary (est. 1966)....... | 1,951,521 |
| Leningrad, U.S.S.R. (est. 1968)...... | 3,755,000 | Karachi, Pakistan (census 1961)...... | 1,912,598 |
| Detroit, Mich.-Windsor, Ont. (a)..... | 3,731,074 | Madras, India (est. 1966)........... | 1,896,122 |
| Philadelphia, Pa. (census 1960)....... | 3,635,228 | Canton, China (est. 1958).......... | 1,867,000 |
| Tientsin, China (est. 1958).......... | 3,278,000 | Athens, Greece (census 1961)........ | 1,852,709 |
| Berlin, E. & W. Germany (est. 1966).. | 3,269,577 | Hamburg, W. Germany (est. 1966).... | 1,847,267 |
| Victoria, Hong Kong (by-census 1966).. | 3,014,900 | | |

*New York-Northeastern New Jersey urbanized area, including the 5 boroughs of New York City plus all or part of the counties of Nassau, Putnam, Rockland, Suffolk and Westchester in New York State and all or part of the counties of Bergen, Essex, Hudson, Middlesex, Morris, Passaic, Somerset and Union in New Jersey. (a) U. S. data, 1960; Canadian data, 1961.

## Area and Population of the World

Source: Statistical Office of the United Nations, June, 1968

| Continent | Area[1] (km2)* | Midyear '67 estimated population | Continent | Area[1] (km2)* | Midyear '67 estimated population |
|---|---|---|---|---|---|
| Africa............ | 30,312,924 | 328,134,000 | Oceania .......... | 8,510,947 | 18,127,000 |
| America, North[2].... | 24,246,904 | 304,439,000 | USSR............ | 22,402,200 | 235,543,000 |
| America, South..... | 17,842,516 | 174,246,000 | | | |
| Asia[3]............. | 27,530,116 | 1,907,481,000 | World.......... | 135,774,513 | 3,419,420,000 |
| Europe[4].......... | 4,928,906 | 451,450,000 | | | |

*One square kilometer (km2) equals 0.386 sq. mi. [1]Including inland waters, but not some uninhabited polar regions and islands. [2]Hawaii, Central America and Caribbean Islands included in N. A. [3]Excluding USSR but including all of Turkey. [4]Excluding USSR and European part of Turkey.

# U. S. Cities with Standard Metropolitan Statistical Areas

**POPULATION OF 228 SMSA'S AND THEIR CENTRAL CITIES**

Areas over 1,000,000 population are numbered according to rank in 1965 *1966 provisional figures

Source: Bureau of the Census

| Standard Metropolitan Statistical Area | 1965 est. (1,000) | 1960 Metropol. area total | 1960 In central cities | 1950 Metropol. area total | 1950 In central cities |
|---|---|---|---|---|---|
| Abilene, Texas | 126 | 120,377 | 90,368 | 85,517 | 45,570 |
| Akron, Ohio | *652 | 605,367 | 290,351 | 473,986 | 274,605 |
| Albany, Ga. | *701 | 75,680 | 55,890 | 43,617 | 31,155 |
| Albany-Schenectady-Troy, N. Y. | 697 | 657,503 | 278,800 | 589,359 | 299,091 |
| Albuquerque, N. Mex. | 288 | 262,199 | 201,189 | 145,673 | 96,815 |
| Allentown-Bethlehem-Easton, Pa.-N. J. | *516 | 492,168 | 215,710 | 437,824 | 208,728 |
| Altoona, Pa. | 137 | 137,270 | 69,407 | 139,154 | 77,177 |
| Amarillo, Texas | 168 | 149,493 | 137,969 | 87,140 | 74,246 |
| Anaheim-Santa Ana-Garden Gr., Calif. (25) | *1,164 | 703,925 | 288,772 | 216,224 | 60,089 |
| Anderson, Ind. | 130 | 125,819 | 49,061 | 103,911 | 46,820 |
| Ann Arbor, Mich. | 187 | 172,440 | 67,340 | 134,606 | 48,251 |
| Asheville, N. C. | 143 | 130,074 | 60,192 | 124,403 | 53,000 |
| Atlanta, Ga. (21) | *1,258 | 1,017,188 | 487,455 | 726,989 | 331,314 |
| Atlantic City, N. J. | 179 | 160,880 | 59,544 | 132,399 | 61,657 |
| Augusta, Ga.-S. C. | 237 | 216,639 | 70,626 | 162,013 | 71,508 |
| Austin, Texas | 247 | 212,136 | 186,455 | 160,980 | 132,459 |
| Bakersfield, Calif. | 319 | 291,984 | 56,848 | 228,309 | 34,784 |
| Baltimore, Md. (12) | *1,980 | 1,803,745 | 939,024 | 1,405,399 | 949,708 |
| Baton Rouge, La. | 255 | 230,058 | 152,419 | 158,436 | 125,629 |
| Bay City, Mich. | 109 | 107,042 | 53,604 | 88,461 | 52,523 |
| Beaumont-Port Arthur, Texas | 313 | 306,016 | 211,456 | 235,650 | 151,544 |
| Billings, Mont. | 84 | 79,016 | 52,851 | 55,875 | 31,834 |
| Biloxi (Gulfport) Miss. | ..... | 119,489 | 74,257 | 84,073 | 60,084 |
| Binghamton, N. Y. | 297 | 283,600 | 75,941 | 246,834 | 80,674 |
| Birmingham, Ala. | *734 | 721,207 | 340,887 | 558,928 | 326,037 |
| Bloomington-Normal, Ill. | 99 | 83,877 | 49,628 | 76,577 | 43,935 |
| Boise City, Idaho | 99 | 93,460 | 34,481 | 70,649 | 34,393 |
| Boston, Mass. (6) | *3,201 | 3,109,158 | 791,329 | 2,410,572 | 801,444 |
| Bridgeport, Stamford, Norwalk, Conn. | 746 | 653,589 | 156,748 | 410,784 | 158,709 |
| Brockton, Mass. | 296 | 149,458 | 72,813 | 119,728 | 62,860 |
| Brownsville-Harlingen-San Benito, Texas | 151 | 151,098 | 105,669 | 125,170 | 72,566 |
| Buffalo, N. Y. (16) | *1,323 | 1,306,957 | 532,759 | 1,089,230 | 580,132 |
| Canton, Ohio | 356 | 340,345 | 113,631 | 283,194 | 116,912 |
| Cedar Rapids, Iowa | 148 | 136,899 | 92,035 | 104,274 | 72,296 |
| Champaign-Urbana, Ill. | 133 | 132,436 | 76,877 | 106,100 | 62,397 |
| Charleston, S. C. | 296 | 254,578 | 65,925 | 195,107 | 70,174 |
| Charleston, W. Va. | 245 | 252,925 | 85,796 | 239,629 | 73,501 |
| Charlotte, N. C. | 360 | 316,781 | 201,564 | 239,086 | 134,042 |
| Chattanooga, Tenn.-Ga. | 292 | 283,169 | 130,009 | 246,453 | 131,041 |
| Chicago, Ill. (see also consolidated areas) (3) | *6,632 | 6,220,913 | 3,550,404 | 5,177,868 | 3,620,962 |
| Cincinnati, Ohio-Ky. (17) | *1,353 | 1,268,479 | 502,550 | 1,023,245 | 503,998 |
| Cleveland, Ohio (11) | *2,004 | 1,909,483 | 876,050 | 1,532,574 | 914,808 |
| Colorado Springs, Colo. | 176 | 143,742 | 70,194 | 74,523 | 45,472 |
| Columbia, S. C. | 289 | 260,828 | 97,433 | 186,844 | 86,914 |
| Columbus, Ga.-Ala. | 260 | 217,985 | 116,779 | 170,541 | 79,611 |
| Columbus, Ohio | *851 | 754,885 | 471,316 | 563,040 | 375,901 |
| Corpus Christi, Texas | 286 | 266,594 | 167,690 | 656,471 | 108,287 |
| Dallas, Texas (19) | *1,352 | 1,119,410 | 679,684 | 743,501 | 434,462 |
| Davenport, Ia.-Rock Island-Moline, Ill. | 339 | 319,375 | 183,549 | 280,748 | 160,656 |
| Dayton, Ohio | *803 | 727,121 | 262,332 | 545,723 | 243,872 |
| Decatur, Ill. | 122 | 118,257 | 78,004 | 98,853 | 66,269 |
| Denver, Colo. (26) | *1,081 | 929,383 | 493,887 | 612,128 | 415,786 |
| Des Moines, Iowa | 271 | 266,315 | 208,982 | 226,010 | 177,965 |
| Detroit, Mich. (5) | *4,060 | 3,762,360 | 1,670,144 | 3,016,197 | 1,849,568 |
| Dubuque, Iowa | 87 | 80,048 | 56,606 | 71,337 | 49,671 |
| Duluth-Superior, Minn.-Wis. | 267 | 276,596 | 140,447 | 252,777 | 139,836 |
| Durham, N. C. | 123 | 154,965 | 78,302 | 101,639 | 71,311 |
| El Paso, Texas | 344 | 314,070 | 276,687 | 194,968 | 130,485 |
| Erie, Pa. | 255 | 250,682 | 138,440 | 219,388 | 130,803 |
| Eugene, Ore. | 194 | 162,890 | 50,977 | 125,776 | 35,879 |
| Evansville, Ind.-Ky. | 223 | 222,890 | 141,543 | 212,664 | 128,636 |
| Fall River, Mass.-R. I. | ..... | 138,156 | 99,942 | 137,298 | 111,963 |
| Fargo-Moorhead, N. Dak.-Minn. | 110 | 106,027 | 69,596 | 89,240 | 53,126 |
| Fayetteville, N. C. | 193 | 148,418 | 47,106 | 96,006 | 34,715 |
| Fitchburg-Leominster, Mass. | ..... | 90,158 | 70,950 | 80,528 | 66,766 |
| Flint, Mich. | *461 | 416,239 | 196,940 | 306,757 | 163,143 |
| Fort Lauderdale-Hollywood, Fla. | 441 | 333,946 | 118,885 | 83,933 | 50,679 |
| Fort Smith, Ark. | 154 | 135,110 | 52,991 | 141,978 | 47,942 |
| Fort Wayne, Ind. | 259 | 232,196 | 161,776 | 183,722 | 133,607 |
| Fort Worth, Texas | *638 | 573,215 | 356,268 | 392,643 | 278,778 |
| Fresno, Calif. | *409 | 365,945 | 133,929 | 276,515 | 91,669 |
| Gadsden, Ala. | 94 | 96,980 | 58,088 | 93,892 | 55,725 |
| Galveston-Texas City, Texas | 157 | 140,364 | 99,240 | 113,066 | 83,188 |
| Gary-Hammond-East Chicago, Ind. | *599 | 573,548 | 347,687 | 408,228 | 275,768 |
| Grand Rapids, Mich. | *505 | 461,906 | 177,313 | 362,043 | 176,515 |
| Great Falls, Mont. | 82 | 73,418 | 55,244 | 53,027 | 39,214 |
| Green Bay, Wis. | 137 | 125,082 | 62,888 | 98,214 | 52,735 |
| Greensboro-Winston-Salem-High Point, N. C. | *571 | 520,249 | 292,772 | 410,129 | 202,173 |
| Greenville, S. C. | 267 | 255,806 | 66,188 | 208,210 | 58,161 |
| Hamilton-Middletown, Ohio | 208 | 199,076 | 114,469 | 147,203 | 91,646 |
| Harrisburg, Pa. | *392 | 371,653 | 79,697 | 317,023 | 89,544 |
| Hartford, New Britain, Conn. | *777 | 689,555 | 162,178 | 420,009 | 177,397 |
| Honolulu, Hawaii | *585 | 500,409 | 294,194 | 353,020 | 248,034 |
| Houston Texas | (14) *1,740 | 1,418,323 | 938,219 | 806,701 | 596,163 |
| Huntington-Ashland, W. Va.-Ky.-Ohio | 260 | 254,780 | 114,910 | 245,795 | 117,484 |
| Huntsville, Ala. | 224 | 153,861 | 72,365 | 108,669 | 16,437 |
| Indianapolis, Ind. | *1,027 | 944,475 | 476,258 | 703,129 | 427,173 |
| Jackson, Mich. | 137 | 131,994 | 50,720 | 107,925 | 51,088 |
| Jackson, Miss. | 250 | 221,367 | 144,422 | 171,045 | 98,271 |
| Jacksonville, Fla. | *500 | 455,411 | 201,030 | 304,029 | 204,517 |
| Jersey City, N. J. | *616 | 610,734 | 276,101 | 647,437 | 299,017 |
| Johnstown, Pa. | 270 | 280,733 | 53,949 | 291,354 | 63,232 |
| Kalamazoo, Mich. | 181 | 169,712 | 82,089 | 126,707 | 57,704 |

| Standard Metropolitan Statistical Area | 1965 est. (1,000) | 1960 Metropol. area total | 1960 In central cities | 1950 Metropol. area total | 1950 In central cities |
|---|---|---|---|---|---|
| Kansas City, Mo.-Kans.................. (22) | *1,209 | 1,092,545 | 475,539 | 848,655 | 456,622 |
| Kenosha, Wis........................... | 114 | 100,615 | 67,899 | 75,238 | 54,368 |
| Knoxville, Tenn........................ | *388 | 368,080 | 111,827 | 337,105 | 124,769 |
| Lafayette, La.......................... | 98 | 84,656 | 40,400 | 57,743 | 33,541 |
| Lafayette-West Lafayette, Ind......... | 96 | 89,122 | 55,010 | 74,473 | 47,441 |
| Lake Charles, La...................... | 135 | 145,475 | 63,392 | 89,635 | 41,272 |
| Lancaster, Pa......................... | 289 | 278,359 | 61,055 | 234,717 | 63,774 |
| Lansing, Mich......................... | 336 | 298,949 | 107,807 | 244,159 | 92,129 |
| Laredo, Texas......................... | 76 | 64,791 | 60,678 | 56,141 | 51,910 |
| Las Vegas, Nev........................ | 232 | 127,016 | 64,405 | 48,289 | 24,624 |
| Lawrence-Haverhill, Mass.-N. H........ | .... | 199,136 | 117,279 | 190,428 | 127,816 |
| Lawton, Okla.......................... | 99 | 90,803 | 61,697 | 55,165 | 34,757 |
| Lewiston-Auburn, Me................... | 91 | 70,295 | 65,253 | 68,426 | 64,108 |
| Lexington, Ky......................... | 159 | 131,906 | 62,810 | 100,746 | 55,534 |
| Lima, Ohio............................ | 112 | 160,862 | 51,037 | 88,183 | 50,246 |
| Lincoln, Nebr......................... | 161 | 155,272 | 128,521 | 119,742 | 98,884 |
| Little Rock-North Little Rock, Ark..... | 279 | 271,936 | 165,845 | 196,685 | 136,310 |
| Lorain-Elyria, Ohio................... | 240 | 217,500 | 112,714 | 148,162 | 81,509 |
| Los Angeles-Long Beach, Calif. ........ (2) | *6,789 | 6,038,771 | 2,823,183 | 4,151,687 | 2,221,125 |
| Louisville, Ky.-Ind................... | *775 | 725,139 | 390,639 | 576,900 | 369,129 |
| Lubbock, Texas........................ | 185 | 156,271 | 128,691 | 101,048 | 71,747 |
| Lynchburg, Va......................... | 119 | 110,701 | 54,790 | 96,936 | 47,727 |
| Macon, Ga............................. | 201 | 180,403 | 69,764 | 135,043 | 70,252 |
| Madison, Wis.......................... | 260 | 222,095 | 126,706 | 169,357 | 96,056 |
| Manchester, N. H...................... | 205 | 102,861 | 88,282 | 93,338 | 82,732 |
| Mansfield, Ohio....................... | 126 | 117,761 | 47,325 | 91,305 | 43,564 |
| McAllen-Pharr-Edinburg, Tex........... | 202 | 180,904 | 65,540 | 160,446 | 41,140 |
| Memphis, Tenn......................... | *752 | 674,583 | 497,524 | 529,577 | 396,000 |
| Miami, Fla............................ (27) | *1,081 | 935,047 | 291,688 | 495,084 | 249,276 |
| Midland, Texas........................ | 67 | 67,717 | 62,625 | 25,785 | 21,713 |
| Milwaukee, Wis........................ (20) | *1,331 | 1,278,850 | 741,324 | 980,309 | 637,392 |
| Minneapolis-St. Paul, Minn........... (15) | *1,629 | 1,482,030 | 796,283 | 1,151,053 | 833,067 |
| Mobile, Ala........................... | *385 | 363,389 | 194,856 | 272,102 | 129,009 |
| Monroe, La............................ | 112 | 101,663 | 52,219 | 74,713 | 38,572 |
| Montgomery, Ala....................... | 207 | 199,734 | 134,393 | 170,614 | 106,525 |
| Muncie, Ind........................... | 117 | 110,938 | 68,603 | 90,242 | 58,479 |
| Muskegon-Muskegon Heights, Mich...... | 153 | 149,943 | 66,037 | 121,545 | 67,257 |
| Nashville, Tenn....................... | *523 | 463,628 | 170,874 | 381,609 | 174,307 |
| New Bedford, Mass..................... | 411 | 143,176 | 102,477 | 141,984 | 109,189 |
| New Haven, Conn....................... | 704 | 320,836 | 152,048 | 273,049 | 164,443 |
| New London-Groton-Norwich, Conn...... | 216 | 170,981 | 72,688 | 134,612 | 68,184 |
| New Orleans, La....................... (28) | *1,044 | 907,123 | 627,525 | 712,393 | 570,445 |
| New York, N. Y. (includes 5 boroughs of New York City plus Nassau, Rockland, Suffolk and Westchester Counties, N. Y.—see also consolidated areas below)..................... (1) | *11,410 | 10,694,632 | 7,781,984 | 9,555,943 | 7,891,957 |
| New York, NE N.J. (SCA)............... | 15,821 | 14,759,429 | ...... | ...... | ...... |
| Newark, N. J.......................... (13) | *1,862 | 1,689,420 | 405,220 | 1,468,458 | 438,776 |
| Newport News-Hampton, Va.............. | 272 | 224,503 | 202,920 | 154,977 | 143,222 |
| Norfolk-Portsmouth, Va................ | *637 | 578,507 | 419,642 | 446,200 | 293,552 |
| Odessa, Texas......................... | 93 | 90,995 | 80,338 | 42,102 | 29,495 |
| Ogden, Utah........................... | 120 | 110,744 | 70,197 | 83,319 | 57,112 |
| Oklahoma City, Okla................... | *588 | 511,833 | 324,253 | 392,439 | 243,504 |
| Omaha, Nebr.-Iowa..................... | *520 | 457,873 | 301,598 | 366,395 | 251,117 |
| Orlando, Fla.......................... | 372 | 318,487 | 88,135 | 141,833 | 52,367 |
| Oxnard-Ventura, Calif................. | 318 | 199,138 | 69,379 | 114,647 | 38,101 |
| Paterson-Clifton-Passaic, N. J....... (18) | *1,318 | 1,186,873 | 279,710 | 876,232 | 261,549 |
| Pensacola, Fla........ .............. | 224 | 203,376 | 56,752 | 131,260 | 43,479 |
| Peoria, Ill........................... | 320 | 313,412 | 103,162 | 271,847 | 111,856 |
| Philadelphia, Pa.-N. J................ (4) | *4,690 | 4,342,897 | 2,002,512 | 3,671,048 | 2,071,605 |
| Phoenix, Ariz......................... | *831 | 663,510 | 439,170 | 331,770 | 106,818 |
| Pine Bluff, Ark....................... | 86 | 81,373 | 44,037 | 76,075 | 37,162 |
| Pittsburgh, Pa........................ (9) | *2,376 | 2,405,435 | 604,332 | 2,213,236 | 576,806 |
| Pittsfield, Mass...................... | 144 | 76,772 | 57,879 | 68,636 | 53,348 |
| Portland, Maine....................... | 197 | 139,122 | 72,566 | 133,983 | 77,634 |
| Portland, Ore.-Wash................... | *908 | 821,897 | 372,676 | 704,829 | 373,628 |
| Providence-Pawtucket, R. I.-Mass...... | *736 | 821,101 | 357,003 | 763,902 | 330,110 |
| Provo-Orem, Utah...................... | 118 | 106,991 | 54,441 | 81,912 | 37,288 |
| Pueblo, Colo.......................... | 119 | 118,707 | 91,181 | 90,188 | 63,685 |
| Racine, Wis........................... | 160 | 141,781 | 89,144 | 109,585 | 71,193 |
| Raleigh, N. C......................... | 195 | 169,082 | 93,931 | 136,450 | 65,676 |
| Reading, Pa........................... | 283 | 275,414 | 98,177 | 255,740 | 109,320 |
| Reno, Nev............................. | 113 | 84,743 | 51,470 | 50,205 | 32,497 |
| Richmond, Va.......................... | *493 | 436,044 | 219,958 | 350,035 | 230,310 |
| Roanoke, Va........................... | 173 | 158,803 | 97,110 | 133,407 | 91,921 |
| Rochester, N. Y....................... | *820 | 732,588 | 318,611 | 615,044 | 332,488 |
| Rockford, Ill......................... | 247 | 230,091 | 126,706 | 169,455 | 92,927 |
| Sacramento, Calif..................... | *749 | 625,503 | 191,667 | 259,429 | 137,572 |
| Saginaw, Mich......................... | 208 | 190,752 | 98,265 | 153,515 | 92,918 |
| St. Joseph, Mo........................ | 95 | 90,581 | 79,673 | 96,826 | 78,588 |
| St. Louis, Mo.-Ill.................... (10) | *2,284 | 2,104,669 | 750,026 | 1,755,334 | 856,796 |
| Salem, Ore............................ | 172 | 147,411 | 49,142 | 127,718 | 43,140 |
| Salinas-Monterey, Calif............... | 222 | 198,351 | 51,575 | 130,498 | 30,122 |
| Salt Lake City, Utah.................. | *526 | 447,795 | 189,454 | 305,762 | 182,121 |
| San Angelo, Texas..................... | 73 | 64,630 | 58,815 | 58,929 | 52,093 |
| San Antonio, Texas.................... | *832 | 716,168 | 587,718 | 525,852 | 408,442 |
| San Bernardino-Riverside-Ontario, Calif. (29) | *1,040 | 809,782 | 222,871 | 451,688 | 132,604 |
| San Diego, Calif...................... (24) | *1,168 | 1,033,011 | 573,224 | 556,808 | 334,387 |
| San Francisco-Oakland, Calif.......... (7) | *2,958 | 2,648,762 | 1,107,864 | 2,135,934 | 1,159,932 |
| San Jose, Calif....................... | *928 | 642,315 | 204,196 | 290,547 | 95,280 |
| Santa Barbara, Calif.................. | 243 | 168,962 | 58,768 | 98,220 | 44,913 |
| Savannah, Ga.......................... | 192 | 188,299 | 149,245 | 151,481 | 119,638 |
| Scranton, Pa.......................... | 226 | 234,531 | 111,443 | 257,396 | 125,536 |
| Seattle-Everett, Wash................. (23) | *1,214 | 1,107,213 | 597,391 | 844,572 | 467,591 |
| Shreveport, La........................ | 289 | 281,481 | 164,372 | 216,686 | 127,206 |
| Sioux City, Iowa...................... | 114 | 120,017 | 89,159 | 114,318 | 83,991 |
| Sioux Falls, S. Dak................... | 94 | 86,575 | 65,466 | 70,910 | 52,696 |
| South Bend, Ind....................... | 270 | 271,057 | 132,445 | 234,526 | 115,911 |
| Spokane, Wash......................... | 267 | 278,333 | 181,608 | 221,561 | 161,721 |
| Springfield, Ill...................... | 153 | 146,539 | 83,271 | 131,484 | 81,628 |
| Springfield, Mo....................... | 140 | 126,276 | 95,865 | 104,823 | 66,731 |
| Springfield, Ohio..................... | 147 | 131,440 | 82,723 | 111,661 | 76,508 |

| Standard Metropolitan Statistical Area | 1965 est. (1,000) | 1960 | | 1950 | |
|---|---|---|---|---|---|
| | | Metropol. area total | In central cities | Metropol. area total | In central cities |
| Springfield-Chicopee-Holyoke, Mass........... | *547 | 493,999 | 288,705 | 422,163 | 266,271 |
| Steubenville-Weirton, Ohio-W. Va............ | 170 | 167,756 | 60,696 | 157,787 | 59,877 |
| Stockton, Calif............................. | 273 | 249,989 | 86,321 | 200,750 | 70,853 |
| Syracuse, N. Y............................. | *613 | 563,781 | 216,038 | 465,114 | 220,583 |
| Tacoma, Wash.............................. | 343 | 321,590 | 147,979 | 275,876 | 143,673 |
| Tallahassee, Fla........................... | 83 | 74,225 | 48,174 | 51,590 | 27,237 |
| Tampa-St. Petersburg, Fla.................. | *883 | 772,453 | 456,268 | 409,143 | 221,419 |
| Terre Haute, Ind.......................... | 167 | 172,069 | 72,500 | 172,468 | 64,214 |
| Texarkana, Texas-Ark...................... | 100 | 91,657 | 50,001 | 94,580 | 40,628 |
| Toledo, Ohio.............................. | *664 | 630,647 | 318,003 | 530,822 | 303,616 |
| Topeka, Kans.............................. | 149 | 141,286 | 119,484 | 105,418 | 78,791 |
| Trenton, N. J............................. | 296 | 266,392 | 114,167 | 229,781 | 128,009 |
| Tucson, Ariz.............................. | 307 | 265,660 | 212,892 | 141,216 | 45,454 |
| Tulsa, Okla............................... | *441 | 418,974 | 261,685 | 327,900 | 182,740 |
| Tuscaloosa, Ala........................... | 118 | 109,047 | 63,370 | 94,092 | 46,396 |
| Tyler, Texas.............................. | 93 | 86,350 | 51,230 | 74,701 | 38,968 |
| Utica-Rome, N. Y.......................... | 346 | 330,771 | 152,056 | 284,262 | 143,213 |
| Vallejo-Napa, Calif........................ | 239 | 200,487 | 83,047 | 151,436 | 39,617 |
| Vineland, N. J. (Cumberland County)....... | ...... | 106,850 | 77,747 | 88,597 | 42,574 |
| Waco, Texas.............................. | 156 | 150,091 | 97,808 | 130,194 | 84,706 |
| Washington, D. C.-Md.-Va.............(8) | *2,615 | 2,064,090 | 763,956 | 1,464,089 | 802,178 |
| Waterloo, Iowa............................ | 124 | 122,482 | 71,755 | 100,448 | 65,198 |
| West Palm Beach, Fla...................... | 281 | 228,106 | 56,208 | 114,688 | 43,162 |
| Wheeling, W. Va.-Ohio..................... | 188 | 190,342 | 53,400 | 196,305 | 58,891 |
| Wichita, Kans............................. | *391 | 381,626 | 254,698 | 253,291 | 168,279 |
| Wichita Falls, Texas....................... | 130 | 129,638 | 101,724 | 105,309 | 68,042 |
| Wilkes-Barre-Hazleton, Pa................. | 346 | 346,972 | 95,607 | 392,241 | 112,317 |
| Wilmington, Del.-N. J...................... | *466 | 414,565 | 95,827 | 301,743 | 110,356 |
| Wilmington, N. C.......................... | 95 | 92,000 | 44,013 | 82,150 | 45,043 |
| Worcester, Mass........................... | 608 | 328,898 | 186,587 | 303,037 | 203,486 |
| York, Pa.................................. | 290 | 290,242 | 54,504 | 246,934 | 59,953 |
| Youngstown-Warren, Ohio.................. | *525 | 509,006 | 226,337 | 416,544 | 218,186 |
| Puerto Rico (3 areas)..................... | | 818,241 | 596,810 | 679,858 | 515,641 |
| Mayaguez............................. | | 83,850 | 50,147 | 87,307 | 58,944 |
| Ponce................................ | | 145,586 | 114,286 | 126,810 | 99,492 |
| San Juan............................. | | 647,979 | 432,377 | 465,741 | 357,205 |

## STANDARD CONSOLIDATED AREAS OF NEW YORK AND CHICAGO

| Standard Consolidated Areas combining metropolitan areas (SMSA) | July 1, 1966 estimate | 1960 | 1950 | Increase 1950 to 1960 |
|---|---|---|---|---|
| New York-Northeastern New Jersey........ | 15,902,000 | 14,759,429 | 12,911,994 | 1,847,435 |
| New York, N. Y., SMSA................. | 11,410,000 | 10,694,633 | 9,555,943 | 1,138,690 |
| Newark, N. J., SMSA.................. | 1,862,000 | 1,689,420 | 1,468,458 | 220,962 |
| Jersey City, N. J., SMSA.............. | 616,000 | 610,734 | 647,437 | −36,703 |
| Paterson-Clifton-Passaic, N. J. SMSA...... | 1,318,000 | 1,186,873 | 876,232 | 310,641 |
| Middlesex County, N. J................. | 512,000 | 433,856 | 264,872 | 168,984 |
| Somerset County, N. J................. | 183,000 | 143,913 | 99,052 | 44,861 |
| Chicago-Northwestern Indiana............ | 7,331,000 | 6,794,461 | 5,586,096 | 1,208,365 |
| Chicago, Ill., SMSA................... | 6,732,000 | 6,220,913 | 5,177,868 | 1,043,045 |
| Gary-Hammond-East Chicago, Ind., SMSA.. | 599,000 | 573,548 | 408,228 | 165,320 |

# New Housing Units Started in U. S.
### Source: Bureau of the Census

| | Inc. Farm | | Non-Farm | |
|---|---|---|---|---|
| | 1966 | 1967p | 1966 | 1967p |
| Total, private and public | 1,196,200 | 1,321,900 | 1,172,800 | 1,298,800 |
| Private............... | 1,165,000 | 1,291,600 | 1,141,500 | 1,268,400 |
| Public............... | 30,900 | 30,300 | 30,900 | 30,300 |
| Metropolitan.......... | 808,400 | 920,300 | 807,300 | 919,700 |
| Private............. | 787,700 | 902,900 | 786,600 | 902,300 |
| Public............. | 20,600 | 17,400 | 20,600 | 17,400 |
| Nonmetropolitan........ | 387,800 | 401,600 | 365,400 | 379,000 |
| Private............. | 377,300 | 388,700 | 354,900 | 366,100 |
| Public............. | 10,300 | 12,900 | 10,300 | 12,900 |
| Type of Structure: | | | | |
| 1-family............... | 779,500 | 844,900 | 756,200 | 821,800 |
| 2-family............... | 40,600 | 47,800 | 40,600 | 47,800 |
| 3- or more family....... | 376,100 | 429,200 | 375,900 | 429,200 |
| Regions: | | | | |
| Northeast.............. | 215,700 | 223,500 | 215,400 | 223,300 |
| North Central......... | 297,400 | 343,900 | 290,100 | 337,300 |
| South................ | 482,800 | 531,500 | 467,000 | 515,300 |
| West................. | 200,500 | 223,000 | 200,300 | 222,900 |

### VALUATION OF ALL PRIVATE CONSTRUCTION
Authorized by building permits in 3,014 selected permit issuing places.

| | 1966 Total | 1967 Total (prelim.) |
|---|---|---|
| All private construction ......................... | $22,031,300,000 | $23,811,900,000 |
| Private residential construction ................. | $10,535,500,000 | $12,070,900,000 |

Estimated value of new construction put in place (including all types of construction, private and public), in the United States, including Alaska and Hawaii, for 1966 amounted to $74,371,000. p-Preliminary.

# Value of New Construction Put in Place in U. S.
### Source: Bureau of the Census

| Values in billions of dollars | Value put in place | | | | Percentage change | |
|---|---|---|---|---|---|---|
| | Annually | | First 4 mos. | | 1966 to 1967 | 1967 to 1968[2] |
| | 1966 | 1967 | 1967 | 1968[1] | | |
| Total new construction...... | 74,371 | 74,936 | 20,497 | 22,650 | +0.8 | +10.5 |
| Private construction........ | 50,446 | 49,583 | 13,466 | 15,537 | −1.7 | +15.4 |
| Private residential buildings (non farm)............... | 23,815 | 23,579 | 5,708 | 7,580 | −1.0 | +32.8 |
| Public construction........ | 23,925 | 25,353 | 7,031 | 7,113 | +6.0 | + 1.2 |

[1]Preliminary. [2]First four months.

# Population and Area of U. S. and Outlying Areas

Source: Bureau of the Census

| | Population | | Gross area (land and water) |
|---|---|---|---|
| | 1960 | 1950 | |
| Total............................. | 183,285,009 | 154,233,234 | 3,628,150 |
| United States............................. | 179,323,175 | 151,325,798 | 3,615,211 |
| Conterminous United States................. | 178,464,236 | 150,697,361 | 3,022,387 |
| Alaska................................ | 226,167 | 128,643 | 586,400 |
| Hawaii............................... | 632,772 | 499,794 | 6,424 |
| Commonwealth of Puerto Rico............. | 2,349,544 | 2,210,703 | 3,435 |
| Outlying areas of sovereignty or jurisdiction..... | 237,869 | 216,188 | 9,504 |
| Possessions............................. | 123,151 | 106,219 | 463 |
| Guam............................... | 67,044 | 59,498 | 212 |
| Virgin Islands of the U. S............... | 32,099 | 26,665 | 133 |
| American Samoa....................... | 20,051 | 18,937 | 76 |
| Midway Islands....................... | 2,356 | 416 | 2 |
| Wake Island.......................... | 1,097 | 349 | 3 |
| Canton Island and Enderbury Island...... | 320 | 272 | 27 |
| Johnston Island and Sand Island.......... | 156 | 46 | (a) |
| Swan Islands......................... | 28 | 36 | 1 |
| Other (b)............................ | (b) | (b) | (c) 9 |
| *Canal Zone.......................... | 42,122 | 52,822 | 553 |
| Corn Islands (h)...................... | 1,872 | 1,304 | 4 |
| Trust Territory of the Pacific Islands (d).... | 76,836 | 54,843 | 8,484 |
| United States population abroad (e).......... | 1,374,421 | 481,545 | .............. |
| Federal employees...................... | 647,730 | 328,505 | .............. |
| Armed Forces........................ | 609,720 | 301,595 | .............. |
| Civilians............................ | 38,010 | 26,910 | .............. |
| Dependents of Federal employees.......... | 506,393 | 107,350 | .............. |
| Crews of merchant vessels................ | 32,464 | 45,690 | .............. |
| Other citizens........................ | (f) 187,834 | (g) | .............. |

*Under U. S. jurisdiction by treaty with Panama.
(a) less than 0.5 sq. mi.

(b) The territory under U. S. sovereignty also includes Palmyra Island, Kingman Reef; Howland, Baker and Jarvis Islands; Tutuila, the Manua Islands, and all others of the Samoa group east of longitude 171° W., together with Swains Island and Navassa Island. U. S. claims to sovereignty over the following western Pacific islands are disputed by the United Kingdom: Caroline Atoll, Christmas, Flint, Malden, Starbuck, Vostok, Funafuti Atoll, Nukufetau Atoll, Nukulailai Atoll, Nurakita, Birnie Atoll, Gardner Atoll, Hull Atoll, McKean Atoll, Sydney Atoll, Phoenix Atoll. Also disputed are sovereignty over Canton and Enderbury Islands. New Zealand disputes U. S. claims to the following atolls: Atafu, Fakaofu, Nukonono, Danger, Manahiki, Rakahanga and Penrhyn, population not enumerated.

(c) Area is for Navassa (2 sq. mi.), Baker, Howland, and Jarvis (combined area 3 sq. mi.), and Palmyra (4 sq. mi.). Areas of other islands listed in footnote (b) not available.

(d) Under United Nations Trusteeship System with U. S. as administering authority.

(e) Excludes citizens temporarily abroad on private business, travel, etc.; these were enumerated at home as absent from their households.

(f) Citizens abroad for extended periods enumerated voluntarily and probably less complete than other categories of Americans abroad. (g) Not available. (h) Leased (1914) from Rep. of Nicaragua for 99 yrs.

# Population and Zip Codes

| Zip code | Place | 1960 | 1950 | Zip code | Place | 1960 | 1950 |
|---|---|---|---|---|---|---|---|
| | **AMERICAN SAMOA** | | | | **PUERTO RICO—Continued** | | |
| 96920 | American Samoa... | 20,051 | 18,937 | 00653 | Guanica............ | 4,130 | 4,833 |
| | **CANAL ZONE** | | | 00654 | Guayama........... | 19,183 | 19,408 |
| | Canal Zone........ | 42,122 | 52,822 | 00656 | Guayanilla.......... | 3,067 | 3,113 |
| | Balboa............ | 3,139 | 4,162 | 00657 | Guaynabo........... | 3,343 | 2,157 |
| | Gamboa........... | 3,489 | 3,074 | 00658 | Gurabo............ | 3,957 | 4,419 |
| | Paraiso............ | 3,113 | 1,503 | 00659 | Hatillo............. | 2,582 | 2,482 |
| | Rainbow City...... | 3,688 | 5,726 | 00661 | Humacao........... | 8,005 | 10,851 |
| | **GUAM** | | | 00662 | Isabela............ | 7,302 | 6,895 |
| 96910 | Guam............. | 67,044 | 59,498 | 00665 | Juana Diaz......... | 4,618 | 4,743 |
| | Agana Hgts......... | 3,210 | 858 | 00666 | Juncos............. | 6,247 | 8,285 |
| | New Agat City...... | 2,596 | 1,340 | 00669 | Lares.............. | 4,216 | 3,836 |
| | Sinajana........... | 2,861 | 3,069 | 00671 | Las Piedros......... | 3,147 | 3,150 |
| | Tamuning.......... | 5,380 | 1,053 | 00672 | Loiza.............. | 3,097 | 2,872 |
| | **PUERTO RICO** | | | 00701 | Manati............ | 9,682 | 10,092 |
| | Puerto Rico........ | 2,349,544 | 2,210,703 | 00708 | Mayaguez.......... | 50,147 | 58,944 |
| 00601 | Adjuntas........... | 5,318 | 5,262 | 00718 | Naguabo........... | 3,296 | 4,442 |
| 00602 | Aguada............ | 3,759 | 3,178 | 00719 | Naranjito.......... | 2,719 | 2,358 |
| 00603 | Aguadilla.......... | 15,943 | 18,276 | 00720 | Orocovis........... | 3,005 | 2,674 |
| 00609 | Aibonito........... | 5,477 | 5,126 | 00731 | Ponce............. | 114,286 | 99,492 |
| 00612 | Arecibo............ | 28,828 | 28,659 | 00745 | Rio Grande......... | 2,763 | 2,623 |
| 00615 | Arroyo............ | 3,741 | 4,980 | 00747 | Sabana Grande..... | 3,318 | 4,867 |
| ..... | Bahomamey........ | 2,888 | ........ | 00751 | Salinas............ | 3,666 | 4,367 |
| 00618 | Barranquitas....... | 4,684 | 4,268 | 00753 | San German........ | 7,790 | 8,872 |
| 00619 | Bayamon........... | 15,109 | 20,171 | 00936* | San Juan.......... | 432,377 | 224,767 |
| 00623 | Cabo Rojo......... | 3,086 | 4,797 | 00754 | San Lorenzo........ | 5,551 | 6,745 |
| 00625 | Caguas............ | 32,015 | 33,759 | 00755 | San Sebastian....... | 4,019 | 5,206 |
| 00630 | Carolina........... | 3,075 | 5,041 | 00757 | Santa Isabel........ | 4,772 | 4,117 |
| 00632 | Catano............ | 8,276 | 9,182 | 00761 | Utuado............ | 9,870 | 9,693 |
| 00633 | Cayey............. | 19,738 | 18,429 | 00762 | Vega Alta.......... | 3,182 | 3,492 |
| 00638 | Ciales............. | 3,275 | 3,482 | 00763 | Vega Baja.......... | 3,718 | 5,536 |
| 00639 | Cidra............. | 3,191 | 3,146 | 00767 | Yabucoa........... | 3,734 | 5,258 |
| 00640 | Coamo............ | 12,146 | 11,592 | 00768 | Yauco............. | 8,996 | 9,801 |
| 00642 | Comerio........... | 5,232 | 5,031 | | **VIRGIN ISLANDS** | | |
| 00643 | Corozal........... | 3,166 | 2,428 | | Virgin Islands...... | 32,099 | 26,665 |
| 00647 | Ensenda........... | 3,229 | 4,730 | 00820 | St. Croix Island..... | 14,973 | 12,103 |
| 00648 | Fajardo........... | 12,409 | 15,336 | 00820 | Christiansted City,... | 5,137 | 4,112 |
| 00617 | Florida Adentro.... | 2,955 | 1,710 | 00801 | St. John Island..... | 925 | 749 |
| 00617 | Florida Afuera...... | 3,250 | ........ | 00801 | St. Thomas Island | 16,201 | 13,813 |
| | | | | 00830 | Charlotte Amalie City | 12,880 | 11,469 |

*Check your local postmaster for the correct ZIP code number for a specific address in San Juan.

## Educational Attainment by Age, Race and Sex

Source: Bureau of the Census

| Age, race and sex March, 1967 | Total population | None | Elementary school | | | High school | | College | | | Median years completed |
|---|---|---|---|---|---|---|---|---|---|---|---|
| | | | 1 to 4 years | 5 to 7 years | 8 years | 1 to 3 years | 4 years | 1 to 3 years | 4 years | 5 yrs. or more | |
| | | | | | (in thousands) | | | | | | |
| **White** | | | | | | | | | | | |
| Total, 14 years and over | 124,503 | 1,323 | 3,426 | 10,895 | 18,132 | 27,306 | 39,040 | 13,333 | 7,278 | 3,770 | 12.0 |
| 14 to 17 years | 12,496 | 42 | 36 | 1,778 | 3,331 | 7,209 | 91 | 9 | | | 9.4 |
| 18 and 19 years | 5,833 | 12 | 13 | 108 | 130 | 1,927 | 2,827 | 817 | | | 12.3 |
| 20 to 24 years | 11,917 | 49 | 41 | 290 | 412 | 1,740 | 5,168 | 3,193 | 838 | 186 | 12.7 |
| 25 years and over | 94,257 | 1,220 | 3,336 | 8,719 | 14,260 | 16,431 | 30,955 | 9,314 | 6,439 | 3,584 | 12.1 |
| 25 to 29 years | 10,233 | 34 | 68 | 331 | 501 | 1,642 | 4,547 | 1,529 | 1,053 | 528 | 12.6 |
| 30 to 34 years | 9,463 | 34 | 114 | 413 | 614 | 1,648 | 4,103 | 1,160 | 914 | 464 | 12.5 |
| 35 to 44 years | 21,223 | 115 | 425 | 1,187 | 1,797 | 4,035 | 8,610 | 2,289 | 1,768 | 997 | 12.4 |
| 45 to 54 years | 20,234 | 132 | 489 | 1,614 | 2,873 | 3,962 | 7,268 | 1,957 | 1,216 | 724 | 12.1 |
| 55 to 64 years | 15,874 | 210 | 681 | 2,080 | 3,476 | 2,896 | 3,813 | 1,360 | 824 | 534 | 10.5 |
| 65 years and over | 17,230 | 695 | 1,559 | 3,094 | 4,999 | 2,248 | 2,614 | 1,019 | 664 | 337 | 8.7 |
| **Male, 14 years and over** | 59,419 | 668 | 1,809 | 5,560 | 8,919 | 12,799 | 16,398 | 6,617 | 3,929 | 2,719 | 12.0 |
| 14 to 17 years | 6,350 | 27 | 22 | 998 | 1,742 | 3,519 | 38 | 4 | | | 9.3 |
| 18 and 19 years | 2,776 | 8 | 7 | 55 | 67 | 1,002 | 1,236 | 401 | | | 12.2 |
| 20 to 24 years | 5,472 | 20 | 24 | 164 | 207 | 747 | 2,065 | 1,713 | 396 | 136 | 12.8 |
| 25 years and over | 44,820 | 614 | 1,757 | 4,342 | 6,905 | 7,531 | 13,060 | 4,500 | 3,534 | 2,582 | 12.1 |
| 25 to 29 years | 4,985 | 17 | 25 | 172 | 279 | 788 | 2,004 | 789 | 521 | 390 | 12.6 |
| 30 to 34 years | 4,638 | 13 | 62 | 216 | 314 | 720 | 1,739 | 618 | 574 | 382 | 12.6 |
| 35 to 44 years | 10,400 | 58 | 237 | 644 | 955 | 1,920 | 3,604 | 1,147 | 1,078 | 759 | 12.4 |
| 45 to 54 years | 9,826 | 73 | 266 | 841 | 1,515 | 1,871 | 3,104 | 976 | 694 | 488 | 12.1 |
| 55 to 64 years | 7,563 | 136 | 379 | 1,050 | 1,688 | 1,332 | 1,634 | 605 | 385 | 354 | 10.6 |
| 65 years and over | 7,408 | 317 | 788 | 1,419 | 2,154 | 900 | 975 | 365 | 282 | 209 | 8.5 |
| **Female, 14 yrs. and over** | 65,084 | 655 | 1,617 | 5,335 | 9,213 | 14,507 | 22,642 | 6,716 | 3,348 | 1,051 | 12.1 |
| 14 to 17 years | 6,146 | 15 | 14 | 781 | 1,589 | 3,690 | 53 | 5 | | | 9.5 |
| 18 and 19 years | 3,057 | 4 | 6 | 53 | 64 | 925 | 1,591 | 415 | | | 12.3 |
| 20 to 24 years | 6,445 | 29 | 17 | 126 | 205 | 993 | 3,103 | 1,480 | 442 | 50 | 12.6 |
| 25 years and over | 49,437 | 608 | 1,580 | 4,375 | 7,355 | 8,900 | 17,895 | 4,816 | 2,906 | 1,001 | 12.1 |
| 25 to 29 years | 5,248 | 17 | 43 | 158 | 222 | 854 | 2,543 | 741 | 532 | 137 | 12.5 |
| 30 to 34 years | 4,825 | 21 | 52 | 197 | 300 | 928 | 2,364 | 542 | 340 | 82 | 12.4 |
| 35 to 44 years | 10,823 | 58 | 189 | 543 | 842 | 2,115 | 5,006 | 1,142 | 690 | 238 | 12.3 |
| 45 to 54 years | 10,408 | 59 | 223 | 772 | 1,358 | 2,091 | 4,164 | 982 | 522 | 236 | 12.2 |
| 55 to 64 years | 8,311 | 74 | 302 | 1,030 | 1,788 | 1,564 | 2,179 | 755 | 440 | 180 | 10.8 |
| 65 years and over | 9,822 | 379 | 771 | 1,675 | 2,845 | 1,348 | 1,639 | 654 | 382 | 128 | 8.7 |
| **Nonwhite** | | | | | | | | | | | |
| Total, 14 years and over | 15,090 | 445 | 1,469 | 2,569 | 1,917 | 4,068 | 3,143 | 905 | 356 | 217 | 9.8 |
| 14 to 17 years | 1,977 | 2 | 27 | 486 | 519 | 933 | 10 | | | | 8.9 |
| 18 and 19 years | 858 | 2 | 5 | 49 | 41 | 425 | 282 | 54 | | | 11.3 |
| 20 to 24 years | 1,648 | 5 | 29 | 88 | 103 | 493 | 633 | 250 | 36 | 10 | 12.2 |
| 25 years and over | 10,607 | 435 | 1,409 | 1,945 | 1,254 | 2,216 | 2,218 | 600 | 320 | 207 | 9.4 |
| 25 to 29 years | 1,401 | 7 | 16 | 109 | 100 | 388 | 537 | 127 | 66 | 50 | 12.1 |
| 30 to 34 years | 1,291 | 8 | 38 | 138 | 87 | 336 | 458 | 130 | 62 | 32 | 12.1 |
| 35 to 44 years | 2,642 | 45 | 185 | 414 | 332 | 700 | 640 | 178 | 86 | 63 | 10.5 |
| 45 to 54 years | 2,222 | 48 | 332 | 485 | 334 | 441 | 388 | 101 | 54 | 39 | 8.7 |
| 55 to 64 years | 1,592 | 92 | 359 | 449 | 225 | 239 | 129 | 44 | 39 | 15 | 7.3 |
| 65 years and over | 1,459 | 235 | 479 | 550 | 176 | 112 | 66 | 20 | 13 | 8 | 5.1 |
| **Male, 14 years and over** | 7,087 | 258 | 832 | 1,235 | 933 | 1,838 | 1,337 | 379 | 155 | 120 | 9.5 |
| 14 to 17 years | 987 | | 20 | 270 | 257 | 439 | 1 | | | | 8.8 |
| 18 and 19 years | 411 | | 5 | 24 | 26 | 232 | 107 | 17 | | | 10.9 |
| 20 to 24 years | 754 | 3 | 17 | 42 | 57 | 234 | 274 | 107 | 15 | 4 | 12.1 |
| 25 years and over | 4,936 | 255 | 791 | 897 | 592 | 932 | 955 | 255 | 141 | 115 | 8.9 |
| 25 to 29 years | 657 | 6 | 9 | 53 | 51 | 171 | 248 | 57 | 24 | 37 | 12.2 |
| 30 to 34 years | 596 | 6 | 32 | 77 | 47 | 135 | 196 | 58 | 27 | 18 | 12.0 |
| 35 to 44 years | 1,210 | 23 | 123 | 192 | 168 | 316 | 240 | 79 | 40 | 28 | 9.9 |
| 45 to 54 years | 1,046 | 29 | 191 | 227 | 158 | 163 | 195 | 42 | 23 | 18 | 8.5 |
| 55 to 64 years | 767 | 53 | 192 | 222 | 100 | 94 | 58 | 15 | 23 | 10 | 6.9 |
| 65 years and over | 660 | 138 | 244 | 126 | 68 | 53 | 18 | 4 | 4 | 4 | 4.1 |
| **Female, 14 yrs. and over** | 8,003 | 187 | 638 | 1,334 | 984 | 2,230 | 1,806 | 526 | 200 | 98 | 10.2 |
| 14 to 17 years | 991 | 2 | 8 | 216 | 262 | 494 | 8 | | | | 9.0 |
| 18 and 19 years | 447 | 2 | | 25 | 15 | 192 | 175 | 37 | | | 11.8 |
| 20 to 24 years | 894 | 2 | 11 | 46 | 46 | 259 | 360 | 143 | 21 | 6 | 12.2 |
| 25 years and over | 5,670 | 180 | 617 | 1,047 | 662 | 1,285 | 1,262 | 346 | 179 | 92 | 9.8 |
| 25 to 29 years | 744 | 1 | 7 | 56 | 49 | 217 | 289 | 70 | 41 | 13 | 12.1 |
| 30 to 34 years | 695 | 2 | 6 | 61 | 41 | 201 | 262 | 73 | 36 | 14 | 12.1 |
| 35 to 44 years | 1,433 | 22 | 62 | 221 | 164 | 384 | 399 | 99 | 46 | 35 | 10.9 |
| 45 to 54 years | 1,175 | 19 | 141 | 258 | 176 | 278 | 193 | 59 | 31 | 21 | 9.0 |
| 55 to 64 years | 825 | 39 | 167 | 227 | 125 | 145 | 71 | 29 | 16 | 5 | 7.7 |
| 65 years and over | 798 | 97 | 234 | 224 | 107 | 60 | 48 | 16 | 9 | 4 | 5.9 |

## Incidence of Poverty for Families

Source: Bureau of the Census (in thousands)

| 1966 | Total | Below Level No. | % | 1966 | Total | Below Level No. | % |
|---|---|---|---|---|---|---|---|
| All families | 48,922 | 6,086 | 12.4 | Female head | 5,172 | 1,810 | 35.0 |
| Male head | 43,750 | 4,276 | 9.8 | White | 4,010 | 1,111 | 27.7 |
| White | 40,007 | 3,264 | 8.2 | No children | 1,936 | 256 | 13.2 |
| Below age 65 | 34,626 | 2,164 | 6.2 | With children | 2,074 | 855 | 41.2 |
| 65 and over | 5,381 | 1,100 | 20.4 | 1 child | 827 | 244 | 29.5 |
| | | | | 2 children | 607 | 226 | 37.2 |
| Employed in March 1967 | 33,254 | 1,712 | 5.1 | 3 children | 332 | 184 | 55.4 |
| White collar, skilled | | | | 4 children | 177 | 101 | 57.1 |
| craftsmen | 21,961 | 670 | 3.1 | 5 children or more | 131 | 100 | 76.3 |
| Semiskilled operatives | 6,369 | 365 | 5.7 | Nonwhite | 1,162 | 699 | 60.2 |
| Service workers | 1,781 | 139 | 7.8 | No children | 275 | 74 | 26.9 |
| Laborers | 1,658 | 280 | 16.9 | With children | 887 | 625 | 70.5 |
| Farmers | 1,485 | 258 | 17.4 | 1 child | 221 | 109 | 49.3 |
| | | | | 2 children | 220 | 140 | 63.6 |
| Nonwhite | 3,743 | 1,012 | 27.0 | 3 children | 135 | 104 | 77.0 |
| Below age 65 | 3,318 | 808 | 24.4 | 4 children | 116 | 101 | 87.1 |
| 65 and over | 425 | 204 | 48.0 | 5 children or more | 195 | 171 | 87.7 |

As applied to 1966 incomes the poverty level of nonfarm residents ranges from $1,560 for a woman 65 or over living alone to $5,440 for a family of 7 or more; it was $3,335 for a nonfarm family of four.

# Marine Disasters Since 1861; Major War Losses

Figures show lives lost. Only more serious disasters are listed. See also Chronology.

(B)—burned, (C)—collision, (D)—damaged, (E)—exploded, (F)—foundered at sea, (G)—ran aground, (M)—sunk by mine, (S)—sunk in storm, (T)—torpedoed, (V)—vanished, (W)—wrecked. Braz.—Brazilian, Br.—British, Fr.—French, Ger.—German, It.—Italian, Jap.—Japanese, Sp.—Spanish, Sw.—Swedish.

### CIVIL WAR 1861-65
**1862**
Mar. 8 Cumberland, Congress. (Fed.) sunk by Merrimac (Conf.)
Mar. 9 Battle of **Merrimac** (Conf.) and **Monitor** (Fed.)—5-hr. battle ended in a draw: Merrimac burned by Conf. in May, to prevent capture
Dec. 31 Monitor (S) off Cape Hatteras
**1863**
Feb. 7 Orpheus (W) off New Zealand...... 190
Apr. 27 Anglo-Saxon (W) off Cape Race.... 237
**1864**
June 19 Alabama (Conf.) sunk by Kearsarge (Fed.)
Feb. 7 Housatonic (Fed.) (T) by the H. L. Hunley (Conf.) off Charleston, S. C. The Hunley swamped and its crew of 9 was lost: **first recorded sinking of warship by submarine**
**1865**
Apr. 27 Sultana (E) on Mississippi River....1,450
Aug. 24 Eagle Speed (F) near Calcutta...... 265
**1866**
Jan. 11 London (F) in Bay of Biscay....... 230
Jan. 30 Missouri (E) on Ohio River........ 100
Oct. 3 Evening Star (F) from New York... 250
**1867**
Oct. 29 Rhone, Wye and 50 other vessels (W) at St. Thomas, West Indies by hurricane.....1,000
**1868**
Apr. 9 Sea Bird (B) on Lake Michigan..... 100
Apr. 17 United Kingdom (V)............... 80
Dec. 4 America; United States (B) Ohio R... 72
**1869**
Oct. 27 Stonewall (B) below Cairo, Ill..... 200
**1870**
Jan. 24 Oneida (C) off Yokohama.......... 115
Jan. 28 City of Boston (V) in Atlantic..... 191
Sept. 7 Br. warship Captain (F) off Spain... 472
Oct. 19 Cambria lost off Inishtrahull....... 170
**1871**
Jan. 28 H. R. Arthur (E).................. 87
July 30 Westfield (ferry) (E) N. Y. harbor.. 100
**1872**
Nov. 7 **Mary Celeste** left New York for Genoa; found abandoned in Atlantic 4 weeks later; crew never heard from
**1873**
Jan. 22 Northfleet (C) off Dungeness...... 300
Apr. 1 Br. Atlantic (W) off Nova Scotia.... 547
Nov. 23 Ville de Havre (C) in Atlantic...... 230
**1874**
Dec. 6 Cospatrick (B)................... 470
**1875**
May 7 Schiller (W) on Scilly Islands........ 200
Nov. 4 Pacific (C) off Cape Flattery....... 236
Dec. 6 Deutschland (W) mouth of Thames.. 157
**1877**
July 15 Eten (W) off Valparaiso.......... 100
Nov. 24 Huron (W) off North Carolina...... 100
Nov. .. Atacama (W) off Caldera, Chile.... 104
**1878**
Jan. 31 Metropolis (W) off North Carolina... 100
Mar. 24 Eurydice (F) near Isle of Wight.... 300
Sept. 3 Princess Alice (C) on Thames River 700
**1879**
Feb. 12-16 13 fishing schooners (F) off N. F... 144
Dec. 2 Borusia sunk off Spain............. 174
**1880**
Jan. 31 Atlanta (V) from Bermuda......... 290
Oct. 16 Alpena (F) Lake Michigan......... 60
Nov. 24 Uncle Joseph (C) off Spezzia....... 250
**1881**
Apr. 29 Tararua (W) off New Zealand..... 131
May 24 Victoria capsized in Thames River, Canada................................ 200
June .. U. S. Naval vessel **Jeanette** crushed in Arctic and sunk 500 miles off Siberian coast. Cmdr. G. W. De Long and 21 others lost; 11 survived, including Lt. G. W. Melville. The vessel had been in the ice pack since Sept., 1879. It had sailed from San Francisco in July, 1879, for the North Pole, having been bought and outfitted by James Gordon Bennett
Aug. 30 Teuton (W) off Cape of Good Hope.. 200
**1882**
Sept. 14 Asia (F) near Sault Ste. Marie...... 98
**1883**
Jan. 19 Ger. Cambria (C) iceberg.......... 389
July 3 Daphne capsized in Clyde.......... 124
**1884**
Jan. 18 City of Columbus (W) off Mass..... 103
Apr. 3 Daniel Steinman (W) off N. S...... 131
Apr. 18 Pomona; State of Florida (C)...... 150
July 22 Sp. Gigon; British Lexham (C)..... 150
**1887**
Jan. 20 Kapunda; Ada Melmore (C) Brazil.. 300
Nov. 19 W. A. Scholten (C) in Eng. Channel.. 134
**1888**
Aug. 14 Geiser; Thingvalla (C)............. 105

Sept. 12 It. steamer; La France (C)........ 89
**1889**
Mar. 16 U. S. warships Trenton, Vandalia and Nipsic; Ger. Adler and Eber (W) at Apia, Samoan Islands, by hurricane.................. 147
**1890**
Jan. 2 Persia (W) on Corsica............. 130
Feb. 17 Br. Duberg (W) in China Sea...... 400
Mar. 1 Quetta (W) off Cape York......... 124
Sept. 19 Turkish frigate Ertogrul (F) off Japan 540
Nov. 10 British cruiser Serpent (S) off Spain 167
Dec. 27 Shanghai (B) in China Sea.......... 100
**1891**
Mar. 17 Utopia (C) off Gibraltar........... 574
Apr. 22 Blanco Encalada (E) in Caldera Bay 200
**1892**
Jan. 13 Namchow (W) in China Sea........ 414
May 22 Braz. warship sunk, La Plata R..... 120
Oct. 28 Roumania (W) off Portugal........ 113
**1893**
Feb. 8 Trinacria (W) off coast of Spain.... 115
Feb. 11 Naronic (V) Liverpool to New York
June 22 Br. battleship Victoria (C) off Syria 350
**1894**
Feb. 2 Kearsarge (W) on Roncadof Reef
Nov. 1 Wairapa (W) off New Zealand...... 134
**1895**
Jan. 30 Ger. Elbe; Br. Crathie (C)......... 335
Mar. 11 Sp. Reina Regenta (F) in Atlantic... 400
**1896**
June 17 Drummond Castle (W) off France.... 250
**1898**
Feb. 15 U. S. battleship **Maine** (E) in Havana harbor................................ 269

### SPANISH-AMERICAN WAR
May 1 **Battle of Manila Bay**—Spanish Reina Cristina; Castilla; cruisers Isla de Cuba and Isla de Luzon; gunboats Don Juan de Austria, Don Antonio de Ulloa and Marques del Duero, under Adm. Patricio Montojo, destroyed by Commodore George Dewey's fleet; Sp., 167 killed, 214 wounded; U. S., 7 wounded
July 3 **Battle of Santiago de Cuba**—Spanish cruisers Maria Teresa, Almirante Oquendo and Vizcaya set afire and run aground west of Santiago; cruiser Cristobal Colon beached at mouth of Rio Turquino. Sp. forces, under Adm. Pascual Cervera, 353 killed, 151 wounded; U. S., under Actg. Rear-Adm. William T. Sampson and Commodore Winfield S. Schley, 1 killed
July 4 Fr. La Bourgoyne; Br. Cromartyshire (C).......................... 560
July 4 Sp. Reina Mercedes scuttled at Santiago
July 5 Sp. warship Alfonso XII sunk off Cuba
July .. Spanish cruiser Jorge Juan sunk
Oct. 14 Mohegan (W) off the Lizard........ 170
Nov. 26 Portland lost off Cape Cod......... 157
**1900**
June 30 Main, Bremen and Saale (B) at Hoboken, N. J.......................... 145
**1901**
Feb. 22 Rio de Janeiro (W) at San Francisco 128
Apr. 1 Turkish Asian (W) in Red Sea...... 180
Aug. 14 Islander, with $3,000,000 in gold, struck iceberg in Steven's Passage, Alaska....... 70
Dec. 2 Br. Condor (V) off Esquimalt, B. C. 104
**1902**
July 21 Primus (C) on the Elbe........... 112
**1903**
June 7 French Libau (C) near Marseilles... 150

### RUSSO-JAPANESE WAR 1904-05
**1904**
Feb. 9 Russian cruisers Variag and Korietz sunk off Chemulpo, Korea, by Japanese
Apr. 13 Russian battleship Petropavlovsk (M) off Port Arthur.................... 600
May 15 Jap battleships Hatsuse and Yashima (M), cruiser Yoshino rammed by sister ship and sunk
June 15 Gen. Slocum (B) at Hell Gate, N. Y...1,030
June 20 Russian submarine Dolphin sunk.... 23
June 28 Norge (W) on Rockall Reef......... 590
**1905**
May 27 **Battle of Tsushima Bay**—Jap. fleet, under Adm. Heihachiro Togo, destroyed Russian fleet under Adm. Ziniry P. Rojdestvensky including battleships Kniaz Suvaroff, Alexander III, Oslisbya, Navarin, Sissoi Velikland Borodino; cruisers Dmitri Donski, Adm. Nakhimoff, Vladimir Monomach, Adm. Oushakoff Zhemchug, Izumrud and Svietlana: Russia lost 10,000 men. Japan lost 3 torpedo boats; casualties under 1,000
Sept. 23 Jap. warship Mikasa.............. 599
**1906**
Jan. 21 Braz. Aquidaban (E) off Brazil..... 212
Jan. 22 Valencia lost off Vancouver Island.. 129
Aug. 4 Italian Sirio (W) off Cape Palos..... 350

**1907**

| | | |
|---|---|---|
| Feb. 12 | Larchmont sunk off Long Island..... | 131 |
| Feb. 21 | Br. Berlin off Hook of Holland..... | 100 |
| Feb. 24 | Austrian Imperatrix (W)........... | 137 |
| Mar. 12 | French battleship Jena (E)......... | 117 |
| July 20 | Columbia; San Petro (C) off Calif.... | 100 |
| Nov. 26 | Turkish Kaptan sunk in North Sea | 110 |

**1908**

| | | |
|---|---|---|
| Mar. 23 | Jap. Matsu Maru (C) near Hakodate | 300 |
| Apr. 30 | Jap. Matsu Shima (E) off Pescadores | 200 |
| July 28 | Ying King (F) off Hong Kong...... | 300 |
| Nov. 6 | Taish (S)........................ | 150 |
| Nov. 27 | San Pablo sunk off Philippines...... | 100 |

**1909**

Jan. 23 White Star liner Republic rammed and sunk by It. Florida off Nantucket light. All but 6 passengers saved by "CQD" (before SOS) sent by Republic's wireless operator Jack Binns; **first time radio was used in sea rescue**

Aug. 1 Br. Waratah (V) from London...... 300

**1910**

Feb. 9 Fr. Gen. Chanzy (W) off Minorca... 200

**1911**

Sept. 25 Fr. battleship Liberte (E) at Toulon 285

**1912**

| | | |
|---|---|---|
| Jan. 11 | Russ (F) in Black Sea............ | 172 |
| Mar. 5 | Spanish Principe de Asturias...... | 500 |
| Mar. 28 | British Yongala (S) off Australia... | 130 |
| Apr. 8 | Nile steamer (C) near Cairo Egypt.. | 200 |
| Apr. 14-15 | White Star liner **Titanic** hit iceberg in North Atlantic............ | 1,517 |
| Sept. 23 | Russian Obnevka sunk in Dvina R... | 115 |
| Sept. 28 | Jap. Kickermaru sunk off Japan.... | 1,000 |

**1913**

Mar. 1 Br. Calvados lost in Sea of Marmora 200
Mar. 5 Ger. destroyer S-178; cruiser Yorck (C) near Helgoland.............. 66
Oct. 9 Volturno (E) in midocean......... 135
Nov. 9 Storm destroyed on Lake Superior the steamers Henry B. Smith, 26; and Leafield, 18; on Lake Huron the steamers John A. McGean, 23; Charles Price, 28; Isaac M. Scott, 26; Hydrus, 24; Argus, 24; James Carruthers, 22; Regina, 25; and Wexford, 24.

**1914**

Jan. 30 S.S. Monroe (C) off Virginia...... 41

**WORLD WAR I 1914-1918**

Mar. 31 Southern Cross (W) Belle Isle Strait 173
May 29 Canadian Empress of Ireland (C) St. Lawrence River..............1,024
Aug. 26 German Kaiser Wilhelm der Grosse sunk off Africa
Aug. 28 German cruisers Ariadne, Coln and Mainz sunk by British
Sept. 12 German cruiser Hela sunk by British sub off Helgoland
Sept. 18 Francis H. Leggett (W) Columbia R. 80
Sept. 22 British cruisers Aboukir, Cressy and Hogue by German submarine.....1,400
Oct. 15 British cruiser Hawke by submarine off Aberdeen coast
Oct. 26 British battleship Audacious (M) off Lough Swilly
Nov. 1 British cruisers Good Hope and Monmouth sunk in Battle of Coronel
Nov. 4 German cruiser Karlsruhe (E)
Nov. 9 German cruiser Emden sunk off Cocos Is.
Nov. 17 German cruiser Yorck (M) off Jade River
Nov. 26 Br. battleship Bulwark (E) at Sheerness
Dec. 8 German cruisers Scharnhorst, Leipzig, Gneisenau and Nurnberg sunk in Battle of Falkland Island.......1,800
Dec. .. French battleship Jean Bart (T) in Med.

**1915**

Jan. 1 British battleship Formidable (T)
Jan. 24 German cruiser Blucher sunk off Dogger Bank.................... 792
Mar. 14 German cruiser Dresden blown up by crew
Mar. 18 British battleships Irresistible and Ocean (T) in Dardanelles and sunk; Inflexible (T) and beached
Mar. 25 U.S. sub F-4, off Honolulu Harbor.. 21
May 7 Cunard Line steamship **Lusitania**, bound from New York to England, sunk in 18 minutes after a German submarine attack off the Old Head of Kinsale, southeast tip of Ireland.......1,198
May 13 British Goliath (T) by Turkish destroyer
May 25 British battleship Triumph (T)
May 27 British battleship Majestic (T)
July 11 German cruiser Konigsberg sunk by British in Rufiji River
July 18 Italian cruiser Giuseppe Garibaldi (T) in Mediterranean
July 24 Eastland overturned in Chicago River 812
Aug. 13 Marowijne in Gulf of Mexico....... 97
Aug. 16 Dredges San Jacinto and Sam Houston (W) off Galveston, Tex....... 106
Nov. 7 Italian Ancona (T) in Mediterranean 206

**1916**

Jan. 6 British battleship King Edward VII (M) off Cape Wrath
Jan. 22 Pollentia (F) in mid-Atlantic
Feb. 3 Daijin Maru sunk in Pacific........ 160
Feb. 26 French cruiser Provence in Mediterranean....................3,100

May 31 **Battle of Jutland**—British cruisers Queen Mary, 1,265; Indefatigable, 1,017: Defence; Invincible, 1,000; Black Prince; Ger. battleship Pommern; cruisers Wiesbaden, Rostock, Elbing and Lutzow, Br. Grand Fleet, under Adm. Sir John R. Jellicoe and Vice-Adm. Sir David Beatty, lost 14 ships, 6,097 men; Ger. High Seas Fleet under Vice-Adms. Reinhard Scheer and Franz von Hipper, lost 11 ships, 2,545 men
June 5 British cruiser Hampshire (M) in Orkneys
Aug. 19 British cruisers Nottingham and Falmouth (T)
Aug. 29 U. S. cruiser Memphis (W) at Santo Domingo.................... 43
Aug. 29 Chinese Hsin Yu sunk off China....1,000
Aug. 29 Jap. Wakatsu Maru (W) off Japan.. 105
Nov. 3 Connemara; Retriever (C) Irish Sea 92
Nov. 21 Br. Britannic (T) Aegean Sea...... 50

**1917**

Jan. 25 British cruiser Laurentic (M) off Ireland...................... 350
Apr. 15 Br. Arcadian (T) in Mediterranean 279
July 9 British warship Vanguard (E) at Scapa Flow................. 800
Oct. 17 U. S. transport Antilles (T)........ 70
Oct. .. Russian battleship Slava sunk in Baltic
Dec. 6 Fr. Mont Blanc, carrying 3,000 tons of T.N.T., exploded in Halifax harbor when rammed by Belgian relief steamer Imo. Over 1,600 died and thousands were injured in the blast, and fire which devastated the northern part of the city. Property damage $50,000,000
Dec. 6 U. S. destroyer Jacob Jones (T) off Scilly Islands.................. 64
Dec. 30 Br. Aragon (T) in Mediterranean... 610

**1918**

Jan. 20 German warship Breslau (M) off Imbros Island
Jan. 21 Br. Louvain (T) in Mediterranean.. 224
Feb. 1 French La Dive (T) in Mediterranean 110
Feb. 5 British Tuscania (T) off Ireland..... 213
Feb. 24 Florizel (W) near Cape Race, N. F.. 92
Apr. 25 Chinese Kiang-Kwan (C) off Hankow 500
May 1 City of Athens (C) off Delaware.... 66
May 10 Br. Santa Anna (T) in Mediterranean 638
May 23 British Moldavia (T) in Atlantic..... 53
May 26 Leasowe Castle (T) in Mediterranean 101
May 31 U. S. troopship Pres. Lincoln (T).. 29
June .. U.S.S. Cyclops (V) left Barbados Mar. 4...................... 309
June 27 Br. Llandovery Castle (T)......... 234
July 6 Columbia sunk in Illinois River..... 87
July 12 Jap. battleship Kawachi (E), Tokayama Bay................. 500
July 14 Fr. Djamnah (T) in Mediterranean 442
July 19 U. S. cruiser San Diego (M) off Fire Island.................... 50
Aug. 3 British Warilda (T) off England.... 123
Sept. 5 U. S. troopship Mt. Vernon........ 36
Sept. 12 British Galway Castle (T) in Atlantic 189
Sept. 26 Tampa (T) off England............ 118
Sept. 30 Ticonderoga (T) in Atlantic........ 213
Oct. 6 British Otranto (C) off Scotland..... 431
Oct. 10 Irish Leinster (T) in St. George's Channel.................... 480
Oct. 25 Canadian Princess Sophia sunk off Alaska.................... 398
Nov. 10 British battleship Britannia (T) off Cape Trafalgar

**1919**

Jan. 1 British yacht Iolaire off Scotland.... 270
Jan. 17 French Chaonia lost in Straits of Messina.................... 460
June 4 Br. sub L-55, off Kronstadt........ 41
Sept. 9 Spanish Valbanera lost off Florida.... 500

**1921**

| | | |
|---|---|---|
| | Spanish Santa Isabel (S) near Villagarcia.................... | 214 |
| Mar. 18 | Hongkong hit rock near Swatow, China.................... | 1,000 |

**1922**

May 20 British Egypt (C) off France........ 98
Aug. 26 Jap. cruiser Niitaka (S) off Kamchatka.................... 300
Aug. 29 Chilean Itata (S) off Copumbo..... 301

**1923**

Mar. 10 Greek Alexander sunk off Piraeus... 150
Apr. 30 Mossamedes (G) at Cape Frio, Africa 220
Aug. 21 Jap sub at dock, Kobe............ 85
Sept. 3 U. S. destroyers Delphy, S. P. Lee, Chauncey, Fuller, Woodbury, Nicholas and Young (W) off Honda Point, Calif............ 22

**1924**

Jan. 10 Br. sub L-24 (C) off Portland, Eng.. 48
Mar. 19 Jap. sub No. 43, (C) off Sasebo.... 49

**1925**

Mar. 12 Jap. Uwajima Maru off Takashima... 103
Aug. 26 It. sub (V) off Sicily............. 50
Sept. 25 U.S. sub S-51 (C) with steamer City of Rome off Black Island........ 34
Nov. 11 Br. sub M-1 (C) in English Channel. 69
Apr. 27 Chichibu (G) off Horomushiro, Jap. 230
Aug. 28 Buryvestnik hit pier at Cronstadt, Russia.................... 300
Oct. 16 Troopship (E) in Yangtze Sea......1,200

**1927**

Aug. 25 Jap destroyers Warabi and Ashi off Bungo Straits............. 129

Oct. 25 Italian Principessa Mafalda (E) off Porto Seguro, Brazil.......... 314

Dec. 17 U. S. sub S-4 (C) off Provincetown, Mass..................... 40

**1928**

July 7 Chilean Angames (S) Araunco Bay... 291

Aug. 6 It. sub F-14 (C) in Adriatic Sea..... 31

Oct. 3 Fr. sub Ondine, off Portugal........ 43

Nov. 12 British Vestris (S) off Virginia...... 113

**1929**

Apr. 22 Jap. Toyo Kuni Maru (W) on Rocky Cape Erino................... 103

Aug. 30 San Juan (C) off Santa Cruz, Calif. 70

Dec. 21 Chinese Lee Cheong near Hong Kong 300

**1931**

Mar. 11 Chinese steamer (E) in Yangtze River 300

May 22 Russian sub No. 9, Gulf of Finland.. 35

June 14 French St. Philibert (S) off St. Nazaire 450

**1932**

Jan. 26 Br. sub M-2, off Portland Bill, Eng. 60

Sept. 9 Observation (E) East River, N. Y. C. 72

Dec. 5 Jap. destroyer Sawarab (S) off Formosa.................... 105

**1933**

Jan. 4 French L'Atlantique (B) in English Channel................. 17

**1934**

Jan. 21 Chinese Weltung (B) on Yangtze R. 216

Mar. 12 Jap. Tomozuru upset west of Nagasaki................... 103

Sept. 8 Morro Castle (B) off Asbury Park, N. J................... 125

**1935**

Jan. 24 Mohawk; Talisman (C) off N. J..... 45

July 3 Jap. Midori Maru (C) in Inland Sea 104

**1936**

Dec. 12 Sp. sub (T) off Malaga........... 47

**1937**

Dec. 12 U. S. Panay, bombed by Jap., Yangtze River................. 2

**1938**

May 5 French Lafayette (B) in dry dock at Havre

**WORLD WAR II 1939-45**

**1939**

Feb. 2 Jap. sub I-36, Bungo Channel...... 81

Apr. 19 French Paris (B) at Le Havre

May 23 U. S. sub Squalus sunk off Portsmouth, N. H............... 26

June 1 British sub Thetis sunk in Irish Sea. 99

June 15 Fr. sub Phenix, off Indo-China...... 63

Sept. 3 Br. Athenia (T) west of Hebrides.... 112

Sept. 17 Br. aircraft carrier Courageous (T).. 515

Oct. 14 British battleship Royal Oak (T).... 786

Dec. 17 German battleship Graf Spee blown up by crew 3 mi. off Uruguay

**1940**

June 8 British aircraft carrier Glorious off Narvik.....................1,204

June 16 Fr. Champlain sunk in Fr. port

June 17 Br. Lancastria (T) off St. Nazaire...2,500

July 3 French battleships Bretagne and Provence sunk. Dunkerque run aground by British off N. Africa

Oct. 26 Empress of Britain (T) off Ireland.. 45

Nov. 3 Laurentic (T)

**1941**

Apr. 23 British Rajputana (T)............. 40

May .. Italian Conte Rosso (T) off Sicily

May 24 British battleship Hood off Greenland by German battleship Bismarck

May 27 Bismarck off Brest by British......2,300

June 16 U. S. sub 0-9 in test dive off Maine... 33

July 13 Georgic destroyed in Suez port...... 737

Oct. 31 U. S. destroyer Reuben James (T) North Atlantic............... 100

Nov. 13 British aircraft carrier Ark Royal in Mediterranean

Nov. 25 British battleship Barham (T) in Mediterranean............... 800

Dec. 2 Australian cruiser Sydney off Australia..................... 645

Dec. 7 Pearl Harbor. *Consult Index*

Dec. 9 British battleship Prince of Wales and cruiser Repulse by Jap. off Malay Peninsula

Dec. 16 British cruiser Galatea (T) in Mediterranean................. 460

**1942**

Feb. 2 Swedish Amerikaland off Cape Hatteras

Feb. 9 French Normandie (B) at pier, New York City............... 1

Feb. 18 U. S. destroyer Truxton and cargo ship Pollus (G) off Newfoundland 204

Mar. 1 U. S. cruiser Houston, Sundra Strait, Battle of Java Sea............ 644

Apr. 5 Br. cruisers Dorsetshire, Cornwall, by Jap. planes off Ceylon...... 425

Apr. 8 Br. aircraft carrier Hermes, destroyer Vampire, in Indian Ocean by Jap. 315

Apr. 8 Greek Enderania sunk off Turkey.... 211

May 8 U. S. aircraft carrier Lexington in Coral Sea battle.............. 150

June 4 Jap. aircraft carriers Akagi (220), Kaga (800), Hiryu (415) and Soryu (718) in Battle of Midway

June 7 U. S. aircraft carrier Yorktown off Midway Island

Aug. 9 U. S. cruisers Quincy (370), Vincennes (332) and Astoria (216) sunk in Solomons

Aug. 22 U. S. destroyer Ingraham (C) in Atlantic.................. 218

Sept. 9 U.S.C.G. Muskeget (V) in Atlantic.. 120

Sept. 15 U. S. aircraft carrier Wasp (T) in Solomons................. 180

Oct. 2 British cruiser Curacao (C) off Eng. 335

Oct. 26 Pres. Coolidge (M) in South Pacific.. 5

Oct. 26 U. S. aircraft carrier Hornet (D) in battle of Santa Cruz Island, later sunk (new Hornet launched Aug. 30, 1943)

Oct. .. Duchess of Athol (T) in Atlantic

Oct. .. Viceroy of India (T) in Atlantic

Nov. 8 British aircraft carrier Avenger off North Africa................ 507

Nov. 13 Jap. battleship Hiyei, off Solomons

Nov. 15 Jap. battleship Kirishima, off Solomons

Dec. 6 British Ceramic (T) off Azores...... 500

**1943**

Jan. .. U. S. sub Argonaut by Jap. near New Britain Island............... 102

Jan. 30 U.S. cruiser Chicago (T) in Solomons

Feb. 3 U. S. S. Dorchester (T) off Greenland 600

In one of the most heroic acts of the war, **4 chaplains** aboard the Dorchester gave their lifebelts to soldiers aboard the transport, linked their arms and prayed as they went down with the ship. They were Clark V. Poling and George L. Fox, Protestants; John P. Washington, Roman Catholic; and Alexander D. Goode, Jewish.

Mar. 15 Empress of Canada (T) off Freetown, West Africa................. 400

June 8 Jap. battleship Mutsu (E) off Japan

June 13 U.S.C.G. Escanaba (E) in Atlantic.. 103

Sept. 9 Italian battleship Roma (W) by Axis planes

Sept. 11 Conte di Savola bombed by Germany in Venice harbor

Sept. 14 It. Conte Verde scuttled at Shanghai

Oct. 20 Navy tankers (C) off Palm Beach, Fla. 88

Nov. 26 Br. Rohna bombed off Algeria......1,015

Dec. 26 Ger. Scharnhorst (T) off Norway by British

**1944**

Jan. 3 U.S.S. Turner (E) off N. Y. Harbor. 138

Mar. 9 U.S.S. Leopold (T) in Atlantic...... 171

Apr. 20 U. S. S. Paul Hamilton (T) off Algiers 504

May 29 U. S. aircraft carrier Block Island (T), in western Atlantic............ 10

June 19 Jap. aircraft carriers Shokaki, Taiho in 1st Battle of Philippine Sea by U. S. sub

July 17 Two munitions ships (E) Port Chicago, Calif.................. 322

Sept. 8 It. Rex in Trieste Harbor by Br. planes

Oct. 24 U. S. carrier Princeton (E) off Leyte

Oct. 24 Jap. battleship Musashi sunk by U. S. planes

Oct. 25 Jap. battleships Fuso, Yamashiro; cruisers Suzuya, Chaikuma, Chokai, Mogami, and aircraft carriers Chiyoda, Zuikaku, Zuiho and Chitose sunk by U. S. Navy in 2nd Battle of Philippine Sea

Nov. 12 German battleship Tirpitz off Norway

Nov. 21 Jap. battleship Kongo off China by U. S. sub

Nov. 24 Swedish Hansa (E) off Gotland...... 100

Nov. 29 Jap. aircraft carrier Shanano off Jap. by U. S. sub

Dec. 18 U. S. destroyers Spence, 318; Monaghan, 245, and Hull, 202 (S) in Pacific

Dec. 24 Belgian Leopoldville (T) enroute to Cherbourg.................. 764

**1945**

Jan. 29 U. S. S. Serpens (E) off Guadalcanal.................. 196

Jan. 30 German Wilhelm Gustloff sunk off Danzig with refugees..........6,000

Mar. 19 U. S. aircraft carrier Franklin (D), made port................. 832

Apr. 7 Jap. battleship Yamato (72,809 tons) off Kyushu Island by U. S. planes....3,033

Apr. 9 U. S. Liberty ship (E) Bari, Italy... 360

Apr. 9 German battleship Adm. Scheer by R.A.F. at Kiel

Apr. 16 German battleship Luetzow by R.A.F.

May 11 U. S. aircraft carrier Bunker Hill (D) 373

July 8 Brazilian cruiser Baia (E) in Atlantic 300

July 24 Jap. battleship Hyuga, cruiser Tone, and aircraft carriers Amagi, Kaiyo sunk off Kure by U. S. planes

July 28 Jap. battleships Haruna, Ise; cruisers Aoba, Izumo and Iwate sunk off Kure by U. S. planes

July 31 U. S. cruiser Indianapolis (T) Philippine Sea (last major loss WW II).. 880

**1947**

Jan. 19 Greek Himera (M) off Athens....... 392

Apr. 16 French Grandcamp (E) in Texas City harbor................... 510

July 17 Ferry Randas (S) Bombay, India.... 625

Nov. 25 U. S. freighter Clarksdale Victory off Br. Columbia.............. 49

**1948**

Jan. 28 Jap. Joo Maru (M) Okayama, Jap.. 250

June 11 Danish Kobenhavn (M) in Kattegat Sound............ 150
Dec. 3 Kiangya (E) in China Sea........... 1,100

**1949**
Jan. 27 Taiping: collier (C) off South China.. 600
Sept. 17 Canadian Noronic (B) at Toronto... 119

**1950**
Jan. 12 Br. sub. Truculent (C) Thames Estuary.................. 65
June 19 Br. Indian Enterprise (E) Red Sea.. 72
Aug. 25 U.S. hospital ship Benevolence, U.S. freighter Mary Luckenbach (C) off San Francisco.............. 24

**1951**
Apr. 16 Br. sub Affray, Eng. Channel....... 75
May 17 Fr. LST Adour (E) Nhatrang, Indo-China..................... 78
June 12 U. S. destroyer Walke (D) off Korea 26
Sept. 1 Fishing boat Pelican (S) Montauk... 45
Sept. 17 Fr. landing ship (M) Cochin, China. 68

**1952**
Jan. 9 Freighter Pennsylvania (S) Pacific.. 45
Jan. 10 Freighter Flying Enterprise (S) off Lizard Pt..................... 1
Apr. 21 U.S. cruiser St. Paul (D) off Korea. 34
Apr. 26 U. S. destroyer Hobson (C) with aircraft carrier Wasp in Atlantic.. 176
Sept. 24 Fr. sub La Sibylle lost off Toulon... 48

**1953**
Jan. 9 South Korean Chang Tyong-Ho (F) off Pusan, Korea............. 249
Jan. 31 Princess Victoria (S) off N. Ireland 133
Apr. 4 Turkish sub Dumlupinar (C) with Sw Naboland, Dardanelles...... 81
Aug. 1 Fr. Monique (V) near New Caledonia. 120
Oct. 16 U. S. aircraft carrier Leyte (D) in Boston harbor............... 37

**1954**
Mar. 26 Sp. Guadalete (S) in Mediterranean 133
May 26 U.S. aircraft carrier Bennington (D) 75 mi. south of Newport, R. I.... 103
Sept. 26 Jap. ferry Toya Maru (S) Tsugaru Strait, Japan................ 1,172
Oct. 7 U.S. Mornackite (S) off Virginia.... 37

**1955**
May 11 Jap. ferry Shiun Maru (C) Inland Sea, Japan.................. 173
June 16 Br. sub Sidon (E) Portland, Eng.... 13

**1956**
Jan. 18 Tanker Salem Maritime (E) Lake Charles, La.................. 52
July 25 It. liner Andrea Doria and Sw. liner Stockholm (C) off Nantucket.... 51
Sept. 16 U.S. Freighter Perlagia (S) off Norway 32

**1957**
July 14 U.S.S.R. Eshghabad (G) Caspian Sea 270
Sept. 21 W. Ger. bark Pamir (S) off Azores.. 80

**1958**
Jan. 26 Jap. ferry Nankai Maru (V) Inland Sea....................... 170
Mar. 1 Turkish ferry Uskudar capsized off Izmit, Turkey................ 361
Nov. 18 U.S. freighter Carl D. Bradley (S), Lake Michigan.............. 33

**1959**
Jan. 30 Danish passenger-freighter Hans Hedtoft hit iceberg, Greenland... 95
Aug. 22 Philippine Pilar II (S) off Palawan... 90

**1960**
Dec. 14 Yugoslav tanker Peter Zoranic, Gr. tanker World Harmony (C) in Bosporus...................... 53
Dec. 19 U.S. aircraft carrier Constellation (B), Brooklyn Navy Yard........ 50

**1961**
Apr. 8 Br. liner Dara (B), Persian Gulf.... 212
July 8 Portuguese Save (G) off Mozambique 259
Sept. 3 Vencedor capsized off Colombia..... 100

**1962**
Jan. 8 Yugoslav Saba, Br. Dorington Court (C), English Channel............ 28
Nov. 18 Norwegian Tharald Brovig, Jap Munakata Maru (C), Japan....... 39

**1963**
Feb. 3 U.S. tanker Marine Sulphur Queen (V) Gulf of Mexico............ 39
Apr. 10 U.S. Navy atomic submarine Thresher sank N. Atlantic.......... 129
July 11 Argentine Ciudad de Asuncion (B), River Plate.................. 53
Dec. 23 Greek liner Lakonia (B) Atlantic.... 155

**1964**
Feb. 10 Australian destroyer Voyager (C) Pacific..................... 82
Nov. 19 Launch capsized, Chenab River, India 125
Nov. 26 Norwegian tanker Stolt Dagali, Israeli liner Shalom (C) off N.J......... 19

**1965**
Mar. 18 Boat loaded with pilgrims (S) Gobindsagar Lake, India.......... 100
Nov. 2 Cuban refugee boat sank off Mexico.. 39
Nov. 13 Cruise ship Yarmouth Castle (B) off Nassau.................... 89

**1966**
Jan. 10 Sp. freighter Monte Palomares (S) N. Atlantic................. 32
Jan. 25 Indonesian Permina (S) Sumatra... 89
May 16 Philippine Pioneer Cebu (S)...... 132
June 16 U. S. tanker Texaco Massachusetts, Br. tanker Alva Cape (C) N. Y.
July 31 Br. launch Darwin (V) off Br. coast.. 31
Oct. 22 U. S. freighter Golden State, Philippine Pioneer Leyte (C) Manila Bay 71
Oct. 26 U. S. aircraft carrier Oriskany caught fire, Gulf of Tonkin........... 43
Dec. 8 Greek ferryship Heraklion (S) Aegean 264

**1967**
Jan. 14 Korean ferry Hanil-Ho (C) off Korea 72
Feb. 21 Canadian trawler Cape Bonnie (W), Halifax Harbor............... 15
May 23 Greek tanker Circe (E), Mediterranean................. 38
July 29 USN carrier Forrestal (B), N. Vietnam.................... 134
Oct. 9 U.S. freighter Panoceanic Fait (S), N. Pacific.................. 34

# Major Railroad Wrecks in the United States

Source: Federal Railroad Admin., Bureau of Railroad Safety
Date, Location and Number of Persons Killed. *See also Chronology*

| Date | Location | Killed |
|---|---|---|
| 1876 Dec. 29 | Ashtabula, Ohio | 92 |
| 1880 Aug. 11 | Mays Landing, N. J. | 40 |
| 1887 Aug. 10 | Chatsworth, Ill. | 81 |
| 1888 Oct. 10 | Mud Run, Pa. | 55 |
| 1896 July 30 | Atlantic City, N. J. | 60 |
| 1903 Dec. 23 | Laurel Run, Pa. | 53 |
| 1904 Aug. 7 | Eden, Colo. | 96 |
| 1904 Sept. 24 | New Market, Tenn. | 56 |
| 1906 Mar. 16 | Florence, Colo. | 35 |
| 1906 Oct. 28 | Atlantic City, N. J. | 40 |
| 1906 Dec. 30 | Washington, D. C. | 53 |
| 1907 Jan. 2 | Volland, Kans. | 33 |
| 1907 Jan. 19 | Fowler, Ind. | 29 |
| 1907 Feb. 16 | New York City | 22 |
| 1907 Mar. 23 | Colton, Calif. | 26 |
| 1907 July 20 | Salem, Mich. | 33 |
| 1907 Sept. 15 | Canaan, N. H. | 24 |
| 1910 Mar. 1 | Wellington, Wash. | 96 |
| 1910 Mar. 21 | Green Mountain, Ia. | 55 |
| 1911 Aug. 25 | Manchester, N. Y. | 29 |
| 1912 July 4 | East Corning, N. Y. | 39 |
| 1912 July 5 | Ligonier, Pa. | 23 |
| 1913 Sept. 2 | North Haven, Conn. | 21 |
| 1914 Aug. 5 | Tipton Ford, Mo. | 43 |
| 1914 Sept. 15 | Lebanon, Mo. | 28 |
| 1916 Mar. 29 | Amherst, Ohio | 27 |
| 1917 Feb. 27 | Mount Union, Pa. | 20 |
| 1917 Sept. 28 | Kellyville, Okla. | 23 |
| 1917 Dec. 20 | Shepherdsville, Ky. | 46 |
| 1918 June 22 | Ivanhoe, Ind. | 68 |
| 1918 July 9 | Nashville, Tenn. | 101 |
| 1918 Nov. 1 | Brooklyn, Malbone St. Tunnel | 97 |
| 1919 Jan. 12 | South Byron, N. Y. | 22 |
| 1919 July 1 | Dunkirk, N. Y. | 12 |
| 1919 Dec. 20 | Onawa, Maine | 23 |
| 1921 Feb. 27 | Porter, Ind. | 37 |
| 1921 Dec. 5 | Woodmont, Pa. | 27 |
| 1922 Aug. 5 | Sulphur Springs, Mo. | 34 |
| 1922 Dec. 13 | Humble, Tex. | 22 |
| 1923 Sept. 27 | Lockett, Wyo. | 31 |
| 1925 June 16 | Hackettstown, N. J. | 50 |
| 1925 Oct. 27 | Victoria, Miss. | 21 |
| 1926 Sept. 5 | Waco, Colo. | 30 |
| 1928 Aug. 24 | I. R. T. subway, N. Y., Times Sq. | 18 |
| 1938 June 19 | Saugus, Mont. | 47 |
| 1939 Aug. 12 | Harney, Nev. | 24 |
| 1940 Apr. 19 | Little Falls, N. Y. | 31 |
| 1940 July 31 | Cuyahoga Falls, Ohio | 43 |
| 1942 Dec. 27 | Almonte, Ontario | 36 |
| 1943 Aug. 29 | Wayland, N. Y. | 27 |
| 1943 Sept. 6 | Frankford Junction, Philadelphia. | 79 |
| 1943 Dec. 16 | Bet. Rennert and Buie, N. C. | 72 |
| 1944 July 6 | High Bluff, Tenn. | 35 |
| 1944 Aug. 4 | Near Stockton, Ga. | 47 |
| 1944 Sept. 14 | Dewey, Ind. | 29 |
| 1944 Dec. 31 | Bagley, Utah | 50 |
| 1945 Aug. 9 | Michigan, N. Dak. | 34 |
| 1946 Apr. 25 | Naperville, Ill. | 45 |
| 1947 Feb. 18 | Gallitzin, Pa. | 24 |
| 1950 Feb. 17 | Rockville Centre, N. Y. | 31 |
| 1950 Sept. 11 | Coshocton, Ohio | 33 |
| 1950 Nov. 22 | Richmond Hill, N. Y. | 79 |
| 1951 Feb. 6 | Woodbridge, N. J. | 84 |
| 1951 Nov. 12 | Wyuta, Wyo. | 17 |
| 1951 Nov. 25 | Woodstock, Ala. | 17 |
| 1953 Mar. 27 | Conneaut, Ohio | 21 |
| 1956 Jan. 22 | Los Angeles, Calif. | 30 |
| 1956 Feb. 28 | Swampscott, Mass. | 13 |
| 1956 Sept. 5 | Springer, N. M. | 20 |
| 1957 June 11 | Vroman, Colo. | 12 |
| 1958 Sept. 15 | Elizabethport, N. J. | 48 |
| 1960 Mar. 14 | Bakersfield, Calif. | 14 |
| 1962 July 28 | Steelton, Pa. | 19 |
| 1966 Dec. 28 | Everett, Mass. | 13 |

World's worst wreck occurred Dec. 12, 1917, Modane, France, passenger train derailed, 543 killed.

# Major Earthquakes

Source: United States Coast and Geodetic Survey. *See also Chronology.*

| Year | Place | Deaths | Year | Place | Deaths |
|---|---|---|---|---|---|
| 1057 | China, Chihli | 25,000 | 1923 Sept. 1 | Japan, Tokyo | 143,000 |
| 1268 | Asia Minor, Silicia | 60,000 | 1932 Dec. 26 | China, Kansu | 70,000 |
| 1290 Sept. 27 | China, Chihli | 100,000 | 1933 Mar. 10 | Long Beach, Calif. | 115 |
| 1293 May 20 | Japan, Kamarkura | 30,000 | 1935 May 31 | India, Quetta | 60,000 |
| 1531 Jan. 26 | Portugal, Lisbon | 30,000 | 1939 Jan. 24 | Chile, Chillan | 30,000 |
| 1556 Jan. 24 | China, Shensi | 830,000 | 1939 Dec. 27 | Turkey, Erzincan | 23,000 |
| 1667 Nov | Caucasia, Shemaka | 80,000 | 1946 May 31 | Eastern Turkey | 1,300 |
| 1693 Jan. 11 | Italy, Catania | 60,000 | 1948 Dec. 21 | Japan, Honshu | 2,000 |
| 1737 Oct. 11 | India, Calcutta | 300,000 | 1948 June 28 | Japan, Fukui | 5,131 |
| 1755 June 7 | Persia, northern | 40,000 | 1949 Aug. 5 | Ecuador, Pelileo | 6,000 |
| 1755 Nov. 1 | Portugal, Lisbon | 60,000 | 1950 Aug. 15 | India, Assam | 1,500 |
| 1783 Feb. 4 | Italy, Calabria | 50,000 | 1953 Mar. 18 | Northwestern Turkey | 1,200 |
| 1797 Feb. 4 | Ecuador, Quito | 41,000 | 1954 Sept. 9-12 | Northern Algeria | 1,657 |
| 1811 Dec. 16 | U.S. New Madrid, Mo. | | 1956 June 10-17 | Northern Afghanistan | 2,000 |
| 1819 June 16 | India, Cutch | 1,543 | 1957 July 2 | Northern Iran | 2,500 |
| 1822 Sept. 5 | Asia Minor, Aleppo | 22,000 | 1957 Dec. 4 | Outer Mongolia | 1,200 |
| 1828 Dec. 28 | Japan, Echigo | 30,000 | 1957 Dec. 13 | Western Iran | 2,000 |
| 1868 Aug. 13-15 | Peru and Ecuador | 25,000 | 1960 Feb. 29 | Morocco, Agadir | 12,000 |
| 1875 May 16 | Venezuela, Colombia | 16,000 | 1960 May 21-30 | Southern Chile | 5,700 |
| 1896 June 15 | Japan, Sea wave | 22,000 | 1962 Sept. 1 | Northwestern Iran | 10,000 |
| 1897 June 12 | India, Assam | 1,542 | 1963 July 26 | Yugoslavia, Skopje | 1,100 |
| 1906 Apr. 18 | Calif., San Francisco | 700 | 1964 Mar. 27 | Alaska | 131 |
| 1906 Aug. 16 | Chile, Valparaiso | 1,500 | 1966 Aug. 19 | Eastern Turkey | 2,529 |
| 1908 Dec. 28 | Italy, Messina | 75,000 | 1967 July 29 | Northern Venezuela | 236 |
| 1915 Jan. 13 | Italy, Avezzano | 29,970 | 1968 Jan. 15 | Sicily | 146 |
| 1920 Dec. 16 | China, Kansu | 180,000 | 1968 May 15 | Japan, N. Honshu | 47 |

# Explosions

Date, Location, Number of Deaths—See also Marine Disasters, Fires and Chronology

| | | | | | | |
|---|---|---|---|---|---|---|
| 1910 Oct. | 1 | Los Angeles Times Bldg | 21 | 1959 Apr. 10 World War II bomb, Philippines. | 38 |
| 1913 Mar. | 7 | Dynamite, Baltimore harbor | 55 | 1959 June 2 Gas truck, Penn. Turnpike | 10 |
| 1915 Sept. | 27 | Gasoline tank car, Ardmore, Okla. | 47 | 1959 June 28 Rail tank cars, Meldrin, Ga. | 25 |
| 1916 July | 22 | San Francisco parade | 10 | 1959 Aug. 7 Dynamite truck, Roseburg, Ore. | 13 |
| 1917 Apr. | 10 | Munitions plant, Eddystone, Pa. | 133 | 1959 Nov. 29 Jamurl Bazar, India, explosives.. | 46 |
| 1917 Dec. | 6 | Halifax Harbor, Canada | 1,600 | 1959 Dec. 13 Dortmund, Ger., 2 apt. bldgs. | 26 |
| 1918 July | 2 | Explosives, Split Rock, N. Y. | 50 | 1960 Mar. 4 Belgian munition ship, Havana. | 100 |
| 1918 Oct. | 4 | Shell plant, Morgan Station, N. J. | 64 | 1960 Oct. 4 Chemical plant, Kingsport, Tenn. | 10 |
| 1919 May | 22 | Food plant, Cedar Rapids, Iowa | 44 | 1960 Oct. 25 Gas, Windsor, Ont., store | 11 |
| 1920 Sept. | 16 | Wall St., New York, bomb | 30 | 1962 Jan. 18 Gas pipeline, Alberta, Canada... | 19 |
| 1924 Jan. | 3 | Food plant, Pekin, Ill. | 42 | 1962 Mar. 3 Gasoline truck, Syria | 31 |
| 1937 Mar. | 18 | New London, Tex., school | 294 | 1962 Oct. 3 Telephone Co. office, New York.. | 23 |
| 1940 Sept. | 11 | Hercules Powder, Kenvil, N. J. | 51 | 1963 Jan. 2 Packing plant, Terre Haute, Ind. | 16 |
| 1942 June | 5 | Ordnance plant, Elwood, Ill. | 49 | 1963 Mar. 9 Dyn. plant, Modderfontain, S. Af. | 45 |
| 1944 Apr. | 14 | Bombay, India, harbor | 700 | 1963 Aug. 13 Explosives dump, Gauhiti, India.. | 32 |
| 1944 July | 17 | Port Chicago, Calif., pier | 322 | 1963 Oct. 31 State Fair Coliseum, Indianapolis | 73 |
| 1944 Oct. | 21 | Liquid gas tank, Cleveland | 135 | 1964 July 23 Bone, Algeria, harbor, munitions. | 100 |
| 1947 Apr. | 16 | Texas City, Tex., pier | 561 | 1965 Mar. 4 Gas pipeline Natchitoches, Ala... | 17 |
| 1948 July | 28 | Farben works, Ludwigshafen,Ger. | 184 | 1965 Aug. 9 Missile silo, Searcy, Ark. | 53 |
| 1950 May | 19 | Munition barges, S. Amboy, N. J | 30 | 1965 Oct. 21 Bridge, Tila Bund, Pakistan..... | 80 |
| 1956 Aug. | 7 | Dynamite trucks, Call, Colombia.1,100 | | 1965 Oct. 30 Marketplace, Cartagena, Col. | 48 |
| 1956 Dec. | 3 | Brooklyn, N. Y., pier | 10 | 1965 Nov. 24 Armory, Keokuk, Iowa. | 20 |
| 1957 Dec. | 5 | Villa Rica, Ga., gas line | 17 | 1966 Oct. 13 Chemical plant, La Salle, Que. | 11 |
| 1958 Apr. | 18 | Sunken munitions ship, Okinawa. | 40 | 1967 Feb. 17 Chemical plant, Hawthorne, N.J.. | 11 |
| 1958 May | 22 | Nike missiles, Leonardo, N. J. | 10 | 1967 Apr. 25 Apartment bldg., Moscow | 20 |

# Major Kidnaping Crimes

**Charles B. Ross,** 4, in Germantown, Pa., **July 1, 1874.** $20,000 not delivered. Boy never found. abductors shot while committing burglary.

**Edward A. Cudahy, Jr.,** 16, in Omaha, Neb., **Dec. 18, 1900.** Returned Dec. 20 after $25,000 ransom paid. Pat Crowe confessed.

**Robert Franks,** 13, in Chicago, **May 22, 1924,** by two youths, Loeb and Leopold, who killed boy. Demand for $10,000 ignored. Loeb died in prison, Leopold paroled 1958, freed Mar. 16, 1963.

**Marian Parker,** 12, in Los Angeles. **Dec. 15, 1927,** returned dead after $1,500 paid. William E. Hickman convicted, hanged.

**Charles A. Lindbergh, Jr.,** 20 mos. old, in Hopewell, N. J., **Mar. 1, 1932;** found dead May 12. Ransom of $50,000 was paid to man identified as Bruno Richard Hauptmann, 35, paroled German convict who entered U.S. illegally. Hauptmann passed ransom bill and $14,000 marked money was found in his garage. He was convicted after spectacular trial at Flemington, and electrocuted in Trenton, N. J., prison, Apr. 3, 1936.

**William A. Hamm, Jr.,** 39, in St. Paul, **June 15, 1933.** $100,000 paid. Alvin Karpis given life.

**Charles F. Urschel,** in Oklahoma City, **July 22, 1933.** Released July 31 after $200,000 paid. Geo. (Machine Gun) Kelly and 5 others given life.

**Edward G. Bremer,** 37, St. Paul, Minn., **Jan. 17, 1934.** Released Feb. 7 after $200,000 paid. Two given life.

**George Weyerhaeuser,** 9, in Tacoma, Wash., **May 24, 1935.** Returned home June 1 after $200,000 paid. Kidnapers given 20 to 60 years.

**Charles Mattson,** 10, in Tacoma, Wash., **Dec. 27, 1936.** Found dead Jan. 11, 1937. Kidnaper asked $28,000, failed to contact, escaped.

**Arthur Fried,** in White Plains, N.Y., **Dec. 4, 1937.** Body not found. Two kidnapers executed.

**Peter Levine,** 12. in New Rochelle, N.Y., **Feb. 24, 1938.** Dismembered body found May 29. $30,-000 ransom not paid. Kidnapers escaped.

**Robert C. Greenlease,** 6, son of a Kansas City, Mo., motor car dealer, taken from school Sept. 28, 1953, and held for $600,000. Body found Oct. 7, when Mrs. Bonnie Brown Heady and Carl A. Hall were arrested. They pleaded guilty and were executed Dec. 18. Two arresting officers—Louis Shoulders and Elmer Dolan—were sentenced to 3 yrs. and 2 yrs., respectively, for perjury in describing recovery of $300,000 of the ransom. Hall claimed he had over $590,000 when arrested.

**Evelyn Smith,** 23, in Phoenix, Ariz., **June 9,** 1954. Released unharmed June 10, after $75,000 was paid.

**Peter Weinberger,** 32 days old, Westbury, L.I., N.Y., July 4, 1956, for $2,000 ransom, not paid. Child found dead. Angelo John LaMarca, 31, convicted, executed.

**Cynthia Ruotolo,** 6 wks. old, taken from carriage in front of Hamden, Conn., store Sept. 1, 1956. Body found Sept. 6 in lake two miles away.

**Lee Crary,** 8, in Everett, Wash., Sept. 22, 1957, for $10,000 ransom, not paid. Escaped after 3 days, led police to George E. Collins, convicted.

**Eric Peugeot,** 4, taken from playground at St. Cloud golf course, Paris, Apr. 12, 1960. Released unharmed 3 days later after payment of undisclosed sum to kidnaper who had demanded $100,000. Raymond Rolland and Pierre-Marie Larcher sentenced to 20 years in prison Oct. 31, 1962, as kidnapers.

**Frank Sinatra, Jr.,** 19, from hotel room in Lake Tahoe, Calif., Dec. 8, 1963. Released Dec. 11 after his father paid $240,000 ransom. John W. Irwin, Barry W. Keenan and Joseph C. Amsler convicted, sentenced to prison; most of ransom recovered.

**Madeleine Dassault,** plane-maker's wife, in Paris, May 23, 1964; found safe next day; 3 arrested.

**Daniel Jesse Goldman,** 18, abducted Mar. 18, 1966, from his home near Bal Harbour, Fla.

**Mrs. Betty Hill,** 42, was held prisoner in her Boulder, Colo., home Jan. 6, 1967, by an intruder who released her shortly afterward when her husband paid $50,000 ransom.

**Kenneth King,** 11, was abducted from his bedroom in Beverly Hills, Calif. Apr. 3, 1967, but was freed unharmed 3 days later after his father paid $250,000 ransom.

*See also Chronology.*

# Floods, Hurricanes, Other Storms

Date, Location, Number of Deaths—*See also Tornadoes and Chronology*
(B)—Blizzard, (F)—Flood, (H)—Hurricane, (S)—Other Storms, (T)—Typhoon, (TW)—Tidal Wave

| Date | Event | Deaths | Date | Event | Deaths |
|---|---|---|---|---|---|
| 1887 | (F), Hwang-ho R., China.. | 900,000 | 1959 Dec. 2 | (F), Frejus, France....... | 412 |
| 1888 Mar. 11-14 | (B), Eastern U. S........ | 400 | 1960 May 23-24 | (TW), Hawaii, Japan, Okinawa.............. | 237 |
| 1889 May 31 | (F), Johnstown, Pa...... | 2,200 | 1960 Sept. 4-12 | (H), Donna, Caribbean, eastern U.S........... | 148 |
| 1900 Sept. 8 | (H, TW), Galveston, Tex.. | 5,000 | 1960 Oct. 10 | (TW), East Pakistan...... | 6,000 |
| 1911 | (F), Yangtze R., China.... | 100,000 | 1960 Oct. 31 | (TW), East Pakistan...... | 4,000 |
| 1913 Mar. 25-27 | (F), Ohio, Indiana........ | 732 | 1961 July 19 | (F), Charleston, W. Va..... | 19 |
| 1913 | (F), Brazos, Tex........ | 500 | 1961 Sept. 11 | (H), Carla, Tex., La...... | 40 |
| 1915 Aug. 17 | (H), Galveston, Tex..... | 275 | 1961 Oct. 31 | (H), Hattie, Br. Honduras. | 400 |
| 1926 Sept. 16-22 | (H), Florida, Alabama... | 372 | 1962 Feb. 17 | (F), German North Sea coast | 343 |
| 1926 Oct. 20 | (H), Cuba.............. | 600 | 1962 Sept. 27 | (F), Barcelona, Spain...... | 445 |
| 1928 Mar. 13 | (F), collapse of St. Francis Dam, Santa Paula, Calif. | 450 | 1963 May 28-29 | (S), East Pakistan........ | 10,000 |
| 1928 Sept. 12-17 | (H), W. Indies, Fla...... | 4,000 | 1963 Oct. 4-8 | (H), Flora, Cuba, Haiti... | 6,000 |
| 1930 Sept. 3 | (H), San Domingo....... | 2,000 | 1963 Oct. 9 | (F), Collapse of Vaiont Dam, northern Italy.... | 1,800 |
| 1937 Jan. 22 | (F), Ohio, Miss. Valleys... | 250 | 1963 Nov. 14-15 | (F), Haiti.............. | 500 |
| 1938 Sept. 21 | (H), New England...... | 600 | 1964 Oct. 4-7 | (H), Hilda, Louisiana..... | 36 |
| 1942 Oct. 15-16 | (H), Bengal, India........ | 11,000 | 1964 Nov. 12 | (F), South Vietnam....... | 7,000 |
| 1942 Nov. 6 | (TW), Bengal, India....... | 10,000 | 1965 May 11 | (S), East Pakistan....... | 17,000 |
| 1944 Sept. 12-16 | (H), N. C. to New England. | 389 | 1965 June 1-2 | (S), East Pakistan........ | 30,000 |
| 1951 Aug. | (F), Manchuria....... | 1,800 | 1965 June 11 | (F), Sanderson, Tex....... | 10 |
| 1953 Jan. 31- Feb. 1 | (S), high tides, Western Europe.............. | 2,000 | 1965 Sept. 7-10 | (H), Betsy, Fla., Miss., La. | 74 |
| 1953 Sept. 25-27 | (T), Viet Nam & Japan... | 1,300 | 1965 Dec. 15 | (S), East Pakistan........ | 10,000 |
| 1954 Aug. 30 | (H), Carol. Northeast U. S. | 68 | 1966 Jan. 31 | (S), Eastern U. S......... | 166 |
| 1954 Sept. 11 | (H), Edna, N.E.U.S., Canada | 23 | 1966 June 4-10 | (H), Alma, Honduras, S.E., U. S................. | 51 |
| 1954 Oct. 12-16 | (H), Hazel, East U. S., Haiti | 347 | 1966 Sept. 24-30 | (H), Inez, Caribbean islands.............. | 293 |
| 1955 Aug. 12-13 | (H), Connie, Carolinas, Va., Md............... | 43 | 1966 Nov. 4 | (B), Midwest, eastern U. S. | 37 |
| 1955 Aug. 18-19 | (H), Diane, Eastern U. S.. | 400 | 1966 Nov. 4-6 | (F), Venice, Florence, Italy | 113 |
| 1955 Sept. 19 | (H), Hilda, Mexico....... | 200 | 1967 Jan. 12 | (S), Northern Mexico .... | 34 |
| 1955 Sept. 22-28 | (H), Janet, Caribbean... | 500 | 1967 Jan. 18-24 | (F), Eastern Brazil ...... | 894 |
| 1955 Oct. | (F), India and Pakistan ... | 1,700 | 1967 Jan. 26-27 | (B), Lower Gt. Lakes area. | 80 |
| 1956 Feb. 1-29 | (B), Western Europe...... | 1,000 | 1967 Feb. 17-23 | (F), Rio de Janeiro....... | 224 |
| 1957 June 27-30 | (H), Audrey—La., Tex.... | 430 | 1967 Mar. 19 | (F), Rio de Janeiro....... | 436 |
| 1958 Feb. 15-16 | (B), Northeastern U.S..... | 171 | 1967 July 9 | (T), Billie, Southern Japan. | 347 |
| 1959 Sept. 17-19 | (T), Sarah, Far East...... | 2,000 | 1967 Sept. 5-23 | (H), Beulah, Carib., Mex., Tex................. | 54 |
| 1959 Sept. 26-27 | (T), Vera, Honshu, Japan.. | 4,466 | 1967 Dec. 12-20 | (B), Southwest U. S....... | 51 |
| 1959 Oct. 27 | (H), Mazanillo. Mexico..... | 1,500 | | | |
| 1959 Nov. 1 | (F), Western Mexico..... | 2,000 | | | |

# Chief Political Assassinations Since 1865

**1865**—April 14. Abraham Lincoln, President of the United States, in Washington; died April 15.

**1881**—Mar. 13. Alexander II, of Russia—July 2. James A. Garfield, President of the United States, in Washington; died Sept. 19.

**1893**—Oct. 28. Carter H. Harrison, Sr., Mayor of Chicago.

**1894**—June 24. Marie Francois Sadi-Carnot, President of France.

**1900**—Jan. 30. William Goebel, Governor of Kentucky—July 29. Humbert I, King of Italy.

**1901**—Sept. 6. William McKinley, President of the United States, in Buffalo; died Sept. 14. Leon Czolgosz executed for the crime Oct. 29.

**1903**—June 11. King Alexander I and Queen Draga of Serbia by army officers at Belgrade.

**1913**—Feb. 23. Francisco I. Madero, President of Mexico and Jose Pino Suarez, the Vice-President—March 18. George, King of Greece.

**1914**—June 28. Archduke Francis Ferdinand of Austria-Hungary and his wife, Countess Sophie Chotek, Duchess of Hohenberg, in Sarajevo, Bosnia (later part of Yugoslavia), by Gavrillo Princip.

**1918**—July 12. Grand Duke Michael of Russia, at Perm—July 16. Nicholas II, abdicated Czar of Russia; his wife, the Czarina Alexandra; their son, Czarevitch Alexis, and their daughters, Grand Duchesses Olga, Tatiana, Marie, Anastasia, and 4 members of their household were murdered in cold blood by Bolsheviki at Ekaterinburg—Dec. 14. Pres. Sidonio Paes of Portugal, in Lisbon.

**1920**—May 20. Gen. Venustiano Carranza, President of Mexico, in Tiaxcaltenago.

**1923**—July 20. Gen. Francisco "Pancho" Villa, ex-rebel leader, in Parral, Mexico.

**1928**—July 17. Gen. Alvaro Obregon, President-elect of Mexico, in San Angel, Mexico.

**1933**—Feb. 15. In Miami, Fla., Joseph Zangara, anarchist, shot at President-elect Franklin D. Roosevelt, but a woman seized his arm, and the bullet fatally wounded Mayor Anton J. Cermak, of Chicago, who died March 6. Zangara was electrocuted on March 20, 1933.

**1934**—July 25. In Vienna, Engelbert Dollfuss, Chancellor of Austria, by Nazi, in the chancellery. Otto Planetta convicted and hanged—Oct. 9. In Marseilles, King Alexander I of Yugoslavia and French Foreign Minister Jean Louis Barthou.

**1935**—Sept. 8. U. S. Senator Huey P. Long, shot in Baton Rouge, La., by Dr. Carl Austin Weiss, who was slain by Long's bodyguards.

**1940**—Aug. 20. Leon Trotsky (Leba Bronstein), 63, exiled Russian war minister, near Mexico City. Killer, identified as Ramon Mercador del Rio, a Spaniard, served 20 years in Mexican prison.

**1942**—Dec. 24. Adm. Jean F. Darlan, 61, Algiers.

**1948**—Jan. 30. Mohandas K. Gandhi, 78, shot in New Delhi, India, by Nathuran Vinayak Godse, 36—Sept. 17. Count Folke Bernadotte, U. N. Mediator for Palestine, ambushed in Jerusalem.

**1950**—Nov. 13. Col. C. Delgado Chalbaud, President of Venezuela, in Caracas.

**1955**—Jan. 2. Jose Antonio Remon, President of Panama, by machine gun at race track, Panama.

**1956**—Sept. 21. Anastasio Somoza, President of Nicaragua, in Leon; died Sept. 29.

**1957**—July 26. President Carlos Castillo Armas of Guatemala, in Guatemala City by one of his own guards, who then committed suicide.

**1958**—July 14. King Faisal of Iraq; his uncle, Crown Prince Abdul Illah, and July 15, Premier Nuri as-Said, by rebels in Baghdad.

**1959**—Sept. 25. Prime Minister S. W. R. D. Bandaranaike of Ceylon, by Buddhist monk in Colombo.

**1960**—Aug. 29. Premier Hazza Majali of Jordan and 10 others killed by time bomb in his office.

**1961**—Jan. 17. Ex-Premier Patrice Lumumba of the Congo, ex-Youth Minister Maurice Mpolo and Senate Vice President Joseph Okito in Katanga Province—May 30. Dominican dictator Rafael Leonidas Trujillo Molina shot to death by assassins near Ciudad Trujillo.

**1963**—Jan. 13. President Sylvanus Olympio of Togo, by ex-soldiers at Lome—Nov. 22. U. S. President John F. Kennedy fatally shot in Dallas, Tex.; Lee Harvey Oswald accused.

**1965**—Jan. 21. Irani Premier Hassan Ali Mansour fatally wounded by assassin in Teheran; 4 executed. Feb. 21. Malcolm X, Negro nationalist, fatally shot in New York City; 3 sentenced to life.

**1966**—Sept. 6. Prime Minister Hendrik F. Verwoerd of South Africa stabbed to death in parliament at Capetown by drifter later ruled insane.

**1968**—Apr. 4. Rev. Dr. Martin Luther King, Jr., fatally shot in Memphis, Tenn.; suspect James Earl Ray captured in London—June 5. Sen. Robert F. Kennedy (D., N. Y.) shot by assassin in Los Angeles, died next day; Sirhan Sirhan, resident alien, charged with murder.

*See also Chronology.*

## ASSASSINATION ATTEMPTS

**1910**—Aug. 6. New York City Mayor Wm. J. Gaynor shot and seriously wounded by discharged city employee on liner about to leave for Europe.

**1912**—Oct. 14. Former U. S. President Theodore Roosevelt shot and seriously wounded by demented man in Milwaukee.

**1950**—Nov. 1. In an attempt to assassinate President Truman, two men identified as members of a Puerto Rican nationalist movement—Griselio Torresola and Oscar Collazo—tried to shoot their way into Blair House. Torresola was killed, and a guard, Pvt. Leslie Coffelt was fatally shot, Collazo, wounded, recovered and was tried and convicted Mar. 7, 1951 for the murder of Coffelt. His death sentence was commuted to life imprisonment by President Truman, July 24, 1952.

*See also Chronology.*

# Some Notable Aircraft Disasters Since 1937

### See also Chronology

| Year | | | Aircraft | Site of accident | Deaths |
|---|---|---|---|---|---|
| 1937 | May | 6 | Ger. zeppelin Hindenburg...... | Burned at Mooring, Lakehurst, N. J......... | 36 |
| 1944 | Aug. | 23 | U. S. Air Force B-24.......... | Hit school, Freckelton, England............. | 76[1] |
| 1945 | July | 28 | U. S. Army B-25............. | Hit Empire State bldg., N. Y. C............ | 14[1] |
| 1946 | May | 20 | U. S. Army C-45............. | Struck Manhattan Co. bldg., N. Y. C........ | 5 |
| 1949 | Nov. | 1 | Eastern Air Lines DC-4........ | Rammed by Bolivian P-38, Wash., D. C...... | 55 |
| 1950 | Mar. | 12 | Chartered Avro Tudor......... | Crashed near Cardiff, Wales............... | 80 |
| 1950 | June | 24 | Northwest Airlines DC-4....... | Exploded in storm over Lake Michigan...... | 58 |
| 1950 | Aug. | 31 | TWA Constellation............ | Crashed, burned, near Cairo, Egypt........ | 55 |
| 1951 | Dec. | 16 | Miami Airlines C-46........... | Plunged into Elizabeth River, N. J......... | 56 |
| 1952 | Jan. | 22 | American Airlines Convair...... | Crashed in Elizabeth, N. J................ | 30[1] |
| 1952 | Feb. | 11 | National Airlines DC-6........ | Crashed in Elizabeth, N. J................ | 33[1] |
| 1952 | Dec. | 20 | U. S. Air Force C-124......... | Fell, burned, Moses Lake, Wash........... | 87 |
| 1953 | Mar. | 3 | Canadian Pacific Comet jet.... | Karachi, Pakistan..................... | 11[2] |
| 1953 | June | 18 | U. S. Air Force C-124......... | Crashed, burned near Tokyo.............. | 129 |
| 1953 | July | 12 | Transocean Air Lines DC-6B... | Crashed into ocean east of Wake Isl....... | 58 |
| 1955 | Mar. | 22 | U. S. Navy DC-6............. | Hit cliff near Honolulu, T. H............. | 66 |
| 1955 | Aug. | 11 | 2 USAF Flying Boxcars....... | Collided near Stuttgart, Germany......... | 66 |
| 1955 | Oct. | 6 | United Air Lines DC-4........ | Hit mountain west of Laramie, Wyo....... | 66 |
| 1955 | Nov. | 1 | United Air Lines DC-6B....... | Exploded, crashed near Longmont, Colo.... | 44[3] |
| 1956 | June | 20 | Venezuelan Super-Const....... | Crashed in Atlantic off Asbury Park, N. J.. | 74 |
| 1956 | June | 30 | TWA Super-Const., United DC-7 | Collided over Grand Canyon, Arizona..... | 128 |
| 1956 | Oct. | 10 | Military Air Transport C-118... | Disappeared 150 miles north of Azores..... | 59 |
| 1956 | Dec. | 9 | Trans-Canada North Star...... | Crashed in mountains, British Columbia.... | 62 |
| 1957 | Mar. | 21 | Military Air Transport C-97... | Disappeared over Pacific................ | 67 |
| 1957 | Aug. | 11 | Maritime Central Airways DC-4. | Crashed in swamp near Quebec........... | 79 |
| 1958 | Feb. | 1 | MATS C-118, USN P2V Neptune | Collided over Los Angeles................ | 48 |
| 1958 | Apr. | 21 | United Airlines DC-7, USAF jet. | Collided near Las Vegas, Nev............. | 49 |
| 1958 | May | 18 | Belgian Sabena DC-6B......... | Crashed at Casablanca, Morocco.......... | 65 |
| 1958 | Aug. | 14 | KLM Super-Constellation...... | Plunged into sea 130 mi. w. of Ireland..... | 99 |
| 1958 | Oct. | 17 | Soviet TU-104 jet airliner...... | Crashed near Kanash, 400 mi. e. of Moscow. | 75 |
| 1959 | Feb. | 3 | Amer. Airlines Lockheed Electra | Crashed in East River, New York City...... | 65 |
| 1959 | June | 26 | TWA Super-Constellation...... | Crashed in storm near Milan, Italy........ | 68 |
| 1960 | Feb. | 25 | USN transport & Arg. airliner... | Collided in air near Rio de Janeiro........ | 61 |
| 1960 | Mar. | 17 | Northwest Airlines Electra..... | Exploded over Tell City, Ind............. | 63 |
| 1960 | July | 27 | Sikorsky S-58 helicopter....... | Crashed in Chicago suburbs.............. | 13[5] |
| 1960 | Oct. | 4 | Eastern Air Lines Electra...... | Crashed after takeoff from Boston........ | 61 |
| 1960 | Dec. | 16 | United DC-8 jet, TWA Super-Constellation............... | Collided over New York City............. | 134[6] |
| 1960 | Dec. | 17 | U. S. Air Force C-131 Convair... | Crashed into Munich street car.......... | 53[1] |
| 1961 | Feb. | 15 | Sabena Airlines Boeing 707..... | Crashed at Berg, Belgium............... | 73[1] |
| 1961 | May | 10 | Air France Starliner.......... | Crashed in Sahara Desert............... | 79 |
| 1961 | July | 12 | Czech Ilyushin-18............ | Hit power line, Casablanca.............. | 72 |
| 1961 | July | 19 | Argentine Airlines DC-6....... | Crashed at Azul, Brazil................. | 67 |
| 1961 | Aug. | 9 | Cunard Eagle Airways Viking... | Crashed in North Sea off Norway......... | 39[7] |
| 1961 | Sept. | 1 | TWA Constellation............ | Crashed at Hinsdale, Ill................ | 78 |
| 1961 | Sept. | 10 | President Airlines DC-6........ | Crashed at Shannon, Ireland............ | 83 |
| 1961 | Nov. | 8 | Imperial Airlines Constellation.. | Crashed near Richmond, Va............. | 77[8] |
| 1962 | Mar. | 1 | Amer. Airlines Boeing 707 jet... | Crashed after takeoff, New York City..... | 95 |
| 1962 | Mar. | 4 | Br. Caledonian Airlines DC-7C.. | Crashed near Douala, Cameroun......... | 111 |
| 1962 | Mar. | 16 | Flying Tiger Super-Const...... | Vanished in western Pacific............. | 107 |
| 1962 | June | 3 | Air France Boeing 707 jet...... | Crashed on takeoff from Paris........... | 130 |
| 1962 | June | 22 | Air France Boeing 707 jet...... | Crashed in storm, Guadeloupe, W. I....... | 113 |
| 1962 | July | 7 | Italian Alitalia airliner....... | Crashed in storm 50 miles n.e. of Bombay.. | 94 |
| 1962 | Nov. | 27 | Brazilian Varig Boeing 707 jet.. | Crashed and burned in Lima, Peru........ | 97 |
| 1963 | Feb. | 1 | Mid. E. Viscount, Turk. AF C-47 | Collided over Ankara, Turkey........... | 95 |
| 1963 | June | 3 | Chartered Northw. Airlines DC-7 | Crashed in Pacific off British Columbia.... | 101 |
| 1963 | Sept. | 2 | Swissair Caravelle Jetliner..... | Crashed after takeoff from Zurich, Switz... | 80 |
| 1963 | Nov. | 29 | Trans-Canada Airlines DC-8F... | Crashed after takeoff from Montreal....... | 118 |
| 1963 | Dec. | 8 | Pan American Boeing 707....... | Crashed near Elkton, Md............... | 82 |
| 1964 | Feb. | 25 | Eastern Air Lines DC-8........ | Crashed in Lake Pontchartrain, La....... | 58 |
| 1964 | Feb. | 29 | Br. Eagle Bristol Britannia..... | Crashed near Innsbruck, Austria......... | 83 |
| 1964 | Mar. | 1 | Paradise Airline Constellation... | Crashed in snow storm, Lake Tahoe, Calif... | 85 |
| 1964 | May | 7 | Pacific Airlines F-27.......... | Crashed near Dublin, Calif.............. | 44[9] |
| 1964 | May | 11 | U.S. MATS C-135 Stratolifter... | Crashed at Clark AFB, Philippines........ | 75 |
| 1965 | Feb. | 8 | Eastern Air Lines DC-7B...... | Plunged into Atlantic after takeoff, New York. | 84 |
| 1965 | May | 20 | Pakistani Boeing 720-B........ | Crashed at Cairo, Egypt, Airport......... | 121 |
| 1965 | June | 25 | U. S. Air Force C-135 transport. | Crashed after takeoff from Los Angeles...... | 84 |
| 1965 | Aug. | 16 | United Airlines Boeing 727..... | Plunged into Lake Michigan near Chicago..... | 30 |
| 1965 | Aug. | 24 | U. S. Marine Corps transport... | Crashed after takeoff from Hong Kong....... | 58 |
| 1965 | Nov. | 8 | American Airlines Boeing 727 ... | Crashed in storm near Cincinnati, Ohio..... | 58 |
| 1965 | Nov. | 11 | United Airlines Boeing 727..... | Crashed, burned in landing at Salt Lake City.. | 42 |
| 1965 | Dec. | 4 | TWA Boeing 707, Eastern shuttle | Collided over Danbury, Conn............ | 4 |
| 1966 | Jan. | 24 | Air India Boeing 707 jetliner.... | Crashed on Mont Blanc, Switzerland...... | 117 |
| 1966 | Feb. | 4 | All-Nippon Boeing 727........ | Plunged into Tokyo Bay................ | 133[4] |
| 1966 | Mar. | 4 | Canadian Pacific DC-8........ | Crashed in landing at Tokyo Airport...... | 64 |
| 1966 | Mar. | 5 | BOAC Boeing 707 jetliner..... | Crashed on Japan's Mount Fuji......... | 124 |
| 1966 | Apr. | 22 | Military-chartered Electra..... | Crashed in storm near Ardmore, Okla...... | 82 |
| 1966 | Aug. | 6 | Braniff BAC-111 jetliner...... | Crashed near Falls City, Nebr........... | 42 |
| 1966 | Sept. | 1 | Britannia 102 turboprop....... | Crashed near Ljubljana, Yugoslavia...... | 97 |
| 1966 | Nov. | 24 | Bulgarian Tabson Ilyushin-18... | Crashed near Bratislava, Czechoslovakia... | 82 |
| 1966 | Dec. | 24 | U. S. military-chartered CL-44.. | Crashed into village in South Vietnam..... | 129[1] |
| 1967 | Mar. | 5 | Lake Airlines Convair 580..... | Crashed in storm near Kenton, Ohio...... | 38 |
| 1967 | Mar. | 9 | TWA DC-9, twin-engine Beechcraft................ | Collided in air at Urbana, Ohio.......... | 26 |
| 1967 | Mar. | 30 | Delta Air Lines DC-8......... | Hit motel at New Orleans............... | 18[1] |
| 1967 | Apr. | 20 | Swiss Brittania turboprop..... | Crashed at Nicosia, Cyprus............. | 126 |
| 1967 | June | 3 | Chartered British DC-4....... | Crashed into Mont Canigou, France...... | 88 |
| 1967 | June | 4 | Chartered British Argonaut.... | Crashed at Stockport, England.......... | 72 |
| 1967 | June | 23 | Mohawk Airlines BAC-111..... | Crashed near Blossburg, Pa............. | 34 |
| 1967 | June | 24 | Two U. S. Marine helicopters... | Collided in air at Camp Lejeune, N. C..... | 22 |
| 1967 | July | 19 | Piedmont Boeing 727, Cessna 310 | Collided in air, Hendersonville, N. C...... | 82 |
| 1967 | Oct. | 12 | British-Cypriot Mark IV Comet.. | Crashed into sea off Turkey............. | 66 |
| 1967 | Nov. | 20 | TWA Convair 880............ | Crashed in snowstorm at Cincinnati...... | 68 |
| 1967 | Dec. | 8 | Peruvian Faucett DC-4........ | Crashed near Huanuco, Peru........... | 66 |

[1]Including those on the ground and in buildings. [2]First fatal crash of commercial jet plane. [3]Caused by bomb planted by John G. Graham in insurance plot to kill his mother, a passenger. [4]Worst disaster involving single plane. [5]First crash of commercial helicopter. [6]Worst commercial air disaster; dead included all 84 aboard jet, all 44 aboard other plane and 6 on ground. [7]Including 34 English schoolboys. [8]Including 74 Army recruits. [9]Tape recording indicated pilot was shot.

# Fires
### Date, Location and Number of Persons Killed—*See also Chronology*

| Date | Location | Killed | Date | Location | Killed |
|---|---|---|---|---|---|
| 1871 Oct. 8 | Chicago, $196,000,000 loss | 250 | 1949 Apr. 5 | Hospital, Effingham, Ill. | 77 |
| 1871 Oct. 9 | Peshtigo, Wis., forest fire | 1,182 | 1950 Jan. 7 | Davenport, Iowa, Mercy Hospital | 41 |
| 1876 Dec. 5 | Brooklyn (N. Y.) Theater | 295 | 1953 Mar. 29 | Largo, Fla., nursing home | 35 |
| 1877 Jan. 20 | St. John, N. B., Canada | 100 | 1953 Apr. 16 | Chicago, metalworking plant | 35 |
| 1881 Dec. 8 | Ring Theater, Vienna | 850 | 1957 Feb. 17 | Home for Aged, Warrenton, Mo. | 72 |
| 1883 Jan. 10 | Milwaukee, Newhall Hotel | 71 | 1957 Nov. 16 | Niagara Falls, N. Y., tenement | 18 |
| 1887 May 25 | Opera, Comique, Paris | 200 | 1958 Mar. 19 | New York City loft building | 24 |
| 1887 Sept. 4 | Exeter, Eng., theater | 200 | 1958 Nov. 8 | Tenement, Montreal, Can. | 21 |
| 1894 Sept. 1 | Hickley, Minn., forest fire | 413 | 1958 Dec. 1 | Parochial school, Chicago | 95 |
| 1897 May 4 | Charity bazaar, Paris | 150 | 1958 Dec. 16 | Store, Bogota, Colombia | 83 |
| 1899 Mar. 17 | Windsor Hotel, New York | 45 | 1959 Mar. 5 | School near Little Rock, Ark. | 24 |
| 1900 June 30 | Hoboken, N. J., docks | 326 | 1959 June 23 | Resort hotel, Stalheim, Norway | 34 |
| 1902 Sept. 20 | Church, Birmingham, Ala. | 115 | 1960 Mar. 12 | Pusan, Korea, chemical plant | 68 |
| 1903 Dec. 30 | Iroquois Theater, Chicago | 602 | 1960 June 11 | Liverpool, Eng., store | 22 |
| 1904 Feb. 7 | Baltimore, Md. | none | 1960 July 14 | Mental hospital, Guatemala City | 225 |
| 1905 Mar. 20 | Brockton, Mass., shoe factory | 50 | 1961 Mar. 13 | Movie theater, Amude, Syria | 152 |
| 1908 Jan. 13 | Rhoads Thea., Boyertown, Pa. | 170 | 1961 Jan. 6 | Thomas Hotel, San Francisco | 20 |
| 1908 Mar. 4 | School, Collinwood, Ohio | 176 | 1961 May 15 | Tenement, Hong Kong | 25 |
| 1911 Mar. 25 | Triangle factory, New York | 145 | 1961 Dec. 8 | Hospital, Hartford, Conn. | 16 |
| 1913 July 22 | Binghamton, N. Y., factory | 35 | 1961 Dec. 17 | Circus, Niterol, Brazil | 323 |
| 1914 Mar. 9 | Mo. Athletic Club, St. Louis | 37 | 1963 May 4 | Theater, Dicurbel, Senegal | 64 |
| 1918 Apr. 13 | Norman, Okla., state hospital | 38 | 1963 Nov. 18 | Surfside Hotel, Atlantic City, N. J. | 25 |
| 1918 Oct. 12 | Cloquet, Minn., forest fire | 400 | 1963 Nov. 23 | Hotel home, Fitchville, Ohio | 63 |
| 1919 June 20 | Mayaguez Theater, San Juan | 150 | 1963 Dec. 29 | Roosevelt Hotel, Jacksonville, Fla. | 22 |
| 1923 May 17 | School, Camden, S. C. | 76 | 1964 May 8 | Apartment building, Manila | 30 |
| 1924 Dec. 24 | School, Hobart, Okla. | 35 | 1964 Dec. 18 | Nursing home, Fountaintown, Ind. | 20 |
| 1929 May 15 | Crile Hospital, Cleveland, Ohio | 124 | 1965 Mar. 1 | Apartment, LaSalle, Canada | 28 |
| 1930 Apr. 21 | Penitentiary, Columbus, Ohio | 320 | 1965 Dec. 20 | Jewish center, Yonkers, N. Y. | 12 |
| 1931 July 24 | Pittsburgh, Pa., home for aged | 48 | 1966 Mar. 11 | Numata, Jap., 2 ski resorts | 31 |
| 1936 Apr. 6 | Gainesville, Ga., hardware Co. | 57 | 1966 Apr. 23 | Lapinlahti, Finland, hospital | 29 |
| 1938 May 16 | Atlanta, Ga., Terminal Hotel | 35 | 1966 Aug. 13 | Melbourne, Austr., hotel | 29 |
| 1940 Apr. 23 | Dance hall, Natchez, Miss. | 198 | 1966 Sept. 12 | Anchorage, Alaska, hotel | 14 |
| 1942 Nov. 28 | Cocoanut Grove, Boston | 491 | 1966 Oct. 17 | N. Y. City bldg. (firemen) | 12 |
| 1943 Sept. 7 | Gulf Hotel, Houston | 55 | 1966 Dec. 7 | Erzurum, Turkey, barracks | 68 |
| 1944 July 6 | Ringling Circus, Hartford | 168 | 1967 Feb. 7 | Restaurant, Montgomery, Ala. | 25 |
| 1946 June 5 | LaSalle Hotel, Chicago | 61 | 1967 May 22 | Store, Brussels, Belgium | 322 |
| 1946 Dec. 7 | Winecoff Hotel, Atlanta | 119 | 1967 July 16 | State prison, Jay, Fla. | 37 |
| 1946 Dec. 12 | New York, ice plant, tenement | 37 | | | |

# Principal Mine Disasters in the U. S.
### ALL COAL MINES UNLESS OTHERWISE DESIGNATED
Source: Bureau of Mines. *See also Chronology.*

| Date | Location | Killed | Date | Location | Killed |
|---|---|---|---|---|---|
| Sept. 6, 1869* | Plymouth, Pa. | 110 | Feb. 8, 1923 | Dawson, N. Mex. | 120 |
| Mar. 13, 1884 | Pocahontas, Va. | 112 | Mar. 8, 1924 | Castle Gate, Utah | 171 |
| Jan. 27, 1891 | Mammoth, Pa. | 109 | Apr. 28, 1924 | Benwood, W. Va. | 119 |
| Jan. 7, 1892 | Krebs, Okla. | 100 | May 19, 1928 | Mather, Pa. | 195 |
| May 1, 1900 | Scofield, Utah | 200 | Dec. 23, 1932 | Moweaqua, Ill. | 54 |
| May 19, 1902 | Coal Creek, Tenn. | 184 | Jan. 10, 1940 | Bartley, W. Va. | 91 |
| July 10, 1902 | Johnstown, Pa. | 112 | July 15, 1940 | Portage, Pa. | 63 |
| June 30, 1903 | Hanna, Wyo. | 169 | Feb. 27, 1943 | Red Lodge, Mont. | 74 |
| Jan. 25, 1904 | Cheswick, Pa. | 179 | Mar. 25, 1947 | Centralia, Ill. | 111 |
| Feb. 20, 1905 | Virginia City, Ala. | 112 | Dec. 21, 1951 | West Frankfort, Ill. | 119 |
| Dec. 6, 1907 | Monongah, W. Va. | 361 | Feb. 4, 1957 | Bishop, Va. | 37 |
| Dec. 19, 1907 | Jacobs Creek, Pa. | 239 | Oct. 27, 1958 | Bishop, Va. | 22 |
| Nov. 28, 1908 | Marianna, Pa. | 154 | Mar. 2, 1961 | Terre Haute, Ind. | 22 |
| Nov. 13, 1909 | Cherry, Ill. | 259 | Dec. 6, 1962 | Carmichaels, Pa. | 37 |
| Apr. 8, 1911 | Littleton, Ala. | 128 | Apr. 25, 1963 | Dola, W. Va. | 22 |
| Oct. 22, 1913 | Dawson, N. Mex. | 263 | Aug. 27, 1963*** | Moab, Utah | 18 |
| Apr. 28, 1914 | Eccles, W. Va. | 181 | Dec. 28, 1965 | Redstone, Colo. | 9 |
| Mar. 2, 1915 | Layland, W. Va. | 112 | June 1, 1966 | Dora, Pa. | 5 |
| Apr. 27, 1917 | Hastings, Colo. | 121 | July 23, 1966 | Mt. Hope, W. Va. | 7 |
| June 8, 1917** | Butte, Mont. | 163 | Mar. 5, 1968**** | Calumet, La. | 21 |
| Nov. 6, 1922 | Spangler, Pa. | 77 | | | |

World's worst mine disaster killed 1,549 workers in the Honkeiko Colliery in Manchuria Apr. 26, 1942.
*Anthracite mine. **Metal mine. ***Potash mine. ****Salt mine.

# Principal Tornadoes Since 1900
### Source: Weather Bureau, United States Department of Commerce. *See also Chronology.*

| Date | Place | Dead | Date | Place | Dead |
|---|---|---|---|---|---|
| 1900 Nov. 20 | Ark., Miss., Tenn. | 73 | 1942 Mar. 16 | Central to N.E. Miss. | 75 |
| 1903 June 1 | Gainesville, Ga. | 98 | 1942 Apr. 27 | Rogers & Mayes Co., Okla. | 52 |
| 1905 May 10 | Snyder. Okla. | 87 | 1944 June 23 | Ohio, Pa., W. Va., Md. | 150 |
| 1908 Apr. 24 | Lamar Co.-Wayne Co., Miss. | 100 | 1945 Apr. 12 | Okla.-Ark. | 102 |
| 1909 Mar. 8 | Dallas-Monroe Co., Ark. | 64 | 1946 Jan. 4 | N. E. Texas | 30 |
| 1913 Mar. 23 | Omaha. Nebr. | 95 | 1947 Apr. 9 | Texas, Okla. & Kans. | 169 |
| 1916 June 5 | Ark. (series of tornadoes) | 83 | 1948 Mar. 19 | Bunker Hill & Gillespie, Ill. | 33 |
| 1917 Mar. 23 | New Albany, Ind. | 45 | 1949 Jan. 3 | La. & Ark. | 58 |
| 1917 May 26 | Mattoon-Charleston, Ill. | 101 | 1952 Mar. 21, 22 | Ark., Mo., Tenn. (series of tornadoes) | 208 |
| 1917 May 27 | Tennessee, Kentucky | 70 | 1953 May 11 | Waco, Texas | 114 |
| 1918 Aug. 21 | Tyler, Minn. | 36 | 1953 June 8 | Flint to Lakeport, Mich. | 116 |
| 1919 June 22 | Fergus Falls, Minn. | 59 | 1953 June 9 | Central & Eastern, Mass. | 90 |
| 1920 Mar. 28 | Ala.-Ga. | 50 | 1953 Dec. 5 | Vicksburg, Miss. | 38 |
| 1920 Apr. 20 | Mississippi, Alabama | 87 | 1955 May 25 | Udall, Kans. | 80 |
| 1920 May 2 | Louisiana, Miss. | 64 | 1957 May 20 | Williamsburg, Kans. to Ruskin Heights, Mo. | 48 |
| 1921 Apr. 15 | Texas, Arkansas | 61 | 1958 June 4 | Northwestern Wisconsin | 30 |
| 1924 Apr. 30 | Central S. C. | 67 | 1959 Feb. 10 | St. Louis, Mo. | 21 |
| 1924 June 28 | Lorain, Sandusky, Ohio | 85 | 1960 May 5, 6 | S. E. Oklahoma, Arkansas | 30 |
| 1925 Mar. 18 | Mo., Ill., Ind. | 689 | 1961 May 5 | Le Flore Co., Okla. | 16 |
| 1925 Nov. 25 | Belleville to Portland, Ark. | 53 | 1962 Mar. 31 | Milton, Fla. | 17 |
| 1927 Apr. 12 | Rock Springs, Tex. | 74 | 1964 Apr. 12 | Kans., Mo., Iowa, Tex. | 13 |
| 1927 May 9 | Arkansas, Poplar Bluff, Mo. | 92 | 1964 Oct. 8 | Larose, La. | 22 |
| 1927 Sept. 29 | St. Louis, Mo. | 72 | 1965 Apr. 11 | Ind., Ill., Mich., Wis. | 271 |
| 1929 Apr. 25 | S.E.-Central Ga. | 40 | 1966 Mar. 3 | Jackson, Miss. | 57 |
| 1930 May 6 | Hill & Ellis Co., Tex. | 41 | 1966 Mar. 3 | Mississippi, Alabama | 61 |
| 1932 Mar. 21 | Ala. (series of tornadoes) | 268 | 1966 June 8 | Kansas | 17 |
| 1936 Apr. 5 | Tupelo, Miss. | 216 | 1967 April 21 | Illinois | 33 |
| 1936 Apr. 6 | Gainesville, Ga. | 203 | | | |
| 1938 Sept. 29 | Charleston, S. C. | 32 | | | |

## Americans of the Past

### AMERICAN MILITARY AND NAVAL LEADERS

Classified according to major service. (N) signifies Navy; (M) signifies Marine Corps

#### WAR OF INDEPENDENCE

| Born | Died | Name |
|---|---|---|
| 1737 | 1789 | Allen, Ethan |
| 1741 | 1801 | Arnold, Benedict |
| 1745 | 1803 | Barry, John (N) |
| 1749 | 1833 | Buford, Abraham |
| 1752 | 1818 | Clark, Geo. Rogers |
| 1739 | 1812 | Clinton, George |
| 1728 | 1806 | Gates, Horatio |
| 1742 | 1786 | Greene, Nathanael |
| 1757 | 1804 | Hamilton, Alex. |
| 1737 | 1814 | Heath, William |
| 1728 | 1777 | Herkimer, Nich. |
| 1718 | 1802 | Hopkins, Esek (N) |
| 1747 | 1792 | Jones, John Paul (N) |
| 1756 | 1806 | Knox, Henry R. |
| 1731 | 1782 | Lee, Charles |
| 1758 | 1818 | Lee, Henry |
| 1732 | 1794 | Lee, Rich. Henry |
| 1733 | 1810 | Lincoln, Benj. |
| 1733 | 1795 | Marion, Francis |
| 1737 | 1775 | Montgomery, Richard |
| 1736 | 1802 | Morgan, Daniel |
| 1730 | 1805 | Moultrie, Wm. |
| 1739 | 1817 | Pickens, Andrew |
| 1745 | 1829 | Pickering, Tim. |
| 1718 | 1790 | Putnam, Israel |
| 1733 | 1804 | Schuyler, Phillip |
| 1728 | 1822 | Stark, John |
| 1736 | 1818 | St. Clair, Arthur |
| 1726 | 1783 | Stirling (Alexander) |
| 1740 | 1795 | Sullivan, John |
| 1734 | 1832 | Sumter, Thomas |
| 1727 | 1800 | Ward, Artemas |
| 1740 | 1775 | Warren, Joseph |
| 1732 | 1799 | Washington, George |
| 1745 | 1796 | Wayne, Anthony |

#### Foreign Officers in the War

| Born | Died | Name |
|---|---|---|
| 1723 | 1788 | DeGrasse, Francois (N) |
| 1721 | 1780 | DeKalb, Johann |
| 1746 | 1817 | Kosciuszko, Thaddeus |
| 1757 | 1834 | LaFayette, Marquis de |
| 1748 | 1779 | Pulaski, James |
| 1725 | 1807 | Rochambeau, Jean de |
| 1730 | 1794 | Steuben, F. W von |

#### WAR OF 1812

| Born | Died | Name |
|---|---|---|
| 1774 | 1833 | Bainbridge, Wm. (N) |
| 1775 | 1828 | Brown, Jacob J. |
| 1772 | 1840 | Chauncey, Isaac (N) |
| 1786 | 1836 | Crockett, David |
| 1751 | 1829 | Dearborn, Henry |
| 1779 | 1820 | Decatur, Stephen (N) |
| 1773 | 1841 | Harrison, Wm. Henry |
| 1793 | 1863 | Houston, Sam |
| 1773 | 1843 | Hull, Isaac (N) |
| 1773 | 1825 | Hull, William |
| 1767 | 1845 | Jackson, Andrew |
| 1781 | 1813 | Lawrence, James (N) |
| 1783 | 1825 | Macdonough, Thos. |
| 1785 | 1819 | Perry, Oliver H. (N) |
| 1779 | 1813 | Pike, Zebulon M. |
| 1780 | 1843 | Porter, David |
| 1773 | 1838 | Rogers, John (N) |
| 1764 | 1839 | Van Rensselaer, S. |
| 1757 | 1825 | Wilkinson, Jas. |

#### MEXICAN WAR

| Born | Died | Name |
|---|---|---|
| 1794 | 1848 | Kearny, Stephen |
| 1804 | 1869 | Pierce, Franklin |
| 1786 | 1866 | Scott, Winfield |
| 1780 | 1861 | Sloat, John D. (N) |
| 1784 | 1850 | Taylor, Zachary |

#### CIVIL WAR: UNION

| Born | Died | Name |
|---|---|---|
| 1805 | 1871 | Anderson, Robert |
| 1832 | 1900 | Averell, William W. |
| 1816 | 1894 | Banks, Nath. P. |
| 1821 | 1875 | Blair, Francis P., Jr. |
| 1818 | 1898 | Buell, Don Carlos |
| 1826 | 1863 | Buford, John |
| 1824 | 1881 | Burnside, Ambrose |
| 1818 | 1893 | Butler, Benj. F. |
| 1817 | 1873 | Canby, Edw R. |
| 1828 | 1900 | Cox, John B. |
| 1819 | 1893 | Crittenden, Thomas L. |
| 1828 | 1890 | Crook, George |
| 1842 | 1874 | Cushing, William B. (N) |
| 1839 | 1876 | Custer, Geo. A. |
| 1809 | 1870 | Dahlgren, John (N) |
| 1819 | 1893 | Doubleday, Abner |
| 1803 | 1865 | DuPont, Saml. (N) |
| 1837 | 1863 | Farnsworth, Elon J. |
| 1801 | 1870 | Farragut, David G. (N) |
| 1828 | 1890 | Fisk, Clinton B. |
| 1806 | 1863 | Foote, Andrew (N) |
| 1823 | 1903 | Franklin, W. B. |
| 1813 | 1890 | Fremont, John C. |
| 1831 | 1881 | Garfield, James A. |
| 1805 | 1877 | Goldsborough, L.M. (N) |
| 1822 | 1876 | Granger, Gordon |
| 1822 | 1885 | Grant, Ulysses S. |
| 1826 | 1911 | Grierson, Benjamin H. |
| 1815 | 1872 | Halleck, Hy. W. |
| 1824 | 1886 | Hancock, W. S. |
| 1822 | 1893 | Hayes, Rutherford B. |
| 1830 | 1887 | Hazen, William B. |
| 1805 | 1880 | Heintzelman, S. P. |
| 1814 | 1879 | Hooker, Jos. |
| 1830 | 1909 | Howard, Oliver O. |
| 1802 | 1886 | Hunter, David |
| 1815 | 1882 | Hurlbut, S. A. |
| 1815 | 1862 | Kearny, Philip |
| 1826 | 1886 | Logan, John A. |
| 1818 | 1861 | Lyon, Nathaniel |
| 1826 | 1885 | McClelian, Geo. B. |
| 1812 | 1900 | McClernand, John |
| 1831 | 1903 | McCook, Alexander M. |
| 1818 | 1885 | McDowell, Irvin |
| 1828 | 1864 | McPherson, Jas. |
| 1815 | 1872 | Meade, Geo. G. |
| 1818 | 1883 | Ord, Edward O. C. |
| 1827 | 1900 | Parke, John G. |
| 1813 | 1885 | Phelps, John W. |
| 1822 | 1892 | Pope, John |
| 1813 | 1891 | Porter, David D. (N) |
| 1822 | 1901 | Porter, Fitz John |
| 1819 | 1901 | Prentiss, Benj. |
| 1809 | 1890 | Radford, William (N) |
| 1820 | 1863 | Reynolds, John F. |
| 1819 | 1892 | Rodgers, C. R. P. (N) |
| 1819 | 1898 | Rosecrans, Wm. S. |
| 1831 | 1906 | Schofield, John |
| 1813 | 1864 | Sedgwick, John |
| 1831 | 1888 | Sheridan, Phillip |
| 1820 | 1891 | Sherman, Wm. T. |
| 1806 | 1879 | Shields, James |
| 1825 | 1914 | Sickles, Daniel E. |
| 1824 | 1902 | Sigel, Franz |
| 1827 | 1894 | Slocum, Henry W. |
| 1807 | 1862 | Smith, Charles F. |
| 1824 | 1903 | Smith, William F. |
| 1797 | 1865 | Sumner, Edwin |
| 1822 | 1880 | Sykes, George |
| 1816 | 1876 | Thomas, Geo. H. |
| 1839 | 1881 | Upton, Emory |
| 1807 | 1864 | Wadsworth, Jas. S. |
| 1821 | 1863 | Wainwright, J. M. |
| 1827 | 1905 | Wallace, Lew |
| 1830 | 1882 | Warren, G. K. |
| 1835 | 1884 | Weitzel, Godfrey |
| 1837 | 1925 | Wilson, James H. |
| 1818 | 1897 | Worden, John L. (N) |
| 1820 | 1899 | Wright, Horatio G. |

#### CIVIL WAR: CONFEDERATE

| Born | Died | Name |
|---|---|---|
| 1817 | 1863 | Armistead, Lewis |
| 1809 | 1893 | Barron, Saml. |
| 1818 | 1893 | Beauregard, P. |
| 1817 | 1876 | Bragg, Braxton |
| 1821 | 1875 | Breckinridge, John C. |
| 1800 | 1874 | Buchanan, Fr. (N) |
| 1823 | 1914 | Buckner, Simon B. |
| 1798 | 1839 | Cooper, Samuel |
| 1816 | 1894 | Early, Jubal A. |
| 1817 | 1872 | Ewell, Rich. S. |
| 1806 | 1863 | Floyd, John B. |
| 1821 | 1877 | Forrest, Nathan B. |
| 1818 | 1883 | Gorgas, Josiah |
| 1832 | 1904 | Gordon, John B. |
| 1818 | 1902 | Hampton, Wade |
| 1815 | 1873 | Hardee, William J. |
| 1825 | 1865 | Hill, Ambrose P. |
| 1821 | 1889 | Hill, Daniel H. |
| 1831 | 1879 | Hood, John B. |
| 1823 | 1895 | Imoden, John D. |
| 1820 | 1898 | Jackson, Henry R. |
| 1824 | 1863 | Jackson, Thos. J. |
| 1803 | 1862 | Johnston, Albert S. |
| 1807 | 1891 | Johnston, Jos. E. |
| 1824 | 1893 | Kirby-Smith, E. |
| 1807 | 1870 | Lee, Robert E. |
| 1833 | 1908 | Lee, Stephen D. |
| 1821 | 1904 | Longstreet, Jas. |
| 1810 | 1871 | Magruder, J. B. |
| 1822 | 1900 | Maury, D. H. |
| 1806 | 1873 | Maury, M. F. (N) |
| 1825 | 1895 | Maxey, Samuel B. |
| 1821 | 1897 | McLaws, Lafayette |
| 1825 | 1864 | Morgan, John H. |
| 1833 | 1916 | Mosby, John |
| 1814 | 1881 | Pemberton, J. C. |
| 1825 | 1875 | Pickett, Geo. E. |
| 1806 | 1878 | Pillow, G. J. |
| 1806 | 1864 | Polk, Leonidas |
| 1809 | 1867 | Price, Sterling |
| 1809 | 1877 | Semmes, Raphael (N) |
| 1816 | 1886 | Sibley, H. H. |
| 1833 | 1864 | Stuart, J. E. B. |
| 1822 | 1898 | Taliaferro, W.B. |
| 1826 | 1879 | Taylor, Richard |
| 1827 | 1890 | Terry, Alfred H. |
| 1820 | 1863 | Van Dorn, Earl |
| 1836 | 1906 | Wheeler, Joseph |

#### SPANISH-AMERICAN

| Born | Died | Name |
|---|---|---|
| 1842 | 1914 | Chaffee, Adna R. |
| 1837 | 1917 | Dewey, Geo. (N) |
| 1846 | 1912 | Evans, Robley D. (N) |
| 1865 | 1917 | Funston, Frederick |
| 1858 | 1928 | Goethals, Geo. W. |
| 1870 | 1937 | Hobson, Richm'd P. (N) |
| 1843 | 1899 | Lawton, Henry W. |
| 1835 | 1905 | Lee, Fitzhugh |
| 1845 | 1912 | MacArthur, Arthur |
| 1839 | 1925 | Miles, Nelson A. |
| 1840 | 1903 | Sampson, Wm. T. (N) |
| 1839 | 1911 | Schley, W. S. (N) |
| 1835 | 1906 | Shafter, Wm. R. |
| 1845 | 1923 | Sigsbee, Chas. D. (N) |
| 1836 | 1906 | Wheeler, Jos. |
| 1860 | 1927 | Wood, Leonard |

#### WORLD WAR I

| Born | Died | Name |
|---|---|---|
| 1859 | 1930 | Allen, Henry T. |
| 1855 | 1932 | Benson, Wm. S. (N) |
| 1853 | 1930 | Bliss, Tasker H. |
| 1861 | 1947 | Bullard, Robt. L. |
| 1864 | 1935 | Capps, Wash. L. |
| 1857 | 1927 | Dickman, Joseph T. |
| 1879 | 1951 | Drum, Hugh A. |
| 1860 | 1931 | Edwards, Clarence |
| 1868 | 1958 | Ely, Hanson E. |
| 1880 | 1967 | Foulois, Benj. D. |
| 1866 | 1947 | Harbord, Jas. G. |
| 1879 | 1960 | Hines, Frank T. |
| 1860 | 1963 | Hodges, Henry C., Jr. |
| 1863 | 1938 | Jones, Hilary P. (N) |
| 1867 | 1942 | Lejeune, John A. (M) |
| 1857 | 1935 | Liggett, Hunter |
| 1880 | 1964 | MacArthur, Douglas |
| 1865 | 1955 | March, Peyton C. |
| 1856 | 1937 | Mayo, Henry T. (N) |
| 1862 | 1930 | Menoher, Chas. T. |
| 1879 | 1936 | Mitchell, Wm. (Billy) |
| 1874 | 1961 | O'Ryan, John F. |
| 1860 | 1948 | Pershing, John J. |
| 1869 | 1957 | Pratt, Wm. V. (N) |
| 1858 | 1936 | Sims, Wm. S. (N) |
| 1862 | 1954 | Wilson, Henry B. (N) |
| 1887 | 1964 | York, Alvin C. (Sgt.) |

#### WORLD WAR II, KOREA

| Born | Died | Name |
|---|---|---|
| 1886 | 1950 | Arnold, Henry H. |
| 1878 | 1967 | Bloch, Claude C. (N) |
| 1888 | 1950 | Buchanan, Pat (N) |
| 1887 | 1945 | Buckner, Simon, Jr. |
| 1890 | 1958 | Chennault, Claire L. |
| 1886 | 1961 | Eichelberger, R. L. |
| 1896 | 1967 | Fechteler, Wm. M. (N) |
| 1883 | 1959 | Halsey, Wm. F. (N) |
| 1878 | 1952 | Haskell, Wm. N. |
| 1892 | 1966 | Hobbs, Leland |
| 1887 | 1966 | Hodges, Courtney |
| 1891 | 1967 | Jones, Albert M. |
| 1878 | 1956 | King, Ernest J. (N) |
| 1875 | 1959 | Leahy, Wm. D. (N) |
| 1880 | 1964 | MacArthur, Douglas |
| 1887 | 1947 | Mitscher, Marc A. (N) |
| 1880 | 1959 | Marshall, Geo. C. |
| 1885 | 1966 | Nimitz, Chester |
| 1896 | 1959 | Parks, Floyd L. |
| 1885 | 1945 | Patton, Geo. S., Jr. |
| 1887 | 1944 | Roosevelt, Theo., Jr. |
| 1896 | 1951 | Sherman Forrest P. (N) |
| 1882 | 1967 | Smith, Holland M. (M) |
| 1895 | 1961 | Smith, W. Bedell |
| 1883 | 1946 | Stilwell, Jos. W. |
| 1884 | 1955 | Towers, John H. (N) |
| 1899 | 1954 | Vandenberg, Hoyt S. |
| 1883 | 1953 | Wainwright, J. M. |
| 1889 | 1950 | Walker, Walton H. |
| 1876 | 1959 | Yarnell, Hy. E (N) |

# AMERICAN WRITERS OF THE PAST
### Novelists, Poets, Historians, Journalists, Publishers, Biographers

## A

**Charles Francis Adams**, biographer, diplomat, 1807-1886.

**Charles Francis Adams**, historian, lawyer, 1835-1915.

**Franklin P. Adams**, journalist, 1881-1960.

**Henry Adams**, historian, philosopher, 1838-1918.

**James Truslow Adams**, historian, 1878-1949.

**Samuel Hopkins Adams**, novelist, magazine writer, 1871-1958. It Happened One Night.

**George Ade**, humorist, dramatist, 1866-1944.

**Louisa May Alcott**, novelist, writer of children's books, 1832-1888. Little Women.

**Thomas Bailey Aldrich**, author, editor, 1836-1907.

**Henry M. Alden**, editor, 1836-1919. Harper's Magazine.

**Horatio Alger**, author of "rags-to-riches" boys' books, 1832-1899.

**James Lane Allen**, novelist, 1849-1925.

**Gertrude Atherton**, novelist, 1857-1948. Black Oxen.

**Mary Austin**, novelist, playwright, 1868-1934.

## B

**Irving Bacheller**, novelist, journalist, 1859-1950. Eben Holden.

**Ray Stannard Baker**, biographer, historian, 1870-1946.

**George Bancroft**, historian, diplomat, 1800-1891.

**Joel Barlow**, poet, diplomat, 1754-1812.

**Margaret Ayer Barnes**, novelist, 1886-1967. Years of Grace.

**Bruce Barton**, author, advertising executive, 1875-1967. The Man Nobody Knows.

**Rex Beach**, novelist, 1877-1949. The Auction Block.

**Charles A. Beard**, historian, 1874-1948.

**Mary Ritter Beard**, historian, 1876-1958.

**Lucius M. Beebe**, journalist, author, 1902-1966. N. Y. Herald Tribune.

**Edward Bellamy**, novelist, journalist, 1850-1898. Looking Backward: 2000-1887.

**Robert C. Benchley**, humorist, journalist, 1889-1945.

**Stephen Vincent Benét**, poet, novelist, 1898-1943.

**William Rose Benét**, poet, novelist, 1886-1950.

**James Gordon Bennett**, journalist, 1795-1872. Founded N. Y. Herald.

**James Gordon Bennett, Jr.**, journalist, 1841-1918. N. Y. Herald, Evening Telegram.

**Albert J. Beveridge**, historian, politician, 1862-1927.

**Ambrose Bierce**, short-story writer, journalist, 1842-1914.

**Earl Derr Biggers**, novelist, 1884-1933. Created Charlie Chan.

**Samuel Bowles II**, journalist, author, 1826-1878. Springfield Republican.

**Gamaliel Bradford**, biographer, 1863-1932.

**Anne Bradstreet**, poet, 1612-1672.

**Arthur Brisbane**, journalist, 1864-1936. N. Y. Sun, Evening Sun, World and Hearst newspapers.

**Louis Bromfield**, novelist, essayist, 1896-1956.

**Van Wyck Brooks**, historian, critic, 1886-1963.

**Heywood Broun**, journalist, 1888-1939. N. Y. Morning Telegraph, Tribune, World.

**Orestes Brownson**, editor, clergyman, 1803-1876.

**Katharine Brush**, novelist, 1902-1952. Young Man of Manhattan.

**William Cullen Bryant**, poet, editor, 1794-1878.

**Henry C. Bunner**, journalist, poet, 1855-1896. Editor of Puck.

**Ned Buntline**, author of dime novels, 1823-1886. Gave "Buffalo Bill" Cody his nickname.

**Edgar Rice Burroughs**, novelist, 1875-1950. Tarzan of the Apes.

**Struthers Burt**, novelist, poet, 1882-1954.

## C

**George W. Cable**, novelist, essayist, 1844-1925.

**Henry Seidel Canby**, editor, critic, 1878-1961. Saturday Review of Literature.

**Will Carleton**, poet, journalist, 1845-1912. Over the Hill to the Poorhouse.

**Rachel Carson**, marine biologist, author, 1907-1964. Silent Spring.

**Amon G. Carter**, newspaper publisher, 1880-1955. Ft. Worth Star-Telegram.

**Willa Cather**, novelist, essayist, 1876-1947. O Pioneers!

**Madison Cawein**, poet, 1865-1914.

**John Vance Cheney**, poet, librarian, 1848-1922.

**Robert W. Chambers**, novelist, artist, 1865-1933. The Rogue's Moon.

**Winston Churchill**, novelist, 1871-1947. The Crisis.

**Raymond Clapper**, journalist, 1892-1944.

**Irvin S. Cobb**, humorist, journalist, 1876-1944.

**James Fenimore Cooper**, novelist, 1789-1851. Leather-Stocking Tales.

**Royal Cortissoz**, journalist, author, 1869-1948. N. Y. Herald Tribune.

**Thomas B. Costain**, novelist, journalist, 1885-1965. The Black Rose.

**Hart Crane**, poet, 1899-1932.

**Stephen Crane**, novelist, short-story writer, 1871-1900. The Red Badge of Courage.

**Francis Marion Crawford**, novelist, 1854-1909.

**Frank Crowninshield**, editor, author, 1872-1947.

**E. E. Cummings**, poet, painter, 1894-1963.

**Cyrus H. K. Curtis**, magazine, newspaper publisher, 1850-1933.

**George William Curtis**, journalist, author, 1824-1892.

**James Oliver Curwood**, novelist, 1878-1927. God's Country and the Woman.

## D

**Charles A. Dana**, editor, 1819-1879. New York Sun.

**Richard H. Dana**, author, lawyer, 1815-1882. Two Years Before the Mast.

**Josephus Daniels**, journalist, statesman, 1862-1948. Raleigh News & Observer.

**Elmer Davis**, journalist, radio commentator, 1890-1958.

**Richard Harding Davis**, journalist, novelist, 1864-1916.

**Robert H. (Bob) Davis**, journalist, editor, 1869-1942. N. Y. Evening Sun.

**Bernard De Voto**, historian, editor, 1897-1955.

**Michael H. De Young**, newspaper editor, 1849-1925. San Francisco Chronicle.

**Emily Dickinson**, poet, 1830-1886.

**Thomas Dixon**, novelist, clergyman, 1864-1946. The Clansman.

**J. Frank Dobie**, author, educator, 1888-1964.

**Hilda Doolittle (H. D.)**, poet, 1886-1961.

**Joseph Rodman Drake**, poet, 1795-1820.

**Theodore Dreiser**, novelist, editor, 1871-1945. An American Tragedy.

**Orvil E. Dryfoos**, newspaper publisher, 1912-1963. New York Times.

**Paul L. Dunbar**, poet, noevlist, 1872-1906.

## E

**Edward Eggleston**, novelist, clergyman, 1837-1902. The Hoosier Schoolmaster.

**Ralph Waldo Emerson**, poet, essayist, 1803-1882.

**John Erskine**, novelist, educator, 1879-1951. The Private Life of Helen of Troy.

## F

**Martha Farquharson**, author of juveniles, 1828-1909. Elsie Dinsmore series.

**William Faulkner**, novelist, 1897-1962. Sanctuary.

**Edna Ferber**, novelist, 1887-1968. Show Boat, Saratoga Trunk.

**Arthur D. Ficke**, poet, novelist, 1883-1945.

**Eugene Field**, poet, journalist, 1850-1895. Little Boy Blue; Wynken, Blynken and Nod.

**James T. Fields**, editor, author, 1817-1881. Atlantic Monthly.

**Joseph Fields**, stage and screen writer, 1895-1966. Co-author of My Sister Eileen.

**Dorothy Canfield Fisher**, novelist, writer of juveniles, 1879-1958.

**John Fiske**, historian, philosopher, 1842-1901.

**F. Scott Fitzgerald**, novelist, short-story writer, 1896-1940. The Great Gatsby.

**John Gould Fletcher**, poet, critic, 1886-1950.

**Esther Forbes**, children's author, 1891-1967. Johnny Tremain.

**Kathryn Forbes**, novelist, 1909-1966. Mama's Bank Account.

**Paul Leicester Ford**, novelist, historian, 1865-1902. The Honorable Peter Stirling.

**Gene Fowler**, journalist, author, 1890-1960. Good Night, Sweet Prince.

**John W. Fox, Jr.**, novelist, 1863-1919. The Little Shepherd of Kingdom Come.

**Douglas S. Freeman**, historian, editor, 1886-1953. Richmond News Leader.

**Mary E. W. Freeman**, short-story writer, 1852-1930.

**Philip Freneau**, poet, journalist, 1752-1832.

**Robert Frost**, poet, 1875-1963.

## G

**Zona Gale**, novelist, dramatist, 1874-1938.

**Frank E. Gannett**, newspaper publisher, 1876-1957. Gannett Newspapers.

**Hamlin Garland**, novelist, 1860-1940. Main-Traveled Roads.

**Ellen Glasgow**, novelist, 1874-1945.

**Susan Glaspell**, novelist, dramatist, 1882-1948.

**Edwin L. Godkin**, journalist, 1831-1902. Founded The Nation.

**Henry W. Grady**, journalist, orator, 1850-1889. Atlanta Constitution.

**Horace Greeley**, journalist, politician, 1811-1872. N. Y. Tribune.

**Zane Grey**, novelist, 1875-1939. Riders of the Purple Sage.

**Gilbert H. Grosvenor**, editor, geographer, 1875-1966. National Geographic Magazine.

**Edgar A. Guest**, poet, 1881-1959. A Heap of Livin'.

**Louise I. Guiney**, poet, essayist, 1861-1920.

**Arthur Guiterman**, poet, 1871-1943.

## H

**Edward Everett Hale**, author, clergyman, 1822-1909. The Man Without a Country.

**James Norman Hall**, novelist, 1887-1951. Co-author Mutiny on the Bounty.

**Fitz-Greene Halleck**, poet, 1790-1867.

**Dashiell Hammett**, writer of detective fiction, 1894-1961. The Thin Man.

**Norman Hapgood**, magazine editor, author, 1868-1937.

**Joel Chandler Harris**, short-story

writer, 1848-1908. Uncle Remus and Br'er Rabbit.

Bret Harte, short-story writer, poet, 1836-1902. The Luck of Roaring Camp.

George B. M. Harvey, journalist, diplomat, 1864-1928.

Nathaniel Hawthorne, novelist, 1804-1864. The Scarlet Letter.

John M. Hay, historian, diplomat, 1838-1905. Abraham Lincoln: A History.

Lafcadio Hearn, author, 1850-1904.

William Randolph Hearst, newspaper publisher, 1863-1951.

Ben Hecht, novelist, playwright, journalist, 1894-1964.

Ernest Hemingway, novelist, short-story writer, 1899-1961. A Farewell to Arms.

Burton J. Hendrick, biographer, journalist, 1871-1949.

O. Henry (W. S. Porter), short-story writer, 1862-1910. The Gift of the Magi.

Joseph Hergesheimer, novelist, 1880-1954. Java Head.

Marguerite Higgins, journalist, 1920-1966.

Robert Hillyer, poet, novelist, 1895-1962.

Alice Tisdale Hobart, novelist, 1882-1967. Oil for the Lamps of China.

Samuel Hoffenstein, poet, 1890-1947.

Charles Fenno Hoffman, poet, editor, 1806-1884.

Oliver Wendell Holmes, poet, novelist, 1809-1894.

Mark DeWolfe Hopper, historian, 1906-1967.

Roy W. Howard, newspaper publisher, editor, 1883-1964. Scripps-Howard Newspapers.

Ed Howe, journalist, author, 1853-1937.

Julia Ward Howe, poet, reformer, 1819-1910. The Battle Hymn of the Republic.

William Dean Howells, novelist, critic, 1837-1920.

Elbert Hubbard, author, editor, 1856-1915. A Message to Garcia.

Frank (Kin) Hubbard, humorist, caricaturist, 1868-1930.

Langston Hughes, poet, playwright, 1902-1967.

Rupert Hughes, novelist, playwright, 1872-1956.

Frazier (Spike) Hunt, journalist, war correspondent, 1885-1967.

## I

Washington Irving, essayist, historian, 1783-1859.

Wallace Irwin, journalist, humorist, 1875-1959.

Will Irwin, journalist, author, 1873-1948.

## J

Henry James, novelist, critic, 1843-1916.

Robinson Jeffers, poet, dramatist, 1887-1962.

Sarah Orne Jewett, novelist, short-story writer, 1849-1909.

James Weldon Johnson, poet, anthologist, 1871-1938.

## K

H. V. Kaltenborn, editor, radio commentator, 1878-1965.

Clarence Budington Kelland, novelist, short-story writer, 1881-1964.

Francis Scott Key, poet, 1779-1843. The Star-Spangled Banner.

Dorothy Kilgallen, journalist, radio-TV personality, 1913-1965.

Bernard Kilgore, journalist, 1908-1967. Wall Street Journal.

Joyce Kilmer, poet, 1886-1918. Trees.

Willard M. Kiplinger, journalist, 1891-1967. Changing Times.

## L

Oliver La Farge, novelist, 1901-1963. Laughing Boy.

William M. Laffan, newspaper publisher, 1848-1900. New York Sun, N. Y. Evening Sun.

Benson Young Landis, editor, 1897-1966. Yearbook of American Churches.

Sidney Lanier, poet, critic, 1842-1881.

Ring Lardner, short-story writer, journalist, 1885-1933.

Victor F. Lawson, journalist, 1850-1925. Chicago Daily News.

Emma Lazarus, poet, essayist, 1849-1887. The New Colossus.

Charles Godfrey Leland, poet, journalist, 1824-1903.

William Ellery Leonard, poet, educator, 1876-1944.

Fulton Lewis, Jr., radio news commentator, 1903-1966.

Ludwig Lewisohn, novelist, critic, 1883-1955.

Vachel Lindsay, poet, 1879-1931.

Jack London, novelist, journalist, 1876-1916. The Call of the Wild.

Benson John Lossing, historian, artist, 1813-1891. Pictorial Field Book of the Revolution.

Elijah P. Lovejoy, journalist, abolitionist, 1802-1837.

Amy Lowell, poet, critic, 1874-1925.

James Russell Lowell, poet, editor, 1819-1891.

Henry R. Luce, publisher, 1898-1967. Time, Life, Fortune magazines.

## M

Edwin Markham, poet, 1852-1940. The Man with the Hoe.

John P. Marquand, novelist, 1893-1960. The late George Apley.

Don Marquis, humorist, journalist, 1878-1937. The Old Soak.

Edgar Lee Masters, poet, biographer, 1869-1950. Spoon River Anthology.

S. S. McClure, editor, publisher, 1857-1949.

Joseph Medill McCormick, journalist, politician, 1877-1925. Chicago Tribune.

Robert R. McCormick, editor, publisher, 1880-1955. Chicago Tribune.

Carson McCullers, novelist, 1917-1967. The Heart Is a Lonely Hunter.

John B. McMaster, historian, 1852-1932.

Joseph Medill, journalist, 1823-1899. Chicago Tribune.

Herman Melville, novelist, poet, 1819-1891. Moby Dick.

Henry L. Mencken, editor, author, 1880-1956. Baltimore Sun, American Mercury.

Edna St. Vincent Millay, poet, 1892-1950.

Joaquin Miller, poet, 1839-1913.

Max Miller, novelist, 1889-1967. I Cover the Waterfront.

Margaret Mitchell, novelist, journalist, 1900-1949. Gone With the Wind.

William Vaughn Moody, poet, dramatist, 1869-1910.

Clement C. Moore, poet, educator, 1779-1863. A Visit from Saint Nicholas.

Christopher Morley, journalist, novelist, 1890-1957. Kitty Foyle.

John L. Motley, historian, diplomat, 1814-1877.

Edward R. Murrow, radio-TV commentator, 1908-1965.

## N

William Rockhill Nelson, journalist, 1841-1915. Kansas City Star.

John G. Nicolay, biographer, 1832-1901. Abraham Lincoln: A History.

Charles B. Nordhoff, novelist, 1887-1947. Co-author Mutiny on the Bounty.

Frank Norris, novelist, journalist, 1870-1902.

Frank Norris, novelist, 1907-1967. Tower in the West.

Kathleen Norris, novelist, 1880-1966.

Frank B. Noyes, newspaper executive, 1863-1948. Associated Press.

## O

Adolph S. Ochs, journalist, 1858-1935. New York Times.

Fremont Older, journalist, 1856-1935. San Francisco Call-Bulletin.

James Oppenheim, poet, novelist, 1882-1932.

## P

Clementine Paddleford, food editor, 1900-1967. N. Y. Herald Tribune.

Thomas (Tom) Paine, author, political theorist, 1737-1809. Common Sense.

Dorothy Parker, poet, short-story writer, 1893-1967.

Francis Parkman, historian, 1823-1893.

James K. Paulding, poet, novelist, 1778-1860.

John Howard Payne, poet, dramatist, 1791-1852. Home, Sweet Home.

Frederick Palmer, war correspondent, 1873-1958.

Alicia Patterson, journalist, 1906-1963. Newsday.

Eleanor Medill Patterson, journalist, 1884-1948. Washington Times-Herald.

Joseph Medill Patterson, publisher, 1879-1946. Founded N. Y. Daily News.

Josephine P. Peabody, poet, dramatist, 1874-1922.

David G. Phillips, journalist, novelist, 1867-1911.

Edgar Allan Poe, poet, short-story writer, critic, 1809-1849.

Ernest Poole, journalist, novelist, 1880-1950.

William H. Prescott, historian, 1796-1859.

Joseph Pulitzer, journalist, 1847-1911. St. Louis Post-Dispatch, N. Y. World.

Joseph Pulitzer, journalist, 1885-1955. St. Louis Post-Dispatch.

Ralph Pulitzer, journalist, 1879-1939. St. Louis Post-Dispatch, N. Y. World.

Ernie Pyle, journalist, war correspondent, 1900-1945.

## R

James G. Randall, historian, 1881-1953.

Burton Rascoe, journalist, author, 1892-1957.

Marjorie Kinnan Rawlings, novelist, 1896-1953. The Yearling.

Thomas Buchanan Read, poet, painter, 1822-1872. Sheridan's Ride.

Lizette Woodworth Reese, poet, 1856-1935.

Ogden M. Reid, journalist, 1882-1947. N. Y. Herald Tribune.

Whitelaw Reid, journalist, diplomat, 1837-1912. N. Y. Tribune.

Quentin Reynolds, journalist, author, 1902-1965.

James Ford Rhodes, historian, 1848-1927.

Alice Hegan Rice, novelist, 1870-1952. Mrs. Wiggs of the Cabbage Patch.

Cale Young Rice, poet, novelist, 1872-1943.

Grantland Rice, journalist, 1880-1954.

John C. Ridpath, historian, educator, 1840-1900.

James Whitcomb Riley, poet, 1849-1916.

Mary Roberts Rinehart, novelist, dramatist, 1876-1958. The Circular Staircase (The Bat).

Elizabeth Madox Roberts, novelist, 1886-1941.

Kenneth Roberts, novelist, 1885-1957. Northwest Passage.

Roy A. Roberts, journalist, 1887-1967. Kansas City Star.

Edwin Arlington Robinson, poet, 1869-1935.

Theodore Roethke, poet, 1908-1963.

Robert Ruark, journalist, author, 1915-1965.

Damon Runyon, short-story writer, journalist, 1884-1946. Guys and Dolls.

## S

**Carl Sandburg**, poet, biographer, 1878-1967.

**George Santayana**, poet, essayist, philosopher, 1863-1952.

**Lew Sarett**, poet, 1888-1954.

**Edward W. Scripps**, newspaper publisher, 1854-1926.

**Robert P. Scripps**, newspaper publisher, 1895-1938. Scripps-Howard Newspapers .

**Alan Seeger**, poet, 1888-1916. I Have a Rendezvous with Death.

**Ernest Thompson Seton**, author, naturalist, 1860-1946. Wild Animals I Have Known.

**Odell Shepard**, author, politician, 1884-1967. Pedlar's Progress.

**Frank Dempster Sherman**, poet, educator, 1860-1916.

**Lydia H. Sigourney**, poet, 1791-1865.

**Edward Rowland Sill**, poet, educator, 1841-1887.

**Lillian Smith**, novelist, 1897-1966. Strange Fruit.

**Samuel Francis Smith**, poet, clergyman, 1808-1895. America.

**Jared Sparks**, historian, educator, 1789-1866.

**Keats Speed**, newspaper editor, 1880-1952. New York Sun.

**Burt L. Standish (Gilbert Patten)**, author, 1866-1945. Frank Merriwell series.

**Frank L. Stanton**, poet, journalist, 1857-1927. Mighty Lak' a Rose.

**Lincoln Steffens**, editor, author, 1866-1936. The Shame of the Cities.

**Edmund C. Stedman**, poet, critic, 1883-1908.

**Gertrude Stein**, author, 1874-1946. Three Lives.

**George Sterling**, poet, 1869-1926.

**Wallace Stevens**, poet, insurance executive, 1879-1955.

**Frank R. Stockton**, novelist, short-story writer, 1834-1902. The Lady or the Tiger?

**Richard H. Stoddard**, poet, critic, 1825-1903.

**Melville E. Stone**, journalist, 1848-1929. Associated Press.

**Harriet Beecher Stowe**, novelist, 1811-1896. Uncle Tom's Cabin.

**Edward Stratemeyer**, author, 1862-1930. Creator of such series as the Rover Boys, Bobbsey Twins, Tom Swift.

**Gene Stratton-Porter**, novelist, 1863-1924. A Girl of the Limberlost.

**Mark Sullivan**, journalist, author, 1874-1952.

**Herbert Bayard Swope**, journalist, 1882-1958. N. Y. World.

## T

**John B. Tabb**, poet, 1845-1909.

**Genevieve Taggard**, poet, 1894-1948.

**Booth Tarkington**, novelist, 1869-1946. Seventeen.

**Bayard Taylor**, poet, novelist, 1825-1878. The Bedouin Love Song.

**Bert (B. L. T.) Taylor**, newspaper columnist, 1866-1921.

**Edward Taylor**, poet, c. 1642-1729.

**Sara Teasdale**, poet, 1884-1933.

**Albert Payson Terhune**, novelist, journalist, 1872-1942. Lad: A Dog.

**Dorothy Thompson**, journalist, author, 1894-1961.

**James Thurber**, humorist, artist, 1894-1961. The New Yorker.

**Eunice Tietjens**, poet, novelist, 1884-1944.

**Ridgely Torrence**, poet, dramatist, 1875-1950.

**Charles Hanson Towne**, poet, editor, 1877-1949.

**George A. Townsend**, journalist, war correspondent, 1841-1914.

**Frederick J. Turner**, historian, educator, 1861-1932.

**Mark Twain (Samuel Clemens)**, novelist, humorist, 1835-1910. The Adventures of Huckleberry Finn.

## V

**Carl Van Doren**, historian, critic, educator, 1885-1950.

**Henry Van Dyke**, poet, educator, essayist, 1852-1933.

**Hendrik Willem Van Loon**, historian, journalist, 1882-1944.

**Varl Van Vechten**, novelist, music critic, 1880-1964.

**Oswald G. Villard**, editor, author, 1872-1949. The Nation.

## W

**Herbert W. Walker**, journalist, 1895-1967. Newspaper Enterprise Association.

**Lew Wallace**, novelist, diplomat, 1827-1905. Ben Hur.

**Artemus Ward (Charles F. Browne)**, humorist, 1834-1867.

**Henry Watterson**, editor, author, 1840-1921. Louisville Courier-Journal.

**Thurlow Weed**, journalist, politician, 1797-1882. Albany Evening Journal.

**Nathanael West**, novelist, 1903-1940.

**Edith Wharton**, novelist, 1862-1937. The Age of Innocence.

**Stewart Edward White**, novelist, 1873-1946.

**William Allen White**, editor, author, 1868-1944. Emporia (Kan.) Gazette.

**Walt Whitman**, poet, 1819-1892.

**John Greenleaf Whittier**, poet, journalist, 1809-1892.

**Kate Douglas Wiggin**, children's author, educator, 1856-1923. Rebecca of Sunnybrook Farm.

**Ella Wheeler Wilcox**, poet, 1850-1919.

**Ben Ames Williams**, novelist, 1889-1953.

**William Carlos Williams**, poet, physician, 1883-1963.

**Nathaniel P. Willis**, novelist, author, 1806-1867.

**Lyle C. Wilson**, journalist, 1899-1967. United Press International.

**Thomas Wolfe**, novelist, 1900-1938. Look Homeward, Angel.

**Samuel Woodworth**, poet, dramatist, 1784-1842. The Old Oaken Bucket.

**Alexander Woollcott**, journalist, critic, 1887-1943.

**Harold Bell Wright**, novelist, 1872-1944. The Shepherd of the Hills.

**Richard Wright**, novelist, 1908-1960. Native Son.

**Elinor Wylie**, poet, novelist, 1885-1928.

## Z

**John Peter Zenger**, journalist, printer, 1697-1746. N. Y. Weekly Journal.

## AMERICAN PAINTERS OF THE PAST

| Born | Died | Name | Born | Died | Name | Born | Died | Name |
|---|---|---|---|---|---|---|---|---|
| 1852 | 1911 | Abbey, Edwin A. | 1848 | 1892 | Harnett, Wm. Michael | 1778 | 1860 | Peale, Rembrandt |
| 1856 | 1915 | Alexander, John W. | 1854 | 1929 | Harrison, L. Birge | 1851 | 1914 | Pearce, Charles S. |
| 1779 | 1843 | Allston, Washington | 1828 | 1901 | Hart, James M. | 1912 | 1956 | Pollock, Jackson |
| 1780 | 1851 | Audubon, John James | 1877 | 1943 | Hartley, Marsden | 1857 | 1923 | Potter, Edward C. |
| 1855 | 1942 | Beaux, Cecelia | 1860 | 1935 | Hassam, Childe | 1853 | 1911 | Pyle, Howard |
| 1852 | 1917 | Beckwith, J. Carroll | 1872 | 1930 | Hawthorne, Charles W. | 1861 | 1909 | Remington, Frederic |
| 1882 | 1925 | Bellows, George W. | 1813 | 1894 | Healy, G. P. A. | 1854 | 1922 | Rice, William M. J. |
| 1828 | 1902 | Bierstadt, Albert | 1865 | 1929 | Henri, Robert | 1838 | 1905 | Richards, William T. |
| 1856 | 1943 | Birch, Reginald B. | 1823 | 1890 | Hicks, Thomas | 1864 | 1926 | Russell, Charles M. |
| 1848 | 1936 | Blashfield, Edwin H. | 1880 | 1966 | Hofmann, Hans | 1847 | 1917 | Ryder, Albert P. |
| 1847 | 1928 | Bridgman, F. A. | 1836 | 1910 | Homer, Winslow | 1856 | 1925 | Sargent, John S. |
| 1859 | 1920 | Browne, Charles Francis | 1882 | 1967 | Hopper, Edward | 1859 | 1926 | Sewell, Amanda B. |
| 1855 | 1941 | Brush, George de Forest | 1840 | 1895 | Hovenden, Thomas | 1860 | 1924 | Sewell, Robert V. V. |
| 1855 | 1926 | Cassatt, Mary | 1824 | 1879 | Hunt, William M. | 1832 | 1928 | Shattuck, Aaron |
| 1796 | 1872 | Catlin, George | 1816 | 1906 | Huntington, Daniel | 1871 | 1951 | Sloan, John |
| 1860 | 1925 | Chapman, Carlton T. | 1801 | 1846 | Inman, Henry | 1847 | 1926 | Steele, Theodore C. |
| 1849 | 1916 | Chase, William M. | 1825 | 1894 | Inness, George | 1835 | 1922 | Story, George H. |
| 1855 | 1925 | Coffin, Wm. A. | 1813 | 1894 | Isham, Samuel | 1856 | 1919 | Story, Julian |
| 1848 | 1888 | Cole, Thos. | 1824 | 1906 | Johnson, Eastman | 1755 | 1828 | Stuart, Gilbert |
| 1840 | 1928 | Colman, Charles C. | 1874 | 1939 | Johnson, Frank Tenney | 1852 | 1941 | Stuart, Jas. E. |
| 1737 | 1815 | Copley, John S. | 1848 | 1927 | Jones, H. Bolton | 1783 | 1872 | Sully, Thomas |
| 1849 | 1924 | Craig, Thomas B. | 1835 | 1910 | La Farge, John | 1861 | 1930 | Symons, Gardner |
| 1845 | 1918 | Crowninshield, Frederic | 1807 | 1889 | Lambdin, James Reid | 1849 | 1921 | Thayer, Abbott H. |
| 1843 | 1909 | Currier, J. Frank | 1816 | 1868 | Leutz, Emmanuel | 1862 | 1938 | Tarbell, Edmund C. |
| 1898 | 1946 | Curry, John Steuart | 1866 | 1955 | Leigh, William R. | 1850 | 1899 | Truesdell, Gaylord S. |
| 1862 | 1928 | Davies, Arthur B. | 1880 | 1940 | Lie, Jonas | 1756 | 1843 | Trumbull, John |
| 1856 | 1933 | Davis, Charles H. | 1852 | 1924 | Loomis, Chester | 1849 | 1925 | Tryon, Dwight N. |
| 1861 | 1918 | Day, Frank Miles | 1867 | 1933 | Luks, George B. | 1853 | 1902 | Twachtman, John H. |
| 1883 | 1935 | Demuth, Charles | 1872 | 1953 | Marin, John | 1776 | 1852 | Vanderlyn, John |
| 1856 | 1926 | Drake, Will H. | 1898 | 1954 | Marsh, Reginald | 1836 | 1923 | Vedder, Elihu |
| 1796 | 1886 | Durand, A. B. | 1836 | 1897 | Martin, Homer | 1856 | 1935 | Volk, Stephen A. D. |
| 1848 | 1919 | Duveneck, Frank | 1860 | 1932 | Melchers, Gari | 1861 | 1940 | Wough, Fred'k J. |
| 1844 | 1916 | Eakins, Thomas | 1858 | 1925 | Metcalf, Willard L. | 1856 | 1928 | Webb, J. Louis |
| 1845 | 1921 | Earle, Lawrence C. | 1842 | 1922 | Miller, Charles H. | 1849 | 1903 | Weeks, Edwin L. |
| 1871 | 1956 | Feininger, Lyonel | 1829 | 1901 | Moran, Edward | 1852 | 1917 | Weir, J. Alden |
| 1808 | 1884 | Freeman, James E. | 1863 | 1935 | Moran, Percy | 1841 | 1926 | Weir, John F. |
| 1822 | 1884 | Fuller, George | 1837 | 1926 | Moran, Thomas | 1738 | 1820 | West, Benjamin |
| 1867 | 1934 | Fuller, Henry Brown | 1860 | 1961 | Moses, Grandma | 1834 | 1903 | Whistler, J. A. M. |
| 1838 | 1928 | Gay, Edward | 1858 | 1928 | Mowbray, H. Siddons | 1892 | 1942 | Wood, Grant |
| 1818 | 1918 | Griswold, C. C. | 1907 | 1947 | Murch, Walter T. | 1823 | 1903 | Wood, Thomas W. |
| 1893 | 1959 | Grosz, George | 1847 | 1918 | Nicoll, J. C. | 1836 | 1892 | Wyant, Alexander H. |
| 1861 | 1927 | Grover, Oliver Dennett | 1835 | 1907 | Noble, Thomas S. | 1882 | 1945 | Wyeth, Newell |
| 1865 | 1931 | Hale, Philip L. | 1741 | 1827 | Peale, Chas. W. | 1830 | 1923 | Yewell, George H. |

## AMERICAN ETCHERS, ENGRAVERS, ILLUSTRATORS, CARTOONISTS

| Born | Died | Name | Born | Died | Name | Born | Died | Name |
|------|------|------|------|------|------|------|------|------|
| 1887 | 1953 | Arms, John Taylor | 1851 | 1906 | French, Edwin D. | 1840 | 1902 | Nast, Thomas |
| 1856 | 1909 | Bacher, Otto Henry | 1851 | 1928 | Frost, Arthur B. | 1863 | 1928 | Outcault, Richard F. |
| 1862 | 1951 | Benson, Frank W. | 1868 | 1945 | Gibson, Chas. Dana | 1870 | 1966 | Parrish, Maxfield |
| 1875 | 1920 | Briggs, Clare | 1866 | 1925 | Keller, Arthur I. | 1741 | 1827 | Peale, Charles, W. |
| 1881 | 1966 | Brown, Arthur Wm. | 1861 | 1933 | Kemble, E. W. | 1857 | 1926 | Pennell, Joseph |
| 1776 | 1820 | Charles, William | 1838 | 1895 | Keppler, Joseph | 1861 | 1933 | Platt, Charles A. |
| 1873 | 1952 | Christy, H. Chandler | 1876 | 1952 | Kirby, Rollin | 1853 | 1911 | Pyle, Howard |
| 1852 | 1931 | Cole, Timothy | 1872 | 1934 | McCay, Winsor | 1877 | 1952 | Robinson, Boardman |
| 1822 | 1888 | Darley, Felix O. C. | 1870 | 1949 | McCutcheon, John T. | 1833 | 1909 | Smillie, James D. |
| 1796 | 1886 | Durand, Asher Brown | 1858 | 1938 | McDougall, Walt | 1887 | 1935 | Smith, Sidney |
| 1901 | 1966 | Edson, Gus | 1884 | 1954 | McManus, George | 1885 | 1952 | Webster, H. T. |
| 1885 | 1954 | Fisher, H. C. (Bud) | 1860 | 1919 | Mielatz, C. F. Wm. | 1887 | 1966 | Westover, Russ |
| 1878 | 1960 | Flagg, Jas. Mont. | 1869 | 1935 | Mielziner, Leo | 1852 | 1916 | Wolf, Henry |
| 1884 | 1964 | Fox, Fontaine | 1874 | 1948 | Morgan, Wallace | | | |

## AMERICAN BUSINESS LEADERS, PHILANTHROPISTS

| Born | Died | Name | Born | Died | Name | Born | Died | Name |
|------|------|------|------|------|------|------|------|------|
| 1884 | 1966 | Arden, Elizabeth | 1834 | 1916 | Green, Henrietta (Hetty) | 1795 | 1869 | Peabody, George |
| 1832 | 1901 | Armour, Phillip D. | 1828 | 1905 | Guggenheim, Meyer | 1830 | 1891 | Pratt, Charles |
| 1764 | 1848 | Astor, John Jacob | 1837 | 1904 | Hanna, Marcus A. | 1808 | 1896 | Pratt, Enoch |
| 1875 | 1967 | Babson, Roger | 1874 | 1940 | Harkness, Edward S. | 1831 | 1897 | Pullman, Geo. M. |
| 1870 | 1965 | Baruch, Bernard M. | 1848 | 1909 | Harriman, Edward | 1839 | 1937 | Rockefeller, John D. |
| 1813 | 1924 | Belmont, August | 1865 | 1957 | Hartford, Geo L. A. | 1874 | 1960 | Rockefeller, J. D., Jr. |
| 1786 | 1844 | Biddle, Nicholas | 1839 | 1897 | Havemeyer, Theo. | 1862 | 1932 | Rosenwald, Julius |
| 1835 | 1919 | Carnegie, Andrew | 1838 | 1916 | Hill, James J. | 1740 | 1785 | Salomon, Haym |
| 1821 | 1905 | Cooke, Jay | 1795 | 1873 | Hopkins, Johns | 1847 | 1920 | Schiff, Jacob H. |
| 1791 | 1883 | Cooper, Peter | 1821 | 1900 | Huntington, C. P. | 1875 | 1966 | Sloan, Alfred P. |
| 1822 | 1888 | Crocker, Charles | 1882 | 1967 | Jergens, Andrew | 1845 | 1912 | Straus, Isidor |
| 1865 | 1951 | Dawes, Chas. G. | 1874 | 1956 | Jones, Jesse H. | 1848 | 1931 | Straus, Nathan |
| 1834 | 1928 | Depew, Chauncey M. | 1882 | 1967 | Kaiser, Henry J. | 1839 | 1903 | Swift, Gustavus |
| 18/6 | 1893 | Drexel, Anthony J. | 1879 | 1948 | Knudsen, Wm. K. | 1845 | 1920 | Vail, Theo. N. |
| 1856 | 1925 | Duke, James B. | 1867 | 1966 | Kresge, S.S. | 1794 | 1877 | Vanderbilt, Cornelius |
| 1739 | 1817 | duPont, Pierre S. | 1863 | 1955 | Kress, Samuel H. | 1843 | 1899 | Vanderbilt, Cornelius |
| 1890 | 1962 | Fairless, Benjamin | 1868 | 1948 | Lamont, Robert P. | 1821 | 1885 | Vanderbilt, Wm. H. |
| 1835 | 1906 | Field, Marshall | 1870 | 1948 | Lamont, Thos. W. | 1849 | 1920 | Vanderbilt, Wm. K. |
| 1860 | 1937 | Filene, Edward A. | 1880 | 1952 | Lasker, Albert D. | 1835 | 1900 | Villard, Henry |
| 1863 | 1947 | Ford, Henry | 1878 | 1963 | Lehman, Herbert H. | 1838 | 1922 | Wanamaker, John |
| 1879 | 1952 | Fox, William | 1874 | 1938 | Mackay, Clarence | 1871 | 1937 | Warburg, Felix M. |
| 1846 | 1927 | Gary, Elbert H. | 1831 | 1902 | Mackay, John W. | 1874 | 1956 | Watson, Thomas J. |
| 1885 | 1966 | Gifford, Walter S. | 1855 | 1937 | Mellon, Andrew W. | 1875 | 1957 | Weir, Ernest T. |
| 1919 | 1964 | Gilbert, A. C. | 1825 | 1910 | Mills, Darius | 1841 | 1904 | Whitney, Wm. C. |
| 1885 | 1966 | Gimbel, Bernard F. | 1837 | 1913 | Morgan, J. Pierpont | 1868 | 1951 | Wiggin, Albert H. |
| 1750 | 1831 | Girard, Stephen | 1868 | 1943 | Morgan, J. P., Jr. | 1890 | 1961 | Wilson, Chas. Erwin |
| 1877 | 1965 | Girdler, Tom M. | 1734 | 1806 | Morris, Robert | 1852 | 1919 | Woolworth, Frank |
| 1836 | 1892 | Gould, Jay | 1887 | 1963 | Olds, Irving S. | | | |

## AMERICAN INVENTORS OF THE PAST

| Born | Died | Name | Born | Died | Name | Born | Died | Name |
|------|------|------|------|------|------|------|------|------|
| 1891 | 1954 | Armstrong, Edwin | 1882 | 1945 | Goddard, Robert H. | 1809 | 1884 | McCormick, Cyrus H. |
| 1847 | 1922 | Bell, Alex. Graham | 1800 | 1860 | Goodyear, Chas. | 1854 | 1899 | Mergenthaler, Ottmar |
| 1874 | 1961 | De Forrest, Lee | 1803 | 1855 | Gorrie, John | 1791 | 1872 | Morse, S. F. B. |
| 1862 | 1938 | Duryea, Charles E. | 1835 | 1901 | Gray, Elisha | 1831 | 1897 | Pullman, George M. |
| 1870 | 1967 | Duryea, J. Frank | 1896 | 1964 | Hazeltine, L. Alan | 1743 | 1792 | Runsey, Jas. |
| 1854 | 1932 | Eastman, Geo. | 1797 | 1878 | Henry, Jos. | 1856 | 1943 | Tesla, Nikola |
| 1847 | 1931 | Edison, Thos. A. | 1812 | 1886 | Hoe, Richard M. | 1853 | 1937 | Thomson, Elihu |
| 1803 | 1889 | Ericsson, John | 1819 | 1869 | Howe, Elias | 1846 | 1914 | Westinghouse, Geo. |
| 1743 | 1798 | Fitch, John | 1866 | 1945 | Lake, Simon | 1765 | 1825 | Whitney, Eli |
| 1765 | 1815 | Fulton, Robert | 1881 | 1957 | Langmuir, Irving | 1871 | 1948 | Wright, Orville |
| 1818 | 1903 | Gatling, Rich. J. | 1826 | 1886 | Loomis, Mahlon | 1867 | 1912 | Wright, Wilbur |

## AMERICAN SCIENTISTS, PHYSICIANS, ENGINEERS OF THE PAST

| Born | Died | Name | Born | Died | Name | Born | Died | Name |
|------|------|------|------|------|------|------|------|------|
| 1838 | 1916 | Abbe, Cleveland | 1706 | 1790 | Franklin, Benjamin | 1852 | 1931 | Michelson, Albert A. |
| 1876 | 1945 | Albee, Fred H. | 1884 | 1967 | Funk, Casimir | 1903 | 1966 | Millikan, Clark |
| 1807 | 1873 | Agassiz, Louis | 1839 | 1903 | Gibbs, Josiah W. | 1868 | 1953 | Millikan, Robert |
| 1832 | 1867 | Baird, Spencer | 1858 | 1928 | Goethals, Geo. W. | 1866 | 1945 | Morgan, Thos. H. |
| 1785 | 1853 | Beaumont, Wm. | 1854 | 1920 | Gorgas, Wm. C. | 1819 | 1868 | Morton, W. T. G. |
| 1889 | 1967 | Bigelow, Henry B. | 1863 | 1914 | Hall, Charles M. | 1890 | 1967 | Muller, Hermann J. |
| 1899 | 1964 | Blalock, Alfred | 1883 | 1964 | Hess, Victor F. | 1904 | 1967 | Oppenheimer, J. Robert |
| 1773 | 1838 | Bowditch, Nath. | 1865 | 1958 | Jackson, Chevalier | 1883 | 1962 | Papanicolaou, Geo. N. |
| 1848 | 1908 | Brooks, Wm. K. | 1834 | 1913 | Klebs, Edwin | 1903 | 1967 | Pincus, Gregory |
| 1868 | 1939 | Cabot, Richard C. | 1834 | 1906 | Langley, Samuel P. | 1851 | 1902 | Reed, Walter S. |
| 1873 | 1944 | Carrel, Alexis | 1881 | 1957 | Langmuir, Irving | 1846 | 1927 | Remsen, Ira |
| 1864 | 1943 | Carver, Geo. W. | 1884 | 1964 | Lanza, Anthony J. | 1871 | 1910 | Ricketts, Howard T. |
| 1877 | 1954 | Compton, Karl T. | 1901 | 1958 | Lawrence, Ernest O. | 1745 | 1813 | Rush, Benjamin |
| 1869 | 1939 | Cushing, Harvey W. | 1815 | 1878 | Long, Crawford | 1877 | 1967 | Schick, Bela |
| 1872 | 1946 | Davis, John S. | 1806 | 1873 | Maury, Matthew F. | 1813 | 1883 | Sims, James M. |
| 1927 | 1961 | Dooley, Thomas | 1865 | 1939 | Mayo, Charles H. | 1865 | 1923 | Steinmetz, Chas. |
| 1901 | 1965 | Du Mont, Allen | 1861 | 1939 | Mayo, Wm. J. | 1898 | 1964 | Szilard, Leo |
| 1820 | 1887 | Eads, James P. | 1845 | 1913 | McBurney, Chas. | 1894 | 1964 | Wiener, Norbert |
| 1879 | 1955 | Einstein, Albert | 1899 | 1966 | Menninger, Wm. C. | 1844 | 1930 | Wiley, Harvey W. |

## AMERICAN SCULPTORS OF THE PAST

| Born | Died | Name | Born | Died | Name | Born | Died | Name |
|------|------|------|------|------|------|------|------|------|
| 1887 | 1964 | Archipenko, Alexander | 1877 | 1953 | Fraser, James E. | 1875 | 1955 | Milles, Carl |
| 1819 | 1911 | Ball, Thomas | 1790 | 1852 | Frazee, John | 1873 | 1940 | O'Connor, Andrew |
| 1863 | 1938 | Barnard, George Grey | 1850 | 1931 | French, Daniel C. | 1844 | 1920 | O'Donovan, William |
| 1865 | 1925 | Bartlett, Paul W. | 1862 | 1929 | Grafly, Charles | 1870 | 1935 | Paulding, John |
| 1867 | 1915 | Bitter, Karl T. | 1805 | 1852 | Greenough, Horatio | 1805 | 1873 | Powers, Hiram |
| 1871 | 1941 | Borglum, Gutzon | 1887 | 1967 | Hoffman, Malvina | 1867 | 1917 | Pratt, Bela |
| 1868 | 1922 | Borglum, Solon H. | 1830 | 1908 | Hosmer, Harriet | 1868 | 1929 | Quinn, Edmond T. |
| 1871 | 1924 | Brenner, Victor D. | 1865 | 1925 | Jaegers, Albert | 1829 | 1904 | Rogers, John |
| 1865 | 1919 | Brooks, Richard E. | 1875 | 1951 | Keck, Charles | 1756 | 1833 | Rush, William |
| 1814 | 1886 | Brown, Henry K. | 1843 | 1907 | Kemeys, Edward | 1848 | 1907 | St. Gaudens, Augustus |
| 1857 | 1935 | Bush-Brown, H. K. | 1882 | 1935 | Lachaise, Gaston | 1871 | 1922 | Shrady, Henry M. |
| 1870 | 1945 | Calder, Alexander S. | 1877 | 1963 | Lawrie, Lee | 1906 | 1965 | Smith, David |
| 1860 | 1920 | Clark, Thomas S. | 1871 | 1935 | Lukeman, Henry A. | 1860 | 1936 | Taft, Lorado |
| 1814 | 1857 | Crawford, Thomas | 1863 | 1937 | MacMonnies, Fred W. | 1830 | 1910 | Ward, J. Q. A. |
| 1861 | 1944 | Dallin, Cyrus | 1885 | 1966 | Manship, Paul | 1870 | 1952 | Weinman, Adolph A. |
| 1884 | 1952 | Davidson, Jo | 1858 | 1927 | Marling, Philip | 1877 | 1942 | Whitney, Gertrude |
| 1878 | 1960 | Evans, Rudulph | 1879 | 1947 | McCartan, Edward | 1877 | 1957 | Young, Mahonri M. |
| 1895 | 1942 | Flannagan, John | 1883 | 1962 | Mestrovic, Ivan | 1863 | 1949 | Zolnay, Geo. Julian |

## AMERICAN EDUCATORS AND RELIGIOUS LEADERS

| Born | Died | Name | Born | Died | Name | Born | Died | Name |
|---|---|---|---|---|---|---|---|---|
| | | **EDUCATORS** | 1827 | 1908 | Norton, Chas. Eliot | 1900 | 1968 | Fry, Franklin C. |
| 1897 | 1967 | Allport, Gordon | 1855 | 1902 | Palmer, Alice Freeman | 1805 | 1879 | Garrison, Wm. Lloyd |
| 1829 | 1916 | Angell, James B. | 1804 | 1894 | Peabody, Eliz. P. | 1834 | 1921 | Gibbons, James |
| 1870 | 1949 | Angell, James R. | 1870 | 1964 | Pound, Roscoe | 1867 | 1938 | Hayes, Patrick J. |
| 1811 | 1900 | Barnard, Henry | 1855 | 1916 | Royce, Hosiah | 1748 | 1830 | Hicks, Elias |
| 1827 | 1911 | Bascom, John | 1774 | 1821 | Seton, Elizabeth | 1879 | 1964 | Holmes, John Haynes |
| 1862 | 1947 | Butler, Nich. Murray | 1885 | 1963 | Seymour, Charles | 1886 | 1968 | Holt, Ivan Lee |
| 1847 | 1909 | Canfield, Jas. H. | 1779 | 1864 | Silliman, Benj. | 1590 | 1643 | Hutchinson, Anne |
| 1807 | 1874 | Cornell, Ezra | 1859 | 1934 | Smith, Theobald | 1843 | 1926 | Kohler, Kaufmann |
| 1862 | 1948 | Cross, Wilbur | 1886 | 1967 | Stace, Walter T. | 1866 | 1949 | Manning, Wm. T. |
| 1859 | 1952 | Dewey, John | 1840 | 1910 | Sumner, Wm. Graham | 1663 | 1728 | Mather, Cotton |
| 1868 | 1963 | DuBois, Wm. E. | 1858 | 1915 | Washington, Booker T. | 1837 | 1899 | Moody, Dwight L. |
| 1834 | 1926 | Eliot, Chas. W. | 1832 | 1918 | White, Andrew D. | 1711 | 1787 | Muhlenberg, H. M. |
| 1863 | 1940 | Finley, John H. | 1787 | 1870 | Willard, Emma | 1891 | 1963 | Oxnam, G. Bromley |
| 1903 | 1967 | Gassner, John W. | 1864 | 1935 | Williams, Walter | 1810 | 1860 | Parker, Theodore |
| 1831 | 1908 | Gilman, Daniel C. | | | | 1842 | 1933 | Parkhurst, C. H. |
| 1906 | 1963 | Griswold, A. Whitney | | | **RELIGIOUS LEADERS** | 1884 | 1968 | Poling, Daniel A. |
| 1844 | 1924 | Hall, G. Stanley | 1835 | 1922 | Abbott, Lyman | 1729 | 1796 | Seabury, Samuel |
| 1856 | 1906 | Harper, William R. | 1745 | 1816 | Asbury, Francis | 1882 | 1968 | Shipler, Guy E. |
| 1802 | 1887 | Hopkins, Mark | 1813 | 1887 | Beecher, Henry Ward | 1881 | 1968 | Silver, Eliezer |
| 1842 | 1910 | James, William | 1775 | 1863 | Beecher, Lyman | 1805 | 1844 | Smith, Joseph |
| 1797 | 1849 | Lyon, Mary | 1835 | 1893 | Brooks, Phillips | 1889 | 1967 | Spellman, Francis |
| 1800 | 1873 | McGuffey, Wm. H. | 1582 | 1658 | Bulkeley, Peter | 1863 | 1935 | Sunday, Wm. (Billy) |
| 1796 | 1859 | Mann, Horace | 1802 | 1867 | Bushnell, Horace | 1832 | 1902 | Talmadge, T. Dewitt |
| 1738 | 1791 | Manning, James | 1780 | 1842 | Channing, Wm. Ellery | 1886 | 1965 | Tillich, Paul |
| 1872 | 1964 | Meiklejohn, Alexander | 1584 | 1652 | Cotton, John | 1599 | 1683 | Williams, Roger |
| 1886 | 1964 | Mott, Frank L. | 1752 | 1817 | Dwight, Timothy | 1874 | 1949 | Wise, Stephen S. |
| 1818 | 1901 | Muhlenberg, Fred. A. | 1821 | 1910 | Eddy, Mary Baker | 1801 | 1877 | Young, Brigham |
| 1869 | 1946 | Neilson, Wm. A. | 1703 | 1758 | Edwards, Jonathan | | | |

## AMERICAN REFORMERS, SOCIAL-ECONOMIC LEADERS OF THE PAST

| Born | Died | Name | Born | Died | Name | Born | Died | Name |
|---|---|---|---|---|---|---|---|---|
| 1860 | 1935 | Addams, Jane | 1805 | 1879 | Garrison, Wm. L. | 1846 | 1911 | Nation, Carry |
| 1847 | 1902 | Altgeld, Peter | 1839 | 1897 | George, Henry | 1811 | 1886 | Noyes, John H. |
| 1820 | 1906 | Anthony, Susan B. | 1837 | 1927 | Gerry, Elbridge T. | 1801 | 1877 | Owen, Robt. Dale |
| 1867 | 1961 | Balch, Emily G. | 1850 | 1924 | Gompers, Samuel | 1810 | 1860 | Parker, Theodore |
| 1821 | 1912 | Barton, Clara H. | 1873 | 1952 | Green, William | 1811 | 1884 | Phillips, Wendell |
| 1809 | 1890 | Brisbane, Albert | 1887 | 1946 | Hillman, Sidney | 1849 | 1914 | Riis, Jacob A. |
| 1800 | 1859 | Brown, John | 1869 | 1933 | Hillquit, Morris | 1883 | 1967 | Sanger, Margaret |
| 1859 | 1947 | Catt, Carrie Chapman | 1801 | 1876 | Howe, Samuel G. | 1797 | 1874 | Smith, Gerrit |
| 1855 | 1926 | Debs, Eugene | 1855 | 1925 | LaFollette, Robt. M. | 1816 | 1902 | Stanton, Eliz. Cady |
| 1802 | 1887 | Dix, Dorothea | 1882 | 1947 | La Guardia, Fiorello | 1818 | 1893 | Stone, Lucy |
| 1817 | 1895 | Douglass, Frederick | 1793 | 1880 | Mott, Lucretia | 1867 | 1960 | Townsend, Francis E. |
| | | | 1886 | 1952 | Murray, Philip | 1839 | 1898 | Willard, Frances E. |

## AMERICAN EXPLORERS, NATURALISTS OF THE PAST

| Born | Died | Name | Born | Died | Name | Born | Died | Name |
|---|---|---|---|---|---|---|---|---|
| | | **EXPLORERS** | 1844 | 1881 | De Long, G. W. | 1779 | 1813 | Pike, Zebulon M. |
| 1884 | 1960 | Andrews, Roy C. | 1877 | 1948 | Dickey, H. S. | 1793 | 1864 | Schoolcraft, Hy. R. |
| 1875 | 1946 | Bartlett, Robert A. | 1880 | 1951 | Ellsworth, Lincoln | 1798 | 1876 | Walker, Joseph R. |
| 1875 | 1956 | Bingham, Hiram | 1813 | 1890 | Fremont, John C. | 1802 | 1847 | Whitman, Marcus |
| 1796 | 1878 | Bonneville, Benj. | 1844 | 1935 | Greely, Adolphus W. | 1798 | 1877 | Wilkes, Charles |
| 1734 | 1820 | Boone, Daniel | 1884 | 1937 | Johnson, Martin | | | |
| 1796 | 1836 | Bowie, James | 1894 | 1953 | Johnson, Osa | | | **NATURALISTS** |
| 1804 | 1881 | Bridger, James | 1820 | 1857 | Kane, Elisha K. | 1864 | 1926 | Akeley, Carl Ethan |
| 1888 | 1957 | Byrd, Richard E. | 1774 | 1809 | Lewis, Meriwether | 1780 | 1851 | Audubon, John J. |
| 1809 | 1868 | Carson, Kit | 1784 | 1864 | Long, Stephen H. | 1849 | 1926 | Burbank, Luther |
| 1770 | 1838 | Clark, William | 1799 | 1877 | Palmer, Nathaniel | 1837 | 1921 | Burroughs, John |
| 1775 | 1813 | Colter, John | 1856 | 1920 | Peary, Robt. E. | 1838 | 1914 | Muir, John |
| 1865 | 1940 | Cook, Frederick A. | 1834 | 1902 | Powell, John W. | 1817 | 1862 | Thoreau, Henry D. |
| | | | | | | 1766 | 1813 | Wilson, Alexander |

# American Architects and Some of Their Achievements

**Max Abramovitz**, b. 1908. Philharmonic Hall at Lincoln Center, N.Y.

**Henry Bacon**, (1866–1924) Lincoln Memorial.

**Marcel Breuer**, b. Pecs, Hungary, 1902. Whitney Museum of American Art, N. Y. (with Hamilton Smith).

**Charles Bulfinch**, (1763–1844) State House, Boston; Capitol, Washington, (part).

**Daniel H. Burnham**, (1846–1912) Union Station, Washington; Flatiron, New York.

**Ralph Adams Cram**, (1863–1942) Cathedral of St. John the Divine, New York; U. S. Military Academy (part).

**Alexander J. Davis**, (1803–1892) Sub-treasury, N. Y.; capitols of Indiana, North Carolina, Illinois, Ohio.

**William F. Gibbs**, (1886–1967) Designed liner United States.

**Cass Gilbert**, (1859–1934) Custom House, Woolworth Bldg., New York; Capitol, St. Paul.

**Bertrand Goldberg**, b. 1913. Marina City Towers, Chicago.

**Bertram G. Goodhue**, (1869–1924) Capitol, Lincoln, Nebr.; St. Thomas, St. Bartholomew, N. Y.

**Wallace K. Harrison**, b. 1895. Metropolitan Opera House at Lincoln Center, N.Y.

**Thomas Hastings**, (1860–1929) Public Library, Frick Mansion, New York.

**James Hoban**, (1762–1831) The White House.

**Raymond Hood**, (1881–1934) Rockefeller Center (part); McGraw-Hill, N. Y.; Tribune, Chicago.

**Richard M. Hunt**, (1828–1896) Metropolitan Museum (part); The Breakers, Newport.

**William Le Baron Jenney**, (1832–1907) Home Insurance, Chicago (demolished).

**Philip C. Johnson**, b. 1906. N.Y. State Theater at Lincoln Center, N.Y.

**Albert Kahn**, (1869–1942) Athletic Club Bldg., General Motors Bldg., New York.

**Christopher Grant LaFarge**, (1862–1938) Chapel, West Point; Cathedral Seattle

**Benjamin H. Latrobe**, (1764–1820) U. S. Capitol (part).

**Charles F. McKim**, (1847–1909) Public Library, Boston; Columbia Univ. (part).

**Ludwig Mies van der Rohe**, b. Aachen, Germany, 1886. Seagram Building, N. Y. (with Philip C. Johnson).

**Robert Mills**, (1781–1855) Washington Monument.

**Frederick L. Olmsted**, (1822–1903) Central Park, New York; Fairmount Park, Philadelphia.

**Ieoh Ming Pei**, b. Canton, China, 1917. Kips Bay Plaza, N.Y.; Earth Sciences Building (M.I.T.) Cambridge, Mass.

**John Russell Pope**, (1874–1937) National Gallery, Washington.

**James Renwick, Jr.**, (1818–1895) Grace Church, St. Patrick's Cathedral, New York; Smithsonian, Corcoran Galleries, Washington.

**Henry H. Richardson**, (1838–1886) Trinity, Boston.

**James Gamble Rogers**, (1867–1947) Columbia-Presbyterian Medical Center, New York; Northwestern Univ., Chicago (part).

**Eero Saarinen**, (1910–1961) Gateway to the West arch, St. Louis; Trans World Flight Center, N.Y.

**Edward Durell Stone**, b. 1902. U.S. Embassy, New Delhi, India; (H. Hartford) Gallery of Modern Art, N.Y.

**Louis H. Sullivan**, (1856–1924) Auditorium, Chicago.

**Richard Upjohn**, (1802–1878) Trinity Ch., N. Y.

**Stanford White**, (1853–1906) Washington Arch, First Madison Square Garden, New York.

**Frank Lloyd Wright**, (1869–1959) Imperial Hotel, Tokyo; Guggenheim Museum, New York.

# American Composers of Operas, Light Operas and Musicals

**Samuel Barber,** b. 1910. Vanessa; Antony and Cleopatra.

**Irving Berlin,** b. Russia. May 11, 1888. Ziegfeld Follies; Music Box Revue, 1921-1924; Face the Music, 1932; As Thousands Cheer, 1933; Louisiana Purchase, 1940; This Is The Army, 1942; Annie Get Your Gun, 1946; Miss Liberty, 1949; Call Me Madam, 1950; Mr. President, 1962. Wrote songs, God Bless America, White Christmas.

**Leonard Bernstein,** b. 1918. Trouble in Tahiti; On the Town; Wonderful Town; West Side Story.

**Marc Blitzstein,** 1905-1964. The Cradle Will Rock; No for an Answer; Regina; Reuben, Reuben.

**Jerry Bock,** b. 1928. Mr. Wonderful, 1956; Fiorello, 1959; Fiddler on the Roof, 1964.

**Charles Wakefield Cadman,** 1881-1946. Shanewis; A Witch of Salem; The Willow Tree; The Land of the Misty Water; The Garden of Death; The Garden of Mystery; Tabasco.

**George W. Chadwick,** 1854-1931. Judith.

**Frederick S. Converse,** 1871-1940. The Pipe of Desire; The Sacrifice.

**Aaron Copland,** b. 1900. The Tender Land.

**Walter J. Damrosch,** 1862-1950. The Scarlet Letter; Cyrano de Bergerac; The Man Without A Country; The Opera Cloak.

**Reginald DeKoven,** 1861-1920. The Begum; Don Quixote; Robin Hood; The Fencing Master; The Algerian; The Mandarin; The Knickerbockers; The Tzigane; Rob Roy; The Highwayman; The Three Dragoons; Papa's Wife; The Little Duchess; Maid Marian; Red Feather; Happy Land; The Student King; The Golden Butterfly; Her Little Highness; The Canterbury Pilgrims.

**Carlisle Floyd.** Susannah; Wuthering Heights; The Passion of Jonathan Wade.

**Rudolf Friml,** b. Prague 1884, naturalized U. S. 1925. The Firefly, 1912; High Jinks, 1913; Katinka, 1916; June Love, 1920; Rose Marie, 1923; Vagabond King, 1925; Bird of Paradise, 1930.

**George Gershwin,** 1898-1937, Lady Be Good, 1924; Oh Kay, 1924; Strike Up the Band, 1927; Funny Face, 1927; Treasure Girl, 1928; Show Girl, 1929; Of Thee I Sing, 1931; Porgy and Bess, 1935.

**Louis Gruenberg,** 1884-1964. The Emperor Jones; Green Mansions; Jack and the Beanstalk; Volpone, Helena's Husband, Antony & Cleopatra.

**Henry K. Hadley,** 1871-1937. Azora; Cleopatra's Night.

**Howard Hanson,** b. 1896. Merry Mount.

**Victor Herbert,** b. Dublin, Feb. 1, 1859, d. New York, N. Y., May 26, 1924. Operas: Natoma, 1911; Madeline, 1914. Operettas: Wizard of the Nile, 1895; The Fortune Teller, 1898; Cyrano de Bergerac, The Ameer, The Viceroy, The Idol's Eye, The Singing Girl, Babette; Mlle. Modiste, 1905; Babes in Toyland, 1903; The Red Mill, 1906; Naughty Marietta, 1910; Sweethearts, 1913; Princess Pat, 1915; Eileen, 1917.

**Jerry Herman,** b. 1931. Milk and Honey, 1961; Hello, Dolly!, 1964; Mame, 1966.

**Jerome Kern,** 1885-1945. Sally, 1920; Sunny, 1925; Show Boat, 1930; Cat and the Fiddle, 1931; Music in the Air, 1932; Roberta, 1933.

**Burton Lane,** b. New York, N. Y., 1912. Three's a Crowd; Finian's Rainbow; On a Clear Day You Can See Forever.

**Frank Loesser,** b. New York, N. Y., 1910. Guys and Dolls; Where's Charley?; The Most Happy Fella. Many songs including Kiss the Boys Goodbye, A Touch of Texas, Praise the Lord and Pass the Ammunition. Jingle, Jangle, Jingle.

**Frederick Loewe,** b. Austria. With Alan Jay Lerner, librettist, The Day Before Spring; Brigadoon; Paint Your Wagon; My Fair Lady; Camelot.

**Gian-Carlo Menotti,** b. Italy, 1911. Amelia Goes to the Ball. The Old Maid and the Thief, The Island God, The Medium, The Telephone, The Consul, Amahl and the Night Visitors, Maria Golovin, The Saint of Bleecker Street; The Unicorn, the Gorgon & the Manticore; The Last Superman; Labyrinth.

**Douglas S. Moore,** b. 1893. Giants in the Earth; The Ballad of Baby Doe; Sister Carrie.

**Horatio W. Parker,** 1863-1919. Mona; Fairyland.

**Cole Porter,** 1893-1964. Hitchy Koo, 1919; Fifty Million Frenchmen, 1929; The Gay Divorce, 1932; Anything Goes, 1934; Jubilee, 1935; DuBarry Was a Lady, 1939; Panama Hattie, 1940; Mexican Hayride, 1943; Kiss Me Kate, 1948; Can Can, 1953; Silk Stockings, 1955.

**Richard Rodgers,** b. 1902. Garrick Gaieties, 1925; Dearest Enemy, 1925; Connecticut Yankee, 1927, revised 1943; Present Arms, 1928; America's Sweetheart, 1931; On Your Toes, 1936; Babes in Arms, 1937; The Boys from Syracuse, 1938; By Jupiter, 1942; Oklahoma!, 1943; Carousel, 1945; Allegro, 1947; South Pacific, 1949; The King & I, 1951; Me & Juliet, 1953; Pipe Dream, 1955; Flower Drum Song, 1958; The Sound of Music, 1959; No Strings, 1962; Do I hear a Waltz?, 1965.

**Sigmund Romberg,** b. Hungary, 1887; d. New York, 1951. Maytime, 1917; The Student Prince, 1924; Desert Song, 1926; Blossom Time, 1926; New Moon, 1927; many others.

**Harold Rome,** b. Hartford, Conn., 1908. Pins and Needles; Call Me Mister; Wish You Were Here; Fanny; Destry Rides Again; I Can Get It For You Wholesale.

**John Philip Sousa,** 1854-1932. The Smugglers; Desiree; Queen of Hearts; El Capitan; The Bride-Elect; The Charlatan, Chris and the Wonderful Lamp.

**Igor F. Stravinsky,** b. Russia, 1882. Le Rossignol, 1914; Oedipus Rex, 1927; The Rake's Progress, 1951; L'Histoire du Soldat, 1956.

**Julie Styne,** b. London, Eng., 1905. High Button Shoes; Gentlemen Prefer Blondes; Bells Are Ringing; Say Darling; Gypsy; Funny Girl.

**Deems Taylor,** 1885-1966. The King's Henchmen; Peter Ibbetson.

**Virgil Thomson,** b. 1886. Four Saints in Three Acts; The Mother of Us All.

**Kurt Weill,** 1900-1950. (Ger.-Amer.) Three-Penny Opera; Down in the Valley; The Protagonist; The Man Who Says Yes; Lady in the Dark; Knickerbocker Holiday; One Touch of Venus; Lost in the Stars; Street Scene.

**Meredith Willson,** b. 1902. The Music Man, 1957.

**Vincent Youmans,** 1898-1946. Two Little Girls in Blue, 1921; Wildflower, 1923; Hit the Deck, 1927; Rainbow, 1928; Smiles, 1930; Through the Years, 1932; Take a Chance, 1932.

# Notable Americans of the Present

Statesmen, Authors, Military Men and Other Prominent Persons Not Listed in Other Categories.

| Name Birthplace | Birthdate | Name Birthplace | Birthdate |
|---|---|---|---|
| Acheson, Dean (Middletown, Conn.) | 4/11/93 | Buckley, William F. (New York, N. Y.) | 11/24/25 |
| Albee, Edward (Washington, D. C.) | 3/12/28 | Bunche, Ralph (Detroit, Mich.) | 8/ 7/04 |
| Albert, Carl (McAlester, Okla.) | 5/10/08 | Bundy, McGeorge (Boston, Mass.) | 3/30/19 |
| Alsop, Joseph W., Jr. (Avon, Conn.) | 10/11/10 | Caldwell, Erskine (Coweta Co., Ga.) | 12/17/03 |
| Alsop, Stewart (Avon, Conn.) | 5/17/14 | Capote, Truman (New Orleans, La.) | 9/30/24 |
| Alston, Walter (Butler Co., Ohio) | 12/ 1/11 | Case, Clifford (Franklin Park, N. J.) | 4/16/04 |
| Arcaro, Eddie (Cincinnati, Ohio) | 2/19/16 | Casper, Billy (San Diego, Calif.) | 6/24/31 |
| Ashe, Arthur (Richmond, Va.) | 7/10/43 | Celler, Emmanuel (Brooklyn, N. Y.) | 5/ 6/88 |
| Baker, Russell (Loudoun Co., Va.) | 8/14/25 | Chamberlain, Wilt (Philadelphia, Pa.) | 8/21/36 |
| Baldwin, Faith (New Rochelle, N. Y.) | 10/ 1/93 | Church, Frank (Boise, Idaho) | 7/25/24 |
| Baldwin, James (New York, N. Y.) | 8/ 2/24 | Clark, Ramsey (Dallas, Texas) | 12/18/27 |
| Ball, George (Des Moines, Iowa) | 12/21/09 | Clay, Cassius (Louisville, Ky.) | 1/18/42 |
| Belli, Melvin (Sonora, Calif.) | 7/29/07 | Clay, Lucius D. (Marietta, Ga.) | 4/23/97 |
| Bellow, Saul (Quebec, Canada) | 7/10/15 | Cohn, Roy (New York, N. Y.) | 2/20/27 |
| Benton, Thomas Hart (Neosho, Mo.) | 4/15/89 | Collins, Leroy (Tallahassee, Fla.) | 3/10/09 |
| Berra, Yogi (St. Louis, Mo.) | 5/12/25 | Conant, James B., (Dorchester, Mass.) | 3/26/93 |
| Bishop, Jim (Jersey City, N. J.) | 11/21/07 | Connally, John B. (Floresville, Tex.) | 2/28/17 |
| Bliss, Ray C. (Akron, Ohio) | 12/16/07 | Cooper, John Sherman (Somerset, Ky.) | 8/23/01 |
| Bowles, Chester (Springfield, Mass.) | 4/ 5/01 | Dempsey, Jack (Manassa, Colo.) | 6/24/95 |
| Bradley, Omar N. (Clark, Mo.) | 2/12/93 | Dewey, Thomas E. (Owosso, Mich.) | 3/24/02 |
| Braun, Wernher von (Wirsitz, Germany) | 3/23/12 | DiMaggio, Joe (Martinez, Calif.) | 11/25/14 |
| Brewster, Kingman (Toledo, Ohio) | 5/ 7/31 | Dirksen, Everett M. (Pekin, Ill.) | 1/ 4/96 |
| Brooke, Edward (Washington, D. C.) | 10/26/19 | Dodd, Thomas (Norwich, Conn.) | 5/15/07 |
| Brown, Edmund (Pat) (San Fran. Calif.) | 4/21/05 | Dominick, Peter (Stamford, Conn.) | 7/7/15 |
| Buchwald, Art (Mt. Vernon, N. Y.) | 10/20/25 | Doolittle, James H. (Alameda, Calif.) | 12/14/96 |
| Buck, Pearl S. (Hillsboro, W. Virginia) | 6/26/92 | Dos Passos, John (Chicago, Ill.) | 1/14/96 |

| Name | Birthplace | Birthdate |
|---|---|---|
| Douglas, Paul (Salem, Mass.) | | 3/26/92 |
| Drury, Allan (Houston, Texas) | | 9/2/18 |
| Dubinsky, David (Brest-Litovsk, Poland) | | 2/22/92 |
| Dulles, Allen W. (Watertown, N. Y.) | | 4/7/93 |
| Durocher, Leo (West Springfield, Mass.) | | 7/27/06 |
| Eisenhower, Dwight D. (Denison, Texas) | | 10/14/90 |
| Eisenhower, Mamie (Boone, Iowa) | | 11/14/96 |
| Eisenhower, Milton, S. (Abilene, Kans.) | | 9/15/99 |
| Fadiman, Clifton (Brooklyn, N. Y.) | | 5/15/04 |
| Farley, James A. (Grassy Point, N. Y.) | | 5/30/88 |
| Farmer, James (Marshall, Texas) | | 1/12/20 |
| Fong, Hiram (Honolulu, Hawaii) | | 10/1/07 |
| Ford, Gerald R. (Omaha, Nebr.) | | 7/14/13 |
| Fortas, Abe (Memphis, Tenn.) | | 6/19/10 |
| Fowler, Henry H. (Roanoke, Va.) | | 9/5/08 |
| Freeman, Orville L. (Minneapolis, Minn.) | | 5/9/18 |
| Fulbright, J. William (Sumner, Mo.) | | 4/9/05 |
| Funston, Keith (Waterloo, Iowa) | | 10/12/10 |
| Galbraith, John Kenneth (Ontario, Can.) | | 10/15/08 |
| Gardner, Erle Stanley (Malden, Mass.) | | 7/17/89 |
| Gavin, James (New York, N. Y.) | | 3/22/07 |
| Getty, J. Paul (Minneapolis, Minn.) | | 12/15/92 |
| Glenn, John (Cambridge, Ohio) | | 7/18/21 |
| Goldberg, Arthur J. (Chicago, Ill.) | | 8/8/08 |
| Goldwater, Barry M. (Phoenix, Ariz.) | | 1/1/09 |
| Graham, Billy (Charlotte, N. C.) | | 11/7/18 |
| Grange, Red (Forksville, Pa.) | | 6/13/04 |
| Harriman, W. Averell (New York, N. Y.) | | 11/15/91 |
| Hatfield, Mark O. (Dallas, Ore.) | | 7/12/22 |
| Heller, Walter (Buffalo, N. Y.) | | 8/27/15 |
| Hershey, Lewis B. (Steuben Co., Ind.) | | 9/12/93 |
| Hogan, Ben (Dublin, Tex.) | | 8/13/12 |
| Hoover, J. Edgar (Washington, D. C.) | | 1/1/95 |
| Hughes, Howard (Houston, Tex.) | | 12/24/05 |
| Hughes, Richard (Florence, N.J.) | | 8/10/09 |
| Humphrey, Hubert (Wallace, So. Dakota) | | 5/27/11 |
| Javits, Jacob K. (New York, N. Y.) | | 5/18/04 |
| Johnson, Luci Baines (Mrs. Patrick Nugent) | | 7/2/47 |
| Johnson, Lynda Bird (Mrs. Charles Robb) | | 3/19/44 |
| Johnson, Lyndon B. (Stonewall, Texas) | | 8/27/08 |
| Johnson, Mrs. Lyndon B. (Karnack, Tex.) | | 12/22/12 |
| Jones, James (Robinson, Ill.) | | 11/6/21 |
| Katzenbach, Nicholas deB. (Phila., Pa.) | | 1/17/22 |
| Kennedy, Caroline | | 11/27/57 |
| Kennedy, Edward M. (Brookline, Mass.) | | 2/22/32 |
| Kennedy, Jacqueline (Southampton, N. Y.) | | 7/28/29 |
| Kennedy, John Fitzgerald, Jr. | | 11/25/60 |
| Kerr, Walter (Evanston, Ill.) | | 7/8/13 |
| Kheel, Theodore (New York, N. Y.) | | 5/9/14 |
| Kieran, John (New York, N. Y.) | | 8/2/92 |
| Kirk, Grayson (Jefferson, Ohio) | | 10/12/03 |
| Koufax, Sandy (Brooklyn, N. Y.) | | 12/30/35 |
| Landon, Alfred (West Middlesex, Pa.) | | 9/9/87 |
| Lawrence, David (Philadelphia, Pa.) | | 12/25/88 |
| Lemnitzer, Lyman L. (Honesdale, Pa.) | | 8/29/99 |
| Lindbergh, Anne Morrow (Englewood, N. J.) | | 1906 |
| Lindbergh, Charles A. (Detroit, Mich.) | | 2/4/02 |
| Lindsay, John V. (New York, N. Y.) | | 11/24/21 |
| Lippmann, Walter (New York, N. Y.) | | 9/23/89 |
| Lodge, Henry Cabot (Nahant, Mass.) | | 7/5/02 |
| Long, Russell B. (Shreveport, La.) | | 11/3/18 |
| Louis, Joe (Lafayette, Ala.) | | 5/13/14 |
| Lowell, Robert (Boston, Mass.) | | 3/1/17 |
| Luce, Clare Booth (New York, N. Y.) | | 4/10/03 |
| MacLeish, Archibald (Glencoe, Ill.) | | 5/7/92 |
| Mailer, Norman (Long Branch, N. J.) | | 1/31/23 |
| Manchester, William (Attleboro, Mass.) | | 4/1/22 |
| Mansfield, Mike (New York, N. Y.) | | 3/16/03 |
| Mantle, Mickey (Spavinaw, Okla.) | | 10/20/31 |
| Marciano, Rocky (Brockton, Mass.) | | 9/1/24 |
| Marshall, Thurgood (Baltimore, Md.) | | 7/2/08 |
| Mays, Willie (Fairfield, Ala.) | | 5/6/31 |
| McCarthy, Eugene (Watkins, Minn.) | | 3/29/16 |
| McCormack, John W. (Boston, Mass.) | | 12/21/91 |
| McGinley, Phyllis (Ontario, Ore.) | | 3/21/05 |
| McKissick, Floyd (Asheville, N. C.) | | 3/9/22 |
| McClellan, John J. (Sheridan, Ark.) | | 2/25/96 |
| McNamara, Robert S. (San Francisco) | | 6/9/16 |
| Meany, George (New York, N. Y.) | | 8/16/94 |
| Menotti, Gian-Carlo (Cadegliano, Italy) | | 7/7/11 |
| Michener, James A. (New York, N. Y.) | | 2/3/07 |
| Miller, Arthur (New York, N. Y.) | | 10/17/15 |
| Mills, Wilbur (Kensett, Ark.) | | 5/24/09 |
| Moore, Marianne (St. Louis, Mo.) | | 11/15/87 |
| Morse, Wayne (Madison, Wisc.) | | 10/20/00 |
| Morton, Thruston (Louisville, Ky.) | | 8/19/07 |
| Moses, Robert (New Haven, Conn.) | | 12/18/88 |
| Moyers, Bill D. (Hugo, Okla.) | | 6/5/34 |
| Murphy, George (New Haven, Conn.) | | 7/4/04 |
| Musial, Stan (Donora, Pa.) | | 11/21/20 |
| Namath, Joe (Beaver Falls, Pa.) | | 5/31/43 |
| Nash, Ogden (Rye, N. Y.) | | 8/19/02 |
| Nicklaus, Jack (Columbus, Ohio) | | 1/21/40 |
| Niebuhr, Reinhold (Wright City, Mo.) | | 6/21/92 |
| Nixon, Richard (Yorba Linda, Calif.) | | 1/9/13 |
| Nizer, Louis (London, Eng.) | | 2/6/02 |
| O'Brien, Lawrence F. (Springfield, Mass.) | | 7/7/17 |
| O'Dwyer, Paul (Ireland) | | 6/29/07 |
| O'Hara, John (Pottsville, Pa.) | | 1/31/05 |
| O'Malley, Walter (Bronx, N. Y.) | | 10/9/03 |
| Paley, William S. (Chicago, Ill.) | | 9/28/01 |
| Palmer, Arnold (Youngstown, Pa.) | | 9/10/29 |
| Patterson, Floyd (Waco, No. Car.) | | 1/4/35 |
| Pauling, Linus (Portland, Ore.) | | 2/28/01 |
| Peale, Norman Vincent (Bowersville, Ohio) | | 5/31/98 |
| Pearson, Drew (Evanston, Ill.) | | 12/13/97 |
| Pegler, Westbrook (Minneapolis, Minn.) | | 8/2/94 |
| Percy, Charles H. (Pensacola, Fla.) | | 9/27/19 |
| Perleman, S. J. (Brooklyn, N. Y.) | | 2/1/04 |
| Pike, James A. (Okla. City, Okla.) | | 2/14/13 |
| Porter, Katherine Ann (Indian Creek, Tex.) | | 5/15/94 |
| Powell, Adam Clayton (New Haven) | | 11/29/08 |
| Rafferty, Max (New Orleans, La.) | | 5/7/17 |
| Randolph, A. Philip (Crescent City, Fla.) | | 4/15/89 |
| Reagan, Ronald (Tampico, Ill.) | | 2/6/11 |
| Reston, James (Clydebank, Scotland) | | 11/3/09 |
| Reuther, Walter P. (Wheeling, W. Va.) | | 9/1/07 |
| Rhodes, James (Jackson Co., Ohio) | | 9/13/09 |
| Rickover, Hyman (Makowa, Poland) | | 1/27/00 |
| Robertson, Oscar (Charlotte, Tenn.) | | 11/24/38 |
| Robinson, Jackie (Cairo, Ga.) | | 1/31/19 |
| Rockefeller, David (New York, N. Y.) | | 6/12/15 |
| Rockefeller, John D. 3rd (New York, N.Y.) | | 3/21/06 |
| Rockefeller, Laurance S. (New York, N.Y.) | | 5/26/10 |
| Rockefeller, Nelson A. (Bar Harbor, Me.) | | 7/8/08 |
| Rockefeller, Winthrop S. (New York, N.Y.) | | 5/1/12 |
| Rockwell, Norman (New York, N. Y.) | | 2/3/94 |
| Romney, George W. (Chihuahua, Mexico) | | 7/8/07 |
| Roosevelt, Elliot (New York, N. Y.) | | 9/23/10 |
| Roosevelt, Franklin D., Jr. (Canada) | | 8/17/14 |
| Rusk, Dean (Cherokee Co., Ga.) | | 2/9/09 |
| Russell, Richard B. (Winder, Ga.) | | 11/2/97 |
| Ryun, Jim (Wichita, Kansas) | | 4/29/47 |
| Salinger, J. D. (New York, N. Y.) | | 1/1/19 |
| Salinger, Pierre (San Francisco, Calif.) | | 6/14/25 |
| Salk, Jonas (New York, N.Y.) | | 10/28/14 |
| Sarnoff, David (Uzlian, Minsk, Russia) | | 2/27/91 |
| Schlesinger, Arthur Jr. (Columbus, Ohio) | | 10/15/17 |
| Scranton, William W. (Madison, Conn.) | | 7/19/17 |
| Seaborg, Glenn T. (Ishpeming, Mich.) | | 4/19/12 |
| Sheen, Fulton J. (El Paso, Ill.) | | 5/8/95 |
| Shirer, William L. (Chicago, Ill.) | | 2/23/04 |
| Shoemaker, Willie (Fabens, Texas) | | 8/19/31 |
| Shor, Toots (Philadelphia, Pa.) | | 5/6/05 |
| Shriver, Sargent (Westminster, Md.) | | 11/9/15 |
| Sinclair, Upton (Baltimore, Md.) | | 9/20/78 |
| Smith, H. Allen (McLeansboro, Ill.) | | 12/19/07 |
| Smith, Margaret Chase (Skowhegan, Me.) | | 12/14/97 |
| Sorenson, Theodore (Lincoln, Neb.) | | 5/8/28 |
| Spillane, Mickey (Brooklyn, N. Y.) | | 3/9/18 |
| Spock, Benjamin (New Haven, Conn.) | | 5/2/03 |
| Stassen, Harold (West St. Paul, Minn.) | | 4/13/07 |
| Steinbeck, John (Salinas, Calif.) | | 2/27/02 |
| Stengel, Casey (Kansas City, Mo.) | | 7/30/91 |
| Taft, Robert Jr., (Cincinnati, Ohio) | | 2/26/17 |
| Taylor, Maxwell D. (Keytesville, Mo.) | | 8/26/01 |
| Thomas, Lowell (Woodington, Ohio) | | 4/6/92 |
| Thompson, Llewellyn (Las Animas, Colo.) | | 8/24/04 |
| Thurmond, J. Strom (Edgefield, S. C.) | | 12/5/02 |
| Tower, John (Houston, Texas) | | 9/29/25 |
| Truman, Harry S. (Lamar, Mo.) | | 5/6/84 |
| Truman, Mrs. Harry (Independence, Mo.) | | 2/13/85 |
| Truman, Margaret (Independence, Mo.) | | 2/17/24 |
| Tunney, Gene (New York, N. Y.) | | 5/25/98 |
| Udall, Stewart L. (St. Johns, Ariz.) | | 1/31/20 |
| Unitas, John (Pittsburgh, Pa.) | | 5/7/33 |
| Unruh, Jesse (Newton, Kansas) | | 9/30/22 |
| Vanderbilt, Alfred G. (London, Eng.) | | 9/22/12 |
| Van Buren, Abigail (Sioux City, Iowa) | | 7/4/18 |
| Veeck, Bill (Chicago, Ill.) | | 2/9/14 |
| Vidal, Gore (West Point, N. Y.) | | 10/3/25 |
| Wagner, Robert F. (New York, N. Y.) | | 4/20/10 |
| Walcott, Jersey Joe (Merchantville, N.J.) | | 1/31/14 |
| Walker, Mickey (Elizabeth, N.J.) | | 7/13/01 |
| Wallace, George (Clio, Ala.) | | 8/25/19 |
| Warren, Earl (Los Angeles, Calif.) | | 3/19/91 |
| Warren, Robert Penn (Guthrie, Ky.) | | 4/24/05 |
| Westmoreland, William (Spartanburg S.C.) | | 3/26/14 |
| White, Paul Dudley (Roxbury, Mass.) | | 6/6/86 |
| White, Theodore (Boston, Mass.) | | 5/6/15 |
| Wilder, Thornton (Madison, Wisc.) | | 4/17/97 |
| Wilkins, Roy (St. Louis, Mo.) | | 8/30/01 |
| Williams, John J. (Frankford, Del.) | | 5/17/04 |
| Williams, Ted (San Diego, Calif.) | | 10/30/18 |
| Williams, Tennessee (Columbus, Miss.) | | 3/26/14 |
| Wirtz, W. Willard (De Kalb, Ill.) | | 3/14/12 |
| Wouk, Herman (New York, N.Y.) | | 5/27/15 |
| Wylie, Philip (Beverly, Mass.) | | 5/12/02 |
| Yarborough, Ralph (Chandler, Tex.) | | 6/8/03 |
| Yastrzemski, Carl (Southampton, N.Y.) | | 8/22/39 |
| Yorty, Sam (Lincoln, Neb.) | | 10/1/09 |
| Young, Whitney (Lincoln Ridge, Ky.) | | 7/31/21 |

## Modern American Playwrights and Some of Their Plays

George Abbott, b. 1887. Co-author Three Men on a Horse, The Boys from Syracuse, Damn Yankees.

Edward F. Albee, b. 1928. Who's Afraid of Virginia Woolf?, Tiny Alice, A Delicate Balance.

Maxwell Anderson, 1888-1959. What Price Glory? Winterset, Saturday's Children, High Tor, Key Largo.

Philip Barry, 1896-1949. The Animal Kingdom, Holiday, The Philadelphia Story.

Abe Burrows, b. 1910. Co-author Guys and Dolls, How to Succeed in Business Without Really Trying.

Mary C. Chase, b. 1907. Harvey.

Paddy Chayefsky, b. 1923. Middle of the Night, The Tenth Man, Gideon, The Passions of Josef D.

Marc Connelly, b. 1890. The Green Pastures.

Russell Crouse, 1893-1966. Co-author State of the Union, Life With Father, Call Me Madam, The Sound of Music, Mr. President.

Edna Ferber, b. 1887. Co-author Dinner at Eight, Stage Door.

Paul Green, b. 1894. In Abraham's Bosom, Wilderness Road.

Moss Hart, 1904-1961. Co-author Once in a Lifetime; You Can't Take It With You.

Ben Hecht, 1884-1964. Co-author The Front Page.

Lillian Hellman, b. 1907. The Children's Hour, The Little Foxes, Watch on the Rhine.

Sidney Howard, 1881-1939. The Silver Cord, Yellow Jack, They Knew What They Wanted.

William Inge, b. 1913. Come Back, Little Sheba; Picnic, Bus Stop, The Dark at the Top of the Stairs, A Loss of Roses.

George S. Kaufman, 1889-1961. Co-author Dinner at Eight, Stage Door, You Can't Take It With You, The Man Who Came to Dinner.

George Kelly, b. 1887. The Show-off, Craig's Wife.

Jean Kerr, b. 1923. Mary, Mary; Poor Richard.

Joseph Kesselring, 1902-1967. Arsenic and Old Lace.

Sidney Kingsley, b. 1906. Men in White, The Patriots, Dead End, Darkness at Noon.

Howard Lindsay, 1889-1968. Co-author State of the Union, Life With Father, Call Me Madam, The Sound of Music, Mr. President.

Charles MacArthur, 1895-1956. Co-author The Front Page.

Archibald MacLeish, b. 1892. J.B.

Carson McCullers, b. 1917. Member of the Wedding.

Arthur Miller, b. 1915. All My Sons, Death of a Salesman, Crucible, View from the Bridge, After the Fall, Incident at Vichy, The Price.

Anne Nichols, 1891-1966. Abie's Irish Rose.

Clifford Odets, 1906-1963. Waiting for Lefty, Awake and Sing, Golden Boy, The Country Girl.

Eugene O'Neill, 1888-1953. The Long Voyage Home, The Emperor Jones, Anna Christie, Desire Under the Elms, Strange Interlude, Mourning Becomes Electra; Ah, Wilderness; The Iceman Cometh, Long Day's Journey Into Night.

John Patrick, b. 1905. The Hasty Heart, Teahouse of the August Moon.

Elmer Rice, 1892-1967. The Adding Machine, Street Scene, Counsellor-at-Law, Dream Girl.

Lynn Riggs, 1889-1954. Green Grow the Lilacs.

William Saroyan, b. 1908. My Heart's in the Highlands, The Time of Your Life.

Doré Schary, b. 1905. Sunrise at Campobello.

Murray Schisgal, b. 1926. The Typists and the Tiger, Luv.

Robert Sherwood, 1896-1955. Reunion in Vienna, The Petrified Forest, Idiot's Delight, There Shall Be No Night, Abe Lincoln in Illinois.

Samuel A. Taylor, b. 1912. The Happy Time, The Pleasure of His Company, co-author Sabrina Fair and No Strings.

John Van Druten, 1901-1957. The Voice of the Turtle; I Remember Mama; Bell, Book and Candle; I Am a Camera.

Thornton Wilder, b. 1897. Our Town, The Skin of Our Teeth, The Matchmaker.

Tennessee Williams, b. 1914. The Glass Menagerie, A Streetcar Named Desire, Cat on a Hot Tin Roof, The Night of the Iguana, The Milk Train Doesn't Stop Here Anymore.

## Entertainment Personalities of the Past

| Born | Died | Name | Born | Died | Name | Born | Died | Name |
|---|---|---|---|---|---|---|---|---|
| | | **A** | 1882 | 1942 | Barrymore, John | 1905 | 1965 | Bow, Clara |
| 1892 | 1948 | Achron, Isador | 1878 | 1954 | Barrymore, Lionel | 1874 | 1946 | Bowes, Maj. Edward |
| 1873 | 1953 | Adair, Jean | 1848 | 1905 | Barrymore, Maurice | 1893 | 1939 | Brady, Alice |
| 1872 | 1953 | Adams, Maude | 1897 | 1963 | Barthelmess, Richard | 1873 | 1948 | Braithwaite, Lillian |
| 1928 | 1968 | Adams, Nick | 1891 | 1962 | Barton, James | 1871 | 1936 | Breese, Edmund |
| 1855 | 1952 | Adler, Jacob P. | 1878 | 1947 | Barton, John | 1898 | 1964 | Brendel, El |
| 1858 | 1953 | Adler, Sarah Levitzka | 1873 | 1941 | Bates, Blanche | 1901 | 1948 | Breneman, Tom |
| 1898 | 1933 | Adoree, Renee | 1888 | 1954 | Bates, Florence | 1875 | 1948 | Brian, Donald |
| 1879 | 1945 | Ainley, Henry | 1873 | 1951 | Bauer, Harold | 1891 | 1951 | Brice, Fanny |
| 1909 | 1964 | Albertson, Frank | 1893 | 1951 | Baxter, Warner | 1866 | 1952 | Broadhurst, George |
| 1885 | 1952 | Alda, Frances | 1880 | 1928 | Bayes, Nora | 1891 | 1959 | Broderick, Helen |
| 1894 | 1956 | Allen, Fred | 1904 | 1965 | Beatty, Clyde | 1898 | 1965 | Brokenshire, Norman |
| 1906 | 1964 | Allen, Gracie | 1873 | 1928 | Beban, George | 1904 | 1951 | Bromberg, J. Edward |
| 1869 | 1948 | Allen, Viola | 1887 | 1955 | Beecher, Janet | 1814 | 1880 | Brougham, John |
| 1883 | 1950 | Allgood, Sara | 1884 | 1946 | Beery, Noah | 1904 | 1957 | Brown, John |
| 1886 | 1954 | Anderson, John Murray | 1889 | 1949 | Beery, Wallace | 1895 | 1953 | Bruce, Nigel |
| 1859 | 1940 | Anderson, Mary | 1903 | 1931 | Beiderbecke, Bix | 1881 | 1948 | Bryant, Charles |
| 1915 | 1967 | Andrews, Laverne | 1854 | 1931 | Belasco, David | 1878 | 1961 | Buchan, Annabelle |
| 1876 | 1958 | Anglin, Margaret | 1851 | 1917 | Bell, Digby | 1891 | 1957 | Buchanan, Jack |
| 1866 | 1931 | Arbuckle, Maclyn | 1906 | 1964 | Bendix, William | 1886 | 1957 | Buck, Gene |
| 1868 | 1946 | Arliss, George | 1905 | 1965 | Bennett, Constance | 1904 | 1965 | Bunce, Alan |
| 1879 | 1951 | Armstrong, Harry | 1873 | 1944 | Bennett, Richard | 1863 | 1915 | Bunny, John |
| 1890 | 1956 | Arnold, Edward | 1879 | 1946 | Bent, Marion | 1912 | 1967 | Burnette, Smiley |
| 1869 | 1950 | Arthur, Julia | 1870 | 1947 | Bentley, Irene | 1896 | 1956 | Burns, Bob |
| 1871 | 1936 | Asche, Oscar | 1867 | 1944 | Beresford, Harry | 1882 | 1941 | Burr, Henry |
| 1885 | 1946 | Atwill, Lionel | 1899 | 1966 | Berg, Gertrude | 1802 | 1860 | Burton, William E. |
| 1845 | 1930 | Auer, Leopold | 1875 | 1938 | Bergere, Valerie | 1883 | 1966 | Bushman, Francis X. |
| 1905 | 1967 | Auer, Mischa | 1863 | 1927 | Bernard, Sam | 1896 | 1946 | Butterworth, Charles |
| 1898 | 1940 | Ayres, Agnes | 1845 | 1923 | Bernhardt, Sarah | 1872 | 1943 | Byron, Arthur |
| | | | 1893 | 1943 | Bernie, Ben | 1843 | 1920 | Byron, Oliver D. |
| | | **B** | 1889 | 1967 | Bickford, Charles | | | |
| 1864 | 1922 | Bacon, Frank | 1911 | 1960 | Bjoerling, Jussi | | | **C** |
| 1859 | 1953 | Bailey, Frankie | 1882 | 1951 | Blaney, Charles E. | 1886 | 1955 | Cahill, Lilly |
| 1847 | 1906 | Bailey, James A. | 1900 | 1943 | Bledsoe, Jules | 1874 | 1933 | Cahill, Marie |
| 1903 | 1951 | Bailey, Mildred | 1872 | 1928 | Blinn, Holbrook | 1895 | 1956 | Calhern, Louis |
| 1893 | 1968 | Bainter, Fay | 1888 | 1959 | Blore, Eric | 1858 | 1942 | Calve, Emma |
| 1895 | 1957 | Baker, Belle | 1899 | 1957 | Bogart, Humphrey | 1865 | 1940 | Campbell, Mrs. Patrick |
| 1876 | 1948 | Baker, Lee | 1885 | 1965 | Boland, Mary | 1892 | 1964 | Cantor, Eddie |
| 1898 | 1963 | Baker, Phil | 1963 | 1960 | Bond, Ward | 1878 | 1947 | Carey, Harry |
| 1882 | 1956 | Bancroft, George | 1866 | 1932 | Bonstelle, Jessie | 1866 | 1959 | Carhart, Georgiana |
| 1890 | 1952 | Banks, Leslie | 1833 | 1893 | Booth, Edwin | 1876 | 1941 | Carle, Richard |
| 1897 | 1950 | Banks, Monty | 1796 | 1852 | Booth, Junius Brutus | 1897 | 1954 | Carney, "Uncle Don" |
| 1890 | 1955 | Bara, Theda | 1894 | 1953 | Bordoni, Irene | 1873 | 1946 | Carr, Alexander |
| 1810 | 1891 | Barnum, Phineas T. | 1888 | 1960 | Bori, Lucrezia | 1880 | 1961 | Carrillo, Leo |
| 1858 | 1891 | Barrett, Lawrence | 1867 | 1943 | Bosworth, Hobart | 1905 | 1965 | Carroll, Nancy |
| 1882 | 1912 | Barrison, Mabel | 1869 | 1913 | Boucicault, Aubrey | 1910 | 1963 | Carson, Jack |
| 1879 | 1959 | Barrymore, Ethel | 1821 | 1890 | Boucicault, Dion | 1862 | 1937 | Carter, Mrs. Leslie |

| orn | Died | Name | Born | Died | Name | Born | Died | Name |
|---|---|---|---|---|---|---|---|---|
| 1879 | 1927 | Carus, Emma | 1905 | 1956 | Dorsey, Tommy | 1884 | 1936 | Glendinning, Ernest |
| 1873 | 1921 | Caruso, Enrico | 1907 | 1959 | Douglas, Paul | 1884 | 1938 | Gluck, Alma |
| 1887 | 1918 | Castle, Vernon | 1858 | 1944 | Downing, Robert | 1870 | 1938 | Godowsky, Leopold |
| 1874 | 1944 | Cavalieri, Lina | 1889 | 1956 | Draper, Ruth | 1886 | 1954 | Goetz, E. Ray |
| 1887 | 1950 | Cavanaugh, Hobart | 1881 | 1965 | Dresser, Louise | 1874 | 1955 | Golden, John |
| 1868 | 1949 | Cawthorn, Joseph | 1869 | 1934 | Dressler, Marie | 1857 | 1919 | Goodwin, Nat C. |
| 1873 | 1938 | Chaliapin, Feod | 1820 | 1897 | Drew, Mrs. John | 1884 | 1940 | Gordon, C. Henry |
| 1919 | 1961 | Chandler, Jeff | 1853 | 1927 | Drew, John (son) | 1887 | 1940 | Gordon, Vera |
| 1883 | 1930 | Chaney, Lon | 1879 | 1920 | Drew, Sydney | 1869 | 1944 | Gottschalk, Ferdinand |
| 1893 | 1940 | Chase, Charlie | 1909 | 1951 | Duchin, Eddy | 1829 | 1869 | Gottschalk, Louis |
| 1886 | 1962 | Chase, Pauline | 1900 | 1964 | Dumke, Ralph | 1879 | 1954 | Greenstreet, Sydney |
| 1893 | 1961 | Chatterton, Ruth | 1873 | 1954 | Duncan, Augustin | 1857 | 1936 | Greet, Ben |
| 1872 | 1931 | Cherry, Charles | 1877 | 1927 | Duncan, Isadora | 1883 | 1944 | Grey, Jane |
| 1861 | 1923 | Chevalier, Albert | 1905 | 1967 | Dunn, James | 1873 | 1950 | Grey, Katherine |
| 1900 | 1951 | Christians, Mady | 1873 | 1947 | Dupree, Minnie | 1874 | 1948 | Griffith, David Wark |
| 1888 | 1960 | Clark, Bobby | 1907 | 1968 | Duryea, Dan | 1858 | 1934 | Griffith, Ann |
| 1887 | 1940 | Clark, Marguerite | 1859 | 1924 | Duse, Eleanora | 1868 | 1944 | Guilbert, Yvette |
| 1850 | 1924 | Claxton, Kate | | | | 1885 | 1957 | Guitry, Sacha |
| 1885 | 1948 | Clayton, Bessie | | | **E** | 1875 | 1959 | Gwenn, Edmund |
| 1874 | 1931 | Clayton, Herbert | 1894 | 1929 | Eagels, Jeanne | | | |
| 1887 | 1950 | Clayton, Lou | 1896 | 1930 | Eames, Clare | | | **H** |
| 1874 | 1939 | Clemmons, Katherine | 1865 | 1952 | Eames, Emma | 1888 | 1942 | Hackett, Charles |
| 1920 | 1966 | Clift, Montgomery | 1875 | 1937 | Earle, Virginia | 1800 | 1871 | Hackett, James H. |
| 1857 | 1934 | Cline, Maggie | 1902 | 1948 | Eaton, Mary | 1869 | 1926 | Hackett, James K. |
| 1900 | 1937 | Clive, Colin | 1881 | 1929 | Eddinger, Wallace | 1902 | 1958 | Hackett, Raymond |
| 1880 | 1940 | Clive, Edward E. | 1901 | 1967 | Eddy, Nelson | 1898 | 1939 | Haig, Emma |
| 1892 | 1967 | Clyde, Andy | 1868 | 1931 | Edeson, Robert | 1870 | 1943 | Haines, Robert T. |
| 1883 | 1954 | Coates, Albert | 1893 | 1954 | Edwards, Alan | 1892 | 1950 | Hale, Alan |
| 1877 | 1961 | Coburn, Charles D. | 1879 | 1945 | Edwards, Gus | 1872 | 1933 | Hale, Louise Closser |
| 1887 | 1934 | Cody, Lew | 1829 | 1905 | Eldridge, Louisa | 1847 | 1919 | Hammerstein, Oscar |
| 1838 | 1899 | Coghlan, Charles | 1874 | 1950 | Elliott, Gertrude | 1895 | 1960 | Hammerstein, Oscar, 2nd |
| 1851 | 1932 | Coghlan, Rose | 1871 | 1940 | Elliott, Maxine | 1879 | 1955 | Hampden, Walter |
| 1878 | 1942 | Cohan, George M. | 1855 | 1942 | Elsler, Effie | 1873 | 1958 | Handy, W. C. |
| 1876 | 1916 | Cohan, Josephine | 1810 | 1884 | Elsler, Fanny | 1924 | 1964 | Haney, Carol |
| 1919 | 1965 | Cole, Nat (King) | 1891 | 1967 | Elman, Mischa | 1893 | 1964 | Hardwicke, Sir Cedric |
| 1878 | 1955 | Collier, Constance | 1883 | 1941 | Eltinge, Julian | 1892 | 1957 | Hardy, Oliver |
| 1866 | 1944 | Collier, William, Sr. | 1841 | 1891 | Emmett, J. K. | 1883 | 1939 | Hare, T. E. (Ernie) |
| 1866 | 1910 | Collins, Lottie | 1881 | 1955 | Enesco, George | 1865 | 1940 | Harlan, Otis |
| 1891 | 1958 | Colman, Ronald | 1903 | 1967 | Erwin, Stuart | 1911 | 1937 | Harlow, Jean |
| 1908 | 1934 | Columbo, Russ | 1881 | 1951 | Errol, Leon | 1872 | 1946 | Harned, Virginia |
| 1907 | 1944 | Compton, Betty | 1857 | 1945 | Evans, Charles E. | 1844 | 1911 | Harrigan, Edward |
| 1888 | 1933 | Conners, Barry | 1913 | 1967 | Evelyn, Judith | 1866 | 1912 | Harris, Henry B. |
| 1887 | 1949 | Connolly, Walter | | | | 1905 | 1944 | Harris, Mildred |
| 1876 | 1937 | Conquest, Ida | | | **F** | 1864 | 1935 | Harrison, R. B. |
| 1855 | 1949 | Conried, Heinrich | 1883 | 1939 | Fairbanks, Douglas | 1895 | 1943 | Hart, Lorenz |
| 1890 | 1964 | Conroy, Frank | 1870 | 1929 | Farnum, Dustin | 1870 | 1946 | Hart, William S. |
| 1854 | 1896 | Conway, Minnie | 1876 | 1953 | Farnum, William | 1907 | 1955 | Hartman, Grace |
| 1901 | 1961 | Cook, Donald | 1882 | 1967 | Farrar, Geraldine | 1876 | 1945 | Harwood, John |
| 1890 | 1959 | Cook, Joe | 1865 | 1935 | Farren, George F. | 1855 | 1903 | Haworth, Joseph |
| 1893 | 1958 | Cook, Phil | 1881 | 1910 | Faust, Lotta | 1874 | 1957 | Haye, Helen |
| 1901 | 1961 | Cooper, Gary | 1868 | 1940 | Faversham, William | 1896 | 1937 | Healy, Ted |
| 1876 | 1951 | Cossart, Ernest | 1861 | 1939 | Fawcett, George | 1879 | 1936 | Heggie, O. P. |
| 1906 | 1959 | Costello, Lou | 1897 | 1960 | Fay, Frank | 1873 | 1918 | Held, Anna |
| 1877 | 1950 | Costello, Maurice | 1895 | 1962 | Fazenda, Louise | 1885 | 1955 | Hempel, Frieda |
| 1875 | 1933 | Courtenay, William | 1887 | 1936 | Fenwick, Irene | 1879 | 1942 | Herbert, Henry |
| 1869 | 1930 | Courtleigh, William | 1885 | 1961 | Ferguson, Elsie | 1887 | 1951 | Herbert, Hugh |
| 1896 | 1941 | Courtney, Fay | 1849 | 1930 | Ferguson, Wm. J. | 1868 | 1952 | Herford, Beatrice |
| 1890 | 1950 | Cowl, Jane | 1905 | 1950 | Field, Sidney | 1883 | 1950 | Herne, Crystal |
| 1847 | 1924 | Crabtree, Lotta | 1867 | 1941 | Fields, Lew | 1840 | 1901 | Herne, James A. |
| 1845 | 1928 | Crane, William H. | 1884 | 1941 | Fields, Stanley | 1857 | 1943 | Herne, Katherine |
| 1875 | 1945 | Craven, Frank | 1879 | 1946 | Fields, W. C. | 1863 | 1937 | Heron, Bijou |
| 1880 | 1942 | Crews, Laura Hope | 1869 | 1947 | Fischer, Alice | 1886 | 1956 | Hersholt, Jean |
| 1865 | 1944 | Crosman, Henrietta | 1865 | 1932 | Fiske, Minnie Maddern | 1895 | 1942 | Hibbard, Edna |
| 1893 | 1966 | Crouse, Russell | 1888 | 1961 | Fitzgerald, Barry | 1857 | 1927 | Hillard, Robert C. |
| 1878 | 1968 | Currie, Finlay | 1874 | 1941 | Fitzgerald, Cissy | 1865 | 1929 | Hitchcock, Raymond |
| 1909 | 1953 | Curtis, Alan | 1895 | 1962 | Flagstad, Kirsten | 1874 | 1932 | Hodge, William |
| 1816 | 1876 | Cushman, Charlotte | 1831 | 1891 | Florence, W. J. | 1914 | 1955 | Hodiak, John |
| | | | 1909 | 1950 | Flynn, Errol | 1876 | 1957 | Hofmann, Josef |
| | | **D** | 1880 | 1942 | Fokine, Michel | 1870 | 1944 | Holland, Mildred |
| 1864 | 1942 | Dalton, Charles | 1853 | 1937 | Forbes-Robertson | 1923 | 1965 | Holliday, Judy |
| 1875 | 1927 | Daly, Arnold | 1899 | 1965 | Ford, Wallace | 1888 | 1951 | Holt, Jack |
| 1838 | 1899 | Daly, Augustin | 1859 | 1933 | Forrest, Arthur | 1871 | 1947 | Homer, Louise |
| 1924 | 1965 | Dandridge, Dorothy | 1806 | 1872 | Forrest, Edwin | 1878 | 1950 | Hopkins, Arthur |
| 1893 | 1941 | Danforth, William | 1872 | 1913 | Fox, Della | 1884 | 1953 | Hopkins, Charles R. |
| 1894 | 1963 | Daniel, Henry | 1854 | 1928 | Foy, Eddie | 1858 | 1935 | Hopper, DeWolf |
| 1860 | 1935 | Daniels, Frank | 1876 | 1941 | Franklin, Irene | 1874 | 1959 | Hopper, Edna Wallace |
| 1921 | 1965 | Darnell, Linda | 1893 | 1966 | Frawley, William | 1890 | 1966 | Hopper, Hedda |
| 1894 | 1967 | Darwell, Jane | 1885 | 1938 | Frederick, Pauline | 1881 | 1965 | Howard, Eugene |
| 1815 | 1877 | Davenport, E. L. | 1870 | 1955 | Friganza, Trixie | 1874 | 1926 | Houdini, Harry |
| 1858 | 1932 | Davenport, Eva | 1890 | 1958 | Frisco, Joe | 1867 | 1961 | Howard, Joe. |
| 1829 | 1891 | Davenport, Mrs. E. L. | 1860 | 1915 | Frohman, Charles | 1893 | 1943 | Howard, Leslie |
| 1850 | 1898 | Davenport, Fanny | 1851 | 1940 | Frohman, Daniel | 1886 | 1955 | Howard, Tom |
| 1866 | 1949 | Davenport, Harry | 1881 | 1950 | Fulton, Maude | 1886 | 1949 | Howard, Willie |
| 1900 | 1961 | Davies, Marion | 1885 | 1947 | Fyffe, Will | 1882 | 1947 | Huberman, B. |
| 1908 | 1961 | Davis, Joan | | | | 1886 | 1957 | Hull, Josephine |
| 1931 | 1955 | Dean, James | | | **G** | 1886 | 1957 | Hume, Benita |
| 1859 | 1933 | De Angelis, Jefferson | 1901 | 1960 | Gable, Clark | 1907 | 1967 | Humphrey, Doris |
| 1881 | 1950 | DeCordoba, Pedro | 1873 | 1929 | Gallagher, Ed. | 1895 | 1958 | Humphrey, Doris |
| 1905 | 1968 | Dekker, Albert | 1900 | 1955 | Gallagher, Richard | 1895 | 1945 | Hunter, Glenn |
| 1898 | 1965 | Demarco, Tony | 1898 | 1940 | Galli, Rosina | 1901 | 1962 | Huning, Ted |
| 1881 | 1959 | DeMille, Cecil B. | 1889 | 1963 | Galli-Curci, Amelita | 1884 | 1950 | Huston, Walter |
| 1891 | 1967 | Denny, Reginald | 1877 | 1967 | Garden, Mary | | | |
| 1878 | 1949 | Desmond, William | 1913 | 1952 | Garfield, John | | | **I** |
| 1878 | 1930 | Destinn, Emmy | 1893 | 1963 | Gaxton, Wm. | 1881 | 1934 | Illington, Margaret |
| 1865 | 1950 | de Wolfe, Elsie | 1904 | 1954 | George, Gladys | 1892 | 1950 | Ingram, Rex |
| 1917 | 1945 | Dickson, Gloria | 1879 | 1961 | George, Grace | 1838 | 1905 | Irving, Henry |
| 1879 | 1947 | Digges, Dudley | 1892 | 1962 | Gibson, Hoot | 1871 | 1944 | Irving, Isabel |
| 1890 | 1944 | Dinehart, Alan | 1890 | 1957 | Gigli, Beniamino | 1872 | 1914 | Irving, Laurence |
| 1901 | 1966 | Disney, Walt | 1897 | 1936 | Gilbert, John | 1867 | 1937 | Irwin, Edward |
| 1895 | 1949 | Dix, Richard | 1855 | 1937 | Gillette, William | 1859 | 1930 | Irwin, Flo |
| 1859 | 1943 | Dixey, Henry E. | 1854 | 1921 | Gillman, Ada | 1862 | 1938 | Irwin, May |
| 1856 | 1924 | Dockstader, Lew | 1867 | 1943 | Gilmore, Frank | | | |
| 1892 | 1941 | Dolly, Jennie | 1879 | 1939 | Gilpin, Charles | | | **J** |
| 1905 | 1958 | Donat, Robert | 1898 | 1968 | Gish, Dorothy | 1875 | 1942 | Jackson, Joe |
| 1887 | 1928 | Dooley, Johnny | 1886 | 1959 | Gleason, James | 1843 | 1910 | James, Louis |
| 1904 | 1957 | Dorsey, Jimmy | 1888 | 1947 | Gleason, Lucille | 1889 | 1956 | Janis, Elsie |
| | | | | | | 1886 | 1950 | Jannings, Emil |
| | | | | | | 1829 | 1905 | Jefferson, Joseph |

| Born | Died | Name |
|---|---|---|
| 1859 | 1923 | Jefferson, Thomas |
| 1872 | 1943 | Jeffreys, Ellis |
| 1862 | 1930 | Jewett, Henry |
| 1892 | 1962 | Johnson, Chic |
| 1878 | 1952 | Johnson, Edward |
| 1886 | 1935 | Johnsson, Moffet |
| 1888 | 1950 | Jolson, Al |
| 1889 | 1940 | Jones, Billy |
| 1889 | 1942 | Jones, Buck |
| 1846 | 1931 | Jones, Frank |
| 1911 | 1965 | Jones, Spike |
| 1890 | 1955 | Joyce, Alice |

**K**

| Born | Died | Name |
|---|---|---|
| 1874 | 1939 | Kalich, Bertha |
| 1878 | 1965 | Kaltenborn, Hans V. |
| 1910 | 1966 | Kane, Helen |
| 1811 | 1868 | Kean, Charles |
| 1806 | 1880 | Kean, Mrs. Charles |
| 1787 | 1833 | Kean, Edmund |
| 1885 | 1945 | Keane, Doris |
| 1896 | 1966 | Keaton, Buster |
| 1858 | 1929 | Keenan, Frank |
| 1830 | 1873 | Keene, Laura |
| 1841 | 1898 | Keene, Thomas W. |
| 1899 | 1960 | Keith, Ian |
| 1899 | 1956 | Kelly, Paul |
| 1873 | 1939 | Kelly, Walter C. |
| 1823 | 1895 | Kemble, Agnes |
| 1775 | 1854 | Kemble, Charles |
| 1809 | 1893 | Kemble, Fannie |
| 1848 | 1935 | Kendal, Dame Madge |
| 1843 | 1917 | Kendal, Wm. H. |
| 1926 | 1959 | Kendall, Kay |
| 1890 | 1948 | Kennedy, Edgar |
| 1885 | 1965 | Kennedy, Tom |
| 1886 | 1945 | Kent, William |
| 1880 | 1947 | Kerrigan, J. Warren |
| 1882 | 1956 | Kibbee, Guy |
| 1902 | 1966 | Kiepura, Jan |
| 1888 | 1964 | Kilbride, Percy |
| 1863 | 1933 | Kilgour, Joseph |
| 1899 | 1965 | King, Alexander |
| 1894 | 1944 | King, Charles |
| 1889 | 1938 | Kohler, Fred |
| 1874 | 1947 | Kolker, Henry |
| 1897 | 1957 | Korngold, Erich W. |
| 1920 | 1962 | Kovacs, Ernie |
| 1893 | 1954 | Kraus, Clemens |
| 1861 | 1950 | Kyle, Howard |

**L**

| Born | Died | Name |
|---|---|---|
| 1862 | 1932 | Lackaye, Wilton |
| 1913 | 1964 | Ladd, Alan |
| 1895 | 1967 | Lahr, Bert |
| 1904 | 1948 | Landi, Elissa |
| 1919 | 1948 | Landis, Carole |
| 1884 | 1944 | Langdon, Harry |
| 1856 | 1929 | Langtry, Lillian |
| 1921 | 1959 | Lanza, Mario |
| 1881 | 1940 | Lasky, Jesse L. |
| 1870 | 1950 | Lauder, Harry |
| 1885 | 1937 | Laughlin, Anna |
| 1899 | 1962 | Laughton, Chas. |
| 1890 | 1965 | Laurel, Stan |
| 1892 | 1954 | Laurie, Joe, Jr. |
| 1872 | 1945 | LaVerne, Lucille |
| 1898 | 1952 | Lawrence, Gertrude |
| 1890 | 1929 | Lawrence, Margaret |
| 1907 | 1952 | Lee, Canada |
| 1848 | 1929 | Lehmann, Lilli |
| 1896 | 1950 | Lehr, Lew |
| 1883 | 1949 | Leiber, Fritz |
| 1913 | 1967 | Leigh, Vivien |
| 1852 | 1908 | Leighton, Margaret |
| 1894 | 1931 | Leitzel, Lillian |
| 1831 | 1905 | Lemoyne, W. J. |
| 1870 | 1941 | Leonard, Eddie |
| 1881 | 1955 | Levy, Ethel |
| 1875 | 1925 | Lewis, Ada |
| 1847 | 1930 | Lewis, Arthur |
| 1888 | 1931 | Lewis, Bertha |
| 1903 | 1966 | Lewis, Fulton, Jr. |
| 1874 | 1944 | Lhevinne, Josef |
| 1889 | 1952 | Lincoln, Elmo |
| 1820 | 1887 | Lind, Jenny |
| 1889 | 1968 | Lindsay, Howard |
| 1869 | 1952 | Lipman, Clara |
| 1876 | 1922 | Lloyd, Marie |
| 1892 | 1957 | Lockhart, Gene |
| 1876 | 1943 | Loftus, Cissie (Marie) |
| 1909 | 1942 | Lombard, Carole |
| 1890 | 1950 | Lord, Pauline |
| 1886 | 1968 | Lorne, Marion |
| 1904 | 1964 | Lorre, Peter |
| 1914 | 1962 | Lovejoy, Frank |
| 1866 | 1937 | Lowell, Helen |
| 1892 | 1947 | Lubitsch, Ernst |
| 1885 | 1956 | Lugosi, Bela |
| 1853 | 1932 | Lupino, George |
| 1893 | 1942 | Lupino, Stanley |
| 1897 | 1957 | Lyman, Abe |
| 1885 | 1954 | Lytell, Bert |
| 1867 | 1936 | Lytton, Henry |

**M**

| Born | Died | Name |
|---|---|---|
| 1907 | 1965 | MacDonald, Jeanette |
| 1863 | 1931 | Mack, Andrew |
| 1878 | 1934 | Mack, Willard |
| 1861 | 1946 | Macy, George Carleton |
| 1896 | 1967 | Mahoney, Will |
| 1865 | 1931 | Mann, Louis |
| 1876 | 1953 | Mannering, Mary |
| 1933 | 1967 | Mansfield, Jayne |
| 1857 | 1907 | Mansfield, Richard |
| 1854 | 1927 | Mantell, Robert B. |
| 1897 | 1951 | Margetson, Arthur |
| 1865 | 1950 | Marlowe, Julia |
| 1890 | 1966 | Marshall, Herbert |
| 1864 | 1943 | Marshall, Tully |
| 1891 | 1961 | Marx, Chico |
| 1893 | 1964 | Marx, Arthur (Harpo) |
| 1860 | 1898 | Mather, Margaret |
| 1869 | 1960 | Matthews, A. E. |
| 1875 | 1955 | Mattson, Edith W. |
| 1862 | 1951 | Maude, Cyril |
| 1886 | 1927 | Maurice (M. Mouvet) |
| 1879 | 1948 | May, Edna |
| 1885 | 1957 | Mayer, Louis B. |
| 1853 | 1944 | Mayhew, Kate |
| 1875 | 1934 | Mayhew, Stella |
| 1869 | 1932 | Mayne, Frank G. |
| 1839 | 1896 | Mayo, Frank |
| 1884 | 1951 | Mayo, Margaret |
| 1884 | 1945 | McCormack, John |
| 1907 | 1962 | McCormick, Myron |
| 1888 | 1931 | McCoy, Bessie |
| 1832 | 1885 | McCullough, John |
| 1883 | 1936 | McCullough, Paul |
| 1895 | 1952 | McDaniel, Hattie |
| 1866 | 1951 | McGlynn, Frank |
| 1879 | 1949 | McIntyre, Frank J. |
| 1857 | 1937 | McIntyre, James |
| 1879 | 1937 | McKinley, Mabel |
| 1886 | 1959 | McLaglen, Victor |
| 1866 | 1932 | McNaughton, Tom |
| 1867 | 1927 | McRae, Bruce |
| 1888 | 1946 | Meek, Donald |
| 1879 | 1936 | Meighan, Thomas |
| 1861 | 1931 | Melba, Nellie |
| 1904 | 1961 | Melton, James |
| 1890 | 1963 | Menjou, Adolphe |
| 1835 | 1868 | Menken, Ada |
| 1902 | 1966 | Menken, Helen |
| 1882 | 1939 | Mercer, Beryl |
| 1880 | 1946 | Merivale, Phillip |
| 1909 | 1944 | Miller, Glenn |
| 1860 | 1926 | Miller, Henry |
| 1898 | 1936 | Miller, Marilyn |
| 1895 | 1927 | Mills, Florence |
| 1903 | 1955 | Minnevitch, Borrah |
| 1917 | 1955 | Miranda, Carmen |
| 1875 | 1957 | Mitchell, Grant |
| 1832 | 1918 | Mitchell, Maggie |
| 1892 | 1962 | Mitchell, Thomas |
| 1880 | 1940 | Mix, Tom |
| 1845 | 1909 | Modjeska, Helena |
| 1860 | 1935 | Moissi, Alexander |
| 1861 | 1932 | Monroe, George W. |
| 1926 | 1962 | Monroe, Marilyn |
| 1875 | 1964 | Monteux, Pierre |
| 1824 | 1861 | Montez, Lola |
| 1919 | 1951 | Montez, Maria |
| 1886 | 1935 | Moore, Florence |
| 1903 | 1947 | Moore, Grace |
| 1861 | 1931 | Moore, Mary |
| 1885 | 1955 | Moore, Tom |
| 1876 | 1962 | Moore, Victor |
| 1882 | 1949 | Moran, George |
| 1884 | 1952 | Moran, Polly |
| 1871 | 1948 | Moreno, Marguerite |
| 1890 | 1949 | Morgan, Frank |
| 1900 | 1941 | Morgan, Helen |
| 1888 | 1956 | Morgan, Ralph |
| 1866 | 1953 | Morley, Victor |
| 1849 | 1925 | Morris, Clara |
| 1914 | 1959 | Morris, Wayne |
| 1845 | 1906 | Morrison, Lewis |
| 1897 | 1967 | Muni, Paul |
| 1894 | 1953 | Munn, Frank |
| 1906 | 1955 | Munson, Ona |
| 1885 | 1965 | Murray, Mae |
| 1908 | 1965 | Murrow, Edward R. |

**N**

| Born | Died | Name |
|---|---|---|
| 1888 | 1950 | Nash, Florence |
| 1865 | 1945 | Nash, George |
| 1879 | 1945 | Nazimova, Alla |
| 1846 | 1905 | Neilson, Ada |
| 1848 | 1880 | Neilson, Adelaide |
| 1885 | 1967 | Nesbit, Evelyn |
| 1868 | 1957 | Neilson-Terry, Julia |
| 1870 | 1951 | Nethersole, Olga |
| 1874 | 1948 | Niblo, Fred |
| 1890 | 1950 | Nijinsky, Vaslav |
| 1898 | 1930 | Normand, Mabel |
| 1879 | 1959 | Norworth, Jack |
| 1893 | 1951 | Novello, Ivor |

**O**

| Born | Died | Name |
|---|---|---|
| 1898 | 1943 | O'Connell, Hugh |
| 1881 | 1959 | O'Connor, Una |
| 1872 | 1937 | O'Dell, Maude |
| 1878 | 1945 | O'Hara, Fiske |
| 1880 | 1938 | Oland, Warner |
| 1860 | 1932 | Olcott, Chauncey |
| 1885 | 1942 | Oliver, Edna May |
| 1892 | 1963 | Olsen, Ole |
| 1847 | 1920 | O'Neill, James |
| 1887 | 1949 | Ouspenskaya, Maria |

**P**

| Born | Died | Name |
|---|---|---|
| 1860 | 1941 | Paderewski, Ignace |
| 1889 | 1954 | Pallette, Eugene |
| 1881 | 1940 | Pasternack, Josef A. |
| 1843 | 1919 | Patti, Adelina |
| 1840 | 1889 | Patti, Carlotta |
| 1885 | 1931 | Pavlowa, Anna |
| 1868 | 1934 | Payton, Corse |
| 1917 | 1966 | Pearce, Alice |
| 1885 | 1950 | Pemberton, Brock |
| 1899 | 1962 | Pendleton, Nat |
| 1904 | 1941 | Penner, Joe |
| 1888 | 1957 | Percy, Esme |
| 1892 | 1937 | Perkins, Osgood |
| 1893 | 1956 | Peters, Brandon |
| 1893 | 1931 | Phillips, Norma |
| 1915 | 1963 | Piaf, Edith |
| 1893 | 1957 | Pinza, Ezio |
| 1900 | 1963 | Pitts, Zasu |
| 1893 | 1964 | Porter, Cole |
| 1904 | 1963 | Powell, Dick |
| 1869 | 1931 | Power, F. Tyrone |
| 1914 | 1958 | Power, Tyrone E. |
| 1872 | 1935 | Powers, Eugene |
| 1900 | 1964 | Price, George E. |
| 1873 | 1943 | Price, Kate |
| 1856 | 1919 | Primrose, George |
| 1879 | 1956 | Prouty, Jed |
| 1871 | 1942 | Pryor, Arthur |
| 1908 | 1944 | Purcell, Dick |
| 1897 | 1958 | Purviance, Edna |

**R**

| Born | Died | Name |
|---|---|---|
| 1873 | 1943 | Rachmaninoff, Sergei |
| 1906 | 1946 | Ragland, John (Rags) |
| 1890 | 1967 | Rains, Claude |
| 1893 | 1963 | Raisa, Rosa |
| 1900 | 1947 | Rankin, Arthur |
| 1892 | 1967 | Rathbone, Basil |
| 1883 | 1953 | Rawlinson, Herbert |
| 1891 | 1943 | Ray, Charles |
| 1852 | 1901 | Reed, Roland |
| 1860 | 1916 | Rehan, Ada |
| 1893 | 1923 | Reid, Wallace |
| 1873 | 1943 | Reinhardt, Max |
| 1870 | 1940 | Richman, Charles |
| 1872 | 1961 | Ring, Blanche |
| 1888 | 1958 | Risdon, Elizabeth |
| 1821 | 1905 | Ristori, Adelaide |
| 1874 | 1930 | Ritchie, Adele |
| 1903 | 1966 | Ritz, Al |
| 1910 | 1938 | Roberti, Lyda |
| 1861 | 1928 | Roberts, Theodore |
| 1878 | 1949 | Robinson, Bill |
| 1859 | 1912 | Robinson, Frederic |
| 1865 | 1942 | Robson, May |
| 1894 | 1958 | Rodzinsky, Artur |
| 1879 | 1935 | Rogers, Will |
| 1897 | 1937 | Roland, Ruth |
| 1887 | 1951 | Romberg, Sigmund |
| 1880 | 1962 | Rooney, Pat |
| 1899 | 1966 | Rose, Billy |
| 1882 | 1936 | Rothafel, S. L. (Roxy) |
| 1878 | 1953 | Ruffo, Titta |
| 1864 | 1936 | Russell, Annie |
| 1861 | 1922 | Russell, Lillian |

**S**

| Born | Died | Name |
|---|---|---|
| 1885 | 1936 | Sale (Chic), Charles |
| 1844 | 1908 | Sarasate, P. M. |
| 1879 | 1954 | Scheff, Fritzi |
| 1892 | 1930 | Schenck, Joe |
| 1895 | 1964 | Schildkraut, Joseph |
| 1865 | 1930 | Schildkraut, Rudolph |
| 1889 | 1965 | Schipa, Tito |
| 1882 | 1951 | Schnabel, Artur |
| 1910 | 1949 | Schumann, Henrietta |
| 1861 | 1936 | Schumann-Heink, E. |
| 1866 | 1945 | Scott, Cyril |
| 1914 | 1965 | Scott, Zachary |
| 1843 | 1896 | Scott-Siddons, Mrs. |
| 1873 | 1935 | Sears, Zelda |
| 1902 | 1965 | Selznick, David O. |
| 1858 | 1935 | Sembrich, Marcella |
| 1889 | 1928 | Semon, Larry |
| 1884 | 1960 | Sennett, Mack |
| 1856 | 1933 | Seymour, William |
| 1867 | 1954 | Shannon, Effie |
| 1907 | 1941 | Shannon, Peggy |
| 1881 | 1951 | Shattuck, Arthur |

(Continued on bottom page 676)

## Canadians of the Past

### STATESMEN

| Born | Died | Name |
|---|---|---|
| 1821 | 1893 | Abbott, John |
| 1878 | 1943 | Aberhart, William |
| 1804 | 1858 | Baldwin, Robert |
| 1870 | 1957 | Bennett, Richard B. |
| 1854 | 1937 | Borden, Robert |
| 1823 | 1917 | Bowell, Mackenzie |
| 1818 | 1880 | Brown, George |
| 1875 | 1940 | Buchan, John |
| 1814 | 1873 | Cartier, George |
| 1817 | 1893 | Galt, Alexander T. |
| 1869 | 1953 | Hepburn, Mitchell F. |
| 1804 | 1873 | Howe, Joseph |
| 1874 | 1950 | King, W. Mackenzie |
| 1841 | 1919 | Laurier, Wilfrid |
| 1815 | 1891 | MacDonald, John A. |
| 1887 | 1967 | Massey, Vincent |
| 1795 | 1861 | Mackenzie, Wm. Lyon |
| 1822 | 1905 | McDougall, William |
| 1825 | 1868 | McGee, Thomas D'Arcy |
| 1874 | 1960 | Meighen, Arthur |
| 1820 | 1914 | Strathcona (Smith) |
| 1844 | 1894 | Thompson, John |
| 1855 | 1927 | Tupper, Charles H. |
| 1888 | 1967 | Vanier, George P. |

### AUTHORS

| Born | Died | Name |
|---|---|---|
| 1748 | 1784 | Alline, Henry |
| 1850 | 1931 | Beauchemin, Nerce |
| 1913 | 1966 | Allen, Ralph |
| .... | 1931 | Beck, L. Adams |
| 1861 | 1924 | Blake, W. H. |
| 1827 | 1916 | Bourassa, Napoleon |
| 1840 | 1901 | Buies, Arthur |
| 1861 | 1918 | Campbell, W. Wilfred |
| 1861 | 1929 | Carman, W. Bliss |
| 1831 | 1904 | Casgrain, Henri-R. |
| 1858 | 1946 | Chapais, Thomas |
| 1850 | 1917 | Chapman, Wm. |
| 1820 | 1890 | Chauveau, Pierre |
| 1885 | 1953 | Chopin, Rene |
| 1850 | 1887 | Crawford, Isabella |
| 1827 | 1879 | Cremazie, Octave |
| 1831 | 1904 | Cosgrain, Abbe R. |
| 1865 | 1945 | Dantin, Louis |
| .... | 1936 | Doughty, Arthur G. |
| 1854 | 1907 | Drummond, W. H. |
| 1862 | 1932 | Duncan, Sara, J. |
| 1799 | 1859 | Fallon, Etienne |
| 1805 | 1865 | Ferland, Jean |
| 1839 | 1908 | Frechette, Louis H. |
| 1809 | 1866 | Garneau, Francis X. |
| 1786 | 1871 | Gaspe, Philippe de |
| 1824 | 1882 | Gerin-Lajoie, Ant. |
| 1871 | 1918 | Gill, Charles |
| 1860 | 1937 | Gordon, Chas. W. (Ralph Connor) |
| 1878 | 1967 | Groulx, Lionel A. |
| 1871 | 1948 | Grove, Frederick |
| 1842 | 1910 | Hannay, James |
| 1796 | 1865 | Haliburton, Thos. C. |
| 1816 | 1876 | Heavysege, Charles |
| 1880 | 1913 | Hemon, Louis |
| 1766 | 1844 | Heriot, George |
| 1894 | 1952 | Innis, H. A. |
| 1881 | 1943 | Kennedy, W. P. M. |
| 1859 | 1931 | Kingsford, Wm. |
| 1817 | 1906 | Kirby, William |
| 1862 | 1913 | Johnson, Pauline |
| 1871 | 1960 | Laberge, Albert |
| 1861 | 1899 | Lampman, Archibald |
| 1871 | 1936 | Laut, Agnes |
| 1869 | 1944 | Leacock, Stephen |
| 1837 | 1918 | Lemay, Pamphile |
| 1857 | 1954 | Lighthall, William |
| 1909 | 1957 | Lowry, Malcolm |
| 1853 | 1931 | Lucas, L. P. |
| 1878 | 1924 | Lozeau, Albert |
| 1876 | 1951 | Mac Innes, Tom |
| 1840 | 1927 | Mair, Charles |
| 1844 | 1945 | Marmette, Joseph |
| 1864 | 1936 | Marquis, Thomas H. |
| 1882 | 1958 | Martin, Chester |
| 1872 | 1918 | McCrae, John |
| 1820 | 1907 | McMullen, John |
| 1874 | 1942 | Montgomery, Lucy |
| 1889 | 1963 | Morin, Paul |
| 1879 | 1941 | Nelligan, Emile |
| 1737 | 1818 | Odell, Jonathan |
| 1895 | 1960 | Panneton, Philippe |
| 1862 | 1932 | Parker, Gilbert |
| 1883 | 1922 | Pickthall, Marj. |
| 1883 | 1964 | Pratt, Edwin J. |
| 1749 | 1809 | Quesnel, Joseph |
| 1796 | 1852 | Richardson, John |
| 1860 | 1943 | Roberts, Chas. G. D. |
| 1885 | 1961 | Roche, Mazo de la |
| 1839 | 1920 | Routhier, Adolph |
| 1870 | 1943 | Roy, Camille |
| 1858 | 1913 | Roy, Joseph E. |
| 1822 | 1893 | Sangster, Charles |
| 1862 | 1944 | Scott, Duncan C. |
| 1874 | 1958 | Service, Robt. W. |
| 1859 | 1931 | Short, Adam |
| 1878 | 1941 | Skelton, O. D. |
| 1823 | 1910 | Smith, Goldwin |
| 1841 | 1923 | Sulte, Benjamin |
| 1888 | 1951 | Trotter, R. G. |

### PAINTERS

| Born | Died | Name |
|---|---|---|
| 1740 | 1794 | Beaucort, Francois |
| 1871 | 1945 | Carr, Emily |
| 1769 | 1819 | Field, Robert |
| 1810 | 1894 | Fowler, Daniel |
| 1812 | 1901 | Jacobi, Otto |
| 1810 | 1871 | Kane, Paul |
| 1812 | 1872 | Krieghoff, Cornelius |
| 1789 | 1855 | Legare, Joseph |
| 1882 | 1953 | Milne, David |
| 1832 | 1809 | O'Brien, Lucius |
| 1859 | 1892 | Peel, Paul |
| 1804 | 1895 | Plamondon, Antoine |
| 1798 | 1849 | Valentine, William |

### SCIENCE, INDUSTRY

| Born | Died | Name |
|---|---|---|
| 1810 | 1882 | Allan, Hugh |
| 1891 | 1941 | Banting, Fredk. G. |
| 1877 | 1943 | Beatty, Edward W. |
| 1889 | 1966 | Hilton, Hugh G. |
| 1798 | 1875 | Logan, Wm. |
| 1849 | 1919 | Osler, Wm. |
| 1876 | 1935 | Macleod, John J. R. |
| 1863 | 1892 | Stairs, Wm. Grant |
| 1902 | 1967 | Zimmerman, Adam |

## Entertainment Personalities of the Past

(continued from page 675)

| Born | Died | Name |
|---|---|---|
| 1860 | 1929 | Shaw, Mary |
| 1861 | 1940 | Shea, Thomas E. |
| 1868 | 1949 | Shean, Al |
| 1892 | 1951 | Shepley, Ruth |
| 1915 | 1967 | Sheridan, Ann |
| 1848 | 1908 | Sheridan, John F. |
| 1885 | 1934 | Sherman, Lowell |
| 1854 | 1955 | Sherwin, Amy |
| 1883 | 1953 | Shubert, Lee |
| 1755 | 1831 | Siddons, Mrs. Sarah |
| 1882 | 1930 | Sills, Milton |
| 1878 | 1946 | Sis Hopkins (Melville) |
| 1891 | 1934 | Skelly, Hal |
| 1858 | 1942 | Skinner, Otis |
| 1870 | 1952 | Skipworth, Alison |
| 1863 | 1948 | Smith, C. Aubrey |
| 1826 | 1881 | Sothern, Edward A. |
| 1859 | 1933 | Sothern, Edward H. |
| 1884 | 1957 | Sothern, Harry |
| 1854 | 1932 | Sousa, John Philip |
| 1884 | 1957 | Sparks, Ned |
| 1876 | 1948 | Speaks, Oley |
| 1888 | 1953 | Spooner, Cecil |
| 1875 | 1953 | Spooner, Edna May |
| 1855 | 1940 | Spooner, Mary G. |
| 1886 | 1958 | Squire, Ronald |
| 1873 | 1937 | Standing, Guy |
| 1898 | 1950 | Starr, Muriel |
| 1871 | 1956 | Stephenson, Henry |
| 1900 | 1941 | Stephenson, James |
| 1883 | 1939 | Sterling, Ford |
| 1882 | 1928 | Stevens, Emily A. |
| 1896 | 1961 | Stewart, Anita |
| 1873 | 1959 | Stone, Fred |
| 1879 | 1953 | Stone, Lewis |
| 1871 | 1954 | Straus, Oskar |
| 1911 | 1960 | Sullavan, Margaret |
| 1903 | 1956 | Sullivan, Francis L. |
| 1862 | 1934 | Summerville, Amelia |

### T

| Born | Died | Name |
|---|---|---|
| 1897 | 1957 | Talmadge, Norma |
| 1878 | 1947 | Tanguay, Eva |
| 1899 | 1934 | Tashman, Lilyan |
| 1873 | 1940 | Tate, Harry |
| 1885 | 1966 | Taylor, Deems |
| 1887 | 1946 | Taylor, Laurette |
| 1878 | 1938 | Tearle, Conway |
| 1884 | 1953 | Tearle, Godfrey |
| 1892 | 1937 | Tell, Alma |
| 1881 | 1934 | Tellegen, Lou |
| 1864 | 1942 | Tempest, Marie |
| 1910 | 1963 | Templeton, Alec |
| 1865 | 1939 | Templeton, Fay |
| 1848 | 1928 | Terry, Ellen |
| 1874 | 1940 | Tetrazzini, Luisa |
| 1857 | 1914 | Thomas, Brandon |
| 1892 | 1960 | Thomas, John Charles |
| 1835 | 1905 | Thomas, Theodore |
| 1835 | 1911 | Thompson, Denman |
| 1861 | 1938 | Thornton, James |
| 1869 | 1936 | Thurston, Howard |
| 1896 | 1960 | Tibbett, Lawrence |
| 1887 | 1940 | Tinney, Frank |
| 1909 | 1958 | Todd, Michael |
| 1874 | 1947 | Toler, Sidney |
| 1878 | 1933 | Torrence, Ernest |
| 1867 | 1957 | Toscanini, Arturo |
| 1900 | 1967 | Tracy, Spencer |
| 1853 | 1917 | Tree, Herbert Beerbohm |
| 1883 | 1942 | Tucker, Richard |
| 1884 | 1966 | Tucker, Sophie |
| 1879 | 1945 | Turner, Clara |
| 1887 | 1946 | Turner, Florence |
| 1874 | 1940 | Turpin, Ben |
| 1908 | 1959 | Twelvetrees, Helen |

### V

| Born | Died | Name |
|---|---|---|
| 1895 | 1926 | Valentino, Rudolph |
| 1882 | 1927 | Valli, Vallie |
| 1870 | 1950 | Van, Billy B. |
| 1894 | 1943 | Veidt, Conrad |
| 1885 | 1944 | Vivian, Robert |
| 1886 | 1957 | Von Stroheim, Erich |

### W

| Born | Died | Name |
|---|---|---|
| 1874 | 1946 | Waldron, Charles D. |
| 1904 | 1966 | Walker, June |
| 1919 | 1951 | Walker, Robert |
| 1904 | 1943 | Waller, Thomas (Fats) |
| 1873 | 1915 | Walsh, Blanche |
| 1876 | 1962 | Walter, Bruno |
| 1878 | 1936 | Walthall, Henry B. |
| 1872 | 1952 | Ward, Fannie |
| 1855 | 1935 | Ward, Sallie |
| 1877 | 1939 | Ware, Helen |
| 1866 | 1951 | Warfield, David |
| 1876 | 1958 | Warner, H. B. |
| 1911 | 1960 | Warren, Leonard |
| 1878 | 1964 | Warwick, Robert |
| 1867 | 1945 | Watson, Billy |
| 1879 | 1962 | Watson, Lucile |
| 1890 | 1965 | Watson, Minor |
| 1896 | 1966 | Webb, Clifton |
| 1867 | 1942 | Weber, Joe |
| 1900 | 1950 | Weill, Kurt |
| 1876 | 1926 | Welch, Ben |
| 1873 | 1918 | Welch, Joe |
| 1880 | 1952 | Wenrich, Percy |
| 1883 | 1953 | Werrenrath, Reinald |
| 1859 | 1934 | West, Basil |
| 1879 | 1942 | Westley, Helen |
| 1895 | 1968 | Wheeler, Bert |
| 1889 | 1938 | White, Pearl |
| 1890 | 1967 | Whiteman, Paul |
| 1869 | 1942 | Whiteside, Walker |
| 1852 | 1943 | Whiting, George |
| 1865 | 1948 | Whitty, Dame May |
| 1895 | 1948 | William, Warren |
| 1877 | 1922 | Williams, Bert |
| 1867 | 1918 | Williams, Evan |
| 1923 | 1953 | Williams, Hank |
| 1872 | 1942 | Williams, Hattie |
| 1854 | 1935 | Wilson, Francis |
| 1904 | 1959 | Withers, Grant |
| 1881 | 1931 | Wolheim, Louis |
| 1888 | 1963 | Woolley, Monty |
| 1889 | 1938 | Woolsey, Robert |
| 1881 | 1956 | Wycherly, Margaret |
| 1844 | 1919 | Wyndham, Charles |
| 1886 | 1966 | Wynn, Ed |
| 1906 | 1964 | Wynyard, Diana |

### Y

| Born | Died | Name |
|---|---|---|
| 1874 | 1929 | Yeamans, Lydia |
| 1869 | 1938 | Yohe, May |
| 1891 | 1960 | Young, Clara Kimball |
| 1887 | 1953 | Young, Roland |
| 1900 | 1956 | Young, Victor |

### Z

| Born | Died | Name |
|---|---|---|
| 1869 | 1932 | Ziegfeld, Florenz |

## Entertainment Personalities—Where and When Born

Actors, Actresses, Composers, Dancers, Musicians, Producers, Radio-TV Performers, Singers

| Name | Birthplace | Born |
|---|---|---|
| **A** | | |
| Abbott, Bud (Wm.) | Atlantic City, N. J. | 1898 |
| Abbott, George | Salamanca, N. Y. | 1887 |
| Abel, Walter | St. Paul, Minn. | 1898 |
| Abner (Norris Goff) | Cove, Ark. | 1906 |
| Ackermann, Bettye | Cottageville, S. Car. | 1928 |
| Adam, Noelle | La Rochelle, France | 1935 |
| Adams, Don | New York, N. Y. | 1927 |
| Adams, Edith | Kingston, Pa. | 1929 |
| Adams, Julie | Waterloo, Iowa | 1928 |
| Addams, Dawn | Suffolk, Eng. | 1930 |
| Adler, Kurt H. | Vienna, Austria | 1905 |
| Adler, Larry | Baltimore, Md. | 1914 |
| Adler, Luther | New York, N. Y. | 1903 |
| Adrian, Max | Ireland | 1903 |
| Agar, John | Chicago, Ill. | 1921 |
| Aherne, Brian | Worcestershire, Eng. | 1902 |
| Albanese, Licia | Bari, Italy | 1913 |
| Alberghetti, Anna | Pesaro, Italy | 1936 |
| Albert, Eddie | Rock Island, Ill. | 1908 |
| Albright, Lola | Akron, Ohio | 1925 |
| Alda, Robert | New York, N. Y. | 1914 |
| Alexander, Ben | Goldfield, Nev. | 1911 |
| Alexander, Katherine | Arkansas | 1901 |
| Allan, Elizabeth | England | 1910 |
| Allbritton, Louise | Oklahoma City, Okla. | 1920 |
| Allen, Mel | Birmingham, Ala. | 1913 |
| Allen, Steve | New York, N. Y. | 1921 |
| Allen, Woody | Brooklyn, N. Y. | 1935 |
| Allister, Claud | London, Eng. | 1893 |
| Allison, Fran | Leporte City, Iowa | |
| Allyson, June | Westchester, N. Y. | 1923 |
| Alpert, Herb | Los Angeles, Calif. | 1937 |
| Ameche, Don | Kenosha, Wis. | 1908 |
| Ames, Ed. | Boston, Mass. | |
| Ames, Leon | Portland, Ind. | 1903 |
| Amos (F. F. Gosden) | Richmond, Va. | 1904 |
| Amsterdam, Morey | Chicago, Ill. | 1912 |
| Anderson, Judith | Adelaide, Australia | 1898 |
| Anderson, Marian | Philadelphia, Pa. | 1902 |
| Anderson, Mary | Birmingham, Ala. | 1922 |
| Anderson, Michael, Jr. | London, Eng. | 1943 |
| Anderson, Warner | Brooklyn, N. Y. | 1911 |
| Andress, Ursula | Switzerland | 1938 |
| Andrews, Dana | Collins, Miss. | 1912 |
| Andrews, Edward | Griffin, Ga. | 1915 |
| Andrews, Julie | Walton, England | 1935 |
| Andrews, Maxene | Minneapolis, Minn. | 1918 |
| Andrews, Patty | Minneapolis, Minn. | 1920 |
| Andy (C. J. Correll) | Peoria, Ill. | 1890 |
| Angel, Heather | Oxford, Eng. | 1909 |
| Angeli, Pier | Caglieri, Sardinia | 1932 |
| Anka, Paul | Canada | 1942 |
| Ann-Margret | Stockholm, Sweden | 1941 |
| Annabella | Paris, France | 1912 |
| Ansara, Michael | Lowell, Mass. | 1922 |
| Archer, John | Osceola, Calif. | 1915 |
| Arden, Eve | Mill Valley, Calif. | 1912 |
| Arkin, Alan | New York, N. Y. | 1935 |
| Arlen, Harold | Buffalo, N. Y. | 1905 |
| Arlen, Richard | Charlottesville, Va. | 1900 |
| Armstrong, Louis | New Orleans, La. | 1900 |
| Armstrong, Robert | Saginaw, Mich. | 1896 |
| Arnaz, Desi | Santiago, Cuba | 1917 |
| Arness, James | Minneapolis, Minn. | 1923 |
| Arnold, Eddy | Nashville, Tenn. | 1918 |
| Arquette, Cliff | Toledo, Ohio | 1905 |
| Arrau, Claudio | Chillau, Chile | 1904 |
| Arroyo, Martina | New York, N. Y. | 1937 |
| Arthur, Jean | New York, N. Y. | 1908 |
| Ashley, Elizabeth | Ocala, Fla. | 1940 |
| Astaire, Fred | Omaha, Nebr. | 1900 |
| Astin, John | Baltimore, Md. | 1930 |
| Astor, Mary | Quincy, Ill. | 1906 |
| Aumont, Jean-Pierre | Paris, France | 1913 |
| Austin, Gene | Texas | 1901 |
| Autry, Gene | Tioga, Texas | 1907 |
| Avalon, Frankie | Philadelphia, Pa. | 1940 |
| Ayres, Lew | Minneapolis, Minn. | 1908 |
| **B** | | |
| Bacall, Lauren | New York, N. Y. | 1924 |
| Baccaloni, Salvatore | Rome, Italy | 1900 |
| Backus, Jim | Cleveland, Ohio | 1913 |
| Baclanova, Olga | Moscow, Russia | 1899 |
| Baer, Jr., Max | Oakland, Calif. | 1938 |
| Baez, Joan | Staten Island, N. Y. | 1941 |
| Bailey, Pearl | Newport News, Va. | 1918 |
| Bailey, Raymond | San Francisco, Calif. | 1905 |
| Baird, William B. | Grand Island, Nebr. | 1904 |
| Baker, Carroll | Johnstown, Pa. | 1931 |
| Baker, Diane | Hollywood, Calif. | 1938 |
| Baker, Josephine | St. Louis, Mo. | 1907 |
| Baker, Kenny | Monrovia, Calif. | 1912 |
| Bakewell, William | Hollywood, Calif. | 1908 |
| Balanchine, George | St. Petersburg, Russia | 1904 |
| Ball, Lucille | Jamestown, N. Y. | 1911 |
| Ballard, Kaye | West Cleveland, Ohio | 1926 |
| Balsam, Martin | New York, N. Y. | 1923 |
| Bampton, Rose | Cleveland, Ohio | 1909 |
| Bancroft, Anne | New York, N. Y. | 1931 |
| Bankhead, Tallulah | Huntsville, Ala. | 1903 |
| Bannon, Ian | Airdrie, Scotland | 1928 |
| Barber, Red | Columbus, Miss. | 1908 |
| Barbirolli, John | London, Eng. | 1899 |
| Bardot, Brigitte | Paris, France | 1934 |
| Bari, Lynn | Roanoke, Va. | 1917 |
| Barker, Lex | Rye, N. Y. | 1919 |
| Barlow, Howard | Urbana, Ill. | 1892 |
| Barnett, Vincent | Pittsburgh, Pa. | 1902 |
| Barrat, Robert | New York, N. Y. | 1891 |
| Barrault, Jean-Louis | Le Vesinet, France | 1919 |
| Barrett, Sheila | Washington, D. C. | 1909 |
| Barrie, Mona | London, Eng. | 1909 |
| Barrie, Wendy | Hong Kong, China | 1913 |
| Barry, Gene | New York, N. Y. | 1922 |
| Barry, Jack | Lindenhurst, N. Y. | 1918 |
| Barrymore, John, Jr. | Beverly Hills, Calif. | 1932 |
| Bartholomew, Freddie | London, England | 1924 |
| Bartok, Eva | Budapest, Hungary | 1929 |
| Basehart, Richard | Zanesville, Ohio | 1915 |
| Basie, Count (Wm.) | Red Bank, N. J. | 1904 |
| Baum, Kurt | Cologne, Germany | 1908 |
| Bavier, Frances | New York, N. Y. | 1903 |
| Baxter, Anne | Michigan City, Ind. | 1923 |
| Beal, John | Joplin, Mo. | 1909 |
| Bean, Orson | Cambridge, Mass. | 1928 |
| Beatles, The | | |
| Harrison, George | Liverpool, Eng. | 1943 |
| Lennon, John | Liverpool, Eng. | 1940 |
| McCartney, Paul | Allerton, Eng. | 1942 |
| Starr, Ringo | Dingle, Eng. | 1940 |
| Beatty, Robert | Hamilton, Ont. | 1909 |
| Beatty, Warren | Richmond, Va. | 1937 |
| Becker, Sandy | New York, N. Y. | 1922 |
| Beery, Noah, Jr. | New York, N. Y. | 1916 |
| Begley, Ed | Hartford, Conn. | 1901 |
| Belafonte, Harry | New York, N. Y. | 1927 |
| Bell, James | Suffolk, Va. | 1891 |
| Bellamy, Ralph | Chicago, Ill. | 1905 |
| Belmondo, Jean-Paul | Neuilly-sur-Seine, Fr. | 1933 |
| Bennett, Joan | Palisades, N. J. | 1910 |
| Bennett, Tony | Astoria, N. Y. | 1926 |
| Benny, Jack | Waukegan, Ill. | 1894 |
| Bentley, John | Warwickshire, Eng. | 1916 |
| Benzell, Mimi | Bridgeport, Conn. | 1924 |
| Bergen, Candice | Beverly Hills, Calif. | 1946 |
| Bergen, Edgar | Chicago, Ill. | 1903 |
| Bergen, Polly | Knoxville, Tenn. | 1930 |
| Bergerac, Jacques | France | 1927 |
| Bergman, Ingrid | Stockholm, Sweden | 1917 |
| Bergner, Elisabeth | Vienna, Austria | 1900 |
| Berle, Milton | New York, N. Y. | 1908 |
| Berlin, Irving | Temun, Russia | 1888 |
| Berlinger, Warren | Brooklyn, N. Y. | 1937 |
| Berman, Shelley | Chicago, Ill. | 1926 |
| Bernardi, Hershel | New York, N. Y. | 1923 |
| Bernstein, Leonard | Lawrence, Mass. | 1918 |
| Best, Edna | Hove, England | 1900 |
| Bethune, Zina | New York, N. Y. | 1945 |
| Bikel, Theodore | Vienna, Austria | 1924 |
| Bing, Rudolf | Vienna, Austria | 1902 |
| Bishop, Joey | Philadelphia, Pa. | 1919 |
| Bishop, Julie | Denver, Colo. | 1917 |
| Black, Frank | Philadelphia, Pa. | 1894 |
| Blackmer, Sidney | Salisbury, N. C. | 1898 |
| Blaine, Vivian | Newark, N. J. | 1924 |
| Blair, Janet | Blair, Pa. | 1921 |
| Blair, June | San Francisco, Calif. | 1937 |
| Blanc, Mel | San Francisco, Calif. | 1908 |
| Bloch, Ray | Alsace-Lorraine | 1902 |
| Blocker, Dan | Bowie County, Tex. | 1928 |
| Blondell, Joan | New York, N. Y. | 1909 |
| Bloom, Claire | London, Eng. | 1931 |
| Blue, Ben | Montreal, Canada | 1901 |
| Blyth, Ann | Mt. Kisco, N. Y. | 1928 |
| Blythe, Betty | Los Angeles, Calif. | 1900 |
| Boehm, Karl | Graz, Austria | 1895 |
| Bogarde, Dirk | London, Eng. | 1921 |
| Boles, John | Greenville, Tex. | 1900 |
| Bolger, Ray | Dorchester, Mass. | 1904 |
| Bond, Sheila | New York, N. Y. | 1928 |
| Bondi, Beulah | Chicago, Ill. | 1892 |
| Boone, Pat | Jacksonville, Fla. | 1934 |
| Boone, Richard | Los Angeles, Calif. | 1916 |
| Booth, Shirley | New York, N. Y. | 1907 |
| Borge, Victor | Copenhagen, Denmark | 1909 |
| Borgnine, Ernest | Hamden, Conn. | 1918 |
| Bosley, Tom | Chicago, Ill. | 1927 |
| Boswell, Connee | New Orleans, La. | |
| Bowman, Lee | Cincinnati, Ohio | 1914 |
| Boyd, Stephen | Belfast, Ireland | 1928 |
| Boyd, William | Cambridge, Ohio | 1898 |
| Boyer, Charles | Figeac, France | 1899 |
| Bracken, Eddie | Astoria, L. I., N. Y. | 1920 |
| Brand, Neville | Kewanee, Ill. | 1921 |
| Brando, Marlon | Omaha, Nebr. | 1924 |
| Brasselle, Keefe | Elyria, Ohio | 1923 |
| Brazzi, Rossano | Bologna, Italy | 1916 |
| Brennan, Eileen | Los Angeles, Calif. | 1937 |
| Brennan, Walter | Swampscott, Mass. | 1894 |
| Brent, Evelyn | Tampa, Fla. | 1899 |

| Name | Birthplace | Born |
|---|---|---|
| Brent, George | Dublin, Ireland | 1904 |
| Brewer, Teresa | Toledo, Ohio | 1932 |
| Brian, David | New York, N. Y. | 1914 |
| Bridges, Lloyd | San Leandro, Calif. | 1913 |
| Brinkley, David | Wilmington, N. Car. | 1920 |
| Britt, May | Sweden | 1936 |
| Britton, Barbara | Long Beach, Calif. | 1923 |
| Brook, Clive | London, England | 1891 |
| Brooks, Louise | Cherryvale, Kans. | 1906 |
| Brooks, Phyllis | Boise, Idaho | 1914 |
| Brooks, Stephen | Columbus, Ohio | 1942 |
| Brown, Jimmy | Manhasset, L. I. | 1936 |
| Brown, Joe E. | Holgate, Ohio | 1892 |
| Brown, Johnny Mack | Dothan, Ala. | 1904 |
| Brown, Vanessa | Vienna, Austria | 1928 |
| Brownlee, John | Geelong, Australia | 1901 |
| Brubeck, Dave | Concord, Calif. | 1920 |
| Bruce, Carol | Brooklyn, N. Y. | 1919 |
| Bruce, Virginia | Minneapolis, Minn. | 1910 |
| Bryant, Anita | Barnsdale, Okla. | 1941 |
| Brynner, Yul | Sakhalin, U.S.S.R. | 1917 |
| Bubbles, John | Louisville, Ky. | 1903 |
| Buchanan, Edgar | Humansville, Mo. | 1903 |
| Buchholz, Horst | Berlin, Germany | 1933 |
| Burke, Billie | Washington, D. C. | 1885 |
| Burke, Paul | New Orleans, La. | 1926 |
| Burnett, Carol | San Antonio, Texas | 1934 |
| Burns, David | New York, N. Y. | 1902 |
| Burns, George | New York, N. Y. | 1896 |
| Burr, Raymond | Westminster, B. C. | 1917 |
| Burrows, Abe | New York, N. Y. | 1910 |
| Burton, Richard | South Wales | 1925 |
| Bushell, Anthony | Kent, Eng. | 1904 |
| Buttons, Red | New York, N. Y. | 1919 |
| Buzzell, Eddie | Brooklyn, N. Y. | 1897 |
| Byington, Spring | Colo. Springs, Colo. | 1898 |
| **C** | | |
| Cabot, Bruce | Carlsbad, N. Mex. | |
| Cabot, Susan | Boston, Mass. | 1927 |
| Caesar, Irving | New York, N. Y. | 1895 |
| Caesar, Sid | Yonkers, N. Y. | 1922 |
| Cagney, James | New York, N. Y. | 1904 |
| Cagney, Jeanne | New York City | 1919 |
| Cahn, Sammy | New York, N. Y. | 1913 |
| Caine, Michael | London, Eng. | 1933 |
| Calhoun, Rory | Los Angeles, Calif. | 1923 |
| Callan, Michael | Philadelphia, Pa. | 1940 |
| Callas, Maria | New York, N. Y. | 1923 |
| Calloway, Cab | Rochester, N. Y. | 1907 |
| Calvert, Phyllis | London, Eng. | 1917 |
| Calvet, Corinne | Paris, France | 1926 |
| Cambridge, Godfrey | New York, N. Y. | 1933 |
| Cameron, Rod | Calgary, Alb., Canada | 1912 |
| Campbell, Glen | Delight, Ark. | 1937 |
| Canary, David | Elwood, Ind. | 1938 |
| Canova, Judy | Jacksonville, Fla. | 1916 |
| Cantinflas | Mexico City, Mex. | 1911 |
| Capp, Al | New Haven, Conn. | 1909 |
| Capra, Frank R. | Palermo, Italy | 1897 |
| Cardinale, Claudia | Italy | 1939 |
| Carey, Macdonald | Sioux City, Ia. | 1913 |
| Carey, Phil | Hackensack, N. J. | 1925 |
| Carle, Frankie | Providence, R. I. | 1903 |
| Carlisle, Kitty | New Orleans, La. | 1914 |
| Carlson, Richard | Albert Lea, Minn. | 1914 |
| Carmichael, Hoagy | Bloomington, Ind. | 1899 |
| Carne, Judy | Northampton, Eng. | 1939 |
| Carney, Art | Mt. Vernon, N. Y. | 1918 |
| Carnovsky, Morris | St. Louis, Mo. | 1898 |
| Caron, Leslie | France | 1931 |
| Carradine, John | New York, N. Y. | 1906 |
| Carroll, Diahann | Bronx, N. Y. | 1935 |
| Carroll, Leo G. | Weedon, England | 1892 |
| Carroll, Madeleine | W. Bromwich, Eng. | 1906 |
| Carroll, Pat | Shreveport, La. | 1927 |
| Carson, Jeannie | Yorkshire, Eng. | 1929 |
| Carson, Johnny | Corning, Iowa | 1925 |
| Carson, Mindy | New York City | 1927 |
| Casadesus, Gaby | Marseilles, France | 1902 |
| Casadesus, Robert | Paris, France | 1899 |
| Casals, Pablo | Vendrell, Spain | 1876 |
| Case, Anna | Clinton, N. J | 1889 |
| Cash, Johnny | Kingsland, Ark. | 1932 |
| Cass, Peggy | Boston, Mass. | 1926 |
| Cassavetes, John | New York, N. Y. | 1929 |
| Cassidy, Jack | New York | 1927 |
| Cassidy, Ted | Pittsburgh, Pa. | 1932 |
| Castle, Irene | New Rochelle, N. Y. | 1894 |
| Caulfield, Joan | West Orange, N. J. | 1922 |
| Cavallaro, Carmen | New York, N. Y. | 1913 |
| Cavett, Dick | Gibbon, Nebr. | 1936 |
| Cerf, Bennett | New York, N. Y. | 1898 |
| Chamberlain, Dick | Beverly Hills, Calif. | 1935 |
| Champion, Gower | Geneva, Ill. | 1920 |
| Champion, Marge | Los Angeles, Calif. | 1926 |
| Chaney, Lon, Jr. | Okla. City, Okla. | 1915 |
| Channing, Carol | Seattle, Wash. | 1922 |
| Chaplin, Charles | London, England | 1889 |
| Chaplin, Charles, Jr. | California | 1925 |
| Chaplin, Sydney | Beverly Hills, Calif. | 1926 |
| Charisse, Cyd | Amarillo, Texas | 1923 |
| Charles, Ray | Albany, Ga. | 1932 |
| Chase, Ilka | New York, N. Y. | 1905 |
| Chayefsky, Paddy | New York City | 1923 |
| Chevalier, Maurice | nr. Paris, France | 1888 |
| Christian, Linda | Tampico, Mexico | 1924 |
| Christie, Audrey | Chicago, Ill. | 1912 |
| Christie, Julie | India | 1941 |
| Churchill, Sarah | London, England | 1916 |
| Cilento, Diane | Queensland, Aust. | 1933 |
| Claire, Ina | Washington, D. C. | 1892 |
| Clark, Dane | New York, N. Y. | 1915 |
| Clark, Dick | Mt. Vernon, N. Y. | 1929 |
| Clark, Fred | Lincoln, Calif. | 1914 |
| Clark, Petula | Ewell, Surrey, Eng. | 1932 |
| Clayton, Jan | Tularosa, N. Mex. | 1925 |
| Cliburn, Van | Shreveport, La. | 1935 |
| Clooney, Rosemary | Maysville, Ky. | 1928 |
| Cobb, Lee J. | New York, N. Y. | 1911 |
| Coburn, James | Laurel, Nebr. | 1928 |
| Coca, Imogene | Philadelphia, Pa. | 1920 |
| Cohen, Myron | Grodno, Poland | 1902 |
| Colbert, Claudette | Paris, France | 1907 |
| Cole, Dennis | Detroit, Mich. | 1943 |
| Cole, Tina | Hollywood, Calif. | 1943 |
| Collinge, Patricia | Dublin, Ireland | 1894 |
| Collins, Dorothy | Windsor, Ontario | 1926 |
| Collins, Joan | London, England | 1933 |
| Collyer, Bud | New York, N. Y. | 1908 |
| Colonna, Jerry | Boston, Mass. | 1903 |
| Como, Perry | Canonsburg, Pa. | 1912 |
| Conklin, Chester | Oskaloosa, Ia. | 1888 |
| Conklin, Peggy | Dobbs Ferry, N. Y. | 1912 |
| Connelly, Marc | McKeesport, Pa. | 1890 |
| Conner, Nadine | Compton, Calif. | 1913 |
| Conners, Michael | Fresno, Calif. | 1925 |
| Connery, Sean | Edinburgh, Scotland | 1930 |
| Connors, Chuck | Brooklyn, N. Y. | 1921 |
| Conrad Robert | Chicago, Ill. | 1935 |
| Considine, Tim | Los Angeles, Calif. | 1940 |
| Conte, Richard | New York, N. Y. | 1914 |
| Converse, Frank | St. Louis, Mo. | 1938 |
| Conway, Gary | Boston, Mass. | 1938 |
| Conway, Shirl | Franklinville, N. Y. | 1916 |
| Conway, Tim | Chagrin Falls, Ohio | 1933 |
| Coogan, Jackie | Los Angeles, Calif. | 1914 |
| Cook, Barbara | Atlanta, Ga. | 1928 |
| Cooke, Alistair | England | 1908 |
| Cooper, Ben | Hartford, Conn. | 1933 |
| Cooper, Gladys | Lewisham, England | 1891 |
| Cooper, Jackie | Los Angeles, Calif. | 1921 |
| Cooper, Melville | Birmingham, England | 1896 |
| Coots, J. Fred | Brooklyn, N. Y. | 1897 |
| Copland, Aaron | Brooklyn, N. Y. | 1900 |
| Corey, Wendell | Dracut, Mass. | 1914 |
| Cornell, Don | New York, N. Y. | 1921 |
| Cornell, Katharine | Berlin, Germany | 1898 |
| Cortez, Ricardo | Vienna, Austria | 1899 |
| Cosby, Bill | Philadelphia, Pa. | 1938 |
| Costello, Dolores | Pittsburgh, Pa. | 1905 |
| Cotsworth, Staats | Oak Park, Ill. | 1908 |
| Cotten, Joseph | Petersburg, Va. | 1905 |
| Courtenay, Tom | Hull, England | 1937 |
| Cowan, Jerome | New York City | 1897 |
| Coward, Noel | Teddington, England | 1899 |
| Cox, Wally | Detroit, Mich. | 1924 |
| Crabbe, Buster | Oakland, Calif. | 1910 |
| Crain, Jeanne | Barstow, Calif. | 1925 |
| Crane, Les | New York, N. Y. | 1934 |
| Crawford, Broderick | Philadelphia, Pa. | 1911 |
| Crawford, Joan | San Antonio, Tex. | 1908 |
| Crenna, Richard | Los Angeles, Calif. | 1927 |
| Crisp, Donald | London, England | 1880 |
| Cronkite, Walter | St. Joseph, Mo. | 1916 |
| Cronyn, Hume | London, Ont. | 1911 |
| Crooks, Richard | Trenton, N. J. | 1900 |
| Crosby, Bing (Harry) | Tacoma, Wash. | 1904 |
| Crosby, Bob | Spokane, Wash. | 1913 |
| Cross, Milton | New York, N. Y. | 1897 |
| Crowley, Pat | Scranton, Pa. | 1929 |
| Cugat, Xavier | Barcelona, Spain | 1900 |
| Cullen, William | Pittsburgh, Pa. | 1920 |
| Culp, Robert | Berkeley, Calif. | 1931 |
| Cummings, Constance | Seattle, Wash. | 1910 |
| Cummings, Robert | Joplin, Mo. | 1910 |
| Cummings, Vicki | Northampton, Mass. | 1919 |
| Cummings, Peggy | Prestatyn, No. Wales | 1925 |
| Curtis, Ken | Lamar, Colo. | 1916 |
| Curtis, Tony | New York, N. Y. | 1925 |
| Cushing, Peter | Surrey, Eng. | 1913 |
| **D** | | |
| Dagmar (Egnor) | Huntington, W. Va. | 1926 |
| Dahl, Arlene | Minneapolis, Minn. | 1927 |
| Dailey, Dan | New York, N. Y. | 1917 |
| Dalrymple, Jean | Morristown, N. J. | 1910 |
| Daly, James | Wisconsin Rapids, Wis. | 1918 |
| Daly, John | Johannesburg, So. Afr. | 1914 |
| Damita, Lili | Paris, France | 1907 |
| Damone, Vic | Brooklyn, N. Y. | 1928 |
| Dana, Bill | Quincy, Mass. | 1924 |
| Daniels, Bebe | Dallas, Tex. | 1901 |
| Daniels, William | Brooklyn, N. Y. | 1927 |
| Danilova, Alexandra | Peterhof, Russia | 1907 |
| Danton, Ray | New York, N. Y. | 1931 |
| Darcel, Denise | Paris, France | 1925 |
| Darin, Bobby | Bronx, N. Y. | 1935 |

| Name | Birthplace | Born | Name | Birthplace | Born |
|---|---|---|---|---|---|
| Darren, James | Philadelphia, Pa | 1936 | **F** | | |
| Darrieux, Danielle | Bordeaux, France | 1917 | Fabian (Forte) | Philadelphia, Pa | 1943 |
| Darrow, Henry | New York, N. Y | 1933 | Fabray, Nanette | San Diego, Calif | 1922 |
| Da Silva, Howard | Cleveland, Ohio | 1909 | Fadiman, Clifton | Brooklyn, N. Y | 1904 |
| Dassin, Jules | Middletown, Conn | 1913 | Fairbanks, Doug., Jr. | New York, N. Y | 1909 |
| Dauphine, Claude | Corbeil, Fr | 1905 | Faith, Percy | Toronto, Ont | 1908 |
| Davidson, John | Pittsburgh, Pa | 1941 | Falk, Peter | New York, N. Y | 1927 |
| Davis, Bette | Lowell, Mass | 1908 | Falkenburg, Jinx | Barcelona, Spain | 1919 |
| Davis, Sammy, Jr. | New York, N. Y | 1925 | Farmer, Frances | Seattle, Wash | 1915 |
| Davis, Ossie | Waycross, Ga | 1917 | Farr, Felicia | Westchester, N. Y | 1932 |
| Dawn, Hazel | Ogden, Utah | 1898 | Farrell, Charles | Onset Bay, Mass | 1901 |
| Day, Dennis | New York, N. Y | 1917 | Farrell, Eileen | Willimantic, Conn | 1920 |
| Day, Doris | Cincinnati, Ohio | 1924 | Farrell, Frank | New York, N. Y | 1912 |
| Day, Laraine | Roosevelt, Utah | 1920 | Farrell, Glenda | Enid, Okla | 1904 |
| Dean, Jimmy | Plainview, Texas | 1928 | Farrow, Mia | Los Angeles, Calif | 1945 |
| De Camp, Rosemary | Prescott, Ariz | 1913 | Faye, Alice | New York, N. Y | 1915 |
| De Carlo, Yvonne | Vancouver, B. C | 1924 | Feeney, Joe | Grand Island, Nebr | 1931 |
| Dee, Frances | Los Angeles, Calif | 1907 | Feldon, Barbara | Pittsburgh, Pa | 1939 |
| Dee, Joey | Passaic, N. J | 1940 | Fellini, Federico | Rimini, Italy | 1920 |
| Dee, Sandra | Bayonne, N. J | 1942 | Fellows Edith | Boston, Mass | 1923 |
| DeFore, Don | Cedar Rapids, Iowa | 1917 | Fenton, Leslie | England | 1903 |
| DeHaven, Gloria | Los Angeles, Calif | 1926 | Fernandel | Marseilles, France | 1903 |
| de Havilland, Olivia | Tokyo, Japan | 1916 | Ferrer, Jose | Santurce, P. R | 1912 |
| Della Chiesa, Vivienne | Chicago, Ill | 1920 | Ferrer, Mel | Elberon, N. J | 1917 |
| Delon, Alain | France | 1935 | Fetchit, Stepin | Key West, Fla | 1902 |
| Del Rio, Dolores | Durango, Mexico | 1905 | Fiedler, Arthur | Boston, Mass | 1894 |
| Demarest, William | St. Paul | 1892 | Field, Betty | Boston, Mass | 1918 |
| De Mille, Agnes | New York, N. Y | 1905 | Field, Sally | Pasadena, Calif | 1946 |
| Dempster, Carol | Duluth, Minn | 1901 | Fields, Gracie | Rochdale, England | 1898 |
| Denning, Richard | Poughkeepsie, N. Y | 1914 | Fields, Shep | Brooklyn, N. Y | 1910 |
| Dennis, Sandy | Lincoln, Nebr | 1936 | Finney, Albert | Salford, Eng | 1936 |
| Denver, Bob | New Rochelle, N. Y | 1935 | Fisher, Eddie | Philadelphia, Pa | 1928 |
| Derek, John | Hollywood, Calif | 1926 | Fitzgerald, Ed | Troy, N. Y | 1898 |
| De Sica, Vittorio | Italy | 1902 | Fitzgerald, Ella | Newport News, Va | 1918 |
| Desmond, Johnny | Detroit, Mich | 1923 | Fitzgerald, Geraldine | Dublin, Ireland | 1914 |
| Devine, Andy | Flagstaff, Ariz | 1905 | Fitzgerald, Pegeen | Norcatur, Kans | 1910 |
| de Wilde, Brandon | New York, N. Y | 1942 | Fleming, Rhonda | Hollywood, Calif | 1922 |
| de Wolfe, Billy | Wollaston, Mass | | Flippen, Jay C | Little Rock, Ark | 1899 |
| Dickinson, Angie | Kulm, No. Dakota | 1936 | Flynn, Joe | Youngstown, Ohio | 1926 |
| Dietrich, Marlene | Berlin, Germany | 1901 | Foch, Nina | Leyden, Neth | 1924 |
| Diller, Phyllis | Lima, Ohio | 1917 | Fonda, Henry | Grand Island, Nebr | 1905 |
| Dillman, Bradford | San Francisco, Calif | 1930 | Fonda, Jane | New York, N. Y | 1937 |
| Dixon, Ivan | New York, N. Y | 1931 | Fonda, Peter | New York, N. Y | 1939 |
| Dixon, Jean | Waterbury, Conn | 1905 | Fontaine, Frank | Cambridge, Mass | 1920 |
| Donahue, Troy | New York, N. Y | 1936 | Fontaine, Joan | Tokyo, Japan | 1917 |
| Donald, Peter | Bristol, England | 1918 | Fontanne, Lynn | London, England | 1887 |
| Donlevy, Brian | Portadown, Ireland | 1903 | Fonteyn, Margot | Reigate, England | 1919 |
| Donnelly, Ruth | Trenton, N. J | 1896 | Foran, Dick | Flemington, N. J | 1910 |
| Dors, Diana | Swindon, England | 1931 | Ford, Glenn (Ernie) | Ford Town, Tenn | 1919 |
| d'Orsay, Fifi | Montreal, Que | 1908 | Ford, Edw. "Senator" | Brooklyn, N. Y | 1887 |
| Douglas, Donna | Baywood, La | 1939 | Ford, Glenn | Quebec, Canada | 1916 |
| Douglas, Kirk | Amsterdam, N. Y | 1916 | Ford, Paul | Baltimore, Md | 1901 |
| Douglas, Melvyn | Macon, Ga | 1901 | Ford, Ruth | Hazelhurst, Miss | |
| Douglas, Mike | Chicago, Ill | 1925 | Forrest, Sally | San Diego, Calif | 1928 |
| Dowling, Eddie | Providence, R. I | 1895 | Forrest, Steve | Huntsville, Tex | 1925 |
| Downey, Morton | Wallingford, Conn | 1902 | Forsythe, John | Penns Grove, N. J | 1918 |
| Downs, Hugh | Akron, Ohio | 1921 | Foster, Norman | Richmond, Ind | 1900 |
| Dragonette, Jessica | Calcutta, India | | Foster, Preston | Ocean City, N. J | 1904 |
| Drake, Alfred | Bronx, N. Y | 1914 | Foster, Susanna | Chicago, Ill | 1925 |
| Drake, Betsy | Paris, France | 1923 | Fox, James | London, England | 1939 |
| Draper, Paul | Florence, Italy | 1911 | Foy, Eddie, Jr. | New Rochelle, N. Y | 1905 |
| Drew, Ellen | Kansas City, Mo | 1915 | Francescatti, Zino | Marseilles, France | 1904 |
| Dru, Joanne | Logan, W. Va | 1923 | Franciosa, Anthony | New York City | 1928 |
| Drury, James | New York N.Y. | 1934 | Francis, Arlene | Boston, Mass | 1908 |
| Duff, Howard | Bremerton, Wash | 1917 | Francis, Connie | Newark, N. J | 1938 |
| Duke, Patty | New York, N. Y | 1946 | Franciscus, James | Clayton, Mo | 1934 |
| Dunaway, Faye | Tallahassee, Fla | 1941 | Frankenheimer, John | Malba, L. I., N. Y | 1930 |
| Duncan, Todd | Danville, Ky | 1900 | Freeman, Mona | Baltimore, Md | 1926 |
| Duncan, Vivian | Los Angeles, Calif | 1902 | Friml, Rudolf | Prague, Austria | 1884 |
| Dunham, Katherine | Chicago, Ill | 1910 | Froman, Jane | St. Louis, Mo | 1911 |
| Dunne, Irene | Louisville, Ky | 1904 | Furness, Betty | New York, N. Y | 1916 |
| Dunninger, Joseph | New York, N. Y | 1898 | **G** | | |
| Durante, Jimmy | New York, N. Y | 1893 | | | |
| Durbin, Deanna | Winnipeg, Canada | 1922 | Gabin, Jean | Villette, Paris, France | 1904 |
| Dvorak, Ann | New York, N. Y | 1912 | Gabor, Eva | Hungary | 1929 |
| Dylan, Bob | Duluth, Minn | 1941 | Gabor, Zsa Zsa | Hungary | 1923 |
| | | | Gahagan, Helen | Boonton, N. J | 1900 |
| **E** | | | Galloway, Don | Brooksville, Ky | 1937 |
| Eastwood, Clint | San Francisco, Calif | 1930 | Gam, Rita | Pittsburgh, Pa | 1928 |
| Eaton, Shirley | London, Eng | 1937 | Gambling, John A | New York City | 1930 |
| Ebsen, Buddy | Belleville, Ill | 1908 | Gambling, John B | Norwich, Eng | 1897 |
| Eckstine, Billy | Pittsburgh, Pa | 1914 | Ganz, Rudolph | Zurich, Switzerland | 1877 |
| Edelman, Herbert | Brooklyn, N. Y | 1933 | Garbo, Greta | Stockholm, Sweden | 1906 |
| Eden, Barbara | Tuscon, Ariz | 1934 | Gardner, Reginald | Wimbledon, England | 1903 |
| Edwards, Cliff | Hannibal, Mo | | Gardner, Ava | Smithfield, N. C | 1922 |
| Edwards, Douglas | Ada, Okla | 1917 | Gardner, Hy | New York, N. Y | 1904 |
| Edwards, Joan | New York, N. Y | 1920 | Gargan, William | Brooklyn, N. Y | 1905 |
| Edwards, Ralph | Merino, Colo | 1913 | Garland, Beverly | Santa Cruz, Calif | 1930 |
| Edwards, Vincent | Brooklyn, N. Y | 1928 | Garland, Judy | Grand Rapids, Minn | 1923 |
| Egan, Richard | San Francisco, Calif | 1923 | Garner, Errol | Pittsburgh, Pa | 1921 |
| Eggar, Samantha | London, Eng | 1939 | Garner, James | Norman, Okla | 1928 |
| Eggerth, Marta | Budapest, Hungary | 1916 | Garner, Peggy Ann | Canton, Ohio | 1932 |
| Ekberg, Anita | Sweden | 1932 | Garroway, Dave | Schenectady, N. Y | 1913 |
| Eldridge, Florence | Brooklyn, N. Y | 1901 | Garrett, Betty | St. Joseph, Mo | 1919 |
| Ellington, Duke | Washington, D. C | 1899 | Garson, Greer | Co. Down, No. Ireland | 1908 |
| Emerson, Faye | Elizabeth, La | 1917 | Garver, Kathy | Long Beach, Calif | 1948 |
| English, Marla | San Diego, Calif | 1935 | Gary, John | Watertown, N. Y | 1932 |
| Erickson, Leif | Alameda, Calif | 1914 | Gavin, John | Los Angeles, Calif | 1928 |
| Esmond, Jill | London, Eng | 1908 | Gaynor, Janet | Philadelphia, Pa | 1906 |
| Etting, Ruth | David City, Nebr | 1896 | Gaynor, Mitzi | Chicago, Ill | 1931 |
| Evans, Dale | Uvalde, Tex | 1912 | Gazzara, Ben | New York, N. Y | 1930 |
| Evans, Dame Edith | London, Eng | 1888 | Geddes, Barbara Bel | New York, N. Y | 1922 |
| Evans, Maurice | Dorchester, England | 1901 | Geer, Will | Frankfort, Ind | 1902 |
| Ewell, Tom | Owensboro, Ky | 1909 | Genevieve (G. Auger) | Paris, France | 1930 |

| Name | Birthplace | Born | Name | Birthplace | Born |
|---|---|---|---|---|---|
| Genn, Leo | London, England | 1905 | Heifetz, Jascha | Vilna, Russia | 1901 |
| Gentry, Bobby | Chickasaw Co., Miss. | 1944 | Heiss, Carol | Ozone Park, N. Y. | 1939 |
| Gershwin, Ira | New York City | 1896 | Hellman, Lillian | New Orleans, La. | 1905 |
| Gielgud, John | London, England | 1904 | Helmore, Tom | London, England | 1912 |
| Gilbert, Billy | Louisville, Ky. | 1894 | Henderson, Florence | Dale, Ind. | 1934 |
| Gingold, Hermione | London, England | 1897 | Henderson, Marcia | Andover, Mass. | 1932 |
| Gish, Lillian | Springfield, Ohio | 1896 | Henderson, Skitch | Birmingham, England. | 1919 |
| Givot, George | Omaha, Nebr. | 1903 | Henie, Sonja | Oslo, Norway | 1913 |
| Gleason, Jackie | Brooklyn, N. Y. | 1916 | Henreid, Paul | Trieste, Italy | 1908 |
| Gobel, George | Chicago, Ill. | 1920 | Hepburn, Audrey | Brussels, Belgium | 1929 |
| Goddard, Mark | Lowell, Mass. | 1936 | Hepburn, Katharine | Hartford, Conn. | 1909 |
| Goddard, Paulette | Great Neck, N. Y. | 1911 | Herbert, Evelyn | Philadelphia, Pa. | 1898 |
| Godfrey, Arthur | New York, N. Y. | 1903 | Herbert, Holmes | Mansfield, Eng. | 1882 |
| Goldwyn, Samuel | Warsaw, Poland | 1882 | Herlie, Eileen | Glasgow, Scotland | 1920 |
| Goodman, Benny | Chicago, Ill. | 1909 | Herman, Woody | Milwaukee, Wis. | 1913 |
| Gorcey, Leo | New York, N. Y. | 1917 | Hershfield, Harry | Cedar Rapids, Iowa. | 1885 |
| Gordon, Gale | New York City | 1906 | Heston, Charlton | Evanston, Ill. | 1924 |
| Gordon, Kitty | Folkestone, England. | 1878 | Hildegarde | Adell, Wis. | 1906 |
| Gordon, Max | New York, N. Y. | 1892 | Hiller, Wendy | Bramhall, England. | 1912 |
| Gordon, Ruth | Wollaston, Mass. | 1896 | Hines, Jerome | Hollywood, Calif. | 1921 |
| Gore, Lesley | Tenafly, N. J. | 1946 | Hines, Mimi | Vancouver, B. C. | 1933 |
| Gorin, Igor | Ukraine, Russia | 1909 | Hingle, Pat | Texas | 1924 |
| Gorme, Eydie | Bronx, N. Y. | 1931 | Hirt, Al | New Orleans, La. | 1922 |
| Gorshin, Frank | Pittsburgh, Pa. | 1935 | Hitchcock, Alfred | London, England | 1899 |
| Gould, Morton | Richmond Hill, N. Y. | 1913 | Hobart, Rose | New York, N. Y. | 1906 |
| Goulet, Robert | Lawrence, Mass. | 1933 | Hodges, Eddie | Hattiesburg, Miss. | 1947 |
| Grable, Betty | St. Louis, Mo. | 1916 | Holbrook, Hal | Cleveland, Ohio. | 1925 |
| Grady, Don | San Diego, Calif. | 1944 | Holden, Fay | Birmingham, England. | 1895 |
| Graham, Martha | Pittsburgh, Pa. | 1902 | Holden, William | O'Fallon, Ill. | 1918 |
| Grahame, Gloria | Los Angeles, Calif. | 1929 | Holloway, Stanley | London, England | 1890 |
| Grahame, Margot | Canterbury, England. | 1911 | Holloway, Sterling | Cedartown, Ga. | |
| Granger, Farley | San Jose, Calif. | 1925 | Holm, Celeste | New York, N. Y. | 1919 |
| Granger, Stewart | England | 1913 | Holmes, Stuart | Chicago, Ill. | 1887 |
| Granville, Bonita | New York, N. Y. | 1923 | Holt, Tim | Beverly Hills, Calif. | 1918 |
| Grant, Cary | Bristol, England | 1904 | Holtz, Lou | San Francisco, Calif. | 1898 |
| Grant, Katherine | Houston, Tex. | 1933 | Homeier, Skip | Chicago, Ill. | 1930 |
| Grauer, Ben | New York, N. Y. | 1908 | Homolka, Oscar | Vienna, Austria | 1901 |
| Gray, Coleen | Staplehurst, Nebr. | 1922 | Hooks, Robert | Washington, D. C. | 1937 |
| Gray, Dolores | Chicago, Ill. | 1924 | Hope, Bob | London, England | 1904 |
| Grayson, Kathryn | Winston-Salem, N. C. | 1923 | Hopkins, Miriam | Bainbridge, Ga. | 1902 |
| Greco, Buddy | Philadelphia, Pa. | 1926 | Horne, Lena | Brooklyn, N. Y. | 1918 |
| Greco, Jose | Abruzzi, Italy | 1915 | Horowitz, Vladimir | Kiev, Russia | 1904 |
| Greco, Juliette | Paris, France | | Horton, Ed. Everett. | Brooklyn, N. Y. | 1888 |
| Green, Eddie | Baltimore, Md. | 1901 | Horton, Robert | Los Angeles, Calif. | 1924 |
| Green, Martyn | London, England | 1899 | Howard, Clint | Burbank, Calif. | 1959 |
| Green, Mitzi | New York, N. Y. | 1920 | Howard Ronnie | Duncan, Okla. | 1954 |
| Greene, Lorne | Canada | 1916 | Howes, Sally Ann | London, England | 1930 |
| Greenwood, Charlotte. | Philadelphia, Pa. | 1893 | Hudson, Rock | Winnetka, Ill. | 1925 |
| Greenwood, Joan | London, England | 1921 | Hull, Henry | Louisville, Ky. | 1890 |
| Greer, Jane | Washington, D. C. | 1924 | Hull, Warren | Gasport, N. Y. | 1903 |
| Gregory, Dick | St. Louis, Mo. | 1933 | Hunt, Marsha | Chicago, Ill. | 1917 |
| Grey Joel | Cleveland, Ohio | 1932 | Hunter, Ian | Cape Town, S. Africa. | 1900 |
| Griffin, Merv | San Mateo, Calif. | 1925 | Hunter, Kim | Detroit, Mich. | 1922 |
| Griffith, Andy | Mount Airy, N. C. | 1926 | Hunter, Tab | New York, N. Y. | 1931 |
| Griffith, Hugh | Wales | 1912 | Huntley, Chet | Cardwell, Mont. | 1911 |
| Grimes, Tammy | Lynn, Mass. | 1934 | Huston, John | Nevada, Mo. | 1906 |
| Grizzard, George | Roanoke Rapids, N. C. | 1928 | Hutchins, Will | Los Angeles, Calif. | 1932 |
| Grofe, Ferde | New York City | 1892 | Hutchinson, Josephine | Seattle, Wash. | 1916 |
| Guardino, Harry | New York, N. Y. | 1925 | Hutton, Betty | Battle Creek, Mich. | 1921 |
| Guinness, Alec | London, England | 1914 | Hutton, Ina Ray | Chicago, Ill. | 1918 |
| | | | Hyer, Martha | Fort Worth, Texas. | 1929 |
| **H** | | | Hyland, Diana | Cleveland Hts., Ohio. | 1937 |
| Hackett, Buddy | Brooklyn, N. Y. | 1924 | Hyman, Earle | Rocky Mt., N. C. | 1926 |
| Hagen, Uta | Gottingen, Germany. | 1919 | | | |
| Hagman, Larry | Ft. Worth, Tex. | 1931 | **I** | | |
| Halasz, Laszlo | Debrecen, Hungary | 1905 | Inescort, Frieda | Edinburgh, Scotland. | 1901 |
| Hale, Barbara | DeKalb, Ill. | 1922 | Ingels, Marty | Brooklyn, N. Y. | 1936 |
| Haley, Jack | Boston, Mass. | 1902 | Ingram, Rex | Cairo, Ill. | 1895 |
| Hamilton, George | Memphis, Tenn. | 1940 | Ireland, John | Vancouver, B. C. | 1915 |
| Hamilton, Neil | Lynn, Mass. | 1899 | Iturbi, Jose | Valencia, Spain. | 1895 |
| Hampton, Lionel | Birmingham, Ala. | 1914 | Ives, Burl | Hunt, Ill. | 1909 |
| Hampton, Ruth | Throop, Pa. | 1932 | | | |
| Hanson, Howard | Wahoo, Nebr. | 1896 | **J** | | |
| Harding, Ann | Ft. Sam Houston, Tex. | 1904 | Jackson, Mahalia | New Orleans, La. | 1912 |
| Harper, Ron | Turtle Creek, Pa. | 1935 | Jaffe, Sam | New York, N. Y. | 1898 |
| Harris, Barbara | Evanston, Ill. | 1935 | Jagger, Dean | Lima, Ohio | 1903 |
| Harris, Julie | Grosse Pte. Park, Mich. | 1925 | James, Dennis | Jersey City, N. J. | 1917 |
| Harris, Phil | Linton, Ind. | 1906 | James, Harry | Albany, Ga. | 1916 |
| Harris, Richard | Co. Limerick, Ire. | 1933 | Janney, Leon | Ogden, Utah | 1917 |
| Harris, Roy | Oklahoma | 1898 | Janney, William | New York, N. Y. | 1908 |
| Harrison, Noel | London, England | 1933 | Janssen, David | Naponee, Nebr. | 1931 |
| Harrison, Rex | Huyton, England. | 1908 | Jason, Rick | New York, N. Y. | 1926 |
| Hartman, Paul | San Francisco, Calif. | | Jeanmaire, Renee | Paris, France | 1925 |
| Harvey, Laurence | Yonishkis, Lithuania. | 1928 | Jeffreys, Anne | Goldsboro, N. C. | 1923 |
| Hasso, Signe | Stockholm, Sweden. | 1918 | Jenkins, Allen | New York, N. Y. | 1900 |
| Hatton, Raymond | Red Oak, Iowa. | 1892 | Jennings, Peter | Toronto, Canada. | 1937 |
| Haver, June | Rock Island, Ill. | 1926 | Jepson, Helen | Titusville, Pa. | 1907 |
| Havoc, June | Seattle, Wash. | 1916 | Jeritza, Maria | Brunn, Austria | 1887 |
| Hawn, Goldie | Washington, D.C. | 1945 | Jessel, George | New York, N. Y. | 1898 |
| Hayakawa, Sessue | China, Japan | 1890 | Johns, Glynis | Durban, So. Africa. | 1923 |
| Hayden, Russell | Chico, Calif. | 1912 | Johnson, Richard | Essex, England | 1927 |
| Hayden, Sterling | Montclair, N. J. | 1916 | Johnson, Russell | Ashley, Pa. | 1924 |
| Haydon, Julie | Oak Park, Ill. | 1910 | Johnson, Van | Newport, R. I. | 1916 |
| Hayes, Geo. (Gabby) | Wellsville, N. Y. | 1885 | Johnston, Johnny | St. Louis, Mo. | 1916 |
| Hayes, Helen | Washington, D. C. | 1900 | Jones, Alan | Scranton, Pa. | 1907 |
| Hayes, Peter Lind | San Francisco, Calif. | 1916 | Jones, Carolyn | Amarillo, Tex. | 1932 |
| Haymes, Dick | Buenos Aires, Arg'tina | 1918 | Jones, Chris | Jackson, Tenn. | 1941 |
| Hayward, Louis | Johannesburg, S. Afr. | 1909 | Jones, Dean | Morgan, Co., Ala. | 1936 |
| Hayward, Susan | Brooklyn, N. Y. | 1919 | Jones, Grandpa | Henderson Co., Ky. | 1913 |
| Hayworth, Rita | New York, N. Y. | 1919 | Jones, Henry | Philadelphia, Pa. | 1912 |
| Healy, Mary | New Orleans, La. | 1918 | Jones, Jack | Hollywood, Calif. | 1938 |
| Heatherton, Joey | New York, N. Y. | 1944 | Jones, Jennifer | Tulsa, Okla. | 1919 |
| Heatter, Gabriel | New York, N. Y. | 1890 | Jones, Shirley | Smithtown, Pa. | 1934 |
| Heckart, Eileen | Columbus, Ohio | 1919 | Jory, Victor | Dawson, Yukon, Can. | 1902 |
| Heflin, Van | Walters, Okla. | 1910 | Joslyn, Allyn | Milford, Pa. | 1905 |
| | | | Jourdan, Louis | Marseilles, France. | 1921 |

| Name | Birthplace | Born | Name | Birthplace | Born |
|---|---|---|---|---|---|
| Judge, Arline | Bridgeport, Conn. | 1912 | Lennon, Peggy | Los Angeles, Calif. | 1941 |
| Jurado, Katy | Guadalajara, Mex. | 1927 | Leonard, Jack E. | New York, N. Y. | 1911 |
|  |  |  | Leonard, Sheldon | New York, N. Y. | 1907 |
| **K** |  |  | Leontovich, Eugenie | Moscow, Russia | 1894 |
|  |  |  | LeRoy, Mervyn | San Francisco, Calif. | 1900 |
| Kanin, Garson | Rochester, N. Y. | 1912 | Leslie, Joan | Detroit, Mich | 1925 |
| Karloff, Boris | Dulwich, England | 1887 | Lester, Jerry | Chicago, Ill. | 1911 |
| Karns, Roscoe | San Bernardino, Calif. | 1897 | Levant, Oscar | Pittsburgh, Pa. | 1906 |
| Kaye, Buddy | New York, N. Y. | 1918 | Levene, Sam | New York, N. Y. | 1907 |
| Kaye, Danny | Brooklyn, N. Y. | 1913 | Levenson, Sam | New York City | 1911 |
| Kaye, Nora | New York, N. Y. | 1920 | Lewis, Jerry | Newark, N. J. | 1926 |
| Kaye, Sammy | Cleveland, Ohio | 1910 | Lewis, Joe E. | New York, N. Y. |  |
| Kaye, Sonya | Brooklyn, N. Y. | 1934 | Lewis, Monica | Chicago, Ill. | 1925 |
| Kazan, Ella | Constantinople, Turk. | 1909 | Lewis, Robert Q. | New York, N. Y. | 1924 |
| Keel, Howard | Gillesple, Ill. | 1919 | Lewis, Sharl | New York, N. Y. | 1934 |
| Keeler, Ruby | Halifax, N. S. | 1909 | Lewis, Ted | Circleville, Ohio | 1891 |
| Keith, Brian | Bayonne, N. J. | 1921 | Liberace | Milwaukee, Wis. | 1919 |
| Kelley, DeForrest | Atlanta, Ga. | 1920 | Lillie, Beatrice | Toronto, Canada | 1898 |
| Kelly, Gene | Pittsburgh, Pa. | 1912 | Lindfors, Viveca | Uppsala, Sweden | 1920 |
| Kelly, Grace | Philadelphia, Pa. | 1930 | Lindsay, Margaret | Dubuque, Iowa | 1910 |
| Kelly, Jack | Astoria, N. Y. | 1927 | Linkletter, Art | Saskatchewan, Can. | 1912 |
| Kelly, Nancy | Lowell, Mass. | 1921 | Linn, Bambi | Brooklyn, N. Y. | 1926 |
| Kelly, Patsy | Brooklyn, N. Y. | 1914 | Lisi, Virna | Italy | 1937 |
| Kennedy, Arthur | Worcester, Mass. | 1914 | List, Emanuel | Vienna, Austria | 1891 |
| Kennedy, George | New York, N. Y. | 1925 | Lilo (Liliane Lewin) | France | 1925 |
| Kennedy, Madge | Chicago, Ill. |  | Livingstone, Mary | Seattle, Wash. | 1909 |
| Kent, Allegra | Los Angeles, Calif. | 1937 | Lloyd, Harold | Buchard, Nebr. | 1893 |
| Kenton, Stan | Wichita, Kans. | 1912 | Lloyd, Harold, Jr. | California | 1932 |
| Kenyon, Doris | Syracuse, N. Y. | 1897 | Lockhart, June | New York, N. Y. | 1925 |
| Kerr, Deborah | Helensburgh, Scotland | 1921 | Lockwood, Margaret | Karachi, India | 1916 |
| Kerr, John | New York, N. Y. | 1931 | Loder, John | London, England | 1898 |
| Kert, Larry | Los Angeles, Calif. | 1930 | Loesser, Frank | New York, N. Y. | 1910 |
| Keyes, Evelyn | Port Arthur, Tex. | 1925 | Logan, Ella | Glasgow, Scotland | 1913 |
| Kiley, Richard | Chicago, Ill. | 1922 | Logan, Joshua | Texarkana, Texas | 1908 |
| Killan, Victor | Jersey City, N. J. | 1898 | Lollobrigida, Gina | Sublaco, Italy | 1928 |
| King, Alan | New York City | 1926 | Lombardo, Guy | London, Ont., Canada | 1902 |
| King, Dennis | Coventry, England | 1897 | London, George | Montreal, Que. | 1920 |
| King, Henry | Christianburg, Va. | 1896 | London, Julie | Santa Rosa, Calif. | 1926 |
| King, Peggy | Greensburg, Pa. | 1931 | Long, Richard | Chicago, Ill. | 1927 |
| King, Walter Woolf | San Francisco, Calif. | 1899 | Lopez, Perry | New York, N. Y. | 1931 |
| King, Wayne | Savannah, Ill | 1901 | Lopez, Trini | Dallas, Texas | 1938 |
| Kirby, Durwood | Covington, Ky. | 1912 | Lopez, Vincent | Brooklyn, N. Y. | 1895 |
| Kirby, Michael | Canada | 1925 | Loren, Sophia | Rome, Italy | 1934 |
| Kirk, Phyllis | Syracuse, N. Y. | 1929 | Loring, Lynn | New York, N. Y. | 1944 |
| Kirkland, Muriel | Yonkers, N. Y. | 1903 | Losch, Tilly | Vienna, Austria | 1902 |
| Kirsten, Dorothy | Montclair, N. J. | 1919 | Loudon, Dorothy | Boston, Mass. | 1932 |
| Kitchell, Iva | Junction City, Kan. | 1919 | Louise, Anita | New York City | 1917 |
| Kitt, Eartha | Columbia, S. C. | 1928 | Louise, Tina | New York City | 1934 |
| Knotts, Don | Morgantown, W. Va. | 1924 | Love, Bessie | Midland, Tex. | 1898 |
| Knowles, Patric | Horsforth, England | 1911 | Lowe, Edmund | San Jose, Calif. | 1892 |
| Knox, Alexander | Strathroy, Canada | 1907 | Loy, Myrna | Helena, Mont. | 1905 |
| Kollmar, Richard | Ridgewood, N. J. | 1910 | Ludwig, Christa | Berlin, Ger. | 1934 |
| Korman, Harvey | Chicago, Ill. | 1927 | Lukas, Paul | Budapest, Hungary | 1895 |
| Kostelanetz, Andre | St. Petersburg, Rus. | 1910 | Luke, Keye | Canton, China | 1904 |
| Kruger, Otto | Toledo, Ohio | 1885 | Lund (Chester Lauck) | Allene, Ark. | 1902 |
| Krupa, Gene | Chicago, Ill. | 1909 | Lund, John | Rochester, N. Y. | 1913 |
| Kullman, Chas. | New Haven, Conn. | 1902 | Lundigan, William | Syracuse, N. Y. | 1914 |
| Kyser, Kay | Rocky Mount, N. C. | 1905 | Lunt, Alfred | Milwaukee, Wis. | 1893 |
|  |  |  | Lupino, Ida | London, England | 1918 |
| **L** |  |  | Lynde, Paul | Mt. Vernon, Ohio | 1926 |
| Laine, Frankie | Chicago, Ill. | 1913 | Lynn, Diana | Los Angeles, Calif. | 1926 |
| Lake, Veronica | Lake Placid, N. Y. | 1919 | Lynn, Jeffrey | Auburn, Mass. | 1909 |
| Lamarr, Hedy | Vienna, Austria | 1915 | Lynley, Carol | New York City | 1942 |
| Lamas, Fernando | Buenos Aires | 1915 | Lyon, Ben | Atlanta, Ga. | 1901 |
| Lamb, Gil | Minneapolis, Minn. | 1906 | Lyon, Sue | Davenport, Iowa | 1946 |
| Lamour, Dorothy | New Orleans, La. | 1914 |  |  |  |
| Lancaster, Burt | New York, N. Y. | 1913 | **M** |  |  |
| Lanchester, Elsa | London, England | 1902 | MacArthur, James | Los Angeles, Calif. | 1937 |
| Landers, Harry | New York, N. Y. | 1921 | MacGrath, Leueen | England | 1914 |
| Landis, Jessie Royce | Chicago, Ill. | 1904 | Mack, Ted | Greeley, Colo. | 1904 |
| Landon, Michael | Forest Hills, N. Y. | 1937 | MacKenzie, Gisele | Winnipeg, Man. | 1927 |
| Lane, Abbe | Brooklyn, N. Y. | 1932 | MacKay, Jim | Philadelphia, Pa. | 1921 |
| Lang, Harold | Daly City, Calif. | 1924 | MacLaine, Shirley | Richmond, Va. | 1934 |
| Lang, June | Minneapolis, Minn. | 1915 | MacLane, Barton | Columbia, S. C. | 1902 |
| Lange, Hope | Redding Ridge, Conn. | 1933 | MacMahon, Aline | McKeesport, Pa. | 1899 |
| Langford, Frances | Lakeland, Fla. | 1913 | MacMurray, Fred | Kankakee, Ill. | 1908 |
| Lansbury, Angela | London, England | 1925 | MacPhail, Duncan | Gavam, Scotland. | 1884 |
| Lansing, Robert | San Diego, Calif. | 1929 | MacRae, Gordon | East Orange, N. J. | 1921 |
| Lanson, Snooky (Roy) | Memphis, Tenn. | 1919 | MacRae, Shella | London, England | 1924 |
| La Rosa, Julius | Brooklyn, N. Y. | 1930 | Macready, George | Providence, R. I. | 1909 |
| Larrimore, Francine | Verdun, France | 1898 | Madison, Guy | Bakersfield, Calif. | 1922 |
| La Rue, Jack | New York, N. Y. |  | Magnani, Anna | Rome, Italy | 1908 |
| Laurie, Piper | Detroit, Mich. | 1932 | Mahler, Fritz | Vienna, Austria | 1901 |
| Lawford, Peter | London, England | 1925 | Main, Marjorie | Acton, Ind. | 1890 |
| Lawrence, Barbara | Carnegie, Okla. | 1930 | Malbin, Elaine | New York, N. Y. | 1932 |
| Lawrence, Carol | Melrose Park, Ill. | 1932 | Malden, Karl | Gary, Ind. | 1914 |
| Lawrence, Marjorie | Victoria, Australia | 1909 | Malone, Dorothy | Chicago, Ill. | 1925 |
| Lawrence, Steve | Brooklyn, N. Y. | 1935 | Malone, Nancy | New York, N. Y. | 1935 |
| Lawrence, Vicki | Inglewood, Calif. | 1949 | Mangano, Silvana | Italy |  |
| Lederer, Francis | Prague, Czechoslov. | 1906 | March, Fredric | Racine, Wis. | 1897 |
| Lee, Gypsy Rose | Seattle, Wash. | 1914 | March, Hal | San Francisco, Calif. | 1920 |
| (Rose Louise Hovick) |  |  | Margo | Mexico City, Mexico. | 1918 |
| Lee, Lila | New York, N. Y. | 1905 | Markova, Alicia | London, England | 1910 |
| Lee, Michele | Los Angeles, Calif. | 1942 | Marlowe, Hugh | Philadelphia, Pa. | 1914 |
| Lee, Peggy | Jamestown, N. D. | 1920 | Marsh, Joan | Porterville, Calif. | 1915 |
| Lee, Pinky | St. Paul, Minn. |  | Marshall, Brenda | Philippines | 1915 |
| Le Gallienne, Eva | London, England | 1899 | Marshall, E. G. | Owatona, Minn. | 1910 |
| Lehmann, Lotte | Perleberg, Germany | 1895 | Marshall, Everett | Lawrence, Mass. | 1901 |
| Leigh, Janet | Merced, Calif. |  | Marshall, Sarah | London, England | 1933 |
| Leighton, Margaret | Warwickshire, Eng. | 1922 | Martin, Dean | Steubenville, Ohio | 1917 |
| Leinsdorf, Erich | Vienna, Austria | 1912 | Martin, Dewey | Katemey, Texas | 1923 |
| Lemmon, Jack | Boston, Mass. | 1925 | Martin, Dick | Detroit, Mich. | 1928 |
| Lennon, Dianne | Los Angeles, Calif. | 1939 | Martin, Mary | Weatherford, Texas | 1914 |
| Lennon, Janet | Culver City, Calif. | 1946 | Martin, Tony | Oakland, Calif. | 1913 |
| Lennon, Kathy | Santa Monica, Calif. | 1943 | Martinelli, Giovanni | Montagnana, Italy | 1885 |

| Name | Birthplace | Born | Name | Birthplace | Born |
|---|---|---|---|---|---|
| Martini, Nino | Verona, Italy | 1905 | Morison, Patricia | New York, N. Y. | 1919 |
| Marvin, Lee | New York, N. Y. | 1924 | Morley, Robert | Semley, England | 1908 |
| Marx, Herbert (Zeppo) | New York, N. Y. | 1901 | Morris, Chester | New York, N. Y. | 1901 |
| Marx, Julius (Groucho) | New York, N. Y. | 1895 | Morrow, Susan | Teaneck, N. J. | 1932 |
| Mason, James | Huddersfield, England | 1909 | Morrow, Vic | Bronx, N. Y. | 1932 |
| Massey, Curt | Midland, Texas | | Morse, Robert | Newton, Mass. | 1931 |
| Massey, Ilona | Hungary | 1910 | Mostel, Zero (Sam) | Brooklyn, N. Y. | 1915 |
| Massey, Raymond | Toronto, Canada | 1896 | Mowbray, Alan | London, England | 1893 |
| Massine, Leonide | Moscow, Russia | 1896 | Muir, Gavin | Chicago, Ill. | 1909 |
| Mastroianni, Marcello | Italy | 1924 | Muir, Jean | New York, N. Y. | 1911 |
| Mathis, Johnny | San Francisco, Calif. | 1935 | Mulhall, Jack | Wap'ing's Falls, N. Y. | 1894 |
| Matthau, Walter | New York City | 1923 | Mulhare, Edward | Ireland | 1921 |
| Matthews, Jessie | London, England | 1907 | Mundy, Meg | London, England | |
| Mature, Victor | Louisville, Ky. | 1916 | Munsel, Patrice | Spokane, Wash. | 1925 |
| Maxwell, Marilyn | Clarinda, Iowa | 1922 | Murphy, Audie | Texas | 1924 |
| May, Elaine | Philadelphia, Pa. | 1932 | Murphy, Mary | Washington, D. C. | 1931 |
| Maynard, Ken | Mission, Texas | 1895 | Murray, Arthur | New York, N. Y. | 1895 |
| Maynor, Dorothy | Norfolk, Va. | 1910 | Murray, Don | Hollywood, Calif. | 1929 |
| Mayo, Virginia | St. Louis, Mo. | 1920 | Murray, Jan | New York | 1919 |
| McBride, Mary Marg. | Paris, Mo. | 1899 | Murray, Kathryn | Jersey City, N. J. | 1906 |
| McCaffery, J. K. M. | Moscow, Idaho. | 1913 | Murray, Ken | New York, N. Y. | 1903 |
| McCallum, David | Glascow, Scotland | 1933 | Myerson, Bess | Bronx, N. Y. | 1924 |
| McCarey, Leo | Los Angeles, Calif. | 1898 | | | |
| McCarthy, Kevin | Seattle, Wash. | 1915 | **N** | | |
| McClure, Doug | Glendale, Calif. | 1935 | Nabors, Jim | Sylacauga, Ala. | 1933 |
| McCoy, Tim | Saginaw, Mich. | 1891 | Nagel, Conrad | Keokuk, Iowa | 1897 |
| McCrary, Tex (John) | Calvert, Texas | 1910 | Naish, J. Carrol | New York, N. Y. | 1900 |
| McCrea, Joel | Los Angeles, Calif. | 1905 | Nardini, Tom | Los Angeles, Calif. | 1945 |
| McDowall, Roddy | London, England | 1928 | Natwick, Mildred | Baltimore, Md. | 1908 |
| McFarland, George | Dallas, Tex. | 1928 | Neal, Patricia | Packard, Ky. | 1926 |
| McGavin, Darren | San Joaquin, Calif. | 1922 | Neff, Hildegarde | Ulm, Germany | 1925 |
| McGee, Fibber, Jordan | Peoria, Ill. | 1896 | Negri, Pola | Lipno, Poland | 1899 |
| McGee, Frank | Monroe, La. | 1921 | Nelson, Barry | Oakland, Calif. | 1925 |
| McGoohan, Patrick | Astoria, N. Y. | 1928 | Nelson, David | New York, N. Y. | 1936 |
| McGuire Sisters: | | | Nelson, Ed | New Orleans, La. | 1928 |
| Christine | Middletown, Ohio | 1928 | Nelson, Gene | Seattle, Wash. | 1920 |
| Dorothy | Middletown, Ohio | 1930 | Nelson, Harriet | Des Moines | |
| Phyllis | Middletown, Ohio | 1931 | Nelson, Lori | Santa Fe, N. M. | 1933 |
| McGuire, Dorothy | Omaha, Nebr. | 1919 | Nelson, Ozzie | Jersey City, N. J. | 1906 |
| McHugh, Frank | Homestead, Pa. | 1899 | Nelson, Ricky | Teaneck, N. J. | 1940 |
| McKay, Scott | Pleasantville, Iowa | 1915 | Nero, Peter | New York, N. Y. | 1934 |
| McKenna, Siobhan | Belfast, Ireland | 1923 | Nesbit, Cathleen | Cheshire, England | 1889 |
| McLerie, Allyn | Grand Mere, Que.,Can. | 1926 | Nevins, Natalie | Philadelphia, Pa. | 1943 |
| McMahon, Ed | Detroit, Mich. | 1923 | Newhart, Bob | Chicago, Ill. | 1923 |
| McMahon, Horace | So. Norwalk, Conn. | 1907 | Newley, Anthony | England | 1931 |
| McQueen, Steve | Indianapolis, Ind. | 1930 | Newman, Paul | Cleveland, Ohio | 1925 |
| Meadows, Audrey | China | 1929 | Newmar, Julie | California | 1930 |
| Meadows, Jayne | Wu Chang, China | 1925 | Nichols, Mike | Berlin, Ger. | 1931 |
| Meeker, Ralph | Minneapolis, Minn. | 1920 | Niesen, Gertrude | At sea | 1913 |
| Melchior, Lauritz | Copenhagen, Denmark | 1890 | Nillson, Anna Q. | Ystad, Sweden | 1893 |
| Menuhin, Yehudi | New York, N. Y. | 1916 | Nilsson, Birgit | Sweden | |
| Mercer, Johnny | Savannah, Ga. | 1909 | Nimoy, Leonard | Boston, Mass. | 1931 |
| Mercouri, Melina | Greece | 1929 | Niven, David | Scotland | 1911 |
| Meredith, Burgess | Cleveland, Ohio | 1909 | Noble, Ray | Sussex, England | 1908 |
| Merkel, Una | Covington, Ky. | 1903 | Nolan, Doris | New York, N. Y. | 1916 |
| Merman, Ethel | Astoria, N. Y. | 1909 | Nolan, Jeannette | Los Angeles, Calif. | 1911 |
| Merrick, David | Hong Kong | 1911 | Nolan, Lloyd | San Francisco, Calif. | 1902 |
| Merrill, Gary | Hartford, Conn. | 1915 | North, Jay | Hollywood, Calif. | 1953 |
| Merrill, Robert | Brooklyn, N. Y. | 1919 | North, John Ringling | Baraboo, Wis. | 1903 |
| Merriman, Nan | Pittsburgh, Pa. | 1920 | North, Sheree | Los Angeles, Calif. | 1933 |
| Middleton, Guy | Hove, England | 1907 | Novak, Kim | Chicago, Ill. | 1933 |
| Middleton, Ray | Chicago, Ill. | 1907 | Novarro, Ramon | Durango, Mexico | 1905 |
| Mielziner, Jo | Paris, France | 1901 | Nugent, Edward | New York, N. Y. | 1904 |
| Milanov, Zinka | Zagreb, Yugoslavia | 1908 | Nugent, Elliott | Dover, Ohio | 1900 |
| Miles, Vera | near Boise City, Okla. | 1930 | Nureyev, Rudolf | Russia | 1938 |
| Miland, Ray | Neath, Wales | 1908 | Nuyen, France | Marseilles, France | 1939 |
| Miller, Ann | Houston, Tex. | 1923 | | | |
| Miller, Mitch | Rochester, N. Y. | 1911 | **O** | | |
| Miller, Roger | Oklahoma | 1937 | Oakie, Jack | Sedalia, Mo. | 1903 |
| Mills, Hayley | London | 1946 | Oberon, Merle | Tasmania, Australia | 1914 |
| Mills, John | Suffolk, Eng. | 1908 | O'Brian, Hugh | Rochester, N. Y. | 1928 |
| Milstein, Nathan | Odessa, Russia | 1904 | O'Brien, Edmond | New York, N. Y. | 1915 |
| Mimieux, Yvette | Hollywood, Calif. | 1942 | O'Brien, Margaret | Los Angeles, Calif. | 1937 |
| Minnelli, Lisa | California | 1946 | O'Brien, Pat | Milwaukee, Wis. | 1899 |
| Mineo, Sal | New York, N. Y. | 1939 | O'Brien-Moore, Erin | Los Angeles, Calif. | 1908 |
| Mitchell, Cameron | Dallastown, Pa. | 1918 | O'Connor, Donald | Chicago, Ill. | 1925 |
| Mitchell, Guy | Detroit, Mich. | 1925 | O'Donnell, Cathy | Siluria, Ala. | 1923 |
| Mitchum, Robert | Bridgeport, Conn. | 1917 | O'Driscoll, Martha | Tulsa, Okla. | 1922 |
| Moffo, Ann | Wayne, Pa. | | O'Hara, Maureen | Dublin, Ireland | 1920 |
| Monroe, Vaughn | Akron, Ohio | 1912 | O'Herlihy, Dan | Wexford, Ire. | 1928 |
| Montalban, Ricardo | Mexico City, Mex. | 1920 | O'Keefe, Walter | Hartford, Conn. | 1907 |
| Montand, Yves | Monsummano, Italy | 1921 | Olivier, Laurence | Dorking, England | 1904 |
| Montgomery, Eliz. | Hollywood, Calif. | 1933 | O'Malley, J. Pat | Burnley, Eng. | 1901 |
| Montgomery, George | Brady, Mont. | 1916 | O'Neal, Ryan | Los Angeles, Calif. | 1941 |
| Montgomery, Robert | Beacon, N. Y. | 1904 | Ormandy, Eugene | Budapest, Hungary | 1899 |
| Montovani, Annunzio | Venice, Italy | 1905 | O'Shea, Kevin | Chicago, Ill. | 1917 |
| Moore, Colleen | Port Huron, Mich. | 1902 | O'Sullivan, Maureen | Boyle, Ireland | 1911 |
| Moore, Constance | Sioux City, Iowa | 1922 | O'Toole, Peter | Ireland | 1934 |
| Moore, Dickie | Los Angeles, Calif. | 1925 | Owen, Reginald | Wheathampstead,Eng. | 1887 |
| Moore, Garry | Baltimore, Md. | 1915 | Owens, Buck | Sherman, Tex. | 1929 |
| Moore, Mary Tyler | Brooklyn, N. Y. | 1937 | | | |
| Moore, Roger | London, Eng. | 1928 | **P** | | |
| Moore, Terry | Los Angeles, Calif. | 1932 | Paar, Jack | Canton, Ohio | 1918 |
| Moorehead, Agnes | Boston, Mass. | 1906 | Page, Geraldine | Kirksville, Mo. | 1924 |
| Moran, Lois | Pittsburgh, Pa. | 1907 | Page, Patti | Claremore, Okla. | 1927 |
| Moreau, Jeanne | Paris, France | 1929 | Paget, Debra | Denver, Colo. | 1933 |
| Moreno, Rita | Humacao, P. R. | 1931 | Paige, Janis | Tacoma, Wash. | 1923 |
| Morgan, Claudia | Brooklyn, N. Y. | 1912 | Paige, Robert | Indianapolis, Ind. | 1910 |
| Morgan, Dennis | Prentice, Wis. | 1920 | Palance, Jack | Lattimer, Pa. | 1920 |
| Morgan, Harry | Detroit, Mich. | 1915 | Palmer, Betsy | East Chicago, Ind. | 1929 |
| Morgan, Henry | New York, N. Y. | 1915 | Palmer, Gregg | San Francisco, Calif. | 1927 |
| Morgan, Jane | Boston, Mass. | 1920 | Palmer, Lilli | Austria | 1914 |
| Morgan, Russ | Scranton, Pa. | 1904 | Parker, Eleanor | Cedarville, Ohio | 1922 |
| Morgana, Nina | Buffalo, N. Y. | 1895 | Parker, Fess | Ft. Worth, Tex. | 1925 |
| Morini, Erika | Vienna, Austria | 1906 | Parker, Frank | New York, N. Y. | 1906 |

| Name | Birthplace | Born | Name | Birthplace | Born |
|---|---|---|---|---|---|
| Parker, Jean | Deer Lodge, Mont. | 1916 | Reynolds, William | Los Angeles, Calif. | 1931 |
| Parker, Suzy | New York City | 1934 | Rich, Irene | Buffalo, N. Y. | 1897 |
| Perkins, Barbara | Vancouver, Canada | 1942 | Richardson, Ralph | Cheltenham, England | 1902 |
| Parks, Bert | Atlanta, Ga. | 1914 | Richardson, Tony | Shipley, England | 1928 |
| Parks, Larry | Olathe, Kans. | 1914 | Richman, Harry | Cincinnati, Ohio | 1895 |
| Pasternak, Joseph | Hungary | 1901 | Rickles, Don | Long Island, N. Y. | 1928 |
| Paterson, Pat | Bradford, England | 1911 | Ritchard, Cyril | Sydney, N. S. W. | 1898 |
| Patterson, Melody | Los Angeles, Calif. | 1947 | Ritter, Tex | Murvaul Tex. | 1907 |
| Patterson, Neva | Nevada, Iowa | 1922 | Ritter, Thelma | Brooklyn, N. Y. | 1905 |
| Paulsen, Pat | South Bend, Wash. | | Ritz, Harry | Newark, N. J. | 1908 |
| Pavan, Marisa | Cagliari, Sardinia | 1932 | Ritz, Jimmy | Newark, N. J. | 1905 |
| Payne, John | Roanoke, Va. | 1912 | Robards, Jason, Jr. | Chicago, Ill. | 1922 |
| Pearl, Jack | New York, N. Y. | 1895 | Robbins, Jerome | Weehawken, N. J. | 1918 |
| Pearl, Minnie | Centerville, Tenn. | 1912 | Robertson, Cliff | La Jolla, Calif. | 1925 |
| Peck, Gregory | La Jolla, Calif. | 1916 | Robertson, Dale | Oklahoma City, Okla. | 1923 |
| Peerce, Jan | New York, N. Y. | 1904 | Robeson, Paul | Princeton, N. J. | 1898 |
| Pelletier, Wilfred | Montreal, Canada | 1896 | Robinson, Edward G. | Bucharest, Rumania | 1893 |
| Peppard, George | Detroit, Mich. | 1933 | Robinson, Jay | New York, N. Y. | 1930 |
| Perkins, Anthony | Brookline, Mass. | 1932 | Robson, Flora | South Shields, England | 1902 |
| Perkins, Millie | Passaic, N. J. | 1940 | Rochester(E.Anders'n) | Oakland, Calif. | 1905 |
| Perry, Margaret | Denver, Colo. | 1913 | Rockwell, Geo. (Doc.) | Providence R. I. | 1889 |
| Persoff, Nehemiah | Israel | 1920 | Rodgers, Richard | New York, N. Y. | 1902 |
| Peters, Roberta | New York, N. Y. | 1930 | Rogers, Chas. (Buddy) | Olathe, Kans. | 1904 |
| Peters, Jean | Canton, Ohio | 1926 | Rogers, Ginger | Independence, Mo. | 1911 |
| Peterson, Dorothy | Hector, Minn. | 1901 | Rogers, Roy | Cincinnati, Ohio | 1912 |
| Petit, Pascale | France | 1937 | Rogers, Will, Jr. | New York, N. Y. | 1912 |
| Pettet, Joanna | London, Eng. | 1944 | Roland, Gilbert | Juarez, Mexico | 1905 |
| Phillips, Margaret | Wales | 1923 | Roman, Ruth | Boston, Mass. | 1924 |
| Piatigorsky, Gregor | Russia | 1903 | Romero, Cesar | New York, N. Y. | 1907 |
| Piazza, Ben | Little Rock, Ark. | 1934 | Rooney, Mickey | Brooklyn, N. Y. | 1922 |
| Piazza, Marguerite | New Orleans, La. | 1926 | Rose Marie | New York, N. Y. | |
| Pickens, Jane | Macon, Ga. | | Rosenbloom, Maxie | New York, N. Y. | 1906 |
| Pickford, Mary | Toronto, Canada | 1893 | Ross, David | St. Paul, Minn. | 1924 |
| Picon, Molly | New York, N. Y. | 1898 | Ross, Lanny | Seattle, Wash. | 1906 |
| Pidgeon, Walter | E. St. John, N. B. | 1898 | Ross, Shirley | Omaha, Nebr. | |
| Piston, Walter | Rockland, Me. | 1894 | Roth, Lillian | Boston, Mass. | 1910 |
| Pleasence, Donald | Worksop, England | 1919 | Rowan, Dan | Los Angeles, Calif. | 1928 |
| Pieshette, Suzanne | New York City | 1937 | Rubin, Benny | New York, N. Y. | 1899 |
| Plowright, Joan | England | 1929 | Rubinoff, David | Grodno, Russia | 1897 |
| Plummer, Christopher | Toronto, Canada | 1929 | Rubinstein, Artur | Lodz, Poland | 1889 |
| Poitier, Sidney | Miami, Fla. | 1924 | Rudolf, Max | Frankfurt, Germany | 1902 |
| Pollard, Michael | Passaic, N. J. | 1940 | Ruggles, Charles | Los Angeles, Calif. | 1892 |
| Pons, Lily | Cannes, France | 1940 | Rule, Janice | Cincinnati, Ohio | 1931 |
| Ponselle, Carmela | Schenectady, N. Y. | 1892 | Rush, Barbara | Denver, Colo. | 1927 |
| Ponselle, Rosa | Meriden, Conn. | 1897 | Russell, Jane | Bemidji, Minn. | 1921 |
| Porterfield, Robert | Austinville, Va. | 1905 | Russell, Rosalind | Waterbury, Conn. | 1912 |
| Portman, Eric | Yorkshire, England | 1903 | Rutherford, Ann | Toronto, Canada | 1924 |
| Poston, Tom | Columbus, Ohio | 1927 | Rutherford, Margaret | London, England | 1892 |
| Powell, Eleanor | Springfield, Mass. | 1912 | Ryan, Irene | El Paso, Tex. | 1903 |
| Powell, Jane | Portland, Ore. | 1929 | Ryan, Robert | Chicago, Ill. | 1913 |
| Powell, William | Pittsburgh, Pa. | 1892 | Rydell, Bobby | Philadelphia, Pa. | 1942 |
| Powers, Mala | San Francisco, Calif. | 1931 | | | |
| Powers, Stefanie | Hollywood, Calif. | 1942 | **S** | | |
| Preminger, Otto | Vienna, Austria | 1906 | Sahl, Mort | Montreal, Que. | 1927 |
| Prentiss, Paula | San Antonio, Texas | 1939 | Saint, Eva Marie | Newark, N. J. | 1924 |
| Presley, Elvis | Tupelo, Miss. | 1935 | St. John, Jill | Los Angeles, Calif. | 1940 |
| Preston, Robert | Newton Mass. | 1918 | Sales, Soupy | Franklinton, No. Car. | 1926 |
| Price, Leontyne | Laurel, Miss. | 1927 | Sanders, George | St. Petersburg, Russia | 1906 |
| Price, Roger | Charleston, W. Va. | 1920 | Sanderson, Julia | Springfield, Mass. | 1887 |
| Price, Vincent | St. Louis, Mo. | 1911 | Sands, Tommy | Chicago, Ill. | 1937 |
| Prima, Louis | New Orleans, La. | 1911 | Sarnoff, Dorothy | New York. N. Y. | |
| Primus, Pearl | Trinidad, W. I. | 1921 | Saunders, Lori | Kansas City, Mo. | 1941 |
| Prince, William | Nichols, N. Y. | 1913 | Saxon, John | Brooklyn, N. Y. | 1935 |
| Provine, Dorothy | Deadwood, S. D. | 1937 | Sayao, Bidu | Rio de Janeiro, Brazil. | 1908 |
| Prowse, Juliet | Bombay, India | 1937 | Schallert, William | Los Angeles, Calif. | 1925 |
| Pryor, Roger | New York, N. Y. | 1903 | Schary, Dore | Newark, N. J. | 1905 |
| Pyne, Joe | Chester, Pa. | 1924 | Schell, Maria | Vienna, Austria | 1926 |
| | | | Schell, Maximilian | Austria | 1931 |
| **Q** | | | Schenkel, Chris | Bippus, Ind. | 1924 |
| Qualen, John | Vancouver, B. C. | 1899 | Scherman, Thomas | New York, N. Y. | 1917 |
| Quayle, Anthony | Lancashire, England | 1913 | Schippers, Thomas | Kalamazoo, Mich. | 1930 |
| Quillan, Eddie | Philadelphia, Pa. | 1907 | Schneider, Alexander | Vilna, Poland | 1908 |
| Quinn, Anthony | Chihuahua, Mexico | 1915 | Schneider, Romy | Austria | 1938 |
| | | | Schuman, William | New York, N. Y. | 1910 |
| **R** | | | Schwartz, Arthur | Brooklyn, N. Y. | 1900 |
| Raft, George | New York, N. Y. | 1895 | Schwarzkopf, Elisabeth | Jarotschin, Poland | 1915 |
| Rainer, Luise | Vienna, Austria | 1912 | Schofield, Paul | Hurst, Pierpont, Eng. | 1922 |
| Raines, Ella | SnoqualmieFalls,Wash. | 1921 | Scott, Barbara Ann | Canada | 1930 |
| Raitt, John | Santa Ana, Calif. | 1917 | Scott, George C. | Virginia | 1927 |
| Ralston, Esther | Bar Harbor, Maine | 1902 | Scott, Gordon | Portland, Ore. | 1927 |
| Ralston, Vera | Prague, Czechoslov. | 1921 | Scott, Hazel | Trinidad | 1920 |
| Rambeau, Marjorie | San Francisco, Calif. | 1889 | Scott, Henry L. | Tivoli, N. Y. | 1908 |
| Rambo, Jack | Delano, Calif. | 1941 | Scott, Lizabeth | Scranton, Pa. | 1923 |
| Randall, Tony | Tulsa, Okla. | 1920 | Scott, Martha | Jamesport, Mo. | 1916 |
| Ray, Aldo | Pen Argyl, Pa. | 1926 | Scott, Randolph | Orange Co., Va. | 1903 |
| Ray, Johnnie | Dallas, Ore. | 1927 | Seal, Elizabeth | England | 1935 |
| Rayburn, Gene | Christopher, Ill. | 1917 | Seberg, Jean | Marshalltown, Iowa | 1938 |
| Raye, Martha | Butte, Mont. | 1916 | Seeger, Pete | New York, N. Y. | 1919 |
| Raymond, Gene | New York, N. Y. | 1908 | Seeley, Blossom | San Pablo, Calif. | |
| Redford, Robert | Hollywood, Calif. | 1936 | Segal, Vivienne | Philadelphia, Pa. | 1897 |
| Redgrave, Lynn | England | 1943 | Seidel, Toscha | Odessa, Russia | 1899 |
| Redgrave, Michael | Bristol, England | 1908 | Sellers, Peter | Southsea, England | 1925 |
| Redgrave, Vanessa | London, England | 1937 | Serkin, Rudolf | Eger, Austria | 1903 |
| Redman, Joyce | Co. Mayo, Ireland | 1918 | Serling, Rod | Syracuse, N. Y. | 1924 |
| Reed, Donna | Denison, Iowa | 1921 | Sharif, Omar | India | 1933 |
| Reed, Robert | Chicago, Ill. | 1932 | Shatner, William | Montreal, Canada | 1931 |
| Regan, Phil | Brooklyn, N. Y. | 1906 | Shaw, Artie | New York, N. Y. | 1910 |
| Reiner, Carl | Bronx, N. Y. | 1923 | Shaw, Robert | Red Bluff, Calif. | 1916 |
| Remick, Lee | Boston, Mass. | 1935 | Shaw, Victoria | Sydney, N. S. W. | 1935 |
| Renaldo, Duncan | Camden, N. J. | 1904 | Shaw, Winfred | San Francisco, Calif. | 1899 |
| Rennie, Michael | Bradford, England | 1909 | Shawn, Edwin (Ted) | Kansas City, Mo. | 1891 |
| Resnik, Regina | New York, N. Y. | 1923 | Shearer, Moira | Scotland | 1926 |
| Reynolds, Debbie | El Paso, Texas | 1932 | Shearer, Norma | Montreal, Canada | 1904 |
| Reynolds, Joyce | San Antonio, Tex. | 1924 | Sherman, Allan | Chicago, Ill. | 1924 |
| Reynolds, Marjorie | Buhl, Idaho | 1921 | Shirley, Anne | New York, N. Y. | 1918 |

| Name | Birthplace | Born | Name | Birthplace | Born |
|---|---|---|---|---|---|
| Shore, Dinah | Winchester, Tenn. | 1920 | Taylor, Robert | Filley, Nebr. | 1911 |
| Shriner, Herb | Toledo, Ohio | 1918 | Taylor, Rod | Sidney, Australia | 1929 |
| Sidney, Sylvia | New York, N. Y. | 1910 | Tebaldi, Renata | Pesaro, Italy | 1922 |
| Siepi, Cesare | Milan, Italy | 1923 | Temple, Shirley | Santa Monica, Calif. | 1929 |
| Signoret, Simone | Germany | 1921 | Terris, Norma | Columbus, Kans. | 1904 |
| Silvera, Frank | Kingston, Jam., W. I. | 1924 | Terry-Thomas | London, Eng. | 1911 |
| Silvers, Phil | Brooklyn, N. Y. | 1912 | Teyte, Maggie | Wolverhampton, Eng. | 1889 |
| Silvers, Sid | Brooklyn, N. Y. | 1908 | Thaxter, Phillis | Portland, Me. | 1921 |
| Sim, Alastair | Edinburgh, Scotland | 1900 | Thebom, Blanche | Monessen, Pa. | 1919 |
| Simmons, Jean | London, England | 1929 | Thibault, Conrad | Northbridge, Mass. | 1898 |
| Simon, Simone | Marseilles, France | 1914 | Thimes, Roy | Chicago, Ill. | 1937 |
| Sinatra, Frank | Hoboken, N. Y. | 1915 | Thomas, Danny | Deerfield, Mich. | 1914 |
| Singleton, Penny | Philadelphia, Pa. | 1912 | Thomas, Lowell | Woodrington, Ohio | 1892 |
| Skelton, Red (Richard) | Vincennes, Ind. | 1913 | Thomas, Marlo | Detroit, Mich | 1938 |
| Skinner, Cornelia Otis | Chicago, Ill. | 1903 | Thompson, Marshall | Peoria, Ill. | 1926 |
| Skulnik, Menasha | Russia | 1895 | Thorndike, Sybil | Gainsborough, Eng. | 1882 |
| Slezak, Walter | Vienna, Austria | 1902 | Tierney, Gene | Brooklyn, N. Y. | 1920 |
| Smith, Bob | Buffalo, N. Y. | 1917 | Tierney, Lawrence | Brooklyn, N. Y. | 1919 |
| Smith, Connie | Kingsland, Ark. | 1932 | Tiffin, Pamela | Oklahoma City. Okla. | 1942 |
| Smith, Cyril | Peterhead, Scotland | 1892 | Tillstrom Burr | Chicago, Ill | 1917 |
| Smith, Ethel | Pittsburgh, Pa. | 1921 | Tiny Tim | New York, N. Y. | .... |
| Smith, Howard K. | Ferriday, La. | 1914 | Todd, Richard | Dublin, Ireland | 1919 |
| Smith, Kate | Greenville, Va. | 1909 | Toomey, Regis | Pittsburgh, Pa. | 1902 |
| Smith, Lois | Topeka, Kan. | 1931 | Tomlin, Pinky | Durant, Okla. | 1907 |
| Smith, Loring | Stratford, Conn. | 1900 | Torme, Mel | Chicago, Ill. | 1925 |
| Smith, Muriel | New York, N. Y. | 1923 | Torn, Rip | Temple, Tex. | 1931 |
| Smith, Roger | Southgate, Calif. | 1933 | Totter, Audrey | Joliet, Ill. | 1923 |
| Smothers, Dick | New York, N. Y. | 1939 | Tracy, Arthur | Philadelphia, Pa. | 1903 |
| Smothers, Tom | New York, N. Y. | 1937 | Tracy, Lee | Atlanta, Ga. | 1898 |
| Snow, Hank | Nova Scotia | 1914 | Traubel, Helen | St. Louis, Mo. | 1903 |
| Somes, Michael | nr. Stroud, England | 1917 | Treacher, Arthur | Brighton, England | 1894 |
| Sommer, Elke | Berlin, Ger | 1941 | Trevor, Claire | New York, N. Y. | 1909 |
| Sothern, Ann | Valley City, N. Dak. | 1912 | Truex, Ernest | Kansas City, Mo. | 1890 |
| Specht, Bobby | Superior, Wis. | 1921 | Tryon, Tom | Hartford, Conn. | 1926 |
| Spewack, Bella | Hungary | 1899 | Tucker, Forrest | Plainfield, Ind. | 1919 |
| Spewack, Samuel | Russia | 1899 | Tucker, Orrin | St. Louis, Mo. | 1911 |
| Spitalny, Phil | Romanoff, Russia | | Tucker, Richard | Brooklyn, N. Y. | 1915 |
| Spivak, Lawrence | Brooklyn, N. Y. | 1900 | Tucker, Tommy | Souris, N. D. | 1907 |
| Stack, Robert | Los Angeles, Calif | 1919 | Tufts, Sonny | Boston, Mass. | 1911 |
| Stafford, Jo | Coalinga, Calif. | 1918 | Turner, Lana | Wallace, Idaho | 1920 |
| Stamp, Terence | London, England | 1940 | Tushingham, Rita | Liverpool, Eng. | 1942 |
| Stang, Arnold | Chelsea, Mass. | 1925 | **U** | | |
| Stanley, Kim | Tularosa, N. M | 1921 | Uggams, Leslie | New York City | 1943 |
| Stanley, Pat | Cincinnati, Ohio | 1931 | Ulric, Lenore | New Ulm, Minn. | 1894 |
| Stanwyck, Barbara | Brooklyn, N. Y. | 1907 | Umeki, Miyoshi | Hokkaido, Japan | 1929 |
| Stapleton, Maureen | Troy, N. Y. | 1925 | Ure, Mary | Glasgow, Scotland | 1935 |
| Starr, Frances | Oneonta, N. Y. | 1886 | Ustinov, Peter | London, England | 1921 |
| Starr, Kay | Dougherty, Okla | 1924 | **V** | | |
| Steber, Eleanor | Wheeling, W. Va. | 1916 | Vallee, Rudy | Island Pond, Vt. | 1901 |
| Steele, Bob | Pendleton, Ore. | 1907 | Vance, Vivian | Cherryvale, Kans. | 1912 |
| Steele, Karen | Hawaii | 1934 | Van Cleef, Lee | Somerville, N. J. | 1925 |
| Steele, Ted | Hartford, Conn. | 1917 | Van Doren, Mamie | Rowena, S. D. | 1933 |
| Steele, Tommy | London, England | 1937 | Van Dyke, Dick | West Plains, Mo. | 1925 |
| Steiger, Rod | W. Hampton, N. Y. | 1925 | Van Fleet, Jo | Oakland, Calif. | 1922 |
| Sterling, Jan | New York, N. Y. | 1923 | Van Horne, Harriet | Syracuse, N. Y. | 1922 |
| Sterling, Robert | Newcastle, Pa. | 1917 | Varnay, Astrid | Stockholm, Sweden | 1918 |
| Stern, Isaac | Kreminisey, Russia | 1920 | Vaughn, Robert | New York, N. Y. | 1932 |
| Stevens, Connie | Brooklyn, N. Y. | 1938 | Venuta, Benay | San Francisco, Calif. | 1913 |
| Stevens, Inger | Stockholm, Sweden | 1936 | Vera-Ellen | Cincinnati, Ohio. | 1926 |
| Stevens, Mark | Cleveland, Ohio | 1922 | Verdon, Gwen | Culver City, Calif. | 1925 |
| Stevens, Onslow | Los Angeles, Calif. | 1902 | Vernon, Jackie | New York, N. Y. | 1929 |
| Stevens, Risé | New York, N. Y. | 1913 | Vidor, King Louis | Galveston, Tex. | 1895 |
| Stevens, Stella | Yazoo City, Miss. | 1938 | Vinson, Helen | Beaumont, Tex. | 1907 |
| Stewart, Elaine | Montclair, N. J. | 1929 | Vinton, Bobby | Canonsburg, Pa. | 1936 |
| Stewart, James | Indiana, Pa. | 1908 | Von Furstenberg, Betsy | Westphalia, Ger. | 1931 |
| Stickney, Dorothy | Dickinson, N. Dak. | 1903 | Von Sydow, Max | Lund, Sweden | 1929 |
| Stokowski, Leopold | London, England | 1882 | Von Zell, Harry R. | Indianapolis, Ind. | 1906 |
| Stone, Carol | New York, N. Y. | 1916 | Voorhees, Donald | Allentown. Pa. | 1903 |
| Stone, Dorothy | Bensonhurst, N. Y. | 1905 | **W** | | |
| Stone, Ezra | New Bedford, Mass. | 1917 | Wagner, Robert | Detroit, Mich. | 1930 |
| Stone, Harvey | Detroit, Mich | 1911 | Wain, Bea | Bronx, N. Y. | 1917 |
| Stone, Milburn | Burrton, Kans. | 1904 | Waggoner, Lyle | Kansas City, Kansas | 1935 |
| Stone, Paula | New York, N. Y. | 1916 | Walburn, Raymond | Plymouth, Ind. | 1887 |
| Storm, Gale | Bloomington, Tex. | 1922 | Walker, Clint | Hartford, Ill. | 1927 |
| Storrs, Suzanne | Salt Lake City, Utah. | 1934 | Walker, Nancy | Philadelphia, Pa. | 1922 |
| Straight, Beatrice | Old Westbury, N. Y. | 1918 | Wallace, Mike | Brookline, Mass. | 1918 |
| Strasberg, Susan | New York, N. Y. | 1938 | Wallach, Eli | Brooklyn, N. Y. | 1915 |
| Strauss, Robert | New York, N. Y. | 1913 | Wallenstein, Alfred | Chicago, Ill. | 1898 |
| Stravinsky, Igor F. | St. Petersburg, Russia. | 1882 | Walston, Ray | New Orleans, La. | 1918 |
| Streisand, Barbra | Brooklyn, N. Y. | 1942 | Ward, Burt | Los Angeles, Calif. | 1946 |
| Stritch, Elaine | Detroit, Mich | 1925 | Warden, Jack | Newark, N. J. | 1920 |
| Stuart, Gloria | Santa Monica, Calif. | 1911 | Warfield, William | Helena, Ark. | 1929 |
| Sullivan, Barry | New York, N. Y. | 1912 | Waring, Fred | Tyrone, Pa. | 1900 |
| Sullivan, Ed | New York, N. Y. | 1902 | Waters, Ethel | Chester, Pa. | 1900 |
| Sumac, Yma | Peru | 1922 | Watson, Debbie | Culver City, Calif. | 1940 |
| Susskind, David | New York, N. Y. | 1920 | Wayne, David | Traverse City, Mich. | 1916 |
| Sutherland, Joan | Australia | 1926 | Wayne, John | Winterset, Iowa | 1907 |
| Suzuki, Pat | Cressy, Calif. | 1931 | Weaver, Charley | | |
| Swanson, Gloria | Chicago, Ill. | 1899 | (Cliff Arquette) | Toledo, Ohio | 1905 |
| Swarthout, Gladys | Deepwater, Mo. | 1904 | Weaver, Dennis | Joplin, Mo. | 1925 |
| Swayze, John Cameron | Wichita, Kan. | 1906 | Webb, Alan | York, England | 1906 |
| Sweet, Blanche | Chicago, Ill. | 1896 | Webb, Jack | Santa Monica, Calif. | 1920 |
| Swenson, Inga | Sweden | 1935 | Webster, Margaret | New York, N. Y. | 1905 |
| Szell, George | Budapest | 1897 | Weede, Robert | Baltimore, Md. | 1903 |
| Szigeti, Joseph | Budapest, Hungary | 1892 | Weidler, Virginia | Hollywood, Calif. | 1927 |
| **T** | | | Weissmuller, Johnny | Windber, Pa. | 1905 |
| Talbot, Lyle | Pittsburgh, Pa. | 1904 | Welch, Raquel | La Jolla, Calif. | 1942 |
| Talbot, Nita | New York, N. Y. | 1930 | Weld, Tuesday | New York, N. Y. | 1943 |
| Tallchief, Maria | Fairfax, Okla. | 1924 | Welk, Lawrence | nr. Strasburg, N. Dak. | 1903 |
| Talmadge, Constance | Brooklyn, N. Y. | 1900 | Welles, Orson | Kenosha, Wis. | 1915 |
| Tamblyn, Russ | Los Angeles, Calif | 1935 | Wells, Kitty | Nashville, Tenn. | 1919 |
| Tandy, Jessica | London, England | 1909 | Werner, Oskar | Vienna, Austria | 1922 |
| Taurog, Norman | Chicago, Ill. | 1899 | West, Adam | Walla Walla, Wash. | 1929 |
| Taylor, Elizabeth | London, England | 1932 | West, Mae | Brooklyn, N. Y. | 1892 |
| Taylor, Kent | Nashua, Iowa | 1907 | Westman, Nydia | New York City | 1907 |

| Name | Birthplace | Born | Name | Birthplace | Born |
|---|---|---|---|---|---|
| White, Jesse | Buffalo, N. Y. | 1919 | Woodward, Joanne | Thomasville, Ga. | 1932 |
| Whitman, Stuart | San Francisco, Calif. | 1926 | Wray, Fay | Alberta, Canada | 1907 |
| Whitmore, James | White Plains, N. Y. | 1921 | Wright, Martha | Seattle, Wash. | 1926 |
| Widmark, Richard | Sunrise, Minn. | 1914 | Wright, Teresa | New York, N. Y. | 1919 |
| Wilcoxon, Henry | British West Indies | 1905 | Wyatt, Jane | New York | 1913 |
| Wilde, Cornel | New York, N. Y. | 1915 | Wyler, William | Mulhouse, France | 1902 |
| Wilding, Michael | Essex, England | 1912 | Wyman, Jane | St. Joseph, Mo. | 1914 |
| Williams, Andy | Wall Lake, Iowa | 1931 | Wynn, Bessie | Adrian, Mich. | 1876 |
| Williams, Emlyn | Mostyn, Wales | 1905 | Wynn, Keenan | New York, N. Y. | 1916 |
| Williams, Esther | Los Angles, Calif. | 1923 | Wynter, Dana | London | 1930 |
| Willson, Meredith | Mason City, Iowa | 1929 | **Y** | | |
| Wilson, Dolores | Philadelphia, Pa. | 1929 | York, Dick | Ft. Wayne, Ind | 1928 |
| Wilson, Flip | Jersey City, N. J. | 1933 | York, Susannah | London, England | 1942 |
| Wilson, Julie | Omaha, Nebr. | 1924 | Young, Alan | Northumberl'd, Eng. | 1919 |
| Wilson, Marie | Anaheim, Calif. | 1917 | Young, Gig | St. Cloud, Minn. | 1917 |
| Wilson, Nancy | Chillicothe, Ohio | 1937 | Young, Loretta | Salt Lake City, Utah. | 1913 |
| Winchell, Paul | New York, N. Y. | 1924 | Young, Robert | Chicago, Ill. | 1907 |
| Winchell, Walter | New York, N. Y. | 1897 | Young, Stephen | Toronto, Canada | 1939 |
| Windom, William | New York, N. Y. | 1924 | Youngman, Henny | Liverpool, England | 1906 |
| Winninger, Charles | Athens, Wis. | 1884 | Yurka, Blanche | St. Paul, Minn. | 1893 |
| Winters, Jonathan | Dayton, Ohio | 1925 | **Z** | | |
| Winters, Shelley | St. Louis, Mo. | 1922 | Zanuck, Darryl F. | Wahoo, Nebr. | 1902 |
| Winwood, Estelle | Lee, England | 1884 | Zimbalist, Efrem | Rostov, Russia | 1889 |
| Withers, Jane | Atlanta, Ga. | 1927 | Zimbalist, Efrem, Jr. | New York, N. Y. | 1923 |
| Wood, Helen | Clarksville, Tenn. | 1937 | Zimmer, Norma | Larsen, Idaho. | |
| Wood, Natalie | San Francisco, Calif. | 1938 | Zorina, Vera | Berlin, Germany | 1917 |
| Wood, Peggy | Brooklyn, N. Y. | 1892 | Zukor, Adolph | Ricse, Hungary | 1873 |

## Foreign Composers of Light Operas

**Francois Adrien Boieldieu,** 1775-1834. (F.) The Caliph of Bagdad.

**Julius Eichberg,** 1824-1893 (G.) The Rose of Tyrol, A Night in Rome.

**Leo Fall,** 1873-1925. (Aus.) The Rebel, The Happy Farmer, The Dollar Princess, Pompadour, The Girl in the Train.

**Gilbert & Sullivan**—W. S. Gilbert, librettist, 1836-1911; Arthur S. Sullivan, composer, 1842-1900. Thespis, 1871; Trial by Jury, 1875; The Sorcerer, 1877; H. M. S. Pinafore, 1878; The Pirates of Penzance, 1880; Patience, 1881; Iolanthe, 1882; Princess Ida, 1884; The Mikado, 1885; Ruddigore, 1887; The Yeomen of the Guard, 1888; The Gondoliers, 1889; Utopia, Ltd., 1893; The Grand Duke, 1896.

**Emmerich (Imre) Kalman** (1882-1953) Sari, Gipsy Princess, Countess Maritza, Paris in Spring, Marinka.

**Franz Lehar,** 1870-1948. (H.) The Merry Widow, The Count of Luxemburg.

**Karl Milloecker,** 1842-1899, (Aus.) The Beggar Student, 1881, and Poor Jonathan, 1890.

**Jacques Offenbach,** 1819-1880. (F.) Opera: Tales of Hoffmann. Operettas: Orpheus in the Underworld, La Belle Helene, Barbebleue, Grandduchess of Gerolstein, Madame Favart.

**Robert Planquette,** 1848-1903. (F.) The Chimes of Normandy, Rip van Winkle, Paul Jones.

**Oskar Straus,** 1870-1954. (Aus.) A Waltz Dream, The Chocolate Soldier.

**Johann Strauss,** 1825-1899. (Aus.) Cagliostro, Gypsy Baron, Die Fledermaus, Night in Venice, Prince Methusalem. Composed famous waltzes: Beautiful Blue Danube, Roses from the South, Artists' Life, Wine, Woman & Song, Tales from the Vienna Woods.

## Concert Violinists of the Past

| Born | Died | Name | Born | Died | Name | Born | Died | Name |
|---|---|---|---|---|---|---|---|---|
| 1856 | 1943 | Adamowski, T..Pol. | 1889 | 1934 | Kichanski, Paul.Pol. | 1844 | 1908 | Sarasate, P. M..Span. |
| 1845 | 1930 | Auer, Leopold..Hung. | 1875 | 1962 | Kreisler, Fritz..Aus. | 1815 | 1894 | Sivori, Ern......Ital. |
| 1795 | 1876 | Boehm, Jos...Czech. | 1880 | 1940 | Kubelik, Jan....Boh. | 1888 | 1953 | Spalding Albert.U. S. |
| 1810 | 1880 | Bull, Ole.......Nor. | 1790 | 1861 | Lipinski, Karl..Pol. | 1784 | 1859 | Spohr, Ludwig..Ger. |
| 1653 | 1713 | Corelli, Arcang..Ital. | 1840 | 1927 | Lotto, Isdor....... | 1692 | 1770 | Tartini, Gius...Ital. |
| 1891 | 1967 | Elman, Mischa..U.S. | 1722 | 1793 | Nardini, Pietro..Ital. | 1880 | 1953 | Thibaud, Jacq..Fr. |
| 1881 | 1955 | Enesco, Georges.Rum. | 1782 | 1840 | Paganini, Nicolo.Ital. | 1820 | 1881 | Vieuxtemps, H..Belg. |
| 1667 | 1762 | Geminiani, F....Ital. | 1868 | 1920 | Powell, Maud... U. S. | 1753 | 1824 | Viotti, Giovanni. Ital. |
| 1716 | 1796 | Giardini, F. di..Ital. | 1830 | 1898 | Remenyi, Edw..Hung. | 1675 | 1741 | Vivaldi, Antonio. Ital. |
| 1858 | 1937 | Hubay, Jeno....Hung. | 1892 | 1936 | Rigo, Jancsi....Hung. | 1835 | 1880 | Wieniawski, H..Pol. |
| 1882 | 1947 | Huberman, B...Pol. | 1774 | 1830 | Rode, Jacques..Fr. | 1845 | 1908 | Wilhelmj, Aug...Ger. |
| 1831 | 1907 | Joachim, Joseph.Hung. | 1863 | 1946 | Rosé, Arnold...Aus. | 1858 | 1931 | Ysaye, Eugene..Belg. |

## Ancient Greeks and Latins

B. C. years are in black type; A. D. years in light. Herodotus believed that Homer lived in what is now called the 9th century B. C.

### GREEKS

| Born | Died | Name | Subj. | Born | Died | Name | Subj. | Born | Died | Name | Subj. |
|---|---|---|---|---|---|---|---|---|---|---|---|
| 389 | 314 | Aeschines | Orat. | 450 | .... | Empedocles | Philos. | 582 | 500 | Pythagoras | Philos. |
| 525 | 456 | Aeschylus | Dram. | 55 | 135 | Epictetus | Philos. | 600 | .... | Sappho | Poet |
| .... | 550 | Aesop | Tales | 342 | 270 | Epicurus | Philos. | 556 | 469 | Simonides | Poet |
| 563 | 478 | Anacreon | Poet | 480 | 406 | Euripides | Dram. | 469 | 399 | Socrates | Philos. |
| 500 | 428 | Anaxagoras | Philos. | 576 | 480 | Heraclitus | Philos. | 495 | 405 | Sophocles | Dram. |
| 287 | 212 | Archimedes | Physi. | 484 | 424 | Herodotus | Hist. | 63 | 24 | Strabo | Geog. |
| 448 | 380 | Aristophanes | Dram. | .... | 735 | Hesiod | Poet | 600 | 540 | Thales | Philos. |
| 384 | 322 | Aristotle | Philos. | 460 | 377 | Hippocrates | Medic. | 530 | 460 | Themistocles | Philos. |
| .... | 194 | Athenaeus | Antiq. | .... | .... | Homer | Poet | .... | 255 | Theocritus | Poet |
| 460 | 370 | Democritus | Philos. | 342 | 292 | Menander | Dram. | 382 | 287 | Theophrastus | Philos. |
| 310 | 240 | Callimachus | Poet | 522 | 443 | Pindar | Poet | 471 | 401 | Thucydides | Hist. |
| 382 | 322 | Demosthenes | Orat. | 429 | 347 | Plato | Philos. | 280 | .... | Timon | Philos. |
| 50 | 13 | Diodorus | Hist. | 49 | 120 | Plutarch | Biog. | 490 | .... | Zeno | Philos. |
| .... | 7 | Dionysius | Hist. | 207 | 122 | Polybius | Hist. | 430 | 357 | Xenophon | Hist. |

### LATINS

| Born | Died | Name | Subj. | Born | Died | Name | Subj. | Born | Died | Name | Subj. |
|---|---|---|---|---|---|---|---|---|---|---|---|
| 330 | 390 | Ammianus | Hist. | 38 | 65 | Lucan | Poet | 86 | 34 | Sallust | Hist. |
| 125 | 200 | Apuleius | Satir. | 180 | 103 | Lucilius | Satir. | 5 | 65 | Seneca | Moral. |
| 130 | 175 | Aulus Gellius | Satir. | 96 | 52 | Lucretius | Philos. | 25 | 100 | Silius | Poet |
| 475 | 524 | Boethius | Philos. | 43 | 104 | Martial | Poet | 61 | 96 | Statius | Poet |
| 234 | 149 | Cato, (Elder) | Orat. | 100 | 30 | Nepos | Hist. | 70 | 150 | Suetonius | Biog. |
| 87 | 54 | Catullus | Poet | 43 | 18 | Ovid | Poet | 55 | 117 | Tacitus | Hist. |
| 107 | 43 | Cicero | Orat. | 34 | 62 | Persius | Satir. | 185 | 159 | Terence | Dram. |
| 365 | 408 | Claudian | Poet | 254 | 184 | Plautus | Dram. | 54 | 18 | Tibullus | Poet |
| 65 | 8 | Horace | Poet | 23 | 79 | Pliny | Natur. | 70 | 19 | Vergil | Poet |
| 60 | 140 | Juvenal | Satir. | 62 | 113 | Pliny (Younger) | Letters | 70 | 16 | Vitruvius | Arch. |
| 59 | 17 | Livy | Hist. | 35 | 95 | Quintilian | Critic | | | | |

# Foreign Composers and Their Operas

Aus.-Austrian. Br.-British. C.-Czech. F.-French. G.-German. H.-Hungarian. It.-Italian. R.-Russian.

**Daniel Auber,** 1782-1871. **(F.)** The Mute of Portici, Fra Diavolo.

**Michael Wm. Balfe,** 1808-1870. (Dublin-born, English) Maid of Artois, Joan of Arc, Bohemian Girl, Sicilian Bride, Rose of Castile.

**Bela Bartok,** 1881-1945. **(H.)** Duke Bluebeard's Castle.

**Ludwig van Beethoven,** 1770-1827. **(G.)** Fidelio.

**Vincenzo Bellini,** 1801-1835. (It.) La Straniera, Capuletti ed i Montecchi, La Sonnambula, Norma, I Puritani.

**Alban Berg,** 1885-1935, (Aus.), pupil of Arnold Schoenberg and composer in the 12-tone scale, wrote Wozzeck, 1925; Lulu, 1927.

**Hector Berlioz,** 1803-1869. (F.) Benvenuto Cellini, Beatrice & Benedict, Damnation of Faust.

**Sir Henry Rowley Bishop,** 1786-1855, (Br.) in 1823 composed Clari, which includes Home Sweet Home, with words by John Howard Payne.

**Georges Bizet,** 1838-1875. (F.) Carmen, Don Procopio, Fair Maid of Perth, Pearl Fishers.

**Arrigo Boito,** 1842-1918. (It.) Mefistofele.

**Alexander Borodin,** 1834-1887. (R.) Prince Igor.

**Benjamin Britten,** b. 1913. (Br.) Paul Bunyan (with W. H. Auden), 1940; Peter Grimes, 1945; The Rape of Lucretia, 1946; The Turn of the Screw, 1954; A Midsummer Night's Dream, 1960.

**Ferruccio Busoni,** 1866-1924. (It.) Turandot, Arlecchino, Doctor Faust.

**Alfredo Catalani,** 1854-1893. (It.) La Falce, Elda, Dejanire, Edmea, Loreley, La Wally.

**Gustave Charpentier,** 1860-1956. (F.) Louise.

**Maria Luigi Cherubini,** 1760-1842. (It.) Armida, Medea, Iphigenia in Aulis, Ali Baba.

**Domenico Cimarosa,** 1749-1801. (It.) The Secret Marriage.

**Peter Cornelius,** 1824-1874. (G.) Der Barbier von Bagdad, Der Cid.

**Eugene Franci D'Albert,** 1864-1932. (G.) The Lowlands.

**Claude Achille Debussy,** 1862-1918. (F.) Pelleas et Melisande.

**C. P. Leo Delibes,** 1836-1890. (F.) Lakmé, Le Roi l'a Dit, Jean de Nivelle. Ballets: Coppelia, Sylvia.

**Frederick Delius,** 1862-1934, (Br.) lived in Florida and Paris, and wrote symphonic poems on both. Best known for music drama A Village Romeo and Juliet.

**Gaetano Donizetti,** 1797-1848. (It.) Elixir of Love, Lucrezia Borgia, Maria Stuart, Marino Faliero, Lucia di Lammermoor, Daughter of the Regiment, Linda of Chamonix, Don Pasquale.

**Paul Dukas,** 1865-1935. (F.) Ariane et Barbe Bleue.

**Antonin Dvorak,** 1841-1904. (C.) King and Collier, Vanda, The Devil and Kate.

**Manuel de Falla,** 1876-1946, (Sp.) whose ballets El Amor Brujo and the Three-Cornered Hat are standard in repertory, in 1905 wrote La Vida Breve (The Brevity of Life).

**Camille Erlanger,** 1863-1910. (F.) Le Juif Polonais, Aphrodite.

**Frederic Erlanger,** 1868-1943. (F.) Tess of the d'Urbervilles.

**Friedrich von Flotow,** 1812-1883. (G.) Martha, Alessandro Stradella.

**Alberto Franchetti,** 1860-1942. (It.) Cristoforo Colombo, Giove a Pompei.

**John Gay,** 1685-1732, (Br.) poet and satirist, wrote The Beggar's Opera, 1728.

**Umberto Giordano,** 1867-1948 (It.) Andrea Chenier, Fedora, Madame Sans-Gene.

**Mikhail Glinka,** 1803-1857. (R.) A Life for the Czar, Ruslan & Ludmilla.

**Christoph Gluck,** 1714-1787. (G.) Orfeo ed Euridice, Alceste, Iphigenie en Aulide, Iphigenie en Tauride, Armide.

**Benjamin L. P. Godard,** 1849-1895, (F.) wrote half a dozen operas of which Jocelyn (1888) became famous for its Berceuse.

**Karl Goldmark,** 1830-1915, (H.), The Queen of Sheba, 1875; Merlin, 1886.

**Charles Gounod,** 1818-1893. (F.) Faust, Romeo and Juliet.

**Enrique Granados,** 1867-1916. (Spanish) Maria del Carmen, Goyescas.

**George Frederick Handel,** 1685-1759. (German-English) Xerxes, Almira, Armida, Berenice.

**Gustav Holst,** 1874-1934. (Br.) The Perfect Fool, The Tale of the Wandering Scholar.

**Arthur Honegger,** 1892-1955. (F.) Judith, Antigone.

**Engelbert Humperdinck,** 1854-1921. (G.) Hansel and Gretel, Die Koenigskinder.

**Leos Janacek,** 1854-1928. (C.) Jenufa, Katya Kabanova, From the House of the Dead.

**Wilhelm Kienzl,** 1857-1941. (Aus.) The Evangelist.

**Zoltan Kodaly,** b. 1882. (H.) Hary Janos.

**Erich Korngold,** 1897-1957. (Aus.) The Ring of Polykrates, Violanta, The Dead City.

**Edouard V. A. Lalo,** 1823-1892. (F.) Fiesque, Namouna, Le Roi d'Ys.

**Ruggiero Leoncavallo,** 1858-1919. (It.) I Pagliacci, Zaza.

**Albert Lortzing,** 1801-1851. (G.) Czar and Carpenter, The Poacher, Undine.

**Pietro Mascagni,** 1863-1945. (It.) Cavalleria Rusticana, L'Amico Fritz, The Rantzau, Iris, Isabeau.

**Jules Massenet,** 1842-1912. (F.) Herodiade, Manon, The Cid, Werther, Thais, Sapho, Cendrillon, Juggler of Notre Dame, Don Quixote, Cleopatra.

**Giuseppe Mercadante,** 1795-1870. (It.) Elisa e Claudio, Il Giuramento, The Brigands.

**Giacomo Meyerbeer,** 1791-1864. (G.) Robert le Diable, Les Huguenots, Le Prophete, Dinorah, L'Africaine.

**Darius Milhaud,** b. 1892. (F.) Le Pauvre Matelot, Christophe Colombe.

**Italo Montemezzi,** 1875-1952. (It.) L'Amore dei Tre Re, La Nave, La Notte di Zoraima.

**Claudio Monteverdi,** 1567-1643. (It.) Orfeo, Arianna.

**Modest Moussorsky,** 1835-1881 (R.) Boris Godunov, Khovanschina.

**Wolfgang Amadeus Mozart,** 1756-1791. (Aus.) Abduction from the Harem, Marriage of Figaro, Don Giovanni, Cosi fan Tutte, The Magic Flute.

**Otto Nicolai,** 1810-1849. (G.) The Merry Wives of Windsor.

**Amilcare Ponchielli,** 1834-1886. (It.) The Betrothed, La Gioconda, Marion Delorme.

**Serge Prokofiev,** 1891-1953. (R.) The Love for the Three Oranges; Betrothal in a Convent; War and Peace.

**Giacomo Puccini,** 1858-1924. (It.) La Boheme, Manon Lescaut, La Tosca, Madame Butterfly, Girl of the Golden West, La Rondine, Turandot.

**Henry Purcell,** 1658-1695, (Br.) composer of Dido and Aeneas and other classical themes, remains famous for his songs.

**Jean Phillippe Rameau,** 1683-1764, (F.) classical composer of opera and ballet, of which Castor & Pollux is occasionally revived.

**Maurice Ravel,** 1875-1937 (F.) The Spanish Hour.

**Otterino Respighi,** 1879-1936. (It.) La Campana Sommersa, La Fiamma.

**Nickolay Rimsky-Korsakov,** 1844-1908. (R.) Ivan the Terrible, The Snow Maiden, The Czar's Bride, Sadko, Golden Cockerel.

**Gioacchino Rossini,** 1792-1868. (It.) Italian in Algiers, Sigismondo, Barber of Seville, Otello, La Cenerentola, Armida, Lady of the Lake, Semiramide, William Tell.

**Chas. Camille Saint-Saens,** 1835-1921. (F.) Samson and Delilah, Henry VIII, Phyne, Helen.

**Dmitri Shostakovich,** b. 1906, (R.) Operas: Lady Macbeth of Minsk, The Nose. Symphonies.

**Bedrich Smetana,** 1824-1884. (C.) Married for Money, Brandenburger in Bohemia, The Bartered Bride.

**Ethel Mary Smyth,** 1858-1944. (Br.) Fantasio, Der Wald, The Wreckers.

**Richard Strauss,** 1864-1949, (G.) Salome, Elektra, Der Rosenkavalier, Woman without a Shadow, Ariadne on Naxos, Arabella, Egyptian Helen.

**Franz von Suppe,** 1820-1895. (Aus.) Fatinitza, Boccaccio, The Beautiful Galathea.

**Peter Tchaikovsky,** 1840-1893. (R.) Undine, Guardsman, Eugen Onegin, Maid of Orleans, Mazeppa, Pique Dame, Iolanthe.

**Ambroise Thomas,** 1811-1896. (F.) Raymond, Mignon, Hamlet.

**Ludwig Thuille,** 1861-1907. (G.) Theuerdank, Lobetanz.

**Giuseppe Verdi,** 1813-1901. (It.) Aida, Otello, Simon Boccanegra, Macbeth, Force of Destiny, Rigoletto, Ernani, Don Carlo, Il Trovatore, Masked Ball, La Traviata, Falstaff.

**Richard Wagner,** 1813-1883. (G.) Rienzi, Flying Dutchman, Tannhäuser, Meistersinger von Nuremberg, Lohengrin, Das Rheingold, Die Walküre, Siegfried, Götterdämmerung, Tristan and Isolde, Parsifal.

**Karl Maria von Weber,** 1786-1826. (G.) Der Freischütz, Euryanthe, Oberon.

**Jaromir Weinberger,** b. 1896. (C.) Schwanda the Bagpipe Player.

**Wolf-Ferrari, Ermanno,** 1876-1948. (It.) Secret of Suzanne, Jewels of the Madonna.

## Composers of Instrumental and Vocal Music

Adolphe C. Adam, 1893-1856. (F.) *Giselle; Le Postillon de Longjumeau.*

Isaac Albeniz, 1860-1909. (Sp.) *Iberia.*

George Antheil, 1900-1959. (U. S.) *Ballet Mécantique.*

Johan Sebastian Bach, 1685-1750. (G.) *St. Matthew Passion; The Welltempered Clavichord.*

Ernest Ball, 1887-1912. (U. S.) *Mother Machree, When Irish Eyes are Smiling, Love Me and the World is Mine.*

Bela Bartok, 1881-1945. (H.) *Concerto for Orchestra; The Miraculous Mandarin.*

Ludwig Van Beethoven, 1770-1824. (G) *Concertos (Emperor); sonatas (Moonlight, Pastorale, Pathetique); symphonies (Eroica).*

Ernest Bloch, 1880-1959. (Swiss) *Schelomo; Voice in the Wilderness.*

François Boieldieu, 1773-1834. (F.) *Caliph of Bagdad.*

Carrie Jacobs Bond, 1826-1946. (U. S.) *I Love You Truly.*

Johannes Brahms, 1833-1897. (G) *Liebeslieder Waltzes, Rhapsody in E Flat Major, Opus 119 for Piano, Academic Festival Overture; symphonies, quartets.*

Max Bruch, 1838-1920. (G.) *Lorelei.*

Anton Bruckner, 1824-1896. (Aus.) *Symphonies (Romantic); Intermezzo for String Quintet.*

Henry Carey, 1690-1743. (Bro.) *Sally in Our Alley.*

John Alden Carpenter, 1876-1951. (U.S.) *Ballets.*

Emmanuel Chabrier, 1841-1894. (Fr.) *Le Roi Malgré Lui; Espana.*

Cecile Chaminade, 1857-1944. (Fr.) *Scarf Dance.*

Ernest Chausson, 1855-1899. (Fr.) *Chanson Perpetuelle.*

Frederic Chopin, 1810-1849. (P.) *Concertos, Polonaise No. 6 in A Flat Major (Heroic), sonatas.*

Samuel Coleridge-Taylor, 1875-1912. (Br.) *Hiawatha trilogy.*

Francois Couperin, 1668-1733. (F.) *Harpsichord suites.*

Paul Dukas, 1865-1935. (Fr.) *Sorcerer's Apprentice.*

Edward Elgar, 1857-1934. (Br.) *Pomp and Circumstance.*

Georges Enesco, 1881-1955. (Rom.) *Romanian Rhapsody.*

Gabriel Fauré, 1845-1924. (Fr.) *Requiem.*

Stephen Collins Foster, 1826-1864. (U. S.) *My Old Kentucky Home, Old Folks at Home, Jeannie with the Light Brown Hair.*

Cesar Franck, 1822-1890. (Belg.) *D Minor Symphony.*

Edward German, 1862-1936. (Br.) *English Fantasia.*

Alexander Glazunov, 1865-1936. (R.) *Carnival Overture; Raymonda ballet; symphonies.*

Edwin F. Goldman, 1878-1956. (U. S.) Marches.

Eugene F. Goosens, 1893-1962. (Br.) Symphonies, operas.

Louis Gottschalk, 1829-1869. (U. S) *The Dying Poet.*

Percy Grainger, 1882-1961. (Br.) *Country Gardens.*

André Grétry, 1741-1813. (Fr.) *Coeur de Lion.*

Edvard Grieg, 1843-1907. (Nor.) *Peer Gynt Suite; Concerto in A Minor.*

Charles Griffes, 1884-1920. (U. S.) *Lake at Evening.*

Joseph Haydn, 1732-1809. (Aus.) Symphonies *(Clock);* oratorios; chamber music.

Paul Hindemith, 1895-1963. (U. S.) *Das Marienleben;* operas, sonatas.

Vincent d'Indy, 1851-1931. (Fr.) Istar variations.

Charles Ives, 1874-1954. (U. S.) *Third Symphony.*

Rodolphe Kreutzer, 1766-1831. (Fr.) 40 etudes for violin.

Edouard Lalo, 1823-1892. (Fr.) *Le Roi d'Ys.*

Franz Liszt, 1811-1886. (H.) 20 Hungarian Rhapsodies; symphonic poems.

Edward MacDowell, 1861-1908. (U. S.) *To a Wild Rose.*

Gustav Mahler, 1860-1911. (Aus.) *Song of the Earth.*

Lowell Mason, 1792-1872. (U. S.) *Nearer My God to Thee.*

Mendelssohn-Bartholdy, 1809-1847. (G.) *Midsummer Night's Dream.*

Karl Milloecker, 1842-1899. (Aus.) *Beggar Student.*

Victor Nessler, 1841-1890. (G.) *Trumpeter of Säckingen.*

Ethelbert Nevin, 1862-1901. (U. S.) *The Rosary.*

Ignace Paderewski, 1860-1941. (P.) *Minuet in G.*

Giovanni Palestrina, 1524-1594. (It.) Church music.

Gabriel Pierne, 1863-1937. (Fr.) *Cantata Edith.*

Sergei Rachmaninov, 1873-1943. (R.) *Prelude in C Sharp Minor.*

Maurice Ravel, 1875-1937. (Fr.) *Bolero.*

Anton Rubinstein, 1829-1894. (R.) *Caprice Russe.*

Alessandro Scarlatti, 1659-1725. (It.) Cantatas; concertos; operas.

Arnold Schoenberg, 1874-1951. (Aus.) *Pelleas und Melisande.*

Franz Schubert, 1797-1828. (A.) Lieder; symphonies *(Unfinished);* overtures *(Rosamunde).*

Robert Schumann, 1810-1856. (G.) Symphonies *(Rhenish); Kinderszenen.*

Aleksandr Scriabin, 1872-1915. (R.) *Prometheus.*

Jean Sibelius, 1865-1957. (Finn.) *Finlandia, Valse Triste.*

Christian Sinding, 1856-1941. (Nor.) *Rustle of Spring.*

Oley Speaks, 1876-1948. (U. S.) *Sylvia, Road to Mandalay.*

Hector Villa Lobos, 1887-1959. (Brazil.) *Choros.*

William Wallace, 1860-1940. (Scot.) *François Villon.*

Hugo Wolf, 1860-1900. Songs.

## Noted Choreographers and Some of Their Ballets

Frederick Ashton, b. 1906. (Br.) Les Rendezvous, The Wedding Bouquet, Cinderella, Sylvia, Ondine, La Fille Mal Gardee.

George Balanchine, b. 1904. (U. S.) Apollo, Agon, Electronics, Don Quixote.

Agnes de Mille, b. 1908. (U. S.) Black Ritual, Three Virgins and a Devil, Drums Sound in Hackensack, Rodeo, Tally-Ho, Fall River Legend.

Anton Dolin, b. 1904. (Br.) David, Job, Nightingale and the Rose, Rhapsody in Blue, Quintet, Capricioso.

Michel Fokine, 1880-1942. (U. S.) Les Sylphides, Carnaval, Prince Igor, Scheherazade, The Specter of the Rose.

Martha Graham, b. 1902. (U. S.) Frontier, Letter to the World, Appalachian Spring, Deaths and Entrances, Errands into the Maze.

Kurt Jooss, b. 1901. (G.) The Green Table, The Big City, Johann Strauss Tonight, The Seven Heroes, The Mirror.

Serge Lifar, b. 1905. (R.) Alexander the Great, Chota Roustavelli, Endymion, Noir et Blanc, Prometheus.

Catherine Littlefield, 1908-1951. (U. S.) Bolero, The Fairy Doll, Let the Righteous Be Glad, The Sleeping Beauty, The Snow Queen.

Eugene Loring, b. 1914. (U. S.) Billy the Kid, The Great American Goof, Harlequin for President, Prairie, Yankee Clipper.

Leonide Massine, b. 1896. (U. S.) Parade, La Boutique Fantasque, The Three-cornered Hat, Saratoga, Union Pacific, Gaite Parisienne.

Vaslav Nijinsky, 1890-1950. (R.) The Afternoon of a Faun, Jeux, The Rite of Spring, Tyl Eulenspiegel.

Ruth Page, b. 1903. (U. S.) Frankie and Johnny, The Bells, Billy Sunday, Impromptu au Bois, Oak Street Beach, The Story of the Soldier.

Jerome Robbins, b. 1918. (U. S.) Fancy Free, Interplay, Facsimile, Summer Day, Pas de Trois, The Cage, Pied Piper, Ballade, Afternoon of a Faun, Fanfare, Quartette, The Concert.

Arthur Saint-Leon, 1821-1870. (Fr.) Coppelia.

Antony Tudor, b. 1909. (Br.) Dark Elegies, Pillar of Fire, Lilac Garden, Offenbach in the Underworld, Dim Lustre, Romeo and Juliet, Undertow.

Ninette de Valois, b. 1898. (Br.) The Birthday of Oberon, Don Quixote, The Haunted Ballroom, Job, The Rake's rogress, The Wise and Foolish Virgins.

## Rulers of England and Great Britain

| Name | ENGLAND | Began | Died | Age | Rgd |
|------|---------|-------|------|-----|-----|
| | **SAXONS AND DANES** | | | | |
| Egbert..... | King of Wessex, won allegiance of all English.............. | 827 | 839 | .. | 12 |
| Ethelwulf... | Son, King of Wessex, Sussex, Kent, Essex................ | 839 | 858 | .. | 19 |
| Ethelbald... | Son of Ethelwulf, displaced father in Wessex............. | 858 | 860 | .. | 2 |
| Ethelbert... | 2nd son of Ethelwulf, united Kent and Wessex............ | 858 | 866 | .. | 8 |
| Ethelred... | 3rd son, King of Wessex, defeated Danes................. | 866 | 871 | .. | 5 |
| Alfred...... | The Great, 4th son, fought Danes, fortified London....... | 871 | 901 | 52 | 30 |
| Edward..... | The Elder, Alfred's son, united England, claimed Scotland... | 901 | 925 | 55 | 24 |
| Athelstan... | The Glorious, Edward's son, King of Mercia, Wessex...... | 925 | 940 | 45 | 15 |
| Edmund..... | 3rd son of Edward, King of Wessex, Mercia.............. | 940 | 946 | 25 | 6 |
| Edred....... | 4th son of Edward................................... | 946 | 955 | 32 | 9 |
| Edwy....... | The Fair, eldest son of Edmund, King of Wessex......... | 955 | 959 | 18 | 3 |
| Edgar...... | The Peaceful, son of Edmund, ruled all English.......... | 959 | 975 | 32 | 17 |
| Edward..... | The Martyr, son of Edgar, murdered by stepmother........ | 975 | 978 | 17 | 4 |
| Ethelred II. | The Unready, son of Edgar, married Emma of Normandy... | 978 | 1016 | 48 | 37 |
| Edmund..... | Ironside, son of Ethelred II, King of London............. | 1016 | 1016 | 27 | 0 |
| Canute..... | The Dane, gave Wessex to Edmund, married Emma........ | 1017 | 1035 | 40 | 18 |
| Harold I.... | Harefoot, natural son of Canute........................ | 1035 | 1040 | .. | 5 |
| Hardicanute | Son of Canute by Emma; Danish King.................. | 1040 | 1042 | 24 | 2 |
| Edward..... | The Confessor, son of Ethelred II (Canonized 1161)...... | 1042 | 1066 | 62 | 24 |
| Harold II... | Edward's brother-in-law, last Saxon King................ | 1066 | 1066 | 44 | 0 |
| | **HOUSE OF NORMANDY** | | | | |
| William I... | The Conqueror, defeated Harold at Hastings.............. | 1066 | 1087 | 60 | 21 |
| William II.. | Rufus, 3rd son of William I, killed by arrow............. | 1087 | 1100 | 43 | 13 |
| Henry I.... | Beauclerc, youngest son of William I.................... | 1100 | 1135 | 67 | 35 |
| | **HOUSE OF BLOIS** | | | | |
| Stephen ... | Son of Adela, 4th dau. of William I, and Count of Blois........ | 1135 | 1154 | 50 | 19 |
| | **HOUSE OF PLANTAGENET** | | | | |
| Henry II... | Son of Goeffrey Plantagenet (Angevin) by Matilda, dau. of Henry I | 1154 | 1189 | 56 | 35 |
| Richard I... | Coeur de Lion, son of Henry II, crusader................ | 1189 | 1199 | 42 | 10 |
| John....... | Lackland, son of Henry II, signed Magna Carta, 1215..... | 1199 | 1216 | 50 | 17 |
| Henry III... | Son of John, acceded at 9, under regency till 1227........ | 1216 | 1272 | 65 | 56 |
| Edward I... | Longshanks, son of Henry III.......................... | 1272 | 1307 | 68 | 35 |
| Edward II.. | Son of Edward I, deposed by Parliament, 1327............ | 1307 | 1327 | 43 | 20 |
| Edward III. | Of Windsor, son of Edward II.......................... | 1327 | 1377 | 65 | 50 |
| Richard II.. | Grandson of Edw. III, minor until 1389, deposed 1399...... | 1377 | 1400 | 34 | 22 |
| | **HOUSE OF LANCASTER** | | | | |
| Henry IV... | Son of John of Gaunt, Duke of Lancaster, son of Edw. III... | 1399 | 1413 | 47 | 13 |
| Henry V... | Son of Henry IV, victor of Agincourt.................... | 1413 | 1422 | 34 | 9 |
| Henry VI... | Son of Henry V deposed 1461, died in Tower............. | 1422 | 1471 | 49 | 39 |
| | **HOUSE OF YORK** | | | | |
| Edward IV. | Great-grandson of Edward III, son of Duke of York........ | 1461 | 1483 | 41 | 22 |
| Edward V.. | Son of Edward IV, murdered in Tower of London......... | 1483 | 1483 | 13 | 0 |
| Richard III. | Crookback, bro. of Edward IV, fell at Bosworth Field...... | 1483 | 1485 | 35 | 2 |
| | **HOUSE OF TUDOR** | | | | |
| Henry VII. | Son of Edmund Tudor, Earl of Richmond, whose father had married the widow of Henry V; descended from Edward III through his mother, Margaret Beaufort via John of Gaunt. By marriage with dau. of Edward IV he united Lancaster and York............ | 1485 | 1509 | 53 | 24 |
| Henry VIII. | Son of Henry VII *See memorable daies.*................ | 1509 | 1547 | 56 | 38 |
| Edward VI. | Son of Henry VIII, by Jane Seymour, his 3rd queen. Ruled under regents. Was forced to name Lady Jane Grey his successor. Council of State proclaimed her queen July 10, 1553. Mary Tudor won Council, was proclaimed queen July 19, 1553. Mary had Lady Jane Grey beheaded for treason, Feb., 1554............. | 1547 | 1553 | 16 | 6 |
| Mary I.... | Daughter of Henry VIII, by Catharine of Aragon.......... | 1553 | 1558 | 43 | 5 |
| Elizabeth... | Daughter of Henry VIII, by Anne Boleyn, *Designated Elizabeth I in 1952.*......................................... | 1558 | 1603 | 69 | 44 |

### GREAT BRITAIN

| | | Began | Died | Age | Rgd |
|------|---------|-------|------|-----|-----|
| | **HOUSE OF STUART** | | | | |
| James I.... | James VI of Scotland, son of Mary, Queen of Scots. *First to call himself King of Great Britain. This became official with the Act of Union, 1707.*..................................... | 1603 | 1625 | 59 | 22 |
| Charles I... | Only surviving son of James I: beheaded Jan. 30, 1649.......... | 1625 | 1649 | 48 | 24 |
| | **COMMONWEALTH, 1649-1660** | | | | |
| | *Council of State, 1649: Protectorate, 1653* | | | | |
| The Crom- | Oliver Cromwell, Lord Protector........................ | 1653 | 1658 | 59 | .. |
| wells..... | Richard Cromwell, Lord Protector, resigned May 25, 1659........ | 1658 | 1712 | 86 | .. |
| | **HOUSE OF STUART (RESTORED)** | | | | |
| Charles II... | Eldest son of Charles I, died without issue............... | 1660 | 1685 | 55 | 25 |
| James II... | Second son of Charles I. Deposed 1688. Interregnum Dec. 11, 1688, to Feb. 13, 1689................................. | 1685 | 1701 | 68 | 3 |
| William III | Son of William, Prince of Orange, by Mary, daughter of Charles I ⎫ | 1689 | 1702 | 51 | 13 |
| and Mary II | Eldest daughter of James II and wife of William III.......⎭ | | 1694 | 33 | 6 |
| Anne....... | Second daughter of James................................ | 1702 | 1714 | 49 | 12 |
| | **HOUSE OF HANOVER** | | | | |
| George I... | Son of Elector of Hanover, by Sophia, grand-dau. of James I..... | 1714 | 1727 | 67 | 13 |
| George II... | Only son of George I, married Caroline of Brandenburg...... | 1727 | 1760 | 77 | 33 |
| George III.. | Grandson of George II, married Charlotte of Mecklenburg........ | 1760 | 1820 | 81 | 59 |
| George IV.. | Eldest son of George III, Prince Regent, from Feb., 1811..... | 1820 | 1830 | 67 | 10 |
| William IV. | Third son of George III, married Adelaide of Saxe-Meiningen..... | 1830 | 1837 | 71 | 7 |
| Victoria.... | Dau. of Edward, 4th son of George III; married (1840) Prince Albert of Saxe-Coburg and Gotha, who became Prince Consort | 1837 | 1901 | 81 | 63 |
| | **HOUSE OF SAXE-COBURG AND GOTHA** | | | | |
| Edward VII. | Eldest son of Victoria, married Alexandra, Princess of Denmark... | 1901 | 1910 | 68 | 9 |
| | **HOUSE OF WINDSOR** | | | | |
| | *Name adapted July 17, 1917* | | | | |
| George V... | Second son of Edward VII, married Princess Mary of Teck...... | 1910 | 1936 | 70 | 25 |
| Edward VIII | Eldest son of George V; acceded Jan. 20, 1936, abdicated Dec. 11. | 1936 | | | 1 |
| George VI.. | Second son of George V; married Lady Elizabeth Bowes-Lyon..... | 1936 | 1952 | 56 | 15¾ |
| Elizabeth II. | Elder daughter of George VI, acceded Feb. 6, 1952............. | 1952 | .... | .. | .... |

# Rulers of France; Kings, Queens, Presidents

## CAESAR TO CHARLEMAGNE

Julius Caesar subdued the Gauls, native tribes of Gaul (France) 57 to 52 B.C. The Romans ruled 500 years. The Franks, a Teutonic tribe, reached the Somme from the East C. 250 A. D. By the 5th century the Merovingian Franks ousted the Romans. In 451 A. D., with the help of Visigoths, Burgundians and others, they defeated Attila and the Huns at Chalons-sur-Marne.

Childeric I became leader of the Merovingians 458 A. D. His son Clovis I (Chlodwig, Ludwig, Louis) crowned 481, founded the dynasty. After defeating the Alemanni (Germans) 496, he was baptized a Christian and made Paris his capital. His line ruled until Childeric III was deposed, 742.

The West Merovingians were called Neustrians, the eastern Austrasians. Pepin of Herstal (687-714) major domus, or head of the palace, of Austrasia, took over Neustria as dux (leader) of the Franks. Pepin's son, Charles, called Martel (the Hammer) defeated the Saracens at Tours-Poitiers, 732; was succeeded by his son, Pepin the Short, 741, who deposed Childeric III and ruled as king until 768.

His son, **Charlemagne**, or Charles the Great, (742-814), became king of the Franks, 768, with his brother Carloman, who died 771. He ruled France, Germany, parts of Italy, Spain, Austria, enforced Christianity. Was crowned Holy Roman Emperor by Pope Leo III in St. Peter's, Rome, Dec. 25, 800 A. D. Succeeded by son, Louis I, the Pious, 814. At death, 840, Louis left empire to sons, Lothair (Roman emperor); Pepin I (king of Aquitaine); Louis II (of Germany); Charles the Bald (France). They quarreled and by the peace of Verdun, 843, divided the empire.

| A.D. | Name and year of accession |
|---|---|
| | **THE CAROLINGIANS** |
| 840 | Charles I, the Bald, Roman Emperor, 875 |
| 877 | Louis II, the Stammerer, son |
| 879 | Louis III (died 882) and Carloman (bro.) |
| 884 | Charles II, the Fat; Roman Emperor, 881 |
| 888 | Eudes (Odo) elected by nobles. Ceded land to |
| 898 | Charles III,the Simple,son of Louis II,defeated by |
| 922 | Robert, brother of Eudes, killed in war |
| 923 | Rodolph (Raoul) Duke of Burgundy |
| 936 | Louis IV, son of Charles III |
| 954 | Lothair, son, aged 13, defeated by Capet |
| 986 | Louis V, the Sluggard, left no heirs |
| | **THE CAPETS** |
| 987 | Hugh Capet, son of Hugh the Great |
| 996 | Robert (the Wise), his son |
| 1031 | Henry I, his son, last Norman |
| 1060 | Philip I (the Fair), son, king at 14 |
| 1108 | Louis VI (the Fat), son |
| 1137 | Louis VII (the Younger), son |
| 1180 | Philip II (Augustus), son, crowned at Reims |
| 1223 | Louis VIII (the Lion), son |
| 1226 | Louis IX, son, crusader. Louis IX (1214-1270) reigned 44 years, arbitrated disputes with English King Henry III; led crusades, 1248 (captured in Egypt 1250) and 1270, when he died of plague in Tunis. Canonized 1297 as St. Louis |
| 1270 | Philip III (the Hardy), son |
| 1285 | Philip IV (the Fair), son, king at 17 |
| 1314 | Louis X (the Headstrong), son. His posthumous son, John I, lived only 7 days |
| 1316 | Philip V (the Tall), brother of Louis X |
| 1322 | Charles IV (the Fair), brother of Louis X |
| | **HOUSE OF VALOIS** |
| 1328 | Philip VI (of Valois), grandson of Philip III |
| 1350 | John II (the Good), his son, retired to England |
| 1364 | Charles V (the Wise), son |
| 1380 | Charles VI (the Beloved), son |
| 1422 | Charles VII (the Victorious), son. In 1429 Joan of Arc (Jeanne d'Arc) promised Charles to oust the English, who occupied northern France. Joan won at Orleans and Patay and had Charles crowned at Reims July 17, 1429. Joan was captured May 24, 1430, and executed May 30, 1431, at Rouen for heresy. Charles ordered her rehabilitation, effected 1455. Agnes Sorel was Charles' mistress |
| 1461 | Louis XI (the Cruel), son, civil reformer |
| 1483 | Charles VIII (the Affable), son |
| 1498 | Louis XII, great grandson of Charles V |
| 1515 | Francis I, of Angouleme, nephew, son-in-law. Francis I (1494-1547) reigned 32 years, fought 4 big wars, was patron of the arts, aided Cellini, del Sarto, Leonardo da Vinci, Rabelais. Embellished Fontainebleau |
| 1547 | Henry II, son, killed at a joust in a tournament. He was the husband of Catherine de Medici (1519-1589) and the lover of Diane de Poitiers (1499-1566). Catherine was born in Florence, daughter of Lorenzo de Medici. By her marriage to Henry II she became the mother of Francis II, Charles IX, Henry III and Queen Margaret (Reine Margot) wife of Henry IV. She persuaded Charles IX to order |

the massacre of Huguenots on St. Bartholomew, Aug. 24, 1572, the day her daughter was married to Henry of Navarre

| | |
|---|---|
| 1559 | Francis II, son of Henry II. In 1548, Mary, Queen of Scots since infancy, was betrothed when 6 to Francis, aged 4. They were married 1558. Francis died 1560, aged 16; Mary ruled Scotland, abdicated 1567. |
| 1560 | Charles IX, brother of Francis II |
| 1574 | Henry III, brother, assassinated |

### HOUSE OF BOURBON

| | |
|---|---|
| 1589 | Henry IV, of Navarre, assassinated. Henry IV made enemies when he gave tolerance to Protestants by Edict of Nantes, 1598. He was grandson of Queen Margaret of Navarre, literary patron. He married Margaret of Valois, Catherine de Medici's daughter; was divorced; in 1600 married Marie de Medicis, Regent of France, 1610-17 for son, Louis XIII, and was exiled by Richelieu |
| 1610 | Louis XIII (the Just), son. Louis XIII (1601-1643) married Anne of Austria. His ministers were Cardinals Richelieu and Mazarin |
| 1643 | Louis XIV (the Grand Monarch), son. Louis XIV, was king 72 years. He exhausted a prosperous country in wars for thrones and territory. By revoking the Edict of Nantes (1685) he caused the emigration of the Huguenots. He said: "I am the state." His mistresses were Louise de la Valiere, Madame de Montespan and Madame de Maintenon |
| 1715 | Louis XV, great grandson. Louis XV (1710-1774) married a Polish princess. Lost Canada to the English. His favorites, Mme Pompadour and Mme. DuBarry influenced policies. Noted for saying: Apres moi, le deluge. (After me, the deluge.) |
| 1774 | Louis XVI, grandson; married Marie Antoinette, dau. of Empress Maria Therese of Austria. King and queen beheaded by Revolution, 1793. Their son, called Louis XVII. died in prison, never ruled |

### FIRST REPUBLIC

| | |
|---|---|
| 1792 | National Convention of the French Revolution |
| 1795 | Directory, under Barras and others |
| 1799 | Consulate, Napoleon Bonaparte, First Consul In 1802 elected Consul for life |

### FIRST EMPIRE

| | |
|---|---|
| 1804 | Napoleon I, Emperor. Josephine (de Beauharnais) Empress, 1804-09; Marie Louise, Empress, 1810-1814. Her son, Francois (1811-1832) titular King of Rome, later Duke de Reichstadt and "Napoleon II," never ruled. Napoleon abdicated 1814, died 1821. *See Memorable Dates.* |

### BOURBONS RESTORED

| | |
|---|---|
| 1814 | Louis XVIII King: brother of Louis XVI |
| 1824 | Charles X, brother: reactionary, deposed by the July Revolution, 1830 |

### HOUSE OF ORLEANS

| | |
|---|---|
| 1830 | Louis Philippe, the Citizen King |

### SECOND REPUBLIC

| | |
|---|---|
| 1848 | Louis Napoleon, President, nephew of Napoleon I. He became: |

### SECOND EMPIRE

| | |
|---|---|
| 1852 | Napoleon III, Emperor. Eugenie (de Montijo) Empress. Lost Franco-Prussian war, deposed 1870. Son, Prince Imperial (1856-79), died in Zulu War. Eugenie died 1920 |

### THIRD REPUBLIC—PRESIDENTS

| | |
|---|---|
| 1871 | Thiers, Louis Adolphe (1797-1877), historian |
| 1873 | MacMahon, Marshal Patrice M. (1808-1893) |
| 1879 | Grevy, Paul J. (1807-1891), resigned |
| 1887 | Sadi-Carnot, M. (1837-1894), assassinated |
| 1894 | Casimir-Perier, Jean P. P. (1847-1907), resigned |
| 1895 | Faure, Francois Felix (1841-1899) |
| 1899 | Loubet, Emile (1838-1929) |
| 1906 | Fallieres, Armand (1841-1931) |
| 1913 | Poincare, Raymond (1860-1934) |
| 1920 | Deschanel, Paul (1856-1922) resigned |
| 1920 | Millerand, Alexandre (1859-1943) resigned |
| 1924 | Doumergue, Gaston (1863-1937) |
| 1931 | Doumer, Paul (1857-1932) assassinated |
| 1932 | Lebrun, Albert (1871-1950) resigned 1940. |
| | **Vichy** govt. under German armistice: Henry Philippe Petain (1865-1951) Chief of State, 1940-1944 |
| | **Provisional** govt., after liberation: Chas. de Gaulle (1890- ) Oct., 1944-Jan. 21, 1946; Felix Gouin (1884- ) Jan. 23, 1946; Georges Bidault (1899- ) June 24, 1946. |

### FOURTH REPUBLIC—PRESIDENTS

| | |
|---|---|
| 1947 | Auriol, Vincent (1884-1966) |
| 1954 | Coty, Rene (1883-1962) |

### FIFTH REPUBLIC—PRESIDENT

| | |
|---|---|
| 1958 | De Gaulle, Charles Andre M. J., born Nov. 22 1890; elected Dec. 21, 1958, reelected Dec. 19, 1965. |

# Rulers of Middle Europe; Rise and Fall of Dynasties

## CAROLINGIAN DYNASTY

Charles the Great, or Charlemagne, ruled France, Italy and Middle Europe; established Ostmark (later Austria); crowned Roman emperor by pope in Rome, 800 A.D. Died, 814.

Louis I (Ludwig) the Pious, son; crowned by Charlemagne 813, d. 840.

Louis the German, son, succeeded to East Francia (Germany) 843-876.

Charles the Fat, son, inherited East Francia and West Francia (France) 876, reunited empire, crowned emperor by pope, 881, deposed, 887.

Arnulf, nephew, 887-899. Partition of empire.

Louis the Child, 900-911, last direct descendant of Charlemagne.

Conrad I, duke of Franconia, first elected German king, 911-918, founded House of Franconia.

## SAXON DYNASTY; FIRST REICH

Henry I, the Fowler, duke of Saxony, 919-936.

Otto I, the Great, 936-973, son; crowned Holy Roman Emperor by pope, 962.

Otto II, 973-983, son; failed to oust Greeks and Arabs from Sicily.

Otto III, 983-1002, son. Crowned emperor at 16.

Henry II, duke of Bavaria, 1002-1024, great-grandson of Henry the Fowler.

## HOUSE OF FRANCONIA

Conrad II, 1024-1039, son-in-law of Otto I.

Henry III, 1039-1056, son; deposed 3 popes; annexed Burgundy.

Henry IV, 1056-1106, son; regency by his mother, Agnes of Poitou. Banned by Pope Gregory VII, he did penance at Canossa.

Henry V, 1106-1125, son; last of Salic House.

Lothair, duke of Saxony, 1125-1137. Crowned emperor in Rome, 1134.

## HOUSE OF HOHENSTAUFEN

Conrad III, duke of Suabia, 1138-1152. In 2nd Crusade.

Frederick I, Barbarossa, 1152-1190; son of Conrad's brother; in 3rd Crusade.

Henry VI, 1190-1196, took Lower Italy from Normans. Son became king of Sicily.

Philipp of Suabia, 1198-1208, son of Frederick I.

Otto IV, of House of Welf, 1198-1215; deposed.

Frederick II, 1215-1250, son of Henry VI; king of Sicily; crowned king of Jerusalem; in 5th Crusade.

Conrad IV, 1250-1254, son, lost Lower Italy to Charles of Anjou.

Conradin, son, king of Jerusalem and Sicily, was beheaded. Last Hohenstaufen.

Interregnum, 1250-1273. Rose of the Electors.

## TRANSITION

Rudolph of Hapsburg, 1273-1291, defeated King Ottocar II of Bohemia. Bequeathed duchy of Austria to eldest son, Albert.

Adolphus, count of Nassau, 1291-1298, killed in war with Albert of Austria.

Albert I, German king, 1298-1308.

Henry VII, of Luxemburg, 1308-1313, crowned emperor in Rome. Seized Bohemia, 1310.

Louis IV of Bavaria (Wittelsbach), 1314-1347 Also elected was Frederick of Austria, 1314-1330 (Hapsburg). Abolition of papal sanction for election of Holy Roman Emperor.

Charles IV, of Luxemburg, 1347-1378, grandson of Henry VII, German emperor and king of Bohemia, Lombardy, Burgundy; took Mark of Brandenburg.

Wenceslaus, 1378-1400, deposed.

Rupert, Duke of Palatine, 1400-1410.

## HUNGARY

Stephen I, house of Arpad, 907-1038. Crowned king by Pope Silvester II, 1001 A.D., converted Magyars. After several centuries of feuds Charles Robert of Anjou became Charles I, 1308-1342.

Louis I, the Great, son, 1342-1382, joint ruler of Poland with Casimir III, 1370. Defeated Turks.

Mary, daughter, 1385-1395, ruled with husband, Sigismund of Luxemburg, 1387-1437, also king of Bohemia. As bro. of Wenceslaus he succeeded Rupert as Holy Roman Emperor, 1410.

Albert II, 1438-1439, son-in-law of Sigismund; also Roman emperor. *See under Hapsburg.*

Ulaszlo I of Poland, died in battle, 1444.

Ladislaus V, child. John Hunyadi (Hunyadi Janos) guardian, fought Turks, Czechs; died 1456.

Matthias I (Corvinus) son of Hunyadi, 1458-1490. Shared rule of Bohemia, captured Vienna, 1485, annexed Austria, Styria, Carinthia.

Ulaszlo II (King of Bohemia) 1490-1516.

Louis II, son, aged 10. 1516-1526. Wars with Soliman, Turk. In 1527 Hungary was split between Ferdinand I, Archduke of Austria, bro.-in-law of Louis II, and John Zapolya, of Transylvania. After Turkish invasion, 1547, Hungary was split between Ferdinand, Prince John Sigismund (Transylvania) and the Turks.

## HOUSE OF HAPSBURG

Albert V of Austria, Hapsburg, crowned king of Hungary, Jan., 1438, Roman emperor, March, 1438, as Albert II; died 1439.

Frederick III, cousin, 1430-1493. Fought Turks.

Maximilian I, son, 1493-1519. Assumed title of Holy Roman emperor (German), 1508.

Charles V, grandson, 1519-1556. King of Spain with mother co-regent; crowned Roman emperor at Aix 1520. Confronted Luther at Worms; attempted church reform and religious conciliation. Abdicated 1556.

Ferdinand I, king of Bohemia, 1526, of Hungary, 1527; disputed. German king, 1531. Crowned Roman emperor on abdication of Charles V. 1556.

Maximilian II, son, 1564-1576; Rudolph II, son, 1576-1612.

Matthias, brother, 1612-1619, king of Bohemia and Hungary.

Ferdinand II, of Styria, king of Bohemia, 1617, of Hungary, 1618, Roman emperor, 1619. Bohemian Protestants deposed him, elected Frederick V of Palatine, starting Thirty Years War.

Ferdinand III, son, king of Hungary, 1625, Bohemia, 1627, Roman emperor, 1637. Peace of Westphalia, 1648, ended war. Leopold I, 1658-1705; Joseph I, 1705-1711; Charles VI, 1711-1740.

Maria Theresa, daughter, 1740-1780, Archduchess of Austria, queen of Hungary; ousted pretender, Charles VII, crowned 1742; in 1745 obtained election of her husband Francis I as Roman emperor and co-regent (d.1765). Fought Seven Years' War with Frederick II (the Great) of Prussia. Mother of Marie Antoinette, Queen of France.

Joseph II, son, 1765-1790, Roman emperor, reformer; powers restricted by Empress Maria Theresa until her death, 1780. First partition of Poland. Leopold II, 1790-1792.

Francis II, 1792-1835. Fought Napoleon. Proclaimed first hereditary emperor of Austria, 1806. Forced to abdicate as Roman emperor, 1806, last use of title. Ferdinand I, son, 1835-1848, abdicated during revolution.

## AUSTRO-HUNGARIAN MONARCHY

Francis Joseph I, nephew, 1848-1916, emperor of Austria, king of Hungary. Dual monarchy of Austria-Hungary formed, 1867. After assassination of heir, Archduke Francis Ferdinand, June 28, 1914, Austrian diplomacy precipitated World War I.

Charles I, grandnephew, 1916-1918, last emperor of Austria and king of Hungary. Abdicated Nov. 11-13, 1918, died 1922.

## RULERS OF PRUSSIA

Nucleus of Prussia was the Mark of Brandenburg. First margrave was Albert the Bear (Albrecht), 1134-1170. First Hohenzollern margrave was Frederick, burggrave of Nuremberg, 1415-1440.

Frederick William, 1640-1688, the Great Elector. Son, Frederick III, 1688-1713, was crowned Frederick I of Prussia, 1701.

Frederick II. the Great, 1740-1786, annexed Silesia, part of Austria.

Frederick William II, nephew, 1786-1797.

Frederick William III, 1797-1840. Napoleonic wars. Queen Louise.

Frederick William IV, 1840-1861. Uprising of 1848 and first parliament and constitution.

## SECOND AND THIRD REICH

William I, 1861-1888, brother. Annexation of Schleswig and Hanover; Franco-Prussian war, 1870-71, proclamation of German Reich, Jan. 18, 1871, at Versailles; William, German emperor (Deutscher Kaiser); Bismarck, chancellor.

Frederick III, son, 1888.

William II, son, 1888-1918. Led Germany in World War I, abdicated as German emperor and king of Prussia, Nov. 9, 1918. Died in exile in Netherlands June 4, 1941. Minor rulers of Bavaria, Saxony, Wurttemberg also abdicated.

Germany proclaimed a republic at Weimar, July 1, 1919. Presidents: Frederick Ebert, 1919-1925, Paul von Hindenburg-Beneckendorff, 1925, reelected 1932, d. Aug. 2, 1934. Adolf Hitler, chancellor, chosen successor as Leader-Chancellor (Fuehrer & Reichskanzler) of Third Reich. Annexed Austria, March, 1938. Precipitated World War II, 1939-1945. Reported suicide May 1, 1945.

# Roman Rulers

From Romulus to the end of the Empire in the West. Rulers of the Roman Empire in the East sat in Constantinople, and for a brief period in Nicaea, until the capture of Constantinople by the Turks in 1453, when it was succeeded by the Ottoman Empire.

| B.C. | Name | A.D. | Name | A.D. | Name |
|---|---|---|---|---|---|
| | **The Kingdom** | 81 | Domitianus | 314 | Constantinus I and Licinius |
| 753 | Romulus (Quirinus) | 96 | Nerva | 324 | Constantinus I (the Great) |
| 716 | Numa Pompilius | 98 | Trajanus | 337 | Constantinus II, Constans I, |
| 673 | Tullus Hostilius | 117 | Hadrianus | | Constantius II |
| 640 | Ancus Marcius | 138 | Antoninus Pius | 340 | Constantius II and Constans I |
| 616 | L. Tarquinius Priscus | 161 | Marcus Aurelius and Lucius | 350 | Constantius II |
| 578 | Servius Tullius | | Verus | 360 | Julianus II (the Apostate) |
| 534 | L. Tarquinius Superbus | 169 | Marcus Aurelius (alone) | 363 | Jovianus |
| | **The Republic** | 180 | Commodus | | |
| 509 | Consulate established | 193 | Pertinax; Jullanus I | | **West (Rome) and East** |
| 509 | Quaestorship instituted | 193 | Septimius Severus | | **(Constantinople)** |
| 498 | Dictatorship introduced | 211 | Caracalla and Geta | 364 | Valentinianus I (West) and |
| 494 | Plebeian Tribunate created | 212 | Caracalla (alone) | | Valens (East) |
| 494 | Plebeian Aedileship created | 217 | Macrinus | 367 | ValentinianusIwithGratianus |
| 444 | Consular Tribunate organized | 218 | Elagabalus (Heliogabalus) | | (West) and Valens (East) |
| 435 | Censorship instituted | 222 | Alexander Severus | 375 | Gratianus with Valentinianus |
| 366 | Praetorship established | 235 | Maximinus I (the Thracian) | | II (West) and Valens (East) |
| 366 | Curule Aedileship created | 238 | Gordianus I and Gordianus | 378 | Gratianus with Valentinianus |
| 362 | Military Tribunate elective | | II; Pupienus and Balbinus | | II (W.), Theodosius I (E.) |
| 326 | Proconsulate introduced | 238 | Gordianus III | 383 | Valentinianus II (West) and |
| 311 | Naval Duumvirate elective | 244 | Philippus (the Arabian) | | Theodosius I (East) |
| 217 | Dictatorship of Fabius | 249 | Decius | 394 | Theodosius I (the Great) |
| | Maximus | 251 | Gallus and Volusianus | 395 | Honorius (West) and Arca- |
| 133 | Tribunate of Tiberius | 253 | Aemilianus | | dius (East) |
| | Gracchus | 253 | Valerianus and Gallienus | 408 | Honorius (West) and Theo- |
| 123 | Tribunate of Gaius Gracchus | 258 | Gallienus (alone) | | dosius II (East) |
| 82 | Dictatorship of Sulla | 268 | Claudius II (the Goth) | 423 | Valentinianus III (West) and |
| 60 | First Triumvirate formed | 270 | Quintillus | | Theodosius II (East) and |
| | (Caesar,Pompelius,Crassus) | 270 | Aurelianus | 450 | Valentinianus III (West) and |
| 46 | Dictatorship of Caesar | 275 | Tacitus | | Marcianus (East) |
| 43 | Second Triumvirate formed | 276 | Florianus | 455 | Maximus (West); Avitus |
| | (Octavianus, Antonius, | 276 | Probus | | (West); Marcianus (East) |
| | Lepidus) | 282 | Carus | 456 | Avitus (W.), Marcianus (E.) |
| | **The Empire** | 283 | Carinus and Numerianus | 457 | Majorianus (W.), Leo I (E.) |
| 27 | Augustus (Gaius Julius | 284 | Diocletianus | 461 | Severus II (W.), Leo I (E.) |
| | Caesar Octavianus) | 286 | Diocletianus and Maximianus | 467 | Anthemius (W.), Leo I (E.) |
| | | 305 | Galerius and Constantius I | 472 | Olybrius (W.), Leo I (E.) |
| **A.D.** | | 306 | Galerius, Maximinus II, | 473 | Glycerius (W.), Leo I (E.) |
| 14 | Tiberius I | | Severus I | 474 | Julius Nepos (W.), Leo II (E.) |
| 37 | Gaius (Caligula) | 307 | Galerius, Maximinus II, | 475 | Romulus Augustulus (West) |
| 41 | Claudius I | | Constantinus I, Licinius, | | and Zeno (East) |
| 54 | Nero | | Maxentius | 476 | End of Empire in West; Odo- |
| 68 | Galba | 311 | Maximinus II, Constantinus | | vacar, King, drops title of |
| 69 | Galba; Otho; Vitellius | | I, Licinius, Maxentius | | Emperor; murdered by |
| 69 | Vespasianus | 312 | Maximinus II, Constantinus | | King Theodoric of Ostro- |
| 79 | Titus | | I, Licinius | | goths 493 A. D. |

# Rulers of Modern Italy

After the fall of Napoleon in 1814 the Congress of Vienna, 1815, restored Italy as a political patchwork, comprising the Kingdom of Naples & Sicily, the Papal States, and smaller units. Piedmont and Genoa were awarded to Sardinia, ruled by King Victor Emmanuel I of Savoy.

United Italy emerged under the leadership of Camillo, Count di Cavour, (1810-1861) Sardinian prime minister. Agitation was led by Giuseppe Mazzini (1805-1872) and Giuseppe Garibaldi (1807-1882), soldier. Victor Emmanuel I abdicated 1821. After a brief regency for a brother, Charles Albert was King 1831-1849, abdicating when defeated by the Austrians at Novara. Succeeded by Victor Emmanuel II (1820-1878).

In 1859 France forced Austria to cede Lombardy to Sardinia, which gave rights to Savoy and Nice to France. In 1860 Garibaldi led 1,000 volunteers in a spectacular campaign, took Sicily and expelled the King of Naples. In 1860 the House of Savoy annexed Tuscany, Parma, Modena, Romagna, the Two Sicilies, the Marches and Umbria. Victor Emmanuel assumed the title of King of

Italy at Turin Mar. 17, 1861. In 1866 he joined Prussia and Austria in the Triple Alliance and received Venetia from Austria. On Sept. 20, 1870, his troops under Gen. Raffaele Cardorna entered Rome and took over the Papal States, ending the temporal power of the Roman Catholic Church.

Succession. Humbert I, 1878, assassinated 1900; Victor Emmanuel III, 1900, abdicated 1946, died 1947; Humbert II, 1946, ruled a month. In 1921 Benito Mussolini (1883-1945) formed the Fascist party and became prime minister Oct. 31, 1922. He made the King Emperor of Ethiopia, 1937; entered World War II as ally of Hitler. He was deposed July 25, 1943.

At a plebiscite June 2, 1946, Italy voted for a republic. Premier Alcide de Gasperi became Chief of State June 13, 1946. On June 28, 1946, the Constituent Assembly elected Enrico de Nicola, Liberal, Provisional President of the Republic of Italy. Luigi Einaudi was elected President May 11, 1948. Giovanni Gronchi was elected Apr. 29, 1955, inaugurated May 11, 1955. Antonio Segni elected May 6, 1962, Giuseppe Saragat Dec. 28, 1964.

# Rulers of Scotland

The Romans gave the name of Caledonia to present-day Scotland and called the people Caledonians. The Scots, a Celtic race that spoke Gaelic, came from Ireland, then called Scotia. Kenneth I (S. C. MacAlpin) was the first Scot to rule both Scots and Picts, 843 A. D.

Duncan I was the first general ruler, 1034. Macbeth seized the kingdom 1040, was slain by Duncan's son, Malcolm Canmore (Malcolm III), 1058.

Malcolm married Margaret, English princess who had fled from the Normans. Queen Margaret introduced English language and English monastic customs. She was canonized. Her son Edgar, 1097, moved the court to Edinburgh. His brothers Alexander I and David I succeeded. Malcolm IV, grandson of David I, 1153, was followed by his brother, William the Lion, 1165, whose son was Alexander II, 1214. The latter's son, Alexander III, defeated the Norse and regained the Hebrides. When he died, 1286, his granddaughter, Margaret, child of Eric of Norway and grandniece of Edward I of England, known as the Maid of Norway, was chosen ruler, but died on the way, 1290.

John Baliol, 1292-1296. [Interregnum, 10 years].

Robert Bruce (The Bruce), 1306-1329, victor at Bannockburn, 1314.

Robert II, 1316-1390, grandson of Robert Bruce, son of Walter, the Steward of Scotland, was called The Steward, first of the so-called Stuart line.

Robert III, son of Robert II, 1390-1406.

James I, son of Robert III, 1406-1437.

James II, son of James I, 1437-1460.

James III, 1460-1488, eldest son of James II.

James IV, 1488-1513, eldest son of James III.

James V, 1513-1542, eldest son of James IV.

Mary, daughter, born 1542, became queen when 1 week old; was crowned 1543. Married, 1548, Francis, son of Henry II of France, who became king 1559, died 1560. Mary ruled Scots 1561 until abdication, 1567. She also married (2) Henry Stewart, Lord Darnley, and (3) James, Earl of Bothwell. Imprisoned by Elizabeth I; beheaded 1587.

James VI, 1567-1625, son of Mary and Lord Darnley, became King of England on death of Elizabeth in 1603. Although the thrones were thus united, the legislative union of Scotland and England was not effected until the act of Union, May 1, 1707.

# Rulers of Denmark, Sweden, Norway

## DENMARK

Earliest rulers invaded Britain; King Canute, who ruled in London 1017-1035, was most famous. The Valdemars furnished kings until the 15th century. In 1282 the Danes won the first national assembly, Danehof, from King Erik.

Most redoubtable medieval character was Margaret, daughter of Valdemar IV, born 1353, married at 10 to King Haakon VI of Norway. In 1375 she had her infant son Olaf made king of Denmark. After his death, 1387, she was regent of Denmark and Norway. In 1388 Sweden accepted her as sovereign. In 1389 she made her grand-nephew, Duke Erik of Pomerania, titular king of Denmark, Sweden and Norway, with herself as regent. In 1397 she effected the Union of Kalmar of the three kingdoms and had Erik crowned. In 1439 the three kingdoms deposed him and elected Christopher of Bavaria king (Christopher III). On his death, 1448, the union broke up.

Succeeding rulers were unable to enforce their claims as rulers of Sweden until 1520, when Christian II conquered Sweden. He was thrown out 1522, and in 1523 Gustavus Vasa united Sweden. Denmark continued to dominate Norway until the Napoleonic wars, when Frederick VI joined the Napoleonic cause after Britain had destroyed the Danish fleet (1807). In 1814 he was forced to cede Norway to Sweden and Helgoland to Britain, receiving Lauenburg. Successors: 1839—Christian VIII; 1848—Frederick VII; 1863—Christian IX; 1906—Frederick VIII; 1912—Christian X; 1947—Frederick IX.

## SWEDEN

Early kings ruled at Uppsala, but did not dominate the country. Sverker (1134-1156) united the Swedes and Goths. In 1435 Sweden obtained the Riksdag, or parliament. After the Union of Kalmar, 1379, the Danes either ruled or harried the country until Christian II of Denmark conquered it anew. 1520. This led to a rising under Gustavus Vasa, who ruled Sweden 1523-1560, and established an independent kingdom. Charles IX (1594-1611, crowned 1607) conquered Moscow. Gustavus II Adolphus (1611-1633) was called the Great. Later rulers: 1633—Christina; 1654—Charles X; 1660—Charles XI; 1697—Charles XII (invader of Russia and Poland, defeated at Poltava, June 28, 1709); 1718—His sister, Unrika Eleanora, elected queen; 1720—Her husband, Frederick I (of Hesse); 1751—Aldolphus Frederick; 1771—Gustavus III; 1792—Gustavus IV; 1809—Charles XIII. (Union with Norway began, 1814). 1818—Charles XIV. He was Jean Bernadotte, Napoleon's Prince of Ponte Corvo, elected 1810 to succeed Charles XIII. He founded the present dynasty. 1844—Oscar I; 1859—Charles XV; 1872—Oscar II; 1907—Gustavus V; 1950—Gustavus VI Adolf.

## NORWAY

Overcoming many rivals, Harald Haarfager (872-930) conquered Norway, Orkneys and Shetlands. Olaf, great-grandson (995-1000) brought Christianity into Norway, Iceland, Greenland. In 1035 Magnus the Good also became king of Denmark. Haakon V (1299-1319) had married his daughter to Erik of Sweden. Their son, Magnus, became ruler of Norway and Sweden at 6. His son, Haakon VI, married Margaret of Denmark; their son Olaf became king of Norway and Denmark, followed by Margaret's regency and the Union of Kalmar, 1397.

In 1450 Norway became subservient to Denmark. Christian IV (1588-1648) founded Christiania, now Oslo. After Napoleonic wars, when Denmark ceded Norway to Sweden, a strong nationalist movement forced recognition of Norway as an independent kingdom united with Sweden under the Swedish kings, 1814-1905. In 1905 the union was dissolved and Prince Carl of Denmark became Haakon VII. He died Sept. 21, 1957, aged 85; succeeded by son, Olav V, b. July 2, 1903.

# Rulers of the Netherlands and Belgium

## THE NETHERLANDS (HOLLAND)

William Frederick, Prince of Orange, led a revolt against French rule, 1813, and was crowned King of the Netherlands, 1815. Belgium seceded Oct. 4, 1830, after a revolt, and formed a separate government. The change was ratified by the two kingdoms by treaty Apr. 19, 1839.

(1840) William II; (1849) William III; (1890) Wilhelmina (daughter of William III and his second wife Princess Emma of Waldeck); Wilhelmina abdicated Sept. 4, 1948, in favor of daughter Juliana, 39.

## BELGIUM

A national congress elected Prince Leopold of Saxe-Coburg King; he took the throne July 21, 1831, as Leopold I. (1865) Leopold II; (1909) Albert I, nephew of Leopold II; (1934) Leopold III, son of Albert; (1944) Prince Charles, Regent. Leopold returned, 1950, yielded powers to son Baudouin, Prince Royal, Aug. 6, 1950, abdicated July 16, 1951. Baudouin I took throne July 17, 1951.

*For political history prior to 1830 see articles on the Netherlands and Belgium.*

# Rulers of Russia; Premiers of the U. S. S. R.

First ruler to consolidate Slav tribes was Rurik, leader of the Russ, who established himself at Novgorod A. D. 862. He and his immediate successors had Scandinavian affiliations. They moved to Kiev after 972 A. D. and ruled as Dukes of Kiev. In 988 Vladimir was converted and adopted the Byzantine Greek service, later modified by Slav influences. Important as organizer and lawgiver was Yaroslav, 1018-1054, whose daughters married kings of Norway, Hungary and France. His grandson, Vladimir II (Monomachus) 1113-1125), was progenitor of several rulers, but in 1169 Andrew Bogolubski overthrew Kiev and began the line known as **Grand Dukes of Vladimir.**

Of the Grand Dukes of Vladimir Alexander Nevsky, 1245-1263, had a son, Daniel, first to be called **Duke of Muscovy** (Moscow) who ruled 1294-1303. His successors became **Grand Dukes of Muscovy.** After Demetrius III, Donskoi, in 1380 defeated the Tartars, they also became Grand Dukes of All Russia. Independence of the Tartars and considerable territorial expansion was achieved under Ivan III, 1462-1505.

**Czars of Muscovy**—Ivan III was referred to in church ritual as Czar. He married Sofia, niece of the last Byzantine emperor. His successor, Basil, died in 1533 when Basil's "son, Ivan, was only 3. He became Ivan IV, "the Terrible," crowned 1547 as Czar of all the Russias, ruled till 1584. Under the weak rule of his son, Theodore, Boris Godunov had control. The dynasty died, and after years of tribal strife and intervention by Polish and Swedish armies, the Russians united under 17-year-old Michael Romanov, distantly related to the first wife of Ivan IV. He ruled 1613-1645 and established the Romanov line. Fourth ruler after Michael was Peter I.

**Czars, or Emperors of Russia (Romanovs)**—Peter I, 1682-1725, known as Peter the Great, took title of Emperor in 1721. His successors and dates of accession were: Catherine, his widow, 1725, Peter II, his grandson, 1727, d. 1730; Anne, Duchess of Courland, 1730, daughter of Peter the Great's brother, Czar Ivan; Ivan VI, 1740-1741, great grandson of Ivan V, child, kept in prison and murdered 1764; Elizabeth, daughter of Peter I, 1741; Peter III, grandson of Peter I, 1761, deposed 1762 for his consort, Catherine II, former princess of Anhalt Zerbst (German) who is known as Catherine the Great, 1762-1796; Paul I, her son, 1796, killed 1801. Alexander I, son of Paul, 1801-1825, defeated Napoleon; Nicholas I, his brother, 1825; Alexander II, son of Nicholas, 1855, assassinated 1881 by terrorists; Alexander III, son, 1881-1894.

Nicholas II, son, 1894-1917, last Czar of Russia, was forced to abdicate by the Revolution that followed defeat by Germany. The Czar, the Czarina, the Czarevitch (Crown Prince) and the Czar's 4 daughters were murdered by the Bolshevists in Ekaterinburg, July 17, 1918.

**Provisional Government**—Prince Georgi Lvov and Alexander Kerensky, premiers, 1917.

## UNION OF SOVIET SOCIALIST REPUBLICS

Bolshevist Revolution, Nov. 7, 1917, displaced Kerensky; Council of People's Commissars formed, Nicolai Lenin, premier. Lenin died Jan. 21, 1924. Alexei Rykov (executed 1938) and V. M. Molotov held the office, but actual ruler was Joseph Stalin (Joseph Vissarionovich Djugashvili), general secretary of the Central Committee of the Communist Party. Stalin became president of the Council of Ministers (premier) May 7, 1941, and died Mar. 5, 1953. Succeeded by Georgi M. Malenkov, as head of the Council and premier and Nikita S. Khrushchev, first secretary of the Central Committee. Malenkov resigned Feb. 8, 1955, became deputy premier, was dropped July 3, 1957. Marshal Nikolai A. Bulganin became premier. Marshal Georgi K. Zhukov became minister of defense, was dropped Nov. 1, 1957. Bulganin was demoted and Khrushchev became premier Mar. 27, 1958. Khrushchev was ousted Dec. 14-15, 1964, replaced by Leonid I. Brezhnev as first secretary of the party and by Aleksei N. Kosygin as premier.

## Rulers of Modern Spain

From 8th to 11th centuries Spain was dominated by the Moors (Arabs and Berbers). The Christian reconquest established small competing kingdoms of the Asturias, Aragon, Castile, Catalonia, Leon, Navarre and Valencia. In 1474 Isabella (Isabel) b. 1451, became queen of Castile & Leon. Her husband, Ferdinand, b. 1452, inherited Aragon, 1474, with Catalonia, Valencia and the Balearic Islands, became Ferdinand V of Castile. By Isabella's request Pope Sixtus IV established the Inquisition, 1478. Last Moorish kingdom, Granada, fell 1492. Columbus opened New World of colonies, 1492. Isabella died 1504, succeeded by her daughter, Juana "the Mad," but Ferdinand ruled until his death 1516.

Charles I, b. 1500, son of Juana and grandson of Ferdinand & Isabella and of Maximilian I of Hapsburg; succeeded latter as Holy Roman Emperor, Charles V, 1520. Abdicated 1556. Philip II, son, 1556-1598, inherited only Spanish throne; conquered Portugal, fought Turks, persecuted non-Catholics, sent Armada vs. England. Was briefly married to Mary I of England, 1554-1558. Succession: Philip III, 1598-1621; Philip IV, 1621-1665; Charles II, 1665-1700, left Spain to Philip of Anjou, grandson of Louis XIV, who as Philip V, 1700-1746, founded Bourbon dynasty. Ferdinand IV, 1746-1759; Charles III, 1759-1788; Charles IV, 1788-1808, abdicated.

Napoleon now dominated politics and made his brother Joseph King of Spain but the Spanish ousted him finally in 1813. Ferdinand VII, 1814-1833, lost American colonies; succeeded by daughter, Isabella II, aged 3, with wife Maria Christina of Naples regent until 1843. Isabella deposed by revolution, 1868. Prince Amadeo of Savoy, 1870-1873. First republic, 1873-1874. Alphonso XII 1875-1885. His posthumous son was Alphonso XIII, with his mother, Queen Maria Christina regent; Spanish-American war, Spain lost Cuba, gave up Puerto Rico, Philippines, Sulu Isl., Marianas. Alphonso took throne 1902, aged 16, married British Princess Victoria Eugenia of Battenberg. The dictatorship of Primo de Rivera, 1923-30, precipitated the revolution of 1931. Alphonso agreed to leave without formal abdication. The monarchy was abolished and the second republic established, with strong socialist backing. Presidents were Niceto Alcala Zamora, to 1936, when Manuel Anzana was chosen.

In July, 1936, the army in Morocco revolted against the government and General Francisco Franco led the troops into Spain. The revolution succeeded by February, 1939, when Anzana resigned. Franco became chief of state, with provisions that if he is incapacitated the Regency Council by two-thirds vote may propose a king to the Cortes, which must have a two-thirds majority to elect him.

Alphonso XIII died in Rome Feb. 28, 1941, aged 54. His property and citizenship had been restored.

A succession law theoretically restoring the monarchy was approved in a 1947 referendum. A new Constitution, approved by referendum Dec. 14, 1966, affirmed Spain's status as a monarchy under a king or a regent. Pretender to the throne, should the monarchy actually be restored, was Don Juan de Borbon y Battenberg, 3rd son of Alphonso XIII. Also favored above other claimants was Don Juan's son, Prince Juan Carlos.

## Leaders in the South American Wars of Liberation

Simon Bolivar (1783-1830), Jose Francisco de San Martin (1783-1850) and Francisco Antonio Gabriel Miranda (1750-1816) are among the heroes of the early 19th century struggles of South American nations to free themselves from Spain. All three, and their contemporaries, operated in periods of intense factional strife, during which soldiers and civilians suffered.

Miranda, a Venezuelan, who had served with the French in the American Revolution and commanded parts of the French Revolutionary armies in the Netherlands, attempted to start a revolt in Venezuela in 1806 and failed. In 1810, with British and American backing, he returned and was briefly a dictator, until the British withdrew their support. In 1812 he was overcome by the royalists in Venezuela and taken prisoner, dying in a Spanish prison in 1816.

San Martin was born in Argentina and during 1789-1811 served in campaigns of the Spanish armies in Europe and Africa. He first joined the independence movement in Argentina in 1812 and then in 1817 invaded Chile with 4,000 men over the high mountain passes. Here he and General Bernardo O'Higgins (1778-1842) defeated the Spaniards at Chacabuco, 1817, and O'Higgins was named Liberator and became first dictator of Chile, 1817-1823. In 1821 San Martin occupied Lima and Callao, Peru, and became Protector of Peru.

Bolivar, the greatest leader of South American liberation from Spain, was born in Venezuela, the son of an aristocratic family. His organizing and administrative abilities were superior and he foresaw many of the political difficulties of the future. He first served under Miranda in 1812 and in 1813 captured Caracas, where he was named Liberator. Forced out next year by civil strife, he led a campaign that captured Bogota in 1814. In 1817 he was again in control of Venezuela and was named dictator. He organized Nueva Granada with the help of General Francisco de Paula Santander (1792-1840). By joining Nueva Granada, Venezuela and the present terrain of Panama and Ecuador, the republic of Colombia was formed with Bolivar president. After numerous setbacks he decisively defeated the Spaniards in the second battle of Carabobo, Venezuela, June 24, 1821.

In May, 1822, Gen. Antonio Jose de Sucre, Bolivar's trusted lieutenant, took Quito, Bolivar went to Guayaquil to confer with San Martin, who resigned as Protector of Peru and withdrew from politics. With a new army of Colombians and Peruvians Bolivar defeated the Spaniards in a saber battle at Juin in 1824 and cleared Peru.

De Sucre organized Charcas (Upper Peru) as Republica Bolivar (now Bolivia) and acted as president in place of Bolivar, who wrote its constitution. Sucre defeated the Spanish faction of Peru at Ayacucho, Dec. 19, 1824.

Continued civil strife finally caused the Colombian federation to break apart. Santander turned against Bolivar, but the latter defeated him and banished him. In 1828 Bolivar gave up the presidency he had held precariously for 14 years. He became ill from tuberculosis and died Dec. 17, 1830. He was honored as the great liberator and is buried in the national pantheon in Caracas.

# British

## POETS, DRAMATISTS, ESSAYISTS, HISTORIANS, NOVELISTS

| Born | Died | Name | Born | Died | Name | Born | Died | Name |
|---|---|---|---|---|---|---|---|---|
| 1672 | 1719 | Addison, Joseph | 1563 | 1631 | Drayton, Michael | 1828 | 1909 | Meredith, George |
| 1805 | 1882 | Ainsworth, W. H. | 1631 | 1700 | Dryden, John | 1806 | 1873 | Mill, John Stuart |
| 1721 | 1770 | Akenside, Mark | 1834 | 1896 | Du Maurier, Geo. L. | 1882 | 1956 | Milne. A. A. |
| 1904 | 1966 | Allingham, Margery | 1819 | 1880 | Eliot, George | 1608 | 1674 | Milton, John |
| 1832 | 1904 | Arnold, Edwin | 1888 | 1965 | Eliot, T. S. | 1779 | 1852 | Moore, Thomas |
| 1822 | 1888 | Arnold, Matthew | 1620 | 1706 | Evelyn, John | 1838 | 1923 | Morley, John |
| 1515 | 1568 | Ascham, Roger | 1707 | 1754 | Fielding, Henry | 1870 | 1916 | Munro, H. H. (Saki) |
| 1775 | 1817 | Austen, Jane | 1809 | 1883 | Fitzgerald, Edward | 1880 | 1958 | Noyes, Alfred |
| 1561 | 1626 | Bacon, Francis | 1908 | 1964 | Fleming, Ian | 1903 | 1950 | Orwell, George |
| 1214 | 1294 | Bacon, Roger | 1873 | 1939 | Ford, Ford Madox | 1839 | 1894 | Pater, Walter |
| 1762 | 1851 | Baillie, Joanna | 1889 | 1966 | Forester, C. S. | 1785 | 1866 | Peacock, Thomas L. |
| 1860 | 1937 | Barrie, James M. | 1908 | 1967 | Frankau, Pamela | 1632 | 1703 | Pepys, Samuel |
| 1584 | 1616 | Beaumont, Francis | 1867 | 1933 | Galsworthy, John | 1688 | 1744 | Pope, Alexander |
| 673 | 735 | Bede, the Venerable | 1685 | 1732 | Gay, John | 1664 | 1721 | Prior, Matthew |
| 1872 | 1956 | Beerbohm, Max | 1737 | 1794 | Gibbon, Edward | 1863 | 1944 | Quiller-Couch, Arthur T. |
| 1870 | 1953 | Belloc, Hilaire | 1857 | 1903 | Gissing, George | 1552 | 1618 | Raleigh, Sir Walter |
| 1876 | 1931 | Bennett, Arnold | 1728 | 1774 | Goldsmith, Oliver | 1814 | 1884 | Reade, Charles |
| 1748 | 1832 | Bentham, Jeremy | 1716 | 1771 | Gray, Thomas | 1882 | 1957 | Richardson, Dorothy |
| 1662 | 1742 | Bentley, Richard | 1925 | 1967 | Griffin, Gwyn | 1689 | 1761 | Richardson, Samuel |
| 1869 | 1951 | Blackwood, Algernon | 1840 | 1928 | Hardy, Thomas | 1819 | 1900 | Ruskin, John |
| 1740 | 1795 | Boswell, James | 1831 | 1923 | Harrison, Frederic | 1886 | 1967 | Sassoon, Siegfried |
| 1844 | 1930 | Bridges, Robert | 1778 | 1830 | Hazlitt, William | 1771 | 1832 | Scott, Sir Walter |
| 1816 | 1855 | Bronte, Charlotte | 1793 | 1835 | Hemans, Felicia | 1564 | 1616 | Shakespeare, William |
| 1818 | 1848 | Bronte, Emily | 1849 | 1903 | Henley, Wm. Ernest | 1856 | 1950 | Shaw, G. Bernard |
| 1806 | 1861 | Browning, Elizabeth B. | 1591 | 1674 | Herrick, Robert | 1797 | 1851 | Shelley, Mary W. |
| 1812 | 1889 | Browning, Robert | 1588 | 1679 | Hobbes, Thomas | 1792 | 1822 | Shelley, Percy Bysshe |
| 1838 | 1922 | Bryce, James | 1770 | 1835 | Hogg, James | 1751 | 1816 | Sheridan, Richard B. |
| 1628 | 1688 | Bunyan, John | 1886 | 1967 | Holland, Vyvyan | 1554 | 1586 | Sidney, Sir Philip |
| 1729 | 1797 | Burke, Edmund | 1799 | 1845 | Hood, Thomas | 1887 | 1964 | Sitwell, Edith |
| 1759 | 1796 | Burns, Robert | 1859 | 1936 | Housman, Alfred E. | 1771 | 1845 | Smith, Sydney |
| 1788 | 1824 | Byron, (Geo. Gordon) | 1711 | 1776 | Hume, David | 1721 | 1771 | Smollett, Tobias |
| 1777 | 1844 | Campbell, Thomas | 1894 | 1963 | Huxley, Aldous | 1774 | 1843 | Southey, Robert |
| 1795 | 1881 | Carlyle, Thomas | 1825 | 1895 | Huxley, Thos. H. | 1552 | 1599 | Spenser, Edmund |
| 1832 | 1898 | Carroll, Lewis | 1889 | 1967 | Irwin, Margaret | 1672 | 1729 | Steele, Richard |
| 1888 | 1957 | Cary, Joyce | 1803 | 1857 | Jerrold, Douglas W. | 1850 | 1894 | Stevenson, Robert Louis |
| 1340 | 1400 | Chaucer, Geoffrey | 1709 | 1784 | Johnson, Samuel | 1880 | 1932 | Strachey, Lytton |
| 1694 | 1773 | Chesterfield, Earl of | 1573 | 1637 | Jonson, Ben | 1667 | 1745 | Swift, Jonathan |
| 1874 | 1936 | Chesterton, G. K. | 1795 | 1821 | Keats, John | 1837 | 1909 | Swinburne, Algernon C. |
| 1762 | 1835 | Cobbett, William | 1896 | 1967 | Kennedy, Margaret | 1809 | 1892 | Tennyson, Alfred |
| 1804 | 1865 | Cobden, Richard | 1819 | 1875 | Kingsley, Charles | 1811 | 1863 | Thackeray, W. M. |
| 1772 | 1834 | Coleridge, S. T. | 1865 | 1936 | Kipling, Rudyard | 1914 | 1953 | Thomas, Dylan |
| 1670 | 1729 | Congreve, William | 1874 | 1945 | Knoblock, Edward | 1700 | 1748 | Thomson, James |
| 1857 | 1924 | Conrad, Joseph | 1775 | 1834 | Lamb, Charles | 1876 | 1962 | Trevelyan, Geo. M. |
| 1878 | 1957 | Coppard, A. E. | 1332 | 1400 | Langland, William | 1815 | 1882 | Trollope, Anthony |
| 1864 | 1924 | Corelli, Marie | 1885 | 1930 | Lawrence, David H. | 1884 | 1941 | Walpole, Hugh |
| 1731 | 1800 | Cowper, William | 1838 | 1903 | Lecky, W. E. H. | 1593 | 1683 | Walton, Izaak |
| 1809 | 1882 | Darwin, Charles | 1866 | 1947 | LeGallienne, Richard | 1851 | 1920 | Ward, Mrs. Humphry |
| 1669 | 1731 | Defoe, Daniel | 1894 | 1957 | Lewis, Wyndham | 1674 | 1748 | Watts, Isaac |
| 1873 | 1956 | De la Mare, Walter | 1632 | 1704 | Locke, John | 1903 | 1966 | Waugh, Evelyn |
| 1785 | 1859 | De Quincey, Thomas | 1800 | 1859 | Macaulay, Thomas B. | 1866 | 1946 | Wells, H. G. |
| 1812 | 1870 | Dickens, Charles | 1863 | 1947 | Machen, Arthur | 1906 | 1964 | White, T. H. |
| 1804 | 1881 | Disraeli, Benjamin | 1888 | 1923 | Mansfield, Katherine | 1861 | 1947 | Whitehead, Alfred N. |
| 1573 | 1631 | Donne, John | 1564 | 1593 | Marlowe, Christopher | 1770 | 1850 | Wordsworth, William |
| 1868 | 1952 | Douglas, Norman | 1878 | 1967 | Masefield, John | 1882 | 1941 | Woolf, Virginia |
| 1867 | 1900 | Dowson, Ernest | 1583 | 1640 | Massinger, Phillip | 1640 | 1715 | Wycherly, William |
| 1859 | 1930 | Doyle, Arthur Conan | 1874 | 1965 | Maugham, W. Somerset | | | |

## BRITISH PAINTERS AND SCULPTORS

| Born | Died | Name | Born | Died | Name | Born | Died | Name |
|---|---|---|---|---|---|---|---|---|
| 1836 | 1912 | Alma-Tadema, Lawr. | 1755 | 1826 | Flaxman, John | 1806 | 1870 | Maclise, Daniel |
| 1872 | 1898 | Beardsley, Aubrey | 1825 | 1899 | Foster, Myles Birket | 1829 | 1896 | Millais, J. E. |
| 1734 | 1808 | Beauclerk, Lady Diana | 1866 | 1934 | Fry, Roger E. | 1763 | 1804 | Morland, George |
| 1735 | 1839 | Beechey, Wm. | 1727 | 1788 | Gainsborough, Thos. | 1834 | 1896 | Morris, William |
| 1881 | 1967 | Beresford, Frank E. | 1648 | 1721 | Gibbons, Grinling | 1849 | 1933 | Murray, David |
| 1757 | 1827 | Blake, William | 1790 | 1866 | Gibson, John | 1835 | 1910 | Orchardson, W. Q. |
| 1802 | 1828 | Bonington, R. P. | 1817 | 1897 | Gilbert, John | 1878 | 1931 | Orpen, William |
| 1821 | 1893 | Brown, Ford Madox | 1775 | 1802 | Girtin, Thomas | 1839 | 1893 | Pettie, John |
| 1833 | 1898 | Burne-Jones, Edw. | 1786 | 1846 | Haydon, Benj. | 1836 | 1919 | Poynter, E. J. Bt. |
| 1799 | 1883 | Calvert, Edward | 1841 | 1917 | Henry, C. N. | 1756 | 1823 | Raeburn, Henry |
| 1781 | 1841 | Chantrey, F. L. | 1697 | 1764 | Hogarth, William | 1723 | 1792 | Reynolds, Joshua |
| 1896 | 1967 | Charoux, Siegfried | 1758 | 1810 | Hoppner, John | 1734 | 1802 | Romney, George |
| 1850 | 1934 | Collier, John | 1827 | 1910 | Hunt, W. Holman | 1828 | 1882 | Rossetti, D. G. |
| 1776 | 1837 | Constable, John | 1646 | 1725 | Kneller, Godfrey | 1891 | 1959 | Spencer, Stanley |
| 1803 | 1902 | Cooper, Thos. Sidney | 1802 | 1873 | Lanseer, Edwin | 1854 | 1935 | Stokes, Adrian |
| 1782 | 1842 | Cotman, J. S. | 1856 | 1941 | Lavery, John | 1775 | 1851 | Turner, J. M. W. |
| 1768 | 1821 | Crome, John | 1769 | 1830 | Lawrence, Thomas | 1817 | 1904 | Watts, Geo. F. |
| 1793 | 1865 | Eastlake, Charles L. | 1830 | 1896 | Leighton, Fred'k, Lord | 1775 | 1856 | Westmacott, R. |
| 1880 | 1959 | Epstein, Jacob | 1794 | 1859 | Leslie, Charles R. | 1785 | 1841 | Wilkie, David |
| 1787 | 1849 | Etty, William | 1864 | 1941 | Llewellyn, William | 1713 | 1782 | Wilson, Richard |

## BRITISH STATESMEN

| Born | Died | Name | Born | Died | Name | Born | Died | Name |
|---|---|---|---|---|---|---|---|---|
| 1852 | 1928 | Asquith, Herbert H. | 1889 | 1952 | Cripps, Stafford | 1863 | 1945 | Lloyd George, David |
| 1879 | 1964 | Astor, Viscountess | 1599 | 1658 | Cromwell, Oliver | 1876 | 1947 | Lytton, Victor |
| 1883 | 1967 | Atlee, Clement | 1859 | 1925 | Curzon of Kedleston | 1866 | 1937 | MacDonald, J. Ramsay |
| 1867 | 1947 | Baldwin, Stanley | 1804 | 1881 | Disraeli, Benjamin | 1854 | 1925 | Milner, Alfred |
| 1848 | 1930 | Balfour, Arthur J. | 1819 | 1886 | Forster, Wm. E. | 1732 | 1792 | North, Frederick |
| 1879 | 1964 | Beaverbrook, Lord | 1749 | 1806 | Fox. Chas. Jas. | 1784 | 1865 | Palmerston, Henry |
| 1897 | 1960 | Bevan, Aneurin | 1906 | 1963 | Gaitskell, Hugh | 1788 | 1850 | Peel, Robert |
| 1881 | 1951 | Bevin, Ernest | 1809 | 1898 | Gladstone, Wm. E. | 1867 | 1937 | Peel, William |
| 1838 | 1922 | Bryce, James | 1712 | 1770 | Grenville, George | 1759 | 1806 | Pitt, William |
| 1770 | 1827 | Canning, George | 1764 | 1845 | Grey, Charles | 1708 | 1778 | Pitt, W. (Chatham) |
| 1769 | 1822 | Castlereagh, Robt. | 1862 | 1933 | Grey, Edward | 1854 | 1932 | Plunkett, Horace |
| 1864 | 1958 | Cecil, Edgar | 1594 | 1643 | Hampden, John | 1853 | 1902 | Rhodes, Cecil |
| 1863 | 1937 | Chamberlain, Austen | 1732 | 1818 | Hastings, Warren | 1847 | 1929 | Rosebery, Arch. |
| 1836 | 1914 | Chamberlain, Joseph | 1863 | 1935 | Henderson, Arthur | 1792 | 1878 | Russell, John |
| 1869 | 1940 | Chamberlain, Neville | 1853 | 1917 | Jameson, Leander S. | 1830 | 1903 | Salisbury, Robt. |
| 1874 | 1965 | Churchill, Winston | 1858 | 1923 | Law, A. Bonar | 1676 | 1745 | Walpole, Robert |
| 1725 | 1774 | Clive, Robert | | | | | | |

## BRITISH ARMY (A), NAVY (N), AIR FORCE (F), EXPLORATION (E)

| Born | Died | Name | Born | Died | Name | Born | Died | Name |
|---|---|---|---|---|---|---|---|---|
| 1861 | 1936 | Allenby, Edmund (A) | 1535 | 1594 | Frobisher, Martin (E) | 1898 | 1967 | McCreery, Richard (A) |
| 1717 | 1797 | Amherst, Jeffrey (A) | 1721 | 1787 | Gage, Thomas (A) | 1867 | 1948 | Milne, Geo. (A) |
| 1584 | 1622 | Baffin, William (E) | 1833 | 1885 | Gordon, Chas. G. (A) | 1894 | 1967 | Morgan, Frederick (A) |
| 1871 | 1936 | Beatty, David (N) | 1870 | 1963 | Gough, Hubert (A) | 1782 | 1853 | Napier, Charles J. (A) |
| 1873 | 1967 | Boyle, Wm. H. D. (N) | 1896 | 1967 | Graham, Ronald (F) | 1810 | 1890 | Napier, Robert C. (A) |
| 1695 | 1755 | Braddock, Edward (A) | 1541 | 1591 | Grenville, Richard (N) | 1758 | 1805 | Nelson, Horatio (N) |
| 1723 | 1792 | Burgoyne, John (A) | 1861 | 1928 | Haig, Douglas (A) | 1696 | 1785 | Oglethorpe, James (A) |
| 1663 | 1733 | Byng, George (N) | 1853 | 1947 | Hamilton, Ian (A) | 1832 | 1914 | Roberts, Frederick (A) |
| 1675 | 1726 | Cadogan, Wm. (A) | 1795 | 1857 | Havelock, Henry (A) | 1719 | 1792 | Rodney, Geo. (N) |
| 1593 | 1676 | Cavendish, Wm. (A) | 1745 | 1792 | Hearne, Samuel (E) | 1800 | 1862 | Ross, James C. (E) |
| 1873 | 1967 | Chatfield, Alfred (N) | 1536 | 1624 | Howard, Charles (N) | 1868 | 1912 | Scott, Robert F. (E) |
| 1738 | 1795 | Clinton, Henry (A) | 1726 | 1799 | Howe, Richard (N) | 1874 | 1922 | Shackleton, Ernest (E) |
| 1892 | 1959 | Cochrane, Edw. L. (N) | 1729 | 1814 | Howe, William (A) | 1869 | 1966 | Shea, John S. (A) |
| 1770 | 1851 | Codrington, Ed. (N) | 1575 | 1611 | Hudson, Henry (E) | 1841 | 1904 | Stanley, Henry M. (E) |
| 1727 | 1779 | Cook, James (E) | 1883 | 1966 | Humphreys, Noel (E) | 1869 | 1951 | Swinton, Ernest (A) |
| 1738 | 1805 | Cornwallis, Chas. (A) | 1880 | 1959 | Ironside, Wm. E. (A) | 1890 | 1967 | Tedder, Arthur W. (F) |
| 1550 | 1605 | Davis, John (E) | 1859 | 1935 | Jellicoe, John (N) | 1757 | 1798 | Vancouver, George (E) |
| 1540 | 1596 | Drake, Francis (N) | 1715 | 1774 | Johnson, Wm. (A) | 1883 | 1950 | Wavell, Archibald (A) |
| 1877 | 1967 | Ellington, Edward (F) | 1872 | 1945 | Keyes, Roger (N) | 1787 | 1834 | Weddell, James (E) |
| 1841 | 1920 | Fisher, John A. (N) | 1850 | 1916 | Kitchener, H. H. (A) | 1769 | 1852 | Wellington, Duke of (A) |
| 1710 | 1759 | Forbes, John (A) | 1888 | 1935 | Lawrence, T. E. (A) | 1727 | 1759 | Wolfe, James (A) |
| 1786 | 1847 | Franklin, John (E) | 1650 | 1722 | Marlborough, Duke of (A) | | | |
| 1852 | 1925 | French, John (A) | 1871 | 1951 | Maurice, Frederick (A) | | | |

## BRITISH SCIENTISTS, ENGINEERS, PHYSICIANS

| Born | Died | Name | Born | Died | Name | Born | Died | Name |
|---|---|---|---|---|---|---|---|---|
| 1888 | 1967 | Bamforth, Joseph | 1892 | 1964 | Haldane, J. B. S. | 1733 | 1804 | Priestley, Jos. |
| 1813 | 1898 | Bessemer, Henry | 1578 | 1657 | Harvey, Wm. | 1857 | 1932 | Ross, Ronald |
| 1899 | 1966 | Cameron, Roy | 1792 | 1871 | Herschel, John | 1871 | 1937 | Rutherford, Ernest |
| 1881 | 1966 | Campbell, Donald F. | 1738 | 1822 | Herschel, Wm. | 1811 | 1870 | Simpson, Jas. Y. |
| 1731 | 1810 | Cavendish, Henry | 1897 | 1967 | Hinshelwood, Cyril | 1781 | 1848 | Stephenson, Geo. |
| 1905 | 1967 | Cockcroft, John | 1861 | 1947 | Hopkins, Frederick | 1624 | 1689 | Sydenham, Thomas |
| 1832 | 1919 | Crooks, Wm. | 1749 | 1823 | Jenner, Edward | 1820 | 1904 | Thompson, Jos. |
| 1870 | 1966 | Dain, Guy | 1815 | 1898 | Jenner, William | 1824 | 1907 | Thomson, Wm. (Kelvin) |
| 1766 | 1844 | Dalton, John | 1878 | 1967 | Jones, Owen T. | 1820 | 1893 | Tyndall, John |
| 1809 | 1882 | Darwin, Charles | 1827 | 1912 | Lister, Jos. | 1823 | 1913 | Wallace, Alf. Russell |
| 1791 | 1867 | Faraday, Michael | 1831 | 1879 | Maxwell, Jas. Clerk | 1736 | 1819 | Watt, James E. |
| 1881 | 1955 | Fleming, Alexander | 1877 | 1967 | McAlpine, Malcolm | 1802 | 1875 | Wheatstone, Chas. |
| 1849 | 1945 | Fleming, Ambrose | 1663 | 1729 | Newcomen, Thos. | 1901 | 1966 | Whinfield, John R. |
| 1897 | 1966 | Franklin, Kenneth J. | 1642 | 1727 | Newton, Isaac | | | |

## BRITISH RELIGIOUS LEADERS

| Born | Died | Name | Born | Died | Name | Born | Died | Name |
|---|---|---|---|---|---|---|---|---|
| 1117 | 1170 | Becket, Thomas á | 1860 | 1954 | Inge, William Ralph | 1613 | 1667 | Taylor, Jeremy |
| 1685 | 1753 | Berkeley, George | 1874 | 1966 | Johnson, Hewlett | 1484 | 1536 | Tyndale, William |
| 1829 | 1912 | Booth, William B. | 1505 | 1572 | Knox, John | 1703 | 1791 | Wesley, John |
| 1566 | 1644 | Brewster, William | 1491 | 1555 | Latimer, Hugh | 1714 | 1770 | Whitefield, Geo. |
| 1489 | 1556 | Cranmer, Thos. | 1813 | 1873 | Livingstone, David | 1802 | 1865 | Wiseman, Nicholas |
| 1624 | 1691 | Fox, George | 1808 | 1892 | Manning, Henry E. | 1475 | 1530 | Wolsey, Thomas |
| 1554 | 1600 | Hooker, Richard | 1801 | 1890 | Newman, John H. | 1324 | 1384 | Wycliffe, John |

## Poets Laureate of England

There is no authentic record of the origin of the office of Poet Laureate of England. According to Warton, there was a Versificator Regis, or King's Poet, in the reign of Henry III (1216-1272), and he was paid 100 shillings a year. Geoffrey Chaucer (1340-1400) assumed the title of Poet Laureate, and in 1389 got a royal grant of a yearly allowance of wine. In the reign of Edward IV (1461-1483), John Kay held the post. Under Henry VII (1485-1509), Andrew Bernard was the Poet Laureate, and was succeeded under Henry VIII (1509-1547) by John Skelton. Next came Edmund Spenser, who died in 1599; then Samuel Daniel, who died in 1619, and then Ben Jonson (appointed 1619). Sir

William D'Avenant was appointed in 1638. He was a godson of William Shakespeare.

Others were John Dryden, 1670-1688; Thomas Shadwell, 1689; Nahum Tate, 1692; Nicholas Rowe, 1715; the Rev. Laurence Eusden, 1718; Colly Cibber, 1730; William Whitehead, 1758, on the refusal of Gray; Rev. Thomas Warton, 1785, on the refusal of Mason; Henry J. Pye, 1790; Robert Southey, 1813, on the refusal of Sir Walter Scott; William Wordsworth, 1843; Alfred Tennyson, 1850; Alfred Austin, 1896; Robert Bridges, 1913 (died 1930); John Masefield, 1930 (died May 12, 1967).

Cecil Day Lewis was appointed to the post Jan. 1, 1968.

# Germans

## GERMAN ENGINEERS, NATURALISTS, SCIENTISTS, INDUSTRIALISTS

| Born | Died | Name | Born | Died | Name | Born | Died | Name |
|---|---|---|---|---|---|---|---|---|
| 1840 | 1905 | Abbe, Ernst | 1834 | 1919 | Haeckel, Ernst | 1848 | 1896 | Lilienthal, Otto |
| 1193 | 1280 | Albertus, Magnus | 1844 | 1913 | Hagenbeck, George F. | 1734 | 1815 | Mesmer, Franz |
| 1844 | 1929 | Benz, Carl | 1755 | 1843 | Hahnemann, Samuel | 1855 | 1916 | Neisser, Albert |
| 1836 | 1907 | Bergmann, Ernest v. | 1821 | 1894 | Helmholz, Hermann | 1787 | 1854 | Ohm, Geo. S. |
| 1811 | 1899 | Bunsen, Robert | 1857 | 1894 | Hertz, Heinrich | 1871 | 1948 | Opel, Wilh. v. |
| 1873 | 1941 | Burger, Hans | 1769 | 1859 | Humboldt, Alex. v. | 1853 | 1932 | Ostwald, Wilhelm |
| 1834 | 1900 | Daimler, Gottlieb | 1767 | 1835 | Humboldt, Wilh. v. | 1858 | 1947 | Planck, Max |
| 1858 | 1913 | Diesel, Rudolf | 1859 | 1935 | Junkers, Hugo | 1632 | 1694 | Pufendorf, Samuel |
| 1895 | 1964 | Domagk, Gerhard | 1571 | 1630 | Kepler, Johannes | 1845 | 1923 | Roentgen, Wilh. |
| 1861 | 1935 | Duisberg, Carl | 1843 | 1910 | Koch, Robert | 1822 | 1890 | Schliemann, Heinrich |
| 1868 | 1954 | Eckener, Hugo | 1812 | 1887 | Krupp, Alfred | 1816 | 1892 | Siemens, Werner v. |
| 1854 | 1915 | Ehrlich, Paul | 1907 | 1967 | Krupp, Alfried | 1842 | 1926 | Thyssen, Aug. |
| 1686 | 1736 | Fahrenheit, Gabriel | 1900 | 1967 | Kuhn, Richard | 1821 | 1902 | Virchow, Rudolf |
| 1852 | 1919 | Fischer, Emil | 1646 | 1716 | Leibnitz, Gottfried v. | 1866 | 1925 | Wassermann, Aug.v. |
| 1882 | 1964 | Franck, James | 1742 | 1799 | Lichtenberg, Georg | 1853 | 1905 | Wissmann, Hermann v. |
| 1400 | 1468 | Gutenberg, Johannes | 1803 | 1873 | Liebig, Justus v. | 1838 | 1917 | Zeppelin, Ferd. v. |

## GERMAN POLITICAL AND MILITARY LEADERS; ECONOMISTS

| Born | Died | Name | Born | Died | Name | Born | Died | Name |
|---|---|---|---|---|---|---|---|---|
| 1876 | 1967 | Adenauer, Konrad | 1863 | 1932 | Hipper, Franz v. | 1848 | 1916 | Moltke, Helmuth von |
| 1815 | 1898 | Bismarck, Otto v. | 1889 | 1945 | Hitler, Adolf | 1876 | 1960 | Raeder, Erich |
| 1742 | 1819 | Bluecher, Gebh. v. | 1882 | 1946 | Keitel, Wilhelm | 1861 | 1922 | Rathenau, Walter |
| 1856 | 1921 | Bethmann-Hollweg, T. v. | 1887 | 1960 | Kesselring, Alb. | 1891 | 1944 | Rommel, Erwin |
| 1849 | 1929 | Buelow, Bernhar v. | 1871 | 1919 | Liebknecht, Karl | 1876 | 1953 | Rundstedt, Karl v. |
| 1780 | 1831 | Clausewitz, C. v. | 1886 | 1966 | Luckner, Felix V. | 1865 | 1939 | Scheidemann, Philipp |
| 1913 | 1967 | Erler, Fritz | 1865 | 1937 | Ludendorff, Erich | 1833 | 1913 | Schlieffen, Alf. v. |
| 1875 | 1921 | Erzberger, Matthias | 1880 | 1919 | Luxemburg, Rosa | 1878 | 1929 | Stresemann, Gustav |
| 1861 | 1922 | Falkenhayn, E. v. | 1849 | 1945 | Mackensen, Aug. v. | 1849 | 1930 | Tirpitz, Alf. v. |
| 1760 | 1831 | Gneisenau, Aug. | 1818 | 1883 | Marx, Karl | 1832 | 1904 | Waldersee, Alf. v. |
| 1847 | 1934 | Hindenburg, Paul v. | 1800 | 1891 | Moltke, Helmuth von | | | |

## GERMAN AUTHORS, DRAMATISTS, ESSAYISTS, HISTORIANS, POETS

| Born | Died | Name | Born | Died | Name | Born | Died | Name |
|---|---|---|---|---|---|---|---|---|
| 1769 | 1860 | Arndt, Ernst Moritz | 1862 | 1946 | Hauptmann, Gerhart | 1844 | 1900 | Nietzsche, Friedrich |
| 1886 | 1956 | Benn, Gottfried | 1813 | 1863 | Hebbel, Friedrich | 1796 | 1835 | Platten, Aug. v. |
| 1898 | 1956 | Brecht, Bertolt | 1760 | 1826 | Hebel, Johann P. | 1795 | 1886 | Ranke, Leopold, v. |
| 1778 | 1842 | Brentano, Clemens | 1770 | 1831 | Hegel, Georg W. F. | 1810 | 1874 | Reuter, Fritz |
| 1832 | 1908 | Busch, Wilhelm | 1797 | 1856 | Heine, Heinrich | 1763 | 1825 | Richter, Jean Paul |
| 1740 | 1815 | Claudius, Matthias | 1744 | 1803 | Herder, Johann v. | 1875 | 1926 | Rilke, Rainer Maria |
| 1863 | 1920 | Dehmel, Richard | 1877 | 1962 | Hesse, Hermann | 1899 | 1966 | Ropke, Wilhelm |
| 1837 | 1898 | Ebers, Georg | 1776 | 1822 | Hoffman, E. T. A. | 1788 | 1866 | Rueckert, Friedrich |
| 1788 | 1857 | Eichendorff, Jos. | 1770 | 1843 | Hoelderlin, Friedrich | 1494 | 1576 | Sachs, Hans |
| 1820 | 1895 | Engels, Friedrich | 1878 | 1945 | Kaiser, Georg | 1775 | 1854 | Schelling, Frederich v. |
| 1886 | 1933 | Ernst, Paul | 1724 | 1804 | Kant, Immanuel | 1759 | 1805 | Schiller, Friedrich |
| 1170 | 1220 | Eschenbach, Wolfram v. | 1896 | 1966 | Kasack, Hermann | 1767 | 1845 | Schlegel, Aug. W. |
| 1884 | 1958 | Feuchtwanger, Lion | 1777 | 1811 | Kielst, Heinrich v. | 1772 | 1829 | Schlegel, Friedr. |
| 1762 | 1814 | Fichte, Johann G. | 1724 | 1803 | Plopstock, Friedr. | 1768 | 1834 | Schleiermacher, Fredrich |
| 1869 | 1966 | Foerster, Friedrich | 1791 | 1813 | Koerner, Karl Th. | 1788 | 1860 | Schopenhauer, Arthur |
| 1819 | 1898 | Fontane, Theodor | 1875 | 1967 | Kolb, Annette | 1817 | 1888 | Storm, Theodor |
| 1816 | 1895 | Freytag, Gustav | 1646 | 1716 | Leibnitz, Gottfried | 1857 | 1928 | Sudermann, Hermann |
| 1868 | 1933 | George, Stefan | 1729 | 1781 | Lessing, Gotthold | 1893 | 1939 | Toller, Ernst |
| 1607 | 1676 | Gerhardt, Paul | 1844 | 1909 | Liliencron, Detlev v. | 1834 | 1896 | Treitschke, Heinrich v. |
| 1749 | 1832 | Goethe, Johann W. v. | 1881 | 1948 | Ludwig, Emil | 1890 | 1935 | Tucholsky, Kurt |
| 1785 | 1863 | Grimm, Jakob | 1871 | 1950 | Mann, Heinrich | 1787 | 1862 | Uhland, Ludwig |
| 1786 | 1859 | Grimm, Wilhelm | 1875 | 1955 | Mann, Thomas | 1873 | 1934 | Wassermann, Jakob |
| 1890 | 1941 | Hasenclever, Walter | 1804 | 1875 | Moerike, Eduard | 1733 | 1813 | Wieland, Chris. M. |
| 1802 | 1827 | Hauff, Wilhelm | 1817 | 1903 | Mommsen, Theodor | 1855 | 1930 | Wolzogen, Ernst von |

## GERMAN ARTISTS: PAINTERS, SCULPTORS, ARCHITECTS

| Born | Died | Name | Born | Died | Name | Born | Died | Name |
|---|---|---|---|---|---|---|---|---|
| 1480 | 1538 | Altdorfer, Albrecht | 1829 | 1880 | Feuerbach, Anselm | 1837 | 1887 | Marees, Hans v. |
| 1476 | 1545 | Baldung, Hans | 1774 | 1840 | Friedrich, Kaspar | 1815 | 1905 | Menzel, Adolf v. |
| 1870 | 1938 | Barlach, Ernst | 1503 | 1529 | Gruenewald, Matth. | 1803 | 1884 | Richter, Ludwig |
| 1884 | 1950 | Beckmann, Max | 1847 | 1921 | Hildebrand, Adolf v. | 1764 | 1850 | Schadow, Johann |
| 1827 | 1901 | Boecklin, Arnold | 1460 | 1524 | Holbein, Hans (Sr.) | 1781 | 1841 | Schinkel, Karl |
| 1726 | 1801 | Chodowiecki, Dan'l | 1497 | 1543 | Holbein, Hans (Jr.) | 1868 | 1932 | Slevogt, Max |
| 1858 | 1925 | Corinth, Louis | 1877 | 1947 | Kolbe, Georg | 1839 | 1924 | Thoma, Hans |
| 1783 | 1867 | Cornelius, Peter | 1867 | 1945 | Kollwitz, Kaethe | 1848 | 1911 | Uhde, Fritz v. |
| 1472 | 1553 | Cranach, Lucas | 1847 | 1935 | Liebermann, Max | 1455 | 1529 | Vischer, Peter |
| 1471 | 1528 | Duerer, Albrecht | 1880 | 1916 | Marc, Franz | | | |

# French

## FRENCH AUTHORS, CRITICS, POETS, DRAMATISTS, HISTORIANS

| Born | Died | Name | Born | Died | Name | Born | Died | Name |
|---|---|---|---|---|---|---|---|---|
| 1079 | 1142 | Abélard, Pierre | 1651 | 1715 | Fénelon, François de | 1808 | 1855 | Nerval, Gerard de |
| 1717 | 1783 | Alembert, Jean d' | 1821 | 1890 | Feuillet, Octave | 1623 | 1662 | Pascal, Blaise |
| 1880 | 1918 | Apollinaire, Guillaume | 1821 | 1880 | Flaubert, Gustave | 1873 | 1914 | Péguy, Charles |
| 1820 | 1889 | Augier, (Emile) | 1886 | 1914 | Fournier, Alain | 1849 | 1930 | Porto-Riche, Georges de |
| 1902 | 1967 | Ayme, Marcel | 1844 | 1924 | France, Anatole (Jacques-Anatole Thibault) | 1697 | 1763 | Prévost, (L'Abbé) |
| 1799 | 1850 | Balzac, Honoré de | | | | 1871 | 1922 | Proust, Marcel |
| 1823 | 1891 | Banville, Théodore de | 1333 | 1400 | Froissart, Jean | 1495 | 1553 | Rabelais, François |
| 1873 | 1935 | Barbusse, Henri | 1811 | 1872 | Gautier, Théophile | 1639 | 1699 | Racine, Jean |
| 1862 | 1923 | Barrès, Maurice | 1869 | 1951 | Gide, André | 1864 | 1936 | Régnier, Henri de |
| 1821 | 1867 | Baudelaire, Charles | 1882 | 1944 | Giraudoux, Jean | 1823 | 1892 | Renan, Ernest |
| 1732 | 1799 | Beaumarchais, Pierre | 1816 | 1882 | Gobineau, Comte de | 1849 | 1926 | Richepin, Jean |
| 1837 | 1899 | Becque, Henry | 1822 | 1896 | Goncourt, Edmond de | 1854 | 1891 | Rimbaud, Arthur |
| 1780 | 1857 | Béranger, Pierre | 1830 | 1870 | Goncourt, Jules de | 1866 | 1944 | Rolland, Romain |
| 1859 | 1941 | Bergson, Henri | 1787 | 1874 | Guizot, François | 1524 | 1585 | Ronsard, Pierre de |
| 1888 | 1948 | Bernanos, Georges | 1570 | 1631 | Hardy, Alexandre | 1868 | 1918 | Rostand, Edmond |
| 1866 | 1947 | Bernard, Tristan | 1842 | 1905 | Heredia, José-Maria de | 1760 | 1836 | Rouget de Lisle, Claude |
| 1876 | 1953 | Bernstein, Henri | 1857 | 1915 | Hervieu, Paul | 1885 | 1966 | Roure, Remy |
| 1876 | 1967 | Birot, Pierre A. | 1892 | 1955 | Honegger, Arthur | 1712 | 1778 | Rousseau, Jean-Jacques |
| 1636 | 1711 | Boileau, Nicolas | 1802 | 1885 | Hugo, Victor | 1610 | 1703 | Saint-Evremond, de |
| 1627 | 1704 | Bossuet, Jacques | 1848 | 1907 | Huysmans, Joris-Karl | 1900 | 1944 | Saint-Exupéry, Ant. de |
| 1852 | 1935 | Bourget, Paul | 1876 | 1944 | Jacob, Max | 1675 | 1755 | Saint-Simon, Duc de |
| 1867 | 1926 | Boylesve, René | 1868 | 1938 | Jammes, Francis | 1804 | 1869 | Sainte-Beuve, Charles A. |
| 1858 | 1932 | Brieux, Eugène | 1815 | 1888 | Labiche, Eugène | 1567 | 1622 | Sales (Saint François de) |
| 1707 | 1788 | Buffon, Georges | 1530 | 1568 | La Boétie, Etienne de | 1804 | 1876 | Sand, George (Lucile Dupin) |
| 1509 | 1564 | Calvin, Jean | 1645 | 1696 | La Bruyère, Jean de | | | |
| 1913 | 1960 | Camus, Albert | 1757 | 1834 | La Fayette, Marquis de | 1831 | 1908 | Sardou, Victorien |
| 1541 | 1603 | Charron, Pierre | 1621 | 1695 | La Fontaine, Jean de | 1791 | 1861 | Scribe, Eugène |
| 1768 | 1848 | Chateaubriand, Franc | 1860 | 1887 | Laforgue, Jules | 1626 | 1696 | Sévigné, (Mme. de) |
| 1762 | 1794 | Chénier, André | 1744 | 1829 | Lamarck, Jean-Baptiste | 1875 | 1959 | Siegfried, Andre |
| 1889 | 1963 | Cocteau, Jean | 1790 | 1869 | Lamartine, Alphonse de | 1766 | 1817 | Staël, (Mme. de) |
| 1873 | 1954 | Colette, Sidonie | 1613 | 1680 | La Rochefoucauld | 1783 | 1842 | Stendhal, (Beyle) |
| 1445 | 1509 | Comines, Philippe de | 1846 | 1870 | Lautréamont, Comte de | 1839 | 1907 | Sully-Prudhomme, René |
| 1798 | 1857 | Comte, Auguste | 1818 | 1894 | Leconte de Lisle | 1828 | 1893 | Taine, Hippolyte |
| 1743 | 1794 | Condorcet, Marquis de | 1853 | 1914 | Lemaitre, Jules | 1795 | 1856 | Thierry Augustin |
| 1767 | 1830 | Constant, Benjamin | 1668 | 1747 | Lesage, Alain-René | 1805 | 1859 | Tocqueville, A. C. de |
| 1842 | 1908 | Coppée, François | 1850 | 1923 | Loti, Pierre (J. Viaud) | 1871 | 1945 | Valéry, Paul |
| 1845 | 1875 | Corbière, Tristan | 1855 | 1928 | Malherbe, François de | 1889 | 1957 | Vercel, Roger |
| 1606 | 1684 | Corneille, Pierre | 1842 | 1898 | Mallarmé, Stéphane | 1844 | 1896 | Verlaine, Paul |
| 1854 | 1928 | Curel, François de | 1688 | 1763 | Marivaux, Pierre | 1828 | 1905 | Verne, Jules |
| 1769 | 1832 | Cuvier, Georges | 1850 | 1893 | Maupassant, Guy de | 1797 | 1863 | Vigny, Alfred de |
| 1840 | 1897 | Daudet, Alphonse | 1885 | 1967 | Maurois, Andre | 1838 | 1889 | Villiers de l'Isle-Adam |
| 1596 | 1650 | Descartes, René | 1803 | 1870 | Mérimée, Prosper | 1431 | 1484 | Villon, François |
| 1713 | 1784 | Diderot, Denis | 1798 | 1874 | Michelet, Jules | 1597 | 1648 | Voiture, Vincent |
| 1881 | 1958 | Du Gard, Roger M. | 1622 | 1673 | Molière, Jean-Baptiste | 1694 | 1778 | Voltaire, (Arouet) |
| 1803 | 1870 | Dumas, Alexandre | 1533 | 1592 | Montaigne, Michel de | 1840 | 1902 | Zola, Emile |
| 1824 | 1895 | Dumas, Alexandre fils | 1689 | 1755 | Montesquieu, Charles de | | | |
| 1926 | 1967 | Fall, Bernard B. | 1810 | 1857 | Musset, Alfred de | | | |

## FRENCH POLITICAL LEADERS (See also page 689)

| Born | Died | Name | Born | Died | Name | Born | Died | Name |
|---|---|---|---|---|---|---|---|---|
| 1884 | 1966 | Auriol, Vincent | 1620 | 1698 | Frontenac, Louis de | 1602 | 1661 | Mazarin, Jules |
| 1872 | 1950 | Blum, Leon | 1838 | 1882 | Gambetta, Leon | 1749 | 1791 | Mirabeau, Honore |
| 1862 | 1932 | Briand, Aristide | 1859 | 1914 | Jaures, Jean | 1860 | 1934 | Poincare, Raymond |
| 1841 | 1929 | Clemenceau, Georges | 1872 | 1957 | Herriot, Edouard | 1878 | 1966 | Reynaud, Paul |
| 1619 | 1683 | Colbert, Jean-Bapt. | 1883 | 1945 | Laval, Pierre | 1585 | 1642 | Richelieu, Cardinal de |
| 1759 | 1794 | Danton, Georges | 1871 | 1950 | Lebrun, Albert | 1758 | 1794 | Robespierre, Max. |
| 1760 | 1794 | Desmoulins, Camille | 1641 | 1691 | Louvois, Fran. de | 1208 | 1265 | Simon de Montfort |
| 1763 | 1820 | Fouche, Jos. | 1744 | 1793 | Marat, Jean-Paul | 1754 | 1838 | Talleyrand, Chas. de |

## FRENCH PAINTERS AND SCULPTORS

| Born | Died | Name | Born | Died | Name | Born | Died | Name |
|---|---|---|---|---|---|---|---|---|
| 1834 | 1904 | Bartholdi, F. A. | 1877 | 1953 | Dufy, Raoul | 1824 | 1898 | Moreau, Gustave |
| 1848 | 1884 | Bastien-Lepage, J. | 1811 | 1889 | Dupre, Jules | 1830 | 1903 | Pissarro, Camille |
| 1822 | 1899 | Bonheur, Rosa | 1852 | 1931 | Forain, Jean L. | 1594 | 1665 | Poussin, Nicolas |
| 1867 | 1947 | Bonnard, Pierre | 1732 | 1806 | Fragonard, Jean | 1758 | 1823 | Prudhon, Pierre |
| 1703 | 1770 | Boucher, Francois | 1820 | 1876 | Fromentin, Eugene | 1824 | 1898 | Puvis de Chavanne |
| 1825 | 1905 | Bouguereau, W. | 1848 | 1903 | Gauguin, Paul | 1840 | 1916 | Redon, Odilon |
| 1876 | 1957 | Brancusi, C. | 1770 | 1837 | Gérard, F. | 1841 | 1919 | Renoir, P. A. |
| 1882 | 1963 | Braque, Georges | 1791 | 1824 | Gericault, J. L. A. T. | 1840 | 1917 | Rodin, Auguste |
| 1851 | 1933 | Carrier-Belleuse, P. | 1824 | 1904 | Gérôme, J. L. | 1871 | 1958 | Rouault, Georges |
| 1839 | 1906 | Cézanne, Paul | 1628 | 1715 | Girardon, Fr. | 1812 | 1867 | Rousseau, P. E. T. |
| 1699 | 1779 | Chardin, Jean-Bapt. | 1839 | 1883 | Goupil, Jules A. | 1795 | 1858 | Scheffer, Ary |
| 1600 | 1682 | Claude Lorrain | 1725 | 1805 | Greuze, J. B. | 1863 | 1927 | Serusier, Paul |
| 1845 | 1902 | Constant, Benj. | 1741 | 1828 | Houdon, J. A. | 1859 | 1891 | Seurat, Georges |
| 1796 | 1875 | Corot, J. B. C. | 1780 | 1867 | Ingres, J. A. D. | 1863 | 1935 | Signac, Paul |
| 1819 | 1877 | Courbet, Gustave | 1755 | 1841 | Lebrun, Marie | 1839 | 1899 | Sisley, Alfred |
| 1817 | 1878 | Daubigny, C. F. | 1887 | 1965 | Le Corbusier | 1900 | 1955 | Tanguy, Yves |
| 1808 | 1879 | Dumier, Honore | 1798 | 1880 | Lemaire, Ph. H. | 1864 | 1901 | Toulouse-Lautrec |
| 1748 | 1825 | David, Louis J. | 1600 | 1682 | Lorrain, Claude | 1813 | 1865 | Troyon, Constant |
| 1783 | 1856 | David d'Angers, P. J. | 1861 | 1944 | Maillol, Aristide | 1883 | 1955 | Utrillo, Maurice |
| 1834 | 1917 | Degas, H. G. E. | 1832 | 1883 | Manet, Edouard | 1758 | 1835 | Vernet, Carle |
| 1799 | 1863 | Delacroix, Eugene | 1869 | 1954 | Matisse, Henri | 1714 | 1789 | Vernet, Claude, J. |
| 1797 | 1856 | Delaroche, Paul | 1815 | 1891 | Meissonier, J. L. E. | 1789 | 1863 | Vernet, Horace |
| 1880 | 1954 | Derain, Andre | 1815 | 1875 | Millet, J. F. | 1876 | 1958 | Vlaminck, Maurice |
| 1807 | 1876 | Diaz de la Pena, N. V. | 1884 | 1920 | Modigliani, Amadeo | 1868 | 1940 | Vuillard, Edouard |
| 1833 | 1883 | Dore, Gustave | 1840 | 1926 | Monet, Claude | 1684 | 1721 | Watteau, Antoine |

## FRENCH SCIENTISTS, PHYSICIANS

| Born | Died | Name | Born | Died | Name | Born | Died | Name |
|---|---|---|---|---|---|---|---|---|
| 1775 | 1836 | Ampere, Andre-Marie | 1678 | 1761 | Fauchard, Pierre | 1864 | 1948 | Lumière, Louis |
| 1788 | 1878 | Becquerel, A. C. | 1842 | 1925 | Flammarion, Camille | 1852 | 1907 | Moissan, Henri |
| 1852 | 1908 | Becquerel, H. A. | 1778 | 1850 | Gay-Lussac, Joseph | 1745 | 1799 | Montgolfier, Jacques |
| 1827 | 1907 | Berthelot, Marcelin | 1900 | 1958 | Joliot-Curie, Frederic | 1740 | 1810 | Montgolfier, Jos. |
| 1812 | 1878 | Bernard, Claude | 1781 | 1826 | Laennec, Rene | 1807 | 1873 | Nelaton, Auguste |
| 1785 | 1870 | Broglie, A. C. de | 1736 | 1813 | Lagrange, Jos. L. | 1863 | 1933 | Painleve, Paul |
| 1872 | 1936 | Bleriot, Louis | 1744 | 1829 | Lamarck, Jean B. | 1647 | 1714 | Papin, Denis |
| 1825 | 1893 | Charcot, Jean M. | 1749 | 1827 | Laplace, Pierre S. | 1510 | 1590 | Pare, Ambroise |
| 1746 | 1823 | Charles, Jacques | 1743 | 1794 | Lavoisier, Antoine | 1822 | 1895 | Pasteur, Louis |
| 1786 | 1889 | Chevreul, Michel | 1822 | 1900 | Lenoir, Etienne | 1854 | 1912 | Poincare, Henri |
| 1859 | 1906 | Curie, Pierre | 1811 | 1877 | LeVerrier, Urbain | 1850 | 1935 | Richet, Chas. |
| 1890 | 1967 | Danjon, Andre | 1862 | 1954 | Lumière, Auguste | 1875 | 1965 | Schweitzer, Albert |

## FRENCH MILITARY LEADERS AND EXPLORERS

| Born | Died | Name | Born | Died | Name | Born | Died | Name |
|---|---|---|---|---|---|---|---|---|
| 1769 | 1821 | Bonaparte, Napoleon | 1753 | 1800 | Kleber, Jean-Bapt. | 1889 | 1952 | Tassigny, Jean de |
| 1753 | 1823 | Carnot, Lazare | 1757 | 1834 | La Fayette, Marquis de | 1611 | 1675 | Turenne, Vicomte de |
| 1519 | 1572 | Coligny, Gasp. de | 1902 | 1947 | Leclerc, Jacques P. | | | **EXPLORERS** |
| 1621 | 1686 | Conde, Prince de | 1854 | 1934 | Lyautey, Louis H. | 1658 | 1730 | Cadillac, Antoine |
| 1881 | 1942 | Darlan, Jean F. | 1756 | 1817 | Massena, Andre | 1491 | 1557 | Cartier, Jacques |
| 1722 | 1788 | DeGrasse, Francois | 1712 | 1759 | Montcalm, Louis de | 1567 | 1635 | Champlain, Sam'l de |
| 1739 | 1823 | Dumouriez, Chas. F. | 1763 | 1813 | Moreau, Jean V. | 1867 | 1936 | Charcot, Jean B. |
| 1851 | 1929 | Foch, Ferdinand | 1769 | 1815 | Ney, Michel | 1640 | 1701 | Hennepin, Louis |
| 1489 | 1512 | Foix, Gaston de | 1856 | 1951 | Petain, Henri Philippe | 1645 | 1700 | Jolliet, Louis |
| 1894 | 1953 | Fonck, Rene | 1725 | 1807 | Rochambeau, Jean-Bapt. | 1643 | 1687 | LaSalle, Robt. de |
| 1849 | 1916 | Gallieni, Jos. S. | 1579 | 1638 | Rohan, Henri | 1637 | 1675 | Marquette, Jacques |
| 1879 | 1949 | Giraud, Henri H. | 1696 | 1750 | Saxe, Maurice de | | | |
| 1852 | 1931 | Joffre, Jos. | 1769 | 1851 | Soult, Nicolas J. | | | |

# Russians

| Born | Died | Name | Born | Died | Name | Born | Died | Name |
|---|---|---|---|---|---|---|---|---|
| | | **AUTHORS—POETS** | | | **ARTISTS** | 1844 | 1908 | Rimsky-Korsakov, N. |
| 1888 | 1966 | Akhmatova, Anna A. | 1866 | 1924 | Bakst, Leon S. | 1829 | 1894 | Rubinstein, Anton |
| 1871 | 1919 | Andreyev, Leonid | 1866 | 1944 | Kandinsky, Vasili | 1871 | 1915 | Scriabin, Alex. |
| 1878 | 1927 | Artsibashev, Mikhail | 1783 | 1836 | Kiprensky, Orest | 1820 | 1871 | Serov, Alex. |
| 1860 | 1884 | Bashkirtsev, Maria | 1878 | 1927 | Kostodiev, Boris | 1856 | 1915 | Taneyev, Sergei |
| 1880 | 1921 | Blok, Alexander | 1861 | 1900 | Levitan, Isaak | 1840 | 1893 | Tschaikovsky, Peter |
| 1860 | 1904 | Chekhov, Anton | 1844 | 1918 | Repin, Ilya | | | |
| 1821 | 1881 | Dostoievski, Feodor | 1865 | 1911 | Serov, Valentin | | | **POLITICAL LEADERS** |
| 1891 | 1967 | Ehrenburg, Ilya G. | 1842 | 1904 | Vereshchagin, Vasili | 1746 | 1819 | Baranov, Alexander |
| 1809 | 1852 | Gogol, Nicholas V. | 1890 | 1967 | Zadkine, Ossip | 1875 | 1946 | Kalinin, Mikhail |
| 1812 | 1891 | Goncharov, Ivan A. | | | | 1870 | 1924 | Lenin, Vladimir |
| 1868 | 1936 | Gorky, Maxim | | | | 1877 | 1952 | Litvinov, Maxim |
| 1812 | 1870 | Herzen, Alexander | | | | 1845 | 1900 | Muraviev, Michael |
| 1809 | 1842 | Koltsov, Alexei | | | **BALLET-STAGE** | 1744 | 1818 | Novikov, Nicholas |
| 1853 | 1921 | Korolenko, Vladimir | 1872 | 1929 | Diaghilev, Sergei | 1739 | 1791 | Potemkin, G. |
| 1768 | 1844 | Krylov, Ivan | 1898 | 1948 | Eisenstein, Sergei | 1772 | 1839 | Speransky, Michael |
| 1870 | 1938 | Kuprin, Alexander | 1890 | 1950 | Nijinsky, Vaslav | 1879 | 1953 | Stalin, Josef |
| 1814 | 1841 | Lermontov, Michael | 1885 | 1931 | Pavlova, Anna | 1863 | 1911 | Stolypin, Peter |
| 1831 | 1895 | Leskov, Nicholas | 1822 | 1910 | Petipa, Marius | 1879 | 1940 | Trotzky, Leon |
| 1821 | 1897 | Maikov, Apollon | 1863 | 1938 | Stanislavsky, Konst. | | | (Bronstein) |
| 1819 | 1883 | Melnikov, Paul | | | | 1849 | 1915 | Witte, Sergei |
| 1848 | 1936 | Memirovich-Danchenko | | | | | | |
| 1865 | 1942 | Merezhkovvsk, D. S. | | | **COMPOSERS** | | | **SCIENTISTS** |
| 1821 | 1877 | Nekrasov, Nicholas | 1861 | 1906 | Arensky, Anton S. | 1898 | 1967 | Balandin, Aleksei |
| 1824 | 1861 | Nikitin, Vasili | 1846 | 1924 | Arkhangelsky, Alex. | 1857 | 1927 | Bekhterev, Vladimir |
| 1823 | 1886 | Ostrovsky, Alexander | 1836 | 1910 | Balakirev, Mily | 1779 | 1852 | Bellingshausen, F. |
| 1890 | 1960 | Pasternak, Boris | 1834 | 1887 | Borodin, Alex. | 1862 | 1916 | Golitzin, Boris |
| 1857 | 1918 | Piekhanov, Georgi | 1835 | 1919 | Cui, Cesar A. | 1842 | 1921 | Kropotkin, Peter |
| 1799 | 1837 | Pushkin, Alexander | 1813 | 1869 | Dargomizhsky, Alex. | 1711 | 1765 | Lomonosov, Michael |
| 1856 | 1919 | Rozanov, Vasili | 1865 | 1936 | Glazunov, Alex. | 1909 | 1967 | Meltsev, Anatoli |
| 1820 | 1879 | Soloviev, Sergei | 1803 | 1857 | Glinka, Mikhail | 1834 | 1907 | Mendeleyev, Dmitri |
| 1824 | 1919 | Suvorin, Alexei | 1859 | 1935 | Ippolitov-Ivanov, M. | 1845 | 1916 | Metchnikov, Elie |
| 1883 | 1945 | Tolstoy, Alexei | 1855 | 1914 | Liadov, Anatol | 1849 | 1936 | Pavlov, Ivan |
| 1828 | 1910 | Tolstoy, Leo | 1835 | 1881 | Mussorsky, Modest | 1810 | 1881 | Pirogov, Nicholas |
| 1818 | 1883 | Turgenev, Ivan | 1892 | 1953 | Prokofiev, Serge | 1859 | 1905 | Popov, Alexander |
| | | | 1866 | 1920 | Rebikov, Vladimir | 1907 | 1966 | Sisakian, Norayr M. |

# Italians

## AUTHORS, DRAMATISTS, POETS, PHILOSOPHERS, HISTORIANS

| Born | Died | Name | Born | Died | Name | Born | Died | Name |
|---|---|---|---|---|---|---|---|---|
| 1749 | 1803 | Alfieri, Vittorio | 1866 | 1952 | Croce, Benedetto | 1785 | 1873 | Manzoni, Alessandro |
| 1846 | 1900 | Amicis, Edmond de | 1863 | 1938 | D'Annunzio, Gabriele | 1805 | 1872 | Mazzini, Giuseppe |
| 1227 | 1274 | Aquinas, Thomas | 1265 | 1321 | Dante, Alighieri | 1698 | 1782 | Metastasio (P. Trapassi) |
| 1492 | 1556 | Aretino, Pietro | 1817 | 1883 | De Sanctis, Francesco | 1672 | 1750 | Muratori, Ludovico |
| 1474 | 1533 | Ariosto, Ludovico | 1909 | 1967 | Emanuelli, Enrico | 1848 | 1923 | Pareto, Vilfredo |
| 1829 | 1907 | Ascoli, Graziadio | 1842 | 1911 | Fogazzaro, Antonio | 1855 | 1912 | Pascoli, Giovanni |
| 1791 | 1863 | Belli, Giuseppe | 1778 | 1827 | Foscolo, Ugo | 1788 | 1854 | Pellico, Silvio |
| 1313 | 1375 | Boccaccio, Giovanni | 1809 | 1850 | Giusti, Giuseppe | 1304 | 1374 | Petrarch, Francesco |
| 1441 | 1494 | Boiardo, Matteo Maria | 1707 | 1793 | Goldoni, Carlo | 1867 | 1936 | Pirandello, Luigi |
| 1548 | 1599 | Bruno, Giordano | 1713 | 1786 | Gozzi, Gaspare | 1432 | 1484 | Pulci, Luigi |
| 1568 | 1639 | Campanella, Tommaso | 1483 | 1540 | Guicciardini, Francesco | 1626 | 1698 | Redi, Francesco |
| 1835 | 1907 | Carducci, Giosue | 1798 | 1837 | Leopardi, Giacomo | 1544 | 1595 | Tasso, Torquato |
| 1725 | 1798 | Casanova, Giovanni | 1836 | 1909 | Lombroso, Cesare | 1840 | 1922 | Verga, Giovanni |
| 1478 | 1529 | Castiglione, Baldassarre | 1469 | 1527 | Machiavelli, Nicolo | 1668 | 1744 | Vico, Giambattista |
| 1884 | 1966 | Cecchi, Emilio | 1449 | 1515 | Manuzio, Aldo (Aldus) | | | |

## ITALIAN EXPLORERS, SCIENTISTS, POLITICAL LEADERS

| Born | Died | Name | Born | Died | Name | Born | Died | Name |
|---|---|---|---|---|---|---|---|---|
| 1776 | 1856 | Avogadro, Amedo | 1737 | 1798 | Galvani, Luigi | 1859 | 1953 | Nitti, Francesco |
| 1738 | 1794 | Beccaria, Cesare | 1807 | 1882 | Garibaldi, Giuseppe | 1254 | 1324 | Polo, Marco |
| 1835 | 1900 | Beltrami, Eugenio | 1881 | 1954 | Gasperi, Alcide de | 1626 | 1698 | Redi, Francesco |
| 1476 | 1507 | Borgia, Cesare | 1882 | 1955 | Graziani, Rodolfo | 1835 | 1910 | Schiaparelli, Giovanni |
| 16th | Gen | Cabot, John (Cabato) | 1483 | 1540 | Guicciardini, Francesco | 1818 | 1878 | Secchi, Angelo |
| 1826 | 1910 | Cannizzaro, Stanislav | 1628 | 1694 | Malpighi, Marcello | 1872 | 1952 | Sforza, Carlo |
| 1810 | 1861 | Cavour, Camillo Benso | 1874 | 1937 | Marconi, Guglielmo | 1729 | 1799 | Spallanzani, Lazzaro |
| 1451 | 1506 | Columbus, Christopher | 1805 | 1872 | Mazzini, Giuseppe | 1608 | 1647 | Torricelli, Evangelista |
| 1830 | 1903 | Cremona, Luigi | 1389 | 1464 | Medici, Cosimo di (1) | 1485 | 1533 | Verrazano, Giovanni |
| 1881 | 1954 | De Gaspari, Alcide | 1519 | 1534 | Medici, Cosimo di (2) | 1454 | 1512 | Vespucci, Amerigo |
| 1901 | 1954 | Fermi, Enrico | 1449 | 1492 | Medici, Lorenzo di | 1745 | 1827 | Volta, Alessandro |
| 1847 | 1897 | Ferrario, Galileo | 1846 | 1910 | Mosso, Angelo | | | |
| 1564 | 1642 | Galileo (G. Galilei) | 1883 | 1945 | Mussolini, Benito | | | |

## ITALIAN PAINTERS, SCULPTORS AND ARCHITECTS

| Born | Died | Name | Born | Died | Name | Born | Died | Name |
|---|---|---|---|---|---|---|---|---|
| 1404 | 1472 | Alberti, Leon Battista | 1500 | 1571 | Cellini, Benvenuto | 1480 | 1528 | Palma, Jacopo |
| 1512 | 1572 | Alessi, Galeazzo | 1240 | 1302 | Cimabue, Giovanni | 1445 | 1523 | Perugino, Pietro |
| 1447 | 1522 | Amadeo, Giovanni | 1489 | 1534 | Corregio, Antonio da | 1720 | 1778 | Piranesi, Giovanni |
| 1387 | 1455 | Angelico, Fra | 1462 | 1521 | Cosimo, Piero di | 1454 | 1513 | Pinturicchio |
| 1591 | 1666 | Barbieri, Giovanni | 1397 | 1482 | Della Robbia, Luca | 1483 | 1520 | Raphael (Raffaelo) |
| 1475 | 1517 | Bartolomea, Fra | 1486 | 1531 | Del Sarto, Andrea | 1575 | 1642 | Reni, Guido |
| 1426 | 1507 | Bellini, Gentile | 1386 | 1466 | Donatello, Donato | 1400 | 1482 | Robbia, Luca della |
| 1428 | 1516 | Bellini, Giovanni | 1378 | 1455 | Ghiberti, Lorenzo | 1615 | 1673 | Rosa, Salvator |
| 1400 | 1470 | Bellini, Jacopo | 1449 | 1494 | Ghirlandaio, Domenico | 1460 | 1529 | Sansovino, Andrea |
| 1467 | 1516 | Beltraffio, Giovanni | 1477 | 1510 | Giorgone | 1486 | 1570 | Sansovino, Jacopo |
| 1598 | 1680 | Bernini, Gian Lor. | 1260 | 1336 | Giotto, Angelo | 1858 | 1899 | Segantini, Giovanni |
| 1598 | 1680 | Bernini, Lorenzo | 1420 | 1497 | Gozzoli, Benozzo | 1883 | 1966 | Severini, Gino |
| 1445 | 1510 | Botticelli, Sandro | 1406 | 1469 | Lippi, Fra Filippo | 1696 | 1770 | Tiepolo, Giambattista |
| 1444 | 1514 | Bramante, Donato | 1459 | 1504 | Lippi, Filippino | 1518 | 1594 | Tintoretto, Jacopo |
| 1377 | 1446 | Brunelleschi, Filippo | 1827 | 1887 | Mangoni, Giuseppe | 1477 | 1576 | Titian (Tiziano) |
| 1697 | 1768 | Canaletto (Canale) | 1431 | 1506 | Mantegna, Andrea | 1397 | 1475 | Uccello, Paolo |
| 1757 | 1822 | Canova, Antonio | 1401 | 1428 | Masaccio, Tommaso | 1511 | 1574 | Vasari, Giorgio |
| 1570 | 1610 | Caravaggio, Amerghi | 1475 | 1564 | Michelangelo, Buonarroti | 1528 | 1588 | Veronese, Paolo |
| 1450 | 1522 | Carpaccio, Vittore | 1826 | 1901 | Morelli, Domenico | 1435 | 1488 | Verrocchio, Andrea |
| 1881 | 1966 | Carra, Carlo | 1518 | 1580 | Palladio, Andrea | 1452 | 1519 | Vinci, Leonardo da |

# Additional European Personalities of the Past

**A—Artist, C—Composer, E—Explorer, M—Musician, P—Philosopher, S—Scientist, St—Statesman, W—Writer**

| Born | Died | Name | Born | Died | Name | Born | Died | Name |
|---|---|---|---|---|---|---|---|---|
| | | **Austrians** | | | **Belgians** | 1885 | 1962 | Bohr, Niels—S. |
| | | | | | | 1546 | 1601 | Brahe, Tycho—S. |
| | | **AUTHORS** | 1827 | 1879 | De Coster, Chas.—W. | 1842 | 1927 | Brandes, Georg—W. |
| | | | 1822 | 1890 | Franck, Cesar—C. | 1885 | 1962 | Dinesen, Isak—W. |
| 1878 | 1965 | Buber, Martin | 1883 | 1966 | Janssen, Albert E.—St. | 1890 | 1966 | Erichsen, Wolja—S. |
| 1791 | 1872 | Grillparzer, Frans | 1862 | 1949 | Maeterlinck, Maur.—W. | 1893 | 1966 | Friis, Astrid—W. |
| 1874 | 1929 | Hofmannsthal, H. V. | 1857 | 1931 | Mont, Pol de—W. | 1857 | 1919 | Gjellerup, Karl—W. |
| 1883 | 1924 | Kafka, Franz | 1836 | 1924 | Picard, Edmond—W. | 1894 | 1967 | Henningsen, Poul—W. |
| 1874 | 1936 | Kraus, Karl | 1823 | 1883 | Pirmez, Octave—W. | 1684 | 1754 | Holberg, Ludvig—W. |
| 1801 | 1862 | Nestroy, Johann | 1818 | 1902 | Potvin, Chas.—W. | 1884 | 1966 | Host, Oluf—A. |
| 1790 | 1836 | Raimund, Ferdinand | 1873 | 1966 | Theunis, Georges—St. | 1813 | 1855 | Kierkegaard, Soren—P. |
| 1875 | 1926 | Rilke, Rainer Maria | 1861 | 1907 | Van Lerberghe, Ch.—W. | 1894 | 1948 | Moeller, John C.—St. |
| 1862 | 1931 | Schnitzler, Artur | 1855 | 1916 | Verhaeren, Emile—W. | 1777 | 1851 | Oersted, Hans, Ch.—S. |
| 1805 | 1868 | Stifter, Adalbert | | | | 1857 | 1943 | Pontoppidan, H.—W. |
| 1843 | 1914 | Suttner, Berta v. | | | **Czechs; Slovaks** | 1140 | 1206 | Saxo, Grammaticus—W. |
| 1165 | 1227 | Walter v. d. Vogelweide | 1878 | 1932 | Bata, Thos. | 1770 | 1844 | Thorvaldsen, B.—A. |
| 1864 | 1918 | Wedekind, Franz | 1884 | 1948 | Benes, Eduard—St. | | | |
| 1881 | 1932 | Wildgans, Anton | 1762 | 1813 | Bernolak, Anton—W. | | | **Finns** |
| 1890 | 1945 | Werfel, Franz | 1890 | 1938 | Capek, Karel—W. | 1894 | 1966 | Aaltonen, Waelnoe—A. |
| 1881 | 1942 | Zweig, Stefan | 1592 | 1671 | Comenius—St. | 1861 | 1921 | Aho, Juham—W. |
| | | | 1841 | 1904 | Dvorak, Anton—C. | 1844 | 1897 | Canth, Minna—W. |
| | | **ARTISTS** | 1825 | 1904 | Hanslick, Eduard—W. | 1854 | 1905 | Edelfelt, Albert—A. |
| 1657 | 1745 | Altamonte, Martino | 1890 | 1967 | Heyrovsky, Jaroslav—S. | 1865 | 1931 | Gallen-Kallela, A. |
| 1840 | 1884 | Makart, Hans | 1879 | 1952 | Hrozny, Bedrich—S. | 1834 | 1872 | Kivi, Aleksis—W. |
| 1724 | 1796 | Maulpertsch, Franz | 1371 | 1415 | Hus, Jan. | 1802 | 1884 | Lonrot, Elias—W. |
| 1890 | 1918 | Schiele, Egon | 1854 | 1928 | Janacek, Leos—C. | 1867 | 1951 | Mannerheim, Carl—St. |
| 1718 | 1801 | Schmidt, Martin | 1810 | 1836 | Macha, Karel—W. | 1878 | 1951 | Palmgren, Selim—C. |
| 1804 | 1871 | Schwind, Mortiz v. | 1838 | 1916 | Mach, Ernest—S. | 1804 | 1877 | Runeberg, John—W. |
| 1858 | 1899 | Segantini, Gio. | 1879 | 1966 | Masaryk, Alice G.—St. | 1865 | 1957 | Sibelius, Jean—C. |
| 1793 | 1865 | Waldmueller, Ferdinand | 1887 | 1948 | Masaryk, Jan—St. | 1889 | 1964 | Sillanpaa, Frans—W. |
| | | | 1850 | 1937 | Masaryk, Tomas—St. | 1806 | 1881 | Snellman, J. V.—P. |
| | | **SCIENTISTS** | 1848 | 1922 | Myslbek, Josef—S. | 1881 | 1966 | Tanner, Vaino A.—St. |
| 1829 | 1894 | Billroth, Theo. | 1834 | 1891 | Neruda, Jan—W. | 1818 | 1898 | Topeilus, Zacharias—W. |
| 1803 | 1853 | Doppler, Christian J. | 1885 | 1944 | Niederle, Lubor | 1862 | 1939 | Westermarck, Edv.—P. |
| 1856 | 1939 | Freud, Sigmund | 1798 | 1876 | Palacky, Franisek—W. | | | |
| 1727 | 1818 | Jacquin, Nikolas V. | 1878 | 1869 | Purkyne, Jan—S. | | | **Hungarians** |
| 1838 | 1916 | Mach, Ernst | 1845 | 1912 | Siadek, Jos.—W. | 1877 | 1919 | Ady, Andrew—W. |
| 1822 | 1884 | Mendel, J. Gregor | 1824 | 1884 | Smetana, Bedrich—C. | 1823 | 1890 | Andrassy, Gyula—St. |
| 1493 | 1541 | Paracelsus, Theoph. | 1880 | 1919 | Stefanik, Milan—S. | 1846 | 1933 | Apponyi, Albert—St. |
| 1874 | 1929 | Pirquet, Clemens v. | | | | 1817 | 1882 | Arany, John—W. |
| 1793 | 1851 | Ressel, Josef | | | **Danes** | 1881 | 1945 | Bartok, Bela—C. |
| 1887 | 1961 | Schroedinger, Erwin | 1805 | 1875 | Anderson, Hans C.—W. | 1806 | 1849 | Batthany, Lajos—St. |
| 1858 | 1929 | Welsbach (Karl Auer) | 1681 | 1741 | Bering, Vitus J.—E. | | | |

| Born | Died | Name |
|---|---|---|
| 1844 | 1920 | Benczur, Gyula—A. |
| 1803 | 1876 | Deak, Francis—St. |
| 1877 | 1960 | Dohnanyi, Erno—C. |
| 1848 | 1919 | Eotvos, Lorand—S. |
| 1810 | 1893 | Erkel, Ferenc—C. |
| 1885 | 1966 | Hevesy, Georg v.—S. |
| 1868 | 1957 | Horthy, Nicholas—St. |
| 1857 | 1456 | Hunyadi, John—S. |
| 1825 | 1904 | Jokai, Maurus—W. |
| 1887 | 1967 | Kallay, Miklos—St. |
| 1887 | 1967 | Kassak, Lajos—W. |
| 1882 | 1967 | Kodaly, Zoltan—C. |
| 1792 | 1830 | Katona, Joseph—W. |
| 1790 | 1838 | Kolcsey, Ferenc—W. |
| 1802 | 1894 | Kossuth, Louis—St. |
| 1046 | 1095 | Ladislas, St.—St. |
| 1890 | 1967 | Lakatos, Geza—St. |
| 1811 | 1886 | Liszt, Franz—C. |
| 1823 | 1864 | Madach, Emeric—W. |
| 1443 | 1490 | Matthias, Corvin—St. |
| 1847 | 1910 | Mikszath, Kalman—W. |
| 1878 | 1952 | Molnar, Ferenc—W. |
| 1844 | 1901 | Munkacsy, Miholy—A. |
| 1823 | 1849 | Petofi, Sandor—W. |
| 1676 | 1735 | Rakoczi, Francis |
| 1818 | 1865 | Semmelweis, Ignaz—S. |
| 975 | 1038 | St. Stephen (1st king) |
| 1791 | 1860 | Szechenyi, Stephen—St. |
| 1861 | 1918 | Tisza, Stephen—St. |
| 1800 | 1855 | Vorosmarty, M.—W. |
| 1849 | 1924 | Zichy, Geza—C. |

## Irish

### AUTHORS

| Born | Died | Name |
|---|---|---|
| 1824 | 1889 | Allingham, Wm. |
| 1923 | 1964 | Behan, Brendan |
| 1832 | 1916 | Brooke, Stopford A. |
| 1843 | 1913 | Dowden, Edward |
| 1878 | 1957 | Dunsany (E.J.Plunkett) |
| 1878 | 1957 | Gogarty, Oliver St. John |
| 1728 | 1774 | Goldsmith, Oliver |
| 1852 | 1932 | Gregory, Lady |
| 1882 | 1941 | Joyce, James |
| 1905 | 1967 | Kavanagh, Patrick |
| 1891 | 1917 | Ledwidge, Francis |
| 1806 | 1872 | Lever, Charles |
| 1797 | 1868 | Lover, Samuel |
| 1879 | 1949 | Lynd, Robert |
| 1916 | 1967 | Macken, Walter |
| 1852 | 1933 | Moore, George |
| 1779 | 1852 | Moore, Thomas |
| 1828 | 1862 | O'Brien, Fitz-James |
| 1911 | 1966 | O'Brien, Flann |
| 1884 | 1964 | O'Casey, Sean |
| 1903 | 1966 | O'Connor, Frank |
| 1844 | 1881 | O'Shaughnessy, Arthur |
| 1879 | 1916 | Pearse, Padraic |
| 1886 | 1958 | Robinson, Lennox |
| 1867 | 1935 | Russell, George |
| 1856 | 1950 | Shaw, G. Bernard |
| 1751 | 1816 | Sheridan, Richard B. |
| 1866 | 1918 | Sigerson, Dora |
| 1882 | 1950 | Stephens, James |
| 1667 | 1745 | Swift, Jonathan |
| 1871 | 1909 | Synge, John M. |
| 1652 | 1715 | Tate, Nahum |
| 1854 | 1900 | Wilde, Oscar |
| 1865 | 1939 | Yeats, Wm. Butler |

## Netherlands

### DUTCH PAINTERS

| Born | Died | Name |
|---|---|---|
| 1450 | 1516 | Bosch, Hieronymus |
| 1410 | 1475 | Bouts, Dirk |
| 1620 | 1691 | Cuyp, Albert |
| 1613 | 1675 | Douw, Gerard |
| 1622 | 1654 | Fabritius, Carel |
| 1584 | 1666 | Hals, Frans |
| 1638 | 1709 | Hobbema, Meindert |
| 1629 | 1683 | Hooch, Pieter |
| 1682 | 1749 | Huysum, Jan van |
| 1872 | 1944 | Mondrian, Piet |
| 1610 | 1685 | Ostade, Adr. van |
| 1625 | 1654 | Potter, Paul |
| 1606 | 1669 | Rembrandt van Rijn |
| 1625 | 1682 | Ruysdael, Jacob |
| 1626 | 1679 | Steen, Jan |
| 1617 | 1681 | Ter Borch, Gerard |
| 1853 | 1890 | Van Gogh, Vincent |
| 1596 | 1656 | Van Goyen, Jan |
| 1494 | 1533 | Van Leyden, Lucas |
| 1632 | 1675 | Vermeer, Jan |

### FLEMISH PAINTERS

| Born | Died | Name |
|---|---|---|
| 1605 | 1638 | Brouwer, Adriaen |
| 1568 | 1625 | Brueghel, Jan |
| 1614 | 1684 | Coques, Gonzales |
| 1440 | 1482 | Goes, Hugo van der |
| 1648 | 1727 | Huysmans, Cornelis |
| 1656 | 1696 | Huysmans, Jacob |
| 1593 | 1678 | Jordaens, Jacob |
| 1478 | 1533 | Mabuse, Jan |
| 1460 | 1531 | Matsys, Quentin |

| Born | Died | Name |
|---|---|---|
| 1435 | 1495 | Memling, Hans |
| 1577 | 1640 | Rubens, Peter Paul |
| 1579 | 1657 | Snyders, Frans |
| 1582 | 1649 | Teniers, David |
| 1610 | 1694 | Teniers, David (2) |
| 1599 | 1641 | Van Dyck, Anthony |
| 1366 | 1426 | Van Eyck, Hubert |
| 1386 | 1440 | Van Eyck, Jan |
| 1399 | 1464 | Weyden, Rogier v. d. |

## Norwegians

### AUTHORS

| Born | Died | Name |
|---|---|---|
| 1813 | 1896 | Aasen, Ivar |
| 1812 | 1885 | Asbjornsen, Peter |
| 1832 | 1910 | Bjornson, Bjornstjerne |
| 1872 | 1959 | Bojer, Johan |
| 1813 | 1895 | Collett, Camilla |
| 1879 | 1967 | Falkberget, Johan |
| 1851 | 1924 | Garborg, Arne |
| 1859 | 1952 | Hamsun, Knut |
| 1828 | 1906 | Ibsen, Henrik |
| 1849 | 1906 | Kielland, Alex. L. |
| 1865 | 1926 | Kinck, Hans E. |
| 1833 | 1908 | Lie, Jonas |
| 1813 | 1882 | Moe, Jorgen |
| 1810 | 1863 | Munch, Peter |
| 1882 | 1949 | Undset, Sigrid |
| 1807 | 1873 | Welhaven, Johan S. |
| 1808 | 1845 | Wergeland, Henrik |

### EXPLORERS

| Born | Died | Name |
|---|---|---|
| 1872 | 1928 | Amundsen, Roald |
| 1861 | 1930 | Nansen, Fridtjof |
| 1854 | 1930 | Sverdrup, Otto |

## Poles

| Born | Died | Name |
|---|---|---|
| 1880 | 1957 | Asch, Scholem—W. |
| 966 | 1025 | Boleslav, Chrobry—St. |
| 1310 | 1370 | Casimir the Great—St. |
| 1810 | 1849 | Chopin, Fryderyk—C. |
| 1473 | 1543 | Copernicus, Nich—S. |
| 1857 | 1924 | Korzeniowski, C.—W. |
| 1746 | 1817 | Kosciuszko, Gen. T.-St. |
| 1812 | 1859 | Krasinski, Z.—W. |
| 1879 | 1959 | Landowska, Wanda.—M |
| 1756 | 1861 | Lelewel, Joachim—W. |
| 1896 | 1966 | Mackiewicz, Stanislaw —W. |
| 1839 | 1895 | Matejko, Jan.—A. |
| 1798 | 1855 | Mickiewicz, Adam—W. |
| 1901 | 1966 | Mikolajczyk, Stanislaw—St. |
| 1867 | 1904 | Moscicki, Ignace—St. |
| 1860 | 1941 | Paderewski, Ignace—C. |
| 1867 | 1935 | Pilsudski, Jos.—St. |
| 1847 | 1912 | Prus, Boleslaw—W. |
| 1748 | 1779 | Pulaski, Casimir—St. |
| 1868 | 1925 | Reymont, W.—W. |
| 1846 | 1916 | Sienkiewicz, H.—W. |
| 1867 | 1934 | Sklodowska, Marie (Curie)—S. |
| 1809 | 1849 | Slowacki, Juliusz—W. |
| 1892 | 1967 | Smeterlin, Jan—M. |
| 1869 | 1907 | Wyspianski, S.—A. |
| 1542 | 1605 | Zamoyski, Jan—St. |
| 1864 | 1925 | Zeromski, Stefan—W |

## Spanish

### AUTHORS

| Born | Died | Name |
|---|---|---|
| 1833 | 1891 | Alarcon, Pedro de |
| 1874 | 1967 | Azorin (J. M. Ruiz) |
| 1866 | 1954 | Benavente, Jacinto |
| 1180 | 1265 | Berceo, Gonzalo de |
| 1867 | 1928 | Blasco, Ibanez,.V. |
| 1600 | 1681 | Calderón de la Barca |
| 1547 | 1616 | Cervantes, Miguel de |
| 1533 | 1594 | Ercilla y Zuniga |
| 1760 | 1828 | Fernández de Moratin |
| 1899 | 1936 | Garcia Lorca, Federico |
| 1503 | 1536 | Garcilaso de la Vega |
| 1561 | 1627 | Góngora y Argote |
| 1803 | 1839 | Heredia y Campuzano |
| 1881 | 1958 | Jimenez, Juan R. |
| 1528 | 1591 | Leon, Luis de |
| 1877 | 1943 | Leon, Ricardo |
| 1332 | 1407 | Lopez de Ayala |
| 1398 | 1458 | Lopez de Mendoza |
| 1440 | 1479 | Manrique, Jorge |
| 1282 | 1348 | Manuel, Juan |
| 1883 | 1955 | Ortega y Gasse, Jose |
| 1852 | 1921 | Pardo Bazan, Emilia |
| 1833 | 1906 | Pereda, Jose Mario de |
| 1843 | 1929 | Perez Galdos, B. |
| 1580 | 1645 | Quevedo y Villegas, F. |
| 1772 | 1857 | Quintana, Manuel Jose |
| 1465 | 1541 | Rojas, Fernando de |
| 1510 | 1566 | Rueda, Lope de |
| 1580 | 1639 | Ruiz de Alarcon, J. |
| 1864 | 1936 | Unamuno, Miguel de |
| 1503 | 1541 | Valdés, Juan de |
| 1824 | 1905 | Valera y Alcalá |
| 1870 | 1936 | Valle-Inclan, D. del |

| Born | Died | Name |
|---|---|---|
| 1562 | 1635 | Vega, Lope de |
| 1579 | 1644 | Velez de Guevara, L. |

### PAINTERS

| Born | Died | Name |
|---|---|---|
| 1786 | 1827 | Alvarez, Don Jose |
| 1601 | 1667 | Cano, Alonzo |
| 1641 | 1685 | Carreno de Miranda |
| 1838 | 1874 | Fortuny, Mariano |
| 1746 | 1828 | Goya y Lucientes, F. |
| 1815 | 1894 | Madrazo, Federico |
| 1509 | 1586 | Morales, Luis de |
| 1618 | 1682 | Murillo, B. E. |
| 1551 | 1609 | Pantoja de la Cruz, Juan |
| 1560 | 1628 | Ribalta, Francisco de |
| 1588 | 1656 | Ribera, Jose |
| 1520 | 1590 | Sanchez Coello, Alonso |
| 1863 | 1923 | Sorolla y Bastida, J. |
| 1548 | 1614 | Theotocupull, Domenigo. El Greco* |
| 1622 | 1690 | Valdes Leal, Juan |
| 1599 | 1660 | Velasquez, Diego |
| 1870 | 1945 | Zuloaga, Ignacio |

*El Greco (the Greek) was born in Candia, Crete, between 1541-48, studied plainting under Titian in Venice, became a leading Spanish painter and died in Toledo.

## Swedes

| Born | Died | Name |
|---|---|---|
| 1793 | 1866 | Almquist, C. J. L.—W. |
| 1859 | 1927 | Arrhenius, Svante A.—S. |
| 1740 | 1795 | Bellman, C. M.—W. |
| 1885 | 1967 | Berg, Bengt—W. |
| 1869 | 1967 | Bergman, H. H.—W. |
| 1895 | 1948 | Bernadotte, Folke—St. |
| 1779 | 1848 | Berzelius, Jakob—S. |
| 1801 | 1865 | Bremer, Fredrika—W. |
| 1866 | 1945 | Cassel, Gustav—S. |
| 1701 | 1744 | Celsius, Anders—S. |
| 1803 | 1889 | Ericsson, John—S. |
| 1876 | 1966 | Fries, Robert—S. |
| 1860 | 1911 | Froding, Gustav—W. |
| 1783 | 1847 | Geijer, E. G.—W. |
| 1905 | 1961 | Hammarskjold, Dag—St. |
| 1885 | 1946 | Hansson, Per Albin |
| 1865 | 1952 | Hedin, Sven—E. |
| 1891 | 1966 | Josephson, Ragnar—W. |
| 1864 | 1931 | Karlfeldt, Erik Axel—W. |
| 1858 | 1940 | Lagerlof, Selma—W. |
| 1707 | 1778 | Linne, Carl von—S. |
| 1875 | 1955 | Milles, Carl—A. |
| 1843 | 1921 | Montelius, Oscar—W. |
| 1857 | 1949 | Munthe, Axel—W. |
| 1833 | 1896 | Nobel, Alfred B.—S. |
| 1842 | 1919 | Retzius, Gustaf—S. |
| 1828 | 1895 | Rydberg, Viktor—W. |
| 1879 | 1966 | Siren, Osvald—W. |
| 1793 | 1823 | Stagnelius, E. J.—W. |
| 1849 | 1912 | Strindberg, August—W. |
| 1688 | 1772 | Swedenborg, E.—W. |
| 1782 | 1846 | Tegner, Esaias—W. |

## Swiss

### AUTHORS, SCHOLARS

| Born | Died | Name |
|---|---|---|
| 1807 | 1873 | Agassiz, Louis |
| 1818 | 1897 | Burckhardt, Jakob |
| 1828 | 1910 | Dunant, Henri |
| 1848 | 1931 | Forel Auguste |
| 1797 | 1854 | Gotthelf, Jeremias |
| 1708 | 1777 | Haller, Albrecht V. |
| 1875 | 1961 | Jung, Carl Gustav |
| 1819 | 1890 | Keller, Gottfried |
| 1741 | 1801 | Lavater, Johann K. |
| 1825 | 1898 | Meyer, Conrad F. |
| 1493 | 1541 | Paracelsus, Theophrastus |
| 1746 | 1827 | Pestalozzi, Johann H. |
| 1712 | 1778 | Rousseau, Jean Jacques |
| 1740 | 1799 | Saussure, Benedict |
| 1845 | 1924 | Spitteler, Karl |
| 1766 | 1817 | Stael, Madame de |
| 1797 | 1847 | Vinet, Alexandre |

### PAINTERS, SCULPTORS

| Born | Died | Name |
|---|---|---|
| 1827 | 1901 | Boecklin, Arnold |
| 1810 | 1864 | Calame, Alexandre |
| 1741 | 1825 | Fussli (Fuseli), J. H. |
| 1901 | 1966 | Giacometti, Alberto |
| 1806 | 1874 | Gleyre, Charles |
| 1853 | 1918 | Hodler, Ferdinand |
| 1741 | 1807 | Kauffmann, Angelica |
| 1879 | 1940 | Klee, Paul |
| 1702 | 1798 | Liotard, Jean Etienne |
| 1794 | 1835 | Robert, Leopold |

## Ukrainians

| Born | Died | Name |
|---|---|---|
| 1881 | 1946 | Bogomolets, Alex—S. |
| 1866 | 1934 | Hrushevsky, Mich.—W. |
| .... | 1657 | Khmelnitsky, B.—St. |
| .... | 1709 | Mazeppa, Ivan—St. |
| 1842 | 1912 | Lysenko, Nicholas—C. |
| 1871 | 1913 | Ukrainka, Lesya—W. |

# U. S. Passport, Visa and Health Requirements

**Source:** Passport Office, U. S. Dept. of State and U. S. Public Health Service

Passports are issued by the United States Department of State to citizens and nationals of the United States for the purpose of documenting them for their foreign travel and to identify them as Americans. Some countries require a visa, or stamp of approval, to be affixed to the passport by the consulate of the country to be visited, while others waive this formality. Also some countries, which do not require visas, require tourist cards from visitors making a short stay.

Passports may not be used for travel into or through Cuba, Mainland China, North Korea or North Vietnam unless specifically endorsed for such travel.

## HOW TO OBTAIN A PASSPORT

An applicant for a passport who has never been previously issued a passport in his own name, must execute an application in person before a clerk of a Federal court or a State court having naturalization jurisdiction, or before an Agent of the Passport Office or before a diplomatic or consular officer of the U. S. abroad. A spouse who is to be included in the application must appear with the applicant and execute the application. Passport Agents are located at Boston (John F. Kennedy Bldg., Government Center), Chicago (Fed. Office Bldg., 219 S. Dearborn); Honolulu (Fed. Bldg.); Los Angeles (Fed. Office Bldg., 300 N. Los Angeles St.); Miami (51 S.W. First Ave.); New Orleans (U. S. Customs House, 423 Canal St.); New York (630 Fifth Ave.); Philadelphia (401 N. Broad St.); San Francisco (Fed. Office Bldg., 450 Golden Gate Ave.); Seattle (1410 Fifth Ave.); Washington D. C. (Passport Office, 17th and H Sts., N. W.).

An applicant may submit a prior passport in lieu of evidence of citizenship. A native-born citizen must submit an acceptable birth certificate, or baptismal certificate. A notice by appropriate authorities indicating no birth record exists must be submitted with evidence other than birth certificate or baptismal certificate. A baptismal certificate or certified copy of record of baptism showing baptism occurred shortly after birth should bear the full name, date and place of birth, and the seal, name, and location of the church. In the absence of the above, other evidence, such as census records, newspaper files, school records or affidavits of persons having personal knowledge of the facts of birth may be submitted for consideration.

A person in the U. S. who has been issued a passport in his own name within the last eight years may obtain a new passport by filling out, signing and mailing a special application form together with his previous passport, two duplicate signed photographs taken within the last 6 months and the established fee to the nearest Passport Agency or to the Passport Office in Wash., D. C. If, however, an applicant is applying for a passport for the first time, if his prior passport was issued before his 18th birthday, if he wishes to include a person other than himself in the passport, or if he is applying for an official or diplomatic passport, he must execute a regular passport application in person before a clerk of court or Passport Agent.

A naturalized citizen should present his naturalization certificate. A person claiming citizenship through either a native-born or naturalized citizen must submit a certificate of citizenship issued by the Attorney General; or a Consular Report of Birth or Certification of Birth issued by the Dept. of State. If one of the above documents has not been obtained, he must submit evidence of citizenship of the parent(s) through whom citizenship is claimed and evidence which would establish the parent/child relationship. Additionally, if through birth to one American and one alien parent, an affidavit showing periods and places of residence in the United States and abroad, specifying periods in Armed Forces of U. S.; if through naturalization of parents, evidence of admission to the United States for permanent residence.

A married woman must submit evidence of citizenship and, under certain conditions, marriage. Special regulations govern women married prior to Sept. 22, 1922; check a Passport Agency.

The applicant shall establish his identity to the satisfaction of the Clerk of Court or Passport Agent. Proof of identity may be established through a personal knowledge of the applicant by the Clerk or Agent or by an item which contains the signature and either a physical description or photograph of the applicant. The following items of identification are acceptable: Previous United States Passport; naturalization certificate; driver's license; a Federal, state, municipal identification card or pass; an industrial or business identification card or pass.

If the applicant is not able to establish his identity by personal knowledge or by one of the above items, he shall have an identifying witness who has known him at least 2 years. The witness himself must have acceptable identification.

**Aliens**—An alien leaving the U.S. must request passport facilities from his home government. He must have a permit from his local Collector of Internal Revenue, and if he wishes to return he should request a re-entry permit from the Immigration and Naturalization Service if it is required.

**Contract Employees**—Persons traveling because of a contract with the Government must submit with their applications letters from their employer stating position, destination and purpose of travel and Armed Forces contract number when pertinent.

Persons of military draft age may receive passports but should inform their draft boards of their travel plans.

## PHOTOGRAPHS AND FEES

**Photographs**—Two recent duplicate photographs, both signed by the applicant and which are a good likeness, must accompany the passport application. A group photograph is preferred if more than one person is included in the passport. Photographs may be in color or in black and white. They must be full face, printed on a thin, unglazed paper base on a light background and must be no smaller than $2\frac{1}{2}$ x $2\frac{1}{2}$ inches nor larger than 3 x 3 inches in size. They must also be capable of withstanding a mounting temperature of over 200° F.

**Fees**—The passport fee is $10, plus an execution fee of $2 whenever an application is executed in person before a clerk of court, Passport Agent or diplomatic or consular officer abroad. No execution fee is payable where a passport is applied for by mail. All applicants must pay the passport fee and, where applicable, the execution fee unless specifically exempted by law. A person who is proceeding abroad on official Government business should submit a sponsoring letter from his employing Agency instead of the passport fee. This letter will also excuse the payment of an execution fee if an application is executed before a Federal official. Where, however, an application is executed before a clerk of State court the latter is authorized by law to collect and retain the $2 fee. Emergency clearance costs $2 at all Passport Agencies except New York and Philadelphia where it is $1. An emergency service fee of $10 is charged in addition to all other fees where work must be performed after hours. The only other fees are for postage and emergency charges. "A passport is valid for five years. The validity period of all passports outstanding (i.e., unrenewed passports within five year of their issue dates) on Aug. 26, 1968 was automatically extended by Act of Congress to five years from the original date of issue without the need of renewal. Upon expiration, passports may no longer be renewed. New passports must be obtained."

During the calender year 1967 the Passport Office, Dept. of State, issued 1,685,512 new and renewed passports to American citizens.

If passport is lost notify the Passport Office, Dept. of State, Wash., D. C. 20524. If lost abroad, report loss to U. S. Consul.

## FOREIGN REGULATIONS

A visa is an endorsement or a notation, usually rubber stamped in a passport by a representative of the country to be visited. It certifies that the bearer of the passport is to be entitled to enter the country for a certain purpose and length of time. With the exception of the Iron Curtain countries, no visas are required for brief tourist travel to Western European countries. Authoritative visa information can be obtained by writing directly to foreign consular officials. The locations of foreign consular offices in the U. S. may be obtained by consulting the Congressional Directory available in most libraries. (Check appropriate city telephone directories for complete address.)

## HEALTH ADVICE

Smallpox vaccination is required by most countries for entry and by the United States for re-entry. The United States does not require smallpox of travelers whose trips are restricted to Aruba, Bahamas, British Virgin Islands, Canada, Canal Zone, Curacao, Greenland, Iceland, Jamaica, Mexico, and St. Pierre and Miquelon. Vaccination is valid for three years.

Yellow fever is required for entry to certain infected countries and when traveling from infected to "receptive" areas. It can be performed only at certain Centers designated by the Public Health Service, and is valid for 10 years.

Cholera is generally required when traveling to or from infected areas. It is valid for 6 months only.

Smallpox, yellow fever, and cholera vaccinations must be recorded on PHS Form 731, International Certificates of Vaccination. These are generally available from state and local health departments and offices issuing passports (including clerks of courts), or from the Superintendent of Documents, U. S. Government Printing Office, Wash., D. C.

20402, for 10¢ apiece. The traveler and his physician should fill in the requested information, and the certificate then must be stamped to be valid. The stamp usually is applied by the state or local health department to which certificates may be either mailed or taken in person.

The following immunizations are suggested for *all* travelers: typhoid, tetanus, diphtheria, polio, and measles. Travelers to South and Central America (except urban Mexico), Africa, Asia and the South Pacific (except Japan, Australia, New Zealand) should receive Immune Serum Globulin (Human) for protection against hepatitis. Travelers to areas infected with malaria should receive preventive treatment. All travelers are advised to take adequate supplies of any medicines they may need and either an extra pair of or prescription for their glasses.

Specific requirements by country are published in "Immunization Information for International Travel" (Government Printing Office, 40¢). Additional information may be obtained from Foreign Quarantine Program, National Communicable Disease Center, Atlanta, Georgia 30333.

# Liberalized U. S. Immigration Law in Effect

The national origins quota system disappeared from United States immigration procedures July 1, 1968, as provided by the Act. of Oct. 3, 1965, which amended the Immigration and Nationality Act.

The Immigration and Nationality Act, as amended, provides for numerical limitations on immigration from the Eastern and Western Hemispheres. Not subject to any numerical limitations, however, are immigrants who are spouses or children of U. S. citizens, or parents of citizens who are 21 years of age or older; returning residents; certain former U. S. citizens; ministers of religion; and certain long-term U.S. Government employees.

The Act of Oct. 3, 1965, established new controls to protect the American labor market from an influx of skilled and unskilled foreign labor. The primary responsibility was placed on the would-be immigrant to obtain the Secretary of Labor's clearance, prior to the issuance of a visa, establishing that there are not sufficient workers in the U. S. at the alien's designation who are able, willing and qualified to perform the skilled or unskilled labor; and that the employment of the alien will not adversely affect wages and working conditions of U. S. citizens similarly employed.

## EASTERN HEMISPHERE IMMIGRANTS

Persons born in countries of the Eastern Hemisphere and dependent areas thereof are subject to an annual limitation of 170,000. Within this numerical limitation there is an annual limitation of 20,000 for each country and 200 for each dependent area. Applicants are classified as either preference or nonpreference.

The preference visa categories are based on certain relationships to persons in the U. S.; i.e., unmarried sons and daughters of United States citizens, spouses and unmarried sons and daughters of resident aliens, married sons and daughters of U. S. citizens, and brothers and sisters of U. S. citizens (first, second, fourth, and fifth preference, respectively); certain professions and skills (third preference); and certain categories of workers which are in short supply in the U. S. (sixth preference). Spouses and children of preference applicants are entitled to the same preference if accompanying or following to join such persons.

Preference status is based on approved petitions, filed with the Immigration and Naturalization Service, by the applicable relatives or employers. Visa numbers for qualified preference applicants are made available in the order of the preference classes and, within such classes, in the order of the filing dates of the petitions.

Immigrants not entitled to classification within one of the above-mentioned preference groups are nonpreference applicants and receive only those visa numbers not needed by preference applicants.

As the preference categories appear likely to take all but a very few of the 170,000 immigrant visa numbers authorized, most applicants without preference status will be unable to immigrate to the United States in the foreseeable future under existing legislation. Further, a heavy demand in some of the preference classes has resulted in extended waiting periods for many applicants in those classes. Also, the higher preference categories may utilize the entire numerical limitation in some countries and dependent areas, which will prevent any visa numbers becoming available for persons from such countries or areas in any of the lower preference categories for that year.

## WESTERN HEMISPHERE IMMIGRANTS

The Act establishes an annual ceiling of 120,000 on immigration by persons born in independent countries of the Western Hemisphere (Canada, Mexico, Central and South America and the Caribbean Area). Within this over-all ceiling there is no numerical limitation set for indivdual countries, and no preference classes have been established for such applicants. Visas within the 120,000 limitation will be made available to qualified applicants in the chronological order of their priority dates. An applicant's priority is based on the date a labor certification is approved or the date proof is received by the consular officer that a labor certification is not required.

## EXCLUDABLE ALIENS

Among aliens who are excludable are persons mentally retarded, insane, psychopathic, mentally defective, sexual deviates, and those afflicted with any dangerous contagious disease or having a physical defect impairing the ability to earn a living. Also chronic alcoholics, narcotic addicts, paupers, beggars, stowaways and prostitutes. Also persons convicted of crimes such as narcotics trafficking or commercialized vice. Also persons who try to enter the U. S. by fraud, illiterates, and persons who left the U. S. to avoid military service. Also anarchists and those who teach or advocate overthrow of the U. S. Government by force or violence.

For more detailed information consult the nearest office of the U. S. Immigration & Naturalization Service, or any U. S. Consul abroad.

# Great Seal of the United States

The Great Seal of the United States was first adopted by the Continental Congress, June 20, 1782, and by the Federal Government Sept. 16, 1789. The Secretary of State is its custodian. Only one face is used on documents.

A representation of the Great Seal is in the hands of every American citizen who possesses a $1 bill. On the back of the bill both sides of the seal are shown. The face of the seal, on the right hand side of the bill, shows an American eagle with wings and talons outstretched. Above his head is a circle containing 13 "pieces argent," or silver buttons; the eagle's breast holds a shield with 13 stripes; the right talon holds an olive branch and the left talon a bundle of 13 arrows. In its beak the eagle holds a ribbon with the motto E Pluribus Unum—Out of Many, One, referring to the union of the states.

On the reverse the seal shows an unfinished pyramid. Above the pyramid is a "glory" or burst of light, with an eye inside a triangle, referring to the Eternal Eye of God, and above it is the motto Annuit Coeptis, meaning He Has Favored Our Undertaking. The base of the pyramid bears the numerals MDCCLXXVI, or 1776, and below it is the motto Novus Ordo Seclorum, or A New Order of the Ages. The pyramid has 13 steps and signifies the strength of the union.

# Naturalization: How to Become an American Citizen

### Source: The Federal Statutes

A person who desires to be naturalized as a citizen of the United States may obtain the necessary application form as well as detailed information from the nearest office of the Immigration and Naturalization Service or from the clerk of a court handling naturalization cases.

There are no racial bars to naturalization. Women have the same right as men to become naturalized.

An applicant must be at least 18 years old. He must have been a lawful resident of the United States continuously for 5 years. For husbands and wives of U. S. citizens the period is 3 years in most instances. Special provisions apply to certain veterans of the Armed Forces.

An applicant must have been physically present in this country for at least one-half of the required 5 years' residence.

Every applicant for naturalization must:

(1) sign the petition in his own handwriting, if physically able to write;

(2) demonstrate an understanding of the English language, including an ability to read, write, and speak words in ordinary usage in the English language (persons physically unable to do so, and persons who were on December 24, 1952 over 50 years of age and had been residing in the United States for 20 years are excepted).

(3) have been a person of good moral character, attached to the principles of the Constitution, and well disposed to the good order and happiness of the United States for five years just before filing the petition or for whatever other period of residence is required in his case and continue to be such a person until admitted to citizenship; and

(4) demonstrate a knowledge and understanding of the fundamentals of the history, and the principles and form of government, of the U. S.

The petitioner also is obliged to have two credible citizen witnesses. These witnesses must have personal knowledge of the applicant's character, residence, loyalty, and other qualifications.

A person not of good moral character includes a habitual drunkard, an adulterer, a polygamist, a violator of criminal law, a gambler, one who gave false testimony to obtain a benefit under the immigration law, one in prison for 180 days or more, one convicted of murder.

Naturalization is denied to any person who, within 10 years, has been subversive, including communists and others who favor totalitarian government, and who were members of a proscribed organization, unless the petitioner was under 16 or joined under duress.

A law approved Aug. 20, 1958, provides for the expeditious naturalization of alien spouses and adopted children of U.S. citizens who are missionaries or performing religious duties and are stationed abroad.

When the applicant files his petition he pays the court clerk $10. At the preliminary hearing he may be represented by a lawyer or social service agency. There is a 30-day wait. If action is favorable, there is a final hearing before a judge, who administers the following oath of allegiance:

## OATH OF ALLEGIANCE

I hereby declare, on oath, that I absolutely and entirely renounce and abjure all allegiance and fidelity to any foreign prince, potentate, state or sovereignty, of whom or which I have heretofore been a subject or citizen; that I will support and defend the Constitution and laws of the United States of America against all enemies, foreign and domestic; that I will bear true faith and allegiance to the same; that I will bear arms on behalf of the United States when required by the law; that I will perform noncombatant service in the armed forces of the United States when required by the law; that I will perform work of national importance under civilian direction when required by the law, and that I take this obligation freely without any mental reservation or purpose of evasion; so help me God.

---

# Customs Exemptions and Advice to Travelers

United States residents returning after a stay abroad of at least 48 hours are, generally speaking, granted customs exemptions of $100 each. Each returning resident may bring home free of duty articles totaling $100 in retail value in the country of acquisition, subject to limitations on liquors and cigars. These articles must accompany the traveler at the time of his return, must be for his personal or household use, must have been acquired as an incident of his trip, and must be properly declared to Customs. Not more than one quart of alcoholic beverages may be included in the $100 exemption.

If a U. S. resident arrives directly or indirectly from American Samoa, Guam, or the Virgin Islands of the United States, his purchases may be valued up to $200 fair retail value, but not more than $100 of the exemption to be applied to the value of articles acquired elsewhere than in such insular possessions, and one gallon of alcoholic beverages may be included in his exemption, but not more than 1 quart of such beverages may have been acquired elsewhere than in the designated islands.

The exemption for articles acquired in the Virgin Islands of the United States and in Mexico is not conditional upon the 48-hour absence requirement.

In either case, the exemption for alcoholic beverages is accorded only when the returning resident has attained 21 years of age at the time of his arrival. One hundred cigars may be included (except Cuban products) in either the $100 or $200 exemption only if the exemption, or any part of it, has not been used within the preceding 30-day period.

Bona fide gifts costing no more than $10 fair retail value may be mailed to friends at home duty-free; addressee cannot receive in a single day gifts exceeding the $10 limitation.

### PRECAUTIONS FOR TRAVEL

In some cases naturalized United States citizens desiring to visit the countries of their birth, and sometimes their American-born children traveling to those countries, may be subject to military service and other regulations there. The United States Department of State advises such travelers to get specific information from the consulates of the countries concerned before departure.

A Briton who becomes a naturalized United States citizen is considered a British citizen by the British until he makes a formal renunciation of British nationality before British authorities.

A French person who has attained majority loses French nationality by voluntary acquisition of U.S. or other nationality. However, French male persons with military service obligations do not lose French nationality unless authorized by the French Government. Authorization is granted when the applicant acquired a foreign nationality after age 50. A female U. S. citizen who marries a Frenchman acquires French nationality unless prior to her marriage she declined it.

Portugal will recognize U. S. naturalization of a Portuguese if the latter has resided five years in the United States.

Greece regards citizens: (1) former Greek nationals naturalized abroad after 1914 without authorization from Greece; (2) persons born abroad of parents considered by Greece to have Greek nationality, even though they may have acquired citizenship elsewhere; (3) Greeks who were former subjects of Turkish territory, except Istanbul; (4) Greeks formerly of Istanbul who left before Aug. 1, 1929 without Turkish passports.

Israel has two types of visas: visitors' visas and immigration visas. A visitor's visa is limited to 3 mos. and may be renewed. A person who wishes to live in Israel permanently must obtain an immigration visa. This person will be required to give military service if a male between 18 and 49, inclusive, or a female between 18 and 38, inclusive, and must obtain authorization from the Ministry of Defense if he or she desires to leave the country before completing military service. A U. S. citizen who voluntarily joins a foreign army loses his U. S. citizenship unless he has written consent of the U. S. Government to do so. Jews arriving in Israel with immigration visas or obtaining such visas while in Israel are automatically granted Israeli nationality unless they declare to a Consul of Israel or to the Israeli Government that they do not want to be nationals of Israel.

# Immigrants Admitted From All Countries

Source: Immigration and Naturalization Service, U. S. Dept. of Justice

| Year | Number | Year | Number | Year | Number |
|---|---|---|---|---|---|
| 1820 | 8,385 | 1891-1900 | 3,687,564 | 1961 | 271,344 |
| 1821-1830 | 143,439 | 1901-1910 | 8,795,386 | 1962 | 283,763 |
| 1831-1840 | 599,125 | 1911-1920 | 5,735,811 | 1963 | 306,260 |
| 1841-1850 | 1,713,251 | 1921-1930 | 4,107,209 | 1964 | 292,248 |
| 1851-1860 | 2,598,214 | 1931-1940 | 528,431 | 1965 | 296,697 |
| 1861-1870 | 2,314,824 | 1941-1950 | 1,035,039 | 1966 | 323,040 |
| 1871-1880 | 2,812,191 | 1959 | 260,686 | 1967 | 456,614 |
| 1881-1890 | 5,246,613 | 1960 | 265,398 | 1820-1967 | 44,070,927 |

Immigration from the close of the Revolutionary War to 1820 is estimated at 250,000.

# Passports Issued and Renewed

Source: Passport Office, Dept. of State

[Passports are actual count; other data based on a sample. Data refer to number of passports issued, not travelers (except as noted). A single passport may cover more than one trip and more than one person]

| Item | 1950 | 1960 | 1963 | 1964 | 1965 | 1966 | 1967 |
|---|---|---|---|---|---|---|---|
| New and renewed passports.... | 299,665 | 853,087 | 1,055,504 | 1,133,228 | 1,330,290 | 1,547,725 | 1,685,512 |
| **Object of travel:**[1] | | | | | | | |
| Government | (N.A.) | 115,910 | 145,034 | 180,328 | 191,140 | 215,585 | 161,122 |
| Nongovernment | (N.A.) | 737,177 | 910,470 | 952,900 | 1,139,150 | 1,332,140 | 1,524,390 |
| Personal reasons[2] | 141,567 | 321,590 | 436,250 | 366,860 | 487,470 | 483,240 | 638,790 |
| Pleasure[3] | 108,486 | 350,897 | 353,150 | 470,180 | 535,150 | 651,220 | 670,880 |
| Business[4] | 27,364 | 24,540 | 86,000 | 78,300 | 76,210 | 135,250 | 140,700 |
| Education | 13,837 | 31,240 | 26,470 | 30,200 | 31,120 | 51,750 | 61,270 |
| Religion | 4,676 | 6,780 | 6,540 | 5,480 | 6,770 | 8,280 | 7,750 |
| Health | 1,069 | 1,460 | 1,350 | 1,140 | 500 | 710 | 2,280 |
| Other | 2,666 | 670 | 710 | 740 | 1,930 | 1,690 | 2,720 |
| **First area destination:** | | | | | | | |
| Africa | 4,827 | 8,440 | 12,350 | 16,120 | 19,580 | 22,690 | 19,580 |
| Australia and Oceania | 2,059 | 35,220 | 32,650 | 36,880 | 50,750 | 58,450 | 55,510 |
| Europe | 243,771 | 669,662 | 794,964 | 864,598 | 992,800 | 1,115,855 | 1,265,172 |
| Far East | 5,558 | 55,960 | 102,010 | 95,640 | 111,310 | 165,660 | 157,020 |
| North, Central and South America | 33,003 | 58,935 | 70,890 | 72,880 | 99,620 | 120,590 | 126,480 |
| Middle-East | 10,447 | 24,670 | 42,390 | 46,710 | 56,080 | 64,070 | 61,340 |
| Not stated[5] | | 200 | 250 | 400 | 150 | 420 | |
| **Mode of travel—departure:** | | | | | | | |
| Ship | 200,800 | 226,245 | 165,141 | 114,621 | 39,340 | 49,765 | 37,793 |
| Air | 96,565 | 626,842 | 890,363 | 1,018,607 | 1,290,950 | 1,497,960 | 1,647,719 |
| **Sex of traveler:** | | | | | | | |
| Male | 155,595 | 419,615 | 534,490 | 579,520 | 700,080 | 810,850 | 870,383 |
| Female | 144,070 | 433,472 | 521,014 | 553,708 | 630,210 | 736,875 | 815,129 |
| **Citizenship of traveler:** | | | | | | | |
| Native | 174,723 | 710,172 | 918,364 | 1,011,597 | 1,236,797 | 1,374,075 | 1,535,313 |
| Naturalized | 124,942 | 142,915 | 137,140 | 121,631 | 93,493 | 173,650 | 150,199 |

[1] Data not entirely comparable because of changes in classifications in 1956, 1958, and 1961.
[2] Includes "Personal business," "Join husband," "Accompany husband," "Business and pleasure," and "Visit family." [3] Includes "Sightsee," "Vacation," "Visit," and "Tourist." [4] Includes applicants formerly listed under "Employment" and "Commercial business." [5] Beginning 1960, includes applicants who listed "World tour."

# Status of American Woman Who Marries a Foreigner

Source: United Nations

**She will automatically acquire the nationality of:**

| | | | | | |
|---|---|---|---|---|---|
| Afghanistan | Gabon* | Italy | Liechtenstein | Philippines | Spain |
| Austria | Greece* | Ivory Coast* | Monaco | Portugal* | Switzerland |
| Cambodia | Haiti | Jordan | Nepal | Rwanda (e) | Togo* |
| Ethiopia | Iran | Korea (Rep.) | Niger* | Saudi Arabia | Turkey |
| Finland | Iraq | Liberia | Peru | Somalia | |

**Automatically gains husband's nationality if she loses her own:**

| | | | | | |
|---|---|---|---|---|---|
| Belgium* | Cen. African Rep.* | Congo (a) | Rep.* | MalagasyRep.(b) | Tunisia |
| | | Costa Rico (b) | France* | Mauritania* | |
| Cameroon* | China | Dominican | Laos* | Somaliland | |

**May acquire husband's nationality if she chooses:**

| | | | | | |
|---|---|---|---|---|---|
| Algeria (c) | Ghana | Lebanon | New Zealand | Sierra Leone | United Kingdom |
| Andorra | Guyana | Libya | Nicaragua | Sudan | Upper Volta |
| Barbados | Indonesia | Luxemburg | Nigeria | Tanganyika | Venezuela |
| Bolivia | Ireland | Mali | Pakistan | Thailand | Vietnam, Rep. |
| Chad (d) | Jamaica | Mexico | Poland | United Arab | Zambia |
| Ecuador | Kenya | Morocco | San Marino | Rep. | |
| Gambia | Kuwait | Netherlands | Senegal | | |

**May acquire husband's nationality more easily than other aliens:**

| | | | | | |
|---|---|---|---|---|---|
| Australia | Colombia | Hungary | Malta | Syrian Arab | Rep. of S. |
| Brazil | Cuba | India | Norway | Rep. | Africa |
| Burma | Czechoslovakia | Israel | Panama | Trinidad- | Uruguay |
| Canada | Denmark | Japan | Singapore | Tobago | Western Samoa |
| Ceylon | El Salvador | Malawi | Sweden (b) | Uganda | Yugoslavia |
| Chile | Guatemala | Malaysia | | | |

**No effect on her nationality:**

| | | | | |
|---|---|---|---|---|
| | Bulgaria | Honduras | Paraguay | USSR |
| Albania | Argentina | Germany (West) | Iceland | Romania |

*She may decline her husband's nationality. [a] She may acquire her husband's nationality if she resides in the country 5 years following the marriage and unless she declines before the expiration of this date. [b] She may acquire her husband's nationality by declaration. [c] She must formally declare before the marriage that she repudiates her nationality of origin. [d] Applies only to marriages celebrated in Chad. [e] Marriage must be registered in civil office of Rwanda Government, which reserves right to oppose within one year the acquisition of nationality.

# EXPLORATION
## Arctic Operations—1967-1968
Source: National Geographic Society and contemporary records.

A National Geographic Society-National Museum of Canada expedition, under the leadership of Dr. Charles F. Merbs, University of Chicago anthropologist, began excavating historic Thule Eskimo sites along the coast of Roes Welcome Sound and the Wager Bay-Chesterfield Inlet areas in northern Canada to study their culture, burial patterns and gather skeletal remains for analysis. These areas are rich in artifacts.

Thule Eskimos, from which the modern Canadian Eskimo is descended racially and culturally, began migrating from the northern Alaska coast about 1,000 years ago, some settling in the Thule region of Greenland and others along the Hudson Bay's western shore and the Labrador coast.

In March, 1968, five Americans and a Canadian, driving motorized sleds, set out to retrace Commodore Peary's 1909 route to the North Pole. On Apr. 19, after 44 days of travel, all but two of the men reached the Pole, where they spent nearly a day before being picked up by plane and returned to their base camp on Ward Hunt Island.

Guided by Ralph Plaisted, who led a similar but unsuccessful expedition the previous year, the amateur explorers started out 15 miles from where Commodore Peary started. Although the Pole was only 475 miles distant on a straight line measurement from their starting point, they zig-zagged more than 800 miles to reach their destination.

A 4-man British expedition set out from Point Barrow, Alaska, on Feb. 21, 1968, with 4 sleds and 40 dogs for Vest Spitsbergen, north of Norway, via the North Pole, several thousand miles and an estimated 16 months away.

Sponsored by the Royal Geographical Society of Britain, the expedition is led by Wally W. Herbert of York, a veteran polar explorer, accompanied by Capt. K. Hedges of the Royal Army Medical Corps. Alan Gill of Bradford, a photographer, and Dr. Roy M. Koerner of Ohio State University, glaciologist. Cost of the expedition is estimated at $150,000.

The men have been making daily weather observations, gathering data on ice, thickness snow density, measuring the disintegration and ablation of sea ice, sea temperatures and incoming reflected solar radiation, as well as recording physiological and psychological reactions. They are also keeping notes of bears, seals and birds shot and eaten. Little is known of the wanderings of polar bears and what they feed on. Also contemplated is a geophysical traverse across the sub-marine Lomonosov Ridge, during which they will record depth soundings and magnetometer and gravity measurements.

The hike has 5 phases. The first: hard sledding to cover as many miles as possible; the second, a "breather" during the summer, when open water and heavy fog often slowed their progress; the third, more sledding in the autumn, after correcting their course to place them in the best position to take advantage of the winter drift; the fourth, 5 months spent in a hut air-dropped to them; and the final phase begins when they abandon their hut in the spring of 1969 and start on the last leg of their hike.

At the start they had hoped to take advantage of favorable ice drift by using a route a few degrees west of true north to add two miles of travel per day to the 8 they hoped to average. Before starting out several days were spent in a plane looking for the "road" (flat ice on which they travelled east for about 60 miles) for their highway through a 100-mile stretch of shattered inshore ice to the safer polar ice. But shifting ice, winds, ridges 15 feet high, low temperatures and open water were all problems as soon as they set out. They had planned to traverse the 380 miles from Barrow in 4 weeks; they covered 50. By mid-May they were nearly 600 miles north of Point Barrow.

Huskies able to pull sleds long distances were purchased from Eskimos living about 100 miles north of Thule, Greenland. Two types of sleds are in use—the Greenland Eskimo sled (200 lbs.) and the Nansen-type (120 lbs.) with hickory runners. Both are convertible into boats by using skis for ribs and covering the new outline with canvas, thus broadening the beam.

Squadron Leader F. Church, RAF, set up a radio station at Barrow and kept in touch until the men were out of range (about 350 miles), then moved it to the U. S weather station on Fletcher's Ice Island T-3, drifting in the Arctic Ocean. He left T-3 in October, on orders, but hoped to return in Feb. 1969, to follow the men on the remainder of their trip.

Cape Morris Jesup, Greenland, may be an island and not a peninsula—if the findings of an expedition to Greenland are correct.

Sponsored by the Control Data Corporation and the National Broadcasting Company, a four-man team flew to Cape Morris Jesup in early May, the fourth party to visit there since it was discovered by Adm. Peary in 1900. Using surveying instruments, they took readings at a number of points where lines from the sun and the moon intersected.

If their findings and calculations are correct (and they are being reviewed by the Army Map Service, Washington, and the National Geodetic Institute of Denmark) Cape Jesup is a mile north and 12 miles east of where it is shown on maps; it is an island and not a peninsula, and maps of the area will have to be revised. Map revision is important for safe submarine navigation under the polar ice.

The new measurements, if verified, do not reflect unfavorably on the work of early surveyors but come from refinement of surveying equipment and methods.

An average of 7,500 sizable icebergs (frozen fresh water) break off glaciers along the west coast of Greenland each year. Of the 400 that drift south of the 48th parallel, the latitude of Newfoundland, about 40 will drift to the vicinity of the 42nd parallel. Drift speed ranges from 5 to 40 miles per day.

The U. S. Coast Guard has been operating the International Ice Patrol since 1914. Today it maintains continuous aerial reconnaissance over more than 33,000 square miles of the North Atlantic. Seventeen nations underwrite the cost, their payments being related to the tonnage of shipping each has in these waters.

When a pilot sees an iceberg he drops a gallon jug of dye on it, marking it for tracking purposes. No practical way has been found to destroy icebergs. As they approach the Gulf Stream sea temperature rises to more than 60°F. and they melt swiftly, usually within two weeks.

The tallest iceberg recorded was found by the Coast Guard icebreaker *Eastwind* in 1957. The portion above water (550 feet) was about one-eighth of its total mass.

To aid in preserving polar bears (more than 10,000 are estimated to be alive now), the International Union for the Conservation of Nature and Natural Resources has listed this creature with other endangered species, and is gathering information on the size and distribution of polar bear populations and migrations. Theo Larsen has reported on aerial surveying, trapping and tagging carried out on Norway's Svalbard archipelago under the sponsorship of Oslo University and the Norsk Polarinstitutt. The aerial surveys point to a heavier population there than in Alaska. The numerous tracks sighted suggest there is a strong migration of bears eastward from Svalbard in the spring, leading to speculation that there is a connection between the polar bear populations of Svalbard and the western Soviet Arctic. This study began in 1966 and will continue into 1970.

The National Research Council announced that the United States, Canada, Denmark and France have joined in a study to find out how Eskimos have managed to survive in a hostile environment. The study will be under the auspices of the 50-nation International Biological Program.

Scientists, using a Convair jet plane, made a series of flights 8 miles above the Arctic land mass gathering data on the northern lights. NASA reports the flights were coordinated with observations from ground stations, with sounding rocket missions and with observations from its OGO-4 (Orbiting Geophysical Observatory) which is more than 250 miles above the earth. The "how" and "why" of the multicolored auroras, often hundreds of miles long and observed as much as 200 miles above the earth's surface, is unknown.

Several dozen men from the Patuxent Naval Air Station, Maryland, spent several weeks in July, 1968, flying over Arctic areas gathering data for the U. S. Naval Oceanographic Office.

The purpose of the flight (one of many these

men undertake for the Naval Oceanographic Office) is to record sea ice conditions and the distribution and spacing of pack ice, the latter information so important to submariners as well as to the planning of mine and undersea war strategy.

## EARLY EXPLORERS

**1587**—John Davis (England). Davis Strait to Sanderson's Hope, 72°12′N.

**1596**—Willem Barents and Jacob van Heemskerck (Holland). Discovered Bear Island, touched northwest tip of Spitsbergen, 79°49′N., rounded Novaya Zemlya, wintered at Ice Haven.

**1607**—Henry Hudson (England). North along Greenland's east coast to Cape Hold-with-Hope, 73°30′, then north of Spitsbergen to 80°23′. Returning he discovered Hudson's Touches (Jan Mayen).

**1616**—William Baffin and Robert Bylot (England). Baffin Bay to Smith Sound.

**1728**—Vitus Bering (Russia). Proved Asia and America were separate by sailing through strait.

**1733-40**—Great Northern Expedition (Russia). Surveyed Siberian Arctic coast.

**1741**—Vitus Bering (Russia). Sighted Alaska from sea, named Mount St. Elias. His lieutenant, Chirikof, discovered coast.

**1771**—Samuel Hearne (Hudson's Bay Co.). Overland from Prince of Wales Fort (Churchill) on Hudson Bay to mouth of Coppermine River.

**1778**—James Cook (Britain). Through Bering Strait to Icy Cape, Alaska, and North Cape, Siberia.

**1789**—Alexander Mackenzie (North West Co., Britain). Montreal to mouth of Mackenzie River.

**1806**—William Scoresby (Britain). North of Spitsbergen to 81°30′.

**1820-3**—Ferdinand von Wrangel (Russia). Completed a survey of Siberian Arctic coast. His exploration joined that of James Cook at North Cape, confirming separation of the continents.

**1845**—Sir John Franklin (Britain) was one of many to seek the Northwest Passage—an ocean route connecting the Atlantic and Pacific via the Arctic. His two ships, (the Erebus and Terror), were last seen entering Lancaster Sound July 26.

**1888**—Fridtjof Nansen (Norway) Crossed Greenland's icecap. 1893-96—Nansen in Fram drifted from New Siberian Isls. to Spitsbergen; tried Polar dash in 1895, reached Franz Josef Land.

**1896**—Solomon A. Andreé (Sweden) and companion, in June, made first attempt to reach North Pole by balloon; failed and returned in August. On July 11, 1897, Andreé and 2 others started in balloon from Danes Isl., Spitsbergen, to drift across Pole to America, and disappeared. Over 33 years later, Aug. 6, 1930, Dr. Gunnar Horn (Norway) found their frozen bodies on White Isl., 82° 56′ N, 29° 52′ E.

**1903-06**—Roald Amundsen (Norway) first sailed Northwest Passage.

## DISCOVERY OF NORTH POLE

Robert E. Peary began exploring in 1886 on Greenland, when he was 30. With his hq. at McCormick Bay he explored Greenland's coast 1891-92, tried for North Pole 1893, returned with large meteorites. In 1900 he reached northern limit of Greenland and 83° 50′ N.; in 1902 he reached 84° 17′ N; in 1906 he went from Ellesmere Isl. to 87° 06′ N. He sailed in the Roosevelt, July, 1908, to winter off Cape Sheridan, Grant Land. The dash for the North Pole began Mar. 1 from Cape Columbia, Ellesmere Land. Peary reached the Pole, 90° N., April 6, 1909.

Peary had several supporting groups carrying supplies until the last group, under Capt. Robt. A. Bartlett, turned back at 87°47′N. Peary, Matthew Henson and 4 Eskimos proceeded with dog teams and sleds. They crossed Pole several times, finally built an igloo at 90°, remained 36 hours. Started south Apr. 7 at 4 p.m. for Cape Columbia. Eskimos were Coqueeh, Ootah, Eginwah and Seegloo. Adm. Peary died Feb. 20, 1920. Henson, a Negro, born Aug. 8, 1866, died in New York, N. Y., Mar. 9, 1955, aged 88. Ootah, last survivor, died near Thule, Greenland, May, 1955, aged 80.

**1914**—Donald MacMillan (U. S.). Northwest, 200 miles, from Axel Heiberg Island to seek Peary's Crocker Land.

**1915-17**—Vilhjalmur Stefansson (Canada) discovered Borden, Brock, Meighen and Lougheed Islands.

**1918-20**—Amundsen sailed Northeast Passage.

**1926**—Richard E. Byrd and Floyd Bennett (U. S.). reached 87°44′N. in attempt to fly to North Pole from Spitsbergen.

**1926**—Richard E. Byrd and Floyd Bennett (U.S.). First over North Pole by air, May 9.

**1926**—Amundsen, Ellsworth, and Umberto Nobile (Italy) flew from Spitsbergen over North Pole May 12, to Teller, Alaska, in dirigible Norge.

**1928**—Nobile crossed North Pole in airship Italia May 24, crashed May 25. Amundsen lost while trying to effect rescue by plane.

**1928**—Sir Hubert Wilkins and Eielson. Flew from Point Barrow to Spitsbergen, 84°N.

## SUBMARINE RECORDS

On Aug. 3, 1958, the Nautilus, under Comdr. William R. Anderson, became the first ship to cross the North Pole beneath the Arctic ice.

On Aug. 12, 1958, the nuclear submarine Skate, Comdr. James F. Calvert, became the second ship to make an underwater crossing of the North Pole.

In March, 1959, the Skate returned to the Arctic and, on its third attempt broke through at the North Pole, the first time any ship had been on the surface at 90° N.

The nuclear-powered U. S. submarine Seadragon, Comdr. George P. Steele II, made the first east-west underwater transit through the Northwest Passage during August, 1960. It sailed from Portsmouth, N. H., headed between Greenland and Labrador through Baffin Bay, then west through Lancaster Sound and McClure Strait to the Beaufort Sea. Traveling submerged for the most part, the submarine made 850 miles from Baffin Bay to the Beaufort Sea in six days. The vessel made a 300-foot dive to sail under an iceberg in Baffin Bay.

In February, 1960, the nuclear submarine Sargo traveled under the Arctic ice pack to and around the North Pole. The Sargo departed from and returned to Honolulu, and spent 31 days and 4 hours under the ice. The submarine successfully smashed its way through ice three feet thick.

---

# Polar Expeditions—Antarctic, 1967-1968

The water dripping from an ice core into a beaker in a laboratory at the U. S. Naval Academy on July 10, 1968, was originally snow falling on Antarctica while Christ walked the Holy Land.

Army Engineers from the Cold Regions Research and Engineering Laboratory, New Hampshire, who completed the first drilling through the Antarctic Ice Cap, 7,100 feet, removed this 15-foot ice core from 850 feet below the surface of Byrd Station. Scientists determined by radiation measurement and a count of the layers of ice formed by summer thaws that one of the layers was formed the year Christ was born.

Penetration of the Ice Cap, which holds about 9/10ths of the world's fresh water, was accomplished about 1½ miles below the surface. Studies of portions of the core samples of air, volcanic ash, ice and some rock from near the bottom will reveal much about the rate of snowfall, temperature variations and composition of the earth's atmosphere for thousands of years. The isotopes trapped within the samples constitute a historical thermometer and can be compared with established temperature-isotope tables to determine age spans.

If this ice sheet ever melts the Statue of Liberty will have water up to her nose and all major seaports will be flooded for the Oceans will have risen about 200 feet, scientists estimate.

Scientists found dormant algae, fungi and bacteria in soil removed from ice-free Taylor Valley, where there is no snow or ice. Inactive during the winter months' low temperatures, these life forms are activated by summer run-off waters from the glaciers in the mountains above the valleys.

This area—the Dry Valleys of Antarctica—is valued by scientists who are developing equipment capable of detecting life on Mars, for it most nearly duplicates a Mars-like atmosphere.

Ten of 21 men living in isolation under the ice and snow of the South Pole—and removed from contact with the outside world—are the subjects of intensive medical studies directed by two psychiatrists.

Working under a grant from the National Science Foundation, these men submitted to many tests to establish their "normal" physical and mental bases before leaving the United States. Their daily activities are being observed and periodic recordings are made of their brain waves, heart action and electrical resistance of their skin. It has been found that men who live closely for long times under stress are subject to drastic emotional upsets.

January, 1968, saw the completion of an 815-mile two-month traverse across barren Queen Maud Land, between the South Pole and the Princess Ragnhild Coast.

Sponsored by the U. S. Coast and Geodetic Survey and financed by the National Science Foundaton, the personnel of the expedition made the trip on Sno-cats. Their trip began at Plateau Station and ended at a point about 900 miles from the South Pole, and took them through a windswept desert where the temperature was often 50° below zero. A new low temperature mark for U. S. Antarctic bases of —123.1 F. was set at Plateau Station July 20, 1968.

The National Science Foundation reports that the 12-year-old Amundsen-Scott Station, now under 16 feet of drifted snow, will have to be modernized or replaced. Plans are being made to build a new station in the next several years.

McMurdo Station, also a dozen years old, is beset with urban sprawl and renewal plans. Steel structures are replacing the huts and shacks of 1957, with several dozen more to be added in the next 10 years.

For the summer population, which exceeds 1,000 men, there are 3 bars, 3 theaters, a bus line, a gymnasium, a power plant, junk yard and a garbage dump! All water pipes to the buildings must be heated to prevent freezing. On July 26, 1968, a wind velocity of 116.15 mph was recorded, a record for the station.

Antarctic survey ships have been aided by the United States satellite ESSA 3, orbiting 200 miles above the South Pole. Photographs made each day by the satellite were sent to the British Antarctic Survey at Cambridge, where they were studied for the location of open water leads and thick ice.

The International Weddell Sea Oceanographic Expedition, (IWSOE) aided by the U. S. Coast Guard icebreaker Glacier and Argentina's icebreaker San Martin initiated a comprehensive survey of the Weddell Sea, the first major work in the area since Sir Ernest Shackleton visited it in 1915.

Satellite signals relayed to the Glacier were particularly helpful. The signal information as to ice pack and cloud· cover conditions enabled the Glacier to move around with a minimum loss of time and scientists established 70 scientific stations (more than planned), 90% of them in areas where no previous oceanographic data had been obtained.

The signals also enabled the Glacier to navigate these waters with greater than normal precision.

Through the joint cooperation of the British Antarctic Survey, the National Science Foundation and the Scott Polar Research Institute, a three-summer program has been laid out to record airborne radio echo soundings of ice depth over the whole of Antarctica.

During the first season's operations it was found that bottom reflections were generally constant to an ice depth of 6,500 feet, intermittent beyond that. Also, greater depths were recorded in those areas where the surface elevation was more than 11,450 feet. The maximum depth recorded was 13,780 feet, in the vicinity of Sovetskaya station.

## FOREIGN OPERATIONS

Australians set up the Amery Ice Shelf Glaciological Research Station, stocking it with more than 40 tons of materials and supplies and four men who wintered there. This site was selected after radar-mapping the entire 153-mile front of the shelf, a line of 130-foot high ice cliffs.

Four tons of snow—from the "cleanest spot on earth"—were shipped from Plateau Station to Brussels, Belgium.

Dr. E. E. Picciotto, an authority on snow chemistry, will analyze the snow to determine the rate of fall of dust particles to the earth in the hope of gaining insight into the evolution of the earth and the solar system.

A 6-foot core of this snow equals 25 years of history, and its purity greatly exceeds that of the highest quality distilled laboratory water.

Belgian and South African scientists worked together in geological, glaciological and photogrammetrical studies 250 miles to the south of the SANAE base and 560 miles west of Belgium's Roi Baudouin base. Dog teams and tracked vehicles transported the men in the field. Supplies were dropped them by plane.

Chileans continued their marine biology studies by taking another census of marine mammals to ascertain the seal population and the annual loss of same. Such counts have been made since 1965.

Twelve men making up Japan's Ninth Antarctic expedition sought to complete a more than 1,500-mile overland hike from Japan's Showa base to the South Pole by Christmas Day, 1968. Their leader is M. Murayama, director of Tokyo's National Science Museum, a prominent polar researcher and mountaineer.

New Zealanders re-surveyed for the final time the stations set on the McMurdo Ice Shelf in 1963-64, for some markers were buried as much as 5 feet. A major part of the survey work was devoted to measuring surface elevation, from which it is hoped to produce a contour map of the ice shelf, an unknown characteristic of the Shelf.

The USSR established its fifth permanent Antarctic base, Bellinghausen Station, on King George Island in the South Shetland group, joining Britain, Argentina and Chile in the warmest part of Antarctica. The other bases are Vostok, Mirny, Molodezhnaya and Novolazarevskaya.

The United Kingdom's survey and geological research in the vicinity of Palmer Land-Alexander Island was restored with the re-stocking and re-opening of the Fossil Bluff station in George VI Sound, and the establishment of other depots in Palmer Land. Geologists concentrated their work on the nunatak region along western Palmer Land and eastern Alexander Island's Ablation Valley. The surveyors extended their work northwards along George VI Sound. Geophysical studies continued at the observatory on Argentine Island.

A number of small groups continued glaciological studies of the Brunt Ice Shelf.

## EARLY HISTORY

Antarctica has been approached since 1773-75, when Capt. Jas. Cook (Britain) reached 71°10' S. Many sea and landmarks bear names of early explorers, Bellingshausen (Russia), discovered Peter I and Alexander I Islands, 1819-21. Nathaniel Palmer (U. S.) discovered Palmer Peninsula, 60° W. 1820, without realizing that this was a continent. Jas. Weddell (Britain) found Weddell Sea, 74°15' S., 1823.

First to announce existence of the continent of Antarctic was Charles Wilkes (U. S.), who followed the coast for 1,500 mi., 1840. Adelie Coast, 140° E., was found by Dumont d'Urville (France), 1840. Ross Ice Shelf was found by Jas. Clark Ross (Britain), 1841-42.

1895—Leonard Kristensen, Norwegian whaling captain, landed a party on the coast of Victoria Land in Jan. 1895. They were the first ashore on the main continental mass. C. E. Borchgrevink, a member of that party, returned in 1899 with a British expedition, first to winter on Antarctica.

1902-04—Robert F. Scott (Britain) discovered Edward VII Peninsula. In 1902 he reached 82°17' S., 146°33' E. from McMurdo Sound.

1908-09—Ernest Shackleton in 1908 introduced the use of Manchurian ponies in Antarctic sledging. In 1909 he reached 88°23' S., discovering a route on to the plateau by way of the Beardmore Glacier and pioneering the way to the Pole.

## DISCOVERY OF SOUTH POLE

1911—Roald Amundsen (Norway) with four men and dog teams reached the Pole Dec. 14, 1911.

1912—Capt. Scott reached the Pole from Ross Island Jan. 13, 1912, with four companions (Dr. E. A. Wilson, Lt. Bowers, Capt. Oates, and Petty Officer Edgar Evans), where they found Amundsen's tent. Of Scott's party, Oates and Evans died first; Scott, Wilson and Bowers died in a tent around March 29. They were found Nov. 12, 1912.

1928—First man to use an airplane over Antarctica was Hubert Wilkins (Britain).

1929—Richard E. Byrd (U. S.) established Little America on Bay of Whales. On 1600-mi. airplane flight begun Nov. 28 he crossed South Pole Nov. 29 with pilot Bernt Balchen, a radio operator and a photographer. Dropped U. S. flag over Pole, temp. 16° below zero.

1934-35—Richard E. Byrd (U. S.) led second expedition to Little America, which explored 450,000 sq. mi. Byrd wintered alone at an advance weather station in 80°08' S.

1934-37—John Rymill led British Graham Land expedition of 1934-37; discovered that Palmer Peninsula is part of Antarctic mainland.

1940—Richard E. Byrd (U. S.) charted most of coast between Ross Sea and Palmer Peninsula.

1946-47—U. S. Navy undertook Operation Highjump under Rear Admiral Byrd. Ships were commanded by Rear Admiral Richard H. Cruzen. Expedition included 13 ships and 4,000 men. 29

land-based flights from Little America and 35 by seaplanes from tenders, photomapped coastline and penetrated beyond Pole.

**1946-48**—Ronne Antarctic Research Expedition, Comdr. Finn Ronne, USNR, determined the Antarctic to be only one continent, with no strait between Weddell Sea and Ross Sea; discovered 250,000 sq. miles of land by flights to 79°S. Lat., and made 14,000 aerial photographs over 450,000 sq. miles of land. Mrs. Ronne and Mrs. H. Darlington, who accompanied their husbands, were the first women to winter on Antarctica.

**1955-57**—U. S. Navy's Operation Deep Freeze led by Adm. Richard E. Byrd. Supporting U. S. scientific efforts for the International Geophysical Year, the Operation was commanded by Rear Adm. George Dufek. It established five coastal stations fronting the Indian, Pacific, and Atlantic Oceans and also three interior stations; explored more

than 1,000,000 sq. miles in Wilkes Land. Seven Navy men under Adm. Dufek landed by plane at the Pole Oct. 31, 1956, and landed radar reflectors.

**1957-58**—During the International Geophysical Year, July, 1957 through Dec., 1958, scientists from 12 countries conducted ambitious programs of Antarctic research. A network of some 60 stations on the continent and sub-Arctic islands studied oceanography, glaciology, meteorology, seismology, geomagnetism, the ionosphere, cosmic rays, aurora and airglow. A party from Ellsworth IGY station (US) south of Weddell Sea under the direction of Captain Finn Ronne explored beyond 1947 flight and delineated Berkner Island imbedded in the Filchner Ice Shelf. Pensacola Mountains, first sighted by Argentines in Oct., 1955 and seen by U. S. Navy in Jan., 1956, were accurately located. New mountain ranges about 11,000 ft. high were discovered in Edith Ronne Land

---

# Mountaineering, 1968

Source: National Geographic Society, Washington, D. C.

The North Ridge of **Mount Kennedy** (13,905 feet), Canada, was scaled for the first time by 4 Dartmouth College students in July. Their efforts included climbing nearly a mile up a vertical face which did not have a ledge more than a foot wide and working their way around several overhangs. One man was buried by an avalanche of snow and came through it unharmed.

Climbing the North Ridge is considered by some to present more challenges than climbing Mount Everest.

A 72-year-old woman, accompanied by her 77- and 75-year-old brothers, defied sub-zero weather and high winds in mid-August and climbed to the peak of **Mount Whitney** (14,494 feet), California, in 7½ hours.

The efforts of a 10-man Japanese team to scale the unclimbed South Ridge of the Yukon's **Mount Vancouver** (15,750 feet) in mid-June terminated when 3 of the climbers were killed by an avalanche. The 7 survivors returned to Japan.

A 6-man team (5 New Zealanders and an Italian journalist) reached the summit of 12,450 foot **Mount Erebus**, Antarctica, early in January.

The primary purpose of their climb was to gather snow accumulation data for a glaciological study, from stations spaced 1,000 feet apart on the mountain. They also tested a new motorized toboggan being considered for field work.

After spending several hours at the peak the team went on to **Mount Terra Nova**, which they peaked the following day. Lack of fuel prevented their going an additional 15-20 miles to reach the upper slope of Mount Terror, 10,075 feet.

**Mont Blanc**, 15,771 feet, is being used as a cosmic ray filter. Approximately 6 tons of geiger counters and other electronic components have been parked along the sides of the highway tunnel between French Savoy and Italy's Valle d'Aosta to measure the intensity of incoming low angle cosmic rays. The data obtained will be correlated with known vertical arrival figures and, hopefully, this will yield insight into the source of cosmic rays.

At the end of August the government of Nepal partially lifted a ban on the climbing of Himalayan peaks and will now permit the scaling of 38, including **Mount Everest**. The ban was placed in effect in 1965 for security reasons.

A 10-woman Japanese-Indian climbing party scaled 22,028-foot **Kailas**, Tibet, in mid-May. They had planned to climb other Himalayan peaks but a combination of bad weather, the death of one guide and the injury of another cancelled the additional climbs.

Six Australians, 4 of them women, attempted to climb **Mount Everest** at the turn of the year. They climbed as far as Khumbu Glacier, about 18,000 feet, at which point they were forced to turn back for the lack of special equipment needed to climb higher.

## SOME EARLIER RECORDS

**Mt. Everest**, 29,028 ft. (India survey) Nepal-Tibet, was conquered May 29, 1953, when Edmund Hillary, New Zealand, and Tenzing Norkay, a Sherpa of Nepal, scaled its southwest face. They were members of a Royal Geographical Society-Alpine Club expedition. *See note on height of Everest, page 720*.

Two successful climbs were made in May, 1956. Three more occurred in May, 1963, by members of an expedition led by Norman G. Dyhrenfurth,

sponsored by the National Geographic Society.

**Mt. Godwin Austen** (K2), 28,250 ft., Kashmir, was surmounted July 31, 1954.

**Mt. Kanchenjunga**, 28,208 ft., Nepal-Sikkim, was conquered May 25, 1955, by a British team. The final six feet were left unscaled as a concession to the natives.

**Lhotse I**, 27,923 ft., Nepal-Tibet, was scaled May 18, 1956, by a Swiss team.

**Mt. Makalu**, 27,824 ft., Nepal-Tibet, conquered by a French Alpine Club team in May, 1955

**Mt. Dhaulagiri**, 26,810 ft., Nepal, was scaled by a Swiss team on May 13, 1960.

**Mt. Manaslu**, 26,760 ft., Nepal, was climbed May, 1956, by a Japanese team.

**Mt. Cho Oyu**, 26,750 ft., Nepal-Tibet, was climbed Oct. 19, 1954, by 3 Austrians and a Sherpa guide. In 1964 5 W. Germans and 2 Sherpas made camp at 10,000 ft. From there 2 Germans on skis and 2 ski-less Sherpas set out for the peak, a German and a Sherpa reaching it.

**Mt. Nanga Parbat**, 26,660 ft., Kashmir, was scaled July 4, 1953, by an Austrian.

**Mt. Annapurna**, 26,504 ft., Nepal, was conquered by a Frenchman on June 3, 1950.

**Mt. Gasherbrum I**, 26,470 ft., Kashmir, was scaled July 5, 1958.

**Mt. Gosainthan**, 26,291 ft., Tibet. Scaled May 2, 1964, by a Chinese team which reported placing a bust of Mao Tse-tung atop it.

**Mt. Gyachung Kang**, 25,910 ft., Nepal-Tibet peak, was bested in April, 1964, by a Japanese team.

**Mt. Nuptse**, 25,726 ft., Nepal-Tibet, first ascended May 16, 1961, by a British team.

**Mt. Istoro Nal**, 24,240 ft. W. Pakistan peak, was scaled June 8, 1955, by an American team.

**Mt. Api**, 23,399 ft., Nepal, bested by an Italian team in 1954.

**Mt. Kokthang**, 23,000 ft., Sikkim, scaled by an Indian team April 26, 1962.

**Mt. Aconcagua**, 22,834 ft., Argentina, was first scaled in 1897 by Mathias Zurbriggen.

**Mt. Numbur**, 22,800 ft., Nepal, scaled in May, 1963, by a Japanese team.

**Mt. Ama Dablam**, 22,500 ft., Nepal, was first scaled in March, 1961, by a 4-man team.

**Mt. Kangtega**, 22,340 ft., Nepal, was scaled by an American in June, 1963.

**Mt. Thamserku**, 21,730 ft., Nepal, scaled by Edmund Hillary in 1964.

**Mt. McKinley**, Alaska, 20,320 ft. South face climbed first in 1961 by Italian team. Two New Jersey men climbed southeast spur in June, 1962. Six U. S. guides climbed east buttress, May, 1963.

**Mt. Kilimanjaro**, 19,340 ft., Tanzania, Africa, scaled in 1962.

**Mt. St. Elias**, 18,008 ft., Alaska, scaled in 1964 for third time. It was first scaled in 1897 and again in 1946.

**Mt. Eiger**, 13,025 ft., Switz. The difficult mile-high north face was scaled for the first time in the summer of 1964 by a woman and a companion. Other women have scaled it by easier routes. Swiss climbers scaled it in 1963. On Mar. 12, 1961, a German team became the first winter ascent of the north face.

**Aiguille du Midi**, 12,603 ft., France, was scaled in 1964 by 3 Frenchmen in the first successful winter climb up the southwest face.

**Mt. Huntington**, 12,240 ft., Alaska, was scaled for the third time in 1964.

**El Capitan**, 9,920 ft., Yellowstone National Park, was scaled by 2 Americans and a Canadian over its southwest face in 1962.

# Early Explorers of the Western Hemisphere

The first men to discover the New World or Western Hemisphere are believed to have walked across a "land bridge" from Siberia to Alaska, an isthmus since broken by Bering Strait. From Alaska, these ancestors of the Indians spread through North, Central and South America. Anthropologists have placed these crossings at between 18,000 and 14,000 B.C.; but evidence found in 1967 near Pueblo, Mex., indicates mankind reached there as early as 35,000-40,000 years ago.

At first, these people were hunters using flint weapons and tools. In Mexico, about 7000-6000 B.C., they founded farming cultures, developing corn, squash, etc. Eventually, they created complex civilizations—Olmec, Toltec, Aztec and Maya and, in South America, Inca. In what is now the eastern U. S., others created the Hopewell Culture, also based on farming, about 1000 B.C.; remains of it are seen today in large mounds in Ohio and elsewhere.

Norsemen (Norwegian Vikings sailing out of Iceland and Greenland) are credited by most scholars with being the first Europeans to discover America, with at least five voyages around 1000 A.D. to areas they called Helluland, Markland and Vinland—possibly Labrador, Nova Scotia or Newfoundland, and New England.

The remains of a settlement at L'Anse-au-Meadow, near the northern tip of Newfoundland, were uncovered by Dr. and Mrs. Helge Ingstad, Norwegian archeologists, 1960-63, with the aid of a grant from the National Geographic Society. They identified the settlement as Norse. Carbon-14 tests from hearths and the remains of a smithy indicated the site was occupied about 900 A.D. and during several hundred years before and after.

In 1965 Yale University announced the discovery of a map, drawn about 1440 and apparently based on earlier maps, showing an area southwest of Greenland labeled Vinland. The map also bore an inscription crediting the discovery of Vinland to Leif Ericsson and Bjarni (Herjolfsson), who are among leaders named in early Norse sagas describing voyages to Vinland.

Christopher Columbus, most famous of the discoverers, was born at Genoa, Italy, but made his discoveries sailing for the Spanish rulers Ferdinand and Isabella. Dates of his voyages, places he discovered and other information follow:

**1492—First voyage.** Left Palos, Spain, Aug. 3 with 88 men (est.). Discovered San Salvador (Guanahani or Watling Isl., Bahamas) Oct. 12. Also Cuba, Hispaniola (San Domingo); built Fort La Navidad on latter.

**1493—Second voyage, first part,** Sept. 25, with 17 ships, 1,500 men. Discovered Dominica (Lesser Antilles) Nov. 3; Guadaloupe, Montserrat, Antigua, San Martin, Santa Cruz, Puerto Rico, Virgin Isls. Settled Isabella on San Domingo. **Second part** (Columbus having remained in Western Hemisphere), Jamaica, Isle of Pines, La Mona Isl.

**1498—Third voyage.** Left Spain May 30, 1498, 6 ships. Discovered Trinidad. Saw South American continent Aug. 1, 1498, but called it Isla Sancta (Holy Island). Entered Gulf of Paris and landed, first time on continental soil. At mouth of Orinoco Aug. 14 he decided this was mainland.

**1500—Fourth voyage,** 4 caravels, 150 men. St. Lucia, Guanja off Honduras; Cape Gracias a Dios, Honduras; San Juan R. and Laguna de Chiriqui, Costa Rica; Veragua, Puerto Bello, Almirante (Isthmus of Panama).

| A.D. | Explorer | Nationality and Employer | Discovery or Exploration |
|---|---|---|---|
| 1497 | John Cabot | Italian-English | Cape Breton Isl. |
| 1498 | John and Sebastian Cabot | Italian-English | Labrador to Hatteras |
| 1499 | Alonso de Ojeda | Spanish | South American coast, Venezuela |
| 1500, Feb. | Vicente y Pinzon | Spanish | South American coast, Amazon River |
| 1500, Apr. | Pedro Alvarez Cabral | Portuguese | Brazil (for Portugal) |
| 1500–02 | Gaspar Corte-Real | Portuguese | Labrador |
| 1501 | Rodrigo de Bastidas | Spanish | Central America |
| 1513 | Vasco Nunez de Balboa | Spanish | Pacific Ocean |
| 1513 | Juan Ponce de Leon | Spanish | Florida |
| 1515 | Juan de Solis | Spanish | Rio de la Plata |
| 1519 | Alonso de Pineda | Spanish | Mouth of Mississippi River |
| 1519 | Hernando Cortes | Spanish | Mexico |
| 1520 | Fernando Magellan | Portuguese-Spanish | Straits of Magellan, Tierra del Fuego |
| 1524 | Giovanni da Verrazano | Italian-French | Atlantic Coast-New York harbor |
| 1526–27 | Sebastian Cabot | Italian-Spanish | Rio de la Plata (river) |
| 1527 | Panfilo de Narvaez | Spanish | Florida |
| 1531 | Alfonso de Souza | Portuguese | Rio de Janeiro (river) |
| 1532 | Francisco Pizarro | Spanish | Peru |
| 1534 | Jacques Cartier | French | Canada, Mont Real |
| 1536 | Pedro de Mendoza | Spanish | Buenos Aires (river) |
| 1536 | A. N. Cabeza de Vaca | Spanish | Texas coast and interior |
| 1539 | Francisco de Ulloa | Spanish | California coast |
| 1539–41 | Hernando de Soto | Spanish | Mississippi River near Memphis |
| 1539 | Marcos de Niza | Italian-Spanish | Southwest (now U. S.) |
| 1540 | Francisco V. de Coronado | Spanish | Southwest (now U. S.) |
| 1540 | Hernando Alarcon | Spanish | Colorado River |
| 1540 | Garcia de L. Cardenas | Spanish | Grand Canyon of the Colorado |
| 1541 | Francisco de Orellana | Spanish | Amazon River |
| 1541–43 | A. N. Cabeza de Vaca | Spanish | Brazil, Paraguay River |
| 1542 | Juan Rodriquez Cabrillo | Portuguese-Spanish | San Diego harbor |
| 1565 | Pedro Menendez | Spanish | St. Augustine |
| 1573 | Pedro Marquez | Spanish | Chesapeake Bay |
| 1576 | Martin Frobisher | English | Frobisher's Bay, Canada |
| 1577–80 | Francis Drake | English | California coast |
| 1582 | Antonio de Espejo | Spanish | Southwest (named New Mexico) |
| 1584 | Amadas & Barlow (for Raleigh) | English | Virginia |
| 1585–87 | Sir Walter Raleigh's men | English | Roanoke Isl., N. C. |
| 1595 | Sir Walter Raleigh | English | Orinoco River |
| 1602 | Bartholomew Gosnold | English | Martha's Vineyard and Massachusetts |
| 1603–09 | Samuel de Champlain | French | Canadian interior, Lake Champlain |
| 1604 | Samuel de Champlain | French | Mt. Desert Island |
| 1607 | Capt. John Smith | English | Atlantic coast |
| 1609–10 | Henry Hudson | English-Dutch | Hudson River; Hudson Bay |
| 1634 | Jean Nicolet | French | Lake Michigan; Wisconsin |
| 1659–68 | Groseilliers and Radisson | French | Upper Mississippi, Hudson Bay |
| 1669–82 | Robt. Cavelier, de La Salle | French | St. Lawrence to Gulf |
| 1673 | Louis Joliet—Jacques Marquette | French | Upper Mississippi River |
| 1680 | Louis Hennepin | French | Falls of St. Anthony |
| 1687–1711 | Eusebio Francisco Kino | Italian-Spanish | Southwest (now U. S.) |
| 1728–41 | Vitus Bering | Danish-Russian | Bering Strait; Alaska |
| 1731 | V. de la Verendrye | Canadian | Red River, Lake Winnipeg |
| 1766–68 | Jonathan Carver | English | West to St. Pierre River |
| 1769 | Gaspar de Portola | Spanish | Golden Gate Bay |
| 1775 | Bruno Hecata | Spanish | Pacific Coast; Oregon |
| 1778 | Capt. James Cook | English | Pacific coast, north |
| 1792 | George Vancouver | English | Pacific coast, north |
| 1792 | Robert Gray | American | Columbia River |
| 1793 | Alexander Mackenzie | English | Canadian west |
| 1804–06 | Meriwether Lewis, Wm. Clark | American | Missouri-Columbia Rivers |
| 1806 | Zebulon Montgomery Pike | American | Rockies, Pikes Peak |
| 1831–36 | Benj. de Bonneville | American | Rockies, California |
| 1842 | John C Fremont | American | Rockies, Pacific Coast |

# Developments in the Earth Sciences
## United States Geological Survey

**Studying the Earth from Space:** Photographs of the Earth's surface obtained from manned and unmanned satellites are providing scientists with new tools to investigate the Earth and its environment, to record changes in the environment, and to collect data that help to make the best use of the assets of our planet. Scientists of the U. S. Department of Interior's Geological Survey, in cooperation with the National Aeronautics and Space Administration (NASA), recently embarked on a program that will provide for the use of resources data acquired from Earth orbital satellites carrying remote-sensing instruments.

The first data to be applied to large operational resources problems will be acquired by an unmanned satellite. This satellite will use a multispectral television system to transmit pictures to receiving stations on the Earth. Each picture will cover an area 100 miles square with a ground resolution of 100-200 feet. Complete coverage of the globe would be achieved every 18 days. Later satellites will carry new, more highly sophisticated sensing devices to further enhance our ability to study the Earth from space. Sensing devices that may be carried by orbital satellites include photographic-cameras, radar, infrared and microwave imagers and radiometers, gravimeters, and luminescene sensors.

**Hydrology:** Implementation of the satellite program will provide a wide range of information that is important in water-resources planning and management, such as data on the runoff and water retention characteristics of drainage basins, measurements of evapotranspiration, water-surface roughness, the flow of major rivers, and groundwater discharge. It may become possible to determine rates of reservoir sedimentation and the growth of deltas; to assess some aspects of water pollution; and to monitor and assess erosion, sedimentation, and other changes in the hydrologic environment brought about by man's activities.

**Geology:** Satellite photography is unequalled for geologic interpretations of very large areas because geologic structures are easier to see on the synoptic, orbital-height photograph than on a mosaic of hundreds of aerial photographs. This is particularly true of long, linear features such as faults which are sometimes associated with deposits of valuable minerals.

Satellite studies can help in the search for new sources of petroleum by showing the broad, gentle folds in the Earth's crust that commonly serve as reservoirs for petroleum.

Airborne ultraviolet sensors are already helping scientists locate certain types of minerals, such as the highly luminescent phosphates. Infrared images from Nimbus satellites, for example, have provided information on the temperature and emissive characteristics of terrain and water surfaces and on volcanic activity. Radar images can be particularly useful in structural mapping. Because radar is remarkably sensitive to gross roughness, faults, fractures, and folds in the Earth's surface are generally well defined.

**Cartography:** A photomap of the southwestern United States, covering 270,000 square miles and compiled from photos taken by Gemini astronauts, was prepared in 1968. This 1:1,000,000 scale map is part of a program to show the feasibility and economy of evaluating earth features from space.

Space-acquired data about the Earth afford several advantages to map makers; particularly important are speed of data collection and economy of data utilization. Also data from satellites in a circular, sun-synchronous orbit are comparable for the entire earth, and provide a uniformly reliable basis for mapping and charting. By using orbital photography and other remote-sensor data, the publication of a truly up-to-date world map at the scale of 1:1,000,000 will be possible.

**Ecology:** Management and conservation of public lands will be greatly improved through the use of remote-sensing devices because detailed land studies of features or conditions that change with time (such as the distribution, health, and vigor of vegetation) will be supported by general views from space.

**Flood-plain mapping:** Mapping of the parts of flood plains inundated by major floods is a prerequisite to the delineation and possible flood-zoning of these hazard-prone areas. The U. S. Geological Survey has published nearly 100 flood-plain maps and many other maps of this kind have been prepared in limited editions for the use of public officials and other interested citizens. The Survey's flood-mapping program is now being greatly accelerated under a cooperative effort being coordinated by the U. S. Army, Corps of Engineers.

**Urban Hydrology:** In 1968, the Geological Survey published "Water Data for Metropolitan Areas—a summary of data from 222 areas in the United States." For each Metropolitan area the report identifies the principal sources of municipal and industrial water supply, summarizes the principal water problems, and identifies the types of water data currently being collected by the Survey.

**Regional water-resources appraisals:** Comprehensive studies of water resources continued in the basins of the Arkansas, Brazos, Colorado, Patuxent, Potomac, and Willamette Rivers, and a 5-year study of the Delmarva Peninsula (Del.-Md.-Va.) was begun in 1968. These regional appraisals, when completed, will provide a quantitative analysis of the entire hydrologic system of which the river is a part, sufficient to explain and predict the flow characteristics of the river, the influence of ground water, and the effects of human activities upon the system.

**Mineral Resources:** The U. S. Geological Survey is conducting research in a wide variety of geological environments in a search for clues to new sources of ores, fertilizer minerals, fossil fuels and construction materials. These programs consist of field research in the distribution, structure, chemical and physical properties of the rocks of the earth, supported by laboratory research and development of new tools and techniques to aid in discovery of the needed mineral raw materials.

Existing analytical techniques have been extended and new techniques have been developed to determine very low concentrations (background levels) of certain chemical elements in rocks and minerals. Using these newly-developed tools and techniques, Survey scientists are identifying mineral target areas considering to be worthy of more detailed exploration and appraisal by private interests.

**Natural Hazards:** Cities and towns continue to encroach into areas susceptible to natural hazards, chief among which are earthquakes. Ways to live safely in earthquake-prone areas are being sought by the Survey through basic geologic studies of broad areas and intensive research on active fault zones, particularly in the western United States. Scientists from the National Center for Earthquake Research in Menlo Park, Calif., are using a wide array of refined seismographs, tiltmeters, strainmeters, magnetometers, and gravity meters to "take the pulse" of the earth along known zones of crustal weakness. Continued research on the causes and nature of volcanic activity and its dangers is concentrated at the Survey's Hawaiian Volcano Observatory, located on the rim of Kilauea Volcano on the island of Hawaii.

**Research under the sea:** Recognizing the sea floor as a likely target for mineral exploration, the Geological Survey is conducting a broad program of research in cooperation with universities and other Federal agencies, designed to decipher the geologic environment of the continental shelf areas and to identify favorable target areas which may become sources of metals, minerals, and oil and gas. In particular, the shelf areas now under study include the Carolina coastal margins, the sea floor off Washington and Alaska, and the sea floor off Puerto Rico.

**Lunar Geology:** The Geological Survey is carrying out a program of lunar research in support of the goals of the National Aeronautic and Space Administration. The Survey's current work consists of lunar geologic mapping, studies in cosmic chemistry and petrography (meteorite, tektites, and cosmic dust), geologic study of terrestrial analogs of lunar features, and development of research instruments and techniques needed to effectively support manned and unmanned geologic exploration of the lunar surface. Based on interpretations of lunar geology, the Survey has recommended prime sites for the first Apollo moon landing.

**International Cooperation:** For more than 25 years the Geological Survey has provided developing nations with technical assistance in appraising their natural resources and in training their earth scientists at the request of the various foreign governments. During the past year the Geological Survey provided 144 specialists to 35 countries and arranged academic or practical training in the United States for 87 earth scientists and engineers from 25 foreign countries.

**Topographic Mapping:** The principal function of the Topographic Division of the Survey is to produce topographic maps of appropriate scale and accuracy to meet the Nation's many needs for general-purpose maps. The USGS publishes about 30,000 different maps in several standard scales and quadrangle sizes. These maps provide a wealth of information needed for planning and executing various projects. Nearly 8,000,000 copies were distributed in 1968.

**Topographic map revision:** A new "photorevision" technique has been developed by the Survey which will permit topographic maps to be updated more rapidly. Aerial photographs are used to locate various features such as new interstate highways, industrial plants, suburban housing, shopping centers, dams, and relocated streams. No field checking or contour line changes are involved. The newly added data are printed on the map in purple clearly showing the changes and additions which have occurred, thus providing a historical comparison that is useful to city planners, geographers, earth scientists, and engineers.

**"Orthophotomapping"—A New Technique:** Ortho-photomaps have been officially introduced into the National Topographic Program. This new map product, as prepared by the Survey, is a topographic map on which the natural and cultural features are portrayed by color-enhanced photographic images in true position. Cartographic symbols are added as needed for interpretation by map users. In 1968 the last of the 16 orthophotomaps covering the entire Okefenokee Swamp were published. Hence, for the first time in nine decades, an entirely new map product has replaced the standard topographic map.

**National Atlas:** The USGS continues its preparation of a 500-page National Atlas of the United States, which in a single volume will provide an accurate composite record of the physical environment of the nation, its resources, economy, industry, population, history and social culture, and political subdivisions. All pages of this unique reference and research tool were in some phase of preparation in late 1968 and 18 maps had been published and were available for purchase. Publication of the bound volume is planned for the fall of 1969.

**Conservation:** The Federal outer continental shelves off Louisiana, Texas, and California continue to attract the attention of the petroleum industry. Bonuses for the right to explore and develop offshore oil and gas lease tracts amounted to nearly $1.2 billion in fiscal 1968. Recent discoveries on the Arctic Slope of Alaska confirm the existence of large hitherto unknown deposits of petroleum on both state and Federal lands which will substantially increase the nation's energy resources.

## Mineral Production, Value and Royalty (Fiscal Year 1968[a])

| Lands | Oil | Gas | Gas liquids | Other[b] | Value | Royalty |
|---|---|---|---|---|---|---|
| | Bls. | 1,000 cu. ft. | Gallons | Tons | | |
| Public | 189,000,000 | 900,000,000 | 500,000,000 | 25,600,000 | $829,000,000 | $85,000,000 |
| Acquired | 11,000,000 | 28,000,000 | 500,000 | 265,000 | 51,000,000 | 6,000,000 |
| Indian | 31,000,000 | 125,000,000 | 65,000,000 | 11,628,000 | 132,000,000 | 16,000,000 |
| Military | 1,500,000 | 48,000,000 | 50,000,000 | | 13,500,000 | 2,000,000 |
| Outer continental shelf | 260,000,000 | 1,400,000,000 | | 1,900,000 | 1,104,000,000 | 180,000,000 |
| Naval petroleum res. no. 2 | 3,000,000 | 5,000,000 | 14,000,000 | | 10,000,000 | 1,200,000 |
| **Total** | **495,500,000** | **2,506,000,000** | **629,500,000** | **39,393,000** | **2,139,500,000** | **290,400,000** |

[a]Estimated in part. [b]All minerals except petroleum products; includes coal, potassium, sodium, etc.

## The Continental Divide

### Source: U. S. Geological Survey, Department of the Interior

Continental Divide: watershed, created by mountain ranges or table-lands of the Rocky Mountains, from which the drainage is easterly or westerly; the easterly flowing waters reaching the Atlantic Ocean chiefly through the Gulf of Mexico, and the westerly flowing waters reaching the Pacific Ocean through the Columbia River, or through the Colorado River, which flows into the Gulf of California.

The location and route of the Continental Divide across the United States may briefly be described as follows:

Beginning at point of crossing the United States-Mexican boundary, near long. 108° 45' W., the Divide, in a northerly direction, crosses New Mexico along the western edge of the Rio Grande drainage basin, entering Colorado near long. 106° 41'.

Thence by a very irregular route northerly across Colorado along the western summits of the Rio Grande and of the Arkansas, the South Platte, and the North Platte River basins, and across Rocky Mountain National Park, entering Wyoming near long. 106° 52'.

Then in a northwesterly direction, forming the western rims of the North Platte, Big Horn, and Yellowstone River basins, crossing the southwestern portion of Yellowstone National Park.

Thence in a westerly and then a northerly direction forming the common boundary of Idaho and Montana, to a point on said boundary near long. 114° 00' W.

Thence northeasterly and northwesterly through Montana and the Glacier National Park, entering Canada near long. 114° 04' W.

## World's Tallest Known Trees

The world's tallest living thing, the *Howard Libbey Tree*—a California redwood—was found by Dr. Paul A. Zahl, staff member of the National Geographic, on the east bank of Redwood Creek in Humboldt County, Calif., in 1963. When discovered it measured 367.8 ft. high with a girth of 44 ft. Remeasured four years later, it was found to be 367.6 ft. high. The *Harry W. Cole Tree* was originally 367.4 ft. but on remeasurement found to be 365.4 ft., and the *National Geographic Tree* was originally 364.3 ft., but is now 364.5 ft. high.

Only California and a pocket in southern Oregon produce earth's tallest living things—the coast redwoods, *Sequoia sempervirens*. Trees grow in a belt 500 miles long and about 30 miles wide.

Forest monarchs of three other species grow in Pacific Coast States, Australia and Tasmania. They include a 324-foot Douglas Fir (*Pseudotsuga Taxifolia*) at Ryderwood, Wash.; a 322-foot Eucalyptus tree (*Eucalyptus Regnans*) in the Styx River Valley of Tasmania; a 305-foot tree of the same species in Victoria, Australia; the 291-foot McKinley Tree and the 272-foot General Sherman, both redwoods (*Sequoia Gigantea*) in Sequoia National Park, Calif.

| Height | All in California | |
|---|---|---|
| 367.6 | Howard Libbey Tree | In Redwood Creek grove, Humboldt Co. |
| 365.4 | Harry W. Cole Tree | |
| 364.5 | National Geographic Tree | |
| 356.5 | Rockefeller Tree | Humboldt Redwoods State Park |
| 352.6 | Founders Tree | |
| 352.3 | Redwood Creek grove | |

## Undersea Craft to Observe Marine Life in Gulf Stream

Construction continues on the PX-15 mesoscaph, a new undersea craft designed by Dr. Jacques Piccard. In this 48-foot vessel he and several associates will drift for 6 weeks along the west edge of the Gulf Stream, from South Florida to Nova Scotia (about 1,500 miles) at depths up to 2,000 feet, observing marine life through 29 portholes.

# 1968 Oceanographic Events

**Source:** National Geographic Society, Washington, D. C.

The third open-ocean phase of the U. S. Navy's "Man in the Sea" program began in the fall of 1968. In preparation for the use of Sealab III, aquanauts tested experimental salvage techniques, conducted oceanographic and marine biological research and ran a series of physiological and human performance tests on the ocean bottom off San Clemente Island, Calif.

Each of five 8-man diving teams, made up of scientists and Navy divers, spent 12 days in the submerged Sealab III, which was anchored in 600 feet of water. Fifty-seven feet long and 12 feet in diameter, this non-propelled vessel is cylinder-shaped, with two rooms attached to the top of it. The teams travel back and forth between the craft and the mother ship in a special pressurized elevator.

Specially designed equipment, called the Bottom Environmental Sensing System, was lowered to gather bottom data around the Sealab III site. It photographed the bottom, recorded current information, took temperature readings and measured sediment and visibility. The bottom in this area is generally sandy and alternates from smooth and flat to steep and boulder-strewn.

The Glomar Challenger, which has in place of a mast an oil field tower rig that stands 170 feet above the waterline, is drilling into ocean floors at 50 sites around the world to gather data on the oceans and their record of changing climates and evolving life.

First drillings were in the Atlantic Ocean. Core samples were taken from the first 3 borings only because the process is so time-consuming. The ship then moved to the southern half of the Gulf of Mexico to explore an unusual formation there that may be an oil field comparable to the one in the Louisiana-Texas region.

Sonic sounding devices have located under the sediment in the deepest part of the Gulf a number of domes similar to salt domes typical of oil fields. Since these domes have never been tapped, there is uncertainty as to what will happen when the drill penetrates and releases oil which is under great pressure. The highest oil well pressure recorded is 8,000 pounds to the square inch—and some think that if the drill does penetrate an untapped dome where there is oil under such pressure the pipe would be blown out, wrecking the equipment. Others believe that the 6,000 pounds per square inch water pressure at the bottom of the Gulf would dampen any such explosion. But no one knows for sure.

The general plan calls for drilling each hole until the bit wears out, then moving to the next site. Hopefully, the floors can be drilled to 2,500 feet beyond a water depth of as much as 4 miles.

Sound waves emanating from two sonar beacons dropped to the bottom are picked up by hydrophones attached to the ship's hull and the signal is fed into a shipboard computer which controls the position of the ship. A pair of large-diameter tubes pass sideways through the hull, one such pair built into the bow area and another pair in the stern area, and each tube has a computer-controlled propeller. The computer determines the direction and distance the ship is to be rotated and activates the propellers within the tubes to move the ship the required distance; at the same time it controls the main screws to keep the ship headed into the wind and current.

## Guinea Tide

The recently discovered and little-known Guinea Tide, which originates in the Gulf of Guinea, just beneath Africa's western land bulge, is the Atlantic home of the highly prized yellowfin and skipjack tuna. Discovery of the Tide was accidental—it came to light when fishing boats working an area of the Atlantic new to them made repeated substantial catches of yellowfins.

Oceanographers spent 4 months and traveled nearly 18,000 miles on the Bureau of Commercial Fisheries' Undaunted to study this phenomenon. They ascertained that this is a different temperature body of water moving into adjoining water and not a true tide. They also ascertained that its movement is seasonal and powerful; that when it does begin to move it heads southward and has a force as strong as any oceanic tide: its daily speed rate averages 7 to 8 miles and it is centered in a little-traveled and little-fished area.

Pacific waters are also being searched for these fish (abundant until 1966) by the Bureau of Commercial Fisheries, the Scripps Institution of Oceanography and scientists from Chile, Ecuador, Mexico and Peru. The search area is some 7,000,000 miles and extends as much as 3,000 miles from the coast lines of these countries. Information is also being gathered on the unexplained shift of current which occurs every 10 years off the coast of Peru.

Underwater archeological excavation of Port Royal, Jamaica, continues into its fourth year, under the guidance of Robert Marx.

An earthquake in 1692 dropped Port Royal beneath the sea. Marx and his aides have recovered many rare and valuable objects from the bottom—watches, church-warden clay pipes with hallmarks, onion bottles, human hair, and a tobacco leaf.

French archeologists will probe the bottom of St. Ann's Bay, Jamaica, to see whether or not two wrecks under 10 feet of mud are caravels abandoned by Columbus in 1503, on his last trip to the New World.

One of the wrecks was found in 1966 by Marx, who removed from the hulk some wood, nails, ceramics, and flint for analysis.

Columbus' records do not give the exact measurements of the ships, but his general description suggests they were about 70 feet long, drew 9 feet of water, had a 23-foot beam, and carried a crew of 30-40 men.

It is not expected that the hulks will contain highly valuable treasures, but if enough of the keel and ribs can be salvaged reconstruction will be fairly easy.

The oceanographic ships USNS Kane and the USS San Pablo spent the summer surveying the Caribbean and the Gulf of Mexico. The data gathered (which included such things as water chemistry, acoustical measurements, bathymetric, seismic and magnetic measurements, etc.) were fed into a computer. When the data are published they will be released through the Naval Oceanographic Office and the National Oceanographic Data Center in Washington.

For the first time in history a sea-borne IBM computer and a Navy satellite have been joined together in a year-long geological-geophysical study of the Atlantic, Indian and Pacific Oceans. Feeding satellite navigation signals into the computer enabled scientists aboard the research

ship Argo to pin-point scientific data gathered within a tenth of a mile of the ship's exact position. Upon completion of the cruise in March, 1969, the Argo will have traveled 61,000 miles to make this study for the Scripps Institution of Oceanography.

The U. S. Coast and Geodetic Survey ship Oceanographer found 25 new submerged mountains in the South Pacific Ocean, some standing 10,800 feet above the bottom; also a number of north-south fractures (at right angles to those found in the North Pacific), and areas of the ocean basin that are as much as 3,000 feet deeper than expected.

A 180-foot buoy was attached to the top of Cobb Seamount, an underwater "island" about 250 miles west of Washington state. Cobb rises to within about 120 feet of the surface of the Pacific Ocean. Various instruments for gathering weather and oceanographic information have been attached to the 60-foot portion of the buoy above water. Since most of the Pacific Northwest weather passes over this area en route east, the climatological instruments will give advance notice of weather conditions.

### Penetration of Daylight

The Navy Oceanographic Office reports that data gathered by 5 different research submarines show that daylight penetrates the ocean as much as 2,300 feet. Maximum penetration was observed when the research submarine Alvin descended in the Tongue of the Ocean, Bahamas, between 2,100 and 2,300 feet. Personnel working in another vessel reported that natural light at a 600-foot depth off the coast of San Diego, Calif., offered a greater viewing range than the vessel's artificial lighting offered because of the lesser effects of scattering.

Four men in the 40-foot submarine Deep Quest set a new submarine diving record when they descended more than 8,100 feet in Pacific waters, 90 miles southwest of San Diego. An American flag was attached to the outside of the vessel and when it reached bottom one of the men within it actuated a firing mechanism which not only released the flag but drove the flagstaff into the ocean bottom.

The Scottish Oceanographic Laboratory began a 5-year study of the top 300 feet of the North Atlantic Ocean. Cargo and weather ships will tow special equipment about 120,000 miles each year to gather data on temperature, chemical pollution, salinity, plankton, etc. It is hoped that the information gathered will aid the world's food supply.

Scientists are evaluating data gathered pertaining to a 175-mile long sea channel, which they believe once joined the Aleutian Abyssal Plain with the North American continent. They are hopeful that this channel, 3 miles beneath the surface of the Pacific Ocean, will provide substantial new information on the geology of the area. It is thought that the same geological shifts which formed the Aleutian Trench nearly 15,000,000 years ago broke the channel.

A representative of the Woods Hole Oceanographic Institution suggests that legal changes are necessary to encourage private industry to raise food in the sea, for in the United States most fishing grounds are in the public domain. He points out that under 5% of U. S. oyster grounds are privately owned (about 165,-000 acres) but more oysters are harvested from them than from more than 4,000,000 public acres.

An area the size of Long Island Sound, maintained for the raft culture of shellfish, could produce an annual crop of mussel meat equal to the entire World's commercial fish landings.

Minerals of 35 of the major elements can be extracted from sea water or mined economically; means will be found to use tides for power generation, and fish farming will double within the decade and redouble by 1975, predicts Dr. N. Fleming of the United Kingdom's National Institute of Oceanography after an 18-month study of the potential benefits which may be harvested from the sea.

## The Average Rise and Fall of Tides
### Source: Coast and Geodetic Survey, ESSA

| Places | Feet | In. | Places | Feet | In. | Places | Feet | In. |
|---|---|---|---|---|---|---|---|---|
| Balboa, Panama... | 12 | 7 | Mobile, Ala. ...... | 1 | 6 | San Diego, Calif... | 4 | 1 |
| Baltimore, Md..... | 1 | 1 | New London, Conn. | 2 | 7 | Sandy Hook, N. J. | 4 | 7 |
| Boston, Mass...... | 9 | 6 | New Orleans, La... | See Pg. 294 | | San Francisco, Calif. | 4 | 0 |
| Charleston, S. C... | 5 | 2 | Newport, R. I..... | 3 | 6 | Savannah, Ga...... | 7 | 5 |
| Colon, Panama.... | 1 | 1 | New York, N. Y... | 4 | 6 | Seattle, Wash...... | 7 | 7 |
| Eastport, Me...... | 18 | 2 | Old Pt. Comfort, Va. | 2 | 6 | Tampa, Fla. ....... | 2 | 10 |
| Galveston, Tex.... | 1 | 5 | Philadelphia, Pa... | 5 | 11 | Washington, D. C.. | 2 | 11 |
| Key West, Fla..... | 1 | 4 | Portland, Me...... | 9 | 0 | | | |

## U. S. Coastline by States*
### Source: ESSA, Department of Commerce

| State | General coastline[1] | Tidal shoreline[2] | State | General coastline[1] | Tidal shoreline[2] |
|---|---|---|---|---|---|
| Atlantic coast........ | 2,069 | 28,673 | Gulf coast.......... | 1,631 | 17,141 |
| Connecticut.......... | (—) | 618 | Alabama............. | 53 | 607 |
| Delaware............. | 28 | 381 | Florida............... | 770 | 5,095 |
| Florida.............. | 580 | 3,331 | Louisiana............ | 397 | 7,721 |
| Georgia.............. | 100 | 2,344 | Mississippi........... | 44 | 359 |
| Maine .............. | 228 | 3,478 | Texas............... | 367 | 3,359 |
| Maryland ........... | 31 | 3,190 | Pacific coast........ | 7,623 | 40,298 |
| Massachusetts ....... | 192 | 1,519 | Alaska .............. | 5,580 | 31,383 |
| New Hampshire...... | 13 | 131 | California ........... | 840 | 3,427 |
| New Jersey.......... | 130 | 1,792 | Hawaii............... | 750 | 1,052 |
| New York........... | 127 | 1,850 | Oregon............... | 296 | 1,410 |
| North Carolina....... | 301 | 3,375 | Washington........... | 157 | 3,026 |
| Pennsylvania ........ | (—) | 89 | | | |
| Rhode Island........ | 40 | 384 | Arctic coast, Alaska . | 1,060 | 2,521 |
| South Carolina....... | 187 | 2,876 | | | |
| Virginia............. | 112 | 3,315 | United States..... | 12,383 | 88,633 |

*In statute miles (April 1, 1961). (—) Represents zero.
[1] Figures are lengths of general outline of seacoast. Measurements were made with a unit measure of 30 minutes of latitude on charts as near the scale of 1:1,200,000 as possible. Coastline of sounds and bays is included to a point where they narrow to width of unit measure, and includes the distance across at such point.
[2] Figures obtained in 1939-40 with a recording instrument on the largest-scale charts and maps then available. Shoreline of outer coast, offshore islands, sounds, bays, rivers, and creeks is included to the head of tidewater or to a point where tidal waters narrow to a width of 100 feet.

# How Deep Is the Ocean?

Principal Ocean Depths. Source: U. S. Naval Oceanographic Office

| Name of Area | Location | Depth Meters | Fathoms | Feet | Ship and/or Country | Year |
|---|---|---|---|---|---|---|
| **PACIFIC OCEAN** | | | | | | |
| Mariana Trench | 11°21'N, 142°12'E | 11,034 | 6,033 | 36,198 | Vityaz (USSR) | 1957 |
| | 11°19'N, 142°15'E | 10,863 | 5,939 | 35,631 | HMS Challenger | 1951 |
| | 11°20'N, 142°16'E | 10,815 | 5,910 | 35,460 | " " (U. K.) | 1951 |
| | 11°21'N, 142°12'E | 10,912 | 5,967 | 35,800 | Bathyscaph Trieste* | 1960 |
| Tonga Trench | 23°15.3'S, 174°44.7'W | 10,882 | 5,950 | 35,702 | Vityaz (USSR) | 1957 |
| | 24°00'S, 175°00'W | 10,850 | 5,933 | 35,598 | Nat'l Geographic | 1965 |
| | 23°16'S, 174°46'W | 10,633 | 5,814 | 34,884 | US Horizon | 1953 |
| Kuril Trench | 44°15.2'N, 150°34.2'E | 10,542 | 5,764 | 34,587 | Vityaz (USSR) | 1954 |
| | 44°18'N, 150°30'E | 10,382 | 5,677 | 34,062 | Vityaz (USSR) | 1953 |
| Philippine Trench | 10°24'N, 126°40'E | 10,539 | 5,763 | 34,578 | Galatheo (Danish) | 1951 |
| (Mindanao) | 10°27'N, 126°39.5'E | 10,497 | 5,740 | 34,440 | USS Cape Johnson | 1945 |
| Izu Trench | 30°32'N, 142°31'E | 10,374 | 5,673 | 34,038 | USS Ramapo | 1932 |
| | 30°30'N, 132°30'E | 9,985 | 5,459 | 32,721 | Bathymetric Map (USSR) | 1964 |
| | 30°49'N, 142°18'E | 9,441 | 5,159 | 30,954 | Mansyu (Japan) | 1924 |
| Kermadec Trench | 31°52.8'S, 177°20.6'W | 10,047 | 5,494 | 32,964 | Vityaz (USSR) | 1957 |
| | 31°51'S, 177°02'W | 9,994 | 5,465 | 32,790 | Galathea (Danish) | 1952 |
| Bonin Trench | 24°30'N, 143°24'E | 9,156 | 5,005 | 30,032 | Vityaz (USSR) | 1964 |
| | 24°17'N, 143°23'E | 9,150 | 5,002 | 30,012 | USS Salt Lake City | 1945 |
| New Britain Trench | 06°34'S, 153°55'E | 9,140 | 4,998 | 29,988 | Planet (German) | 1910 |
| | 06°18'S, 153°48'E | 9,103 | 4,976 | 29,858 | Bathymetric (USSR) | 1964 |
| | 06°18'S, 153°43'E | 8,936 | 4,886 | 29,316 | USS Blackfin | 1959 |
| Yap Trench | 08°33'N, 138°02'E | 8,527 | 4,662 | 27,976 | Vityaz (USSR) | 1958 |
| | 08°08'N, 137°49'E | 8,028 | 4,390 | 26,340 | USCGC Kukui | 1965 |
| | 07°55'N, 137°39'E | 8,028 | 4,390 | 26,340 | USS Greenfish | 1965 |
| Japan Trench | 36°08'N, 142°43'E | 8,412 | 4,597 | 27,591 | Bathymetric (USSR) | 1964 |
| Palau Trench | 07°40'N, 135°04'E | 8,138 | 4,449 | 26,693 | Stefan (German) | 1905 |
| | 07°31'N, 134°56'E | 7,324 | 4,005 | 24,030 | USCGC Ironwood | 1966 |
| Aleutian Trench | 50°53'N, 176°23'E | 8,100 | 4,429 | 26,574 | USCGC Bering Strait | 1953 |
| | 51°13'N, 174°48'E | 7,882 | 4,276 | 25,656 | USCGC Chelan | 1936 |
| | 50°51'N, 172°16'E | 7,679 | 4,199 | 25,194 | Coast & Geodetic | 1966 |
| | 50°41'N, 177°11'E | 7,666 | 4,192 | 25,152 | " " | 1966 |
| Peru Chile Trench | 23°18'S, 71°41'W | 8,064 | 4,409 | 26,454 | US Spencer F. Baird | 1957 |
| (Atacama Trench) | 23°27'S, 71°21'W | 8,064 | 4,409 | 26,454 | IGY | |
| | 21°00'S, 71°15'W | 7,920 | 4,330 | 25,980 | US Atlantis | 1955 |
| New Hebrides Trench | 20°36'S, 168°37'E | 7,570 | 4,138 | 24,830 | Planet (German) | 1910 |
| Ryukyu Trench | 25°15'N, 128°32'E | 7,507 | 4,105 | 24,629 | Mansyu (Japan) | 1925 |
| | 24°00'N, 126°48'E | 7,181 | 3,926 | 23,554 | Bathymetric (USSR) | 1964 |
| Mid. America Trench | 14°02'N, 93°39'W | 6,669 | 3,642 | 21,852 | USS Epce | 1952 |
| **ATLANTIC OCEAN** | | | | | | |
| Puerto Rico Trench | 19°35'N, 68°17'W | 8,648 | 4,729 | 28,374 | USS Archerfish | 1961 |
| | 19°45'N, 67°49'W | 8,528 | 4,663 | 27,978 | USS Rehoboth | 1955 |
| | 19°44'N, 67°22'W | 8,497 | 4,646 | 27,876 | USS Rehoboth | 1955 |
| | 19°53'N, 66°55'W | 8,476 | 4,635 | 27,810 | USS San Pablo | 1955 |
| | 19°42'N, 67°05'W | 8,381 | 4,583 | 27,498 | US Vema | 1954 |
| Cayman Trench | 19°12'N, 80°00'W | 7,535 | 4,120 | 24,720 | US Vema | 1960 |
| | 18°59'N, 80°12'W | 7,211 | 3,943 | 23,658 | (British Admiralty) | 1955 |
| | 18°59'N, 80°22'W | 7,191 | 3,932 | 23,592 | " " | 1937 |
| | 19°03'N, 80°22'W | 7,491 | 4,096 | 24,576 | (Germany) | 1937 |
| So. Sandwich Trench | 55°14'S, 26°29'W | 8,252 | 4,512 | 27,072 | USS Eltanin | 1963 |
| | 55°08'S, 26°04'W | 8,246 | 4,509 | 27,054 | USS Eltanin | 1963 |
| | 55°08'S, 26°05'W | 8,219 | 4,494 | 26,964 | USS Eltanin | 1963 |
| | 55°07'S, 26°46'W | 8,264 | 4,518 | 27,113 | Meteor (Germany) | 1926 |
| Romanche Gap | 00°16'S, 18°35'W | 7,864 | 4,300 | 25,800 | US Vema | 1957 |
| | 00°13'S, 18°26'W | 7,729 | 4,226 | 25,356 | USS Albatross | 1948 |
| Brazil Basin | 09°10'S, 23°02'W | 5,119 | 3,346 | 20,076 | US Vema | 1956 |
| **INDIAN OCEAN** | | | | | | |
| Java Trench | (no position) | 7,725 | 4,224 | 25,344 | Nat'l Geographic | 1967 |
| | 10°20'S, 110°10'E | 7,450 | 4,073 | 24,442 | (British Admiralty) | 1928 |
| | 10°00'S, 108°05'E | 6,459 | 3,828 | 22,968 | Planet (German) | 1906 |
| Ob Trench | (no position) | 6,874 | 3,759 | 22,553 | Nat'l Geographic | 1967 |
| Vema Trench | (no position) | 6,402 | 3,501 | 21,004 | Nat'l Geographic | 1967 |
| Agulhas Basin | (no position) | 6,195 | 3,388 | 20,325 | Nat'l Geographic | 1967 |
| Diamantina Trench | 35°00'S, 105°35'E | 6,062 | 3,315 | 19,890 | Nat'l Geographic | 1967 |
| **ARCTIC OCEAN** | | | | | | |
| Eurasia Basin | 82°23'N, 19°31'E | 5,450 | 2,980 | 17,880 | Fidor Lithke (USSR) | 1955 |
| **MEDITERRANEAN SEA** | | | | | | |
| Ionian Basin | 36°32'N, 21°06'E | 5,150 | 2,816 | 16,896 | USS Taner | 1955 |
| | 35°51'N, 22°18'E | 5,005 | 2,737 | 16,420 | Calypso (French) | 1955 |

*Deepest descent was made Jan. 23, 1960, when the bathyscaph Trieste of the U. S. Navy dove 35,800 ft. in the Mariana Trench, 250 mi. SW of Guam. On board were Lt. Don Walsh, USN, and Jacques Piccard, whose father built the Trieste. A depth of 31,350 ft. was reached by two Frenchmen, Huot and Willm, in a bathyscaph S of Urup Is. in the Kuriles, July 15, 1962.

## Ocean Area and Average Depth

Four major bodies of water are recognized by geographers and mapmakers. They are: the Pacific, Atlantic, Indian and Arctic Oceans.

The Atlantic and Pacific Oceans are considered divided at the equator into the No. Atlantic and So. Atlantic; the No. Pacific and So. Pacific.

The Arctic Ocean is the name for waters north of the continental land masses in the region of the Arctic Circle. The term Antarctic Ocean is used by some cartographers to describe the waters around Antarctica, but no fixed geographic points locate its northern limits.

| | Sq. Miles | Avg. Depth | | Sq. Miles | Avg. Depth |
|---|---|---|---|---|---|
| Pacific Ocean | 64,186,300 | 13,739 | Hudson Bay | 281,900 | 305 |
| Atlantic Ocean | 33,420,000 | 12,257 | East China Sea | 256,600 | 620 |
| Indian Ocean | 28,350,500 | 12,704 | Andaman Sea | 218,100 | 3,667 |
| Arctic Ocean | 3,662,200 | 4,362 | Black Sea | 196,100 | 3,906 |
| South China Sea | 1,148,500 | 4,802 | Red Sea | 174,900 | 1,764 |
| Caribbean Sea | 971,400 | 8,448 | North Sea | 164,900 | 308 |
| Mediterranean Sea | 969,100 | 4,926 | Baltic Sea | 147,500 | 180 |
| Bering Sea | 873,000 | 4,893 | Yellow Sea | 113,500 | 121 |
| Gulf of Mexico | 582,100 | 5,297 | Gulf of California | 59,100 | 2,375 |
| Sea of Okhotsk | 537,500 | 3,192 | Persian Gulf | ·88,800 | 328 |
| Sea of Japan | 319,100 | 5,468 | | | |

The Malayan Sea is not considered a geographical entity but a term used for convenience for waters between the South Pacific and the Indian Ocean.

# Geologic Time—The Age of the Earth
### by William L. Newman, Geologist, U. S. Geological Survey

The earth is at least four and a half billion years old, according to recent estimates. This vast span of time, called geologic time by earth scientists and believed by some to reach back to the birth of the Solar System itself, is difficult if not impossible to understand in the familiar units of months and years, or even centuries. How then do scientists reckon geologic time and why do they believe the earth is so old?

The evidence for an ancient earth is concealed in the rocks so liberally displayed on the earth's surface. Their ages vary widely but, like pages in a long and complicated history, they record the earth-shaping events of the past such as mountain building, cycles of erosion and deposition, and sea encroachment.

Two scales are used to date the various episodes and to measure the age of the earth—a *relative* time scale, based on the sequence of layering of the rocks and the slow but progressive development of life as displayed by fossils preserved in the rocks; and an *atomic* time scale, based on the natural radioactivity of chemical elements in the rocks.

James Hutton, in 1785, first proposed the most fundamental principle used to determine the relative ages of rocks: the *law of superposition*. He proposed that wherever uncontorted layers of rocks are exposed, the bottommost layer was deposited first and is, therefore, the oldest exposed; each succeeding layer is progressively younger.

William Smith discovered in 1798 that certain layers of rocks contained fossils unlike those in other layers, and that rocks of the same age could be identified by their similar or related fossil assemblages. By combining the study of fossils (paleontology) with the study of rock layers (stratigraphy), geologists are able to match or "correlate" strata of the same age throughout a large region and even throughout the world.

Recurring events in the earth's history such as mountain building and sea encroachment, of which the rock layers themselves are records, comprise units of geologic time even though the actual dates of the events are unknown. Human events are commonly dated in relative terms as having taken place either B.C. or A.D.—broad divisions of time. Shorter spans are measured by the dynasties of ancient Egypt or by the reigns of kings and queens in Europe. Similarly, geologists have divided relative time into *Eras*—broad spans based on the general character of life that existed during those times, and *Periods*—shorter spans based partly on evidence of major disturbances of the earth's crust. Periods are further subdivided into *Epochs*.

The atomic time scale is an outgrowth of Henri Bequerel's discovery in 1896 of the natural radioactive decay of uranium. Radioactive decay is a spontaneous process in which an atom (the parent) loses particles from its nucleus to form an atom (the daughter) of a different element. The rate of decay is conveniently expressed in terms of the atom's *half-life*. The atoms (isotopes) of certain elements decay slowly and several of these are used as atomic clocks:

| Parent (Isotope) | Daughter (Isotope) | Currently accepted Half-life values |
|---|---|---|
| Potassium$^{40}$ | Argon$^{40}$ | 1.3 billion years |
| Rubidium$^{87}$ | Strontium$^{87}$ | 50 billion years |
| Thorium$^{232}$ | Lead$^{208}$ | 14.1 billion years |
| Uranium$^{235}$ | Lead$^{207}$ | 713 million years |

Dating rocks by the atomic clock method is simple in theory but the laboratory procedures are complex. The numbers of parent and daughter atoms in each specimen must be determined in order to tell how long the radioactive process has been going on, or—in other words—the age of the rock. The principal difficulty lies in measuring precisely very tiny amounts of atoms.

Interweaving the relative time scale with atomic time poses certain problems because not all types of rocks can be dated directly by atomic methods. Igneous rocks, such as granite and basalt which crystallize from a molten state, are most useful for this purpose. By bracketing sedimentary rock layers within time zones determined by dating appropriately selected igneous rocks, however, the following time chart combining both relative geologic time and atomic time has been constructed:

### RELATIVE GEOLOGIC TIME

| Era | Period | Epoch | Atomic time* |
|---|---|---|---|
| | Quaternary | Holocene | |
| | | Pleistocene | 2–3 |
| Cenozoic | Tertiary | Pliocene | 12 |
| | | Miocene | 26 |
| | | Oligocene | 37–38 |
| | | Eocene | 53–54 |
| | | Paleocene | 65 |
| Mesozoic | Cretaceous | Late | |
| | | Early | 136 |
| | Jurassic | Late | |
| | | Middle | |
| | | Early | 190–195 |
| | Triassic | Late | |
| | | Middle | |
| | | Early | 225 |
| Palezoic | Permian | Late | |
| | | Early | 280 |
| | Carboniferous Systems — Pennsylvanian | Late | |
| | | Middle | |
| | | Early | — |
| | Carboniferous Systems — Mississippian | Late | |
| | | Early | 345 |
| | Devonian | Late | |
| | | Middle | |
| | | Early | 395 |
| | Silurian | Late | |
| | | Middle | |
| | | Early | 430–440 |
| | Ordovician | Late | |
| | | Middle | |
| | | Early | 500 |
| | Cambrian | Late | |
| | | Middle | |
| | | Early | 570 |
| Precambrian | | | 3,600+ |

*Estimated ages of time boundaries (millions of years)

---

# 12,000,000-year-old Stone Hammer Found by Dr. Leakey
### Source: National Geographic Society, Washington, D. C.

A pre-human African hominid, *Kenyapithecus wickeri*, added animal food to his diet by hammering open skulls and bones to reach brains and marrow, using a crude stone hammer found at Fort Ternan, Kenya, by Dr. Louis S. B. Leakey.

The hammer, which shows considerable damage along two angular edges as a result of usage, is an important mi!estone in our understanding of man's evolution as a toolmaker. Also found at the site were fossil bones of animal skulls and bones which showed evidence of deliberate fracture.

The discoveries were made under a grant from the National Geographic Society, a long-time sponsor of Dr. Leakey's research.

*Homo habilis* had a kit of several kinds of stone tools. However, the much older find suggests that, in time, stone tools made during the Pliocene age will be found, thus dating the start of toolmaking as much as 10,000,000 years before *Homo habilis*.

Work at the site exposed a rich fossil deposit of the Upper Miocene age, also about 12,000,000 years old.

Another discovery was that of a complete fossil elephant, 2,000,000 years old, found in 1967 in the Baringo area of Kenya by the Leakeys' son and daughter-in-law. The brittle fossil stood 13 ft. high at the shoulder, two feet taller than today's largest elephants, and had straight tusks which reached to the ground. It is now in the collection of the Kenya National Museum Centre for Prehistory and Paleontology at Nairobi.

The most famous of discoveries by Dr. and Mrs. Leakey were remains of the three species of hominids found in Olduvai Gorge, Tanzania, where they may have lived alongside one another nearly 1,800,000 years ago. The Gorge is a rich fossil site near Serengeti National Park, cut away by erosion; its cliffs reveal the geological sediments of 2,000,000 years.

# Volcanoes of the World: Eruptions of 1968

**Source:** National Geographic Society, Washington, D. C.

**(E)** Eruption, year in parentheses (R) Rumbling (St) Steaming (D) Dormant

Another volcano in Antarctica made itself known Dec. 4, 1967, when a 10-mile-wide crater-lake began erupting about a mile and a half from the Chilean Antarctic Station on Deception Island, some 600 miles south of Tierra del Fuego. Personnel manning Argentina's, Chile's and Great Britain's stations on the island were forced to flee their buildings and await evacuation by helicopter. Rescue ships could not enter the horseshoe-shaped bay because the water rose and fell rapidly, the heat was intense and the bay was being showered with rock and ash; the helicopters were forced to fly shuttle trips across the bay.

In the month prior to the initial eruption, a seismograph at the Chilean base recorded nearly 350 tremors.

The Chilean station was covered with nearly a foot of ash. One crater was found only three-fourths of a mile from the Chilean base. About two inches of ash settled on the British station.

The eruptions created a new 200-foot-high island in Telefon Bay which measures about a half-mile wide by three-quarters of a mile long and is composed of volcanic ash and scoriae. British scientists are studying this island.

Of particular interest is the fact that penguins and skua gulls fled their rookeries several hours before the men on the island felt the first tremors. Scientists would like to know whether or not their departure was coincidence or if they have an "early warning system" that is better than man-made machines.

Antarctica has been one of the quietest areas on the earth so far as earthquakes and volcanoes are concerned. But this may be changing with the discovery several years ago of the active volcano **Mount Melbourne,** 8,500 feet, nearly 200 miles from **Mount Erebus,** and now Deception's shift from passive to active. Recently made infrared aerial photographs show molten lava in the summit crater of Mount Erebus.

One theory about the change of role is that the harbor area of Deception Island is a water-covered volcano, just as is Crater Lake, Oregon, and that, with the passage of time, enough water seeped through and became so highly heated that it created sufficient steam to cause the eruptions. Another thought is that internal pressures may have caused it to become active.

On July 29, 1968, for the first time in more than 500 years, **Mount Arenal,** 5,032 feet, Costa Rica, erupted, with blasts continuing over several days. Some of the smoke and ash was projected 45,000 feet into the sky and carried as far as 250 miles to the north to fall on Managua, Nicaragua.

Puerto Nuevo, a village of more than 8,000 residents near the base of the volcano and about 50 miles north of San José, was partially destroyed. Nearly 100 persons have been killed by this volcano.

It is estimated that it will take Costa Rica 20 years to recover from the nearly $50,000,000 damages these eruptions have caused.

The U. S. Geological Survey advises that **Mount Shasta** and **Lassen Peak,** Calif., and **Mount St. Helens,** Wash., are volcanoes similar to **Arenal:** dormant, not necessarily dead. It is also believed that **Mount Rainier** erupted about the same time as **Arenal** did 500 or so years ago.

**Mayon,** 8,284 feet, in the Philippines, erupted in 1968, its first eruption since 1947 and its 32nd eruption since 1814. It erupted 82 times in the 10 days following its initial eruption in April, 1968, causing tens of thousands of its residents to leave their homes because of the danger of hot mud flows and floods.

One blast was reportedly so strong that it jolted the recording pen off a nearby seismograph.

Four refugees returning to their homes died from inhaling volcanic ash, causing police to arrest refugees trying to enter the evacuated areas.

Also in the Philippines, 984-foot **Mount Taal,** south of Manila erupted again on Jan. 31, the fourth time in a year.

**Mount Etna** continued its rumblings, with an occasional mild eruption. As of mid-year none of the eruptions had been violent nor had the lava flow threatened nearby towns.

**Kilauea** volcano's Hiiaka crater erupted the morning of Aug. 22 with 75-foot fountains, the first time in history this crater had erupted.

| Name | Location | Ht. Ft. | Name | Location | Ht. Ft. |
|---|---|---|---|---|---|
| **AFRICA** | | | Peuetsagoë (D) | Sumatra | 9,121 |
| Kibo, Kilimanjaro (D) | Tanzania | 19,340 | Avachinskaya (St) | U.S.S.R. | 9,026 |
| Cameroon Mt. (E-1959) | Cameroon | 13,350 | Big Ben (E-1950) | Heard Island | 9,007 |
| Nyiragongo (E-1948) | Rep. of the Congo | 11,385 | Balbi (D) | Solomons | 9,000 |
| | | | Papandajan (St) | Java | 8,602 |
| Nyamlagira (E-1958) | Rep. of the Congo | 10,028 | Gueureudong (E-1924) | Sumatra | 8,497 |
| | | | Asama (E-1965) | Japan | 8,340 |
| Fogo (E-1951) | Cape Verde Is. | 9,281 | Mayon (E-1968) | Philippines | 8,284 |
| Tristan da Cunha (E-1961) | Atlantic Ocean | 6,760 | Sumbing (E-1926) | Sumatra | 8,225 |
| | | | Tandikat (E-1924) | Sumatra | 8,166 |
| San Juan (D) | La Palma, Canary Is. | 2,612 | Yake Dake (E-1963) | Japan | 8,064 |
| | | | Sinabung (St) | Sumatra | 7,913 |
| **ANTARCTICA** | | | Bromo (St) | Java | 7,848 |
| Erebus (St.) | | 12,450 | Idjen (D) | Java | 7,828 |
| Deception Island (E-1967) | | | Ulawun (D) | New Britain | 7,532 |
| Melbourne (St.) | | 8,966 | Ngauruhoe (E-1956) | New Zealand | 7,515 |
| | | | Guntur (D) | Java | 7,379 |
| **ASIA—OCEANIA** | | | Bamus (D) | New Britain | 7,338 |
| Klyuchevskaya (E-1962) | U.S.S.R. | 15,584 | Galunggung (E-1920) | Java | 7,113 |
| Kerintji (St) | Sumatra | 12,484 | Amburombu (E-1924) | Indonesia | 7,051 |
| Fuji (D) | Japan | 12,388 | Sorikmarapi (E-1917) | Sumatra | 7,037 |
| Rindjani (E-1964) | Indonesia | 12,224 | Petarangan (E-1939) | Java | 7,005 |
| Tolbachik (E-1941) | U.S.S.R. | 12,080 | Sibajak (St) | Sumatra | 6,870 |
| Semeru (E-1963) | Java | 12,060 | Tokachi (E-1962) | Japan | 6,813 |
| Ichinskaya | U.S.S.R. | 11,880 | Tangkubanperahu (R) | Java | 6,637 |
| Kronotskaya (D) | U.S.S.R. | 11,575 | Bagana (E-1966) | Solomons | 6,560 |
| Koryakskaya (E-1957) | U.S.S.R. | 11,339 | Tongariro (E-1950) | New Zealand | 6,458 |
| Slamat (E-1953) | Java | 11,247 | Sangeang (E-1953) | Indonesia | 6,394 |
| Raung (St) | Java | 10,932 | Kaba (E-1941) | Sumatra | 6,358 |
| Shiveluch (E-1964) | U.S.S.R. | 10,771 | Awu (E-1966) | Indonesia | 6,102 |
| Dempo (St) | Sumatra | 10,364 | Soputan (E-1947) | Celebes | 5,994 |
| Welirang (D) | Java | 10,354 | Siau (E-1949) | Indonesia | 5,853 |
| Agung (E-1964) | Bali | 10,308 | Kelud (E-1966) | Java | 5,679 |
| Sundoro (D) | Java | 10,285 | Batur (E-1963) | Bali | 5,636 |
| Tjareme (E-1938) | Java | 10,098 | Belerang (St) | Sumatra | 5,636 |
| Gede (E-1949) | Java | 9,705 | Ternate (E-1938) | Halmahera | 5,627 |
| Apo (D) | Philippines | 9,690 | Hibok Hibok (E-1960) | Philippines | 5,619 |
| Merapi (E-1962) | Java | 9,551 | Lewotobi Perampuan | | |
| Bezymyannaya (E-1961) | U.S.S.R. | 9,514 | (E-1935) | Indonesia | 5,591 |
| Marapi (D) | Sumatra | 9,485 | Kirishima (St) | Japan | 5,577 |
| Tambora (D) | Indonesia | 9,353 | Mutu (D) | Indonesia | 5,545 |
| Ruapehu (St.) | New Zealand | 9,175 | Lamongna (St) | Java | 5,482 |

| Name | Location | Ht. Ft. | Name | Location | Ht. Ft. |
|---|---|---|---|---|---|
| **ASIA—OCEANIA (Continued)** | | | Shishaldin (St)......... | Aleutians..... | 9,387 |
| Boleng (E-1950)........ | Indonesia.... | 5,443 | Veniaminof (D)......... | Alaska........ | 8,225 |
| Gamkonora (E-1949)... | Halmahera... | 5,364 | Pavlof (E-1950)........ | Alaska........ | 8,215 |
| Aso (E-1958)........... | Japan........ | 5,223 | Griggs (St)............ | Alaska........ | 7,600 |
| Lewotobi Lakilaki(E-'40) | Indonesia.... | 5,217 | Paricutin (D).......... | Mexico....... | 7,451 |
| Lokon (D)............. | Celebes...... | 5,184 | Mageik (St)............ | Alaska........ | 7,244 |
| Bulusan (E-1966)...... | Philippines.. | 5,115 | Douglas (St)........... | Alaska........ | 7,064 |
| Sarycheva (E-1960).... | Kuril Is..... | 4,960 | Chiginagak (D)........ | Alaska........ | 7,031 |
| Meakan (E-1959)...... | Japan........ | 4,931 | Katmai (E-1962)....... | Alaska........ | 6,715 |
| Ibu (D)............... | Halmahera... | 4,921 | Kukak (St)............ | Alaska........ | 6,700 |
| Karymskaya (E-1963).. | U.S.S.R..... | 4,869 | Makushin (D).......... | Aleutians..... | 6,680 |
| Lewotolo (D).......... | Indonesia.... | 4,757 | Pogromni (E-1964)..... | Aleutians..... | 6,568 |
| Lopevi (E-1960)....... | New Hebrides. | 4,755 | Martin (E-1960)........ | Alaska........ | 6,100 |
| Ambrim (E-1951)...... | New Hebrides. | 4,376 | Trident (E-1963)....... | Alaska........ | 6.010 |
| Mahawu (D)........... | Celebes...... | 4,278 | Tanaga (D)............ | Aleutians..... | 5,925 |
| Long Island (E-1953).. | Bismarck Ar.. | 4,278 | Great Sitkin (St)...... | Aleutians..... | 5,710 |
| Manam (E-1966)...... | Bismarck Ar.. | 4,265 | Cleveland (E-1944)..... | Aleutians..... | 5,675 |
| Tongkoko (D)......... | Celebes...... | 3,770 | Gareloi (D)............ | Aleutians..... | 5,534 |
| Werung (E-1948)...... | Indonesia.... | 3,678 | Korovin (D)........... | Aleutians..... | 4,852 |
| Sakurajima (E-1967)... | Japan........ | 3,668 | Kanaga (D)............ | Aleutians..... | 4,416 |
| Langla (E-1965)....... | New Britain.. | 3,586 | Aniakchak (D)......... | Alaska....... | 4,275 |
| Dukono (E-1950)....... | Halmahera... | 3,566 | Akutan (E-1952)....... | Aleutians..... | 4,275 |
| Lamington (E-1951).... | New Guinea.. | 3,500 | Kiska (1962)........... | Aleutians..... | 4,275 |
| Minami (E-1963)....... | Japan........ | 3,478 | Augustine (E-1935)..... | Alaska....... | 3,927 |
| Yasur (R)............. | New Hebrides. | 3,420 | Little Sitkin (St)...... | Aleutians..... | 3,897 |
| Lolobau (D)........... | Bismarck Ar.. | 3,058 | Okmok (E-1958)........ | Aleutians..... | 3,519 |
| Asuncion (St).......... | Marianas..... | 2,923 | Seguam (D)............ | Aleutians..... | 3,458 |
| Paloé (E-1964)........ | Indonesia.... | 2,871 | Yunaska (D)........... | Aleutians..... | 3,133 |
| Sirung (E-1947)....... | Indonesia.... | 2,828 | Kagamil (D)........... | Aleutians..... | 2,930 |
| O Yama (E-1962)...... | Japan........ | 2,674 | Novarupta (St)........ | Alaska....... | 2,760 |
| Krakatau (E-1953)..... | Indonesia.... | 2,667 | Cerberus (D).......... | Alaska....... | 2,541 |
| Bam Island (D)........ | Bismarck Ar.. | 2,625 | Boquerón (E-1955)..... | Revilla Gigedo | |
| Nila (E-1932).......... | Indonesia.... | 2,562 |  | Is. (Mexico).. | 1,280 |
| Batu Tara (St)........ | Indonesia.... | 2,454 | | | |
| Alamagan (E-1945)..... | Marianas..... | 2,441 | **CENTRAL AMERICA—CARIBBEAN** | | |
| Ruang (E-1949)........ | Indonesia.... | 2,379 | | | |
| Bango (D)............. | New Britain.. | 2,375 | Tajumulco (R).......... | Guatemala.... | 13,812 |
| Tinakula (D).......... | Santa Cruz Is. | 2,200 | Tacaná (R)............ | Guatemala.... | 13,333 |
| Ija (St).............. | Indonesia.... | 2,162 | Acatenango (R)........ | Guatemala.... | 12,992 |
| Banda (D)............ | Indonesia.... | 2,152 | Fuego (E-1967)........ | Guatemala.... | 12,582 |
| Teun (D)............. | Indonesia.... | 2,149 | Santa Maria (R)....... | Guatemala.... | 12,362 |
| Serua (D)............ | Indonesia.... | 2,103 | Atitlan (R)............ | Guatemala.... | 11,565 |
| Mihara (E-1964)...... | Japan........ | 2,028 | Irazú (E-1964)......... | Costa Rica... | 11,260 |
| Pagan (D)............ | Marianas..... | 1,870 | San Pedro (R)......... | Guatemala.... | 9,921 |
| Tofua (D)............ | Tonga Islands. | 1,660 | Poás (St)............. | Costa Rica... | 8,930 |
| Unauna (E-1960)...... | Indonesia.... | 1,640 | Pacaya (E-1965)....... | Guatemala.... | 8,346 |
| Farallon de Pajaros | | | Izalco (E-1967)........ | El Salvador... | 7,828 |
| (E-1952)............ | Marianas..... | 1,096 | San Miguel (E-1957)... | El Salvador... | 6,994 |
| Guguan (D.).......... | Marianas..... | 988 | Ometepe (Concepción) | | |
| Taal (E-1968)......... | Philippines... | 984 | (E-1957)............ | Nicaragua.... | 5,106 |
| Didicas (E-1952)....... | Philippines... | 900 | Arenal (E-1968)....... | Costa Rica... | 5,092 |
| Niuafo'ou (E-1946).... | Tonga Islands. | 853 | Pelée (D)............. | Martinique... | 4,583 |
| Tavurvur (E-1941)..... | New Britain... | 741 | Momotombo (E-1952)... | Nicaragua.... | 4,126 |
| Fonualei (E-1939)...... | Tonga Islands. | 600 | Conchagua (E-1947)... | El Salvador... | 4,100 |
| Matthew Island (D)... | Loyalty Is... | 580 | Soufrière (D).......... | St. Vincent Isl. | 4,048 |
| Anak Krakatau (E-1960) | Indonesia.... | 510 | Telica (E-1965)........ | Nicaragua.... | 3,409 |
| | | | Negro (E-1962)........ | Nicaragua.... | 3,204 |
| **MID-PACIFIC** | | | Santiago (St).......... | Nicaragua.... | 1,969 |
| Mauna Loa (E-1950)... | Hawaii...... | 13,680 | | | |
| Kilauea (E-1968)....... | Hawaii...... | 4,090 | **SOUTH AMERICA** | | |
| | | | Guallatiri (E-1959)..... | Chile........ | 19,882 |
| **EUROPE** | | | Lascar (E-1951)....... | Chile........ | 19,652 |
| | | | Cotopaxi (St).......... | Ecuador..... | 19,347 |
| Etna (E-1968)........ | Sicily, Italy... | 10,958 | Misti (D)............. | Peru........ | 19,031 |
| Askja (E-1961)........ | Iceland...... | 4,954 | Cayambe (D).......... | Ecuador..... | 18,996 |
| Hekla (St)............ | Iceland...... | 4,892 | Tupungatito (E-1959)... | Chile........ | 18,504 |
| Vesuvius (D).......... | Italy........ | 4,190 | Sangay (E-1946)....... | Ecuador..... | 17,159 |
| Katla (E-1918)........ | Iceland...... | 3,182 | Tungurahua (R)........ | Ecuador..... | 16,512 |
| Stromboli (E-1967).... | Italy........ | 3,038 | Cotacachi (E-1955)..... | Ecuador..... | 16,204 |
| Thira (St)............ | Greece...... | 1,860 | Pichincha (D)......... | Ecuador..... | 15,696 |
| Vulcano (D).......... | Italy........ | 1,637 | Purace (E-1950)....... | Colombia.... | 15,604 |
| Surtsey (E-1965)...... | Iceland...... | 568 | Lautaro (St).......... | Chile........ | 11,090 |
| Ilha Nova (E-1958).... | Azores...... | 200 | Llaima (E-1955)....... | Chile........ | 10,239 |
| | | | Villarrica (E-1964)..... | Chile........ | 9,318 |
| **NORTH AMERICA** | | | Osorno (E-1960)....... | Cnile........ | 8,730 |
| Popocatépetl (St)...... | Mexico...... | 17,887 | Shoshuenco (E-1960)... | Chile........ | 7,743 |
| Wrangell (St)......... | Alaska...... | 14,005 | Puyehue (E-1960)...... | Chile........ | 7,349 |
| Colima (St)........... | Mexico...... | 13,993 | Calbuco (E-1961)...... | Chile........ | 6,611 |
| Spurr (E-1953)........ | Alaska...... | 11,069 | Casablanca (E-1960).... | Chile........ | 6,529 |
| Torbert (E-1953)...... | Alaska...... | 10,600 | Cauye (E-1960)........ | Chile........ | 4,692 |
| Lassen (D)........... | California... | 10,457 | Alcedo (E-1954)........ | Galapagos Is.. | 3,599 |
| Redoubt (E-1966)...... | Alaska...... | 10,197 | Rininahue (E-1955)..... | Chile........ | 1,004 |
| Iliamna (St).......... | Alaska...... | 10,092 | | | |

**Mt. Vesuvius,** dominating the Bay of Naples, is the most famous of volcanoes. In August, 79 A. D., it buried Pompeii (c. 20,000 pop.) under hot ash and Herculaneum and Stabiae under mud flows. Three-fifths of Pompeii has been excavated; also part of Herculaneum, most of which lies under Resina. Stabiae lies under Castellammare. There was a big eruption in 1139, and a major one in December, 1631, when 15 towns were destroyed and 4,000 people killed. Minor eruptions have occurred in 1779, 1793, 1872, 1906 and 1944, sometimes with loss of life.

**Krakatau** on an island in the Sunda Strait between Sumatra and Java exploded Aug. 27, 1883, creating a depth of 1,000 ft. in the ocean. The explosion was heard 2,500 mi. away, and tidal waves killed 35,000. In 1927 Krakatau formed the island of Anak Krakatau, which exploded, 1929, depositing an island in the hole caused in 1883.

**Mont Pelée,** Martinique, destroyed St. Pierre and more than 30,000 people May 8, 1902. Eruptions slightly less powerful occurred May 20 and Aug. 30, 1902. A major eruption began Sept. 16, 1929, and lasted 3 years.

**Mt. Agung, 10,308 ft.,** on the island of Bali, erupted in January, March and May, 1963; the last two eruptions claimed a total of more than 1,500 lives and a third of Bali's farm land, and left 85,000 homeless. Bali's **Mt. Batur,** 5,636 ft., erupted in September, 1963, forcing 1,200 persons to leave their homes at its base; rumblings and explosions could be heard for 50 miles.

In Alaska's Valley of 10,000 Smokes, the lowest of **Mt. Trident's** 3 peaks erupted Apr. 1, 1963; the cloud of smoke and dust was visible 100 miles away.

# The Great Lakes

**Source: U. S. Army Engineer District, Lake Survey, Detroit, Mich.**

The Great Lakes form the largest body of fresh water in the world and with their connecting waterways are the largest inland water transportation unit. Draining the great North Central basin of the U. S., they enable shipping to reach the Atlantic via their outlet, the St. Lawrence R., and also the Gulf of Mexico via the Illinois Waterway, from Lake Michigan to the Mississippi R. A third outlet connects with the Hudson R. and thence the Atlantic via the N. Y. State Barge Canal System.

Only one of the lakes, Lake Michigan, is wholly in the United States; the others are shared with Canada. Ships carrying grain, lumber and iron ore move from the shores of Lake Superior to Whitefish Bay at the east end of the lake, thence through the Soo (Sault Ste. Marie) locks, through the St. Mary's River and into Lake Huron. To reach the steel mills at Gary, Ind. and South Chicago, Ill., ore ships move west from Lake Huron to Lake Michigan through the Straits of Mackinac.

Lake Huron discharges its waters into Lake Erie through a narrow waterway, the St. Clair R., Lake St. Clair and the Detroit R. **Lake St. Clair**, a marshy basin, is 26 miles long and 24 miles wide at its maximum. A ship channel has been dredged through the lake. Detroit lies on the east side of Michigan. The Detroit-Canada tunnel provides vehicular access to Canada under Detroit R. and the Ambassador Bridge links Detroit and Windsor.

Lake Superior is 600 feet above mean water level at Father Point, Quebec, on the International Great Lakes Datum (1955). From Duluth, Minn., to the eastern end of Lake Ontario is 1,156 mi.

The Lake Survey is one of the 3 nautical charting agencies of the U. S. Govt. Besides charting, it maintains water level records, makes special hydraulics and hydrology studies, and conducts oceanographic-type research on the Gt. Lakes.

| | Superior | Michigan | Huron | Erie | Ontario |
|---|---|---|---|---|---|
| Length in miles........................... | 350 | 307 | 206 | 241 | 193 |
| Breadth in miles........................... | 160 | 118 | 101 | 57 | 53 |
| Deepest soundings in feet................... | 1,333 | 923 | 750 | 216 | 802 |
| Volume of water in cubic miles.............. | 2,935 | 1,180 | 849 | 110 | 393 |
| Area (sq. miles) water surface—U. S......... | 20,700 | 22,300 | 9,100 | 4,980 | 3,460 |
| Canada........ | 11,100 | ...... | 13,900 | 4,930 | 3,888 |
| **Total Area (sq. miles) U. S. and Canada..** | **31,800** | **22,300** | **23,000** | **9,910** | **7,340** |
| Area (sq. miles) entire drainage basin—U. S.... | 37,400 | 67,900 | 25,300 | 23,700 | 16,800 |
| Canada.... | 42,600 | ...... | 49,500 | 9,880 | 15,300 |
| **Total Area (sq. miles) U. S. and Canada..** | **80,000** | **67,900** | **74,800** | **33,580** | **32,100** |
| Mean surface above mean water level at Father Point, Quebec. average level in feet (108 years). | 600.37 | 578.68 | 578.69 | 570.36 | 244.77 |
| Latitude, North........................... | { 46° 25' / 49° 06' | 41° 37' / 46° 06' | 43° 00' / 46° 17' | 41° 23' / 42° 52' | 43° 11' / 44° 15' |
| Longitude, West........................... | { 84° 22' / 92° 06' | 84° 45' / 88° 02' | 79° 43' / 84° 45' | 78° 51' / 83° 29' | 76° 03' / 79° 53' |
| National boundary line in miles.............. | 282.8 | None | 260.8 | 251.5 | 174.6 |
| United States shore line (Mainland only) miles... | 909 | 1,395 | 564 | 424 | 294 |

# Lakes of the World

**Source: National Geographic Society, Washington, D. C.**

A lake is a body of water surrounded by land. Although some lakes are called seas, they are lakes by definition. The Caspian Sea is bounded by the Soviet Union and Iran and is fed by eight rivers.

| Name | Continent | Area sq. mi. | Length mi. | Depth feet | Elev. feet |
|---|---|---|---|---|---|
| Caspian Sea.......... | Asia-Europe......... | 143,550 | 760 | 3,264 | −92 |
| Superior............. | North America...... | 31,800 | 350 | 1,333 | 600 |
| Victoria............. | Africa.............. | 26,828 | 250 | 265 | 3,720 |
| Aral Sea............. | Asia................ | 25,300 | 280 | 223 | 174 |
| Huron............... | North America...... | 23,000 | 206 | 750 | 579 |
| Michigan............ | North America...... | 22,400 | 307 | 923 | 579 |
| Tanganyika.......... | Africa.............. | 12,700 | 420 | 4,710 | 2,534 |
| Great Bear.......... | North America...... | 12,275 | 192 | 1,356 | 512 |
| Baykal.............. | Asia................ | 11,780 | 395 | 5,315 | 1,493 |
| Nyasa............... | Africa.............. | 11,430 | 360 | 2,226 | 1,550 |
| Great Slave......... | North America...... | 10,980 | 298 | 2,015 | 512 |
| Erie................ | North America...... | 9,910 | 241 | 210 | 570 |
| Winnipeg............ | North America...... | 9,464 | 266 | 60 | 713 |
| Ontario............. | North America...... | 7,600 | 193 | 802 | 245 |
| Ladoga............. | Europe............. | 6,835 | 120 | 738 | 13 |
| Balkhash........... | Asia................ | 6,720 | 373 | 85 | 1,115 |
| Chad............... | Africa.............. | 6,300 | 175 | 24 | 787 |
| Maracaibo.......... | South America...... | 5,127 | 96 | 115 | S. L. |
| Onega.............. | Europe............. | 3,710 | 145 | 361 | 108 |
| Volta............... | Africa.............. | 3,276 | 250 | .... | .... |
| Titicaca............ | South America...... | 3,200 | 122 | 922 | 12,506 |
| Athabasca.......... | North America...... | 3,120 | 208 | 407 | 699 |
| Nicaragua........... | North America...... | 3,100 | 102 | 230 | 105 |
| Eyre................ | Australia........... | 2,970 | 90 | 4 | −52 |
| Rudolf.............. | Africa.............. | 2,473 | 154 | 200 | 1,230 |
| Reindeer............ | North America...... | 2,467 | 143 | .... | 1,150 |
| Issyk Kul........... | Asia................ | 2,355 | 115 | 2,303 | 5,279 |
| Torrens............. | Australia........... | 2,230 | 130 | .... | 106 |
| Vänern............. | Europe............. | 2,156 | 91 | 328 | 144 |
| Winnipegosis........ | North America...... | 2,103 | 141 | 38 | 833 |
| Albert.............. | Africa.............. | 2,075 | 100 | 54 | 2,030 |
| Kariba.............. | Africa.............. | 2,050 | 175 | 390 | 1,590 |
| Nettilling........... | North America...... | 1,956 | 67 | .... | 100 |
| Nipigon............. | North America...... | 1,870 | 72 | 540 | 855 |
| Gairdner............ | Australia........... | 1,840 | 90 | .... | 112 |
| Manitoba............ | North America...... | 1,817 | 140 | 12 | 814 |
| Urmia............... | Asia................ | 1,815 | 90 | 49 | 4,180 |
| Mweru.............. | Africa.............. | 1,770 | 76 | 84 | 3,010 |
| Kyoga.............. | Africa.............. | 1,710 | 50 | 25 | 3,400 |
| Khanka............. | Asia................ | 1,700 | 55 | 33 | 226 |
| Lake of the Woods.... | North America...... | 1,695 | 72 | 69 | 1,060 |
| Koko (Tsing)........ | Asia................ | 1,625 | 68 | 125 | 10,515 |
| Dubawnt............ | North America...... | 1,600 | 69 | .... | 764 |
| Great Salt.......... | North America...... | 1,500 | 75 | 48 | 4,200 |
| Tungt'ing........... | Asia................ | 1,430 | 75 | .... | 36 |
| Van Gölü........... | Asia................ | 1,419 | 80 | 82 | 5,643 |

# The Largest Lake in Each State of the United States

**Source:** National Geographic Society, Washington, D. C.

(*) indicates Reservoir

| State | Largest entirely within state | Largest partly in another state | Shared with | Origin | Area in square miles | Feet above sea level | Maximum depth feet | Shore-line length miles |
|---|---|---|---|---|---|---|---|---|
| Ala... | Wheeler...... | | | Man-made | 104.84 | 556 | 58 | 1,063 |
| | | Guntersville... | Tenn..... | Man-made | 107.97 | 595 | 60 | 962 |
| Alaska | Illamna...... | | | Natural.. | 1,033 | 50 | ......... | 188 |
| Ariz... | San Carlos*.... | | | Man-made | 30.6 | 2,523 | 249 | ......... |
| | | Powell...... | Utah..... | Man-made | 252 | 3,700 | 580 | ......... |
| Ark... | Ouachita...... | | | Man-made | 62.65 | 578 | 207 | 690 |
| | | Bull Shoals.... | Mo...... | Man-made | 111.31 | 695 | 243 | 1,050 |
| Calif.. | Salton Sea.... | | | Natural.. | 360 | −231 | 46 | ......... |
| | | Tahoe...... | Nev.... | Natural.. | 192 | 6,229 | 1,685 | 71 |
| Colo.. | John Martin*... | | | Man-made | 28.72 | 3,765 | 118 | 86 |
| Conn.. | Candlewood... | | | Man-made | 8.46 | 429 | 85 | 65 |
| Del... | Lum's Pond... | | | Man-made | .31 | 44 | 12 | 3.5 |
| Fla... | Okeechobee... | | | Natural.. | 700 | 18.7 | ......... | 110 |
| Ga... | Sidney Lanier. | | | Man-made | 57.96 | 1,035 | 180 | 540 |
| | | Clark Hill*.... | S. C.... | Man-made | 111.09 | 330 | 190 | 1,057 |
| Hawaii | Koloa*...... | | | Man-made | .66 | 233 | 22.5 | 3.3 |
| Idaho. | Pend Oreille... | | | Natural.. | 133 | 2,063 | 1,150 | 111.3 |
| | | Bear...... | Utah.... | Natural.. | 136 | 5,930 | 30 | 51.5 |
| Ill.... | Crab Orchard... | | | Man-made | 10.96 | 405 | 33 | 103 |
| | | Michigan..... | Wis., Ind., Mich. | Natural.. | 22,400 | 578.8 | 923 | 1,660 |
| Ind... | Wawasee...... | | | Natural.. | 4.09 | 859 | 68 | 18 |
| | | Michigan..... | Wis., Ill., Mich. | Natural.. | 22,400 | 578.8 | 923 | 1,660 |
| Iowa.. | Spirit...... | | | Natural.. | 8.84 | 1,402 | | |
| Kan... | Tuttle Creek*.. | | | Man-made | 24.68 | 1,075 | 56 | 112 |
| Ky... | Cumberland... | | | Man-made | 78.51 | 723 | ......... | 1,255 |
| | | Kentucky..... | Tenn.... | Man-made | 247.34 | 375 | 145 | 2,380 |
| La.... | Pontchartrain... | | | Natural.. | 630 | S.L. | 15 | 113 |
| Me... | Moosehead.... | | | Natural.. | 117 | 1,028 | 246 | ......... |
| Md... | Deep Creek... | | | Man-made | 7.03 | 2,462 | | |
| Mass.. | Quabbin*..... | | | Man-made | 38.6 | 530 | 150 | 118 |
| Mich.. | Houghton..... | | | Natural.. | 31.3 | 1,139 | 20 | 30 |
| | | Superior...... | Wis., Ont., Minn. | Natural.. | 31,800 | 600 | 1,333 | 2,980 |
| Minn.. | Red...... | | | Natural.. | 451 | 1,175 | 31 | 123 |
| | | Superior...... | Wis., Ont., Mich. | Natural.. | 31,800 | 600 | 1,333 | 2,980 |
| Miss... | Sardis...... | | | Man-made | 15.31 | 234 | ......... | 60 |
| Mo... | Lake of the Ozarks...... | | | Man-made | 93.75 | ......... | 125 | 1,375 |
| | | Bull Shoals.... | Ark...... | Man-made | 111.31 | 695 | 243 | 1,050 |
| Mont. | Fort Peck*.... | | | Man-made | 382.81 | 2,250 | 220 | 1,600 |
| Nebr.. | McConaughy*.. | | | Man-made | 55 | 3,276 | 150 | 50 |
| Nev... | Pyramid...... | | | Natural.. | 187.5 | 3,800 | 330 | 70 |
| | | Mead...... | Ariz.... | Man-made | 247 | 1,221 | 589 | 550 |
| N. H.. | Winnipesaukee.. | | | Natural.. | 71.55 | 504 | 120 | 128 |
| N. J.. | Hopatcong.... | | | Man-made | 4.19 | 924 | 58 | 35 |
| N. M. | Elephant Butte*...... | | | Man-made | 58.85 | 4,450 | 193 | 250 |
| N. Y.. | Oneida...... | | | Natural.. | 80 | 370 | 50 | 52 |
| | | Erie...... | Mich., Pa., Ohio, Ont. | Natural.. | 9,910 | 570 | 210 | 856 |
| N. C.. | Norman...... | | | Man-made | 50.78 | 760 | 115 | 520 |
| | | John H. Kerr*. | Va...... | Man-made | 76.4 | 300 | 100 | 800 |
| N. D.. | Garrison*..... | | | Man-made | 609.38 | 1,850 | 200 | 1,600 |
| Ohio.. | Grand...... | | | Man-made | 20 | 869 | 12 | 60 |
| | | Erie...... | Mich., Pa., N.Y., Ont. | Natural.. | 9,910 | 570 | 210 | 856 |
| Okla.. | Eufaula*..... | | | Man-made | 160.16 | 585 | 87 | 600 |
| | | Texoma...... | Texas.... | Man-made | 149.06 | 617 | 94 | 540 |
| Ore... | Upper Klamath (incl. Agency Lake)...... | | | Natural.. | 140.63 | 4,139 | 40 | 105 |
| Pa.... | Wallenpaupack. | | | Man-made | 9 | 1,182 | 50 | 45 |
| | | Erie...... | Mich.,N.Y., Ohio. Ont. | Natural.. | 9,910 | 570 | 210 | 856 |
| R. I.. | Scituate*..... | | | Man-made | 5.68 | 284 | 80 | 38 |
| S. C.. | Marion...... | | | Man-made | 157.03 | 75 | 35 | 299 |
| | | Clark Hill*.... | Ga...... | Man-made | 111.09 | 330 | 190 | 1,057 |
| S. D.. | Francis Case... | | | Man-made | 160.31 | 1,375 | 140 | 540 |
| Tenn.. | Watts Bar.... | | | Man-made | 60.31 | 745 | 80 | 783 |
| | | Kentucky..... | Ky...... | Man-made | 247.34 | 375 | 145 | 2,380 |
| Texas. | Texarkana.... | | | Man-made | 46.56 | 225 | 39 | 141 |
| | | Texoma...... | Okla.... | Man-made | 149.06 | 617 | 94 | 540 |
| Utah.. | Great Salt.... | | | Natural.. | 1,500 | 4,200 | 48 | 350 |
| | | Powell...... | Ariz.... | Man-made | 252 | 3,700 | 580 | ......... |
| Vt.... | Bomoseen..... | | | Natural.. | 3.69 | 411 | ......... | ......... |
| | | Champlain.... | N. Y. Que. | Natural.. | 430 | 100 | 399 | ......... |
| Va.... | Smith Mountain...... | | | Man-made | 31.25 | 795 | 200 | 500 |
| | | John H. Kerr*. | N. C..... | Man-made | 76.4 | 300 | 100 | 800 |
| Wash.. | F. D. Roosevelt.. | | | Man-made | 123.44 | 1,288 | 375 | 302 |
| W. Va. | Tygart...... | | | Man-made | 5.37 | 1,010 | ......... | 106 |
| | | Bluestone*.... | Va...... | Man-made | 3.07 | 1,409 | 42 | 33 |
| Wis... | Winnebago.... | | | Natural.. | 215.26 | ......... | 21.6 | 91.96 |
| | | Superior...... | Minn., Mich. Ont. | Natural.. | 31,800 | 600 | 1,333 | 2,980 |
| Wyo.. | Yellowstone.... | | | Natural.. | 137 | 7,735 | ......... | ......... |

# Famous Waterfalls

**Source:** National Geographic Society, Washington, D. C.

Height=total drop in one or more leaps; †=falls of more than one leap; *=falls that diminish greatly seasonally; **=falls that reduce to a trickle or are dry for part of each year. If river names not shown, they are same as the falls. R.=river; L.=lake; (C)=cascade-type. See notes following list.

| Name and Location | Ft. | Name and Location | Ft. | Name and Location | Ft. |
|---|---|---|---|---|---|
| **AFRICA** | | Norway— | | Kentucky | |
| **Angola** | | †Eastern Mardalsfoss.... | 1,696 | Cumberland.......... | 68 |
| Duque de Braganca, | | Highest fall........... | 974 | Maryland | |
| Lucala R............ | 344 | Western Mardalsfoss.... | 1,535 | Great, Potomac R. (C) | 90 |
| Ruacana, Cunene R...... | 406 | (Both on L. Eikesdal). | | Minnesota | |
| **Ethiopia** | | Skjeggedal.......... | 525 | **Minnehaha........ | 54 |
| Baratieri, Ganale | | Skykkje, Skykkjua R.... | 820 | Montana | |
| Dorya R............. | 459 | Vettis, Morkedöla R.... | 1,214 | Missouri............ | 75 |
| Dal Verme, Ganale | | Highest fall......... | 889 | New Jersey | |
| Dorya R............. | 98 | Vöring, Bjorela R....... | 597 | **Passaic............ | 70 |
| Fincha.............. | 508 | Sweden | | New York | |
| *Tesissat, Blue Nile R.... | 140 | †Handöl, Handöl Cr..... | 345 | Taughannock........ | 215 |
| **Lesotho** | | †*Stora Sjöfallet, Lule R. | 130 | Oregon | |
| Maletsunyane........ | 630 | Tannforsen, Are R...... | 120 | †Multnomah......... | 620 |
| **Rhodesia-Zambia** | | Switzerland | | Highest fall........ | 542 |
| *Victoria, Zambezi R..... | 355 | †Giétroz (Glacier) (C)... | 1,640 | Tennessee | |
| **South Africa** | | †Diesbach............. | 394 | Fall Creek.......... | 256 |
| *Aughrabies, Orange R... | 400 | †Giessbach........... | 1,312 | Rock House Creek.... | 125 |
| Howick, Umgeni R...... | 311 | Handegg, Aare R...... | 151 | Washington | |
| *Tugela (5 falls)........ | 3,110 | Iffigen............. | 394 | Fairy Falls.......... | 700 |
| Highest fall........... | 1,350 | Pissevache, La Salanfe R. | 213 | Mt. Rainer Nat. Pk. | |
| **Tanzania-Zambia** | | †Reichenbach......... | 656 | Narada, Paradise R. | 168 |
| *Kalambo.............. | 726 | Rhine.............. | 65 | Sluiskin, Paradise R | 300 |
| **Uganda** | | †Simmen, Simme R..... | 459 | Palouse............ | 198 |
| Murchison, Victoria | | Stäuber............. | 590 | Snoqualmie........ | 270 |
| Nile R............. | 130 | Staubbach........... | 984 | Wisconsin | |
| **Zambia** | | †Trümmelbach....... | 1,312 | Manitou, Black R.... | 165 |
| Chirombo, Ielsa R...... | 880 | | | Wyoming | |
| | | **NORTH AMERICA** | | Yellowstone National Pk. | |
| **ASIA** | | **Canada** | | Tower............. | 132 |
| | | British Columbia | | Yellowstone (upper). | 109 |
| India—**Cauvery........ | 330 | †Takakkaw (Daly | | Yellowstone (lower). | 308 |
| †**Gersoppa (Jog), | | Glacier)......... | 1,650 | Mexico—El Salto....... | 218 |
| Sharavati R.......... | 830 | Highest fall........ | 1,200 | **Juanacatlán, Rio | |
| **Japan** | | Panther, Nigel Cr..... | 600 | Grande de Santiago.... | 66 |
| **Kegon, L. Chuzenji.... | 330 | Labrador | | | |
| Yudaki, L. Yuno........ | 335 | Churchill Falls, | | **SOUTH AMERICA** | |
| | | Churchill, R........ | 245 | | |
| **AUSTRALASIA** | | Mackenzie District | | **Argentina—Brazil** | |
| **Australia** | | Virginia, S. Nahanni R. | 315 | †Iguazú................ | 230 |
| New South Wales | | Quebec | | **Brazil**—Glass............ | 1,325 |
| †Wentworth.......... | 518 | Montmorency........ | 251 | Herval............. | 400 |
| Highest fall........ | 360 | **Canada-United States** | | Paulo Afonso, São Fran- | |
| Wollomombi........ | 1,100 | Ontario-New York | | cisco R............ | 275 |
| Queensland | | Niagara: American... | 193 | Patos-Maribondo, Rio | |
| Coomera............ | 210 | Horseshoe... | 186 | Grande............ | 115 |
| Tully.............. | 450 | **United States** | | Urubupunga, Alto | |
| **New Zealand** | | Arizona | | Paraná R............ | 40 |
| *Bowen (from Glaciers).. | 540 | Mooney, Havasu Cr... | 220 | **Brazil-Paraguay** | |
| Helena............. | 890 | California | | Sete Quedas, or Guaira | |
| Stirling........... | 505 | Feather, Fall R....... | 640 | Alto Paraná R....... | 130 |
| †Sutherland, Arthur R... | 1,904 | Iilllouette.......... | 370 | **Colombia**—Tequendama, | |
| | | Nevada, Merced R.... | 594 | Bogotá R............ | 427 |
| **EUROPE** | | **Ribbon............ | 1,612 | Catarata de Candelas, | |
| Austria—Upper Gastein... | 207 | Silver Strand........ | 1,170 | Cusiana R........... | 984 |
| Lower Gastein........ | 280 | Vernal, Merced R.... | 317 | **Ecuador** | |
| (Both on Ache R.) | | †Yosemite............ | 2,425 | Agoyan, Pastaza R...... | 200 |
| †Golling, Schwarzbach R. | 200 | Bridalveil.......... | 620 | **Guyana** | |
| Krimml (Krimmler)... | 1,250 | *Yosemite (upper)... | 1,430 | Kaieteur, Potaro R..... | 741 |
| France—†Gavarnie (C)... | 1,385 | *Yosemite (lower)... | 320 | King Edward VIII, | |
| Great Britain—Wales | | Colorado | | Semang R............ | 840 |
| Pistyll Cain, Afon Gain R. | 150 | Seven.............. | 266 | King George VI, Utshi | |
| Pistyll Rhaladr........ | 240 | Georgia | | R................. | 1,600 |
| Scotland | | †Tallulah............ | 251 | †Marina, Ipobe R....... | 500 |
| Glomach............ | 370 | Idaho | | Highest fall........ | 300 |
| Iceland—Detti, Jokul R... | 144 | Henry's Fork (upper).. | 96 | Venezuela—†Angel....... | 3,212 |
| Gull, Hvita R......... | 101 | Henry's Fork (lower).. | 70 | Highest fall.......... | 2,648 |
| Italy—Toce (C)......... | 470 | **Shoshone, Snake R.. | 195 | Cuquenán............ | 2,000 |
| | | **Twin, Snake R...... | 125 | | |

The earth has thousands of waterfalls, some of considerable magnitude. Their importance is determined not only by height but volume of flow, steadiness of flow, crest width, whether the water drops sheerly or over a sloping surface, and one leap or a succession of leaps. A series of low falls flowing over a considerable distance is known as a cascade.

Sete Quedas or Guaira is the world's greatest waterfall when its mean annual flow (estimated at 470,-000 cusecs, cubic feet per second) is combined with height. A greater volume of water passes over Stanley Falls, though not one of its seven cataracts, spread over nearly 60 miles of the Congo River, exceeds 10 feet.

Estimated mean annual flow, in cusecs, of other major waterfalls are: Niagara, 212,200; Paulo Afonso, 100,000; Urubupunga, 97,000; Iguazú, 61,600; Patos-Maribondo, 53,000; Victoria, 38,400; Churchill, Labrador, 40,000; and Kaieteur, 23,400.

Cauvery, India, is the most variable of the world's known waterfalls. It fluctuates from a trickle in dry periods to 667,470 cusecs during monsoons.

The Niagara River carries the water of Lake Erie to Lake Ontario, a descent of about 326 feet in 36 miles. It flows over two cataracts at Niagara: the Horseshoe or Canadian Fall and the American Fall. Since the opening of new hydroelectric stations on both the United States and Canadian sides of the river, the height of the falls is constantly changing. As water is taken from the river by these stations the level of the pool below the falls rises and lowers by as much as 30 feet. At their maximum height, which is only at night and during the off-tourist season, the Canadian Fall is 186 feet high and the American Fall 193 feet high.

# Highest and Lowest Continental Altitudes

**Source:** National Geographic Society, Washington, D. C. (In feet)

| Continent | Highest Point | Elevation | Lowest Point | Below Sea Level |
|---|---|---|---|---|
| Asia......... | Mount Everest, Nepal-Tibet......... | 29,028 | Dead Sea, Israel-Jordan.... | 1,296 |
| South America. | Mount Aconcagua, Argentina......... | 22,834 | Salinas Grandes, Peninsula Valdés, Argentina........ | 131 |
| North America. | Mount McKinley, Alaska............. | 20,320 | Death Valley, California.... | 282 |
| Africa....... | Kibo (Kilimanjaro) Tanzania........ | 19,340 | Qattara Depression, Egypt.. | 436 |
| Europe....... | Mount El'brus U.S.S.R. Caucasus Mts. | 18,481 | Caspian Sea, U.S.S.R...... | 92 |
| Antarctica... | Vinson Massif (est.)............... | 16,860 | Sea level................. | ......... |
| Australia.... | Mount Kosciusko, New South Wales... | 7,310 | Lake Eyre, South Australia.. | 52 |

## HEIGHT OF MOUNT EVEREST

Mt. Everest was 29,002 ft. tall when Edmund Hillary and Tenzing Norkey scaled it in 1953. This triangulation figure had been accepted since 1850. In 1954 the Surveyor General of the Republic of India set the height at 29,028 ft., plus or minus 10 ft. because of snow. The National Geographic Society accepts the new figure, but many mountaineering groups still use 29,002 ft.

## HIGH PEAKS IN UNITED STATES, CANADA, MEXICO

| Name | Place | Feet | Name | Place | Feet | Name | Place | Feet |
|---|---|---|---|---|---|---|---|---|
| McKinley........ | Alaska. | 20,320 | La Plata....... | Colo... | 14,336 | Windom......... | Colo... | 14,087 |
| Logan.......... | Can... | 19,850 | Blanca........ | Colo... | 14,317 | Russell........ | Calif.. | 14,086 |
| Citlaltepec | | | Uncompahgre.. | Colo... | 14,309 | Eolus......... | Colo... | 14,084 |
| (Orizaba)..... | Mexico | 18,700 | Crestone...... | Colo... | 14,294 | Columbia...... | Colo... | 14,073 |
| St. Elias...... | Alaska. | 18,008 | Lincoln....... | Colo... | 14,286 | Augusta....... | Alaska- | |
| Popocatepétl... | Mexico | 17,887 | Grays........ | Colo... | 14,270 | | Can. | 14,070 |
| Foraker....... | Alaska. | 17,400 | Antero....... | Colo... | 14,269 | Culebra....... | Colo... | 14,069 |
| Iztaccihuatl.... | Mexico | 17,343 | Torreys...... | Colo... | 14,267 | Missouri...... | Colo... | 14,067 |
| Lucania....... | Can... | 17,147 | Castle........ | Colo... | 14,265 | Humboldt..... | Colo... | 14,064 |
| King.......... | Can... | 17,130 | Evans........ | Colo... | 14,264 | Bierstad...... | Colo... | 14,060 |
| Steele......... | Can... | 16,644 | Quandary..... | Colo... | 14,264 | Sunlight...... | Colo... | 14,059 |
| Bona.......... | Alaska. | 16,500 | Longs........ | Colo... | 14,256 | Split......... | Calif.. | 14,058 |
| Blackburn..... | Alaska. | 16,390 | McArthur..... | Can... | 14,253 | Nauhcampatepetl | | |
| Kennedy...... | Alaska. | 16,286 | Mt. Wilson.... | Colo... | 14,246 | (Perote)....... | Mexico | 14,049 |
| Sanford....... | Alaska. | 16,237 | White........ | Calif.. | 14,246 | Handies....... | Colo... | 14,048 |
| South Buttress.. | Alaska. | 15,885 | North Palisade.. | Calif.. | 14,242 | Middle Palisade.. | Calif.. | 14,040 |
| Wood......... | Can... | 15,885 | Cameron...... | Colo... | 14,238 | Little Bear.... | Colo... | 14,037 |
| Vancouver..... | Alaska- | | Shavano...... | Colo... | 14,229 | Sherman...... | Colo... | 14,036 |
| | Can. | 15,700 | Belford....... | Colo... | 14,197 | Redcloud..... | Colo... | 14,034 |
| Churchill...... | Alaska. | 15,638 | Princeton..... | Colo... | 14,197 | Langley....... | Calif.. | 14,028 |
| Fairweather.... | Alaska. | 15,300 | Yale......... | Colo... | 14,196 | Conundrum.... | Colo... | 14,022 |
| Zinantecatl | | | Crestone Needles. | Colo... | 14,191 | Tyndall....... | Calif.. | 14,018 |
| (Toluca)...... | Mexico | 15,016 | Bross........ | Colo... | 14,172 | Pyramid...... | Colo... | 14,018 |
| Hubbard....... | Alaska- | | Kit Carson.... | Colo... | 14,165 | Wetterhorn.... | Colo... | 14,017 |
| | Can. | 15,015 | Wrangell...... | Alaska. | 14,163 | Wilson........ | Colo... | 14,017 |
| Bear.......... | Alaska. | 14,831 | Shasta....... | Calif.. | 14,162 | Muir......... | Calif.. | 14,015 |
| Walsh......... | Can... | 14,780 | Sill.......... | Calif.. | 14,162 | North Maroon.. | Colo... | 14,014 |
| East Buttress... | Alaska. | 14,730 | El Diente...... | Colo... | 14,159 | San Luis...... | Colo... | 14,014 |
| Matlalcueyetl.. | Mexico | 14,636 | Maroon....... | Colo... | 14,156 | Huron........ | Colo... | 14,005 |
| Hunter........ | Alaska. | 14,573 | Tabeguache... | Colo... | 14,155 | Holy Cross.... | Colo... | 14,005 |
| Alverstone..... | Alaska- | | Oxford....... | Colo... | 14,153 | Sunshine...... | Colo... | 14,001 |
| | Can. | 14,565 | Sneffels...... | Colo... | 14,150 | Grizzly....... | Colo... | 14,000 |
| Browne Tower... | Alaska. | 14,530 | Point Success.... | Wash.. | 14,150 | Colima....... | Mexico | 13,993 |
| Whitney....... | Calif.. | 14,494 | Democrat...... | Colo... | 14,148 | Barnard...... | Calif.. | 13,990 |
| Elbert........ | Colo... | 14,433 | Liberty Cap.... | Wash.. | 14,133 | Stewart....... | Colo... | 13,980 |
| Massive....... | Colo... | 14,421 | Capitol....... | Colo... | 14,130 | Keith......... | Calif.. | 13,977 |
| Harvard....... | Colo... | 14,420 | Lindsey....... | Colo... | 14,125 | Le Conte...... | Calif.. | 13,960 |
| Rainier........ | Wash.. | 14,410 | Pikes Peak..... | Colo... | 14,110 | Meeker....... | Colo... | 13,911 |
| Williamson.... | Calif.. | 14,375 | Snowmass..... | Colo... | 14,092 | Kennedy...... | Can... | 13,905 |

## SOUTH AMERICA

| Peak | Country | Feet | Peak | Country | Feet | Peak | Country | Feet |
|---|---|---|---|---|---|---|---|---|
| Aconcagua, Argentina | | 22,834 | Sajama, Bolivia | | 21,391 | Gen. Manuel Belgrano, | | |
| Bonete, Argentina | | 22,546 | Nacimiento, Argentina | | 21,302 | Argentina | | 20,505 |
| Sargantay, Peru | | 22,542 | Illimani, Bolivia | | 21,201 | Pumasillo, Peru | | 20,492 |
| Ojos del Salado, Argentina- | | | Coropuna, Peru | | 21,079 | Solo, Argentina | | 20,492 |
| Chile | | 22,539 | Laudo, Argentina | | 20,997 | Polleras, Argentina | | 20,456 |
| Tupungato, Argentina- | | | Ancohuma, Bolivia | | 20,958 | Pular, Chile | | 20,423 |
| Chile | | 22,310 | Ausangate, Peru | | 20,945 | Chañi, Argentina | | 20,341 |
| Pissis, Argentina | | 22,241 | Toro, Argentina-Chile | | 20,932 | Aucanquilcha, Chile | | 20,295 |
| Mercedario, Argentina | | 22,211 | Tres Cruces, Argentina- | | | Juncal, Argentina | | 20,276 |
| Huascarán, Peru | | 22,205 | Chile | | 20,853 | Negro, Argentina | | 20,184 |
| Llullaillaco, Argentina-Chile | | 22,057 | Huandoy, Peru | | 20,852 | Quela, Argentina | | 20,128 |
| El Libertador, Argentina | | 22,047 | Parinacota, Bolivia-Chile | | 20,768 | Condoriri, Bolivia | | 20,095 |
| Cachi, Argentina | | 22,047 | Tórtolas, Argentina-Chile | | 20,745 | Palermo, Argentina | | 20,079 |
| Yerupaja, Peru | | 21,758 | Ampato, Peru | | 20,702 | Solimana, Peru | | 20,068 |
| Lincancaur, Argentina- | | | Cóndor, Argentina | | 20,669 | San Juan, Argentina | | 20,049 |
| Chile | | 21,719 | Salcantay, Peru | | 20,574 | Nevada, Argentina-Chile | | 20,023 |
| Galan, Argentina | | 21,654 | Chimborazo, Ecuador | | 20,561 | Antofalla, Argentina | | 20,013 |
| El Muerto, Argentina-Chile | | 21,457 | Huancarhuas, Peru | | 20,531 | Marmolejo, Argentina-Chile | | 20,013 |

The highest point in the West Indies is in the Dominican Republic, Pico Duarte (10,200 ft.)

## EUROPE

| Peak | Feet | Peak | Feet | Peak | Feet | Peak | Feet |
|---|---|---|---|---|---|---|---|
| **Alps** | | Hohberghorn | 13,842 | Fiescherhorn | 13,283 | **Pyrenees** | |
| Mont Blanc | 15,771 | Alphubel | 13,799 | Grünhorn | 13,266 | Aneto | 11,168 |
| Monte Rosa (high- | | Rimpfischhorn | 13,776 | Lauteraarhorn | 13,261 | Posets | 11,073 |
| est peak of group) | 15,203 | Aletschhorn | 13,763 | Dürrenhorn | 13,238 | Perdido | 11,007 |
| Dom | 14,913 | Strahlhorn | 13,747 | Allalinhorn | 13,213 | Maladeta | 10,866 |
| Liskamm | 14,852 | Dent d'Hérens | 13,686 | Weissmies | 13,199 | Vignemale | 10,820 |
| Weisshorn | 14,782 | Breithorn | 13,665 | Lagginhorn | 13,156 | Long | 10,479 |
| Täschhorn | 14,733 | Bishorn | 13,645 | Fletschhorn | 13,110 | Estats | 10,304 |
| Matterhorn | 14,690 | Jungfrau | 13,642 | Zupó | 13,109 | Montcalm | 10,105 |
| Dent Blanche | 14,293 | Ecrins | 13,461 | Adlerhorn | 13,081 | **Caucasus (Europe-Asia)** | |
| Nadelhorn | 14,196 | Mönch | 13,448 | Gletscherhorn | 13,068 | El'brus | 18,481 |
| Grand Combin | 14,154 | Pollux | 13,422 | Schalihorn | 13,040 | Shkara | 17,064 |
| Lenzspitze | 14,088 | Schreckhorn | 13,379 | Scerscen | 13,028 | Dykh Tau | 17,054 |
| Finsteraarhorn | 14,022 | Ober Gabelhorn | 13,330 | Eiger | 13,025 | Kashtan Tau | 16,877 |
| Castor | 13,865 | Gran Paradiso | 13,323 | Jägerhorn | 13,024 | Kazbek | 16,558 |
| Zinalrothorn | 13,849 | Bernina | 13,284 | Rottalhorn | 13,022 | Dzhangi Tau | 16,565 |

## ASIA

| Peak | Country | Feet | Peak | Country | Feet |
|---|---|---|---|---|---|
| Everest | Nepal-Tibet | 29,028 | Pobedy Peak | Sinkiang-U.S.S.R. | 24,406 |
| K2 (Godwin Austen) | Kashmir | 28,250 | Sia Kangri | Kashmir | 24,350 |
| Kanchenjunga | Nepal-Sikkim | 28,208 | Haramosh Peak | Pakistan | 24,272 |
| Lhotse I (Everest) | Nepal-Tibet | 27,923 | Istoro Nal | Pakistan | 24,240 |
| Makalu I | Nepal-Tibet | 27,824 | Tent Peak | Nepal-Sikkim | 24,088 |
| Lhotse II (Everest) | Nepal-Tibet | 27,560 | Chamlang | Nepal | 24,012 |
| Dhaulagiri | Nepal | 26,810 | Kabru | Nepal-Sikkim | 24,002 |
| Manaslu I | Nepal | 26,760 | Alung Gangri | Tibet | 24,000 |
| Cho Oyu | Nepal-Tibet | 26,750 | Chomo Lhari | Tibet-Bhutan | 23,997 |
| Nanga Parbat | Kashmir | 26,660 | Baltoro Kangri | Kashmir | 23,990 |
| Annapurna | Nepal | 26,504 | Muz Tagh | Sinkiang | 23,890 |
| Gasherbrum | Kashmir | 26,470 | Mana | India | 23,860 |
| Broad | Kashmir | 26,400 | Baruntse | Nepal | 23,688 |
| Gosanthain | Tibet | 26,291 | Amne Machin | China | 23,490 |
| Annapurna II | Nepal | 26,041 | Nepal Peak | Nepal-Sikkim | 23,458 |
| Gyachung Kang | Nepal-Tibet | 25,910 | Pumori | Nepal-Tibet | 23,442 |
| Disteghil | Kashmir | 25,868 | Gauri Sankar | Nepal-Tibet | 23,440 |
| Himalchuli | Nepal | 25,801 | Badrinath | India | 23,420 |
| Nuptse (Everest) | Nepal-Tibet | 25,726 | Nunkun | Kashmir | 23,410 |
| Masherbrum | Kashmir | 25,660 | Lenina Peak | U.S.S.R. | 23,405 |
| Nanda Devi | India | 25,645 | Api | Nepal | 23,399 |
| Chomo Lonzo | Nepal-Tibet | 25,640 | Trisul | India | 23,360 |
| Rakaposhi | Kashmir | 25,550 | Kangto | India-Tibet | 23,260 |
| Kamet | India-Tibet | 25,447 | Nyenchhen Thangtha | Tibet | 23,255 |
| Namcha Barwa | Tibet | 25,445 | Tirsuli | India | 23,210 |
| Gurla Mandhata | Tibet | 25,355 | Dunagiri | India | 23,184 |
| Ulugh Muz Tagh | Tibet-Sinkiang | 25,340 | Pauhunri | Sikkim-Tibet | 23,180 |
| Kungur | Sinkiang | 25,325 | Lombo Kangra | Tibet | 23,165 |
| Tirich Mir | Pakistan | 25,230 | Ama Dablam | Nepal | 22,494 |
| Makalu II | Nepal-Tibet | 25,130 | Pyramid | Nepal-Sikkim | 22,430 |
| Minya Konka | China | 24,900 | Cho Polu | Nepal | 22,093 |
| Kula Gangri | Tibet-Bhutan | 24,784 | Lingtren | Nepal-Tibet | 21,972 |
| Changtse (Everest) | Nepal-Tibet | 24,780 | Khumbutse | Nepal-Tibet | 21,785 |
| Muz Tagn Ata | Sinkiang | 24,757 | Hlako Gangri | Tibet | 21,265 |
| Skyang Kangri | Kashmir | 24,750 | Mt. Grosvenor | China | 21,190 |
| Communism Peak | U.S.S.R. | 24,590 | Thagehhab Gangri | Tibet | 20,970 |
| Jongsong Peak | Nepal-Sikkim | 24,472 | Damavand | Iran | 18,934 |
|  |  |  | Ararat | Turkey | 16,946 |

## AFRICA, AUSTRALIA AND OCEANIA

| Mountains and Country | Feet | Mountains and Country | Feet | Mountains and Country | Feet |
|---|---|---|---|---|---|
| Kilimanjaro (2 peaks) |  | Mandala, New Guinea | 15,420 | Gughe, Ethiopia | 13,780 |
| Kibo, Tanzania | 19,340 | Ras Dashan, Ethiopa | 15,158 | Toubkal, Morocco | 13,671 |
| Mawenzi, Tanzania | 16,896 | Meru, Tanzania | 14,979 | Kinabalu, Malaysia | 13,455 |
| Kenya, Kenya | 17,058 | Wilhelm, New Guinea | 14,793 | Lesatima, Kenya | 13,104 |
| Margherita, Uganda- |  | Karisimbi, Rep. of Congo- |  | Kerintji, Sumatra | 12,484 |
| Rep. of Congo | 16,763 | Rwanda | 14,787 | Cook, New Zealand | 12,349 |
| Sukarno, New Guinea | 16,500 | Elgon, Kenya-Uganda | 14,178 | Teide, Canary Isl. | 12,198 |
| Pilimsit, New Guinea | 15,748 | Batu, Ethiopia | 14,131 | Kosciusko, Australia | 7,310 |
| Trikora, New Guinea | 15,585 |  |  |  |  |

## ANTARCTICA

| Peak | Feet | Peak | Feet | Peak | Feet |
|---|---|---|---|---|---|
| Vinson Massif | 16,860 | Miller | 13,648 | Falla | 12,549 |
| Tyree | 16,290 | Long Gables | 13,620 | Rucker | 12,520 |
| Shinn | 15,750 | Dickerson | 13,517 | Goldthwait | 12,510 |
| Gardner | 15,375 | Giovinetto | 13,412 | Morris | 12,500 |
| Epperly | 15,100 | Wade | 13,399 | Erebus | 12,450 |
| Kirkpatrick | 14,855 | Fisher | 13,386 | Campbell | 12,434 |
| Elizabeth | 14,698 | Lister | 13,205 | Don Pedro Christophersen | 12,355 |
| Markham | 14,275 | Wexler | 13,202 | Lysaght | 12,326 |
| Bell | 14,117 | Shear | 13,100 | Huggins | 12,247 |
| Mackellar | 14,098 | Fridtjof Nansen | 13,087 | Sabine | 12,201 |
| Anderson | 13,957 | Odishaw | 13,008 | Astor | 12,175 |
| Bentley | 13,934 | Donaldson | 12,894 | Mohl | 12,172 |
| Kaplan | 13,878 | Ray | 12,808 | Frakes | 12,064 |
| Andrew Jackson | 13,745 | Sellery | 12,779 | Jones | 12,040 |
| Sidley | 13,717 | Waterman | 12,730 | Gjelsvik | 12,008 |
| Ostenso | 13,710 | Anne | 12,703 | Coman | 12,000 |
| Minto | 13,658 | Press | 12,694 |  |  |

# The Seven Wonders of the Ancient World

**The Pyramids of Egypt.** These pyramids, the monumental tombs of ancient Egyptian pharaohs, were constructed 3000 B.C. to 1800 B.C. The oldest is at Sakkara. The largest are at Gizeh, near Cairo. Of these, the Great Pyramid of Cheops has a base covering over 13 acres; originally it was 481 ft. high, each base side was 754.5 ft. long; its size was reduced by removal of the facing stone and top stone, leaving its height 450 ft.

**The Hanging Gardens of Babylon.** Built by Nebuchadnezzar, King of Babylonia, about 600 B.C. in what is now Iraq, the gardens consisted according to legend of 5 terraces, each 50 ft. above the other. No traces remain.

**The Statue of Zeus at Olympia.** This 40-ft. marble statue decorated with ivory and beaten gold, was created by the Greek sculptor Phidias about 432 B.C. Considered the greatest masterpiece of Greek sculpture, the statue stood in the temple of Zeus at Olympia, in the western Peloponnesus, scene of the ancient Olympic games. The statue was removed and destroyed.

**The Temple of Artemis at Ephesus.** South of what is now Izmir, Turkey, the Ionian Greeks erected this famous temple in the latter part of the 4th Century B.C., on the site of earlier temples, the last of which had been destroyed by one Herostatus in 356 B.C., supposedly on the night in which Alexander the Great was born. The new temple had Ionic columns over 60 ft. tall. It was destroyed by the Goths in 262 A.D.

**The Mausoleum at Halicarnassus.** After Prince Mausolus of Caria in SW Asia Minor died, 353 B.C., his widow, Queen Artemisia, built a huge marble tomb, completed about 325 B.C., in his memory at Halicarnassus (Now Bodrum, Turkey). Its name, the Mausoleum, came to be the generic term for monumental tombs. It was destroyed by an earthquake. Fragments of the Greek sculptures from the edifice are on exhibit at the British Museum, London.

**The Colossus of Rhodes.** This huge bronze statue of Helios, the Greek god of the sun (usually identified with Apollo), stood in the harbor of Rhodes on the island of Rhodes, SW of Asia Minor. Constructed by the sculptor Chares, 292-280 B.C., it is variously reported as having been 105 to 117 ft. tall (New York's Statue of Liberty is 111 ft. from heel to top of head). Thrown down by an earthquake, about 224 B.C., it lay prone for hundreds of years before being sold off as scrap.

**The Pharos of Alexandria.** A white marble tower in pyramidal shape, this famous lighthouse was completed about 280 B.C. on the peninsula of Pharos (formerly an island) at Alexandria in Egypt. It was built during the reign of Ptolemy Philadelphus (Ptolemy II) and may have been designed by the architect Sostratus. It is variously reported as having been 400-600 ft. tall. It was destroyed by an earthquake, 1375 A.D.

# Important Islands and Their Areas

**Source:** National Geographic Society, Washington, D. C.
Figure in parentheses shows rank among the world's ten largest islands. Some islands have not been surveyed accurately; in such cases estimated areas are shown. *See footnotes.

| LOCATION-OWNERSHIP | Area in Square Miles |
|---|---|
| **ARCTIC OCEAN** | |
| **Canadian Islands** | |
| Axel Heiberg | 15,779 |
| Baffin (5) | 183,810 |
| Banks | 23,230 |
| Bathurst | 7,609 |
| Devon | 20,861 |
| Ellesmere (9) | 82,119 |
| Melville | 16,369 |
| Prince of Wales | 12,830 |
| Somerset | 9,370 |
| Southampton | 15,700 |
| Victoria (10) | 81,930 |
| **USSR Islands** | |
| Franz Josef Land | 6,400 |
| Novaya Zemlya (two Is.) | 31,900 |
| Wrangell | 2,800 |
| **Norwegian Islands** | |
| Svalbard | 24,100 |
| Nordaust Landet | 5,792 |
| Vest Spitsbergen | 15,251 |
| **ATLANTIC OCEAN** | |
| Anticosti, Canada | 3,043 |
| Ascension, U. K. | 34 |
| Azores, Portugal | 888 |
| Faial | 66.2 |
| São Miguel | 299 |
| Bahamas, U. K. | 4,400 |
| Bermudas, U. K. | 20.46 |
| Block, Rhode Island | 10.8 |
| land only | 9.3 |
| Canaries, Spain | 2,808 |
| Fuerteventura | 670 |
| Gran Canaria | 634 |
| Tenerife | 919 |
| Cape Breton, Canada | 3,970 |
| Cape Verde, Portugal | 1,557 |
| Faeroes, Denmark | 540 |
| Falklands, U. K. | 4,618 |
| Fernando de Noronha (Archipelago), Brazil | 7.2 |
| **British Isles** | |
| Great Britain, main-land (8) | 84,186 |
| Channel Islands | 75 |
| Guernsey | 30 |
| Jersey | 45 |
| Sark | 1.99 |
| Hebrides | 2,662 |
| Ireland island | 32,598 |
| Ireland, republic | 27,138 |
| Northern Ireland | 5,462 |
| Man | 227 |
| Orkneys | 375 |
| Scilly | 6.3 |
| Shetlands | 549 |
| Skye | 670 |
| Wight | 147 |
| Greenland, Denmark (1) | 840,000 |
| Iceland | 39,768 |
| Surtsey | 2.5 |
| Long Island, N. Y. | 1,723 |
| land only | 1,401 |
| Madeiras, Portugal | 308 |
| Marajó, Brazil | 1,553 |
| Martha's Vineyard, Mass. | 108.7 |
| land only | 92.8 |

| LOCATION-OWNERSHIP | Area in Square Miles |
|---|---|
| Mount Desert, Me. | 105.4 |
| land only | 75.9 |
| Nantucket, Mass. | 57 |
| land only | 46.4 |
| Newfoundland, Canada | 43,359 |
| Prince Edward, Canada | 2,184 |
| St. Helena, U. K. | 47 |
| South Georgia, U. K. | 1,470 |
| Tierra del Fuego, Chile and Argentina | 18,800 |
| Tristan da Cunha, U. K. | 40.15 |
| **BALTIC SEA** | |
| Aland, Finland | 572 |
| Bornholm, Denmark | 217 |
| Gotland, Sweden | 1,225 |
| **CARIBBEAN SEA** | |
| Antigua, U. K. | 108 |
| Aruba, Netherlands | 69.9 |
| Barbados | 170 |
| Cuba | 43,038 |
| Isle of Pines | 1,180 |
| Curaçao, Netherlands | 173 |
| Dominica, U. K. | 305 |
| Guadeloupe, France | 687 |
| Hispaniola, (Haiti and Dominican Republic) | 29,530 |
| Jamaica | 4,232 |
| Martinique, France | 425 |
| Puerto Rico, U. S. | 3,435 |
| Tobago | 116 |
| Trinidad | 1,864 |
| Virgins, U. S. | 132 |
| **INDIAN OCEAN** | |
| Andamans, India | 2,508 |
| Ceylon | 25,332 |
| Madagascar (Malagasy Republic) (4) | 230,035 |
| Mauritius | 720 |
| Pemba | 380 |
| Réunion, France | 969 |
| Seychelles, U. K. | 156 |
| Zanzibar | 640 |
| **Persian Gulf** | |
| Bahrain | 231 |
| **MEDITERRANEAN SEA** | |
| Balearics, Spain | 1,936 |
| Corfu, Greece | 246 |
| Corsica, France | 3,367 |
| Crete, Greece | 3,207 |
| Cyprus | 3,572 |
| Elba, Italy | 87.4 |
| Malta | 95 |
| Rhodes, Greece | 545 |
| Sardinia, Italy | 9,194 |
| Sicily, Italy | 9,817 |
| Euboea, Greece | 1,456 |
| **PACIFIC OCEAN** | |
| Aleutians, U. S. | 6,821 |
| Adak | 289 |
| Amchitka | 114 |
| Attu | 318 |
| Kanaga | 135 |
| Kiska | 110 |
| Tanaga | 185 |
| Umnak | 675 |
| Unalaska | 1,064 |
| Unimak | 1,600 |
| Canton, U. S., U. K.* | |
| Carolines, U. S. trust terr., | 463 |
| Christmas, U. S., U. K.* | |

| LOCATION-OWNERSHIP | Area in Square Miles |
|---|---|
| Diomede, Big, U.S.S.R. | 11.3 |
| Diomede, Little, U. S. | 2.4 |
| Easter, Chile | 63.9 |
| Formosa (Taiwan) | 13,885 |
| Funafuti, U. K., U. S.* | |
| Galapagos, Ecuador | 2,868 |
| Guadalcanal, U. K. | 1,130 |
| Hainan, China | 13,000 |
| Hawaiian, U. S.* | 6,439 |
| Hawaii | 4,030 |
| Oahu | 604 |
| Hong Kong, U. K. | 32 |
| Japan | 142,727 |
| Hokkaido | 30,077 |
| Honshu (7) | 88,000 |
| Iwo Jima | 7.8 |
| Kyushu | 13,768 |
| Shikoku | 6,857 |
| Kodiak | 5,363 |
| Marianas, U. S. trust terr., excluding Guam | 184 |
| Guam, U. S. | 212 |
| Marquesas, France | 492 |
| Marshalls, U. S. trust terr. | 69.8 |
| Bikini* | |
| New Caledonia, France | 7,335 |
| New Guinea (2) | 317,000 |
| New Hebrides, U. K.-Fr. | 5,700 |
| New Zealand | 103,736 |
| Chatham | 372 |
| North | 44,281 |
| South | 58,093 |
| Stewart | 670 |
| Okinawa | 485 |
| Philippines | 115,830 |
| Leyte | 2,416 |
| Luzon | 46,636 |
| Mindanao | 39,191 |
| Mindoro | 3,891 |
| Negros | 5,041 |
| Palawan | 5,693 |
| Panay | 4,047 |
| Samar | 5,309 |
| Quemoy, Formosa | 50 |
| Sakhalin, U.S.S.R. | 28,597 |
| Samoas | 1,173 |
| American Samoa | 76 |
| Western Samoa | 1,097 |
| Santa Catalina, Calif. | 74 |
| Tahiti, France | 402 |
| Tasmania, Australia | 26,383 |
| Tongas, U. K. | 269 |
| Vancouver, Canada | 12,408 |
| Vanua Levi (Fiji) | 2,137 |
| Viti Levu (Fiji) | 4,053 |
| **East Indies** | |
| Bali, Indonesia | 2,269 |
| Borneo, Indonesia- Malaysia, U. K. (3) | 287,400 |
| Celebes, Indonesia | 72,987 |
| Java, Indonesia | 48,763 |
| Madura, Indonesia | 2,113 |
| Moluccas, Indonesia | 28,767 |
| New Britain, Aust. | 14,600 |
| New Ireland, Aust. | 3,340 |
| Sumatra, Indonesia (6) | 182,860 |
| Timor | 13,071 |
| Indonesian Timor | 5,800 |
| Portuguese Timor | 5,762 |

**Australia**, often called an island, is a continent. Its mainland area is 2,967,909 sq. mi. Census Bureau gives 6,542 sq. mi. as 1967 preliminary land area of Hawaiian Islands.
**Islands in minor waters:** Manhattan (31 sq. mi.), Staten (64 sq. mi.) and Governors (173 acres), all in New York Harbor, U. S.; Isle Royale (209.9 sq. mi.), Lake Superior, U. S.; Manitoulin (1,068 sq. mi.), Lake Huron, Canada; Penang (110 sq. mi.), Strait of Malacca, Malaysia; Singapore (224 sq. mi.), Singapore Strait, Singapore.
**Atolls:** Bikini (lagoon area, 280 sq. mi., land area 2.87 sq. mi)., U. S. Trust Territory of the Pacific Islands; Canton (lagoon 20 sq. mi.), land 4.3 sq. mi.), U. S. and U. K.; Christmas (lagoon 89 sq. mi., land 184 sq. mi.), U. S. and U. K.; Funafuti (lagoon 84 sq. mi., land 17 sq. mi.), U. S. and U. K.

## Earthquakes Perform Necessary Function

Earthquakes continue to cause damage and loss of life around the globe but scientists point out that they are vital to the continued development of our earth. There are more than 1,200 seismograph stations around the world, which detect 500,000 tremblors a year, the National Geographic Society says. Of these, 100,000 can be heard or felt and some 1,000 cause damage. Scientists assert that this repeated uplifting of the earth's crust, with the quakes that go with it, is essential to life. With mountains constantly eroding, if they were not raised again the world would become a place of stagnant seas and swamps.

No place is immune from the possibility of an earthquake, but four out of five occur around the edge of the Pacific Ocean. A second major trouble zone extends from the West Indies across the Atlantic and Mediterranean to the Himalayas and the East Indies. Today's most widely accepted theory of quakes holds that they are caused by titanic shifts in the earth's crust along cracks or fracture lines called faults. When the rock gives way under the strain at some weak point, often far below the surface, powerful shock waves are released. Some circle the globe; others pass through the earth, at 8 miles a second.

## Important Rivers of the United States

| River | Source, or Upper Limit of Length | Outflow | Miles |
|---|---|---|---|
| Alabama................ | Junction of Coosa and Tallapoosa Rivers, Elmore County, Ala................ | Mobile River............ | 315 |
| Allegheny.............. | Potter County, Pa................ | Ohio River............. | 325 |
| Altamaha.............. | Junction of Oconee and Ocmulgee Rivers, Montgomery County, Ga........ | Atlantic Ocean.......... | 137 |
| Altamaha-Ocmulgee....... | Junction of Yellow and South Rivers, Newton County, Ga................ | Atlantic Ocean.......... | 392 |
| Androscoggin........... | Umbagog Lake, Maine................ | Atlantic Ocean.......... | 171 |
| Apalachicola-Chattahoochee. | Towns County, Ga................ | Gulf of Mexico, Fla..... | 500 |
| Arkansas.............. | Lake County, Colo................ | Mississippi River, Ark.... | 1,450 |
| Big Black (Miss.)......... | Webster County, Miss................ | Mississippi River....... | 330 |
| Big Horn.............. | Junction of Wind and Popo Agie Rivers, Fremont County, Wyo............ | Yellowstone Riv., Mont... | 336 |
| Black (Mo.-Ark.)........ | Junction E.&W. Forks, Reynolds Cty., Mo. | White River............ | 280 |
| Black Warrior........... | Junction of Locust and Mulberry Forks. Jefferson County, Ala............ | Tombigbee River....... | 178 |
| Brazos................ | Junction of Salt and Double Mountain Forks, Stonewall County, Tex........ | Gulf of Mexico....... | 870 |
| Canadian.............. | Colfax County, N. Mex................ | Arkansas Riv., Okla..... | 906 |
| Cape Fear............. | Junction of Haw and Deep Rivers, Chatham County, N. C................ | Atlantic Ocean......... | 202 |
| Cedar (Iowa).......... | Dodge County, Minn................ | Iowa River, Iowa...... | 329 |
| Cheyenne............. | Junction of South Fork and Beaver Creek, Fall River County, S. Dak........ | Missouri River......... | 290 |
| Chippewa............. | Junction of East and West Forks, Sawyer County, Wis................ | Mississippi River....... | 183 |
| Cimarron.............. | Colfax County, N. Mex................ | Arkansas Riv., Okla..... | 600 |
| Clark Fork-Pend Oreille... | Silver Bow County, Mont................ | Columbia R., B. C., Can... | 505 |
| Colorado (Ariz.)........ | Rocky Mountain National Park, Colo.... (90 miles in Mexico)........ | Arizona-Sonora line.... Gulf of Calif........ | 1,360 1,450 |
| Colorado (Texas)....... | Dawson County, Texas................ | Matagorda Bay....... | 840 |
| Columbia.............. | Columbia Lake, British Columbia....... | Pac. Ocean, Bet. Ore. & W.. | 1,214 |
| Columbia, Upper....... | Columbia Lake, British Columbia....... | To mouth of Snake River.. | 890 |
| Colville.............. | Brooks Range................ | Beaufort Sea........ | 350 |
| Connecticut........... | Third Connecticut Lake, N. H......... | L. I. Sound, Conn....... | 407 |
| Coosa................ | Junction of Etowah and Oostanaula Rivers, Floyd County, Ga........ | Alabama River....... | 286 |
| Cumberland........... | Junction of Poor and Clover Forks, Harlan County, Ky................ | Ohio River........ | 687 |
| Delaware.............. | Junction of East and West Branches, at Hancock, N. Y................ | Liston Point at head of Delaware Bay....... | 280 |
| Deschutes............. | Lava Lake, Deschutes County, Oreg...... | Columbia River....... | 250 |
| Des Moines............ | Junction of East and West Forks, Humboldt County, Iowa................ | Mississippi River....... | 327 |
| Dolores.............. | Dolores County, Colo................ | Colorado River....... | 230 |
| Flint................. | Junction of Mud and Camp Creeks, Fayette County, Ga................ | Apalachicola River....... | 265 |
| Fox (Wis.)............ | Columbia County, Wis................ | Green Bay........ | 175 |
| French Broad.......... | Junction of North and West Forks, Transylvania County, N. C................ | Tennessee River........ | 210 |
| Genesee.............. | Potter County, Pa................ | Lake Ontario........ | 144 |
| Gila................. | Catron County, N. Mex................ | Colorado River, Ariz..... | 630 |
| Grand (Mich.)......... | Jackson County, Mich................ | Lake Michigan....... | 260 |
| Green (Ky.)........... | Lincoln County, Ky................ | Ohio River, Ky........ | 360 |
| Green (Utah-Wyo.)....... | Junction of Wells and Trail Creeks, Sublette County, Wyo................ | Colorado River, Utah..... | 730 |
| Gunnison.............. | Junction of Taylor and East Rivers, Gunnison County, Colo................ | Colorado River........ | 150 |
| Holston.............. | Junction of North and South Forks. Sullivan County, Tenn................ | Tennessee River........ | 140 |
| Housatonic............ | Town of Washington, Mass................ | Long Island Sound....... | 148 |
| Hudson............... | Henderson Lake, Essex County, N. Y.... | Upper N. Y. Bay, NY-NJ.. | 306 |
| Humboldt............. | Mouth of Bishop Creek, Elko Co., Nev.... | Humboldt Sink....... | 290 |
| Illinois.............. | Junction of Kankakee and Des Plaines Rivers, Grundy County Ill........ | Mississippi River........ | 273 |
| Iowa................ | Junction of East and West Branches, Wright County, Ia................ | Mississippi River....... | 291 |
| James (N. Dak.-S. Dak.)... | Wells County, North Dakota........ | Missouri River, S. D..... | 710 |
| James (Va.)........... | Junction of Jackson and Cowpasture Rivers, Botetourt County, Va........ | Hampton Roads........ | 340 |
| Jefferson-Beaverhead-Red Rock............. | Source of Red Rock River in Beaverhead County, Mont................ | Missouri River........ | 217 |
| John Day............. | Blue Mountains, Grant County, Oreg...... | Columbia River........ | 281 |
| Kanawha-New.......... | Junction of North and South Forks of New River, Ashe County, N. C....... | Ohio River............ | 352 |
| Kansas.............. | Junction of Smoky Hill and Republican Rivers, Geary County, Kans........ | Missouri River........ | 169 |
| Kennebec............. | Moosehead Lake, Maine................ | Atlantic Ocean........ | 164 |
| Kentucky............. | Junction of North and Middle Forks, Lee County, Ky................ | Ohio River........ | 259 |
| Klamath............. | Lake Ewauna, Klamath Falls, Oreg...... | Pacific Ocean........ | 250 |
| Koyukuk............. | Brooks Range................ | Yukon River........ | 500 |
| Kuskokwim............ | Alaska Range................ | Kuskokwim Bay....... | 550 |
| Licking.............. | Magoffin County, Kentucky........ | Ohio River........ | 350 |
| Little Colorado........ | Latitude 34°, Apache County, Ariz...... | Colorado River........ | 300 |
| Little Missouri........ | Crook County, Wyo................ | Missouri River........ | 560 |
| Merrimack............ | Junction of Pemigewassett and Winnipesaukee Rivers, Franklin, N. H........ | Atlantic Ocean........ | 110 |
| Miami............... | Indian Lake, Logan County, Ohio........ | Ohio River........ | 160 |
| Milk................ | Junction of North and South Forks, Alberta Province................ | Missouri River, Mont..... | 625 |
| Minnesota............ | Big Stone Lake, Minn................ | Mississippi R., St. Paul.... | 332 |
| Mississippi........... | Lake Itasca, Minn................ | Mouth of S W Pass...... | 2,348 |
| Mississippi, Upper...... | Lake Itasca, Minn................ | To mouth of Missouri R.... | 1,171 |
| Mississippi-Missouri-Red Rk. | Source of Red Rock River, Mont........ | Mouth of S W Pass...... | 3,710 |
| Missouri.............. | Junction Jefferson, Madison and Gallatin Rivers, Madison County, Mont....... | Mississippi River........ | 2,315 |
| Missouri-Red Rock........ | Source of Red Rock River, Mont........ | Mississippi River........ | 2,533 |
| Mobile-Alabama-Coosa...... | Junction of Etowah and Oostanaula Rivers, Floyd County, Ga............ | Mobile Bay............ | 639 |

| River | Source, or Upper Limit of Length | Outflow | Miles |
|---|---|---|---|
| Mohawk | Junction of East and West Branches, Oneida County, N. Y. | Hudson River | 148 |
| Monongahela | Junction of West Fork and Tygart Rivers, Marion County, W. Va. | Ohio River | 128 |
| Muskingum | Junction of Tuscarawas and Walhonding Rivers, Coshocton County, Ohio | Ohio River | 110 |
| Neches | Van Zandt County, Tex. | Sabine Lake | 280 |
| Neosho | Morris County, Kans. | Arkansas River, Okla. | 460 |
| Neuse | Junction of Eno and Flat Rivers, Durham County, N. C. | Pamlico Sound | 260 |
| New | Junction of North and South Forks, Ashe County, N. C. | Kanawha River | 255 |
| Niobrara | Niobrara County, Wyo. | Missouri River, Nebr. | 431 |
| Noatak | Brooks Range | Kotzebue Sound | 350 |
| North Canadian | Union County, N. Mex. | Canadian River, Okla. | 760 |
| North Platte | Junction of Grizzly and Little Grizzly Creeks, Jackson County, Colo. | Platte River, Nebr. | 618 |
| Nueces | Edwards County, Tex. | Nueces Bay | 338 |
| Ohio | Junction of Allegheny and Monongahela Rivers, Pittsburgh, Pa. | Mississippi R., Ill.-Ky. | 981 |
| Ohio-Allegheny | Potter County, Pa. | Mississippi River | 1,306 |
| Osage | Junction of Marais des Cygnes River and Little Osage River, Mo. | Missouri River, Mo. | 250 |
| Ouachita | Polk County, Ark. | Red River, La. | 605 |
| Owyhee | Junction of East and South Forks, Owyhee County, Idaho | Snake River | 250 |
| Pearl | Neshoba County, Miss. | Gulf of Mexico, Miss.-La. | 490 |
| Pecos | Mora County, N. Mex. | Rio Grande, Texas | 735 |
| Pee Dee | Junction of Yadkin and Uwharrie Rivers, Montgomery County, N. C. | Winyah Bay | 233 |
| Pee Dee-Yadkin | Watauga County, N. C. | Winyah Bay, S. C. | 435 |
| Penobscot | Junction of East and West Branches, Medway, Maine | Atlantic Ocean | 101 |
| Platte | Junction of North and South Platte Rivers, North Platte, Nebr. | Missouri River, Nebr. | 310 |
| Porcupine | Yukon Territory (Canada) | Yukon River, Alaska | 450 |
| Potomac | Junction of North and South Branches, Hampshire County, W. Va. | Chesapeake Bay | 287 |
| Powder | Junction of South and Middle Forks, Johnson County, Wyo. | Yellowstone River, Mont. | 375 |
| Rappahannock | Fauquier and Rappahannock Counties, Va. | Chesapeake Bay | 185 |
| Red (Okla.-Tex.-La.) | Junction of Prairie Dog Town and North Forks, Okla. | Mississippi River | 1,018 |
| Red River of the North | Junction of Otter Tail and Bois de Sioux Rivers, Wilkin County, Minn. | Lake Winnipeg, Man., Can. | 545 |
| Republican | Junction of North Fork and Arikaree River, Dundy County, Nebr. | Kansas River, Kan. | 445 |
| Rio Grande | San Juan County, Colo. | Gulf of Mexico | 1,885 |
| Roanoke | Junction of North and South Forks, Montgomery County, Va. | Albemarle Sound, N. C. | 380 |
| Rock (Ill.-Wis.) | Washington County, Wis. | Mississippi River, Ill. | 300 |
| Sabine | Junction of South and Caddo Forks, Hunt County, Tex. | Sabine Lake, Tex.-La. | 380 |
| Sacramento | Siskiyou County, Calif. | Suisun Bay | 382 |
| St. Croix (Minn.-Wis.) | Upper St. Croix Lake, Wis. | Mississippi River | 164 |
| St. Francis | Iron County, Mo. | Mississippi River, Ark. | 425 |
| St. Johns (Fla.) | Lake Washington, Brevard County, Fla. | Atlantic Ocean | 276 |
| St. Joseph | Hillsdale County, Mich. | Lake Michigan | 210 |
| Salmon (Idaho) | Custer County, Idaho | Snake River, Idaho | 420 |
| San Joaquin | Junction of South and Middle Forks, Madera County, Calif. | Suisun Bay | 350 |
| San Juan | Silver Lake, Archuleta County, Colo. | Colorado River, Utah | 360 |
| Santee | Junction of Wateree and Congaree Rivers, Richland, S. C. | Atlantic Ocean | 143 |
| Santee-Wateree-Catawba | McDowell County, N. C. | Atlantic Ocean, S. C. | 538 |
| Savannah | Junction of Seneca and Tugaloo Rivers, Anderson County, S. C. | Atlantic Ocean, Ga.-S. C. | 314 |
| Schuylkill | Near Tuscarora, Schuylkill County, Pa. | Delaware River | 131 |
| Scioto | Auglaize County, Ohio | Ohio River | 237 |
| Smoky Hill | Cheyenne County, Colo. | Kansas River, Kan. | 540 |
| Snake | Ocean Plateau, Teton County, Wyo. | Columbia River, Wash. | 1,038 |
| South Fork Shenandoah | Junction of North and South Rivers at Port Republic, Va. | Shenandoah River | 100 |
| South Platte | Junction of South and Middle Forks, Park County, Colo. | Platte River, Nebr. | 424 |
| Susquehanna | Otsego Lake, Otsego County, N. Y. | Chesapeake Bay, Md. | 444 |
| Suwanee | Junction of North and Log Rivers, Charlton County, Ga. | Gulf of Mexico | 190 |
| Tallahatchie | Tippah County, Miss. | Yazoo River, Miss. | 301 |
| Tallapoosa | Near Embry in Paulding County, Ga. | Alabama River | 268 |
| Tanana | Wrangell Mts. (Yukon Territory, Can.) | Yukon River, Alaska | 800 |
| Tar-Pamlico | Person County, N. C. | Pamlico Bay | 215 |
| Tennessee | Junction of French Broad and Holston Rivers, Knox County, Tenn. | Ohio River, Ky. | 652 |
| Tennessee-French Broad | Junction of North and West Forks of FrenchBroad, Transylvania County, N.C. | Ohio River | 862 |
| Tombigbee | Junction of East and West Forks, Monroe County, Miss. | Mobile River, Ala. | 409 |
| Tongue | Junction of North and South Forks, Sheridan County, Wyo. | Yellowstone River | 246 |
| Trinity | Junction of East and West Forks, Kaufman County, Tex. | Galveston Bay, Texas | 360 |
| Wabash | Darke County, Ohio | Ohio River, Ill.-Ind. | 475 |
| Washita | Hemphill County, Tex. | Red River, Okla. | 500 |
| West Branch Penobscot | Junction of North and South Branches, Somerset County, Maine | Penobscot River | 112 |
| White (Ark.-Mo.) | Madison County, Ark. | Mississippi River | 690 |
| Willamette | Junction of Coast and Middle Forks, near Eugene, Ore. | Columbia River | 190 |
| Wisconsin | Le Vieux Desert, Vilas County, Wis. | Mississippi River | 430 |
| Yazoo | Junction of Tallahatchie and Yalobusha Rivers, Leflore County, Miss. | Mississippi River | 188 |
| Yellowstone | Park County, Wyo. | Missouri River, N. D. | 671 |
| Yukon | Junction of Lewes and Pelly Rivers, Yukon Territory, Canada | Bering Sea, Alaska | 1,800 |

# Notable Bridges in the United States

Source: U. S. Coast Guard and other official sources
Asterisk (*) designates Railroad Bridge. Span of a bridge is distance between its supports.

## SUSPENSION

| Year | Bridge | Location | Span |
|---|---|---|---|
| 1964 | Verrazano-Narrows | New York, N. Y. | 4,260 |
| 1937 | Golden Gate | San Fran. Bay | 4,200 |
| 1957 | Mackinac | Sts. of Mackinac | 3,800 |
| 1931 | Geo. Washington | Hudson River | 3,500 |
| 1952 | Tacoma | Washington | 2,800 |
| 1936 | Transbay | San Fran. Bay | 2,310 |
| 1939 | Bronx-Whitestone | East R., N.Y.C. | 2,300 |
| 1951 | Del. Memorial | Wilmington,Del. | 2,150 |
| 1968 | Del. Mem. (new) | Wilmington,Del. | 2,150 |
| 1957 | Walt Whitman | Phila., Pa. | 2,000 |
| 1929 | Ambassador | Detroit-Canada | 1,850 |
| 1961 | Throgs Neck | Long Is. Sound | 1,800 |
| 1926 | Benjamin Franklin | Philadelphia | 1,750 |
| 1924 | Bear Mt., N. Y. | Hudson River | 1,632 |
| 1952 | Chesapeake Bay | SandyPoint,Md. | 1,600 |
| 1903 | Williamsburg | East R., N.Y.C. | 1,600 |
| 1883 | Brooklyn | East R., N.Y.C. | 1,595 |
| 1938 | Thousand Islands | St. Lawrence R. | (note) |
| 1930 | Mid-Hudson, N. Y. | Poughkeepsie | 1,500 |
| 1964 | San Pedro-Ter. Isle | Los Angeles Har. | 1,500 |
| 1909 | Manhattan | East R., N.Y.C. | 1,470 |
| 1936 | Triborough | East R., N.Y.C. | 1,380 |
| 1931 | St. Johns | Portland, Ore. | 1,207 |
| 1929 | Mount Hope | Rhode Island | 1,200 |
| 1939 | Deer Isle | Maine | 1,080 |
| 1931 | Maysville | Ohio River | 1,060 |
| 1867 | Cincinnati | Ohio River | 1,057 |
| 1900 | Miampimi | Mexico | 1,030 |
| 1849 | Wheeling | Ohio River | 1,010 |
| 1929 | Royal Gorge | Colorado | 880 |
| 1933 | Anthony Wayne | Ohio | 782 |
| 1933 | South 10th St. | Pittsburgh, Pa. | 750 |
| 1932 | Waldo-Hancock | Maine | 750 |
| 1935 | Bettendorf, Iowa | Mississippi R. | 710 |
| 1921 | Rondout | Kingston, N.Y. | 705 |

## CANTILEVER

| Year | Bridge | Location | Span |
|---|---|---|---|
| UC | Chester, Pa. | Delaware River | 1,644 |
| 1958 | New Orleans, La. | Mississippi, R. | 1,575 |
| 1936 | Transbay | San Fran. Bay | 1,400 |
| UC | Baton Rouge, La. | Mississippi R. | 1,235 |
| 1955 | Nyack-Tarrytown | Hudson River | 1,212 |
| 1930 | Longview | Columbia River | 1,200 |
| 1909 | Queensboro | East R., N.Y.C. | 1,182 |
| 1927 | Carquinez Strait | California | 1,100 |
| 1958 | Parallel Span | | 1,100 |
| 1957 | Richmond | San Fran. Bay | 1,070 |
| 1929 | Cooper River | Charleston, S.C. | 1,050 |
| 1963 | Newburgh-Beacon | Hudson R., N.Y. | 1,000 |
| 1951 | East St. Louis, Ill. | Mississippi R. | 964 |
| 1940 | Natchez | Mississippi R. | 875 |
| 1938 | Bluewater | Pt. Huron,Mich. | 871 |
| 1954 | St. Petersburg, Fla. | Tampa Bay | 864 |
| 1940 | *Baton Rouge | Mississippi R. | 848 |
| 1899 | *Cornwall | St. Lawrence R. | 843 |
| 1940 | Greenville | Mississippi R. | 840 |
| 1961 | Helena, Ark. | Mississippi R. | 840 |
| 1930 | *Vicksburg | Mississippi R. | 825 |
| 1929 | Louisville | Ohio River | 820 |
| 1935 | Rip Van Winkle | Catskill, N.Y. | 800 |
| 1932 | Lake Union | Seattle | 800 |
| 1938 | Cairo, Ill. | Ohio River | 800 |
| 1940 | Ludlow Ferry | Potomac R. | 800 |
| 1932 | Washington Mem. | Seattle, Wash. | 800 |
| 1936 | North Bend, Oreg. | Coos Bay | 793 |
| 1935 | Huey P. Long | New Orleans | 790 |
| 1916 | *Memphis(Harahan) | Mississippi R. | 790 |
| 1892 | *Memphis | Mississippi R. | 790 |
| 1949 | Memphis-Arkansas | Mississippi R. | 790 |
| 1904 | *Mingo, W. Va. | Ohio River | 769 |
| 1910 | *Beaver, Pa. | Ohio River | 767 |
| 1911 | Sewickley, Pa. | Ohio River | 750 |
| 1928 | Outerbridge,N.Y.C. | Arthur Kill | 750 |
| 1964 | Sunshine, Don'ville | Mississippi, La. | 750 |
| UC | Delair, N. J. | Delaware River | 730 |
| 1940 | Bridge of the Gods | Oregon | 705 |
| 1930 | Cairo, Ill. | Mississippi R. | 700 |
| 1927 | Rim to Rim | Twin Falls, Ida. | 700 |
| 1928 | Goethals, N.Y.C. | Arthur Kill | 672 |
| 1905 | Thebes, Ill. | Mississippi R. | 671 |
| 1957 | Rappahannock | White Stone, Va. | 648 |
| 1960 | Summit | Ches. & Del. Can. | 600 |
| 1959 | Castleton | Hudson R., N.Y. | 600 |

## STEEL ARCH

| Year | Bridge | Location | Span |
|---|---|---|---|
| 1931 | Bayonne, N.J. | Kill van Kull | 1,652 |
| 1959 | Glenn Canyon | Colorado River | 1,028 |
| 1962 | Lewiston-Queenston | Lewiston, N. Y. | 1,000 |
| 1917 | *Hell Gate | East R., N.Y.C. | 977 |
| 1941 | Rainbow | Niagara Falls | 960 |
| 1966 | Lincoln Trail | Cannelton, Ind. | 806 |
| 1936 | Henry Hudson | Harlem River | 800 |
| 1931 | West End | Pittsburgh | 778 |
| 1931 | Croton Lake, N. Y. | Westchester | 750 |
| 1931 | McKees Rocks | Pittsburgh | 750 |
| 1956 | Newark-Bayonne | NewarkBay,N.J. | 670 |
| 1924 | *Michigan Central | Niagara Falls | 640 |

| Year | Bridge | Location | Span |
|---|---|---|---|
| 1938 | Middletown | Connecticut | 600 |
| 1936 | Yaquina Bay | Oregon | 600 |
| 1954 | Captree | Gt.So.Bay,N.Y. | 600 |
| 1963 | Robert Moses | Fire Isl., N.Y. | 600 |
| 1916 | Colorado River | Ariz.-Calif. | 592 |
| 1917 | Cuyahoga River | Cleveland, Ohio | 591 |
| 1949 | Chesapeake City | Ches.&Del.Can. | 540 |
| 1941 | St. Georges | Ches.&Del.Can. | 540 |
| 1874 | Eads, St. Louis | Mississippi R. | 520 |
| 1888 | Washington, N.Y.C. | Harlem River | 509 |
| 1962 | Alex'der Hamilton | Harlem R., N.Y. | 505 |
| 1951 | Hastings, Minn. | Mississippi R. | 502 |
| 1961 | Duluth Harbor | Lake Superior | 500 |
| 1848 | High Bridge,N.Y.C. | Harlem River | 496 |
| 1956 | Wabash Memorial | Mt.Vernon, Ind. | 441 |

## CONCRETE ARCH

| Year | Bridge | Location | Span |
|---|---|---|---|
| 1931 | Westinghouse | Pittsburgh | 425 |
| 1923 | Cappelen | Minneapolis | 400 |
| 1930 | Jack's Run | Pittsburgh | 400 |

## TWIN CONCRETE TRESTLE

| Year | Bridge | Location | Span |
|---|---|---|---|
| 1963 | Slidell, La. | L. Pontchar-train | 28,550[1] |

## CONTINUOUS TRUSS

| Year | Bridge | Location | Span |
|---|---|---|---|
| 1957 | Mackinac | Sts. of Mackinac | 2,082 |
| 1966 | S. N. PearmanMem | Charleston,S.C. | 1,350 |
| 1966 | Astoria, Ore. | Columbia R. | 1,232 |
| UC | Commodore Pt. | Jacksonville, Fla. | 1,088 |
| 1943 | Dubuque, Ia. | Mississippi R. | 845 |
| 1963 | Brent Spence | Ohio River | 831 |
| 1953 | John E. Mathews | Jacksonville, Fla. | 810 |
| 1944 | St. Louis | Mississippi R. | 804 |
| 1957 | Kingston-Rhinecliff | Hudson R., N.Y. | 800 |
| 1931 | Sherman Minton | New Albany, Ind. | 800 |
| 1918 | *Sciotoville | Ohio River | 775 |
| 1964 | John F. Kennedy | Louisville, Ky. | 706 |
| 1966 | Matthew E. Welsh | Mauckport, Ind. | [2]707 |
| 1929 | Chain of Rocks | Mississippi R. | 699 |
| 1956 | Penn.-N.J. T'np'ke | Delaware River | 682 |
| 1938 | Port Arthur-Orange | Texas | 680 |
| 1929 | *Cincinnati | Ohio River | 675 |
| 1928 | CapeGirardeau,Mo. | Mississippi R. | 672 |
| 1946 | Chester, Ill. | Mississippi R. | 670 |
| 1930 | Quincy, Ill. | Mississippi R. | 628 |
| 1934 | Bourne | Cape Cod Canal | 616 |
| 1935 | Sagamore | Cape Cod Canal | 616 |
| 1936 | Meredosia | Illinois River | 567 |
| 1936 | Hannibal, Mo. | Mississippi R. | 562 |
| 1937 | Homestead | Pittsburgh | 553 |
| 1961 | Ship Canal | Seattle, Wash. | 552 |
| 1932 | Pulaski Skyway | Passaic R. N.J. | 550 |
| 1927 | Ross Island | Portland, Ore. | 535 |
| 1935 | South Omaha | Missouri R. | 525 |
| 1962 | Martinez, Calif. | Carquinex Str. | 475 |

## SIMPLE TRUSS

| Year | Bridge | Location | Span |
|---|---|---|---|
| 1917 | *Metropolis | Ohio River | 720 |
| 1929 | *Paducah, Ky. | Ohio River | 716 |
| 1922 | *Tanana River | Nenana, Alaska | 700 |
| 1911 | *MacArthur | St. Louis | 665 |
| 1933 | *Henderson | Ohio River | 665 |
| 1919 | Louisville | Ohio River | 644 |
| 1933 | Atchafalaya | MorganCity,La. | 608 |
| 1924 | *Castleton | Hudson River | 598 |
| 1906 | Elizabethtown | Great Miami R. | 586 |
| 1929 | *Louisville | Ohio River | 546 |
| 1889 | *Cincinnati | Ohio River | 542 |
| 1914 | Pittsburgh | Allegheny R. | 531 |
| 1930 | *Martinez | California | 526 |
| 1927 | Peace, Buffalo | Niagara River | 360 |

## PLATE GIRDER

| Year | Bridge | Location | Span |
|---|---|---|---|
| 1943 | Gold Star | New London | 540 |
| 1963 | Lake Charles B'pass | Louisiana | 399 |
| 1957 | Conn. Turnpike | Quinnipac R. | 387 |
| 1952 | Newark-Kearny | Passaic, R., N.J. | 375 |
| 1952 | Kearny-Secaucus | Hackensack,N.J. | 375 |
| 1966 | LeClaire | LeClaire, Iowa | 370 |
| 1942 | Charter Oak | Hartford, Conn. | 300 |
| 1940 | Lakefront | Cleveland, Ohio | 271 |
| 1966 | Hansen | Hansen, Idaho | 258 |
| 1965 | Susitna River | Alaska | 250 |
| 1940 | Thomas A. Edison | Raritan River | 250 |
| 1954 | Garden St. Pkway | Raritan River | 250 |
| 1965 | Knik River | Alaska | 202 |
| 1964 | Herbert C. Bonner | Oregon, N. C. | 180 |
| 1961 | W'r w Wilson Mem. | Potomac River | 175 |

## VERTICAL LIFT

| Year | Bridge | Location | Span |
|---|---|---|---|
| 1959 | *Arthur Kill | N.Y.-N.J. | 558 |
| 1935 | *Cape Cod Canal | Massachusetts | 544 |
| 1960 | *Delair, N.J. | Delaware River | 542 |
| 1937 | Marine Parkway | New York City | 540 |
| 1931 | Burlington, N.J. | Delaware R. | 534 |
| 1912 | *A-S-B Pratt | Kansas City | 428 |

[1]Length of bridge. [2]Two spans each 707 feet.

| Year | Bridge | Location | Span | Year | Bridge | Location | Span |
|---|---|---|---|---|---|---|---|
| 1945 | *Harry S. Truman. | Kansas City.... | 427 | 1928 | James River...... | Newport News.. | 300 |
| 1932 | *M-K-T R. R..... | Missouri R...... | 414 | 1929 | San Mateo........ | California...... | 300 |
| 1930 | Duluth........... | Minnesota...... | 386 | 1926 | *Missouri Pacific.. | Kragen, Ark.... | 300 |
| 1941 | St. Johns River... | Jack'ville, Fla.. | 386 | 1924 | Piscataqua River.. | Portsm'th, N. H. | 300 |
| 1958 | *Norfolk, Va..... | Elizabeth River. | 384 | | | | |
| 1922 | *Cincinnati....... | Ohio River..... | 365 | | **SWING SPAN** | | |
| 1961 | Corpus Christi, Tex. | Port Aransas- | | 1927 | *Fort Madison.... | Mississippi R... | 525 |
| | R. R.–Highway.. | Corpus Christi | 344 | 1908 | *Willamette R..... | Portland, Ore... | 521 |
| 1933 | Albany-Rensselaer. | Hudson River... | 341 | 1903 | *East Omaha...... | Missouri R..... | 519 |
| 1933 | Troy-Menands.... | Hudson River... | 341 | 1952 | Yorktown........ | York River, Va. | 500 |
| 1941 | Passaic River..... | New Jersey..... | 332 | 1897 | *Duluth, Minn.... | St. Louis Bay.. | 486 |
| 1930 | *Martinez........ | California...... | 328 | 1899 | *C. M. & N. R. R. | Chicago........ | 474 |
| 1929 | *Penn.-Lehigh..... | Newark Bay.... | 322 | 1895 | Sioux City, Ia.... | Missouri R..... | 470 |
| 1920 | *Chattanooga..... | Tennessee R.... | 310 | 1914 | *Coos Bay........ | Oregon........ | 458 |
| 1936 | Triboro, N.Y.C.... | East River..... | 310 | | | | |
| 1936 | Hardin........... | Illinois River.... | 309 | | **FLOATING PONTOON** | | |
| 1957 | Claiborne Ave..... | New Orleans.... | 305 | 1963 | 2nd Lake Wash.... | Seattle, Wash... | 7,998 |
| 1927 | Cochrane......... | Mobile, Ala..... | 300 | 1961 | Hood Canal....... | PtGamble,Wash | 7,014 |
| | | | | 1940 | Lake Washington. | Seattle........ | 6,566 |

## Construction Details of Large Bridges

**Verrazano-Narrows Bridge,** between Staten Island and Brooklyn, N. Y., has a suspension span of 4,260 ft., longest in the world and exceeding the Golden Gate Bridge, San Francisco, by 60 ft. One level in use November, 1964. The name is a compromise; it spans the Narrows and commemorates a visit to New York harbor in April, 1524, deduced from certain general notes left by Giovanni da Verrazano, Italian navigator sailing for Francis I of France. Second level to be opened in 1969.

**Angostura,** suspension type, span 2,336 feet, 1967, at Ciudad Bolivar, Venezuela. Total length 5,507.

**Braga Bridge** over Taunton River between Fall River and Somerset, Mass. It is 5,800 feet long.

**Bendorf Bridge** on the Rhine River, 5 mi. n. of Coblentz, completed 1965, is a 3-span cement girder bridge, 3,378 ft. overall length, 102 ft. wide, with the main span 682 ft.

**Champlain Bridge** at Montreal crossing the St. Lawrence River was opened 1962. It is 4 mi. long. Three other connect Montreal with the South Bank, the Jacques Cartier, Victoria and Mercier bridges.

**Corpus Christi, Texas,** has a high level port entrance bridge. It is a cantilever truss with anchor spans 310 ft. and main span 620 ft., total length approx. 5,862 ft.

**Delaware Memorial Bridge** over Delaware River near Wilmington. A twin suspension bridge paralleling the original 250 ft. upstream has a 2,150-ft. main span suspended from 440-ft. towers.

**Gerald Desmond Bridge** at Long Beach Harbor, Calif., a cantilever, 1,050 feet long.

**Gladesville Bridge** at Sydney, Australia, has the longest concrete arch in the world (1,000 ft. span).

**George Washington Bridge,** New York City, 4th longest suspension bridge in the world, spans the Hudson River between W. 178th St., Manhattan, and Ft. Lee, N. J.; 4,760 ft. between anchorages, two levels, 14 traffic lanes. **Triborough Bridge** connects Manhattan, the Bronx and Queens; project comprises a suspension bridge, a vertical lift bridge, and a fixed bridge, all connected by long viaducts. The famous **Brooklyn Bridge** over the East River, connecting Manhattan and Brooklyn, was completed in 1883, breaking all previous records by spanning 1,595 ft.

**Golden Gate Bridge,** crossing San Francisco Bay, has the second longest single span, 4,200 ft.

**Hampton Roads Bridge-Tunnel, Va.** A crossing completed in 1957 consisting of two man-made islands, two concrete trestle bridges, and one tunnel, under Hampton Roads with a length of 7,479 ft.

**Lake Pontchartrain Causeway,** a concrete trestle bridge, 24 miles long, carries traffic to New Orleans.

**Lake Washington Floating Bridge,** Seattle, is built on 25 floating concrete sections. Floating structure 6,566 feet long. Bridge with approaches 8,583 feet.

**Narragansett Bridge** between Newport and Jamestown, R. I. Total length 11,225 ft., a main suspension span of 1,600 feet, two side suspension spans each 687 feet long.

**New York City bridges,** *see Verrazano-Narrows Bridge and George Washington Bridge above.*

**Oosterscheldebrug,** opened Dec. 15, 1965, is a 3.125-mile causeway for automobiles over a sea arm in Zeeland, the Netherlands. It completes a direct connection between Flushing and Rotterdam.

**Quebec Road,** suspension, span 2,190 feet, 1969, Quebec, Canada.

**Royal Gorge Bridge,** 1,053 ft. above the Arkansas River in Colorado, is the highest bridge above water. Opened Dec. 8, 1929, it is 1,260 ft. long with a main span of 880 ft., width 18 ft.

**San Mateo-Hayward Bridge** across San Francisco Bay is first major orthotropic bridge in U. S. It is 6.7 miles long, 4.9-mile low-level concrete trestle and 1.8 miles high-level steel bridge.

**Seaway Skyway Bridge** across the St. Lawrence River from Ogdensburg, N. Y., to Johnston, Ont., opened 1960, is 13,510 ft. long with approaches and 7,260 ft. between abutments.

**Seven Mile Bridge** is the longest of an expanse of bridges connecting the Florida Keys. It was built by the Florida East Coast Railway between 1904 and 1916, now a state highway.

**Severn Bridge,** with a main span of 3,240 ft., crosses the Severn River, linking England and Wales.

**Straits of Mackinac Bridge,** opened June 28, 1958, is the longest suspension bridge between anchorages and with approaches extends nearly 5 mi. between Mackinaw City and St. Ignace, Mich.

**Sunshine Skyway,** a 15-mile-long bridge-causeway with twin roadbeds that crosses Tampa Bay at St. Petersburg, Fla., a system of twin bridges 864 feet long and 4 smaller bridges with 6 causeways.

**Tagus River Bridge** near Lisbon, Portugal, longest suspension bridge outside the United States, has a 3,323-ft. main span. Opened Aug. 6, 1966, it was named Salazar Bridge for the former premier.

**Thatcher Ferry Bridge,** opened 1962, spans Panama Canal 201 ft. above the water level near Balboa.

**Thomas A. Edison Memorial Bridge** (causeway) across Sandusky Bay between Martin Point and Danbury, Ohio, is 2.67 miles long. The main bridge is 2,044 feet long.

**Thousand Island Bridge, St. Lawrence River.** American span 800 ft.; Canadian 750 ft.

**Woodrow Wilson Memorial Bridge** across the Potomac River at Staunton, Va. is over a mile long.

**Zoo Bridge** across the Rhine at Cologne, with steel box girders, has a main span of 850 ft.

## Land Vehicular Tunnels in United States

over 1,500 feet long

| Name | Location | Lgh. Ft. | Name | Location | Lgh. Ft. |
|---|---|---|---|---|---|
| Straight Creek..... | Route 70, Colorado. | 8,950 | Mall Tunnel....... | Dist. of Columbia.. | 3,400 |
| Copperfield........ | Copperfield, Utah... | 6,989 | Low Level......... | Broadway, Calif.... | 2,944 |
| Sideling Hill....... | Penna. Turnpike... | 6,782 | Kalihi........... | Honolulu, Hawaii... | 2,780 |
| Liberty Tubes...... | Pittsburgh, Pa..... | 6,336 | West Virginia...... | W. Va. Turnpike... | 2,669 |
| Allegheny......... | Penna. Turnpike... | 6,070 | Cross-Town....... | 178 St. N.Y.C..... | 2,414 |
| Zion Natl. Park.... | Rte. 1, Utah...... | 5,766 | F.D. Roosevelt Dr.. | 81-89 Sts. NYC.... | 2,400 |
| Tuscarora......... | Penna. Turnpike... | 5,326 | Battery Park...... | New York City..... | 2,300 |
| Kittatinny........ | Penna. Turnpike... | 4,727 | Battery St........ | Seattle, Wash...... | 2,140 |
| Laurel Hill........ | Penna. Turnpike... | 4,541 | Big Oak Flat...... | Yosemite Natl. Pk. | 2,083 |
| Evans............. | Penna. Turnpike... | 4,379 | Prudential........ | Boston, Mass...... | 1,980 |
| Blue Mountain..... | Penna. Turnpike... | 4,339 | Internatl. Underpass | Los Angeles, Calif... | 1,910 |
| Wawona........... | Yosemite Natl. Pk. | 4,233 | Street-Car........ | Providence, R. I.... | 1,793 |
| Squirrel Hill....... | Pittsburgh, Pa..... | 4,225 | Broadway........ | San Francisco, Calif. | 1,616 |
| Big Walker Mt..... | Route I-77, Va..... | 4,200 | F.D. Roosevelt Dr.. | 42-48 Sts. NYC.... | 1,600 |
| Fort Pitt......... | Pittsburgh, Pa..... | 3,600 | Mt. Baker Ridge (3) | Seattle, Wash...... | 1,577 |
| Rays Hill.......... | Penna. Turnpike... | 3,532 | | | |

# Japanese Plan Undersea Tunnel Linking Hokkaido and Honshu

Preliminary engineering studies began in 1968 on a project for a 22.5-mile undersea tunnel to link Hokkaido, Japan's northern island, with the main Japanese island of Honshu. The tunnel, to be used by electric trains, would be the longest of its kind in the world. Completion by 1975 was contemplated.

Meanwhile, plans were being pushed for construction of a tunnel under the English Channel to link Britain and France. Construction was expected to begin in 1969 and to take 6 years. Two tubes enclosing railroad tracks are planned, with automobiles to be carried on special railroad cars. Cost of the tunnel between Dover and Calais was estimated at $600,000,000. Distance between terminals would be some 40 miles, 20 of it under water.

**Orange-Fish Rivers Tunnel,** expected to be the world's longest, is under construction as part of a $602,000,000 project to irrigate and develop the arid heart of South Africa. Preliminary excavation

for the 51½-mile tunnel began in 1967.

**Canadian Bridge-Tunnel.** The Canadian Government started construction early in 1966 of a $148,-000,000 tunnel-bridge-causeway project across Northumberland Strait linking New Brunswick and Prince Edward Island. The 9-mile crossing will carry both a railway and a highway. Completion is expected in 1971.

**Chesapeake Bay Bridge-Tunnel,** 17.6 mi. long, was opened for traffic April 15, 1964. It has 12½ mi. of concrete trestles 30 ft. above mean low water, 2 one-mile tunnels, 2 steel bridges, 4-manmade islands, 1½ mi. of earthfill causeway and approx. 5½ mi. of approach roadway, most of the latter 28 ft. wide. It connects Cape Charles, on the Eastern Shore of Virginia, with Chesapeake Beach between Norfolk and Virginia Beach on the mainland, thus providing a new route to Florida via the New Jersey Turnpike and U. S. 13. Cost of the project was over $200,000,000.

## Underwater Vehicular Tunnels in United States
### Over 1,000 feet in length

| Name | Location | Waterway | Length Feet |
|------|----------|----------|------------:|
| Bart Trans-Bay Tube | San Francisco | S. F. Bay | 3.6 mile |
| Brooklyn-Battery | New York, N. Y. | East River | 9,117 |
| Holland Tunnel | New York, N. Y. | Hudson River | 8,557 |
| Lincoln Tunnel | New York, N. Y. | Hudson River | 8,216 |
| Harbor Tunnel | Baltimore, Md. | Patapsco River | 7,650 |
| Hampton Roads | Norfolk, Va. | Hampton Roads | 7,479 |
| Queens Midtown | New York, N. Y. | East River | 6,414 |
| Thimble Shoal Channel | Cape Henry, Va. | Chesapeake Bay | 5,738 |
| Sumner Tunnel | Boston, Mass. | Boston Harbor | 5,650 |
| Detroit-Windsor | Detroit, Mich. | Detroit River | 5,135 |
| Chesapeake Channel | Cape Charles, Va. | Chesapeake Bay | 5,450 |
| Callahan Tunnel | Boston, Mass. | Boston Harbor | 5,046 |
| Elizabeth River | Norfolk, Va. | Elizabeth River | 4,194 |
| Posey Tube | Oakland, Calif. | Oakland Estuary | 3,500 |
| Bankhead Tunnel | Mobile, Ala. | Mobile River | 3,109 |
| Baytown Tunnel | Baytown, Tex. | Houston Ship Channel | 3,009 |
| Washburn Tunnel | Houston, Tex. | Ship Channel | 2,936 |
| Harvey Tunnel | Louisiana | Intracoastal Canal | 1,080 |

## World's Longest Railway Tunnels
**Source:** 1967-68 Railway Directory & Year Book. Tunnels over 4 miles in length.

| Tunnel | Date | Length Miles Yd. | Operating Railway | Country |
|--------|------|----------|-------------------|---------|
| | | *UC under construction.* | | |
| Simplon No. II | 1922 | 12  559 | Swiss Fed. & Italian St. | Switz.-Italy |
| Simplon No. I | 1906 | 12  537 | Swiss Fed. & Italian St. | Switz.-Italy |
| Apennine | 1934 | 11  892 | Italian State | Italy |
| Gotthard | 1882 | 9  562 | Swiss Federal | Switzerland |
| Lötschberg | 1913 | 9  140 | Bern-Lötschberg-Simplon | Switzerland |
| Hokuriku | 1962 | 8  1,089 | Japanese National | Japan |
| Mont Cenis (Fréjus) | 1871 | 8  855 | Italian State | France-Italy |
| Cascade | 1929 | 7  1,397 | Great Northern | United States |
| Montana | UC | 7  1,390 | Great Northern | United States |
| Arlberg | 1884 | 6  650 | Austrian Federal | Austria |
| Moffat | 1928 | 6  373 | Denver & Rio Grande | United States |
| Shimizu | 1931 | 6  50 | Japanese National | Japan |
| Kvineshei | 1943 | 5  1,112 | Norwegian State | Norway |
| Rimutaka | 1955 | 5  821 | New Zealand Gov. | New Zealand |
| Ricken | 1910 | 5  608 | Swiss Federal | Switzerland |
| Grenchenberg | 1915 | 5  581 | Swiss Federal | Switzerland |
| Otira | 1923 | 5  564 | New Zealand Gov. | New Zealand |
| Tauern | 1909 | 5  551 | Austrian Federal | Austria |
| Haegebostad | 1943 | 5  467 | Norwegian State | Norway |
| Ronco | 1889 | 5  277 | Italian State | Italy |
| Hauenstein (Lower) | 1916 | 5  95 | Swiss Federal | Switzerland |
| Connaught | 1916 | 5  39 | Canadian Pacific | Canada |
| Karawanken | 1906 | 4  1,683 | Austrian Federal | Austria-Yugo. |
| New Tanna | 1964 | 4  1,663 | Japanese National | Japan |
| Somport | 1928 | 4  1,572 | French National | France-Spain |
| Tanna | 1934 | 4  1,493 | Japanese National | Japan |
| Ulrikken | 1964 | 4  1,338 | Norwegian State | Norway |
| Hoosac | 1875 | 4  1,230 | Boston & Maine | United States |
| Monte Orso | 1927 | 4  1,230 | Italian State | Italy |
| Lupacino | 1958 | 4  1,178 | Italian State | Italy |
| Vivola | 1927 | 4  1,004 | Italian State | Italy |
| Monte Adone | 1934 | 4  760 | Italian State | Italy |
| Jungfrau | 1912 | 4  750 | Jungfrau | Switzerland |
| Borgallo | 1884 | 4  700 | Italian State | Italy |
| Severn | 1886 | 4  628 | Western Region | Great Britain |
| Lusse (Vosges) | 1937 | 4  474 | French National | France |
| Marianopoli | 1885 | 4  42 | Italian State | Italy |
| Turchino | 1894 | 4  10 | Italian State | Italy |

## U. S. Geodetic Datum Point

The geodetic datum point of the United States is the Coast and Geodetic Survey's triangulation station *Meades Ranch* in Osborne County, Kansas, at latitude 39°13′26″.686 N and longitude 98°32′30″.506 W. (Frequently this is referred to as the geodetic center of the U. S., which has no meaning.) This geodetic datum point is a fundamental point from which all latitude and longitude computations originate for North America and Central America.

# Dams and Reservoirs; Water Conservation

Source: Bureau of Reclamation

**Colorado River Storage Project. Morrow Point Dam** on the Gunnison River in Colo. was completed in 1968 by the Bureau of Reclamation. A principal feature of the Curecanti Storage Unit of the Colorado River Storage Project, the concrete dam is 468 feet high and 720 feet long. It is a landmark structure, incorporating three "firsts" for the Bureau: use of a thin-arch, double curvature design; location of the powerplant underground; and a free-fall spillway employing gates at the top of the dam (creating a waterfall twice as high as Niagara Falls). The powerplant is under construction. Also on the Curecanti Unit, the second of the two 30,000 kilowatt generators of the Blue Mesa powerplant went into operation in 1968. **Blue Mesa Dam** on the Gunnison River has been in operation several years. The unit's **Crystal Dam** and powerplant are still to be built. The other three storage units of the CRSP are fully in operation: **Glen Canyon Dam**, reservoir, and powerplant on the Colorado River in Utah and Arizona; **Flaming Gorge Dam**, reservoir, and powerplant on the Green in Utah and Wyoming; and **Navajo Dam** and reservoir in New Mexico and Colorado.

The Azotea Tunnel, a feature of the San Juan-Chama participating project in New Mexico, was "holed through" 1,200 feet beneath the crest of the Continental Divide during the year. It will be capable of conveying water by gravity at the rate of 950 cfs from the tributary streams of the Colorado River basin on the west side of the Rockies into the Rio Grande basin on the east. The project's two other tunnels, which will funnel water to the Azotea, were also virtually completed in 1968. Construction began on **Heron Dam** high up on the eastern slope. It will impound the water from the western slope and release it to flow down the Rio Chama and the Rio Grande for municipal and industrial use in Albuquerque and for the irrigation of farmlands in the Rio Grande basin.

Since authorization of the Colorado River Storage Project in 1956, about $696,000,000 of Federal funds has been converted into dams, reservoirs, powerplants, transmission facilities systems, and other facilities of the five-state project.

**Central Valley Project, California.** Pre-construction work began in 1968 on the Bureau of Reclamation's $200,000,000 Auburn Dam, chief feature of the Auburn-Folsom South Unit of the Central Valley Project. On the North Fork of the American River, this structure will be Reclamation's longest and highest double curvature concrete dam, spanning 3,500 feet at its crest 680 feet above bedrock. Its reservoir, with 2,500,000 acre-feet storage capacity, will yield 390,000 acre-feet of water annually to irrigate 413,000 acres and to supply municipal and industrial water for communities in the area, as well as to furnish recreational and fish and wildlife benefits. A powerplant having an initial capacity of 300,000 kilowatts will be constructed at the toe of the dam. Another unit feature, the 67-mile long Folsom South canal on the American River downstream from the dam will deliver the water to the farmlands and communities and will serve as the first reach of the Eastside division of the Central Valley Project planned for future development.

Three features of the San Luis unit were dedicated in 1968: the 382-foot high **San Luis Dam**, most massive earth-filled dam ever constructed by Reclamation; O'Neill regulating dam; and the San Luis Pumping-Generating plant. This complex will store winter-time run-off from northern California streams. The river-size San Luis Canal will start it on its way to beneficial use in the southern two-thirds of the state. Construction has continued on the gigantic Westlands irrigation system, which has made initial deliveries to farmlands in the San Joaquin Valley. Ultimately this system will contain more than 1,000 miles of pipeline.

The San Luis Unit will make some 1,200,000 acre-feet of irrigation water available to about 614,000 acres of agricultural land and will provide 45,000 acre-feet (14.6 billion gallons) of municipal and industrial water annually. This unit is a unique joint Federal-State development, which not only will serve the Federal irrigation project, but will store and transport California State Water Project water. **Oroville Dam**, chief feature of the State project, was dedicated in 1968. The highest earthfill dam in the world, the 770-foot structure

straddles the Feather River about 60 miles north of Sacramento.

Water deliveries through the 500-mile-long Central Valley project in 1967 reached 2,700,000 acre-feet, largely for irrigating some 1,600,000 acres of land which produce crops valued at nearly $600,000,000. Project powerplants produce about 5.5 billion kilowatt hours a year, and approximately 7,600,000 visitor days' recreation use is recorded at the project's man-made lakes.

**Third Powerplant at Grand Coulee Dam.** Excavation for the third powerplant has commenced and contracts have been let for the first three turbines and generators, largest ever manufactured. These three units are the first of six which will be installed in the Grand Coulee facility to bring its present 2,000,000 kilowatt capacity to 5,600,000. The plan now is to double the capacity of the third powerplant at some future date to bring the total capacity of Grand Coulee to 9,200,000 kilowatts. Congressional authorization will be needed for this addition.

**Fryingpan-Arkansas Project.** Construction continued in 1968 on **Sugar Loaf** and **Ruedi Dams**, major earthfill impoundment structures. The former, east of the Continental Divide, will result in the enlargement of Turquoise Lake from 17,000 to 130,000 acre-feet. Ruedi Dam on the western slope will create a 101,000 acre-foot impoundment on the Fryingpan River, compensating water users in western Colorado for the supply diverted at higher elevations through the Divide Tunnel into Turquoise Lake for use in the Arkansas basin. The 5.3-mile-long tunnel under the Continental Divide and two small shorter tunnels were virtually completed in 1968, and pre-construction work commenced for **Pueblo Dam** and reservoir on the eastern slope. Pueblo Reservoir will impound 357,000 acre-feet of water.

The multiple-purpose Fryingpan-Arkansas Project will provide water for supplemental irrigation of 280,000 acres and for domestic and industrial uses, will generate 111,000 kilowatt hours of hydroelectric power, and will provide flood control, fish and wildlife, and recreation benefits.

**Missouri River Basin Project.** Construction began on the Snake Creek pumping plant, key feature of the Garrison Diversion Unit, which will provide irrigation for 250,000 acres of land in North Dakota, will supply municipal and industrial water to 14 towns and cities, and will provide recreation and fish and wildlife enchancement benefits. The Snake Creek plant will pump water from the reservoir behind the Corp of Engineers **Garrison Dam** on the Missouri into an adjacent lake from where it will be conveyed to the farms and communities.

Two other units of the Missouri River Basin Project were authorized in fiscal year 1968 for construction. **Nebraska Midstate**, which will provide a surface and groundwater supply to irrigate approximately 140,000 acres along the Platte River and will replenish the groundwater which is being rapidly depleted; and Oahe Unit in South Dakota which will pump water from the Corps of Engineers Oahe reservoir on the mainstream to irrigate, in its first stage, about 190,000 acres, furnish municipal and industrial water supply, and provide flood control, recreation opportunities, and fish and wildlife benefits.

**Pacific Northwest-Pacific Southwest Intertie.** The 500-transmission kilovolt line from the Oregon border 94 miles south to Round Mountain in California has been completed by the Bureau of Reclamation and the first electric energy was transported from the Pacific Northwest to the Central Valley project. The intertie, most extensive electrical transmission system ever undertaken in the United States, is being built by Federal, other public, and private utilities to tie together, for their mutual benefit, the transmission systems of 11 western states.

**Southern Nevada Water Project.** Construction began on a 4-mile tunnel through the River Mountains, which lie between the Las Vegas Valley and Lake Mead behind Hoover Dam on the Colorado River. The project will pump water from Mead and distribute it to meet municipal and industrial water needs of Las Vegas, Nellis Air Force Base, and other communities and industries in the area.

**Project "Skywater."** During 1968 the Bureau of Reclamation continued its "Project Skywater," an

extensive program of research in atmospheric water resources. The project, financed by appropriations of $5,015,000 during fiscal 1968 and with $4,750,000 allotted for 1969, involves investigations of weather modification—principally precipitation from clouds when they are transporting large quantities of moisture. The runoff produced by the precipitation obtained from the air masses can be subsequently stored in reservoirs for many beneficial uses on Reclamation projects in the western states. Advances in technology indicate a capability of adding some 475,-000,000 acre-feet of new water annually to the nation's water supply. Production costs of $1 to $4 per acre-foot are expected, with benefits ranging from $5 to $50 and higher per acre-foot.

### Federal Reclamation Program

The Federal Reclamation program was authorized in 1902 to reclaim arid lands of the West by developing irrigation water supplies. The scope of its purpose was subsequently enlarged to include hydropower generation, municipal and industrial water supply, flood control, river regulation, water quality control, fish and wildlife enhancement, and recreation. To provide these benefits the Bureau has completed or has under construction 273 storage dams and dikes, with reservoirs having a combined total capacity of nearly 135,000,000 acre-feet of water; 53 hydroelectric plants with an ultimate installed capacity of 11,300,000 kilowatts; 16,150 circuit miles of transmission line; 98 major pumping plants; 6,800 miles of supply canals; nearly 200 miles of tunnels; and various other physical structures to carry out its prescribed functions.

Nearly unique among Federal programs, Reclamation in large measure pays its own way. Close to 90% of the Federal cost of construction is returned to the Treasury by project beneficiaries. The water-using beneficiaries also assume operation and maintenance of project water delivery systems.

The Bureau of Reclamation markets power from 51 Bureau-built powerplants, 6 Corps of Engineers plants, and the Falcon Plant of the International Boundary and Water Commission. During fiscal year 1968 the Bureau sold 42.6 billion kilowatt-hours of electric power, with revenues of $136,200,-000, including sales associated with power deliveries to Bonneville Power Administration for marketing.

### Power Administration

**Southeastern Power Administration** (Dept. of the Interior) markets power produced at projects controlled by the Corps of Engineers in Virginia, West Virginia, North Carolina, South Carolina, Georgia, Florida, Kentucky, Alabama, Mississippi, and Tennessee. Power is sold to 159 customers from plants in operation at Allatoona, Georgia; Buford, Georgia; Clark Hill, Georgia-South Carolina; Hartwell, Georgia-South Carolina; Jim Woodruff, Georgia-Florida; Walter F. George, Georgia-Alabama; John H. Kerr, Virginia-North Carolina; Philpott, Virginia; Wolf Creek, Kentucky; Barkley, Kentucky; Dale Hollow, Tennessee-Kentucky; Center Hill, Tennessee; Old Hickory, Tennessee; and Cheatham, Tennessee, with a capacity of 1,807,000 kilowatts. Seven plants are under construction with 905,375 kws capacity.

During the year ended June 30, 1968, SEPA sold 6,323,558,728 kilowatt-hours, gross revenue $31,709,-992.37.

**Southwestern Power Administration**, with hq in Tulsa, Okla., is the agency of the Dept. of the Interior designated to market surplus hydroelectric power and energy generated at Federal multiple purpose reservoirs in the southwest. Of 23 hydroelectric plants 15 are in commercial operation, and 8 are under construction.

SPA operates 1,515 miles of high-voltage transmission line and 35 substations and switching stations, including a 161,000 volt interconnection with the Bureau of Reclamation. This inter-tie, the first between federally owned systems, permits interchange of up to 50,000 kw between the two agencies by taking advantage of the daily and seasonal diversities between the two areas served.

During fiscal year 1968, SPA energy sales amounted to 4,462,000,000 kwh, compared to 3,035,598,542 kwh in 1967, an increase of 1,426,401,458 kwh. Gross revenues for 1968 totaled $32,187,197, as opposed to $28,924,961 for the same period in 1966-67, an 11.3% increase. In 1968, 51% of the energy marketed by SPA was sold to REA Cooperatives, 13% to municipalities, 3% to public authorities, 13% to aluminum industry and 20% to private utility companies.

[A kilowatt hour (kwh) represents 1 hour of 1,000 watts. A kilowatt (kw) equals about $1\frac{1}{3}$ horsepower.]

### Tennessee Valley Authority

TVA is a corporate agency of the Federal government, established by Congress in 1933 to develop the Tennessee River system and to aid in the development of other resources of the Tennessee Valley region. This includes work in flood control, navigation, electric power, recreation, agriculture, forestry, and water quality resource development.

TVA has built or acquired 26 major dams on the Tennessee and its tributary rivers, and by agreement with Alcoa controls water releases at 6 of its major dams. These structures make the main stream of the Tennessee navigable over its 650-mile length from Knoxville to the Ohio River, regulate flood waters, and generate hydroelectric power.

TVA is wholesale power supplier to 160 local electric systems serving 2 million customers in parts of 7 states, and sells power directly to several large atomic, military, and industrial installations. Fiscal year 1968 power sales were 85 billion kwh, about 60 times as much electricity as the region used in 1933. Since about 1950, when the region's hydroelectric potential was largely developed, most of the additional generating capacity built to meet this rapid growth in power demands has been in coal-fired steam plants. In 1968 system capacity was 18,000,000 kw, with another 9,500,000 kw in nuclear and coal-fired power plants scheduled for operation by 1974.

The TVA power system is financially self-supporting and self-liquidating and power funds are accounted for separately from funds used for non-power activities. Funds for new power construction are obtained primarily from the earnings of the system and bonds and notes sold in the public markets. U.S. appropriations for power purposes are being repaid to the Treasury on a regular schedule, plus a return on the portion unrepaid. The repayment in 1968 was $15,000,000 and the return, computed at a rate of 4.1% was $46,862,000. Substantial payments are made to state and local governments in lieu of taxes.

At the end of fiscal 1968, TVA had 19,717 employees.

## California State Water Project

Source: California Resources Agency, Department of Water Resources

California's State Water Project is the nation's first statewide water resources development, according to its builder and operator, the California Department of Water Resources. That agency says the California project will move more water a longer distance than any other distribution system; that it is the first water supply system to have recreation features planned from the beginning and built along with delivery works. Its key facility is Oroville Dam, highest dam in the United States.

The project stretches from 5 small dams and reservoirs in Northern California to the terminal reservoir at Perris in Southern California, a distance of about 650 miles.

Water conserved behind the giant embankment at Oroville Dam will move through the Feather and Sacramento River channels to the Sacramento-San Joaquin Delta.

From that point the State Water Project water will travel through the 444-mile-long California Aqueduct for distribution to homes, farms and factories in Central, Coastal and Southern California.

Part of the Calif. Aqueduct contains the San Luis unit, a joint-use facility of dams, pumping plants and canals in which the State and Federal Governments share costs, operation and maintenance.

Water deliveries to the San Joaquin Valley began in 1968 and are scheduled to be made to Castaic Lake in Los Angeles County in 1971 and to Lake Perris in Riverside County in 1972.

Water deliveries have been made since 1962 to water agencies south of San Francisco Bay through the South Bay Aqueduct, first completed aqueduct of the project.

At the Tehachapi Mountains, which the California Aqueduct crosses enroute to Southern California, the Edmonston Pumping Plant will pump more water higher than any other pumping plant in the world—110,000,000 gallons per hour one-third of a mile up—according to the California Department of Water Resources.

# Major World Dams

Source: Bureau of Reclamation. Dept. of the Interior (Revised Oct. 1, 1968). *Replaces existing dam.
Volume in cubic yards. Capacity (Gross) in acre feet. Year of completion. U.C. under construction.
Type A—Arch. B—Buttress. C—Cupola. E—Earthfill. G—Gravity. R—Rockfill. MA—Multi-arch.

| Name of Dam | Type | Year | River and Basin | Country | Height | Crest Length | Volume (1,000) | Res. Cap. (1,000) |
|---|---|---|---|---|---|---|---|---|
| | | | | | Feet | Feet | | |
| Almendra (Villarino) | A,G. | UC | Tormes-Douro | Spain | 623 | 13,284 | 3,275 | 2,005 |
| Alpe Gera | G. | 1965 | Cormor-Adda-Po | Italy | 584 | 1,710 | 2,265 | 53 |
| Beas | E. | UC | Beas-Indus | India | 380 | 5,000 | 44,200 | 6,600 |
| Bhakra | G. | 1963 | Sutlej-Indus | India | 740 | 1,700 | 5,400 | 8,000 |
| Bhumiphol (Yanhee) | G. | 1964 | Ping-Chao Phraya | Thailand | 505 | 1,595 | 1,268 | 9,890 |
| Bratsk | G,E. | 1964 | Angara-Yenisey | USSR | 410 | 16,200 | 21,180 | 137,230 |
| Bullards Bar* | A. | UC | N. Yuba-Sacramento | U.S.A. | 645 | 1,800 | 2,700 | 930 |
| Cabord-Basset | MA. | UC | Zambezi | Mozambique | 508 | 750 | NA | 54,000 |
| Canelles | A. | 1960 | Noguera Ribagorzana | Spain | 492 | 689 | 438 | 549 |
| Castaic | E. | UC | Castaic-Santa Clara | U.S.A. | 335 | 5,200 | 42,600 | 350 |
| Charvak | E,R. | UC | Chirchik-Syr Darya | USSR | 551 | 2,500 | 24,994 | 1,626 |
| Chirkey | C,R. | UC | Sulak | USSR | 764 | 1,109 | 1,604 | 2,250 |
| Cochiti | E. | UC | Rio Grande | U.S.A. | 241 | 28,050 | 53,000 | 602 |
| Contra | A. | 1965 | Verzasca-Ticino-Po | Switzerland | 754 | 1,246 | 863 | 70 |
| Curnera | A. | 1966 | Rein de Curnera | Switzerland | 499 | 1,115 | 824 | 32 |
| Dneprodzerzhinsk | G,E. | 1964 | Dnieper | USSR | 115 | 121,120 | 28,985 | 1,986 |
| Don Pedro* | R. | UC | Tuolumne-San Joaquin | U.S.A. | 580 | 1,900 | 16,535 | 2,030 |
| Dworshak | G. | UC | Clearwater-Columbia | U.S.A. | 693 | 3,302 | 7,200 | 3,453 |
| Flaming Gorge | A. | 1964 | Green-Colorado | U.S.A. | 502 | 1,285 | 987 | 3,789 |
| Fort Peck | E. | 1940 | Missouri | U.S.A. | 250 | 21,026 | 125,600 | 19,100 |
| Fort Randall | E. | 1956 | Missouri | U.S.A. | 165 | 10,700 | 50,200 | 6,100 |
| Garrison | E. | 1956 | Missouri | U.S.A. | 210 | 12,000 | 66,500 | 24,400 |
| Gatun | E. | 1912 | Chagres | Panama | 115 | 7,700 | 22,958 | 4,413 |
| Gepatsch | E. | 1964 | Faggenbach | Austria | 500 | 2,070 | 9,250 | 114 |
| Glen Canyon | A. | 1964 | Colorado | U.S.A. | 710 | 1,560 | 4,901 | 27,000 |
| Gokcekaya (Ciceroz) | CR. | UC | Sakarya | Turkey | 518 | 1,460 | 920 | 746 |
| Gorky | G,E. | 1955 | Volga | USSR | 112 | 42,340 | 7,969 | 7,215 |
| Goschenencraip | E. | 1960 | Goschenerreuss-Rhine | Switzerland | 508 | 1,771 | 12,220 | 61 |
| Grand Coulee | G. | 1942 | Columbia | U.S.A. | 550 | 4,173 | 10,585 | 9,562 |
| Grande Dixence | G. | 1962 | Dixence-Rhone | Switzerland | 932 | 2,296 | 7,792 | 324 |
| Gran Suarna | A. | UC | Navia | Spain | 499 | 1,148 | 884 | 567 |
| Guri | RE. | UC | Caroni | Venezuela | 512 | 2,264 | 3,894 | 14,354 |
| Hirakud | G,E. | 1956 | Mananadi | India | 202 | 15,748 | 25,100 | 6,600 |
| Hoover (Boulder) | G. | 1936 | Colorado | U.S.A. | 726 | 1,244 | 4,400 | 31,250 |
| Hungry Horse | A,G. | 1953 | S.F. Flathead-Columbia | U.S.A. | 564 | 2,115 | 3,086 | 3,468 |
| Idikki | A. | UC | Peryar | India | 560 | 1,100 | 740 | 1,375 |
| Inguri | CR. | UC | Inguri | USSR | 988 | 2,240 | 3,920 | 1,257 |
| Ivankovo | E,G. | 1937 | Volga-Caspian S. | USSR | 98 | 31,398 | 20,207 | 908 |
| Jari | E. | 1967 | Jari-Indus | Pakistan | 234 | 5,700 | 42,000 | 4,500 |
| Kakhovka | E. | 1955 | Dneper | USSR | 121 | 12,467 | 46,617 | 14,755 |
| Kanev | E. | UC | Dneper | USSR | 82 | 52,950 | 49,520 | 139 |
| Karadj | CR. | 1962 | Karadj-Nur | Iran | 584 | 1,300 | 930 | 139 |
| Kariba | A. | 1959 | Zambezi | Rhodesia | 420 | 2,025 | 1,330 | 130,000 |
| Keban | G,R. | UC | Euphrates | Turkey | 672 | 3,592 | 16,782 | 24,724 |
| Kiev | E. | 1964 | Dneper | USSR | 62 | 134,180 | 58,030 | 3,024 |
| King Paul (Kremasta) | E,R. | 1965 | Acheloos | Greece | 525 | 1,496 | 10,202 | 3,648 |
| Kremenchug | E,G. | 1961 | Dneper | USSR | 98 | 35,727 | 36,282 | 10,945 |
| Kurobe No. 4 | A. | 1964 | Kurobe | Japan | 610 | 1,603 | 1,782 | 162 |
| Luzzone | A. | 1963 | Brennodi Luzzone | Switzerland | 682 | 1,738 | 1,786 | 70 |
| Mangla | E. | 1967 | Jhelum-Indus | Pakistan | 380 | 11,000 | 108,300 | 5,900 |
| Manicouagan No. 5 | MA. | 1967 | Manicouagan-St. Law. | Canada | 703 | 4,501 | 2,880 | 115,000 |
| Mauvoisin | C. | 1958 | Drance de Bagnes-Rho. | Switzerland | 777 | 1,706 | 2,655 | 146 |
| Melones* | E,R. | UC | Stanislaus-San Joaquin | U.S.A. | 608 | 1,500 | 17,860 | 2,400 |
| Mica | E,R. | UC | Columbia | Canada | 800 | 2,550 | 40,000 | 19,800 |
| Mingechaur | E. | 1953 | Kurd-Caspian S. | USSR | 262 | 5,085 | 20,400 | 13,000 |
| Montanejos | A. | UC | Mijares | Spain | 554 | 820 | 164 | 203 |
| Monteynard | A. | 1962 | Drac-Isera-Rhone | France | 509 | 705 | 596 | 195 |
| Mossyrock | C. | UC | Cowlitz-Columbia | U.S.A. | 605 | 1,750 | 1,270 | 1,586 |
| Mratinje | A. | UC | Piva-Drina-Danube | Yugoslavia | 721 | 938 | 770 | 722 |
| Nagarjunasagar | G,E. | 1966 | Krishna | India | 406 | 15,326 | 73,572 | 9,177 |
| Nagawado | CA. | UC | Azusa | Japan | 508 | 1,204 | 865 | 100 |
| Navajo | E. | 1963 | San Juan-Colorado | U.S.A. | 402 | 3,648 | 26,841 | 1,709 |
| Nurek | E. | UC | Vakhsh-Amu Darya | USSR | 1,017 | 2,280 | 75,900 | 8,430 |
| Oahe | E. | 1963 | Missouri | U.S.A. | 245 | 9,300 | 92,000 | 23,600 |
| Okutadami | G. | 1961 | Agano-Tadami | Japan | 515 | 1,575 | 2,145 | 487 |
| Oroville | E,R. | UC | Feather-Sacramento | U.S.A. | 770 | 7,600 | 80,325 | 3,484 |
| Pahlevi (Dez) | C. | 1963 | Dez-Karun | Iran | 668 | 757 | 608 | 2,717 |
| Portage Mountain | E. | UC | Peace-Mackenzie | Canada | 600 | 6,700 | 56,680 | 57,000 |
| Portas | A. | UC | Cambia | Spain | 499 | 1,588 | 979 | 609 |
| Roselend | A,B. | 1961 | Doron de Beaufort-Rho. | France | 492 | 2,644 | 1,236 | 152 |
| Sadd-El-Aali (High dam) | R. | UC | Nile | UAR | 364 | 11,808 | 56,287 | 125,600 |
| Sakuma | G. | 1956 | Tenryu | Japan | 510 | 963 | 1,465 | 265 |
| San Luis | E. | 1967 | San Luis-San Joaquin | U.S.A. | 382 | 18,500 | 78,000 | 2,095 |
| Santa Giustina | A. | 1950 | Nace-Adige | Italy | 500 | 407 | 146 | 148 |
| Saratov | E. | UC | Volga-Caspian S. | USSR | 131 | 4,130 | 34,500 | 10,860 |
| Sayansk | A. | UC | Yenisey | USSR | 774 | 3,500 | 11,925 | 12,400 |
| Shasta | G. | 1945 | Sacramento | U.S.A. | 602 | 3,460 | 8,400 | 4,493 |
| Solteira Island | F,G,B | UC | Parana-Rio de la Plata | Brazil | 262 | 20,293 | 32,914 | 17,187 |
| South Saskatchewan | E. | 1966 | So. Saskatchewan | Canada | 223 | 16,700 | 86,328 | 8,000 |
| Speccheri | C. | 1957 | Leno di Vallarsa-Adige | Italy | 514 | 631 | 153 | 8 |
| Suapiti | E. | 1930 | Konkoure | Guinea | 394 | 3,511 | 32,699 | 8,918 |
| Swift | E. | 1958 | Lewis-Columbia | U.S.A. | 512 | 2,100 | 15,431 | 756 |
| Takane No. 1 | B. | UC | Hidd | Japan | 436 | 884 | 438 | 37 |
| Talbingo (Yaiwal) | R. | UC | Tumut | Australia | 530 | 2,300 | 19,000 | 700 |
| Tarbela | E. | UC | Indus | Pakistan | 485 | 9,000 | 159,000 | 11,100 |
| Tignes | A. | 1952 | Isere-Rhone | France | 592 | 1,230 | 831 | 186 |
| Toktogul | CR. | UC | Naryn-Syr-Darya | USSR | 705 | 1,352 | 3,480 | 15,800 |
| Trinity | E. | 1962 | Trinity-Klamath | U.S.A. | 537 | 2,600 | 29,251 | 2,448 |
| Tsimlvanskaya | E,G. | 1952 | Don | USSR | 135 | 43,413 | 44,323 | 17,715 |
| Twin Buttes | E. | 1963 | Concho-Colo. of Texas | U.S.A. | 134 | 42,460 | 21,442 | 641 |
| Ukai | E,G. | UC | Tapti | India | 225 | 16,164 | 33,370 | 6,900 |
| Vaiont | C. | 1961 | Vaiont-Piave | Italy | 858 | 624 | 460 | 137 |
| Vidaru | A. | 1963 | Arges-Danube | Romania | 545 | 1,000 | 654 | 377 |
| Volga—22nd Cong. | E,R,G | 1958 | Volga | USSR | 154 | 13,038 | 33,020 | 27,160 |
| Volga—V. I. Lenin. | E,G. | 1955 | Volga | USSR | 148 | 12,405 | 44,298 | 47,020 |
| Yellowtail | A. | 1966 | Bighorn-Missouri | U.S.A. | 525 | 1,450 | 1,460 | 1,375 |
| Zervrella | A. | 1957 | Valserrhein-Rhine | Switzerland | 495 | 1,653 | 819 | 81 |
| Zeuzier | A. | 1957 | Lienne-Rhone | Switzerland | 512 | 918 | 392 | 41 |

# Major Public and Private Dams and Reservoirs in U. S.

**HEIGHT—OVER 250 FEET, VOLUME—OVER 1,000,000 CUBIC YARDS**
Source: Bureau of Reclamation, Dept. of the Interior Corps of Engineers, U. S. Army
and Tennessee Valley Authority
**Where reservoir name is different it is shown in italics**

**Height**—Difference in elevation in feet, between lowest point in foundation and top of dam, exclusive of parapet or other projections.
**Length**—Overall length of barrier in feet; main dam and its integral features as located between natural abutments.
**Volume**—Total volume in cubic yards of all material in main dam and its appurtenant works.
**Year**—Date structure was originally completed for use. (1) Under construction subject to revision.
**River**—Main stream.
**Purpose:** Irr or I—Irrigation; FC—Flood Control; P—Power Production; N—Navigation; WS—Water Supply; RR—River Regulation; DC—Debris Control.
**Parentheses** after name indicate type of dam as follows: (C)—Concrete; (E)—Earth; (G)—Gravity; (M)—Masonry; (R)—Rock Fill.
*Replacing existing dam.

| Name of dam | State | River | Ht. | Lth. | Vol. (1,000) | Purpose | Yr. |
|---|---|---|---|---|---|---|---|
| Oroville (E) | Calif. | Feather | 770 | 770 | 7,600 | Irr-WS-P-FC | 1968 |
| Hoover (C) *Mead* | Ariz.-Nev. | Colorado | 726 | 1,244 | 4,400 | FC-I-P-RR-N | 1936 |
| Dworshak (C) | Idaho | N. Fork Clearwater | 717 | 3,287 | 6,600 | FC-P-N | (1) |
| Glen Canyon (C) *Powell* | Ariz. | Colorado | 710 | 1,560 | 4,901 | P-RR | 1964 |
| Bullards Bar* | Calif. | North Yuba | 645 | 1,800 | 2,700 | P | (1) |
| New Bullards Bar (C) | Calif. | North Yuba | 635 | 2,220 | 2,600 | I-WS-P | (1) |
| Melones* | Calif. | Stanislaus | 608 | 1,500 | 17,860 | I-P | (1) |
| Mossy Rock (G) | Wash. | Cowlitz | 605 | 1,750 | 1,270 | P | (1) |
| Shasta (C & E) | Calif. | Sacramento | 602 | 3,460 | 8,400 | FC-I-P-RR-N | 1945 |
| Don Pedro* | Calif. | Tuolumne | 580 | 1,900 | 16,535 | I-FC-P | (1) |
| Hungry Horse (C) | Mont. | South Fork Flathead | 564 | 2,115 | 3,086 | Irr-P-FC-N | 1953 |
| Grand Coulee (C) *F. D. Roosevelt* | Wash. | Columbia | 550 | 4,173 | 10,585 | I-P-RR-FC-N | 1942 |
| Ross | Wash. | Skagit | 540 | 1,300 | 909 | F C-P | 1949 |
| Trinity (E) | Calif. | Trinity | 537 | 2,600 | 29,251 | I-P | 1962 |
| Yellowtail (C) | Mont. | Bighorn | 525 | 1,450 | 1,460 | I-P-FC | 1966 |
| Cougar Reservoir (E) | Oreg. | So. Fork McKenzie | 515 | 1,730 | 12,572 | FC-P | 1964 |
| Swift (E) | Wash. | Lewis | 512 | 2,100 | 15,431 | Irr | 1958 |
| Flaming Gorge | Utah | Green | 502 | 1,285 | 987 | | 1964 |
| Fontana (G) | N. C. | Little Tennessee | 480 | 2,365 | 3,576 | FC-P-RR | 1944 |
| New Exchequer (R) | Calif. | Merced | 479 | 1,240 | 5,169 | I-P-RR | 1967 |
| Anderson Ranch (E) | Idaho | South Fork, Boise | 456 | 1,350 | 9,653 | FC-Irr-P | 1950 |
| Detroit (C) | Oreg. | North Santiam | 454 | 1,580 | 1,350 | FC-N-P-Irr-WS-RR | 1953 |
| Carters (R) | Georgia | Coosawattee | 445 | 2,053 | 15,950 | FC-P-RR | (1) |
| Pine Flat (C) | Calif. | Kings | 430 | 1,820 | 2,200 | FC-Irr-RR | 1954 |
| Mud Mt. (Stevens) (E) | Wash. | White | 425 | 700 | 2,300 | FC | 1953 |
| Mammoth Pool (E) | Calif. | San Joaquin | 411 | 820 | 5,355 | P-WS | 1960 |
| Lower Hell Hole (R) | Calif. | Rubicon | 410 | 1,550 | 8,315 | P-I-WS-RR | (1) |
| Union Valley (E) | Calif. | Silver Creek | 408 | 1,800 | 10,000 | P | 1963 |
| Navajo (E) | N. Mex. | San Juan | 402 | 3,648 | 26,841 | I-FC-RR | 1963 |
| Brownlee (G) | Idaho | Snake | 395 | 1,320 | 6,000 | P | 1958 |
| Navajo (G) | N. M. | San Juan | 385 | 3,800 | 27,000 | I-FC-RR | 1963 |
| Summersville (R) | W. Va. | Gauley | 384 | 2,280 | 11,000 | FC-RR | 1966 |
| San Luis (E) | Calif. | San Luis Cr. | 382 | 18,500 | 78,000 | | 1967 |
| Merriman *Rondout* | N. Y. | Rondout Creek | 375 | 3,000 | 8,987 | WS | 1939 |
| Neversink (E) | N. Y. | Neversink | 345 | 3,420 | 11,484 | WS-P-FC-RR | 1954 |
| Lucky Peak (E) | Idaho | Boise | 340 | 2,940 | 6,300 | FC-Irr | 1955 |
| Folsom (C) | Calif. | American | 340 | 10,200 | 9,010 | FC-Irr-P | 1955 |
| Blue Mesa (E) | Colo. | Gunnison | 340 | 770 | 3,040 | I-P-FC | 1966 |
| Green Peter (G) | Oreg. | Mid. Santiam | 340 | 1,350 | 1,145 | I-P-FC-N | 1967 |
| Hills Creek Dam (E) | Oreg. | Mid. Fk. Willamette | 338 | 2,150 | 10,830 | FC-P-WS-N-Irr | 1962 |
| Castaic (E) | Calif. | Castaic Cr. | 335 | 5,200 | 42,600 | WS | (1) |
| Casitas (E) | Calif. | Coyote Creek | 334 | 2,000 | 9,310 | I-WS | 1959 |
| Yale (E) | Wash. | Lewis | 328 | 2,590 | 4,200 | P | 1953 |
| Salt Springs (R) | Calif. | No. Fk., Mokelumne | 328 | 1,300 | 3,000 | P | 1931 |
| Abiquiu (E) | N. M. | Rio Chama | 325 | 1,500 | 7,600 | FC | 1962 |
| San Gabriel (E) | Calif. | San Gabriel | 320 | 1,520 | 10,600 | FC | 1938 |
| Beardsley (E) | Calif. | Stanislaus | 320 | 960 | 3,250 | I P | 1957 |
| Hell's Canyon (R) | Idaho | Snake | 320 | 860 | 3,000 | P | 1967 |
| Friant (C) *Millerton* | Calif. | San Joaquin | 319 | 3,488 | 2,135 | Irr-FC | 1942 |
| Watauga (E) | Tenn. | Watauga | 318 | 900 | 3,578 | FC-P-RR | 1948 |
| Cherry Valley (E) *L. Lloyd* | Calif. | Cherry Creek | 315 | 2,630 | 7,000 | I-WS-P | 1956 |
| Sultan No. 1 (G) | Wash. | Sultan | 310 | ... | ... | ... | 1952 |
| Green Mountain (E) | Colo. | Blue | 309 | 1,150 | 4,360 | Irr-P | 1943 |
| Kensico (G) | N. Y. | Bronx | 307 | 1,843 | 2,975 | WS | 1915 |
| Hiwassee | N. C. | Hiwassee | 307 | 1,376 | 801 | FC-P-RR | 1940 |
| R. D. Bailey (R) | W. Va. | Guyandot | 305 | 1,330 | 6,648 | FC | (1) |
| Downsville (E) | N. Y. | East branch, Delaware | 304 | 3,250 | 10,470 | FC-RR-WS-P | 1955 |
| Upper Baker (G) | Wash. | Baker | 308 | 1,200 | 628 | P | 1959 |
| Granby (E) | Colo. | Colorado | 298 | 861 | 2,974 | Irr-P | 1950 |
| New Croton (G) *Croton* | N. Y. | Croton | 297 | 2,168 | 1,450 | WS | 1905 |
| Courtright (R) | Calif. | Helms Creek | 295 | 862 | 1,560 | P | 1958 |
| Winsor (E) *Quabbin* | Mass. | Swift | 295 | 2,640 | 4,000 | PWS | 1940 |
| Blue River (E) | Oreg. | Blue | 293 | 1,170 | 4,660 | I-FC-N | (1) |
| Wishon (E) | Calif. | N. F., Kings | 290 | 3,350 | 3,700 | P | (1) |
| Lewis Smith (R) | Ala. | Black Warrior | 290 | 2,200 | 4,850 | P | 1961 |
| South Holston (ER) | Tenn. | South Fork, Holston | 285 | 1,600 | 5,995 | FC-P-RR | 1950 |
| Ruedi | Colo. | Fryingpan | 285 | 1,060 | 3,823 | | 1968 |
| Lemon (E) | Colo. | Florida | 284 | 1,360 | 3,042 | | 1963 |
| Laurel River (R) | Ky. | Laurel | 282 | 1,420 | 3,200 | P | (1) |
| Whiskeytown (E) | Calif. | Clear Creek | 282 | 4,070 | 4,535 | I-P | 1964 |
| Cogswell (R) | Calif. | West Fork, San Gabriel | 280 | 484 | 1,044 | FC | 1935 |
| Diablo (E) | Texas | Rio Grande | 280 | 43,240 | 30,000 | I-P-FC | |
| Muddy (E) | Oreg. | Lewis | 280 | 7,400 | 10,600 | FC | (1) |
| Cachuma (E) | Calif. | Santa Ynez | 279 | 3,350 | 6,695 | Irr-FC-WS | 1953 |
| Marshall Ford (C & E) *Travis* | Texas | Colorado (Texas) | 278 | 5,093 | 3,389 | P-FC-RR-N | 1942 |
| Santa Felicia (E) *Piru* | Calif. | Piru Creek | 275 | 1,260 | 3,900 | I-FC | 1955 |
| Dix River (RR) | Ky. | Dix | 275 | 1,080 | 1,747 | P | 1925 |
| Gorge High | Wash. | Skagit | 275 | 670 | 280 | P | 1960 |
| Sly Creek (E) | Calif. | Lost Creek | 271 | 2,100 | 5,232 | I-WS-P | 1961 |
| Palisades (E) | Idaho | South Fork, Snake | 270 | 2,100 | 13,571 | Irr-P-FC | 1957 |
| El Capitan (ER) | Calif. | San Diego | 270 | 1,200 | 2,680 | WS | 1934 |
| Nacimiento (E) | Calif. | Nacimiento | 270 | 1,470 | 3,412 | I-FC | 1957 |

| Name of dam | State | River | Ht. | Lth. | Vol. | Purpose | Yr. |
|---|---|---|---|---|---|---|---|
| Briones (E) | Calif. | Bear Creek | 268 | 2,100 | 9,912 | WS-RR | 1964 |
| Ball Mountain Res. (E) | Vt. | West. | 265 | 915 | 2,135 | FC | 1961 |
| Alcova (E) | Wyo. | North Platte | 265 | 763 | 1,635 | Irr-P | 1938 |
| Norris (G) | Tenn. | Clinch | 265 | 1,860 | 1,184 | FC-P-RR | 1936 |
| Mathews (E) | Calif. | Cajalco Creek | 264 | 6,522 | 9,560 (1,000) | WS | 1938 |
| Quabbin Dike (E) | Mass. | Swift | 264 | 2,140 | 2,500 | WS-P | 1937 |
| Wyman (GE) | Me. | Upper Kennebec | 263 | 2,650 | 2,610 | P | 1930 |
| Table Rock (C & E) | Mo. | White | 261 | 6,423 | 4,620 | FC-P | 1959 |
| Leroy Anderson (ER) | Calif. | Coyote Ck. | 260 | 1,385 | 3,320 | FC | 1950 |
| The Dalles (C & E) | Oreg-Wash | Columbia | 260 | 8,875 | 5,061 | N-P | 1961 |
| Lookout Point (C & E) | Oregon | Middle Fork, Willamette. | 258 | 3,381 | 9,027 | Irr-P-N-FC-WS-RR | 1954 |
| Bull Shoals (G) | Ark. | White | 258 | 2,256 | 2,100 | FC-P | 1952 |
| Wolf Creek (C & E) | Ky. | Cumberland | 258 | 5,736 | 11,569 | FC-P | 1950 |
| John W. Flannagan (R) | Va. | Pound | 258 | 960 | 2,387 | FC | 1966 |
| Gathright (R) | Va. | Jackson | 257 | 1,172 | 2,100 | FC-RR | (1) |
| Greers Ferry Dam (C & E) | Ark. | Little Red | 253 | 1,627 | 4,930 | FC-P | 1962 |
| Olive Bridge (G) | N. Y. | Esopus Creek | 252 | 4,650 | 8,200 | WS | 1915 |
| Ashokan (G) | N. Y. | Esopus Creek | 252 | 4,650 | 2,471 | WS | 1912 |
| Fort Peck (E) | Mont. | Missouri | 251 | 21,026 | 125,628 | FC-P-N-Irr | 1940 |
| Tygart River (G) | W. Va. | Tygart | 250 | 1,921 | 1,380 | FC | 1938 |
| Terminus Reservoir (E) | Calif. | Kaweah | 250 | 2,375 | 6,450 | FC-Irr | 1962 |
| Center Hill (C & E) | Tenn. | Caney Fork | 250 | 2,160 | 3,582 | FC-P | 1951 |
| Nantahala (RR) | N. C. | Nantahala | 250 | 1,042 | 2,265 | P | 1948 |
| Osgood (E) | Colo. | Crystal | 250 | 1,660 | 5,363 | I | (1) |

### International Dams and Reservoirs

**Source:** International Boundary and Water Commission U. S. and Mexico

| | | | | | | | |
|---|---|---|---|---|---|---|---|
| Amistad Dam and Reservoir (C & E) | Tex.-Mex. | Rio Grande | 254 | 32,022 | 20,055 | I-FC | 1969 |
| Falcon Dam and Reservoir (C & E) | Tex.-Mex. | Rio Grande | 150 | 26,294 | 13,242 | I-FC-P | 1954 |

# Non-Federal Hydroelectric Plants in U. S.

### CAPACITIES OF 100,000 KILOWATTS OR MORE AS OF JANUARY 1, 1968

Auxiliary and Pumped Storage Units are not included in Hydroelectric Capacities

**Source:** Federal Power Commission, Bureau of Power

| Plant | State | Owner | Kilowatts |
|---|---|---|---|
| Robert Moses Niagara | N. Y. | Power Authority State of N. Y. | 1,953,900 |
| Robert Moses (Massena) | N. Y. | Power Authority State of N. Y. | 912,000 |
| Wanapum | Wash. | Grant County Dist. No. 2. | 831,250 |
| Priest Rapids | Wash. | Grant County Dist. No. 2 | 788,500 |
| Rocky Reach | Wash. | Chelan County Dist. No. 1. | 711,550 |
| Wells | Wash. | Douglas County PUD No. 1 | 542,010 |
| Conowingo | Md. | Philadelphia Electric Co. | 474,480 |
| Hells Canyon | Ore. | Idaho Power Co. | 391,500 |
| Brownlee | Idaho. | Idaho Power Co. | 360,400 |
| Ross | Wash. | Seattle Dept. of Lighting Co. | 360,000 |
| Cowans Ford | N. C. | Duke Power Co. | 350,000 |
| Upper Smith Mt. | Va. | Appalachian Power Co. | 300,200 |
| Noxon Rapids | Mont. | The Washington Water Power Co. | 282,880 |
| Round Butte | Ore. | Portland Gen. Elec. Co. | 247,050 |
| Safe Harbor | Pa. | Safe Harbor Water Power Corp. | 226,500 |
| Walter Bouldin | Ala. | Alabama Power Co. | 225,000 |
| Rock Island | Wash. | Chelan County Dist. No. 1. | 212,100 |
| Saluda | S. C. | So. Carolina Electric and Gas Co. | 208,750 |
| Swift No. 1 | Wash. | Pacific Power and Light Co. | 204,000 |
| Cabinet Gorge | Idaho. | The Washington Water Power Co. | 200,000 |
| Oxbow | Oreg. | Idaho Power Co. | 190,000 |
| Caribou No. 1 & 2 | Calif. | Pacific Gas and Electric Co. | 184,800 |
| Gaston | N. C. | Virginia Electric and Power Co. | 177,920 |
| Osage | Mo. | Union Electric Co. of Mo. | 172,000 |
| Kerr | Mont. | The Montana Power Co. | 168,000 |
| Lewis Smith | Ala. | Alabama Power Co. | 157,500 |
| James B. Black | Calif. | Pacific Gas and Electric Co. | 154,800 |
| Martin Dam | Ala. | Alabama Power Co. | 154,200 |
| Comerford | N. H. | New England Power Co. | 140,400 |
| S. C. Moore | N. H. | New England Power Co. | 140,400 |
| Merwin | Wash. | Pacific Power and Light Co. | 135,000 |
| D. R. Holm | Calif. | San Francisco Utilities Commission | 135,000 |
| Haas | Calif. | Pacific Gas and Electric Co. | 135,000 |
| Gorge | Wash. | Seattle Department of Lighting Co. | 134,400 |
| Jaybird | Calif. | Sacramento Mun. Util. Dist. | 133,000 |
| Pinopolis | S. C. | So. Carolina Public Service Authority | 132,615 |
| Mammoth Pool | Calif. | Southern California Edison Co. | 129,360 |
| Logan-Martin | Ala. | Alabama Power Co. | 128,250 |
| Balch No. 1 & 2 | Calif. | Pacific Gas and Electric | 128,000 |
| Pit No. 5. | Calif. | Pacific Gas and Electric Co. | 128,000 |
| Keokuk | Iowa. | Union Electric Co. | 124,800 |
| Poe | Calif. | Pacific Gas and Electric Co. | 124,200 |
| Mayfield | Wash. | City of Tacoma | 121,500 |
| Calderwood | Tenn. | Tapoco Inc. | 121,500 |
| Diablo | Wash. | Seattle Department of Lighting Co. | 120,000 |
| Lay Dam | Ala. | Alabama Power Co. | 118,000 |
| Rock Creek | Calif. | Pacific Gas and Electric Co. | 113,400 |
| Cheoah | N. C. | Tapoco Inc. | 110,000 |
| Markham Ferry | Okla. | Grand River Dam Auth. | 108,000 |
| Walters | N. C. | Carolina Power and Light Co. | 108,000 |
| Yale | Wash. | Pacific Power and Light Co. | 108,000 |
| Pelton | Oreg. | Portland General Electric Co. | 108,000 |
| Holtwood | Pa. | Pennsylvania Power and Light Co. | 107,000 |
| Big Creek No. 3. | Calif. | Southern California Edison Co. | 106,500 |
| Pit No. 7. | Calif. | Pacific Gas and Electric Co. | 104,400 |
| Hawks Nest | W. Va. | Union Carbide Corp. | 102,000 |
| Roanoke Rapids | N. C. | Virginia Electric and Power Co. | 100,080 |
| Jordan No. 1. | Ala. | Alabama Power Co. | 100,000 |

# Hydroelectric Stations and Power Plants in U. S.
### Built And Operated By Corps Of Engineers, U S. Army (as of Sept. 25, 1968)

| Project | First power product. | Existing install. (KW) | Under construct. (KW) | Ultimate (KW) |
|---|---|---|---|---|
| Albeni Falls Reservoir, Idaho | 1955 | 42,600 | ............ | 42,600 |
| Allatoona Reservoir, Georgia | 1950 | 74,000 | ............ | 110,000 |
| Barkley Lock and Dam, Kentucky-Tennessee | 1966 | 130,000 | ............ | 130,000 |
| Beaver Reservoir, Arkansas | 1965 | 112,000 | ............ | 112,000 |
| Big Bend Reservoir, South Dakota | 1964 | 468,000 | ............ | 468,000 |
| Blakely Mountain Reservoir, Arkansas | 1955 | 75,000 | ............ | 75,000 |
| Bonneville Dam, Oregon-Washington | 1938 | 518,400 | ............ | 518,400 |
| Broken Bow, Okla | 1969 | ............ | 100,000 | 100,000 |
| Dworshak, Idaho | 1972 | ............ | 400,000 | 1,060,000 |
| Buford Dam, Georgia | 1957 | 86,000 | ............ | 86,000 |
| Bull Shoals Reservoir, Arkansas-Missouri | 1952 | 340,000 | ............ | 340,000 |
| Carters, Ga | 1972 | ............ | 500,000 | 500,000 |
| Center Hill Reservoir, Tennessee | 1950 | 135,000 | ............ | 135,000 |
| Cheatham Lock and Dam, Tennessee | 1959 | 36,000 | ............ | 36.000 |
| Chief Joseph Dam. Washington | 1955 | 1,024,000 | ............ | 1,728,000 |
| Clarence F. Cannon, Missouri | 1974.... | ............ | 54,000 | 54,000 |
| Clark Hill Reservoir, Georgia-South Carolina | 1953 | 280,000 | ............ | 280,000 |
| Cordell Hull, Tenn | 1971 | ............ | 100,000 | 100,000 |
| Cougar Reservoir. Oregon | 1964 | 25,000 | ............ | 60,000 |
| Dale Hollow Reservoir, Tennessee | 1948 | 54,000 | ............ | 54,000 |
| Dardanelle Lock and Dam, Arkansas | 1965 | 124,000 | ............ | 124,000 |
| DeGray, Ark | 1971 | ............ | 68,000 | 108,000 |
| Denison Dam (Lake Texoma), Oklahoma-Texas | 1945 | 70,000 | ............ | 175,000 |
| Detroit Reservoir, Oregon | 1953 | 118,000 | ............ | 118,000 |
| Eufaula Reservoir, Oklahoma | 1964 | 90,000 | ............ | 90,000 |
| Fort Gibson Reservoir, Oklahoma | 1953 | 45,000 | ............ | 67,500 |
| Fort Peck Dam, Montana | 1943 | 165,000 | ............ | 165,000 |
| Fort Randall Reservoir, South Dakota | 1954 | 320,000 | ............ | 320,000 |
| Garrison Reservoir, North Dakota | 1956 | 400,000 | ............ | 400,000 |
| Gavins Point Reservoir, South Dakota-Nebraska | 1956 | 100,000 | ............ | 100,000 |
| Green Peter Reservoir, Oregon | 1967 | 100,000 | ............ | 100,000 |
| Greers Ferry Reservoir, Arkansas | 1964 | 96,000 | ............ | 96,000 |
| Hartwell Reservoir, Georgia-South Carolina | 1962 | 264,000 | ............ | 330,000 |
| Hills Creek Reservoir, Oregon | 1962 | 30,000 | ............ | 30,000 |
| Ice Harbor Lock and Dam, Washington | 1961 | 270,000 | ............ | 602,880 |
| Jim Woodruff Lock and Dam, Georgia-Florida | 1957 | 30,000 | ............ | 30,000 |
| John Day Lock and Dam, Oregon-Washington | 1968 | 270,000 | 1,910,000 | 2,700,000 |
| John H. Kerr Reservoir, North Carolina-Virginia | 1952 | 204,000 | ............ | 204,000 |
| Jones Bluffs, Alabama | 1974 | ............ | 68,000 | 68,000 |
| J, Percy Priest, Tenn | 1968 | ............ | 28,000 | 28,000 |
| Kaysinger Bluff, Missouri | 1974 | ............ | 160,000 | 160,000 |
| Keystone, Okla | 1968 | 70,000 | ............ | 70,000 |
| Laurel River Res., Kentucky | 1973 | ............ | 61,000 | 61,000 |
| Libby, Montana | 1973 | ............ | 420,000 | 800,000 |
| Little Goose, Wash | 1970 | ............ | 405,000 | 810,000 |
| Lookout Point Reservoir, Oregon | 1954 | 135 000 | ............ | 135,000 |
| Lost Creek, Oregon | 1974 | ............ | 49,000 | 49,000 |
| Lower Granite, Washington | 1973 | ............ | 405,000 | 810,000 |
| Lower Monumental Lock & Dam, Washington | 1969 | ............ | 405,000 | 810,000 |
| McNary Lock and Dam, Oregon-Washington | 1953 | 980,000 | ............ | 1,400,000 |
| Millers Ferry, Ala | 1969 | ............ | 75,000 | 75,000 |
| Narrows Reservoir, Arkansas | 1950 | 17,000 | 8,500 | 25,500 |
| New Melones, California | 1974 | ............ | 150,000 | 150,000 |
| Norfork Reservoir, Arkansas-Missouri | 1944 | 70,000 | ............ | 140,000 |
| Oahe Reservoir, South Dakota-North Dakota | 1962 | 595,000 | ............ | 595,000 |
| Old Hickory Lock and Dam, Tennessee | 1957 | 100,000 | ............ | 100,000 |
| Ozark Lock and Dam, Arkansas | 1972 | ............ | 100,000 | 100,000 |
| Philpott Reservoir, Virginia | 1953 | 14,000 | ............ | 14,000 |
| Robert S. Kerr | 1970 | ............ | 110,000 | 110,000 |
| St. Mary's River, Michigan | 1951 | 18,400 | ............ | 18,400 |
| Sam Rayburn, Texas | 1965 | 52,000 | ............ | 52,000 |
| Snettisham, Alaska | 1972 | ............ | 46,700 | 70,000 |
| Stockton, Mo | 1970 | ............ | 45,200 | 45,200 |
| Table Rock Reservoir, Missouri-Arkansas | 1959 | 200,000 | ............ | 200,000 |
| Tenkiller Ferry Reservoir, Oklahoma | 1953 | 34,000 | ............ | 34,000 |
| The Dalles Dam, Oregon-Washington | 1957 | 1,119,000 | 687,800 | 1,806,800 |
| Walter F. George Lock and Dam, Alabama-Georgia | 1963 | 130,000 | ............ | 130,000 |
| Webbers Falls, Oklahoma | 1972 | ............ | 60,000 | 60,000 |
| West Point, Georgia | 1972 | ............ | 73,780 | 108,780 |
| Whitney Reservoir, Texas | 1953 | 30,000 | ............ | 30,000 |
| Wolf Creek Reservoir, Kentucky | 1951 | 270,000 | ............ | 270,000 |

# World's Largest Hydroelectric Generating Plants
### Source: Bureau of Reclamation
UC—Under Construction. NA—Not Available

| Name (Ultimate capacity of 1,000,000 kilowatts or more.) | Present (Megawatts) | Ultimate (Megawatts) | Year of Initial Operation |
|---|---|---|---|
| Sayansk, USSR | NA | 6,300 | UC |
| Krasnoyarsk, USSR | NA | 6,000 | 1967 |
| Grand Coulee, U.S.A | 1.974 | 5,574 | 1941 |
| Churchill Falls, Canada | NA | 4,500 | UC |
| Bratsk, USSR | 4,500 | 4,500 | 1961 |
| Sukhovo, USSR | NA | 4,500 | UC |
| Ust-Illimsk, USSR | 720 | 4,320 | UC |
| Kettle Rapids, Canada | 1,018 | 3,240 | UC |
| Ilha Solteira Island, Brazil | NA | 3,200 | UC |
| John Day, U.S.A | 2,160 | 2,700 | UC |
| Nurek, USSR | NA | 2,700 | UC |
| Volga—22nd Congress, USSR | 2,543 | 2,543 | 1958 |
| Portage Mountain, Canada | 1,150 | 2,300 | UC |
| Iron Gate, Romania-Yugoslavia | NA | 2,160 | UC |
| Volga—V. I. Lenin, USSR | 2,100 | 2,100 | 1955 |
| Sadd-El-Aali, (High Aswan), UAR | 1,750 | 2,100 | 1967 |
| Mica, Canada | NA | 2,000 | UC |
| Robert Moses Niagara, U.S.A | 1,950 | 1,950 | 1961 |
| St. Lawrence Power Dam, Canada-U.S.A | 1,880 | 1,880 | 1958 |
| Guri, Venezuela | 527 | 1,757 | 1967 |

| Name<br>(Ultimate capacity of 1,000,000 kilowatts or more.) | Present<br>(Megawatts) | Ultimate<br>(Megawatts) | Year of<br>Initial<br>Operation |
|---|---|---|---|
| Dalles, U.S.A. | 1,119 | 1,743 | 1957 |
| Chief Joseph, U.S.A. | 1,024 | 1,728 | 1956 |
| Kemano, Canada. | 835 | 1,670 | 1954 |
| Beauharnois, Canada. | 1,586 | 1,641 | 1951 |
| Inguri, USSR. | NA | 1,600 | UC |
| Kariba, Rhodesia-Zambia. | 600 | 1,500 | 1959 |
| Liukiansia, China. | NA | 1,500 | 1963 |
| Tumut—3, Australia. | NA | 1,500 | UC |
| Jupia, Brazil. | NA | 1,400 | 1961 |
| Sir Adam Beck No. 2, Canada. | 900 | 1,370 | 1954 |
| Hoover, U.S.A. | 1,345 | 1,345 | 1936 |
| Wanapum, U.S.A. | 831 | 1,330 | 1963 |
| Manicouagan No. 5, Canada. | NA | 1,320 | UC |
| Saratov, USSR. | NA | 1,300 | UC |
| Priest Rapids, U.S.A. | 789 | 1,262 | 1959 |
| Keban, Turkey. | 620 | 1,240 | UC |
| Rocky Reach, U.S.A. | 775 | 1,215 | 1961 |
| Furnas, Brazil. | 900 | 1,200 | 1963 |
| Toktogul, USSR. | NA | 1,200 | UC |
| Manicouagan No. 3, Canada. | NA | 1,120 | UC |
| Sanmen Hsia, China. | NA | 1,100 | UC |
| Nizhne-Kamskaya, USSR. | NA | 1,090 | UC |
| Dworshak, U.S.A. | NA | 1,060 | UC |
| Bersimis No. 1, Canada. | 1,050 | 1,050 | 1956 |
| Bhakra, India. | 450 | 1,050 | .... |
| Zeya, USSR. | NA | 1,020 | UC |
| Manicouagan No. 2, Canada. | NA | 1,016 | 1965 |
| Mangia, Pakistan. | 300 | 1,000 | UC |
| Chirkey, USSR. | NA | 1,000 | UC |
| Votkinsk, USSR. | NA | 1,000 | 1961 |
| Kettle Rapids, Canada. | NA | 1,000 | UC |

## TVA Hydroelectric Power Plants
### Source: Tennessee Valley Authority

| Projects | State | River | Initial<br>Operation | Generating Capacity KWS | |
|---|---|---|---|---|---|
| | | | | Existing | Ultimate |
| Wilson (a) | Ala. | Tenn. | 1925 | 629,840 | 629,840 |
| Wheeler | Ala. | Tenn. | 1936 | 356,400 | 356,400 |
| Fontana | N. C. | Little Tenn. | 1945 | 202,500 | 202,500 |
| Pickwick Landing | Tenn. | Tenn. | 1938 | 216,000 | 216,000 |
| Kentucky | Ky. | Tenn. | 1944 | 160,000 | 160,000 |
| Watts Bar | Tenn. | Tenn. | 1942 | 150,000 | 150,000 |
| Fort Loudon | Tenn. | Tenn. | 1943 | 128,000 | 128,000 |
| Cherokee | Tenn. | Holston | 1942 | 120,000 | 120,000 |
| Hiwassee | N. C. | Hiwassee | 1940 | 117,100 | 117,100 |
| Douglas | Tenn. | French Broad | 1943 | 112,000 | 112,000 |
| Chickamauga | Tenn. | Tenn. | 1940 | 108,000 | 108,000 |
| Norris | Tenn. | Clinch | 1936 | 100,800 | 100,800 |
| Guntersville | Ala. | Tenn. | 1939 | 97,200 | 97,200 |
| Nickajack | Tenn. | Tenn. | 1968 | 97,200 | 97,200 |
| Apalachia | N. C. | Hiwassee | 1943 | 75,000 | 75,000 |
| Boone | Tenn. | S. Fork Holston | 1953 | 75,000 | 75,000 |
| Melton Hill | Tenn. | Clinch | 1964 | 72,000 | 72,000 |
| Watauga | Tenn. | Watauga | 1949 | 50,000 | 50,000 |
| Tims Ford | Tenn. | Elk | UC | UC | 45,000 |
| Fort Patrick Henry | Tenn. | S. Fork Holston | 1953 | 36,000 | 36,000 |
| South Holston | Tenn. | S. Fork Holston | 1951 | 35,000 | 35,000 |
| Great Falls ab. | Tenn. | Caney | 1916 | 31,860 | 31,860 |
| Ocoee No. 3 | Tenn. | Ocoee | 1943 | 27,000 | 27,000 |
| Ocoee No. 2a | Tenn. | Ocoee | 1913 | 21,000 | 21,000 |
| Blue Ridge a | Ga. | Toccoa | 1931 | 20,000 | 20,000 |
| Ocoee No. 1a | Tenn. | Ocoee | 1912 | 18,000 | 18,000 |
| Nottely | Ga. | Nottely | 1956 | 15,000 | 15,000 |
| Chatuge | N. C. | Hiwassee | 1954 | 10,000 | 10,000 |
| Tellico | Tenn. | Little Tenn. | UC | c | |

UC Under construction. aNot built by TVA. bIn Cumberland Valley. cNo powerhouse, diverts river flow for increased generation at Fort Loudon Dam.

## Hydroelectric Power Plants in U. S.
### BUREAU OF RECLAMATION
#### Capacity of 15,000 Kilowatts or more, June 30, 1967

| State | Project | Name of plant | Year of<br>initial<br>operation | Existing<br>(kilowatts) | Ultimate<br>(kilowatts) |
|---|---|---|---|---|---|
| Ariz.-Nevada | Boulder Canyon | Hoover | 1936 | 1,344,800 | 1,344,800 |
| Ariz.-Nevada | Parker-Davis | Davis | 1951 | 225,000 | 225,000 |
| Arizona | Colorado River Sto. | Glen Canyon | 1964 | 900,000 | 900,000 |
| Ariz.-Cal. | Parker-Davis | Parker | 1942 | 120,000 | 120,000 |
| California | Central Valley | Folsom | 1955 | 162,000 | 162,000 |
| California | Central Valley | Keswick | 1949 | 75,000 | 75,000 |
| California | Central Valley | Shasta | 1944 | 379,000 | 379,000 |
| California | Central Valley | Judge Francis Carr | 1963 | 134,000 | 134,000 |
| California | Central Valley | San Luis | 1967 | 106,000 | 424,000 |
| California | Central Valley | O'Neill | 1967 | 21,000 | 25,200 |
| California | Central Valley | Auburn | 1975 | ............ | 240,000 |
| California | Central Valley | Spring Creek | 1964 | 150,000 | 150,000 |
| California | Central Valley | Trinity | 1964 | 100,350 | 100,350 |
| Colorado | Colo. R. Sto. | Blue Mesa | 1967 | ............ | 60,000 |
| Colorado | Colo.-Big Thompson | Estes | 1950 | 45,000 | 45,000 |
| Colorado | Colo.-Big Thompson | Flatiron | 1954 | 71,500 | 71,500 |
| Colorado | Colo.-Big Thompson | Green Mountain | 1943 | 21,600 | 21,600 |
| Colorado | Colo. River Sto. | Crystal | 1973 | ............ | 28,000 |
| Colorado | Colo. R. Sto. | Morrow Point | 1969 | ............ | 120,000 |
| Colorado | Colo.-Big Thompson | Pole Hill | 1954 | 33,250 | 33,250 |
| Idaho | Boise | Anderson Ranch | 1950 | 27,000 | 40,500 |
| Idaho | Palisades | Palisades | 1957 | 114,000 | 114,000 |
| Montana | Mo. River Basin | Canyon Ferry | 1953 | 50,000 | 50,000 |
| Montana | Hungry Horse | Hungry Horse | 1952 | 285,000 | 285,000 |
| Montana | Mo. River Basin | Yellowtail | 1966 | 250,000 | 250,000 |
| New Mexico | Rio Grande | Elephant Butte | 1940 | 24,300 | 24,300 |
| Oregon | Rogue River Basin | Green Springs | 1960 | 16,000 | 16,000 |
| Utah | Colorado River Sto. | Flaming Gorge | 1963 | 108,000 | 108,000 |

| State | Project | Name of plant | Year of initial operation | Existing (kilowatts) | Ultimate (kilowatts) |
|-------|---------|---------------|---------------------------|----------------------|----------------------|
| Washington.... | Columbia Basin...... | Grand Coulee........ | 1941 | 1,974,000 | 5,574,000 |
| Wyoming...... | Kendrick........... | Alcova............. | 1955 | 36,000 | 36,000 |
| Wyoming...... | Kendrick........... | Seminoe........... | 1939 | 32,400 | 32,400 |
| Wyoming...... | Mo. River Basin..... | Boysen............ | 1952 | 15,000 | 15,000 |
| Wyoming...... | Mo. River Basin..... | Fremont Canyon..... | 1960 | 48,000 | 48,000 |
| Wyoming...... | Mo. River Basin..... | Glendo............ | 1958 | 24,000 | 24,000 |
| Wyoming...... | Mo. River Basin..... | Kortes............ | 1950 | 36,000 | 36,000 |

# Nuclear Power Reactors in U. S.

Source: U. S. Atomic Energy Commission (June 30, 1968)

| State | Site | Cap. (kws) | Utility | Start up |
|-------|------|------------|---------|----------|
| Alabama........... | Browns Ferry..... | 1,065,000 | Tenn. Valley Authority................. | 1970 |
| | Browns Ferry..... | 1,065,000 | Tenn. Valley Authority................. | 1971 |
| | Browns Ferry..... | 1,064,500 | Tenn. Valley Authority................. | 1972 |
| Arkansas.......... | Dardanelle Lake... | 850,000 | Ark. Power & Light Co............... | 1972 |
| California......... | Humboldt Bay.... | 68,500 | Pacific Gas & Elec. Co.............. | 1963 |
| | San Clemente...... | 430,000 | So. Calif. Edison & | |
| | | | San Diego Gas & Elec. Co........ | 1967 |
| | Corral Canyon.... | 462,000 | L. A. Dept. of Water & Power...... | 1973 |
| | Diablo Canyon.... | 1,060,000 | Pacific Gas & Electric Co.......... | 1971 |
| | Sacramento County. | 850,000 | Sacramento Municipal Dist......... | 1973 |
| Colorado.......... | Platteville........ | 330,000 | Public Service Co. of Colorado..... | 1971 |
| Connecticut....... | Haddan Neck...... | 462,000 | Conn. Yankee Atomic Power Co.... | 1967 |
| | Waterford No. 1... | 652,100 | Northeast Utilities................ | 1969 |
| | Waterford No. 2... | 828,000 | Northeast Utilities................ | 1974 |
| Florida........... | Turkey Point No. 3. | 651,500 | Florida Power & Light Co.......... | 1970 |
| | Turkey Point No. 4. | 651,500 | Florida Power & Light Co.......... | 1971 |
| | Red Level......... | 825,000 | Florida Power Corp................ | 1972 |
| | Hutchinson Island.. | 800,000 | Florida Power & Light Co.......... | 1973 |
| Georgia........... | Baxley........... | 786,000 | Georgia Power Co................. | 1973 |
| Illinois........... | Morris No. 1...... | 200,000 | Commonwealth Edison Co.......... | 1959 |
| | Morris No. 2...... | 715,000 | Commonwealth Edison Co.......... | 1968 |
| | Morris No. 3...... | 715,000 | Commonwealth Edison Co.......... | 1969 |
| | Zion No. 1........ | 1,050,000 | Commonwealth Edison Co.......... | 1972 |
| | Zion No. 2........ | 1,050,000 | Commonwealth Edison Co.......... | 1973 |
| | Quad Cities No. 1. | 715,000 | Comm. Ed. Co.—Ia.-Ill. Gas & Elec. Co... | 1970 |
| | Quad Cities No. 2. | 715,000 | Comm. Ed. Co.—Ia.-Ill. Gas & Elec. Co... | 1971 |
| Indiana........... | Burns Harbor..... | 515,000 | No. Indiana Public Service Co...... | 1972 |
| Iowa............. | Cedar Rapids..... | 537,600 | Iowa Electric & Power Co.......... | 1973 |
| Maine............ | Wiscasset........ | 790,000 | Maine Yankee Atomic Power Co.... | 1972 |
| Maryland......... | Lusby............ | 800,000 | Baltimore Gas & Electric.......... | 1973 |
| | Lusby............ | 800,000 | Baltimore Gas & Electric.......... | 1974 |
| Massachusetts..... | Rowe............ | 175,000 | Yankee Atomic Electric Co......... | 1960 |
| | Plymouth......... | 625,000 | Boston Edison Co................. | 1971 |
| Michigan.......... | Big Rock Point.... | 70,400 | Consumers Power Co.............. | 1962 |
| | South Haven...... | 700,000 | Consumers Power Co.............. | 1969 |
| | Lagoona Beach.... | 60,900 | Power Reactor Development Co..... | 1963 |
| | Bridgman......... | 1,060,000 | Indiana & Michigan Electric....... | 1972 |
| | Bridgman......... | 1,054,000 | Indiana & Michigan Electric....... | 1973 |
| | Midland.......... | 650,000 | Consumers Power Co.............. | 1974 |
| | Midland.......... | 650,000 | Consumers Power Co.............. | 1975 |
| Minnesota........ | Elk River........ | 22,000 | Rural Cooperative Power Assoc..... | 1962 |
| | Monticello........ | 471,700 | Northern States Power Co......... | 1970 |
| | Red Wing No. 1... | 550,000 | Northern States Power Co......... | 1972 |
| | Red Wing No. 2... | 550,000 | Northern States Power Co......... | 1974 |
| Nebraska.......... | Fort Calhoun..... | 457,400 | Omaha Public Power District....... | 1971 |
| | Brownville........ | 778,000 | Consumers Public Power........... | 1972 |
| New Jersey........ | Toms River....... | 515,000 | Jersey Central Power & Light Co.... | 1968 |
| | Toms River....... | 800,000 | Jersey Central Power & Light Co.... | 1973 |
| | Artificial Island.... | 1,050,000 | Public Service................... | 1971 |
| | Artificial Island.... | 1,050,000 | Public Service................... | 1973 |
| New York......... | Indian Point No. 1. | 265,000 | Consolidated Edison Co........... | 1962 |
| | Indian Point No. 2. | 873,000 | Consolidated Edison Co........... | 1969 |
| | Indian Point No. 3. | 965,300 | Consolidated Edison Co........... | 1971 |
| | Scriba............ | 500,000 | Niagara Mohawk Power Co......... | 1968 |
| | Easton........... | 765,800 | Niagara Mohawk Power Co......... | 1971 |
| | Rochester........ | 420,000 | Rochester Gas & Electric Co....... | 1969 |
| | Shoreham........ | 523,000 | Long Island Lighting Co........... | 1973 |
| | Lansing.......... | 829,000 | N. Y. State Electric & Gas Co...... | 1973 |
| North Carolina.... | *............... | 1,115,000 | Consolidated Edison.............. | 1973 |
| | *............... | 800,000 | Carolina Power & Light........... | 1973 |
| | *............... | 800,000 | Carolina Power & Light........... | 1974 |
| | *............... | 800,000 | Carolina Power & Light........... | |
| Pennsylvania...... | Peach Bottom No. 1 | 40,000 | Philadelphia Electric Co........... | 1966 |
| | Peach Bottom No. 2 | 1,065,000 | Philadelphia Electric Co........... | 1971 |
| | Peach Bottom No. 3 | 1,065,000 | Philadelphia Electric Co........... | 1973 |
| | *............... | 1,065,000 | Philadelphia Electric Co........... | 1975 |
| | *............... | 1,065,000 | Philadelphia Electric Co........... | 1977 |
| | Shippingport...... | 90,000 | Duquesne Light Co............... | 1957 |
| | Shippingport No. 2 | 783,000 | Duquesne Light Co............... | 1973 |
| | Three Mile Island.. | 831,000 | Metropolitan Edison Co........... | 1971 |
| | *............... | 1,100,000 | Penna. Power & Light............ | 1975 |
| | *............... | 1,100,000 | Penna. Power & Light............ | 1977 |
| Puerto Rico........ | Punta Higuera.... | 16,500 | Puerto Rico Water Resources Authority... | 1964 |
| South Carolina..... | Hartsville........ | 663,000 | Carolina Power & Light Co......... | 1970 |
| | Lake Keowee No. 1. | 841,100 | Duke Power Co.................. | 1971 |
| | Lake Keowee No. 2. | 841,100 | Duke Power Co.................. | 1972 |
| | Lake Keowee No. 3. | 841,100 | Duke Power Co.................. | 1973 |
| South Dakota...... | Sioux Falls....... | 58,500 | Northern States Power Co......... | 1964 |
| Tennessee......... | Sequoyah......... | 1,125,000 | Tenn. Valley Authority............ | 1973 |
| | Sequoyah......... | 1,125,000 | Tenn. Valley Authority............ | 1974 |
| Vermont.......... | Vernon.......... | 513,900 | Vermont Yankee Nuclear Corp..... | 1970 |
| Virginia.......... | Hog Island....... | 783,000 | Virginia Electric & Power Co....... | 1971 |
| | Hog Island....... | 783,000 | Virginia Electric & Power Co....... | 1972 |
| | Louisa County.... | 800,000 | Virginia Electric & Power Co....... | 1974 |
| Washington....... | Richland......... | 790,000 | Washington Public Power Supply System | 1966 |
| Wisconsin......... | Genoa........... | 50,000 | Dairyland Power Cooperative...... | 1966 |
| | Two Creeks No. 1.. | 454,600 | Wisc. Mich. Power Co............ | 1970 |
| | Two Creeks No. 2.. | 454,600 | Wisc. Mich. Power Co............ | 1971 |
| | Carlton.......... | 527,000 | Wisc. Public Service Co........... | 1973 |

Nuclear plant capacity (kilowatts): In operation 2,798,700; being built 22,501,000; planned reactors ordered 34,980,000, reactors not ordered 12,660,000; total 72,939,700     * Site not selected.

## Centennial Planned for Grand Canyon Explorer

The United States will honor one of its most remarkable pioneers, explorer-scientist John Wesley Powell, with a national centennial in 1969.

The one-armed veteran of the Civil War survived boat crashes and near-drowning to make the pioneer exploration of the Green and Colorado Rivers through forbidding canyon country from Wyoming to Nevada. He set out from Green River, Wyo., with 9 men and 4 boats in May, 1869.

Major Powell's bold exploration of the Colorado traversed an unknown region of 56,000 square miles. A self-made scientist, he alone comprehended the potential of the arid West, and made far-reaching contributions to knowledge of its resources and also its Indian tribes.

To pay homage due to this man, the U. S. Department of the Interior, the Smithsonian Institution, and National Geographic Society are joint sponsors of the centennial on the 100th anniversary of Major Powell's journey down the perilous river through the Grand Canyon.

Conquest of the Colorado in 1869 made the former geology teacher a romantic and respected hero. His journals, scientific works and lectures spread his fame.

Major Powell became the most powerful scientist in the nation's capital. He helped found the Interior Department's Geological Survey and the Smithsonian's Bureau of American Ethnology, serving both as director. He helped establish the Geological Society of America and the National Geographic Society.

Soon after Major Powell's death in 1902, the National Geographic wrote: "Few men in the history of the United States have left behind them such a deep and lasting impression on the scientific work of the Nation." Yet knowledge of his adventures and achievements has faded in the 20th century.

## World's Highest Dams

C—Concrete; E—Earth; UC—Under Construction

| Name | Height (ft.) | | Year | Name | Height (ft.) | | Year |
|---|---|---|---|---|---|---|---|
| Nurek, USSR | 1017 | E | UC | Toktogul, USSR | 705 | | UC |
| Inguri, USSR | 988 | C | UC | Manicouagan No. 5, Canada.. | 703 | C | UC |
| Grand Dixence, Switzerland.. | 932 | C | 1962 | Dworshak, U.S.A. | 693 | C | UC |
| Valont, Italy | 858 | C | 1961 | Luzzone, Switzerland | 682 | C | 1963 |
| Mica, Canada | 800 | E | UC | Auburn, U.S.A. | 680 | C | UC |
| Mauvoisin, Switzerland | 777 | C | 1958 | Keban, Turkey | 672 | E | UC |
| Sayansk, USSR | 774 | C | UC | Pahlevi, Iran | 668 | C | 1963 |
| Oroville, U.S.A. | 770 | E | 1968 | Bullards Bar, U.S.A. | 645 | C | UC |
| Chirkey, USSR | 764 | C | UC | Almendra, Spain | 623 | C | UC |
| Contra, Switzerland | 754 | C | 1965 | Kurobe No. 4, Japan | 610 | C | 1964 |
| Bhakra, India | 740 | C | 1962 | Melones, U.S.A. | 608 | E | UC |
| Hoover, U.S.A. | 726 | C | 1936 | Mossyrock, U.S.A. | 605 | C | UC |
| Mratinje, Yugoslavia | 721 | C | UC | Shasta, U.S.A. | 602 | C | 1945 |
| Glen Canyon, U.S.A. | 710 | C | 1964 | Portage Mountain, Canada... | 600 | E | UC |

## World's Largest Dams

**Source: Bureau of Reclamation, Dept. of the Interior**
Based on total volume of structure. All dams listed are predominantly earthfill or rockfill and may contain concrete sections. UC—Under Construction.

| Name | Cubic Yards | Year | Name | Cubic Yards | Year |
|---|---|---|---|---|---|
| Tarbella, Pakistan, | 159,000,000 | UC | Sadd-El-Aall(High Dam), UAR | 56,300,000 | UC |
| Fort Peck, U. S. A. | 125,600,000 | 1940 | Cochiti, U. S. A. | 53,000,000 | UC |
| Mangla, Pakistan | 108,300,000 | 1967 | Fort Randall, U. S. A. | 50,200,000 | 1956 |
| Oahe, U. S. A. | 92,000,000 | 1963 | Kanev, USSR | 49,500,000 | UC |
| South Saskatchewan, Can. | 86,300,000 | 1966 | Kakhovka, USSR | 46,600,000 | 1955 |
| Oroville, U. S. A. | 80,300,000 | UC | Tsimlyansk, USSR | 44,300,000 | 1952 |
| San Luis, U. S. A. | 78,000,000 | 1967 | Volga, V. I. Lenin, USSR | 44,300,000 | 1955 |
| Nurek, USSR | 75,900,000 | UC | Beas, India | 44,200,000 | UC |
| Nagajunasagar, India | 73,600,000 | 1966 | Castaic, U. S. A. | 42,600,000 | UC |
| Garrison, U. S. A. | 66,500,000 | 1956 | Jari, Pakistan | 42,000,000 | 1967 |
| Kiev, USSR | 58,000,000 | 1964 | Mica, Canada | 40,000,000 | UC |
| Gorky, USSR | 58,000,000 | 1955 | Kremenchug, USSR | 36,300,000 | 1961 |
| Portage Mountain, Canada.. | 56,700,000 | UC | Saratov, USSR | 34,500,000 | UC |

## World's Greatest Man-Made Lakes [1]

UC—Under Construction. 1. Formed by dam construction. 2. Represents increase in natural lake.

| Name of dam | Capacity-acre-feet | Year | Name of dam | Capacity-acre-feet | Year |
|---|---|---|---|---|---|
| Owen Falls, Uganda (2) | 166,000,000 | 1954 | Irkutsk, USSR (2) | 37,300,000 | 1956 |
| Bratsk, USSR | 137,200,000 | 1964 | Hoover, U. S. A. | 31,250,000 | 1936 |
| Kariba, Rhodesia-Zambia | 130,000,000 | 1959 | Sunda, Congo | 28,375,000 | 1961 |
| Sadd-El-Aall (High Dam) | 125,600,000 | UC | Volga-22nd Cong., USSR | 27,200,000 | 1958 |
| Akosombo, Ghana | 120,000,000 | 1965 | Glen Canyon, U. S. A. | 27,000,000 | 1964 |
| Manicouagan No. 5, Canada.. | 115,000,000 | 1967 | Zeyskaya, USSR | 26,000,000 | UC |
| Krasnoyarsk, USSR | 59,400,000 | UC | Valerio Trujano, Mexico | 26,000,000 | 1964 |
| Portage Mountain, Canada... | 57,000,000 | UC | Keban, Turkey | 24,700,000 | UC |
| Sanmen Hsia, China | 52,700,000 | 1962 | Garrison, U. S. A. | 24,400,000 | 1956 |
| Ust-Ilim, USSR | 48,100,000 | UC | Iroquois, U. S. A.-Canada (2). | 24,300,000 | 1959 |
| Volga-V. I. Lenin, USSR | 47,000,000 | 1955 | Oahe, U. S. A. | 23,600,000 | 1963 |
| Bukhtarma, USSR | 43,000,000 | 1960 | Rybinsk-Sheksna, USSR | 20,600,000 | 1941 |
| Tankiangkow, China | 41,800,000 | 1962 | | | |

## Size and Dimensions of the Continents

**Source: U. S. Naval Oceanographic Office**

| | Sq. mi. | Miles | | | Sq. mi. | Miles | |
|---|---|---|---|---|---|---|---|
| | | N to S | E to W | | | N to S | E to W |
| No. America (inc. islands).. | 9,300,000 | 5,300 | 4,000 | Africa | 11,500,000 | 5,000 | 4,700 |
| South America | 6,800,000 | 4,750 | 3,100 | Australia | 2,950,000 | 1,970 | 2,400 |
| Europe | 3,750,000 | 2,400 | 3,800 | Antarctica | 5,300,000 | | |
| Asia (inc. islands) | 16,900,000 | 5,300 | 6,000 | | | | |

Fertile regions occupy 33,000,000 sq. mi. Steppes 19,000,000 sq. mi. Deserts 5,000,000 sq. mi.

# Latitude, Longitude and Altitude of United States Cities

**Source:** Coast and Geodetic Survey (ESSA) for geographic position.
Altitudes U. S. Geological Survey and various sources. *Approx. altitude at Downtown Business Area.

| City | Lat. ° ′ ″ | Long. ° ′ ″ | Alt.* Feet |
|---|---|---|---|
| Akron, Ohio | 41 05 00 | 81 30 44 | 874 |
| Albany, N. Y. | 42 39 01 | 73 45 01 | 20 |
| Albuquerque, N. M. | 35 05 01 | 106 39 05 | 4,945 |
| Allentown, Pa. | 40 36 11 | 75 28 06 | 255 |
| Altoona, Pa. | 40 30 55 | 78 24 03 | 1,180 |
| Amarillo, Tex. | 35 12 27 | 101 50 04 | 3,685 |
| Anchorage, Alaska. | 61 10 00 | 149 59 00 | 118 |
| Ann Arbor, Mich. | 42 16 59 | 83 44 52 | 880 |
| Asheville, N. C. | 35 35 42 | 82 33 26 | 1,985 |
| Ashland, Ky. | 38 28 36 | 82 38 23 | 536 |
| Atlanta, Ga. | 33 45 10 | 84 23 37 | 1,050 |
| Atlantic City, N. J. | 39 21 32 | 74 25 53 | 10 |
| Augusta, Ga. | 33 28 20 | 81 58 00 | 143 |
| Augusta, Me. | 44 18 53 | 69 46 29 | 45 |
| Austin, Tex. | 30 16 09 | 97 44 37 | 505 |
| Baltimore, Md. | 39 17 26 | 76 36 45 | 20 |
| Bangor, Me. | 44 48 13 | 68 46 18 | 20 |
| Baton Rouge, La. | 30 26 58 | 91 11 00 | 57 |
| Battle Creek, Mich. | 42 18 58 | 85 10 48 | 820 |
| Bay City, Mich. | 43 36 04 | 83 53 15 | 595 |
| Beaumont, Tex. | 30 05 20 | 94 06 09 | 20 |
| Bellingham, Wash. | 48 54 02 | 122 28 36 | 60 |
| Berkeley, Calif. | 37 52 10 | 122 16 17 | 40 |
| Bethlehem, Pa. | 40 37 16 | 75 22 34 | 235 |
| Billings, Mont. | 45 47 00 | 108 30 04 | 3,120 |
| Binghamton, N. Y. | 42 06 03 | 75 54 47 | 865 |
| Birmingham, Ala. | 33 31 01 | 86 48 36 | 600 |
| Bismarck, N. D. | 46 48 23 | 100 47 17 | 1,674 |
| Boise, Idaho | 43 37 07 | 116 11 58 | 2,704 |
| Boston, Mass. | 42 21 24 | 71 03 25 | 21 |
| Bridgeport, Conn. | 41 10 49 | 73 11 22 | 10 |
| Brockton, Mass. | 42 05 02 | 71 01 25 | 130 |
| Brownsville, Tex. | 25 54 07 | 97 29 58 | 35 |
| Buffalo, N. Y. | 42 52 52 | 78 52 21 | 585 |
| Burlington, Vt. | 44 28 34 | 73 12 46 | 110 |
| Butte, Mont. | 46 01 06 | 112 32 11 | 5,765 |
| Cambridge, Mass. | 42 22 01 | 71 06 22 | 20 |
| Camden, N. J. | 39 56 41 | 75 07 14 | 30 |
| Canton, Ohio | 40 47 50 | 81 22 37 | 1,030 |
| Cedar Rapids, Iowa | 41 58 01 | 91 39 51 | 730 |
| Champaign, Ill. | 40 07 05 | 88 14 43 | 740 |
| Charleston, S. C. | 32 46 35 | 79 55 53 | 9 |
| Charleston, W. Va. | 38 21 01 | 81 37 52 | 601 |
| Charlotte, N. C. | 35 13 14 | 80 50 45 | 720 |
| Chattanooga, Tenn. | 35 02 41 | 85 18 32 | 675 |
| Cheyenne, Wyo. | 41 08 09 | 104 49 07 | 6,100 |
| Chicago, Ill. | 41 52 28 | 87 38 22 | 595 |
| Cincinnati, Ohio | 39 06 07 | 84 30 35 | 550 |
| Cleveland, Ohio | 41 29 51 | 81 41 50 | 660 |
| Colorado Springs | 38 50 07 | 104 49 16 | 5,980 |
| Columbia, Mo. | 38 57 03 | 92 19 46 | 730 |
| Columbia, S. C. | 34 00 02 | 81 02 00 | 190 |
| Columbus, Ga. | 32 28 07 | 84 59 24 | 265 |
| Columbus, Ohio | 39 57 47 | 83 00 17 | 780 |
| Concord, N. H. | 43 12 22 | 71 32 25 | 290 |
| Corpus Christi, Tex. | 27 47 51 | 97 23 45 | 35 |
| Dallas, Tex. | 32 47 09 | 96 47 37 | 435 |
| Davenport, Iowa | 41 31 19 | 90 34 33 | 590 |
| Dayton, Ohio | 39 45 32 | 84 11 43 | 574 |
| Daytona Beach, Fla | 29 12 44 | 81 01 10 | 7 |
| Decatur, Ill. | 39 50 42 | 88 56 47 | 682 |
| Denver, Colo. | 39 44 58 | 104 59 22 | 5,280 |
| Des Moines, Iowa | 41 35 14 | 93 37 00 | 805 |
| Detroit, Mich. | 42 19 48 | 83 02 57 | 585 |
| Dodge City, Kans. | 37 45 17 | 100 01 09 | 2,480 |
| Duluth, Minn. | 46 46 56 | 92 06 25 | 610 |
| Durham, N. C. | 36 00 00 | 78 54 45 | 405 |
| El Paso, Tex. | 31 45 36 | 106 29 11 | 3,695 |
| Elizabeth, N. J. | 40 39 43 | 74 12 59 | 21 |
| Erie, Pa. | 42 07 15 | 80 04 57 | 685 |
| Eugene, Ore. | 44 03 16 | 123 05 30 | 422 |
| Evansville, Ind. | 37 58 20 | 87 34 21 | 385 |
| Fairbanks, Alaska. | 64 48 00 | 147 51 00 | 448 |
| Fall River, Mass. | 41 42 06 | 71 09 18 | 40 |
| Fargo, N. D. | 46 52 30 | 96 47 18 | 900 |
| Flint, Mich. | 43 00 50 | 83 41 33 | 715 |
| Fort Wayne, Ind. | 41 04 21 | 85 08 26 | 790 |
| Fort Worth, Tex. | 32 44 55 | 97 19 44 | 670 |
| Fresno, Calif. | 36 44 12 | 119 47 11 | 285 |
| Gadsden, Ala. | 34 00 57 | 86 00 41 | 555 |
| Galveston, Tex. | 29 18 10 | 94 47 43 | 5 |
| Gary, Ind. | 41 36 12 | 87 20 19 | 590 |
| Grand Rapids | 42 58 03 | 85 40 13 | 610 |
| Green Bay, Wis. | 44 30 48 | 88 00 50 | 590 |
| Greensboro, N. C. | 36 04 17 | 79 47 25 | 839 |
| Greenville, S. C. | 34 50 50 | 82 24 01 | 966 |
| Gulfport, Miss. | 30 22 04 | 89 05 36 | 20 |
| Hamilton, Ohio | 39 23 59 | 84 33 47 | 600 |
| Harrisburg, Pa. | 40 15 43 | 76 52 59 | 365 |
| Hartford, Conn. | 41 46 12 | 72 40 49 | 40 |
| Helena, Mont. | 46 35 33 | 112 02 24 | 4,155 |
| Holyoke, Mass. | 42 12 29 | 72 36 36 | 115 |
| Honolulu | 21 18 22 | 157 51 35 | 21 |
| Houston, Tex. | 29 45 26 | 95 21 37 | 40 |
| Huntington, W. Va. | 38 25 12 | 82 26 33 | 565 |
| Indianapolis, Ind. | 39 46 07 | 86 09 46 | 710 |
| Iowa City, Iowa. | 41 39 37 | 91 31 53 | 685 |
| Jackson, Mich. | 42 14 43 | 84 24 22 | 940 |
| Jackson, Miss. | 32 17 56 | 90 11 06 | 298 |
| Jacksonville, Fla. | 30 19 44 | 81 39 42 | 20 |

| City | Lat. ° ′ ″ | Long. ° ′ ″ | Alt.* Feet |
|---|---|---|---|
| Jersey City, N. J. | 40 43 50 | 74 03 56 | 20 |
| Johnstown, Pa. | 40 19 35 | 78 55 03 | 1,185 |
| Kalamazoo, Mich. | 42 17 29 | 85 35 14 | 755 |
| Kansas City, Kan. | 39 07 04 | 94 38 24 | 750 |
| Kansas City, Mo. | 39 04 56 | 94 35 20 | 750 |
| Kenosha, Wis. | 42 35 43 | 87 50 11 | 610 |
| Key West, Fla. | 24 33 30 | 81 48 12 | 5 |
| Knoxville, Tenn. | 35 57 39 | 83 55 07 | 890 |
| Lafayette, Ind. | 40 25 11 | 86 53 39 | 550 |
| Lancaster, Pa. | 40 02 25 | 76 18 29 | 355 |
| Lansing, Mich. | 42 44 01 | 84 33 15 | 830 |
| Laredo, Tex. | 27 30 22 | 99 30 30 | 440 |
| Las Vegas, Nev. | 36 10 20 | 115 08 37 | 2,030 |
| Lawrence, Mass. | 42 42 16 | 71 10 08 | 65 |
| Lexington, Ky. | 38 02 50 | 84 29 46 | 955 |
| Lima, Ohio | 40 44 35 | 84 06 20 | 865 |
| Lincoln, Nebr. | 40 48 59 | 96 42 15 | 1,150 |
| Little Rock, Ark. | 34 44 42 | 92 16 37 | 300 |
| Long Beach, Calif. | 33 46 14 | 118 11 18 | 35 |
| Lorain, Ohio | 41 28 05 | 82 10 49 | 610 |
| Los Angeles, Calif. | 34 03 15 | 118 14 28 | 340 |
| Louisville, Ky. | 38 14 47 | 85 45 49 | 450 |
| Lowell, Mass. | 42 38 25 | 71 19 14 | 100 |
| Lubbock, Tex. | 33 35 05 | 101 50 33 | 3,195 |
| Macon, Ga. | 32 50 12 | 83 37 36 | 335 |
| Madison, Wis. | 43 04 23 | 89 22 55 | 860 |
| Manchester, N. H. | 42 59 28 | 71 27 41 | 175 |
| Memphis, Tenn. | 35 08 46 | 90 03 10 | 275 |
| Miami, Fla. | 25 46 37 | 80 11 32 | 10 |
| Milwaukee, Wis. | 43 02 19 | 87 54 15 | 635 |
| Minneapolis, Minn. | 44 58 57 | 93 15 43 | 815 |
| Mobile, Ala. | 30 41 36 | 88 02 33 | 5 |
| Moline, Ill. | 41 30 31 | 90 30 49 | 585 |
| Montgomery, Ala. | 32 22 33 | 86 18 31 | 160 |
| Montpelier, Vt. | 44 15 36 | 72 34 41 | 485 |
| Muncie, Ind. | 40 11 28 | 85 23 16 | 950 |
| Nashville, Tenn. | 36 09 33 | 86 46 55 | 450 |
| Newark, N. J. | 40 44 14 | 74 10 19 | 55 |
| New Bedford, Mass. | 41 38 13 | 70 55 41 | 15 |
| New Britain, Conn. | 41 40 08 | 72 46 59 | 200 |
| New Haven, Conn. | 41 18 25 | 72 55 30 | 40 |
| New Orleans, La. | 29 56 53 | 90 04 10 | 5 |
| New York, N. Y. | 40 45 06 | 73 59 39 | 55 |
| Niagara Falls, N. Y. | 43 05 34 | 79 03 26 | 570 |
| Norfolk, Va. | 36 51 10 | 76 17 21 | 10 |
| Oakland, Calif. | 37 48 03 | 122 15 54 | 25 |
| Ogden, Utah | 41 13 31 | 111 58 21 | 4,295 |
| Oklahoma City | 35 28 26 | 97 31 04 | 1,195 |
| Omaha, Nebr. | 41 15 42 | 95 56 14 | 1,040 |
| Orlando, Fla. | 28 32 42 | 81 22 38 | 70 |
| Paducah, Ky. | 37 05 13 | 88 35 56 | 345 |
| Pasadena, Calif. | 34 08 44 | 118 08 41 | 830 |
| Paterson, N. J. | 40 55 01 | 74 10 21 | 100 |
| Pensacola, Fla. | 30 24 51 | 87 12 56 | 15 |
| Peoria, Ill. | 40 41 42 | 89 35 33 | 470 |
| Philadelphia, Pa. | 39 56 58 | 75 09 21 | 100 |
| Phoenix, Ariz. | 33 27 12 | 112 04 28 | 1,090 |
| Pittsburgh, Pa. | 40 26 19 | 80 00 00 | 745 |
| Pittsfield, Mass. | 42 26 53 | 73 15 14 | 1,015 |
| Port Arthur, Texas | 29 52 30 | 93 56 15 | 10 |
| Portland, Me. | 43 39 33 | 70 15 19 | 25 |
| Portland, Ore. | 45 31 06 | 122 40 35 | 77 |
| Portsmouth, Va. | 36 50 07 | 76 18 14 | 10 |
| Providence, R. I. | 41 49 32 | 71 24 41 | 80 |
| Pueblo, Colo. | 38 16 17 | 104 36 33 | 4,690 |
| Racine, Wis. | 42 43 49 | 87 47 12 | 630 |
| Raleigh, N. C. | 35 46 38 | 78 38 21 | 365 |
| Reading, Pa. | 40 20 09 | 75 55 40 | 265 |
| Reno, Nev. | 39 31 27 | 119 48 40 | 4,490 |
| Richmond, Va. | 37 32 15 | 77 26 09 | 160 |
| Roanoke, Va. | 37 16 13 | 79 56 44 | 905 |
| Rochester, Minn. | 44 01 21 | 92 28 03 | 990 |
| Rochester, N. Y. | 43 09 41 | 77 36 21 | 515 |
| Rockford, Ill. | 42 17 07 | 89 05 48 | 715 |
| Sacramento, Calif. | 38 34 57 | 121 29 41 | 30 |
| Saginaw, Mich. | 43 25 52 | 83 56 05 | 595 |
| St. Joseph, Mo. | 39 45 57 | 94 51 02 | 850 |
| St. Louis, Mo. | 38 37 45 | 90 12 22 | 455 |
| St. Paul, Minn. | 44 57 19 | 93 06 07 | 780 |
| St. Petersburg, Fla. | 27 46 18 | 82 38 19 | 20 |
| Salt Lake City | 40 45 23 | 111 53 26 | 4,390 |
| San Angelo, Tex. | 31 27 39 | 100 26 03 | 1,845 |
| San Antonio, Tex. | 29 25 37 | 98 29 06 | 650 |
| San Bernardino | 34 06 30 | 117 17 28 | 1,080 |
| San Diego, Calif. | 32 42 53 | 117 09 21 | 20 |
| San Francisco | 37 46 39 | 122 24 40 | 65 |
| San Jose, Calif. | 37 20 16 | 121 53 24 | 90 |
| Santa Barbara | 34 25 18 | 119 41 55 | 100 |
| Santa Fe, N. M. | 35 41 11 | 105 56 10 | 6,950 |
| Savannah, Ga. | 32 04 42 | 81 05 37 | 20 |
| Schenectady, N. Y. | 42 48 42 | 73 55 42 | 245 |
| Scranton, Pa. | 41 24 32 | 75 39 46 | 725 |
| Seattle, Wash. | 47 36 32 | 122 20 12 | 10 |
| Shreveport, La. | 32 30 46 | 93 44 58 | 204 |
| Sioux City, Iowa | 42 29 46 | 96 24 30 | 1,110 |
| Sioux Falls, S. D. | 43 32 55 | 96 43 35 | 1,395 |
| Somerville, Mass. | 42 23 15 | 71 06 07 | 13 |
| South Bend, Ind. | 41 40 33 | 86 15 01 | 710 |
| Spartanburg, S. C. | 34 57 03 | 81 56 06 | 875 |
| Spokane, Wash. | 47 39 32 | 117 25 33 | 1,890 |

| City | ª Lat. | Long. | Alt.* | City | Lat. | Long. | Alt.* |
|---|---|---|---|---|---|---|---|
| | ° ′ ″ | ° ′ ″ | Feet | | ° ′ ″ | ° ′ ″ | Feet* |
| Springfield, Ill..... | 39 47 58 | 89 38 51 | 610 | Tulsa, Okla........ | 36 09 12 | 95 59 34 | 804 |
| Springfield, Mass... | 42 06 21 | 72 35 32 | 85 | Utica, N. Y........ | 43 06 12 | 75 13 33 | 415 |
| Springfield, Mo.... | 37 13 03 | 93 17 32 | 1,300 | Waco, Tex......... | 31 33 12 | 97 08 00 | 405 |
| Springfield, Ohio... | 39 55 38 | 83 48 29 | 980 | Walla Walla, Wash. | 46 04 08 | 118 20 24 | 936 |
| Stamford, Conn.... | 41 03 09 | 73 32 24 | 35 | Washington, D. C.. | 38 53 51 | 77 00 33 | 25 |
| Steubenville, Ohio.. | 40 21 42 | 80 36 53 | 660 | Waterbury, Conn... | 41 33 13 | 73 02 31 | 260 |
| Stockton, Calif.... | 37 30 | 121 17 16 | 20 | Waterloo, Iowa.... | 42 29 40 | 92 20 20 | 850 |
| Superior, Wis..... | 46 43 14 | 92 06 07 | 630 | Wheeling, W. Va... | 40 04 03 | 80 43 20 | 650 |
| Syracuse, N. Y.... | 43 03 04 | 76 09 14 | 400 | Wichita, Kan..... | 37 41 30 | 97 20 16 | 1,290 |
| Tacoma, Wash.... | 47 14 59 | 122 26 15 | 110 | Wichita Falls, Tex.. | 33 54 34 | 98 29 28 | 945 |
| Tampa, Fla....... | 27 56 58 | 82 27 25 | 15 | Wilkes-Barre, Pa... | 41 14 32 | 75 53 17 | 640 |
| Terre Haute, Ind... | 39 28 03 | 87 24 26 | 496 | Wilmington, Del... | 39 44 46 | 75 32 51 | 135 |
| Toledo, Ohio...... | 41 39 14 | 83 32 39 | 585 | Winston-Salem.... | 36 05 52 | 80 14 42 | 860 |
| Topeka, Kan...... | 39 03 16 | 95 40 23 | 930 | Worcester, Mass... | 42 15 37 | 71 48 17 | 475 |
| Trenton, N. J..... | 40 13 14 | 74 46 13 | 35 | Yonkers, N. Y..... | 40 55 55 | 73 53 54 | 10 |
| Troy, N. Y....... | 42 43 45 | 73 40 58 | 35 | York, Pa.......... | 39 57 35 | 76 43 36 | 370 |
| Tucson, Ariz...... | 32 13 15 | 110 58 08 | 2,390 | Youngstown, Ohio.. | 41 05 57 | 80 39 02 | 840 |

## Highest and Lowest Altitudes in the United States

**Source:** U.S. Geological Survey. (Minus sign means below sea level; elevations are in feet.)

| | Highest Point | | | Lowest Point | | |
|---|---|---|---|---|---|---|
| State | Name | County | Elev. | Name | County | Elev. |
| Alabama......... | Cheaha Mountain... | Cleburne........ | 2,407 | Gulf of Mexico.... | | Sea level |
| Alaska.......... | McKinley (South).. | | 20,320 | Pacific Ocean.. | | Sea level |
| Arizona......... | Humphreys Peak... | Coconino...... | 12,633 | Colorado R.... | Yuma....... | 70 |
| Arkansas........ | Magazine Mountain. | Logan........ | 2,753 | Ouachita R.... | Ashley Union | 55 |
| California*...... | Mount Whitney.... | Inyo-Tulare.... | 14,494 | Death Valley... | Inyo........ | −282 |
| Canal Zone...... | Cerro Galera..... | Balboa District... | 1,205 | Atlantic Ocean.. | | Sea level |
| Colorado........ | Mount Elbert..... | Lake........... | 14,433 | Arkansas R.... | Prowers..... | 3,350 |
| Connecticut..... | Mount Frissell.... | Litchfield...... | 2,380 | L. I. Sound.... | | Sea level |
| Delaware........ | On Ebright Road... | New Castle..... | 442 | Atlantic Ocean.. | | Sea level |
| Dist. of Col..... | Tenleytown...... | N. W. part...... | 410 | Potomac R.... | | 1 |
| Florida.......... | West boundary.... | Walton........ | 345 | Atlantic Ocean.. | | Sea level |
| Georgia......... | Brasstown Bald.... | Towns-Union... | 4,784 | Atlantic Ocean.. | | Sea level |
| Guam........... | Mount Lamlam.... | Agat District... | 1,329 | Pacific Ocean.. | | Sea level |
| Hawaii.......... | Mauna Kea...... | Hawaii........ | 13,796 | Pacific Ocean.. | | Sea level |
| Idaho........... | Borah Peak...... | Custer........ | 12,662 | Snake R....... | Nez Perce... | 710 |
| Illinois.......... | Charles Mound.... | Jo Daviess..... | 1,235 | Mississippi R... | Alexander... | 279 |
| Indiana......... | Franklin Township.. | Wayne........ | 1,257 | Ohio R....... | Posey...... | 320 |
| Iowa............ | Ocheyedan Mound.. | Osceola........ | 1,675 | Mississippi R... | Lee........ | 480 |
| Kansas.......... | Mount Sunflower... | Wallace....... | 4,039 | Verdigris R.... | Montgomery | 680 |
| Kentucky........ | Black Mountain... | Harlan........ | 4,145 | Mississippi R... | Fulton...... | 257 |
| Louisiana........ | Driskill Mountain... | Bienville...... | 535 | New Orleans.... | Orleans..... | −5 |
| Maine........... | Mount Katahdin... | Piscataquis.... | 5,268 | Atlantic Ocean.. | | Sea level |
| Maryland........ | Backbone Mountain. | Garrett........ | 3,360 | Atlantic Ocean.. | | Sea level |
| Massachusetts... | Mount Greylock.... | Berkshire..... | 3,491 | Atlantic Ocean.. | | Sea level |
| Michigan........ | Mount Curwood.... | Baraga....... | 1,980 | Lake Erie...... | | 572 |
| Minnesota....... | Eagle Mountain.... | Cook......... | 2,301 | Lake Superior... | | 602 |
| Mississippi...... | Woodall Mountain.. | Tishomingo.... | 806 | Gulf of Mexico.... | | Sea level |
| Missouri......... | Taum Sauk Mt.... | Iron......... | 1,772 | St. Francis R... | Dunklin.... | 230 |
| Montana........ | Granite Peak..... | Park......... | 12,799 | Kootenai R.... | Lincoln..... | 1,800 |
| Nebraska........ | Johnson Township.. | Kimball....... | 5,426 | S.E. cor. State. | Richardson.. | 840 |
| Nevada.......... | Boundary Peak.... | Esmeralda..... | 13,140 | Colorado R.... | Clark....... | 470 |
| New Hampshire.. | Mt. Washington... | Coos......... | 6,288 | Atlantic Ocean.. | | Sea level |
| New Jersey...... | High Point...... | Sussex........ | 1,803 | Atlantic Ocean.. | | Sea level |
| New Mexico...... | Wheeler Peak.... | Taos......... | 13,161 | Red Bluff Res... | Eddy....... | 2,817 |
| New York....... | Mount Marcy.... | Essex........ | 5,344 | Atlantic Ocean.. | | Sea level |
| North Carolina.. | Mount Mitchell... | Yancey....... | 6,684 | Atlantic Ocean.. | | Sea level |
| North Dakota.... | White Butte..... | Slope........ | 3,506 | Red River..... | Pembina.... | 750 |
| Ohio............ | Campbell Hill.... | Logan........ | 1,550 | Ohio R....... | Hamilton... | 433 |
| Oklahoma....... | Black Mesa...... | Cimarron..... | 4,973 | Little River.... | McCurtain.. | 287 |
| Oregon.......... | Mount Hood...... | Clackamas-H.R. | 11,235 | Pacific Ocean.. | | Sea level |
| Pennsylvania.... | Mt. Davis....... | Somerset...... | 3,213 | Delaware R.... | Delaware... | Sea level |
| Puerto Rico...... | Cerro de Punta... | Ponce........ | 4,389 | Atlantic Ocean.. | | Sea level |
| Rhode Island.... | Jerimoth Hill.... | Providence.... | 812 | Atlantic Ocean.. | | Sea level |
| Samoa.......... | Lata.......... | Tau Island..... | 3,056 | Pacific Ocean.. | | Sea level |
| South Carolina... | Sassafras Mountain.. | Pickens....... | 3,560 | Atlantic Ocean.. | | Sea level |
| South Dakota.... | Harney Peak..... | Pennington.... | 7,242 | Big Stone Lake. | Roberts..... | 962 |
| Tennessee....... | Clingmans Dome... | Sevier........ | 6,643 | Mississippi R... | Shelby..... | 182 |
| Texas........... | Guadalupe Peak... | Culberson..... | 8,751 | Gulf of Mexico.... | | Sea level |
| Utah............ | Kings Peak...... | Duchesne..... | 13,528 | Beaverdam Cr... | Washington. | 2,000 |
| Vermont......... | Mount Mansfield... | Lamoille...... | 4,393 | Lake Champl'n. | Franklin.... | 95 |
| Virginia......... | Mount Rogers.... | Grayson-Smyth.. | 5,729 | Atlantic Ocean.. | | Sea level |
| Virgin Islands.... | Crown Mt...... | Is. St. Thomas... | 1,556 | Atlantic Ocean.. | | Sea level |
| Washington...... | Mount Rainier.... | Pierce........ | 14,410 | Pacific Ocean.. | | Sea level |
| West Virginia.... | Spruce Knob..... | Pendleton..... | 4,862 | Potomac R..... | Jefferson... | 240 |
| Wisconsin....... | Timms Hill...... | Price......... | 1,952 | Lake Michigan.. | | 581 |
| Wyoming........ | Gannett Peak.... | Fremont...... | 13,785 | B. Fourche R... | Crook...... | 3,100 |

*Highest and lowest points in the conterminous U. S. (48 states) are only 85 miles apart.

## Niagara Power Project

With an installed capacity of 2,190,000 kw., the Niagara Power Project of the Power Authority of the State of New York is the largest in the Western World. That huge capacity is reached with the Robert Moses Niagara Power Plant, whose 13 generators have a total capacity of 1,950,000 kw., and the 12 generating units of the Lewiston Pump Generating Plant, total capacity 240,000 kw. First power was delivered as scheduled on Feb. 10, 1961, and the final generating unit was placed on the line Nov. 11, 1962. The project was certified as completed Nov. 30, 1963.

Water for the operation is obtained from the Niagara River, 2½ miles above Niagara Falls. Two huge conduits conveying water under the city of Niagara Falls to the plants 4 miles below the Falls. Under the 1950 treaty with Canada more water may be drawn at night and during winter than during daylight hours of the summer tourist season. Power is sold to municipalities, rural electric cooperatives, industries and private utilities.

Niagara Power Project was financed by $737,000,-000 worth of bonds sold to private investors and no government credit or tax money is used. The bonds are paid from revenue derived from the sale of power.

The Power Authority also financed, built and is operating the United States half of the St. Lawrence Power Project, at Massena, N. Y., which has a total (United States and Canada) installed capacity of 1,824,000 kw.

# NATIONAL DEFENSE
### Data as of Aug. 1, 1968

**Chairman, Joint Chiefs of Staff**
General Earle G. Wheeler (Army)

## ARMY
**Chief of Staff**—General William C. Westmoreland

| Generals of the Army | Date of Rank |
|---|---|
| Bradley, Omar N. | Sept. 20, 1950 |
| Eisenhower, Dwight D. | Dec. 20, 1944 |

### Generals
| | |
|---|---|
| Abrams, Creighton W., Jr. | Sept. 4, 1964 |
| Beach, Dwight E. | July 1, 1965 |
| Besson, Frank S., Jr. | May 27, 1964 |
| Bonesteel, Charles H., 3rd | Sept. 1, 1966 |
| Conway, Theodore J. | Nov. 1, 1966 |
| Goodpaster, Andrew J. | July 3, 1968 |
| Haines, Ralph E., Jr. | June 1, 1967 |
| Lemnitzer, Lyman L. | Mar. 25, 1955 |
| Parker, Theodore W. | July 1, 1963 |
| Polk, James H. | May 31, 1967 |
| Porter, Robert W., Jr. | Mar. 18, 1965 |
| Wood, Robert J. | Sept. 1, 1962 |
| Woolnough, James K. | July 1, 1967 |

### Lieutenant Generals
| | |
|---|---|
| Alger, James D. | Aug. 1, 1967 |
| Betts, Austin W. | Apr. 1, 1966 |
| Bowen, John W. | Sept. 14, 1963 |
| Boyle, Andrew J. | Dec. 1, 1965 |
| Bunker, William B. | May 9, 1966 |
| Carter, Marshall S. | Apr. 1, 1962 |
| Cassidy, William F. | June 30, 1965 |
| Chesarek, Ferdinand J. | Aug. 1, 1966 |
| Collins, Arthur S. | Jan. 6, 1967 |
| Connor, Albert O. | June 28, 1967 |
| Critz, Harry H. | June 1, 1967 |
| Davis, John J. | Oct. 19, 1966 |
| Doleman, Edgar C. | Mar. 18, 1965 |
| Engler, Jean E. | May 27, 1964 |
| Exton, Hugh M. | July 29, 1967 |
| Harrell, Ben | Feb. 28, 1963 |
| Heaton, Leonard D. | Sept. 9, 1959 |
| Hershey, Lewis B. | June 23, 1956 |
| Holmgren, John A. | Aug. 1, 1965 |
| Hutchin, Claire E., Jr. | June 30, 1967 |
| Kelly, John E. | July 3, 1968 |
| Kinnard, Harry W. D. | June 29, 1967 |
| Lampert, James B. | Jan. 7, 1966 |
| Larsen, Stanley R. | July 15, 1966 |
| Lemley, Harry J., Jr. | Sept. 1, 1966 |
| Lincoln, Lawrence J. | July 30, 1964 |
| Mather, George R. | Aug. 18, 1965 |
| Michaelis, John H. | May 7, 1962 |
| Mildren, Frank T. | July 1, 1965 |
| Mock, Vernon P. | June 1, 1965 |
| Palmer, Bruce, Jr. | July 29, 1964 |
| Peers, William R. | June 26, 1968 |
| Rich, Charles W. G. | Aug. 1, 1964 |
| Rosson, William B. | July 28, 1967 |
| Sackton, Frank J. | Aug. 1, 1967 |
| Seaman, Jonathan O. | July 14, 1966 |
| Spivy, Berton E., Jr. | Apr. 1, 1965 |
| Starbird, Alfred D. | Oct. 30, 1962 |
| Throckmorton, John L. | July 31, 1964 |
| Underwood, George V., Jr. | July 1, 1968 |
| Unger, Ferdinand T. | Nov. 1, 1966 |
| Weyand, Frederick | July 1, 1967 |
| York, Robert H. | July 30, 1967 |

## AIR FORCE
**Chief of Staff**—General John P. McConnell

### Generals
| | |
|---|---|
| Brown, George S. | Aug. 1, 1968 |
| Burchinal, David A. | July 31, 1966 |
| Disosway, Gabriel P. | Aug. 1, 1963 |
| Estes, Howell M., Jr. | July 19, 1964 |
| Ferguson, James | July 30, 1966 |
| Holloway, Bruce N. | Aug. 1, 1965 |
| Momyer, William W. | Dec. 13, 1967 |
| Nazzaro, Joseph J. | Feb. 1, 1967 |
| Reeves, Raymond J. | July 29, 1966 |
| Ryan, John D. | Dec. 1, 1964 |
| Stone, William S. | July 28, 1966 |
| Wade, Horace M. | July 31, 1968 |

### Lieutenant Generals
| | |
|---|---|
| Agan, Arthur C. | June 29, 1966 |
| Breitweiser, Robert A. | June 29, 1967 |
| Carroll, Joseph F. | Feb. 1, 1960 |
| Catton, Jack J. | June 26, 1967 |
| Clark, Albert P. | June 21, 1965 |
| Clay, Lucius D., Jr. | June 30, 1968 |
| Compton, Keith K. | June 30, 1964 |
| Davis, Benjamin O., Jr. | Apr. 30, 1965 |
| Dean, Fred M. | Dec. 29, 1963 |
| Donovan, Stanley J. | June 10, 1967 |
| Edmundson, James V. | Feb. 17, 1965 |
| Friedman, Robert J. | Feb. 18, 1965 |

| | |
|---|---|
| Gideon, Francis C. | May 23, 1968 |
| Gillem, Alvan C. 2nd | May 25, 1968 |
| Graham, Gordon M. | July 2, 1968 |
| Hardy, John S. | Nov. 1, 1966 |
| Harrison, Bertram C. | July 1, 1968 |
| Hedlund, Earl C. | June 28, 1967 |
| Holzapple, Joseph R. | May 27, 1964 |
| Kiefer, William B. | Mar. 1, 1967 |
| Klocko, Richard P. | Dec. 13, 1967 |
| Lavelle, John D. | May 29, 1968 |
| Maddux, Sam, Jr. | June 23, 1965 |
| Martin, Glen W. | Sept. 1, 1965 |
| McGehee, Thomas K. | May 28, 1968 |
| McKee, Seth J. | July 12, 1966 |
| McNickle, Marvin L. | June 28, 1966 |
| McPherson, John B. | May 26, 1968 |
| Meyer, John C. | June 12, 1967 |
| Milton, Theodore R. | Feb. 17, 1967 |
| Moore, Joseph H. | June 25, 1965 |
| Moorman, Thomas S. | Dec. 12, 1961 |
| Mundell, Lewis L. | June 22, 1965 |
| O'Neill, John W. | June 27, 1967 |
| Phillips, Samuel C. | May 27, 1968 |
| Pletcher, Kenneth E. | Dec. 1, 1967 |
| Ruegg, Robt. G. | June 11, 1967 |
| Russell, Austin J. | June 30, 1966 |
| Smith, Robert N. | May 24, 1968 |
| Terhune, Charles H., Jr. | May 1, 1967 |
| Warren, Robert J. | July 3, 1968 |
| Wilson, James W. | July 1, 1966 |

## NAVY
**Chief of Naval Operations**
Admiral Thomas H. Moorer

### Admirals
| | |
|---|---|
| Clarey, Bernard A. | Jan. 17, 1968 |
| Galantin, Ignatius J. | May 19, 1967 |
| Holmes, Ephraim P. | June 17, 1967 |
| Hyland, John J. (Aviation) | Dec. 1, 1967 |
| McCain, John S., Jr. | May 1, 1967 |
| Rivero, Horacio, Jr. | July 31, 1964 |
| Wendt, Waldemar F. A. | July 31, 1968 |

### Vice Admirals
| | |
|---|---|
| Ashworth, Frederick L. (Aviation) | May 11, 1966 |
| Baumberger, Walter H. | Mar. 17, 1967 |
| Bennett, Fred. G. | Jan. 17, 1968 |
| Blouin, Francis J. | July 27, 1966 |
| Booth, Charles T. (Aviation) | Apr. 1, 1965 |
| Bowen, Harold G., Jr. | July 7, 1967 |
| Bringle, William F. (Aviation) | Nov. 6, 1967 |
| Caldwell, Turner F., Jr. (Aviation) | Nov. 1, 1967 |
| Chew, John L. | Nov. 25, 1965 |
| Colwell, John B. | Jan. 18, 1964 |
| Connolly, Thomas F. (Aviation) | Nov. 1, 1965 |
| Duncan, Charles K. | June 1, 1965 |
| Ellis, William E. (Aviation) | June 2, 1964 |
| Ensey, Lot. | Sept. 1, 1964 |
| Gayler, Noel A. M. (Aviation) | Sept. 28, 1967 |
| Hayward, John T. (Aviation) | Apr. 25, 1959 |
| Heinz, Luther C. | Sept. 1, 1965 |
| Jackson, Andrew McB. (Aviation) | July 20, 1964 |
| Johnson, Nels C. | May 8, 1967 |
| Lee, John M. | Feb. 17, 1967 |
| Lowrance, Vernon L. | Aug. 31, 1964 |
| Martin, William I. (Aviation) | Apr. 10, 1967 |
| Masterson, Kleber S. | Apr. 17, 1964 |
| Masterton, Paul (Aviation) | Nov. 1, 1967 |
| Mustin, Lloyd M. | Aug. 21, 1964 |
| Needham, Ray C. (Aviation) | Aug. 1, 1963 |
| Ramage, Lawson P. | July 15, 1963 |
| Roeder, Bernard F. | Mar. 25, 1965 |
| Schade, Arnold F. | Nov. 19, 1966 |
| Semmes, Benedict J., Jr. | Apr. 1, 1964 |
| Shifley, Ralph L. (Aviation) | Sept. 1, 1967 |
| Shinn, Allen M. (Aviation) | Nov. 1, 1966 |
| Smith, John V. | June 7, 1968 |
| Strean, Bernard M. (Aviation) | July 31, 1968 |
| Taylor, Rufus L. | June 1, 1966 |
| Tyree, John A., Jr. | July 26, 1968 |

## MARINE
**Corps Commandant, with rank of General**
Chapman, Leonard F., Jr. ... Jan. 1, 1968

### Lieutenant Generals
| | |
|---|---|
| Buse, Henry W., Jr. | Dec. 26, 1964 |
| Cushman, Robt. W., Jr. | June 1, 1967 |
| Fields, Lewis J. | July 1, 1968 |
| Nickerson, Herman, Jr. | Mar. 19, 1968 |
| Van Ryzin, William J. | June 1, 1968 |
| Walt, Lewis W. | Mar. 7, 1967 |
| Weede, Richard G. | July 1, 1967 |

## COAST GUARD
**Commandant, with rank of Admiral**
Smith, Willard J. ... July 1, 1966
**Asst. Commandant, with rank of Vice Admiral**
Trimble, Paul E. ... July 27, 1966

## How the Military Hand Salute Originated

Hand-raising as a formal greeting probably originated with the cavemen, who wanted to prove to one another that they carried no weapons, according to the National Geographic Society. Later an armored knight raised his right arm to lift his helmet visor and to show friendship by keeping his sword hand away from the weapon. Before the 19th Century, British soldiers saluted by tipping their hats. In the modern U. S. military salute the right hand is raised smartly so the forefinger touches the forehead just above and to the right of the right eye, thumb and fingers extended, forearm and wrist at a 45-degree angle. This salute, with variations, is common among military forces around the world.

# Hall of Heroes for Medal of Honor Winners

The names of all recipients of the Medal of Honor, the nation's highest military award for heroism, are now enshrined in a Hall of Heroes in the Pentagon in Washington, D. C. The Hall of Heroes is located in the "A" ring of the Pentagon at the end of the corridor from the Mall entrance. Its walls are lined with plaques bearing the names of the more than 3,200 recipients of the Medal of Honor. When the Hall was dedicated on May 14, 1968, the totals by Service were: Army 2,215, Navy 731, Marine Corps 245, Air Force 46, and Coast Guard 1.

## Medal of Honor Winners in Vietnam War

*(Chronologically through presentation of Oct. 17, 1968)*

Capt. Roger H. C. Donlon, U. S. Army, of Saugerties, N. Y.

*Sgt. Larry F. Pierce, U. S. Army, of Wasco, Calif.

*Pfc. Milton F. Olive 3rd, U. S. Army, of Chicago, Ill.

Lt. Charles Q. Williams, U.S. Army, of Vance, S. C.

*Seabee Marvin Glen Shields, U. S. Navy, of Port Townsend, Wash.

Sgt. Robert E. O'Malley, U. S. Marine Corps, of Woodside, Queens (New York City).

First Lt. Walter J. Marm, Jr., U. S. Army, of Washington, Pa.

Maj. Bernard F. Fisher, U. S. Air Force, of Kuna, Idaho.

*Second Lt. Robert J. Hibbs, U. S. Army, of Cedar Falls, Iowa.

*First Lt. Frank S. Reasoner, U. S. Marine Corps, of Kellogg, Idaho.

*Lance Corp. Joe C. Paul, U. S. Marine Corps, of Vandalia, Ohio.

Capt. Harvey C. Barnum, Jr., U. S. Marine Corps, of Cheshire, Conn.

Specialist 6 Lawrence Joel, U. S. Army, of Winston-Salem, N. C.

*Specialist 4 Daniel Fernandez, U. S. Army, of Los Lunas, N. M.

*Staff Sgt. Peter S. Connor, U. S. Marine Corps, a native of Orange, N. J.

*Sgt. James W. Robinson, Jr., U. S. Army, of Annandale, Va.

Gunnery Sgt. Jimmie E. Howard, U. S. Marine Corps, of San Diego, Calif.

*Staff Sgt. Jimmy G. Stewart, U. S. Army, of Columbus, Ga.

Sgt. David C. Dolby, U. S. Army, of Oaks, Pa.

*First Lt. James A. Gardner, U. S. Army, of Dyersburg, Tenn.

Maj. Howard V. Lee, U. S. Marine Corps, of New York City.

Staff Sgt. Charles B. Morris, U. S. Army, of Galax, Va.

*Capt. Joseph X. Grant, U. S. Army, of Cambridge, Mass.

*Capt. Hilliard A. Wilbanks, U. S. Air Force, of Glen Allan, Miss.

*Seaman David G. Ouellet, U. S. Navy, of Wellesley, Mass.

Maj. Merlyn H. Dethlefsen, U. S. Air Force, of Derby, Kan.

*Sgt. Donald R. Long, U. S. Army, a native of Blackfork, Ohio.

*Pfc. Lewis Albanese, U. S. Army, of Seattle, Wash.

Maj. Robert J. Modrzejewski, U. S. Marine Corps, of Annapolis, Md.

2nd Lt. John J. McGinty, 3rd, U. S. Marine Corps of Laurel Bay, S. C.

*Pfc. Douglas E. Dickey, U. S. Marine Corps, a native of Greenville, Ohio.

Sgt. John F. Baker, Jr., U. S. Army, a native of Davenport, Iowa.

Capt. Robert F. Foley, U. S. Army, a native of Newton, Mass.

Capt. Gerald O. Young, U. S. Air Force, of Anacortes, Wash.

Boatswain's Mate 1st Cl. James E. Williams, U. S. Navy, of Darlington, S. C.

Sgt. Richard A. Pittman, U. S. Marine Corps, of Stockton, Calif.

Specialist 5 Charles C. Hagemeister, U. S. Army, of Lincoln, Neb.

*Specialist 4 Donald W. Evans, Jr., U. S. Army, a native of Covina, Calif.

*1st Lt. George K. Sisler, U. S. Army, of Dexter, Mo.

*Capt. Euripides Rubio, Jr., U. S. Army, of Ponce, Puerto Rico.

*Pfc. Billy L. Lauffer, U. S. Army, of Tucson, Ariz.

*Pfc. James Anderson, Jr., U. S. Marine Corps, of Compton, Calif.

*2nd Lt. John P. Bobo, U. S. Marine Corps, of Niagara Falls, N. Y.

*Sgt. Walter K. Singleton, U. S. Marine Corps, of Memphis, Tenn.

*Pfc. Louis E. Willett, U. S. Army, a native of Brooklyn, N. Y.

Staff Sgt. Delbert O. Jennings, U. S. Army, of Stockton, Calif.

Sgt. Leonard B. Keller, U. S. Army, of Rockford, Ill.

Specialist 4 Raymond R. Wright, U. S. Army, of Mineville, N. Y.

1st Sgt. David H. McNerney, U. S. Army, of Fort Dix, N. J.

Staff Sgt. Kennneth E. Stumpf, U. S. Army, of Menasha, Wis.

*Lance Corp. Roy M. Wheat, U. S. Marine Corps, of Moselle, Miss.

*Sgt. Elmelindo Rodrigues Smith, U. S. Army, a native of Hawaii.

*Pfc. James H. Monroe, U. S. Army, of Wheaton, Ill.

*Awarded posthumously.

### Medal of Honor Awarded to Skipper of U.S.S. Liberty

The Medal of Honor was presented June 11, 1968, to Capt. William L. McGonagle of the U. S. Navy, skipper of the U.S.S. Liberty, which was nearly destroyed by Israeli warplanes and torpedo boats in the Mediterranean Sea in 1967, with the loss of 34 American lives. Secy. of the Navy Paul R. Ignatius said McGonagle "was responsible for saving the lives of many of his crew and for saving the ship."

## The Medal of Honor; Other Top U. S. Military Awards

The Medal of Honor is the highest military award for bravery that can be given to any individual in the United States of America. It is presented to its recipients, usually by the President, "in the name of the Congress of the United States," and for this reason it is often called the Congressional Medal of Honor.

The law, as amended in 1963, provides that the President may award the Medal of Honor to any person who, while a member of the armed forces, "distinguished himself conspicuously by gallantry and intrepidity at the risk of his life above and beyond the call of duty—(1) while engaged in an action against an enemy of the United States; (2) while engaged in military operations involving conflict with an opposing foreign force; or (3) while serving with friendly foreign forces engaged in an armed conflict against an opposing armed force in which the United States is not a belligerent party."

Criteria for awarding the medal to officers or enlisted men of the Army, Navy, Marine Corps, Air Force and Coast Guard are identical, although the actual medals vary slightly in design. On rare occasions, Congress has enacted special legislation to award the Medal of Honor for individual exploits in peacetime. The Navy Medal of Honor has been awarded for heroism by noncombatants on several occasions.

**Distinguished Service Cross, Navy Cross, Air Force Cross.** These decorations, all ranked on the same level, may be awarded to a person who, while serving in any capacity with the Army, Navy, Marine Corps or Air Force, "distinguishes himself by extraordinary heroism not justifying the award of a Medal of Honor."

**Distinguished Service Medal.** Awarded to any person who, while serving with the armed forces in any capacity, "distinguishes himself by exceptionally meritorious service to the United States in a duty of great responsibility."

**Silver Star.** Awarded to a person who, while serving in any capacity with the armed forces, "is cited for gallantry in action that does not warrant a Medal of Honor or Distinguished Service Cross."

**Other Awards.** Lesser awards for heroism or extraordinary achievement include the Bronze Star, Distinguished Flying Cross, Soldiers Medal, Navy and Marine Corps Medal, and Airman's Medal. The Purple Heart, originally for bravery, is now given to those wounded in action.

# United States Army
### Source: Department of the Army
### ARMY MILITARY PERSONNEL ON ACTIVE DUTY[a]

| June 30 (b) | Total strength | Commissioned officers | | | Warrant officers | | Enlisted personnel | | |
|---|---|---|---|---|---|---|---|---|---|
| | | Total | Male | Female (c) | Male (d) | Female | Total | Male | Female |
| 1930...... | 138,452 | 13,062 | 12,255 | 807 | 1,089 | ....... | 124,301 | 124,301 | ....... |
| 1935...... | 138,569 | 12,646 | 12,043 | 603 | 825 | ....... | 125,098 | 125,098 | ....... |
| 1940...... | 267,767 | 17,563 | 16,624 | 939 | 763 | ....... | 249,441 | 249,441 | ....... |
| 1942...... | 3,074,184 | 203,137 | 190,662 | 12,475 | 3,285 | ....... | 2,867,762 | 2,867,762 | ....... |
| 1943...... | 6,993,102 | 557,657 | 521,435 | 36,222 | 21,919 | 0 | 6,413,526 | 6,358,200 | 55,326 |
| 1944...... | 7,992,868 | 740,077 | 692,351 | 47,726 | 36,893 | 10 | 7,215,888 | 7,144,601 | 71,287 |
| 1945...... | 8,266,373 | 835,403 | 772,511 | 62,892 | 56,216 | 44 | 7,374,710 | 7,283,930 | 90,780 |
| 1946...... | 1,889,690 | 257,300 | 240,643 | 16,657 | 9,826 | 18 | 1,622,546 | 1,605,847 | 16,699 |
| 1950...... | 591,487 | 67,784 | 63,375 | 4,409 | 4,760 | 22 | 518,921 | 512,370 | 6,551 |
| 1954...... | 1,403,011 | 116,483 | 110,728 | 5,755 | 11,673 | 52 | 1,274,803 | 1,268,016 | 6,787 |
| 1955...... | 1,107,606 | 111,347 | 106,173 | 5,174 | 10,552 | 48 | 985,659 | 977,943 | 7,716 |
| 1956...... | 1,024,075 | 107,273 | 102,441 | 4,832 | 11,047 | 44 | 905,711 | 897,941 | 7,770 |
| 1957...... | 996,243 | 100,051 | 95,520 | 4,531 | 11,093 | 43 | 885,056 | 877,900 | 7,156 |
| 1958...... | 897,224 | 93,597 | 89,246 | 4,351 | 11,080 | 39 | 792,508 | 785,434 | 7,074 |
| 1959...... | 860,148 | 91,048 | 86,756 | 4,292 | 10,603 | 39 | 758,458 | 750,621 | 7,837 |
| 1960...... | 871,348 | 91,056 | 86,832 | 4,224 | 10,141 | 39 | 770,112 | 761,833 | 8,279 |
| 1961...... | 856,853 | 90,006 | 85,853 | 4,213 | 9,817 | 38 | 756,932 | 748,372 | 8,560 |
| 1962...... | 1,064,647 | 105,225 | 100,920 | 4,305 | 10,777 | 48 | 948,597 | 939,876 | 8,721 |
| 1963...... | 974,070 | 98,622 | 94,810 | 3,812 | 9,640 | 40 | 865,768 | 857,476 | 8,292 |
| 1964...... | 971,384 | 100,640 | 96,905 | 3,735 | 10,193 | 37 | 860,514 | 852,556 | 7,958 |
| 1965...... | 967,049 | 101,812 | 98,029 | 3,783 | 10,285 | 23 | 854,924 | 846,409 | 8,520 |
| 1966...... | 1,197,468 | 106,468 | 102,347 | 4,121 | 11,296 | 22 | 1,079,682 | 1,070,503 | 9,170 |
| 1967...... | 1,440,120 | 127,400 | 122,700 | 4,700 | 16,090 | 34 | 1,296,600 | 1,256,900 | 9,709 |
| 1968...... | 1,567,408 | 145,988 | 139,680 | 6,308 | 20,158 | 27 | 1,401,727 | 1,391,016 | 10,711 |

(a) Represents strength of the active Army, including Philippine Scouts, retired Regular Army personnel on extended active duty, and National Guard and Reserve personnel on extended active duty; excludes U.S. Military Academy cadets, contract surgeons, and National Guard and Reserve personnel not on extended active duty.

(b) Data for 1930 to 1947 include personnel in the Army Air Forces and its predecessors (Air Service and Air Corps).

(c) Includes: Women Doctors, Dentists and Medical Service Corps Officers for 1946 and subsequent years, Women in the Army Nurse Corps for all years, and the Women's Army Corps and Women's Medical Specialists Corps (dieticians, physical therapists and occupational specialists) for 1943 and subsequent years.

(d) Includes Army field clerks and field clerks, Quartermaster Corps as follows: 1925, 377. Act of Congress approved April 27, 1926, directed the appointment as warrant officers, of field clerks still in active service. Includes Flight Officers as follows: 1943, 5,700, 1944, 13,615, 1945, 31,117, 1946, 2,580.

### ARMY EXPENDITURES FOR MILITARY FUNCTIONS (a)
#### (in millions of dollars)

| Fiscal year | Amount | Fiscal year | Amount | Fiscal year | Amount | Fiscal year | Amount |
|---|---|---|---|---|---|---|---|
| 1935..... | 366 | 1947..... | 8,027 | 1955..... | 8,901 | 1962..... | 11,427 |
| 1940..... | 669 | 1949..... | 6,482 | 1956..... | 8,703 | 1963..... | 11,499 |
| 1942..... | 14,805 | 1950..... | 3,985 | 1957..... | 9,063 | 1964..... | 12,050 |
| 1943..... | 42,573 | 1951..... | 7,478 | 1958..... | 9,051 | 1965..... | 11,600 |
| 1944..... | 49,289 | 1952..... | 15,708 | 1959..... | 9,467 | 1966..... | 14,810 |
| 1945..... | 49,750 | 1953..... | 16,241 | 1960..... | 9,392 | 1967..... | 21,012 |
| 1946..... | 27,176 | 1954..... | 12,910 | 1961..... | 10,130 | 1968..... | 25,251 |

(a) Excludes expenditures for all civil functions as defined in "The Budget of the United States Government." Data for fiscal years to 1947 include all Army Air Force expenditures.

---

# U. S. Army Insignia and Chevrons
### Source: Department of the Army

**Grade**    **Insignia**

**General of the Armies**

(General John J. Pershing, the only person to have held this rank, was authorized to prescribe his own insignia, but never wore in excess of four stars. The rank originally was established by Congress for George Washington in 1799, but no record has been found to show that the appointment was made.)

**General of the Army**....Five silver stars fastened together in a circle and the coat of arms of the United States in gold color metal with shield and crest enameled

**General** ................Four silver stars
**Lieutenant General** ....Three silver stars
**Major General** ........Two silver stars
**Brigadier General** .....One silver star
**Colonel** ................Silver eagle
**Lieutenant Colonel** ....Silver oak leaf
**Major** ..................Gold oak leaf
**Captain** ................Two silver bars
**First Lieutenant** ......One silver bar
**Second Lieutenant** ....One gold bar

#### Warrant officers
Grade Four—Silver bar with three enamel brown bands
Grade Three—Silver bar with two enamel brown bands
Grade Two—Gold bar with three enamel brown bands
Grade One—Gold bar with two enamel brown bands

#### Non-commissioned officers
Sergeant Major of the Army (E-9). Three chevrons above the three arcs with a five-pointed star between the chevrons and arcs.

Sergeant Major (E-9). Three chevrons above the three arcs with a five-pointed star between the chevrons and arcs.

First Sergeant (E-8). Three chevrons above three arcs with a lozenge between the chevrons and arcs.

Master Sergeant (E-8). Three chevrons above three arcs.

Platoon Sergeant or Sergeant First Class (E-7). Three chevrons above two arcs.

Staff Sergeant (E-6). Three chevrons above one arc.

Sergeant (E-5). Three chevrons.
Corporal (E-4). Two chevrons.

#### Specialists
Specialist Nine (E-9). Three arcs above the eagle device and two chevrons below.

Specialist Eight (E-8). Three arcs above the eagle device and one chevron below.

Specialist Seven (E-7). Three arcs above the eagle device.

Specialist Six (E-6). Two arcs above the eagle device.

Specialist Five (E-5). One arc above the eagle device.

Specialist Four (E-4). Eagle device only.

#### Other Enlisted
Private First Class (E-3). One chevron above one arc.

Private (E-2). One chevron.
Private (E-1). None.

# U. S. Navy Insignia

**NAVY**
Stripes and corps device are of gold embroidery.
*Stripes*
Fleet Admiral......1 two inch with 4 one-half inch.
Admiral ..........1 two inch with 3 one-half inch.
Vice Admiral......1 two inch with 2 one-half inch.
Rear Admiral......1 two inch with 1 one-half inch.
Commodore
(war time only)..1 two inch.
Captain ..........4 one-half inch.
Commander ......3 one-half inch.
Lieut. Commander..2 one-half inch, with 1 one quarter inch between.
Lieutenant ......2 one-half inch.
Lieutenant (j.g.)...1 one-half inch with 1 one quarter inch above.
Ensign ..........1 one-half inch.
Warrant Officers—One ½″ (¼″ for warrant officer W-1) broken with ½″ intervals of blue as follows:
Chief Warrant Officer W-4—1 break

Chief Warrant Officer W-3—2 breaks, 2″ apart
Chief Warrant Officer W-2—3 breaks, 2″ apart
Warrant Officer W-1—3 breaks, 2″ apart
(on ¼″ gold)
Enlisted personnel....A rating badge worn on the left arm, consisting of a spread eagle and chevrons, with the appropriate specialty centered between.

**MARINE CORPS**
Marine Corps and Army have similar insignia except for color and fewer Marine Corps subdivisions. Its distinctive cap and collar ornament is the combination of the American eagle, anchor and globe.

**COAST GUARD**
Coast Guard insignia follow Navy custom, with certain minor changes such as the officer cap insignia. The Coast Guard shield is worn on both sleeves of officers and on the right sleeve of all enlisted men.

## United States Navy Personnel on Active Duty
Source: Department of the Navy (*Excludes Nurses)

| June 30 | Officers* | Nurses | Enlisted | Off. Cand. | Total |
|---|---|---|---|---|---|
| 1940................. | 13,162 | 442 | 144,824 | 2,569 | 160,997 |
| 1945................. | 320,293 | 11,086 | 2,988,207 | 61,231 | 3,380,817 |
| 1950................. | 42,687 | 1,954 | 331,860 | 5,037 | 381,538 |
| 1955................. | 72,423 | 2,104 | 579,864 | 6,304 | 660,695 |
| 1960................. | 67,456 | 2,103 | 544,040 | 4,385 | 617,984 |
| 1965................. | 75,996 | 1,870 | 587,183 | 6,399 | 671,448 |
| 1966................. | 77,757 | 2,048 | 658,635 | 6,765 | 745,205 |
| 1967................. | 79,574 | 2,328 | 663,831 | 5,886 | 751,619 |
| 1968................. | 81,970 | 2,355 | 673,610 | 6,422 | 764,357 |

## United States Naval Expenditures
Source: Department of the Navy

| Fiscal year | Total amount expended | Shipbuilding, conversion and modernizations | Aircraft and missile procurement | Military construction | All other expenditures |
|---|---|---|---|---|---|
| 1940.............. | $885,769,794 | $328,819,394 | $24,011,998 | $72,503,151 | $460,435,251 |
| 1945.............. | 29,380,421,832 | 7,228,192,871 | 3,541,009,589 | 1,576,096,922 | 17,035,122,450 |
| 1950.............. | 4,065,484,778 | 281,328,056 | 452,723,233 | 86,054,932 | 3,245,378,557 |
| 1955.............. | 9,637,637,835 | 903,303,717 | 1,834,511,038 | 238,631,005 | 6,661,192,075 |
| 1960.............. | 11,848,690,002 | 1,380,031,231 | 2,027,098,025 | 284,928,383 | 8,228,632,362 |
| 1966.............. | 16,514,579,307 | 1,482,321,612 | 2,520,357,140 | 451,006,848 | 12,060,893,707 |
| 1967.............. | 19,291,496,288 | 1,398,414,838 | 3,006,902,022 | 522,638,470 | 14,363,540,958 |
| 1968.............. | 22,106,320,837 | 1,355,850,877 | 3,642,007,920 | 92,966,944 | 17,015,495,096 |

## Marine Corps Personnel on Active Duty
Source: Department of the Navy (Navy Comptroller as of June 30)

| Yr. | Officers | Enl. | Total | Yr. | Officers | Enl. | Total | Yr. | Officers | Enl. | Total |
|---|---|---|---|---|---|---|---|---|---|---|---|
| 1955... | 18,417 | 186,753 | 205,170 | 1965... | 17,258 | 172,955 | 190,213 | 1967... | 23,592 | 261,677 | 285,269 |
| 1960... | 16,203 | 154,242 | 170,621 | 1966... | 20,512 | 241,204 | 261,716 | 1968... | 24,555 | 282,697 | 307,252 |

## Primary U. S. Military Training Centers

### ARMY

| Name—P.O. Address | Zip | Nearest City | Name—P.O. Address | Zip | Nearest City |
|---|---|---|---|---|---|
| Fort Benning, Ga........ | 31905 | Columbus | Fort Knox, Ky........... | 40121 | Louisville |
| Fort Bliss, Texas........ | 79906 | El Paso | Fort Leonard Wood, Mo... | 65475 | Jefferson City |
| Fort Bragg, N. C........ | 28307 | Fayetteville | Fort Lewis, Wash....... | 98433 | Olympia |
| Fort Campbell, Ky....... | 42223 | Clarksville, Tenn. | Fort McClellan, Ala...... | 36205 | Anniston |
| Fort Dix, N. J.......... | 08640 | Trenton | Fort Ord, Calif......... | 93941 | Monterey |
| Fort Gordon, Ga........ | 30905 | Augusta | Fort Polk, La.......... | 71459 | Leesville |
| Fort Huachuca, Ariz.... | 85613 | Tucson | Fort Sam Houston, Tex... | 78234 | San Antonio |
| Fort Jackson, S. C...... | 29207 | Columbia | Fort Sill, Okla........ | 73503 | Lawton |

### NAVY

| Name | Zip | Nearest City | Name | Zip | Nearest City |
|---|---|---|---|---|---|
| Bainbridge, Md. (Waves).. | 21905 | Baltimore | San Diego, Calif......... | 92136 | San Diego |
| Great Lakes, Ill.......... | 60088 | Waukegan | Orlando, Fla`.......... | 32813 | Orlando |

### MARINE CORPS

| Name | Zip | Nearest City | Name | Zip | Nearest City |
|---|---|---|---|---|---|
| Camp LeJeune, N. C..... | 28542 | Fayetteville | Camp Pendleton, Calif.... | 92055 | Los Angeles |
| Parris Island, S. C...... | 29905 | Beaufort | San Diego, Calif......... | 92140 | San Diego |

### AIR FORCE

| Name | Zip | Nearest City | Name | Zip | Nearest City |
|---|---|---|---|---|---|
| Maxwell AFB, Ala........ | 36112 | Montgomery | MacDill AFB, Fla........ | 33608 | Tampa |
| Randolph AFB, Tex...... | 78148 | San Antonio | Nellis AFB, Nev........ | 89110 | Las Vegas |
| Edwards AFB, Calif..... | 93523 | Rosamond | Pope AFB, N. C........ | 28308 | Fayetteville |
| Eglin AFB, Fla.......... | 32542 | Valparaiso | Shaw AFB, S. C........ | 29152 | Sumter |
| Kirtland AFB, N. M..... | 87117 | Albuquerque | Vandenberg AFB, Calif... | 93437 | Lompoc |
| Holloman AFB, N. M..... | 88330 | Alamogordo | Keesler AFB, Miss........ | 39534 | Biloxi |
| Lackland AFB, Tex...... | 78236 | San Antonio | | | |

## Armed Services Appoint Senior Enlisted Adviser

The U. S. Army, Navy and Air Force in 1966-67 each created a new position of senior enlisted adviser whose primary job is to represent the point of view of his services' enlisted men and women on matters of welfare, morale and any problem concerning enlisted personnel. The senior adviser will have direct access to the military chief of his branch of service and policy-making bodies. The Marine Corps has had such a position for many years.

The senior enlisted adviser for each of the four Military Departments is:

**Army**—Sgt. Major of the Army George W. Dunaway.

**Navy**—Master Chief Gunner's Mate Delbert D. Black.

**Air Force**—Chief Master Sgt. of the Air Force Paul W. Airey.

**Marines**—Sgt. Major Herbert J. Sweet.

# United States Air Force

Source: Department of the Air Force

The Army Air Forces were started Aug. 1, 1907, as the Aeronautical Division of the Signal Corps, U. S. Army. The division consisted of one officer and two enlisted men, and it was more than a year before it carried out its first mission in an airplane of its own. When the U. S. entered World War I (April 6, 1917), the Aviation Service, as it was called then, had 55 planes and 65 officers, only 35 of whom were fliers. On the day the Japanese struck at Pearl Harbor (Dec. 7, 1941), the Army Air Forces, as they had been renamed six months previously, had 10,329 planes, of which only 2,846 were suited for combat service. But when the Army's air arm reached its peak during World War II (in July, 1944), it had 79,908 of all types of aircraft and (in May, 1945) 43,248 combat aircraft and (in March, 1944) 2,411,294 officers and enlisted men. The Air Force was established under the Armed Services Unification Act of July 26, 1947.

## USAF PERSONNEL AT HOME AND OVERSEAS—OFFICERS AND ENLISTED MEN

| June 30 | Continental U. S. | Overseas | Total | June 30 | Continental U. S. | Overseas | Total |
|---|---|---|---|---|---|---|---|
| 1940 | 40,229 | 10,936 | 51,165 | 1962 | 664,752 | 219,273 | 884,025 |
| 1945 | 1,153,373 | 1,128,886 | 2,282,259 | 1963 | 659,194 | 210,237 | 869,431 |
| 1950 | 317,816 | 93,461 | 411,277 | 1964 | 655,605 | 200,295 | 855,900 |
| 1955 | 689,635 | 270,311 | 959,946 | 1965 | 635,430 | 189,232 | 824,662 |
| 1957* | 651,674 | 268,161 | 919,835 | 1966 | 641,957 | 245,396 | 887,353 |
| 1960[1] | 607,383 | 207,369 | 814,752 | 1967 | 617,632 | 279,862 | 897,494 |
| 1961 | 617,020 | 204,131 | 821,151 | 1968 | 616,163 | 285,035 | 901,198 |

*Since 1957 continental U. S. includes Air Force Academy Cadets as follows: (1957) 504; (1960) 1,949; (1961) 2,267; (1962) 2,520; (1963) 2,660; (1964) 2,838; (1965) 2,907; (1966) 3,152; (1967) 3,361; (1968) 3,652.

[1]Since 1960 Overseas includes Alaska and Hawaii. All figures include Mobilized Personnel. Officers 2,158, enlisted 13,484.

## USAF MILITARY PERSONNEL

| June 30 | Officers & Airmen | Male Commissioned Officers | | | | Total Warrant Officers |
|---|---|---|---|---|---|---|
| | | USAF (reg.) & RA | USAFR & ORC | ANG & NG | AFUS & AUS | |
| 1950 | 411,277 | 19,735 | 33,585 | 14 | 55 | 2,085 |
| 1955 | 959,946 | 23,463 | 105,587 | 984 | 2 | 3,961 |
| 1960 | 814,752 | 49,584 | 72,115 | 248 | 3 | 4,069 |
| 1964 | 855,900 | 59,610 | 67,143 | 330 | 67 | 2,808 |
| 1965 | 824,662 | 62,076 | 62,537 | 280 | 54 | 2,532 |
| 1966 | 887,353 | 62,146 | 66,158 | 215 | 126 | 2,079 |
| 1967 | 897,494 | 62,876 | 72,297 | 151 | 161 | 1,689 |
| 1968 | 901,198 | 64,595 | 73,519 | 1,392 | 185 | 1,367 |

### FEMALE COMMISSIONED OFFICERS, AND ENLISTED PERSONNEL

| June 30 | Female commissioned officers | | | | Female WO | Enlisted personnel | | |
|---|---|---|---|---|---|---|---|---|
| | Total | WAF | Nurses | WMSC[1] | | Total | Male | Female |
| 1950 | 1,525 | 303 | 1,143 | 79 | 7 | 354,271 | 350,489 | 3,782 |
| 1960 | 3,858 | 679 | 3,020 | 159 | 5 | 685,063 | 679,412 | 5,651 |
| 1965 | 4,099 | 708 | 3,185 | 206 | 1 | 690,177 | 685,436 | 4,741 |
| 1966 | 4,189 | 696 | 3,271 | 222 | ........ | 756,629 | 751,579 | 5,050 |
| 1967 | 4,670 | 762 | 3,678 | 230 | ........ | 762,009 | 756,821 | 5,188 |
| 1968 | 4,991 | 893 | 3,863 | 235 | ........ | 761,507 | 755,384 | 6,123 |

[1]Since 1957 Includes Male Nurses and Male Medical Specialists.

## Military Units, U. S. Army and Air Force

**Army units. Squad.** In infantry usually ten men under a staff sergeant. **Platoon.** Small military unit usually under a lieutenant. **Company.** Headquarters and three more platoons under a captain. **Battalion.** (Battalion-size unit in the cavalry is a squadron.) Headquarters and three or more companies (Company in the artillery is a battery; in the cavalry it is a troop), under a lieutenant colonel. **Squadron.** Headquarters and three or more troops of cavalry under a colonel (in time of war the Infantry Brigade is commanded by the brigadier general). **Division.** Headquarters and three infantry brigades with artillery and auxiliary troops under a major general. **Army Corps.** Two to five divisions with corps troops under a lieutenant general. **Army.** Headquarters and two or more corps with auxiliary troops under a general.

**Air Force Units. Flight.** Small components of a squadron organized for special purpose such as medical evacuation flights. **Squadron.** The basic organized unit of the Air Force, used by operational as well as support forces but not limited by numbers of personnel assigned; two to three tactical squadrons are assigned to a tactical wing. **Group.** Terminology used for special tactical forces and for many support elements. They do not necessarily have subordinate units assigned. **Wing.** Used for tactical and support forces. A tactical wing usually has two to three operational squadrons assigned. **Division.** An organizational component of operational numbered Air Forces consisting of two to three wings, also used to designate numerous support and research components. **Air Force.** An intermediate echelon of command directly under the headquarters of a large operational command, usually with four to seven subordinate divisions. **Major command.** A major subdivision of the Air Force that is assigned a major segment of the USAF mission, usually two to four subordinate Air Force elements in operational command.

# National Guard of the United States

Source: National Guard Bureau, Washington, D.C. 20310

The National Guard of the United States originated with the Old North Regiment of the Colonial Militia in Massachusetts in 1636. It is the oldest military force in the country and has participated in all U.S. wars and conflicts from the Revolutionary War to the Vietnam war.

Today the Army and Air National Guard total over 450,000 men, serving in over 3,790 Army and Air National Guard units in more than 2,700 communities in all 50 States, Puerto Rico and the District of Columbia.

By act of Congress, the Guard is the primary reserve of the U. S. Army and Air Force. In peacetime, it is commanded by the State governors and serves in State emergencies, disasters, and civil disturbances.

The Army National Guard as of June 30, 1968, had Federal equipment and vehicles valued at $1.6 billion and a Federal budget appropriation of approximately $89,000,000. The Air National Guard had Federal equipment and aircraft valued at $2 billion and a budget of about $370,670,000. The States provide substantial support to the Guard each year in various types of indirect support such as donation of land, police and fire protection, and maintenance of roads.

Besides being a reserve force available for war and civil emergencies, the Guard is now a full-time partner in the air defense network in the NIKE Hercules missile sites around key cities and in the fighter-interceptor planes and pilots on round-the-clock runway alert.

The National Guard is administered by the National Guard Bureau, a joint office of the Departments of the Army and the Air Force, in the Pentagon. Chief of the Bureau is Major General Winston P. Wilson of Arkansas, first Air National Guard general to hold the office.

# United States Military Academy, West Point, N. Y.

The United States Military Academy is located on the Hudson River some fifty miles from New York City. The service rendered to the nation by the Academy has been widely acclaimed during its 167 years in existence. Its graduates are loyal to its ideals of "Duty, Honor, Country."

The Academy was established on March 16, 1802 with the first class, numbering 10 cadets, entering on July 4, 1802. West Point has been a military post since Jan. 20, 1778.

Requirements for admission to the Military Academy differ somewhat from those for admission to a civilian college in that each prospective cadet must first be designated a candidate from one of the sources of nomination listed below. Usually the candidate obtains his nomination either from the Representative in Congress from his Congressional district or from one of his Senators.

Admission to the Military Academy may be gained only by appointment to one of the cadetships authorized by law. Graduation of the senior class normally leaves about 1000 vacant cadetships each year and candidates may be nominated for these vacancies only during the year preceding the admission day in the first week in July. The cadetships authorized are allocated among the various sources of nomination as follows:

## CONGRESSIONAL

| | |
|---|---:|
| 435 Representatives (5 each) | 2175 |
| 100 Senators (5 each) | 500 |
| Other: | |
| Vice Presidential | 5 |
| District of Columbia | 5 |
| Canal Zone | 1 |
| Puerto Rico | 6 |
| Guam, Virgin Islands, American Samoa | 1 |

## COMPETITIVE

| | | |
|---|---|---:|
| Army: | | |
| Regular Components | Annually | 85 |
| Reserve Components | Annually | 85 |
| Presidential | Annually | 100 |
| Sons of Veterans | Annually | 20 |
| Honor Military and Honor Naval Schools | Annually | 13 |
| Sons of Medal of Honor Winners | | Unlimited |
| Foreign Cadets | | 24 |

(The number of cadetships under the competitive category shown above will not be fully implemented until the early 1970s.)

For each vacancy from a State or Congressional District 10 candidates may be nominated by one of two methods. Either the Principal-Alternate method whereby candidates are listed in order of Priority as Principal, 1st, 2nd, 3rd, 4th, 5th Alternate etc., or the Congressional Competitive method whereby the best qualified nominee is selected by the Academic Board, USMA may be used. Selection of candidates is left to Senator or Representative.

Candidates must be U. S. citizens, and must not have reached 22nd birthday, good moral character, and must never have been married. After being designated candidates, they take three types of examination: academic, medical, and physical aptitude. The academic qualification for admission is determined by an analysis of the candidate's scholastic record and his performance on tests of the College Entrance Examination Board. The tests are: scholastic aptitude, achievement in English composition and mathematics.

Congressional candidates may offer for admission their scores on any of the College Board examinations; all competitive candidates, however, must take tests at specified dates in the year prior to entrance. All candidates also must qualify in a thorough medical examination and a test of physical aptitude designed to measure strength, agility, endurance, and muscular coordination. Upon receipt of a nomination, the candidate may immediately take the medical examination and thereby satisfy the medical entrance requirement. All three examinations are given in December, January and March at designated military installations located in this country and in certain foreign countries. Candidates should consult the USMA catalogue for test dates.

Prospective cadets who completed their entrance examinations are notified of the results of the examinations and their eligibility for admission beginning Jan. 1 thru Apr. 15. Those fully qualified and for whom a vacancy exists report to West Point in the first week in July. Upon admission each cadet takes the oath of allegiance and agrees to serve as a commissioned officer for not less than 5 years immediately following graduation.

All expenses necessary to the education and training of cadets at the U. S. Military Academy are borne by the Government. Cadets, as members of the Regular Army, receive pay and allowances as provided by law (currently in excess of $2,000 per year, plus rations). From this pay, cadets are required to purchase uniforms, textbooks, and some incidental items. To defray the cost of the initial issues of uniforms and equipment a deposit of $300 is requested.

Summer periods are primarily devoted to practical military instruction but approximately 4 weeks' leave is granted cadets each summer after completion of their first year. The academic year runs from September through May. Upon successful completion of the 4-year course, the graduate receives the B.S. degree and is commissioned a 2d Lieutenant in the Regular Army.

In addition to U. S. citizens, the Secretary of the Army is authorized to permit not exceeding four Filipinos (one for each entering class), to be designated by the President of the Republic of the Philippines, to receive instruction at the Academy.

The act of June 26, 1946 (as amended) authorizes the President of the United States to permit not exceeding 20 persons at a time from the American republics to receive instruction at the Academy, provided not more than three from any one country are there at the same time.

Citizens of other foreign countries have been permitted from time to time to attend the Military Academy upon specific authorization of the United States Congress in each case but are not entitled by reason of their graduation therefrom to appointment to any office or position in the United States.

The Superintendent of the Military Academy is Maj. Gen. S. W. Koster, U. S. A., the Dean of the Academic Board is Brig. Gen. John R. Jannarone, U. S. A., the Commandant of Cadets is Brig. Gen. Bernard W. Rogers, U. S. A.

Requests for information and for the Academy catalog should be sent to the Director of Admissions, U. S. Military Academy, West Point, N. Y. 10996.

# United States Naval Academy at Annapolis

The United States Naval Academy was established as the Naval School Oct. 10, 1845 at Annapolis, Maryland. It was renamed the U. S. Naval Academy in 1850. A four-year course was adopted a year later. From the first, the faculty has been composed about equally of officers and civilians.

The Academy is the undergraduate college of the U. S. Navy. Its purpose is to educate and train young men for careers in the naval service. Leadership and character development and physical fitness are stressed. The Academy is accredited by the Middle States Association of Colleges and Secondary Schools. Graduates of its 4-year course are awarded the Bachelor of Science degree and are commissioned ensigns in the U. S. Navy or second lieutenants in the U. S. Marine Corps.

The head and Superintendent is a Rear Admiral. A navy captain commands the 4,200-man Brigade of Midshipmen. The Academic Dean and head of the academic program is a civilian. Religious activities are headed by a senior navy chaplain.

The basic curriculum consists of a core curriculum (85%) devoted to basic courses in science, naval science, engineering, social sciences, and the humanities plus electives (15%) in the area of the midshipman's selected minor or major (23 minors/ 23 majors offered). Provision is made for validation of previous college-level work. In addition,

superior students may carry more than the required number of courses. Over 300 electives are offered.

Selected seniors, Trident Scholars, pursue independent study and research programs under a faculty advisor. In addition, graduate-level courses are offered which are creditable toward advanced degrees following graduation.

Majors offered include: Aerospace Engineering, Mechanical Engineering, Naval Engineering, History, Literature, Foreign Affairs, Politics and Economics, French, German, Italian, Portuguese, Russsian, Spanish, Applied Mathematics, Theoretical Mathematics, Oceanography, Management, Operations Analysis, Chemistry, Physics, Applied Science, Electrical Science, and Systems Engineering (Weapons).

To have basic eligibility for admission a candidate must be: A citizen of the United States; of good moral character; at least 17 and not yet 22 years of age on July 1st of their entering year; a high school graduate or its equivalent; and unmarried and not previously married.

If basically eligible, candidates must: Obtain a nomination; qualify academically; qualify medically and physically; be selected for appointment. They may qualify academically by submitting an acceptable secondary record and acceptable scores on College Entrance Examination Board aptitude

(verbal and math) and achievement (Eng. composition and either Math I or II) tests, or, in the case of certain Congressional nominees, by presenting an acceptable secondary record and an acceptable transcript for one year of college.

Physically, candidates must be at least 5'4" and not over 6'6" tall. They must have 20/20 vision in both eyes. (The Academy will consider granting a limited number of waivers to 6'8" in height and to 20/100 in vision (correctable to 20/20 for candidates with outstanding academic and leadership accomplishments.)

The primary avenues to selection for appointment as midshipmen follow:

85, yearly, from regular armed forces personnel.
85, yearly, from Navy and Marine Corps reserves.
100, annually, to sons of regular members of the armed forces, active, retired, or deceased.
150, annually, selected from qualified congressional alternates.
20, annually, from honor military schools (10) and NROTC units, contract students only (10).
40 sons of deceased or disabled veterans may be at the Academy at any one time. Eligibility is limited to sons of veterans killed in action, or dead or with service-connected disability rated at 100% from wounds, injuries, or disease contracted in or aggravated by active service.

Congressman, the Vice President, the District (D. C.) Commissioner, and the Resident Commissioner of Puerto Rico may each have 5 midshipmen at the Academy at any one time. Congressmen may nominate 10 candidates for each vacancy. Over half of the 1,350 appointments as midshipmen made annually originate from these sources.

In addition there are limited numbers of appointments available (annually) from the Philippines (4); the Canal Zone (1); Virgin Islands/ Guam/American Samoa (1); and the American republics (20).

The President appoints the best-qualified of the 40 sons of deceased veterans, and the 100 best-qualified sons of officers and enlisted men in the regular Armed Services. He also appoints sons of Medal of Honor holders.

The Secretary of the Navy awards the 170 (85+ 85) appointments to regular and reserve personnel, and the 150 to alternate congressional nominees,

all on a competitive, best-qualified basis. He may also make a limited number of additional appointments each year, to bring the Brigade to authorized strength, from among qualified congressional and competitive nominees, all on a best-qualified basis.

On being appointed a midshipman, candidates must subscribe (with consent of parent or guardian if a minor) to serve for at least six years (5 on active duty) following their graduation and commissioning. In addition, each civilian appointee assumes a separate 6-year military obligation under the Universal Military Service and Training Act under which he may be transferred to the Naval or Marine Corps Reserve if separated from the Academy prior to graduation. Those having an enlisted or officer status prior to appointment and who are separated prior to graduation must fulfill the military obligation assumed at the time of their initial enlistment, induction or appointment. Academy time counts toward fulfillment of total military obligation, but does not serve in place of required service under draft.

Tuition, board and lodging, and medical care are provided. Midshipmen receive $171.10 per month for books, uniforms, and personal needs. Midshipmen may not marry while at the Academy.

For full information write: Dean of Admissions, Naval Academy, Annapolis, Md. 21402 or the Chief of Naval Personnel, Navy Dept., Wash., D. C. 20370.

## Naval Academy Museum

The Naval Academy Museum is headed by a navy captain reporting directly to the Superintendent. The Museum serves as inspiration to the men of the Brigade by providing tangible evidence of some of the most glorious episodes in the nation's history. In addition, its collection of more than 50,000 items provides an important reference source for the study of naval history by faculty, midshipmen, and other interested scholars. Among the many original documents are the contracts for building our first naval ships; letters of John Paul Jones; and memorials of steamboat inventors John Fitch, James Rumsey, and Robert Fulton. In addition, the museum is well-known for its distinguished Rogers Collection of Ship Models; seascapes by Edward Moran; and the Beverly R. Robinson collection of over 1,000 historic naval prints.

# United States Air Force Academy

The United States Air Force Academy, the nation's newest service academy, is located at the foot of the Rampart Range of the Rocky Mountains near Colorado Springs, Colo. Established April 1, 1954, the Academy occupied temporary quarters on Lowry Air Force Base in Denver till moved to the permanent campus in 1958. The first class of cadets was graduated in June, 1959.

Most of the Academy's graduates have gone on to Air Force pilot training. A percentage of each class has entered institutions of higher learning for graduate work in technical and professional fields.

To enter the Academy immediately after graduation from high school, a student should apply to nominating authorities during the spring months of his junior year. To qualify, an applicant must be at least 17 and not yet 22 on July 1 of the year he enters the Academy; be a male citizen of the United States, morally and physically fit, and must never have been married.

A resident of the United States who meets the eligibility requirements may apply for a nomination by writing to a U. S. Senator from his state or a U. S. Representative from his Congressional district. In such a letter the applicant should state briefly his qualifications, parents' name, place of residence, and educational background. Approximately 85% of the vacancies in each class are reserved for Congressional nominees.

Each member of Congress may nominate one principal and 9 alternate candidates for each existing vacancy. If the principal candidate qualifies on the entrance examinations, he will be selected. If he does not pass the examination, the

first qualified alternate will be chosen or a Senator or Representative may authorize the Academy to select the best qualified of his 10 candidates on a competitive basis.

Candidates are selected under several other nominating categories, primarily sons of career members of the armed forces and members of the Regular and Reserve components of the Air Force.

All candidates will be required to take the following examinations, usually scheduled from December through April: physical aptitude; the College Entrance Examination Board tests; and the Air Force medical examination.

Cadets spend four years at the Air Force Academy engaging in scientific and liberal arts studies, along with military training. Upon graduation they receive a Bachelor of Science degree, with a major in one or more of 28 fields of study, and a second lieutenant's commission in the Regular Air Force. Those physically qualified may elect to undergo a course in pilot or navigator training after graduation.

Cadets receive their education, quarters, medical and dental care at Government expense. In addition, they receive $171.60 per month for books, clothing, and personal expenses.

The Cadets in the first class chose the falcon as the mascot of the Academy.

Superintendent of the Academy is Lt. Gen. Thomas S. Moorman, USAF. Commandant of Cadets is Brig. Gen. Robin Olds, USAF. Dean of the Faculty is Brig. Gen. William T. Woodyard, USAF.

Requests for catalog and information should go to Registrar, U. S. Air Force Academy, Colo. 80840.

# U. S. Coast Guard Academy

The United States Coast Guard Academy, New London, Conn., was founded in 1876. The administration building is named Hamilton Hall in honor of Alexander Hamilton, first Secretary of the Treasury, who founded the Coast Guard (1790).

The Academy's four-year course embraces engineering, military science, cultural and other professional subjects. Cadets are paid $1,823.40 a year with rations and are credited with the sum of $600 to defray the cost of their initial clothing and equipment, this sum to be deducted subsequently

from their pay. In addition each cadet upon appointment is required to deposit $300 with the Superintendent of the Academy to help defray additional clothing and equipment costs. Cadets are appointed solely on the basis of a nationwide competition which begins with December college board tests.

Upon graduation, a Cadet receives a bachelor of science degree and is commissioned by the President as an Ensign in the Coast Guard, receiving the same pay and allowances as an officer of similar rank in the other armed services.

# The United States Marine Corps in 1968

On Jan. 1, 1968, Gen. Leonard F. Chapman, Jr., became Commandant of the Marine Corps.

By September, Corps strength was more than 307,000 with approximately 84,000 Marines in Vietnam. In their 4th year of fighting in Vietnam, Marines fought numerous sustained actions against Vietcong and North Vietnamese (NVA) forces in the northern provinces of South Vietnam. They inflicted heavy losses in the enemy-initiated Tet Offensive, notably in the battle of Hue. The 70-day action at the Khe Sanh prevented an estimated 20,000 North Vietnamese soldiers from gaining free access to the northern provinces. In February, because of the enemy's increased activity, the 27th Marine Regiment was deployed from Camp Pendleon to Vietnam temporarily. In August, Marines crossed the DMZ for the first time since July of 1967 in pursuit of fleeing NVA troops. As of September, 14 Marines had earned the Medal of Honor for heroism.

The Marines in Vietnam were members of the III Marine Amphibious Force (III MAF), comprised of the 1st and 3rd Marine Division reinforced by part of the 5th Marine Division, the heavily 1st Marine Aircraft Wing, and a Force Logistics Command. III MAF was the major part of Fleet Marine Force, Pacific (FMFPac), headquartered in Hawaii. Other FMPac subordinate commands included the Okinawa-based 9th Marine Amphibious Brigade, which, in turn, was the parent unit for Special Landing Forces based aboard Navy 7th Fleet ships in the China Sea; the 1st Marine Brigade in Hawaii; and the California-based 3rd Marine Aircraft Wing, 5th Marine Division, and Force Troops, FMFPac (combat support units).

The Marine Corps' second complete air/ground team is Fleet Marine Force, Atlantic (FMFLant),

headquartered in Norfolk. Va. Its major elements include the 2nd Marine Division; 2nd Marine Aircraft Wing; and Force Troops, FMFLant, all based in North Carolina. FMFLant landing teams are constantly deployed with Navy ships in the Mediterranean and Caribbean, and as a defense force for the Naval Base, Guantanamo Bay, Cuba.

Marines returning from Vietnam raised the combat-experience level of the Corps and of the 48,000-man Marine Corps Reserve. The 4th Marine Aircraft Wing is the air/ground team of the Marine Corps Reserve, available for combat if called upon.

Recruit Depots at Parris Island, S.C., and San Diego, Calif, gave approximately 89,000 recruits 8 weeks of "boot camp." At the major Marine Corps bases—Camp Lejeune, N. C. and Camp Pendleton, Calif.—new Marines received an additional two to 4 weeks of individual combat, basic specialist, and Vietnam-oriented training. Officer candidate and basic officer classes were conducted at the Marine Corps Development and Education Command, Quantico, Va., and 2,881 officer candidates were commissioned.

Basic flight training was given at Naval Air Stations in Pensacola, Fla., and Corpus Christi, Tex.; and, since 1967, with all Air Force Air Training Command bases. A total of 665 Marine student pilots received their wings in 1968. In addition, Marine pilots received helicopter flight training at Army training bases in Texas and Georgia. Advanced aviation training was provided by Marine Aircraft Wings and Marine Air Stations at Cherry Point, N.C., and El Toro, Calif., and by the Marine Air Reserve Training Command at Glenview, Ill.

In 1968, a formal Computer Sciences School was established at Marine Corps Development and Education Command, Quantico.

# United States Merchant Marine Academy

The United States Merchant Marine Academy—the fifth permanent Federal Academy for officer training—has an authorized peacetime complement of approximately 1000 Midshipmen from every state in the Union, Puerto Rico, District of Columbia, Canal Zone, Guam, American Samoa, and the Virgin Islands.

On completion of courses, graduates receive their original Merchant Marine license as deck or engineer officers qualified to serve in any ship in the United States Merchant Marine. Graduates also receive B.S. degrees and commissions as Ensigns in the U. S. Naval Reserve.

Appointments to the Academy are governed by a state and territory quota based on population. All candidates must be nominated by a member of Congress to compete for appointment, possess a minimum of 15 units from accredited schools, qualify in a national competitive examination, and pass a Naval Officer physical examination and security investigation. Each Member of Congress may nominate up to 10 candidates for each class.

A candidate must be an unmarried male citizen

of the U. S., not less than 17 years of age and not over 22 by July 1 of the year in which admission is sought. He must be of good moral character, sound constitution and not less than 5 ft. 4 in. or more than 6 ft. 6 in. in height. A candidate for appointment as a deck midshipman must have minimum uncorrected visual acuity of at least 20/40 in one eye and 20/70 in the other; as an engineering midshipman he must have at least 20/50 in one eye and 20/70 in the other. All candidates must have corrected visual acuity of 20/20 in each eye and normal color perception. Waivers for failure to meet physical requirements will not be granted.

Under Federal legislation the Academy is authorized to admit students from American republics for the four-year program. Enrollment is limited to 12 students at any time.

The Academy grounds at Kings Point, N. Y., covers 65 acres on the north shore of Long Island. The Superintendent of the Academy is Rear Admiral Gordon McLintock, USMS.

Requests for further information should be addressed to the Admission Office, U. S. Merchant Marine Academy, Kings Point, N. Y. 11024.

# Personal Salutes and Honors

The national salute is 21 guns. It is also the salute to a national flag. The salute to the Union, commemorative of the Declaration of Independence and consisting of one gun for each State, will be fired at noon on July 4 at every post provided with suitable artillery.

A 21-gun salute on arrival and departure, with 4 ruffles and flourishes, is rendered to the President of the United States, to an ex-President and to a President-elect. The national anthem or *Hail to the Chief*, as appropriate, is played for the President, and the national anthem for the others. A 21-gun salute on arrival and departure, with 4 ruffles and flourishes, also is rendered to the sovereign or chief of state of a foreign country or a member of a reigning royal family; the national anthem of his or her country is played. The music is considered an inseparable part of the salute and will immediately follow the ruffles and flourishes without pause.

| Rank | Salute—guns | | Ruffles flourishes | Music |
|---|---|---|---|---|
| | Arrive | Leave | | |
| Vice President of United States, Speaker of House | 19 | .. | 4 | March |
| American or foreign ambassador | 19 | .. | 4 | Nat. anthem, of official |
| Premier or prime minister | 19 | .. | 4 | Nat. anthem of official |
| Secretary of Defense, Army, Navy or Air Force | 19 | 19 | 4 | March |
| Other Cabinet members, Senate President pro tempore, Governor, or Chief Justice of U. S. | 19 | .. | 4 | March |
| Chairman, Joint Chiefs of Staff | 19 | 19 | 4 | General's |
| Army Chief of Staff, Chief of Naval Operations, Air Force Chief of Staff, Marine Commandant | 19 | 19 | 4 | or |
| Army General; Air Force General; Fleet Admiral | 19 | 19 | 4 | Admiral's |
| Generals, Admirals | 17 | 17 | 4 | March |
| Assistant Secretaries of Defense, Army, Navy or Air Force | 17 | 17 | 4 | March |
| Chairman of a Committee of Congress | 17 | .. | 4 | March |

**Other salutes** (on arrival only) include 15 guns for American envoys or ministers and foreign envoys or ministers accredited to the United States; 15 guns for a lieutenant general or vice admiral; 13 guns for a major general or rear admiral; 13 guns for American ministers resident and ministers resident accredited to the U. S.; 11 guns for a brigadier general or commodore; 11 guns for American charges d'affaires and like officials accredited to U. S.; and 11 guns for consuls general accredited to U. S.

# Women's Branches of the U. S. Military Service

## WOMEN'S ARMY CORPS

Colonel Elizabeth P. Hoisington, GS, Director, Department of the Army, Pentagon, Wash., D. C.

The Women's Army Corps, an outgrowth of the WAAC in World War II, was established as a component of the Regular Army and Army Reserve by Congress in 1948. The WAC makes available to the Army volunteer womanpower, trained in noncombat occupational skills to support the peacetime forces and to serve as a base upon which use of the nation's womanpower could be rapidly expanded in time of emergency. To be eligible for membership, applicants must be U. S. citizens (or have been lawfully admitted for permanent residence), have no dependents under 18 and meet certain specific standards. Enlistment is open to women between the ages of 18 to 34 inclusive, who have high school diplomas or equivalent. Students in their junior year of college may apply for the 4-week College Junior summer training program. Outstanding students of the program may be further selected for participation during their senior year of college in the Student Officer Program. Graduates of accredited colleges and universities, ages 20 to 30, may apply for direct appointment and active duty as officers. Enlisted women may also become officers through attendance at Officer Candidate School. Basic training for officers and enlisted women is given at the U. S. WAC Center and School, Fort McClellan, Alabama. In addition, WAC members receive advanced training along with men in the Army Service Schools.

## ARMY NURSE CORPS

Colonel Anna Mae Hays, Chief, Army Nurse Corps, Office of The Surgeon General, Department of the Army, Main Navy Building, Washington, D. C., 20315.

The Army Nurse Corps, established in 1901 as a part of the Army Medical Service, is the oldest of the women's services in the Armed Forces. An officer corps of registered professional nurses, its proud history includes significant and courageous contributions to our Nation in two world wars and in the Korean and Vietnamese Conflicts. Army nurses serve in ranks from second lieutenant to colonel, based upon qualifications and length of service. Male nurses have been commissioned in the Corps since 1955.

Graduates of hospital or university schools of nursing accredited by the National League for Nursing and/or acceptable to The Surgeon General, who are currently registered to practice nursing in one state of the United States or in Puerto Rico may apply for a commission provided they are less than 35 years of age and U. S. citizens or have been admitted for permanent residence.

The Registered Nurse Student Program is available to nurses who can complete requirements for a baccalaureate or higher degree within 24 months. Participants receive pay and allowances of a commissioned officer and are obligated to serve on active duty for a period not to exceed three years.

The Army Student Nurse Program offers financial assistance to students enrolled in a hospital or university school of nursing. Participants in hospital programs in nursing may receive a maximum of 12 months financial assistance and are obligated to serve two years as an Army Nurse Corps officer following licensure to practice nursing. Participants in university programs of nursing may receive a maximum of 24 months of financial assistance. These participants are commissioned as officers six months prior to graduation and following graduation and licensure and are obligated to serve as Army Nurse Corps officers for a period not to exceed three years.

The Walter Reed Army Institute of Nursing Program offers a unique opportunity to a limited number of high school graduates annually to acquire a baccalaureate degree in nursing. Selected candidates enroll in an accredited college of their choice for the first two years and transfer to the University of Maryland School of Nursing for the final two years to complete the requirements for a bachelor of science degree and obtain state licensure. Candidates are commissioned second lieutenants in the Army Nurse Corps and incur a three year obligation to serve on active duty.

Educational opportunities for Army Nurse Corps officers on active duty are available in advanced clinical specialization and education through pro-

fessional programs, postgraduate short courses and workshops conducted at military installations and civilian institutions.

Army nurses serve throughout the world wherever American troops are stationed.

## ARMY MEDICAL SPECIALIST CORPS

Colonel Mary Lipscomb Hamrick, Chief, Army Medical Specialist Corps, Office of the Surgeon General, Dept. of the Army, Wash., D. C. 20315.

The Women's Medical Specialist Corps was established as a Regular Army component of the Medical Department in 1947. The name was changed to Army Medical Specialist Corps in 1955, when male dietitians, physical and occupational therapists were authorized for its Reserve Section. Regular Army commissions were established for male officers in 1966.

Direct commissions are available to qualified U. S. citizens with a bachelor's degree, who have completed the required specialty training and are under 35. Applicants with academic degrees may enroll for professional training courses offered by the Army Medical Dept. The dietetic internship and physical therapy course take 12 months; a 9-month clinical affiliation program in occupational therapy is available to students who have completed the didactic portion at an approved school.

Financial assistance during the last 2 years in approved colleges is available to qualified students in dietetic and occupational therapy courses. Participants are commissioned in the AMSC on graduation, and serve on active duty for 3 or 4 years.

Summer practicums, with no service obligation incurred, are available to college students in home economics, physical and occupational therapy courses at selected Army hospitals.

AMSC officers serve in Army hospitals in the United States and overseas.

## NAVY AND NAVAL RESERVE

Capt. Rita Lenihan, Assistant Chief of Naval Personnel for Women and Director of the WAVES, Bureau of Naval Personnel, Navy Department, Washington, D. C. 20370.

WAVES is the popular name for the women in the United States Navy.

Women officers in the Navy must hold a baccalaureate degree to qualify for a commission and are required to serve on active duty for two years. They are assigned to duty in the Naval Shore Establishment in the same fields in which male officers serve, including personnel management, comptrollership, computer programming, intelligence and logistics. Staff officers (Medical Corps, Supply Corps, Medical Service Corps and Judge Advocate General Corps) are assigned duty in their specialties.

Enlisted women in the Navy must be a high school graduate and enlist for at least 3 years. There are over 20 different ratings open to enlisted women, including such specialties as: air traffic control, data processing, electronics, journalism, photography, radio and communications, weather forecasting, and yeoman (secretarial) duties.

Assignment of WAVES is made interchangeably with Navy men, excepting duties at sea. WAVES may not be assigned to duty aboard Navy ships other than hospital ships and transports, nor may they serve in aircraft engaged in combat missions. They are, however, assigned to duty overseas.

All provisions of law relating to pay, money allowances, leave, and other benefits applicable to male personnel also apply to women.

## NURSE CORPS, USN AND USNR

Captain Veronica M. Bulshefski, NC, USN, Director, Navy Nurse Corps, Bureau of Medicine and Surgery, Navy Department, Washington, D. C.

Navy Nurse Corps officers provide nursing care of patients, supervise and instruct hospital corpsmen and other nursing personnel. They serve in hospitals, dispensaries, Hospital Corps Schools, at domestic and overseas stations, and aboard USS Hospital Ships.

Female or male applicants for direct appointments between ages 20 to 34, must be registered professional nurses who meet eligibility requirements for commission in the Navy. All appointments are made in the Nurse Corps, U. S. Naval Reserve in ranks of ensign, lieutenant (j.g.), or lieutenant, depending on education, professional experience and age.

The Navy Nurse Corps Candidate Program provides financial assistance to those qualified junior and senior nursing students and registered nurses who are matriculated in a nurse baccalaureate de-

gree or higher degree program in approved universities. Students participating in the program receive tuition, fees, allowances for books and pay, quarters, and subsistence commensurate with the grade in which they serve. Six months prior to completion of degree requirements, students are commissioned as Ensign, 1905, USNR and receive the base pay and allowance of that rank. Following graduation participants will be ordered to the U. S. Naval Schools Command, Newport, R. I., for a 4 week indoctrination course after which they will be commissioned in the Naval Reserve as Nurse Corps officers (2905). The graduate will be commissioned to the grade of ensign, lieutenant (j.g.) or lieutenant (s.g.) depending on education, professional experience and age. Candidates serve on active duty for 2 years for one year of subsidized education or 3 years for more than one year of subsidized education.

## WOMEN IN THE U. S. AIR FORCE (WAF)

Colonel Jeanne M. Holm, Director, Hq USAF, the Pentagon, Washington, D. C. 20330.

During World War II, 40,000 women served as members of the Air WAC on duty with the Army Air Corps and Army Air Forces. In September, 1947, the separate Department of the Air Force was established. The following year the Women's Armed Services Integration Act of 1948 authorized the appointment and enlistment of women in the Regular Air Force and the Air Force Reserve.

The WAF is not a constituted corps or a separate program but is an integral part of the Air Force military personnel program. In most cases, WAF are completely interchangeable with their male contemporaries on a job-for-job basis and the same general Air Force policies are equally applicable to men and women. Women in the Air Force serve at Air Force installations all over the U. S. and at many overseas locations, including Southeast Asia.

During 1968 there was 900 WAF officers and 6,500 enlisted women. By the mid-1970s, approximately 14,000 will be serving.

## AIR FORCE NURSE CORPS

Colonel Ethel A. Hoefly, Chief, Office of the Surgeon General, USAF, Washington, D. C. 20333.

The Air Force Nurse Corps was established as an integral part of the Air Force Medical Service in 1949. The majority of Air Force Nurses are on duty in Air Force hospitals as general duty staff nurses. Others work in specialties such as, anesthesia, operating room, psychiatry, obstetrics, research, aerospace, or teaching. A limited number are assigned as flight nurses in the aeromedical evacuation of patients by air. A selected number of nurses are enrolled in both military and civilian schools and universities for advanced professional education. Nurses in the Air Force are assigned on a world wide basis.

An applicant must be a citizen, at least 20 but not more than 35 years of age; physically qualified for military nursing; a graduate of a school of nursing offering a minimum 3-year basic curriculum, acceptable to the Surgeon General, USAF, and registered to practice professional nursing. The rank she receives depends on professional experience and educational background. Initial appointments to the Regular Air Force are made from Reserve Nurses on active duty. Air Force Nurses have rank and pay as officers in the USAF.

## AIR FORCE MEDICAL SPECIALISTS

Col. Frances G. Ballentine, Chief, Office of the Surgeon General, USAF, Washington, D. C. 20333.

The Medical Specialists as a corps was organized 1949 when the USAF Medical Service was established. In 1965 all medical specialists were transferred to the Biomedical Sciences Corps which was organized as a new corps within the Office of the Surgeon General. Air Force dietitians, occupational therapists and physical therapists continue to be identified as medical specialists within the new Biomedical Sciences Corps.

Initial appointments are made in the USAF Reserve. Eligibility for commissions require that the applicant must be a citizen, physically and educationally qualified, between 21 and 35 years of age.

The educational requirements for appointment require a minimum of a baccalaureate degree and completion of approved courses in the candidate's specialty.

Applicants between 21 and 28 years of age may be commissioned as Second Lieutenants for the purpose of completing an approved dietetic internship, physical or occupational therapy courses (not to exceed 12 months). Initial appointments to the Regular Air Force are selected from Reserve medical specialists on active duty. Air Force Medical Specialists enjoy the rank and pay as commissioned officers in the USAF.

## WOMEN MARINES

The first women in the Marine Corps served for one year during World War I when 305 women, called Marinettes, performed primarily clerical duties in Washington, D. C. During World War II, twenty-five years later, women were again called upon to free Marines to fight. The Women Marine Reserve was authorized on February 13, 1943 and by 1945, a total of 23,145 women had answered the call to perform more than 200 different military duties from typists to parachute riggers to map makers. Following the war, a few volunteers remained on active duty and with the passage of the Womens Armed Services Integration Act of 1948, Women Marines became a component part of the Marine Corps. On June 30, 1968, there were approximately 225 women Marine officers and 2,555 enlisted women serving throughout the continental United States, Hawaii, England, Italy, Germany, Okinawa, Japan and Vietnam.

An applicant for enlistment must be between 18 and 28 years inclusive, a high school graduate or able to complete the General Educational Development test at a high school level, have parents' consent if under 21, and be single with no dependents, though she may marry after training at Parris Island, South Carolina.

Officer candidates must be over 18 to enroll for training and between 21 and 29 to be commissioned. Civilian trainees must receive a baccalaureate degree from an accredited college or university prior to commissioning. Enlisted Women Marines and Women Reservists may apply for officer training if they are college graduates or if they successfully complete an officer's selection test.

The Director of Women Marines, selected every 4 years from the senior women Marine Officers, is a member of the staff at Headquarters Marine Corps, Washington, D. C.

## COAST GUARD SPARS

Headquarters for U. S. Coast Guard is Washington, D. C. Senior SPAR officer on duty is Commander Elizabeth B. Hall, stationed at Cape May, N. J.

The Coast Guard's SPAR organization was established during World War II on November 23, 1942. Recruit training was first at Hunter College, N. Y., then at Palm Beach, Florida. By war's end, approximately 1,000 officers and 10,000 enlisted women were serving in the Coast Guard.

After World War II, the SPARS were largely demobilized, but were reactivated at the outbreak of the Korean War. At that time a number of SPARS returned to active duty to take over specialized jobs. At present, there are nine SPAR officers and 34 enlisted women on active duty throughout the United States.

SPAR recruits must be between 20 and 30 and unmarried. They undergo basic training at the U. S. Naval Training School at Bainbridge, Maryland. On completion of their training, they are given specialized instruction in the Yeoman and Storekeeper rates at the Coast Guard training facility in Groton, Connecticut.

# Public Fallout Shelter Space for 176,000,000 Located

### Source: Office of Civil Defense, Dept. of the Army

Civil defense is a key element of national defense in the nuclear age. The U. S. civil defense effort is centered on providing protection for the population against the radioactive fallout that would accompany a nuclear attack. All the states and thousands of local governments participate in the national effort with guidance and assistance from the

Office of Civil Defense of the Department of Defense. The primary objective is to establish a system of shelters with supporting systems for warning people and sustaining them in shelter during a fallout emergency, for monitoring and reporting fallout and for initiating recovery efforts. In addition to attack preparedness missions, most state and

local civil defense organizations are charged by law with responsibility for preparedness against natural disaster and with the direction of natural disaster control and relief operations.

**Shelters.** By Mid-1968, public fallout shelter space for more than 176,000,000 persons had been located and survival supplies for sustaining almost 80,000,000 persons for up to eight days were stocked in marked public shelters.

These shelters are being established by virtue of the fact that many existing large buildings contain areas with inherent protective features against fallout radiation.

In 1966, the national shelter survey was expanded to include smaller buildings, including private dwellings, to add their shelter potential to the national inventory.

By mid-1968, home surveys had been undertaken in R. I., Maine, Minn., Iowa, Kan., W. Va., Colo., Wyo., N. H., Vt., Idaho, Wis., Wash., Mont., Alaska, S. D., N. D., Utah, Nebr., Mich., Ore., Va., Md., Del., Conn., Mass., Long Island and Dist. of Col.

To encourage the incorporation of shelter in new construction, OCD has developed design techniques which add protective features to structures such as schools, office buildings and public buildings at little or no additional cost, without loss of esthetic values and without interfering with the normal, peacetime use of the shelter area in the buildings.

A Community Shelter Planning (CSP) program, tested in every state in previous years, was deployed in 1966 as an essential part of emergency preparedness. The basic purpose of this program is to develop in each community—with the assistance of local or state planning professionals—practical procedures for making efficient use of the best fallout protection available in the event of attack, get this information to each citizen, and prepare each department of local government to support the plan and meet its responsibilities in time of major disaster. CSP projects are under way in 725 localities involving 60,000,000 people.

**CD Organization.** The Office of Civil Defense was created in 1961 with the transfer of civil defense responsibilities from the Executive Office of the President to the Secretary of Defense. In 1964, OCD was transferred to the Office of the Secretary of the Army. Joseph Romm is the acting national Director of Civil Defense. OCD has eight regional offices and operates a Staff College and three warning centers. The transfer of civil defense functions to the Office of the Secretary of the Army has facilitated plans for support of government by the armed services in a nuclear attack.

## Civil Air Patrol Trains Pilots of Both Sexes

**Civil Air Patrol,** organized in 1941 by civilians to help the Office of Civil Defense, in 1948 became an auxiliary of the United States Air Force, not as an agency of the Government but as a civilian organization of adults and youngsters with interest in aviation and aerospace projects. It provides instruction and training for cadets, who may be male or female from age 13 to 18. It has 2,337 units in the various states and 85,000 members, including 47,000 teenage cadets; nearly 20% of its membership is female. It has a National Commander and Headquarters at Maxwell AFB, Alabama.

# American Military Cemeteries and Memorials on Foreign Soil

Administered by the American Battle Monuments Commission, Washington, D. C.
(Numbers of graves, and numbers of commemorated missing in parentheses)

### WORLD WAR I CEMETERIES

Aisne-Marne, near Belleau (Aisne) France (2288-1060)
Brookwood (Surrey) England (468-563)
Flanders Field, Waregem, Belgium (368-43)
Meuse-Argonne, Romagne (Meuse), France (14,-246-954)
Oise-Aisne, Seringes (Aisne), near Fere-en-Tardenois (Aisne), France (6012-241)
St. Mihiel, Thiaucourt (M. et M.), France (4,152-284)
Somme, Bony (Aisne), France (1837-333)
Suresnes (Seine), France (1541-974). In this cemetery rest also 24 of our unknown Dead of World War II. The World War I chapel was, by the addition of two loggias, converted into a shrine to commemorate our Dead of both Wars. Senior representatives of the American and French governments assemble here on ceremonial occasions to pay homage to our military Dead of these wars.

### MONUMENTS

Andenarde, Belgium.
Bellicourt (Aisne), France.
Brest (Finistère), France.
Cantigny (Somme), France.
Château-Thierry (Aisne), France
Gibraltar.
Kemmel, near Ypres, Belgium.
Montfaucon (Meuse), France.
Montsec (Meuse), France.
Sommepy (Marne), France.
Tours (Indre et Loire), France.

### WORLD WAR II CEMETERIES

Ardennes, near Neuville-en-Condroz, Belgium (5,-271-462)
Brittany, near St. James (Manche), France 4,410-498)
Cambridge, near Cambridge, England, (3,811-5125)
Epinal, near Epinal (Vosges), France (5,255-424)

Florence, near Florence (Tuscany), Italy (4,402-1409)
Henri-Chapelle, near Henri-Chapelle, Belgium (7,989-450)
Lorraine, St. Avold (Moselle), France (10,489-444)
Luxembourg, near Luxembourg (City) (5,076-170)
Manila, near Manila, Republic of the Philippines (17,206-36,279)
Netherlands, Margraten, Holland (8,301-1722)
Normandy, near St. Laurent (Calvados), France (9,386-1557)
North Africa, Carthage, Tunisia (2,840-3724)
Rhône, Draguignan (Var), France (861-293)
Sicily-Rome, Nettuno, Italy (7,862-3094)

To commemorate those who met their deaths in the American coastal waters of the Atlantic and Pacific Oceans the Commission has erected a memorial in Battery Park, New York City, on which are inscribed 4,596 names, and at the Presidio of San Francisco, California, which carries 412 names.

World War II dead are also buried in Sitka National Cemetery, Sitka, Alaska, Puerto Rico National Cemetery, Bayamon, Puerto Rico, and the National Memorial Cemetery of the Pacific, Honolulu, Hawaii. These cemeteries, all on American soil, are under the jurisdiction of The Office of the Chief of Support Services, Department of the Army, Washington, D. C. 20315. At the Honolulu Cemetery the American Battle Monuments Commission has erected a memorial which records the names of 18,093 Missing of World War II and 8,187 Missing resulting from the Korean operations.

The Commission also maintains a cemetery in Mexico City where the remains of 750 Americans who gave their lives in the Mexican War (1846-1848) are buried.

The decoration of graves with natural cut flowers only, is permitted in the cemeteries under the control of The American Battle Monuments Commission. The Commission is glad to assist interested persons in arranging with local florists in foreign countries to furnish such decorations.

# National Cemeteries

Administered by the National Park Service, Department of the Interior.

Antietam (11.36), Sharpsburg, Md.
Battleground (1.03), Washington, D. C.
Fort Donelson (15.34), Dover, Tenn.
Fredericksburg (12.00), Fredericksburg, Va.
Gettysburg (20.58), Gettysburg, Pa.
Poplar Grove (8.72), Petersburg, Va.
Shiloh (10.25), Pittsburgh Landing, Tenn.
Stones River (20.09), Murfreesboro, Tenn.
Vicksburg (117.85), Vicksburg, Miss.

Yorktown (2.91), Yorktown, Va.
The Department of the Army has jurisdiction over 86 other National Cemeteries (3,435 acres) situated in the United States and its possessions.
The American Battle Monuments Commission administers the United States Military Cemeteries and Memorials on foreign soil.
**Arlington National Cemetery, Va.,** contains Tomb of the Unknown Soldier. *See Index.*

## United States Coast Guard

The U. S. Coast Guard dates its origin from Aug. 4, 1790, when the First Congress authorized the construction of a revenue fleet known as the Revenue Marine. The Revenue Marine, later known as the Revenue Cutter Service, ultimately developed into the present-day Coast Guard. However, the modern era of the Service began on Jan. 28, 1915, when Pres. Wilson signed legislation combining the Revenue Cutter Service and the historic Life Saving Service into a single organization to be called the U. S. Coast Guard.

The United States Coast Guard is responsible for a wide range of duties which are concerned with maintaining safety and order upon the high seas and navigable waters subject to the jurisdiction of the United States. The primary purpose of most of these duties is to prevent loss of life and property due to unsafe or illegal practices. The maintenance of safety and order is not limited to enforcement of laws. The Coast Guard also directs a program of education among ship operators and boatmen, and enlists their cooperation in the prevention of marine casualties. This role includes maintenance of more than 44,000 aids to navigation—lighthouses, buoys, bells, etc.— along 40,000 miles of waters; lifesaving activities; removal of derelicts and other menaces to navigation; marine inspection; Oceanographic Research; ice-breaking; medical aid to seamen; law enforcement on the high seas and navigable waters of the United States; the prevention of smuggling; patrol of the North Pacific Ocean and Bering Sea to regulate the taking of fur-bearing sea mammals and fish; aid during flood and hurricanes; maintenance of the International Ice Patrol to report the amount of iceberg drift for the benefit of vessels crossing the North Atlantic; maintaining ocean weather stations; and supervising the engagement, records and discipline of officers and seamen serving in the Merchant Marine. To carry out its many functions, the Coast Guard has a fleet of more than 2,900 floating craft of all types plus 166 fixed and rotary-wing aircraft.

The Coast Guard is administered by the Commandant of the Coast Guard, at Headquarters in Washington, D. C., through a field organization of 12 District Coast Guard Offices in the continental United States, Hawaii and Alaska. A military service constituting a branch of the armed forces of the United States at all times the Coast Guard operates as a service of the Transportation Dept., to which it was transferred on April 1, 1967. Until then it was in the Treasury Dept. In time of war, or on direction of the President it operates as part of the Navy.

The Coast Guard Auxiliary is a nonmilitary organization administered by the Commandant, with more than 25,000 members in about 700 communities. Its primary activity is to assist the Coast Guard in the promotion of safety and efficiency in the operation of small boats.

Training facilities include a recruit receiving center at Cape May, N. J., and at Alameda, Calif., various service schools for enlisted men, the Coast Guard Academy in New London, Conn., for officer candidates, and the Reserve Training Center at Yorktown, Va.

The Search and Rescue Agency has the Commandant of the Coast Guard as its head.

Congress on May 14, 1960, enacted a law to improve Coast Guard organization by (1) increasing present limitation of 4 years applicable to extension of enlistments to 6 years; (2) raising the limitation on 3,000 commissioned officer personnel to 3,500; (3) improving civilian teaching staff and commissioned teaching staff at Coast Guard Academy; (4) providing for increased grade of admiral for officer serving as commandant and of vice admiral for officer serving as asst. commandant; eliminating the position of engineer-in-chief and the term of four years for asst. commandant.

## Coast Guard Personnel on Active Duty

Source: Treasury Department, U. S. Coast Guard

| | Total | Officers[1] | Cadets | Enlisted | | Total | Officers[1] | Cadets | Enlisted |
|---|---|---|---|---|---|---|---|---|---|
| 1940.. | 13,756 | 1,351 | 144 | 12,261 | 1960.. | 30,616 | 4,020 | 405 | 26,191 |
| 1945.. | 171,192 | 12,683 | 219 | 158,290 | 1965.. | 31,700 | 4,425 | 440 | 26,832 |
| 1950.. | 23,190 | 2,906 | 296 | 19,988 | 1967.. | 35,631 | 3,889 | 804 | 30,535 |
| 1955.. | 28,607 | 3,520 | 533 | 24,554 | 1968.. | 36,683 | 5,372 | 799 | 31,311 |

[1]Includes warrant officers.

## Debt Owed U. S. Arising from World War I as of June 30, 1968

Source: Treasury Department

| Country | Original Indebtedness | Interest thru June 30, 1968 | Cumulative Payments | | Unmatured Principal* | Principal and interest due and unpaid* |
|---|---|---|---|---|---|---|
| | | | Principal | Interest | | |
| Armenia...... | $ 11,959,917 | $ 29,185,065 | $ 17 | ............ | ............ | $ 41,144,965 |
| Austria[1]..... | 26,843,148 | 44,058 | 862,668 | ............ | ............ | 26,024,539 |
| Belgium...... | 419,837,630 | 327,200,720 | 19,157,630 | $ 33,033,642 | $ 189,780,000 | 505,067,077 |
| Cuba........ | 10,000,000 | 2,286,751 | 10,000,000 | 2,286,751 | ............ | ............ |
| Czechoslovakia | 185,071,023 | 115,647,578 | 19,829,914 | 304,178 | 83,400,000 | 197,184,509 |
| Estonia...... | 16,466,012 | 22,442,310 | ............ | 1,248,432 | 8,639,000 | 29,020,890 |
| Finland...... | 8,999,999 | 11,637,950 | [2]4,484,999 | [2]11,637,950 | 4,515,000 | ............ |
| France...... | 4,089,689,588 | 3,372,178,164 | 226,039,588 | 260,036,302 | 1,709,919,070 | 5,265,872,791 |
| Great Britain. | 4,802,181,641 | 7,132,031,958 | 434,181,641 | 1,590,672,656 | 2,337,000,000 | 7,572,359,301 |
| Greece...... | [3]34,319,843 | 3,493,628 | 1,049,702 | 3,406,251 | 20,790,141 | 12,567,376 |
| Hungary[4].... | 1,982,555 | 2,841,815 | 73,795 | 482,924 | 1,053,625 | 3,213,816 |
| Italy........ | 2,042,364,319 | 354,784,720 | 37,464,319 | 63,365,560 | 1,127,400,000 | 1,168,919,159 |
| Latvia...... | 6,888,664 | 9,489,578 | 9,200 | 752,349 | 3,648,300 | 11,968,694 |
| Liberia...... | 26,000 | 10,471 | 26,000 | 10,471 | ............ | ............ |
| Lithuania.... | 6,432,465 | 8,827,681 | 234,783 | 1,003,173 | 3,355,037 | 10,667,152 |
| Nicaragua[5]... | 141,950 | 26,625 | 141,950 | 26,625 | ............ | ............ |
| Poland...... | 207,344,297 | 286,609,084 | [6]1,287,297 | 21,359,000 | 111,324,000 | 359,983,084 |
| Rumania..... | 68,359,192 | 53,076,784 | [7]4,498,632 | [7]292,375 | 30,794,000 | 85,850,969 |
| Russia...... | 192,601,297 | 485,719,744 | ............ | [8]8,750,311 | ............ | 669,570,729 |
| Yugoslavia... | 63,577,712 | 27,982,152 | 1,952,712 | 636,059 | 34,138,000 | 54,833,093 |
| **Total......** | **$12,195,087,259** | **$12,245,517,146** | **$761,295,052** | **$1,999,305,017** | **$5,665,756,184** | **$16,014,248,152** |

*To arrive at the total outstanding figure add the figures in the two columns together.

[1]The Federal Republic of Germany has recognized liability for securities falling due between March 12, 1938 and May 8, 1945.

[2]$7,419,970.26 has been made available for educational exchange programs with Finland pursuant to 20 U.S.C. 222-224.

[3]Includes $13,155,921.00 refunded by the agreement of May 28, 1964. The agreement was ratified by Congress Nov. 5, 1966.

[4]Interest payments from December 15, 1932 to June 15, 1937 were paid in pengo equivalent.

[5]The indebtedness of Nicaragua was canceled pursuant to the agreement of April 14, 1938.

[6]Excludes claim allowance of $1,813,428.69 dated December 15, 1929.

[7]Excludes payment of $100,000.00 on June 14, 1940 as a token of good faith.

[8]Principally proceeds from liquidation of Russian assets in the United States.

# Casualties in Principal Wars of the United States
## SEE INDEX FOR VIETNAM CASUALTIES

Data prior to World War I are based upon incomplete records in many cases. Casualty data are confined to dead and wounded personnel and therefore exclude personnel captured or missing in action who were subsequently returned to military control. Dash (—) indicates information is not available.

| Wars | Branch of service | Number serving | Battle deaths | Other deaths | Wounds not mortal[8] | Total |
|------|-------------------|----------------|---------------|--------------|----------------------|-------|
| **Revolutionary War** 1775–1783 | Total | — | 4,435 | — | 6,188 | 10,623 |
| | Army | 184,000 | 4,044 | — | 6,004 | 10,048 |
| | Navy | to | 342 | — | 114 | 456 |
| | Marines | 250,000 | 49 | — | 70 | 119 |
| **War of 1812** 1812–1815 | Total | [9]286,730 | 2,260 | — | 4,505 | 6,765 |
| | Army | — | 1,950 | — | 4,000 | 5,950 |
| | Navy | — | 265 | — | 439 | 704 |
| | Marines | — | 45 | — | 66 | 111 |
| **Mexican War** 1846–1848 | Total | [9]78,718 | 1,733 | 11,550 | 4,152 | 17,435 |
| | Army | — | 1,721 | 11,550 | 4,102 | 17,373 |
| | Navy | — | 1 | — | 3 | 4 |
| | Marines | — | 11 | — | 47 | 58 |
| **Civil War** (Union forces only) 1861–1865 | Total | [9]2,213,363 | 140,414 | 224,097 | 281,881 | 646,392 |
| | Army | 2,128,948 | 138,154 | 221,374 | 280,040 | 639,568 |
| | Navy | } 84,415 | 2,112 | 2,411 | 1,710 | 6,233 |
| | Marines | | 148 | 312 | 131 | 591 |
| Confederate forces (estimate)[1] 1863–1866 | Total | — | 74,524 | 59,297 | — | 133,821 |
| | Army | } 600,000 | — | — | — | — |
| | Navy | to | — | — | — | — |
| | Marines | } 1,500,000 | — | — | — | — |
| **Spanish-American War** 1898 | Total | 306,760 | 385 | 2,061 | 1,662 | 4,108 |
| | Army[4] | 280,564 | 369 | 2,061 | 1,594 | 4,024 |
| | Navy | 22,875 | 10 | 0 | 47 | 57 |
| | Marines | 3,321 | 6 | 0 | 21 | 27 |
| **World War I** April 6, 1917– Nov. 11, 1918 | Total | 4,743,826 | 53,513 | 63,195 | 204,002 | 320,710 |
| | Army[5] | 4,057,101 | 50,510 | 55,868 | 193,663 | 300,041 |
| | Navy | 599,051 | 431 | 6,856 | 819 | 8,106 |
| | Marines | 78,839 | 2,461 | 390 | 9,520 | 12,371 |
| | Coast Gd. | 8,835 | 111 | 81 | — | 192 |
| **World War II** Dec. 7, 1941– Dec. 31, 1946[2] | Total | 16,353,659 | 292,131 | 115,185 | 670,846 | 1,078,162 |
| | Army[6] | 11,260,000 | 234,874 | 83,400 | 565,861 | 884,135 |
| | Navy[7] | 4,183,466 | 36,950 | 25,664 | 37,778 | 100,392 |
| | Marines | 669,100 | 19,733 | 4,778 | 67,207 | 91,718 |
| | Coast Gd. | 241,093 | 574 | 1,343 | — | 1,917 |
| **Korean War** June 25, 1950– July 27, 1953[3] | Total | 5,764,143 | 33,629 | 20,617 | 103,284 | 157,530 |
| | Army | 2,834,000 | 27,704 | 9,429 | 77,596 | 114,729 |
| | Navy | 1,177,000 | 458 | 4,043 | 1,576 | 6,077 |
| | Marines | 424,000 | 4,267 | 1,261 | 23,744 | 29,272 |
| | Air Force | 1,285,000 | 1,200 | 5,884 | 368 | 7,452 |
| | Coast Gd. | 44,143 | | | | |

[1]Authoritative statistics for the Confederate Forces are not available. An estimated 26,000–31,000 Confederate personnel died in Union prisons.
[2]Data are for the period Dec. 1, 1941 through Dec. 31, 1946 when hostilities were officially terminated by Presidential Proclamation, but few battle deaths or wounds not mortal were incurred after the Japanese acceptance of Allied peace terms on Aug. 14, 1945. Numbers serving from Dec. 1, 1941–Aug. 31, 1945 were: Total—14,903,213; Army—10,420,000; Navy—3,883,520; and Marine Corps—599,693.
[3]Tentative final data based upon information available as of Sept. 30, 1954, at which time 24 persons were still carried as missing in action.
[4]Number serving covers the period April 21–Aug. 13, 1898, while dead and wounded data are for the period May 1–Aug. 31, 1898. Active hostilities ceased on Aug. 13, 1898, but ratifications of the treaty of peace were not exchanged between the United States and Spain until April 11, 1899.
[5]Includes Air Service. Battle deaths and wounds not mortal include casualties suffered by American forces in Northern Russia to Aug. 25, 1919 and in Siberia to April 1, 1920. Other deaths cover the period April 1, 1917–Dec. 31, 1918. [6]Includes Army Air Forces.
[7]Battle deaths and wounds not mortal include casualties incurred in Oct. 1941 due to hostile action.
[8]Marine Corps date for World War II, the Spanish-American War and prior wars represent the number of individuals wounded, whereas all other data in this column represent the total number (incidence) of wounds.
[9]As reported by the Commissioner of Pensions in his Annual Report for Fiscal Year 1903.

---

# American Military Action, 1900-1968

1900—Occupation of Puerto Rico (annexed 1899).
1900—2,500 Marines help relieve Peking in Boxer Rebellion.
1900-1902—Occupation of Cuba.
1900-1902—Guerrilla war in Philippines.
1903—Sailors and Marines from U. S. S. Nashville stop Colombian Army at Panama.
1904—Brief intervention in Dominican Republic.
1906-1909—Intervention in Cuba.
1909—Brief intervention in Honduras.
1911—Intervention (to collect customs) in Honduras, Nicaragua, Dominican Republic.
1914—Apr. 21 to Nov. 23. Marines in Vera Cruz; also Atlantic fleet and Brig. Gen. Fredk. Funston.
1914—Marines enter Haiti, stay until 1934.
1916—Gen. John J. Pershing and 12,000 into Northern Mexico to stop raids by Villa, Mar. 15-Nov. 24.
1916-1924—Marines in Dominican Republic.
1917—Apr. 6 to Nov. 11, 1918. War with Germany, Austria-Hungary.
1918-1920—Expedition into Russia, Siberia.
1918-1923—Occupation of Germany.

1922-24—Marines in Nicaragua.
1926-33—Marines in Nicaragua.
1927—1,000 U. S. Marines in China.
1941-1945—War with Japan, Germany, Italy and allies. Army units posted in Japan and West Germany.
1950-1953—U. S. and other U.N. countries aid the Republic of Korea to repel North Korean invaders; U. S. Navy protects Taiwan.
1957—U. S. Fleet to Near East.
1958—Marines and Army units support Lebanon.
1960—Navy patrol in Caribbean to protect Guatemala and Nicaragua.
1961—Army units to Vietnam.
1962—Units of U. S. Navy on Cuban blockade duty. Marines in Thailand.
1962-65—U. S. Military Assistance Command. Vietnam; units of U. S. Army, Navy, Air Force, Marine Corps, Coast Guard.
1965—Marines, U. S. Army units to Dominican Republic.
1965—American commanders in Vietnam authorized to send U.S. Armed Force into combat.

## Casualties of All Belligerents in World War I

Source: U. S. War Department

| Country | Total Mobilized Forces | Killed and Died | Wounded Casualties | Prisoners and Missing | Total Casualties | Per cent |
|---|---|---|---|---|---|---|
| **ALLIES** | Number | Number | Number | Number | Number | |
| Russia.................. | 12,000,000 | 1,700,000 | 4,950,000 | 2,500,000 | 9,150,000 | 76.3 |
| France.................. | 8,410,000 | 1,357,800 | 4,266,000 | 537,000 | 6,160,800 | 73.3 |
| British Commonwealth.. | 8,904,467 | 908,371 | 2,090,212 | 191,652 | 3,190,235 | 35.8 |
| Italy................... | 5,615,000 | 650,000 | 947,000 | 600,000 | 2,197,000 | 39.1 |
| United States.......... | 4,355,000 | 126,000 | 234,300 | 4,500 | 364,800 | 8.0 |
| Japan.................. | 800,000 | 300 | 907 | 3 | 1,210 | .2 |
| Romania............... | 750,000 | 335,706 | 120,000 | 80,000 | 535,706 | 71.4 |
| Serbia................. | 707,343 | 45,000 | 133,148 | 152,958 | 331,106 | 46.8 |
| Belgium............... | 267,000 | 13,716 | 44,686 | 34,659 | 93,061 | 34.9 |
| Greece................ | 230,000 | 5,000 | 21,000 | 1,000 | 27,000 | 11.7 |
| Portugal.............. | 100,000 | 7,222 | 13,751 | 12,318 | 33,291 | 33.3 |
| Montenegro........... | 50,000 | 3,000 | 10,000 | 7,000 | 20,000 | 40.0 |
| **Total............** | **42,188,810** | **5,152,115** | **12,831,004** | **4,121,099** | **22,104,209** | **52.3** |
| **CENTRAL POWERS** | | | | | | |
| Germany.............. | 11,000,000 | 1,773,700 | 4,216,058 | 1,152,800 | 7,142,558 | 64.9 |
| Austria-Hungary....... | 7,800,000 | 1,200,000 | 3,620,000 | 2,200,000 | 7,020,000 | 90.0 |
| Turkey................ | 2,850,000 | 325,000 | 400,000 | 250,000 | 975,000 | 34.2 |
| Bulgaria.............. | 1,200,000 | 87,500 | 152,390 | 27,029 | 266,919 | 22.2 |
| **Total............** | **22,850,000** | **3,386,200** | **8,388,448** | **3,629,829** | **15,404,477** | **67.4** |
| **Grand total......** | **65,038,810** | **8,538,315** | **21,219,452** | **7,750,919** | **37,508,686** | **57.9** |

## Peak Strength of Armed Forces; Battle Deaths in World War II

Source: Peak strength from U. S. Department of the Army. Battle deaths from various sources.

### ALLIES AND ASSOCIATED POWERS

| Country | Peak strength | Battle deaths | Country | Peak strength | Battle deaths |
|---|---|---|---|---|---|
| Australia............. | 680,000 | 23,365 | New Zealand........ | 157,000 | 10,033 |
| Belgium.............. | 650,000 | 7,760 | Norway............. | 45,000 | 1,000 |
| Canada............... | 780,000 | 37,476 | Poland............. | 1,000,000 | 320,000 |
| China................ | 5,000,000 | [2]2,200,000 | So. Africa, Union of... | 140,000 | 6,840 |
| Denmark............. | 25,000 | 3,006 | United Kingdom..... | 5,120,000 | 244,723 |
| France............... | 5,000,000 | 210,671 | United States........ | [3]12,300,000 | 291,557 |
| Greece............... | 414,000 | [2]273,700 | U.S.S.R............ | 12,500,000 | 7,500,000 |
| India................ | 2,150,000 | 24,338 | Yugoslavia.......... | 410,000 | 410,000 |
| Netherlands.......... | 410,000 | 6,238 | | | |

[1]1937-1945 against Japan. [2]Includes 50,000 killed in guerrilla warfare. [3]Peak strength of U. S. Army in World War II—May 31, 1945—8,291,336.

### OTHER POWERS THAT DECLARED WAR ON AXIS

Forces engaged and losses, if any, not available.

| Country | Peak strength | Country | Peak strength | Country | Peak strength | Country | Peak strength |
|---|---|---|---|---|---|---|---|
| Albania........ | 25,000 | Czechoslovakia | 150,000 | Honduras..... | 3,500 | Peru......... | 40,000 |
| Argentina..... | 160,000 | Dom. Republic | 5,000 | Iran.......... | 120,000 | Philippines.... | 200,000 |
| Bolivia........ | 10,000 | Ecuador...... | 9,000 | Iraq.......... | 47,000 | Turkey....... | 850,000 |
| Brazil......... | 200,000 | Egypt........ | 54,000 | Liberia....... | 1,000 | Uruguay...... | 11,000 |
| Chile......... | 60,000 | El Salvador... | 3,500 | Luxembourg... | 1,000 | Venezuela.... | 15,000 |
| Colombia...... | 19,000 | Ethiopia...... | 38,000 | Mexico....... | 70,000 | | |
| Costa Rica.... | 500 | Guatemala.... | 6,000 | Nicaragua..... | 3,500 | | |
| Cuba......... | 20,000 | Haiti........ | 4,000 | Paraguay..... | 10,000 | | |

### AXIS

| Country | Peak strength | Battle deaths | Country | Peak strength | Battle deaths |
|---|---|---|---|---|---|
| Bulgaria............. | 450,000 | 10,000 | Italy................ | 3,750,000 | *77,494 |
| Finland.............. | 250,000 | 82,000 | Japan............... | 6,095,000 | 1,219,000 |
| Germany (inc. Austria). | 10,200,000 | 3,500,000 | Romania............. | 600,000 | 300,000 |
| Hungary............. | 350,000 | 140,000 | *Includes 17,494 on Allied side. | | |

NEUTRALS, Peak Strength—Afghanistan, 92,000; Portugal, 115,000; Saudi Arabia, 8,000; Siam, 126,500; Spain, 850,000; Sweden, 350,000; Switzerland, 650,000.

### ADJUTANT GENERAL'S FIGURES OF CIVIL WAR DEATHS

Figures reported from the Adjutant General's Office previous to the above revision, and accepted for many years, are as follows:

Union Army, according to records in the office of the Adjutant General of the War Department in Washington—killed or died of wounds, 110,070 (6,365 officers, 103,705 men); died of disease, 224,586 (2,795 officers, 221,791 men); other deaths, 24,872 (424 officers, 24,448 men). Totals, 359,528 (9,584 officers, 349,944 men).

Confederate Army, estimated, no official records in the office of the Adjutant General of the War Department in Washington—killed in battle, 52,954 (2,086 officers, 50,868 men); died of wounds, 21,570 (1,246 officers, 20,324 men); died of disease, 59,297 (1,294 officers, 58,003 men). Total, 113,821 (4,626 officers, 129,195 men).

### WORLD WAR II MERCHANT MARINE CASUALTIES

Source: U. S. Coast Guard

Died from direct causes while serving on American flag ships, 845; died in prisoner-of-war camps, 37; listed as missing, 4,780.

There were 572 released prisoners of war, and one prisoner unaccounted for. Another 500 men died while serving on foreign flag ships under U. S. control.

The number of U. S. flag ships lost was 605 of 6,000,000 deadweight tons.

## Death of Last U. S. Cavalry Horse Ends an Era

Chief, a bay gelding who was the last Cavalry horse on the rolls of the United States Army, died May 24, 1968, at Fort Riley, Kan. He was 36 years old and had lived for 18 years in semi-retirement. The Army held an elaborate military funeral to mark the end of an era.

# Veterans' Benefits Further Improved by 1968 Legislation

Source: Veterans Administration, William J. Driver, Administrator, Washington, D. C. 20420

The chief laws in behalf of veterans and their dependents enacted by Congress in 1968 assured that veterans receiving pensions will not suffer pension cuts because of increases in their Social Security benefits, raised the home loan guarantee ceiling from $7,500 to $12,500; and increased compensation payments up to $100 monthly. The year also saw the veteran population of the nation climb by more than 1,000,000 to a total of 26,314,000.

Major veterans legislation was passed in 1966 when all veterans who served in the Armed Forces after Jan. 31, 1955 (official termination of the Korean Conflict) were provided a permanent program of educational assistance and other benefits by the Veterans Readjustment Benefits Act of 1966. In 1967, with the U. S. Armed Forces serving in Vietnam, Congress responded to the President's request to provide war-time benefits to Vietnam veterans as well as increased benefits for older veterans. Public Law 90-77, the Veterans Pension and Readjustment Assistance Act of 1967, became fully effective Oct. 1, 1967.

One of the most popular provisions with young veterans was the increase in educational assistance allowances. The law provides that veterans of active duty in the Armed Forces for more than 180 days, any part of which was after Jan. 1 1955, are entitled to receive monthly educational allowances according to the following table:

| Kind of training | Dependents | | | |
|---|---|---|---|---|
| | None | One | Two | Above 2* |
| School: | | | | |
| Full-time.... | $130 | $155 | $175 | $10 |
| ¾ Time...... | 95 | 115 | 135 | 7 |
| ½ Time..... | 60 | 75 | 85 | 5 |
| Cooperative.. | 105 | 115 | 145 | 7 |

*The amount in column for 2 plus the amount shown for each dependent.

Entitlement is on a basis of one month of schooling for each month of service, up to 36 months, or the equivalent in part-time education. Eligibility ceases at the end of 8 years from the date of the veteran's last release from active duty after Jan. 31, 1955. Entitlement is also extended to any person on active duty in the Armed Forces who has served for at least two years and continues on active duty.

Full-time training consists of 14 semester hours or the equivalent, three-quarter time consists of 10 to 13 semester hours, and half-time is 7 to 9 semester hours or the equivalent. A cooperative program is a full-time program of education consisting of institutional courses and alternate phases of training in a business or industry.

Full education assistance allowances were made available to "educationally disadvantaged" veterans so they can complete high school without reducing their eligibility for advanced educational benefits.

Also, monthly allowances for apprenticeships and on-the-job training have been provided. Payments range from $80 a month for a single veteran to $100 a month when there are two or more dependents. The allowances are reduced for succeeding six-month periods.

Monthly allowances for farm cooperative training cover institutional agricultural courses with a minimum of 12 clock hours per week in addition to related work on the farm. Allowances range from $105 a month for the single veteran to $145 a month when there are two dependents, plus an additional $7 a month for each additional dependent.

Flight training leading to a commercial license was added to educational benefits by the 1967 legislation which authorizes such training at approved flying schools only for veterans who have a private flying license or who have satisfactorily completed the required flying and ground school instruction for a private license. Allowances range from $130 per month for single veterans in full programs to $175 for those with two dependents plus $10 per month for each additional dependent. Unlike ordinary classroom study, flight training allowances are based on cost. VA pays 90% of the ordinary costs of the training up to the limit of a veteran's total eligibility for educational assistance. For each $130 a veteran receives for flight training assistance, his eligibility is charged one month.

Under the current law, eligible veterans and servicemen may obtain GI loans made by private lenders and guaranteed by the VA, for the purchase of homes or farms. In certain rural areas where ordinary lending facilities are not available, direct loans may be made by the VA for the purchase of homes and farmhouses. The effect of the Government's guarantee is intended to be to eliminate or reduce the amount of the down payment the lender normally requires. The VA may guarantee a home loan made by a private lender up to $12,500 or 60% of the loan, whichever is less. The guarantee on a farm real estate loan other than to acquire a home may not exceed $4,000 or 50% of the loan. Not more than $2,000 or 50% of the loan may be guaranteed for non-real estate farm loans. GI loans bear interest not to exceed 6.75%. There is no maximum on the amount of a guaranteed loan, the only limit is on the amount of the guarantee. Direct loans made by the VA may not exceed $17,500.

The law now provides complete hospital service for veterans with service-connected disabilities and care (if beds are available) to veterans of the Spanish-American War, World War I, World War II, and the Korean Conflict and all veterans since that time. Veterans with non-service-connected disabilities are admitted if a bed is available and if they are unable to defray the cost.

The law also provides civil service preference in Federal employment and extends to these veterans job counseling and employment placement service under the supervision of the U. S. Department of Labor.

Unemployment compensation is also administered by the U. S. Department of Labor through State Employment Service offices. The amount of the unemployment pay for which most veterans may become eligible depends upon the laws of the state in which the veteran lives.

Prior laws granted compensation to veterans who are disabled by injury or disease incurred in or aggravated by active service in the line of duty. Payments are based on the degree of disability.

Certain pension payments were increased by the 1967 legislation and various other benefits were also increased.

For the very seriously disabled veterans the VA may provide specially equipped automobiles, as well as prosthetic devices, and grants for the purchase or construction of "wheelchair homes."

# PAY SCALE of the ARMY,
## COMMISSIONED OFFICERS

| Pay grade | Army and Air Force rank | Navy rank | Under 2 | Over 2 | Over 3 | Over 4 | Over 6 | Over 8 | Over 10 |
|---|---|---|---|---|---|---|---|---|---|
| | Rank or pay grade | | Cumulative years of service (Rate per month, dollars) Over 2 years round figures | | | | | | |
| O-10¹ | Chief of Staff....... | | $2208.60 | $2209 | $2209 | $2209 | $2209 | $2209 | $2209 |
| O-10¹ | General*.......... | Admiral*.............. | 1607.70 | 1664 | 1664 | 1664 | 1664 | 1728 | 1728 |
| O-9 | Lieutenant General... | Vice Admiral.......... | 1425.00 | 1462 | 1493 | 1493 | 1493 | 1531 | 1531 |
| O-8 | Major General...... | Rear Admiral (upper half) | 1290.60 | 1329 | 1360 | 1360 | 1360 | 1462 | 1462 |
| O-7 | Brigadier General.... | Rear Admiral (lower half) | 1072.20 | 1145 | 1145 | 1145 | 1196 | 1196 | 1265 |
| O-6 | Colonel........... | Captain.............. | 794.40 | 873 | 930 | 930 | 930 | 930 | 930 |
| O-5 | Lieutenant Colonel... | Commander........... | 635.40 | 746 | 797 | 797 | 797 | 797 | 822 |
| O-4 | Major ............ | Lieutenant Commander... | 536.10 | 652 | 696 | 696 | 696 | 740 | 790 |
| *Commissioned officers with less than 4 years of active service as an enlisted member²* | | | | | | | | | |
| O-3 | Captain........... | Lieutenant........... | 498.30 | 556 | 594 | 658 | 689 | 714 | 753 |
| O-2 | First Lieutenant..... | Lieutenant (junior grade).. | 399.30 | 474 | 569 | 588 | 600 | 600 | 600 |
| O-1 | Second Lieutenant... | Ensign.............. | 343.20 | 379 | 474 | 474 | 474 | 474 | 474 |
| *Commissioned officers with over 4 years of active service as an enlisted member²* | | | | | | | | | |
| O-3 | Captain........... | Lieutenant........... | 583.20 | 611 | 633 | 658 | 689 | 714 | 753 |
| O-2 | First Lieutenant...... | Lieutenant (junior grade). | 521.40 | 533 | 549 | 588 | 600 | 620 | 652 |
| O-1 | Second Lieutenant... | Ensign.............. | 420.30 | 448 | 465 | 474 | 506 | 525 | 544 |

## WARRANT OFFICERS

| | | | | | | | | | |
|---|---|---|---|---|---|---|---|---|---|
| W-4 | Chief Warrant........ | Commissioned Warrant... | 507.30 | 544 | 544 | 556 | 582 | 607 | 632 |
| W-3 | Chief Warrant........ | Commissioned Warrant... | 461.10 | 500 | 500 | 506 | 512 | 550 | 582 |
| W-2 | Chief Warrant........ | Commissioned Warrant... | 403.80 | 436 | 436 | 449 | 474 | 500 | 519 |
| W-1 | Warrant Officer....... | Warrant Officer......... | 336.60 | 386 | 386 | 417 | 436 | 455 | 474 |

## ENLISTED PERSONNEL³

| | | | | | | | | | |
|---|---|---|---|---|---|---|---|---|---|
| E-9⁴ | Sergeant Major **.... | Master Chief Petty Officer. | | | | | | | 576 |
| E-8⁴ | Master Sergeant...... | Senior Chief Petty Officer.. | | | | | | 483 | 497 |
| E-7 | Sgt. 1st Class....... | Chief Petty Officer ...... | 303.90 | 364 | 377 | 391 | 404 | 417 | 430 |
| E-6 | Staff Sergeant....... | Petty Officer, 1st class ... | 261.90 | 318 | 331 | 344 | 358 | 371 | 384 |
| E-5 | Sergeant........... | Petty Officer, 2nd class ... | 226.20 | 278 | 291 | 304 | 324 | 338 | 351 |
| E-4 | Corporal........... | Petty Officer, 3rd class.... | 190.20 | 238 | 251 | 271 | 285 | 285 | 285 |
| E-3 | Private 1st Class..... | Seaman............... | 137.70 | 192 | 205 | 218 | 218 | 218 | 218 |
| E-2 | Private............ | Seaman Apprentice ....... | 113.40 | 159 | 159 | 159 | 159 | 159 | 159 |
| E-1 | Private............ | Seaman Recruit ........ | 109.50 | 145 | 145 | 145 | 145 | 145 | 145 |
| E-1 | (under 4 months)... | (under 4 months)..... | 102.30 | | | | | | |

**The pay scale also applies to:** Coast Guard and Marine Corps, Coast and Geodetic Survey, Public Health Service, National Guard, and the Organized Reserves.

*Four star General or Admiral—personal money allowances of $2,200 per annum, or $4,000 if Chief of Staff or Chief of Naval Operations.
Three star General or Admiral—personal money allowance of $500 per annum.
A senior member of the United Nations Staff (while so serving) receives pay and allowances of a three star General or Admiral plus $2,200 personal money allowance.

**A new title of Chief Master Sergeant created in 1965 rates in E-9 classification.
¹While serving as Chairman of Joint Chiefs of Staff, Chief of Staff of the Army, Chief of Naval Operations, Chief of Staff of the Air Forces, or Commandant of the Marine Corps, basic pay for this grade is $2,493.00 regardless of cumulative years of service.
²First 3 steps not affected by increase of July 1, 1968.
³Air Force enlisted personnel pay grades, E-9, Chief Master Sergeant; E-8, Sr. Master Sergeant; E-7, Master Sergeant; E-6, Technical Sergeant; E-5, Staff Sergeant; E-4 Sergeant; E-3, Airman 1st Class; E-2, Airman; E-1, Basic Airman.
Marine Corps enlisted ranks are as follows: E-9, Sergeant Major and Master Gunnery Sergeant; E-8, First Sergeant and Master Sergeant; E-7, Gunnery Sergeant; E-6, Staff Sergeant; E-5, Sergeant; E-4, Corporal; E-3, Lance Corporal; E-2, Private First Class Marine; E-1, Private.
Marine Corps officer ranks are same as Army and AF.
⁴While serving as Sergeant Major of the Army, Master Chief Petty Officer of the Navy, Chief Master Sergeant of the Air Force, or Sergeant Major of the Marine Corps, basic pay for this grade is $902.40 regardless of cumulative years of service.
⁵Authorized only when government quarters are not available.

## HAZARDOUS DUTY
### Flying Duty (crew member) and Submarine Duty
### Additional Monthly Pay

| | Under 3 yrs. | Over 3 yrs. | Maximum Over—Amt. |
|---|---|---|---|
| O—10 | $165 | $165 | $165 |
| O— 9 | 165 | 165 | 165 |
| O— 8 | 155 | 165 | 165 |
| O— 7 | 150 | 160 | 160 |
| O— 6 | 200 | 215 | 18 yrs.—$245 |
| O— 5 | 190 | 205 | 18 " — 245 |
| O— 4 | 170 | 185 | 18 " — 240 |
| O— 3 | 145 | 155 | 14 " — 205 |
| | Under 2 yrs. | Over 2 yrs. | |
| O— 2 | 115 | 125 | 14 " — 185 |
| O— 1 | 100 | 105 | 14 " — 170 |
| W— 4 | 115 | * | 18 " — 165 |
| W— 3 | 110 | 115 | 14 " — 140 |
| W— 2 | 105 | 110 | 14 " — 135 |
| W— 1 | 100 | 105 | 12 " — 130 |
| E— 9 | 105 | 105 | 105 |
| E— 8 | 105 | 105 | 105 |
| E— 7 | 80 | 85 | 12 yrs.— 105 |
| E— 6 | 70 | 75 | 12 " — 100 |
| E— 5 | 60 | 70 | 12 " — 95 |
| E— 4 | 55 | 65 | 8 " — 80 |
| E— 3 | 55 | 60 | 2 " — 60 |
| E— 2 | 50 | 60 | 2 " — 60 |
| E— 1 | 50 | 55 | 2 " — 55 |

Aviation Cadet under 2 years $50.
*W-4 Under 6 years receives $115.

## INCENTIVE PAY

Officers and Warrant Officers.............$110.00
Enlisted men ............................. 55.00

Types of duties for which these flat rates are payable are as follows—(1) Frequent and regular aerial flights not as a crew member. (2) Parachute jumping as an essential part of military duty. (3) Duty involving intimate contact with leprosy. (4) Duty involving demolition of explosives. (5) Submarine escape training tank duty. (6) Deep sea diving duty (including helium—oxygen diving). (7) Human acceleration or deceleration duty (8) High- or low-pressure chamber duty. (9) Thermal stress duty. (10) Training for assignment to submarines of advanced design or for positions of increased responsibility aboard a submarine.

## SEA AND FOREIGN DUTY

*Defense Secretary designates places where special duty pay may be awarded*
(See Pay Grades listed above)

| | | | |
|---|---|---|---|
| E-9.............. | $22.50 | E-4............... | $13.00 |
| E-8.............. | 22.50 | E-3............... | 9.00 |
| E-7.............. | 22.50 | E-2............... | 8.00 |
| E-6.............. | 20.00 | E-1............... | 8.00 |
| E-5.............. | 16.00 | | |

# NAVY and AIR FORCE (July 1, 1968 see asterisk below)

## COMMISSIONED OFFICERS

| Cumulative years of service (Rate per month, dollars) Round Figures | | | | | | | | Basic allowance for quarters (Subsistence allowances explained below) | |
|---|---|---|---|---|---|---|---|---|---|
| Over 12 | Over 14 | Over 16 | Over 18 | Over 20 | Over 22 | Over 26 | Over 30 | Without dependents | With dependents |
| $2209 | $2209 | $2209 | $2209 | $2209 | $2209 | $2209 | $2209 | $160.20 | $201.00 |
| 1860 | 1860 | 1993 | 1993 | 2126 | 2126 | 2259 | 2259 | 160.20 | 201.00 |
| 1594 | 1594 | 1728 | 1728 | 1860 | 1860 | 1993 | 1993 | 160.20 | 201.00 |
| 1531 | 1531 | 1594 | 1664 | 1728 | 1797 | 1797 | 1797 | 160.20 | 201.00 |
| 1265 | 1329 | 1462 | 1563 | 1563 | 1563 | 1563 | 1563 | 160.20 | 201.00 |
| 930 | 962 | 1113 | 1170 | 1196 | 1265 | 1373 | 1373 | 140.10 | 170.10 |
| 866 | 924 | 993 | 1050 | 1082 | 1120 | 1120 | 1120 | 130.20 | 157.50 |
| 835 | 873 | 911 | 936 | 936 | 936 | 936 | 936 | 120.00 | 145.05 |
| 790 | 810 | 810 | 810 | 810 | 810 | 810 | 810 | 105.00 | 130.05 |
| 600 | 600 | 600 | 600 | 600 | 600 | 600 | 600 | 95.10 | 120.00 |
| 474 | 474 | 474 | 474 | 474 | 474 | 474 | 474 | 85.20 | 110.10 |
| 790 | 822 | 822 | 822 | 822 | 822 | 822 | 822 | 105.00 | 130.05 |
| 677 | 696 | 696 | 696 | 696 | 696 | 696 | 696 | 95.10 | 120.00 |
| 563 | 588 | 588 | 588 | 588 | 588 | 588 | 588 | 85.20 | 110.10 |

## WARRANT OFFICERS

| | | | | | | | | | |
|---|---|---|---|---|---|---|---|---|---|
| 677 | 708 | 734 | 753 | 778 | 866 | 866 | 866 | 120.00 | 145.05 |
| 600 | 620 | 638 | 658 | 683 | 708 | 734 | 734 | 105.00 | 130.05 |
| 537 | 556 | 576 | 594 | 613 | 638 | 638 | 638 | 95.10 | 120.00 |
| 493 | 512 | 531 | 550 | 569 | 569 | 569 | 569 | 85.20 | 110.10 |

## ENLISTED PERSONNEL[3]

| | | | | | | | | Dependents (a) | | | |
|---|---|---|---|---|---|---|---|---|---|---|---|
| | | | | | | | | None [5] | One | Two | Over 2 |
| 589 | 603 | 616 | 630 | 642 | 676 | 742 | 742 | 85.20 | 120.00 | 120.00 | 120.00 |
| 510 | 523 | 537 | 549 | 563 | 596 | 663 | 663 | 85.20 | 120.00 | 120.00 | 120.00 |
| 444 | 464 | 477 | 490 | 497 | 530 | 596 | 596 | 75.00 | 114.90 | 114.90 | 114.90 |
| 404 | 417 | 430 | 437 | 437 | 437 | 437 | 437 | 70.20 | 110.10 | 110.10 | 110.10 |
| 364 | 371 | 371 | 371 | 371 | 371 | 371 | 371 | 70.20 | 105.00 | 105.00 | 105.00 |
| 285 | 285 | 285 | 285 | 285 | 285 | 285 | 285 | 70.20 | 105.00 | 105.00 | 105.00 |
| 218 | 218 | 218 | 218 | 218 | 218 | 218 | 218 | 55.20 | 55.20 | 83.10 | 105.00 |
| 159 | 159 | 159 | 159 | 159 | 159 | 159 | 159 | 55.20 | 55.20 | 83.10 | 105.00 |
| 145 | 145 | 145 | 145 | 145 | 145 | 145 | 145 | | | | |
| ... | ... | ... | ... | ... | ... | ... | ... | 55.20 | 55.20 | 83.10 | 105.00 |

(a) Payable only when serviceman authorizes deduction of a specified amount from his basic pay—$40 to $80 depending on grade.

### BASIC ALLOWANCES FOR SUBSISTENCE

This allowance, the quarters allowance, and any other allowance are not subject to income tax. Officers—Subsistence (food) is paid to all officers regardless of rank.....................$47.88 per month
Enlisted members:
When rations in kind are not available ...........................................$2.57 per day
When permission is granted to mess off the base ......... $1.10 per day or $33.00 per month
When assigned to duty under emergency conditions where
no government messing facilities are available ..................... $3.42 per day (maximum rate)

### FAMILY SEPARATION ALLOWANCE

Under certain conditions of family separation of more than 30 days, members in Pay Grades E-4 (with over 4 years' service) and above will be allowed $30 a month in addition to any other allowances to which he is entitled.

### UNIFORM ALLOWANCE

Enlisted personnel receive an initial uniform allowance valued at $164 to $285, with variations between Services. After 6 months and up to the 36th month, a monthly maintenance allowance of $4.20 is paid. After 36 months the monthly allowance varies between $5.40 and $6.00.

### REENLISTMENT BONUS

Reenlistment bonuses are paid to enlisted personnel, ranging from $400 for third reenlistment to $820 for first reenlistment: maximum cumulative bonus $2,000.

### SPECIAL PAY

Members of the uniformed services entitled to receive basic pay shall, in addition thereto, be entitled to receive incentive pay for the performance of hazardous duty required by competent orders. The President may, in time of war, suspend the payment of incentive pay for the performance of any or all hazardous duty. Officers receive no additional pay for overseas or sea duty.

### DUTY SUBJECT TO HOSTILE FIRE

Except in time of war declared by the Congress, a special pay of $55 a month is allotted to any member of the Uniformed Services during any month in which he was subject to hostile fire.

### MEDICAL AND DENTAL CORPS

Commissioned officers in the Medical, Dental and Veterinary Corps of the Regular Army, Navy and Air Force and commissioned medical, dental, and veterinary officers of the Regular Corps of the Public Health Service receive special pay based on cumulative years of service as follows: 0-2 years, $100; 2 to 6 years, $150; 6 to 10 years, $250; over 10 years $350. These rates are in addition to basic pay and allowance.

### NEW DEFENSE DEPARTMENT PAY POLICY

The Defense Dept. announced June 21, 1965, a new policy under which military men in South Vietnam will be eligible for $55 a month extra in combat pay. The new policy also made special combat pay available to men injured or wounded by hostile fire, explosion of enemy mines, or other hostile action in the Dominican Republic.

# *Military Pay Scale

A pay rise bill for the members of the armed forces was approved in 1967 by Congress and signed by the President. The bill provided for increases in 3 steps, first in Oct. 1, 1967, the second for July 1, 1968 (shown above) and the third April 1, 1969.

# Selective Service System; Military Selective Service Act

Source: Selective Service System, Washington, D. C.

Legislation providing for Selective Service has been in effect continuously since 1948. The induction provisions of the Military Selective Service Act of 1967 were extended until July 1, 1971, by Act of Congress, June 30, 1967.

The Selective Service System registers, classifies, selects and delivers men for induction into the Armed Forces. Most of the needs of the services are met by enlistments. But it is generally recognized that most men who enlist do so in order to choose a time to serve and a service of their choice, as an alternative to later induction. The military services rely on the prospect of induction to prompt enlistments. The Selective Service System, by induction, supplies the balance required to meet service needs.

The System also aids in maintaining the strength and the stability of the Reserve and National Guard. Deferments are provided for continued satisfactory participation in these reserve programs. Sufficient satisfactory participation in the Ready Reserve qualifies a man for Class IV-A as having completed service under the Military Selective Service Act of 1967.

The draft of married men into the Armed Forces was delayed by Pres. Kennedy Sept. 10, 1963. The order changed the sequence of selection so that married non-fathers would be called only after all single men 19-26 had been called. Pres. Johnson on Aug. 26, 1965 changed the order of selection to place childless married men in the same draft classification as single men. This was necessary because the pool of single men was no longer ample to fill draft quotas to meet the increased needs of the Armed Forces.

## STANDBY RESERVE

In addition to helping maintain the active and reserve forces, the Selective Service System has statutory responsibility for the selective recall of the nation's Standby Reserve when their recall to duty is authorized. The System must make and keep current a determination of which individual members of the Standby Reserve are available for recall and which should remain in the civilian economy because of occupations vital to the nation or because recall would result in extreme hardship to dependents. The System is thus responsible for the proper utilization of this segment of the manpower resource, numbering at this time 466,554 men and women as of June 30, 1968.

## DEFERMENTS AND EXEMPTIONS

The law states that selection for service is to be accomplished in a manner "consistent with the maintenance of an effective national economy." The operation of the System had the effect, through the prospect of deferment, of inducing men to prepare for, enter into, and remain in, civilian activities essential to national strength. The Act of 1967 provides for the deferment of persons satisfactorily pursuing a full-time course of instruction at a college, university, or similar institution of learning who request such deferment. Such deferment shall continue until the registrant completes the requirements of his baccalaureate degree, fails to pursue satisfactorily a full-time course of instruction, or attains the age of 24, whichever occurs first.

A registrant who has received a student deferment after July 1, 1967, and has been awarded a baccalaureate degree may not subsequently be classified in I-S (C) or III-A on the sole basis of fatherhood.

After Oct. 1, 1967, only graduate students pursuing medical studies or in other fields identified by the Director of Selective Service after receiving advice from the National Security Council may receive graduate student deferments. Students who entered their second or subsequent year of graduate school without interruption by Oct. 1, 1967 may be deferred for one additional year to earn a master's degree or not to exceed a total of five years to earn a doctorate or professional degree or one additional year whichever is greater.

Deferments also are provided for fathers, extreme hardship to dependents, agricultural and industrial occupations, apprentices, some officials, sole surviving sons, some aliens, and for those physically, mentally, or morally not qualified for military service. Ministers and divinity students are exempted from service but not from registration.

## INDUCTIONS

The number of men inducted since 1948 through June 1968 was 4,213,678 which included 108,632 for the Marine Corps and 30,092 for the Navy. Calls by month since January 1968 were: Jan. 34,000; Feb. 23,300; Mar. 41,000; Apr. 48,000; May 45,900; June 20,000; July 15,000; Aug. 18,300; Sept. 12,200; Oct. 13,800, Nov. 10,000.

Physicians, dentists and allied specialist categories are liable for service under the same conditions that apply to all registrants. The law gives the President authority to order these registrants to active duty involuntarily from the Reserve. It also provides that the Secretary of Defense may requisition registrants by specialty. The prospect of induction of these registrants on special calls influence them to apply for and accept reserve commissions. They are then ordered to two years of active duty as service needs dictate.

## SEQUENCE OF SELECTION

Registrants are selected for induction in the following order: (1) Delinquents 19 and older with the oldest selected first; (2) Volunteers 17-25 in sequence in which they volunteer for induction; (3) Nonvolunteers 19-25 single or married after Aug. 26, 1965, with the oldest selected first; (4) Nonvolunteers 19-25 married on or before Aug. 26, 1965 with the oldest selected first; (5) Nonvolunteers 26 and older with the youngest selected first; (6) Nonvolunteers 18½ to 19 with the oldest selected first.

## CLASSIFICATION

The registrant is placed by the local board in one of the following classes:

**Class I-A:** Available for military service.

**Class I-A-O:** Conscientious objector available for non-combatant military service only.

**Class I-C:** Member of the Armed Forces of the United States, Environmental Science Services Administration, or the Public Health Service.

**Class I-D:** Member of reserve component or student taking military training.

**Class I-O:** Conscientious objector available for civilian work contributing to the maintenance of the national health, safety, or interest.

**Class I-S:** Student deferred by law until graduation from high school or attainment of age of 20, or until end of his academic year at a college or university.

**Class I-W:** Conscientious objector performing civilian work contributing to the maintenance of the national health, safety, or interest, or who has completed such work.

**Class I-Y:** Registrant qualified for military service only in time of war or national emergency.

**Class II-A:** Registrant deferred because of civilian occupation (except agriculture and activity in study).

**Class II-C:** Registrant deferred because of agricultural occupation.

**Class II-S:** Registrant deferred because of activity in study.

**Class III-A:** Registrant with a child or children; and registrant deferred by reason of extreme hardship to dependents.

**Class IV-A:** Registrant who has completed service; sole surviving son.

**Class IV-B:** Officials deferred by law.

**Class IV-C:** Aliens not currently liable for military service.

**Class IV-D:** Ministers of religion or divinity students.

**Class IV-F:** Registrant not qualified for any military service.

**Class V-A:** Registrant over the age of liability for military service.

## SELECTIVE SERVICE SYSTEM

The Selective Service System has a National Headquarters at 1724 F Street N. W., Washington, D. C. 20435; a state hq. in each state and similar hq. for New York City, the District of Columbia, the Virgin Islands, Puerto Rico, Guam, and the Panama Canal Zone—a total of 56. Approximately 4,000 local draft boards of 3 or more unpaid civilians, function one in each county except in sparsely populated areas, or in heavily populated urban areas. An appeal board is situated in each Federal judicial district.

# VITAL STATISTICS

Source: Division of Vital Statistics, National Center for Health Statistics, Public Health Service
U. S. Dept. of Health, Education & Welfare

## First Half-Year, January-June 1968

### BIRTHS

The birth rate and the fertility rate continued to decline during the first half of 1968. Live births during the 6 months totaled 1,645,000, a decrease of 71,000 from the figure for the corresponding 6 months in 1967. The fertility rate for the first half of 1968 was 84.4 births per 1,000 women aged 15-44, or 4% below the rate of 88.4 for the first half of 1967.

### MARRIAGES

An estimated 951,000 marriages were performed in the first half of 1968 or 78,000 more than during the corresponding period in 1967. During June 1968 the marriage rate was 15.7 per 1,000 population, compared with 14.7 for June 1967.

### DIVORCES

The January-June 1968 divorce total for 40 reporting areas was about 208,000, nearly 8% more than were granted for the same period in 1967.

### DEATHS

The death rate for the first half of 1968 was 3.2% higher than the corresponding rate for 1967, due to the relatively high death rates recorded in January and February of 1968.

For the first 6 months of 1968 the infant mortality rate for each month has been lower than the rate observed in the corresponding months of 1967. Cumulatively for this period the 1968 rate was 22.2 per 1,000 live births, a drop of 3.1% from the rate of 22.9 recorded in 1967.

### PROVISIONAL STATISTICS
#### 12 Months Ending with June 1968

| | Number | | Rate | |
|---|---|---|---|---|
| | 1968 | 1967 | 1968 | 1967 |
| Live births | 3,465,000 | 3,582,000 | 17.4 | 18.2 |
| Marriages | 1,990,000 | 1,870,000 | 10.0 | 9.5 |
| Deaths | 1,891,000 | 1,844,000 | 9.5 | 9.4 |
| Infant deaths | 75,600 | 81,700 | 21.8 | 22.8 |
| Population base (in millions) | | | 199.0 | 196.9 |

## Annual Report for the Year 1967
### Provisional Statistics

With only minute changes the general trends observed for several years past continued in 1967. The birth rate decreased by less than 1% for the 10th consecutive year. The marriage rate showed its 5th annual increase. The death rate was .1% upward. The divorce rate was the highest since 1949.

### BIRTHS

The birth and fertility rates continued to decline from their most recent peaks, which were reached in 1957. In 1967 the birth rate was 17.9 births per 1,000 population, and the fertility rate was 87.8 births per 1,000 women 15-44 years of age.

The current decline in fertility (which began in the late 1950's) has been brought about in part by changes in the age pattern of child-bearing. Women who are now 25 years of age are having relatively low birth rates because they had unusually high birth rates when they were younger. At the same time, women who are now under 25 years of age are having relatively low birth rates because they are apparently delaying some births until they are a little older. Also, these younger women may have fewer children altogether than did women who began having their families in the late 1940's and the 1950's.

### MARRIAGE AND DIVORCE

The number of men and women in the United States who marry each year has increased substantially and without interruption since 1962. Not since the close of World War II have marriages reached the current figure of 1,913,000, and not since the end of the Korean Conflict has the marriage rate reached its present level of 9.7 marriages per 1,000 population. The magnitude of the marriage boom is indicated by annual increases in marriages between 1962 and 1967 which have averaged 65,000, well above average annual increases in marriages for any other 5-year period since World War II.

Although marriages have increased both in absolute numbers and in proportion to the total population since 1962, only about 1 of every 14 women of eligible age married during 1967 as compared to 1 of every 8 in 1946. High postwar birth rates resulting in current large numbers of young people of marriageable age are the key factor affecting the upward swing in the number of marriages. Is it likely that there will be a continuing high level of marriages through 1970.

An estimated 534,000 decrees of divorce or annulment were granted in the United States in 1967. Compared with an estimated 494,000 for 1966, this is an increase of 40,000, or 8.0%; the increase in divorce between 1965 and 1966 was only 2.7%. The divorce rate per 1,000 population also increased from 2.5 in 1966 to 2.7 in 1967. The rate for 1967 is the highest national divorce rate since 1949.

### DEATHS

An estimated 1,852,000 deaths occurred in the United States in 1967. This provisional rate is higher than the final rate of 951 deaths per 100,000 for 1966. In turn the final rate for 1966 was higher than that for 1965 (943 deaths per 100,000).

| Rank | Causes of death | Death rate | % of deaths |
|---|---|---|---|
| | All causes | 936.0 | 100.0 |
| 1 | Diseases of heart | 366.2 | 39.1 |
| 2 | Malignant neoplasms | 159.0 | 17.0 |
| 3 | Vascular lesions | 102.6 | 11.0 |
| 4 | Accidents | 55.1 | 5.9 |
| 5 | Influenza and pneumonia | 28.5 | 3.0 |
| 6 | Certain diseases of early infancy | 24.1 | 2.6 |
| 7 | General arteriosclerosis | 19.0 | 2.0 |
| 8 | Diabetes mellitus | 17.4 | 1.9 |
| 9 | Diseases of circulatory system | 15.3 | 1.6 |
| 10 | Other bronchopulmonic diseases | 14.8 | 1.6 |
| | All other causes | 134.0 | 14.3 |

**Diseases of Heart**—The death rate for diseases of heart (the leading cause of death) decreased from 371.2 per 100,000 population in 1966 to an estmated 366.2 in 1967, a reduction of about 1⅓%.

**Malignant Neoplasms**—The death rate for Malignant neoplasms continued to increase, reaching a high of 159.0 per 100,000 population in 1967. This was mainly due to increases in the rates for Malignant neoplasms of respiratory system and Malignant neoplasms of other and unspecified sites.

**Accidents**—The death rate for Accidents was 5% lower in 1967 than in 1966. This reduction was almost entirely due to a decrease in the death rate for Accidents exclusive of motor vehicle accidents while the rate for Motor vehicle accidents remained approximately the same.

**Influenza and Pneumonia**—The death rate for Pneumonia, except pneumonia of newborn, reached its lowest point in more than a decade in 1967, falling to a rate of 27.8 per 100,000 population. The death rate for Influenza, 50% lower than in 1966, was also at its lowest point in several years.

**Other Diseases of Circulatory System**—While the death rate for Diseases of heart showed a slight decline in 1967, the rate for Other diseases of the circulatory system evidenced an increase of almost 5% over 1966. About 40% of the total number of deaths in this category were attributed to its largest component, Aortic aneurysm, nonsyphilitic, and dissecting aneurysm.

**Certain Diseases of Early Infancy**—The death rate for Certain diseases of early infancy decreased from 26.4 per 100,000 population in 1966 to an estimate 24.1 in 1967, a reduction of about 8.7%. This decrease can be only partially explained by the fact that the birth rate is declining since the birth rate fell only 2.7% during the same period.

**Other Bronchopulmonic Diseases**—The death rate for Other bronchopulmonic diseases continued its slow but steady rise, reaching an all time high of 14.8 deaths per 100,000 population in 1967. This was an increase of 2.1% over the rate observed in 1966. Emphysema without mention of bronchitis, the major component, accounted for about 70% of the 1967 deaths in this category.

# Births and Deaths by States

Source: U. S. Dept. of Health, Education, and Welfare, National Center for Health Statistics. Registered by place of occurrence. Excludes fetal deaths.

| Area | Births[1] | | Deaths | | Area | Births[1] | | Deaths | |
|---|---|---|---|---|---|---|---|---|---|
| | 1966 | 1967 | 1966 | 1967 | | 1966 | 1967 | 1966 | 1967 |
| Ala. | 65,808 | 64,353 | 32,847 | 32,352 | Nebr. | 25,450 | 24,218 | 14,824 | 14,678 |
| Alaska | 6,515 | 6,241 | 1,314 | 1,291 | Nev. | 8,655 | 8,500 | 3,467 | 3,499 |
| Ariz. | 32,176 | 32,089 | 13,351 | 13,103 | N. H. | 12,039 | 11,946 | 7,057 | 7,192 |
| Ark. | 34,461 | 33,350 | 19,279 | 19,239 | N. J. | 116,873 | 112,871 | 64,584 | 64,524 |
| Calif. | 350,091 | 340,661 | 159,892 | 159,610 | N. M. | 22,022 | 21,386 | 6,887 | 6,932 |
| Colo. | 36,107 | 37,236 | 16,635 | 16,902 | N. Y. | 322,765 | 309,146 | 187,703 | 186,223 |
| Conn. | 51,289 | 49,046 | 25,847 | 25,823 | N. C. | 92,863 | 92,603 | 42,497 | 42,561 |
| Del. | 10,203 | 9,936 | 4,914 | 4,824 | N. D. | 12,411 | 11,382 | 5,769 | 5,433 |
| D. of C. | 29,103 | 28,589 | 10,863 | 10,430 | Ohio | 190,160 | 184,738 | 98,731 | 98,227 |
| Fla. | 101,643 | 100,167 | 63,889 | 65,386 | Okla. | 39,439 | 39,054 | 24,239 | 24,310 |
| Ga. | 90,504 | 86,302 | 38,239 | 38,085 | Ore. | 32,860 | 31,925 | 19,038 | 18,809 |
| Hawaii | 14,977 | 14,802 | 3,850 | 3,995 | Pa. | 196,927 | 189,261 | 126,557 | 125,251 |
| Idaho | 12,600 | 12,517 | 5,740 | 5,712 | R. I. | 16,837 | 16,288 | 9,488 | 9,378 |
| Ill. | 200,290 | 193,745 | 110,086 | 108,243 | S. C. | 50,609 | 50,005 | 21,878 | 21,507 |
| Ind. | 94,596 | 92,784 | 47,478 | 46,755 | S. D. | 12,525 | 11,379 | 6,524 | 6,351 |
| Iowa | 49,598 | 48,223 | 29,627 | 29,162 | Tenn. | 71,011 | 71,559 | 38,004 | 37,605 |
| Kan. | 34,925 | 33,445 | 21,714 | 21,369 | Texas | 212,271 | 206,104 | 87,343 | 86,436 |
| Ky. | 59,222 | 58,281 | 31,739 | 31,740 | Utah | 23,067 | 23,541 | 6,994 | 6,819 |
| La. | 77,609 | 74,896 | 32,824 | 31,781 | Vt. | 7,870 | 7,540 | 4,619 | 4,572 |
| Me. | 18,105 | 17,896 | 10,996 | 10,899 | Va. | 79,703 | 78,267 | 36,648 | 36,486 |
| Md. | 63,756 | 61,483 | 31,378 | 30,696 | Wash. | 50,116 | 54,912 | 29,004 | 29,677 |
| Mass. | 101,827 | 100,925 | 60,972 | 59,116 | W. Va. | 30,797 | 29,895 | 19,499 | 19,328 |
| Mich. | 164,210 | 162,271 | 74,206 | 74,356 | Wisc. | 79,869 | 75,642 | 40,304 | 39,683 |
| Minn. | 65,960 | 64,534 | 33,766 | 33,247 | Wyo. | 5,792 | 5,406 | 2,667 | 2,743 |
| Miss. | 48,276 | 46,691 | 22,792 | 21,892 | | | | | |
| Mo. | 80,989 | 78,563 | 52,507 | 51,278 | U. S. | 3,629,000 | 3,533,000 | 1,869,000 | 1,852,000 |
| Mont. | 12,526 | 12,107 | 6,814 | 6,518 | | | | | |

[1]Based on a 50-percent sample.

## BIRTHS AND DEATHS IN THE UNITED STATES

Data refer only to events occurring within the United States, including Alaska beginning in 1959 and Hawaii in 1960. Excludes fetal deaths. Rates per 1,000 population enumerated as of April 1 for 1940, 1950, and 1960; estimated as of July 1 for all other years. [1]Births based on a 50 percent sample.

| Year | Births | | | | Deaths | | | |
|---|---|---|---|---|---|---|---|---|
| | Males | Females | Totals | | Males | Females | Totals | |
| | | | Number | Rate | | | Number | Rate |
| 1940 | 1,211,684 | 1,148,715 | 2,360,399 | 17.9 | 791,003 | 626,266 | 1,417,269 | 10.8 |
| 1945 | 1,404,587 | 1,330,869 | 2,735,456 | 19.5 | 788,063 | 613,656 | 1,401,719 | 10.6 |
| 1950 | 1,823,555 | 1,730,594 | 3,554,149 | 23.6 | 827,749 | 624,705 | 1,452,454 | 9.6 |
| 1955 | 2,073,719 | 1,973,576 | 4,047,295 | 24.6 | 872,638 | 656,079 | 1,528,717 | 9.3 |
| 1960[1] | 2,179,708 | 2,078,142 | 4,257,850 | 23.7 | 975,648 | 736,334 | 1,711,982 | 9.5 |
| 1964[1] | 2,060,162 | 1,967,328 | 4,027,490 | 21.0 | 1,017,778 | 780,273 | 1,798,051 | 9.4 |
| 1965[1] | 1,927,054 | 1,833,304 | 3,760,358 | 19.4 | 1,035,200 | 792,936 | 1,828,136 | 9.4 |
| 1966 | 1,845,862 | 1,760,412 | 3,606,274 | 18.4 | 1,052,827 | 810,322 | 1,863,149 | 9.5 |
| 1967 (p) | ...... | ...... | 3,533,000 | 17.9 | ...... | ...... | 1,852,000 | 9.4 |

# Marriages, Divorces and Rates in the United States

Source: U. S. Dept. of Health, Education and Welfare. National Center for Health Statistics. Data refer only to events occurring within the United States, including Alaska beginning with 1959 and Hawaii with 1960. Rates per 1,000 population.

| Year | Marriages[1] | | Divorces[2] | | Year | Marriages[1] | | Divorces[2] | |
|---|---|---|---|---|---|---|---|---|---|
| | No. | Rate | No. | Rate[3] | | No. | Rate | No. | Rate[3] |
| 1890 | 570,000 | 9.0 | 33,461 | 0.5 | 1940 | 1,595,879 | 12.1 | 264,000 | 2.0 |
| 1895 | 620,000 | 8.9 | 40,387 | 0.6 | 1945 | 1,612,992 | 12.2 | 485,000 | 3.5 |
| 1900 | 709,000 | 9.3 | 55,751 | 0.7 | 1950 | 1,667,231 | 11.1 | 385,144 | 2.6 |
| 1905 | 842,000 | 10.0 | 67,976 | 0.8 | 1955 | 1,531,000 | 9.3 | 377,000 | 2.3 |
| 1910 | 948,166 | 10.3 | 83,045 | 0.9 | 1960 | 1,523,000 | 8.5 | 393,000 | 2.2 |
| 1915 | 1,007,595 | 10.0 | 104,298 | 1.0 | 1963 | 1,654,000 | 8.8 | 428,000 | 2.3 |
| 1920 | 1,274,476 | 12.0 | 170,505 | 1.6 | 1964 | 1,725,000 | 9.0 | 450,000 | 2.4 |
| 1925 | 1,188,334 | 10.3 | 175,449 | 1.5 | 1965 | 1,800,000 | 9.3 | 479,000 | 2.5 |
| 1930 | 1,126,856 | 9.2 | 195,961 | 1.6 | 1966 (p.) | 1,844,000 | 9.4 | 494,000 | 2.5 |
| 1935 | 1,327,000 | 10.4 | 218,000 | 1.7 | 1967 (p.) | 1,913,000 | 9.7 | 534,000 | 2.7 |

[1]Includes estimates and marriage licenses for some states for all years. [2]Includes reported annulments. [3]Divorce rates for 1945, based on population including armed forces overseas. (p) Provisional.

## MARRIAGES AND DIVORCES BY STATES

Data: Divorce 1964, Marriages 1966[1], by place of occurrence. Divorces include reported annulments.

| State | Marriages[1] 1967 | Divorces 1965 | State | Marriages[1] 1967 | Divorces 1965 | State | Marriages[1] 1967 | Divorces 1965 |
|---|---|---|---|---|---|---|---|---|
| Alabama | 42,518 | 11,036 | Louisiana | 31,461 | [3]4,623 | Oklahoma | 35,031 | 11,864 |
| Alaska | 2,579 | 1,118 | Maine | 9,162 | 2,521 | Oregon | 14,355 | 6,219 |
| Arizona | 14,737 | 8,575 | Maryland | 50,431 | 6,978 | Pennsylvania | 85,898 | 16,578 |
| Arkansas | 21,923 | 6,622 | Massachusetts | 40,977 | 7,848 | Rhode Island | 6,515 | 1,193 |
| California | 147,378 | 69,926 | Michigan | 84,701 | 20,305 | S. Carolina | 51,553 | 3,018 |
| Colorado | 21,845 | [2]6,700 | Minnesota | 27,973 | 4,893 | S. Dakota | 9,040 | 1,015 |
| Connecticut | 22,490 | 3,733 | Mississippi | 23,280 | 5,730 | Tennessee | 49,586 | 11,143 |
| Delaware | 3,586 | 740 | Missouri | 43,765 | 13,185 | Texas | 124,191 | 41,323 |
| Dist. of Col. | 7,593 | 1,328 | Montana | 5,503 | 2,002 | Utah | 10,220 | 2,872 |
| Florida | 55,835 | 23,574 | Nebraska | 13,000 | 2,520 | Vermont | 3,924 | 601 |
| Georgia | 54,690 | 12,043 | Nevada | 86,329 | 9,996 | Virginia | 48,701 | 8,889 |
| Hawaii | 7,339 | 1,111 | N. Hampshire | 9,313 | 1,573 | Washington | 38,497 | 11,518 |
| Idaho | 14,100 | 2,874 | New Jersey | 49,255 | 5,632 | West Virginia | 14,208 | 3,852 |
| Illinois | 105,535 | 24,654 | New Mexico | 8,443 | [3]3,662 | Wisconsin | 30,330 | 5,232 |
| Indiana | 52,269 | [2]18,520 | New York | 147,438 | 8,187 | Wyoming | 3,693 | 1,414 |
| Iowa | 22,342 | 5,258 | N. Carolina | 45,189 | 11,150 | | | |
| Kansas | 19,964 | 5,816 | N. Dakota | 4,942 | 720 | U. S. | 1,913,000 | 479,000 |
| Kentucky | 28,583 | 8,276 | Ohio | 80,650 | 25,780 | | | |

[1]Provisional. Data represent marriages reported, marriage intentions filed, or marriage licenses issued. [2]Data estimated. [3]Data incomplete.

# Deaths and Death Rates for Selected Causes

Source: National Center for Health Statistics, Public Health Service,
U. S. Dept. of Health, Education and Welfare

Rates per 100,000 population.

| 1967* Cause of death | Number | Rate | 1967* Cause of death | Number | Rate |
|---|---|---|---|---|---|
| All Causes.................. | 1,852,000 | 936.0 | Nonrheumatic chronic endo- | | |
| Tuberculosis, all forms....... | 6,560 | 3.3 | carditis and other myo- | | |
| Tuberculosis of respiratory system | 6,010 | 3.0 | cardial degeneration....... | 52,500 | 26.5 |
| Tuberculosis, other forms........ | 550 | 0.3 | Other diseases of heart....... | 32,550 | 16.5 |
| Syphilis and its sequelae.......... | 1,110 | 1.1 | Hypertensive heart disease... | 49,880 | 25.2 |
| Dysentery, all forms........ | 100 | 0.1 | Other hypertensive disease.... | 12,070 | 6.1 |
| Scarlet fever and streptococcal sore | | | General arteriosclerosis...... | 37,670 | 19.0 |
| throat............ | 70 | 0.0 | Other diseases of circulatory | | |
| Diphtheria........ | 20 | 0.0 | system................... | 30,190 | 15.3 |
| Whooping cough........ | 40 | 0.0 | Chronic and unspecified nephritis | | |
| Meningococcal infections........... | 660 | 0.3 | and other renal sclerosis...... | 9,490 | 4.8 |
| Acute poliomyelitis.......... | ..... | ..... | Influenza and pneumonia, except | | |
| Measles............ | 60 | 0.0 | pneumonia of newborn......... | 56,460 | 28.5 |
| Infectious hepatitis.... | 710 | 0.4 | Influenza.......... | 1,450 | 0.7 |
| Other infective and parasitic diseases | 5,190 | 2.6 | Pneumonia, except pneumonia of | | |
| Malignant neoplasms, incl. neoplasms | | | newborn.................. | 55,010 | 27.8 |
| of lymphatic and hematopoietic | | | Bronchitis................. | 5,830 | 2.9 |
| tissues................. | 314,630 | 159.0 | Other bronchopulmonix diseases.... | 29,320 | 14.8 |
| Malignant neoplasm of buccal cav- | | | Ulcer of stomach and duodenum.... | 10,180 | 5.1 |
| ity and pharynx............. | 6,770 | 3.4 | Appendicitis............... | 1,760 | 0.9 |
| Malignant neoplasm of digestive | | | Hernia and intestinal obstruction... | 10,090 | 5.1 |
| organs and peritoneum, not spec- | | | Gastritis, duodenitis, enteritis, and | | |
| ified as secondary........ | 95,170 | 48.1 | colitis, except diarrhea of newborn. | 7,800 | 3.9 |
| Malignant neoplasm of respiratory | | | Cirrhosis of liver......... | 27,410 | 13.9 |
| system, not specified as secondary | 59,160 | 29.9 | Cholelithiasis, cholecystitis, and | | |
| Malignant neoplasm of breast..... | 28,960 | 14.6 | cholangitis. ....... | 3,960 | 2.0 |
| Malignant neoplasm of genital | | | Acute nephritis, and nephritis with | | |
| organs................ | 40,130 | 20.3 | edema including nephrosis....... | 910 | 0.5 |
| Malignant neoplasm of urinary | | | Infections of kidney.............. | 8,590 | 4.3 |
| organs................... | 14,760 | 7.5 | Hyperplasia of prostate......... | 2,920 | 1.5 |
| Malignant neoplasm of other and | | | Deliveries and complications of preg- | | |
| unspecified sites.............. | 38,430 | 19.4 | nancy, childbirth, and the puer- | | |
| Leukemia and aleukemia......... | 14,510 | 7.3 | perium................... | 1,020 | 0.5 |
| Lymphosarcoma and other neo- | | | Abortion........... | 170 | 0.1 |
| plasms of lymphatic and hema- | | | Other complications.......... | | |
| topoietic tissues.......... | 16,740 | 8.5 | Congenital malformations........ | 850 | 0.4 |
| Benign neoplasms and neoplasms of | | | Certain diseases of early infancy.... | 17,070 | 8.6 |
| unspecified nature.............. | 5,090 | 2.6 | Birth injuries, postnatal asphyxia, | | |
| Asthma..................... | 3,960 | 2.0 | and atelectasis............ | 47,760 | 24.1 |
| Diabetes Mellitus................ | 34,430 | 17.4 | Infections of newborn.......... | | |
| Anemias................ | 3,270 | 1.7 | Other diseases peculiar to early | 19,880 | 10.0 |
| Meningitis, except meningococcal and | | | infancy, and immaturity un- | 3,380 | 1.7 |
| Tuberculosis................ | 1,940 | 1.0 | qualified.......... | 24,500 | 12.4 |
| Major cardiovascular-renal diseases.. | 1,016,950 | 514.0 | Symptoms, senility, and ill-defined | | |
| Diseases of cardiovascular system.. | 1,007,460 | 509.2 | conditions.............. | 24,470 | 12.4 |
| Vascular lesions affecting central | | | All other diseases.............. | 57,690 | 29.2 |
| nervous system............. | 202,940 | 102.6 | Accidents.................. | 108,960 | 55.1 |
| Diseases of heart............ | 724,590 | 366.2 | Motor vehicle accidents....... | 53,140 | 26.9 |
| Rheumatic fever and chronic | | | Nonmotor vehicle accidents.... | 55,820 | 28.2 |
| rheumatic heart disease.... | 14,120 | 7.1 | Accidents in the home........... | 21,550 | 10.9 |
| Arteriosclerotic heart disease | | | Other nonmotor vehicle accidents. | 34,270 | 17.3 |
| including coronary disease.. | 575,540 | 290.9 | Suicide................. | 20,700 | 10.5 |
| | | | Homicide.................. | 13,100 | 6.6 |

Due to rounding estimates of deaths, figures may not add to totals. *Provisional.

---

# Principal Types of Accidental Deaths

Source: National Center for Health Statistics, Data for 1967 are National Safety Council estimates

| Year | All types | Motor vehicle | Falls | Burns | Drown- ing | Fire- arms | Machin- ery | Poison gases | Other poisons |
|---|---|---|---|---|---|---|---|---|---|
| 1960........ | 93,806 | 38,137 | 19,023 | 7,645 | 6,529 | 2,334 | 1,951 | 1,253 | 1,679 |
| 1963........ | 100,669 | 43,564 | 19,335 | 8,172 | 6,347 | 2,263 | 1,965 | 1,489 | 2,061 |
| 1964........ | 105,000 | 47,700 | 18,941 | 7,379 | 6,709 | 2,275 | 1,945 | 1,360 | 2,100 |
| 1965........ | 108,004 | 49,163 | 19,984 | 7,347 | 6,799 | 2,344 | 2,054 | 1,526 | 2,110 |
| 1966........ | 113,563 | 53,041 | 20,066 | 8,084 | 7,084 | 2,558 | 2,070 | 1,648 | 2,283 |
| 1967 (est.)... | 112,000 | 53,100 | 19,800 | 7,700 | 6,800 | 2,800 | 2,100 | 1,600 | 2,400 |

## DEATH RATES PER 100,000 POPULATION

| 1960........ | 52.1 | 21.2 | 10.6 | 4.2 | 3.6 | 1.3 | 1.1 | 0.7 | 0.9 |
|---|---|---|---|---|---|---|---|---|---|
| 1963........ | 53.4 | 23.1 | 10.2 | 4.3 | 3.4 | 1.2 | 1.0 | 0.8 | 1.1 |
| 1964........ | 54.9 | 24.9 | 9.9 | 3.9 | 3.5 | 1.2 | 1.0 | 0.8 | 1.1 |
| 1965........ | 55.7 | 25.4 | 10.3 | 3.8 | 3.5 | 1.2 | 1.1 | 0.8 | 0.1 |
| 1966........ | 58.0 | 27.1 | 10.2 | 4.1 | 3.6 | 1.3 | 1.1 | 0.8 | 1.2 |
| 1967 (est.)... | 56.6 | 26.8 | 10.0 | 3.9 | 3.4 | 1.4 | 1.1 | 0.8 | 1.2 |

## ACCIDENTAL INJURIES BY SEVERITY OF INJURY

| 1967 Severity of injury | Total* | Motor vehicle | Work | Home | Public Non-motor vehicle |
|---|---|---|---|---|---|
| All injuries.............. | 10,900,000 | 1,950,000 | 2,200,000 | 4,350,000 | 2,500,000 |
| Deaths.............. | 112,000 | 53,100 | 14,200 | 28,500 | 20,000 |
| Nonfatal injuries........ | 10,800,000 | 1,900,000 | 2,200,000 | 4,300,000 | 2,500,000 |
| Permanent impairments.... | 400,000 | 160,000 | 90,000 | 110,000 | 60,000 |
| Temporary total disabilities | 10,400,000 | 1,750,000 | 2,100,000 | 4,200,000 | 2,450,000 |

## CERTAIN COSTS OF ACCIDENTAL INJURIES, 1967

| Total............ | $13,000,000,000 | $7,300,000,000 | $3,200,000,000 | $1,500,000,000 | $1,200,000,000 |
|---|---|---|---|---|---|
| Wage loss............... | 6,000,000,000 | 2,700,000,000 | 1,500,000,000 | 1,000,000,000 | 950,000,000 |
| Medical expense........ | 2,200,000,000 | 700,000,000 | 800,000,000 | 500,000,000 | 250,000,000 |
| Overhead cost of insurance.. | 4,800,000,000 | 3,900,000,000 | 900,000,000 | 10,000,000 | 10,000,000 |

*Duplications between motor-vehicle, work and home are eliminated in total.

# Marriage Information

Source: Compiled by William E. Mariano: Council on Marriage Relations, Inc.,
110 East 42 St., New York, N. Y. 10017 (as of Oct. 15, 1968)

Marriageable age, by states, for both males and females with and without consent of parents or guardians. But in most states, the court has authority, in an emergency, to marry young couples below the ordinary age of consent, where due regard for their morals and welfare so requires.

| State | With consent | | Without consent | | Blood test | | Wait for license | Wait after license |
| | Men | Women | Men | Women | Required | Other state accepted | | |
|---|---|---|---|---|---|---|---|---|
| Alabama (b) | 17 | 14 | 21 | 18 | Yes | Yes | None | None |
| Alaska | 18 | 16 | 21 | 18 | Yes | ........ | 3 days | None |
| Arizona | 18 | 16 | 21 | 18 | Yes | Yes | (g) | None |
| Arkansas | 18 | 16 | 21 | 18 | Yes | No | 3 days | None |
| California | 18 | 16 | 21 | 18 | Yes | Yes | None | None |
| Colorado | 16 | 16 | 21 | 18 | Yes | Yes | None | None |
| Connecticut | 16 | 16 | 21 | 21 | Yes | Yes | 4 days | None |
| Delaware | 18 | 16 | 21 | 18 | Yes | No | None | (c) |
| District of Columbia | 18 | 16 | 21 | 18 | Yes | Yes | 4 days | None |
| Florida | 18 | 16 | 21 | 21 | Yes | Yes | 3 days | None |
| Georgia | 18 | 16 | 19 | 18 | Yes | Yes | None(b) | None |
| Hawaii | 18 | 16 | 20 | 20 | Yes | No | 3 days | None |
| Idaho | 18 | 16 | 21 | 18 | Yes | Yes | None(i) | None |
| Illinois (a) | 18 | 16 | 21 | 18 | Yes | Yes | None | None |
| Indiana | 18 | 16 | 21 | 18 | Yes | No | 3 days | None |
| Iowa | 18 | 16 | 21 | 18 | Yes | No | 3 days | None |
| Kansas | 18 | 18 | 21 | 18 | Yes | Yes | 3 days | None |
| Kentucky | 18 | 16 | 18 | 18 | Yes | No | 3 days | None |
| Louisiana (a) | 18 | 16 | 21 | 21 | Yes | No | None | 72 hours |
| Maine | 16 | 16 | 21 | 18 | Yes | Yes | 5 days | None |
| Maryland | 18 | 16 | 21 | 18 | None | None | 48 hours | None |
| Massachusetts | 18 | 16 | 21 | 18 | Yes | Yes | 3 days | None |
| Michigan | 18 | 16 | 18 | 18 | Yes | No | 3 days | None |
| Minnesota | 18 | 16 | 21 | 18 | None | ........ | 5 days | None |
| Mississippi (b) | 17 | 15 | 21 | 18 | Yes | ........ | 3 days | None |
| Missouri | 15 | 15 | 21 | 18 | Yes | ........ | 3 days | None |
| Montana | 18 | 16 | 21 | 18 | Yes | Yes | 5 days | None |
| Nebraska | 18 | 16 | 21 | 21 | Yes | Yes | None | None |
| Nevada | 18 | 16 | 21 | 18 | None | None | None | None |
| New Hampshire (a) | 14(e) | 13(e) | 20 | 18 | Yes | ........ | 5 days | None |
| New Jersey (a) | 18 | 16 | 21 | 18 | Yes | Yes | 72 hours | None |
| New Mexico | 18 | 16 | 21 | 18 | Yes | No | 3 days | None |
| New York | 16 | 14 | 21 | 18 | Yes | No | None | 24 hrs. (h) |
| North Carolina | 16 | 16 | 18 | 18 | Yes | No | None | None |
| North Dakota (a) | 18 | 15 | 21 | 18 | Yes | No | None | None |
| Ohio (a) | 18 | 16 | 21 | 21 | Yes | No | 5 days | None |
| Oklahoma | 18 | 15 | 21 | 18 | Yes | No | None(i) | ** |
| Oregon | 18(e) | 15(e) | 21 | 18 | Yes | No | 7 days | None |
| Pennsylvania | 16 | 16 | 21 | 21 | Yes | No | 3 days | None |
| Rhode Island (a) (b) | 18 | 16 | 21 | 21 | Yes | No | none | None |
| South Carolina | 16 | 14 | 18 | 18 | None | None | 24 hrs. | None |
| South Dakota | 18 | 16 | 21 | 18 | Yes | No | None | None |
| Tennessee (b) | 16 | 16 | 21 | 21 | Yes | Yes | 3 days | None |
| Texas | 16 | 14 | 21 | 18 | Yes | Yes | (b) | None |
| Utah | 16 | 14 | 21 | 18 | Yes | Yes | None | None |
| Vermont (a) | 18 | 14(e) | 21 | 18 | Yes | ........ | None | 5 days |
| Virginia | 18 | 16 | 21 | 21 | Yes | Yes | None | None |
| Washington | 17 | 17 | 21 | 18 | (d) | ........ | 3 days | None |
| West Virginia | 18 | 16 | 21 | 21 | Yes | No | 3 days | None |
| Wisconsin | 18 | 16 | 21 | 18 | Yes | Yes | 5 days | None |
| Wyoming | 18 | 16 | 21 | 21 | Yes | Yes | None | None |
| Puerto Rico | 18 | 16 | 21 | 21 | (f) | None | None | None |
| Virgin Islands | 16 | 14 | 21 | 18 | None | None | None | 8 days |

(a) Special laws applicable to non-residents. (b) Special laws applicable to those under 21 years; Alabama—bond required if male is under 21, female under 18. (c) 24 hours if one or both parties resident of state; 96 hours if both parties are non-residents. (d) None, but male must file affidavit. (e) Parental consent plus Court's consent required. (f) None, but a medical certificate is required. (g) Wait for license from time blood test is taken; Arizona, 48 hours. (h) Marriage may not be solemnized within 3 days from date of blood test. (i) If either under 21: Idaho, 3 days; Oklahoma, 72 hrs.

# Wedding Anniversaries

The traditional names for wedding anniversaries go back many years in social usage. As such names as wooden, crystal, silver and golden were applied it was considered proper to present the married pair with gifts made of these products or of something related. While the list of permissible gifts is extensive, gifts are most appropriate when retaining a suggestion of the originals. Thus the wooden anniversary may call for anything of wood, including furniture, but as the years mount the gifts become more valuable until the 60th or diamond anniversary, calls for diamonds. The traditional list follows, with a few allowable revisions in parenthesis.

1st—Paper
2nd—Cotton
3rd—Leather
4th—Linen, (silk)
5th—Wood

6th—Iron
7th—Wool, copper
8th—Bronze
9th—Pottery, (china)
10th—Tin, (aluminum)

11th—Steel
12th—Silk
13th—Lace
14th—Ivory
15th—Crystal

20th—China
25th—Silver
30th—Pearl
35th—Coral
40th—Ruby

45th—Sapphire
50th—Gold
55th—Emerald
60th—Diamond

# Birth Stones

Source: Retail Jewelers of America, Inc.

| Month | Ancient | Modern | Month | Ancient | Modern | Month | Ancient | Modern |
|---|---|---|---|---|---|---|---|---|
| January | Garnet | Garnet | May | Agate | Emerald | September | Chrysolite | Sapphire |
| February | Amethyst | Amethyst | June | Emerald | Pearl, Moonstone or Alexandrite | October | Aquamarine | Opal or Tourmaline |
| March | Jasper | Bloodstone or Aquamarine | July | Onyx | Ruby | November | Topaz | Topaz |
| April | Sapphire | Diamond | August | Carnelian | Sardonyx or Peridot | December | Ruby | Turquoise or Zircon |

The term precious stones actually applies only to diamonds, rubies, sapphires and emeralds. All others are semiprecious. Precious gems are minerals brought to perfection by the lapidary's art. The pearl, often a gem of great value, is not a precious stone.

# Grounds for Divorce

**Source:** Compiled by William E. Mariano: Council on Marriage Relations, Inc., 110 East 42nd Street, New York 17, N. Y. Persons contemplating divorce should study latest decisions or secure legal advice before initiating proceedings since different interpretations or exceptions in each case can change the conclusion reached. Some states apply statutes strictly, others are more lenient.

| State | Adultery | Cruelty | Desertion | Non-support | Alcoholism | Felony | Impotency | Pregnancy at marriage | Drug addiction | Fraudulent contract | Other causes | Residence time | Time between interlocutory and final decrees |
|---|---|---|---|---|---|---|---|---|---|---|---|---|---|
| Alabama | x | x | x | x | x | x | x | x | x | .... | A-Q-K-W | 1 year* | None-R |
| Alaska | x | x | x | x | x | x | x | .... | x | .... | F-K-B | 1 year | None |
| Arizona | x | x | x | x | x | x | x | .... | x | .... | X | 1 year | None |
| Arkansas | x | x | x | x | x | x | x | .... | x | .... | B-Y-K-DD | 3 months* | None |
| California | x | x | x | x | x | x | .... | .... | .... | .... | K | 1 year | 1 year |
| Colorado | x | x | x | x | x | x | .... | .... | x | .... | K-W | 1 year* | None |
| Connecticut | x | x | x | .... | x | x | .... | .... | .... | x | K-F | 3 years* | None |
| Delaware | x | x | x | .... | x | x | x | .... | .... | .... | K-Y-DD-FF | 2 years | 3 months |
| Dist. of Columbia | x | .... | x | .... | .... | x | .... | .... | .... | .... | Y-Z | 1 year | None |
| Florida | x | x | x | .... | x | .... | x | .... | x | .... | A-M-BB-DD | 6 months | None |
| Georgia | x | x | .... | x | x | x | x | x | .... | x | K-M-AA | 6 months | None-U |
| Hawaii | x | x | x | x | x | x | x | .... | .... | .... | K-Z-B | 1 | 1 |
| Idaho | x | x | x | x | x | x | .... | .... | .... | .... | X-K | 6 weeks | None |
| Illinois | x | x | x | .... | x | x | x | .... | x | .... | A-C-DD-EE | 1 year* | None |
| Indiana | x | x | x | x | x | x | .... | .... | .... | .... | K | 1 year* | None |
| Iowa | x | x | x | x | x | x | .... | x | .... | .... | | 1 year* | None-S |
| Kansas | x | x | x | x | x | x | .... | .... | x | x | K | 1 year* | None-T |
| Kentucky | x | x | x | .... | x | x | x | x | x | x | C-D-E-X-K | 1 year | None |
| Louisiana | x | .... | .... | .... | x | .... | .... | .... | .... | .... | X-Z | 1 year* | None |
| Maine | x | x | x | x | x | x | .... | .... | x | .... | | 6 months | None |
| Maryland | x | .... | x | .... | .... | x | x | .... | .... | .... | Y-K | 1 year | None |
| Massachusetts | x | x | x | x | .... | x | x | .... | x | .... | Y-K | 5 years* | 6 mos. |
| Michigan | x | x | x | x | x | x | .... | .... | .... | .... | | 1 year* | None |
| Minnesota | x | x | x | .... | x | x | x | .... | .... | .... | K-W | 1 year | None-T |
| Mississippi | x | x | x | x | x | x | x | x | .... | .... | K-M-DD | 1 year* | None-U |
| Missouri | x | x | x | x | x | x | x | .... | .... | .... | B-J | 1 year | None |
| Montana | x | x | x | .... | x | .... | .... | .... | .... | .... | K | 1 year | None* |
| Nebraska | x | x | x | x | x | x | .... | .... | .... | .... | K | 2 years* | 6 months |
| Nevada | x | x | x | .... | x | x | x | .... | .... | .... | F-K-Y | 6 weeks | None |
| New Hampshire | x | x | x | x | x | x | x | .... | .... | .... | D | 1 year* | None |
| New Jersey | x | x | x | .... | .... | .... | .... | .... | .... | .... | | 2 years* | 3 months |
| New Mexico | x | x | x | x | x | x | .... | .... | .... | .... | K-F | 1 year* | None |
| New York | x | x | x | .... | .... | x | .... | .... | .... | .... | X-Z | 1 year* | 3 mos.* |
| North Carolina | x | .... | .... | .... | .... | .... | x | x | .... | .... | Q-K-X | 6 months | None |
| North Dakota | x | x | x | x | x | x | .... | .... | .... | .... | K | 1 year | None-U |
| Ohio | x | x | x | x | x | x | .... | .... | .... | .... | K | 1 year | None |
| Oklahoma | x | x | x | .... | x | x | x | .... | .... | x | BB-CC-DD | 1 year | None |
| Oregon | x | x | x | .... | x | x | x | .... | .... | x | F-K-BB-CC | 6 months | 6 months |
| Pennsylvania | x | x | x | .... | .... | x | x | .... | .... | x | B-M-DD | 1 year* | None |
| Rhode Island | x | x | x | x | x | x | x | .... | x | .... | H-X | 2 years* | 6 months |
| South Carolina | x | x | x | .... | x | .... | .... | .... | .... | .... | | 1 year | None |
| South Dakota | x | x | x | x | x | x | .... | .... | .... | .... | | 1 year* | None |
| Tennessee | x | x | x | x | x | x | x | x | .... | .... | K | 2 years | None |
| Texas | x | x | x | .... | x | x | .... | .... | .... | .... | A-B-DD-EE | 2 years | None |
| Utah | x | x | x | x | .... | x | x | .... | .... | .... | K-X | 1 year | None-N |
| Vermont | x | x | x | x | .... | x | .... | .... | .... | .... | W-K | 6 months | 6 mos.-O* |
| Virginia | x | .... | x | .... | .... | x | x | x | .... | .... | I-B | 1 year | None-U* |
| Washington | x | x | x | x | x | x | x | .... | .... | x | B-K-Y | 1 year | None |
| West Virginia | x | x | x | x | x | x | .... | .... | x | .... | | 2 years*2 | None-R-U |
| Wisconsin | x | x | x | x | x | x | .... | .... | .... | .... | X-W | 2 years | 1 year |
| Wyoming | x | x | x | x | x | x | x | x | .... | .... | B-J-K | 60 days | |

*Exceptions are to be noted. ¹Determined by court order. ²No minimum residence required in adultery cases. A—Violence. B—Indignities. C—Loathsome disease. D—Joining religious order disbelieving in marriage. E—Unchaste behavior after marriage. F—Incompatibility. H—Any gross misbehavior or wickedness. I—Wife being a prostitute. J—Husband being a vagrant. K—5 years insanity; exceptions: 18 months Alaska; 2 years Georgia, Nevada, Oregon, Washington and Wyoming; 3 years Arkansas, California, Colorado, Kansas, Hawaii, Maryland, Mississippi; 6 years Idaho. M—Consanguinity. N—In cruelty cases, one year to remarry. O—Plaintiff, six months; defendant, two years to remarry. P—If guilty spouse is sentenced to infamous punishment. Q—Crime against nature. R—Sixty days to remarry. S—One year to remarry; Hawaii; one year with minor child. T—Six months to remarry; in Kansas 30 days. U—Adultery cases, remarriage in discretion of Court. W—Separation for three years after decree for same. In Alabama four years. In Minnesota two years and Wisconsin five years. X—Separation no cohabitation—five years. Exceptions: Louisiana, Virginia, Wyoming and New York (under agreement) two years; Texas 3 years and Rhode Island 10 years. Y—Separation no cohabitation—three years. Exception: North Carolina, one year if caused by criminal act of defendant; Dist. of Columbia and Nevada, one year; Maryland, 18 mos.; Washington, two years. Z—Separation for two years after decree for same, District of Columbia and Louisiana one year. AA—Mental incapacity at time of marriage. BB—Procurement of out-of-state divorce. CC—Gross neglect of duty. DD—Bigamy. EE—Attempted homicide. FF—Plaintiff under age at time of marriage.

The plaintiff can invariably remarry in the same State where he or she procured a decree of divorce for annulment. Not so the defendant, who is barred, in certain States for some offenses. After a period of time has elapsed even the offender can apply for special permission.

The U. S. Supreme Court in a 5 to 4 opinion, ruled April 18, 1949, that one-sided quick divorces could be challenged as illegal if notice of the action was not served on the divorced partner within the divorcing States, excepting where the partner was represented at the proceedings.

**Enoch Arden Laws.** Disappearance and unknown to be alive—Connecticut 7 years absence; New Hampshire, 2 years; New York, 5 years (called dissolution); Vermont, 7 years.

# Blue Cross Hospitalization Plans in U. S. and Canada

**Source:** Blue Cross Association, Enrollment as of Jan. 1, 1968

| State | Plans | Number | State | Plans | Number | State | Plans | Number |
|---|---|---|---|---|---|---|---|---|
| Alabama | 1 | 841,683 | Missouri | 2 | 1,575,171 | Health Service Inc. | 1 | 129,518 |
| Arizona | 1 | 241,134 | Montana | 1 | 42,091 | Jamaica | 1 | 12,692 |
| Arkansas | 1 | 325,328 | Nebraska | 1 | 272,378 | Puerto Rico | 1 | N/A |
| California | 2 | 2,839,022 | N. H. & Vt | 1 | 400,431 | **Canadian Provinces** | | |
| Colorado | 1 | 756,824 | New Jersey | 1 | 3,045,695 | | | |
| Connecticut | 1 | 1,490,783 | New Mexico | 1 | 112,896 | Alberta | 1 | 302,445 |
| Delaware | 1 | 359,456 | New York | 8 | 10,443,198 | New Brunswick, | | |
| Dist. of Col | 1 | 1,204,040 | North Carolina | 2 | 1,303,548 | Newfoundland, | | |
| Florida | 1 | 1,066,650 | North Dakota | 1 | 239,095 | Nova Scotia, | | |
| Georgia | 2 | 672,181 | Ohio | 7 | 5,057,705 | Prince Edward | | |
| Idaho | 1 | 105,831 | Oklahoma | 1 | 550,089 | Island | 1 | 431,076 |
| Illinois | 2 | 2,782,653 | Oregon | 1 | 381,674 | Ontario | 1 | 2,702,464 |
| Indiana | 1 | 1,822,214 | Pennsylvania | 5 | 6,044,466 | Quebec | 1 | 925,320 |
| Iowa-S. Dak | 2 | 925,367 | Rhode Island | 1 | 701,948 | | | |
| Kansas | 1 | 663,413 | South Carolina | 1 | 338,284 | **48 States, District of Columbia, 7 Canadian Provinces, Jamaica, Puerto Rico** | | |
| Kentucky | 1 | 1,021,046 | Tennessee | 2 | 1,138,880 | | | |
| Louisiana | 2 | 743,618 | Texas | 1 | 2,042,069 | | | |
| Maine | 1 | 384,585 | Utah | 1 | 290,944 | | | |
| Maryland | 1 | 1,188,005 | Virginia | 2 | 1,026,845 | | | |
| Massachusetts | 1 | 3,144,951 | Wash. & Alaska | 1 | 339,004 | | | |
| Michigan | 1 | 4,586,704 | West Virginia | 4 | 339,542 | | | |
| Minnesota | 1 | 810,133 | Wisconsin | 1 | 1,185,106 | Total | 82 | 69,895,423 |
| Mississippi | 1 | 459,956 | Wyoming | 1 | 85,272 | | | |

Blue Cross Plans are local non-profit organizations that provide hospital service to members. Enrollment as of Dec. 31, 1967 constituted 33.1% of the population of the United States served by Blue Cross and 26.7% of the seven provinces served by the four Canadian Plans. During 1967, Blue Cross paid $3.5 billion to hospitals for 13,-500,000 hospital admissions and outpatient visits and 58,100,000 days of care. This amount represents 90% of total earned income, the remainder being allocated to operating expenses (5.4% of total income); 4.6% was added to reserves.

Blue Cross Plans provide services for periods ranging from 21 to 730 days at full benefits, plus occasionally a period of partial benefits ranging from 30 to 245 days. All plans provide board and room, general nursing care, use of operating and delivery rooms, routine laboratory service, routine drugs and medications, routine dressings and casts. Many of the plans cover the following services in varying degrees: special diets, emergency room care, anesthesia, X-Ray, electrocardiograms, basal metabolism tests, physical therapy, oxygen therapy, pathology, special drugs and medications, and other hospital services.

Members of one Plan moving into the area of another Plan usually must transfer their membership. A reciprocal program, the Inter-Plan Service Benefits Bank, supplemented by schedules of benefits in non-member hospitals, assures receipt of care in any recognized general hospital in the world. Health Service, Incorporated, a Blue Cross-owned stock company, provides a means for enrollment of employees of national firms. Medical and surgical care are available through non-profit prepayment Plans, most of which are known as Blue Shield Plans.

# Blue Shield Medical-Surgical Plans

**Source:** John W. Castellucci, Executive Vice-President.

National Association of Blue Shield Plans as of March 31, 1968

| State | Plans | Number | State | Plans | Number | State | Plans | Number |
|---|---|---|---|---|---|---|---|---|
| Alabama | 1 | 243,756 | Mississippi | 1 | 434,969 | West Virginia | 7 | 368,383 |
| Arizona | 1 | 824,149 | Missouri | 2 | 1,250,197 | Wisconsin | 2 | 1,503,266 |
| Arkansas | 1 | 326,251 | Montana | 1 | 97,266 | Wyoming | 1 | 84,247 |
| California | 1 | 1,341,026 | Nebraska | 1 | 268,029 | Puerto Rico | 1 | 129,049 |
| Colorado | 1 | 718,685 | N. Hampshire | 1 | 414,585 | Medical Indemnity of America | 1 | 176,602 |
| Connecticut | 1 | 1,245,395 | New Jersey | 1 | 2,947,437 | | | |
| Delaware | 1 | 333,544 | New Mexico | 1 | 111,728 | **Canada** | | |
| Dist. of Col | 1 | 1,150,627 | New York | 7 | 8,035,429 | | | |
| Florida | 1 | 1,055,139 | North Carolina | 1 | 1,274,146 | Alberta | 1 | 637,649 |
| Georgia | 2 | 600,462 | North Dakota | 1 | 228,365 | British Columbia | 1 | 736,367 |
| Hawaii | 1 | 336,080 | Ohio | 2 | 4,104,347 | Manitoba | 1 | 622,170 |
| Idaho | 1 | 43,542 | Oklahoma | 1 | 551,452 | Maritime Prov | 1 | 397,888 |
| Illinois | 2 | 2,350,147 | Oregon | 1 | 178,082 | Ontario | 2 | 1,794,566 |
| Indiana | 1 | 1,788,750 | Pennsylvania | 1 | 5,311,571 | Quebec | 1 | 899,828 |
| Iowa | 1 | 782,632 | Rhode Island | 1 | 684,642 | Saskatchewan | 2 | ......... |
| Kansas | 1 | 672,432 | South Carolina | 1 | 332,416 | **47 States, Dist. Of Columbia, Puerto Rico, and Canadian Provinces** | | |
| Kentucky | 1 | 960,387 | South Dakota | 1 | 72,852 | | | |
| Maine | 1 | 349,696 | Tennessee | 2 | 1,052,941 | | | |
| Maryland | 1 | 1,003,144 | Texas | 1 | 2,015,078 | | | |
| Massachusetts | 1 | 3,076,849 | Utah | 1 | 277,050 | | | |
| Michigan | 1 | 4,383,562 | Virginia | 2 | 1,028,888 | Total 1968 | 82 | 62,951,957 |
| Minnesota | 1 | 640,338 | Washington | 7 | 705,933 | Total 1967 | 84 | 60,479,873 |

Blue Shield Plans offer prepaid coverage for medical-surgical expenses. They are nonprofit in operation and are approved by local medical societies or physician communities. Total underwritten enrollment consisted of 29.3% of the population of the United States served by the 72 U. S. Blue Shield Plans on March 31, 1968. Canadian enrollment consisted of 26.5% of the population served by the 9 Canadian Blue Shield Plans. The underwritten enrollment of the Blue Shield Plan in Puerto Rico amounted to 5.5% of the population. During the first quarter of 1968, Blue Shield paid $411,758,702 for medical care of Blue Shield members. This amount represented 87.7% of total income, 9.5% was devoted to operating expense and 2.8% was added to reserves.

Blue Shield Plans provide paid-in-full, service and indemnity benefits. Paid-in-full programs provide benefits without any income limitations. Service programs provide paid-in-full benefits, providing the subscriber is within certain income limitations. On the average, income limits are $6,000 for individuals and $7,500 for families. When the member's annual income exceeds the income limits, payments are made as indemnities toward the cost of covered services. Indemnity benefits provide cash allowances toward the cost of services.

Basic Blue Shield benefits include medical service, surgical and obstetrical care, laboratory examinations, radiology and anesthesia. In addition, many Plans provide coverage for medical examinations, assistant surgeons' fees, and consultants' services. New benefit areas such as prescription drugs, home and office care, dental care and others have been implemented by some Plans and are being widely studied by others.

Members of one Plan moving into the area of another must usually transfer their membership. The majority of Blue Shield Plans are coordinated with Blue Cross Plans.

# Health Insurance Coverage by Insurance Companies
Source: Health Insurance Institute, New York, N. Y.

At the beginning of 1968 insurance companies writing health insurance policies in the U. S. provided hospital expense protection to a net total of 100,298,000 persons. At the beginning of 1967, there were 1,045 companies writing these policies. Many of these companies were licensed to operate in all 50 states and the District of Columbia, some were licensed to operate in several states, and a few were licensed in only one state. In 1940, they covered some 3,700,000 persons with hospital insurance.

There have been significant increases in four other types of health insurance provided by insurance companies—surgical expense insurance, regular medical expense insurance, major medical expense insurance, and loss of income insurance. As of Dec. 31, 1967, insurance companies provided protection against the cost of surgery to 93,618,000 persons, compared with 2,280,000 in 1940. Coverage under regular medical insurance, which pays for doctor's calls and other non-surgical care by doctors, was held by 64,604,000 persons at the end of 1967 compared with 200,000 in 1944, the first

year insurance companies offered regular medical expense protection. Major medical expense insurance, which normally provides benefits of $10,000 or more to pay for virtually all types of medical services, covered 62,226,000 persons at the end of 1967, compared with 108,000 in 1951, the first year major medical insurance was introduced nationally. Disability income insurance, which replaces income lost as a result of sickness or injury, protected through insurance company policies a total of 43,512,000 workers at the close of 1967 compared with 14,369,000 in 1946.

In 1967 insurance companies paid out $6,029,-000,000 in health insurance benefits. This total included $1,211,000 in loss of income benefit payments.

The Health Insurance Council in its 22nd annual survey of the extent of voluntary health insurance coverage in the United States, reported that at the end of 1967 insurance companies, Blue Cross-Blue Shield and other health care plans, provided hospital insurance to 162,853,000 persons and paid out $11,037,000 in benefits.

## Average Future Lifetime in United States
Source: U. S. Dept. of Health, Education and Welfare, National Center for Health Statistics, 1966 Data

| Age interval | Number living[1] | Average remaining lifetime[2] | | | | |
|---|---|---|---|---|---|---|
| | | Total | White | | Nonwhite | |
| | | | Male | Female | Male | Female |
| 0-1 | 100,000 | 70.1 | 67.6 | 74.7 | 60.7 | 67.4 |
| 1-5 | 97,639 | 70.8 | 68.2 | 75.1 | 62.4 | 68.8 |
| 5-10 | 97,276 | 67.1 | 64.4 | 71.3 | 58.8 | 65.2 |
| 10-15 | 97,063 | 62.2 | 59.6 | 66.4 | 54.0 | 60.4 |
| 15-20 | 96,863 | 57.3 | 54.7 | 61.5 | 49.2 | 55.5 |
| 20-25 | 96,368 | 52.6 | 50.1 | 56.7 | 44.6 | 50.7 |
| 25-30 | 95,727 | 48.0 | 45.5 | 51.8 | 40.3 | 46.0 |
| 30-35 | 95,072 | 43.3 | 40.8 | 47.0 | 36.0 | 41.4 |
| 35-40 | 94,258 | 38.6 | 36.2 | 42.2 | 31.9 | 37.0 |
| 40-45 | 93,118 | 34.1 | 31.6 | 37.5 | 28.0 | 32.8 |
| 45-50 | 91,390 | 29.7 | 27.2 | 32.9 | 24.2 | 28.8 |
| 50-55 | 88,753 | 25.5 | 23.1 | 28.5 | 20.8 | 25.0 |
| 55-60 | 84,779 | 21.5 | 19.3 | 24.2 | 17.6 | 21.3 |
| 60-65 | 79,029 | 17.9 | 15.9 | 20.2 | 14.9 | 18.1 |
| 65-70 | 71,298 | 14.6 | 12.9 | 16.3 | 12.4 | 15.2 |
| 70-75 | 60,781 | 11.6 | 10.3 | 12.8 | 11.0 | 13.4 |
| 75-80 | 48,078 | 9.0 | 8.0 | 9.6 | 9.8 | 11.2 |
| 80-85 | 34,040 | 6.7 | 6.1 | 6.9 | 8.4 | 9.2 |
| 85 and over | 19,855 | 4.7 | 4.4 | 4.7 | 6.7 | 7.0 |

[1]Of 100,000 born alive, number living at beginning of age interval.
[2]Average number of years of life remaining at beginning of age interval.

### YEARS OF LIFE EXPECTED AT BIRTH*

| Year | Total | Male | Female | Year | Total | Male | Female |
|---|---|---|---|---|---|---|---|
| 1967[1] | 70.5 | 67.0 | 74.2 | 1935 | 61.7 | 59.9 | 63.9 |
| 1966 | 70.1 | 66.7 | 73.8 | 1930 | 59.7 | 58.1 | 61.6 |
| 1965 | 70.2 | 66.8 | 73.7 | 1925 | 59.0 | 57.6 | 60.6 |
| 1960 | 69.7 | 66.6 | 73.1 | 1920 | 54.1 | 53.6 | 54.6 |
| 1955 | 69.5 | 66.6 | 72.7 | 1915 | 54.5 | 52.5 | 56.8 |
| 1950 | 68.2 | 65.6 | 71.1 | 1910 | 50.0 | 48.4 | 51.8 |
| 1945 | 65.9 | 63.6 | 67.9 | 1905 | 48.7 | 47.3 | 50.2 |
| 1940 | 62.9 | 60.8 | 65.2 | 1900 | 47.3 | 46.3 | 48.3 |

*Based on Death-Registration States 1900-1925, and United States 1930-1966. [1]Provisional.

## Average Weight of Americans by Height and Age
Source: Society of Actuaries; from its 1959 report on a 4-year study of 5,000,000 persons
The figures represent weights in ordinary indoor clothing and shoes, and heights with shoes.

| MEN | | | | | | WOMEN | | | | | |
|---|---|---|---|---|---|---|---|---|---|---|---|
| Height | 20-24 | 25-29 | 30-39 | 40-49 | 50-59 | Height | 20-24 | 25-29 | 30-39 | 40-49 | 50-59 |
| 5'0" | 122 | 128 | 131 | 134 | 136 | 4'10" | 102 | 107 | 115 | 122 | 125 |
| 5'1" | 125 | 131 | 134 | 137 | 139 | 4'11" | 105 | 110 | 117 | 124 | 127 |
| 5'2" | 128 | 134 | 137 | 140 | 142 | 5'0" | 108 | 113 | 120 | 127 | 130 |
| 5'3" | 132 | 138 | 141 | 144 | 145 | 5'1" | 112 | 116 | 123 | 130 | 133 |
| 5'4" | 136 | 141 | 145 | 148 | 149 | 5'2" | 115 | 119 | 126 | 133 | 136 |
| 5'5" | 139 | 144 | 149 | 152 | 153 | 5'3" | 118 | 122 | 129 | 136 | 140 |
| 5'6" | 142 | 148 | 153 | 156 | 157 | 5'4" | 121 | 125 | 132 | 140 | 144 |
| 5'7" | 145 | 151 | 157 | 161 | 162 | 5'5" | 125 | 129 | 135 | 143 | 148 |
| 5'8" | 149 | 155 | 161 | 165 | 166 | 5'6" | 129 | 133 | 139 | 147 | 152 |
| 5'9" | 153 | 159 | 165 | 169 | 170 | 5'7" | 132 | 136 | 142 | 151 | 156 |
| 5'10" | 157 | 163 | 170 | 174 | 175 | 5'8" | 136 | 140 | 146 | 155 | 160 |
| 5'11" | 161 | 167 | 174 | 178 | 180 | 5'9" | 140 | 144 | 150 | 159 | 164 |
| 6'0" | 166 | 172 | 179 | 183 | 185 | 5'10" | 144 | 148 | 154 | 164 | 169 |
| 6'1" | 170 | 177 | 183 | 187 | 189 | 5'11" | 149 | 153 | 159 | 169 | 174 |
| 6'2" | 174 | 182 | 188 | 192 | 194 | 6'0" | 154 | 158 | 164 | 174 | 180 |
| 6'3" | 178 | 186 | 193 | 197 | 199 | | | | | | |
| 6'4" | 181 | 190 | 199 | 203 | 205 | | | | | | |

## Flower of the Month
**January**—Carnation or Snowdrop. **February**—Violet or Primrose. **March**—Jonquil or Daffodil. **April** —Sweet Pea or Daisy. **May**—Lily of the Valley or Hawthorn. **June**—Rose or Honeysuckle. **July**—Larkspur or Water Lily. **August**—Poppy or Gladiolus. **September**—Aster or Morning Glory. **October**—Calendula or Cosmos. **November**—Chrysanthemum. **December**—Narcissus or Holly.
**Baby Colors**—Blue for boys. Pink for girls.

# Estimated Number of Illegitimate Births

**Source:** Division of Statistics, Natl. Center for Health Statistics, U. S. Dept. H.E.W.

### Ratio Per 1,000 Unmarried Women

| | | | 1965[1] | 1964[1] | 1960[1] | 1950 | 1940 |
|---|---|---|---|---|---|---|---|
| 15-44 years[2] | (total) | | 23.5 | 23.0 | 21.6 | 14.1 | 7.1 |
| 15-44 " | (white) | | 11.6 | 11.0 | 9.2 | 6.1 | 3.6 |
| 15-44 " | (non-white) | | 97.6 | 97.2 | 98.3 | 71.2 | 35.6 |

[1]Based on a 50% sample of births. [2]Rates computed by relating total births, regardless of age of mother, to women, 15-44.

Only 34 states and the District of Columbia currently report illegitimacy. Among the nonreporting states are New York, California and Massachusetts, together account for 21% of all births in 1964. To obtain national estimates all states are grouped into geographic divisions. The ratio per 1,000 of illegitimate births reported for each division is then assumed to be the same for nonreporting states.

| 1964 State | Total | White | Negro | Other | 1964 State | Total | White | Negro | Other |
|---|---|---|---|---|---|---|---|---|---|
| | Number of illegitimate births | | | | | Number of illegitimate births | | | |
| **Total** | **195,068** | **73,692** | **118,512** | **2,864** | Nev. | 526 | 302 | 198 | 26 |
| Ala. | 9,162 | 950 | 8,210 | 2 | N. J. | 7,096 | 2,850 | 4,238 | 8 |
| Alaska | 420 | 116 | 12 | 292 | N. Car. | 10,874 | 1,988 | 8,662 | 224 |
| Del. | 1,194 | 316 | 874 | 4 | N. Dak. | 506 | 418 | 2 | 86 |
| Dis. of Col. | 4,648 | 412 | 4,232 | 4 | Ohio | 12,780 | 6,790 | 5,962 | 28 |
| Florida | 12,384 | 3,346 | 9,022 | 16 | Ore. | 1,690 | 1,492 | 152 | 46 |
| Hawaii | 1,138 | 314 | 22 | 802 | Pa. | 12,966 | 6,222 | 6,494 | 250 |
| Ill. | 17,096 | 5,666 | 11,386 | 44 | R. I. | 640 | 498 | 142 | — |
| Ind. | 5,772 | 3,554 | 2,214 | 4 | S. Car. | 7,266 | 808 | 6,456 | 2 |
| Iowa | 1,862 | 1,636 | 224 | 2 | S. Dak. | 796 | 444 | 6 | 346 |
| Kansas | 1,864 | 1,210 | 632 | 22 | Tenn. | 8,040 | 2,002 | 6,036 | 2 |
| Ky. | 4,140 | 2,370 | 1,768 | 2 | Texas | 14,906 | 6,578 | 8,320 | 8 |
| La. | 9,524 | 1,094 | 8,424 | 6 | Utah | 460 | 436 | 16 | 8 |
| Maine | 876 | 856 | 6 | 14 | Va. | 8,684 | 2,466 | 6,218 | — |
| Mich. | 9,800 | 5,330 | 4,444 | 26 | Wash. | 2,906 | 2,444 | 276 | 186 |
| Minn. | 3,570 | 3,100 | 218 | 252 | W. Va. | 2,486 | 1,980 | 506 | — |
| Miss. | 8,690 | 494 | 8,176 | 20 | Wis. | 3,606 | 2,686 | 826 | 94 |
| Mo. | 6,430 | 2,306 | 4,122 | 2 | Wyo. | 270 | 218 | 16 | 36 |

# Patients in State and County Mental Hospitals

**Source:** National Institute of Mental Health. Average daily number of resident patients, 1967

| State | No. | State | No. | State | No. | State | No. |
|---|---|---|---|---|---|---|---|
| Alabama | 7,726 | Indiana | 10,753 | Nevada | 534 | Tennessee | 7,147 |
| Alaska | 179 | Iowa | 1,685 | New Hampshire | 2,174 | Texas | 15,193 |
| Arizona | 1,202 | Kansas | 2,411 | New Jersey | 18,446 | Utah | 533 |
| Arkansas | 2,088 | Kentucky | 4,563 | New Mexico | 644 | Vermont | 1,161 |
| California | 23,284 | Louisiana | 5,665 | New York | 82,876 | Virginia | 11,583 |
| Colorado | 2,528 | Maine | 2,785 | North Carolina | 8,803 | Washington | 3,308 |
| Connecticut | 7,117 | Maryland | 8,426 | North Dakota | 1,373 | West Virginia | 5,240 |
| Delaware | 1,456 | Massachusetts | 15,936 | Ohio | 21,281 | Wisconsin | 13,005 |
| Dist. of Col. | 5,765 | Michigan | 16,789 | Oklahoma | 4,285 | Wyoming | 550 |
| Florida | 9,931 | Minnesota | 5,583 | Oregon | 2,485 | | |
| Georgia | 10,996 | Mississippi | 5,138 | Pennsylvania | 34,370 | **Total** | |
| Hawaii | 720 | Missouri | 9,538 | Rhode Island | 1,941 | | |
| Idaho | 713 | Montana | 1,428 | South Carolina | 6,137 | | **438,587** |
| Illinois | 26,682 | Nebraska | 2,933 | South Dakota | 1,498 | | |

*Provisional data. [1]Excludes data from one hospital.

The above data was based on reports from 304 of 306 State and County hospitals. The full-time personnel was estimated at 218,948 and the expenditures $1,415,480,302. The average daily expenditures per patient based on the resident patient population of hospitals reporting expenditures was $8.84.

# Patients Under Care by Type of Facility in United States

**Source:** National Institute of Mental Health Data for 1967 (Provisional data)

| Type of Facility | Facilities Reporting | Residents July 1, 1966 | Total Admissions | Deaths in Hosps. | Net Live Releases[1] | Residents June30,1967 |
|---|---|---|---|---|---|---|
| State and County Hosps. | 304 of 306 | 452,793 | 348,561 | 39,608 | 335,737 | 426,009 |
| Private Mental Hosps[2] | 148 of 174 | | 43,804[3] | | | 12,173[4] |
| Public Inst. for Mentally Retarded | 165 of 165 | 192,774 | 15,714 | 3,635 | 11,665 | 193,188 |
| Outpatient Psychiatric Clinics[5] | 1867 of 2259 | 452,332[6] | 393,324 | | 515,804[6] | 529,852[6] |

*Provisional data. [1]Net release alive from hospital is defined as the excess number of patients released alive from the hospital over those returning to the hospital from all leave statuses. National data on placements and returns from extramural care are not available but net releases may be computed from less detailed movement data as: Net Live Releases = Resident Patients beginning of year + All Admissions, minus Deaths in Hospitals, minus Resident Patients end of year. [2]For 1966, only data on first admissions and resident patients collected. [3]This is the number of first admissions (admissions with no prior psychiatric experience) reported by 152 of 174 hospitals. [4]As of December 31, 1966. [5]Includes clinics of the Veterans Administration. [6]Patients on the books of the clinics. [7]Patients terminated from the clinic rolls.

# Selected Statistics on State and County Mental Hospitals

**Source:** National Institute of Mental Health

| Year | Total Admitted[1] | First[2] | Readmissions[3] | Net Releases[4] | Deaths in Hospital | Resident end of year | Expense per Patient[5] |
|---|---|---|---|---|---|---|---|
| 1950 | 152,286 | 114,054 | 38,232 | 99,659 | 41,280 | 512,501 | $779.61 |
| 1955 | 178,003 | 122,284 | 55,719 | 126,498 | 44,384 | 558,922 | 1,116.59 |
| 1960 | 234,791 | 140,015 | 94,776 | 191,386 | 49,748 | 535,540 | 1,702.41 |
| 1965 | 314,027 | 144,090 | 169,937 | 285,760 | 43,964 | 475,202 | 2,503.99 |
| 1966 | 327,014 | 162,627[7] | 161,308[7] | 308,636 | 42,753 | 452,273 | 2,810.31 |
| 1967[6] | 348,561 | 136,986[8] | 178,587[8] | 335,737 | 39,608 | 462,009 | 3,226.05 |

[1]Excludes transfers. [2]Beginning with 1962, this category was changed to Admissions with No Prior Psychiatric Inpatient Experience. [3]Prior admissions to hospitals in same state system and all other admissions. [4]Net Releases=resident patients beginning of year, plus all admissions (excluding transfers) minus deaths in hospital, minus resident patients end of year. [5]Per average daily resident patient population. [6]Provisional data including estimates for under-reporting wherever possible. [7]N. Y. changed its definition and reported first admissions to the N. Y. Hosp. system. [8]Excludes N. Y. and Michigan.

# Purchases and Ownership of Life Insurance in U. S.
## and Assets of U. S. Life Insurance Companies
### Legal Reserve Life Insurance Companies
Source: Division of Statistics & Research, Institute of Life Insurance
In millions of dollars.

| Year | Purchases of Life Insurance[1] | | | | Insurance in Force | | | | | Assets |
| | Ordi-nary | Group | Indus-trial | Total | Ordi-nary | Group | Indus-trial | Credit | Total | |
|---|---|---|---|---|---|---|---|---|---|---|
| 1940...... | $6,689 | $691 | $3,350 | $10,730 | $79,346 | $14,938 | $20,866 | $380 | $115,530 | $30,802 |
| 1945...... | 9,859 | 1,265 | 3,430 | 14,554 | 101,550 | 22,172 | 27,675 | 365 | 151,762 | 44,797 |
| 1950...... | 17,326 | 6,068 | 5,402 | 28,796 | 149,071 | 47,793 | 33,415 | 3,889 | 234,168 | 64,020 |
| 1955...... | 30,827 | 11,258 | 6,342 | 48,427 | 216,600 | 101,300 | 39,682 | 14,750 | 372,332 | 90,432 |
| 1960...... | 52,883 | 14,645 | 6,880 | 74,408 | 340,268 | 175,434 | 39,563 | 31,183 | 586,448 | 119,576 |
| 1962...... | 56,998 | 15,533 | 7,046 | 79,577 | 389,150 | 209,178 | 39,638 | 38,011 | 675,977 | 133,291 |
| 1963...... | 64,267 | 18,152 | 7,154 | 89,573 | 418,856 | 228,540 | 39,672 | 43,555 | 730,623 | 141,121 |
| 1964...... | 74,012 | 23,684 | 7,312 | 15,008 | 455,860 | 252,182 | 39,833 | 49,933 | 797,808 | 149,470 |
| 1965...... | 83,485 | 51,385 | 7,296 | 142,166 | 497,630 | 306,113 | 39,818 | 56,993 | 900,554 | 158,884 |
| 1966...... | 88,963 | 26,219 | 7,078 | 121,990 | 538,992 | 343,362 | 39,663 | 62,672 | 984,689 | 167,022 |
| 1967...... | 94,699 | 38,761 | 7,152 | 140,612 | 582,565 | 391,089 | 39,215 | 66,952 | 1,079,821 | 177,361 |
| 1968(6 mos.) | 51,100 | 16,400 | 3,400 | 70,900 | n. a. | n. a. | n. a. | n. a. | 1,130,000* | 182,000* |

*Estimate. n. a. Not available. [1]Figures exclude credit life insurance.

# Motor Vehicle Traffic Deaths by States
Source: State traffic authorities

| Place of accidents | Number 1967 | 1966 | Mil. death rate* 1967 | 1966 | Place of accidents | Number 1967 | 1966 | Mil. death rate* 1967 | 1966 |
|---|---|---|---|---|---|---|---|---|---|
| Alabama........ | 1,099 | 1,061 | 6.9 | 7.0 | Nebraska....... | 445 | 425 | 5.2 | 5.1 |
| Alaska......... | 53 | 74 | 6.0 | 8.9 | Nevada......... | 181 | 212 | 6.0 | 7.3 |
| Arizona........ | 572 | 643 | 6.2 | 7.4 | New Hampshire. | 160 | 148 | 4.2 | 4.1 |
| Arkansas....... | 640 | 673 | 6.8 | 7.3 | New Jersey..... | 1,168 | 1,127 | 3.3 | 3.3 |
| California...... | 4,803 | 4,830 | 4.9 | 5.0 | New Mexico..... | 450 | 431 | 7.3 | 7.2 |
| Colorado....... | 587 | 601 | 5.4 | 5.8 | New York....... | 2,902 | 2,812 | 4.8 | 4.8 |
| Connecticut.... | 441 | 409 | 3.1 | 3.0 | North Carolina.. | 1,747 | 1,724 | 7.1 | 7.4 |
| Delaware...... | 136 | 131 | 5.0 | 5.0 | North Dakota... | 200 | 209 | 5.6 | 6.0 |
| Dist. of Col..... | 131 | 97 | 5.1 | 3.8 | Ohio........... | 2,520 | 2,605 | 5.0 | 5.3 |
| Florida........ | 1,777 | 1,819 | 5.6 | 6.0 | Oklahoma...... | 879 | 799 | 5.9 | 5.5 |
| Georgia........ | 1,614 | 1,605 | 6.7 | 7.0 | Oregon........ | 658 | 678 | 5.8 | 6.2 |
| Hawaii......... | 135 | 116 | 5.2 | 4.6 | Pennsylvania... | 2,331 | 2,180 | 4.4 | 4.3 |
| Idaho.......... | 276 | 266 | 6.8 | 6.8 | Rhode Island... | 104 | 109 | 2.5 | 2.7 |
| Illinois........ | 2,493 | 2,522 | 4.9 | 5.2 | South Carolina.. | 913 | 968 | 7.1 | 7.9 |
| Indiana........ | 1,570 | 1,574 | 5.6 | 5.9 | South Dakota... | 224 | 265 | 5.5 | 6.5 |
| Iowa.......... | 817 | 904 | 6.0 | 6.9 | Tennessee...... | 1,250 | 1,272 | 6.9 | 7.4 |
| Kansas........ | 664 | 733 | 5.0 | 5.7 | Texas......... | 3,367 | 3,406 | 5.8 | 6.2 |
| Kentucky...... | 1,028 | 1,086 | 6.2 | 7.0 | Utah.......... | 275 | 330 | 5.2 | 6.4 |
| Louisiana...... | 1,217 | 1,238 | 8.4 | 8.9 | Vermont....... | 132 | 126 | 6.0 | 6.0 |
| Maine......... | 261 | 234 | 5.0 | 4.6 | Virginia........ | 1,223 | 1,106 | 5.4 | 5.1 |
| Maryland...... | 807 | 756 | 4.5 | 4.4 | Washington.... | 874 | 828 | 4.9 | 5.0 |
| Massachusetts.. | 867 | 900 | 3.8 | 4.1 | West Virginia... | 584 | 517 | 7.5 | 6.9 |
| Michigan...... | 2,123 | 2,298 | 4.8 | 5.3 | Wisconsin...... | 1,149 | 1,126 | 5.5 | 5.6 |
| Minnesota..... | 962 | 983 | 5.2 | 5.5 | Wyoming...... | 143 | 153 | 5.3 | 5.8 |
| Mississippi..... | 908 | 847 | 9.1 | 9.0 | Puerto Rico..... | 488 | 407 | 11.3 | 10.1 |
| Missouri....... | 1,318 | 1,379 | 5.5 | 6.0 | Virgin Islands... | .... | 4 | .... | .... |
| Montana....... | 319 | 276 | 8.1 | 7.1 | Guam......... | 17 | 25 | 6.1 | 11.4 |

*The mileage death rate is the number of deaths per 100,000,000 vehicle-miles.

# Transportation Accident Death Rates
Source: Interstate Commerce Commission; Civil Aeronautics Board and National Safety Council

| Kind of Transportation Passenger Deaths in 1967 | Passenger Miles | Passenger Deaths | Rate Per 100,000,000 Passenger Miles | 1965-67 Average Death Rate |
|---|---|---|---|---|
| Automobiles and taxis[1]............ | 1,480,000,000,000 | 35,300 | 2.40 | 2.40 |
| Automobiles on turnpikes............ | 39,000,000,000 | 440 | 1.10 | 1.20 |
| Buses............................. | 66,000,000,000 | 130 | 0.20 | 0.19 |
| Railroad passenger trains............ | 15,200,000,000 | 13 | 0.09 | 0.10 |
| Scheduled air transport planes (domestic) | 78,910,000,000 | 226 | 0.29 | 0.25 |

[1]Drivers of passenger automobiles are considered passengers.

# Deaths in Civil Aviation Accidents
Source: National Safety Council (NTSB & FAA)

| Year | Total deaths* | Scheduled flights (passengers) | | | | General aviation | |
| | | Domestic | | International | | | |
| | | No. | Rate** | No. | Rate** | No. | Rate**[1] |
|---|---|---|---|---|---|---|---|
| 1960.............. | 1,286 | 297 | 0.93 | 10 | 0.12 | 787 | 24 |
| 1963.............. | 1,157 | 48 | 0.12 | 73 | 0.59 | 893 | 23 |
| 1964.............. | 1,250 | 65 | 0.14 | 94 | 0.63 | 1,086 | 24 |
| 1965.............. | 1,279 | 205 | 0.38 | 21 | 0.12 | 1,029 | 21 |
| 1966.............. | 1,423 | 59 | 0.09 | 0 | 0.00 | 1,151 | 17 |
| 1967 (prel.)...... | 1,472 | 226 | 0.29 | 0 | 0.00 | 1,186 | 16 |

*Includes some deaths not shown separately—crew members in scheduled operations and persons not in planes killed in airplane accidents. Excludes deaths in military plane accidents.
**Rates are the number of deaths per 100,000,000 passenger miles. [1](NSC estimate) Pilots and other crew members are considered passengers for general aviation only.

# Federal Bureau of Investigation

The Federal Bureau of Investigation (FBI) is an activity of the Department of Justice, and is located at 9th St. and Pennsylvania Ave., Washington, D. C. It investigates all violations of Federal laws except those specifically assigned to some other agency by legislative action, such violations including counterfeiting, and internal revenue, postal and customs violations. It also investigates espionage, sabotage, treason and other matters affecting internal security, as well as kidnaping, transportation of stolen goods across state lines, interstate traffic in prostitution and violations of the Federal bank and atomic energy laws.

The FBI collects and classifies police and crime reports for the nation. The Identification Division had 189,154,682 fingerprint cards on file Sept. 1, 1967. While this division is of great usefulness in detecting criminals, it serves a wider purpose in recording the fingerprints of many other citizens who voluntarily make this record.

The FBI has 58 field divisions in the principal cities of the country. Consult telephone directories *for location and phone numbers.*

An applicant for the position of Special Agent of the FBI must be at least 23 and under 41 years old

and graduate of a state-accredited resident law school or from a resident four-year college with a major in accounting with at least three years of practical accounting and/or auditing experience. An agent gets 14 weeks of training, during which he learns techniques of investigation and arrest and recognition of evidence.

J. Edgar Hoover has been director since 1924. He was born in Washington, D. C. in 1895, and was graduated from George Washington U. in 1916.

## U. S. Govt. Crime Reports

Source: Federal Bureau of Investigation

| Offense | 1967 | Percent over 1966 |
|---|---|---|
| Murder | 12,090 | +10.8 |
| Forcible rape | 27,100 | +7.0 |
| Robbery | 202,050 | +28.4 |
| Aggravated assault | 253,300 | +9.3 |
| Burglary | 1,605,700 | +15.7 |
| Larceny $50 and over | 1,047,100 | +17.0 |
| Auto theft | 654,900 | +17.6 |
| **Total** | **3,802,300** | **+16.5** |

# 21% Increase in Crime in U. S. Reported in 1968

The Federal Bureau of Investigation's Uniform Crime Reports have disclosed that crime in United States cities, suburbs and rural areas increased an average of 21% during the first 6 months of 1968 when compared to the corresponding period of 1967.

Crimes of violence increased 21% as a group, with individual increases of 29% in robbery, 17% in murder, 14% in aggravated assault and 15% in forcible rape, according to the crime reports voluntarily submitted to the FBI by law enforcement agencies throughout the country.

In crimes against property, which as a group increased 20%, auto theft was up 24%, burglary 17% and larceny $50 and over 23% in the 6 months, the FBI said.

All cities when grouped by population size reported increases ranging from 17% in cities under 10,000 population to 24% in cities 250,000 to 500,000 inhabitants. The increase was 21% in suburban areas and rural areas reported a jump of 14%. The upward trend was consistent for all geographic areas of the country, according to the reports.

## Crime Index Trends by Geographic Region
(January-June, 1968 over 1967 in Percentage)

| Region | Total | Murder | Forcible rape | Robbery | Aggravated assault | Burglary | Larceny $50 and over | Auto theft |
|---|---|---|---|---|---|---|---|---|
| Northeastern States | +27 | +18 | +5 | +49 | +7 | +22 | +26 | +34 |
| North Central States | +17 | +12 | +13 | +10 | +10 | +13 | +24 | +20 |
| Southern States | +18 | +16 | +19 | +30 | +15 | +16 | +20 | +18 |
| Western States | +20 | +26 | +22 | +29 | +24 | +18 | +22 | +22 |

## Locations of Federal Detention Areas
Source: U. S. Bureau of Prisons

**Penitentiaries:** Atlanta, Ga.; Leavenworth, Kans.; Lewisburg, Pa.; McNeil Island, Wash.; Marion, Ill.; Terre Haute, Ind. **Reformatories:** El Reno, Okla.; Petersburg, Va.; Women, Alderson, W. Va. **Medical center:** Springfield, Mo.; Hospital; Maintenance unit. **Prison camps:** Eglin Air Force Base, Florida; Montgomery, Ala.; Safford, Ariz. **Correctional Institutions:** Danbury, Conn.; La Tuna, Tex.; Lompoc, Calif.; Texarkana, Tex.; Milan, Mich.; Tallahassee, Fla.; Seagoville, Tex.; Terminal Island, Calif.; Sandstone, Minn. **Detention headquarters center:** New York City; Florence, Arizona. **Institutions for juvenile and youth offenders:** Ashland, Ky.; Englewood, Colo.; Morgantown, W. Va. **Community Treatment Centers:** Detroit, Mich.; Chicago, Ill.; Los Angeles, Calif.; Kansas City, Mo.; Atlanta, Ga.; Houston, Texas; Oakland, Calif.; New York City.

### Prisoners in State and Federal Prisons and Reformatories

| | | | | | |
|---|---|---|---|---|---|
| 1940 | 173,706 | 1955 | 185,780 | 1961 | 220,149 | 1964 | 214,336 |
| 1945 | 133,649 | 1959 | 207,446 | 1962 | 218,830 | 1965 | 210,895 |
| 1950 | 166,123 | 1960 | 212,953 | 1963 | 217,283 | 1966 | 199,654 |

## Arrests in 1967 by Sex
Source: Federal Bureau of Investigation, Dept. of Justice
Compiled from reports of 4,566 police agencies. Estimated 1967 population in area 145,927,000

| Offense charged | Male | Female | Offense charged | Male | Female |
|---|---|---|---|---|---|
| Criminal homicide: | | | Sex offenses (except forcible | | |
| (a) Murder and nonnegligent | | | rape and prostitution) | 46,569 | 6,972 |
| manslaughter | 7,650 | 1,495 | Narcotic drug laws | 87,097 | 13,982 |
| (b) Manslaughter by negligence | 2,720 | 302 | Gambling | 77,388 | 7,384 |
| Forcible rape | 12,659 | | Offenses against family and | | |
| Robbery | 56,689 | 3,100 | children | 51,140 | 4,997 |
| Aggravated assault | 93,343 | 13,849 | Driving under the influence | 262,925 | 18,227 |
| Burglary—breaking or entering | 229,752 | 9,709 | Liquor laws | 185,149 | 24,592 |
| Larceny—theft | 340,355 | 106,944 | Drunkenness | 1,408,594 | 109,215 |
| Auto theft | 113,227 | 5,006 | Disorderly conduct | 476,022 | 74,447 |
| Other assaults | 205,342 | 24,586 | Vagrancy | 96,354 | 10,393 |
| Arson | 7,499 | 559 | All other offenses (except traffic) | 564,604 | 90,311 |
| Forgery and counterfeiting | 26,515 | 6,947 | Suspicion | 79,357 | 16,437 |
| Fraud | 44,678 | 13,514 | Curfew and loitering law | | |
| Embezzlement | 4,904 | 1,169 | violations | 77,457 | 17,415 |
| Stolen property: buying, receiving, possessing | 26,489 | 2,131 | Runaways | 67,043 | 62,489 |
| Vandalism | 102,540 | 6,759 | **Total** | **4,829,918** | **688,502** |
| Weapons: carrying, possessing, etc | 66,979 | 4,705 | **Total (all)** | **5,518,420** | |
| Prostitution and commercialized vice | 8,878 | 30,866 | | | |

# Secret Service Protects Major National Candidates

United States Secret Service protection was extended to all major Presidential and Vice Presidential candidates by legislation passed by Congress and signed by President Johnson June 6, 1968. The Secret Service, an agency of the Treasury Dept., protects the President and members of his immediate family, the President-elect, the Vice President and the Vice President-elect. The Service is also authorized to protect a former President and his wife during his lifetime and the person of a widow and minor children of a former President.

The Secret Service detects and arrests persons committing any offense against U. S. laws relating to coins, obligations and securities of the U. S. and foreign governments.

During fiscal 1968 the Service arrested 1,370 persons for violating the counterfeiting laws and recovered more than $13,0000,000 in counterfeit currency, an all-time high in both categories. The loss to the public amounted to over $2,860,000. Coin counterfeiting in the U. S. increased from $15,000 in fiscal 1967 to about $26,000 in fiscal 1968.

Forged Government-check cases investigated by the Service during fiscal 1968 numbered 52,667 and involved an amount of more than $5,500,000. A total of 2,422 persons were arrested for Government-check violations.

The Service also investigated 11,505 cases involving the forgery and fraudulent negotiation of U. S. Savings Bonds having a value at maturity of $1,242,000. The Service made 146 arrests in connection with these crimes.

# INTERPOL (International Criminal Police Organization)

The United States is one of 101 countries that are members of INTERPOL, the International Criminal Police Organization. United States participation in INTERPOL was authorized by Congress in 1958. Because of the Treasury Dept.'s activities in the suppression of counterfeiting, smuggling and the narcotics traffic, all of which have international ramifications, that department was designated as U. S. representative to INTERPOL.

Each member nation has one vote at a general assembly of INTERPOL held annually at a site chosen by the delegates at the previous year's assembly. The chairman of the U. S. delegation attending such meetings is the Special Assistant to the Secretary of the Treasury (for Enforcement).

INTERPOL dates from 1914, but World War I brought suspension of all its activities until 1923. The organization's first constitution was drawn up in that year. Files on international criminals were built up gradually to a point where their value to the police of member nations became apparent. During World War II the files disappeared from Vienna, where the General Secretariat of INTERPOL was located.

The organization was reconstituted at the end of World War II. The General Secretariat was moved to Paris and is now located in the Parisian suburb of Saint-Cloud. Information concerning thousands of international criminals is received there, sorted and disseminated to INTERPOL National Central Bureaus in the member countries. Besides handling voluminous mail, the General Secretariat receives and transmits over 118,000 messages a year over its radio network.

INTERPOL does not employ any investigators as such. The General Secretariat refers inquiries to the appropriate National Central Bureau. Also, the National Central Bureaus correspond between themselves and send copies of their correspondence to the Secretary General in Paris.

In the United States all inquiries, both incoming and outgoing, are channeled through the National Central Bureau in Washington. Investigations required in this country are conducted by the U. S. Secret Service, Customs Agency Service, and Internal Revenue Service, all agencies of the Treasury Dept. Frequently, also, inquiries are referred by the National Central Bureau at Washington to police and other enforcement agencies on the municipal, county, state and Federal levels for investigation.

## Police Roster

Police officers and civilian employees in large cities as of Jan. 1, 1968

| City | Officers | Civilian | City | Officers | Civilian | City | Officers | Civilian |
|---|---|---|---|---|---|---|---|---|
| New York.... | 27,462 | 2,643 | Cleveland...... | 2,199 | 270 | Houston...... | 1,436 | 294 |
| Chicago....... | 11,428 | 1,487 | St. Louis...... | 2,058 | 612 | New Orleans... | 1,299 | 219 |
| Philadelphia.... | 7,393 | 697 | Milwaukee..... | 1,893 | 128 | Seattle....... | 984 | 160 |
| Los Angeles.... | 5,383 | 1,663 | San Francisco.. | 1,763 | 298 | Kansas City.... | 938 | 297 |
| Detroit........ | 4,356 | 472 | Pittsburgh..... | 1,548 | 21 | Indianapolis... | 918 | 118 |
| Baltimore...... | 3,039 | 332 | Dallas......... | 1,436 | 230 | Cincinnati..... | 923 | 129 |
| Washington.... | 2,726 | 347 | Newark........ | 1,388 | 275 | Jersey City.... | 860 | 215 |
| Boston........ | 2,495 | 193 | Buffalo........ | 1,310 | 217 | Denver....... | 844 | 162 |

# Maximum Penalties for First Degree Murder
## INCLUDING CAPITAL PUNISHMENT
Imprisonment for life may be imposed instead of death in all states.

| | | | |
|---|---|---|---|
| Alabama.... | Electrocution | Maine...... Life Imprisonment | Pennsylvania Electrocution |
| Alaska...... | Life Imprisonment | Maryland.... Lethal Gas | Rhode Island Life Imprisonment |
| Arizona..... | Lethal Gas | Mass........ Electrocution | So. Carolina.. Electrocution |
| Arkansas.... | Electrocution | Michigan.... Life Imprisonment | So. Dakota.. Electrocution |
| California.... | Lethal Gas | Minnesota... Life Imprisonment | Tennessee ... Electrocution |
| Colorado.... | Lethal Gas | Mississippi... Lethal Gas | Texas....... Electrocution |
| Connecticut.. | Electrocution | Missouri..... Lethal Gas | Utah........ Hanging or Shooting |
| Delaware.... | Hanging | Montana.... Hanging | Vermont(b).. Life Imprisonment |
| Dist. of Col.. | Electrocution | Nebraska.... Electrocution | Virginia..... Electrocution |
| Florida...... | Electrocution | Nevada..... Lethal Gas | Washington.. Hanging |
| Georgia..... | Electrocution | New Hamp.. Hanging | W. Virginia... Life Imprisonment |
| Hawaii...... | Life Imprisonment | New Jersey.. Electrocution | Wisconsin... Life Imprisonment |
| Idaho....... | Hanging | New Mexico. Lethal Gas | Wyoming.... Lethal Gas |
| Illinois...... | Electrocution | New York (a) Life Imprisonment | U. S. Govt... Death or Life |
| Indiana..... | Electrocution | No. Carolina. Lethal Gas | Am. Samoa.. Hanging |
| Iowa....... | Life Imprisonment | No. Dakota.. Life Imprisonment | Canal Zone.. Hanging |
| Kansas...... | Hanging | Ohio........ Electrocution | Guam....... Life Imprisonment |
| Kentucky... | Electrocution | Oklahoma... Electrocution | Puerto Rico.. Life Imprisonment |
| Louisiana... | Electrocution | Oregon...... Life Imprisonment | Virgin Islands Life Imprisonment |

(a) the death penalty applicable to persons for killing a peace officer acting in the line of duty and to convicts under life sentence for killing a guard or inmate. (b) Electrocution for killing of prison personnel or unrelated second offense.

## Murders, Robberies, Burglaries and Auto Thefts

**Source: Uniform Crime Reports (FBI)**

Index of Crime in 1967 as reported or estimated in the Standard Metropolitan Statistical Areas of over 500,000 population. *Includes manslaughter.

| | Murder* | Robbery | Burglary | Auto theft | | Murder* | Robbery | Burglary | Auto theft |
|---|---|---|---|---|---|---|---|---|---|
| Akron, Ohio | 24 | 709 | 4,939 | 3,703 | Milwaukee, Wis. | 50 | 765 | 6,766 | 5,789 |
| Albany-Schenectady-Troy | 17 | 245 | 4,228 | 1,926 | Minneapolis-St. Paul, Minn. | 34 | 2,280 | 18,353 | 8,602 |
| Allentown-Bethlehem-Easton | 7 | 110 | 2,182 | 643 | Nashville, Tenn. | 66 | 648 | 6,194 | 2,920 |
| Anaheim-Santa Ana-Garden Gr. | 21 | 699 | 15,162 | 3,353 | Newark, N.J. | 114 | 2,852 | 22,977 | 10,096 |
| Atlanta, Georgia | 171 | 1,187 | 10,870 | 4,059 | New Haven-Waterbury, Conn. | 16 | 150 | 6,405 | 3,127 |
| Baltimore, Md. | 225 | 7,008 | 25,199 | 12,280 | New Orleans, La. | 144 | 2,234 | 12,232 | 7,075 |
| Birmingham, Ala. | 96 | 468 | 6,791 | 1,984 | New York, N.Y. | 821 | 37,282 | 171,589 | 68,299 |
| Bost.-Lowell-Lawrence | 105 | 2,165 | 20,595 | 25,798 | Norfolk-Ports., Va. | 57 | 827 | 7,498 | 2,723 |
| Bridgeport-Stamford-Norwalk | 17 | 336 | 6,331 | 3,148 | Oklahoma City, Okla. | 41 | 377 | 5,540 | *1,724 |
| Buffalo, N.Y. | 37 | 1,120 | 9,791 | 6,723 | Omaha, Nebr.-Iowa | 34 | 501 | 4,789 | 2,196 |
| Chicago, Ill. | 647 | 20,080 | 46,436 | 39,635 | Paterson-Clifton-Passaic, N.J. | 30 | 638 | 7,877 | 4,208 |
| Cinc.-Ohio-Ky.-Ind. | 93 | 861 | 8,399 | 2,994 | Philadelphia, Pa. | 300 | 696 | 27,679 | 13,757 |
| Cleveland, Ohio | 173 | 3,892 | 11,900 | 13,737 | Phoenix, Ariz. | 50 | 900 | 12,796 | 4,866 |
| Columbus, Ohio | 45 | 921 | 8,712 | 3,364 | Pittsburgh, Pa. | 72 | 2,325 | 13,011 | 10,677 |
| Dallas, Tex. | 155 | 1,108 | 12,688 | 5,087 | Portland, Ore.-Wash. | 28 | 1,130 | 11,049 | 3,996 |
| Dayton, Ohio | 74 | 993 | 6,117 | 2,520 | Providence-Pawtucket-Warwick | 16 | 250 | 6,789 | 5,198 |
| Denver, Colo. | 44 | 1,164 | 10,494 | 4,809 | Richmond, Va. | 50 | 487 | 6,036 | 2,332 |
| Detroit, Mich. | 366 | 14,032 | 59,700 | 24,351 | Rochester, N.Y. | 40 | 503 | 4,649 | 1,299 |
| Ft. Lauderdale-Hollywood, Fla. | 65 | 613 | 6,796 | 1,683 | Sacramento, Calif. | 44 | 666 | 8,516 | 3,616 |
| Ft. Worth, Texas | 102 | 606 | 6,855 | 2,774 | St. Louis, Mo.-Ill. | 249 | 4,000 | 24,169 | 11,590 |
| Gary-Ham'd-E. Chi. | 48 | 1,427 | 4,862 | 4,221 | Salt Lake City, Utah | 20 | 324 | 5,070 | 1,589 |
| Grand Rapids, Mich. | 20 | 453 | 4,923 | 1,374 | San Antonio, Texas | 85 | 489 | 9,827 | 2,935 |
| Greensboro-High Point, N.C. | 48 | 257 | 3,617 | 1,100 | San Bernardino-Riverside-Ont. | 40 | 652 | 14,993 | 3,226 |
| | | | | | San Diego, Calif. | 40 | 634 | 8,113 | 3,480 |
| Hartford-New Britain-Bristol | 29 | 381 | 5,481 | 2,306 | San Francisco-Oakland | 181 | 6,834 | 51,409 | 21,229 |
| Honolulu, Hawaii | 17 | 144 | 7,857 | 2,888 | San Jose, Calif. | 23 | 398 | 9,597 | 3,036 |
| Houston, Texas | 299 | 3,438 | 20,829 | 8,794 | Seattle-Ever't, Wash. | 60 | 1,228 | 13,421 | 5,236 |
| Indianapolis, Ind. | 69 | 1,376 | 10,827 | 6,173 | Springfield-Chicopee-Holyoke | 13 | 116 | 2,553 | 2,417 |
| Jacksonville, Fla. | 50 | 1,188 | 9,013 | 1,725 | Syracuse, N.Y. | 22 | 407 | 4,812 | 1,090 |
| Jersey City, N.J. | 33 | 423 | 3,310 | 4,855 | Tampa-St. Petersburg | 73 | 1,218 | 14,105 | 2,625 |
| Kan. City, Mo.-Kan. | 103 | 2,764 | 15,067 | 6,760 | Toledo, Ohio-Mich. | 40 | 1,121 | 5,388 | 2,107 |
| Los Angeles-Long Beach, Calif. | 496 | 16,538 | 125,220 | 48,493 | Washington, D.C.-Md.-Va. | 230 | 7,061 | 30,745 | 15,791 |
| Louisville, Ky.-Ind. | 77 | 1,030 | 7,634 | 5,862 | Worcester, Mass. | 16 | 211 | 4,786 | 3,360 |
| Memphis, Tenn.-Ark. | 83 | 879 | 9,453 | 2,374 | Youngstown-Warren, Ohio | 27 | 458 | 3,103 | 1,795 |
| Miami, Fla. | 133 | 3,286 | 16,876 | 5,427 | | | | | |

## Building Fire Losses By Causes

**Source: National Fire Protection Assn. Copyright 1968**

These are estimated figures intended to show the relative order of magnitude of fire losses by cause. These figures by themselves do not show the relative safety in utilization of various types of materials, devices, fuels or services. They are approximations based on experience in typical states.

| 1967 | Number of fires | | Losses | |
|---|---|---|---|---|
| Heating and cooking | | 128,600 | | $127,000,000 |
| Equipment, defective or overheated | 69,200 | | $73,300,000 | |
| Chimneys, flues defective or overheated | 23,300 | | 17,200,000 | |
| Hot ashes and coals | 7,700 | | 8,500,000 | |
| Combustibles near heaters | 28,400 | | 28,000,000 | |
| Smoking and matches | | 160,100 | | 75,300,000 |
| Electrical | | 144,600 | | 193,600,000 |
| Fixed services, fires due to wiring, equipment, etc. | 87,400 | | 135,300,000 | |
| Power-consuming appliances | 57,200 | | 58,300,000 | |
| Rubbish, source of ignition unknown | | 23,800 | | 16,300,000 |
| Flammable liquid fires and explosions not reported in heating and cooking | | 51,300 | | 59,400,000 |
| Open flames and sparks | | 65,500 | | 95,700,000 |
| Sparks on roof | 2,900 | | 1,600,000 | |
| Welding and cutting | 5,800 | | 16,500,000 | |
| Sparks from machinery, friction | 11,100 | | 12,200,000 | |
| Thawing pipes | 3,200 | | 5,100,000 | |
| Miscellaneous open flames and sparks | 42,500 | | 60,300,000 | |
| Lightning | | 21,100 | | 30,600,000 |
| Children and matches | | 84,000 | | 59,700,000 |
| Exposure | | 22,200 | | 33,800,000 |
| Incendiary, suspicious | | 44,100 | | 141,700,000 |
| Spontaneous ignition | | 18,100 | | 27,200,000 |
| Gas fires and explosions not reported in heating and cooking | | 7,500 | | 17,000,000 |
| Explosions, miscellaneous and unclassified | | 6,000 | | 24,500,000 |
| Fireworks, firecrackers and rockets | | 3,000 | | 1,400,000 |
| Miscellaneous known causes | | 56,900 | | 88,900,000 |
| Unknown or undetermined | | 124,100 | | 630,900,000 |
| **Totals** | | **960,900** | | **$1,623,000,000** |

## Annual Fire Losses in the United States

**Source: National Insurance Actuarial and Statistical Assn.**

| Year | Loss | Year | Loss | Year | Loss | Year | Loss |
|---|---|---|---|---|---|---|---|
| 1920 | $447,886,677 | 1950 | $648,909,000 | 1956 | $ 989,290,000 | 1962 | $1,265,002,000 |
| 1925 | 559,418,184 | 1951 | 730,084,000 | 1957 | 1,023,190,000 | 1963 | 1,405,558,000 |
| 1930 | 501,980,624 | 1952 | 815,134,000 | 1958 | 1,056,266,000 | 1964 | 1,367,128,000 |
| 1935 | 235,263,401 | 1953 | 903,400,000 | 1959 | 1,047,073,000 | 1965 | 1,455,631,000 |
| 1940 | 285,878,697 | 1954 | 870,984,000 | 1960 | 1,107,824,000 | 1966 | 1,496,755,000 |
| 1945 | 484,274,000 | 1955 | 885,218,000 | 1961 | 1,209,042,000 | 1967 | 1,706,717,000 |

# AGRICULTURE
## Farms in United States by State—Number, Acreage, Value
Source: Bureau of the Census (Census of 1964)

| State | Farms | Land in Farms | Value of land and Buildings Per Farm | Per Acre | State | Farms | Land in Farms | Value of land and Buildings Per Farm | Per Acre |
|---|---|---|---|---|---|---|---|---|---|
| | No. | Acres | Dollars | Dollars | | No. | Acres | Dollars | Dollars |
| U.S........ | 3,157,857 | 1,110,187,000 | 50,646 | 143.81 | E. S. | | | | |
| New | | | | | Central.... | 468,155 | 64,508,797 | 22,235 | 181.07 |
| England... | 41,957 | 7,744,494 | | | Kentucky... | 133,038 | 16,265,180 | 22,235 | 181.07 |
| Maine..... | 12,875 | 2,590,022 | 19,979 | 100.06 | Tennessee.. | 133,446 | 15,266,213 | 20,509 | 178.94 |
| N. Hamp... | 4,648 | 903,197 | 25,402 | 132.12 | Alabama... | 92,530 | 15,225,797 | 20,552 | 124.57 |
| Vermont... | 9,247 | 2,524,371 | 29,733 | 109.22 | Mississippi. | 109,141 | 17,751,607 | 24,322 | 150.34 |
| Mass...... | 8,019 | 901,789 | 43,492 | 386.06 | W. S. | | | | |
| R. Island.. | 1,100 | 103,801 | 46,030 | 484.94 | Central.... | 436,200 | 204,760,125 | | |
| Conn...... | 6,068 | 721,314 | 67,429 | 560.67 | Arkansas... | 79,898 | 16,565,299 | 36,734 | 177.51 |
| Middle | | | | | Louisiana.. | 62,466 | 10,411,045 | 38,636 | 232.86 |
| Atlantic.. | 160,237 | 24,234,888 | | | Oklahoma.. | 88,726 | 36,077,472 | 49,212 | 120.72 |
| New York.. | 66,510 | 12,275,308 | 32,797 | 176.96 | Texas...... | 205,110 | 141,706,309 | 77,756 | 111.53 |
| New Jersey. | 10,641 | 1,155,597 | 73,487 | 662.42 | | | | | |
| Pa........ | 83,086 | 10,803,983 | 29,836 | 228.35 | Mountain. | 134,115 | 268,002,843 | | |
| E. N. | | | | | Montana... | 27,020 | 65,833,760 | 103,271 | 42.30 |
| Central... | 573,605 | 99,486,458 | | | Idaho..... | 29,661 | 15,301,513 | 68,178 | 131.71 |
| Ohio...... | 120,381 | 17,619,167 | 43,373 | 295.42 | Wyoming... | 9,038 | 37,052,632 | 115,355 | 28.13 |
| Indiana.... | 108,082 | 17,933,226 | 51,645 | 309.84 | Colorado... | 29,798 | 38,255,626 | 90,183 | 70.23 |
| Illinois.... | 132,822 | 29,957,501 | 80,894 | 356.94 | N. Mexico.. | 14,206 | 47,646,966 | 117,042 | 34.93 |
| Michigan... | 93,504 | 13,598,992 | 34,027 | 232.82 | Arizona.... | 6,477 | 40,559,493 | 330,549 | 52.78 |
| Wisconsin.. | 118,816 | 20,377,572 | 26,765 | 154.71 | Utah...... | 15,759 | 12,867,081 | 57,747 | 70.66 |
| W. N. | | | | | Nevada.... | 2,156 | 10,482,772 | 182,436 | 37.65 |
| Central... | 703,782 | 283,603,322 | | | | | | | |
| Minnesota.. | 131,163 | 30,804,980 | 39,075 | 166.14 | Pacific[1] | 166,183 | 76,572,765 | | |
| Iowa...... | 154,162 | 33,758,321 | 59,553 | 271.77 | Washington. | 45,574 | 19,052,538 | 64,304 | 154.22 |
| Missouri... | 147,315 | 32,691,618 | 33,451 | 150.38 | Oregon.... | 39,757 | 20,509,302 | 59,079 | 114.71 |
| No. Dakota. | 48,836 | 42,717,360 | 58,450 | 66.78 | California.. | 80,852 | 37,010,925 | 214,650 | 468.40 |
| So. Dakota | 49,703 | 45,567,263 | 56,615 | 61.60 | Alaska..... | 382 | 1,959,440 | 47,150 | 9.17 |
| Nebraska.. | 80,163 | 47,792,663 | 65,268 | 109.39 | Hawaii..... | 4,864 | 2,354,454 | 98,936 | 204.82 |
| Kansas.... | 92,440 | 50,271,117 | 66,397 | 121.55 | | | | | |
| S. Atlantic | 468,377 | 76,959,414 | | | | | | | |
| Delaware.. | 4,401 | 717,013 | 53,443 | 321.74 | | | | | |
| Maryland.. | 20,760 | 3,180,696 | 64,999 | 422.18 | **Puerto Rico and Possessions** | | | | |
| Virginia... | 80,354 | 12,001,860 | 27,572 | 182.64 | | | | | |
| W. Virginia. | 34,504 | 5,278,592 | 13,882 | 90.52 | | | | | |
| N. Carolina. | 148,202 | 14,381,724 | 24,442 | 252.37 | Puerto Rico | 44,829 | N.A. | N.A. | N.A. |
| S. Carolina. | 56,248 | 8,101,417 | 24,948 | 171.08 | Guam...... | 2,529 | 30,099 | N.A. | N.A. |
| Georgia.... | 83,366 | 17,886,931 | 29,155 | 183.59 | Am. Samoa[2] | 2,135 | 11,521 | N.A. | N.A. |
| Florida.... | 40,542 | 15,411,181 | 109,053 | 285.71 | Virgin Isl.. | 466 | 39,539 | 166,441 | 1961.65 |

N.A.—not available. [1]Except Hawaii and Alaska. [2]Not enumerated in 1964.

## Index Numbers of Prices Received by Farmers
Source: Economic Research Service; Department of Agriculture Index (1910-14 = 100 per cent)

| Year | All Farm Products | All Crops | Livestock[1] | Food Grains | Feed Grains and Hay | Feed Grains | Cotton | Tobacco | Oil-bearing Crops | Fruit | Commercial Vegetables[3] | Potatoes, Sweetpot.[3] | Meat Animals | Dairy Products | Poultry and Eggs | Wool |
|---|---|---|---|---|---|---|---|---|---|---|---|---|---|---|---|---|
| 1910.. | 104 | 105 | 102 | 109 | 96 | 97 | 118 | 84 | 120 | 100 | .... | 83 | 101 | 100 | 104 | 117 |
| 1915.. | 99 | 96 | 102 | 127 | 105 | 110 | 76 | 82 | 106 | 82 | .... | 86 | 102 | 101 | 101 | 126 |
| 1920.. | 211 | 235 | 190 | 249 | 202 | 209 | 262 | 233 | 208 | 188 | ... | 294 | 171 | 202 | 222 | 214 |
| 1925.. | 156 | 164 | 149 | 171 | 132 | 139 | 186 | 168 | 147 | 165 | 153 | 170 | 139 | 156 | 162 | 221 |
| 1930.. | 125 | 115 | 134 | 93 | 106 | 109 | 104 | 140 | 111 | 149 | 128 | 162 | 133 | 142 | 128 | 119 |
| 1935.. | 109 | 103 | 114 | 97 | 107 | 112 | 98 | 171 | 127 | 89 | 116 | 72 | 115 | 114 | 116 | 110 |
| 1940.. | 100 | 90 | 109 | 84 | 85 | 86 | 83 | 134 | 103 | 81 | 122 | 89 | 108 | 120 | 98 | 160 |
| 1945.. | 207 | 202 | 211 | 172 | 167 | 168 | 179 | 360 | 228 | 228 | 240 | 207 | 207 | 229 | 198 | 232 |
| 1950.. | 258 | 233 | 280 | 224 | 193 | 198 | 282 | 402 | 276 | 194 | 211 | 166 | 340 | 249 | 186 | 341 |
| 1955.. | 232 | 231 | 234 | 228 | 183 | 187 | 272 | 437 | 249 | 202 | 223 | 178 | 246 | 247 | 191 | 242 |
| 1960.. | 239 | 222 | 253 | 203 | 152 | 151 | 254 | 500 | 214 | 244 | 230 | 203 | 296 | 259 | 160 | 235 |
| 1964.. | 237 | 239 | 236 | 190 | 167 | 166 | 262 | 490 | 256 | 306 | 248 | 230 | 270 | 256 | 142 | 299 |
| 1965.. | 248 | 233 | 261 | 164 | 174 | 173 | 245 | 513 | 265 | 246 | 261 | 295 | 319 | 261 | 145 | 261 |
| 1966(r).. | 267 | 237 | 292 | 185 | 180 | 180 | 215 | 552 | 293 | 258 | 285 | 195 | 356 | 294 | 161 | 275 |
| 1967.. | 253 | 224 | 277 | 177 | 174 | 174 | 191 | 555 | 276 | 225 | 284 | 193 | 336 | 305 | 132 | 223 |

[1]Livestock and livestock products. [2]For fresh market and processing beg. 1952. [3]Including dry edible beans.

## Average Farm Wages

| Cal. yr. | Per month Incl. board | Excl. board | Per day Incl. board | Excl. board | Cal. yr. | Per month Incl. board | Excl. board | Per day Incl. board | Excl. board | Cal. yr. | Per month Incl. board | Excl. board | Per day Incl. board | Excl. board |
|---|---|---|---|---|---|---|---|---|---|---|---|---|---|---|---|
| 1910 | $21.00 | $28.00 | $1.05 | $1.35 | 1930 | $37.50 | $48.00 | $1.80 | 62.15 | 1940 | $27.50 | $37.50 | $1.30 | $1.60 |
| 1920 | 51.00 | 65.00 | 2.80 | 3.30 | 1935 | 22.00 | 30.50 | 1.10 | 1.35 | 1945 | 79.00 | 101.00 | 3.85 | 4.35 |

### NEW SERIES

| Calendar year | Per month With house | With board & room | Per week With board & room | Without board or room | Per day With house | With board & room | Without board or room | Per hour With house | Without board or room |
|---|---|---|---|---|---|---|---|---|---|
| 1950....... | $121.00 | $99.00 | $23.50 | $31.00 | $3.50 | $4.45 | $4.50 | $.63 | $.69 |
| 1955....... | 154.00 | 123.00 | 29.75 | 38.00 | 4.20 | 5.40 | 5.30 | .74 | .82 |
| 1959....... | 186.00 | 144.00 | 34.75 | 44.50 | 5.10 | 6.30 | 6.40 | .85 | .95 |
| 1960....... | 192.00 | 149.00 | 35.50 | 45.75 | 5.30 | 6.50 | 6.60 | .88 | .97 |
| 1962....... | 200.00 | 155.00 | 37.00 | 47.75 | 5.60 | 6.70 | 6.90 | .92 | 1.01 |
| 1963....... | 206.00 | 159.00 | 37.50 | 48.50 | 5.70 | 6.90 | 7.10 | .94 | 1.05 |
| 1964....... | 212.00 | 162.00 | 38.50 | 49.50 | 5.90 | 7.10 | 7.30 | .97 | 1.08 |
| 1965....... | 223.00 | 171.00 | 40.25 | 51.50 | 6.20 | 7.40 | 7.60 | 1.03 | 1.14 |
| 1966....... | 243.00 | 185.00 | 43.50 | 55.75 | 6.70 | 8.00 | 8.20 | 1.10 | 1.23 |
| 1967....... | 262.00 | 199.00 | 47.50 | 60.50 | 7.50 | 8.60 | 9.00 | 1.18 | 1.33 |

## Average Prices Received by U. S. Farmers

**Source:** Economic Research Service; Department of Agriculture

The figures represent dollars per 100 lbs. for hogs, beef cattle, veal calves, sheep, lamb and milk (wholesale); dollars per head for milk cows; cents per lb. for milk fat (in cream), chickens, broilers, turkeys and wool; cents for eggs per dozen. *Revised

| Year [1] | Hogs | Cattle (beef) | Calves (veal) | Sheep | Lambs | Cows (milk) | Milk (wholesale) | Milk fat (in cream) | Chickens | Broilers | Turkeys | Eggs | Wool |
|---|---|---|---|---|---|---|---|---|---|---|---|---|---|
| 1930 | 8.84 | 7.71 | 9.68 | 4.74 | 7.76 | 74.20 | 2.21 | 34.5 | 18.4 | 3 | 20.2 | 23.7 | 19.5 |
| 1935 | 8.65 | 6.04 | 7.16 | 3.75 | 7.28 | 46.90 | 1.72 | 28.1 | 15.3 | 20.0 | 20.1 | 23.4 | 19.3 |
| 1940 | 5.39 | 7.56 | 8.83 | 3.95 | 8.10 | 61.00 | 1.82 | 28.0 | 13.9 | 17.3 | 15.2 | 18.0 | 28.4 |
| 1945 | 14.00 | 12.10 | 13.00 | 6.38 | 13.10 | 111.00 | 3.19 | 50.3 | 27.0 | 29.5 | 33.7 | 37.7 | 41.9 |
| 1950 | 18.00 | 23.30 | 26.30 | 11.60 | 25.10 | 198.00 | 3.89 | 62.0 | 24.9 | 27.4 | 32.9 | 36.3 | 62.1 |
| 1955 | 15.00 | 15.60 | 16.80 | 5.78 | 18.40 | 146.00 | 4.01 | 57.8 | 23.4 | 25.2 | 30.2 | 39.5 | 42.8 |
| 1958 | 19.60 | 21.90 | 25.30 | 7.20 | 21.00 | 210.00 | 4.13 | 59.3 | 17.7 | 18.5 | 23.9 | 38.5 | 36.4 |
| 1959 | 14.10 | 22.60 | 26.70 | 6.00 | 18.70 | 233.00 | 4.16 | 60.1 | 15.3 | 16.1 | 23.9 | 31.4 | 43.3 |
| 1960 | 15.30 | 20.40 | 22.90 | 5.61 | 17.90 | 223.00 | 4.21 | 60.5 | 16.3 | 16.9 | 25.4 | 36.0 | 42.0 |
| 1962 | 16.30 | 21.30 | 25.10 | 5.67 | 17.80 | 221.00 | 4.10 | 59.4 | 14.6 | 15.2 | 21.6 | 33.8 | 47.7 |
| 1963 | 14.90 | 19.90 | 24.00 | 5.80 | 18.10 | 215.00 | 4.10 | 59.5 | 14.1 | 14.6 | 22.3 | 34.5 | 48.5 |
| 1964 | 14.80 | 18.00 | 20.40 | 5.96 | 19.90 | 209.00 | 4.15 | 60.2 | 13.7 | 14.2 | 21.0 | 33.8 | 53.2 |
| 1965* | 20.60 | 19.90 | 22.10 | 6.34 | 22.80 | 212.00 | 4.23 | 61.1 | 14.4 | 15.0 | 22.2 | 33.7 | 47.1 |
| 1966 | 22.80 | 22.20 | 26.00 | 6.84 | 23.40 | 246.00 | 4.81 | 67.2 | 14.7 | 15.3 | 23.1 | 39.1 | 52.1 |
| 1967 | 18.90 | 22.30 | 26.30 | 6.35 | 22.10 | 260.00 | 5.02 | 66.2 | 12.7 | 13.3 | 19.5 | 31.2 | 39.8 |

The figures represent cents per bushel for oats; cents per lb. for cotton and peanuts; dollars per bushel for wheat, corn, barley, soybeans and apples; dollars per 100 lbs. for rice, sorghum and potatoes; dollars per ton for cottonseed and baled hay.

| Crop year [2] | Wheat | Corn | Cotton | Oats | Barley | Rice | Soy-beans | Sor-ghum | Peanuts | Cotton-seed | Hay | Potatoes | Apples |
|---|---|---|---|---|---|---|---|---|---|---|---|---|---|
| 1930 | .663 | .550 | 9.46 | 31.1 | .420 | 1.74 | 1.34 | 1.02 | 3.46 | 22.00 | 11.00 | 1.47 | ... |
| 1935 | .827 | .632 | 11.08 | 25.7 | .376 | 1.60 | .714 | .973 | 3.12 | 30.50 | 7.60 | .980 | .63 |
| 1940 | .674 | .601 | 9.53 | 29.8 | .393 | 1.80 | .892 | .873 | 3.33 | 21.70 | 9.78 | .850 | .72 |
| 1945 | 1.49 | 1.23 | 22.51 | 65.0 | 1.01 | 3.98 | 2.08 | 2.14 | 8.27 | 51.10 | 20.30 | 2.30 | 2.80 |
| 1950 | 2.00 | 1.52 | 39.90 | 78.8 | 1.19 | 5.09 | 2.47 | 1.88 | 10.9 | 86.60 | 21.10 | 1.50 | 1.64 |
| 1955 | 1.99 | 1.35 | 32.27 | 60.0 | .920 | 4.81 | 2.22 | 1.75 | 11.7 | 44.60 | 22.50 | 1.77 | 2.03 |
| 1958 | 1.75 | 1.12 | 33.09 | 57.8 | .900 | 4.68 | 2.00 | 1.78 | 10.6 | 43.80 | 18.80 | 1.31 | 1.87 |
| 1959 | 1.76 | 1.04 | 31.56 | 64.6 | .860 | 4.59 | 1.96 | 1.53 | 9.56 | 38.80 | 22.30 | 2.27 | 4.95 |
| 1960 | 1.74 | .997 | 30.08 | 59.8 | .838 | 4.55 | 2.13 | 1.49 | 10.0 | 42.50 | 21.70 | 2.00 | 6.09 |
| 1962 | 2.04 | 1.10 | 31.74 | 62.4 | .915 | 5.04 | 2.34 | 1.82 | 11.0 | 47.90 | 21.80 | 1.66 | 5.68 |
| 1963 | 1.85 | 1.09 | 32.02 | 62.2 | .897 | 5.01 | 2.51 | 1.74 | 11.2 | 50.70 | 24.60 | 1.78 | 5.16 |
| 1964 | 1.37 | 1.15 | 29.62 | 63.1 | .915 | 4.90 | 2.62 | 1.88 | 11.2 | 47.10 | 23.90 | 3.50 | 5.35 |
| 1965 | 1.35 | 1.16 | 28.03 | 62.2 | 1.02 | 4.93 | 2.54 | 1.76 | 11.4 | 46.70 | 23.20 | 2.54 | 5.37 |
| 1966 | 1.63 | 1.29 | 20.64 | 66.5 | 1.05 | 4.95 | 2.75 | 1.82 | 11.3 | 65.90 | 25.00 | 2.05 | 6.04 |
| 1967 | 1.39 | 1.05 | 25.40 | 66.1 | 1.00 | 4.92 | 2.49 | 1.79 | 11.4 | 55.20 | 24.50 | 1.90 | 6.80 |

[1] Weighted calendar year prices for livestock and livestock products other than wool. 1943 through 1963, wool prices are weighted on marketing year basis. [2] Weighted crop year prices. Crop years are as follows: Apples, June-May; wheat, oats, barley, hay and potatoes, July-June; cotton, rice, peanuts and cottonseed, August-July; soybeans, September-August; and corn and sorghum grain, October-September. [3] Prices for apples are quoted in cents per pound beginning in 1959. Quoted prior as dollars per bushel (48 lbs.).

## Farm Income—Cash Receipts from Marketings (in $1,000)

| 1967 State | Crops | Live-Stock | Govt. Pay. | Total | 1967 State | Crops | Live-Stock | Govt. Pay. | Total |
|---|---|---|---|---|---|---|---|---|---|
| Ala... | $169,078 | $424,776 | $89,180 | $683,034 | Neb.. | $572,990 | $1,162,431 | $134,514 | $1,869,935 |
| Alask. | 1,101 | 3,159 | 70 | 4,330 | Nev.. | 11,613 | 45,770 | 1,687 | 59,070 |
| Ariz... | 288,116 | 239,403 | 46,785 | 574,304 | N.H.. | 11,905 | 44,185 | 675 | 56,765 |
| Ark... | 426,683 | 424,577 | 103,289 | 954,549 | N.J.. | 156,169 | 101,807 | 4,201 | 256,177 |
| Calif. | 2,331,754 | 1,547,457 | 110,289 | 3,989,500 | N.Mex. | 96,378 | 221,041 | 33,315 | 350,734 |
| Colo... | 200,299 | 684,984 | 57,606 | 942,889 | N.Y.. | 295,586 | 698,517 | 20,215 | 1,014,318 |
| Conn.. | 66,400 | 93,444 | 887 | 160,731 | N.C.. | 816,593 | 463,141 | 61,696 | 1,341,430 |
| Del... | 44,574 | 87,379 | 1,567 | 133,520 | N.Dak. | 435,615 | 281,773 | 130,850 | 848,238 |
| Fla... | 732,780 | 329,432 | 17,643 | 1,079,855 | Ohio.. | 538,031 | 696,266 | 70,355 | 1,304,652 |
| Ga... | 456,904 | 576,209 | 77,825 | 1,110,938 | Okla.. | 263,031 | 543,691 | 112,097 | 918,819 |
| Ha... | 161,611 | 37,349 | 8,554 | 207,514 | Ore... | 294,566 | 229,077 | 22,627 | 546,270 |
| Ida... | 292,817 | 227,081 | 37,070 | 556,968 | Pa... | 230,844 | 657,441 | 21,191 | 909,476 |
| Ill... | 1,308,084 | 1,224,145 | 97,674 | 2,629,903 | R.I... | 9,176 | 10,361 | 76 | 19,613 |
| Ind... | 639,499 | 752,091 | 77,317 | 1,468,907 | S.C.. | 281,037 | 143,799 | 57,437 | 482,273 |
| Ia... | 890,541 | 2,546,951 | 142,839 | 3,580,331 | S.D.. | 218,265 | 705,795 | 65,944 | 990,004 |
| Kans. | 528,338 | 951,919 | 212,379 | 1,692,636 | Tenn. | 242,612 | 358,696 | 73,783 | 675,091 |
| Ken.. | 440,049 | 380,812 | 41,527 | 862,388 | Tex.. | 1,153,007 | 1,368,976 | 462,163 | 2,984,146 |
| La... | 378,030 | 216,044 | 55,463 | 649,537 | Utah. | 45,220 | 145,371 | 8,954 | 199,545 |
| Me... | 79,356 | 133,041 | 2,145 | 214,542 | Vt.... | 14,023 | 122,908 | 1,715 | 138,646 |
| Md... | 108,564 | 219,523 | 5,217 | 333,304 | Va... | 239,562 | 272,924 | 17,582 | 530,068 |
| Mass. | 68,595 | 87,453 | 656 | 156,704 | Wash. | 528,248 | 253,431 | 52,321 | 834,000 |
| Mich. | 399,689 | 455,642 | 56,039 | 911,370 | W.Va. | 20,701 | 72,978 | 3,884 | 97,563 |
| Minn. | 594,016 | 1,236,728 | 95,251 | 1,925,995 | Wis.. | 207,931 | 1,212,178 | 41,227 | 1,461,336 |
| Miss. | 396,630 | 384,246 | 146,914 | 927,790 | Wyo.. | 34,550 | 166,267 | 11,098 | 211,915 |
| Mo... | 447,082 | 895,350 | 115,838 | 1,458,270 | Total | | | | |
| Mont. | 220,813 | 267,156 | 69,098 | 557,067 | U.S. | $18,383,056 | $24,405,175 | $3,078,829 | $45,867,060 |

## Cooperative Farm Credit System

Loans outstanding to farmers and farmer's cooperatives from banks and associations supervised by the Farm Credit Administration

| Year ended Dec. 31 | Farm mortgage loans Federal land banks | Farm production loans Production Credit ass'ns | Loans to co-operatives by banks for cooperatives | FICB loans and discounts other than interagency | Total |
|---|---|---|---|---|---|
| 1945 | $1,027,587,000 | $198,887,000 | $157,545,000 | $29,912,000 | $1,413,931,000 |
| 1950 | 946,469,000 | 455,472,000 | 344,979,000 | 70,020,000 | 1,816,940,000 |
| 1955 | 1,437,165,000 | 653,478,000 | 370,683,000 | 70,785,000 | 2,592,111,000 |
| 1960 | 2,563,772,000 | 1,490,138,000 | 648,859,000 | 91,951,000 | 4,794,720,000 |
| 1964 | 3,718,169,000 | 2,296,248,000 | 957,826,000 | 131,751,000 | 7,103,994,000 |
| 1965 | 4,280,675,000 | 2,595,480,000 | 1,055,163,000 | 146,091,000 | 8,080,389,000 |
| 1966 | 4,957,836,000 | 3,042,333,000 | 1,289,819,000 | 162,473,000 | 9,452,461,000 |
| 1967 | 5,609,265,000 | 3,550,971,000 | 1,506,383,000 | 181,781,000 | 10,848,400,000 |

# Production of Chief United States Crops

Source: Economic Research Service; Department of Agriculture

| Year | Corn, grain | Oats | Barley | Sorghums for grain | All Wheat | Rye | Buckwheat | Flaxseed | Cotton Lint | Cotton Seed |
|---|---|---|---|---|---|---|---|---|---|---|
| | 1,000 bushels | 1,000 bushels | 1,000 bushels | 1,000 bushels | 1,000 bushels | 1,000 bushels | 1,000 bushels | 1,000 bushels | 1,000 bales | 1,000 tons |
| 1960... | 3,906,949 | 1,153,332 | 429,065 | 619,954 | 1,354,709 | 33,108 | 847 | 30,402 | 14,272 | 5,886 |
| 1961... | 3,597,803 | 1,010,314 | 392,441 | 480,208 | 1,232,359 | 27,336 | 864 | 22,178 | 14,318 | 5,978 |
| 1962... | 3,606,311 | 1,012,197 | 427,726 | 510,284 | 1,091,958 | 40,698 | 828 | 32,230 | 14,867 | 6,139 |
| 1963... | 4,019,238 | 965,510 | 392,833 | 585,394 | 1,146,821 | 29,178 | 952 | 31,041 | 15,334 | 6,192 |
| 1964... | 3,484,265 | 852,257 | 386,059 | 489,796 | 1,283,371 | 32,476 | 1,020 | 24,401 | 15,182 | 6,237 |
| 1965... | 4,084,342 | 926,851 | 392,279 | 672,698 | 1,315,613 | 33,223 | 2 | 35,402 | 14,956 | 6,116 |
| 1966[1]... | 4,117,355 | 801,327 | 393,186 | 714,992 | 1,311,702 | 27,725 | 2 | 23,390 | 9,575 | 3,960 |
| 1967... | 4,722,164 | 781,867 | 370,246 | 765,617 | 1,524,349 | 24,075 | 2 | 19,931 | 7,618 | 3,133 |

| Year | Tobacco | All Hay | Sorghums for forage | Beans dry edible | Peas dry field | Peanuts | Soybeans | Potatoes | Sweet potatoes | Five seed crops |
|---|---|---|---|---|---|---|---|---|---|---|
| | 1,000 lbs. | 1,000 tons | 1,000 tons | 1,000 cwt. | 1,000 cwt. | 1,000 lbs. | 1,000 bushels | 1,000 cwt. | 1,000 cwt. | 1,000 lbs. |
| 1960... | 1,944,175 | 118,158 | 3,861 | 17,411 | 3,274 | 1,718,011 | 555,085 | 257,425 | 15,445 | 372,376 |
| 1961... | 2,061,392 | 116,957 | 3,384 | 19,672 | 3,559 | 1,657,099 | 678,554 | 293,594 | 15,213 | 315,257 |
| 1962... | 2,314,782 | 121,759 | 3,991 | 17,942 | 5,075 | 1,719,320 | 669,186 | 266,703 | 19,362 | 306,605 |
| 1963... | 2,343,799 | 117,537 | 4,285 | 19,982 | 4,889 | 1,942,088 | 699,165 | 271,730 | 15,831 | 340,688 |
| 1964... | 2,227,347 | 118,778 | 4,147 | 17,375 | 4,880 | 2,099,144 | 700,921 | 239,403 | 15,284 | 330,385 |
| 1965... | 1,854,568 | 125,536 | 4,451 | 16,457 | 4,076 | 2,383,971 | 845,608 | 289,783 | 18,748 | 303,144 |
| 1966[1].. | 1,888,497 | 121,027 | 4,273 | 19,962 | 3,721 | 2,410,391 | 928,481 | 306,902 | 13,697 | 284,611 |
| 1967... | 2,007,314 | 126,361 | 4,317 | 15,472 | 3,751 | 2,508,865 | 972,701 | 305,906 | 14,212 | 239,371 |

| Year | Sugar cane Sugar and seed | Sirup | Sorgo sirup | Sugar beets | Pecans | Almonds | Walnuts | Filberts | Oranges and Tangerines | Grapefruit |
|---|---|---|---|---|---|---|---|---|---|---|
| | 1,000 tons | 1,000 gallons | 1,000 gallons | 1,000 tons | 1,000 tons | 1,000 tons | 1,000 tons | 1,000 tons | 1,000 boxes | 1,000 boxes |
| 1960........ | 7,720 | 3,519 | 1,943 | 16,421 | 93.8 | 53.0 | 72.8 | 9.0 | 121,535 | 43,380 |
| 1961........ | 9,861 | 3,303 | 2,000 | 17,704 | 126.8 | 66.4 | 67.5 | 11.8 | 141,095 | 42,910 |
| 1962........ | 10,074 | 2,702 | 2 | 18,250 | 37.6 | 48.0 | 79.9 | 7.8 | 106,715 | 34,740 |
| 1963........ | 13,885 | 2,814 | 2 | 23,328 | 188.2 | 59.7 | 83.1 | 7.0 | 96,055 | 34,210 |
| 1964........ | 14,360 | 2,989 | 2 | 23,389 | 89.3 | 75.4 | 90.2 | 8.1 | 124,610 | 41,030 |
| 1965........ | 12,945 | 2,923 | 2 | 20,918 | 125.6 | 72.9 | 80.3 | 7.7 | 144,750 | 46,700 |
| 1966[1]..... | 13,365 | 2,121 | 2 | 20,342 | 80.0 | 85.1 | 96.0 | 12.2 | 195,010 | 55,580 |
| 1967........ | 14,982 | 2,201 | 2 | 19,366 | 103.7 | 79.0 | 76.8 | 7.5 | 132,900 | 41,700 |

[1]Revised. [2]Discontinued.

# Harvested Acreage of Principal Crops

Source: Economic Research Service; Department of Agriculture. In thousands of acres.

| State | Harvested acreage of 59 crops (exc. duplications)[1] Average 1961-65 | 1966 | 1967 | State | Harvested acreage of 59 crops (exc. duplications)[1] Average 1961-65 | 1966 | 1967 |
|---|---|---|---|---|---|---|---|
| Alabama.......... | 3,161 | 2,653 | 2,674 | Nebraska......... | 16,271 | 15,730 | 16,851 |
| Alaska........... | | | | Nevada.......... | 466 | 399 | 457 |
| Arizona.......... | 1,080 | 961 | 1,067 | New Hampshire.... | 189 | 169 | 161 |
| Arkansas......... | 6,167 | 6,465 | 6,843 | New Jersey........ | 580 | 553 | 544 |
| California........ | 6,527 | 6,428 | 6,720 | New Mexico....... | 1,033 | 981 | 1,059 |
| Colorado......... | 5,327 | 5,753 | 5,334 | New York......... | 4,695 | 4,643 | 4,555 |
| Connecticut....... | 218 | 200 | 187 | North Carolina..... | 4,431 | 4,198 | 4,449 |
| Delaware......... | 473 | 502 | 527 | North Dakota...... | 17,639 | 17,856 | 18,802 |
| Florida........... | 1,197 | 1,298 | 1,403 | Ohio............. | 9,131 | 9,239 | 9,591 |
| Georgia.......... | 3,946 | 3,547 | 3,909 | Oklahoma........ | 8,532 | 8,506 | 8,965 |
| Hawaii........... | | | | Oregon.......... | 2,651 | 2,668 | 2,826 |
| Idaho............ | 3,666 | 3,677 | 3,977 | Pennsylvania...... | 4,645 | 4,506 | 4,548 |
| Illinois........... | 20,065 | 20,770 | 21,533 | Rhode Island...... | 31 | 27 | 27 |
| Indiana.......... | 10,397 | 10,654 | 11,065 | South Carolina..... | 2,495 | 2,226 | 2,348 |
| Iowa............ | 20,497 | 20,752 | 21,591 | South Dakota...... | 14,398 | 14,353 | 15,034 |
| Kansas.......... | 19,211 | 19,291 | 20,230 | Tennessee........ | 3,758 | 3,763 | 3,929 |
| Kentucky........ | 3,636 | 3,669 | 3,786 | Texas............ | 20,378 | 18,291 | 19,196 |
| Louisiana........ | 2,534 | 2,856 | 3,268 | Utah............ | 1,041 | 1,067 | 1,105 |
| Maine........... | 630 | 585 | 554 | Vermont......... | 729 | 686 | 652 |
| Maryland......... | 1,503 | 1,497 | 1,520 | Virginia.......... | 2,757 | 2,607 | 2,727 |
| Massachusetts..... | 241 | 218 | 207 | Washington....... | 4,099 | 4,189 | 4,548 |
| Michigan......... | 6,577 | 6,248 | 6,327 | West Virginia...... | 782 | 728 | 743 |
| Minnesota........ | 17,757 | 17,504 | 18,618 | Wisconsin........ | 9,221 | 9,254 | 9,300 |
| Mississippi....... | 4,427 | 4,391 | 4,795 | Wyoming........ | 1,773 | 1,690 | 1,878 |
| Missouri......... | 11,308 | 11,421 | 11,849 | | | | |
| Montana......... | 8,059 | 8,061 | 8,654 | United States... | 290,329 | 287,728 | 300,933 |

[1]Includes artichokes, asparagus, barley, beans (dry edible), beans (lima), beans (snap), beets, broccoli, brussels sprouts, cabbage, cabbage (sauerkraut), carrots, cauliflower, celery, corn (all), corn (broom), corn (sweet), cotton, cowpeas (for peas), cucumbers, eggplant, escarole, flaxseed, garlic, hay (all), kale, lettuce, melons (all, incl. cantaloupes, honeydews, muskmelons, and watermelons), oats, onions, peas (dry field), peas (green), peanuts (harvested for nuts), peppers (green), potatoes (sweet), potatoes (white), rice, rye, shallots, sorghums (for grain), sorghums (for forage and silage), soybeans (for beans), spinach, sugar beets, sugarcane (all), sweetclover seed, timothy seed, tobacco, tomatoes, and wheat (spring and winter).

Alfalfa seed, red clover seed and Lespedeza seed are included in the count of crops; partially duplicated in acreage.

# Better Wheat Seed Available to Midwest Farmers

Purdue University has announced that seed of a new soft red winter wheat, yielding 6 bushels an acre more than the next best variety of this pastry flour grain, will be available to Midwest farmers in the Fall of 1969. Development of the new wheat, named Arthur after the first head of Purdue's botany and plant pathology department, took over 35 years of research and breeding.

# Visible Supply of Wheat, Corn and Oats in United States

**Source:** Chicago Board of Trade

| Year | Wheat (1,000 bushels) Date | Largest | Date | Smallest | Corn (1,000 bushels) Date | Largest | Date | Smallest | Oats (1,000 bushels) Date | Largest | Date | Smallest |
|---|---|---|---|---|---|---|---|---|---|---|---|---|
| 1940.. | Sept. 28 | 173,573 | June 22 | 85,098 | Dec. 28 | 63,064 | June 8 | 23,010 | Jan. 6 | 10,425 | July 20 | 2,022 |
| 1945.. | Sept. 22 | 143,662 | May 26 | 52,847 | Mar. 3 | 20,678 | Sept. 8 | 3,391 | Oct. 20 | 45,741 | Apr. 7 | 6,512 |
| 1950.. | Oct. 21 | 228,758 | May 27 | 147,197 | Dec. 30 | 54,442 | Oct. 28 | 35,386 | Sept. 23 | 19,052 | Apr. 29 | 1,007 |
| 1955.. | Oct. 1 | 423,351 | May 7 | 335,864 | Feb. 12 | 51,310 | Aug. 13 | 17,507 | Sept. 10 | 37,505 | June 11 | 12,521 |
| 1960.. | Sept. 12 | 544,934 | June 13 | 363,634 | Dec. 19 | 138,220 | Aug. 15 | 81,302 | Oct. 24 | 30,542 | July 5 | 5,211 |
| 1963.. | Sept. 3 | 430,852 | June 3 | 302,382 | Dec. 16 | 130,791 | Oct. 14 | 59,352 | Sept. 23 | 28,468 | July 1 | 6,820 |
| 1964.. | Aug. 17 | 374,907 | June 1 | 268,688 | Dec. 7 | 117,623 | Sept. 8 | 44,659 | Sept. 28 | 24,140 | July 20 | 9,743 |
| 1965.. | Aug. 6 | 334,477 | May 7 | 222,208 | Feb. 12 | 119,679 | Sept. 24 | 56,299 | Oct. 8 | 29,684 | July 2 | 6,611 |
| 1966.. | Jan. 7 | 255,261 | Dec. 30 | 139,563 | Dec. 30 | 136,499 | Jun. 17 | 64,914 | Sept. 23 | 39,527 | June 17 | 11,781 |
| 1967.. | Sept. 15 | 210,167 | June 9 | 94,813 | April 7 | 156,467 | Oct. 13 | 44,787 | Oct. 13 | 30,624 | July 21 | 14,656 |

**CONTACT (SPOT) PRICES OF WHEAT, CORN AND OATS AT CHICAGO**

| Year | Wheat Low Month | Dols. | Wheat High Month | Dols. | Corn Low Month | Dols. | Corn High Month | Dols. | Oats Low Month | Dols. | Oats High Month | Dols. |
|---|---|---|---|---|---|---|---|---|---|---|---|---|
| 1940..... | Aug. | 0.69¾ | April | 1.16 | July | 0.55½ | May | 0.78¾ | Aug. | 0.28 | April | 0.46 |
| 1945..... | Aug. | 1.60½ | Nov. | 1.80½ | July | 1.10¼ | July[1] | 1.34 | Aug. | 0.58¾ | Dec. | 0.87 |
| 1950..... | Aug. | 2.06 | Dec. | 2.44 | Jan. & Feb. | 1.30 | Sept. | 2.42 | Jan. | 0.72¼ | Dec. | 1.05½ |
| 1955..... | Aug. | 1.83¾ | Jan. | 2.39½ | Oct. | 1.05¾ | Jan. | 1.59¾ | Sept. | 0.57 | Jan. | 0.88¾ |
| 1960..... | July | 1.83¾ | March | 2.26 | Nov. | 0.88 | May | 1.25 | Nov. | 0.60¾ | Jan. | 0.82 |
| 1962,.... | Feb. | 2.02¾ | July | 2.25¼ | Jan. | 1.03 | May[2] | 1.19¼ | Oct. | 0.64½ | Dec. | 0.79 |
| 1963..... | July | 1.79 | Nov. | 2.33¼ | Nov. | 1.11 | Sept. | 1.38½ | Aug. | 0.62 | Jan. | 0.79¼ |
| 1964..... | July | 1.43¾ | Jan. | 2.25½ | Oct. | 1.11½ | Sept. | 1.32¾ | July[3] | 0.62 | Dec. | 0.78½ |
| 1965..... | July | 1.45 | Nov. | 1.69 | Oct. | 1.09¼ | May | 1.39 | July | 0.68 | Apr. | 0.80¼ |
| 1966.... | April | 1.61¼ | July | 2.03 | Mar. | 1.22 | Aug. | 1.54½ | Aug. | 0.72¼ | June | 0.80¼ |
| 1967.... | Nov. | 1.45¼ | March | 1.83½ | Nov. | 0.99 | Feb.[4] | 1.45¼ | Aug. | 0.66¾ | Jan. | 0.81½ |

[1]July and September. [2]May and December. [3]June and July. [4]Feb. and April.

**LOW AND HIGH PRICES OF RYE AT CHICAGO (CENTS)**

| Yr. | Month | Cts. | Month | Cts. | Yr. | Month | Cts. | Month | Cts. | Yr. | Month | Cts. | Month | Cts. |
|---|---|---|---|---|---|---|---|---|---|---|---|---|---|---|
| 1940 | June | 38⅛ | April | 75¼ | 1959 | July | 132 | Mar. | 149¾ | 1963 | July | 129½ | Nov. | 162 |
| 1945 | April | 133 | Nov. | 185 | 1960 | Oct. | 118½ | Feb. | 132½ | 1964 | Nov. | 123¼ | Aug. | 132¼ |
| 1950 | Aug. | 142¼ | Dec. | 178½ | 1961 | Aug. | 132¼ | Nov. | 164½ | 1965 | Sept | 122 | Sept. | 122 |
| 1955 | Aug. | 100¼ | Feb. | 135 | 1962 | Sept. | 121¾ | Dec. | 133½ | 1966 | Oct. | 124½ | Jan. | 132 |

# Farmers' Marketing, Farm Supply, Related Service Cooperatives

**Source:** Farmer Cooperative Service, U. S. Dept. of Agriculture (Marketing Season 1965-66[1])

A marketing season includes the period during which the farm products of a specified year are moved into the channels of trade. Marketing seasons overlap.

| State | Cooperatives | Memberships | Net business[2] | State | Cooperatives | Memberships | Net business[2] |
|---|---|---|---|---|---|---|---|
| | No. | No. | $1,000 | | No. | No. | $1,000 |
| Alabama...... | 62 | 82,275 | 91,192 | Nebraska..... | 366 | 268,455 | 460,909 |
| Alaska........ | 2 | 405 | 2,655 | Nevada....... | 3 | 230 | 5,083 |
| Arizona....... | 13 | 76,595 | 108,871 | New Hamp.... | 8 | 2,960 | 29,315 |
| Arkansas...... | 106 | 86,060 | 256,772 | New Jersey.... | 58 | 25,215 | 116,807 |
| California..... | 356 | 89,720 | [2]1,798,974 | New Mexico... | 29 | 8,555 | 43,750 |
| Colorado...... | 99 | 51,155 | 155,688 | New York..... | 322 | 128,500 | 774,023 |
| Connecticut... | 20 | 5,520 | 68,453 | North Carolina | 39 | 295,420 | 257,588 |
| Delaware...... | 9 | 11,120 | 16,562 | North Dakota. | 503 | 251,680 | 420,500 |
| Florida....... | 108 | 48,375 | 388,515 | Ohio.......... | 237 | 280,895 | 620,729 |
| Georgia....... | 76 | 179,235 | 241,767 | Oklahoma..... | 165 | 137,730 | 280,036 |
| Hawaii........ | 26 | 2,215 | [2]15,063 | Oregon....... | 103 | 63,665 | 260,993 |
| Idaho......... | 79 | 54,705 | 151,493 | Pennsylvania.. | 160 | 126,995 | 443,087 |
| Illinois....... | 391 | 430,275 | 858,868 | Rhode Island.. | 1 | 730 | 13,083 |
| Indiana....... | 128 | 427,155 | 502,752 | South Carolina. | 23 | 72,615 | 67,370 |
| Iowa.......... | 532 | 431,395 | 989,495 | South Dakota. | 293 | 189,250 | 248,200 |
| Kansas....... | 315 | 219,890 | 522,304 | Tennessee..... | 131 | 156,790 | 127,814 |
| Kentucky...... | 84 | 191,830 | 157,836 | Texas......... | 511 | 184,255 | 803,645 |
| Louisiana..... | 95 | 15,405 | 98,948 | Utah.......... | 54 | 32,880 | 101,915 |
| Maine........ | 16 | 9,755 | 46,644 | Vermont...... | 21 | 9,470 | 98,579 |
| Maryland...... | 46 | 47,520 | 128,378 | Virginia...... | 143 | 198,440 | 219,991 |
| Massachusetts. | 28 | 9,325 | 78,611 | Washington... | 170 | 115,360 | 387,076 |
| Michigan...... | 174 | 145,420 | 422,383 | West Virginia.. | 69 | 42,620 | 39,304 |
| Minnesota.... | 1,015 | 616,705 | 1,022,042 | Wisconsin..... | 611 | 389,170 | 808,135 |
| Mississippi.... | 130 | 124,445 | 334,409 | Wyoming..... | 32 | 12,720 | 24,496 |
| Missouri...... | 190 | 395,820 | 387,192 | | | | |
| Montana...... | 177 | 79,355 | 138,212 | U. S........ | 8,329 | 6,826,275 | $15,636,507 |

[1]Preliminary. [2]Volume of a sugar cooperative with headquarters in California whose business originated in Hawaii was included in California.

# Production and Consumption of Meat and Lard

**Source:** Economic Research Service; Department of Agriculture (in million lbs.)

| Year | Beef Production | Beef Consumption | Veal Production | Veal Consumption | Lamb and Mutton Production | Lamb and Mutton Consumption | Pork (exclud. Lard) Production | Pork (exclud. Lard) Consumption | All Meats Production | All Meats Consumption | Lard Production | Lard Consumption |
|---|---|---|---|---|---|---|---|---|---|---|---|---|
| 1935.... | 6,608 | 6,770 | 1,023 | 1,087 | 877 | 923 | 5,919 | 6,155 | 14,427 | 14,935 | 1,276 | 1,221 |
| 1940.... | 7,175 | 7,257 | 981 | 981 | 876 | 873 | 10,044 | 9,701 | 19,076 | 18,812 | 2,288 | 1,901 |
| 1945.... | 10,276 | 7,665 | 1,664 | 1,534 | 1,054 | 943 | 10,697 | 8,598 | 23,691 | 18,740 | 2,066 | 1,509 |
| 1950.... | 9,534 | 9,529 | 1,230 | 1,206 | 597 | 596 | 10,714 | 10,390 | 22,075 | 21,721 | 2,631 | 1,891 |
| 1955.... | 13.569 | 13.313 | 1,578 | 1,531 | 758 | 753 | 10,990 | 10,833 | 26,895 | 26,430 | 2,660 | 1,639 |
| 1960.... | 14,573 | 15,147 | 1,109 | 1,093 | 768 | 852 | 11,606 | 11,565 | 28,236 | 28,657 | 2,562 | 1,358 |
| 1965.... | 18,724 | 19,057 | 1,020 | 992 | 651 | 716 | 11,140 | 11,234 | 31,535 | 31,999 | 2,045 | 1,225 |
| 1966 ... | 19,725 | 20,139 | 910 | 881 | 650 | 771 | 11,337 | 11,241 | 32,622 | 33,032 | 1,929 | 1,076 |
| 1967.... | 20,212 | 20,716 | 792 | 749 | 646 | 759 | 12,581 | 12,506 | 34,231 | 34,730 | 2,077 | 1,056 |

# Grain, Hay, Potato, Cotton, Tobacco Production
### Source: Economic Research Service; Department of Agriculture (Preliminary)

| 1967 State | Barley 1,000 bushels | Corn, grain 1,000 bushels | Cotton lint[1] 1,000 bales | All Hay 1,000 tons | Oats 1,000 bushels | Potatoes[2] Irish 1,000 cwt. | Rye 1,000 bushels | Tobacco 1,000 pounds | All Wheat 1,000 bushels |
|---|---|---|---|---|---|---|---|---|---|
| Alabama | ..... | 37,840 | 197 | 780 | 1,050 | 2,630 | ..... | 1,008 | 2,688 |
| Alaska | | | | | | | | | |
| Arizona | 12,000 | 777 | 454 | 1,122 | ..... | 2,725 | ..... | ..... | 2,450 |
| Arkansas | 128 | 2,688 | 497 | 1,357 | 4,307 | 184 | ..... | ..... | 18,838 |
| California | 75,400 | 18,480 | 1,040 | 7,579 | 3,995 | 33,488 | ..... | ..... | 11,718 |
| Colorado | 10,992 | 20,736 | | 2,888 | 2,988 | 11,790 | 224 | ..... | 38,310 |
| Connecticut | | | | 239 | | 1,312 | | 8,970 | |
| Delaware | 1,078 | 15,403 | | 75 | 132 | 1,700 | 234 | ..... | 1,064 |
| Florida | | 22,450 | 7 | 274 | 407 | 4,778 | | 31,590 | 960 |
| Georgia | 279 | 88,856 | 228 | 845 | 3,500 | | 1,240 | 150,294 | 3,380 |
| Hawaii | | | | | | | | | |
| Idaho | 25,921 | 1,782 | | 3,714 | 2,976 | 63,900 | 192 | ..... | 56,905 |
| Illinois | 782 | 1,091,500 | | 3,867 | 44,718 | 412 | 588 | ..... | 76,396 |
| Indiana | 462 | 447,804 | | 1,894 | 14,352 | 2,340 | 437 | 13,833 | 48,396 |
| Iowa | 184 | 930,155 | | 7,132 | 92,326 | 493 | 100 | ..... | 1,690 |
| Kansas | 2,160 | 72,080 | | 5,282 | 5,796 | 128 | 405 | ..... | 221,620 |
| Kentucky | 1,512 | 93,440 | 1 | 2,947 | 760 | 266 | 192 | 400,060 | 7,854 |
| Louisiana | | 6,280 | 428 | 644 | 1,558 | 179 | | 115 | 2,600 |
| Maine | | | | 461 | 1,395 | 38,160 | | | |
| Maryland | 4,600 | 43,132 | | 710 | 1,200 | 416 | 416 | 36,300 | 5,967 |
| Massachusetts | | | | 282 | | 1,216 | | 3,200 | |
| Michigan | 840 | 91,455 | | 3,300 | 24,486 | 8,948 | 874 | ..... | 40,320 |
| Minnesota | 34,638 | 355,896 | | 7,583 | 157,232 | 13,488 | 1,904 | ..... | 33,795 |
| Mississippi | | 17,640 | 1,054 | 1,096 | 3,300 | 270 | | | 13,860 |
| Missouri | 888 | 198,168 | 59 | 5,642 | 8,580 | 286 | 340 | 4,652 | 53,824 |
| Montana | 37,022 | 476 | | 3,864 | 5,180 | 1,476 | 95 | ..... | 119,136 |
| Nebraska | 700 | 329,230 | | 6,604 | 19,618 | 2,223 | 1,320 | ..... | 88,112 |
| Nevada | 986 | | 4 | 809 | 50 | 192 | | | 1,240 |
| New Hampshire | | | | 234 | | 252 | | | |
| New Jersey | 1,008 | 6,336 | | 383 | 473 | 4,560 | 243 | ..... | 1,950 |
| New Mexico | 816 | 720 | 157 | 963 | | 520 | | | 3,948 |
| New York | 588 | 21,252 | | 5,845 | 22,308 | 17,773 | 406 | ..... | 10,000 |
| North Carolina | 3,024 | 107,160 | 44 | 654 | 6,716 | 2,116 | 360 | 834,675 | 8,432 |
| North Dakota | 85,824 | 4,914 | | 4,145 | 61,272 | 13,452 | 4,028 | ..... | 176,828 |
| Ohio | 552 | 255,960 | | 2,936 | 24,400 | 3,134 | 288 | 20,992 | 51,476 |
| Oklahoma | 3,841 | 1,080 | 194 | 3,065 | 3,360 | 39 | 559 | ..... | 88,689 |
| Oregon | 8,645 | 740 | | 2,325 | 3,760 | 13,252 | 288 | ..... | 31,988 |
| Pennsylvania | 9,900 | 81,048 | | 4,035 | 20,250 | 9,120 | 558 | 38,850 | 17,280 |
| Rhode Island | | | | 27 | | 1,140 | | | |
| South Carolina | 644 | 22,287 | 179 | 390 | 3,420 | 175 | 399 | 165,722 | 3,024 |
| South Dakota | 13,079 | 93,024 | | 4,913 | 109,600 | 590 | 6,450 | ..... | 73,061 |
| Tennessee | 465 | 44,631 | 145 | 1,951 | 1,845 | 368 | 95 | 110,258 | 8,526 |
| Texas | 1,350 | 18,658 | 2,767 | 3,774 | 6,615 | 4,329 | 350 | ..... | 53,216 |
| Utah | 7,500 | | | 1,665 | 1,281 | 1,463 | | | 8,649 |
| Vermont | | | | 1,063 | 296 | 288 | | | |
| Virginia | 5,967 | 35,332 | | 1,532 | 2,860 | 4,046 | 490 | 131,986 | 6,790 |
| Washington | 9,492 | 1,530 | | 2,345 | 1,665 | 22,090 | 330 | ..... | 118,464 |
| West Virginia | 517 | 3,584 | | 912 | 615 | 355 | | 3,515 | 660 |
| Wisconsin | 1,950 | 136,240 | | 10,268 | 107,177 | 13,266 | 460 | 16,127 | 2,358 |
| Wyoming | 4,512 | 1,400 | | 1,946 | 4,048 | 578 | 210 | ..... | 7,687 |
| **Total U.S.** | **370,246** | **4,722,164** | **7,455** | **126,361** | **781,867** | **305,906** | **24,075** | **1,972,147** | **1,524,349** |

# Grain Receipts at Western Grain Centers
### Source: Chicago Board of Trade. (In bushels)

| 1966 | Wheat | Corn | Oats | Rye | Barley | Soy Beans | Total |
|---|---|---|---|---|---|---|---|
| Chicago | 35,156,000 | 99,659,000 | 4,427,000 | 457,000 | 9,171,000 | 37,846,000 | 186,716,000 |
| Duluth | 87,712,000 | 27,693,000 | 24,227,000 | 1,832,000 | 23,193,000 | 5,151,000 | 169,808,000 |
| Enid | 35,670,000 | | 22,000 | | 4,000 | | 35,696,000 |
| Hutchinson | 59,359,000 | 541,000 | | | | | 59,900,000 |
| Indianapolis | 781,000 | 11,946,000 | 5,000 | | | 1,193,000 | 13,925,000 |
| Kansas City | 110,557,000 | 37,116,000 | 1,482,000 | 75,000 | 202,000 | 13,165,000 | 162,597,000 |
| Milwaukee | 1,035,000 | 16,919,000 | 784,000 | 38,000 | 22,421,000 | 792,000 | 41,989,000 |
| Minneapolis | 122,366,000 | 43,138,000 | 33,886,000 | 6,348,000 | 77,320,000 | 10,173,000 | 293,211,000 |
| Omaha | 29,462,000 | 32,823,000 | 2,750,000 | 258,000 | 52,000 | 5,716,000 | 71,061,000 |
| Peoria | 48,000 | 32,000,000 | 64,000 | | | 172,000 | 33,048,000 |
| Salina | 22,804,000 | 171,000 | | | | 2,000 | 22,977,000 |
| Sioux City | 3,864,000 | 8,420,000 | 11,198,000 | 93,000 | 46,000 | 12,566,000 | 36,187,000 |
| St. Joseph | 4,033,000 | 16,389,000 | 4,954,000 | | | 6,854,000 | 32,230,000 |
| St. Louis | 40,485,000 | 57,555,000 | 997,000 | 50,000 | 676,000 | 5,886,000 | 105,649,000 |
| Toledo | 35,358,000 | 37,216,000 | 3,978,000 | 32,000 | 9,000 | 23,011,000 | 99,604,000 |
| Wichita | 18,255,000 | 297,000 | 9,000 | | 84,000 | 9,392,000 | 28,037,000 |
| **Totals** | **606,945,000** | **421,883,000** | **88,763,000** | **9,943,000** | **133,182,000** | **131,919,000** | **1,392,635,000** |

NOTE: Sioux City, Peoria and Enid are rail receipts only.

### GRAIN ELEVATOR CAPACITIES IN VARIOUS CITIES
#### In bushels over 10,000,000. As of Jan. 1, 1968

| Cities | Capacity Bushels | Cities | Capacity Bushels | Cities | Capacity Bushels | Cities | Capacity Bushels |
|---|---|---|---|---|---|---|---|
| Albany | 13,500,000 | Fort Worth | 89,184,000 | Oklahoma City | 3,716,000 | Seattle & Tacoma | 13,250,000 |
| Amarillo | 32,930,000 | Galveston | 9,300,000 | | | Sioux City | 13,406,000 |
| Baltimore | 12,800,000 | Houston | 27,986,000 | CouncilBluffs | 33,597,000 | Toledo | 39,000,000 |
| Buffalo | 51,090,000 | Hutchinson | 50,963,000 | Peoria | 8,570,000 | Wichita | 92,665,000 |
| *Chicago | 79,597,000 | Indianapolis | 19,385,000 | Philadelphia | 4,825,000 | | |
| Cincinnati | 5,458,000 | Kansas City | 113,753,000 | Portland | 1,500,000 | **CANADA** | |
| Dallas | 5,000,000 | Lincoln | 43,342,000 | Portland, Ore & Col. River | 39,135,000 | Baie Comeau | 12,898,000 |
| Decatur | 24,400,000 | Lubbock | 62,504,000 | Salina | 58,000,000 | Ft. William & Port Arthur | 106,601,000 |
| Des Moines | 14,525,000 | Memphis | 12,586,000 | San Fran. & Bay Region | 12,608,000 | Midland | 12,666,000 |
| Duluth and Superior | 77,439,000 | Milwaukee | 28,850,000 | St. Joseph | 23,707,000 | Montreal | 22,262,000 |
| Enid | 66,637,000 | Minneapolis | 152,954,000 | St. Louis | 30,564,000 | Vancouver | 21,806,500 |
| Evansville | 7,742,000 | New Orleans | 12,300,000 | | | | |
| Fort Dodge | 2,389,000 | Norfolk | 10,560,000 | | | | |

*Chicago has 29 elevators. Public storage capacity 59,190,000 bu.; Private storage 20,407,000 bu. Total 79,597,000 bu.

# Nutritive Value of Foods (Calories, Proteins, Etc.)

**Source:** Home and Garden Bulletin No. 72. U. S. Department of Agriculture.

Available for 25¢ from Supt. of Documents, U. S. Government Printing Office, Washington, D. C. 20402

| Food | Measure | Water (percent) | Food energy (calories) | Protein (grams) | Fat (grams) Total lipid | Carbohydrates (grams) | Calcium (milligrams) | Iron (milligrams) | Vitamin A value (int'l units) | Ascorbic Acid |
|---|---|---|---|---|---|---|---|---|---|---|
| **MILK, CREAM, CHEESE** | | | | | | | | | | |
| Cow's milk, fluid, whole | 1 cup | 87 | 160 | 9 | 9 | 12 | 288 | 0.1 | 350 | 2 |
| Cow's milk, fluid, nonfat (skim) | 1 cup | 90 | 90 | 9 | T. | 13 | 298 | .1 | 10 | 2 |
| Cream, half-and-half | 1 cup | 80 | 325 | 8 | 28 | 11 | 261 | .1 | 1,160 | 2 |
| Cream, light, table or coffee | 1 cup | 72 | 505 | 7 | 49 | 10 | 245 | .1 | 2,030 | 2 |
| Cheese, blue mold (Roquefort-type) | 1 oz. | 40 | 105 | 6 | 9 | 1 | 89 | .1 | 350 | 0 |
| Cheese, cheddar or American | 1″ cube | 37 | 70 | 4 | 5 | 1 | 128 | .2 | 220 | 0 |
| Cheese, cottage, creamed | 1 oz. | 78 | 30 | 4 | 1 | 1 | 27 | .1 | 50 | 0 |
| **EGGS (LARGE)** | | | | | | | | | | |
| Eggs, raw, whole | 1 egg | 74 | 80 | 6 | 6 | T. | 27 | 1.1 | 590 | 0 |
| Eggs, boiled | 2 eggs | 74 | 160 | 13 | 12 | 1 | 54 | 2.3 | 1,180 | 0 |
| Eggs, scrambled with milk and fat | 1 egg | 72 | 110 | 7 | 8 | 1 | 51 | 1.1 | 690 | 0 |
| **MEAT, POULTRY** | | | | | | | | | | |
| Bacon, broiled or fried, crisp | 2 pcs. | 8 | 100 | 5 | 8 | 1 | 2 | .5 | 0 | .... |
| Beef, braised or pot-roasted | 3 oz. | 53 | 245 | 23 | 16 | 0 | 10 | 2.9 | 30 | .... |
| Beef, hamburger, broiled | 3 oz. | 54 | 245 | 21 | 17 | 0 | 9 | 2.7 | 30 | .... |
| Beef roast, such as rib | 3 oz. | 40 | 375 | 17 | 34 | 0 | 8 | 2.2 | 70 | .... |
| Beef roast, such as round | 3 oz. | 62 | 165 | 25 | 7 | 0 | 11 | 3.2 | 10 | .... |
| Beef steak, broiled, as sirloin | 3 oz. | 44 | 330 | 20 | 27 | 0 | 9 | 2.5 | 50 | .... |
| Beef steak, broiled, as round | 3 oz. | 55 | 220 | 24 | 13 | 0 | 10 | 3.0 | 20 | .... |
| Chicken, broiled without bone | 3 oz. | 71 | 115 | 20 | 3 | 0 | 8 | 1.4 | 80 | .... |
| Chicken, ½ breast fried with bone | 3.3 oz. | 58 | 155 | 25 | 5 | 1 | 9 | 1.3 | 70 | .... |
| Chicken leg, fried, with bone | 2.1 oz. | 55 | 90 | 12 | 4 | T. | 6 | .9 | 50 | .... |
| Lamb chop, thick, broiled | 4.8 oz. | 47 | 400 | 25 | 33 | 0 | 10 | 1.5 | .... | .... |
| Lamb, leg, roasted | 3 oz. | 54 | 235 | 22 | 16 | 0 | 9 | 1.4 | .... | .... |
| Lamb, shoulder, roasted | 3 oz. | 50 | 285 | 18 | 23 | 0 | 9 | 1.0 | .... | .... |
| Liver, beef, fried | 2 oz. | 57 | 130 | 15 | 6 | 3 | 6 | 5.0 | 30,280 | 15 |
| Pork ham, smoked, cooked | 3 oz. | 54 | 245 | 18 | 19 | 0 | 8 | 2.2 | 0 | .... |
| Pork chop, thick | 3.5 oz. | 42 | 260 | 16 | 21 | 0 | 8 | 2.2 | 0 | .... |
| Pork roast, oven-cooked | 3 oz. | 46 | 310 | 21 | 24 | 0 | 9 | 2.7 | 0 | .... |
| Sausage, frankfurter, cooked | One | 58 | 155 | 6 | 14 | 1 | 3 | .8 | .... | .... |
| Veal cutlet, broiled | 3 oz. | 60 | 185 | 23 | 9 | 0 | 9 | 2.7 | .... | .... |
| Veal roast, medium done | 3 oz. | 55 | 230 | 23 | 14 | 0 | 10 | 2.9 | .... | .... |
| **FISH** | | | | | | | | | | |
| Bluefish, baked or broiled | 3 oz. | 68 | 135 | 22 | 4 | 0 | 25 | .6 | 40 | .... |
| Clams, raw, meat only | 3 oz. | 82 | 65 | 11 | 1 | 2 | 59 | 5.2 | 90 | 8 |
| Crabmeat, canned or cooked | 3 oz. | 77 | 85 | 15 | 2 | 1 | 38 | .7 | .... | .... |
| Oysters, meat only, raw | 1 cup | 85 | 160 | 20 | 4 | 8 | 226 | 13.2 | 740 | .... |
| Oyster stew, 3-4 oysters | 1 cup | 84 | 200 | 11 | 12 | 11 | 269 | 3.3 | 640 | .... |
| Salmon, pink, canned | 3 oz. | 71 | 120 | 17 | 5 | 0 | 167 | .7 | 60 | .... |
| Sardines, canned in oil | 3 oz. | 62 | 175 | 20 | 9 | 0 | 372 | 2.5 | 190 | .... |
| Shrimp, canned, meat only | 3 oz. | 70 | 100 | 21 | 1 | 1 | 98 | 2.6 | 50 | .... |
| Swordfish, broiled | 3 oz. | 65 | 150 | 24 | 5 | 0 | 23 | 1.1 | 1,750 | .... |
| Tuna, canned in oil | 3 oz. | 61 | 170 | 24 | 7 | 0 | 7 | 1.6 | 70 | .... |
| **VEGETABLES & PRODUCTS** | | | | | | | | | | |
| Asparagus, cooked, cut spears | 1 cup | 94 | 35 | 4 | T. | 6 | 37 | 1.0 | 1,580 | 46 |
| Asparagus, canned, green spears | Six | 92 | 20 | 2 | T. | 3 | 18 | 1.8 | 770 | 14 |
| Asparagus, bleached spears | Six | 92 | 20 | 2 | T. | 4 | 15 | 1.0 | 80 | 14 |
| Beans, lima, immature, cooked | 1 cup | 71 | 180 | 12 | 1 | 32 | 75 | 4.0 | 450 | 28 |
| Beans, snap, green, cooked | 1 cup | 92 | 30 | 2 | T. | 7 | 62 | .8 | 680 | 16 |
| Beans, snap, green, canned | 1 cup | 94 | 45 | 2 | T. | 10 | 81 | 2.9 | 690 | 9 |
| Beets, cooked, diced | 1 cup | 91 | 50 | 2 | T. | 12 | 23 | .8 | 40 | 11 |
| Broccoli spears, cooked | 1 cup | 91 | 40 | 5 | T. | 7 | 132 | 1.2 | 3,750 | 135 |
| Brussels sprouts cooked | 1 cup | 88 | 45 | 5 | 1 | 8 | 42 | 1.4 | 680 | 113 |
| Cabbage, raw, shredded | 1 cup | 92 | 25 | 1 | T. | 5 | 49 | .4 | 130 | 47 |
| Cabbage, raw, coleslaw | 1 cup | 83 | 120 | 1 | 9 | 9 | 52 | .5 | 180 | 35 |
| Cabbage, cooked | 1 cup | 94 | 35 | 2 | T. | 7 | 75 | .5 | 220 | 56 |
| Carrots, raw, 5½ by 1 in | One | 88 | 20 | 1 | T. | 5 | 18 | .4 | 5,500 | 4 |
| Cauliflower, cooked, flower-buds | 1 cup | 93 | 25 | 3 | T. | 5 | 25 | .8 | 70 | 66 |
| Corn, cooked, ear 5 by 1¾ in | 1 ear | 74 | 70 | 3 | 1 | 16 | 2 | .5 | 310 | 7 |
| Corn, canned | 1 cup | 81 | 170 | 5 | 2 | 40 | 10 | 1.0 | 690 | 13 |
| Lettuce, looseleaf head 4 in. diameter | 1 head | 95 | 30 | 3 | T. | 6 | 77 | 4.4 | 2,130 | 18 |
| Lettuce, compact 4¾ in. diameter | 1 head | 96 | 60 | 4 | 1 | 13 | 91 | 2.3 | 1,500 | 29 |
| Peas, green, cooked | 1 cup | 82 | 115 | 9 | 1 | 19 | 37 | 2.9 | 860 | 33 |
| Peas, green, canned | 1 cup | 83 | 165 | 9 | 1 | 31 | 50 | 4.2 | 1,120 | 22 |
| Potatoes, medium, baked | One | 75 | 90 | 3 | T. | 21 | 9 | .7 | T. | 20 |
| Potatoes, medium, boiled in skin | One | 80 | 105 | 3 | T. | 23 | 10 | .8 | T. | 22 |
| Potatoes, French-fried, cooked | 10 pcs. | 45 | 155 | 2 | 7 | 20 | 9 | .7 | T. | 12 |
| Potatoes, French-fried, frozen | 10 pcs. | 53 | 125 | 2 | 5 | 19 | 5 | 1.0 | T. | 12 |
| Potatoes, mashed, milk and butter | 1 cup | 80 | 185 | 4 | 8 | 24 | 47 | .8 | 330 | 18 |
| Potato chips, medium | Ten | 2 | 115 | 1 | 8 | 10 | 8 | .4 | T. | 3 |
| Spinach, cooked | 1 cup | 92 | 40 | 5 | 1 | 6 | 167 | 4.0 | 14,580 | 50 |
| Spinach, canned, drained | 1 cup | 91 | 45 | 5 | 1 | 6 | 212 | 4.7 | 14,400 | 24 |
| Squash, summer, diced, cooked | 1 cup | 96 | 30 | 2 | T. | 7 | 52 | .8 | 820 | 21 |
| Squash, winter, baked, mashed | 1 cup | 81 | 130 | 4 | 1 | 32 | 57 | 1.6 | 8,610 | 27 |
| Tomatoes, raw, medium | One | 94 | 35 | 2 | T. | 7 | 20 | .8 | 1,350 | 34 |
| Tomatoes, canned | 1 cup | 94 | 50 | 2 | T. | 10 | 15 | 1.2 | 2,180 | 40 |
| Tomato juice, canned | 1 cup | 94 | 45 | 2 | T. | 10 | 17 | 2.2 | 1,940 | 39 |
| **FRUITS & PRODUCTS** | | | | | | | | | | |
| Apples, medium, raw | One | 85 | 70 | T. | T. | 18 | 8 | .4 | 50 | 3 |
| Apple juice, bottled or canned | 1 cup | 88 | 120 | T. | T. | 30 | 15 | 1.5 | ..... | 2 |
| Applesauce, canned, sweetened | 1 cup | 76 | 230 | 1 | T. | 60 | 10 | 1.3 | 100 | 3 |
| Bananas, raw, 6 by 1½ in | One | 76 | 85 | 1 | T. | 23 | 8 | .7 | 190 | 10 |
| Cantaloupe, raw, medium | Half | 91 | 60 | 1 | T. | 14 | 27 | .8 | 6,540 | 63 |
| Grapefruit, raw, medium, white | Half | 89 | 55 | 1 | T. | 14 | 22 | .6 | 10 | 52 |
| Grapefruit, raw, medium, pink | Half | 89 | 60 | 1 | T. | 15 | 23 | .6 | 640 | 52 |
| Grapefruit juice, fresh | 1 cup | 90 | 95 | 1 | T. | 23 | 22 | .5 | ..... | 92 |
| Grapefruit juice, canned, unsweetened | 1 cup | 89 | 100 | 1 | T. | 24 | 20 | 1.0 | 20 | 84 |
| Grape juice, bottled | 1 cup | 83 | 165 | 1 | T. | 42 | 28 | .8 | ..... | T. |
| Lemons, raw, medium | One | 90 | 20 | 1 | T. | 6 | 18 | .4 | 10 | 38 |
| Lemon juice, fresh | 1 cup | 91 | 60 | 1 | T. | 20 | 17 | .5 | 40 | 113 |
| Lemon juice, canned, unsweetened | 1 cup | 92 | 55 | 1 | T. | 19 | 17 | .5 | 40 | 102 |

| Food | Measure | Water (percent) | Food energy (calories) | Protein (grams) | Fat (grams) Total lipid | Carbohydrates (grams) | Calcium (milligrams) | Iron (milligrams) | Vitamin A value (int'l units) | Ascorbic Acid |
|---|---|---|---|---|---|---|---|---|---|---|
| Oranges, raw, Calif. navel | One | 85 | 60 | 2 | T. | 16 | 49 | 0.5 | 240 | 75 |
| Oranges, Florida, all varieties | One | 86 | 75 | 1 | T. | 19 | 67 | .3 | 310 | 70 |
| Orange juice, fresh, Calif. | 1 cup | 88 | 115 | 2 | 1 | 26 | 27 | .7 | 500 | 122 |
| Orange juice, fresh, Fla., early | 1 cup | 90 | 100 | 1 | T. | 23 | 25 | .5 | 490 | 127 |
| Orange juice, frozen, water added | 1 cup | 88 | 110 | 2 | T. | 27 | 22 | .2 | 500 | 112 |
| **GRAIN PRODUCTS** | | | | | | | | | | |
| Biscuits, baking powder | One | 27 | 140 | 3 | 6 | 17 | 46 | .6 | T. | T. |
| Bread, cracked wheat | 1 loaf | 35 | 1,190 | 39 | 10 | 236 | 399 | 5.0 | T. | T. |
| Bread, enriched French or Vienna | 1 loaf | 31 | 1,315 | 41 | 14 | 251 | 195 | 10.0 | T. | 0 |
| Bread, American type | 1 loaf | 36 | 1,100 | 41 | 5 | 236 | 340 | 7.3 | 0 | 0 |
| Bread, white, enriched, 2% non-fat dry milk solids | 1 loaf | 36 | 1,225 | 39 | 15 | 229 | 318 | 10.9 | T. | T. |
| Bread, whole wheat | 1 loaf | 36 | 1,105 | 48 | 14 | 216 | 449 | 10.4 | T. | T. |
| Crackers, saltines | Two | 4 | 35 | 1 | 1 | 6 | 2 | .1 | 0 | 0 |
| Crackers, plain soda | Two | 4 | 50 | 1 | 1 | 8 | 2 | .2 | 0 | 0 |
| Doughnuts, cake type | One | 24 | 125 | 1 | 6 | 16 | 13 | .4 | 30 | T. |
| Macaroni, enriched cooked tender | 1 cup | 72 | 155 | 5 | 1 | 32 | 11 | 1.3 | 0 | 0 |
| Pancakes, wheat, 4 in. diameter | 1 cake | 50 | 60 | 2 | 2 | 9 | 27 | .4 | 30 | T. |
| Pancakes, buckwheat, 4 in. diameter | 1 cake | 58 | 55 | 2 | 2 | 6 | 59 | .4 | 60 | T. |
| Pie, apple, 1/7 of 9 in. diameter | 1 cut | 48 | 345 | 3 | 15 | 51 | 11 | .4 | 40 | 1 |
| Pie, cherry, 1/7 of 9 in. diameter | 1 cut | 47 | 355 | 4 | 15 | 52 | 19 | .4 | 590 | 1 |
| Pie, custard, 1/7 of 9 in. diameter | 1 cut | 58 | 280 | 8 | 14 | 30 | 125 | .8 | 300 | 0 |
| Pie, lemon meringue, 1/7 of 9 in. diameter | 1 cut | 47 | 305 | 4 | 12 | 45 | 17 | .6 | 200 | 4 |
| Pie, mince, 1/7 of 9 in. diameter | 1 cut | 43 | 365 | 3 | 16 | 56 | 38 | 1.4 | T. | 1 |
| Pie, pumpkin, 1/7 of 9 in. diameter | 1 cut | 59 | 275 | 5 | 15 | 32 | 66 | .6 | 3,210 | 0 |
| Pizza (cheese), 1/8 of 14 in. diameter | 1 cut | 45 | 185 | 7 | 6 | 27 | 107 | .7 | 290 | 4 |
| Popcorn, popped | 1 cup | 3 | 65 | 1 | 3 | 8 | 1 | .3 | ..... | 0 |
| Spaghetti, enriched, cooked until tender | 1 cup | 72 | 155 | 5 | 1 | 32 | 11 | 1.3 | 0 | 0 |
| Spaghetti with meatballs and sauce | 1 cup | 70 | 335 | 19 | 12 | 39 | 125 | 3.8 | 1,600 | 22 |
| Waffles, enriched flour | One | 41 | 210 | 7 | 7 | 28 | 85 | 1.3 | 250 | T. |
| **FATS, OILS** | | | | | | | | | | |
| Butter | 1 cup | 16 | 1,625 | 1 | 184 | 1 | 45 | .0 | 7,500 | 0 |
| Lard | 1 cup | 0 | 1,985 | 0 | 220 | 0 | 0 | .0 | 0 | 0 |
| Vegetable fats | 1 cup | 0 | 1,770 | 0 | 200 | 0 | 0 | .0 | 0 | 0 |
| Margarine | 1 cup | 16 | 1,635 | 1 | 184 | 1 | 45 | .0 | 7,500 | 0 |
| Salad dressing, French | 1 tbs. | 39 | 60 | T. | 6 | 3 | 2 | .1 | ..... | ..... |
| Salad dressing, Mayonnaise | 1 tbs. | 15 | 110 | T. | 12 | 1 | 3 | .1 | 40 | ..... |
| Salad dressing, 1,000 island | 1 tbs. | 32 | 75 | T. | 8 | 2 | 2 | .1 | 50 | T. |
| **SUGARS, SWEETS** | | | | | | | | | | |
| Candy, milk chocolate, sweetened | 1 oz. | 1 | 150 | 2 | 9 | 16 | 65 | .3 | 80 | T. |
| Candy, plain fudge | 1 oz. | 8 | 115 | 1 | 3 | 21 | 22 | .3 | T. | T. |
| Chocolate syrup | 1 tbs. | 32 | 50 | T. | T. | 13 | 3 | .3 | ..... | 0 |
| Honey, strained or extracted | 1 tbs. | 17 | 65 | T. | 0 | 17 | 1 | .1 | 0 | T. |
| Jams, marmalades, preserves | 1 tbs. | 29 | 55 | T. | T. | 14 | 4 | .2 | T. | T. |
| Jellies | 1 tbs. | 29 | 55 | T. | T. | 14 | 4 | .3 | T. | 1 |
| Sugar, granulated cane or beet | 1 cup | T. | 770 | 0 | 0 | 199 | 0 | .2 | 0 | 0 |
| Sugar, brown, firm-packed | 1 cup | 2 | 820 | 0 | 0 | 212 | 187 | 7.5 | 0 | 0 |
| **MISCELLANEOUS** | | | | | | | | | | |
| Ginger ale | 1 cup | 92 | 80 | 0 | 0 | 18 | ..... | ..... | 0 | 0 |
| Cola type beverage | 1 cup | 90 | 95 | 0 | 0 | 24 | ..... | ..... | 0 | 0 |
| Chili sauce | 1 tbs. | 68 | 20 | T. | T. | 4 | 3 | .1 | 240 | 3 |
| Soup, bean with pork, canned | 1 cup | 84 | 170 | 8 | 6 | 22 | 62 | 2.2 | 650 | 2 |
| Soup, beef noodle, canned | 1 cup | 93 | 70 | 4 | 3 | 7 | 8 | 1.0 | 50 | T. |
| Soup, beef bouillon, broth, cons., canned | 1 cup | 96 | 30 | 5 | 0 | 3 | T. | .5 | T. | ..... |
| Soup, chicken noodle, canned | 1 cup | 93 | 65 | 4 | 2 | 8 | 10 | .5 | 50 | T. |
| Soup, clam chowder, canned | 1 cup | 92 | 85 | 2 | 3 | 13 | 36 | 1.0 | 920 | ..... |
| Soup, vegetable with beef broth, canned | 1 cup | 92 | 80 | 3 | 2 | 14 | 20 | .8 | 3,250 | ..... |

T. indicates a trace.

# Recommended Daily Dietary Allowances

**Source:** Home and Garden Bulletin No. 72. U. S. Department of Agriculture

The Recommended Daily Dietary Allowances are amounts of nutrients recommended by the Food and Nutrition Board of the National Research Council as adequate for maintenance of good nutrition in healthy persons in the U. S. Calorie allowances apply to persons engaged in moderate physical activity; they are excessive for persons in sedentary occupation.

| Person | Age in years | Weight in pounds | Height in inches | Food energy (calories) | Protein (grams) | Calcium (grams) | Iron (milligrams) | Vitamin A (inter'l units) | Thiamin (milligrams) | Riboflavin (milligrams) | Niacin (milligrams) | Ascorbic acid (milligrams) | Vitamin D (int'l units) |
|---|---|---|---|---|---|---|---|---|---|---|---|---|---|
| Men | 18-35 | 154 | 69 | 2,900 | 70 | .8 | 10 | 5,000 | 1.2 | 1.7 | 19 | 70 | .... |
|  | 35-55 | 154 | 69 | 2,600 | 70 | .8 | 10 | 5,000 | 1.0 | 1.6 | 17 | 70 | .... |
|  | 55-75 | 154 | 69 | 2,200 | 70 | .8 | 10 | 5,000 | .9 | 1.3 | 15 | 70 | .... |
| Women | 18-35 | 128 | 64 | 2,100 | 58 | .8 | 15 | 5,000 | .8 | 1.3 | 14 | 70 | .... |
|  | 35-55 | 128 | 64 | 1,900 | 58 | .8 | 15 | 5,000 | .8 | 1.2 | 13 | 70 | .... |
|  | 55-75 | 128 | 64 | 1,600 | 58 | .8 | 10 | 5,000 | .8 | 1.2 | 13 | 70 | .... |
| Pregnant (last 4½ mos.) | | | | +200 | +20 | +.5 | +5 | +1,000 | +.2 | +.3 | +3 | +30 | 400 |
| Lactating | | | | +1,000 | +40 | +.5 | +5 | +3,000 | +.4 | +.6 | +7 | +30 | 400 |
| Boys | 9-12 | 72 | 55 | 2,400 | 60 | 1.1 | 15 | 4,500 | 1.0 | 1.4 | 16 | 70 | 400 |
|  | 12-15 | 98 | 61 | 3,000 | 75 | 1.4 | 15 | 5,000 | 1.2 | 1.8 | 20 | 80 | 400 |
|  | 15-18 | 134 | 68 | 3,400 | 85 | 1.4 | 15 | 5,000 | 1.4 | 2.0 | 22 | 80 | 400 |
| Girls | 9-12 | 72 | 55 | 2,200 | 55 | 1.1 | 15 | 4,500 | .9 | 1.3 | 15 | 80 | 400 |
|  | 12-15 | 103 | 62 | 2,500 | 62 | 1.3 | 15 | 5,000 | 1.0 | 1.5 | 17 | 80 | 400 |
|  | 15-18 | 117 | 64 | 2,300 | 58 | 1.3 | 15 | 5,000 | .9 | 1.3 | 15 | 70 | 400 |
| Children | 1-3 | 29 | 34 | 1,300 | 32 | .8 | 8 | 2,000 | .7 | .8 | 9 | 40 | 400 |
|  | 3-6 | 40 | 42 | 1,600 | 40 | .8 | 10 | 2,500 | .6 | 1.0 | 11 | 50 | 400 |
|  | 6-9 | 53 | 49 | 2,100 | 52 | .8 | 12 | 3,500 | .8 | 1.3 | 14 | 60 | 400 |
| Infants | 0-1 | 18 | ... | lb. x 52 ÷7 | lb. x 1.1 ±0.2 | .7 | lb. x 0.45 | 1,500 | .4 | .6 | 6 | 30 | 400 |

# Civilian Consumption of Major Food Commodities per Person
Source: Economic Research Service; Department of Agriculture

| Commodity[1] | Avg. 1957-59 | 1966 | 1967 prel. | Commodity | Avg. 1957-59 | 1966 | 1967 Prel. |
|---|---|---|---|---|---|---|---|
| | lbs. | lbs. | lbs. | Citrus............ | 34.0 | 29.0 | 31.7 |
| **Meats (carcass wt.)...** | 156.6 | 170.5 | 177. | Apples (com.)..... | 21.0 | 15.9 | 16.2 |
| Beef.............. | 82.1 | 104.0 | 105.9 | Other (exc. melons).. | 40.5 | 36.3 | 32.8 |
| Veal.............. | 7.1 | 4.5 | 3.8 | Processed: | | | |
| Lamb and mutton... | 4.4 | 4.0 | 3.9 | Canned fruit...... | 22.4 | 23.0 | 22.5 |
| Pork (exc. lard).... | 63.0 | 58.0 | 63.9 | Canned juice..... | 13.5 | 11.6 | 11.7 |
| **Fish** (edible wt.).... | 10.5 | 10.6 | 10.6 | Frozen (inc. juices) | 8.6 | 8.1 | 10.1 |
| **Poultry products** | | | | Dried.......... | 3.3 | 3.0 | 2.9 |
| Eggs (farm basis)— | | | | **Vegetables** | | | |
| number........... | 356 | 313 | 324 | Fresh[2]........... | 104.1 | 95.6 | 96.4 |
| Chicken (ready to | | | | Canned, excl. pota- | | | |
| cook)........... | 27.5 | 36.0 | 37.1 | toes & sweetpot.. | 43.3 | 47.3 | 48.9 |
| Turkey (ready to | | | | Frozen, excl. pot.... | 6.6 | 9.3 | 9.9 |
| cook)........... | 6.0 | 7.8 | 8.6 | Potatoes, fresh equiv. | 106.9 | 113.3 | 115.0 |
| **Dairy products** | | | | Sweetpotatoes, fresh | | | |
| Cheese........... | 7.9 | 9.8 | 9.9 | equivalent...... | 8.3 | 5.9 | 5.6 |
| Condensed and | | | | **Grains** | | | |
| evap. milk....... | 14.8 | 9.7 | 9.1 | Cornmeal and flour.. | 7.4 | 5.6 | 5.5 |
| Fluid milk and cream | | | | Corn syrup........ | 9.4 | 14.0 | 14.0 |
| (milk equiv.)...... | 337 | 296 | 286 | Corn sugar........ | 3.6 | 4.5 | 4.6 |
| Ice cream (prod. wt.) | 18.4 | 18.1 | 18.1 | Wheat flour[3]........ | 120 | 111 | 112 |
| **Fats and Oils—Total,** | | | | Wheat cereals...... | 2.8 | 2.9 | 2.9 |
| **fat content.....** | 45.3 | 49.3 | 49.3 | Rice, milled....... | 5.4 | 7.3 | 7.3 |
| Butter (actual wt.).. | 8.2 | 5.7 | 5.5 | **Other** | | | |
| Margarine (act. wt.) | 8.9 | 10.5 | 10.5 | Coffee (green beans). | 15.7 | 14.5 | 14.7 |
| Lard.............. | 9.3 | 5.5 | 5.4 | Tea............. | .58 | .69 | .67 |
| Shortening........ | 11.4 | 15.9 | 15.9 | Cocoa beans....... | 3.5 | 4.2 | 4.2 |
| Other edible fats | | | | Peanuts (shelled)... | 4.6 | 5.4 | 5.9 |
| and oils.......... | 10.8 | 14.8 | 15.2 | Dry edible beans.... | 7.7 | 6.3 | 7.0 |
| **Fruits** | | | | Melons.......... | 25.1 | 21.9 | 21.5 |
| Fresh............. | 95.5 | 81.2 | 80.7 | Sugar (refined)..... | 96.1 | 97.4 | 97.1 |

[1]Quantity in pounds except for eggs. Data on calendar year basis except for dried fruits, which are on pack-year basis, fresh citrus fruits and peanuts on a crop-year basis, and rice on August 1 year. Fresh citrus fruits begins in previous October and rice year begins in previous August. [2]Commercial production for sale as fresh produce. [3]Includes white, whole wheat, and semolina flour.

# Agricultural Products, Production and Exports
Source: Foreign Agricultural Service, Dept. of Agriculture

| Commodity[1] | Unit | Production United States | Production World Total | Production % U.S. | Exports United States | Exports World Total | Exports % U.S. |
|---|---|---|---|---|---|---|---|
| Wheat, grain only...... | Mil. Bu. | 1,312 | 10,490 | 12.5 | 684 | 1,853 | 36.9 |
| Oats.................. | Mil. Bu. | 801 | 3,142 | 25.4 | 17 | 85 | 20.0 |
| Corn for grain.......... | Mil. Bu. | 4,117 | 8,948 | 46.0 | 524 | 989 | 53.0 |
| Barley................. | Mil. Bu. | 393 | 4,636 | 8.5 | 45 | 327 | 13.8 |
| Soybeans.............. | Mil. Bu. | 928 | 1,279 | 72.6 | [2]263 | [2]3296 | 88.9 |
| Rice, milled[4]........... | 1,000 M. T. | 3,858 | 163,000 | 2.4 | 1,779 | 7,090 | 25.1 |
| Lard.................. | Mil. lbs. | 1,929 | 7,470 | 25.8 | 189 | 683 | 27.7 |
| Tallow and grease....... | Mil. lbs. | 5,037 | 8,660 | 58.2 | 2,238 | 3,460 | 64.7 |
| Tobacco, unmftd........ | Mil. lbs. | 1,972 | 10,140 | 19.4 | 572 | 1,801 | 31.8 |
| Edible veg. oils........ | 1,000 S.T. | [5]5,587 | 18,500 | 30.2 | [6]2,185 | [7]4,790 | 45.6 |
| Cotton................. | [8]1,000 Bls. | 9,575 | 48,287 | 19.8 | 4,832 | 17,847 | 27.1 |

[1]Crop year 1966-67 as follows: Wheat, oats and barley year beginning July 1; corn, Oct. 1; soybeans, Sept. 1; rice and cotton, Aug. 1; other commodities on calendar year 1967 and partially estimated. [2]Excludes Alaska, Hawaii and Puerto Rico except for exports. [3]Calendar year. [4]Includes estimates for China Mainland. [5]Excludes Communist Asia and USSR. [6]United States oil production figures include oil equivalent of exported oilseeds. [7]Excludes re-exports and exports of oil produced from imported oilseeds. [8]Exports from producing countries. [9]Bales of 500 pounds gross weight.

# Egg Production in the U. S.
Source: Economic Research Service; Department of Agriculture (in millions of eggs)

| State | 1966 | 1967 | State | 1966 | 1967 | State | 1966 | 1967 | State | 1966 | 1963 | State | 1966 | 1967 |
|---|---|---|---|---|---|---|---|---|---|---|---|---|---|---|
| Ala... | 2,387 | 2,645 | Idaho. | 222 | 224 | Minn.. | 2,379 | 2,463 | N. D.. | 307 | 306 | Vt.... | 133 | 129 |
| Alas.. | 10 | 9 | Ill.... | 1,800 | 1,921 | Miss... | 2,338 | 2,508 | Ohio.. | 2,283 | 2,365 | Wash.. | 1,007 | 1,121 |
| Ariz.. | 223 | 243 | Ind... | 2,443 | 2,545 | Mo.... | 1,340 | 1,419 | Okla.. | 506 | 541 | W. Va. | 1,007 | 1,094 |
| Ark... | 2,737 | 3,134 | Ia.... | 3,589 | 3,507 | Mont. | 188 | 201 | Ore... | 509 | 511 | W. Va. | 329 | 345 |
| Calif.. | 7,664 | 8,078 | Kan... | 958 | 962 | Nebr.. | 1,224 | 1,282 | Pa.... | 3,205 | 3,165 | Wis... | 1,392 | 1,385 |
| Colo.. | 246 | 309 | Ky.... | 673 | 720 | Nev... | 8 | 7 | R. I.. | 80 | 79 | Wyo.. | 45 | 44 |
| Conn.. | 839 | 844 | La.... | 755 | 804 | N. H.. | 389 | 379 | S. C... | 1,114 | 1,234 | | | |
| Del... | 131 | 131 | Me.... | 1,095 | 1,175 | N. J.. | 1,191 | 1,189 | S. D... | 1,361 | 1,384 | U. S... | 66,484 | 70,161 |
| Fla... | 1,999 | 2,199 | Md.... | 311 | 324 | N. M.. | 153 | 145 | Tenn.. | 1,011 | 1,172 | | | |
| Ga.... | 4,501 | 4,981 | Mass.. | 531 | 531 | N. Y.. | 2,302 | 2,374 | Texas. | 2,737 | 2,943 | | | |
| Ha'i... | 188 | 196 | Mich.. | 1,567 | 1,665 | N. C.. | 2,717 | 2,949 | Utah.. | 283 | 280 | | | |

Gross income from farm eggs (1966) $2,165,083,000; (1967) $1,822,726,000. Prices received by farmers per dozen (1966) 39.1¢, (1967) 31.0¢. Gross income from farm chickens (1966) $111,543,000; (1967) $101,767,000. Commercial broilers produced (1966) 2,571,576,000, gross income $1,371,648,000; (1967) 2,592,586,000, gross income $1,223,062,000. Gross income from eggs and chickens (includes commercial broilers) (1966) $3,648,274,000; (1967) $3,147,555,000. Chickens on farms on Jan. 1, (1967) 428,746,000, value $513,082,000.

# Farm Employment—Annual Averages
Source: Economic Research Service; Department of Agriculture
Index (1910-14 = 100 per cent)

| Yr. | Total Aver. No. (1,000) | Total Index % | Family Aver. No. (1,000) | Family Index % | Hired Aver. No. (1,000) | Hired Index % | Yr. | Total Aver. No. (1,000) | Total Index % | Family Aver. No. (1,000) | Family Index % | Hired Aver. No. (1,000) | Hired Index] % |
|---|---|---|---|---|---|---|---|---|---|---|---|---|---|---|
| 1915. | 13,592 | 100 | 10,140 | 100 | 3,452 | 102 | 1945. | 10,000 | 74 | 7,581 | 78 | 2,119 | 62 |
| 1920. | 13,432 | 99 | 10,041 | 99 | 3,391 | 100 | 1950. | 9,926 | 73 | 7,597 | 75 | 2,329 | 69 |
| 1925. | 13,036 | 96 | 9,715 | 96 | 3,321 | 96 | 1955. | 8,364 | 62 | 6,347 | 62 | 2,017 | 59 |
| 1930. | 12,497 | 92 | 9,307 | 92 | 3,190 | 94 | 1960. | 7,057 | 52 | 5,172 | 52 | 1,885 | 55 |
| 1935. | 12,733 | 94 | 9,855 | 97 | 2,878 | 85 | 1966. | 5,214 | 38 | 3,854 | 38 | 1,360 | 40 |
| 1940. | 10,979 | 81 | 8,300 | 82 | 2,679 | 79 | 1967. | 4,903 | 36 | 3,650 | 36 | 1,253 | 37 |

# U. S. Imports of Coffee

Source: Bureau of the Census, Dept. of Commerce

| Origin 1967 | Pounds | Value | Origin 1967 | Pounds | Value |
|---|---|---|---|---|---|
| **Coffee Crude** | | | **Coffee, Roasted or Ground (Continued)** | | |
| Brazil | 802,832,080 | $278,285,945 | Indonesia | 22,046 | 4,983 |
| Colombia | 405,128,779 | 163,205,087 | Italy | 4,950 | 4,620 |
| Angola | 195,972,165 | 59,387,054 | Jamaica | 4,440 | 4,397 |
| Ethiopia | 140,040,629 | 47,520,419 | Zustralia | 4,170 | 4,133 |
| Uganda | 139,514,330 | 42,307,753 | Canada | 5,400 | 3,000 |
| Salvador | 112,896,246 | 40,468,530 | Switzerland | 3,960 | 1,677 |
| Guatemala | 93,403,630 | 34,467,573 | United Kingdom | 1,440 | 1,569 |
| Indonesia | 149,930,847 | 33,821,229 | Sweden | 882 | 614 |
| Ivory Coast | 91,269,886 | 27,465,843 | Costa Rica | 1,521 | 562 |
| Ecuador | 61,824,498 | 20,431,166 | | | |
| Burundi Rwanda | 57,295,020 | 20,290,119 | **Total** | **4,355,208** | **$1,580,310** |
| Peru | 59,193,801 | 20,212,739 | | | |
| Costa Rica | 42,869,196 | 16,107,890 | **Coffee Substitutes (A Mixture** | | |
| Cameroon | 50,429,091 | 15,884,871 | **of Coffee with Substitutes)** | | |
| Venezuela | 37,499,712 | 13,662,741 | Switzerland | 26,542 | $50,619 |
| Malagasy | 45,757,786 | 13,306,457 | West Germany | 32,489 | 27,877 |
| Dominion Republic | 33,535,093 | 11,692,484 | Netherlands | 33,000 | 5,948 |
| Nicaragua | 23,016,263 | 8,368,069 | France | 2,520 | 5,044 |
| Honduras | 18,335,226 | 6,529,045 | United Kingdom | 5,435 | 4,424 |
| Tanzania | 16,920,333 | 5,796,373 | Italy | 1,309 | 957 |
| India | 18,327,172 | 5,625,252 | Bulgaria | 2,017 | 273 |
| Kenya | 15,037,736 | 5,204,468 | | | |
| Haiti | 11,620,510 | 3,793,711 | **Total** | **106,295** | **$96,046** |
| Guinea | 11,661,152 | 3,550,231 | | | |
| New Guinea | 9,110,901 | 3,284,844 | **Chicory Roots, Crude** | | |
| Liberia | 7,600,563 | 2,156,016 | Poland | 4,354,460 | $114,181 |
| Congo | 5,506,620 | 1,851,526 | Costa Rica | 15,212 | 5,903 |
| Bolivia | 4,329,272 | 1,417,894 | Belgium | 43,210 | 3,600 |
| Malaysia | 4,617,115 | 1,379,974 | | | |
| Paraguay | 4,252,410 | 1,187,016 | **Total** | **4,412,882** | **$123,684** |
| Ghana | 4,163,437 | 1,118,255 | | | |
| Trinidad | 2,666,604 | 718,707 | **Chicory, Ground or Otherwise** | | |
| Surinam | 2,220,589 | 716,990 | France | 3,994,700 | $323,818 |
| Nigeria | 2,362,761 | 681,713 | Belgium | 1,188,750 | 75,428 |
| French Somaliland | 1,423,385 | 479,029 | Canada | 50,000 | 3,600 |
| Panama | 1,055,239 | 378,178 | | | |
| Switzerland | 764,940 | 370,881 | **Total** | **5,233,450** | **$402,846** |
| Sierra Leone | 953,700 | 285,925 | | | |
| Arabia | 485,158 | 193,464 | **Coffee Extracts, Essences & Concentrates** | | |
| Rep. of South Africa | 582,276 | 174,450 | United Kingdom | 1,440 | $1,573 |
| Singapore | 382,245 | 95,619 | Switzerland | 687 | 614 |
| Other West Africa | 297,997 | 92,748 | Israel | 282 | 600 |
| British Honduras | 223,633 | 75,128 | Australia | 105 | 289 |
| Argentina | 198,414 | 61,875 | | | |
| Guyana | 201,073 | 59,057 | **Total** | **2,514** | **$3,076** |
| Togo | 187,298 | 47,305 | | | |
| South Asia | 77,205 | 22,083 | **Coffee, Instant or Soluble** | | |
| Aden | 44,312 | 17,430 | Brazil | 22,453,221 | $23,502,184 |
| Jamaica | 3,187 | 2,709 | France | 1,723,223 | 3,395,674 |
| | | | Salvador | 1,028,834 | 1,014,269 |
| **Total** | **2,819,044,381** | **$962,679,289** | Guatemala | 860,887 | 783,974 |
| | | | Mexico | 700,703 | 690,630 |
| **Coffee, Roasted or Ground** | | | Nicaragua | 228,239 | 276,765 |
| Mexico | 2,444,482 | $1,029,819 | Argentina | 178,083 | 192,330 |
| Arabia | 455,896 | 151,151 | Italy | 91,108 | 98,850 |
| Paraguay | 463,638 | 100,038 | West Germany | 85,937 | 96,821 |
| Ethiopia | 220,504 | 75,085 | United Kingdom | 7,535 | 7,936 |
| Brazil | 235,486 | 67,641 | Israel | 4,980 | 7,134 |
| Burundi Rwanda | 216,161 | 38,883 | Jamaica | 750 | 2,342 |
| Colombia | 77,161 | 30,625 | Switzerland | 840 | 1,879 |
| Peru | 74,690 | 27,435 | Canada | 1,820 | 1,700 |
| Uganda | 112,055 | 26,692 | | | |
| West Germany | 6,326 | 7,386 | **Total** | **27,366,323** | **$30,073,024** |

# Farm-Mortgage Debt Outstanding by Lender Groups

Source: Farm Production Economics Division, U. S. Department of Agriculture

| Year (Jan. 1) | Total farm-mortgage debt[1] | Amounts held by principal lender groups | | | | |
|---|---|---|---|---|---|---|
| | | Federal land banks[2] | Farmers Home Administration[3] | Life insurance companies[4] | Commercial and savings banks[5] | Individuals and others[6] |
| | $1,000 | $1,000 | $1,000 | $1,000 | $1,000 | $1,000 |
| 1960 | 12,073,580 | 2,334,792 | 437,016 | 2,819,542 | 1,625,024 | 4,857,203 |
| 1961 | 12,812,210 | 2,538,425 | 481,610 | 2,974,609 | 1,686,139 | 5,131,427 |
| 1962 | 13,890,875 | 2,802,275 | 566,175 | 3,161,757 | 1,784,619 | 5,576,049 |
| 1963 | 15,159,843 | 3,023,149 | 585,263 | 3,391,183 | 2,053,369 | 6,106,879 |
| 1964 | 16,792,450 | 3,280,842 | 601,397 | 3,778,537 | 2,356,130 | 6,775,544 |
| 1965 | 18,880,151 | 3,685,501 | 615,463 | 4,284,921 | 2,662,479 | 7,631,787 |
| 1966 | 21,168,703 | 4,234,021 | 627,109 | 4,798,970 | 2,933,814 | 8,574,789 |
| 1967 | 23,283,052 | 4,908,094 | 581,589 | 5,210,915 | 3,164,223 | 9,418,231 |
| 1968 (prelim.) | 25,472,074 | 5,552,844 | 532,702 | 5,540,876 | 3,537,172 | 10,308,480 |

[1]Excludes Alaska, Hawaii, Territories and possessions.
[2]Includes regular mortgages, purchase-money mortgages, and sales contracts.
[3]Direct farm loans only. Includes farm-purchase, farm-enlargement, farm-development and loans primarily for refinancing purposes, project-liquidation, rural-housing (excludes nonfarm), and soil and water loans to individuals, and loans for these purposes from State Corporation trust funds.
[4]Estimates based on direct reports from life insurance companies and official reports submitted to State insurance commissioners. Includes legal reserve companies only and regular mortgages, purchase-money mortgages, and unpaid principal sales contracts. Beginning 1965, excludes sales contracts.
[5]All operating banks. Includes bank holdings of soil and water loans and farm-ownership loans insured by the Farmers Home Administration.
[6]The amounts shown are residuals or differences between the amounts reported by institutional lenders and the estimates of total farm-mortgage debt. They may be taken as a rough measure of the farm-mortgage debt held by individuals and other nonreporting lenders.

## Fire Season on Forest Lands

Source: Forest Service, U. S. Dept. of Agriculture (As of Sept. 30, 1968)

Periods of above normal fire danger in some far western areas during 1968 increased the total National Forest protection area burned to above that of the previous year.

Arizona and New Mexico National Forests experienced a very severe fire season for the 2nd year in a row, with losses in excess of 40,000 acres—more than twice the five-year average. In the Northwest, warm, dry weather produced high fire dangers during July and early Aug., then eased abruptly in mid-August with the advent of unseasonably wet weather, but not before nearly 50,000 acres had burned in the National Forests across Washington, Oregon, Idaho, and Montana. Serious problems developed early in California, with a fire in June which blackened more than 50,000 acres on the Angeles National Forest and adjacent areas, and continued into the Fall. Fire losses generally were near or below normal in the rest of the country.

The National Forest protected area burned in 1968 through September 30, totaled approximately 205,000 acres. In 1967, losses for the same period amounted to 182,000 acres, and for the full year, 204,000 acres.

### Forest Fires in 1967

On all Federal, State and private forest lands during 1967 a total of 125,025 fires were reported, an increase of 2,525 over the 122,500 fires reported during 1966. Acreage burned on all lands totalled 4,-658,586 acres, an increase of 84,197 acres above the 4,574,389 acres burned over in 1966.

Through carelessness or incendiarism, man continues to cause the largest portion of all forest fires. During 1967, 103,427 fires or 91% of the 113,762 fires reported as having burned on protected lands, were man-caused. Lightning caused 10,-335 fires or 9% of the total protected area fires. Causes of the 11,263 fires which occurred on unprotected land are unknown.

More than 479,000,000 acres of State and private forest land are protected under the Federal-State Cooperative Fire Control Program. The area qualifying for protec-tion under this program is now in excess of 517,000,000 acres. The goal of the cooperative program is to bring protection to the nearly 38,000,000 acres not now receiving protection. All States participate in the Cooperative Forest Fire Protection effort.

### National Forest System

Administered by the Forest Service, U.S. Dept. of Agriculture, the National Forest System is made up of 154 National Forests, 19 National Grasslands, and other minor acreages which total 186,799,021 acres in 45 States, Puerto Rico, and the Virgin Islands. All lands within the National Forest System are managed under two guiding principles: multiple use—the management of lands to make each area yield the combination of uses best suited to public needs; and sustained yield—maintenance of a continuous supply of all forest resources through wise use, management, and protection.

National Forest lands which supply water for agriculture, industry, recreation, and domestic use, for example, also are managed to prevent erosion and help control floods, yet there also may be camping, skiing, and timber harvesting on the same land.

The scenic beauty and recreation opportunities available on National Forests yearly draw millions of Americans to these lands to hunt, fish, camp, picnic, boat, swim, hike, ski, and to make pack trips into the wilderness. Use reached 150 million visitor days during calendar year 1967.

**Record State & Private Protected Lands:**

| Group 1967 | Number of fires | Acres burned |
|---|---|---|
| Rocky Mountain...... | 4,681 | 387,192 |
| Pacific.............. | 5,553 | 93,652 |
| North Central........ | 9,843 | 163,273 |
| Southern............. | 70,774 | 1,215,012 |
| Eastern.............. | 11,416 | 66,977 |
| Total............. | 102,267 | 1,926,106 |

**Record on State & Private Unprotected Lands:**

| | Number of fires | Acres burned |
|---|---|---|
| Rocky Mountain...... | 1,493 | 232,750 |
| North Central........ | 3,642 | 350,840 |
| Southern............. | 6,128 | 1,806,794 |
| Total............. | 11,263 | 2,390,384 |

## National Forest Areas

Source: Forest Service, Department of Agriculture. (In Acres) Data as of June 30, 1966

| States | Area[1] | States | Area[1] | States | Area[1] | States | Area[1] |
|---|---|---|---|---|---|---|---|
| Alabama.... | 631,623 | Kansas...... | 107,255 | New Mexico. | 9,154,803 | Utah....... | 7,994,405 |
| Alaska...... | 20,735,040 | Kentucky... | 524,554 | New York... | 13,779 | Vermont.... | 233,463 |
| Arizona..... | 11,436,320 | Louisiana.... | 593,291 | N. Carolina.. | 1,125,278 | Virgin Isl.... | 147 |
| Arkansas.... | 2,434,629 | Maine...... | 50,016 | N. Dakota... | 1,104,958 | Virginia..... | 1,486,830 |
| California... | 19,988,665 | Mass........ | 1,651 | Ohio........ | 119,082 | Washington.. | 9,700,193 |
| Colorado.... | 14,347,827 | Michigan.... | 2,615,748 | Oklahoma... | 286,854 | W. Virginia.. | 910,238 |
| Connecticut.. | 10 | Minnesota... | 2,782,763 | Oregon..... | 15,468,906 | Wisconsin... | 1,475,671 |
| Florida...... | 1,075,702 | Mississippi... | 1,134,266 | Pa.......... | 475,961 | Wyoming.... | 9,167,571 |
| Georgia..... | 794,405 | Missouri.... | 1,389,911 | Puerto Rico.. | 27,916 | | |
| Idaho....... | 20,341,503 | Montana.... | 16,670,543 | S. Carolina.. | 587,753 | Total..... | 186,799,021 |
| Illinois...... | 220,183 | Nebraska.... | 349,399 | S. Dakota ... | 1,982,188 | | |
| Indiana..... | 138,661 | Nevada..... | 5,062,932 | Tennessee... | 602,057 | | |
| Iowa........ | 360 | N. Hamp.... | 678,477 | Texas....... | 775,292 | | |

[1]Includes National Grasslands, land utilization projects and other special areas administered by the Forest Service.

## Conservation Concept Needs Broader Definition in Modern Day

In the light of the growing threat of air and water pollution, officials of the U. S. Department of Agriculture believe that most current dictionaries carry wholly inadequate definitions of the word "conservation." The conservation movement sprang directly from the forest movement in the United States, in large measure under the leadership of Gifford Pinchot (1865-1964), American forestry expert and pioneering chief of the Division of Forestry (now the Forest Service of the Dept. of Agriculture). Pinchot is credited with being among the first to realize that the use and misuse of all natural resources are interdependent, that conservation of these natural resources is essential to the national and individual welfare. He was the originator of the present-day concept of conservation—"the use of the earth for the good of man"—which he and President Theodore Roosevelt planted on the American scene. The original concept was broadened by Secy. of Agriculture Orville L. Freeman, who stressed in 1966 the need for "the conservation of man's total environment."

# Animals in Natural Settings in U. S. Zoos
Source: Edward R. Ricciuti, Curator Publications & Public Relations, N. Y. Zoological Society

Not far from the Bronx Zoo's famed "African Plains," a roughly circular building, massive but gracefully simple and clean in architecture, unfailingly provokes comment and expectant glances from zoo visitors. This is the "World of Darkness," scheduled for opening in spring 1969. In recent years probably no other zoo exhibits complex has created such widespread public interest before opening.

The World of Darkness is an exhibits building centered on a key zoological fact: that many—if not the majority—of the Earth's higher animals are most active after dark.

In this and in other respects the World of Darkness represents a challenging concept of zoo exhibition that has taken hold in the nation's leading zoos. These zoos are no longer places where the citizen goes merely to stare at wild animals enclosed in barren cages. True, the animals are still there. So are many cages, which present views obstructed by steel bars and wire. But the bars and wire are going the way of the cigar-store Indian. They are as foreign to modern zoo planning as the birch switch is to contemporary education.

The best zoos are no longer content to present animals in a vacuum. Instead, the new type of zoo exhibit is aimed at teaching man about the relationship between animals and the rest of nature. This means presenting animals in their natural environment and building exhibits around important scientific principles.

Instead of the "Big Cat Building," today's zoo planners are more likely to conceive an "African Forest," or a "Life in the Marsh" exhibit. Zoos around the United States are striving to present animals in natural settings so like the wild that visitors will be able to appreciate the animal in the context of its environment.

During the year, for example, the Bronx Zoo (October) opened a large North American outdoor exhibit where polar bears and Kodiak bears—world's largest living land carnivores—roam a landscaped panorama and live in dens hewn out of natural rock. There are no bars—only moats separate visitor and bear.

A series of exhibits at the Milwaukee Zoo illustrates the relationship of predator and prey. Lions range what appear to be the same African savannahs as zebras. Jaguars, great spotted cats of the New World, seem to share the same landscape with inoffensive tapirs. Tigers prowl with deer browsing not far away. Actually prey and predator are separated by moats, but these are hidden from public view.

At the San Diego zoo, visitors readily can appreciate how various wild sheep have adapted to a mountainous environment. These agile creatures live in an exhibit on a rocky hillside, that for its appearance could be in a wilderness half a world away from crowded southern California. Also in San Diego, aardvarks are to be seen in a natural-appearing tunnel exhibit, and visitors may walk through vast cages where brilliant tropical birds fly about.

The reptile house at Brookfield Zoo has several exhibits that illustrate the various ecological niches occupied by different animals. Brookfield's reptile house has several "mixed exhibits"—each containing a group of animals interested in different kinds of living quarters.

Several species of tropical birds live in a swamp exhibit with different reptiles, including green iguanas and a pair of boa constrictors. Cottontop marmosets—small monkeys—scamper about the treetops in this exhibit.

Ultimately, this type of zoo exhibit is aimed at interpreting the living world of nature for zoo visitors, especially urban dwellers who seldom if ever chance to see vast stretches of forest, unmarred seashore, or silent deserts. Zoos have a new sense of mission in this regard for, zoo professionals believe, when man begins to understand the place of living creatures in nature, humanity will better understand man's own position in the natural scheme of things.

At the same time, particularly since the nation's major zoos are in or near large cities, zoo planners design their exhibit areas so that these will improve the quality of urban living.

The need for more sophisticated exhibits has brought a new kind of specialist into the zoological park field. This is the professional trained in graphic arts. A forerunner in promoting this field was the Arizona-Sonora Desert Museum, really more like a zoo than a museum. The Bronx Zoo in 1964 established a Department of Exhibition and Graphic Arts. Since then Chicago's Brookfield Zoo and the Philadelphia Zoo have created similar departments. Other zoos are using consultants or are planning similar departments.

To educate and entertain, modern zoo exhibits depend on a variety of media: graphics, electronics, and the printed word. Inside the Bronx Zoo's Aquatic Birds Building visitors look out over a wild beach, listen to the sound of surf upon shore, and watch shore birds skitter along the water's edge picking up morsels of food. A "wave machine" sends ripples through the water. Better yet, the only thing between visitors and birds is air. There are no bars, not even glass, in this exhibit.

A graphic display on the wall opposite the seashore exhibits tells visitors where they can see shore birds within a 2-hour drive of Manhattan—while around the corner other graphics detail the biology of flight.

By combining the talents of the exhibits specialists with those of zoologists (many of whom have had to become part-time exhibit designers) modern zoos are helping man to understand his world.

Outside of the exhibits field, of course, there were many important developments in United States zoos during the year. Here are some of these, taken from the pages of ANIMAL KINGDOM, national magazine of zoos and aquariums published by the New York Zoological Society:

—Twin orangutans were born in February at Seattle's Woodland Park Zoo.

—The Woodland Park Zoo also obtained five sea otters from an expedition sent to Amchitka Island in the Aleutians.

—The Bronx Zoo added a third takin to its collection, the only group of these rare animals in the western world. These shaggy, horned "goat-antelopes" are native to southern Asia.

—Snow leopard cubs—two of them—were born at the Oklahoma City Zoo, offspring of that zoo's female, "Tanya," and the Bronx Zoo's "Bowser II."

—The Philadelphia Zoo put the first zoo monorail into operation (scheduled for fall). The monorail, traveling some 15 feet above ground, takes visitors on a 15-minute tour of the zoo.

—A black rhinoceros was born at Oklahoma City Zoo in May.

—Twenty-two reticulated pythons, first of their kind from zoo-bred animals in the United States, were hatched at the Bronx Zoo from eggs produced in February.

## Aquariums

Killer whales, so-called "wolves of the sea," were to be attractions at several of the nation's aquariums during the year. These huge sea mammals were scheduled for appearance at the New York Aquarium, the Seattle Marine Aquarium, ABC Marine World, Marineland of the Pacific, Sea World, and the Miami Seaquarium.

The Seattle aquarium supplied a 5,800-pound female killer whale, "Lupa," to the New York Aquarium. Lupa was airlifted cross country by jet freighter. During the trip she was cradled in a sling-like stretcher suspended within the aircraft. A battery-operated pump sprayed cold water over the whale during the flight.

The whale was hauled from the John F. Kennedy International Airport to the New York Aquarium, Coney Island, on a flatbed truck. A huge crane lifted the 18-foot-long sea mammal into her exhibit pool.

An aquarium—the New England Aquarium—was opened at Boston's Central Wharf, overlooking Boston Harbor.

This large new institution is operated by the New England Aquarium Corporation. Construction began in 1965. The aquarium has a large variety of marine animals on display in well-designed settings.

## A Collection of Animal Collectives

The English language boasts an abundance of nouns used to describe groups of things, particularly pairs or aggregations of animals. Some of these words have fallen into comparative disuse, but many of them are still in service, helping to enrich the vocabularies of those who like their language to be precise, who tire of hearing a group referred to as "a bunch of," or who enjoy the sound of words that aren't overworked.

Here is a lexicon of some of these "collectives":

| | | |
|---|---|---|
| band of gorillas | exaltation of larks | pair of horses |
| bed of clams, oysters | flight of birds | pod of whales, seals |
| bevy of quail, swans | flock of sheep, geese | pride of lions |
| brace of ducks | gaggle of geese | school of fish |
| brood of chicks | gam of whales | sedge or siege of cranes, bitterns |
| cast of hawks | gang of elks | shoal of fish, pilchards |
| cete of badgers | grist of bees | skein of geese |
| charm of goldfinches | herd of curlews, elephants, etc. | skulk of foxes |
| chattering of choughs | hive of bees | sleuth of bears |
| cloud of gnats | horde of gnats | sounder of boars, swine |
| clowder of cats | husk of hares | span of mules |
| clutch of chicks | kindle or kendle of kittens | spring of teals |
| clutter of cats | leap of leopards | swarm of bees |
| colony of ants | leash of greyhounds, foxes | team of ducks, horses |
| congregation of plovers | litter of pigs | tribe of goats |
| covert of coots | murder of crows | troop of kangaroos, monkeys |
| covey of quail, partridge | muster of peacocks | volery of birds |
| down of hares | mute of hounds | watch of nightingales |
| draught of fish | nest of vipers | wing of plovers |
| drift of swine | nest, nide or nye of pheasants | yoke of oxen |
| drove of cattle, sheep | pack of hounds, wolves | |

## Gestation, Longevity and Incubation

Note: The figures on gestation, incubation and longevity given below are averages based on estimates by leading authorities. The potential life span of mammals is rarely attained in nature. The longevity figures for wild animals listed below were based on experience with such animals in zoos.

| Animal | Gestation (days) | Longevity (years) | Animal | Gestation (days) | Longevity (years) | Animal | Gestation (days) | Longevity (years) |
|---|---|---|---|---|---|---|---|---|
| Ass | 365 | 24 | Elephant | 645 | 47 | Pig | 112 | 14 |
| Baboon | 187 | 27 | Elk | 250 | 22 | Puma | 90 | 11 |
| Badger | 60 | 15 | Fox | 52 | 8 | Rabbit | 37 | 5 |
| Bat | | 6 | Giraffe | 425 | 10 | Rhinoceros | 450 | 27 |
| Bear | | | Goat (dom.) | 151 | | Sea Lion | 350 | 19 |
| Black | 219 | 19 | Goat (mtn.) | 184 | 9 | Sheep | 154 | 13 |
| Grizzly | 225 | 31 | Gorilla | 257 | 25 | Squirrel | 44 | 8 |
| Polar | 240 | 31 | Guinea Pig | 68 | 4 | Tiger | 105 | 19 |
| Beaver | 122 | 13 | Horse | 330 | 27 | Whale | 365 | 37 |
| Buffalo | 278 | 20 | Kangaroo | 42 | 19 | Wolf | 63 | 12 |
| Camel | 406 | 20 | Leopard | 98 | 17 | Zebra | 365 | 20 |
| Cat (domestic) | 63 | 15 | Lion | 100 | 15–29 | **Incubation Time** | | |
| Chimpanzee | 231 | 30 | Monkey | 164 | 7 | Chicken | 21 | |
| Chipmunk | 31 | 7 | Moose | 240 | 8 | Duck | 30 | |
| Cow | 284 | 18 | Mouse | | | Goose | 30 | |
| Deer | 201 | 17 | (meadow) | 21 | 4 | Pigeon | 18 | |
| Dog | 61 | 16 | Opossum | 14–17 | 4 | Turkey | 26 | |

## Things Looking Up for the Whooping Crane

The successful hatching at the Patuxent Wildlife Research Center, Laurel, Md., in 1968 of all the whooping crane eggs taken from the Canadian wilds late in May was hailed by Secy. of the Interior Stewart L. Udall as a "major success in man's battle to preserve this rare bird."

The only known flock of wild whooping cranes has its winter home at the Aransas National Wildlife Refuge in Texas. In 1938, when the official count began, only 18 were known to exist. By 1941, the number returning to Aransas for the winter had dropped to 15. Then conservation efforts turned the tide, and a new record number of 48 left Aransas in 1968 for summer nesting grounds near the Arctic

Circle. In addition, there are at least 22 cranes in captivity, bringing the total to around 70.

The 1968 egg-hunting expedition to the nesting grounds near the Arctic Circle was staged by the Canadian Wildlife Service and the Interior Dept.'s Bureau of Sport Fisheries and Wildlife. Nine whooper eggs and one newly hatched whooper were removed from nests. Four young whoopers had been raised successfully at Patuxent from the first egg-hunting expedition, a year earlier.

A baby whooper being raised at Patuxent was hatched successfully in 1967 by a mating pair at the San Antonio Zoo, the only breeding adult whoopers in captivity.

## Livestock on Farms in the United States

Source: Economic Research Service; Department of Agriculture

| Year On Jan. 1 | All Cattle | Milk Cows | All* Sheep | Hogs | Horses and Mules | Year On Jan. 1 | All Cattle | Milk Cows | Stock Sheep | Hogs | Horses and Mules |
|---|---|---|---|---|---|---|---|---|---|---|---|
| | 1,000 | 1,000 | 1,000 | 1,000 | 1,000 | | 1,000 | 1,000 | 1 000 | 1,000 | 1,000 |
| 1890...... | 60,014 | 16,544 | 48,105 | 51,055 | 20,995 | 1957..... | 92,860 | 15,000 | 44,518 | 48,130 | 18,054 |
| 1900...... | 59,739 | 19,450 | 50,239 | 48,072 | 24,211 | 1958..... | 91,176 | 21,265 | 27,167 | 51,517 | 3,354 |
| 1910...... | 58,993 | 21,455 | 40,743 | 60,159 | 25,742 | 1959..... | 93,322 | 20,132 | 28,108 | 58,045 | 3,142 |
| 1920...... | 70,400 | 22,575 | 38,543 | 55,770 | 22,569 | 1960..... | 96,236 | 19,527 | 28,849 | 59,026 | ** |
| 1925...... | 63,373 | 23,032 | 51,565 | 55,705 | 19,124 | 1961†..... | 97,700 | 19,271 | 28,320 | 55,560 | ** |
| 1930...... | 61,003 | 26,082 | 46,139 | 39,066 | 16,683 | 1962†¹..... | 100,369 | 18,963 | 26,719 | 56,619 | ** |
| 1935...... | 68,846 | 24,940 | 46,266 | 61,165 | 14,478 | 1963†..... | 104,488 | 18,379 | 25,122 | 57,993 | ** |
| 1940...... | 68,309 | 27,770 | 39,609 | 59,373 | 11,950 | 1964†..... | 107,903 | 17,647 | 23,455 | 56,757 | ** |
| 1945...... | 85,573 | 23,853 | 26,132 | 56,937 | 7,781 | 1965†..... | 109,000 | 16,981 | 21,543 | 50,792 | ** |
| 1950...... | 77,963 | 23,462 | 27,137 | 50,474 | 4,309 | 1966†..... | 108,862 | 15,987 | 21,456 | 47,414 | ** |
| 1955...... | 96,592 | 22,912 | 26,890 | 55,354 | 3,928 | 1967†..... | 108,645 | 15,198 | 20,661 | 53,249 | ** |
| 1956...... | 95,900 | 22,325 | 26,348 | 51,897 | 3,574 | 1968²..... | 108,813 | 14,662 | 19,184 | 54,263 | ** |

*Stock sheep reported beginning with the year 1935. **Discontinued. †Revised.
¹Estimates for Alaska & Hawaii included in the United States totals beginning with 1961.
²The total estimated value on farms as of Jan. 1, 1967 was as follows (average value per head in parentheses): All cattle $16,183,380,000 ($149); milk cows $3,679,000,000 ($251); stock sheep $367,407,000 ($19.20); hogs $1,610,510,000 ($29.70); chickens $466,598,000 ($1.10); turkeys $34,121,000 ($4.68).

# Fish and Game Regulations

## All 50 States, D.C., and 10 Canadian Provinces

### Compiled by the World Almanac from official state and province sources

These regulations are the latest available for this edition of the World Almanac and indicate what the sportsman may expect to find. Because of possible changes, local exceptions and additional details, copies of current regulations should be obtained from the agencies listed below with each state. Some states have fish or game possession limits which further restrict daily limits. Some have special licenses for juveniles and others. Some require training in safe handling of firearms.

Seasons and bag limits on migratory game birds (ducks, geese, woodcock, etc.) are set by the U. S. Secretary of the Interior; some states have additional restrictions. Persons 16 and over must have a $3 Federal Duck Stamp (obtainable at post offices) to hunt migratory waterfowl, in addition to a state license. Details are obtainable from state offices (shown below) and the U. S. Fish & Wildlife Service, Washington, D.C. 20240. In Canada, migratory bird regulations are set by the Canadian Wildlife Service, Dept. of Northern Affairs and Natural Resources, Ottawa.

### ALABAMA

**FISH:** Res. lic. $2.15; non-res. $5, 7-days $2. No closed season, no size lim. Daily lim. varies 3-50.
**GAME:** Res. $3 (state) or $1 (c unty); non-res. $25.15, 7-days $10.15, small game $7.15. Deer: opens early Nov. for 1 mo. in some areas, 2 in others; antlered bucks only 1 a day. Turkey: early Nov.-early Jan., Mar. 20-Apr. 25, some counties; Mar. 20-Apr. 25 only, in others; 1 gobbler a day, 5 per season. Racoon, opossum, Oct. 15-Feb. 28, no limit. Fox, beaver, bobcat, no lim., no closed seas. Details: Dept. of C nservation, Game & Fish Div., Montgomery, 36104.

### ALASKA

**FISH:** Res. lic. $5; non-res. $10. Open season year 'round, with local exceptions. Freshwater daily lim. 10 in some areas, 15 in others, exceptions. Saltwater, no bag lims., some exceptions.
**GAME:** Res. $7; non-res. $10; plus non-res. big game tags $10 to $150 each. Big game seasons open Aug. or Sept., run for several months, some exceptions. Bag lims.: moose 1; deer 4 most areas; caribou no closed season, no lim. most areas; elk 1; mt. goat 2; mt. sheep 1; brown or grizzly bear 1; black bear 3; polar 1; wolf, wolverine, no lim. most areas; fur animals, no lim. most areas; small game, 5-20 daily; walrus, no closed seas., no lim., some areas (1 adult bull for non-res.); seals, sea lion, porpoise, beluga, no closed seas., no lim. Details: Dept. of Fish and Game, Subport Bldg., Juneau 99801.

### ARIZONA

**FISH:** Res. lic. $3 plus $2 for trout; non-res. $9 plus $6 for trout, 5-days $3 plus $2; other, special licenses. No closed season. No daily lims. except black bass 10; striped bass 3; trout, salmon, grayling, total 10; catfish 25, some exceptions.
**GAME:** Res. $5, fish-game $9; non-res. $20, fish-game $25, arch. $15. Plus big game tags. Deer: 1 per yr.; guns, 2 wks. in Nov.; arch., 2 wks. in Sept. Elk, antelope: 1 each in 3 yrs. Buffalo (res. only), bighorn: 1 each in lifetime. Turkey: 9 days in Oct., 1 only. Quail: Oct. and Dec.-Jan., 15 daily. Details: Game & Fish Dept., Ariz. State Bldg., Phoenix 85007.

### ARKANSAS

**FISH:** Res. lic. $3.50; non-res. $6, 14-days $3.50. No closed seas. Daily lim.: trout, walleye, sauger, 6; black bass 10; crappie 20; catfish 10; white bass 25; bream, sunfish, perch 50; pickerel 6; total 75 game fish daily.
**GAME:** Res. $3.50; non-res. $20, including deer and turkey $30. Turkey: gun and arch., part of Oct.; 2 gobblers per year. Deer: gun, 6 days in Nov., 6 in Dec., arch., Oct. 1-Jan. 31; 1 per period, 2 yer yr. Squirrel, rabbit, Oct. 1-Oct. 31, 8 each daily. Quail: Dec. 1-mid Feb., 8 daily. Details: Game & Fish Commission, Little Rock 72201.

### CALIFORNIA

**FISH:** Res. lic. $3; non-res. $10, 10-days $3, 3-days ocean, $1. Plus stamp inland, $1. Most freshwater, no closed seas. with exceptions; daily lims. on most fish. Trout: south, all year; rest, May-Nov.; daily lims. 10 summer, 5 winter. Saltwater: some lims., seasons.
**GAME:** Res. $4, deer tag $2; non-res. $25, deer tag $10. Plus bear tag $1; pheasant tags, $2. Deer: early seas. some areas, part Aug.-part Sept.; late, other areas, part Sept.-Oct., some areas 1, some 2 bucks per yr. Bear, late Sept.-early Jan., 2 per seas. Pheasant: mostly late Nov.-early Dec., 2 male daily, 10 per seas. Quail: most areas Nov.-Jan., 10 daily. Details: Dept. of Fish & Game, 1416 9th St., Sacramento 95814.

### COLORADO

**FISH:** Res. lic. $6; non-res. $10, 10-days $5. No closed seas., no min. length, except some areas. Trout: min. lengths some waters; 6 daily, some areas 10. Pike: 6 daily. Bass: 10 daily. Crappie, white bass, etc. 30 daily.
**GAME:** Res. (deer, elk, small game, bear, mtn. lion, fish) $30; non-res. (same group) $135, small game $15 (some single lic. for single game). Big game seas. opens 3rd Sat. in Oct. Details: Game, Fish & Parks Dept., 6060 Broadway, Denver 80216.

### CONNECTICUT

**FISH:** Res. lic. $4.35; non-res. $6.35, 3-days $1.85. Most streams, mid Apr.-Oct. 31: trout, kokanee, char, 8 daily, no more than 5 trout or char; black bass, pickerel, no lim.; northern pike, min. 20", 6 daily. Lakes and ponds mostly mid Apr.-late Feb. Trout, northern pike, same as streams; pickerel, min. 15", 6 daily; black bass, min. 12", 6 daily.
**GAME:** Res. $4.35; non-res. $11.35; fish-game res. $6.35, non-res. $15.35; arch.-deer $5.35. Deer: Nov.-Dec.; arch., 1 per seas.; farmland, shotgun or arch., 1 per permit, 2 per seas., Dec. Pheasant, ruffed grouse: late Oct.-early Dec., 2 daily, 10 seas. Gray squirrel: late Oct.-early Jan., 8 daily, 40 seas.; cottontail, same seas.; 3 daily, 25 seas. Quail: late Oct.-early Nov., 2 daily, 10 seas. Details: Board of Fisheries & Game, State Office Bldg., Hartford 06115.

### DELAWARE

**FISH:** Res. lic. $2.20, trout stamp $2.10; non-res., $7.50, trout stamp $2.10. No closed seas., min. lengths or daily lims., some exceptions. Trout: mid Apr.-mid Nov., 4 daily. Bass: min. 10", 6 daily, no closed season.
**GAME:** Res. $3.20; non-res. $20. Deer: shotgun; New Castle Co., 2 days Nov., Kent and Sussex Cos., 5 days Nov., 3 days Jan., lim. 1 per season; longbow, Sept. 15-early Nov. Pheasant: usually late Nov.-early Jan., 2 males daily. Generally, daily lims. are 4 animals and 8 local game birds. Board of Game & Fish Commissioners, Dover 19901.

### DISTRICT OF COLUMBIA

**FISH:** No restrictions, except prohibited in some waters. Details: Chief, Metropolitan Police, Washington, D. C. 20001.
**GAME:** Hunting forbidden.

### FLORIDA

**FISH:** Res. lic. $3; non-res. $8, 5-days $2.25, 14-days $3.25. Freshwater: no closed seas., no min. lengths. Daily lims.: bl. bass 10, white 30, pickerel 15; bream, perch, red-fin pike, 50 total. Saltwater: some closed seas., some min. lengths.
**GAME:** Res. $2 (co.) $7.50 (state); non-res. $26.50, 10-days $11.50. Deer: part Nov.-part Jan., 2 bucks per day, 3 per seas. Turkey: part Nov.-part Jan., 2 per day, 3 per seas.; part Mar.-part Apr., 1 gobbler per day, 2 per seas. Quail: part Nov.-part Feb., 12 daily. Details: Game & Fresh Water Fish Commission, Tallahassee 32304.

### GEORGIA

**FISH:** Res. lic. $2.25; non-res. $7.25, 5-days $2.25. Plus $1 daily for trout in management areas. No closed seas. except trout, open Apr. 1-Oct. 15 in northern Ga. Daily lims.: bass 15; bream 50; muskie 2; perch, crappie, 40 each; trout, walleye, shad, 8 each. Total 50 daily. Channel cat, no lim. A few local length lims on trout, bass.
**GAME:** Res. $3.25, arch., $3.25; non-res. $25.25 (arch., same), 10-days $12.50. Deer: seas. by areas,

mostly 2 bucks only; arch. seas. starts earlier, 2 of either sex. Ruffed grouse: mid Oct.-late Feb., 3 daily. Rabbit: late Nov.-late Feb., 5 daily in no., 10 in so. Turkey: seas. by areas, mostly 1 per seas. Bear: some cos., Nov.-Dec., 1 per seas. Details: Game & Fish Commission, 401 State Capitol, Atlanta 30334.

## HAWAII

**FISH:** Res. lic. $3.75; non-res. $7.50, 30-days $3.75. No closed seas. for bass, min. 9″, 10 daily; tucunare, min. 12″, 3 daily; oscar, min. 10″, 3 daily; channel cat, no min., 3 daily. Trout: min. 6″, 10 daily, only in seas. on Kauai. Saltwater: some restrictions on octopus, lobster, crabs, mullet, etc.

**GAME:** Lic. $7.50; non-res. $15. No open seas. for migratory birds and some others. General game bird seas., Nov.-part Jan. For axis deer, wild goat, pig, sheep, regulations differ in management areas. Details: Div. of Fish & Game, 530 S. Hotel St., Honolulu 96813.

## IDAHO

**FISH:** Res. lic. $4; fish-game $6; non-res. $15. 7-days $5. General seas. June-Oct., some exceptions, some areas open all year, spec. permit for salmon, steelhead, sturgeon. Bass, sunfish, perch, no lims. Salmon, 2 daily, 10 per yr.; sturgeon, 1, 2; steelhead 2, 20. Trout 15 or 7 lbs. daily. Exceptions in some areas.

**GAME:** Res. $3 plus deer tag $2, elk $3, mt. goat $10, mt. sheep $10; non-res. fish-game $100, one deer or bear, $25, birds $25. Bear, no closed seas. but exceptions, 1 per yr. Elk mostly part Oct.-part Nov., 1 per yr. Deer mostly part Oct.-part Nov., 1 per yr. Pheasant part Oct.-part Nov., lims. vary. Rabbits, Sept.-Feb., 5 daily. Details: Fish & Game Dept., P. O. Box 25, Boise 83707.

## ILLINOIS

**FISH:** Res., non-res. lic. $2.25. Pickerel, northern pike, 5 daily, min. 20″; walleye pike, saugers, bass, 10 daily; trout, 8 daily. No lims., no closed seas.: lake trout, perch, sunfish, etc.

**GAME:** Res. $3.25; non-res. reciprocal with state of res. Deer (shotgun, rifled slug): 6 days in fall, 1 per seas.; arch., Oct., part Nov., part Dec., 1 per seas. Squirrel: mostly Aug.-mid Nov., 5 daily. Rabbit, late Nov.-Jan., 5 daily. Mid-Nov.-Dec. 31: cock pheasant, 2 daily; quail, 8; Hung. partridge, 2. Details: Dept. of Conservation, State Office Bldg., Springfield 62706.

## INDIANA

**FISH:** Res. lic. fish-game $4; non-res. fish $4.50, 14-days $3, fish-game $16. Plus trout stamp $2. Trout (in lakes) no closed seas., min. 7″, 5 daily; (streams) open May-Oct., min. 7″, 10 daily. No closed seas., no min., length: bass, 6 of all kinds total (except rock) daily; bluegill, sunfish, crappies, rock bass, 25 total daily; walleye, northern pike, 6 of each daily.

**GAME:** Lic. see above. Plus res. deer $5.50; non-res. $25.50. Deer: gun, late Nov.-early Dec., 1 buck; arch., late Oct.-early Nov., 1 either sex. Rabbit, part Nov.-part Jan., 5 daily. Part Nov.-part Dec., quail 10 daily, Hung. partridge 5; pheasant 2. Part Nov.-Jan.: opossum, mink, raccoon, muskrat, no lim. Details: Div. of Fish & Game, Room 605, State Office Bldg., Indianapolis 46209.

## IOWA

**FISH:** Res. lic. $3, fish-game $5; non-res., $5, 6 days $3. One day, $1. Plus trout stamp $3. No closed seas., no lim.: gar, shad, sunfish, bluegill, rock and yellow bass. No closed seas.: perch 25 daily, catfish 8, trout 6, largemouth, smallmouth bass, 5 each, walleye, sauger, 5 daily; northern pike 3.

**GAME:** Res. $3; non-res., same as charged non-res. by own state (min. $5). Plus deer (res. only) $10. Deer: shotgun, 2-4 days in Nov., 1 per yr.; bow-arrow, part Oct.-part Nov., 1 per yr. Pheasants: usually part Nov.-Dec., 3 cocks daily. Quail: part Oct.-Jan., 8 daily. Rabbit: part Sept.-part Feb., 10 daily. Raccoon: part Oct.-Feb., no lim. Details: Conservation Commission, E. 7th and Court Sts., Des Moines 50308.

## KANSAS

**FISH:** Res. lic. $3, fish-game $6; non-res. $5, 10-days $3. No closed seas., no min. length. Black bass, catfish, total 10 daily; walleye, sauger, 5; northern pike, 3.

**GAME:** Res. $3; non-res. $15. Plus game birds $1; spec. perm. for deer. Deer: gun, 5 days Dec., 1 only; arch., Oct.-Nov. Part Nov.-part Dec.: quail 8 daily; pheasant, some areas, 2 male daily. Prairie chicken: some areas, 5 days in Nov., 2

daily. Rabbit: varied seas., 10 daily. Details: Forestry, Fish & Game Commission, Box 1028, Pratt 67124.

## KENTUCKY

**FISH:** Res. lic. $4.25; non-res. $7.50, 10-days $3.25; Ohio Riv. for res. of Ohio, Ind., Ill., $4.25. No closed seas. Daily lim.: black bass, sauger, walleye, 10; rainbow trout, muskie, northern pike, 5; crappie, striped bass, 60; rock bass 15. Length lims. on black bass, walleye, muskie.

**GAME:** Res. $4.25; non-res. $25.50. Plus big game $10.50 (non-res. from states barring non-res. from deer-hunting may not hunt deer). Deer: arch., designated cos., Oct. and Dec.; firearms, designated cos., 5 days Nov. (buck only): 1 per yr. Grouse: Dec.-Feb., 4 daily. Squirrel: late Aug.-Nov., some areas also Dec.; 6 daily. Seas. opens in Nov.: quail 10 daily, rabbit 8. Details: Fish and Wildlife Resources Dept., State Office Bldg., Annex, Frankfort 40601.

## LOUISIANA

**FISH:** Res. non-res. $5, 7-day $2. No closed seas. Daily lim.: black bass 15; yellow, white bass, 25; crappie 50; sunfish 100.

**GAME:** Res. $2; non-res. $25 min., 5-days $5 min. Deer: by areas, parts of Nov., Dec., Jan., 1 daily, 5 per year, mostly bucks only; arch., part Oct., part Jan. Turkey: Mar. 29-Apr. 20, few areas, 2 per yr. Quail: Nov. 28-Feb. 28, 10 daily. Rabbit: Oct. 5-Feb. 16, 8 daily. Squirrel: Oct. 5-Jan. 10, 8 daily. Details: Wild Life and Fisheries Commission, 400 Royal St., New Orleans 70130.

## MAINE

**FISH:** Res. lic. fish-game $7.25; non-res. $11, 15-days $7.75, 3-days $5. General open seas.: lakes-ponds, Apr.-Sept.; streams, Apr.-mid Aug.; rivers, Apr.-mid Sept.; except black bass starts late June. Local exceptions. Daily lim.: salmon (14″ min.), trout (6″), togue (14″), black bass (10″), total of 8 with total wght. 7.5 lbs.; pickerel 10; white perch mostly no lim.; some exceptions. Ice fishing in some areas.

**GAME:** Res. $4, arch. $5.25; non-res. small game $17.25, big game $33.25, arch.-deer $15.25. Deer: by zones, mostly late Oct.-Nov., 1 per yr. Bear, June-Dec. Rabbit, mostly Oct.-Feb., 4 daily. Gray squirrel, Oct.-part Nov., 4 daily. Partridge, pheasant, usualy Oct.-part Nov., 4 part., 2 pheas. daily. No closed seas.: fox, bobcat. Details: Dept. of Inland Fisheries & Game, State Office Bldg., Augusta 04330.

## MARYLAND

**FISH:** Res. lic. $3; non-res. $10, 3 days $3. Plus trout stamp $1. Trout: mid-Apr. to mid Mar., min. 7″, 7 daily. Walleye: Apr.-mid Nov., 14″, 5. No closed seas.: large, small mouth bass, 9″, total 10 (5 in state impoundments); pickerel 14″, 5; northern pike 20″, 2; muskie 30″, 2; rock bass 14″, no lim.; all others, no restrictions.

**GAME:** Res. $6.50 (statewide), $3 (co.); non-res. $25. Plus deer and turkey stamp $5.50. Deer: firearms, late Nov.-early Dec.; arch. mid Sept.-early Jan.; 1 per yr. Turkey, some cos. only, last 2 wks. Oct., 1 per yr. Nov. 1-Jan. 15, daily lims.: pheasant 2 (male), grouse 2, rabbit 4. Nov. 15-Feb. 1; quail, 6 daily. Sept. 11-Apr. 1: raccoon, opossum, no lim. Details: Game & Inland Fish Dept., State Office Bldg., Annapolis 21404.

## MASSACHUSETTS

**FISH:** Res. lic. $5.25, women $4.25; non-res. $9.75, 7-days $5.25. Brook, brown or rainbow trout: ponds, lakes (6 daily), most rivers, streams, (12 daily); 3rd Sat. in Apr.-3rd Sat. in Oct.; also most ponds, lakes, 3rd Sun. in Oct.-Feb. 28, 2 daily. From 3rd Sat. in Apr. to Feb. 28: lake trout (18″), 2 daily; black bass 10″, northern pike 20″, perch, pickerel 14″, 5 each daily.

**GAME:** Res. $5.25, sporting $8.25; non-res. $16.25. Plus arch. stamp for deer $1.10. Late Oct.-late Nov.; pheasant, 2 cocks daily, 6 per yr.; quail, 5 daily, 25 per yr. Deer: shotgun, 6 days in Dec., arch. part Nov., total 1 per yr. Opossum: late Sept.-late Dec., no lim. Grouse: part Oct.-part Jan., 3 daily, 15 per yr. Black bear: late Oct.-late Dec., 1 per yr. Details: Div. of Fisheries & Game, 100 Cambridge St., Boston 02202.

## MICHIGAN

**FISH:** Res. lic. $3; non-res. $6, 7-days $5. Plus trout stamps. Brook, brown rainbow trout: Apr.-Nov., min. 7″, 5 daily in lakes, 10 in streams, and total not over 10 lbs. Open most of yr.: lake trout, muskie (30″ min.), 2 each inland waters; northern

pike (20″ min.), walleye (13″), 5 daily inland waters, total 10 Great Lakes. Large, small mouth bass, mostly June-Dec., 10″, 5 daily. Sturgeon: some areas, 42″, Jan.-Feb., 2 per yr.

**GAME:** Res. small game $3.10, deer $5.10, arch.-deer $5.10, bear $5.10; non-res. small game $20.10, deer $35.10, arch.-deer $15.10, bear $25.10. Bear: Upper Peninsula only, part Sept.-part Nov., 1 per yr. Deer: firearms, last half Nov., 1 male, 3″ antlers; arch., Oct., part Nov., Dec., 1 either sex. Season differs in Upper and Lower Penin.: rabbits, ruffed grouse, 5 daily, pheasants 2 daily. Details: Dept. of Conservation, Lansing 48926.

### MINNESOTA

**FISH:** Res. lic. $2.25, hus.-wife $2.75; non-res. $5.25, hus.-wife $9, 3-days $3. Mid May-mid Feb.: northern pike 3 daily; walleye, sauger, total 6 daily; muskie, 1 daily, min. 30″. June 1-mid Feb.: large, small mouth bass, 6 daily. May-mid Sept.: lake trout, 3 daily. Season by areas: trout. No closed seas.: catfish, 5 daily.

**GAME:** Res. small game $3, arch.-deer $5, gun-deer $5; non-res. small game $26, arch.-deer $10.25, gun-deer $50.25. Deer: gun, 9 days in Nov., some areas; arch., Oct. and part-Dec., some areas; total 1 per yr. Part Oct., part Nov.: partridge, ruffed grouse, sharptail grouse, male pheasant, 3 each daily. Details: Dept. of Conservation, Centennial Office Bldg., St. Paul 55101.

### MISSISSIPPI

**FISH:** Res. lic. $3, 3-days $1, fish-game $5; non-res. fish $6, 3-days $1.50. No closed seas., no length lim. Daily lim.: black bass 15, sauger 15; striped bass, crappie 30 each; sunfish 50; total 75.

**GAME:** Res. $3.50, plus deer and turkey $2, arch.-deer $3; non-res. (all game) $25 plus $2 deer and turkey, 3-days (no deer, turkey) $6. Bobwhite: Dec.-mid Feb., 10 daily. Rabbit: part Oct.-part Feb., 8. Squirrel: part Oct.-part Jan., 8. Turkey: part Mar., part Apr., mostly 1 gobbler daily, 3 per lic. yr. Deer (area restrictions): gun-arch., parts of Nov., Dec., Jan., 1 buck with 4″ antlers per seas.; arch., part Oct.-part Nov., 1 either sex per seas. Details: Game & Fish Commission, Box 451, Jackson 39205.

### MISSOURI

**FISH:** Res. lic. $4.30, fish-game $7.80; non-res. $6.30, 14-days $4.30. Plus trout permit $2.30. No closed seas. except black bass, some areas (closed Mar. 1-May 29) and walleye, sauger, some areas (closed Mar. 15-Apr. 15). Daily lim.: black bass, in streams 6, in impoundments 10; white, rock, yellow, striped bass, 15; channel, blue cat, 10; flathead cat 5; walleye 4; crappie 30; trout, kokanee, 5; muskie 1; pike 2.

**GAME:** Res. $4.30, arch.-deer $5.30, firearms-deer $5.30, turkey $5.30; non-res. small game $20.30, turkey $25.30, firearms-deer $25.30, arch. $10.30. Deer: firearms, 5 days Nov., 7 days Dec., 1 per yr.; arch., opens Oct. 1, 1 per yr. Rabbit: May 30-Mar. 1, 10 daily. Squirrel: May 30-Dec. 31, 6 daily. Pheasant: some areas only, Nov. 10-Dec. 10, 1 male daily. Turkey: 1 male per yr. Details: Missouri Conservation Commission, Jefferson City 65101.

### MONTANA

**FISH:** Res. lic. $4; non-res. $15, 6-days $5. General seas. mid May-late Nov.; some areas open all yr., some closed all yr. General daily lim.: trout, char, grayling, total of 10, total 10 lbs.; whitefish, 20; walleye, sauger, northern pike, bass, total of 15, total 15 lbs.; kokanee salmon, 10. No lim. on other fish.

**GAME:** Res. (fish, birds, 1 deer, elk, black bear) $20, spec. licenses $3-$25; non-res. (fish, birds, 2 deer, 1 elk, 1 black bear) $150, spec. licenses $10-$50. Deer, elk, grizzly: late Oct.-late Nov., 1 each per yr. (some areas 2 deer). Black bear: mid Mar.-late Nov., 1 per yr. Special seas., drawings for antelope, mt. goat, bighorn, moose. Details: Fish & Game Dept., Helena 59601.

### NEBRASKA

**FISH:** Res. lic. $3.50, fish-game $7; non-res., $6, 5-days $2.50. No closed seas. except spec. areas. Daily lim.: trout 5; large, small mouth bass, total 10; walleye and sauger, total 8; channel catfish 10, flathead 4, northern pike (24″ min.) 6, paddlefish 2, bait minnows 100; others, no lim.

**GAME:** Res., small game $4, deer $10, antelope $10, turkey $5; non-res., small game $25, deer $25, antelope $25, turkey $15. Plus game bird stamp $1. Pheasant: early Nov.-mid Jan., 3 cocks daily.

Quail: early Nov.-mid Jan., 6 or 8 daily, by region. Grouse: part Sept., Oct., Nov., 3 daily. Deer: firearm, 9 days in Nov.; arch., parts of Oct., Nov., Dec., 1 daily, 1 total in possession (including storage). Turkey: 9 days in Nov., 1 daily, 1 in poss. Details: Game Commission, Lincoln 68509.

### NEVADA

**FISH:** Res. lic. $5; non-res. $10, 5-days $3.50. No closed seas. (local exceptions). Trout, char, salmon, whitefish, 10 daily; other game fish, total 15 daily, except no lim. on yellow perch, crappie, sunfish, bluegill, Sacramento perch.

**GAME:** Res. $5; non-res. $35. Plus spec. fees for various big game. Most big game hunting restricted by areas, quotas, drawings. Antelope, elk, for res. only. Details: Fish & Game Commission, Box 10678, Reno 89510.

### NEW HAMPSHIRE

**FISH:** Res. lic. $4.50, fish-game $7; non-res. $8.75, 15-days $5.75. Early May-Oct. 15: Brown, rainbow trout, 10 fish or 5 lbs. daily; golden trout, 5 fish or 5 lbs. daily. No closed seas.: bass, 5 daily; pickerel, 10 or 10 lbs. daily; bullhead, 40 daily; walleye, min. 12″, 10 lbs. daily; white and yellow perch, no lim.

**GAME:** Res. $4, arch., $3; non-res. $25.25, arch., $10. Deer: part Nov.-Dec. 1, arch., part Dec.; 1 per yr. Ruffed grouse: Oct. 1-Dec. 1, 4 daily, 25 per yr. Pheasant: Oct., 2 daily, 10 per yr. Gray squirrel: Oct.-part Nov., 5 daily. Hare (3 daily), rabbit (5 daily), Oct. 1-Mar. 15, total 5 daily. Bear: Sept. 1-Dec. 3, no lim. Details: Fish & Game Dept., Concord 03301.

### NEW JERSEY

**FISH:** Res. lic. $4.15, trout stamp $2; non-res. $7.15, 3-days $3.65, trout stamp $5. Trout: closed seas. usually Mar.-part Apr., 6 daily, some areas fly only. No closed seas. in unfrozen waters: small, large mouth bass, min. 9″, total 5 daily; pike-perch (min. 12″), pickerel, 10 each daily. No restrictions: rock, white, calico bass; white, yellow perch; crappie, sunfish, catfish, carp, eels.

**GAME:** Res. $5.15, arch. $5.15; non-res. $15.15, arch. $15.15. Usual seas.: Deer: arch., Oct.-part Nov., 1 per seas. either sex; firearms or arch., 1 wk. in Dec., 1 per seas., antler min. 3″. Bear: arch., Oct.-part Nov., firearm or arch., 1 wk. in Dec.; 1 per seas. Pheasant: part Nov., part Dec., 2 male daily. Parts of Nov., Dec., Jan., Feb.; 7 quail, 3 grouse, 5 squirrel, 4 cottontail rabbits, 1 hare daily. Details: Div. of Fish & Game, Box 1809, Trenton 08625.

### NEW MEXICO

**FISH:** Res. lic. $5.50, 1-day $2, hunt-fish $12; non-res. $10, 5 days $5.25, 1-day $2. General rules: Trout: early May-Nov. 30, north of Highway 66; all yr. so. of 66; 12 daily. No closed seas.: black bass 12 daily, walleye 12, northern pike (min. 18″) 6, catfish 15, crappie 40, white bass 40. No lim.: perch, bullheads, bluegills, sunfish.

**GAME:** Res. deer-bear-turkey-squirrel $7.50, big game-birds $9, birds $5, antelope $10, elk $15, sheep $20; non res. deer-bear-turkey-squirrel $50.25, sheep $100, arch., deer $15, birds $17, antelope $40, elk $50. Fall seasons by areas: deer, bear, turkey, several weeks; antelope 2 days; elk 9 days; bag lim., 1 each per yr. Prairie chicken: 2 days, 4 per yr. Coyotes, mt. lion, fox: no closed seas. Details: Game & Fish Dept., State Capitol, Santa Fe 87501.

### NEW YORK

**FISH:** Res. lic. $3.25, fish-game $5.75; non-res. $5.50, 6-day $4.25. Apr. 1-Sept. 30: trout, any size, 10 daily; lake trout, landlocked salmon, min 15″, 3 trout, 2 salmon daily. Black bass: June 21-Nov. 30, 10″, 6 daily. May 1-Mar. 1: walleye any size, pickerel 12″, northern pike 18″, 10 each daily. Rock and white bass, sunfish, yellow and white perch, no closed seas., no lim. Local exceptions to most rules.

**GAME:** Res. $3.25, deer-bear $3.25; non-res. $10.75, deer-bear $10. Arch. stamp (deer-bear) $3.25. Small game upstate usually opens early Oct.; squirrel 5 daily, ruffed grouse 4, pheasant 2, rabbit 6, raccoon (no lim.), quail 4; L. I. usually month later, dif. lims. Deer: Oct. 25-1st Tues. Dec., north zone; 3rd Mon. Nov.-1st Tues. Dec., south zone. Bear: same as deer, north zone, part Nov.-part Dec. in some other counties; 1 deer, 1 bear per yr., no seas. L. I. Details: Conservation Dept., Albany, N. Y. 12226.

## NORTH CAROLINA

**FISH:** Res. lic. $4.25 (statewide), $1.65 (co.), fish-game $6.25, plus mt. trout waters $1.25; non-res. $8.25, 5-days $3.75, 1-day $1.65, plus mt. trout $3.25. Trout: part Apr.-part Sept., 7 daily. No closed seas.: muskie, 2 daily, min. 26"; small, large mouth, spotted bass, 8 total daily, min. 10"; walleye, sauger, 10", 8 daily. Kokanee salmon, part Nov.-part Sept., 7 daily. Others, no closed seas.

**GAME:** Res. $4.25 (statewide), $1.65 (co.); non-res. $22, 6-days $17.75. Bear: mostly Oct. 18-Jan. 1, 1 daily, 2 per seas. Deer: seas. varies by areas, mostly parts of Oct., Nov., Dec.; 1 male with antlers daily, 2 per seas. Late Nov.-mid Feb.: quail, 8 daily, 100 per seas.; turkey, 1 daily, 2 per seas.; pheasant, no lim. some areas, no open seas others. Mid Nov.-mid Feb.: raccoon, 1 daily, 20 per seas.; rabbit, 5 daily, 75 per seas.; opossum, no lim. Details: Wildlife Resources Commission, Box 2919, Raleigh 27602.

## NORTH DAKOTA

**FISH:** Res. lic. $3; non-res. $5, 7-days $2. Early May to late Mar. Daily lim.: large or small mouth bass, trout (except some areas), walleye, sauger, 5 each daily; pike 3, muskie 1. No seas. or lim.: catfish, sunfish, etc. Some ice fishing.

**GAME:** Res. small game $2, deer-gun $6, deer-arch. $6; non-res. small game $25, deer-gun $50, deer-arch, $25; other spec. permits. Deer: gun, 10 days in Nov., 1 per yr.; arch., part Aug.-part Nov., part Dec., 1 only. Partridge: part Sept.-part Dec., 4 daily, 12 seas. Game & Fish Dept., Bismarck 58501.

## OHIO

**FISH:** Res. lic. $4.35; non-res. $6.35, 15-days $4.35. No closed seas., no min. length or bag limits; some exceptions. Ice fishing permitted.

**GAME:** Res. $4.35; non-res. $20.35. Plus deer permit $5.35. Deer (1 per seas.): gun, by zones, 2-6 days Dec.; arch., part Oct.-part Dec. Quail (6 daily), pheasant (2 daily), partridge (2 daily): part Nov., part Dec., part Jan. Rabbit (4 daily), mid Nov.-late Jan. Ruffed grouse (3 daily), mid Oct.-late Feb. Details: Natural Resources Dept., Wildlife Div., Columbus 43212.

## OKLAHOMA

**FISH:** Res. lic. $3.25, fish-game $6; non-res. $3.25. No closed seas. except some areas. No min. length except walleye, sauger 15". Daily lim.: black bass, 10; trout 6, catfish 15, walleye 5, crappie 37; rock bass, no lim.

**GAME:** Res. $3.25; non-res. small game $15, big $25. Deer: gun, 9 days in Nov., 1 buck; arch., 30 days Oct. 19-Nov. 17, 1. Quail: mid Nov.-mid Jan., 3 days each wk., 10 daily. Turkey: 9 days in Apr., 1 tom; 5 days in Nov., 1 tom. Pheasant: some counties only. Details: Wildlife Conservation Dept., 1801 No. Lincoln Blvd., Oklahoma City 73105.

## OREGON

**FISH:** Res. lic. $6, fish-game $10, non-res. $15, 10-days $7, 1-day $1.50. Plus salmon-steelhead card, $1. No closed seas., sunfish, perch, crappies, catfish (100 daily, total 50 lbs.), black bass (12 daily, only over 17"), shad (10 daily), sturgeon (3 daily, 36"-72"). Late Apr.-Oct. 31 most areas: steelhead and salmon under 20", trout, 10 daily, only 5 over 12"; steelhead and salmon over 20", 2 daily; also, winter seas. by areas.

**GAME:** Res. $5; non-res. $35. Plus antelope (res. only), deer, elk tags and fees. Deer: part of Oct. 1. Elk: part of Nov., 1. Bear: most areas no lim. Blue, ruffed grouse: part Oct., 3 daily. Pheasant: part Oct.-part Nov., 2 cocks daily. Details: State Game Commission, 1634 S.W. Alder St., Portland 97208.

## PENNSYLVANIA

**FISH:** Res. lic. $5.20; non-res. $9.70, 5-days $5.20. Trout: mostly part Apr. to part Sept., min. 6", 6-8 daily. Small, large mouth bass: mid June to mid Mar., min. 9", total 6 daily. Pickerel, walleye: early May-mid Mar., min. 15", 6 each daily. Northern pike: early May to mid Mar., min. 24", 2 daily. Spec. rules for winter fishing.

**GAME:** Res. $5.20; non-res. $25.35, 3-days (regulated shooting grnds.) $3.15. Bear: 6 days late Nov., 1 per seas. Deer: antlered, 2 wks. early Dec.; no antlers, 3 days in Dec.; arch., either sex, Oct., late Dec.-part Jan.; total 1 deer. Small game seas. opens late Oct.: turkey, 1 per seas.; ruffed grouse, 2 daily, 10 per yr.; squirrels, 6, 30; rabbits, 4, 20; male pheasant, 2, 8; quail, 4, 20. Details: Penn. Game Commission, P. O. Box 1567, Harrisburg 17120.

## RHODE ISLAND

**FISH:** Res. lic. $3.25; non-res. $7.25, 3-days $3.25. Large, small mouth bass: Apr. 20-Feb. 28, 6 daily. Pickerel, same, min. 12", 10 daily. Trout: Apr. 20-Nov. 30, 6 daily; Dec. 1-Feb. 28, 2 daily. No closed seas., no lim.: yellow, white perch; sunfish, bullhead, carp, striped bass (min. 16").

**GAME:** Res. $3.25, deer $5; non-res. $10.25, deer $20. Deer: arch., part Oct. and part Dec.-Jan., 1 per seas.; shotgun 6 days Dec., 1 per seas. Partridge (2 daily), preasant (2): parts Oct., Nov., Dec., Jan. Fox, woodchuck: no lim. Raccoon: Oct. 10-Jan. 31, 2 per night. Details: Dept. of Natural Resources, Veterans Memorial Bldg., Providence 02903.

## SOUTH CAROLINA

**FISH:** Res. lic. $1.10; non-res. $10.25, 10-days $3.10. Extra fees, some lakes. No closed seas. Daily lim.: bass, rockfish, trout, total 10 plus 25 other game fish; exceptions in some areas.

**GAME:** Res. $4.25 (state), $1.35 (co.); non-res. $22.25, 3-days, $11.25. Most areas, late in yr.: turkey, 2 gobblers daily, 5 per seas.; deer 1 to 5, by areas, per seas. Quail: most areas Thanksgiving to Mar. 1, mostly 10 daily. Squirrels: mostly Sept. 15-Feb. 15, mostly 10 daily. Fox: no closed seas. Details: Div. of Game, Box 167, Columbia 29202.

## SOUTH DAKOTA

**FISH:** Res. lic. $3; non-res. $6, 5-days $2. No closed seas. most of state. Daily lim., most of state: largemouth bass, catfish, sturgeon, 10 each; walleye, sauger, total 8; northern pike, 6; rock bass, crappie, perch, bluegill, sunfish, 50 each; trout, 5 in E, 12 in W.

**GAME:** Res. 50 cents, turkey $2, big game $7.50, small game $2; non-res. 50 cents, big game $35, small game $25, turkey $5. Turkey: mid Oct.-mid Nov., 1 per seas. Deer: gun, part of Nov., 1 buck only; arch., Oct. or Nov., part Dec., by areas, 1 per seas. Pheasant: late Oct. by areas, 2 male daily some areas, 3 others. Grouse, partridge, early fall, some cos., 3 daily. Details: Dept. of Game, Fish & Parks, Pierre 57501.

## TENNESSEE

**FISH:** Res. lic. fish-game $5; non-res. fish $5, 10-days $2. Plus trout $2. No closed seas. Daily lim.: black bass 10, walleye 5, sauger 15, trout (min. 6" for brook trout) 7, muskie (min. 25") 3; crappie, pickerel, bluegill, white-yellow bass, no lim.

**GAME:** Res. fish-game $5; non-res. game $15, 3-days $6. Plus big game $5. Bear: some cos., part Oct., 1 per yr. Turkey: part Apr., part May, 1 gobbler per yr. Deer: arch., part Oct., 1 either sex; gun-arch., part Nov., part Dec., 1 buck with antlers per yr. Rabbit: late Nov.-Feb. 15, 5 daily. Quail: late Nov.-Feb. 15, 8 daily. Ruffed grouse: Nov.-Feb., 3 daily. Bear, boar, Oct., 1 each. Details: Game & Fish Commission, 706 Church St., Nashville 37203.

## TEXAS

**FISH:** Res. or non-res. llc. $2.15. No closed seas. General daily lim.: black bass, 15, min. 7", not more than 10 over 11"; white bass 25, white perch 25, catfish 25. Some exceptions.

**GAME:** Res. $3.15; non-res. $25. Seas. by counties. Quail, 12 daily; squirrel, 10; javelina (peccary), 2 per seas. Deer: mostly part Nov.-Dec., lim. per yr. varies by areas, 1 to 4. Turkey: mostly late Nov.-Dec., 2 per yr. Bear: some areas, late Nov.-Dec., 1 per yr. Details: Parks & Wildlife Dept., Austin 78701.

## UTAH

**FISH:** Res. lic. $5; non-res. $15, 2-days $2.50. General seas., June-Nov. 30. Daily lim.: trout 8, black bass 10, white bass 15, grayling 15, crappie 10, walleye 5, catfish 25. No lim. on length.

**GAME:** Res. fish-game $10, deer $5, birds $4.50; non-res. deer $50, birds $20. Deer: late Oct., 1 only; arch., earlier seas., 1. Seas. opens: pheasant, quail, early Nov.; grouse, partridge, late Sept. Elk, moose, antelope, buffalo, big horn: res. only, drawings for permits. Details: Fish & Game Div., 1596 West North Temple, Salt Lake City 84116.

## VERMONT

**FISH:** Res. lic. $1.75, fish-game $3.50; non-res. $6.25, 3-days $2.25, 14-days $4.25, fish-game $26. Last Sat. in Apr.-Sept. 30: trout, min. 6", 5 lbs. 12 fish daily; lake trout, salmon, min. 15", total 2 daily. Mid June-Nov. 30, black bass, min. 10", 10 daily. Last Sat. in Apr.-Mar. 15: walleye, pike-

perch, min. 12″, total 10 daily; muskie, northern pike, pickerel, min. 12″, total 10 daily.

**GAME:** Res. $2.25, arch. $1; non-res. $22, small game $10.50, arch. $3.50. Deer: gun-arch., 16 days starting 2nd Sat. in Nov., min. antler 3″; arch., 16 days starting 2nd Sat. in Oct.; 1 per seas. Part Sept.-part Nov.: rabbit, 3 daily, gray squirrel 4, partridge 4, chukar 4, pheasant 2, quail 4. Turkey, Oct., 1. Details: Fish & Game Dept., Montpelier 05602.

## VIRGINIA

**FISH:** Res. lic. $3.50 (state), $2 (co.); non-res. $10, 3-days $1.50; plus trout, stocked waters, res. $1, non-res. $5. Seas. all year except trout (mostly early Apr.-Dec. 31. 8 daily). Large, small mouth, spotted bass; total 8 daily. Pickerel, walleye, 8 daily. Northern pike, muskie; min. 26″, 2 daily. Crappie, rock bass, sunfish, total 25 daily.

**GAME:** Res. $3.50 (state), $2 (co.); non-res. $15.75. Plus deer-bear-turkey: res. $2; non-res. $10. Deer: seas. by areas, 1 (some areas 2) per yr. Bear: mostly mid Nov.-late Dec., 1 per seas. Quail (8 daily, 125 per yr.), grouse (3 daily, 15 per yr.), rabbit (6 daily, 75 per yr.): mostly mid Nov.-Jan. 30. Turkey: mostly mid Nov.-mid Dec., 2 per yr. Details: Commission of Game & Inland Fisheries, Box 1642, Richmond 23213.

## WASHINGTON

**FISH:** Res. lic. $5.50 (state), $4 (co.), fish-game $9; non-res. $15, 7-days $4. General summer seas.: mid. Apr.-Oct. 31; winter, Dec.-Mar. Catfish, perch, crappie, sunfish: no catch lim., no min. size. All other game fish, 6″. Daily lim.: bass, 20 lb.; trout, 6″, 12; steelhead 2, whitefish 15.

**GAME:** Res. $5.50; non-res. $35. Plus deer, res. $2, non-res. no extra; res. elk $7.50, non-res. elk $25; res. goat $7.50, non-res. $25. Pheasant: part Oct-part Nov., 3 cocks daily. Quail: part Oct.-late Jan. in east, part Oct.-early Nov. in west, 10 daily. Deer: mostly part Oct., 1 buck with antlers. Elk: part Nov., 1 bull with antlers; some areas, 1 either sex. Bear: mostly Sept.-Nov., no lim. in west; 1 in east. Mt. goat, sheep; controlled hunts by drawing, 1 per yr. Cougar, 1 per yr. Details: Dept. of Game, 600 N. Capitol Way, Olympia 98502.

## WEST VIRGINIA

**FISH:** Res. lic. $3.25, fish-game $5.25; non-res. $10.25, 6 days $3.25. Open seas. all yr. Daily lim.: trout, black bass, channel catfish, 8 each. Muskie, no lim., min. 26″. Others, no lim.

**GAME:** Res. $3.25; non-res. $20.25, arch. only and fish $5.25. Turkey: 1 in fall seas., 1 in spring. Bear (gun): part Nov., part Dec. Deer and bear (bow): Oct. 12-Dec. 31. Deer (gun): Nov. 25-Dec. 7. Lim.: deer 1 per seas.; bear, 1 per yr. Grouse: Oct. 12-Feb. 22, 4 daily. Raccoon: Oct. 12-Jan. 26, 2 nightly. Details: Dept. of Natural Resources, Charleston 25305.

## WISCONSIN

**FISH:** Res. lic. $3; non-res. $6, 15-days (hus.-wife) $7. Seasons mostly start late spring, end late winter. Daily lim.: bass, walleye, sauger, northern pike, mostly 5; muskie 1, min. 30″; trout (mid May-mid Sept.) mostly 10, min. 6″. No closed seas., no min. length: white, yellow, rock bass, no lim. most areas; crappie, perch, sunfish, total 50 daily.

**GAME:** Res. small game $4, deer $5; non-res. $25, including deer $50, arch-deer $15. Deer: fire-arms, seas by zones, mostly 1 wk. in Nov.; 1 antlered buck per seas. most areas. Bear: fire-arms, same seas., 1 per yr. Arch.: parts of Sept., Oct., Nov., Dec.; 1 deer either sex, 1 bear. Ruffed grouse: Oct. in no., Oct.-part Dec. in so., 3 daily. Pheasant: part Oct.-part Nov., 2 males daily (1 daily 1st 2 days). Details: Conservation Dept., Box 450, Madison 53701.

## WYOMING

**FISH:** Res. lic. $3; non-res. $12, 5-days $4. Some areas all year. Daily lim. mostly 10 fish or 8 lbs.

**GAME:** Res. spec. fees $2-$15 for various game; non-res. small game $5, general lic. $125, spec. fees $15-$75. No closed seas.: bobcat, coyote, mt. lion, lynx. Other seas. mostly in fall by areas. Lic. quotas on antelope, elk; moose, mt. sheep, 1 every 3 yrs. Birds: fall seas. bag lim. by areas. Details: Game & Fish Commission, Box 1589, Cheyenne 82001.

# CANADA

## ALBERTA

**FISH:** Res. (Canada) lic., $3; non-res. $10. No closed seas. Daily lim.: trout, grayling, total 10; pike, walleye, sauger, goldeye, total 15: kokanee 10, lake trout 5, perch no lim. No min. lengths.

**GAME:** Res. $2; non-res. Canadian big game $75; alien big game $150. Plus special fees for most game. Spring and fall seas.: grizzly, 1 only; black or brown bear, 2. Fall seas. by area units: 1 only per yr. of deer, elk, moose, caribou; bighorn, 1 male per yr.; mt. goat, 1 per yr.; partridge, 7 daily; ptarmigan, blue grouse, 5 each daily; sharp-tail, spruce, ruffed grouse, varied lims. by zones. Details: Fish & Wildlife Div., Dept. of Lands & Forests, Edmonton.

## BRITISH COLUMBIA

**FISH:** Res. (Canada) lic. $3; alien $10, 3-days $3.50. Most areas no closed season. Daily lim.: northern pike, walleye, bass, 10 each; salmon 2 over 20″, total 8; kokanee 25. Only 40 steelhead per yr. (alien $5).

**GAME:** Res. $4; non-res. Canadian $15; alien $25. Plus big game tag fees. Plus non-res. big game trophy fees for all big game killed. Seasons set by areas. Seas. lim.: grizzly, elk, caribou, moose, sheep (max only), 1 each; mt. goat mostly 2; deer 2 some areas, 3 others; black bear. Daily lim.: grouse, mostly 15; sharptail grouse mostly 6; partridge 10; quail mostly 15; pheasant mostly 3 male. Details: Fish & Wildlife Branch, Dept. of Recreation & Conservation, Victoria.

## MANITOBA

**FISH:** Res. (Canada) lic. $2.25; others $6.50. No min. lengths. Mostly mid May-Mar. 31: small, large mouth bass, 6 daily; muskie 1; walleye, northern pike, sauger, 8 each; brown, lake trout, 5 each; rainbow, 10. Split seas.: brook trout, 2 or 10.

**GAME:** Res. (Can.) game birds $2.25; others $25. Deer: res. $5, res. (Can.) $25, others $40. Moose: res. $15, res. (Can. reciprocal) $25, others $100. Deer: mostly Nov., 1 only. Moose: late Sept.-Nov. 30, 1 per seas. Ptarmigan: Sept.-mid Feb., 10 daily. Sharptail grouse (3-6 daily), partridge (2 daily); both mostly part of Oct. Ruffed, spruce grouse; fall by areas, 6 or 8 daily. Details: Dept. of Mines & Natural Resources, Norquay Bldg., Winnipeg 1.

## NEW BRUNSWICK

**FISH:** Res. lic. (hus.-wife) $2.50, including salmon $5; non-res. $7.50, including salmon $25.50. Also, spec. licenses. Salmon: mostly mid May to early fall, 4 daily. Trout (20 daily), landlocked salmon (10 daily, min. 14″), mid Apr.-mid Sept. Black bass: June 16-Sept. 30 (15 daily, min. 10″). Pickerel, perch, no lim.

**GAME:** Res. $4.50, birds-rabbit $2.50; non-res. $35.50, birds-only $25.50. Deer: Oct.-Nov., 2 per yr. either sex. Bear: Apr. 1-Aug. 30, Oct. 1-Nov. 30, 2 per seas. Grouse: Oct.-part Nov., 6 daily. Moose (res. only, $15 lic.), 1 per yr. Details: Fish & Wildlife Branch, Natural Resources Dept., Fredericton.

## NEWFOUNDLAND

**FISH:** Res. salmon lic. $5; non-res. $30, 14-days $20, 1-day $5. Non-res. trout $5. Salmon: May 24-Sept. 15, 4 daily, 21 per wk., art. fly only. Rainbow trout, June 1-Sept. 15; other "trout" (including char, northern pike) in certain rivers, May 24-Sept. 15, elsewhere Jan. 15-Sept. 30; 24 daily or 10 lbs. (only 4 lake trout daily).

**GAME:** Res., moose $15, caribou $15, bear $10, ptarmigan $2, hare $1; non-res., moose $75, caribou $100, bear $10, ptarmigan $5, hare $5. Bear, moose: seas. by areas, 1 each. Caribou: restricted no. of lic., 1 stag. Hare: Oct. 1-Dec., no lim. Ptarmigan: late Sept.-Nov., 50 per seas. Details: Fish—Federal Dept. of Fisheries, Box 5667, St. John's; Game—Dir. of Wildlife, Dept. of Mines, Agriculture & Resources, St. John's.

## NOVA SCOTIA

**FISH:** Res. lic. $1; non-res. $5. Atlantic salmon: mostly late spring to fall, 3 daily, 15 per wk. Trout: mid Apr.-mid Sept., 15 daily (speckled, brown, 6″ min.; gray 15″; rainbow, May 15-Oct. 31, 8″). Smallmouth bass: July 1-Oct. 31, 10 daily, min 9″.

**GAME:** Res. big game $4, small game $2, moose $15; non-res.small game $15, big game $40. Pheasant: mostly Oct.-Nov., 2 male daily. Partridge: same seas., 5 daily. Deer: mid Oct.-late Nov., 1 per seas. some areas, 2 in others. Bear: same seas., no lim. Moose: res. only, by lottery, late Sept., 1 only. Details: Conservation Div., Dept. of Lands & Forests, Box 516, Kentville.

## ONTARIO

**FISH:** Res. (of Ont., Man., Sask.) lic. $3.25 (needed in parks and Lake Superior only); non-res. $6.50, 3-days $3.25. Black bass: mostly late June to late Fall, 6 daily. Pike: all yr., 6 daily. Maskinonge: all yr., 2 daily, min. 28". Trout, mostly all yr.: rainbow, brown, 5 each daily; brook, 15 or 10 lbs. daily. Sturgeon: mostly June 15-May 14, 1 daily.

**Game:** Res. (of Ont., Man., Sask.) general $3, bear-deer $10, bear-moose $15, spring bear (Jan.-June) $5.25; non-res. bear-birds-small game $21, including deer $36, including moose $101, spring bear (Apr.-June) $10.50. Black bear: Sept. 1-June 30, no lim. Fox, raccoon; no closed seas., no lim. Fall seas. by areas: deer, moose, total 1 each; ruffed, spruce grouse, total 5 daily; sharptail grouse, ptarmigan, total 5 daily; partridge 8; squirrel 10. Details: Dept. of Lands & Forests, Parliament Bldgs., Toronto.

## PRINCE EDWARD ISLAND

**FISH:** Res. lic. $2; non-res. $3. Speckled trout: Apr. 15-Sept. 30, 20 daily. Rainbow trout: some lakes June 1-Oct. 31, 20 daily; elsewhere included in speckled trout seas., and lim. Salmon: May 15-Oct. 31, 6 daily, 21 per wk., art. fly only.

**GAME:** Res. $2; non-res. $10. Ruffed grouse: Oct.-Nov., 3 daily. Hare: mid Nov.-mid Jan., 5 daily. Fox: June-Feb., no lim. Details: Fish & Wildlife Div., Dept. of Fisheries, Charlottetown.

## QUEBEC

**FISH:** Res. lic. $1.10 (lakes, salmon rivers); non-res. $15.50 (all fish), $5.25 (3-days), $5.25 (no salmon). Large, small mouth bass: late June to freeze-up, mostly 10 each daily; Atlantic salmon: summer, 2-6 daily, min. 12". Rainbow, brown, lake trout: late Apr.-mid Sept., 6 each. Other trout: late Apr.-mid Sept., total 25 daily.

**GAME:** Res. small game $3.25, spec. big game fees $2.10 to $12.50; non-res. small game $15.50, deer-bear $25.50, all game $101. Deer, moose: by areas, part Sept., part Oct., 1 each per yr. Grouse, partridge: late Sept.-late Nov., 5 daily total. Bear: no lim. Details: Dept. of Tourism, Fish & Game, Parliament Bldgs., Quebec City.

## SASKATCHEWAN

**FISH:** Res. (Canada) lic. $2; others $10, no-trout-or-grayling waters $5. Mostly May 4-Apr. 15: northern pike, pickerel, goldeye, whitefish, sauger, grayling, 8 each daily; brook, rainbow, brown trout, total 5; lake trout 5, sturgeon 1. July 20-Apr. 15: large mouth bass 5.

**GAME:** Res. (Canada) game bird $3; non-res. $26. Deer: res. $6, res. (Can.) $21, others $36. Moose: res. $10, res. (Can.) $25, others $100. Deer: mostly Nov., 1 per yr. (2 some areas). Moose: some areas 2 per seas., some areas 1. Bear: spring and fall seasons, 2 per yr., special fees. Partridge: part Sept.-part Nov., 6 daily. Same seas: ruffed, spruce grouse, 6 each daily; sharptail grouse 4-6 daily. Details: Dept. of Natural Resources, Regina.

# Time of Tides at Points on Atlantic Coast

**Source: Coast and Geodetic Survey, ESSA**

**See also Tides and Their Causes Page 294**

To be added or subtracted from Time of Tides tables at New York City, as shown below.

| Location | | H. M. | Location | | H. M. | Location | | H. M. |
|---|---|---|---|---|---|---|---|---|
| Annapolis, Md. | add | 9 10 | Marblehead, Mass. | add | 2 40 | Point Lookout, Md. | add | 5 15 |
| Atlantic City, N. J. | sub. | 1 10 | Miami Beach, Fla. | sub. | 0 20 | Portland, Me. | add | 2 30 |
| Baltimore, Md. | add | 10 55 | Nahant, Mass. | add | 2 40 | Portsmouth, N. H. | add | 2 50 |
| Bar Harbor, Me. | add | 2 10 | New Bedford, Mass. | sub. | 0 55 | Providence, R. I. | sub. | 0 55 |
| Beaufort, S. C. | add | 0 30 | Newburyport, Mass. | add | 3 20 | Richmond, Va. | add | 8 45 |
| Block Is. Hbr., R. I. | sub. | 1 05 | New Haven, Conn. | add | 2 45 | Rockport, Mass. | add | 2 35 |
| Boston, Mass. | add | 2 40 | New London, Conn. | add | 1 10 | Salem, Mass. | add | 2 45 |
| Bridgeport, Conn. | add | 2 50 | Newport, R. I. | sub. | 1 05 | Sandy Hook, N. J. | sub. | 0 40 |
| Cape May, N. J. | sub. | 0 45 | Norfolk, Va. | add | 0 55 | Savannah, Ga. | add | 0 20 |
| Charleston, S. C. | sub. | 0 35 | Old Pt. Comfort, Va. | add | 0 20 | Southport, N. C. | sub. | 0 30 |
| Gloucester. Mass. | add | 2 35 | Philadelphia, Pa. | add | 6 00 | Washington, D. C. | add | 12 25 |
| Jacksonville, Fla. | add | 1 25 | Plymouth, Mass. | add | 2 55 | Wilmington, N. C. | add | 2 05 |

# Tide Tables for 1969 (at New York City)

Time meridian 75° W. 0000 is midnight. 1200 is noon. All hours greater than 1200 are p.m. Heights are reckoned from the datum of soundings on charts of the locality which is mean low water.

**Time and Height of High and Low Waters at the Battery—Eastern STANDARD Time**

### JANUARY

| Day | Time h. m. | Ht. ft. |
|---|---|---|
| 1 W | 00 24 | 0.0 |
| | 06 42 | 4.5 |
| | 13 06 | -0.2 |
| | 19 06 | 3.4 |
| 2 Th | 01 06 | 0.0 |
| | 07 24 | 4.6 |
| | 13 54 | -0.3 |
| | 19 48 | 3.5 |
| 3 F | 01 48 | 0.0 |
| | 08 00 | 4.6 |
| | 14 30 | -0.4 |
| | 20 30 | 3.5 |
| 4 Sa | 02 30 | 0.0 |
| | 08 36 | 4.6 |
| | 15 12 | -0.4 |
| | 21 06 | 3.5 |
| 5 Su | 03 06 | 0.0 |
| | 09 12 | 4.5 |
| | 15 48 | -0.4 |
| | 21 48 | 3.5 |
| 6 M | 03 42 | 0.1 |
| | 09 48 | 4.4 |
| | 16 18 | -0.4 |
| | 22 30 | 3.5 |
| 7 Tu | 04 06 | 0.1 |
| | 10 24 | 4.2 |
| | 16 48 | -0.3 |
| | 23 06 | 3.6 |
| 8 W | 04 42 | 0.2 |
| | 11 00 | 4.1 |
| | 17 18 | -0.2 |
| | 23 42 | 3.7 |

### January (cont.)

| Day | Time h. m. | Ht. ft. |
|---|---|---|
| 9 Th | 05 18 | 0.2 |
| | 11 42 | 4.0 |
| | 17 48 | -0.1 |
| 10 F | 00 24 | 3.8 |
| | 06 06 | 0.3 |
| | 12 24 | 3.8 |
| | 18 30 | 0.0 |
| 11 Sa | 01 06 | 4.0 |
| | 07 24 | 0.4 |
| | 13 18 | 3.7 |
| | 19 30 | 0.1 |
| 12 Su | 02 06 | 4.1 |
| | 08 54 | 0.4 |
| | 14 18 | 3.5 |
| | 20 54 | 0.0 |
| 13 M | 03 06 | 4.3 |
| | 10 00 | 0.1 |
| | 15 30 | 3.4 |
| | 22 0? | -0.1 |
| 14 Tu | 04 18 | 4.5 |
| | 11 06 | -0.1 |
| | 16 48 | 3.5 |
| | 23 06 | -0.3 |
| 15 W | 05 24 | 4.8 |
| | 12 00 | -0.5 |
| | 18 00 | 3.7 |
| 16 Th | 00 06 | -0.5 |
| | 06 24 | 5.1 |
| | 13 00 | -0.8 |
| | 19 00 | 3.9 |

### January (cont.)

| Day | Time h. m. | Ht. ft. |
|---|---|---|
| 17 F | 01 00 | -0.7 |
| | 07 24 | 5.3 |
| | 13 54 | -1.0 |
| | 19 54 | 4.2 |
| 18 Sa | 02 00 | -0.9 |
| | 08 12 | 5.4 |
| | 14 42 | -1.2 |
| | 20 42 | 4.4 |
| 19 Su | 02 48 | -1.0 |
| | 09 06 | 5.3 |
| | 15 30 | -1.3 |
| | 21 36 | 4.4 |
| 20 M | 03 42 | -0.9 |
| | 10 00 | 5.2 |
| | 16 12 | -1.2 |
| | 22 30 | 4.5 |
| 21 Tu | 04 30 | -0.8 |
| | 10 48 | 4.9 |
| | 17 00 | -1.0 |
| | 23 24 | 4.4 |
| 22 W | 05 18 | -0.5 |
| | 11 42 | 4.5 |
| | 17 42 | -0.7 |
| 23 Th | 00 12 | 4.3 |
| | 06 06 | -0.1 |
| | 12 30 | 4.1 |
| | 18 30 | -0.3 |
| 24 F | 01 00 | 4.2 |
| | 07 06 | 0.2 |
| | 13 12 | 3.8 |
| | 19 24 | 0.0 |

### January (cont.)

| Day | Time h. m. | Ht. ft. |
|---|---|---|
| 25 Sa | 01 48 | 4.1 |
| | 08 12 | 0.4 |
| | 14 06 | 3.4 |
| | 20 24 | 0.2 |
| 26 Su | 02 36 | 3.9 |
| | 09 18 | 0.5 |
| | 15 00 | 3.1 |
| | 21 24 | 0.3 |
| 27 M | 03 36 | 3.9 |
| | 10 12 | 0.5 |
| | 16 00 | 3.0 |
| | 22 18 | 0.4 |
| 28 Tu | 04 30 | 3.9 |
| | 11 06 | 0.3 |
| | 17 06 | 3.0 |
| | 23 06 | 0.3 |
| 29 W | 05 30 | 4.0 |
| | 11 54 | 0.1 |
| | 18 00 | 3.1 |
| | 23 54 | 0.3 |
| 30 Th | 06 18 | 4.2 |
| | 12 42 | -0.1 |
| | 18 48 | 3.3 |
| 31 F | 00 42 | 0.1 |
| | 07 00 | 4.4 |
| | 13 24 | -0.3 |
| | 19 30 | 3.5 |
| **FEBRUARY** | | |
| 1 Sa | 01 30 | 0.0 |
| | 07 42 | 4.5 |
| | 14 06 | -0.4 |
| | 20 06 | 3.7 |

### February (cont.)

| Day | Time h. m. | Ht. ft. |
|---|---|---|
| 2 Su | 02 12 | -0.1 |
| | 08 18 | 4.6 |
| | 14 48 | -0.5 |
| | 20 42 | 3.8 |
| 3 M | 02 48 | -0.2 |
| | 08 54 | 4.6 |
| | 15 18 | -0.6 |
| | 21 18 | 3.9 |
| 4 Tu | 03 24 | -0.3 |
| | 09 24 | 4.5 |
| | 15 54 | -0.5 |
| | 21 54 | 4.0 |
| 5 W | 03 54 | -0.3 |
| | 10 00 | 4.4 |
| | 16 18 | -0.5 |
| | 22 24 | 4.1 |
| 6 Th | 04 30 | -0.2 |
| | 10 36 | 4.2 |
| | 16 48 | -0.4 |
| | 23 06 | 4.2 |
| 7 F | 05 06 | -0.1 |
| | 11 18 | 4.0 |
| | 17 18 | -0.3 |
| | 23 54 | 4.2 |
| 8 Sa | 05 48 | 0.1 |
| | 12 06 | 3.8 |
| | 17 54 | -0.1 |
| 9 Su | 00 42 | 4.3 |
| | 06 54 | 0.3 |
| | 12 54 | 3.6 |
| | 18 54 | 0.1 |

## February (cont.)

| Day | Time h. m. | Ht. ft. |
|---|---|---|
| 10 M | 01 36 | 4.3 |
|  | 08 30 | 0.3 |
|  | 14 00 | 3.4 |
|  | 20 24 | 0.2 |
| 11 Tu | 02 42 | 4.3 |
|  | 09 48 | 0.2 |
|  | 15 18 | 3.3 |
|  | 21 48 | 0.1 |
| 12 W | 04 00 | 4.4 |
|  | 10 48 | 0.0 |
|  | 16 42 | 3.4 |
|  | 22 54 | -0.1 |
| 13 Th | 05 18 | 4.7 |
|  | 11 48 | -0.4 |
|  | 17 48 | 3.7 |
|  | 23 54 | -0.4 |
| 14 F | 06 18 | 4.9 |
|  | 12 42 | -0.7 |
|  | 18 48 | 4.1 |
| 15 Sa | 00 54 | -0.7 |
|  | 07 12 | 5.2 |
|  | 13 36 | -0.9 |
|  | 19 36 | 4.4 |
| 16 Su | 01 48 | -0.9 |
|  | 08 00 | 5.3 |
|  | 14 24 | -1.1 |
|  | 20 30 | 4.7 |
| 17 M | 02 36 | -1.0 |
|  | 08 48 | 5.2 |
|  | 15 06 | -1.2 |
|  | 21 12 | 4.8 |
| 18 Tu | 03 24 | -1.0 |
|  | 09 36 | 5.0 |
|  | 15 48 | -1.1 |
|  | 22 00 | 4.8 |
| 19 W | 04 06 | -0.8 |
|  | 10 18 | 4.7 |
|  | 16 24 | -0.8 |
|  | 22 48 | 4.7 |
| 20 Th | 04 48 | -0.5 |
|  | 11 06 | 4.3 |
|  | 17 06 | -0.5 |
|  | 23 36 | 4.5 |
| 21 F | 05 36 | -0.1 |
|  | 11 54 | 4.0 |
|  | 17 48 | -0.1 |
| 22 Sa | 00 18 | 4.3 |
|  | 06 24 | 0.3 |
|  | 12 36 | 3.6 |
|  | 18 30 | 0.3 |
| 23 Su | 01 06 | 4.1 |
|  | 07 24 | 0.6 |
|  | 13 24 | 3.3 |
|  | 19 30 | 0.6 |
| 24 M | 01 54 | 3.9 |
|  | 08 36 | 0.7 |
|  | 14 18 | 3.0 |
|  | 20 36 | 0.8 |
| 25 Tu | 02 48 | 3.7 |
|  | 09 36 | 0.7 |
|  | 15 18 | 2.9 |
|  | 21 42 | 0.8 |
| 26 W | 03 48 | 3.7 |
|  | 10 36 | 0.5 |
|  | 16 30 | 2.9 |
|  | 22 36 | 0.7 |
| 27 Th | 04 54 | 3.8 |
|  | 11 24 | 0.3 |
|  | 17 30 | 3.2 |
|  | 23 30 | 0.5 |
| 28 F | 05 48 | 4.1 |
|  | 12 12 | 0.1 |
|  | 18 18 | 3.5 |

### MARCH

| Day | Time h. m. | Ht. ft. |
|---|---|---|
| 1 Sa | 00 18 | 0.3 |
|  | 06 30 | 4.3 |
|  | 12 54 | -0.2 |
|  | 19 00 | 3.8 |
| 2 Su | 01 06 | 0.0 |
|  | 07 12 | 4.5 |
|  | 13 36 | -0.4 |
|  | 19 36 | 4.1 |

## March (cont.)

| Day | Time h. m. | Ht. ft. |
|---|---|---|
| 3 M | 01 48 | -0.2 |
|  | 07 48 | 4.6 |
|  | 14 12 | -0.5 |
|  | 20 12 | 4.3 |
| 4 Tu | 02 24 | -0.4 |
|  | 08 24 | 4.7 |
|  | 14 48 | -0.6 |
|  | 20 42 | 4.5 |
| 5 W | 03 00 | -0.5 |
|  | 09 00 | 4.6 |
|  | 15 18 | -0.6 |
|  | 21 18 | 4.6 |
| 6 Th | 03 36 | -0.6 |
|  | 09 36 | 4.5 |
|  | 15 48 | -0.5 |
|  | 21 54 | 4.7 |
| 7 F | 04 12 | -0.5 |
|  | 10 18 | 4.3 |
|  | 16 18 | -0.4 |
|  | 22 36 | 4.7 |
| 8 Sa | 04 54 | -0.3 |
|  | 11 00 | 4.0 |
|  | 16 54 | -0.2 |
|  | 23 30 | 4.7 |
| 9 Su | 05 42 | -0.1 |
|  | 11 54 | 3.8 |
|  | 17 36 | 0.0 |
| 10 M | 00 24 | 4.6 |
|  | 06 48 | 0.2 |
|  | 12 54 | 3.6 |
|  | 18 36 | 0.3 |
| 11 Tu | 01 24 | 4.4 |
|  | 08 18 | 0.4 |
|  | 14 00 | 3.4 |
|  | 20 18 | 0.5 |
| 12 W | 02 36 | 4.4 |
|  | 09 30 | 0.2 |
|  | 15 18 | 3.4 |
|  | 21 42 | 0.4 |
| 13 Th | 03 54 | 4.4 |
|  | 10 36 | 0.0 |
|  | 16 36 | 3.7 |
|  | 22 48 | 0.1 |
| 14 F | 05 06 | 4.6 |
|  | 11 30 | -0.3 |
|  | 17 42 | 4.1 |
|  | 23 48 | -0.3 |
| 15 Sa | 06 06 | 4.8 |
|  | 12 24 | -0.6 |
|  | 18 36 | 4.5 |
| 16 Su | 00 42 | -0.5 |
|  | 06 54 | 5.0 |
|  | 13 12 | -0.8 |
|  | 19 24 | 4.8 |
| 17 M | 01 30 | -0.8 |
|  | 07 42 | 5.1 |
|  | 13 54 | -0.9 |
|  | 20 06 | 5.0 |
| 18 Tu | 02 18 | -0.9 |
|  | 08 24 | 5.0 |
|  | 14 36 | -0.9 |
|  | 20 48 | 5.1 |
| 19 W | 03 00 | -0.8 |
|  | 09 06 | 4.8 |
|  | 15 18 | -0.8 |
|  | 21 30 | 5.0 |
| 20 Th | 03 42 | -0.7 |
|  | 09 48 | 4.5 |
|  | 15 54 | -0.5 |
|  | 22 12 | 4.9 |
| 21 F | 04 24 | -0.4 |
|  | 10 36 | 4.1 |
|  | 16 30 | -0.2 |
|  | 22 54 | 4.6 |
| 22 Sa | 05 00 | -0.1 |
|  | 11 18 | 3.8 |
|  | 17 00 | 0.2 |
|  | 23 36 | 4.4 |
| 23 Su | 05 48 | 0.3 |
|  | 12 06 | 3.5 |
|  | 17 30 | 0.5 |

## March (cont.)

| Day | Time h. m. | Ht. ft. |
|---|---|---|
| 24 M | 00 18 | 4.1 |
|  | 06 36 | 0.6 |
|  | 12 48 | 3.3 |
|  | 18 12 | 0.9 |
| 25 Tu | 01 06 | 3.9 |
|  | 07 48 | 0.8 |
|  | 13 42 | 3.1 |
|  | 19 42 | 1.2 |
| 26 W | 02 00 | 3.8 |
|  | 09 00 | 0.8 |
|  | 14 42 | 3.0 |
|  | 21 06 | 1.2 |
| 27 Th | 03 00 | 3.7 |
|  | 10 00 | 0.7 |
|  | 15 54 | 3.1 |
|  | 22 06 | 1.0 |
| 28 F | 04 06 | 3.8 |
|  | 10 48 | 0.5 |
|  | 16 54 | 3.4 |
|  | 23 00 | 0.8 |
| 29 Sa | 05 06 | 4.0 |
|  | 11 36 | 0.2 |
|  | 17 42 | 3.7 |
|  | 23 48 | 0.4 |
| 30 Su | 05 54 | 4.2 |
|  | 12 18 | 0.0 |
|  | 18 24 | 4.1 |
| 31 M | 00 24 | 0.1 |
|  | 06 36 | 4.4 |
|  | 12 54 | -0.2 |
|  | 19 00 | 4.5 |

### APRIL

| Day | Time h. m. | Ht. ft. |
|---|---|---|
| 1 Tu | 01 18 | -0.2 |
|  | 07 18 | 4.6 |
|  | 13 36 | -0.4 |
|  | 19 36 | 4.8 |
| 2 W | 02 00 | -0.5 |
|  | 07 54 | 4.6 |
|  | 14 12 | -0.5 |
|  | 20 12 | 5.1 |
| 3 Th | 02 42 | -0.6 |
|  | 08 30 | 4.6 |
|  | 14 48 | -0.5 |
|  | 20 48 | 5.2 |
| 4 F | 03 18 | -0.7 |
|  | 09 12 | 4.5 |
|  | 15 24 | -0.4 |
|  | 21 30 | 5.2 |
| 5 Sa | 04 00 | -0.6 |
|  | 10 00 | 4.3 |
|  | 16 00 | -0.3 |
|  | 22 18 | 5.1 |
| 6 Su | 04 48 | -0.4 |
|  | 10 54 | 4.1 |
|  | 16 42 | -0.1 |
|  | 23 12 | 5.0 |
| 7 M | 05 36 | -0.1 |
|  | 11 54 | 3.9 |
|  | 17 30 | 0.2 |
| 8 Tu | 00 18 | 4.8 |
|  | 06 48 | 0.1 |
|  | 13 00 | 3.7 |
|  | 18 48 | 0.5 |
| 9 W | 01 24 | 4.6 |
|  | 08 06 | 0.3 |
|  | 14 06 | 3.7 |
|  | 20 18 | 0.6 |
| 10 Th | 02 30 | 4.5 |
|  | 09 18 | 0.2 |
|  | 15 18 | 3.8 |
|  | 21 36 | 0.4 |
| 11 F | 03 42 | 4.4 |
|  | 10 18 | 0.0 |
|  | 16 24 | 4.1 |
|  | 22 36 | 0.2 |
| 12 Sa | 04 48 | 4.5 |
|  | 11 06 | -0.2 |
|  | 17 24 | 4.5 |
|  | 23 30 | -0.1 |
| 13 Su | 05 42 | 4.6 |
|  | 11 54 | -0.4 |
|  | 18 12 | 4.8 |

## April (cont.)

| Day | Time h. m. | Ht. ft. |
|---|---|---|
| 14 M | 00 24 | -0.4 |
|  | 06 36 | 4.7 |
|  | 12 42 | -0.5 |
|  | 19 00 | 5.1 |
| 15 Tu | 01 12 | -0.5 |
|  | 07 18 | 4.7 |
|  | 13 24 | -0.5 |
|  | 19 42 | 5.3 |
| 16 W | 02 00 | -0.6 |
|  | 08 00 | 4.6 |
|  | 14 06 | -0.5 |
|  | 20 18 | 5.3 |
| 17 Th | 02 42 | -0.6 |
|  | 08 42 | 4.4 |
|  | 14 48 | -0.4 |
|  | 21 00 | 5.2 |
| 18 F | 03 18 | -0.4 |
|  | 09 24 | 4.2 |
|  | 15 24 | -0.1 |
|  | 21 36 | 5.0 |
| 19 Sa | 04 00 | -0.2 |
|  | 10 06 | 3.9 |
|  | 15 54 | 0.1 |
|  | 22 18 | 4.7 |
| 20 Su | 04 36 | 0.0 |
|  | 10 48 | 3.7 |
|  | 16 24 | 0.5 |
|  | 22 54 | 4.5 |
| 21 M | 05 18 | 0.3 |
|  | 11 36 | 3.5 |
|  | 16 54 | 0.8 |
|  | 23 36 | 4.2 |
| 22 Tu | 06 00 | 0.6 |
|  | 12 24 | 3.3 |
|  | 17 24 | 1.1 |
| 23 W | 00 24 | 4.1 |
|  | 07 00 | 0.8 |
|  | 13 18 | 3.2 |
|  | 18 18 | 1.3 |
| 24 Th | 01 12 | 3.9 |
|  | 08 12 | 0.8 |
|  | 14 12 | 3.3 |
|  | 20 24 | 1.4 |
| 25 F | 02 06 | 3.8 |
|  | 09 12 | 0.8 |
|  | 15 06 | 3.4 |
|  | 21 30 | 1.2 |
| 26 Sa | 03 06 | 3.8 |
|  | 10 06 | 0.6 |
|  | 16 00 | 3.7 |
|  | 22 24 | 0.9 |
| 27 Su | 04 12 | 3.9 |
|  | 10 48 | 0.4 |
|  | 16 54 | 4.0 |
|  | 23 12 | 0.5 |
| 28 M | 05 06 | 4.1 |
|  | 11 30 | 0.2 |
|  | 17 42 | 4.5 |
| 29 Tu | 00 00 | 0.2 |
|  | 05 54 | 4.3 |
|  | 12 12 | 0.0 |
|  | 18 24 | 4.9 |
| 30 W | 00 48 | -0.2 |
|  | 06 42 | 4.4 |
|  | 12 54 | -0.2 |
|  | 19 00 | 5.2 |

### MAY

| Day | Time h. m. | Ht. ft. |
|---|---|---|
| 1 Th | 01 30 | -0.4 |
|  | 07 24 | 4.5 |
|  | 13 36 | -0.3 |
|  | 19 42 | 5.5 |
| 2 F | 02 18 | -0.6 |
|  | 08 06 | 4.5 |
|  | 14 18 | -0.4 |
|  | 20 24 | 5.6 |
| 3 Sa | 03 06 | -0.7 |
|  | 08 54 | 4.4 |
|  | 15 00 | -0.3 |
|  | 21 12 | 5.6 |
| 4 Su | 03 48 | -0.7 |
|  | 09 48 | 4.3 |
|  | 15 48 | -0.2 |
|  | 22 06 | 5.4 |

## May (cont.)

| Day | Time h. m. | Ht. ft. |
|---|---|---|
| 5 M | 04 42 | -0.5 |
|  | 10 54 | 4.1 |
|  | 16 36 | 0.0 |
|  | 23 12 | 5.2 |
| 6 Tu | 05 36 | -0.3 |
|  | 11 54 | 4.1 |
|  | 17 36 | 0.3 |
| 7 W | 00 12 | 5.0 |
|  | 06 36 | -0.1 |
|  | 13 00 | 4.1 |
|  | 18 48 | 0.6 |
| 8 Th | 01 12 | 4.8 |
|  | 07 48 | 0.0 |
|  | 14 00 | 4.1 |
|  | 20 12 | 0.6 |
| 9 F | 02 18 | 4.6 |
|  | 08 54 | 0.0 |
|  | 15 00 | 4.3 |
|  | 21 18 | 0.5 |
| 10 Sa | 03 18 | 4.5 |
|  | 09 48 | -0.1 |
|  | 16 00 | 4.5 |
|  | 22 18 | 0.2 |
| 11 Su | 04 18 | 4.4 |
|  | 10 42 | -0.2 |
|  | 17 00 | 4.8 |
|  | 23 12 | 0.0 |
| 12 M | 05 18 | 4.4 |
|  | 11 30 | -0.2 |
|  | 17 48 | 5.0 |
| 13 Tu | 00 06 | -0.1 |
|  | 06 06 | 4.4 |
|  | 12 12 | -0.2 |
|  | 18 30 | 5.2 |
| 14 W | 00 48 | -0.2 |
|  | 06 54 | 4.3 |
|  | 12 54 | -0.2 |
|  | 19 12 | 5.3 |
| 15 Th | 01 36 | -0.3 |
|  | 07 36 | 4.2 |
|  | 13 36 | -0.1 |
|  | 19 54 | 5.3 |
| 16 F | 02 18 | -0.3 |
|  | 08 18 | 4.1 |
|  | 14 18 | 0.0 |
|  | 20 30 | 5.2 |
| 17 Sa | 03 00 | -0.2 |
|  | 09 00 | 3.9 |
|  | 14 54 | 0.2 |
|  | 21 06 | 5.0 |
| 18 Su | 03 42 | -0.1 |
|  | 09 42 | 3.8 |
|  | 15 30 | 0.4 |
|  | 21 42 | 4.8 |
| 19 M | 04 18 | 0.1 |
|  | 10 30 | 3.6 |
|  | 16 06 | 0.7 |
|  | 22 24 | 4.6 |
| 20 Tu | 05 06 | 0.3 |
|  | 11 18 | 3.5 |
|  | 16 30 | 0.9 |
|  | 23 06 | 4.4 |
| 21 W | 05 36 | 0.5 |
|  | 12 06 | 3.5 |
|  | 17 06 | 1.1 |
|  | 23 48 | 4.2 |
| 22 Th | 06 18 | 0.6 |
|  | 12 48 | 3.5 |
|  | 17 48 | 1.3 |
| 23 F | 00 30 | 4.1 |
|  | 07 12 | 0.7 |
|  | 13 36 | 3.6 |
|  | 19 12 | 1.4 |
| 24 Sa | 01 18 | 4.0 |
|  | 08 18 | 0.7 |
|  | 14 18 | 3.8 |
|  | 20 42 | 1.3 |
| 25 Su | 02 12 | 3.9 |
|  | 09 06 | 0.6 |
|  | 15 06 | 4.0 |
|  | 21 42 | 1.0 |

## May (cont.) / JUNE

| Day | Time h. m. | Ht. ft. |
|---|---|---|
| 26 M | 03 06 | 3.9 |
|  | 09 54 | 0.5 |
|  | 16 00 | 4.4 |
|  | 22 36 | 0.6 |
| 27 Tu | 04 12 | 4.0 |
|  | 10 42 | 0.3 |
|  | 16 54 | 4.7 |
|  | 23 24 | 0.3 |
| 28 W | 05 12 | 4.1 |
|  | 11 24 | 0.1 |
|  | 17 42 | 5.1 |
| 29 Th | 00 18 | 0.0 |
|  | 06 06 | 4.2 |
|  | 12 12 | -0.1 |
|  | 18 30 | 5.5 |
| 30 F | 01 06 | -0.3 |
|  | 06 54 | 4.3 |
|  | 13 06 | -0.2 |
|  | 19 18 | 5.7 |
| 31 Sa | 02 00 | -0.6 |
|  | 07 48 | 4.4 |
|  | 13 54 | -0.3 |
|  | 20 06 | 5.8 |
| **JUNE** | | |
| 1 Su | 02 48 | -0.7 |
|  | 08 42 | 4.4 |
|  | 14 48 | -0.3 |
|  | 21 00 | 5.8 |
| 2 M | 03 36 | -0.7 |
|  | 09 42 | 4.4 |
|  | 15 36 | -0.2 |
|  | 22 00 | 5.6 |
| 3 Tu | 04 30 | -0.6 |
|  | 10 48 | 4.4 |
|  | 16 30 | 0.0 |
|  | 23 00 | 5.4 |
| 4 W | 05 24 | -0.5 |
|  | 11 48 | 4.4 |
|  | 17 30 | 0.2 |
| 5 Th | 00 00 | 5.2 |
|  | 06 18 | -0.3 |
|  | 12 42 | 4.5 |
|  | 18 36 | 0.4 |
| 6 F | 01 00 | 4.9 |
|  | 07 24 | -0.1 |
|  | 13 42 | 4.6 |
|  | 19 48 | 0.5 |
| 7 Sa | 01 54 | 4.6 |
|  | 08 24 | 0.0 |
|  | 14 36 | 4.7 |
|  | 21 00 | 0.5 |
| 8 Su | 02 48 | 4.4 |
|  | 09 18 | 0.0 |
|  | 15 30 | 4.7 |
|  | 21 54 | 0.4 |
| 9 M | 03 48 | 4.2 |
|  | 10 12 | 0.0 |
|  | 16 30 | 4.9 |
|  | 22 48 | 0.3 |
| 10 Tu | 04 48 | 4.0 |
|  | 11 00 | 0.1 |
|  | 17 18 | 5.0 |
|  | 23 42 | 0.2 |
| 11 W | 05 42 | 4.0 |
|  | 11 42 | 0.1 |
|  | 18 06 | 5.1 |
| 12 Th | 00 30 | 0.1 |
|  | 06 30 | 4.0 |
|  | 12 24 | 0.2 |
|  | 18 48 | 5.2 |
| 13 F | 01 12 | 0.1 |
|  | 07 12 | 3.9 |
|  | 13 12 | 0.3 |
|  | 19 30 | 5.2 |
| 14 Sa | 02 00 | 0.0 |
|  | 07 54 | 3.9 |
|  | 13 54 | 0.4 |
|  | 20 06 | 5.1 |
| 15 Su | 02 42 | 0.0 |
|  | 08 36 | 3.8 |
|  | 14 36 | 0.5 |
|  | 20 42 | 5.0 |

## June (cont.) / JULY

| Day | Time h. m. | Ht. ft. |
|---|---|---|
| 16 M | 03 18 | 0.0 |
|  | 09 24 | 3.8 |
|  | 15 12 | 0.6 |
|  | 21 24 | 4.9 |
| 17 Tu | 04 00 | 0.0 |
|  | 10 06 | 3.7 |
|  | 15 48 | 0.7 |
|  | 22 00 | 4.7 |
| 18 W | 04 36 | 0.1 |
|  | 10 54 | 3.7 |
|  | 16 18 | 0.9 |
|  | 22 36 | 4.5 |
| 19 Th | 05 06 | 0.3 |
|  | 11 36 | 3.7 |
|  | 16 54 | 1.0 |
|  | 23 12 | 4.4 |
| 20 F | 05 42 | 0.4 |
|  | 12 12 | 3.8 |
|  | 17 30 | 1.1 |
|  | 23 54 | 4.3 |
| 21 Sa | 06 12 | 0.5 |
|  | 12 54 | 4.0 |
|  | 18 18 | 1.2 |
| 22 Su | 00 36 | 4.2 |
|  | 07 00 | 0.6 |
|  | 13 30 | 4.1 |
|  | 19 42 | 1.2 |
| 23 M | 01 24 | 4.0 |
|  | 07 54 | 0.6 |
|  | 14 12 | 4.4 |
|  | 21 00 | 1.0 |
| 24 Tu | 02 12 | 3.9 |
|  | 08 54 | 0.5 |
|  | 15 06 | 4.6 |
|  | 22 00 | 0.7 |
| 25 W | 03 18 | 3.9 |
|  | 09 54 | 0.4 |
|  | 16 06 | 4.9 |
|  | 23 00 | 0.4 |
| 26 Th | 04 30 | 3.9 |
|  | 10 48 | 0.2 |
|  | 17 12 | 5.2 |
|  | 23 54 | 0.1 |
| 27 F | 05 36 | 4.0 |
|  | 11 42 | 0.1 |
|  | 18 06 | 5.6 |
| 28 Sa | 00 48 | -0.2 |
|  | 06 36 | 4.2 |
|  | 12 42 | -0.1 |
|  | 19 00 | 5.8 |
| 29 Su | 01 42 | -0.5 |
|  | 07 36 | 4.4 |
|  | 13 42 | -0.2 |
|  | 19 54 | 5.9 |
| 30 M | 02 36 | -0.7 |
|  | 08 30 | 4.5 |
|  | 14 36 | -0.3 |
|  | 20 48 | 5.9 |
| **JULY** | | |
| 1 Tu | 03 24 | -0.8 |
|  | 09 30 | 4.6 |
|  | 15 30 | -0.3 |
|  | 21 48 | 5.8 |
| 2 W | 04 12 | -0.8 |
|  | 10 30 | 4.7 |
|  | 16 24 | -0.2 |
|  | 22 42 | 5.5 |
| 3 Th | 05 00 | -0.6 |
|  | 11 24 | 4.3 |
|  | 17 18 | 0.8 |
|  | 23 42 | 5.0 |
| 4 F | 05 54 | -0.4 |
|  | 12 24 | 4.9 |
|  | 18 18 | 0.3 |
| 5 Sa | 00 36 | 4.9 |
|  | 06 48 | -0.1 |
|  | 13 12 | 4.9 |
|  | 19 24 | 0.5 |
| 6 Su | 01 24 | 4.6 |
|  | 07 48 | 0.1 |
|  | 14 06 | 4.9 |
|  | 20 30 | 0.6 |

## July (cont.)

| Day | Time h. m. | Ht. ft. |
|---|---|---|
| 7 M | 02 18 | 4.2 |
|  | 08 42 | 0.3 |
|  | 15 00 | 4.8 |
|  | 21 30 | 0.7 |
| 8 Tu | 03 12 | 3.9 |
|  | 09 36 | 0.4 |
|  | 15 54 | 4.8 |
|  | 22 24 | 0.7 |
| 9 W | 04 12 | 3.7 |
|  | 10 24 | 0.5 |
|  | 16 48 | 4.8 |
|  | 23 12 | 0.5 |
| 10 Th | 05 12 | 3.7 |
|  | 11 12 | 0.5 |
|  | 17 42 | 4.9 |
| 11 F | 00 06 | 0.4 |
|  | 06 06 | 3.7 |
|  | 12 00 | 0.5 |
|  | 18 24 | 5.0 |
| 12 Sa | 00 48 | 0.3 |
|  | 06 54 | 3.8 |
|  | 12 48 | 0.6 |
|  | 19 06 | 5.1 |
| 13 Su | 01 36 | 0.2 |
|  | 07 36 | 3.9 |
|  | 13 30 | 0.6 |
|  | 19 48 | 5.1 |
| 14 M | 02 18 | 0.1 |
|  | 08 18 | 3.9 |
|  | 14 18 | 0.6 |
|  | 20 24 | 5.1 |
| 15 Tu | 03 00 | 0.0 |
|  | 09 00 | 4.0 |
|  | 14 54 | 0.6 |
|  | 21 00 | 5.0 |
| 16 W | 03 36 | 0.0 |
|  | 09 42 | 4.0 |
|  | 15 30 | 0.6 |
|  | 21 36 | 4.9 |
| 17 Th | 04 06 | 0.0 |
|  | 10 18 | 4.1 |
|  | 16 06 | 0.7 |
|  | 22 12 | 4.7 |
| 18 F | 04 36 | 0.1 |
|  | 10 54 | 4.1 |
|  | 16 36 | 0.8 |
|  | 22 48 | 4.6 |
| 19 Sa | 05 00 | 0.3 |
|  | 11 36 | 4.2 |
|  | 17 06 | 0.8 |
|  | 23 18 | 4.4 |
| 20 Su | 05 30 | 0.4 |
|  | 12 06 | 4.4 |
|  | 17 48 | 0.9 |
| 21 M | 00 00 | 4.3 |
|  | 06 00 | 0.5 |
|  | 12 48 | 4.5 |
|  | 18 42 | 1.0 |
| 22 Tu | 00 48 | 4.1 |
|  | 06 48 | 0.6 |
|  | 13 36 | 4.7 |
|  | 20 12 | 1.0 |
| 23 W | 01 42 | 3.9 |
|  | 07 54 | 0.6 |
|  | 14 30 | 4.8 |
|  | 21 30 | 0.8 |
| 24 Th | 02 42 | 3.8 |
|  | 09 18 | 0.6 |
|  | 15 36 | 5.0 |
|  | 22 36 | 0.6 |
| 25 F | 04 06 | 3.8 |
|  | 10 24 | 0.4 |
|  | 16 48 | 5.2 |
|  | 23 30 | 0.3 |
| 26 Sa | 05 24 | 4.0 |
|  | 11 30 | 0.2 |
|  | 17 54 | 5.5 |
| 27 Su | 00 30 | -0.1 |
|  | 06 30 | 4.3 |
|  | 12 30 | 0.0 |
|  | 18 48 | 5.8 |

## July (cont.) / AUGUST

| Day | Time h. m. | Ht. ft. |
|---|---|---|
| 28 M | 01 24 | -0.4 |
|  | 07 24 | 4.6 |
|  | 13 30 | -0.2 |
|  | 19 42 | 5.9 |
| 29 Tu | 02 18 | -0.6 |
|  | 08 18 | 4.9 |
|  | 14 24 | -0.4 |
|  | 20 36 | 5.9 |
| 30 W | 03 06 | -0.8 |
|  | 09 12 | 5.0 |
|  | 15 18 | -0.4 |
|  | 21 30 | 5.8 |
| 31 Th | 03 48 | -0.8 |
|  | 10 06 | 5.1 |
|  | 16 06 | -0.3 |
|  | 22 24 | 5.5 |
| **AUGUST** | | |
| 1 F | 04 36 | -0.6 |
|  | 11 00 | 5.2 |
|  | 16 54 | -0.1 |
|  | 23 12 | 5.2 |
| 2 Sa | 05 18 | -0.4 |
|  | 11 48 | 5.1 |
|  | 17 48 | 5.1 |
| 3 Su | 00 06 | 4.8 |
|  | 06 06 | 5.0 |
|  | 12 42 | 5.0 |
|  | 18 48 | 0.6 |
| 4 M | 00 54 | 4.4 |
|  | 07 00 | 0.3 |
|  | 13 30 | 4.9 |
|  | 19 54 | 0.8 |
| 5 Tu | 01 48 | 4.0 |
|  | 08 00 | 0.6 |
|  | 14 18 | 4.7 |
|  | 20 54 | 0.9 |
| 6 W | 02 36 | 3.7 |
|  | 09 00 | 0.8 |
|  | 15 12 | 4.6 |
|  | 21 54 | 0.9 |
| 7 Th | 03 42 | 3.5 |
|  | 09 54 | 0.9 |
|  | 16 12 | 4.6 |
|  | 22 48 | 0.8 |
| 8 F | 04 42 | 3.5 |
|  | 10 48 | 0.9 |
|  | 17 12 | 4.7 |
|  | 23 36 | 0.7 |
| 9 Sa | 05 42 | 3.6 |
|  | 11 36 | 0.8 |
|  | 18 00 | 4.8 |
| 10 Su | 00 24 | 0.5 |
|  | 06 30 | 3.8 |
|  | 12 24 | 0.8 |
|  | 18 42 | 5.0 |
| 11 M | 01 12 | 0.3 |
|  | 07 18 | 4.0 |
|  | 13 12 | 0.6 |
|  | 19 24 | 5.1 |
| 12 Tu | 01 54 | 0.1 |
|  | 07 54 | 4.2 |
|  | 13 54 | 0.5 |
|  | 20 00 | 5.1 |
| 13 W | 02 30 | 0.0 |
|  | 08 30 | 4.4 |
|  | 14 36 | 0.4 |
|  | 20 36 | 5.1 |
| 14 Th | 03 06 | -0.1 |
|  | 09 06 | 4.5 |
|  | 15 12 | 0.4 |
|  | 21 06 | 5.0 |
| 15 F | 03 36 | 0.0 |
|  | 09 42 | 4.5 |
|  | 15 42 | 0.4 |
|  | 21 42 | 4.8 |
| 16 Sa | 04 06 | 0.1 |
|  | 10 12 | 4.6 |
|  | 16 12 | 0.5 |
|  | 22 12 | 4.6 |

## August (cont.) / SEPTEMBER

| Day | Time h. m. | Ht. ft. |
|---|---|---|
| 17 Su | 04 30 | 0.2 |
|  | 10 48 | 4.7 |
|  | 16 48 | 0.5 |
|  | 22 48 | 4.5 |
| 18 M | 04 54 | 0.3 |
|  | 11 24 | 4.8 |
|  | 17 24 | 0.7 |
|  | 23 30 | 4.2 |
| 19 Tu | 05 24 | 0.4 |
|  | 12 12 | 4.8 |
|  | 18 18 | 0.9 |
| 20 W | 00 24 | 4.0 |
|  | 06 06 | 0.6 |
|  | 13 06 | 4.9 |
|  | 19 48 | 1.0 |
| 21 Th | 01 18 | 3.8 |
|  | 07 12 | 0.8 |
|  | 14 06 | 4.9 |
|  | 21 12 | 0.9 |
| 22 F | 02 30 | 3.7 |
|  | 09 00 | 0.8 |
|  | 15 18 | 4.9 |
|  | 22 18 | 0.6 |
| 23 Sa | 04 00 | 3.8 |
|  | 10 18 | 0.6 |
|  | 16 36 | 5.1 |
|  | 23 18 | 0.3 |
| 24 Su | 05 18 | 4.1 |
|  | 11 24 | 0.3 |
|  | 17 42 | 5.4 |
| 25 M | 00 12 | -0.1 |
|  | 06 18 | 4.5 |
|  | 12 24 | 0.0 |
|  | 18 42 | 5.7 |
| 26 Tu | 01 06 | -0.4 |
|  | 07 12 | 4.9 |
|  | 13 18 | -0.3 |
|  | 19 30 | 5.8 |
| 27 W | 01 54 | -0.6 |
|  | 08 00 | 5.2 |
|  | 14 12 | -0.5 |
|  | 20 18 | 5.8 |
| 28 Th | 02 42 | -0.7 |
|  | 08 48 | 5.4 |
|  | 15 00 | -0.5 |
|  | 21 06 | 5.6 |
| 29 F | 03 24 | -0.7 |
|  | 09 36 | 5.5 |
|  | 15 42 | -0.4 |
|  | 21 54 | 5.3 |
| 30 Sa | 04 06 | -0.5 |
|  | 10 24 | 5.4 |
|  | 16 30 | -0.1 |
|  | 22 42 | 5.0 |
| 31 Su | 04 48 | -0.2 |
|  | 11 12 | 5.2 |
|  | 17 18 | 0.2 |
|  | 23 30 | 4.6 |
| **SEPTEMBER** | | |
| 1 M | 05 24 | 0.2 |
|  | 12 06 | 5.0 |
|  | 18 06 | 0.6 |
| 2 Tu | 00 24 | 4.2 |
|  | 06 12 | 0.6 |
|  | 12 48 | 4.8 |
|  | 19 12 | 1.0 |
| 3 W | 01 12 | 3.8 |
|  | 07 12 | 1.0 |
|  | 13 42 | 4.6 |
|  | 20 18 | 1.1 |
| 4 Th | 02 06 | 3.6 |
|  | 08 24 | 1.2 |
|  | 14 36 | 4.4 |
|  | 21 24 | 1.1 |
| 5 F | 03 06 | 3.4 |
|  | 09 30 | 1.3 |
|  | 15 36 | 4.3 |
|  | 22 18 | 1.0 |
| 6 Sa | 04 06 | 3.5 |
|  | 10 24 | 1.2 |
|  | 16 36 | 4.4 |
|  | 23 12 | 0.7 |

## September (cont.)

| Day | Time h. m. | Ht. ft. |
|---|---|---|
| 7 Su | 05 18 | 3.7 |
|  | 11 12 | 1.0 |
|  | 17 30 | 4.6 |
|  | 23 54 | 0.5 |
| 8 M | 06 06 | 4.0 |
|  | 12 00 | 0.8 |
|  | 18 18 | 4.8 |
| 9 Tu | 00 36 | 0.3 |
|  | 06 48 | 4.3 |
|  | 12 48 | 0.6 |
|  | 18 54 | 5.0 |
| 10 W | 01 18 | 0.1 |
|  | 07 24 | 4.5 |
|  | 13 30 | 0.4 |
|  | 19 30 | 5.0 |
| 11 Th | 01 54 | 0.0 |
|  | 08 00 | 4.7 |
|  | 14 06 | 0.2 |
|  | 20 06 | 5.0 |
| 12 F | 02 30 | -0.1 |
|  | 08 30 | 4.9 |
|  | 14 48 | 0.1 |
|  | 20 36 | 5.0 |
| 13 Sa | 03 00 | -0.1 |
|  | 09 00 | 5.0 |
|  | 15 24 | 0.1 |
|  | 21 12 | 4.8 |
| 14 Su | 03 30 | 0.0 |
|  | 09 36 | 5.1 |
|  | 15 54 | 0.1 |
|  | 21 42 | 4.6 |
| 15 M | 04 00 | 0.1 |
|  | 10 12 | 5.1 |
|  | 16 30 | 0.3 |
|  | 22 24 | 4.4 |
| 16 Tu | 04 24 | 0.2 |
|  | 10 54 | 5.0 |
|  | 17 12 | 0.5 |
|  | 23 12 | 4.1 |
| 17 W | 05 00 | 0.4 |
|  | 11 48 | 5.0 |
|  | 18 12 | 0.7 |
| 18 Th | 00 12 | 3.9 |
|  | 05 48 | 0.7 |
|  | 12 48 | 4.9 |
|  | 19 36 | 0.9 |
| 19 F | 01 24 | 3.7 |
|  | 07 12 | 0.9 |
|  | 14 00 | 4.8 |
|  | 21 00 | 0.8 |
| 20 Sa | 02 42 | 3.7 |
|  | 09 06 | 0.9 |
|  | 15 12 | 4.8 |
|  | 22 06 | 0.5 |
| 21 Su | 04 00 | 3.9 |
|  | 10 18 | 0.6 |
|  | 16 24 | 5.0 |
|  | 23 00 | 0.2 |
| 22 M | 05 06 | 4.3 |
|  | 11 18 | 0.3 |
|  | 17 30 | 5.2 |
|  | 23 54 | -0.1 |
| 23 Tu | 06 06 | 4.8 |
|  | 12 12 | -0.1 |
|  | 18 24 | 5.4 |
| 24 W | 00 42 | -0.4 |
|  | 06 54 | 5.2 |
|  | 13 00 | -0.3 |
|  | 19 12 | 5.5 |
| 25 Th | 01 30 | -0.6 |
|  | 07 36 | 5.5 |
|  | 13 54 | -0.5 |
|  | 20 00 | 5.4 |
| 26 F | 02 12 | -0.6 |
|  | 08 24 | 5.6 |
|  | 14 36 | -0.5 |
|  | 20 42 | 5.2 |
| 27 Sa | 02 54 | -0.6 |
|  | 09 06 | 5.6 |
|  | 15 24 | -0.4 |
|  | 21 24 | 4.9 |

## September (cont.)

| Day | Time h. m. | Ht. ft. |
|---|---|---|
| 28 Su | 03 36 | -0.4 |
|  | 09 54 | 5.4 |
|  | 16 06 | -0.1 |
|  | 22 12 | 4.6 |
| 29 M | 04 12 | 0.0 |
|  | 10 36 | 5.2 |
|  | 16 48 | 0.2 |
|  | 23 00 | 4.2 |
| 30 Tu | 04 48 | 0.3 |
|  | 11 24 | 4.9 |
|  | 17 36 | 0.6 |
|  | 23 48 | 3.9 |

### OCTOBER

| Day | Time h. m. | Ht. ft. |
|---|---|---|
| 1 W | 05 24 | 0.8 |
|  | 12 18 | 4.6 |
|  | 18 30 | 0.9 |
| 2 Th | 00 42 | 3.6 |
|  | 06 12 | 1.1 |
|  | 13 00 | 4.4 |
|  | 19 36 | 1.1 |
| 3 F | 01 36 | 3.4 |
|  | 07 30 | 1.4 |
|  | 13 54 | 4.2 |
|  | 20 48 | 1.1 |
| 4 Sa | 02 36 | 3.4 |
|  | 08 54 | 1.5 |
|  | 14 54 | 4.1 |
|  | 21 42 | 0.9 |
| 5 Su | 03 36 | 3.4 |
|  | 09 54 | 1.3 |
|  | 15 54 | 4.1 |
|  | 22 36 | 0.7 |
| 6 M | 04 36 | 3.7 |
|  | 10 48 | 1.1 |
|  | 16 48 | 4.3 |
|  | 23 18 | 0.5 |
| 7 Tu | 05 30 | 4.0 |
|  | 11 30 | 0.8 |
|  | 17 36 | 4.5 |
| 8 W | 00 00 | 0.3 |
|  | 06 12 | 4.4 |
|  | 12 18 | 0.5 |
|  | 18 18 | 4.7 |
| 9 Th | 00 42 | 0.1 |
|  | 06 48 | 4.7 |
|  | 13 00 | 0.2 |
|  | 19 00 | 4.8 |
| 10 F | 01 18 | -0.1 |
|  | 07 18 | 5.0 |
|  | 13 42 | 0.0 |
|  | 19 30 | 4.8 |
| 11 Sa | 01 54 | -0.2 |
|  | 07 54 | 5.2 |
|  | 14 18 | -0.2 |
|  | 20 06 | 4.7 |
| 12 Su | 02 24 | -0.2 |
|  | 08 24 | 5.3 |
|  | 15 00 | -0.2 |
|  | 20 42 | 4.6 |
| 13 M | 03 00 | -0.1 |
|  | 09 00 | 5.4 |
|  | 15 36 | -0.2 |
|  | 21 24 | 4.4 |
| 14 Tu | 03 30 | -0.1 |
|  | 09 48 | 5.3 |
|  | 16 18 | -0.1 |
|  | 22 12 | 4.2 |
| 15 W | 04 12 | 0.1 |
|  | 10 36 | 5.2 |
|  | 17 06 | 0.2 |
|  | 23 12 | 3.9 |
| 16 Th | 04 54 | 0.4 |
|  | 11 42 | 5.0 |
|  | 18 06 | 0.4 |
| 17 F | 00 24 | 3.8 |
|  | 05 54 | 0.7 |
|  | 12 48 | 4.8 |
|  | 19 30 | 0.5 |
| 18 Sa | 01 30 | 3.8 |
|  | 07 30 | 0.9 |
|  | 13 54 | 4.7 |
|  | 20 42 | 0.5 |

## October (cont.)

| Day | Time h. m. | Ht. ft. |
|---|---|---|
| 19 Su | 02 42 | 3.9 |
|  | 09 00 | 0.7 |
|  | 15 06 | 4.7 |
|  | 21 48 | 0.2 |
| 20 M | 03 48 | 4.2 |
|  | 10 06 | 0.4 |
|  | 16 12 | 4.7 |
|  | 22 42 | 0.0 |
| 21 Tu | 04 48 | 4.5 |
|  | 11 06 | 0.1 |
|  | 17 12 | 4.8 |
|  | 23 30 | -0.3 |
| 22 W | 05 48 | 4.9 |
|  | 11 54 | -0.2 |
|  | 18 06 | 4.9 |
| 23 Th | 00 18 | -0.5 |
|  | 06 30 | 5.3 |
|  | 12 48 | -0.4 |
|  | 18 54 | 5.0 |
| 24 F | 01 00 | -0.5 |
|  | 07 18 | 5.5 |
|  | 13 36 | -0.5 |
|  | 19 36 | 4.9 |
| 25 Sa | 01 42 | -0.5 |
|  | 08 00 | 5.5 |
|  | 14 18 | -0.5 |
|  | 20 18 | 4.7 |
| 26 Su | 02 24 | -0.4 |
|  | 08 42 | 5.4 |
|  | 15 00 | -0.4 |
|  | 21 00 | 4.4 |
| 27 M | 03 06 | -0.2 |
|  | 09 18 | 5.2 |
|  | 15 42 | -0.2 |
|  | 21 42 | 4.1 |
| 28 Tu | 03 42 | 0.1 |
|  | 10 00 | 5.0 |
|  | 16 24 | 0.1 |
|  | 22 24 | 3.8 |
| 29 W | 04 18 | 0.4 |
|  | 10 48 | 4.7 |
|  | 17 06 | 0.4 |
|  | 23 24 | 3.6 |
| 30 Th | 04 48 | 0.7 |
|  | 11 36 | 4.4 |
|  | 17 54 | 0.6 |
| 31 F | 00 12 | 3.4 |
|  | 05 30 | 1.1 |
|  | 12 24 | 4.2 |
|  | 18 54 | 0.8 |

### NOVEMBER

| Day | Time h. m. | Ht. ft. |
|---|---|---|
| 1 Sa | 01 06 | 3.3 |
|  | 06 24 | 1.3 |
|  | 13 12 | 4.0 |
|  | 20 00 | 0.9 |
| 2 Su | 02 00 | 3.3 |
|  | 08 06 | 1.4 |
|  | 14 06 | 3.9 |
|  | 21 00 | 0.8 |
| 3 M | 02 54 | 3.4 |
|  | 09 12 | 1.3 |
|  | 15 00 | 3.9 |
|  | 21 48 | 0.6 |
| 4 Tu | 03 48 | 3.7 |
|  | 10 12 | 1.0 |
|  | 16 00 | 3.9 |
|  | 22 36 | 0.4 |
| 5 W | 04 42 | 4.0 |
|  | 11 00 | 0.7 |
|  | 16 48 | 4.0 |
|  | 23 18 | 0.2 |
| 6 Th | 05 24 | 4.3 |
|  | 11 42 | 0.3 |
|  | 17 36 | 4.2 |
|  | 23 54 | 0.0 |
| 7 F | 06 06 | 4.7 |
|  | 12 30 | 0.0 |
|  | 18 24 | 4.3 |
| 8 Sa | 00 36 | -0.1 |
|  | 06 42 | 5.1 |
|  | 13 12 | -0.2 |
|  | 19 00 | 4.4 |

## November (cont.)

| Day | Time h. m. | Ht. ft. |
|---|---|---|
| 9 Su | 01 12 | -0.3 |
|  | 07 24 | 5.3 |
|  | 14 00 | -0.4 |
|  | 19 42 | 4.4 |
| 10 M | 01 54 | -0.3 |
|  | 08 00 | 5.5 |
|  | 14 42 | -0.5 |
|  | 20 24 | 4.3 |
| 11 Tu | 02 36 | -0.3 |
|  | 08 42 | 5.5 |
|  | 15 24 | -0.5 |
|  | 21 12 | 4.2 |
| 12 W | 03 18 | -0.3 |
|  | 09 36 | 5.4 |
|  | 16 12 | -0.5 |
|  | 22 12 | 4.0 |
| 13 Th | 04 00 | -0.1 |
|  | 10 36 | 5.2 |
|  | 17 06 | -0.3 |
|  | 23 18 | 3.9 |
| 14 F | 04 54 | 0.1 |
|  | 11 36 | 5.0 |
|  | 18 00 | -0.1 |
| 15 Sa | 00 24 | 3.9 |
|  | 06 06 | 0.4 |
|  | 12 42 | 4.8 |
|  | 19 12 | 0.0 |
| 16 Su | 01 24 | 4.0 |
|  | 07 30 | 0.5 |
|  | 13 42 | 4.6 |
|  | 20 18 | 0.0 |
| 17 M | 02 24 | 4.1 |
|  | 08 48 | 0.4 |
|  | 14 48 | 4.4 |
|  | 21 24 | -0.1 |
| 18 Tu | 03 30 | 4.3 |
|  | 09 48 | 0.2 |
|  | 15 48 | 4.4 |
|  | 22 18 | -0.2 |
| 19 W | 04 24 | 4.6 |
|  | 10 48 | 0.0 |
|  | 16 48 | 4.3 |
|  | 23 06 | -0.4 |
| 20 Th | 05 24 | 4.9 |
|  | 11 36 | -0.2 |
|  | 17 42 | 4.3 |
|  | 23 48 | -0.4 |
| 21 F | 06 12 | 5.1 |
|  | 12 30 | -0.4 |
|  | 18 30 | 4.3 |
| 22 Sa | 00 36 | -0.4 |
|  | 06 54 | 5.2 |
|  | 13 12 | -0.4 |
|  | 19 18 | 4.2 |
| 23 Su | 01 18 | -0.4 |
|  | 07 36 | 5.2 |
|  | 14 00 | -0.4 |
|  | 20 00 | 4.1 |
| 24 M | 02 00 | -0.4 |
|  | 08 18 | 5.1 |
|  | 14 42 | -0.4 |
|  | 20 36 | 3.9 |
| 25 Tu | 02 42 | -0.1 |
|  | 08 54 | 5.0 |
|  | 15 24 | -0.3 |
|  | 21 24 | 3.7 |
| 26 W | 03 18 | 0.1 |
|  | 09 36 | 4.7 |
|  | 16 00 | -0.2 |
|  | 22 06 | 3.5 |
| 27 Th | 03 54 | 0.3 |
|  | 10 18 | 4.5 |
|  | 16 42 | 0.0 |
|  | 23 00 | 3.4 |
| 28 F | 04 30 | 0.6 |
|  | 11 00 | 4.3 |
|  | 17 24 | 0.2 |
|  | 23 48 | 3.3 |
| 29 Sa | 05 06 | 0.8 |
|  | 11 42 | 4.1 |
|  | 18 06 | 0.4 |

## November (cont.)

| Day | Time h. m. | Ht. ft. |
|---|---|---|
| 30 Su | 00 36 | 3.3 |
|  | 05 42 | 1.0 |
|  | 12 24 | 3.9 |
|  | 19 00 | 0.5 |

### DECEMBER

| Day | Time h. m. | Ht. ft. |
|---|---|---|
| 1 M | 01 18 | 3.3 |
|  | 06 54 | 1.1 |
|  | 13 12 | 3.8 |
|  | 20 00 |  |
| 2 Tu | 02 06 | 3.4 |
|  | 08 24 | 1.1 |
|  | 13 54 | 3.7 |
|  | 20 54 | 0.5 |
| 3 W | 02 48 | 3.0 |
|  | 09 24 | 1.0 |
|  | 14 48 | 3.6 |
|  | 21 42 | 0.5 |
| 4 Th | 03 42 | 3.9 |
|  | 10 18 | 3.6 |
|  | 15 48 | 3.6 |
|  | 22 24 | 0.2 |
| 5 F | 04 36 | 4.2 |
|  | 11 06 | 0.3 |
|  | 16 48 | 3.7 |
|  | 23 12 | 0.0 |
| 6 Sa | 05 24 | 4.6 |
|  | 11 54 | -0.1 |
|  | 17 48 | 3.8 |
|  | 23 54 | -0.2 |
| 7 Su | 06 12 | 5.0 |
|  | 12 48 | -0.4 |
|  | 18 36 | 3.9 |
| 8 M | 00 42 | -0.4 |
|  | 06 54 | 5.2 |
|  | 13 36 | -0.6 |
|  | 19 24 | 4.0 |
| 9 Tu | 01 30 | -0.5 |
|  | 07 42 | 5.4 |
|  | 14 24 | -0.8 |
|  | 20 12 | 4.1 |
| 10 W | 02 18 | -0.6 |
|  | 08 30 | 5.4 |
|  | 15 12 | -0.9 |
|  | 21 06 | 4.1 |
| 11 Th | 03 12 | -0.6 |
|  | 09 30 | 5.4 |
|  | 16 00 | -0.9 |
|  | 22 06 | 4.1 |
| 12 F | 04 00 | -0.5 |
|  | 10 30 | 5.2 |
|  | 16 54 | -0.8 |
|  | 23 12 | 4.1 |
| 13 Sa | 04 54 | -0.3 |
|  | 11 30 | 5.0 |
|  | 17 48 | -0.6 |
| 14 Su | 00 12 | 4.1 |
|  | 06 00 | -0.1 |
|  | 12 24 | 4.7 |
|  | 18 48 | -0.4 |
| 15 M | 01 06 | 4.2 |
|  | 07 12 | 0.1 |
|  | 13 24 | 4.5 |
|  | 19 48 | -0.3 |
| 16 Tu | 02 00 | 4.3 |
|  | 08 24 | 0.1 |
|  | 14 18 | 4.2 |
|  | 20 48 | -0.3 |
| 17 W | 03 00 | 4.3 |
|  | 09 24 | 0.1 |
|  | 15 18 | 3.9 |
|  | 21 48 | -0.3 |
| 18 Th | 04 00 | 4.4 |
|  | 10 24 | 0.0 |
|  | 16 18 | 3.8 |
|  | 22 36 | -0.3 |
| 19 F | 04 54 | 4.6 |
|  | 11 18 | -0.1 |
|  | 17 18 | 3.7 |
|  | 23 24 | -0.3 |
| 20 Sa | 05 48 | 4.7 |
|  | 12 06 | -0.2 |
|  | 18 12 | 3.7 |
| 21 Su | 00 12 | -0.3 |
|  | 06 36 | 4.8 |
|  | 12 54 | -0.3 |
|  | 18 54 | 3.7 |

## December (cont.)

| Day | Time h. m. | Ht. ft. |
|---|---|---|
| 22 M | 00 54 | -0.2 |
|  | 07 18 | 4.8 |
|  | 13 42 | -0.4 |
|  | 19 42 | 3.6 |
| 23 Tu | 01 42 | -0.2 |
|  | 07 54 | 4.8 |
|  | 14 24 | -0.4 |
|  | 20 24 | 3.6 |
| 24 W | 02 24 | -0.1 |
|  | 08 36 | 4.7 |
|  | 15 06 | -0.4 |
|  | 21 06 | 3.5 |
| 25 Th | 03 00 | 0.0 |
|  | 09 12 | 4.6 |
|  | 15 42 | -0.4 |
|  | 21 48 | 3.5 |
| 26 F | 03 36 | 0.1 |
|  | 09 54 | 4.4 |
|  | 16 18 | -0.3 |
|  | 22 30 | 3.4 |
| 27 Sa | 04 12 | 0.3 |
|  | 10 30 | 4.2 |
|  | 16 54 | -0.2 |
|  | 23 12 | 3.4 |
| 28 Su | 04 42 | 0.4 |
|  | 11 06 | 4.0 |
|  | 17 24 | 0.0 |
|  | 23 54 | 3.4 |
| 29 M | 05 12 | 0.5 |
|  | 11 42 | 3.9 |
|  | 18 00 | 0.1 |
| 30 Tu | 00 30 | 3.5 |
|  | 05 54 | 0.7 |
|  | 12 24 | 3.7 |
|  | 18 30 | 0.2 |
| 31 W | 01 06 | 3.6 |
|  | 06 54 | 0.8 |
|  | 13 00 | 3.6 |
|  | 19 24 | 0.3 |

# Time of Tides at Points on Pacific Coast

**Source: Coast and Geodetic Survey, Environmental Science Services Administration**

**See also Tides and Their Causes on Page 294**

The chart below can be used to approximate the time of high or low tide at stations listed by adding or subtracting the mean time difference shown on the chart from the times shown in the tide tables for San Francisco. San Francisco is a semidiurnal station (two highs and two low tides per day), as are most of the other stations shown. However, at a few of these stations the tide becomes diurnal on occasion (one high and one low tide per day); on such occasions it is not possible to make a correct prediction by referring times to San Francisco.

|  | H. M. |  | H. M. |  | H. M. |
|---|---|---|---|---|---|
| Aberdeen, Wash. .... | add 1 45 | Juneau, Alaska ..... | add 2 25 | Sacramento, Cal. ..... | add 8 35 |
| Anchorage, Alaska .. | add 6 55 | Ketchikan, Alaska .. | add 2 00 | Salina Cruz, Mexico.. | add 3 00 |
| Astoria, Ore. ...... | add 1 55 | Kodiak, Alaska ...... | add 1 10 | San Diego, Cal. ...... | sub 2 20 |
| Balboa, Canal Zone .. | sub 8 15 | Long Beach, Cal. .... | sub 2 15 | Santa Barbara, Cal... | sub 1 55 |
| Cordova, Alaska .... | add 0 35 | Los Angeles ....... | sub 2 20 | Seattle, Wash. ...... | add 5 30 |
| Crescent City, Cal. ... |  0 00 | Massacre Bay, Alaska | add 4 20 | Sitka, Alaska ...... | add 2 05 |
| Dutch Harbor, Alaska | add 4 50 | Midway Islands .... | add 5 20 | Stockton, Cal. ...... | add 7 15 |
| Honolulu ....... | add 5 15 | Portland, Ore. ...... | add 8 10 | Vancouver, B.C. ...... | add 6 30 |
| Humboldt Bay, Cal... | add 0 30 | Port Townsend, Wash. | add 4 40 | Victoria, B.C. ...... | add 3 35 |

# Tide Tables for 1969 (at San Francisco)

Time meridian 120°W. 0000 is midnight. 1200 is noon. All hours greater 1200 are p.m. Heights are reckoned from the datum of soundings on charts of the locality which is mean low water.

**Time and Height of High and Low Waters at Golden Gate—Pacific STANDARD Time**

## JANUARY / FEBRUARY / MARCH

| Day | Time h. m. | Ht. ft. |
|---|---|---|
| 1 W | 03 00 | 3.3 |
|  | 09 24 | 5.9 |
|  | 16 42 | -0.6 |
|  | 23 54 | 4.4 |
| 2 Th | 03 42 | 3.4 |
|  | 09 54 | 5.9 |
|  | 17 12 | -0.8 |
| 3 F | 00 30 | 4.5 |
|  | 04 18 | 3.4 |
|  | 10 30 | 5.9 |
|  | 17 48 | -0.8 |
| 4 Sa | 01 12 | 4.5 |
|  | 05 00 | 3.4 |
|  | 11 06 | 5.9 |
|  | 18 24 | -0.8 |
| 5 Su | 01 48 | 4.5 |
|  | 05 42 | 3.4 |
|  | 11 36 | 5.8 |
|  | 18 54 | -0.7 |
| 6 M | 02 18 | 4.6 |
|  | 06 24 | 3.3 |
|  | 12 12 | 5.6 |
|  | 19 24 | -0.5 |
| 7 Tu | 02 54 | 4.6 |
|  | 07 12 | 3.1 |
|  | 13 00 | 5.3 |
|  | 20 00 | -0.2 |
| 8 W | 03 18 | 4.8 |
|  | 08 12 | 2.9 |
|  | 13 48 | 4.8 |
|  | 20 36 | 0.2 |
| 9 Th | 03 48 | 5.0 |
|  | 09 18 | 2.5 |
|  | 14 48 | 4.3 |
|  | 21 12 | 0.8 |
| 10 F | 04 18 | 5.2 |
|  | 10 30 | 1.9 |
|  | 16 06 | 3.8 |
|  | 21 54 | 1.4 |
| 11 Sa | 04 54 | 5.5 |
|  | 11 42 | 1.3 |
|  | 17 48 | 3.5 |
|  | 22 42 | 2.0 |
| 12 Su | 05 30 | 5.8 |
|  | 12 48 | 0.5 |
|  | 19 30 | 3.5 |
|  | 23 42 | 2.5 |
| 13 M | 06 18 | 6.1 |
|  | 13 48 | -0.2 |
|  | 21 00 | 3.8 |
| 14 Tu | 00 36 | 2.9 |
|  | 07 12 | 6.4 |
|  | 14 48 | -0.9 |
|  | 22 06 | 4.1 |
| 15 W | 01 48 | 3.1 |
|  | 08 06 | 6.6 |
|  | 15 36 | -1.4 |
|  | 22 54 | 4.5 |
| 16 Th | 02 48 | 3.2 |
|  | 09 06 | 6.8 |
|  | 16 30 | -1.7 |
|  | 23 42 | 4.7 |
| 17 F | 03 48 | 3.1 |
|  | 10 00 | 6.9 |
|  | 17 18 | -1.8 |
| 18 Sa | 00 24 | 5.0 |
|  | 04 42 | 2.9 |
|  | 10 54 | 6.8 |
|  | 18 00 | -1.7 |
| 19 Su | 01 06 | 5.1 |
|  | 05 42 | 2.7 |
|  | 11 48 | 6.5 |
|  | 18 42 | -1.4 |
| 20 M | 01 48 | 5.3 |
|  | 06 36 | 2.5 |
|  | 12 42 | 6.1 |
|  | 19 24 | -0.9 |
| 21 Tu | 02 24 | 5.4 |
|  | 07 42 | 2.3 |
|  | 13 36 | 5.5 |
|  | 20 06 | -0.2 |
| 22 W | 03 00 | 5.5 |
|  | 08 42 | 2.0 |
|  | 14 36 | 4.8 |
|  | 20 42 | 0.5 |
| 23 Th | 03 42 | 5.6 |
|  | 09 54 | 1.7 |
|  | 15 42 | 4.2 |
|  | 21 24 | 1.2 |
| 24 F | 04 24 | 5.6 |
|  | 11 06 | 1.3 |
|  | 17 00 | 3.7 |
|  | 22 06 | 1.9 |
| 25 Sa | 05 06 | 5.6 |
|  | 12 12 | 1.0 |
|  | 18 36 | 3.5 |
|  | 22 54 | 2.5 |
| 26 Su | 05 54 | 5.6 |
|  | 13 18 | 0.6 |
|  | 20 06 | 3.6 |
|  | 23 54 | 2.9 |
| 27 M | 06 36 | 5.5 |
|  | 14 12 | 0.2 |
|  | 21 18 | 3.9 |
| 28 Tu | 00 54 | 3.2 |
|  | 07 30 | 5.6 |
|  | 14 54 | -0.1 |
|  | 22 06 | 4.1 |
| 29 W | 01 54 | 3.3 |
|  | 08 18 | 5.6 |
|  | 15 42 | -0.3 |
|  | 22 48 | 4.3 |
| 30 Th | 02 42 | 3.3 |
|  | 09 00 | 5.7 |
|  | 16 18 | -0.5 |
|  | 23 24 | 4.4 |
| 31 F | 03 30 | 3.2 |
|  | 09 42 | 5.8 |
|  | 16 48 | -0.7 |
| **FEBRUARY** |  |  |
| 1 Sa | 00 00 | 4.5 |
|  | 04 06 | 3.1 |
|  | 10 18 | 5.9 |
|  | 17 24 | -0.7 |
| 2 Su | 00 36 | 4.6 |
|  | 04 48 | 3.0 |
|  | 10 54 | 5.9 |
|  | 17 54 | -0.7 |
| 3 M | 01 00 | 4.7 |
|  | 05 24 | 2.8 |
|  | 11 30 | 5.7 |
|  | 18 18 | -0.5 |
| 4 Tu | 01 24 | 4.8 |
|  | 06 12 | 2.5 |
|  | 12 12 | 5.5 |
|  | 18 54 | -0.2 |
| 5 W | 01 48 | 4.9 |
|  | 07 00 | 2.2 |
|  | 12 54 | 5.1 |
|  | 19 24 | 0.3 |
| 6 Th | 02 12 | 5.1 |
|  | 07 48 | 1.8 |
|  | 13 48 | 4.6 |
|  | 19 54 | 0.8 |
| 7 F | 02 48 | 5.3 |
|  | 08 48 | 1.4 |
|  | 14 54 | 4.1 |
|  | 20 30 | 1.5 |
| 8 Sa | 03 12 | 5.5 |
|  | 09 54 | 1.0 |
|  | 16 18 | 3.7 |
|  | 21 12 | 2.1 |
| 9 Su | 03 54 | 5.7 |
|  | 11 12 | 0.6 |
|  | 18 00 | 3.5 |
|  | 22 00 | 2.6 |
| 10 M | 04 42 | 5.8 |
|  | 12 24 | 0.0 |
|  | 19 42 | 3.6 |
|  | 23 12 | 3.1 |
| 11 Tu | 05 42 | 6.0 |
|  | 13 30 | -0.5 |
|  | 21 00 | 4.0 |
| 12 W | 00 24 | 3.3 |
|  | 06 54 | 6.1 |
|  | 14 30 | -0.9 |
|  | 21 54 | 4.3 |
| 13 Th | 01 42 | 3.2 |
|  | 08 00 | 6.3 |
|  | 15 24 | -1.3 |
|  | 22 36 | 4.6 |
| 14 F | 02 48 | 3.0 |
|  | 09 06 | 6.5 |
|  | 16 12 | -1.4 |
|  | 23 12 | 4.9 |
| 15 Sa | 03 48 | 2.6 |
|  | 10 00 | 6.5 |
|  | 16 54 | -1.3 |
|  | 23 54 | 5.1 |
| 16 Su | 04 42 | 2.2 |
|  | 10 54 | 6.4 |
|  | 17 36 | -1.1 |
| 17 M | 00 24 | 5.3 |
|  | 05 36 | 1.9 |
|  | 11 48 | 6.1 |
|  | 18 12 | -0.6 |
| 18 Tu | 01 00 | 5.5 |
|  | 06 24 | 1.5 |
|  | 12 36 | 5.6 |
|  | 18 48 | 0.0 |
| 19 W | 01 30 | 5.6 |
|  | 07 18 | 1.3 |
|  | 13 30 | 5.0 |
|  | 19 24 | 0.7 |
| 20 Th | 02 00 | 5.6 |
|  | 08 12 | 1.1 |
|  | 14 30 | 4.5 |
|  | 20 00 | 1.4 |
| 21 F | 02 42 | 5.5 |
|  | 09 12 | 0.9 |
|  | 15 36 | 4.0 |
|  | 20 36 | 2.0 |
| 22 Sa | 03 18 | 5.4 |
|  | 10 12 | 0.8 |
|  | 16 48 | 3.7 |
|  | 21 18 | 2.5 |
| 23 Su | 04 00 | 5.3 |
|  | 11 24 | 0.7 |
|  | 18 24 | 3.6 |
|  | 22 06 | 3.0 |
| 24 M | 04 48 | 5.1 |
|  | 12 30 | 0.6 |
|  | 19 54 | 3.7 |
|  | 23 24 | 3.2 |
| 25 Tu | 05 54 | 5.1 |
|  | 13 30 | 0.3 |
|  | 20 48 | 3.9 |
| 26 W | 00 36 | 3.3 |
|  | 06 54 | 5.1 |
|  | 14 18 | 0.1 |
|  | 21 42 | 4.2 |
| 27 Th | 01 42 | 3.2 |
|  | 07 54 | 5.3 |
|  | 15 06 | -0.1 |
|  | 22 12 | 4.4 |
| 28 F | 02 36 | 3.0 |
|  | 08 42 | 5.4 |
|  | 15 42 | -0.3 |
|  | 22 48 | 4.5 |
| **MARCH** |  |  |
| 1 Sa | 03 12 | 2.8 |
|  | 09 24 | 5.6 |
|  | 16 12 | -0.4 |
|  | 23 12 | 4.7 |
| 2 Su | 03 54 | 2.5 |
|  | 10 06 | 5.6 |
|  | 16 42 | -0.4 |
|  | 23 36 | 4.8 |
| 3 M | 04 36 | 2.1 |
|  | 10 48 | 5.6 |
|  | 17 12 | -0.2 |
| 4 Tu | 00 00 | 4.9 |
|  | 05 12 | 1.7 |
|  | 11 30 | 5.4 |
|  | 17 42 | 0.1 |
| 5 W | 00 24 | 5.1 |
|  | 05 54 | 1.3 |
|  | 12 12 | 5.2 |
|  | 18 12 | 0.5 |

## March (cont.)

| Day | Time h. m. | Ht. ft. |
|---|---|---|
| 6 Th | 00 48 | 5.2 |
| | 06 42 | 0.9 |
| | 13 00 | 4.8 |
| | 18 42 | 1.1 |
| 7 F | 01 12 | 5.4 |
| | 07 36 | 0.5 |
| | 14 00 | 4.4 |
| | 19 18 | 1.6 |
| 8 Sa | 01 42 | 5.6 |
| | 08 24 | 0.3 |
| | 15 06 | 4.0 |
| | 19 54 | 2.2 |
| 9 Su | 02 18 | 5.6 |
| | 09 30 | 0.1 |
| | 16 36 | 3.7 |
| | 20 36 | 2.7 |
| 10 M | 03 06 | 5.7 |
| | 10 48 | -0.1 |
| | 18 12 | 3.7 |
| | 21 42 | 3.2 |
| 11 Tu | 04 06 | 5.6 |
| | 12 00 | -0.4 |
| | 19 42 | 3.9 |
| | 23 12 | 3.4 |
| 12 W | 05 24 | 5.6 |
| | 13 12 | -0.6 |
| | 20 42 | 4.3 |
| 13 Th | 00 42 | 3.2 |
| | 06 48 | 5.7 |
| | 14 12 | -0.8 |
| | 21 24 | 4.6 |
| 14 F | 02 00 | 2.9 |
| | 08 00 | 5.8 |
| | 15 00 | -0.9 |
| | 22 00 | 4.9 |
| 15 Sa | 02 54 | 2.3 |
| | 09 06 | 5.9 |
| | 15 48 | -0.8 |
| | 22 36 | 5.2 |
| 16 Su | 03 48 | 1.8 |
| | 10 00 | 5.8 |
| | 16 24 | -0.5 |
| | 23 06 | 5.4 |
| 17 M | 04 36 | 1.3 |
| | 10 54 | 5.7 |
| | 17 06 | -0.1 |
| | 23 42 | 5.5 |
| 18 Tu | 05 24 | 0.8 |
| | 11 48 | 5.4 |
| | 17 36 | 0.5 |
| 19 W | 00 12 | 5.5 |
| | 06 12 | 0.5 |
| | 12 36 | 5.0 |
| | 18 06 | 1.1 |
| 20 Th | 00 36 | 5.6 |
| | 06 54 | 0.2 |
| | 13 30 | 4.6 |
| | 18 42 | 1.7 |
| 21 F | 01 06 | 5.5 |
| | 07 42 | 0.2 |
| | 14 24 | 4.2 |
| | 19 12 | 2.2 |
| 22 Sa | 01 36 | 5.4 |
| | 08 30 | 0.2 |
| | 15 24 | 3.9 |
| | 19 42 | 2.6 |
| 23 Su | 02 18 | 5.2 |
| | 09 24 | 0.3 |
| | 16 36 | 3.7 |
| | 20 36 | 3.0 |
| 24 M | 02 54 | 4.9 |
| | 10 30 | 0.4 |
| | 18 00 | 3.7 |
| | 21 36 | 3.2 |
| 25 Tu | 03 48 | 4.7 |
| | 11 36 | 0.4 |
| | 19 18 | 3.9 |
| | 23 00 | 3.4 |
| 26 W | 05 00 | 4.6 |
| | 12 36 | 0.3 |
| | 20 12 | 4.1 |

## March (cont.)

| Day | Time h. m. | Ht. ft. |
|---|---|---|
| 27 Th | 00 30 | 3.2 |
| | 06 12 | 4.7 |
| | 13 30 | 0.2 |
| | 20 48 | 4.3 |
| 28 F | 01 30 | 3.0 |
| | 07 18 | 4.8 |
| | 14 12 | 0.0 |
| | 21 24 | 4.5 |
| 29 Sa | 02 12 | 2.6 |
| | 08 12 | 4.9 |
| | 14 54 | 0.0 |
| | 21 54 | 4.7 |
| 30 Su | 03 00 | 2.2 |
| | 09 06 | 5.0 |
| | 15 30 | 0.0 |
| | 22 18 | 4.9 |
| 31 M | 03 36 | 1.6 |
| | 09 54 | 5.1 |
| | 16 00 | 0.2 |
| | 22 42 | 5.1 |

### APRIL

| Day | Time h. m. | Ht. ft. |
|---|---|---|
| 1 Tu | 04 18 | 1.1 |
| | 10 36 | 5.1 |
| | 16 30 | 0.5 |
| | 23 00 | 5.3 |
| 2 W | 05 00 | 0.5 |
| | 11 24 | 5.0 |
| | 17 00 | 0.9 |
| | 23 24 | 5.5 |
| 3 Th | 05 42 | 0.0 |
| | 12 18 | 4.8 |
| | 17 30 | 1.4 |
| | 23 54 | 5.7 |
| 4 F | 06 24 | -0.4 |
| | 13 12 | 4.5 |
| | 18 06 | 1.9 |
| 5 Sa | 00 24 | 5.8 |
| | 07 12 | -0.7 |
| | 14 12 | 4.3 |
| | 18 48 | 2.4 |
| 6 Su | 00 54 | 5.8 |
| | 08 12 | -0.8 |
| | 15 24 | 4.1 |
| | 19 30 | 2.9 |
| 7 M | 01 42 | 5.7 |
| | 09 12 | -0.7 |
| | 16 48 | 3.9 |
| | 20 30 | 3.2 |
| 8 Tu | 02 36 | 5.5 |
| | 10 24 | -0.7 |
| | 18 06 | 4.1 |
| | 21 48 | 3.4 |
| 9 W | 03 54 | 5.3 |
| | 11 36 | -0.6 |
| | 19 18 | 4.4 |
| | 23 36 | 3.3 |
| 10 Th | 05 18 | 5.1 |
| | 12 42 | -0.6 |
| | 20 06 | 4.7 |
| 11 F | 01 00 | 2.8 |
| | 06 42 | 5.1 |
| | 13 42 | -0.5 |
| | 20 42 | 5.0 |
| 12 Sa | 02 06 | 2.2 |
| | 08 00 | 5.1 |
| | 14 30 | -0.3 |
| | 21 18 | 5.3 |
| 13 Su | 03 00 | 1.5 |
| | 09 06 | 5.1 |
| | 15 12 | 0.1 |
| | 21 54 | 5.5 |
| 14 M | 03 48 | 0.8 |
| | 10 00 | 5.0 |
| | 15 48 | 0.6 |
| | 22 24 | 5.7 |
| 15 Tu | 04 30 | 0.2 |
| | 10 48 | 4.9 |
| | 16 24 | 1.1 |
| | 22 54 | 5.8 |
| 16 W | 05 12 | -0.2 |
| | 11 48 | 4.7 |
| | 17 00 | 1.6 |
| | 23 18 | 5.7 |

## April (cont.)

| Day | Time h. m. | Ht. ft. |
|---|---|---|
| 17 Th | 05 54 | -0.4 |
| | 12 42 | 4.5 |
| | 17 24 | 2.1 |
| | 23 48 | 5.7 |
| 18 F | 06 30 | -0.5 |
| | 13 30 | 4.3 |
| | 18 00 | 2.5 |
| 19 Sa | 00 18 | 5.5 |
| | 07 12 | -0.5 |
| | 14 24 | 4.1 |
| | 18 36 | 2.8 |
| 20 Su | 00 48 | 5.3 |
| | 07 54 | -0.3 |
| | 15 24 | 4.0 |
| | 19 12 | 3.1 |
| 21 M | 01 18 | 5.1 |
| | 08 48 | -0.1 |
| | 16 24 | 3.9 |
| | 20 00 | 3.3 |
| 22 Tu | 02 00 | 4.8 |
| | 09 42 | 0.1 |
| | 17 30 | 3.9 |
| | 21 12 | 3.4 |
| 23 W | 02 54 | 4.6 |
| | 10 42 | 0.2 |
| | 18 30 | 4.1 |
| | 22 42 | 3.4 |
| 24 Th | 04 06 | 4.4 |
| | 11 42 | 0.2 |
| | 19 18 | 4.3 |
| 25 F | 00 00 | 3.2 |
| | 05 18 | 4.3 |
| | 12 30 | 0.2 |
| | 19 54 | 4.5 |
| 26 Sa | 00 36 | 2.7 |
| | 06 36 | 4.3 |
| | 13 12 | 0.3 |
| | 20 24 | 4.8 |
| 27 Su | 01 54 | 2.1 |
| | 07 42 | 4.3 |
| | 13 54 | 0.4 |
| | 20 54 | 5.0 |
| 28 M | 02 36 | 1.5 |
| | 08 42 | 4.4 |
| | 14 30 | 0.7 |
| | 21 18 | 5.3 |
| 29 Tu | 03 18 | 0.7 |
| | 09 42 | 4.5 |
| | 15 06 | 1.0 |
| | 21 42 | 5.6 |
| 30 W | 04 00 | 0.0 |
| | 10 36 | 4.5 |
| | 15 42 | 1.4 |
| | 22 06 | 5.8 |

### MAY

| Day | Time h. m. | Ht. ft. |
|---|---|---|
| 1 Th | 04 42 | -0.6 |
| | 11 30 | 4.6 |
| | 16 18 | 1.8 |
| | 22 36 | 6.0 |
| 2 F | 05 24 | -1.1 |
| | 12 24 | 4.6 |
| | 17 00 | 2.3 |
| | 23 06 | 6.2 |
| 3 Sa | 06 12 | -1.4 |
| | 13 24 | 4.5 |
| | 17 42 | 2.7 |
| | 23 48 | 6.2 |
| 4 Su | 07 06 | -1.5 |
| | 14 24 | 4.4 |
| | 18 24 | 3.0 |
| 5 M | 00 30 | 6.1 |
| | 08 00 | -1.5 |
| | 15 30 | 4.4 |
| | 19 24 | 3.3 |
| 6 Tu | 01 24 | 5.8 |
| | 09 00 | -1.3 |
| | 16 36 | 4.4 |
| | 20 36 | 3.4 |
| 7 W | 02 30 | 5.5 |
| | 10 06 | -1.0 |
| | 17 42 | 4.6 |
| | 22 12 | 3.3 |

## May (cont.)

| Day | Time h. m. | Ht. ft. |
|---|---|---|
| 8 Th | 03 42 | 5.0 |
| | 11 06 | -0.7 |
| | 18 36 | 4.8 |
| | 23 42 | 2.9 |
| 9 F | 05 12 | 4.7 |
| | 12 06 | -0.3 |
| | 19 18 | 5.1 |
| 10 Sa | 01 00 | 2.2 |
| | 06 36 | 4.5 |
| | 13 00 | 0.1 |
| | 20 00 | 5.4 |
| 11 Su | 02 06 | 1.4 |
| | 07 54 | 4.4 |
| | 13 48 | 0.6 |
| | 20 36 | 5.6 |
| 12 M | 02 54 | 0.7 |
| | 09 06 | 4.4 |
| | 14 30 | 1.1 |
| | 21 06 | 5.8 |
| 13 Tu | 03 42 | 0.0 |
| | 10 06 | 4.4 |
| | 15 12 | 1.7 |
| | 21 36 | 5.9 |
| 14 W | 04 18 | -0.5 |
| | 11 06 | 4.4 |
| | 15 48 | 2.2 |
| | 22 06 | 5.9 |
| 15 Th | 05 00 | -0.8 |
| | 11 54 | 4.4 |
| | 16 18 | 2.5 |
| | 22 36 | 5.8 |
| 16 F | 05 36 | -0.9 |
| | 12 42 | 4.4 |
| | 16 54 | 2.9 |
| | 23 06 | 5.7 |
| 17 Sa | 06 12 | -0.9 |
| | 13 36 | 4.3 |
| | 17 30 | 3.1 |
| | 23 36 | 5.6 |
| 18 Su | 06 54 | -0.8 |
| | 14 18 | 4.2 |
| | 18 06 | 3.2 |
| 19 M | 00 06 | 5.4 |
| | 07 30 | -0.6 |
| | 15 06 | 4.2 |
| | 18 48 | 3.4 |
| 20 Tu | 00 42 | 5.2 |
| | 08 18 | -0.4 |
| | 16 00 | 4.2 |
| | 19 36 | 3.5 |
| 21 W | 01 18 | 4.9 |
| | 09 00 | -0.2 |
| | 16 48 | 4.2 |
| | 20 42 | 3.5 |
| 22 Th | 02 12 | 4.6 |
| | 09 48 | -0.1 |
| | 17 36 | 4.3 |
| | 22 06 | 3.4 |
| 23 F | 03 12 | 4.3 |
| | 10 36 | 0.2 |
| | 18 12 | 4.6 |
| | 23 24 | 3.0 |
| 24 Sa | 04 30 | 4.0 |
| | 11 24 | 0.4 |
| | 18 48 | 4.8 |
| 25 Su | 00 36 | 2.4 |
| | 05 48 | 3.8 |
| | 12 06 | 0.7 |
| | 19 18 | 5.1 |
| 26 M | 01 24 | 1.7 |
| | 07 18 | 3.8 |
| | 12 54 | 1.1 |
| | 19 48 | 5.4 |
| 27 Tu | 02 12 | 0.8 |
| | 08 30 | 3.9 |
| | 13 36 | 1.5 |
| | 20 12 | 5.7 |
| 28 W | 03 00 | 0.0 |
| | 09 36 | 4.0 |
| | 14 18 | 1.9 |
| | 20 48 | 6.1 |

## May (cont.)

| Day | Time h. m. | Ht. ft.* |
|---|---|---|
| 29 Th | 03 42 | -0.7 |
| | 10 36 | 4.2 |
| | 15 00 | 2.3 |
| | 21 18 | 6.3 |
| 30 F | 04 30 | -1.4 |
| | 11 36 | 4.4 |
| | 15 48 | 2.6 |
| | 22 00 | 6.5 |
| 31 Sa | 05 12 | -1.8 |
| | 12 30 | 4.5 |
| | 16 36 | 2.9 |
| | 22 42 | 6.6 |

### JUNE

| Day | Time h. m. | Ht. ft. |
|---|---|---|
| 1 Su | 06 06 | -2.0 |
| | 13 24 | 4.6 |
| | 17 24 | 3.1 |
| | 23 30 | 6.6 |
| 2 M | 06 54 | -2.0 |
| | 14 18 | 4.7 |
| | 18 18 | 3.2 |
| 3 Tu | 00 18 | 6.3 |
| | 07 48 | -1.8 |
| | 15 12 | 4.8 |
| | 19 24 | 3.3 |
| 4 W | 01 18 | 5.9 |
| | 08 42 | -1.4 |
| | 16 06 | 4.9 |
| | 20 36 | 3.2 |
| 5 Th | 02 24 | 5.4 |
| | 09 36 | -0.9 |
| | 16 54 | 5.1 |
| | 22 12 | 2.9 |
| 6 F | 03 36 | 4.8 |
| | 10 30 | -0.3 |
| | 17 48 | 5.3 |
| | 23 36 | 2.3 |
| 7 Sa | 05 00 | 4.3 |
| | 11 18 | 0.3 |
| | 18 30 | 5.5 |
| 8 Su | 00 48 | 1.6 |
| | 06 30 | 4.0 |
| | 12 12 | 1.0 |
| | 19 12 | 5.7 |
| 9 M | 01 48 | 0.9 |
| | 07 54 | 3.9 |
| | 13 00 | 1.6 |
| | 19 48 | 5.9 |
| 10 Tu | 02 42 | 0.2 |
| | 09 12 | 4.0 |
| | 13 48 | 2.2 |
| | 20 24 | 6.0 |
| 11 W | 03 24 | -0.3 |
| | 10 12 | 4.1 |
| | 14 30 | 2.6 |
| | 21 00 | 6.0 |
| 12 Th | 04 12 | -0.7 |
| | 11 06 | 4.3 |
| | 15 12 | 2.9 |
| | 21 30 | 6.0 |
| 13 F | 04 48 | -0.9 |
| | 11 54 | 4.3 |
| | 15 48 | 3.2 |
| | 22 06 | 5.9 |
| 14 Sa | 05 30 | -0.9 |
| | 12 42 | 4.4 |
| | 16 30 | 3.3 |
| | 22 42 | 5.8 |
| 15 Su | 06 00 | -0.9 |
| | 13 24 | 4.4 |
| | 17 06 | 3.4 |
| | 23 12 | 5.7 |
| 16 M | 06 36 | -0.8 |
| | 14 06 | 4.4 |
| | 17 42 | 3.4 |
| | 23 42 | 5.6 |
| 17 Tu | 07 12 | -0.7 |
| | 14 42 | 4.4 |
| | 18 30 | 3.4 |
| 18 W | 00 12 | 5.4 |
| | 07 48 | -0.6 |
| | 15 18 | 4.4 |
| | 19 18 | 3.4 |

## June (cont.) / July

| Day | Time h. m. | Ht. ft. |
|---|---|---|
| 19 Th | 01 00 | 5.1 |
| | 08 24 | -0.3 |
| | 16 00 | 4.5 |
| | 20 18 | 3.3 |
| 20 F | 01 48 | 4.8 |
| | 09 00 | 0.0 |
| | 16 30 | 4.7 |
| | 21 24 | 3.1 |
| 21 Sa | 02 36 | 4.4 |
| | 09 36 | 0.4 |
| | 17 06 | 4.9 |
| | 22 42 | 2.6 |
| 22 Su | 03 54 | 3.9 |
| | 10 18 | 0.8 |
| | 17 36 | 5.1 |
| | 23 48 | 2.0 |
| 23 M | 05 24 | 3.6 |
| | 11 06 | 1.3 |
| | 18 06 | 5.4 |
| 24 Tu | 00 48 | 1.2 |
| | 07 00 | 3.5 |
| | 11 54 | 1.8 |
| | 18 42 | 5.8 |
| 25 W | 01 48 | 0.4 |
| | 08 30 | 3.6 |
| | 12 42 | 2.3 |
| | 19 18 | 6.1 |
| 26 Th | 02 36 | -0.4 |
| | 09 42 | 3.9 |
| | 13 36 | 2.7 |
| | 20 00 | 6.4 |
| 27 F | 03 24 | -1.1 |
| | 10 42 | 4.2 |
| | 14 30 | 2.9 |
| | 20 54 | 6.7 |
| 28 Sa | 04 18 | -1.6 |
| | 11 30 | 4.5 |
| | 15 30 | 3.1 |
| | 21 42 | 6.9 |
| 29 Su | 05 06 | -1.9 |
| | 12 24 | 4.7 |
| | 16 24 | 3.1 |
| | 22 30 | 6.9 |
| 30 M | 05 54 | -2.0 |
| | 13 06 | 4.9 |
| | 17 18 | 3.1 |
| | 23 24 | 6.8 |

### JULY

| Day | Time h. m. | Ht. ft. |
|---|---|---|
| 1 Tu | 06 42 | -1.9 |
| | 13 54 | 5.0 |
| | 18 18 | 3.0 |
| 2 W | 00 18 | 6.4 |
| | 07 30 | -1.6 |
| | 14 36 | 5.2 |
| | 19 24 | 2.9 |
| 3 Th | 01 12 | 5.9 |
| | 08 12 | -1.1 |
| | 15 24 | 5.4 |
| | 20 36 | 2.6 |
| 4 F | 02 18 | 5.3 |
| | 09 00 | -0.4 |
| | 16 06 | 5.5 |
| | 21 48 | 2.3 |
| 5 Sa | 03 24 | 4.6 |
| | 09 48 | 0.4 |
| | 16 48 | 5.7 |
| | 23 12 | 1.8 |
| 6 Su | 04 48 | 4.0 |
| | 10 30 | 1.2 |
| | 17 30 | 5.8 |
| 7 M | 00 24 | 1.2 |
| | 06 24 | 3.7 |
| | 11 24 | 1.9 |
| | 18 18 | 5.8 |
| 8 Tu | 02 24 | 0.6 |
| | 08 00 | 3.7 |
| | 12 12 | 2.5 |
| | 19 00 | 5.9 |
| 9 W | 02 18 | 0.1 |
| | 07 12 | 3.9 |
| | 13 06 | 2.9 |
| | 19 48 | 5.9 |

## July (cont.)

| Day | Time h. m. | Ht. ft. |
|---|---|---|
| 10 Th | 03 06 | -0.3 |
| | 10 12 | 4.1 |
| | 14 00 | 3.2 |
| | 20 30 | 5.9 |
| 11 F | 03 48 | -0.5 |
| | 11 00 | 4.3 |
| | 14 48 | 3.3 |
| | 21 12 | 5.9 |
| 12 Sa | 04 30 | -0.7 |
| | 11 42 | 4.4 |
| | 15 36 | 3.4 |
| | 21 48 | 5.9 |
| 13 Su | 05 06 | -0.8 |
| | 12 18 | 4.5 |
| | 16 12 | 3.4 |
| | 22 30 | 5.9 |
| 14 M | 05 42 | -0.8 |
| | 12 54 | 4.6 |
| | 16 54 | 3.3 |
| | 23 00 | 5.9 |
| 15 Tu | 06 12 | -0.7 |
| | 13 30 | 4.6 |
| | 17 30 | 3.3 |
| | 23 30 | 5.8 |
| 16 W | 06 42 | -0.6 |
| | 14 00 | 4.7 |
| | 18 12 | 3.1 |
| 17 Th | 00 12 | 5.5 |
| | 07 12 | -0.4 |
| | 14 30 | 4.7 |
| | 19 00 | 3.0 |
| 18 F | 00 48 | 5. |
| | 07 42 | -0.2 |
| | 14 54 | 4.8 |
| | 19 54 | 2.8 |
| 19 Sa | 01 36 | 4.8 |
| | 08 12 | 0.4 |
| | 15 24 | 5.0 |
| | 20 54 | 2.4 |
| 20 Su | 02 30 | 4.3 |
| | 08 48 | 0.9 |
| | 15 48 | 5.2 |
| | 22 00 | 2.0 |
| 21 M | 03 42 | 3.9 |
| | 09 24 | 1.5 |
| | 16 18 | 5.4 |
| | 23 12 | 1.4 |
| 22 Tu | 05 12 | 3.5 |
| | 10 06 | 2.1 |
| | 17 00 | 5.7 |
| 23 W | 00 18 | 0.8 |
| | 07 00 | 3.4 |
| | 11 00 | 2.6 |
| | 17 42 | 6.0 |
| 24 Th | 01 18 | 0.1 |
| | 08 30 | 3.7 |
| | 12 06 | 3.0 |
| | 18 42 | 6.2 |
| 25 F | 02 18 | -0.6 |
| | 09 36 | 4.0 |
| | 13 18 | 3.2 |
| | 19 36 | 6.5 |
| 26 Sa | 03 12 | -1.1 |
| | 10 30 | 4.4 |
| | 14 18 | 3.2 |
| | 20 36 | 6.7 |
| 27 Su | 04 00 | -1.5 |
| | 11 18 | 4.7 |
| | 15 18 | 3.1 |
| | 21 36 | 6.9 |
| 28 M | 04 48 | -1.7 |
| | 12 00 | 4.9 |
| | 16 18 | 2.9 |
| | 22 30 | 6.9 |
| 29 Tu | 05 36 | -1.7 |
| | 12 36 | 5.2 |
| | 17 18 | 2.6 |
| | 23 24 | 6.7 |
| 30 W | 06 18 | -1.4 |
| | 13 18 | 5.4 |
| | 18 12 | 2.4 |

## July (cont.) / August

| Day | Time h. m. | Ht. ft. |
|---|---|---|
| 31 Th | 00 18 | 6.3 |
| | 07 00 | -0.9 |
| | 13 54 | 5.6 |
| | 19 12 | 2.1 |

### AUGUST

| Day | Time h. m. | Ht. ft. |
|---|---|---|
| 1 F | 01 12 | 5.7 |
| | 07 42 | -0.2 |
| | 14 30 | 5.7 |
| | 20 12 | 1.8 |
| 2 Sa | 02 12 | 5.1 |
| | 08 18 | 0.5 |
| | 15 12 | 5.8 |
| | 21 24 | 1.5 |
| 3 Su | 03 24 | 4.4 |
| | 09 00 | 1.3 |
| | 15 48 | 5.8 |
| | 22 30 | 1.2 |
| 4 M | 04 42 | 3.9 |
| | 09 42 | 2.0 |
| | 16 30 | 5.7 |
| | 23 42 | 0.9 |
| 5 Tu | 06 12 | 3.7 |
| | 10 30 | 2.7 |
| | 17 24 | 5.6 |
| 6 W | 00 48 | 0.5 |
| | 07 42 | 3.8 |
| | 11 30 | 3.1 |
| | 18 18 | 5.6 |
| 7 Th | 01 48 | 0.2 |
| | 09 00 | 4.0 |
| | 12 42 | 3.3 |
| | 19 12 | 5.6 |
| 8 F | 02 42 | 0.0 |
| | 09 54 | 4.3 |
| | 13 42 | 3.4 |
| | 20 06 | 5.7 |
| 9 Sa | 03 30 | -0.2 |
| | 10 36 | 4.5 |
| | 14 42 | 3.3 |
| | 20 54 | 5.8 |
| 10 Su | 04 06 | -0.4 |
| | 11 12 | 4.6 |
| | 15 24 | 3.2 |
| | 21 12 | 5.9 |
| 11 M | 04 42 | -0.5 |
| | 11 42 | 4.6 |
| | 16 00 | 3.1 |
| | 22 12 | 5.9 |
| 12 Tu | 05 12 | -0.5 |
| | 12 12 | 4.8 |
| | 16 42 | 2.9 |
| | 22 48 | 5.8 |
| 13 W | 05 36 | -0.4 |
| | 12 36 | 4.9 |
| | 17 18 | 2.7 |
| | 23 24 | 5.7 |
| 14 Th | 06 06 | -0.2 |
| | 13 06 | 4.9 |
| | 18 00 | 2.4 |
| 15 F | 00 06 | 5.5 |
| | 06 30 | 0.1 |
| | 13 30 | 5.0 |
| | 18 42 | 2.1 |
| 16 Sa | 00 48 | 5.1 |
| | 07 00 | 0.6 |
| | 13 48 | 5.2 |
| | 19 30 | 1.8 |
| 17 Su | 01 36 | 4.7 |
| | 07 30 | 1.1 |
| | 14 12 | 5.3 |
| | 20 24 | 1.4 |
| 18 M | 02 30 | 4.2 |
| | 08 00 | 1.7 |
| | 14 42 | 5.5 |
| | 21 24 | 1.1 |
| 19 Tu | 03 48 | 3.8 |
| | 08 42 | 2.2 |
| | 15 18 | 5.7 |
| | 22 30 | 0.7 |
| 20 W | 05 24 | 3.6 |
| | 09 24 | 2.8 |
| | 16 06 | 5.8 |
| | 23 48 | 0.3 |

## August (cont.) / September

| Day | Time h. m. | Ht. ft. |
|---|---|---|
| 21 Th | 07 06 | 3.6 |
| | 10 24 | 3.2 |
| | 17 00 | 5.9 |
| 22 F | 01 00 | -0.1 |
| | 08 30 | 3.9 |
| | 11 54 | 3.4 |
| | 18 18 | 6.1 |
| 23 Sa | 02 00 | -0.6 |
| | 09 30 | 4.3 |
| | 13 12 | 3.3 |
| | 19 30 | 6.3 |
| 24 Su | 02 54 | -0.9 |
| | 10 06 | 4.6 |
| | 14 18 | 3.1 |
| | 20 36 | 6.5 |
| 25 M | 03 42 | -1.1 |
| | 10 48 | 5.0 |
| | 15 24 | 2.7 |
| | 21 36 | 6.6 |
| 26 Tu | 04 30 | -1.1 |
| | 11 24 | 5.3 |
| | 16 18 | 2.2 |
| | 22 30 | 6.5 |
| 27 W | 05 12 | -0.9 |
| | 12 00 | 5.5 |
| | 17 12 | 1.8 |
| | 23 24 | 6.3 |
| 28 Th | 05 48 | -0.4 |
| | 12 30 | 5.7 |
| | 18 00 | 1.3 |
| 29 F | 06 24 | 0.2 |
| | 13 06 | 5.8 |
| | 18 54 | 1.0 |
| 30 Sa | 01 12 | 5.3 |
| | 07 00 | 0.8 |
| | 13 36 | 5.9 |
| | 19 48 | 0.8 |
| 31 Su | 01 12 | 4.8 |
| | 07 36 | 1.5 |
| | 14 12 | 5.8 |
| | 20 42 | 0.7 |

### SEPTEMBER

| Day | Time h. m. | Ht. ft. |
|---|---|---|
| 1 M | 03 18 | 4.3 |
| | 08 12 | 2.2 |
| | 14 48 | 5.6 |
| | 21 48 | 0.6 |
| 2 Tu | 04 36 | 4.0 |
| | 09 00 | 2.8 |
| | 15 36 | 5.5 |
| | 22 54 | 0.6 |
| 3 W | 06 00 | 3.9 |
| | 09 54 | 3.2 |
| | 16 30 | 5.3 |
| 4 Th | 00 06 | 0.6 |
| | 07 00 | 4.0 |
| | 11 12 | 3.4 |
| | 17 30 | 5.2 |
| 5 F | 01 12 | 0.4 |
| | 08 12 | 4.2 |
| | 12 36 | 3.5 |
| | 18 42 | 5.2 |
| 6 Sa | 02 06 | 0.3 |
| | 09 18 | 4.4 |
| | 13 36 | 3.3 |
| | 19 42 | 5.3 |
| 7 Su | 03 00 | 0.1 |
| | 09 54 | 4.6 |
| | 14 30 | 3.1 |
| | 20 30 | 5.4 |
| 8 M | 03 24 | 0.0 |
| | 10 24 | 4.8 |
| | 15 12 | 2.8 |
| | 21 18 | 5.5 |
| 9 Tu | 03 48 | -0.1 |
| | 10 54 | 4.9 |
| | 15 48 | 2.5 |
| | 22 00 | 5.6 |
| 10 W | 04 30 | 0.0 |
| | 11 18 | 5.0 |
| | 16 24 | 2.1 |
| | 23 48 | 0.3 |

## September (cont.) / October

| Day | Time h. m. | Ht. ft. |
|---|---|---|
| 11 Th | 05 00 | 0.2 |
| | 11 42 | 5.1 |
| | 17 06 | 1.7 |
| | 23 18 | 5.4 |
| 12 F | 05 24 | 0.5 |
| | 12 06 | 5.3 |
| | 17 42 | 1.3 |
| 13 Sa | 00 00 | 5.2 |
| | 05 54 | 0.9 |
| | 12 24 | 5.4 |
| | 18 24 | 0.9 |
| 14 Su | 00 48 | 4.9 |
| | 06 24 | 1.4 |
| | 12 48 | 5.5 |
| | 19 12 | 0.6 |
| 15 M | 01 42 | 4.5 |
| | 06 54 | 2.0 |
| | 13 12 | 5.7 |
| | 20 00 | 0.3 |
| 16 Tu | 02 42 | 4.2 |
| | 07 24 | 2.5 |
| | 13 42 | 5.8 |
| | 21 00 | 0.2 |
| 17 W | 04 00 | 3.9 |
| | 08 06 | 2.9 |
| | 14 30 | 5.8 |
| | 22 06 | 0.1 |
| 18 Th | 05 36 | 3.8 |
| | 09 06 | 3.3 |
| | 15 24 | 5.7 |
| | 23 18 | -0.1 |
| 19 F | 07 06 | 4.0 |
| | 10 30 | 3.5 |
| | 16 42 | 5.6 |
| 20 Sa | 00 36 | -0.3 |
| | 08 12 | 4.3 |
| | 12 06 | 3.5 |
| | 18 06 | 5.7 |
| 21 Su | 01 36 | -0.5 |
| | 08 54 | 4.7 |
| | 13 24 | 3.1 |
| | 19 24 | 5.8 |
| 22 M | 02 30 | -0.6 |
| | 09 30 | 5.0 |
| | 14 30 | 2.5 |
| | 20 36 | 5.9 |
| 23 Tu | 03 18 | -0.5 |
| | 10 06 | 5.3 |
| | 15 24 | 1.9 |
| | 21 36 | 5.9 |
| 24 W | 04 00 | -0.2 |
| | 10 42 | 5.6 |
| | 16 18 | 1.2 |
| | 22 30 | 5.8 |
| 25 Th | 04 36 | 0.2 |
| | 11 12 | 5.8 |
| | 17 06 | 0.7 |
| | 23 30 | 5.6 |
| 26 F | 05 12 | 0.7 |
| | 11 42 | 6.0 |
| | 17 48 | 0.3 |
| 27 Sa | 00 24 | 5.3 |
| | 05 48 | 1.3 |
| | 12 12 | 6.0 |
| | 18 36 | 0.0 |
| 28 Su | 01 18 | 4.9 |
| | 06 24 | 1.9 |
| | 12 42 | 5.9 |
| | 19 24 | -0.1 |
| 29 M | 02 12 | 4.6 |
| | 06 54 | 2.5 |
| | 13 18 | 5.8 |
| | 20 12 | 0.0 |
| 30 Tu | 03 12 | 4.3 |
| | 07 36 | 2.9 |
| | 13 54 | 5.5 |
| | 21 06 | 0.2 |

### OCTOBER

| Day | Time h. m. | Ht. ft. |
|---|---|---|
| 1 W | 04 30 | 4.1 |
| | 08 24 | 3.3 |
| | 14 36 | 5.2 |
| | 22 12 | 0.4 |

### October (cont.)

| Day | Time h. m. | Ht. ft. |
|---|---|---|
| 2 Th | 05 42 | 4.1 |
|  | 09 24 | 3.5 |
|  | 15 30 | 4.9 |
|  | 23 12 | 0.5 |
| 3 F | 06 54 | 4.2 |
|  | 10 54 | 3.6 |
|  | 16 42 | 4.8 |
| 4 Sa | 00 18 | 0.5 |
|  | 07 48 | 4.4 |
|  | 12 18 | 3.4 |
|  | 18 00 | 4.7 |
| 5 Su | 01 12 | 0.4 |
|  | 08 30 | 4.6 |
|  | 13 24 | 3.1 |
|  | 19 06 | 4.8 |
| 6 M | 01 54 | 0.3 |
|  | 09 06 | 4.8 |
|  | 14 12 | 2.7 |
|  | 20 06 | 4.9 |
| 7 Tu | 02 36 | 0.4 |
|  | 09 30 | 5.0 |
|  | 14 54 | 2.2 |
|  | 20 54 | 4.9 |
| 8 W | 03 06 | 0.4 |
|  | 10 00 | 5.2 |
|  | 15 30 | 1.7 |
|  | 21 42 | 5.0 |
| 9 Th | 03 36 | 0.7 |
|  | 10 18 | 5.3 |
|  | 16 06 | 1.2 |
|  | 22 30 | 5.0 |
| 10 F | 04 12 | 1.0 |
|  | 10 42 | 5.5 |
|  | 16 42 | 0.6 |
|  | 23 18 | 4.9 |
| 11 Sa | 04 42 | 1.4 |
|  | 11 06 | 5.7 |
|  | 17 24 | 0.1 |
| 12 Su | 00 06 | 4.8 |
|  | 05 12 | 1.8 |
|  | 11 24 | 5.8 |
|  | 18 06 | -0.3 |
| 13 M | 01 00 | 4.7 |
|  | 05 42 | 2.3 |
|  | 11 54 | 6.0 |
|  | 18 54 | -0.6 |
| 14 Tu | 01 54 | 4.5 |
|  | 06 2⸱ | 2.7 |
|  | 12 24 | 6.0 |
|  | 19 42 | -0.7 |
| 15 W | 03 00 | 4.3 |
|  | 07 00 | 3.1 |
|  | 13 06 | 6.0 |
|  | 20 42 | -0.6 |
| 16 Th | 04 18 | 4.2 |
|  | 07 48 | 3.4 |
|  | 14 00 | 5.8 |
|  | 21 48 | -0.6 |
| 17 F | 05 30 | 4.3 |
|  | 09 12 | 3.6 |
|  | 15 06 | 5.5 |
|  | 23 00 | -0.5 |
| 18 Sa | 06 36 | 4.5 |
|  | 10 48 | 3.5 |
|  | 16 30 | 5.3 |
| 19 Su | 00 06 | -0.4 |
|  | 07 30 | 4.8 |
|  | 12 24 | 3.1 |
|  | 18 00 | 5.1 |
| 20 M | 01 06 | -0.2 |
|  | 08 12 | 5.1 |
|  | 13 36 | 2.4 |
|  | 19 24 | 5.1 |

### October (cont.)

| Day | Time h. m. | Ht. ft. |
|---|---|---|
| 21 Tu | 01 54 | 0.0 |
|  | 08 48 | 5.5 |
|  | 14 30 | 1.7 |
|  | 20 36 | 5.1 |
| 22 W | 02 36 | 0.4 |
|  | 09 24 | 5.8 |
|  | 15 24 | 0.9 |
|  | 21 36 | 5.1 |
| 23 Th | 03 18 | 0.9 |
|  | 09 54 | 6.0 |
|  | 16 12 | 0.2 |
|  | 22 36 | 5.0 |
| 24 F | 04 00 | 1.4 |
|  | 10 24 | 6.1 |
|  | 16 54 | -0.3 |
|  | 23 36 | 4.9 |
| 25 Sa | 04 36 | 1.9 |
|  | 10 54 | 6.1 |
|  | 17 36 | -0.6 |
| 26 Su | 00 24 | 4.8 |
|  | 05 12 | 2.4 |
|  | 11 24 | 6.1 |
|  | 18 18 | -0.7 |
| 27 M | 01 24 | 4.6 |
|  | 05 42 | 2.8 |
|  | 11 54 | 5.9 |
|  | 19 00 | -0.6 |
| 28 Tu | 02 12 | 4.5 |
|  | 06 24 | 3.1 |
|  | 12 30 | 5.7 |
|  | 19 48 | -0.4 |
| 29 W | 03 06 | 4.3 |
|  | 07 00 | 3.4 |
|  | 13 06 | 5.4 |
|  | 20 30 | -0.2 |
| 30 Th | 04 06 | 4.3 |
|  | 07 54 | 3.5 |
|  | 13 48 | 5.1 |
|  | 21 24 | 0.0 |
| 31 F | 05 06 | 4.3 |
|  | 09 00 | 3.6 |
|  | 14 36 | 4.8 |
|  | 22 24 | 0.2 |

### NOVEMBER

| Day | Time h. m. | Ht. ft. |
|---|---|---|
| 1 Sa | 06 06 | 4.4 |
|  | 10 30 | 3.6 |
|  | 15 48 | 4.5 |
|  | 23 18 | 0.4 |
| 2 Su | 06 54 | 4.6 |
|  | 11 54 | 3.3 |
|  | 17 06 | 4.3 |
| 3 M | 00 06 | 0.5 |
|  | 07 30 | 4.8 |
|  | 12 54 | 2.9 |
|  | 18 18 | 4.2 |
| 4 Tu | 00 54 | 0.6 |
|  | 08 06 | 5.0 |
|  | 13 42 | 2.3 |
|  | 19 30 | 4.2 |
| 5 W | 01 30 | 0.8 |
|  | 08 30 | 5.3 |
|  | 14 30 | 1.6 |
|  | 20 30 | 4.3 |
| 6 Th | 02 12 | 1.1 |
|  | 08 54 | 5.5 |
|  | 15 06 | 0.9 |
|  | 21 30 | 4.4 |
| 7 F | 02 42 | 1.5 |
|  | 09 18 | 5.7 |
|  | 15 48 | 0.2 |
|  | 22 24 | 4.5 |

### November (cont.)

| Day | Time h. m. | Ht. ft. |
|---|---|---|
| 8 Sa | 03 24 | 1.8 |
|  | 09 42 | 5.9 |
|  | 16 24 | -0.4 |
|  | 23 18 | 4.6 |
| 9 Su | 04 00 | 2.2 |
|  | 10 12 | 6.2 |
|  | 17 06 | -0.9 |
| 10 M | 00 12 | 4.6 |
|  | 04 36 | 2.6 |
|  | 10 42 | 6.3 |
|  | 17 54 | -1.2 |
| 11 Tu | 01 06 | 4.6 |
|  | 05 18 | 2.9 |
|  | 11 18 | 6.4 |
|  | 18 42 | -1.4 |
| 12 W | 02 06 | 4.5 |
|  | 06 00 | 3.2 |
|  | 12 00 | 6.3 |
|  | 19 30 | -1.4 |
| 13 Th | 03 00 | 4.5 |
|  | 06 54 | 3.4 |
|  | 12 54 | 6.1 |
|  | 20 30 | -1.2 |
| 14 F | 04 06 | 4.6 |
|  | 07 54 | 3.6 |
|  | 13 48 | 5.8 |
|  | 21 30 | -0.9 |
| 15 Sa | 05 00 | 4.7 |
|  | 09 24 | 3.5 |
|  | 15 00 | 5.3 |
|  | 22 30 | -0.6 |
| 16 Su | 06 00 | 5.0 |
|  | 11 06 | 3.2 |
|  | 16 24 | 4.9 |
|  | 23 30 | -0.2 |
| 17 M | 06 42 | 5.3 |
|  | 12 24 | 2.5 |
|  | 17 54 | 4.5 |
| 18 Tu | 00 24 | 0.3 |
|  | 07 24 | 5.6 |
|  | 13 30 | 1.7 |
|  | 19 24 | 4.4 |
| 19 W | 01 12 | 0.8 |
|  | 08 00 | 5.9 |
|  | 14 30 | 0.8 |
|  | 20 36 | 4.4 |
| 20 Th | 02 00 | 1.4 |
|  | 08 36 | 6.1 |
|  | 15 18 | 0.1 |
|  | 21 48 | 4.5 |
| 21 F | 02 42 | 1.9 |
|  | 09 12 | 6.2 |
|  | 16 06 | -0.5 |
|  | 22 48 | 4.5 |
| 22 Sa | 03 24 | 2.4 |
|  | 09 42 | 6.2 |
|  | 16 42 | -0.8 |
|  | 23 42 | 4.6 |
| 23 Su | 04 00 | 2.8 |
|  | 10 18 | 6.2 |
|  | 17 24 | -1.0 |
| 24 M | 00 30 | 4.6 |
|  | 04 36 | 3.1 |
|  | 10 48 | 6.1 |
|  | 18 06 | -1.0 |
| 25 Tu | 01 18 | 4.5 |
|  | 05 18 | 3.3 |
|  | 11 24 | 5.9 |
|  | 18 42 | -0.9 |

### November (cont.)

| Day | Time h. m. | Ht. ft. |
|---|---|---|
| 26 W | 02 06 | 4.5 |
|  | 05 54 | 3.4 |
|  | 12 00 | 5.7 |
|  | 19 24 | -0.7 |
| 27 Th | 02 54 | 4.4 |
|  | 06 36 | 3.5 |
|  | 12 36 | 5.4 |
|  | 20 06 | -0.4 |
| 28 F | 03 42 | 4.4 |
|  | 07 30 | 3.6 |
|  | 13 18 | 5.1 |
|  | 20 48 | -0.2 |
| 29 Sa | 04 30 | 4.5 |
|  | 08 36 | 3.6 |
|  | 14 06 | 4.8 |
|  | 21 30 | 0.0 |
| 30 Su | 05 12 | 4.6 |
|  | 09 54 | 3.4 |
|  | 15 00 | 4.5 |
|  | 22 12 | 0.3 |

### DECEMBER

| Day | Time h. m. | Ht. ft. |
|---|---|---|
| 1 M | 05 48 | 4.8 |
|  | 11 06 | 3.1 |
|  | 16 12 | 4.1 |
|  | 22 54 | 0.6 |
| 2 Tu | 06 24 | 5.0 |
|  | 12 18 | 2.6 |
|  | 17 30 | 3.8 |
|  | 23 42 | 1.0 |
| 3 W | 06 54 | 5.2 |
|  | 13 12 | 1.9 |
|  | 18 54 | 3.7 |
| 4 Th | 00 30 | 1.4 |
|  | 07 24 | 5.5 |
|  | 14 00 | 1.1 |
|  | 20 18 | 3.8 |
| 5 F | 01 12 | 1.8 |
|  | 07 54 | 5.8 |
|  | 14 42 | 0.3 |
|  | 21 24 | 4.0 |
| 6 Sa | 01 54 | 2.2 |
|  | 08 24 | 6.1 |
|  | 15 24 | -0.4 |
|  | 22 24 | 4.2 |
| 7 Su | 02 36 | 2.6 |
|  | 09 00 | 6.3 |
|  | 16 12 | -1.0 |
|  | 23 18 | 4.4 |
| 8 M | 03 24 | 2.9 |
|  | 09 36 | 6.6 |
|  | 16 54 | -1.5 |
| 9 Tu | 00 12 | 4.5 |
|  | 04 12 | 3.1 |
|  | 10 18 | 6.7 |
|  | 17 42 | -1.7 |
| 10 W | 01 00 | 4.7 |
|  | 05 00 | 3.2 |
|  | 11 06 | 6.7 |
|  | 18 30 | -1.8 |
| 11 Th | 01 54 | 4.8 |
|  | 05 54 | 3.3 |
|  | 11 54 | 6.6 |
|  | 19 18 | -1.7 |
| 12 F | 02 42 | 4.9 |
|  | 06 54 | 3.3 |
|  | 12 48 | 6.2 |
|  | 20 12 | -1.4 |
| 13 Sa | 03 30 | 5.0 |
|  | 08 00 | 3.2 |
|  | 13 54 | 5.7 |
|  | 21 00 | -0.9 |

### December (cont.)

| Day | Time h. m. | Ht. ft. |
|---|---|---|
| 14 Su | 04 24 | 5.2 |
|  | 09 24 | 3.0 |
|  | 15 00 | 5.1 |
|  | 21 54 | -0.4 |
| 15 M | 05 06 | 5.4 |
|  | 10 54 | 2.5 |
|  | 16 18 | 4.5 |
|  | 22 48 | 0.3 |
| 16 Tu | 05 54 | 5.7 |
|  | 12 12 | 1.8 |
|  | 17 48 | 4.1 |
|  | 23 36 | 1.0 |
| 17 W | 06 36 | 5.9 |
|  | 13 18 | 1.0 |
|  | 19 24 | 3.9 |
| 18 Th | 00 30 | 1.7 |
|  | 07 18 | 6.0 |
|  | 14 12 | 0.3 |
|  | 20 48 | 4.0 |
| 19 F | 01 18 | 2.3 |
|  | 07 54 | 6.1 |
|  | 15 12 | -0.3 |
|  | 21 54 | 4.2 |
| 20 Sa | 02 06 | 2.8 |
|  | 08 36 | 6.2 |
|  | 15 54 | -0.7 |
|  | 22 54 | 4.4 |
| 21 Su | 02 54 | 3.1 |
|  | 09 12 | 6.2 |
|  | 16 36 | -0.9 |
|  | 23 42 | 4.5 |
| 22 M | 03 36 | 3.3 |
|  | 09 54 | 6.1 |
|  | 17 12 | -1.0 |
| 23 Tu | 00 24 | 4.5 |
|  | 04 18 | 3.4 |
|  | 10 30 | 6.0 |
|  | 17 48 | -1.0 |
| 24 W | 01 06 | 4.6 |
|  | 04 54 | 3.4 |
|  | 11 06 | 5.9 |
|  | 18 24 | -0.9 |
| 25 Th | 01 48 | 4.6 |
|  | 05 36 | 3.4 |
|  | 11 42 | 5.7 |
|  | 19 00 | -0.7 |
| 26 F | 02 24 | 4.6 |
|  | 06 18 | 3.4 |
|  | 12 18 | 5.5 |
|  | 19 36 | -0.5 |
| 27 Sa | 03 00 | 4.6 |
|  | 07 06 | 3.4 |
|  | 12 54 | 5.2 |
|  | 20 06 | -0.2 |
| 28 Su | 03 36 | 4.7 |
|  | 08 06 | 3.3 |
|  | 13 36 | 4.9 |
|  | 20 42 | 0.1 |
| 29 M | 04 06 | 4.8 |
|  | 09 06 | 3.0 |
|  | 14 24 | 4.4 |
|  | 21 18 | 0.5 |
| 30 Tu | 04 36 | 5.0 |
|  | 10 18 | 2.7 |
|  | 15 30 | 4.0 |
|  | 21 54 | 1.0 |
| 31 W | 05 12 | 5.2 |
|  | 11 24 | 2.1 |
|  | 16 54 | 3.6 |
|  | 22 36 | 1.5 |

## Harvest Moon and Hunter's Moon

The Harvest Moon, the full moon nearest to the Autumnal equinox, ushers in a period of several successive days when the moon rises soon after sunset. This phenomenon gives farmers in north temperate latitudes extra hours of light in which to harvest their crops before frost and winter come —hence the name. In 1969 it falls on Sept. 25.

The next full moon after Harvest Moon is called the Hunter's Moon, accompanied by a similar phenomenon but less marked.

# SPORTS OF 1968
## WORLD SERIES
### Tigers Defeat Cardinals in Seven Games
### Composite Box Score
## DETROIT TIGERS

| | G | AB | R | H | 2B | 3B | HR | RBI | BB | SO | Bat. Avg. | PO | A | E | Fldg. Avg. |
|---|---|---|---|---|---|---|---|---|---|---|---|---|---|---|---|
| Dick McAuliffe, 2b...... | 7 | 27 | 5 | 6 | 0 | 0 | 1 | 3 | 4 | 6 | .222 | 11 | 16 | 0 | 1.000 |
| Mickey Stanley, ss...... | 7 | 28 | 4 | 6 | 0 | 1 | 0 | 0 | 2 | 4 | .214 | 15 | 16 | 2 | .939 |
| Al Kaline, rf........ | 7 | 29 | 6 | 11 | 2 | 0 | 2 | 8 | 0 | 7 | .379 | 18 | 0 | 0 | 1.000 |
| Norm Cash, 1b....... | 7 | 26 | 5 | 10 | 0 | 0 | 1 | 5 | 3 | 5 | .385 | 59 | 6 | 2 | .970 |
| Willie Horton, lf....... | 7 | 23 | 6 | 7 | 1 | 1 | 1 | 3 | 5 | 6 | .304 | 5 | 1 | 1 | .857 |
| Jim Northrup, cf....... | 7 | 28 | 6 | 7 | 0 | 1 | 2 | 8 | 1 | 5 | .250 | 22 | 0 | 2 | .917 |
| Bill Freehan, c......... | 7 | 24 | 0 | 2 | 1 | 0 | 0 | 2 | 4 | 8 | .083 | 45 | 6 | 2 | .962 |
| Don Wert, 3b......... | 6 | 17 | 1 | 2 | 0 | 0 | 0 | 2 | 6 | 5 | .118 | 5 | 14 | 0 | 1.000 |
| Ed Mathews.......... | 2 | 3 | 0 | 1 | 0 | 0 | 0 | 0 | 1 | 1 | .333 | 0 | 1 | 1 | .500 |
| Dick Tracewski, 3b...... | 2 | 0 | 1 | 0 | 0 | 0 | 0 | 0 | 0 | 0 | .000 | 0 | 0 | 0 | .000 |
| Dennis McLain, p....... | 3 | 6 | 0 | 0 | 0 | 0 | 0 | 0 | 0 | 4 | .000 | 0 | 3 | 1 | .750 |
| John Matchick ......... | 3 | 3 | 0 | 0 | 0 | 0 | 0 | 0 | 0 | 1 | .000 | 0 | 0 | 0 | .000 |
| Pat Dobson, p......... | 3 | 0 | 0 | 0 | 0 | 0 | 0 | 0 | 0 | 0 | .000 | 1 | 0 | 0 | 1.000 |
| Gates Brown......... | 1 | 1 | 0 | 0 | 0 | 0 | 0 | 0 | 0 | 0 | .000 | 0 | 0 | 0 | .000 |
| Don McMahon, p....... | 2 | 0 | 0 | 0 | 0 | 0 | .0 | 0 | 0 | 0 | .000 | 1 | 0 | 0 | 1.000 |
| Mickey Lolich, p....... | 3 | 12 | 2 | 3 | 0 | 0 | 1 | 2 | 1 | 5 | .250 | 1 | 4 | 0 | 1.000 |
| Ray Oyler, ss......... | 4 | 0 | 0 | 0 | 0 | 0 | 0 | 0 | 0 | 0 | .000 | 2 | 0 | 0 | 1.000 |
| Earl Wilson, p......... | 1 | 1 | 0 | 0 | 0 | 0 | 0 | 0 | 0 | 1 | .000 | 0 | 2 | 0 | 1.000 |
| Daryl Patterson, p....... | 2 | 0 | 0 | 0 | 0 | 0 | 0 | 0 | 0 | 0 | .000 | 0 | 1 | 0 | 1.000 |
| Wayne Comer........... | 1 | 1 | 0 | 1 | 0 | 0 | 0 | 0 | 0 | 0 | 1.000 | 0 | 0 | 0 | .000 |
| John Hiller, p......... | 2 | 0 | 0 | 0 | 0 | 0 | 0 | 0 | 0 | 0 | .000 | 1 | 0 | 0 | 1.000 |
| Jim Price............ | 2 | 2 | 0 | 0 | 0 | 0 | 0 | 0 | 0 | 0 | .000 | 0 | 0 | 0 | .000 |
| Joe Sparma, p.......... | 1 | 0 | 0 | 0 | 0 | 0 | 0 | 0 | 0 | 0 | .000 | 0 | 0 | 0 | .000 |
| Fred Lasher, p......... | 1 | 0 | 0 | 0 | 0 | 0 | 0 | 0 | 0 | 0 | .000 | 0 | 1 | 0 | 1.000 |
| Totals................ | 7 | 231 | 34 | 56 | 4 | 3 | 8 | 33 | 27 | 59 | .242 | 186 | 71 | 11 | .959 |

## ST. LOUIS CARDINALS

| | G | AB | R | H | 2B | 3B | HR | RBI | BB | SO | Bat. Avg. | PO | A | E | Fldg. Avg. |
|---|---|---|---|---|---|---|---|---|---|---|---|---|---|---|---|
| Lou Brock, lf............ | 7 | 28 | 6 | 13 | 3 | 1 | 2 | 5 | 3 | 4 | .464 | 13 | 0 | 1 | .929 |
| Curt Flood, cf.......... | 7 | 28 | 4 | 8 | 1 | 0 | 0 | 2 | 2 | 2 | .286 | 13 | 0 | 0 | 1.000 |
| Roger Maris, rf......... | 6 | 19 | 5 | 3 | 1 | 0 | 0 | 1 | 3 | 3 | .158 | 8 | 0 | 0 | 1.000 |
| Orlando Cepeda, 1b..... | 7 | 28 | 2 | 7 | 0 | 0 | 2 | 6 | 2 | 3 | .250 | 48 | 4 | 0 | 1.000 |
| Tim McCarver, c........ | 7 | 27 | 3 | 9 | 0 | 2 | 1 | 4 | 3 | 2 | .333 | 61 | 1 | 0 | 1.000 |
| Mike Shannon, 3b....... | 7 | 29 | 3 | 8 | 1 | 0 | 1 | 4 | 1 | 5 | .276 | 5 | 10 | 1 | .938 |
| Julian Javier, 2b........ | 7 | 27 | 1 | 9 | 1 | 0 | 0 | 3 | 3 | 4 | .333 | 15 | 14 | 0 | 1.000 |
| Dal Maxvill, ss......... | 1 | 22 | 1 | 0 | 0 | 0 | 0 | 0 | 3 | 5 | .000 | 15 | 14 | 0 | 1.000 |
| Bob Gibson, p........ | 3 | 8 | 2 | 1 | 0 | 0 | 1 | 2 | 1 | 2 | .125 | 2 | 0 | 0 | 1.000 |
| Ron Davis, rf.......... | 2 | 7 | 0 | 0 | 0 | 0 | 0 | 0 | 0 | 0 | .000 | 5 | 0 | 0 | 1.000 |
| Nelson Briles, p........ | 2 | 4 | 0 | 0 | 0 | 0 | 0 | 0 | 0 | 4 | .000 | 0 | 1 | 0 | 1.000 |
| Steve Carlton, p........ | 2 | 0 | 0 | 0 | 0 | 0 | 0 | 0 | 0 | 0 | .000 | 1 | 0 | 0 | 1.000 |
| Ron Willis, p.......... | 3 | 0 | 0 | 0 | 0 | 0 | 0 | 0 | 0 | 0 | .000 | 1 | 0 | 0 | .000 |
| Phil Gagliano......... | 2 | 2 | 0 | 1 | 0 | 0 | 0 | 0 | 0 | 1 | .500 | 0 | 0 | 0 | .000 |
| Joe Hoerner, p........ | 3 | 2 | 0 | 1 | 0 | 0 | 0 | 0 | 0 | 0 | .500 | 0 | 1 | 0 | 1.000 |
| Ray Washburn, p........ | 2 | 3 | 0 | 0 | 0 | 0 | 0 | 0 | 0 | 0 | .000 | 0 | 0 | 0 | .000 |
| Ed Spiezio........... | 1 | 1 | 0 | 1 | 0 | 0 | 0 | 0 | 0 | 0 | 1.000 | 0 | 0 | 0 | .000 |
| Dick Schofield ......... | 2 | 0 | 0 | 0 | 0 | 0 | 0 | 0 | 0 | 0 | .000 | 0 | 0 | 0 | .000 |
| Larry Jaster, p......... | 1 | 0 | 0 | 0 | 0 | 0 | 0 | 0 | 0 | 0 | .000 | 0 | 0 | 0 | .000 |
| Dick Hughes, p........ | 1 | 0 | 0 | 0 | 0 | 0 | 0 | 0 | 0 | 0 | .000 | 0 | 0 | 0 | .000 |
| Dave Ricketts.......... | 1 | 1 | 0 | 1 | 0 | 0 | 0 | 0 | 0 | 0 | 1.000 | 0 | 1 | 0 | 1.000 |
| Wayne Granger, p....... | 1 | 0 | 0 | 0 | 0 | 0 | 0 | 0 | 0 | 0 | .000 | 0 | 0 | 0 | .000 |
| Bob Tolan........... | 1 | 1 | 0 | 0 | 0 | 0 | 0 | 0 | 0 | 1 | .000 | 0 | 0 | 0 | .000 |
| John Edwards.......... | 1 | 1 | 0 | 0 | 0 | 0 | 0 | 0 | 0 | 1 | .000 | 0 | 0 | 0 | .000 |
| Mel Nelson, p......... | 1 | 0 | 0 | 0 | 0 | 0 | 0 | 0 | 0 | 0 | .000 | 0 | 0 | 0 | .000 |
| Totals................ | 7 | 239 | 27 | 61 | 7 | 3 | 7 | 27 | 21 | 40 | .255 | 186 | 48 | 2 | .991 |

## Pitching Summary
### DETROIT TIGERS

| | G | CG | IP | H | R | BB | SO | HB | WP | W | L | Pct. | ER | ERA |
|---|---|---|---|---|---|---|---|---|---|---|---|---|---|---|
| Dennis McLain .................. | 3 | 1 | 16⅔ | 18 | 8 | 4 | 13 | 0 | 0 | 1 | 2 | .333 | 6 | 3.18 |
| Pat Dobson ..................... | 3 | 0 | 4⅔ | 5 | 2 | 1 | 0 | 0 | 0 | 0 | 0 | .000 | 2 | 3.60 |
| Don McMahon ................. | 2 | 0 | 2 | 4 | 3 | 0 | 1 | 0 | 0 | 0 | 0 | .000 | 5 | 18.00 |
| Mickey Lolich .................. | 3 | 3 | 27 | 20 | 5 | 6 | 21 | 1 | 0 | 3 | 0 | 1.000 | 5 | 1.67 |
| Earl Wilson .................... | 1 | 0 | 4⅓ | 4 | 3 | 6 | 3 | 0 | 0 | 0 | 1 | .000 | 3 | 6.75 |
| Daryl Patterson ................ | 2 | 0 | 3 | 1 | 0 | 1 | 0 | 0 | 0 | 0 | 0 | .000 | 0 | 0.00 |
| John Hiller .................... | 2 | 0 | 2 | 6 | 4 | 3 | 1 | 0 | 0 | 0 | 0 | .000 | 4 | 18.00 |
| Fred Lasher ................... | 1 | 0 | 2 | 1 | 0 | 0 | 1 | 0 | 0 | 0 | 0 | .000 | 0 | 0.00 |
| Joe Sparma ..................... | 1 | 0 | ⅓ | 2 | 2 | 0 | 0 | 0 | 0 | 0 | 0 | .000 | 2 | 54.00 |
| Totals ..................... | 7 | 4 | 62 | 61 | 27 | 21 | 40 | 1 | 0 | 4 | 3 | .571 | 24 | 3.48 |

### ST. LOUIS CARDINALS

| | G | CG | IP | H | R | BB | SO | HB | WP | W | L | Pct. | ER | ERA |
|---|---|---|---|---|---|---|---|---|---|---|---|---|---|---|
| Bob Gibson ..................... | 3 | 3 | 27 | 18 | 5 | 4 | 35 | 0 | 0 | 2 | 1 | .667 | 5 | 1.67 |
| Nelson Briles ................... | 2 | 0 | 11⅓ | 13 | 7 | 4 | 7 | 0 | 0 | 0 | 1 | .000 | 7 | 5.73 |
| Steve Carlton ................... | 2 | 0 | 4 | 7 | 3 | 1 | 3 | 0 | 0 | 0 | 0 | .000 | 3 | 6.75 |
| Ron Willis ..................... | 3 | 0 | 4⅓ | 2 | 4 | 4 | 1 | 0 | 0 | 0 | 0 | .000 | 4 | 9.00 |
| Joe Hoerner .................... | 3 | 0 | 4⅔ | 5 | 4 | 5 | 3 | 0 | 0 | 1 | 1 | .000 | 2 | 3.85 |
| Ray Washburn ................... | 2 | 0 | 7⅓ | 7 | 8 | 7 | 6 | 0 | 0 | 1 | 1 | .500 | 8 | 9.82 |
| Larry Jaster ................... | 1 | 0 | 0 | 2 | 3 | 1 | 0 | 0 | 0 | 0 | 0 | .000 | 3 | * |
| Dick Hughes .................... | 1 | 0 | ⅓ | 2 | 0 | 0 | 0 | 0 | 0 | 0 | 0 | .000 | 0 | 0.00 |
| Wayne Granger .................. | 1 | 0 | 2 | 0 | 0 | 1 | 2 | 0 | 0 | 0 | 0 | .000 | 0 | 0.00 |
| Mel Nelson .................... | 1 | 0 | 1 | 0 | 0 | 0 | 1 | 0 | 0 | 0 | 0 | .000 | 0 | 0.00 |
| Totals ..................... | 7 | 3 | 62 | 56 | 34 | 27 | 59 | 3 | 0 | 3 | 4 | .429 | 32 | 4.65 |

*Gave up three earned runs in no innings pitched.

## Composite Score by Innings

| | | | | | | | | | | |
|---|---|---|---|---|---|---|---|---|---|---|
| Detroit ........................................... | 0 | 3 | 13 | 3 | 2 | 3 | 7 | 0 | 3—34 |
| St. Louis .......................................... | 5 | 0 | 2 | 5 | 4 | 1 | 4 | 4 | 2—27 |

## 1968 World Series Box Scores
### Lolich Notches Three Wins for Tigers

The Detroit Tigers became world baseball champions by defeating the St. Louis Cardinals in the 1968 World Series, 4 games to 3. Led by left-hander Mickey Lolich, who won 3 games in the series, the Tigers were forced to win the final three games after falling behind, 3 games to 1. Lolich, by starting, finishing and winning 3 games in one World Series duplicated the feat performed one year earlier by Bob Gibson of the Cardinals.

# FIRST GAME
### Busch Memorial Stadium, St. Louis, Oct. 2

## DETROIT TIGERS

| | AB | R | H | RBI | PO | A |
|---|---|---|---|---|---|---|
| McAuliffe, 2b | 4 | 0 | 0 | 0 | 3 | 0 |
| Stanley, ss | 4 | 0 | 2 | 0 | 3 | 2 |
| Kaline, rf | 4 | 0 | 1 | 0 | 2 | 0 |
| Cash, 1b | 4 | 0 | 0 | 0 | 7 | 1 |
| Horton, lf | 4 | 0 | 0 | 0 | 2 | 0 |
| Northrup, cf | 3 | 0 | 0 | 0 | 2 | 0 |
| Freehan, c | 2 | 0 | 0 | 0 | 4 | 1 |
| Wert, 3b | 2 | 0 | 1 | 0 | 0 | 0 |
| bMathews, ph | 1 | 0 | 0 | 0 | 0 | 0 |
| Tracewski, 3b | 0 | 0 | 0 | 0 | 0 | 0 |
| McLain, p | 1 | 0 | 0 | 0 | 0 | 2 |
| aMatchick, ph | 1 | 0 | 0 | 0 | 0 | 0 |
| Dobson, p | 0 | 0 | 0 | 0 | 0 | 0 |
| cBrown, ph | 1 | 0 | 0 | 0 | 0 | 0 |
| McMahon, p | 0 | 0 | 0 | 0 | 1 | 0 |
| **Totals** | 31 | 0 | 5 | 0 | 24 | 7 |

## ST. LOUIS CARDINALS

| | AB | R | H | RBI | PO | A |
|---|---|---|---|---|---|---|
| Brock, lf | 4 | 1 | 1 | 2 | 2 | 0 |
| Flood, cf | 4 | 0 | 1 | 0 | 1 | 0 |
| Maris, rf | 3 | 1 | 0 | 0 | 1 | 0 |
| Cepeda, 1b | 4 | 0 | 0 | 0 | 1 | 1 |
| McCarver, c | 3 | 1 | 1 | 0 | 17 | 1 |
| Shannon, 3b | 4 | 1 | 2 | 1 | 0 | 0 |
| Javier, 2b | 3 | 0 | 1 | 2 | 2 | 0 |
| Maxvill, ss | 2 | 0 | 0 | 0 | 2 | 0 |
| Gibson, p | 2 | 0 | 0 | 0 | 1 | 0 |
| **Totals** | 29 | 4 | 6 | 4 | 27 | 2 |

a-Grounded out for McLain in 6th.
b-Struck out for Wert in 8th.
c-Flied out for Dobson in 8th.

| | | | | | | |
|---|---|---|---|---|---|---|
| Detroit (A.) | 0 0 0 | 0 0 0 | 0 0 0—0 |
| St. Louis (N.) | 0 0 3 | 0 0 1 | 0 x—4 |

| | IP | H | R | ER | BB | SO |
|---|---|---|---|---|---|---|
| McLain (L.) | 5 | 3 | 3 | 2 | 3 | 3 |
| Dobson | 2 | 2 | 1 | 1 | 1 | 0 |
| McMahon | 1 | 1 | 0 | 0 | 0 | 0 |
| Gibson (W.) | 9 | 5 | 0 | 0 | 1 | 17 |

Errors—Freehan, Horton, Cash. Left on bases—Detroit 5, St. Louis 6. Two-base hit—Kaline. Three-base hit—McCarver. Home run—Brock. Stolen bases—Brock; Javier, Flood. Sacrifice—Gibson.

**How runs were scored**—Three in Cardinals fourth: Maris and McCarver walked. Shannon singled to left, scoring Maris. When Horton bobbled the ball, McCarver went to third and Shannon to second. Javier singled to right, scoring both runners.

One in Cardinal seventh: Brock homered.

**Umpires**—Gorman (N.) plate; Honochick (A.) first base; Landes (N.) second base; Kinnamon (A.) third base; Harvey (N.) left field; Haller (A.) right field. Time of game—2:29. Attendance—54,692.

# SECOND GAME
### Busch Memorial Stadium, St. Louis, Oct. 3

## DETROIT TIGERS

| | AB | R | H | RBI | PO | A |
|---|---|---|---|---|---|---|
| McAuliffe, 2b | 5 | 0 | 2 | 2 | 1 | 5 |
| Stanley, ss-cf | 5 | 0 | 1 | 0 | 0 | 3 |
| Kaline, rf | 5 | 2 | 2 | 0 | 2 | 0 |
| Cash, 1b | 5 | 2 | 3 | 1 | 11 | 0 |
| Horton, lf | 3 | 2 | 2 | 1 | 0 | 0 |
| Oyler, ss | 0 | 0 | 0 | 0 | 0 | 0 |
| Northrup, cf-lf | 5 | 1 | 1 | 0 | 4 | 0 |
| Freehan, c | 4 | 0 | 0 | 0 | 9 | 1 |
| Wert, 3b | 2 | 0 | 0 | 1 | 0 | 2 |
| Lolich, p | 4 | 1 | 2 | 2 | 0 | 0 |
| **Totals** | 38 | 8 | 13 | 7 | 27 | 11 |

## ST. LOUIS CARDINALS

| | AB | R | H | RBI | PO | A |
|---|---|---|---|---|---|---|
| Brock, lf | 3 | 1 | 1 | 0 | 0 | 0 |
| Javier, 2b | 4 | 0 | 2 | 0 | 2 | 2 |
| Flood, cf | 3 | 0 | 1 | 0 | 2 | 0 |
| Cepeda, 1b | 4 | 0 | 2 | 1 | 7 | 0 |
| Shannon, 3b | 4 | 0 | 0 | 0 | 1 | 3 |
| McCarver, c | 4 | 0 | 0 | 0 | 7 | 0 |
| Davis, rf | 4 | 0 | 0 | 0 | 4 | 0 |
| Maxvill, ss | 3 | 0 | 0 | 0 | 4 | 3 |
| Briles, p | 2 | 0 | 0 | 0 | 0 | 0 |
| Carlton, p | 0 | 0 | 0 | 0 | 0 | 0 |
| Willis, p | 0 | 0 | 0 | 0 | 0 | 0 |
| aGagliano, ph | 1 | 0 | 0 | 0 | 0 | 0 |
| Hoerner, p | 0 | 0 | 0 | 0 | 0 | 0 |
| **Totals** | 32 | 1 | 6 | 1 | 27 | 8 |

a-Grounded out for Willis in 8th.

| | | | | | | |
|---|---|---|---|---|---|---|
| Detroit (A.) | 0 1 1 | 0 0 3 | 1 0 2—8 |
| St. Louis (N.) | 0 0 0 | 0 0 1 | 0 0—1 |

| | IP | H | R | ER | BB | SO |
|---|---|---|---|---|---|---|
| Lolich (W.) | 9 | 6 | 1 | 1 | 2 | 9 |
| Briles (L.) | 5 | 7 | 4 | 4 | 1 | 2 |
| Carlton | 1 | 4 | 2 | 2 | 1 | 1 |
| Willis | 2 | 1 | 0 | 0 | 2 | 2 |
| Hoerner | 1 | 1 | 2 | 0 | 3 | 1 |

Errors—Stanley, Shannon. Double plays—Stanley, McAuliffe and Cash; Maxvill and Cepeda; Javier, Maxvill and Cepeda. Left on bases—Detroit 11, St. Louis 6. Home runs—Horton, Lolich, Cash. Stolen bases—Brock 2. Sacrifice—Oyler.

**How runs were scored**—One in Tiger second: Horton hit a home run.

One in Tiger third: Lolich hit a home run.

Three in Tiger sixth: Cash hit a home run. Horton and Northrup singled. Wert walked. McAuliffe singled to center, scoring Horton and Northrup.

One in Cardinal sixth: Brock walked and stole second. Flood had an infield hit, Brock taking third. Cepeda singled, scoring Brock.

One in Tiger seventh: Kaline and Cash singled. Horton walked. Northrup hit into a double play, as Kaline scored.

Two in Tiger ninth: Kaline singled. Cash was safe on Shannon's error. Kaline taking second. Oyler sacrificed the runners to second and third. With two out, Freehan was intentionally passed loading the bases. Wert walked, forcing in a run. Lolich walked, forcing in a run.

**Umpires**—Honochick (A.) plate; Landes (N.) first base; Kinnamon (A.) second base; Harvey (N.) third base; Haller (A.) left field foul line; Gorman (N.) right field foul line. Time of game—2:41. Attendance—54,692.

# THIRD GAME
### Tiger Stadium, Detroit, Oct. 5

## ST. LOUIS CARDINALS

| | AB | R | H | RBI | PO | A |
|---|---|---|---|---|---|---|
| Brock, lf | 4 | 1 | 3 | 0 | 5 | 0 |
| Flood, cf | 4 | 2 | 2 | 1 | 1 | 0 |
| Maris, rf | 3 | 2 | 1 | 0 | 2 | 0 |
| Cepeda, 1b | 5 | 1 | 1 | 3 | 10 | 0 |
| McCarver, c | 5 | 1 | 2 | 3 | 5 | 0 |
| Shannon, 3b | 4 | 0 | 2 | 0 | 0 | 1 |
| Javier, 2b | 4 | 0 | 1 | 0 | 2 | 5 |
| Maxvill, ss | 4 | 0 | 0 | 0 | 2 | 2 |
| Washburn, p | 3 | 0 | 0 | 0 | 0 | 1 |
| Hoerner, p | 2 | 0 | 1 | 0 | 0 | 0 |
| **Totals** | 38 | 7 | 13 | 7 | 27 | 9 |

## DETROIT TIGERS

| | AB | R | H | RBI | PO | A |
|---|---|---|---|---|---|---|
| McAuliffe, 2b | 4 | 2 | 2 | 1 | 0 | 1 |
| Stanley, ss | 3 | 0 | 0 | 0 | 0 | 2 |
| Kaline, rf | 4 | 1 | 1 | 2 | 1 | 0 |
| Cash, 1b | 3 | 0 | 0 | 0 | 8 | 1 |
| Horton, lf | 2 | 0 | 0 | 0 | 1 | 0 |

| | AB | R | H | RBI | PO | A |
|---|---|---|---|---|---|---|
| Northrup, cf | 4 | 0 | 0 | 0 | 7 | 0 |
| Freehan, c | 3 | 0 | 0 | 0 | 6 | 2 |
| Wert, 3b | 4 | 0 | 0 | 0 | 3 | 2 |
| Wilson, p | 1 | 0 | 0 | 0 | 0 | 2 |
| Dobson, p | 0 | 0 | 0 | 0 | 0 | 0 |
| aMatchik, ph | 1 | 0 | 0 | 0 | 0 | 0 |
| McMahon, p | 0 | 0 | 0 | 0 | 0 | 0 |
| Patterson, p | 0 | 0 | 0 | 0 | 0 | 0 |
| bComer, ph | 1 | 0 | 1 | 0 | 0 | 0 |
| Hiller, p | 0 | 0 | 0 | 0 | 1 | 0 |
| cPrice, ph | 1 | 0 | 0 | 0 | 0 | 0 |
| Totals | 30 | 3 | 4 | 3 | 27 | 10 |

a-Struck out for Dobson in 5th.
b-Singled for Patterson in 7th.
c-Flied out for Hiller in 9th.

| | | | | | | | | | |
|---|---|---|---|---|---|---|---|---|---|
| St. Louis (N) | 0 | 0 | 0 | 4 | 0 | 3 | 0—7 |
| Detroit (A) | 0 | 2 | 0 | 1 | 0 | 0 | 0—3 |

| | IP | H | R | ER | BB | SO |
|---|---|---|---|---|---|---|
| Washburn (W.) | 5⅓ | 3 | 3 | 3 | 4 | 3 |
| Hoerner | 3⅔ | 1 | 0 | 0 | 1 | 2 |
| Wilson (L.) | 4⅓ | 4 | 3 | 3 | 6 | 3 |
| Dobson | ⅔ | 2 | 1 | 1 | 0 | 0 |
| McMahon | 1 | 0 | 0 | 0 | 0 | 1 |
| Patterson | 1 | 0 | 0 | 0 | 0 | 0 |
| Hiller | 2 | 4 | 0 | 0 | 1 | 1 |

Double play—Freehan, Wert. Left on bases—St. Louis 11, Detroit 6. Doubles—Flood, Maris. Home runs—Kaline, McCarver, McAuliffe, Cepeda. Stolen bases—Brock 3.

**How runs were scored**—Two in Tiger third: Kaline hit a home run with a man on.

Four in Cardinal fifth: Brock singled and stole second. Flood doubled, scoring Brock. Maris walked. McCarver hit a three-run homer.

One in Tiger fifth: McAuliffe hit a home run.

Three in Cardinal seventh: Flood singled. Maris doubled, sending Flood to third. Cepeda hit a three-run homer.

Umpires—Landes (N.) plate; Kinnamon (A.) first base; Harvey (N.) second base; Haller (A.) third base; Gorman (N.) left field; Honochick (A.) right field. Time—3:17. Attendance—53,634.

# FOURTH GAME
### Tiger Stadium, Detroit, Oct. 6
## ST. LOUIS CARDINALS

| | AB | R | H | RBI | PO | A |
|---|---|---|---|---|---|---|
| Brock, lf | 5 | 2 | 3 | 4 | 2 | 0 |
| Flood, cf | 5 | 1 | 1 | 0 | 3 | 0 |
| Maris, rf | 5 | 1 | 0 | 1 | 0 | 0 |
| Cepeda, 1b | 4 | 0 | 1 | 0 | 9 | 1 |
| McCarver, c | 5 | 1 | 3 | 1 | 10 | 0 |
| Shannon, 3b | 5 | 1 | 2 | 2 | 1 | 0 |
| Javier, 2b | 4 | 1 | 2 | 0 | 0 | 2 |
| Maxvill, ss | 4 | 1 | 0 | 2 | 1 | 1 |
| Gibson, p | 3 | 2 | 1 | 2 | 0 | 0 |
| Totals | 40 | 10 | 13 | 10 | 27 | 4 |

## DETROIT TIGERS

| | AB | R | H | RBI | PO | A |
|---|---|---|---|---|---|---|
| McAuliffe, 2b | 4 | 0 | 0 | 0 | 2 | 4 |
| Stanley, ss | 4 | 0 | 0 | 0 | 3 | 3 |
| Kaline, rf | 4 | 0 | 2 | 0 | 1 | 0 |
| Cash, 1b | 4 | 0 | 1 | 0 | 10 | 1 |
| Horton, lf | 3 | 0 | 0 | 1 | 1 | 0 |
| Northrup, cf | 4 | 1 | 1 | 1 | 5 | 0 |
| Mathews, 3b | 2 | 0 | 1 | 0 | 0 | 1 |
| Freehan, c | 3 | 0 | 0 | 0 | 4 | 1 |
| McLain, p | 1 | 0 | 0 | 0 | 0 | 0 |
| Sparma, p | 0 | 0 | 0 | 0 | 0 | 0 |
| Patterson, p | 0 | 0 | 0 | 0 | 0 | 1 |
| aPrice, ph | 1 | 0 | 0 | 0 | 0 | 0 |
| Lasher, p | 0 | 0 | 0 | 0 | 0 | 1 |
| Hiller, p | 0 | 0 | 0 | 0 | 0 | 0 |
| Dobson, p | 0 | 0 | 0 | 0 | 1 | 0 |
| Totals | 31 | 1 | 5 | 1 | 27 | 12 |

a-Struck out for Patterson in 5th.
b-Flied out for Lasher in 7th.

| | | | | | | | | | | |
|---|---|---|---|---|---|---|---|---|---|---|
| St. Louis (N) | 2 | 0 | 2 | 2 | 0 | 0 | 4 | 0—10 |
| Detroit (A) | 0 | 0 | 0 | 1 | 0 | 0 | 0—1 |

| | IP | H | R | ER | BB | SO |
|---|---|---|---|---|---|---|
| Gibson (W.) | 9 | 5 | 1 | 1 | 2 | 10 |
| McLain (L.) | 2⅔ | 6 | 4 | 3 | 1 | 3 |
| Sparma | ⅓ | 2 | 2 | 2 | 0 | 0 |
| Patterson | 2 | 1 | 0 | 0 | 1 | 1 |
| Lasher | 2 | 1 | 0 | 0 | 1 | 1 |
| Hiller | 2 | 4 | 3 | 2 | 0 | 0 |
| Dobson | 2 | 1 | 0 | 0 | 0 | 0 |

Errors—McLain, Freehan, Mathews, Northrup. Double play—Cepeda, Maxvill. Left on base—St. Louis 7, Detroit 5. Doubles—Kaline, Shannon, Javier, Brock. Triples—McCarver, Brock. Home runs—Brock, Gibson, Northrup. Stolen base—Brock.

**How runs were scored**—Two in Cardinal first: Brock hit a home run. Maris was safe at first on an error. McCarver singled. Shannon singled, scoring Maris.

Two in Cardinal third: Flood singled. McCarver tripled, scoring Flood. Shannon doubled, scoring McCarver.

Two in Cardinal fourth: Gibson hit a home run. Brock tripled. Maris grounded out, scoring Brock.

One in Tiger fourth: Northrup hit a home run.

Four in Cardinal eighth: Shannon was safe at first on an error. Javier doubled, sending Shannon to third. Maxvill walked. Gibson walked, forcing in a run. Brock doubled, clearing the bases.

Umpires—Kinnamon (A.) plate; Harvey (N.) first base; Haller (A.) second base; Gorman (N.) third base; Honochick (A.) left field; Landes (N.) right field. Time—2:34. Attendance 53,634.

# FIFTH GAME
### Tiger Stadium, Detroit, Oct. 7
## ST. LOUIS CARDINALS

| | AB | R | H | RBI | PO | A |
|---|---|---|---|---|---|---|
| Brock, lf | 5 | 1 | 3 | 0 | 2 | 0 |
| Javier, 2b | 4 | 0 | 2 | 0 | 2 | 1 |
| Flood, cf | 0 | 0 | 0 | 0 | 1 | 0 |
| Cepeda, 1b | 4 | 1 | 1 | 1 | 3 | 0 |
| Shannon, 3b | 4 | 1 | 2 | 2 | 7 | 0 |
| McCarver, c | 4 | 0 | 0 | 1 | 1 | 2 |
| Davis, rf | 3 | 0 | 1 | 0 | 6 | 0 |
| aGagliano, ph | 1 | 0 | 0 | 0 | 1 | 0 |
| Maxvill, ss | 1 | 0 | 0 | 0 | 0 | 0 |
| bSpiezio, ph | 3 | 0 | 0 | 0 | 1 | 2 |
| cSchofield, pr | 1 | 0 | 1 | 0 | 0 | 0 |
| Briles, p | 0 | 0 | 0 | 0 | 0 | 0 |
| Hoerner, p | 2 | 0 | 0 | 0 | 0 | 2 |
| Willis, p | 0 | 0 | 0 | 0 | 0 | 0 |
| dMaris, ph | 1 | 0 | 0 | 0 | 0 | 0 |
| Totals | 35 | 3 | 9 | 3 | 24 | 7 |

## DETROIT TIGERS

| | AB | R | H | RBI | PO | A |
|---|---|---|---|---|---|---|
| McAuliffe, 2b | 4 | 1 | 1 | 0 | 2 | 3 |
| Stanley, ss, cf | 3 | 1 | 1 | 0 | 2 | 3 |
| Kaline, rf | 4 | 0 | 2 | 2 | 3 | 0 |
| Cash, 1b | 2 | 0 | 2 | 0 | 7 | 1 |
| Horton, lf | 4 | 1 | 1 | 0 | 1 | 1 |
| Oyler, ss | 0 | 0 | 0 | 0 | 1 | 0 |
| Northrup, cf, lf | 3 | 0 | 1 | 1 | 2 | 0 |
| Freehan, c | 4 | 0 | 0 | 0 | 9 | 1 |
| Wert, 3b | 3 | 0 | 0 | 0 | 0 | 0 |
| Lolich, p | 4 | 1 | 1 | 0 | 1 | 2 |
| Totals | 31 | 5 | 9 | 5 | 27 | 11 |

a-Flied out for Davis in 9th.
b-Singled for Maxvill in 9th.
c-Ran for Spiezio in 9th.
d-Struck out for Willis in 9th.

| | | | | | | | | | | |
|---|---|---|---|---|---|---|---|---|---|---|
| St. Louis (N) | 3 | 0 | 0 | 0 | 0 | 0 | 0 | 0 | 0—3 |
| Detroit (A) | 0 | 0 | 0 | 2 | 0 | 0 | 3 | 0 | x—5 |

| | IP | H | R | ER | BB | SO |
|---|---|---|---|---|---|---|
| Briles | 6⅓ | 6 | 3 | 3 | 3 | 5 |
| Hoerner (L.) | 0 | 3 | 2 | 2 | 1 | 0 |
| Willis | 1⅔ | 0 | 0 | 0 | 1 | 0 |
| Lolich (W.) | 9 | 9 | 3 | 3 | 1 | 7 |

Errors—Cash. Double play—Shannon, Javier, Cepeda. Left on base—St. Louis 7, Detroit 7. Doubles—Brock 2. Triples—Stanley, Horton. Home run—Cepeda. Stolen base—Cash. Sacrifice—Cash.

**How runs were scored**—Three in Cardinal first: Brock doubled. Flood singled, scoring Brock. Cepeda hit a home run.

Two in Tiger fourth: Stanley tripled and scored on Cash's sacrifice fly. Horton tripled. Northrup singled, scoring Horton.

Three in Tiger seventh: Lolich singled. McAuliffe singled. Stanley walked, filling the bases. Kaline singled, scoring Lolich and McAuliffe. Cash singled, scoring Stanley.

Umpires—Harvey (N.), plate; Haller (A.), first base; Gorman (N.) second base; Honochick (A.), third base; Landes (N.) left field; Kinnamon (A.) right field.

Time of game—2:43. Attendance—53,634.

## SIXTH GAME

Busch Memorial Stadium, St. Louis, Oct. 9

### DETROIT TIGERS

| | AB | R | H | RBI | PO | A |
|---|---|---|---|---|---|---|
| McAuliffe, 2b | 2 | 2 | 0 | 0 | 3 | 1 |
| Stanley, ss, cf | 5 | 2 | 2 | 2 | 1 | 1 |
| Kaline, rf | 4 | 3 | 3 | 4 | 7 | 0 |
| Cash, 1b | 4 | 2 | 3 | 5 | 5 | 0 |
| Horton, lf | 3 | 2 | 2 | 2 | 0 | 0 |
| Oyler, ss | 0 | 0 | 0 | 0 | 0 | 0 |
| Northrup, cf, lf | 5 | 1 | 2 | 4 | 1 | 0 |
| Freehan, c | 4 | 0 | 1 | 1 | 7 | 0 |
| Wert, 3b | 3 | 1 | 0 | 0 | 2 | 2 |
| McLain, p | 4 | 0 | 0 | 0 | 1 | 1 |
| Totals | 34 | 13 | 12 | 13 | 27 | 5 |

### ST. LOUIS CARDINALS

| | AB | R | H | RBI | PO | A |
|---|---|---|---|---|---|---|
| Brock, lf | 4 | 0 | 1 | 0 | 1 | 0 |
| Flood, cf | 4 | 0 | 0 | 0 | 0 | 0 |
| Maris, rf | 4 | 1 | 2 | 0 | 2 | 0 |
| Cepeda, 1b | 4 | 0 | 2 | 0 | 7 | 2 |
| McCarver, c | 4 | 0 | 1 | 0 | 8 | 0 |
| Shannon, 3b | 4 | 0 | 1 | 0 | 1 | 2 |
| Javier, 2b | 4 | 0 | 1 | 1 | 3 | 2 |
| Maxvill, ss | 4 | 0 | 0 | 0 | 4 | 5 |
| Washburn, p | 0 | 0 | 0 | 0 | 0 | 0 |
| Jaster, p | 0 | 0 | 0 | 0 | 0 | 0 |
| Willis, p | 0 | 0 | 0 | 0 | 0 | 0 |
| Hughes, p | 0 | 0 | 0 | 0 | 0 | 0 |
| aRicketts | 1 | 0 | 1 | 0 | 0 | 0 |
| Carlton, p | 0 | 0 | 0 | 0 | 1 | 1 |
| bTolan | 1 | 0 | 0 | 0 | 0 | 0 |
| Granger, p | 0 | 0 | 0 | 0 | 0 | 1 |
| cEdwards | 1 | 0 | 0 | 0 | 0 | 0 |
| Nelson, p | 0 | 0 | 0 | 0 | 0 | 0 |
| Totals | 35 | 1 | 9 | 1 | 27 | 13 |

a-Singled for Hughes in 3d.
b-Struck out for Carlton in 6th.
c-Struck out for Granger in 8th.

| | | | | | | |
|---|---|---|---|---|---|---|
| Detroit (A.) | 0 | 2 | 10 | 0 | 1 | 0 0 0—13 |
| St. Louis (N.) | 0 | 0 | 0 | 0 | 0 | 0 0 1— 1 |

| | IP | H | R | ER | BB | SO |
|---|---|---|---|---|---|---|
| McLain (W.) | 9 | 9 | 1 | 1 | 0 | 7 |
| Washburn (L.) | 2 | 4 | 5 | 5 | 3 | 3 |
| Jaster | 0 | 2 | 3 | 3 | 1 | 0 |
| Willis | 2⅓ | 1 | 4 | 4 | 2 | 0 |
| Hughes | ⅓ | 2 | 0 | 0 | 0 | 0 |
| Carlton | 3 | 3 | 1 | 1 | 0 | 2 |
| Granger | 3 | 3 | 1 | 1 | 0 | 1 |
| Nelson | 1 | 0 | 0 | 0 | 0 | 1 |

Errors—Brock, Stanley. Double plays—Maxvill, Javier, Cepeda; Stanley, McAuliffe, Cash; Maxvill, Javier, Cepeda; Granger, Maxvill, Cepeda. Left on bases—Detroit 5, St. Louis 7. Double—Horton. Home runs—Northrup, Kaline. Sacrifice—McLain.

How runs were scored—Two in Tiger second: Cash walked. Horton doubled, scoring Cash. Freehan singled, scoring Horton.

Ten in Tiger third: McAuliffe walked. Stanley singled. Kaline singled, scoring McAuliffe. Cash singled, scoring Stanley. Horton walked. Northrup hit a grand slam homer. Freehan walked. Wert was hit by a pitch. McAuliffe walked. Kaline singled, scoring two runs. Cash and Horton followed with run-scoring singles.

One in Tiger fifth: Kaline hit a home run.

One in Cardinal ninth: Maris and Cepeda singled. Javier singled, scoring Maris.

Umpires—Haller (A.), plate; Gorman (N.), first base; Honochick (A.), second base; Landes (N.), third base; Kinnamon (A.), left field; Harvey (N.), right field.

Time of game—2:26. Attendance—54,692.

## SEVENTH GAME

Busch Memorial Stadium, St. Louis, Oct. 10

### DETROIT TIGERS

| | AB | R | H | RBI | PO | A |
|---|---|---|---|---|---|---|
| McAuliffe, 2b | 4 | 0 | 0 | 0 | 1 | 3 |
| Stanley, ss, cf | 4 | 0 | 1 | 0 | 5 | 2 |
| Kaline, rf | 4 | 0 | 0 | 0 | 2 | 0 |
| Cash, 1b | 4 | 1 | 1 | 0 | 11 | 2 |
| Horton, lf | 4 | 1 | 2 | 0 | 0 | 0 |
| Oyler, ss | 0 | 0 | 0 | 0 | 1 | 0 |
| bTracewski | 0 | 1 | 0 | 0 | 0 | 0 |
| Northrup, cf, lf | 4 | 1 | 2 | 2 | 1 | 0 |
| Freehan, c | 4 | 0 | 1 | 1 | 6 | 0 |
| Wert, 3b | 3 | 0 | 1 | 1 | 0 | 6 |
| Lolich, p | 4 | 0 | 0 | 0 | 0 | 2 |
| Totals | 35 | 4 | 8 | 4 | 27 | 15 |

### ST. LOUIS CARDINALS

| | AB | R | H | RBI | PO | A |
|---|---|---|---|---|---|---|
| Brock, lf | 3 | 0 | 1 | 0 | 1 | 0 |
| Javier, 2b | 4 | 0 | 0 | 0 | 3 | 2 |
| Flood, cf | 4 | 0 | 2 | 0 | 3 | 0 |
| Cepeda, 1b | 3 | 0 | 0 | 0 | 7 | 0 |
| Shannon, 3b | 4 | 1 | 1 | 1 | 1 | 2 |
| McCarver, c | 3 | 0 | 1 | 0 | 8 | 0 |
| Maris, rf | 2 | 0 | 0 | 0 | 3 | 0 |
| Maxvill, ss | 2 | 0 | 0 | 0 | 0 | 1 |
| aGagliano | 1 | 0 | 0 | 0 | 0 | 0 |
| Schofield, ss | 0 | 0 | 0 | 0 | 1 | 0 |
| Gibson, p | 3 | 0 | 0 | 0 | 0 | 0 |
| Totals | 30 | 1 | 5 | 1 | 27 | 5 |

a-Grounded out for Maxvill in 8th.
b-Ran for Horton in 9th.

| | | | | | | |
|---|---|---|---|---|---|---|
| Detroit (A.) | 0 | 0 | 0 | 0 | 0 | 0 3 0 1—4 |
| St. Louis (N.) | 0 | 0 | 0 | 0 | 0 | 0 0 0 1—1 |

| | IP | H | R | ER | BB | SO |
|---|---|---|---|---|---|---|
| Lolich (W.) | 9 | 5 | 1 | 1 | 3 | 4 |
| Gibson (L.) | 9 | 8 | 4 | 4 | 1 | 8 |

Error—Northrup. Double play—Stanley, Cash. Left on bases—Detroit 5, St. Louis 5. Double—Freehan. Triple—Northrup. Home run—Shannon. Stolen base—Flood.

How runs were scored—Three in Tiger seventh: Cash and Horton singled. Northrup tripled, scoring Cash and Horton. Freehan doubled, scoring Northrup.

One in Tiger ninth: Horton singled. Northrup singled. Wert singled, scoring a run.

One in Cardinal ninth: Shannon hit a home run.

Umpires—Gorman (N.) plate; Honochick (A.) first base; Landes (N.) second base; Kinnamon (A.) third base; Harvey (N.) left field foul line; Haller (A.) right field foul line.

Time of game—2:07. Attendance—54,692.

## World Series Attendance and Receipts Since 1947

| Yr. | Clubs | G. | Atten. | Rcpts. | Yr. | Clubs | G. | Atten. | Rcpts. |
|---|---|---|---|---|---|---|---|---|---|
| 1947 | N. Y. (A.)-Brooklyn (N.) | 7 | 389,763 | 2,137,549 | 1958 | N. Y. (A.)-Milw. (N.) | 7 | 393,909 | 2,397,223 |
| 1948 | Clevel'd (A.)-Boston (N.) | 6 | 358,362 | 1,633,685 | 1959 | L. A. (N.)-Chicago (A) (*) | 6 | 420,784 | 2,626,973 |
| 1949 | N. Y. (A.)-Brooklyn (N.) | 5 | 236,710 | 1,129,627 | 1960 | Pitts (N)-N. Y. (A.) | 7 | 349,813 | 2,230,627 |
| 1950 | New York (A.)-Phila. (N.) | 4 | 196,009 | 953,669 | 1961 | N. Y. (A.)-Cincinnati(N). | 5 | 223,247 | 1,480,095 |
| 1951 | New York (A.)-N. Y. (N.) | 6 | 341,977 | 1,633,457 | 1962 | N. Y. (A.)-San Fran. (N.) | 7 | 376,864 | 2,878,891 |
| 1952 | N. Y. (A.)-Brooklyn (N.) | 7 | 340,906 | 1,622,753 | 1963 | L. A. (N)-N. Y. (A.) | 4 | 247,279 | 1,995,190 |
| 1953 | N. Y. (A.)-Brooklyn (N.) | 6 | 307,350 | 1,779,269 | 1964 | St. Louis (N)-N. Y. (A.). | 7 | 321,807 | 2,243,187 |
| 1954 | New York (A.)-Clev. (A.). | 4 | 251,507 | 1,566,203 | 1965 | L. A. (N)-Minn. (A). | 7 | 364,326 | 2,975,041 |
| 1955 | Brooklyn (N)-N.Y. (A.) | 7 | 362,310 | 2,337,515 | 1966 | L. A. (N.)-Balt. (A) (**). | 4 | 220,791 | 2,047,142 |
| 1956 | N. Y. (A.)-Brooklyn (N.) | 7 | 345,903 | 2,173,254 | 1967 | St. Louis (N)-Bos. (A.). | 7 | 304,085 | 2,350,607 |
| 1957 | Milw. (N.)-N. Y. (A.) | 7 | 394,712 | 2,475,978 | 1968 | St. Louis (N)-Det. (A.). | 7 | 379,670 | 3,018,113 |

Receipts since 1948 do not include fees for radio and television rights. This revenue customarily goes to players' pension fund. *Attendance record. **Receipts record for 4-game Series.

## How Players Shared 1968 World Series Money

From the player pool of the 1968 World Series (derived from receipts of the first 4 games only), members of the winning Detroit Tigers received $10,936.66 each and the losing St. Louis Cardinals got $7,078.71 each. Both winners' and losers' shares were far below the World Series records—$12,794 each for the winning Los Angeles Dodgers in 1963 and $8,189 each for the losing Dodgers in 1966.

# 17 Records Broken, 35 Tied in 1968 World Series

## INDIVIDUAL RECORDS BROKEN

Most home runs, pitcher as batter, total Series—2, Bob Gibson, St. Louis.

Fewest hits, Series, 0, Dal Maxvill, St. Louis, 22 at bats.

Most games won, consecutive, total Series—7, Gibson.

Most complete games won, consecutive, total Series—7, Gibson.

Most complete games, consecutive, total Series—8, Gibson.

Most strikeouts, game—17, Gibson, Oct. 2.

Most strikeouts, Series—35, Gibson.

Most putouts, catcher, Series—61, Tim McCarver, St. Louis.

Fewest putouts, first baseman, game—1, Orlando Cepeda, St. Louis, Oct. 2.

## INDIVIDUAL RECORDS TIED

Hitting home run, first Series at bat—Mickey Lolich, Detroit, Oct. 3.

Most hits, Series—13, Lou Brock, St. Louis.

Most total bases, Series—24, Brock.

Most long hits, Series—6, Lou Brock.

Hitting in each game—Brock.

Fewest runs scored, Series—0, Bill Freehan, Detroit.

Fewest bases on balls, Series—0, Al Kaline, Detroit.

Most stolen bases, total Series—14, Brock.

Most stolen bases, Series—7, Brock.

Most stolen bases, game—3, Brock, Oct. 5.

Home run, bases full, game—Jim Northrup, Detroit, Oct. 9.

Most RBI, inning—4, Northrup, 3d inning, Oct. 9.

Most hits, inning—2, Al Kaline and Norm Cash, Detroit, 3d inning, Oct. 9.

Most runs scored, inning—2, Dick McAuliffe, Mickey Stanley and Kaline, Detroit, 3d inning, Oct. 9.

Most at bats, inning—2, Stanley, Kaline, Cash and Northrup, Detroit, 3d inning, Oct. 9.

Most bases on balls, inning—2, McAuliffe, 3d inning, Oct. 9.

Most games won, Series—3, Mickey Lolich, Detroit.

Most games won, no losses, Series—3, Lolich.

Most games lost, Series—2, Dennis McLain, Detroit.

Most complete games, Series—3, Gibson, Lolich.

Most innings, one or more strikeouts, game, 9, Gibson, Oct. 2.

Most chances, catcher, game, 18, McCarver, Oct. 2.

Most chances, catcher, inning—3, McCarver, 2d inning and 9th inning, Oct. 2.

Most putouts, shortstop, inning—3, Stanley, 6th inning, Oct. 10.

## CLUB RECORDS BROKEN

Most strikeouts, club, game—17, Detroit, Oct. 2.

Most strikeouts, club, Series—59, Detroit.

Most strikeouts, both clubs, Series—99 (Detroit 59 vs. St. Louis 40).

Most batsmen hit by pitch club, game—3, Detroit by St. Louis, Oct. 9.

Fewest two-base hits, both clubs, Series—11 (Detroit 4 vs. St. Louis 7).

Fewest sacrifice hits, both clubs, Series—3 (St. Louis 1 vs. Detroit 2).

Fewest assists, club, Series—48, St. Louis.

Fewest assists, club, game—2, St. Louis, Oct. 2.

## CLUB RECORDS TIED

Most home runs, by pitchers as batters, Series—2 (St. Louis 1 vs. Detroit 1).

Most strikeouts, both clubs, inning—5 (Detroit 3 vs. St. Louis 2, 2d inning, Oct. 2).

Most pinch-hitters, club, inning—3, St. Louis, 9th inning, Oct. 7.

Most three-base hits, both clubs, Series—6 (Detroit 3 vs. St. Louis 3).

Fewest two-base hits, club, Series—4, Detroit.

Fewest stolen bases, club, Series—0, Detroit.

Fewest sacrifice hits, club, Series—1, St. Louis.

Most runs scored, inning—10, Detroit, 3d inning, Oct. 9.

Most batsmen facing pitcher, inning—15, Detroit, 3d inning, Oct. 9.

Most RBI, inning—10, Detroit, 3d inning, Oct. 9.

Most pitchers used, inning—4, St. Louis, 3d inning, Oct. 9.

# Baseball World Championships, 1903-1968

| Yr. | Winners | Won | Losers | Won | Yr. | Winners | Won | Losers | Won |
|---|---|---|---|---|---|---|---|---|---|
| 1903 | Boston, A. L... | 5 | Pittsb'gh, N. L. | 3 | 1936 | N. Y., A. L... | 4 | N. Y., N. L.... | 2 |
| 1904 | N. Y., N. L... | refused play | Boston., A. L. | | 1937 | N. Y., A. L... | 4 | N. Y., N. L.... | 1 |
| 1905 | N. Y., N. L... | 4 | Phila., A. L.... | 1 | 1938 | N. Y., A. L... | 4 | Chicago, N. L.. | 0 |
| 1906 | Chicago, A. L.. | 4 | Chicago, N. L.. | 2 | 1939 | N. Y., A. L... | 4 | Cincinnati, N.L. | 0 |
| 1907* | Chicago, N. L.. | 4 | Detroit, A. L... | 0 | 1940 | Cinc., N. L..... | 4 | Detroit, A. L... | 3 |
| 1908 | Chicago, N. L.. | 4 | Detroit, A. L... | 1 | 1941 | N. Y., A. L... | 4 | B'klyn, N. L... | 1 |
| 1909 | Pittsb'gh, N. L. | 4 | Detroit, A. L... | 3 | 1942 | St. Louis, N. L. | 4 | N. Y., A. L.... | 1 |
| 1910 | Phila., A. L... | 4 | Chicago, N. L.. | 1 | 1943 | N. Y., A. L... | 4 | St. Louis, N. L.. | 1 |
| 1911 | Phila., A. L... | 4 | N. Y., N. L.... | 2 | 1944 | St. Louis, N. L. | 4 | St. Louis A. L.. | 2 |
| 1912* | Boston, A. L... | 4 | N. Y., N. L.... | 3 | 1945 | Detroit, A. L... | 4 | Chicago, N. L.. | 3 |
| 1913 | Phila., A. L... | 4 | N. Y., N. L.... | 1 | 1946 | St. Louis, N. L. | 4 | Boston, A. L... | 3 |
| 1914 | Boston, N. L... | 4 | Phila., A. L... | 0 | 1947 | N. Y., A. L... | 4 | B'klyn, N. L... | 3 |
| 1915 | Boston, A. L... | 4 | Phila., N. L... | 1 | 1948 | Cleveland, A. L. | 4 | Boston, N. L... | 2 |
| 1916 | Boston, A. L... | 4 | B'klyn, N. L... | 1 | 1949 | N. Y., A. L... | 4 | B'klyn, N. L... | 1 |
| 1917 | Chicago, A. L.. | 4 | N. Y., N. L.... | 2 | 1950 | N. Y., A. L... | 4 | Phila., N. L... | 0 |
| 1918 | Boston, A. L... | 4 | Chicago, N. L.. | 2 | 1951 | N. Y., A. L... | 4 | N. Y., N. L.... | 2 |
| 1919 | Cincin., N. L... | 5 | Chicago, A. L.. | 3 | 1952 | N. Y., A. L... | 4 | B'klyn, N. L... | 3 |
| 1920 | Clevel'd, A. L.. | 5 | B'klyn, N. L... | 2 | 1953† | N. Y., A. L... | 4 | B'klyn, N. L... | 2 |
| 1921 | N. Y., N. L... | 5 | N. Y., A. L.... | 3 | 1954 | N. Y., N. L... | 4 | Cleve., A. L... | 0 |
| 1922* | N. Y., N. L... | 4 | N. Y., A. L.... | 0 | 1955 | B'klyn., N. L... | 4 | N. Y., A. L.... | 3 |
| 1923 | N. Y., A. L... | 4 | N. Y., N. L.... | 2 | 1956 | N. Y., A. L... | 4 | B'klyn, N. L... | 3 |
| 1924 | Wash., A. L... | 4 | N. Y., N. L.... | 3 | 1957 | Milw., N. L.... | 4 | N. Y., A. L.... | 3 |
| 1925 | Pittsb'gh, N. L. | 4 | Wash., A. L... | 3 | 1958 | N. Y., A. L... | 4 | Milw., N. L.... | 3 |
| 1926 | St. Louis, N. L.. | 4 | N. Y., A. L... | 3 | 1959 | LosAngeles,N.L. | 4 | Chicago, A. L.. | 2 |
| 1927 | N. Y., A. L... | 4 | Pitts., N. L.... | 0 | 1960 | Pittsb'gh, N. L. | 4 | N. Y., A. L.... | 3 |
| 1928 | N. Y., A. L... | 4 | St.Louis, N. L... | 0 | 1961 | N. Y., A. L... | 4 | Cincinnati. N.L. | 1 |
| 1929 | Phila., A. L... | 4 | Chicago, N. L.. | 1 | 1962 | N. Y., A. L... | 4 | San Fran., N. L. | 3 |
| 1930 | Phila., A. L... | 4 | St. Louis, N. L.. | 2 | 1963 | L. A., N. L..... | 4 | N. Y., A. L.... | 0 |
| 1931 | St. Louis N.L... | 4 | Phila., A. L... | 3 | 1964 | St. Louis, N. L. | 4 | N. Y., A. L.... | 3 |
| 1932 | N. Y., A. L... | 4 | Chicago, N. L.. | 0 | 1965 | L. A., N. L.... | 4 | Minn., A. L... | 3 |
| 1933 | N. Y., N. L... | 4 | Wash., A. L... | 1 | 1966 | Balt., A. L..... | 4 | L. A., N. L.... | 0 |
| 1934 | St. Louis, N. L.. | 4 | Detroit, A. L... | 3 | 1967 | St. Louis, N. L.. | 4 | Boston, A. L... | 3 |
| 1935 | Detroit, A. L... | 4 | Chicago, N. L.. | 2 | 1968 | Detroit, A. L... | 4 | St. Louis, N. L.. | 3 |

* One tie game. † First major league club to win five world championships in succession.

# ALL-TIME HOME RUN LEADERS

| Player | HR. | Player | HR. | Player | HR. |
|---|---|---|---|---|---|
| Babe Ruth | 714 | Ralph Kiner | 369 | Ken Boyer | 282 |
| Willie Mays | 587 | Joe DiMaggio | 361 | Ted Kluszewski | 279 |
| Mickey Mantle | 536 | John Mize | 359 | Rudy York | 277 |
| Jimmy Foxx | 534 | Yogi Berra | 358 | Roger Maris | 275 |
| Ted Williams | 521 | Joe Adcock | 336 | Willie McCovey | 268 |
| Ed Mathews | 512 | Hank Greenberg | 331 | Vic Wertz | 266 |
| Mel Ott | 511 | Roy Sievers | 318 | Norm Cash | 260 |
| Henry Aaron | 510 | Al Kaline | 314 | Bobby Thomson | 264 |
| Lou Gehrig | 493 | Al Simmons | 307 | Joe Gordon | 253 |
| Stan Musial | 475 | Rogers Hornsby | 302 | Larry Doby | 253 |
| Ernie Banks | 474 | Chuck Klein | 300 | Fred Williams | 251 |
| Frank Robinson | 418 | Robert Johnson | 288 | Leon Goslin | 248 |
| Duke Snider | 407 | Hank Sauer | 288 | Bob Allison | 247 |
| Harmon Killebrew | 397 | Del Ennis | 288 | Vernon Stephens | 247 |
| Rocco Colavito | 374 | Frank Thomas | 286 | Hack Wilson | 244 |
| Gil Hodges | 370 | Orlando Cepeda | 284 | | |

# Major League Pennant Winners, 1901-1968

## NATIONAL LEAGUE — AMERICAN LEAGUE

| Year | Winner | Won | Lost | Per Cent | Manager | Year | Winner | Won | Lost | Per Cent | Manager |
|---|---|---|---|---|---|---|---|---|---|---|---|
| 1901 | Pittsburgh | 90 | 49 | .647 | Clarke | 1901 | Chicago | 83 | 53 | .610 | Griffith |
| 1902 | Pittsburgh | 103 | 36 | .741 | Clarke | 1902 | Philadelphia | 83 | 53 | .610 | Mack |
| 1903 | Pittsburgh | 91 | 49 | .650 | Clarke | 1903 | Boston | 91 | 47 | .659 | J. J. Collins |
| 1904 | New York | 106 | 47 | .693 | McGraw | 1904 | Boston | 95 | 59 | .617 | Collins |
| 1905 | New York | 105 | 48 | .686 | McGraw | 1905 | Philadelphia | 92 | 56 | .622 | Mack |
| 1906 | Chicago | 116 | 36 | .763 | Chance | 1906 | Chicago | 93 | 58 | .616 | Jones |
| 1907 | Chicago | 107 | 45 | .704 | Chance | 1907 | Detroit | 92 | 58 | .613 | Jennings |
| 1908 | Chicago | 99 | 55 | .643 | Chance | 1908 | Detroit | 90 | 63 | .588 | Jennings |
| 1909 | Pittsburgh | 110 | 42 | .724 | Clarke | 1909 | Detroit | 98 | 54 | .645 | Jennings |
| 1910 | Chicago | 104 | 50 | .675 | Chance | 1910 | Philadelphia | 102 | 48 | .680 | Mack |
| 1911 | New York | 99 | 54 | .647 | McGraw | 1911 | Philadelphia | 101 | 50 | .669 | Mack |
| 1912 | New York | 103 | 48 | .682 | McGraw | 1912 | Boston | 105 | 47 | .691 | Stahl |
| 1913 | New York | 101 | 51 | .664 | McGraw | 1913 | Philadelphia | 96 | 57 | .627 | Mack |
| 1914 | Boston | 94 | 59 | .614 | Stallings | 1914 | Philadelphia | 99 | 53 | .651 | Mack |
| 1915 | Philadelphia | 90 | 62 | .592 | Moran | 1915 | Boston | 101 | 50 | .669 | Carrigan |
| 1916 | Brooklyn | 94 | 60 | .610 | Robinson | 1916 | Boston | 91 | 63 | .591 | Carrigan |
| 1917 | New York | 98 | 56 | .636 | McGraw | 1917 | Chicago | 100 | 54 | .649 | Rowland |
| 1918 | Chicago | 84 | 45 | .651 | Mitchell | 1918 | Boston | 75 | 51 | .595 | Barrow |
| 1919 | Cincinnati | 96 | 44 | .686 | Moran | 1919 | Chicago | 88 | 52 | .629 | Gleason |
| 1920 | Brooklyn | 93 | 60 | .604 | Robinson | 1920 | Cleveland | 98 | 56 | .636 | Speaker |
| 1921 | New York | 94 | 56 | .614 | McGraw | 1921 | New York | 98 | 55 | .641 | Huggins |
| 1922 | New York | 93 | 61 | .604 | McGraw | 1922 | New York | 94 | 60 | .610 | Huggins |
| 1923 | New York | 95 | 58 | .621 | McGraw | 1923 | New York | 98 | 54 | .645 | Huggins |
| 1924 | New York | 93 | 60 | .608 | McGraw | 1924 | Washington | 92 | 62 | .597 | Harris |
| 1925 | Pittsburgh | 95 | 58 | .621 | McKechnie | 1925 | Washington | 96 | 55 | .636 | Harris |
| 1926 | St. Louis | 89 | 65 | .578 | Hornsby | 1926 | New York | 91 | 63 | .591 | Huggins |
| 1927 | Pittsburgh | 94 | 60 | .610 | Bush | 1927 | New York | 110 | 44 | .714 | Huggins |
| 1928 | St. Louis | 95 | 59 | .617 | McKechnie | 1928 | New York | 101 | 53 | .656 | Huggins |
| 1929 | Chicago | 98 | 54 | .645 | McCarthy | 1929 | Philadelphia | 104 | 46 | .693 | Mack |
| 1930 | St. Louis | 92 | 62 | .597 | Street | 1930 | Philadelphia | 102 | 52 | .662 | Mack |
| 1931 | St. Louis | 101 | 53 | .656 | Street | 1931 | Philadelphia | 107 | 45 | .704 | Mack |
| 1932 | Chicago | 90 | 64 | .584 | Grimm | 1932 | New York | 107 | 47 | .695 | McCarthy |
| 1933 | New York | 91 | 61 | .599 | Terry | 1933 | Washington | 99 | 53 | .651 | Cronin |
| 1934 | St. Louis | 95 | 58 | .621 | Frisch | 1934 | Detroit | 101 | 53 | .656 | Cochrane |
| 1935 | Chicago | 100 | 54 | .649 | Grimm | 1935 | Detroit | 93 | 58 | .616 | Cochrane |
| 1936 | New York | 92 | 62 | .597 | Terry | 1936 | New York | 102 | 51 | .667 | McCarthy |
| 1937 | New York | 95 | 57 | .625 | Terry | 1937 | New York | 102 | 52 | .662 | McCarthy |
| 1938 | Chicago | 89 | 63 | .586 | Hartnett | 1938 | New York | 99 | 53 | .651 | McCarthy |
| 1939 | Cincinnati | 97 | 57 | .630 | McKechnie | 1939 | New York | 106 | 45 | .702 | McCarthy |
| 1940 | Cincinnati | 100 | 53 | .654 | McKechnie | 1940 | Detroit | 90 | 64 | .584 | Baker |
| 1941 | Brooklyn | 100 | 54 | .649 | Durocher | 1941 | New York | 101 | 53 | .656 | McCarthy |
| 1942 | St. Louis | 106 | 48 | .688 | Southworth | 1942 | New York | 103 | 51 | .669 | McCarthy |
| 1943 | St. Louis | 105 | 49 | .682 | Southworth | 1943 | New York | 98 | 56 | .636 | McCarthy |
| 1944 | St. Louis | 105 | 49 | .682 | Southworth | 1944 | St. Louis | 89 | 65 | .578 | Sewell |
| 1945 | Chicago | 98 | 56 | .636 | Grimm | 1945 | Detroit | 88 | 65 | .575 | O'Neill |
| 1946 | St. Louis | 98 | 58 | .628 | Dyer | 1946 | Boston | 104 | 50 | .675 | Cronin |
| 1947 | Brooklyn | 94 | 60 | .610 | Shotton | 1947 | New York | 97 | 57 | .630 | Harris |
| 1948 | Boston | 91 | 62 | .595 | Southworth | 1948 | Cleveland | 97 | 58 | .626 | Boudreau |
| 1949 | Brooklyn | 97 | 57 | .630 | Shotton | 1949 | New York | 97 | 57 | .630 | Stengel |
| 1950 | Philadelphia | 91 | 63 | .591 | Sawyer | 1950 | New York | 98 | 56 | .636 | Stengel |
| 1951 | New York | 98 | 59 | .624 | Durocher | 1951 | New York | 98 | 56 | .636 | Stengel |
| 1952 | Brooklyn | 96 | 57 | .627 | Dressen | 1952 | New York | 95 | 59 | .617 | Stengel |
| 1953 | Brooklyn | 105 | 49 | .682 | Dressen | 1953 | New York* | 99 | 52 | .656 | Stengel |
| 1954 | New York | 97 | 57 | .630 | Durocher | 1954 | Cleveland | 111 | 43 | .721 | Lopez |
| 1955 | Brooklyn | 98 | 55 | .641 | Alston | 1955 | New York | 96 | 58 | .623 | Stengel |
| 1956 | Brooklyn | 93 | 61 | .604 | Alston | 1956 | New York | 97 | 57 | .630 | Stengel |
| 1957 | Milwaukee | 95 | 59 | .617 | Haney | 1957 | New York | 98 | 56 | .636 | Stengel |
| 1958 | Milwaukee | 92 | 62 | .597 | Haney | 1958 | New York | 92 | 62 | .597 | Stengel |
| 1959 | Los Angeles | 88 | 68 | .564 | Alston | 1959 | Chicago | 94 | 60 | .610 | Lopez |
| 1960 | Pittsburgh | 95 | 59 | .617 | Murtaugh | 1960 | New York | 97 | 57 | .630 | Stengel |
| 1961 | Cincinnati | 93 | 61 | .604 | Hutchinson | 1961 | New York | 109 | 53 | .673 | Houk |
| 1962 | San Francisco | 103 | 62 | .624 | Dark | 1962 | New York | 96 | 66 | .593 | Houk |
| 1963 | Los Angeles | 99 | 63 | .611 | Alston | 1963 | New York | 104 | 57 | .646 | Houk |
| 1964 | St. Louis | 93 | 69 | .574 | Keane | 1964 | New York | 99 | 63 | .611 | Berra |
| 1965 | Los Angeles | 97 | 65 | .599 | Alston | 1965 | Minnesota | 102 | 60 | .630 | Mele |
| 1966 | Los Angeles | 95 | 67 | .586 | Alston | 1966 | Baltimore | 97 | 63 | .606 | Bauer |
| 1967 | St. Louis | 101 | 60 | .627 | Schoendienst | 1967 | Boston | 92 | 70 | .568 | Williams |
| 1968 | St. Louis | 97 | 65 | .599 | Schoendienst | 1968 | Detroit | 103 | 59 | .636 | Smith |

*First major league team to win pennant five years in succession.

## Professional Baseball Government

William D. Eckert, a retired lieutenant general of the United States Air Force, was elected commissioner of baseball Nov. 17, 1965, for a 7-year-term at an annual salary of $65,000. He succeeded Commissioner Ford C. Frick, who retired after serving in the post since 1952.

Commissioner—William D. Eckert.
Secretary-Treasurer—Charles Segar.
Director of Public Relations and Promotions—Joseph L. Reichler.
Executive Asst. Public Relations & Promotions—Monte Irvin.
Office—680 Fifth Ave., New York, N. Y. 10019.

### NATIONAL LEAGUE
President, secretary, treasurer—Warren C. Giles.
Director of Public Relations—David J. Grote.

Office—2601 Carew Tower, Cincinnati, Ohio.

### AMERICAN LEAGUE
Pres., sec., treas.—Joseph Edward Cronin.
Executive Assistant—Bob Holbrook.
Office—520 Boylston Street, Boston 16, Mass.

### NATIONAL ASSOCIATION
President—Philip Piton.
Director, Public Relations—Daniel F. O'Brien.
Office—720 East Broad Street, Columbus 15, Ohio.

## 1968 Amateur Softball Association

| Division | Champion |
|---|---|
| Men's Fast Pitch | Bombers, Clearwater, Fla. |
| Woman's Fast Pitch | Brakettes, Stratford, Conn. |
| Men's Open Slow Pitch | County Sports, Levittown, N.Y. |
| Men's Industrial Slow | Lycoming, Stratford, Conn. |
| Woman's Slow Pitch | Escue Pontiac, Cinn., Ohio |
| 16" Slow Pitch | Sobles, Chicago, Ill. |

# National League Records, 1968

## FINAL STANDING OF CLUBS

| | St. Louis | San Francisco | Chicago | Cincinnati | Atlanta | Pittsburgh | Los Angeles | Philadelphia | New York | Houston | Won | Lost | Percentage | Games Behind |
|---|---|---|---|---|---|---|---|---|---|---|---|---|---|---|
| St. Louis *Cardinals* | — | 8 | 9 | 11 | 13 | 12 | 9 | 10 | 12 | 13 | 97 | 65 | .599 | — |
| San Francisco *Giants* | 10 | — | 9 | 10 | 9 | 11 | 9 | 9 | 11 | 10 | 88 | 74 | .543 | 9 |
| Chicago *Cubs* | 9 | 9 | — | 7 | 10 | 10 | 12 | 9 | 8 | 10 | 84 | 78 | .519 | 13 |
| Cincinnati *Reds* | 7 | 8 | 11 | — | 8 | 10 | 9 | 11 | 9 | 9 | 83 | 79 | .512 | 14 |
| Atlanta *Braves* | 5 | 9 | 8 | 10 | — | 8 | 9 | 11 | 12 | 10 | 81 | 81 | .500 | 16 |
| Pittsburgh *Pirates* | 6 | 7 | 8 | 8 | 12 | — | 8 | 9 | 9 | 13 | 80 | 82 | .494 | 17 |
| Los Angeles *Dodgers* | 9 | 9 | 6 | 9 | 9 | 10 | — | 10 | 7 | 7 | 76 | 86 | .469 | 21 |
| Philadelphia *Phillies* | 8 | 9 | 9 | 7 | 7 | 9 | 8 | — | 10 | 9 | 76 | 86 | .469 | 21 |
| New York *Mets* | 6 | 7 | 10 | 8 | 6 | 9 | 11 | 8 | — | 8 | 73 | 89 | .451 | 24 |
| Houston *Astros* | 5 | 8 | 8 | 9 | 7 | 5 | 11 | 9 | 10 | — | 72 | 90 | .444 | 25 |

## CLUB BATTING

| | g. | ab. | r. | h. | hr. | sb. | pct. |
|---|---|---|---|---|---|---|---|
| Cincinnati | 163 | 5764 | 690 | 1573 | 106 | 59 | .273 |
| Pittsburgh | 163 | 5569 | 583 | 1404 | 80 | 130 | .252 |
| Atlanta | 163 | 5552 | 514 | 1399 | 80 | 82 | .252 |
| St. Louis | 162 | 5561 | 583 | 1383 | 73 | 110 | .249 |
| Chicago | 163 | 5459 | 612 | 1319 | 130 | 41 | .242 |
| San Francisco | 163 | 5442 | 599 | 1301 | 108 | 50 | .239 |
| Philadelphia | 162 | 5372 | 543 | 1253 | 100 | 58 | .233 |
| Houston | 162 | 5336 | 510 | 1233 | 66 | 44 | .231 |
| Los Angeles | 162 | 5354 | 470 | 1233 | 67 | 58 | .230 |
| New York | 163 | 5503 | 473 | 1252 | 81 | 73 | .228 |

## CLUB PITCHING

| | g. | cg. | ip. | h. | r. | bb. | so. | era. |
|---|---|---|---|---|---|---|---|---|
| St. Louis | 162 | 63 | 1479 | 1282 | 472 | 375 | 972 | 2.49 |
| Los Ang. | 162 | 38 | 1449 | 1293 | 509 | 414 | 993 | 2.69 |
| San Fran. | 163 | 77 | 1469 | 1302 | 529 | 343 | 943 | 2.71 |
| New York | 163 | 45 | 1483 | 1250 | 499 | 429 | 1017 | 2.72 |
| Pittsburgh | 163 | 42 | 1487 | 1322 | 532 | 484 | 896 | 2.75 |
| Atlanta | 163 | 44 | 1474 | 1325 | 549 | 362 | 871 | 2.92 |
| Houston | 162 | 50 | 1447 | 1362 | 588 | 479 | 1023 | 3.26 |
| Phila. | 162 | 42 | 1448 | 1416 | 615 | 427 | 935 | 3.36 |
| Chicago | 163 | 46 | 1453 | 1399 | 611 | 393 | 890 | 3.41 |
| Cin. | 163 | 24 | 1490 | 1399 | 673 | 573 | 963 | 3.56 |

## INDIVIDUAL BATTING

### Leaders—450 or More At Bats

| Player—Club | g. | ab. | h. | hr. | rbi. | sb. | pct. |
|---|---|---|---|---|---|---|---|
| ‡Rose, Cin. | 149 | 626 | 210 | 10 | 49 | 3 | .335 |
| †Alou, Pitts. | 146 | 558 | 185 | 0 | 52 | 18 | .332 |
| Alou, Atlanta | 160 | 662 | 210 | 11 | 57 | 12 | .317 |
| Johnson, Cin. | 149 | 603 | 188 | 2 | 58 | 16 | .312 |
| Flood, St. Louis | 150 | 618 | 186 | 5 | 60 | 11 | .301 |
| Jones, New York | 146 | 509 | 151 | 14 | 55 | 23 | .297 |
| Beckert, Chicago | 155 | 643 | 189 | 4 | 37 | 6 | .294 |
| †McCovey, S. F. | 148 | 523 | 153 | 36 | 105 | 4 | .293 |

## INDIVIDUAL PITCHING

### Leaders—162 or More Innings

| Pitcher—Club | g. | ip. | h. | bb. | so. | w. | l. | era. |
|---|---|---|---|---|---|---|---|---|
| Gibson, St. L. | 34 | 305 | 198 | 62 | 268 | 22 | 9 | 1.12 |
| Bolin, S. Fran. | 34 | 177 | 128 | 46 | 126 | 10 | 5 | 1.98 |
| †Veale, Pitts. | 36 | 245 | 187 | 94 | 171 | 13 | 14 | 2.06 |
| †*Koosman, N. Y. | 35 | 264 | 221 | 69 | 178 | 19 | 12 | 2.08 |
| Blass, Pitts. | 33 | 220 | 191 | 57 | 132 | 18 | 6 | 2.13 |
| Drysdale, L.A. | 31 | 239 | 201 | 56 | 155 | 14 | 12 | 2.15 |
| Seaver, N. Y. | 36 | 278 | 224 | 48 | 205 | 16 | 12 | 2.20 |
| Washburn, St. L. | 31 | 215 | 191 | 47 | 124 | 14 | 8 | 2.26 |

*Individual Batting (over 100 at-bats)  Individual Pitching (over 50 innings)*

## ATLANTA BRAVES

| Batting | g. | ab. | r. | h. | hr. | rbi. | sb. | pct. |
|---|---|---|---|---|---|---|---|---|
| Alou | 160 | 662 | 72 | 210 | 11 | 57 | 12 | .317 |
| Millan | 149 | 570 | 49 | 165 | 1 | 33 | 6 | .289 |
| H. Aaron | 160 | 606 | 84 | 174 | 29 | 86 | 28 | .287 |
| †Francona | 122 | 346 | 32 | 99 | 2 | 47 | 3 | .286 |
| Torre | 115 | 424 | 45 | 115 | 10 | 55 | 1 | .271 |
| R. Johnson | 75 | 202 | 16 | 53 | 0 | 12 | 0 | .262 |
| T. Aaron | 98 | 283 | 21 | 69 | 1 | 25 | 3 | .244 |
| ‡Martinez | 113 | 356 | 34 | 82 | 0 | 12 | 6 | .230 |
| Boyer | 71 | 273 | 19 | 62 | 4 | 17 | 2 | .227 |
| †Jackson | 105 | 358 | 37 | 81 | 1 | 19 | 16 | .226 |
| *†Lum | 122 | 232 | 22 | 52 | 3 | 21 | 3 | .224 |
| Tillman | 86 | 236 | 16 | 52 | 5 | 20 | 0 | .220 |
| D. Johnson | 127 | 342 | 29 | 71 | 8 | 33 | 0 | .208 |

| Pitching | g. | cg. | ip. | h. | bb. | so. | w. | l. | era. |
|---|---|---|---|---|---|---|---|---|---|
| Upshaw | 52 | 0 | 117 | 98 | 24 | 74 | 8 | 7 | 2.46 |
| Niekro | 37 | 15 | 257 | 228 | 45 | 140 | 14 | 12 | 2.56 |
| Jarvis | 34 | 14 | 256 | 201 | 50 | 157 | 16 | 12 | 2.60 |
| †Kelley | 31 | 1 | 98 | 87 | 45 | 73 | 2 | 4 | 2.76 |
| Raymond | 39 | 0 | 60 | 56 | 18 | 38 | 3 | 5 | 2.85 |
| *†Stone | 17 | 2 | 75 | 64 | 19 | 52 | 7 | 4 | 2.88 |
| *Britton | 34 | 2 | 90 | 80 | 34 | 61 | 4 | 6 | 3.10 |
| *Reed | 35 | 6 | 201 | 189 | 49 | 111 | 11 | 10 | 3.36 |
| Pappas | 37 | 3 | 184 | 181 | 32 | 118 | 12 | 13 | 3.47 |
| K. Johns'n | 31 | 1 | 135 | 145 | 25 | 56 | 5 | 8 | 3.47 |

## CHICAGO CUBS

| Batting | g. | ab. | r. | h. | hr. | rbi. | sb. | pct. |
|---|---|---|---|---|---|---|---|---|
| Beckert | 155 | 643 | 98 | 189 | 4 | 37 | 8 | .294 |
| †Williams | 163 | 642 | 91 | 185 | 30 | 98 | 4 | .288 |
| †Smith | 55 | 142 | 13 | 39 | 5 | 25 | 0 | .275 |
| †Spangler | 88 | 177 | 21 | 48 | 2 | 18 | 0 | .271 |
| Santo | 162 | 577 | 86 | 142 | 26 | 98 | 3 | .246 |
| Banks | 150 | 552 | 71 | 136 | 32 | 83 | 2 | .246 |
| Johnson | 62 | 205 | 14 | 50 | 1 | 14 | 3 | .244 |
| Phillips | 143 | 440 | 49 | 106 | 13 | 33 | 9 | .241 |
| ‡Kessinger | 160 | 655 | 63 | 157 | 1 | 32 | 9 | .240 |
| Hundley | 160 | 553 | 40 | 125 | 7 | 65 | 1 | .226 |
| Hickman | 75 | 188 | 22 | 42 | 5 | 23 | 1 | .223 |

**(Chicago, cont.)**

| Pitching | g. | cg. | ip. | h. | bb. | so. | w. | l. | era. |
|---|---|---|---|---|---|---|---|---|---|
| Regan | 73 | 0 | 135 | 119 | 26 | 67 | 12 | 5 | 2.27 |
| Jenkins | 40 | 20 | 308 | 255 | 65 | 260 | 20 | 15 | 2.63 |
| Hands | 38 | 11 | 259 | 221 | 36 | 148 | 16 | 10 | 2.88 |
| †Holtzman | 34 | 6 | 215 | 201 | 76 | 151 | 11 | 14 | 3.35 |
| *Nye | 27 | 6 | 133 | 145 | 34 | 74 | 7 | 12 | 3.79 |
| Lamabe | 42 | 0 | 61 | 68 | 24 | 29 | 3 | 2 | 4.28 |
| Niekro | 34 | 2 | 177 | 204 | 59 | 65 | 14 | 10 | 4.32 |

## CINCINNATI REDS

| Batting | g. | ab. | r. | h. | hr. | rbi. | sb. | pct. |
|---|---|---|---|---|---|---|---|---|
| ‡Rose | 149 | 626 | 94 | 210 | 10 | 49 | 3 | .335 |
| Johnson | 149 | 603 | 79 | 188 | 2 | 58 | 16 | .312 |
| May | 146 | 559 | 78 | 162 | 22 | 80 | 4 | .290 |
| Helms | 127 | 507 | 35 | 146 | 2 | 47 | 5 | .288 |
| Perez | 160 | 625 | 93 | 176 | 18 | 92 | 3 | .282 |
| *Bench | 154 | 564 | 67 | 155 | 15 | 82 | 1 | .275 |
| †Pinson | 130 | 499 | 60 | 135 | 5 | 48 | 17 | .271 |
| †Ruiz | 85 | 139 | 15 | 36 | 0 | 9 | 4 | .259 |
| †Whitfield | 87 | 171 | 15 | 44 | 6 | 32 | 0 | .257 |
| †Jones | 103 | 234 | 40 | 59 | 10 | 34 | 2 | .252 |
| Cardenas | 137 | 452 | 45 | 106 | 7 | 41 | 2 | .235 |
| Woodward | 68 | 143 | 15 | 33 | 0 | 11 | 2 | .231 |

| Pitching | g. | cg. | ip. | h. | bb. | so. | w. | l. | era. |
|---|---|---|---|---|---|---|---|---|---|
| Nolan | 23 | 4 | 150 | 105 | 49 | 111 | 9 | 4 | 2.40 |
| Abern'thy | 78 | 0 | 136 | 111 | 55 | 63 | 10 | 7 | 2.45 |
| Carroll | 68 | 0 | 144 | 130 | 39 | 73 | 7 | 8 | 2.69 |
| Culver | 42 | 5 | 226 | 229 | 84 | 116 | 11 | 16 | 3.23 |
| †Arrigo | 36 | 5 | 205 | 181 | 77 | 140 | 12 | 10 | 3.34 |
| Maloney | 38 | 8 | 207 | 183 | 80 | 182 | 16 | 10 | 3.61 |
| Kelso | 35 | 0 | 54 | 56 | 15 | 38 | 4 | 1 | 4.00 |
| Cloninger | 25 | 2 | 110 | 96 | 59 | 73 | 5 | 6 | 4.09 |
| Ritchie | 28 | 0 | 57 | 68 | 13 | 32 | 2 | 3 | 4.58 |
| †McCool | 30 | 0 | 51 | 59 | 41 | 30 | 3 | 4 | 4.94 |
| Lee | 44 | 0 | 65 | 70 | 36 | 31 | 2 | 4 | 5.12 |

*Rookie  †Left handed  ‡Switch hitter

## HOUSTON ASTROS

| Batting | g. | ab. | r. | h. | hr. | rbi. | sb. | pct. |
|---|---|---|---|---|---|---|---|---|
| †Staub ........ | 161 | 591 | 54 | 172 | 6 | 72 | 2 | .291 |
| Wynn ........ | 156 | 542 | 85 | 146 | 26 | 67 | 11 | .269 |
| Rader ........ | 98 | 333 | 42 | 89 | 6 | 43 | 2 | .267 |
| Menke ........ | 150 | 542 | 56 | 135 | 6 | 56 | 5 | .249 |
| Bateman ..... | 111 | 350 | 28 | 87 | 4 | 33 | 1 | .249 |
| Gotay ........ | 75 | 165 | 9 | 41 | 1 | 11 | 1 | .248 |
| *Herrera ..... | 27 | 100 | 9 | 24 | 0 | 7 | 0 | .240 |
| †Miller ....... | 79 | 257 | 35 | 61 | 6 | 28 | 6 | .237 |
| *Watson ...... | 45 | 140 | 13 | 32 | 2 | 8 | 1 | .229 |
| Aspromonte .. | 124 | 409 | 25 | 92 | 1 | 46 | 1 | .225 |
| *Torres ...... | 128 | 466 | 44 | 104 | 1 | 24 | 2 | .223 |
| Simpson ...... | 85 | 233 | 36 | 46 | 6 | 19 | 4 | .197 |
| ‡Thomas ..... | 90 | 201 | 14 | 39 | 1 | 11 | 2 | .194 |
| Adlesh ....... | 40 | 104 | 3 | 19 | 0 | 4 | 0 | .183 |

| Pitching | g. | cg. | ip. | h. | bb. | so. | w. | l. | era. |
|---|---|---|---|---|---|---|---|---|---|
| *Ray ......... | 41 | 1 | 81 | 65 | 25 | 72 | 2 | 3 | 2.67 |
| †Cuellar ..... | 28 | 11 | 171 | 152 | 45 | 133 | 8 | 11 | 2.74 |
| †Lemaster ... | 33 | 7 | 224 | 231 | 72 | 146 | 10 | 15 | 2.85 |
| Buzhardt .... | 39 | 0 | 84 | 72 | 35 | 37 | 4 | 4 | 3.11 |
| Giusti ....... | 37 | 12 | 251 | 226 | 67 | 187 | 11 | 14 | 3.19 |
| Wilson ....... | 33 | 9 | 209 | 187 | 69 | 176 | 13 | 16 | 3.23 |
| Dierker ...... | 32 | 10 | 234 | 207 | 89 | 161 | 12 | 15 | 3.31 |
| *Dukes ...... | 43 | 3 | 53 | 62 | 28 | 37 | 2 | 2 | 4.25 |

## LOS ANGELES DODGERS

| Batting | g. | ab. | r. | h. | hr. | rbi. | sb. | pct. |
|---|---|---|---|---|---|---|---|---|
| †Haller ...... | 144 | 474 | 37 | 135 | 4 | 53 | 1 | .285 |
| Boyer ........ | 83 | 221 | 20 | 60 | 6 | 41 | 2 | .271 |
| †Gabrielson .. | 108 | 304 | 38 | 82 | 10 | 35 | 1 | .270 |
| †Crawford .... | 61 | 175 | 25 | 44 | 4 | 14 | 1 | .251 |
| †Davis ....... | 160 | 643 | 86 | 161 | 7 | 31 | 36 | .250 |
| ‡Parker ...... | 135 | 468 | 42 | 112 | 3 | 27 | 4 | .239 |
| ‡Lefebvre .... | 84 | 286 | 23 | 68 | 5 | 31 | 0 | .238 |
| †Fairly ...... | 141 | 441 | 32 | 103 | 4 | 44 | 0 | .234 |
| ‡Popovich .... | 134 | 418 | 35 | 97 | 2 | 25 | 1 | .232 |
| Bailey ....... | 105 | 322 | 24 | 73 | 8 | 39 | 2 | .227 |
| Savage ....... | 64 | 134 | 7 | 28 | 2 | 7 | 1 | .209 |
| Colavito ..... | 40 | 113 | 8 | 23 | 3 | 11 | 0 | .204 |
| †*Fairey ..... | 99 | 156 | 17 | 31 | 1 | 10 | 1 | .199 |
| *Versalles .... | 122 | 403 | 29 | 79 | 2 | 24 | 6 | .196 |
| *Alcaraz ..... | 41 | 106 | 4 | 16 | 2 | 5 | 1 | .151 |

| Pitching | g. | cg. | ip. | h. | bb. | so. | w. | l. | era. |
|---|---|---|---|---|---|---|---|---|---|
| *Bill'ham .... | 50 | 0 | 71 | 54 | 30 | 46 | 3 | 0 | 2.03 |
| Grant ........ | 37 | 1 | 95 | 77 | 19 | 35 | 6 | 4 | 2.08 |
| Drysdale .... | 31 | 12 | 239 | 201 | 56 | 155 | 14 | 12 | 2.15 |
| †Brewer ..... | 54 | 0 | 76 | 59 | 33 | 75 | 8 | 3 | 2.49 |
| Sutton ....... | 35 | 7 | 208 | 179 | 59 | 162 | 11 | 15 | 2.60 |
| Singer ....... | 37 | 12 | 256 | 227 | 78 | 227 | 13 | 17 | 2.88 |
| Purdin ....... | 35 | 0 | 56 | 42 | 21 | 38 | 2 | 3 | 3.05 |
| †Osteen ..... | 39 | 5 | 254 | 267 | 54 | 119 | 12 | 18 | 3.08 |
| †Kekich ..... | 25 | 1 | 115 | 116 | 46 | 84 | 2 | 10 | 3.99 |

## NEW YORK METS

| Batting | g. | ab. | r. | h. | hr. | rbi. | sb. | pct. |
|---|---|---|---|---|---|---|---|---|
| Jones ........ | 146 | 509 | 63 | 151 | 14 | 55 | 23 | .297 |
| Grote ........ | 124 | 404 | 29 | 114 | 3 | 31 | 2 | .282 |
| Charles ...... | 117 | 369 | 41 | 102 | 15 | 53 | 5 | .276 |
| †*Boswell .... | 75 | 284 | 37 | 74 | 4 | 11 | 7 | .261 |
| Swoboda ..... | 132 | 450 | 46 | 109 | 11 | 59 | 7 | .242 |
| ‡Shamsky .... | 116 | 345 | 30 | 82 | 12 | 48 | 1 | .238 |
| ‡Stahl ....... | 53 | 183 | 15 | 43 | 3 | 10 | 3 | .235 |
| ‡Kranepool .. | 126 | 373 | 29 | 86 | 3 | 20 | 0 | .231 |
| †Martin ..... | 78 | 244 | 20 | 55 | 3 | 10 | 0 | .225 |
| †Harrelson .. | 111 | 402 | 38 | 88 | 0 | 14 | 4 | .219 |
| Agee ......... | 132 | 368 | 30 | 80 | 5 | 17 | 13 | .217 |
| Linz ......... | 78 | 258 | 19 | 54 | 0 | 17 | 1 | .209 |
| Goossen ..... | 38 | 106 | 4 | 22 | 0 | 6 | 0 | .208 |
| †*Collins .... | 58 | 154 | 12 | 31 | 1 | 13 | 0 | .201 |
| Buchek ...... | 73 | 192 | 8 | 35 | 1 | 11 | 1 | .182 |
| ‡Weis ....... | 90 | 274 | 15 | 47 | 1 | 14 | 3 | .172 |
| ‡Bosch ...... | 50 | 111 | 14 | 19 | 3 | 7 | 1 | .171 |

| Pitching | g. | cg. | ip. | h. | bb. | so. | w. | l. | era. |
|---|---|---|---|---|---|---|---|---|---|
| *†Koosman | 35 | 17 | 264 | 221 | 69 | 178 | 19 | 12 | 2.08 |
| Seaver .... | 36 | 14 | 278 | 224 | 48 | 205 | 16 | 12 | 2.20 |
| *McAndrew | 12 | 2 | 79 | 66 | 17 | 46 | 4 | 7 | 2.28 |
| Koonce ... | 55 | 0 | 97 | 80 | 32 | 50 | 6 | 4 | 2.41 |
| Taylor ... | 58 | 0 | 77 | 64 | 18 | 50 | 1 | 5 | 2.69 |
| Selma .... | 33 | 4 | 170 | 148 | 54 | 117 | 9 | 10 | 2.75 |
| Cardwell . | 29 | 5 | 180 | 156 | 50 | 83 | 7 | 13 | 2.95 |
| *Ryan .... | 21 | 3 | 134 | 93 | 75 | 133 | 6 | 9 | 3.09 |
| †Jackson . | 25 | 0 | 93 | 88 | 17 | 60 | 3 | 7 | 3.68 |
| Frisella .. | 19 | 0 | 51 | 53 | 17 | 47 | 2 | 4 | 3.88 |

## PHILADELPHIA PHILLIES

| Batting | g. | ab. | r. | h. | hr. | rbi. | sb. | pct. |
|---|---|---|---|---|---|---|---|---|
| Sutherland .. | 67 | 138 | 16 | 38 | 0 | 15 | 0 | .275 |
| †Gonzalez ... | 121 | 416 | 45 | 110 | 3 | 38 | 6 | .264 |
| Allen ........ | 152 | 521 | 88 | 137 | 33 | 90 | 7 | .263 |
| Pena ......... | 138 | 500 | 56 | 130 | 1 | 38 | 3 | .260 |
| †Briggs ...... | 110 | 338 | 36 | 86 | 7 | 31 | 6 | .254 |
| Taylor ....... | 145 | 547 | 59 | 137 | 3 | 38 | 22 | .250 |

| | | | |
|---|---|---|---|
| *Rookie | †Left handed | ‡Switch hitter | |

## (Philadelphia, cont.)

| Batting | g. | ab. | r. | h. | hr. | rbi. | sb. | pct. |
|---|---|---|---|---|---|---|---|---|
| †Callison .... | 121 | 398 | 46 | 97 | 14 | 40 | 4 | .244 |
| †White ...... | 127 | 385 | 34 | 92 | 9 | 40 | 0 | .239 |
| Rojas ........ | 152 | 621 | 53 | 144 | 9 | 48 | 4 | .232 |
| Joseph ....... | 66 | 155 | 20 | 34 | 3 | 12 | 0 | .219 |
| Lock ......... | 99 | 248 | 26 | 52 | 8 | 34 | 3 | .210 |
| †Dalrymple .. | 85 | 241 | 19 | 50 | 3 | 26 | 1 | .207 |
| Ryan ......... | 96 | 296 | 12 | 53 | 1 | 15 | 0 | .179 |

| Pitching | g. | cg. | ip. | h. | bb. | so. | w. | l. | era. |
|---|---|---|---|---|---|---|---|---|---|
| L. Jackson .. | 34 | 12 | 244 | 229 | 60 | 126 | 13 | 17 | 2.77 |
| †Fryman .... | 34 | 10 | 214 | 198 | 64 | 151 | 12 | 14 | 2.78 |
| †Short ...... | 42 | 9 | 270 | 236 | 81 | 202 | 19 | 13 | 2.93 |
| †G. Jckson .. | 33 | 1 | 61 | 59 | 20 | 49 | 1 | 6 | 2.95 |
| Wagner ..... | 44 | 0 | 78 | 69 | 31 | 44 | 4 | 4 | 3.00 |
| *Johnson .... | 16 | 2 | 81 | 82 | 29 | 40 | 4 | 4 | 3.22 |
| Farrell ...... | 54 | 0 | 83 | 83 | 32 | 57 | 4 | 6 | 3.47 |
| Boozer ....... | 38 | 0 | 69 | 76 | 15 | 49 | 2 | 2 | 3.65 |
| *James ...... | 29 | 1 | 116 | 112 | 46 | 83 | 4 | 4 | 4.27 |
| Wise ......... | 30 | 7 | 182 | 210 | 38 | 97 | 9 | 15 | 4.55 |

## PITTSBURGH PIRATES

| Batting | g. | ab. | r. | h. | hr. | rbi. | sb. | pct. |
|---|---|---|---|---|---|---|---|---|
| †Alou ........ | 146 | 558 | 59 | 185 | 0 | 52 | 18 | .332 |
| Clemente .... | 132 | 502 | 74 | 146 | 18 | 57 | 2 | .291 |
| Mota ......... | 111 | 331 | 35 | 93 | 1 | 33 | 4 | .281 |
| Clendenon ... | 158 | 584 | 63 | 150 | 17 | 87 | 10 | .257 |
| *Patek ....... | 61 | 208 | 31 | 53 | 2 | 18 | 18 | .255 |
| Mazeroski ... | 143 | 506 | 36 | 127 | 3 | 42 | 3 | .251 |
| †Stargell .... | 128 | 435 | 57 | 103 | 24 | 67 | 5 | .237 |
| Pagan ........ | 79 | 163 | 24 | 36 | 4 | 21 | 2 | .221 |
| May .......... | 138 | 416 | 26 | 91 | 1 | 33 | 0 | .219 |
| †Kolb ........ | 73 | 119 | 16 | 26 | 2 | 6 | 2 | .218 |

| Pitching | g. | cg. | ip. | h. | bb. | so. | w. | l. | era. |
|---|---|---|---|---|---|---|---|---|---|
| Kline ........ | 56 | 0 | 113 | 94 | 31 | 48 | 12 | 5 | 1.67 |
| *†Walker .... | 39 | 0 | 63 | 42 | 38 | 66 | 0 | 3 | 2.00 |
| †Veale ....... | 36 | 13 | 245 | 187 | 94 | 171 | 13 | 14 | 2.06 |
| *Ellis ........ | 33 | 12 | 220 | 191 | 57 | 132 | 18 | 6 | 2.13 |
| Blass ......... | 26 | 2 | 104 | 82 | 38 | 52 | 6 | 5 | 2.42 |
| Face ......... | 43 | 0 | 52 | 46 | 7 | 34 | 2 | 4 | 2.60 |
| *Moose ...... | 38 | 3 | 171 | 136 | 41 | 126 | 8 | 12 | 2.74 |
| Sisk ......... | 33 | 0 | 96 | 101 | 35 | 40 | 5 | 5 | 3.38 |
| McBean ..... | 36 | 9 | 193 | 204 | 63 | 100 | 9 | 12 | 3.59 |
| Bunning .... | 27 | 3 | 160 | 168 | 48 | 95 | 4 | 14 | 3.88 |

## ST. LOUIS CARDINALS

| Batting | g. | ab. | r. | h. | hr. | rbi. | sb. | pct. |
|---|---|---|---|---|---|---|---|---|
| Flood ........ | 150 | 618 | 71 | 186 | 5 | 60 | 11 | .301 |
| *Brock ....... | 159 | 660 | 92 | 184 | 6 | 51 | 62 | .279 |
| Shannon ..... | 156 | 576 | 62 | 153 | 15 | 79 | 1 | .266 |
| Javier ....... | 139 | 519 | 54 | 135 | 4 | 52 | 10 | .260 |
| †Maris ....... | 100 | 310 | 25 | 79 | 5 | 45 | 0 | .255 |
| †McCarver .. | 128 | 434 | 35 | 110 | 5 | 48 | 4 | .253 |
| Maxvill ...... | 151 | 459 | 51 | 116 | 1 | 24 | 0 | .253 |
| Cepeda ...... | 157 | 600 | 71 | 149 | 16 | 73 | 8 | .248 |
| ‡Edwards .... | 85 | 230 | 14 | 55 | 3 | 29 | 1 | .239 |
| †Tolan ....... | 92 | 278 | 28 | 64 | 5 | 17 | 9 | .230 |
| Gagliano ..... | 53 | 105 | 13 | 24 | 0 | 13 | 0 | .229 |
| ‡Schofield ... | 69 | 127 | 14 | 28 | 1 | 8 | 1 | .220 |
| Davis ........ | 85 | 296 | 33 | 60 | 1 | 17 | 1 | .203 |

| Pitching | g. | cg. | ip. | h. | bb. | so. | w. | l. | era. |
|---|---|---|---|---|---|---|---|---|---|
| Gibson ....... | 34 | 28 | 305 | 198 | 62 | 268 | 22 | 9 | 1.12 |
| Washburn ... | 31 | 8 | 215 | 191 | 47 | 124 | 14 | 8 | 2.26 |
| Briles ....... | 33 | 13 | 244 | 251 | 55 | 141 | 19 | 11 | 2.80 |
| *Nelson ...... | 18 | 1 | 53 | 49 | 9 | 16 | 2 | 1 | 2.89 |
| †Carlton .... | 34 | 10 | 232 | 214 | 61 | 162 | 13 | 11 | 2.99 |
| Willis ........ | 48 | 0 | 64 | 50 | 28 | 39 | 2 | 3 | 3.38 |
| †Jaster ...... | 31 | 3 | 154 | 153 | 38 | 70 | 9 | 13 | 3.51 |
| Hughes ...... | 25 | 0 | 64 | 45 | 21 | 50 | 2 | 2 | 3.52 |

## SAN FRANCISCO GIANTS

| Batting | g. | ab. | r. | h. | hr. | rbi. | sb. | pct. |
|---|---|---|---|---|---|---|---|---|
| †McCovey .... | 148 | 523 | 81 | 153 | 36 | 105 | 4 | .293 |
| Mays ......... | 148 | 498 | 84 | 144 | 23 | 79 | 12 | .289 |
| Dietz ........ | 98 | 301 | 21 | 82 | 6 | 38 | 1 | .272 |
| †*Marshall .. | 76 | 174 | 17 | 46 | 1 | 16 | 2 | .264 |
| Alou ......... | 119 | 420 | 26 | 110 | 0 | 39 | 1 | .262 |
| Hart ......... | 136 | 480 | 67 | 124 | 23 | 78 | 3 | .258 |
| *Bonds ....... | 81 | 307 | 55 | 78 | 9 | 35 | 16 | .254 |
| Hunt ......... | 148 | 529 | 79 | 132 | 2 | 28 | 6 | .250 |
| Hiatt ........ | 90 | 224 | 14 | 52 | 4 | 33 | 0 | .232 |
| Davenport ... | 113 | 272 | 27 | 61 | 1 | 17 | 0 | .224 |
| †Cline ....... | 116 | 291 | 37 | 65 | 1 | 28 | 0 | .223 |
| ‡Lanier ...... | 151 | 486 | 37 | 100 | 0 | 27 | 2 | .206 |
| *Johnson .... | 67 | 174 | 11 | 33 | 1 | 7 | 1 | .190 |

| Pitching | g. | cg. | ip. | h. | bb. | so. | w. | l. | era. |
|---|---|---|---|---|---|---|---|---|---|
| Bolin ........ | 34 | 6 | 177 | 128 | 46 | 126 | 10 | 5 | 1.98 |
| Linzy ........ | 57 | 0 | 95 | 76 | 27 | 36 | 9 | 8 | 2.08 |
| Marichal ..... | 38 | 30 | 326 | 295 | 46 | 218 | 26 | 9 | 2.43 |
| Perry ........ | 39 | 19 | 291 | 240 | 58 | 174 | 16 | 15 | 2.44 |
| ‡Sadecki .... | 38 | 13 | 254 | 225 | 70 | 206 | 12 | 18 | 2.91 |
| †McCor'ick .. | 38 | 9 | 198 | 196 | 49 | 120 | 12 | 14 | 3.59 |

# American League Records, 1968

## FINAL STANDING OF CLUBS

| | Detroit | Baltimore | Cleveland | Boston | New York | Oakland | Minnesota | California | Chicago | Washington | Won | Lost | Percentage | Games Behind |
|---|---|---|---|---|---|---|---|---|---|---|---|---|---|---|
| Detroit *Tigers*............. | — | 10 | 12 | 12 | 10 | 13 | 10 | 13 | 13 | 10 | 103 | 59 | .636 | — |
| Baltimore *Orioles*.......... | 8 | — | 7 | 9 | 13 | 9 | 10 | 10 | 11 | 14 | 91 | 71 | .562 | 12 |
| Cleveland *Indians*......... | 6 | 11 | — | 8 | 10 | 6 | 14 | 11 | 13 | 7 | 86 | 75 | .534 | 16½ |
| Boston *Red Sox*........... | 6 | 9 | 10 | — | 10 | 8 | 9 | 9 | 14 | 11 | 86 | 76 | .531 | 17 |
| New York *Yankees*........ | 8 | 5 | 8 | 8 | — | 10 | 6 | 12 | 12 | 14 | 83 | 79 | .512 | 20 |
| Oakland *Athletics*........ | 5 | 9 | 12 | 10 | 8 | — | 10 | 13 | 8 | 7 | 82 | 80 | .506 | 21 |
| Minnesota *Twins*......... | 8 | 8 | 4 | 9 | 12 | 8 | — | 11 | 8 | 11 | 79 | 83 | .488 | 24 |
| California *Angels*......... | 5 | 8 | 7 | 9 | 6 | 5 | 7 | — | 8 | 12 | 67 | 95 | .414 | 36 |
| Chicago *White Sox*........ | 5 | 7 | 5 | 4 | 6 | 10 | 10 | 10 | — | 10 | 67 | 95 | .414 | 36 |
| Washington *Senators*........ | 8 | 4 | 10 | 7 | 4 | 11 | 7 | 6 | 8 | — | 65 | 96 | .404 | 37½ |

## CLUB BATTING

| | g. | ab. | r. | h. | hr. | sb. | pct. |
|---|---|---|---|---|---|---|---|
| Oakland ..... | 163 | 5405 | 569 | 1300 | 94 | 148 | .241 |
| Minnesota .. | 162 | 5374 | 562 | 1274 | 105 | 98 | .237 |
| Boston ...... | 162 | 5303 | 614 | 1253 | 125 | 76 | .236 |
| Detroit ..... | 164 | 5490 | 671 | 1292 | 185 | 27 | .235 |
| Cleveland ... | 162 | 5414 | 516 | 1266 | 75 | 114 | .234 |
| Chicago .... | 162 | 5405 | 463 | 1233 | 71 | 90 | .228 |
| California ... | 162 | 5331 | 498 | 1209 | 83 | 62 | .227 |
| Baltimore .. | 162 | 5275 | 579 | 1187 | 133 | 79 | .225 |
| Washington | 161 | 5400 | 524 | 1207 | 124 | 30 | .224 |
| New York ... | 164 | 5308 | 536 | 1137 | 109 | 90 | .214 |

## CLUB PITCHING

| | g. | cg. | ip. | h. | bb. | so. | era. |
|---|---|---|---|---|---|---|---|
| Balt. ..... | 162 | 53 | 1451 | 1111 | 497 | 501 | 1041 | 2.65 |
| Clev. ..... | 162 | 48 | 1464 | 1086 | 504 | 540 | 1158 | 2.66 |
| Detroit | 164 | 59 | 1490 | 1180 | 492 | 486 | 1112 | 2.71 |
| Chicago .. | 162 | 20 | 1468 | 1290 | 527 | 451 | 830 | 2.75 |
| New York | 164 | 45 | 1467 | 1308 | 531 | 424 | 830 | 2.79 |
| Minn. ..... | 162 | 46 | 1433 | 1224 | 546 | 413 | 996 | 2.89 |
| Oakland .. | 163 | 45 | 1456 | 1219 | 544 | 505 | 999 | 2.97 |
| Boston .. | 162 | 55 | 1447 | 1302 | 611 | 522 | 978 | 3.34 |
| Calif. ..... | 162 | 29 | 1437 | 1235 | 615 | 518 | 867 | 3.44 |
| Wash. ..... | 161 | 26 | 1440 | 1402 | 665 | 518 | 827 | 3.64 |

## INDIVIDUAL BATTING

**Leaders—450 or More At Bats**

| Player—Club | g. | ab. | r. | h. | hr. | rbi. | sb. | pct. |
|---|---|---|---|---|---|---|---|---|
| †Yastrzemski, Bost. | 157 | 539 | 162 | 23 | 74 | 13 | .301 |
| Cater, Oakland .. | 147 | 504 | 146 | 6 | 62 | 8 | .290 |
| †Oliva, Minn. ... | 128 | 470 | 136 | 18 | 68 | 10 | .289 |
| Horton, Detroit .. | 143 | 512 | 146 | 36 | 85 | 0 | .285 |
| †Uhlaender, Minn. | 140 | 488 | 138 | 7 | 52 | 16 | .283 |
| †Davalillo, Calif. | 144 | 519 | 144 | 3 | 31 | 25 | .277 |
| Campaneris, Oak. | 159 | 642 | 177 | 4 | 38 | 62 | .276 |
| Harrelson, Boston | 150 | 535 | 147 | 35 | 109 | 2 | .275 |
| F. Howard, Wash. | 158 | 598 | 164 | 44 | 106 | 0 | .274 |

## INDIVIDUAL PITCHING

**Leaders—162 or More Innings**

| Pitcher—Club | g. | ip. | h. | bb. | so. | w. | l. | era. |
|---|---|---|---|---|---|---|---|---|
| Tiant, Clev. .... | 34 | 258 | 152 | 73 | 264 | 21 | 9 | 1.60 |
| †McDowell, Clev. | 38 | 269 | 180 | 110 | 283 | 15 | 14 | 1.81 |
| †McNally, Balt. | 35 | 273 | 175 | 55 | 202 | 22 | 10 | 1.95 |
| McLain, Det. .... | 41 | 336 | 241 | 63 | 280 | 31 | 6 | 1.96 |
| †John, Chicago . | 25 | 177 | 135 | 49 | 117 | 10 | 5 | 1.98 |
| *Bahnsen, N. Y. | 37 | 267 | 216 | 68 | 161 | 17 | 12 | 2.06 |
| Nash, Oakland . | 34 | 229 | 185 | 55 | 170 | 13 | 13 | 2.28 |
| Horlen, Chicago | 35 | 224 | 197 | 70 | 102 | 12 | 14 | 2.37 |

## Individual Batting (over 100 at-bats)

## BALTIMORE ORIOLES

| Batting | g. | ab. | r. | h. | hr. | rbi. | sb. | pct. |
|---|---|---|---|---|---|---|---|---|
| ‡Buford ...... | 130 | 426 | 65 | 120 | 15 | 46 | 28 | .282 |
| F. Robinson .. | 130 | 421 | 69 | 113 | 15 | 52 | 11 | .268 |
| B. Robinson .. | 162 | 608 | 65 | 154 | 17 | 75 | 1 | .253 |
| †Powell ...... | 154 | 550 | 60 | 137 | 22 | 85 | 7 | .249 |
| Johnson ..... | 145 | 504 | 50 | 122 | 9 | 56 | 7 | .242 |
| Etchebarren .. | 74 | 189 | 20 | 44 | 5 | 20 | 0 | .233 |
| †Valentine /.. | 84 | 192 | 20 | 41 | 5 | 12 | 1 | .214 |
| Blair ........ | 141 | 421 | 48 | 89 | 7 | 38 | 4 | .211 |
| Belanger ..... | 145 | 472 | 40 | 98 | 2 | 21 | 10 | .208 |
| *†Hendricks .. | 79 | 183 | 19 | 37 | 7 | 23 | 0 | .202 |
| ‡Blefary ...... | 137 | 451 | 50 | 90 | 15 | 39 | 6 | .200 |
| *Motton ...... | 83 | 217 | 27 | 43 | 8 | 25 | 1 | .198 |
| *†May ....... | 83 | 152 | 15 | 29 | 0 | 7 | 3 | .191 |

| Pitching | g. | cg. | ip. | h. | bb. | so. | w. | l. | era. |
|---|---|---|---|---|---|---|---|---|---|
| Drabowsky | 45 | 0 | 61 | 35 | 25 | 46 | 4 | 4 | 1.92 |
| †McNally .. | 35 | 18 | 273 | 175 | 55 | 202 | 22 | 10 | 1.95 |
| Watt .... | 59 | 0 | 84 | 63 | 35 | 70 | 5 | 5 | 2.25 |
| *Nelson .. | 19 | 0 | 71 | 49 | 26 | 70 | 4 | 3 | 2.41 |
| Bunker .. | 18 | 2 | 71 | 59 | 14 | 44 | 2 | 0 | 2.41 |
| Hardin .. | 35 | 16 | 244 | 188 | 70 | 159 | 18 | 13 | 2.51 |
| Phoebus .. | 36 | 9 | 241 | 186 | 105 | 195 | 15 | 15 | 2.61 |
| *Leonhard | 28 | 5 | 126 | 95 | 57 | 60 | 7 | 7 | 3.14 |
| ‡Brabender | 37 | 3 | 125 | 116 | 48 | 92 | 6 | 7 | 3.31 |
| †Richert .. | 36 | 0 | 62 | 51 | 11 | 46 | 6 | 3 | 3.48 |

## BOSTON RED SOX

| Batting | g. | ab. | r. | h. | hr. | rbi. | sb. | pct. |
|---|---|---|---|---|---|---|---|---|
| †Yastrze'ski .. | 157 | 539 | 90 | 162 | 23 | 74 | 13 | .301 |
| †Tartabull ... | 72 | 140 | 24 | 39 | 0 | 6 | 2 | .279 |
| Harrelson .... | 150 | 535 | 79 | 147 | 35 | 109 | 2 | .275 |
| Andrews ..... | 147 | 536 | 77 | 145 | 7 | 45 | 3 | .271 |
| ‡Smith ...... | 155 | 558 | 78 | 148 | 15 | 70 | 22 | .265 |
| Howard ...... | 71 | 203 | 22 | 49 | 5 | 17 | 1 | .241 |
| †Jones ....... | 111 | 353 | 38 | 83 | 5 | 29 | 1 | .235 |
| Petrocelli ... | 123 | 406 | 41 | 95 | 12 | 46 | 0 | .234 |
| Foy .......... | 150 | 515 | 65 | 116 | 10 | 60 | 26 | .225 |
| Gibson ....... | 76 | 231 | 15 | 52 | 3 | 20 | 1 | .225 |
| †Robinson .... | 76 | 105 | 6 | 23 | 1 | 15 | 1 | .219 |
| Adair ........ | 74 | 208 | 18 | 45 | 2 | 12 | 0 | .216 |
| Scott ........ | 124 | 350 | 23 | 60 | 3 | 25 | 3 | .171 |

| Pitching | g. | cg. | ip. | h. | bb. | so. | w. | l. | era. |
|---|---|---|---|---|---|---|---|---|---|
| Santiago .. | 18 | 7 | 124 | 96 | 42 | 87 | 9 | 4 | 2.25 |
| Morehead | 11 | 3 | 55 | 52 | 20 | 28 | 1 | 4 | 2.45 |
| †Lyle .... | 49 | 0 | 66 | 67 | 14 | 55 | 6 | 1 | 2.86 |

## BOSTON RED SOX (cont.)

| Pitching | g. | cg. | ip. | h. | bb. | so. | w. | l. | era. |
|---|---|---|---|---|---|---|---|---|---|
| Culp ....... | 35 | 11 | 216 | 166 | 82 | 190 | 16 | 6 | 2.92 |
| ‡Landis ... | 38 | 0 | 60 | 47 | 30 | 58 | 3 | 3 | 3.00 |
| †Ellsworth . | 31 | 10 | 196 | 196 | 37 | 106 | 16 | 7 | 3.03 |
| Bell ....... | 35 | 9 | 199 | 177 | 67 | 105 | 11 | 11 | 3.17 |
| †Pizarro .. | 19 | 6 | 108 | 97 | 44 | 84 | 6 | 8 | 3.58 |
| Waslewski | 34 | 2 | 105 | 108 | 40 | 59 | 4 | 7 | 3.69 |
| Stange ... | 50 | 1 | 103 | 89 | 25 | 54 | 5 | 5 | 3.84 |
| Lonborg .. | 23 | 4 | 113 | 88 | 59 | 73 | 6 | 10 | 4.30 |
| Stephenson | 23 | 2 | 69 | 81 | 42 | 51 | 2 | 8 | 5.61 |

## CALIFORNIA ANGELS

| Batting | g. | ab. | r. | h. | hr. | rbi. | sb. | pct. |
|---|---|---|---|---|---|---|---|---|
| †Davalillo ..... | 144 | 519 | 49 | 144 | 3 | 31 | 25 | .277 |
| Morton ....... | 81 | 163 | 13 | 44 | 1 | 18 | 2 | .270 |
| †Johnstone ... | 41 | 115 | 11 | 30 | 0 | 3 | 2 | .261 |
| Reichardt ..... | 151 | 534 | 62 | 136 | 21 | 73 | 8 | .255 |
| †Satriano ..... | 111 | 297 | 19 | 75 | 8 | 35 | 0 | .253 |
| Knoop ........ | 152 | 494 | 48 | 123 | 3 | 39 | 3 | .249 |
| Fregosi ....... | 159 | 615 | 77 | 150 | 9 | 49 | 9 | .244 |
| Rodriguez .... | 76 | 223 | 14 | 54 | 1 | 16 | 0 | .242 |
| †Repoz ....... | 133 | 375 | 30 | 90 | 13 | 54 | 8 | .240 |
| †Mincher ..... | 120 | 399 | 35 | 94 | 13 | 48 | 0 | .236 |
| †Kirkpatrick .. | 89 | 161 | 23 | 37 | 1 | 15 | 1 | .230 |
| Schaal ....... | 60 | 219 | 22 | 46 | 2 | 16 | 5 | .210 |
| Hinton ....... | 116 | 267 | 28 | 52 | 7 | 23 | 3 | .195 |
| ‡Rodgers ..... | 91 | 258 | 13 | 49 | 1 | 14 | 2 | .190 |
| †Causey ...... | 63 | 111 | 8 | 18 | 0 | 7 | 0 | .162 |

| Pitching | g. | cg. | ip. | h. | bb. | so. | w. | l. | era. |
|---|---|---|---|---|---|---|---|---|---|
| *Murphy .. | 15 | 3 | 99 | 67 | 28 | 56 | 5 | 6 | 2.09 |
| *Me'smith | 28 | 2 | 81 | 44 | 35 | 74 | 4 | 2 | 2.22 |
| †Pattin ... | 52 | 0 | 84 | 67 | 37 | 66 | 4 | 4 | 2.79 |
| †Brunet .. | 39 | 8 | 245 | 191 | 68 | 131 | 13 | 17 | 2.87 |
| McGlothlin | 40 | 8 | 208 | 187 | 60 | 135 | 10 | 15 | 3.55 |
| Clark ..... | 21 | 0 | 94 | 74 | 54 | 60 | 1 | 11 | 3.73 |
| †Wright .. | 42 | 2 | 127 | 123 | 43 | 73 | 10 | 6 | 3.90 |
| Ellis ...... | 42 | 3 | 164 | 151 | 56 | 93 | 9 | 9 | 4.01 |
| *‡B'meier .. | 55 | 0 | 72 | 65 | 24 | 31 | 1 | 4 | 4.25 |
| Rojas ..... | 38 | 0 | 55 | 55 | 15 | 33 | 4 | 3 | 4.25 |

## CHICAGO WHITE SOX

| Batting | g. | ab. | r. | h. | hr. | rbi. | sb. | pct. |
|---|---|---|---|---|---|---|---|---|
| Davis ........ | 132 | 456 | 30 | 122 | 8 | 50 | 4 | .268 |
| *Melton ...... | 34 | 109 | 5 | 29 | 2 | 16 | 1 | .266 |
| Aparicio ..... | 157 | 622 | 56 | 164 | 4 | 36 | 18 | .264 |
| †Wagner ..... | 107 | 211 | 19 | 55 | 1 | 24 | 2 | .261 |

*Rookie    †Left handed    ‡Switch hitter

## CHICAGO WHITE SOX (cont.)

| Batting | g. | ab. | r. | h. | hr. | rbi. | sb. | pct. |
|---|---|---|---|---|---|---|---|---|
| Alomar | 132 | 363 | 40 | 92 | 0 | 11 | 20 | .253 |
| Berry | 153 | 504 | 49 | 127 | 7 | 32 | 6 | .252 |
| Josephson | 128 | 434 | 35 | 107 | 6 | 45 | 2 | .247 |
| Williams | 63 | 134 | 6 | 32 | 1 | 8 | 0 | .239 |
| †McCraw | 136 | 478 | 51 | 112 | 9 | 44 | 20 | .234 |
| Kenworthy | 58 | 122 | 2 | 27 | 0 | 2 | 0 | .221 |
| McNertney | 74 | 169 | 18 | 37 | 3 | 18 | 0 | .219 |
| *Bradford | 102 | 281 | 32 | 61 | 5 | 24 | 8 | .217 |
| †Ward | 125 | 399 | 43 | 86 | 15 | 50 | 4 | .216 |
| Hansen | 126 | 362 | 35 | 71 | 9 | 32 | 0 | .196 |
| *†Voss | 61 | 167 | 14 | 26 | 2 | 15 | 5 | .156 |

| Pitching | g. | cg. | ip. | h. | bb. | so. | w. | l. | era. |
|---|---|---|---|---|---|---|---|---|---|
| Wilhelm | 72 | 0 | 94 | 69 | 24 | 72 | 4 | 4 | 1.72 |
| †Wood | 88 | 5 | 159 | 127 | 33 | 73 | 13 | 12 | 1.82 |
| †John | 25 | 5 | 177 | 135 | 49 | 117 | 10 | 5 | 1.98 |
| Locker | 70 | 0 | 90 | 78 | 27 | 62 | 5 | 4 | 2.30 |
| Horlen | 35 | 4 | 224 | 197 | 70 | 102 | 12 | 14 | 2.37 |
| Fisher | 35 | 2 | 181 | 176 | 48 | 80 | 8 | 13 | 2.98 |
| Priddy | 35 | 2 | 114 | 106 | 41 | 64 | 3 | 11 | 3.63 |
| †Peters | 31 | 6 | 163 | 146 | 60 | 110 | 4 | 13 | 3.75 |
| *Carlos | 29 | 0 | 122 | 121 | 37 | 57 | 4 | 14 | 3.91 |
| Ribant | 31 | 0 | 56 | 62 | 27 | 27 | 2 | 4 | 4.34 |

## CLEVELAND INDIANS

| Batting | g. | ab. | r. | h. | hr. | rbi. | sb. | pct. |
|---|---|---|---|---|---|---|---|---|
| †Maye | 109 | 299 | 20 | 84 | 4 | 27 | 0 | .281 |
| Azcue | 115 | 357 | 23 | 100 | 4 | 22 | 1 | .280 |
| Cardenal | 157 | 582 | 78 | 150 | 7 | 44 | 40 | .258 |
| Johnson | 65 | 202 | 25 | 52 | 5 | 23 | 6 | .257 |
| Horton | 133 | 477 | 57 | 119 | 14 | 59 | 3 | .249 |
| †Sims | 122 | 361 | 48 | 90 | 11 | 44 | 1 | .249 |
| †Snyder | 106 | 298 | 32 | 72 | 3 | 28 | 1 | .242 |
| Fuller | 97 | 244 | 14 | 59 | 0 | 18 | 2 | .242 |
| Brown | 154 | 495 | 43 | 116 | 6 | 35 | 1 | .234 |
| *Nelson | 87 | 189 | 26 | 44 | 0 | 19 | 22 | .233 |
| Alvis | 131 | 452 | 38 | 101 | 8 | 37 | 5 | .223 |
| Harper | 129 | 235 | 26 | 51 | 6 | 26 | 11 | .217 |
| Salmon | 103 | 276 | 24 | 59 | 3 | 12 | 7 | .214 |
| †Hall | 98 | 236 | 19 | 49 | 2 | 16 | 2 | .208 |

| Pitching | g. | ip. | h. | bb. | so. | w. | l. | era. |
|---|---|---|---|---|---|---|---|---|
| Tiant | 34 | 19 | 258 | 152 | 73 | 264 | 21 | 9 | 1.60 |
| *Romo | 40 | 0 | 83 | 43 | 32 | 54 | 5 | 3 | 1.63 |
| †McDowell | 38 | 11 | 269 | 180 | 110 | 283 | 15 | 14 | 1.81 |
| Williams | 44 | 6 | 194 | 163 | 51 | 147 | 13 | 11 | 2.55 |
| Fisher | 54 | 0 | 95 | 87 | 17 | 44 | 4 | 2 | 2.84 |
| Siebert | 31 | 8 | 206 | 145 | 88 | 146 | 12 | 10 | 2.97 |
| *†Paul | 36 | 0 | 92 | 72 | 35 | 86 | 5 | 8 | 3.91 |
| Hargan | 32 | 4 | 158 | 139 | 80 | 78 | 8 | 15 | 4.16 |

## DETROIT TIGERS

| Batting | g. | ab. | r. | h. | hr. | rbi. | sb. | pct. |
|---|---|---|---|---|---|---|---|---|
| Kaline | 102 | 327 | 50 | 94 | 10 | 52 | 6 | .287 |
| Horton | 143 | 512 | 68 | 146 | 36 | 85 | 0 | .285 |
| †Northrup | 154 | 580 | 76 | 153 | 21 | 90 | 4 | .264 |
| Freehan | 155 | 540 | 73 | 142 | 25 | 84 | 1 | .263 |
| †Cash | 127 | 411 | 50 | 108 | 25 | 63 | 1 | .263 |
| Stanley | 154 | 583 | 88 | 151 | 11 | 60 | 4 | .259 |
| †McAuliffe | 151 | 570 | 95 | 142 | 16 | 56 | 8 | .249 |
| *†Matchick | 80 | 227 | 18 | 46 | 3 | 14 | 0 | .203 |
| Wert | 150 | 536 | 43 | 107 | 12 | 37 | 0 | .200 |
| Price | 64 | 132 | 12 | 23 | 3 | 13 | 0 | .174 |
| Tracewski | 90 | 212 | 30 | 33 | 4 | 15 | 3 | .156 |
| Oyler | 111 | 215 | 13 | 29 | 1 | 12 | 0 | .135 |

| Pitching | g. | cg. | ip. | h. | bb. | so. | w. | l. | era. |
|---|---|---|---|---|---|---|---|---|---|
| McLain | 41 | 28 | 336 | 241 | 63 | 280 | 31 | 6 | 1.96 |
| McMahon | 45 | 0 | 82 | 53 | 30 | 65 | 5 | 2 | 1.98 |
| *Patterson | 38 | 0 | 68 | 53 | 27 | 49 | 2 | 3 | 2.12 |
| †Hiller | 39 | 4 | 128 | 92 | 51 | 78 | 9 | 6 | 2.39 |
| Dobson | 47 | 2 | 125 | 89 | 48 | 92 | 5 | 8 | 2.66 |
| Wilson | 34 | 10 | 224 | 192 | 65 | 168 | 13 | 12 | 2.85 |
| †Lolich | 39 | 8 | 220 | 178 | 65 | 197 | 17 | 9 | 3.19 |
| Sparma | 34 | 7 | 182 | 169 | 77 | 110 | 10 | 10 | 3.71 |

## MINNESOTA TWINS

| Batting | g. | ab. | r. | h. | hr. | rbi. | sb. | pct. |
|---|---|---|---|---|---|---|---|---|
| †Oliva | 128 | 470 | 54 | 136 | 18 | 68 | 10 | .289 |
| †Uhlaender | 140 | 488 | 52 | 138 | 7 | 52 | 16 | .283 |
| †Carew | 127 | 461 | 46 | 126 | 1 | 42 | 12 | .273 |
| Tovar | 157 | 613 | 89 | 167 | 6 | 47 | 35 | .272 |
| †Reese | 123 | 332 | 40 | 86 | 4 | 28 | 3 | .259 |
| Allison | 145 | 468 | 63 | 116 | 22 | 52 | 9 | .248 |
| *†Look | 59 | 118 | 7 | 29 | 0 | 9 | 0 | .246 |
| Quilici | 97 | 229 | 22 | 56 | 1 | 22 | 0 | .245 |
| Rollins | 93 | 203 | 14 | 49 | 6 | 30 | 3 | .241 |
| Kostro | 63 | 108 | 9 | 26 | 0 | 9 | 0 | .241 |
| †Roseboro | 135 | 380 | 31 | 82 | 8 | 39 | 2 | .216 |
| Killebrew | 100 | 296 | 40 | 62 | 17 | 40 | 0 | .209 |
| *†Holt | 70 | 106 | 9 | 22 | 0 | 8 | 0 | .208 |
| Clark | 104 | 227 | 14 | 42 | 1 | 13 | 3 | .185 |
| Hernandez | 83 | 199 | 13 | 35 | 2 | 17 | 5 | .176 |

*Rookie   †Left handed   ‡Switch hitter

## MINNESOTA TWINS (cont.)

| Pitching | g. | cg. | ip. | h. | bb. | so. | w. | l. | era. |
|---|---|---|---|---|---|---|---|---|---|
| Perry | 32 | 3 | 139 | 113 | 26 | 69 | 8 | 6 | 2.27 |
| Chance | 43 | 15 | 292 | 224 | 63 | 234 | 16 | 16 | 2.53 |
| Wrth'ton | 54 | 0 | 76 | 67 | 32 | 57 | 4 | 5 | 2.61 |
| Miller | 45 | 0 | 72 | 65 | 24 | 41 | 0 | 3 | 2.75 |
| †Kaat | 30 | 9 | 208 | 192 | 40 | 129 | 14 | 12 | 2.94 |
| *†Per'noski | 66 | 0 | 87 | 86 | 39 | 68 | 8 | 7 | 3.10 |
| †Merritt | 38 | 11 | 259 | 207 | 52 | 182 | 12 | 16 | 3.24 |
| Boswell | 34 | 7 | 190 | 148 | 86 | 143 | 10 | 13 | 3.32 |
| †R...land | 28 | 0 | 62 | 55 | 23 | 36 | 4 | 1 | 3.48 |

## NEW YORK YANKEES

| Batting | g. | ab. | r. | h. | hr. | rbi. | sb. | pct. |
|---|---|---|---|---|---|---|---|---|
| ‡White | 159 | 577 | 89 | 154 | 17 | 62 | 20 | .267 |
| †Pepitone | 108 | 380 | 41 | 93 | 15 | 56 | 8 | .245 |
| Kosco | 131 | 466 | 47 | 112 | 15 | 59 | 2 | .240 |
| Robinson | 108 | 342 | 34 | 82 | 6 | 40 | 7 | .240 |
| †Mantle | 144 | 435 | 57 | 103 | 18 | 54 | 6 | .237 |
| †Clarke | 148 | 579 | 52 | 133 | 2 | 26 | 20 | .230 |
| *Cox | 135 | 437 | 33 | 100 | 7 | 41 | 3 | .229 |
| †Gibbs | 123 | 422 | 31 | 90 | 3 | 29 | 9 | .213 |
| ‡Michael | 61 | 116 | 8 | 23 | 1 | 8 | 3 | .198 |
| ‡Tresh | 152 | 507 | 60 | 99 | 11 | 52 | 10 | .195 |
| *Fernandez | 51 | 135 | 15 | 23 | 7 | 30 | 1 | .170 |
| Howser | 85 | 150 | 24 | 23 | 0 | 3 | 0 | .153 |

| Pitching | g. | cg. | ip. | h. | bb. | so. | w. | l. | era. |
|---|---|---|---|---|---|---|---|---|---|
| McDaniel | 24 | 0 | 51 | 30 | 12 | 43 | 4 | 1 | 1.76 |
| *Bahnsen | 37 | 10 | 267 | 216 | 68 | 161 | 17 | 12 | 2.06 |
| †Hamilton | 40 | 0 | 51 | 37 | 13 | 42 | 2 | 2 | 2.12 |
| Stot'myre | 36 | 19 | 279 | 243 | 65 | 140 | 21 | 12 | 2.45 |
| Peterson | 36 | 6 | 212 | 187 | 29 | 114 | 12 | 11 | 2.63 |
| Verbanic | 42 | 2 | 97 | 104 | 41 | 39 | 6 | 7 | 3.15 |
| Womack | 45 | 0 | 62 | 53 | 29 | 28 | 3 | 7 | 3.19 |
| †Barber | 20 | 3 | 128 | 127 | 64 | 88 | 6 | 5 | 3.23 |
| Talbot | 29 | 1 | 99 | 89 | 42 | 67 | 1 | 9 | 3.36 |
| †Downing | 15 | 1 | 61 | 54 | 20 | 40 | 3 | 3 | 3.54 |
| M'bouquet | 17 | 2 | 89 | 92 | 13 | 32 | 6 | 7 | 4.45 |

## OAKLAND ATHLETICS

| Batting | g. | ab. | r. | h. | hr. | rbi. | sb. | pct. |
|---|---|---|---|---|---|---|---|---|
| Cater | 147 | 504 | 53 | 146 | 6 | 62 | 8 | .290 |
| Campaneris | 159 | 642 | 87 | 177 | 4 | 38 | 62 | .276 |
| †Monday | 148 | 482 | 56 | 132 | 8 | 49 | 15 | .274 |
| Hershberger | 99 | 245 | 22 | 67 | 5 | 32 | 8 | .273 |
| Bando | 162 | 605 | 67 | 152 | 9 | 67 | 13 | .251 |
| †Jackson | 154 | 553 | 83 | 138 | 29 | 74 | 14 | .250 |
| ‡Kubiak | 48 | 120 | 10 | 30 | 0 | 8 | 1 | .250 |
| Pagliaroni | 66 | 199 | 19 | 49 | 6 | 20 | 0 | .246 |
| Green | 76 | 202 | 19 | 47 | 6 | 18 | 3 | .233 |
| ‡Donaldson | 126 | 363 | 37 | 80 | 2 | 27 | 5 | .220 |
| †Webster | 66 | 196 | 17 | 42 | 3 | 23 | 3 | .214 |
| Duncan | 82 | 244 | 15 | 47 | 7 | 28 | 1 | .193 |
| *Gosger | 89 | 150 | 7 | 27 | 0 | 6 | 3 | .180 |
| *Rudi | 68 | 181 | 10 | 32 | 1 | 12 | 1 | .177 |

| Pitching | g. | cg. | ip. | h. | bb. | so. | w. | l. | era. |
|---|---|---|---|---|---|---|---|---|---|
| Nash | 34 | 12 | 229 | 185 | 55 | 170 | 13 | 3 | 2.28 |
| Segui | 52 | 0 | 83 | 51 | 32 | 71 | 6 | 5 | 2.39 |
| Odom | 32 | 9 | 231 | 179 | 93 | 143 | 16 | 10 | 2.49 |
| †Lindblad | 47 | 0 | 56 | 51 | 14 | 42 | 4 | 3 | 2.73 |
| Dobson | 35 | 11 | 225 | 197 | 80 | 109 | 12 | 14 | 3.00 |
| Krausse | 36 | 2 | 185 | 146 | 62 | 104 | 10 | 11 | 3.11 |
| *Sprague | 47 | 0 | 68 | 51 | 34 | 34 | 3 | 4 | 3.31 |
| Hunter | 36 | 11 | 234 | 210 | 69 | 174 | 13 | 13 | 3.35 |
| Aker | 54 | 0 | 76 | 72 | 33 | 42 | 4 | 4 | 4.14 |

## WASHINGTON SENATORS

| Batting | g. | ab. | r. | h. | hr. | rbi. | sb. | pct. |
|---|---|---|---|---|---|---|---|---|
| F. Howard | 158 | 598 | 79 | 164 | 44 | 106 | 0 | .274 |
| *Alyea | 53 | 150 | 18 | 40 | 6 | 23 | 0 | .267 |
| McMullen | 151 | 557 | 66 | 137 | 20 | 62 | 1 | .246 |
| †B. Allen | 121 | 373 | 33 | 90 | 6 | 39 | 2 | .241 |
| †Stroud | 105 | 306 | 41 | 73 | 4 | 23 | 10 | .239 |
| †Epstein | 123 | 385 | 40 | 90 | 13 | 33 | 1 | .234 |
| *†Unser | 156 | 635 | 66 | 146 | 1 | 30 | 11 | .230 |
| Cullen | 119 | 269 | 24 | 62 | 3 | 29 | 0 | .230 |
| H. Allen | 68 | 128 | 16 | 28 | 1 | 9 | 0 | .219 |
| Peterson | 94 | 226 | 20 | 46 | 3 | 18 | 2 | .204 |
| †Bryan | 40 | 108 | 7 | 22 | 3 | 8 | 2 | .204 |
| Casanova | 96 | 322 | 19 | 63 | 4 | 26 | 0 | .196 |
| †French | 59 | 165 | 9 | 32 | 1 | 10 | 1 | .194 |
| Bowens | 57 | 115 | 14 | 22 | 4 | 7 | 0 | .191 |
| Brinkman | 77 | 193 | 12 | 36 | 0 | 6 | 0 | .187 |
| *‡Coggins | 62 | 171 | 15 | 30 | 0 | 7 | 1 | .175 |

| Pitching | g. | cg. | ip. | h. | bb. | so. | w. | l. | era. |
|---|---|---|---|---|---|---|---|---|---|
| Pascual | 31 | 8 | 201 | 180 | 59 | 111 | 13 | 12 | 2.69 |
| Hannan | 25 | 4 | 140 | 147 | 50 | 75 | 10 | 6 | 3.02 |
| Higgins | 58 | 0 | 99 | 80 | 44 | 64 | 4 | 4 | 3.09 |
| Coleman | 33 | 12 | 223 | 212 | 51 | 139 | 12 | 16 | 3.27 |
| †Moore | 32 | 0 | 118 | 116 | 42 | 56 | 4 | 6 | 3.36 |
| Humphreys | 56 | 0 | 93 | 78 | 30 | 57 | 5 | 7 | 3.68 |
| Bosman | 47 | 0 | 140 | 140 | 38 | 66 | 2 | 9 | 3.79 |
| †Bertaina | 27 | 1 | 127 | 133 | 69 | 80 | 7 | 13 | 4.68 |
| B. Howard | 23 | 0 | 80 | 92 | 49 | 42 | 1 | 6 | 4.73 |
| Ortega | 31 | 1 | 116 | 115 | 62 | 57 | 5 | 12 | 4.97 |

## Champion Batters and Their Averages

| Yr. | NATIONAL LEAGUE Player | Club | Aver. | Yr. | AMERICAN LEAGUE Player | Club | Aver. |
|---|---|---|---|---|---|---|---|
| 1943 | Stan Musial | St. Louis | .357 | 1943 | Luke Appling | Chicago | .328 |
| 1944 | Dixie Walker | Brooklyn | .357 | 1944 | Lou Boudreau | Cleveland | .327 |
| 1945 | Phil Cavarretta | Chicago | .355 | 1945 | George Stirnweiss | New York | .309 |
| 1946 | Stan Musial | St. Louis | .365 | 1946 | Mickey Vernon | Washington | .353 |
| 1947 | Harry Walker | Philadelphia | .363 | 1947 | Ted Williams | Boston | .343 |
| 1948 | Stan Musial | St. Louis | .376 | 1948 | Ted Williams | Boston | .369 |
| 1949 | Jackie Robinson | Brooklyn | .342 | 1949 | George Kell | Detroit | .343 |
| 1950 | Stan Musial | St. Louis | .346 | 1950 | Billy Goodman | Boston | .354 |
| 1951 | Stan Musial | St. Louis | .355 | 1951 | Ferris Fain | Philadelphia | .344 |
| 1952 | Stan Musial | St. Louis | .336 | 1952 | Ferris Fain | Philadelphia | .327 |
| 1953 | Carl Furillo | Brooklyn | .344 | 1953 | Mickey Vernon | Washington | .337 |
| 1954 | Willie Mays | New York | .345 | 1954 | Roberto Avila | Cleveland | .341 |
| 1955 | Richie Ashburn | Philadelphia | .338 | 1955 | Al Kaline | Detroit | .340 |
| 1956 | Hank Aaron | Milwaukee | .328 | 1956 | Mickey Mantle | New York | .353 |
| 1957 | Stan Musial | St. Louis | .351 | 1957 | Ted Williams | Boston | .388 |
| 1958 | Richie Ashburn | Philadelphia | .350 | 1958 | Ted Williams | Boston | .328 |
| 1959 | Hank Aaron | Milwaukee | .355 | 1959 | Harvey Kuenn | Detroit | .353 |
| 1960 | Dick Groat | Pittsburgh | .325 | 1960 | Pete Runnels | Boston | .320 |
| 1961 | Roberto Clemente | Pittsburgh | .351 | 1961 | Norm Cash | Detroit | .361 |
| 1962 | Tommy Davis | Los Angeles | .346 | 1962 | Pete Runnels | Boston | .326 |
| 1963 | Tommy Davis | Los Angeles | .326 | 1963 | Carl Yastrzemski | Boston | .321 |
| 1964 | Roberto Clemente | Pittsburgh | .339 | 1964 | Tony Oliva | Minnesota | .323 |
| 1965 | Roberto Clemente | Pittsburgh | .329 | 1965 | Tony Oliva | Minnesota | .321 |
| 1966 | Matty Alou | Pittsburgh | .342 | 1966 | Frank Robinson | Baltimore | .316 |
| 1967 | Roberto Clemente | Pittsburgh | .357 | 1967 | Carl Yastrzemski | Boston | .326 |
| 1968 | Pete Rose | Cincinnati | .335 | 1968 | Carl Yastrzemski | Boston | .301 |

## Home Run Leaders

| Year | NATIONAL LEAGUE | Year | AMERICAN LEAGUE |
|---|---|---|---|
| 1943 | Bill Nicholson, Chicago.............29 | 1943 | Rudy York, Detroit.................34 |
| 1944 | Bill Nicholson, Chicago.............33 | 1944 | Nick Etten, New York...............22 |
| 1945 | Tommy Holmes, Boston..............28 | 1945 | Vern Stephens, St. Louis...........24 |
| 1946 | Ralph Kiner, Pittsburgh............23 | 1946 | Hank Greenberg, Detroit............44 |
| 1947 | Ralph Kiner, Pitts.; John Mize, N.Y..51 | 1947 | Ted Williams, Boston...............32 |
| 1948 | Ralph Kiner, Pitts.; John Mize, N.Y..40 | 1948 | Joe DiMaggio, New York.............39 |
| 1949 | Ralph Kiner, Pittsburgh............54 | 1949 | Ted Williams, Boston...............43 |
| 1950 | Ralph Kiner, Pittsburgh............47 | 1950 | Al Rosen, Cleveland................37 |
| 1951 | Ralph Kiner, Pittsburgh............42 | 1951 | Gus Zernial, Chicago-Philadelphia..33 |
| 1952 | Ralph Kiner, Pittsburgh;          | 1952 | Larry Doby, Cleveland..............32 |
|      | Hank Sauer, Chicago.......37 | 1953 | Al Rosen, Cleveland................43 |
| 1953 | Ed Mathews, Milwaukee.............47 | 1954 | Larry Doby, Cleveland..............32 |
| 1954 | Ted Kluszewski, Cincinnati.........49 | 1955 | Mickey Mantle, New York............37 |
| 1955 | Willie Mays, New York..............51 | 1956 | Mickey Mantle, New York............52 |
| 1956 | Duke Snider, Brooklyn..............43 | 1957 | Roy Sievers, Washington............42 |
| 1957 | Hank Aaron, Milwaukee.............44 | 1958 | Mickey Mantle, New York............42 |
| 1958 | Ernie Banks, Chicago...............47 | 1959 | Rocky Colavito, Cleveland, |
| 1959 | Ed Mathews, Milwaukee.............46 |  | Harmon Killebrew, Washington..42 |
| 1960 | Ernie Banks, Chicago...............41 | 1960 | Mickey Mantle, New York............40 |
| 1961 | Orlando Cepeda, San Francisco.......46 | 1961 | Roger Maris, New York..............61 |
| 1962 | Willie Mays, San Francisco..........49 | 1962 | Harmon Killebrew, Minnesota........48 |
| 1963 | Hank Aaron, Milwaukee; | 1963 | Harmon Killebrew, Minnesota........45 |
|      | Willie McCovey, San Francisco.....44 | 1964 | Harmon Killebrew, Minnesota........49 |
| 1964 | Willie Mays, San Francisco..........47 | 1965 | Tony Conigliaro, Boston............32 |
| 1965 | Willie Mays, San Francisco..........52 | 1966 | Frank Robinson, Baltimore..........49 |
| 1966 | Hank Aaron, Atlanta................44 | 1967 | Carl Yastrzemski, Boston; |
| 1967 | Hank Aaron, Atlanta................39 |  | Harmon Killebrew, Minn...........44 |
| 1968 | Willie McCovey, San Francisco.......36 | 1968 | Frank Howard, Wash................44 |

**All-time Major League Record (154-game Season)—60—Babe Ruth, New York Yankees (A.), 1927. (162-game Season)—61—Roger Maris, New York Yankees, 1961.** Prior to the 1931 season a batted ball that bounced into the stands was a home run (now a ground-rule double). None of Babe Ruth's record 60 homers bounced into the stands.

## Runs Batted In Leaders

| Yr. | NATIONAL LEAGUE Batter, Club | RBI | Yr. | AMERICAN LEAGUE Batter, Club | RBI |
|---|---|---|---|---|---|
| 1947 | John Mize, New York | 138 | 1947 | Ted Williams, Boston | 114 |
| 1948 | Stan Musial, St. Louis | 131 | 1948 | Joe DiMaggio, New York | 155 |
| 1949 | Ralph Kiner, Pittsburgh | 127 | 1949 | Ted Williams, Vern Stephens, Boston. | 159 |
| 1950 | Del Ennis, Philadelphia | 126 | 1950 | Walt Dropo, Boston |  |
| 1951 | Monte Irvin, New York | 121 |  | Vern Stephens, Boston | 144 |
| 1952 | Hank Sauer, Chicago | 121 | 1951 | Gus Zernial, Chi.-Phila. | 129 |
| 1953 | Roy Campanella, Brooklyn | 142 | 1952 | Al Rosen, Cleveland | 105 |
| 1954 | Ted Kluszewski, Cincinnati | 141 | 1953 | Al Rosen, Cleveland | 145 |
| 1955 | Duke Snider, Brooklyn | 136 | 1954 | Larry Doby, Cleveland | 126 |
| 1956 | Stan Musial, St. Louis | 109 | 1955 | Ray Boone, Detroit, |  |
| 1957 | Hank Aaron, Milwaukee | 132 |  | Jack Jensen, Boston | 116 |
| 1958 | Ernie Banks, Chicago | 129 | 1956 | Mickey Mantle, New York | 130 |
| 1959 | Ernie Banks, Chicago | 143 | 1957 | Roy Sievers, Washington | 114 |
| 1960 | Hank Aaron, Milwaukee | 126 | 1958 | Jack Jensen, Boston | 122 |
| 1961 | Orlando Cepeda, San Francisco | 142 | 1959 | Jack Jensen, Boston | 112 |
| 1962 | Tommy Davis, Los Angeles | 153 | 1960 | Roger Maris, New York | 112 |
| 1963 | Hank Aaron, Milwaukee | 130 | 1961 | Roger Maris, New York | 142 |
| 1964 | Ken Boyer, St. Louis | 119 | 1962 | Harmon Killebrew, Minn. | 126 |
| 1965 | Deron Johnson, Cincinnati | 130 | 1963 | Dick Stuart, Boston | 118 |
| 1966 | Hank Aaron, Atlanta | 127 | 1964 | Brooks Robinson, Baltimore | 118 |
| 1967 | Orlando Cepeda, St. Louis | 111 | 1965 | Rocky Colavito, Cleveland | 108 |
| 1968 | Willie McCovey, San Francisco | 105 | 1966 | Frank Robinson, Baltimore | 122 |
|  |  |  | 1967 | Carl Yastrzemski, Boston | 121 |
|  |  |  | 1968 | Ken Harrelson, Boston | 109 |

## American Legion Junior Baseball World Champions

| | | |
|---|---|---|
| 1952—Cincinnati, Ohio | 1957—Cincinnati, Ohio | 1961—Phoenix, Ariz. | 1965—Charlotte, N. C. |
| 1953—Yakima, Wash. | 1958—Cincinnati, Ohio | 1962—St. Louis, Mo. | 1966—Oakland, Calif. |
| 1954—San Diego, Calif. | 1959—Detroit, Mich. | 1963—Long Beach, Calif. | 1967—Tuscaloosa, Ala. |
| 1955—Cincinnati, Ohio | 1960—New Orleans, La. | 1964—Upland, Calif. | 1968—Memphis, Tenn. |
| 1956—St. Louis, Mo. |  |  |  |

# Major League No-Hit Games Since 1938
## (Complete Nine-inning Games)

| Date | Pitcher | Club | Score |
|------|---------|------|-------|
| 1938—June 11 | Johnny Vander Meer | Cincinnati-Boston N | 3-0 |
| 1938—June 15 | Johnny Vander Meer | Cincinnati-Brooklyn N (night game) | 6-0 |
| 1938—Aug. 27 | Monte Pearson | New York-Cleveland A (2nd game) | 13-0 |
| 1940—April 16 | Bob Feller | Cleveland-Chicago A (opening day) | 1-0 |
| 1940—April 30 | Tex Carleton | Brooklyn-Cincinnati N | 3-0 |
| 1941—Aug. 20 | Lon Warneke | St. Louis-Cincinnati N | 2-0 |
| 1944—April 27 | Jim Tobin | Boston-Brooklyn N | 2-0 |
| 1944—May 15 | Clyde Shoun | Cincinnati-Boston N | 1-0 |
| 1945—Sept. 9 | Dick Fowler | hiladelphia-St. Louis A | 1-0 |
| 1946—April 23 | Ed Head | Brooklyn-Boston N | 5-0 |
| 1946—April 30 | Bob Feller | Cleveland-New York A | 1-0 |
| 1947—June 18 | Ewell Blackwell | Cincinnati-Boston N (night game) | 6-0 |
| 1947—July 10 | Don Black | Cleveland-Philadelphia A | 3-0 |
| 1947—Sept. 3 | Bill McCahan | Philadelphia-Washington A | 3-0 |
| 1948—June 30 | Bob Lemon | Cleveland-Detroit A | 2-0 |
| 1948—Sept. 9 | Rex Barney | Brooklyn-New York N (night game) | 2-0 |
| 1950—Aug. 11 | Vern Bickford | Boston-Brooklyn N (night game) | 7-0 |
| 1951—May 6 | Cliff Chambers | Pittsburgh-Boston N (2nd game) | 3-0 |
| 1951—July 1 | Bob Feller | Cleveland-Detroit A (1st game) | 2-1 |
| 1951—July 12 | Allie Reynolds | New York-Cleveland A (night game) | 1-0 |
| 1951—Sept. 28 | Allie Reynolds | New York-Boston A (first game) | 8-0 |
| 1952—May 15 | Virgil Trucks | Detroit-Washington A | 1-0 |
| 1952—June 19 | Carl Erskine | Brooklyn-Chicago N | 5-0 |
| 1952—Aug. 25 | Virgil Trucks | Detroit-New York A | 1-0 |
| 1953—May 6 | Bobo Holloman | St. Louis-Philadelphia A (night game) | 6-0 |
| 1954—June 12 | Jim Wilson | Milwaukee-Philadelphia N | 2-0 |
| 1955—May 12 | Sam Jones | Chicago-Pittsburgh N | 4-0 |
| 1956—May 12 | Carl Erskine | Brooklyn-New York N | 3-0 |
| 1956—July 14 | Mel Parnell | Boston-Chicago A | 4-0 |
| 1956—Sept. 25 | Sal Maglie | Brooklyn-Philadelphia N (night game) | 5-0 |
| 1956—Oct. 8 | Don Larsen (1) | New York-Brooklyn N | 2-0 |
| 1957—Aug. 20 | Bob Keegan | Chicago-Washington A | 6-0 |
| 1958—July 20 | Jim Bunning | Detroit-Boston A | 3-0 |
| 1958—Sept. 20 | Hoyt Wilhelm | Baltimore-New York A | 1-0 |
| 1959—May 26 | Harvey Haddix (2) | Pittsburgh-Milwaukee N | 0-2 |
| 1960—May 15 | Don Cardwell | Chicago-St. Louis N (2nd game) | 4-0 |
| 1960—Aug. 18 | Lew Burdette | Milwaukee-Philadelphia N | 1-0 |
| 1960—Sept. 16 | Warren Spahn | Milwaukee-Philadelphia N | 4-0 |
| 1961—April 28 | Warren Spahn | Milwaukee-San Francisco N (night) | 1-0 |
| 1962—May 5 | Bo Belinsky | Los Angeles-Baltimore A (night game) | 2-0 |
| 1962—June 26 | Earl Wilson | Boston-Los Angeles A (night game) | 2-0 |
| 1962—June 30 | Sandy Koufax | Los Angeles-New York N (night game) | 5-0 |
| 1962—Aug. 1 | Bill Monbouquette | Boston-Chicago A (night game) | 1-0 |
| 1962—Aug. 26 | Jack Kralick | Minnesota-Kansas City A | 3-0 |
| 1963—May 11 | Sandy Koufax | Los Angeles-San Francisco N (night) | 8-0 |
| 1963—May 17 | Don Nottebart | Houston-Philadelphia N (night) | 4-1 |
| 1963—June 15 | Juan Marichal | San Francisco-Houston N | 1-0 |
| 1964—April 23 | Ken Johnson (3) | Houston-Cincinnati N | 0-1 |
| 1964—June 4 | Sandy Koufax | Los Angeles-Philadelphia N | 3-0 |
| 1964—June 21 | Jim Bunning (4) | Philadelphia-New York N | 6-0 |
| 1965—June 14 | Jim Maloney (5) | Cincinnati-New York N (night) | 0-1 |
| 1965—Aug. 19 | Jim Maloney (6) | Cincinnati-Chicago N (1st game) | 1-0 |
| 1965—Sept. 9 | Sandy Koufax (4) | Los Angeles-Chicago N | 1-0 |
| 1965—Sept. 16 | Dave Morehead | Boston-Cleveland A | 2-0 |
| 1966—June 10 | Sonny Siebert | Cleveland-Washington A (night) | 2-0 |
| 1967—Apr. 30 | S. Barber, Stu Miller (7) | Baltimore-Detroit A | 0-2 |
| 1967—June 18 | Don Wilson | Houston-Atlanta N | 2-0 |
| 1967—Aug. 25 | Dean Chance | Minnesota-Cleveland A | 2-1 |
| 1967—Sept. 10 | Joe Horlen | Chicago-Detroit A | 4-0 |
| 1968—April 27 | Tom Phoebus | Baltimore-Boston A | 6-0 |
| 1968—May 8 | Jim Hunter (4) | Oakland-Minnesota A | 4-0 |
| 1968—July 29 | George Culver | Cincinnati-Philadelphia N (night) | 6-1 |
| 1968—Sept. 17 | Gaylord Perry | San Francisco-St. Louis N (night) | 1-0 |
| 1968—Sept. 18 | Ray Washburn | St. Louis-San Francisco N | 2-0 |

(1) Perfect game and first World Series no-hitter. (2) Pitched 12 perfect innings. He allowed one hit in the 13th and lost the game. (3) Lost game on two errors in ninth inning. (4) Perfect game. (5) Maloney pitched ten hitless innings, then allowed two hits in the eleventh. Struck out eighteen batters. (6) Ten innings. (7) Barber pitched 8⅔ innings, Miller ⅓ of an inning. Detroit scored two 9th-inning runs on a wild pitch and an error.

# Leading Pitchers—Earned-Run Average
Based on 10 complete games through 1950 then 154 innings until A. L. expanded in '61, N. L. in '62, then 162 innings. Bob Gibson of the Cardinals set NL record in 1968 with a 1.12 ERA.

| | NATIONAL LEAGUE | | | | | AMERICAN LEAGUE | | | |
|---|---|---|---|---|---|---|---|---|---|
| Yr. | Pitcher, Club | G | IP | ERA | Yr. | Pitcher, Club | G | IP | ERA |
| 1947 | Warren Spahn, Boston | 40 | 290 | 2.33 | 1947 | Spud Chandler, New York | 17 | 128 | 2.46 |
| 1948 | Harry Brecheen, St. Louis | 33 | 233 | 2.24 | 1948 | Gene Bearden, Cleveland | 37 | 230 | 2.43 |
| 1949 | Dave Koslo, New York | 38 | 212 | 2.50 | 1949 | Mel Parnell, Boston | 39 | 295 | 2.78 |
| 1950 | Jim Hearn, St. L.-N. Y. | 22 | 134 | 2.49 | 1950 | Early Wynn, Cleveland | 32 | 214 | 3.20 |
| 1951 | Chet Nichols, Boston | 33 | 156 | 2.88 | 1951 | Saul Rogovin, Det.-Chi. | 27 | 217 | 2.78 |
| 1952 | Hoyt Wilhelm, New York | 71 | 159 | 2.43 | 1952 | Allie Reynolds, New York | 35 | 244 | 2.07 |
| 1953 | Warren Spahn, Milwaukee | 35 | 266 | 2.10 | 1953 | Ed Lopat, New York | 25 | 178 | 2.43 |
| 1954 | John Antonelli, New York | 39 | 259 | 2.29 | 1954 | Mike Garcia, Cleveland | 45 | 259 | 2.64 |
| 1955 | Bob Friend, Pittsburgh | 44 | 200 | 2.84 | 1955 | Billy Pierce, Chicago | 33 | 206 | 1.97 |
| 1956 | Lew Burdette, Milwaukee | 39 | 256 | 2.71 | 1956 | Whitey Ford, New York | 31 | 226 | 2.47 |
| 1957 | Johnny Podres, Brooklyn | 31 | 196 | 2.66 | 1957 | Bobby Shantz, New York | 30 | 173 | 2.45 |
| 1958 | Stu Miller, San Francisco | 41 | 182 | 2.47 | 1958 | Whitey Ford, New York | 30 | 219 | 2.01 |
| 1959 | Sam Jones, San Francisco | 50 | 271 | 2.82 | 1959 | Hoyt Wilhelm, Baltimore | 32 | 226 | 2.19 |
| 1960 | Mike McCormick, San Fran. | 40 | 253 | 2.70 | 1960 | Frank Baumann, Chicago | 47 | 185 | 2.68 |
| 1961 | Warren Spahn, Milwaukee | 38 | 263 | 3.01 | 1961 | Dick Donovan, Washington | 32 | 169 | 2.40 |
| 1962 | Sandy Koufax, Los Angeles | 28 | 184 | 2.54 | 1962 | Hank Aguirre, Detroit | 42 | 216 | 2.21 |
| 1963 | Sandy Koufax, Los Angeles | 40 | 311 | 1.88 | 1963 | Gary Peters, Chicago | 41 | 243 | 2.33 |
| 1964 | Sandy Koufax, Los Angeles | 29 | 223 | 1.74 | 1964 | Dean Chance, Los Angeles | 46 | 278 | 1.56 |
| 1965 | Sandy Koufax, Los Angeles | 43 | 336 | 2.04 | 1965 | Sam McDowell, Cleveland | 42 | 274 | 2.17 |
| 1966 | Sandy Koufax, Los Angeles | 41 | 323 | 1.73 | 1966 | Gary Peters, Chicago | 29 | 204 | 2.03 |
| 1967 | Phil Niekro, Atlanta | 46 | 207 | 1.87 | 1967 | Joe Horlen, Chicago | 35 | 258 | 2.06 |
| 1968 | Bob Gibson, St. Louis | 34 | 305 | 1.12 | 1968 | Luis Tiant, Cleveland | 34 | 258 | 1.60 |

Earned-run average is computed by multiplying the number of earned runs allowed by 9, then dividing by the number of innings pitched.

# Members of National Baseball Hall of Fame and Museum

The shrine of organized baseball, dedicated June 12, 1939 is located in Cooperstown, N. Y.

Alexander, Grover Cleveland
Anson (Cap), Adrian O.
Appling, Lucius B.
Baker (Home Run), J. Frank
Barrow, Edward G.
Bender (Chief), Charles
Bresnahan, Roger
Brouthers, Dan
Brown (Three Finger), Mordecai P.
Bulkeley, Morgan C.
Burkett, Jesse C.
Carey, Max George
Cartwright, Alexander J., Jr.
Chadwick, Henry
Chance, Frank L.
Chesbro, John D.
Clarke, Fred
Clarkson, John G.
Cobb, Tyrus R.
Cochrane (Mickey), Gordon S.
Collins, Edward T.
Collins, James
Comiskey, Charles A.
Connolly, Thomas H.
Crawford (Wahoo), Samuel E.
Cronin, Joseph Edward
Cummings (Candy), W. A.
Cuyler (Kiki), Hazen
Dean (Dizzy), Jay Hanna
Delahanty, Ed
Dickey, William M.
DiMaggio, Joseph Paul
Duffy, Hugh
Evers, John J.
Ewing (Buck), William B.
Faber, Urban C.
Feller, Robert William

Flick, Elmer H.
Foxx, James E.
Frisch, Frank
Galvin (Pud), James
Gehrig (Lou), Henry Louis
Gehringer, Charles
Goslin (Goose), Leon
Greenberg, Henry Benjamin
Griffith, Clark C.
Grimes, Burleigh A.
Grove (Lefty), Robert M.
Hamilton, William Robert
Hartnett (Gabby), Charles L.
Heilmann, Harry Edwin
Hornsby, Rogers
Hubbell, Carl
Huggins, Miller J.
Jennings, Hugh
Johnson, Byron B.
Johnson, Walter P.
Keefe, Timothy J.
Keeler, William
Kelly (King), Mike J.
Klem, William J.
Lajoie, Napoleon
Landis, Kenesaw M.
Lyons, Theodore A.
Mack, Connie
Manush, Henry E.
Maranville (Rabbit), Walter J
Mathewson, Christy
McCarthy, Joseph V.
McCarthy, Thomas F.
McGinnity, Joseph J.
McGraw, John J.
McKechnie, William Boyd
Medwick, Joe

Nichols (Kid), Charles A.
O'Rourke, James H.
Ott (Mel), Melvin T.
Pennock, Herbert J.
Plank, Edward S.
Radbourne (Old Hoss), Charlie
Rice (Sam), Edgar C.
Rickey, Branch
Rixey, Eppa
Robinson, Jackie
Robinson, Wilbert
Roush, Edd J.
Ruffing (Red), Charles
Ruth (Babe), George H.
Schalk, Raymond W.
Simmons (Al), Aloysius Harry
Sisler, George H.
Spalding, Albert G.
Speaker (Tris), Tristram E.
Stengel (Casey), Charles D.
Terry, William H.
Tinker, Joseph B.
Traynor (Pie), Harold J.
Vance (Dazzy), Arthur Charles
Waddell (Rube), George Edward
Wagner (Honus), John Peter
Wallace, Roderick J.
Walsh, Edward A.
Waner, Lloyd
Waner, Paul Glee
Ward, John Montgomery
Wheat, Zachariah Davis
Williams, Theodore
Wright, George
Wright, Harry
Young (Cy), Denton T.

# Most Valuable Player Awards

Source: Baseball Writers' Association.

| NATIONAL LEAGUE | | AMERICAN LEAGUE | |
|---|---|---|---|
| Year Player | Club | Year Player | Club |
| 1936—Carl Hubbell | New York | 1936—Lou Gehrig | New York |
| 1937—Joe Medwick | St. Louis | 1937—Charley Gehringer | Detroit |
| 1938—Ernie Lombardi | Cincinnati | 1938—Jimmy Foxx | Boston |
| 1939—Bucky Walters | Cincinnati | 1939—Joe DiMaggio | New York |
| 1940—Frank McCormick | Cincinnati | 1940—Hank Greenberg | Detroit |
| 1941—Dolph Camilli | Brooklyn | 1941—Joe DiMaggio | New York |
| 1942—Mort Cooper | St. Louis | 1942—Joe Gordon | New York |
| 1943—Stan Musial | St. Louis | 1943—Spurgeon Chandler | New York |
| 1944—Martin Marion | St. Louis | 1944—Hal Newhouser | Detroit |
| 1945—Phil Cavarretta | Chicago | 1945—Hal Newhouser | Detroit |
| 1946—Stan Musial | St. Louis | 1946—Ted Williams | Boston |
| 1947—Bob Elliott | Boston | 1947—Joe DiMaggio | New York |
| 1948—Stan Musial | St. Louis | 1948—Lou Boudreau | Cleveland |
| 1949—Jackie Robinson | Brooklyn | 1949—Ted Williams | Boston |
| 1950—Jim Konstanty | Philadelphia | 1950—Phil Rizzuto | New York |
| 1951—Roy Campanella | Brooklyn | 1951—Yogi Berra | New York |
| 1952—Hank Sauer | Chicago | 1952—Bobby Shantz | Philadelphia |
| 1953—Roy Campanella | Brooklyn | 1953—Al Rosen | Cleveland |
| 1954—Willie Mays | New York | 1954—Yogi Berra | New York |
| 1955—Roy Campanella | Brooklyn | 1955—Yogi Berra | New York |
| 1956—Don Newcombe | Brooklyn | 1956—Mickey Mantle | New York |
| 1957—Henry Aaron | Milwaukee | 1957—Mickey Mantle | New York |
| 1958—Ernie Banks | Chicago | 1958—Jackie Jensen | Boston |
| 1959—Ernie Banks | Chicago | 1959—Nellie Fox | Chicago |
| 1960—Dick Groat | Pittsburgh | 1960—Roger Maris | New York |
| 1961—Frank Robinson | Cincinnati | 1961—Roger Maris | New York |
| 1962—Maury Wills | Los Angeles | 1962—Mickey Mantle | New York |
| 1963—Sandy Koufax | Los Angeles | 1963—Elston Howard | New York |
| 1964—Ken Boyer | St. Louis | 1964—Brooks Robinson | Baltimore |
| 1965—Willie Mays | San Francisco | 1965—Zoilo Versalles | Minnesota |
| 1966—Roberto Clemente | Pittsburgh | 1966—Frank Robinson | Baltimore |
| 1967—Orlando Cepeda | St. Louis | 1967—Carl Yastrzemski | Boston |

# Rookie of the Year Award

Source: Baseball Writers' Assn.
1947—Combined Selection—Jackie Robinson, Brooklyn, 1b
1948—Combined Selection—Alvin Dark, Boston, N. L., ss

| Year | National League | Year | American League |
|---|---|---|---|
| 1949—Don Newcombe, Brooklyn, p | | 1949—Roy Sievers, St. Louis, of | |
| 1950—Sam Jethroe, Boston, of | | 1950—Walt Dropo, Boston, 1b | |
| 1951—Willie Mays, N. Y., of | | 1951—Gil McDougald, N. Y., 3b | |
| 1952—Joe Black, Brooklyn, p | | 1952—Harry Byrd, Phil., p | |
| 1953—Jim Gilliam, Brooklyn, 2b | | 1953—Harvey Kuenn, Detroit, ss | |
| 1954—Wally Moon, St. Louis, of | | 1954—Bob Grim, N. Y., p | |
| 1955—Bill Virdon, St. Louis, of | | 1955—Herb Score, Cleveland, p | |
| 1956—Frank Robinson, Cinn., of | | 1956—Luis Aparicio, Chicago, ss | |
| 1957—Jack Sanford, Phil., p | | 1957—Tony Kubek, N. Y., if-of | |
| 1958—Orlando Cepeda, S. F., 1b | | 1958—Albie Pearson, Wash., of | |
| 1959—Willie McCovey, S. F., 1b | | 1959—Bob Allison, Wash., of | |
| 1960—Frank Howard, Los Angeles, of | | 1960—Ron Hansen, Balt., ss | |
| 1961—Billy Williams, Chicago, of | | 1961—Don Schwall, Boston, p | |
| 1962—Ken Hubbs, Chicago, 2b | | 1962—Tom Tresh, N. Y., if-of | |
| 1963—Pete Rose, Cinn., 2b | | 1963—Gary Peters, Chicago, p | |
| 1964—Richie Allen, Phil., 3b | | 1964—Tony Oliva, Minn., of | |
| 1965—Jim Lefebvre, L. A., 2b | | 1965—Curt Blefary, Balt., of | |
| 1966—Tommy Helms, Cinn., 3b | | 1966—Tommie Agee, Chicago, of | |
| 1967—Tom Seaver, N. Y., p | | 1967—Rod Carew, Minn., 2b | |

# Major League Baseball Attendance

| NATIONAL LEAGUE | | | | AMERICAN LEAGUE | | | |
|---|---|---|---|---|---|---|---|
| | 1968 | 1967 | 1966 | | 1968 | 1967 | 1966 |
| St. Louis........ | 2,011,177 | 2,100,838 | 1,712,980 | Detroit......... | 2,031,847 | 1,445,184 | 1,124,293 |
| New York...... | 1,781,657 | 1,565,492 | 1,932,693 | Boston.......... | 1,940,588 | 1,692,349 | 811,172 |
| Los Angeles.... | 1,581,093 | 1,662,599 | 2,617,029 | Minnesota...... | 1,143,257 | 1,483,421 | 1,259,374 |
| Houston........ | 1,312,887 | 1,333,862 | 1,872,108 | New York....... | 1,125,124 | 1,141,714 | 1,124,648 |
| Atlanta........ | 1,126,540 | 1,362,849 | 1,539,801 | California...... | 1,025,956 | 1,301,557 | 903,359 |
| Chicago........ | 1,043,409 | 977,984 | 635,891 | Baltimore...... | 868,709 | 858,822 | 1,203,366 |
| San Francisco.... | 837,220 | 1,243,400 | 1,657,192 | Cleveland...... | 857,994 | 685,698 | 903,359 |
| Cincinnati...... | 733,354 | 952,788 | 742,958 | Oakland........ | 838,501 | 652,246 | 733,929 |
| Pittsburgh...... | 693,485 | 904,121 | 1,196,618 | Chicago........ | 798,914 | 966,284 | 990,016 |
| Philadelphia..... | 664,546 | 824,252 | 1,108,201 | Washington..... | 542,052 | 770,868 | 576,260 |
| **Total** | **11,785,368** | **12,927,185** | **15,015,471** | **Total** | **11,172,942** | **10,883,915** | **10,166,738** |

| Previous Years | | | | Previous Years | |
|---|---|---|---|---|---|
| 1965—13,581,136 | | 1962—11,360,169 | 1965—8,860,764 | | 1962—10,015,056 |
| 1964—12,045,190 | | 1961— 8,731,502 | 1964— 9,235,151 | | 1961—10,163,016 |
| 1963—11,382,277 | | 1960—10,684,963 | 1963—10,015,056 | | 1960— 9,226,526 |

## MAJOR LEAGUE ATTENDANCE RECORDS

**All-time Season Record, Both Leagues**—25,203,229—set in 1966.
**All-time Season Record, One Club**—2,755,184—Los Angeles Dodgers, 1962.
**Record Attendance, Six-Game World Series**—420,784—1959 Series between Los Angeles Dodgers and Chicago White Sox. (Exceeded seven-game Series record.)
**Record Attendance, World Series Game**—92,706—fifth game, 1959 Series, Los Angeles, Oct. 6.
**Record Attendance, Regular Season Game**—84,587—Municipal Stadium, Cleveland, Ohio, Sept. 12, 1954, in doubleheader between Cleveland Indians and New York Yankees. Cleveland won both, 4 to 1 and 3 to 2. (Including the pass list of 1,976, overall attendance was 86,563.)
**Attendance, Regular-Season Single Game**—78,672—Los Angeles Memorial Coliseum, April 18, 1958, in opening game between Los Angeles Dodgers and San Francisco Giants.
**Exhibition Game**—93,103—Game honoring Roy Campanella; New York Yankees vs. Los Angeles Dodgers, Los Angeles Coliseum, May 7, 1959.

# 1968 All-Major League Baseball Team

The following is the second annual All-Players All-Star Baseball Team as selected by the players of both leagues in a poll conducted by Newspaper Enterprise Assn. Players could not vote for members of their own team.

| Name | Team | Votes |
|---|---|---|
| **First Base** | | |
| Willie McCovey, San Francisco (NL) | | 264 |
| Rusty Staub, Houston (NL) | | 84 |
| Ernie Banks, Chicago (NL) | | 76 |
| Boog Powell, Baltimore (AL) | | 17 |
| Orlando Cepeda, St. Louis (NL) | | 6 |
| Mickey Mantle, New York (AL) | | 3 |
| **Second Base** | | |
| Tommy Helms, Cincinnati (NL) | | 187 |
| Rod Carew, Minnesota (AL) | | 96 |
| Glenn Beckert, Chicago (NL) | | 74 |
| Dick McAuliffe, Detroit (AL) | | 69 |
| Mike Andrews, Boston (AL) | | 55 |
| Ken Boswell, New York (NL) | | 20 |
| Bill Mazeroski, Pittsburgh (NL) | | 19 |
| Felix Millan, Atlanta (NL) | | 7 |
| Cookie Rojas, Philadelphia (NL) | | 5 |
| Julian Javier, St. Louis (NL) | | 4 |
| **Third Base** | | |
| Brooks Robinson, Baltimore (AL) | | 171 |
| Ron Santo, Chicago (NL) | | 162 |
| Mike Shannon, St. Louis (NL) | | 58 |
| Tony Perez, Cincinnati (NL) | | 43 |
| Richie Allen, Philadelphia (NL) | | 18 |
| Maury Wills, Pittsburgh (NL) | | 14 |
| Jim Hart, San Francisco (NL) | | 12 |
| Bobby Cox, New York (AL) | | 11 |
| Ed Charles, New York (NL) | | 3 |
| Ron Clark, Minnesota (AL) | | 2 |
| **Shortstop** | | |
| Jim Fregosi, California (AL) | | 156 |
| Luis Aparicio, Chicago (AL) | | 101 |
| Don Kessinger, Chicago (NL) | | 32 |
| Gene Alley, Pittsburgh (NL) | | 16 |
| Campy Campaneris, Oakland (AL) | | 11 |
| Dal Maxvill, St. Louis (NL) | | 7 |
| Rico Petrocelli, Boston (AL) | | 2 |
| Zoilo Versalles, Los Angeles (NL) | | 2 |
| **Outfield** | | |
| Curt Flood, St. Louis (NL) | | 242 |
| Pete Rose, Cincinnati (NL) | | 214 |
| Ken Harrelson, Boston (AL) | | 190 |
| Frank Howard, Washington (AL) | | 132 |
| Willie Horton, Detroit (AL) | | 60 |

| Name | Team | Votes |
|---|---|---|
| Matty Alou, Pittsburgh (NL) | | 44 |
| Billy Williams, Chicago (NL) | | 39 |
| Tony Oliva, Minnesota (AL) | | 34 |
| Henry Aaron, Atlanta (NL) | | 27 |
| Carl Yastrzemski, Boston (AL) | | 26 |
| Lou Brock, St. Louis (NL) | | 21 |
| Willie Mays, San Francisco (NL) | | 19 |
| Bobby Bonds, San Francisco (NL) | | 9 |
| Alex Johnson, Cincinnati (NL) | | 3 |
| Rick Monday, Oakland (AL) | | 2 |
| Joe Pepitone, New York (AL) | | 2 |
| Reggie Smith, Boston (AL) | | 1 |
| Roberto Clemente, Pittsburgh (NL) | | 1 |
| Del Unser, Washington (AL) | | 1 |
| Jose Tartabull, Boston (AL) | | 1 |
| **Catcher** | | |
| Bill Freehan, Detroit (AL) | | 174 |
| John Bench, Cincinnati (NL) | | 126 |
| Tom Haller, Los Angeles (NL) | | 95 |
| Tim McCarver, St. Louis (NL) | | 74 |
| Joe Torre, Atlanta (NL) | | 62 |
| Jerry Grote, New York (NL) | | 15 |
| Joe Azcue, Cleveland (AL) | | 9 |
| Mike Ryan, Philadelphia (NL) | | 4 |
| **Starting Pitcher** | | |
| Denny McLain, Detroit (AL) | | 164 |
| Bob Gibson, St. Louis (NL) | | 150 |
| Juan Marichal, San Francisco (NL) | | 132 |
| Jerry Koosman, New York (NL) | | 9 |
| Don Drysdale, Los Angeles (NL) | | 6 |
| Luis Tiant, Cleveland (AL) | | 4 |
| **Relief Pitcher** | | |
| Phil Regan, Chicago (NL) | | 178 |
| Ted Abernathy, Cincinnati (NL) | | 142 |
| Hoyt Wilhelm, Chicago (AL) | | 44 |
| Wilbur Wood, Chicago (AL) | | 39 |
| Ron Kline, Pittsburgh (NL) | | 27 |
| Joe Hoerner, St. Louis (NL) | | 26 |
| Frank Linzy, San Francisco (NL) | | 10 |
| Fred Lasher, Detroit (AL) | | 8 |
| Steve Hamilton, New York (AL) | | 8 |
| Lindy McDaniel, New York (AL) | | 6 |
| Bob Locker, Chicago (AL) | | 5 |
| Moe Drabowsky, Baltimore (AL) | | 2 |
| Cecil Upshaw, Atlanta (NL) | | 2 |

## Cy Young Award Winners

| | | |
|---|---|---|
| 1956—Don Newcombe, Dodgers | 1961—Whitey Ford, Yankees | 1966—Sandy Koufax, Dodgers |
| 1957—Warren Spahn, Braves | 1962—Don Drysdale, Dodgers | 1967—(NL) Mike McCormick, Giants |
| 1958—Bob Turley, Yankees | 1963—Sandy Koufax, Dodgers | (AL) Jim Lonborg, Red Sox |
| 1959—Early Wynn, White Sox | 1964—Dean Chance, Angels | 1968—(NL) Bob Gibson, Cardinals |
| 1960—Vernon Law, Pirates | 1965—Sandy Koufax, Dodgers | (AL) Dennis McLain, Tigers |

## 1968 Little League World Series

The 22nd annual Little League World Series was won by Wakayama (Japan) as they defeated Richmond (Virginia) by the score of 1-0 on Aug. 24, 1968, at Williamsport, Pa. This was the second straight year that a Japanese team won the Little League title. West Tokyo was the winner in 1967.

# Minor League Pennant Winners in 1968
## *Major League Affiliations in Parentheses*

### INTERNATIONAL LEAGUE

| Club | W. | L. | Pct. | G.B. | Club | W. | L. | Pct. | G.B. |
|---|---|---|---|---|---|---|---|---|---|
| Toledo (Tigers) | 83 | 64 | .565 | ... | Syracuse (Yankees) | 72 | 75 | .490 | 11 |
| Columbus (Pirates) | 82 | 64 | .562 | ½ | Louisville (Red Sox) | 72 | 75 | .490 | 11 |
| Rochester (Orioles) | 77 | 69 | .527 | 5½ | Buffalo (Senators) | 66 | 81 | .449 | 17 |
| Jacksonville (Mets) | 75 | 71 | .514 | 7½ | Richmond (Braves) | 59 | 87 | .404 | 23½ |

#### Batting Averages
(over 250 at bats)

| Player—Club | g. | ab. | h. | hr. | rbi. | pct. | Player—Club | g. | ab. | h. | hr. | rbi. | pct. |
|---|---|---|---|---|---|---|---|---|---|---|---|---|---|
| Rettenmund, Rochester | 114 | 393 | 130 | 22 | 59 | .331 | O'Brien, Lou | 129 | 471 | 124 | 12 | 60 | .263 |
| Christian, Toledo | 123 | 473 | 151 | 5 | 57 | .319 | Brown, Toledo | 110 | 350 | 92 | 13 | 54 | .263 |
| Reynolds, Jacksonville | 114 | 404 | 129 | 9 | 50 | .319 | Valdespino, Richmond | 74 | 255 | 67 | 7 | 25 | .263 |
| Sanguillen, Columbus | 105 | 377 | 119 | 8 | 60 | .316 | Crowley, Rochester | 75 | 271 | 71 | 8 | 34 | .262 |
| Jimenez, Columbus | 139 | 499 | 157 | 14 | 77 | .315 | Lopez, Buffalo | 117 | 353 | 91 | 13 | 53 | .258 |
| Oliver, Columbus | 132 | 473 | 149 | 14 | 74 | .315 | Stone, Rochester | 120 | 460 | 118 | 5 | 42 | .257 |
| Regan, Syracuse | 119 | 424 | 129 | 11 | 39 | .304 | Green, Toledo | 95 | 288 | 74 | 5 | 28 | .257 |
| Demeter, Rochester | 111 | 369 | 111 | 10 | 63 | .301 | Lehrer, Louisville | 145 | 516 | 132 | 3 | 53 | .256 |
| Sorrell, Jacksonville | 117 | 384 | 115 | 9 | 56 | .299 | Alyea, Buffalo | 87 | 297 | 75 | 31 | 61 | .253 |
| Chance, Buffalo | 140 | 509 | 149 | 29 | 84 | .293 | Walrath, Buffalo | 102 | 345 | 87 | 7 | 30 | .252 |
| Ferraro, Syracuse | 118 | 440 | 129 | 4 | 41 | .293 | Harrison, Richmond | 146 | 522 | 131 | 25 | 83 | .251 |
| Woods, Toledo | 137 | 500 | 146 | 16 | 58 | .292 | Heise, Jacksonville | 114 | 415 | 104 | 2 | 29 | .251 |
| Thomas, Louisville | 136 | 475 | 137 | 6 | 52 | .288 | | | | | | | |
| Calero, Louisville | 131 | 467 | 134 | 8 | 66 | .287 | | | | | | | |
| Floyd, Rochester | 102 | 359 | 103 | 6 | 52 | .287 | | | | | | | |
| Otis, Jacksonville | 139 | 500 | 143 | 15 | 70 | .286 | **Pitching Records** | | | | | | |
| de la Hoz, Richmond | 81 | 308 | 88 | 9 | 33 | .286 | (over 100 innings) | | | | | | |
| Derrick, Toledo | 132 | 456 | 129 | 11 | 74 | .283 | | | | | | | |
| Smith, Columbus | 131 | 491 | 138 | 9 | 52 | .281 | Pitcher—Club | g. | ip. | so. | w. | l. | era. |
| Pfeil, Jacksonville | 143 | 560 | 157 | 8 | 49 | .280 | Scherman, Toledo | 30 | 102 | 69 | 8 | 2 | 1.76 |
| Billings, Buffalo | 130 | 387 | 107 | 11 | 35 | .276 | Cisco, Louisville | 29 | 204 | 157 | 11 | 12 | 2.21 |
| Hebner, Columbus | 104 | 381 | 105 | 6 | 51 | .276 | Cox, Buffalo | 60 | 104 | 65 | 7 | 5 | 2.34 |
| Hiller, Columbus | 84 | 273 | 75 | 3 | 36 | .275 | McAndrew, Jacksonville | 23 | 117 | 117 | 8 | 3 | 2.54 |
| Spriggs, Columbus | 138 | 521 | 143 | 6 | 34 | .274 | Beene, Rochester | 48 | 114 | 100 | 8 | 7 | 2.68 |
| Kelly, Richmond | 101 | 385 | 105 | 3 | 28 | .273 | Magrini, Syracuse | 26 | 153 | 105 | 8 | 10 | 2.71 |
| Lahoud, Louisville | 101 | 326 | 89 | 8 | 40 | .273 | Shellenback, Columbus | 25 | 142 | 90 | 9 | 8 | 2.85 |
| Tracy, Jacksonville | 75 | 368 | 73 | 6 | 40 | .272 | Gentry, Jacksonville | 30 | 198 | 156 | 12 | 8 | 2.91 |
| Fiore, Rochester | 108 | 376 | 102 | 19 | 62 | .271 | Rooker, Toledo | 25 | 190 | 206 | 14 | 8 | 2.91 |
| Garrido, Richmond | 121 | 456 | 123 | 6 | 40 | .270 | Lasko, Syracuse | 33 | 166 | 126 | 8 | 7 | 2.93 |
| Boehmer, Syracuse | 144 | 518 | 139 | 10 | 75 | .268 | Marshall, Toledo | 31 | 211 | 190 | 15 | 9 | 2.94 |
| Kennedy, Syr-Col | 140 | 471 | 126 | 8 | 57 | .268 | Connors, Jacksonville | 23 | 112 | 63 | 8 | 5 | 2.97 |
| Campbell, Toledo | 97 | 339 | 90 | 26 | 64 | .265 | Jones, Buffalo | 25 | 185 | 184 | 12 | 8 | 3.02 |
| | | | | | | | Radatz, Toledo | 24 | 101 | 103 | 6 | 7 | 3.63 |
| | | | | | | | Gelnar, Columbus | 25 | 183 | 97 | 10 | 10 | 3.10 |
| | | | | | | | Closter, Syracuse | 23 | 122 | 110 | 7 | 8 | 3.10 |
| | | | | | | | Roberts, Columbus | 27 | 193 | 133 | 18 | 5 | 3.17 |

### PACIFIC COAST LEAGUE

| EASTERN DIVISION | | | | | WESTERN DIVISION | | | | |
|---|---|---|---|---|---|---|---|---|---|
| Club | W. | L. | Pct. | G.B. | Club | W. | L. | Pct. | G.B. |
| Tulsa (Cardinals) | 95 | 53 | .642 | .... | Spokane (Dodgers) | 85 | 60 | .586 | .... |
| San Diego (Phillies) | 76 | 70 | .521 | 18 | Hawaii (White Sox) | 78 | 69 | .531 | 8½ |
| Phoenix (Giants) | 76 | 71 | .517 | 18½ | Portland (Indians) | 72 | 71 | .500 | 12½ |
| Denver (Twins) | 73 | 72 | .503 | 20½ | Seattle (Angels) | 71 | 76 | .483 | 15 |
| Indianapolis (Reds) | 66 | 78 | .458 | 27 | Tacoma (Cubs) | 65 | 83 | .439 | 21½ |
| Oklahoma City (Astros) | 61 | 84 | .421 | 32½ | Vancouver (Athletics) | 58 | 88 | .397 | 27½ |

#### Batting Averages
(over 250 at bats)

| Player—Club | g. | ab. | h. | hr. | rbi. | pct. | Player—Club | g. | ab. | h. | hr. | rbi. | pct. |
|---|---|---|---|---|---|---|---|---|---|---|---|---|---|
| Hicks, Tulsa | 117 | 407 | 149 | 23 | 85 | .366 | Rowe, Vancouver | 90 | 256 | 70 | 3 | 16 | .273 |
| Piniella, Portland | 88 | 331 | 105 | 13 | 62 | .317 | McKnight, Phoenix | 136 | 489 | 133 | 14 | 75 | .272 |
| Sizemore, Spokane | 81 | 258 | 81 | 0 | 34 | .314 | Nagelson, Portland | 118 | 371 | 101 | 15 | 56 | .272 |
| Kelly, Denver | 108 | 396 | 121 | 3 | 31 | .306 | Glover, Denver | 101 | 324 | 88 | 2 | 29 | .272 |
| Scheinblum, Portland | 122 | 457 | 139 | 14 | 78 | .304 | W. Williams, S-H | 106 | 305 | 83 | 3 | 25 | .272 |
| Money, San Diego | 127 | 482 | 146 | 9 | 59 | .303 | Mashore, Indianapolis | 123 | 477 | 129 | 9 | 41 | .270 |
| Burda, Phoenix | 119 | 445 | 134 | 7 | 51 | .301 | Lewis, San Diego | 123 | 423 | 114 | 16 | 57 | .270 |
| Fosse, Portland | 103 | 339 | 102 | 9 | 42 | .301 | Wicker, Tulsa | 109 | 386 | 104 | 9 | 40 | .269 |
| Gutierrez, Phoenix | 139 | 531 | 158 | 0 | 52 | .298 | Freese, Tac-Haw | 83 | 271 | 73 | 6 | 42 | .269 |
| Oliver, Denver | 137 | 515 | 153 | 20 | 93 | .297 | Boccabella, Tacoma | 73 | 268 | 72 | 16 | 43 | .296 |
| Nettles, Denver | 130 | 451 | 134 | 22 | 83 | .297 | Jones, Tacoma | 146 | 523 | 140 | 24 | 76 | .268 |
| McRae, Indianapolis | 119 | 444 | 131 | 16 | 65 | .295 | James, Spokane | 113 | 395 | 106 | 5 | 44 | .268 |
| Hague, Tulsa | 147 | 529 | 155 | 23 | 99 | .293 | | | | | | | |
| Barry, San Diego | 130 | 441 | 129 | 9 | 59 | .293 | | | | | | | |
| Laboy, Tulsa | 142 | 527 | 154 | 15 | 100 | .292 | **Pitching Records** | | | | | | |
| Mason, Phoenix | 111 | 424 | 123 | 1 | 28 | .290 | (over 100 innings) | | | | | | |
| J. Miller, Spokane | 131 | 463 | 133 | 12 | 70 | .287 | | | | | | | |
| Gaines, Den-Haw | 125 | 414 | 119 | 8 | 38 | .287 | Pitcher—Club | g. | ip. | so. | w. | l. | era. |
| Werhas, San Diego | 122 | 426 | 122 | 8 | 65 | .286 | Mikkelsen, Tulsa | 26 | 184 | 136 | 16 | 4 | 1.91 |
| Geiger, Tulsa | 124 | 406 | 116 | 14 | 50 | .286 | Moeller, Spokane | 33 | 227 | 141 | 15 | 9 | 2.22 |
| Klimchock, Portland | 118 | 432 | 123 | 9 | 53 | .285 | Coates, Seattle | 32 | 213 | 189 | 17 | 10 | 2.28 |
| Huntz, Tulsa | 114 | 504 | 143 | 10 | 74 | .284 | Strahler, Spokane | 27 | 137 | 108 | 7 | 9 | 2.30 |
| Mooring, Denver | 127 | 402 | 114 | 8 | 43 | .284 | R. Robertson, Phoenix | 34 | 258 | 216 | 18 | 9 | 2.34 |
| Conde, Indianapolis | 97 | 308 | 87 | 2 | 39 | .283 | Taylor, Tulsa | 34 | 230 | 128 | 18 | 7 | 2.35 |
| Cowan, San Diego | 143 | 564 | 158 | 19 | 73 | .280 | Foster, Spokane | 16 | 104 | 87 | 8 | 5 | 2.60 |
| Etheridge, Phoenix | 113 | 399 | 111 | 4 | 46 | .278 | Meyer, Vancouver | 27 | 130 | 137 | 6 | 9 | 2.63 |
| Sinnerud, Okla. City | 96 | 299 | 83 | 6 | 32 | .278 | Raffo, San Diego | 34 | 148 | 86 | 11 | 7 | 2.68 |
| E. Johnson, Okla. City | 129 | 466 | 129 | 19 | 73 | .277 | Sherrod, Tacoma | 25 | 168 | 82 | 11 | 11 | 2.79 |
| McGuire, Seattle | 109 | 376 | 104 | 3 | 44 | .277 | O. Pena, Port-Sea | 56 | 132 | 99 | 7 | 6 | 2.80 |
| Johnstone, Seattle | 84 | 314 | 87 | 13 | 56 | .277 | Lersch, San Diego | 26 | 174 | 114 | 11 | 8 | 2.84 |
| Napoleon, Ha-Den. | 96 | 271 | 75 | 9 | 35 | .277 | Tsitouris, Indianapolis | 17 | 111 | 76 | 7 | 8 | 2.92 |
| Hutton, Spokane | 132 | 439 | 121 | 6 | 54 | .276 | Everitt, Spokane | 33 | 240 | 201 | 17 | 10 | 2.93 |
| Sprague, Portland | 86 | 314 | 86 | 2 | 19 | .274 | Belinsky, Hawaii | 29 | 176 | 181 | 9 | 14 | 2.97 |
| LaRose, Tacoma | 120 | 436 | 119 | 4 | 31 | .273 | G. Woodson, Portland | 34 | 163 | 112 | 13 | 10 | 3.04 |
| Breeden, Tulsa | 118 | 407 | 111 | 5 | 44 | .273 | Fisher, Hawaii | 24 | 140 | 56 | 8 | 9 | 3.09 |
| | | | | | | | J. Pena, Indianapolis | 42 | 194 | 178 | 11 | 14 | 3.15 |
| | | | | | | | Wynne, Hawaii | 28 | 152 | 98 | 9 | 12 | 3.20 |
| | | | | | | | Garibaldi, Phoenix | 30 | 182 | 128 | 10 | 9 | 3.21 |

## Minor League Player of the Year

Tolia (Tony) Solaita, 20, a native of Samoa, has been named Minor League Player of the Year for 1968. A lefthanded hitting first baseman, Solaita batted .302 and hit 49 home runs for High Point-Thomasville in the Carolina League before being called up by the New York Yankees late in the season. He received the Topps Award and the J.G. Taylor Spink Memorial Award. For his selection as the outstanding player in his league he also received a George M. Trautman Memorial Plaque.

# Minor League Final Standings
### Major League Affiliations in parentheses

## Class AA

### EASTERN LEAGUE

| Club | W | L | Pct. | GB |
|---|---|---|---|---|
| Pittsfield (Red Sox) | 84 | 55 | .604 | .... |
| Reading (Phillies) | 81 | 59 | .579 | 3½ |
| Elmira (Orioles) | 77 | 63 | .550 | 7½ |
| Binghamton (Yankees) | 67 | 72 | .482 | 17 |
| York (Pirates) | 58 | 82 | .414 | 26½ |
| Waterbury (Indians) | 52 | 88 | .371 | 32½ |

### SOUTHERN LEAGUE

| Club | W | L | Pct. | GB |
|---|---|---|---|---|
| Asheville (Reds) | 86 | 54 | .614 | .... |
| Montgomery (Tigers) | 80 | 57 | .584 | 4½ |
| Charlotte (Twins) | 72 | 68 | .514 | 14 |
| Birmingham (Athletics) | 66 | 74 | .471 | 20 |
| Savannah (Senators) | 57 | 79 | .419 | 27 |
| Evansville (White Sox) | 55 | 84 | .396 | 30½ |

### TEXAS LEAGUE
#### Eastern Division

| Club | W | L | Pct. | GB |
|---|---|---|---|---|
| Arkansas (Cardinals) | 82 | 58 | .586 | .... |
| Shreveport (Braves) | 78 | 62 | .557 | 4 |
| Memphis (Mets) | 67 | 69 | .493 | 13 |
| Dallas-Ft. Worth (Astros) | 60 | 79 | .432 | 21½ |

#### Western Division

| Club | W | L | Pct. | GB |
|---|---|---|---|---|
| El Paso (Angels) | 77 | 60 | .562 | .... |
| Albuquerque (Dodgers) | 70 | 69 | .504 | 8 |
| Amarillo (Giants) | 67 | 71 | .486 | 10½ |
| San Antonio (Cubs) | 53 | 86 | .381 | 25 |

## Class A

### CALIFORNIA LEAGUE

| Club | W | L | Pct. | GB |
|---|---|---|---|---|
| Fresno (Giants) | 43 | 26 | .623 | .... |
| Stockton (Orioles) | 38 | 32 | .543 | 5½ |
| San Jose (Angels) | 36 | 34 | .514 | 7½ |
| Lodi (Cubs) | 35 | 35 | .500 | 8½ |
| Modesto (Cardinals) | 34 | 36 | .486 | 9½ |
| Visalia (Mets) | 33 | 37 | .471 | 10½ |
| Reno (Indians) | 30 | 39 | .435 | 13 |
| Bakersfield (Dodgers) | 30 | 40 | .429 | 13½ |

### CAROLINA LEAGUE
#### Eastern Division

| Club | W | L | Pct. | GB |
|---|---|---|---|---|
| Raleigh-Durham (Mets) | 81 | 56 | .591 | .... |
| Tidewater (Phillies) | 79 | 58 | .577 | 2 |
| Peninsula (Athletics) | 76 | 62 | .551 | 5½ |
| Wilson (Twins) | 70 | 67 | .511 | 11 |
| Rocky Mount (Tigers) | 69 | 71 | .493 | 13½ |
| Kinston (Yankees) | 59 | 76 | .437 | 21 |

#### Western Division

| Club | W | L | Pct. | GB |
|---|---|---|---|---|
| *Salem (Pirates) | 84 | 54 | .609 | .... |
| Lynchburg (White Sox) | 68 | 71 | .489 | 16½ |
| H.P.-Thomasville (Co-op) | 68 | 71 | .489 | 16½ |
| Greensboro (Astros) | 61 | 78 | .439 | 23½ |
| Burlington (Senators) | 56 | 81 | .409 | 27½ |
| Winston-Salem (Red Sox) | 55 | 81 | .400 | 28 |

*Salem won regular-season pennant on basis of highest percentage.*

### FLORIDA STATE LEAGUE
#### Eastern Division

| Club | W | L | Pct. | GB |
|---|---|---|---|---|
| *Miami (Orioles) | 87 | 55 | .613 | .... |
| Cocoa (Astros) | 74 | 65 | .532 | 11½ |
| Daytona Beach (Dodgers) | 73 | 70 | .510 | 14½ |
| Ft. Lauderdale (Yanks) | 62 | 75 | .453 | 22½ |
| West Palm Beach (Braves) | 59 | 77 | .434 | 25 |

#### Western Division

| Club | W | L | Pct. | GB |
|---|---|---|---|---|
| Orlando (Twins) | 81 | 59 | .579 | .... |
| St. Petersburg (Cards) | 80 | 63 | .559 | 2½ |
| Tampa (Reds) | 74 | 62 | .544 | 5 |
| Lakeland (Tigers) | 58 | 81 | .417 | 22½ |
| Leesburg (Athletics) | 51 | 92 | .357 | 31½ |

*Miami won regular-season pennant on basis of highest percentage.*

### MIDWEST LEAGUE

| Club | W | L | Pct. | GB |
|---|---|---|---|---|
| Decatur (Giants) | 40 | 21 | .656 | .... |
| Quincy (Cubs) | 35 | 26 | .574 | 5 |
| Waterloo (Red Sox) | 33 | 28 | .541 | 7 |
| Appleton (White Sox) | 31 | 29 | .517 | 8½ |
| Cedar Rapids (Cards) | 31 | 31 | .500 | 9½ |
| Quad Cities (Angels) | 30 | 31 | .492 | 10 |
| Wisconsin Rapids (Twins) | 30 | 31 | .492 | 10 |
| Burlington (Athletics) | 26 | 35 | .426 | 14 |
| Clinton (Pirates) | 26 | 35 | .426 | 14 |
| Dubuque (Royals) | 22 | 37 | .373 | 17 |

### NYP LEAGUE

| Club | W | L | Pct. | GB |
|---|---|---|---|---|
| Auburn (Twins) | 49 | 27 | .645 | .... |
| Oneonta (Yankees) | 43 | 34 | .558 | 6½ |
| Williamsport (Co-op) | 40 | 35 | .533 | 8½ |
| Newark (Pilots) | 38 | 36 | .514 | 10 |
| Batavia (Tigers) | 37 | 38 | .493 | 11½ |
| Geneva (Senators) | 38 | 40 | .487 | 12 |
| Jamestown (Red Sox) | 31 | 44 | .413 | 17½ |
| Corning (Royals) | 27 | 49 | .355 | 22 |

### NORTHERN LEAGUE

| Club | W | L | Pct. | GB |
|---|---|---|---|---|
| St. Cloud (Twins) | 43 | 27 | .614 | .... |
| Mankato (Mets) | 42 | 27 | .609 | ½ |
| Sioux Falls (Reds) | 41 | 29 | .586 | 2 |
| Duluth-Superior (White Sox) | 31 | 39 | .443 | 12 |
| Huron (Phillies) | 26 | 43 | .377 | 16½ |
| Aberdeen (Orioles) | 26 | 44 | .371 | 17 |

### NORTHWEST LEAGUE

| Club | W | L | Pct. | GB |
|---|---|---|---|---|
| Tri-City (Dodgers) | 45 | 30 | .600 | .... |
| Eugene (Phillies) | 41 | 32 | .562 | 3 |
| Medford (Giants) | 34 | 43 | .442 | 12 |
| Lewiston (Cardinals) | 30 | 45 | .400 | 15 |

# Record of All-Star Baseball Games, 1933-1968

All-Star games are played annually by teams composed of players from the American and National Leagues. Formerly the teams were selected by a nationwide poll of fans, but beginning in 1958 the procedure was changed to one in which the players, coaches and managers make the selections. From the receipts of the game, plus radio and television receipts of the world series, $4,100,000 goes into the players' pension fund. The game was not played in 1945.

| Game | Year | Winner | Score | Location | Game | Year | Winner | Score | Location |
|---|---|---|---|---|---|---|---|---|---|
| 1st | 1933 | American | 4-2 | Chicago | 21st | 1954 | American | 11-9 | Cleveland |
| 2nd | 1934 | American | 9-7 | New York | 22nd[2] | 1955 | National | 6-5 | Milwaukee |
| 3rd | 1935 | American | 4-1 | Cleveland | 23rd | 1956 | National | 7-3 | Washington |
| 4th | 1936 | National | 4-3 | Boston | 24th | 1957 | American | 6-5 | St. Louis |
| 5th | 1937 | American | 8-3 | Washington | 25th | 1958 | American | 4-3 | Baltimore |
| 6th | 1938 | National | 4-1 | Cincinnati | 26th | 1959 | National | 5-4 | Pittsburgh |
| 7th | 1939 | American | 3-1 | New York | 27th | 1959 | American | 5-3 | Los Angeles |
| 8th | 1940 | National | 4-0 | St. Louis | 28th | 1960 | National | 5-3 | Kansas City |
| 9th | 1941 | American | 7-5 | Detroit | 29th | 1960 | National | 6-0 | New York |
| 10th | 1942 | American | 3-1 | New York | 30th[3] | 1961 | National | 5-4 | San Francisco |
| 11th* | 1943 | American | 5-3 | Philadelphia | 31st | 1961 | Called-Rain | 1-1 | Boston |
| 12th* | 1944 | National | 7-1 | Pittsburgh | 32nd[3] | 1962 | National | 3-1 | Washington |
| 13th | 1946 | American | 12-0 | Boston | 33rd | 1962 | American | 9-4 | Chicago |
| 14th | 1947 | American | 2-1 | Chicago | 34th | 1963 | National | 5-3 | Cleveland |
| 15th | 1948 | American | 5-2 | St. Louis | 35th | 1964 | National | 7-4 | New York |
| 16th | 1949 | American | 11-7 | New York | 36th | 1965 | National | 6-5 | Minnesota |
| 17th[1] | 1950 | National | 4-3 | Chicago | 37th[3] | 1966 | National | 2-1 | St. Louis |
| 18th | 1951 | National | 8-3 | Detroit | 38th[4] | 1967 | National | 2-1 | Anaheim |
| 19th | 1952 | National | 3-2 | Philadelphia | 39th* | 1968 | National | 1-0 | Houston |
| 20th | 1953 | National | 5-1 | Cincinnati | | | | | |

[1]14 innings. [2]12 innings. [3]10 innings. [4]15 innings. *Night game.

# Home Run Distances in Baseball Parks

| AMERICAN LEAGUE | | Ft. from plate to fence | | | NATIONAL LEAGUE | | Ft. from plate to fence | | |
|---|---|---|---|---|---|---|---|---|---|
| Team | Name of park | RF | CF | LF | Team | Name of park | RF | CF | LF |
| New York..... | Yankee Stadium.... | 296 | 461 | 301 | Atlanta........ | Atlanta Stadium.... | 330 | 402 | 330 |
| Boston....... | Fenway Park..... | 302 | 420 | 315 | New York..... | Shea Stadium...... | 341 | 410 | 341 |
| Cleveland.... | Municipal Stadium.. | 320 | 410 | 320 | Houston....... | Astrodome........ | 340 | 406 | 340 |
| Detroit...... | Tiger Stadium..... | 325 | 440 | 340 | San Francisco... | Candlestick Park... | 335 | 410 | 335 |
| Chicago...... | White Sox Park.... | 352 | 415 | 352 | Los Angeles.... | Dodger Stadium.... | 330 | 410 | 330 |
| Baltimore.... | Memorial Stadium... | 309 | 410 | 309 | Chicago....... | Wrigley Field..... | 353 | 400 | 355 |
| Oakland...... | Oak.-Alameda Co... | 330 | 410 | 330 | Pittsburgh.... | Forbes Field...... | 300 | 457 | 365 |
| Minnesota.... | Metropolitan Stad.. | 330 | 425 | 346 | Cincinnati.... | Crosley Field..... | 366 | 387 | 328 |
| California.... | Anaheim Stadium... | 333 | 406 | 333 | St. Louis..... | Busch Mem. Stad.. | 330 | 414 | 330 |
| Washington... | D. C. Stadium.... | 335 | 410 | 335 | Philadelphia... | Connie Mack Stad.. | 329 | 447 | 334 |

## Baseball Parks Seating Capacity

| | | | |
|---|---|---|---|
| Astrodome (Houston, Tex.)............ | 44,500 | Forbes Field, Pittsburgh, Pa......... | 35,000 |
| Anaheim Stadium.................... | 43,204 | Kansas City (Mo.) Municipal Stadium..... | 32,561 |
| Atlanta (Ga.), Stadium............... | 51,383 | Memorial Stadium, Baltimore......... | 52,185 |
| Busch Memorial Stadium, St. Louis, Mo... | 49,450 | Metropolitan Sta., Bloomington, Minn.... | 45,181 |
| Candlestick Park, San Francisco....... | 42,500 | Milwaukee County Stadium........... | 43,826 |
| Cleveland (Ohio) Municipal Stadium...... | 76,977 | Oakland-Alameda County Coliseum...... | 50,000 |
| White Sox Park, Chicago............. | 46,550 | Shea Sta., Queens, N. Y. C........... | 56,000 |
| Connie Mack Stad., Philadelphia, Pa..... | 33,608 | Tiger Stadium, Detroit, Mich......... | 53,089 |
| Crosley Field, Cincinnati, Ohio........ | 29,468 | Washington (D. C.) Stadium.......... | 45,016 |
| Dodger Stadium, (Chavez Ravine), L. A... | 56,000 | Wrigley Field, Chicago, Ill.......... | 36,644 |
| Fenway Park, Boston, Mass........... | 33,375 | Yankee Stadium, New York, N. Y....... | 67,000 |

## McLain Wins 31 Games

Dennis McLain of the Detroit Tigers became in 1968 the first pitcher in 34 years to win 30 games in the major leagues. A complete list of hurlers who have won 30 or more games since 1900 follows.

| | | | |
|---|---|---|---|
| 1968—Dennis McLain, Detroit Tigers | 31 | 1912—Joe Wood, Boston Red Sox | 34 |
| 1934—Dizzy Dean, St. Louis Cardinals | 34 | 1910—Jack Coombs, Philadelphia Athletics | 31 |
| 1931—Lefty Grove, Philadelphia Athletics | 31 | 1908—Ed Walsh, Chicago White Sox | 40 |
| 1920—Jim Bagby, Cleveland Indians | 31 | 1905—Christy Mathewson, New York Giants | 37 |
| 1917—Grover Cleveland Alexander, Philadelphia Phillies | 31 | 1905—Christy Mathewson, New York Giants | 31 |
| | | 1904—Christy Mathewson, New York Giants | 33 |
| 1916—Grover Cleveland Alexander, Philadelphia Phillies | 33 | 1904—Joe McGinnity, New York Giants | 35 |
| | | 1904—Jack Chesbro, New York Yankees | 41 |
| 1915—Grover Cleveland Alexander, Philadelphia Phillies | 31 | 1903—Christy Mathewson, New York Giants | 30 |
| | | 1903—Joe McGinnity, New York Giants | 31 |
| 1913—Walter Johnson, Washington Senators | 36 | 1902—Cy Young, Boston Red Sox | 32 |
| 1912—Walter Johnson, Washington Senators | 32 | 1901—Cy Young, Boston Red Sox | 32 |

## Jim Hunter Pitches a Perfect Game

Jim (Catfish) Hunter of the Oakland Athletics became the 10th pitcher in baseball history to hurl a perfect game when he retired all 27 Minnesota Twin batters at Oakland, Calif., on May 8, 1968. The game was witnessed by 6,298 spectators. A list of perfect game hurlers since 1880 follows:

| Year | Pitcher | Club | Date | Score |
|---|---|---|---|---|
| 1880........... | John L. Richmond....... | Worcester vs. Cleveland, (N.)......... | June 12........ | 1—0 |
| | John M. Ward.......... | Providence vs. Buffalo (N.)........... | June 17........ | 5—0 |
| 1904........... | Denton T. Young...... | Boston vs. Philadelphia (A.)......... | May 5.......... | 3—0 |
| 1908........... | Adrian C. Joss........ | Cleveland vs. Chicago (A.).......... | Oct. 2......... | 1—0 |
| 1917........... | *Ernest G. Shore...... | Boston vs. Washington (A.).......... | June 23........ | 4—0 |
| 1922........... | C. C. Robertson...... | Chicago vs. Detroit (A.)............ | April 30....... | 2—0 |
| 1956........... | †Donald J. Larsen..... | New York (A.) vs. Brooklyn (N.)..... | Oct. 8......... | 2—0 |
| 1964........... | James P. Bunning...... | Philadelphia vs. New York (N.)...... | June 21........ | 6—0 |
| 1965........... | Sanford Koufax....... | Los Angeles vs. Chicago (N.)....... | Sept. 9........ | 1—0 |
| 1968........... | Jim Hunter.......... | Oakland vs. Minnesota (A.).......... | May 8.......... | 4—0 |

*Babe Ruth, the starting pitcher, was banished from the game after walking the first batter. That batter was caught stealing and Shore retired the next 26 batters.

†World Series game.

# Playing Cards and Dice Chances

### POKER HANDS (Four-Suit)

| Hand | Number Possible | Odds Against |
|---|---|---|
| Royal Flush | 4 | 649,739 to 1 |
| Other Straight Flush | 36 | 72,192 to 1 |
| Four of a kind | 624 | 4,164 to 1 |
| Full House | 3,744 | 693 to 1 |
| Flush | 5,108 | 508 to 1 |
| Straight | 10,200 | 254 to 1 |
| Three of a kind | 54,912 | 46 to 1 |
| Two Pairs | 123,552 | 20 to 1 |
| One Pair | 1,098,240 | 4 to 3 (1.37 to 1) |
| Nothing | 1,302,540 | 1 to 1 |
| **Total** | **2,598,960** | |

### BRIDGE

**Perfect hand**—In dealing a hand of 13 cards from 52, the probability of drawing a perfect hand—13 spades—is 1 in 635,013,559,600.

**One suit**—Chances of drawing 13 cards of one suit are 1 in 158,753,389,900.

### PINOCHLE AUCTION

**Odds Against Finding in "Widow" of Three Cards**

| Open Places | Odds Against |
|---|---|
| 1 .................................... | 5 to 1 |
| 2 .................................... | 2 to 1 |
| 3 .................................... | Even |
| 4 .................................... | 3 to 2 for |
| 5 .................................... | 2 to 1 for |

### DICE

**Totals Probabilities on Two Dice**

| Total | Odds Against (Single toss) |
|---|---|
| 2 ............................ | 35 to 1 |
| 3 ............................ | 17 to 1 |
| 4 ............................ | 11 to 1 |
| 5 ............................ | 8 to 1 |
| 6 ............................ | 31 to 5 |
| 7 ............................ | 5 to 1 |
| 8 ............................ | 31 to 5 |
| 9 ............................ | 8 to 1 |
| 10 ........................... | 11 to 1 |
| 11 ........................... | 17 to 1 |
| 12 ........................... | 35 to 1 |

**Probabilities of Consecutive Winning Plays**

| No. Consecutive Wins | By 7, 11, or Point |
|---|---|
| 1 ............................ | 244 in 495 |
| 2 ............................ | 24 in 100 |
| 3 ............................ | 3 in 25 |
| 4 ............................ | 1 in 16 |
| 5 ............................ | 1 in 34 |
| 6 ............................ | 1 in 70 |
| 7 ............................ | 1 in 141 |
| 8 ............................ | 1 in 287 |
| 9 ............................ | 1 in 582 |
| 10 ........................... | 1 in 1,131 |

# U. S. Tennis Championships

## MEN'S SINGLES

| Year | Champion | Final Opponent | Year | Champion | Final Opponent |
|---|---|---|---|---|---|
| 1938 | J. Donald Budge | C. Gene Mako | 1953 | Tony Trabert | E. Victor Seixas, Jr. |
| 1939 | R. L. Riggs | W. Van Horn | 1954 | E. Victor Seixas, Jr. | Rex Hartwig |
| 1940 | D. McNeill | R. L. Riggs | 1955 | Tony Trabert | Ken Rosewall |
| 1941 | R. L. Riggs | F. L. Kovacs | 1956 | Kenneth Rosewall | Lewis Hoad |
| 1942 | F. R. Schroeder, Jr. | F. A. Parker | 1957 | Malcolm Anderson | Ashley Cooper |
| 1943 | Lieut. (J G.)—J. R. Hunt | (C. G. Seaman) | 1958 | Ashley Cooper | Malcolm Anderson |
| | | J. A. Kramer | 1959 | Neale A. Fraser | Alejandro Olmedo |
| 1944 | Sgt. Frank Parker | W. F. Talbert | 1960 | Neale A. Fraser | Rodney Laver |
| 1945 | Sgt. Frank Parker | W. F. Talbert | 1961 | Roy Emerson | Rodney Laver |
| 1946 | John Kramer | Thomas Brown, Jr. | 1962 | Rodney Laver | Roy Emerson |
| 1947 | John Kramer | Frank Parker | 1963 | Rafael Osuna | F. A. Froehling, 3d |
| 1948 | Richard Gonzales | Eric Sturgess | 1964 | Roy Emerson | Fred Stolle |
| 1949 | Richard Gonzales | F. R. Schroeder, Jr | 1965 | Manuel Santana | Cliff Drysdale |
| 1950 | Arthur Larsen | Herbert Flam | 1966 | Fred Stolle | John Newcombe |
| 1951 | Frank Sedgman | E. Victor Seixas, Jr. | 1967 | John Newcombe | Clark Graebner |
| 1952 | Frank Sedgman | Gardnar Mulloy | 1968 | Arthur Ashe | Robert Lutz |

## MEN'S DOUBLES

| Year | Doubles Champions | Year | Doubles Champions |
|---|---|---|---|
| 1937... | H. Henkle and Baron G. Von Cramm (Ger.) | 1953... | Rex Hartwig and Mervyn Rose |
| 1938... | J. D. Budge and C. G. Mako | 1954... | E. Victor Seixas, Jr. and Tony Trabert |
| 1939... | A. K. Quist & J. E. Bromwich (Aust.) | 1955... | Kosei Kamo and Atsushi Miyagi |
| 1940... | J. A. Kramer and F. R. Schroeder, Jr. | 1956... | Lewis Hoad and Kenneth Rosewall |
| 1941... | J. A. Kramer and F. R. Schroeder, Jr. | 1957... | Ashley Cooper and Neale Fraser |
| 1942... | Lt. G. Mulloy and W. F. Talbert | 1958... | Hamilton Richardson and Alejandro Olmedo |
| 1943... | J. Kramer and Frank Parker | 1959... | Neale A. Fraser and Roy Emerson |
| 1944... | Lt. W. D. McNeill and a/c R. Falkenburg | 1960... | Neale A. Fraser and Roy Emerson |
| 1945... | Lt. G. Mulloy and W. F. Talbert | 1961... | Dennis Ralston and Chuck McKinley |
| 1946... | G. Mulloy and W. F. Talbert | 1962... | Rafael Osuna and Antonio Palafox |
| 1947... | J. A. Kramer and F. R. Schroeder, Jr. | 1963... | Dennis Ralston and Chuck McKinley |
| 1948... | G. Mulloy and W. F. Talbert | 1964... | Dennis Ralston and Chuck McKinley |
| 1949... | John Bromwich and William Sidwell | 1965... | Roy Emerson and Fred Stolle |
| 1950... | John E. Bromwich and Frank Sedgman | 1966... | Roy Emerson and Fred Stolle |
| 1951... | Frank Sedgman & Kenneth McGregor (Aust.) | 1967... | John Newcombe and Tony Roche |
| 1952... | Mervyn Rose and E. Victor Seixas, Jr. | 1968... | Robert Lutz and Stan Smith |

## WOMEN'S SINGLES, DOUBLES, MIXED DOUBLES

| Yr. | Singles Champions | Doubles Champions | Mixed Doubles Champions |
|---|---|---|---|
| 1938 | Miss Alice Marble | Miss A. Marble & Mrs. S. P. Fabyan | Miss A. Marble & J. D. Budge |
| 1939 | Miss Alice Marble | Miss A. Marble & Mrs. S. P. Fabyan | Miss Alice Marble & H. C. Hopman |
| 1940 | Miss Alice Marble | Miss A. Marble & Miss S. Palfrey | Miss Alice Marble & R. L. Riggs |
| 1941 | Mrs. E. T. Cooke | Mrs. E. T. Cooke & Miss M. Osborne | Mrs. E. T. Cooke & J. A. Kramer |
| 1942 | Miss Pauline Betz | Misses A. L. Brough & M. Osborne. | Miss A. L. Brough & F. R. Schroeder, Jr. |
| 1943 | Miss Pauline Betz | Misses A. L. Brough & M. Osborne. | Miss M. Osborne & W. F. Talbert |
| 1944 | Miss Pauline Betz | Misses A. L. Brough & M. Osborne. | Miss M. Osborne & W. F. Talbert |
| 1945 | Mrs. E. T. Cooke | Misses A. L. Brough & M. Osborne. | Miss M. Osborne & W. F. Talbert |
| 1946 | Miss Pauline Betz | Misses A. L. Brough & M. Osborne. | Miss M. Osborne & W. F. Talbert |
| 1947 | Miss A. L. Brough | Misses A. L. Brough & M. Osborne. | Miss A. L. Brough & J. Bromwich |
| 1948 | Mrs. M. O. du Pont | Miss A. L. Brough & Mrs. M. O. du Pont | Miss A. L. Brough & T. Brown, Jr. |
| 1949 | Mrs. M. O. du Pont | Miss A. L. Brough & Mrs. M. O. du Pont | Miss A. L. Brough & E. Sturgess |
| 1950 | Mrs. M. O. du Pont | Miss A. L. Brough & Mrs. M. O. du Pont | Mrs. M. O. du Pont & Kenneth MacGregor |
| 1951 | Maureen Connolly | Doris Hart and Shirley Fry | Doris Hart & Frank Sedgman |
| 1952 | Maureen Connolly | Doris Hart and Shirley Fry | Doris Hart & Frank Sedgman |
| 1953 | Maureen Connolly | Doris Hart and Shirley Fry | Doris Hart & E. Victor Seixas, Jr. |
| 1954 | Doris Hart | Doris Hart and Shirley Fry | Doris Hart & E. Victor Seixas, Jr. |
| 1955 | Doris Hart | A. Louise Brough and Mrs. Margaret du Pont | Doris Hart & E. Victor Seixas, Jr. |
| 1956 | Shirley J. Fry | A. Louise Brough and Mrs. Margaret du Pont | Mrs. Margaret du Pont and Kenneth Rosewall |
| 1957 | Althea Gibson | A. Louise Brough and Mrs. Margaret du Pont | Althea Gibson and Gardnar Mulloy |
| 1958 | Althea Gibson | Darlene Hard and Jeanne Arth | Mrs. M O. du Pont and Neale Fraser |
| 1959 | Maria E. Bueno | Darlene Hard and Jeanne Arth | Mrs. M. O. du Pont and Neale Fraser |
| 1960 | Darlene R. Hard | Darlene R. Hard and Maria Bueno. | Mrs. M. O. du Pont and Neale Fraser |
| 1961 | Darlene R. Hard | Darlene Hard and Lesley Turner. | Margaret Smith and Robert Mark |
| 1962 | Margaret Smith | Maria Bueno and Darlene Hard. | Margaret Smith and Fred Stolle |
| 1963 | Maria E. Bueno | Margaret Smith and Robyn Ebbern. | Margaret Smith and Kenneth Fletcher |
| 1964 | Maria E. Bueno | Billie Jean Moffitt & Karen Susman | Margaret Smith & John Newcombe |
| 1965 | Margaret Smith | Mrs. Carol Gardner & Nancy Richey | Margaret Smith & Fred Stolle |
| 1966 | Maria Bueno | Maria Bueno & Nancy Richey | Donna Floyd Fales & Owen Davidson |
| 1967 | Billie Jean King | Rosemary Casals & Billie Jean King | Billie Jean King & Owen Davidson |
| 1968 | Mrs. Margaret S. Court | Maria Bueno & Mrs. M. S. Court | Mary Ann Eisel & Peter Curtis |

## CLAY COURT CHAMPIONS

| Yr. | Champion | Doubles Champions | Yr. | Champion | Doubles Champions |
|---|---|---|---|---|---|
| 1948 | R. A. Gonzales. | S. Match-T. Chambers | 1958 | Bernard Bartzen | B. MacKay-S. Giammalva |
| 1949 | R. A. Gonzales. | E. V. Seixas-S. Match | 1959 | B. Bartzen | B Bartzen-G. Golden |
| 1950 | Herbert Flam | H. Flam-A. Larsen | 1960 | Barry MacKay. | Bob Hewitt-Marty Mulligan |
| 1951 | Tony Trabert | T. Trabert-H. Richardson | 1961 | B. Bartzen | C. McKinley-R. D. Ralston |
| 1952 | Arthur Larsen | G. Golden-A. Larsen | 1962 | Chuck McKinley | R. Earnhart-M. Riessen |
| 1953 | E. Vic Seixas, Jr. | B. Bartzen-G. Golden | 1963 | Chuck McKinley | M. Riessen-C. Graebner |
| 1954 | B. Bartzen | T. Trabert-E. V. Seixas, Jr. | 1964 | Dennis Ralston. | C. McKinley-D. Ralston |
| 1955 | Tony Trabert | T. Trabert-H. Richardson | 1965 | Dennis Ralston. | C. Graebner-M. Riessen |
| 1956 | Herbert Flam | P. Contreras-A. Olmedo | 1966 | Cliff Richey. | D. Ralston-C. Graebner |
| 1957 | E. Victor Seixas, Jr. | Ashley Cooper-Neale Fraser | 1967 | Arthur Ashe | M. Riessen-C. Graebner |
| | | | 1968 | Clark Graebner | Robert Lutz and Stan Smith |

## MEN'S INDOOR CHAMPIONS

| Yr. | Singles | Doubles | Yr. | Singles | Doubles |
|---|---|---|---|---|---|
| 1949 | R. A. Gonzales | Wm. Talbert and D. McNeill | 1960 | Barry MacKay | Andres Gimeno-Manuel Santana |
| 1950 | Don McNeill | Wm Talbert and D. McNeill | 1961 | Richard Savitt | C. Crawford-R Holmberg |
| 1951 | William Talbert | Wm. Talbert and D. McNeill | 1962 | Chas McKinley | R. Laver-C. McKinley |
| 1952 | Richard Savitt | Wm. Talbert and Budge Patty | 1963 | Dennis Ralston | D. Ralston-C. McKinley |
| 1953 | Arthur Larsen | A. Larsen and K. Nielsen | 1964 | Chas. McKinley | M. Santana-J. L. Arilla |
| 1954 | Sven Davidson | W. F. Talbert and Tony Trabert | 1965 | Jan Erik Lundquist | D. Ralston-C. McKinley |
| 1955 | Tony Traber | E. V. Seixas, Jr. and T. Trabert | | | |
| 1956 | Ulf Schmidt | S. Giammalva & E. V. Seixas, Jr | 1966 | C. Pasarell | B. Lutz-S. Smith |
| 1957 | Kurt Nielsen | Grant Golden-Barry MacKay | 1967 | C. Pasarell | A. Ashe-C.Pasarell |
| 1958 | Richard Savitt | Grant Golden-Barry MacKay | 1968 | Cliff Richey | Thomas Koch and Tom Okker |
| 1959 | Alex Olmedo | Alex Olmedo-Barry MacKay | | | |

## WOMEN'S INDOOR CHAMPIONS

| Yr. | Champion | Doubles Champions | Yr. | Champion | Doubles Champions |
|---|---|---|---|---|---|
| 1948 | Mrs. P. C. Todd | Miss D Hart and Miss B. Scofield | 1959 | Lois Felix | Lois Felix and Katharine Hubbell |
| 1949 | Miss G Moran | Miss G. Moran and Mrs. R. A. Buck | 1960 | Carole Wright | Mrs. Richard A. Buck and Ruth Jeffery |
| 1950 | Miss Nancy Chaffee | Miss Nancy Chaffee and Mrs. R. A. Buck | 1961 | Janet S. Hopps | Janet S. Hopps and Kay Hubbell |
| 1951 | Miss Nancy Chaffee | Miss Nancy Chaffee and Mrs. Richard Buck | 1962 | Carole Wright | Ruth Jeffery and Belmar Gunderson |
| 1952 | Mrs. Nancy Chaffee Kiner | Mrs. Nancy Chaffee Kiner and Mrs. Patricia Todd | 1963 | Carol Hanks | Carol Hanks and Mary Ann Eisel |
| 1953 | Mrs. Thelma Long | Mrs. Thelma Long and Mrs. Barbara Davidson | 1964 | Mary Ann Eisel | Mary Ann Eisel & Katharine Hubbell |
| 1954 | Mrs. Dorothy W. Levine | Mrs. Dorothy W. Levine and Mrs. Barbara Ward | 1965 | Nancy Richey | Carol Hanks Aucamp and Mary Ann Eisel |
| 1955 | Katharine Hubbell | K. Hubbell and R. Jeffery | 1966 | Billie Jean King | Billie Jean King & Rosemary Casals |
| 1956 | Lois Felix | L. Felix and K. Hubbell | 1967 | Billie Jean King | Carol Hanks Aucamp & Mary Ann Eisel |
| 1957 | Mrs. Dorothy Levine | Mrs Dorothy Levine and Nancy O'Connell | 1968 | Billie Jean King | Billie Jean King & Rosemary Casals |
| 1958 | Nancy O'Connell | Carol Hanks and Nancy O'Connell | | | |

## NATIONAL INTERCOLLEGIATE CHAMPIONS

| Yr. | Singles | College | Doubles | College |
|---|---|---|---|---|
| 1948 | Harry Likas | San Franc. U | F. Kovaleski & B. Bartzen | Wm. & Mary |
| 1949 | Jack Tuero | Tulane | J. Brinks and Fred Fisher | Washington |
| 1950 | Herbert Flam | U. C. L. A. | H. Flam and W. E. Garrett | U. C. L. A. |
| 1951 | Tony Trabert | Cincinnati | Earl Cochell and Hugh Stewart | So. California |
| 1952 | Hugh Stewart | So. California | Hugh Ditzler and Cliff Mayne | California |
| 1953 | Hamilton Richardson | Tulane | Lawrence Huebner and Robert Perry | U. C. L. A. |
| 1954 | Hamilton Richardson | Tulane | Robert Perry and Ron Livingston | U. C. L. A. |
| 1955 | Jose Aguero | Tulane | Pancho Contreras and Joaquin Reyes | So. California |
| 1956 | Alejandro Olmedo | So. California | Alejandro Olmedo and Pancho Contreras | So. California |
| 1957 | Barry MacKay | Michigan | Crawford Henry and Ronald Holmberg | Tulane |
| 1958 | Alejandro Olmedo | So. California | Alejandro Olmedo and Edward Atkinson | So. California |
| 1959 | Whitney Reed | San Jose State | Ronald Holmberg and Crawford Henry | Tulane |
| 1960 | Larry Nagler | U. C. L. A. | Larry Nagler and Allen Fox | U. C. L. A. |
| 1961 | Allen Fox | U. C. L. A. | Rafael Osuna and Ramsey Earnhart | So. California |
| 1962 | Rafael Osuna | So. California | Rafael Osuna and Ramsey Earnhart | So. California |
| 1963 | Dennis Ralston | So. California | Dennis Ralston and Rafael Osuna | So. California |
| 1964 | Dennis Ralston | So. California | Dennis Ralston and Bill Bond | So. California |
| 1965 | Arthur Ashe | U. C. L. A. | Arthur Ashe and Ian Crookenden | U. C. L. A. |
| 1966 | Charles Pasarell | U. C. L. A. | Charles Pasarell and Ian Crookenden | U. C. L. A. |
| 1967 | Bob Lutz | So. Calif. | Stan Smith & Bob Lutz | So. Calif. |
| 1968 | Stan Smith | So. Calif. | Stan Smith & Bob Lutz | So. Calif. |

# British (Wimbledon) Champions

### Inaugurated 1877

| Year | Men's singles | Women's singles | Year | Men's singles | Women's singles |
|---|---|---|---|---|---|
| 1953 | Victor Seixas | Maureen Connolly | 1961 | Rodney Laver | Angela Mortimer |
| 1954 | Jaroslav Drobny | Maureen Connolly | 1962 | Rodney Laver | Karen Hantze Susman |
| 1955 | Tony Trabert | Louise Brough | 1963 | Chuck McKinley | Margaret Smith |
| 1956 | Lewis Hoad | Shirley Fry | 1964 | Roy Emerson | Maria Bueno |
| 1957 | Lewis Hoad | Althea Gibson | 1965 | Roy Emerson | Margaret Smith |
| 1958 | Ashley Cooper | Althea Gibson | 1966 | Manuel Santana | Billie Jean King |
| 1959 | Alex Olmedo | Maria Bueno | 1967 | John Newcombe | Billie Jean King |
| 1960 | Neale Fraser | Maria Bueno | 1968 | Rod Laver | Billie Jean King |

# Other Tennis Championships in 1968

**Australian Championships**, Melbourne, Australia—Men's Singles: Bill Bowrey; Men's Doubles: Crealy-Stone; Women's Singles: Billie Jean King; Women's Doubles: Karen Krantzcke-Kerry Melville.

**Eastern Grass Court Championships**, South Orange, N. J.—Men's Singles: Charles Pasarell; Women's Singles: Mary Ann Eisel; Women's Doubles: Mary Ann Eisel-Valerie Ziegenfuss.

**French Championships**, Paris, France—Men's Singles: Ken Rosewall; Men's Doubles: Ken Rosewall-Fred Stolle; Women's Singles: Nancy Richey; Women's Doubles: Francoise Durr-Ann Haydon Jones.

**Italian Championships**, Rome, Italy—Men's Singles: Tom Okker; Men's Doubles: Marty Riessen-Tom Okker; Women's Singles: Lesley Turner

Bowrey; Women's Doubles: Margaret Smith Court-Virginia Wade.

**Pennsylvania Grass Court Championships**—Men's Singles: Arthur Asne; Men's Doubles: Arthur Ashe-Marty Riessen; Women's Singles: Kristy Pigeon; Women's Doubles: Mary Ann Eisel-Valerie Ziegenfuss.

**Women's Collegiate Championships**, Carlton College, Northfield, Minn.—Singles: Emilie Burrer; Doubles: Emilie Burrer-Becky Vest.

**Wightman Cup Matches** (Women's Team of U. S. & England)—Great Britain defeated U. S. 4-3. Series standing since 1932: U. S. 33, Great Britain 7.

**Federation Cup**—(Women's Team of all Nations) Paris, France—Final Round: Australia d. Netherlands 3-0.

# Davis Cup International Tennis—Challenge Round

| Yr. | Winner | Loser | Score | Yr. | Winner | Loser | Score | Yr. | Winner | Loser | Score |
|---|---|---|---|---|---|---|---|---|---|---|---|
| 1900 | U. S. | Brit. Isles. | 5-0 | 1925 | U. S. | France | 5-0 | 1949 | U. S. | Australia | 4-1 |
| 1902 | U. S. | Brit. Isles. | 3-2 | 1926 | U. S. | France | 4-1 | 1950 | Australia | U. S. | 4-1 |
| 1903 | British | U. S. | 4-1 | 1927 | France | U. S. | 3-2 | 1951 | Australia | U. S. | 3-2 |
| 1904 | British | Belgium. | 5-0 | 1928 | France | U. S. | 4-1 | 1952 | Australia | U. S. | 4-1 |
| 1905 | British | U. S. | 5-0 | 1929 | France | U. S. | 3-2 | 1953 | Australia | U. S. | 3-2 |
| 1906 | British | U. S. | 5-0 | 1930 | France | U. S. | 4-1 | 1954 | U. S. | Australia | 3-2 |
| 1907 | Australia | British | 3-2 | 1931 | France | England | 3-2 | 1955 | Australia | U. S. | 5-0 |
| 1908 | Australia | U. S. | 3-2 | 1932 | France | U. S. | 3-2 | 1956 | Australia | U. S. | 5-0 |
| 1909 | A'str'lasia | U. S. | 5-0 | 1933 | Gt. Britain | France | 3-2 | 1957 | Australia | U. S. | 3-2 |
| 1911 | A'str'lasia | U. S. | 5-0 | 1934 | Gt. Britain | U. S. | 4-1 | 1958 | U. S. | Australia | 3-2 |
| 1912 | British | Austr'lasia | 3-2 | 1935 | Gt. Britain | U. S. | 5-0 | 1959 | Australia | U. S. | 3-2 |
| 1913 | U. S. | British | 3-2 | 1936 | Gt. Britain | Australia | 3-2 | 1960 | Australia | Italy | 4-1 |
| 1914 | A'str'lasia | British | 3-2 | 1937 | U. S. | England | 4-1 | 1961 | Australia | Italy | 5-0 |
| 1919 | A'str'lasia | British | 4-1 | 1938 | U. S. | Australia | 3-2 | 1962 | Australia | Mexico | 5-0 |
| 1920 | U. S. | Austr'lasia | 5-0 | 1939 | Australia | U. S. | 3-2 | 1963 | U. S. | Australia | 3-2 |
| 1921 | U. S. | Japan | 5-0 | 1940-1945—(Not played) | | | | 1964 | Australia | U. S. | 3-2 |
| 1922 | U. S. | Australia | 4-1 | 1946 | U. S. | Australia | 5-0 | 1965 | Australia | Spain | 4-1 |
| 1923 | U. S. | Australia | 4-1 | 1947 | U. S. | Australia | 4-1 | 1966 | Australia | India | 4-1 |
| 1924 | U. S. | Australia | 5-0 | 1948 | U. S. | Australia | 5-0 | 1967 | Australia | Spain | 4-1 |

# National Junior Tennis Champions

## JUNIOR OUTDOOR SINGLES

1958 Earl Buchholz, Jr.
1959 Dennis Ralston
1960 William Lenoir
1961 Charles Pasarell
1962 Mike Belkin
1963 Cliff Richey
1964 Stanley Smith
1965 Robert Lutz
1966 Steve Ayoyer
1967 Jeff Borowiak
1968 Bob McKinley

## JUNIOR OUTDOOR DOUBLES

1958—Earl Buchholz, Jr. and Chuck McKinley
1959—Chuck McKinley and Martin Riessen
1960—Frank Froehling and William Lenoir
1961—Clark Graebner and Charles Pasarell
1962—Jackie Cooper and Mickey Schad
1963—Jack Jackson and John Pickens
1964—Dean Penero and Jeff Brown
1965—Marcello Lara and Jasjit Singh
1966—Alberto Carrero and Stan Pasarell
1967—Zan Guerry and Antonio Ortiz
1968—Bob McKinley and F. D. Robbins

## BOYS' 16 OUTDOOR SINGLES

1958 Clark Graebner
1959 James Beste
1960 Mike Belkin
1961 Bill Harris
1962 Cliff Richey
1963 Bill Harris
1964 Alberto Carrero
1965 Zan Guerry
1966 Erik van Dillen
1967 Richard Stockton
1968 Jimmy Connors

## BOYS' 16 OUTDOOR DOUBLES

1958—Clark Graebner and Warren Daane
1959—Charles Pasarell and Jorge de Jesus
1960—Frank Froehling and William Lenoir
1961—Jeff Brown and Dean Penero
1962—Jackie Cooper and Mickey Schad
1963—Roy Barth and Robert Lutz
1964—William Davidson and James Rombeau
1965—Mike Estep and George Taylor
1966—Dick Stockton and Erik van Dillen
1967—Mike Machette and Dick Stockton
1968—James Hagey and Robert Kreiss

## GIRLS' OUTDOOR SINGLES

1958 Sally Moore
1959 Karen Hantze
1960 Karen Hantze
1961 Victoria Palmer
1962 Victoria Palmer
1963 Julie Heldman
1964 Mary Ann Eisel
1965 Peaches Bartkowicz
1966 Pam Richmond
1967 Peaches Bartkowicz
1968 Kristy Pigeon

## GIRLS' OUTDOOR DOUBLES

1958—Karen Hantze and Helene Weill
1959—Karen Hantze and Kathy Chabot
1960—Karen Hantze and Kathy Chabot
1961—Victoria Palmer and Judy Alvarez
1962—Jane Albert and Mary Arfaras
1963—Stephanie DeFina and Jane Albert
1964—Mary Ann Eisel and Wendy Overton
1965—Peaches Bartkowicz and Valerie Ziegenfuss
1966—Peaches Bartkowicz and Valerie Ziegenfuss
1967—Peaches Bartkowicz and Valerie Ziegenfuss
1968—Kristy Pigeon and Denise Carter

## GIRLS' 16 OUTDOOR SINGLES

1959 Victoria Palmer
1960 Julie Heldman
1961 Janie Albert
1962 Kathy Blake
1963 Jane Bartkowicz
1964 Jane Bartkowicz
1965 Peaches Bartkowicz
1966 Linda Tuero
1967 Kristien Kemmer
1968 Janet Newberry

## GIRLS' 16 OUTDOOR DOUBLES

1959—Victoria Palmer and Margaret Taylor

1960—Patty Barth and Margaret Taylor
1961—Janie Albert and Jean Danilovich
1963—Rosemary Casals and Pixie Lamm
1964—Patsy Rippy and Paulette Verzin
1965—Peaches Bartkowicz and Valerie Ziegenfuss
1966—Linda Tuero and Connie Capozzi
1967—Gail Hansen and Patty Ann Reese
1968—Kristine Kemmer and Janet Newberry

## JUNIOR INDOOR SINGLES

1958 Chuck McKinley
1959 Chuck McKinley
1960 Arthur Ashe, Jr.
1961 Arthur Ashe, Jr.
1962 Gary Pilser
1963 Cliff Richey
1964 Frank Conner
1965 Armistead Neely
1966 Jeff Borowiak
1967 Don Lutz

## JUNIOR INDOOR DOUBLES

1958—Chuck McKinley and Raymond Senkowski
1959—Chuck McKinley and Clifford Buchholz
1960—Frank Froehling III and Butch Newman
1961—Cliff Buchholz and Butch Newman
1962—Bill Brown and Gary Rieser
1963—Bill Brown and Gary Rieser
1964—John Good and Brian Marcus
1965—Dick Dell and Turner Howard
1966—Jeff Borowiak and Mike Estep
1967—Don Lutz and John Fort

## BOYS' 16 INDOOR SINGLES

1958 Clifford Buchholz
1959 Karl Hedrick
1960 Martin Schad
1961 Cliff Richey
1962 Cliff Richey
1963 Chuck Brainard
1964 Jasjit Singh
1965 Jeff Borowiak
1966 George Taylor
1967 Dick Stockton

## BOYS' 16 INDOOR DOUBLES

1958—Claude Bakewell and James Parker
1959—Martin Schad and Jackie Cooper
1960—John Pickens and Martin Schad
1961—Jeff Brown and Cliff Richey
1962—Cliff Richey and Steve Stockton
1963—Chuck Brainard and John Towner
1964—Leo Estopare and Dan Oram
1965—Bob Alloo and Leo Estopare
1966—Jack Hughes and Robin Sandage
1967—Dick Stockton and Mike Machette

## GIRLS' INDOOR SINGLES

1958 Bonnie Mencher
1959 Justina Bricka
1960 Sue Behlmar
1961 Alice B. Christer
1962 Yale Stockwell
1963 Yale Stockwell
1964 Carolyn Clarke
1965 Vicki Rogers
1966 Judy Dixon
1967 Andrea Voikos

## GIRLS' INDOOR DOUBLES

1958—Susan Behlmar and Bonnie Mencher
1959—Justina Bricka and Sue Behlmar
1960—Sue Behlmar and Heidi Lincoln
1961—Virginia Gilbane and Joanne Swanson
1962—Duane Horan and Joanne Swanson
1963—Yale Stockwell and Roberta Zimman
1964—Carolyn Clarke and Susan Mabrey
1965—Charlotte Atwater and Carolyn Clarke
1966—Evelyn Haase and Bonnie Logan
1967—Connie Capozzi and Marjorie Gengler

## GIRLS' 16 INDOOR SINGLES

1959 Virginia Gilbane
1960 Barbara Menoff
1961 Yale Stockwell
1962 Yale Stockwell
1963 Marilyn Ashner
1964 Carolyn Clarke
1965 Vicki Rogers
1966 Andrea Voikos
1967 Andrea Voikos

# Indianapolis Speedway Winners

## DISTANCE 500 MILES (Inaugurated 1911)

| Year | Car and driver | Time | MPH | Year | Car and driver | Time | MPH |
|------|----------------|------|-----|------|----------------|------|-----|
| 1954 | Fuel Injection Special, Billy Vukovich | 3:49:17.27 | 130.840 | 1961 | Bowes Seal Fast Spec., A. J. Foyt | 3:35:37.4 | 139.130 |
| 1955 | John Zink Special, Bob Sweikert | 3:53:59.53 | 128.209 | 1962 | Leader Card Spec., Rodger Ward | 3:33:50.33 | 140.292 |
| 1956 | John Zink Special, Pat Flaherty | 3:53:00.00 | 128.490 | 1963 | Agajanian-Willard Battery Special, Parnelli Jones | 3:29:35.40 | 143.137 |
| 1957 | Belond Exhaust Special, Sam Hanks | 3:41:14.25 | 135.601 | 1964 | Sheraton-Thompson, A. J. Foyt | 3:23:35.83 | 147.350 |
| 1958 | Belond A P.Special, Jimmy Bryan | 3:44:13.00 | 133.791 | 1965 | Lotus Powered by Ford, Jimmy Clark | 3:19:05.34 | 150.686 |
| 1959 | Leader Card Special, Rodger Ward | 3:40:49.20 | 135.857 | 1966 | American Red Ball Spec., Graham Hill | 3:27:52.53 | 144.317 |
| 1960 | Ken-Paul Special, Jim Rathmann | 3:36:11.36 | 138.775 | 1967 | Sheraton-Thompson Spl., A. J. Foyt | 3:18:24.42 | 151.207 |
| | | | | 1968 | Rislone Spl., Bobby Unser | 3:16:13.76 | 152.882 |

(1) Race stopped at 345 miles, rain. Race Record—152.882 mph—Bobby Unser, 1968.

# World Drivers' Championship

| Year | Driver (car) | Year | Driver (car) | Year | Driver (car) |
|------|--------------|------|--------------|------|--------------|
| 1950 | G. Farina (Alfa Romeo) | 1957 | J. Fangio (Maserati) | 1963 | J. Clark (Lotus-Climax) |
| 1951 | J. Fangio (Alfa Romeo) | 1958 | J. Hawthorn (Ferrari) | 1964 | J. Surtees (Ferrari) |
| 1952 | A. Ascari (Ferrari) | 1959 | J. Brabham | 1965 | J. Clark (Lotus-Climax) |
| 1953 | A. Ascari (Ferrari) | | (Cooper-Climax) | 1966 | J. Brabham (Brabham-Repco) |
| 1954 | J. Fangio (Mercedes & Maserati) | 1960 | J. Brabham (Cooper-Climax) | | |
| 1955 | J. Fangio (Mercedes) | 1961 | P. Hill (Ferrari) | 1967 | D. Hulme (Brabham-Repco) |
| 1956 | J. Fangio (Lancia-Ferrari) | 1962 | G. Hill (BRM) | | |

# American Road Race of Champions

Sponsored by Newspaper Enterprise Assn. and Nine Flags—Daytona Beach, Fla., Nov. 25-26, 1967. Determines National Class Champions of Sports Car Club of America.

| Class | Driver (Car) | Class | Driver (Car) | Class | Driver (Car) |
|-------|--------------|-------|--------------|-------|--------------|
| A Prod. | R. Smith (Cobra) | C Sports | J. Hansen (Lola) | Formula | |
| B Prod. | F.VanBeuren (M'tang) | D Sports | W. Koch (Koch) | Vee | R. Campbell (Zink) |
| C Prod. | A. Johnson (Porsche) | E Sports | R.Mitchell(Elva-BMW) | Sedan A | J. McComb (Mustang) |
| D Prod. | J. Thompson (Yenko) | F Sports | P. Jett (Lotus 23B) | Sedan B | V. Provenzano (Alfa Romeo GTA) |
| E Prod. | L. Midgley (TR-3) | G Sports | C. Gibson (Lotus 23) | | |
| F Prod. | R. Sharp (Datsun) | H Sports | J. Iglehart (Bobsy) | Sedan C | R. McDaniel (Austin Cooper) |
| G Prod. | J. Truitt (A-H Sprite) | Formulas | | | |
| H Prodd. | R. LaPeer (A-H Sprite) | A, B, C | C. Dietrich (McLaren) | Sedan D | D. Parkinson (Fiat Abarth) |

# World's Land Speed Records
## Evolution of the Mile Record

| Date | Driver | Car | MPH | Date | Driver | Car | MPH |
|------|--------|-----|-----|------|--------|-----|-----|
| 12/18/98 | Chasseloup-Laubat | Jeantaud | 39.24 | 3/29/27 | Seagrave | Sunbeam | 203.790 |
| 4/29/99 | Jenatzy | Jamais Contente Jenatzy | 65.79 | 4/22/28 | Keech | White Triplex | 207.552 |
| | | | | 3/11/29 | Seagrave | Irving-Napier | 231.446 |
| 11/17/02 | Augieres | Mars | 77.13 | 2/ 5/31 | Campbell | Napier-Campbell | 246.086 |
| 11/ 5/03 | Duray | Gabron-Brillie | 84.73 | 2/24/32 | Campbell | Napier-Campbell | 253.96 |
| 12/30/04 | Barras | Darracq | 109.65 | 2 22/33 | Campbell | Napier-Campbell | 272.109 |
| 1/25/05 | B.wden | Mercedes | 109.75 | 9/ 3/35 | Campbell | Bluebird Spl. | 301.13 |
| 1/26/06 | Marriott | Stanley (Steam) | 127.659 | 11/19/37 | Eyston | Thunderbolt #1 | 311.42 |
| 3/16/10 | Oldfield | Benz | 131.724 | 9/16/38 | Eyston | Thunderbolt #1 | 357.5 |
| 4/23/11 | Burman | Benz | 141.732 | 8/23/39 | Cobb | Railton | 368.9 |
| 2/12/19 | DePalma | Packard | 149.875 | 9/16/47 | Cobb | Railton-Mobil | 394.2 |
| 4/27/20 | Milton | Duesenberg | 156.046 | 8/ 5/63 | Breedlove | Spirit of America | 407.45 |
| 4/28/26 | Parry-Thomas | Thomas Spl. | 170.624 | 10/27/64 | Arfons | Green Monster | 536.71 |
| | | | | 11/15/65 | Breedlove | Spirit of America | 600.601 |

# National Automobile Champions (U. S. Auto Club)

| | | | |
|---|---|---|---|
| 1950 Henry Banks | 1955 Bob Sweikert | 1959 Rodger Ward | 1963 A. J. Foyt |
| 1951 Tony Bettenhausen | 1956 Jimmy Bryan | 1960 A. J. Foyt | 1964 A. J. Foyt |
| 1952 Chuck Stevenson | 1957 Jimmy Bryan | 1961 A. J. Foyt | 1965 Mario Andretti |
| 1953 Sam Hanks | 1958 Tony Bettenhausen | 1962 Rodger Ward | 1966 Mario Andretti |
| 1954 Jimmy Bryan | | | 1967 A. J. Foyt |

# Daytona 500 Winners

| Year | Driver (Car) | Avg. MPH | Year | Driver (Car) | Avg. MPH |
|------|--------------|----------|------|--------------|----------|
| 1959 | L. Petty (Oldsmobile) | 135.521 | *1965 | F. Lorenzen (Ford) | 141.539 |
| 1960 | J. Johnson (Chevrolet) | 124.740 | **1966 | R. Petty (Plymouth) | 160.627 |
| 1961 | M. Panch (Pontiac) | 149.601 | 1967 | M. Andretti (Ford) | 146.926 |
| 1962 | F. Roberts (Pontiac) | 152.529 | 1968 | C. Yarborough (Mercury) | 143.251 |
| 1963 | T. Lund (Ford) | 151.566 | *332.5 miles because of rain. | | |
| 1964 | R. Petty (Plymouth) | 154.334 | **495 miles because of rain. | | |

# Canadian-American Challenge Cup

| Year | Driver (Car) |
|------|--------------|
| 1966 | J. Surtees (Lola T-70 Chev.) |
| 1967 | B. McLaren (McLaren M6A Chev.) |

# Trans-American Championship

| | Over 2-Liter | Under 2-Liter |
|------|--------------|---------------|
| 1966 | Ford Motor Co. | Alfa-Romeo |
| 1967 | Ford Motor Co. | Porsche |
| 1968 | Chevrolet Div. | Porsche |

# Grand National Champions (NASCAR)
## National Assn. of Stock Car Auto Racing

| Year | Driver (Car) | Year | Driver (Car) | Year | Driver (Car) |
|------|--------------|------|--------------|------|--------------|
| 1949 | R. Byron (Oldsmobile) | 1956 | E. Baker (Chrysler-Dodge) | 1963 | J. Weatherly (Pontiac-Mercury) |
| 1950 | W. Rexford (Oldsmobile) | 1957 | E. Baker (Chevrolet) | | |
| 1951 | H. Thomas (Ply.-Hudson) | 1958 | L. Petty (Oldsmobile) | 1964 | R. Petty (Plymouth) |
| 1952 | T. Flock (Hudson) | 1959 | L. Petty (Olds.-Plymouth) | 1965 | N. Jarrett (Ford) |
| 1953 | H. Thomas (Hudson) | 1960 | R. White (Chevrolet) | 1966 | D. Pearson (Dodge) |
| 1954 | L. Petty (Chrysler) | 1961 | N. Jarrett (Chevrolet) | 1967 | R. Petty (Plymouth) |
| 1955 | T. Flock (Chrysler) | 1962 | J. Weatherly (Pontiac) | 1968 | D. Pearson (Ford) |

# Trotting and Pacing Records

**Source:** Larry Evans, United States Trotting Association. Records to Oct. 15, 1968

## TROTTING RECORDS

Asterisk (*) denotes that record was made in a race.

### One Mile Records

#### (Mile Track)

**All-age Stallion**—*1:55⅗—Noble Victory, Du Quoin, Ill., Sept. 1, 1966.

**All-age Mare**—1:56¾—Rosalind, Lexington, Ky. Oct. 4, 1938.

**All-age Gelding**—1:55¼—Greyhound, Lexington, Ky., Sept. 29, 1938.

**Yearling Colt**—2:15¾—Airdale, Lexington, Ky., Oct. 2, 1912.

**Yearling Filly**—2:15⅕—Rilda Rose, Lexington, Ky., Oct. 6, 1955.

**Two-year-old Colt**—*1:58⅖—Nevele Pride, Lexington, Ky., Oct. 4, 1967.

**Two-year-old Filly**—1:58⅗—Impish, Lexington, Ky., Sept. 29, 1961.

**Two-year-old Gelding**—2:02⅗—Record Mat, Lexington, Ky., Oct. 8, 1957; *Argo Kid, Lexington, Ky., Oct. 3, 1963.

**Three-year-old Colt**—*1:56⅗—Nevele Pride, Indianapolis, Ind., Aug. 31, 1968.

**Three-year-old Filly**—1:58—Yankee Lass, Lexington, Ky., Oct. 20, 1957; Emily's Pride, Lexington, Ky., Oct. 8, 1958; Expresson, Lexington, Ky., Oct. 12, 1959; Worth Seein, Lexington, Ky., Oct. 4, 1962.

**Three-year-old Gelding**—*1:59—Senator Frost, Inglewood, Calif., Nov. 19, 1958.

**Four-year-old Stallion**—*1:55⅗—Noble Victory, Du Quoin, Ill., Sept. 1, 1966.

**Four-year-old Mare**—1:57⅕—Fresh Yankee, Lexington, Ky., Oct. 3, 1967.

**Four-year-old Gelding** — *1:57¼ — Greyhound, Springfield, Ill., Aug. 21, 1936.

#### (Half-Mile Track)

**All-age Stallion**—1:58⅗—Matastar, Delaware, Ohio, Sept. 16, 1963. *1:58⅗—Speedy Rodney, Yonkers, N. Y., Sept. 2, 1966.

**All-age Mare**, *1:59⅕—Armbro Flight, Delaware, Ohio, Sept. 20, 1965.

**All-age Gelding**—1:59¾—Greyhound, Goshen, N. Y., July 16, 1937.

**Two-year-old Colt**—*2:00⅕—Ayres, Delaware, Ohio, 1963.

**Two-year-old Filly**—*2:03⅗—Impish, Delaware, Ohio, 1961.

**Two-year-old Gelding**—*2:05⅗—Mustard Seed, Saratoga Springs, N. Y., 1965.

**Three-year-old Colt**—*2:00⅖—Snow Speed, Delaware, Ohio, Sept. 18, 1968.

**Three-year-old Filly**—*1:59⅕—Armbro Flight, Delaware, Ohio, 1965.

**Three-year-old Gelding**—*2:01⅘—Bonus Boy, Saratoga Springs, N. Y., 1966.

**Four-year-old Stallion**—*1:59—Noble Victory, Saratoga Springs, N. Y., 1966.

**Four-year-old Mare** — *2:00⅖ — Flamboyant, Yonkers, N. Y., Aug. 2, 1968.

**Four-year-old Gelding**—*2:01⅖—Sleepy Play, Wilmington, Del., 1966.

### Odd Distances

**1-1/16 Miles**—*2:05⅗—Senator Frost, Inglewood, Calif., Oct. 17, 1959, and Dartmouth, Westbury, N. Y. Sept. 26, 1964.

**1-1/16 Miles, Half-mile Track**—*2:08⅗—Perfect Freight, Westbury, N. Y., 1966.

**1-3/16 Miles**—*2:22⅘—Scotch Victor, Inglewood, Calif., Nov. 6, 1954.

**1¼ Miles** — *2:30⅗ — Pronto Don, Inglewood, Calif., Nov. 24, 1951.

**1¼ Miles, Half-mile Track**—*2:31⅖—Speedy Scot, Westbury, N. Y., 1964; Noble Victory, Westbury, N. Y., 1966.

**1½ Miles** — 3:02½ — Greyhound, Indianapolis, Ind., Sept. 14, 1937.

**1½ Miles, Half-mile Track**—3:05⅗—Duke Rodney, Yonkers, N. Y., July 2, 1964.

**2 Miles**—4:06—Greyhound, Indianapolis, Ind., Sept. 19, 1939.

**2 Miles, Half-mile Track**—*4:10⅘—Pronto Don, Westbury, N.Y., Sept. 13, 1951.

**Fastest Two Heats**—*1:57⅖; *1:56⅗—Nevele Pride, Indianapolis, Aug. 31, 1968.

**Fastest Two Heats, Half-Mile Track**—*1:58⅘, *2:00⅗—Speedy Rodney, Goshen, N. Y., 1966.

**Fastest Three Heats**—2:01, 2:00¼, 2.00—Greyhound, Goshen, N.Y., Aug. 13, 1936; 2:02, 2:00, 1:59¼—Rosalind, Lexington, Ky., Sept. 30, 1937.

## PACING RECORDS

### One Mile Records

#### (Mile Track)

**All-age Stallion**—1:53⅗—Bret Hanover, Lexington, Ky., Oct. 7, 1966.

**All-age Mare**—*1:56⅖—Tarport Lib, Lexington, Ky., Oct. 7, 1966.

**All-age Gelding**—1:57⅖—Cardigan Bay, Inglewood, Calif., Oct. 30, 1965.

**Two-year-old Colt**—*1:57—Bullet Hanover, Indianapolis, Ind., Sept. 9, 1959.

**Two-year-old Filly**—1:57⅕—Timely Beauty, Lexington, Ky., Oct. 15, 1962.

**Two-year-old Gelding**—*1:59⅘—Corsican, Lexington, Ky., Oct. 1. 1957.

**Three-year-old Colt**—*1:55—Bret Hanover, Indianapolis, Ind., 1965.

**Three-year-old Filly**—*1:56⅖—Tarport Lib, Lexington, Ky., 1966.

**Three-year-old Gelding** — *1:59 — Frisco Creed, Inglewood, Calif., Nov. 9, 1955; Egyptian Pride, Philadelphia, Pa., June 26, 1963; Royal Gene Pick, Vernon, N. Y., 1966. 1:59—Tarport Jimmy, Lexington, Ky., 1961.

**Four-year-old Stallion**—1:53⅗—Bret Hanover, Lexington, Ky., 1966.

**Four-year-old Mare**—1:56⅘—Dottie's Pick, Inglewood, Calif., Nov. 16, 1956.

**Four-year-old Gelding**—*1:57⅘—Ace of Spades, Inglewood, Calif., Nov. 9, 1961.

#### (Half-Mile Track)

**All-age Stallion**—1:55⅗—Adios Butler, Delaware, Ohio, Sept. 21, 1961.

**All-age Mare**—*1:59⅕—Countess Adios, Delaware, Ohio, Sept. 19, 1960.

**All-age Gelding**—*1:58⅕—Cardigan Bay, Yonkers, N. Y., July 16, 1964.

**Two-year-old Colt**—1:59⅘—Laverne Hanover, Saratoga Springs, N. Y., June 24, 1968.

**Two-year-old Filly** — *2:01⅖ — Good Counsel, Delaware, Ohio, 1956.

**Two-year-old Gelding**—*2:02⅗—Corsican, Saratoga Springs, N. Y., 1957.

**Three-year-old Colt**—*1:57—Bret Hanover, Delaware, Ohio, Sept. 23, 1965.

**Three-year-old Filly**—*1:59⅕—Countess Adios, Delaware, Ohio, 1960.

**Three-year-old Gelding**—*2:00⅗—Skipper Gene, Maywood, Ill., 1965.

**Four-year-old Stallion**—*1:57⅘—Bye Bye Byrd, Westbury, N. Y., 1959.

**Four-year-old Mare** — *1:59⅘ — Adios Claire, Westbury, N. Y., 1959

**Four-year-old Gelding**—*1.59⅖—Meadow Elva, Yonkers, N. Y., Sept. 27, 1968.

### Odd Distances

**1¼ Miles**—*2:30⅖—Dr. Stanton, Arcadia, Calif., May 15, 1948.

**1¼ Miles, Half-mile Track**—*2:29⅗—Irvin Paul, Westbury, N. Y., Sept. 1, 1962.

**1-1/16 Miles**—*2:03⅕—Adios Vic, Inglewood, Calif., Oct. 23, 1965.

**1-1/16 Miles, Half-mile Track**—*2:06⅖—Amortizer, Westbury, N.Y., June 29, 1956.

**1⅛ miles**—*2:11⅕—Adios Butler, Inglewood, Calif., Nov. 4, 1961; Irvin Paul, Inglewood, Calif., 1962.

**1½ Miles**, *3:05⅖—Right Time, Inglewood, Calif., 1961; and K. D. Senator, E. Boston, Mass., 1963.

**1½ Miles, Half-mile Track**—*3:03—Tarquinius, Westbury, N. Y., Sept. 12, 1964.

**2 Miles**—4:17—Dan Patch, Macon, Ga., 1903.

**2 Miles, Half-Mile Track**—*4:08⅘—Irvin Paul, Yonkers, N. Y., June 28, 1962.

**Fastest Two Heats**—*1:55⅖, 1:56⅕—Adios Harry, Vernon, N.Y., July 8, 1955.

**Fastest Three Heats**—*1:58¼, 1:58½, 1:59¼—Her Ladyship. Syracuse, N.Y., Aug. 31, 1938.

# Winners of Famous Harness Stakes

## THE HAMBLETONIAN (3-year-old trotters)

| Yr. Winner | Best Time | Value | Yr. Winner | Best Time | Value |
|---|---|---|---|---|---|
| 1939—Peter Astra | 2:04¼ | $40,502 | 1954—Newport Dream | 2:02⅘ | $106,830 |
| 1940—Spencer Scott | 2:02 | 43,658 | 1955—Scott Frost | 2:00⅗ | 86,863 |
| 1941—Bill Gallon | 2:05 | 38,729 | 1956—The Intruder | 2:01⅖ | 98,591 |
| 1942—The Ambassador | 2:04 | 38,954 | 1957—Hickory Smoke | 2:00⅕ | 111,126 |
| 1943—Volo Song | 2:02½ | 42,298 | 1958—Emily's Pride | 1:59⅘ | 106,719 |
| 1944—Yankee Maid | 2:04 | 33,577 | 1959—Diller Hanover | 2:01⅕ | 125,284 |
| 1945—Titan Hanover | 2:04 | 50,190 | 1960—Blaze Hanover | 1:59⅗ | 144,590 |
| 1946—Chestertown | 2:02½ | 50,905 | 1961—Harlan Dean | 1:58⅖ | 131,573 |
| 1947—Hoot Mon | 2:00 | 46.267 | 1962—A.C.'s Viking | 1:59⅗ | 116,312 |
| 1948—Demon Hanover | 2:02 | 59.941 | 1963—Speedy Scot | 1:58 | 115,549 |
| 1949—Miss Tilly | 2:01⅖ | 69,791 | 1964—Ayres | 1:56⅘ | 115,281 |
| 1950—Lusty Song | 2:02 | 75,209 | 1965—Egyptian Candor | 2:04⅗ | 122,245 |
| 1951—Mainliner | 2:02⅗ | 95,263 | 1966—Kerry Way | 1:58⅘ | 122,540 |
| 1952—Sharp Note | 2:02⅗ | 87,657 | 1967—Speedy Streak | 2:00 | 122,650 |
| 1953—Helicopter | 2:01⅗ | 117.118 | 1968—Nevele Pride | 1:59⅖ | 116,190 |

| Year | FOX STAKE 2-yr.-old pacers | | LITTLE BROWN JUG 3-yr.-old pacers | | HORSEMAN STAKE 2-yr.-old trotters | | KENTUCKY FUTURITY 3-yr.-old trotters | |
|---|---|---|---|---|---|---|---|---|
| | Winner | Time | Winner | Time | Winner | Time | Winner | Time |
| 1961 | Coffee Break | 1:58⅕ | Henry T. Adios | 1:58⅘ | Safe Mission | 2:03⅗ | Duke Rodney | 1:58⅕ |
| 1962 | (rained out) | | Lehigh Hanover | 1:58⅘ | (rained out) | | Safe Mission | 1:59⅕ |
| 1963 | Race Time | 1:58 | Overtrick | 1:57⅕ | Smart Rodney | 2:03⅗ | Speedy Scot | 1:57⅕ |
| 1964 | Bret Hanover | 1:58 | Vicar Hanover | 2:01 | Noble Victory | 2:00⅕ | Ayres | 1:58⅕ |
| 1965 | Romeo Hanover | 1:59 | Bret Hanover | 1:57 | Kerry Way | 2:02⅘ | Armbro Flight | 1:59 |
| 1966 | Best of All | 1:59⅖ | Romeo Hanover | 1:59⅗ | Kimberly Dutchess | 2:04⅗ | Governor Armbro | 2:00⅖ |
| 1967 | Golden Money Maker | 1:58⅘ | Best of All | 1:59 | Nevele Pride | 2:02⅕ | Speed Model | 1:59⅗ |
| 1968 | Laverne Hanover | 1:59⅘ | Rum Customer | 1:59⅗ | Nevele Major | 2:02⅗ | Nevele Pride | 1:57 |

## OTHER HARNESS RACING WINNERS IN 1968

| Event | Winner | Best time | Value |
|---|---|---|---|
| The Dexter Cup (3-year-old) (trot) | Nevele Pride | 2:02 2-5 | $166,746 |
| Yonkers Futurity (3-year-old) (trot) | Nevele Pride | 2:03 3-5 | 150,000 |
| The Colonial (3-year-old) (trot) | Nevele Pride | 1:59 | 100,000 |
| Roosevelt International Trot (1¼ miles) | Roquepine | 2:38 3-5 | 100,000 |
| The Empire (1¼ miles) (pace) | Romulus Hanover | 2:34 4-5 | 100,000 |
| The Hilltop (1¼ miles) (trot) | Flamboyant | 2:36 | 100,000 |
| Realization (4-year-old) (trot) (1 1/16 miles) | Flamboyant | 2:12 | 99,561 |
| The Adios (3-year-old) (pace) | Bye And Large | 2:00 1-5 | 93,920 |
| American-National Maturity (4-year-old) (pace) | Best of All | 1:57 1-5 | 85,318 |
| American-National Maturity (4-year-old) (trot) | Proven Freight | 2:02 | 71,151 |
| N. Y. State Fair Open Pace (3-year-olds) | Chester J. P. | 2:03 1-5 | 64,580 |
| Ill. Colt Stake (2-year-old) (pace) | Active Don | 2:00 | 58,800 |
| Ill. Colt Stake (3-year-old) (pace) | Shoestring | 1:59 3-5 | 53,350 |
| N. Y. State Fair Open Trot (3-year-olds) | Fine Shot | 2:04 1-5 | 52,000 |
| The International (1½ miles) (pace) | Cardinal King | 3:06 | 50,000 |
| Good Time (1¼ miles) (pace) | Cardinal King | 2:32 2-5 | 50,000 |
| N. H. Sweepstakes Inv. (3-year-old) (pace) | Nob Hill | 2:01 4-5 | 50,000 |
| National Championship (1½ miles) (pace) | Cardinal King | 3:05 4-5 | 50,000 |
| The Ed Sullivan (pace) | Romulus Hanover | 2:00 | 50,000 |
| The Washington Park Inv. Pace | Nardin's Byrd | 2:05 3-5 | 50,000 |
| The Summer Classic (pace) | True Duane | 1:58 | 50,000 |
| American Trotting Championship (1¼ miles) | Carlisle | 2:34 2-5 | 50,000 |
| The United Nations (1½ miles) (trot) | Earl Laird | 3:17 2-5 | 50,000 |
| The Gotham (1¼ miles) (trot) | Carlisle | 2:35 1-5 | 50,000 |
| The Midwest Derby (pace) | Careless Time | 2:02 1-5 | 50,000 |
| The Lawrence B. Sheppard (2-year-old) (pace) | Hammerin Hank | 2:03 | 50,000 |

## LEADING DRIVERS

| Yr. | Races Won | | Grand Circuit | | Money Won | |
|---|---|---|---|---|---|---|
| 1956 | Bill Haughton | 167 | Joe O'Brien | $242,787 | Bill Haughton | $572,945 |
| 1957 | Bill Haughton | 156 | John Simpson | 367,670 | Bill Haughton | 586,950 |
| 1958 | Bill Haughton | 176 | Joe O'Brien | 267,342 | Bill Haughton | 816,659 |
| 1959 | William Gilmour | 165 | Joe O'Brien | 263,636 | Bill Haughton | 711,435 |
| 1960 | Del Insko | 156 | Del Miller | 338,594 | Del Miller | 567,282 |
| 1961 | Bob Farrington | 201 | Jimmy Arthur | 248,211 | Stanley Dancer | 674,723 |
| 1962 | Bob Farrington | 203 | Stanley Dancer | 306,454 | Stanley Dancer | 760,343 |
| 1963 | Donald Busse | 201 | Ralph Baldwin | 299,899 | Bill Haughton | 790,086 |
| 1964 | Bob Farrington | 312 | Stanley Dancer | 269,080 | Stanley Dancer | 1,051,538 |
| 1965 | Bob Farrington | 310 | Joe O'Brien | 304,791 | Bill Haughton | 889,943 |
| 1966 | Bob Farrington | 283 | George Sholty | 293,531 | Stanley Dancer | 1,218,403 |
| 1967 | Bob Farrington | 277 | Bill Haughton | 448,294 | Bill Haughton | 1,305,773 |

## Queen's Plate

The Queen's Plate (known as King's Plate during reign of male), Canada's most famous thoroughbred race, is the oldest continuously run stakes race in North America. Originated in 1860 over 1⅛ miles (now 1¼ miles) for 3-year-olds, Canadian-foaled, race is staged under Royal tutelage for trophy and 50 gold sovereigns plus purse. Trophy is not a plate but a foot-high gold cup valued at $5,000. However, race is identified as a plate race because of 17th Century English tradition of awarding plates.

| Year Winner Jockey | Time | Dollars | Year Winner Jockey | Time | Dollars |
|---|---|---|---|---|---|
| 1950—McGill, C. Rogers | 1:52.2 | $14,290 | 1960—Victoria Park, A. Gomez | 2:02 | $42,750 |
| 1951—Major Factor, A. Bavington | 1:53 | 16,152 | 1961—Blue Light, H. Dittfach | 2:05 | 46,475 |
| 1952—Epigram, G. Robillard | 1:58.3 | 17,022 | 1962—Flaming Page, J. Fitzsimmons | 2:04.3 | 51,225 |
| 1953—Canadiana, E. Arcaro | 1:52.1 | 20,592 | 1963—Canebora, M. Ycaza | 2:04 | 54,850 |
| 1954—Collisteo, C. Rogers | 1:52 | 22,452 | 1964—Northern Dancer, W. Hartack | 2:02.1 | 49,234 |
| 1955—Ace Marine, G. Walker | 1:52.2 | 25,514 | 1965—Whistling Sea, T. Inouye | 2:03.2 | 47,852 |
| 1956—Canadian Champ, D. Stevenson | 1:55 | 25,430 | 1966—Titled Hero, A. Gomez | 2:03.3 | 52,173 |
| 1957—Lyford Cay, A. Gomez | 2:02.3 | 26,210 | 1967—Jammed Lovely, J. Fitzsimmons | 2:03 | 51,821 |
| 1958—Caledon Beau, A. Coy | 2:04.1 | 26,151 | 1968—Merger, W. Harris | 2:05.2 | 53,641 |
| 1959—New Providence, R. Ussery | 2:04.4 | 51,767 | | | |

## Kentucky Derby, 3 Yr. Olds
**Churchill Downs, Louisville, Ky.**
Inaugurated 1875. Distance 1¼ miles; 1½ miles until 1896

| Yr. | Winner, weight | Time | Doll'rs | Yr. | Winner, weight | Time | Doll'rs |
|---|---|---|---|---|---|---|---|
| 1875.. | Aristides (100) | 2.37 3-4 | 2,850 | 1922.. | Morvich (126) | 2.04 3-5 | 53,775 |
| 1876.. | Vagrant (97) | 2.38 1-4 | 2,950 | 1923.. | Zev (126) | 2.05 2-5 | 53,600 |
| 1877.. | Baden Baden (100) | 2.38 | 3,300 | 1924.. | Black Gold (126) | 2.05 1-5 | 52,775 |
| 1878.. | Day Star (100) | 2.37 1-4 | 4,050 | 1925.. | Flying Ebony (126) | 2.07 3-5 | 52,950 |
| 1879.. | Lord Murphy (100) | 2.37 | 3,550 | 1926.. | Bubbling Over (126) | 2.03 4-5 | 50,075 |
| 1880.. | Fonso (105) | 2.37 1-2 | 3,800 | 1927.. | Whiskery (126) | 2.06 | 51,000 |
| 1881.. | Hindoo (105) | 2.40 | 4,410 | 1928.. | Reigh Count (126) | 2.10 2-5 | 55,375 |
| 1882.. | Apollo (102) | 2.40 1-4 | 4,560 | 1929.. | Clyde Van Dusen (126) | 2.10 4-5 | 53,950 |
| 1883.. | Leonatus (105) | 2.43 | 3,760 | 1930.. | Gallant Fox (126) | 2.07 3-5 | 50,725 |
| 1884.. | Buchanan (110) | 2.40 1-4 | 3,990 | 1931.. | Twenty Grand (126) | 2.01 4-5 | 48,725 |
| 1885.. | Joe Cotton (110) | 2.37 1-5 | 4,630 | 1932.. | Burgoo King (126) | 2.05 1-5 | 52,350 |
| 1886.. | Ben Ali (118) | 2.36 1-2 | 4,890 | 1933.. | Broker's Tip (126) | 2.06 4-5 | 48,925 |
| 1887.. | Montrose (118) | 2.39 1-4 | 4,200 | 1934.. | Cavalcade (126) | 2.04 | 28,175 |
| 1888.. | Macbeth II (115) | 2.38 1-4 | 4,740 | 1935.. | Omaha (126) | 2.05 | 39,525 |
| 1889.. | Spokane (118) | 2.34 1-2 | 4,970 | 1936.. | Bold Venture (126) | 2.03 3-5 | 37,725 |
| 1890.. | Riley (118) | 2.45 | 5,460 | 1937.. | War Admiral (126) | 2.03 1-5 | 52,050 |
| 1891.. | Kingman (122) | 2.52 1-2 | 4,680 | 1938.. | Lawrin (126) | 2.04 4-5 | 47,050 |
| 1892.. | Azra (122) | 2.41 1-2 | 4,230 | 1939.. | Johnstown (126) | 2.03 2-5 | 46,350 |
| 1893.. | Lookout (122) | 2.39 1-4 | 4,090 | 1940.. | Gallahadion (126) | 2.05 | 60,150 |
| 1894.. | Chant (122) | 2.41 | 4,020 | 1941.. | Whirlaway (126) | 2.01 2-5 | 61,275 |
| 1895.. | Halma (122) | 2.37 1-2 | 2,970 | 1942.. | Shut Out (126) | 2.04 2-5 | 64,225 |
| 1896.. | Ben Brush (117) | 2.07 3-4 | 4,850 | 1943.. | Count Fleet (126) | 2.04 | 60,725 |
| 1897.. | Typhoon II (117) | 2.12 1-2 | 4,850 | 1944.. | Pensive (126) | 2.04 1-5 | 64,675 |
| 1898.. | Plaudit (117) | 2.09 | 4,850 | 1945.. | Hoop, Jr. (126) | 2.07 | 64,850 |
| 1899.. | Manuel (117) | 2.12 | 4,850 | 1946.. | Assault (126) | 2.06 3-5 | 96,400 |
| 1900.. | Lieut. Gibson (117) | 2.06 1-4 | 4,850 | 1947.. | Jet Pilot (126) | 2.06 3-5 | 92,160 |
| 1901.. | His Eminence (117) | 2.07 3-4 | 4,850 | 1948.. | Citation (126) | 2.05 2-5 | 83,400 |
| 1902.. | Alan-a-Dale (117) | 2.08 3-4 | 4,850 | 1949.. | Ponder (126) | 2.04 1-5 | 91,600 |
| 1903.. | Judge Himes (117) | 2.09 | 4,850 | 1950.. | Middleground (126) | 2.01 3-5 | 92,650 |
| 1904.. | Elwood (117) | 2.08 1-2 | 4,850 | 1951.. | Count Turf (126) | 2.02 3-5 | 98,050 |
| 1905.. | Agile (122) | 2.10 3-4 | 4,850 | 1952.. | Hill Gail (126) | 2.01 3-5 | 96,300 |
| 1906.. | Sir Huon (117) | 2.08 4-5 | 4,850 | 1953.. | Dark Star (126) | 2.02 | 90,050 |
| 1907.. | Pink Star (117) | 2.12 3-5 | 4,850 | 1954.. | Determine (126) | 2.03 | 102,050 |
| 1908.. | Stone Street (117) | 2.15 1-5 | 4,850 | 1955.. | Swaps (126) | 2.01 4-5 | 108,400 |
| 1909.. | Wintergreen (117) | 2.08 1-5 | 4,850 | 1956.. | Needles (126) | 2.03 2-5 | 123,450 |
| 1910.. | Donau (117) | 2.06 2-5 | 4,850 | 1957.. | Iron Liege (126) | 2.02 1-5 | 107,950 |
| 1911.. | Meridian (117) | 2.05 | 4,850 | 1958.. | Tim Tam (126) | 2.05 | 116,400 |
| 1912.. | Worth (117) | 2.09 2-5 | 4,850 | 1959.. | Tomy Lee (126) | 2.02 1-5 | 119,650 |
| 1913.. | Donerail (117) | 2.04 4-5 | 5,475 | 1960.. | Venetian Way (126) | 2.02 2-5 | 114,850 |
| 1914.. | Old Rosebud (114) | 2.03 2-5 | 9,125 | 1961.. | Carry Back (126) | 2.04 | 120,500 |
| 1915*. | Regret (112) | 2.05 2-5 | 11,450 | 1962.. | Decidedly (126) | 2.00 2-5 | 119,650 |
| 1916.. | George Smith (117) | 2.04 | 9,750 | 1963.. | Chateaugay (126) | 2.01 4-5 | 108,900 |
| 1917.. | Omar Khayyam (117) | 2.04 3-5 | 16,600 | 1964.. | Northern Dancer (126) | 2.00 | 114,300 |
| 1918.. | Exterminator (114) | 2.10 4-5 | 14,700 | 1965.. | Lucky Debonair (126) | 2.01 1-5 | 112,000 |
| 1919.. | Sir Barton (112½) | 2.09 4-5 | 20,825 | 1966.. | Kauai King (126) | 2.02 | 120,500 |
| 1920.. | Paul Jones (126) | 2.09 | 30,375 | 1967.. | Proud Clarion (126) | 2.00 3-5 | 119,700 |
| 1921.. | Behave Yourself (126) | 2.04 1-5 | 38,450 | 1968.. | (A) Forward Pass (126) | 2.02 1-5 | 122,600 |

(A) This race was won by Dancer's Image, who was disqualified after chemical tests disclosed he had run with a pain-killing drug, phenylbutazone, in his system. All wagers were paid on Dancer's Image and the winning time is for that horse.

The Kentucky Derby has been won five times by one jockey—Eddie Arcaro, 1938, 1941, 1945, 1948 and 1952; four times by Bill Hartack, 1957, 1960, 1962 and 1964; and three times by each of three jockeys—Isaac Murphy, 1884, 1890 and 1891; Earle Sande, 1923, 1925 and 1930, and Willie Shoemaker, 1955, 1959, 1965. *Regret only filly ever to win the Derby.

## Preakness
**Pimlico, Baltimore, Md. (1873); 1-3/16 Miles, 3 Yr. Olds**

| Yr. | Winner, weight | Time | Doll'rs | Yr. | Winner, weight | Time | Doll'rs |
|---|---|---|---|---|---|---|---|
| 1933.. | Head Play (126) | 2.02 | 26,850 | 1951.. | Bold (126) | 1.56 2-5 | 83,100 |
| 1934.. | High Quest (126) | 1.58 1-5 | 25,175 | 1952.. | Blue Man (126) | 1.57 2-5 | 86,135 |
| 1935.. | Omaha (126) | 1.58 2-5 | 25,325 | 1953.. | Native Dancer (126) | 1.57 4-5 | 65,200 |
| 1936.. | Bold Venture (126) | 1.59 | 27,325 | 1954.. | Hasty Road (126) | 1.57 2-5 | 91,600 |
| 1937.. | War Admiral (126) | 1.58 2-5 | 45,600 | 1955.. | Nashua (126) | 1.54 3-5 | 67,550 |
| 1938.. | Dauber (126) | 1.59 4-5 | 51,875 | 1956.. | Fabius (126) | 1.58 2-5 | 84,250 |
| 1939.. | Challedon (126) | 1.59 4-5 | 53,710 | 1957.. | Bold Ruler (126) | 1.56 1-5 | 65,250 |
| 1940.. | Bimelech (126) | 1.58 3-5 | 53,230 | 1958.. | Tim Tam (126) | 1.57 1-5 | 97,900 |
| 1941.. | Whirlaway (126) | 1.58 4-5 | 49,365 | 1959.. | Royal Orbit (126) | 1.57 | 136,200 |
| 1942.. | Alsab (126) | 1.57 | 58,175 | 1960.. | Bally Ache (126) | 1.57 3-5 | 121,000 |
| 1943.. | Count Fleet (126) | 1.57 2-5 | 43,190 | 1961.. | Carry Back (126) | 1.57 3-5 | 125,000 |
| 1944.. | Pensive (126) | 1.59 1-5 | 60,075 | 1962.. | Greek Money (126) | 1.56 1-5 | 135,000 |
| 1945.. | Polynesian (126) | 1.58 4-5 | 66,170 | 1963.. | Candy Spots (126) | 1.56 1-5 | 127,500 |
| 1946.. | Assault (126) | 2.01 2-5 | 96,620 | 1964.. | Northern Dancer (126) | 1.56 4-5 | 142,200 |
| 1947.. | Faultless (126) | 1.59 | 98,005 | 1965.. | Tom Rolfe (126) | 1.56 1-5 | 125,400 |
| 1948.. | Citation (126) | 2.02 2-5 | 91,870 | 1966.. | Kauai King (126) | 1.55 2-5 | 129,000 |
| 1949.. | Capot (126) | 1.56 | 79,985 | 1967.. | Damascus (126) | 1.55 1-5 | 141,500 |
| 1950.. | Hill Prince (126) | 1.59 1-5 | 56,110 | 1968.. | Forward Pass (126) | 1.56 4 | 142,700 |

## Belmont Stakes
**(1867); 1½ Miles, 3 Yr. Olds, Belmont Park, Elmont, L. I., N. Y.**
Run at Jerome Park prior to 1890; Morris Park, 1890-1905. Distance 1⅝ miles prior to 1874; 1½ miles, 1874-1889; 1¼ miles, 1890-1892; 1⅛ miles, 1893-1894; 1¼ miles, 1895; 1⅜ miles, 1896-1925; increased to 1½ miles, 1926. Run at 1¼ miles, 1904 and 1905. Not run 1911 or 1912. Aqueduct, 1963-1967.

| Year | Winner, weight | Time | Dollars | Year | Winner, weight | Time | Dollars |
|---|---|---|---|---|---|---|---|
| 1939.. | Johnstown (126) | 2.29 3-5 | 37,020 | 1954.. | High Gun (126) | 2.30 4-5 | 89,000 |
| 1940.. | Bimelech (126) | 2.29 3-5 | 35,030 | 1955.. | Nashua (126) | 2.29 | 83,700 |
| 1941.. | Whirlaway (126) | 2.31 | 39,770 | 1956.. | Needles (126) | 2.29 4-5 | 83,600 |
| 1942.. | Shut Out (126) | 2.29 1-5 | 44,520 | 1957.. | Gallant Man (126) | 2.26 3-5 | 77,300 |
| 1943.. | Count Fleet (126) | 2.28 1-5 | 35,340 | 1958.. | Cavan (126) | 2.30 1-5 | 73,440 |
| 1944.. | Bounding Home (126) | 2.32 1-5 | 55,000 | 1959.. | Sword Dancer (126) | 2.28 2-5 | 93,525 |
| 1945.. | Pavot (126) | 2.30 1-5 | 52,675 | 1960.. | Celtic Ash (126) | 2.29 3-5 | 96,785 |
| 1946.. | Assault (126) | 2.30 4-5 | 75,400 | 1961.. | Sherluck (126) | 2.29 1-5 | 104,900 |
| 1947.. | Phalanx (126) | 2.29 2-5 | 78,900 | 1962.. | Jaipur (126) | 2.28 4-5 | 109,550 |
| 1948.. | Citation (126) | 2.28 1-5 | 77,700 | 1963.. | Chateaugay (126) | 2.30 1-5 | 101,700 |
| 1949.. | Capot (126) | 2.30 1-5 | 60,900 | 1964.. | Quadrangle (126) | 2.28 2-5 | 110,850 |
| 1950.. | Middleground (126) | 2.28 3-5 | 61,350 | 1965.. | Hail To All (126) | 2.28 2-5 | 104,150 |
| 1951.. | Counterpoint (126) | 2.29 | 82,000 | 1966.. | Amberoid (126) | 2.29 2-5 | 117,700 |
| 1952.. | One Count (126) | 2.30 1-5 | 82,400 | 1967.. | Damascus (126) | 2.28 4-5 | 104,950 |
| 1953.. | Native Dancer (126) | 2.28 3-5 | 82,500 | 1968.. | Stage Door Johnny (126) | 2.27 1-5 | 117,700 |

## Horse Racing Revenues to States in 1967

| State | Racing days Thorough-bred | Harness | Attendance Thorough-bred | Harness | Pari-mutuel turnover Thorough bred | Harness | *Revenue to state Thorough-bred | Harness |
|---|---|---|---|---|---|---|---|---|
| Ariz...... | 107 | 13 | 338,502 | 35,209 | $17,877,051 | $282,572 | $954,967 | $12,575 |
| Ark...... | 43 | | 451,155 | | 31,250,200 | | 2,071,707 | |
| Calif..... | 316 | 65 | 5,275,554 | 631,493 | 491,991,737 | 54,067,243 | 38,481,031 | 3,568,207 |
| Colo...... | 71 | | 325,182 | | 14,507,281 | | 489,607 | |
| Del....... | 55 | 205 | 618,533 | 1,128,608 | 54,515,185 | 63,297,696 | 3,433,871 | 2,961,993 |
| Fla....... | 201 | 93 | 1,432,545 | 230,450 | 177,275,294 | 11,080,053 | 15,220,270 | 922,578 |
| Idaho.... | 62 | | 61,695 | | 1,682,952 | | 98,001 | |
| Ill....... | 307 | 357 | 3,636,286 | 3,027,306 | 310,590,158 | 211,603,523 | 23,708,950 | 14,094,587 |
| Ky....... | 206 | 193 | 1,419,041 | 663,338 | 92,923,229 | 17,036,143 | 4,452,596 | 731,018 |
| La....... | 179 | | 1,603,643 | | 69,139,164 | | 3,968,037 | |
| Me....... | 48 | 157 | 209,844 | 350,000 | 6,787,844 | 10,302,127 | 484,742 | 721,528 |
| Md....... | 164 | 126 | 1,746,380 | 495,770 | 172,146,494 | 24,690,992 | 9,863,611 | 1,583,205 |
| Mass..... | 89 | 90 | 862,199 | 730,033 | 74,720,992 | 36,849,239 | 5,737,124 | 2,343,497 |
| Mich..... | 163 | 218 | 1,867,803 | 888,923 | 149,762,003 | 67,690,788 | 12,896,193 | 3,861,527 |
| Mont..... | 60 | | 139,513 | | 1,262,970 | | | |
| Nebr..... | 163 | | 1,014,038 | | 52,631,799 | | 2,040,498 | |
| N. H...... | 53 | 222 | 601,962 | 1,003,298 | 54,756,956 | 49,103,808 | 4,500,036 | 3,175,327 |
| N. J...... | 168 | 90 | 2,956,603 | 587,776 | 301,410,852 | 46,153,225 | 28,088,319 | 3,120,700 |
| N. M...... | 187 | | 681,571 | | 22,630,940 | | 567,221 | |
| N. Y...... | 355 | 984 | 7,044,464 | 8,970,124 | 689,878,653 | 721,319,079 | 77,200,682 | 70,314,792 |
| Ohio..... | 400 | 397 | 1,782,512 | 1,492,470 | 124,310,733 | 62,543,684 | 9,499,394 | 3,756,153 |
| Ore...... | 60 | | 346,731 | | 14,121,093 | | 927,243 | |
| Pa....... | | 248 | | 1,786,103 | | 117,934,895 | | 6,839,270 |
| R. I...... | 143 | | 1,323,386 | | 109,185,902 | | 9,947,832 | |
| S. D...... | 49 | | 70,987 | | 4,116,930 | | 131,591 | |
| Vt....... | 119 | 48 | 379,090 | 117,277 | 23,068,858 | 6,947,409 | 1,441,986 | 287,817 |
| Wash..... | 141 | | 327,732 | | 37,716,747 | | 1,905,912 | |
| W. Va.... | 488 | | 2,009,638 | | 140,830,408 | | 8,273,689 | |
| **Totals** | **4,397** | **3,561** | **38,526,589** | **22,343,639** | **$3,241,092,425** | **$1,518,936,315** | **$266,385,121** | **$119,347,809** |

*Fairs and Quarter-horse Racing—A number of states received additional revenues from county fairs and quarter-horse racing: California, $2,777,738; Colorado, $107,402; Idaho, $5,821; Maine, $227,732; Maryland, $1,644,337; Massachusetts, $668,371; New Hampshire, $41,757; New Mexico, $173,969; Ohio, $51,821; Oregon, $41,692; South Dakota, $9,997; Washington, $5,860.

### TOTAL RACING REVENUE TO STATES BY YEARS (DOLLARS)

| | | | | | |
|---|---|---|---|---|---|
| 1945 | 65,265,405.48 | 1952 | 142,489,696.00 | 1960 | 258,039,365.00 |
| 1946 | 94,035,859.47 | 1953 | 167,426,465.00 | 1961 | 264,858,077.00 |
| 1947 | 97,926,984.16 | 1954 | 178,015,828.00 | 1962 | 287,930,030.00 |
| 1948 | 95,803,363.95 | 1955 | 186,969,588.00 | 1963 | 316,570,791.00 |
| 1949 | 95,327,052.96 | 1956 | 207,456,272.00 | 1964 | 350,095,928.00 |
| 1950 | 98,366,166.67 | 1957 | 216,747,621.00 | 1965 | 369,892,036.00 |
| 1951 | 117,250,564.00 | 1958 | 222,049,651.00 | 1966 | 388,452,125.00 |
| | | 1959 | 243,388,655.00 | 1967 | 394,381,913.00 |

## LEADING MONEY-WINNING HORSES OF THE WORLD

| Horse | Sts. | 1st | 2nd | 3rd | Amt. won | Horse | Sts. | 1st | 2nd | 3rd | Amt. won |
|---|---|---|---|---|---|---|---|---|---|---|---|
| Kelso........... | 62 | 39 | 12 | 2 | $1,977,396 | Hill Rise........... | 39 | 13 | 6 | 8 | $634,599 |
| Round Table..... | 66 | 43 | 8 | 5 | 1,749,869 | Bardstown....... | 31 | 18 | 7 | 1 | 628,752 |
| Buckpasser...... | 31 | 25 | 4 | 1 | 1,462,014 | Jaipur........... | 19 | 10 | 6 | 0 | 618,926 |
| Nashua......... | 30 | 22 | 4 | 1 | 1,288,565 | Prove It......... | 25 | 15 | 4 | 1 | 613,820 |
| Carry Back...... | 61 | 21 | 11 | 11 | 1,241,165 | Tosmah.......... | 39 | 23 | 6 | 2 | 612,591 |
| Damascus (a)... | 31 | 21 | 7 | 3 | 1,176,781 | Olden Times..... | 54 | 17 | 10 | 5 | 603,875 |
| Citation....... | 45 | 32 | 10 | 2 | 1,085,760 | †In Reality...... | 19 | 10 | 8 | 0 | 601,024 |
| Native Diver.... | 81 | 37 | 7 | 12 | 1,026,500 | Needles......... | 21 | 11 | 3 | 3 | 600,355 |
| Swoon's Son.... | 51 | 30 | 10 | 3 | 970,605 | Terrang......... | 66 | 15 | 9 | 12 | 599,285 |
| Dr. Fager (a)... | 21 | 17 | 2 | 1 | 965,592 | Mark-Ye-Well... | 40 | 14 | 2 | 4 | 581,910 |
| Roman Brother.. | 42 | 16 | 10 | 5 | 943,473 | Northern Dancer.. | 18 | 14 | 2 | 2 | 580,806 |
| Stymie......... | 131 | 35 | 33 | 28 | 918,485 | Oil Capitol...... | 80 | 19 | 10 | 9 | 580,756 |
| T. V. Lark...... | 72 | 19 | 13 | 6 | 902,194 | Forward Pass (a).. | 23 | 10 | 4 | 2 | 580,631 |
| Swaps......... | 25 | 19 | 2 | 2 | 848,900 | Determine....... | 44 | 18 | 7 | 9 | 573,360 |
| Sword Dancer... | 39 | 15 | 7 | 4 | 829,610 | Tom Fool....... | 30 | 21 | 7 | 1 | 570,165 |
| Candy Spots.... | 22 | 12 | 5 | 1 | 824,718 | Whirlaway...... | 60 | 32 | 15 | 9 | 561,161 |
| Mongo......... | 46 | 22 | 10 | 4 | 820,766 | Quadrangle..... | 26 | 10 | 5 | 6 | 559,386 |
| Armed......... | 81 | 41 | 20 | 10 | 817,475 | Old Hat........ | 80 | 35 | 18 | 9 | 556,401 |
| Find.......... | 110 | 22 | 27 | 27 | 803,615 | On Trust....... | 88 | 23 | 19 | 13 | 554,125 |
| Gun Bow....... | 42 | 17 | 8 | 4 | 798,722 | Rejected........ | 47 | 11 | 10 | 2 | 549,500 |
| Crimson Satan.. | 58 | 18 | 9 | 9 | 796,077 | Affectionately... | 52 | 18 | 8 | 6 | 546,660 |
| Native Dancer... | 22 | 21 | 1 | 0 | 785,240 | Tompion........ | 39 | 11 | 11 | 6 | 545,173 |
| Cicada......... | 42 | 23 | 8 | 6 | 783,674 | Summer Tan.... | 28 | 11 | 12 | 2 | 542,796 |
| First Landing... | 37 | 19 | 9 | 2 | 779,577 | Promised Land... | 77 | 21 | 10 | 16 | 541,707 |
| Bold Ruler..... | 33 | 23 | 4 | 2 | 764,204 | Hasty Road..... | 28 | 14 | 5 | 3 | 541,402 |
| Bally Ache..... | 31 | 16 | 9 | 4 | 758,522 | Ponder......... | 41 | 14 | 7 | 4 | 541,275 |
| Bald Eagle..... | 23 | 9 | 5 | 3 | 676,442 | Clem........... | 47 | 12 | 8 | 13 | 535,681 |
| Assault........ | 42 | 18 | 6 | 7 | 675,470 | Dedicate....... | 43 | 12 | 9 | 5 | 533,200 |
| Tom Rolfe..... | 31 | 16 | 5 | 5 | 671,297 | †Successor...... | 22 | 6 | 6 | 6 | 527,379 |
| Social Outcast... | 58 | 18 | 9 | 6 | 668,300 | Eddie Schmidt... | 101 | 20 | 10 | 18 | 526,292 |
| †Straight Deal... | 74 | 19 | 15 | 7 | 658,463 | Porterhouse..... | 70 | 19 | 8 | 12 | 519,460 |
| Intentionally... | 34 | 18 | 7 | 2 | 652,258 | Bold Lad....... | 19 | 14 | 2 | 1 | 516,465 |
| Hillsdale...... | 41 | 23 | 6 | 4 | 646,935 | Gallant Man.... | 26 | 14 | 4 | 1 | 510,358 |
| Crozier........ | 54 | 10 | 12 | 3 | 641,733 | Talent Show.... | 116 | 16 | 15 | 22 | 507,030 |
| Never Bend.... | 23 | 13 | 4 | 2 | 641,524 | Bobby Brocato... | 88 | 21 | 16 | 14 | 504,515 |
| Ridan......... | 23 | 13 | 6 | 2 | 635,074 | | | | | | |

(a) Record to Oct. 15, 1968. †Not including 1968 record.

## Triple Crown Turf Winners, Owners and Jockeys
### (Kentucky Derby, Preakness and Belmont Stakes)

| Year | Horse | Owner | Jockey | Year | Horse | Owner | Jockey |
|---|---|---|---|---|---|---|---|
| 1919 | Sir Barton | J. K. L. Ross | J. Loftus | 1941 | Whirlaway | Warren Wright | E. Arcaro |
| 1930 | Gallant Fox | W. Woodward | E. Sande | 1943 | Count Fleet | Mrs. J. D. Hertz | J. Longden |
| 1935 | Omaha | W. Woodward | W. Sanders | 1946 | Assault | R. J. Kleberg | W. Mehrtens |
| 1937 | War Admiral | S. D. Riddle | C. Kurtsinger | 1948 | Citation | Warren Wright | E. Arcaro |

## 1968 LEADING JOCKEYS

| | Money Won | | As of Oct. 1, 1968 | | Races Won | | | |
|---|---|---|---|---|---|---|---|---|
| Jockey | Mts. | 1st | Pct. | Amt. Won | Jockey | Mts. | 1st | Pct. | Amt. Won |
| Baeza, B. | 938 | 176 | .188 | $2,223,196 | Cordero, A. | 1,179 | 233 | .198 | $1,884,657 |
| Pincay, L. | 1,064 | 212 | .199 | 2,037,538 | Pineda, A. | 1,468 | 221 | .151 | 1,450,635 |
| Cordero, A. | 1,179 | 233 | .198 | 1,884,657 | Cusimano, G. J. | 1,170 | 216 | .185 | 902,240 |
| Ycaza, M. | 630 | 119 | .189 | 1,705,499 | Pincay, L. | 1,064 | 212 | .199 | 2,037,538 |
| Rotz, J. L. | 939 | 154 | .164 | 1,572,577 | Manganello, M. | 1,020 | 208 | .204 | 534,206 |
| Belmonte, E. | 962 | 151 | .157 | 1,564,847 | Moyers, L. | 1,204 | 198 | .164 | 746,685 |
| Lambert, J. | 1,017 | 186 | .183 | 1,472,899 | Perret, C. | 1,312 | 197 | .150 | 985,960 |
| Pineda, A. | 1,468 | 221 | .151 | 1,450,635 | Whited, D. | 1,070 | 191 | .179 | 638,611 |
| Velasquez, J. | 1,018 | 184 | .181 | 1,258,677 | Lambert, J. | 1,017 | 186 | .183 | 1,472,899 |
| Sellers, J. | 948 | 145 | .153 | 1,230,839 | Rini, A. | 1,091 | 185 | .169 | 350,399 |
| Pierce, D. | 1,058 | 165 | .156 | 1,229,332 | Velasquez, J. | 1,018 | 184 | .181 | 1,258,677 |
| Blum, W. | 1,237 | 171 | .138 | 1,152,702 | Lopez, J. | 1,353 | 184 | .136 | 739,591 |
| Fires, E. | 1,033 | 151 | .146 | 1,100,171 | Grubb, R. | 916 | 181 | .198 | 788,336 |
| Baltazar, C. | 1,126 | 162 | .144 | 1,099,092 | Baeza, B. | 938 | 176 | .188 | 2,223,196 |
| Turcotte, R. | 1,009 | 127 | .126 | 1,086,998 | Marquez, C. | 763 | 173 | .226 | 268,972 |
| Perret, C. | 1,312 | 197 | .150 | 985,960 | Holmes, D. | 1,059 | 172 | .162 | 555,864 |

## Annual Leading Jockey

| | RACES WON | | | | MONEY WON | | | |
|---|---|---|---|---|---|---|---|---|
| Year | Jockey | Mounts | Wins | Year | Jockey | Mounts | Wins | Amt. Won |
| 1953 | W. Shoemaker | 1,683 | 485 | 1954 | W. Shoemaker | 1,251 | 380 | 1,876,760 |
| 1954 | W. Shoemaker | 1,251 | 380 | 1955 | E. Arcaro | 820 | 158 | 1,864,796 |
| 1955 | W. Hartack | 1,702 | 417 | 1956 | W. Hartack | 1,387 | 347 | 2,343,955 |
| 1956 | W. Hartack | 1,387 | 347 | 1957 | W. Hartack | 1,238 | 341 | 3,060,501 |
| 1957 | W. Hartack | 1,238 | 341 | 1958 | W. Shoemaker | 1,133 | 300 | 2,961,693 |
| 1958 | W. Shoemaker | 1,133 | 300 | 1959 | W. Shoemaker | 1,285 | 347 | 2,843,133 |
| 1959 | W. Shoemaker | 1,285 | 347 | 1960 | W. Shoemaker | 1,227 | 274 | 2,123,961 |
| 1960 | W. Hartack | 1,402 | 307 | 1961 | W. Shoemaker | 1,256 | 304 | 2,690,819 |
| 1961 | J. Sellers | 1,394 | 328 | 1962 | W. Shoemaker | 1,126 | 311 | 2,916,844 |
| 1962 | R. Ferraro | 1,755 | 352 | 1963 | W. Shoemaker | 1,203 | 271 | 2,526,925 |
| 1963 | W. Blum | 1,704 | 360 | 1964 | W. Shoemaker | 1,056 | 246 | 2,649,553 |
| 1964 | W. Blum | 1,577 | 324 | 1965 | B. Baeza | 1,245 | 270 | 2,582,702 |
| 1965 | J. Davidson | 1,582 | 319 | 1966 | B. Baeza | 1,341 | 289 | 2,951,220 |
| 1966 | A. Gomez | 996 | 318 | 1967 | B. Baeza | 1,064 | 256 | 3,088,888 |
| 1967 | J. Velasquez | 1,939 | 438 | | | | | |

## 1968 LEADING TRAINERS

| | Money Won | | As of Oct. 1, 1968 | | Races Won | | | |
|---|---|---|---|---|---|---|---|---|
| Trainer | Sts. | 1st | Pct. | Amt. Won | Trainer | Sts. | 1st | Pct. | Amt. Won |
| Maloney, J. W. | 134 | 36 | .269 | $963,694 | Hammond, E. | 1,052 | 176 | .167 | $329,542 |
| Whittingham, C. | 464 | 75 | .162 | 795,594 | Van Berg, J. | 835 | 168 | .201 | 598,519 |
| Forrest, H. | 140 | 32 | .228 | 740,994 | Smithers, A. G. | 630 | 117 | .186 | 294,161 |
| Hirsch, M. | 181 | 44 | .243 | 671,384 | Cavalaris, L., Jr. | 450 | 112 | .249 | 641,104 |
| Millerick, M. E. | 401 | 73 | .182 | 656,842 | Smith, J. R. | 576 | 103 | .179 | 310,471 |
| Cavalaris, L., Jr. | 450 | 112 | .249 | 641,104 | Smith, D. | 495 | 102 | .206 | 323,708 |
| Neloy, E. A. | 179 | 42 | .224 | 635,287 | Winick, A. N. | 582 | 100 | .172 | 582,550 |
| Carroll, D. W. | 601 | 66 | .110 | 611,455 | Baird, D. | 495 | 94 | .190 | 97,672 |
| Van Berg, J. | 835 | 168 | .201 | 598,519 | Maxwell, P. | 337 | 86 | .253 | 114,961 |
| Winick, A. N. | 582 | 100 | .172 | 582,550 | Bishop, W. H. | 818 | 86 | .105 | 309,689 |
| Nerud, J. A. | 178 | 25 | .140 | 570,723 | Jacobson, H. | 383 | 82 | .214 | 385,408 |
| Burch, E. | 184 | 28 | .152 | 533,403 | Delp, G. G. | 409 | 79 | .193 | 330,181 |
| Resseguet, W., Jr. | 528 | 75 | .142 | 519,442 | Ramirez, J. | 328 | 77 | .235 | 90,327 |
| Yowell, J. | 229 | 36 | .157 | 480,330 | Irwin, R. L. | 429 | 75 | .175 | 271,494 |
| King, E. W. | 278 | 34 | .122 | 464,698 | Threewitt, N. | 437 | 75 | .171 | 369,173 |

## Annual Leading Trainer

| | RACES WON | | | | MONEY WON | | | |
|---|---|---|---|---|---|---|---|---|
| Year | Trainer | No. of Starts | No. of Wins | Amount won | Year | Trainer | No. of Starts | No. of Wins | Amount won |
| 1952 | R. H. McDaniel. | | 168 | 573,837 | 1953 | H. Trotsek | | 54 | 1,028,873 |
| 1953 | R. H. McDaniel. | | 211 | 751,957 | 1954 | W. Molter | | 136 | 1,107,860 |
| 1954 | R. H. McDaniel. | | 206 | 834,390 | 1955 | J. Fitzsimmons | | 66 | 1,270,055 |
| 1955 | F. H. Merrill, Jr. | | 154 | 298,794 | 1956 | W. Molter | | 142 | 1,227,402 |
| 1956 | V. R. Wright | | 177 | 532,344 | 1957 | H. A. Jones | | 70 | 1,150,910 |
| 1957 | V. R. Wright | | 192 | 527,271 | 1958 | W. Molter | | 69 | 1,116,544 |
| 1958 | F. H. Merrill, Jr. | | 171 | 320,827 | 1959 | W. Molter | | 71 | 847,290 |
| 1959 | V. R. Wright | | 172 | 534,319 | 1960 | H. Jacobs | | 97 | 748,349 |
| 1960 | F. H. Merrill, Jr. | | 143 | 344,459 | 1961 | H. A. Jones | | 62 | 759,856 |
| 1961 | V. R. Wright | | 178 | 442,650 | 1962 | M. A. Tenney | | 58 | 1,099,474 |
| 1962 | W. H. Bishop | | 162 | 544,261 | 1963 | M. A. Tenney | 192 | 40 | 860,703 |
| 1963 | H. Jacobson | 688 | 140 | 730,418 | 1964 | W. C. Winfrey | 287 | 61 | 1,350,534 |
| 1964 | H. Jacobson | 730 | 169 | 801,869 | 1965 | H. Jacobs | 610 | 91 | 1,331,628 |
| 1965 | H. Jacobson | 886 | 200 | 863,721 | 1966 | E. A. Neloy | 282 | 93 | 2,456,250 |
| 1966 | L. C. Cavalaris | 635 | 175 | 763,201 | 1967 | E. A. Neloy | 262 | 72 | 1,776,089 |
| 1967 | E. Hammond | 996 | 200 | 325,905 | | | | | |

## Largest Winnings By One Horse in a Year

| Year | Horse | Dollars | Year | Horse | Dollars | Year | Horse | Dollars |
|---|---|---|---|---|---|---|---|---|
| 1937 | Seabiscuit | 168,580 | 1948 | Citation | 709,470 | 1959 | Sword Dancer | 537,004 |
| 1938 | Stagehand | 189,710 | 1949 | Ponder | 321,825 | 1960 | Bally Ache | 455,045 |
| 1939 | Challedon | 174,535 | 1950 | Noor | 346,940 | 1961 | Carry Back | 565,349 |
| 1940 | Bimelich | 111,005 | 1951 | Counterpoint | 250,525 | 1962 | Never Bend | 402,969 |
| 1941 | Whirlaway | 272,386 | 1952 | Crafty Admiral | 277,225 | 1963 | Candy Spots | 604,481 |
| 1942 | Shut Out | 238,972 | 1953 | Native Dancer | 513,425 | 1964 | Gun Bow | 580,100 |
| 1943 | Count Fleet | 174,055 | 1954 | Determine | 327,700 | 1965 | Buckpasser | 568,096 |
| 1944 | Pavot | 179,040 | 1955 | Nashua | 752,550 | 1966 | Buckpasser | 669,078 |
| 1945 | Busher | 273,735 | 1956 | Needles | 440,850 | 1967 | Damascus | 817,941 |
| 1946 | Assault | 424,195 | 1957 | Round Table | 600,258 | 1968* | Forward Pass | 546,674 |
| 1947 | Armed | 376,325 | 1958 | Round Table | 662,780 | | | |

*Through Oct. 1.

# Major Stakes Races 1968

| Event | Track | Added Value | Winner | Dist. Furl. | Time | Jockey |
|---|---|---|---|---|---|---|
| **3 YEAR OLDS AND UP** | | | | | | |
| Aqueduct Stakes | Aqueduct | 100,000 | Damascus | 9 | 1:48.2 | B. Baeza |
| Arlington Classic | Arlington | 100,000 | Exclusive Native | 8 | 1:36 | I. Valenzuela |
| Benj. Lindheimer Hdcp. | Arlington | 100,000 | War Censor | 9½ | 1:57.2 | E. Fires |
| Bowling Green Hdcp. | Belmont | 50,000 | High Hat | 12 | 2:29.4 | E. Belmonte |
| Brooklyn Hdcp. | Aqueduct | 100,000 | Damascus | 10 | 1:59.1 | M. Ycaza |
| Californian | Hollywood Park | 100,000 | Dr. Fager | 8½ | 1:40.4 | B. Baeza |
| Carter Hdcp. | Belmont | 50,000 | In Reality | 7 | 1:21.4 | J. Velasquez |
| Dixie Hdcp. | Pimlico | 50,000 | High Hat | 12 | 2:29.4 | R. Broussard |
| Donn Hdcp. | Gulfstream | 50,000 | Favorable Turn | 9 | 1:48.1 | E. Belmonte |
| Excelsior Hdcp. | Aqueduct | 50,000 | Peter Piper | 9 | 1:48 | J. Velasquez |
| Grey Lag Hdcp. | Aqueduct | 75,000 | Bold Hour | 9 | 1:48.4 | J. Rotz |
| Gulfstream Park Hdcp. | Gulfstream | 100,000 | Gentleman James | 10 | 2:02.1 | R. Grubb |
| Haskell Hdcp. | Monmouth | 100,000 | Bold Hour | 10 | 2:03 | W. Boland |
| Hialeah Turf Cup | Hialeah | 75,000 | He's A Smoothie | 12 | 2:32.4 | B. Baeza |
| Jockey Gold Cup | Belmont | 100,000 | Quicken Tree | 16 | 3:22.4 | B. Hartack |
| John B. Campbell Hdcp. | Bowie | 100,000 | In Reality | 8½ | 1:42 | C. Baltazar |
| Manhattan Hdcp. | Belmont | 50,000 | Quicken Tree | 12 | 2:28 | B. Hartack |
| Man O' War Stakes | Belmont | 100,000 | Czar Alexander | 12 | 2:30.4 | J. Velasquez |
| Massachusetts Hdcp. | Suffolk | 50,000 | Out Of The Way | 10 | 2:02.4 | J. Rotz |
| Metropolitan Hdcp. | Belmont | 100,000 | In Reality | 8 | 1:35 | J. Rotz |
| Michigan Mile | Detroit | 100,000 | No Double | 9 | 1:49 | Heath |
| Roseben Hdcp. | Aqueduct | 50,000 | Dr. Fager | 7 | 1:21.2 | J. Rotz |
| San Juan Capistrano Hdcp. | Santa Anita | 125,000 | Niarkos | 14 | 2:47.4 | A. Pineda |
| Santa Anita Hdcp. | Santa Anita | 100,000 | Mr. Right | 10 | 2:04.3 | Yanez |
| Seminole Hdcp. | Hialeah | 50,000 | Favorable Turn | 9 | 1:47.1 | E. Belmonte |
| Suburban Hdcp. | Aqueduct | 100,000 | Dr. Fager | 10 | 1:59.3 | B. Baeza |
| Sunset Hdcp. | Hollywood Park | 100,000 | Fort Marcy | 12 | 2:26.3 | L. Pincay |
| Tidal Hdcp. | Aqueduct | 50,000 | More Scents | 9 | 1:47.3 | A. Cordero |
| U.N. Hdcp. | Atlantic City | 100,000 | Dr. Fager | 9½ | 1:55.1 | B. Baeza |
| Westchester Stakes | Aqueduct | 50,000 | R. Thomas | 8 | 1:35.2 | J. Nichols |
| *Whitney Hdcp. | Saratoga | 50,000 | Dr. Fager | 9 | 1:48.2 | B. Baeza |
| Widener Hdcp. | Hialeah | 100,000 | Sette Bello | 10 | 2:01.3 | E. Fires |
| William DuPont Hdcp. | Delaware | 50,000 | Damascus | 8½ | 1:43.3 | B. Baeza |
| Woodward Stakes | Belmont | 100,000 | Mr. Right | 12 | 2:03 | H. Gustines |
| *4 year olds and up. | | | | | | |
| **3 YEAR OLDS AND UP, FILLIES AND MARES** | | | | | | |
| Barbara Fritchie Hdcp. | Bowie | 50,000 | Too Bald | 7 | 1:21.4 | M. Ycaza |
| Beldame Stakes | Aqueduct | 75,000 | Gamely | 9 | 1:49.3 | L. Pincay |
| Black Helen Hdcp. | Hialeah | 50,000 | Treacherous | 9 | 1:49 | H. Gustines |
| Delaware Hdcp. | Delaware | 100,000 | Politely | 10 | 2:02.4 | A. Cordero |
| Matchmaker Stakes | Atlantic City | 100,000 | Politely | 8½ | 1:55.1 | A. Cordero |
| Santa Margarita | Santa Anita | 100,000 | Gamely | 9 | 1:49 | M. Ycaza |
| Sheepshead Bay Hdcp. | Aqueduct | 40,000 | Ludham | 9½ | 1:54.4 | J. Vasquez |
| | | 40,000 | Politely | 9½ | 1:55.2 | A. Cordero |
| Top Flight Hdcp. | Aqueduct | 50,000 | Americo Lady | 9 | 1:49 | J. Velasquez |
| **3 YEAR OLDS** | | | | | | |
| American Derby | Arlington | 100,000 | Forward Pass | 9 | 1:48.4 | I. Valenzuela |
| Belmont Stakes | Belmont | 125,000 | Stage Dr. Jo'ny | 12 | 2:27.1 | H. Gustines |
| Dwyer Hdcp. | Aqueduct | 75,000 | Stage Dr. Jo'ny | 10 | 2:01.3 | H. Gustines |
| Flamingo | Hialeah | 100,000 | Wise Exchange | 9 | 1:49.1 | E. Belmonte |
| Florida Derby | Gulfstream | 100,000 | Forward Pass | 9 | 1:49 | D. Brumfield |
| Gotham | Aqueduct | 50,000 | Verbatim | 8 | 1:34 | J. Rotz |
| Governors Gold Cup | Bowie | 100,000 | Dancer's Image | 8½ | 1:42.4 | R. Ussery |
| Hollywood Derby | Hollywood | 100,000 | Poleax | 10 | 1:59.4 | B. Hartack |
| Jerome Hdcp. | Belmont | 50,000 | Iron Ruler | 8 | 1:35.1 | J. Velasquez |
| Jersey Derby | Garden State | 100,000 | Out Of The Way | 9 | 1:49 | E. Belmonte |
| Kentucky Derby | Churchill Downs | 125,000 | Forward Pass | 10 | 2:02.1 | I. Valenzuela |
| Lawrence Realization | Belmont | 50,000 | Funny Fellow | 13 | 2:41.1 | B. Baeza |
| Preakness | Pimlico | 150,000 | Forward Pass | 9½ | 1:56.4 | I. Valenzuela |
| Santa Anita Derby | Santa Anita | 100,000 | Alley Fighter | 9 | 1:49 | L. Pincay |
| Saratoga Hdcp. | Belmont | 50,000 | Stage Dr. Jo'ny | 8 | 1:35.2 | H. Gustines |
| Travers Stakes | Saratoga | 75,000 | Chompion | 10 | 2:04.4 | J. Cruquet |
| Withers Stakes | Aqueduct | 50,000 | Call Me Prince | 8 | 1:35.1 | W. Boland |
| Wood Memorial | Aqueduct | 100,000 | Dancer's Image | 9 | 1:49 | R. Ussery |
| **3 YEAR OLDS, FILLIES** | | | | | | |
| Acorn Stakes | Belmont | 50,000 | Dark Mirage | 8 | 1:34.4 | M. Ycaza |
| Alabama Stakes | Saratoga | 50,000 | Gay Matelda | 10 | 2:04.2 | J. Rotz |
| Coaching C. Amer. Oaks | Belmont | 100,000 | Dark Mirage | 10 | 2:01.4 | M. Ycaza |
| Gazelle Hdcp. | Aqueduct | 50,000 | Another Nell | 9 | 1:50.4 | C. Perret |
| Kentucky Oaks | Churchill Downs | 50,000 | Dark Mirage | 8½ | 1:44.3 | M. Ycaza |
| Monmouth Oaks | Monmouth | 50,000 | Dark Mirage | 9 | 1:51.2 | M. Ycaza |
| Mother Goose Stakes | Belmont | 75,000 | Dark Mirage | 9 | 1:49.2 | M. Ycaza |
| Pucker Up Stakes | Arlington | 50,000 | Another Nell | 8 | 1:34 | C. Perret |
| **2 YEAR OLDS** | | | | | | |
| Arch Ward Stakes | Arlington | 50,000 | Trusty Pro | 6 | 1:10.2 | J. Lopez |
| Arlington-Wash. Futurity | Arlington | 150,000 | Strong Strong | 7 | 1:22.4 | D. Gargen |
| Champagne Stakes | Belmont | 125,000 | Top Knight | 8 | 1:35.1 | M. Ycaza |
| Cowdin Stakes | Belmont | 50,000 | King Emperor | 7 | 1:22.3 | B. Baeza |
| Futurity | Belmont | 75,000 | Top Knight | 6½ | 1:16.1 | M. Ycaza |
| Sapling Hdcp. | Monmouth | 50,000 | Reviewer | 5 | 1:10.2 | B. Baeza |
| **2 YEAR OLDS, FILLIES** | | | | | | |
| Arl'ton-Wash. Lassie Stks. | Arlington | 150,000 | Process Scot | 6½ | 1:17.2 | C. Baltazar |
| Frizette Stakes | Belmont | 75,000 | Shuvee | 8 | 1:37 | J. Davidson |
| Matron Stakes | Aqueduct | 50,000 | Gallant Bloom | 6 | 1:10.2 | E. Belmonte |
| Selima Stakes | Laurel | 50,000 | Shuvee | 8½ | 1:44.4 | R. Turcotte |
| Sorority Stakes | Monmouth | 100,000 | Big Advance | 6 | 1:11 | B. Baeza |
| Spinway Stakes | Saratoga | 50,000 | Queen's Double | 6 | 1:11.2 | B. Baeza |

## Record of Citation

| Year | Age | Starts | 1st | 2nd | 3rd | Unpl. | Won | Year | Age | Starts | 1st | 2nd | 3rd | Unpl. | Won |
|---|---|---|---|---|---|---|---|---|---|---|---|---|---|---|---|
| 1947. | 2 | 9 | 8 | 1 | 0 | 0 | $155,680 | 1950. | 5 | 9 | 2 | 7 | 0 | 0 | $73,480 |
| 1948. | 3 | 20 | 19 | 1 | 0 | 0 | 709,470 | 1951. | 6 | 7 | 3 | 1 | 2 | 1 | 147,130 |
| 1949. | 4 | (Did not start due to injuries) | | | | | | Tot. | | 45 | 32 | 10 | 2 | 1 | $1,085,760 |

Citation was retired at age of 6, July 19, 1951. His last winning race, the Hollywood Gold Cup, Inglewood, Calif., July 14, 1951, brought his total winnings to $1,085,760. A bay colt by Bull Lea–Hydroplane II, he was bred and owned by the Calumet Farm.

# Skeet Shooting Championships in 1968
## NATIONAL SKEET SHOOTING ASSOCIATION
### Bucyrus, Kansas, July 27-Aug. 3

**OPEN INDIVIDUAL CHAMPIONS**

**All-Around**—James A. Bellows, Lackland AFB. Tex., 547 x 550.
**12 Gauge—(Co-Champions)**—Allen F. Buntrock, Fallon, Nev., 250 x 250; Thomas J. Heffron Jr., Groton, N. Y., 250 x 250.
**20 Gauge**—James (Mike) Martin, South Bend, Ind., 100 x 100.
**28 Gauge**—T/Sgt. Cecil H. Trammell, Lackland AFB, Tex., 100 x 100.
**.410 Gauge**—Carl N. Poston Sr., Chattanooga, Tenn., 98 x 100.

**SPECIAL EVENTS—12 GAUGE**

**Military Individual**—Allen F. Buntrock, Fallon, Nev., 250 x 250.
**Civilian**—Thomas J. Heffron Jr., Groton, N. Y., 250 x 250.
**Collegiate**—Jay I. Gerlich, West Des Moines, Iowa, 250 x 250.
**Junior Lady**—Michelle V. Keithley, Northridge, Calif., 97 x 100.
**Sub-Junior**—Tito Killian, San Antonio, Tex., 99 x 100.
**Western Open**—John L. Davis, Jr., Columbia, S. C., 100 x 100.
**Eastern Open**—Richard C. Bienapfl, Minneapolis, Minn., 100 x 100.
**Referees' Championship**—Richard W. Smith, Auburn, N. Y., 100 x 100.

**LADY CHAMPIONS**

**All-Around**—Mrs. Philip D. Armour Jr., Coral Gables, Fla., 533 x 550.
**12 Gauge**—Mrs. Sallie H. Durbin, Kirkwood, Mo., 249 x 250.
**20 Gauge**—Miss Leslee Nelson, Bloomington, Minn., 100 x 100.
**28 Gauge**—Mrs. Philip D. Armour Jr., Coral Gables, Fla., 99 x 100.
**.410 Gauge**—Helen L. Donn, Fort Smith, Ark., 94 x 100.

**VETERAN CHAMPIONS**

**All-Around**—George T. Vicknair, Baton Rouge, La., 529 x 550.
**12 Gauge**—Carl B. Stutzman, Peoria, Ill., 249 x 250.
**20 Gauge**—Carl B. Stutzman, Peoria, Ill., 99 x 100.
**28 Gauge**—George T. Vicknair, Baton Rouge, La., 99 x 100.
**.410 Gauge**—R. B. Ross, Brownwood, Tex., 92 x 100.

**SENIOR CHAMPIONS**

**All-Around**—Ted V. Hannaford, Warren, Mich., 539 x 550.
**12 Gauge**—Claude W. Purbaugh, Monrovia, Calif., 250 x 250.
**20 Gauge**—Tom Jones, Birmingham, Ala., 100 x 100.
**28 Gauge**—Ted V. Hannaford, 99 x 100.
**.410 Gauge**—Ted V. Hannaford, 97 x 100.

**SUB-SENIOR CHAMPIONS**

**All-Around**—Charles F. Garberson, Los Angeles, Calif., 539 x 550.
**12 Gauge**—Charles F. Garberson, 250 x 250.
**20 Gauge**—Chesley J. Crites, Detroit, Mich., 100 x 100.
**28 Gauge**—Paul Guillory, Lake Charles, La., 99 x 100.
**.410 Gauge**—Alex H. Kerr, Beverly Hills, Calif., 98 x 100.

**JUNIOR CHAMPIONS**

**All-Around**—Steve Pakis, Hot Springs, Ark., 541 x 550.
**12 Gauge**—Michael V. Keithley, Northridge, Calif., 250 x 250.
**20 Gauge**—Chuck Mayhew, Dallas, Tex., 100 x 100.
**28 Gauge**—Steve Pakis, Hot Springs, Ark., 99 x 100.
**.410 Gauge**—Gus Blass III, Little Rock, Ark., 97 x 100.

**INDUSTRY CHAMPIONS**

**All-Around**—Barney C. Hartman, St. Lambert, P. Q. 547 x 550.
**12 Gauge**—Barney C. Hartman, 250 x 250.
**20 Gauge**—Barney C. Hartman, 100 x 100.
**28 Gauge**—Fred D. Missildine, Sea Island, Ga., 100 x 100.
**.410 Gauge**—Barney C. Hartman, 99 x 100.

**TWO-MAN TEAMS**

**All-Around**—James A. Bellows and T/Sgt. Cecil H. Trammell, Lackland AFB, Tex., 1089 x 1100.
**12 Gauge**—Kenny Barnes, Jr., Bakersfield, and Charles F. Garberson, Los Angeles, Calif., 500 x 500.
**20 Gauge**—2nd Lt. Allen W. Morrison and Lt. Kenneth L. Wilson, Quantico, Va., 200 x 200.
**28 Gauge**—James A. Bellows and T/Sgt. Cecil H. Trammell, 200 x 200.
**.410 Gauge**—Charles H. Collins, Hixson, and Carl N. Poston Sr., Chattanooga, Tenn., 196 x 200.

**HUSBAND AND WIFE TEAMS**

**All-Around**—John R. and Sallie H. Durbin, Kirkwood, Mo., 1072 x 1100.
**12 Gauge**—John R. and Sallie H. Durbin, 499 x 500.
**20 Gauge**—John R. and Sallie H. Durbin, 197 x 200.
**28 Gauge**—Fred and Esther Schmitt, Peoria, Ill., 191 x 200.
**.410 Gauge**—John R and Sallie H. Durbin, 187 x 200.

**CHAMPION OF CHAMPIONS**

**Champion, 4 guns, 25 Targets each**—James W. Austin, Honolulu, Hawaii, 100 x 100.

# Trapshooting Championships in 1968
## 69th GRAND AMERICAN TOURNAMENT
### Vandalia, Ohio, Aug. 19-24

**Grand American Handicap**

| | |
|---|---|
| **Men**—Denton Childers, Rochester, Mich. | 100x100 |
| **Women**—Rosemary Miller, New Castle, Del. | 98x100 |
| **Juniors**—Mike Meader, Luna Pier, Mich | 100x100 |
| **Sub-Juniors**—Brad Sleeter, Markham, Ill. | 99x100 |
| **Veterans**—Henry Bullock, Milmay, N. J. | 98x100 |
| **Industry**—Foster Mosher, Pewaukee, Wis. | 97x100 |
| **Jimmy Robinson Trophy to High Canadian**—Ron Scondo, Glen Williams, Ont. | 99x100 |
| **High Past Winner Trophy**—Oscar Scheske, Belleville, Ill. | 96x100 |

**Preliminary Handicap**

| | |
|---|---|
| **Men**—John Morelli, Pittsburgh, Pa. | 100x100 |
| **Women**—Booge Mercer, Chatsworth, Ill. | 97x100 |
| **Juniors**—John Morelli, Pittsburgh, Pa. | 100x100 |
| **Veterans**—W. L. Acker, Dallas, Tex. | 96x100 |
| **Industry**—Larry French Jr., Salt Lake City, Utah | 97x100 |

**Clay Target Championships**

| | |
|---|---|
| **Men**—Bueford Bailey, Big Springs, Neb. | 200x200 |
| **Women**—Loral I. Delaney, Anoka, Minn. | 199x200 |
| **Juniors**—Doug Bedwell, Brazil, Ind. | 200x200 |
| **Sub-Juniors**—W. R. Jacobsen, Clearwater, Fla. | 200x200 |
| **Veterans**—J. O. Bates, Ft. Worth, Tex. | 198x200 |
| **Industry**—Walt Langhorst, Salt Lake City, Utah | 199x200 |
| **Class AA**—Don Beler, Cincinnati, O. | 200x200 |
| **Class A**—Tony Vasaturo, Brooklyn, N. Y. | 200x200 |
| **Class B**—Clifford Sweeney, Greensboro, Pa. | 199x200 |
| **Class C**—Mel Meyers, Cincinnati, O. | 199x200 |
| **Class D**—Randy Gates, Needles, Calif. | 198x200 |

**Introductory Singles**

| | |
|---|---|
| **Men**—Jack Morris, San Antonio, Tex. | 200x200 |
| **Women**—Loral I. Delaney, Anoka, Minn. | 197x200 |

| | |
|---|---|
| **Junior**—Doug Bedwell, Brazil, Ind. | 199x200 |
| **Industry**—Lee Davidson, Tipp City, O. | 200x200 |
| **Veterans**—Oz Conrad, Stillwater, Minn. | 97x100 |
| **Husband & Wife**—Ed and Mary Beranek, Strongsville, O. | 392x400 |
| **Parent & Child**—Gene and Garland Sears, El Reno, Okla. | 394x400 |
| **Brothers**—Fred and Tony Vasaturo, Staten Island & Brooklyn, N. Y. | 396x400 |

**Champion of Champions**

| | |
|---|---|
| **Men**—Mark Huff, Minot, N. D. | 100x100 |
| **Women**—Nadine Ljutic, Yakima, Wash. | 99x100 |
| **Junior**—W. David Iseley, Gaston, Ind. | 100x100 |
| **Zone**—Southwestern | 989x1000 |

**Doubles Championships**

| | |
|---|---|
| **Men**—Hugh Driggs, Palmyra, Mich. | 100x100 |
| **Women**—Marian Harrison, Los Angeles | 92x100 |
| **Juniors**—Jim Burke, Los Alamitos, Calif. | 98x100 |
| **Veterans**—Walter Johnson, Inglewood, Calif. | 94x100 |
| **Industry**—Walt Langhorst, Salt Lake City, Utah | 98x100 |

**Vandalia Handicap**

| | |
|---|---|
| **Men**—Pete Kennedy, Cranston, R. I. | 99x100 |
| **Women**—Linda Goachee, Ft. Myers, Fla. | 98x100 |
| **Juniors**—Robert Green, Flint, Mich | 97x100 |
| **Veterans**—George Tony, Indianapolis | 94x100 |
| **Industry**—Lee Davidson, Tipp City, O. | 95x100 |

**High Over-All**

| | |
|---|---|
| **Men**—Hugh Driggs, Palmyra, Mich. | 985x1000 |
| **Women**—Loral I. Delaney, Anoka, Minn. | 949x1000 |
| **Junior**—Doug Bedwell, Brazil, Ind. | 980x1000 |
| **Veteran**—J. O. Bates, Ft. Worth, Tex. | 953x1000 |
| **Industry**—Lee Davidson, Tipp City, O. | 971x1000 |
| **All-Around**—Hugh Driggs | 395x 400 |

# COLLEGE BASKETBALL
## Final Standings in 1967-1968 Season

### IVY LEAGUE

| | Conference Games W. L. | All Games W. L. |
|---|---|---|
| Columbia | 12 2 | 23 5 |
| Princeton | 12 2 | 20 6 |
| Yale | 8 6 | 15 9 |
| Dartmouth | 6 8 | 16 |
| Cornell | 6 8 | 14 11 |
| Pennsylvania | 4 10 | 9 17 |
| Brown | 4 10 | 9 14 |
| Harvard | 4 10 | 7 14 |

### YANKEE

| | Conference Games W. L. | All Games W. L. |
|---|---|---|
| Rhode Island | 8 2 | 15 11 |
| Massachusetts | 8 2 | 14 12 |
| Connecticut | 7 3 | 11 13 |
| Vermont | 5 5 | 12 12 |
| Maine | 2 8 | 7 17 |
| New Hampshire | 0 10 | 1 22 |

### METROPOLITAN

| | Conference Games W. L. | All Games W. L. |
|---|---|---|
| St. Peter's | 8 0 | 24 4 |
| Long Island | 7 1 | 22 |
| Wagner | 5 3 | 20 7 |
| Fairleigh Dickinson | 4 4 | 10 12 |
| Iona | 4 4 | 13 9 |
| Seton Hall | 4 4 | 9 15 |
| Manhattan | 3 5 | 8 11 |
| Hofstra | 1 7 | 13 12 |
| St. Francis (N. Y.) | 0 8 | 7 16 |

### ATLANTIC COAST

| | Conference Games W. L. | All Games W. L. |
|---|---|---|
| North Carolina | 12 2 | 28 4 |
| Duke | 11 3 | 22 6 |
| So. Carolina | 9 5 | 15 7 |
| No. Carolina St. | 8 6 | 16 10 |
| Virginia | 5 9 | 9 16 |
| Maryland | 4 10 | 8 16 |
| Clemson | 3 11 | 4 20 |
| Wake Forest | 3 11 | 5 21 |

### SOUTHERN

| | Conference Games W. L. | All Games W. L. |
|---|---|---|
| Davidson | 9 1 | 24 5 |
| West Virginia | 9 2 | 19 9 |
| Citadel | 6 5 | 11 14 |
| Virginia Military | 8 7 | 9 17 |
| Furman | 6 6 | 13 13 |
| Richmond | 8 8 | 12 13 |
| East Carolina | 6 7 | 9 16 |
| William & Mary | 4 10 | 6 17 |
| G. Washington | 2 12 | 5 19 |

### SOUTHEASTERN

| | Conference Games W. L. | All Games W. L. |
|---|---|---|
| Kentucky | 15 3 | 22 5 |
| Tennessee | 12 5 | 20 6 |
| Vanderbilt | 12 6 | 20 6 |
| Georgia | 11 7 | 17 8 |
| Florida | 11 5 | 15 10 |
| Louisiana State | 8 10 | 14 12 |
| Auburn | 8 9 | 13 13 |
| Mississippi St. | 5 13 | 9 17 |
| Mississippi | 4 14 | 7 17 |
| Alabama | 3 15 | 10 16 |

### OHIO VALLEY

| | Conference Games W. L. | All Games W. L. |
|---|---|---|
| Murray State | 10 4 | 16 8 |
| East Tennessee | 10 4 | 19 8 |
| W. Kentucky | 9 5 | 18 7 |
| Morehead State | 8 6 | 12 9 |
| Mid. Tennessee | 7 7 | 15 9 |
| E. Kentucky | 6 8 | 10 14 |
| Tenn. Tech | 4 10 | 9 17 |
| Austin Peay | 2 12 | 8 16 |

### MID-AMERICAN

| | Conference Games W. L. | All Games W. L. |
|---|---|---|
| Bowling Green | 10 2 | 18 7 |
| Marshall | 9 3 | 17 8 |
| Toledo | 8 4 | 15 8 |
| W. Michigan | 7 5 | 11 13 |
| Miami (O.) | 4 8 | 11 12 |
| Kent State | 3 9 | 9 15 |
| Ohio | 3 9 | 7 16 |

### BIG TEN

| | Conference Games W. L. | All Games W. L. |
|---|---|---|
| Ohio State | 10 4 | 21 8 |
| Iowa | 10 4 | 16 9 |
| Purdue | 9 5 | 15 9 |
| Northwestern | 8 6 | 13 10 |
| Wisconsin | 7 7 | 13 11 |
| Michigan St. | 6 8 | 12 12 |
| Illinois | 6 8 | 11 13 |
| Michigan | 6 8 | 11 13 |
| Indiana | 4 10 | 10 14 |
| Minnesota | 4 10 | 7 17 |

### MISSOURI VALLEY

| | Conference Games W. L. | All Games W. L. |
|---|---|---|
| Louisville | 14 2 | 21 7 |
| Bradley | 12 4 | 19 9 |
| Cincinnati | 11 5 | 18 8 |
| Drake | 9 7 | 18 8 |
| St. Louis | 9 7 | 15 11 |
| Wichita State | 7 9 | 12 14 |
| Tulsa | 5 11 | 11 12 |
| N. Texas State | 3 13 | 8 18 |
| Memphis State | 2 14 | 8 17 |

### BIG EIGHT

| | Conference Games W. L. | All Games W. L. |
|---|---|---|
| Kansas State | 11 3 | 19 9 |
| Kansas | 10 4 | 22 8 |
| Nebraska | 8 6 | 15 10 |
| Oklahoma | 8 6 | 13 13 |
| Iowa State | 8 6 | 12 13 |
| Missouri | 5 9 | 10 16 |
| Oklahoma State | 3 11 | 10 16 |
| Colorado | 3 11 | 9 16 |

### SOUTHWEST

| | Conference Games W. L. | All Games W. L. |
|---|---|---|
| Texas Christian | 9 5 | 15 11 |
| Baylor | 8 6 | 15 9 |
| Texas A. & M. | 8 6 | 14 10 |
| Texas | 8 6 | 11 13 |
| Arkansas | 7 7 | 10 14 |
| Rice | 6 8 | 8 16 |
| Texas Tech | 5 9 | 9 15 |
| So. Methodist | 5 9 | 6 18 |

### WESTERN ATHLETIC

| | Conference Games W. L. | All Games W. L. |
|---|---|---|
| New Mexico | 8 2 | 23 5 |
| Wyoming | 5 5 | 18 9 |
| Utah | 5 5 | 17 9 |
| Brigham Young | 4 6 | 13 12 |
| Arizona | 4 6 | 11 13 |
| Arizona State | 4 6 | 11 17 |

### PACIFIC EIGHT

| | Conference Games W. L. | All Games W. L. |
|---|---|---|
| UCLA | 14 0 | 29 1 |
| So. California | 11 3 | 18 8 |
| Washington St. | 8 6 | 16 9 |
| California | 7 7 | 15 9 |
| Oregon State | 5 9 | 12 13 |
| Stanford | 5 9 | 10 15 |
| Washington | 4 10 | 12 14 |
| Oregon | 2 12 | 7 19 |

### WEST COAST ATHLETIC

| | Conference Games W. L. | All Games W. L. |
|---|---|---|
| Santa Clara | 13 1 | 21 3 |
| Loyola (Calif.) | 11 3 | 19 6 |
| San Francisco | 10 4 | 18 10 |
| San Jose State | 8 6 | 13 12 |
| Pacific (Calif.) | 5 9 | 16 10 |
| UC-S. Barbara | 3 11 | 9 17 |
| St. Mary's (Cal.) | 3 11 | 4 20 |
| Pepperdine | 2 12 | 9 17 |

### INDIANA COLLEGIATE

| | Conference Games W. L. | All Games W. L. |
|---|---|---|
| Indiana State | 9 3 | 23 8 |
| DePauw | 9 3 | 16 8 |
| Evansville | 8 4 | 20 8 |
| Butler | 6 6 | 11 14 |
| Ball State | 5 7 | 10 12 |
| Valparaiso | 3 9 | 10 15 |
| St. Joseph's | 2 10 | 9 14 |

### OHIO

| | Conference Games W. L. | All Games W. L. |
|---|---|---|
| Denison | 11 2 | 18 5 |
| Baldwin-Wallace | 11 2 | 19 9 |
| Kenyon | 10 2 | 23 5 |
| Otterbein | 9 3 | 13 8 |
| Wooster | 8 4 | 14 8 |
| Wittenberg | 8 5 | 13 13 |
| Marietta | 6 6 | 8 12 |
| Heidelberg | 5 7 | 11 9 |
| Ohio Wesleyan | 5 8 | 9 14 |
| Hiram | 4 9 | 9 13 |
| Capital | 3 10 | 6 16 |
| Muskingum | 3 10 | 3 16 |
| Oberlin | 3 9 | 7 11 |
| Mt. Union | 1 6 | 6 17 |

### SOUTHWESTERN

| | Conference Games W. L. | All Games W. L. |
|---|---|---|
| Jackson State | 12 2 | 24 3 |
| Alcorn A & M | 12 2 | | |
| Southern Univ. | 9 5 | 17 6 |
| Arkansas AM & N | 8 6 | 18 7 |
| Prairie View | 6 8 | 13 12 |
| Texas Southern | 5 9 | 11 12 |
| Grambling | 4 10 | 11 14 |
| Wiley | 0 14 | 4 21 |

### FAR WESTERN

| | Conference Games W. L. | All Games W. L. |
|---|---|---|
| UC Davis | 12 2 | 16 11 |
| San Francisco State | 11 3 | 16 10 |
| Sacramento St. | 9 5 | 16 10 |
| Hayward State | 7 7 | 10 14 |
| Nevada | 6 8 | 8 18 |
| Chico State | 4 10 | 6 17 |
| Humboldt St. | 4 10 | — — |
| Somona State | 3 11 | 9 17 |

### OTHER MAJOR TEAMS

| | W. L. | | W. L. | | W. L. | | W. L. |
|---|---|---|---|---|---|---|---|
| Air Force | 9 15 | Duquesne | 18 7 | Loyola (La.) | 11 14 | St. Francis (Pa.) | 19 6 |
| American | 14 12 | Fairfield | 16 10 | Marquette | 22 6 | St. John's | |
| Army | 20 5 | Florida State | 19 8 | Miami (Fla.) | 17 11 | (N. Y.) | 19 8 |
| Boston College | 17 8 | Fordham | 19 8 | Navy | 9 11 | St. Joseph's |  |
| Boston Univ. | 10 14 | Georgetown | | New Mexico St. | 23 6 | (Pa.) | 17 9 |
| Bucknell | 12 11 | (D. C.) | 11 12 | New York | 8 16 | Seattle | 14 13 |
| Butler | 11 14 | Georgia Tech | 12 13 | Niagara | 12 12 | So. Illinois | 13 11 |
| Canisius | 8 17 | Gettysburg | 14 11 | No. Illinois | 10 14 | Syracuse | 11 14 |
| Centenary | 3 23 | Hardin- | | Notre Dame | 21 9 | Temple | 19 9 |
| Colgate | 10 16 | Simmons | 10 16 | Oklahoma City | 20 7 | Texas (El Paso) | 14 9 |
| Colorado St. | 11 13 | Holy Cross | 15 8 | Penn State | 10 10 | Tulane | 12 12 |
| Creighton | 8 17 | Houston | 31 2 | Pittsburgh | 7 15 | Utah State | 14 11 |
| Dayton | 21 9 | Jacksonville | 13 13 | Portland | 5 21 | Villanova | 19 9 |
| Delaware | 16 7 | Lafayette | 5 19 | Providence | 11 14 | Virginia Tech | 11 11 |
| Denver | 11 14 | LaSalle | 20 8 | Rider | 10 14 | W. Texas State | 10 11 |
| DePaul | 13 12 | Lehigh | 12 11 | Rutgers | 14 10 | Xavier (O.) | 10 16 |
| Detroit | 13 12 | Loyola (Ill.) | 15 9 | St. Bonaventure | 23 2 | | |

# Basketball Champions by Years

| | National Invitation Tournament | | | | National Collegiate A. A. | | |
|---|---|---|---|---|---|---|---|
| | Winner | | Runner-up | | Winner | | Runner-up |
| 1954.... | Holy Cross.........71 | Duquesne..........62 | | La Salle...........92 | | Bradley..........76 |
| 1955.... | Duquesne..........70 | Dayton............58 | | San Francisco.....77 | | La Salle..........63 |
| 1956.... | Louisville.........93 | Dayton............80 | | San Francisco.....83 | | Iowa.............71 |
| 1957.... | Bradley...........84 | Memphis State.....83 | | North Carolina....54 | | Kansas...........53 |
| 1958.... | Xavier............78 | Dayton............74 | | Kentucky..........84 | | Seattle...........72 |
| 1959.... | St. John's.........76 | Bradley...........71 | | California.........71 | | West Virginia.....70 |
| 1960.... | Bradley...........88 | Providence.........72 | | Ohio State........75 | | California.........55 |
| 1962.... | Providence........62 | St. Louis..........59 | | Cincinnati........70 | | Ohio State........65 |
| 1962.... | Dayton...........73 | St. John's.........67 | | Cincinnati........71 | | Ohio State........69 |
| 1963.... | Providence........81 | Canisius..........66 | | Loyola (Chicago)...60 | | Cincinnati........58 |
| 1964.... | Bradley...........86 | New Mexico........54 | | UCLA.............98 | | Duke.............83 |
| 1965.... | St. John's.........55 | Villanova..........51 | | UCLA.............91 | | Michigan..........80 |
| 1966.... | Brigham Young.....97 | NYU..............84 | | Texas Western.....72 | | Kentucky..........65 |
| 1967.... | Southern Illinois...71 | Marquette.........56 | | UCLA.............79 | | Dayton...........64 |
| 1967.... | Dayton...........61 | Kansas...........48 | | UCLA.............78 | | North Carolina.....55 |

## NCAA Individual Statistics
### (University Division)

#### SCORING

| | G. | FG. | FT. | Pt. | Avg. |
|---|---|---|---|---|---|
| Maravich, Louisiana St. | 26 | 432 | 274 | 1138 | 43.8 |
| Murphy, Niagara..... | 24 | 337 | 242 | 916 | 38.2 |
| Hayes, Houston...... | 33 | 519 | 176 | 1214 | 36.8 |
| Travis, Oklahoma City | 27 | 324 | 160 | 808 | 29.9 |
| Portman, Creighton... | 25 | 303 | 132 | 738 | 29.5 |
| Mount, Purdue....... | 24 | 259 | 165 | 683 | 28.5 |
| Hill, W. Texas State... | 21 | 237 | 99 | -573 | 27.3 |
| Halimon, Utah State.. | 25 | 256 | 159 | 671 | 26.8 |
| Foster, Miami (O.)... | 23 | 230 | 157 | 617 | 26.8 |
| Walk, Florida........ | 25 | 239 | 185 | 663 | 26.5 |
| Lanier, St. Bonaventure | 25 | 272 | 112 | 656 | 26.2 |
| Alcindor, UCLA...... | 28 | 294 | 146 | 734 | 26.2 |
| Powell, Loyola (La.)... | 25 | 263 | 125 | 651 | 26.0 |
| Williams, Iowa....... | 25 | 219 | 194 | 632 | 25.3 |
| Hollines, Denver...... | 25 | 241 | 144 | 626 | 25.0 |
| Webster, St. Peter's.. | 28 | 279 | 142 | 700 | 25.0 |
| Allen, Bradley....... | 28 | 258 | 170 | 686 | 24.5 |
| Smith, Iowa State.... | 25 | 197 | 210 | 604 | 24.2 |
| Platkowski, Bowl. Grn. | 25 | 263 | 75 | 601 | 24.0 |
| Jackson, Utah....... | 26 | 247 | 128 | 622 | 23.9 |
| Stone, Marshall...... | 25 | 238 | 116 | 592 | 23.7 |
| Quick, Xavier........ | 26 | 218 | 179 | 615 | 23.7 |
| Hayes, Boston U..... | 24 | 194 | 177 | 565 | 23.5 |
| Hochstein, Holy Cross. | 22 | 166 | 185 | 517 | 23.5 |
| May, Dayton......... | 30 | 239 | 223 | 701 | 23.4 |
| Sludut, Holy Cross.... | 23 | 216 | 102 | 534 | 23.2 |
| McCarter, Drake..... | 26 | 252 | 99 | 603 | 23.2 |
| Brown, Middle Tenn.. | 24 | 229 | 98 | 556 | 23.2 |
| Tolmie, Navy........ | 20 | 177 | 107 | 461 | 23.1 |
| Stephenson, Maine.... | 24 | 215 | 123 | 553 | 23.0 |

#### FIELD GOAL PERCENTAGE
##### (Minimum 130 Scored)

| | G. | FG. | FGA. | Pct. |
|---|---|---|---|---|
| Allen, Bradley.......... | 28 | 258 | 394 | .655 |
| Hunt, Army........... | 22 | 154 | 248 | .621 |
| Alcindor, UCLA........ | 28 | 294 | 480 | .613 |
| Unseld, Louisville...... | 28 | 234 | 382 | .613 |
| Sorenson, Ohio State.... | 29 | 196 | 329 | .596 |
| Sidle, Oklahoma....... | 26 | 189 | 321 | .589 |
| Webster, St. Peter's..... | 28 | 279 | 477 | .585 |
| Lanier, St. Bonaventure.. | 25 | 272 | 466 | .584 |

#### FREE THROW PERCENTAGE
##### (Minimum 90 Scored)

| | G. | FT. | FTA. | Pct. |
|---|---|---|---|---|
| Heiser, Princeton...... | 26 | 117 | 130 | .990 |
| Ward, Centenary...... | 26 | 94 | 106 | .887 |
| Carpenter, Pacific..... | 26 | 96 | 109 | .881 |
| Luchini, Marquette..... | 29 | 107 | 124 | .863 |
| Williams, Rice........ | 24 | 113 | 131 | .863 |
| Garrett, So. Illinois.... | 24 | 100 | 116 | .862 |
| Montgomery, Wk Forest. | 25 | 134 | 157 | .854 |
| Wininger, Butler...... | 24 | 97 | 114 | .851 |

#### REBOUNDS

| | G. | No. | Avg. |
|---|---|---|---|
| Walk, Florida .......... | 25 | 494 | 19.8 |
| Smith, Eastern Kentucky... | 24 | 472 | 19.7 |
| Hayes, Houston ........ | 33 | 624 | 18.9 |
| Unseld, Louisville....... | 28 | 513 | 18.3 |
| Cunningham, Murray State. | 23 | 410 | 17.8 |
| Lewis, St. Francis (Pa.).... | 25 | 443 | 17.7 |
| Wilson, Idaho State...... | 24 | 420 | 17.5 |
| Cowens, Florida State..... | 27 | 456 | 16.9 |

## NEA All-America Team, 1968

The following is the 1968 college All-America team selected for Newspaper Enterprise Assn. by the 12 NBA coaches and their talent scouts.

| First Team | | Second Team | |
|---|---|---|---|
| **Name** | **School** | **Name** | **School** |
| Lew Alcindor, UCLA | | Larry Miller, North Carolina | |
| Elvin Hayes, Houston | | Calvin Murphy, Niagara | |
| Pete Maravich, LSU | | Jo Jo White, Kansas | |
| Don May, Dayton | | Bob Lanier, St. Bonaventure | |
| Westley Unseld, Louisville | | Don Smith, Iowa State | |

### SPECIAL MENTION

Lucius Allen, UCLA; Mike Lewis, Duke; Butch Beard, Louisville; Henry Logan, Western Carolina; Charlie Scott, North Carolina; Simmie Hill, West Texas State; Mervin Jackson, Utah; Shaler Halimon, Utah State; Ron Williams, West Virginia; Tom Boerwinkle, Tennessee; Harry Hollines, Denver.

## Basketball Hall of Fame
### Springfield, Mass.

The Naismith Memorial Basketball Hall of Fame was incorporated in 1959 to serve as a memorial to James Naismith, who invented the game of basketball for students of the School for Christian Workers (now Springfield College) in December, 1891, at Springfield, Mass. The following persons have been enshrined in the Basketball Hall of Fame for outstanding contributions to basketball:

#### College Players

Harold (Bud) Foster, Wisconsin; Victor Hanson, Syracuse; Charles (Chuck) Hyatt, Pittsburgh; Robert Kurland, Oklahoma State; Angelo (Hank) Luisetti, Stanford; Branch McCracken, Indiana; C. Edward Macauley, St. Louis; George Mikan, DePaul; Charles (Stretch) Murphy, Purdue; H. O. (Pat) Page, Chicago; Andy Phillip, Illinois; John Roosma, U. S. Military Academy; John Schommer, Chicago; Christian Steinmetz, Wisconsin; J. A. (Cat) Thompson, Montana State; John R. Wooden, Purdue.

#### Professional Players

Bennie Borgmann, Nat Holman, Joe Lapchick, John (Honey) Russell, Barney Sedran, Edward A. Wachter.

#### AAU Players

Forrest S. DeBernardi, Robert (Ace) Gruenig, Jack McCracken.

#### Coaches

Ernest A. Blood, Howard G. Cann, Dr. H. Clifford Carlson, Everett S. Dean, Amory T. Gill, Howard A. Hobson, Alvin F. Julian, Frank Keaney, George E. Keogan, Ward (Piggy) Lambert, Kenneth Loeffler, Dr. Walter E. Meanwell, Leonard D. Sacns.

#### Referees

George Hepbron, George Hoyt, Matthew P. Kennedy, Ernest Quigley, David Tobey, David Walsh.

#### Contributors

Dr. Forrest C. (Phog) Allen, Walter A. Brown, John W. Bunn, Clair F. Bee, Dr. Luther Gulick, Edward J. Hickox, Paul D. Hinkle, Edward S. (Ned) Irish, R. William Jones, William G. Mokray, Ralph Morgan, Frank (Pop) Morgenweck, Dr. James Naismith, John J. O'Brien, Sr., Harold Olsen, H. V. Porter, William Reid, Lynn St. John, A. A. Schabinger, Amos Alonzo Stagg, Oswald Tower, Arthur L. Trester.

# NATIONAL BASKETBALL ASSOCIATION

| Eastern Division | W. | L. | Pct. | Pts. | Op. | Western Division | W. | L. | Pct. | Pts. | Op. |
|---|---|---|---|---|---|---|---|---|---|---|---|
| Philadelphia | 62 | 20 | .756 | 10051 | 9346 | St. Louis | 56 | 26 | .683 | 9266 | 9042 |
| Boston | 54 | 28 | .659 | 9523 | 9186 | Los Angeles | 52 | 30 | .634 | 9937 | 9477 |
| New York | 43 | 39 | .524 | 9523 | 9374 | San Francisco | 43 | 39 | .524 | 9598 | 9647 |
| Detroit | 40 | 42 | .488 | 9725 | 9889 | Chicago | 29 | 53 | .354 | 8982 | 9310 |
| Cincinnati | 39 | 43 | .476 | 9562 | 9631 | Seattle | 23 | 59 | .280 | 9732 | 10261 |
| Baltimore | 36 | 46 | .439 | 9627 | 9659 | San Diego | 15 | 67 | .183 | 9215 | 9919 |

**Eastern Divisional Championship**—Boston defeated Philadelphia, 4 games to 3.
**Western Divisional Championship**—Los Angeles defeated San Francisco, 4 games to 0.
**Championship Series**—Boston defeated Los Angeles, 4 games to 2.

| Individual Scoring Leaders | FG | FT | Pts. | Avg.* | Field Goal Percentage Leaders (A) | FG | FGA | Pct. |
|---|---|---|---|---|---|---|---|---|
| Bing, Detroit | 835 | 472 | 2142 | 27.1 | Chamberlain, Philadelphia | 819 | 1377 | .595 |
| Baylor, Los Angeles | 757 | 488 | 2002 | 26.0 | Bellamy, New York | 511 | 944 | .541 |
| Chamberlain, Philadelphia | 819 | 354 | 1992 | 24.3 | Lucas, Cincinnati | 707 | 1361 | .519 |
| Monroe, Baltimore | 742 | 507 | 1991 | 24.3 | West, Los Angeles | 476 | 926 | .514 |
| Greer, Philadelphia | 777 | 422 | 1976 | 24.1 | Chappell, Detroit | 235 | 458 | .513 |
| Robertson, Cincinnati | 660 | 576 | 1896 | 29.2 | Robertson, Cincinnati | 660 | 1321 | .500 |
| Hazzard, Seattle | 733 | 428 | 1894 | 23.9 | Hawkins, Los Angeles | 389 | 779 | .499 |
| Lucas, Cincinnati | 707 | 346 | 1760 | 21.4 | Dischinger, Detroit | 394 | 797 | .494 |
| Beaty, St. Louis | 639 | 455 | 1733 | 21.1 | Nelson, Boston | 312 | 632 | .494 |
| LaRusso, San Francisco | 602 | 522 | 1726 | 21.8 | Boozer, Chicago | 622 | 1265 | .492 |
| | | | | | Finkel, San Diego | 242 | 492 | .492 |

| Leaders in Rebounds | G. | No. | Avg.* | Free Throw Percentage Leaders (A) | FT | FTA | Pct. | Leaders in Assists | G. | No. | Avg.* |
|---|---|---|---|---|---|---|---|---|---|---|---|
| Chamberlain, Phil. | 82 | 1952 | 23.8 | Robertson, Cinn. | 576 | 660 | .873 | Chamberlain, Phil. | 82 | 702 | 8.6 |
| Lucas, Cinn. | 82 | 1560 | 19.0 | Siegfried, Boston | 236 | 272 | .868 | Wilkens, St. Louis | 82 | 679 | 8.3 |
| Russell, Boston | 78 | 1451 | 18.6 | Gambee, San Diego | 321 | 379 | .847 | Robertson, Cinn. | 65 | 633 | 9.7 |
| C. Lee, S. F. | 82 | 1141 | 13.9 | Hetzel, S. F. | 395 | 474 | .833 | Bing, Detroit | 79 | 509 | 6.4 |
| Thurmond, S. F. | 51 | 1121 | 22.0 | Smith, Cinn | 320 | 386 | .829 | Hazzard, Seattle | 79 | 493 | 6.2 |
| Scott, Baltimore | 81 | 1111 | 13.7 | S. Jones, Boston | 311 | 376 | .827 | Williams, San Diego | 79 | 391 | 4.9 |
| Bridges, St. Louis | 82 | 1102 | 13.4 | Robinson, Chicago | 288 | 352 | .818 | Attles, S. F. | 67 | 390 | 5.8 |
| DeBusschere, Det. | 80 | 1081 | 13.5 | Havlicek, Boston | 368 | 453 | .812 | Havlicek, Boston | 82 | 384 | 4.7 |
| Reed, N. Y. | 81 | 1073 | 13.2 | West, L. A. | 391 | 482 | .811 | Rodgers, Chi.-Cinn. | 78 | 380 | 4.9 |
| Bellamy, N. Y. | 82 | 961 | 11.7 | Russell, N. Y. | 282 | 349 | .808 | Greer, Phil. | 82 | 372 | 4.5 |

*Per game (A) minimum 220.

## Podoloff Trophy Winners

Wilt Chamberlain of Philadelphia was selected as the winner of the Maurice Podoloff Trophy for the third straight year as the Most Valuable Player in the N. B. A. for the 1967-68 season. The award was determined in a poll of all players on the twelve teams conducted by Newspaper Enterprise Association.

1956—Bob Pettit, St. Louis
1957—Bob Cousy, Boston
1958—Bill Russell, Boston
1959—Bob Pettit, St. Louis
1960—Wilt Chamberlain, Philadelphia
1961—Bill Russell, Boston
1962—Bill Russell, Boston

1963—Bill Russell, Boston
1964—Oscar Robertson, Cincinnati
1965—Bill Russell, Boston
1966—Wilt Chamberlain, Philadelphia
1967—Wilt Chamberlain, Philadelphia
1968—Wilt Chamberlain, Philadelphia

## N. B. A. SCORING LEADERS

| Yr. | Scoring Champion | Pts. | Avg. | Yr. | Scoring Champion | Pts. | Avg. |
|---|---|---|---|---|---|---|---|
| 1947 | Joe Fulks, Philadelphia | 1,389 | 23.2 | 1958 | George Yardley, Detroit | 2,001 | 27.8 |
| 1948 | Max Zaslofsky, Chicago | 1,007 | 21.0 | 1959 | Bob Pettit, St. Louis | 2,105 | 29.2 |
| 1949 | George Mikan, Minneapolis | 1,698 | 28.3 | 1960 | Wilt Chamberlain, Philadelphia | 2,707 | 37.9 |
| 1950 | George Mikan, Minneapolis | 1,865 | 27.4 | 1961 | Wilt Chamberlain, Philadelphia | 3,033 | 38.4 |
| 1951 | George Mikan, Minneapolis | 1,932 | 28.4 | 1962 | Wilt Chamberlain, Philadelphia | 4,029 | 50.4 |
| 1952 | Paul Arizin, Philadelphia | 1,674 | 25.4 | 1963 | Wilt Chamberlain, San Francisco | 3,586 | 44.8 |
| 1953 | Neil Johnston, Philadelphia | 1,564 | 22.3 | 1964 | Wilt Chamberlain, San Francisco | 2,948 | 36.5 |
| 1954 | Neil Johnston, Philadelphia | 1,759 | 24.4 | 1965 | Wilt Chamberlain, San Fran., Phila. | 2,534 | 34.7 |
| 1955 | Neil Johnston, Philadelphia | 1,631 | 22.7 | 1966 | Wilt Chamberlain, Philadelphia | 2,649 | 33.5 |
| 1956 | Bob Pettit, St. Louis | 1,849 | 25.7 | 1967 | Rick Barry, San Francisco | 2,775 | 35.6 |
| 1957 | Paul Arizin, Philadelphia | 1,817 | 25.6 | 1968 | Dave Bing, Detroit | 2,142 | 27.1 |

## NBA CHAMPIONS 1948-1968

| Year | Regular Season Eastern Division | Western Division | Playoffs Winner | Loser |
|---|---|---|---|---|
| 1948 | Philadelphia | St. Louis | Baltimore | Philadelphia |
| 1949 | Washington | Rochester | Minneapolis | Washington |
| 1950 | Syracuse | Minneapolis | Minneapolis | Syracuse |
| 1951 | Philadelphia | Minneapolis | Rochester | New York |
| 1952 | Syracuse | Rochester | Minneapolis | New York |
| 1953 | New York | Minneapolis | Minneapolis | New York |
| 1954 | New York | Minneapolis | Minneapolis | Syracuse |
| 1955 | Syracuse | Ft. Wayne | Syracuse | Ft. Wayne |
| 1956 | Philadelphia | Ft. Wayne | Philadelphia | Ft. Wayne |
| 1957 | Boston | St. Louis | Boston | St. Louis |
| 1958 | Boston | St. Louis | St. Louis | Boston |
| 1959 | Boston | St. Louis | Boston | Minneapolis |
| 1960 | Boston | St. Louis | Boston | St. Louis |
| 1961 | Boston | St. Louis | Boston | St. Louis |
| 1962 | Boston | Los Angeles | Boston | Los Angeles |
| 1963 | Boston | Los Angeles | Boston | Los Angeles |
| 1964 | Boston | San Francisco | Boston | San Francisco |
| 1965 | Boston | Los Angeles | Boston | Los Angeles |
| 1966 | Philadelphia | Los Angeles | Boston | Los Angeles |
| 1967 | Philadelphia | San Francisco | Philadelphia | San Francisco |
| 1968 | Philadelphia | St. Louis | Boston | Los Angeles |

# AMERICAN BASKETBALL ASSOCIATION

| Eastern Division | W. | L. | Pct. | Pts. | Op. | Western Division | W. | L. | Pct. | Pts. | Op. |
|---|---|---|---|---|---|---|---|---|---|---|---|
| Pittsburgh... | 54 | 24 | .692 | 8731 | 8479 | New Orleans . | 48 | 30 | .615 | 8712 | 8334 |
| Minnesota... | 50 | 28 | .641 | 8469 | 8163 | Dallas....... | 46 | 32 | .590 | 8576 | 8470 |
| Indiana...... | 38 | 40 | .487 | 8546 | 8530 | Denver..... | 45 | 33 | .577 | 8244 | 7914 |
| Kentucky.... | 36 | 42 | .462 | 8150 | 8207 | Houston..... | 29 | 49 | .372 | 8074 | 8407 |
| New Jersey... | 36 | 42 | .462 | 8641 | 8768 | Anaheim..... | 25 | 53 | .321 | 8704 | 9057 |
| | | | | | | Oakland ..... | 22 | 56 | .282 | 8642 | 9160 |

**Eastern Divisional Championship**—Pittsburgh defeated Minnesota, 4 games to 1.
**Western Divisional Championship**—New Orleans defeated Dallas, 4 games to 1.
**Championship Series**—Pittsburgh defeated New Orleans, 4 games to 3.

| Scoring Leaders | FG | FT | Pts. | Avg. | Free Throw % Leaders | | Pct. | Leaders in Assists | | No. | Avg. |
|---|---|---|---|---|---|---|---|---|---|---|---|
| C. Hawkins, Pitts.. | 633 | 603 | 1875 | 26.8 | C. Beasley, Dal... | | 87.2 | L. Brown, N. O. .... | | 506 | 6.5 |
| D. Moe, N. O. .... | 662 | 551 | 1884 | 24.2 | B. Lloyd, N. J... | | 85.4 | C. Hagan, Dal...... | | 276 | 4.9 |
| L. Tart, Oak.-N. J. | 632 | 451 | 1718 | 23.5 | J. Beasley, Dal... | | 84.2 | S. Chubin, Ana..... | | 364 | 4.7 |
| D. Carrier, Ky..... | 559 | 395 | 1765 | 22.9 | T. Jackson, N. J.. | | 82.9 | C. Hawkins, Pitts... | | 316 | 4.5 |
| L. Jones, Den...... | 594 | 530 | 1742 | 22.9 | M. Nowell, N. J... | | 82.6 | R. Brown, Ind...... | | 327 | 4.3 |
| M. Daniels, Minn... | 668 | 390 | 1729 | 22.2 | D. Carrier, Ky.... | | 82.5 | M. McHartley, Dal. | | 230 | 4.0 |
| W. Somerset, Hous.. | 434 | 359 | 1326 | 21.7 | L. Dampier, Ky... | | 82.3 | A. Heyman, Pitts... | | 272 | 3.7 |
| C. Williams, Pitts.. | 591 | 290 | 1625 | 20.8 | A. Becker, Hous . | | 82.0 | C. Beasley, Dal..... | | 290 | 3.7 |
| L. Dampier, Ky.... | 582 | 209 | 1487 | 20.7 | L. Brown, N. O... | | 81.3 | B. Leibowitz, Pitts.- | | | |
| F. Lewis, Ind...... | 526 | 465 | 1565 | 20.6 | S. Chubin, Ana.... | | 81.1 | N. J.-Oakland..... | | 300 | 3.7 |
| | | | | | | | | W. Somerset, Hous.. | | 225 | 3.7 |

| 2-Pt. F. G. % Leaders | FG | FGA | Pct. | 3-Pt. F. G. % Leaders | | FG | Pct. | Leaders in Rebounds | | No. | Avg. |
|---|---|---|---|---|---|---|---|---|---|---|---|
| T. Washington, Pitts. | 310 | 594 | 52.2 | D. Carrier, Ky.... | | 84 | 35.7 | M. Daniels, Minn.... | | 1213 | 15.6 |
| C. Hawkins, Pitts.... | 633 | 1214 | 52.1 | R. Perry, Minn.... | | 62 | 34.8 | C. Hawkins, Pitts... | | 945 | 13.5 |
| B. Netolicky, Ind.... | 468 | 927 | 50.5 | C. Vaughn, Pitts.. | | 137 | 33.4 | J. Beasley, Dal..... | | 982 | 12.8 |
| C. Beasley, Dal...... | 371 | 745 | 49.8 | J. Rayl, Ind...... | | 57 | 32.6 | I. Harge, Pitt.-Oak.. | | 1038 | 12.7 |
| A. Robbins, N. O..... | 446 | 912 | 49.5 | L. Selvage, Ana... | | 147 | 32.0 | A. Robbins, N. O.... | | 894 | 12.2 |
| D. Anderson, N. J.... | 463 | 938 | 49.4 | B. Warley, Ana... | | 52 | 31.3 | J. Hadnot, Oak...... | | 936 | 12.2 |
| J. Beasley, Dal...... | 622 | 1262 | 49.3 | H. Hale, Hous..... | | 35 | 31.3 | J. Ligon, Ky....... | | 929 | 11.9 |
| C. Hagan, Dal....... | 371 | 756 | 49.1 | T. Jackson, N. J.. | | 91 | 30.1 | B. Netolicky, Ind.... | | 819 | 11.5 |
| C. Powell, Dal....... | 532 | 1085 | 49.0 | C. Williams, Pitts. | | 51 | 28.7 | D. Anderson, N. J... | | 856 | 11.0 |
| J. Hammond, Den..... | 224 | 458 | 48.9 | L. Dampier, Ky... | | 38 | 26.8 | T. Washington, Pitts. | | 672 | 10.7 |

## ABA Champions

| | Regular Season | | Playoffs | |
|---|---|---|---|---|
| Year | Eastern Division | Western Division | Winner | Loser |
| 1968 | Pittsburgh | New Orleans | Pittsburgh | New Orleans |

## ABA Most Valuable Player

Connie Hawkins of Pittsburgh was selected as the Most Valuable Player in the ABA for the 1967-68 season. The award was determined in a poll of sports writers taken by the U. S. Basketball Writers Association.

## Biddy Basketball Champions

Biddy basketball competition, with scaled down courts, equipment and shorter periods of play, is open to boys up to 12 and girls up to 13. Local, regional and national tournaments are held annually under jurisdiction of Biddy Basketball national headquarters, Scranton, Pa. National champions have been:

| Winner | Runner-up | | Winner | Runner-up |
|---|---|---|---|---|
| 1957..... New Orleans, La..45 | Atlantic City, N.J.42 | 1963..... | New Orleans, La.. 44 | New York, N. Y.. 43 |
| 1958..... Bridgeport, Conn.49 | Puerto Rico......46 | 1964..... | Chester, Pa...... 61 | Jersey City, N. J..55 |
| 1959..... Bridgeport, Conn.50 | New Orleans, La..36 | 1965..... | New York, N. Y. 37 | New Orleans, La..32 |
| 1960..... Gary, Ind .......51 | Jersey City, N.J..47 | 1966..... | New Orleans, La..53 | Jersey City, N. J..38 |
| 1961..... Jefferson, La.....42 | Wichita, Kan.....42 | 1967..... | Wichita, Kans....41 | New Orleans, La..38 |
| 1962..... Wichita, Kansas..41 | Jefferson, La.....40 | 1968..... | Augusta, Ga.....46 | Dallas, Tex......41 |

**Mr. Biddy Basketball, 1968**—James White, Augusta, Ga.

# Fencing Championships in 1968

### 76th ANNUAL U. S. NATIONAL CHAMPIONSHIPS
Miami, Florida, June 22-30

**Foil**—Heizaburo Okawa, Mori; Jeffrey Checkes, N. Y. Fencers Club; Herbert Cohen, N. Y. Fencers Club.
**Epee**—Paul Pesthy, New York AC; David Micahnik, Csiszar; Robert Beck, Unattached.
**Sabre**—A. Jack Keane, New York AC; Alex Orban, New York AC; Thomas Balla, Csiszar.

**Women**—Janice Romary, Mori; Harriet King, Lucia; Maxine Mitchell, Los Angeles FC.
**Foil Team**—Salle Santelli, N. Y.
**Epee Team**—Salle Csiszar, Phila.
**Sabre Team**—New York Athletic Club.
**Women's Team**—Salle Santelli, N. Y.
**Martini & Rossi Trophy**—New York A.C.

### 71st ANNUAL INTERCOLLEGIATE FENCING ASS'N. CHAMPIONSHIPS
Princeton, N. J., March 15, 16

**Foil**—Jeffrey Kostler, Columbia; Arthur Baer, Columbia; John McKay, Columbia.
**Epee**—Burt Pearlman, Columbia; George Mosin, NYU; Van Wolosin, NYU.
**Sabre**—Frank Lowy, Columbia; Todd Makler.

Penn; Norman Braslow, Penn.
**Foil Team**—NYU and Columbia tied.
**Epee Team**—NYU.
**Sabre Team**—Pennsylvania.
**Three-weapon Team**—NYU.

### MARTINI & ROSSI INTERNATIONAL TOURNAMENT
NYAC, April 19-21

**Foil**—Adam Lisewski, Poland; Jeff Checkes, USA; Christian Noel, France.
**Epee**—Zoltan Nemere, Hungary; James Melcher, USA; Paul Pesthy, USA.

**Sabre**—Jerzy Pawlowski, Poland; Tibor Pesza, Hungary; Marcel Parent, France.
**Match of Nations**—Poland.

### 24th ANNUAL NCAA FENCING CHAMPIONSHIPS

**Foil**—Gerard Esponda, U. of San Francisco.
**Epee**—Don Sieja, Cornell.

**Sabre**—Todd Makler, Penn.
**Team Trophy**—Columbia.

### 40th INTERCOLLEGIATE WOMEN'S FENCING ASSOCIATION CHAMPIONSHIPS
Fairleigh Dickinson, Teaneck, N. J.

**Individual**—Karen Denton, Cornell; Nelda Latham, CCNY; Ann O'Donnell, J. C. State.

**Team**—Cornell University.

# Hockey Champions in 1967-68
## NATIONAL HOCKEY LEAGUE
### Final Standings

| EAST DIVISION | W | L | T | Pts. | GF | GA | WEST DIVISION | W | L | T | Pts. | GF | GA |
|---|---|---|---|---|---|---|---|---|---|---|---|---|---|
| Montreal | 42 | 22 | 10 | 236 | 167 | 94 | Philadelphia | 31 | 32 | 11 | 173 | 179 | 73 |
| New York | 39 | 23 | 12 | 226 | 183 | 90 | Los Angeles | 31 | 33 | 10 | 200 | 224 | 72 |
| Boston | 37 | 27 | 10 | 259 | 216 | 84 | St. Louis | 27 | 31 | 16 | 177 | 191 | 70 |
| Chicago | 32 | 26 | 16 | 212 | 222 | 80 | Minnesota | 27 | 32 | 15 | 191 | 226 | 69 |
| Toronto | 33 | 31 | 10 | 209 | 176 | 76 | Pittsburgh | 27 | 34 | 13 | 195 | 216 | 67 |
| Detroit | 27 | 35 | 12 | 245 | 257 | 66 | Oakland | 15 | 42 | 17 | 153 | 219 | 47 |

### LEADING SCORERS

| | GP | G | A | Pts. | PIM | | GP | G | A | Pts. | PIM |
|---|---|---|---|---|---|---|---|---|---|---|---|
| Stan Mikita, Chi. | 72 | 40 | 47 | 87 | 14 | Bobby Rousseau, Mtl. | 74 | 19 | 46 | 65 | 47 |
| Phil Esposito, Bos. | 74 | 35 | 49 | 84 | 21 | Fred Stanfield, Bos. | 73 | 20 | 44 | 64 | 10 |
| Gordie Howe, Det. | 74 | 39 | 43 | 82 | 53 | Yvan Cournoyer, Mtl. | 64 | 28 | 32 | 60 | 23 |
| Jean Ratelle, N. Y. | 74 | 32 | 46 | 78 | 18 | Mike Walton, Tor. | 73 | 30 | 29 | 59 | 48 |
| Rod Gilbert, N. Y. | 73 | 29 | 48 | 77 | 12 | Andy Bathgate, Pitt. | 74 | 20 | 39 | 59 | 55 |
| Bobby Hull, Chi. | 71 | 44 | 31 | 75 | 39 | Bob Nevin, N. Y. | 74 | 28 | 30 | 58 | 20 |
| Norm Ullman, Det., Tor. | 71 | 35 | 37 | 72 | 28 | Ed Joyal, L. A. | 74 | 23 | 34 | 57 | 20 |
| Alex Delvecchio, Det. | 74 | 22 | 48 | 70 | 14 | Wayne Connelly, Minn. | 74 | 35 | 21 | 56 | 40 |
| Johnny Bucyk, Bos. | 72 | 30 | 39 | 69 | 8 | Ken Hodge, Bos. | 74 | 25 | 31 | 56 | 31 |
| Ken Wharram, Chi. | 74 | 27 | 42 | 69 | 18 | Dean Prentice, Det. | 69 | 17 | 38 | 55 | 42 |
| Jean Beliveau, Mtl. | 59 | 31 | 37 | 68 | 28 | Red Berenson, N.Y., St. L. | 74 | 24 | 30 | 54 | 24 |
| John McKenzie, Bos. | 74 | 28 | 38 | 66 | 107 | Ted Hampson, Det., Oak. | 71 | 17 | 37 | 54 | 14 |
| Phil Goyette, N. Y. | 73 | 25 | 40 | 65 | 10 | | | | | | |

### ADDITIONAL PLAYERS BY DIVISION

| EAST | GP | G | A | Pts. | PIM | WEST | GP | G | A | Pts. | PIM |
|---|---|---|---|---|---|---|---|---|---|---|---|
| Doug Mohns, Chi. | 65 | 24 | 29 | 53 | 53 | Ray Cullen, Minn. | 67 | 28 | 25 | 53 | 18 |
| Frank Mahovlich, Tor., Det. | 63 | 26 | 26 | 52 | 32 | Andre Boudrias, Minn. | 74 | 18 | 35 | 53 | 42 |
| | | | | | | Gerry Melnyk, St. L. | 73 | 15 | 35 | 50 | 14 |
| Gilles Tremblay, Mtl. | 71 | 23 | 28 | 51 | 8 | Lou Angotti, Phil. | 70 | 12 | 37 | 49 | 35 |
| Bob Pulford, Tor. | 74 | 20 | 30 | 50 | 40 | Dave Balon, Minn. | 73 | 15 | 32 | 47 | 84 |
| Tom Williams, Bos. | 68 | 18 | 32 | 50 | 14 | Mike McMahon, Minn. | 74 | 14 | 33 | 47 | 71 |
| Derek Sanderson, Bos. | 71 | 24 | 25 | 49 | 98 | Bill Flett, L. A. | 73 | 26 | 20 | 46 | 97 |
| Don Marshall, N. Y. | 70 | 19 | 30 | 49 | 2 | Lowell MacDonald, L. A. | 74 | 21 | 24 | 45 | 12 |
| Ron Ellis, Tor. | 74 | 28 | 20 | 48 | 8 | Gerry Ehman, Oak. | 73 | 19 | 25 | 44 | 20 |
| Dave Keon, Tor. | 67 | 11 | 37 | 48 | 4 | Ab McDonald, Pitt. | 74 | 22 | 21 | 43 | 38 |
| Dick Duff, Mtl. | 66 | 25 | 21 | 46 | 21 | Gary Dornhoefer, Phil. | 65 | 13 | 30 | 43 | 134 |
| Floyd Smith, Det., Tor. | 63 | 24 | 22 | 46 | 14 | Leon Rochefort, Phil. | 74 | 21 | 21 | 42 | 16 |
| Ralph Backstrom, Mtl. | 70 | 20 | 25 | 45 | 14 | Parker MacDonald, Minn. | 69 | 19 | 23 | 42 | 22 |
| Paul Henderson, Det., Tor. | 63 | 18 | 26 | 44 | 43 | Art Stratton, Pitt., Phil. | 70 | 16 | 25 | 41 | 20 |
| Claude Provost, Mtl. | 73 | 14 | 30 | 44 | 26 | Bill Hicke, Oak. | 52 | 21 | 19 | 40 | 32 |
| Ted Green, Bos. | 72 | 7 | 36 | 43 | 133 | Ted Irvine, L. A. | 73 | 18 | 22 | 40 | 26 |
| Eddie Shack, Bos. | 70 | 23 | 19 | 42 | 107 | Gord Labossiere, L. A. | 68 | 13 | 27 | 40 | 31 |
| Jacques Lemaire, Mtl. | 69 | 22 | 20 | 42 | 16 | Ken Schinkel, Pitt. | 57 | 14 | 25 | 39 | 19 |
| Gary Bergman, Det. | 74 | 13 | 28 | 41 | 109 | Bill White, L. A. | 74 | 11 | 27 | 38 | 100 |
| Vic Hadfield, N. Y. | 59 | 20 | 19 | 39 | 45 | Earl Ingarfield, Pitt. | 50 | 15 | 22 | 37 | 12 |
| Gary Jarrett, Det. | 68 | 18 | 21 | 39 | 20 | Ed Hoekstra, Phil. | 70 | 15 | 21 | 36 | 6 |
| Bruce MacGregor, Det. | 71 | 15 | 24 | 39 | 13 | Real Lemieux, L. A. | 74 | 12 | 23 | 35 | 60 |
| Pat Stapleton, Chi. | 67 | 4 | 34 | 38 | 34 | Charlie Burns, Oak. | 73 | 9 | 26 | 35 | 20 |
| Murray Oliver, Tor. | 74 | 16 | 21 | 37 | 18 | Val Fonteyne, Pitt. | 69 | 6 | 28 | 34 | 0 |
| Pierre Pilote, Chi. | 74 | 1 | 36 | 37 | 69 | Gene Ubriaco, Pitt. | 65 | 18 | 15 | 33 | 16 |
| Ed Westfall, Bos. | 73 | 14 | 22 | 36 | 38 | Bill Goldsworthy, Minn. | 68 | 14 | 19 | 33 | 68 |
| Eric Nesterenko, Chi. | 71 | 11 | 25 | 36 | 37 | Wally Boyer, Oak. | 74 | 13 | 20 | 33 | 44 |
| Pit Martin, Chi. | 63 | 16 | 19 | 35 | 36 | Noel Price, Pitt. | 70 | 6 | 27 | 33 | 48 |
| Orland Kurtenbach, N. Y. | 73 | 15 | 20 | 35 | 82 | Frank St. Marseille, St. L. | 56 | 16 | 16 | 32 | 12 |
| Jim Neilson, N. Y. | 67 | 6 | 29 | 35 | 60 | Paul Andrea, Pitt. | 65 | 11 | 21 | 32 | 2 |
| George Armstrong, Tor. | 62 | 13 | 21 | 34 | 4 | Brit Selby, Phil. | 56 | 15 | 15 | 30 | 24 |
| Dennis Hull, Chi. | 74 | 18 | 15 | 33 | 34 | Bill Sutherland, Phil. | 60 | 20 | 9 | 29 | 6 |
| John Ferguson, Mtl. | 61 | 15 | 18 | 33 | 117 | Billy Harris, Oak. | 62 | 12 | 17 | 29 | 2 |
| Kent Douglas, Oak., Det. | 76 | 11 | 21 | 32 | 126 | Don McKenney, St. L. | 39 | 5 | 24 | 29 | 4 |
| Bobby Orr, Bos. | 46 | 11 | 20 | 31 | 63 | Don Blackburn, Phil. | 67 | 9 | 20 | 29 | 23 |
| Pete Stemkowski, Tor., Det. | 73 | 10 | 21 | 31 | 86 | Terry Crisp, St. L. | 73 | 9 | 20 | 29 | 10 |
| J. C. Tremblay, Mtl. | 73 | 4 | 26 | 30 | 18 | Billy Dea, Pitt. | 73 | 16 | 12 | 28 | 6 |
| Harry Howell, N. Y. | 74 | 5 | 24 | 29 | 62 | Terry Gray, L. A. | 65 | 12 | 16 | 28 | 22 |
| Jim Pappin, Tor. | 58 | 13 | 15 | 28 | 37 | Jean-Paul Parise, Tor., Minn. | 44 | 11 | 17 | 28 | 27 |
| Henri Richard, Mtl. | 54 | 9 | 19 | 28 | 16 | Forbes Kennedy, Phil. | 73 | 10 | 18 | 28 | 130 |
| Tim Horton, Tor. | 69 | 4 | 23 | 27 | 82 | Keith McCreary, Pitt. | 70 | 14 | 12 | 26 | 44 |
| Dallas Smith, Bos. | 74 | 4 | 23 | 27 | 65 | Bill McCreary, St. L. | 70 | 13 | 13 | 26 | 22 |
| Ron Stewart, St. L., N. Y. | 74 | 14 | 12 | 26 | 30 | Pat Hannigan, Phil. | 65 | 11 | 15 | 26 | 36 |
| Arnie Brown, N. Y. | 74 | 1 | 25 | 26 | 83 | Claude Laforge, Phil. | 63 | 9 | 16 | 25 | 36 |
| Brian Conacher, Tor. | 64 | 11 | 14 | 25 | 31 | Howie Menard, L. A. | 35 | 9 | 15 | 24 | 32 |
| Jacques Laperriere, Mtl. | 72 | 4 | 21 | 25 | 84 | Larry Cahan, Oak. | 74 | 9 | 15 | 24 | 80 |
| Red Fleming, N. Y. | 73 | 17 | 7 | 24 | 132 | Gary Sabourin, St. L. | 50 | 13 | 10 | 23 | 50 |
| Chico Maki, Chi. | 60 | 8 | 16 | 24 | 4 | Howie Hughes, L. A. | 74 | 9 | 14 | 23 | 20 |
| Doug Jarrett, Chi. | 74 | 4 | 19 | 23 | 48 | Bob Wall, L. A. | 71 | 5 | 18 | 23 | 66 |
| Bernie Geoffrion, N. Y. | 59 | 5 | 16 | 21 | 11 | Alain Caron, Oak. | 58 | 9 | 13 | 22 | 18 |
| Ted Harris, Mtl. | 67 | 5 | 16 | 21 | 78 | Leo Boivin, Pitt. | 73 | 9 | 13 | 22 | 74 |
| Gilles Marotte, Chi. | 73 | 0 | 21 | 21 | 122 | John Miszuk, Phil. | 74 | 5 | 17 | 22 | 79 |
| Camille Henry, N. Y. | 36 | 8 | 12 | 20 | 0 | Brian Campbell, L. A. | 44 | 6 | 15 | 21 | 16 |
| Glen Sather, Bos. | 65 | 8 | 12 | 20 | 34 | Bob Dillabough, Pitt. | 47 | 7 | 12 | 19 | 13 |
| Larry Hillman, Tor. | 55 | 3 | 17 | 20 | 13 | Larry Popein, Oak. | 47 | 5 | 14 | 19 | 12 |
| Marcel Pronovost, Tor. | 70 | 3 | 17 | 20 | 48 | Joe Watson, Phil. | 73 | 5 | 14 | 19 | 56 |
| Wayne Carleton, Tor. | 65 | 8 | 11 | 19 | 34 | George Swarbrick, Oak. | 49 | 13 | 5 | 18 | 62 |
| Howie Young, Det. | 62 | 2 | 17 | 19 | 112 | Doug Robinson, L. A. | 34 | 9 | 9 | 18 | 6 |
| Doug Roberts, Det. | 37 | 8 | 9 | 17 | 12 | Ron Schock, S. L. | 55 | 9 | 9 | 18 | 17 |
| Garry Unger, Tor., Det. | 28 | 6 | 11 | 17 | 6 | Bob Rivard, Pitt. | 27 | 5 | 12 | 17 | 4 |
| Rod Selling, N. Y. | 71 | 5 | 11 | 16 | 44 | Milan Marcetta, Minn. | 36 | 4 | 13 | 17 | 6 |
| Bart Crashley, Det. | 57 | 2 | 14 | 16 | 18 | Ed Van Impe, Phil. | 67 | 4 | 13 | 17 | 141 |
| Don Awrey, Bos. | 74 | 3 | 12 | 15 | 150 | Dale Rolfe, L. A. | 68 | 3 | 13 | 16 | 84 |
| Serge Savard, Mtl. | 67 | 2 | 13 | 15 | 34 | | | | | | |
| Allan Stanley, Tor. | 64 | 1 | 13 | 14 | 16 | | | | | | |
| Skip Krake, Bos. | 68 | 5 | 7 | 12 | 13 | | | | | | |
| Gary Doak, Bos. | 59 | 2 | 10 | 12 | 100 | | | | | | |
| Mickey Redmond, Mtl. | 41 | 6 | 5 | 11 | 4 | | | | | | |
| Jimmy Peters, Det. | 45 | 5 | 6 | 11 | 8 | | | | | | |
| Terry Harper, Mtl. | 57 | 3 | 8 | 11 | 66 | | | | | | |
| Claude Larose, Mtl. | 42 | 2 | 9 | 11 | 28 | | | | | | |

# STANLEY CUP PLAYOFF RESULTS
## (BEST 4 OUT OF 7 GAMES)

**Series "A"**
Apr. 4 at Montreal—Montreal 2, Boston 1
Apr. 6 at Montreal—Montreal 5, Boston 3
Apr. 9 at Boston—Montreal 5, Boston 2
Apr. 11 at Boston—Montreal 3, Boston 2
Montreal won series "A" 4 games to 0.

**Series "B"**
Apr. 4 at New York—Chicago 1, New York 3
Apr. 9 at New York—Chicago 1, New York 2
Apr. 11 at Chicago—Chicago 7, New York 4
Apr. 13 at Chicago—Chicago 3, New York 1
Apr. 14 at New York—Chicago 2, New York 1
Apr. 16 at Chicago—Chicago 4, New York 1
Chicago won series "B" 4 games to 2.

**Series "C"**
Apr. 4 at Philadelphia—St. Louis 1, Philadelphia 0
Apr. 6 at Philadelphia—St. Louis 3, Philadelphia 4
Apr. 10 at St. Louis—St. Louis 3, Philadelphia 2
Apr. 11 at St. Louis—St. Louis 5, Philadelphia 2
Apr. 13 at Philadelphia—St. Louis 1, Philadelphia 6
Apr. 16 at St. Louis—St. Louis 1, Philadelphia 2
Apr. 18 at Philadelphia—St. Louis 3, Philadelphia 1
St. Louis won series "C" 4 games to 3.

**Series "D"**
Apr. 4 at Los Angeles—Minnesota 1, Los Angeles 2
Apr. 6 at Los Angeles—Minnesota 0, Los Angeles 2
Apr. 9 at Minnesota—Minnesota 7, Los Angeles 5
Apr. 11 at Minnesota—Minnesota 3, Los Angeles 2

Apr. 13 at Los Angeles—Minnesota 2, L. A. 3
Apr. 16 at Minnesota—Minnesota 4, Los Angeles 3
Apr. 18 at Los Angeles—Minnesota 9, L. A. 4
Minnesota Won series "D" 4 games to 3.

**Series "E"**
Apr. 18 at Montreal—Montreal 9, Chicago 2
Apr. 20 at Montreal—Montreal 4, Chicago 1
Apr. 23 at Chicago—Montreal 4, Chicago 2
Apr. 25 at Chicago—Montreal 1, Chicago 2
Apr. 28 at Montreal—Montreal 4, Chicago 3
Montreal won series "E" 4 games to 1.

**Series "F"**
Apr. 21 at St. Louis—St. Louis 5, Minnesota 3
Apr. 22 at Minnesota—St. Louis 2, Minnesota 3
Apr. 25 at St. Louis—St. Louis 1, Minnesota 3
Apr. 27 at St. Louis—St. Louis 4, Minnesota 3
*(Played at St. Louis: Minnesota home game)*
Apr. 29 at St. Louis—St. Louis 3, Minnesota 2
May 1 at Minnesota—St. Louis 1, Minnesota 4
May 3 at St. Louis—St. Louis 2, Minnesota 1
St. Louis won series "F" 4 games to 3.

**Series "G"**
May 5 at St. Louis—Montreal 3, St. Louis 2
May 7 at St. Louis—Montreal 1, St. Louis 0
May 9 at Montreal—Montreal 4, St. Louis 3
May 11 at Montreal—Montreal 3, St. Louis 2
Montreal won Stanley Cup 4 games to 0.

## 1968 STANLEY CUP SCORING

| | GP | G | A | Pts. | PIM | | GP | G | A | Pts. | PIM |
|---|---|---|---|---|---|---|---|---|---|---|---|
| Bill Goldsworthy, Minn. | 14 | 8 | 7 | 15 | 12 | Bobby Hull, Chi. | 11 | 4 | 6 | 10 | 15 |
| Milan Marcetta, Minn. | 14 | 7 | 7 | 14 | 4 | Mike McMahon, Minn. | 14 | 3 | 7 | 10 | 4 |
| Dickie Moore, St. L. | 18 | 7 | 7 | 14 | 15 | Claude Provost, Mtl. | 13 | 2 | 8 | 10 | 10 |
| Yvan Cournoyer, Mtl. | 13 | 6 | 8 | 14 | 4 | Parker MacDonald, Minn. | 14 | 4 | 5 | 9 | 2 |
| Jacques Lemaire, Mtl. | 13 | 7 | 6 | 13 | 6 | Larry Keenan, St. L. | 18 | 4 | 5 | 9 | 4 |
| Frank St. Marseille, St. L. | 18 | 5 | 8 | 13 | 0 | Pit Martin, Chi. | 11 | 3 | 6 | 9 | 2 |
| Dave Balon, Minn. | 14 | 4 | 9 | 13 | 14 | J. C. Tremblay, Mtl. | 13 | 3 | 6 | 9 | 2 |
| Stan Mikita, Chi. | 11 | 5 | 7 | 12 | 6 | Andre Boudrias, Minn. | 14 | 3 | 6 | 9 | 8 |
| Wayne Connelly, Minn. | 14 | 8 | 3 | 11 | 2 | Henri Richard, Mtl. | 13 | 4 | 4 | 8 | 4 |
| Jean Beliveau, Mtl. | 10 | 7 | 4 | 11 | 6 | John Ferguson, Mtl. | 13 | 3 | 5 | 8 | 25 |

# Stanley Cup Champions

| | | | |
|---|---|---|---|
| 1937—Detroit Red Wings | 1946—Montreal Canadiens | 1954—Detroit Red Wings | 1962—Toronto Maple Leafs |
| 1938—Chicago Black Hawks | 1947—Toronto Maple Leafs | 1955—Detroit Red Wings | 1963—Toronto Maple Leafs |
| 1939—Boston Bruins | 1948—Toronto Maple Leafs | 1956—Montreal Canadiens | 1964—Toronto Maple Leafs |
| 1940—New York Rangers | 1949—Toronto Maple Leafs | 1957—Montreal Canadiens | 1965—Montreal Canadiens |
| 1941—Boston Bruins | 1950—Detroit Red Wings | 1958—Montreal Canadiens | 1966—Montreal Canadiens |
| 1942—Toronto Maple Leafs | 1951—Toronto Maple Leafs | 1959—Montreal Canadiens | 1967—Toronto Maple Leafs |
| 1943—Detroit Red Wings | 1952—Detroit Red Wings | 1960—Montreal Canadiens | 1968—Montreal Canadiens |
| 1944—Montreal Canadiens | 1953—Montreal Canadiens | 1961—Chicago Black Hawks | |
| 1945—Toronto Maple Leafs | | | |

# HOCKEY TROPHY WINNERS

| ROSS TROPHY<br>Leading Scorer | NORRIS TROPHY<br>Best Defenseman | CALDER TROPHY<br>Best Rookie |
|---|---|---|
| 1968—Stan Mikita, Chicago | Bobby Orr, Boston | Derek Sanderson, Boston |
| 1967—Stan Mikita, Chicago | Harry Howell, New York | Bobby Orr, Boston |
| 1966—Bobby Hull, Chicago | Jacques Laperriere, Montreal | Brit Selby, Toronto |
| 1965—Stan Mikita, Chicago | Pierre Pilote, Chicago | Roger Crozier, Detroit |
| 1964—Stan Mikita, Chicago | Pierre Pilote, Chicago | Jacques Laperriere, Montreal |
| 1963—Gordie Howe, Detroit | Pierre Pilote, Chicago | Kent Douglas, Toronto |
| 1962—Bobby Hull, Chicago | Doug Harvey, New York | Bobby Rousseau, Montreal |
| 1961—Bernie Geoffrion, Can. | Doug Harvey, Montreal | Dave Keon, Toronto |
| 1960—Bobby Hull, Chicago | Doug Harvey, Montreal | Bill (Red) Hay, Chicago |
| 1959—Dickie Moore, Canadiens | Tom Johnson, Montreal | Ralph Backstrom, Montreal |

| HART TROPHY<br>M. V. P. | VEZINA TROPHY<br>Leading Goalie | LADY BYNG TROPHY<br>Sportsmanship |
|---|---|---|
| 1968—Stan Mikita, Chicago | Worsley, Vachon, Montreal | Stan Mikita, Chicago |
| 1967—Stan Mikita, Chicago | Hall, De Jordy, Chicago | Stan Mikita, Chicago |
| 1966—Bobby Hull, Chicago | Hodge, Worsley, Montreal | Alex Delvecchio, Detroit |
| 1965—Bobby Hull, Chicago | Sawchuck, Bower, Toronto | Bobby Hull, Chicago |
| 1964—Jean Beliveau, Montreal | Charlie Hodge, Montreal | Ken Wharram, Chicago |
| 1963—Gordie Howe, Detroit | Glenn Hall, Chicago | Dave Keon, Toronto |
| 1962—Jacques Plante, Montreal | Jacques Plante, Montreal | Dave Keon, Toronto |
| 1961—Bernie Geoffrion, Mont. | Johnny Bower, Toronto | Red Kelly, Toronto |
| 1960—Gordie Howe, Detroit | Jacques Plante, Montreal | Don McKenney, Boston |
| 1959—Andy Bathgate, New York | Jacques Plante, Montreal | Alex Delvecchio, Detroit |

# All-Star Teams 1968

| Position | First Team | Second Team |
|---|---|---|
| Goal | Gump Worsley, Montreal | Ed Giacomin, New York |
| Defense | Bobby Orr, Boston | J. C. Tremblay, Montreal |
| Defense | Tim Horton, Toronto | Jim Neilson, New York |
| Center | Stan Mikita, Chicago | Phil Esposito, Boston |
| Right Wing | Gordie Howe, Detroit | Rod Gilbert, New York |
| Left Wing | Bobby Hull, Chicago | John Buyck, Boston |

## AMERICAN HOCKEY LEAGUE
### Final Standings
### EASTERN DIVISION

|  | W | L | T | Pts. | GF | GA |
|---|---|---|---|---|---|---|
| Hershey Bears.... | 34 | 30 | 8 | 76 | 274 | 248 |
| Springfield Kings.. | 31 | 33 | 8 | 70 | 247 | 275 |
| Providence Reds.. | 30 | 33 | 9 | 69 | 235 | 272 |
| Baltimore Clippers. | 28 | 34 | 10 | 66 | 235 | 255 |

### WESTERN DIVISION

|  | W | L | T | Pts. | GF | GA |
|---|---|---|---|---|---|---|
| Rochester Amer... | 38 | 25 | 9 | 85 | 273 | 233 |
| Quebec Aces...... | 33 | 28 | 11 | 77 | 277 | 240 |
| Buffalo Bisons.... | 32 | 28 | 12 | 76 | 239 | 223 |
| Cleveland Barons.. | 28 | 30 | 14 | 70 | 236 | 255 |

## ONTARIO JUNIOR LEAGUE
### Final Standings

|  | W | L | T | Pts. | GF | GA |
|---|---|---|---|---|---|---|
| Kitchener Rangers. | 38 | 10 | 6 | 82 | 326 | 175 |
| Montreal Canadiens | 39 | 12 | 3 | 81 | 261 | 170 |
| Hamilton Red Wgs. | 31 | 13 | 10 | 72 | 235 | 162 |
| Niagara Falls Flyers | 32 | 15 | 7 | 71 | 255 | 169 |
| Toronto Marlboros. | 31 | 17 | 6 | 68 | 273 | 179 |
| St. Catharines Black Hawks ... | 21 | 30 | 3 | 45 | 200 | 211 |
| London Nationals . | 17 | 31 | 6 | 40 | 177 | 262 |
| Peterboro Petes .. | 13 | 30 | 11 | 37 | 183 | 243 |
| Oshawa Generals.. | 12 | 37 | 5 | 29 | 177 | 310 |
| Ottawa 67's...... | 6 | 45 | 3 | 15 | 105 | 329 |

## WESTERN HOCKEY LEAGUE
### Final Standings

|  | W | L | T | Pts. | GF | GA |
|---|---|---|---|---|---|---|
| Portland Buckaroos | 40 | 26 | 6 | 86 | 246 | 168 |
| Seattle Totems .... | 35 | 30 | 7 | 77 | 297 | 199 |
| San Diego Gulls .. | 31 | 36 | 5 | 67 | 241 | 236 |
| Phoenix Road Run. | 28 | 40 | 4 | 60 | 215 | 276 |
| Vancouver Canucks | 26 | 41 | 5 | 57 | 213 | 258 |

## CENTRAL HOCKEY LEAGUE
### Final Standings
### NORTHERN DIVISION

|  | W | L | T | Pts. | GF | GA |
|---|---|---|---|---|---|---|
| Tulsa Oilers....... | 37 | 22 | 11 | 85 | 278 | 241 |
| Kansas City Blues. | 31 | 29 | 10 | 72 | 249 | 243 |
| Memphis So. Stars. | 24 | 34 | 12 | 60 | 206 | 244 |
| Omaha Knights .. | 14 | 46 | 10 | 38 | 167 | 272 |

### SOUTHERN DIVISION

|  | W | L | T | Pts. | GF | GA |
|---|---|---|---|---|---|---|
| Okla. City Blazers. | 38 | 20 | 12 | 88 | 245 | 174 |
| Ft. Worth Wings. . | 34 | 25 | 11 | 79 | 245 | 199 |
| Dallas Blk Hawks . | 30 | 29 | 11 | 71 | 230 | 251 |
| Houston Apollos... | 28 | 31 | 11 | 67 | 220 | 216 |

# Soccer in 1968
## North American Soccer League, 1968
### Final Standings

### Eastern Conference
#### Atlantic Division

|  | W | L | T | BP | Pts | GF | GA |
|---|---|---|---|---|---|---|---|
| Atlanta ......... | 18 | 7 | 6 | 48 | 174 | 50 | 32 |
| Washington ... | 15 | 10 | 7 | 56 | 167 | 63 | 53 |
| New York ..... | 12 | 8 | 12 | 56 | 164 | 62 | 54 |
| Baltimore ..... | 13 | 16 | 3 | 41 | 128 | 42 | 43 |
| Boston ........ | 9 | 17 | 6 | 49 | 121 | 51 | 69 |

#### Lakes Division

|  | W | L | T | BP | Pts | GF | GA |
|---|---|---|---|---|---|---|---|
| Cleveland ..... | 14 | 7 | 11 | 58 | 175 | 62 | 44 |
| Chicago ........ | 13 | 10 | 9 | 59 | 164 | 68 | 68 |
| Toronto ....... | 13 | 13 | 6 | 48 | 144 | 55 | 69 |
| Detroit ....... | 6 | 21 | 4 | 40 | 88 | 48 | 65 |

### Western Conference
#### Gulf Division

|  | W | L | T | BP | Pts | GF | GA |
|---|---|---|---|---|---|---|---|
| Kansas City ... | 16 | 11 | 5 | 47 | 158 | 61 | 43 |
| Houston ....... | 14 | 12 | 6 | 48 | 150 | 58 | 41 |
| St. Louis ...... | 12 | 14 | 6 | 40 | 130 | 47 | 59 |
| Dallas ......... | 2 | 26 | 4 | 28 | 52 | 28 | 109 |

#### Pacific Division

|  | W | L | T | BP | Pts | GF | GA |
|---|---|---|---|---|---|---|---|
| San Diego ...... | 18 | 8 | 6 | 60 | 186 | 65 | 38 |
| Oakland ........ | 18 | 8 | 6 | 59 | 185 | 71 | 38 |
| Los Angeles ... | 11 | 13 | 8 | 49 | 139 | 55 | 52 |
| Vancouver ..... | 12 | 15 | 5 | 49 | 136 | 51 | 60 |

Each victory worth 6 points. Tie—3 points. Loss—none. 1 Bonus Point (BP) awarded for each goal up to a maximum of 3 per game.
**Eastern Conference Championship**—Atlanta Defeated Cleveland 3 goals to 2 (2 games).
**Western Conference Championship**—San Diego defeated Kansas City 2 goals to 1 (2 games).
**Championship Series**—Atlanta defeated San Diego 3 goals to 0 (2 games).
**Attendance**—Total for 292 games, 1,550,588 (5,310 average per game).

### Leading Scorers

|  | GP | G | A | Pts |
|---|---|---|---|---|
| John Kowalik, Chi. .......... | 28 | 30 | 9 | 69 |
| Cirilo Fernandez, S. D. ...... | 29 | 30 | 7 | 67 |
| Ilija Mitic, Oak. ............ | 28 | 18 | 12 | 48 |
| Henri Klein, Van. .......... | 26 | 20 | 4 | 44 |
| Iris DeBrito, Tor. .......... | 24 | 21 | 2 | 44 |
| Eric Barber, K. C. .......... | 31 | 17 | 8 | 42 |
| Casey Frankiewicz, St. L. .... | 31 | 16 | 7 | 39 |
| Pete Sulincevski, Chi. ....... | 30 | 16 | 7 | 39 |
| Carlos Metidieri, L. A. ....... | 32 | 16 | 5 | 37 |
| Enrique Mateos, Clev. ....... | 31 | 16 | 4 | 36 |
| Selimir Milosevic, Oak. ...... | 22 | 17 | 1 | 35 |
| Dieter Perau, N. Y. ......... | 32 | 13 | 7 | 33 |

### International Matches Sponsored by NASL Teams in NASL Cities

Feb. 17 at Vancouver—Bonsucesso (Argentina 3, Vancouver 1.
Feb. 25 at Vancouver—Racing (Argentina) 4, Vancouver 0.
Mar. 3 at San Francisco—Guadalajara (Mexico) 1, Oakland 0 (OT).
Mar. 24 at San Diego—San Diego 5, Club America (Mexico) 1.
May 27 at Atlanta—Atlanta 3, Manchester City (England) 1.
May 30 at Kansas City—Kansas City 1, Dunfermline (Scotland) 1.
June 9 at Oakland—Oakland 3, Manchester City 0.
Dunfermline 3, St. Louis 1.
June 13 at Kansas City—Borussia Dortmund (Germany) 3, Kansas city 1.
June 15 at Atlanta—Atlanta 3, Manchester City 1.

June 19 at Vancouver—Borussia Dortmund 2, Vancouver 1.
June 21 at New York—Santos (Brazil) 4, Napoli (Italy) 2.
June 28 at Toronto—Santos 5, Napoli 2.
June 30 at St. Louis—Santos 3, St. Louis 2.
July 4 at Kansas City—Santos 4, Kansas City 1.
July 8 at Boston—Santos 7, Boston 1.
July 10 at Cleveland—Cleveland 2, Santos 1.
July 11 at New York—New York 5, Santos 3.
July 14 at Washington—Santos 3, Washington 1.
July 19 at Chicago—Gornik-Zabrze 3, Chicago 2.
Aug. 21 at New York—Real Madrid 4, New York 1.
Aug. 28 at Atlanta—Santos 6, Atlanta 2.
Aug. 30 at Oakland—Santos 3, Oakland 1.
Sept. 1 at New York—Santos 3, Benfica 3.
Sept. 22 at Oakland—Oakland 2, Israel national team 1.

## The World Cup

The World Cup, emblematic of international soccer supremacy, was won by England on July 20, 1966, by defeating West Germany, 4-2 in overtime. For this eighth tournament, 14 teams besides England and West Germany were entered. The others were Argentina, Bulgaria, Chile, France, Hungary, No. Korea, Mexico, Portugal, Spain, Switzerland, the Soviet Union, Italy, Uruguay and Brazil. Winners and sites of previous World Cup play follow:

| Year | Winner | Site | Year | Winner | Site |
|---|---|---|---|---|---|
| 1930 | Uruguay | Uruguay | 1954 | W. Germany | Switzerland |
| 1934 | Italy | Italy | 1958 | Brazil | Sweden |
| 1938 | Italy | France | 1962 | Brazil | Chile |
| 1950 | Uruguay | Brazil | 1966 | England | England |

# Table Tennis Championships in 1968
## 38TH UNITED STATES OPEN CHAMPIONSHIPS
### Detroit, Mich., Mar. 15-17

**Men's Singles**—Dal Joon Lee, Columbus, Ohio.
**Women's Singles**—Vi Nesukaitis, Toronto.
**Mixed Doubles**—Dell Sweeris & Connie Sweeris, Grand Rapids, Mich.
**Women's Doubles**—Barbara Kaminsky, Lanham, Md. & Vi Nesukaitis, Toronto.
**Men's Doubles**—Bernie Bukiet, New York & Dell Sweeris, Grand Rapids, Mich.
**Senior Women Over 40**—Velta Adminis, Toronto.
**Senior Men Over 40**—Chuck Burns, Detroit.
**Esquire Men Over 50**—Max Marinko, Toronto.
**Sr. Esquire Men Over 60**—Simon Ratner, Silver Spring, Md.
**Sr. Men's Doubles Over 40**—Bernie Bukiet, New York & Fran Delaney, Stratford, Conn.
**Esquire Men's Doubles Over 50**—Sol Schiff, New York & Bill Cross, North Brunswick, N. J.

**Junior Boys Under 17**—Surasek Koakiettavecchi, Thailand.
**Boys Under 15**—Mitchell Sealtiel, Trenton, N. J.
**Boys Under 13**—Gary Adelman, Roslyn, N. Y.
**Junior Miss Under 17**—Vi Nesukaitis, Toronto.
**Girls Under 15**—Wendy Hicks, Santa Barbara, Calif.
**Girls Under 13**—Angelita Rosal, San Diego, Calif.
**Boys Doubles Under 17**—Dan LeBaron, Grand Rapids, Mich. & John Tannehill, Middleport, Ohio.
**Boys Doubles Under 15**—Alton Everett, Phoenix & Raymond Martinez, San Diego, Calif.
**Boys Doubles Under 13**—John Quick, Orlando, Fla. & Chris Sylvan, Ft. Lauderdale, Fla.
**Junior Miss Doubles Under 17**—Vi Nesukaitis, Toronto & Shirley Gero, Montreal.
**Junior Mixed Doubles Under 17**—Bob Bisno, L. A. & Vi Nesukaitis, Toronto.

# Badminton Championships in 1968
## UNITED STATES OPEN CHAMPIONS
### Fullerton, Calif., Apr. 10-13

**Men's Singles**—Channarong Ratanasaengsuang, Thailand, def. Jim Poole, Louisiana, 15-7, 15-11.
**Men's Doubles**—Don Paup, California & Jim Poole, Louisiana, def. Eiichi Sakai & Takeshi Miyanaga, Japan, 15-8, 15-18, 17-15.
**Woman's Singles**—Miss Tyna Barinaga, Arizona, def. Miss Dot O'Neil, Connecticut, 11-2, 11-6.

**Women's Doubles**—Mrs. Helen Tibbetts, California & Miss Tyna Barinaga, Arizona, def. Miss Doris Haase & Mrs. Lois Alston, California, 15-4, 8-15, 15-12.
**Mixed Doubles**—Larry Saben & Mrs. Carlene Starkey, California, def. Jim Poole, Louisiana, & Miss Tyna Barinaga, Arizona, 15-5, 15-4.

### ALL-ENGLAND WORLD CHAMPIONSHIPS
### Wembley, England, March 20-23

**Men's Singles**—Rudy Hartano, Indonesia, def. Tan Aik Huang, Malaysia, 15-12, 15-9.
**Men's Doubles**—Erland Kops & Henning Borch, Denmark, def. Ng Boon Bee & Tan Yee Khan, Malaysia, 15-6, 15-4.
**Women's Singles**—Mrs. Eva Twedberg, Sweden, def. Miss Minarni, Indonesia, 11-6, 11-2.

**Women's Doubles**—Miss Minarni & Miss Retno Koestijah, Indonesia, def. Miss Noriko Takagi & Miss Hiroe Amano, Japan, 15-5, 15-8.
**Mixed Doubles**—Tony Jordan & Miss Sue Pound, England, def. Robert McCoig & Mrs. Muriel Woodcock, Scotland, 15-6, 15-6.

# Archery Championships in 1968
## 23rd ANNUAL NATIONAL FIELD ARCHERY CHAMPIONSHIP TOURNAMENT
### Salinas, Calif., July 29-Aug. 2

**Bare Bow**

**Open Men**—David Hughes, Irving, Texas, 2593.
**Amateur Men**—Norman Coon, Otis A.F.B. Mass., 2397.
**Open Women**—Mary Ellen Durham, Ft. Pierce, Fla., 1964.
**Amateur Women**—Eunice Schewe, Roscoe, Ill., 2038.
**Youth Boy**—Chris Labucki, Westfield, Mass., 2216.
**Youth Girl**—Rosemary Peterson, Jersey City, N. J., 1773.

**Freestyle**

**Open Men**—Clarence Kozlowski, Coalinga, Calif., 2615.
**Amateur Men**—Don Snipes, Spring Valley, Calif., 2524.
**Open Women**—Ann Butz, Suffern, New York, 2384.
**Amateur Women**—Diane Vetrecin, Chula Vista, Calif., 2277.
**Youth Boy**—Stephen Lieberman, Reading, Pa., 2515.
**Youth Girl**—Megan MacDonald, Anaheim, Calif., 1433.

### NATIONAL ARCHERY ASSOCIATION CHAMPIONSHIP

**Men's Amateur**—Hardy Ward, Mt. Pleasant, Tex.
**Intermediate Boys**—Dennis Israel, Sheridan, Ind.
**Junior Boy**—Judd Myers, Waterloo, Iowa.
**Cadet Boy**—George C. Ruth, Columbia, Pa.

**Women's Amateur**—Victoria L. Cook, Minneapolis, Minn.
**Intermediate Girl**—Cynthia E. Slade, Oxford, Miss.
**Junior Girl**—Pamela Slade, Oxford, Miss.

# Crane Wins Pocket Billiard Championship

Irving Crane of Rochester, N. Y., won his fourth world pocket billiard championship by defeating Luther Lassiter, the defending champion, in a playoff match at the Statler Hilton Hotel, N. Y., on Apr. 20, 1968. Crane was awarded $3,000 for his victory. Lassiter's second-place finish netted him $1,500. The following is the final standing of the championship event.

| | W | L | | W | L |
|---|---|---|---|---|---|
| Irving Crane, Rochester, N. Y. | 11 | 3 | Jack Colavita, West Caldwell, N. J. | 6 | 8 |
| Luther Lassiter, Elizabeth City, N. C. | 11 | 3 | Danny Gartner, Newark, N. J. | 5 | 9 |
| Steve Mizerak, Jr., Perth Amboy, N. J. | 10 | 4 | Jimmy Relihan, Springfield, Mass. | 5 | 9 |
| Frank McGown, Brooklyn, N. Y. | 10 | 4 | Cicero Murphy, Brooklyn, N. Y. | 4 | 10 |
| Lou Butera, West Pittston, Pa. | 9 | 5 | Petey Margo, Union City, N. J. | 3 | 11 |
| Joe Balsis, Minersville, Pa. | 9 | 5 | Bill Amodeo, Baldwin, L. I. | 3 | 11 |
| Art Cranfield, Syracuse, N. Y. | 8 | 6 | Onofrio Lauri, Seaford, L. I. | 3 | 11 |
| Dallas West, Rockford, Ill. | 7 | 7 | | | |

# Helms World Trophy Winners

The Helms World Trophy Award, instituted in 1949, recognizing the six foremost amateur athletes of the six continents, is an annual project of the Helms Athletic Foundation, Los Angeles, Calif. Selections are retroactive to 1896, year of the first modern Olympiads. The trophy itself, made of bronze, silver and gold and standing six feet high, bears the names of those honored. Those chosen receive silver plaques commemorating their recognition.

### WORLD TROPHY WINNERS, 1967

| Continent | Winner | Country | Sport |
|---|---|---|---|
| North America | Randy Matson | United States | Track and Field |
| South America | Jose Silvio Fiolo | Brazil | Swimming |
| Europe | Liesel Westermann | West Germany | Track and Field |
| Africa | Naftali Temu | Kenya | Track and Field |
| Asia | Kenji Kimihara | Japan | Marathon |
| Australasia | Judy Pollock | Australia | Track and Field |

# World Swimming Records

### Approved by International Swimming Federation to Sept. 15, 1968

Under a F.I.N.A. decision of May 1, 1957, only records made in 55-yards or 50-meter pools are accepted as world marks. A number of new records await confirmation.

## MEN'S FREESTYLE

| Distance | Time | Holder | Country | Where made | Date |
|---|---|---|---|---|---|
| 100 meters | 0:52.6 | Ken Walsh | U.S.A. | Winnipeg, Canada | July 27, 1967 |
|  |  | Zac Zorn | U.S.A. | Long Beach, Calif. | Sept. 2, 1968 |
| 110 yards | 0:53.5 | R. B. McGregor | Gt. Britain | Blackpool, Eng. | Sept. 10, 1966 |
| 200 meters | 1:54.3 | Don Schollander | U.S.A. | Long Beach, Calif. | Aug. 30, 1968 |
| 220 yards | 1:57 | Don Schollander | U.S.A. | Vancouver, B. C. | Aug. 27, 1966 |
| 400 meters | 4:06.5 | Ralph Hutton | Canada | Lincoln, Nebr. | Aug. 1, 1968 |
| 440 yards | 4:12.2 | Greg Charlton | U.S.A. | Vancouver, B. C. | Aug. 26, 1966 |
| 800 meters | 8:34.3 | Mike Burton | U.S.A. | Long Beach, Calif. | Sept. 3, 1968 |
| 880 yards | 8:55.5 | Murray Rose | Australia | Vancouver, B. C. | Sept. 5, 1964 |
| 1,500 meters | 16:08.5 | Mike Burton | U.S.A. | Long Beach, Calif. | Sept. 3, 1968 |
| 1,650 yards | 17:11.0 | Jon Konrads | Australia | Sydney, Aust. | Feb. 27, 1960 |

## MEN'S BREASTSTROKE—SURFACE STROKE

| | | | | | |
|---|---|---|---|---|---|
| 100 meters | 1:06.2 | Nikolai Pankin | USSR. | Moscow, USSR | Apr. 18, 1968 |
| 110 yards | 1:08.2 | Ian O'Brien | Australia | Kingston, Jamaica | Aug. 12, 1966 |
| 200 meters | 2:27.4 | Vladimir Kosinsky | USSR. | Kalev, Estonia | Apr. 3, 1968 |
| 220 yards | 2:28 | Ian O'Brien | Australia | Kingston, Jamaica | Aug. 6, 1966 |

## MEN'S BUTTERFLY

| | | | | | |
|---|---|---|---|---|---|
| 100 meters | 0:55.6 | Mark Spitz | U.S.A. | Long Beach, Calif. | Aug. 30, 1968 |
| 110 yards | 0:56.3 | Mark Spitz | U.S.A. | London, Eng. | Sept. 30, 1967 |
| 200 meters | 2:05.7 | Mark Spitz | U.S.A. | Berlin, Germany | Oct. 8, 1967 |
| 220 yards | 2:08.4 | Kevin Berry | Australia | Sydney, Aust. | Jan. 12, 1963 |

## MEN'S BACKSTROKE

| | | | | | |
|---|---|---|---|---|---|
| 100 meters | 0:58.4 | Roland Matthes | E. Germany | Leipzig, E. Germany | Sept. 21, 1967 |
| 110 yards | 1:00.1 | Roland Matthes | E. Germany | Leipzig, E. Germany | Sept. 20, 1967 |
| 200 meters | 2:07.5 | Roland Matthes | E. Germany | Leipzig, E. Germany | Aug. 14, 1968 |
| 220 yards | 2:12 | Peter Reynolds | Australia | Kingston, Jamaica | Aug. 9, 1966 |

## MEN'S INDIVIDUAL MEDLEY

| | | | | | |
|---|---|---|---|---|---|
| 200 meters | 2:10.6 | Charles Hickcox | U.S.A. | Long Beach, Calif. | Aug. 31, 1968 |
| 400 meters | 4:39.0 | Charles Hickcox | U.S.A. | Long Beach, Calif. | Aug. 30, 1968 |
| 440 yards | 4:46.8 | Michael Holthaus | W. Germany | London, Eng. | Aug. 20, 1968 |

## MEN'S FREESTYLE RELAYS

| | | | | | |
|---|---|---|---|---|---|
| 400 m. (4x100) | 3:32.5 | Nat'l team (Zorn, Rerych, Walsh, Schollander) | U.S.A. | Long Beach, Calif. | Sept. 3, 1968 |
| 440 yds. (4x110) | 3:35.6 | Nat'l team (Wenden, Dickson, Ryan, Windle) | Australia | Kingston, Jamaica | Aug. 11, 1966 |
| 800 m. (4x200) | 7:52.1 | Nat'l team (Clark, Saari, Ilman, Schollander) | U.S.A. | Tokyo, Japan | Oct. 18, 1964 |
| 880 yds. (4x220) | 7:59.5 | Nat'l team (Wenden, Reynolds, Dickson, Windle) | Australia | Kingston, Jamaica | Aug. 5, 1966 |

## MEN'S MEDLEY RELAYS

| | | | | | |
|---|---|---|---|---|---|
| 400 m. (4x100) | 3:56.5 | Nat'l team (Matthes, Henninger, Gregor, Weigand) | E. Germany | Leipzig, E. Germany | Nov. 8, 1967 |
| 440 yds. (4x110) | 4:03.2 | Nat'l team (Reynolds, O'Brien, Dunn, Wenden) | Australia | Kingston, Jamaica | Aug. 12, 1966 |

## WOMEN'S FREESTYLE

| | | | | | |
|---|---|---|---|---|---|
| 100 meters | 0:58.9 | Dawn Fraser | Australia | Sydney, Aust. | Feb. 29, 1964 |
| 110 yards | 0:59.5 | Dawn Fraser | Australia | Melbourne, Aust. | Nov. 24, 1962 |
| 200 meters | 2:06.7 | Debbie Meyer | U.S.A. | Los Angeles, Calif. | Aug. 24, 1968 |
| 220 yards | 2:11.6 | Dawn Fraser | Australia | Sydney, Aust. | Feb. 27, 1960 |
| 400 meters | 4:24.5 | Debbie Meyer | U.S.A. | Los Angeles, Calif. | Aug. 25, 1968 |
| 440 yards | 4:38.8 | Kathy Wainwright | Australia | Kingston, Jamaica | Aug. 12, 1966 |
| 800 meters | 9:10.4 | Debbie Meyer | U.S.A. | Los Angeles, Calif. | Aug. 28, 1968 |
| 880 yards | 9:44.1 | Debbie Meyer | U.S.A. | London, England | Sept. 30, 1967 |
| 1,500 meters | 17:31.2 | Debbie Meyer | U.S.A. | Los Angeles, Calif. | July 21, 1968 |
| 1,650 yards | 18:47.8 | Angela Coughlan | Canada | Hamilton, Ont. | July 27, 1968 |

## WOMEN'S BREASTSTROKE—SURFACE STROKE

| | | | | | |
|---|---|---|---|---|---|
| 100 meters | 1:14.2 | Catie Ball | U.S.A. | Los Angeles, Calif. | Aug. 25, 1968 |
| 110 yards | 1:17 | Catie Ball | U.S.A. | London, Eng. | Sept. 30, 1967 |
| 200 meters | 2:38.5 | Catie Ball | U.S.A. | Los Angeles, Calif. | Aug. 26, 1968 |
| 220 yards | 2:46.9 | Catie Ball | U.S.A. | London, Eng. | Sept. 30, 1967 |

## WOMEN'S BUTTERFLY

| Distance | Time | Holder | Country | Where made | Date |
|---|---|---|---|---|---|
| 100 meters | 1:04.5 | Ada Kok | Netherlands | Budapest | Aug. 14, 1965 |
| 110 yards | 1:05.1 | Ada Kok | Netherlands | Blackpool, Eng. | May 30, 1967 |
| 200 meters | 2:21 | Ada Kok | Netherlands | Blackpool, Eng. | Aug. 25, 1967 |
| 220 yards | 2:21 | Ada Kok | Netherlands | Blackpool, Eng. | Aug. 25, 1967 |

## WOMEN'S BACKSTROKE

| | | | | | |
|---|---|---|---|---|---|
| 100 meters | 1:06.4 | Karen Muir | So. Africa | Montreuil, France | Apr. 6, 1968 |
| 110 yards | 1:06.7 | Karen Muir | So. Africa | Kimberley, S. Africa | Jan. 30, 1968 |
| 200 meters | 2:23.8 | Karen Muir | So. Africa | Los Angeles, Calif. | July 21, 1968 |
| 220 yards | 2:24.1 | Karen Muir | So. Africa | Kimberley, S. Africa | Jan. 29, 1968 |

**World Swimming Records continued**     **WOMEN'S INDIVIDUAL MEDLEY**

| | | | | | |
|---|---|---|---|---|---|
| 200 meters | 2:23.4 | Claudia Kolb | U. S. A. | Los Angeles, Calif. | Aug. 25, 1968 |
| 400 meters | 5:04.7 | Claudia Kolb | U. S. A. | Los Angeles, Calif. | Aug. 24, 1968 |
| 440 yards | 5:25.1 | Mary Ellen Olcese | U. S. A. | Cardiff, Wales | Aug. 21, 1965 |

**WOMEN'S FREESTYLE RELAYS**

| | | | | | |
|---|---|---|---|---|---|
| 400 m. (4x100) | 4:03.5 | Santa Clara, S. C. (Gustavson, Ryan, Fritz, Watson) | U. S. A. | Philadelphia, Pa. | Aug. 19, 1967 |
| 440 yds. (4x110) | 4:10.8 | Nat'l team (Tanner, Hughes, Kennedy, Lay) | Canada | Kingston, Jamaica | Aug. 5, 1966 |

**WOMEN'S MEDLEY RELAYS**

| | | | | | |
|---|---|---|---|---|---|
| 400 m. (4x00) | 4:30 | Nat'l team (Moore, Ball, Daniel, Fordyce) | U. S. A. | Winnipeg, Canada | July 30, 1967 |
| 440 yds. (4x110) | 4:37.4 | Nat'l team (Watson, Ball, Daniel, Barkman) | U. S. A. | London, Eng. | Sept. 30, 1967 |

# Swimming Championships in 1968

## MEN'S NATIONAL AAU SHORT COURSE CHAMPIONSHIPS
### Greenville, N. C., Apr. 11-13

**100 Yd.** Freestyle—Don Havens, USC. **Time—0:45.67.**

**200 Yd.** Freestyle—Bill Burrell, Indiana. **Time—1:43.46.**

**500 Yd.** Freestyle—Trevor Charlton, Pasadena City College. **Time—4:37.29.**

**1,650 Yd.** Freestyle—Mike Burton, Arden Hills. **Time—16:04.56.**

**100 Yd.** Breaststroke—Ken Merten, LAAC. **Time—0:58.83.**

**200 Yd.** Breaststroke—Brian Job. **Time—2:08.00.**

**100 Yd.** Backstroke—Charles Hickcox, Indiana. **Time—0:52.51.**

**200 Yd.** Backstroke—Charles Hickcox. **Time—1:54.93.**

**100 Yd.** Butterfly—Mark Spitz. **Time—0:49.72.**

**200 Yd.** Butterfly—Mark Spitz. **Time—1:51.50.**

**200 Yd.** Individual Medley—Charles Hickcox. **Time—1:53.30.**

**400 Yd.** Individual Medley—Gary Hall. **Time—4:10.07.**

**400 Yd.** Medley Relay—Yale (Bettendorf, Buckley, Waples, Job) **Time—3:30.41.**

**400 Yd.** Freestyle Relay—Phillips 66 (MacMillan, Hammer, Grimm, Zorn). **Time—3:04.70.**

**800 Yd.** Freestyle Relay—Indiana (Burrell, Windle, Utley, Hickcox). **Time—6:55.11.**

## WOMEN'S NATIONAL AAU SHORT COURSE CHAMPIONSHIPS
### Pittsburgh, Pa., Apr. 17-20

**100 Yd.** Freestyle—Jane Barkman, Vesper BC. **Time—0:52.1.**

**200 Yd.** Freestyle—Debbie Meyer, Arden Hills. **Time—1:52.1.**

**500 Yd.** Freestyle—Debbie Meyer. **Time—4:54.1.**

**1,650 Yd.** Freestyle—Debbie Meyer. **Time—17:04.4.**

**100 Yt.** Breaststroke—Jan Henne, Santa Clara SC. **Time—1:07.0.**

**200 Yd.** Breaststroke—Sharon Wickman, Olympic Club. **Time—2:25.2.**

**100 Yd.** Backstroke—Kaye Hall, Tacoma SC. **Time—0:59.3.**

**200 Yd.** Backstroke—Kaye Hall. **Time—2:10.8.**

**100 Yd.** Butterfly—Ellie Daniel, Vesper BC. **Time—0:58.2.**

**200 Yd.** Butterfly—Ellie Daniel. **Time—2:06.6.**

**200 Yd.** Individual Medley—Claudia Kolb, Santa Clara SC. **Time—2:08.5.**

**400 Yd.** Individual Medley—Claudia Kolb. **Time—4:32.2.**

**400 Yd.** Medley Relay—Santa Clara SC (Swaggerty, Henne, Kolb, Gustavson). **Time—4:02.4.**

**400 Yd.** Freestyle Relay—Santa Clara SC (Henne, Watson, Ryan, Gustavson). **Time—3:32.6.**

**800 Yd.** Freestyle Relay—Santa Clara SC (Gustavson, Henne, Ryan, Kolb). **Time—7:42.7.**

## NATIONAL AAU LONG COURSE CHAMPIONSHIPS
### Lincoln, Nebr., Aug. 1-4

**Men**

**100 Meter** Freestyle—Mark Spitz, Santa Clara SC. **Time—0:53.6.**

**200 Meter** Freestyle—Mark Spitz. **Time—1:57.**

**400 Meter** Freestyle—Ralph Hutton, Foothills AC, Calif. **Time—4:06.5.**

**1500 Meter** Freestyle—Mike Burton, Arden Hills. **Time—16:29.4.**

**200 Meter** Backstroke—Jack Horsley, Red Shield Triton SC. **Time—2:12.2.**

**100 Meter** Breaststroke—Mike Dirksen, Oregon. **Time—1:08.8.**

**100 Meter** Butterfly—Mark Spitz. **Time—0:57.**

**200 Meter** Individual Medley—Juan Bello, Peru. **Time—2:14.1.**

**400 Meter** Individual Medley—Gary Hall, Phillips 66. **Time—4:48.**

**400 Meter** Medley Relay—Santa Clara SC (Haywood, Job, Spitz, Schollander). **Time—4:00.3.**

**400 Meter** Freestyle Relay—Los Angeles AC (Johnson, Kidder, Saari, Havens). **Time—3:35.3.**

**Team Champion**—Santa Clara SC, 168 points.

**Women**

**100 Meter** Freestyle—Jane Barkman, Vesper BC, Philadelphia. **Time—1:00.1.**

**200 Meter** Freestyle—Eadie Wetzel, Lake Forest SC. **Time—2:08.8.**

**400 Meter** Freestyle—Debbie Meyer, Arden Hills, Calif. **Time—4:26.7.**

**1500 Meter** Freestyle—Debbie Meyer. **Time—17:38.5.**

**100 Meter** Breaststroke—Catie Ball, Jacksonville, Fla. **Time—1:15.7.**

**200 Meter** Backstroke—Karen Muir, So. Africa. **Time—2:24.3.**

**100 Meter** Butterfly—Ellie Daniel, Vesper BC. **Time—1:06.9.**

**200 Meter** Individual Medley—Claudia Kolb, Santa Clara SC. **Time—2:27.5.**

**400 Meter** Individual Medley—Sue Pedersen, Arden Hills, Calif. **Time—5:10.3.**

**400 Meter** Medley Relay—Santa Clara SC (Swaggerty, Henne, Kolb, Gustavson). **Time—4:33.8.**

**400 Meter** Freestyle Relay—Santa Clara SC. **Time—4:02.1.**

**Team Champion**—Santa Clara SC, 201 points.

# National AAU Indoor Diving Championships in 1968

### Held at Greenville & Pittsburgh during Swimming Championships

**Men**

**One-Meter Diving**—Jim Henry, Indiana Aquatic Club. 485. 5 pts.

**Three-Meter Diving**—Win Young, Indiana Aquatic Club. 456.15 pts.

**Ten-Meter Diving**—Larry Andreason, Los Alamitos, Calif. 445.38 pts.

**Women**

**One-Meter Diving**—Keala O'Sullivan, Oahu, Hawaii. 415.89 pts.

**Three-Meter Diving**—Lesley Bush, Princeton, N. J. 407.01 pts.

**Platform Diving**—Lesley Bush, Princeton, N. J. 288.29 pts.

# 1968 Winter Olympic Games

**Grenoble, France, Feb. 6-18**

A record total of 1,272 men and women athletes from 37 nations participated in 35 events in the tenth Winter Olympic Games held at Grenoble, France.

### MEDAL STANDINGS

| | Gold | Silver | Bronze |
|---|---|---|---|
| Norway | 6 | 6 | 2 |
| Soviet Union | 5 | 5 | 3 |
| France | 4 | 3 | 2 |
| Italy | 4 | 0 | 0 |
| Austria | 3 | 4 | 4 |
| Netherlands | 3 | 3 | 3 |
| Sweden | 3 | 2 | 3 |
| West Germany | 2 | 2 | 3 |
| United States | 1 | 5 | 1 |
| Finland | 1 | 2 | 2 |
| East Germany | 1 | 2 | 2 |
| Czechoslovakia | 1 | 2 | 1 |
| Canada | 1 | 1 | 1 |
| Switzerland | 0 | 2 | 4 |
| Romania | 0 | 0 | 1 |

### FIGURE SKATING

**Men**—Wolfgang Schwartz, Austria, **1,904.1 pts.;** Tim Wood, U.S.A., **1,891.6 pts.;** 3, Patrick Pera, France, **1,864.5 pts.**

**Women**—Peggy Fleming, U.S.A., **1,970.5 pts.;** Gabiele Seyfert, E. Germany, **1,882.3 pts.;** Hana Maskova, Czech., **1,828.8 pts.**

**Pairs**—Ludmila Beloussova & Oleg Protopopov, USSR, **315 pts.;** Tatiana Joukchestervina & Alexandre Gorelik, USSR, **312.3 pts.;** Margot Glockshuber & Wolfgang Danne, W. Germany, **304.4 pts.**

### SPEED SKATING—MEN

**500 Meters**—Erhard Keller, W. Germany; Magne Thomassen, Norway and Terry McDermott, U.S.A. (tie for second). **Time—0:40.3.**

**1,500 Meters**—Cornelis Verberk, Holland; Art Schenk, Holland and Ivar Eriksen, Norway (tie for second). **Time—2:03.4.**

**5,000 Meters**—F. Anton Maier, Norway; Cornelis Verberk, Holland; Petrus Nottet, Holland. **Time—7:22.4.**

**10,000 Meters**—Johnny Hoeglin, Sweden; F. Anton Maier, Norway; Derjan Sandler, Sweden. **Time—15:23.6.**

### SPEED SKATING—WOMEN

**500 Meters**—Ludmila Titova, USSR; Mary Meyers, U.S.A., Dianne Holum, U.S.A. and Jennifer Fish, U.S.A. (3 way tie for second). **Time—0:46.1.**

**1,000 Meters**—Carolina Geijssen, Holland; Ludmila Titova, USSR; Dianne Holum, U.S.A. **Time—1:32.6.**

**1,500 Meters**—Kaija Mustonen, Finland; Carolina Geijssen, Holland; Christina Kaiser, Holland. **Time—2:22.4.**

**3,000 Meters**—Johanna Schut, Holland; Kaija Mustonen, Finland; Christina Kaiser, Holland. **Time—4.56.2.**

### SKIING—MEN

**Downhill**—Jean Claude Killy, France; Guy Perillat, France; J. Daniel Daetwyler, Switzerland. **Time—1:59.85.**

**Slalom**—Jean Claude Killy, France; T. Herbert Huber, Austria; Alfred Matt, Austria. **Time—99.73.**

**Giant Slalom**—Jean Claude Killy, France; Willy Favre, Switzerland; Heinrich Messner, Austria. **Time—3:29.28.**

**15 Km. Cross Country**—Harald Groenningen, Norway; Erro Maentyranta, Finland; Gunnar Larsson, Sweden. **Time—47:54.2.**

**30 Km. Cross Country**—Franco Nones, Italy; Odd Martinsen, Norway; Erro Maentyranta, Finland. **Time—1:35:39.2.**

**50 Km. Cross Country**—Ole Ellefsaeter, Norway; Vlatches Vedenine, USSR; Josef Haas, Switzerland. **Time—2:28:45.8.**

**90 Meter Jumping**—Vladimir Beloussov, USSR; Jiri Raska, Czech.; Lars Grini, Norway. **Points—231.3.**

**70 Meter Jumping**—Jiri Raska, Czech.; Reinhold Bachler, Austria; Baldur Premil, Austria. **Points—216.5.**

**15 Km. Cross Country & 70 Meter Jump**—Franz Keller, W. Germany; Alois Kaelin, Switzerland; Andreas Kunz, E. Germany. **Points—449.04.**

**40 Km. Relay**—Norway (Martinsen, Tyldum, Groenningen, Ellefsaeter); Sweden; Finland. **Time—2:08:33.5.**

**Biathlon**—Magnar Solberg, Norway; Alexandre Tikhonov, USSR; Vladimir Goundartsev, USSR. **Time—1:13:45.9.**

**Biathlon Relay**—USSR (Tikhonov, Pousanov, Mamatov, Goundartsev); **Norway; Sweden. Time—2:13:02.4.**

### SKIING—WOMEN

**Downhill**—Olga Pall, Austria; Isabelle Mir, France; Christl Haas, Austria. **Time—1:40.87.**

**Slalom**—Marielle Goitschel, France; Nancy Greene, Canada; Annie Famose, France. **Time—85.86.**

**Giant Slalom**—Nancy Greene, Canada; Annie Famose, France; Fernande Bochatay, Switzerland. **Time—1:51.97.**

**5 Km. Cross Country**—Toini Gustafsson, Sweden; Galina Koulakova, USSR; Alevtina Koltchina, USSR. **Time—16:45.2.**

**10 Km. Cross Country**—Toini Gustafsson, Sweden; Berit Moerdre, Norway; Inger Aufles, Norway. **Time—36:46.5.**

**15 Km. Relay**—Norway (Aufles, Damon, Moerdre); Sweden; USSR. **Time—57:30.**

### BOBSLEIGH

**Two-Man**—Italy (Eugenio Monti, Luciano De-Paolis); W. Germany; Rumania. **Time—4:41.54.**

**Four-Man**—Italy (Eugenio Monti, Luciano De-Paolis, Roberto Zandonella, Mario Armano); Austria; Switzerland. **Time—2:17.39.**

### LUGE

**Men's Single**—Manfred Schmid, Austria; Thomas Koehler, E. Germany; Klaus Bonsack, E. Germany. **Time—2:52.48** (3 runs).

**Men's Doubles**—Klaus Bonsack & Thomas Koehler, E. Germany; Manfred Schmid & Ewald Walch, Austria; Wolfgang Winkler & Fritz Nachmann, W. Germany. **Time—1:35.85** (2 runs).

**Woman's Single**—Erica Lechner, Italy; Christa Schmuck, W. Germany; Angelika Duenhaupt, W. Germany. **Time—2:28.66** (3 runs).

### ICE HOCKEY

1, USSR (6 wins, 1 loss); 2, Czech (5 wins, 1 tie, 1 loss); 3, Canada (5 wins, 2 losses).

# Olympic Winter Games Champions, 1924-1968

## SITES AND UNOFFICIAL WINNERS OF GAMES

**1924—Chamonix, France (Norway)**
**1928—St. Moritz, Switzerland (Norway)**
**1932—Lake Placid, N. Y. (U. S.)**
**1936—Garmisch-Partenkirchen (Norway)**
**1948—St. Moritz (Sweden)**
1952—Oslo, Norway **(Norway)**
1956—Cortina d'Ampezzo, Italy **(USSR)**
1960—Squaw Valley, Calif. **(USSR)**
1964—Innsbruck, Austria (USSR)
1968—Grenoble, France (Norway)
1972—Sapporo, Japan (scheduled)

### BIATHLON

| | Time |
|---|---|
| 1960—Klas Lestander, Sweden | 1:33:21.6 |
| 1964—Vladimir Melanin, USSR | 1:20:26.8 |
| 1968—Magnar Solberg, Norway | 1:13:45.9 |

### BOBSLEDDING

#### 4-MAN BOB

| (Driver in parentheses) | Time |
|---|---|
| 1924—Switzerland (Edward Scherrer) | 5:45.54 |
| *1928—United States (William Fiske) | 3:20.5 |
| 1932—United States (William Fiske) | 7:53.68 |
| 1936—Switzerland (Pierre Musy) | 5:19.85 |
| 1948—United States (Edward Rimkus) | 5:20.1 |
| 1952—Germany (Andreas Ostler) | 5:07.84 |
| 1956—Switzerland (Franz Kapus) | 5:10.44 |
| 1964—Canada (Victor Emery) | 4:14.46 |
| 1968—Italy (Eugenio Monti) | 2:17.39 |

*Five-man bobsled

#### 2-MAN BOB

| | Time |
|---|---|
| 1932—U.S.A. (Hubert Stevens) | 8:14.74 |
| 1936—U.S.A. (Ivan Brown) | 5:29.29 |
| 1948—Switzerland (F. Endrich) | 5:29.2 |
| 1952—Germany (Andreas Ostler) | 5:24.54 |
| 1956—Italy (Dalla Costa) | 5:30.14 |
| 1964—Great Britain (Antony Nash) | 4:21.90 |
| 1968—Italy (Eugenio Monti) | 4:41.54 |

### FIGURE SKATING

#### MEN'S SINGLES

1908—Ulrich Sachow, Sweden
1920—Gillis Grafström, Sweden
1924—Gillis Grafström, Sweden
1928—Gillis Grafström, Sweden
1932—Karl Schaefer, Austria
1936—Karl Schaefer, Austria
1948—Richard T. Button, U.S.A.
1952—Richard T. Button, U.S.A.
1956—Hayes Alan Jenkins, U.S.A.
1960—David W. Jenkins, U.S.A.
1964—Manfred Schnelldorfer, Germany
1968—Wolfgang Schwartz, Austria

#### WOMEN'S SINGLES

1908—Madge Syers, Great Britain

1920—Magda Julin-Mauroy, Sweden
1924—Mrs. Heima von Szabo-Planck, Austria
1928—Sonja Henie, Norway
1932—Sonja Henie, Norway
1936—Sonja Henie, Norway
1948—Barbara Ann Scott, Canada
1952—Jeanette Altwegg, Great Britain
1956—Tenley E. Albright, U.S.A.
1960—Carol Heiss, U.S.A.
1964—Sjoukje Dijkstra, Holland
1968—Peggy Fleming, U.S.A.

## PAIRS

1908—Anna Hübler & Heinrich Burger, Germany
1920—Ludovika & Walter Jakobsson, Finland
1924—Helene Engelman & Alfred Berger, Austria
1928—Andrée Joly & Pierre Brunet, France
1932—Andrée Joly & Pierre Brunet, France
1936—Maxie Herber & Ernest Baier, Germany
1948—Micheline Lannoy & Pierre Baugniet, Belgium
1952—Ria and Paul Falk, Germany
1956—Elizabeth Schwarz & Kurt Oppelt, Austria
1960—Barbara Wagner & Robert Paul, Canada
1964—Ludmila Beloussova & Oleg Protopopov, USSR
1968—Ludmila Beloussova & Oleg Protopopov, USSR

## ALPINE SKIING
### MEN'S DOWNHILL

| | | Time |
|---|---|---|
| 1948—Henri Oreiller, France | | 2:55.0 |
| 1952—Zeno Colo, Italy | | 2:30.8 |
| 1956—Anton Sailer, Austria | | 2:52.2 |
| 1960—Jean Vuarnet, France | | 2:06.0 |
| 1964—Egon Zimmermann, Austria | | 2:18.1 |
| 1968—Jean Claude Killy, France | | 1:59.85 |

### MEN'S GIANT SLALOM

| | | Time |
|---|---|---|
| 1952—Stein Eriksen, Norway | | 2:25.0 |
| 1956—Anton Sailer, Austria | | 3:00.1 |
| 1960—Roger Staub, Switzerland | | 1:48.3 |
| 1964—François Bonlieu, France | | 1:46.7 |
| 1968—Jean Claude Killy, France | | 99.73 |

### MEN'S SLALOM

| | | Time |
|---|---|---|
| 1948—Edi Reinalter, Switzerland | | 2:10.3 |
| 1952—Othmar Schneider, Austria | | 2:00.0 |
| 1956—Anton Sailer, Austria | | 194.7 pts. |
| 1960—Ernst Hinterseer, Austria | | 2:08.9 |
| 1964—Josef Stiegler, Austria | | 2:11.1 |
| 1968—Jean Claude Killy, France | | 3:29.28 |

### WOMEN'S DOWNHILL

| | | Time |
|---|---|---|
| 1948—Hedi Schlunegger, Switzerland | | 2:28.3 |
| 1952—Trude Jochum-Beiser, Austria | | 1:47.1 |
| 1956—Madeline Berthod, Switzerland | | 1:40.7 |
| 1960—Heidi Biebl, Germany | | 1:37.6 |
| 1964—Christl Haas, Austria | | 1:55.3 |
| 1968—Olga Pall, Austria | | 1:40.87 |

### WOMEN'S GIANT SLALOM

| | | Time |
|---|---|---|
| 1952—Andrea Mead Lawrence, U.S.A. | | 2:06.8 |
| 1956—Ossi Reichert, Germany | | 1:56.5 |
| 1960—Yvonne Ruegg, Switzerland | | 1:39.9 |
| 1964—Marielle Goitschel, France | | 1:52.2 |
| 1968—Marielle Goitschel, France | | 85.86 |

### WOMEN'S SLALOM

| | | Time |
|---|---|---|
| 1948—Gretchen Fraser, U.S.A. | | 1:57.2 |
| 1952—Andrea Mead Lawrence, U.S.A. | | 2:10.6 |
| 1956—Renée Colliard, Switzerland | | 112.3 pts. |
| 1960—Anne Heggtveigt, Canada | | 1:49.6 |
| 1964—Christine Goitschel, France | | 1:35.11 |
| 1968—Nancy Greene, Canada | | 1:51.97 |

## NORDIC SKIING
### MEN'S CROSS-COUNTRY EVENTS
#### 15 Kilometers (9.3 miles) or Equivalent

| | | Time |
|---|---|---|
| 1924—Thorleif Haug, Norway | | 1:14:31.0 |
| 1928—Johan Gröttumsbraaten, Norway | | 1:37:01.0 |
| 1932—Sven Utterström, Sweden | | 1:23:07.0 |
| 1936—Erik-August Larsson, Sweden | | 1:14:38.0 |
| 1948—Martin Lundström, Sweden | | 1:13:50.0 |
| 1956—Hallgeir Brenden, Norway | | 49:39.0 |
| 1960—Haakon Brusveen, Norway | | 51:55.0 |
| 1960—Haakon Brusveen, Norway | | 0:51:55.0 |
| 1964—Eero Mantyranta, Finland | | 1:30:50.7 |
| 1968—Harald Groenningen, Norway | | 47:54.2 |

(Note: Approx. 18-kilo course 1924-1952)

#### 30 Kilometers (18.6 miles)

| | | Time |
|---|---|---|
| 1956—Veikko Hakulinen, Finland | | 1:44:06.0 |
| 1960—Sixten Jernberg, Sweden | | 1:51:03.9 |
| 1964—Eero Mantyranta, Finland | | 50.54.1 |
| 1968—Franco Nones, Italy | | 1:35:39.2 |

#### 50 Kilometers (31 miles)

| | | Time |
|---|---|---|
| 1924—Thorleif Haug, Norway | | 3:44:32.0 |
| 1928—Per Erik Hedlund, Sweden | | 4:52:03.0 |
| 1932—Veli Saarinen, Finland | | 4:28:00.0 |
| 1936—Elis Viklund, Sweden | | 3:30:11.0 |
| 1948—Nils Karlsson, Sweden | | 3:47:48.0 |
| 1952—Veikko Hakulinen, Finland | | 3:33:33.0 |
| 1956—Sixten Jernberg, Sweden | | 2:50:27.0 |
| 1960—Kaleiv Hamalainen, Finland | | 2:59:06.3 |
| 1964—Sixten Jernberg, Sweden | | 2:43:52.6 |
| 1968—Ole Ellefsaeter, Norway | | 2:28:45.8 |

#### 40 Kil meter Cross-Country Relay

| | | Time |
|---|---|---|
| 1936—Finland, Norway, Sweden | | 2:41:33.0 |
| 1948—Sweden, Finland, Norway | | 2:32:08.0 |
| 1952—Finland, Norway, Sweden | | 2:20:16.0 |
| 1956—USSR, Finland, Sweden | | 2:15:30.0 |

| | | |
|---|---|---|
| 1960—Finland, Norway, USSR | | 2:18:45.6 |
| 1964—Sweden, Finland, USSR | | 2:18:34.6 |
| 1968—Norway, Sweden, Finland | | 2:08.33.5 |

#### 15 Km. Cross-Country & Jumping

| | | Points |
|---|---|---|
| 1924—Thorleif Haug, Norway | | 453.800 |
| 1928—Johan Gröttumsbraaten, Norway | | 427.800 |
| 1932—Johan Gröttumsbraaten, Norway | | 446.200 |
| 1936—Oddbjorn Hagen, Norway | | 430.300 |
| 1948—Heikki Hasu, Finland | | 448.800 |
| 1952—Simon Slattvik, Norway | | 451.621 |
| 1960—Sverre Stenersen, Norway | | 455.000 |
| 1960—Georg Thoma, Germany | | 457.952 |
| 1964—Tormod Knutsen, Norway | | 469.280 |
| 1968—Franz Keller, W. Germany | | 449.04 |

#### Ski Jumping (90 meters)

| | | Points |
|---|---|---|
| 1924—Jacob T. Thams, Norway | | 227.5 |
| 1928—Alfred Andersen, Norway | | 230.5 |
| 1932—Birger Ruud, Norway | | 228.0 |
| 1936—Birger Ruud, Norway | | 232.0 |
| 1948—Petter Hugsted, Norway | | 228.1 |
| 1952—A. Bergmann, Norway | | 226.0 |
| 1956—Antti Hyvarinen, Finland | | 227.0 |
| 1960—Helmut Recknagel, Germany | | 227.2 |
| 1964—Toralf Engan, Norway | | 230.7 |
| 1968—Vladimir Beloussov, USSR | | 231.3 |

#### Ski Jumping (70 meters)

| | | Points |
|---|---|---|
| 1964—Veikko Kankkonen, Finland | | 229.9 |
| 1968—Jiri Raska, Czech. | | 216.5 |

## WOMEN'S EVENTS
### 5 Kilometers (approx. 3.1 miles)

| | | Time |
|---|---|---|
| 1964—Claudia Boyarskikh, USSR | | 17:50.5 |
| 1968—Toini Gustafsson, Sweden | | 16:45.2 |

### 10 Kilometers (6.2 miles)

| | | Time |
|---|---|---|
| 1952—Lydia Wideman, Finland | | 41:40.0 |
| 1956—Lyubob Kosyreva, USSR | | 38:11.0 |
| 1960—Maria Gusakova, USSR | | 39:46.6 |
| 1964—Claudia Boyarskikh, USSR | | 40:24.3 |
| 1968—Toini Gustafsson, Sweden | | 36:46.5 |

### 15 Kilometer Cross-Country Relay

| | | Time |
|---|---|---|
| 1956—Finland, USSR, Sweden | | 1:09:01.0 |
| 1960—Sweden, USSR, Finland | | 1:04:21.4 |
| 1964—USSR, Sweden, Finland | | 59:20.2 |
| 1968—Norway, Sweden, USSR | | 57:30 |

## SPEED SKATING
### MEN'S EVENTS
#### 500 Meters

| | | Time |
|---|---|---|
| 1924—Charles Jewtraw, U.S.A. | | 0:44.0 |
| 1928—Clas Thunberg, Finland & Bernt Evensen, Norway (tie) | | 0:43.4 |
| 1932—John A. Shea, U.S.A. | | 0:43.4 |
| 1936—Ivar Ballangrud, Norway | | 0:43.4 |
| 1948—Finn Helgesen, Norway | | 0:43.1 |
| 1952—Kenneth Henry, U.S.A. | | 0:43.2 |
| 1956—Evgeniy Grishin, USSR | | 0:40.2 |
| 1960—Evgeniy Grishin, USSR | | 0:40.2 |
| 1964—R. Terrence McDermott, U.S.A. | | 0:40.1 |
| 1968—Erhard Keller, W. Germany | | 0:40.3 |

#### 1,500 Meters

| | | Time |
|---|---|---|
| 1924—Clas Thunberg, Finland | | 2:20.8 |
| 1928—Clas Thunberg, Finland | | 2:21.1 |
| 1932—John A. Shea, U.S.A. | | 2:57.2 |
| 1936—Charles Mathiesen, Norway | | 2:19.2 |
| 1948—Sverre Farstad, Norway | | 2:17.6 |
| 1952—Hjalmar Anderson, Norway | | 2:20.4 |
| 1956—Evgeniy Grishin, USSR | | 2:08.6 |
| 1960—Roald Edgar Aas, Norway & Evgeny Grishin, USSR (tie) | | 2:10.4 |
| 1964—Ants Anston, USSR | | 2:10.3 |
| 1968—Cornelis Verkerk, Holland | | 2:03.4 |

#### 5,000 Meters

| | | Time |
|---|---|---|
| 1924—Clas Thunberg, Finland | | 8:39.0 |
| 1928—Ivar Ballangrud, Norway | | 8:50.5 |
| 1932—Irving Jaffee, U.S.A. | | 9:40.8 |
| 1936—Ivar Ballangrud, Norway | | 8:19.6 |
| 1948—Reidar Liakleb, Norway | | 8:29.4 |
| 1952—Hjalmar Anderson, Norway | | 8:10.6 |
| 1956—Boris Shilkov, USSR | | 7:48.7 |
| 1960—Viktor Kosichkin, USSR | | 7:51.3 |
| 1964—Knut Johannesen, Norway | | 7:38.4 |
| 1968—F. Anton Maier, Norway | | 7:22.4 |

#### 10,000 Meters

| | | Time |
|---|---|---|
| 1924—Julius Skutnabb, Finland | | 18:04.8 |
| 1928—Event not held, thawing of ice | | |
| 1932—Irving Jaffe, U.S.A. | | 19:13.6 |
| 1936—Ivar Ballangrud, Norway | | 17:24.3 |
| 1948—Ake Seyffarth, Norway | | 17:26.3 |
| 1952—Hjalmar Anderson, Norway | | 16:45.8 |
| 1956—Sigvard Ericsson, Sweden | | 16:35.9 |
| 1960—Knut Johannesen, Norway | | 15:46.6 |
| 1964—Jonny Nilsson, Sweden | | 15:50.1 |
| 1968—Johnny Hoeglin, Sweden | | 15:23.6 |

## WOMEN'S EVENTS
### 500 Meters

| | | Time |
|---|---|---|
| 1960—Helga Haase, Germany | | 0:45.9 |
| 1964—Lydia Skoblikova, USSR | | 0:45.0 |
| 1968—Ludmila Titova, USSR | | 0:46.1 |

### 1,000 Meters

| | | Time |
|---|---|---|
| 1960—Klara Guseva, USSR | | 1:34.1 |
| 1964—Lydia Skoblikova, USSR | | 1:33.2 |
| 1968—Carolina Geijssen, Holland | | 1:32.6 |

### 1,500 Meters

| | | Time |
|---|---|---|
| 1960—Lydia Skoblikova, USSR | | 2:52.2 |
| 1964—Lydia Skoblikova, USSR | | 2:22.6 |

1968—Kaija Mustonen, Finland ............2:22.4

**3,000 Meters** — **Time**
1960—Lydia Skoblikova, USSR ............5:14.3
1964—Lydia Skoblikova, USSR ............5:14.9
1968—Johanna Schut, Holland ............4:56.2

### ICE HOCKEY
(Three medal winners, in order)
1920—Canada, U.S.A., Czechoslovakia
1924—Canada, U.S.A., Great Britain
1928—Canada, Sweden, Switzerland
1932—Canada, U.S.A., Germany
1936—Great Britain, Canada, U.S.A.
1948—Canada, Czechoslovakia, Switzerland
1952—Canada, U.S.A., Sweden

1956—USSR, U.S.A., Canada
1960—U.S.A., Canada, USSR
1964—USSR, Sweden, Czechoslovakia
1968—USSR, Czechoslovakia, Canada

### LUGE

**MEN'S SINGLES** — **Time**
1964—Thomas Kohler, Germany ........3:25.77
1968—Manfred Schmid, Austria ........2:52.48

**MEN'S DOUBLES** — **Time**
1964—Austria ............................1:41.62
1968—East Germany ....................1:35.85

**WOMEN'S SINGLES** — **Time**
1964—Ortun Enderlein, Germany ........3:24.67
1968—Erica Lechner, Italy ................2:28.66

## Figure Ice-Skating Championships in 1968

### UNITED STATES CHAMPIONSHIPS
Philadelphia, Pa., Jan. 18-21

**Senior Men**—Tim Wood, Detroit Skating Club.
**Senior Ladies**—Peggy Fleming, Broadmoor Skating Club.
**Senior Pairs**—Cynthia & Ronald Kauffman, Seattle Skating Club.
**Dance Championship**—Judy Schwomeyer, Winter Club of Indianapolis, & James Sladky, Genesee Figure Skating Club.
**Junior Men**—Kenneth Shelley, Arctic Blades Figure Skating Club.

**Junior Ladies**—Barbara Ray, Burlingame, Calif.
**Junior Pairs**—Tisha Baird, Philadelphia Skating Club & Humane Society, & Richard Inglesi, City of Ardmore, Pa.
**Silver Dance**—Joan Bitterman & Brad Hislop, Seattle Skating Club.
**Novice Men**—Dean Hiltzik, Metropolitan Figure Skating Club.
**Novice Ladies**—Pegeen Naughton, Long Island Figure Skating Club.

### WORLD CHAMPIONSHIPS
Geneva, Switzerland, Feb. 27-Mar. 3

**Men**—Emmerich Danzer, Austria.
**Ladies**—Peggy Fleming, United States.
**Pairs**—Ludmila Beloussova & Oleg Protopopov, Soviet Union.

**Dance**—Diane Towler & Bernard Ford, Great Britain.

## United States Sectional Championships

### EASTERN CHAMPIONSHIPS
South Weymouth, Mass., Dec. 28-30, 1967

**Senior Ladies**—Wendy Jones, Hershey Figure Skating Club.
**Gold Dance**—Ann & Harvey Millier, Philadelphia Skating Club & Humane Society.
**Junior Men**—Richard Inglesi, City of Ardmore, Pa.
**Junior Ladies**—Lise Gantz, Philadelphia Skating Club & Humane Society.
**Junior Pairs**—Tisha Baird, Philadelphia Skating Club & Humane Society, & Richard Inglesi, City of Ardmore, Pa.
**Silver Dance**—Mary Bonacci, Rye Figure Skating Club, & Roger Bennett, Southern Connecticut Figure Skating Club.
**Novice Men**—James Webb, The Skating Club of Boston.
**Novice Ladies**—Melissa Militano, Long Island Figure Skating Club.
**Novice Pairs**—Karen Cohen, North Jersey Figure Skating Club, & George Magill, Laurelton Pines Figure Skating Club.
**Bronze Dance**—Sally West & Malcolm McKown, Bay Path Figure Skating Club.
**Intermediate Men**—Thomas Lombard, Philadelphia Skating Club & Humane Society.
**Intermediate Ladies**—Ellen Kinney, Rye Figure Skating Club.
**Veterans Dance**—Katrine Neil, Essex Skating Club, & Charles Lally, Garden State Skating Club.

### MIDWESTERN CHAMPIONSHIPS
Green Bay, Wis., Jan. 4-6

**Senior Men**—Duane Maki, Detroit Skating Club.
**Senior Ladies**—Janet Lynn, Wagon Wheel Figure Skating Club.
**Senior Pairs**—Joanne Heckert & Gary Clark, Lansing Skating Club.
**Gold Dance**—Vicky Camper & Eugene Heffron, Detroit Skating Club.
**Junior Men**—John Baldwin, Broadmoor Skating Club.
**Junior Ladies**—Wen-An Sun, Broadmoor Skating Club.

**Junior Pairs**—Susan & Will Smith, Tulsa Figure Skating Club.
**Silver Dance**—Caren Cady & Warren Danner, Winter Club of Indianapolis.
**Novice Men**—Tim Flynn, Denver Figure Skating Club.
**Novice Ladies**—Barbara Freyer, Winter Club of Indianapolis.
**Novice Pairs**—Nancy & Roger Glenn, Wagon Wheel Figure Skating Club.
**Bronze Dance**—Jane Pankey & Richard Horne, Detroit Skating Club.
**Intermediate Men**—Tom Van Camp, Lansing Skating Club.
**Intermediate Ladies**—Kris Sherard, Wagon Wheel Figure Skating Club.

### PACIFIC COAST CHAMPIONSHIPS
Portland, Ore., Nov. 30-Dec. 2, 1967

**Senior Men**—J. Misha Petkevich, Great Falls Figure Skating Club.
**Senior Ladies**—Dawn Glab, Arctic Blades Figure Skating Club.
**Senior Pairs**—Jo Jo Starbuck & Kenneth Shelley, Arctic Blades Figure Skating Club.
**Gold Dance**—Gaie Shoman & Roger Berry, Los Angeles Figure Skating Club.
**Junior Men**—Atoy Wilson, Los Angeles Figure Skating Club.
**Junior Ladies**—Barbara Ray, City of Burlingame, Calif.
**Junior Pairs**—Jill Ritchie & Ralph Meredith, Overlake Skating Club.
**Silver Dance**—Joan Bitterman & Brad Hislop, Seattle Skating Club.
**Novice Men**—Bob Stephens, Los Angeles Figure Skating Club.
**Novice Ladies**—Teri Beckerman, Los Angeles Figure Skating Club.
**Novice Pairs**—Diane Puckett, Lakewood Winter Club, & Rollie Arthur, City of Tacoma.
**Bronze Dance**—Denese Abden-Nur & Jack Danks, Los Angeles Figure Skating Club.
**Intermediate Men**—James Demogines, Los Angeles Figure Skating Club.
**Intermediate Ladies**—Sylvia Mennine, All Year Figure Skating Club.

## 1968 Canadian Figure Skating Champions

**Senior Men's**—Jay Humphry.
**Senior Ladies'**—Karen Magnussen.
**Senior Pairs**—Bette & John McKilligan.
**Senior Dance**—Joni Graham & Don Philips.
**Junior Ladies'**—Judy Williams.

**Junior Men's**—Patrick McKilligan.
**Junior Dance**—Mary Church & Tom Falls.
**Novice Men's Singles**—Steven Sugar.
**Novice Ladies' Singles**—Madeleine Begg.

## Rodeo Cowboy All Around Champions
Source: Rodeo Cowboys Association, Inc.

| | | | | |
|---|---|---|---|---|
| 1954 | Buck Rutherford, Lenapah, Okla. ....$40,404 | | 1961 | Benny Reynolds, Melrose, Mont.......$31,309 |
| 1955 | Casey Tibbs, Ft. Pierre, S. D.........42.065 | | 1962 | Tom Nesmith, Bethel, Okla.............32,611 |
| 1956 | Jim Shoulders, Henryetta, Okla.......43,381 | | 1963 | Dean Oliver, Boise, Idaho.............31,329 |
| 1957 | Jim Shoulders, Henryetta, Okla.......33,299 | | 1964 | Dean Oliver, Boise, Idaho.............31,150 |
| 1958 | Jim Shoulders, Henryetta, Okla.......33,212 | | 1965 | Dean Oliver, Boise, Idaho.............33,163 |
| 1959 | Jim Shoulders, Henryetta, Okla.......32,905 | | 1966 | Larry Mahan, Brooks, Oregon..........40,358 |
| 1960 | Harry Tompkins, Dublin, Texas.......32,522 | | 1967 | Larry Mahan, Brooks, Oregon.........51.996 |

# National Roller Skating Champions in 1968
## U. S. AMATEUR ROLLER SKATING ASSOCIATION
### Cleveland, Ohio, July 21-27

**Senior Men**—Jackie Courtney, Marion, Ind.
**Senior Ladies**—Kathleen Schreiber, Levittown, N. Y.
**Senior Dance**—Thomas Straker & Bonnie Lambert, Livonia, Mich.
**Senior Mixed Pairs**—Jack Courtney & Sheryl Trueman, Marion, Ind.
**Senior Ladies Pairs**—Kathleen Schreiber & Karen Seekamp, Levittown, N. Y.
**Senior Fours**—Terry Neeley, Barbara Grimes, William Spooner and Donna Presson, Bladensburg, Md.
**Junior Men**—Rick Gunning, Frankfort, Ind.
**Junior Ladies**—Karen Seekamp, Levittown, N. Y.
**Junior Dance**—Richard Horne & Jane Pankey, Livonia, Mich.
**Junior Mixed Pairs**—Tim Abell-Gigi Leleu, Harvey, Ill.
**Intermediate Men Singles**—Richard Veliko, Levittown, N. Y.
**Intermediate Ladies Singles**—Nancy Buehl, South Amboy, N. J.
**Intermediate Men Figures**—Wally Sloan, Summit, Ill.
**Intermediate Ladies Figures**—Karen Ehman, Bay Shore, N. Y.

**Intermediate Dance**—Thomas LeVan & Patti Seipp, Melrose Park, Ill.
**Intermediate Mixed Pairs**—Richard Veliko & Nancy Buehl, Levittown, N. Y.
**Intermediate Ladies Pairs**—Melody Gerdon & Bonnie Murphy, Bay Shore, N. Y.
**Intermediate Fours**—Michael Maslan, Mary Klein, Wally Sloan and Judy Mueller, Summit, Ill.
**Senior Veteran Dance**—Earl King & Nancy King, Bay Shore, N. Y.
**Junior Veteran Dance**—George Burghardt & Mary Burghardt, Levittown, N. Y.

### Speed Events

**Senior Men**—Don Rogers, Pomona, Calif.
**Senior Ladies**—Linda Barber, Grandville, Mich.
**Senior Men Relays**—Michael Figard & Doug Kraai, Grand Rapids, Mich.
**Senior Ladies Relay**—Vickie Duffy & Barbara Skelton, Indianapolis, Ind.
**Junior Men**—Dan Lees, Granville, Mich.
**Junior Ladies**—Vickie Duffy, Indianapolis, Ind.
**Intermediate Men**—Joseph Aidukas, Bayonne, N. J.
**Intermediate Ladies**—Suzanne Ardale, South Amboy, N. J.

# North American Amateur Roller Skating Championships, 1968
### Lincoln, Neb.

**Senior Men's Singles**—Michael Jacques, Norwood, Mass.
**Senior Ladies Singles**—Darlene Barile, Agawam, Mass.
**Intermediate Men's Singles**—Joseph Polinski, Lakewood, N. J.
**Intermediate Ladies Singles**—Gail Robovitsky, Clawson, Mich.
**Novice Men's Singles**—Raymond Phillips, Norwood, Mass.
**Novice Ladies Singles**—Robyn White, Pontiac, Mich.
**Senior Men's Figure**—Richard Gustafson, New Britain, Conn.
**Senior Ladies Figure**—Carol Langlois, New Britain, Conn.
**Intermediate Men's Figure**—Richard Hodgekinson, Detroit, Mich.
**Intermediate Ladies Figure**—Debra Jackson, Carmichaels, Calif.
**Novice Men's Figure**—Garry Crow, Arnold, Mich.
**Novice Ladies Figure**—Colleen Hanley, Clawson, Mich.
**Senior Pairs**—Gail Robovitsky, Ron Robovitsky, Clawson, Mich.
**Intermediate Pairs**—P. J. Gormley, Sandi Barton, Elmhurst, Ill.

**Novice Pairs**—David Ripp Weaver, Beth Benbow, Dayton, Ohio.
**Senior Fours**—Dennis Collier, Karen Marshall, Richard Toon, Judy Jerue, San Leandro, Calif.
**Novice Fours**—John Gustafson, Ray Lenty, Mary O'Mara, Laura O'Mara, Vancouver, Wash.
**Queen Contest**—Carol Moore, Fort Lauderdale, Fla.
**Senior Dance**—Adolph Wacker, Linda Mottice, San Leandro, Calif.
**Intermediate Dance**—Ronald Miner, Sandra Boston, Indianapolis.
**Novice Dance**—Darcy Clay, Mike Fleming, Whittier, Calif.
**Junior Dance**—Donna Shaw, Ronald Milton, Norwood, Mass.

### Speed Events

**Senior Men**—Malcolm Williamson, Irving, Texas.
**Senior Ladies**—Sharon Van Lue, Glendora, Calif.
**Intermediate Men**—Pat Bergin, Irving, Texas.
**Intermediate Ladies**—Jan Irvin, Fort Worth, Texas.
**Junior Boys**—Randy Wardlaw, Pontiac, Mich.
**Junior Girls**—Susie Johnson, Fort Worth, Texas.
**Men's Relay**—Mike Layport, Pat Layport, Jeff McDermott, Mark Cole, Santa Ana, Calif.

# Water Ski Championships in 1968
## 26th ANNUAL NATIONAL CHAMPIONSHIPS
### Canton, Ohio, Aug. 2-25

**Men's Overall**—Mike Suyderhoud, San Anselmo, Calif., 2848 points.
**Men's Slalom**—Mike Suyderhoud, 44 buoys.
**Men's Jumping**—Mike Suyderhoud, 156 ft.
**Men's Tricks**—Alan Kempton, Tampa, Fla., 4310 points.
**Women's Overall**—Liz Allan, Winter Park, Fla., 3000 points.
**Women's Slalom**—Liz Allan, 45 buoys.
**Women's Jumping**—Liz Allan, 109 ft.
**Women's Tricks**—Liz Allan, 3605 points.
**Sr. Men's Overall**—Bill Stevenson, Greenville, S. C., 2625 points.
**Sr. Men's Slalom**—Art Smrekar, Richmond, Calif., 45 buoys.
**Sr. Men's Jumping**—Joe Hessell, Xenia, Ohio, 103 ft.
**Sr. Men's Tricks**—Al Tyll, Bantam, Conn., 4297 points.
**Sr. Women's Overall**—Thelma Salmas, Novato, Calif., 2864 points.
**Sr. Women's Slalom**—Thelma Salmas, 38 buoys.
**Sr. Women's Jumping**—Fran Mooney, Miami, Fla., 76 ft.
**Sr. Women's Tricks**—Artis Price, Mundelein, Ill., 2304 points.

**Boys' Overall**—Ricky McCormick, Independence, Mo., 2686 points.
**Boys' Slalom**—Kris LaPoint, Castro Valley, Calif., 46½ buoys.
**Boys' Jumping**—Frankie Dees, Cypress Gardens, Fla., 123 ft.
**Boys' Tricks**—Ricky McCormick, 4907 points.
**Girls' Overall**—Linda Leavengood, Coral Gables, Fla., 2539 points.
**Girls' Slalom**—Lisa St. John, Falls River Mills, Calif., 52 buoys.
**Girls' Jumping**—Linda Leavengood, 107 ft.
**Girls' Tricks**—Lisa St. John, 3420 points.
**Jr. Boys' Overall**—Wayne Grimditch, Pompano Beach, Fla., 2882 points.
**Jr. Boys' Slalom**—Bob LaPoint, Castro Valley, Calif., 55 buoys.
**Jr. Boys' Jumping**—Wayne Grimditch, 102 ft.
**Jr. Boys' Tricks**—Wayne Grimditch, 3506 pts.
**Jr. Girls' Overall**—Whitney Ballentine, Anderson, S. C., 2451 points.
**Jr. Girls' Slalom**—Whitney Ballentine, 40½ buoys.
**Jr. Girls' Jumping**—Paula Clower, Grant, Ala., 74 ft.
**Jr. Girls' Tricks**—Janie Peckinpaugh, Muncie, Ind., 1972 points.

## 10th ANNUAL MASTERS TOURNAMENT
### Callaway Gardens, Ga., July 12-14

**Men's Overall**— Frankie Dees, Cypress Gardens, Fla., 2705 points.
**Men's Slalom**—Kris LaPoint, Castro Valley, Calif., 47 buoys.
**Men's Jumping**—Mike Suyderhoud, San Anselmo, Calif., 155 ft.

**Men's Tricks**—Alan Kempton, Tampa, Fla., 4846 points.
**Women's Overall**—Elizabeth Allan, Winter Park, Fla., 3000 points.
**Women's Slalom**—Elizabeth Allan, 51 buoys.
**Women's Jumping**—Elizabeth Allan, 110 ft.
**Women's Tricks**—Elizabeth Allan, 4140 points.

# Intercollegiate Rowing Association Records

### ONONDAGA LAKE, SYRACUSE, N. Y.
### UNIVERSITY EIGHT-OAR CREWS (Course four miles)

| Year | Winner | Time | Second | Third | Fourth | Fifth |
|------|--------|------|--------|-------|--------|-------|
| 1952.... | Navy (a) .......... | 15:08.1 | Princeton..... | Cornell ...... | Wisconsin..... | California |
| 1953.... | Navy (a).......... | 15:29.6 | Cornell ...... | Washington.... | Wisconsin.... | Columbia |
| 1954.... | Navy (a).......... | 16:04.4 | Cornell ...... | Washington.... | Wisconsin.... | California |
| 1955.... | Cornell (a)....... | 15:49.9 | Pennsylvania | Navy...... | Washington.. | Stanford |
| 1956.... | Cornell (a)....... | 16:22.4 | Navy...... | Wisconsin.... | Washington.... | Stanford |
| 1957.... | Cornell (a)....... | 15:26.6 | Pennsylvania.. | Stanford ...... | Princeton...... | Syracuse |
| 1958.... | Cornell (a)....... | 17:12.1 | Navy...... | Syracuse | Princeton...... | California |
| 1959.... | Wisconsin(a)...... | 18:01.7 | Syracuse | Navy...... | California.... | Washington |
| 1960.... | California (a)..... | 15:57.0 | Navy | Washington... | Brown...... | Cornell-Penn |
| 1961.... | California (a)..... | 16:49.2 | Cornell ...... | M I T...... | Washington.... | Penn |
| 1962.... | Cornell(a)........ | 17:02.9 | Washington.... | California.... | Wisconsin.... | Penn |
| 1963.... | Cornell (a)....... | 17:24.0 | Navy...... | M. I. T...... | California.... | Wisconsin |
| 1964.... | California (b)..... | 6:31.1 | Washington.... | Cornell...... | Princeton...... | M.I.T. |
| 1965.... | Navy (a) ........ | 16:51.3 | Cornell........ | Washington.... | Rutgers ...... | Brown |
| 1966.... | Wisconsin (a).... | 16:03.4 | Navy...... | Princeton..... | Brown...... | Penn |
| 1967.... | Penn (a) ........ | 16:13.9 | Wisconsin ...... | Cornell...... | Princeton...... | Navy |
| 1968 .... | Penn (b)......... | 6:15.6 | Washington.... | Princeton ..... | Northeastern.. | Rutgers |

Course record for four miles—18:12.6 (California in 1939).
(a) Race at 3 miles. (b) Race at 2,000 meters.

# Yale-Harvard Rowing

The Yale-Harvard rowing contests were begun in 1852. The original race, the first intercollegiate athletic event, was an 8-oared race with coxswain rowed over a two-mile course at Center Harbor, Lake Winnepesaukee. From 1859 through 1875 coxswains were dispensed with and the 6-oared boats were steered by a rudder controlled by the bow oar. In races at various sites. The two colleges returned to eight oars with cox for their first four-mile race, June 30, 1876, on the Connecticut River at Springfield, Mass., Yale winning in 22 m. 2 sec. The course was changed to the Thames River at New London, Conn., in 1878.

The race was omitted in 1917, but in 1918 a two-mile race was rowed on the Housatonic River, Derby, Conn., on June 1, which Harvard won, time 10 m. 58 sec. From 1852 to 1923 inclusive Yale won 30 races and Harvard 30.

Yale-Harvard freshmen eights began their contests in 1899 on the Thames, Harvard winning. The 1902 race was a dead heat.

### VARSITY EIGHTS (Four miles)

| Date | Won by | Time Winner | Time Loser | Date | Won by | Time Winner | Time Loser |
|------|--------|-------------|------------|------|--------|-------------|------------|
| 1951...... | Harvard...... | 21:26.0 | 21:48.2 | 1960...... | Harvard...... | 19:41.6 | 20:08.3 |
| 1952...... | Yale........... | 22:49.0 | 22:52.8 | 1961...... | Harvard...... | 22:00.0 | 22:29.5 |
| 1952...... | Harvard....... | 20:09.0 | 20:20.0 | 1962...... | Yale........ | 21:26.0 | 21:27.0 |
| 1954...... | Yale........... | 21:58.4 | 22:02.0 | 1963...... | Harvard...... | 19:47.0 | 20:15.0 |
| 1955...... | Yale........... | 20:05.0 | ........... | 1964...... | Harvard...... | 20:48.2 | 21:06.0 |
| 1956...... | Yale........... | 19:26.0 | | 1965...... | Harvard...... | 19:41.6 | 20:21.0 |
| 1957...... | Yale........... | 20:35.0 | 21:03.0 | 1966...... | Harvard...... | 19:44.0 | |
| 1958...... | Yale........... | 22:39.0 | 22:52.0 | 1967...... | Harvard...... | 22:43.4 | 23:08.2 |
| 1959...... | Yale........... | 19:52.0 | 20:02.0 | 1968...... | Harvard...... | 20 21 0 | |

Downstream and course record—19:21.4 (Harvard in 1948). Upstream record—19:44.0 (Harvard in 1966). Varsity victories—Yale 47; Harvard 56.

# Oxford-Cambridge Boat Race

### Inaugurated, 1841. Course, 4¼ miles

| Yr. | Date | Winner | Time | Yr. | Date | Winner | Time | Yr. | Date | Winner | Time |
|-----|------|--------|------|-----|------|--------|------|-----|------|--------|------|
| 1945 | Feb. 24 | Cambridge.. | | 1953 | Mar. 28 | Cambridge.. | 19:54 | 1961 | Arpil 1 | Cambridge... | 19:22 |
| 1946 | Mar. 30 | Oxford..... | 19:54 | 1954 | Apr. 3 | Oxford..... | 20:22 | 1962 | April 7 | Cambridge.. | 19:46 |
| 1947 | Mar. 29 | Cambridge.. | 23:01 | 1955 | Mar. 26 | Cambridge.. | 19:10 | 1963 | Mar. 23 | Oxford...... | 19:20 |
| 1948 | Mar. 27 | Cambridge.. | 17:50 | 1956 | Mar. 24 | Cambridge.. | 18:36 | 1964 | Mar. 28 | Cambridge.. | 19:18 |
| 1949 | Mar. 26 | Cambridge.. | 18:57 | 1957 | Mar. 30 | Cambridge.. | 19:01 | 1965 | April 3 | Oxford...... | 18:07 |
| 1950 | April 1 | Cambridge.. | 20:15 | 1958 | Apr. 5 | Cambridge.. | 18:15 | 1966 | Mar. 26 | Oxford...... | 19:12 |
| 1951 | Mar. 26 | Cambridge.. | 20:50 | 1959 | Mar. 28 | Oxford...... | 18:52 | 1967 | Mar. 25 | Oxford...... | 18:52 |
| 1952 | Mar. 29 | Oxford..... | 20:23 | 1960 | April 2 | Oxford...... | 18:59 | 1968 | Mar. 30 | Cambridge.. | 18:22 |

Recapitulation (Races of 1940, 1943, 1944 not counted) 1941-1942—no races on account of war. Cambridge 62, Oxford 51, dead heat 1 (1877).
Course Record—17:50—Set by Cambridge in 1948.

# Amateur Rowing Championships in 1968

### 94th NATIONAL CHAMPIONSHIPS
### New York, N. Y., Aug. 9-10

Quarter Mile Dash—Jim Dietz, NYAC, New York City. Time—1:15.0.

150 Lb. Quarter Mile—Larry Klecatsky, Bachelors Barge, Phila. Time—1:17.5.

150 Lb. Single Sculls—Larry Klecatsky, Bachelors Barge, Phila. Time—7:44.5.

150 Lb. Double Sculls—Bachelors Barge, Phila. Time—7:04.6.

150 Lb. Quadruple Sculls—Detroit B. C., Detroit, Mich. Time—6:42.8.

150 Lb. Four Oared Shell With Cox.—St. Catharine, Ontario. Time—7:03.5.

150 Lb. Eight Oared Shell—St. Catharine, Ontario. Time—6:16.0.

Association Single Sculls—Thos. McKibbon, Long Beach, Calif. Time—7:29.0.

Intermediate Eight Oared Shells—Ecorse B. C., Ecorse, Mich. Time—6:29.6.

Intermediate Four Oared Shell With Cox.—Vesper B. C., Phila. Time—6:59.0.

Quadruple Sculls—Potomac B. C., Wash., D. C. Time—6:36.0.

Pair Oared Shell With Cox.—Potomac B. C., Wash., D. C. Time—7:27.2.

Pair Oared Shell Without Cox.—Potomac B. C., Wash., D. C. Time—6:56.7.

Four Oared Shell With Cox.—Vesper B. C., Phila., Pa. Time—6:34.6.

Four Oared Shell Without Cox.—Vesper B. C., Phila. Time—6:29.0.

Championship Single Sculls—Thos. McKibbon, Long Beach, Calif. Time—7:22.7.

Eight Oared Shells—St. Catharine, Ontario. Time—6:00.0.

Double Sculls—Vesper B. C., Phila. Time—6:38.0.

Barnes Trophy—Vesper B. C. 110½ Points.

## Crew Racing Regattas in 1968

| Date | Site | Distance | Winner | Second | Winner's time |
|------|------|----------|--------|--------|---------------|
| Mar. 30 | Philadelphia, Pa. | 2,000 meters | Temple | Fordham | 6:24 |
| Apr. 6 | Princeton, N. J. | 2,000 meters | Princeton | Rutgers | 6:03.4 |
| Apr. 13 | Harlem River, N.Y. | 2,000 meters | MIT | Columbia | 6:42.4 |
| Apr. 13 | Orchard Beach, N. Y. (Grimaldi Cup) | 2,000 meters | Holy Cross | Villanova | 6:48.1 |
| Apr. 13 | Annapolis, Md. | 2,000 meters | Princeton | Navy | 7:15 |
| Apr. 20 | Princeton, N. J. (Platt Cup) | 2,000 meters | Cornell | Princeton | 6:12 |
| Apr. 20 | Harlem River, N. Y. (Childs Cup) | 2,000 meters | Penn | Princeton | 5:22.8 |
| Apr. 27 | Boston, Mass. | 2,000 meters | Northeastern | Brown | 6:31.7 |
| Apr. 27 | Princeton, N. J. (Compton Cup) | 2,000 meters | Harvard | Princeton | 6:13.3 |
| May 4 | Derby, Conn. (Carnegie Cup) | 2,000 meters | Princeton | Yale | 5:39 |
| May 4 | Annapolis, Md. (Adams Cup) | 2,000 meters | Harvard | Penn | 6:05.7 |
| May 4 | Marietta, Ohio (Mid-Am Regatta) | 2,000 meters | Marietta | Purdue | 5:42.3 |
| May 11 | Philadelphia, Pa. (Dad Vail Regatta) | 2,000 meters | Georgetown | Temple | 6:00.6 |
| May 18 | Ithaca, N. Y. (Madeira Cup) | 2,000 meters | Penn | Cornell | 6:08 |
| May 18 | Seattle, Wash. (West. Spring Regatta) | 2,000 meters | Wash. | UCLA, Stanford (tie) | 5:56.7 |

## Royal Canadian Henley Regatta

1968—St. Catharines Rowing Club, 395 points; Hamilton Leanders, 145 points; Buffalo West Side, 116½ points.

1967—St. Catharines Rowing Club, 214½ points; Ecorse, Michigan Boat Club, 136½ points; Hamilton Leander Rowing Club, 136 points.

1966—St. Catharines Rowing Club, 268½ points; Philadelphia Undine Rowing Club, 160 points; New York Rowing Club, 119 points.

1965—St. Catharines Rowing Club, 254 points; Detroit Boat Club, 232½ points; Toronto Argonauts Rowing Club, 182½ points.

## International Yacht Races for the America's Cup

Competition for the America's Cup grew out of the first contest to establish a world yachting championship, one of the carnival features of the London Exposition of 1851. The race, open to all classes of yachts all over the world, covered a 60-mile course around the Isle of Wight; the prize was a cup worth about $500, donated by the Royal Yacht Squadron of England, known as the "America's Cup" because it was first won by the United States yacht America. Successive efforts of British and Australian yachtsmen have failed to win the famous trophy, which remains in the United States. On Sept. 19, 1967, the 12-meter yacht Intrepid won a fourth straight victory over Australia's challenger, Dame Pattie, to keep the symbol of world sailing supremacy in the United States. The U. S. yacht was skippered by Emil (Bus) Mosbacher, Jr., of White Plains, N. Y., and designed by Olin Stephens of Scarsdale, N. Y. Dame Pattie was skippered by Jock Sturrock and designed by Warwick Hood of Australia.

### WINNERS OF THE AMERICA'S CUP

| | | | |
|---|---|---|---|
| 1851 America. | 1881 Mischief (2 races) | 1901 Columbia (3 races) | ish) (2 races) |
| 1870 Magic. | 1885 Puritan (2 races) | 1903 Reliance (3 races) | 1937 Ranger (4 races) |
| 1871 Columbia (2 races); | 1886 Mayflower (2 races) | 1920 Resolute (best of 7 | 1958 Columbia (4 races) |
| Sappho (2 races); | 1887 Volunteer (2 races) | races) | 1962 Weatherly (4-1) |
| Livonia (British) (1 | 1893 Vigilant (3 races) | 1930 Enterprise (4 races) | 1964 Constellation (4-0) |
| race) | 1895 Defender (3 races) | 1934 Rainbow (4 races); | 1967 Intrepid (4-0) |
| 1876 Madeleine (2 races) | 1899 Columbia (3 races) | Endeavour II (Brit- | |

## North American Yachting Championships in 1968

James Hunt of South Dartmouth, Mass., won the Mallory Cup, symbolic of the men's sailing championship, on Aug. 30. He had a total of 48¾ points for the four-day, eight-race series on San Francisco Bay. Richard Rose of Seattle placed second with 43½ points.

The Adams Cup, symbolic of the women's sailing championship, was won by June Methot of the Monmouth Boat Club, Red Bank, N. J., on Aug. 28. She had a total of 50 points in the event, held on Barnegat Bay. Martha McDougle of San Francisco was second with 41½ points.

## Power Boat Racing Champions

### GOLD CUP Distance: 90 miles

| Year | Boat | Owner | Driver | Winner's fastest heat | Site |
|------|------|-------|--------|----------------------|------|
| 1949 | My Sweetie | E. Gregory-E. Schoenherr | Bill Cantrell | 78.64 | Detroit, Mich. |
| 1950 | Slo-Mo-Shun IV | S. S. Sayres | Ted Jones | 80.99 | Detroit, Mich. |
| 1951 | Slo-Mo-Shun V | S. S. Sayres | Lou Fageol | 91.766 | Seattle. Wash. |
| 1952 | Slo-Mo-Shun IV | S. S. Sayres | Stanley Dollar | 84.355 | Seattle. Wash. |
| 1953 | Slo-Mo-Shun IV | S. S. Sayres | Fageol-Taggart | 95.268 | Seattle. Wash. |
| 1954 | Slo-Mo-Shun V | S. S. Sayres | Lou Fageol | 99.784 | Seattle. Wash. |
| 1955 | Gale V | Joseph A. Schoenith | Lee Schoenith | 100.954 | Seattle. Wash. |
| 1956 | Miss Thriftway | Willard Rhodes | Bill Muncey | | Detroit, Mich. |
| 1957 | Miss Thriftway | Willard Rhodes | Bill Muncey | 109.828 | Seattle. Wash. |
| 1958 | Hawaii Kai III | Edgar Kaiser | Jack Regas | 108.734 | Seattle. Wash. |
| 1959 | Maverick | W. T. Waggoner, Jr. | Bill Stead | 106.278 | Seattle. Wash. |
| 1961 | Miss Century 21 | Willard Rhodes | Bill Muncey | 102.399 | Reno, Nev. |
| 1962 | Miss Century 21 | Willard Rhodes | Bill Muncey | 101.446 | Seattle. Wash. |
| 1963 | Miss Bardahl | Ole Bardahl | Ron Musson | 114.650 | Detroit, Mich. |
| 1964 | Miss Bardahl | Ole Bardahl | Ron Musson | 108.104 | Detroit, Mich. |
| 1965 | Miss Bardahl | Ole Bardahl | Ron Musson | 110.655 | Seattle. Wash. |
| 1966 | Tahoe Miss | Harrah's | Mira Slovak | 97.861 | Detroit, Mich. |
| 1967 | Miss Bardahl | Ole Bardahl | Bill Schumacher | 104.691 | Seattle. Wash. |
| 1968 | Miss Bardahl | Ole Bardahl | Bill Schumacher | | Detroit, Mich. |

# World Record Fish Caught by Rod and Reel

**Source:** Salt-water: International Game Fish Association. Fresh-water: Field & Stream Magazine.
Records confirmed to August 10, 1968

**SALT-WATER FISH. All-tackle records, both men and women.**

| Species | Weight | Length | Girth | Where caught | Date | Angler |
|---|---|---|---|---|---|---|
| Albacore | 69 lbs. | 3' 6" | 32½" | St. Helena | Apr. 7, 1956 | P. Allen |
| | 69 lbs. 1 oz. | 4' ¼" | 33¼" | Hudson Canyon, N. J. | Oct. 8, 1961 | Walter C. Timm |
| | 69 lbs. 2 oz. | 3' 10" | 32' | Montauk, N. Y. | Aug. 21, 1964 | Lary R. Kranz |
| Amberjack | 149 lbs. | 5' 11" | 41¾" | Bermuda | June 21, 1964 | Peter Simons |
| Barracuda, Great | 103 lbs. 4 oz. | 5' 6" | 31¼" | Bahama Islands | 1932 | C. E. Benet |
| Bass, Cal. Black Sea | 557 lbs. 3 oz. | 7' 4¼" | 78" | Catalina Is., Calif. | July 1, 1962 | R. M. Lane |
| Bass, Cal. White Sea | 83 lbs. 12 oz. | 5' 5½" | 34" | San Felipe, Mexico | Mar. 31, 1953 | L. C. Baumgardner |
| Bass, Channel | 83 lbs. | 4' 4" | 29" | Cape Charles, Va. | Aug. 5, 1949 | Zack Waters, Jr. |
| Bass, Giant Sea | 680 lbs. | 7' 1½" | 66" | Fernandina Beach, Fla. | May 20, 1961 | Lynn Joyner |
| Bass, Sea | 8 lbs. | 1' 10" | 19" | Nantucket Sound, Mass. | May 13, 1951 | H. R. Rider |
| Bass, Striped | 73 lbs. | 5' | 30½" | Vineyard Sound, Mass. | Aug. 17, 1913 | C. B. Church |
| Blackfish (or Tautog) | 21 lbs. 6 oz. | 2' 7½" | 23½" | Cape May, N.J. | June 12, 1954 | R. N. Sheafer |
| Bluefish | 24 lbs. 3 oz. | 3' 5" | 22" | San Miguel, Azores | Aug. 27, 1953 | M. A. da Silva Veloso |
| Bonefish | 19 lbs. | 3' 3⅝" | 17" | Zululand, S. Africa | May 26, 1962 | Brian W. Batchelor |
| Bonito, Oceanic | 39 lbs. 15 oz. | 3' 3" | 28" | Walker Cay, Bahamas | Jan. 21, 1952 | F. Drowley |
| Cobia | 102 lbs. | 5' 10" | 34" | Cape Charles, Va. | July 3 1938 | J. E. Stansbury |
| Cod | 81 lbs. | 4' 6⅞" | 35½" | Brielle, N. J | Mar. 15, 1967 | Joseph Chesla |
| Dolphin | 76 lbs. 12 oz. | 5'10½" | 35" | Bimini, Bahamas | May 28, 1964 | Charles Costello |
| Drum, Black | 98½ lbs. | 4' 5" | 40" | Willis Wharf, Virginia | June 12, 1967 | Gary Hilton Kelley |
| Flounder, Summer | 22 lbs. 1 oz. | 3' 1" | 35" | Caleta Horcon, Chile | Dec. 8, 1965 | F. I. Aguirrezabal |
| Kingfish (Tanguigue) | 81 lbs. | 5' 11½" | 29¼" | Karachi, Pakistan | Aug. 27, 1960 | G. Rusinak |
| Marlin, Black | 1,560 lbs. | 14' 6" | 81" | Cabo Blanco, Peru | Aug. 4, 1953 | A. C. Glassell, Jr. |
| Marlin, Blue | 845 lbs. | 13' 1" | 71" | St. Thomas, Virgin Is. | July 4, 1968 | Elliot J. Fishman |
| Marlin, Pacific Blue | 1100 lbs. | 13' 9½" | 79½" | Le Morne, Mauritius | Feb. 20, 1966 | Andre D'Hotman De Villiers |
| | 1100 lbs. | 14'4¾" | 72½" | Kailua, Kona Hawaii | May 23, 1967 | Hale L. Erickson |
| Marlin, Striped | 465 lbs. | 10' 6" | 65" | Mayor Is., N. Z. | Feb. 27, 1948 | James Black |
| Marlin, White | 161 lbs. | 8' 8" | 33" | Miami Beach | 1938 | L. F. Hooper |
| Permit | 50 lbs. | 3' 7" | 34½" | Miami, Fla. | Mar. 27, 1965 | Robert E. Miller |
| Pollack | 43 lbs. | 4' | 29" | Brielle, N. J. | Oct. 21, 1964 | Philip Barlow |
| Rainbow Runner | 30 lbs. 15 oz. | 3' 11" | 22" | Kauai, Hawaii | Apr. 27, 1963 | Holbrook Goodale |
| Roosterfish | 114 lbs. | 5' 4" | 33" | La Paz, Mex. | June 1, 1960 | Abe Sackheim |
| Sailfish, Atlantic | 141 lbs. 1 oz. | 8' 5" | ........ | Ivory Coast, Africa | Jan. 26, 1961 | Tony Burnand |
| Sailfish, Pacific | 221 lbs. | 10' 9" | ........ | Santa Cruz Is., Galapagos | Feb. 12, 1947 | C. W. Stewart |
| Shark, Blue | 410 lbs. | 11' 6" | 52" | Rockport, Mass. | Sept. 1, 1960 | R. C. Webster |
| | 410 lbs. | 11' 2" | 52½" | Rockport, Mass. | Aug. 17, 1967 | Martha Webster |
| Shark, Mako | 1,000 lbs. | 12' | ........ | Mayor Island, N. Z. | Mar. 14, 1943 | B. D. H. Ross |
| Shark, Man-Eater or White | 2,664 lbs. | 16' 10" | 9' 6" | Ceduna, So. Australia | Apr. 21, 1959 | Alfred Dean |
| Shark, Porbeagle | 400 lbs. 8 oz. | 7' 9½" | 57½" | Fire Island, N. Y. | May 16, 1965 | James T. Kirkup |
| Shark, Thresher | 922 lbs. | ........ | ........ | Bay of Islands, N. Z. | Mar. 21, 1937 | W. W. Dowding |
| Shark, Tiger | 1,780 lbs. | 13'10½" | 103" | Cherry Grove, S. C. | June 14, 1964 | Walter Maxwell |
| Snook, or Robalo | 52 lbs. 6 oz. | 4' 1½" | 26" | Lapaz, Mexico | Jan. 9, 1963 | Jane Haywood |
| Swordfish | 1,182 lbs. | 14'11¼" | 78" | Iquique, Chile | May 7, 1953 | L. Marron |
| Tarpon | 283 lbs. | 7' 2⅝" | ........ | L. Maracaibo, Venezuela | Mar. 19, 1956 | M. Salazar |
| Tuna, Allison (Yellowfin) | 269 lbs. 8 oz. | 6' 9" | 53" | Kauai, Hawaii | May 30, 1962 | Henry Nishikawa |
| Tuna, Atlantic Big-Eyed | 295 lbs. | 6' 6½" | 40" | San Miguel, Azores | July 8, 1960 | Dr. Arsenio Cordeiro |
| Tuna, Pacific Big-Eyed | 435 lbs. | 7' 9" | 63½" | Cabo Blanco, Peru | Apr. 17, 1957 | Dr. Russel Lee |
| Tuna, Blackfin | 36 lbs. | 3' ¼" | 28⅛" | Bermuda | July 14, 1963 | Joseph E. Baptiste, Jr. |
| | 36 lbs. 4 oz. | 3' 1½" | 28' ⅛" | Challenger Bk., Bermuda | Aug. 6, 1966 | Raymond C. McPherson |
| Tuna, Bluefin | 977 lbs. | 9' 8" | 94½" | St. Ann Bay, N. S. | Sept. 4, 1950 | D. M. Hodgson |

| Species | Weight | Length | Girth | Where caught | Date | Angler |
|---|---|---|---|---|---|---|
| Wahoo | 149 lbs. | 6′ 7¾″ | 37½″ | Cat Cay, Bahamas | June 15, 1962 | John Pirovano |
| Weakfish | 19 lbs. 8 oz. | 3′ 1″ | 23¾″ | Trinidad, W. Indies | Apr. 13, 1962 | Dennis B. Hall |
| Weakfish, Spotted | 15 lbs. 3 oz. | 2′ 10½″ | 20½″ | Fort Pierce, Fla. | Jan. 13, 1949 | C. W. Hubbard |
| Yellowtail | 111 lbs. | 5′ 2″ | 38″ | Bay of Islands, New Zealand | June 11, 1961 | A. F. Plim |
| **FRESH-WATER FISH** | | | | | | |
| Black Bass, Large-mouth | 22 lbs. 4 oz. | 32½″ | 28½ | Montgomery Lake, Ga. | June 2, 1932 | George W. Perry |
| Black Bass, Small-mouth | 11 lbs. 15 oz. | 27″ | 21⅔ | Dale Hollow Lake, Ky. | July 9, 1955 | David L. Hayes |
| Bass, Redeye | 6 lbs. ½ oz. | 20½″ | 15 4/5″ | Hallawakee Creek, Ala. | Mar. 24, 1967 | Thomas Sharpe |
| Bass, White | 5 lbs. 2 oz. | 19″ | 15½″ | Grenada Dam, Miss. | July 9, 1960 | Eddy Vaughn |
| Black Bullhead | 8 lbs. | 24″ | 17¾″ | Lake Waccabuc, N. Y. | Aug. 1, 1951 | Kani Evans |
| Bass, Spotted | 8 lbs. | 24″ | 18¼″ | Smith Lake, Ala. | Mar. 7, 1966 | Bob Hamilton |
| Bluegill | 4 lbs. 12 oz. | 15″ | 18¼″ | Ketona Lake, Ala. | Apr. 9, 1950 | T. S. Hudson |
| Carp | 55 lbs. 5 oz. | 42″ | 31″ | Clearwater Lake, Minn. | July 10, 1952 | Frank J. Ledwein |
| Catfish, Blue | 97 lbs. | 57″ | 37″ | Missouri River, S. D. | Sept. 16, 1959 | E. B. Elliott |
| Catfish, Channel | 58 lbs. | 47½″ | 29⅛″ | Santee-Cooper Res., S. C. | July 7, 1964 | W. B. Whaley |
| Char, Arctic | 27 lbs. 4 oz. | 40¼″ | 26¼″ | Tree River, N. W. T. | Sept. 2, 1963 | Wm. Murphy |
| Crappie, Black | 5 lbs. | 19¼″ | 18⅝″ | Santee-Cooper Res. S. C. | Mar. 15, 1957 | Paul E. Foust |
| Crappie, White | 5 lbs. 3 oz. | 21″ | 19″ | Enid Dam, Miss. | July 31, 1957 | Fred L. Bright |
| Dolly Varden | 32 lbs. | 40½″ | 29¾″ | L. Pend Oreille, Idaho | Oct. 27, 1949 | N. L. Higgins |
| Gar, Alligator | 279 lbs. | 93″ | ........ | Rio Grande R., Texas | Dec. 2, 1951 | Bill Valverde |
| Gar, Longnose | 50 lbs. 5 oz. | 72¼″ | 22¼″ | Trinity River, Texas | July 30, 1954 | Townsend Miller |
| Grayling, Arctic | 5 lbs. | 21″ | 11″ | Great Slave Lake, N.W.T | Aug. 5, 1959 | W. G. Clark |
| Muskellunge | 69 lbs. 15 oz. | 64½″ | 31¾″ | St Lawrence River, N. Y. | Sept. 22, 1957 | Arthur Lawton |
| Perch, White | 4 lbs. 12 oz. | 19½″ | 13″ | Messalonskee Lake, Maine | June 4, 1949 | Mrs. Earl Small |
| Perch, Yellow | 4 lbs. 3½ oz. | ........ | ........ | Bordentown, N. J. | May 1865 | Dr. C. C. Abbot |
| Pickerel, Chain | 9 lbs. 6 oz. | 31″ | 14″ | Homerville, Ga. | Feb. 17, 1961 | Baxley Mc-Quaig, Jr. |
| Pike, Northern | 46 lbs. 2 oz. | 52½″ | 25″ | Sacandaga Res., N. Y | Sept 15, 1940 | Peter Dubuc |
| Salmon, Atlantic | 79 lbs. 2 oz. | ........ | ........ | Tanaelv, Nor. | 1928 | Henrik Henriksen |
| Salmon, Chinook | 92 lbs. | 58½″ | 36″ | Skeena River, B. C. | July 19, 1959 | H. Wichmann |
| Salmon, Silver | 31 lbs. | ........ | ........ | Cowichan Bay, B. C. | Oct. 11, 1947 | Mrs. Lee Hall-berg |
| Salmon, Landlocked | 22 lbs. 8 oz. | 36″ | est. 20″ | Sebago Lake, Maine | Aug. 1, 1907 | Edward Blakely |
| Sauger | 8 lbs. 5 oz. | 28″ | ........ | Niobrara, Nebr. | Oct. 22, 1961 | Mrs. Betty Tepner |
| Sturgeon, White | 360 lbs. | 111″ | 86″ | Snake River, Idaho | April 24, 1956 | Willard Cravens |
| Sunfish, Redear | 2 lbs. 15 oz. | 14″ | 15¾″ | Ponte Vedra Beach, Fla. | Mar. 6, 1965 | Ronald D. Gray, Jr. |
| Trout, Brook | 14½ lbs. | 31½″ | 11½″ | Nipigon River Ontario | July, 1916 | Dr. W. J. Cook |
| Trout, Brown | 39½ lbs. | ........ | ........ | Loch Awe, Scotland | 1866 | W. Muir |
| Trout, Cutthroat | 41 lbs. | 39″ | ........ | Pyramid Lake, Nev. | Dec., 1925 | J. Skimmerhorn |
| Trout, Golden | 11 lbs. | 28″ | 16″ | Cook's Lake, Wyo. | Aug 5, 1948 | Charles S. Reed |
| Trout, Lake | 63 lbs. 2 oz. | 51½″ | 32¾″ | Lake Superior | May 25, 1952 | Hubert Hammers |
| Trout, Rainbow or Steelhead | 37 lbs. | 40½″ | 28″ | Lake Pend Oreille, Idaho | Nov. 25 1947 | Wes Hamlet |
| Trout, Sunapee | 11 lbs. 8 oz. | 33″ | 17¼″ | Lake Sunapee, N. H. | Aug. 1, 1954 | Ernest Theo-haris |
| Walleye | 25 lbs. | 41″ | 29″ | Old Hickory Lake, Tenn. | Aug. 1, 1960 | Mabry Harper |
| Whitefish, Mountain | 5 lbs. | 19″ | 14″ | Athabasca R., Alberta | June 3, 1963 | Orville Welch |

## Angling and Casting Championships in 1968

### AMERICAN CASTING ASSOCIATION

**Men's Combined (fresh water)**

**All Around**—Zack Willson Jr., St. Charles, Mo.
**All Distance**—Zack Willson Jr., 3,445 ft.
**All Accuracy**—Zack Willson Jr., 391 pts.
**Distance Baits**—B. L. Farley, San Antonio, Tex., 2,429 ft.
**Distance Flies**—Zack Willson Jr., 1,062 ft.
**Accuracy Baits**—Zack Willson Jr., 196 pts.
**Accuracy Flies**—Jim Green, Stanton, Calif., 198 pts.

**Men's Single Events (fresh water)**

**⅜ oz. Distance**—Ed Lanser, St. Louis, Mo., 365 ft. Avg.
**⅝ oz. Distance**—Zack Willson, 448⅓ ft. Avg.
**Trout Fly Distance**—Dick Ward, Springfield, Va., 161 ft. Avg.
**Salmon Fly Distance**—William Peters, Toledo, O., 198⅔ ft. Avg.
**Dry Fly Accuracy**—George Applegren, Arlington Heights, Ill., 99 pts.
**Wet Fly Accuracy**—Jim Green, Stanton, Calif., 100 pts.
**⅜ oz. Accuracy**—Zack Willson Jr., 97 pts.
**⅝ oz. Accuracy**—Zack Willson Jr., 99 pts.

**Women's Single Events (fresh water)**

**All Accuracy**—Donna Monty, Toronto, Ontario, 345 pts.
**Accuracy Baits**—Donna Monty, 180 pts.
**Accuracy Flies**—Elsie Seiffert, Hartford, Conn., 186 pts.
**Dry Fly Accuracy**—Elsie Seiffert, 92 pts.
**Wet Fly Accuracy**—Elsie Seiffert, 94 pts.
**⅜ oz. Accuracy**—Donna Monty, 91 pts.
**⅝ oz. Accuracy**—Donna Monty, 89 pts.

# Boxing Champions by Classes

### As of Oct. 15, 1968

Heavyweight .............................. *Vacant*[1]
Light-Heavyweight (175 lbs.) ............... Bob Foster, Washington, D. C.
Middleweight (160 lbs.) .................... Nino Benvenuti, Italy
Welterweight (147 lbs.) ................... Curtis Cokes, Dallas, Tex.
Junior Welterweight (140 lbs.) ............ Paul Fujii, Honolulu
Lightweight (135 lbs.) .................... Teo Cruz, Dom. Republic
Junior Lightweight (130 lbs.) ............. Hiroshi Kobayashi, Japan
Featherweight (126 lbs.) .................. Sho Saijvo, Japan
Bantamweight (118 lbs.) ................... Lionel Rose, Australia
Flyweight (112 lbs.) ...................... Chartchai Chionoi, Thailand

[1]Jimmy Ellis is officially recognized as the heavyweight champion by the majority of state boxing commissions. The remainder recognize Joe Frazier. Ring magazine continues to regard Cassius Clay as champion.

# Ring Champions by Years

## HEAVYWEIGHTS

| | |
|---|---|
| 1882-1892 | John L. Sullivan (A) |
| 1892-1897 | James J. Corbett (B) |
| 1897-1899 | Robert Fitzsimmons |
| 1899-1905 | James J. Jeffries (C) |
| 1905-1906 | Marvin Hart |
| 1906-1908 | Tommy Burns |
| 1908-1915 | Jack Johnson |
| 1915-1919 | Jess Willard |
| 1919-1926 | Jack Dempsey |
| 1926-1928 | Gene Tunney* |
| 1928-1930 | Vacant |
| 1930-1932 | Max Schmeling |
| 1932 | Jack Sharkey |
| 1933 | Primo Carnera |
| 1934 | Max Baer |
| 1935-1936 | James J. Braddock |
| 1937-1949 | Joe Louis* |
| 1949-1951 | Ezzard Charles |
| 1951-1952 | Joe Walcott |
| 1952-1956 | Rocky Marciano* |
| 1956-1959 | Floyd Patterson |
| 1959 | Ingemar Johansson |
| 1960-1962 | Floyd Patterson |
| 1962-1963 | Sonny Liston |
| 1964-1969 | Cassius Clay* (D) |

(A) London Prize Ring (bare knuckle champion).
(B) First Marquis of Queensberry Champion.
(C) Jeffries abandoned the title (1905) and designated Marvin Hart and Jack Root as logical contenders and agreed to referee a fight between them, the winner to be declared champion. Hart defeated Root in 12 rounds (1905) and in turn was defeated by Tommy Burns (1906) who immediately laid claim to the title. Jack Johnson defeated Burns (1908) and was recognized as champion. He clinched the title by defeating Jeffries in an attempted comeback (1910).
(D) Title declared vacant by the World Boxing Assn. and other groups in 1967 after Clay's refusal to fulfill his military obligation.

## LIGHT HEAVYWEIGHTS

| | |
|---|---|
| 1903 | Jack Root, George Gardner |
| 1903-1905 | Bob Fitzsimmons |
| 1905-1912 | Philadelphia Jack O'Brien* |
| 1912-1916 | Jack Dillon |
| 1916-1920 | Battling Levinsky |
| 1920-1922 | Georges Carpentier |
| 1922 | Gene Tunney (outpointed Levinsky and gained American title) |
| 1922 | Harry Greb (outpointed Tunney for American title) |
| 1923 | Battling Siki (knocked out Carpentier for world title) |
| 1923 | Gene Tunney* (outpointed Greb) |
| 1923-1925 | Mike McTigue (outpointed Siki for world title) |
| 1925 | Paul Berlenbach (outpointed McTigue) |
| 1926-1927 | Jack Delaney* (outpointed Berlenbach) |
| 1927-1929 | Tommy Loughran* (outpointed McTigue) |
| 1930-1934 | Maxey Rosenbloom (outpointed Jimmy Slattery, recognized as champion by the New York State Athletic Commission. National Boxing Association vacated Rosenbloom's title) |
| 1934-1935 | Bob Olin (outpointed Rosenbloom, recognized in New York as champion) |
| 1935-1939 | John Henry Lewis* |
| 1939-1939 | Melio Bettina (defeated Jack Fox in elimination tournament to gain title vacated by Lewis) |
| 1939-1941 | Billy Conn* |
| 1941 | Anton Christoforidis (won NBA elimination tourney for title) |
| 1941-1949 | Gus Lesnevich, Freddie Mills. |
| 1949-1950 | Freddie Mills |
| 1950-1952 | Joey Maxim |
| 1953-1960 | Archie Moore |
| 1961 | Harold Johnson (NBA); Archie Moore (New York, Mass.) |
| 1962-1963 | Harold Johnson |
| 1963-1965 | Willie Pastrano |
| 1965-1966 | Jose Torres |

*Abandoned title.

| | |
|---|---|
| 1966-1968 | Dick Tiger |
| 1968 | Bob Foster |

## MIDDLEWEIGHTS

| | |
|---|---|
| 1884-1891 | Jack "Nonpareil" Dempsey |
| 1891-1897 | Bob Fitzsimmons* |
| 1897-1907 | Tommy Ryan* |
| 1907-1908 | Stanley Ketchel, Billy Papke |
| 1908-1910 | Stanley Ketchel |
| 1911-1913 | Claimed by Billy Papke, Frank Klaus, Mike Gibbons. Ed McGoorty and George Chip |
| 1913 | Frank Klaus, George Chip |
| 1914-1917 | Al McCoy |
| 1917-1920 | Mike O'Dowd |
| 1920-1923 | Johnny Wilson |
| 1923-1926 | Harry Greb |
| 1926 | Tiger Flowers, Mickey Walker |
| 1926-1931 | Mickey Walker* |
| 1931-1932 | Gorilla Jones (NBA), Ben Jeby (New York) |
| 1932-1937 | Marcel Thil (NBA) |
| 1933 | Lou Brouillard (New York), Vince Dundee (New York) |
| 1934 | Teddy Yarosz (New York) |
| 1935 | Babe Risko (New York) |
| 1936-1937 | Freddie Steele (NBA and New York) |
| 1938 | Al Hostak (NBA), Solly Krieger (NBA). Fred Apostoli (New York) |
| 1939-1940 | Al Hostak (NBA) |
| 1939 | Fred Apostoli (New York), Ceferino Garcia (New York) |
| 1940 | Tony Zale (NBA), Ken Overlin (New York) |
| 1941 | Tony Zale (NBA), Billy Soose (New York) |
| 1942-1947 | Tony Zale |
| 1947-1948 | Rocky Graziano |
| 1948 | Tony Zale, Marcel Cerdan |
| 1949 | Marcel Cerdan, Jake LaMotta |
| 1950 | Jake LaMotta |
| 1951 | Ray Robinson (universal); Randy Turpin; Ray Robinson* |
| 1952 | Ray Robinson* |
| 1953-1955 | Carl (Bobo) Olson |
| 1955-1956 | Ray Robinson |
| 1957 | Gene Fullmer, Ray Robinson, Carmen Basilio |
| 1958 | Carmen Basilio, Ray Robinson |
| 1959 | Gene Fullmer (NBA); Ray Robinson (New York) |
| 1960 | Gene Fullmer (NBA); Paul Pender (New York and Mass.) |
| 1961 | Gene Fullmer (NBA); Terry Downes (New York, Mass., Europe) |
| 1962 | Gene Fullmer, Dick Tiger (NBA); Paul Pender (New York and Mass.)* |
| 1963 | Dick Tiger (universal). |
| 1963-1965 | Joey Giardello |
| 1965-1966 | Dick Tiger |
| 1966-1967 | Emile Griffith |
| 1967 | Nino Benvenuti |
| 1967-1968 | Emile Griffith |
| 1968 | Nino Benvenuti |

## WELTERWEIGHTS

| | |
|---|---|
| 1892 | Danny Needham, Mysterious Billy Smith |
| 1892-1894 | Mysterious Billy Smith |
| 1894-1896 | Tommy Ryan |
| 1896 | Kid McCoy (outgrew class) |
| 1900 | Mysterious Billy Smith, Rube Ferns Matty Matthews |
| 1901 | Matty Matthews, Rube Ferns |
| 1901-1904 | Joe Walcott |
| 1904-1906 | Dixie Kid, Joe Walcott, Honey Mellody |
| 1907-1911 | Mike Sullivan |
| 1911-1915 | Vacant |
| 1915-1919 | Ted Lewis, Jack Britton |
| 1919-1922 | Jack Britton |
| 1922-1926 | Mickey Walker |
| 1926 | Pete Latzo |
| 1927-1929 | Joe Dundee |
| 1929 | Jackie Fields |
| 1930 | Jackie Fields, Jack Thompson, Tommy Freeman |
| 1931 | Freeman, Thompson, Lou Brouillard |
| 1932 | Jackie Fields |
| 1933 | Young Corbett, Jimmy McLarnin |

| | |
|---|---|
| 1934 | Barney Ross, Jimmy McLarnin |
| 1935 | Jimmy McLarnin, Barney Ross |
| 1936-1938 | Barney Ross |
| 1938-1939 | Henry Armstrong |
| 1940 | Fritzi Zivic |
| 1941-1946 | Fred Cochrane |
| 1946-1947 | Marty Servo*; Ray Robinson (A) |
| 1947-1950 | Ray Robinson |
| 1951 | Ray Robinson (England)*; Johnny Bratton (NBA); Kid Gavilan |
| 1952-1954 | Kid Gavilan |
| 1954-1955 | Johnny Saxton |
| 1955 | Tony De Marco; Carmen Basilio |
| 1956 | Carmen Basilio, Johnny Saxton, Carmen Basilio |
| 1957 | Carmen Basilio* |
| 1958 | Virgil Akins; Don Jordan |
| 1959 | Don Jordan |
| 1960 | Benny Paret |
| 1961 | Emile Griffith, Benny Paret |
| 1962 | Benny Paret, Emile Griffith |
| 1963 | Luis Rodriguez, Emile Griffith |
| 1964-1966 | Emile Griffith* (B) |
| 1966 | Curtis Cokes |

(A) Robinson gained the title by defeating Tommy Bell in an elimination agreed to by the NY Commission and the NBA. Both claimed Robinson waived his title when he won the middleweight crown from LaMotta in 1951. Gavilan defeated Bratton in an elimination to find a successor.

(B) Title became vacant when Griffith won the middleweight title.

### LIGHTWEIGHTS

| | |
|---|---|
| 1885-1896 | Jack McAuliffe* (American champion) |
| 1896-1899 | Kid Lavigne |
| 1899-1902 | Frank Erne |
| 1901-1908 | Joe Gans |
| 1908-1910 | Battling Nelson |
| 1910-1912 | Ad Wolgast |
| 1912-1914 | Willie Ritchie |
| 1914-1917 | Freddie Welsh |
| 1917-1924 | Benny Leonard* |
| 1925 | Jimmy Goodrich, Rocky Kansas |
| 1926-1930 | Sammy Mandell |
| 1930 | Al Singer, Tony Canzoneri |
| 1930-1933 | Tony Canzoneri |
| 1933-1935 | Barney Ross* |
| 1935 | Tony Canzoneri |
| 1936 | Tony Canzoneri, Lou Ambers |
| 1937 | Lou Ambers |
| 1938 | Henry Armstrong |
| 1939 | Lou Ambers |
| 1940 | Lew Jenkins |
| 1941-1943 | Sammy Angott |
| 1943 | Beau Jack (New York), Bob Montgomery, Beau Jack (New York) |
| 1944-1947 | Bob Montgomery (New York) S. Angott (NBA), J. Zurita (NBA) |
| 1945-1951 | Ike Williams (NBA; later universal) |
| 1951-1952 | James Carter |
| 1952 | Lauro Salas, James Carter |
| 1953-1954 | James Carter |
| 1954 | Paddy De Marco; James Carter |
| 1955 | James Carter; Bud Smith |
| 1956 | Bud Smith, Joe Brown |
| 1957-1962 | Joe Brown |
| 1962-1965 | Carlos Ortiz |
| 1965 | Ismael Laguana |
| 1965-1968 | Carlos Ortiz |
| 1968 | Teo Cruz |

### FEATHERWEIGHTS

| | |
|---|---|
| 1892-1900 | George Dixon (A) |
| 1900-1901 | Terry McGovern |
| 1901-1904 | Young Corbett |
| 1904-1908 | Tommy Sullivan |
| 1908-1912 | Abe Attell |
| 1912-1922 | Johnny Kilbane |
| 1923 | Johnny Kilbane, Eugene Criqui, Johnny Dundee |
| 1923-1925 | Johnny Dundee |
| 1925-1927 | Kid Kaplan* |
| 1927-1928 | Benny Bass |
| 1928 | Tony Canzoneri, Andre Routis |
| 1929-1932 | C. Battalino* |
| 1932-1934 | Tommy Paul (NBA), Freddie Miller (NBA) |
| 1934-1936 | Freddie Miller |
| 1936-1937 | Petey Sarron |
| 1937 | P. Sarron, Henry Armstrong* |
| 1938-1940 | Joey Archibald (B) |
| 1940-1941 | Harry Jeffra |

*Abandoned title.

| | |
|---|---|
| 1941 | Joey Archibald, Chalky Wright |
| 1941-1942 | Chalky Wright |
| 1942-1948 | Willie Pep |
| 1948-1949 | Sandy Saddler |
| 1949-1950 | Willie Pep |
| 1950-1954 | Sandy Saddler |
| 1952-1954 | Interim champion: Percy Bassett |
| 1955-1956 | Sandy Saddler* |
| 1957-1959 | Hogan (Kid) Bassey |
| 1959-1962 | Davey Moore |
| 1963-1964 | Sugar Ramos |
| 1964-1967 | Vicente Saldivar* |
| 1968 | Sho Saijyo |

(A) Claim disputed.

(B) After Petey Scalzo knocked out Archibald (Dec. 5, 1938) in an overweight match and was refused a title bout, the NBA named Scalzo champion. The NBA title succession was: Petey Scalzo, 1938-1941; Richard Lemos, 1941; Jackie Wilson, 1941-1943; Jackie Callura, 1943; Phil Terranova, 1943-1944; Sal Bartolo, 1944-1946.

### BANTAMWEIGHTS

| | |
|---|---|
| 1890-1892 | George Dixon* |
| 1892-1894 | Vacant |
| 1894-1899 | Jimmy Barry* |
| 1899-1900 | Terry McGovern* |
| 1901-1902 | Harry Harris* |
| 1902-1903 | Harry Forbes |
| 1903-1904 | Frankie Neil |
| 1904 | Joe Bowker*, Digger Stanley (Eng.), Jimmy Walsh (U.S.) |
| 1905-1907 | Jimmy Walsh* |
| 1907-1910 | Vacant |
| 1910-1914 | Johnny Coulon |
| 1914-1917 | Kid Williams |
| 1917-1920 | Pete Herman |
| 1920-1921 | Joe Lynch |
| 1921 | Pete Herman, Johnny Buff |
| 1922 | Johnny Buff, Joe Lynch |
| 1922-1924 | Joe Lynch |
| 1924 | Abe Goldstein, Eddie Martin |
| 1925 | Eddie Martin, Charley (Phil) Rosenberg |
| 1925-1926 | Charley (Phil) Rosenberg |
| 1927-1928 | Bud Taylor* (NBA only) |
| 1929-1935 | Al Brown |
| 1935-1936 | Baltazar Sangchili |
| 1936 | Tony Marino, Sixto Escobar |
| 1937 | Sixto Escobar, Harry Jeffra |
| 1938-1940 | Sixto Escobar* |
| 1940-1942 | Lou Salica |
| 1942-1947 | Manuel Ortiz |
| 1947 | Harold Dade, Manuel Ortiz |
| 1948-1950 | Manuel Ortiz |
| 1950-1952 | Vic Toweel |
| 1952 | Vic Toweel, Jimmy Carruthers |
| 1953-1954 | Jimmy Carruthers* |
| 1954-1955 | Robert Cohen (NBA) |
| 1955 | Raul Macias (NBA); Robert Cohen (New York and World Committee) |
| 1956 | Mario D'Agata (New York and World Committee); Raul Macias (NBA) |
| 1957 | Alphonse Halimi (New York and World Committee); Raul Macias (NBA) |
| 1958-1959 | Alphonse Halimi (universal) |
| 1959-1960 | Jose Becerra* |
| 1961-1965 | Eder Jofre (universal) |
| 1965-1968 | Fighting Harada |
| 1968 | Lionel Rose |

### FLYWEIGHTS

| | |
|---|---|
| 1916-1923 | Jimmy Wilde |
| 1923-1925 | Pancho Villa |
| 1925-1927 | Fidel La Barba* |
| 1927-1930 | Izzy Schwartz (New York only) |
| 1930 | Midget Wolgast (New York); Frankie Genaro (NBA) |
| 1931-1932 | Young Perez (defeated Frankie Genaro) |
| 1932-1935 | Jackie Brown |
| 1935-1938 | Benny Lynch* |
| 1939-1943 | Peter Kane* |
| 1943-1943 | Vacant |
| 1943-1947 | Jackie Patterson |
| 1947-1950 | Rinty Monaghan* |
| 1950-1952 | Dado Marino |
| 1952-1954 | Yoshio Shirai |
| 1954-1960 | Pascual Perez |
| 1960-1962 | Pone Kingpetch |
| 1962 | Masahika Harada |
| 1963 | Pone Kingpetch, Hiroyuki Ebihara |
| 1964-1965 | Pone Kingpetch |
| 1965-1966 | Salvatore Burruni |
| 1966 | Walter McGowen |
| 1966 | Chartchai Chionoi |

## AAU Senior Boxing Championships in 1968

### Maumee, Ohio, Apr. 4-6

106 lbs.—Harlan Marbley, Washington, D. C.
112 lbs.—Kenneth Bazer, New Iberia, La.
119 lbs.—Sam Goss, Trenton, N. J.
126 lbs.—George McCarvey, Hyattsville, Md.
132 lbs.—Ronnie Harris, Canton, Ohio.
139 lbs.—Joe Louis Valdez, Houston, Texas.

147 lbs.—Michael Colbert, Portland, Ore.
156 lbs.—William Beeler, Louisville, Ky.
165 lbs.—Alfred Jones, Detroit, Mich.
178 lbs.—Leonard Hutchins, Detroit, Mich.
Heavyweight—George Foreman, Pleasanton, Calif.
Team—Pacific.

# Major Professional Boxing Bouts in 1968

### Nov. 13, 1967—Oct. 14, 1968

| Date | Winner, weight | Loser, weight | Round | Site |
|---|---|---|---|---|
| | **1967** | | | |
| Nov. 13 | Brian London, 198 | Zora Folley, 212 | D-10 | Liverpool, Eng. |
| Nov. 16 | Danny Perez, 156 | Jose Stable, 155 | D-10 | New York, N. Y. |
| Nov. 16 | Paul Fuji, 140 | Willi Quatour, 137 | KO-4 | Tokyo |
| *Nov. 17 | Dick Tiger, 168 | Roger Rouse, 174 | KO-12 | Las Vegas |
| Nov. 17 | Eduardo Corletti | Everett Copeland | KO-5 | Turin, Italy |
| Nov. 18 | Buster Mathis, 242 | Roberto Davila, 207 | KO-7 | Stockholm, Sweden |
| Nov. 27 | Roger Russell | Leotis Martin | D-10 | Philadelphia |
| Dec. 2 | Jimmy Ellis, 194 | Oscar Bonavena, 206 | D-12 | Louisville, Ky. |
| Dec. 6 | Bobby Foster, 179 | Sonny Moore, 205 | KO-2 | Washington, D. C. |
| Dec. 11 | Lionel Rose, 117 | Rocky Gattellari, 114 | KO-13 | Sydney, Aust. |
| *Dec. 14 | Kiroshi Kabayashi, 129 | Teshiaki Numata, 129 | KO-12 | Tokyo |
| Dec. 15 | Luis Rodriguez, 152 | Benny Briscoe, 155 | D-10 | New York, N. Y. |
| Dec. 15 | Emile Griffith, 157 | Remo Golfarini, 161 | KO-6 | Rome, Italy |
| Dec. 18 | Joe Frazier, 210 | Marion Comer, 180 | KO-3 | Boston |
| | **1968** | | | |
| Jan. 20 | Nino Benvenuti, 159 | Charlie Austin, 159 | D-10 | Rome, Italy |
| Jan. 28 | Piero Tomasoni, 193 | Bob Stallings, 197 | D-10 | Milan, Italy |
| *Jan. 29 | Chartchai Chionoi, 109 | Efren Torres, 111 | KO-13 | Mexico City |
| Feb. 3 | Harold Johnson, 170 | Lothar Stengel, 168 | D-10 | Frankfurt, Germany |
| Feb. 3 | Jerry Quarry, 193 | Thad Spencer, 200 | KO-12 | Oakland, Calif. |
| Feb. 5 | Curtis Cokes | Jean Josselin | D-10 | Paris |
| Feb. 6 | Luis Rodriguez, 154 | Charlie Austin, 159 | KO-6 | Miami |
| Feb. 16 | Oscar Bonavena | Felipe Marich | KO-6 | Argentina |
| Feb. 16 | Roscoe Bell, 152 | Ray Malon, 149 | KO-2 | Orlando, Fla. |
| Feb. 19 | Joe Harris, 155 | Dick Di Veronica, 153 | D-10 | Philadelphia |
| Feb. 19 | Ken Buchanan, 131 | Maurice Cullen, 135 | KO-11 | London |
| Feb. 23 | Moses Harrell, 200 | Pedro Sanchez, 209 | KO-3 | Orlando, Fla. |
| Feb. 26 | Johnny Pritchett | Leslie McAteer | D-15 | Nottingham, Eng. |
| *Feb. 27 | Lionel Rose, 117 | Fighting Harada, 117 | D-15 | Tokyo |
| Feb. 29 | Roberto Davila, 197 | Brian London, 197 | KO-6 | Liverpool, Eng. |
| Mar. 3 | Percy Pugh, 142 | Jerry Pellegrini, 146 | D-15 | New Orleans |
| Mar. 4 | Joe Frazier, 204 | Buster Mathis, 243 | KO-11 | New York |
| *Mar. 4 | Nino Benvenuti, 160 | Emile Griffith, 154 | D-15 | New York |
| Mar. 7 | Renaldo Victoria, 139 | Roosevelt Ware, 147 | D-10 | Portland, Maine |
| Mar. 8 | Roscoe Bell, 152 | Dennis Riggs, 160 | KO-4 | Orlando, Fla. |
| Mar. 15 | Curtis Cokes, 154 | Jimmy Lester, 155 | D-10 | Oakland, Calif. |
| Mar. 15 | Lavelle Franklin, 135 | Jimmy Fields, 134 | KO-2 | Los Angeles |
| Mar. 26 | Luis Rodriguez, 154 | Carl Moore, 157 | D-10 | Miami Beach |
| *Mar. 29 | Paul Rojas, 126 | Enrique Higgins, 125 | D-15 | Los Angeles |
| Mar. 29 | Jim Beattie, 250 | Orville Qualls, 240 | KO-3 | Detroit |
| Apr. 1 | Jose Torres, 175 | Bobby Dunlop, 173 | KO-6 | Sydney, Aust. |
| Apr. 2 | Paul Fuji, 143 | Roberto Cruz, 142 | KO-9 | Sapparo, Japan |
| Apr. 5 | Leotis Martin, 193 | Karl Mildenberger, 205 | KO-7 | Frankfurt, Germany |
| Apr. 5 | Sandro Mazzinghi, 157 | Bob Cassidy, 157 | KO-2 | Rome, Italy |
| Apr. 9 | Howard Winston | Jimmy Anderson | D-10 | Wembley, Eng. |
| Apr. 15 | Ismael Laguna, 135 | Bud Anderson, 138 | KO-9 | Philadelphia |
| *Apr. 16 | Curtis Cokes, 145 | Willie Ludick, 146 | KO-5 | Dallas, Tex. |
| Apr. 19 | Jose Gonzalez, 161 | Vincente Rondon, 160 | KO-8 | New York |
| Apr. 19 | Jim Beattie, 251 | Willie Richardson, 192 | D-10 | St. Paul, Minn. |
| *Apr. 27 | Jimmy Ellis | Jerry Quarry | D-15 | Oakland, Calif. |
| Apr. 30 | Buster Mathis, 247 | Mel Turnbow, 238 | KO-7 | Cincinnati |
| May 7 | Luis Rodriguez, 156 | Teddy Wright, 165 | D-10 | Miami Beach, Fla. |
| May 17 | Jose Gonzalez, 161 | Jimmy Ramos, 160 | D-10 | New York, N. Y. |
| *May 24 | Bob Foster, 173 | Dick Tiger, 168 | KO-4 | New York |
| *May 26 | Sandro Mazzinghi, 151 | Kim Ki-Soo, 151 | D-15 | Milan, Italy |
| May 27 | Art Hernandez | Rudy Rodriguez | D-10 | Milwaukee |
| May 28 | Leotis Martin, 202 | Thad Spencer, 193 | KO-9 | London |
| June 7 | Nino Benvenuti, 161 | Yoshiaki Alasaka, 170 | KO-2 | Rome |
| June 11 | Emile Griffith | Andy Heilman | D-12 | Oakland, Calif. |
| *June 24 | Joe Frazier, 203 | Manuel Ramos, 208 | KO-2 | New York |
| June 25 | Al Jones | Matt Blow | D-10 | Miami Beach, Fla. |
| June 25 | Cleveland Williams | Les Borden | KO-1 | Houston |
| June 25 | Terry Lee, 171 | Ronnie Wilson, 165 | D-10 | San Diego |
| June 29 | Teo Cruz, 134 | Carlos Ortiz, 135 | D-15 | Santo Domingo |
| *July 2 | Lionel Rose | Takao Sakurai | D-15 | Tokyo |
| July 3 | Art Davis, 156 | Jerry Weakland | KO-2 | Las Vegas |
| July 5 | Nino Benvenuti, 164 | Jimmy Ramos, 163 | KO-4 | Turin, Italy |
| July 5 | Curtis Cokes | Joseph Sishi | KO-5 | Durban, So. Africa |
| July 6 | Sonny Liston, 219 | Henry Clark, 215 | KO-7 | San Francisco |
| July 17 | Ismael Laguna, 136 | Victor Melendez, 136 | D-10 | New York |
| July 23 | Den Morton, 204 | Wayne Kindred, 196 | KO-6 | Los Angeles |
| July 24 | Alvin Lewis, 215 | Eduardo Corletti, 195 | KO-2 | Detroit |
| July 24 | Jose Legra, 125 | Howard Winstone, 125 | KO-5 | Porthcawl, Wales |
| July 24 | Buster Mathis, 226 | Jim Beattie, 244 | KO-7 | Bloomington, Minn. |
| Aug. 1 | Bob Herrington, 166 | Lloyd Bozeman, 174 | D-10 | Portland, Maine |
| Aug. 6 | Cleveland Williams, 211 | Jean-Claude Roy, 186 | D-10 | Houston |
| Aug. 6 | Emile Griffith, 157 | Joe Harris, 160 | D-12 | Philadelphia |
| Aug. 12 | Jack Bodell, 204 | Mel Turnbow, 241 | KO-6 | Blackpool, Eng. |
| Aug. 13 | Al Jones, 200 | Jim Howard | KO-6 | Miami Beach, Fla. |
| Aug. 17 | Stan Hayward, 152 | Johnny Brooks, 153 | D-10 | New Orleans |
| Aug. 20 | Ismael Laguna, 136 | Lloyd Marshall, 132 | KO-9 | New York |
| Aug. 20 | Benny Briscoe, 161 | Jose Gonzalez, 161 | D-10 | New York |
| Aug. 20 | Antonio Amaya, 136 | Frankie Narvaez, 136 | D-10 | New York |
| Aug. 28 | Lionel Rose, 120 | Jose Medel, 120 | D-10 | Los Angeles |
| Sept. 4 | Fighting Harada | Noluo Chiba | KO-7 | Sano, Japan |
| Sept. 9 | Bob Foster, 177 | Roger Rouse, 177 | KO-5 | Washington |
| Sept. 11 | Frank De Paula, 175 | Jimmy McDermott, 171 | KO-4 | New York |
| Sept. 13 | Johnny Famechon, 124 | Billy McCrandle, 122 | KO-12 | Melbourne |
| *Sept. 14 | Jimmy Ellis, 163 | Floyd Patterson | D-15 | Stockholm, Sweden |
| Sept. 17 | Nino Benvenuti, 163 | Art Hernandez, 164 | D-10 | Toronto |
| Sept. 17 | George Chuvalo, 207 | Vic Brown, 193 | KO-3 | Toronto |
| Sept. 26 | Buster Mathis, 223 | James Woody, 203 | KO-6 | New York, N. Y. |
| Sept. 26 | George Chuvalo, 208 | Manuel Ramos | KO-5 | New York, N. Y. |
| *Sept. 27 | Sho Saijyo, 125 | Paul Rojas, 126 | D-15 | Los Angeles |
| *Sept. 27 | Teo Cruz, 135 | Mando Ramus | D-15 | Los Angeles |
| Oct. 9 | Joe Shaw | Pete Toro | D-10 | New York, N. Y. |
| Oct. 14 | Sonny Liston, 221 | Sonny Moore, 295 | KO-3 | Phoenix, Ariz. |

*Indicates championship bout.

# History of Heavyweight Championship Bouts

1889—July 8—John L. Sullivan beat Jake Kilrain, 75 rounds, Richburg, Miss. (Last championship bare knuckles bout.)

*1892—Sept. 7—James J. Corbett defeated John L. Sullivan, 21 rounds, New Orleans. (Used big gloves for first time.)

1894—Jan. 25—James J. Corbett ko'd Charley Mitchell, 3 rounds, Jacksonville, Fla.

*1897—March 17—Bob Fitzsimmons defeated James J. Corbett, 14 rounds, Carson City, Nev.

*1899—June 9—James J. Jeffries beat Bob Fitzsimmons, 11 rounds, Coney Island, N. Y.

1899—Nov. 3—James J. Jeffries beat Tom Sharkey, 25 rounds, Coney Island, N. Y.

1900—May 11—James J. Jeffries knocked out James J. Corbett, 23 rounds, Coney Island, N. Y.

1901—Nov. 15—James J. Jeffries, ko'd Gus Ruhlin, 5 rounds, San Francisco.

1902—July 25—James J. Jeffries knocked out Bob Fitzsimmons, 8 rounds, San Francisco, Cal.

1903—Aug. 14—James J. Jeffries knocked out James J. Corbett, 10 rounds, San Francisco, Cal.

1904—Aug. 26—James J. Jeffries knocked out Jack Munroe, 2 rounds, San Francisco, Cal.

*1905—James J. Jeffries retired, July 3—Marvin Hart knocked out Jack Root, 12 rounds, Reno. Jeffries refereed and presented the title to the victor. Jack O'Brien also claimed the title.

*1906—Feb. 23—Tommy Burns defeated Marvin Hart, 20 rounds, Los Angeles, Cal.

1906—Nov. 28—Philadelphia Jack O'Brien and Tommy Burns, 20 rounds, draw, Los Angeles.

1907—May 8—Tommy Burns defeated Jack O'Brien, 20 rounds, Los Angeles, Cal.

1907—July 4—Tommy Burns knocked out Bill Squires, 1 round, Colma, Cal.

1907—Dec. 2—Tommy Burns knocked out Gunner Moir, 10 rounds, London.

1908—Feb. 10—Tommy Burns knocked out Jack Palmer, 4 rounds, London.

1908—March 17—Tommy Burns knocked out Jem Roche, 1 round, Dublin.

1908—April 18—Tommy Burns knocked out Jewey Smith, 5 rounds, Paris.

1908—June 13—Tommy Burns knocked out Bill Squires, 8 rounds, Paris.

1908—Aug. 24—Tommy Burns knocked out Bill Squires, 13 rounds, Sydney, New South Wales.

1908—Sept. 2—Tommy Burns knocked out Bill Lang, 2 rounds, Melbourne, Australia.

*1908—Dec. 26—Jack Johnson stopped Tommy Burns, 14 rounds, Sydney, Australia. Police halted contest.

1909—May 19—Jack Johnson and Jack O'Brien, 6 rounds, draw, Philadelphia.

1909—June 30—Jack Johnson and Tony Ross, 6 rounds, draw, Pittsburgh, Pa.

1909—Sept. 9—Jack Johnson and Al Kaufman, 10 rounds, no decision, San Francisco, Cal.

1909—Oct. 16—Jack Johnson knocked out Stanley Ketchell, 12 rounds, Colma, Cal.

1910—July 4—Jack Johnson knocked out Jim Jeffries, 15 rounds, Reno, Nev. (Jeffries came back from retirement.)

1912—July 4—Jack Johnson won on points from Jim Flynn, 9 rounds, Las Vegas, N. M., (contest stopped by police).

1913—Nov. 28—Jack Johnson knocked out Andre Spaul, 2 rounds, Paris.

1913—Dec. 9—Jack Johnson and Jim Johnson, 10 rounds, draw, Paris. (Bout called a draw when Jack Johnson declared he had broken his arm.)

1914—June 27—Jack Johnson won from Frank Moran, 20 rounds, Paris.

*1915—April 5—Jess Willard knocked out Jack Johnson, 26 rounds, Havana, Cuba.

1916—March 25—Jess Willard and Frank Moran, 10 rounds (no decision), New York City.

*1919—July 4—Jack Dempsey knocked out Jess Willard, Toledo, O. (Willard failed to answer bell for fourth round.)

1920—Sept. 6—Jack Dempsey knocked out Billy Miske, 3 rounds, Benton Harbor, Mich.

1920—Dec. 14—Jack Dempsey knocked out Bill Brennan, 12 rounds, New York City.

1921—July 2—Jack Dempsey knocked out Georges Carpenter, 4 rounds, Boyle's Thirty Acres, Jersey City, N. J., (Carpenter had held the so called white heavyweight title since July 16, 1914, in a series established in 1913, after Jack Johnson's exile in Europe late in 1912.)

1923—July 4—Jack Dempsey won on points from Tom Gibbons, 15 rounds, Shelby, Mont.

1923—Sept. 14—Jack Dempsey knocked out Luis Firpo, 2 rounds, New York City.

*1926—Sept. 23—Gene Tunney beat Jack Dempsey, 10 rounds, decision, Philadelphia.

1927—Sept. 22—Gene Tunney beat Jack Dempsey, 10 rounds, decision, Chicago.

1928—July 26—Gene Tunney knocked out Tom Heeney, 11 rounds, Yankee Stadium, New York; soon afterward he announced his retirement.

*1930—June 12—Max Schmeling of Germany defeated Jack Sharkey in fourth round when Sharkey fouled Schmeling in a bout which was generally considered to have resulted in the election of a successor to Gene Tunney, New York.

1931—July 3—Max Schmeling knocked out Young Stribling, 15 rounds in Cleveland.

*1932—June 21—Jack Sharkey defeated Max Schmeling, 15 rounds, decision, New York City.

*1933—June 29—Primo Carnera knocked out Jack Sharkey, six rounds, New York City.

1933—Oct. 22—Carnera defeated Paulino Uzcudun, 15 rounds, in Rome.

1934—March 1—Primo Carnera defeated Tommy Loughran in 15 rounds in Miami.

*1934—June 14—Max Baer knocked out Primo Carnera, eleven rounds, New York City.

*1935—June 13—James J. Braddock defeated Max Baer, 15 rounds, New York City.

*1937—June 22—Joe Louis knocked out James J. Braddock, 8 rounds, Chicago.

1937—Aug. 30—Joe Louis defeated Tommy Farr, 15 rounds, decision, New York City.

1938—Feb. 23—Joe Louis knocked out Nathan Mann, 3 rounds, New York City.

1938—April 1—Joe Louis knocked out Harry Thomas, 5 rounds, New York City.

1938—June 22—Joe Louis knocked out Max Schmeling, one round, New York City.

1939—January 25—Joe Louis knocked out John H. Lewis, 1 round, New York City.

1939—April 17—Joe Louis knocked out Jack Roper, 1 round, Los Angeles.

1939—June 28—Joe Louis knocked out Tony Galento, 4 rounds, New York City.

1939—September 20—Joe Louis knocked out Bob Pastor, 11 rounds, Detroit, Mich.

1940—February 9—Joe Louis defeated Arturo Godoy, 15 rounds, decision, New York City.

1940—March 29—Joe Louis knocked out Johnny Paychek, 2 rounds, New York City.

1940—June 20—Joe Louis knocked out Arturo Godoy, 8 rounds, New York City.

1940—Dec. 16—Joe Louis knocked out Al McCoy, 6 rounds, Boston.

1941—Jan. 31—Joe Louis knocked out Red Burman, 5 rounds, New York City.

1941—Feb. 17—Joe Louis knocked out Gus Dorazio, 2 rounds, Philadelphia.

1941—March 21—Joe Louis knocked out Abe Simon, 13 rounds, Detroit, Mich.

1941—April 8—Joe Louis knocked out Tony Musto, 9 rounds, St. Louis, Mo.

1941—May 23—Joe Louis beat Buddy Baer, 7 rounds, Washington, D C., on a disqualification.

1941—June 18—Joe Louis knocked out Billy Conn, 13 rounds, New York City.

1941—Sept. 29—Joe Louis knocked out Lou Nova, 6 rounds, New York City.

1942—Jan. 9—Joe Louis knocked out Buddy Baer, 1 round, New York City.

1942—March 27—Joe Louis knocked out Abe Simon, 6 rounds, New York City.

1946—June 19—Joe Louis knocked out Billy Conn, 8 rounds, New York City.

1946—Sept. 18—Joe Louis knocked out Tami Mauriello, 1 round, New York City.

1947—Dec. 5—Joe Louis defeated Joe Walcott in a 15-round bout by a split decision, New York City.

1948—June 25—Joe Louis knocked out Joe Walcott, 11 rounds, New York City.

*1949—June 22—Following Joe Louis' retirement Ezzard Charles defeated Joe Walcott by a unanimous decision, 15 rounds, Chicago, Ill. (N.B.A. recognition only).

1949—Aug. 10—Ezzard Charles knocked out Gus Lesnevich, seven rounds, New York City.

1949—Oct. 14—Ezzard Charles knocked out **Pat** Valentino, eight rounds, San Francisco (clinched American title).

1950—Aug. 15—Ezzard Charles knocked out Freddy Beshore, 14 rounds, Buffalo, N. Y.

1950—Sept. 27—Ezzard Charles defeated Joe Louis in latter's attempted comeback, 15 rounds, New York City (universal recognition).

1950—Dec. 5—Ezzard Charles knocked out **Nick** Barone, 11 rounds, Cincinnati, Ohio.

1951—Jan. 12—Ezzard Charles knocked out **Lee** Oma, 10 rounds, New York, N.Y.

1951—March 7—Ezzard Charles outpointed Joe Walcott, 15 rounds, Detroit, Mich.

1951—May 30—Ezzard Charles outpointed Joey Maxim, light heavyweight champion, 15 rounds, Chicago.

*1951—July 18—Joe Walcott knocked out Ezzard Charles, 7th round, Pittsburgh, Pa.

1952—June 5—Joe Walcott outpointed Ezzard Charles, 15 rounds, Philadelphia, Pa.

*1952—Sept. 23—Rocky Marciano knocked out Joe Walcott, 13th round, Philadelphia, Pa.

1953—May 15—Rocky Marciano knocked out Joe Walcott, first round, Chicago, Ill.

1953—Sept. 24—Rocky Marciano knocked out Roland LaStarza, 11th round, Polo Grounds, New York, N.Y.

1954—June 17—Rocky Marciano outpointed Ezzard Charles, 15 rounds, Yankee Stadium, New York, N. Y.

1954—Sept. 17—Rocky Marciano knocked out Ezzard Charles, 8th round, Yankee Stadium, New York, N. Y.

1955—May 16—Rocky Marciano knocked out Don Cockell, 9th round, Kezar Stadium, San Francisco, Calif.

1955—Sept. 21—Rocky Marciano knocked out Archie Moore, 9th round, Yankee Stadium, N.Y. Marciano retired undefeated, Apr. 27, 1956.

*1956—Nov. 30—Floyd Patterson, a contender, knocked out **Archie Moore**, 5th round, **Chicago**, Ill., gaining the championship.

1957—July 29—Floyd Patterson knocked out Hurricane Jackson, 10th round, Polo Grounds, New York, N.Y.

1957—Aug. 22—Floyd Patterson knocked **out** Pete Rademacher, 6th round, Seattle, Wash.

1958—Aug. 18—Floyd Patterson ko'd Roy Harris, 12th round, Los Angeles, Calif.

1959—May 1—Floyd Patterson knocked out **Brian** London, 11 rounds, Indianapolis, Ind.

*1959—June 26—Ingemar Johansson, Sweden, ko'd Floyd Patterson, 3rd round, Yankee Stadium, New York City.

*1960—June 20—Floyd Patterson knocked out Ingemar Johansson, 5th round, Polo Grounds, New York, N. Y. (First heavyweight in boxing history to regain title.)

1961—Mar. 13—Floyd Patterson knocked out Ingemar Johansson, 6th round, Convention Hall, Miami Beach, Fla.

1961—Dec. 4—Floyd Patterson knocked out Tom McNeeley, 4th round, Toronto, Ont., Canada.

*1962—Sept. 25—Sonny Liston knocked out Floyd Patterson, first round, Comiskey Park, Chicago, Ill.

1963—July 22—Sonny Liston knocked out Floyd Patterson, first round, Las Vegas, Nevada.

*1964—Feb. 25—Cassius Clay knocked out Sonny Liston, 7th round, Miami Beach, Fla.

1965—May 26—Cassius Clay knocked out Sonny Liston, first round, Lewiston, Maine.

1965—Nov. 11—Cassius Clay knocked out Floyd Patterson, twelfth round, Las Vegas, Nev.

1966—Mar. 29—Cassius Clay outpointed George Chuvalo, 15 rounds, Toronto, Ont.

1966—May 21—Cassius Clay knocked out Henry Cooper, sixth round, London, Eng.

1966—Aug. 6—Cassius Clay knocked out Brian London, third round, London, Eng.

1966—Sept. 10—Cassius Clay knocked out Karl Mildenberger, twelfth round, Frankfurt, Germany.

1966—Nov. 14—Cassius Clay knocked out Cleveland Williams, third round, Houston, Tex.

1967—Feb. 6—Cassius Clay outpointed Ernie Terrell, 15 rounds, Houston, Tex.

1967—March 22—Cassius Clay knocked out Zora Folley, seventh round, **New York.**

*Title changed hands.

# Edward J. Neil Trophy and Walker Award

The Edward J. Neil Memorial Trophy is awarded annually by the Boxing Writers' Assn. of N. Y. to the one who has done the most for boxing in the preceding year. The plaque is in memory of Edward J. Neil, an AP sportswriter killed in 1938 while covering the Spanish revolution. James J. Walker Memorial Award to an individual for long and meritorious service to boxing. Recent winners:

1958—Archie Moore, light heavyweight champion. Walker Award: Sam Taub, writer and announcer.

1959—Ingemar Johansson, heavyweight champion. Walker Award: Marv Jenson, boxing manager.

1960—Floyd Patterson, heavyweight champion. Walker Award: Ned Brown.

1961—Gene Fullmer, N.B.A. world middleweight champion. Walker Award: Dr. Alexander Schiff, New York State Athletic Commission.

1962—Dick Tiger, world middleweight champion. Walker Award: Dr. Mal Stevens.

1963—Emile Griffith, world welterweight champion. Walker Award: Harry Markson, boxing dir.,

Madison Sq. Garden.

1964—Willie Pastrano, world light-heavyweight champion. Walker Award: Mickey Walker, former welterweight and middleweight champion.

1965—Cassius Clay, world heavyweight champion. Walker Award: Jack Cuddy, former boxing writer for U.P.I.

1966—Dick Tiger, world light-heavyweight champion. Walker Award: Nat Fleischer, editor Ring Magazine and The Ring Record Book and Boxing Encyclopedia.

1967—Carlos Ortiz, world lightweight champion. Walker Award: Joe Louis, former world heavyweight **champion.**

## Sports Arenas

| Name and location | Cap.* | Name and location | Cap.* |
|---|---|---|---|
| Ak-Sar-Ben Field, Omaha, Neb. | 14,000 | Mid-South Coliseum, Memphis. | 12,000 |
| Atlantic City Audit., Atlantic City, N. J. | 40,000 | Milwaukee Arena. | 12,500 |
| Baltimore Civic Center. | 12,348 | Montreal Forum. | 14,097 |
| Boston Garden. | 13,909 | New Orleans Municipal Audit. | 9,100 |
| Charlotte Coliseum. | 13,500 | Oakland-Alameda County Coliseum. | 15,000 |
| Chicago Stadium. | 17,374 | Oklahoma City State Fair Arena. | 10,000 |
| Cincinnati Gardens. | 11,438 | Olympia, Detroit. | 13,208 |
| Cleveland Arena. | 10,000 | Olympic Auditorium, Los Angeles. | 10,500 |
| Convention Hall, Philadelphia. | 9,200 | Onondaga Cty. War Mem., Syracuse, N. Y. | 7,500 |
| Cobo Arena, Detroit. | 11,009 | Penn Palestra, Philadelphia. | 9,200 |
| Cow Palace, San Francisco. | 17,000 | Pittsburgh Civic Arena. | 12,500 |
| Dallas Memorial Auditorium. | 11,000 | Portland Memorial Coliseum. | 10,500 |
| Freedom Hall, Louisville, Ky. | 20,000 | Reynolds Coliseum, Raleigh, N. C. | 12,400 |
| International Amphitheatre, Chicago. | 9,500 | Rhode Island Audit., Providence. | 7,150 |
| Hobart Arena, Troy, Ohio. | 6,000 | St. Louis Arena. | 14,039 |
| Kiel Auditorium, St. Louis. | 10,574 | Sam Houston Coliseum, Houston. | 13,000 |
| Long Beach Arena, Calif. | 11,168 | San Diego Intl. Sports Arena. | 14,000 |
| Los Angeles Forum. | 17,500 | San Francisco Civic Audit. | 7,500 |
| Los Angeles Sports Arena. | 15,333 | Seattle Center Coliseum. | 12,595 |
| Louisville Convention Center. | 7,000 | Spectrum, Phil. | 16,000 |
| Madison Square Garden. | 19,500 | Uline Arena, Washington, D. C. | 11,000 |
| Maple Leaf Gardens, Toronto. | 15,600 | Veterans Memorial Audit., Des Moines, Ia. | 15,000 |
| Metropolitan Sports Center, Bloomington, Minn. | 14,400 | Veterans Memorial Coliseum, Phoenix, Ariz. | 10,294 |
| | | Washington Coliseum. | 5,300 |
| Miami Beach Convention Hall. | 12,000 | Will Rogers Coliseum, Ft. Worth, Texas. | 7,000 |

*Normal seating capacity.

## Madison Square Garden Hall of Fame

The new Madison Square Garden Center, above Pennsylvania Station in New York City, includes a Hall of Fame which initially honors 88 performers and personalities who made important contributions in the 88 years of earlier Gardens (1879-1967). The Garden Hall of Famers, classified by category, follow:

**BASKETBALL**
Elgin Baylor
Clair Bee
Bill Bradley
Howard Cann
Wilt Chamberlain
Bob Cousy
Tom Gola
Nat Holman
Pat Kennedy
Bob Kurland
Joe Lapchick
Jerry Lucas
Hank Luisetti
Bob Pettit
Oscar Robertson
Bill Russell

**BIKE RACE**
Alfred Goullet
Reggie McNamara

**BOWLING**
Don Carter
Billy Golembiewski

**BOXING**
Henry Armstrong
Bill Corum

Jack Dempsey
James A. Farley
Mike Jacobs
Benny Leonard
Joe Louis
Rocky Marciano
William Muldoon
Ray Robinson
John L. Sullivan

**CIRCUS, RODEO**
Gene Autry
P. T. Barnum
Buffalo Bill Cody
Emmett Kelly
John Ringling North
John Ringling
Roy Rogers
Jim Shoulders
May Wirth

**DOG SHOW**
Anne Rogers Clark
Dr. Samuel Milbank
Percy Roberts

**HOCKEY**
Frank Boucher

King Clancy
Bill Cook
Gordie Howe
Bobby Hull
Ching Johnson
Howie Morenz
Lester Patrick
Maurice Richard
Eddie Shore

**HORSE SHOW**
John McE. Bowman
Loula Long Combs
Maj. Gen. Guy V. Henry
Wm. H. Vanderbilt

**ICE SHOW**
Sonja Henie
Ronnie Robertson
Roy Shipstad

**TENNIS**
Don Budge
Suzanne Lenglen
Bill Tilden

**TRACK**
Glenn Cunningham
Ron Delany

John McHugh
Loren Murchison
Paavo Nurmi
Joie Ray
Bob Richards
James E. Sullivan
Emil Von Elling
Pete Waters
Bernie Wefers

**WRESTLING**
Jack Curley
Frank Gotch
Strangler Lewis
Jim Londos

**BUILDERS**
Asa S. Bushnell
Irving Mitchell Felt
Daniel J. Ferris
Bernard F. Gimbel
Stanton Griffis
Edward S. (Ned) Irish
John Reed Kilpatrick
Paul H. Pilgrim
George L. (Tex) Rickard
Fred Schmertz

## Curling Events in 1968

**The Douglas Medal**, Hastings on Hudson, N. Y. Jan. 4-7. N. Y. Caledonian C.C., Vern Hambly, skip. **The Griffith Medal**, Brae Burn C.C., Bud Chandler, skip. **The Williamson Medal**, Albany C.C., Peter Anderson, skip.

**The Holland Bowl**, Petersham, Mass. Jan. 11-14. Border C.C. #1, M. W. MacDonald, skip. **The McGregor Trophy**, Border C.C. #2, A. Joyal, skip. **The Holt Trophy**, Norfolk C.C., W. Hill, skip.

**The Mitchell Gold Medal**, Utica, N. Y. Jan. 11-14. Utica C.C. #6, Arthur Cobb, skip. **The Allen Memorial Medal**, Utica C.C. #2, Ed Boerger, skip. **The Country Club Cup**, Marmora C.C., V. Glover, skip. **The Dewar Trophy**, Utica C.C. #1, Joseph Brindisi, skip.

**The Governor's Bowl**, Albany, N. Y. Jan. 18-21. Plainfield C.C., R. A. Fuller, skip. **The Patroon Plate**, Albany C.C., Joseph Lisuzzo, skip. **The Fort Orange Trophy**, Schenectady C.C., Henry Parker, skip.

**The Dykes Memorial Medal**, Rochester, N. Y. Jan. 19-21. Schenectady C.C., C. Hequembourg, skip. **The Brookline Trophy**, Nashua C.C., W. Zechel, skip. **The Davies Bowl**, Mahopac C.C., Wm. Switzer, skip.

**The Ardsley Medal**, Ardsley, N. Y., and Hastings on Hudson, N. Y. Feb. 1-4. N. Y. Caledonian C.C., Vern Hambly, skip. **The Mahopac Medal**, St. Andrew's Golf Club, Don McKay, skip. **The N. Y. Caledonian Medal**, Brae Burn C.C., Wheat Kittredge, skip.

**The Nutmeg Stone**, Darien, Conn. Feb. 8-11. Nutmeg C.C., Don McLeod, skip. **The Bartlett Medal**, N. Y. Caledonian C.C., Gerry Wade, skip.

**The Ardsley Shield**, Nashua C.C., W. Bickford, skip. **The Consolation**, Utica C.C., Monty Mead, skip.

**U. S. Women's Curling Assn. National Championships**, Duluth, Minn. Feb. 14-17. St. Paul Bonnie Spielers, Joanne Schwab, skip.

**The Howard Stockton Cup**, Brookline, Mass. Feb. 22-25. Brae Burn C.C., Bud Chandler, skip. **The Clyde Park Cup**, Montreal Thistle, Jim McAvity, skip. **The Primrose Cup**, The Country Club, Dick Hallowell, skip.

**The Eddison Medal**, Ardsley on Hudson, N. Y. Feb. 23-25. N. Y. Caledonian C.C., Vern Hambly, skip. **The St. Andrew's Medal**, Montreal Thistle C.C., J. Mewman, skip. **The Nutmeg Jug**, Schenectady C.C., Gordon Link, skip.

**The Gordon Championship Rink Medal**, Schenectady, N. Y. Feb. 29-Mar. 3. Buffalo C.C., W. Vance, skip. **The Emmet Memorial Medal**, Rochester C.C., W. J. Dulmage, skip. **The Mohawk Trophy**, Petersham C.C., Art Hamm, skip.

**U. S. Men's Curling Association National Championships**, Madison, Wis. Mar. 4-9. Wisconsin, Bud Somerville, skip.

**The McDonald Brier Canadian Championships**, Kelowna B.C., Mar. 4-8. Calgary C.C., Ron Northcott, skip.

**The Gordon International Medal**, Hastings on Hudson, Ardsley, N. Y., Darien, Conn. Mar. 15-16. Canada defeated United States by 84 stones.

**The Silver Broom World's Championship**, Pointe Claire, Mar. 20-24, won by Canada, Roy Northcott, skip.

## 16th North American Canoeing Championships
### Philadelphia, Pa., Aug. 18, 1968

**Canoe Singles**—Chris Hook, Canada.
**Canoe Doubles**—Canada (Jim Reardon & Dean Oldershaw).
**Kayak Singles**—John Pickett, United States.

**Kayak Doubles**—United States (Bob Harris & Bill Bragg).

**Point Score**—Canada 53; United States 51.

## Amateur Wrestling in 1968
### NATIONAL AAU CHAMPIONSHIPS
#### Lincoln, Neb., Apr. 11-16

**Freestyle**
**114.5 Lbs.**—Arthur Chavez, San Francisco Olympic Club.
**125.5 Lbs.**—Rich Sofman, New York Athletic Club.
**138.5 Lbs.**—Masamitsu Ichiguchi, New York Athletic Club.
**154 Lbs.**—Bobby Douglas, Michigan Wrestling Club.
**171.5 Lbs.**—Mike Gallego, San Francisco Olympic Club.
**191.5 Lbs.**—Russ Camilleri, San Francisco Olympic Club.
**213.5 Lbs.**—Henk Schenk, U. S. Army.
**Heavyweight**—Larry Kristoff, Mayor Daley Youth Foundation.
**Outstanding Wrestler**—Russ Camilleri.

**Outstanding Sportsman**—Mike Young, Brigham Young.
**Team Champions**—San Francisco Olympic Club.
**Greco-Roman**
**114.5 Lbs.**—Arthur Chavez, San Francisco Olympic Club.
**125.5 Lbs.**—Ikeni Yamamoto, Japan.
**138.5 Lbs.**—Jim Hezewinkel, U. S. Army.
**154 Lbs.**—Fred Lett, Michigan Wrestling Club.
**171.5 Lbs.**—Larry Lyden, Minnesota OWA.
**191.5 Lbs.**—Wayne Baughman, U. S. Air Force.
**213.5 Lbs.**—Jess Lewis, Oregon State.
**Heavyweight**—Bob Johnson, Minnesota OWA.
**Outstanding Wrestler**—Jim Hazewinkel.
**Outstanding Sportsman**—Steve Garner, Marshfield, Oregon.
**Team Champions**—Minnesota Olympic Wrestling Assn.

# Golf Records

## AMERICAN (UNITED STATES) GOLF CHAMPIONS

| Yr. | United States Open | National Amateur | Natl Women's Amateur | Yr. | United States Open | National Amateur | Natl Women's Amateur |
|---|---|---|---|---|---|---|---|
| 1900 | Harry Vardon | W. J. Travis | F. C. Griscom | 1935 | S. Parks, Jr. | W. L. Little, Jr. | Glenna C. Vare |
| 1901 | W. Anderson | W. J. Travis | G. Hecker | 1936 | Tony Manero | John Fischer | Pamela Barton |
| 1902 | L. Auchterlonie | L. N. James | G. Hecker | 1937 | R. Guldahl | J. Goodman | Mrs. E. L. Page |
| 1903 | W. Anderson | W. J. Travis | Bessie Anthony | 1938 | R. Guldahl | W. Turnesa | Patty Berg |
| 1904 | W. Anderson | H. C. Egan | G. M. Bishop | 1939 | B. Nelson | M. Ward | Betty Jameson |
| 1905 | W. Anderson | H. C. Egan | P. Mackay | 1940 | L. Little | R. Chapman | Betty Jameson |
| 1906 | Alex Smith | E. M. Byers | H. S. Curtis | 1941 | C. Wood | M. Ward | Mrs. F. Newell |
| 1907 | Alex Ross | J. D. Travers | M. Curtis | 1942-45 | (Not played) | | |
| 1908 | Fred McLeod | J. D. Travers | K. C. Harley | 1946 | L. Mangrum | T. Bishop | Mrs. B. Zaharias |
| 1909 | G. Sargent | R. A. Gardner | D. I. Campbell | 1947 | L. Worsham | R. Riegel | Louise Suggs |
| 1910 | Alex Smith | W. Fownes, Jr. | D. I. Campbell | 1948 | Ben Hogan | W. Turnesa | Grace Lenczyk |
| 1911 | J. McDermott | H. H. Hilton | M. Curtis | 1949 | C. Middlecoff | Charles Coe | Mrs. D. Porter |
| 1912 | J. McDermott | J. D. Travers | M. Curtis | 1950 | Ben Hogan | Sam Urzetta | Beverly Hanson |
| 1913 | F. Ouimet | J. D. Travers | G. Ravenscroft | 1951 | Ben Hogan | W. Maxwell | Dorothy Kirby |
| 1914 | Walter Hagen | F. Ouimet | Mrs. H. A. Jackson | 1952 | Julius Boros | Jack Westland | Mrs. J. Pung |
| 1915 | J. D. Travers | R. Gardner | Mrs. C. H. Vanderbeck | 1953 | Ben Hogan | Gene Littler | Mary Faulk |
| 1916 | C. Evans, Jr. | C. Evans, Jr. | Alexa Stirling | 1954 | Ed Furgol | Arnold Palmer | B. Romack |
| 1917-1918 | (Not played) | | | 1955 | Jack Fleck | Harvie Ward | Pat Lesser |
| 1919 | Walter Hagen | S. D. Herron | Alexa Stirling | 1956 | C. Middlecoff | Harvie Ward | M. Stewart |
| 1920 | Edward Ray | C. Evans, Jr. | Alexa Stirling | 1957 | Dick Mayer | Lt. H. Robbins | J. Gunderson |
| 1921 | Jas. Barnes | T. Gullford | M. Hollins | 1958 | Tommy Bolt | Charles Coe | Anne Quast |
| 1922 | G. Sarazen | J. Sweetser | Glenna Collett | 1959 | Bill Casper, Jr. | Jack Nicklaus | B. McIntire |
| 1923 | R. T. Jones, Jr. | M. R. Marston | E. Cummings | 1960 | Arnold Palmer | Deane Beman | Jo Anne Gunderson |
| 1924 | C. Walker | R. T. Jones, Jr. | Mrs. D. C. Hurd | | | | |
| 1925 | W. Macfarlane | R. T. Jones, Jr. | Glenna Collett | 1961 | Gene Littler | Jack Nicklaus | Mrs. Anne Q. Decker |
| 1926 | R. T. Jones, Jr. | G. Von Elm | Mrs. G. Stetson | | | | |
| 1927 | T. Armour | R. T. Jones, Jr. | Mrs. M. Horn | 1962 | Jack Nicklaus | Labron Harris, Jr. | Jo Anne Gunderson |
| 1928 | J. Farrell | R. T. Jones, Jr. | Glenna Collett | | | | |
| 1929 | R. T. Jones, Jr. | H. R. Joh'n, Jr. | Glenna Collett | 1963 | Julius Boros | Deane Beman | Anne Q. Welts |
| 1930 | R. T. Jones, Jr. | R. T. Jones, Jr. | Glenna Collett | 1964 | Ken Venturi | Wm. Campbell | Barbara McIntire |
| 1931 | Wm. Burke | F. Ouimet | Helen Hicks | 1965 | Gary Player | Robert Murphy, Jr. | Jean Ashley |
| 1932 | Gene Sarazen | C.R.Somerville | Virg. Van Wie | 1966 | Billy Casper | Gary Cowan | Jo Anne Carner |
| 1933 | John Goodman | G. Dunlap, Jr. | Virg. Van Wie | 1967 | Jack Nicklaus | Bob Dickson | Lou Dill |
| 1934 | O. Dutra | W. L. Little, Jr. | Virg. Van Wie | 1968 | Lee Trevino | Bruce Fleisher | Jo Anne Carner |

## Masters Golf Tournament Champions
### Augusta, Ga.

| Year | Winner | Score | Year | Winner | Score | Year | Winner | Score |
|---|---|---|---|---|---|---|---|---|
| 1934 | Horton Smith | 284 | 1947 | Jimmy Demaret | 281 | 1958 | Arnold Palmer | 284 |
| 1935 | Gene Sarazen* | 281 | 1948 | Claude Harmon | 279 | 1959 | Art Wall, Jr. | 284 |
| 1936 | Horton Smith | 285 | 1949 | Sam Snead | 282 | 1960 | Arnold Palmer | 282 |
| 1937 | Byron Nelson | 283 | 1950 | Jimmy Demaret | 283 | 1961 | Gary Player | 280 |
| 1938 | Henry Picard | 285 | 1951 | Ben Hogan | 280 | 1962 | Arnold Palmer* | 280 |
| 1939 | Ralph Guldahl | 279 | 1952 | Sam Snead | 286 | 1963 | Jack Nicklaus | 286 |
| 1940 | Jimmy Demaret | 280 | 1953 | Ben Hogan | 274 | 1964 | Arnold Palmer | 276 |
| 1941 | Craig Wood | 280 | 1954 | Sam Snead* | 289 | 1965 | Jack Nicklaus | 271 |
| 1942 | Byron Nelson* | 280 | 1955 | Cary Middlecoff | 279 | 1966 | Jack Nicklaus* | 288 |
| 1943-1945 | (Not played) | | 1956 | Jack Burke | 289 | 1967 | Gay Brewer, Jr. | 280 |
| 1946 | Herman Keiser | 282 | 1957 | Doug Ford | 283 | 1968 | Bob Goalby | 277 |

*Won Playoff

## Professional Golfers' Association Championships

| Year | Winner | Year | Winner | Year | Winner | Year | Winner |
|---|---|---|---|---|---|---|---|
| 1945 | Byron Nelson | 1951 | Sam Snead | 1957 | Lionel Hebert | 1963 | Jack Nicklaus |
| 1946 | Ben Hogan | 1952 | James Turnesa | 1958 | Dow Finsterwald | 1964 | Bob Nichols |
| 1947 | J. Ferrier (Aust.) | 1953 | Walter Burkemo | 1959 | Bob Rosburg | 1965 | Dave Marr |
| 1948 | Ben Hogan | 1954 | Melvin Harbert | 1960 | Jay Herbert | 1966 | Al Geiberger |
| 1949 | Sam Snead | 1955 | Doug Ford | 1961 | Jerry Barber | 1967 | Don January |
| 1950 | Chandler Harper | 1956 | Jack Burke | 1962 | Gary Player | 1968 | Julius Boros |

## U. S. Women's Open Golf Champions

| Year | Winner | Year | Winner | Year | Winner |
|---|---|---|---|---|---|
| 1948 | Mrs. M. D. Zaharias | 1955 | Fay Crocker | 1962 | Murle Lindstrom |
| 1949 | Louise Suggs | 1956 | Mrs. K. Cornelius | 1963 | Mary Mills |
| 1950 | Mrs. M. D. Zaharias | 1957 | Betsy Rawls | 1964 | Mickey Wright |
| 1951 | Betsy Rawls | 1958 | Mickey Wright | 1965 | Carol Mann |
| 1952 | Louise Suggs | 1959 | Mickey Wright | 1966 | Sandra Spuzich |
| 1953 | Betsy Rawls | 1960 | Betsy Rawls | 1967 | Catherine Lacoste (a) |
| 1954 | Mrs. M. D. Zaharias | 1961 | Mickey Wright | 1968 | Susie Maxwell Berning |

(a) Amateur

## Professional Golfers' Association Hall of Fame

Established in 1940 to honor those who have made outstanding contributions to the game by their lifetime playing ability.

| | | | |
|---|---|---|---|
| Anderson, Willie | Dutra, Olin | Little, W. Lawson | Sarazen, Gene |
| Armour, Tommy | Evans, Chick | Mangrum, Lloyd | Shute, Denny |
| Barnes, Jim | Farrell, Johnny | McDermott, John | Smith, Alex |
| Brady, Mike | Ghezzi, Vic | McLeod, Fred | Smith, Horton |
| Burke, Billy | Guldahl, Ralph | Nelson, Byron | Smith, MacDonald |
| Cooper, Harry | Hagen, Walter | Ouimet, Francis | Snead, Sam |
| Cruickshank, Bobby | Harrison, E. J. | Picard, Henry | Travers, Jerry |
| Demaret, Jimmy | Hogan, Ben | Revolta, Johnny | Travis, Walter |
| Diegel, Leo | Hutchison, Jock, Sr. | Runyan, Paul | Wood, Craig |
| Dudley, Edward | Jones, Bob | | |

# Open and Invitation Golf Tournaments in 1968

## MEN

| Date | Event | Winner | Score | Prize |
|------|-------|--------|-------|-------|
| Jan. 14 | Bing Crosby Tournament, Pebble Beach, Calif. | Johnny Pott | *285 | $16,000 |
| Jan. 21 | Kaiser International Open, Napa, Calif. | Kermit Zarley | 273 | 25,000 |
| Jan. 28 | Los Angeles Open | Billy Casper | 274 | 20,000 |
| Feb. 4 | Bob Hope Desert Classic, Palm Springs, Calif. | Arnold Palmer | *348 | 20,000 |
| Feb. 11 | Andy Williams—San Diego Open | Tom Weiskopf | 273 | 30,000 |
| Feb. 18 | Phoenix Open | George Knudson | 272 | 20,000 |
| Feb. 25 | Tucson Open | George Knudson | 273 | 20,000 |
| Mar. 10 | Doral Open, Miami, Fla. | Gardner Dickinson | 275 | 20,000 |
| Mar. 17 | Florida Citrus Open, Orlando | Dan Sikes | 274 | 23,000 |
| Mar. 25 | Pensacola Open, Fla. | George Archer | 268 | 14,000 |
| Mar. 31 | Greater Jacksonville Open | Tony Jacklin | 273 | 20,000 |
| Apr. 8 | Greater Greensboro Open, N. C. | Billy Casper | 267 | 27,500 |
| Apr. 14 | Masters Golf Tournament, Augusta, Ga. | Bob Goalby | 277 | 20,000 |
| Apr. 21 | Tournament of Champions, Las Vegas | Don January | 276 | 30,000 |
| Apr. 21 | Azalea Open, Wilmington, N. C. | Steve Reid | *271 | 5,000 |
| Apr. 28 | Byron Nelson Golf Classic, Dallas, Tex. | Miller Barber | 270 | 20,000 |
| May 5 | Champions Golf Tournament, Houston | Roberto de Vicenzo | 274 | 20,000 |
| May 12 | Greater New Orleans Open | George Archer | 271 | 20,000 |
| May 19 | Colonial National Invitational Tournament, Ft. Worth | Billy Casper | 275 | 25,000 |
| May 26 | Memphis Open | Bob Lunn | 268 | 20,000 |
| June 2 | Atlanta Golf Classic | Bob Lunn | 280 | 23,000 |
| June 9 | Indianapolis Open | Billy Casper | 280 | 20,000 |
| June 17 | U. S. Open Golf Championship, Rochester, N. Y. | Lee Trevino | 275 | 30,000 |
| June 23 | Canadian Open, Toronto | Bob Charles | 274 | 25,000 |
| June 30 | Cleveland Open | Dave Stockton | 276 | 22,000 |
| July 7 | Buick Open, Grand Blanc, Mich. | Tom Weiskopf | 280 | 25,000 |
| July 14 | Greater Milwaukee Open | Dave Stockton | 275 | 40,000 |
| July 21 | Professional Golfers Assn. Championship, San Antonio | Julius Boros | 281 | 25,000 |
| July 28 | Minnesota Golf Classic | Dan Sikes | 272 | 20,000 |
| Aug. 4 | Western Open, Chicago | Jack Nicklaus | 273 | 26,000 |
| Aug. 11 | American Golf Classic, Akron | Jack Nicklaus | *280 | 25,000 |
| Aug. 18 | Westchester Golf Classic, Harrison, N. Y. | Julius Boros | 272 | 50,000 |
| Aug. 25 | Philadelphia Golf Classic | Bob Murphy | *276 | 20,000 |
| Sept. 2 | Thunderbird Classic, Clifton, N. J. | Bob Murphy | 277 | 30,000 |
| Sept. 8 | Greater Hartford Open, Conn. | Billy Casper | 266 | 20,000 |
| Sept. 8 | World Series of Golf, Akron | Gary Player | *143 | 50,000 |
| Sept. 15 | Kemper Open, Sutton, Mass. | Arnold Palmer | 276 | 30,000 |
| Oct. 5 | Alcan Open Tournament Southport, Eng. | Gay Brewer | 283 | 55,000 |
| Oct. 20 | Sahara Invitation Tournament, Las Vegas | Chi Chi Rodriguez | *274 | 20,000 |

## WOMEN

| Date | Event | Winner | Score | Prize |
|------|-------|--------|-------|-------|
| Mar. 17 | Orange Blossom Open, St. Petersburg | Kathy Whitworth | 213 | $1,875 |
| Mar. 31 | Palm Beach County Open, Fla. | Mickey Wright | 215 | 1,875 |
| Apr. 14 | O'Sullivan Tournament, Winchester, Va. | Marilyn Smith | 216 | 1,875 |
| Apr. 21 | Lady Carling Open, Atlanta | Carol Mann | 200 | 2,350 |
| Apr. 28 | Raleigh Invitational | Carol Mann | 214 | 2,250 |
| May 5 | Shreveport Kiwanis Tournament, La. | Carol Mann | 217 | 1,725 |
| May 12 | Tall City Open, Midland, Tex. | Mickey Wright | 204 | 2,625 |
| May 26 | Dallas Civitan Open | Kathy Whitworth | 209 | 2,775 |
| June 9 | Bluegrass Invitational Tournament, Louisville | Carol Mann | 210 | 2,100 |
| June 23 | Ladies PGA Tournament, Sutton, Mass. | Sandy Post | *294 | 3,000 |
| June 30 | Lady Carling Open, Baltimore | Kathy Whitworth | 214 | 3,000 |
| July 7 | United States Open, Reading, Pa. | Susie Maxwell Berning | 289 | 5,000 |
| July 14 | Pabst Open, Columbus, Ohio | Carol Mann | 206 | 4,200 |
| July 21 | Buckeye Savings Tournament, Cincinnati | Carol Mann | 209 | 2,775 |
| Aug. 12 | Concord Open, Kiamesha Lake, N Y. | Shirley Englehorn | 229 | 4,275 |
| Aug. 18 | Holiday Inn Invitational, St. Louis | Kathy Whitworth | 206 | 2,260 |
| Sept. 1 | Willow Park Open, Calgary, Alberta | Carol Mann | 205 | 2,250 |
| Sept. 8 | Pacific Golf Tournament, Eugene, Ore. | Sandra Haynie | 213 | 1,875 |
| Sept. 15 | Shirley Englehorn Invitational, Caldwell, Idaho | Carol Mann | 208 | 1,725 |
| Sept. 22 | Kings River Open, Kingsburg, Calif. | Kathy Whitworth | 208 | 2,250 |

*Won playoff of tie

## BRITISH OPEN GOLF CHAMPIONS

| Year | Winner | Year | Winner | Year | Winner | Year | Winner |
|------|--------|------|--------|------|--------|------|--------|
| 1905. | James Braid | 1926. | R. T. Jones, Jr. (U. S.) | 1940–45 | (Not played) | 1959. | Gary Player |
| 1906. | James Braid | | | 1946. | S. Snead (U. S.) | 1960. | Kel Nagle (Aust.) |
| 1907. | Arnaud Massy | 1927. | R. T. Jones, Jr. (U. S.) | 1947. | F. Daly (Ireland) | 1961. | Arnold Palmer (U. S.) |
| 1908. | James Braid | | | 1948. | T. H. Cotton | | |
| 1909. | J. H. Taylor | 1928. | W. Hagen (U. S.) | 1949. | Bobby Locke (So. Africa) | 1962. | Arnold Palmer (U. S.) |
| 1910. | James Braid | 1929. | W. Hagen (U. S.) | | | | |
| 1911. | H. Vardon | 1930. | R. T. Jones, Jr. (U. S.) | 1950. | Bobby Locke (So. Africa) | 1963. | Bob Charles (N.Z.) |
| 1912. | Ed. Ray | | | | | 1964. | Tony Lema (U. S.) |
| 1913. | J. H. Taylor | 1931. | T. Armour (U. S.) | 1951. | Max Faulkner | 1965. | Peter Thomson |
| 1914. | H. Vardon | 1932. | G. Sarazen (U. S.) | 1952. | Bobby Locke (Africa) | 1966. | Jack Nicklaus (U.S.) |
| 1915–1919 | (Not played) | 1933. | D. Shute (U. S.) | | | 1967. | Roberto de Vicenzo (Arg.) |
| 1920. | George Duncan | 1934. | T. H. Cotton | 1953. | Ben Hogan (U. S.) | | |
| 1921. | Jock Hutchison | 1935. | A. Perry | 1954. | P. Thomson (Aust.) | 1968. | Gary Player (So. Africa) |
| 1922. | Walter Hagen (U.S.) | 1936. | Alf. Padgham | 1955. | Peter Thomson | | |
| 1923. | A. H. Havers | 1937. | T. H. Cotton | 1956. | Peter Thomson | | |
| 1924. | W. Hagen (U. S.) | 1938. | Whitecomb R. A. | 1957. | Bobby Locke | | |
| 1925. | J. Barnes (U. S.) | 1939. | D. Burton | 1958. | Peter Thomson | | |

## BRITISH AMATEUR GOLF CHAMPIONS

| Year | Winner | Year | Winner | Year | Winner | Year | Winner |
|------|--------|------|--------|------|--------|------|--------|
| 1908. | E. A. Lassen | 1926. | J. Sweetser (U. S.) | 1940–45 | (Not played) | 1956. | John Beharrell |
| 1909. | R. Maxwell | 1927. | Dr. W. Tweddell | 1946. | J. Bruen | 1957. | Reid Jack |
| 1910. | John Ball | 1928. | T. P. Perkins | 1947. | W. Turnesa | 1958. | Joseph Carr |
| 1911. | H. H. Hilton | 1929. | C. Tolley | 1948. | F. Stranahan (U.S.) | 1959. | DeaneBeman(U.S.) |
| 1912. | John Ball | 1930. | R.T.Jones,Jr.(U.S.) | 1949. | Sam McCready | 1960. | Joseph Carr |
| 1913. | H. H. Hilton | 1931. | E. Martin-Smith | 1950. | Frank Stranahan (U. S.) | 1961. | Michael Bonallack |
| 1914. | J. L. C. Jenkins | 1932. | J. De Forest | | | 1962. | Richard Davies (U. S.) |
| 1915–1919 | (Not played) | 1933. | M. Scott | 1951. | Dick Chapman (U.S.) | | |
| 1920. | Cyril J. Tolley | 1934. | W.L.Little,Jr.(U.S.) | | | 1963. | Michael Lunt |
| 1921. | W. I. Hunter | 1935. | W.L.Little,Jr.(U.S.) | 1952. | H. Ward (U. S.) | 1964. | Gordon Clark |
| 1922. | E. W. Holderness | 1936. | H. Thomson | 1953. | Joseph Carr | 1965. | Mike Bonallack |
| 1923. | R. Wethered | 1937. | R.Sweeny,(U.S.bn) | 1954. | Doug Bachli (Aust.) | 1966. | Bobby Cole |
| 1924. | E. W. Holderness | 1938. | C. Yates (U. S.) | 1955. | Lt. Joseph Conrad (U. S.) | 1967. | Bob Dickson (U.S.) |
| 1925. | R. Harris | 1939. | A. Kyle | | | 1968. | Mike Bonallack |

## CANADIAN OPEN GOLF CHAMPIONS

| Year | Winner | Year | Winner | Year | Winner | Year | Winner |
|---|---|---|---|---|---|---|---|
| 1940. | S. Snead | 1948. | C. Congdon | 1955. | ArnoldPalmer(U.S.) | 1962. | Ted Kroll (U. S.) |
| 1941. | S. Snead | 1949. | E.J.Harrison(U.S.) | 1956. | DougSanders(U.S.) | 1963. | Doug Ford (U.S.) |
| 1942. | C. Wood | 1950. | Jim Ferrier (U. S.) | 1957. | GeorgeBayer(U.S.) | 1964. | Kel Nagle (Aust.) |
| 1943-44 | (Not played) | 1951. | Jim Ferrier (U. S.) | 1958. | WesEllis,Jr. (U.S.) | 1965. | Gene Littler (U.S.) |
| 1945. | Byron Nelson | 1952. | J. Palmer (U.S.) | 1959. | Doug Ford (U.S.) | 1966. | D.Massengale(U.S.) |
| 1946. | G. Fazio | 1953. | DaveDouglas(U.S.) | 1960. | Art Wall, Jr. (U.S.) | 1967. | Billy Casper (U.S.) |
| 1947. | R. Locke (S. Af.) | 1954. | Pat Fletcher | 1961. | Jacky Cupit (U.S.) | 1968. | Bob Charles (N.Z.) |

## CANADIAN AMATEUR GOLF CHAMPIONS

| Year | Winner | Year | Winner | Year | Winner | Year | Winner |
|---|---|---|---|---|---|---|---|
| 1939. | K. Black | 1950. | W. Mawhinney | 1957. | Nick Weslock | 1963. | Nick Weslock |
| 1940-45 | (Not played) | 1951. | Walter McElroy | 1958. | Bruce Castator | 1964. | Nick Weslock |
| 1946. | H. Nartell | 1952. | L. Bouchey (U. S.) | 1959. | John Johnston | 1965. | George Henry |
| 1947. | F. Stranahan (U.S.) | 1953. | Don Cherry (U. S.) | 1960. | Keith Alexander | 1966. | Nick Weslock |
| 1948. | F. Stranahan (U.S.) | 1954. | H. Ward, Jr. (U.S.) | 1961. | Gary Cowan | 1967. | Stuart Jones |
| 1949. | R. Chapman (U.S.) | 1955. | Moe Norman | 1962. | Reg Taylor | 1968. | Jim Doyle |

## International Curtis Cup Golf Match

### UNITED STATES VS. GREAT BRITAIN—WOMEN'S AMATEUR (BIENNIAL)

**Series Standing—United States 11, Great Britain 2, 2 ties**

| Year | Series Record | Year | Series Record |
|---|---|---|---|
| 1948 | United States 6½; Great Britain 2½ | 1960 | United States 6½; Great Britain 2½ |
| 1950 | United States 7½; Great Britain 1½ | 1962 | United States 8; Great Britain 1 |
| 1952 | Great Britain 5; United States 4 | 1964 | United States 10½; Great Britain 7½ |
| 1954 | United States 6; Great Britain 3 | 1966 | United States 13; Great Britain 5 |
| 1956 | Great Britain 5; United States 4 | 1968 | United States 10½; Great Britain 7½ |
| 1958 | Great Britain 4½; United States 4½ | | |

## Ryder Cup Matches

### UNITED STATES VS. GREAT BRITAIN—PROFESSIONAL (BIENNIAL)

**Series Standing—United States 14, Great Britain 3**

| Series Record | |
|---|---|
| 1951—United States 9½; Great Britain 2½ | 1959—United States 8½; Great Britain 3½ |
| 1953—United State 6½; Great Britain 5½ | 1961—United States 14½; Great Britain 9½ |
| 1955—United States 8; Great Britain 4 | 1963—United States 23; Great Britain 9 |
| 1957—Great Britain 7; United States 4 | 1965—United States 19½; Great Britain 12½ |
| | 1967—United States 23½; Great Britain 8½ |

## International Walker Cup Golf Match

### UNITED STATES VS. GREAT BRITAIN—MEN'S AMATEUR (BIENNIAL)

**Series Standing—United States 19, Great Britain 1, 1 tie**

| Year | Series record | Year | Series record |
|---|---|---|---|
| 1947.. | United States 8; Great Britain 4 | 1959.. | United States 9; Great Britain 3 |
| 1949.. | United States 10; Great Britain 2 | 1961.. | United States 11; Great Britain 1 |
| 1951.. | United States 6; Great Britain 3 (3 halved) | 1963.. | United States 9; Great Britain 3 |
| 1953.. | United States 9; Great Britain 3 | 1965.. | United States 11; Great Britain 11 |
| 1955.. | United States 10; Great Britain 2 | 1967.. | United States 13; Great Britain 7 |
| 1957.. | United States 8; Great Britain 3 | | |

## Contract Bridge Championships in 1967-1968

### Winners of Major Events at 3 National Tournaments
#### Fall 1967—Spring and Summer 1968
**Source: American Contract Bridge League**

**Board-a-Match Teams**—Edgar Kaplan, Alvin Roth, William Root, all New York, N. Y.; Arthur Robinson, Strafford, Pa.; Robert Jordan, Bala Cynwyd, Pa.; Norman Kay, Philadelphia, Pa.

**Men's Teams**—Ira Corn, William Eisenberg, Robert Goldman, Michael Lawrence, Robert Wolff, all Dallas, Texas; James Jacoby, Richardson, Texas.

**Women's Teams**—Bee Schenken, New York, N. Y.; Sallie Johnson, Westport, Conn.; Peggy Solomon, Philadelphia, Pa.; Mary Jane Farell, Beverly Hills, Calif.

**Mixed Teams**—Oswald Jacoby, Dallas, Texas; Helen Sobel Smith, Detroit, Mich.; James Jacoby, Richardson, Texas; Minda Brachman, Dallas, Texas.

**Spingold Knockout Teams**—George Rapee, Edgar Kaplan, New York, N. Y.; Sidney Lazard, New Orleans, La.; Eric Murray, Sammy Kehela, both Toronto, Ont., Canada.

**Vanderbilt Knockout Teams**—Edgar Kaplan, Alvin Roth, William Root, all New York, N. Y.; Norman Kay, Philadelphia, Pa.; Arthur Robinson, Strafford, Pa.; Robert Jordan, Bala Cynwyd, Pa.

**Blue Ribbon Pairs**—Sammy Kehela, Wolf Lebovic, both Toronto, Ont., Canada.

**Life Masters Men's Pairs**—Peter Pender, San Franscisco, Calif.; Harlow Lewis, Philadelphia, Pa.

**Life Masters Women's Pairs**—Mrs. Nancy Gruver, Ellicott City, Md.; Mrs. Sue Sachs, Baltimore, Md.

**Life Masters Pairs**—William Eisenberg, Robert Goldman, both Dallas, Texas.

**Men's Pairs**—Kyle Larsen, San Francisco, Calif.; Edmond Lazarus, Pikesville, Md.

**Women's Pairs**—Hermine Baron, Los Angeles, Calif.; Rhoda Walsh, Bel Air, Calif.

**Mixed Pairs**—Trudy Machlin, Silver Spring, Md.; Kit Woolsey, Washington, D. C.

**Open Pairs**—Dick Spero, New York, N. Y.; Ronald Blau, Bellmore, N. Y.

**Senior and Advanced Senior Masters Pairs**—John Landon, Rochester, N. Y.; Henry Greenberg, St. Paul, Minn.

**1968 World Bridge Olympiad**, Deauville, France—Italy (Walter Avarelli, Giorgio Belladonna, Massimo D'Alelio, Pietro Forquet, Benito Garozzo, Camillo Pabis Ticci; Angelo Tracanella, non-playing captain).

## Senior National AAU Weightlifting Championships in 1968
### York, Pa., June 8-9

| Class | Winner | Total (lbs.) |
|---|---|---|
| Bantam (123½) | Fernando Baez, Puerto Rico | 740 |
| Featherweight (132¼) | Walter Imahara, New Orleans AC | 795 |
| Lightweight (148¾) | Steve Mansour, Detroit | 820 |
| Light-heavyweight (181¾) | Joe Puleo, Detroit | 1025 |
| Middle-heavyweight (198¼) | Phil Grappaldi, Bellville, N. J. | 1055 |
| 242 lb. class | Joe Murry, New Orleans | 1035 |
| Heavyweight | Bob Bednarski, York Barbell Club | 1280 |

# Ski Championships in 1968

**Source:** Gloria C. Chadwick, Secy., United States Ski Association

## UNITED STATES SKI ASSN. CHAMPIONSHIPS

### NATIONAL ALPINE CHAMPIONSHIPS

Crystal Mountain, Wash., Mar. 8-10
**Men's Downhill**—Scott Henderson, Canada. **Time** —106.510.
**Men's Slalom**—Rick Chaffee, U. S. A. **Time**—97.190.
**Men's Giant Slalom**—Rick Chaffee, U. S. A. **Time** —140.780.
**Women's Downhill**—Ann Black, U. S. A. **Time**—114.040.
**Women's Slalom**—Judy Nagel, U. S. A. **Time**—97.680.
**Women's Giant Slalom**—Marilyn Cochran, U.S.A. **Time**—136.300.

### ROCH CUP CHAMPIONSHIPS

Aspen, Colo., Mar. 15-17
**Men's Downhill**—Gerhard Nenning, Austrian. **Time**—119.49.
**Men's Slalom**—Bill Kidd, U. S. A. **Time**—126.18.
**Men's Giant Slalom**—Reinhard Tritcher, Austrian. **Time**—154.00.

**Men's Combined**—Bill Kidd, U. S. A. **Total Pts.** —14.27.
**Women's Downhill**—Nancy Greene, Canada. **Time** —133.29.
**Women's Slalom**—Nancy Greene, Canada. **Time** —88.48.
**Women's Giant Slalom**—Nancy Greene, Canada. **Time**—126.02.
**Women's Combined**—Nancy Greene, Canada.

### NCAA CHAMPIONSHIPS

Steamboat Springs, Colo., Mar. 21-23
**Downhill**—Barney Pett, Ft. Lewis. **Time**—1:37.30.
**Cross Country**—Clark Matis, Colorado. **Time**—56.21.
**Two Run Slalom**—Dennis McCoy, Denver. **Time** —1:36.32.
**Jumping**—Peter Robes, Wyoming. 221.2 p ints.
**Team Standing**—Wyoming, 383.9 points; Denver, 376.2 points; Dartmouth, 369.5 points.

# American Ski Jumping Records

| Year | Skier | Site | Distance Feet |
|---|---|---|---|
| 1910 | Oscar Gunderson | Chippewa Falls, Wis. | 138 |
| 1910 | August Nordby | Ishpeming, Mich. | 140 |
| 1911 | Anders Haugen | Ironwood, Mich. | 152 |
| 1913 | Ragnar Omtvedt | Ironwood, Mich. | 169 |
| 1913 | Lars Haugen | Steamboat Springs, Colo. | 185 |
| 1916 | Ragnar Omtvedt | Steamboat Springs, Colo. | 192 |
| 1917 | Henry Hall | Steamboat Springs, Colo. | 203 |
| 1919 | Anders Haugen | Dillon, Colo. | 213 |
| 1919 | Lars Haugen | Steamboat Springs, Colo. | 214 |
| 1932 | Glen Armstrong | Salt Lake City, Utah | 224 |
| 1932 | Hans Beck | Lake Placid, N. Y. | 235 |
| 1934 | John Elvrum | Big Pines, Calif. | 240 |
| 1937 | Alf Engen | Salt Lake City, Utah | 242 |
| 1939 | Alf Engen | Iron Mountain, Mich. | 251 |
| 1939 | Robert Roecker | Iron Mountain, Mich. | 257 |
| 1941 | Alf Engen | Iron Mountain, Mich. | 267 |
| 1941 | Torger Tokle | Leavenworth, Wash. | 273 |
| 1941 | Torger Tokle | Hyak, Wash. | 288 |
| 1942 | Torger Tokle | Iron Mountain, Mich. | 289 |
| 1949 | Sverre Kongsgaard | Hyak, Wash. | 290 |
| 1949 | Joe Perrault | Iron Mountain, Mich. | 293 |
| 1949 | Matti Pietikainen | Iron Mountain, Mich. | 294 |
| 1949 | Joe Perrault | Iron Mountain, Mich. | 297 |
| 1950 | Gorden Wren | Steamboat Springs, Colo. | 297 |
| 1950 | Billy Olson | Iron Mountain, Mich. | 297 |
| 1951 | Ansten Samuelstuen | Steamboat Springs, Colo. | 316 |
| 1960 | James Brennan | Iron Mountain, Mich. | 316 |
| 1962 | John Balfanz | Westby, Wis. | 317 |
| 1962 | Pekka Tirkkonen | Iron Mountain, Mich. | 317 |
| 1963 | Eugene Kotlarek | Steamboat Springs, Colo. | 318-322 |
| 1965 | Toralf Engan | Leavenworth, Wash. | 324 |
| 1965 | John Balfanz | Iron Mountain, Mich. | 325 |
| 1967 | Bjorn Wirkola | Leavenworth, Wash. | 335 |

# Speed Ice-Skating Championships in 1968

## UNITED STATES NATIONAL OUTDOOR CHAMPIONSHIPS

St. Paul, Minn., Jan. 27-28, 1968

**Senior Men**
⅙ Mile—Pete Cefalu, Wis. **Time**—0:23.2.
440 Yds.—Bobby Fenn, U. S. Army. **Time**—0:36.4.
880 Yds.—Pete Cefalu, Wis. **Time**—1:14.0.
¾ Mile—Pete Cefalu, Wis. **Time**—2:08.2.
1 Mile—Bobby Fenn, U. S. Army. **Time**—2:49.1.
2 Miles—Pete Cefalu, Wis. **Time**—6:12.8.
5 Miles—Bobby Fenn, U. S. Army. **Time**—15:20.8.

**Champion**—Peter Cefalu, Wis., 20 Pts.
**Senior W men**
⅙ Mile—Mary Blair, Wis. **Time**—0:26.8.
440 Yds.—Helen Lutsch, Ill. **Time**—0:41.2.
880 Yds.—Helen Lutsch. **Time**—1:34.1.
¾ Mile—Helen Lutsch. **Time**—2:25.2.
1 Mile—Helen Lutsch. **Time**—3:09.5.
**Champion**—Helen Lutsch, 20 Pts.

## UNITED STATES NATIONAL INDOOR CHAMPIONSHIPS

St. Louis, Mo., Mar. 2-3, 1968

**Senior Men**
440 Yds.—Pete Cefalu, Wis. **Time**—0:39.4.
880 Yds.—John Keith, So. Calif. **Time**—1:18.6.
¾ Mile—John Keith. **Time**—2:00.7.
1 Mile—Bill Lanigan, Mid Atlantic. **Time**—2:43.1.
2 Miles—Bill Lanigan. **Time**—5:50.3.

**Champion**—John Keith, So. Calif., 16 Pts.
**Senior W men**
440 Yds.—Diane Layton, Ill. **Time**—0:43.5.
880 Yds.—Sally Blatchford, Ill. **Time**—1:28.1.
¾ Mile—Mary Blair, Wis. **Time**—2:19.7.
1 Mile—Sally Blatchford, Ill. **Time**—3:08.8.
**Champion**—Mary Blair, Wis., 11 Pts.

## UNITED STATES OPEN INDOOR CHAMPIONSHIPS

Flushing, N. Y., Mar. 9, 1968

**Senior Men**
440 Yds.—Bill Lanigan, Mid Atlantic. **Time**—0:38.9.
880 Yds.—Bill Lanigan. **Time**—1:18.8.
¾ Mile—Bill Lanigan. **Time**—2:00.5.
1 Mile—Bill Lanigan. **Time**—2:44.3.
2 Miles—Bill Lanigan. **Time**—5:45.8.
**Champion**—Bill Lanigan, 25 Pts.

**Senior Women**
440 Yds.—Sally Blatchford, Ill. **Time**—0:43.3.
880 Yds.—Cathy Crowe, Mo. **Time**—1:29.6.
¾ Mile—Cathy Crowe. **Time**—2:17.0.
1 Mile—Sally Blatchford. **Time**—3:11.2.
**Co-Champion**—Sally Blatchford and Cathy Crowe, 13 Pts. each.

# American Bowling Congress Championships, 1968
### Cincinnati, Ohio

## REGULAR DIVISION
### Individual

1. Wayne Kowalski, Revere, Mass., 279, 241, 218—738.
2. Gary Lewis, Chicago, Ill., 279, 196, 259—734.
3. Jim Robinette, Alexandria, Va., 254, 247, 232—733.

Runners-up—Ronnie Moore, Louisville, Ky.—718; Douglas Sigler Jr., Metairie, La.—714; Ron Babjar, Eugene, Ore.—710; Edward Hughes, Elmira, N. Y.—701; Lary Everhart, Lexington, N. C.—701; Don Smith, Dayton, Ohio—699; Frank Cutrie, Syracuse, N. Y.—697.

### All-Events

1. Vince Mazzanti, Philadelphia, 732, 600, 639—1971.
2. Ronnie Moore, Louisville, Ky.—546, 688, 718—1952.
3. Gary Lewis, Chicago, Ill., 592, 620, 734—1946.

Runners-up—Alfred Gatena, Dubuque, Iowa—1942; Randall L. Bare, Roanoke, Va.—1935; Dean Bundy, Ft. Dodge, Iowa—1925; Tony Ciocco, Kalamazoo, Mich.—1923; Mike Stranney, Milwaukee, Wis.—1921; Ray Redmer, Detroit, Mich.—1911; Roger Hutton, Joliet, Ill.—1910.

### Doubles

1. Rich Stark, Glenwood Springs, Colo., 233, 232, 247—712; Walt Roy, Glenwood Springs, Colo., 175, 226, 212—613. Aggregate 1325.
2. Tie—Louis Abdoo, Farmington, Mich., 194, 195, 192—581; Alexander Wasik, Farmington Mich., 257, 235, 242—734. Aggregate 1315.
2. Tie—Jim Todd, Seattle, Wash., 269, 214, 206—689; Earl Anthony, Seattle, Wash., 186, 194, 246—626. Aggregate 1315.

Runners-up—Ronnie Moore-Jim Ewald Jr., Louisville, Ky.—1304; Tim Crabtree-Jack Campbell, Louisville, Ky.—1301; Ted Bakatselos-Don Wray, Detroit, Mich.—1296; Ernie Kovach-Dennis Taylor, Cleveland, Ohio—1292; Wally Gay-Dave Brown, Buffalo, N. Y.—1291; Vince Larroque-Rube Scheidt, Alexandria, Va.—1289; Chuck Clay-John Koenig, Chicago, Ill.—1297; Clarence Fath-Stan Warman, Cincinnati, Ohio—1287.

### Teams

1. Dave's Auto Supply, Philadelphia, Pa.—Dan Spada, 212, 198, 223—633; Harry Hartman, 194, 202, 234—630; Charles Faino, 238, 193, 186—617; Bud Stoudt, 193, 186, 221—600; Jack Winters, 187, 226, 191—604. Aggregate 3084.
2. Food Fair Stores, Philadelphia, Pa.—Peter Gabriel, 214, 179, 194—587; John Till, 188, 229, 178—595; Vince Mazzanti, 227, 278, 227—732; Don DiCicco, 170, 203, 213—586; Joe Ostroski, 191, 191, 182—564. Aggregate 3064.
3. Washtenaw Lanes, Ann Arbor, Mich.—Donald Biegel, 235, 182, 204—621; James Wilbanks, 203, 178, 220—601; James Deck, 202, 181, 192—575; Larry Durham, 222, 201, 201—624; William Fite, 224, 205, 193—622. Aggregate 3043.

## CLASSIC DIVISION
### Individual

1. Dave Davis, Phoenix, Ariz., 275, 235, 231—741.
2. Charles Pezzano, Paterson, N. J., 223, 235, 233—691.
3. Vince Lucci Sr., Trenton, N. J., 247, 215, 210—672.

Runners-up—Joe Joseph, Lansing, Mich.—670; Therm Davis, Chicago, Ill.—699; Lou Frantz Sr., Louisville, Ky.—688; Jim Stefanich, Joliet, Ill.—667; Tom Harnisch, Buffalo, N. Y.—657; Jim Godman, Burbank, Calif.—657; John Barnhill, Inkster, Mich.—653.

### All Events

1. Jim Stefanich, Joliet, Ill., 664, 652, 667—1983.
2. Jim Schroeder, Buffalo, N. Y., 626, 674, 644—1944.
3. Lou Frantz Sr., Louisville, Ky., 601, 668, 668—1937.

Runners-up—Al Thompson, Cleveland, Ohio—1926; Jimmy Certain, Huntsville, Ala.—1925; Bob Strampe, Detroit, Mich.—1918; Joe Joseph, Lansing, Mich.—1913; Mike Totsky, Detroit, Mich.—1903; Tim Harahan, Encino, Calif.—1877; Therm Davis, Chicago, Ill.—1873.

### Doubles

1. Bill Tucker, Los Angeles, Calif., 216, 300, 181—697; Don Johnson, Kokomo, Ind., 190, 223, 219—632. Aggregate 1329.
2. Bob Reams, Birmingham, Ala., 204, 203, 224—631; Carl Lundquist, Jackson, Miss., 206, 247, 213—666. Aggregate 1297.
3. Lou Frantz Sr., Louisville, Ky., 242, 246, 180—668; Bob Ramirez, Los Angeles, Calif., 173, 222, 233—628. Aggregate 1296.

Runners-up—Jimmy Mack-Jim Stefanich, Joliet, Ill.—1294; Dave Soutar-Bob Strampe, Detroit, Mich.—1292; Dale Seavoy-Al Thompson, Detroit, Mich.—1288; Ray Bluth, St. Louis-Jimmy Certain, Huntsville, Ala.—1288; Billy Welu, St. Louis-Andy Marzich, Los Angeles, Calif.—1283; Al Kaelin-Lou Frantz Jr., Louisville, Ky.—1280; Chuck Wagner-Fred Johnson, Chicago, Ill.—1279.

### Teams

1. Bowl-Rite Supply, Joliet, Ill.—Donald McCune, 597, 646—1243; Jim Mack, 593, 644—1237; Therm Davis, 576, 703—1297; Tim Harahan, 629, 413—1042; Jim Stefanich, 664, 630—1294; Steve Buel, 190—190. Aggregate 6285.
2. Brownstone, Newton, Mass.—Don Carter, 634, 640—1274; Carmen Salvino, 644, 584—1228; Ray Bluth, 620, 643—1263; John Guenther, 623, 612—1235; Les Schissler, 550, 597—1147. Aggregate 6147.
3. Drewry's Beer, Detroit, Mich.—Bill Schlicker, 689, 607—1296; Bill Srock, 526—526; Walt Pych, 598—598; Joe Joseph, 645, 585—1230; Jack Curry, 613, 555—1168; Jim Schroeder, 626, 596—1222.

## Other Bowling Championships in 1968

**27th Annual National All-Star Championship,** Garden City, L. I., N. Y., May 18-25—Jim Stefanich, Joliet, Ill., average 219-30, prize $15,000. Women, Dotty Fothergill, Attleboro, Mass., average 211, prize $5,000.

**National Intercollegiate Championships,** Cincinnati, Ohio, Mar. 31. Doubles—Pat Holseth, U. of Minnesota and Jerry Steere, Florida State; Singles—Jack Connaughton, LaCrosse (Wis.) State U.; All Events—Jack Connaughton, LaCrosse (Wis.) State U.

**Invitational Bowling Tournament of the Americas,** Miami, Fla. July 23-28—Men: (singles) Benjamin Corona, Mexico; (doubles) Peter Hoyles & Charles Mile, Canada. Women: (singles) Janice Sue Reichley, U. S.; (doubles) Janice Sue Reichley & Jodie McCullough, U. S.

## Masters Bowling Tournament Champions

| Year | Winner | Runner-up | W. | L. | Ave. |
|------|--------|-----------|----|----|------|
| 1957 | Dick Hoover, Akron, Ohio | Bill Lillard, Chicago, Ill. | 9 | 1 | 216-39 |
| 1958 | Tom Hennessey, St. Louis, Mo. | Lou Frantz, Louisville, Ky. | 7 | 0 | 209-15 |
| 1959 | Ray Bluth, St. Louis, Mo. | Bill Golembiewski, Detroit, Mich. | 7 | 0 | 214-26 |
| 1960 | Bill Golembiewski, Detroit, Mich. | Steve Nagy, St. Louis, Mo. | 7 | 0 | 206-13 |
| 1961 | Don Carter, St. Louis, Mo. | Dick Hoover, St. Louis, Mo. | 8 | 1 | 211-18 |
| 1962 | Billy Golembiewski, Detroit, Mich. | Ron Winger, Los Angeles, Calif. | 7 | 0 | 223-12 |
| 1963 | Harry Smith, St. Louis, Mo. | Bobby Meadows, Dallas, Texas | 7 | 0 | 219-3 |
| 1964 | Billy Welu, St. Louis, Mo. | Harry Smith, Baltimore, Md. | 7 | 0 | 227 |
| 1965 | Billy Welu, St. Louis, Mo. | Don Ellis, Houston, Tex. | 9 | 1 | 202-12 |
| 1966 | Bob Strampe, Detroit | Al Thompson, Cleveland | 7 | 0 | 219-8 |
| 1967 | Lou Scalia, Miami, Fla. | Bill Johnson, New Orleans | 7 | 0 | 216-9 |
| 1968 | Pete Tountas, Tucson, Ariz. | Buzz Fazio, Detroit, Mich. | 9 | 1 | 220-15 |

## MASTERS TOURNAMENT RECORDS

### High Series

| | |
|---|---|
| Don Carter, St. Louis, Mo., 1962 | 1,084 |
| Ray Bluth, St. Louis, Mo., 1962 | 1,051 |
| Wayne Zahn, Atlanta, Ga., 1966 | 1,038 |
| Tony Lindemann, Detroit, Mich., 1958 | 1,021 |
| Don Johnson, Kokomo, Ind., 1967 | 1,019 |
| Don Carter, St. Louis, Mo., 1963 | 1,017 |
| Joe Joseph, Detroit, Mich., 1961 | 1,013 |
| Dick Weber, St. Louis, Mo., 1962 | 1,006 |
| Pete Tountas, Chicago, Ill., 1964 | 1,006 |
| Don Carter, St. Louis, Mo., 1959 | 1,005 |

### High Game

| | |
|---|---|
| Al Horn, Jr., Los Angeles, Calif., 1961 | 300 |
| Don Carter, St. Louis, Mo., 1962 | 300 |
| Ray Bluth, St. Louis, Mo., 1962 | 300 |
| Bob Hart, Erie, Pa., 1967 | 300 |
| Steve Nagy, Cleveland, Ohio, 1952 | 299 |
| J D. Myres, Casper, Wyo., 1962 | 298 |
| Bob Christensen, Phoenix, Ariz., 1962 | 298 |
| Therm Gibson, Detroit, Mich., 1963 | 298 |
| Jim Desmond, Fairbanks, Alaska, 1964 | 296 |
| Jim Erlandson, Nampa, Idaho, 1955 | 290 |

# American Bowling Congress Champions and Records

| Yr. | Individual | All Events | Two-Man Team | Five-Man Team |
|---|---|---|---|---|
| 1959 | Ed Lubanski, Detroit, Mich............764 | Ed Lubanski, Detroit, Mich............2,116 | Gib Fischbach-Barney Vehige, St. Louis, Mo..1,372 | Pfeiffer Beer. Detroit, Mich....3,243 |
| 1960 | Paul Kulbaga, Cleveland, Ohio.......726 | Vince Lucci, Trenton, N. J.......1,985 | Andy Marzich-Dick Jensen, Los Angeles, Calif.....1,369 | A & A Asphalt, Detroit Mich....3,096 |
| 1961 | Lyle Spooner, St. Cloud, Minn.....726 | Luke Karen, Detroit, Mich......1,960 | Joseph Macaluso-Eugene Hering, Irvington, N. J.1,342 | Meyerland Builders, Houston, Texas...3,134 |
| 1962 | Andy Renaldy, Youngstown, Ohio 720 | Billy Young, Tulsa, Okla...........2,015 | John Gribin-Gary Madison, Riverside, Calif..1,376 | Strike 'n Spare, Chicago, Ill......3,128 |
| 1963 | Fred Dellelo, Oneonta, N. Y.............744 | Bus Oswalt, Fort Wayne, Ind.....2,055 | Bus Oswalt-Gerry Schmidt, Fort Wayne, Ind.......1,337 | Old Fitzgerald Chicago...3,180 |
| 1964 | Jim Stefanich, Chicago, Ill.............726 | Les Zikes, Chicago, Ill............2,001 | Pat Russo-Tony Russo, Teaneck, N. J.......1,343 | 300 Bowl, Pontiac Mich....3,117 |
| 1965 | Ken Roeth, Dubuque, Iowa............700 | Tom Hathaway, Los Angeles, Calif...1,922 | Buzz Bosler-Dan Siak, Milwaukee, Wis.....1,300 | C & C McDermitt, Pittsburgh, Pa.3,074 |
| 1966 | Don Chapman, Scranton, Pa............761 | John Wilcox, Jr., Williamsport, Pa.2,004 | Tony Lolacano, Bob Kwiecien, Detroit, Mich.........1,351 | Plaza Lanes, Sault Ste. Marie, Ont., Canada..3,066 |
| 1967 | Frank Perry, Lorain, Ohio............723 | Gary Lewis, Chicago, Ill............2,010 | Mark Kugiltsch, Ron Wheeler, Milwaukee, Wisc.....1,357 | Pinky's Bowl, Milw'k..3,327 |
| 1968 | Wayne Kowalski, Revere, Mass. 778 | Vince Mazzanti, Philadelphia....1,971 | Rich Stark, Walt Roy, Glenwood Springs, Colo................1,325 | Dave's Auto Supply, Philadelphia..3,084 |

## OFFICIAL RECORDS OF ANNUAL ABC TOURNAMENTS

| Type of record | Holder of record | Tourn. Yr. | Score |
|---|---|---|---|
| High team total.......... | Ace Mitchell Shur-Hooks, Akron, Ohio.......... | 1966 | 3,357 |
| High team game.......... | Falstaff Beer, San Antonio, Texas.......... | 1958 | 1,226 |
| High doubles score.......... | John Klares-Steve Nagy, Cleveland, Ohio.... | 1952 | 1,453 |
| High doubles game.......... | John Gworek-Henry Kmidowski, Buffalo. N. Y... | 1946 | 544 |
| High singles total.......... | Lee Jouglard, Detroit, Mich.......... | 1951 | 775 |
| High all events score...... | Jack Winters, Philadelphia, Pa.......... | 1962 | 2,147 |
| High team all events...... | Falstaff Beer, St. Louis, Mo.......... | 1958 | 9,608 |
| High life-time pin total...... | Bill Doehrman, Ft. Wayne, Indiana............ | 1908 to 1968 | 96,307 |

## RECORD AVERAGES FOR CONSECUTIVE TOURNAMENTS

| No. in row | Name of record holder | Span | Games | Average |
|---|---|---|---|---|
| Two............ | Steve Nagy, Cleveland Ohio........... | 1951–52 | 18 | 224.09 |
| Three............ | Steve Nagy, Cleveland, Ohio........... | 1951–53 | 27 | 221.02 |
| Four............ | Bob Strampe, Detroit, Mich........... | 1964–67 | 48 | 215.40 |
| Five............ | Bob Strampe, Detroit, Mich........... | 1964–68 | 57 | 215.28 |
| Ten............ | Bob Strampe, Detroit, Mich........ | 1959–68 | 108 | 208.27 |

## ALL-TIME RECORDS FOR LEAGUE AND TOURNAMENT PLAY

| Type of record | Holder of record | Year | Score | Style of competition |
|---|---|---|---|---|
| High team total...... | Budweiser Beer, St. Louis, Mo........... | 1958 | 3,858 | League |
| High team game...... | Hook Grip Five, Lodi, N. J........... | 1950 | 1,342 | League |
| High doubles total..... | Lou Celestino-Jim Troyano, Paterson, N.J. | 1963 | 1,609 | League |
| High doubles game..... | Tom Dorn-Ron Spohn, Columbus, O..... | 1965 | 587 | League |
| High individual total.... | Albert Brandt, Lockport, N. Y........... | 1939 | 886 | League |
| High all events score... | Frank Benkovic, Milwaukee, Wis........ | 1932 | 2,259 | Tournament |

## BOWLERS WITH FIVE OR MORE SANCTIONED 300 GAMES

| | | |
|---|---|---|
| Elvin Mesger, Sullivan, Mo.... 20 | Jerry Woji, Milwaukee, Wis... 7 | Donald Bartz, Milwaukee..... 5 |
| George Billick, Old Forge, Pa.. 17 | Ray Schanen, Milwaukee...... 7 | Dean Briggs, Tulsa, Okla...... 5 |
| Dick Weber, St. Louis, Mo..... 15 | Salvatore Bivona, Paterson, N.J..... 6 | *Charley Daw, Milwaukee.... 5 |
| Al Faragalli, Wayne, N.J..... 13 | | Johnny Fehr, Indianapolis, Ind. 5 |
| Walter Ward, Cleveland, O..... 12 | Bob Ramirez, Los Angeles.... 6 | Russell Fields, San Jose, Cal... 5 |
| Don Carter, Tarzana, Calif..... 12 | Lou Campi, Dumont, N. J.... 6 | Andy Grilli, Milwaukee, Wis... 5 |
| *Hank Marino, Milwaukee..... 11 | Ed Davis, Milford, N. J..... 6 | Don Hooper, Anaheim, Cal.... 5 |
| Frank Clause, Old Forge, Pa.... 11 | Don Dubro, St. Louis, Mo..... 6 | Paul Krumske, Chicago, Ill.... 5 |
| Ed Lubanski, Detroit, Mich..... 11 | *Bill Flynn, Cleveland, O..... 6 | Paul Kulbaga, Cleveland, O... 5 |
| Ray Bluth, St. Louis. Mo..... 10 | Sam Garofalo, St. Louis, Mo.... 6 | Fred Lening, Yardley, Pa..... 5 |
| Pat Patterson, St. Louis, Mo... 10 | Casey Jones, Plymouth, Wis.. 6 | Bill Lenzen, Chicago, Ill...... 5 |
| Boss Bosco, Akron, O....... 9 | Joe Joseph, Lansing, Mich..... 6 | Tony Lindemann, Detroit...... 5 |
| Al Savas, Milwaukee, Wis..... 9 | Pete Kozloski, Plains, Pa...... 6 | Vince Lucci, Trenton, N. J.... 5 |
| Lou Foxie, Paterson, N.J..... 9 | Steve Nagy, Cleveland, O..... 6 | Paul Marian, Chicago, Ill..... 5 |
| Dave Soutar, Detroit, Mich.... 9 | Frank Pollak, Pittsburgh, Pa.. 6 | Norm Meyers, Los Angeles.... 5 |
| Dennis Wright, Milwaukee..... 8 | Wayne Pinkalla, Milwaukee... 6 | Larry Oakar, Cleveland, O..... 5 |
| Ray Eklund, Milwaukee, Wis.. 8 | Robert Pinkalla, Milwaukee... 6 | Don Osep, Milwaukee, Wis.... 5 |
| Walter King, Detroit, Mich..... 8 | Harold Schaefer, St. Louis.... 6 | Ken Rothermich, St. Louis.... 5 |
| Junie McMahon, Lodi, N.J.... 8 | Harry Smith, Redwood City, Calif......... 6 | Art Scheer, St. Louis, Mo..... 5 |
| Tom Hennessey, St. Louis, Mo. 8 | Bob Strampe, Detroit, Mich... 6 | Frank Sosplrato, Cleveland, O.. 5 |
| Eddie Botten, Union City, N.J. 7 | Jerry Tharp, St. Louis, Mo..... 6 | Jim Sturm, Cleveland, O..... 5 |
| Dick Hoover, Akron, O..... 7 | George Tomek, Plymouth, Pa. 6 | Ed Winchester, Philadelphia,.. 5 |
| Howard Holmes, Los Angeles. 7 | Stephen Tomek, Plymouth, Pa. 6 | Bill Bunetta, Fresno, Calif... 5 |
| Ken McKenzie, Dallas, Texas. 7 | | |

*Bowled two 300 games in official 3-game series.

## GENERAL BOWLING FIGURES FOR UNITED STATES

| | 1967-68 | 1966-67 | 1965-66 | 1964-65 | 1963-64 |
|---|---|---|---|---|---|
| Total alley beds............... | 147,526 | 151,731 | 156,219 | 159,079 | 158,996 |
| Number bowling establishments.... | 9,707 | 10,070 | 10,457 | 10,752 | 10,839 |
| Total, ABC teams............ | 1,203,479 | 1,217,454 | 1,248,423 | 1,264,650 | 1,268,048 |
| Number of bowlers, all types...... | 29,000,000 | 29,000,000 | 29,000,000 | 29,000,000 | 28,000,000 |

# Professional Bowlers Association Tournaments: 1968

| Date | Event | Purse | Winner | Winner's share |
|------|-------|-------|--------|----------------|
| Jan. 6 | North Phoenix Jaycee Open | $40,000 | Dick Ritger | $6,000 |
| Jan. 13 | Showboat Invitational, Las Vegas | 55,000 | Bill Allen | 10,000 |
| Jan. 20 | San Jose Open, Calif. | 50,000 | Bill Allen | 7,000 |
| Jan. 27 | Denver PBA Open | 40,000 | Dave Soutar | 6,000 |
| Feb. 24 | Tampa Bay Sertoma PBA Open | 40,000 | Jim Stefanich | 6,000 |
| Mar. 2 | Buckeye Open, Toledo, Ohio | 50,000 | Jim Stefanich | 6,000 |
| Mar. 9 | Miller High Life Open, Milwaukee | 60,000 | Johnny Guenther | 10,000 |
| Mar. 16 | Greater Buffalo PBA Open | 45,000 | Bob Strampe | 6,000 |
| Mar. 23 | Ebonite Gold Cup Open, Mountainside, N. J. | 60,000 | Teata Semiz | 8,000 |
| Mar. 30 | New Orleans Lions PBA Open | 40,000 | Dick Ritger | 6,000 |
| Apr. 6 | Firestone Tournament of Champions, Akron | 100,000 | Dave Davis | 25,000 |
| Apr. 13 | Mobile Sertoma PBA Open | 40,000 | Jim Stefanich | 6,000 |
| June 8 | Seattle Open | 30,000 | Billy Hardwick | 3,000 |
| June 15 | Portland Open | 30,000 | Jim Stefanich | 3,000 |
| June 22 | Fresno Open | 32,000 | Jim Stefanich | 3,000 |
| June 30 | Squirt Tucson Open | 30,000 | Tim Harahan | 3,000 |
| July 7 | El Paso Open | 30,000 | Mike Durbin | 3,000 |
| July 14 | Fort Worth Open | 30,000 | Don McCune | 3,000 |
| July 21 | Houston Sertoma Open | 30,000 | Wayne Zahn | 3,000 |
| Aug. 11 | Grand Haven Open, Mich. | 32,000 | Bill Allen | 3,000 |
| Aug. 18 | Waukegan Open, Illinois | 36,000 | Bob Strampe | 3,000 |
| Sept. 2 | Rochester Open, N. Y. | 32,000 | Tim Harahan | 3,000 |
| Sept. 8 | Portsmouth-Norfolk Open, Va. | 30,000 | Don Johnson | 3,000 |
| Sept. 15 | Altoona Jaycee Open, Pa. | 30,000 | Jim Godman | 3,000 |
| Sept. 22 | Newark Kiwanis Open, N. J. | 30,000 | Bill Allen | 3,000 |
| Sept. 29 | Mercury Open, Edison, N. J. | 40,000 | Wayne Zahn | 3,000 |

## PBA Leading Money Winners

Total winnings are from PBA, ABC Masters and BPAA All-Star tournaments only, and do not include numerous other tournaments nor earnings from special television shows and matches.

| Year | Player | Total money | Year | Player | Total money |
|------|--------|-------------|------|--------|-------------|
| 1959 | Dick Weber | $ 7,672 | 1964 | Bob Strampe | $33,592 |
| 1960 | Don Carter | 22,525 | 1965 | Dick Weber | 47,675 |
| 1961 | Dick Weber | 26,280 | 1966 | Wayne Zahn | 54,720 |
| 1962 | Don Carter | 49,972 | 1967 | Dave Davis | 54,165 |
| 1963 | Dick Weber | 46,333 | 1968 | Jim Stefanich (A) | 64,790 |

(a) As of Sept. 16, 1968.

## The $100,000 Firestone Tournament of Champions

This is professional bowling's richest tournament and has been held each year since its inception in 1965, in Akron, Ohio, the home of the Professional Bowlers Association. First prize is $25,000. The tournament is limited to champions of PBA events and recognized major tournaments.

| Year | Winner | Year | Winner | Year | Winner | Year | Winner |
|------|--------|------|--------|------|--------|------|--------|
| 1965 | Billy Hardwick | 1966 | Wayne Zahn | 1967 | Jim Stefanich | 1968 | Dave Davis |

# Woman's International Bowling Congress Champions

| Yr. | Individual | All Events | Two-Woman Teams | Five-Woman Teams |
|-----|------------|-----------|-----------------|------------------|
| 1965 | Doris Rudell, Whittier, Calif. ...659 | Donna Zimmerman, Norwalk, Calif...1,833 | Betty Remmick-Mary Ann White, Denver, Colo...1,263 | Belmont Bowl Pro Shop, Chicago, Ill...2,929 |
| 1966 | Gloria Bouvia, Portland, Ore...675 | Kate Helbig, Mohnton, Pa...1,835 | Pat Spence-Martha Morgan, Hampton, Va...1,231 | Gossard Girls, Chicago, Ill...2,755 |
| 1967 | Glorian Paeth, Pt. Huron, Mich...652 | Carol Miller, Milwaukee, Wisc...1,862 | Elaine Liburdi-Joan Oleske, Union City & Lyndhurst, N. J...1,252 | The Orphans, Los Angeles...2,970 |
| 1968 | Norma Parks, Raytown, Md...691 | Janice Reichley, Waco, Tex...1,889 | Pauline Stickler-Mary Lou Graham, Miami...1,250 | Hudepohl Beer, Cincinnati...2,923 |

## RECORDS OF 300 GAMES IN WIBC SANCTIONED PLAY

**Season**

**1967-68**—Lois Cook, Park Rapids, Minn.; Dee Dungca, Gardena, Calif.; Barbara Flis, Middletown, R. I.; Jeanette Hayakawa, San Francisco; Barbara Hite, Arnold, Mo.; Pauline Huffman, Lexington, Ky.; Sally Huslin, Andalusia, Pa.; Linda Land, St. Petersburg, Fla.; Jeanne Martin, Seattle; Elizabeth Pepper, Auburn, N. Y.; Lorelie Pippin, San Jose, Calif.; Marlene Rettig, Holgate, Ohio; Jeannine Ritchie, Raytown, Mo.; and Donna Webster, Seattle.

**1966-67**—Donna Crisler, Carbondale, Kan.; Doreen Daneri, Daly City, Calif.; Pat Dwyer, Medford, Ore.; Bonnie Flint, Placerville, Calif.; Nancy Forry, Ephrata, Pa.; Eva Frank, Norfolk, Neb.; Elois Gray, Harrisburg, Pa.; Mildred Martorella, Rochester, N. Y.; Dorothy Kaleel, Houston, Tex.; Arlis Kuess, Big Bend, Wis.; Shirley Mansfield, San Antonio, Tex.; Shirley Miner, Covina, Calif.; Shirley Music, Gardena, Calif.; Connie Pick, Bellflower, Calif.; Jane Shira, Bothell, Wash.; Nancy Sillmann, Fullerton, Pa.; Arlene Van Hekken, Holland, Mich.; Barbara White, Lockport, N. Y.; Dolores Witte, Brownsville, Tex.

**1965-66**—Dione Agnone, LaCrescenta, Calif.; Virginia Celli, Jacksonville, Fla.; Betty Dart, Grand Forks AFB, N. Dak.; Joanne Doyle, Redwood City, Calif.; Mildred L. Gibson, Tulsa, Okla.; Winona Gums, N. Highlands, Calif.; Joan Holm, Chicago, Ill.; Janet Hoodenpyl, Orangevale, Calif.; Betty Knecht, Minneapolis, Minn.; Betty Mivelaz, Tujunga, Calif.; Marty Parish, Corpus Christi, Tex.; Nan Poquette, E. Lansing, Mich.; Ruth Retz, Benton Harbor, Mich.; Margarette Uncles, Silver Springs, Md.; Sylvia Wagstaff, Zanesville, Ohio; Margaret M. Wilson, Lemay, Mo.

## Checker Champions

Source: U. S. Checker Assn., New York, N. Y.

**World Freestyle**—Enrique Freeman, New York, N. Y.

**U. S. Straight**—Walter Hellman, Gary, Indiana.

**Eastern U. S. Straight**—Harold Fryer, Brooklyn, N. Y.

**Southern U. S. Straight**—Ronald P. Johnson, Jackson, Tenn. and K. D. Hanson, Fremont, Calif. (co-champions).

**Central U. S. Straight**—Eugene Frazier, Parsons, Kansas.

**Western U. S. Straight**—Millard Hopper, Los Angeles.

## National Duckpin Bowling Champions, 1968
### Source: Natl. Duckpin Bowling Congress

Men's Singles—Andy Constantinople, New Haven, Conn., 489.

Women's Singles—Mary Ann Mitchell, Avon, Conn., 467.

Men's Doubles—George Haugh-Robert Cleary, Baltimore, Md., 919.

Women's Doubles—Doris Short-Jean Stewart, Baltimore, Md., 780.

Men's Teams—Valley Oilers, Portland, Conn., 2085.

Women's Teams—Johnny's New & Used Cars, Baltimore, Md., 1849.

Men's All Events—Lindset Hammonds, Washington, D. C., 1324.

Women's All Events—Mary Ann Mitchell, Avon, Conn., 1202.

Mixed Doubles—Beverly Conner-Randy Tull, Baltimore, Md., 859.

## 23rd Annual Rubberband Duckpin Bowling Championships
### Heidelberg, Pa., Mar. 30-May 19, 1968

Men's Singles—Richard Pander, New Brighton, Pa., 632.

Women's Singles—Salina Connor, Jean Stewart, both of Baltimore, Md., (tie), 529.

Men's Doubles—Anthony Rullo-James Stoner, Pittsburgh, Pa., 1,179.

Women's Doubles—Ruth Kratz-Selina Connor, Baltimore, Md., 1,033.

Men's All Events—Robert Vosel, Bridgeville, Pa., 1,691.

Women's All Events—Beverly Connor, Baltimore, Md., 1,561.

Men's Team Event—Cappelli's No. 1, Bridgeville, Pa., 2,567.

Women's Team Event—Phil-Mar Major Girls, Baltimore, Md., 2,311.

Mixed Team Event (3 men & 3 women)—MacNab, No. 1, McKeesport, Pa., 3,037.

Mixed Double Event (One Man & One Woman)—Audrey Palm 486-Norman Henning 624, McKeesport, Pa., 1,110.

# Lawn Bowls Championships in 1968
## NATIONAL OPEN TOURNAMENT, AMERICAN LAWN BOWLS ASS'N
### Milwaukee, Wis., July 13-17

Rettie Memorial Trophy—Milwaukee West LBC (Gerhardt, Hansen, Arnold Prachthauser, Donald Prachthauser).

Chicago Cup—Gary, Indiana LBC (McGaffney, Brown, Milligan, Withers).

Wisconsin Cup—Lakeside LBC, Chicago (Savage, Ibe, Stewart, Davis).

California Trophy (Doubles)—Detroit LBC (Sneddon, Stephen).

Lakeside Trophy (Doubles)—(Esch, Veitch).

Western New York Trophy (Doubles)—Detroit LBC (Sneddon, Johnson).

National Open Singles Trophy—James Grainger, Toronto, Canada.

Metropolitan Trophy (Singles)—Alex Veitch, Oakland, Calif.

Pacific Northwest Trophy (Singles)—Ralph Welton, Milwaukee, Wis.

United States Championships, A.L.B.A. Buck Hill Falls, Pa., Sept. 3-7 (Singles)—George Dunn, Niagara Falls, N. Y. (Doubles)—James F. Candelet and Robert Smart, Smithfield Avenue LBC, Pawtucket, R. I.

# Lacrosse Champions in 1968

27th Annual All Star Game—Hempstead, New York, June 15th, North 9, South 8.

National Intercollegiate Champion (Wingate Trophy)—Johns Hopkins University.

Mideastern Division (Cyrus C. Miller Trophy)—Johns Hopkins University.

Ivy League Champion—Cornell University.

South Atlantic Division (Strobhar Trophy)—Washington College.

Central Atlantic Division (Moore Trophy)—Penn State University.

New York Metropolitan Div. (Lydecker Trophy)—C. W. Post College.

Central New York Division (Cox Trophy)—Syracuse University.

Northern New York Division (Morrill Trophy)—Hartwick College.

Northeastern Division (Taylor Trophy)—Amherst College.

Colonial Division—Nichols College.

Midwest Division (Hixson Trophy)—Denison University.

Rocky Mountain Division—Air Force Academy.

### 1968 ALL AMERICA LACROSSE TEAM

Goal ............... Milton E. Hilliard (Cornell)

Goal ................... Malcolm Ogilvie (Navy)

Defense ............... Carl Tamulevich (Navy)

Defense ....... Michael A. Clark (Johns Hopkins)

Defense ................... Peter Coy (Virginia)

Midfield .................. John McIntosh (Navy)

Midfield ............ Stephen Pfeiffer (Maryland)

Midfield .... Charles Goodell, (Johns Hopkins)

Attack ....... Joseph W. Cowan (Johns Hopkins)

Attack ...... Downman McCarty (Johns Hopkins)

Attack ................... Peter Cramblot (Army)

### ALL STAR LACROSSE SERIES RECORD

| | | |
|---|---|---|
| 1951—North 12, South 11 | 1957—North 14, South 10 | 1963—South 14, North 11 |
| 1952—South 15, North 7 | 1958—South 26, North 6 | 1964—American 12, National 10 |
| 1953—South 12, North 9 | 1959—South 10, North 9 | 1965—North 15, South 10 |
| 1954—North 13, South 11 | 1960—South 15, North 12 | 1966—South 13, North 5 |
| 1955—South 12, North 11 | 1961—South 12, North 9 | 1967—North 7, South 5 |
| 1956—South 20, North 10 | 1962—South 14, North 4 | 1968—North 9, South 8 |

# World Horseshoe Pitching Champions
## (Men)

| Year | Champion Home | W. | L. | Ringer Pct. | Year | Champion Home | W. | L. | Ringer Pct. |
|---|---|---|---|---|---|---|---|---|---|
| 1961 | Harold Reno Sabina, Ohio | 34 | 1 | .838 | 1965 | Elmer Hohl, Wellesley, Ont., Can. | 32 | 3 | .846 |
| 1962 | Paul Focht Dayton, Ohio | 32 | 3 | .818 | 1966 | Curt Day Frankfort, Ind. | 26 | 2 | .866 |
| 1963 | John Monasmith Yakima, Wash. | 32 | 3 | .823 | 1967 | Dan Kuchcinski, Erie, Pa. | 34 | 1 | .844 |
| 1964 | Harold Reno Sabina, Ohio | 32 | 3 | .841 | 1968 | Elmer Hohl, Wellesley, Ont. | 35 | 0 | .885 |

## National Ladies Champions

| Year | Champion | R. Pct. |
|---|---|---|
| 1961 | Vicki (Chapelle) Winston, Lamonte, Mo.... | .549 |
| 1962 | Sue Gillespie, Portland, Ind............... | .653 |
| 1963 | Vicki (Chapelle) Winston, Lamonte, Mo.... | .586 |
| 1964 | Sue Gillespie, Portland, Ind............... | .811 |
| 1965 | Sue Gillespie, Portland, Ind............... | .759 |
| 1966 | Vicki (Chapelle) Winston, Lamonte, Mo.... | .725 |
| 1967 | Vicki (Chapelle) Winston, Lamonte, Mo.... | .736 |
| 1968 | Lorraine Thomas, Lockport, N.Y.......... | .746 |

## World Junior Champions

| Champion | R. Pct. |
|---|---|
| Gary Roberts, Lucasville, O........ | .500 |
| Gary Roberts, Lucasville, O........ | .624 |
| Gary Roberts, Lucasville, O........ | .628 |
| Gary Roberts, Lucasville, O........ | .679 |
| Ross Stevenson, Baden, Ont........ | .651 |
| Mark Seibold, Huntington, Ind.... | .756 |
| Farron Eisemann, Riverton, Wyo... | .736 |
| Farron Eisemann, Riverton, Wyo... | .785 |

# World Track and Field Records

**Source:** International Amateur Athletic Federation; record approved to Oct. 1, 1968
*Asterisk indicates pending record. A number of new records await confirmation

## Men
## RUNNING

| Event | Record | Holder | Country | Date | Where made |
|---|---|---|---|---|---|
| 100 yds...... | 9.1 s............. | Bob Hayes....... | U. S. A...... | June 21, 1963 | St. Louis, Mo. |
| | | James Hines...... | U. S. A...... | May 13, 1967 | Houston, Tex. |
| | | Charlie Greene... | U. S. A...... | June 15, 1967 | Provo, Utah |
| 220 yds........ | 19.5 s............. | Tommie Smith... | U. S. A...... | May 7, 1966 | San Jose, Calif. |
| | (Straight course) | | | | |
| 220 yds........ | 20.0 s............. | Tommie Smith... | U. S. A...... | May 11, 1966 | Sacramento, Calif. |
| | (Turn) | | | | |
| 440 yds....... | 44.8 s............. | Tommie Smith... | U. S. A...... | May 20, 1967 | San Jose, Calif. |
| 880 yds....... | 1 m., 45.1 s....... | Peter Snell...... | New Zealand | Feb. 3, 1962 | Christchurch, N.Z. |
| 1 mile........ | 3 m., 51.1 s....... | Jim Ryun....... | U. S. A...... | June 23, 1967 | Bakersfield, Calif. |
| 2 miles........ | 8 m., 19.8 s....... | Ron Clarke...... | Australia..... | June 27, 1967 | Sweden |
| | *8 m., 19.6 s...... | Ron Clarke...... | Australia..... | Aug. 24, 1968 | London, Eng. |
| 3 miles........ | 12 m., 52.4 s...... | Ron Clarke...... | Australia..... | July 10, 1965 | London, Eng. |
| 6 miles........ | 26 m., 47.0 s...... | Ron Clarke...... | Australia..... | July 14, 1965 | Oslo, Norway |
| 10 miles....... | 47 m., 12.8 s...... | Ron Clarke...... | Australia..... | Mar. 3, 1965 | Mentone, Aust. |
| 15 miles....... | 1 h., 12 m., 48.2 s.. | Ron Hill........ | Gt. Britain.. | July 21, 1965 | Bolton, Eng. |
| 1 hour........ | 12 mi., 1,006 yds.. | Ron Clarke...... | Australia..... | Oct. 27, 1965 | Victoria, Aust. |

## RUNNING—METRIC DISTANCES

| 100 meters..... | 10.0 s............. | Armin Hary..... | Germany..... | June 21, 1960 | Zurich, Switzerland |
| | | Harry Jerome..... | Canada...... | July 15, 1960 | Saskatchewan, Canada |
| | | Horacio Esteves... | Venezuela.... | Aug. 15, 1964 | Caracas, Venez. |
| | | Bob Hayes....... | U. S. A...... | Oct. 15, 1964 | Tokyo, Japan |
| | | Jim Hines....... | U. S. A...... | May 27, 1967 | Modesto, Calif. |
| | *9.9 s............. | Jim Hines....... | U. S. A...... | June 20, 1968 | Sacramento, Calif. |
| | *9.9 s............. | Charlie Greene... | U. S. A...... | June 20, 1968 | Sacramento, Calif. |
| 200 meters.... | 19.5 s............. | Tommie Smith... | U. S. A...... | May 7, 1966 | San Jose, Calif. |
| | (Straight course) | | | | |
| 200 meters.... | 20.0 s............. | Tommie Smith... | U. S. A...... | May 11, 1966 | Sacramento, Calif. |
| | (Turn) | | | | |
| | *19.7 s............. | John Carlos..... | U. S. A...... | Sept. 12, 1968 | S. Lake Tahoe, Cal. |
| 400 meters.... | 44.5 s............. | Tommie Smith... | U. S. A...... | May 20, 1967 | San Jose, Calif. |
| | *44 s............. | Lee Evans...... | U. S. A...... | Sept. 14, 1968 | S. Lake Tahoe, Cal. |
| 800 meters.... | 1 m., 44.3 s....... | Peter Snell...... | New Zealand | Feb. 3, 1962 | Christchurch, N.Z. |
| 1,000 meters... | 2 m., 16.2 s....... | Juergen May..... | E. Germany.. | July 20, 1965 | Erfurt, Germany |
| 1,500 meters... | | Franz-Joseph Kemper....... | W. Germany.. | Sept. 21, 1966 | Hanover, Ger. |
| | 3 m., 33.1 s | Jim Ryun....... | U. S. A...... | July 8, 1967 | Los Angeles, Cal. |
| 2,000 meters... | *4 m., 56.2 s | Michel Jazy..... | France...... | Oct. 12, 1966 | Paris, France |
| 3,000 meters... | 7 m., 39.6 s........ | Kipchoge Keino.. | Kenya...... | Aug. 27, 1965 | Halsingborg |
| 5,000 meters... | 13 m., 24.2 s........ | Kipchoge Keino.. | Kenya...... | Nov. 30, 1965 | Auckland, N. Z. |
| 10,000 meters... | 27 m., 39.4 s........ | Ron Clarke...... | Australia..... | July 14, 1965 | Oslo, Norway |
| 15,000 meters... | 44 m., 54.6 s........ | Emil Zatopek.... | Czechoslovakia | Sept. 29, 1951 | Stara Boleslav, Czecho. |
| 20,000 meters... | 59 m., 22.8 s........ | Ron Clarke...... | Australia..... | Oct. 27, 1965 | Victoria, Aust. |
| 25,000 meters... | 1 h., 15 m., 22.6 s.. | Ron Hill........ | Gr. Britain.. | July 21, 1965 | Bolton, Eng. |
| 30,000 meters... | 1 h., 32 m., 34.6 s.. | T. F. K. Johnston.. | Gr. Britain.. | Oct. 16, 1965 | Thames, Eng. |
| 3,000 meter stpl. | 8 m., 26.4 s........ | Gaston Roelants.. | Belgium...... | Aug. 7, 1965 | Brussels, Belgium |

## HURDLES (10 hurdles)

| 120 yards..... | 13.2 s............. | Martin Lauer..... | Germany..... | July 7, 1959 | Zurich, Switz. |
| | | Lee Calhoun..... | U. S. A...... | Aug. 21, 1960 | Berne, Switz. |
| | | Earl McCullouch... | U. S. A...... | July 16, 1967 | Minneapolis, |
| 220 yards...... | 21.9 s............. | Don Styron...... | U. S. A...... | Apr. 2, 1960 | Baton Rouge |
| 440 yards...... | 49.3 s............. | G. C. Potgieter... | South Africa.. | Apr. 16, 1960 | Bloemfontein, S. A. |
| 110 meters.... | 13.2 s............. | Martin Lauer..... | Germany..... | July 7, 1959 | Zurich, Switz. |
| | | Lee Calhoun..... | U. S. A...... | Aug. 21, 1960 | Berne, Switz. |
| | | Earl McCullouch... | U. S. A...... | July 16, 1967 | Minneapolis |
| 200 meters.... | 21.9 s............. | Don Styron...... | U. S. A...... | Apr. 2, 1960 | Baton Rouge |
| 200 meters.... | 22.5 s............. | Martin Lauer..... | Germany..... | July 7, 1959 | Zurich, Switz. |
| | (Turn) | Glenn Davis..... | U. S. A...... | Aug. 20, 1960 | Berne, Switz. |
| 400 meters..... | 49.1 s............. | Rex Cawley..... | U. S. A...... | Sept. 13, 1964 | Los Angeles, Calif. |

## RELAY RACES

| Event | Record | Holder | Country | Date | Where made |
|---|---|---|---|---|---|
| 440 yds. (4x110) (2 turns) | 38.6 s........ | Univ. of Southern Calif............ (McCullouch, Kuller, Simpson, Miller) | U. S. A...... | June 17, 1967.. | Provo, Utah |
| 880 yds. (4x220)...... | 1 m., 22.1 s... | San Jose State Coll. (Shackelford, Talmadge, Evans, Smith) | U. S. A...... | May 13, 1967.. | Fresno, Calif |
| 1 mile (4x440)........ | 3 m., 04.5 s... | Arizona State Un.... (M. Barrick, H. Carr, R. Freeman, U. Williams) | U. S. A...... | Apr. 27, 1963.. | Walnut, Calif. |
| | | Southern Univ. Track Club......... (R. Johnson, A. Gates, E. Mason, T. Lewis) | U. S. A...... | May 29, 1965.. | Modesto, Calif. |
| 2 miles (4x880)........ | 7 m., 17.4 s... | U. of Southern Calif. (J. Link, D. Best, D. Buck, D. Carr) | U. S. A...... | May 13, 1966.. | Los Angeles, Calif. |
| 4 miles (4x1) (mile)... | 16 m., 09.0 s.. | Univ. of Oregon... (A San Romani, Jr., V. Reeve, K. Forman, D. Burleson) | U. S. A...... | May 12, 1962.. | Fresno, Calif. |

## RELAY RACES—METRIC DISTANCES

| | | | | | |
|---|---|---|---|---|---|
| 400 mtrs. (4x100) | 38.6 s. | Univ. of So. Calif. (McCullouch, Kuller, Simpson, Miller) | U. S. A. | June 17, 1967. | Provo, Utah |
| 800 mtrs. (4x200) | 1 m., 22.1 s. | San Jose State Coll. (Shackelford, Talmadge, Evans, Smith) | U. S. A. | May, 13 1967. | Fresno, Calif. |
| 1,600 mtrs. (4x400) | 3 m., 00.7 s. | Nat'l team (O. Cassell, M. Larrabee, U. Williams, H. Carr) | U. S. A. | Oct. 21, 1964. | Tokyo, Japan |
| | *2 m., 59.6 s. | Natl. team (Frey, Evans, Smith, Lewis) | U. S. A. | July 24, 1966. | Los Angeles |
| 3,200 mtrs. (4x800) | 7 m., 15.8 s. | Nat'l team (A. Baaillieux, A. Langenus, E. Leva, R. Moens) | Belgium | Aug. 8, 1956. | Brussels, Belgium |
| 6,000 mtrs. (4x1,500) | 14 m., 49.0 s. | French Nat'l team (Vervoort, Nicolas, Jazy, Wadoux) | France | June 25, 1965. | Paris, France |

## FIELD EVENTS

| | | | | | |
|---|---|---|---|---|---|
| High jump | 7 ft., 5¾ in. | Valery Brumel | USSR | July 21, 1963. | Moscow, Russia |
| Long jump | 27 ft., 4¾ in. | Ralph Boston | U. S. A. | May 29, 1965. | Modesto, Calif. |
| Triple jump | 55 ft., 10¼ in. | Josef Schmidt | Poland | Aug. 5, 1960. | Olsztyn, Poland |
| Pole vault | 17 ft., 7¾ in. | Paul Wilson | U. S. A. | June 23, 1967. | Bakersfield, Calif. |
| | *17 ft. 9 in. | Bob Seagren | U. S. A. | Sept. 12, 1968. | So. Lake Tahoe, Calif. |
| 16 lb. shot put | 71 ft., 5½ in. | Randy Matson | U. S. A. | Apr. 22, 1967. | College Sta., Texas |
| Discus throw | 213 ft., 11¾ in. | Ludvik Danek | Czecho. | Oct. 12, 1965. | Czecho. |
| | *218 ft. 4 in. | Jay Silvester | U. S. A. | May 25, 1968. | Modesto, Calif. |
| Javelin throw | 300 ft., 11 in. | Terje Pedersen | Norway | Sept. 2, 1964. | Oslo, Norway |
| | *301 ft. 9¼ in. | Janis Lusis | USSR | June 23, 1968. | Saartjarvi, Finland |
| 16 lb. hammer throw. | 241 ft., 11 in. | G. Zsivotsky | Hungary | Sept. 4, 1965. | Hungary |
| Decathlon | 8,319 pts. | Kurt Bendlin | W. Germany | May 13-14, 1967 | Heidelberg, Germany |

## WALKING

| | | | | | |
|---|---|---|---|---|---|
| 20 miles | 2 h., 31 m., 33.0 s. | A Vedjakov | USSR | Aug. 23, 1958 | Moscow, USSR |
| 30 miles | 4 h., 02 m., 33 s. | Christian Hohne | E. Germany | May 16, 1965 | Potsdam |

## WALKING—METRIC DISTANCES

| | | | | | |
|---|---|---|---|---|---|
| 20,000 meters | 1 h., 27 m., 05.0 s. | V. Golubnichiy | USSR | Sept, 23, 1958 | Simferopol, USSR |
| 30,000 meters | 2 h., 17 m., 16.8 s. | A. Egorov | USSR | July 15, 1959 | Leningrad, USSR |
| 50,000 meters | 4 h., 10 m., 51.8 s. | Christian Hohne | E. Germany | May 16, 1965 | Potsdam |
| 2 hours | 16 miles, 743 yds. | A. Egorov | USSR | July 15, 1959 | Leningrad |

# Women

## RUNNING

| | | | | | |
|---|---|---|---|---|---|
| 100 yards | 10.3 s. | Marlene Mathews | Australia | Mar. 10, 1958. | Sydney |
| | | Wyomia Tyus | U. S. A. | July 17, 1965. | Kingston, Jam. |
| 220 yards | 22.9 s. | Mary Burvill | Australia | Feb. 22, 1964. | Perth, Australia |
| 440 yards | 52.4 s. | Judy Amoore | Australia | Feb. 2, 1965. | Perth, Australia |
| 880 yards | 2 m., 02.0 s. | D. Willis | Australia | Mar. 3, 1962. | Perth, Australia |
| 60 meters | 7.2 s. | Betty Cuthbert | Australia | Feb. 27, 1960. | Sydney, Australia |
| 100 meters | 11.1 s. | I. Bochkareva | USSR | Aug. 28, 1961. | Moscow |
| | | Irena Kirszenstein | Poland | July 9, 1965. | Prague |
| | | Eva Klobukovska | Poland | July 9, 1965. | |
| | | Wyomia Tyus | U. S. A. | July 31, 1965. | Kiev, USSR |
| | | Barbara Ferrell | U. S. A. | Feb. 7, 1967 | Santa Barbara, Cal. |
| | | L. Samotyesova | USSR | Aug. 15, 1968. | Moscow |
| | | Margaret Bailes | U. S. A. | Aug. 18, 1968. | Aurora, Colo. |
| 200 meters | 22.7 s. | Irena Kirszenstein | Poland | Aug. 8, 1965. | Warsaw, Poland |
| 400 meters | 51.9 s. | Shin Guen Dan | North Korea. | Oct. 23, 1962. | Pyongyang, No. Korea |
| 800 meters | 2 m., 1.1 s. | Ann Packer | Gr. Britain | Oct. 20, 1964. | Tokyo, Japan |
| | *2 m., 0.5 s. | Vera Nikolic | Yugoslavia | July 20, 1968. | London, Eng. |

## HURDLES

| | | | | | |
|---|---|---|---|---|---|
| 80 meters | 10.3 s. | Irena Press | USSR | Oct. 24, 1965. | USSR |

## FIELD EVENTS

| | | | | | |
|---|---|---|---|---|---|
| High jump | 6 ft., 3 in. | I. Balas | Rumania | July 15, 1961. | Sofia, Bulg. |
| Long jump | 22 ft., 2¼ in. | Mary Rand | Gr. Britain | Oct. 14, 1964. | Tokyo, Japan |
| Shot put | 61 ft. | Tamara Press | USSR | Sept. 19, 1965. | Kassel, Germany |
| Discus throw | 195 ft., 10½ in. | Tamara Press | USSR | Aug. 11, 1965. | Moscow |
| Javelin | 204 ft., 8½ in. | Elena Gorchakova | USSR | Oct. 16, 1964. | Tokyo, Japan |
| Pentathlon | 5,246 pts. | Irena Press | USSR | Oct. 16-17, 1964. | Japan |

## RELAY RACES

| | | | | | |
|---|---|---|---|---|---|
| 440 yards (4x110).... | 45.2 s........ | Nat'l team......... (M. Cobb, M. Rand, D. Arden, D. Hyman) | Gr. Britain... | Aug. 5, 1963.. | London, England |
| 400 mtrs. (4x100)..... | 43.6 s........ | Nat'l team......... (T. Ciepla, I. Kirszenstein, H. Gorecka, E. Klobukowska) | Poland....... | Oct. 21, 1964.. | Tokyo, Japan |
| 800 mtrs. (4x200)..... | 1 m., 35.1 s... | Nat'l team......... (R. Lace, V. Laslovskaya, G. Popova, M. Itkina) | USSR......... | July 14, 1963.. | Moscow, USSR |
| 880 yds. (4x220)...... | 1 m., 36.0 s... | Nat'l team......... (H. Sadau, G. Birke-meyer, B. Mayer, C. Studnick) | E. Germany.. | July 26, 1958.. | Leipzig, Germany |
| 1½ miles (3x880)..... | 6 m., 25.2 s... | Nat'l team......... (Sterling, Lowe Piercy) | Gr. Britain... | July 30, 1967.. | Budapest |
| 2,400 mtrs. (3x800)... | 6 m., 20 s.... | Nat'l team......... (Sterling, Lowe Piercy) | Gr. Britain... | Aug. 28, 1967.. | London |

## National Interscholastic Track and Field Records

### Source: National Federation of State High School Athletic Associations
Records approved to Nov., 1968

| Event | Record | Holder | School | Site and year |
|---|---|---|---|---|
| 100 yds......... | 0:09.3........ | William Gaines...... | Clearview Regional H. S., Mullica Hill, O.... | Deptford, Ohio, 1967 |
| 220 yds......... | 0:20.2........ | Forrest O. Beaty..... | Herbert Hoover H. S. Glendale, Calif...... | Chaffey, Calif., 1961 |
| 440 yds......... | 0:46.1........ | Ulis C. Williams...... | Compton (Calif.) Senior H. S........ | Ontario, Calif., 1961 |
| 880 yds......... | 1:48.8........ | Richard J. Joyce..... | Sierra H. S., Whittier, Calif........ | Bakersfield, Calif., 1965 |
| 1 mile.......... | 3:58.3........ | James Ryun........ | Wichita East H. S., Wichita, Kan..... | Wichita, Kan., 1965 |
| 2 mile.......... | 8:48.3........ | Rick Evan Riley..... | Ferris H. S., Spokane, Wash........ | Pullman, Wash., 1966 |
| 120 yd. high hdles. | 0:13.5........ | Richmond M. Flowers, Jr............. | Sidney Lanier H. S., Montgomery, Ala... | Mobile, Ala., 1965 |
| | | William Tipton...... | Central H. S., Pontiac, Mich........ | Saginaw, Mich., 1967 |
| 180 yd. low hurdles | 0:18.1........ | Donald Castronovo... | Oceanside H. S., Oceanside, N. Y.... | Ithaca, N. Y., 1964 |
| | | Steve Caminiti...... | Crespi Carmelite H. S., Encino, Calif..... | Encino, Calif., 1964 |
| | | Earl McCullouch..... | Polytechnic H. S., Long Beach, Calif... | Norwalk, Calif., 1964 |
| High jump....... | 7 ft. 1¼ in... | Otis Halley........ | Union H.S., Wasco, Calif....... | Bakersfield, Calif., 1968 |
| Long jump....... | 25 ft. 7 in.... | Jerry Proctor........ | John Muir H. S., Pasa-dena, Calif...... | Ontario, Calif., 1967 |
| Pole vault (indoor) | 16 ft. ¾ in... | Paul Wilson......... | Warren H. S., Down-ey, Calif...... | Los Angeles, Calif., 1965 |
| Pole vault (out.).. | 16 ft. 6¾ in... | Paul Wilson......... | Warren H. S., Down-ey, Calif...... | Westminster, Calif., 1965 |
| Triple jump...... | 49 ft. 3½ in... | Warren L. Rockwell, Jr. | Wheatley H. S., Old Westbury, N. Y... | Great Neck, N. Y., 1964 |
| Shot put (12 lbs.).. | 72 ft. 3¼ in... | Sam Walker......... | W. W. Samuel H. S., Dallas, Tex....... | Corpus Christi, Tex., 1968 |
| Discus.......... | 199 ft. 10½ in.. | Leon Miller.......... | Hilliard H. S., Hilliard, Ohio.......... | Worthington, Ohio, 1967 |
| Javelin.......... | 252 ft. 8 in.... | Mark Murro......... | Essex Catholic H. S., Newark, N. J..... | Dover, N. J., 1967 |
| 440 yd. relay..... | 0:41.1........ | Anderson, Beasley, Copeland, Williams.. | Kirkpatrick H. S., Ft. Worth, Tex..... | Austin, Tex., 1968 |
| 880 yd. relay..... | 1:25.4........ | Jackson, James, Reed, Hill............ | White Plains (N. Y.) H. S............ | Jamaica, N. Y., 1966 |
| 1 mile relay...... | 3:11.8........ | Bouche, Bradley, Bow-man, Grant....... | Memorial H. S., Hous-ton, Texas....... | Baytown, Texas, 1967 |
| 2 mile relay..... | 7:41.9........ | Menta, Jakosa, Bow-man, Grant........ | Proviso West H. S., Hillside, Ill........ | Glen Ellyn, Ill., 1965 |
| Sprint medley relay (1 mile)........ | 3:23.3........ | Korson, Brake, Prince, Morton......... | Memorial H. S., Hous-ton, Texas....... | Houston, Texas, 1967 |

## James E. Sullivan Memorial Trophy Winners

The James E. Sullivan Memorial Trophy, inaugurated in 1930, is awarded annually by the AAU to the athlete who "by his or her performance, example and influence as an amateur, has done the most during the year to advance the cause of sportsmanship."

| Year | Name | Sport | Points | Year | Name | Sport | Points |
|---|---|---|---|---|---|---|---|
| 1942.. | Cornelius Warmerdam.. | Track.... | 1,101 | 1955.. | Harrison Dillard....... | Track.... | 1,375 |
| 1943.. | Gilbert Dodds........ | Track.... | 860 | 1956.. | Patricia K. McCormick. | Diving.... | 1,889 |
| 1944.. | Ann Curtis.......... | Swimming | 694 | 1957.. | Bobby Joe Morrow.... | Track.... | 1,583 |
| 1945.. | Felix A. Blanchard.... | Football.. | 923 | 1958.. | Glenn Davis......... | Track.... | 1,868 |
| 1946.. | Arnold Tucker....... | Football.. | 597 | 1959.. | Parry O'Brien....... | Track.... | 1,318 |
| 1947.. | John B Kelly, Jr...... | Rowing... | 663 | 1960.. | Rafer Johnson....... | Decathlon. | 1,611 |
| 1948.. | Robert B. Mathias.... | Track.... | 1,491 | 1961.. | Wilma Rudolph Ward.. | Track.... | 1,627 |
| 1949.. | Richard T. Button.... | Skating.. | 947 | 1962.. | James T. Beatty..... | Track.... | 2,459 |
| 1950.. | Fred Wilt.......... | Track.... | 1,197 | 1963.. | John T. Pennel...... | Track.... | 1,115 |
| 1951.. | Rev. Robt. E. Richards.. | Track.... | 1,263 | 1964.. | Don Schollander..... | Swimming. | 2,161 |
| 1952.. | Horace Ashenfelter... | Track.... | 1,112 | 1965.. | Bill Bradley........ | Basketball | 852 |
| 1953.. | Dr. Sammy Lee...... | Diving... | 1,676 | 1966.. | Jim Ryun.......... | Track.... | 3,838 |
| 1954.. | Mal Whitfield........ | Track.... | 1,689 | 1967.. | Randy Matson....... | Track.... | 787 |

# American Track and Field Records

**Source:** Amateur Athletic Union. Records are those set by an American citizen anywhere in the world. Indoor records are for tracks not more than 220 yards per lap unless otherwise noted. A number of new records await confirmation. Italics indicate record pending.

## OUTDOOR

| Distance | Time | Holder | Where made | Date |
|---|---|---|---|---|
| 100 yards | 9.1 s. | Bob Hayes | St. Louis, Mo | June 21, 1963 |
| | | Charlie Green | Provo, Utah | June 17, 1967 |
| | | Jim Hines | Houston, Tex. | May 13, 1967 |
| 220 yards | 19.5 s. | Tommie Smith | San Jose, Calif. | May 7, 1966 |
| 220 yards (turn) | 20.0 s. | Tommie Smith | Sacramento, Calif. | May 11, 1966 |
| 300 yards | 30.2 s. | C. W. Paddock | Redlands, Calif. | Apr. 23, 1921 |
| | | Cliff Bourland | Los Angeles, Calif. | Apr. 17, 1943 |
| 440 yards | 44.8 s. | Tommie Smith | San Jose, Calif. | May 20, 1967 |
| 600 yards | 1 m., 08.5 s. | Willie Atterbury | Columbus, Ohio | Apr. 20, 1957 |
| 880 yards | 1 m., 44.9 s. | Jim Ryun | Terre Haute, Ind | June 10, 1966 |
| 1,000 yards | 2:06.8 s. | Wade Bell | Eugene, Ore. | July 5, 1967 |
| 1,320 yards | 2 m., 54.8 s. | Jim Grelle | Woodland Hills, Calif. | Aug. 29, 1964 |
| 1 mile | 3 m., 51.1 s. | Jim Ryun | Bakersfield, Calif. | June 23, 1967 |
| 2 miles | 8 m., 25.2 s. | Jim Ryun | Los Angeles, Calif. | May 13, 1966 |
| | 8 m., 22.2 s. | *George Young* | *San Diego, Calif.* | *June 1, 1968* |
| 3 miles | 12 m., 53.0 s. | Gerry Lindgren | Seattle, Wash. | May 14, 1966 |
| 4 miles | 18 m., 27.4 s. | Peter McArdle | Yonkers, N. Y. | May 3, 1964 |
| 5 miles | 23 m., 13.4 s. | Peter McArdle | Yonkers, N. Y. | May 3, 1964 |
| 6 miles | 27 m., 11.6 s. | Billy Mills | San Diego, Calif. | June 27, 1965 |
| | | Gerry Lindgren | San Diego, Calif. | June 27, 1965 |
| 7 miles | 33 m., 45.8 s. | George Brown | St. Paul, Minn. | Sept. 18, 1966 |
| 8 miles | 38 m., 43.4 s. | George Brown | St. Paul, Minn. | Sept. 18, 1966 |
| 9 miles | 43 m., 43.8 s. | George Brown | St. Paul, Minn. | Sept. 18, 1966 |
| 10 miles | 48 m., 28.0 s. | Buddy Edelen | Hurlingham Park, Eng. | April 18, 1963 |
| 15 miles | 1 h., 18 m., 10.8 s. | Ron Daws | St. Paul, Minn. | Sept. 18, 1965 |
| 20 miles | 1 h., 46 m., 13.0 s. | Lou Castagnola | Arlington, Va. | Jan. 22, 1967 |
| 1 hour | 12 mi., 232 yds. | Mike Kimball | Alameda, Calif. | Aug. 5, 1967 |
| 2 hours | 21 mi., 1,738 yds. | Lou Castagnola | Arlington, Va. | Jan. 22, 1967 |

## METRIC DISTANCES—OUTDOOR

| 100 meters | 10.0 s. | Bob Hayes | Tokyo, Japan | Oct. 15, 1964 |
|---|---|---|---|---|
| | 10.0 s. | Jim Hines | Modesto, Calif. | May 27, 1967 |
| | *9.9 s.* | *Jim Hines* | *Sacramento, Calif.* | *June 20, 1968* |
| | *9.9 s.* | *Charlie Greene* | *Sacramento, Calif.* | *June 20, 1968* |
| 200 meters | 19.5 s. | Tommie Smith | San Jose, Calif. | May 7, 1966 |
| (straightaway) | | | | |
| 200 meters | 20.0 s. | Tommie Smith | Sacramento, Calif. | May 11, 1966 |
| | *19.7 s.* | *John Carlos* | *So. Lake Tahoe, Calif.* | *Sept. 14, 1968* |
| 300 meters | 33.0 s. | Andrew Stanfield | Orebro, Sweden | Aug. 18, 1949 |
| 400 meters | 44.5 s. | Tommie Smith | San Jose, Calif. | May 20, 1967 |
| (two turns) | *44.0 s.* | *Lee Evans* | *So. Lake Tahoe, Calif.* | *Sept. 14, 1968* |
| 500 meters | 1 m., 01 s. | Mal Whitfield | Antwerp, Belgium | July 25, 1949 |
| 600 meters | 1 m., 17.0 s. | Jack Yerman | Buffalo, N. Y. | Aug. 23, 1959 |
| 800 meters | 1 m., 44.9 s. | Jim Ryun | Terre Haute, Ind | June 10, 1966 |
| 1,000 meters | 2 m., 19.3 s. | Tom Courtney | Goteborg, Sweden | July 4, 1954 |
| 1,500 meters | 3 m., 33.1 s. | Jim Ryun | Los Angeles, Calif. | July 8, 1967 |
| 2,000 meters | 5 m., 07.4 s. | Jim Grelle | Sidney, Aust. | Mar. 18, 1966 |
| 3,000 meters | 7 m., 54.2 s. | Jim Beatty | Avranches, France | Aug. 15, 1962 |
| 5,000 meters | 13 m., 38.0 s. | Bob Schul | Compton, Calif. | June 5, 1964 |
| | | Gerry Lindgren | Los Angeles, Calif. | June 4, 1966 |
| 6,000 meters | 17 m., 49.6 s. | Van Nelson | St. Paul, Minn. | Sept. 18, 1966 |
| 7,000 meters | 21 m., 08.8 s. | Bob Scharf | Wash., D.C. | May 30, 1966 |
| 8,000 meters | 23 m., 54.4 s. | George Brown | St. Paul, Minn. | Sept. 18, 1966 |
| 9,000 meters | 27 m., 13.6 s. | Robert Scharf | Washington, D. C. | May 30, 1966 |
| 10,000 meters | 28 m., 17.6 s. | Billy Mills | Augsburg, Germany | Aug. 12, 1965 |
| 15,000 meters | 45 m., 16.8 s. | L. G. Edelen | London, Eng. | Apr. 13, 1963 |
| 20,000 meters | 1 hr., 2 m., 25.6 s. | Ken Moore | Eugene, Ore. | Mar. 11, 1966 |
| 25,000 meters | 1 hr., 22 m., 14.2 s. | Ron Daws | St. Paul, Minn. | Sept. 18, 1965 |
| 30,000 meters | 1 hr., 45 m., 28.4 s. | Richard Halmes | Arlington, Va. | Jan. 20, 1963 |

## INDOOR

| 60 yards | 5.9 s. | Bob Hayes | New York, N. Y. | Feb. 22, 1964 |
|---|---|---|---|---|
| | | Sam Perry | New York, N. Y. | Jan. 28, 1965 |
| | | Darrel Newman | San Francisco, Calif. | Feb. 26, 1965 |
| | | Charles Greene | Los Angeles, Calif. | Jan. 22, 1966 |
| | | Bill Gaines | Albuquerque, N. M. | Mar. 4, 1966 |
| | | Jim Hines | Albuquerque, N. M. | Jan. 28, 1967 |
| 100 yards | 9.5 s. | David Sime | Washington, D. C. | Jan. 21, 1956 |
| 220 yards | 22.2 s. | Theo. P. Ellison | Brooklyn, N. Y. | Mar. 1, 1935 |
| 300 yards | 30.5 s. | James Lingel | Buffalo, N. Y. | Feb. 14, 1953 |
| 440 yards | 46.2 s. | Tommie Smith | Louisville, Ky. | Feb. 18, 1967 |
| | 47.0 s. | *Larry James* | *Detroit, Mich.* | *Mar. 15, 1968* |
| 600 yards | 1 m., 9.0 s. | Martin McGrady | Louisville, Ky. | Feb. 12, 1966 |
| 880 yards | 1 m., 48.9 s. | Dave Patrick | Detroit, Mich. | Mar. 10, 1967 |
| 1,000 yards | 2 m., 7.9 s. | Ernie Cunliffe | Boston, Mass. | Jan. 28, 1961 |
| 1,320 yards | 3 m., 01.2 s. | Joseph M. Deady | New York, N. Y. | Jan. 7, 1956 |
| 1 mile | 3 m., 56.4 s. | Tom O'Hara | Chicago, Ill. | Mar. 6, 1964 |
| 2 miles | 8 m., 30.8 s. | James F. Beatty | Chicago, Ill. | Mar. 9, 1963 |
| 3 miles | 13 m., 16.2 s. | Tracy Smith | Oakland, Calif. | Mar. 5, 1967 |
| | 13 m., 15 s. | *Tracy Smith* | *Toronto, Ont.* | *Mar. 1, 1968* |
| 4 miles | 19 m., 39.8 s. | G. V. Bonhag | New York, N. Y. | Feb. 5, 1910 |
| 5 miles | 24 m., 59.4 s. | G. V. Bonhag | New York, N. Y. | Mar. 16, 1909 |
| 6 miles | 30 m., 42 s. | G. V. Bonhag | New York, N. Y. | Mar. 20, 1909 |
| 7 miles | 35 m., 50.6 s. | G. V. Bonhag | New York, N. Y. | Mar. 20, 1909 |
| 10 miles | 54 m., 21.2 s. | L. Tewanima | New York, N. Y. | Mar. 27, 1909 |
| 25 miles | 2 h., 44 m., 50 s. | M. Maloney | New York, N. Y. | Jan. 8, 1909 |

## METRIC DISTANCES—INDOOR

| 60 meters | 6.6 s. | Jesse Owens | New York, N. Y. | Feb. 23, 1935 |
|---|---|---|---|---|
| | | Ben Johnson | New York, N. Y. | Feb. 26, 1938 |
| | | Ben Johnson | New York, N. Y. | Feb. 23, 1935 |
| | | Herbert Thompson | New York, N. Y. | Feb. 25, 1939 |
| 100 meters | 10.7 s. | Robt. Rodenkirchen | Brooklyn, N. Y. | Jan. 8, 1938 |
| 200 meters | 22.2 s. | Theo. P. Ellison | Brooklyn, N. Y. | Mar. 1, 1935 |
| 400 meters | 46.2 s. | Tommie Smith | Louisville, Ky. | Feb. 18, 1967 |
| 500 meters | 1 m., 02.9 s. | Mal Whitfield | New York, N. Y. | Feb. 28, 1953 |
| 600 meters | 1 m., 20.3 s. | James B. Herbert | New York, N. Y. | Feb. 26, 1938 |

## METRIC DISTANCES—INDOOR continued

| | | | | | |
|---|---|---|---|---|---|
| 800 meters | 1 m., 47.4 s. | Ted Nelson | Berlin, Germany | Apr. 9, 1965 |
| 1,000 meters | 2 m., 26.4 s. | Lloyd Hahn | New York, N. Y. | Mar. 26, 1927 |
| 1,500 meters | 3 m., 43.6 s. | Tom O'Hara | New York, N. Y. | Feb. 27, 1964 |
| 2,000 meters | 5 m., 16.8 s. | Jim Beatty | Chicago, Ill. | Mar. 9, 1963 |
| 3,000 meters | 7 m., 56.6 s. | Billy Mills | Berlin, Germany | Apr. 7, 1965 |
| 4,000 meters | 11 m., 27.4 s. | Horace Ashenfelter | New York, N. Y. | Feb. 20, 1935 |
| 5,000 meters | 14 m., 30.9 s. | Donald Lash | New York, N. Y. | Feb. 25, 1939 |

## RACE WALKING—OUTDOOR

| | | | | |
|---|---|---|---|---|
| 1 mile | 6 m., 29.6 s. | F. P. Murray | New York, N. Y. | Oct. 27, 1883 |
| 2 miles | 13 m., 29.2 s. | Rudolp Haluza | Walnut, Calif. | Apr. 16, 1966 |
| 3 miles | 21:03.8 s. | Ronald O. Laird | Santa Monica, Calif. | July 1, 1967 |
| 4 miles | 28 m., 34.0 s. | Ronald Zinn | Chicago, Ill. | Oct. 31, 1964 |
| 5 miles | 36 m., 4.2 s. | Ronald Zinn | Chicago, Ill. | Oct. 31, 1964 |
| 9 miles | 1 h., 5 m., 45.6 s. | Ronald O. Laird | Walnut, Calif. | May 16, 1964 |
| 10 miles | 1 hr., 13 m., 17.6 s. | Ronald O. Laird | Walnut, Calif. | May 16, 1964 |
| 15 miles | 1 h., 57 m., 36.0 s. | Ronald O. Laird | San Diego, Calif. | Feb. 20, 1966 |
| 20 miles | 2 h., 40 m., 12.0 s. | Ronald O. Laird | Chicago, Ill. | Oct. 27, 1963 |
| 25 miles | 3 h., 39 m., 36.8 s. | Ronald O. Laird | San Diego, Calif. | Feb. 25, 1966 |
| 1 hour | 8 mi., 420 yds. | Ronald O. Laird | Walnut, Calif. | May 16, 1964 |
| 2 hours | 15 mi., 125 ft., 6 in. | Ronald O. Laird | Chicago, Ill. | Oct. 27, 1963 |

## RELAY RACING

(Long track—More than 220 yards per lap.
*Denotes indoor record.)
**400 meters (4x100)—39.0s.,** United States National Team (Drayton, Ashworth, Stebbins, Hayes), Tokyo, Oct. 21, 1964. U. S. National Team (McCullouch, Bright, Copeland, Hines), Los Angeles, Calif., July 8, 1967.
**440 yards (4x110)—(2 turns)—39.6s.,** Southern Univ. (Nair, Harris, Johnson, Anderson), Modesto, Calif., May 28, 1966. 39s *Santa Clara Valley Youth Village (Gaines, Clayton, Williams, Smith). Los Angeles, June 7, 1968.*
**800 meters (4x200)—1m. 22.1s.,** San Jose State (Talmadge, Shakelford, Evans, Smith), Fresno, Calif., May 13, 1967.
**880 yards (4x220)—1m. 22.1s.,** San Jose State Coll., Fresno, Calif., May 13, 1967. *1m. 31.6s.* (7 turns), Henry Snyder H. S., Jersey City, N. J. (Harry Smith, Howard Smith, Branch, Cox), New York, N. Y., Feb. 1, 1958.
**1000 meters medley relay (100, 200, 300, 400)—1m, 50s.,** United States Team (Whitfield, Dixon, Ault, Stanfield), Basle, Switzerland, Aug. 20, 1960.
**1000 yards sprint medley (440, 100, 220, 300)—*1m. 51.3s.,* No. Carolina Coll. (McCray, Tate, Johnson, Roberts), New York, N. Y., Feb. 22, 1964.
**1600 meters (4x400)—2m. 59.6 s.,** United States Team (Frey, Evans, Smith, Lewis), Los Angeles, Calif., July 24, 1966.
**1 mile (4x440)—3m. 3.5s.,** San Jose State, Fresno, Calif., May 13, 1967. *3m. 10.2s.,* Southern Univ. (Mason, Gates, Johnson, Ford), Louisville, Ky., 1967.
**Two miles (4x880)—7m. 17.4s.,** Univ. of So. Calif. (Link, Bess, Buck, Carr), Los Angeles, Calif., May 13, 1966. *7m. 25.6s.,* 49er T. C. (Von Ruden, Davis, McCalla, Taylor), Albuquerque, N. M., Jan. 28, 1967. *7m. 23.8* Villanova *(Hamilton, Messenger, Murphy, Patrick), Louisville, Feb. 18, 1968.*
**4 miles (4x1 mile)—*17m. 21.7s.,** Univ. of Pennsylvania (Venzke, Coan, McKniff, Dean), Buffalo, N. Y., Mar. 11, 1933.
**6,000-meter relay—15m. 26.2s.,** United States team (Ryun, Dellinger, Young, Schul), Osaka, Japan, Oct. 25, 1964.
**2,900 meters medley (400, 200, 800, 1,500)—6m. 58.9s.,** U. S. Army Team (H. Bright, G. Brown, H. Cryer, W. Druetzler). Buffalo, N. Y., June 28, 1953. *7m, 8.3s,* New York A. C. (Stribling, O'Sullivan, Venzke, Graves), New York, N. Y., Feb. 25, 1939.
**Medley (440, 220, 880, mile)—7m. 18.4 s.,** Univ. of Chicago T. C. (Caffey, Johnson, Wheeler, Coleman), Buffalo, N. Y., Aug. 18, 1957. *7m. 25 3s,* New York University (Francis, Fangboner, Gares, MacMitchell), New York City, Feb. 22, 1941.
**2½ miles distance medley (880, 440, 1320, 1 mile)—9m. 33.8s.,** Kansas Univ. (Grindal, Peck, Yergovich, Ryun), Des Moines, Iowa, Apr. 29, 1967.

## HURDLE RACING

**60 yards: High hurdles—*6.8s.,** Hayes Jones, Baltimore, Md., Feb. 29, 1964. *6.5s.,* George Byers, Kansas City, Mo., Mar. 1, 1968.
**65 meters: High hurdles—*8.3s.,** Allan Tolmich, New York City, Feb. 22, 1941.
**70 yards: High hurdles—*8.0s.,** Hayes Jones, Detroit, at Louisville, Ky., Feb. 17, 1962.
**120 yards: High hurdles—13.2s.,** Lee Calhoun, Berne, Switzerland, Aug. 21, 1960. Earl McCullouch, Minneapolis, Minn., July 16, 1967.
**110 meters: High hurdles—13.2s.,** Lee Calhoun, Berne, Switzerland, Aug. 21, 1960. Earl McCullouch, Minneapolis, July 16, 1967. *15.8s.,* Sol Furth, Brooklyn, N. Y., Jan. 16, 1932.
**200 meters: Low hurdles—21.9s.,** Donald A. Styron, Baton Rouge, La., Apr. 2, 1960. Around turn—22.5s., Glenn Davis, Berne, Switzerland, Aug. 20, 1960.
**220 yards: Low hurdles—21.9s.,** Donald A. Styron, Baton Rouge, La., Apr. 2, 1960. Around turn—22.7s., Charles Tidwell, Berkeley, Calif., June 13, 1958.
**400 meters: Intermediate hurdles—49.1s.,** Rex Cawley, Los Angeles, Calif., Sept. 13, 1964.
**440 yards: Intermediate hurdles—49.6s.,** Rex Cawley, Albuquerque, N. M., June 15, 1963.

## STEEPLECHASE

**3,000 meters—8m. 32.4s.,** Pat Traynor, Dusseldorf, Ger., Aug. 17, 1967.
**2 miles—9m. 49.6s.,** Charles Jones, Dayton, Ohio, June 22, 1957. *9m. 35.4s.,* Joseph P. McCluskey, New York, N. Y., Feb. 22, 1941.

## JUMPING

**Standing high jump—5 ft. 5¾ in.,** Leo Goehring, Travers Island, N. Y., June 14, 1913. *5 ft. 6 in.,* Harold M. Osborn, St. Louis, Mo., April 4, 1936.
**Running high jump—7 ft. 3¾ in.,** John Thomas, Stanford, Calif., July 1, 1960. *7 ft. 3 in.,* John Thomas, Boston, Mass., Jan. 28, 1961; *John Rambo, San Francisco, Calif., Jan. 7, 1967.
**Standing broad jump—11 ft. 4⅞ in.,** Ray C. Ewry, St. Louis, Aug. 29, 1904.
**Long jump—27 ft. 4¾ in.,** Ralph Boston, Modesto, Calif., May 29, 1965. *26 ft. 11½ in.,* Bob Beamon, Oakland, Calif., Mar. 4, 1967. *27 ft. 2¾ in. Bob Beamon, Detroit, Mar. 15, 1968.*
**Triple Jump—54 ft. 11 in.,** Art Walker, Los Angeles, Calif., July 23, 1966. *54 ft. 9½ in.,* Art Walker, Albuquerque, N. M., Mar. 5, 1966.

## POLE VAULT

**17 ft. 7¾ in.,** Paul Wilson, Bakersfield, Calif., June 23, 1967. *17 ft. 9 in. Bob Seagren, So. Lake Tahoe, Calif., Sept. 12, 1968. *17 ft. 3 in.,* Bob Seagren, Cleveland, Ohio, Feb. 18, 1967. 17 ft. 4¼ in., Bob Seagren, New York, N. Y., Jan 25, 1968.*

## 16-LB. HAMMER THROW

Weight (including handle), 16 lbs., entire length 4 feet thrown from 7-foot circle—235 ft. 11 in., Ed Burke, Bakersfield, Calif., June 22, 1967.

## PUTTING 16-LB. SHOT

**71 ft. 5½ in.,** Randy Matson, College Station, Tex., Apr. 22, 1967. *67 ft. 10 in.,* Neal Steinhauer, Portland, Ore., Jan. 28, 1967.

## DISCUS THROW

Weight., 4 lbs. 6½ oz. From 8 ft. 2½ in. circle—210 ft. 6 in., Jay Sylvester, Long Beach, Calif., June 5, 1965. 218 ft. 4 in., *Jay Silvester, Modesto, Calif., May 25, 1968*

## JAVELIN THROW

**284 ft.,** John Tushaus, Los Angeles, Calif., May 13, 1966.

## THROWING WEIGHTS

**56-lb. weight for distance,** thrown with both hands from a 7-ft. circle without follow—48 ft. ¾ in., George Frenn, Pasadena, Calif., June 4, 1967.
**56-lb. weight for height—16 ft. 11¼ in.,** P. Donovan, San Francisco, Calif., Feb. 20, 1914.
**35-lb. weight for distance—68 ft. 7½ in.,** George Frenn, Berkeley, Calif., Mar. 4, 1967. Harold Connolly, New York, N. Y., Feb. 20, 1960.

## ALL-ROUND TRACK AND FIELD RECORD

**8,265 points,** Tom Pagani, Baltimore, Md., Aug. 5, 1962.

## DECATHLON

**8,230 pts.,** Russ Hodges, Los Angeles, Calif., July 23-24, 1966.

## PENTATHLON

**3,765 points,** Bill Toomey, Westbrook, Me., July 8, 1964.

## 61st Annual Wanamaker Millrose Games
### Madison Square Garden, New York, N.Y., Jan. 25, 1968

60 Yds.—Lennox Miller, USC. Time—0:06.2.
500 Yds.—Larry James, Villanova. Time—0:56.1.
600 Yds.—Marty McGrady, Santa Clara. Time—1:10.1.
880 Yds.—Ralph Doubell, Australia. Time—1:53.2.
1,000 Yds.—Byron Dyce, NYU. Time—2:10.1.
Wanamaker Mile—Preston Davis, U.S. Army. Time—4:03.9.

Three Miles—George Young, Casa Grande, Ariz. Time—13:31.8.
60 Yd. High Hurdles—Leon Coleman, So. Calif. Striders. Time—0:07.2.
Women's 880 Yds.—Madeline Manning, Tenn. State. Time—2:13.8.
Pole Vault—Bob Seagren, USC. 17 ft. 4¼ in.
High Jump—John Thomas, Boston AA. 6 ft. 10 in.

## 79th Annual Boston Athletic Association Games
### Boston, Mass. Jan. 27, 1968

50 Yds.—Lennox Miller, USC. Time—0:05.3.
440 Yds.—Vince Mathews, J.C. Smith. Time—0:48.8.
600 Yds.—Tom Farrell, U.S. Army. Time—1:11.1.
1,000 Yds.—Ralph Doubell, Australia. Time—2:08.0.
One Mile—Sam Bair, Kent State. Time—4:01.9.
Two Miles—George Young, Casa Grande, Ariz. Time—8:44.8.
45 Yd. High Hurdles—Erv Hall, Villanova. Time—0:05.5.

One Mile Walk—Steve Hayden, Long Island AC. Time—6:49.4
One Mile Relay—Villanova (Davis, Nichter, James, Prince). Time—3:17.8.
Pole Vault—Bob Seagren, USC. 17 ft. ¾ in.
High Jump—John Thomas, Boston AA. 6 ft. 10 in.
Shot Put—Dick Benka, Harvard. 54 ft. ½ in.
Long Jump—John Pistel, Amherst. 23 ft. 4 in.
35-lb. Weight Throw—Bob Narcessian, Rhode Island. 59 ft. 8¼ in.

## 49th Annual Knights of Columbus Indoor Track Meet
### Madison Square Garden, Feb. 2, 1968

60 Yds.—Bill Gaines, Santa Clara. Time—0:06.2.
500 Yds.—Jim Kemp, U.S. Army. Time—0:56.2.
600 Yds.—Martin McGrady, Santa Clara. Time—1:10.8.
880 Yds.—Ralph Doubell, Australia. Time—1:51.5.
1,000 Yds.—Bob Zieminski, Georgetown DC. Time—2:11.0.

One Mile—Sam Bair, Kent State. Time—4:03.8.
Two Miles—Bill Clark, Quantico Marines. Time—8:53.6.
60 Yd. High Hurdles—Erv Hall, Villanova. Time—0:07.1
Pole Vault—Bob Seagren, USC. 16 ft. 6¾ in.
High Jump—John Hartfield, Houston Striders. 7 ft.

## 9th Los Angeles Times Indoor Track & Field Meet
### Los Angeles, Calif., Feb. 10, 1968

60 Yds.—Charles Greene, Cornhuskers TC. Time—0:06.0.
440 Yards—Lee Evans, San Jose State. Time—0:47.8.
500 Yds.—Jim Kemp, U.S. Army. Time—0:57.5.
600 Yds.—Martin McGrady, Santa Clara. Time—1:10.9.
1,000 Yds.—Ralph Doubell, Australia. Time—2:08.2.
One Mile—Tim Danielson, San Diego. Time—4:06.1.
Two Miles—George Young, Casa Grande, Ariz. Time—8:31.8.
60 Yd. High Hurdles—Earl McCullouch, USC. Time—0:06.9.
One Mile Relay—U.S. Army (Webster, Jones, Tobler, Kemp). Time—3:16.1.
Two Mile Relay—U.S. Army (Burleson, Daugherty, Delaney, Mitchell). Time—7:40.4.

One Mile Walk—Ron Laird, NYAC. Time—6:26.3.
Pole Vault—John Vaughn, UCLA. 17 ft. ½ in.
High Jump—Valentine Gavrilo, USSR. 7 ft. 2 in.
Long Jump—Tonu Lepik, USSR. 25 ft. 8½ in.
Shot Put—George Woods, Pacific Coast Club. 65 ft. 2½ in.

### Women's Events

60 Yds.—Barbara Ferrell, L.A. Mercurettes. Time—0:06.7.
440 Yds.—Kathy Hammond, Will's Spikettes. Time—0:56.0.
880 Yds.—Madeline Manning, Tenn. State. Time—2:10.9.
60 Yd High Hurdles—Cherrie Sherrard, Laurel TC. Time—0:07.7.
High Jump—Eleanor Montgomery, Tenn. State. 5 ft. 10 in.
Long Jump—Tatyana Talishova, USSR. 20 ft. 2½ in.

## New York Athletic Club Track Meet
### Madison Square Garden, Feb. 16, 1968

60 Yds.—Lennox Miller, Univ. of So. Calif. Time—0:06.1.
500 Yds.—Hardee McAlhaney, Tenn. Time—0:57.8.
600 Yds.—Bill Ellis, Catholic Univ. Time—1:11.2.
880 Yds.—Preston Davis, U. S. Army. Time—1:54.8.
Baxter Mile—Sam Bair, Kent State. Time—4:05.6.
Two Miles—George Young, Casa Grande, Ariz. Time—8:38.8.

60 Yd. High Hurdles—Richmond Flowers, Tenn. Time—0:07.1.
One Mile Walk—Ron Laird, NYAC. Time—6:22.2.
Pole Vault—Bob Seagren, Univ. of So. Calif. 16 ft. 6 in.
Long Jump—Bob Beamon, Univ. of Texas. 26 ft. 3½ in.
High Jump—Richard Fosbury, Oregon St. 7 ft.
Women's Broad Jump—Joan Henry, Montreal. 18 ft. 10 in.
Women's High Jump—Frazetta Parham, Los Angeles. 5 ft. 6 in.

## NAIA National Track & Field Championships
### Albuquerque, New Mexico, May 31-June 1, 1968

100 Meters—Oliver Ford, Southern (La.). Time—0:10.1.
200 Meters—Andrew Hopkins, Stephen F. Austin (Tex.). Time—0:20.9.
400 Meters—Hal Francis, Arkansas AM&N. Time—0:45.6.
800 Meters—Earl Goldman, Arkansas AM&N. Time—1:48.6.
1500 Meters—John Mason, Fort Hays State (Kan.). Time—3:46.5.
5000 Meters—David Ellis, Eastern Michigan. Time—14:25.2.
10,000 Meters—Van Nelson, St. Cloud State (Minn.). Time—30:58.2.
110 Meter High Hurdles—Gerald Cerulla, Eastern Michigan. Time—0:13.7.
400 Meter Hurdles—Jeff Bennett, Oklahoma Christian. Time—0:51.3.
3000 Meter Steeplechase—Pat McMahon, Oklahoma Baptist. Time—9:26.7.
440 Yard Relay—Stephen F. Austin (Hopkins, Malone, Cramer, Moore). Time—0:40.1.

Mile Relay—Prairie View A&M (Newhouse, Dotson, Johnson, Boggess). Time—3:06.5.
Discus—Phillip Gary, Kentucky State. 161 ft. 2 in.
Hammer—August Zilincar, Monmouth (N. J.). 196 ft. 7 in.
High Jump—Nick Martinez, Northern Arizona. 6 ft. 10 in.
Javelin—Dave VanderGriend, Western Washington State. 238 ft. 4 in.
Long Jump—Jerry Proctor, Redlands (Calif.). 26 ft. 1½ in.
Pole Vault—Larry Ashley, Northeast Louisiana State. 160 ft. ¼ in.
Shot Put—James Bagby, Prairie View A&M. 57 ft. 7 in.
Triple Jump—Henry Granger, Pittsburgh State (Kan.). 49 ft. ½ in.
Team Points—Prairie View A&M (Tex.), 47; Arkansas AM&N, 45 1/6; Eastern Michigan, 42; Southern (La.) 38 1/3; Emporia State (Kan.). 32.

# 80th Annual AAU Indoor Track and Field Championships
## Oakland, Calif., Feb. 23-24, 1968

### Men's Division
60 Yds.—Bill Gaines, Santa Clara. Time—0:06.0.
600 Yds.—Martin McGrady, Santa Clara. Time—1:09.2.
1,000 Yds.—Tom Von Ruden, U. S. Army. Time—2:10.7.
One Mile—Preston Davis, U. S. Army. Time—4:06.0.
Three Miles—George Young, Unatt. Time—13:17.7.
60 Yd. Hurdles—Earl McCullouch, So. Calif. Time—0:06.9.
One Mile Walk—Ron Laird, NYAC. Time—6:16.9.
One Mile Relay—U. S. Army (Webster, Jones, Tobler, Kemp). Time—3:17.1.
Triple Jump—Charles Craig, Pacific Coast Club. 54 ft. 1¾ in.
Pole Vault—Dennis Phillips, Oregon State. 17 ft. ¾ in.
Long Jump—Bob Beamon, Univ. of Texas, El Paso. 26 ft. 11½ in.
High Jump—Valentin Gavrilov, USSR. 7 ft. 1 in.
Shot Put—George Woods, Pacific CC. 66 ft. 3¼ in.
35-lb. Weight Throw—Ed Burke, Striders. 65 ft. 3½ in.
Team Standings—Pacific Coast Club, 30; So. Calif. Striders, 27; Santa Clara Valley Youth Village, 20; New York AC, 13; Southern Calif., 11.

### Women's Division
60 Yds.—Barbara Ferrell, L. A. Mercurettes. Time—0:06.7.
220 Yds.—Vilma Charleton, Crown Cities TC. Time—0:25.1.
440 Yds.—Lois Drinkwater, Valley of the Sun. Time—0:56.5.
One Mile—Doris Brown, Falcon TC. Time—4:59.1.
880 Yds.—Madeline Manning, Tenn. State. Time—2:11.8.
60 Yds. Hurdles—Pat VanWolvelaere, Angles TC. Time—0:07.4.
Spring Relay—Tennessee State (Tyus, Daniel, Dennis, Render). Time—1:10.8.
Spring Medley Relay—Los Angeles Mercurettes (Scott, Wilson, DeBusk, Ferrell). Time—1:45.1.
Shot Put—Maren Seidler, Shore AC. 48 ft. 9 in.
Basketball Throw—Barbara Friedrick, Shore AC. 135 ft.
Long Jump—Tatiana Talisheva, USSR. 20 ft. 4½ in.
High Jump—Eleanor Montgomery, Tenn. State. 5 ft. 10½ in.
Team Standings—Tennessee State, 24; Los Angeles Mercurettes, 19; Crown Cities TC, 16; Valley of the Sun, 10; Falcon TC, 9.

# 6th Annual Telegram-Maple Leaf Indoor Games
## Toronto, Ontario, March 2, 1968

### Men's Division
50 yd. Hurdles—Willie Davenport, Southern University. Time—0:05.9.
50 Yds.—Charles Green, Nebraska. Time—0:05.2.
600 Yds.—Frank Tomeo, New York. Time—1:10.5.
1,000 Yds.—Bill Crothers, Toronto. Time—2:10.9.
Canadian Mile—Jim Irons, Toronto. Time—4:18.6.
Invitational Mile—Dave Bailey, Toronto. Time—4:05.2.
High Jump—Otis Burrell, University of Nevada. 7 ft.
Pole Vault—Denis Phillips, Oregon State University. 16 ft. 6 in.
Shot Put—Jay Silvester, Utah. 64 ft. 5 in.
One-Mile Relay—Toronto East York (Brereton,

McMann, Brooks, Powell). Time—3:25.9.
Two-Mile Relay—University of Toronto (Field, Davis, Bailey, Richards). Time—7:59.3.
Three-Mile Run—Tracy Smith, U. S. Army. Time—13:15.2.

### Women's Division
50 Yd. Hurdles—Mamie Rollins, Chicago. Time—0:06.5.
50 Yds.—Wyomia Tyus, Tennessee State University. Time—0:05.8.
300 Yds.—Wyomia Tyus, Tennessee State University. Time—0:35.9.
880 Yds.—Doris Brown, Seattle. Time—2:11.4.
High Jump—Pat Winslow, Iowa State University. 5 ft. 6 in.

# 59th Annual Drake Relays
## Des Moines, Iowa, April 26-27, 1968

100 Yds.—Clyde Glosson, Trinity. Time—0:09.5.
120 Yd. High Hurdles—Mike Butler, Wisconsin. Time—0:13.8.
440 Yds.—Charles Benson, Southern Illinois. Time—0:46.7.
440 Yd. Hurdles—Jesse Ball, Prairie View. Time—0:51.7.
College-University Mile—Al Van Troba, Abeline Christian. Time—4:04.3.
Invitational Mile—Sam Bair, Kent State. Time—4:06.2.
Two Miles—Ed Norris, Kent State. Time—8:52.2.
Three Miles—Van Nelson, St. Cloud State. Time—13:17.4.
Six Miles—Van Nelson. Time—28:22.1.
High Jump—Stan Cury, Baylor. 6. ft. 9 in.
Shot Put—James Bagby, Prairie View. 58 ft. 3 in.
Pole Vault—Martin Rollins, Texas A. & M. 15 ft. 6 in.
Javelin—Bill Skinner, Tennessee. 239 ft. 2 in.
Triple Jump—Lennox Burgher, Nebraska. 52 ft. 11 in.
Long Jump—Hal Oswalt, Oklahoma State. 24 ft. 7¼ in.

Discus Throw—John Morton, Florida. 178 ft. 3 in.
Invitational Discus Throw—Parry O'Brien. 180 ft. 2 in.

## University Relays
440 Yds.—Oklahoma (W. Long, Smith, Brown, G. Long). Time—0:40.5.
880 Yds.—Ohio Univ. (Smith, Fuller, Hosler, Taylor). Time—1:23.7.
One Mile—Texas (McKaniel, Matina, Canada, Morton). Time—3:05.2.
Two Miles—Kansas (Grindal, Ferrell, McClain, Ryun). Time—7:21.8.
Four Miles—Drake (Compson, Hoffert, Hunt, Evans). Time—16:39.7.
Sprint Medley—Kansas State (Collins, Heer, Holbrook, Swenson).—Time—3:19.5.
Distance Medley—Kansas (Grindal, Olison, McClain, Ryun). Time—9:41.9.
480 Yd. Shuttle High Hurdles—Kansas (Byers, Gaines, Adams, Stevens). Time—0:56.7.

# 4th Annual NCAA Indoor Track and Field Championships
## Detroit, Mich., March 15-16, 1968. Sponsored by The Detroit News

60 Yds.—Jim Green, Kentucky. Time—0:06.0.
440 Yds.—Larry James, Villanova. Time—0:47.0.
600 Yds.—Tom Albright, Colgate. Time—1:10.6.
880 Yds.—Dave Patrick, Villanova. Time—1:52.0.
1,000 Yds.—Ray Arrington, Wisconsin. Time—2:09.3.
One Mile—Jim Ryun, Kansas. Time—4:06.8.
Two Miles—Jim Ryun, Kansas. Time—8:38.9.
60 Yd. High Hurdles—Richmond Flowers, Tennessee. Time—0:07.0.
One Mile Relay—Villanova (Nichter, Davis, Prince, James). Time—3:14.4.

Two Mile Relay—Harvard (Burns, Shaw, Baker, McKelvey). Time—7:26.8.
Medley Relay—Villanova (Messenger, Whitehead, Donnelly, Murphy). Time—9:49.5.
Long Jump—Bob Beamon, Texas-El Paso. 27 ft. 2¾ in.
Shot Put—John Vanreenen, Washington State. 62 ft. 1 in.
35 lb. Weight Throw—Bob Narcessian, Rhode Island. 66 ft. 5¾ in.
Pole Vault—Paul Wilson, USC. 16 ft. 8 in.
Team Champion—Villanova, 35½ pts.; Southern Calif., 25 pts.; Oklahoma, 17 pts.

## 47th NCAA Outdoor Championships
### Berkeley, Calif., June 13-15, 1968

**100 Meters**—Lennox Miller, Southern Calif. Time—0:10.1.
**200 Meters**—Emmett Taylor, Ohio Univ. **Time**—0:20.8.
**400 Meters**—Lee Evans, San Jose State. **Time**—0:45.0.
**800 Meters**—Byron Dyce, NYU. **Time**—1:47.3.
**1,500 Meters**—Dave Patrick, Villanova. **Time**—3:39.9.
**5,000 Meters**—Gerry Lindgren, Washington State. **Time**—13.57.2.
**10,000 Meters**—Gerry Lindgren. **Time**—29.41.
**110 Meter High Hurdles**—Earl McCullouch, So. Calif. **Time**—0:13.4.
**400 Meter Hurdles**—Dave Hemery, Boston Univ. **Time**—0:49.8.
**3,000 Meter Stepplechase**—Kerry Pearce, Texas-El Paso. **Time**—8:50.8.
**440 Yard Relay**—Southern Calif. **Time**—0:39.5.
**One Mile Relay**—Villanova. **Time**—3:08.6.
**High Jump**—Dick Fosbury, Oregon State. **7 ft. 2¼ in.**
**Pole Vault**—Jon Vaugh, UCLA. 17 ft. ½ in.
**Long Jump**—Pertti Pousi, Brigham Young Univ. 26 ft. 3¼ in.
**Triple Jump**—Lennox Burgher, Nebraska. 53 ft. 1¼ in.
**Shot Put**—Steve Marcus, UCLA. 61 ft. 7¾ in.
**Discus**—John Van Reenen, Wash. St. 194 ft. 10 in.
**Hammer Throw**—Bob Narcessian, Rhode Island. 202 ft. 1 in.
**Javelin**—Carl O'Donnell, Washington State. 258 ft. 11 in.
**Team**—Southern California, 58 pts.

## 80th Annual AAU Outdoor Track and Field Championships
### Sacramento, Calif., June 20-21, 1968

**100 Meters**—Charlie Greene, Huskers AA. **Time**—0:10.0.
**200 Meters**—Tommie Smith, Santa Clara. **Time**—0:20.3.
**400 Meters**—Lee Evans, Santa Clara Valley Youth Village. **Time**—0:45.0.
**800 Meters**—Wade Bell, Oregon TC. **Time**—1:45.4.
**1,500 Meters**—John Mason, Ft. Hays State. **Time**—3:43.1.
**5,000 Meters**—Bob Day, So. Calif. Striders. **Time**—13:50.4.
**10,000 Meters**—Tracy Smith, U. S. Army. **Time**—28:47.
**110 Meter Hurdles**—Earl McCullouch. **Time**—0:13.5.
**400 Meter Hurdles**—Ron Whitney, So. Calif. Striders. **Time**—0:49.6.
**3,000 Meter Walk**—Don DeNoon. **Time**—12:37.9.
**3,000 Meter Steeplechase**—George Young. **Time**—8:30.5.
**Discus Throw**—Jay Silvester. 203 ft. 9 in.
**Triple Jump**—Art Walker, So. Calif. Striders. 53 ft. 9¼ in.
**Javelin**—Frank Covelli, Pacific Coast Club. 269 ft. 6 in.
**High Jump**—Ed Hanks, Brigham Young. 6 ft. 11 in.
**Hammer Throw**—Ed Burke, So. Calif. Striders. 217 ft. 2 in.
**Shot Put**—Randy Matson, Houston Striders. 67 ft. 5 in.
**Pole Vault**—Dick Railsback, So. Calif. Striders. 17 ft. ¼ in.
**Long Jump**—Bob Beamon, Houston Striders. 27 ft. 4 in.
**Highest Point Score**—So. Calif. Striders.

## Decathlon and Pentathlon National Champions
### DECATHLON
100 meters, long jump, shot put, high jump, 400 meters, 110 meter high-hurdles, discus, pole vault, javelin and 1500 meters.

| Year | Champion | Affiliation | Points |
|------|----------|-------------|--------|
| 1962 | C. K. Yang | U. C. L. A.; Rep. of China | 8249 |
| 1963 | Steve Pauly | Oregon State University | 7852 |
| 1964 | C. K. Yang | Pasadena A. A.; Rep. of China | 8641 |
| *1965 | Bill Toomey | Pasadena A. A. | 7764 |
| 1966 | Bill Toomey | Pasadena A. A. | 8234 |
| 1967 | Bill Toomey | Southern California Striders | 7880 |
| 1968 | Bill Toomey | Southern Calif. Striders | 8037 |

*New scoring system adopted.

### PENTATHLON
Long jump, discus, javelin, 200 meters and 1,500 meters.

| 1962 | Paul Herman | Westmont College, Santa Barbara, Calif. | 3389 |
|------|-------------|------------------------------------------|------|
| 1963 | Bill Toomey | Santa Clara Valley Youth Village | 3365 |
| 1964 | Bill Toomey | Stanford Univ. | 3687 |
| 1965 | Jim Miller | Colorado | 3091 |
| 1966 | Jeff Bannister | Gorham, Maine | 3512 |
| 1967 | Lynn Baker | Univ. of Colorado | 3448 |
| 1968 | Joe Hilbe | Chico Track Club | 3456 |

## 72nd Annual Boston Marathon
### Boston, Mass., April 19, 1968

Ambrose Burfoot of Wesleyan Univ. covered the traditional marathon distance of 26 miles 385 yards in 2 hours 22 minutes 17 seconds to win the 1968 Boston Marathon. Finishing second was Lt. Bill Clark of the Marine Corps. It was the first 1, 2 American finish in 23 years. The event drew a record field of 890 starters. The leading finishers follow:

| | | | |
|---|---|---|---|
| 1—Ambrose J. Burfoot, Wesleyan | 2:22:17 | 10—August Muhrcke, Milrose A. A. | 2:34:15 |
| 2—Lieut. Bill Clark, U. S. Marines | 2:22:49 | 11—Edward Winrow, New York A. C. | 2:35:12 |
| 3—Alfred Penaloza, Mexico | 2:25:06 | 12—Bruce C. Labudde, Georgia St. | 2:35:47 |
| 4—Pablo Garrido, Mexico | 2:25:07 | 13—Ronald C. Wallingford, Canada | 2:37:03 |
| 5—Ron Daws, Twin Cities T. C. | 2:29:17 | 14—Arthur W. Coolidge, Boston A. A. | 2:37:42 |
| 6—Robert D. Dienes, Occidental | 2:30:13 | 15—John J. Kelley, Boston A. A. | 2:37:43 |
| 7—Jose Garcia Gaspar, Mexico | 2:30:29 | 16—James A. Daley Jr., No. Medford | 2:38:05 |
| 8—Mikko Ala-Lempilampi, Finland | 2:31:35 | 17—Raymond T. Hall, Conn. C. A. A. | 2:38:09 |
| 9—D. McFadzean, Scotland | 2:32:27 | 18—Morris Aarbo, Edmonton, Alberta | 2:39:02 |

## National Spearfishing Champions

| Men | Women |
|-----|-------|
| 1960—Long Beach Neptunes | 1960—Mermaids |
| 1961—Long Beach Neptunes | 1961—Connecticut Council |
| 1962—Florida Skin Divers Association | 1962—Southeast Council |
| 1963—Florida Skin Divers Association | 1963—Oregon Council |
| 1964—Greater Los Angeles Council | 1964—Washington Council |
| 1965—Central California Council | 1965—Oregon Council |
| 1966—Greater Los Angeles Council | 1966—Florida Skin Divers Association |
| 1967—Washington Council | 1967—Los Angeles Council |
| 1968—Central California Council | 1968—Washington Council |

# National Football League
*Final 1967 Standings*

## Eastern Conference

### Century Division

|  | W | L | T | PF | PA |
|---|---|---|---|---|---|
| Cleveland | 9 | 5 | 0 | 334 | 297 |
| New York | 7 | 7 | 0 | 369 | 379 |
| St. Louis | 6 | 7 | 1 | 333 | 356 |
| Pittsburgh | 4 | 9 | 1 | 281 | 320 |

### Capitol Division

|  | W | L | T | PF | PA |
|---|---|---|---|---|---|
| Dallas | 9 | 5 | 0 | 342 | 268 |
| Philadelphia | 6 | 7 | 1 | 351 | 409 |
| Washington | 5 | 6 | 3 | 347 | 353 |
| New Orleans | 3 | 11 | 0 | 233 | 379 |

## Western Conference

### Central Division

|  | W | L | T | PF | PA |
|---|---|---|---|---|---|
| Green Bay | 9 | 4 | 1 | 332 | 209 |
| Chicago | 7 | 6 | 1 | 239 | 218 |
| Detroit | 5 | 7 | 2 | 260 | 259 |
| Minnesota | 3 | 8 | 3 | 233 | 294 |

### Coastal Division

|  | W | L | T | PF | PA |
|---|---|---|---|---|---|
| Los Angeles* | 11 | 1 | 2 | 398 | 196 |
| Baltimore | 11 | 1 | 2 | 394 | 198 |
| San Francisco | 7 | 7 | 0 | 273 | 337 |
| Atlanta | 1 | 12 | 1 | 175 | 422 |

*Won division title by outscoring Baltimore in their two meetings.

# American Football League
*Final 1967 Standings*

## Eastern Division

|  | W | L | T | PF | PA |
|---|---|---|---|---|---|
| Houston | 9 | 4 | 1 | 258 | 199 |
| New York | 8 | 5 | 1 | 371 | 329 |
| Buffalo | 4 | 10 | 0 | 237 | 285 |
| Miami | 4 | 10 | 0 | 219 | 407 |
| Boston | 3 | 10 | 1 | 280 | 389 |

## Western Division

|  | W | L | T | PF | PA |
|---|---|---|---|---|---|
| Oakland | 13 | 1 | 0 | 468 | 233 |
| Kansas City | 9 | 5 | 0 | 408 | 254 |
| San Diego | 8 | 5 | 1 | 360 | 352 |
| Denver | 3 | 11 | 0 | 256 | 409 |

# Jim Thorpe Trophy Winners

The Jim Thorpe Trophy winner is picked by a Newspaper Enterprise Assn. poll of all NFL players. It goes to the most valuable NFL player and is the oldest and highest professional football award.

| Year | Player and Team | Year | Player and Team |
|---|---|---|---|
| 1955 | Harlon Hill, Chicago Bears | 1962 | Jim Taylor, Green Bay Packers |
| 1956 | Frank Gifford, N. Y. Giants | 1963 | (tie) Jim Brown, Cleveland Browns and |
| 1957 | John Unitas, Baltimore Colts |  | Y. A. Tittle, N. Y. Giants |
| 1958 | Jim Brown, Cleveland Browns | 1964 | Lenny Moore, Baltimore Colts |
| 1959 | Charley Conerly, N. Y. Giants | 1965 | Jim Brown, Cleveland Browns |
| 1960 | Norm Van Brocklin, Philadelphia Eagles | 1966 | Bart Starr, Green Bay Packers |
| 1961 | Y. A. Tittle, N. Y. Giants | 1967 | John Unitas, Baltimore Colts |

# Green Bay Wins Super Bowl Game

The second professional football game between the champions of the National and American Leagues resulted in a 33-14 victory by the National League Champion Green Bay Packers over the Oakland Raiders on Jan. 14, 1968. The game was played at the Orange Bowl in Miami before 75,546 spectators plus an estimated 50,000,000 television viewers. For their victory each Packer received $15,000, with $7,500 going to each losing Raider, in addition to the money the players received for winning their respective league championships.

## SCORING

| | | | | |
|---|---|---|---|---|
| Green Bay Packers | 3 | 13 | 10 | 7—33 |
| Oakland Raiders | 0 | 7 | 0 | 7—14 |

G.B.—FG, Chandler, 39.
G.B.—FG, Chandler, 20.
G.B.—Dowler, 62, pass from Starr (Chandler, kick).
Oak.—Miller, 23, pass from Lamonica (Blanda, kick).
G.B.—FG, Chandler, 43.
G.B.—Anderson, 2, run (Chandler, kick).
G.B.—FG, Chandler, 31.
G.B.—Adderley, 60, return of interception (Chandler, kick).
Oak.—Miller, 23, pass from Lamonica (Blanda, kick).

## GAME STATISTICS

|  | Packers | Raiders |
|---|---|---|
| First downs | 19 | 16 |
| Rushing yardage | 163 | 105 |
| Passing yardage | 162 | 186 |
| Return yardage | 144 | 139 |
| Passes | 13-24 | 15-34 |
| Interceptions by | 1 | 0 |
| Punts | 6-39 | 6-44 |
| Fumbles lost | 0 | 2 |
| Yards penalized | 12 | 31 |

## INDIVIDUAL STATISTICS

Rushes—G.B.: Wilson, 17 for 65 yards; Anderson, 14 for 48; William, 8 for 36; Starr, 1 for 14; Mercein, 1 for 0. Oak.: Dixon, 12 for 52; Todd, 2 for 37; Banaszak, 6 for 16.
Passing—G.B.: Starr, 13 of 24 for 202 yards. Oak.: Lamonica, 15 of 34 for 208.
Receptions—G.B.: Dale, 4 for 43 yards; Fleming,

4 for 35; Anderson, 2 for 18; Dowler, 2 for 71; McGee, 1 for 35. Oak.: Miller, 5 for 84; Biletnikoff, 2 for 10; Banaszak, 4 for 69; Cannon, 2 for 25; Dixon, 1 for 3; Wells, 1 for 17.

## PLAYERS

### GREEN BAY PACKERS

Ends—Dowler, Dale, Fleming, Davis, Aldridge, Long, McGee, Capo, B. Brown.
Tackles—Skoronski, Gregg, Kostelnik, Jordan, Weatherwax.
Guards—Gillingham, Kramer, Thurston.
Centers—Hyland, Bowman.
Linebackers—Robinson, Nitschke, Caffey, Crutcher, Flanigan.
Quarterbacks—Starr, Bratkowski.
Offensive Backs—Anderson, Wilson, Williams, Mercein.
Defensive Backs—Adderley, Jeter, T. Brown, Wood, Rowser, Hart.
Kicker—Chandler.

### OAKLAND RAIDERS

Ends—Miller, Biletnikoff, Cannon, Lassiter, Davidson, Wells, Kocourek, Herock, Oats.
Tackles—Svihus, Schuh, Birdwell, Keating, Kruse, Archer, Sligh.
Guards—Upshaw, Hawkins, Harvey.
Center—J. Otto.
Linebackers—Laskey, Conners, G. Otto, Williamson, Budness, Benson.
Quarterback—Lamonica.
Offensive Backs—Banaszak, Dixon, Todd, Hagberg.
Defensive Backs—McCloughan, W. Brown, Grayson, Powers, Williams, Bird.
Kickers—Blanda, Eischeid.

# Super Bowl

| Year | Winner | Loser | Site |
|---|---|---|---|
| 1967 | Green Bay Packers, 35 | Kansas City Chiefs, 10 | Memorial Coliseum, Los Angeles |
| 1968 | Green Bay Packers, 33 | Oakland Raiders, 14 | Orange Bowl, Miami |

## NATIONAL FOOTBALL LEAGUE

| Year | Winners (W-L-T) (East) | Winners (W-L-T) (West) | Playoff |
|---|---|---|---|
| 1933 | New York Giants (11-3-0) | Chicago Bears (10-2-1) | Chicago Bears 23, New York 21 |
| 1934 | New York Giants (8-5-0) | Chicago Bears (13-0-0) | New York 30, Chicago Bears 13 |
| 1935 | New York Giants (9-3-0) | Detroit Lions (7-3-2) | Detroit 26, New York 7 |
| 1936 | Boston Redskins (7-5-0) | Green Bay Packers (10-1-1) | Green Bay 21, Boston 6 |
| 1937 | Washington Redskins (8-3-0) | Chicago Bears (9-1-1) | Wash. 28, Chicago Bears 21 |
| 1938 | New York Giants (8-2-1) | Green Bay Packers (8-3-0) | New York 23, Green Bay 17 |
| 1939 | New York Giants (9-1-1) | Green Bay Packers (9-2-0) | Green Bay 27, New York 0 |
| 1940 | Washington Redskins (9-2-0) | Chicago Bears (8-3-0) | Chicago Bears 73, Wash. 0 |
| 1941 | New York Giants (8-3-0) | Chicago Bears (10-1-1) (A) | Chicago Bears 37, New York 9 |
| 1942 | Wash. Redskins (10-1-1) | Chicago Bears (11-0-0) | Wash. 14, Chicago Bears 6 |
| 1943 | Wash. Redskins (6-3-1) (A) | Chicago Bears (8-1-1) | Chicago Bears 41, Wash. 21 |
| 1944 | New York Giants (8-1-1) | Green Bay Packers (8-2-0) | Green Bay 14, New York 7 |
| 1945 | Wash. Redskins (8-2-0) | Cleveland Rams (9-1-0) | Cleveland 15, Washington 14 |
| 1946 | New York Giants (7-3-1) | Chicago Bears (8-2-1) | Chicago Bears 24, New York 14 |
| 1947 | Philadelphia Eagles (8-4-0) (A) | Chicago Cardinals (9-3-0) | Chicago Cardinals 28, Phila. 21 |
| 1948 | Philadelphia Eagles (9-2-1) | Chicago Cardinals (11-1-0) | Phila. 7, Chicago Cardinals 0 |
| 1949 | Philadelphia Eagles (11-1-0) | Los Angeles Rams (8-2-2) | Philadelphia 14, Los Angeles 0 |
| 1950 | Cleveland Browns (10-2-0) (A) | Los Angeles Rams (9-3-0) (A) | Cleveland 30, Los Angeles 28 |
| 1951 | Cleveland Browns (11-1-0) | Los Angeles Rams (8-4-0) | Los Angeles 24, Cleveland 17 |
| 1952 | Cleveland Browns (8-4-0) | Detroit Lions (9-3-0) (A) | Detroit 17, Cleveland 7 |
| 1953 | Cleveland Browns (11-1-0) | Detroit Lions (10-2-0) | Detroit 17, Cleveland 16 |
| 1954 | Cleveland Browns (9-3-0) | Detroit Lions (9-2-1) | Cleveland 56, Detroit 10 |
| 1955 | Cleveland Browns (9-2-1) | Los Angeles Rams (8-3-1) | Cleveland 38, Los Angeles 14 |
| 1956 | New York Giants (8-3-1) | Chicago Bears (9-2-1) | New York 47, Chicago Bears 7 |
| 1957 | Cleveland Browns (9-2-1) | Detroit Lions (8-4-0) (A) | Detroit 59, Cleveland 14 |
| 1958 | New York Giants (9-3-0) (A) | Baltimore Colts (9-3-0) | Baltimore 23, New York 17 (B) |
| 1959 | New York Giants (10-2-0) | Baltimore Colts (9-3-0) | Baltimore 31, New York 16 |
| 1960 | Philadelphia Eagles (10-2-0) | Green Bay Packers (8-4-0) | Philadelphia 17, Green Bay 13 |
| 1961 | New York Giants (10-3-1) | Green Bay Packers (11-3-0) | Green Bay 37, New York 0 |
| 1962 | New York Giants (12-2-0) | Green Bay Packers (13-1-0) | Green Bay 16, New York 7 |
| 1963 | New York Giants (11-3-0) | Chicago Bears (11-1-2) | Chicago 14, New York 10 |
| 1964 | Cleveland Browns (10-3-1) | Baltimore Colts (12-2-0) | Cleveland 27, Baltimore 0 |
| 1965 | Cleveland Browns (11-3-0) | Green Bay Packers (10-3-1) (A) | Green Bay 23, Cleveland 12 |
| 1966 | Dallas Cowboys (10-3-1) | Green Bay Packers (12-2-0) | Green Bay 34, Dallas 27 |

(A) Won divisional playoff. (B) Won at 8:15 sudden death overtime period.

| Year | Conference | Division | Winners (W-L-T) | Playoffs |
|---|---|---|---|---|
| 1967 | East | Century | Cleveland (9-5-0) | Dallas 52, Cleveland 14 |
| | | Capitol | Dallas (9-5-0) | |
| | West | Central | Green Bay (9-4-1) | Green Bay 28, L.A. 7 |
| | | Coastal | Los Angeles (11-1-2) (A) | Green Bay 21, Dallas 17 |

(A) Won division title by outscoring Baltimore in their two meetings.

## PASSING LEADERS

| Year | Player | Atts. | Com. | YG. |
|---|---|---|---|---|
| 1933 | Harry Newman, N. Y. | 132 | 53 | 963 |
| 1934 | Arnie Herber, G. B. | 115 | 42 | 799 |
| 1935 | Ed Danowski, N. Y. | 113 | 57 | 795 |
| 1936 | Arnie Herber, G. B. | 173 | 77 | 1239 |
| 1937 | Sammy Baugh, Wash. | 171 | 81 | 1127 |
| 1938 | Ed Danowski, N. Y. | 129 | 70 | 848 |
| 1939 | Parker Hall, Cleve. | 208 | 106 | 1227 |
| 1940 | Sammy Baugh, Wash. | 177 | 111 | 1367 |
| 1941 | Cecil Isbell, G. B. | 206 | 117 | 1479 |
| 1942 | Cecil Isbell, G. B. | 268 | 146 | 2021 |
| 1943 | Sammy Baugh, Wash. | 239 | 133 | 1754 |
| 1944 | Frank Filchock, Wash. | 147 | 84 | 1139 |
| 1945 | Sammy Baugh, Wash. | 182 | 128 | 1669 |
| 1946 | Bob Waterfield, L. A. | 251 | 127 | 1747 |
| 1947 | Sammy Baugh, Wash. | 354 | 210 | 2938 |
| 1948 | Tommy Thompson, Phila. | 246 | 141 | 1965 |
| 1949 | Sammy Baugh, Wash. | 255 | 145 | 1903 |
| 1950 | Norm Van Brocklin, L. A. | 233 | 127 | 2061 |
| 1951 | Bob Waterfield, L. A. | 176 | 88 | 1566 |
| 1952 | Norm Van Brocklin, L. A. | 205 | 113 | 1736 |
| 1953 | Otto Graham, Cleve. | 258 | 167 | 2722 |
| 1954 | Norm Van Brocklin, L. A. | 260 | 139 | 2637 |
| 1955 | Otto Graham, Cleve. | 185 | 98 | 1721 |
| 1956 | Ed Brown, Bears | 168 | 96 | 1667 |
| 1957 | Tom O'Connell, Cleve. | 110 | 63 | 1229 |
| 1958 | Eddie LeBaron, Wash. | 145 | 79 | 1365 |
| 1959 | Charley Conerly, N. Y. | 194 | 113 | 1706 |
| 1960 | Milt Plum, Cleve. | 250 | 151 | 2297 |
| 1961 | Milt Plum, Cleve. | 302 | 177 | 2416 |
| 1962 | Bart Starr, G. B. | 285 | 178 | 2438 |
| 1963 | Y. A. Tittle, N. Y. | 367 | 221 | 3145 |
| 1964 | Bart Starr, G. B. | 272 | 163 | 2144 |
| 1965 | Rudy Bukich, Chi. | 312 | 176 | 2641 |
| 1966 | Bart Starr, G. B. | 251 | 156 | 2257 |
| 1967 | Sonny Jurgensen, Wash. | 508 | 288 | 3747 |

## PASS-RECEIVING LEADERS

| Year | Player | Ct. | YG. |
|---|---|---|---|
| 1933 | John Kelley, Bklyn. | 21 | 219 |
| 1934 | Joe Carter, Phila. | 16 | 237 |
| 1935 | Tod Goodwin, N. Y. | 26 | 432 |
| 1936 | Don Hutson, G. B. | 34 | 526 |
| 1937 | Don Hutson, G. B. | 41 | 552 |
| 1938 | Gaynell Tinsley, Cards. | 41 | 516 |
| 1939 | Don Hutson, G. B. | 34 | 846 |
| 1940 | Don Looney, Phila. | 58 | 707 |
| 1941 | Don Hutson, G. B. | 58 | 738 |
| 1942 | Don Hutson, G. B. | 74 | 1211 |
| 1943 | Don Hutson, G. B. | 47 | 776 |
| 1944 | Don Hutson, G. B. | 58 | 866 |
| 1945 | Don Hutson, G. B. | 47 | 834 |
| 1946 | Jim Benton, L. A. | 63 | 981 |
| 1947 | Jim Keane, Bears | 64 | 910 |
| 1948 | Tom Fears, L. A. | 51 | 698 |
| 1949 | Tom Fears, L. A. | 77 | 1013 |
| 1950 | Tom Fears, L. A. | 84 | 1116 |
| 1951 | Elroy Hirsch, L. A. | 66 | 1495 |
| 1952 | Mac Speedie, Cleve. | 62 | 911 |
| 1953 | Pete Pihos, Phila. | 63 | 1049 |
| 1954 | Pete Pihos, Phila. | 60 | 872 |
| | Billy Wilson, S. F. | 60 | 830 |
| 1955 | Pete Pihos, Phila. | 62 | 864 |
| 1956 | Billy Wilson, S. F. | 60 | 889 |
| 1957 | Billy Wilson, S. F. | 52 | 757 |
| 1958 | Ray Berry, Balt. | 56 | 794 |
| | Pete Retzlaff, Phila. | 56 | 766 |
| 1959 | Ray Berry, Balt. | 66 | 959 |
| 1960 | Ray Berry, Balt. | 74 | 1298 |
| 1961 | Jim Phillips, L. A. | 78 | 1092 |
| 1962 | Bobby Mitchell, Wash. | 72 | 1384 |
| 1963 | Bobby Conrad, Cards. S. L. | 73 | 967 |
| 1964 | Johnny Morris, Bears. | 93 | 1200 |
| 1965 | Dave Parks, S. F. | 80 | 1344 |
| 1966 | Charlie Taylor, Wash. | 72 | 1119 |
| 1967 | Charlie Taylor, Wash. | 70 | 990 |

## SCORING LEADERS

| Year | Player | Pts. | Year | Player | Pts. |
|---|---|---|---|---|---|
| 1933 | Strong, N. Y., Presnell, Ports. | 64 | 1950 | Doak Walker, Det. | 128 |
| 1934 | Jack Manders, Bears (Chi.) | 79 | 1951 | Elroy Hirsch, L. A. | 102 |
| 1935 | Earl Clark, Det. | 55 | 1952 | Gordie Soltau, San Fran. | 94 |
| 1936 | Earl Clark, Det. | 73 | 1953 | Gordie Soltau, San Fran. | 114 |
| 1937 | Jack Manders, Bears. | 69 | 1954 | Bobby Walston, Phila. | 114 |
| 1938 | Clark Hinkle, G. B. | 58 | 1955 | Doak Walker, Det. | 96 |
| 1939 | Andy Farkas, Wash. | 68 | 1956 | Bobby Layne, Det. | 99 |
| 1940 | Don Hutson, G. B. | 57 | 1957 | Sam Baker, Wash., Lou Groza, Cleve. | 77 |
| 1941 | Don Hutson, G. B. | 95 | 1958 | Jimmy Brown, Cleve. | 108 |
| 1942 | Don Hutson, G. B. | 138 | 1959 | Paul Hornung, G. B. | 94 |
| 1943 | Don Hutson, G. B. | 117 | 1960 | Paul Hornung, G. B. | 176 |
| 1944 | Don Hutson, G. B. | 85 | 1961 | Paul Hornung, G. B. | 146 |
| 1945 | Steve Van Buren, Phila. | 110 | 1962 | Jim Taylor, G. B. | 114 |
| 1946 | Ted Fritsch, G. B. | 100 | 1963 | Don Chandler, N. Y. | 106 |
| 1947 | Pat Harder, Cards (Chi.) | 102 | 1964 | Lenny Moore, Balt. | 120 |
| 1948 | Pat Harder, Cards (Chi.) | 110 | 1965 | Gale Sayers, Chi. | 132 |
| 1949 | Pat Harder, Cards (Chi.) | 102 | 1966 | Bruce Gossett, L. A. | 113 |
| | Gene Roberts, N. Y. | 102 | 1967 | Jim Bakken, S. L. | 117 |

## RUSHING LEADERS

| Year | Player | YG. | Atts. | Year | Player | YG. | Atts. |
|---|---|---|---|---|---|---|---|
| 1933 | Cliff Battles, Bos | 737 | 146 | 1951 | Eddie Price, N. Y. | 971 | 271 |
| 1934 | Beattie Feathers, Bears (Chi.) | 1004 | 101 | 1952 | Dan Towler, L. A. | 894 | 156 |
| 1935 | Doug Russell, Cards (Chi.) | 499 | 140 | 1953 | Joe Perry, San Fran. | 1018 | 192 |
| 1936 | Tuffy Leemans, N. Y. | 830 | 206 | 1954 | Joe Perry, San Fran. | 1049 | 173 |
| 1937 | Cliff Battles, Wash. | 874 | 216 | 1955 | Alan Ameche, Balt. | 961 | 213 |
| 1938 | Whizzer White, Pitts | 567 | 152 | 1956 | Rick Casares, Bears (Chl) | 1126 | 234 |
| 1939 | Bill Osmanski, Bears (Chi.) | 699 | 121 | 1957 | Jimmy Brown, Cleve. | 942 | 202 |
| 1940 | Whizzer White, Det. | 514 | 146 | 1958 | Jimmy Brown, Cleve. | 1527 | 257 |
| 1941 | Pug Manders, Bklyn | 486 | 111 | 1959 | Jimmy Brown, Cleve. | 1329 | 290 |
| 1942 | Bill Dudley, Pitts. | 696 | 162 | 1960 | Jimmy Brown, Cleve. | 1257 | 215 |
| 1943 | Bill Paschal, N. Y. | 572 | 147 | 1961 | Jimmy Brown, Cleve. | 1408 | 305 |
| 1944 | Bill Paschal, N. Y. | 737 | 196 | 1962 | Jim Taylor, G. B. | 1474 | 272 |
| 1945 | Steve Van Buren, Phil. | 832 | 143 | 1963 | Jimmy Brown, Cleve. | 1863 | 291 |
| 1946 | Bill Dudley, Pitts. | 604 | 146 | 1964 | Jimmy Brown, Cleve. | 1446 | 280 |
| 1947 | Steve Van Buren, Phila. | 1008 | 217 | 1965 | Jimmy Brown, Cleve. | 1544 | 289 |
| 1948 | Steve Van Buren, Phila. | 845 | 201 | 1966 | Gale Sayers, Chi | 1231 | 229 |
| 1949 | Steve Van Buren, Phila. | 1146 | 263 | 1967 | Leroy Kelly, Cleve. | 1205 | 235 |
| 1950 | Marion Motley, Cleve. | 810 | 140 | | | | |

# AMERICAN FOOTBALL LEAGUE

| Year | Eastern Division | Western Division | Playoff |
|---|---|---|---|
| 1960 | Houston Oilers (10-4-0) | L. A. Chargers (10-4-0) | Houston 24, Los Angeles 16 |
| 1961 | Houston Oilers (10-3-1) | San Diego Chargers (12-2-0) | Houston 10, San Diego 3 |
| 1962 | Houston Oilers (11-3-0) | Dallas Texans (11-3-0) | Dallas 20, Houston 17 (b) |
| 1963 | Boston Patriots (8-6-1) (a) | San Diego Chargers (11-3-0) | San Diego 51, Boston 10 |
| 1964 | Buffalo Bills (12-2-0) | San Diego Chargers (8-5-1) | Buffalo 20, San Diego 7 |
| 1965 | Buffalo Bills (10-3-1) | San Diego Chargers (9-2-3) | Buffalo 23, San Diego 0 |
| 1966 | Buffalo Bills (9-4-1) | Kansas City Chiefs (11-2-1) | Kansas City 31, Buffalo 7 |
| 1967 | Houston Oilers (9-4-1) | Oakland Raiders (13-1-0) | Oakland 40, Houston 7 |

(a) Won divisional playoff. (b) Won at 2:45 of second overtime period.

## League Leaders

### SCORING LEADERS

| Year | Player | Pts. |
|---|---|---|
| 1960 | Gene Mingo, Denver | 123 |
| 1961 | Gino Cappelletti, Boston | 147 |
| 1962 | Gene Mingo, Denver | 137 |
| 1963 | Gino Cappelletti, Boston | 113 |
| 1964 | Gino Cappelletti, Boston | 155 |
| 1965 | Gino Cappelletti, Boston | 132 |
| 1966 | Gino Cappelletti, Boston | 119 |
| 1967 | George Blanda, Oakland | 116 |

### RUSHING LEADERS

| Year | Player | YG | Atts. |
|---|---|---|---|
| 1960 | Abner Haynes, Dallas | 875 | 156 |
| 1961 | Billy Cannon, Houston | 948 | 200 |
| 1962 | Cookie Gilchrist, Buffalo | 1096 | 214 |
| 1963 | Clem Daniels, Oakland | 1098 | 214 |
| 1964 | Cookie Gilchrist, Buffalo | 981 | 230 |
| 1965 | Paul Lowe, San Diego | 1121 | 222 |
| 1966 | Jim Nance, Boston | 1458 | 299 |
| 1967 | Jim Nance, Boston | 1216 | 269 |

### PASSING LEADERS

| Year | Player | Atts. | Com. | YG |
|---|---|---|---|---|
| 1960 | Jack Kemp, L. A. | 406 | 211 | 3018 |
| 1961 | George Blanda, Hous. | 362 | 187 | 3330 |
| 1962 | Len Dawson, Dallas | 310 | 189 | 2749 |
| 1963 | Tobin Rote, San Diego | 287 | 170 | 2510 |
| 1964 | Len Dawson, K. C. | 354 | 199 | 2879 |
| 1965 | Jack Hadl, San Diego | 348 | 174 | 2798 |
| 1966 | Len Dawson, Kansas City | 284 | 159 | 2527 |
| 1967 | Daryle Lamonica, Oakland | 425 | 220 | 3228 |

### PASS-RECEIVING LEADERS

| Year | Player | Ct. | YG |
|---|---|---|---|
| 1960 | Lionel Taylor, Denver | 92 | 1235 |
| 1961 | Lionel Taylor, Denver | 100 | 1176 |
| 1962 | Lionel Taylor, Denver | 77 | 908 |
| 1963 | Lionel Taylor, Denver | 78 | 1101 |
| 1964 | Charlie Hennigan, Houston | 101 | 1561 |
| 1965 | Lionel Taylor, Denver | 85 | 1131 |
| 1966 | Lance Alworth, San Diego | 73 | 1383 |
| 1967 | George Sauer, N.Y. | 75 | 1189 |

## Professional Football Attendance

### AMERICAN LEAGUE

| | 1967 | 1966 | 1965 |
|---|---|---|---|
| Boston | 162,481 | 190,138 | 143,098 |
| Buffalo | 280,461 | 299,127 | 306,875 |
| Denver | 231,801 | 192,769 | 219,812 |
| Houston | 185,129 | 177,896 | 230,857 |
| Kansas City | 315,006 | 259,071 | 150,169 |
| Miami | 197,710 | 182,428 | |
| New York | 437,036 | 415,768 | 384,144 |
| Oakland | 276,488 | 253,508 | 136,427 |
| San Diego | 297,312 | 189,664 | 202,402 |
| **Total** | 2,383,424 | 2,160,369 | 1,782,584 |

### NATIONAL LEAGUE

| | 1967 | 1966 | 1965 |
|---|---|---|---|
| Atlanta | 384,891 | 395,679 | |
| Baltimore | 418,143 | 418,143 | 416,361 |
| Chicago | 320,550 | 327,587 | 321,283 |
| Cleveland | 544,807 | 544,250 | 557,283 |
| Dallas | 460,476 | 473,373 | 388,912 |
| Detroit | 368,443 | 358,181 | 362,769 |
| Green Bay | 352,586 | 349,442 | 348,334 |
| Los Angeles | 419,997 | 438,432 | 282,333 |
| Minnesota | 304,901 | 315,837 | 321,119 |
| New Orleans | 528,242 | | |
| New York | 440,043 | 439,905 | 439,813 |
| Philadelphia | 424,868 | 407,196 | 400,564 |
| Pittsburgh | 271,522 | 249,331 | 228,954 |
| St. Louis | 316,923 | 317,166 | 213,862 |
| San Francisco | 253,286 | 249,892 | 275,284 |
| Washington | 353,149 | 348,094 | 349,503 |
| **Total** | 6,162,827 | 5,542,508 | 4,906,374 |

## PRO FOOTBALL'S HALL OF FAME
### Canton, Ohio

| | | | |
|---|---|---|---|
| Cliff Battles | Otto Graham | Bobby Layne | Dan Reeves |
| Sammy Baugh | Red Grange | Sid Luckman | Art Rooney |
| Chuck Bednarik | Joe Guyon | Link Lyman | Ken Strong |
| Bert Bell | George Halas | Tim Mara | Joe Stydahar |
| Charles Bidwill | Ed Healey | George Marshall | Jim Thorpe |
| Paul Brown | Mel Hein | George McAfee | George Trafton |
| Joe Carr | Pete Henry | John (Blood) McNally | Charlie Trippi |
| Guy Chamberlin | Arnold Herber | Mike Michalske | Emlen Tunnell |
| Dutch Clark | Clarke Hinkle | Wayne Millner | Clyde (Bulldog) Turner |
| Jim Conzelman | Elroy Hirsch | Marion Motley | Steve Van Buren |
| Art Donovan | Cal Hubbard | Bronco Nagurski | Bob Waterfield |
| Paddy Driscoll | Don Hutson | Ernie Nevers | Alex Wojciechowicz |
| Bill Dudley | Walt Kiesling | Steve Owen | |
| Dr. Daniel Fortmann | Curly Lambeau | Hugh (Shorty) Ray | |

## Professional Football Player Draft

The following are the first round picks of the second combined National Football League-American Football League player draft.

1—**Minnesota**—Ron Yary, offensive tackle, Southern California.

2—**Cincinnati**—Bob Johnson, center, Tennessee.

3—**Atlanta**—Claude Humphrey, defensive tackle, Tennessee A&I.

4—**San Diego**—Russ Washington, offensive tackle, Missouri.

5—**Green Bay**—Fred Carr, linebacker, University of Texas at El Paso.

6—**Boston**—Dennis Byrd, defensive tackle, North Carolina State.

7—**New Orleans**—Kevin Hardy, defensive end-tackle, Notre Dame.

8—**Miami**—Larry Csonka, fullback, Syracuse.

9—**Buffalo**—Haven Moses, flanker, San Diego State.

10—**Pittsburgh**—Mike Taylor, defensive tackle, Southern California.

11—**Minnesota**—Greg Landry, quarterback, Massachusetts.

12—**Washington**—Jim Smith, defensive back, Oregon.

13—**St. Louis**—MacArthur Lane, halfback, Utah State.

14—**Philadelphia**—Tim Rossovich, defensive end, Southern California.

15—**San Francisco**—Forrest Blue, center, Auburn.

16—**Chicago**—Mike Hull, fullback, Southern California.

17—**New York (AFL)**—Lee White, fullback, Weber State.

18—**San Diego**—Jim Hill, defensive back, Tennessee A&I.

19—**Kansas City**—Maurice (Mo.) Moorman, offensive tackle, Texas A&M.

20—**Dallas**—Dennis Homan, flanker, Alabama.

21—**Cleveland**—Marvin Upshaw, defensive end, Trinity (Tex.)

22—**Kansas City**—George Daney, offensive guard, Texas-El Paso.

23—**Baltimore**—John Williams, offensive tackle, Minnesota.

24—**Detroit**—Earl McCullouch, split end, Southern California.

25—**Oakland**—Eldridge Dickey, quarterback, Tennessee A&I.

26—**Green Bay**—Bill Lueck, offensive guard, Arizona.

27—**Miami**—Doug Crusan, offensive tackle, Indiana.

## Canadian Football League (Grey Cup)

Winners of Eastern and Western divisions meet in championship game for Grey Cup (donated by Governor-General Earl Grey in 1909). Canadian football features three downs, 110-yard field, each team dressing 32 players of which 12 can be on field at one time. Each team allowed 14 U. S. imports, who usually dominate the sport.

1948—Calgary Stampeders 12, Ottawa Rough Riders 7

1949—Montreal Alouettes 28, Calgary Stampeders 15

1950—Toronto Argonauts 13, Winnipeg Blue Bombers 0

1951—Ottawa Rough Riders 21, Saskatchewan Roughriders 14

1952—Toronto Argonauts 21, Edmonton Eskimos 11

1953—Hamilton Tiger-Cats 12, Winnipeg Blue Bombers 6

1954—Edmonton Eskimos 26, Montreal Alouettes 25

1955—Edmonton Eskimos 34, Montreal Alouettes 19

1956—Edmonton Eskimos 50, Montreal Alouettes 27

1957—Hamilton Tiger-Cats 32, Winnipeg Blue Bombers 7

1958—Winnipeg Blue Bombers 35, Hamilton Tiger-Cats 28

1959—Winnipeg Blue Bombers 21, Hamilton Tiger-Cats 7

1960—Ottawa Rough Riders 16, Edmonton Eskimos 6

1961—Winnipeg Blue Bombers 21, Hamilton Tiger-Cats 14

1962—Winnipeg Blue Bombers 28, Hamilton Tiger-Cats 27

1963—Hamilton Tiger-Cats 21, British Columbia Lions 10

1964—British Columbia Lions 34, Hamilton Tiger-Cats 24

1965—Hamilton Tiger-Cats 22, Winnipeg Blue Bombers 16

1966—Saskatchewan Roughriders 29, Ottawa Rough Riders 14

1967—Hamilton Tiger-Cats 24, Saskatchewan Roughriders 1

## Continental Football League

The Continental League Championship game was played Dec. 10, 1967, at Anaheim, Calif. The score was Orlando (Fla.) Panthers 38, Orange County (Calif.) Ramblers 14. Don Jonas threw 5 touchdown passes for Orlando.

# Stadiums

For stadiums that house a major league baseball team see Index. For college stadiums see page 866.

| Name and location | Cap.* | Name and location | Cap.* |
|---|---|---|---|
| American Legion Memorial, Charlotte, N. C. | 22,315 | Long Beach (Calif.) Veterans Memorial | 15,000 |
| Balboa Stadium, San Diego, Calif. | 34,500 | Los Angeles Memorial Coliseum | 920,00 |
| Bears Stadium, Denver, Colo. | 34,643 | Mississippi Memorial Stadium, Jackson | 46,000 |
| Bowman Grey Stad., Winston-Salem, N. C. | 16,841 | Orange Bowl, Miami, Fla. | 70,369 |
| Buffalo War Memorial Stadium | 44,500 | Ottawa Stadium, Ottawa, Canada | 27,872 |
| Columbus (Ga.) Memorial Stadium | 35,000 | Portland Civic Stadium | 29,010 |
| Cotton Bowl, Dallas, Tex. | 75,504 | Richmond (Va.) City Stadium | 22,009 |
| Empire Stadium, Vancouver | 32,759 | Roanoke (Va.) Victory Stadium | 30,000 |
| Gator Bowl, Jacksonville, Fla. | 70,000 | Rose Bowl, Pasadena, Calif. | 100,570 |
| John F. Kennedy Stadium, Phil. | 105,000 | Rubber Bowl, Akron, Ohio | 35,007 |
| Kansas City Municipal Stadium | 40,106 | San Diego Stadium | 50,000 |
| Kentucky Exposition Stadium, Louisville | 21,000 | Sicks Seattle Stadium | 10,500 |
| Kezar Stadium, San Francisco | 60,000 | Soldier Field, Chicago | 77,110 |
| Ladd Memorial Stadium, Mobile, Ala. | 40,605 | Sugar Bowl, New Orleans, La. | 80,982 |
| Lambeau Field, Green Bay, Wisc. | 50,180 | Tampa Stadium, Tampa, Fla. | 45,005 |
| Legion Stadium, Birmingham, Ala. | 68,821 | Wood Memorial Stad., Sioux Falls, S. D. | 10,000 |

*Normal permanent seating capacity.

## 31st Annual Soap Box Derby

Branch Lew, 11, of Muncie, Ind., won the 31st All-American Soap Box Derby at Akron, Ohio Aug. 24, 1968, besting a field of 243 contestants from 46 states and from Canada, Venezuela, the Philippines, Okinawa and West Germany for the $7,500 college scholarship. Ronald Alber, 14, of the Bay Area (Fremont), Calif. was awarded a $5,000 scholarship for second, and Dennis Jett Puckett, 11, of De-Kalb County (Decatur), Ga., received a $4,000 scholarship for third place. A total of $30,000 in scholarships was awarded to the first 9 place finishers by Chevrolet, national derby sponsor. Each of the 243 contestants received a $500 United States Savings Bond for victory in his hometown race.

# College Football Stadiums

| Name and location | Cap.* | Name and location | Cap.* |
|---|---|---|---|
| Alabama Univ. of (Denny) University, Ala. | 56,000 | Missouri, U. of, (Memorial), Columbia, Mo. | 55,000 |
| Angelo St. Coll. (San Angelo Stad.), Tex. | 17,133 | Nebraska, Un. of, (Memorial), Lincoln | 63,444 |
| Arizona State Univ. (Sun Devil) | 42,350 | New Mexico St. U., (Memorial Stad.), | |
| Arizona, Univ. of, Tucson (Varsity) | 40,000 | Univ. Park | 20,000 |
| Arkansas, Univ. of (Razorback Stad.) | | New Mexico, Un. of, Albuquerque | 30,000 |
| Fayetteville | 45,000 | North Carolina St. U., (Carter Stad.), | |
| Auburn Univ., (Cliff Hare Stad.), Auburn, | | Raleigh | 41,000 |
| Ala. | 45,000 | North Carolina, Un. of, (Kenan), Chapel Hill | 46,000 |
| Baylor Univ., Waco, Texas | 49,000 | No. Texas St. Univ. (Fouts Field), Denton | 20,000 |
| Boston Coll. (Alumni Stad.), Boston, Mass. | 26,000 | Northern Ill. Univ. Stad., DeKalb | 20,000 |
| Boston Univ. (Nickerson Field), Boston | 15,500 | Northwestern Univ., (Dyche), Evanston, Ill. | 55,000 |
| Bowling Green State Univ. (Perry Field) O. | 23,000 | Notre Dame Stad., South Bend, Ind. | 59,000 |
| Brigham Young Univ. Stad., Utah | 30,000 | Ohio State Univ., (Ohio Stad.), Columbus. | 83,000 |
| Brown State, Providence, R. I. | 17,851 | Ohio U., (Don Peden), Athens | 17,500 |
| Bucknell (Memorial Stad.), Lewisburg, Pa. | 18,000 | Okla. State U., (Lewis Stad.), Stillwater | 40,000 |
| Butler U., (Butler Bowl), Indianapolis, Ind. | 21,000 | Okla., Un. of, (Owen Field), Norman | 61,826 |
| Calif., Un. of (Memorial Stad.), Berkeley. | 76,780 | Old Dominion Coll., (Foreman), Norfolk, Va. | 30,000 |
| Central St.(Wantland Stad.),Edmond,Okla. | 20,000 | Oreg. St. Univ., (Parker Stad.), Corvallis. | 40,750 |
| Cincinnati Un. of (Nippert), Ohio | 28,000 | Oreg., Un. of, (Autzen Stad.), Eugene | 41,000 |
| Citadel (Hagood Stad.), Charleston, S. C. | 22,500 | Pacific, Univ. of the, (Pacific Mem.), | |
| Clemson Univ. (Memorial Stad.), S. C. | 43,451 | Stockton, Calif. | 35,000 |
| Coe (Kingston) Cedar Rapids, Iowa | 15,000 | Penn. St. Univ., (Beaver Stad.), Pa. | 46,284 |
| Colgate Univ. (Andy Kerr Stad.) | | Penn., Un. of,(Franklin Field), Phila. | 60,546 |
| Hamilton, N. Y. | 16,528 | Pittsburgh, Univ. of, (Pitt. Stad.), Pa. | 60,000 |
| Colorado St. Univ Stad., Ft. Collins | 30,000 | Princeton Un., (Palmer), Princeton, N. J. | 45,725 |
| Colorado, Un. of (Folsom), Boulder, Colo. | 50,516 | Purdue Un., (Ross-Ade), Lafayette, Ind. | 62,000 |
| Columbia Univ., (Baker Field), N. Y., N. Y. | 32,000 | Rice Stad., Houston, Texas | 70,000 |
| Conn., Univ. of (Memorial Stad.), Storrs | 15,500 | Rutgers Stad., New Brunswick, N. J. | 24,000 |
| Cornell Un. (Schellkopf Field), Ithaca, N. Y. | 34,000 | San Diego St. Coll., (Aztec Bowl) | 14,500 |
| Dartmouth Coll., (Memorial Field), | | San Jose St. Coll., (Spartan Stad.) | 17,900 |
| Hanover, N. H. | 13,900 | So. Car., Un. of, (Carolina), Columbia | 42,338 |
| Dayton, Univ. of (Baujan Field) | 13,888 | So. Mississippi, U. of, (Faulkner Field), | |
| Delaware, Univ. of (Delaware Stad.) | 13,500 | Hattiesburg | 16,000 |
| Detroit Univ, of (Titan Stad.), Mich. | 20,000 | So. Univ., A&M Stad., Baton Rouge, La. | 18,000 |
| Drake Stad., Des Moines, Iowa | 18,000 | Stanford Stad., Stanford, Calif. | 89,000 |
| Duke Univ., (Wade Stad.), Durham, N.C. | 57,000 | Syracuse, (N. Y.), Univ., (Archbold) | 40,696 |
| E. Carolina (Ficklen Stad.), Greenville | 20,000 | Tampa, Univ. of, (Tampa Stad.), Fla. | 50,000 |
| E. Texas St. (Memorial Stad.) | 13,000 | Temple Stad., Phil. | 20,500 |
| Eastern Kentucky (Hanger Field), Richmond | 18,200 | Tenn. A&I St. Univ. (Hale), Nashville | 16,000 |
| Evansville, Univ. of (Reitz Bowl), Ind. | 13,000 | Tenn., Un. of, (Neyland), Knoxville | 61,000 |
| Florida State, (Campbell), Tallahassee | 42,000 | Texas A. & M., U., (Kyle Field), Coll. Sta. | 48,080 |
| Florida, Un. of, (Florida Field), Gainesville. | 60,000 | Texas Christian U., (Carter Stad.), Ft. Worth | 47,000 |
| Fresno St. Coll. (Ratcliffe Stad.), Calif. | 13,000 | Texas So. Un., (Jeppesen Stad.), Houston | 20,000 |
| Georgia Inst. of Tech., (Grant Field) Atlanta | 60,000 | Texas Tech. Coll., (Jones Stad.), Lubbock | 42,500 |
| Georgia, Un. of, (Sanford), Athens | 60,000 | Texas, Un. of, (Memorial), Austin | 66,000 |
| Grambling Coll., (Tiger Stad.), La. | 15,000 | Texas, Univ. of, (Sun Bowl), El Paso | 30,000 |
| Harvard Univ., Boston, Mass. | 37,289 | Toledo, Univ. of (Glass Bowl), Ohio | 16,500 |
| Hawaii, Univ. of, (Honolulu Stad.) | 25,000 | Trinity U., (Alamo Stad.), San Antonio,Tex. | 25,000 |
| Holy Cross (Fitton Field) Worcester, Mass. | 22,000 | Tulane Stad. (Sugar Bowl), New Orleans, La | 80,985 |
| Idaho, Un. of (Neale), Moscow, Idaho | 13,888 | Tulsa, Univ. of, (Skelly), Tulsa, Okla. | 40,000 |
| Illinois, Un. of (Memorial) | 71,227 | U.S. Air Force Acad., (Falcon Stad.), Colo. | 40,828 |
| Illinois St. Univ. (Hancock Field), Normal. | 15,000 | U.S. Military Academy (Michie), | |
| Indiana St. (Municipal), Terre Haute | 25,000 | West Point, N. Y. | 32,000 |
| Indiana Univ. (Mem. Stad.), Bloomington. | 48,000 | U.S. Naval Academy, Annapolis, Md | 29,000 |
| Iowa St. U., (Clyde Williams Field), Ames. | 33,000 | Utah State U. (Romney Stad.), Logan | 20,000 |
| Iowa, Univ. of, (Iowa Stad.), Iowa City. | 59,400 | Utah, Un. of, (Ute Stad.), Salt Lake City. | 28,800 |
| Kan. St. Univ., Manhattan | 35,000 | Vanderbilt U., (Dudley Field), Nashville. | 34,000 |
| Kansas, Un. of, (Memorial), Lawrence | 51,500 | Va. Poly Inst., (Lane), Blacksburg | 35,000 |
| Kent St. U., (Memorial Stad.), Ohio | 20,000 | Virginia, Un. of, (Scott), Charlottesville, Va. | 30,000 |
| Kentucky, Un. of, (McLean), Lexington | 38,000 | Wake Forest Un., Winston-Salem, N.C.. | 30,000 |
| Lafayette Coll., (Fisher Stad.), Easton, Pa. | 17,000 | Wash. St. U., (Rogers Field), Pullman | 23,000 |
| Lamar St. Coll. of Tech., (Cardinal Stad), | | Washington Stad., Un. of, Seattle | 55,500 |
| Beaumont, Tex | 17,300 | Weber St. Coll. Stad., Ogden, Utah | 18,000 |
| Lehigh Univ., (Taylor), Bethlehem, Pa. | 17,307 | West Texas State Univ., (Buffalo), Canyon | 20,000 |
| La. Poly. Inst., (Tech. Stad.), Ruston. | 27,500 | W. Va. U., (Mountaineer Fld.), Morgantown | 35,000 |
| La. State Un., (Tiger), Baton Rouge | 67,800 | Western Kentucky Univ., (Smith Stad.) | 20,000 |
| Marquette Stad., Milwaukee, Wis. | 20,000 | Western Mich. U., (Waldo Stad.), | |
| Maryland, Un. of, (Byrd), College Park | 33,000 | Kalamazoo | 20,500 |
| Memphis St. Univ., (Memorial Stad.) | 50,150 | Wichita St. U., (Veterans Field) | 16,500 |
| Miami Univ., (Miami Field) | 14,900 | William & Mary, Coll. of, (Cary), Williams- | |
| Michigan State, Univ., (Spartan Stadium) | 76,000 | burg, Va. | 15,000 |
| Michigan, Univ. of, (Mich. Stad.) | | Wisconsin, Univ. of, (Camp Randall) | 76,483 |
| Ann Arbor | 101,001 | Wyoming, U. of, (War Memorial), Laramie | 18,671 |
| Minnesota, Un. of, (Memorial), Minn. | 63,430 | Xavier Stad., Cincinnati | 15,000 |
| Miss. St. Univ., (Scott Field) | 34,000 | Yale Bowl, New Haven, Conn. | 70,874 |
| Miss. Un. of, (Hemingway), University | 34,500 | | |

*Normal seating capacity.

# Heisman Trophy Winners
## (Outstanding College Football Player)

| | | | | |
|---|---|---|---|---|
| 1936 | Larry Kelley, Yale, E | | 1952 | Billy Vessels, Oklahoma, HB |
| 1937 | Clinton Frank, Yale, QB | | 1953 | John Lattner, Notre Dame, HB |
| 1938 | David O'Brien, Texas Christian, QB | | 1954 | Alan Ameche, Wisconsin, FB |
| 1939 | Nile Kinnick, Iowa, QB | | 1955 | Howard Cassady, Ohio State, HB |
| 1940 | Tom Harmon, Michigan, HB | | 1956 | Paul Hornung, Notre Dame, QB |
| 1941 | Bruce Smith, Minnesota, HB | | 1957 | John Crow, Texas A & M, HB |
| 1942 | Frank Sinkwich, Georgia, HB | | 1958 | Pete Dawkins, Army, HB |
| 1943 | Angelo Bertelli, Notre Dame, QB | | 1959 | Billy Cannon, Louisiana State, HB |
| 1944 | Leslie Horvath, Ohio State, QB | | 1960 | Joe Bellino, Navy, HB |
| 1945 | Felix Blanchard, Army, FB | | 1961 | Ernest Davis, Syracuse, HB |
| 1946 | Glenn Davis, Army, HB | | 1962 | Terry Baker, Oregon State, QB |
| 1947 | John Lujack, Notre Dame, QB | | 1963 | Roger Staubach, Navy, QB |
| 1948 | Doak Walker, Southern Methodist, HB | | 1964 | John Huarte, Notre Dame, QB |
| 1949 | Leon Hart, Notre Dame, E | | 1965 | Mike Garrett, Southern California, HB |
| 1950 | Vic Janowicz, Ohio State, HB | | 1966 | Steve Spurrier, Florida, QB |
| 1951 | Richard Kazmaier, Princeton, HB | | 1967 | Gary Beban, UCLA, QB |

# Atlantic Coast League

The Atlantic Coast League Championship game was played Nov. 25, 1967, at Mount Vernon, N. Y. The score was Virginia Sailors 20, Westchester Bulls 14.

# College Football Hall of Fame

### RUTGERS UNIVERSITY, NEW BRUNSWICK, N. J.

## PLAYERS

**Name—Sch—Pos—Last Yr Pl'd**

A. Agase, Purdue/Ill., G, '46
F. Albert, Stanford, QB, '41
C. Aldrich, Tex. Christ., C, '38
J. Alexander, Syracuse, G, '20
C. E. Bacon, Wesleyan, QB, '12
S. Barnes, Calif., E, '21
C. Barrett, Cornell, QB, '15
B. Baston, Minn., E, '16
G. Battles, W.Va., Wes., HB, '31
S. Baugh, Tex. Christ., HB, '36
J. Bausch, Kansas, HB, '30
J. Berwanger, Chicago, QB, '35
F. Blanchard, Army, FB, '46
L. Bomar, Vanderbilt, E-HB, '24
A. Booth, Yale, HB, '31
F. Borries, Navy, HB, '34
B. Boynton, Wms., QB, '20
G. Brown, Yale, G, '00
J. Brown, Jr., Navy, G-T, '13
J. M. Brown, Ala., HB, '25
C. Cagle, SW La./Army, HB, '29
D. Campbell, Harvard, E, '01
J. Cannon, Notre Dame, G, '29
E. Carideo, Notre Dame, QB, '30
C. Carney, Illinois, E, '21
H. Carpenter, Va. Poly, HB, '05
C. Carroll, Washington, HB, '28
E. Casey, Harvard, HB, '19
G. Chamberlain, Nebr., E-HB, '15
P. Christman, Mo., HB, '40
E. Clark, Colo. Col., QB, '29
C. Conerly, Mississippi, QB, '47
G. Connor, Holy Cross/Notre Dame, T, '47
W. Corbus, Stanford, G, '33
H. Cowan, Princeton, T, '89
T. Coy, Yale, FB, '09
J. Crowley, Notre Dame, HB, '24
S. Cutter, Navy, T, '34
G. Dalrymple, Tulane, E, '31
C. Daly, Harvard/Army, QB, '02
G. Davis, Army, HB, '46
F. DesJardien, Chicago, C, '14
J. DeWitt, Princeton, G, '03
B. Dodd, Tenn., QB, '30
N. Dougherty, Tenn., G, '09
M. Drury, So. Calif., QB, '27
B. Dudley, Va., HB, '41
W. Eckersall, Chicago, QB, '06
R. Evans, Kansas, HB, '47
B. Feathers, Tenn., HB, '33
W. Fesler, Ohio State, E, '30
F. Fish, Harvard, T, '09
A. Flowers, Davidson/Ga. Tech, HB, '20
C. Frank, Yale, HB, '37
B. Friedman, Mich., QB, '26
E. Garbisch, Army, C, '24
C. Gelbert, Penn, E-HB, '96
W. Gilbert, Auburn, C, '36
G. Gipp, Notre Dame, FB, '20
M. Goldberg, Pitts., HB, '38
O. Graham, Northw'n, HB, '43
H. Grange, Ill., HB, '25
R. Grayson, Stanford, FB, '35
M. Gulick, Toledo & Hobart, QB, '29
E. Hale, Miss. Col., HB, '21
T. Hamilton, Navy, B, '25
H. Hardwick, Harv'd, E-HB, '14
T. Hare, Penn., G, '00
C. Harley, Ohio State, FB, '19

T. Harmon, Mich., HB, '40
H. Harpster, Car. Tech, QB, '28
E. Hart, Princeton, FB-T, '11
H. Hazel, Rutgers, FB, '24
W. Heffelfinger, Yale, G, '91
M. Hein, Wash. St., C, '30
W. Henry, Wash. & Jeff., T, '19
R. Herwig, California, C, '37
W. Heston, Mich., HB, '04
H. Hickman, Tenn., G, '31
D. Hill, Duke, C, '38
F. Hinkey, Yale, '94
C. Hinkle, Vanderbilt, C, '37
J. Hitchcock, Auburn, HB, '32
J. Hogan, Yale, T, '04
J. Holland, Cornell, E, '38
W. Hollenback, Penn., HB, '08
C. Hubbard, Geneva/Centenary, E, '26
J. Hubbard, Amherst, HB, '06
A. Hubert, Alabama, FB, '25
W. Humble, Rice, G, '46
J. Hunt, Tex. A&M, HB-QB, '27
D. Hutson, Ala., E, '34
C. Isbell, Purdue, B, '37
H. Joesting, Minn., FB, '27
F. Juhan, Univ. of the South, C, '10
C. Justice, No. Car., HB, '49
K. Kavanaugh, La. State, E, '39
E. Kaw, Cornell, HB, '22
D. Kazmaier, Princeton, HB, '51
J. Keck, Princeton, T, '21
H. Ketcham, Yale, C-G, '13
J. Kilpatrick, Yale, E, '10
J. Kimbrough, Tex.A&M, FB, '40
F. Kinard, Miss., T, '37
P. King, Princeton, QB, '93
N. Kinnick, Iowa, HB, '39
H. Kipke, Mich., HB, '23
E. Layden, Notre Dame, FB, '24
B. Layne, Texas, FB-HB-QB, '47
L. Lea, Princeton, E, '95
J. Leech, Va. Military, HB, '20
J. Locke, Iowa, FB, '22
S. Luckman, Columbia, QB, '38
J. Lujack, Notre Dame, QB, '47
F. Lund, Minn., HB, '34
G. McAfee, Duke, HB, '39
J. McCormick, Princ., FB, '07
E. McEver, Tenn., HB, '31
J. McEwan, Minn./Army, C, '16
B. McFadden, Clemson, HB, '39
T. McClung, Yale, HB, '91
J. McGovern, Minn., QB, '10
G. McLaren, Pitts., FB, '18
A. McMillin, Centre, QB, '21
R. McWhorter, Ga., HB, '13
E. Mahan, Harvard, FB, '15
W. Mallory, Yale, FB, '23
J. Mauthe, Penn. St., HB, '12
L. Mercer, Penn., E, '12
A. Mickal, LSU, HB, '35
E. Miller, Notre Dame, T, '24
J. Minds, Penn., T-FB, '97
C. Montgomery, Col., QB, '33
F. Muller, Calif., E, '22
B. Nagurski, Minn., T-FB, '29
E. Nevers, Stanford, FB, '25
M. Newell, Harvard, T, '93
A. Oberlander, D'tm'th, HB, '25
D. O'Brien, Tex.Christ., HB, '38
P. O'Dea, Wisconsin, FB, '99

E. Oliphant, Purdue/Army, HB, '17
B. Oosterbaan, Mich., E, '27
C. Parker, Duke, HB, '36
V. Pazzetti, Wesleyan/Lehigh, QB, '12
R. Peck, Pitts., C, '16
S. Pennock, Harvard, G, '14
G. Pfann, Cornell, QB, '23
H. Phillips, U. of the So., G, '04
J. Pingel, Mich. State, HB, '38
P. Pinos, Indiana, E-FB, '45
E. Pinckert, So. Calif., HB, '31
F. Pollard, Brown, HB, '16
H. Pund, Ga. Tech., C, '28
C. Reeds, Okla., FB, '13
R. Reynolds, Stanford, T, '35
G. Rinehart, Lafayette, G, '97
I. Rodgers, W. Va., FB, '19
A. Rosenberg, So. Cal., G, '34
K. Rote, So. Meth., HB, '50
J. Routt, Tex. A&M, G, '37
G. Sauer, Nebraska, FB, '33
W.Schoonover, Arkansas, E., '29
D. Schreiner, Wis., E, '42
A. Schulz, Michigan, C, '08
F. Schwab, Lafayette, G, '22
P. Schwegler, Wash., T, '31
T. Shevlin, Yale, E, '05
C. Simons, Tulane, HB, '34
F. Sington, Alabama, T, '30
F. Sinkwich, Georgia, HB, '42
F. Slater, Iowa, T, '21
H. Smith, So. Calif., G, '39
N. Snow, Michigan, HB, '01
C. Spears, Dartmouth, G, '15
W. Spears, Vanderbilt, QB, '27
E. Sprackling, Brown, QB, '11
A. Stagg, Yale, E, '89
H. Stein, Pittsburgh, T, '21
K. Strong, N.Y.U., FB, '28
H. Stuhldreher, N.D., QB, '24
R. Suffridge, Tennessee, G, '40
J. Thorpe, Carlisle, HB, '12
B. Ticknor, Harvard, C, '30
G. Tinsley, La. State, E, '36
E. Tipton, Duke, B, '38
C. Trippi, Ga., HB, '46
E. Tryon, Colgate, HB, '25
C. Turner, Hardin-Sim., C, '39
N. Van Brocklin, Oregon, QB, '48
D. Walker, So. Meth., HB, '49
A. Walsh, Notre Dame, C, '24
K. Washington, UCLA, HB, '39
H. Weekes, Columbia, HB, '02
E. Weir, Nebraska, T, '25
J. Weller, Princeton, G, '35
B. West, Colgate, T, '19
C. Wharton, Penn., G, '96
B. White Colorado HB, '38
D. Whitmire, Ala./Navy, T, '44
E. Widseth, Minnesota, T, '36
R. Wildung, Minnesota, T, '42
J. Williams, Rice, E, '49
G. Wilson, Washington, HB, '25
A. Wistert, Mich., T, '42
F. Wistert, Michigan, T, '33
A. Wojciechowicz, Ford, C, '36
A. Wyant, Buck/Chi., G, '94
C. Young, Wash. & Lee, HB, '16
C. Young, Ill., HB, '46

## COACHES

William A. Alexander
Ike Armstrong
Madison Bell
Hugo Bezdek
Dana Bible
Bernard W. Bierman
Earl H. Blaik
Charles W. Caldwell, Jr.
Walter Camp
Frank W. Cavanaugh
Herbert Crisler
Gilmour Dobie
Michael J. Donahue
Charles (Gus) Dorais
Donald B. Faurot
Edward Hall
Richard C. Harlow
Percy P. Haughton
John W. Heisman

Robert A. Higgins
Howard H. Jones
L. MaC. (Biff) Jones
Thomas (Tad) Jones
Andrew Kerr
George E. Little
Lou Little
Daniel McGugin
DeOrmand (Tuss) McLaughry
L. R. (Dutch) Meyer
Bernie H. Moore
Ray Morrison
Clarence Munn
Earl (Greasy) Neale
Robert R. Neyland
Frank (Buck) O'Neil
Bennie Owen
E. N. Robinson

Knute K. Rockne
E. L. (Dick) Romney
William W. Roper
Clark D. Shaughnessy
Andrew L. Smith
Carl Snavely
Amos Alonzo Stagg
John (Jock) Sutherland
Frank W. Thomas
W. Wallace Wade
Lynn (Pappy) Waldorf
Glenn S. (Pop) Warner
E. E. (Tad) Wieman
John W. Wilce
Henry L. Williams
George W. Woodruff
Fielding H. Yost
Robert Zuppke

# Records of Post-Season Football Games

Figures in parentheses after games denote attendance.

### ROSE BOWL
**Jan. 1        Pasadena, Calif.**
1948—Michigan 49, Southern California 0 (93,000)
1949—Northwestern 20, California 14 (93,000)
1950—Ohio State 17, California 14 (100,963)
1951—Michigan 14, California 6 (98,939)
1952—Illinois 40, Stanford 7 (96,825)
1953—Southern California 7, Wisconsin 0 (100,000)
1954—Michigan State 28, U.C.L.A. 20 (100,000)
1955—Ohio State 20, So. California 7 (89,191)
1956—Michigan State 17, U.C.L.A. 14 (100,809)
1957—Iowa 35, Oregon State 19 (97,126)
1958—Ohio State 10, Oregon 7 (100,000)
1959—Iowa 38, California 12 (98,297)
1960—Washington 44, Wisconsin 8 (100,809)
1961—Washington 17, Minnesota 7 (97,314)
1962—Minnesota 21, U.C.L.A. 3 (98,214)
1963—So. California 42, Wisconsin 37 (98,698)
1964—Illinois 17, Washington 7 (96,957)
1965—Michigan 34, Oregon State 7 (100,423)
1966—U.C.L.A. 14, Michigan State 12 (100,087)
1967—Purdue 14, Southern Calif. 13 (101,455)
1968—So. Calif. 14, Indiana 3 (102,946)

### SUGAR BOWL
**Jan. 1        New Orleans, La.**
1954—Georgia Tech 42, West Virginia 19 (75,000)
1955—Navy 21, Mississippi 0 (82,000)
1956—Georgia Tech 7, Pittsburgh 0 (80,175)
1957—Baylor 13, Tennessee 7 (81,000)
1958—Mississippi 39, Texas 7 (82,000)
1959—Louisiana State 7, Clemson 0 (82,000)
1960—Mississippi 21, Louisiana State 0 (83,000)
1961—Mississippi 14, Rice 6 (82,851)
1962—Alabama 10, Arkansas 3 (82,910)
1963—Mississippi 17, Arkansas 13 (82,900)
1964—Alabama 12, Mississippi 7 (80,785)
1965—Louisiana State 13, Syracuse 10 (65,000)
1966—Missouri 20, Florida 18 (67,421)
1967—Alabama 34, Nebraska 7 (82,000)
1968—Louisiana State 20, Wyoming 13 (78,963)

### ORANGE BOWL
**Jan. 1        Miami, Fla.**
1954—Oklahoma 7, Maryland 0 (68,718)
1955—Duke 34, Nebraska 7 (68,750)
1956—Oklahoma 20, Maryland 6 (76,561)
1957—Colorado 27, Clemson 21 (72,552)
1958—Oklahoma 48, Duke 21 (76,318)
1959—Oklahoma 21, Syracuse 6 (75,281)
1960—Georgia 14, Missouri 0 (75,280)
1961—Missouri 21, Navy 14 (71,218)
1962—Louisiana State 25, Colorado 7 (62,381)
1963—Alabama 17, Oklahoma 0 (73,280)
1964—Nebraska 13, Auburn 7 (72,647)
1965—Texas 21, Alabama 17 (72,647)
1966—Alabama 39, Nebraska 28 (74,214)
1967—Florida 27, Georgia Tech 12 (72,426)
1968—Oklahoma 26, Tennessee 24 (77,993)

### SUN BOWL
**Jan. 1        El Paso, Tex.**
1954—Texas Western 37, Miss. Southern 14 (9,500)
1955—Texas Western 47, Florida State 20 (14,000)
1956—Wyoming 21, Texas Tech. 14 (14,500)
1957—George Washington 13, Texas Western 0 (13,500)
1958—Louisville 34, Drake 20 (12,000)
1959—Wyoming 14, Hardin-Simmons 6 (13,000)
1959, Dec. 31—N. M. St. 28, No. Texas St. 8
1960, Dec. 31—N. M. St. 20, Utah St. 14 (16,000)
1961—Dec. 31—Villanova 17, Wichita 9 (15,000)

1962, Dec. 31—W. Texas St. 15, Ohio U. 14 (16,000)
1963, Dec. 31—Oregon 21, So. Methodist 14 (26,500)
1964, Dec. 26—Georgia 7, Texas Tech 0 (28,000)
1965, Dec. 31—Texas Western 13, Texas Christian 12 (27,450)
1966, Dec. 24—Wyoming 28, Florida St. 20 (24,381)
1967, Dec. 30—Texas (El Paso) 14, Mississippi 7 (34,685)

### COTTON BOWL
**Jan. 1        Dallas, Texas**
1955—Georgia Tech 14, Arkansas 6 (75,504)
1956—Mississippi 14, Texas Christian 13 (76,504)
1957—Texas Christian 28, Syracuse 27 (68,000)
1958—Navy 20, Rice 7 (75,504)
1959—Air Force Acad. 0, Texas Christian 0 (75,504)
1960—Syracuse 23, Texas 14 (75,504)
1961—Duke 7, Arkansas 6 (74,000)
1962—Texas 12, Mississippi 7 (75,504)
1963—Louisiana State 13, Texas 0 (75,504)
1964—Texas 28, Navy 6 (75,504)
1965—Arkansas 10, Nebraska 7 (75,504)
1966—Louisiana St. 14, Arkansas 7 (76,200)
1966, Dec. 31—Georgia 24, S.M.U. 9 (75,400)
1968—Texas A & M 20, Alabama 16 (75,000)

### BLUE AND GRAY (NORTH-SOUTH)
**(Dec.)        Montgomery, Ala.**
1957—South 21, North 20
1958—North 16, South 0 (21,000)
1959—North 20, South 8 (20,000)
1960—North 35, South 7 (12,000)
1961—South 9, North 7 (18,000)
1962—North 10, South 6 (20,000)
1963—South 21, North 14 (20,000)
1964—North 10, South 6 (16,000)
1965—South 23, North 19 (18,000)
1966—North 14, South 9 (18,000)
1967—North 22, South 16 (23,350)

### SHRINE ALL-STAR GAME
**(EAST-WEST)**
**San Francisco**
1957, West 27, East 13
1958, Dec. 27—East 26, West 14 (60,000)
1960, Jan. 2—West 21, East 14 (60,000)
1960, Dec. 31—East 7, West 0 (59,000)
1961, Dec. 30—West 21, East 8 (59,000)
1962, Dec. 29—East 25, West 19 (59,000)
1963, Dec. 28—East 6, West 6 (60,128)
1965, Jan. 2—West 11, East 7 (60,000)
1965, Dec. 31—West 22, East 7 (56,121)
1966, Dec. 31—East 45, West 32 (52,741)
1967, Dec. 30—East 16, West 14 (49,000)

### GATOR BOWL
**Jacksonville, Fla.**
1954, Jan. 1—Texas Tech 35, Auburn 13
1954, Dec. 31—Auburn 33, Baylor 13
1955, Dec. 31—Vanderbilt 25, Auburn 13
1956—Dec. 29—Georgia Tech 21, Pittsburgh 14
1957, Dec. 28—Tennessee 3, Texas A & M 0
1958, Dec. 27—Mississippi 7, Florida 3
1960, Jan. 2—Arkansas 14, Georgia Tech 7
1960, Dec. 31—Florida 13, Baylor 12
1961, Dec. 30—Penn State 30, Georgia Tech 15
1962, Dec. 29—Florida 17, Penn State 7
1963, Dec. 28—North Carolina 35, Air Force Academy 0 (50,018)
1965, Jan. 2—Fla. State 36, Okla. 19 (50,408)
1965, Dec. 31—Ga. Tech 31, Texas Tech 21 (60,127)
1966, Dec. 31—Tennessee 18, Syracuse 12 (60,312)
1967, Dec. 30—Penn State 17, Florida State 17 (68,019)

### OTHER GAMES OF POST-1967 FOOTBALL SEASON

**Orange Blossom Classic,** Miami, Fla., Dec. 2—Grambling 28, Florida A & M 25. **Camellia Bowl,** Sacramento, Calif., Dec. 9—San Diego State 27, San Francisco State 6. **NAIA Bowl,** Morgantown, W. Va., Dec. 9—Fairmont State 28, Eastern Washington State 21. **Liberty Bowl,** Memphis, Tenn., Dec. 16—North Carolina State 14, Georgia 7. **Tangerine Bowl,** Orlando, Fla., Dec. 16—Tennessee (Martin Branch) 25, West Chester (Pa.) 8. **Pecan Bowl,** Abilene, Tex., Dec. 16—Texas (Arlington) 13, North Dakota State 0. **Bluebonnet Bowl,** Houston Tex., Dec. 23—Colorado 31, Miami (Fla.) 21. **All Star Shrine Game,** Miami, Fla., Dec. 25—North 24, South 0. **Senior Bowl,** Mobile, Ala., Jan. 6—South 34, North 21. **Hula Bowl,** Honolulu, Hawaii, Jan. 6—North 50, South 6.

# College Football Coach of the Year

**(Football Writers Assn.)**

| Year | Coach | School | Year | Coach | School |
|---|---|---|---|---|---|
| 1946 | Earl Blaik | Army | 1957 | Wayne Woodrow Hayes | Ohio State |
| 1947 | H. O. (Fritz) Crisler | Michigan | 1958 | Paul F. Dietzel | L.S.U. |
| 1948 | Bennie G. Oosterbaan | Michigan | 1959 | Floyd B. Schwartzwalder | Syracuse |
| 1949 | Charles B. (Bud) Wilkinson | Univ. of Okla. | 1960 | None picked | |
| 1950 | Charles Caldwell | Princeton | 1961 | Paul Bryant | Alabama |
| 1951 | Charles (Chuck) Taylor | Stanford | 1962 | John McKay | U. S. C. |
| 1952 | Clarence L. (Biggie) Munn | Mich. State | 1963 | Darrell Royal | Texas |
| 1953 | James M. Tatum | Maryland | 1964 | Ara Parseghian | Notre Dame |
| 1954 | Henry R. (Red) Sanders | U.C.L.A. | 1965 | Tommy Prothro | U. C. L. A. |
| 1955 | Hugh Duffy Daugherty | Mich. State | 1966 | Tom Cahill | Army |
| 1956 | Bowden Wyatt | Tennessee | 1967 | John Pont | Indiana |

# College Football Scores in 1968

## SCORES, NICKNAMES AND COLORS OF LEADING AMERICAN COLLEGES

### *Results not available for inclusion in this edition

**ADELBERT**
Red Cats
*Red and White*
0—Allegheny ......16
11—Grove City ......14
24—Wash. & Jeff....20
13—John Carroll....23
6—Bethany ........24
0—Thiel ...........40
7—Carne-Mellon ...28
7—Case Tech .......2

**AIR FORCE**
Falcons
*Silver and Blue*
20—Florida .........23
10—Wyoming ........3
13—Stanford .......24
26—Navy ...........20
31—Colo. St. Univ...0
27—Pittsburgh .....14
25—No. Carolina ...15
10—Arizona ........14
28—Tulsa ..........8
58—Colorado .......35

**AKRON**
Zips
*Blue and Gold*
32—Butler ..........7
41—Indiana State ..13
9—Tampa ..........24
7—Eastern Mich. ..16
27—Bradley ........13
31—Eastern Kentucky 20
46—Illinois State ...0
59—Baldwin-Wallace .0
14—W. Kentucky ...14
42—Youngstown ....13

**ALABAMA**
Crimson Tide
*Crimson and White*
14—Va. Tech. ......7
17—Southern Miss. ..14
8—Mississippi .....10
31—Vanderbilt .......7
7—Tennessee ......10
21—Clemson .......14
20—Miss. St. ......13
16—L.S.U. .........7
16—Miami (Fla.) ...6
*Nov. 30—Auburn

**ALBRIGHT**
Lions
*Red and White*
9—Lycoming .......0
14—Juniata ........7
7—Springfield .....30
21—Gettysburg ....20
10—Dela. Valley ...6
28—Drexel Tech. ...0
12—Moravian ......9
7—Lebanon Valley ..0
28—Upsala .........7

**ALFRED**
Saxons
*Purple and Gold*
17—Brockport St. ...0
0—C. W. Post .....34
16—St. Lawrence ...0
7—Hobart .........14
7—Rochester ......33
28—Cortland St. ...45
7—Union ..........21

**ALLEGHENY**
Gators
*Blue and Gold*
16—Adelbert ........0
29—Bethany .......24
14—John Carroll ...13
18—C'rnegie-Mell'n .48
40—Wash. & Jeff. ..20
60—Case Tech .....18
35—Thiel ..........32
42—Rochester ......0

**AMERICAN INT'L**
Yellow Jackets
*Gold and White*
27—Coast Guard ...14
7—Amherst .......34
13—Northeastern ...30
50—Bates ..........19
14—Springfield ....14
14—Cent. Conn. St. ..14
40—South'n Conn. ..22
28—Bridgeport .....31

**AMHERST**
Lord Jeffs
*Purple and White*
14—Springfield ....28
34—Amer Int'l .....7
33—Bowdoin ........3
26—Rochester ......0
58—Wesleyan ......13
42—Tufts ..........6
31—Trinity ........3
24—Williams .......17

**ARIZONA**
Wildcats
*Red and Blue*
21—Iowa St. .......12
19—New Mexico ....14
25—Tex., El Paso ...0
19—Brigham Young ..3
13—Indiana .......16
28—Wash. St. .....14
14—Air Force ......10
16—Utah ..........15
14—Wyoming .......7
*Nov. 30—Arizona St.

**ARIZONA STATE**
Sun Devils
*Maroon and Gold*
55—Wisconsin .......7
31—Texas, El Paso ..19
13—Wyoming .......27
41—Washington State 14
9—Oregon St. .....28
63—New Mexico ....18
59—Utah ..........21
47—Brigham Young ..12
66—San Jose St. ....0
*Nov. 30—Arizona

**ARKANSAS**
Razorbacks
*Cardinal and White*
32—Okla. St. .......15
56—Tulsa ..........13
17—Texas Christian ..7
35—Baylor .........19
29—Texas .........39
17—No. Texas St. ...15
25—Texas A.&M. ...22
46—Rice ...........21
35—S. M. U. .......29
42—Texas Tech ......7

**ARMY**
Cadets
*Black, Gold and Grey*
34—The Citadel ....14
13—Vanderbilt .....17
3—Missouri ........7
10—California ......7
24—Rutgers ........0
57—Duke ..........25
24—Penn St. ......28
58—Boston Coll. ...25
26—Pittsburgh ......0
*Nov. 30—Navy

**AUBURN**
Tigers
*Orange and Blue*
28—S. M. U. .......37
26—Miss. St. .......0
26—Kentucky ........7
21—Clemson .......10
20—Georgia Tech. ..21
14—Miami (Fla.) ....6
24—Florida ........13
28—Tenn. .........14
3—Georgia ........17
*Nov. 30—Alabama

**BALDWIN-WALLACE**
Yellow Jackets
*Brown and Gold*
14—Findlay .........0
48—UW Milwaukee ..8
26—Youngstown .....6
68—Oberlin .........0
49—Otterbein .......0
14—Wittenberg .....7
26—Ohio Wesleyan ..20
19—Akron .........59
28—Ohio Northern ...0

**BALL STATE**
Cardinal and White
20—Northern Ill. ...40
8—Bowling Green ..62
26—Valparaiso .....11
26—Evansville ......7
7—Eastern Mich. ..43
17—DePauw ........12
24—Butler .........21
14—Indiana St. ....20
46—St. Joseph's .....6

**BATES**
Bobcats
*Garnet*
18—Middlebury ......0
32—Norwich ........7
19—Trinity (Conn.) ..48
20—Worcester Tech. .30
19—Amer. Int'l .....50
52—Acadia ..........4
14—Bowdoin ........0
21—Colby .........12
43—Bridgewater St. ..7

**BAYLOR**
Bears
*Green and Gold*
36—Indiana ........40
10—Michigan St. ...28
16—L. S. U. .......48
19—Arkansas .......35
10—Texas A.&M. ....7
14—T. C. U. .......47
26—Texas .........47
42—Texas Tech. ....28
17—S. M. U. .......33
*Nov. 30—Rice

**BOSTON COLLEGE**
Eagles
*Maroon and Gold*
49—Navy ...........15
31—Buffalo ........15
28—Villanova ......15
14—Tulane .........28
0—Penn St. .......29
25—Army ..........58
45—V. M. I. .......13
21—Massachusetts ...6
*Nov. 30—Holy Cross

**BOSTON UNIV.**
Terriers
*Scarlet and White*
0—Colgate ........28
6—Maine ..........3
7—Temple .........7
21—Massachusetts ...7
7—Holy Cross ......7
33—Conn. .........23
6—Rhode Island ...7
13—Delaware .......11
10—Buffalo ........13

**BOWDOIN**
Polar Bears
*White*
10—Worcester Tech. .14
14—Wesleyan ......27
3—Amherst ........33
7—Williams .......14
17—Colby ..........9
41—Bates ..........14
6—Tufts ...........7

**BOWLING GREEN**
Falcons
*Orange and Brown*
62—Ball St. ........8
20—Dayton ........14
17—W. Michigan ...10
0—Toledo .........0
30—Kent St. .......7
7—Miami (O.) .....51
54—Marshall ......28
27—Ohio Univ. ....28
6—No. Illinois .....7
44—Xavier .........14

**BRADLEY**
Braves
*Red and White*
6—Central Mich. ...41
19—Evansville ......27
14—Western Ill. ....13
22—SE Missouri ....19
37—Eastern Ill. ....28
16—Wheaton ........7
0—Pensacola NAS ..35
21—UW Milwaukee ...7
26—Illinois State ...42

**BRIDGEPORT**
Purple Knights
*Purple and White*
8—Trenton St. ......7
19—Northeastern ...42
7—Cent. Conn. St. ..14
6—So. Conn. ......18
20—Montclair St. ...3
16—Hofstra ........30
16—Ithaca .........15
16—Glassboro St. ...6
31—Amer. Int'l .....28

**BRIGHAM YOUNG**
Cougars
*Royal Blue and White*
17—W. Michigan ....7
20—Iowa St. .......28
17—Wyoming .......20
3—Arizona ........19
25—Texas, El Paso ..31
21—Utah ..........30
8—Utah St. .......34
12—Arizona St. ....47
35—New Mexico .....6
*Nov. 30—San Jose St.

**BROWN**
Bruins
*Seal Brown and White*
10—Rhode Island ....9
13—Pennsylvania ...17
13—Yale ..........35
0—Dartmouth ......48
27—Colgate ........19
7—Princeton ......50
0—Cornell ........31
7—Harvard ........31
20—Columbia .......46

**BUCKNELL**
Bisons
*Orange and Blue*
22—Davidson .......13
10—Penn ..........27
0—Harvard ........59
29—Temple ........26
7—Gettysburg .....12
13—Lafayette ......10
42—Maine ..........21
34—Colgate ........38
31—Lehigh ........27
12—Delaware .......38

**BUFFALO**
Bulls
*Royal Blue and White*
10—Iowa St. .......28
21—Kent St. .......13
23—Massachusetts ...0
12—Boston Coll. ...31
29—Delaware .......17
7—Villanova ......28
10—Holy Cross ......9
50—Temple ........40
20—North'n Ill. .....7
13—Boston Univ. ...10

**BUTLER**
Bulldogs
*Blue and White*
7—Akron ..........32
0—Western Ky. ...35
12—Indiana St. ....28
49—St. Joseph's ...14
7—Valparaiso .....10
7—Evansville ......44
21—Ball State .....24
7—De Pauw .......30
26—Wabash ........8

**CALIFORNIA**
Golden Bears
*Blue and Gold*
21—Michigan .......7
10—Colorado ........0
46—San Jose St. ....0
7—Army ..........10
39—U.C.L.A. .......15
43—Syracuse ........0
7—Washington ......0
17—So. Calif. ......35
36—Oregon ..........8
0—Stanford .......20
*Nov. 30—Hawaii

### CARLETON
### Carls
*Maize and Blue*
14—Monmouth ......20
8—Lawrence ...... 7
17—Coe .......... 6
13—Beloit ........35
7—St. Olaf ......38
6—Cornell Col. ..35
9—Ripon .........35
20—Knox ..........12

### CARNEGIE-MELLON
### Tartans
*Carnegie Plaid*
28—Thiel .........42
28—Oberlin .......28
6—Grove City ....10
48—Allegheny .....18
7—F. & M. ...... 6
38—Johns Hopkins .53
28—Adelbert ...... 0
26—Wash. & Jeff. . 9

### CASE INST. OF TECH
### Roughriders
*Brown and White*
14—Bethany .......69
7—John Carroll ..29
14—Thiel .........47
8—Wash. & Jeff. .31
6—Wilmington ....27
18—Allegheny .....60
2—Adelbert ...... 7

### CHATTANOOGA
### Moccasins
*Navy Blue and Gold*
41—Austin Peay ...13
32—Jacksonville ..14
28—Mid. Tenn. ....15
35—Wofford .......14
16—E. Tennessee .. 6
3—The Citadel ... 9
20—Tenn. Tech. ... 6
16—Mississippi ...33
31—Furman ........14
40—Samford ....... 7

### CINCINNATI
### Bearcats
*Red and Black*
10—Texas Tech ....10
7—Xavier ........14
33—Houston .......71
31—Tampa .........28
40—Wichita St. ...27
27—Tulsa .........28
34—No. Texas St. .55
37—Louisville .... 7
48—Ohio Univ. ....60
23—Miami (Ohio) ..21

### CITADEL
### Bulldogs
*Blue and White*
14—Army ..........34
28—Lehigh ........12
31—Furman ........12
16—Richmond ......21
13—V.M.I. ........ 8
9—Chattanooga ...31
3—Davidson ......17
0—West Virginia .17
24—Wm. & Mary ...21
14—East Carolina .23

### CLEMSON
### Tigers
*Purple and Orange*
20—Wake Forest ...20
13—Georgia .......31
21—Georgia Tech. .24
10—Auburn ........21
39—Duke ..........22
14—Alabama .......21
24—No. Caro. St. .19
16—Maryland ......21
24—North Carolina 14
3—South Carolina  7

### COAST GUARD
### Cadets
*Blue and White*
0—Springfield ...29
14—Amer. Int'l. ..27
22—Norwich .......26
26—Wesleyan ......23
7—Southwestern ..33
0—Worcester Tech 36
21—Trinity .......47
14—Rochester .....42
35—R. P. I. ......20
*Nov. 30—PMC Colleges

### COE
### Kohawks
*Crimson and Gold*
6—Lawrence .....42
6—Beloit ........ 7
6—Carleton ......17
19—St. Olaf ...... 6
33—Cornell Coll. .10
13—Ripon .........17
43—Knox ..........14
34—Grinnell ......28

### COLBY
### Mules
*Blue and Grey*
9—Norwich .......32
0—R.P.I. ........ 6
8—Northeastern ..38
7—Springfield ...14
6—Trinity .......35
0—Bowdoin .......17
0—Maine Maritime  6
12—Bates .........21

### COLGATE
### Red Raiders
*Maroon*
28—Boston U. ..... 0
0—Cornell .......17
14—Yale ..........49
14—Holy Cross .... 6
14—Princeton ..... 7
19—Brown .........21
27—Lehigh ........13
38—Bucknell ......34
10—Lafayette .....14
34—Rutgers .......55

### COLORADO
### Buffaloes
*Silver and Gold*
28—Oregon ........ 7
0—California ....10
28—Iowa St. ......18
14—Missouri ......27
37—Kansas St. ....14
41—Oklahoma ......27
14—Kansas ........27
17—Oklahoma St. ..34
0—Nebraska ......22
35—Air Force .....58

### COLORADO STATE
### Rams
*Green and Gold*
21—New Mex. ......13
0—Kansas St. ....21
12—No. Tex. St. ..17
13—Texas Tech ....43
37—Wichita St. ...15
0—Air Force .....31
0—Pacific .......31
14—Wyoming .......46
17—W. Texas St. .. 7
19—Texas (El Paso) 23

### COLUMBIA
### Lions
*Columbia Blue & White*
14—Lafayette .....36
16—Princeton .....24
14—Harvard .......44
7—Yale ..........29
17—Rutgers .......21
34—Cornell .......25
19—Dartmouth .....31
7—Pennsylvania .13
46—Brown .........20

### CONNECTICUT
### Huskies
*Flag Blue and White*
21—Vermont ....... 0
14—Yale ..........31
10—N. Hampshire ..17
18—Davidson ......30
29—Maine ......... 0
27—Massachusetts .20
23—Boston U. .....33
15—Rutgers .......27
35—Rhode Island .. 6
24—Holy Cross ....27

### CORNELL
### Big Red
*Carnelian and White*
17—Colgate ....... 0
17—Rutgers .......16
8—Pennsylvania .14
0—Harvard .......10
3—Yale ..........25
25—Columbia ......34
31—Brown ......... 9
6—Dartmouth .....27
13—Princeton .....41

### DARTMOUTH
### Indians
*Oak Green*
21—New Hamp. ..... 0
17—Holy Cross ....29
7—Princeton .....34
48—Brown ......... 0
7—Harvard .......22
27—Yale ..........47
31—Columbia ......19
27—Cornell ....... 6
21—Pennsylvania .26

### DAVIDSON
### Wildcats
*Red and Black*
13—Bucknell ......22
14—Richmond ......24
14—Virginia ......41
30—Connecticut ...18
28—Furman ........ 7
21—The Citadel ...28
17—V.M.I. ........21
24—Wofford ....... 9
20—Vanderbilt ....53

### DAYTON
### Flyers
*Red and Blue*
14—Kent St. ......10
57—St. Joseph's .. 0
14—Bowling Green .20
28—Louisville ....14
11—So. Illinois ..18
12—Ohio Univ. ....42
25—Xavier ........27
0—Miami (O) .....14
10—Toledo ........ 3
35—Temple ........17

### DELAWARE
### Blue Hens
*Blue and Gold*
35—Hofstra ....... 0
0—Villanova .....16
28—Massachusetts .23
17—Buffalo .......29
28—W. Chester St.  0
50—Temple ........27
14—Rutgers .......23
37—Lehigh ........13
41—Boston Univ. .13
38—Bucknell ......12

### DENISON
### Big Red
*Red and White*
0—Calif. St. (Pa.) 36
21—Washington (Mo.) 12
28—Wabash ........12
3—Mt. Union ..... 6
0—Wooster .......28
23—Oberlin ....... 6
7—Muskingum .....13
6—Wittenberg ....48
8—Ohio Wesleyan .44

### DEPAUW
### Tigers
*Old Gold*
10—Wheaton ....... 6
20—St. Joseph's .. 6
3—Valparaiso .... 7
22—Evansville ....21
12—Ball State ....17
17—Centre ........10
30—Butler ........ 7
17—Indiana State .41
18—Wabash ........ 7

### DICKINSON
### Red Devils
*Red and White*
6—Leb. Valley ...49
11—Swarthmore ....21
37—Haverford .....13
7—F. & M. .......24
0—Muhlenberg ....48
0—Wilkes ........28
14—Ursinus .......47
6—Johns Hopkins .47

### DRAKE
### Bulldogs
*White and Blue*
30—Northern Ariz. 14
26—Wichita State .23
31—Quantico ......33
26—Wichita State .23
19—Northern Iowa .21
32—U. Neb. Omaha .14
0—Southern Ill. .21
28—South Dakota ..49
38—So. Dak. State 20
38—Louisville ....37

### DREXEL TECH
### Dragons
*Blue and Gold*
21—Lehigh ........59
7—Tufts .........28
23—Juniata .......20
0—R.P.I. ........10
0—Lafayette .....27
0—Albright ......28
35—PMC Colleges ..13
42—Western Md. ...14

### DUKE
### Blue Devils
*Royal Blue and White*
14—So. Carolina .. 7
10—Michigan ......31
30—Maryland ......28
20—Virginia ......50
22—Clemson .......39
25—Army ..........57
46—Ga. Tech. .....30
15—No. Caro. S. ..17
18—Wake Forest ... 3
14—No. Carolina ..25

### EAST CAROLINA
### Pirates
*Purple and Gold*
37—Parsons ....... 7
0—William & Mary 14
7—Louisiana Tech 35
0—So. Miss. .....65
7—Richmond ......31
24—Furman ........33
21—Tampa .........28
14—Marshall ......20
23—The Citadel ...14
*Nov. 30—E. Tenn. St.

### FLORIDA
### Gators
*Orange and Blue*
23—Air Force .....20
9—Florida State . 3
31—Mississippi St. 14
24—Tulane ........ 3
7—No. Carolina .22
14—Vanderbilt ....14
13—Auburn ........24
0—Georgia .......51
16—Kentucky ......14
*Nov. 30—Miami (Fla.)

### FLORIDA STATE
### Seminoles
*Garnet and Gold*
24—Maryland ......14
3—Florida ....... 9
20—Texas A. & M. .14
7—Memphis State .10
35—South Carolina 28
22—Virginia Tech .40
27—Miss. State ...14
48—No. Carolina State 7
42—Wake Forest ...24
*Nov. 29—Houston

### FRANKLIN & MARSHALL
### Diplomats
*Blue and White*
17—Ursinus ....... 0
17—Johns Hopkins . 6
12—Swarthmore .... 3
24—Dickinson ..... 7
6—Carn.-Mellon .. 7
19—Lebanon Valley 17
31—Haverford ..... 0
13—Muhlenberg ....18

### FRESNO STATE
### Bulldogs
*Cardinal and Blue*
23—Idaho State ...38
21—San Jose State 25
30—Portland State 14
35—San Fern. State 12
17—Cal Poly (SLO)  0
42—L. A. State ...20
12—San Diego State 42
34—Long Beach St. 28
37—Montana State .16
10—Pacific ....... 7

### FURMAN
### Paladin
*Purple and White*
12—Miss. Coll. ...21
13—Presbyterian .. 9
7—Wofford .......13
12—The Citadel ...31
0—Richmond ......34
7—Davidson ......28
13—E. Carolina ...24
12—Samford .......17
14—Chattanooga ...31
*Nov. 28—Wofford

## GENEVA
### Golden Tornadoes
*Gold and White*
7—Frostburg State .. 7
7—Clarion State ....42
7—Westminster ....27
6—Juniata ..........33
0—Waynesburg .....49
0—Grove City ......9
7—Edinboro State ..31
12—Bridgewater St. ..17

## GEORGIA
### Bulldogs
*Red and Black*
17—Tennessee .......17
31—Clemson .........13
21—South Carolina ..20
21—Mississippi .....7
32—Vanderbilt ......6
35—Kentucky ........14
10—Houston .........10
51—Florida .........0
17—Auburn ..........3
*Nov. 30—Georgia Tech

## GEORGIA TECH
### Yellow Jackets
*White and Old Gold*
17—T. C. U. .........6
7—Miami (Fla.) ....10
24—Clemson .........21
7—Tennessee .......24
21—Auburn ..........20
23—Tulane ..........19
30—Duke ............46
15—Navy ............35
6—Notre Dame .....34
*Nov. 30—Georgia

## GETTYSBURG
### Bullets
*Orange and Blue*
10—Hofstra .........26
8—Kings Point .....26
21—C. W. Post ......22
22—Tufts ...........28
20—Albright ........21
12—Bucknell ........0
13—Lehigh ..........34
0—Lafayette ......37
11—Temple ..........30

## GRAMBLING
### Tigers
*Black and Gold*
13—Alcorn A & M ...9
7—Morgan State ...8
22—Prairie View ...14
30—Tennessee State .21
28—Mississippi Valley 13
33—Jackson State ...33
28—Texas Southern ..18
46—Ark. A.M.&N. ...20
37—Wiley ...........6
34—Southern U. ....32
*Nov. 30—Sugar Cup Classic

## GROVE CITY
### Wolverines
*Crimson and White*
20—Brockport .......12
13—Adrian ..........33
14—Adelbert ........11
10—Carnegie-Mellon .6
7—Thiel ...........13
42—Geneva ..........0
32—Hobart ..........27
10—Bethany .........7

## HAMILTON
### Continentals
*Buff and Blue*
6—Rochester ......14
35—R. P. I. ........32
10—Hobart ..........12
18—Middlebury ......14
6—St. Lawrence ...14
8—Wesleyan ........10
12—Kenyon ..........9
13—Union ...........22

## HARVARD
### The Crimson
*Crimson*
27—Holy Cross ......20
59—Bucknell ........0
21—Columbia ........14
10—Cornell .........0
22—Dartmouth .......14
28—Pennsylvania ...6
7—Princeton ......7
31—Brown ...........24
29—Yale ............29

## HAVERFORD
### Fords
*Scarlet and Black*
6—Muhlenberg .....32
13—Dickinson .......37
0—Johns Hopkins ..42
6—Juniata .........58
0—F. & M. .........31
13—Ursinus .........53
17—Swarthmore .....6

## HOBART
### Statesmen
*Purple and Orange*
6—Upsala ..........7
6—St. Lawrence ...42
12—Hamilton ........10
14—Alfred ..........7
6—Union ...........14
27—Grove City ......32
21—R. P. I. ........7
0—Muskingum ......6

## HOFSTRA
### Flying Dutchmen
*Blue and Gold*
26—Gettysburg ......10
0—Delaware ........35
34—Albion ..........14
0—Lafayette ......7
12—Temple ..........20
30—Bridgeport ......16
9—Kings Point ....13
7—Maine ...........42
26—Wagner ..........7
*Nov. 28—C. W. Post

## HOLY CROSS
### Crusaders
*Royal Purple*
20—Harvard .........27
29—Dartmouth .......17
6—Colgate .........14
9—Boston U. ......7
9—Buffalo .........10
6—Syracuse ........47
47—Massachusetts ..13
14—Rutgers .........41
27—Connecticut ....24
*Nov. 30—Boston College

## HOUSTON
### Cougars
*Scarlet and White*
54—Tulane ..........7
20—Texas ...........20
71—Cincinnati ......33
17—Oklahoma State ..21
29—Mississippi .....7
10—Georgia .........10
27—Memphis State ..7
77—Idaho ...........3
100—Tulsa ...........6
*Nov. 29—Florida State

## IDAHO
### Vandals
*Silver and Gold*
14—Montana State ..17
7—Washington State 14
35—Idaho State .....15
31—Pacific (Calif.) ..14
56—Montana .........45
8—Oregon .........23
7—Washington .....37
50—Weber State .....42
35—San Jose State ..17
3—Houston ........77

## IDAHO STATE
### Bengals
*Orange and Black*
52—Portland State ..30
38—Fresno State ....23
15—Idaho ...........35
14—Montana State ..31
23—Montana .........13
16—Weber State .....23
20—Boise ...........27
22—So. Dakota State 41
16—Neb. (Omaha) ...13

## ILLINOIS
### Fighting Illini
*Orange and Blue*
7—Kansas ..........47
0—Missouri ........44
10—Indiana .,.......28
10—Minnesota ......17
0—Notre Dame .....58
24—Ohio State ......31
17—Purdue ..........35
0—Michigan .......36
14—Northwestern ...0
13—Iowa ...........37

## INDIANA
### Fightin' Hoosiers
*Cream and Crimson*
40—Baylor ..........36
20—Kansas ..........38
28—Illinois ........14
38—Iowa ...........34
22—Michigan ........27
16—Arizona .........13
21—Wisconsin .......20
24—Michigan State ..22
6—Minnesota ......20
35—Purdue ..........38

## IOWA
### Hawkeyes
*Gold and Black*
21—Oregon State ...20
17—T. C. U. ........28
28—Notre Dame .....51
34—Indiana .........38
41—Wisconsin .......0
14—Purdue ..........44
35—Minnesota ......28
68—Northwestern ...34
27—Ohio State ......33
37—Illinois ........13

## IOWA STATE
### Cyclones
*Cardinal and Gold*
28—Buffalo .........10
12—Arizona .........21
28—Brigham Young ..20
18—Colorado ........28
23—Kansas State ...14
7—Oklahoma .......42
25—Kansas ..........46
13—Nebraska .......54
7—Missouri .......42
17—Oklahoma State .26

## ITHACA
### Bombers
*Blue and Gold*
6—W. Chest. State .28
6—Cent. Conn. State 37
21—Cortland State ..34
21—Susquehanna ....34
19—Wilkes ..........28
14—C. W. Post .....27
15—Bridgeport .....13
17—Monticello State .13

## JACKSON STATE
### Tigers
*Blue and White*
8—Prairie View ...10
6—Alcorn A & M ...30
14—Arkansas AM&N ..15
16—Southern Univ. ..30
33—Grambling .......35
23—Wiley ...........7
0—Texas Southern .14
21—Bishop ..........15
32—Miss. Valley ...7

## JOHN CARROLL
### Blue Streaks
*Blue and Gold*
30—Wash. & Jeff. ...8
29—Case Tech ......7
13—Allegheny .......14
0—Ashland ........45
23—Adelbert .......3
22—Betheny (W. Va.) 13
14—Findlay .........20
6—Thiel ..........12

## JOHNS HOPKINS
### Blue Jays
*Gold and Sable*
30—Muhlenberg .....28
6—F. & M. .........27
35—Ursinus .........20
42—Haverford .......0
13—Rand-Macon .....28
53—Carnegie-Mellon .38
34—Swarthmore .....15
47—Dickinson .......6
46—West. Maryland .23

## JUNIATA
### Indians
*Blue and Gold*
35—Westminster ....27
7—Albright .......14
20—Drexel Tech ....23
33—Geneva ..........6
7—Lycoming .......7
58—Haverford .......6
45—Susquehanna ....8
55—St. Lawrence ...0
27—Moravian ........20

## KANSAS
### Jayhawks
*Crimson and Blue*
47—Illinois ........7
28—Indiana .........20
68—New Mexico .....7
23—Nebraska .......13
49—Oklahoma State .14
46—Iowa State Univ. 25
27—Colorado ........14
23—Oklahoma .......27
38—Kansas State ...29
21—Missouri .......19

## KANSAS STATE
### Wildcats
*Purple and White*
21—Colo. State U. ..0
9—Penn State .....25
34—Virginia Tech ..19
14—Iowa State .....23
14—Colorado ........37
20—Missouri .......56
20—Oklahoma .......35
12—Nebraska .......0
24—Kansas ..........38
14—Oklahoma State .14

## KENT STATE
### Golden Flashes
*Blue and Gold*
10—Dayton ..........24
13—Buffalo .........21
7—Ohio Univ. .....31
0—Miami (O.) .....24
0—W. Michigan ....14
7—Bowling Green ..30
12—Toledo ..........28
9—Louisville .....23
36—Marshall ........12
7—Xavier ..........23

## KENTUCKY
### Wildcats
*Blue and White*
12—Missouri ........6
14—Mississippi .....30
7—Auburn ..........26
35—Oregon State ...34
3—L. S. U. .......13
14—Georgia .........35
0—W. Virginia ....16
0—Vanderbilt .....6
14—Florida .........16
7—Tennessee ......24

## KINGS POINT
### Mariners
*Blue and Gold*
26—Gettysburg .....8
31—Adelphi ........0
19—Union ..........13
37—Army "B" .......7
16—C. W. Post .....7
7—Wagner .........7
13—Hofstra .........9
0—Lafayette ......7
43—Jersey City State 7

## LAFAYETTE
### Leopards
*Maroon and White*
7—Rutgers ........37
36—Columbia ........14
7—Hofstra .........0
27—Washington & Lee 7
27—Drexel Tech ....0
10—Bucknell ........13
37—Gettysburg .....0
7—Kings Point ....0
14—Colgate .........10
6—Lehigh .........21

## LEBANON VALLEY
### Flying Dutchmen
*Blue and White*
49—Dickinson .......6
28—Ursinus .........6
39—Muhlenberg .....29
7—Moravian .......28
17—F. & M. .........19
0—Albright .......6
16—Wilkes ..........23
21—PMC Colleges ...6

## LEHIGH
### Engineers
*Brown and White*
59—Drexel Tech ....21
12—The Citadel .....28
14—Wittenberg .....37
26—Rutgers .........29
0—Penn ...........34
34—Gettysburg .....13
35—Delaware ........37
27—Bucknell .......13
21—Lafayette ......6

## LOUISIANA STATE
### Fighting Tigers
*Purple and Gold*
13—Texas A. & M. ...12
21—Rice .........7
48—Baylor .........16
0—Miami (Fla.) ...30
13—Kentucky .........3
10—T. C. U. .........7
24—Mississippi .........27
7—Alabama .........16
20—Mississippi State 16
34—Tulane .........10

## LOUISVILLE
### Cardinals
*Cardinal Red and Black*
33—So. Illinois ......10
14—Dayton .........28
16—Tulsa .........7
13—Marshall .........8
21—Wichita State ...14
23—Kent State .........9
7—Cincinnati .........37
14—No. Texas State .36
37—Drake .........38
*Nov. 30—Memphis St.

## LYCOMING
### Warriors
*Blue and Gold*
0—Albright .........9
10—Wagner .........7
3—Delaware Valley .39
29—W. Maryland ...37
7—Juniata .........22
13—Susquehanna ...17
8—Upsala .........39
13—Muhlenberg ...21

## MAINE
### Black Bears
*Blue and White*
3—Massachusetts ...21
3—Boston Univ. ...6
28—Vermont .........7
17—New Hampshire .42
0—Connecticut .........29
21—Rhode Island ...14
21—Bucknell .........42
42—Hofstra .........7

## MARSHALL
### Thundering Herd
*Green and White*
7—Morehead State .7
8—Ohio Univ. .........38
12—Toledo .........35
20—Xavier .........6
0—Miami (O.) .........46
5—Louisville .........13
12—W. Michigan ...40
52—Bowling Green ...7
12—Kent State .........36
0—East Carolina ...49

## MARYLAND
### Terrapins
*Black and Gold*
14—Florida State ...24
14—Syracuse .........32
3—Duke .........20
33—North Carolina ...24
21—South Carolina ...19
11—No. Caro. State .31
14—Wake Forest ...38
0—Clemson .........16
13—Penn State .........57
23—Virginia .........28

## MASSACHUSETTS
### Redmen
*Maroon and White*
21—Maine .........3
0—Buffalo .........23
23—Delaware .........14
7—Boston Univ. ...21
9—Rhode Island ...7
0—Connecticut .........27
49—Vermont .........0
13—Holy Cross .........47
0—New Hampshire .13
6—Boston College ...21

## MEMPHIS STATE
### Tigers
*Blue and Grey*
7—Mississippi .........21
17—Tennessee .........24
30—No. Texas State .12
42—W. Texas State ...7
10—Florida State ...20
29—So. Mississippi ...9
32—Tulsa .........6
7—Houston .........23
40—Wichita State ...18
*Nov. 30 Louisville

## MIAMI (FLA.)
### Hurricanes
*Orange, Green & White*
28—Northwestern ...7
10—Georgia Tech ...7
3—So. California ...28
30—L. S. U. .........0
13—Virginia Tech ...8
6—Auburn .........31
48—Pittsburgh .........0
7—Penn State .........22
6—Alabama .........14
*Nov. 30—Florida

## MIAMI (OHIO)
### Redskins
*Red and White*
28—Xavier (Ohio) ...7
20—Pacific .........21
28—W. Michigan ...0
34—Kent State .........0
46—Marshall .........0
7—Ohio Univ. .........24
31—Bowling Green ...7
21—Toledo .........17
14—Dayton .........0
21—Cincinnati .........23

## MICHIGAN
### Wolverines
*Maize and Blue*
7—California .........21
31—Duke .........10
32—Navy .........9
28—Michigan State .14
27—Indiana .........22
33—Minnesota .........20
35—Northwestern ...0
36—Illinois .........0
34—Wisconsin .........9
14—Ohio State .........50

## MICHIGAN STATE
### Spartans
*Green and White*
14—Syracuse .........10
28—Baylor .........10
39—Wisconsin .........0
14—Michigan .........28
13—Minnesota .........14
21—Notre Dame ...17
20—Ohio State .........25
22—Indiana .........24
0—Purdue .........9
31—Northwestern ...14

## MIDDLEBURY
### Panthers
*Blue and White*
0—Bates .........18
40—Wesleyan .........42
20—Worcester Tech ...25
14—Williams .........48
14—Hamilton .........18
35—R. P. I. .........0
24—Norwich .........24
18—Vermont .........49

## MINNESOTA
### Gophers
*Maroon and Gold*
20—So. California ...29
14—Nebraska .........17
24—Wake Forest ...19
17—Illinois .........10
14—Michigan State ...13
20—Michigan .........33
28—Iowa .........35
27—Purdue .........13
20—Indiana .........6
23—Wisconsin .........15

## MISSISSIPPI
### Rebels
*Cardinal Red & Navy Blue*
21—Memphis State ...7
30—Kentucky .........14
10—Alabama .........8
7—Georgia .........21
21—So. Mississippi .13
17—Houston .........29
27—L. S. U. .........24
33—Chattanooga ...16
0—Tennessee .........31
*30—Mississippi State

## MISSISSIPPI STATE
### Bulldogs
*Maroon and White*
13—Louisiana Tech .20
0—Auburn .........26
14—Florida .........3
14—So. Mississippi .47
28—Texas Tech .........28
17—Tampa .........24
13—Alabama .........20
14—Florida State ...27
16—LSU .........20
*Nov. 30—Mississippi

## MISSOURI
### Tigers
*Old Gold and Black*
6—Kentucky .........12
44—Illinois .........0
7—Army .........3
27—Colorado .........14
16—Nebraska .........14
56—Kansas State ...20
42—Oklahoma State .7
42—Iowa State .........7
14—Oklahoma .........28
19—Kansas .........21

## MONTANA
### Grizzlies
*Copper, Silver, Gold*
37—North Dakota .12
0—South Dakota ...21
58—Portland State ...0
3—Utah State .........50
45—Idaho .........56
13—Idaho State .........23
24—Montana State ...29
16—Weber State ...20
0—Northern Arizona.18

## MONTANA STATE
### Bobcats
*Blue and Gold*
17—Idaho .........14
17—Portland State ...6
22—San Diego State .34
20—West Texas State.35
31—Idaho State .........14
14—Weber State ...20
20—Northern Ariz. ...15
29—Montana .........24
41—North Dakota ...7
16—Fresno State ...37

## MONTCLAIR STATE
### Indians
*Scarlet and White*
14—Cortland State ...21
14—Delaware State ...34
58—Curry (Mass.) ...6
6—Cent. Conn. State 3
3—Bridgeport .........20
10—So. Conn. St. ...36
7—Trenton State ...15
3—Ithaca .........17
20—Glassboro State ...27

## MORAVIAN
### Greyhounds
*Blue and Grey*
7—Delaware Valley .22
0—Wilkes .........40
6—Wagner .........20
2—PMC Coll. .........7
28—Lebanon Valley .7
9—Albright .........12
27—Upsala .........9
20—Juniata .........27
47—Muhlenberg ...15

## MORGAN STATE
### Bears
*Blue and Orange*
27—N. C. College ...7
19—Maryland State ..18
24—Virginia Union ...0
38—Delaware State .3
6—No. Caro. A&T ...7
46—Hampton .........14
34—Norfolk State ...7
25—Virginia State ...0

## MUHLENBERG
### Mules
*Cardinal and Grey*
28—Johns Hopkins .30
32—Haverford .........6
29—Lebanon Valley .39
45—Ursinus .........6
48—Dickinson .........6
55—Swarthmore ...6
21—Lycoming .........13
18—Frank. & Marsh. 13
15—Moravian .........47

## NAVY
### Midshipmen
*Navy Blue and Gold*
6—Penn State .........31
15—Boston College ...49
9—Michigan .........32
20—Air Force .........16
17—Pittsburgh .........26
0—Virginia .........24
14—Notre Dame ...45
35—Georgia Tech ...15
6—Syracuse .........44
*Nov. 30—Army

## NEBRASKA
### Cornhuskers
*Scarlet and Cream*
13—Wyoming .........10
31—Utah .........9
17—Minnesota .........14
13—Kansas .........23
17—Missouri .........16
21—Oklahoma State .0
24—Iowa State .........13
0—Kansas State ...12
22—Colorado .........6
0—Oklahoma .........47

## NEVADA
### Wolf Pack
*Blue and Silver*
13—Williamette .........40
17—UC Santa Barb'ra 13
48—San Francisco ...23
15—Chicago State ...0
7—Hayward State .7
14—Sacramento State 17
17—Humboldt State ...20
24—UC Davis .........25
21—San Francisco St. 7
0—Hawaii .........21

## NEW HAMPSHIRE
### Wildcats
*Blue and White*
0—Dartmouth .........21
17—Connecticut .........10
42—Maine .........17
10—Vermont .........12
26—Northeastern ...3
27—Rhode Island ...7
17—Springfield .........10
16—Massachusetts ...0

## NEW MEXICO
### Lobos
*Cherry and Silver*
13—Colorado State U. .21
5—Texas, El Paso ...44
8—Arizona .........19
7—Kansas .........68
7—Utah .........30
24—San Jose State ...55
6—Wyoming .........35
28—Arizona State ...63
6—New Mexico State 33
6—Brigham Young ...35

## NEW MEXICO STATE
### Aggies
*Crimson and White*
12—Utah State .........28
20—No. Texas State ...47
21—Texas (Arl.) ...20
16—Lamar Tech ...14
14—Texas (El Paso) ...30
27—No. Illinois .........13
14—West Texas State 23
47—Wichita State ...21
33—New Mexico ...6
*Nov. 28—La. Tech

## NORTH CAROLINA
### Tar Heels
*Carolina Blue & White*
6—No. Caro. State .38
27—South Carolina ...32
8—Vanderbilt .........7
24—Maryland .........33
22—Florida .........7
31—Wake Forest ...48
15—Air Force .........28
6—Virginia .........41
14—Clemson .........24
25—Duke .........14

## NO. CAROLINA STATE
### Wolfpack
*Red and White*
10—Wake Forest ...6
38—North Carolina ...6
14—Oklahoma .........28
11—S. M. U. .........35
36—South Carolina ...12
19—Virginia .........0
31—Maryland .........11
19—Clemson .........24
7—Duke .........15
7—Florida State ...48

## NORTHEASTERN
### Huskies
*Red and Black*
22—C. W. Post .........28
42—Bridgeport .........19
38—Colby .........8
30—American Intnl. ...7
10—Springfield .........7
3—New Hampshire .26
0—E. Michigan .........41
20—Cortlandt State ...17
41—Temple .........26

## N. TEXAS STATE
### Eagles
*Green and White*

| | |
|---|---|
| 47—New Mexico State | 20 |
| 17—Colo. State Univ. | 12 |
| 12—Memphis State | 30 |
| 17—No. Michigan | 3 |
| 20—Tulsa | 17 |
| 15—Arkansas | 17 |
| 55—Cincinnati | 34 |
| 34—Texas (El Paso) | 31 |
| 36—Louisville | 14 |
| 44—Wichita State | 6 |

## NORTHWESTERN
### Wildcats
*Purple and White*

| | |
|---|---|
| 7—Miami (Fla.) | 28 |
| 7—So. California | 24 |
| 6—Purdue | 43 |
| 7—Notre Dame | 27 |
| 21—Ohio State | 45 |
| 13—Wisconsin | 10 |
| 0—Michigan | 35 |
| 34—Iowa | 68 |
| 0—Illinois | 14 |
| 14—Michigan State | 31 |

## NORWICH
### Cadets
*Maroon and Gold*

| | |
|---|---|
| 32—Colby | 7 |
| 0—Bates | 32 |
| 26—Coast Guard | 22 |
| 13—Me. Maritime | 9 |
| 10—St. Lawrence | 6 |
| 7—Vermont | 20 |
| 24—Middlebury | 24 |
| 35—Worcester Tech | 12 |

## NOTRE DAME
### Fighting Irish
*Gold and Blue*

| | |
|---|---|
| 45—Oklahoma | 21 |
| 22—Purdue | 37 |
| 51—Iowa | 28 |
| 27—Northwestern | 7 |
| 58—Illinois | 8 |
| 17—Michigan State | 21 |
| 45—Navy | 14 |
| 56—Pittsburgh | 7 |
| 34—Georgia Tech | 6 |
| *Nov. 30—So. California | |

## OBERLIN
### Yeomen
*Crimson and Gold*

| | |
|---|---|
| 20—Hiram | 17 |
| 28—Carnegie-Mellon | 28 |
| 0—Baldwin-Wall. | 68 |
| 42—Lake Forest | 22 |
| 6—Denison | 23 |
| 16—Kenyon | 34 |
| 0—Ohio Wesleyan | 64 |
| 21—Wooster | 23 |

## OHIO STATE
### Buckeyes
*Scarlet and Grey*

| | |
|---|---|
| 35—S. M. U. | 14 |
| 21—Oregon | 6 |
| 13—Purdue | 0 |
| 45—Northwestern | 21 |
| 31—Illinois | 24 |
| 25—Michigan State | 20 |
| 43—Wisconsin | 8 |
| 33—Iowa | 27 |
| 50—Michigan | 14 |

## OHIO UNIV.
### Bobcats
*Green and White*

| | |
|---|---|
| 48—Marshall | 8 |
| 31—Kent State | 7 |
| 40—Toledo | 31 |
| 41—William & Mary | 7 |
| 24—Miami (O.) | 7 |
| 42—Dayton | 12 |
| 34—W. Michigan | 27 |
| 28—Bowling Green | 27 |
| 60—Cincinnati | 48 |
| 28—No. Illinois | 13 |

## OHIO WESLEYAN
### Battling Bishops
*Red and Black*

| | |
|---|---|
| 14—Albion | 7 |
| 35—Heidelberg | 7 |
| 43—Wooster | 7 |
| 19—Muskingum | 3 |
| 39—Wabash | 0 |
| 20—Baldwin-Wallace | 26 |
| 64—Oberlin | 0 |
| 24—Mt. Union | 11 |
| 44—Denison | 8 |

## OKLAHOMA
### Sooners
*Crimson and White*

| | |
|---|---|
| 21—N*tre Dame | 45 |
| 28—No. Caro. State | 14 |
| 28—Texas | 26 |
| 42—Iowa State | 7 |
| 27—Colorado | 41 |
| 35—Kansas State | 20 |
| 21—Kansas | 23 |
| 28—Missouri | 14 |
| 47—Nebraska | 0 |
| *Nov. 30—Oklahoma St. | |

## OKLAHOMA STATE
### Cowboys
*Orange and Black*

| | |
|---|---|
| 15—Arkansas | 32 |
| 3—Texas | 31 |
| 21—Houston | 17 |
| 14—Kansas | 49 |
| 20—Nebraska | 21 |
| 7—Missouri | 42 |
| 34—Colorado | 17 |
| 26—Iowa State U. | 17 |
| 14—Kansas State | 21 |
| *Nov. 30—Oklahoma | |

## OREGON
### Ducks
*Green and Yellow*

| | |
|---|---|
| 7—Colorado | 28 |
| 12—Stanford | 28 |
| 6—Ohio State | 21 |
| 3—Washington | 0 |
| 23—Idaho | 6 |
| 4—Utah | 8 |
| 13—So. California | 20 |
| 27—Washington State | 13 |
| 8—California | 36 |
| 19—Oregon State | 41 |

## OREGON STATE
### Beavers
*Orange and Black*

| | |
|---|---|
| 20—Iowa | 21 |
| 24—Utah | 14 |
| 35—Washington | 21 |
| 34—Kentucky | 35 |
| 28—Arizona State | 9 |
| 16—Washington State | 8 |
| 29—Stanford | 7 |
| 45—UCLA | 21 |
| 13—So. California | 17 |
| 41—Oregon | 19 |

## PACIFIC
### Tigers
*Orange and Black*

| | |
|---|---|
| 21—Miami (O.) | 20 |
| 7—W. Texas State | 23 |
| 14—Idaho | 31 |
| 30—Santa Clara | 22 |
| 13—Utah State | 7 |
| 31—Colo. State U. | 0 |
| 28—San Jose State | 0 |
| 27—Calif. (Santa Barb.) | 21 |
| 0—Stanford | 24 |
| 3—Fresno State | 10 |

## PENNSYLVANIA
### Quakers
*Red and Blue*

| | |
|---|---|
| 27—Bucknell | 10 |
| 17—Brown | 13 |
| 10—Cornell | 8 |
| 34—Lehigh | 0 |
| 19—Princeton | 14 |
| 6—Harvard | 28 |
| 13—Yale | 30 |
| 13—Columbia | 7 |
| 26—Dartmouth | 21 |

## PENN STATE
### Nittany Lions
*Blue and White*

| | |
|---|---|
| 31—Navy | 6 |
| 25—Kansas State | 9 |
| 31—West Virginia | 20 |
| 21—U. C. L. A. | 6 |
| 29—Boston College | 0 |
| 22—Miami (Fla.) | 7 |
| 57—Maryland | 13 |
| 65—Pittsburgh | 9 |
| *Dec. 7—Syracuse | |

## PMC COLLEGES
### Cadets
*Red, White, Yellow*

| | |
|---|---|
| 0—W. Maryland | 30 |
| 6—Upsala | 21 |
| 6—Moravian | 2 |
| 7—Trinity | 45 |
| 13—Drexel Tech | 35 |
| 0—Wilkes | 34 |
| 22—Swarthmore | 9 |
| 6—Lebanon Valley | 21 |
| *Nov. 30—Coast Guard | |

## PITTSBURGH
### Panthers
*Blue and Gold*

| | |
|---|---|
| 7—U. C. L. A. | 63 |
| 14—W. Virginia | 38 |
| 14—Wm. & Mary | 38 |
| 17—Syracuse | 50 |
| 16—Navy | 17 |
| 14—Air Force | 27 |
| 0—Miami (Fla.) | 48 |
| 7—Notre Dame | 56 |
| 0—Army | 26 |
| 9—Penn St. | 65 |

## PORTLAND STATE
### Vikings
*Green and White*

| | |
|---|---|
| 30—Idaho State | 52 |
| 16—Montana State | 17 |
| 0—Montana | 58 |
| 14—Fresno State | 30 |
| 12—Weber State | 28 |
| 19—Eastern Wash. | 13 |
| 27—Western Wash. | 20 |
| 20—San Fernando St. | 62 |
| 47—Simon Fraser | 16 |
| 13—Southern Oregon | 6 |

## PRINCETON
### Tigers
*Orange and Black*

| | |
|---|---|
| 14—Rutgers | 20 |
| 21—Columbia | 16 |
| 34—Dartmouth | 7 |
| 7—Colgate | 14 |
| 14—Penn | 19 |
| 50—Brown | 7 |
| 7—Harvard | 9 |
| 17—Yale | 42 |
| 41—Cornell | 13 |

## PURDUE
### Boiler Makers
*Old Gold and Black*

| | |
|---|---|
| 44—Virginia | 6 |
| 37—Notre Dame | 22 |
| 43—Northwestern | 6 |
| 0—Ohio St. | 13 |
| 28—Wake Forest | 27 |
| 44—Iowa | 14 |
| 35—Illinois | 17 |
| 9—Minnesota | 27 |
| 9—Michigan State | 0 |
| 38—Indiana | 35 |

## RPI
### Fightin' Engineers
*Red and White*

| | |
|---|---|
| 14—St. Lawrence | 10 |
| 6—Colby | 0 |
| 32—Hamilton | 35 |
| 14—Drexel Tech | 24 |
| 14—Union | 20 |
| 0—Middlebury | 35 |
| 14—Worcester Tech | 23 |
| 7—Hobart | 21 |
| 20—Coast Guard | 34 |

## RHODE ISLAND
### Rams
*Blue and White*

| | |
|---|---|
| 0—Temple | 28 |
| 9—Brown | 10 |
| 33—So. Conn. St. | 8 |
| 52—Vermont | 10 |
| 14—Massachusetts | 9 |
| 14—Maine | 21 |
| 6—N. Hampshire | 27 |
| 6—Boston Univ. | 20 |
| 6—Connecticut | 35 |

## RICE
### Owls
*Blue and Grey*

| | |
|---|---|
| 35—Washington | 35 |
| 7—L. S. U. | 21 |
| 0—Tennessee | 52 |
| 24—S. M. U. | 32 |
| 14—Texas | 38 |
| 15—Texas Tech | 38 |
| 21—Arkansas | 46 |
| 14—Texas A. & M. | 24 |
| 14—Texas Christian | 24 |
| *Nov. 30—Baylor | |

## RICHMOND
### Spiders
*Red and Blue*

| | |
|---|---|
| 14—Toledo | 31 |
| 0—W. Virginia | 17 |
| 21—The Citadel | 16 |
| 34—Furman | 14 |
| 31—E. Carolina | 7 |
| 35—V. M. I. | 0 |
| 18—Virginia Tech. | 31 |
| 33—So. Miss. | 0 |
| 31—Wm. & Mary | 6 |

## ROCHESTER
### Yellowjackets
*Yellow and Blue*

| | |
|---|---|
| 14—Hamilton | 6 |
| 6—Williams | 7 |
| 7—Union | 21 |
| 0—Amherst | 26 |
| 33—Alfred | 0 |
| 37—St. Lawrence | 7 |
| 42—C*ast Guard | 14 |
| 19—Allegheny | 42 |

## RUTGERS
### Scarlet Knights
*Scarlet*

| | |
|---|---|
| 37—Lafayette | 7 |
| 20—Princeton | 14 |
| 16—Cornell | 17 |
| 29—Lehigh | 26 |
| 0—Army | 24 |
| 28—Columbia | 17 |
| 23—Delaware | 14 |
| 27—Connecticut | 14 |
| 41—Holy Cross | 14 |
| 55—Colgate | 34 |

## SACRAMENTO STATE
### Hornets
*Green and Gold*

| | |
|---|---|
| 13—Calif. Poly | 7 |
| 26—C. P. Pomona | 13 |
| 13—Humboldt St. | 20 |
| 24—UC Davis | 7 |
| 13—San Fran. St. | 14 |
| 17—Nevada | 14 |
| 14—Chico St. | 0 |
| 16—Hayward St. | 14 |
| 76—San Francisco | 0 |
| 26—Calif. Western | 14 |

## ST. LAWRENCE
### Larries
*Scarlet and Brown*

| | |
|---|---|
| 10—R. P. I. | 14 |
| 6—Union | 7 |
| 42—Hobart | 6 |
| 0—Alfred | 16 |
| 0—Norwich | 10 |
| 13—Hamilton | 6 |
| 7—Rochester | 37 |
| 7—Juniata | 35 |

## SAN DIEGO STATE
### Aztecs
*Scarlet and Black*

| | |
|---|---|
| 23—U. Tex. Arlington | 18 |
| 40—Northern Ill. | 21 |
| 34—Montana State | 22 |
| 42—Tex. Southern | 23 |
| 37—L. A. State | 14 |
| 48—San Jose State | 6 |
| 42—Fresno State | 12 |
| 69—Southern Miss. | 7 |
| 13—Tennessee State | 13 |
| *Nov. 30—Utah State | |

## UNIV. SAN FRAN.
### Dons
*Green and Gold*

| | |
|---|---|
| 0—Oregon Tech | 0 |
| 0—Nevada Southern | 23 |
| 13—Nevada | 48 |
| 10—Redlands | 20 |
| 10—St. Mary's | 13 |
| 0—Loyola | 38 |
| 0—Hayward St. | 33 |
| 26—UC Riverside | 42 |
| 0—Sacramento St. | 76 |

## SAN JOSE STATE
### Spartans
*Gold and White*

| | |
|---|---|
| 20—Stanford | 68 |
| 25—Fresno St. | 21 |
| 0—California | 46 |
| 55—New Mexico | 24 |
| 6—San Diego St. | 48 |
| 0—Pacific (Calif.) | 28 |
| 17—Idaho | 35 |
| 0—Washington St. | 46 |
| 0—Arizona St. | 66 |
| *Nov. 30—Brigham Young | |

## SOUTH CAROLINA
### Fighting Gamecocks
*Garnet and Black*

| | |
|---|---|
| 7—Duke | 14 |
| 32—No. Carolina | 27 |
| 20—Georgia | 21 |
| 12—No. Caro. St. | 36 |
| 19—Maryland | 21 |
| 28—Florida St. | 35 |
| 49—Virginia | 28 |
| 34—Wake Forest | 21 |
| 6—Virginia Tech | 17 |
| 7—Clemson | 3 |

### SOUTH DAKOTA
**Coyotes**
*Vermillion and White*
28—Mankato St. .....14
21—Montana ..........0
17—North Dakota ...15
13—No. Dakota St. ..35
35—Morningside .....13
13—Northern Iowa ...7
49—Drake ...........28
33—Augustana .......0
35—Colorado St. ....14

### SO. DAKOTA STATE
**Jackrabbits**
*Yellow and Blue*
12—Weber State .....27
3—No. Dakota State 21
42—Morningside .....0
0—Northern Iowa ...38
16—North Dakota ....0
23—South Dakota ....55
23—Youngstown ......0
47—Augustana .......27
41—Idaho State .....22
20—Drake ...........28

### SO. CALIFORNIA
**Trojans**
*Cardinal and Gold*
29—Minnesota .......20
7—Northwestern ....7
21—Miami (Fla.) ....3
27—Stanford ........24
7—Washington ......0
20—Oregon .........13
35—California ......17
17—Oregon St. .....13
14—UCLA ...........16
*Nov. 30—Notre Dame

### SO. CONN. STATE
**Pioneers**
*Blue and White*
0—E. Michigan .....40
0—Trenton St. .....0
8—Rhode Island ...33
18—Bridgeport ......6
0—Glassboro St. ...0
36—Montclair St. ..10
20—C. W. Post .....21
22—American Intl. ..40
7—Cent. Conn. St. .6

### SOUTHERN ILLINOIS
**Salukis**
*Maroon and White*
10—Louisville ......0
3—Tulsa ..........30
24—Lamar Tech .....7
18—Dayton .........17
0—Drake ..........0
15—Youngstown .....18
3—Northern Mich. .20
20—Tampa .........23
68—Southwest Mo. ..6

### SMU
**Mustangs**
*Red and Blue*
37—Auburn .........28
14—Ohio St. .......35
35—No. Carol. St. .14
21—T. C. U. ......14
32—Rice ...........24
39—Texas Tech .....18
7—Texas .........38
36—Texas A. & M. .23
29—Arkansas ......35
33—Baylor .........17

### SOUTHERN MISS.
**Southerners**
*Black and Gold*
27—SE Louisiana ...15
14—Alabama ........17
65—E. Carolina ....0
47—Miss. St. ......14
13—Mississippi ....21
7—Memphis State ..29
20—Louisiana Tech. .0
7—San Diego St. ..68
7—Richmond .......33
21—Tampa ..........0

### SOUTHERN UNIV.
**Jaguars**
*Blue and Gold*
3—Texas Southern . 6
26—Prairie View ....0
27—Miss. Valley ....0
14—Arkansas AM&N ..24
30—Jackson State ..16
14—Alcorn A&M .....18
0—Tenn. State ....16
2—Wiley ..........0
14—Florida A&M ...33
32—Grambling ......34

### SPRINGFIELD
**Chiefs**
*Maroon and White*
29—Coast Guard .....0
28—Amherst ........14
30—Albright ........7
48—Colby ...........7
7—Northeastern ....0
14—Amer. Int'l .....0
28—Wagner ..........7
10—New Hampshire ..17
42—Tufts ...........3

### STANFORD
**Indians**
*Cardinal*
68—San Jose St. ...20
20—Oregon .........12
24—Air Force ......13
24—So. Calif. .....27
21—Wash. St. ......21
17—U. C. L. A. ....20
7—Oregon St. .....29
35—Washington .....20
24—Pacific .........0
20—California ......0

### SUSQUEHANNA
**Crusaders**
*Orange and Maroon*
27—Otterbein ......26
6—Western Md. ....32
13—Bloomsburg .....13
6—Ithaca .........21
9—Upsala .........16
15—Lycoming .......13
0—Juniata ........40
6—Wagner .........16
7—Delaware Valley .14

### SWARTHMORE
**Little Quakers**
*Garnet*
0—Wooster ........37
21—Dickinson ......11
3—F. & M. ........12
0—Ursinus ........28
6—Muhlenberg .....55
15—Johns Hopkins ..34
9—PMC Colleges ...22
6—Haverford ......17

### SYRACUSE
**Orangemen**
*Orange*
10—Michigan St. ...14
32—Maryland .......14
20—U. C. L. A. .....7
50—Pittsburgh .....17
0—California ......43
47—Holy Cross .....0
31—Wm. & Mary .....0
44—Navy ...........6
0—West Virginia ..23
*Dec. 7—Penn State

### TAMPA
**Spartans**
*Red, Gold, Black*
18—UC Santa Barbara 7
24—Akron ...........9
17—Tulane .........14
28—Cincinnati .....31
21—Eastern Mich. ...0
24—Mississippi St. .21
22—Northern Mich. .19
28—East Carolina ..21
23—Southern Ill. ..20
7—Southern Miss. .21

### TEMPLE
**Owls**
*Cherry and White*
28—Rhode Island ....0
26—Wayne St. ......6
0—Boston Univ. ....7
26—Bucknell .......29
16—Hofstra ........12
27—Delaware .......50
40—Buffalo ........50
30—Gettysburg .....11
26—Northeastern ...41
7—Dayton .........35

### TENNESSEE
**Volunteers**
*Orange and White*
17—Georgia ........17
24—Memphis St. ....17
52—Rice ...........0
24—Georgia Tech. ...7
10—Alabama .........9
42—U. C. L. A. ....18
14—Auburn .........28
31—Mississippi .....0
24—Kentucky .......7
*Nov. 30—Vanderbilt

### TENNESSEE STATE
**Tigers**
*Blue and White*
40—Kentucky State ..7
21—Parsons ........12
11—Texas Southern .10
22—Grambling ......30
13—Florida A&M ....32
16—Southern Univ. ..0
58—Morris Brown ...6
13—San Diego State .13

### TEXAS
**Longhorns**
*Orange and White*
20—Houston ........20
22—Texas Tech. ....31
31—Oklahoma St. ....3
26—Oklahoma .......20
39—Arkansas .......29
38—Rice ...........14
38—S. M. U. ........7
47—Baylor .........26
47—Texas Christian .21
*Nov. 28—Texas A&M

### TEXAS A&M
**Aggies**
*Maroon and White*
12—L. S. U. .......13
35—Tulane ..........3
14—Florida St. ....20
16—Texas Tech .....21
27—T. C. U. ........7
9—Baylor .........10
22—Arkansas .......25
23—SMU ............36
24—Rice ...........14
*Nov. 28—Texas

### TEXAS CHRISTIAN
**Horned Frogs**
*Purple and White*
7—Georgia Tech. ..17
28—Iowa ...........17
7—Arkansas .......17
14—S. M. U. .......21
7—Texas A&M ......27
7—L. S. U. .......10
47—Baylor .........14
14—Texas Tech. ....31
21—Texas ..........47
24—Rice ...........14

### U. TEXAS—EL PASO
**Miners**
*Orange and White*
14—Calif. (S. B.) ..14
44—New Mexico .....15
19—Arizona St. ....31
0—Arizona ........25
21—Long Beach St. .22
30—New Mexico St. .14
31—Brigham Young ...0
31—No. Texas State .34
19—Wyoming ........26
23—Colo. St. Univ. .19

### TEXAS TECH
**Red Raiders**
*Scarlet and Black*
10—Cincinnati .....10
31—Texas .........22
43—Colo. St. Univ. .13
21—Texas A. & M. ..16
28—Miss. State ....20
18—S. M. U. .......39
38—Rice ...........15
31—Texas Christian .14
28—Baylor .........42
7—Arkansas ......42

### THIEL
**Tomcats**
*Old Gold and Blue*
42—Carn.-Mellon ...28
34—Wash. & Jeff. ...6
47—Case Tech. .....14
13—Grove City ......7
14—Bethany ........23
40—Adelbert ........0
32—Allegheny ......35
12—John Carroll ....0

### TOLEDO
**Rockets**
*Blue and Gold*
31—Richmond .......14
45—Villanova ......21
35—Marshall .......12
31—Ohio U. ........40
0—Bowling Green ...0
30—W. Michigan .....6
17—Miami (Ohio) ...21
10—Xavier (Ohio) ..20
3—Dayton .........10

### TRINITY (CONN.)
**Bantams**
*Blue and Gold*
14—Williams .......31
48—Bates ..........19
7—Tufts ..........3
35—Colby ...........6
45—PMC Coll. .......7
47—Coast Guard ...21
3—Amherst ........31
19—Wesleyan .......17

### TUFTS
**Jumbos**
*Brown and Blue*
28—Drexel Tech .....7
28—Gettysburg .....22
3—Trinity .........7
17—Wagner .........10
30—Williams .......28
6—Amherst ........42
7—Bowdoin .........6
3—Springfield ....42

### TULANE
**Green Wave**
*Olive Green & Sky Blue*
7—Houston ........54
3—Texas A. & M. ..35
14—Tampa ..........17
3—Florida ........24
28—Boston Coll. ...14
19—Ga. Tech. ......23
7—Vanderbilt .....21
25—Tulsa ..........15
47—Virginia .......63
10—L. S. U. .......34

### TULSA
**Golden Hurricane**
*Blue, Crimson, Gold*
13—Arkansas .......56
30—So. Illinois ....3
7—Louisville .....16
17—No. Texas State .20
34—Cincinnati .....27
6—Memphis State ..32
15—Tulane .........25
8—Air Force ......28
6—Houston .......100
*Nov. 28—Wichita State

### UNION
**Dutchmen**
*Garnet*
7—St. Lawrence ....6
13—Kings Point ....19
21—Rochester .......7
24—R.P.I. .........14
1—Hobart .........6
17—Williams ........7
21—Alfred ..........7
22—Hamilton .......13

### UCLA
**Bruins**
*Navy Blue and Gold*
63—Pittsburgh ......7
31—Washington State 21
7—Syracuse .......20
6—Penn State .....21
15—California ......39
20—Stanford .......17
18—Tennessee ......42
21—Oregon State ...45
0—Washington ......6
16—So. California .28

### UPSALA
**Vikings**
*Blue and Grey*
7—Hobart ..........6
8—Wagner .........34
21—PMC Coll. .......6
16—Susquehanna .....9
7—Wilkes ..........9
39—Lycoming ........6
9—Moravian .......27
0—Albright .......28

### URSINUS
**Bears**
*Red, Old Gold, Black*
0—Frank. & Marsh. 17
6—Leb. Valley ....28
20—J. Hopkins .....35
6—Muhlenberg .....45
28—Swarthmore ......0
5—Delaware Valley .24
47—Dickinson ......14
35—Haverford ......13

## UTAH
**Redskins, Utes**
*Crimson and White*

| | |
|---|---|
| 0—Nebraska | 31 |
| 21—Oregon State | 24 |
| 17—Washington State | 14 |
| 30—New Mexico | 7 |
| 9—Wyoming | 20 |
| 6—Oregon | 14 |
| 30—Brigham Young | 21 |
| 21—Arizona State | 59 |
| 15—Arizona | 16 |
| 13—Utah State | 28 |

## UTAH STATE
**Aggies**
*Navy Blue and White*

| | |
|---|---|
| 28—New Mexico State | 12 |
| 3—Wyoming | 48 |
| 38—Wichita State | 0 |
| 50—Montana | 28 |
| 20—Wisconsin | 0 |
| 7—Pacific | 18 |
| 20—W. Texas State | 10 |
| 34—Brigham Young | 8 |
| 28—Utah | 13 |
| *Nov. 30 San Diego State | |

## VANDERBILT
**Commodores**
*Black and Gold*

| | |
|---|---|
| 25—V. M. I. | 12 |
| 17—Army | 13 |
| 7—No. Carolina | 8 |
| 7—Alabama | 31 |
| 2—Georgia | 32 |
| 14—Florida | 14 |
| 21—Tulane | 7 |
| 6—Kentucky | 0 |
| 53—Davidson | 20 |
| *Nov. 30—Tennessee | |

## VERMONT
**Catamounts**
*Green and Gold*

| | |
|---|---|
| 0—Connecticut | 21 |
| 9—Wilkes | 31 |
| 1—Maine | 28 |
| 0—Rhode Island | 52 |
| 12—New Hampshire | 10 |
| 0—Norwich | 7 |
| 0—Massachusetts | 49 |
| 49—Middlebury | 18 |
| 10—C. W. Post | 25 |

## VILLANOVA
**Wildcats**
*Blue and White*

| | |
|---|---|
| 21—Toledo | 45 |
| 16—Delaware | 0 |
| 19—V. M. I. | 13 |
| 7—Boston College | 28 |
| 28—Buffalo | 7 |
| 21—Xavier | 10 |
| 12—Wm. & Mary | 33 |
| 27—Quantico | 13 |
| 20—West Virginia | 30 |
| 63—W. Chester State | 3 |

## VIRGINIA
**Cavaliers**
*Orange and Blue*

| | |
|---|---|
| 6—Purdue | 44 |
| 47—V. M. I. | 0 |
| 41—Davidson | 14 |
| 50—Duke | 20 |
| 24—No. Carolina St. | 19 |
| 24—Navy | 31 |
| 28—So. Carolina | 49 |
| 41—No. Carolina | 6 |
| 63—Tulane | 47 |
| 28—Maryland | 23 |

## VMI
**Keydets**
*Red, White & Yellow*

| | |
|---|---|
| 12—Vanderbilt | 25 |
| 0—Virginia | 47 |
| 13—Villanova | 19 |
| 7—W. Virginia | 14 |
| 8—The Citadel | 13 |
| 0—Wm. & Mary | 20 |
| 0—Richmond | 35 |
| 13—Davidson | 7 |
| 13—Boston College | 45 |
| 23—Virginia Tech. | |

## VIRGINIA TECH
**Gobblers**
*Orange and Maroon*

| | |
|---|---|
| 7—Alabama | 14 |
| 12—Wm. & Mary | 0 |
| 19—Kansas State | 34 |
| 7—Wake Forest | 6 |
| 8—Miami (Fla.) | 13 |
| 27—W. Virginia | 12 |
| 40—Florida State | 22 |
| 31—Richmond | 18 |
| 23—So. Carolina | 6 |
| *Nov. 28—V. M. I. | |

## WAGNER
**Seahawks**
*Green and White*

| | |
|---|---|
| 0—Lycoming | 10 |
| 31—Upsala | 8 |
| 20—Moravian | 6 |
| 10—Tufts | 17 |
| 0—Kings Point | 24 |
| 7—Springfield | 28 |
| 18—Susquehanna | 6 |
| 26—Hofstra | 7 |
| 7—Wittenberg | 45 |

## WAKE FOREST
**Demon Deacons**
*Old Gold and Black*

| | |
|---|---|
| 6—No. Carolina St. | 10 |
| 20—Clemson | 20 |
| 19—Minnesota | 24 |
| 6—Virginia Tech. | 7 |
| 27—Purdue | 28 |
| 48—No. Carolina | 31 |
| 38—Maryland | 14 |
| 11—So. Carolina | 34 |
| 3—Duke | 18 |
| 24—Florida State | 42 |

## WASH. & JEFF.
**Presidents**
*Red and Black*

| | |
|---|---|
| 8—John Carroll | 30 |
| 7—Thiel | 34 |
| 20—Adelbert | 24 |
| 31—Case Tech | 8 |
| 20—Allegheny | 14 |
| 6—Wayne State | 40 |
| 21—Bethany | 56 |
| 6—Carnegie-Mellon | 26 |

## WASHINGTON & LEE
**Generals**
*Royal Blue and White*
—Guilford ...........

| | |
|---|---|
| 21—Rand-Macon | 45 |
| 0—Centre | 10 |
| 7—Lafayette | 27 |
| 0—Hamp.-Sydney | 7 |
| 27—Bridgewater | 13 |
| 16—Sewanee | 7 |
| 7—Southwest. Tenn. | 38 |
| 14—Wash. (Mo.) | 3 |

## WASHINGTON STATE
**Cougars**
*Crimson and Grey*

| | |
|---|---|
| 14—Idaho | 14 |
| 21—U. C. L. A. | 31 |
| 14—Utah | 17 |
| 14—Arizona State | 41 |
| 21—Stanford | 21 |
| 8—Oregon State | 16 |
| 14—Arizona | 28 |
| 13—Oregon | 27 |
| 46—San Jose St. | 0 |
| 24—Washington | 0 |

## WASHINGTON
**Huskies**
*Purple and Gold*

| | |
|---|---|
| 35—Rice | 35 |
| 21—Wisconsin | 17 |
| 21—Oregon State | 35 |
| 0—Oregon | 17 |
| 7—So. California | 14 |
| 7—California | 7 |
| 20—Stanford | 35 |
| 0—UCLA | 0 |
| 0—Washington St. | 24 |

## WAYNE STATE
**Tartars**
*Forest Green & Old Gold*

| | |
|---|---|
| 23—Michigan Tech | 13 |
| 6—Temple | 26 |
| 13—U. Ill. Chicago | 0 |
| 6—Ferris State | 16 |
| 7—Augustana (S.D.) | 34 |
| 61—Wash. (Mo.) | 29 |
| 14—Wash. & Jeff | 6 |
| 19—Eastern Ill. | 60 |
| 6—Central Mich. | 35 |

## WAYNESBURG
**Yellow Jackets**
*Orange and Black*

| | |
|---|---|
| 14—Fairmont State | 41 |
| 28—Slippery Rock | 7 |
| 19—Ohio Northern | 0 |
| 27—California State | 26 |
| 17—Ashland | 16 |
| 49—Geneva | 0 |
| 55—W. Va. Wes'n | 13 |
| 39—Westminster | 7 |
| 69—Lock Haven | 0 |

## WESLEYAN
**Cardinals**
*Cardinal Red and Black*

| | |
|---|---|
| 42—Middlebury | 40 |
| 27—Bowdoin | 14 |
| 23—Coast Guard | 26 |
| 29—Worcester Tech | 6 |
| 13—Amherst | 58 |
| 10—Hamilton | 8 |
| 26—Williams | 24 |
| 17—Trinity | 19 |

## WESTERN MARYLAND
**Terrors**
*Green & Gold*

| | |
|---|---|
| 36—Susquehanna | 6 |
| 30—PMC | 0 |
| 37—Lycoming | 29 |
| 30—Shepherd | 7 |
| 29—Hamp.-Sydney | 3 |
| 14—Rand.-Macon | 41 |
| 25—Delaware Valley | 34 |
| 14—Drexel | 42 |
| 23—Johns Hopkins | 46 |

## W. MICHIGAN
**Broncos**
*Brown and Gold*

| | |
|---|---|
| 20—Arkansas State | 0 |
| 7—Brigham Young | 17 |
| 0—Miami (Ohio) | 28 |
| 10—Bowling Green | 17 |
| 14—Kent State | 0 |
| 6—Toledo | 30 |
| 40—Marshall | 12 |
| 27—Ohio U. | 34 |
| 36—W. Tex. St. | 53 |

## WESTMINSTER
**Titans**
*Blue and White*

| | |
|---|---|
| 34—Slippery Rock | 12 |
| 27—Juniata | 35 |
| 21—Heidelberg | 7 |
| 27—Geneva | 7 |
| 20—Bethany | 7 |
| 20—Mt. Union | 6 |
| 28—Glenville | 13 |
| 7—Waynesburg | 39 |

## W. TEXAS STATE
**Buffaloes**
*Maroon and White*

| | |
|---|---|
| 45—Lamar Tech | 7 |
| 26—Wichita State | 0 |
| 23—Pacific (Calif.) | 7 |
| 35—Montana State | 20 |
| 21—Memphis State | 42 |
| 41—Texas (Arl.) | 0 |
| 10—Utah State | 20 |
| 23—New Mexico | 14 |
| 53—W. Michigan | 36 |
| 22—Colorado State | 17 |

## W. VIRGINIA
**Mountaineers**
*Old Gold and Blue*

| | |
|---|---|
| 17—Richmond | 0 |
| 38—Pittsburgh | 14 |
| 20—Penn State | 31 |
| 14—V. M. I. | 7 |
| 20—William & Mary | 0 |
| 12—Virginia Tech | 27 |
| 16—Kentucky | 35 |
| 17—The Citadel | 0 |
| 30—Villanova | 20 |
| 23—Syracuse | 6 |

## WICHITA STATE
**Shockers**
*Yellow and Black*

| | |
|---|---|
| 0—W. Texas State | 26 |
| 0—Utah State | 38 |
| 23—Drake | 26 |
| 15—Colo. St. Univ. | 37 |
| 27—Cincinnati | 40 |
| 14—Louisville | 21 |
| 21—New Mexico St. | 47 |
| 18—Memphis St. | 40 |
| 6—No. Texas St. | 44 |
| *Nov. 28—Tulsa | |

## WILKES
**Colonels**
*Blue and Gold*

| | |
|---|---|
| 31—Vermont | 9 |
| 40—Moravian | 0 |
| 31—Delaware Valley | 3 |
| 28—Ithaca | 19 |
| 9—Upsala | 7 |
| 28—Dickinson | 0 |
| 34—PMC Colleges | 0 |
| 23—Lebanon Valley | 16 |

## WILLIAM & MARY
**Indians**
*Green, Gold and Silver*

| | |
|---|---|
| 14—E. Carolina | 0 |
| 0—Virginia Tech | 12 |
| 3—Pittsburgh | 14 |
| 0—Ohio Univ. | 41 |
| 0—West Virginia | 20 |
| 20—V. M. I. | 0 |
| 33—Villanova | 12 |
| 0—Syracuse | 31 |
| 21—The Citadel | 24 |
| 6—Richmond | 31 |

## WILLIAMS
**Ephmen**
*Purple and Gold*

| | |
|---|---|
| 31—Trinity | 14 |
| 7—Rochester | 6 |
| 48—Middlebury | 14 |
| 14—Bowdoin | 7 |
| 28—Tufts | 30 |
| 7—Union | 17 |
| 24—Wesleyan | 26 |
| 17—Amherst | 24 |

## WISCONSIN
**Badgers**
*Cardinal and White*

| | |
|---|---|
| 7—Arizona State | 55 |
| 17—Washington | 21 |
| 0—Michigan State | 39 |
| 0—Utah State | 20 |
| 0—Iowa | 41 |
| 10—Northwestern | 13 |
| 0—Utah State | 20 |
| 8—Ohio St. | 43 |
| 9—Michigan | 34 |
| 15—Minnesota | 23 |

## WORCESTER TECH
**Engineers**
*Maroon and Grey*

| | |
|---|---|
| 14—Bowdoin | 10 |
| 25—Middlebury | 20 |
| 30—Bates | 20 |
| 6—Wesleyan | 29 |
| 36—Coast Guard | 0 |
| 23—R. P. I. | 21 |
| 12—Norwich | 35 |

## WYOMING
**Cowboys**
*Brown and Gold*

| | |
|---|---|
| 10—Nebraska | 13 |
| 48—Utah State | 3 |
| 3—Air Force | 10 |
| 27—Arizona State | 13 |
| 20—Brigham Young | 17 |
| 20—Utah | 9 |
| 35—New Mexico | 6 |
| 46—Colorado State | 13 |
| 26—Texas, El Paso | 19 |
| 7—Arizona | 14 |

## XAVIER
**Musketeers**
*Blue and White*

| | |
|---|---|
| 7—Miami (Ohio) | 28 |
| 28—Quantico | 12 |
| 14—Cincinnati | 17 |
| 30—Marshall | 20 |
| 10—No. Illinois | 20 |
| 10—Villanova | 21 |
| 27—Dayton | 25 |
| 20—Toledo | 10 |
| 23—Kent St. | 7 |
| 14—Bowling Green | 44 |

## YALE
**Bulldogs**
*Yale Blue*

| | |
|---|---|
| 31—Connecticut | 14 |
| 49—Colgate | 14 |
| 35—Brown | 13 |
| 29—Columbia | 7 |
| 25—Cornell | 13 |
| 47—Dartmouth | 27 |
| 30—Penn | 13 |
| 42—Princeton | 17 |
| 29—Harvard | 29 |

## YOUNGSTOWN STATE
**Penguins**
*Red and White*

| | |
|---|---|
| 18—Gusta. Adolphus | 14 |
| 21—Central Michigan | 24 |
| 6—Baldwin-Wallace | 22 |
| 38—Pensacola Navy | 58 |
| 25—Morehead State | 35 |
| 20—South Dakota St. | 23 |
| 7—Southern Illinois | 15 |
| 14—Eastern Kentucky | 14 |
| 13—Akron | 42 |

## NAIA National Championships

Source: National Assn. of Intercollegiate Athletics

| Date 1968 | Event | Site | Champion |
|---|---|---|---|
| June 4-8 | Tennis | Kansas City, Mo. | Redlands (Calif.) |
| June 4-7 | Golf | Bemidji, Minn. | Indiana Univ. (Pa.) |
| June 3-7 | Baseball | St. Joseph, Mo. | William Jewell (Mo.) |
| June 1 | Outdoor Track | Albuquerque, N. M. | Prairie View A&M (Tex.) |
| Apr. 26-27 | Bowling | Kansas City, Mo. | La Crosse State (Wisc.) |
| Mar. 21-23 | Gymnastics | Hays, Kansas | Northwestern La. State. |
| Mar. 14-16 | Swimming | St. Cloud, Minn. | Eastern Michigan |
| Mar. 11-16 | Basketball | Kansas City, Mo. | Central State (Ohio) |
| Mar. 8-9 | Ice Hockey | St. Paul, Minn. | Bemidji State (Minn.) |
| Mar. 7-9 | Wrestling | Alamosa, Colo. | Adams State (Colo.) |
| Jan. 19-20 | Indoor Track | Kansas City, Mo. | Prairie View A&M (Tex.) |
| **1967** | | | |
| Dec. 9 | Football | Morgantown, West Virginia | Fairmont State (W. Va.) |
| Nov. 25 | Cross Country | Omaha, Nebr. | Eastern Michigan |
| Nov. 24-25 | Soccer | Quincy, Ill. | Quincy (Ill.) |

## Evolution of the World Record for the One Mile Run

The table below shows how the world record for the one-mile run has been lowered in the past 103 years.

| Time | Individual | Year | Time | Individual | Year |
|---|---|---|---|---|---|
| 4:56 | Charles Lawes, Britain | 1864 | 4:07.6 | Jack Lovelock, New Zealand | 1933 |
| 4:36.5 | Richard Webster, Britain | 1865 | 4:06.8 | Glenn Cunningham, U. S. | 1934 |
| 4:29 | William Chinnery, Britain | 1868 | 4:06.4 | Sydney Wooderson, Britain | 1937 |
| 4:28.8 | W. C. Gibbs, Britain | 1868 | 4:06.2 | Gunder Haegg, Sweden | 1942 |
| 4:26 | Walter Slade, Britain | 1874 | 4:06.2 | Arne Andersson, Sweden | 1942 |
| 4:24.5 | Walter Slade, Britain | 1875 | 4:04.6 | Gunder Haegg, Sweden | 1942 |
| 4:23.2 | Walter George, Britain | 1880 | 4:02.6 | Arne Andersson, Sweden | 1943 |
| 4:21.4 | Walter George, Britain | 1882 | 4:01.6 | Arne Andersson, Sweden | 1944 |
| 4:19.4 | Walter George, Britain | 1882 | 4:01.4 | Gunder Haegg, Sweden | 1945 |
| 4:18.4 | Walter George, Britain | 1884 | 3:59.4 | Roger Bannister, Britain | 1954 |
| 4:18.2 | Fred Bacon, Scotland | 1894 | 3:58 | John Landy, Australia | 1954 |
| 4:17 | Fred Bacon, Scotland | 1895 | 3:57.2 | Derek Ibbotson, Britain | 1957 |
| 4:15.6 | Thomas Conneff, U. S. | 1895 | 3:54.5 | Herb Elliott, Australia | 1958 |
| 4:15.4 | John Paul Jones, U. S. | 1911 | 3:54.4 | Peter Snell, New Zealand | 1962 |
| 4:14.6 | John Paul Jones, U. S. | 1913 | 3:54.1 | Peter Snell, New Zealand | 1964 |
| 4:12.6 | Norman Taber, U. S. | 1915 | 3:53.6 | Michel Jazy, France | 1965 |
| 4:10.4 | Paavo Nurmi, Finland | 1923 | 3:51.3 | Jim Ryun, U. S. | 1966 |
| 4:09.2 | Jules Ladoumegue, France | 1931 | 3:51.1 | Jim Ryun, U. S. | 1967 |

## Rifle and Pistol Championships in 1968

Source: National Rifle Association of America

**National Pistol Championship**—Maj. Franklin C. Green, San Antonio, Texas, 2635-111X.

**National Trophy Individual Pistol Match**—S/Sgt. Arnold Vitarbo, New York City, N. Y., 293-12X.

**National Smallbore Rifle Prone Championship**—Army Capt. Donald Adams, Halifax, Va., 6395-508X.

**National Women's Smallbore Rifle Prone Championship**—Marianne Jensen, Saginaw, Mich., 6386-499X.

**National Smallbore Rifle Prone Junior Title**—Sue Lausten, Livonia, Mich., 6376-442X.

**National Smallbore Rifle Position Championship**—Army Maj. Lones Wigger, Carter, Montana, 1560-84X.

**National Smallbore Rifle Position Women's Title**—Army Capt. Margaret Thompson, Topeka, Kansas, 1539-67X.

**National Smallbore Rifle Position Junior Title**—William P. Schweitzer, Lancaster, Penn., 1533-66X.

**National Service Rifle Championship**—Lt. David A. Luke, U. S. Marine Corps, 1555-41X.

**National High Power Rifle Championship**—Middleton Tompkins, Long Beach, Calif., 1568-55X.

**National High Power Women's Rifle Championship**—Margaret Thompson, Topeka, Kansas, 1515-31X.

## Quarter Horse Racing

The richest horse race in the world, the all American Futurity is run each Labor Day at Ruidoso Downs, Ruidoso, New Mexico. It is open to 2-year-old Quarter Horses. The distance of the event is 400 yards, and the weight is 119 pounds.

| Year | Winner | Weight | Time | Value to Winner | Jockey | Owner |
|---|---|---|---|---|---|---|
| 1959 | Galobar | 116 | 20.5 | $64,843 | C. Lambert | Hugh Huntley |
| 1960 | Tonto Bars Hank | 119 | 20.2 | 65,122 | C. Perner | Milo and C. G. Whitcomb |
| 1961 | Pokey Bar | 119 | 20.1 | 101,212 | K. Chapman | Hugh Huntley |
| 1962 | Hustling Man | 119 | 20.3 | 96,425 | C. Detiege | J. B. Ferguson |
| 1963 | Goetta | 116 | 20.40 | 127,500 | C. Smith | Hugh Huntley |
| 1964 | Decketta | 119 | 20.30 | 134,030 | B. Morris | W. W. Wilson |
| 1965 | Savannah Jr. | 120 | 20.30 | 192,730 | J. Wallace | J. R. and R. E. Cates |
| 1966 | Go Dick Go | 119 | 20.27 | 198,300 | B. Nesmith | Joe V. Leitner |
| 1967 | Laico Bird | 119 | 20.11 | 228,300 | B. Harmon | F. H. Jones, Jr. |
| 1968 | Three Oh's | 119 | 20.06 | 160,372 | J. Nicodemus | Donald G. Strole |

## AAU Gymnastics Championships in 1968

Long Beach, Calif.

### Men's Events

**All-Around**—Makoto Sakamoto, Univ. of Southern Calif.
**Floor Exercise**—Toby Towson, Michigan State.
**Rings**—Steve Cohen, Philadelphia.
**Parallel Bars**—Makoto Sakamoto.
**Side Horse**—John Russo, Wis.
**Long Horse**—Makoto Sakamoto.
**Horizontal Bar**—Makoto Sakamoto.
**Trampoline**—Dave Jacobs, Michigan Univ.

**Tumbling**—Doug Roger, Pasadena, Calif.

### Women's Events

**All-Around**—Linda Metheny, Tusculo, Ill.
**Vault**—Joyce Tanac, Seattle.
**Free Exercise**—Linda Metheny.
**Balance Beam**—Linda Metheny.
**Uneven Bars**—Doris Brause, New Haven, Conn.
**Tumbling**—Judy Wills, Southern Illinois Univ.
**Trampoline**—Judy Wills.

# Dog Show

Six main classes of dogs are presently recognized: Sporting dogs—Pointers, Retrievers, Setters, Spaniels, Weimaraners; the Hound group; Working dogs, including boxers, collies, Doberman pinschers, Shepherds, mastiffs; the Terrier group; the Toy group, including Chihuahuas, Toy Spaniels, Papillons, Pekingese, Pomeranians, Yorkshires; Non-sporting group—Boston Terriers, bulldogs, Chow Chows, Dalmatians, Keeshonden, Poodles, etc. In all, 115 different breeds are recognized and shown in the United States

Poodles remained the No. 1 breed in the United States for the eighth straight year according to 1967 pure-bred registration figures released in 1968 by the American Kennel Club. A record 885,800 individual dogs were registered, an increase of 10.1% over the previous year.

### WESTMINSTER KENNEL CLUB
Madison Square Garden, New York, N. Y.

| Year | Best-in-show | Breed | Owner |
|---|---|---|---|
| 1956... | Ch. Wilber White Swan | Toy poodle | Mrs. Bertha Smith |
| 1957... | Ch. Shirkhan of Grandeur | Afghan hound | Sunny Shay & Dorothy Chenade |
| 1958... | Ch. Puttencove Promise | Standard poodle | Mr. & Mrs. George Putnam |
| 1959... | Ch. Fontclair Festoon | Miniature poodle | Clarence Dillon |
| 1960... | Ch. Chik T'Sun of Caversham | Pekingese | Mr. and Mrs. C. C. Venable |
| 1961... | Ch. Cappoquin Little Sister | Toy poodle | Florence Michelson |
| 1962... | Ch. Elfinbrook Simon | West Highland terrior | Florence and Barbara Worcester |
| 1963... | Ch. Wakefield's Black Knight | English springer spaniel | Mrs. W. J. S. Borie |
| 1964... | Ch. Courtenay Fleetfoot | Whippet | Mrs. Margaret P. Newcombe |
| 1965... | Ch. Carmichael's Fanfare | Scottish terrier | Mr. and Mrs. Charles C. Stalter |
| 1966... | Ch. Zeloy Mooremaides Magic | Wire Fox terrier | Marion G. Bunker |
| 1967... | Ch. Bardene Bingo | Scottish terrier | E. H. Stuart |
| 1968.... | Ch. Stingray of Derryabah | Lakeland terrier | Mr. and Mrs. James A. Farrell, Jr. |

# Tour de France Bicycle Race

Jan Janssen of the Netherlands won the 1968 Tour de France bicycle race by only a 38-second margin in the 2,937.5-mile event which covered 25 days, ending July 21. The victor's over-all time was 133 hrs., 49 min., 42 sec. Herman Van Springel of Belgium finished second.

# 18th Chess Olympiad

The Soviet Union won the Hamilton Russell trophy at the 18th Chess Olympiad in Lugano, Switzerland, on Nov. 7, 1968. Yugoslavia finished second, followed by Bulgaria, United States and West Germany. The International Team Tournament championship was the 9th straight victory for the Russians.

# Polo Records
## UNITED STATES POLO RECORDS

### National Open Tournament

1958 Dallas Circle F 7, Solocup 5
1959 Dallas Circle F 8, Aurora (Buffalo) 7
1960 Oak Brook CCC 8, Royal Palm 5
1961 Milwaukee 13, Beaver Ridge Farm (Detroit, Mich.) 9
1962 Santa Barbara 8, Royal Palm 7
1963 Tulsa 7, Oakland (Calif.) Crescents 6
1964 Oak Brook 10, Solo Cup Crescents 9
1965 Oak Brook 11, Bunn Tyco Chicago 9
1966 Tulsa 10, Fountain Grove 5
1967 Bunntyco-Oakbrook 8, Milwaukee 2
1968 Midland 9, Milwaukee 0

### National 20-Goal Tournament

1958 Meadow Brook 9, Aiken 7
1959 Dallas Circle F 11, Meadow Brook 5
1960 Royal Palm 6, Circle F 4
1961 Royal Palm 9, Milwaukee 4

1962 Milwaukee 8, Santa Barbara 7
1963 Oak Brook 10, Tulsa 7
1964 Oak Brook 8, Tulsa 5
1965 Santa Barabara-Oak Brook 7, Milwaukee 2
1966 Sunny Climes 9, Oak Brook 7
1967 Milwaukee 11, Keswick-Blue Ridge 7
1968 Oak Brook 12, Keswick Sunnny Climes 9

### Intercollegiate Championship

1958 Cornell 22, Yale 4
1959 Cornell 14, Virginia 5
1960 Yale 11, Cornell 6
1961 Cornell 10, Yale 4
1962 Cornell 14, Yale 5
1963 Cornell 11, Yale 4
1964 Yale 12, Cornell 9
1965 Yale 12, Cornell 3
1966 Cornell 12, Yale 10
1967 Yale 12, Cornell 11
1968 Yale 17, Cornell 13

### OTHER POLO TOURNAMENTS IN 1968

National 16-Goal Tournament—Milwaukee 11, Midland 8.
National Inter-Circuit Tournament—Midland 7, Keswick Sunny Climes 3.
National 12-Goal Tournament—Midland 7, Keswick Sunny Climes 3.

# National AAU Handball Championships

Billy Yambrick, St. Paul, Minn., won the 1968 AAU 4 wall handball singles championship in a competition held in New York City. Rudy and Oscar Obert from the New York AC were the doubles champions. Bob Brady and Bob McGuire, San Francisco, Calif., won the masters doubles.

# Bobsled Championships in 1968
Lake Placid, N. Y., Jan. 28-Mar. 3, 1968

Two-Man North American Championships—Malone Bobsled Club (Charles McDonald and John Handly). Time—5:05.92.

Four-Man North American Championships—U. S. Air Force Bobsled Team (Lester Fenner, Al Lowe, Allan Hachigian, John DeZalia). Time—4:40.22.

Two-Man National AAU Championships—U. S. Air Force Bobled Team (Gary Sheffield, Howard Siler). Time—4:40.71.

Four-Man National AAU Championships—U. S. Air Force Bobsled Team (Fenner, DeZalla, Lowe, Hachigian). Time—4:33.26.

# Grey Cup Symbolizes Canadian Pro Football Championship

The Grey Cup, donated by Governor-General Earl Grey in 1909, is symbolic of the championship of the Canadian Football League. Each year the winners of the league's Western and Eastern divisions meet to contest for the coveted cup in one of Canada's top professional sports events.

# 1968 Olympic Games
## Mexico City, Oct. 12-27, 1968

Competing in the games of the 19th modern Olympiad, held in Mexico City Oct. 12-27, 1968, were 7,226 athletes from 119 nations. Although it had been feared that the high altitude of Mexico City would have an adverse effect on the athletes, the performances were generally superior and the breaking of world and Olympic records became almost commonplace. The United States won the unofficial team title by taking 107 medals; the Soviet Union won 91. The medal totals by nations and results of major events follow:

| | Gold | Silver | Bronze | Total | | Gold | Silver | Bronze | Total |
|---|---|---|---|---|---|---|---|---|---|
| United States | 45 | 28 | 34 | 107 | Cuba | 0 | 4 | 0 | 4 |
| Soviet Union | 29 | 31 | 31 | 91 | Finland | 1 | 2 | 1 | 4 |
| Hungary | 10 | 10 | 12 | 32 | Mongolia | 0 | 1 | 3 | 4 |
| East Germany | 9 | 9 | 7 | 25 | Sweden | 2 | 1 | 1 | 4 |
| Japan | 11 | 7 | 7 | 25 | Brazil | 0 | 1 | 2 | 3 |
| West Germany | 5 | 10 | 10 | 25 | New Zealand | 1 | 0 | 2 | 3 |
| Poland | 5 | 2 | 11 | 18 | Argentina | 0 | 0 | 2 | 2 |
| Australia | 5 | 7 | 5 | 17 | Belgium | 0 | 1 | 1 | 2 |
| Italy | 3 | 4 | 9 | 16 | Norway | 1 | 1 | 0 | 2 |
| Rumania | 4 | 6 | 5 | 15 | Ethiopia | 1 | 1 | 0 | 2 |
| France | 7 | 3 | 5 | 15 | South Korea | 0 | 1 | 1 | 2 |
| Czechoslovakia | 7 | 2 | 4 | 13 | Tunisia | 1 | 0 | 1 | 2 |
| Britain | 5 | 5 | 3 | 13 | Turkey | 2 | 0 | 0 | 2 |
| Bulgaria | 2 | 4 | 3 | 9 | Uganda | 0 | 1 | 1 | 2 |
| Kenya | 3 | 4 | 2 | 9 | Cameroons | 0 | 1 | 0 | 1 |
| Mexico | 3 | 3 | 3 | 9 | Greece | 0 | 0 | 1 | 1 |
| Denmark | 1 | 4 | 3 | 8 | India | 0 | 0 | 1 | 1 |
| Yugoslavia | 3 | 3 | 2 | 8 | Jamaica | 0 | 1 | 0 | 1 |
| Netherlands | 3 | 3 | 1 | 7 | Pakistan | 1 | 0 | 0 | 1 |
| Iran | 2 | 1 | 2 | 5 | Taiwan | 0 | 0 | 1 | 1 |
| Switzerland | 0 | 1 | 4 | 5 | Venezuela | 1 | 0 | 0 | 1 |
| Canada | 1 | 3 | 1 | 5 | Silver medal in team pursuit cycling is pending. | | | | |
| Austria | 0 | 2 | 2 | 4 | | | | | |

## TRACK AND FIELD—MEN

**100 Meters**—1, Jim Hines, United States; 2, Lennox Miller, Jamaica; 3, Charlie Greene, United States. **Time—0:09.9** (world record).

**200 Meters**—1, Tommie Smith, United States; 2, Peter Norman, Australia; 3, John Carlos, United States. **Time—0:19.8** (world record).

**400 Meters**—1, Lee Evans, United States; 2, Larry James, United States; 3, Ron Freeman, United States. **Time—0:43.8** (world record).

**800 Meters**—1, Ralph Doubell, Australia; 2, Wilson Kiprugut, Kenya; 3, Tom Farrell, United States. **Time—1:44.3** (ties world record).

**1,500 Meters**—1, Kipchoge Keino, Kenya; 2, Jim Ryun, United States; 3, Bobo Tummler, W. Germany. **Time—3:34.9** (Olympic record).

**5,000 Meters**—1, Mohammed Gammoudi, Tunisia; 2 Kipchoge Keino, Kenya; 3, Naftali Temu, Kenya. **Time—14:05.0.**

**10,000 meters**—1, Naftali Temu, Kenya; 2, Mamo Wolde, Ethiopia; 3, Mohammed Gammoudi, Tunisia. **Time—29:27.4.**

**3,000 Meter Steeplechase**—1, Amos Biwatt, Kenya; 2, Benjamin Kogo, Kenya; 3, George Young, United States. **Time—8:51.0.**

**Marathon**—1, Mamo Wolde, Ethiopia; 2, Kenji Kimihara, Japan; 3, Mike Ryan, New Zealand. **Time—2:20:26.4.**

**20-Km. Walk**—Vladimir Golubnichiy, USSR; 2, Jose Pedraza, Mexico; 3, Nickolay Smago, USSR. **Time—1:35:58.4.**

**50-Km. Walk**—1, Christoph Hohne, E. Germany; 2, Antal Kiss, Hungary; 3, Larry Young, United States. **Time—4:20:13.6.**

**110 Meter Hurdles**—1 Willie Davenport, United States; 2, Ervin Hall, United States; 3, Eddy Ottoz, Italy. **Time—0:13.3** (Olympic record).

**400 Meter Hurdles**—1, Dave Hemery, Great Britain; 2, Gerhard Hennige, W. Germany; 3, John Sherwood, Great Britain. **Time—0:48.1** (world record).

**400 Meter Relay**—1, United States (Greene, Pender, R. Smith, Hines) 2, Cuba; 3, France. **Time—0:38.2** (world record).

**1,600 Meter Relay**—1, United States (Matthews, Freeman, James, Evans); 2, Kenya; 3, W. Germany. **Time—2:56.1** (world record).

**High Jump**—1, Dick Fosbury, United States; 2, Ed Caruthers, United States; 3, Valentin Gavrilov, USSR. **7 ft. 4¼ in.** (Olympic record).

**Long Jump**—1, Bob Beamon, United States; 2, Klaus Beer, E. Germany; 3, Ralph Boston, United States. **29 ft. 2½ in.** (world record).

**Pole Vault**—1, Bob Seagren, United States; 2, Claus Schiprowski, W. Germany; 3, Wolfgang Nordwig, E. Germany. **17 ft. 8½ in.** (world record).

**Hammer Throw**—1, Gyula Zsivotsky, Hungary; 2, Rimuald Klim, USSR; 3, Lazar Lovasz, Hungary. **240 ft. 8 in.** (Olympic record).

**Discus**—1, Al Oerter, United States; 2, Luther Milde, E. Germany; 3, Ludvik Danek, Czech. **212 ft. 6½ in.** (Olympic record).

**Triple Jump**—1, Victor Saneev, USSR; 2, Nelson Prudencio, Brazil; 3, Giuseppe Gentile, Italy. **57 ft. ¾ in.** (world record).

**Shot Put**—1, Randy Matson, United States; 2,

George Woods, United States; 3, Eduard Guschin, USSR. **67 ft. 4¾ in.** (Olympic record).

**Javelin**—1, Yanis Lusis, USSR; 2, Jorma Kinnunen, Finland; 3, Gergely Kulcsar, Hungary. **295 ft. 7¼ in.** (Olympic record).

**Decathlon**—1, Bill Toomey, United States; 2, Hans Walde, W. Germany; 3, Kurt Bendlin, W. Germany. **8,193 Pts.**

## TRACK AND FIELD—WOMEN

**100 Meters**—Wyomia Tyus, United States; 2, Barbara Ferrell, United States; 3, Irena Szewinska, Poland. **Time—0:11.0** (world record).

**200 Meters**—1, Irena Szewinska, Poland; 2 Raelene Boyle, Australia; 3, Jennifer Lamy, Australia. **Time—0:22.5** (world record).

**400 Meters**—1, Colette Besson, France; 2, Lillian Board, Great Britain; 3, Natalia Pechenkina, USSR. **Time—0:52.0** (ties Olympic record).

**800 Meters**—1, Madeline Manning, United States; 2, Ilona Silai, Romania; 3, Maria Gommers, Netherlands. **Time—2:00.9.**

**80 Meter Hurdles**—1, Maureen Caird, Australia; 2, Pam Kilborn, Australia; 3, Chi Cheng, Taiwan. **Time—0:10.3** (ties world record).

**400 Meter Relay**—1, United States (Ferrell, Bailes, Netter, Tyus); 2, Cuba; 3, USSR. **Time—0:42.8** (world record).

**High Jump**—1, Miloslava Rezkova, Czech.; 2, Antonina Okorokova, USSR; 3, Valentina Kozyr, USSR. **5 ft. 11¾ in.**

**Long Jump**—1, Viorica Viscopoleanu, Romania; 2, Sheila Sherwood, Great Britain; 3, Tatiana Talysheva, USSR. **22 ft. 4½ in.** (world record).

**Shot Put**—1, Margarita Gummel, E. Germany; 2, Marita Lange, E. Germany; 3, Nadezhda Chizhova, USSR. **64 ft. 4 in.** (world record).

**Discus**—1, Lia Manoliu, Romania; 2, Kiesel Westerman, W. Germany; 3, Kleiber Konstek, Hungary. **191 ft. 2½ in.** (Olympic record).

**Javelin**—1, Angela Nemeth, Hungary; 2, Mihaela Penes, Romania; 3, Eva Jenko, Austria. **198 ft. ½ in.**

**Pentathlon**—1, Ingred Becker, W. Germany; 2, Liese Prokop, Austria; 3, Anna Toth Kovacs, Hungary. **5,098 Pts.**

## SWIMMING—MEN

**100 Meter Freestyle**—1, Mike Wenden, Australia; 2, Ken Walsh, United States; 3, Mark Spitz, United States. **Time—0:52.2** (world record).

**200 Meter Freestyle**—1, Mike Wenden, Australia; 2, Don Schollander, United States; 3, John Nelson, United States. **Time—1:55.2** (Olympic record).

**400 Meter Freestyle**—1, Mike Burton, United States; 2, Ralph Hutton, Canada; 3, Alain Mosconi, France. **Time—4:09.0** (Olympic record).

**1,500 Meter Freestyle**—1, Mike Burton, United States; 2, J. Kinsella, United States; 3, G. Brough, Australia. **Time—16:38.9** (Olympic record).

**100 Meter Breaststroke**—1, Don McKenzie, United States; 2, Cladimir Kosinsky, USSR; 3, Pankin, USSR. **Time—1:07.7** (Olympic record).

**200 Meter Breaststroke**—1, Felipe Munoz, Mexico; 2, Cladimir Kosinsky, USSR; 3, Brian Job, United States. **Time—2:28.7.**

**100 Meter Butterfly**—1, Doug Russell, United

# Beamon's Record-Breaking Jump Is Sensation of Olympics

Of the many record-breaking performances in the 1968 Olympics at Mexico City the most phenomenal, in the eyes of most experts, was the long jump of 29 ft. 2½ inches by Bob Beamon. Beamon's leap, made on his first attempt in the finals, shattered the world record of 27 ft. 4¾ inches. Klaus Beer of East Germany took second with 26 ft. 10½ inches and world record holder Ralph Boston of the U. S. finished third with 26 ft. 9¼ inches. All 3 bettered the Olympic record of 26 ft. 7¾ inches held by Boston.

The fact that Beamon's prodigious leap exceeded the world record by nearly two feet seemed incredible in view of the history of the long jump mark. Jesse Owens' world record of 26 ft. 8¼ inches had stood for 25 years when Boston broke it in 1960. The USSR's Igor Ter-Ovanesyan topped that in 1962, Boston set the record at 27 ft. 4¾ inches in 1965, and Ter-Ovanesyan equalled that unofficially in 1967. But Boston and Ter-Ovanesyan had increased the world mark by only 8½ inches in 8 years of effort until Beamon came along. Beamon, 22, from Jamaica, Queens, in New York City, attends the University of Texas at El Paso.

## SWIMMING—MEN Cont'd

States; 2, Mark Spitz, United States; 3, Ross Wales, United States. **Time—0:55.9** (Olympic record).

**200 Meter Butterfly**—1, Carl Robbie, United States; 2, Martyn Woodroffe, Great Britain; 3, John Ferris, United States. **Time—2:08.7.**

**100 Meter Backstroke**—1, Roland Matthes, E. Germany; 2, Charles Hickcox, United States; 3, Ron Mills, United States. **Time—0:58.7** (Olympic record).

**200 Meter Backstroke**—1, Roland Matthes, E. Germany; 2, Mitchel Ivey, United States; 3, Jack Horsley, United States. **Time—2:09.6** (Olympic record).

**200 Meter Individual Medley**—1, Charles Hickcox, United States; 2, Greg Buckingham, United States; 3, John Ferris, United States. **Time—2:12.0** (Olympic record).

**400 Meter Individual Medley**—1, Charles Hickcox, United States; 2, Gary Hall, United States; 3, Michael Holthaus, W. Germany. **Time—4:48.4.**

**400 Meter Freestyle Relay**—United States (Spitz, Zorn, Reyreh, Walsh); 2, USSR; 3, Australia. **Time—3:31.7** (world record).

**800 Meter Freestyle Relay**—1, United States (Nelson, Reryck, Spitz, Schollander); 2, Australia; 3, USSR. **Time—7:52.3.**

**400 Meter Medley Relay**—1, United States (Hickcox, Russell, McKenzie, Walsh); 2, East Germany; 3, USSR. **Time—3:54.9** (world record).

**Springboard Diving**—1, Bernard Wrightson, United States; 2, Klaus DiBiasi, Italy; 3, James Henry, United States. **170.15 points.**

**Platform Diving**—1, DiBiasi, Italy; 2, Gaxiola, Mexico; 3, Young, United States.

### SWIMMING—WOMEN

**100 Meter Freestyle**—1, Jan Henne, United States; 2, Sue Pedersen, United States; 3, Linda Gustavson, United States. **Time—1:00.0.**

**200 Meter Freestyle**—Debbie Meyer, United States; 2, Jan Henne, United States; 3, Jane Barkman, United States. **Time—2:10.5** (Olympic record).

**400 Meter Freestyle**—1, Debbie Meyer, United States; 2, Linda Gustavson, United States; 3, Karen Moras, Australia. **Time—4:31.8** (Olympic record).

**800 Meter Freestyle**—1, Debbie Meyer, United States; 2, Pam Kruse, United States; 3, Maria Ramirez, Mexico. **Time—9:24.0** (Olympic record).

**100 Meter Breaststroke**—1, Djurdjica Biedov, Yugoslavia; 2, Galina Prozumenshikova, USSR; 3, Sharon Wichman. **Time—1:15.8** (Olympic record).

**200 Meter Breaststroke**—1, Sharon Wichman, United States; 2, Djurdjica Biedov, Yugoslavia; 3, Galina Prozumenshikova, USSR. **Time—2:44.4** (Olympic record).

**100 Meter Butterfly**—1, Lynette McClements, Australia; 2, Ellie Daniel, United States; 3, Susie Shields, United States. **Time—1:05.5.**

**200 Meter Butterfly**—1, Ada Kok, Netherlands; 2, Helga Lindner, E. Germany; 3, Ellie Daniel, United States. **Time—2:24.7** (Olympic record).

**100 Meter Backstroke**—1, Kaye Hall, United States; 2, Elaine Tanner, Canada; 3, Jane Swagerty, United States. **Time—1:06.2** (world record).

**200 Meter Backstroke**—1, Pokey Watson, United States; 2, Elaine Tanner, Canada; 3, Kaye Hall, United States. **Time—2:24.8** (Olympic record).

**200 Meter Individual Medley**—1, Claudia Kolb, United States; Susan Pedersen; Jan Henne, United States. **Time—2:24.7** (Olympic record).

**400 Meter Individual Medley**—1, Claudia Kolb, United States; 2, Lynn Vidali, United States; 3, Sabine Steinbach, E. Germany. **Time—5:08.5** (Olympic record).

**400 Meter Freestyle Relay**—United States (Barkman, Gustavson, Pedersen, Henne); 2, East Germany; 3, Canada. **Time—**4:02.5 (Olympic record).

**400 Meter Medley Relay**—1, United States (Hall, Daniel, Ball, Pedersen); 2, Australia; 3, W. Germany. **Time—4:28.3** (world record).

**Spring Board Diving**—1, Sue Gossick, United States; 2, Tamara Pogozheva, USSR; 3, Keala O'Sullivan, United States. **150.77 points.**

**Platform Dive**—1, Duchkova, Czech.; 2, Lobanova, USSR; 3, Peterson, United States.

## BASKETBALL

**Final Standings**—1, United States; 2, Yugoslavia; 3, USSR.

## BOXING

**Bantamweight**—Valery Sokolov, USSR.
**Light Flyweight**—Francisco Rodriguez, Venezuela.
**Flyweight**—Ricardo Delgado, Mexico.
**Featherweight**—Antonio Roldan, Mexico.
**Lightweight**—Ronnie Harris, United States.
**Light Welterweight**—Jerzy Kulej, Poland.
**Welterweight**—Manfred Wolke, East Germany.
**Light Middleweight**—Boris Lagutin, USSR.
**Middleweight**—Cristopher Finnegan, Britain.
**Light Heavyweight**—Dan Pozdniak, USSR.
**Heavyweight**—George Foreman, United States.

## CANOEING

**Kayak Singles**—Mihaly Hesz, Hungary. **Time—**4:02.63.
**Kayak Pairs**—USSR (Shaparenko, Morozov). **Time—**3:37.54.
**Kayak Fours**—Norway (Amundsen, Soby, Berger, Johansen).
**Canadian Singles**—Tibor Tatai, Hungary. **Time—**4:36.14.
**Canadian Doubles**—Romania (Patzaichim, Covaliov). **Time—**4:07.18.
**Women's Kayak Singles**—Ludmila Pinaeva, USSR. **Time—2:11.09.**
**Women's Kayak Doubles**—West Germany (Zimmerman, Esser). **Time—1:56.44.**

## CYCLING

**Road Race** (121¾ **Miles**)—Piefranco Vianelli, Italy.
**100 Km. Road Race**—Netherlands.
**4 Man Team Sprint**—Denmark.
**Tandem Sprint**—France.
**1,000 Meter Time Trial**—Pierre Trentin, France.
**Scratch Sprint**—Daniel Morelon, France.
**4,000 Meter Individual Pursuit**—Daniel Rebillard, France.

## EQUESTRIAN

**Jumping**—William Steinkraus, United States.
**Three-day Event**—Jean Jacques Guyon, France.
**Dressage**—Ivan Kzimov, USSR.
**Dressage Team**—W. Germany.
**Team Three-day Event**—Great Britain.
**Grand Prix Team Jumping**—Canada.

## FENCING

**Fail**—Ion Drimba, Romania.
**Saber**—Jerzy Pawlowski, Poland.
**Epee**—Gyozo Kulcsar, Hungary.
**Women's Foil**—Elene Novikova, USSR.
**Team Foil**—France.
**Team Saber**—USSR.
**Team Epee**—Hungary.
**Women's Team Foil**—USSR.

## FIELD HOCKEY

**Final Standings**—1, Pakistan; 2, Australia; 3, India.

## GYMNASTICS—MEN

**All-Around**—Sawato Kato, Japan.
**Floor Exercise**—Sawato Kato, Japan.
**Pommeled Horse**—Miroslav Cerar, Yugoslavia.
**Rings**—Akinori Nakayama, Japan.
**Long Horse**—Mikhail Voronin, USSR.
**Parallel Bars**—Akinori Nakayama, Japan.
**Horizontal Bar**—(tie) Mikhail Voronin, USSR; and Akinori Nakayama, Japan.
**Team**—Japan.

## GYMNASTICS—WOMEN

**All-Around**—Vera Caslavska, Czech.
**Long Horse Vault**—Vera Caslavska, Czech.
**Uneven Parallel Bars**—Vera Caslavska, Czech.
**Balance Beam**—Natalia Kuchinskaya, USSR.
**Floor Exercise**—(tie) Vera Caslavska, Czech; and Larissa Petrik, USSR.
**Team**—USSR.

## MODERN PENTATHLON

**Individual**—Bjoern Ferm, Sweden.
**Team**—Hungary.

### ROWING
**Coxed Fours**—New Zealand.
**Coxless Pairs**—East Germany.
**Eights**—West Germany.
**Single Sculls**—Jan Wienese, Netherlands.
**Double Sculls**—USSR.
**Coxed Pair**—Italy.
**Coxless Fours**—East Germany.

### SHOOTING
**Small Bore Rifle (Prone)**—Jan Kurka, Czech.
**Free Pistol**—Grigory Kosykh, USSR.
**Trapshooting**—Robert Braithwaite, Great Britain.
**Skeetshooting**—Evgeny Petrov, USSR.
**Small Bore Rifle (3 Positions)**—Bernard Klinger, West Germany.
**Free Rifle**—Gary Anderson, United States.
**Rapid Fire Pistol**—Josef Zapedzki, Poland.

### SOCCER
**Final Standings**—1, Hungary; 2, Bulgaria; 3, Japan.

### VOLLEYBALL
**Men's Final Standings**—1, USSR; 2, Japan; 3, Czech.
**Women's Final Standings**—1, USSR; 2, Japan; 3, Poland.

### WATER POLO
**Final Standings**—1, Yugoslavia; 2, USSR; 3, Hungary.

### WEIGHTLIFTING
**Bantamweight**—Mohammed Nassiri, Iran, 809¾.
**Featherweight**—Yosjinobu Miyake, Japan, 865.
**Lightweight**—Waldemar Baszanowski, Poland, 964½.

**Middleweight**—Victor Kurentsov, USSR, 1,046¾.
**Light Heavyweight**—Boris Selitsky, USSR, 1,068¾.
**Middle Heavyweight**—Kaarlo Kangasniemi, Finland, 1,140½.
**Heavyweight**—Leonid Zhabotinsky, USSR, 1,262.

### WRESTLING
*Free-Style*
**Flyweight**—Shigeo Nakata, Japan.
**Bantamweight**—Yojiro Uetake, Japan.
**Featherweight**—Masaaki Kanedo, Japan.
**Lightweight**—Abdollah Movahed, Iran.
**Welterweight**—Mahmud Atalay, Turkey.
**Middleweight**—Boris Gurevich, USSR.
**Light Heavyweight**—Ahmet Ayuk, Turkey.
**Heavyweight**—Aleksandr Medved, USSR.

*Greco-Roman*
**Bantamweight**—Jaros Varga, Hungary.
**Flyweight**—Peter Kirov, Bulgaria.
**Featherweight**—Roman Rurua, USSR.
**Lightweight**—Muneji Munemura, Japan.
**Welterweight**—Rudolph Vesper, East Germany.
**Middleweight**—Lothar Metz, East Germany.
**Light Heavyweight**—Boyan Radev, Bulgaria.
**Heavyweight**—Istvan Kozma, Hungary.

### YACHTING
**5.5 Meter Class**—Sweden.
**Finn**—USSR.
**Dragon**—United States.
**Star**—United States.
**Flying Dutchman**—Great Britain.

## Olympic Games Champions 1896—1968
### TRACK AND FIELD—MEN

**60-Meters Run**
1900 Alvin Kraenzlein, United States .............7s
1904 Archie Hahn, United States .............7s

**100-Meters Run**
1896 Thomas Burke, United States .............12s
1900 F. W. Jarvis, United States.........10 4-5s
1904 Archie Hahn, United States .............11s
1906 Archie Hahn, United States .. 11-5s
1908 Reginald Walker, South Africa....10 4-5s
1912 Ralph Craig, United States.........10 4-5s
1920 Charles Paddock, U. S. .............10 4-5s
1924 Harold Abrahams, Great Britain......10.6s
1928 Percy Williams, Canada .............10.8s
1932 Eddie Tolan, United States...........10.3s
1936 Jesse Owens, United States..........10.3s
1948 Harrison Dillard, United States......10.3s
1952 Lindy Remigino, United States.......10.4s
1956 Bobby Morrow, United States.........10.5s
1960 Armin Hary, Germany .............10.2s
1964 Bob Hayes, United States ..........10.0s
1968 Jim Hines, United States .............9.9s

**200-Meters Run**
1900 J. W. B. Tewksbury, United States.. 22 1-5s
1904 Archie Hahn, United States ...... 21 3-5s
1908 Robert Kerr, Canada ...............22 2-5s
1912 Ralph Craig, United States.........21.7s
1920 Allan Woodring, United States .......22s
1924 Jackson Scholz, United States .......21.6s
1928 Percy Williams, Canada .............21 4-5s
1932 Eddie Tolan, United States...........21.2s
1936 Jesse Owens, United States..........20.7s
1948 Mel Patton, United States..........21.1s
1952 Andrew Stanfield, United States......20.7s
1956 Bobby Morrow, United States ........20.6s
1960 Livio Berruti, Italy .............20.5s
1964 Henry Carr, United States ..........20.3s
1968 Tommie Smith, United States ...........19.8s

**400-Meters Run**
1896 Thomas Burke, United States.......54 1-5s
1900 Maxey Long, United States..........49 2-5s
1904 Harry Hillman, United States .......49 1-5s
1906 Paul Pilgrim, United States .......53 1-5s
1908 Wyndham Halswelle, Great Britain,
 walkover ...........................50s
1912 Charles Reidpath, United States......48.2s
1920 Bevil Rudd, South Africa.........49 3-5s
1924 Eric Liddell, Great Britain..........47.6s
1928 Ray Barbuti, United States ....... 47 4-5s
1932 William Carr, United States ........46.2s
1936 Archie Williams, United States ......46.5s
1948 Arthur Wint, Jamaica, B.W.I. ........46.2s
1952 George Rhoden, Jamaica, B.W.I.......45.9s
1956 Charles Jenkins, United States ......46.7s
1960 Otis Davis, United States ..........44.9s
1964 Michael Larrabee, United States......45.1s
1968 Lee Evans, United States .............43.8s

**800-Meters Run**
1896 Edwin Flack, Great Britain.........2m. 11s
1900 Alfred Tysoe, Great Britain.......2m. 1 2-5s
1904 James Lightbody, United States.... 1m. 56s
1906 Paul Pilgrim, United States .....2m. 1 1-5s
1908 Mel Sheppard, United States.....1m. 52 4-5s
1912 James Meredith, United States.. 1m. 51.9s
1920 Albert Hill, Great Britain.......1m. 53 2-5s

1924 Douglas Lowe, Great Britain......1m. 52.4s
1928 Douglas Lowe, Great Britain .....1m. 51 4-5s
1932 Thomas Hampson, Great Britain ...1m. 49.8s
1936 John Woodruff, United States......1m. 52.9s
1948 Mal Whitfield, United States ......1m. 49.2s
1952 Mal Whitfield, United States ......1m. 49.2s
1956 Thomas Courtney, United States 1m 47.7s
1960 Peter Snell, New Zealand ..........1m. 46.3s
1964 Peter Snell, New Zealand .........1m. 45.1s
1968 Ralph Doubell, Australia .........1m. 44.3s

**1,500-Meters Run**
1896 Edwin Flack, Great Britain......4m. 33 1-5s
1900 Charles Bennett, Great Britain ...... 4m. 6s
1904 James Lightbody, United States..4m. 5 2-5s
1906 James Lightbody, United States.....4m. 12s
1908 Mel Sheppard, United States....4m. 3 2-5s
1912 Arnold Jackson, Great Britain .....3m. 56.8s
1920 Albert Hill, Great Britain........4m. 1 4-5s
1924 Paavo Nurmi, Finland ...........3m. 53.6s
1928 Harry Larva, Finland .........3m. 53 1-5s
1932 Luigi Beccali, Italy .............3m. 51.2s
1936 Jack Lovelock, New Zealand......3m. 47.8s
1948 Henri Eriksson, Sweden .........3m. 49.8s
1952 Joseph Barthel, Luxemburg .......3m. 45.2s
1956 Ron Delany, Ireland ...........3m. 41.2s
1960 Herb Elliott, Australia .........3m. 35.6s
1964 Peter Snell, New Zealand .......3m. 38.1s
1968 Kipchoge Keino, Kenya .........3m. 34.9s

**3,000-Meters Steeplechase**
1920 Percy Hodge, Great Britain......10m. 2 2-5s
1924 Willie Ritola, Finland .......... 9m. 33.6s
1928 Toivo Loukola, Finland .......9m. 21 4-5s
1922 Volnari Iso-Hollo, Finland ...... 10m. 33.4s
 (About 3450 mtrs. extra lap by error)
1936 Volnari Iso-Hollo, Finland ....... 9m. 3.8s
1948 Thure Sjoestrand, Sweden ........ 9m. 4.6s
1952 Horace Ashenfelter, United States..8m. 45.4s
1956 Chris Brasher, Great Britain .... 8m. 42.2s
1960 Zdzislaw Krzyszkowiak, Poland ....8m. 34.2s
1964 Gaston Roelants, Belgium ........8m. 30.8s
1968 Amos Biwott, Kenya ...............8m. 51s

**5,000-Meters Run**
1912 Hannes Kolehmainen, Finland .....14m. 36.6s
1920 Joseph Guillemot France .....14m. 55⅗s
1924 Paavo Nurmi, Finland ...........14m. 31.2s
1928 Willie Ritola, Finland ..........14m. 38s
1932 Lauri Lehtinen, Finland .........14m. 30s
1936 Gunnar Hooker, Finland ........14m. 22.2s
1948 Gaston Reiff, Belgium .........14m. 17.6s
1952 Emil Zatopek, Czechoslovakia....14m. 6.0s
1956 Vladimir Kuts, USSR............13m. 39.6s
1960 Murray Halberg, New Zealand ...13m. 43.4s
1964 Bob Schul, United States .......13m. 48.8s
1968 Mohamed Gammoudi, Tunisia .....14m. 05.0s

**Cross-Country**
1912 Hannes Kolehmainen, Finland ... 45m. 11.6s

**5-Mile Run**
1906 H. Hawtrey, Great Britain ........26m. 26½s
1908 Emil Voigt, Great Britain .....25m. 11 1-5s

**10,000-Meters Run**
1912 Hannes Kolehmainen, Finland ...31m. 20.8s
1920 Paavo Nurmi, Finland...........31m.45.8s
1924 Willie Ritola, Finland..........30m. 23.2s

| | | |
|---|---|---|
| 1928 | Paavo Nurmi, Finland | 30m. 18 4-5s |
| 1932 | Janusz Kusocinski, Poland | 30m. 11.4s |
| 1936 | Ilmari Salminen, Finland | 30m. 15.4s |
| 1948 | Emil Zatopek, Czechoslovakia | 29m. 59.6s |
| 1952 | Emil Zatopek, Czechoslovakia | 29m. 17.0s |
| 1956 | Vladimir Kuts, USSR | 28m. 45.6s |
| 1960 | Pytor Bolotnikov, USSR | 28m. 32.2s |
| 1964 | Billy Mills, United States | 28m. 24.4s |
| 1968 | Naftali Temu, Kenya | 29m. 27.4s |

**Marathon**

| | | |
|---|---|---|
| 1896 | Spyros Loues, Greece | 2h. 55m. 20s |
| 1900 | Michel Teato, France | 2h. 59m |
| 1904 | Thomas Hicks, United States | 3h, 28m. 53s |
| 1906 | W. J. Sherring, Canada | 2h. 51m. 23 3-5s |
| 1908 | John J. Hayes, United States | 2h. 55m. 18.4s |
| 1912 | Kenneth McArthur, South Africa | 2h. 36m. 54.8s |
| 1920 | Hannes Kolehmainen, Finland | 2h. 32m. 35 4-5s |
| 1924 | Albin Stenroos, Finland | 2h. 41m. 22.6s |
| 1928 | El Ouafi, France | 2h. 32m. 57s |
| 1932 | Juan Zabala, Argentina | 2h. 31m. 36s |
| 1936 | Kitei Son, Japan | 2h. 29m. 19.2s |
| 1948 | Delfo Cabera, Argentina | 2h. 34m. 51.6s |
| 1952 | Emil Zatopek, Czechoslovakia | 2h. 23m. 03.2s |
| 1956 | Alain Mimoun, France | 2h. 25m. |
| 1960 | Abebe Bikila, Ethiopia | 2h. 15m. 15.2s |
| 1964 | Abebe Bikila, Ethiopia | 2h. 12m. 11.2s |
| 1968 | Mamo Wolde, Ethiopia | 2h. 20m. 26.4s |

**10,000-Meters Cross-Country**

| | | |
|---|---|---|
| 1920 | Paavo Nurmi, Finland | 27m. 15s |
| 1924 | Paavo Nurmi, Finland | 32m. 54.8s |

**1,500-Meters Walk**

| | | |
|---|---|---|
| 1906 | George V Bonhag, United States | 7m. 12 3-5s |

**3,000-Meters Walk**

| | | |
|---|---|---|
| 1920 | Ugo Frigerio, Italy | 13m. 14 1-5s |

**3,500-Meters Walk**

| | | |
|---|---|---|
| 1908 | George Larner, Great Britain | 14m. 55s |

**10,000-Meters Walk**

| | | |
|---|---|---|
| 1912 | George Goulding, Canada | 46m. 28.4s |
| 1920 | Ugo Frigerio, Italy | 48m. 6 1-5s |
| 1924 | Ugo Frigerio, Italy | 47m. 49s |
| 1948 | John Mikaelsson, Sweden | 45m. 13.2s |
| 1952 | John Mikaelsson, Sweden | 45m. 02.8s |

**20,000-Meters Walk**

| | | |
|---|---|---|
| 1956 | Leonid Spirine, USSR | 1h. 31m. 27.4s |
| 1960 | Vladimir Golubnichiy, USSR | 1h. 34m. 7.2s |
| 1964 | Kenneth Mathews, Great Britain | 1h. 29m. 34.0s |
| 1968 | Vladimir Golubnichiy, USSR | 1h. 35m. 58.4s |

**50,000 Meters Walk**

| | | |
|---|---|---|
| 1932 | Thos. W. Green, Great Britain | 4h. 50m. 10s |
| 1936 | Harold Whitlock, Great Britain | 4h. 30m. 41.4s |
| 1948 | John Lundgren, Sweden | 4h. 41m. 52s |
| 1952 | Giuseppe Bordoni, Italy | 4h. 28m. 07.8s |
| 1956 | Norman Read, New Zealand | 4h. 30m. 42.8s |
| 1960 | Donald Thompson, Great Britain | 4h. 25m. 30s |
| 1964 | Abdon Pamich, Italy | 4h. 11m. 11.2s |
| 1968 | Christoph Hohne, E. Germany | 4h. 20m. 13.6s |

**110-Meters Hurdles**

| | | |
|---|---|---|
| 1896 | Thomas Curtis, United States | 17 3-5s |
| 1900 | Alvin Kraenzlein, United States | 15 2-5s |
| 1964 | Frederick Schule, United States | 16s |
| 1906 | R. G. Leavitt, United States | 16 1-5s |
| 1908 | Forrest Smithson, United States | 15s |
| 1912 | Frederick Kelly, United States | 15.1s |
| 1920 | Earl Thomson, Canada | 14 4-5s |
| 1924 | Daniel Kinsey, United States | 15s |
| 1928 | Sydney Atkinson, South Africa | 14.8s |
| 1932 | George Saling, United States | 14.6s |
| 1936 | Forrest Towns, United States | 14.2s |
| 1948 | William Porter, United States | 13.9s |
| 1952 | Harrison Dillard, United States | 13.7s |
| 1956 | Lee Calhoun, United States | 13.5s |
| 1960 | Lee Calhoun, United States | 13.8s |
| 1964 | Hayes Jones, United States | 13.6s |
| 1968 | Willie Davenport, United States | 13.3s |

**200-Meters Hurdles**

| | | |
|---|---|---|
| 1900 | Alvin Kraenzlein, United States | 25 2-5s |
| 1904 | Harry Hillman, United States | 24 3-5s |

**400-Meters Hurdles**

| | | |
|---|---|---|
| 1900 | J. W. B. Tewksbury, United States | 57 3-5s |
| 1904 | Harry Hillman, United States | 53s |
| 1908 | Charles Bacon, United States | 55s |
| 1920 | Frank Loomis, United States | 54s |
| 1924 | F. Morgan Taylor, United States | 52.6s |
| 1928 | Lord Burghley, Great Britain | 53 2-5s |
| 1932 | Robert Tisdall, Ireland | 51.8s |
| 1936 | Glenn Hardin, United States | 52.4s |
| 1948 | Roy Cochran, United States | 51.1s |
| 1952 | Charles Moore, United States | 50.8s |
| 1956 | Glenn Davis, United States | 50.1s |
| 1960 | Glenn Davis, United States | 49.3s |
| 1964 | Rex Cawley, United States | 49.6s |
| 1968 | Dave Hemery, Great Britain | 48.1s |

**Standing High Jump**

| | | |
|---|---|---|
| 1900 | Ray Ewry, United States | 5ft. 5in |
| 1904 | Ray Ewry, United States | 4ft. 11in |
| 1906 | Ray Ewry, United States | 5ft. 1 5-8in |
| 1908 | Ray Ewry, United States | 5ft. 2in |
| 1912 | Platt Adams, United States | 5ft. 4 1-4in |

**Running High Jump**

| | | |
|---|---|---|
| 1896 | Ellery Clark, United States | 5ft. 11 1-4in |
| 1900 | Irving Baxter, United States | 6ft. 2 4-5in |
| 1904 | Samuel Jones, United States | 5ft. 11in |
| 1906 | Con Leahy, Ireland | 5ft. 9 7-8in |
| 1908 | Harry Porter, United States | 6ft. 3in |
| 1912 | Almer W. Richards, United States | 6ft. 4in |
| 1920 | Richard Landon, United States | 6ft. 4 3-8in |
| 1924 | Harold Osborn, United States | 6ft. 6in |
| 1928 | Robert W. King, United States | 6ft. 4 3-8in |
| 1932 | Duncan McNaughton, Canada | 6ft. 5⅝in |
| 1936 | Cornelius Johnson, United States | 6ft. 7 15-16in |
| 1948 | John L. Winter, Australia | 6ft. 6in |
| 1952 | Walter Davis, United States | 6ft. 8.32in |
| 1956 | Charles Dumas, United States | 6ft. 11¼in |
| 1960 | Robert Shavlakadze, USSR | 7ft. 1in |
| 1964 | Valery Brumel, USSR | 7ft. 1⅞in |
| 1968 | Dick Fosbury, United States | 7ft. 4¼in |

**Standing Broad Jump**

| | | |
|---|---|---|
| 1900 | Ray Ewry, United States | 10ft. 6 2-5in |
| 1904 | Ray Ewry, United States | 11ft. 4 7-8in |
| 1906 | Ray Ewry, United States | 10ft. 10in |
| 1908 | Ray Ewry, United States | 10ft. 11 1-4in |
| 1912 | Constantin Tsicilitras, Greece | 11ft. 3-4in |

**Long Jump**

| | | |
|---|---|---|
| 1896 | Ellery Clark, United States | 20ft. 9 3-4in |
| 1900 | Alvin Kraenzlein, United States | 23ft. 6 7-8in |
| 1904 | Myer Prinstein, United States | 24ft. 1in |
| 1906 | Myer Prinstein, United States | 23ft. 7 1-2in |
| 1908 | Frank Irons, United States | 24ft. 6 1-2in |
| 1912 | Albert Gutterson, United States | 24ft. 11 1-4in |
| 1920 | Wm. Petterssen, Sweden | 23ft. 5 1-2in |
| 1924 | DeHart Hubbard, United States | 24ft. 5 1-8in |
| 1928 | Edward B. Hamm, United States | 25ft. 4 3-4in |
| 1932 | Edward Gordon, United States | 25ft. 3-4in |
| 1936 | Jesse Owens, United States | 26ft. 5 5-16in |
| 1948 | William Steele, United States | 25ft. 8in |
| 1952 | Jerome Biffle, United States | 24ft. 10.03in |
| 1956 | Gregory Bell, United States | 25ft. 8¼in |
| 1960 | Ralph Boston, United States | 26ft. 7¾in |
| 1964 | Lynn Davies, Great Britain | 26ft. 5¾in |
| 1968 | Bob Beamon, United States | 29ft. 2½in. |

**400-Meters Relay**

| | | |
|---|---|---|
| 1912 | Great Britain | 42.4s |
| 1920 | United States | 42 1-5s |
| 1924 | United States | 41s |
| 1928 | United States | 41s |
| 1932 | United States | 40s |
| 1936 | United States | 39.8s |
| 1948 | United States | 40.3s |
| 1952 | United States | 40.1s |
| 1956 | United States | 39.5s |
| 1960 | Germany (U. S. disqual.) | 39.5s |
| 1964 | United States | 39.0s |
| 1968 | United States | 38.2s |

**1,600 Meters Relay**

| | | |
|---|---|---|
| 1908 | United States | 3m. 27 1-5s |
| 1912 | United States | 3m. 16.6s |
| 1920 | Great Britain | 3m. 22 1-5s |
| 1924 | United States | 3m. 16s |
| 1928 | United States | 3m. 14 1-5s |
| 1932 | United States | 3m. 8.2s |
| 1936 | Great Britain | 3m. 9s |
| 1948 | United States | 3m. 10.4s |
| 1952 | Jamaica, B.W.I. | 3m. 03.9s |
| 1956 | United States | 3m. 04.8s |
| 1960 | United States | 3m. 02.2s |
| 1964 | United States | 3m. 00.7s |
| 1968 | United States | 2m. 56.1s |

**Pole Vault**

| | | |
|---|---|---|
| 1896 | William Hoyt, United States | 10ft. 9¾in |
| 1900 | Irving Baxter, United States | 10ft. 9 9-10in |
| 1904 | Charles Dvorak, United States | 11ft. 6in |
| 1906 | Fernand Gouder, France | 11ft. 6in |
| 1908 | A. C. Gilbert, United States; Edward Cook Jr., United States | 12ft. 2in |
| 1912 | Harry Babcock, United States | 12ft. 11 1-2in |
| 1920 | Frank Foss, United States | 13ft. 5in |
| 1924 | Lee Barnes, United States; Glenn Graham, United States | 12ft. 11 1-2in |
| 1928 | Sabin W. Carr, United States | 13ft. 9 1-2in |
| 1932 | William Miller, United States | 14ft. 1 7-8in |
| 1936 | Earle Meadows, United States | 14ft. 3 1-4in |
| 1948 | Guinn Smith, United States | 14ft. 1¼in |
| 1952 | Robert Richards, United States | 14ft. 11¼ in |
| 1956 | Robert Richards, United States | 14ft. 11½in |
| 1960 | Don Bragg, United States | 15ft. 5⅛in |
| 1964 | Fred Hansen, United States | 16ft. 8½in |
| 1968 | Bob Seagren, United States | 17ft. 8½in |

**16-Lb. Hammer Throw**

| | | |
|---|---|---|
| 1900 | John Flannagan, United States | 167ft. 4in |
| 1904 | John Flannagan, United States | 168ft. 1in |
| 1908 | John Flannagan, United States | 170ft. 4 1-4in |
| 1912 | Matt McGrath, United States | 179ft. 7 1-8in |
| 1920 | Pat Ryan, United States | 173ft. 5 5-8in |
| 1924 | Fred Tootell, United States | 174ft. 10 1-8in |
| 1928 | Patrick O'Callaghan, Ireland | 168ft. 7 3-8in |
| 1932 | Patrick O'Callaghan, Ireland | 176ft. 11 1-8in |
| 1936 | Karl Hein, Germany | 185 ft. 4 3-16in |
| 1948 | Imre Nemeth, Hungary | 183ft. 11½in |
| 1952 | Jozsef Csermak, Hungary | 197ft. 11.67in |
| 1956 | Harold Connolly, United States | 207ft. 3½in |

1960 Vasily Rudenkov, USSR............220ft. 2in
1964 Romuald Klim, USSR............228ft. 9½in
1968 Gyula Zsivotsky, Hungary ..........240ft. 8in

**Discus Throw**

1896 Robt. Garrett, United States....95ft. 7 1-2in
1900 Rudolf Bauer, Hungary......118ft. 2 9-10in
1904 Martin Sheridan, United States 128ft. 10 1-2in
1906 Martin Sheridan, United States..136ft. 1-3in
1908 Martin Sheridan, United States....134ft. 2in
1912 Armas Taipale, Finland.............148 4in
Right and left hand—Armas Taipale
Finland ..................271ft. 10 1-4in
1920 Elmer Niklander, Finland.....146ft. 7 1-4in
1924 Clarence Houser, United States ..151ft. 5⅛in
1928 Clarence Houser, United States ..155ft. 3in
1932 John Anderson, United States..162ft. 4 7-8in
1936 Ken Carpenter, United States..165ft. 7 3-8in
1948 Adolfo Consolini, Italy............173ft. 2in
1952 Sim Iness, United States........180ft. 6.85in
1956 Al Oerter, United States..........184ft. 11in
1960 Al Oerter, United States..........194ft. 2in
1964 Al Oerter, United States.........200ft. 1½in
1968 Al Oerter, United States .........212ft. 6½in

**Standing Hop, Step and Jump**

1900 Ray Ewry, United States .........34ft. 8½in
1904 Ray Ewry, United States .........34ft. 7¼in

**Triple Jump**

1896 James Connolly, United States ..........45ft
1900 Myer Prinstein, United States...47ft. 4 1-4in
1904 Myer Prinstein, United States.......... 47ft
1906 P. G. O'Connor, Ireland ............46ft. 2in
1908 Timothy Ahearne, Great Britain .48ft. 11¼in.
1912 Gustaf Lindblom, Sweden .........48ft.5⅛in
1920 Vilho Tuulos, Finland ..............47ft. 7in
1924 Archie Winter, Australia ........50ft. 11¼in
1928 Mikio Oda, Japan...................49ft. 11in
1932 Chuhei Nambu, Japan...............51ft. 7in
1936 Naoto Tajima, Japan.. .........52ft. 5 7-8in
1948 Arne Ahman, Sweden .............50ft. 6¼in
1952 Adhemar da Silva, Brazil.........53ft. 2.59in
1956 Adhemar da Silva, Brazil.........53ft. 7½in
1960 Jozef Schmidt, Poland ...............55ft. 1¾in
1964 Jozef Schmidt, Poland ...........55ft. 3½in
1968 Victor Saneev, USSR ...............57ft. ¾in

**16-Lb. Shot Put**

1896 Robt. Garrett, United States.... 36ft. 2in
1900 Robt. Sheldon, United States ..46ft. 3 1-8in
1904 Ralph Rose, United States..........48ft. 7in
1906 Martin Sheridan, United States 40ft. 4 4-5in
1908 Ralph Rose, United States......46ft. 7 1-2in
1912 Pat McDonald, United States.........50ft. 4in
Right and left hand—Ralph Rose,
United States .. .........90ft. 5 1-2in
1920 Ville Porhola, Finland.........48ft. 7 1-8in
1924 Clarence Houser, United States ..49ft. 2 3-8in
1928 John Kuck, United States........52ft. 3-4in
1932 Leo Sexton, United States......52ft. 6 3-16in
1936 Hans Woelke, Germany.......53ft. 1 13-16in
1948 Wilbur Thompson, United States.. 56ft. 2in
1952 Parry O'Brien United States......57ft. 1.43in
1956 Parry O'Brien, United States.......60ft. 11in
1960 William Nieder, United States ....64ft. 6¾in
1964 Dallas Long, United States .......66ft. 8½in
1968 Randy Matson, United States .....67ft. 4¾in

**Discus Throw—Greek Style**

1906 Werner Jaevinen, Finland.........115ft. 4in
1908 Martin Sheridan, United States ....124ft. 8in

**Javelin Throw**

1906 Erik Lemming, Sweden.............175ft. 6in
1908 Erik Lemming, Sweden..........178ft. 7 1-2in
Held in middle—Erik Lemming,
Sweden ..................179ft. 10 1-2in
1912 E. Lemming, Sweden..........198ft. 11 1-4in
Both hands, Julius Saaristo
Finland ......................358ft. 11 7-8in
1920 Jonni Myyra, Finland.. .........215ft. 9¾in
1924 Jonni Myyra, Finland..........206ft. 6 3-4in
1928 Eric Lundquist, Sweden........218ft. 6 1-8in
1932 Matti Jarvinen, Finland............238ft. 7in
1936 Gerhard Stoeck, Germany.....235ft. 8 5-16in
1948 Kaj T. Rautavaara, Finland....228ft. 10½in
1952 Cy Young, United States........242ft. 0.79in
1956 Egil Danielsen, Norway..........281ft. 2¼in
1960 Viktor Tsibulenko, USSR ........277ft. 8⅜in
1964 Pauli Nevala, Finland............271ft. 2½in
1968 Yanis Lusis, USSR ...............295ft. 7¼in

**Modern Pentathlon**

1952 Lars Hall, Sweden ....................32 pts
1956 Lars Hall, Sweden ..................4,833 pts
1960 Ferenc Nemeth, Hungary ..........5,024 pts
1964 Ferenc Torok, Hungary ...........5,116 pts
1968 Bjoern Ferm, Sweden ...............4,964 pts

**Decathlon (A)**

1912 Hugo Wieslander, Sweden ........7,724.49 pts
1920 Helge Loveland, Norway ........6,804.35 pts
1924 Harold Osborn, United States..7,710.775 pts
1928 Paavo Yrjola, Finland ...........8,056.20 pts
1932 James Bausch, United States ....8,462.23 pts
1936 Glenn Morris, United States........7,900 pts
1948 Robert Mathias, United States......7,139 pts
1952 Robert Mathias, United States......7,887 pts
1956 Milton Campbell, United States....7,937 pts
1960 Rafer Johnson, United States......8,392 pts
1964 Willi Holdorf, Germany ............7,887 pts
1968 Bill Toomey, United States ..........8,193 pts
(A) Former point system, 1936-1960

## TRACK AND FIELD—WOMEN

**100-Meter Run**

1928 Elizabeth Robinson, United States......12.2s
1932 Stella Walsh, Poland ....................11.9s
1936 Helen Stephens, United States .........11.5s
1948 Francina Blankers-Koen, Netherlands...11.9s
1952 Marjorie Jackson, Australia..............11.5s
1956 Betty Cuthbert, Australia.................11.5s
1960 Wilma Rudolph, United States..........11.0s
1964 Wyomia Tyus, United States............11.4s
1968 Wyomia Tyus, United States............11.0s

**200-Meter Run**

1948 Francina Blankers-Koen, Netherlands...24.4s
1952 Marjorie Jackson, Australia..............23.7s
1956 Betty Cuthbert, Australia.................23.4s
1960 Wilma Rudolph, United States..........24.0s
1964 Edith McGuire, United States...........23.0s
1968 Irene Szswinska, Poland..................22.5s

**400-Meter Run**

1964 Betty Cuthbert, Australia.....................52s
1968 Colette Besson, France ........................52s

**800-Meter Run**

1928 Linda Radke, Germany.............2m. 16.8s
1960 Ljudmila Shevcova, USSR ...........2m. 4.3s
1964 Ann Packer, Great Britain..........2m. 1.1s
1968 Madeline Manning, United States...2m. 0.9s

**400-Meter Relay**

1928 Canada .......................................48.4s
1932 United States ...............................47.0s
1936 United States ...............................46.9s
1948 Netherlands ..................................47.5s
1952 United States ...............................45.9s
1956 Australia .....................................44.5s
1960 United States ...............................44.5s
1964 Poland .........................................43.6s
1968 United States.................................42.8s

**80-Meter Hurdles**

1932 Mildred Didrikson, United States.......11.7s
1936 Trebisonda Villa, Italy ...................11.7s
1948 Francina Blankers-Koen, Netherlands...11.2s
1952 Shirley Strickland de la Hunty, Australia 10.9s
1956 Shirley Strickland de la Hunty, Australia 10.7s
1960 Irina Press, USSR ..........................10.8s
1964 Karin Balzer, Germany .....................10.5s
1968 Maureen Caird, Australia..................10.3s

**High Jump**

1928 Ethel Catherwood, Canada ...........5ft. 3in
1932 Jean Shiley, United States..........5ft. 5¼in
1936 Ibolya Csak, Hungary ...................5ft. 3in
1948 Alice Coachman, United States.....5ft. 6⅛in
1952 Esther Brand, South Africa..........5ft. 5¾in
1956 Mildred L. McDaniel, United States 5ft. 9¼in
1960 Iolanda Balas, Romania ..............6ft. ¼in
1964 Iolanda Balas, Romania ..............6ft. 2⅞in
1968 Miloslava Rezkova, Czech..........5ft. 11¾in

**Discus Throw**

1928 Helena Konopacka, Poland......129ft. 11⅞in
1932 Lillian Copeland, United States.....133ft. 2in
1936 Gisela Mauermayer, Germany..156ft. 3 3/16in
1948 Micheline Ostermeyer, France....137ft. 6½in
1952 Nina Romaschkova, USSR.........168ft. 8½in
1956 Olga Fikotova, Czechoslovakia....176ft. 1½in
1960 Nina Ponomareva, USSR...........180ft. 8¼in
1964 Tamara Press, USSR ...........187ft. 10½in
1968 Lia Manoliu, Romania...........191ft. 2½in

**Javelin Throw**

1932 Mildred Didrikson, United States...143ft. 4in
1936 Tilly Fleischer, Germany........148ft. 2¾in
1948 Herma Bauma, Austria..............149ft. 6in
1952 Dana Zatopekova, Czechoslovakia...165ft. 7in
1956 Inessa Janzeme, USSR..............176ft. 8in
1960 Elvira Ozolina, USSR..............183ft. 8in
1964 Mihaela Penes, Romania .........198ft. 7½in
1968 Angela Nemeth, Hungary...........198ft. ½in

**Shot Put**

1948 Micheline Ostermeyer, France....45ft. 1½in
1952 Galina Zybina, USSR..............50ft. 1½in
1956 T. Tishkyevich, USSR.................54ft. 5in
1960 Tamara Press, USSR...............56ft. 9⅞in
1964 Tamara Press, USSR...............59ft. 6¼in
1968 Margarita Gummel, E. Germany....64ft. 4in

**Long Jump**

1948 Olga Gyarmati, Hungary...........18ft. 8¼in
1962 Yvette Williams, New Zealand....20ft. 5¾in
1956 E. Krzeskinska, Poland...........20ft. 9¾in
1960 Vyera Krepina, USSR.............20ft. 10¾in
1964 Mary Rand, Great Britain..........22ft. 2¼in
1968 V. Viscopoleanu, Romania.........22ft. 4½in

**Pentathlon**

1964 Irina Press, USSR ................5,246 pts.
1968 Ingred Becker, W. Germany .......5,098 pts.

# Olympic Games Records

The modern Olympic Games, first held in Athens, Greece, in 1896, were the result of efforts by Baron Pierre de Coubertin, a French educator, to promote interest in education and culture, also to foster better international understanding through the universal medium of youth's love of athletics.

His source of inspiration for the Olympic Games was the ancient Greek Olympic Games, most notable of the four Panhellenic celebrations. The games were combined patriotic, religious and athletic festivals held every four years. The first such recorded festival was that held in 776 B.C., the date from which the Greeks began to keep their calendar by "Olympiads," or four-year spans between the games.

The first Olympiad is said to have consisted merely of a 200-yard foot race near the small city of Olympia, but the games gained in scope and became demonstrations of national pride. Only Greek citizens—amateurs—were permitted to participate. Winners received laurel, wild olive and palm wreaths and were accorded many special privileges. Under the Roman emperors, the games deteriorated into professional carnivals and circuses. Emperor Theodosius banned them in 394 A.D.

Baron de Coubertin enlisted 9 nations to send athletes to the first modern Olympics in 1896; now more than 100 nations compete. Winter Olympic Games were started in 1924.

## SITES AND UNOFFICIAL WINNERS OF GAMES

| | | | | | | | |
|---|---|---|---|---|---|---|---|
| 1896 | Athens (U. S.) | 1912 | Stockholm (U. S.) | 1936 | Berlin (Germany) | 1964 | Tokyo (U. S.) |
| 1900 | Paris (U. S.) | 1920 | Antwerp (U. S.) | 1948 | London (U. S.) | 1968 | Mexico City (U. S.) |
| 1904 | St. Louis (U. S.) | 1924 | Paris (U. S.) | 1952 | Helsinki (U. S.) | | |
| 1906 | Athens (U. S.) | 1928 | Amsterdam (U. S.) | 1956 | Melbourne (USSR) | 1972 | Munich (scheduled) |
| 1908 | London (U. S.) | 1932 | Los Angeles (U. S.) | 1960 | Rome (USSR) | | |

## TRACK AND FIELD—MEN

| Event | Record | Holder | Nation | Site, date |
|---|---|---|---|---|
| 100-meter run | 9.9 s | Jim Hines | United States | Mexico City 1968 |
| 200-meter run | 19.8 s | Tommie Smith | United States | Mexico City 1968 |
| 400-meter run | 43.8 s | Lee Evans | United States | Mexico City 1968 |
| 800-meter run | 1 m., 44.3 s | Ralph Doubell | Australia | Mexico City 1968 |
| 1500-meter run | 3 m., 34.9 s | Kipchoge Keino | Kenya | Mexico City 1968 |
| 5000-meter run | 13 m., 39.6 s | Vladimir Kuts | USSR | Melbourne 1956 |
| 10,000-meter run | 28 m., 24.4 s | Billy Mills | United States | Tokyo 1964 |
| Marathon | 2 h., 12 m., 11.2 s | Abebe Bikila | Ethiopia | Tokyo 1964 |
| 50,000-meter walk | 4 h., 11 m., 12.4 s | Abdon Pamich | Italy | Tokyo 1964 |
| 110-meter hurdles | 13.3 s | Willie Davenport | United States | Mexico City 1968 |
| 400-meter hurdles | 48.1 s | Dave Hemery | Great Britain | Mexico City 1968 |
| 3,000-meter stpl | 8 m., 30.8 s | Gaston Roelants | Belgium | Tokyo 1964 |
| High jump | 7 ft., 4¼ in. | Dick Fosbury | United States | Mexico City 1968 |
| Long jump | 29 ft., 2½ in. | Bob Beamon | United States | Mexico City 1968 |
| Triple jump | 57 ft., ¾ in. | Victor Saneev | USSR | Mexico City 1968 |
| Pole vault | 17 ft., 8½ in. | Bob Seagren | United States | Mexico City 1968 |
| Discus | 212 ft., 6½ in. | Al Oerter | United States | Mexico City 1968 |
| Javelin | 295 ft., 7¼ in. | Yanis Lusis | USSR | Mexico City 1968 |
| 16-lb. shot put | 67 ft., 4¾ in. | Randy Matson | United States | Mexico City 1968 |
| 16-lb. hammer | 240 ft., 8 in. | Gyula Zsivotsky | Hungary | Mexico City 1968 |
| Decathlon | 8,193 Points | Bill Toomey | United States | Mexico City 1968 |

400-meter relay—38.2s.—United States (Greene, Pender, R. Smith, Hines), Mexico City, 1968.
1600-meter relay—2 m. 56.1 s.—United States (Matthews, Freeman, James, Evans), Mexico City, 1968.

## TRACK AND FIELD—WOMEN

| | | | | |
|---|---|---|---|---|
| 100-meter run | 11.0 s | Wyomia Tyus | United States | Mexico City 1968 |
| 200-meter run | 22.5 s | Irena Szewinska | Poland | Mexico City 1968 |
| 400-meter run | 52.0 s | Betty Cuthbert | Australia | Tokyo 1964 |
| | | Colette Besson | France | Mexico City 1968 |
| 800-meter run | 2 m., 0.9 s | Madeline Manning | United States | Mexico City 1968 |
| 80-meter hurdles | 10.3 s | Maureen Caird | Australia | Mexico City 1968 |
| High jump | 6 ft., 2⅞ in. | Iolanda Balas | Romania | Tokyo 1964 |
| Long jump | 22 ft., 4½ in. | V. Viscopoleanu | Romania | Mexico City 1968 |
| Discus | 191 ft., 2½ in. | Lia Manoliu | Romania | Mexico City 1968 |
| Javelin | 198 ft., 7½ in | Mihaela Penes | Romania | Tokyo 1964 |
| Shot put | 64 ft., 4 in. | Margarita Gummel | E. Germany | Mexico City 1968 |
| Pentathlon | 5,246 Points | Irena Press | USSR | Tokyo 1964 |

400-meter relay—42.8s. United States (Ferrell, Bailes, Netter, Tyus), Mexico City, 1968.

## SWIMMING—MEN

| | | | | |
|---|---|---|---|---|
| 100-meter freestyle | 52.2 s | Mike Wenden | Australia | Mexico City 1968 |
| 200-meter freestyle | 1 m., 55.2 s | Mike Wenden | Australia | Mexico City 1968 |
| 400-meter freestyle | 4 m., 09.0 s | Mike Burton | United States | Mexico City 1968 |
| 1,500-meter freestyle | 16 m., 38.9 s | Mike Burton | United States | Mexico City 1968 |
| 100-meter backstroke | 58.7 s | Roland Matthes | E. Germany | Mexico City 1968 |
| 200-meter backstroke | 2 m., 09.6 s | Roland Matthes | E. Germany | Mexico City 1968 |
| 100-m. breaststroke | 1 m., 07.7 s | Don McKenzie | United States | Mexico City 1968 |
| 200-m. breaststroke | 2 m., 27.8 s | Ian O'Brien | Australia | Tokyo 1964 |
| 100-meter butterfly | 55.9 s | Doug Russell | United States | Mexico City 1968 |
| 200-meter butterfly | 2 m., 6.6 s | Kevin Berry | Australia | Tokyo 1964 |
| 200-meter medley | 2 m., 12 s | Charles Hickcox | United States | Mexico City 1968 |
| 400-meter medley | 4 m., 45.4 s | Dick Roth | United States | Tokyo 1964 |

400-meter freestyle relay, 3:31.7—United States (Spitz, Zorn, Reyrch, Walsh), 1968.
800-meter freestyle relay, 7:52.1—United States (Clark, Saari, Ilman, Schollander), 1964.
400-meter medley relay, 3:54.9—United States (Hickcox, Russell, McKenzie, Walsh), 1968.

## SWIMMING—WOMEN

| | | | | |
|---|---|---|---|---|
| 100-meter freestyle | 59.5 s | Dawn Fraser | Australia | Tokyo 1964 |
| 200-meter freestyle | 2 m., 10.5 s | Debbie Meyer | United States | Mexico City 1968 |
| 400-meter freestyle | 4 m., 31.8 s | Debbie Meyer | United States | Mexico City 1968 |
| 800-meter freestyle | 9 m., 24 s | Debbie Meyer | United States | Mexico City 1968 |
| 100-meter backstroke | 1 m., 06.2 s | Kaye Hall | United States | Mexico City 1968 |
| 200-meter backstroke | 2 m., 24.8 s | Pokey Watson | United States | Mexico City 1968 |
| 100-m. breaststroke | 1 m., 15.8 s | Djurdjica Biedov | Yugoslavia | Mexico City 1968 |
| 200-m. breaststroke | 2 m., 44.4 s | Sharon Wichman | United States | Mexico City 1968 |
| 100-meter butterfly | 1 m., 4.7 s | Sharon Stouder | United States | Tokyo 1964 |
| 200-meter butterfly | 2 m., 24.7 s | Ada Kok | Netherlands | Mexico City 1968 |
| 200-meter medley | 2 m., 24.7 s | Claudia Kolb | United States | Mexico City 1968 |
| 400-meter medley | 5 m., 08.5 s | Claudia Kolb | United States | Mexico City 1968 |

400-meter freestyle relay—4:02.5—United States (Barkman, Gustavson, Pedersen, Henne), 1968.
400-meter medley relay—4:28.3—United States (Hall, Daniel, Ball, Pedersen), 1968.

# ELECTION STATISTICS

## Popular and Electoral Vote for President, 1968

### Latest figures compiled by United Press International from official and unofficial returns.

| States | Electoral vote | | | Popular vote | | | | |
|---|---|---|---|---|---|---|---|---|
| | Nixon | Hum-phrey | Wal-lace | Nixon | Hum-phrey | Wal-lace | Other | Total |
| Ala. | ..... | ....... | 10 | 146,923 | 196,579 | 691,425 | 4,002 | 1,038,929 |
| Alaska | 3 | ....... | ....... | 36,428 | 34,501 | 9,887 | ....... | 80,816 |
| Ariz. | 5 | ....... | ..... | 255,970 | 166,742 | 45,066 | 2,762 | 470,540 |
| Ark. | ..... | ....... | 6 | 186,547 | 183,317 | 236,504 | ....... | 606,368 |
| Calif. | 40 | ....... | ..... | 3,409,554 | 3,187,364 | 482,162 | 26,992 | 7,106,072 |
| Colo. | 6 | ....... | ..... | 409,262 | 336,272 | 60,691 | 1,274 | 807,499 |
| Conn. | ..... | 8 | ..... | 569,942 | 661,595 | 78,931 | ....... | 1,310,468 |
| Del. | 3 | ....... | ....... | 95,479 | 88,471 | 28,285 | ....... | 212,235 |
| D. of C. | ..... | 3 | ....... | 31,012 | 139,556 | ....... | ....... | 170,568 |
| Fla. | 14 | ....... | ....... | 886,804 | 676,794 | 624,207 | ....... | 2,187,805 |
| Ga. | ..... | ....... | 12 | 365,722 | 333,062 | 535,389 | ....... | 1,234,173 |
| Hawaii | ..... | 4 | ....... | 91,440 | 141,300 | 3,465 | ....... | 236,205 |
| Idaho | 4 | ....... | ....... | 164,029 | 88,835 | 36,058 | ....... | 288,922 |
| Ill. | 26 | ....... | ....... | 2,137,239 | 2,008,319 | 385,058 | ....... | 4,530,616 |
| Ind. | 13 | ....... | ..... | 1,057,784 | 806,259 | 243,030 | 6,124 | 2,113,197 |
| Iowa | 9 | ....... | ....... | 616,776 | 477,445 | 66,258 | 900 | 1,161,379 |
| Kan. | 7 | ....... | ....... | 468,172 | 299,890 | 87,453 | ....... | 855,515 |
| Ky. | 9 | ....... | ....... | 458,905 | 395,097 | 190,493 | ....... | 1,044,495 |
| La. | ..... | ....... | 10 | 259,715 | 317,929 | 537,045 | ....... | 1,114,689 |
| Me. | ..... | 4 | ....... | 164,560 | 212,950 | 6,232 | ....... | 382,742 |
| Md. | ..... | 10 | ....... | 514,357 | 584,891 | 179,945 | ....... | 1,279,193 |
| Mass. | ..... | 14 | ....... | 762,477 | 1,458,058 | 85,556 | ....... | 2,306,091 |
| Mich. | ..... | 21 | ....... | 1,330,749 | 1,567,310 | 320,344 | 3,981 | 3,222,384 |
| Minn. | ..... | 10 | ....... | 620,687 | 807,122 | 66,948 | 3,198 | 1,497,955 |
| Miss. | ..... | ....... | 7 | 88,214 | 149,419 | 414,402 | ....... | 652,035 |
| Mo. | 12 | ....... | ....... | 807,635 | 785,908 | 205,129 | ....... | 1,798,672 |
| Mont. | 4 | ....... | ....... | 130,119 | 109,218 | 18,548 | ....... | 257,885 |
| Nebr. | 5 | ....... | ....... | 303,968 | 163,531 | 42,604 | ....... | 510,103 |
| Nev. | 3 | ....... | ....... | 71,961 | 58,999 | 20,071 | ....... | 151,031 |
| N. H. | 4 | ....... | ....... | 154,903 | 130,589 | 11,173 | 525 | 297,190 |
| N. J. | 17 | ....... | ....... | 1,325,465 | 1,264,206 | 262,164 | 23,683 | 2,875,518 |
| N. M. | 4 | ....... | ....... | 168,473 | 129,451 | 25,602 | 1,966 | 325,492 |
| N. Y. | ..... | 43 | ....... | 2,980,420 | 3,356,999 | 349,205 | 24,963 | 6,711,587 |
| N. C. | 13 | ....... | ....... | 619,434 | 456,968 | 490,609 | ....... | 1,567,011 |
| N. D. | 4 | ....... | ....... | 138,667 | 94,319 | 14,244 | 198 | 247,428 |
| Ohio | 26 | ....... | ....... | 1,785,318 | 1,692,213 | 468,591 | ....... | 3,946,122 |
| Okla. | 8 | ....... | ....... | 449,697 | 301,658 | 191,731 | ....... | 943,086 |
| Ore. | 6 | ....... | ....... | 403,491 | 355,875 | 49,151 | ....... | 808,517 |
| Pa. | ..... | 29 | ....... | 1,991,784 | 2,203,946 | 368,275 | 11,377 | 4,575,382 |
| R. I. | ..... | 4 | ....... | 115,929 | 239,497 | 14,967 | 480 | 370,873 |
| S. C. | 8 | ....... | ....... | 260,558 | 196,889 | 211,754 | ....... | 669,201 |
| S. D. | 4 | ....... | ....... | 147,438 | 117,505 | 13,209 | ....... | 278,152 |
| Tenn. | 11 | ....... | ....... | 467,232 | 350,941 | 421,044 | 87 | 1,238,404 |
| Texas | ..... | 25 | ....... | 1,227,199 | 1,267,317 | 581,717 | ....... | 3,076,233 |
| Utah | 4 | ....... | ....... | 238,637 | 157,072 | 27,052 | 274 | 423,035 |
| Vt. | 3 | ....... | ....... | 85,128 | 70,449 | 4,953 | 550 | 161,080 |
| Va. | 12 | ....... | ....... | 595,607 | 443,873 | 322,203 | 1,432 | 1,363,115 |
| Wash. | ..... | 9 | ....... | 520,491 | 561,675 | 85,713 | 2,273 | 1,170,152 |
| W. Va. | ..... | 7 | ....... | 306,601 | 373,382 | 72,022 | ....... | 752,005 |
| Wis. | 12 | ....... | ....... | 809,997 | 748,804 | 127,835 | 2,934 | 1,689,570 |
| Wyo. | 3 | ....... | ....... | 70,093 | 44,893 | 11,059 | ....... | 126,045 |
| **Total U.S.** | **302** | **191** | **45** | **31,304,992** | **30,994,354** | **9,825,459** | **119,975** | **72,244,780** |

## Major National Convention Cities since 1856

### (Number in parentheses)

Atlantic City, N. J., (1)—Dem., 1964.
Baltimore, Md., (3)—Rep., 1864; Dem., 1872, 1912.
Charleston, S. C., (1)—Dem., 1860.
Chicago, Ill., (24)—Rep., 1860, 1868, 1880, 1884, 1888, 1904, 1908, 1912, 1916, 1920, 1932, 1944, 1952, 1960. Dem., 1864, 1884, 1892, 1896, 1932, 1940, 1944, 1952, 1956, 1968.
Cincinnati, O., (3)—Rep., 1876; Dem., 1856, 1880.
Cleveland, O., (2)—Rep., 1924, 1936.
Denver, Col., (1)—Dem., 1908.
Houston, Tex., (1)—Dem., 1928.

Kansas City, Mo., (2)—Rep., 1928; Dem., 1900.
Los Angeles, Calif., (1)—Dem., 1960.
Miami, Fla. (1)—Rep., 1968.
Minneapolis, Minn., (1)—Rep., 1892.
New York City, (2)—Dem., 1868, 1924.
Philadelphia, Pa., (7)—Rep., 1856, 1872, 1900, 1940, 1948; Dem., 1936, 1948.
St. Louis, Mo., (5)—Rep., 1896; Dem., 1876, 1888, 1904, 1916.
San Francisco, Calif., (3)—Rep., 1956, 1964; Dem., 1920.

# United States Senate Election Returns by States, 1968

Source: Compiled from United Press International official and unofficial returns as of Nov. 20, 1968

Asterisk (*) denotes incumbent

| State | Senator Elected | | Vote Cast | Losing Candidate | | Vote Cast |
|---|---|---|---|---|---|---|
| Alabama | James B. Allen | (D) | 638,774 | Perry O. Hooper | (R) | 202,227 |
| Alaska[1] | Mike Gravel | (D) | 35,754 | Elmer Rasmuson | (R) | 29,469 |
| Arizona | Barry Goldwater | (R) | 264,659 | Roy Elson | (D) | 201,963 |
| Arkansas | J. William Fulbright | (D)* | 344,548 | Charles T. Bernard | (R) | 236,723 |
| California[2] | Alan Cranston | (D) | 3,615,261 | Max Rafferty | (R) | 3,275,679 |
| Colorado | Peter H. Dominick | (R)* | 460,686 | Steve McNichols | (D) | 326,667 |
| Connecticut | Abraham Ribicoff | (D)* | 648,899 | Edwin H. May, Jr. | (R) | 545,755 |
| Florida | Edward J. Gurney | (R) | 1,131,449 | LeRoy Collins | (D) | 892,637 |
| Georgia | Herman E. Talmadge | (D)* | 880,650 | Earl Patton | (R) | 255,108 |
| Hawaii | Daniel K. Inouye | (D)* | 189,202 | Wayne C. Thiessen | (R) | 34,004 |
| Idaho | Frank Church | (D)* | 163,848 | George V. Hansen | (R) | 108,449 |
| Illinois | Everett M. Dirksen | (R)* | 2,263,263 | William G. Clark | (D) | 1,990,022 |
| Indiana | Birch Bayh | (D)* | 1,061,456 | William D. Ruckelshaus | (R) | 983,430 |
| Iowa | Harold E. Hughes | (D) | 574,298 | David Stanley | (R) | 568,021 |
| Kansas | Robert J. Dole | (R) | 479,185 | William I. Robinson | (D) | 310,435 |
| Kentucky | Marlow W. Cook | (R) | 480,167 | Katherine Peden | (D) | 445,471 |
| Maryland[3] | C. McC. Mathias | (R) | 535,131 | Daniel B. Brewster | (D)* | 434,972 |
| Missouri | Thomas F. Eagleton | (D) | 850,960 | Thomas B. Curtis | (R) | 810,491 |
| Nevada | Alan Bible | (D)* | 81,925 | M. Edward Fike | (R) | 67,903 |
| New Hampshire | Norris Cotton | (R)* | 170,163 | John W. King | (D) | 116,816 |
| New York[4] | Jacob K. Javits | (R)* | 3,323,574 | Paul O'Dwyer | (D) | 2,144,476 |
| North Carolina | Sam J. Ervin, Jr. | (D)* | 842,635 | Robert V. Somers | (R) | 556,659 |
| North Dakota | Milton R. Young | (R)* | 154,966 | Herschel Lashkowitz | (D) | 90,699 |
| Ohio | William B. Saxbe | (R) | 1,918,330 | John J. Gilligan | (D) | 1,803,660 |
| Oklahoma | Henry L. Bellmon | (R) | 470,120 | A. S. Mike Monroney | (D)* | 419,658 |
| Oregon | Robert W. Packwood | (R) | 408,726 | Wayne Morse† | (D)* | 405,144 |
| Pennsylvania | Richard S. Schweiker | (R) | 2,218,144 | Joseph S. Clark | (D)* | 2,048,349 |
| South Carolina | Ernest F. Hollings | (D)* | 397,407 | Marshall J. Parker | (R) | 245,879 |
| South Dakota | George McGovern | (D)* | 156,454 | Archie Gubbrud | (R) | 118,992 |
| Utah | Wallace F. Bennett | (R)* | 223,758 | Milton L. Weilenman | (D) | 192,457 |
| Vermont | George D. Aiken | (R)* | 157,154 | Unopposed | | |
| Washington | Warren G. Magnuson | (D)* | 722,915 | Jack Metcalf | (R) | 390,947 |
| Wisconsin | Gaylord Nelson | (D)* | 1,017,711 | Jerris Leonard | (R) | 632,939 |

[1]Ernest Gruening, Independent 13,386. [2]Paul Jacobs, Peace and Freedom, 91,254. [3]George P. Mahoney, Independent, 147,787. [4]James L. Buckley, Conservative, 1,109,087. †Morse demanded a recount.

# Election Returns for Governors by States, 1968

Source: Compiled from United Press International official and unofficial returns as of Nov. 20, 1968

Asterisk (*) denotes incumbent

| State | Governor Elected | | Vote Cast | Losing Candidate | | Vote Cast |
|---|---|---|---|---|---|---|
| Arizona | John R. Williams | (R)* | 270,873 | Sam Goddard | (D) | 200,258 |
| Arkansas | Winthrop Rockefeller | (R)* | 317,107 | Marion H. Crank | (D) | 291,099 |
| Delaware | Russell W. Peterson | (R) | 104,216 | Charles L. Terry Jr. | (D)* | 101,907 |
| Illinois | Richard B. Ogilvie | (R) | 2,201,623 | Samuel H. Shapiro | (D)* | 2,071,102 |
| Indiana | Edgar D. Whitcomb | (R) | 1,082,276 | Robert L. Rock | (D) | 956,816 |
| Iowa | Robert D. Ray | (R) | 612,676 | Paul Franzenburg | (D) | 520,734 |
| Kansas | Robert B. Docking | (D)* | 438,566 | Rick Harman | (R) | 401,741 |
| Missouri | Warren E. Hearnes | (D)* | 1,014,581 | Lawrence K. Roos | (R) | 640,805 |
| Montana | Forrest Anderson | (D) | 118,999 | Tim M. Babcock | (R)* | 93,117 |
| New Hampshire | Walter R. Peterson | (R) | 149,902 | Emile R. Bussiere | (D) | 135,378 |
| New Mexico | David F. Cargo | (R)* | 159,495 | Fabian Chavez | (D) | 156,693 |
| North Carolina | Robert W. Scott | (D) | 821,232 | James C. Gardner | (R) | 737,075 |
| North Dakota | William L. Guy | (D)* | 135,954 | Robert P. McCarney | (R) | 108,381 |
| Rhode Island | Frank Licht | (D) | 191,053 | John H. Chafee | (R)* | 178,557 |
| South Dakota | Frank Farrar | (R) | 158,762 | Robert Chamberlin | (D) | 116,994 |
| Texas | Preston Smith | (D) | 1,659,478 | Paul Eggers | (R) | 1,252,952 |
| Utah | Calvin L. Rampton | (D)* | 288,979 | Carl W. Buehner | (R) | 134,754 |
| Vermont | Deane C. Davis | (R) | 89,211 | John J. Daley | (D) | 71,908 |
| Washington | Daniel J. Evans | (R)* | 617,596 | John J. O'Connell | (D) | 516,224 |
| West Virginia | Arch A. Moore | (R) | 376,962 | J. M. Sprouse | (D) | 363,776 |
| Wisconsin | Warren P. Knowles | (R)* | 892,680 | Bronson LaFollette | (D) | 790,577 |

# Party Nominees for President and Vice President

Asterisk (*) denotes winning ticket

| | Democratic | | | Republican | |
|---|---|---|---|---|---|
| Year | President | Vice President | | President | Vice President |
| 1900 | William J. Bryan | Adlai E. Stevenson | | William McKinley* | Theodore Roosevelt |
| 1904 | Alton B. Parker | Henry G. Davis | | Theodore Roosevelt* | Charles W. Fairbanks |
| 1908 | William J. Bryan | John W. Kern | | William H. Taft* | James S. Sherman |
| 1912 | Woodrow Wilson* | Thomas R. Marshall | | William H. Taft | James S. Sherman |
| 1916 | Woodrow Wilson* | Thomas R. Marshall | | Charles E. Hughes | Charles W. Fairbanks |
| 1920 | James M. Cox | Franklin D. Roosevelt | | Warren G. Harding* | Calvin Coolidge |
| 1924 | John W. Davis | Charles W. Bryan | | Calvin Coolidge* | Charles G. Dawes |
| 1928 | Alfred E. Smith | Joseph T. Robinson | | Herbert Hoover* | Charles Curtis |
| 1932 | Franklin D. Roosevelt* | John N. Garner | | Herbert Hoover | Charles Curtis |
| 1936 | Franklin D. Roosevelt* | John N. Garner | | Alfred M. Landon | Frank Knox |
| 1940 | Franklin D. Roosevelt* | Henry A. Wallace | | Wendell L. Willkie | Charles McNary |
| 1944 | Franklin D. Roosevelt* | Harry S. Truman | | Thomas E. Dewey | John W. Bricker |
| 1948 | Harry S. Truman* | Alben W. Barkley | | Thomas E. Dewey | Earl Warren |
| 1952 | Adlai E. Stevenson | John J. Sparkman | | Dwight D. Eisenhower* | Richard M. Nixon |
| 1956 | Adlai E. Stevenson | Estes Kefauver | | Dwight D. Eisenhower* | Richard M. Nixon |
| 1960 | John F. Kennedy* | Lyndon B. Johnson | | Richard M. Nixon | Henry Cabot Lodge |
| 1964 | Lyndon B. Johnson* | Hubert H. Humphrey | | Barry M. Goldwater | William E. Miller |
| 1968† | Hubert H. Humphrey | Edmund S. Muskie | | Richard M. Nixon* | Spiro T. Agnew |

[1]Died Oct. 30 and the Republican National Committee named Nicholas Murray Butler.
†1968 Third party candidates were George C. Wallace and Gen. Curtis E. LeMay.

# Major Parties' Popular and Electoral Vote for President

**(F) Federalist; (D) Democrat; (R) Republican; (DR) Democrat Republican; (NR) National Republican; (W) Whig; (P) People's; (Pr) Progressive; (SR) States' Rights**

Asterisk (*)—See notes below for various years. ᵖpreliminary

| Year | President Elected | Popular Vote | Electoral Vote | Losing Candidate | Popular Vote | Electoral Vote |
|------|------------------|-------------|---------------|-----------------|-------------|---------------|
| 1789 | George Washington (F).... | Unknown | 69 | No opposition............... | | |
| 1792 | George Washington (F).... | Unknown | 132 | No opposition............... | | |
| 1796 | John Adams (F)........... | Unknown | 71 | Thomas Jefferson (DR).... | Unknown | 68 |
| 1800 | Thomas Jefferson (DR).... | Unknown | 73 | Aaron Burr (DR)......... | Unknown | 73 |
| | Elected by House of Representatives (due to tie vote) | | | | | |
| 1804 | Thomas Jefferson (DR).... | Unknown | 162 | Charles Pinckney (F).... | Unknown | 14 |
| 1808 | James Madison (DR)...... | Unknown | 122 | Charles Pinckney (F).... | Unknown | 47 |
| 1812 | James Madison (DR)...... | Unknown | 128 | DeWitt Clinton (F)...... | Unknown | 89 |
| 1816 | James Monroe (DR)...... | Unknown | 183 | Rufus King (F)......... | Unknown | 34 |
| 1820 | James Monroe (DR)...... | Unknown | 231 | John Quincy Adams (DR).. | Unknown | 1 |
| 1824 | John Quincy Adams (NR).. | 105,321 | 84 | Andrew Jackson (D)...... | 155,872 | 99 |
| | Elected by House of Representatives (no candidate having polled a majority) | | | Henry Clay (DR)........ | 46,587 | 37 |
| | | | | William H. Crawford (DR) | 44,282 | 41 |
| 1828 | Andrew Jackson (D)...... | 647,231 | 178 | John Quincy Adams (NR).. | 509,097 | 83 |
| 1832 | Andrew Jackson (D)...... | 687,502 | 219 | Henry Clay (DR)........ | 530,189 | 49 |
| | First national convention for Presidential candidates | | | | | |
| 1836 | Martin Van Buren (D)..... | 762,678 | 170 | William H. Harrison (W)... | 548,007 | 73 |
| 1840* | William H. Harrison (W)... | 1,275,017 | 234 | Martin Van Buren (D)..... | 1,128,702 | 60 |
| | (Died April 4, 1841) | | | | | |
| 1844 | James K. Polk (D)....... | 1,337,243 | 170 | Henry Clay (W)......... | 1,299,068 | 105 |
| 1848* | Zachary Taylor (W)...... | 1,360,101 | 163 | Lewis Cass (D).......... | 1,220,544 | 127 |
| | (Died July 9, 1850) | | | | | |
| 1852 | Franklin Pierce (D)...... | 1,601,474 | 254 | Winfield Scott (W)...... | 1,386,578 | 42 |
| 1856 | James C. Buchanan (D)... | 1,927,995 | 174 | John C. Fremont (R)..... | 1,391,555 | 114 |
| 1860 | Abraham Lincoln (R)..... | 1,866,352 | 180 | Stephen A. Douglas (D)... | 1,375,157 | 12 |
| | | | | John C. Breckinridge (D).. | 845,763 | 72 |
| | | | | John Bell (Const. Union).. | 589,581 | 39 |
| 1864* | Abraham Lincoln (R)..... | 2,216,067 | 212 | George McClellan (D)..... | 1,808,725 | 21 |
| | (Died April 15, 1865) | | | | | |
| 1868 | Ulysses S. Grant (R)...... | 3,015,071 | 214 | Horatio Seymour......... | 2,709,615 | 80 |
| 1872 | Ulysses S. Grant (R)...... | 3,597,070 | 286 | Horace Greeley (D-L)...... | 2,834,079 | ...... |
| | | | | (Died Nov. 29, 1872) | | |
| 1876* | Rutherford B. Hayes (R)... | 4,033,950 | 185 | Samuel J. Tilden (D)...... | 4,284,757 | 184 |
| 1880* | James A. Garfield (R)..... | 4,449,053 | 214 | Winfield S. Hancock (D)... | 4,442,030 | 155 |
| | (Died Sept. 19, 1881) | | | | | |
| 1884 | Grover Cleveland (D)...... | 4,911,017 | 219 | James G. Blaine (R)...... | 4,848,334 | 182 |
| 1888* | Benjamin Harrison (R).... | 5,444,337 | 233 | Grover Cleveland (D)...... | 5,540,050 | 168 |
| 1892 | Grover Cleveland (D)...... | 5,554,414 | 277 | Benjamin Harrison (R).... | 5,190,802 | 145 |
| | | | | James Weaver (D)....... | 1,027,329 | 22 |
| 1896 | William McKinley (R)..... | 7,035,638 | 271 | William J. Bryan (D-P).... | 6,467,946 | 176 |
| 1900* | William McKinley (R)..... | 7,219,530 | 292 | William J. Bryan (D)..... | 6,358,071 | 155 |
| | (Died Sept. 14, 1901) | | | | | |
| 1904 | Theodore Roosevelt (R)... | 7,628,834 | 336 | Alton B. Parker (D)...... | 5,084,491 | 140 |
| 1908 | William H. Taft (R)...... | 7,679,006 | 321 | William J. Bryan (D)..... | 6,409,106 | 162 |
| 1912 | Woodrow Wilson (D)...... | 6,286,214 | 435 | Theodore Roosevelt (Pr)... | 4,216,020 | 88 |
| | | | | William H. Taft (R)...... | 3,483,922 | 8 |
| 1916 | Woodrow Wilson (D)...... | 9,129,606 | 277 | Charles E. Hughes (R).... | 8,538,221 | 254 |
| 1920* | Warren G. Harding (R).... | 16,152,200 | 404 | James M. Cox (D)........ | 9,147,353 | 127 |
| | (Died Aug. 2, 1923) | | | | | |
| 1924 | Calvin Coolidge (R)...... | 15,725,016 | 382 | John W. Davis (D)....... | 8,385,586 | 136 |
| | | | | Robert M. LaFollette (Pr).. | 4,822,856 | 13 |
| 1928 | Herbert Hoover (R)...... | 21,392,190 | 444 | Alfred E. Smith (D)...... | 15,016,443 | 87 |
| 1932 | Franklin D. Roosevelt (D).. | 22,821,857 | 472 | Herbert Hoover (R)...... | 15,761,841 | 59 |
| 1936 | Franklin D. Roosevelt (D).. | 27,751,597 | 523 | Alfred Landon (R)....... | 16,679,583 | 8 |
| 1940 | Franklin D. Roosevelt (D).. | 27,243,466 | 449 | Wendell Wilkie (R)...... | 22,304,755 | 82 |
| 1944* | Franklin D. Roosevelt (D).. | 25,602,505 | 432 | Thomas E. Dewey (R).... | 22,006,278 | 99 |
| | (Died April 12, 1945) | | | | | |
| 1948 | Harry S. Truman (D)...... | 24,105,812 | 303 | Thomas E. Dewey (R).... | 21,970,065 | 189 |
| | | | | J. Strom Thurmond (SR)... | 1,169,021 | 39 |
| | | | | Henry A. Wallace (Pr)..... | 1,157,172 | ...... |
| 1952 | Dwight D. Eisenhower (R).. | 33,936,252 | 442 | Adlai E. Stevenson (D)... | 27,314,992 | 89 |
| 1956* | Dwight D. Eisenhower (R).. | 35,585,316 | 457 | Adlai E. Stevenson (D)... | 26,031,322 | 73 |
| 1960* | John F. Kennedy (D)..... | 34,227,096 | 303 | Richard M. Nixon (R).... | 34,108,546 | 219 |
| 1964 | Lyndon B. Johnson (D).... | 43,126,506 | 486 | Barry M. Goldwater (R)... | 27,176,799 | 52 |
| 1968ᴾ | Richard M. Nixon (R)..... | 31,304,992 | 302 | Hubert H. Humphrey (D).. | 30,994,354 | 191 |
| | | | | George C. Wallace (3rd party) | 9,825,459 | 45 |

**1840**—President Harrison died on April 4, 1841, and Vice President Tyler became President.

**1848**—President Taylor died in office on July 9, 1850, was succeeded by Vice President Fillmore.

**1864**—President Lincoln was shot April 14, 1865 at Ford's Theatre, Washington, by actor J. Wilkes Booth, and died April 15, whereupon Vice President Andrew Johnson became President.

**1876**—Florida, Louisiana, Oregon and South Carolina election returns were disputed. A board of Commissioners, referred to as The Electoral Commission, was created by act of Congress (approved Jan. 29, 1877) for the purpose of deciding disputed cases in the 1876 presidential election. It was in session from Feb. 1 to March 2, 1877 and its decisions resulted in the seating of Hayes, the Republican candidate who received the disputed 22 electoral votes. The members of. the commission voted on party lines—8 Republicans and 7 Democrats. Congress, in joint session (March 2, 1877) declared Hayes and Wheeler elected President and Vice President by an electoral vote of 185 for Hayes and 184 for Tilden. The Senate was Republican. The House, which was Democratic, resolved and declared as a separate body (March 3) that Tilden and Hendricks were elected on the face of the returns.

**1880**—President Garfield was shot July 2, 1881, at Washington, D. C., by Charles J. Guiteau of New York and died Sept. 19, whereupon Vice President Chester A. Arthur became President.

**1888**—On the result of the popular vote Cleveland had more votes than Harrison but the 233 electoral votes cast for Harrison against the 168 for Cleveland elected Harrison president.

**1900**—President McKinley was shot, Sept. 6, 1901, at the Pan American Exposition, Buffalo, N. Y. He died on Sept. 14, and Vice President Theodore Roosevelt became President. The assassin, Leon Czolgosz, was executed Oct. 29, 1901.

**1920**—President Harding died at San Francisco, Calif., Aug. 2, 1923, and was succeeded by Vice President Calvin Coolidge.

**1944**—President Roosevelt died at Warm Springs, Ga., on April 12, 1945, whereupon Vice President Harry S. Truman became President.

**1956**—Democrats elected 74 electors but one from Alabama refused to vote for Stevenson, voted for Walter B. Jones.

**1960**—Sen. Harry F. Byrd (D.-Va.) received 15 electoral votes; 6 from unpledged Alabama Democrats, 8 from unpledged Mississippi Democrats, and 1 from defecting Oklahoma Republican elector.

# PRESIDENTIAL ELECTION RETURNS BY STATES

Compiled by the World Almanac from official and unofficial returns collected by United Press International.

## Alabama

| County | 1968 | | | 1964 | |
| | Humphrey (D) | Nixon (R) | Wallace (I) | Democrat (†) | Goldwater (R) |
|---|---|---|---|---|---|
| Autauga.... | 1,404 | 534 | 4,614 | 485 | 2,969 |
| Baldwin.... | 1,938 | 2,279 | 14,352 | 2,506 | 10,870 |
| Barbour.... | 3,614 | 376 | 8,916 | 902 | 3,853 |
| Bibb....... | 542 | 235 | 3,412 | 525 | 2,623 |
| Blount..... | 296 | 1,820 | 5,682 | 2,397 | 4,442 |
| Bullock.... | 1,707 | 180 | 1,689 | 1,121 | 1,516 |
| Butler..... | 3,585 | 957 | 10,952 | 971 | 4,002 |
| Calhoun.... | 4,192 | 2,752 | 17,691 | 6,170 | 10,635 |
| Chambers... | 2,552 | 1,076 | 6,854 | 2,529 | 4,630 |
| Cherokee... | 336 | 246 | 3,258 | 1,847 | 1,693 |
| Chilton.... | 729 | 2,267 | 8,686 | 1,706 | 5,202 |
| Choctaw.... | 1,189 | 53 | 2,742 | 413 | 2,497 |
| Clarke..... | 1,284 | 479 | 8,164 | 926 | 4,460 |
| Clay ...... | 392 | 725 | 3,267 | 1,176 | 2,815 |
| Cleburne... | 172 | 484 | 3,426 | 660 | 2,156 |
| Coffee..... | 1,010 | 605 | 6,897 | 1,206 | 4,910 |
| Colbert.... | 1,377 | 1,862 | 11,060 | 5,562 | 5,267 |
| Conecuh.... | 750 | 144 | 3,732 | 615 | 2,782 |
| Coosa..... | 646 | 426 | 2,821 | 738 | 1,978 |
| Covington.. | 775 | 884 | 11,163 | 1,627 | 7,554 |
| Crenshaw... | 694 | 288 | 4,448 | 805 | 3,008 |
| Cullman.... | 568 | 4,646 | 10,963 | 5,078 | 7,152 |
| Dale...... | 882 | 588 | 7,646 | 949 | 4,970 |
| Dallas..... | 4,955 | 1,098 | 9,317 | 709 | 5,888 |
| DeKalb..... | 361 | 1,947 | 2,896 | 4,910 | 6,746 |
| Elmore..... | 1,780 | 808 | 9,016 | 1,217 | 6,363 |
| Escambia... | 902 | 520 | 7,571 | 1,911 | 5,623 |
| Etowah..... | 3,716 | 4,836 | 20,989 | 8,853 | 12,894 |
| Fayette.... | 681 | 848 | 4,787 | 1,279 | 3,203 |
| Franklin... | 635 | 2,437 | 5,707 | 3,097 | 4,025 |
| Geneva.... | 273 | 194 | 5,209 | 1,070 | 4,502 |
| Greene..... | 1,171 | 64 | 749 | 589 | 1,124 |
| Hale...... | 1,444 | 223 | 2,346 | 552 | 1,898 |
| Henry..... | 941 | 94 | 4,129 | 585 | 2,896 |
| Houston.... | 1,504 | 874 | 14,557 | 1,395 | 10,353 |
| Jackson.... | 936 | 1,084 | 7,845 | 3,100 | 2,730 |
| Jefferson.. | 55,029 | 38,167 | 102,161 | 38,328 | 100,756 |
| Lamar..... | 298 | 339 | 4,957 | 1,028 | 2,734 |
| Lauderdale. | 2,727 | 3,350 | 19,202 | 6,582 | 5,978 |
| Lawrence... | 1,009 | 577 | 5,992 | 1,802 | 1,809 |
| Lee....... | 2,881 | 2,607 | 7,594 | 1,785 | 5,914 |
| Limestone.. | 891 | 824 | 7,800 | 3,016 | 2,377 |
| Lowndes.... | 1,095 | 244 | 1,881 | 309 | 1,548 |
| Macon..... | 3,865 | 206 | 1,036 | 2,941 | 1,858 |
| Madison.... | 9,679 | 12,941 | 28,263 | 13,193 | 14,279 |
| Marengo.... | 2,711 | 483 | 4,338 | 793 | 3,677 |
| Marion.... | 353 | 1,426 | 6,387 | 1,669 | 3,966 |
| Marshall... | 988 | 2,683 | 12,637 | 4,405 | 5,712 |
| Mobile..... | 21,070 | 9,660 | 58,438 | 20,351 | 49,493 |
| Monroe.... | 1,370 | 587 | 4,472 | 846 | 3,870 |
| Montg'm'y. | 27,357 | 7,255 | 37,980 | 7,368 | 23,015 |
| Morgan.... | 1,917 | 2,941 | 16,719 | 5,360 | 7,013 |
| Perry ..... | 2,264 | 264 | 2,490 | 519 | 2,046 |
| Pickens.... | 1,388 | 317 | 4,168 | 744 | 3,416 |
| Pike...... | 1,664 | 704 | 5,921 | 782 | 4,373 |
| Randolph... | 615 | 740 | 4,744 | 1,845 | 3,127 |
| Russell.... | 3,597 | 707 | 7,569 | 1,535 | 4,877 |
| St. Clair... | 934 | 1,548 | 6,647 | 1,946 | 6,037 |
| Shelby .... | 1,178 | 3,140 | 8,390 | 1,952 | 4,813 |
| Sumter..... | 1,928 | 234 | 1,486 | 404 | 1,653 |
| Talladega.. | 2,478 | 1,463 | 10,807 | 3,700 | 8,946 |
| Tallapoosa. | 1,255 | 1,139 | 8,180 | 1,720 | 5,530 |
| Tuscaloosa. | 2,356 | 1,486 | 7,704 | 5,763 | 13,227 |
| Walker.... | 1,508 | 2,062 | 11,192 | 6,107 | 8,582 |
| Washington. | 546 | 163 | 4,057 | 1,200 | 2,803 |
| Wilcox..... | 1,129 | 199 | 1,723 | 157 | 1,789 |
| Winston.... | 272 | 2,192 | 3,032 | 1,487 | 3,438 |
| **Totals...** | **191,687** | **138,064** | **643,518** | **209,848** | **479,085** |

†The Democratic electors were unpledged, thus no Johnson vote appears.

### ALABAMA VOTE SINCE 1920

1920 (Pres.), Cox, Dem., 163,254; Harding, Rep., 74,690; Watkins, Proh., 757; Debs, Soc., 2,369.
1924 (Pres.), Davis, Dem., 112,966; Coolidge, Rep., 45,005; LaFollette, Prog., 8,084; Faris, Proh., 538.
1928 (Pres.), Smith, Dem., 127,797; Hoover, Rep., 120,725; Thomas, Soc., 460.
1932 (Pres.), Roosevelt, Dem., 207,910; Hoover, Rep., 34,675; Foster, Com., 406; Thomas, Soc., 2,030; Upshaw, Proh., 13.
1936 (Pres.), Roosevelt, Dem. 238,195; Landon, Rep., 35,358; Colvin, Proh., 719; Browder, Com., 679; Lemke, Union, 549; Thomas, Soc., 242.
1940 (Pres.), Roosevelt, Dem., 250,726; Willkie, Rep., 42,174; Babson, Proh., 698; Browder, Com., 509; Thomas, Soc., 100.
1944 (Pres.), Roosevelt, Dem., 198,918; Dewey, Rep., 44,540; Watson, Proh., 1,095; Thomas, Soc., 190.
1948 (Pres.), Thurmond, States' Rights, 171,443; Dewey, Rep., 40,930; Wallace, Prog., 1,522; Watson, Proh., 1,085.
1952 (Pres.), Eisenhower, Rep., 149,231; Stevenson, Dem., 275,075; Hamblen, Proh., 1,814.
1956 (Pres.), Stevenson, Dem., 280,844; Eisenhower, Rep., 195,694; Independent electors, 20,323.
1960 (Pres.), Kennedy, Dem., 324,050; Nixon, Rep., 237,981; Faubus, States' Rights, 4,367; Decker, Proh., 2,106; King, Afro-Americans, 1,485; Scattering, 236.
1964 (Pres.), Dem., 209,848; Goldwater, Rep., 479,085; Scattering, 105.
1968 (Pres.), Nixon, Rep., 138,064; Humphrey, Dem., 191,687; Wallace, 3rd party, 643,518.

## Alaska

| Election District | 1968 | | | 1964 | |
| | Humphrey (D) | Nixon (R) | Wallace (I) | Johnson (D) | Goldwater (R) |
|---|---|---|---|---|---|
| No. 1...... | 1,807 | 2,125 | 513 | 3,041 | 1,554 |
| No. 2...... | 829 | 934 | 113 | 1,378 | 464 |
| No. 3...... | 1,201 | 1,093 | 146 | 1,745 | 651 |
| No. 4...... | 2,729 | 2,487 | 358 | 3,762 | 1,545 |
| No. 5...... | 644 | 579 | 134 | 1,056 | 250 |
| No. 6...... | 635 | 877 | 280 | 990 | 495 |
| No. 7...... | 890 | 1,071 | 349 | 1,242 | 963 |
| No. 8...... | 12,953 | 13,583 | 3,843 | 13,537 | 9,051 |
| No. 9...... | 449 | 371 | 88 | 674 | 264 |
| No. 10..... | 1,686 | 1,666 | 887 | 1,627 | 1,000 |
| No. 11..... | 854 | 983 | 242 | 1,183 | 399 |
| No. 12..... | 263 | 296 | 54 | 731 | 124 |
| No. 13..... | 539 | 579 | 94 | 931 | 267 |
| No. 14..... | 992 | 670 | 123 | 1,601 | 214 |
| No. 15..... | 615 | 742 | 281 | 1,366 | 600 |
| No. 16..... | 4,561 | 5,699 | 1,656 | 6,410 | 4,340 |
| No. 17..... | 915 | 733 | 93 | 1,149 | 252 |
| No. 18..... | 898 | 778 | 102 | 1,371 | 420 |
| No. 19..... | 557 | 272 | 63 | 635 | .77 |
| * | 557 | 1,001 | 312 | | |
| **Totals...** | **34,574** | **36,539** | **9,731** | **44,329** | **22,930** |

*Ballot cast for President only by voters ineligible to vote in local elections.

### ALASKA VOTE SINCE 1960

1960 (Pres.), Kennedy, Dem., 29,809; Nixon, Rep., 30,953.
1964 (Pres.), Johnson, Dem., 44,329; Goldwater, Rep., 22,930.
1968 (Pres.), Nixon, Rep., 36,539; Humphrey, Dem., 34,574; Wallace, 3rd party, 9,731.

## Arizona

| County | 1968 | | | 1964 | |
| | Humphrey (D) | Nixon (R) | Wallace (I) | Johnson (D) | Goldwater (R) |
|---|---|---|---|---|---|
| Apache..... | 1,668 | 2,092 | 402 | 2,042 | 1,849 |
| Cochise.... | 6,597 | 7,619 | 2,392 | 9,045 | 7,644 |
| Coconino... | 3,414 | 6,772 | 1,049 | 5,270 | 5,756 |
| Gila....... | 4,831 | 3,610 | 1,222 | 6,821 | 3,713 |
| Graham.... | 1,726 | 2,327 | 859 | 2,783 | 2,655 |
| Greenlee... | 2,434 | 1,026 | 276 | 3,147 | 1,132 |
| Maricopa... | 82,532 | 151,515 | 24,432 | 122,042 | 143,114 |
| Mohave.... | 2,109 | 3,208 | 883 | 2,243 | 2,091 |
| Navajo.... | 2,926 | 4,590 | 1,442 | 4,770 | 4,870 |
| Pima...... | 39,786 | 49,479 | 7,221 | 54,120 | 46,995 |
| Pinal...... | 7,409 | 6,883 | 1,869 | 9,911 | 6,956 |
| Santa Cruz. | 1,551 | 1,697 | 240 | 1,955 | 1,503 |
| Yavapai.... | 3,989 | 8,296 | 1,837 | 5,747 | 7,749 |
| Yuma...... | 5,770 | 6,856 | 1,941 | 7,857 | 6,548 |
| **Totals...** | **166,742** | **255,970** | **45,066** | **237,753** | **242,535** |

### ARIZONA VOTE SINCE 1920

1920 (Pres.), Cox, Dem., 29,546; Harding, Rep., 37,016; Watkins, Proh., 4; Debs, Soc., 222; Christensen, Farm.-Lab., 15.
1924 (Pres.), Coolidge, Rep., 30,516; Davis, Dem., 26,235; LaFollette, Prog., 17,210.
1928 (Pres.), Hoover, Rep., 52,533; Smith, Dem., 38,537; Foster, Com., 184.
1932 (Pres.), Roosevelt, Dem., 79,264; Hoover, Rep., 36,104; Thomas, Soc., 2,030; Foster, Com., 406.
1936 (Pres.), Roosevelt, Dem., 86,722; Landon, Rep., 33,433; Lemke, Union, 3,307; Colvin, Proh., 384; Thomas, Soc., 317.
1940 (Pres.), Roosevelt, Dem., 95,267; Willkie, Rep., 54,030; Babson, Proh., 742.

**Arizona (cont'd)**

1944 (Pres.), Roosevelt, Dem., 80,926; Dewey, Rep., 56,287; Watson, Proh., 421.
1948 (Pres.), Truman, Dem., 95,251; Dewey, Rep., 77,597; Wallace, Prog., 3,310; Watson, Proh., 786; Teichert, Soc. Lab., 121.
1952 (Pres.), Eisenhower, Rep., 152,042; Stevenson, Dem., 108,528.
1956 (Pres.), Eisenhower, Rep., 176,990; Stevenson, Dem., 112,880; Andrews, Ind., 303.
1960 (Pres.), Kennedy, Dem., 176,781; Nixon, Rep., 221,241; Hass, Soc. Lab., 469.
1964 (Pres.), Johnson, Dem., 237,753; Goldwater, Rep., 242,535; Hass, Soc. Labor, 482.
1968 (Pres.), Nixon, Rep., 255,970; Humphrey, Dem., 166,742; Wallace, 3rd party, 45,066; scattered, 2,762.

## Arkansas

| County | 1968 | | | 1964 | |
|---|---|---|---|---|---|
| | Hum-phrey (D) | Nixon (R) | Wallace (I) | John-son (D) | Gold-water (R) |
| Arkansas... | 2,028 | 1,838 | 3,777 | 3,200 | 3,769 |
| Ashley...... | 1,920 | 1,555 | 4,363 | 2,901 | 3,742 |
| Baxter...... | 1,952 | 3,401 | 1,513 | 2,900 | 1,986 |
| Benton...... | 4,088 | 8,104 | 4,036 | 5,655 | 5,977 |
| Boone....... | 1,907 | 3,349 | 2,169 | 3,770 | 2,857 |
| Bradley..... | 1,457 | 802 | 2,546 | 2,229 | 1,852 |
| Calhoun..... | 688 | 287 | 1,215 | 1,409 | 889 |
| Carroll..... | 1,303 | 2,605 | 1,174 | 2,005 | 2,105 |
| Chicot...... | 2,595 | 865 | 2,187 | 2,916 | 1,972 |
| Clark....... | 2,713 | 1,643 | 2,785 | 4,127 | 1,884 |
| Clay........ | 1,663 | 2,410 | 1,657 | 3,280 | 1,999 |
| Cleburne.... | 1,202 | 1,301 | 1,675 | 2,645 | 1,221 |
| Cleveland... | 407 | 312 | 1,751 | 1,121 | 1,026 |
| Columbia... | 2,487 | 1,916 | 3,843 | 3,485 | 4,009 |
| Conway..... | 2,560 | 1,973 | 1,958 | 4,205 | 2,378 |
| Craighead... | 3,738 | 5,047 | 6,742 | 8,334 | 5,163 |
| Crawford.... | 1,511 | 2,655 | 2,821 | 3,537 | 3,294 |
| Crittenden.. | 3,475 | 2,454 | 4,657 | 4,168 | 4,065 |
| Cross....... | 1,555 | 1,093 | 3,056 | 2,421 | 2,147 |
| Dallas...... | 1,253 | 629 | 1,725 | 1,779 | 1,625 |
| Desha....... | 1,918 | 954 | 2,497 | 3,294 | 1,930 |
| Drew........ | 1,324 | 1,040 | 2,307 | 1,980 | 2,109 |
| Faulkner.... | 3,756 | 2,791 | 4,375 | 6,116 | 3,259 |
| Franklin.... | 1,149 | 1,333 | 2,111 | 2,685 | 1,580 |
| Fulton...... | 983 | 1,186 | 1,052 | 1,704 | 846 |
| Garland..... | 5,655 | 7,674 | 6,955 | 1,591 | 9,952 |
| Grant....... | 852 | 627 | 2,194 | 1,678 | 1,308 |
| Greene...... | 2,197 | 2,856 | 3,021 | 14,742 | 2,271 |
| Hempstead.. | 2,322 | 1,783 | 3,136 | 3,355 | 2,493 |
| Hot Spring.. | 2,137 | 1,780 | 4,139 | 4,543 | 2,911 |
| Howard..... | 1,061 | 1,286 | 1,657 | 1,320 | 1,640 |
| Indep'nce... | 2,289 | 2,782 | 2,770 | 4,455 | 2,470 |
| Izard....... | 958 | 931 | 1,109 | 1,736 | 726 |
| Jackson..... | 2,051 | 1,356 | 3,525 | 4,651 | 2,141 |
| Jefferson.... | 8,843 | 4,758 | 9,826 | 12,872 | 9,968 |
| Johnson..... | 1,747 | 1,637 | 1,693 | 3,127 | 1,535 |
| Lafayette... | 1,207 | 673 | 1,664 | 1,484 | 1,476 |
| Lawrence... | 1,613 | 1,788 | 2,813 | 3,498 | 2,013 |
| Lee......... | 2,125 | 834 | 1,907 | 2,335 | 1,668 |
| Lincoln..... | 1,209 | 488 | 2,084 | 2,468 | 1,410 |
| Little River. | 1,092 | 745 | 1,473 | 2,040 | 1,141 |
| Logan....... | 1,998 | 2,341 | 2,160 | 3,604 | 2,265 |
| Lonoke...... | 2,014 | 1,677 | 4,002 | 3,818 | 3,636 |
| Madison..... | 1,173 | 1,929 | 830 | 2,715 | 1,997 |
| Marion...... | 990 | 1,385 | 877 | 1,661 | 1,088 |
| Miller...... | 1,310 | 1,221 | 2,789 | 5,190 | 4,253 |
| Mississippi.. | 4,993 | 4,369 | 6,141 | 8,678 | 6,213 |
| Monroe..... | 1,783 | 804 | 2,406 | 2,258 | 1,968 |
| Montgom'y. | 649 | 867 | 992 | 1,358 | 932 |
| Nevada..... | 1,308 | 840 | 1,773 | 2,190 | 1,406 |
| Newton..... | 852 | 1,467 | 567 | 1,374 | 1,357 |
| Ouachita.... | 4,603 | 2,209 | 5,031 | 7,056 | 5,572 |
| Perry....... | 631 | 731 | 911 | 1,320 | 1,048 |
| Phillips..... | 5,039 | 2,151 | 4,279 | 5,818 | 3,963 |
| Pike........ | 655 | 1,104 | 1,541 | 1,531 | 1,241 |
| Poinsett.... | 1,672 | 2,140 | 4,074 | 5,635 | 3,031 |
| Polk........ | 1,325 | 2,059 | 1,812 | 2,575 | 2,022 |
| Pope........ | 2,578 | 3,319 | 2,769 | 4,972 | 2,651 |
| Prairie..... | 918 | 678 | 2,008 | 1,812 | 1,476 |
| Pulaski..... | 26,141 | 26,017 | 25,279 | 40,535 | 38,212 |
| Randolph... | 1,365 | 1,237 | 1,610 | 2,680 | 1,312 |
| St. Francis.. | 3,248 | 1,608 | 4,184 | 3,651 | 3,094 |
| Saline...... | 3,091 | 2,659 | 5,469 | 5,605 | 3,628 |
| Scott....... | 1,000 | 1,162 | 1,238 | 1,838 | 1,121 |
| Searcy...... | 719 | 1,877 | 720 | 1,508 | 11,649 |
| Sebastian... | 6,029 | 11,367 | 8,222 | 10,299 | 13,110 |
| Sevier...... | 1,208 | 1,280 | 1,557 | 2,123 | 1,249 |
| Sharp....... | 1,023 | 1,126 | 1,299 | 1,810 | 1,215 |
| Stone....... | 749 | 967 | 963 | 1,374 | 942 |
| Union....... | 4,421 | 4,919 | 7,853 | 6,948 | 8,472 |
| Van Buren.. | 1,149 | 1,325 | 1,224 | 2,054 | 1,270 |
| Washington. | 6,131 | 10,697 | 5,115 | 10,166 | 6,856 |
| White....... | 3,179 | 3,888 | 5,054 | 6,566 | 5,023 |
| Woodruff... | 1,270 | 625 | 1,734 | 2,307 | 1,366 |
| Yell........ | 1,513 | 1,819 | 1,949 | 3,407 | 1,527 |
| **Totals.** | **.183,317** | **186,547** | **236,504** | **314,197** | **243,264** |

1920 (Pres.), Cox, Dem., 107,408; Harding, Rep., 71,117; Debs, Soc., 5,111.
1924 (Pres.), Davis, Dem., 84,795; Coolidge, Rep., 40,564; LaFollette, Prog., 13,173.
1928 (Pres.), Smith, Dem., 119,196; Hoover, Rep., 77,751; Thomas, Soc., 429; Foster, Com., 317.
1932 (Pres.), Roosevelt, Dem., 189,602; Hoover, Rep., 28,467; Thomas, Soc., 1,269; Harvey, Ind., 1,049; Foster, Com., 175.
1936 (Pres.), Roosevelt, Dem., 146,765; Landon, Rep., 32,039; Thomas, Soc., 446; Browder, Com., 164; Lemke, Union, 4.
1940 (Pres.), Roosevelt, Dem., 158,622; Willkie, Rep., 42,121; Babson, Proh., 793; Thomas, Soc., 305.
1944 (Pres.), Roosevelt, Dem., 148,965; Dewey, Rep., 63,551; Thomas, Soc., 438.
1948 (Pres.), Truman, Dem., 149,659; Dewey, Rep., 50,959; Thurmond, States' Rights, 40,068; Thomas, Soc., 1,037; Wallace, Prog., 751; Watson, Proh., 1.
1952 (Pres.), Eisenhower, Rep., 177,155; Stevenson, Dem., 226,300; Hamblen, Proh., 886; MacArthur, Christian Nationalist, 458; Hass, Soc. Lab., 1.
1956 (Pres.), Stevenson, Dem., 213,277; Eisenhower, Rep., 186,287; Andrews, Ind., 7,008.
1960 (Pres.), Kennedy, Dem., 215,049; Nixon, Rep., 184,508; National States' Rights, 28,952.
1964 (Pres.), Johnson, Dem., 314,197; Goldwater, Rep. 243,264; Kasper, Nat'l States Rights, 2,965.
1968 (Pres.), Nixon, Rep., 186,547; Humphrey, Dem., 183,317; Wallace, 3rd party, 236,504.

## California

| County | 1968 | | | 1964 | |
|---|---|---|---|---|---|
| | Hum-phrey (D) | Nixon (R) | Wallace (I) | John-son (D) | Gold-water (R) |
| Alameda.... | 218,305 | 152,376 | 28,262 | 283,833 | 142,998 |
| Alpine...... | 83 | 150 | 20 | 91 | 124 |
| Amador.... | 2,404 | 2,269 | 660 | 3,410 | 1,682 |
| Butte....... | 12,883 | 22,223 | 3,888 | 20,831 | 19,574 |
| Calaveras... | 2,183 | 3,042 | 643 | 3,145 | 2,244 |
| Colusa...... | 1,858 | 2,361 | 344 | 2,790 | 1,811 |
| ContraCosta | 101,448 | 97,243 | 18,287 | 113,071 | 65,011 |
| Del Norte... | 2,232 | 2,371 | 493 | 3,652 | 2,075 |
| El Dorado... | 6,050 | 7,464 | 1,673 | 8,810 | 5,775 |
| Fresno...... | 65,153 | 59,901 | 11,291 | 89,375 | 46,792 |
| Glenn....... | 2,461 | 3,838 | 806 | 3,937 | 3,351 |
| Humboldt... | 16,348 | 16,696 | 2,743 | 25,515 | 12,909 |
| Imperial.... | 7,182 | 9,985 | 1,985 | 11,143 | 10,330 |
| Inyo........ | 2,314 | 3,641 | 714 | 3,161 | 2,751 |
| Kern........ | 45,588 | 53,965 | 12,426 | 64,174 | 45,014 |
| Kings....... | 8,643 | 7,826 | 1,640 | 13,073 | 5,753 |
| Lake........ | 3,831 | 4,537 | 902 | 4,680 | 3,616 |
| Lassen...... | 2,930 | 2,553 | 712 | 4,072 | 2,124 |
| Los Angeles. | 1,194,- 230 | 1,231,- 579 | 147,349 | 1,568,- 300 | 1,161,- 067 |
| Madera..... | 6,932 | 6,229 | 1,122 | 9,391 | 4,461 |
| Marin...... | 36,241 | 41,381 | 3,794 | 46,462 | 28,682 |
| Mariposa... | 1,188 | 1,496 | 302 | 1,704 | 1,264 |
| Mendocino.. | 7,933 | 8,300 | 1,550 | 11,869 | 6,322 |
| Merced..... | 14,453 | 11,615 | 2,248 | 19,431 | 8,814 |
| Modoc...... | 1,264 | 1,727 | 350 | 1,972 | 1,386 |
| Mono....... | 465 | 1,130 | 156 | 666 | 850 |
| Monterey... | 28,261 | 33,669 | 4,800 | 40,093 | 24,579 |
| Napa....... | 14,704 | 14,245 | 3,467 | 19,580 | 11,567 |
| Nevada..... | 4,607 | 6,051 | 1,067 | 6,397 | 4,899 |
| Orange..... | 146,982 | 310,247 | 32,776 | 176,539 | 224,196 |
| Placer...... | 14,034 | 12,411 | 2,566 | 18,256 | 9,389 |
| Plumas..... | 2,961 | 2,097 | 529 | 4,019 | 1,686 |
| Riverside... | 61,122 | 83,393 | 12,426 | 80,528 | 51,758 |
| Sacramento. | 117,997 | 96,526 | 16,106 | 149,668 | 77,871 |
| San Benito.. | 2,809 | 2,961 | 501 | 3,779 | 2,449 |
| S.Bernardino | 89,372 | 111,913 | 21,177 | 123,012 | 92,145 |
| San Diego... | 166,105 | 258,545 | 32,967 | 211,508 | 214,445 |
| S. Francisco. | 162,579 | 92,170 | 17,325 | 230,758 | 92,994 |
| San Joaquin. | 41,559 | 46,785 | 8,827 | 59,210 | 36,546 |
| San Luis Obispo.. | 14,888 | 17,713 | 2,193 | 22,252 | 14,906 |
| San Mateo.. | 106,351 | 98,005 | 14,652 | 140,978 | 77,916 |
| San Barbara | 37,305 | 49,670 | 5,051 | 48,381 | 38,020 |
| Santa Clara. | 173,066 | 163,082 | 18,721 | 202,249 | 117,420 |
| Santa Cruz.. | 20,490 | 25,362 | 3,464 | 26,714 | 18,836 |
| Shasta...... | 14,510 | 11,821 | 2,815 | 19,142 | 9,178 |
| Sierra...... | 559 | 548 | 85 | 828 | 413 |
| Siskiyou.... | 6,592 | 6,314 | 1,088 | 9,126 | 5,186 |
| Solano...... | 25,931 | 16,114 | 5,405 | 34,930 | 15,263 |
| Sonoma..... | 32,817 | 37,673 | 5,771 | 44,354 | 27,677 |
| Stanislaus... | 31,306 | 29,576 | 3,953 | 43,078 | 21,973 |
| Sutter...... | 4,624 | 8,665 | 1,218 | 6,787 | 7,241 |
| Tehama..... | 4,572 | 5,198 | 1,216 | 6,928 | 4,529 |
| Trinity..... | 1,913 | 1,426 | 432 | 2,175 | 1,252 |
| Tulare...... | 22,181 | 29,316 | 4,580 | 33,974 | 22,527 |
| Tuolumne... | 3,913 | 4,330 | 865 | 4,939 | 2,861 |
| Ventura..... | 47,790 | 59,693 | 8,233 | 57,805 | 40,264 |
| Yolo........ | 15,751 | 11,063 | 1,733 | 18,266 | 7,976 |
| Yuba....... | 4,461 | 5,371 | 1,296 | 6,766 | 4,964 |
| **Totals...** | **3,186,- 270** | **3,407,- 851** | **481,665** | **4,171,- 877** | **2,879,- 108** |

## California (cont'd)

### CALIFORNIA VOTE SINCE 1920

1920 (Pres.). Cox, Dem., 229,191; Harding, Rep., 624,992; Watkins, Proh., 25,204; Debs, Soc., 64,076.

1924 (Pres.). Coolidge, Rep., 733,250; Davis, Dem., 105,514; LaFollette, Prog., 424,649; Faris, Proh., 18,365.

1928 (Pres.). Hoover, Rep., Proh., 1,162,323; Smith, Dem., 614,365; Thomas, Soc., 19,595; Varney, Proh., 14,394 (incl. in Hoover vote); Foster, Com., 216 (incl. 194 for Gitlow).

1932 (Pres.). Roosevelt, Dem., 1,324,157; Hoover, Rep., 847,902; Thomas, Soc., 63,299; Upshaw, Proh., 20,637; Harvey, Liberty, 9,827; Foster, Com., 1,023.

1936 (Pres.). Roosevelt, Dem., 1,766,836; Landon, Rep., 836,431; Colvin, Proh., 12,917; Thomas, Soc., 11,325; Browder, Com., 10,877.

1940 (Pres.). Roosevelt, Dem., 1,877,618; Wilkie, Rep., 1,351,419; Thomas, Prog., 16,506; Browder, Com., 13,586; Babson, Proh., 9,400.

1944 (Pres.). Roosevelt, Dem., 1,988,564; Dewey, Rep., 1,512,965; Watson, Proh., 14,770; Thomas, Soc., 3,923; Teichert, Soc. Lab., 327.

1948 (Pres.). Truman, Dem., 1,913,134; Dewey, Rep., 1,895,269; Wallace, Prog., 190,381; Watson, Proh., 16,926; Thomas, Soc., 3,459; Thurmond, States' Rights, 1,228; Teichert, Soc. Lab., 195; Dobbs, Soc. Workers, 133.

1952 (Pres.). Eisenhower, Rep., 2,897,310; Stevenson, Dem., 2,197,548; Hallinan, Prog., 24,106; Hamblen, Proh., 15 653; MacArthur, (Tenny Ticket) 3,326; (Kellems Ticket) 178; Hass, Soc. Lab., 273; Hoopes, Soc., 206; Scattered, 3,249.

1956 (Pres.). Eisenhower, Rep., 3,027,668; Stevenson, Dem., 2,420,136; Holtwick, Proh., 11,119; Andrews, Constitution, 6,087; Hass, Soc. Lab., 300; Hoopes, Soc., 123; Dobbs, Soc. Workers, 96; Smith, Christian Nat'l., 8; Scattered, 819.

1960 (Pres.). Kennedy, Dem., 3,224,099; Nixon, Rep. 3,259,722; Decker, Proh., 21,706; Hass, Soc. Lab., 1,051.

1964 (Pres.). Johnson, Dem., 4,171,877; Goldwater, Rep., 2,879,108; Hass, Soc. Labor, 489; DeBerry, Soc. Worker, 378; Munn, Proh., 305; Hensley, Universal, 19; Scattering, 5,410.

1968 (Pres.). Nixon, Rep., 3,407,851; Humphrey, Dem., 3,186,270; Wallace, 3rd party, 481,665; scattered, 26,992.

# Colorado

| County | 1968 | | | 1964 | |
| | Hum- phrey (D) | Nixon (R) | Wal- lace (I) | John- son (D) | Gold- water (R) |
|---|---|---|---|---|---|
| Adams | 25,333 | 24,121 | 5,329 | 35,498 | 15,652 |
| Alamosa | 1,574 | 2,277 | 287 | 2,481 | 1,488 |
| Arapahoe | 18,569 | 33,712 | 3,891 | 27,940 | 23,071 |
| Archuleta | 409 | 486 | 83 | 632 | 370 |
| Baca | 734 | 144 | 340 | 1,366 | 1,241 |
| Bent | 1,122 | 1,234 | 276 | 1,737 | 937 |
| Boulder | 17,392 | 27,578 | 2,495 | 22,737 | 17,373 |
| Chaffee | 1,460 | 1,726 | 258 | 2,463 | 1,476 |
| Cheyenne | 392 | 664 | 136 | 735 | 676 |
| Clear Creek | 660 | 994 | 175 | 1,086 | 676 |
| Conejos | 1,489 | 1,366 | 117 | 2,033 | 1,031 |
| Costilla | 938 | 477 | 20 | 1,284 | 299 |
| Crowley | 565 | 775 | 196 | 967 | 690 |
| Custer | 204 | 423 | 77 | 406 | 358 |
| Delta | 2,327 | 3,692 | 618 | 143,927 | 2,879 |
| Denver | 106,081 | 92,013 | 11,404 | 3,480 | 73,238 |
| Dolores | 217 | 392 | 131 | 496 | 322 |
| Douglas | 857 | 1,909 | 327 | 1,442 | 1,336 |
| Eagle | 927 | 1,048 | 160 | 1,299 | 644 |
| Elbert | 484 | 1,043 | 185 | 857 | 924 |
| El Paso | 21,226 | 32,067 | 6,805 | 27,844 | 23,822 |
| Fremont | 2,960 | 4,247 | 823 | 5,181 | 3,875 |
| Garfield | 2,271 | 3,157 | 591 | 3,196 | 2,282 |
| Gilpin | 248 | 358 | 99 | 363 | 233 |
| Grand | 433 | 1,167 | 217 | 902 | 814 |
| Gunnison | 876 | 1,421 | 157 | 1,540 | 903 |
| Hinsdale | 43 | 127 | 22 | 94 | 107 |
| Huerfano | 1,934 | 1,133 | 150 | 2,734 | 895 |
| Jackson | 177 | 474 | 51 | 384 | 354 |
| Jefferson | 32,254 | 52,278 | 6,461 | 43,162 | 33,395 |
| Kiowa | 423 | 689 | 112 | 701 | 570 |
| Kit Carson | 1,026 | 1,977 | 232 | 1,906 | 1,516 |
| Lake | 1,550 | 1,025 | 287 | 2,362 | 681 |
| LaPlata | 2,526 | 4,269 | 673 | 4,442 | 3,550 |
| Larimer | 9,148 | 18,435 | 1,810 | 12,776 | 11,636 |
| Las Animas | 4,679 | 2,545 | 353 | 6,591 | 1,833 |
| Lincoln | 809 | 1,407 | 247 | 1,327 | 1,104 |
| Logan | 2,521 | 4,334 | 736 | 4,222 | 3,497 |
| Mesa | 8,775 | 10,745 | 2,076 | 12,716 | 8,317 |
| Mineral | 125 | 116 | 33 | 204 | 89 |
| Moffat | 765 | 1,785 | 322 | 1,657 | 1,438 |
| Montezuma | 1,349 | 2,461 | 545 | 2,686 | 2,035 |
| Montrose | 2,397 | 3,556 | 753 | 4,009 | 2,678 |
| Morgan | 2,306 | 4,598 | 584 | 4,271 | 3,228 |
| Otero | 3,863 | 4,726 | 713 | 5,999 | 3,605 |
| Ouray | 250 | 401 | 120 | 456 | 358 |

## Colorado (cont'd)

| County | 1968 | | | 1964 | |
| | Hum- phrey (D) | Nixon (R) | Wal- lace (I) | John- son (D) | Gold- water (R) |
|---|---|---|---|---|---|
| Park | 286 | 601 | 134 | 515 | 493 |
| Phillips | 723 | 1,237 | 211 | 1,243 | 1,012 |
| Pitkin | 728 | 1,135 | 137 | 958 | 540 |
| Prowers | 2,335 | 2,745 | 506 | 3,759 | 2,044 |
| Pueblo | 27,189 | 16,596 | 3,797 | 34,933 | 13,103 |
| Rio Blanco | 502 | 1,294 | 204 | 1,134 | 1,015 |
| Rio Grande | 1,562 | 2,442 | 174 | 2,161 | 1,699 |
| Routt | 1,080 | 1,591 | 291 | 1,853 | 1,095 |
| Saguache | 648 | 823 | 97 | 1,099 | 622 |
| San Juan | 134 | 165 | 59 | 275 | 129 |
| San Miguel | 336 | 422 | 60 | 636 | 332 |
| Sedgwick | 546 | 1,006 | 100 | 942 | 895 |
| Summit | 301 | 536 | 95 | 483 | 344 |
| Teller | 403 | 721 | 249 | 685 | 577 |
| Washington | 699 | 1,634 | 352 | 1,341 | 1,434 |
| Weld | 10,420 | 17,097 | 2,174 | 17,268 | 12,204 |
| Yuma | 1,175 | 2,529 | 330 | 2,145 | 2,007 |
| **Totals** | **335,715** | **408,146** | **60,447** | **476,024** | **296,767** |

### COLORADO VOTE SINCE 1920

1920 (Pres.). Cox, Dem., 104,936; Harding, Rep., 173,248; Watkins, Proh., 2,807; Debs, Soc., 8,046; Christensen, Farm-Lab., 3,016.

1924 (Pres.). Coolidge, Rep., 195,171; Davis, Dem., 75,238; LaFollette, Prog., 57,368; Faris, Proh., 966; Foster, Workers, 562; Johns, Soc. Lab., 378.

1928 (Pres.). Hoover, Rep., 253,872; Smith, Dem., 133,131; Thomas, Soc., 3,472; Foster, Com., 675; Farm.-Lab., 1,092.

1932 (Pres.). Roosevelt, Dem., 250,877; Hoover, Rep., 189,617; Thomas, Soc., 14,018; Upshaw, Proh., 1,928.

1936 (Pres.). Roosevelt, Dem., 295,081; Landon, Rep., 181,267; Lemke, Union, 9,962; Thomas, Soc., 1,593; Browder, Com., 497; Aiken, Soc. Labor, 336.

1940 (Pres.). Roosevelt, Dem., 265,554; Wilkie, Rep., 279,576; Thomas, Soc., 1,899; Babson, Proh., 1,597; Browder, Com., 378.

1944 (Pres.). Roosevelt, Dem., 234,331; Dewey, Rep., 268,731; Thomas, Soc., 1,977.

1948 (Pres.). Truman, Dem., 267,288; Dewey, Rep., 239,714; Wallace, Prog., 6,115; Thomas, Soc., 1,678; Dobbs, Soc. Workers, 228; Teichert, Soc. Lab., 214.

1952 (Pres.). Eisenhower. Rep., 379,782; Stevenson, Dem., 245,504; MacArthur, Constitution, 2,181; Hallinan, Prog., 1,919; Hoopes, Soc., 365; Hass, Soc. Lab., 352.

1956 (Pres.). Eisenhower, Rep., 394,479; Stevenson, Dem., 263,997; Hass, Soc. Lab., 3,308; Andrews, Ind., 759; Hoopes, Soc., 531.

1960 (Pres.). Kennedy, Dem., 330,629; Nixon, Rep., 402,242; Hass, Soc. Lab., 2,803; Dobbs, Soc. Workers, 572.

1964 (Pres.). Johnson, Dem., 476,024; Goldwater, Rep., 296,767; Hass, Soc. Labor, 302; DeBerry, Soc. Worker, 2 537; Munn, Proh., 1,356.

1968 (Pres.). Nixon, Rep., 408,146; Humphrey, Dem., 335,715; Wallace, 3rd party, 60,447. scattered, 1,274.

# Connecticut

| County | 1968 | | | 1964 | |
| | Hum- phrey (D) | Nixon (R) | Wal- lace (I) | John- son (D) | Gold- water (R) |
|---|---|---|---|---|---|
| Fairfield | 139,364 | 173,108 | 21,477 | 194,782 | 125,576 |
| Hartford | 190,865 | 151,794 | 16,779 | 240,971 | 88,811 |
| Litchfield | 29,340 | 31,429 | 3,526 | 40,172 | 20,834 |
| Middlesex | 23,727 | 21,999 | 2,706 | 30,517 | 14,697 |
| New Haven | 159,653 | 130,501 | 23,985 | 218,743 | 97,656 |
| New London | 41,507 | 37,116 | 4,879 | 54,551 | 24,391 |
| Tolland | 18,007 | 16,666 | 1,918 | 22,195 | 9,951 |
| Windham | 19,098 | 14,162 | 1,380 | 25,238 | 9,080 |
| **Totals** | **621,561** | **556,721** | **76,650** | **826,269** | **390,996** |

### CONNECTICUT VOTE SINCE 1920

1920 (Pres.). Cox, Dem., 120,721; Harding, Rep., 229,238; Watkins, Proh., 1,771; Debs., Soc., 10,350; Christensen, Farm-Lab., 1,947.

1924 (Pres.). Coolidge, Rep., 246,322; Davis, Dem., 110,184; LaFollette, Prog., 42,416; Johns, Soc. Lab., 1,373.

1928 (Pres.). Hoover, Rep., 296,614; Smith, Dem., 252,040; Thomas, Soc., 3,019; Foster, Com., 730; Reynolds, Soc. Lab., 622.

1932 (Pres.). Roosevelt, Dem., 281,632; Hoover, Rep., 288,420; Thomas, Soc., 22,767.

1936 (Pres.). Roosevelt, Dem., 382,129; Landon, Rep., 278,685; Lemke, Union, 21,805; Thomas, Soc., 5,683; Browder, Com., 1,193.

1940 (Pres.). Roosevelt, Dem., 417,621; Wilkie,

## Connecticut (cont'd)

Rep., 361,021; Browder, Com., 1,091; Aiken, Soc. Lab., 971; Willkie, Union, 798.
1944 (Pres.), Roosevelt, Dem., 435,146; Dewey, Rep., 390,527; Thomas, Soc., 5,097; Teichert, Soc. Lab., 1,220.
1948 (Pres.), Truman, Dem., 423,297; Dewey, Rep., 437,754; Wallace, Prog., 13,713; Thomas, Soc., 6,964; Teichert, Soc. Lab., 1,184; Dobbs, Soc. Workers, 606.
1952 (Pres.), Eisenhower, Rep., 611,012; Stevenson, Dem., 481,649; Hoopes, Soc., 2,244; Hallinan, Peoples, 1,466; Hass, Soc. Lab., 535; Write-in, 5.
1956 (Pres.), Eisenhower, Rep., 711,837; Stevenson, Dem., 405,079; Scattered, 205.
1960 (Pres.), Kennedy, Dem., 657,055; Nixon, Rep., 565,813.
1964 (Pres.), Johnson, Dem., 826,269; Goldwater, Rep., 390,996; Scattered, 1,313.
1968 (Pres.), Nixon, Rep., 556,721; Humphrey, Dem., 621,561; Wallace, 3rd party, 76,650; scattered, 1,302.

## Delaware

| County | 1968 | | | 1964 | |
| | Humphrey (D) | Nixon (R) | Wallace (I) | Johnson (D) | Goldwater (R) |
|---|---|---|---|---|---|
| New Castle (Inc. Wilmington)... | 67,395 | 68,630 | 17,050 | 91,752 | 54,767 |
| Kent...... | 8,972 | 10,818 | 4,712 | 12,981 | 9,006 |
| Sussex...... | 11,689 | 15,533 | 5,760 | 17,971 | 14,305 |
| **Totals...** | **88,056** | **94,981** | **27,522** | **122,704** | **78,078** |

### DELAWARE VOTE SINCE 1920

1920 (Pres.), Cox, Dem., 39,911; Harding, Rep., 52,858; Watkins, Proh., 986; Debs. Soc., 988; Christensen, Farm-Lab., 93.
1924 (Pres.), Coolidge, Rep., 52,441; Davis, Dem., 33,445; LaFollette, Prog. & Soc., 4,979.
1928 (Pres.), Hoover, Rep., 68,860; Smith, Dem., 36,643.
1932 (Pres.), Hoover, Rep., 57,074; Roosevelt, Dem., 54,319; Thomas, Soc., 1,376; Foster, Com., 133.
1936 (Pres.), Roosevelt, Dem., 69,702; Landon, Rep., 54,014; Lemke, Union, 442; Thomas, Soc., 179; Browder, Com., 52.
1940 (Pres.), Roosevelt, Dem., 74,599; Willkie, Rep., 61,440; Babson, Proh., 220; Thomas, Soc., 115.
1944 (Pres.), Roosevelt, Dem., 68,166; Dewey, Rep., 56,747; Watson, Proh., 294; Thomas, Soc., 154.
1948 (Pres.), Truman, Dem., 67,813; Dewey, Rep., 69,688; Wallace, Prog., 1,050; Watson, Proh., 343; Thomas, Soc., 250; Teichert, Soc. Lab., 29.
1952 (Pres.). Eisenhower. Rep., 90,059; Stevenson, Dem., 83,315; Hass, Soc. Lab., 242; Hamblen, Proh., 234; Hallinan, Prog., 155; Hoopes, Soc., 20.
1956 (Pres.), Eisenhower. Rep., 98,057; Stevenson, Dem., 79,421; Holtwick, Proh., 400; Hass, Soc. Lab., 110.
1960 (Pres.), Kennedy, Dem.. 99,590; Nixon. Rep., 96,373; Faubus, States' Rights, 354; Decker, Proh., 284; Hass, Soc. Lab., 82.
1964 (Pres.). Johnson, Dem.. 122,704; Goldwater, Rep., 78,078; Hass, Soc. Lab., 113; Munn, Proh., 425.
1968 (Pres.), Nixon, Rep., 88,056; Humphrey, Dem.. 94,981; Wallace, 3rd party, 27,522.

## District of Columbia

| County | 1968 | | | 1964 | |
| | Humphrey (D) | Nixon (R) | Wallace (I) | Johnson (D) | Goldwater (R) |
|---|---|---|---|---|---|
| Dist. of C... | 139,566 | 31,012 | ...... | 169,796 | 28,801 |
| **Totals...** | **139,566** | **31,012** | ...... | **169,796** | **28,801** |

### DISTRICT OF COLUMBIA

1964 (Pres.), Johnson, Dem., 169,796; Goldwater, Rep., 28,801.
1968 (Pres.), Nixon, Rep., 31,012; Humphrey, Dem., 139,566.

## Florida

| County | 1968 | | | 1964 | |
| | Humphrey (D) | Nixon (R) | Wallace (I) | Johnson (D) | Goldwater (R) |
|---|---|---|---|---|---|
| Alachua.... | 10,060 | 9,670 | 8,696 | 13,483 | 11,151 |
| Baker...... | 487 | 294 | 1,962 | 1,137 | 1,121 |
| Bay........ | 4,020 | 5,121 | 15,161 | 7,846 | 12,849 |

## Florida (cont'd)

| County | 1968 | | | 1964 | |
| | Humphrey (D) | Nixon (R) | Wallace (I) | Johnson (D) | Goldwater (R) |
|---|---|---|---|---|---|
| Bradford ... | 1,173 | 718 | 2,840 | 2,320 | 1,987 |
| Brevard.... | 18,281 | 37,124 | 21,909 | 24,833 | 24,551 |
| Broward.... | 56,613 | 106,122 | 31,992 | 68,406 | 85,264 |
| Calhoun.... | 398 | 356 | 2,375 | 980 | 1,793 |
| Charlotte.. | 3,647 | 6,056 | 2,270 | 4,831 | 4,163 |
| Citrus..... | 1,775 | 2,767 | 2,606 | 2,521 | 2,329 |
| Clay...... | 1,954 | 3,251 | 4,046 | 3,114 | 3,805 |
| Collier.... | 2,230 | 5,362 | 2,952 | 2,877 | 3,581 |
| Columbia... | 1,750 | 1,553 | 4,046 | 3,249 | 4,145 |
| Dade....... | 176,689 | 135,222 | 53,391 | 208,941 | 117,480 |
| De Soto.... | 937 | 1,103 | 2,054 | 1,777 | 1,986 |
| Dixie...... | 325 | 217 | 1,546 | 923 | 908 |
| Duval...... | 54,341 | 51,585 | 60,559 | 79,365 | 81,116 |
| Escambia... | 16,281 | 15,089 | 37,000 | 25,371 | 32,414 |
| Flagler.... | 601 | 360 | 817 | 940 | 718 |
| Franklin... | 699 | 529 | 1,909 | 1,366 | 1,419 |
| Gadsden.... | 3,274 | 1,537 | 4,446 | 4,556 | 5,207 |
| Gilchrist.. | 208 | 183 | 1,119 | 711 | 540 |
| Glades..... | 230 | 261 | 600 | 441 | 541 |
| Gulf....... | 711 | 364 | 2,725 | 1,659 | 2,001 |
| Hamilton... | 820 | 337 | 1,574 | 1,302 | 1,158 |
| Hardee..... | 703 | 1,278 | 2,529 | 1,908 | 2,321 |
| Hendry..... | 791 | 900 | 1,638 | 1,352 | 1,650 |
| Hernando... | 1,524 | 2,053 | 2,387 | 2,320 | 2,337 |
| Highlands.. | 2,582 | 4,560 | 3,475 | 4,203 | 4,747 |
| Hillsborough | 45,848 | 49,441 | 46,913 | 71,289 | 50,616 |
| Holmes..... | 312 | 377 | 4,700 | 1,193 | 3,225 |
| Indian River | 3,179 | 6,518 | 3,022 | 5,122 | 6,191 |
| Jackson.... | 2,472 | 1,236 | 8,622 | 4,386 | 7,064 |
| Jefferson.. | 1,066 | 459 | 1,567 | 1,504 | 1,684 |
| Lafayette.. | 215 | 137 | 1,125 | 545 | 648 |
| Lake....... | 4,599 | 11,763 | 8,442 | 7,773 | 12,897 |
| Lee........ | 7,978 | 14,376 | 8,741 | 10,204 | 12,886 |
| Leon....... | 10,440 | 9,288 | 12,878 | 10,927 | 15,181 |
| Levy....... | 767 | 745 | 2,449 | 1,986 | 1,580 |
| Liberty.... | 242 | 154 | 1,322 | 377 | 910 |
| Madison.... | 1,378 | 650 | 2,703 | 2,121 | 2,822 |
| Manatee.... | 8,286 | 18,247 | 8,214 | 13,074 | 17,147 |
| Marion..... | 5,798 | 7,468 | 9,600 | 9,112 | 10,879 |
| Martin..... | 2,580 | 5,179 | 2,471 | 3,621 | 4,292 |
| Monroe..... | 5,534 | 5,094 | 4,271 | 8,936 | 4,842 |
| Nassau..... | 1,598 | 1,301 | 3,634 | 2,731 | 3,134 |
| Okaloosa... | 3,059 | 5,525 | 12,237 | 7,890 | 9,961 |
| Okeechobee. | 542 | 862 | 1,604 | 1,016 | 1,316 |
| Orange..... | 22,548 | 50,874 | 27,247 | 38,248 | 48,884 |
| Osceola.... | 1,870 | 4,172 | 3,462 | 3,531 | 4,516 |
| Palm Beach. | 32,837 | 62,191 | 21,894 | 43,836 | 49,614 |
| Pasco...... | 6,292 | 9,743 | 6,966 | 8,135 | 7,606 |
| Pinellas... | 68,205 | 109,235 | 33,814 | 98,381 | 80,414 |
| Polk....... | 15,898 | 27,839 | 31,540 | 29,355 | 35,906 |
| Putnam..... | 2,920 | 2,955 | 5,150 | 4,995 | 5,072 |
| St. Johns.. | 2,748 | 3,880 | 4,682 | 4,357 | 7,450 |
| St. Lucie.. | 5,232 | 7,281 | 4,410 | 7,748 | 7,204 |
| Santa Rosa. | 1,600 | 2,567 | 8,549 | 3,570 | 5,983 |
| Sarasota... | 10,127 | 30,160 | 7,041 | 13,937 | 21,917 |
| Seminole... | 6,120 | 10,821 | 7,275 | 9,125 | 10,078 |
| Sumter..... | 1,277 | 910 | 2,879 | 2,259 | 1,631 |
| Suwannee... | 1,182 | 845 | 3,955 | 2,393 | 3,002 |
| Taylor..... | 941 | 794 | 3,318 | 1,708 | 2,661 |
| Union...... | 290 | 179 | 1,192 | 740 | 710 |
| Volusia.... | 24,987 | 28,024 | 17,209 | 34,901 | 24,988 |
| Wakulla.... | 440 | 247 | 1,668 | 753 | 1,270 |
| Walton..... | 1,064 | 963 | 5,135 | 2,449 | 3,753 |
| Washington. | 722 | 528 | 3,682 | 1,500 | 2,725 |
| **Totals...** | **676,794** | **886,804** | **624,207** | **948,540** | **905,941** |

### FLORIDA VOTE SINCE 1920

1920 (Pres.), Cox, Dem., 90,515; Harding, Rep., 44,853; Watkins, Proh., 5,124; Debs. Soc., 5,189.
1924 (Pres.), Davis, Dem., 62,083; Coolidge, Rep., 30,633; LaFollette, Prog., 8,625; Faris, Proh., 5,498; Nations, Amer., 2,315.
1928 (Pres.), Hoover, Rep., 144,168; Smith, Dem., 101,764; Thomas, Soc., 4,036; Foster, Com., 3,704.
1932 (Pres.), Roosevelt, Dem., 206,307; Hoover, Rep., 69,170; Thomas, Soc., 775.
1936 (Pres.), Roosevelt, Dem., 249,117; Landon, Rep., 78,248; Thomas, Soc., 775.
1940 (Pres.), Roosevelt, Dem., 359,334; Willkie, Rep., 126,158.
1944 (Pres.), Roosevelt, Dem., 339,377; Dewey, Rep., 143,215.
1948 (Pres.), Truman, Dem., 281,988; Dewey, Rep., 194,280; Thurmond, States' Rights, 89,755; Wallace, Prog., 11,620.
1952 (Pres.), Eisenhower, Rep., 544,036; Stevenson, Dem., 444,950; Scattered, 351.
1956 (Pres.), Eisenhower, Rep., 643,849; Stevenson, Dem., 480,371.
1960 (Pres.), Kennedy, Dem., 748,700; Nixon, Rep., 795,476.
1964 (Pres.), Johnson, Dem., 948,540; Goldwater, Rep., 905,941.
1968 (Pres.), Nixon, Rep., 886,804; Humphrey, Dem., 676,794; Wallace, 3rd party, 624,207.

## Georgia

| County | 1968 Humphrey (D) | Nixon (R) | Wallace (I) | 1964 Johnson (D) | Goldwater (R) |
|---|---|---|---|---|---|
| Appling.... | 760 | 795 | 2,678 | 1,562 | 2,597 |
| Atkinson... | 686 | 288 | 1,554 | 811 | 1,157 |
| Bacon...... | 279 | 586 | 1,935 | 1,179 | 2,136 |
| Baker...... | 548 | 99 | 1,067 | 600 | 914 |
| Baldwin.... | 2,109 | 2,318 | 2,678 | 2,740 | 3,430 |
| Banks...... | 296 | 398 | 1,434 | 1,258 | 548 |
| Barrow..... | 1,070 | 1,372 | 2,731 | 2,277 | 2,316 |
| Bartow..... | 2,149 | 2,041 | 4,052 | 4,635 | 2,813 |
| Ben Hill.... | 876 | 661 | 1,833 | 1,523 | 2,089 |
| Berrien..... | 451 | 566 | 2,810 | 2,658 | 4,073 |
| Bibb....... | 10,579 | 13,490 | 17,308 | 17,831 | 25,641 |
| Bleckley.... | 396 | 756 | 2,458 | 978 | 2,578 |
| Brantley.... | 317 | 237 | 1,709 | 909 | 1,231 |
| Brooks..... | 787 | 589 | 2,404 | 1,027 | 2,342 |
| Bryan...... | 560 | 381 | 1,426 | 857 | 1,433 |
| Bulloch.... | 1,788 | 2,113 | 3,953 | 2,720 | 4,823 |
| Burke...... | 1,676 | 1,416 | 1,802 | 1,208 | 3,034 |
| Butts...... | 959 | 584 | 1,490 | 1,534 | 1,261 |
| Calhoun.... | 697 | 234 | 979 | 289 | 1,066 |
| Camden.... | 1,146 | 751 | 1,988 | 1,693 | 1,802 |
| Candler.... | 587 | 552 | 1,624 | 795 | 1,710 |
| Carroll..... | 2,326 | 3,135 | 6,509 | 4,794 | 4,984 |
| Catoosa.... | 901 | 2,043 | 6,449 | 2,922 | 4,143 |
| Charlton.... | 455 | 332 | 1,157 | 574 | 1,179 |
| Chatham... | 18,178 | 18,013 | 17,206 | 23,176 | 33,141 |
| Chat'hoc'ee. | 148 | 70 | 303 | 191 | 243 |
| Chattooga.. | 1,255 | 1,087 | 3,024 | 3,986 | 1,476 |
| Cherokee... | 1,434 | 2,675 | 3,351 | 3,189 | 3,398 |
| Clarke..... | 5,543 | 5,800 | 3,452 | 7,519 | 4,875 |
| Clay....... | 516 | 133 | 608 | 360 | 544 |
| Clayton.... | 3,489 | 8,182 | 11,601 | 5,869 | 10,489 |
| Clinch..... | 334 | 304 | 1,142 | 706 | 1,084 |
| Cobb....... | 8,755 | 18,649 | 17,805 | 16,647 | 20,863 |
| Coffee..... | 1,331 | 1,241 | 3,785 | 2,719 | 4,392 |
| Colquitt.... | 1,119 | 1,882 | 6,325 | 2,563 | 6,493 |
| Columbia... | 905 | 1,636 | 2,207 | 1,428 | 2,575 |
| Cook....... | 603 | 521 | 2,438 | 1,337 | 2,058 |
| Coweta..... | 1,204 | 2,442 | 3,781 | 3,712 | 3,656 |
| Crawford... | 489 | 246 | 886 | 723 | 957 |
| Crisp...... | 1,017 | 935 | 3,271 | 1,756 | 3,337 |
| Dade...... | 282 | 615 | 2,460 | 1,227 | 1,378 |
| Dawson.... | 246 | 509 | 845 | 932 | 639 |
| Decatur.... | 1,729 | 749 | 4,576 | 2,011 | 5,060 |
| De Kalb.... | 27,796 | 52,485 | 23,954 | 37,154 | 49,409 |
| Dodge..... | 1,230 | 1,055 | 3,406 | 2,376 | 3,285 |
| Dooly..... | 879 | 454 | 1,803 | 1,471 | 1,662 |
| Dougherty.. | 3,831 | 5,611 | 9,317 | 5,248 | 12,776 |
| Douglas.... | 1,241 | 1,848 | 4,159 | 2,501 | 3,315 |
| Early...... | 785 | 327 | 2,797 | 771 | 2,398 |
| Echols..... | 56 | 53 | 533 | 184 | 396 |
| Effingham.. | 635 | 769 | 2,561 | 680 | 2,679 |
| Elbert..... | 1,216 | 914 | 3,252 | 3,172 | 1,887 |
| Emanuel.... | 1,508 | 1,297 | 3,307 | 2,279 | 3,311 |
| Evans..... | 492 | 543 | 1,475 | 799 | 1,572 |
| Fannin..... | 1,134 | 3,096 | 1,095 | 2,834 | 3,433 |
| Fayette.... | 551 | 867 | 1,888 | 896 | 1,349 |
| Floyd...... | 4,036 | 7,470 | 10,001 | 8,750 | 9,849 |
| Forsyth.... | 647 | 1,389 | 2,397 | 1,682 | 1,471 |
| Franklin.... | 766 | 600 | 2,691 | 2,758 | 864 |
| Fulton..... | 77,847 | 64,153 | 36,995 | 93,540 | 73,150 |
| Gilmer..... | 690 | 2,074 | 1,259 | 2,159 | 2,167 |
| Glascock... | 47 | 185 | 733 | 134 | 836 |
| Glynn..... | 3,247 | 3,725 | 5,331 | 5,712 | 7,341 |
| Gordon.... | 1,161 | 1,815 | 3,077 | 3,260 | 2,317 |
| Grady..... | 1,425 | 561 | 3,817 | 1,887 | 2,983 |
| Greene.... | 1,635 | 652 | 1,223 | 2,698 | 1,093 |
| Gwinnett... | 3,226 | 5,350 | 8,909 | 6,705 | 6,823 |
| Habersham.. | 1,070 | 1,611 | 3,008 | 3,412 | 1,595 |
| Hall...... | 3,160 | 4,902 | 5,530 | 8,003 | 4,296 |
| Hancock... | 2,165 | 381 | 1,104 | 1,074 | 925 |
| Haralson.. | 771 | 1,451 | 3,251 | 2,186 | 3,129 |
| Harris..... | 1,072 | 1,021 | 1,851 | 940 | 2,165 |
| Hart...... | 979 | 586 | 3,208 | 3,142 | 1,166 |
| Heard..... | 356 | 303 | 1,153 | 1,061 | 807 |
| Henry..... | 2,317 | 2,017 | 3,604 | 3,583 | 3,125 |
| Houston... | 2,831 | 4,285 | 7,339 | 4,258 | 6,532 |
| Irwin..... | 474 | 430 | 1,955 | 1,740 | 2,017 |
| Jackson.... | 1,537 | 1,139 | 3,473 | 3,953 | 1,664 |
| Jasper..... | 835 | 456 | 926 | 848 | 1,075 |
| Jeff Davis... | 376 | 577 | 1,958 | 745 | 1,875 |
| Jefferson... | 1,879 | 1,227 | 2,040 | 1,253 | 2,950 |
| Jenkins.... | 704 | 574 | 1,249 | 908 | 1,509 |
| Johnson.... | 446 | 381 | 2,041 | 682 | 1,940 |
| Jones..... | 1,105 | 693 | 1,770 | 1,380 | 1,805 |
| Lamar..... | 790 | 575 | 1,440 | 1,548 | 1,570 |
| Lanier..... | 277 | 241 | 1,024 | 661 | 719 |
| Laurens.... | 3,451 | 2,738 | 6,649 | 3,828 | 5,295 |
| Lee....... | 673 | 389 | 1,201 | 244 | 1,041 |
| Liberty.... | 1,572 | 592 | 1,365 | 2,212 | 1,458 |
| Lincoln.... | 491 | 408 | 1,270 | 353 | 943 |
| Long...... | 574 | 156 | 1,037 | 1,336 | 246 |
| Lowndes... | 2,402 | 3,073 | 5,679 | 4,363 | 6,811 |
| Lumpkin... | 396 | 687 | 1,048 | 1,189 | 855 |
| Macon..... | 954 | 598 | 1,559 | 1,076 | 1,723 |
| Madison.... | 621 | 600 | 2,529 | 2,341 | 1,190 |
| Marion.... | 247 | 186 | 849 | 365 | 719 |
| McDuffie... | 991 | 1,324 | 1,709 | 1,124 | 2,657 |

| Georgia (cont'd) County | 1968 Humphrey (D) | Nixon (R) | Wallace (I) | 1964 Johnson (D) | Goldwater (R) |
|---|---|---|---|---|---|
| Mcintosh... | 943 | 315 | 841 | 1,193 | 795 |
| Meriwether.. | 1,760 | 1,120 | 2,571 | 2,423 | 2,250 |
| Miller..... | 171 | 249 | 1,862 | 274 | 1,658 |
| Mitchell.... | 1,255 | 731 | 3,647 | 1,197 | 3,265 |
| Monroe..... | 1,028 | 770 | 1,422 | 1,578 | 1,665 |
| Montg'm'y.. | 503 | 352 | 1,433 | 878 | 1,409 |
| Morgan.... | 973 | 616 | 1,391 | 1,654 | 1,485 |
| Murray.... | 818 | 1,278 | 1,750 | 2,426 | 1,064 |
| Muscogee... | 7,591 | 11,193 | 15,804 | 12,446 | 21,025 |
| Newton.... | 1,996 | 1,660 | 3,017 | 3,620 | 2,678 |
| Oconee..... | 414 | 713 | 1,405 | 1,073 | 1,241 |
| Oglethorpe.. | 483 | 383 | 1,737 | 864 | 1,126 |
| Paulding... | 1,023 | 789 | 3,054 | 2,513 | 1,916 |
| Peach..... | 1,362 | 904 | 1,638 | 1,585 | 1,970 |
| Pickens.... | 677 | 1,659 | 1,392 | 1,930 | 1,955 |
| Pierce..... | 368 | 446 | 2,446 | 982 | 1,981 |
| Pike...... | 632 | 345 | 1,442 | 946 | 1,064 |
| Polk...... | 2,007 | 1,729 | 4,240 | 4,555 | 3,288 |
| Pulaski.... | 514 | 595 | 1,569 | 953 | 1,762 |
| Putnam.... | 972 | 594 | 1,177 | 1,018 | 1,196 |
| Quitman... | 198 | 90 | 459 | 230 | 377 |
| Rabun..... | 590 | 680 | 1,407 | 1,796 | 551 |
| Randolph.. | 1,028 | 502 | 1,438 | 962 | 1,656 |
| Richmond.. | 11,770 | 1,493 | 9,532 | 13,545 | 21,481 |
| Rockdale.. | 1,213 | 1,195 | 2,215 | 1,972 | 1,503 |
| Schley..... | 309 | 164 | 619 | 377 | 577 |
| Screven.... | 1,411 | 916 | 1,830 | 1,446 | 2,260 |
| Seminole... | 369 | 201 | 1,922 | 427 | 1,294 |
| Spalding... | 2,949 | 3,077 | 4,953 | 5,466 | 4,763 |
| Stephens... | 1,035 | 1,295 | 2,802 | 3,483 | 1,371 |
| Stewart.... | 489 | 233 | 932 | 373 | 1,037 |
| Sumter.... | 1,701 | 1,383 | 3,489 | 1,727 | 3,774 |
| Talbot..... | 510 | 317 | 688 | 627 | 679 |
| Taliaferro... | 678 | 232 | 508 | 628 | 337 |
| Tattnall.... | 957 | 852 | 3,405 | 1,648 | 3,264 |
| Taylor..... | 691 | 393 | 1,626 | 1,097 | 1,372 |
| Telfair..... | 992 | 616 | 2,367 | 1,872 | 1,914 |
| Terrell..... | 1,275 | 545 | 1,798 | 569 | 1,921 |
| Thomas.... | 2,583 | 2,261 | 5,039 | 3,257 | 6,306 |
| Tift....... | 1,187 | 1,692 | 3,942 | 2,286 | 4,650 |
| Toombs.... | 896 | 1,397 | 3,405 | 1,685 | 3,543 |
| Towns..... | 770 | 1,492 | 589 | 1,289 | 1,140 |
| Treutlen... | 341 | 474 | 1,081 | 1,331 | 722 |
| Troup..... | 2,896 | 3,239 | 6,232 | 6,032 | 5,277 |
| Turner.... | 412 | 419 | 1,845 | 719 | 1,672 |
| Twiggs.... | 812 | 336 | 1,167 | 786 | 1,178 |
| Union..... | 974 | 1,221 | 906 | 2,135 | 1,473 |
| Upson..... | 1,480 | 1,494 | 3,579 | 3,275 | 3,103 |
| Walker.... | 1,930 | 3,664 | 8,725 | 5,454 | 5,939 |
| Walton.... | 1,552 | 1,399 | 4,047 | 2,350 | 2,874 |
| Ware...... | 2,255 | 2,047 | 5,895 | 5,189 | 4,948 |
| Warren.... | 582 | 406 | 767 | 384 | 1,070 |
| Washington. | 1,443 | 1,247 | 2,029 | 1,830 | 2,296 |
| Wayne..... | 980 | 1,313 | 3,422 | 2,182 | 3,619 |
| Webster.... | 147 | 72 | 494 | 144 | 457 |
| Wheeler.... | 488 | 251 | 934 | 980 | 849 |
| White..... | 435 | 762 | 1,157 | 1,520 | 840 |
| Whitfield... | 2,723 | 4,828 | 3,954 | 7,330 | 4,646 |
| Wilcox.... | 465 | 381 | 1,822 | 900 | 1,794 |
| Wilkes.... | 953 | 873 | 1,709 | 1,437 | 1,652 |
| Wilkinson.. | 829 | 685 | 1,870 | 963 | 2,172 |
| Worth..... | 719 | 638 | 3,048 | 862 | 3,157 |
| **Totals** ... | **333,062** | **365,722** | **535,389** | **522,557** | **616,600** |

### GEORGIA VOTE SINCE 1920

1920 (Pres.), Cox, Dem., 107,162; Harding, Rep., 43,720; Deb, Soc., 465.

1924 (Pres.), Davis, Dem., 123,200; Coolidge, Rep., 30,300; LaFollette, Prog., 12,691; Faris, Proh., 231; Nations, Amer., 155.

1928 (Pres.), Smith, Dem., 129,602; Hoover, Rep., 63,498; Hoover (anti-Smith, Dem.), 35,871; Hoover total, 99,369; Thomas, Soc., 124; Foster, Com., 64.

1932 (Pres.), Roosevelt, Dem., 234,118; Hoover, Rep., 19,863; Upshaw, Proh., 1,125; Thomas, Soc., 461; Foster, Com., 23.

1936 (Pres.), Roosevelt, Dem., 255,364; Landon, Rep., 36,942; Colvin, Proh., 660; Lemke, Union, 141; Thomas, Soc., 68.

1940 (Pres.), Roosevelt, Dem., 265,194; Willkie, Rep., 23,934; Ind. Dem., 22,428; total, 46,362; Babson, Proh., 983.

1944 (Pres.), Roosevelt, Dem., 268,187; Dewey, Rep., 56,506; Watson, Proh., 36.

1948 (Pres.), Truman, Dem., 254,646; Dewey, Rep., 76,691; Thurmond, States' Rights, 85,055; Wallace, Prog., 1,636; Watson, Proh., 732.

1952 (Pres.), Eisenhower, Rep., 198,979; Stevenson, Dem., 456,823; Liberty Party, 1.

1956 (Pres.), Stevenson, Dem., 444,388; Eisenhower, Rep., 222,778; Andrews, Ind., (Write-in), 1,754.

1960 (Pres.), Kennedy, Dem., 458,638; Nixon, Rep., 274,472; Write-ins, 239.

1964 (Pres.), Johnson, Dem., 522,557; Goldwater, Rep., 616,600.

1968 (Pres.), Nixon, Rep., 365,722; Humphrey, Dem., 333,062; Wallace, 3rd party, 535,389.

# Hawaii

| County | 1968 Humphrey (D) | Nixon (R) | Wallace (I) | 1964 Johnson (D) | Goldwater (R) |
|---|---|---|---|---|---|
| Hawaii..... | 15,819 | 9,625 | 283 | 20,011 | 4,962 |
| Honolulu.. | 108,141 | 71,259 | 2,794 | 121,859 | 33,536 |
| Kauai...... | 7,043 | 4,136 | 155 | 8,713 | 1,971 |
| Maui....... | 10,297 | 6,380 | 233 | 12,666 | 3,553 |
| **Totals...** | **141,300** | **91,440** | **3,465** | **163,249** | **44,022** |

## HAWAII VOTE SINCE 1960

1960 (Pres.), Kennedy, Dem., 92,410; Nixon, Rep., 92,295.

1964 (Pres.), Johnson, Dem., 163,249; Goldwater, Rep., 44,022.

1968 (Pres.), Nixon, Rep., 91,440; Humphrey, Dem., 141,300; Wallace, 3rd party, 3,465.

# Idaho

| County | 1968 Humphrey (D) | Nixon (R) | Wallace (I) | 1964 Johnson (D) | Goldwater (R) |
|---|---|---|---|---|---|
| Ada........ | 10,391 | 26,708 | 5,441 | 19,639 | 25,404 |
| Adams..... | 360 | 844 | 237 | 750 | 689 |
| Bannock.... | 9,083 | 10,234 | 1,978 | 13,483 | 7,825 |
| Bear Lake.. | 1,058 | 1,865 | 165 | 1,857 | 1,409 |
| Benewah.... | 1,126 | 1,108 | 245 | 1,796 | 981 |
| Bingham.... | 2,990 | 6,505 | 1,190 | 5,231 | 5,364 |
| Blaine..... | 815 | 1,337 | 332 | 1,293 | 1,161 |
| Boise...... | 205 | 450 | 154 | 450 | 414 |
| Bonner..... | 2,889 | 2,895 | 741 | 4,328 | 2,975 |
| Bonneville. | 5,189 | 13,643 | 2,308 | 9,637 | 10,736 |
| Boundary... | 893 | 1,084 | 330 | 1,418 | 1,065 |
| Butte...... | 521 | 691 | 100 | 848 | 649 |
| Camas..... | 118 | 271 | 93 | 258 | 316 |
| Canyon..... | 5,432 | 14,519 | 3,019 | 10,601 | 13,466 |
| Caribou.... | 727 | 1,731 | 327 | 1,422 | 1,303 |
| Cassia..... | 1,175 | 4,163 | 988 | 2,608 | 4,009 |
| Clark...... | 87 | 271 | 49 | 186 | 262 |
| Clearwater. | 1,888 | 1,292 | 343 | 2,446 | 767 |
| Custer..... | 385 | 711 | 327 | 714 | 720 |
| Elmore..... | 826 | 1,445 | 473 | 2,310 | 1,857 |
| Franklin... | 831 | 2,510 | 1,583 | 2,400 |  |
| Fremont.... | 962 | 2,297 | 667 | 1,970 | 1,945 |
| Gem........ | 1,183 | 2,314 | 500 | 2,328 | 1,979 |
| Gooding.... | 1,018 | 2,349 | 861 | 1,848 | 2,527 |
| Idaho...... | 1,829 | 2,256 | 672 | 3,188 | 1,990 |
| Jefferson.. | 1,021 | 3,149 | 971 | 2,061 | 2,740 |
| Jerome..... | 871 | 2,409 | 720 | 1,828 | 3,113 |
| Kootenai... | 6,200 | 7,078 | 1,402 | 8,215 | 6,096 |
| Latah...... | 2,966 | 3,042 | 553 | 5,249 | 3,475 |
| Lemhi...... | 547 | 1,476 | 533 | 1,067 | 1,496 |
| Lewis...... | 927 | 697 | 177 | 1,557 | 1,432 |
| Lincoln.... | 350 | 972 | 223 | 617 | 969 |
| Madison.... | 904 | 2,971 | 513 | 1,949 | 2,101 |
| Minidoka... | 1,332 | 3,182 | 1,140 | 2,827 | 3,111 |
| Nez Perce.. | 6,502 | 5,016 | 1,051 | 9,245 | 3,912 |
| Oneida..... | 460 | 1,114 | 110 | 768 | 1,111 |
| Owyhee..... | 562 | 1,385 | 377 | 1,168 | 1,216 |
| Payette.... | 637 | 1,476 | 731 | 2,508 | 2,764 |
| Power...... | 582 | 1,222 | 224 | 1,161 | 966 |
| Shoshone... | 3,850 | 3,078 | 652 | 5,194 | 2,884 |
| Teton...... | 376 | 694 | 128 | 598 | 675 |
| Twin Falls. | 3,943 | 11,387 | 2,776 | 7,638 | 11,518 |
| Valley..... | 522 | 1,149 | 297 | 1,126 | 980 |
| Washington. | 1,033 | 2,020 | 451 | 1,952 | 1,730 |
| **Totals...** | **85,566** | **157,010** | **35,024** | **148,920** | **143,557** |

## IDAHO VOTE SINCE 1920

1920 (Pres.), Cox, Dem., 46,579; Harding, Rep., 88,975; Watkins, Proh., 9; Debs, Soc., 38; Christensen, Farm-Lab., 6.

1924 (Pres.), Coolidge, Rep., 69,879; LaFollette, Prog., 54,160; Davis, Dem., 24,256.

1928 (Pres.), Hoover, Rep., 99,848; Smith, Dem., 53,074; Thomas, Soc., 1,308.

1932 (Pres.), Roosevelt, Dem., 109,479; Hoover, Rep., 71,312; Harvey, Lib., 4,712; Thomas, Soc., 526; Foster, Com., 491.

1936 (Pres.), Roosevelt, Dem., 125,683; Landon, Rep., 66,256; Lemke, Union, 7,684.

1940 (Pres.), Roosevelt, Dem., 127,842; Willkie, Rep., 106,553; Thomas, Soc., 497; Browder, Com., 276.

1944 (Pres.), Roosevelt, Dem., 107,399; Dewey, Rep., 100,137; Watson, Proh., 503; Thomas, Soc., 282.

1948 (Pres.), Truman, Dem., 107,370; Dewey, Rep., 101,514; Wallace, Prog., 4,972; Watson, Proh., 628; Thomas, Soc., 332.

1952 (Pres.), Eisenhower, Rep., 180,707; Stevenson, Dem., 95,081; Hallinan, Prog., 443; Write-in, 23.

1956 (Pres.), Eisenhower, Rep., 166,979; Stevenson, Dem., 105,868; Andrews, Ind., 126; Write-in, 16.

## Idaho (cont'd)

1960 (Pres.), Kennedy, Dem., 138,853; Nixon, Rep., 161,597.

1964 (Pres.), Johnson, Dem., 148,920; Goldwater, Rep., 143,557.

1968 (Pres.), Nixon, Rep., 157,010; Humphrey, Dem., 85,566; Wallace, 3rd party, 35,024.

# Illinois

| County | 1968 Humphrey (D) | Nixon (R) | Wallace (I) | 1964 Johnson (D) | Goldwater (R) |
|---|---|---|---|---|---|
| Adams..... | 11,474 | 17,364 | 3,082 | 18,321 | 13,993 |
| Alexander... | 2,929 | 2,540 | 1,443 | 4,763 | 2,895 |
| Bond....... | 2,516 | 3,675 | 758 | 3,815 | 3,058 |
| Boone...... | 2,801 | 5,936 | 783 | 3,694 | 5,053 |
| Brown...... | 1,275 | 1,607 | 247 | 2,083 | 1,355 |
| Bureau..... | 6,304 | 11,216 | 1,171 | 9,086 | 9,552 |
| Calhoun.... | 1,329 | 1,542 | 199 | 1,805 | 1,288 |
| Carroll.... | 2,558 | 5,275 | 440 | 4,062 | 4,487 |
| Cass...... | 3,307 | 3,411 | 395 | 4,424 | 2,836 |
| Champaign. | 18,425 | 26,027 | 3,857 | 25,792 | 22,010 |
| Christian. | 8,465 | 7,476 | 1,695 | 11,898 | 6,153 |
| Clark..... | 2,813 | 4,809 | 949 | 4,464 | 4,403 |
| Clay...... | 2,878 | 4,429 | 672 | 4,551 | 3,665 |
| Clinton... | 4,454 | 6,460 | 1,174 | 7,339 | 4,692 |
| Coles...... | 7,332 | 10,446 | 1,931 | 11,377 | 8,876 |
| Cook...... | 1,134,980 | 931,018 | 181,876 | 1,537,181 | 895,718 |
| Crawford.. | 3,383 | 5,870 | 774 | 5,624 | 4,834 |
| Cumberland. | 1,828 | 2,671 | 505 | 3,056 | 2,251 |
| De Kalb... | 6,852 | 14,419 | 1,182 | 10,257 | 11,791 |
| De Witt... | 2,823 | 4,247 | 762 | 4,371 | 3,605 |
| Douglas... | 2,824 | 5,058 | 652 | 4,695 | 4,223 |
| Du Page... | 47,692 | 122,934 | 13,730 | 66,229 | 98,871 |
| Edgar..... | 3,565 | 6,301 | 1,316 | 5,966 | 5,527 |
| Edwards... | 1,095 | 2,633 | 403 | 1,991 | 2,262 |
| Effingham. | 4,496 | 6,697 | 777 | 6,782 | 5,044 |
| Fayette... | 4,010 | 4,448 | 939 | 6,295 | 4,492 |
| Ford...... | 2,216 | 5,233 | 550 | 3,427 | 4,650 |
| Franklin.. | 9,229 | 8,164 | 1,632 | 13,581 | 7,620 |
| Fulton.... | 9,354 | 9,582 | 1,249 | 13,030 | 7,785 |
| Gallatin.. | 1,980 | 1,802 | 404 | 2,845 | 1,394 |
| Greene.... | 3,094 | 3,944 | 652 | 4,781 | 3,128 |
| Grundy.... | 3,414 | 6,634 | 1,082 | 5,246 | 5,522 |
| Hamilton.. | 1,951 | 2,912 | 643 | 3,133 | 2,561 |
| Hancock... | 3,720 | 6,867 | 791 | 6,199 | 5,557 |
| Hardin.... | 1,199 | 1,492 | 187 | 1,639 | 1,324 |
| Henderson. | 1,635 | 2,224 | 288 | 2,271 | 1,863 |
| Henry..... | 8,455 | 12,524 | 1,725 | 12,085 | 10,644 |
| Iroquois.. | 3,897 | 10,954 | 1,225 | 7,029 | 9,423 |
| Jackson... | 8,992 | 9,180 | 1,572 | 12,165 | 7,013 |
| Jasper.... | 2,012 | 2,944 | 728 | 3,406 | 2,614 |
| Jefferson. | 6,476 | 7,367 | 1,667 | 9,653 | 6,248 |
| Jersey.... | 3,266 | 3,781 | 971 | 3,936 | 3,041 |
| Jo Daviess. | 3,228 | 5,563 | 607 | 4,818 | 4,607 |
| Johnson... | 1,143 | 2,405 | 421 | 1,770 | 2,217 |
| Kane...... | 26,205 | 53,444 | 6,150 | 40,703 | 46,391 |
| Kankakee.. | 14,155 | 19,464 | 3,569 | 20,792 | 16,082 |
| Kendall... | 2,228 | 7,184 | 780 | 3,430 | 5,710 |
| Knox...... | 8,707 | 14,216 | 2,394 | 15,000 | 12,850 |
| Lake...... | 44,409 | 68,999 | 8,738 | 62,785 | 58,840 |
| LaSalle... | 22,885 | 25,975 | 2,549 | 30,923 | 21,216 |
| Lawrence.. | 3,205 | 4,873 | 903 | 5,136 | 4,176 |
| Lee....... | 4,736 | 9,587 | 925 | 7,315 | 8,445 |
| Livingston. | 5,229 | 11,963 | 929 | 8,476 | 10,239 |
| Logan..... | 4,552 | 8,638 | 1,029 | 7,712 | 6,805 |
| Macon..... | 23,369 | 21,027 | 5,163 | 35,045 | 17,957 |
| Macoupin.. | 10,750 | 10,262 | 2,325 | 15,227 | 8,430 |
| Madison... | 46,287 | 39,613 | 14,164 | 65,115 | 30,009 |
| Marion.... | 7,737 | 8,134 | 1,680 | 12,363 | 7,060 |
| Marshall.. | 2,455 | 3,897 | 313 | 3,561 | 3,209 |
| Mason..... | 3,365 | 3,899 | 572 | 4,857 | 2,833 |
| Massac.... | 1,934 | 3,578 | 926 | 3,396 | 3,078 |
| McDonough. | 3,785 | 8,496 | 628 | 6,144 | 6,907 |
| McHenry... | 10,898 | 27,245 | 2,701 | 18,014 | 22,503 |
| McLean.... | 12,779 | 22,284 | 2,351 | 19,550 | 19,120 |
| Menard.... | 1,640 | 2,980 | 372 | 2,491 | 2,322 |
| Mercer.... | 3,143 | 4,844 | 607 | 4,410 | 4,220 |
| Monroe.... | 2,922 | 5,056 | 1,247 | 4,605 | 5,936 |
| Montgomery. | 7,323 | 7,547 | 1,231 | 10,581 | 6,425 |
| Morgan.... | 5,300 | 8,900 | 1,138 | 9,235 | 7,240 |
| Moultrie.. | 2,447 | 3,094 | 571 | 3,733 | 2,493 |
| Ogle...... | 4,399 | 12,196 | 1,060 | 6,917 | 10,430 |
| Peoria.... | 30,937 | 37,021 | 5,648 | 47,360 | 33,327 |
| Perry..... | 4,449 | 5,383 | 1,181 | 6,639 | 4,287 |
| Piatt..... | 2,447 | 3,973 | 636 | 3,897 | 3,141 |
| Pike...... | 4,491 | 5,034 | 684 | 6,576 | 4,113 |
| Pope...... | 732 | 1,307 | 224 | 1,117 | 1,329 |
| Pulaski... | 2,076 | 1,741 | 815 | 3,332 | 1,716 |
| Putnam.... | 988 | 1,351 | 162 | 1,359 | 1,131 |
| Randolph.. | 5,960 | 7,685 | 1,392 | 9,199 | 5,803 |
| Richland.. | 2,495 | 4,871 | 853 | 4,239 | 3,901 |
| Rock Island. | 34,531 | 30,440 | 5,060 | 41,759 | 23,714 |
| St. Clair. | 50,594 | 34,492 | 15,260 | 74,005 | 28,226 |
| Saline.... | 5,985 | 6,857 | 961 | 8,337 | 5,691 |
| Sangamon.. | 29,542 | 36,510 | 6,586 | 43,073 | 33,077 |
| Schuyler.. | 1,475 | 2,760 | 346 | 2,504 | 2,417 |
| Scott..... | 1,252 | 1,971 | 325 | 1,952 | 1,627 |
| Shelby.... | 4,528 | 5,487 | 1,115 | 7,088 | 4,281 |
| Stark..... | 1,128 | 2,292 | 239 | 1,776 | 2,117 |

## Illinois (cont'd)

| County | 1968 Humphrey (D) | Nixon (R) | Wallace (I) | 1964 Johnson (D) | Goldwater (R) |
|---|---|---|---|---|---|
| Stephenson.. | 7,040 | 11,821 | 1,050 | 10,854 | 9,252 |
| Tazewell.... | 20,715 | 22,969 | 4,563 | 28,561 | 17,170 |
| Union....... | 3,603 | 3,889 | 871 | 5,208 | 3,142 |
| Vermilion... | 23,475 | 30,752 | 7,730 | 24,765 | 19,506 |
| Wabash..... | 2,244 | 3,529 | 614 | 3,721 | 2,905 |
| Warren..... | 3,085 | 5,877 | 824 | 4,670 | 5,258 |
| Washington.. | 2,093 | 4,791 | 672 | 3,670 | 3,840 |
| Wayne...... | 2,989 | 5,537 | 747 | 5,198 | 4,745 |
| White...... | 3,837 | 5,351 | 761 | 5,963 | 4,000 |
| Whiteside... | 8,132 | 15,177 | 1,179 | 12,536 | 12,940 |
| Will....... | 43,630 | 31,576 | 12,595 | 49,663 | 38,619 |
| Williamson.. | 9,744 | 11,887 | 1,816 | 14,613 | 9,130 |
| Winnebago.. | 36,702 | 47,646 | 6,176 | 48,834 | 39,920 |
| Woodford... | 4,005 | 7,876 | 856 | 5,914 | 6,248 |
| **Totals...** | **2,008,-** 319 | **2,137,-** 239 | **385,065** | **2,796,-** 833 | **1,905,-** 946 |

### ILLINOIS VOTE SINCE 1920

1920 (Pres.), Cox, Dem., 534,395; Harding, Rep., 1,420,480; Watkins, Proh., 11,216; Debs, Soc., 74,747; Christensen, Farm-Lab., 49,630.

1924 (Pres.), Coolidge, Rep., 1,453,321; Davis, Dem., 576,975; LaFollete, Prog., 432,027; Johns, Soc. Lab., 2,334; Foster, Workers, 2,622; Faris, Proh., 2,367; Wallace, Comm. Land., 421.

1928 (Pres.), Hoover, Rep., 1,768,141; Smith, Dem., 1,313,817; Thomas, Soc., 19,138; Reynolds, Soc. Lab., 1,812; Foster, Com., 381.

1932 (Pres.), Roosevelt, Dem., 1,882,304; Hoover, Rep., 1,432,756; Thomas, Soc., 67,258; Foster, Com., 15,582; Upshaw, Proh., 6,388; Reynolds, Soc. Lab., 3,638.

1936 (Pres.), Roosevelt, Dem., 2,282,999; Landon, Rep., 1,570,393; Lemke, Union, 89,439; Thomas, Soc., 7,530; Colvin, Proh., 3,439; Aiken, Soc. Lab., 1,921.

1940 (Pres.), Roosevelt, Dem., 2,149,934; Willkie, Rep., 2,047,240; Thomas, Soc., 10,914; Babson, Proh., 9,190.

1944 (Pres.), Roosevelt, Dem., 2,079,479; Dewey, Rep., 1,939,314; Teichert, Soc. Lab., 9,677; Watson, Proh., 7,411; Thomas, Soc., 180.

1948 (Pres.), Truman, Dem., 1,994,715; Dewey, Rep., 1,961,103; Watson, Proh., 11,959; Thomas, Soc., 11,522; Teichert, Soc. Lab., 3,118.

1952 (Pres.), Eisenhower, Rep., 2,457,327; Stevenson, Dem., 2,013,920; Hass, Soc. Lab., 9,363; Write-in, 448.

1956 (Pres.), Eisenhower, Rep., 2,623,327; Stevenson, Dem., 1,775,682; Hass, Soc. Lab., 8,342; Write-in, 56.

1960 (Pres.), Kennedy, Dem., 2,377,846; Nixon, Rep., 2,368,988; Hass, Soc. Lab., 10,560; Write-in, 15.

1964 (Pres.), Johnson, Dem., 2,796.833; Goldwater, Rep., 1,905,946; Write-in, 62.

1968 (Pres.), Nixon, Rep., 2,137,239; Humphrey, Dem., 2,008,319; Wallace, 3rd party, 385,065.

## Indiana

| County | 1968 Humphrey (D) | Nixon (R) | Wallace (I) | 1964 Johnson (D) | Goldwater (R) |
|---|---|---|---|---|---|
| Adams..... | 4,667 | 5,774 | 762 | 6,637 | 4,230 |
| Allen...... | 40,411 | 59,211 | 9,121 | 50,706 | 49,284 |
| Barthol'mew | 8,268 | 13,628 | 2,438 | 12,940 | 11,026 |
| Benton..... | 1,854 | 3,326 | 400 | 2,940 | 2,886 |
| Blackford... | 2,898 | 3,052 | 534 | 4,210 | 2,552 |
| Boone...... | 4,118 | 7,905 | 1,346 | 6,716 | 7,419 |
| Brown...... | 1,327 | 1,881 | 587 | 2,135 | 1,390 |
| Carroll..... | 2,816 | 4,796 | 918 | 4,789 | 3,896 |
| Cass...... | 7,142 | 9,441 | 1,601 | 11,148 | 7,735 |
| Clark...... | 11,493 | 10,305 | 4,982 | 17,330 | 7,701 |
| Clay....... | 3,956 | 5,743 | 1,569 | 6,528 | 5,412 |
| Clinton..... | 5,714 | 7,929 | 1,033 | 8,353 | 7,157 |
| Crawford... | 1,536 | 2,132 | 589 | 2,514 | 1,828 |
| Daviess.... | 4,071 | 7,036 | 1,274 | 6,528 | 6,319 |
| Dearborn... | 4,842 | 6,208 | 1,704 | 7,699 | 5,473 |
| Decatur.... | 3,602 | 5,474 | 731 | 5,564 | 4,702 |
| DeKalb..... | 4,790 | 7,650 | 931 | 7,559 | 6,210 |
| Delaware... | 19,532 | 23,554 | 6,349 | 28,469 | 20,022 |
| Dubois..... | 6,725 | 5,865 | 905 | 10,114 | 3,800 |
| Elkhart.... | 14,222 | 24,484 | 3,440 | 21,679 | 19,870 |
| Fayette.... | 4,575 | 5,286 | 1,413 | 6,713 | 4,637 |
| Floyd...... | 10,671 | 9,714 | 3,266 | 15,656 | 7,834 |
| Fountain... | 3,237 | 5,110 | 1,280 | 5,574 | 4,666 |
| Franklin... | 2,386 | 3,468 | 775 | 4,021 | 2,956 |
| Fulton..... | 2,561 | 5,145 | 757 | 4,374 | 4,410 |
| Gibson..... | 6,777 | 7,645 | 1,497 | 10,507 | 5,865 |
| Grant...... | 10,938 | 16,170 | 3,602 | 17,574 | 14,688 |
| Greene..... | 5,493 | 6,525 | 1,419 | 8,574 | 5,919 |
| Hamilton... | 4,586 | 14,250 | 2,202 | 7,553 | 12,060 |
| Hancock.... | 3,902 | 7,516 | 1,896 | 6,573 | 6,370 |

## Indiana (cont'd)

| County | 1968 Humphrey (D) | Nixon (R) | Wallace (I) | 1964 Johnson (D) | Goldwater (R) |
|---|---|---|---|---|---|
| Harrison... | 3,725 | 4,410 | 1,557 | 5,949 | 3,671 |
| Hendricks.. | 6,155 | 12,597 | 3,231 | 8,857 | 11,497 |
| Henry...... | 8,045 | 11,626 | 2,366 | 12,374 | 10,184 |
| Howard..... | 11,026 | 15,905 | 4,507 | 17,809 | 12,897 |
| Huntington.. | 6,238 | 9,002 | 1,250 | 9,308 | 7,838 |
| Jackson.... | 5,140 | 7,710 | 1,891 | 8,572 | 6,285 |
| Jasper..... | 2,201 | 4,996 | 1,003 | 3,995 | 4,497 |
| Jay........ | 4,290 | 5,460 | 918 | 6,781 | 4,439 |
| Jefferson... | 4,635 | 5,731 | 1,196 | 6,694 | 4,808 |
| Jennings.... | 2,996 | 4,416 | 1,214 | 4,307 | 3,469 |
| Johnson.... | 5,946 | 12,089 | 3,021 | 10,099 | 10,472 |
| Knox...... | 7,297 | 8,369 | 2,053 | 12,678 | 7,612 |
| Kosciusko... | 5,342 | 12,633 | 1,700 | 8,759 | 10,488 |
| La Grange.. | 1,691 | 3,328 | 380 | 2,818 | 2,785 |
| Lake...... | 99,897 | 77,911 | 35,099 | 134,978 | 73,722 |
| LaPorte.... | 15,780 | 20,295 | 4,587 | 22,220 | 16,270 |
| Lawrence... | 5,349 | 8,830 | 1,995 | 8,677 | 8,186 |
| Madison.... | 23,886 | 28,726 | 6,613 | 33,325 | 24,171 |
| Marion..... | 115,715 | 162,503 | 32,043 | 152,418 | 143,015 |
| Marshall.... | 5,385 | 9,290 | 1,685 | 8,397 | 7,895 |
| Martin..... | 2,315 | 2,512 | 604 | 3,137 | 2,000 |
| Miami..... | 5,019 | 7,295 | 1,294 | 7,667 | 6,270 |
| Monroe..... | 10,789 | 13,752 | 2,361 | 11,918 | 10,309 |
| Montgom'y.. | 4,752 | 9,085 | 1,309 | 8,042 | 7,823 |
| Morgan..... | 4,042 | 8,944 | 3,122 | 7,011 | 8,347 |
| Newton..... | 1,453 | 3,145 | 483 | 2,547 | 2,780 |
| Noble...... | 5,075 | 6,699 | 1,253 | 7,621 | 5,682 |
| Ohio....... | 991 | 1,053 | 243 | 1,397 | 905 |
| Orange..... | 2,918 | 4,666 | 915 | 4,490 | 4,187 |
| Owen...... | 1,932 | 2,898 | 776 | 3,339 | 2,788 |
| Parke...... | 2,472 | 3,738 | 907 | 4,034 | 3,570 |
| Perry...... | 4,343 | 4,211 | 547 | 6,226 | 3,090 |
| Pike....... | 2,953 | 3,087 | 745 | 4,519 | 2,703 |
| Porter..... | 8,914 | 17,328 | 6,126 | 12,975 | 14,480 |
| Posey...... | 3,889 | 5,045 | 1,204 | 6,164 | 3,573 |
| Pulaski..... | 2,071 | 3,361 | 681 | 3,408 | 3,202 |
| Putnam..... | 3,692 | 5,873 | 1,826 | 6,275 | 5,331 |
| Randolph... | 3,962 | 7,238 | 1,431 | 6,804 | 6,551 |
| Ripley..... | 3,787 | 5,389 | 1,215 | 5,933 | 4,587 |
| Rush....... | 2,636 | 5,004 | 761 | 4,450 | 4,507 |
| St. Joseph.. | 47,414 | 47,114 | 11,948 | 65,844 | 39,872 |
| Scott...... | 2,796 | 2,671 | 784 | 4,205 | 1,992 |
| Shelby..... | 5,417 | 8,574 | 2,205 | 9,078 | 7,310 |
| Spencer.... | 3,767 | 4,603 | 612 | 4,834 | 3,980 |
| Starke..... | 3,208 | 4,011 | 1,097 | 4,838 | 3,466 |
| Steuben.... | 2,268 | 4,762 | 577 | 3,999 | 4,075 |
| Sullivan.... | 4,453 | 4,266 | 1,135 | 7,351 | 3,867 |
| Switzerland.. | 1,466 | 1,515 | 452 | 2,231 | 1,390 |
| Tippecanoe.. | 14,528 | 24,352 | 2,000 | 20,257 | 9,036 |
| Tipton..... | 2,646 | 4,270 | 861 | 4,410 | 3,663 |
| Union...... | 920 | 1,691 | 404 | 1,463 | 1,531 |
| Vanderb'gh. | 31,326 | 38,231 | 7,737 | 45,796 | 27,231 |
| Vermillion.. | 3,845 | 3,607 | 1,175 | 5,957 | 3,397 |
| Vigo...... | 20,328 | 20,814 | 5,386 | 27,606 | 19,001 |
| Wabash.... | 4,598 | 8,611 | 836 | 7,485 | 6,905 |
| Warren..... | 1,375 | 2,475 | 483 | 2,261 | 2,154 |
| Warrick.... | 4,784 | 5,742 | 1,503 | 7,222 | 4,376 |
| Washington.. | 2,936 | 3,891 | 1,143 | 4,943 | 3,598 |
| Wayne..... | 10,686 | 17,335 | 4,240 | 15,269 | 15,342 |
| Wells...... | 3,827 | 5,361 | 882 | 5,945 | 4,018 |
| White...... | 3,395 | 5,932 | 995 | 5,407 | 5,015 |
| Whitley.... | 3,848 | 5,684 | 1,120 | 5,798 | 4,896 |
| **Totals...** | **806,259** | **1,057,-** 784 | **243,030** | **1,170,-** 848 | **911,118** |

### INDIANA VOTE SINCE 1920

1920 (Pres.), Cox, Dem., 511,364; Harding, Rep., 696,370; Watkins, Proh., 13,462; Debs, Soc., 24,703; Christensen, Farm-Lab., 16,499.

1924 (Pres.), Coolidge, Rep., 703,042; Davis, Dem., 492,245; LaFollette, Prog., 71,700; Faris, Proh., 4,416; Foster, Workers, 987.

1928 (Pres.), Hoover, Rep., 848,290; Smith, Dem., 562,691; Varney, Proh., 5,496; Thomas, Soc., 3,871; Reynolds, Soc. Lab., 645.

1932 (Pres.), Roosevelt, Dem., 862,054; Hoover, Rep., 677,184; Thomas, Soc., 21,388; Upshaw, Proh., 10,399; Foster, Com., 2,187; Reynolds, Soc. Lab., 2,070.

1936 (Pres.), Roosevelt, Dem., 943,974; Landon, Rep., 691,570; Lemke, Union, 19,407; Thomas, Soc., 3,856; Browder, Com., 1,090.

1940 (Pres.), Roosevelt, Dem., 874,063; Willkie, Rep., 899,466; Babson, Proh., 6,437; Thomas, Soc., 2,075; Aiken, Soc. Lab., 706.

1944 (Pres.), Roosevelt, Dem., 781,403; Dewey, Rep., 875,891; Watson, Proh., 12,574; Thomas, Soc., 2,223.

1948 (Pres.), Truman, Dem., 807,833; Dewey, Rep., 821,079; Watson, Proh., 14,711; Wallace, Prog., 9,649; Thomas, Soc., 2,179; Teichert, Soc. Lab., 763.

1952 (Pres.), Eisenhower, Rep., 1,136,259; Stevenson, Dem., 801,530; Hamblen, Proh., 15,335; Hallinan, Prog., 1,222; Hass, Soc. Lab., 979.

1956 (Pres.), Eisenhower, Rep., 1,182,811; Stevenson, Dem., 783,908; Holtwick, Proh., 6,554; Hass, Soc. Lab., 1,334.

1960 (Pres.), Kennedy, Dem., 952,358; Nixon, Rep.,

**Indiana (cont'd)**

1,175,120; Decker, Proh., 6,746; Hass, Soc. Lab., 1,136.
1964 (Pres.), Johnson, Dem., 1,170,848; Goldwater, Rep., 911,118; Munn, Proh., 8,266; Hass, Soc. Lab. 1,374.
1968 (Pres.), Nixon, Rep., 1,057,784; Humphrey, Dem., 806,259; Wallace, 3rd party, 243,030; scattered, 6,124.

# Iowa

| County | 1968 | | | 1964 | |
|---|---|---|---|---|---|
| | Humphrey (D) | Nixon (R) | Wallace (I) | Johnson (D) | Goldwater (R) |
| Adair..... | 1,558 | 2,785 | 234 | 2,851 | 1,953 |
| Adams..... | 1,096 | 1,868 | 260 | 1,941 | 1,321 |
| Allamakee.. | 2,250 | 4,449 | 407 | 3,504 | 3,691 |
| Appanoose.. | 3,005 | 3,497 | 540 | 4,960 | 2,872 |
| Audubon... | 1,720 | 2,592 | 198 | 3,011 | 1,871 |
| Benton..... | 3,944 | 5,016 | 596 | 6,614 | 3,453 |
| Black Hawk. | 20,997 | 25,591 | 2,611 | 30,716 | 19,774 |
| Boone..... | 5,217 | 5,258 | 517 | 7,699 | 3,543 |
| Bremer..... | 2,481 | 5,604 | 423 | 5,045 | 3,880 |
| Buchanan... | 3,670 | 4,541 | 457 | 5,213 | 1,876 |
| Buena Vista. | 3,051 | 5,177 | 384 | 5,245 | 3,747 |
| Butler..... | 1,673 | 4,701 | 252 | 3,370 | 3,462 |
| Calhoun.... | 2,261 | 3,715 | 336 | 4,407 | 2,422 |
| Carroll..... | 4,809 | 3,927 | 412 | 7,807 | 2,387 |
| Cass...... | 2,136 | 5,223 | 370 | 4,006 | 4,182 |
| Cedar..... | 2,551 | 4,494 | 410 | 4,617 | 3,106 |
| Cerro Gordo | 8,553 | 10,662 | 1,019 | 13,156 | 7,884 |
| Cherokee... | 2,705 | 4,436 | 340 | 4,336 | 3,180 |
| Chickasaw.. | 2,971 | 3,067 | 286 | 4,454 | 2,632 |
| Clarke..... | 1,655 | 2,059 | 286 | 2,659 | 1,546 |
| Clay...... | 2,840 | 4,235 | 369 | 4,631 | 2,999 |
| Clayton.... | 3,168 | 5,133 | 541 | 5,624 | 3,923 |
| Clinton.... | 9,489 | 11,902 | 1,233 | 14,267 | 8,219 |
| Crawford... | 2,832 | 4,286 | 539 | 5,024 | 2,999 |
| Dallas..... | 5,062 | 5,549 | 640 | 7,447 | 3,763 |
| Davis..... | 1,904 | 2,016 | 350 | 2,966 | 1,424 |
| Decatur.... | 2,063 | 2,246 | 249 | 3,331 | 1,542 |
| Delaware... | 2,760 | 4,650 | 412 | 4,623 | 3,427 |
| Des Moines. | 10,158 | 8,458 | 1,281 | 13,894 | 5,830 |
| Dickinson.. | 2,286 | 3,472 | 302 | 3,490 | 2,443 |
| Dubuque... | 18,664 | 14,197 | 1,701 | 23,695 | 10,104 |
| Emmet..... | 2,163 | 3,448 | 224 | 3,487 | 2,611 |
| Fayette.... | 4,030 | 6,929 | 634 | 6,900 | 5,567 |
| Floyd..... | 2,971 | 4,792 | 390 | 5,317 | 3,721 |
| Franklin... | 1,777 | 3,605 | 239 | 3,582 | 2,452 |
| Fremont.... | 1,584 | 2,385 | 398 | 2,703 | 2,044 |
| Greene..... | 2,208 | 3,208 | 269 | 3,825 | 2,141 |
| Grundy.... | 1,675 | 4,664 | 293 | 3,582 | 3,215 |
| Guthrie.... | 2,063 | 3,349 | 280 | 3,962 | 2,169 |
| Hamilton... | 3,058 | 4,607 | 301 | 5,195 | 3,127 |
| Hancock... | 2,131 | 3,544 | 245 | 3,857 | 2,269 |
| Hardin..... | 3,229 | 5,335 | 407 | 5,459 | 3,828 |
| Harrison... | 2,410 | 3,867 | 525 | 4,575 | 3,203 |
| Henry..... | 2,532 | 4,613 | 503 | 4,223 | 3,247 |
| Howard.... | 2,427 | 3,141 | 247 | 3,841 | 2,360 |
| Humboldt.. | 1,940 | 3,239 | 217 | 3,376 | 2,250 |
| Ida....... | 1,463 | 2,753 | 208 | 2,905 | 1,977 |
| Iowa...... | 2,586 | 4,115 | 351 | 4,261 | 2,828 |
| Jackson.... | 3,412 | 4,533 | 482 | 5,130 | 3,066 |
| Jasper..... | 6,556 | 7,903 | 732 | 10,216 | 5,321 |
| Jefferson... | 2,411 | 4,130 | 377 | 4,135 | 2,755 |
| Johnson.... | 13,541 | 11,484 | 736 | 14,717 | 6,860 |
| Jones...... | 3,414 | 4,511 | 475 | 5,511 | 3,154 |
| Keokuk.... | 2,807 | 3,588 | 328 | 4,790 | 2,597 |
| Kossuth.... | 4,392 | 5,350 | 283 | 6,893 | 3,776 |
| Lee....... | 7,967 | 8,822 | 1,232 | 12,244 | 6,321 |
| Linn...... | 29,570 | 30,865 | 3,182 | 40,106 | 21,845 |
| Louisa.... | 1,632 | 2,529 | 323 | 2,624 | 1,845 |
| Lucas..... | 1,942 | 2,543 | 290 | 3,310 | 1,935 |
| Lyon...... | 1,403 | 4,198 | 151 | 2,747 | 3,185 |
| Madison... | 2,187 | 3,151 | 328 | 3,518 | 2,250 |
| Mahaska... | 3,721 | 5,669 | 592 | 6,396 | 3,787 |
| Marion.... | 4,618 | 6,491 | 583 | 7,911 | 3,903 |
| Marshall... | 6,362 | 9,402 | 819 | 9,815 | 6,323 |
| Mills..... | 1,215 | 2,913 | 531 | 2,463 | 2,424 |
| Mitchell... | 2,103 | 3,533 | 179 | 3,868 | 2,489 |
| Monona.... | 2,184 | 2,980 | 405 | 3,971 | 2,208 |
| Monroe.... | 2,225 | 2,143 | 298 | 3,186 | 1,588 |
| Montgomery | 1,892 | 4,155 | 425 | 3,489 | 3,101 |
| Muscatine.. | 4,726 | 7,361 | 643 | 8,020 | 5,547 |
| O'Brien.... | 2,146 | 5,594 | 322 | 4,295 | 4,336 |
| Osceola.... | 1,421 | 2,531 | 160 | 2,498 | 1,798 |
| Page...... | 2,127 | 5,307 | 634 | 4,402 | 4,775 |
| Palo Alto... | 2,874 | 3,114 | 234 | 4,441 | 2,206 |
| Plymouth... | 3,239 | 6,236 | 557 | 5,691 | 4,920 |
| Pocahontas. | 2,363 | 2,939 | 254 | 3,988 | 2,079 |
| Polk...... | 52,604 | 52,241 | 9,523 | 74,194 | 37,280 |
| Pot'w'tamie. | 9,485 | 16,038 | 2,838 | 17,569 | 14,208 |
| Poweshiek.. | 3,250 | 4,470 | 362 | 5,213 | 3,109 |
| Ringgold... | 1,247 | 1,986 | 256 | 2,260 | 1,571 |
| Sac....... | 2,207 | 4,182 | 280 | 4,358 | 2,937 |
| Scott..... | 24,646 | 25,777 | 4,143 | 31,526 | 19,488 |
| Shelby.... | 2,395 | 3,386 | 319 | 4,148 | 2,928 |
| Sioux..... | 2,181 | 10,010 | 382 | 4,145 | 8,078 |
| Story..... | 9,456 | 13,327 | 728 | 12,329 | 8,188 |
| Tama...... | 3,769 | 4,956 | 472 | 6,057 | 3,543 |
| Taylor..... | 1,501 | 2,765 | 368 | 2,780 | 2,162 |
| Union..... | 2,137 | 3,365 | 324 | 3,751 | 2,502 |

**Iowa (cont'd)**

| County | 1968 | | | 1964 | |
|---|---|---|---|---|---|
| | Humphrey (D) | Nixon (R) | Wallace (I) | Johnson (D) | Goldwater (R) |
| Van Buren.. | 1,356 | 2,334 | 239 | 2,555 | 1,700 |
| Wapello.... | 9,375 | 7,825 | 1,355 | 13,971 | 5,524 |
| Warren..... | 4,613 | 5,619 | 919 | 6,639 | 3,679 |
| Washington. | 2,679 | 4,899 | 349 | 4,587 | 3,315 |
| Wayne..... | 1,723 | 2,553 | 283 | 3,062 | 1,994 |
| Webster.... | 8,570 | 9,358 | 966 | 13,005 | 6,576 |
| Winnebago.. | 2,168 | 3,543 | 202 | 3,677 | 2,331 |
| Winneshiek. | 3,364 | 5,605 | 344 | 5,811 | 3,941 |
| Woodbury.. | 18,337 | 21,163 | 2,168 | 26,841 | 17,347 |
| Worth..... | 1,815 | 2,383 | 214 | 2,936 | 1,777 |
| Wright..... | 2,959 | 4,291 | 239 | 4,998 | 2,831 |
| Totals... | 477,445 | 616,776 | 66,258 | 733,030 | 449,148 |

**IOWA VOTE SINCE 1920**

1920 (Pres.), Cox, Dem., 227,921; Harding, Rep., 634,674; Watkins, Proh., 4,197; Debs, Soc., 16,981; Christensen, Farm-Lab., 10,321.
1924 (Pres.), Coolidge, Rep., 537,635; LaFollette, Prog., 272,243; Davis, Dem., 162,600; Foster, Workers, 4,037.
1928 (Pres.), Hoover, Rep., 623,818; Smith, Dem., 378,936; Thomas, Soc., 2,960; Webb, Farm-Lab., 3,088; Foster, Com., 328; Reynolds, Soc. Lab., 230.
1932 (Pres.), Roosevelt, Dem., 598,019; Hoover, Rep., 414,433; Thomas, Soc., 20,467; Upshaw, Proh., 2,111; Coxey, Farm-Lab., 1,094; Foster, Com., 559.
1936 (Pres.), Roosevelt, Dem., 621,756; Landon, Rep., 487,977; Lemke, Union, 29,687; Thomas, Soc., 1,373; Colvin, Proh., 1,182; Browder, Com., 506; Aiken, Soc. Lab., 252.
1940 (Pres.), Roosevelt, Dem., 578,800; Willkie, Rep., 632,370; Babson, Proh., 2,284; Browder, Com., 1,524; Aiken, Soc. Lab., 452.
1944 (Pres.), Roosevelt, Dem., 499,876; Dewey, Rep., 547,267; Watson, Proh., 3,752; Thomas, Soc., 1,511; Teichert, Soc. Lab., 193.
1948 (Pres.), Truman, Dem., 522,380; Dewey, Rep., 494,018; Wallace, Prog., 12,125; Teichert, Soc. Lab., 4,274; Watson, Proh., 3,382; Thomas, Soc., 1,829; Dobbs, Soc. Workers, 256.
1952 (Pres.), Eisenhower, Rep., 808,906; Stevenson, Dem., 451,513; Hallinan, Prog., 5,085; Hamblen, Proh., 2,882; Hoopes, Soc., 219; Hass, Soc. Lab., 139; Scattering, 29.
1956 (Pres.), Eisenhower, Rep., 729,187; Stevenson, Dem., 501,858; Andrews (A.C.P. of Iowa), 3,202; Hoopes, Soc., 192; Hass, Soc. Lab., 125.
1960 (Pres.), Kennedy, Dem., 550,565; Nixon, Rep., 722,381; Hass, Soc. Lab., 230; Write-in, 634.
1964 (Pres.), Johnson, Dem., 733,030; Goldwater, Rep., 449,148; Hass, Soc. Lab., 182; DeBerry, Soc. Worker, 159; Munn, Proh., 1,902; Scattering, 118.
1968 (Pres.), Nixon, Rep., 616,776; Humphrey, Dem., 477,445; Wallace, 3rd party, 66,258; scattering, 806.

# Kansas

| County | 1968 | | | 1964 | |
|---|---|---|---|---|---|
| | Humphrey (D) | Nixon (R) | Wallace (I) | Johnson (D) | Goldwater (R) |
| Allen...... | 1,997 | 3,520 | 497 | 3,369 | 2,841 |
| Anderson... | 1,242 | 2,168 | 397 | 2,058 | 1,692 |
| Atchison... | 3,318 | 3,643 | 888 | 5,037 | 3,147 |
| Barber..... | 1,027 | 2,023 | 282 | 1,845 | 1,758 |
| Barton..... | 4,464 | 6,700 | 1,017 | 7,340 | 4,826 |
| Bourbon... | 2,241 | 3,985 | 743 | 3,980 | 3,290 |
| Brown..... | 1,199 | 3,748 | 463 | 2,386 | 3,213 |
| Butler..... | 6,052 | 7,893 | 1,655 | 9,061 | 6,364 |
| Chase..... | 462 | 1,038 | 154 | 886 | 902 |
| Chautauqua. | 478 | 1,537 | 329 | 1,163 | 1,463 |
| Cherokee... | 3,930 | 4,211 | 1,054 | 5,720 | 3,730 |
| Cheyenne.. | 412 | 1,418 | 172 | 886 | 1,147 |
| Clark..... | 446 | 920 | 210 | 881 | 777 |
| Clay...... | 936 | 3,385 | 454 | 1,806 | 3,030 |
| Cloud..... | 2,132 | 3,242 | 412 | 3,314 | 2,680 |
| Coffey..... | 933 | 2,223 | 367 | 1,594 | 1,998 |
| Comanche.. | 451 | 906 | 85 | 818 | 694 |
| Cowley.... | 5,019 | 8,071 | 1,751 | 7,593 | 7,092 |
| Crawford... | 7,132 | 7,294 | 1,774 | 10,282 | 6,286 |
| Decatur.... | 652 | 1,654 | 206 | 1,314 | 1,382 |
| Dickinson.. | 2,399 | 5,511 | 675 | 4,070 | 4,704 |
| Doniphan... | 658 | 2,402 | 425 | 1,866 | 1,952 |
| Douglas.... | 2,173 | 3,372 | 697 | 9,416 | 7,825 |
| Edwards.... | 832 | 1,242 | 182 | 1,427 | 932 |
| Elk....... | 503 | 1,537 | | 994 | 1,267 |
| Ellis..... | 3,829 | 3,924 | 555 | 5,553 | 2,440 |
| Ellsworth... | 1,060 | 1,776 | 246 | 2,118 | 1,406 |
| Finney.... | 2,520 | 3,295 | 496 | 3,639 | 2,201 |
| Ford...... | 3,191 | 4,645 | 935 | 5,221 | 3,481 |
| Franklin... | 2,524 | 4,875 | 825 | 4,410 | 3,725 |
| Geary..... | 2,228 | 2,954 | 625 | 3,419 | 2,259 |
| Gove...... | 538 | 1,018 | 164 | 1,022 | 774 |

## Kansas (cont'd)

| County | 1968 Humphrey (D) | Nixon (R) | Wallace (I) | 1964 Johnson (D) | Goldwater (R) |
|---|---|---|---|---|---|
| Graham.... | 597 | 1,308 | 243 | 1,193 | 1,194 |
| Grant..... | 618 | 1,121 | 217 | 1,023 | 723 |
| Gray...... | 617 | 852 | 148 | 1,136 | 648 |
| Greeley.... | 227 | 465 | 82 | 469 | 387 |
| Greenwood.. | 1,122 | 2,937 | 385 | 2,048 | 2,717 |
| Hamilton.. | 410 | 751 | 170 | 726 | 685 |
| Harper.... | 1,015 | 2,351 | 288 | 1,813 | 1,969 |
| Harvey.... | 3,349 | 6,682 | 789 | 5,306 | 4,979 |
| Haskell.... | 476 | 762 | 285 | 820 | 570 |
| Hodgeman.. | 387 | 756 | 130 | 821 | 607 |
| Jackson.... | 1,225 | 2,678 | 501 | 1,971 | 2,334 |
| Jefferson.. | 1,355 | 2,781 | 929 | 2,066 | 2,380 |
| Jewell.... | 703 | 1,703 | 215 | 1,601 | 1,895 |
| Johnson.... | 24,656 | 51,078 | 6,221 | 31,213 | 37,672 |
| Kearny.... | 423 | 721 | 95 | 737 | 563 |
| Kingman.... | 1,201 | 2,318 | 319 | 2,226 | 1,917 |
| Kiowa..... | 491 | 1,484 | 123 | 970 | 1,135 |
| Labette.... | 3,973 | 5,478 | 1,286 | 6,208 | 4,761 |
| Lane...... | 305 | 781 | 112 | 773 | 586 |
| Leavenw'th. | 5,593 | 7,109 | 2,010 | 7,479 | 5,544 |
| Lincoln.... | 583 | 1,723 | 217 | 1,316 | 1,373 |
| Linn...... | 893 | 2,250 | 419 | 1,725 | 1,939 |
| Logan..... | 411 | 1,121 | 221 | 957 | 967 |
| Lyon...... | 4,020 | 6,553 | 847 | 6,197 | 5,184 |
| Marion.... | 1,494 | 4,287 | 303 | 2,792 | 3,481 |
| Marshall.... | 1,949 | 3,835 | 731 | 3,334 | 3,432 |
| McPherson.. | 2,881 | 6,430 | 534 | 5,173 | 4,483 |
| Meade..... | 569 | 1,481 | 191 | 1,179 | 1,290 |
| Miami..... | 2,739 | 3,614 | 1,013 | 4,620 | 2,907 |
| Mitchell.... | 1,199 | 2,486 | 259 | 1,898 | 1,951 |
| Mont'gm'y.. | 5,206 | 9,695 | 2,455 | 8,553 | 8,437 |
| Morris.... | 976 | 1,938 | 313 | 1,605 | 1,683 |
| Morton.... | 369 | 589 | 200 | 938 | 609 |
| Nemaha.... | 1,925 | 3,008 | 628 | 3,260 | 2,391 |
| Neosho.... | 2,724 | 3,950 | 784 | 4,795 | 3,458 |
| Ness...... | 769 | 1,352 | 192 | 1,562 | 1,034 |
| Norton.... | 841 | 2,543 | 188 | 1,449 | 2,245 |
| Osage..... | 1,864 | 3,157 | 792 | 2,737 | 2,681 |
| Osborne.... | 793 | 2,073 | 301 | 1,659 | 1,700 |
| Ottawa.... | 777 | 1,740 | 253 | 1,535 | 1,491 |
| Pawnee.... | 1,418 | 2,037 | 300 | 2,577 | 1,468 |
| Phillips.... | 844 | 2,567 | 340 | 1,804 | 2,164 |
| Pott'atomie. | 1,363 | 3,267 | 490 | 2,432 | 2,606 |
| Pratt...... | 1,490 | 2,670 | 435 | 2,594 | 2,493 |
| Rawlins.... | 553 | 1,438 | 286 | 959 | 1,292 |
| Reno...... | 9,877 | 11,808 | 1,710 | 14,936 | 8,829 |
| Republic.... | 1,187 | 2,846 | 240 | 2,222 | 2,414 |
| Rice...... | 2,198 | 3,297 | 386 | 3,665 | 2,390 |
| Riley...... | 4,258 | 8,296 | 772 | 5,597 | 6,396 |
| Rooks..... | 1,012 | 2,252 | 307 | 1,923 | 1,985 |
| Rush...... | 884 | 1,471 | 217 | 1,778 | 1,098 |
| Russell.... | 1,361 | 3,177 | 290 | 2,505 | 2,435 |
| Saline..... | 6,285 | 9,327 | 1,259 | 9,725 | 6,533 |
| Scott..... | 500 | 1,385 | 193 | 1,018 | 1,143 |
| Sedgwick.... | 42,649 | 58,153 | 11,691 | 66,372 | 52,592 |
| Seward.... | 1,291 | 3,065 | 550 | 2,520 | 2,910 |
| Shawnee.... | 20,877 | 29,649 | 6,577 | 30,626 | 25,736 |
| Sheridan.... | 563 | 1,002 | 144 | 1,028 | 808 |
| Sherman.... | 954 | 1,803 | 388 | 1,522 | 1,463 |
| Smith..... | 943 | 2,563 | 283 | 1,809 | 2,026 |
| Stafford.... | 1,205 | 1,851 | 253 | 2,087 | 1,516 |
| Stanton.... | 287 | 541 | 61 | 500 | 459 |
| Stevens.... | 528 | 1,157 | 296 | 1,006 | 992 |
| Sumner.... | 3,582 | 5,630 | 1,116 | 5,574 | 4,760 |
| Thomas.... | 1,074 | 1,971 | 241 | 1,793 | 1,528 |
| Trego..... | 623 | 1,211 | 225 | 1,177 | 974 |
| Wabaunsee. | 695 | 1,979 | 402 | 1,287 | 1,839 |
| Wallace.... | 431 | 608 | 144 | 496 | 516 |
| Washington. | 1,131 | 3,177 | 332 | 2,015 | 2,654 |
| Wichita.... | 364 | 757 | 130 | 662 | 529 |
| Wilson..... | 1,276 | 3,340 | 660 | 2,592 | 2,919 |
| Woodson.... | 639 | 1,449 | 207 | 1,128 | 1,279 |
| Wyandotte.. | 33,309 | 22,180 | 11,301 | 43,442 | 20,553 |
| **Totals...** | **294,443** | **461,772** | **86,489** | **464,028** | **386,579** |

### KANSAS VOTE SINCE 1920

1920 (Pres.), Cox, Dem., 185,464; Harding, Rep., 369,268; Debs, Soc., 15,511.
1924 (Pres.), Coolidge, Rep., 407,671; Davis, Dem., 156,319; LaFollette, Prog., 98,461.
1928 (Pres.), Hoover, Rep., 513,672; Smith, Dem., 193,003; Thomas, Soc., 6,206; Foster, Com., 320.
1932 (Pres.), Roosevelt, Dem., 424,204; Hoover, Rep., 349,498; Thomas, Soc., 18,276.
1936 (Pres.), Roosevelt, Dem., 464,520; Landon Rep., 397,727; Thomas, Soc., 2,766; Lemke, Union, 494.
1940 (Pres.), Roosevelt, Dem., 364,725; Willkie, Rep., 489,169; Babson, Proh., 4,056; Thomas, Soc., 2,347.
1944 (Pres.), Roosevelt, Dem., 287,458; Dewey, Rep., 442,096; Watson, Proh., 2,609; Thomas, Soc., 1,613.
1948 (Pres.), Truman, Dem., 351,902; Dewey, Rep., 423,039; Watson, Proh., 6,468; Wallace, Prog., 4,603; Thomas, Soc., 2,807.
1952 (Pres.), Eisenhower, Rep., 616,302; Stevenson,

## Kansas (cont'd)

Dem., 273,296; Hamblen, Proh., 6,038; Hoopes, Soc., 530.
1956 (Pres.), Eisenhower, Rep., 566,878; Stevenson, Dem., 296,317; Holtwick, Proh., 3,048.
1960 (Pres.), Kennedy, Dem., 363,213; Nixon, Rep., 561,474; Decker, Proh., 4,138.
1964 (Pres.), Johnson, Dem., 464,028; Goldwater, Rep., 386,579; Munn, Proh., 5,393; Hass, Soc. Labor, 1,901.
1968 (Pres.), Nixon, Rep., 461,772; Humphrey, Dem., 294,443; Wallace, 3rd party, 86,489.

# Kentucky

| County | 1968 Humphrey (D) | Nixon (R) | Wallace (I) | 1964 Johnson (D) | Goldwater (R) |
|---|---|---|---|---|---|
| Adair...... | 1,362 | 3,239 | 856 | 2,854 | 3,052 |
| Allen...... | 927 | 2,952 | 905 | 2,023 | 2,309 |
| Anderson... | 1,334 | 1,594 | 657 | 2,491 | 1,085 |
| Ballard.... | 1,632 | 4,568 | 1,197 | 2,867 | 519 |
| Barren.... | 3,494 | 4,205 | 2,140 | 6,420 | 2,936 |
| Bath...... | 1,394 | 1,277 | 657 | 2,571 | 1,009 |
| Bell...... | 4,138 | 4,909 | 1,200 | 6,979 | 4,185 |
| Boone..... | 2,725 | 4,081 | 2,240 | 5,077 | 3,430 |
| Bourbon... | 2,566 | 1,848 | 1,023 | 4,068 | 1,222 |
| Boyd...... | 7,744 | 8,118 | 2,351 | 11,436 | 6,941 |
| Boyle..... | 2,663 | 2,715 | 1,356 | 4,976 | 1,972 |
| Bracken... | 1,067 | 1,115 | 548 | 1,958 | 686 |
| Breathitt... | 2,933 | 1,332 | 444 | 4,714 | 691 |
| Breckinr'ge. | 1,979 | 2,683 | 1,014 | 3,733 | 2,167 |
| Bullitt.... | 2,135 | 1,965 | 2,180 | 3,900 | 1,417 |
| Butler.... | 691 | 2,637 | 635 | 1,555 | 2,429 |
| Caldwell... | 1,436 | 2,139 | 1,426 | 2,831 | 1,738 |
| Calloway... | 3,811 | 2,619 | 2,094 | 7,290 | 1,576 |
| Campbell.. | 9,639 | 13,422 | 4,680 | 16,012 | 12,209 |
| Carlisle... | 1,145 | 479 | 807 | 1,565 | 282 |
| Carroll.... | 1,765 | 868 | 514 | 2,592 | 491 |
| Carter.... | 2,306 | 3,137 | 890 | 4,136 | 2,821 |
| Casey..... | 879 | 3,698 | 649 | 1,875 | 3,457 |
| Christian... | 4,281 | 3,788 | 4,527 | 8,727 | 3,882 |
| Clark..... | 2,367 | 2,700 | 1,824 | 4,205 | 2,019 |
| Clay...... | 1,147 | 4,608 | 356 | 3,098 | 3,223 |
| Clinton.... | 568 | 2,572 | 280 | 994 | 2,351 |
| Crittenden.. | 838 | 1,941 | 748 | 1,627 | 1,863 |
| Cumberland. | 646 | 2,116 | 355 | 1,348 | 794 |
| Daviess.... | 9,831 | 10,074 | 5,004 | 15,253 | 1,350 |
| Edmonson.. | 679 | 2,280 | 516 | 1,022 | 8,603 |
| Elliott.... | 1,359 | 514 | 271 | 2,026 | 1,323 |
| Estill..... | 1,265 | 2,236 | 675 | 2,105 | 1,996 |
| Fayette.... | 16,529 | 24,138 | 7,728 | 25,317 | 18,739 |
| Fleming.... | 1,372 | 2,174 | 611 | 2,678 | 1,668 |
| Floyd..... | 8,310 | 3,598 | 1,080 | 11,644 | 2,352 |
| Franklin... | 6,296 | 3,966 | 2,630 | 10,130 | 320 |
| Fulton.... | 1,204 | 1,079 | 1,526 | 2,493 | 2,169 |
| Gallatin... | 685 | 413 | 304 | 1,246 | 1,267 |
| Garrard... | 1,189 | 1,386 | 675 | 2,092 | 1,828 |
| Grant..... | 1,085 | 2,205 | 941 | 2,461 | 1,068 |
| Graves.... | 5,052 | 3,851 | 3,901 | 9,958 | 2,389 |
| Grayson... | 1,748 | 3,507 | 668 | 2,920 | 2,974 |
| Green..... | 4,689 | 4,677 | 1,365 | 2,160 | 2,110 |
| Greenup... | 4,594 | 4,533 | 1,314 | 6,680 | 4,045 |
| Hancock... | 882 | 1,049 | 419 | 1,423 | 756 |
| Hardin.... | 4,332 | 5,057 | 3,745 | 7,460 | 3,744 |
| Harlan.... | 6,387 | 4,572 | 2,099 | 9,394 | 4,025 |
| Harrison... | 2,373 | 1,637 | 839 | 4,179 | 1,054 |
| Hart...... | 1,658 | 2,817 | 1,002 | 3,313 | 1,961 |
| Henderson.. | 4,927 | 3,373 | 2,124 | 8,022 | 734 |
| Henry..... | 1,978 | 1,271 | 711 | 3,521 | 2,838 |
| Hickman... | 880 | 623 | 1,154 | 2,149 | 613 |
| Hopkins... | 4,397 | 3,632 | 3,592 | 7,954 | 3,328 |
| Jackson.... | 304 | 3,054 | 277 | 920 | 2,654 |
| Jefferson... | 90,252 | 95,941 | 35,561 | 146,023 | 80,951 |
| Jessamine.. | 1,334 | 2,338 | 1,440 | 2,485 | 1,968 |
| Johnson.... | 2,118 | 4,049 | 331 | 3,053 | 3,075 |
| Kenton.... | 14,656 | 17,263 | 7,612 | 23,103 | 15,630 |
| Knott..... | 3,335 | 1,098 | 430 | 4,739 | 482 |
| Knox...... | 2,244 | 4,382 | 944 | 4,150 | 3,583 |
| Larue..... | 1,241 | 1,861 | 776 | 2,742 | 1,195 |
| Laurel.... | 1,756 | 6,161 | 1,216 | 3,633 | 5,008 |
| Lawrence... | 1,825 | 1,947 | 476 | 2,703 | 1,745 |
| Lee....... | 674 | 1,339 | 285 | 1,376 | 1,162 |
| Leslie..... | 813 | 2,550 | 232 | 1,795 | 1,071 |
| Letcher.... | 3,446 | 3,142 | 874 | 5,420 | 2,632 |
| Lewis..... | 1,086 | 2,760 | 491 | 2,047 | 2,230 |
| Lincoln.... | 1,702 | 2,534 | 1,086 | 3,307 | 1,958 |
| Livingston.. | 1,272 | 1,079 | 953 | 2,147 | 821 |
| Logan..... | 3,339 | 3,402 | 1,881 | 6,234 | 2,232 |
| Lyon...... | 719 | 580 | 618 | 1,412 | 583 |
| Madison... | 3,884 | 5,325 | 2,558 | 6,877 | 4,266 |
| Magoffin... | 1,927 | 1,967 | 229 | 2,498 | 1,327 |
| Marion.... | 2,359 | 1,555 | 818 | 4,265 | 1,075 |
| Marshall... | 3,301 | 2,432 | 2,254 | 5,968 | 1,676 |
| Martin.... | 759 | 1,943 | 136 | 1,694 | 1,567 |
| Mason.... | 2,772 | 2,661 | 1,131 | 4,502 | 2,430 |
| McCracken. | 9,741 | 5,887 | 5,809 | 16,178 | 4,547 |
| McCreary.. | 759 | 2,680 | 479 | 1,428 | 2,233 |
| McLean.... | 1,373 | 1,372 | 1,055 | 2,576 | 1,173 |
| Meade.... | 1,857 | 1,333 | 863 | 3,076 | 1,050 |
| Menifee... | 554 | 509 | 247 | 1,076 | 318 |
| Mercer.... | 1,950 | 2,432 | 1,227 | 3,564 | 1,737 |

| Kentucky (cont'd) | 1968 | | | 1964 | |
|---|---|---|---|---|---|
| County | Humphrey (D) | Nixon (R) | Wallace (I) | Johnson (D) | Goldwater (R) |
| Metcalfe.... | 697 | 4,086 | 550 | 1,967 | 1,272 |
| Monroe.... | 680 | 3,977 | 550 | 1,713 | 3,293 |
| Montgom'y. | 1,408 | 2,115 | 980 | 3,039 | 544 |
| Morgan.... | 2,179 | 1,305 | 373 | 3,293 | 549 |
| Muhlenb'g.. | 3,688 | 3,853 | 2,229 | 6,421 | 3,300 |
| Nelson.... | 3,574 | 2,409 | 1,114 | 5,586 | 1,683 |
| Nicholas.... | 911 | 725 | 413 | 1,742 | 625 |
| Ohio...... | 1,695 | 3,504 | 1,260 | 3,303 | 2,977 |
| Oldham.... | 1,399 | 1,655 | 937 | 2,622 | 1,253 |
| Owen...... | 1,608 | 827 | 697 | 2,980 | 401 |
| Owsley.... | 303 | 1,417 | 157 | 571 | 1,168 |
| Pendleton.. | 1,156 | 1,614 | 760 | 2,495 | 1,313 |
| Perry...... | 4,611 | 3,993 | 983 | 6,728 | 3,213 |
| Pike...... | 11,585 | 8,777 | 1,868 | 14,140 | 7,073 |
| Powell.... | 934 | 1,157 | 625 | 1,622 | 999 |
| Pulaski.... | 2,822 | 8,079 | 1,707 | 5,840 | 7,384 |
| Robertson.. | 406 | 416 | 186 | 734 | 381 |
| Rockcastle.. | 868 | 3,072 | 644 | 1,631 | 2,820 |
| Rowan..... | 1,898 | 2,017 | 541 | 2,824 | 1,554 |
| Russell.... | 961 | 3,035 | 718 | 1,729 | 2,527 |
| Scott...... | 1,868 | 1,753 | 1,142 | 3,289 | 1,334 |
| Shelby.... | 2,579 | 2,287 | 1,185 | 4,933 | 1,385 |
| Simpson.... | 1,045 | 511 | 406 | 3,168 | 969 |
| Spencer.... | 564 | 733 | 448 | 1,422 | 522 |
| Taylor..... | 1,367 | 3,032 | 1,554 | 3,082 | 2,592 |
| Todd...... | 1,082 | 1,433 | 1,932 | 2,738 | 1,359 |
| Trigg...... | 1,330 | 1,100 | 1,180 | 2,790 | 915 |
| Trimble.... | 1,045 | 511 | 406 | 1,881 | 291 |
| Union..... | 2,596 | 1,371 | 1,084 | 3,934 | 1,229 |
| Warren.... | 5,200 | 8,084 | 4,355 | 9,887 | 5,619 |
| Washington. | 1,644 | 1,828 | 658 | 2,790 | 1,567 |
| Wayne..... | 1,467 | 3,055 | 475 | 2,737 | 2,382 |
| Webster.... | 2,114 | 1,446 | 1,337 | 3,741 | 1,211 |
| Whitley.... | 2,134 | 5,639 | 1,650 | 4,782 | 4,775 |
| Wolfe..... | 1,151 | 744 | 277 | 2,018 | 569 |
| Woodford.. | 1,646 | 1,901 | 894 | 2,974 | 1,216 |
| **Totals...** | **395,097** | **458,905** | **190,493** | **669,659** | **372,977** |

### KENTUCKY VOTE SINCE 1920

1920 (Pres.), Cox, Dem., 456,497; Harding, Rep., 452, 480; Watkins, Proh., 3,325; Debs, Soc., 6,409.
1924 (Pres.), Coolidge, Rep., 398,966; Davis, Dem., 374,855; LaFollette, Prog., 38,465; Johns, Soc Lab., 1,499; Nations, Amer., 1,299; Wallace Comm. Land, 248.
1928 (Pres.), Hoover, Rep., 558,064; Smith, Dem., 381,070; Thomas, Soc., 837; Reynolds, Soc. Lab., 340; Foster, Com., 293.
1932 (Pres.), Roosevelt, Dem., 580,574; Hoover, Rep., 394,716; Upshaw, Proh., 2,252; Thomas, Soc., 3,853; Reynolds, Soc. Lab., 1,396; Foster, Com., 272.
1936 (Pres.), Roosevelt, Dem., 541,944; Landon, Rep., 369,702; Lemke, Union, 12,501; Colvin, Proh., 929; Thomas, Soc., 627; Aiken, Soc. Lab., 294; Browder, Com., 204.
1940 (Pres.), Roosevelt, Dem., 557,222; Willkie, Rep., 410,384; Babson, Proh., 1,443; Thomas, Soc., 1,014.
1944 (Pres.), Roosevelt, Dem., 472,589; Dewey, Rep., 392,448; Watson, Proh., 2,023; Thomas, Soc., 535; Teichert, Soc. Lab., 326.
1948 (Pres.), Truman, Dem., 466,756; Dewey, Rep., 341,210; Thurmond, States' Rights, 10,411; Wallace, Prog., 1,567; Thomas, Soc., 1,284; Watson, Proh., 1,245; Teichert, Soc. Lab., 185.
1952 (Pres.), Eisenhower, Rep., 495,029; Stevenson, Dem., 495,729; Hemblen, Proh., 1,161; Haas, Soc. Lab., 893; Hallinan, Proh., 336.
1956 (Pres.), Eisenhower, Rep., 572,192; Stevenson, Dem., 476,453; Byrd, States' Rights, 2,657; Holtwick, Proh., 2,145; Hass, Soc. Lab., 358.
1960 (Pres.), Kennedy, Dem., 521,855; Nixon, Rep., 602,607.
1964 (Pres.), Johnson, Dem., 669,659; Goldwater, Rep., 372,977; John Kasper, Nat'l States Rights, 3,469.
1968 (Pres.), Nixon, Rep., 458,905; Humphrey, Dem., 395,097; Wallace, 3rd party, 190,493.

### Louisiana

| Louisiana (cont'd) | 1968 | | | 1964 | |
|---|---|---|---|---|---|
| County | Humphrey (D) | Nixon (R) | Wallace (I) | Johnson (D) | Goldwater (R) |
| Caldwell.... | 606 | 490 | 2,364 | 609 | 2,534 |
| Cameron... | 467 | 469 | 1,759 | 1,576 | 871 |
| Catahoula.. | 771 | 757 | 2,677 | 560 | 2,387 |
| Claiborne... | 1,503 | 1,116 | 3,318 | 482 | 3,917 |
| Concordia... | 2,012 | 981 | 4,529 | 809 | 4,022 |
| De Soto ... | 3,184 | 960 | 4,097 | 1,254 | 3,954 |
| E. Baton Rouge... | 21,772 | 21,770 | 35,951 | 26,152 | 36,964 |
| East Carroll. | 1,926 | 746 | 1,699 | 263 | 1,486 |
| E. Feliciana. | 1,402 | 464 | 2,225 | 486 | 1,900 |
| Evangeline.. | 2,658 | 1,547 | 7,636 | 6,163 | 3,975 |
| Franklin.... | 691 | 1,052 | 5,394 | 759 | 5,470 |
| Grant...... | 941 | 1,106 | 3,470 | 1,454 | 3,292 |
| Iberia..... | 5,513 | 5,448 | 8,071 | 8,141 | 8,196 |
| Iberville.... | 3,796 | 1,252 | 4,273 | 4,445 | 3,432 |
| Jackson.... | 1,530 | 1,061 | 3,979 | 1,552 | 4,521 |
| Jefferson... | 20,433 | 29,732 | 41,650 | 31,804 | 37,161 |
| Jeff. Davis.. | 2,563 | 2,180 | 4,814 | 4,966 | 3,673 |
| Lafayette... | 7,983 | 10,669 | 11,723 | 14,487 | 12,398 |
| Lafourche.. | 5,422 | 4,742 | 10,157 | 12,045 | 6,164 |
| La Salle.... | 629 | 1,040 | 3,328 | 864 | 4,319 |
| Lincoln.... | 2,070 | 2,645 | 4,125 | 1,714 | 5,766 |
| Livingston.. | 1,400 | 947 | 9,907 | 3,509 | 5,508 |
| Madison.... | 2,357 | 603 | 2,298 | 417 | 2,061 |
| Morehouse.. | 1,793 | 1,763 | 5,377 | 891 | 6,222 |
| Natchitoches | 1,801 | 2,326 | 5,238 | 2,975 | 5,525 |
| Orleans.... | 72,693 | 48,225 | 58,884 | 82,045 | 81,049 |
| Ouachita... | 5,174 | 9,354 | 14,009 | 4,174 | 21,024 |
| Plaquemines | 1,155 | 972 | 6,437 | 775 | 4,904 |
| Pte. Coupee. | 3,141 | 857 | 3,512 | 2,247 | 2,327 |
| Rapides.... | 8,816 | 10,228 | 16,725 | 9,992 | 18,122 |
| Red River... | 749 | 407 | 2,305 | 334 | 2,235 |
| Richland... | 1,017 | 1,031 | 4,415 | 747 | 4,498 |
| Sabine..... | 1,163 | 1,153 | 4,638 | 2,081 | 4,165 |
| St. Bernard. | 2,488 | 3,486 | 13,058 | 6,175 | 8,055 |
| St. Charles.. | 3,070 | 1,675 | 4,383 | 5,085 | 2,715 |
| St. Helena.. | 1,351 | 219 | 1,802 | 706 | 1,319 |
| St. James... | 2,929 | 773 | 2,744 | 4,214 | 1,467 |
| St. John.... | 3,242 | 933 | 3,240 | 3,958 | 1,694 |
| St. Landry.. | 8,835 | 3,389 | 12,354 | 11,807 | 10,920 |
| St. Martin.. | 3,321 | 1,625 | 4,759 | 4,675 | 2,793 |
| St. Mary... | 5,312 | 4,586 | 6,761 | 7,327 | 5,530 |
| St.Tammany | 4,486 | 4,874 | 11,479 | 6,694 | 7,883 |
| Tangipahoa. | 5,006 | 2,930 | 13,090 | 7,169 | 9,732 |
| Tensas.... | 845 | 503 | 1,281 | 192 | 1,655 |
| Terrebonne. | 4,590 | 5,190 | 8,814 | 8,577 | 6,729 |
| Union..... | 1,338 | 1,117 | 4,297 | 1,155 | 4,344 |
| Vermilion... | 3,748 | 3,352 | 7,629 | 9,204 | 4,984 |
| Vernon.... | 1,286 | 1,469 | 5,026 | 3,564 | 3,696 |
| Washington. | 3,016 | 1,688 | 11,070 | 4,825 | 7,438 |
| Webster.... | 2,782 | 2,495 | 8,646 | 1,755 | 8,177 |
| W. Baton Rouge.... | 1,994 | 667 | 2,534 | 1,892 | 1,835 |
| West Carroll | 388 | 583 | 3,579 | 395 | 3,017 |
| W. Feliciana | 12,404 | 2,992 | 10,468 | 223 | 897 |
| Winn...... | 1,230 | 1,070 | 4,015 | 1,193 | 4,366 |
| **Totals...** | **317,814** | **259,688** | **536,779** | **387,068** | **509,225** |

### LOUISIANA VOTE SINCE 1920

1920 (Pres.) Cox, Dem., 87,519; Harding, Rep., 38,538.
1924 (Pres.), Davis, Dem., 93,218; Coolidge, Rep., 24,670; LaFollette, Prog., 4,063.
1928 (Pres.), Smith, Dem., 164,655; Hoover, Rep., 51,160.
1932 (Pres.), Roosevelt, Dem., 249,418; Hoover, Rep., 18,863.
1936 (Pres.), Roosevelt, Dem., 292,894; Landon, Rep., 36,791.
1940 (Pres.), Roosevelt, Dem., 319,751; Willkie, Rep., 52,446.
1944 (Pres.), Roosevelt, Dem., 281,564; Dewey, Rep., 67,750.
1948 (Pres.), Thurmond, States' Rights, 204,290; Truman, Dem., 136,344; Dewey, Rep., 72,657; Wallace, Prog., 3,035.
1952 (Pres.) Eisenhower, Rep., 306,925; Stevenson, Dem., 345,027.
1956 (Pres.), Eisenhower, Rep., 329,047; Stevenson, Dem., 243,977; Andrews, States' Rights, 44,520.
1960 (Pres.), Kennedy, Dem., 407,339; Nixon, Rep., 230,980; States' Rights (unpledged) 169,572.
1964 (Pres.), Johnson, Dem., 387,068; Goldwater, Rep., 509,225.
1968 (Pres.), Nixon, Rep., 259,688; Humphrey, Dem., 317,814; Wallace, 3rd party, 536,779.

### Louisiana

| County | 1968 | | | 1964 | |
|---|---|---|---|---|---|
| | Humphrey (D) | Nixon (R) | Wallace (I) | Johnson (D) | Goldwater (R) |
| Acadia .... | 4,123 | 3,185 | 9,833 | 9,463 | 6,706 |
| Allen....... | 1,986 | 1,011 | 4,393 | 3,787 | 2,704 |
| Ascension.. | 3,199 | 1,334 | 6,001 | 4,829 | 3,197 |
| Assumption. | 2,085 | 1,223 | 2,898 | 3,056 | 2,112 |
| Avoyelles... | 2,973 | 2,459 | 6,760 | 5,102 | 4,874 |
| Beauregard. | 1,646 | 1,437 | 4,039 | 3,049 | 3,349 |
| Bienville... | 1,768 | 851 | 3,466 | 855 | 3,740 |
| Bossier.... | 2,680 | 3,727 | 9,217 | 1,937 | 9,822 |
| Caddo...... | 17,811 | 21,242 | 28,439 | 10,158 | 42,197 |
| Calcasieu.. | 14,751 | 9,590 | 20,274 | 23,285 | 17,046 |

### Maine

| County | 1968 | | | 1964 | |
|---|---|---|---|---|---|
| | Humphrey (D) | Nixon (R) | Wallace (I) | Johnson (D) | Goldwater (R) |
| Androscog'n. | 26,819 | 10,390 | 524 | 30,080 | 7,441 |
| Aroostook... | 15,024 | 13,920 | 273 | 17,552 | 9,994 |

## Maine (cont'd)

| County | 1968 Hum-phrey (D) | Nixon (R) | Wal-lace (I) | 1964 John-son (D) | Gold-water (R) |
|---|---|---|---|---|---|
| Cumberland. | 44,728 | 32,272 | 1,074 | 50,844 | 22,365 |
| Franklin.... | 4,307 | 4,127 | 159 | 5,784 | 2,887 |
| Hancock.... | 4,979 | 8,956 | 324 | 7,415 | 6,304 |
| Kennebec... | 21,769 | 16,120 | 532 | 24,813 | 11,307 |
| Knox...... | 1,272 | 1,831 | 69 | 7,022 | 4,404 |
| Lincoln..... | 3,621 | 5,659 | 231 | 5,099 | 3,984 |
| Oxford..... | 10,870 | 8,095 | 377 | 13,616 | 5,340 |
| Penobscot... | 24,320 | 20,005 | 663 | 28,766 | 14,449 |
| Piscataquis. | 3,519 | 3,245 | 158 | 4,781 | 2,473 |
| Sagadahoc.. | 5,553 | 4,180 | 179 | 7,006 | 2,733 |
| Somerset.... | 8,210 | 6,485 | 316 | 10,694 | 4,541 |
| Waldo...... | 3,513 | 4,784 | 227 | 5,397 | 3,324 |
| Washington. | 5,528 | 5,532 | 215 | 9,312 | 3,816 |
| York...... | 28,818 | 18,959 | 911 | 34,083 | 13,339 |
| **Totals ...** | **212,950** | **164,56** | **6,232** | **262,264** | **118,701** |

### MAINE VOTE SINCE 1920

1920 (Pres.), Cox, Dem., 58,961; Harding, Rep., 136,355; Watkins, Proh., 1; Debs, Soc., 2,214.
1924 (Pres.), Coolidge, Rep., 138,440; Davis, Dem., 41,964; LaFollette, Prog., 11,382; Johns, Soc. Lab., 406.
1928 (Pres.), Hoover, Rep., 179,923; Smith, Dem., 81,179; Thomas, Soc., 1,068.
1932 (Pres.), Roosevelt, Dem., 128,907; Hoover Rep., 166,631; Thomas, Soc., 2,439; Reynolds, Soc. Lab., 255; Foster, Com., 162.
1936 (Pres.), Landon, Rep., 168,823; Roosevelt, Dem., 126,333; Lemke, Union, 7,581; Thomas, Soc., 783; Colvin, Proh., 334; Browder, Com., 257; Aiken, Soc. Lab., 129.
1940 (Pres.), Roosevelt, Dem., 156,478; Willkie, Rep., 165,951; Browder, Com., 411.
1944 (Pres.), Roosevelt, Dem., 140,631; Dewey, Rep., 155,434; Teichert, Soc. Lab., 335.
1948 (Pres.), Truman, Dem., 111,916; Dewey, Rep., 150,234; Wallace, Prog., 1,884; Thomas, Soc., 547; Teichert, Soc. Lab., 206.
1952 (Pres.), Eisenhower, Rep., 232,353; Stevenson, Dem., 118,806; Hallinan, Prog., 332; Hass, Soc. Lab., 156; Hoopes, Soc., 138; Scattered, 1.
1956 (Pres.), Eisenhower, Rep., 249,238; Stevenson, Dem., 102,468.
1960 (Pres.), Kennedy, Dem., 181,159; Nixon, Rep., 240,608.
1964 (Pres.), Johnson, Dem., 262,264; Goldwater, Rep., 118,701.
1968 (Pres.), Nixon, Rep., 164,560; Humphrey, Dem., 212,950; Wallace, 3rd party, 6,232.

# Maryland

| County | 1968 Hum-phrey (D) | Nixon (R) | Wal-lace (I) | 1964 John-son (D) | Gold-water (R) |
|---|---|---|---|---|---|
| Allegany.... | 13,227 | 13,561 | 5,172 | 20,425 | 12,384 |
| A. Arundel.. | 24,907 | 35,582 | 15,523 | 37,981 | 26,725 |
| Balto. Co.... | 80,798 | 108,930 | 29,283 | 117,153 | 77,870 |
| Balto. City.. | 175,989 | 80,538 | 33,022 | 240,716 | 76,089 |
| Calvert..... | 2,032 | 1,946 | 1,471 | 3,335 | 1,765 |
| Caroline.... | 1,654 | 3,053 | 1,386 | 3,710 | 2,696 |
| Carroll..... | 4,658 | 11,888 | 3,085 | 8,451 | 8,332 |
| Cecil....... | 4,442 | 6,282 | 3,182 | 7,854 | 5,330 |
| Charles..... | 4,267 | 4,493 | 3,173 | 6,546 | 3,455 |
| Dorchester.. | 2,714 | 4,183 | 3,270 | 4,564 | 5,327 |
| Frederick... | 8,316 | 15,084 | 4,348 | 14,548 | 9,264 |
| Garrett..... | 1,933 | 4,021 | 818 | 3,515 | 3,624 |
| Harford.... | 9,914 | 15,799 | 4,978 | 13,550 | 9,968 |
| Howard..... | 5,752 | 9,957 | 2,796 | 8,185 | 6,833 |
| Kent....... | 2,243 | 3,145 | 1,146 | 4,113 | 2,008 |
| Montgom'y. | 84,213 | 78,948 | 14,514 | 103,113 | 52,554 |
| Pr. George's. | 71,524 | 73,269 | 32,867 | 81,806 | 46,413 |
| Qu'nAnne's. | 1,969 | 2,888 | 1,298 | 4,052 | 1,955 |
| St. Mary's.. | 3,280 | 3,348 | 2,547 | 5,831 | 2,878 |
| Somerset.... | 2,373 | 3,541 | 1,889 | 4,527 | 3,155 |
| Talbot..... | 2,532 | 4,713 | 1,352 | 4,671 | 3,693 |
| Washington. | 11,266 | 15,257 | 6,737 | 19,858 | 12,756 |
| Wicomico... | 5,190 | 8,352 | 4,272 | 8,695 | 7,448 |
| Worcester... | 2,046 | 3,541 | 1,871 | 3,713 | 2,973 |
| **Totals ...** | **527,245** | **508,329** | **179,998** | **730,912** | **385,495** |

### MARYLAND VOTE SINCE 1920

1920 (Pres.), Cox, Dem., 180,626; Harding, Rep., 236,117; Debs, Soc., 8,876; Christensen, 3rd Party, 1,645; Cox, Lab., 1,178.
1924 (Pres.), Coolidge, Rep., 162,414; Davis, Dem., 148,072; LaFollette, Prog., 47,157; Johns, Soc. Lab., 987.
1928 (Pres.), Hoover, Rep., 301,479; Smith, Dem., 223,626; Thomas, Soc., 1,701; Reynolds, Soc. Lab., 906; Foster, Com., 636.
1932 (Pres.), Roosevelt, Dem., 314,314; Hoover, Rep., 184,184; Thomas, Soc., 10,489; Reynolds,

## Maryland (cont'd)

Soc. Lab., 1,036; Foster, Com., 1,031.
1936 (Pres.), Roosevelt, Dem., 389,612; Landon, Rep., 231,435; Thomas, Soc., 1,629; Aiken, Soc. Lab., 1,305; Browder, Com., 915.
1940 (Pres.), Roosevelt, Dem., 384,546; Willkie, Rep., 269,534; Thomas, Soc., 4,093; Browder, Com., 1,274; Aiken, Lab., 657.
1944 (Pres.), Roosevelt, Dem., 315,490; Dewey, Rep., 292,949.
1948 (Pres.), Truman, Dem., 286,521; Dewey, Rep., 294,814; Wallace, Prog., 9,983; Thomas, Soc., 2,941; Thurmond, States' Rights, 2,476; Wright, Write-in 2,294.
1952 (Pres.), Eisenhower, Rep., 499,424; Stevenson, Dem., 395,337; Hallinan, Prog., 7,313.
1956 (Pres.), Eisenhower, Rep., 559,738; Stevenson, Dem., 372,613.
1960 (Pres.), Kennedy, Dem., 565,808; Nixon, Rep., 489,538.
1964 (Pres.), Johnson, Dem., 730,912; Goldwater, Rep., 385,495; Write-in, 50.
1968 (Pres.), Nixon, Rep., 508,329; Humphrey, Dem., 527,245; Wallace, 3rd party, 179,998.

# Massachusetts

| County | 1968 Hum-phrey (D) | Nixon (R) | Wal-lace (I) | 1964 John-son (D) | Gold-water (R) |
|---|---|---|---|---|---|
| Barnstable.. | 16,480 | 24,182 | 1,235 | 20,101 | 15,133 |
| Berkshire... | 41,509 | 24,110 | 2,766 | 48,839 | 15,160 |
| Bristol..... | 119,160 | 56,638 | 6,983 | 146,885 | 39,230 |
| Dukes...... | 1,540 | 1,576 | 75 | 2,187 | 1,015 |
| Essex...... | 171,896 | 100,435 | 9,226 | 210,135 | 71,653 |
| Franklin.... | 12,066 | 12,325 | 913 | 17,106 | 8,344 |
| Hampden... | 110,535 | 54,723 | 9,652 | 133,085 | 44,299 |
| Hampshire.. | 28,217 | 17,823 | 2,354 | 32,058 | 11,385 |
| Middlesex... | 366,550 | 170,078 | 13,153 | 439,790 | 134,729 |
| Nantucket.. | 744 | 991 | 52 | 1,197 | 587 |
| Norfolk..... | 158,149 | 108,173 | 11,015 | 186,488 | 68,612 |
| Plymouth... | 67,536 | 54,548 | 5,249 | 82,007 | 37,941 |
| Suffolk..... | 202,368 | 48,992 | 15,063 | 257,161 | 40,251 |
| Worcester... | 165,670 | 87,883 | 7,820 | 209,383 | 61,388 |
| **Totals ...** | **1,458,-058** | **762,477** | **85,556** | **1,786,-422** | **549,727** |

### MASSACHUSETTS VOTE SINCE 1920

1920 (Pres.), Cox, Dem., 276,691; Harding, Rep., 681,153; Debs, Soc., 32,267.
1924 (Pres.), Coolidge, Rep., 703,489; Davis, Dem., 280,884; LaFollette, Prog., 141,225; Foster, Workers, 2,637; Johns, Soc. Lab., 1,668.
1928 (Pres.), Smith, Dem., 792,758; Hoover, Rep., 775,566; Thomas, Soc., 6,262; Foster, Com., 2,464; Reynolds, Soc. Lab., 773.
1932 (Pres.), Roosevelt, Dem., 800,148; Hoover, Rep., 736,959; Thomas, Soc., 34,305; Foster, Com., 4,821; Reynolds, Soc. Lab., 2,668; Upshaw, Proh., 1,142.
1936 (Pres.), Roosevelt, Dem., 942,716; Landon, Rep, 768,613; Lemke, Union, 118,639; Thomas, Soc., 5,111; Browder, Com., 2,930; Aiken, Soc. Lab., 1,305; Colvin, Proh., 1,032.
1940 (Pres.), Roosevelt, Dem., 1,076,522; Willkie, Rep., 939,700; Thomas, Soc., 4,091; Browder, Com., 1,806; Aiken, Soc. Lab., 1,492; Babson, Proh., 1,370.
1944 (Pres.), Roosevelt, Dem., 1,035,296; Dewey, Rep., 921,350; Teichert, Scc. Lab., 2,780; Watson, Proh., 973.
1948 (Pres.), Truman, Dem., 1,151,788; Dewey, Rep., 909,370; Wallace, Prog., 38,157; Teichert, Soc. Lab., 5,535; Watson, Proh., 1,663.
1952 (Pres.), Eisenhower, Rep., 1,292,325; Stevenson, Dem., 1,083,525; Hallinan, Prog., 4,636; Hass, Soc. Lab., 1,957; Hamblen, Proh., 886; Scattered, 69; Blanks, 41,150.
1956 (Pres.), Eisenhower, Rep., 1,393,197; Stevenson, Dem., 948,190; Hass, Soc. Lab., 5,573; Holtwick. Proh., 1,205; Others, 341.
1960 (Pres.), Kennedy, Dem., 1,487,174; Nixon, Rep., 976,750; Hass, Soc. Lab., 3,892; Decker, Proh., 1,633; Others, 31; Blank and void 26,024.
1964 (Pres.), Johnson, Dem., 1,786,422; Goldwater, Rep., 549,727; Hass, Soc. Lab., 4,755; Munn, Proh., 3,735; scattered 159; Blank, 48,104.
1968 (Pres.), Nixon, Rep., 762,477; Humphrey, Dem., 1,458,058; Wallace, 3rd party, 85,556.

# Michigan

| County | 1968 Hum-phrey (D) | Nixon (R) | Wal-lace (I) | 1964 John-son (D) | Gold-water (R) |
|---|---|---|---|---|---|
| Alcona ..... | 833 | 1,313 | 263 | 1,611 | 1,199 |
| Alger....... | 1,927 | 1,400 | 174 | 2,743 | 1,010 |

## Michigan (cont'd)

| County | 1968 Humphrey (D) | Nixon (R) | Wallace (I) | 1964 Johnson (D) | Goldwater (R) |
|---|---|---|---|---|---|
| Allegan | 7,818 | 15,736 | 2,452 | 11,934 | 11,223 |
| Alpena | 3,558 | 6,610 | 512 | 7,508 | 3,954 |
| Antrim | 1,690 | 3,002 | 342 | 2,684 | 2,172 |
| Arenac | 1,572 | 2,089 | 298 | 2,436 | 1,413 |
| Baraga | 1,680 | 1,508 | 116 | 2,568 | 1,160 |
| Barry | 5,088 | 8,227 | 1,598 | 8,102 | 5,509 |
| Bay | 20,351 | 17,620 | 2,170 | 29,754 | 11,896 |
| Benzie | 1,152 | 2,238 | 219 | 1,983 | 1,674 |
| Berrien | 21,275 | 32,021 | 9,175 | 33,653 | 26,387 |
| Branch | 4,518 | 7,070 | 1,037 | 7,858 | 5,110 |
| Calhoun | 25,256 | 23,468 | 5,887 | 32,939 | 18,987 |
| Cass | 5,616 | 6,997 | 2,256 | 8,789 | 5,925 |
| Charlevoix | 2,446 | 3,697 | 557 | 3,757 | 2,664 |
| Cheboygan | 2,608 | 3,162 | 607 | 4,028 | 2,342 |
| Chippewa | 4,207 | 5,284 | 745 | 6,537 | 4,098 |
| Clare | 1,981 | 3,419 | 619 | 2,927 | 2,258 |
| Clinton | 5,329 | 9,082 | 1,495 | 8,932 | 5,891 |
| Crawford | 845 | 1,266 | 187 | 1,464 | 696 |
| Delta | 6,625 | 5,005 | 664 | 10,046 | 4,434 |
| Dickinson | 6,284 | 5,862 | 532 | 7,921 | 3,365 |
| Eaton | 8,347 | 14,185 | 2,272 | 12,590 | 8,919 |
| Emmet | 2,624 | 4,405 | 446 | 4,197 | 2,731 |
| Genesee | 69,521 | 56,041 | 22,566 | 100,346 | 48,311 |
| Gladwin | 1,668 | 2,840 | 311 | 2,725 | 1,941 |
| Gogebic | 5,839 | 4,140 | 434 | 7,945 | 3,350 |
| Gd. Tr'v'rse | 4,741 | 8,960 | 901 | 7,475 | 6,198 |
| Gratiot | 4,040 | 8,404 | 949 | 7,383 | 5,369 |
| Hillsdale | 3,793 | 8,507 | 1,107 | 6,564 | 6,420 |
| Houghton | 6,988 | 6,639 | 385 | 9,761 | 5,024 |
| Huron | 3,608 | 8,743 | 92 | 7,349 | 6,263 |
| Ingham | 34,252 | 41,579 | 5,621 | 53,685 | 32,965 |
| Ionia | 6,055 | 8,625 | 1,270 | 10,362 | 5,698 |
| Iosco | 2,633 | 4,068 | 744 | 4,336 | 2,704 |
| Iron | 4,130 | 3,292 | 340 | 6,011 | 2,399 |
| Isabella | 4,060 | 6,467 | 637 | 7,040 | 4,672 |
| Jackson | 17,147 | 25,158 | 5,146 | 28,219 | 20,944 |
| Kalamazoo | 26,437 | 39,796 | 7,398 | 40,789 | 27,105 |
| Kalkaska | 751 | 1,152 | 288 | 1,220 | 862 |
| Kent | 61,589 | 85,614 | 11,354 | 86,860 | 66,831 |
| Keweenaw | 602 | 525 | 65 | 860 | 370 |
| Lake | 1,483 | 1,094 | 202 | 1,978 | 794 |
| Lapeer | 5,237 | 8,867 | 2,071 | 8,595 | 6,010 |
| Leelanau | 1,562 | 2,798 | 292 | 2,369 | 2,070 |
| Lenawee | 10,552 | 16,275 | 2,197 | 16,815 | 11,381 |
| Livingston | 5,223 | 6,843 | 1,815 | 9,698 | 6,723 |
| Luce | 823 | 1,383 | 88 | 1,459 | 871 |
| Mackinac | 1,751 | 2,507 | 317 | 2,748 | 1,967 |
| Macomb | 113,460 | 61,125 | 28,923 | 131,450 | 44,684 |
| Manistee | 3,641 | 3,989 | 603 | 5,520 | 2,918 |
| Marquette | 11,086 | 8,750 | 784 | 14,045 | 6,615 |
| Mason | 1,395 | 1,726 | 208 | 5,993 | 3,842 |
| Mecosta | 2,738 | 7,381 | 625 | 4,214 | 3,454 |
| Menominee | 4,877 | 4,600 | 630 | 7,119 | 3,545 |
| Midland | 7,473 | 14,483 | 1,851 | 12,587 | 9,020 |
| Missaukee | 736 | 2,161 | 290 | 1,288 | 1,786 |
| Monroe | 18,866 | 15,683 | 4,867 | 26,528 | 11,499 |
| Montcalm | 5,299 | 8,293 | 1,245 | 8,970 | 5,181 |
| M'ntm'r'ncy | 810 | 1,279 | 260 | 1,369 | 863 |
| Muskegon | 21,561 | 25,035 | 4,782 | 36,769 | 22,146 |
| Newaygo | 3,046 | 6,134 | 925 | 5,457 | 4,931 |
| Oakland | 154,526 | 156,538 | 32,850 | 182,797 | 114,025 |
| Oceana | 1,828 | 3,644 | 723 | 3,773 | 2,958 |
| Ogemaw | 1,644 | 2,526 | 445 | 2,812 | 1,609 |
| Ontonagon | 2,462 | 2,300 | 177 | 3,485 | 1,658 |
| Osceola | 1,509 | 3,705 | 583 | 2,891 | 2,779 |
| Oscoda | 563 | 1,124 | 159 | 930 | 784 |
| Otsego | 2,856 | 1,846 | 236 | 2,245 | 1,214 |
| Ottawa | 12,259 | 33,356 | 3,409 | 20,151 | 24,512 |
| Presque Isle | 2,300 | 2,565 | 385 | 3,565 | 1,770 |
| Roscommon | 1,639 | 2,635 | 430 | 2,345 | 1,722 |
| Saginaw | 29,950 | 34,304 | 6,098 | 45,309 | 28,146 |
| St. Clair | 16,147 | 21,066 | 5,249 | 24,662 | 17,011 |
| St. Joseph | 5,404 | 10,426 | 1,696 | 9,284 | 7,307 |
| Sanilac | 5,075 | 9,113 | 1,683 | 6,266 | 7,590 |
| Schoolcraft | 1,868 | 1,745 | 205 | 2,675 | 1,397 |
| Shiawassee | 8,674 | 11,450 | 2,374 | 13,676 | 7,786 |
| Tuscola | 4,698 | 10,405 | 1,652 | 9,374 | 7,509 |
| Van Buren | 7,294 | 10,664 | 2,554 | 11,336 | 8,120 |
| Washtenaw | 32,225 | 35,554 | 7,412 | 42,089 | 25,595 |
| Wayne | 651,020 | 266,737 | 104,368 | 831,674 | 260,901 |
| Wexford | 2,832 | 4,364 | 517 | 4,414 | 3,016 |
| **Totals** | **1,567,- 310** | **1,330,- 749** | **320,344** | **2,136,- 615** | **1,060,- 152** |

### MICHIGAN VOTE SINCE 1920

1920 (Pres.), Cox, Dem., 233,450; Harding, Rep., 762,865; Watkins, Proh., 9,646; Debs, Soc., 28,947; Christensen, Farm.-Lab., 10,372.

1924 (Pres.), Coolidge, Rep., 874,631; Davis, Dem., 152,238; LaFollette, Prog., 122,014; Faris, Proh., 6,085; Johns, Soc. Lab., 5,330.

1928 (Pres.), Hoover, Rep., 965,396; Smith, Dem., 396,762; Thomas, Soc., 3,516; Foster, Com., 2,881; Proh, 2,728; Soc. Lab., 799.

1932 (Pres.), Roosevelt, Dem., 871,700; Hoover, Rep., 739,894; Thomas, Soc., 39,205; Foster, Com., 9,318; Upshaw, Proh., 2,893; Reynolds, Soc. Lab., 1,041; Harvey, Lib., 217.

## Michigan (cont'd)

1936 (Pres.), Roosevelt, Dem., 1,016,794; Landon, Rep., 699,733; Lemke, Union, 75,795; Thomas, Soc., 8,208; Browder, Com., 3,384; Aiken. Soc. Lab., 600; Colvin, Proh., 579.

1940 (Pres.), Roosevelt, Dem., 1,032,991; Willkie, Rep., 1,039,917; Thomas, Soc., 7,593; Browder, Com., 2,834; Babson, Proh., 1,795; Aiken. Soc. Lab., 795

1944 (Pres.), Roosevelt, Dem., 1,106,899; Dewey, Rep., 1,084,423; Watson, Proh., 6,503; Thomas, Soc., 4,598; Smith, America First, 1,530; Teichert, Soc. Lab., 1,264.

1948 (Pres.), Truman, Dem., 1,003,448; Dewey, Rep., 1,038,595; Wallace, Prog., 46,515; Watson, Proh., 13,052; Thomas, Soc., 6,063; Teichert, Soc. Lab., 1,263; Dobbs, Soc. Workers, 672.

1952 (Pres.), Eisenhower, Rep., 1,551,529; Stevenson, Dem., 1,230,657; Hamblen, Proh., 10,331; Hallinan, Prog., 3,922; Hass, Soc. Lab., 1,495; Dobbs, Soc. Workers, 655; Scattered, 3.

1956 (Pres.), Eisenhower, Rep., 1,713,647; Stevenson, Dem., 1,359,898; Holtwick, Proh., 6,923.

1960 (Pres.), Kennedy, Dem., 1,687,269, Nixon, Rep., 1,620,428; Dobbs, Soc. Workers, 4,347; Decker, Proh., 2,029; Daly, Tax Cut, 1,767; Hass, Soc. Lab., 1,718; Ind. American, 539.

1964 (Pres.), Johnson, Dem., 2,136,615; Goldwater, Rep., 1,060,152; DeBerry, Soc. Worker, 3,817; Hass.. Soc. Lab., 1,704; Proh. (no candidate listed), 669; Scattering, 145.

1968 (Pres.), Nixon, Rep., 1,330,749; Humphrey, Dem., 1,567,310; Wallace, 3rd party, 320,344; scattered, 3,981.

# Minnesota

| County | 1968 Humphrey (D) | Nixon (R) | Wallace (I) | 1964 Johnson (D) | Goldwater (R) |
|---|---|---|---|---|---|
| Aitkin | 3,094 | 3,094 | 286 | 3,874 | 2,000 |
| Anoka | 30,556 | 16,358 | 3,073 | 31,714 | 13,201 |
| Becker | 4,875 | 4,728 | 568 | 6,453 | 3,751 |
| Beltrami | 5,034 | 3,912 | 599 | 5,967 | 3,184 |
| Benton | 4,025 | 3,470 | 514 | 4,679 | 2,838 |
| Big Stone | 2,119 | 1,645 | 176 | 2,831 | 1,331 |
| Blue Earth | 9,254 | 9,571 | 686 | 10,687 | 8,009 |
| Brown | 4,585 | 7,039 | 703 | 6,069 | 5,851 |
| Carlton | 8,538 | 3,016 | 444 | 9,552 | 2,780 |
| Carver | 4,590 | 6,649 | 528 | 5,123 | 5,424 |
| Cass | 3,569 | 3,888 | 486 | 4,635 | 3,110 |
| Chippewa | 3,701 | 3,195 | 243 | 4,550 | 2,806 |
| Chisago | 4,102 | 3,053 | 492 | 4,347 | 2,525 |
| Clay | 7,987 | 7,910 | 640 | 10,161 | 6,085 |
| Clearwater | 2,046 | 1,284 | 217 | 2,596 | 1,137 |
| Cook | 777 | 853 | 96 | 976 | 764 |
| Cottonwood | 3,046 | 4,050 | 293 | 4,090 | 3,423 |
| Crow Wing | 7,411 | 6,687 | 672 | 9,197 | 5,131 |
| Dakota | 28,416 | 19,290 | 2,142 | 28,391 | 13,856 |
| Dodge | 2,437 | 3,064 | 201 | 3,138 | 2,474 |
| Douglas | 4,826 | 5,464 | 536 | 6,040 | 4,122 |
| Faribault | 4,335 | 5,662 | 379 | 5,946 | 4,817 |
| Fillmore | 3,918 | 6,257 | 426 | 5,813 | 4,824 |
| Freeborn | 8,671 | 7,315 | 558 | 10,554 | 6,136 |
| Goodhue | 7,220 | 8,283 | 451 | 9,035 | 6,539 |
| Grant | 1,982 | 1,929 | 179 | 2,631 | 1,734 |
| Hennepin | 105,357 | 99,986 | 7,204 | 241,020 | 154,736 |
| Houston | 2,703 | 4,450 | 521 | 3,885 | 3,433 |
| Hubbard | 1,920 | 2,720 | 304 | 2,553 | 2,283 |
| Isanti | 3,439 | 2,429 | 451 | 4,026 | 1,982 |
| Itasca | 10,512 | 4,898 | 780 | 12,054 | 4,137 |
| Jackson | 3,515 | 2,886 | 359 | 4,576 | 2,441 |
| Kanabec | 2,154 | 1,847 | 240 | 2,666 | 1,348 |
| Kandiyohi | 7,639 | 5,086 | 658 | 9,108 | 4,011 |
| Kittson | 1,894 | 1,436 | 179 | 2,790 | 1,153 |
| Koochiching | 4,697 | 2,104 | 299 | 5,878 | 1,602 |
| LacQuiParle | 2,937 | 2,672 | 212 | 3,934 | 2,236 |
| Lake | 4,266 | 1,351 | 263 | 4,704 | 1,205 |
| L'k o' Woods | 875 | 607 | 69 | 1,266 | 489 |
| Le Sueur | 5,094 | 4,189 | 292 | 6,117 | 3,191 |
| Lincoln | 2,109 | 1,732 | 187 | 3,024 | 1,393 |
| Lyon | 5,317 | 4,331 | 306 | 6,649 | 3,165 |
| McLeod | 4,861 | 6,619 | 576 | 5,755 | 5,545 |
| Mahnomen | 1,508 | 893 | 201 | 1,967 | 648 |
| Marshall | 3,161 | 2,367 | 418 | 4,594 | 1,893 |
| Martin | 4,271 | 7,115 | 580 | 5,575 | 6,529 |
| Meeker | 4,213 | 4,044 | 438 | 5,270 | 3,099 |
| Mille Lacs | 3,494 | 2,990 | 399 | 4,369 | 2,474 |
| Morrison | 6,111 | 4,612 | 612 | 7,492 | 3,515 |
| Mower | 11,022 | 7,736 | 692 | 13,573 | 6,510 |
| Murray | 2,662 | 2,906 | 316 | 3,822 | 2,325 |
| Nicollet | 4,244 | 4,671 | 312 | 5,121 | 3,605 |
| Nobles | 5,171 | 4,451 | 477 | 6,431 | 3,517 |
| Norman | 2,828 | 1,981 | 200 | 3,631 | 1,662 |
| Olmsted | 13,417 | 17,292 | 1,103 | 16,195 | 12,699 |
| Otter Tail | 7,400 | 12,483 | 802 | 9,997 | 10,542 |
| Pennington | 2,998 | 2,247 | 212 | 3,894 | 1,630 |
| Pine | 4,044 | 2,591 | 463 | 5,123 | 2,279 |
| Pipestone | 2,234 | 3,241 | 260 | 3,365 | 2,481 |
| Polk | 8,330 | 6,074 | 700 | 11,052 | 5,039 |
| Pope | 2,592 | 2,504 | 265 | 3,549 | 2,213 |

## Minn. (cont'd)

| County | 1968 | | | 1964 | |
|---|---|---|---|---|---|
| | Humphrey (D) | Nixon (R) | Wallace (I) | Johnson (D) | Goldwater (R) |
| Ramsey .... | 122,568 | 64,068 | 8,543 | 133,948 | 56,898 |
| Red Lake... | 1,467 | 718 | 130 | 1,861 | 573 |
| Redwood .. | 3,680 | 5,134 | 462 | 4,722 | 4,546 |
| Renville.... | 4,535 | 4,821 | 543 | 6,072 | 4,340 |
| Rice....... | 7,785 | 7,037 | 477 | 9,299 | 5,518 |
| Rock....... | 2,084 | 3,056 | 232 | 2,896 | 2,389 |
| Roseau..... | 2,649 | 2,048 | 326 | 3,636 | 1,651 |
| St. Louis.... | 72,267 | 25,981 | 3,255 | 79,529 | 25,246 |
| Scott....... | 6,656 | 4,632 | 540 | 7,248 | 3,311 |
| Sherburne.. | 3,481 | 2,737 | 369 | 3,787 | 2,132 |
| Sibley...... | 2,540 | 4,290 | 361 | 3,577 | 3,854 |
| Stearns..... | 15,990 | 15,422 | 2,081 | 19,063 | 13,009 |
| Steele...... | 4,631 | 6,193 | 358 | 6,022 | 4,882 |
| Stevens..... | 2,247 | 2,560 | 246 | 2,910 | 2,220 |
| Swift...... | 3,716 | 2,476 | 247 | 4,380 | 2,132 |
| Todd....... | 3,992 | 4,883 | 572 | 5,673 | 4,006 |
| Traverse.... | 1,669 | 1,277 | 137 | 2,247 | 1,073 |
| Wabasha... | 3,452 | 4,081 | 346 | 4,367 | 3,133 |
| Wadena.... | 2,198 | 2,912 | 269 | 2,908 | 2,418 |
| Waseca..... | 3,057 | 4,292 | 244 | 3,633 | 3,570 |
| Washington. | 16,449 | 10,921 | 1,527 | 18,108 | 8,850 |
| Watonwan.. | 2,701 | 3,446 | 278 | 3,615 | 2,823 |
| Wilkin .... | 1,946 | 2,037 | 181 | 2,751 | 1,636 |
| Winona.... | 8,627 | 7,998 | 781 | 11,397 | 6,345 |
| Wright..... | 8,793 | 6,321 | 627 | 8,687 | 5,476 |
| Yellow Med. | 3,587 | 3,060 | 406 | 4,707 | 2,751 |
| **Totals ...** | **857,738** | **658,643** | **68,931** | **991,117** | **5596,24** |

### MINNESOTA VOTE SINCE 1920

1920 (Pres.), Cox, Dem., 142,994; Harding, Rep., 519,421; Watkins, Proh., 11,489; Debs, Soc., 56,106.

1924 (Pres.), Coolidge, Rep., 420,759; LaFollette, Prog., 339,192; Davis, Dem., 55,913; Foster, Workers, 4,427; Johns, Soc. Lab., 1,855.

1928 (Pres.), Hoover, Rep., 560,977; Smith, Dem., 396,451; Thomas, Soc., 6,774; Foster, Com., 4,853; Industrial, 1,921.

1932 (Pres.), Roosevelt, Dem., 600,806; Hoover, Rep., 363,959; Thomas, Soc., 25,476; Foster, Com., 6,101; Coxey, Farm.-Lab., 5,731; Reynolds, Ind., 770.

1936 (Pres.), Roosevelt, Dem., 698,811; Landon, Rep., 350,461; Lemke, Union, 74,296; Thomas, Soc., 2,872; Browder, Com., 2,574.; Aiken, Soc., 961.

1940 (Pres.), Roosevelt, Dem., 644,196; Willkie, Rep., 596,274; Thomas, Soc., 5,454; Browder, Com., 2,711; Aiken, Ind., 2,553.

1944 (Pres.), Roosevelt, Dem., 589,864; Dewey, Rep., 527,416; Thomas, Soc., 5,073; Teichert, Ind., Gov't., 3,176.

1948 (Pres.), Truman, Dem., 692,966; Dewey, Rep., 483,617; Wallace, Prog., 27,866; Thomas, Soc., 4,646; Teichert, Soc. Lab., 2,525; Dobbs, Soc. Workers, 606.

1952 (Pres.), Eisenhower, Rep., 763,211; Stevenson, Dem., 608,458; Hallinan, Prog., 2,666; Hass, Soc. Lab., 2,383; Hamblen, Proh., 2,147; Dobbs, Soc. Workers, 618.

1956 (Pres.), Eisenhower, Rep., 719,302; Stevenson, Dem., 617,525; Hass, Soc. Lab. (Ind. Gov.), 2,080; Dobbs, Soc. Workers, 1,098.

1960 (Pres.), Kennedy, Dem., 779,933; Nixon, Rep., 757,915; Dobbs, Soc. Workers, 3,077; Industrial Gov., 962.

1964 (Pres.), Johnson, Dem., 991,117; Goldwater, Rep., 559,624; DeBerry, Soc. Workers, 1,177; Hass, Industrial Gov., 2,544.

1968 (Pres.), Nixon, Rep., 658,643; Humphrey, Dem., 857,738; Wallace, 3rd party, 68,931; scattered 2,443.

## Mississippi

| County | 1968 | | | 1964 | |
|---|---|---|---|---|---|
| | Humphrey (D) | Nixon (R) | Wallace (I) | Johnson (D) | Goldwater (R) |
| Adams..... | 5,271 | 1,475 | 6,812 | 1,093 | 5,900 |
| Alcorn..... | 1,122 | 1,760 | 6,304 | 1,917 | 3,376 |
| Amite...... | 1,533 | 393 | 3,206 | 103 | 2,742 |
| Attala...... | 1,588 | 599 | 4,776 | 263 | 4,409 |
| Benton..... | 853 | 185 | 1,630 | 236 | 934 |
| Bolivar..... | 4,696 | 1,790 | 5,018 | 731 | 4,680 |
| Calhoun.... | 276 | 394 | 4,823 | 294 | 3,224 |
| Carroll..... | 925 | 138 | 2,131 | 98 | 2,043 |
| Chickasaw.. | 720 | 381 | 4,062 | 279 | 3,133 |
| Choctaw.... | 417 | 211 | 2,543 | 150 | 2,096 |
| Claiborne... | 2,129 | 230 | 1,143 | 84 | 1,226 |
| Clarke..... | 878 | 298 | 4,214 | 253 | 3,591 |
| Clay....... | 1,438 | 510 | 3,654 | 226 | 2,848 |
| Coahoma... | 5,308 | 1,884 | 3,556 | 964 | 4,172 |
| Copiah..... | 2,724 | 704 | 4,951 | 239 | 4,506 |

## Miss. (cont'd)

| County | 1968 | | | 1964 | |
|---|---|---|---|---|---|
| | Humphrey (D) | Nixon (R) | Wallace (I) | Johnson (D) | Goldwater (R) |
| Covington.. | 691 | 445 | 3,668 | 392 | 3,033 |
| De Soto.... | 1,898 | 1,092 | 5,346 | 461 | 2,928 |
| Forrest..... | 2,957 | 3,294 | 9,975 | 1,128 | 9,291 |
| Franklin.... | 752 | 231 | 2,429 | 91 | 2,211 |
| George..... | 214 | 171 | 3,992 | 242 | 2,797 |
| Greene..... | 449 | 132 | 2,744 | 216 | 1,851 |
| Grenada.... | 2,050 | 718 | 4,335 | 155 | 3,643 |
| Hancock.... | 904 | 1,065 | 4,072 | 1,501 | 2,548 |
| Harrison.... | 4,670 | 6,542 | 18,157 | 5,393 | 19,350 |
| Hinds...... | 14,880 | 13,488 | 32,366 | 5,058 | 36,801 |
| Holmes..... | 3,881 | 520 | 3,008 | 110 | 3,115 |
| Humphreys. | 1,219 | 258 | 2,151 | 84 | 1,863 |
| Issaquena.. | 527 | 44 | 534 | 34 | 456 |
| Itawamba.. | 417 | 569 | 5,204 | 1,127 | 2,140 |
| Jackson.... | 2,236 | 2,942 | 15,261 | 2,371 | 11,357 |
| Jasper...... | 987 | 373 | 3,100 | 236 | 2,994 |
| Jefferson... | 2,121 | 144 | 1,112 | 69 | 1,258 |
| Jeff. Davis.. | 1,465 | 297 | 2,614 | 235 | 2,351 |
| Jones...... | 2,476 | 3,242 | 12,276 | 1,981 | 12,123 |
| Kemper.... | 655 | 167 | 2,530 | 191 | 2,185 |
| Lafayette... | 1,578 | 1,235 | 3,329 | 720 | 3,202 |
| Lamar..... | 351 | 546 | 4,422 | 304 | 3,372 |
| Lauderdale.. | 3,195 | 2,328 | 14,842 | 1,583 | 13,291 |
| Lawrence... | 740 | 329 | 2,825 | 236 | 2,373 |
| Leake...... | 1,295 | 453 | 4,568 | 170 | 4,343 |
| Lee........ | 1,912 | 2,529 | 9,232 | 2,409 | 5,165 |
| Leflore..... | 4,386 | 1,514 | 5,732 | 380 | 5,589 |
| Lincoln..... | 1,585 | 1,057 | 7,276 | 437 | 6,750 |
| Lowndes.... | 2,229 | 1,968 | 6,829 | 533 | 6,135 |
| Madison.... | 4,225 | 812 | 3,833 | 251 | 3,283 |
| Marion..... | 1,722 | 763 | 5,848 | 505 | 5,469 |
| Marshall.... | 2,907 | 577 | 2,794 | 342 | 2,250 |
| Monroe.... | 1,506 | 1,167 | 7,856 | 985 | 5,627 |
| Montg'm'y. | 896 | 475 | 2,988 | 149 | 3,181 |
| Neshoba.... | 867 | 531 | 6,417 | 293 | 5,431 |
| Newton.... | 799 | 542 | 5,561 | 238 | 4,735 |
| Noxubee.... | 1,387 | 232 | 2,040 | 70 | 1,980 |
| Oktibbeha.. | 1,826 | 1,276 | 4,127 | 390 | 3,795 |
| Panola..... | 2,743 | 1,098 | 4,133 | 413 | 4,002 |
| Pearl River. | 926 | 1,298 | 6,050 | 735 | 4,009 |
| Perry...... | 439 | 227 | 2,541 | 279 | 1,775 |
| Pike....... | 2,848 | 1,428 | 5,711 | 543 | 6,418 |
| Pontotoc ... | 599 | 733 | 4,798 | 702 | 2,699 |
| Prentiss.... | 440 | 723 | 5,055 | 1,013 | 2,289 |
| Quitman.... | 1,499 | 434 | 2,454 | 336 | 2,065 |
| Rankin..... | 1,979 | 1,126 | 9,238 | 332 | 7,541 |
| Scott....... | 1,064 | 635 | 5,091 | 238 | 4,729 |
| Sharkey.... | 972 | 275 | 1,167 | 128 | 1,116 |
| Simpson.... | 1,070 | 873 | 5,024 | 271 | 4,949 |
| Smith...... | 352 | 437 | 4,367 | 238 | 4,045 |
| Stone...... | 342 | 258 | 2,140 | 179 | 1,776 |
| Sunflower... | 2,360 | 1,021 | 3,881 | 251 | 4,127 |
| Tal'hatchie.. | 722 | 300 | 218 | 255 | 3,126 |
| Tate....... | 1,162 | 605 | 2,823 | 283 | 2,390 |
| Tippah..... | 660 | 599 | 4,622 | 974 | 2,482 |
| Tishomingo. | 335 | 617 | 456 | 977 | 1,934 |
| Tunica..... | 1,133 | 413 | 783 | 99 | 945 |
| Union...... | 594 | 965 | 5,198 | 1,237 | 2,939 |
| Walthall.... | 1,233 | 387 | 3,189 | 154 | 3,014 |
| Warren..... | 4,503 | 2,392 | 7,523 | 1,631 | 7,409 |
| Washington. | 5,527 | 3,496 | 6,280 | 2,004 | 5,611 |
| Wayne..... | 739 | 247 | 4,081 | 276 | 3,539 |
| Webster.... | 299 | 321 | 3,494 | 237 | 2,884 |
| Wilkinson... | 2,175 | 270 | 1,499 | 103 | 1,473 |
| Winston.... | 911 | 508 | 4,635 | 237 | 3,922 |
| Yalobusha.. | 865 | 559 | 2,688 | 259 | 2,385 |
| Yazoo..... | 2,165 | 950 | 4,945 | 204 | 4,801 |
| **Totals ...** | **149,419** | **88,214** | **414,402** | **52,618** | **356,528** |

### MISSISSIPPI VOTE SINCE 1920

1920 (Pres.), Cox, Dem., 69,277; Harding, Rep., 11,576; Debs, Soc., 1,639.

1924 (Pres.), Davis, Dem., 100,475; Coolidge, Rep., 8,546; LaFollette, Prog., 3,494.

1928 (Pres.) Smith, Dem., 124,539; Hoover, Rep., 27,153.

1932 (Pres.), Roosevelt, Dem., 140,168; Hoover, Rep., 5,180; Thomas, Soc., 686.

1936 (Pres.), Roosevelt, Dem., 157,318; Landon, Rep., Howard faction, 2,760; Rowlands faction, 1,675; total, 4,435; Thomas, Soc., 329.

1940 (Pres.), Roosevelt, Dem., 168,252; Willkie, Ind. Rep., 4,550; Rep., 2,814; total, 7,364; Thomas, Soc., 103.

1944 (Pres.), Roosevelt, Dem., 158,515; Dewey, Rep., 3,742; Reg. Dem., 9,964; Ind. Rep., 7,859; Texas, Rep., 1,082.

1948 (Pres.), Thurmond, States' Rights, 167,538; Truman, Dem., 19,384; Dewey, Rep., 5,043; Wallace, Prog., 225.

1952 (Pres.), Eisenhower, Ind. vote pledged to Rep. candidate, 112,966; Stevenson, Dem., 172,566.

1956 (Pres.), Stevenson, Dem., 144,498; Eisenhower, Rep., 56,372; Black and Tan Grand Old Party, 4,313; total, 60,685; Byrd, Independent, 42,966.

1960 (Pres.), Democratic unpledged electors, 116,-248; Kennedy, Dem., 108,362; Nixon, Rep., 73,561. *Mississippi's victorious slate of 8 unpledged

## Mississippi (cont'd)

Democratic electors cast their votes for Sen. Harry F. Byrd (D.-Va.).
1964 (Pres.), Johnson, Dem., 52,618; Goldwater, Rep., 356,528.
1968 (Pres.), Nixon, Rep., 88,214; Humphrey, Dem., 149,419; Wallace, 3rd party, 414,402.

# Missouri

| County | 1968 Humphrey (D) | Nixon (R) | Wallace (I) | 1964 Johnson (D) | Goldwater (R) |
|---|---|---|---|---|---|
| Adair | 2,645 | 4,624 | 592 | 4,235 | 3,573 |
| Andrew | 2,005 | 3,398 | 358 | 3,211 | 2,594 |
| Atchison | 1,759 | 2,259 | 340 | 2,870 | 1,653 |
| Andrain | 4,806 | 5,005 | 1,024 | 7,387 | 3,316 |
| Barry | 3,397 | 5,537 | 758 | 5,307 | 4,757 |
| Barton | 1,832 | 2,928 | 499 | 3,173 | 2,332 |
| Bates | 3,370 | 4,087 | 801 | 5,162 | 3,514 |
| Benton | 1,345 | 2,899 | 498 | 2,030 | 2,477 |
| Bollinger | 1,693 | 2,283 | 588 | 2,792 | 2,125 |
| Boone | 11,768 | 11,844 | 2,015 | 14,758 | 7,695 |
| Buchanan | 15,949 | 16,168 | 2,755 | 24,164 | 11,501 |
| Butler | 4,386 | 6,312 | 2,755 | 7,710 | 5,616 |
| Caldwell | 1,490 | 2,631 | 430 | 2,475 | 2,125 |
| Callaway | 3,772 | 4,225 | 1,273 | 5,916 | 2,983 |
| Camden | 1,646 | 3,700 | 641 | 2,522 | 2,607 |
| Cape Girar. | 6,654 | 10,237 | 2,360 | 11,431 | 8776 |
| Carroll | 2,473 | 3,680 | 645 | 4,069 | 2,994 |
| Carter | 738 | 861 | 289 | 1,232 | 761 |
| Cass | 4,468 | 5,271 | 1,938 | 6,355 | 3,665 |
| Cedar | 1,218 | 2,935 | 430 | 2,347 | 2,478 |
| Chariton | 2,373 | 2,404 | 509 | 3,862 | 1,932 |
| Christian | 1,586 | 4,019 | 633 | 2,646 | 3,232 |
| Clark | 1,489 | 2,111 | 341 | 2,223 | 1,660 |
| Clay | 17,386 | 19,299 | 6,881 | 23,993 | 13,997 |
| Clinton | 2,503 | 2,671 | 600 | 3,598 | 1,800 |
| Cole | 5,876 | 11,473 | 1,608 | 8,127 | 10,068 |
| Cooper | 2,797 | 4,115 | 479 | 4,201 | 3,530 |
| Crawford | 2,108 | 3,555 | 671 | 3,444 | 2,660 |
| Dade | 917 | 2,270 | 417 | 1,641 | 1,931 |
| Dallas | 1,257 | 2,835 | 465 | 1,983 | 2,268 |
| Daviess | 1,589 | 2,330 | 323 | 2,739 | 1,874 |
| DeKalb | 1,452 | 2,112 | 285 | 2,347 | 1,679 |
| Dent | 1,789 | 2,338 | 457 | 2,860 | 1,788 |
| Douglas | 978 | 2,836 | 312 | 1,593 | 2,280 |
| Dunklin | 5,063 | 4,359 | 2,903 | 8,467 | 3,465 |
| Franklin | 7,566 | 9,824 | 1,950 | 13,464 | 8,313 |
| Gasconade | 1,130 | 4,398 | 353 | 2,126 | 3,672 |
| Gentry | 2,189 | 2,435 | 208 | 3,198 | 1,677 |
| Greene | 19,669 | 32,638 | 6,751 | 30,130 | 23,989 |
| Grundy | 1,976 | 3,213 | 419 | 3,363 | 2,411 |
| Harrison | 1,688 | 3,092 | 412 | 2,787 | 2,516 |
| Henry | 3,514 | 3,824 | 682 | 5,761 | 3,083 |
| Hickory | 537 | 1,484 | 209 | 854 | 1,157 |
| Holt | 1,211 | 2,030 | 379 | 1,871 | 1,726 |
| Howard | 2,333 | 1,825 | 507 | 3,507 | 1,339 |
| Howell | 2,762 | 5,631 | 1,449 | 4,968 | 4,632 |
| Iron | 1,755 | 1,605 | 491 | 2,730 | 1,050 |
| Jackson | 112,154 | 90,986 | 28,780 | 161,290 | 78,766 |
| Jasper | 10,667 | 16,794 | 3,166 | 18,045 | 15,481 |
| Jefferson | 13,230 | 11,709 | 6,104 | 18,916 | 7,887 |
| Johnson | 3,484 | 4,834 | 1,018 | 6,412 | 4,348 |
| Knox | 1,257 | 1,562 | 350 | 2,085 | 1,305 |
| Laclede | 2,948 | 4,849 | 848 | 4,517 | 3,848 |
| Lafayette | 4,372 | 6,404 | 983 | 7,400 | 5,493 |
| Lawrence | 3,710 | 6,834 | 898 | 6,383 | 6,047 |
| Lewis | 2,067 | 2,038 | 537 | 3,281 | 1,239 |
| Lincoln | 3,009 | 3,190 | 1,291 | 4,993 | 2,271 |
| Linn | 3,933 | 3,795 | 513 | 5,735 | 2,883 |
| Livingston | 3,455 | 3,809 | 518 | 5,320 | 2,703 |
| McDonald | 2,177 | 3,013 | 678 | 3,488 | 3,055 |
| Macon | 3,474 | 3,816 | 821 | 5,389 | 2,837 |
| Madison | 1,521 | 2,164 | 615 | 2,718 | 1,756 |
| Maries | 1,185 | 1,438 | 403 | 2,063 | 1,183 |
| Marion | 5,420 | 4,737 | 1,223 | 8,314 | 3,605 |
| Mercer | 783 | 1,406 | 125 | 1,284 | 1,040 |
| Miller | 1,727 | 4,425 | 725 | 2,858 | 3,784 |
| Mississippi | 2,257 | 1,419 | 1,565 | 4,015 | 1,665 |
| Moniteau | 1,687 | 3,204 | 586 | 2,624 | 2,758 |
| Monroe | 2,776 | 1,349 | 516 | 4,103 | 928 |
| Montg'm'y. | 1,901 | 2,903 | 623 | 3,289 | 2,610 |
| Morgan | 1,649 | 2,916 | 504 | 2,468 | 2,742 |
| N. Madrid. | 4,195 | 2,317 | 2,984 | 7,415 | 2,583 |
| Newton | 5,085 | 7,442 | 1,490 | 8,139 | 6,660 |
| Nodaway | 4,494 | 4,736 | 635 | 6,690 | 3,789 |
| Oregon | 1,676 | 1,163 | 625 | 2,908 | 992 |
| Osage | 1,927 | 3,595 | 445 | 2,608 | 2,712 |
| Ozark | 607 | 1,970 | 304 | 1,064 | 1,540 |
| Pemiscot | 2,562 | 2,166 | 2,970 | 5,083 | 2,658 |
| Perry | 1,958 | 3,858 | 462 | 3,456 | 2,837 |
| Pettis | 6,329 | 6,738 | 1,539 | 8,987 | 5,409 |
| Phelps | 4,218 | 5,579 | 1,055 | 5,776 | 3,755 |
| Pike | 3,191 | 3,068 | 802 | 5,273 | 1,944 |
| Platte | 4,685 | 4,836 | 1,815 | 6,143 | 3,059 |
| Polk | 2,170 | 4,145 | 614 | 3,353 | 3,288 |
| Pulaski | 2,303 | 2,555 | 718 | 3,383 | 1,856 |
| Putnam | 952 | 1,971 | 169 | 1,484 | 1,547 |
| Ralls | 1,900 | 1,175 | 478 | 2,847 | 758 |
| Randolph | 4,811 | 3,582 | 893 | 6,988 | 2,485 |
| Ray | 3,464 | 2,535 | 1,062 | 5,189 | 1,734 |
| Reynolds | 1,624 | 1,970 | 559 | 1,835 | 530 |

## Missouri (cont'd)

| County | 1968 Humphrey (D) | Nixon (R) | Wallace (I) | 1964 Johnson (D) | Goldwater (R) |
|---|---|---|---|---|---|
| Ripley | 1,438 | 1,972 | 675 | 2,688 | 1,684 |
| St. Charles. | 10,374 | 13,533 | 5,752 | 14,530 | 9,020 |
| St. Clair | 1,496 | 2,301 | 411 | 2,593 | 1,961 |
| St. Francois. | 6,379 | 7,501 | 1,867 | 10,567 | 5,690 |
| Ste. Genev. | 2,207 | 1,937 | 440 | 3,768 | 1,316 |
| St. Louis | 165,325 | 189,022 | 39,103 | 213,658 | 134,962 |
| St. Louis Cy. | 143,217 | 58,202 | 19,474 | 207,958 | 59,604 |
| Saline | 4,633 | 4,841 | 535 | 7,308 | 3,635 |
| Schuyler | 969 | 1,291 | 168 | 1,449 | 1,072 |
| Scotland | 1,340 | 1,554 | 211 | 2,187 | 1,215 |
| Scott | 4,313 | 3,850 | 2,464 | 7,512 | 3,212 |
| Shannon | 1,216 | 1,048 | 446 | 2,312 | 904 |
| Shelby | 2,045 | 1,693 | 358 | 3,156 | 1,212 |
| Stoddard | 3,151 | 3,919 | 1,751 | 5,944 | 3,014 |
| Stone | 1,096 | 2,992 | 451 | 1,835 | 2,377 |
| Sullivan | 1,907 | 2,332 | 225 | 2,695 | 2,052 |
| Taney | 1,219 | 3,289 | 424 | 2,544 | 2,741 |
| Texas | 3,104 | 4,035 | 981 | 4,934 | 2,902 |
| Vernon | 3,557 | 3,590 | 787 | 5,955 | 3,077 |
| Warren | 1,033 | 2,669 | 565 | 1,903 | 2,323 |
| Washington. | 2,290 | 2,540 | 778 | 3,908 | 2,286 |
| Wayne | 1,714 | 2,136 | 643 | 3,005 | 2,019 |
| Webster | 2,547 | 4,118 | 572 | 3,824 | 3,341 |
| Worth | 853 | 924 | 126 | 1,373 | 831 |
| Wright | 1,337 | 3,576 | 487 | 3,292 | 3,466 |
| **Totals** | **790,661** | **812,470** | **204,375** | **1,164,-344** | **653,535** |

## MISSOURI VOTE SINCE 1920

1920 (Pres.), Cox, Dem., 574,799; Harding, Rep., 727,162; Watkins, Proh., 5,142; Debs, Soc., 20,242; Christensen. F.-Lab., 3,291.

1924 (Pres.), Coolidge, Rep., 648,486; Davis, Dem., 572,753; LaFollette, Prog., 84,160; Faris, Proh., 1,418; Johns, Soc. Lab., 909; Wallace, Comm. Land, 259.

1928 (Pres.), Hoover, Rep., 834,080; Smith, Dem., 662,562; Thomas, Soc., 3,739; Reynolds, Soc. Lab., 340.

1932 (Pres.), Roosevelt, Dem., 1,025,406; Hoover, Rep., 564,713; Thomas, Soc., 16,374; Upshaw, Proh., 2,429; Foster, Com., 568; Reynolds, Soc. Lab., 404.

1936 (Pres.), Roosevelt, Dem., 1,111,403; Landon, Rep., 697,891; Lemke, Union, 14,630; Thomas, Soc., 3,454; Colvin, Proh., 908; Browder, Com., 417; Aiken, Soc. Lab., 292.

1940 (Pres.), Roosevelt, Dem., 958,476; Willkie, Rep., 871,009; Thomas, Soc., 2,226; Babson, Prch., 1,809; Aiken, Soc. Lab., 209.

1944 (Pres.), Roosevelt, Dem., 807,357; Dewey, Rep., 761,175; Thomas, Soc., 1,750; Watson, Proh., 1,175; Teichert, Soc. Lab., 221.

1948 (Pres.), Truman, Dem., 917,315; Dewey, Rep., 655,039; Wallace, Prog., 3,998; Thomas, Soc., 2,222.

1952 (Pres.), Eisenhower, Rep., 959,429; Stevenson, Dem., 929,830; Hallinan, Prog., 987; Hamblen, Proh., 885; MacArthur, Christian Nationalist, 302; America First, 233; Hoopes, Soc., 227; Hass, Soc. Lab. 169.

1956 (Pres.), Stevenson, Dem., 918,273; Eisenhower, Rep., 914,299.

1960 (Pres.), Kennedy, Dem., 972,201; Nixon, Rep., 962,221.

1964 (Pres.), Johnson, Dem., 1,164,344; Goldwater, Rep., 653,535.

1968 (Pres.), Nixon, Rep., 812,470; Humphrey, Dem., 790,661; Wallace, 3rd party, 204,375.

# Montana

| County | 1968 Humphrey (D) | Nixon (R) | Wallace (I) | 1964 Johnson (D) | Goldwater (R) |
|---|---|---|---|---|---|
| Beaverhead. | 368 | 935 | 205 | 1,469 | 1,754 |
| Big Horn | 897 | 1,308 | 167 | 2,509 | 1,481 |
| Blaine | 837 | 1,044 | 129 | 1,742 | 961 |
| Broadwater. | 439 | 671 | 108 | 595 | 609 |
| Carbon | 1,352 | 1,972 | 288 | 2,098 | 1,535 |
| Carter | 269 | 624 | 110 | 453 | 576 |
| Cascade | 12,170 | 10,014 | 1,319 | 17,609 | 8,986 |
| Chauteau | 1,216 | 1,695 | 247 | 1,827 | 1,444 |
| Custer | 1,760 | 2,831 | 275 | 2,790 | 2,302 |
| Daniels | 688 | 826 | 69 | 987 | 742 |
| Dawson | 1,687 | 2,537 | 217 | 2,691 | 1,938 |
| Deer Lodge. | 4,208 | 1,554 | 310 | 4,835 | 1,415 |
| Fallon | 477 | 990 | 97 | 765 | 827 |
| Fergus | 1,793 | 2,711 | 533 | 3,300 | 2,980 |
| Flathead | 4,406 | 5,891 | 1,225 | 8,015 | 6,325 |
| Gallatin | 3,392 | 6,920 | 617 | 6,443 | 5,621 |
| Garfield | 79 | 265 | 65 | 384 | 509 |
| Glacier | 1,723 | 1,643 | 295 | 2,218 | 1,458 |
| Gold'n Val'y | 62 | 171 | 18 | 352 | 252 |

| Montana (cont'd) | 1968 | | | 1964 | |
|---|---|---|---|---|---|
| County | Hum-phrey (D) | Nixon (R) | Wal-lace (I) | John-son (D) | Gold-water (R) |
| Granite..... | 502 | 626 | 135 | 658 | 527 |
| Hill........ | 3,386 | 2,970 | 305 | 4,491 | 2,101 |
| Jefferson.... | 820 | 796 | 152 | 967 | 662 |
| Judith Basin | 616 | 814 | 106 | 822 | 678 |
| Lake....... | 415 | 778 | 200 | 3,148 | 2,828 |
| Lewis&Clark | 4,560 | 6,702 | 632 | 7,506 | 6,155 |
| Liberty..... | 390 | 675 | 83 | 619 | 533 |
| Lincoln..... | 910 | 808 | 217 | 3,140 | 1,554 |
| Madison.... | 511 | 959 | 188 | 1,125 | 1,276 |
| McCone.... | 589 | 739 | 82 | 891 | 615 |
| Meagher.... | 218 | 543 | 102 | 405 | 506 |
| Mineral.... | 367 | 329 | 88 | 901 | 368 |
| Missoula.... | 5,985 | 5,512 | 1,000 | 12,900 | 8,065 |
| Musselshell. | 795 | 958 | 111 | 1,189 | 823 |
| Park....... | 1,825 | 3,033 | 460 | 2,824 | 2,619 |
| Petroleum... | 108 | 211 | 36 | 210 | 190 |
| Phillips..... | 1,100 | 1,353 | 177 | 1,612 | 1,242 |
| Pondera.... | 1,149 | 1,531 | 205 | 1,759 | 1,110 |
| Powder Riv. | 258 | 699 | 118 | 449 | 649 |
| Powell..... | 270 | 317 | 48 | 1,896 | 1,140 |
| Prairie..... | 270 | 640 | 30 | 488 | 555 |
| Ravalli..... | 1,824 | 2,830 | 598 | 3,300 | 2,350 |
| Richland.... | 1,399 | 2,381 | 228 | 2,320 | 1,784 |
| Roosevelt... | 1,334 | 1,524 | 104 | 2,463 | 1,612 |
| Rosebud.... | 416 | 703 | 124 | 1,212 | 1,105 |
| Sanders.... | 530 | 1,115 | 193 | 1,836 | 1,163 |
| Sheridan.... | 1,275 | 1,471 | 115 | 1,905 | 837 |
| Silver Bow.. | 12,595 | 5,471 | 1,117 | 15,751 | 4,873 |
| Stillwater... | 686 | 1,347 | 177 | 1,130 | 1,140 |
| Sweet Grass. | 336 | 1,043 | 100 | 653 | 856 |
| Teton...... | 1,228 | 1,697 | 179 | 1,808 | 1,308 |
| Toole...... | 1,048 | 1,408 | 249 | 1,649 | 1,223 |
| Treasure.... | 188 | 298 | 41 | 285 | 251 |
| Valley...... | 1,927 | 2,289 | 393 | 3,032 | 2,077 |
| Wheatland.. | 525 | 673 | 101 | 790 | 583 |
| Wibaux..... | 252 | 347 | 56 | 427 | 308 |
| Yellowstone. | 10,718 | 17,360 | 1,899 | 17,446 | 15,571 |
| **Totals...** | **99,538** | **117,272** | **16,383** | **164,246** | **113,032** |

#### MONTANA VOTE SINCE 1920

1920 (Pres.), Cox, Dem., 57,372; Harding, Rep., 109,430; Christensen, F.-Lab., 12,204.
1924 (Pres.), Coolidge, Rep., 74,138; LaFollette, Prog., 61,105; Davis, Dem., 33,805; Foster, Workers, 357; Johns, Soc. Lab., 247.
1928 (Pres.), Hoover, Rep. 113,300; Smith, Dem. 78,578; Thomas, Soc., 1,667; Foster, Com., 563.
1932 (Pres.), Roosevelt, Dem., 127,286; Hoover, Rep., 78,078; Thomas, Soc., 7,891; Foster, Com., 1,775; Harvey, Lib., 1,449.
1936 (Pres.), Roosevelt, Dem., 159,690; Landon, Rep., 63,598; Lemke, Union, 5,549; Thomas, Soc., 1,066; Browder, Com., 385; Colvin, Proh., 224.
1940 (Pres.), Roosevelt, Dem., 145,698; Willkie, Rep., 99,579; Thomas, Soc.,1,443; Babson, Proh., 664; Browder, Com., 489.
1944 (Pres.), Roosevelt, Dem., 112,556; Dewey, Rep., 93,163; Thomas, Soc., 1,296; Watson, Proh., 340.
1948 (Pres.), Truman, Dem., 119,071; Dewey, Rep., 96,770; Wallace, Prog., 7,313; Thomas, Soc., 695; Watson, Proh., 429.
1952, (Pres.), Eisenhower, Rep., 157,394; Stevenson, Dem., 106,213; Hallinan, Prog., 723; Hamblen, Proh., 548; Hoopes, Soc., 159.
1956 (Pres.), Eisenhower, Rep., 154,933; Stevenson, Dem., 116,238.
1960 (Pres.), Kennedy, Dem., 134,891; Nixon, Rep., 141,841; Decker, Proh., 456; Dobbs, Soc. Workers, 391.
1964 (Pres.), Johnson, Dem., 164,246; Goldwater, Rep., 113,032; Kasper, Nat'l States Rights, 519; Munn, Proh., 499; DeBerry, Soc. Worker, 332.
1968 (Pres.), Nixon, Rep., 117,272; Humphrey, Dem., 99,538; Wallace, 3rd party, 16,383.

## Nebraska

| County | 1968 | | | 1964 | |
|---|---|---|---|---|---|
| | Hum-phrey (D) | Nixon (R) | Wal-lace (I) | John-son (D) | Gold-water (R) |
| Adams..... | 3,219 | 6,449 | 572 | 6,441 | 5,586 |
| Antelope.... | 905 | 2,676 | 348 | 2,004 | 2,566 |
| Arthur..... | 43 | 205 | 15 | 126 | 243 |
| Banner..... | 63 | 330 | 68 | 196 | 357 |
| Blaine...... | 60 | 330 | 24 | 195 | 326 |
| Boone..... | 916 | 2,091 | 281 | 1,905 | 1,893 |
| Box Butte.. | 978 | 2,532 | 233 | 1,968 | 2,725 |
| Boyd...... | 416 | 1,174 | 238 | 908 | 1,100 |
| Brown..... | 344 | 1,258 | 155 | 885 | 1,272 |
| Buffalo.... | 2,765 | 6,454 | 686 | 5,436 | 5,425 |
| Burt...... | 893 | 2,507 | 244 | 2,074 | 2,459 |
| Butler..... | 1,501 | 1,563 | 315 | 2,293 | 1,642 |
| Cass...... | 1,697 | 3,042 | 586 | 3,975 | 2,947 |
| Cedar..... | 1,397 | 2,746 | 328 | 3,104 | 2,299 |
| Chase...... | 344 | 1,102 | 186 | 907 | 1,081 |

| Nebraska (cont'd) | 1968 | | | 1964 | |
|---|---|---|---|---|---|
| County | Hum-phrey (D) | Nixon (R) | Wal-lace (I) | John-son (D) | Gold-water (R) |
| Cherry ..... | 536 | 1,989 | 206 | 1,428 | 2,244 |
| Cheyenne... | 920 | 2,534 | 386 | 2,689 | 3,129 |
| Clay....... | 898 | 2,167 | 176 | 2,001 | 1,879 |
| Colfax..... | 889 | 2,183 | 305 | 2,207 | 1,972 |
| Cuming.... | 890 | 3,107 | 284 | 2,265 | 3,064 |
| Custer..... | 1,342 | 4,072 | 379 | 3,475 | 3,916 |
| Dakota..... | 1,478 | 2,227 | 268 | 2,654 | 1,906 |
| Dawes..... | 689 | 2,391 | 252 | 1,569 | 2,518 |
| Dawson.... | 1,522 | 4,943 | 358 | 3,790 | 4,577 |
| Deuel...... | 229 | 920 | 75 | 533 | 972 |
| Dixon...... | 862 | 1,973 | 171 | 1,912 | 1,845 |
| Dodge..... | 3,618 | 7,703 | 782 | 6,731 | 6,812 |
| Douglas.... | 49,591 | 65,659 | 15,158 | 77,480 | 61,613 |
| Dundy..... | 244 | 950 | 117 | 712 | 911 |
| Fillmore.... | 1,261 | 2,120 | 186 | 2,497 | 1,936 |
| Franklin.... | 606 | 1,384 | 140 | 1,409 | 1,241 |
| Frontier.... | 305 | 1,093 | 134 | 841 | 1,090 |
| Furnas..... | 1,330 | 1,017 | 132 | 1,669 | 2,011 |
| Gage...... | 3,590 | 5,229 | 560 | 6,411 | 4,035 |
| Garden..... | 205 | 1,047 | 94 | 559 | 1,106 |
| Garfield.... | 174 | 741 | 59 | 483 | 761 |
| Gosper.... | 215 | 673 | 57 | 512 | 547 |
| Grant...... | 77 | 291 | 17 | 199 | 304 |
| Greeley.... | 694 | 840 | 138 | 1,305 | 775 |
| Hall....... | 4,349 | 7,995 | 767 | 8,273 | 6,715 |
| Hamilton... | 878 | 2,453 | 130 | 1,986 | 2,105 |
| Harlan..... | 549 | 1,312 | 197 | 1,195 | 1,283 |
| Hayes..... | 122 | 472 | 70 | 362 | 503 |
| Hitchcock.. | 355 | 1,080 | 170 | 946 | 1,149 |
| Holt....... | 1,206 | 3,171 | 415 | 2,739 | 3,194 |
| Hooker..... | 36 | 321 | 10 | 137 | 335 |
| Howard.... | 969 | 1,219 | 180 | 2,025 | 1,019 |
| Jefferson... | 1,489 | 2,637 | 251 | 2,804 | 2,275 |
| Johnson.... | 722 | 1,458 | 205 | 1,554 | 1,312 |
| Kearney.... | 796 | 1,735 | 176 | 1,767 | 1,352 |
| Keith...... | 660 | 1,999 | 167 | 1,784 | 1,927 |
| Keya Paha.. | 105 | 491 | 45 | 320 | 506 |
| Kimball.... | 381 | 1,394 | 229 | 1,242 | 1,573 |
| Knox...... | 1,088 | 3,013 | 345 | 2,617 | 2,752 |
| Lancaster... | 22,770 | 31,379 | 2,785 | 34,503 | 23,887 |
| Lincoln..... | 3,203 | 5,588 | 727 | 6,446 | 4,811 |
| Logan...... | 121 | 339 | 50 | 296 | 267 |
| Loup...... | 60 | 308 | 35 | 176 | 348 |
| McPherson. | 40 | 229 | 33 | 104 | 219 |
| Madison.... | 2,279 | 6,787 | 592 | 4,661 | 6,155 |
| Merrick.... | 813 | 1,929 | 204 | 1,741 | 1,798 |
| Morrill..... | 139 | 408 | 106 | 1,228 | 1,649 |
| Nance..... | 648 | 1,248 | 163 | 1,323 | 1,155 |
| Nemaha.... | 915 | 2,073 | 272 | 2,084 | 1,936 |
| Nuckolls.... | 1,086 | 1,792 | 161 | 2,181 | 1,546 |
| Otoe...... | 1,463 | 3,691 | 451 | 3,169 | 3,626 |
| Pawnee.... | 551 | 1,131 | 201 | 1,111 | 1,166 |
| Perkins.... | 340 | 1,101 | 118 | 877 | 912 |
| Phelps..... | 742 | 2,816 | 241 | 2,153 | 2,440 |
| Pierce..... | 645 | 2,330 | 192 | 1,631 | 1,965 |
| Platte...... | 2,815 | 5,550 | 738 | 5,160 | 4,705 |
| Polk....... | 668 | 1,714 | 195 | 1,730 | 1,607 |
| Red Willow. | 1,080 | 2,901 | 333 | 2,416 | 2,740 |
| Richardson.. | 1,500 | 2,922 | 491 | 3,245 | 2,850 |
| Rock...... | 142 | 749 | 87 | 376 | 835 |
| Saline..... | 2,473 | 2,230 | 336 | 4,125 | 1,780 |
| Sarpy...... | 3,357 | 5,574 | 1,865 | 5,581 | 4,418 |
| Saunders... | 1,935 | 3,292 | 542 | 4,172 | 3,345 |
| Scotts Bluff. | 2,496 | 6,916 | 885 | 6,368 | 6,965 |
| Seward..... | 1,592 | 2,812 | 248 | 3,347 | 2,221 |
| Sheridan.... | 428 | 2,138 | 223 | 1,156 | 2,440 |
| Sherman.... | 748 | 718 | 143 | 1,632 | 762 |
| Sioux...... | 155 | 540 | 60 | 379 | 698 |
| Stanton.... | 397 | 1,341 | 146 | 1,014 | 1,299 |
| Thayer..... | 1,019 | 2,200 | 165 | 2,298 | 2,132 |
| Thomas.... | 72 | 332 | 29 | 212 | 319 |
| Thurston... | 773 | 1,255 | 201 | 1,700 | 1,194 |
| Valley..... | 811 | 1,928 | 163 | 1,545 | 1,657 |
| Washington. | 1,102 | 2,688 | 382 | 2,701 | 2,638 |
| Wayne..... | 736 | 2,446 | 184 | 1,630 | 2,359 |
| Webster.... | 750 | 1,415 | 176 | 1,657 | 1,191 |
| Wheeler.... | 132 | 309 | 44 | 248 | 317 |
| York...... | 1,185 | 3,731 | 251 | 2,832 | 3,410 |
| **Totals...** | **163,592** | **301,312** | **42,288** | **307,307** | **276,847** |

#### NEBRASKA VOTE SINCE 1920

1920 (Pres.), Cox, Dem., 119,608; Harding, Rep., 247,498; Watkins, Proh., 5,947; Debs, Soc., 9,600.
1924 (Pres.), Coolidge, Rep., 218,585; Davis, Dem., 137,289; LaFollette, Prog., 106,701; Faris, Proh., 1,594.
1928 (Pres.), Hoover, Rep., 349,745; Smith, Dem., 197,959; Thomas, Soc., 3,434.
1932 (Pres.), Roosevelt, Dem., 359,082; Hoover, Rep., 201,177; Thomas, Soc., 9,876.
1936 (Pres.), Roosevelt, Dem., 347,454; Landon, Rep., 248,731; Lemke, Union, 12,847.
1940 (Pres.), Roosevelt, Dem., 263,677; Willkie, Rep., 352,201.
1944 (Pres.), Roosevelt, Dem., 233,246; Dewey, Rep., 329,880.
1948 (Pres.), Truman, Dem., 224,165; Dewey, Rep., 264,774.

**Nebraska (cont'd)**

1952 (Pres.), Eisenhower, Rep., 421,603; Stevenson, Dem., 188,057.
1956 (Pres.), Eisenhower, Rep., 378,108; Stevenson, Dem., 199,029.
1960 (Pres.), Kennedy, Dem., 232,542; Nixon, Rep., 380,553.
1964 (Pres.), Johnson, Dem., 307,307; Goldwater, Rep., 276,847.
1968 (Pres.), Nixon, Rep., 301,312; Humphrey, Dem., 163,592; Wallace, 3rd party, 42,288.

## Nevada

| County | 1968 | | | 1964 | |
|---|---|---|---|---|---|
| | Humphrey (D) | Nixon (R) | Wallace (I) | Johnson (D) | Goldwater (R) |
| Churchill ... | 1,211 | 1,953 | 575 | 1,565 | 1,607 |
| Clark ...... | 32,173 | 30,005 | 9,960 | 40,760 | 23,921 |
| Douglas.... | 670 | 1,790 | 327 | 1,010 | 1,127 |
| Elko ...... | 1,686 | 2,986 | 559 | 2,785 | 1,856 |
| Esmeralda.. | 118 | 138 | 97 | 187 | 131 |
| Eureka..... | 149 | 277 | 64 | 285 | 243 |
| Humboldt... | 885 | 1,282 | 353 | 1,421 | 1,106 |
| Lander..... | 302 | 461 | 147 | 391 | 338 |
| Lincoln..... | 414 | 655 | 144 | 785 | 440 |
| Lyon...... | 939 | 1,526 | 444 | 1,327 | 1,397 |
| Mineral.... | 1,242 | 927 | 700 | 1,440 | 927 |
| Nye....... | 699 | 976 | 500 | 1,276 | 822 |
| Ormsby.... | 1,170 | 3,159 | 662 | 2,129 | 1,997 |
| Pershing.... | 466 | 567 | 180 | 738 | 486 |
| Storey...... | 182 | 222 | 50 | 261 | 172 |
| Washoe..... | 14,662 | 23,467 | 4,933 | 20,170 | 18,350 |
| White Pine.. | 2,062 | 1,570 | 376 | 2,809 | 1,174 |
| **Totals ...** | **58,999** | **71,961** | **20,071** | **79,339** | **56,094** |

### NEVADA VOTE SINCE 1920

1920 (Pres.), Cox, Dem., 9,851; Harding, Rep., 15,479; Debs, Soc., 1,864.
1924 (Pres.), Coolidge, Rep., 11,243; LaFollette, Prog., 9,769; Davis, Dem., 5,909.
1928 (Pres.), Hoover, Rep., 18,327; Smith, Dem., 14,090.
1932 (Pres.), Roosevelt, Dem., 28,756; Hoover, Rep., 12,674.
1936 (Pres.), Roosevelt, Dem., 31,925; Landon, Rep., 11,923.
1940 (Pres.), Roosevelt, Dem., 31,945; Willkie, Rep., 21,229.
1944 (Pres.), Roosevelt, Dem., 29,623; Dewey, Rep., 24,611.
1948 (Pres.), Truman, Dem., 31,291; Dewey, Rep., 29,357; Wallace, Prog., 1,469.
1952 (Pres.), Eisenhower, Rep., 50,502; Stevenson, Dem., 31,688.
1956 (Pres.), Eisenhower, Rep., 56,049; Stevenson, Dem., 40,640.
1960 (Pres.), Kennedy, Dem., 54,880; Nixon, Rep., 52,387.
1964 (Pres.), Johnson, Dem., 79,339; Goldwater, Rep., 56,094.
1968 (Pres.), Nixon, Rep., 71,961; Humphrey, Dem., 58,999; Wallace, 3rd party, 20,071.

## New Hampshire

| County | 1968 | | | 1964 | |
|---|---|---|---|---|---|
| | Humphrey (D) | Nixon (R) | Wallace (I) | Johnson (D) | Goldwater (R) |
| Belknap.... | 4,942 | 8,642 | 454 | 8,024 | 5,908 |
| Carroll ..... | 2,163 | 6,795 | 348 | 4,058 | 4,957 |
| Cheshire ... | 9,135 | 10,702 | 441 | 13,626 | 5,958 |
| Coos...... | 8,261 | 6,822 | 399 | 11,956 | 4,823 |
| Grafton .... | 7,813 | 12,881 | 727 | 12,566 | 8,461 |
| Hill'boro'gh | 45,423 | 42,409 | 4,231 | 58,237 | 29,503 |
| Merrimack.. | 12,711 | 19,289 | 1,201 | 19,818 | 12,564 |
| Rockingh'm. | 21,195 | 28,842 | 2,333 | 27,256 | 19,498 |
| Strafford.... | 13,129 | 12,427 | 650 | 17,737 | 8,342 |
| Sullivan.... | 5,817 | 6,094 | 389 | 8,787 | 3,975 |
| **Totals ...** | **130,589** | **154,903** | **11,173** | **182,065** | **104,029** |

### NEW HAMPSHIRE VOTE SINCE 1920

1920 (Pres.), Cox, Dem., 62,662; Harding, Rep., 95,196; Debs, Soc., 1,234.
1924 (Pres.), Coolidge, Rep., 98,575; Davis, Dem., 57,201; LaFollette, Prog., 8,993.
1928 (Pres.), Hoover, Rep., 115,404; Smith, Dem., 80,715; Thomas, Soc., 455; Foster, Com., 173.
1932 (Pres.), Roosevelt, Dem., 100,680; Hoover, Rep., 103,629; Thomas, Soc., 947; Foster, Com., 264.
1936 (Pres.), Roosevelt, Dem., 108,460; Landon, Rep., 104,642; Lemke, Union, 4,819; Browder, Com., 193.

**New Hampshire (cont'd)**

1940 (Pres.), Roosevelt, Dem., 125,292; Willkie, Rep., 110,127.
1944 (Pres.), Roosevelt, Dem., 119,663; Dewey, Rep., 109,916; Thomas, Soc., 46.
1948 (Pres.), Truman, Dem., 107,995; Dewey, Rep., 121,299; Wallace, Prog., 1,970; Thomas, Soc., 86; Teichert, Soc. Lab., 83; Thurmond, States' Rights, 7.
1952 (Pres.), Eisenhower, Rep., 166,287; Stevenson, Dem., 106,663.
1956 (Pres.), Eisenhower, Rep., 176,519; Stevenson, Dem., 90,364; Andrews, Const., 111.
1960 (Pres.), Kennedy, Dem., 137,772; Nixon, Rep., 157,989.
1964 (Pres.), Johnson, Dem., 182,065; Goldwater, Rep., 104,029.
1968 (Pres.), Nixon, Rep., 154,903; Humphrey, Dem., 130,589; Wallace, 3rd party, 11,173; scattered 525.

## New Jersey

| County | 1968 | | | 1964 | |
|---|---|---|---|---|---|
| | Humphrey (D) | Nixon (R) | Wallace (I) | Johnson (D) | Goldwater (R) |
| Atlantic.... | 35,581 | 32,807 | 7,528 | 50,945 | 25,626 |
| Bergen..... | 162,182 | 224,911 | 23,663 | 234,849 | 157,899 |
| Burlington.. | 41,651 | 46,177 | 11,635 | 57,638 | 31,215 |
| Camden.... | 87,347 | 77,642 | 23,111 | 124,620 | 60,844 |
| Cape May .. | 9,664 | 14,970 | 3,498 | 14,943 | 11,390 |
| Cumberland. | 21,661 | 18,388 | 5,356 | 33,593 | 12,611 |
| Essex ..... | 185,440 | 140,084 | 26,823 | 277,042 | 116,172 |
| Gloucester.. | 27,438 | 30,596 | 10,626 | 40,305 | 23,702 |
| Hudson..... | 124,939 | 91,324 | 23,138 | 200,051 | 69,515 |
| Hunterdon.. | 8,755 | 15,851 | 2,749 | 15,091 | 10,173 |
| Mercer..... | 63,218 | 45,354 | 16,104 | 86,985 | 35,081 |
| Middlesex... | 103,339 | 96,513 | 24,136 | 151,196 | 63,370 |
| Monmouth.. | 69,669 | 87,311 | 13,047 | 95,320 | 61,367 |
| Morris..... | 52,398 | 85,512 | 9,659 | 73,684 | 55,024 |
| Ocean..... | 26,909 | 41,995 | 8,520 | 36,892 | 25,985 |
| Passaic..... | 74,442 | 79,862 | 16,617 | 113,919 | 63,114 |
| Salem...... | 11,172 | 11,407 | 3,647 | 17,846 | 8,682 |
| Somerset... | 27,580 | 42,459 | 7,331 | 43,659 | 28,416 |
| Sussex...... | 8,325 | 18,043 | 2,843 | 14,349 | 11,836 |
| Union ..... | 109,674 | 110,309 | 19,963 | 164,989 | 82,999 |
| Warren..... | 12,822 | 13,950 | 2,197 | 19,755 | 8,822 |
| **Totals ...** | **1,264,-206** | **1,325,-465** | **262,164** | **1,867,-671** | **963,843** |

### NEW JERSEY VOTE SINCE 1920

1920 (Pres.), Cox, Dem., 258,229; Harding, Rep., 611,670; Watkins, Proh., 4,711; Debs, Soc., 27,217; Christensen, Farm Lab., 2,173.
1924 (Pres.), Coolidge, Rep., 676,277; Davis, Dem., 298,043; LaFollette, Prog., 109,028; Faris, Proh., 1,660; Foster, Workers, 1,560; Johns, Soc. Lab., 358.
1928 (Pres.), Smith, Dem., 616,517; Hoover, Rep., 926,050; Foster, Com., 1,257; Reynolds, Soc. Lab., 500.
1932 (Pres.), Roosevelt, Dem., 806,630; Hoover, Rep., 775,684; Thomas, Soc., 42,998; Foster, Com., 2,915; Reynolds, Soc. Lab., 1,062; Upshaw, Proh., 774.
1936 (Pres.), Roosevelt, Dem., 1,083,549; Landon, Rep., 719,421; Lemke, Union, 9,405; Thomas, Soc., 3,895; Browder, Com., 1,590; Colvin, Proh., 916; Aiken, Soc. Lab., 346.
1940 (Pres.), Roosevelt, Dem., 1,016,404; Willkie, Rep., 944,876; Browder, Com., 8,814; Thomas, Soc., 2,823; Babson, Proh., 851; Aiken, Soc. Lab., 446.
1944 (Pres.), Roosevelt, Dem., 987,874; Dewey, Rep., 961,335; Teichert, Soc. Lab., 6,939; Watson, Nat'l Proh., 4,255; Thomas, Soc., 3,385.
1948 (Pres.), Truman, Dem., 895,455; Dewey, Rep., 981,124; Wallace, Prog., 42,683; Watson, Proh., 10,593; Thomas, Soc., 10,521; Dobbs, Soc. Workers, 5,825; Teichert, Soc. Lab., 3,354.
1952 (Pres.), Eisenhower, Rep., 1,373,613; Stevenson, Dem., 1,015,902; Hoopes, Soc., 8,593; Hass, Soc. Lab., 5,815; Hallinan, Prog., 5,589; Krajewski, Poor Man's, 4,203; Dobbs, Soc. Workers, 3,850; Hamblen, Proh., 989.
1956 (Pres.), Eisenhower, Rep., 1,606,942; Stevenson, Dem., 850,337; Holtwick, Proh., 9,147; Hass, Soc. Lab., 6,736; Andrews, Conservative, 5,317; Dobbs, Soc. Workers, 4,004; Krajewski, American Third Party, 1,829.
1960 (Pres.), Kennedy, Dem., 1,385,415; Nixon, Rep., 1,363,324; Dobbs, Soc. Workers, 11,402; Lee, Conservative, 8,708; Hass, Soc. Lab., 4,262.
1964 (Pres.), Johnson, Dem., 1,867,671; Goldwater, Rep., 963,843; DeBerry, Soc. Workers, 8,181; Hass, Soc. Labor, 7,075.
1968 (Pres.), Nixon, Rep., 1,325,465; Humphrey, Dem., 1,264,206; Wallace, 3rd party, 262,164; scattered, 23,683.

## New Mexico

| County | 1968 Humphrey (D) | Nixon (R) | Wallace (I) | 1964 Johnson (D) | Goldwater (R) |
|---|---|---|---|---|---|
| Bernalillo... | 40,456 | 55,553 | 4,886 | 55,036 | 42,583 |
| Catron..... | 273 | 686 | 128 | 624 | 584 |
| Chaves..... | 3,512 | 8,866 | 1,423 | 8,650 | 8,419 |
| Colfax..... | 2,477 | 2,212 | 262 | 3,367 | 1,636 |
| Curry..... | 2,915 | 5,583 | 1,750 | 5,228 | 5,120 |
| De Baca.... | 345 | 658 | 130 | 674 | 559 |
| Dona Ana... | 7,633 | 10,797 | 1,461 | 10,748 | 7,280 |
| Eddy..... | 6,088 | 7,160 | 1,672 | 11,216 | 6,747 |
| Grant..... | 3,817 | 2,907 | 793 | 5,253 | 2,042 |
| Guadalupe.. | 1,041 | 1,089 | 60 | 1,649 | 1,058 |
| Harding.... | 287 | 423 | 37 | 431 | 473 |
| Hidalgo.... | 678 | 606 | 257 | 995 | 628 |
| Lea..... | 4,746 | 7,405 | 3,020 | 8,862 | 7,033 |
| Lincoln.... | 803 | 2,003 | 287 | 1,565 | 1,761 |
| Los Alamos.. | 2,556 | 3,447 | 268 | 3,767 | 1,895 |
| Luna..... | 1,438 | 1,932 | 490 | 2,286 | 1,665 |
| McKinley... | 4,491 | 4,376 | 547 | 6,913 | 2,965 |
| Mora..... | 1,069 | 1,105 | 35 | 1,509 | 1,014 |
| Otero..... | 3,998 | 4,492 | 1,700 | 6,035 | 3,498 |
| Quay..... | 1,399 | 2,123 | 567 | 2,333 | 2,161 |
| Rio Arriba.. | 4,798 | 3,939 | 269 | 6,787 | 2,906 |
| Roosevelt.. | 1,547 | 3,254 | 738 | 2,875 | 2,732 |
| Sandoval... | 2,598 | 1,944 | 126 | 3,332 | 1,077 |
| San Juan.. | 5,032 | 7,748 | 2,302 | 6,901 | 6,808 |
| San Miguel. | 4,069 | 4,008 | 160 | 5,767 | 2,714 |
| Santa Fe... | 9,544 | 9,307 | 492 | 12,616 | 5,834 |
| Sierra..... | 930 | 1,624 | 251 | 1,633 | 1,501 |
| Socorro.... | 1,869 | 2,211 | 172 | 2,597 | 1,774 |
| Taos..... | 2,992 | 3,113 | 116 | 4,204 | 2,006 |
| Torrance... | 974 | 1,316 | 188 | 1,446 | 1,183 |
| Union..... | 654 | 1,199 | 267 | 1,159 | 1,232 |
| Valencia... | 5,415 | 5,572 | 708 | 7,757 | 3,950 |
| **Totals...** | **130,444** | **168,658** | **25,592** | **194,017** | **131,838** |

### NEW MEXICO VOTE SINCE 1920

1920 (Pres.), Cox, Dem., 46,668; Harding, Rep., 57,634; Christensen, F.-Lab., 1,097.
1924 (Pres.), Coolidge, Rep., 54,745; Davis, Dem., 48,542; LaFollette, Prog., 9,543.
1928 (Pres.), Hoover, Rep., 69,645; Smith, Dem., 48,211; Foster, Com., 158.
1932 (Pres.), Roosevelt, Dem., 95,089; Hoover, Rep., 54,217; Thomas, Soc., 1,776; Harvey, Lib. 389; Foster, Com., 135.
1936 (Pres.), Roosevelt, Dem., 105,838; Landon, Rep., 61,710; Lemke, Union, 942; Thomas, Soc., 343; Browder, Com., 43.
1940 (Pres.), Roosevelt, Dem., 103,699; Wilkie, Rep., 79,315.
1944 (Pres.), Roosevelt, Dem., 81,389; Dewey, Rep., 70,688; Watson, Proh., 148.
1948 (Pres.), Truman, Dem., 105,464; Dewey, Rep., 80,303; Wallace, Prog., 1,037; Watson, Proh., 127; Thomas, Soc., 83; Teichert, Soc. Lab., 49.
1952 (Pres.), Eisenhower, Rep., 132,170; Stevenson, Dem., 105,661; Hamblen, Proh, 297; Hallinan, Ind. Prog., 225; MacArthur, Christian National, 220; Hass, Soc. Lab., 35.
1956 (Pres.), Eisenhower, Rep., 146,788; Stevenson, Dem., 106,098; Holtwick, Proh., 607; Andrews, Ind., 364; Hass, Soc. Lab., 69.
1960 (Pres.), Kennedy, Dem., 156,027; Nixon, Rep., 153,733; Decker, Proh., 777; Hass, Soc. Lab., 570.
1964 (Pres.), Johnson, Dem., 194,017; Goldwater, Rep., 131,838; Hass, Soc. Labor, 1,217; Munn, Proh., 543.
1968 (Pres.), Nixon, Rep., 168,658; Humphrey, Dem., 130,444; Wallace, 3rd party, 25,592.

## New York

| County | 1968 Humphrey (D) | Nixon (R) | Wallace (I) | 1964 John son (D-L*) | Goldwater (R) |
|---|---|---|---|---|---|
| Albany..... | 76,452 | 52,219 | 4,946 | 114,827 | 32,224 |
| Alleghany.. | 4,911 | 10,957 | 821 | 10,329 | 7,688 |
| Broome..... | 36,852 | 46,501 | 4,348 | 59,021 | 32,048 |
| Cattaraugus | 12,356 | 16,395 | 1,595 | 21,994 | 10,907 |
| Cayuga..... | 14,541 | 16,084 | 1,808 | 24,090 | 11,453 |
| Chautauqua | 26,416 | 28,477 | 3,194 | 42,924 | 19,069 |
| Chemung... | 15,801 | 20,586 | 2,793 | 26,332 | 14,716 |
| Chenango.. | 5,714 | 11,852 | 675 | 11,553 | 7,293 |
| Clinton..... | 10,383 | 11,784 | 901 | 18,398 | 6,078 |
| Columbia.. | 7,832 | 13,836 | 1,362 | 14,516 | 9,023 |
| Cortland... | 5,752 | 10,301 | 726 | 11,110 | 6,149 |
| Delaware... | 5,366 | 12,341 | 1,123 | 11,686 | 8,359 |
| Dutchess .. | 30,985 | 44,881 | 5,615 | 50,179 | 29,503 |
| Erie..... | 244,449 | 163,067 | 32,457 | 344,910 | 125,962 |
| Essex..... | 3,932 | 9,291 | 773 | 10,739 | 5,837 |

**New York (cont'd)**

| County | 1968 Humphrey (D) | Nixon (R) | Wallace (I) | 1964 John son (D) | Goldwater (R) |
|---|---|---|---|---|---|
| Franklin.... | 6,624 | 8,126 | 262 | 12,467 | 4,846 |
| Fulton..... | 8,831 | 11,781 | 978 | 15,846 | 7,278 |
| Genesee.... | 9,534 | 12,420 | 1,126 | 15,713 | 8,114 |
| Greene..... | 6,183 | 9,997 | 827 | 10,034 | 7,842 |
| Hamilton... | 765 | 2,120 | 162 | 1,603 | 1,269 |
| Herkimer... | 10,711 | 14,913 | 1,352 | 20,136 | 10,159 |
| Jefferson... | 13,305 | 18,182 | 819 | 25,175 | 10,718 |
| Lewis..... | 3,179 | 5,459 | 368 | 6,584 | 3,185 |
| Livingston.. | 6,761 | 11,284 | 756 | 13,481 | 7,120 |
| Madison.... | 6,985 | 13,542 | 1,008 | 14,313 | 8,558 |
| Monroe.... | 142,003 | 142,902 | 10,663 | 205,226 | 80,099 |
| Montgom'y. | 11,563 | 12,470 | 1,123 | 19,370 | 8,471 |
| Niagara.... | 41,307 | 38,679 | 6,247 | 67,260 | 28,663 |
| Oneida.... | 44,154 | 51,968 | 5,582 | 73,359 | 39,737 |
| Onondaga.. | 82,494 | 93,168 | 8,394 | 128,630 | 63,205 |
| Ontario.... | 11,000 | 16,717 | 1,055 | 19,922 | 10,847 |
| Orange.... | 27,241 | 44,795 | 6,280 | 48,244 | 30,610 |
| Orleans.... | 4,883 | 8,760 | 635 | 9,304 | 5,567 |
| Oswego.... | 14,448 | 19,763 | 1,885 | 24,788 | 12,415 |
| Otsego..... | 7,752 | 13,267 | 1,075 | 15,190 | 8,643 |
| Putnam.... | 8,178 | 12,623 | 2,076 | 12,636 | 9,219 |
| Rensselaer.. | 30,618 | 34,487 | 3,415 | 51,170 | 20,814 |
| Rockland... | 39,146 | 42,808 | 5,260 | 46,173 | 26,187 |
| St. Law'ce.. | 15,361 | 20,532 | 1,026 | 29,173 | 12,102 |
| Saratoga... | 17,188 | 25,185 | 2,009 | 29,264 | 13,364 |
| Schenec'dy. | 34,526 | 33,036 | 3,175 | 51,892 | 21,848 |
| Schoharie.. | 4,229 | 6,224 | 705 | 7,187 | 4,193 |
| Schuyler... | 2,032 | 4,049 | 515 | 4,326 | 2,925 |
| Seneca..... | 5,151 | 6,966 | 568 | 8,890 | 4,473 |
| Steuben.... | 12,163 | 24,199 | 2,199 | 24,634 | 15,988 |
| Sullivan.... | 9,207 | 11,349 | 744 | 16,728 | 8,006 |
| Tioga..... | 5,156 | 10,158 | 1,060 | 10,411 | 7,147 |
| Tompkins... | 10,359 | 13,733 | 1,211 | 16,103 | 9,070 |
| Ulster..... | 20,056 | 33,770 | 3,995 | 35,486 | 23,749 |
| Warren..... | 6,492 | 12,925 | 792 | 12,772 | 7,834 |
| Washington | 6,612 | 12,535 | 916 | 13,826 | 8,160 |
| Wayne..... | 8,793 | 17,025 | 1,165 | 18,729 | 10,586 |
| Wyoming... | 4,431 | 8,407 | 770 | 8,866 | 6,099 |
| Yates..... | 2,113 | 5,513 | 389 | 4,983 | 3,675 |
| **Outside** | | | | | |
| N. Y. C... | 1,203,-266 | 1,354,-359 | 145,724 | 1,922,-602 | 899,394 |
| Nassau.... | 279,184 | 329,674 | 30,197 | 382,590 | 248,886 |
| Suffolk.... | 117,002 | 208,483 | 29,976 | 180,598 | 144,350 |
| Westchester | 172,344 | 201,017 | 21,386 | 243,723 | 149,052 |
| N. Y. Suburban.. | 567,998 | 741,562 | 81,517 | 806,911 | 542,288 |
| Bronx..... | 275,851 | 141,368 | 21,819 | 403,014 | 135,780 |
| Kings..... | 488,649 | 246,251 | 33,531 | 684,839 | 229,291 |
| New York. | 370,574 | 135,795 | 13,077 | 503,848 | 120,125 |
| Queens.... | 414,853 | 308,737 | 44,399 | 541,418 | 274,351 |
| Richmond.. | 34,829 | 54,671 | 9,073 | 50,524 | 42,330 |
| **Greater N. Y. C...** | 1,584,-756 | 886,822 | 121,899 | 2,183,-643 | 801,877 |
| **Totals...** | 3,356,-999 | 2,980,-420 | 348,205 | 4,913,-156 | 2,243,-559 |
| **Dem. Total** | | | | 4,570,-724 | |
| **Liberal....** | | | | 342,432 | |

*Democratic and Liberal.

### NEW YORK VOTE SINCE 1920

1920 (Pres.), Cox, Dem., 731,238; Harding, Rep., 1,871,167; Watkins, Proh., 19,653; Debs, Soc. 203,201; Christensen, F.-Lab., 18,413.
1924 (Pres.), Davis, Dem., 950,796; Coolidge, Rep., 1,820,058; LaFollette, Prog., 268,510; LaFollette, Soc., 198,783; Johns, Soc. Lab., 9,928; Foster, Workers, 8,228.
1928 (Pres.), Hoover, Rep., 2,193,344; Smith, Dem., 2,089,863; Thomas, Soc., 107,332; Reynolds, Soc. Lab., 4,206; Foster, Com., 10,884.
1932 (Pres.), Roosevelt, Dem., 2,534,959; Hoover, Rep., 1,937,963; Thomas, Soc., 177,397; Foster, Com., 27,956; Reynolds, Soc. Lab., 10,339.
1936 (Pres.), Roosevelt, Dem., 3,018,298; American Lab., 274,924; total, 3,293,222; Landon, Rep., 2,180,670; Thomas, Soc., 86,879; Browder, Com., 35,609.
1940 (Pres.), Roosevelt, Dem., 2,834,500; American Lab., 417,418; total 3,251,918; Willkie, Rep., 3,027,478; Thomas, Soc., 18,950; Babson, Proh., 3,250.
1944 (Pres.), Roosevelt, Dem., 2,478,598; American Lab., 496,405; Liberal, 329,325; total, 3,304,238; Dewey, Rep., 2,987,647; Teichert, Ind. Gov't, 14,352; Thomas, Soc., 10,553.
1948 (Pres.), Truman, Dem., 2,557,642; Liberal, 222,562; total, 2,780,204; Dewey, Rep., 2,841,163; Wallace. Amer. Lab., 509,559; Thomas, Soc., 40,879; Teichert, Ind. Gov't, 2,729; Dobbs, Soc. Workers, 2,675.
1952 (Pres.), Eisenhower, Rep., 3,952,815; Stevenson, Dem., 2,687,890, Liberal, 416,711; total,

**New York (cont'd)**

3,104,601; Hallinan, American Lab., 64,211;
Hoopes, Soc., 2,664; Dobbs, Soc. Workers, 2,212;
Hass, Ind. Gov't, 1,560; Scattering, 178; Blank
and void, 87,813.
1956 (Pres.), Eisenhower, Rep., 4,340,340; Stevenson, Dem., 2,458,212; Liberal, 292,557; total,
2,750,769. Write-in votes for Andrews, 1,027;
Werdel, 492; Hass, 150; Hoopes, 82; Others, 476.
1960 (Pres.), Kennedy, Dem., 3,423,909; Liberal,
406,176; total, 3,830,085. Nixon, Rep., 3,446,419;
Dobbs, Soc. Workers, 14,319; Scattering, 256;
Blank and void, 88,896.
1964 (Pres.) Johnson, Dem., 4,913,156; Goldwater,
Rep., 2,243,559; Hass, Soc. Labor, 6,085; DeBerry,
Soc. Worker, 3,215; Scattering, 188; Blank and
Void, 151,383.
1968 (Pres.), Nixon, Rep., 2,980,420; Humphrey,
Dem., 3,356,999; Wallace, 3rd party, 348,205;
scattered, 18,131.

## North Carolina

| County | 1968 Hum-phrey (D) | Nixon (R) | Wal-lace (I) | 1964 John-son (D) | Gold-water (R) |
|---|---|---|---|---|---|
| Alamance... | 8,241 | 12,310 | 13,139 | 15,397 | 15,177 |
| Alexander... | 1,834 | 4,379 | 2,203 | 3,722 | 3,760 |
| Alleghany... | 1,102 | 1,695 | 904 | 2,368 | 1,573 |
| Anson...... | 2,969 | 1,474 | 3,571 | 4,144 | 1,721 |
| Ashe........ | 3,426 | 4,894 | 888 | 4,965 | 4,191 |
| Avery....... | 631 | 3,197 | 690 | 1,523 | 2,653 |
| Beaufort... | 3,232 | 2,669 | 5,686 | 6,090 | 3,595 |
| Bertie...... | 3,207 | 811 | 3,108 | 3,332 | 931 |
| Bladen..... | 2,754 | 1,746 | 3,897 | 4,516 | 2,169 |
| Brunswick.. | 2,972 | 2,404 | 3,358 | 4,240 | 3,721 |
| Buncombe.. | 14,624 | 21,031 | 11,889 | 31,623 | 19,372 |
| Burke...... | 5,704 | 11,068 | 5,892 | 12,815 | 10,081 |
| Cabarrus... | 5,501 | 13,226 | 6,538 | 11,921 | 13,178 |
| Caldwell... | 4,746 | 10,433 | 5,095 | 10,846 | 8,733 |
| Camden.... | 707 | 180 | 1,100 | 870 | 534 |
| Carteret... | 3,762 | 4,593 | 3,061 | 6,231 | 4,289 |
| Caswell.... | 2,137 | 1,036 | 2,851 | 2,513 | 1,793 |
| Catawba... | 6,974 | 18,393 | 7,285 | 15,814 | 17,116 |
| Chatham... | 3,532 | 3,845 | 3,239 | 5,295 | 4,111 |
| Cherokee... | 2,402 | 3,768 | 915 | 3,823 | 3,106 |
| Chowan.... | 1,201 | 798 | 1,696 | 1,696 | 787 |
| Clay....... | 847 | 1,390 | 293 | 1,457 | 1,286 |
| Cleveland.. | 5,661 | 7,298 | 9,649 | 10,876 | 7,874 |
| Columbus.. | 4,243 | 3,881 | 6,693 | 9,004 | 4,471 |
| Craven..... | 4,240 | 2,991 | 6,509 | 7,422 | 4,691 |
| Cumberland | 9,938 | 9,143 | 9,539 | 13,864 | 9,093 |
| Currituck... | 738 | 363 | 1,471 | 1,455 | 741 |
| Dare....... | 700 | 1,035 | 844 | 1,476 | 867 |
| Davidson... | 7,594 | 16,678 | 11,544 | 13,735 | 17,292 |
| Davie...... | 1,502 | 3,866 | 2,515 | 3,086 | 4,460 |
| Duplin..... | 3,451 | 2,724 | 6,082 | 7,169 | 3,821 |
| Durham.... | 16,563 | 12,705 | 13,542 | 22,874 | 15,264 |
| Edgecombe | 5,243 | 3,198 | 5,861 | 7,834 | 3,932 |
| Forsyth..... | 20,281 | 31,623 | 15,681 | 31,615 | 30,276 |
| Franklin.... | 2,855 | 1,375 | 5,525 | 4,554 | 2,097 |
| Gaston..... | 10,100 | 18,741 | 13,973 | 20,197 | 17,129 |
| Gates...... | 1,151 | 406 | 1,227 | 1,702 | 556 |
| Graham.... | 1,061 | 1,570 | 363 | 1,737 | 1,398 |
| Granville... | 2,638 | 1,837 | 4,071 | 4,596 | 2,624 |
| Greene..... | 1,560 | 650 | 2,906 | 2,712 | 901 |
| Guilford.... | 25,604 | 38,996 | 19,751 | 39,969 | 35,635 |
| Halifax..... | 4,927 | 3,148 | 7,116 | 8,952 | 4,757 |
| Harnett.... | 4,007 | 5,184 | 6,531 | 7,477 | 5,883 |
| Haywood... | 5,703 | 6,205 | 3,898 | 10,664 | 5,575 |
| Henderson.. | 3,053 | 9,334 | 3,861 | 6,066 | 8,780 |
| Hertford... | 3,275 | 1,125 | 2,203 | 3,953 | 994 |
| Hoke....... | 2,185 | 812 | 1,545 | 2,254 | 779 |
| Hyde....... | 769 | 401 | 533 | 1,127 | 514 |
| Iredell..... | 4,878 | 10,557 | 9,021 | 11,231 | 12,892 |
| Jackson.... | 2,956 | 3,747 | 1,080 | 4,905 | 3,183 |
| Johnston... | 4,492 | 6,764 | 9,212 | 10,326 | 7,523 |
| Jones...... | 1,225 | 361 | 1,780 | 2,129 | 776 |
| Lee........ | 2,524 | 2,586 | 3,711 | 4,730 | 2,753 |
| Lenoir..... | 3,853 | 3,844 | 8,036 | 7,617 | 5,617 |
| Lincoln.... | 4,044 | 6,188 | 3,161 | 7,304 | 5,869 |
| Macon..... | 2,070 | 3,295 | 1,162 | 3,774 | 2,900 |
| Madison... | 2,201 | 3,130 | 1,034 | 3,829 | 3,336 |
| Martin..... | 3,118 | 1,221 | 3,818 | 4,821 | 1,511 |
| McDowell.. | 2,543 | 4,740 | 3,018 | 6,314 | 4,174 |
| Mecklenb'g | 31,102 | 56,325 | 20,070 | 49,582 | 46,589 |
| Mitchell.... | 819 | 3,778 | 603 | 1,736 | 3,263 |
| Montgom'y. | 2,410 | 3,070 | 2,259 | 3,933 | 3,385 |
| Moore...... | 3,583 | 5,322 | 3,263 | 6,384 | 5,162 |
| Nash....... | 5,283 | 4,602 | 9,230 | 9,163 | 6,396 |
| New Han'er. | 7,750 | 10,020 | 9,291 | 12,584 | 12,140 |
| Northampton | 4,072 | 860 | 2,986 | 5,046 | 1,187 |
| Onslow..... | 3,281 | 3,444 | 5,542 | 5,955 | 3,771 |
| Orange..... | 8,366 | 6,097 | 3,845 | 9,206 | 5,785 |
| Pamlico.... | 1,280 | 745 | 1,447 | 1,864 | 1,036 |
| Pasquotank. | 2,564 | 1,430 | 3,597 | 4,269 | 2,380 |
| Pender..... | 1,942 | 1,007 | 2,720 | 3,205 | 1,961 |
| Perquimans. | 1,023 | 468 | 1,554 | 1,458 | 941 |
| Person..... | 2,644 | 2,138 | 4,065 | 4,742 | 2,162 |
| Pitt........ | 7,696 | 5,745 | 9,167 | 11,317 | 5,149 |
| Polk....... | 1,523 | 2,550 | 1,484 | 3,013 | 2,765 |
| Randolph... | 5,351 | 13,450 | 6,892 | 10,639 | 13,739 |

| No. Carolina (cont'd) County | 1968 Hum-phrey (D) | Nixon (R) | Wal-lace (I) | 1964 John-son (D) | Gold-water (R) |
|---|---|---|---|---|---|
| Richmond.. | 4,257 | 2,865 | 5,457 | 8,516 | 3,123 |
| Robeson... | 8,248 | 4,526 | 6,441 | 13,796 | 3,591 |
| Rockingham | 6,774 | 8,095 | 9,324 | 11,432 | 9,063 |
| Rowan..... | 8,074 | 15,207 | 9,220 | 14,934 | 14,804 |
| Rutherford.. | 4,622 | 7,785 | 4,476 | 9,541 | 7,115 |
| Sampson... | 4,797 | 6,597 | 4,527 | 8,067 | 7,634 |
| Scotland.... | 2,252 | 1,717 | 2,016 | 3,844 | 1,229 |
| Stanly...... | 4,199 | 9,428 | 4,706 | 7,931 | 8,924 |
| Stokes...... | 2,374 | 4,781 | 3,410 | 4,898 | 4,664 |
| Surry...... | 5,088 | 9,638 | 4,103 | 9,810 | 7,970 |
| Swain...... | 1,227 | 1,494 | 537 | 2,294 | 1,534 |
| Transylvania | 2,210 | 4,033 | 2,365 | 4,483 | 3,547 |
| Tyrrell..... | 581 | 291 | 415 | 996 | 374 |
| Union...... | 3,630 | 5,290 | 4,761 | 7,208 | 4,229 |
| Vance...... | 3,852 | 2,252 | 5,244 | 5,186 | 3,452 |
| Wake...... | 20,979 | 28,928 | 17,250 | 31,653 | 22,542 |
| Warren..... | 2,293 | 796 | 2,294 | 2,849 | 1,909 |
| Washington. | 1,898 | 1,016 | 1,866 | 2,505 | 1,144 |
| Watauga... | 2,952 | 5,081 | 1,060 | 4,031 | 3,932 |
| Wayne..... | 5,338 | 5,678 | 8,709 | 9,791 | 7,555 |
| Wilkes..... | 4,497 | 11,195 | 2,876 | 9,176 | 11,014 |
| Wilson..... | 4,173 | 4,053 | 7,903 | 7,238 | 5,002 |
| Yadkin..... | 1,443 | 5,885 | 2,397 | 3,638 | 5,860 |
| Yancey..... | 2,215 | 2,448 | 752 | 3,714 | 2,004 |
| **Totals ....** | **464,113** | **627,192** | **496,188** | **800,139** | **624,844** |

### NORTH CAROLINA VOTE SINCE 1920

1920 (Pres.), Cox, Dem., 305,447; Harding, Rep.,
232,848; Watkins, Proh., 17; Debs, Soc., 446.
1924 (Pres.), Davis, Dem., 284,270; Coolidge, Rep.,
191,753; LaFollette, Prog., 6,651; Faris, Proh., 13.
1928 (Pres.), Hoover, Rep., 348,923; Smith, Dem.,
286,227.
1932 (Pres.), Roosevelt, Dem., 497,566; Hoover,
Rep., 208,344; Thomas, Soc., 5,591.
1936 (Pres.), Roosevelt, Dem., 616,141; Landon,
Rep., 223,283; Thomas, Soc., 21; Browder, Com.,
11; Lemke, Union, 2.
1940 (Pres.), Roosevelt, Dem., 609,015; Wilkie,
Rep., 213,633.
1944 (Pres.), Roosevelt, Dem., 527,399; Dewey,
Rep., 263,155.
1948 (Pres.), Truman, Dem., 459,070; Dewey, Rep.,
258,572; Thurmond, States' Rights, 69,652; Wallace, Prog., 3,915.
1952 (Pres.), Eisenhower, Rep., 558,107; Stevenson,
Dem., 652,803.
1956 (Pres.), Eisenhower, Rep., 575,062; Stevenson,
Dem., 590,530.
1960 (Pres.), Kennedy, Dem., 713,136; Nixon, Rep.,
655,420.
1964 (Pres.), Johnson, Dem., 800,139; Goldwater,
Rep., 624,844.
1968 (Pres.), Nixon, Rep., 627,192; Humphrey,
Dem., 464,113; Wallace, 3rd party, 496,188.

## North Dakota

| County | 1968 Hum-phrey (D) | Nixon (R) | Wal-lace (I) | 1964 John-son (D) | Gold-water (R) |
|---|---|---|---|---|---|
| Adams..... | 641 | 1,020 | 116 | 1,010 | 877 |
| Barnes..... | 2,623 | 3,831 | 348 | 4,007 | 2,987 |
| Benson..... | 1,772 | 1,707 | 164 | 2,566 | 1,489 |
| Billings.... | 174 | 395 | 69 | 348 | 340 |
| Bottineau... | 1,520 | 2,631 | 230 | 2,546 | 2,060 |
| Bowman.... | 559 | 927 | 156 | 1,070 | 756 |
| Burke...... | 808 | 1,239 | 132 | 1,454 | 974 |
| Burleigh... | 5,139 | 10,661 | 818 | 8,120 | 7,239 |
| Cass....... | 10,819 | 15,240 | 1,167 | 15,674 | 12,972 |
| Cavalier... | 1,631 | 1,953 | 257 | 2,810 | 1,417 |
| Dickey..... | 1,098 | 2,087 | 161 | 1,818 | 1,808 |
| Divide..... | 914 | 1,032 | 102 | 1,498 | 779 |
| Dunn...... | 772 | 1,207 | 169 | 1,351 | 1,079 |
| Eddy....... | 893 | 1,018 | 76 | 1,337 | 747 |
| Emmons.... | 756 | 1,991 | 311 | 1,556 | 1,759 |
| Foster..... | 897 | 1,119 | 123 | 1,315 | 927 |
| Golden Val.. | 348 | 735 | 115 | 640 | 722 |
| Grand Forks | 7,695 | 9,802 | 1,332 | 10,740 | 7,367 |
| Grant...... | 488 | 1,648 | 157 | 1,063 | 1,421 |
| Griggs..... | 1,008 | 1,110 | 109 | 1,505 | 885 |
| Hettinger... | 638 | 1,424 | 163 | 1,275 | 1,188 |
| Kidder..... | 548 | 1,204 | 192 | 1,047 | 1,104 |
| La Moure... | 1,269 | 2,008 | 189 | 2,145 | 1,604 |
| Logan...... | 459 | 1,416 | 135 | 951 | 1,187 |
| McHenry... | 1,595 | 2,226 | 281 | 2,643 | 1,728 |
| McIntosh... | 342 | 2,258 | 129 | 950 | 1,891 |
| McKenzie... | 935 | 1,625 | 164 | 1,584 | 1,352 |
| McLean.... | 2,050 | 2,764 | 216 | 3,339 | 2,204 |
| Mercer..... | 730 | 2,039 | 169 | 1,310 | 1,540 |
| Morton..... | 3,156 | 4,465 | 489 | 5,173 | 2,955 |
| Mountrail... | 1,662 | 1,494 | 212 | 2,548 | 1,131 |
| Nelson..... | 1,477 | 1,526 | 157 | 2,186 | 1,101 |
| Oliver..... | 269 | 616 | 85 | 548 | 469 |
| Pembina.... | 1,686 | 2,574 | 335 | 3,198 | 1,961 |

| No. Dakota (cont'd) | 1968 | | | 1964 | |
|---|---|---|---|---|---|
| County | Humphrey (D) | Nixon (R) | Wallace (I) | Johnson (D) | Goldwater (R) |
| Pierce...... | 1,048 | 1,700 | 229 | 1,893 | 1,178 |
| Ramsey.... | 2,384 | 3,189 | 269 | 3,572 | 2,409 |
| Ransom.... | 1,286 | 1,943 | 153 | 2,063 | 1,647 |
| Renville. ... | 880 | 851 | 84 | 1,356 | 640 |
| Richland.... | 3,098 | 4,224 | 443 | 4,525 | 3,425 |
| Rolette...... | 1,870 | 1,211 | 172 | 2,566 | 892 |
| Sargent.... | 1,308 | 1,386 | 154 | 1,840 | 1,189 |
| Sheridan.... | 350 | 1,295 | 79 | 724 | 1,187 |
| Sioux...... | 525 | 482 | 58 | 695 | 314 |
| Slope...... | 238 | 379 | 64 | 436 | 329 |
| Stark...... | 2,577 | 4,365 | 500 | 4,270 | 2,888 |
| Steele...... | 991 | 952 | 88 | 1,404 | 796 |
| Stutsman... | 3,532 | 5,162 | 477 | 5,463 | 3,990 |
| Towner.... | 990 | 1,109 | 124 | 1,628 | 788 |
| Traill...... | 1,740 | 2,692 | 243 | 2,614 | 2,312 |
| Walsh...... | 2,948 | 3,410 | 453 | 4,911 | 2,454 |
| Ward...... | 7,105 | 9,079 | 896 | 10,871 | 6,798 |
| Wells...... | 1,265 | 2,266 | 247 | 2,314 | 1,875 |
| Williams... | 3,263 | 3,980 | 483 | 5,352 | 3,076 |
| **Totals...** | **94,319** | **138,667** | **14,244** | **149,784** | **108,207** |

### NORTH DAKOTA VOTE SINCE 1920

1920 (Pres.), Cox, Dem., 37,422; Harding, Rep., 160,072; Debs, Soc., 8,282.

1924 (Pres.), Coolidge, Rep., 94,931; LaFollette, Prog., 89,922; Davis, Dem., 13,858; Foster, Workers, 370.

1928 (Pres.), Hoover, Rep., 131,441; Smith, Dem., 106,648; Thomas, Soc., 842; Foster, Com., 936.

1932 (Pres.), Roosevelt, Dem., 178,350; Hoover, Rep., 71,772; Harvey, Lib., 1,817; Thomas, Soc., 3,521; Foster, Com., 830.

1936 (Pres.), Roosevelt, Dem., 163,148; Landon, Rep., 72,751; Lemke, Union, 36,708; Thomas, Soc., 552; Browder, Com., 360; Colvin, Proh., 197.

**1940 (Pres.), Roosevelt, Dem., 124,036; Willkie,** Rep., 154,590; Thomas, Soc., 1,279; Knutson, Com., 545; Babson, Proh., 325.

1944 (Pres.), Roosevelt, Dem., 100,144; Dewey, Rep., 118,535; Thomas, Soc., 943; Watson, Proh., 549.

1948 (Pres.), Truman, Dem., 95,812; Dewey, Rep., 115,139; Wallace, Prog., 8,391; Thomas, Soc., 1,000; Thurmond, States' Rights, 374.

1952 (Pres.), Eisenhower, Rep., 191,712; Stevenson, Dem., 76,694; MacArthur, Christian Nationalist, 1,075; Hallinan, Prog., 344; Hamblen, Proh., 302.

1956 (Pres.), Eisenhower, Rep., 156,766; Stevenson, Dem., 96,742; Andrews, American, 483.

1960 (Pres.), Kennedy, Dem., 123,963; Nixon, Rep., 154,310; Dobbs, Soc. Workers, 158.

1964 (Pres.), Johnson, Dem., 149,784; Goldwater, Rep., 108,207; DeBerry, Soc. Worker, 224; Munn, Proh., 174.

1968 (Pres.), Nixon, Rep., 138,667; Humphrey, Dem., 94,319; Wallace, 3rd party, 14,244; scattered, 198.

# Ohio

| County | 1968 | | | 1964 | |
|---|---|---|---|---|---|
| | Humphrey (D) | Nixon (R) | Wallace (I) | Johnson (D) | Goldwater (R) |
| Adams..... | 2,685 | 3,978 | 1,049 | 5,005 | 3,702 |
| Allen...... | 10,808 | 22,956 | 4,198 | 18,990 | 19,897 |
| Ashland.... | 4,547 | 9,744 | 1,321 | 8,493 | 7,308 |
| Ashtabula.. | 16,736 | 17,052 | 2,751 | 24,104 | 13,183 |
| Athens..... | 7,350 | 7,736 | 1,207 | 10,653 | 6,211 |
| Auglaize.... | 5,550 | 9,368 | 1,527 | 8,632 | 7,954 |
| Belmont.... | 22,673 | 11,322 | 2,475 | 28,180 | 9,693 |
| Brown..... | 3,621 | 4,700 | 2,307 | 6,983 | 3,904 |
| Butler..... | 23,649 | 35,962 | 14,208 | 42,278 | 31,413 |
| Carroll..... | 3,119 | 4,634 | 1,091 | 5,050 | 3,655 |
| Champaign . | 4,294 | 6,963 | 1,651 | 7,138 | 5,588 |
| Clark...... | 24,029 | 23,745 | 6,714 | 34,275 | 19,112 |
| Clermont... | 9,041 | 15,506 | 7,868 | 16,523 | 13,367 |
| Clinton..... | 2,978 | 6,259 | 1,829 | 6,514 | 6,082 |
| Columbiana. | 19,384 | 19,952 | 3,876 | 28,706 | 15,827 |
| Coshocton.. | 5,012 | 7,254 | 1,279 | 8,332 | 5,965 |
| Crawford... | 6,736 | 11,903 | 2,373 | 11,968 | 8,970 |
| Cuyahoga.. | 358,488 | 235,769 | 71,014 | 492,911 | 196,436 |
| Darke..... | 7,360 | 10,922 | 2,013 | 12,433 | 8,581 |
| Defiance.... | 6,226 | 7,353 | 925 | 8,707 | 5,048 |
| Delaware... | 4,056 | 9,029 | 2,557 | 8,080 | 8,395 |
| Erie...... | 11,390 | 13,023 | 2,437 | 15,968 | 9,981 |
| Fairfield.... | 9,540 | 14,785 | 4,127 | 15,611 | 11,480 |
| Fayette.... | 2,964 | 5,235 | 1,962 | 6,128 | 4,567 |
| Franklin... | 101,112 | 148,884 | 37,470 | 154,527 | 131,345 |
| Fulton..... | 3,338 | 7,816 | 1,033 | 5,604 | 5,973 |
| Gallia...... | 2,660 | 5,139 | 1,039 | 4,740 | 4,408 |
| Geauga.... | 4,784 | 11,795 | 3,230 | 12,212 | 9,423 |
| Greene..... | 14,922 | 17,012 | 5,899 | 21,276 | 14,571 |
| Guernsey... | 5,814 | 7,342 | 1,692 | 9,503 | 6,429 |

| Ohio (cont'd) | 1968 | | | 1964 | |
|---|---|---|---|---|---|
| County | Humphrey (D) | Nixon (R) | Wallace (I) | Johnson (D) | Goldwater (R) |
| Hamilton... | 133,359 | 182,440 | 46,243 | 199,127 | 161,179 |
| Hancock.... | 6,912 | 15,030 | 2,656 | 11,547 | 11,610 |
| Hardin..... | 4,180 | 6,963 | 1,794 | 7,324 | 5,679 |
| Harrison.... | 3,593 | 3,532 | 1,874 | 5,159 | 2,928 |
| Henry..... | 3,256 | 6,970 | 799 | 5,845 | 5,094 |
| Highland... | 3,831 | 6,495 | 2,208 | 7,281 | 5,985 |
| Hocking.... | 3,701 | 4,001 | 1,004 | 5,951 | 2,858 |
| Holmes..... | 1,898 | 3,350 | 479 | 3,559 | 2,106 |
| Huron..... | 5,495 | 8,044 | 1,451 | 10,780 | 7,655 |
| Jackson.... | 4,023 | 6,044 | 1,048 | 7,056 | 4,949 |
| Jefferson... | 21,306 | 12,926 | 3,736 | 33,039 | 11,784 |
| Knox...... | 5,729 | 9,070 | 1,696 | 11,222 | 7,258 |
| Lake...... | 27,930 | 28,454 | 9,120 | 38,552 | 23,282 |
| Lawrence... | 8,672 | 9,782 | 2,470 | 12,635 | 7,757 |
| Licking.... | 15,041 | 19,673 | 5,402 | 23,364 | 15,096 |
| Logan..... | 4,790 | 8,462 | 1,647 | 8,484 | 6,683 |
| Lorain..... | 42,607 | 34,141 | 8,819 | 55,755 | 26,683 |
| Lucas..... | 91,477 | 89,883 | 17,234 | 128,110 | 57,782 |
| Madison.... | 2,880 | 5,882 | 1,631 | 5,242 | 4,945 |
| Mahoning.. | 68,464 | 42,996 | 12,189 | 90,934 | 33,775 |
| Marion.... | 8,648 | 12,887 | 2,771 | 14,400 | 10,050 |
| Medina.... | 9,195 | 14,089 | 3,587 | 14,729 | 10,221 |
| Meigs...... | 2,835 | 5,528 | 775 | 5,133 | 3,373 |
| Mercer..... | 6,901 | 6,313 | 1,100 | 10,081 | 4,373 |
| Miami..... | 13,228 | 16,997 | 3,348 | 19,379 | 12,985 |
| Monroe.... | 3,109 | 2,683 | 567 | 4,776 | 1,944 |
| Montgomery | 95,201 | 84,000 | 26,095 | 126,633 | 71,979 |
| Morgan.... | 1,794 | 3,032 | 450 | 3,053 | 2,281 |
| Morrow.... | 2,195 | 4,901 | 1,509 | 4,572 | 4,194 |
| Muskingum. | 13,100 | 15,267 | 3,378 | 20,792 | 11,635 |
| Noble...... | 1,726 | 2,615 | 587 | 2,925 | 2,250 |
| Ottawa.... | 6,319 | 7,150 | 1,647 | 9,618 | 5,639 |
| Paulding... | 2,716 | 4,074 | 907 | 4,465 | 3,254 |
| Perry...... | 4,812 | 4,817 | 1,088 | 7,816 | 3,895 |
| Pickaway... | 3,536 | 6,690 | 2,296 | 7,310 | 5,317 |
| Pike...... | 3,445 | 3,241 | 1,427 | 5,331 | 2,567 |
| Portage.... | 16,340 | 15,061 | 5,889 | 23,308 | 10,842 |
| Preble..... | 3,807 | 6,546 | 2,173 | 7,574 | 5,839 |
| Putnam.... | 3,530 | 7,189 | 1,380 | 7,014 | 5,221 |
| Richland... | 14,987 | 23,484 | 5,301 | 24,799 | 18,833 |
| Ross...... | 6,873 | 11,277 | 4,087 | 12,704 | 9,623 |
| Sandusky... | 8,581 | 11,696 | 1,745 | 13,481 | 8,254 |
| Scioto..... | 13,835 | 15,214 | 3,167 | 21,559 | 13,465 |
| Seneca..... | 8,966 | 12,030 | 2,006 | 14,518 | 9,536 |
| Shelby..... | 6,479 | 7,248 | 1,499 | 10,004 | 5,190 |
| Stark...... | 57,714 | 68,414 | 16,855 | 88,704 | 53,632 |
| Summit.... | 99,977 | 82,591 | 26,182 | 142,319 | 68,000 |
| Trumbull... | 40,365 | 32,576 | 9,275 | 54,342 | 27,059 |
| Tuscarawas. | 15,632 | 14,306 | 2,740 | 23,623 | 9,962 |
| Union..... | 2,431 | 6,415 | 1,392 | 4,985 | 5,504 |
| Van Wert... | 4,359 | 7,850 | 1,329 | 7,695 | 6,194 |
| Vinton..... | 1,608 | 2,219 | 414 | 2,618 | 1,919 |
| Warren.... | 6,855 | 12,755 | 6,585 | 12,406 | 10,982 |
| Washington. | 6,922 | 11,888 | 1,697 | 11,193 | 8,873 |
| Wayne.... | 8,891 | 15,156 | 1,924 | 14,806 | 9,890 |
| Williams... | 4,501 | 8,059 | 970 | 7,547 | 5,653 |
| Wood...... | 10,887 | 16,210 | 2,947 | 16,304 | 12,142 |
| Wyandot... | 2,923 | 5,265 | 910 | 5,273 | 4,139 |
| **Totals...** | **1,692,-213** | **1,785,-318** | **468,591** | **2,498,-331** | **1,470,-865** |

### OHIO VOTE SINCE 1920

1920 (Pres.), Cox, Dem., 780,037; Harding, Rep., 1,182,022; Watkins, Proh., 294; Debs, Soc., 57,147.

1924 (Pres.), Coolidge, Rep., 1,176,130; Davis, Dem., 477,888; LaFollette, Prog., 357,948; Johns, Soc. Lab., 3,025; Wallace, Comm. Land., 1,246.

1928 (Pres.), Hoover, Rep., 1,627,546; Smith, Dem., 864,210; Thomas, Soc., 8,683; Foster, Com., 2,836; Reynolds, Soc. Lab., 1,515; Varney, Proh., 3,556.

1932 (Pres.), Roosevelt, Dem., 1,301,695; Hoover, Rep., 1,227,679; Thomas, Soc., 64,094; Upshaw, Proh., 7,421; Foster, Com., 7,221; Reynolds, Soc. Lab., 1,968.

1936 (Pres.), Roosevelt, Dem., 1,747,122; Landon, Rep., 1,127,709; Lemke, Union, 132,212; Browder, Com., 5,251; Thomas, Soc., 117; Aiken, Soc. Lab., 14.

1940 (Pres.), Roosevelt, Dem., 1,733,139; Willkie, Rep., 1,586,773.

1944 (Pres.), Roosevelt, Dem., 1,570,763; Dewey, Rep., 1,582,293.

1948 (Pres.), Truman, Dem., 1,452,791; Dewey, Rep., 1,445,684; Wallace, Prog., 37,596.

1952 (Pres.), Eisenhower, Rep., 2,100,391; Stevenson, Dem., 1,600,367.

1956 (Pres.), Eisenhower, Rep., 2,262,610; Stevenson, Dem., 1,439,655.

1960 (Pres.), Kennedy, Dem., 1,944,248; Nixon, Rep., 2,217,611.

1964 (Pres.), Johnson, Dem., 2,498,331; Goldwater, Rep., 1,470,865.

1968 (Pres.), Nixon, Rep., 1,785,318; Humphrey, Dem., 1,692,213; Wallace, 3rd party, 468,591.

## Oklahoma

| County | Hum-phrey (D) 1968 | Nixon (R) 1968 | Wal-lace (I) 1968 | John-son (D) 1964 | Gold-water (R) 1964 |
|---|---|---|---|---|---|
| Adair | 1,549 | 2,877 | 1,000 | 3,003 | 2,859 |
| Alfalfa | 864 | 2,232 | 310 | 1,730 | 2,450 |
| Atoka | 1,400 | 1,131 | 1,613 | 2,459 | 1,424 |
| Beaver | 624 | 2,114 | 339 | 1,508 | 1,982 |
| Beckham | 2,354 | 2,935 | 1,550 | 4,115 | 2,557 |
| Blaine | 1,285 | 3,046 | 732 | 2,384 | 2,741 |
| Bryan | 3,215 | 2,727 | 2,264 | 5,934 | 2,652 |
| Caddo | 4,212 | 4,712 | 1,858 | 7,447 | 3,724 |
| Canadian | 3,577 | 5,891 | 2,525 | 5,747 | 5,193 |
| Carter | 5,807 | 5,127 | 3,414 | 10,645 | 4,986 |
| Cherokee | 2,554 | 3,971 | 1,866 | 4,449 | 3,467 |
| Choctaw | 2,268 | 1,414 | 1,751 | 3,969 | 1,718 |
| Cimarron | 436 | 1,121 | 527 | 878 | 1,225 |
| Cleveland | 8,425 | 12,132 | 4,415 | 11,599 | 9,656 |
| Coal | 963 | 669 | 625 | 1,613 | 721 |
| Comanche | 8,081 | 9,238 | 5,879 | 13,585 | 7,936 |
| Cotton | 1,192 | 1,016 | 905 | 2,216 | 1,123 |
| Craig | 2,098 | 2,686 | 1,229 | 3,838 | 2,541 |
| Creek | 5,151 | 6,934 | 3,913 | 9,836 | 6,355 |
| Custer | 2,717 | 4,709 | 936 | 4,464 | 3,362 |
| Delaware | 2,129 | 3,168 | 1,402 | 3,702 | 2,743 |
| Dewey | 773 | 1,508 | 540 | 1,617 | 1,438 |
| Ellis | 533 | 1,601 | 426 | 1,120 | 1,452 |
| Garfield | 5,631 | 13,925 | 2,836 | 10,175 | 12,297 |
| Garvin | 3,844 | 3,786 | 2,670 | 7,013 | 3,470 |
| Grady | 4,760 | 4,242 | 2,117 | 7,593 | 3,569 |
| Grant | 1,047 | 2,403 | 437 | 2,120 | 1,992 |
| Greer | 1,419 | 1,225 | 830 | 2,671 | 1,247 |
| Harmon | 1,097 | 644 | 403 | 1,665 | 602 |
| Harper | 517 | 1,482 | 353 | 1,240 | 1,355 |
| Haskell | 1,563 | 1,516 | 1,013 | 2,542 | 1,355 |
| Hughes | 2,578 | 1,897 | 1,170 | 4,477 | 1,692 |
| Jackson | 3,371 | 2,247 | 1,786 | 5,894 | 2,366 |
| Jefferson | 1,628 | 780 | 701 | 2,555 | 811 |
| Johnston | 1,216 | 1,048 | 974 | 2,370 | 1,065 |
| Kay | 6,131 | 12,651 | 2,145 | 11,296 | 12,033 |
| Kingfisher | 1,226 | 3,558 | 720 | 2,512 | 3,117 |
| Kiowa | 2,219 | 2,418 | 977 | 3,686 | 2,206 |
| Latimer | 523 | 311 | 233 | 2,297 | 849 |
| Le Flore | 3,880 | 3,870 | 3,189 | 7,105 | 3,904 |
| Lincoln | 2,304 | 3,855 | 1,969 | 5,046 | 3,854 |
| Logan | 2,508 | 3,960 | 1,687 | 4,279 | 3,787 |
| Love | 931 | 677 | 766 | 1,863 | 663 |
| McClain | 1,842 | 2,047 | 1,647 | 3,638 | 1,638 |
| McCurtain | 2,944 | 2,793 | 2,878 | 5,982 | 2,981 |
| McIntosh | 1,759 | 1,532 | 1,423 | 3,497 | 1,428 |
| Major | 594 | 2,550 | 357 | 1,291 | 2,436 |
| Marshall | 1,191 | 1,209 | 986 | 2,318 | 1,101 |
| Mayes | 2,858 | 4,220 | 2,421 | 6,421 | 4,157 |
| Murray | 1,773 | 1,454 | 1,027 | 3,083 | 1,236 |
| Muskogee | 9,021 | 8,707 | 4,596 | 16,330 | 8,508 |
| Noble | 1,412 | 2,911 | 618 | 2,713 | 2,157 |
| Nowata | 1,315 | 2,160 | 1,114 | 2,644 | 2,142 |
| Okfuskee | 1,777 | 1,686 | 981 | 2,905 | 1,629 |
| Oklahoma | 58,719 | 89,515 | 32,544 | 90,641 | 83,660 |
| Okmulgee | 6,089 | 4,709 | 3,728 | 10,195 | 4,704 |
| Osage | 3,919 | 5,499 | 2,408 | 7,395 | 5,695 |
| Ottawa | 4,820 | 5,000 | 1,421 | 7,589 | 4,090 |
| Pawnee | 1,343 | 2,437 | 990 | 2,389 | 2,278 |
| Payne | 4,492 | 7,949 | 2,123 | 8,906 | 7,936 |
| Pittsburg | 6,112 | 3,978 | 3,730 | 9,903 | 3,555 |
| Pontotoc | 4,291 | 4,161 | 2,425 | 7,449 | 4,166 |
| Pottawatomie | 6,721 | 6,899 | 3,873 | 10,884 | 6,841 |
| Pushmataha | 1,232 | 1,225 | 1,287 | 2,563 | 1,332 |
| Roger Mills | 720 | 1,102 | 601 | 1,345 | 926 |
| Rogers | 2,665 | 4,631 | 3,141 | 5,449 | 4,202 |
| Seminole | 3,889 | 3,711 | 2,142 | 6,582 | 3,676 |
| Sequoyah | 2,618 | 2,797 | 2,158 | 4,304 | 2,846 |
| Stephens | 5,244 | 5,508 | 3,570 | 9,272 | 5,323 |
| Texas | 1,176 | 3,729 | 946 | 2,500 | 3,339 |
| Tillman | 1,771 | 1,748 | 1,372 | 3,354 | 2,001 |
| Tulsa | 32,748 | 81,476 | 28,443 | 61,454 | 76,770 |
| Wagoner | 2,183 | 3,187 | 2,262 | 3,957 | 2,840 |
| Washington | 4,641 | 12,812 | 3,091 | 8,571 | 12,382 |
| Washita | 1,771 | 2,592 | 858 | 3,339 | 2,147 |
| Woods | 1,549 | 3,557 | 517 | 2,750 | 2,886 |
| Woodward | 1,444 | 3,748 | 663 | 2,934 | 3,094 |
| **Totals** | **297,243** | **442,693** | **197,167** | **519,834** | **412,665** |

### OKLAHOMA VOTE SINCE 1920

1920 (Pres.), Cox, Dem., 215,808; Harding, Rep., 243,464; Debs, Soc., 25,679.

1924 (Pres.), Davis, Dem., 259,798; Coolidge, Rep., 226,242; LaFollette, Prog., 41,141; Johns, Soc. Lab., 5,234.

1928 (Pres.), Hoover, Rep., 394,046; Smith, Dem., 219,174; Thomas, Soc., 3,924; Farm-Lab., 1,283.

1932 (Pres.), Roosevelt, Dem., 515,468; Hoover, Rep., 188,165.

1936 (Pres.), Roosevelt, Dem., 501,069; Landon, Rep., 245,122; Thomas, Soc., 2,221; Colvin, Proh., 1,328.

1940 (Pres.), Roosevelt, Dem., 474,313; Willkie, Rep., 348,872; Babson, Proh., 3,027.

### Oklahoma (cont'd)

1944 (Pres.), Roosevelt, Dem., 401,549; Dewey, Rep., 319,424; Watson, Proh., 1,663.

1948 (Pres.), Truman, Dem., 452,782; Dewey, Rep., 268,817.

1952 (Pres.), Eisenhower, Rep., 518,045; Stevenson, Dem., 430,939.

1956 (Pres.), Eisenhower, Rep., 473,769; Stevenson, Dem., 385,581.

1960 (Pres.), Kennedy, Dem., 370,111; Nixon, Rep., 533,039.

1964 (Pres.), Johnson, Dem., 519,834; Goldwater, Rep., 412,665.

1968 (Pres.), Nixon, Rep., 442,693; Humphrey, Dem., 297,243; Wallace, 3rd party, 197,167.

## Oregon

| County | Hum-phrey (D) 1968 | Nixon (R) 1968 | Wal-lace (I) 1968 | John-son (D) 1964 | Gold-water (R) 1964 |
|---|---|---|---|---|---|
| Baker | 2,464 | 3,311 | 480 | 3,903 | 2,670 |
| Benton | 6,538 | 11,654 | 749 | 8,971 | 7,250 |
| Clackamas | 26,770 | 30,413 | 3,371 | 35,711 | 21,299 |
| Clatsop | 6,243 | 5,810 | 651 | 8,371 | 4,023 |
| Columbia | 6,064 | 4,208 | 728 | 7,728 | 2,489 |
| Coos | 10,710 | 8,033 | 1,682 | 16,109 | 5,032 |
| Crook | 1,681 | 1,727 | 256 | 2,419 | 1,161 |
| Curry | 1,934 | 2,323 | 436 | 3,195 | 1,467 |
| Deschutes | 4,859 | 5,599 | 738 | 6,947 | 3,148 |
| Douglas | 9,186 | 13,339 | 3,584 | 15,909 | 9,806 |
| Gilliam | 436 | 619 | 65 | 775 | 442 |
| Grant | 934 | 1,632 | 239 | 1,877 | 1,149 |
| Harney | 1,036 | 1,612 | 196 | 1,577 | 1,172 |
| Hood River | 2,385 | 2,597 | 413 | 3,564 | 1,786 |
| Jackson | 12,764 | 19,575 | 2,469 | 19,486 | 14,598 |
| Jefferson | 1,160 | 1,659 | 180 | 1,739 | 1,197 |
| Josephine | 4,351 | 8,456 | 1,800 | 6,857 | 6,918 |
| Klamath | 5,629 | 9,604 | 1,735 | 9,066 | 8,530 |
| Lake | 730 | 1,538 | 229 | 1,419 | 1,304 |
| Lane | 32,940 | 36,905 | 5,420 | 49,785 | 24,139 |
| Lincoln | 5,009 | 5,031 | 659 | 7,101 | 3,200 |
| Linn | 10,032 | 12,604 | 1,648 | 14,926 | 8,382 |
| Malheur | 2,021 | 5,447 | 892 | 3,798 | 4,177 |
| Marion | 22,232 | 30,295 | 2,745 | 32,091 | 18,897 |
| Morrow | 797 | 1,068 | 102 | 1,470 | 627 |
| Multnomah | 124,629 | 106,630 | 11,053 | 161,040 | 81,683 |
| Polk | 4,961 | 6,997 | 591 | 7,292 | 4,319 |
| Sherman | 384 | 646 | 59 | 859 | 494 |
| Tillamook | 3,609 | 3,261 | 394 | 5,246 | 2,318 |
| Umatilla | 6,402 | 8,975 | 956 | 10,689 | 6,138 |
| Union | 3,409 | 3,796 | 521 | 4,929 | 2,553 |
| Wallowa | 1,006 | 1,527 | 194 | 1,790 | 1,055 |
| Wasco | 3,918 | 3,842 | 514 | 5,890 | 2,695 |
| Washington | 22,943 | 34,184 | 2,566 | 29,081 | 20,813 |
| Wheeler | 242 | 443 | 27 | 458 | 340 |
| Yamhill | 5,487 | 7,936 | 819 | 8,949 | 5,508 |
| **Totals** | **355,875** | **403,491** | **49,151** | **501,017** | **282,779** |

### OREGON VOTE SINCE 1920

1920 (Pres.), Cox, Dem., 80,019; Harding, Rep., 143,592; Watkins, Proh., 3,595; Debs, Soc., 9,801.

1924 (Pres.), Coolidge, Rep., 142,579; LaFollette, Prog., 68,403; Davis, Dem., 67,589; Johns, Soc. Lab., 917.

1928 (Pres.), Hoover, Rep., 205,341; Smith, Dem., 109,223; Thomas, Soc., 2,720; Reynolds, Soc. Labor, 1,564; Foster, Com., 1,094.

1932 (Pres.), Roosevelt, Dem., 213,871; Hoover, Rep., 136,019; Thomas, Soc., 15,450; Reynolds, Soc. Lab., 1,730; Foster, Com., 1,681.

1936 (Pres.), Roosevelt, Dem., 266,733; Landon, Rep., 122,706; Lemke, Union, 21,831; Thomas, Soc., 2,143; Aiken, Soc. Lab., 500; Browder, Com., 104; Colvin, Proh., 4.

1940 (Pres.), Roosevelt, Dem., 258,415; Willkie, Rep., 219,555; Aiken, Soc. Lab., 2,487; Thomas, Soc., 398; Browder, Com., 191; Babson, Proh., 154.

1944 (Pres.), Roosevelt, Dem., 248,635; Dewey, Rep., 225,365; Thomas, Soc., 3,785; Watson, Proh., 2,362.

1948 (Pres.), Truman, Dem., 243,147; Dewey, Rep., 260,904; Wallace, Prog., 14,978; Thomas, Soc., 5,051.

1952 (Pres.), Eisenhower, Rep., 420,815; Stevenson, Dem., 270,579; Hallinan, Ind., 3,665.

1956 (Pres.), Eisenhower, Rep., 406,393; Stevenson, Dem., 329,204.

1960 (Pres.), Kennedy, Dem., 367,402; Nixon, Rep., 408,060.

1964 (Pres.), Johnson, Dem., 501,017; Goldwater, Rep., 282,779; Write-in, 2,509.

1968 (Pres.), Nixon, Rep., 403,491; Humphrey, Dem., 355,875; Wallace, 3rd party, 49,151.

# Pennsylvania

| County | Humphrey (D) | Nixon (R) | Wallace (I) | Johnson (D) | Goldwater (R) |
|---|---|---|---|---|---|
| | 1968 | 1968 | 1968 | 1964 | 1964 |
| Adams | 5,940 | 10,875 | 1,392 | 11,148 | 8,617 |
| Allegheny | 354,917 | 250,061 | 79,441 | 475,207 | 241,707 |
| Armstrong | 13,712 | 13,529 | 2,152 | 21,098 | 10,618 |
| Beaver | 44,720 | 27,271 | 7,811 | 60,492 | 23,174 |
| Bedford | 4,656 | 10,053 | 1,230 | 9,165 | 7,968 |
| Berks | 49,138 | 51,143 | 7,707 | 73,444 | 36,726 |
| Blair | 15,499 | 26,578 | 3,750 | 26,157 | 24,301 |
| Bradford | 6,207 | 11,890 | 1,286 | 10,714 | 10,434 |
| Bucks | 56,056 | 66,412 | 16,648 | 78,287 | 50,243 |
| Butler | 19,026 | 20,800 | 4,032 | 27,267 | 17,360 |
| Cambria | 40,295 | 32,082 | 4,196 | 55,183 | 26,281 |
| Cameron | 1,059 | 1,725 | 144 | 1,904 | 1,376 |
| Carbon | 10,366 | 9,396 | 891 | 15,416 | 7,309 |
| Centre | 10,827 | 15,269 | 1,321 | 16,556 | 9,481 |
| Chester | 6,599 | 12,077 | 2,258 | 47,940 | 40,280 |
| Clarion | 5,292 | 7,862 | 918 | 9,235 | 6,143 |
| Clearfield | 12,131 | 13,740 | 2,075 | 19,211 | 11,338 |
| Clinton | 6,178 | 6,305 | 579 | 10,038 | 4,298 |
| Columbia | 7,135 | 10,134 | 1,511 | 13,885 | 8,982 |
| Crawford | 11,093 | 14,349 | 1,735 | 18,212 | 10,664 |
| Cumberland | 15,034 | 31,837 | 4,773 | 26,633 | 23,665 |
| Dauphin | 24,801 | 47,033 | 7,339 | 46,119 | 42,718 |
| Delaware | 104,112 | 128,997 | 24,488 | 147,189 | 111,189 |
| Elk | 6,697 | 5,960 | 911 | 10,455 | 4,354 |
| Erie | 50,056 | 40,434 | 4,540 | 72,944 | 31,393 |
| Fayette | 32,568 | 17,884 | 6,087 | 45,155 | 16,127 |
| Forest | 644 | 1,121 | 123 | 1,249 | 900 |
| Franklin | 11,106 | 18,312 | 4,420 | 19,332 | 13525 |
| Fulton | 1,049 | 2,121 | 592 | 2,180 | 1,747 |
| Greene | 8,051 | 4,763 | 1,027 | 11,412 | 3,896 |
| Huntingdon | 4,038 | 7,959 | 921 | 7,435 | 6,571 |
| Indiana | 11,973 | 14,349 | 2,061 | 17,568 | 11,706 |
| Jefferson | 6,669 | 9,820 | 1,204 | 10,851 | 8,373 |
| Juniata | 2,274 | 3,884 | 492 | 4,138 | 3,087 |
| Lackawanna | 56,576 | 36,997 | 2,916 | 88,131 | 31,272 |
| Lancaster | 27,077 | 62,162 | 7,313 | 53,041 | 52,243 |
| Lawrence | 20,567 | 17,620 | 3,518 | 29,092 | 15,998 |
| Lebanon | 9,274 | 21,003 | 2,488 | 15,882 | 17,891 |
| Lehigh | 43,003 | 45,717 | 3,827 | 60,377 | 32,245 |
| Luzerne | 76,328 | 54,398 | 6,341 | 106,397 | 43,895 |
| Lycoming | 16,068 | 22,543 | 2,588 | 25,879 | 19,011 |
| McKean | 6,116 | 9,965 | 667 | 10,950 | 7,948 |
| Mercer | 22,378 | 22,226 | 2,921 | 32,199 | 18,153 |
| Mifflin | 5,537 | 7,762 | 821 | 8,811 | 6,006 |
| Monroe | 6,774 | 9,004 | 1,212 | 10,622 | 6,281 |
| Montg'm'y | 99,992 | 136,239 | 14,988 | 135,657 | 102,714 |
| Montour | 2,181 | 3,153 | 420 | 3,683 | 2,527 |
| North'mpt'n | 41,748 | 30,788 | 3,028 | 58,818 | 21,048 |
| North'berl'd | 16,720 | 21,567 | 2,373 | 28,082 | 17,046 |
| Perry | 2,869 | 6,468 | 1,192 | 6,054 | 5,354 |
| Philadelphia | 518,751 | 249,742 | 62,391 | 670,645 | 239,733 |
| Pike | 1,548 | 3,474 | 396 | 2,753 | 2,651 |
| Potter | 1,806 | 3,767 | 431 | 3,652 | 3,232 |
| Schuylkill | 34,154 | 35,624 | 4,131 | 50,560 | 26,386 |
| Snyder | 680 | 2,641 | 277 | 4,199 | 5,195 |
| Somerset | 11,918 | 17,536 | 1,905 | 17,934 | 14,817 |
| Sullivan | 983 | 1,507 | 169 | 1,690 | 1,344 |
| Susqueh'na | 4,178 | 8,126 | 840 | 7,838 | 6,567 |
| Tioga | 8,977 | 3,410 | 1,027 | 7,415 | 7,064 |
| Union | 2,078 | 6,205 | 554 | 4,262 | 4,944 |
| Venango | 8,136 | 11,702 | 1,102 | 13,065 | 9,873 |
| Warren | 6,216 | 8,484 | 641 | 10,598 | 5,965 |
| Washington | 43,572 | 20,462 | 7,860 | 63,482 | 24,127 |
| Wayne | 2,500 | 6,356 | 607 | 5,781 | 6,512 |
| Westmorel'd | 75,404 | 47,167 | 13,066 | 107,131 | 41,493 |
| Wyoming | 2,297 | 4,917 | 489 | 4,268 | 3,864 |
| York | 32,646 | 50,148 | 7,884 | 58,787 | 33,677 |
| **Totals** | 2,168,-970 | 1,934,-924 | 360,438 | 3,130,-954 | 1,673,-657 |

### PENNSYLVANIA VOTE SINCE 1920

1920 (Pres.), Cox, Dem., 503,202; Harding, Rep., 1,218,215; Watkins, Proh., 42,612; Debs, Soc., 70,021; Christensen, Lab., 15,642.

1924 (Pres.), Coolidge, Rep., 1,401,481; Davis, Dem., 409,192; LaFollette, Soc., 93,441; Labor, 214,126; Nations, Amer., 13,035; Faris, Proh., 9,779; Foster, Workers, 2,735.

1928 (Pres.), Hoover, Rep., 2,055,382; Smith, Dem., 1,067,586; Thomas, Soc., 18,647; Foster, Labor, (Workers, 2,687; Com., 2,039), 4,726.

1932 (Pres.), Roosevelt, Dem., 1,295,948; Hoover, Rep., 1,453,540; Thomas, Soc., 91,119; Upshaw, Proh., 11,319; Foster, Com., 5,658; Cox, Jobless, 725; Reynolds, Indust., 659.

1936 (Pres.), Roosevelt, Dem., 2,353,788; Landon, Rep., 1,690,300; Lemke, Royal Oak, 67,467; Thomas, Soc., 14,375; Colvin, Proh., 6,691; Browder, Com., 4,060; Aiken, Ind., Lab., 1,424.

1940 (Pres.), Roosevelt, Dem., 2,171,035; Willkie, Rep., 1,889,848; Thomas, Soc., 10,967; Browder, Com., 4,519; Aiken, Ind., Gov., 1,518.

1944 (Pres.), Roosevelt, Dem., 1,940,479; Dewey, Rep., 1,835,054; Thomas, Soc., 11,721; Watson,

## Pennsylvania (cont'd)

Proh., 5,750; Teichert, Ind. Gov., 1,789.

1948 (Pres.), Truman, Dem., 1,752,426; Dewey, Rep., 1,902,197; Wallace, Prog., 55,161; Thomas, Soc., 11,325; Watson, Proh., 10,338; Dobbs, Militant Workers, 2,133; Teichert, Ind. Gov., 1,461.

1952 (Pres.), Eisenhower, Rep., 2,415,789; Stevenson, Dem., 2,146,269; Hamblen, Proh., 8,771; Hallinan, Prog., 4,200; Hoopes, Soc., 2,684; Dobbs, Militant Workers, 1,502; Hass, Ind. Gov., 1,347; Scattered, 155.

1956 (Pres.), Eisenhower, Rep., 2,585,252; Stevenson, Dem., 1,981,769; Haas, Soc. Lab., 7,447; Dobbs, Militant Workers, 2,035.

1960 (Pres.), Kennedy, Dem., 2,556,282; Nixon, Rep., 2,439,956; Hass, Soc. Lab., 7,185; Dobbs, Soc. Workers, 2,678; Scattering 440.

1964 (Pres.), Johnson, Dem., 3,130,954; Goldwater, Rep., 1,673,657; De Berry, Soc. Worker, 10,456; Hass, Soc. Labor, 5,092; Scattering, 2,531.

1968 (Pres.), Nixon, Rep., 1,934,924; Humphrey, Dem., 2,168,970; Wallace, 3rd party, 360,438.

# Rhode Island

| County | Humphrey (D) | Nixon (R) | Wallace (I) | Johnson (D) | Goldwater (R) |
|---|---|---|---|---|---|
| | 1968 | 1968 | 1968 | 1964 | 1964 |
| Bristol | 11,161 | 6,912 | 457 | 14,306 | 4,466 |
| Kent | 165,372 | 67,484 | 10,017 | 44,476 | 12,297 |
| Newport | 12,954 | 10,699 | 1,185 | 19,782 | 7,078 |
| Providence | 34,530 | 21,446 | 2,406 | 219,465 | 43,432 |
| Washington | 15,480 | 9,588 | 902 | 17,434 | 7,342 |
| **Totals** | 239,497 | 115,929 | 14,967 | 315,463 | 74,615 |

### RHODE ISLAND VOTE SINCE 1920

1920 (Pres.), Cox, Dem., 55,062; Harding, Rep., 107,463; Watkins, Proh., 510; Debs, Soc., 4,351.

1924 (Pres.), Coolidge, Rep., 125,286; Davis, Dem., 76,606; LaFollette, Prog., 7,628; Foster, Workers, 280; Johns, Soc. Lab., 268.

1928 (Pres.), Smith, Dem., 118,973; Hoover, Rep., 117,522; Reynolds, Soc. Lab., 416; Foster, Com., 283.

1932 (Pres.), Roosevelt, Dem., 146,604; Hoover, Rep., 115,266; Thomas, Soc., 3,138; Foster, Com., 546; Reynolds, Soc. Lab., 433; Upshaw, Proh., 183.

1936 (Pres.), Roosevelt, Dem., 165,238; Landon, Rep., 125,031; Lemke, Union, 19,569; Aiken, Soc. Lab., 929; Browder, Com., 411.

1940 (Pres.), Roosevelt, Dem., 182,182; Willkie, Rep., 138,653; Browder, Com., 239; Babson, Proh., 74.

1944 (Pres.), Roosevelt, Dem., 175,356; Dewey, Rep., 123,487; Watson, Proh., 433.

1948 (Pres.), Truman, Dem., 188,736; Dewey, Rep., 135,787; Wallace, Prog., 2,619; Thomas, Soc., 429; Teichert, Soc. Lab., 131.

1952 (Pres.), Eisenhower, Rep., 210,935; Stevenson, Dem., 203,293; Hallinan, Prog., 187; Hass, Soc. Lab., 83.

1956 (Pres.), Eisenhower, Rep., 225,819; Stevenson, Dem., 161,790.

1960 (Pres.), Kennedy, Dem., 258,032; Nixon, Rep., 147,502.

1964 (Pres.), Johnson, Dem., 315,463; Goldwater, Rep., 74,615.

1968 (Pres.), Nixon, Rep., 115,929; Humphrey, Dem., 239,497; Wallace, 3rd party, 14,967.

# South Carolina

| County | Humphrey (D) | Nixon (R) | Wallace (I) | Johnson (D) | Goldwater (R) |
|---|---|---|---|---|---|
| | 1968 | 1968 | 1968 | 1964 | 1964 |
| Abbeville | 1,425 | 1,213 | 3,201 | 2,689 | 1,448 |
| Aiken | 6,329 | 12,309 | 8,754 | 7,622 | 17,467 |
| Allendale | 1,548 | 1,012 | 829 | 772 | 1,740 |
| Anderson | 3,792 | 4,131 | 10,569 | 11,670 | 8,398 |
| Bamberg | 1,845 | 1,327 | 1,618 | 1,419 | 2,366 |
| Barnwell | 1,716 | 1,849 | 2,357 | 1,382 | 3,670 |
| Beaufort | 3,565 | 2,179 | 1,192 | 2,747 | 3,432 |
| Berkeley | 5,134 | 4,021 | 4,810 | 3,537 | 6,100 |
| Calhoun | 1,214 | 881 | 612 | | 1,591 |
| Charleston | 18,019 | 23,939 | 13,037 | 14,564 | 32,509 |
| Cherokee | 2,012 | 2,953 | 5,607 | 4,258 | 3,627 |
| Chester | 2,865 | 2,862 | 2,762 | 3,882 | 2,915 |
| Chesterfield | 3,180 | 2,564 | 4,324 | 4,634 | 2,449 |
| Clarendon | 3,606 | 2,201 | 2,097 | 832 | 2,960 |
| Colleton | 2,488 | 2,756 | 2,544 | 2,051 | 4,637 |
| Darlington | 4,102 | 8,796 | 3,826 | 5,010 | 6,717 |
| Dillon | 2,211 | 2,396 | 2,132 | 2,773 | 2,742 |
| Dorchester | 4,030 | 3,316 | 3,509 | 1,604 | 5,109 |
| Edgefield | 1,225 | 1,698 | 1,007 | 824 | 2,489 |

## So. Carolina (cont'd)

| County | 1968 Humphrey (D) | 1968 Nixon (R) | 1968 Wallace (I) | 1964 Johnson (D) | 1964 Goldwater (R) |
|---|---|---|---|---|---|
| Fairfield.... | 3,011 | 1,619 | 1,336 | 2,628 | 1,997 |
| Florence.... | 8,522 | 12,059 | 9,399 | 7,157 | 10,346 |
| Georgetown.. | 4,110 | 3,269 | 2,642 | 3,423 | 4,705 |
| Greenville... | 12,928 | 31,652 | 15,241 | 17,275 | 29,358 |
| Greenwood... | 3,936 | 5,188 | 6,225 | 5,479 | 5,653 |
| Hampton.... | 2,105 | 1,670 | 1,375 | 1,439 | 2,259 |
| Horry...... | 3,933 | 6,341 | 6,860 | 5,444 | 5,293 |
| Jasper...... | 1,411 | 633 | 1,091 | 1,002 | 1,593 |
| Kershaw.... | 2,538 | 4,078 | 3,960 | 3,168 | 5,617 |
| Lancaster... | 3,151 | 4,874 | 4,886 | 4,970 | 4,742 |
| Laurens.... | 2,997 | 4,756 | 4,182 | 4,365 | 5,081 |
| Lee........ | 2,150 | 1,218 | 2,113 | 1,156 | 2,489 |
| Lexington... | 3,892 | 11,626 | 8,274 | 4,807 | 12,041 |
| Marion..... | 2,816 | 2,499 | 1,477 | 2,046 | 3,197 |
| Marlboro... | 2,303 | 2,139 | 2,145 | 2,422 | 1,864 |
| McCormick. | 1,059 | 464 | 759 | 498 | 939 |
| Newberry... | 2,485 | 4,726 | 3,607 | 3,222 | 5,571 |
| Oconee..... | 1,983 | 2,610 | 4,689 | 5,560 | 2,712 |
| Orangeburg. | 8,959 | 5,142 | 7,343 | 5,607 | 10,456 |
| Pickens..... | 2,014 | 6,872 | 4,321 | 3,506 | 5,882 |
| Richland... | 18,277 | 26,215 | 7,154 | 17,939 | 27,306 |
| Saluda..... | 1,209 | 1,541 | 2,135 | 1,409 | 2,524 |
| Spartanburg | 11,392 | 17,760 | 16,738 | 20,034 | 18,411 |
| Sumter..... | 6,374 | 5,764 | 4,754 | 3,775 | 7,729 |
| Union...... | 2,271 | 3,011 | 4,590 | 3,892 | 3,815 |
| Williamsburg | 5,106 | 3,029 | 2,652 | 2,248 | 4,810 |
| York....... | 5,651 | 7,400 | 6,653 | 8,346 | 7,292 |
| **Totals...** | **196,889** | **260,558** | **211,754** | **215,700** | **309,048** |

### SOUTH CAROLINA VOTE SINCE 1920

1920 (Pres.), Cox, Dem., 64,170; Harding, Rep., 2,244; Debs, Soc., 26.

1924 (Pres.), Davis, Dem., 49,008; Coolidge, Rep., 1,123; LaFollette, Prog., 620.

1928 (Pres.), Smith, Dem., 62,700; Anti-Smith, 2,670; Hoover, Rep., 3,188; Thomas, Soc., 44.

1932 (Pres.), Roosevelt, Dem., 102,347; Hoover, Rep., 1,978; Thomas, Soc., 82.

1936 (Pres.), Roosevelt, Dem., 113,791; Landon, Rep., Tolbert faction (953), Hambright faction (693), total, 1,646.

1940 (Pres.), Roosevelt, Dem., 95,470; Willkie, Rep., 1,727.

1944 (Pres.), Roosevelt, Dem., 90,601; Dewey, Rep., 4,547; Southern Democrats, 7,799; Watson, Proh., 365; Rep. (Tolbert faction), 63.

1948 (Pres.), Thurmond, States' Rights, 102,607; Truman, Dem., 34,423; Dewey, Rep., 5,386; Wallace, Prog., 154; Thomas, Soc., 1.

1952 (Pres.), Eisenhower ran on two tickets. Under State law vote cast for two Eisenhower slates of electors could not be combined. Eisenhower, Ind., 158,289; Rep., 9,793; total, 168,082; Stevenson, Dem., 173,004; Hamblen, Proh., 1.

1956 (Pres.), Stevenson, Dem., 136,372; Byrd, Ind., 88,509; Eisenhower, Rep., 75,700; Andrews, Ind., 2.

1960 (Pres.), Kennedy, Dem., 198,129; Nixon, Rep., 188,558; Write-in, 1.

1964 (Pres.), Johnson, Dem., 215,700; Goldwater, Rep., 309,048; Write-ins: Nixon, 1; Wallace, 5; Powell, 1; Thurmond, 1.

1968 (Pres.), Nixon, Rep., 260,558; Humphrey, Dem., 196,889; Wallace, 3rd party, 211,754.

## South Dakota

| County | 1968 Humphrey (D) | 1968 Nixon (R) | 1968 Wallace (I) | 1964 Johnson (D) | 1964 Goldwater (R) |
|---|---|---|---|---|---|
| Aurora..... | 1,060 | 1,033 | 130 | 1,555 | 871 |
| Beadle..... | 5,338 | 4,214 | 288 | 5,968 | 4,051 |
| Bennett.... | 457 | 665 | 111 | 775 | 624 |
| Bon Homme. | 1,773 | 2,411 | 209 | 2,494 | 1,784 |
| Brookings... | 3,202 | 4,674 | 205 | 4,191 | 3,692 |
| Brown...... | 7,291 | 6,665 | 560 | 9,107 | 5,524 |
| Brule...... | 1,425 | 1,240 | 153 | 2,205 | 968 |
| Buffalo..... | 265 | 261 | 28 | 501 | 278 |
| Butte...... | 1,017 | 2,091 | 196 | 1,863 | 1,877 |
| Campbell... | 245 | 1,216 | 73 | 411 | 1,162 |
| Chas. Mix.. | 2,369 | 2,099 | 207 | 3,488 | 1,625 |
| Clark...... | 1,325 | 1,596 | 118 | 1,771 | 1,511 |
| Clay....... | 2,006 | 2,299 | 131 | 2,599 | 1,802 |
| Codington.. | 4,235 | 3,929 | 279 | 5,353 | 3,593 |
| Corson..... | 821 | 1,108 | 80 | 1,328 | 1,034 |
| Custer..... | 727 | 1,143 | 194 | 1,176 | 1,142 |
| Davison.... | 3,284 | 3,574 | 251 | 4,861 | 2,789 |
| Day....... | 2,463 | 2,061 | 182 | 3,235 | 1,914 |
| Deuel...... | 1,076 | 1,398 | 151 | 1,524 | 1,317 |
| Dewey..... | 721 | 941 | 123 | 1,259 | 981 |
| Douglas.... | 592 | 1,613 | 77 | 1,149 | 1,189 |
| Edmunds... | 1,225 | 1,534 | 181 | 1,708 | 1,442 |
| Fall River.. | 965 | 1,843 | 286 | 1,706 | 2,026 |

## So. Dakota (cont'd)

| County | 1968 Humphrey (D) | 1968 Nixon (R) | 1968 Wallace (I) | 1964 Johnson (D) | 1964 Goldwater (R) |
|---|---|---|---|---|---|
| Faulk...... | 819 | 997 | 204 | 1,225 | 974 |
| Grant...... | 1,889 | 2,259 | 211 | 2,583 | 1,854 |
| Gregory.... | 1,267 | 1,810 | 251 | 1,995 | 1,644 |
| Haakon.... | 377 | 759 | 109 | 662 | 795 |
| Hamlin.... | 1,147 | 1,649 | 129 | 1,561 | 1,525 |
| Hand...... | 1,136 | 1,650 | 226 | 1,563 | 1,466 |
| Hanson.... | 826 | 901 | 72 | 1,232 | 802 |
| Harding.... | 266 | 564 | 65 | 487 | 489 |
| Hughes..... | 1,668 | 3,204 | 343 | 2,606 | 2,732 |
| Hutchinson. | 1,412 | 3,503 | 175 | 2,189 | 2,884 |
| Hyde...... | 499 | 708 | 113 | 736 | 666 |
| Jackson.... | 267 | 481 | 98 | 480 | 445 |
| Jerauld.... | 745 | 1,002 | 56 | 999 | 857 |
| Jones...... | 358 | 562 | 88 | 548 | 415 |
| Kingsbury.. | 1,491 | 2,298 | 146 | 2,005 | 2,126 |
| Lake....... | 2,294 | 2,876 | 188 | 2,988 | 2,417 |
| Lawrence... | 2,425 | 4,185 | 335 | 3,468 | 3,743 |
| Lincoln.... | 1,961 | 3,259 | 222 | 2,836 | 2,740 |
| Lyman..... | 643 | 1,063 | 131 | 1,057 | 862 |
| Marshall.... | 1,518 | 1,476 | 130 | 2,181 | 1,756 |
| McCook.... | 1,653 | 1,959 | 188 | 723 | 1,891 |
| McPherson.. | 389 | 1,975 | 126 | 2,063 | 1,183 |
| Meade..... | 1,522 | 2,392 | 343 | 2,323 | 2,140 |
| Mellette.... | 407 | 611 | 79 | 658 | 525 |
| Miner...... | 1,255 | 1,045 | 92 | 1,679 | 945 |
| Minnehaha.. | 16,334 | 19,984 | 1,175 | 20,929 | 16,766 |
| Moody..... | 1,614 | 1,689 | 157 | 2,301 | 1,461 |
| Pennington. | 7,249 | 9,562 | 1,166 | 9,881 | 8,926 |
| Perkins.... | 869 | 1,498 | 114 | 1,255 | 1,409 |
| Potter..... | 780 | 1,273 | 149 | 1,260 | 954 |
| Roberts.... | 2,651 | 2,225 | 337 | 3,567 | 1,931 |
| Sanborn.... | 956 | 1,024 | 8 | 1,401 | 912 |
| Shannon.... | 1,202 | 533 | 61 | 3,120 | 1,953 |
| Spink...... | 2,669 | 2,068 | 178 | 750 | 549 |
| Stanley..... | 440 | 572 | 98 | 596 | 667 |
| Sully...... | 356 | 676 | 93 | 2,241 | 1,937 |
| Todd....... | 987 | 686 | 91 | 2,184 | 2,846 |
| Tripp...... | 1,366 | 2,242 | 245 | 2,828 | 1,727 |
| Turner..... | 1,325 | 1,596 | 118 | 1,952 | 1,849 |
| Union...... | 2,014 | 2,212 | 225 | 3,747 | 3,208 |
| Walworth... | 1,276 | 2,204 | 182 | 554 | 447 |
| Washaba'gh. | 203 | 224 | 22 | 1,748 | 557 |
| Yankton.... | 2,753 | 3,978 | 392 | 1,274 | 723 |
| Ziebach.... | 348 | 446 | 55 | 348 | 211 |
| **Totals..** | **117,505** | **147,438** | **13,209** | **163,010** | **130,108** |

### SOUTH DAKOTA VOTE SINCE 1920

1920 (Pres.), Cox, Dem., 35,938; Harding, Rep., 110,692; Watkins, Proh., 900; F.-Lab., 34,707.

1924 (Pres.), Coolidge, Rep., 101,299; LaFollette, Prog., 75,355; Davis, Dem., 27,214.

1928 (Pres.), Hoover, Rep., 157,660; Smith, Dem., 102,660; Thomas, Soc., 443; Foster, Com., 232; Farm-Lab., 927.

1932 (Pres.), Roosevelt, Dem., 183,515; Hoover, Rep., 99,212; Harvey, Lib., 3,333; Thomas, Soc., 1,551; Upshaw, Proh., 463; Foster, Com., 364.

1936 (Pres.), Roosevelt, Dem., 160,137; Landon, Rep., 125,977; Lemke, Union, 10,338.

1940 (Pres.), Roosevelt, Dem., 131,862; Willkie, Rep., 177,065.

1944 (Pres.), Roosevelt, Dem., 96,711; Dewey, Rep., 135,365.

1948 (Pres.), Truman, Dem., 117,653; Dewey, Rep., 129,651; Wallace, Prog., 2,801.

1952 (Pres.), Eisenhower, Rep., 203,857; Stevenson, Dem., 90,426.

1956 (Pres.), Eisenhower, Rep., 171,569; Stevenson, Dem., 122,288.

1960 (Pres.), Kennedy, Dem., 128,070; Nixon, Rep., 178,417.

1964 (Pres.), Johnson, Dem., 163,010; Goldwater, Rep., 130,108.

1968 (Pres.), Nixon, Rep., 147,438; Humphrey, Dem., 117,505; Wallace, 3rd party, 13,209.

## Tennessee

| County | 1968 Humphrey (D) | 1968 Nixon (R) | 1968 Wallace (I) | 1964 Johnson (D) | 1964 Goldwater (R) |
|---|---|---|---|---|---|
| Anderson.... | 7,198 | 10,233 | 4,323 | 12,146 | 8,860 |
| Bedford.... | 2,415 | 1,869 | 4,098 | 5,610 | 2,272 |
| Benton..... | 1,059 | 1,468 | 2,255 | 2,611 | 1,363 |
| Bledsoe..... | 957 | 1,477 | 732 | 1,412 | 1,431 |
| Blount..... | 5,176 | 12,753 | 4,407 | 8,459 | 11,876 |
| Bradley.... | 2,762 | 6,924 | 4,159 | 5,693 | 6,717 |
| Campbell.... | 2,268 | 4,024 | 1,367 | 4,412 | 4,232 |
| Cannon.... | 809 | 780 | 1,464 | 2,190 | 746 |
| Carroll..... | 1,932 | 3,757 | 3,298 | 4,056 | 3,734 |
| Carter..... | 2,160 | 9,467 | 3,009 | 5,326 | 8,472 |
| Cheatham.. | 778 | 669 | 2,497 | 2,750 | 803 |
| Chester..... | 849 | 1,408 | 2,037 | 1,763 | 1,767 |
| Claiborne... | 1,392 | 3,097 | 884 | 2,581 | 2,852 |

## Tennessee (cont'd)

| County | 1968 Humphrey (D) | Nixon (R) | Wallace (I) | 1964 Johnson (D) | Goldwater (R) |
|---|---|---|---|---|---|
| Clay | 667 | 814 | 451 | 1,196 | 622 |
| Cocke | 950 | 5,645 | 1,159 | 2,109 | 5,084 |
| Coffee | 3,040 | 3,337 | 4,794 | 6,837 | 3,012 |
| Crockett | 703 | 932 | 2,865 | 1,817 | 1,873 |
| Cumberl'd | 1,423 | 3,115 | 1,471 | 3,073 | 2,975 |
| Davidson | 44,543 | 44,175 | 47,889 | 79,387 | 45,335 |
| Decatur | 877 | 1,409 | 1,544 | 1,813 | 1,429 |
| DeKalb | 847 | 1,532 | 1,516 | 2,291 | 1,402 |
| Dickson | 2,034 | 1,291 | 3,475 | 4,724 | 1,281 |
| Dyer | 2,033 | 2,826 | 5,842 | 4,717 | 4,517 |
| Fayette | 2,236 | 740 | 2,570 | 2,636 | 2,922 |
| Fentress | 671 | 2,026 | 808 | 1,550 | 1,969 |
| Franklin | 2,489 | 1,700 | 4,939 | 6,029 | 2,262 |
| Gibson | 3,962 | 4,093 | 7,233 | 8,119 | 4,614 |
| Giles | 2,203 | 1,264 | 3,966 | 4,940 | 1,378 |
| Grainger | 761 | 2,788 | 596 | 1,309 | 2,634 |
| Greene | 2,947 | 7,957 | 2,753 | 5,916 | 6,913 |
| Grundy | 1,307 | 618 | 1,642 | 2,775 | 686 |
| Hamblen | 2,390 | 6,382 | 2,259 | 4,607 | 5,196 |
| Hamilton | 23,441 | 29,302 | 32,080 | 38,546 | 40,200 |
| Hancock | 731 | 3,001 | 596 | 687 | 1,517 |
| Hardeman | 1,709 | 1,171 | 2,924 | 2,675 | 2,450 |
| Hardin | 1,153 | 2,910 | 2,325 | 2,620 | 3,025 |
| Hawkins | 2,213 | 6,217 | 1,798 | 4,191 | 5,712 |
| Haywood | 1,709 | 1,152 | 2,757 | 2,290 | 2,407 |
| Henderson | 1,230 | 3,591 | 2,086 | 1,955 | 3,133 |
| Henry | 3,149 | 2,068 | 3,439 | 5,874 | 2,261 |
| Hickman | 1,152 | 760 | 2,473 | 2,877 | 1,019 |
| Houston | 636 | 232 | 941 | 1,572 | 287 |
| Humphreys | 1,391 | 866 | 2,095 | 3,230 | 916 |
| Jackson | 1,122 | 673 | 908 | 2,291 | 551 |
| Jefferson | 1,494 | 5,494 | 1,199 | 2,600 | 4,923 |
| Johnson | 450 | 3,107 | 375 | 927 | 2,889 |
| Knox | 24,528 | 47,202 | 18,277 | 42,463 | 42,797 |
| Lake | 737 | 409 | 1,262 | 1,667 | 736 |
| Lauderdale | 2,108 | 1,080 | 3,566 | 3,847 | 1,880 |
| Lawrence | 2,191 | 4,343 | 3,993 | 5,449 | 4,590 |
| Lewis | 1,088 | 455 | 997 | 2,061 | 388 |
| Lincoln | 1,848 | 1,167 | 4,214 | 4,861 | 1,728 |
| Loudon | 1,581 | 4,299 | 1,996 | 3,365 | 4,148 |
| McMinn | 2,889 | 6,098 | 2,535 | 5,207 | 5,624 |
| McNairy | 1,377 | 2,979 | 2,872 | 2,994 | 3,109 |
| Macon | 530 | 2,173 | 1,041 | 1,446 | 1,846 |
| Madison | 5,517 | 6,143 | 9,420 | 10,573 | 10,932 |
| Marion | 1,661 | 1,959 | 2,784 | 3,775 | 2,728 |
| Marshall | 1,527 | 1,202 | 3,379 | 3,989 | 1,340 |
| Maury | 3,401 | 3,048 | 8,148 | 7,716 | 4,605 |
| Meigs | 493 | 729 | 442 | 916 | 824 |
| Monroe | 2,926 | 4,749 | 1,222 | 4,100 | 4,349 |
| M'tgomery | 5,538 | 3,248 | 5,638 | 10,178 | 2,814 |
| Moore | 346 | 224 | 856 | 1,034 | 264 |
| Morgan | 968 | 1,803 | 1,028 | 1,957 | 1,842 |
| Obion | 2,235 | 2,420 | 4,680 | 5,672 | 2,802 |
| Overton | 1,592 | 1,255 | 1,176 | 3,258 | 1,155 |
| Perry | 726 | 519 | 784 | 1,440 | 514 |
| Pickette | 405 | 884 | 199 | 728 | 935 |
| Polk | 1,454 | 1,808 | 754 | 2,113 | 1,685 |
| Putnam | 3,541 | 3,693 | 3,073 | 6,309 | 2,993 |
| Rhea | 1,301 | 2,428 | 2,237 | 2,637 | 2,730 |
| Roane | 3,258 | 6,033 | 3,898 | 6,108 | 5,735 |
| Robertson | 2,315 | 1,802 | 3,904 | 5,784 | 1,797 |
| Rutherford | 4,921 | 4,168 | 7,773 | 9,580 | 4,088 |
| Scott | 991 | 2,406 | 734 | 2,007 | 2,406 |
| Sequatchie | 549 | 663 | 1,011 | 1,162 | 804 |
| Sevier | 1,112 | 7,629 | 1,476 | 2,995 | 6,821 |
| Shelby | 82,602 | 73,403 | 76,971 | 111,496 | 100,527 |
| Smith | 1,443 | 1,089 | 1,831 | 2,934 | 1,084 |
| Stewart | 1,041 | 443 | 1,057 | 2,444 | 441 |
| Sullivan | 9,783 | 20,251 | 9,991 | 19,496 | 17,703 |
| Sumner | 4,376 | 4,519 | 7,592 | 9,102 | 3,437 |
| Tipton | 2,071 | 1,422 | 4,943 | 3,821 | 3,073 |
| Trousdale | 694 | 252 | 649 | 1,270 | 205 |
| Unicoi | 910 | 3,327 | 843 | 2,000 | 2,731 |
| Union | 527 | 1,956 | 449 | 1,091 | 1,770 |
| Van Buren | 282 | 327 | 507 | 865 | 293 |
| Warren | 2,046 | 1,858 | 3,814 | 5,027 | 1,754 |
| Washington | 4,930 | 12,882 | 4,925 | 10,253 | 10,612 |
| Wayne | 926 | 2,417 | 1,208 | 1,178 | 2,510 |
| Weakley | 1,988 | 2,858 | 4,525 | 5,161 | 2,684 |
| White | 1,584 | 1,423 | 1,750 | 2,987 | 1,199 |
| Williamson | 2,063 | 2,788 | 4,867 | 5,075 | 2,707 |
| Wilson | 2,916 | 2,736 | 5,648 | 6,267 | 2,707 |
| **Totals** | **352,834** | **474,086** | **425,237** | **635,047** | **508,965** |

### TENNESSEE VOTE SINCE 1920

1920 (Pres.), Cox, Dem., 206,558; Harding, Rep., 219,829; Debs, Soc., 2,239.

1924 (Pres.), Davis, Dem., 158,404; Coolidge, Rep., 130,882; LaFollette, Prog., 10,656; Farris, Proh., 115.

1928 (Pres.), Hoover, Rep. 195,388; Smith, Dem., 167,343; Thomas, Soc., 631; Foster, Com., 111.

1932 (Pres.), Roosevelt, Dem., 259,817; Hoover, Rep., 126,806; Upshaw, Proh., 1,995; Thomas, Soc., 1,786; Foster, Com., 234.

1936 (Pres.), Roosevelt, Dem., 327,083; Landon, Rep., 146,516; Thomas, Soc., 685; Colvin, Proh., 632; Browder, Com., 319; Lemke, Union, 296.

## Tennessee (cont'd)

1940 (Pres.), Roosevelt, Dem., 351,601; Willkie, Rep., 169,153; Babson, Proh., 1,606; Thomas, Soc., 463.

1944 (Pres.), Roosevelt, Dem., 308,707; Dewey, Rep., 200,311; Watson, Proh., 882; Thomas, Soc., 892.

1948 (Pres.), Truman, Dem., 270,402; Dewey, Rep., 202,914; Thurmond, States' Rights, 73,815; Wallace, Prog., 1,864; Thomas, Soc., 1,288.

1952 (Pres.), Eisenhower, Rep., 446,147; Stevenson, Dem., 443,710; Hamblen, Proh., 1,432; Hallinan, Prog., 885; MacArthur, Christian Nationalist, 379.

1956 (Pres.), Eisenhower, Rep., 462,288; Stevenson, Dem., 456,507; Andrews, Ind., 19,820; Holtwick, Proh., 789.

1960 (Pres.), Kennedy, Dem., 481,453; Nixon, Rep., 556,577; Faubus, States' Rights, 11,304; Decker, Proh., 2,458.

1964 (Pres.), Johnson, Dem., 635,047; Goldwater, Rep., 508,965; Write-in, 34.

1968 (Pres.), Nixon, Rep., 474,086; Humphrey, Dem., 352,834; Wallace, 3rd party, 425,237.

# Texas

| County | 1968 Humphrey (D) | Nixon (R) | Wallace (I) | 1964 Johnson (D) | Goldwater (R) |
|---|---|---|---|---|---|
| Anderson | 3,447 | 2,828 | 3,196 | 4,809 | 3,362 |
| Andrews | 575 | 852 | 789 | 2,133 | 1,442 |
| Angelina | 5,174 | 4,645 | 6,111 | 8,194 | 5,262 |
| Aransas | 711 | 672 | 267 | 1,492 | 602 |
| Archer | 1,308 | 636 | 413 | 1,766 | 441 |
| Armstrong | 301 | 434 | 206 | 544 | 365 |
| Atascosa | 2,522 | 1,805 | 811 | 3,224 | 1,283 |
| Austin | 1,299 | 1,971 | 1,084 | 2,365 | 1,545 |
| Bailey | 820 | 1,174 | 563 | 1,503 | 1,056 |
| Bandera | 535 | 842 | 423 | 876 | 762 |
| Bastrop | 2,687 | 1,455 | 975 | 3,912 | 1,130 |
| Baylor | 1,064 | 657 | 443 | 1,403 | 389 |
| Bee | 2,957 | 1,995 | 589 | 3,314 | 1,509 |
| Bell | 11,893 | 5,705 | 3,547 | 14,557 | 2,938 |
| Bexar | 95,237 | 72,726 | 16,138 | 108,658 | 53,469 |
| Blanco | 575 | 577 | 200 | 1,197 | 290 |
| Borden | 157 | 117 | 112 | 266 | 152 |
| Bosque | 1,817 | 1,373 | 727 | 2,690 | 1,024 |
| Bowie | 5,555 | 5,282 | 6,354 | 10,368 | 7,018 |
| Brazoria | 11,439 | 10,631 | 8,026 | 15,917 | 8,477 |
| Brazos | 6,299 | 6,899 | 2,437 | 7,998 | 4,003 |
| Brewster | 958 | 790 | 342 | 1,251 | 358 |
| Briscoe | 528 | 411 | 219 | 966 | 342 |
| Brooks | 1,952 | 571 | 176 | 2,299 | 400 |
| Brown | 3,996 | 3,096 | 1,606 | 5,214 | 2,207 |
| Burleson | 1,678 | 541 | 694 | 2,527 | 617 |
| Burnet | 1,872 | 1,459 | 643 | 2,585 | 821 |
| Caldwell | 2,889 | 1,402 | 837 | 3,560 | 1,034 |
| Calhoun | 2,641 | 1,672 | 1,072 | 3,398 | 1,031 |
| Callahan | 1,437 | 921 | 737 | 2,178 | 849 |
| Cameron | 15,238 | 10,814 | 1,754 | 16,056 | 9,531 |
| Camp | 1,272 | 555 | 1,074 | 1,841 | 729 |
| Carson | 904 | 1,211 | 571 | 1,574 | 1,044 |
| Cass | 2,536 | 1,930 | 2,883 | 3,603 | 2,681 |
| Castro | 1,181 | 1,033 | 623 | 1,865 | 626 |
| Chambers | 1,217 | 1,061 | 1,329 | 1,921 | 1,023 |
| Cherokee | 3,242 | 2,670 | 3,795 | 5,485 | 3,043 |
| Childress | 1,093 | 1,045 | 621 | 1,977 | 952 |
| Clay | 1,573 | 936 | 665 | 2,357 | 659 |
| Cochran | 633 | 548 | 449 | 1,260 | 497 |
| Coke | 563 | 387 | 208 | 900 | 366 |
| Coleman | 1,449 | 1,507 | 1,153 | 2,670 | 1,434 |
| Collin | 5,923 | 6,494 | 4,063 | 7,833 | 3,341 |
| Coll'sworth | 746 | 712 | 475 | 1,145 | 724 |
| Colorado | 1,976 | 2,296 | 1,163 | 3,650 | 1,918 |
| Comal | 2,338 | 3,676 | 724 | 3,644 | 2,223 |
| Comanche | 1,970 | 1,284 | 708 | 2,851 | 962 |
| Concho | 468 | 318 | 156 | 948 | 307 |
| Cooke | 2,716 | 3,797 | 1,412 | 4,083 | 3,117 |
| Coryell | 2,987 | 1,698 | 1,302 | 3,679 | 877 |
| Cottle | 792 | 268 | 266 | 1,122 | 230 |
| Crane | 498 | 493 | 712 | 919 | 637 |
| Crockett | 571 | 498 | 279 | 799 | 409 |
| Crosby | 1,574 | 865 | 401 | 2,278 | 611 |
| Culberson | 329 | 298 | 145 | 473 | 314 |
| Dallam | 588 | 990 | 430 | 1,058 | 700 |
| Dallas | 123,828 | 183,759 | 55,266 | 166,472 | 137,065 |
| Dawson | 1,521 | 2,091 | 900 | 3,171 | 1,691 |
| Deaf Smith | 1,545 | 2,474 | 791 | 2,094 | 1,793 |
| Delta | 1,037 | 370 | 475 | 1,619 | 339 |
| Denton | 7,463 | 8,222 | 3,188 | 9,137 | 4,335 |
| De Witt | 1,871 | 2,599 | 784 | 3,286 | 2,283 |
| Dickens | 811 | 428 | 295 | 1,324 | 339 |
| Dimmit | 762 | 487 | 268 | 1,184 | 501 |
| Donley | 543 | 816 | 268 | 1,068 | 708 |
| Duval | 3,978 | 384 | 121 | 4,432 | 353 |
| Eastland | 1,329 | 1,420 | 582 | 4,692 | 2,049 |
| Ector | 5,312 | 10,557 | 8,671 | 10,826 | 11,497 |
| Edwards | 148 | 409 | 82 | 337 | 371 |
| Ellis | 5,431 | 3,794 | 2,841 | 7,278 | 2,779 |
| El Paso | 32,658 | 30,347 | 5,111 | 35,050 | 20,687 |
| Erath | 2,915 | 2,210 | 941 | 3,851 | 1,642 |
| Falls | 2,990 | 1,395 | 1,364 | 3,933 | 1,216 |

| Texas (cont'd) | 1968 | | | 1964 | |
|---|---|---|---|---|---|
| County | Humphrey (D) | Nixon (R) | Wallace (I) | Johnson (D) | Goldwater (R) |
| Fannin..... | 3,931 | 1,585 | 1,661 | 5,976 | 1,219 |
| Fayette..... | 1,833 | 2,380 | 1,562 | 3,630 | 2,036 |
| Fisher...... | 1,560 | 555 | 268 | 2,108 | 454 |
| Floyd....... | 1,305 | 1,465 | 847 | 2,383 | 1,229 |
| Foard...... | 594 | 216 | 168 | 833 | 146 |
| Fort Bend... | 4,494 | 4,676 | 2,447 | 6,186 | 3,493 |
| Franklin... | 1,001 | 481 | 507 | 1,520 | 424 |
| Freestone... | 2,066 | 958 | 1,069 | 2,816 | 1,074 |
| Frio........ | 1,330 | 795 | 307 | 1,507 | 607 |
| Gaines..... | 1,087 | 1,401 | 1,037 | 2,045 | 1,153 |
| Galveston... | 25,263 | 14,902 | 9,787 | 30,672 | 12,365 |
| Garza...... | 662 | 615 | 383 | 1,254 | 567 |
| Gillespie.... | 725 | 2,945 | 432 | 2,264 | 1,695 |
| Glasscock... | 106 | 169 | 172 | 179 | 183 |
| Goliad...... | 690 | 707 | 156 | 990 | 549 |
| Gonzales.... | 1,939 | 1,476 | 1,013 | 3,348 | 1,190 |
| Gray....... | 2,374 | 5,994 | 2,426 | 3,633 | 5,011 |
| Grayson.... | 10,379 | 8,043 | 4,612 | 14,207 | 5,500 |
| Gregg...... | 5,733 | 9,278 | 8,109 | 8,741 | 11,761 |
| Grimes..... | 1,473 | 1,076 | 976 | 2,229 | 1,014 |
| Guadalupe.. | 3,530 | 4,330 | 1,241 | 4,568 | 2,731 |
| Hale....... | 3,293 | 4,696 | 2,309 | 5,910 | 3,666 |
| Hall....... | 1,038 | 753 | 449 | 1,785 | 667 |
| Hamilton... | 1,116 | 1,266 | 452 | 2,048 | 1,006 |
| Hansford... | 392 | 1,359 | 437 | 860 | 1,193 |
| Hardeman... | 1,145 | 873 | 531 | 1,835 | 697 |
| Hardin..... | 2,894 | 1,968 | 3,879 | 5,143 | 1,987 |
| Harris..... | 182,522 | 203,957 | 90,270 | 227,819 | 154,401 |
| Harrison.... | 4,345 | 3,013 | 4,708 | 6,351 | 5,568 |
| Hartley.... | 299 | 597 | 264 | 565 | 437 |
| Haskell..... | 1,888 | 713 | 610 | 2,903 | 512 |
| Hayes...... | 3,546 | 2,013 | 643 | 3,780 | 1,279 |
| Hemphill... | 400 | 699 | 201 | 649 | 563 |
| Henderson.. | 3,119 | 2,310 | 2,497 | 4,697 | 1,988 |
| Hidalgo.... | 20,087 | 14,457 | 2,569 | 22,110 | 11,563 |
| Hill....... | 3,315 | 1,769 | 1,761 | 5,130 | 1,557 |
| Hockley.... | 2,489 | 2,316 | 1,492 | 4,049 | 1,674 |
| Hood....... | 763 | 383 | 247 | 1,661 | 423 |
| Hopkins.... | 2,700 | 1,859 | 1,932 | 4,133 | 1,518 |
| Houston.... | 2,782 | 1,391 | 2,062 | 3,681 | 1,675 |
| Howard.... | 3,897 | 3,805 | 2,789 | 6,083 | 3,272 |
| Hudspeth... | 289 | 285 | 132 | 438 | 224 |
| Hunt....... | 4,488 | 4,416 | 3,220 | 6,567 | 3,302 |
| Hutchinson.. | 2,416 | 4,813 | 2,909 | 4,625 | 5,358 |
| Irion...... | 187 | 211 | 92 | 351 | 199 |
| Jack...... | 1,133 | 968 | 509 | 1,594 | 847 |
| Jackson.... | 1,698 | 1,438 | 1,145 | 2,775 | 1,168 |
| Jasper..... | 3,436 | 1,859 | 2,906 | 3,600 | 1,919 |
| Jeff Davis... | 239 | 191 | 66 | 304 | 174 |
| Jefferson.... | 29,039 | 25,983 | 21,809 | 44,584 | 28,771 |
| Jim Hogg... | 1,276 | 223 | 53 | 1,375 | 152 |
| Jim Wells... | 6,304 | 2,827 | 913 | 6,849 | 1,988 |
| Johnson.... | 5,330 | 4,372 | 2,882 | 6,381 | 3,251 |
| Jones...... | 2,370 | 1,676 | 931 | 3,622 | 1,295 |
| Karnes..... | 2,277 | 1,342 | 790 | 3,178 | 993 |
| Kaufman... | 3,311 | 2,431 | 2,350 | 4,766 | 1,922 |
| Kendall.... | 538 | 1,569 | 364 | 970 | 1,200 |
| Kenedy.... | 100 | 76 | 7 | 115 | 30 |
| Kent....... | 303 | 143 | 188 | 563 | 115 |
| Kerr....... | 1,878 | 3,692 | 1,073 | 2,894 | 2,706 |
| Kimble..... | 463 | 640 | 264 | 862 | 520 |
| King....... | 109 | 44 | 71 | 180 | 34 |
| Kinney..... | 333 | 198 | 68 | 439 | 155 |
| Kleberg.... | 4,358 | 2,413 | 592 | 4,568 | 1,652 |
| Knox...... | 1,222 | 580 | 325 | 1,773 | 439 |
| Lamar..... | 4,485 | 3,496 | 2,916 | 6,303 | 2,594 |
| Lamb...... | 2,267 | 2,595 | 1,460 | 4,318 | 2,022 |
| Lampasas... | 1,423 | 935 | 470 | 2,224 | 744 |
| LaSalle..... | 645 | 324 | 112 | 988 | 223 |
| Lavaca..... | 2,165 | 1,698 | 1,451 | 4,031 | 1,480 |
| Lee........ | 1,283 | 1,075 | 631 | 1,884 | 923 |
| Leon....... | 1,545 | 669 | 880 | 2,373 | 642 |
| Liberty.... | 3,469 | 2,746 | 3,395 | 5,357 | 2,884 |
| Limestone... | 2,796 | 1,485 | 1,402 | 3,777 | 1,478 |
| Lipscomb... | 279 | 1,079 | 187 | 589 | 763 |
| Live Oak... | 922 | 931 | 484 | 1,423 | 795 |
| Llano...... | 1,292 | 1,079 | 464 | 1,727 | 655 |
| Loving..... | 18 | 23 | 40 | 46 | 32 |
| Lubbock.... | 15,385 | 25,598 | 9,074 | 22,057 | 17,372 |
| Lynn....... | 1,333 | 1,005 | 548 | 2,281 | 745 |
| Madison... | 994 | 608 | 765 | 1,298 | 644 |
| Marion..... | 1,260 | 637 | 957 | 1,372 | 927 |
| Martin..... | 390 | 343 | 539 | 892 | 402 |
| Mason..... | 560 | 789 | 169 | 941 | 590 |
| Matagorda.. | 3,595 | 3,094 | 1,770 | 4,143 | 2,407 |
| Maverick... | 1,570 | 771 | 165 | 2,113 | 545 |
| McCulloch.. | 1,350 | 947 | 259 | 2,100 | 655 |
| McLennan.. | 22,393 | 15,963 | 8,273 | 28,429 | 10,892 |
| McMullen.. | 160 | 169 | 99 | 267 | 175 |
| Medina.... | 2,754 | 2,216 | 868 | 3,408 | 1,583 |
| Menard.... | 362 | 491 | 118 | 588 | 397 |
| Midland.... | 4,756 | 12,889 | 5,675 | 8,646 | 11,906 |
| Milam..... | 3,269 | 1,614 | 1,525 | 4,368 | 1,334 |
| Mills...... | 722 | 645 | 296 | 1,228 | 495 |
| Mitchell.... | 1,689 | 893 | 499 | 2,420 | 737 |
| Montague... | 2,555 | 1,736 | 914 | 3,746 | 1,106 |
| Montgomery | 3,732 | 4,023 | 4,644 | 4,989 | 3,167 |
| Moore..... | 1,359 | 2,183 | 1,258 | 2,393 | 1,762 |
| Morris..... | 1,707 | 1,054 | 1,323 | 2,366 | 1,218 |
| Motley..... | 397 | 415 | 295 | 678 | 324 |

| Texas (cont'd) | 1968 | | | 1964 | |
|---|---|---|---|---|---|
| County | Humphrey (D) | Nixon (R) | Wallace (I) | Johnson (D) | Goldwater (R) |
| Nac'doches. | 3,349 | 3,235 | 3,198 | 4,524 | 2,976 |
| Navarro.... | 4,571 | 1,810 | 1,887 | 6,811 | 2,139 |
| Newton.... | 1,476 | 555 | 1,509 | 2,211 | 738 |
| Nolan...... | 2,644 | 1,717 | 1,077 | 3,540 | 1,610 |
| Nueces..... | 38,449 | 20,330 | 6,769 | 40,426 | 14,048 |
| Ochiltree... | 432 | 2,138 | 492 | 920 | 1,814 |
| Oldham.... | 237 | 320 | 230 | 397 | 269 |
| Orange..... | 6,485 | 5,886 | 8,845 | 9,390 | 6,216 |
| Palo Pinto. | 3,447 | 2,415 | 1,179 | 3,791 | 1,748 |
| Panola..... | 1,708 | 1,586 | 2,650 | 2,608 | 2,818 |
| Parker..... | 4,301 | 3,068 | 1,934 | 5,270 | 2,175 |
| Parmer.... | 833 | 1,539 | 730 | 1,556 | 1,216 |
| Pecos...... | 1,592 | 1,524 | 897 | 2,068 | 1,393 |
| Polk....... | 1,916 | 1,013 | 1,712 | 2,492 | 1,199 |
| Potter..... | 7,460 | 11,755 | 4,821 | 12,850 | 11,505 |
| Presidio.... | 966 | 481 | 132 | 1,156 | 431 |
| Rains...... | 558 | 340 | 306 | 893 | 272 |
| Randall.... | 4,060 | 11,400 | 3,128 | 6,016 | 7,843 |
| Reagan.... | 370 | 454 | 288 | 614 | 406 |
| Real....... | 277 | 290 | 136 | 487 | 255 |
| Red River.. | 2,245 | 1,305 | 1,554 | 3,391 | 1,257 |
| Reeves..... | 1,456 | 1,300 | 748 | 2,340 | 1,251 |
| Refugio.... | 1,699 | 1,114 | 486 | 2,319 | 772 |
| Roberts.... | 90 | 311 | 113 | 198 | 297 |
| Robertson.. | 2,742 | 894 | 869 | 3,350 | 895 |
| Rockwall... | 778 | 614 | 582 | 1,305 | 445 |
| Runnels.... | 1,448 | 1,707 | 737 | 2,645 | 1,480 |
| Rusk...... | 4,065 | 3,819 | 4,703 | 6,528 | 5,488 |
| Sabine..... | 1,078 | 455 | 935 | 1,801 | 428 |
| San Augustine. | 817 | 506 | 1,137 | 1,173 | 760 |
| San Jacinto. | 1,235 | 381 | 693 | 1,680 | 343 |
| San Patricio. | 6,375 | 3,266 | 1,764 | 7,176 | 2,188 |
| San Saba... | 1,140 | 535 | 465 | 1,859 | 418 |
| Schleicher.. | 378 | 396 | 178 | 514 | 388 |
| Scurry..... | 2,031 | 1,745 | 1,086 | 3,381 | 1,741 |
| Shackelford.. | 673 | 557 | 277 | 934 | 487 |
| Shelby..... | 294 | 302 | 565 | 3,487 | 2,220 |
| Sherman.... | 307 | 723 | 376 | 462 | 629 |
| Smith...... | 8,897 | 12,079 | 9,595 | 12,474 | 12,960 |
| Somervell... | 384 | 312 | 203 | 641 | 210 |
| Starr...... | 3,922 | 1,374 | 71 | 4,056 | 678 |
| Stephens... | 1,239 | 1,287 | 525 | 1,753 | 1,119 |
| Sterling.... | 151 | 170 | 54 | 243 | 140 |
| Stonewall... | 635 | 213 | 262 | 978 | 219 |
| Sutton..... | 351 | 412 | 147 | 694 | 357 |
| Swisher.... | 1,760 | 1,177 | 623 | 2,410 | 315 |
| Tarrant.... | 71,982 | 73,977 | 26,026 | 97,092 | 56,593 |
| Taylor..... | 9,107 | 13,366 | 4,340 | 13,366 | 9,220 |
| Terrell..... | 201 | 250 | 149 | 364 | 294 |
| Terry...... | 1,635 | 1,948 | 864 | 3,034 | 1,928 |
| Throck-morton... | 618 | 317 | 126 | 883 | 44 |
| Titus...... | 2,317 | 1,572 | 1,886 | 3,528 | 1,627 |
| Tom Green. | 6,879 | 9,705 | 3,082 | 9,767 | 6,667 |
| Travis..... | 39,685 | 34,309 | 8,798 | 44,058 | 19,838 |
| Trinity..... | 1,146 | 636 | 997 | 1,654 | 763 |
| Tyler...... | 1,204 | 1,020 | 1,444 | 1,818 | 1,216 |
| Upshur.... | 2,360 | 1,439 | 2,667 | 4,027 | 2,222 |
| Upton...... | 463 | 664 | 459 | 958 | 636 |
| Uvalde..... | 1,338 | 1,604 | 592 | 2,358 | 1,963 |
| Val Verde.. | 3,095 | 1,675 | 462 | 3,555 | 1,346 |
| Van Zandt.. | 2,706 | 1,954 | 2,090 | 4,047 | 1,614 |
| Victoria.... | 6,042 | 6,352 | 2,336 | 8,141 | 4,201 |
| Walker..... | 2,392 | 1,950 | 1,452 | 2,877 | 1,557 |
| Waller..... | 1,684 | 950 | 797 | 2,167 | 980 |
| Ward...... | 1,318 | 1,544 | 1,364 | 2,221 | 1,730 |
| Washington.. | 1,686 | 3,244 | 677 | 2,938 | 2,019 |
| Webb...... | 9,417 | 2,103 | 304 | 10,073 | 1,094 |
| Wharton.... | 3,317 | 3,227 | 1,354 | 6,234 | 2,775 |
| Wheeler.... | 812 | 1,176 | 570 | 1,440 | 1,138 |
| Wichita.... | 15,382 | 11,942 | 6,082 | 19,131 | 8,585 |
| Wilbarger... | 1,998 | 1,909 | 1,292 | 3,200 | 1,539 |
| Willacy.... | 1,930 | 1,416 | 465 | 2,152 | 1,230 |
| Williamson.. | 5,528 | 2,923 | 1,669 | 7,430 | 1,766 |
| Wilson..... | 2,071 | 843 | 386 | 3,472 | 718 |
| Winkler.... | 938 | 1,391 | 1,248 | 2,059 | 1,617 |
| Wise....... | 2,174 | 1,915 | 1,040 | 3,852 | 1,386 |
| Wood...... | 2,129 | 2,046 | 2,025 | 3,528 | 2,068 |
| Yoakum.... | 615 | 1,123 | 724 | 1,415 | 859 |
| Young..... | 2,482 | 1,860 | 1,004 | 3,395 | 1,600 |
| Zapata..... | 909 | 251 | 52 | 1,009 | 135 |
| Zavala..... | 1,307 | 693 | 214 | 1,784 | 598 |
| **Totals...** | **1,245,-116** | **1,207,-417** | **575,517** | **1,663,-185** | **958,566** |

**TEXAS VOTE SINCE 1920**

1920 (Pres.), Cox, Dem., 288,767; Harding, Rep., 114,269; Debs, Soc., 8,121; Rep. (Black and Tan), 27,247; Amer. Party, 47,968.

1924 (Pres.) Davis, Dem., 484,605; Coolidge, Rep., 130,023; LaFollette, Prog., 42,881.

1928 (Pres.) Hoover, Rep., 367,036; Smith, Dem., 341,032; Thomas, Soc., 722; Foster, Com., 209.

1932 (Pres.), Roosevelt, Dem., 760,348; Hoover, Rep., 97,959; Thomas, Soc., 4,450; Harvey, Lib., 324; Foster, Com., 207; Jackson Party, 104.

1936 (Pres.), Roosevelt, Dem., 734,485; Landon, Rep., 103,874; Lemke, Union, 3,281; Thomas,

## Texas (cont'd)

Soc., 1,075; Colvin, Proh., 514; Browder, Com., 253.
1940 (Pres.). Roosevelt, Dem., 840,151; Willkie, Rep., 199,152; Babson, Proh., 925; Thomas, Soc., 728; Browder, Com., 212.
1944 (Pres.). Roosevelt, Dem., 821,605; Dewey, Rep., 191,425; Texas Regulars, 135,439; Watson, Proh., 1,017; Thomas, Soc., 594; America First, 250.
1948 (Pres.). Truman, Dem., 750,700; Dewey, Rep., 282,240; Thurmond, States' Rights, 106,909; Wallace, Prog., 3,764; Watson, Proh., 2,758; Thomas, Soc., 874.
1952 (Pres.). Eisenhower, Rep., 1,102,878; Stevenson, Dem., 969,228; Hamblen, Proh., 1,983; MacArthur, Christian Nationalist, 833; MacArthur, Constitution, 730; Hallinan, Prog., 294.
1956 (Pres.). Eisenhower, Rep., 1,080,619; Stevenson, Dem., 859,958; Andrews, Ind., 14,591.
1960 (Pres.). Kennedy, Dem., 1,167,932; Nixon, Rep., 1,121,699; Sullivan, Constitution, 18,169; Decker, Proh., 3,870; Write-in, 175.
1964 (Pres.). Johnson, Dem., 1,663,185; Goldwater, Rep., 958,566; Lightburn, Constitution, 5,060.
1968 (Pres.). Nixon, Rep., 1,207,417; Humphrey, Dem., 1,245,116; Wallace, 3rd party. 575,517.

## Utah

| County | 1968 | | | 1964 | |
|---|---|---|---|---|---|
| | Humphrey (D) | Nixon (R) | Wallace (I) | Johnson (D) | Goldwater (R) |
| Beaver..... | 745 | 989 | 158 | 1,189 | 792 |
| Box Elder... | 3,093 | 7,767 | 907 | 5,113 | 6,851 |
| Cache..... | 4,327 | 11,911 | 1,040 | 6,627 | 9,326 |
| Carbon..... | 4,349 | 2,618 | 271 | 5,672 | 2,130 |
| Daggett.... | 97 | 152 | 42 | 170 | 112 |
| Davis..... | 10,715 | 21,165 | 2,805 | 14,177 | 14,477 |
| Duchesne... | 796 | 1,678 | 236 | 1,320 | 1,251 |
| Emery..... | 1,019 | 1,223 | 161 | 1,434 | 1,103 |
| Garfield... | 314 | 1,033 | 139 | 658 | 821 |
| Grand..... | 707 | 1,435 | 215 | 1,145 | 1,130 |
| Iron....... | 1,157 | 3,343 | 514 | 2,053 | 2,522 |
| Juab....... | 906 | 1,199 | 95 | 1,319 | 926 |
| Kane....... | 147 | 814 | 174 | 340 | 784 |
| Millard.... | 976 | 2,318 | 220 | 1,462 | 1,973 |
| Morgan..... | 551 | 1,022 | 130 | 835 | 572 |
| Piute...... | 172 | 411 | 60 | 273 | 361 |
| Rich....... | 183 | 525 | 39 | 326 | 435 |
| Salt Lake.. | 77,258 | 101,557 | 9,389 | 103,926 | 78,118 |
| San Juan... | 680 | 1,393 | 262 | 993 | 1,371 |
| Sanpete.... | 1,696 | 3,304 | 307 | 2,547 | 2,620 |
| Sevier..... | 1,167 | 3,190 | 384 | 1,948 | 2,617 |
| Summit..... | 961 | 1,787 | 113 | 1,497 | 1,331 |
| Tooele..... | 3,885 | 3,199 | 694 | 5,239 | 2,515 |
| Uintah..... | 1,150 | 3,039 | 398 | 2,142 | 2,438 |
| Utah....... | 16,762 | 28,899 | 3,800 | 19,420 | 20,934 |
| Wasatch.... | 939 | 1,612 | 86 | 1,430 | 1,105 |
| Washington. | 975 | 3,226 | 796 | 1,789 | 2,501 |
| Wayne..... | 248 | 511 | 54 | 412 | 407 |
| Weber...... | 20,102 | 36,078 | 3,491 | 29,666 | 20,262 |
| **Totals...** | **156,077** | **247,398** | **26,980** | **219,628** | **181,785** |

### UTAH VOTE SINCE 1920

1920 (Pres.), Cox, Dem., 56,639; Harding, Rep., 81,555; Debs, Soc., 3,159; F.-Lab., 4,475.
1924 (Pres.), Coolidge, Rep., 77,327; Davis, Dem., 47,001; LaFollette, Prog., 33,662.
1928 (Pres.), Hoover, Rep., 94,618; Smith, Dem., 80,985; Thomas, Soc., 954; Foster, Com., 47.
1932 (Pres.), Roosevelt, Dem., 116,750; Hoover, Rep., 84,795; Thomas, Soc., 4,087; Foster, Com., 947.
1936 (Pres.), Roosevelt, Dem., 150,246; Landon, Rep., 64,555; Lemke, Union, 1,121; Thomas, Soc., 432; Browder, Com., 280; Colvin, Proh., 43.
1940 (Pres.), Roosevelt, Dem., 154,277; Willkie, Rep., 93,151; Thomas, Soc., 200; Browder, Com., 191.
1944 (Pres.), Roosevelt, Dem., 150,088; Dewey, Rep., 97,891; Thomas, Soc., 340.
1948 (Pres.), Truman, Dem., 149,151; Dewey, Rep., 124,402; Wallace, Prog., 2,679; Dobbs, Soc. Workers, 73.
1952 (Pres.), Eisenhower, Rep., 194,190; Stevenson, Dem., 135,364.
1956 (Pres.), Eisenhower, Rep., 215,631; Stevenson, Dem., 118,364.
1960 (Pres.), Kennedy, Dem., 169,248; Nixon, Rep., 205,361; Dobbs, Soc. Workers, 100.
1964 (Pres.), Johnson, Dem., 219,628; Goldwater, Rep., 181,785.
1968 (Pres.), Nixon, Rep., 247,398; Humphrey, Dem., 156,077; Wallace, 3rd party, 26,980.

# Vermont

| County | 1968 | | | 1964 | |
|---|---|---|---|---|---|
| | Humphrey (D) | Nixon (R) | Wallace (I) | Johnson (D) | Goldwater (R) |
| Addison.... | 2,913 | 5,007 | 303 | 4,781 | 3,499 |
| Bennington | 4,966 | 5,929 | 421 | 7,222 | 3,890 |
| Caledonia.. | 3,204 | 4,995 | 254 | 5,730 | 3,266 |
| Chittenden. | 16,637 | 14,660 | 794 | 21,492 | 8,962 |
| Essex...... | 1,003 | 1,009 | 58 | 1,673 | 747 |
| Franklin... | 5,997 | 5,217 | 353 | 8,823 | 3,260 |
| Grand Isle. | 730 | 754 | 72 | 993 | 506 |
| Lamoille... | 1,239 | 2,962 | 141 | 2,375 | 2,038 |
| Orange..... | 1,862 | 4,130 | 209 | 3,917 | 2,723 |
| Orleans.... | 2,695 | 4,057 | 274 | 4,892 | 3,029 |
| Rutland.... | 9,051 | 10,314 | 764 | 13,244 | 7,167 |
| Washington | 7,287 | 9,384 | 501 | 11,994 | 5,750 |
| Windham.... | 5,332 | 6,916 | 374 | 8,370 | 4,184 |
| Windsor.... | 6,990 | 9,794 | 435 | 12,168 | 5,847 |
| **Totals...** | **70,446** | **85,128** | **4,953** | **107,674** | **54,868** |

### VERMONT VOTE SINCE 1920

1920 (Pres.), Cox, Dem., 20,919; Harding, Rep., 68,212; Watkins, Proh., 774.
1924 (Pres.), Coolidge, Rep., 80,498; Davis, Dem., 16,124; LaFollette, Prog., 5,964; Faris, Proh., 326.
1928 (Pres.), Hoover, Rep., 90,404; Smith, Dem., 44,440; Varney, Proh., 338.
1932 (Pres.), Roosevelt, Dem., 56,266; Hoover, Rep., 78,984; Thomas, Soc., 1,533; Foster, Com., 195.
1936 (Pres.), Landon, Rep., 81,023; Roosevelt, Dem., 62,124; Browder, Com., 405.
1940 (Pres.), Roosevelt, Dem., 64,269; Willkie, Rep., 78,371; Browder, Com., 411.
1944 (Pres.), Roosevelt, Dem., 53,820; Dewey, Rep., 71,527.
1948 (Pres.), Truman, Dem., 45,557; Dewey, Rep., 75,926; Wallace, Prog., 1,279; Thomas, Soc., 585.
1952 (Pres.), Eisenhower, Rep., 109,717; Stevenson, Dem., 43,355; Hallinan, Prog., 282; Hoopes, Soc., 185.
1956 (Pres.), Eisenhower, Rep., 110,390; Stevenson, Dem., 42,549; Scattered, 39.
1960 (Pres.), Kennedy, Dem., 69,186; Nixon, Rep., 98,131.
1964 (Pres.), Johnson, Dem., 107,674; Goldwater, Rep., 54,868.
1968 (Pres.), Nixon, Rep., 85,128; Humphrey, Dem., 70,446; Wallace, 3rd party, 4,953; scattered, 550.

# Virginia

| County | 1968 | | | 1964 | |
|---|---|---|---|---|---|
| | Humphrey (D) | Nixon (R) | Wallace (I) | Johnson (D) | Goldwater (R) |
| Accomack... | 2,466 | 3,231 | 3,460 | 3,528 | 3,144 |
| Albemarle.. | 2,257 | 4,513 | 1,677 | 3,062 | 3,255 |
| Alleghany.. | 986 | 1,653 | 1,152 | 1,580 | 1,101 |
| Amelia..... | 826 | 859 | 832 | 884 | 1,348 |
| Amherst.... | 1,414 | 2,431 | 2,199 | 2,730 | 2,675 |
| App'matt'x. | 756 | 1,744 | 1,512 | 1,339 | 2,444 |
| Arlington.. | 26,105 | 28,161 | 6,746 | 33,567 | 20,485 |
| Augusta.... | 2,028 | 6,313 | 2,483 | 4,039 | 4,327 |
| Bath....... | 494 | 872 | 529 | 770 | 516 |
| Bedford.... | 2,141 | 3,989 | 4,176 | 3,806 |
| Bland...... | 560 | 938 | 361 | 851 | 717 |
| Botetourt.. | 1,272 | 2,599 | 1,267 | 2,377 | 2,098 |
| Brunswick.. | 1,910 | 1,141 | 2,084 | 18,833 | 2,560 |
| Buchanan... | 5,249 | 3,666 | 975 | 4,756 | 2,349 |
| Buck'h'm... | 984 | 1,026 | 1,185 | 1,182 | 1,547 |
| Campbell... | 1,985 | 5,780 | 4,425 | 3,401 | 5,713 |
| Caroline... | 2,165 | 1,629 | 1,084 | 2,064 | 1,166 |
| Carroll.... | 1,773 | 4,924 | 959 | 2,517 | 3,617 |
| Charles C'y | 1,457 | 320 | 176 | 1,023 | 323 |
| Charlotte.. | 945 | 1,042 | 2,163 | 1,191 | 1,974 |
| Chesterf'd. | 5,714 | 21,992 | 11,493 | 8,376 | 17,486 |
| Clarke..... | 768 | 1,127 | 742 | 1,136 | 1,068 |
| Craig...... | 419 | 580 | 256 | 767 | 477 |
| Culpeper... | 1,239 | 2,229 | 1,217 | 1,886 | 1,775 |
| Cumberl'd.. | 978 | 844 | 607 | 871 | 1,099 |
| Dickenson.. | 3,320 | 3,407 | 634 | 3,485 | 2,143 |
| Dinwiddie.. | 1,552 | 1,451 | 2,245 | 2,182 | 2,096 |
| Essex...... | 896 | 792 | 528 | 760 | 789 |
| Fairfax.... | 44,746 | 57,650 | 14,705 | 48,680 | 30,755 |
| Fauquier... | 2,099 | 2,845 | 1,536 | 3,506 | 2,101 |
| Floyd...... | 715 | 2,275 | 537 | 1,144 | 1,836 |
| Fluvanna... | 772 | 1,137 | 725 | 1,008 | 823 |
| Franklin... | 2,025 | 3,042 | 3,219 | 3,447 | 2,279 |
| Frederick.. | 1,611 | 3,697 | 2,137 | 2,580 | 2,585 |
| Giles...... | 2,038 | 2,721 | 1,368 | 3,133 | 1,952 |
| Gloucester. | 1,210 | 1,619 | 1,525 | 1,949 | 1,631 |
| Goochland.. | 1,389 | 1,216 | 837 | 1,452 | 1,241 |
| Grayson.... | 1,926 | 3,563 | 1,090 | 3,238 | 3,015 |
| Greene..... | 255 | 856 | 433 | 460 | 641 |
| Greensville. | 1,367 | 529 | 1,256 | 2,262 | 2,245 |

## Virginia (cont'd)

| County | 1968 Humphrey (D) | Nixon (R) | Wallace (I) | 1964 Johnson (D) | Goldwater (R) |
|---|---|---|---|---|---|
| Halifax..... | 2,199 | 2,634 | 4,235 | 2,198 | 3,928 |
| Hanover.... | 2,029 | 5,148 | 3,038 | 2,864 | 4,879 |
| Henrico.... | 8,500 | 34,218 | 11,700 | 12,779 | 29,286 |
| Henry...... | 4,235 | 3,946 | 6,900 | 5,295 | 2,844 |
| Highland ... | 284 | 619 | 166 | 476 | 511 |
| Isle of Wi'ht | 1,977 | 1,312 | 2,328 | 2,656 | 1,737 |
| James City.. | 1,521 | 1,443 | 1,083 | 1,744 | 1,092 |
| King George | 882 | 568 | 614 | 1,085 | 644 |
| King & Q'n.. | 730 | 829 | 632 | 786 | 699 |
| King Wm... | 764 | 1,045 | 615 | 904 | 1,065 |
| Lancaster... | 1,134 | 1,640 | 876 | 1,245 | 1,663 |
| Lee....... | 4,198 | 4,366 | 762 | 5,151 | 3,463 |
| Loudoun.... | 3,262 | 4,577 | 2,110 | 4,278 | 2,594 |
| Louisa...... | 1,288 | 1,509 | 1,146 | 1,731 | 1,369 |
| Lunenburg.. | 1,252 | 1,181 | 1,626 | 1,128 | 1,847 |
| Madison.... | 478 | 1,188 | 763 | 862 | 1,060 |
| Mathews.... | 691 | 1,309 | 773 | 1,137 | 1,149 |
| Mecklenb'g. | 2,667 | 2,750 | 4,022 | 3,238 | 4,976 |
| Middlesex... | 575 | 809 | 655 | 973 | 1,019 |
| Montgom'y. | 2,700 | 7,098 | 1,719 | 3,872 | 4,604 |
| Nansem'nd.. | 4,173 | 2,101 | 3,721 | 4,804 | 2,590 |
| Nelson...... | 1,120 | 1,130 | 1,206 | 1,635 | 893 |
| New Kent... | 765 | 526 | 609 | 684 | 677 |
| N'th'mton.. | 1,418 | 1,410 | 1,229 | 1,516 | 1,586 |
| No'th'berl'd. | 1,077 | 1,438 | 965 | 988 | 1,423 |
| Nottoway... | 1,529 | 1,514 | 1,673 | 2,138 | 2,353 |
| Orange..... | 580 | 1,727 | 1,050 | 1,508 | 1,595 |
| Page........ | 2,125 | 3,667 | 995 | 2,606 | 2,804 |
| Patrick..... | 1,953 | 2,609 | 1,876 | 2,306 | 1,468 |
| Pitts'lvania. | 5,340 | 5,041 | 9,367 | 5,228 | 7,120 |
| Powhatan... | 1,004 | 722 | 929 | 969 | 1,182 |
| Prince Ed... | 1,567 | 1,857 | 1,224 | 1,512 | 2,545 |
| Prince Geo.. | 1,272 | 1,559 | 1,920 | 1,502 | 1,790 |
| Pr. Will'm.. | 5,246 | 7,994 | 5,160 | 5,611 | 3,343 |
| Pulaski..... | 2,497 | 4,409 | 1,346 | 3,620 | 3,101 |
| Rapp'h'nock | 330 | 498 | 307 | 675 | 449 |
| Richmond... | 397 | 878 | 445 | 636 | 901 |
| Roanoke.... | 3,903 | 12,440 | 4,746 | 8,808 | 10,714 |
| Rockbridge. | 845 | 2,320 | 1,037 | 2,599 | 2,200 |
| Rock'gham.. | 2,111 | 7,729 | 1,809 | 4,205 | 4,155 |
| Russell..... | 3,564 | 3,857 | 1,369 | 4,330 | 3,012 |
| Scott....... | 3,138 | 5,345 | 1,510 | 4,720 | 4,533 |
| Shenandoah. | 1,654 | 5,482 | 1,511 | 3,184 | 3,981 |
| Smyth...... | 2,631 | 5,297 | 1,809 | 4,113 | 3,830 |
| So'th'mton.. | 1,803 | 1,376 | 2,068 | 2,566 | 1,520 |
| Spots'v'nia.. | 1,647 | 1,676 | 1,589 | 2,097 | 1,261 |
| Stafford.... | 1,698 | 2,572 | 2,197 | 2,489 | 1,888 |
| Surry....... | 1,126 | 523 | 708 | 1,131 | 1,004 |
| Sussex...... | 1,541 | 1,105 | 1,135 | 1,234 | 1,537 |
| Tazewell.... | 4,729 | 4,424 | 2,017 | 6,081 | 3,231 |
| Warren..... | 1,513 | 2,296 | 1,479 | 2,494 | 1,886 |
| Washington. | 3,243 | 6,663 | 3,090 | 5,070 | 4,146 |
| Westm'l'nd. | 1,156 | 1,402 | 943 | 1,312 | 1,181 |
| Wise....... | 6,497 | 5,483 | 1,848 | 7,220 | 3,309 |
| Wythe..... | 1,765 | 3,638 | 1,375 | 2,879 | 2,958 |
| York....... | 1,409 | 2,519 | 2,576 | 3,385 | 2,992 |
| **Total Counties...** | **252,844** | **380,804** | **200,852** | **331,679** | **308,879** |
| **City** | | | | | |
| Alexandria.. | 14,351 | 13,265 | 4,131 | 16,828 | 8,825 |
| Bristol..... | 1,531 | 1,930 | 911 | 2,429 | 1,289 |
| Buena Vista. | 387 | 814 | 456 | 691 | 459 |
| Ch'l'tt'ville. | 3,831 | 5,601 | 1,764 | 5,205 | 4,415 |
| Chesapeake. | 6,709 | 6,203 | 11,061 | 9,532 | 9,038 |
| Clft'n F'rge. | 734 | 925 | 462 | 1,252 | 850 |
| ColonialH'ts | 650 | 2,650 | 2,106 | 1,198 | 2,420 |
| Covington... | 1,195 | 1,551 | 846 | 2,055 | 1,149 |
| Danville.... | 4,498 | 6,796 | 5,391 | 4,539 | 7,900 |
| Emporia.... | 657 | 812 | 716 | | |
| Fairfax..... | 2,149 | 2,961 | 959 | 2,835 | 1,924 |
| Falls Church | 1,877 | 1,885 | 494 | 2,371 | 1,329 |
| Franklin.... | 790 | 1,000 | 510 | 1,257 | 783 |
| Fred'cksb'g . | 2,036 | 2,142 | 878 | 2,410 | 1,511 |
| Galax...... | 748 | 1,257 | 304 | 717 | 697 |
| Hampton.... | 11,309 | 10,532 | 10,689 | 13,542 | 8,731 |
| Harris'nb'g.. | 1,036 | 2,859 | 453 | 1,765 | 1,820 |
| Hopewell... | 1,568 | 2,942 | 2,092 | 2,498 | 3,183 |
| Lexington... | 734 | 1,170 | 177 | | |
| Lynchburg.. | 4,335 | 9,913 | 3,649 | 6,758 | 10,044 |
| Martinsville. | 2,727 | 2,618 | 1,856 | 2,943 | 1,805 |
| N'p't News. | 13,786 | 12,565 | 10,115 | 15,296 | 10,584 |
| Norfolk.... | 28,683 | 22,288 | 14,502 | 32,388 | 18,429 |
| Norton..... | 555 | 495 | 215 | 824 | 372 |
| Petersburg.. | 10,508 | 6,198 | 6,834 | 4,521 | 3,253 |
| Portsmouth. | 15,736 | 9,402 | 12,127 | 16,073 | 8,420 |
| Radford.... | 1,206 | 2,077 | 461 | 1,850 | 1,505 |
| Richmond .. | 32,856 | 26,375 | 8,539 | 35,662 | 27,196 |
| Roanoke.... | 9,156 | 16,147 | 5,070 | 15,314 | 13,164 |
| Salem...... | 1,369 | 3,945 | 1,507 | | |
| So. Boston.. | 620 | 1,298 | 659 | 636 | 1,206 |
| Staunton.... | 1,729 | 4,434 | 1,054 | 2,705 | 2,969 |
| Suffolk..... | 1,044 | 1,277 | 1,039 | 1,579 | 1,463 |
| Virginia B'h. | 10,036 | 16,218 | 10,915 | 12,892 | 10,529 |
| Waynesboro. | 1,446 | 3,302 | 816 | 2,369 | 2,107 |
| Wil'msburg | 991 | 1,156 | 247 | 1,171 | 906 |
| Winchester.. | 1,358 | 2,708 | 770 | 2,254 | 2,180 |
| **Total, Ct's** | **194,831** | **209,711** | **124,575** | **226,359** | **172,455** |
| **Co's & Cit's** | **447,675** | **590,515** | **325,427** | **558,038** | **481,334** |

## Virginia (cont'd)

### VIRGINIA VOTE SINCE 1920

1920 (Pres.), Cox, Dem., 141,670; Harding, Rep., 87,456; Watkins, Proh., 826; Debs, Soc., 807; Christensen, Farm.-Lab., 240.

1924 (Pres.), Davis, Dem., 139,797; Coolidge, Rep., 73,359; LaFollette, Prog., 10,379; Johns, Soc. Lab., 191.

1928 (Pres.), Hoover, Rep., 164,609; Smith, Dem., 140,146; Thomas, Soc., 250; Reynolds, Soc. Lab., 180; Foster, Com., 173.

1932 (Pres.), Roosevelt, Dem., 203,979; Hoover, Rep., 89,637; Thomas, Soc., 2,382; Upshaw, Proh., 1,843; Foster, Com., 86; Cox. Ind., 15.

1936 (Pres.), Roosevelt, Dem., 234,980; Landon, Rep., 98,366; Colvin, Proh., 594; Thomas, Soc., 313; Lemke, Union, 233; Browder, Com., 98.

1940 (Pres.), Roosevelt, Dem., 235,961; Willkie, Rep., 109,363; Babson, Proh., 882; Thomas, Soc., 282; Browder, Com., 71; Aiken, Soc. Lab., 48.

1944 (Pres.), Roosevelt, Dem., 242,276; Dewey, Rep., 145,243; Watson, Proh., 459; Thomas, Soc., 417; Teichert, Soc. Lab., 90.

1948 (Pres.), Truman, Dem., 200,786; Dewey, Rep., 172,070; Thurmond, States' Rights, 43,393; Wallace, Prog., 2,047; Thomas, Soc., 726; Teichert, Soc. Lab., 234.

1952 (Pres.), Eisenhower, Rep., 349,037; Stevenson, Dem., 268,677; Hass, Soc. Lab., 1,160; Hoopes, Social Dem., 504; Hallinan, Prog., 311.

1956 (Pres.), Eisenhower, Rep., 386,459; Stevenson, Dem., 267,760; Andrews, States' Rights, 42,964; Hoopes, Soc. Dem., 444; Hass, Soc. Lab., 351.

1960 (Pres.), Kennedy, Dem., 362,327; Nixon, Rep., 404,521; Coiner, Conservative, 4,204; Hass, Soc. Lab., 397.

1964 (Pres.), Johnson, Dem., 558,038; Goldwater, Rep. 481,334; Hass, Soc. Lab., 2,895.

1968 (Pres.), Nixon, Rep., 590,515; Humphrey, Dem., 447,675; Wallace, 3rd party, 325,427; scattered 1,432.

# Washington

| County | 1968 Humphrey (D) | Nixon (R) | Wallace (I) | 1964 Johnson (D) | Goldwater (R) |
|---|---|---|---|---|---|
| Adams..... | 1,162 | 2,318 | 275 | 2,027 | 2,241 |
| Asotin..... | 2,495 | 2,002 | 384 | 3,657 | 1,777 |
| Benton..... | 9,795 | 12,898 | 2,703 | 16,650 | 11,708 |
| Chelan..... | 6,172 | 8,003 | 1,109 | 10,295 | 7,406 |
| Clallam.... | 6,412 | 5,190 | 1,086 | 9,265 | 4,175 |
| Clark...... | 20,077 | 16,092 | 2,076 | 29,341 | 12,300 |
| Columbia... | 683 | 1,056 | 149 | 1,138 | 1,048 |
| Cowlitz.... | 12,563 | 9,837 | 1,375 | 17,605 | 6,708 |
| Douglas.... | 2,538 | 2,934 | 586 | 3,728 | 2,643 |
| Ferry...... | 519 | 535 | 162 | 931 | 526 |
| Franklin... | 3,620 | 3,678 | 1,130 | 6,375 | 3,615 |
| Garfield.... | 598 | 848 | 140 | 781 | 751 |
| Grant..... | 5,098 | 6,072 | 1,340 | 8,352 | 6,065 |
| Grays H'bor | 11,452 | 6,296 | 1,109 | 17,145 | 5,744 |
| Island..... | 2,853 | 3,399 | 550 | 3,946 | 3,044 |
| Jefferson... | 2,020 | 1,496 | 346 | 3,012 | 1,432 |
| King...... | 202,957 | 193,402 | 28,409 | 268,216 | 177,598 |
| Kitsap..... | 20,465 | 13,429 | 2,610 | 26,904 | 10,702 |
| Kittitas.... | 3,519 | 3,670 | 474 | 5,383 | 3,200 |
| Klickitat... | 2,204 | 2,066 | 289 | 3,819 | 1,850 |
| Lewis...... | 7,956 | 7,966 | 1,197 | 12,070 | 6,933 |
| Lincoln.... | 1,505 | 2,684 | 289 | 2,299 | 2,911 |
| Mason..... | 4,216 | 2,766 | 564 | 5,514 | 2,549 |
| O kanogan.. | 3,878 | 3,901 | 945 | 6,554 | 3,931 |
| Pacific..... | 3,526 | 2,276 | 326 | 5,056 | 1,789 |
| Pend Oreille | 1,203 | 956 | 192 | 1,978 | 985 |
| Pierce..... | 67,452 | 45,357 | 10,201 | 84,566 | 40,164 |
| San Juan... | 556 | 897 | 81 | 906 | 839 |
| Skagit..... | 9,717 | 9,041 | 1,363 | 14,162 | 8,138 |
| Skamania... | 1,129 | 834 | 160 | 1,758 | 653 |
| Snohomish.. | 40,892 | 33,810 | 6,326 | 55,013 | 25,902 |
| Spokane.... | 45,872 | 47,039 | 7,519 | 62,092 | 49,387 |
| Stevens.... | 2,674 | 3,044 | 831 | 4,266 | 3,302 |
| Thurston... | 12,737 | 11,958 | 2,129 | 17,578 | 9,351 |
| Wahkiakum. | 834 | 571 | 117 | 1,175 | 446 |
| Walla Walla | 5,280 | 8,753 | 911 | 9,481 | 8,102 |
| Whatcom... | 12,539 | 12,769 | 2,067 | 20,297 | 10,900 |
| Whitman... | 4,573 | 6,872 | 620 | 6,760 | 6,765 |
| Yakima.... | 17,865 | 24,576 | 3,573 | 29,604 | 22,786 |
| **Totals...** | **561,675** | **520,491** | **85,713** | **779,699** | **470,366** |

### WASHINGTON VOTE SINCE 1916

1916 (Pres.), Wilson, Dem., 183,388; Hughes, Rep., 167,244; Hanly, Proh., 6,868; Benson, Soc., 22,800.

1920 (Pres.), Cox, Dem., 84,298; Harding, Rep., 223,137; Watkins, Proh., 3,790; Debs, Soc., 8,913; Christensen, Farm.-Lab., 77,246.

1924 (Pres.), Coolidge, Rep., 220,224; LaFollette, Prog., 150,727; Davis, Dem., 42,842; Nations, Amer., 5,991; Johns, Soc. Lab., 1,004; Foster, Workers, 761.

## Washington (cont'd)

1928 (Pres.), Hoover, Rep., 335,884; Smith, Dem., 156,772; Thomas, Soc., 2,614; Reynolds, Soc. Lab., 4,068; Foster, Com., 1,541.

1932 (Pres.), Roosevelt, Dem., 353,260; Hoover, Rep., 208,645; Harvey, Lib., 30,308; Thomas, Soc., 17,080; Foster, Com., 2,972; Upshaw, Proh., 1,540; Reynolds, Soc. Lab., 1,009.

1936 (Pres.), Roosevelt, Dem., 459,579; Landon, Rep., 206,892; Lemke, Union, 17,463; Thomas, Soc., 3,496; Browder, Com., 1,907; Pellsy, Christian, 1,598; Colvin, Proh., 1,041; Aiken, Soc. Lab., 362.

1940 (Pres.), Roosevelt, Dem., 462,145; Willkie, Rep., 322,123; Thomas, Soc., 4,586; Browder, Com., 2,626; Babson, Proh., 1,686; Aiken, Soc. Lab., 667.

1944 (Pres.), Roosevelt, Dem., 486,774; Dewey, Rep., 361,689; Thomas, Soc., 3,824; Watson, Proh., 2,396; Teichert, Soc. Lab., 1,645.

1948 (Pres.), Truman, Dem., 476,165; Dewey, Rep., 386,315; Wallace, Prog., 31,692; Watson, Proh., 6,117; Thomas, Soc., 3,534; Teichert, Soc. Lab., 1,133; Dobbs, Soc. Workers, 103.

1952 (Pres.), Eisenhower, Rep., 599,107; Stevenson, Dem., 492,845; MacArthur, Christian Nationalist, 7,290; Hallinan, Prog., 2,460; Hass, Soc. Lab., 633; Hoopes, Soc., 254; Dobbs, Soc. Workers, 119.

1956 (Pres.), Eisenhower, Rep., 620,430; Stevenson, Dem., 523,002; Hass, Soc. Lab., 7,457.

1960 (Pres.), Kennedy, Dem., 599,298; Nixon, Rep., 629,273; Hass, Soc. Lab., 10,895; Curtis, Constitution, 1,401; Dobbs, Soc. Workers, 705.

1964 (Pres.), Johnson, Dem., 779,699; Goldwater, Rep., 470,366; Hass, Soc. Labor, 7,772; DeBerry, Freedom Soc., 537.

1968 (Pres.), Nixon, Rep., 520,491; Humphrey, Dem., 561,675; Wallace, 3rd party, 85,713; scattered, 1,783.

### West Virginia

| County | 1968 Humphrey (D) | Nixon (R) | Wallace (I) | 1964 Johnson (D) | Goldwater (R) |
|---|---|---|---|---|---|
| Barbour.... | 3,051 | 3,107 | 424 | 4,758 | 2,533 |
| Berkeley.... | 3,507 | 4,811 | 1,665 | 8,628 | 5,457 |
| Boone...... | 6,354 | 2,959 | 913 | 8,609 | 2,467 |
| Braxton .... | 3,267 | 2,440 | 384 | 4,787 | 1,867 |
| Brooke...... | 7,195 | 3,949 | 1,399 | 9,834 | 3,364 |
| Cabell...... | 18,909 | 19,388 | 4,618 | 28,437 | 16,957 |
| Calhoun.... | 1,684 | 1,612 | 318 | 2,626 | 1,275 |
| Clay...... | 1,916 | 1,474 | 349 | 3,182 | 1,366 |
| Doddridge.. | 844 | 1,861 | 146 | 1,587 | 1,581 |
| Fayette.... | 13,723 | 4,818 | 1,828 | 19,990 | 4,051 |
| Gilmer..... | 1,581 | 1,401 | 214 | 2,832 | 1,116 |
| Grant...... | 786 | 2,936 | 256 | 1,494 | 2,464 |
| Greenbrier.. | 5,550 | 5,094 | 1,465 | 10,112 | 4,549 |
| Hampshire.. | 1,546 | 1,699 | 564 | 3,381 | 1,473 |
| Hancock.... | 8,972 | 5,115 | 2,053 | 14,001 | 5,009 |
| Hardy...... | 1,767 | 1,768 | 490 | 2,996 | 1,308 |
| Harrison.... | 17,849 | 13,100 | 1,978 | 25,683 | 9,986 |
| Jackson..... | 2,549 | 4,019 | 699 | 5,022 | 4,359 |
| Jefferson.... | 3,122 | 2,711 | 447 | 5,901 | 1,901 |
| Kanawha... | 46,352 | 41,784 | 11,517 | 70,511 | 38,383 |
| Lewis...... | 3,155 | 4,031 | 637 | 5,248 | 2,979 |
| Lincoln..... | 3,668 | 2,875 | 416 | 5,852 | 3,436 |
| Logan...... | 13,355 | 4,700 | 1,838 | 16,999 | 3,776 |
| Marion..... | 16,120 | 9,434 | 1,714 | 22,047 | 7,707 |
| Marshall.... | 7,549 | 6,104 | 1,189 | 11,757 | 6,175 |
| Mason..... | 3,699 | 4,217 | 691 | 6,511 | 4,467 |
| McDowell... | 12,796 | 3,999 | 2,029 | 18,046 | 3,684 |
| Mercer..... | 11,314 | 8,580 | 2,872 | 18,298 | 8,905 |
| Mineral.... | 3,449 | 3,843 | 950 | 6,344 | 3,801 |
| Mingo..... | 8,591 | 3,861 | 1,119 | 12,266 | 3,154 |
| Monongalia.. | 4,290 | 3,091 | 482 | 17,358 | 6,473 |
| Monroe..... | 2,377 | 2,911 | 531 | 3,367 | 2,385 |
| Morgan..... | 1,014 | 2,243 | 461 | 1,820 | 1,866 |
| Nicholas.... | 4,843 | 3,662 | 839 | 6,878 | 2,628 |
| Ohio...... | 13,096 | 10,936 | 1,880 | 21,178 | 12,006 |
| Pendleton... | 1,921 | 949 | 158 | 2,498 | 1,296 |
| Pleasants... | 1,522 | 1,534 | 204 | 2,287 | 1,339 |
| Pocahontas.. | 1,835 | 1,936 | 422 | 3,317 | 1,716 |
| Preston.... | 3,552 | 4,930 | 476 | 6,264 | 4,015 |
| Putnam.... | 4,150 | 4,402 | 1,110 | 6,910 | 4,165 |
| Raleigh.... | 14,585 | 7,055 | 2,414 | 23,606 | 6,952 |
| Randolph.... | 4,330 | 3,582 | 705 | 8,012 | 2,984 |
| Ritchie..... | 1,279 | 2,993 | 284 | 2,244 | 2,717 |
| Roane...... | 2,635 | 3,779 | 424 | 3,820 | 3,451 |
| Summers.... | 2,993 | 1,846 | 683 | 5,037 | 1,962 |
| Taylor..... | 2,951 | 3,004 | 466 | 4,442 | 2,292 |
| Tucker..... | 1,752 | 1,498 | 332 | 2,664 | 1,314 |
| Tyler...... | 1,125 | 2,590 | 260 | 2,275 | 2,522 |
| Upshur..... | 1,878 | 3,816 | 417 | 3,774 | 3,606 |
| Wayne..... | 6,101 | 3,541 | 1,879 | 11,578 | 5,340 |
| Webster.... | 2,533 | 1,253 | 278 | 3,755 | 936 |
| Wetzel..... | 3,691 | 3,660 | 732 | 6,329 | 3,215 |
| Wirt...... | 819 | 1,050 | 140 | 1,286 | 899 |
| Wood...... | 8,624 | 11,617 | 2,316 | 21,560 | 14,947 |
| Wyoming... | 6,596 | 3,936 | 1,005 | 9,188 | 3,377 |
| **Totals...** | **334,856** | **269,504** | **64,635** | **538,087** | **253,953** |

### WEST VIRGINIA VOTES SINCE 1920

1920 (Pres.), Cox, Dem., 220,789; Harding, Rep., 282,007; Watkins, Proh., 1,528; Debs, Soc., 5,618.

1924 (Pres.), Coolidge, Rep., 288,635; Davis, Dem., 257,232; LaFollette, Prog., 36,723; Nations, Amer., 1,072.

1928 (Pres.), Hoover, Rep., 375,551; Smith, Dem., 263,748; Thomas, Soc., 1,313; Varney, Proh., 1,703; Foster, Com., 401.

1932 (Pres.), Roosevelt, Dem., 405,124; Hoover, Rep., 330,731; Thomas, Soc., 5,133; Upshaw, Proh., 2,342; Foster, Com., 444.

1936 (Pres.), Roosevelt, Dem., 502,582, Landon, Rep., 325,358; Colvin, Proh., 1,173; Thomas, Soc., 832.

1940 (Pres.), Roosevelt, Dem., 495,662; Willkie, Rep., 372,414.

1944 (Pres.), Roosevelt, Dem., 392,777; Dewey, Rep., 322,819.

1948 (Pres.), Truman, Dem., 429,188; Dewey, Rep., 316,251; Wallace, Prog., 3,311.

1952 (Pres.), Eisenhower, Rep., 419,970; Stevenson, Dem., 453,578.

1956 (Pres.), Eisenhower, Rep., 449,297; Stevenson, Dem., 381,534.

1960 (Pres.), Kennedy, Dem., 441,786; Nixon, Rep., 395,995.

1964 (Pres.), Johnson, Dem., 538,087; Goldwater, Rep., 253,953.

1968 (Pres.), Nixon, Rep., 269,504; Humphrey, Dem., 334,856; Wallace, 3rd party, 64,635.

### Wisconsin

| County | 1968 Humphrey (D) | Nixon (R) | Wallace (I) | 1964 Johnson (D) | Goldwater (R) |
|---|---|---|---|---|---|
| Adams..... | 1,614 | 1,691 | 461 | 2,262 | 1,219 |
| Ashland.... | 4,147 | 2,557 | 401 | 5,383 | 2,198 |
| Barron..... | 5,183 | 7,526 | 867 | 8,332 | 5,701 |
| Bayfield.... | 3,036 | 2,333 | 323 | 3,875 | 1,886 |
| Brown..... | 21,615 | 30,133 | 4,341 | 30,851 | 21,134 |
| Buffalo..... | 2,122 | 2,992 | 413 | 3,663 | 2,091 |
| Burnett..... | 2,010 | 2,056 | 414 | 2,921 | 1,536 |
| Calumet.... | 3,609 | 5,792 | 792 | 5,356 | 3,905 |
| Chippewa... | 7,335 | 7,772 | 1,282 | 10,911 | 6,277 |
| Clark...... | 4,601 | 6,325 | 1,398 | 7,781 | 4,897 |
| Columbia... | 6,698 | 8,633 | 1,067 | 10,093 | 6,253 |
| Crawford... | 2,391 | 3,316 | 419 | 3,930 | 2,726 |
| Dane...... | 59,951 | 39,917 | 3,771 | 68,118 | 27,124 |
| Dodge..... | 8,948 | 14,909 | 1,875 | 15,497 | 10,772 |
| Door...... | 2,728 | 5,647 | 535 | 4,416 | 4,289 |
| Douglas.... | 12,506 | 5,656 | 930 | 15,237 | 4,579 |
| Dunn...... | 4,392 | 5,415 | 709 | 6,475 | 3,964 |
| Eau Claire.. | 12,302 | 11,799 | 1,169 | 15,775 | 8,700 |
| Florence.... | 718 | 821 | 157 | 1,029 | 596 |
| Fond du Lac | 12,563 | 18,184 | 1,934 | 18,040 | 12,708 |
| Forest..... | 1,470 | 1,264 | 412 | 2,479 | 1,069 |
| Grant...... | 5,414 | 10,789 | 1,054 | 9,309 | 7,872 |
| Green...... | 3,501 | 6,502 | 641 | 5,548 | 5,364 |
| Green Lake.. | 2,299 | 4,893 | 488 | 3,893 | 3,871 |
| Iowa...... | 2,897 | 4,005 | 509 | 4,620 | 3,275 |
| Iron....... | 1,913 | 1,137 | 262 | 2,514 | 963 |
| Jackson.... | 2,293 | 3,172 | 529 | 3,818 | 2,532 |
| Jefferson.... | 8,716 | 12,478 | 1,470 | 13,295 | 8,741 |
| Juneau..... | 2,595 | 3,828 | 712 | 4,583 | 2,976 |
| Kenosha.... | 21,427 | 17,088 | 3,486 | 30,522 | 14,767 |
| Kewaunee.. | 2,622 | 4,467 | 703 | 4,792 | 2,980 |
| La Crosse... | 11,570 | 17,433 | 2,214 | 16,625 | 13,135 |
| Lafayette... | 2,853 | 4,084 | 470 | 4,471 | 3,194 |
| Langlade... | 3,064 | 3,712 | 718 | 5,077 | 2,994 |
| Lincoln..... | 3,858 | 4,793 | 670 | 5,883 | 3,894 |
| Manitowoc.. | 15,288 | 13,562 | 1,790 | 21,927 | 9,849 |
| Marathon... | 18,063 | 16,907 | 3,051 | 24,603 | 12,766 |
| Marinette... | 6,415 | 7,134 | 1,223 | 9,657 | 5,332 |
| Marquette... | 1,228 | 2,374 | 279 | 1,927 | 1,881 |
| Menominee.. | 531 | 179 | 30 | 947 | 78 |
| Milwaukee.. | 206,108 | 160,117 | 34,456 | 288,577 | 149,962 |
| Monroe..... | 4,012 | 6,938 | 1,056 | 6,385 | 5,126 |
| Oconto..... | 3,737 | 5,680 | 1,141 | 6,360 | 4,420 |
| Oneida..... | 4,435 | 5,077 | 941 | 6,431 | 3,909 |
| Outagamie.. | 14,224 | 25,080 | 2,956 | 21,556 | 18,595 |
| Ozaukee.... | 7,246 | 12,155 | 1,505 | 9,517 | 8,581 |
| Pepin...... | 1,263 | 1,493 | 231 | 2,154 | 1,069 |
| Pierce..... | 4,783 | 4,990 | 453 | 6,351 | 3,291 |
| Polk...... | 5,179 | 5,583 | 656 | 7,215 | 3,754 |
| Portage.... | 10,024 | 6,181 | 900 | 11,887 | 4,579 |
| Price...... | 2,794 | 3,096 | 621 | 4,299 | 2,406 |
| Racine..... | 27,045 | 28,028 | 7,457 | 37,785 | 21,434 |
| Richland... | 2,288 | 4,141 | 485 | 4,315 | 3,204 |
| Rock...... | 20,567 | 25,229 | 3,655 | 28,257 | 20,372 |
| Rusk...... | 2,559 | 2,666 | 726 | 4,176 | 2,214 |
| St. Croix... | 6,807 | 6,595 | 735 | 8,864 | 4,565 |
| Sauk...... | 6,406 | 8,608 | 1,019 | 9,288 | 6,345 |
| Sawyer..... | 1,830 | 2,475 | 435 | 2,591 | 2,012 |
| Shawano... | 3,602 | 8,444 | 1,181 | 6,560 | 6,519 |
| Sheboygan.. | 20,170 | 17,764 | 1,181 | 26,410 | 12,968 |
| Taylor..... | 2,910 | 3,043 | 959 | 4,624 | 2,261 |
| Trempealeau | 3,971 | 4,861 | 747 | 6,320 | 3,264 |

| Wisconsin (cont'd) | 1968 | | | 1964 | |
|---|---|---|---|---|---|
| County | Hum-phrey (D) | Nixon (R) | Wal-lace (I) | John-son (D) | Gold-water (R) |
| Vernon..... | 3,666 | 5,824 | 1,062 | 6,242 | 4,640 |
| Vilas...... | 1,798 | 3,339 | 598 | 2,841 | 2,827 |
| Walworth.. | 7,505 | 15,040 | 1,755 | 11,746 | 12,225 |
| Washburn.. | 2,273 | 2,425 | 384 | 3,181 | 1,865 |
| Washington. | 8,104 | 12,439 | 2,065 | 11,563 | 9,191 |
| Waukesha.. | 31,947 | 47,557 | 6,921 | 39,796 | 35,502 |
| Waupaca... | 3,978 | 10,606 | 1,206 | 6,990 | 8,381 |
| Waushara.. | 1,652 | 4,187 | 566 | 3,004 | 3,437 |
| Winnebago. | 18,605 | 25,361 | 3,045 | 23,636 | 21,084 |
| Wood...... | 10,921 | 11,795 | 1,695 | 15,378 | 8,388 |
| Totals ... | 748,895 | 810,092 | 126,762 | 1,050,- 424 | 638,495 |

### WISCONSIN VOTE SINCE 1920

1920 (Pres.), Cox, Dem., 113,422; Harding, Rep., 498,576; Watkins, Proh., 8,647; Debs, Soc., 85,041.

1924 (Pres.), LaFollette, Prog., 453,678; Coolidge, Rep., 311,614; Davis, Dem., 68,115; Foster, Workers, 3,773; Faris, Proh., 2,918; Johns, Soc. Lab., 411; Wallace, Comm. Land, 270.

1928 (Pres.); Hoover, Rep., 544,205; Smith, Dem., 450,259; Thomas, Soc., 18,213; Foster, Com., 1,528; Reynolds, Soc Lab., 381; Varney, Proh., 2,245.

1932 (Pres.), Roosevelt, Dem., 707,410; Hoover, Rep., 347,741; Thomas, Soc., 53,379; Foster, Com., 3,112; Upshaw, Proh., 2,672; Reynolds, Soc. Lab., 494.

1936 (Pres.), Roosevelt, Dem., 802,984; Landon, Rep., 380,828; Lemke, Union, 60,297; Thomas, Soc., 10,626; Browder, Com., 2,197; Colvin, Proh., 1,071; Aiken, Soc. Lab., 557.

1940 (Pres.), Roosevelt, Dem., 704,821; Willkie, Rep., 679,260; Thomas, Soc., 15,071; Browder, Com., 2,394; Babson, Proh., 2,148; Aiken, Soc. Lab., 1,882.

1944 (Pres.), Roosevelt, Dem., 650,413; Dewey, Rep., 674,532; Thomas, Soc., 13,205; Teichert, Soc. Lab., 1,002.

1948 (Pres.), Truman, Dem., 647,310; Dewey, Rep., 590,959; Wallace, Prog., 25,282; Thomas, Soc., 12,547; Teichert, Soc. Lab., 399; Dobbs, Soc. Workers, 303.

1952 (Pres.), Eisenhower, Rep., 979,744; Stevenson, Dem., 622,175; Hallinan, Ind., 2,174; Dobbs, Ind., 1,350; Hoopes, Ind., 1,157; Hass, Ind., 770.

1956 (Pres.), Eisenhower, Rep. 954,844; Stevenson, Dem., 586,768; Andrews, Ind., 6,918; Hoopes, Soc., 754; Hass, Soc. Lab., 710; Dobbs, Soc. Workers, 564.

1960 (Pres.), Kennedy, Dem., 830,805; Nixon, Rep., 895,175; Dobbs, Soc. Workers, 1,792; Hass, Soc. Lab., 1,310.

1964 (Pres.), Johnson, Dem., 1,050,424; Goldwater, Rep., 638,495; DeBerry, Soc. Worker, 1,692; Haas, Soc. Lab., 1,204.

1968 (Pres.), Nixon, Rep., 810,092; Humphrey, Dem., 748,895; Wallace, 3rd party, 126,762; scattered, 2,934.

## Wyoming

| | 1968 | | | 1964 | |
|---|---|---|---|---|---|
| County | Hum-phrey (D) | Nixon (R) | Wal-lace (I) | John-son (D) | Gold-water (R) |
| Albany..... | 4,079 | 4,422 | 578 | 6,019 | 2,923 |
| Big Horn... | 1,201 | 2,771 | 353 | 2,690 | 2,668 |
| Campbell... | 558 | 1,694 | 290 | 1,196 | 1,606 |
| Carbon..... | 2,725 | 2,532 | 388 | 4,322 | 2,160 |
| Converse... | 492 | 1,460 | 232 | 1,250 | 1,559 |
| Crook...... | 318 | 1,250 | 175 | 780 | 1,214 |
| Fremont.... | 3,077 | 5,399 | 885 | 5,985 | 4,809 |
| Goshen..... | 1,529 | 2,774 | 468 | 2,749 | 2,604 |
| Hot Springs. | 703 | 1,273 | 170 | 1,380 | 1,228 |
| Johnson.... | 398 | 1,737 | 217 | 852 | 1,640 |
| Laramie.... | 9,411 | 9,832 | 1,615 | 16,059 | 8,563 |
| Lincoln..... | 1,247 | 2,029 | 285 | 2,273 | 1,811 |
| Natrona.... | 5,900 | 10,578 | 2,092 | 11,167 | 10,135 |
| Niobrara... | 250 | 1,136 | 104 | 843 | 1,122 |
| Park....... | 1,852 | 4,072 | 605 | 3,745 | 3,698 |
| Platte...... | 1,035 | 1,613 | 319 | 1,890 | 1,470 |
| Sheridan... | 2,671 | 5,163 | 612 | 4,747 | 4,491 |
| Sublette.... | 310 | 1,152 | 226 | 791 | 900 |
| Sweetwater. | 4,101 | 2,731 | 637 | 5,969 | 1,944 |
| Teton...... | 461 | 1,419 | 169 | 968 | 1,081 |
| Uinta...... | 1,199 | 1,510 | 175 | 1,929 | 1,186 |
| Washakie... | 748 | 2,038 | 198 | 1,695 | 1,713 |
| Weston..... | 628 | 1,512 | 266 | 1,419 | 1,473 |
| Totals ... | 44,893 | 70,093 | 11,059 | 80,718 | 61,998 |

### WYOMING VOTE SINCE 1920

1920 (Pres.), Cox, Dem., 17,429; Harding, Rep., 35,091; Watkins, Proh., 265; Debs, Soc., 1,288; Christensen, F.-Lab., 2,180.

1924 (Pres.), Coolidge, Rep., 41,858; LaFollette, Prog., 25,174; Davis, Dem., 12,868.

1928 (Pres.), Hoover, Rep., 52,748; Smith, Dem., 29,299; Thomas, Soc., 788.

1932 (Pres.), Roosevelt, Dem., 54,370; Hoover, Rep., 39,583; Thomas, Soc., 2,829; Foster, Com., 180.

1936 (Pres.), Roosevelt, Dem., 62,624; Landon, Rep., 38,739; Lemke, Union, 1,653; Thomas, Soc., 200; Browder, Com., 91; Colvin, Proh., 75.

1940 (Pres.), Roosevelt, Dem., 59,287; Willkie, Rep., 52,633; Babson, Proh., 172; Thomas, Soc., 148.

1944 (Pres.), Roosevelt, Dem., 49,419; Dewey, Rep., 51,921.

1948 (Pres.), Truman, Dem., 52,354; Dewey, Rep., 47,947; Wallace, Prog., 931; Thomas, Soc., 137; Teichert, Soc. Lab., 56.

1952 (Pres.), Eisenhower, Rep., 81,047; Stevenson, Dem., 47,934; Hamblen, Proh., 194; Hoopes, Soc., 40; Hass, Soc. Lab., 36.

1956 (Pres.), Eisenhower, Rep., 74,573; Stevenson, Dem., 49,554.

1960 (Pres.), Kennedy, Dem., 63,331; Nixon, Rep., 77,451.

1964 (Pres.), Johnson, Dem., 80,718; Goldwater, Rep., 61,998.

1968 (Pres.), Nixon, Rep., 70,093; Humphrey, Dem., 44,893; Wallace, 3rd party, 11,059.

## The Electoral College

The President and the Vice President of the United States are the only elective Federal officials not elected by direct vote of the people. They are elected by the members of the Electoral College, an institution that has survived since the founding of the nation despite more than 100 attempts in Congress to alter or abolish it. In the elections of 1824, 1876 and 1888 the Presidential candidate receiving the largest popular vote failed to win a majority of the electoral votes.

On Presidential election day, the first Tuesday after the first Monday in November of every fourth year, each state chooses as many electors as it has Senators and Representatives in Congress. In 1964 for the first time, as provided by the 23rd Amendment to the Constitution, the District of Columbia voted for 3 electors. Thus, with 100 Senators and 435 Representatives, there are 538 members of the Electoral College, with a majority of 270 electoral votes needed to elect the President and Vice President.

Political parties customarily nominate their lists of electors at their respective state conventions. An elector cannot be a member of Congress or any person holding Federal office.

Some states print the names of the candidates for President and Vice President at the top of the ballot while others list only the names of the electors. In either case, the electors of the party receiving the highest vote are elected. The electors meet on the first Monday after the second Wednesday in December in their respective state capitals or in some other place prescribed by State Legislatures. By long-established custom they vote for their party nominee, thus giving all the state's electoral votes to him, although the Constitution does not require them to do so. The only constitutional requirement is that at least one of the persons each elector votes for shall not be an inhabitant of that elector's home state.

Certified and sealed lists of the votes of the electors in each state are mailed to the President of the U. S. Senate. He opens them in the presence of the members of the Senate and House of Representatives in a joint session held on Jan. 6 (the next day if that falls on a Sunday), and the electoral votes of all the states are then counted. If no candidate for President has a majority, the House of Representatives chooses a President from among the three highest candidates, with all Representatives from each state combining to cast one vote for that state. If no candidate for Vice President has a majority, the Senate chooses from the top two, Senators voting as individuals.

# THE NINETY-FIRST CONGRESS, FIRST SESSION

### As of Nov. 15, 1968
The Congress must meet annually on Jan. 3, unless it has, by law, appointed a different day

## The Senate

Terms are for 6 years and end January 3 of the year preceding name. Annual salary $30,000.
To be eligible for the U. S. Senate, a person must be at least 30 years of age, a citizen of the United States for at least 9 years, and a resident of the state from which he is chosen.

Democrats, 58; Republicans, 42. Total, 100. (*) Asterisk designates senior Senator.

| Terms Expire | SENATORS | P. O. Address |
|---|---|---|
| | **ALABAMA** | |
| 1975 | James B. Allen......Dem., | Gadsden |
| 1973 | John Sparkman*......Dem., | Huntsville |
| | **ALASKA** | |
| 1975 | Mike Gravel......Dem., | Anchorage |
| 1973 | E. L. (Bob) Bartlett*..Dem., | Juneau |
| | **ARIZONA** | |
| 1975 | Barry Goldwater....Rep., | Scottsdale |
| 1971 | Paul J. Fannin*......Rep., | Phoenix |
| | **ARKANSAS** | |
| 1975 | J. William Fulbright. Dem., | Fayetteville |
| 1973 | John L. McClellan*...Dem., | Camden |
| | **CALIFORNIA** | |
| 1975 | Alan Cranston......Dem., | Los Angeles |
| 1971 | George Murphy*.....Rep., | Beverly Hills |
| | **COLORADO** | |
| 1975 | Peter H. Dominick....Rep., | Englewood |
| 1973 | Gordon Allott*......Rep., | Lamar |
| | **CONNECTICUT** | |
| 1975 | Abraham Ribicoff....Dem., | Hartford |
| 1971 | Thomas J. Dodd*.....Dem., | West Hartford |
| | **DELAWARE** | |
| 1973 | J. Caleb Boggs......Rep., | Wilmington |
| 1971 | John J. Williams*....Rep., | Millsboro |
| | **FLORIDA** | |
| 1975 | Edward J. Gurney....Rep., | Winter Park |
| 1971 | Spessard L. Holland*..Dem., | Bartow |
| | **GEORGIA** | |
| 1975 | Herman E. Talmadge..Dem., | Lovejoy |
| 1973 | Richard B. Russell*...Dem., | Winder |
| | **HAWAII** | |
| 1971 | Hiram L. Fong*......Rep., | Honolulu |
| 1969 | Daniel K. Inouye....Dem., | Honolulu |
| | **IDAHO** | |
| 1975 | Frank Church*......Dem., | Boise |
| 1973 | Len B. Jordan.......Rep., | Boise |
| | **ILLINOIS** | |
| 1975 | Everett M. Dirksen*..Rep., | Pekin |
| 1973 | Charles H. Percy.....Rep., | Kenilworth |
| | **INDIANA** | |
| 1975 | Birch Bayh........Dem., | Indianapolis |
| 1971 | Vance Hartke*......Dem., | Evansville |
| | **IOWA** | |
| 1975 | Harold E. Hughes....Dem., | Ida Grove |
| 1973 | Jack Miller*.......Rep., | Sioux City |
| | **KANSAS** | |
| 1975 | Robert J. Dole......Rep., | Russell |
| 1973 | James B. Pearson*....Rep., | Prairie Village |
| | **KENTUCKY** | |
| 1975 | Marlow W. Cook.....Rep., | Maryhill |
| 1973 | John Sherman Cooper*......Rep., | Somerset |
| | **LOUISIANA** | |
| 1975 | Russell B. Long.....Dem., | Baton Rouge |
| 1973 | Allen J. Ellender*.....Dem., | Houma |
| | **MAINE** | |
| 1973 | Margaret Chase Smith*......Rep., | Skowhegan |
| 1971 | Edmund S. Muskie....Dem., | Waterville |
| | **MARYLAND** | |
| 1975 | C. McC. Mathias, Jr...Rep., | Frederick |
| 1971 | Joseph D. Tydings*...Dem., | Havre De Grace |
| | **MASSACHUSETTS** | |
| 1973 | Edward W. Brooke....Rep., | Newton Center |
| 1971 | Edward M. Kennedy*..Dem., | Boston |
| | **MICHIGAN** | |
| 1973 | Robert P. Griffin.....Rep., | Traverse City |
| 1971 | Philip A. Hart*......Dem., | Mackinac Is. |
| | **MINNESOTA** | |
| 1973 | Walter F. Mondale....Dem., | Minneapolis |
| 1971 | Eugene J. McCarthy*..Dem., | St. Paul |
| | **MISSISSIPPI** | |
| 1973 | James O. Eastland*...Dem., | Doddsville |
| 1971 | John Stennis......Dem., | DeKalb |
| | **MISSOURI** | |
| 1975 | Thomas F. Eagleton...Dem., | St. Louis |
| 1971 | Stuart Symington*....Dem., | St. Louis |

| Terms Expire | SENATORS | P. O. Address |
|---|---|---|
| | **MONTANA** | |
| 1973 | Lee Metcalf........Dem., | Helena |
| 1971 | Mike Mansfield*.....Dem., | Missoula |
| | **NEBRASKA** | |
| 1973 | Carl T. Curtis......Rep., | Minden |
| 1971 | Roman L. Hruska*....Rep., | Omaha |
| | **NEVADA** | |
| 1975 | Alan Bible*........Dem., | Reno |
| 1971 | Howard W. Cannon...Dem., | Las Vegas |
| | **NEW HAMPSHIRE** | |
| 1975 | Norris Cotton*......Rep., | Concord |
| 1973 | Thomas J. McIntyre...Dem., | Laconia |
| | **NEW JERSEY** | |
| 1973 | Clifford P. Case*.....Rep., | Rahway |
| 1971 | H. A. Williams, Jr....Dem., | Westfield |
| | **NEW MEXICO** | |
| 1973 | Clinton P. Anderson*..Dem., | Albuquerque |
| 1971 | Joseph M. Montoya...Dem., | Santa Fe |
| | **NEW YORK** | |
| 1975 | Jacob K. Javits*.....Rep., | New York City |
| 1971 | Charles E. Goodell....Rep., | Jamestown |
| | **NORTH CAROLINA** | |
| 1975 | Sam J. Ervin, Jr.*....Dem., | Morganton |
| 1973 | B. Everett Jordan....Dem., | Saxapahaw |
| | **NORTH DAKOTA** | |
| 1975 | Milton R. Young*.....Rep., | La Moure |
| 1971 | Quentin N. Burdick...Dem., | Fargo |
| | **OHIO** | |
| 1975 | William B. Saxbe.....Rep., | Mechanicsburg |
| 1971 | Stephen M. Young*....Dem., | Shaker Heights |
| | **OKLAHOMA** | |
| 1975 | Henry Bellmon......Rep., | Billings |
| 1973 | Fred R. Harris*......Dem., | Lawton |
| | **OREGON** | |
| 1975 | Robert W. Packwood [1].Rep., | Portland |
| 1973 | Mark O. Hatfield*....Rep., | Salem |
| | **PENNSYLVANIA** | |
| 1975 | Richard S. Schweiker..Rep., | Worcester |
| 1971 | Hugh Scott*.......Rep., | Philadelphia |
| | **RHODE ISLAND** | |
| 1973 | Claiborne Pell......Dem., | Newport |
| 1971 | John O. Pastore*.....Dem., | Providence |
| | **SOUTH CAROLINA** | |
| 1975 | Ernest F. Hollings....Dem., | Charleston |
| 1973 | Strom Thurmond*....Rep., | Aiken |
| | **SOUTH DAKOTA** | |
| 1975 | George McGovern....Dem., | Mitchell |
| 1973 | Karl E. Mundt*......Rep., | Madison |
| | **TENNESSEE** | |
| 1973 | Howard H. Baker, Jr..Rep., | Knoxville |
| 1971 | Albert Gore*.......Dem., | Carthage |
| | **TEXAS** | |
| 1973 | John G. Tower......Rep., | Wichita Falls |
| 1971 | Ralph Yarborough*...Dem., | Austin |
| | **UTAH** | |
| 1975 | Wallace F. Bennett*...Rep., | Salt Lake City |
| 1971 | Frank E. Moss......Dem., | Salt Lake City |
| | **VERMONT** | |
| 1975 | George D. Aiken*....Rep., | Putney |
| 1971 | Winston L. Prouty....Rep., | Newport |
| | **VIRGINIA** | |
| 1973 | William B. Spong, Jr...Dem., | Portsmouth |
| 1971 | Harry F. Byrd, Jr.*...Dem., | Winchester |
| | **WASHINGTON** | |
| 1975 | Warren G. Magnuson*.Dem., | Seattle |
| 1971 | Henry M. Jackson....Dem., | Everett |
| | **WEST VIRGINIA** | |
| 1973 | Jennings Randolph*...Dem., | Elkins |
| 1971 | Robert C. Byrd......Dem., | Sophia |
| | **WISCONSIN** | |
| 1975 | Gaylord Nelson......Dem., | Madison |
| 1971 | William Proxmire*....Dem., | Madison |
| | **WYOMING** | |
| 1973 | Clifford P. Hansen....Rep., | Jackson |
| 1971 | Gale W. McGee*.....Dem., | Laramie |

**90th Congress Senate Officials—Subject to change in 91st Congress January 1969**

President pro Tempore—Carl Hayden[2]
Chaplain—Rev. Frederick Brown Harris, D.D.
Secretary of the Senate—Francis R. Valeo
Chief Clerk—Darrell St. Claire
Sergeant at Arms—Robert G. Dunphy

Majority Floor Leader—Mike Mansfield
Majority Whip—Russell B. Long
Majority Secretary—J. Stanley Kimmitt
Minority Floor Leader—Everett M. Dirksen
Minority Whip—Thomas H. Kuchel[3]
Minority Secretary—J. Mark Trice

[1]Recount demanded by incumbent Sen. Wayne Morse. [2]Retiring. [3]Defeated in primary.

# The House of Representatives

### As of Nov. 15, 1968

Members elected to serve to Jan. 3, 1971. Annual salary $30,000. Speaker of House $43,000 and $10,000 for expenses, all taxable.

To be eligible for the House of Representatives, a person must be at least 25 years of age, a citizen of the United States for at least 7 years, and a resident of the state from which he is chosen.

(*) Served in the Ninetieth Congress. (†) Designates women members in the House.

**Democrats, 243; Republicans, 192; Total 435.**

| Districts | Representatives | P. O. Address |
|---|---|---|
| **ALABAMA** | | |
| 1 | W. Jack Edwards*........ Rep.. | Mobile |
| 2 | William L. Dickinson*... Rep.. | Montgomery |
| 3 | George W. Andrews*..... Dem.. | Union Springs |
| 4 | Bill Nichols*........... Dem.. | Sylacauga |
| 5 | Walter Flowers......... Dem.. | Tuscaloosa |
| 6 | John H. Buchanan*..... Rep.. | Birmingham |
| 7 | Tom Bevill*............ Dem.. | Jasper |
| 8 | Robert E. Jones, Jr.*... Dem.. | Scottsboro |
| **ALASKA** | | |
| | Howard W. Pollock*.... Rep.. | Anchorage |
| **ARIZONA** | | |
| 1 | John J. Rhodes*........ Rep.. | Mesa |
| 2 | Morris K. Udall*....... Dem.. | Tucson |
| 3 | Sam Steiger*........... Rep.. | Prescott |
| **ARKANSAS** | | |
| 1 | Bill Alexander......... Dem.. | Osceola |
| 2 | Wilbur D. Mills*....... Dem.. | Kensett |
| 3 | John P. Hammerschmidt*. Rep.. | Harrison |
| 4 | David Pryor*........... Dem.. | Camden |
| **CALIFORNIA** | | |
| 1 | Don Clausen*.......... Rep... | Crescent City |
| 2 | Harold T. Johnson*..... Dem.. | Roseville |
| 3 | John E. Moss*......... Dem.. | Sacramento |
| 4 | Robert L. Leggett*..... Dem.. | Vallejo |
| 5 | Phillip Burton*........ Dem.. | San Francisco |
| 6 | William S. Maillard*.... Rep.. | San Francisco |
| 7 | Jeffery Cohelan*....... Dem.. | Berkeley |
| 8 | George P. Miller*...... Dem.. | Alameda |
| 9 | Don Edwards*.......... Dem.. | San Jose |
| 10 | Charles S. Gubser*..... Rep.. | Gilroy |
| 11 | Paul N. McCloskey, Jr.* Rep.. | Portola Valley |
| 12 | Burt L. Talcott*....... Rep.. | Salinas |
| 13 | Charles M. Teague*.... Rep.. | Ojai |
| 14 | Jerome R. Waldie*..... Dem.. | Antioch |
| 15 | John J. McFall*........ Dem.. | Manteca |
| 16 | B. F. Sisk*............ Dem.. | Fresno |
| 17 | Glenn M. Anderson*.... Dem.. | Torrance |
| 18 | R. B. (Bob) Mathias*... Rep.. | Visalia |
| 19 | Chet Holifield*........ Dem.. | Montebello |
| 20 | H. Allen Smith*........ Rep.. | Glendale |
| 21 | Augustine F. Hawkins*.. Dem.. | Los Angeles |
| 22 | James C. Corman*...... Dem.. | Van Nuys |
| 23 | Del Clawson*.......... Rep.. | Compton |
| 24 | Glenard P. Lipscomb*... Rep.. | Los Angeles |
| 25 | Charles E. Wiggins*.... Rep.. | El Monte |
| 26 | Thomas M. Rees*...... Dem.. | Beverly Hills |
| 27 | Edwin Reinecke*....... Rep.. | Tujunga |
| 28 | Alphonzo Bell*......... Rep.. | Beverly Hills |
| 29 | George E. Brown, Jr.*.. Dem.. | Monterey Park |
| 30 | Edward R. Roybal*..... Dem.. | Los Angeles |
| 31 | Charles H. Wilson*..... Dem.. | Los Angeles |
| 32 | Craig Hosmer*......... Rep.. | Long Beach |
| 33 | Jerry L. Pettis*....... Rep.. | Loma Linda |
| 34 | Richard T. Hanna*..... Dem.. | Fullerton |
| 35 | James B. Utt*......... Rep.. | Santa Ana |
| 36 | Bob Wilson*........... Rep.. | San Diego |
| 37 | Lionel Van Deerlin*.... Dem.. | San Diego |
| 38 | John V. Tunney*....... Dem.. | Riverside |
| **COLORADO** | | |
| 1 | Byron G. Rogers*...... Dem.. | Denver |
| 2 | Donald G. Brotzman*... Rep.. | Boulder |
| 3 | Frank E. Evans*....... Dem.. | Pueblo |
| 4 | Wayne N. Aspinall*.... Dem.. | Palisade |
| **CONNECTICUT** | | |
| 1 | Emilio Q. Daddario*.... Dem.. | Hartford |
| 2 | William L. St. Onge*... Dem.. | Putnam |
| 3 | Robert N. Giaimo*..... Dem.. | North Haven |
| 4 | Lowell P. Weicker, Jr.. Rep.. | Greenwich |
| 5 | John S. Monagan*...... Dem.. | Waterbury |
| 6 | Thomas J. Meskill*.... Rep.. | New Britain |
| **DELAWARE—At Large** | | |
| | William V. Roth, Jr.*.. Rep.. | Wilmington |
| **FLORIDA** | | |
| 1 | Robert L. F. Sikes*.... Dem.. | Crestview |
| 2 | Don Fuqua*........... Dem.. | Altha |
| 3 | Charles E. Bennett*.... Dem.. | Jacksonville |
| 4 | William Chappell, Jr.... Dem.. | Ocala |
| 5 | Louis Frey, Jr.*....... Rep.. | Winter Park |
| 6 | Sam Gibbons*......... Dem.. | Tampa |
| 7 | James A. Haley*....... Dem.. | Sarasota |
| 8 | William C. Cramer*.... Rep.. | St. Petersburg |
| 9 | Paul G. Rogers*....... Dem.. | West Palm Beach |
| 10 | J. Herbert Burke*..... Rep.. | Hollywood |
| 11 | Claude Pepper*........ Dem.. | Miami |
| 12 | Dante B. Fascell*...... Dem.. | Miami |
| **GEORGIA** | | |
| 1 | G. Elliott Hagan*...... Dem.. | Sylvania |
| 2 | Maston O'Neal*........ Dem.. | Bainbridge |
| 3 | Jack Brinkley*......... Dem.. | Columbus |
| 4 | Benjamin B. Blackburn* Rep.. | Atlanta |
| 5 | S. Fletcher Thompson*. Rep.. | East Point |
| 6 | John J. Flynt, Jr.*..... Dem.. | Griffin |
| 7 | John W. Davis*........ Dem.. | Summerville |
| 8 | William S. Stuckey*.... Dem.. | Eastman |

| Districts | Representatives | P. O. Address |
|---|---|---|
| **GEORGIA (continued)** | | |
| 9 | Phil M. Landrum*...... Dem.. | Jasper |
| 10 | Robert G. Stephens, Jr.* Dem.. | Athens |
| **HAWAII—At Large** | | |
| | Spark M. Matsunaga*... Dem.. | Honolulu |
| | Patsy T. Mink*†....... Dem.. | Pahu |
| **IDAHO** | | |
| 1 | James A. McClure*..... Rep.. | Payette |
| 2 | Orval H. Hansen....... Rep.. | Idaho Falls |
| **ILLINOIS** | | |
| 1 | William L. Dawson*.... Dem.. | Chicago |
| 2 | Abner J. Mikva........ Dem.. | Chicago |
| 3 | William T. Murphy*.... Dem.. | Chicago |
| 4 | Edward J. Derwinski*... Rep.. | Chicago |
| 5 | John C. Kluczynski*.... Dem.. | Chicago |
| 6 | Daniel J. Ronan*...... Dem.. | Chicago |
| 7 | Frank Annunzio*....... Dem.. | Chicago |
| 8 | Daniel Rostenkowski*... Dem.. | Chicago |
| 9 | Sidney R. Yates*...... Dem.. | Chicago |
| 10 | Harold R. Collier*..... Rep.. | Berwyn |
| 11 | Roman C. Pucinski*.... Dem.. | Chicago |
| 12 | Robert McClory*....... Rep.. | Lake Bluff |
| 13 | Donald Rumsfeld*...... Rep.. | Glenview |
| 14 | John N. Erlenborn*..... Rep.. | Elmhurst |
| 15 | Charlotte T. Reid†*.... Rep.. | Aurora |
| 16 | John B. Anderson*..... Rep.. | Rockford |
| 17 | Leslie C. Arends*...... Rep.. | Melvin |
| 18 | Robert H. Michel*..... Rep.. | Peoria |
| 19 | Tom Railsback*........ Rep.. | Moline |
| 20 | Paul Findley*......... Rep.. | Pittsfield |
| 21 | Kenneth J. Gray*...... Dem.. | West Frankfort |
| 22 | William L. Springer*... Rep.. | Champaign |
| 23 | George E. Shipley*..... Dem.. | Olney |
| 24 | Melvin Price*......... Dem.. | St. Louis |
| **INDIANA** | | |
| 1 | Ray J. Madden*....... Dem.. | Gary |
| 2 | Earl F. Landgrebe..... Rep.. | South Bend |
| 3 | John Brademas*....... Dem.. | South Bend |
| 4 | E. Ross Adair*........ Rep.. | Fort Wayne |
| 5 | Richard L. Roudebush*. Rep.. | Noblesville |
| 6 | William G Bray*...... Rep.. | Martinsville |
| 7 | John T. Myers*........ Rep.. | Covington |
| 8 | Roger H. Zion*........ Rep.. | Evansville |
| 9 | Lee H. Hamilton*...... Dem.. | Columbus |
| 10 | David W. Dennis....... Rep.. | Richmond |
| 11 | Andrew Jacobs, Jr.*... Dem.. | Indianapolis |
| **IOWA** | | |
| 1 | Fred Schwengel*....... Rep.. | Davenport |
| 2 | John C. Culver*....... Dem.. | Marion |
| 3 | H. R. Gross*.......... Rep.. | Waterloo |
| 4 | John Kyl*............. Rep.. | Bloomfield |
| 5 | Neal Smith*........... Dem.. | Altoona |
| 6 | Wiley Mayne*......... Rep.. | Sioux City |
| 7 | William J. Scherle*.... Rep.. | Henderson |
| **KANSAS** | | |
| 1 | Keith G. Sebelius...... Rep.. | Norton |
| 2 | Chester L. Mize*...... Rep.. | Atchison |
| 3 | Larry Winn, Jr.*...... Rep.. | Leawood |
| 4 | Garner E. Shriver*.... Rep.. | Wichita |
| 5 | Joe Skubitz*.......... Rep.. | Pittsburg |
| **KENTUCKY** | | |
| 1 | Frank A. Stubblefield*. Dem.. | Murray |
| 2 | William H. Natcher*... Dem.. | Bowling Green |
| 3 | William O. Cowger*.... Rep.. | Louisville |
| 4 | Marion G. Snyder*..... Rep.. | Jeffersontown |
| 5 | Tim Lee Carter*....... Rep.. | Tompkinsville |
| 6 | John C. Watts*........ Dem.. | Nicholasville |
| 7 | Carl D. Perkins*...... Dem.. | Hindman |
| **LOUISIANA** | | |
| 1 | F. Edward Hebert*..... Dem.. | New Orleans |
| 2 | Hale Boggs*.......... Dem.. | New Orleans |
| 3 | Patrick T. Caffery..... Dem.. | New Iberia |
| 4 | Joe D. Waggonner, Jr.* Dem.. | Plain Dealing |
| 5 | Otto E. Passman*...... Dem.. | Monroe |
| 6 | John R. Rarick*....... Dem.. | St. Francisville |
| 7 | Edwin W. Edwards*.... Dem.. | Crowley |
| 8 | Speedy O. Long*....... Dem.. | Jena |
| **MAINE** | | |
| 1 | Peter N. Kyros*....... Dem.. | Portland |
| 2 | William D. Hathaway*.. Dem.. | Auburn |
| **MARYLAND** | | |
| 1 | Rogers C. B. Morton*.. Rep.. | Easton |
| 2 | Clarence D. Long*..... Dem.. | Ruxton |
| 3 | Edward A. Garmatz*... Dem.. | Baltimore |
| 4 | George H. Fallon*..... Dem.. | Baltimore |
| 5 | Lawrence J. Hogan..... Rep.. | Hyattsville |
| 6 | J. Glenn Beall, Jr..... Rep.. | Frostburg |
| 7 | Samuel N. Friedel*.... Dem.. | Baltimore |
| 8 | Gilbert Gude*......... Rep.. | Bethesda |
| **MASSACHUSETTS** | | |
| 1 | Silvio O. Conte*....... Rep.. | Pittsfield |
| 2 | Edward P. Boland*..... Dem.. | Springfield |
| 3 | Philip J. Philbin*..... Dem.. | Clinton |
| 4 | Harold D. Donohue*.... Dem.. | Worcester |
| 5 | F. Bradford Morse*.... Rep.. | Lowell |

| Districts | Representatives | P. O. Address |
|---|---|---|
| **MASSACHUSETTS (continued)** | | |
| 6 | William H. Bates*......Rep... | Salem |
| 7 | Torbert H. Macdonald*..Dem... | Malden |
| 8 | Thomas P. O'Neill, Jr.*..Dem... | Cambridge |
| 9 | John W. McCormack*...Dem... | Dorchester |
| 10 | Margaret M. Heckler†*..Rep... | Wellesley |
| 11 | James A. Burke*.......Dem... | Milton |
| 12 | Hastings Keith*.......Rep... | W. Bridgewater |
| **MICHIGAN** | | |
| 1 | John Conyers, Jr.*.....Dem... | Detroit |
| 2 | Marvin L. Esch*.......Rep... | Ann Arbor |
| 3 | Garry Brown*.........Rep... | Schoolcraft |
| 4 | Edward Hutchinson*...Rep... | Fennville |
| 5 | Gerald R. Ford, Jr.*...Rep... | Grand Rapids |
| 6 | Chas. E. Chamberlain*..Rep... | East Lansing |
| 7 | Donald W. Reigle, Jr.*..Rep... | Flint |
| 8 | James Harvey*........Rep... | Saginaw |
| 9 | Guy Vander Jagt*......Rep... | Cadillac |
| 10 | Elford A. Cederberg*..Rep... | Bay City |
| 11 | Philip E. Ruppe*......Rep... | Houghton |
| 12 | James G. O'Hara*.....Dem... | Utica |
| 13 | Charles C. Diggs, Jr.*..Dem... | Detroit |
| 14 | Lucien N. Nedzi*......Dem... | Detroit |
| 15 | William D. Ford*......Dem... | Taylor |
| 16 | John D. Dingell*.......Dem... | Detroit |
| 17 | Martha W. Griffiths*†...Dem... | Detroit |
| 18 | William S. Broomfield*..Rep... | Royal Oak |
| 19 | Jack H. McDonald*.....Rep... | Detroit |
| **MINNESOTA** | | |
| 1 | Albert H. Quie*.......Rep... | Dennison |
| 2 | Ancher Nelson*.......Rep... | Hutchinson |
| 3 | Clark MacGregor*.....Rep... | Plymouth Village |
| 4 | Joseph E. Karth*......Dem... | St. Paul |
| 5 | Donald M. Fraser*.....Dem... | Minneapolis |
| 6 | John M. Zwach*.......Rep... | Walnut Grove |
| 7 | Odin Langen*.........Rep... | Kennedy |
| 8 | John A. Blatnik*......Dem... | Chisholm |
| **MISSISSIPPI** | | |
| 1 | Thomas G. Abernethy*..Dem... | Okolona |
| 2 | Jamie L. Whitten*.....Dem... | Charleston |
| 3 | Charles H. Griffin*....Dem... | Utica |
| 4 | G. V. Montgomery.....Dem... | Meridian |
| 5 | William M. Colmer*....Dem... | Pascagoula |
| **MISSOURI** | | |
| 1 | William L. Clay*......Dem... | St. Louis |
| 2 | James W. Symington...Dem... | Clayton |
| 3 | Leonor K. Sullivan*†..Dem... | St. Louis |
| 4 | William J. Randall*....Dem... | Independence |
| 5 | Richard W. Bolling*...Dem... | Kansas City |
| 6 | W. R. Hull, Jr.*......Dem... | Weston |
| 7 | Durward G. Hall*.....Rep... | Springfield |
| 8 | Richard H. Ichord*....Dem... | Houston |
| 9 | William L. Hungate*...Dem... | Troy |
| 10 | Bill D. Burlison*......Dem... | Cape Girardeau |
| **MONTANA** | | |
| 1 | Arnold Olsen*........Dem... | Helena |
| 2 | James F. Battin*......Rep... | Billings |
| **NEBRASKA** | | |
| 1 | Robert V. Denney*....Rep... | Fairbury |
| 2 | Glenn Cunningham*....Rep... | Omaha |
| 3 | David T. Martin*......Rep... | Kearney |
| **NEVADA—At Large** | | |
| | Walter S. Baring*.....Dem... | Reno |
| **NEW HAMPSHIRE** | | |
| 1 | Louis C. Wyman*......Rep... | Manchester |
| 2 | James C. Cleveland*...Rep... | New London |
| **NEW JERSEY** | | |
| 1 | John E. Hunt*........Rep... | Pitman |
| 2 | C. W. Sandman, Jr.*...Rep... | Cape May |
| 3 | James J. Howard*.....Dem... | Wall |
| 4 | Frank Thompson, Jr.*..Dem... | Trenton |
| 5 | PeterH.B.Frelinghuysen*Rep... | Morristown |
| 6 | William T. Cahill*.....Rep... | Collingswood |
| 7 | William B. Widnall*...Rep... | Saddle River |
| 8 | Charles S. Joelson*....Dem... | Paterson |
| 9 | Henry Helstoski*......Dem... | E. Rutherford |
| 10 | Peter W. Rodino, Jr.*..Dem... | Newark |
| 11 | Joseph G. Minish*.....Dem... | West Orange |
| 12 | Florence P. Dwyer†*...Rep... | Elizabeth |
| 13 | Cornelius E. Gallagher*..Dem... | Bayonne |
| 14 | Dominick V. Daniels*..Dem... | Jersey City |
| 15 | Edward J. Patten*.....Dem... | Perth Amboy |
| **NEW MEXICO—At Large** | | |
| | Manuel Lujan, Jr.....Rep... | Albuquerque |
| | Ed Forenan..........Dem... | Las Cruces |
| **NEW YORK** | | |
| 1 | Otis G. Pike*.........Dem... | Riverhead |
| 2 | James R. Grover, Jr.*..Rep... | Babylon |
| 3 | Lester L. Wolff*......Dem... | Great Neck |
| 4 | John W. Wydler*......Rep... | Garden City |
| 5 | Allard K. Lowenstein...Dem... | New York City |
| 6 | Seymour Halpern*.....Rep... | Forest Hills |
| 7 | Joseph P. Addabbo*...Dem... | Ozone Park |
| 8 | Benj. S. Rosenthal*...Dem... | Elmhurst |
| 9 | James J. Delaney*.....Dem... | L. I. City |
| 10 | Emanuel Celler*......Dem... | Brooklyn |
| 11 | Frank J. Brasco*......Dem... | Brooklyn |
| 12 | Shirley Chisholm†.....Dem... | Brooklyn |
| 13 | Bertram L. Podell*....Dem... | Brooklyn |
| 14 | John J. Rooney*......Dem... | Brooklyn |
| 15 | Hugh L. Carey*.......Dem... | Brooklyn |
| 16 | John M. Murphy*......Dem... | Staten Island |
| 17 | Edward I. Koch*......Dem... | New York City |
| 18 | Adam C. Powell*......Dem... | New York City |

| Districts | Representatives | P. O. Address |
|---|---|---|
| **NEW YORK (continued)** | | |
| 19 | Leonard Farbstein*....Dem... | New York City |
| 20 | William Fitts Ryan*...Dem... | New York City |
| 21 | James H. Scheuer*....Dem... | Bronx |
| 22 | Jacob H. Gilbert*.....Dem... | New York City |
| 23 | Jonathan B. Bingham*..Dem... | Bronx |
| 24 | Mario Biaggi.........Dem... | Bronx |
| 25 | Richard L. Ottinger*...Dem... | Pleasantville |
| 26 | Ogden R. Reid*.......Rep... | Purchase |
| 27 | Martin B. McKneally...Rep... | Newburgh |
| 28 | Hamilton Fish, Jr.....Rep... | Millbrook |
| 29 | Daniel E. Button*.....Rep... | Albany |
| 30 | Carleton J. King*.....Rep... | Saratoga Springs |
| 31 | Robert C. McEwen*...Rep... | Ogdensburg |
| 32 | Alexander Pirnie*.....Rep... | New Hartford |
| 33 | Howard Robison*.....Rep... | Owego |
| 34 | James M. Hanley*.....Dem... | Syracuse |
| 35 | Samuel S. Stratton*...Dem... | Amsterdam |
| 36 | Frank J. Horton*.....Rep... | Rochester |
| 37 | Barber B. Conable, Jr.*.Rep... | Alexander |
| 38 | James F. Hastings.....Rep... | Allegany |
| 39 | Richard D. McCarthy*..Dem... | Buffalo |
| 40 | Henry P. Smith*......Rep... | N. Tonawanda |
| 41 | Thaddeus J. Dulski*...Dem... | Buffalo |
| **NORTH CAROLINA** | | |
| 1 | Walter B. Jones*......Dem... | Farmville |
| 2 | L. H. Fountain*......Dem... | Tarboro |
| 3 | David N. Henderson*...Dem... | Wallace |
| 4 | Nick Galifianakis*....Dem... | Durham |
| 5 | Wilmer Mizell........Dem... | Winston-Salem |
| 6 | L. Richardson Preyer..Dem... | Greensboro |
| 7 | Alton Lennon*........Dem... | Wilmington |
| 8 | Earl B. Ruth.........Rep... | Salisbury |
| 9 | Charles R. Jonas*.....Rep... | Lincolnton |
| 10 | James T. Broyhill*....Rep... | Arden |
| 11 | Roy A. Taylor*......Dem... | Black Mountain |
| **NORTH DAKOTA** | | |
| 1 | Mark Andrews*.......Rep... | Mapleton |
| 2 | Thomas S. Kleppe*....Rep... | Bismarck |
| **OHIO** | | |
| 1 | Robert Taft, Jr.*......Rep... | Mapleton |
| 2 | Donald D. Clancy*....Rep... | Cincinnati |
| 3 | Charles W. Whalen, Jr.*.Rep... | Dayton |
| 4 | William M. McCulloch*.Rep... | Piqua |
| 5 | Delbert L. Latta*.....Rep... | Bowling Green |
| 6 | William H. Harsha*...Rep... | Portsmouth |
| 7 | Clarence J. Brown, Jr.*.Rep... | Urbana |
| 8 | Jackson E. Betts*.....Rep... | Findlay |
| 9 | Thomas L. Ashley*....Dem... | Waterville |
| 10 | Clarence E. Miller*...Rep... | Lancaster |
| 11 | J. William Stanton*...Rep... | Painesville |
| 12 | Samuel L. Devine*....Rep... | Columbus |
| 13 | Charles A. Mosher*...Rep... | Oberlin |
| 14 | William H. Ayres*....Rep... | Akron |
| 15 | Chalmers P. Wylie*...Rep... | Columbus |
| 16 | Frank T. Bow*.......Rep... | Canton (R.F.D.) |
| 17 | John M. Ashbrook*....Rep... | Johnstown |
| 18 | Wayne L. Hays*......Dem... | Flushing |
| 19 | Michael J. Kirwan*....Dem... | Youngstown |
| 20 | Michael A. Feighan*...Dem... | Cleveland |
| 21 | Louis Stokes.........Dem... | Shaker Heights |
| 22 | Charles A. Vanik*.....Dem... | Cleveland |
| 23 | William E. Minshall*..Rep... | Cleveland |
| 24 | Donald E. Lukens*....Rep... | Middletown |
| **OKLAHOMA** | | |
| 1 | Page Belcher*........Rep... | Enid |
| 2 | Ed Edmondson*.......Dem... | Muskogee |
| 3 | Carl Albert*.........Dem... | McAlester |
| 4 | Tom Steed*..........Dem... | Shawnee |
| 5 | John Jarman*........Dem... | Oklahoma City |
| 6 | John N. Happy Camp...Rep... | Waukomis |
| **OREGON** | | |
| 1 | Wendell Wyatt*......Rep... | Astoria |
| 2 | Al Ullman*..........Dem... | Baker |
| 3 | Edith Green*†.......Dem... | Portland |
| 4 | John R. Dellenback*...Rep... | Medford |
| **PENNSYLVANIA** | | |
| 1 | William A. Barrett*...Dem... | Philadelphia |
| 2 | Robert N. C. Nix*....Dem... | Philadelphia |
| 3 | James A. Byrne*......Dem... | Philadelphia |
| 4 | Joshua Eilberg*......Dem... | Philadelphia |
| 5 | William J. Green*.....Dem... | Philadelphia |
| 6 | Gus Yatron..........Dem... | Reading |
| 7 | Lawrence G. Williams*.Rep... | Springfield |
| 8 | Edward B. Biester, Jr.*.Rep... | Furlong |
| 9 | G. Robert Watkins*...Rep... | West Chester |
| 10 | Joseph M. McDade*...Rep... | Scranton |
| 11 | Daniel J. Flood*......Dem... | Wilkes-Barre |
| 12 | J. Irving Whalley*....Rep... | Windber |
| 13 | R. Lawrence Coughlin..Rep... | Villanova |
| 14 | William S. Moorhead*..Dem... | Pittsburgh |
| 15 | Fred B. Rooney*......Dem... | Bethlehem |
| 16 | Edwin D. Eshleman*...Rep... | Lancaster |
| 17 | Herman T. Schneebeli*.Rep... | Williamsport |
| 18 | Robert J. Corbett*....Rep... | Pittsburgh |
| 19 | George A. Goodling*...Rep... | Loganville |
| 20 | Joseph Gaydos*......Dem... | McKeesport |
| 21 | John H. Dent*........Dem... | Jeannette |
| 22 | John P. Saylor*......Rep... | Johnstown |
| 23 | Albert W. Johnson*...Rep... | Smethport |
| 24 | Joseph P. Vigorito*...Dem... | Erie |
| 25 | Frank M. Clark*......Dem... | Bessemer |
| 26 | Thomas E. Morgan*...Dem... | Fredericktown |
| 27 | Jame G. Fulton*......Rep... | Pittsburgh |

| Districts | Representatives | P. O. Address |
|---|---|---|
| **RHODE ISLAND** | | |
| 1 F. J. St. Germain* | Dem. | Woonsocket |
| 2 Robert O. Tiernan* | Dem. | Warwick |
| **SOUTH CAROLINA** | | |
| 1 L. Mendel Rivers* | Dem. | Charleston |
| 2 Albert Watson* | Rep. | Columbia |
| 3 W. J. Bryan Dorn* | Dem. | Greenwood |
| 4 James R. Mann* | Dem. | Greenville |
| 5 Thomas S. Gettys* | Dem. | Rock Hill |
| 6 John L. McMillan* | Dem. | Florence |
| **SOUTH DAKOTA** | | |
| 1 Ben Reifel* | Rep. | Aberdeen |
| 2 E. Y. Berry* | Rep. | McLaughlin |
| **TENNESSEE** | | |
| 1 James H. Quillen* | Rep. | Kingsport |
| 2 John J. Duncan* | Rep. | Knoxville |
| 3 W. E. (Bill) Brock* | Rep. | Chattanooga |
| 4 Joe L. Evins* | Dem. | Smithville |
| 5 Richard Fulton* | Dem. | Nashville |
| 6 William R. Anderson* | Dem. | Waverly |
| 7 Ray Blanton* | Dem. | Adamsville |
| 8 Robert A. Everett* | Dem. | Union City |
| 9 Dan Kuykendall* | Rep. | Memphis |
| **TEXAS** | | |
| 1 Wright Patman* | Dem. | Texarkana |
| 2 John Dowdy* | Dem. | Athens |
| 3 Jim Collins* | Rep. | Grand Prairie |
| 4 Ray Roberts* | Dem. | McKinney |
| 5 Earle Cabell* | Dem. | Dallas |
| 6 Olin E. Teague* | Dem. | College Station |
| 7 George Bush* | Rep. | Houston |
| 8 Bob Eckhardt* | Dem. | Houston |
| 9 Jack Brooks* | Dem. | Beaumont |
| 10 J. J. Pickle* | Dem. | Austin |
| 11 W. R. Poage* | Dem. | Waco |
| 12 Jame C. Wright* | Dem. | Ft. Worth |
| 13 Graham B. Purcell* | Dem. | Wichita Falls |
| 14 John Young* | Dem. | Corpus Christi |
| 15 Eligio De La Garza* | Dem. | Mission |
| 16 Richard C. White* | Dem. | El Paso |
| 17 Omar Burleson* | Dem. | Anson |
| 18 Robert Price* | Rep. | Pampa |
| 19 George H. Mahon* | Dem. | Lubbock |
| 20 Henry B. Gonzalez* | Dem. | San Antonio |
| 21 O. C. Fisher* | Dem. | San Angelo |
| 22 Bob Casey* | Dem. | Houston |
| 23 Abraham Kazen, Jr.* | Dem. | Laredo |

| Districts | Representatives | P. O. Address |
|---|---|---|
| **UTAH** | | |
| 1 Lawrence J. Burton* | Rep. | Ogden |
| 2 Sherman P. Lloyd* | Rep. | Salt Lake City |
| **VERMONT—At Large** | | |
| Robert T. Stafford* | Rep. | Rutland City |
| **VIRGINIA** | | |
| 1 Thomas N. Downing* | Dem. | Newport News |
| 2 G. William Whitehurst* | Rep. | Norfolk |
| 3 David E. Satterfield* | Dem. | Richmond |
| 4 Watkins M. Abbitt* | Dem. | Appomattox |
| 5 W. C. Daniel | Dem. | Danville |
| 6 Richard H. Poff* | Rep. | Radford |
| 7 John O. Marsh, Jr.* | Dem. | Strasburg |
| 8 William L. Scott* | Rep. | Fairfax |
| 9 William C. Wampler* | Rep. | Bristol |
| 10 Joel T. Broyhill* | Rep. | Arlington |
| **WASHINGTON** | | |
| 1 Thomas M. Pelly* | Rep. | Seattle |
| 2 Lloyd Meeds* | Dem. | Everett |
| 3 Julia B. Hansen*† | Dem. | Cathlamet |
| 4 Catherine May*† | Rep. | Yakima |
| 5 Thomas S. Foley* | Dem. | Spokane |
| 6 Floyd V. Hicks* | Dem. | Tacoma |
| 7 Brock Adams* | Dem. | Seattle |
| **WEST VIRGINIA** | | |
| 1 Robert H. Mollohan* | Dem. | Fairmont |
| 2 Harley O. Staggers* | Dem. | Keyser |
| 3 John M. Slack, Jr.* | Dem. | Charleston |
| 4 Ken Hechler* | Dem. | Huntington |
| 5 James Kee* | Dem. | Bluefield |
| **WISCONSIN** | | |
| 1 Henry C. Schadeberg* | Rep. | Burlington |
| 2 Robert Kastenmeier* | Dem. | Watertown |
| 3 Vernon W. Thomson* | Rep. | Richland Center |
| 4 Clement J. Zablocki* | Dem. | Milwaukee |
| 5 Henry S. Reuss* | Dem. | Milwaukee |
| 6 William A. Steiger* | Rep. | Oshkosh |
| 7 Melvin R. Laird* | Rep. | Marshfield |
| 8 John W. Byrnes* | Rep. | Green Bay |
| 9 Glenn R. Davis* | Rep. | New Berlin |
| 10 Alvin E. O'Konski* | Rep. | Mercer |
| **WYOMING—At Large** | | |
| John Wold | Rep. | Casper |
| **PUERTO RICO** | | |
| **Resident Commissioner** | | |
| Jorge Luis Cordova-Diaz | | San Juan |

**90th Congress House Officials—Subject to change in 91st Congress January 1969**

The Speaker—John W. McCormack
Parliamentarian—Lewis Deschler
Chaplain—Rev. Edward G. Latch, D.D.
Majority Leader—Carl Albert
Majority Whip—Hale Boggs

Minority Leader—Gerald R. Ford
Minority Whip—Leslie C. Arends
Clerk of the House—W. Pat Jennings
Sergeant at Arms—Zeake W. Johnson, Jr.
Doorkeeper—William M. Miller
Postmaster—H. H. Morris

## Speakers of the House of Representatives

Party designations: A. American; D, Democratic; DR, Democratic Republican; F. Federalist;
R, Republican; W, Whig. *Served only one day.

| Name | Party, State | Tenure | Name | Party, State | Tenure |
|---|---|---|---|---|---|
| Frederick A. C. Muhlenberg | F, Pa. | 1789-1791 | Galusha A. Grow | R, Pa. | 1861-1863 |
| Jonathan Trumbull | F, Conn. | 1791-1793 | Schuyler Colfax | R, Ind. | 1863-1869 |
| Frederick A. C. Muhlenberg | F, Pa. | 1793-1795 | *Theodore M. Pomeroy | R, N. Y. | 1869-1869 |
| Jonathan Dayton | F, N. J. | 1795-1799 | James G. Blaine | R, Me. | 1869-1875 |
| Theodore Sedgwick | F, Mass. | 1799-1801 | Michael C. Kerr | D, Ind. | 1875-1876 |
| Nathaniel Macon | DR, N. C. | 1801-1807 | Samuel J. Randall | D, Pa. | 1876-1881 |
| Joseph B. Varnum | DR, Mass. | 1807-1811 | Joseph W. Keifer | R, Ohio. | 1881-1883 |
| Henry Clay | DR, Ky. | 1811-1814 | John G. Carlisle | D, Ky. | 1883-1889 |
| Langdon Cheves | DR, S. C. | 1814-1815 | Thomas B. Reed | R, Me. | 1889-1891 |
| Henry Clay | DR, Ky. | 1815-1820 | Charles F. Crisp | D, Ga. | 1891-1895 |
| John W Taylor | DR, N. Y. | 1820-1821 | Thomas B. Reed | R, Me. | 1895-1899 |
| Philip P. Barbour | DR, Va. | 1821-1823 | David B. Henderson | R, Iowa. | 1899-1903 |
| Henry Clay | DR, Ky. | 1823-1825 | Joseph G. Cannon | R, Ill. | 1903-1911 |
| John W. Taylor | D, N. Y. | 1825-1827 | Champ Clark | D, Mo. | 1911-1919 |
| Andrew Stevenson | D, Va. | 1827-1834 | Frederick H. Gillett | R, Mass. | 1919-1925 |
| John Bell | D, Tenn. | 1834-1835 | Nicholas Longworth | R, Ohio. | 1925-1931 |
| James K. Polk | D, Tenn. | 1835-1839 | John N. Garner | D, Tex. | 1931-1933 |
| Robert M. T. Hunter | D, Va. | 1839-1841 | Henry T. Rainey | D, Ill. | 1933-1935 |
| John White | W, Ky. | 1841-1843 | Joseph W Byrns | D, Tenn. | 1935-1936 |
| John W. Jones | D, Va. | 1843-1845 | William B. Bankhead | D, Ala. | 1936-1940 |
| John W. Davis | D, Ind. | 1845-1847 | Sam Rayburn | D, Tex. | 1940-1947 |
| Robert C. Winthrop | W, Mass. | 1847-1849 | Joseph W. Martin, Jr. | R, Mass. | 1947-1949 |
| Howell Cobb | D, Ga. | 1849-1851 | Sam Rayburn | D, Tex. | 1949-1953 |
| Linn Boyd | D, Ky. | 1851-1855 | Joseph W. Martin, Jr. | R, Mass. | 1953-1955 |
| Nathaniel P. Banks | A, Mass. | 1856-1857 | Sam Rayburn | D, Tex. | 1955-1961 |
| James L. Orr | D, S. C. | 1857-1859 | John W McCormack | D, Mass. | 1962- |
| William Pennington | R, N. J. | 1860-1861 | | | |

## Wallace Tops 3rd Party Candidates Numerically But Not Percentage-Wise

George C. Wallace, running for President in 1968 as a 3rd party candidate, garnered more votes than any other such candidate ever did. But he did not top the percentages of the total vote rolled up by some earlier 3rd spot runners.

His high numerical total was achieved mainly because he was on the ballot in 50 states and because 1968 saw more voters at the polls than any previous Presidential election.

In 1912, former President Theodore Roosevelt, Progressive, won 27.4% of the popular vote and 88 electoral votes; in 1924, Robert M. La Follette, Progressive, had 17% and 13 electoral votes; in 1948, Strom Thurmond, States' Rights, took 2.4% and 39 electoral votes while Henry A. Wallace also got 2.4% but no electoral votes; in 1968, George Wallace won 13.2% and 45 electoral votes.

# GOVERNORS AND STATE GOVERNMENT OFFICIALS

| State | Capital | Governor | Party | Term Years | Term Expires | Annual Salary |
|---|---|---|---|---|---|---|
| Alabama | Montgomery | Albert P. Brewer | Dem. | 4 | Jan. 1971 | $25,000 |
| Alaska | Juneau | Walter J. Hickel | Rep. | 4 | Jan. 1971 | 27,500 |
| Arizona | Phoenix | John R. Williams | Rep. | 2 | Jan. 1971 | 22,500 |
| Arkansas | Little Rock | Winthrop Rockefeller | Rep. | 2 | Jan. 1971 | 10,000 |
| California | Sacramento | Ronald Reagan | Rep. | 4 | Jan. 1971 | 44,100 |
| Colorado | Denver | John A. Love | Rep. | 4 | Jan. 1971 | 20,000 |
| Connecticut | Hartford | John N. Dempsey | Dem. | 4 | Jan. 1971 | 35,000 |
| Delaware | Dover | Russell W. Peterson | Rep. | 4 | Jan. 1973 | 25,000 |
| Florida | Tallahassee | Claude R. Kirk, Jr. | Rep. | 4 | Jan. 1971 | 36,000 |
| Georgia | Atlanta | Lester G. Maddox | Dem. | 4 | Jan. 1971 | 42,500 |
| Hawaii | Honolulu | John A. Burns | Dem. | 4 | Jan. 1971 | 33,500 |
| Idaho | Boise | Don Samuelson | Rep. | 4 | Jan. 1971 | 17,500 |
| Illinois | Springfield | Richard B. Ogilvie | Rep. | 4 | Jan. 1973 | 45,000 |
| Indiana | Indianapolis | Edgar D. Whitcomb | Rep. | 4 | Jan. 1973 | 25,000 |
| Iowa | Des Moines | Robert D. Ray | Rep. | 2 | Jan. 1971 | 30,000 |
| Kansas | Topeka | Robert B. Docking | Dem. | 2 | Jan. 1971 | 20,000 |
| Kentucky | Frankfort | Louie B. Nunn | Rep. | 4 | Dec. 1971 | 30,000 |
| Louisiana | Baton Rouge | John J. McKeithen | Dem. | 4 | May 1972 | 20,000 |
| Maine | Augusta | Kenneth M. Curtis | Dem. | 4 | Jan. 1971 | 20,000 |
| Maryland | Annapolis | Spiro T. Agnew* | Rep. | 4 | Jan. 1971 | 25,000 |
| Massachusetts | Boston | John A. Volpe | Rep. | 4 | Jan. 1971 | 35,000 |
| Michigan | Lansing | George W. Romney | Rep. | 4 | Jan. 1971 | 40,000 |
| Minnesota | St. Paul | Harold LeVander | Rep. | 4 | Jan. 1971 | 27,500 |
| Mississippi | Jackson | John Bell Williams | Dem. | 4 | Jan. 1972 | 25,000 |
| Missouri | Jefferson City | Warren E. Hearnes | Dem. | 4 | Jan. 1973 | 37,500 |
| Montana | Helena | Forrest H. Anderson | Dem. | 4 | Jan. 1973 | 23,250 |
| Nebraska | Lincoln | Norbert T. Tiemann | Rep. | 4 | Jan. 1971 | 18,000 |
| Nevada | Carson City | Paul Laxalt | Rep. | 4 | Jan. 1971 | 25,000 |
| New Hampshire | Concord | Walter R. Peterson, Jr. | Rep. | 2 | Jan. 1971 | 30,000 |
| New Jersey | Trenton | Richard J. Hughes | Dem. | 4 | Jan. 1970 | 35,000 |
| New Mexico | Santa Fe | David F. Cargo | Rep. | 2 | Jan. 1971 | 17,500 |
| New York | Albany | Nelson A. Rockefeller | Rep. | 4 | Jan. 1971 | 50,000 |
| North Carolina | Raleigh | Robert W. Scott | Dem. | 4 | Jan. 1973 | 35,000 |
| North Dakota | Bismarck | William L. Guy | Dem. | 4 | Jan. 1973 | 18,000 |
| Ohio | Columbus | James A. Rhodes | Rep. | 4 | Jan. 1971 | 40,000 |
| Oklahoma | Oklahoma City | Dewey F. Bartlett | Rep. | 4 | Jan. 1971 | 25,000 |
| Oregon | Salem | Tom McCall | Rep. | 4 | Jan. 1971 | 25,000 |
| Pennsylvania | Harrisburg | Raymond P. Shafer | Rep. | 4 | Jan. 1971 | 45,000 |
| Rhode Island | Providence | Frank Licht | Dem. | 2 | Jan. 1971 | 30,000 |
| South Carolina | Columbia | Robert E. Mc Nair | Dem. | 4 | Jan. 1971 | 25,000 |
| South Dakota | Pierre | Frank Farrar | Rep. | 2 | Jan. 1971 | 18,000 |
| Tennessee | Nashville | Buford Ellington | Dem. | 4 | Jan. 1971 | 18,500 |
| Texas | Austin | Preston Smith | Dem. | 2 | Jan. 1971 | 40,000 |
| Utah | Salt Lake City | Calvin L. Rampton | Dem. | 4 | Jan. 1973 | 18,000 |
| Vermont | Montpelier | Deane C. Davis | Rep. | 2 | Jan. 1971 | 25,000 |
| Virginia | Richmond | Mills E. Godwin, Jr. | Dem. | 4 | Jan. 1970 | 30,000 |
| Washington | Olympia | Daniel J. Evans | Rep. | 4 | Jan. 1973 | 32,500 |
| West Virginia | Charleston | Arch A. Moore | Rep. | 4 | Jan. 1973 | 25,000 |
| Wisconsin | Madison | Warren P. Knowles | Rep. | 2 | Jan. 1971 | 25,000 |
| Wyoming | Cheyenne | Stanley K. Hathaway | Rep. | 4 | Jan. 1971 | 20,000 |
| **Possessions** | | | | | | |
| American Samoa | Pago Pago | Owen S. Aspinall | Dem. | (a) | .......... | 24,500 |
| Guam | Agana | Manuel F. L. Guerrero | Dem. | 4 | Mar. 1971 | 25,890 |
| Puerto Rico | San Juan | Luis Ferré | Prog. | 4 | Jan. 1973 | 25,000 |
| Virgin Islands | Charlotte Amalie | Ralph M. Palewonsky | Dem. | (†) | .......... | 28,000 |

*Successor picked by Legislature Jan. 1969; (a) Appointed by Interior Dept.; (†) Appointed by President.

## Governments of States and Possessions

**Compiled by World Almanac from statistics supplied by the Secretaries of State.**

Below appears the makeup of each state's government as constituted after 1968 elections except in Arkansas, Illinois, Maine, New Hampshire, North Dakota, Tennessee, and Vermont. In those states, as well as American Samoa and Puerto Rico, an asterisk indicates that information may be outdated because of elections or new appointments. All the governors are listed as after 1968 elections.

### Alabama

Governor—Albert P. Brewer, D., $25,000.
Lt. Governor—Vacant, $32 per legislative day, plus annual salary of $300 per month.
Sec. of State—Mabel S. Amos, D., $15,000.
Atty. General—MacDonald Gallion, D., $18,000.
Treasurer—Mrs. Agnes Baggett, D., $15,000.
Auditor—Melba Till Allen, D., $15,000.
Supt. of Educ.—Ernest Stone, D., $15,000.
Comm. of Agric.—Richard Beard, D., $15,000.
LEGISLATURE
Meets odd years, 1st Tues. in May, at Montgomery. Members receive $30 per day during legislative sessions, annual salary of $300 per month, plus 10¢ per mile travel allowance (one round trip between home and Capitol).
Senate—Dem., 34; Rep., 1. Total, 35.
House—Dem., 106. Total, 106.

### Alaska

Governor—Walter J. Hickel, R., $27,000.
Sec. of State—Keith Miller, R., $23,700.
Administration—Robert W. Ward, $23,700.
Education—Dr. Clifford R. Hartman, $23,700.
Health & Walfare—J. Scott McDonald, $23,700.
Law—G. Kent Edwards, $23,700.
LEGISLATURE
Meets annually, in January, at Juneau, for as long as may be necessary. First session in odd years. Members receive $6,000 per year plus $35 per day while in session. $500 allowance for secretarial services, plus one round trip first class airfare from residence to Juneau.
Senate—Rep., 11; Dem., 9. Total, 20.
House—Dem., 22; Rep., 18. Total, 40.

### Arizona

Governor—John R. Williams, R., $22,500.
Sec. of State—Wesley Nelson, D., $13,000.
Atty. General—Gary Nelson, R., $16,800.
Treasurer—Morris A. Herring R., $10,800.
LEGISLATURE
Meets annually, in January, at Phoenix. Members receive $1,800 for each regular session, plus expenses and travel allowance; $20 per day for special sessions.
Senate—Dem., 13; Rep., 17. Total, 30.
House—Dem., 26; Rep., 34. Total, 60.

### Arkansas

Governor—Winthrop Rockefeller, R., $10,000.
*Lt. Governor—Footsie Britt, R., $2,500.
*Sec. of State—Kelly Bryant, D., $5,000.
*Auditor—Jimmy Jones, D., $5,000.
*Atty. General—Joseph Purcell, D., $6,000.
*Treasurer—Mrs. Nancy J. Hall, D., $5,000.
GENERAL ASSEMBLY
Meets odd year, in January, at Little Rock. Members receive $2,400 for each two-year period. $20 a day while in session, plus 5¢ a mile travel expense.
*Senate—Dem., 35 (total).
*House—Dem., 97; Rep., 3. Total, 100.

### California

Governor—Ronald Reagan, R., $44,100.
Lt. Governor—Robert H. Finch, R., $25,000.
Sec. of State—Frank M. Jordan, R., $25,000.
Controller—Houston I. Flourney, R., $25,000.
Atty. General—Thomas C. Lynch, D., $32,000.
Treasurer—Ivy Baker Priest, R., $25,000.
Supt. Public Instr.—Max Rafferty, N.P., $25,000.

## LEGISLATURE

Meets in annual general sessions, unlimited as to duration. Members receive $16,000 per year plus mileage and $21 daily expenses while in session. Daily expenses on interim business: $25.
Senate—Dem., 20; Rep., 20. Total, 40.
Assembly—Dem., 39; Rep. 41. Total, 80.

## Colorado

Governor—John A. Love, R., $20,000.
Lt. Governor—Mark Hogan, D., $4,800.
Sec. of State—Byron Anderson, R., $10,000.
Auditor—John R. Proctor, R., $18,500.
Atty. General—Duke W. Dunbar, R., $15,000.
Treasurer—Virginia Blue, R., $10,000.

### GENERAL ASSEMBLY

Meets annually, in January, at Denver. Members receive $3,600 annually plus $25 per session day with a maximum of 140 days in two years.
Senate—Dem., 11; Rep., 24. Total, 35.
House—Dem., 27; Rep., 38. Total, 65.

## Connecticut

Governor—John N. Dempsey, D., $35,000.
Lt. Governor—A. R. Frassinelli, D., $10,000.
Sec. of State—Mrs. Ella T. Grasso, D., $15,000.
Treasurer—Gerald A. Lamb, D., $15,000.
Comptroller—Louis I. Gladstone, D., $15,000.
Atty. General—Robert K. Killian, D., $20,000.

### GENERAL ASSEMBLY

Meets odd years, in January, at Hartford. Members receive $3,250 salary plus $750 for expenses per term and travel allowance of 10¢ per mile.
Senate—Dem., 24; Rep., 12. Total, 36.
House—Dem., 110; Rep., 67. Total, 177.

## Delaware

Governor—Russell W. Peterson, R., $25,000.
Lt. Governor—Eugene D. Bookhammer, R., $9,000.
Auditor—George Cripps, R., $12,000.
Atty. General—David P. Buckson, R., $15,000.
Treasurer—Daniel J. Ross, R., $12,000.

### GENERAL ASSEMBLY

Meets annually at Dover, odd years in January, even years in February. Members receive $6,000 per year.
Senate—Dem., 6; Rep., 13. Total, 19.
House—Dem., 13; Rep., 26. Total, 39.

## Florida

Governor—Claude R. Kirk, Jr., R., $36,000.
Sec. of State—Tom Adams, D., $32,000.
Comptroller—Fred O. Dickinson, Jr., D., $29,000.
Atty. General—Earl Faircloth, D., $29,000.
Treasurer—Broward Williams, D., $29,000.
Supt. Publ. Instr.—Floyd T. Christian, D., $29,000.
Comm. of Agric.—Doyle Conner, D., $29,000.

### LEGISLATURE

Meets annually, in April, at Tallahassee. Members receive $1,200 per year plus $300 expense allowance per month during session.
Senate—Dem., 32; Rep., 16. Total, 48.
House—Dem., 77; Rep., 42. Total, 119.

## Georgia

Governor—Lester G. Maddox, D., $42,500.
Lt. Governor—George T. Smith, D., $20,000.
Sec. of State—Ben W. Fortson, Jr., D., $22,500.
Comptroller General—James L. Bentley, Jr., R., $22,500.
Atty. General—Arthur K. Bolton, D., $26,000.

### GENERAL ASSEMBLY

Meets annually, at Atlanta. Members receive $4,200 per year, and during session an additional $25 per day for expenses.
Senate—Dem., 48; Rep., 6; Ind., 1; Run-off, 1. Total, 56.
House—Dem., 168; Rep., 26; Run-off, 1. Total, 195.

## Hawaii

Governor—John A. Burns, D., $33,500.
Lt. Governor—Thomas P. Gill, D., $27,500.
Comptroller—KeNam Kim, D., $18,000-$22,000[1].
Atty. General—Bert T. Kobayashi, D., $18,500-$25,000[1].
Dir. of Finance—Andrew T. F. Ing, D., $18,500-$25,000[1].
Supt. of Education—Ralph H. Kiyosaki, Ind., $18,500-$25,000[†].
Dir. of Health—Dr. Walter B. Quisenberry, D., $18,500-$25,000[1].
[1]Governor determines specific salary.
[†]Bd. of Education sets specific salary.

### LEGISLATURE

Meets annually, in January, at Honolulu. Members receive $12,000 per year plus allowance for expenses.
Senate—Dem., 16; Rep., 9. Total, 25.
House—Dem., 39; Rep., 12. Total, 51.

## Idaho

Governor—Don Samuelson, R., $17,500.
Lt. Governor—Jack M. Murphy, R., $3,600, plus $30 per day expenses sessions of legislature. In absence of Governor acts in his stead and draws regular pay of Governor.
Sec. of State—Pete T. Cenarrusa, R., $12,500.
Treasurer—Marjorie Ruth Moon, D., $12,500.
Atty. General—Allan G. Shepard, R., $12,500.
Auditor—Joe R. Williams, D., $12,500.
Supt. Publ. Instr.—D. F. Engelking, D., $12,500.

### LEGISLATURE

Meets annually, on second Monday in January, at Boise. Members receive $10 per day served, plus $25 per day expenses.
Senate—Rep., 22; Dem., 13. Total, 35.
House—Rep., 39; Dem., 31. Total, 70.

## Illinois

Governor—Richard B. Ogilvie, R., $45,000.
Lieut. Governor—Paul Simon, D., $16,000.
Sec. of State—Paul Powell, D., $20,000.
Auditor—Michael J. Howlett, D., $20,000.
Atty. General—William J. Scott, R., $20,000.
Treasurer—Adlai E. Stevenson, 3rd., D., $30,000.
Supt. Public Instr.—Ray Page, R., $30,000.

### GENERAL ASSEMBLY

Meets odd years, in January, at Springfield. Members receive $18,000 for the biennium.
*Senate—Rep., 38; Dem., 20. Total, 58.
*House—Rep., 99; Dem., 78. Total, 177.

## Indiana

Governor—Edgar D. Whitcomb, R., $25,000.
Lt. Governor—Richard E. Folz, R., $16,500.
also $1,800 per year as President of Senate, plus $5 per day during legislative sessions.
Sec. of State—William N. Salin, R., $16,500.
Auditor—Trudy S. Etherton, R., $16,500.
Atty. General—Theodore L. Sendak, R., $18,000.
Treasurer—John K. Snyder, R., $16,500.
Supt. Publ. Instr.—Richard D. Wells, R., $18,000.

### GENERAL ASSEMBLY

Meets odd years, in January, at Indianapolis. Members receive $1,800 per year, and 8¢ per mile for one round trip per week.
Senate—Rep., 35; Dem., 15. Total, 50.
House—Rep., 73; Dem., 27. Total, 100.

## Iowa

Governor—Robert D. Ray, R., $30,000.
Lt. Governor—Roger W. Jepsen, R., $80 per day while in session.
Sec. of State—Melvin D. Synhorst, R., $16,000.
Auditor—Lloyd R. Smith, R., $16,000.
Atty. General—Richard C. Turner, R., $21,000.
Treasurer—Maurice E. Baringer, R., $16,000.
Sec. of Agriculture—L. B. Liddy, R., $16,000.

### GENERAL ASSEMBLY

Meets annually, in January, at Des Moines. Members receive $40 per day for the session.
Senate—Dem., 16; Rep., 45. Total, 61.
House—Dem., 38; Rep., 86. Total, 124.

## Kansas

Governor—Robert Docking, D., $20,000.
Lt. Governor—James H. De Coursey, Jr., D., $8,000.
Sec. of State—Mrs. E. M. Shanahan, R., $12,650.
Auditor—Clay E. Hedrick, R., $12,650.
Atty. General—Kent Frizzell, R., $17,500.
Treasurer—Walter H. Perry, R., $12,650.
Comm. of Insurance—Frank Sullivan, R., $16,500.

### LEGISLATURE

Meets annually in January, at Topeka. Members receive $10 a day plus $25 a day expenses, total not to exceed $3,150 for a regular or $1,050 for a special or budget session; also an expense allowance between sessions and mileage.
Senate—Rep., 32; Dem., 8. Total, 40.
House—Rep., 87; Dem., 38. Total, 125.

## Kentucky

Governor—Louie B. Nunn, R., $30,000.
Lt. Gov.—Wendell Ford, D., $20,000, plus additional compensation when acting in place of Governor.
Sec. of State—Elmer Begley, R., $18,000.
Auditor—Clyde Conley, R., $18,000.
Atty. Gen.—John Breckinridge, D., $20,000.
Treasurer—Thelma Stovall, D., $18,000.
Supt. Public Instr.—Wendell Butler, D., $20,000.
Comm. of Agric.—Robert Miller, R., $18,000.

### GENERAL ASSEMBLY

Meets even years, in January, at Frankfort. Members receive $25 per day during session; presiding officers, $30. All members also receive $25 per day for expenses.
Senate—Dem., 24; Rep., 14. Total, 38.
House—Dem., 57; Rep., 43. Total, 100.

## Louisiana

Governor—John J. McKeithen, D., $20,000.
Lt. Governor—C. C. Aycock, D., $16,500.
Sec. of State—Wade O. Martin, Jr., D., $18,700.
Atty. General—J. P. F. Gremillion, D., $18,700.
Treasurer—Mary Evelyn Parker, D., $14,850.
Supt. of Education—William J. Dodd, D., $18,700.

## LEGISLATURE

Meets even years (60 calendar days) and odd years (30 calendar days) in May, at Baton Rouge. Members receive $50 per day and mileage during the 60 days session of 10c a mile for 8 round trips. When the Legislature is not in session, members receive $250 per month as an expense allowance.

Senate—Dem., 39 (total).
House—Dem., 105 (total).

## Maine

Governor—Kenneth Curtis, D., $20,000.
Sec. of State—Joseph T. Edgar, R.
Atty. General—James S. Erwin, R.
Commissioner of Finance—Maurice F. Williams.
Auditor—Armand G. Sansoucy.

### LEGISLATURE

Meets odd years, in Jan., at Augusta. Members receive $2,000 per session; presiding officers, $2,300.
*Senate—Dem., 10; Rep., 24. Total, 34.
*House—Dem., 55; Rep., 96. Total, 151.

## Maryland

Governor—Spiro T. Agnew, R., $25,000.
*Note—Legislature to choose successor to Vice President-elect Agnew in January, 1969.*
Sec. of State—C. Stanley Blair, R., $12,000.
Auditor—Howard F. Wiedy, R., $16,000.
Comptroller—Louis L. Goldstein, D., $20,000.
Atty. General—Francis B. Burch, D., $20,000.
Treasurer—John A. Luetkemeyer, D., $2,500.

### GENERAL ASSEMBLY

Meets 70 days annually on the 3rd Wednesday in January, at Annapolis. Members receive $2,400 per year; Speaker of House and President of Senate, each $2,650 per year.
Senate—Dem., 35; Rep., 8. Total, 43.
House—Dem., 117; Rep., 25. Total, 142.

## Massachusetts

Governor—John A. Volpe, R., $35,000.
Lt. Governor—Francis W. Sargent, R., $20,000.
Sec. of the Commonwealth—John F. X. Davoren, D., $20,000.
Atty. General—Elliot L. Richardson, R., $25,000.
Auditor—Thaddeus Buczko, D., $20,000.
Treasurer—Robert O. Crane, D., $20,000.

### GENERAL COURT (LEGISLATURE)

Meets each January in Boston. Salaries indefinite pending action of new Legislature.
Senate—Dem., 27; Rep., 13. Total, 40.
House—Dem., 173; Rep., 67. Total, 240.

## Michigan

Governor—George W. Romney, R., $40,000.
Lt. Governor—William H. Milliken, R., $22,500.
Sec. of State—James M. Hare, D., $30,000.
Atty. General—Frank J. Kelley, D., $30,000.

### LEGISLATURE

Meets annually, in January, at Lansing. Members receive $12,500 per year plus $2,500 expense allowance.
Senate—Rep., 20; Dem., 18. Total, 38.
House—Rep., 53; Dem., 57. Total, 110.

## Minnesota

Governor—Harold LeVander, R., $27,500.
Lt. Governor—James B. Goetz, R., $9,600.
Sec. of State—Joseph L. Donovan, DFL, $20,500.
Auditor—Stafford King, R., $20,500.
Atty. General—Douglas M. Head, R., $22,000.
Treasurer—Val Bjornson, R., $20,500.
(Democratic-Farmer-Labor is the legal name of the Democratic Party in Minnesota.)

### LEGISLATURE

Meets odd years, in January, at St. Paul. Members receive $4,800 per year plus expense allowance during session.
Senate—67, elected without party designation.
House—135, elected without party designation.

## Mississippi

Governor—John Bell Williams, D., $25,000.
Lt. Gov.—Charles Sullivan, D., $8,500 per regular legislative session, plus expense allowance.
Sec. of State—Heber Ladner, D., $16,000.
Auditor—W. H. (Hamp) King, D., $16,000.
Atty. Gen.—Joe T. Patterson, D., $16,500.
Treasurer—Evelyn Gandy, D., $16,000.
Supt. Public Educ.—Garvin Johnson, D., $16,000.

### LEGISLATURE

Meets annually in January, at Jackson. Members receive $5,000 per regular session, plus travel allowance and $100 per month while not in session.
Senate—Dem., 52; Rep., 0. Total 52.
House—Dem., 122; Rep., 0. Total, 122.

## Missouri

Governor—Warren E. Hearnes, D., $37,500.
Lt. Governor—William S. Morris, D., $16,000.
Sec. of State—James C. Kirkpatrick, D., $20,000.
Auditor—Haskell Holman, D., $20,000.
Atty. General—John C. Danforth, R., $25,000.
Treasurer—M. E. Morris, D., $20,000.

### GENERAL ASSEMBLY

Meets odd years, in January, at Jefferson City. Members receive $4,800 per year and $10 per day for expenses plus mileage allowance.
Senate—Dem., 23; Rep., 11. Total, 34.
House—Dem., 109; Rep., 54. Total, 163.

## Montana

Governor—Forrest H. Anderson, D., $23,250.
Lt. Governor—Thomas L. Judge, D., 60 days Legislative pay at $25.00 per day, plus $15 per day for expenses; average governor's pay while serving as governor.
Sec. of State—Frank Murray, D., $10,500.
Auditor—E. V. (Sonny) Omholt, R., $10,500.
Atty. General—Bob Woodahl, R., $15,500.
Treasurer—Alex B. Stephenson, R., $10,500.
Supt. Public Instr.—Dolores Colburg, D., $13,750.

### LEGISLATIVE ASSEMBLY

Meets odd years, in January, at Helena. Members receive $20 per day plus $15 per day for expenses while in session.
Senate—Dem., 30; Rep., 25. Total, 55.
House—Dem., 46; Rep., 58. Total, 104.

## Nebraska

Governor—Norbert T. Tiemann, R., $18,000.
Lt. Governor—John E. Everroad, R., $6,000.
Sec. of State—Frank Marsh, R., $12,500.
Auditor—Ray C. Johnson, R., $12,500.
Atty. General—Clarence A. Meyer, R., $16,000.
Treasurer—Wayne Swanson, R., $12,500.

### LEGISLATURE

Meets odd years in January, at Lincoln. Members receive salary of not more than $200 per month plus traveling expenses for one round trip to and from session.
Unicameral body composed of 49 members who are elected on a nonpartisan ballot and are classed as Senators.

## Nevada

Governor—Paul Laxalt, R., $25,000.
Lt. Governor—Ed Fike, R., $4,500 plus $40 per day when acting as Governor and President of the Senate during legislative sessions.
Sec. of State—John Koontz, D., $15,000.
Controller—Wilson McGowen, R., $15,000.
Atty. General—Harvey Dickerson, D., $18,000.
Treasurer—Michael Mirabelli, D., $15,000.

### LEGISLATURE

Meets odd years in January, at Carson City. Newly elected members receive $40 per day for 60 days (20 days for special sessions). Holdover senators $25 per day with same limitations. All members receive per diem of $25 per day for 60 days (20 days special session) and $15 per day in excess of these limitations. Travel allowance of 10c per mile.
Senate—Dem., 11; Rep., 9. Total, 20.
Assembly—Dem., 18; Rep., 22. Total, 40.

## New Hampshire

Governor—Walter R. Peterson, Jr., R., $30,000.
*Sec. of State—Robert L. Stark, R., $13,500-$15,000 (A).
*Comptroller—Leonard S. Hill, D., $16,000-$17,500 (A).
*Atty. General—George S. Pappagianis, D., $16,000-$17,500 (A).
(A) Salary depends on number of years served.

### GENERAL COURT (LEGISLATURE)

Meets odd years, in January, at Concord. Members receive $200; presiding officers $250.
Senate—Rep., 15; Dem., 9. Total, 24.
House—Rep., 255; Dem., 145. Total, 400.

## New Jersey

Governor—Richard J. Hughes, D., $35,000.
Sec. of State—Robert J. Burkhardt, D., $23,000.
Atty. Gen.—Arthur J. Sills, D., $25,000.
Treasurer—John A. Kervick, D., $25,000.
Auditor—George B. Harper, R., $12,000.

### LEGISLATURE

Meets anually, in January, at Trenton. Members receive $7,500 per year, except President of Senate and Speaker of Assembly who receive ⅓ more by virtue of their office.
Senate—Dem., 9; Rep., 31. Total, 40.
Assembly—Dem., 22; Rep., 58. Total, 80.

## New Mexico

Governor—David F. Cargo, R., $17,500.
Lt. Governor—E. Lee Francis, R., $40 per day when presiding over Senate.
Sec. of State—Ernestine D. Evans, D., $12,500.
Auditor—Harold G. Thompson, R., $7,200.
Atty. General—James A. Maloney, D., $17,500.

Treasurer—Jesse D. Kornegay, D., $12,500.
Comm. Public Lands—Alex J. Armijo, D., $15,000.

### LEGISLATURE

Meets in January, at Santa Fe, odd years for 60 days, even years for 30 days. Members receive $20 per day while in session.
Senate—Dem., 25; Rep., 17. Total, 42.
House—Dem., 44; Rep., 26. Total, 70.

## New York

Governor—Nelson A. Rockefeller, R., $50,000.
Lt. Governor—Malcolm Wilson, R., $30,000.
Sec. of State—John P. Lomenzo, R., $34,765.
Comptroller—Arthur Levitt, D., $40,000.
Atty. General—Louis J. Lefkowitz, R., $40,000.

### LEGISLATURE

Meets annually, in January, at Albany. Members receive $15,000 per year.
Senate—Rep., 33; Dem., 24. Total, 57.
Assembly—Rep., 76; Dem., 72; Con., 2. Total, 150.

## North Carolina

Governor—Robert W. Scott, D., $35,000.
Lt. Governor—H. Pat Taylor, Jr., D., $5,000 per year, plus $20 per day not to exceed 120 days per regular session, $4,000 per year expense allowance.
Sec. of State—Thad Eure, D., $20,000.
Auditor—Henry L. Bridges, D., $20,000.
Atty. General—Robert Morgan, D., $20,000.
Treasurer—Edwin Gill, D., $20,000.
Supt. Public Instr.—Craig Phillips, D., $20,000.

### GENERAL ASSEMBLY

Meets odd years in January, at Raleigh. Members receive $15 per day not to exceed 120 days, and subsistence and travel allowances while in session.
Senate—Dem., 38; Rep., 12. Total, 50.
House—Dem., 91; Rep., 29. Total, 120.

## North Dakota

Governor—William L. Guy, D., $18,000 plus $6,000 per year expense allowance.
*Lt. Governor—Charles Tighe, D., $1,600.
*Sec. of State—Ben Meier, R., $6,000.
*Auditor—Curtis Olson, R., $6,000.
Atty. General—Helgi Johanneson, R., $8,500.
*Treasurer—Walter Christensen, D., $6,000.
*Supt. Public Instruction—M. F. Peterson, N-P., $7,200. All state officers receive $5,000 per year for expenses except the Lt. Gov. who receives $400 for expenses.

### LEGISLATIVE ASSEMBLY

Meets odd years, in January at Bismarck. Members receive $5 per day, plus $25 per day expense allowance while in session, plus $35 per month when not in session.
*Senate—Rep., 44; Dem., 5. Total, 49.
*House—Rep., 83; Dem., 15. Total, 98.

## Ohio

Governor—James A. Rhodes, R., $40,000.
Lt. Governor—John W. Brown, R., $17,000.
Sec. of State—Ted W. Brown, R., $25,000.
Auditor—Roger Cloud, R., $25,000.
Treasurer—John D. Herbert, R., $25,000.
Supt. Public Instr.—Martin W. Essex, $25,000.

### GENERAL ASSEMBLY

Meets annually, in January, at Columbus. Second session commencing not later than Mar. 15 of year following each regular session. Members receive $12,750 per year plus travel allowance.
Senate—Rep., 21; Dem., 12. Total, 33.
House—Rep., 64; Dem., 35. Total, 99.

## Oklahoma

Governor—Dewey Bartlett, R., $25,000.
Lt. Governor—George Nigh, D., $9,000.
Sec. of State—John Rogers, D., $12,600.
Auditor—Joe Bailey Cobb, D., $9,200.
Atty. General—G. T. Blankenship, R., **$16,500.**
Treasurer—Leo Winters, D., $12,600.
Supt. Public Instr.—Dr. D. D. Creech, R., $16,500.

### LEGISLATURE

Meets each year in January, at Oklahoma City. Members receive the sum of $8,400 per annum.
Senate—Dem., 38; Rep., 10. Total, 48.
House—Dem., 76; Rep., 23. Total, 99.

## Oregon

Governor—Tom McCall, R., $25,000.
Sec. of State—Clay Myers, R., $21,000.
Atty. General—Lee Johnson, R., $21,000.
Treasurer—Robert W. Straub, D., $21,000.
Supt. Public Instr.—Dale Parnell, (N-P) $20,000.

### LEGISLATIVE ASSEMBLY

Meets odd years, in January, at Salem. Members receive $250 monthly and $20 expenses per day during any session.
Senate—Dem., 16; Rep., 14. Total, 30.

House—Dem., 22; Rep., 38. Total, 60.

## Pennsylvania

Governor—Raymond P. Shafer, R., $45,000.
Lt. Governor—Raymond Broderick, R., $32,500.
Sec. of State—Joseph J. Kelley, Jr., $25,000.
Auditor of State—Mrs. Grace M. Sloan, D., $32,500.
Atty. General—William Sennett, R., $32,500.
Treasurer—Thomas Z. Minehart, D., $32,500.

### GENERAL ASSEMBLY

Meets annually, in January, at Harrisburg. Members receive $7,200 per year plus $4,800 for expenses.
Senate—Rep., 27; Dem., 23. Total, 50.
House—Rep., 95; Dem., 108. Total, 203.

## Rhode Island

Governor—Frank Licht, D., $30,000.
Lt. Governor—J. Joseph Garrahy, D., $12,000.
Sec. of State—August P. La France, D., $18,000.
Atty. General—Herbert F. DeSimone, R., $22,000.
Treasurer—Raymond H. Hawksley, D., $18,000.

### GENERAL ASSEMBLY

Meets annually, in Jan., at Providence. Members receive $5 per day for 60 days (the Speaker, $10), also travel allowance of 8¢ per mile.
Senate—Dem., 36; Rep., 9; In doubt, 5. Total, 50.
House—Dem., 74; Rep., 21; In doubt, 5. Total, 100.

## South Carolina

Governor—Robert E. McNair, D, $25,000
Sec. of State—O. Frank Thornton, D., **$20,000.**
Comptroller General—Henry Mills, D., $20,000.
Atty. General—Daniel R. McLeod, D., $20,000.
Treasurer—G. L. Patterson, Jr., D., $20,000.
Supt. of Educ.—Cyril B. Busbee, D., $20,000.
Comm. of Agric.—William L. Harrelson, D., $20,000.

### GENERAL ASSEMBLY

Meets annually, in January, at Columbia, Members receive $4,000 per year plus expense allowance of $15 per day and travel and postage allowance.
Senate—Dem., 47; Rep., 3. Total, 50.
House—Dem., 121; Rep., 3. Total, 124.

## South Dakota

Governor—Frank Farrar, R., $18,000.
Lt. Governor—James Abdnor, R., $2,400.
Sec. of State—Miss Alma Larson, R., $10,800.
Treasurer—Neal Strand, R., $10,800.
Atty. General—Gordon Mydland, R., $14,000.
Auditor—Alice Kundert, R., $10,800.
Comm. of Schools and Public Lands—Dr. Gordon A. Diedtrich, $10,800.

### LEGISLATURE

Meets annually in January, at Pierre. Members receive $1,800 for 45 day session in odd-numbered years, and $1,200 for 30 day session in even-numbered years, plus 7¢ per mile travel allowance. For special session, $10 per day for each day of attendance.
Senate—Rep., 27; Dem., 8. Total, 35.
House—Rep., 59; Dem., 16. Total, 75.

## Tennessee

Governor—Buford Ellington, D., $18,500.
Lt. Governor—Frank C. Gorrell, D., receives regular legislative salary.
*Sec. of State—Joe C. Carr, D., $17,500.
*Comptroller—William Snodgrass, D., $17,500.
*Treasurer—Charlie Worley, D., $17,500.
Atty. General—George F. McCanless, D., $20,000.

### GENERAL ASSEMBLY

Meets odd years, in January, at Nashville. Members receive $150 per month plus expenses for each day in session (not to exceed 105 days).
Senate—Dem., 20; Rep., 13. Total, 33.
House—Dem., 49; Rep., 49; Ind., 1. Total, 99.

## Texas

Governor—Preston Smith, D., $40,000.
Lt. Governor—Ben Barnes, D., same salary as State Senator while presiding over Senate, plus living quarters: Governor's salary when acting as Governor.
Sec. of State—Roy R. Barrera, D., $24,000.
Comptroller—Robert S. Calvert, D., $26,000.
Atty. General—Crawford C. Martin, D., $27,500.
Treasurer—Jesse James, D., $26,000.

### LEGISLATURE

Meets odd years, in January, at Austin. Members receive annual salary not exceeding $4,800 plus per diem while in session and travel allowance.
Senate—Dem., 29; Rep., 2. Total, 31.
House—Dem., 142; Rep., 8. Total, 150.

## Utah

Governor—Calvin L. Rampton, D., $18,000.
Sec. of State—Clyde L. Miller, D., $13,000.
Auditor—Sherman J. Preece, R., $12,000.

Atty. General—Vernon B. Romney, R., $13,000.
Treasurer—Golden L. Allen, R., $12,000.

### LEGISLATURE

Meets annually in January at Salt Lake City. While in session members receive $25 per diem, expenses of $15 per diem, plus mileage.
Senate—Rep., 20; Dem., 8. Total, 28.
House—Rep., 48; Dem., 21. Total, 69.

## Vermont

Governor—Deane C. Davis, R., $25,000.
Lt. Governor—Thomas L. Hayes, R., $12,000.
Sec. of State—Richard C. Thomas, R., $13,000.
Auditor—Robert T. King, R., $15,000.
Atty. General—James L. Jeffords, R., $19,000.
Treasurer—Frank Davis, R., $15,000.

### GENERAL ASSEMBLY

Meets odd years, in January, at Montpelier. Members receive $150 weekly, while in session, with a limit of $4,500 for a regular session and $30 per day for special session, with specified expenses.
*Senate—Rep., 22; Dem., 8. Total, 30.
*House—Rep., 91; Dem., 54; Rep. & Dem., 2; Dem. Rep., 1; Ind., 2. Total, 150.

## Virginia

Governor—Mills E. Godwin, Jr., D., $30,000.
Lt. Governor—Fred G. Pollard, D., $2,100 each biennial session of Legislature, plus $3,000 per year for expenses.
Sec. of the Commonwealth—Miss Martha Bell Conway, D., $14,500.
Atty. General—Robert Y. Button, D., $22,000.
Treasurer—Lewis H. Vaden, D., $17,500.
Auditor of Public Accts.—Joseph S. James, D., $17,500.

### GENERAL ASSEMBLY

Meets even years in January, at Richmond. Members receive $2,100 per regular 60 day biennial session plus $1,200 for expenses.
Senate—Dem., 34; Rep., 6. Total, 40.
House—Dem., 85; Rep., 15. Total, 100.

## Washington

Governor—Daniel J. Evans, R., $32,500.
Lt. Governor—John A. Cherberg, D., $10,000.
Sec. of State—A. L. "Lud" Kramer, R., $15,000.
Auditor—R. V. Graham, D., $16,500.
Atty. General—John G. McCutcheon, D., $23,000.
Treasurer—Robert S. O'Brien D., $15,000.
Supt. Public Lands—Bert Cole, D., $16,500.
Comm. Public Lands—Bert Cole, D., $16,500.

### LEGISLATURE

Meets odd years in January, at Olympia. Members receive $3,600 annually, plus $25 per day while in session for subsistence and lodging.
Senate—Dem., 27; Rep., 22. Total, 49.
House—Dem., 43; Rep., 56. Total, 99.

## West Virginia

Governor—Arch A. Moore, Jr., R., $25,000.
Sec. of State—John D. Rockefeller IV, D., $17,000.
Auditor—Denzil L. Gainer, D., $18,500.
Atty. General—Chauncey Browning, Jr., D., $18,500.
Treasurer—John H. Kelly, D., $17,500.
Comm. Agric.—Gus R. Douglass, D., 17,000.

### LEGISLATURE

Meets annually in January, at Charleston. Members receive $1,500 per year.
Senate—Dem., 22; Rep., 12. Total, 34.
House—Dem., 63; Rep., 37. Total, 100.

## Wisconsin

Governor—Warren P. Knowles, R., $25,000.
Lt. Governor—Jack B. Olson, R., $15,000 per biennium.
Sec. of State—Robert C. Zimmerman, R., $13,500.
*State Treasurer—Harold W. Clemens, R., $13,500.
Atty. General—Robert W. Warren, R., $20,000.
Supt. of Schools—William C. Kahl N-P., $20,000.

### LEGISLATURE

Meets odd years, in January at Madison. Members receive $8,400 annually plus $15.00 per day expenses for attendance each day.
Senate—Rep., 23; Dem., 10. Total,33.
Assembly—Rep., 52; Dem., 48. Total, 100.

## Wyoming

Governor—Stanley K. Hathaway, R., $20,000.
Sec. of State—Mrs. Thyra Thomson, R., $15,000.
Auditor—Everett Copenhaver, R., $15,000.
Atty. General—James E. Barrett, $14,400.
Treasurer—Mrs. Minnie Mitchell, R., $15,000.
Supt. Public Instr.—K. H. Roberts, R., $15,000.

### LEGISLATURE

Meets odd years in January, at Cheyenne. Members receive $12 per day while in session, plus $20 per day for expenses, and 8¢ a mile travel allowance.
Senate—Rep., 19; Dem., 11. Total, 30.
House—Rep., 44; Dem., 16; Contested, 1. Total, 61.

## American Samoa

Governor—Owen S. Aspinall, $24,500.
*Secretary—Alvin R. Mangnall, $15,150.
*Special Assistant to the Governor—Mundey Johnston.
*Directors: (Salaries $10,000 to $18,000).
  Agriculture—Thomas G. Hatakeyama.
  Administrative Services—M. W. Bales.
  Education—Dr. Roy D. Cobb.
  Legal Affairs and Public Safety—Charles H. Habernigg.
  Medical Services—Dr. Allen Service.
  Port Administrator—Fred J. Urhle.
  Public Safety Commissioner—Vacant.
  Secretary of Samoan Affairs—High Chief Le'iato, T.
  Public Works—A. P. Pratt.

### LEGISLATURE

Composed of a Senate of 19 members and a House of Representatives of 20 members. Meets annually, in March, at Fagatogo. Members receive $600 annually, plus $15 per day on special session called by the Governor on budget hearings, these hearings not to exceed 10 days.

## Guam

Governor—Manuel F. L. Guerrero, $25,890.
Sec. of Guam—Denver Dickerson, $22,085.
Directors: (Salaries $11,750 to $17,750).
  Agriculture—Francisco B. Aguon.
  Atty. General—Paul Abbate.
  Chief Commissioner—Vincente Q. Sanchez.
  Commerce—Paul Souder.
  Education—L. P. Martin.
  Finance—Joaquin Guerrero.
  Labor and Personnel—Charles F. Toves.
  Land Management—Frank I. San Nicolas.
  Public Health and Welfare—Dr. Robert G. Atwood.
  Public Safety—Major Jose C. Quintanilla.
  Public Works—Fred M. Poole.
  Washinngton Rep—Antonio B. Won Pat.
    $25,000 (elected at large).

### LEGISLATURE

Meets annually at Agana. Salary $6,000 per annum.

## Puerto Rico

Governor—Luis Ferré, N-P., 25,000.
*Secretaries of:
Agriculture—Miguel Hernandez Agosto, $19,000.
Commerce—Geraro Baquero, $19,000.
Education—Angel Quintero Alfaro, $19,000.
Health—Manuel A. Torres Aguiar, M.D., $19,000.
Justice—Jose C. Aponte, $19,000.
Labor—Alfredo Nazario, $19,000.
Public Works—Francisco Lizardi, $19,000.
State—Guillermo Irizarry, $19,500.
Treasury—Jorge Font Saldana, 19,000.

### LEGISLATIVE ASSEMBLY

Composed of a Senate of 32 members and a House of Representatives of 64 members. Meets annually, in January, at San Juan, members receive $5,400 plus expense and travel allowances while in session.

## Virgin Islands

Governor—Ralph M. Paiewonsky, $28,000.
Government Secretary—Cyril E. King, $25,000.
Comptroller—C. Loring Jetton, $24,393.
Atty. General—Francisco Corneiro, $23,075.
Budget Director—Magdalena Bryan, $23,075.
Commissioners:
  Agriculture—Walter I. M. Hodge, $17,511.
  Commerce—Dr. Albert Prendergast, $21,098.
  Education—Dr. Arthur Richards, $20,439.
  Finance—Reuben Wheatley, $17,511.
  Health—Dr. Roy A. Anduze, $20,439.
  Housing & Community Renewal—Elmo D. Roebuck, $18,641.
  Labor—Melville Stevens, $18,641.
  Property & Procurement—Mario Lewis, $19,711.
  Public Safety—Otis L. Felix, $19,206.
  Public Works—James W. Huston, $23,075.
  Social Welfare—Macon M. Berryman, $19,771.

### LEGISLATURE

Unicameral Legislature of 15 members meets each year in January for 60 days, at Charlotte Amalie. Each member receives $9,000 annually, plus allowance for expenses and travel.

# Mayors and City Managers of Larger United States Cities

## AS OF JANUARY, 1969

*Asterisk before name denotes city manager. All others are mayors. For mayors, dates are those of expiration of term, for city managers, they are dates of appointment.

D., Democrat; R., Republican; Ind., Independent; N-P, Non-Partisan.

| City | Mayor or (*) City Manager | Term |
|---|---|---|
| Abilene, Tex.... | *H. P. Clifton........ | 1963, July |
| Abington, Pa... | *Fred F. Schaefer.... | 1958, June |
| Akron, Ohio.... | John S. Ballard, R.... | 1971, Dec. |
| Alameda, Calif.. | *H. D. Weller...... | 1957, Oct. |
| Albany, Ga..... | *S. A. Roos....... | 1961, Aug. |
| Albany, N. Y.. | E. Corning, 2d, D.... | 1969, Dec. |
| Albuquerque,.. | *Richard Wilson.... | 1968, Aug. |
| Alexandria, La.. | W. G. Bowdon, Jr., D. | 1969, June |
| Alexandria, Va.. | *Albert M. Hair, Jr... | 1962, June |
| Alhambra, Calif. | *Harry S. Scott... | 1968, Sept. |
| Allen Park, Mich. | Leo L. Paluch, D.... | 1969, Apr. |
| Allentown, Pa... | Ray B. Bracy, D..... | 1970, Jan. |
| Alton, Ill...... | C. Wiseman, Jr., D... | 1969, May |
| Altoona, Pa.... | William H. Prosser, R. | 1972, Jan. |
| Amarillo, Tex... | *John S. Stiff....... | 1963, Sept. |
| Amherst, N. Y.. | Harry Jones, R...... | 1970, Jan. |
| Anaheim, Calif.. | *Keith A. Murdoch... | 1958, Nov. |
| Anchorage, Alas. | *Robert E. Sharp.... | 1968, Apr. |
| Anderson, S. C.. | *Richard A. Bolin ... | 1968, Aug. |
| Ann Arbor, Mich. | *G. C. Larcom, Jr.... | 1956, Apr. |
| Appleton, Wis... | G. L. Buckley, N-P... | 1972, Apr. |
| Arcadia, Calif... | *Lyman H. Cozad... | 1966, Sept. |
| Arlington, Mass. | *Donald R. Marquis.. | 1966, Nov. |
| Arlington, Tex.. | *Herman J. Veselka... | 1966, Apr. |
| Arlington, Va... | *Bert Johnson...... | 1962, Dec. |
| Asheville, N. C.. | *P. E. Horton, 3rd... | 1968, Sept. |
| Atlanta, Ga.... | Ivan Allen Jr., N-P... | 1969, Dec. |
| Atlantic City.. | R. S. Jackson, Jr.... | 1972, May |
| Auburn, N. Y... | *Bruce L. Clifford.... | 1966, Aug. |
| Augusta, Ga.... | Geo. Sancken, Jr., N-P | 1970, Jan. |
| Aurora, Colo.... | *Robert O. Wright... | 1959, Apr. |
| Aurora, Ill..... | Albert D. McCoy, N-P | 1969, Apr. |
| Austin, Tex.... | *Robert H. Tinstman. | 1967, Sept. |
| Bakersfield, Cal.. | *Harold E. Bergen.... | 1966, Apr. |
| Baltimore, Md.. | T. J. Alesandro, D.... | 1971, Dec. |
| Bangor, Me..... | *Merle F. Goff...... | 1966, Dec. |
| Baton Rouge, La. | W. W. Dumas, D.... | 1972, Dec. |
| Bay City, Mich.. | *W. Larry Collins ... | 1968, Oct. |
| Bayonne, N. J.. | F. G. Fitzpatrick, D.. | 1970, June |
| Beaumont, Tex.. | *O. C. Galloway.... | 1968, June |
| Belleville, Ill... | Chas. E. Nichols, N-P. | 1969, Apr. |
| Belleville, N. J.. | Kenneth Smith, D... | 1972, May |
| Berkeley, Calif.. | *William C. Hanley... | 1967, Feb. |
| Berwyn, Ill..... | George Dolezal, R.... | 1969, Apr. |
| Bethlehem, Pa.. | H. G. Payrow, Jr., R.. | 1970, June |
| Beverly, Mass... | James Vitale, D..... | 1969, Dec. |
| Binghamton,N.Y. | J. W. Esworthy, R... | 1969, Dec. |
| Biloxi, Miss.... | Daniel Guice, D..... | 1969, July |
| Birmingham, Ala. | George Seibels, R.... | 1971, Dec. |
| Bloomfield, N. J. | *H. Joseph North.... | 1967, Oct. |
| Bloomington, Ill. | *S. W. McAllister.... | 1966, July |
| Bloomington, Minn. | *John Pidgeon...... | 1967, Dec. |
| Boston, Mass... | Kevin White, D..... | 1971, Dec. |
| Boulder, Colo... | *Ted Tedesco...... | 1967, June |
| Bridgeport, Ct.. | Hugh C. Curran, D... | 1969, Nov. |
| Bristol, Conn... | Henry J. Wojtusik, D. | 1969, Dec. |
| Brockton, Mass | John E. Sullivan, D... | 1969, Dec. |
| Brookline, Mass. | Board of Selectmen | ...... |
| Brownsville, Tex. | *A. B. Westbrook.... | 1962, Jan. |
| Buena Park, Calif. | *George M. Bahner... | 1966, May |
| Buffalo, N. Y... | Frank A. Sedita, D... | 1969, Dec. |
| Burbank, Calif.. | *Joseph N. Baker.... | 1968, Mar. |
| Burlington, Vt.. | Francis J. Cain, D.... | 1969, Apr. |
| Cambridge, Mass | *J. A. DeGugliemo.... | 1966, Jan. |
| Camden, N. J .. | Alfred R. Pierce, D... | 1969, July |
| Canton, Ohio.. | Stanley A. Cmich, R.. | 1971, Dec. |
| Casper, Wyo.... | *Henry Rolfes, Jr.... | 1959, Jan. |
| Cedar Rapids Ia | Frank A. Bosh, N-P... | 1969, Dec. |
| Champaign, Ill.. | *Warren B. Browning. | 1962, Dec. |
| Charleston, S. C. | J. Palmer Gaillard, D. | 1971, Dec. |
| Charleston,w.Va | Elmer H. Dodson, R.. | 1971, Apr. |
| Charlotte, N. C. | *William J. Veeder... | 1959, Aug. |
| Chattanooga, | Ralph H. Kelley, D... | 1971, Apr. |
| Chester, Pa..... | John Nacrelli, R..... | 1969, Dec. |
| Chesapeake, Va.. | *G. Robert House, Jr. | 1968, Oct. |
| Chicago, Ill.... | Richard J. Daley, D... | 1971, Dec. |
| Chicopee, Mass. | Richard Demers, D... | 1969, Dec. |
| Chula Vista, Calif. | *Fred A. Ross....... | 1963, Aug. |
| Cicero, Ill..... | John Karner, R...... | 1972, Apr. |
| Cincinnati, Ohio. | *Richard L. Krabach.. | 1968, June |
| Cleveland, Ohio. | Carl B. Stokes, D.... | 1969, Nov. |
| Cleveland Hights | *William C. Lahman.. | 1964, Oct. |
| Clifton, N. J.... | *William Holster..... | 1956, Dec. |
| Colo. Spgs., Colo. | *George H. Fellows... | 1966, Oct. |
| Columbia, Mo... | *Don F. Allard...... | 1962, Feb. |
| Columbia, S. C.. | *Carey C. Burnett... | 1961, Sept. |
| Columbus, Ga... | *Ralph A. Sayers.... | 1960, June |
| Columbus, Ohio. | M. Sensenbrenner, D.. | 1972, Jan. |
| Commerce, Calif. | *Lawrence O'Rourke.. | 1960, Mar. |
| Compton, Calif.. | *James C. Johnson... | 1968, Sept. |
| Concord, Calif.. | *F. A. Stewart...... | 1960, Jan. |
| Concord, N. H.. | *James E. Henchey... | 1968, Feb. |
| Corpus Christi.. | *R. Marvin Townsend. | 1968, Jan. |
| Costa Mesa, Cal. | *Arthur R. McKenzie. | 1965, Aug. |
| CouncilBluffs, Ia. | *M. Don Harmon.... | 1968, Feb. |
| Covington, Ky.. | *Robert F. Wray.... | 1968, Jan. |
| Cranston, R. I.. | James DiPrete, Jr. R. | 1971, Jan. |
| Cuyahoga Falls, Ohio. | D. R. Ackerman, R... | 1969, Dec. |
| Dallas, Tex.... | *W. S. McDonald.... | 1966, July |
| Daly City, Calif. | *Edward Frank..... | 1960, Mar. |
| Danville, Ill.... | Albert Gardner, R.... | 1971, Apr. |
| Danville, Va.... | *Frank A. Faison.... | 1967, Feb. |
| Davenport, Ia... | John H. Jebens, R.... | 1969, Dec. |
| Dayton, Ohio... | *Graham Watt..... | 1967, Mar. |
| Daytona Bch., Fla. | *Charles E. Jackson... | 1966, Aug. |
| Dearborn, Mich. | O. L. Hubbard, N-P... | 1971, Jan. |
| Decatur, Ill.... | *W. Robert Semple... | 1967, Nov. |
| Denver, Colo... | T. G. Currigan, D.... | 1971, July |
| Des Moines, Ia.. | *Tom Chenoweth.... | 1964, Jan. |
| Des Plaines, Ill.. | Herbert Behrel, N-P... | 1969, Apr. |
| Detroit, Mich... | J. P. Cavanagh, N-P.. | 1970, Jan. |
| Dubuque, Ia.... | *Gilbert D. Chavenelle | 1960, June |
| Duluth, Minn... | Ben Boo, N-P...... | 1971, Apr. |
| Durham, N. C.. | *I. Harding Hughes, Jr. | 1963, Feb. |
| E. Cleveland, O.. | *G. T. Apthorp..... | 1962, Aug. |
| E. Detroit, Mich. | *Chas. H. Beaublen... | 1951, July |
| E. Hartford, Conn. | E. G. Atwood, R.... | 1969, Nov. |
| E. Orange...... | J. W. Kelly, Jr., D... | 1969, Dec. |
| E. Point, Ga.... | R. E. Brown, R..... | 1972, Dec. |
| E. Providence, R. I. | *Pete A. Pakey..... | 1967, Sept. |
| E. St. Louis, Ill.. | Alvin G. Fields, N-P.. | 1971, Apr. |
| Eau Claire, Wis. | *Walter C. Kane.... | 1968, Jan. |
| Edison, N. J .... | A. M. Yelenscics, D... | 1969, Dec. |
| El Cajon, Calif.. | *Robt. M. Applegate. | 1958, Sept. |
| Elgin, Ill....... | *Robert L. Brunton... | 1962, Jan. |
| Elizabeth, N. J.. | Thomas G. Dunn, D.. | 1972, Dec. |
| Elkhart, Ind.... | John W. Weaver, R... | 1971, Dec. |
| Elmhurst, Ill.... | *Robert T. Palmer... | 1953, Aug. |
| Elmira, N. Y... | *Lawrence E. Eyres... | 1968, July |
| El Paso, Tex.... | J. F. Williams, N-P... | 1969, Apr. |
| Elyria, O...... | L. P. Reichlin, D.... | 1971, Dec. |
| Enid, Okla..... | *Waldo M. Porr..... | 1961, Sept. |
| Erie, Pa....... | Louis J. Tullio, D.... | 1970, Jan. |
| Euclid, Ohio.... | Kenneth J. Sims, N-P. | 1971, Nov. |
| Eugene, Ore.... | *Hugh McKinley..... | 1960, Oct. |
| Evanston, Ill... | *Wayne F. Anderson. | 1962, Oct. |
| Evansville, Ind.. | Frank McDonald, D.. | 1971, Dec. |
| Everett, Wash... | A. F. Alexander, N-P.. | 1970, Apr. |
| Fairfield, Conn.. | J. J. Sullivan, D..... | 1969, Nov. |
| Fair Lawn, N. J. | *George Pellack..... | 1960, June |
| Fargo, N. Dak.. | H. I. Lashkowitz, D... | 1970, Apr. |
| Fayet'ville, N. C. | *Gilbert W. Ray..... | 1949, Jan. |
| Florissant, Mo... | James J. Eagen D.... | 1971, Apr. |
| Flint, Mich.... | *Thomas Kay...... | 1963, Mar. |
| Ft. Lauderdale.. | *Robert H. Bubier... | 1963, Mar. |
| Ft. Smith, Ark.. | Jack Freeze, N-P.... | 1970, Dec. |
| Ft. Wayne, Ind. | Harold S. Zeis, R.... | 1971, Dec. |
| Ft. Worth, Tex.. | *Howard McMahan... | 1967, May |
| Framingham, Mass. | Board of Selectmen ... | ...... |
| Fresno, Calif... | *Neil Goedhard.... | 1968, May |
| Fullerton, Calif.. | *W. F. Cornett, Jr.... | 1966, Oct. |
| Gadsden, Ala... | L. L. Gilliland, D.... | 1970, Sept. |
| Galesburg, Ill... | *Thomas B. Herring.. | 1960. Nov. |
| Galveston, Tex.. | *John Unverferth.... | 1967, July |
| Gardena, Calif.. | *John Ghormley..... | 1966, Aug. |
| Garden Grove, Calif. | *Dudley N. Lapham.. | 1961, Oct. |
| Garfield Hgts., O. | F. W. Petrancek, D... | 1969, Dec. |
| Garland, Tex... | *C. E. Duckworth... | 1965, Jan. |
| Gary, Ind..... | R. G. Hatcher, D.... | 1971, Nov. |
| Gastonia, N. C.. | *Peter F. Lydens.... | 1966, Sept. |
| Glendale, Calif.. | *C. E. Perkins..... | 1952, Apr. |
| Gr. Rapids,Mich. | *Julian H. Orr...... | 1968, Apr. |
| Granite City, Ill. | Donald Partney, D... | 1969, Apr. |
| Great Falls, Mont. | J. J. McLaughlin, D.. | 1969, May |
| Green Bay, Wis. | Don A. Tilleman, N-P | 1971, May |
| Greensboro,N.C. | John Turner....... | 1968, May |
| Greenville, Miss. | Patrick Dunne, D.... | 1972, Jan. |
| Greenville, S. C.. | *Aaron Marsh...... | 1967, Apr. |
| Greenwich, Ct... | John F. Taintor, R... | 1969, Dec. |
| Hagerstown, Md. | Herman L. Mills, R... | 1968, Apr. |
| Hamden, Conn.. | William Adams, Jr. D | 1970, Jan. |
| Hamilton, Ohio.. | *C. R. Lukens...... | 1964. Feb. |
| Hammond, Ind.. | Joseph E. Klen, D... | 1971, Dec. |
| Hampton, Va... | *C. E. Johnson..... | 1956, May |
| Harlingen, Tex.. | *John Clary....... | 1968, Mar. |
| Harrisburg, Pa.. | Albert H. Straub R.. | 1972, Jan. |
| Hartford, Conn.. | *Elisha C. Freedman. | 1963, May |
| Haverhill, Mass. | James Waldron, N-P.. | 1969, Dec. |
| Hayward, Calif.. | *Raymond E. Doran. | 1960, Apr. |

| City | Mayor or (*) City Manager | Term |
|---|---|---|
| Hialeah, Fla.... | Henry Milander, N-P.. | 1969, Nov. |
| High Point, N.C. | *Harold R. Cheek.... | 1960, Mar. |
| Highland Park, Mich.... | Robert Blackwell, R... | 1971, Nov. |
| Hollywood, Fla.. | *Joseph W. Watson.. | 1952, June |
| Holyoke, Mass.. | William Taupier, D... | 1970, Jan. |
| Honolulu, Hawaii | Frank F. Fasi, D.... | 1973, Jan. |
| Houston, Tex.... | Louie Welch, D.... | 1970, Jan. |
| Huntington, W. Va.... | *Edward A. Ewing... | 1964, Feb. |
| Huntsville, Ala. | Joe W. Davis, N-P.... | 1972, Oct. |
| Hutchinson, Kan. | *George W. Pyle.... | 1967, Aug. |
| Independence, Mo.... | *Lyle Alberg..... | 1968, Sept. |
| Indianapolis, Ind. | Richard Lugar, R... | 1972, Jan. |
| Inglewood, Calif. | *Douglas W. Ayres... | 1968, Apr. |
| Inkster, Mich... | *Ralph A. DeSantis... | 1966, Aug. |
| Iowa City, Iowa. | *Frank R. Smiley... | 1967, Feb. |
| Irving, Tex.... | *Morris M. Howard.. | 1960, Apr. |
| Irvington, N.J. | Harry Stevenson, N-P | 1970, July |
| Jackson, Mich.. | *Paul L. White.... | 1965, Jan. |
| Jackson, Miss. | Allen Thompson, D.. | 1969, July |
| Jacksonville, Fla. | Hans Tanzler, Jr., D.. | 1971, June |
| Jamestown, N.Y. | Charles Magnuson, R. | 1969, Dec. |
| Janesville, Wis.. | *Karl A. Samek..... | 1967, Sept. |
| Jersey City, N.J. | T. J. Whelan, N-P... | 1969, July |
| Johnstown, Pa.. | K. O. Tompkins, R... | 1972, Jan. |
| Joplin, Mo.... | *Robert E. Metzinger. | 1968, Mar. |
| Kalamazoo, Mich | *James Caplinger.... | 1968, July |
| Kan. City, Kan. | J. H. McDowell, N-P.. | 1972, Apr. |
| Kan. City, Mo.. | *John L. Taylor.... | 1968, Feb. |
| Kearny, N.J. | Joseph M. Healey, D. | 1969, Dec. |
| Kenosha, Wis... | *John A. Serpe..... | 1966, June |
| Kettering, O... | *Ervin L. Welch.... | 1954, Dec. |
| Key West, Fla. | *Charles C. Ryan.... | 1968, May |
| Knoxville, Tenn. | Leonard Rogers, D.. | 1971, Dec. |
| Kokomo, Ind.. | John W. Miller, R..... | 1972, Jan. |
| LaCrosse, Wis.. | Warren Loveland, N-P | 1969, Apr. |
| Lafayette, La.. | J. R. Bertrand, D... | 1972, May |
| Lake Chas., La. | James Sudduth, D.... | 1969, June |
| Lakeland, Fla.. | *Robert V. Youkey... | 1960, Jan. |
| Lakewood, Cal. | *Marshall W. Julian.. | 1962, Jan. |
| Lakewood, Ohio. | Robert M. Lawther, R | 1971, Dec. |
| Lancaster, Pa.. | T. J. Monaghan, D.... | 1969, Dec. |
| Lansing, Mich.. | Max Murninghan, N-P | 1969, Apr. |
| Laredo, Tex.... | J. C. Martin, Jr., N-P.. | 1970, May |
| Las Vegas, Nev. | *Arthur R. Trelease... | 1964, Nov. |
| Lawton, Okla.. | Wayne Gilley, D.... | 1969, May |
| Lexington, Ky.. | *John R. Cook, Jr.... | 1952, May |
| Lewiston, Me.. | John Beliveau, D.... | 1970, Jan. |
| Lima, Ohio.... | C. P. Morris, N-P.... | 1969, Nov. |
| Lincoln, Nebr.. | Sam Schwartzkop, N-P | 1971, May |
| LincolnPk., Mich. | Robt. DeMars, D.... | 1969, Apr. |
| Linden, N.J. | John Gregorio, D.... | 1970, Dec. |
| Little Rock, Ark. | *E. Jack Murphy (act) | 1968, Sept. |
| Livonia, Mich.. | Harvey Moelke, R.... | 1970, Apr. |
| Long Beach, Cal. | *John R. Mansell.... | 1961, Mar. |
| Longview, Tex. | *Harry G. Mosley.... | 1952, July |
| Los Angeles, Cal. | Samuel W. Yorty, N-P | 1969, June |
| Louisville, Ky.. | K. A. Schmied, R.... | 1969, Dec. |
| Lowell, Mass... | *Charles Gallagher... | 1966, Dec. |
| L. Merion, Pa.. | *Thomas B. Fulweiler. | 1968, Jan. |
| Lubbock, Tex... | *W. R. Blackwell.... | 1967, Feb. |
| Lynchburg, Va. | *Robert D. Morrison.. | 1949, Sept. |
| Lynn, Mass.... | Irving E. Kane, N-P.. | 1970, Jan. |
| Madison, Wis.. | Otto Festge, N-P.... | 1969, Apr. |
| Malden, Mass... | Walter Kelliher, N-P.. | 1969, Dec. |
| Manchester, Ct. | *Robt. B. Weiss..... | 1966, Jan. |
| Mansfield, Ohio. | Robert Lemley, D.... | 1971, Dec. |
| Marion, Ohio.. | Eugene Yazel, R.... | 1971, Dec. |
| McKeesport, Pa. | Albert Elko, D...... | 1969, Dec. |
| Medford, Mass.. | *Howard H. Reed.... | 1962, May |
| Memphis, Tenn. | Henry Loeb, N-P.... | 1971, Dec. |
| Meridian, Miss. | *Joel W. Forrester... | 1959, July |
| Mesa, Ariz.... | *J. A. Petrie...... | 1952, June |
| Miami, Fla.... | *M. L. Reese...... | 1960, Mar. |
| Miami Bch., Fla. | *J. C. Duffield..... | 1967, Sept. |
| Middletown, O.. | *Dan W. Kothe..... | 1964, June |
| Midland, Tex... | *James W. Brown.... | 1964, Nov. |
| Midwest City, Okla.... | *W. D. Baker...... | 1966, May |
| Milford, Conn.. | Alan Jepson, D..... | 1969, Nov. |
| Milwaukee, Wis. | Henry W. Maier, N-P. | 1972, Apr. |
| Minneapolis... | Arthur Naftalin D... | 1969, July |
| Mobile, Ala.... | Lambert Mims..... | 1969, Oct. |
| Modesto, Calif.. | *John C. Keefe..... | 1963, Apr. |
| Moline, Ill.... | James F. Arndt, R.... | 1969, May |
| Monroe, La.... | W. L. Howard, D.... | 1972, July |
| Monterey Park, Calif.... | *William Woollett, Jr. | 1965, Aug. |
| Montgomery, Ala. | Earl D. James, D..... | 1971, Oct. |
| Mt. Vernon, N.Y. | August Petrillo, R.... | 1971, Dec. |
| Muncie, Ind... | Paul Cooley, D..... | 1971, Dec. |
| Muskegon, Mich. | *George F. Liddle... | 1942, May |
| Muskogee, Okla. | *Vacant........ | |
| Nashua, N.H... | Dennis Sullivan, N-P. | 1969, Dec. |
| Nashville, Tenn. | C. Beverly Briley, D.. | 1971, Aug. |
| New Bedford, Mass....... | E. F. Harrington, D... | 1969, Dec. |
| New Britain, Conn...... | Paul J. Manafort, R... | 1969, Nov. |
| New Brunswick, N.J..... | Patricia Q. Sheehan, N-P.. | 1971, May |
| New Haven, Ct. | Richard C. Lee, D... | 1969, Dec. |
| New Kensington, Pa....... | Lenus H. Hileman, D. | 1970, Jan. |
| New Orleans, La. | Victor H. Schiro, D... | 1970, May |
| New Rochelle, N.Y....... | *Murray Fuerst...... | 1965, Feb. |
| New York, N.Y. | John V. Lindsay, R... | 1969, Dec. |
| Newark, N.J. .. | Hugh Addonizio, N-P. | 1970, July |
| Newark, Ohio.. | J. H. Alexander, R.... | 1972, Jan. |
| Newport, R.I.. | *B. Cowles Mallory... | 1968, Feb. |
| Newport News. | *W. E. Lawson, Jr.... | 1965, Sept. |
| Newton, Mass.. | Monte Basbas, N-P... | 1969, Dec. |
| Niagara Falls.. | *Donald J. O'Hara... | 1967, Jan. |
| Norfolk, Va.... | *Thos. F. Maxwell.... | 1956, Feb. |
| Norman, Okla.. | *Jerry M. Smith..... | 1968, Feb. |
| Norwalk, Calif. | *M. D. McKeown.... | 1968, Sept. |
| Norwalk, Conn. | Frank N. Zullo, D.... | 1969, Nov. |
| Norwich, Conn. | *Thomas H. Hissom... | 1967, July |
| Oak Park, Ill.. | *Harris Stevens..... | 1962, June |
| Oak Pk., Mich. | *Donald F. McIntyre. | 1967, Aug. |
| Oakland, Calif. | *Jerome Keithley.... | 1966, |
| Oak Ridge, Tenn. | *Carlton E. McMullin. | 1962, Apr. |
| Odessa, Tex.... | *Ronald J. Neighbors. | 1968, Nov. |
| Ogden, Utah... | *Samuel B. Hood..... | 1962, Feb. |
| Okla. City, Okla. | *Robert Oldland..... | 1967, Sept. |
| Omaha, Nebr... | A. W. Sorensen, N-P.. | 1969, May |
| Ontario, Calif. | *H. K. Hunter...... | 1966, Jan. |
| Orange, N.J. .. | John F. Monica, R.... | 1971, June |
| Orlando, Fla... | Carl Langford N-P... | 1972, Oct. |
| Oshkosh, Wis.. | *Angus Crawford.... | 1966, Feb. |
| Owensboro, Ky.. | *Max N. Rhoads.... | 1959, Aug. |
| Oxnard, Calif.. | *Paul E. Wolven..... | 1953, Feb. |
| Palo Alto, Cal.. | *George E. Morgan... | 1966, Feb. |
| Parkersburg, W.Va....... | Glen B. Gainer, Jr. D. | 1971, Apr. |
| Parma, Ohio... | John Petruska, D..... | 1971, Dec. |
| Pasadena, Calif. | *John D. Phillips.... | 1966, Oct. |
| Pasadena, Tex. | Clyde Doyal, D..... | 1969, Apr. |
| Passaic, N.J. .. | *Theodore Janescek.. | 1967, Sept. |
| Paterson, N.J. | Lawrence Kramer, R.. | 1969, Nov. |
| Pawtucket, R.I. | Robt. F. Burns, N-P.. | 1971, Jan. |
| Pensacola, Fla. | *William H. Law, Jr.. | 1965, Oct. |
| Peoria, Ill..... | *Leonard H. Caro.... | 1964, Apr. |
| Perth Amboy, N.J....... | James Flynn, Jr., D... | 1970, May |
| Petersburg, Va. | *Roy F. Ash....... | 1950, Jan. |
| Philadelphia, Pa. | James H. J. Tate, D.. | 1972, Dec. |
| Phoenix, Ariz.. | *Robert Coop...... | 1964, Dec. |
| Pico Rivera, Cal. | *Robert B. Carleson.. | 1965, Jan. |
| Pine Bluff, Ark.. | A. T. Franks, N-P.... | 1968, Dec. |
| Pittsburgh, Pa. | Joseph M. Barr, D.... | 1969, Dec. |
| Plainfield, N.J. | Frank Blatz, Jr., R... | 1970, Jan. |
| Pomona, Calif.. | *Frederick W. Sharp.. | 1949, Aug. |
| Pontiac, Mich.. | *Joseph A. Warren... | 1964, Aug. |
| Port Arthur, Tex. | *George E. Dibrell... | 1962, Oct. |
| Port Huron, Mich. | *Gerald R. Bouchard. | 1965, Apr. |
| Portland, Me... | *John Menario..... | 1967, June |
| Portland, Ore.. | Terry Schrunk, N-P... | 1973, Jan. |
| Portsmouth, O.. | *Huxley Kennedy.... | 1967, Feb. |
| Portsmouth, Va. | *A. P. Johnson, Jr.... | 1958, Sept. |
| Poughkeepsie.. | *James Mulcare..... | 1968, Sept |
| Providence, R.I. | J. A. Doorley, Jr., D.. | 1971, Jan. |
| Provo, Utah.... | Verl G. Dixon, R.... | 1969, Dec. |
| Pueblo, Colo... | *George H. Fellows... | 1959, July |
| Quincy, Ill..... | Wes W. Olson, R.... | 1969, Apr. |
| Quincy, Mass.. | James McIntyre, R.... | 1970, Jan. |
| Racine, Wis ... | William H. Beyer, N-P | 1969, Apr. |
| Raleigh, N. C .. | *William H. Carper... | 1950, Sept. |
| Rapid City, S.D. | Henry Baker, N-P.... | 1969, May |
| Reading, Pa.... | V. R. H. Yarnell, D... | 1972, Jan. |
| Redondo Beach, Calif....... | *F. E. Hopkins...... | 1954, June |
| Redwood City, Calif....... | *Howard C. Ullrich... | 1965, Dec. |
| Reno, Nev.... | *Joe E. Latimore.... | 1960, Oct. |
| Revere, Mass... | G. V. Coletta, D..... | 1969, Dec. |
| Richfield, Minn. | *Wayne Burggraaff... | 1968, Dec. |
| Richmond, Calif. | *Kenneth Smith..... | 1967, Sept. |
| Richmond, Va.. | *Alan Kiepper...... | 1967, Sept. |
| Riverside, Calif. | *John B. Wentz..... | 1963, Dec. |
| Roanoke, Va... | *Julian F. Hirst..... | 1965, Oct. |
| Rochester, Minn. | Alex. P. Smekta, N-P. | 1969, Apr. |
| Rochester, N.Y. | *Seymour Scher..... | 1965, Dec. |
| Rock Island, Ill. | *Raymond P. Botch... | 1961, Jan. |
| Rockford, Ill... | B. T. Schleicher, R... | 1969, Apr. |
| Rome, N.Y.... | Wm. A. Valentine, R. | 1971, Dec. |
| Roseville, Mich. | *James Bottomley... | 1968, July |
| Roswell, N.M.. | *H. E. McMinn..... | 1964, May |
| Royal Oak, Mich. | *Bruce W. Love..... | 1961, June |
| Sacramento, Cal. | *E. A. Fairbairn..... | 1964, July |
| Saginaw, Mich.. | *E. H. Potthoff, Jr... | 1961, July |
| St. Clair Shores, Mich....... | *Donald J. Harm.... | 1962, Jan. |
| St. Joseph, Mich. | D. A. Merrifield, N-P. | 1970, Apr. |
| St. Louis, Mo.. | A. J. Cervantes, D.... | 1969, Apr. |
| St. Louis Park, Minn....... | *Chris Cherches.... | |
| St. Paul, Minn. | Thomas R. Byrne, D.. | 1970, June |
| St. Petersburg. | *Lynn H. Andrews... | 1961, Nov. |
| Salem, Mass... | F. X. Collins, N-P.... | 1970, Jan. |
| Salem, Ore.... | *Robert S. Moore.... | 1968, Aug. |
| Salina, Kan.... | Norris D. Olson..... | 1964, May |
| Salt Lake City.. | J. Bracken Lee, R.... | 1971, Jan. |
| San Angelo, Tex. | *H. D. Howard...... | 1958, July |

| City | Mayor or (*) City Manager | Term | City | Mayor or (*) City Manager | Term |
|---|---|---|---|---|---|
| San Antonio,Tex. | *Gerald Henckel, J..R | 1967, Dec. | Troy, N. Y..... | *Sidney C. Smith..... | 1967, May |
| San Bernardino.. | Al C. Ballard, D..... | 1969, May | Tucson, Ariz.... | *Roger O'Mara...... | 1966, Sept |
| San Diego, Calif. | *Walter Hahn, Jr.... | 1966, Dec. | Tulsa, Okla..... | J. M. Hewgley, Jr.. R. | 1970, Apr. |
| San Francisco... | Joseph Alioto, D .... | 1972, Jan. | Tuscaloosa, Ala. | G. Van Tassel, D..... | 1969, Oct. |
| San Jose, Calif.. | *Anthony P. Hamann. | 1950, Mar. | Tyler, Tex...... | *Robert Hayes....... | 1967, Dec. |
| San Leandro.... | *Wesley McClure.... | 1948, May | Union, N. J.... | F. E. Biertuempfel, R. | 1969, Dec. |
| San Mateo, Calif. | *Arthur B. Sullivan... | 1946, Jan. | University City, Mo. | *Chas. T. Henry..... | 1959, Jan. |
| Santa Ana, Calif. | *Carl J. Thornton.... | 1951, Aug. | Utica, N. Y..... | Dominick Assaro, D... | 1969, Nov. |
| Santa Barbara.. | *Clifford Petrie...... | 1968, Dec. | Vallejo, Calif... | *D. R. Sollenberger... | 1967, June |
| Santa Monica, Calif. | *Perry Scott........ | 1964, Oct. | Valley Stream, N. Y. | Charles J. Monica, R. | 1970, Apr. |
| Santa Rosa,Calif. | *George Minturn.... | 1961, Sept. | Vineland, N. J.. | Henry Garton, R..... | 1972, June |
| Savannah, Ga... | *Picot B. Floyd...... | 1967, May | Waco, Tex,..... | *Elmer A. Roberts.... | 1964, July |
| Scottsdale, Ariz. | *W. V. Donaldson.... |  | Warren, Mich... | Ted Bates, R....... | 1969, Apr. |
| Scranton, Pa... | J. J. Walsh, D...... | 1968, July | Warwick, R. I... | Philip Noel, D....... | 1970, Jan. |
| Seattle, Wash... | J. D. Braman, N-P... | 1965, Apr. | Wash., D. C.... | Bd. of Commissioners | .......... |
| Shaker Hghts.,O. | Paul K. Jones, R..... | 1970, Jan. | Waterbury, Ct.. | George P. Harlamon, R | 1969, Dec. |
| Sheboygan, Wis. | J. R. Browne, R.... | 1970, Jan. | Waterloo, Ia.... | Lloyd Turner, N-P ... | 1970, Jan. |
| Shreveport, La.. | Clyde E. Fant, D.... | 1971, Dec. | Watertown,Mass | Board of Selectmen |  |
| Sioux City, Ia.. | *Buford M. Watson... | 1969, Apr. | Waukegan, Ill... | Robert Sabonjian, N-P | 1969, May |
| Sioux Falls, S. D. | M. E. Schirmer, N-P. | 1970, Nov. | Wauwatosa,Wis. | Ervin A. Meier, N-P.. | 1972, Apr. |
| Skokie, Ill...... | *Gordon E. Thorn... | 1967, July | West Allis, Wis.. | Arnold Klentz, N-P... | 1972, Apr. |
| Somerville,Mass. | J. F. Brennan, D.... | 1969, May | W. Covina, Cal.. | *George Aiassa...... | 1958, May |
| South Bend, Ind. | Lloyd M. Allen, R.... | 1966, Oct. | W. Hartford, Ct. | *Richard H. Custer... | 1962, Aug. |
| So. Gate, Calif.. | *Carl H. Zeise...... | 1969, Dec. | W. Haven, Conn. | A. F. Zarnowski, R.... | 1969, Dec. |
| So. San Francisco Calif. | *Vacant.......... | 1966, Oct. | W.NewYork,N.J. | J. R. Armellino, D.... | 1971, May |
| Spartanb'g, S. C. | *Lott T. Rogers..... | 1958, Oct. | W. Orange, N. J. | Louis P. Falcone, N-P | 1970, June |
| Spokane, Wash.. | *F. Sylvin Fulwiler... | 1963, Aug. | W. Palm Beach . | *William H. Tyre..... | 1966, Aug. |
| Springfield, Ill.. | Nelson Howarth, N-P. | 1971, Apr. | Wheeling, W. Va. | *Thomas W. Lewis... | 1968, Oct. |
| Springfield,Mass. | F. H. Freedman, R ... | 1969, Dec. | White Plains, N. Y. | Richard S. Hendey, R. | 1969, Dec. |
| Springfield, Mo.. | *D. A. Burkhalter... | 1966, May | Wichita, Kan.... | *Ralph Wulz........ | 1968, Sept. |
| Springfield, Ohio. | *Alfred Stodzas..... | 1968, Nov. | Wichita Falls, Tex. | *L. Jack Davis....... | 1963, Jan. |
| Stamford, Conn. | Bruno Giordano, D... | 1969, Dec. | Wilkes-Barre,Pa. | *F. E. Wegner....... | 1968, Apr. |
| Stockton, Calif.. | *Frank Fargo....... | 1963, Jan. | Wilmington, Del. | Hal Haskell, R....... | 1973, Jan. |
| Stratford, Conn. | *Richard E. Blake.... | 1963, Aug. | Wilmington,N.C. | *E. C. Brandon, Jr... | 1962, May |
| Sunnyvale, Cal.. | *John E. Dever..... | 1967, Aug. | Winston-Salem.. | *John M. Gold....... | 1951, Aug. |
| Syracuse, N. Y.. | Wm. F. Walsh, R.... | 1969, Dec. | Woodbridge,N.J. | *George Meholick .... | 1968, Feb. |
| Tacoma, Wash.. | *David D. Rowlands.. | 1956, June | Woonsocket, R.I. | A. Edgar Lussier, N-P. | 1969, Apr. |
| Tallahassee, Fla. | *Arvah B. Hopkins... | 1952, Feb. | Worcester, Mass. | *Francis J. McGrath.. | 1951, Apr. |
| Tampa, Fla..... | Dick Greco, Jr., D... | 1971, Sept. | Wyoming, Mich. | *Charles Thompson... | 1966, Nov. |
| Taunton, Mass.. | B. A. Friedman, N-P.. | 1969, Dec. | Yakima, Wash.. | *Craig McMicken.... | 1967, Sept. |
| Teaneck, N. J... | *Werner H. Schmid... | 1959, Mar. | Yonkers, N. Y.. | *Elder Gunter ...... | 1968, Aug. |
| Terre Haute,Ind. | Leland Larrison, R... | 1971, Dec. | York, Pa....... | John L. Snyder, R.... | 1970, Jan. |
| Toledo, Ohio.... | *William J. Gross.... | 1968, Apr. | Youngstown, O.. | Anthony B. Flask, D.. | 1969, Dec. |
| Topeka, Kan.... | Charles Wright, N-P.. | 1969, Apr. | Zanesville, Ohio. | *Samuel Grey....... | 1962, Dec. |
| Torrance, Calif.. | *Edward J. Ferraro... | 1964, Feb. |  |  |  |
| Trenton, N. J... | C. J. Armenti, N-P... | 1970, July |  |  |  |

# Qualifications for Voting by States

Data as of June 30, 1968

A voter must be at least 21 years of age (18 in Georgia and Kentucky, 19 in Alaska, 20 in Hawaii), a citizen; not a convict. Most states require registration. The Voting Rights Act of 1965 suspended literacy tests and other devices to determine qualification of voters in any state or county that had them in force on Nov. 1, 1964, and where less than 50% of the voting age population was registered on that date or voted in the Presidential election.

| State | Previous Residence Required in | | | State | Previous Residence Required in | | |
|---|---|---|---|---|---|---|---|
|  | State | County | Precinct |  | State | County | Precinct |
| Alabama...... | 1 yr. | 6 mos. | 3 mos. | Montana...... | 1 yr. | 30 days | 30 days |
| Alaska....... | (b) 1 yr. | .......... | (a) 30 days | Nebraska..... | (b) 6 mos. | 40 days | 10 days |
| Arizona....... | (b) 1 yr. | 30 days | 30 days | Nevada...... | 6 mos. | 30 days | 10 days |
| Arkansas..... | 1 yr. | 6 mos. | 30 days | New Hampshire | 6 mos. | 6 mos. | 6 mos. |
| California.... | (b) 1 yr. | 90 days | 54 days | New Jersey... | 6 mos. | 40 days | .......... |
| Colorado..... | (b) 1 yr. | 90 days | 20 days | New Mexico.. | 1 yr. | 90 days | 30 days |
| Connecticut.. | (b) 6 mos. | (c) 6 mos. | ........ | New York.... | (b) 3 mos. | 3 mos. | 3 mos. |
| Delaware.... | 1 yr. | 3 mos. | 30 days | North Carolina. | (b) 1 yr. | .......... | 30 days |
| Dist. of Col.... | 1 yr. | ........ | ...... | North Dakota.. | 1 yr. | 90 days | 30 days |
| Florida....... | 1 yr. | 6 mos. | 6 mos. | Ohio......... | (b) 1 yr. | 40 days | 40 days |
| Georgia....... | 1 yr. | 6 mos. | ...... | Oklahoma..... | 6 mos. | 2 mos. | 20 days |
| Hawaii....... | 1 yr. | ........ | 3 mos. | Oregon...... | (b) 6 mos. | .......... | 2 mos. |
| Idaho........ | (b) 6 mos. | 30 days | 30 days | Pennsylvania.. | 90 days | .......... | (f) 6 mos. |
| Illinois....... | (b) 1 yr. | 90 days | 30 days | Rhode Island.. | 1 yr. | 6 mos. | 3 mos. |
| Indiana...... | 6 mos. | (d) 60 days | 30 days | South Carolina. | 1 yr. | 90 days | 30 days |
| Iowa......... | 6 mos. | 60 days | 10 days | South Dakota.. | 1 yr. | 90 days | 30 days |
| Kansas....... | (b) 6 mos. | 30 days | 30 days | Tennessee.... | 1 yr. | 3 mos. | .... |
| Kentucky..... | 1 yr. | 6 mos. | (e) | Texas........ | 1 yr. | 6 mos | .... |
| Louisiana..... | 1 yr. | 6 mos. | (f) 3 mos. | Utah........ | 1 yr. | 4 mos. | 60 days |
| Maine........ | 6 mos. | 6 mos. | .... | Vermont..... | 1 yr. | 90 days | 90 days |
| Maryland.... | 1 yr. | ....... | (f) 6 mos. | Virginia...... | 1 yr. | 6 mos. | 30 days |
| Massachusetts. | 1 yr. | 6 mos. | .... | Washington... | (b) 1 yr. | 90 days | 30 days |
| Michigan..... | 6 mos. | ....... | 30 days | West Virginia.. | 1 yr. | 60 days | 30 days |
| Minnesota.... | (b) 6 mos. | ...... | (g) 30 days | Wisconsin.... | 6 mos. | .......... | 10 days |
| Mississippi.... | 2 yrs. | 1 yr. | (h) 1 yr. | Wyoming..... | 1 yr. | 60 days | 10 days |
| Missouri...... | (b) 1 yr. | 60 days | 60 days |  |  |  |  |

(a) Election district. (b) Residence requirement reduced for qualified voters from another state when voting for President and Vice President. (c) Town. (d) Township. (e) 4 months in municipality for municipal elections. (f) Municipality. (g) With certain exceptions. (h) 6 months for ordained ministers and their wives if minister is in charge of a church.

## POST OFFICES IN UNITED STATES

As of June 30, 1968 there was a total of 32,261 post offices throughout the United States and Possessions. Of this number 4,953 were First Class; 7,357 Second Class; 12,912 Third Class, and 7,039 Fourth Class.

# POSTAL INFORMATION
## United States Domestic Rates
### FIRST CLASS

Letters written, and matter sealed against inspection, 6¢ for each ounce or fraction. U. S. Postal cards: single 5¢; double 10¢; private postal cards, same.

Exception: Drop letters when deposited for local delivery at offices not having letter-carrier service and not collected or delivered by rural or star route carriers may be sent at other than the first class rate.

First class includes written matter, namely letters, postal cards, post cards (private mailing cards) and all other matter wholly or partly in writing, whether sealed or unsealed, except manuscripts for books, periodical articles and music, manuscript copy accompanying proofsheets or corrected proofsheets of the same and the writing authorized by law on matter of other classes. Also matter sealed or closed against inspection. Bills and statements of accounts.

### GREETING CARDS

Under the new regulations in effect January 1968 greeting cards (unsealed) and other single-piece mailings cost 6¢ for the first 2 ounces and 2¢ for each additional ounce or fraction.

### AIRMAIL

Air postal or post card 8¢ each, letters and packages (up to 7 ounces) 10¢ an ounce. Airmail other than cards weight under 2 ounces, 10¢ per ounce plus 2¢ per piece, weight over 2 ounces, 10¢ an ounce plus 5¢ per piece. Over 7 ounces air parcel post rates plus 5¢ per piece. This is in the U. S. its territories and possessions, also to Armed Forces outside the U. S. when addressed APO or FPO, New York, N. Y., San Francisco, Calif. or Seattle, Wash. May be certified, registered, sent C.O.D. or special delivery.

### SECOND CLASS

Single copy mailings by general public 5¢ for first 2 ounces and 1¢ for each additional ounce. There are special rates for publications, newspapers and bulk mailing, consult local postmasters for rates and permit.

### THIRD CLASS

Third Class (limit up to but not including 16 ounces): Mailable matter not in 1st and 2nd classes.

Single mailing: Greeting cards (unsealed), small parcels, printed matter, booklets and catalogs, 6¢ the first 2 ounces and 2 cents for each additional ounce or fraction.

Bulk material: Books, catalogs of 24 pages or more, seeds, cuttings, bulbs, roots, scions and plants; 16¢ for first pound and 16 cents for each additional pound or fraction.

Other matter: Newsletters, shoppers' guides, advertising circulars: 22 cents a pound. Subject to a minimum rate for which Post Office should be consulted. Separate rates for some nonprofit organizations. Bulk mailing fee, $30 per calendar year. Apply to postmaster for permit.

### PARCEL POST—FOURTH CLASS

Fourth Class or Parcel Post (16 ounces and over): Merchandise, printed matter, etc., may be sealed.

On parcels weighing less than 10 lbs. and measuring more than 84 inches, but not more than 100 inches in length and girth combined, the minimum postage charge shall be the zone charge applicable to a 10-pound parcel.

### PRIORITY MAIL

First-class mail of more than 13 ounces and airmail of more than 7 ounces have been merged into a "Priority Mail (Heavy Pieces)" service. First-class and airmail weighing up to one pound is charged 80¢ as Priority Mail regardless of its domestic destination. The most expeditious handling and transportation available will be used for fastest delivery.

### FORWARDING ADDRESSES

The law that increased postal rates established the return address service for all classes of mail. (First time for first-class mail.) The mailer, in order to obtain a forwarding address, must endorse the envelope or cover "Address Correction Requested." The destination post office then will determine whether a forwarding address has been left on file and provide it for a fee of 10¢.

### SPECIAL HANDLING

Fourth class parcels will be handled and delivered as expeditiously as practicable (but not special delivery) upon payment, in addition to the regular postage: Up to 2 lbs., 25¢; over 2 lbs. and up to 10 lbs., 35¢; over 10 lbs., 50¢. Such parcels must be endorsed, Special Handling.

### SPECIAL DELIVERY

First class mail, up to 2 lbs., 30c; over 2 lbs. and up to 10 lbs., 45c; over 10 lbs., 60c. 2nd, 3rd and 4th class mail up to 2 lbs., 55c; over 2 lbs. and up to 10 lbs., 65c; over 10 lbs., 80c.

### AIR MAIL PARCEL POST

Air Parcel Post (over 7 ounces to 70 lbs.): Packages not to exceed 100 inches in length and girth combined, including written and other matter of the first class, whether sealed or unsealed, fractions of a pound being charged as a full pound. Ten cents an ounce or fraction for all domestic air mail up to and including 7 ounces regardless of distance or zone.

Rates according to zone apply between the U. S. and Puerto Rico and Virgin Isles.

Parcels weighing less than 10 pounds, measuring over 84 inches but not exceeding 100 inches in length and girth combined are chargeable with a minimum rate equal to that for a 10 pound parcel for the zone to which addressed.

## Air Mail Parcel Post

| Zones | To 1 lb. | 1½ | 2 | 2½ | 3 | 3½ | 4 | 4½ | 5 | Each lb. or fract. over 5 |
|---|---|---|---|---|---|---|---|---|---|---|
| 1, 2, 3 | $0.80 | $0.98 | $1.16 | $1.40 | $1.64 | $1.88 | $2.12 | $2.36 | $2.60 | $0.48 |
| 4 | .80 | 1.02 | 1.23 | 1.48 | 1.73 | 1.98 | 2.23 | 2.48 | 2.73 | .50 |
| 5 | .80 | 1.07 | 1.34 | 1.62 | 1.90 | 2.18 | 2.46 | 2.74 | 3.02 | .56 |
| 6 | .80 | 1.14 | 1.47 | 1.79 | 2.11 | 2.43 | 2.75 | 3.07 | 3.39 | .64 |
| 7 | .80 | 1.18 | 1.55 | 1.91 | 2.27 | 2.63 | 2.99 | 3.35 | 3.71 | .72 |
| 8 | .80 | 1.24 | 1.68 | 2.08 | 2.48 | 2.88 | 3.28 | 3.68 | 4.08 | .80 |

**Registry.** All mailable matter prepaid with postage at the first-class or airmail rate may be registered. The mailer is required to declare the value of mail presented for registration.

**Insurance** is applicable to 3rd and 4th class matter. Matter for sale addressed to prospective purchasers who have not ordered it or authorized its sending will not be insured.

**C.O.D.: Unregistered**—is applicable to 3rd and 4th class matter and sealed domestic mail of any class bearing postage at the 1st class rate. Such mail must be based on bona fide orders or be in conformity with agreements between senders and addressees. **Registered**—For details consult postmaster.

**Certified** mail service is available for any matter having no intrinsic value on which 1st class or air mail postage is paid. Receipt is furnished at time of mailing and evidence of delivery obtained. The fee is 30c in addition to postage. Return receipt, restricted delivery and special delivery are available upon payment of additional fees. No indemnity.

### REGISTERED, INSURED, C. O. D., CERTIFIED

| Indemnity and fees | Regis-tration | Insur-ance | C.O.D. |
|---|---|---|---|
| Indemnity to $10. | .75 | .20 | .60 |
| 10.01 to 15...... | .75 | .20 | .70 |
| 15.01 to 25..... | .75 | .30 | .70 |
| 25.01 to 50..... | .75 | .30 | .80 |
| 50.01 to 100.... | .75 | .40 | .90 |
| 100.01 to 150.... | 1.00 | .50 | 1.00 |
| 150.01 to 200.... | 1.00 | .60 | 1.00 |
| 200.01 to 400.... | 1.25 | | |
| 400.01 to 600.... | 1.50 | Limit $200. | |
| 600.01 to 800.... | 1.75 | | |
| 800.01 to 1,000.. | 2.00 | | |

Consult postmaster for registry rates on articles valued above $1,000.

### MONEY ORDERS

Money Orders: Must be purchased at the money order window of the post office or one of its stations. Maximum amount for which a single order may be issued, $100.

**Domestic fees:** From 1c to $10, 25c; $10.01 to $50, 35c; $50.01 to $100, 40c. Payable in the U.S., incl. Puerto Rico, Virgin Islands, Guam and Tutuila (Samoa).

**Fees for sending money abroad:** 1c to $10, 45c; $10.01 to $50, 65c; $50.01 to $100, 75c.

## Parcel Post Rate Schedule (Effective Oct. 19, 1968)

| 1lb., not exceeding | Local | 1 & 2 | 3 | 4 | 5 | 6 | 7 | 8 |
|---|---|---|---|---|---|---|---|---|
| 2 | $0.50 | $0.60 | $0.60 | $0.65 | $0.70 | $0.80 | $0.85 | $0.90 |
| 3 | .50 | .65 | .70 | .75 | .85 | .95 | 1.05 | 1.15 |
| 4 | .55 | .70 | .75 | .85 | .95 | 1.10 | 1.20 | 1.35 |
| 5 | .55 | .75 | .80 | .90 | 1.15 | 1.25 | 1.40 | 1.60 |
| 6 | .55 | .80 | .90 | 1.00 | 1.15 | 1.40 | 1.55 | 1.75 |
| 7 | .60 | .90 | .95 | 1.10 | 1.30 | 1.50 | 1.75 | 1.95 |
| 8 | .60 | .95 | 1.00 | 1.15 | 1.40 | 1.65 | 1.90 | 2.15 |
| 9 | .65 | 1.00 | 1.05 | 1.25 | 1.50 | 1.80 | 2.05 | 2.35 |
| 10 | .65 | 1.05 | 1.15 | 1.35 | 1.65 | 1.90 | 2.25 | 2.55 |
| 11 | .65 | 1.10 | 1.20 | 1.40 | 1.75 | 2.00 | 2.40 | 2.75 |
| 12 | .70 | 1.15 | 1.25 | 1.50 | 1.85 | 2.15 | 2.55 | 2.90 |
| 13 | .70 | 1.20 | 1.35 | 1.55 | 1.95 | 2.25 | 2.70 | 3.10 |
| 14 | .75 | 1.25 | 1.40 | 1.65 | 2.05 | 2.40 | 2.85 | 3.25 |
| 15 | .75 | 1.30 | 1.45 | 1.75 | 2.15 | 2.50 | 3.00 | 3.45 |
| 16 | .75 | 1.35 | 1.55 | 1.80 | 2.25 | 2.60 | 3.15 | 3.60 |
| 17 | .80 | 1.40 | 1.60 | 1.90 | 2.35 | 2.75 | 3.30 | 3.80 |
| 18 | .80 | 1.45 | 1.65 | 1.95 | 2.45 | 2.85 | 3.45 | 4.00 |
| 19 | .85 | 1.50 | 1.75 | 2.05 | 2.55 | 2.95 | 3.60 | 4.15 |
| 20 | .85 | 1.55 | 1.80 | 2.10 | 2.65 | 3.10 | 3.75 | 4.35 |

(Consult postmaster for parcels over 20 pounds or measuring more than 72 inches, length and girth.)

### CATALOGS

| Bulk Mailings* | Local | 1 & 2 | 3 | 4 | 5 | 6 | 7 | 8 |
|---|---|---|---|---|---|---|---|---|
| Piece rate........... | 17¢ | 21¢ | 21¢ | 21¢ | 21¢ | 21¢ | 21¢ | 22¢ |
| Bulk lb. rate.. | 1.9¢ | 3.0¢ | 3.6¢ | 4.6¢ | 5.7¢ | 7.1¢ | 8.7¢ | 10.4¢ |

*Minimum Quantity. Each mailing must consist of 300 or more individually addressed pieces.

### Individual Piece Mailings

| Weight lbs. | Local | 1 & 2 | 3 | 4 | 5 | 6 | 7 | 8 |
|---|---|---|---|---|---|---|---|---|
| 1.5 | $0.23 | $0.29 | $0.30 | $0.31 | $0.33 | $0.35 | $0.38 | $0.41 |
| 2 | .24 | .30 | .32 | .33 | .36 | .39 | .42 | .46 |
| 2.5 | .25 | .32 | .33 | .36 | .39 | .42 | .46 | .51 |
| 3 | .26 | .33 | .35 | .38 | .42 | .46 | .51 | .57 |
| 3.5 | .27 | .35 | .37 | .40 | .44 | .49 | .55 | .62 |
| 4 | .28 | .36 | .39 | .42 | .47 | .53 | .59 | .67 |
| 4.5 | .29 | .38 | .41 | .45 | .50 | .56 | .64 | .72 |
| 5 | .30 | .39 | .42 | .46 | .53 | .60 | .58 | .77 |
| 6 | .32 | .42 | .46 | .51 | .59 | .67 | .77 | .88 |
| 7 | .34 | .45 | .50 | .56 | .64 | .74 | .85 | .98 |
| 8 | .36 | .48 | .53 | .60 | .70 | .81 | .94 | 1.09 |
| 9 | .38 | .51 | .57 | .65 | .76 | .88 | 1.04 | 1.19 |
| 10 | .39 | .54 | .60 | .69 | .81 | .95 | 1.12 | 1.29 |

### Zone Mileage

| | | | |
|---|---|---|---|
| 1 & 2—Up to 150 | 4—300-600 | 6—1,000-1,400 | 8—Over 1,800 |
| 3—150-300 | 5—600-1,000 | 7—1,400-1,800 | |

### CATALOGS

**Educational Materials (Limit 70 lbs.)**

Complete books with 24 or more pages, at least 22 of which are printed consisting wholly of reading matter or scholarly bibliography with no advertising other than incidental announcements of books, 16mm films, film catalogs (except when mailed to commercial theatres), printed music, printed objective test materials, sound recordings including incidental announcements of recordings, and guides or scripts for use with such recordings; manuscripts for books, periodical articles and music permanently processed educational reference charts; and certain medical information, all zones: 12¢ first lb. 6¢ each additional lb.

### Library Rate (Limit 70 lbs.)

The special Library Rate of 5¢ first lb., 2¢ each additional lb. or fraction thereof, applies to the following when loaned or exchanged between schools, colleges, public libraries and certain nonprofit organizations; books, printed music, bound academic theses, periodicals, sound recordings and certain other library materials. The Library Rate applies to the following when sent to or from schools, colleges, libraries and non-profit groups; 16mm films, filmstrips, transparencies, slides, microfilms, sound recordings, scientific or mathematical kits or instruments, and certain catalogs and guides. Maximum size 100 inches length and girth combined. (See your postmaster.)

# INTERNATIONAL RATES FOR ORDINARY SURFACE MAIL,
## AIR MAIL AND SURFACE PARCEL POST (In effect May 1, 1967)

Aerogrammes—13 cents each to all countries.

Air Mail Post Cards (single)—13 cents each to all countries except Canada and Mexico (6¢).

| Country | Ordinary surface mail (not over 1 oz.) | Air Service — Letters and letter packages (per ½ oz.) | Air Service — Other Articles First 2 oz. | Air Service — Other Articles Each add'l 2 oz. or fraction | Air Service — Parcel Post First 4 oz. | Air Service — Parcel Post Each add'l 4 oz. or fraction | Surface Parcel Post First 2 lbs. | Surface Parcel Post Each add'l pound or fraction | Max. wt. for parcel post (surface or air) Lbs. |
|---|---|---|---|---|---|---|---|---|---|
| Aden......... | 13¢ | 25¢ | $0.60 | $0.30 | $1.78 | $0.69 | $1.10 | $0.35 | 22 |
| Afghanistan.... | 13 | 25 | .60 | .30 | 2.00 | .75 | 1.10 | .35 | 22 |
| Albania........ | 13 | ³20 | .50 | .20 | 2.12 | .49 | 1.10 | .35 | 22 |
| Algeria........ | 13 | 20 | .50 | .20 | 1.72 | .50 | 1.10 | .35 | 44 |
| Andorra....... | 13 | 20 | .50 | .20 | 1.77 | .44 | 1.10 | .35 | 44 |
| Anguilla....... | 13 | 15 | .40 | .10 | 1.13 | .23 | 1.00 | .30 | 22 |
| Antigua....... | 13 | 15 | .40 | .10 | 1.13 | .23 | 1.00 | .30 | 22 |
| Argentina...... | 13 | ⁴15 | .50 | .20 | 1.56 | .67 | 1.10 | .35 | 44 |
| Aruba........ | 13 | 15 | .40 | .10 | 1.32 | .28 | 1.00 | .30 | 44 |
| Ascension Isl... | 13 | 15 | .50 | .20 | ........ | ........ | 1.10 | .35 | 22 |
| Australia....... | 13 | 25 | .60 | .30 | 1.66 | .76 | 1.10 | .35 | 22 |
| Austria........ | 13 | 20 | .50 | .20 | 1.71 | .46 | 1.10 | .35 | 44 |
| Azores........ | 13 | 20 | ²50 | .20 | 1.24 | .35 | 1.10 | .35 | 22 |
| Bahamas...... | 13 | 15 | .40 | .10 | 1.39 | .16 | 1.00 | .30 | 22 |
| Bahrein....... | 13 | 25 | .60 | .30 | 1.54 | .65 | 1.10 | .35 | 22 |
| Barbados...... | 13 | 15 | .40 | .10 | 1.21 | .32 | 1.00 | .30 | 22 |
| Barbuda....... | 13 | 15 | .40 | .10 | 1.13 | .23 | 1.00 | .30 | 22 |
| Belgium....... | 13 | 20 | .50 | .20 | 1.53 | .42 | 1.10 | .35 | 44 |
| Bermuda...... | 13 | 15 | .40 | .10 | 1.12 | .22 | 1.00 | .30 | 33 |
| Bhutan........ | 13 | ³25 | ²60 | .30 | ........ | ........ | ........ | ........ | ........ |
| Bolivia........ | 13 | ³15 | ²50 | .20 | 1.57 | .43 | 1.10 | .35 | 44 |
| Bonaire....... | 13 | 15 | .40 | .10 | 1.32 | .28 | 1.00 | .30 | 44 |
| Botswana...... | 13 | 25 | .60 | .30 | 1.69 | .80 | 1.10 | .35 | 22 |
| Brazil........ | 13 | ³15 | .50 | .20 | 1.87 | .49 | 1.10 | .35 | ⁴44 |
| Br. Honduras... | 13 | 15 | .40 | .10 | 1.20 | .30 | 1.00 | .30 | 22 |
| Brit. Virgin Isl.. | 13 | 15 | .40 | .10 | 1.13 | .23 | 1.00 | .30 | 22 |
| Brunei........ | 13 | 25 | .60 | .30 | 1.91 | .93 | 1.10 | .35 | 22 |
| Bulgaria....... | 13 | 20 | .50 | .20 | 1.36 | .47 | 1.10 | .35 | 22 |
| Burma........ | 13 | 25 | ²60 | .30 | 2.10 | .91 | 1.10 | .35 | 22 |
| Burundi....... | 13 | 25 | .60 | .30 | 1.75 | .67 | 1.10 | .35 | 22 |
| Cambodia...... | 13 | 25 | .60 | .30 | ........ | ........ | 1.10 | .35 | 22 |
| Cameroon...... | 13 | 25 | .60 | .30 | 1.77 | .58 | 1.10 | .35 | 22 |
| Canada....... | 6 | ¹10 | (²5) | ........ | ........ | ........ | ⁶1.00 | .30 | ⁷25 |
| Cape Verde Isl. | 13 | 25 | ²60 | .30 | 1.73 | .51 | 1.10 | .35 | 22 |
| Cen. Africa Rep. | 13 | 25 | .60 | .30 | 1.75 | .67 | 1.10 | .35 | 44 |
| Ceylon........ | 13 | 25 | .60 | .30 | 2.12 | .81 | 1.10 | .35 | 44 |
| Chad......... | 13 | 25 | .60 | .30 | 1.75 | .67 | 1.10 | .35 | 44 |
| Chile........ | 13 | 15 | ²50 | .20 | 1.85 | .55 | 1.10 | .35 | 22 |
| China, Rep.... | 13 | ⁴25 | .60 | .30 | 1.56 | .66 | 1.10 | .35 | 44 |
| China, Cont.... | 13 | ³25 | ²60 | .30 | ........ | ........ | ........ | ........ | ........ |
| Colombia...... | 13 | ³15 | ²50 | .20 | 1.82 | .31 | 1.10 | .35 | 44 |
| Comoro Islands. | 13 | 25 | .60 | .30 | 1.99 | .91 | 1.10 | .35 | 44 |
| Congo (Brazza.) | 13 | 25 | .60 | .30 | 1.75 | .67 | 1.10 | .35 | 44 |
| Congo (Leopold.) | 13 | 25 | .60 | .30 | 1.75 | .67 | 1.10 | .35 | 44 |
| Corsica....... | 13 | 20 | .50 | .20 | 1.89 | .42 | 1.10 | .35 | 44 |
| Costa Rica..... | 13 | 15 | .40 | .10 | 1.31 | .26 | 1.00 | .30 | 44 |
| Cuba......... | 13 | 15 | ²40 | .10 | 1.51 | .32 | 1.00 | .30 | 22 |
| Curacao....... | 13 | 15 | .40 | .10 | 1.32 | .28 | 1.00 | .30 | 44 |
| Cyprus........ | 13 | 25 | .60 | .30 | 1.83 | .54 | 1.10 | .35 | 44 |
| Czechoslovakia. | 13 | 20 | .50 | .20 | 1.38 | .48 | 1.10 | .35 | 44 |
| Dahomey...... | 13 | 25 | .60 | .30 | 1.60 | .54 | 1.10 | .35 | 44 |
| Denmark...... | 13 | 20 | .50 | .20 | 1.35 | .45 | 1.10 | .35 | 44 |
| Dominica...... | 13 | 15 | .40 | .10 | 1.52 | .30 | 1.00 | .30 | 22 |
| Dominican R... | 13 | ³15 | .40 | .10 | 1.42 | .23 | 1.00 | .30 | 44 |
| Ecuador....... | 13 | ⁴15 | .50 | .20 | 1.76 | .30 | 1.10 | .35 | 44 |
| El Salvador.... | 13 | 15 | ⁴40 | .10 | 1.40 | .27 | 1.00 | .30 | 44 |
| Estonia........ | 13 | ³25 | ⁴60 | .30 | 1.81 | .60 | 1.10 | .35 | 44 |
| Ethiopia....... | 13 | 25 | .60 | .30 | 1.80 | .69 | 1.10 | .35 | 44 |
| Falkland Isl.... | 13 | 15 | .50 | .20 | 1.90 | .54 | 1.10 | .35 | 22 |
| Faroe Islands.. | 13 | 20 | .50 | .20 | 1.35 | .45 | 1.10 | .35 | 44 |
| Fernando Po... | 13 | ³25 | .60 | .30 | 1.64 | .62 | 1.10 | .35 | 44 |
| Fiji Islands.... | 13 | 25 | .60 | .30 | 1.77 | .56 | 1.10 | .35 | 22 |
| Finland....... | 13 | 20 | .50 | .20 | 1.38 | .49 | 1.10 | .35 | 44 |
| France, incl. Monaco..... | 13 | 20 | .50 | .20 | 1.89 | .42 | 1.10 | .35 | 44 |
| French Guiana.. | 13 | 15 | .50 | .20 | 1.39 | .35 | 1.10 | .35 | 44 |
| Fr. Polynesia... | 13 | 25 | .60 | .30 | 1.71 | .48 | 1.10 | .35 | 44 |
| Fr. Somaliland.. | 13 | 25 | .60 | .30 | 1.84 | .65 | 1.10 | .35 | 44 |
| Gabon Rep.... | 13 | 25 | .60 | .30 | 1.75 | .67 | 1.10 | .35 | 44 |
| Gambia....... | 13 | 25 | .60 | .30 | 1.52 | .48 | 1.10 | .35 | 22 |
| Germany, incl. Saar........ | 13 | 20 | .50 | .20 | 1.34 | .44 | 1.10 | .35 | ⁴44 |
| Ghana........ | 13 | 25 | .60 | .30 | 1.85 | .58 | 1.10 | .35 | 22 |
| Gibraltar...... | 13 | 20 | .50 | .20 | 1.37 | .47 | 1.10 | .35 | 22 |
| Gilbert and Ellice..... | 13 | 25 | ²60 | .30 | 1.69 | .63 | 1.10 | .35 | 22 |
| Great Britain... | 13 | 20 | .50 | .20 | 1.32 | .42 | 1.10 | .35 | 22 |
| Greece........ | 13 | 20 | .50 | .20 | 1.66 | .53 | 1.10 | .35 | 22 |
| Greenland...... | 13 | 20 | .50 | .20 | 1.49 | .59 | 1.10 | .35 | 44 |
| Grenada....... | 13 | 15 | .40 | .10 | 1.52 | .30 | 1.00 | .30 | 44 |
| Guadeloupe.... | 13 | 15 | .40 | .10 | 1.27 | .23 | 1.00 | .30 | 44 |
| Guatemala.... | 13 | ⁴15 | ²40 | .10 | 1.59 | .29 | 1.00 | .30 | 44 |
| Guinea....... | 13 | 25 | .60 | .30 | 1.56 | .61 | 1.10 | .35 | 44 |
| Guyana....... | 13 | 15 | .50 | .20 | 1.54 | .31 | 1.00 | .30 | 22 |
| Haiti........ | 13 | 15 | ²40 | .10 | 1.43 | .22 | 1.00 | .30 | 44 |
| Honduras...... | 13 | 15 | .40 | .10 | 1.35 | .29 | 1.00 | .30 | ⁴44 |
| Hong Kong.... | 13 | 25 | .60 | .30 | 1.68 | .79 | 1.10 | .35 | 22 |
| Hungary....... | 13 | 20 | .50 | .20 | 1.37 | .48 | 1.10 | .35 | 44 |

| Country | Ordinary surface mail (not over 1 oz.) | Letters and letter packages (per ½ oz.) | Air Service | | | | Surface Parcel Post | | Max. wt. for parcel post (surface or air) Lbs. |
|---|---|---|---|---|---|---|---|---|---|
| | | | Other Articles | | Parcel Post | | | | |
| | | | First 2 oz. | Each add'l 2 oz. or fraction | First 4 oz. | Each add'l 4 oz. or fraction | First 2 lbs. | Each add'l pound or fraction | |
| Iceland | 13¢ | 20¢ | [2].50 | .20 | 1.69 | .35 | 1.10 | .35 | 44 |
| India | 13 | 25 | [4].60 | .30 | 1.70 | .80 | 1.10 | .35 | [4]44 |
| Indonesia | 13 | 25 | .60 | .30 | 2.21 | .96 | 1.10 | .35 | 22 |
| Iran | 13 | 25 | .60 | .30 | 1.70 | .61 | 1.10 | .35 | 44 |
| Iraq | 13 | 25 | .60 | .30 | 1.89 | .60 | 1.10 | .35 | 44 |
| Ireland (Eire) | 13 | 20 | .50 | .20 | 1.31 | .42 | 1.10 | .35 | 22 |
| Israel | 13 | 25 | .60 | .30 | 1.86 | .57 | 1.10 | .35 | 22 |
| Italy | 13 | [3]20 | .50 | .20 | 1.67 | .49 | 1.10 | .35 | 44 |
| Ivory Coast | 13 | 25 | .60 | .30 | 1.56 | .60 | 1.10 | .35 | 44 |
| Jamaica | 13 | 15 | .40 | .10 | 1.50 | .20 | 1.00 | .30 | 22 |
| Japan | 13 | [4]25 | [4].60 | .30 | 1.39 | .50 | 1.10 | .35 | 22 |
| Jordan | 13 | 25 | .60 | .30 | 1.73 | .56 | 1.10 | .35 | 22 |
| Kenya | 13 | 25 | .60 | .30 | 1.86 | .69 | 1.10 | .35 | 22 |
| Korea | 13 | [4]25 | .60 | .30 | 1.43 | .54 | 1.10 | .35 | 22 |
| Kuwait | 13 | 25 | .60 | .30 | 1.52 | .63 | 1.10 | .35 | 22 |
| Laos | 13 | 25 | .60 | .30 | 2.13 | .86 | 1.10 | .35 | 22 |
| Latvia | 13 | [3]25 | [4].60 | .30 | 1.81 | .60 | 1.10 | .35 | 44 |
| Lebanon | 13 | 25 | .60 | .30 | 1.73 | .56 | 1.10 | .35 | [4]44 |
| Leeward Isl | 13 | 15 | .40 | .10 | 1.13 | .23 | 1.00 | .30 | 44 |
| Lesotho | 13 | 25 | .60 | .30 | 1.69 | .80 | 1.10 | .35 | 22 |
| Liberia | 13 | 25 | .60 | .30 | 1.42 | .53 | 1.10 | .35 | 22 |
| Libya | 13 | 20 | .50 | .20 | 1.71 | .54 | 1.10 | .35 | 44 |
| Liechtenstein | 13 | 20 | .50 | .20 | 1.52 | .43 | 1.10 | .35 | 44 |
| Lithuania | 13 | [3]25 | [4].60 | .30 | 1.81 | .60 | 1.10 | .35 | 44 |
| Luxembourg | 13 | 20 | .50 | .20 | 1.57 | .41 | 1.10 | .35 | 44 |
| Macao | 13 | 25 | .60 | .30 | 2.04 | .79 | 1.10 | .35 | 22 |
| Madagascar | 13 | 25 | .60 | .30 | 1.96 | .77 | 1.10 | .35 | 44 |
| Madeira Isl | 13 | 20 | [2].50 | .20 | 1.34 | .45 | 1.10 | .35 | 22 |
| Malawi | 13 | 25 | .60 | .30 | 1.69 | .79 | 1.10 | .35 | 22 |
| Malaysia | 13 | 25 | .60 | .30 | 2.05 | .90 | 1.10 | .35 | 22 |
| Maldive Isl | 13 | [3]25 | [2].60 | .30 | ......... | ..... | 1.10 | .35 | 22 |
| Mali | 13 | 25 | .60 | .30 | 2.20 | .52 | 1.10 | .35 | 44 |
| Malta | 13 | 20 | .50 | .20 | 1.65 | .49 | 1.10 | .35 | 22 |
| Martinique | 13 | 15 | .40 | .10 | 1.27 | .23 | 1.00 | .30 | 44 |
| Mauritania | 13 | 25 | .60 | .30 | 1.50 | .49 | 1.10 | .35 | 44 |
| Mauritius | 13 | 25 | .60 | .30 | 1.91 | .82 | 1.10 | .35 | 22 |
| Mexico[4] | 6 | [1]10 | .40 | .10 | 1.12 | .22 | 1.00 | .30 | 44 |
| Montserrat | 13 | 15 | .40 | .10 | 1.13 | .23 | 1.00 | .30 | 44 |
| Morocco | 13 | 20 | .50 | .20 | 1.67 | .49 | 1.10 | .35 | 44 |
| Muscat | 13 | 25 | .60 | .30 | 1.54 | .65 | 1.10 | .35 | 22 |
| Nepal | 13 | [3]25 | [2].60 | .30 | 1.69 | .80 | 1.10 | .35 | 22 |
| Netherlands | 13 | 20 | .50 | .20 | 1.50 | .42 | 1.10 | .35 | 44 |
| Neth. Antilles | 13 | 15 | .40 | .10 | 1.32 | .28 | 1.00 | .30 | 44 |
| Nevis | 13 | 15 | .40 | .10 | 1.13 | .23 | 1.00 | .30 | 22 |
| New Caledonia | 13 | 25 | .60 | .30 | 1.78 | .59 | 1.10 | .35 | 44 |
| New Guinea | 13 | 25 | .60 | .30 | 1.73 | .84 | 1.10 | .35 | 22 |
| New Hebrides | 13 | 25 | .60 | .30 | 1.68 | .59 | 1.10 | .35 | 44 |
| New Zealand | 13 | 25 | .60 | .30 | 1.89 | .67 | 1.10 | .35 | 22 |
| Nicaragua | 13 | 15 | .40 | .10 | 1.32 | .26 | 1.00 | .30 | 44 |
| Niger | 13 | 25 | .60 | .30 | 2.19 | .50 | 1.10 | .35 | 44 |
| Nigeria | 13 | 25 | .60 | .30 | 2.00 | .59 | 1.10 | .35 | 22 |
| Norway | 13 | 20 | .50 | .20 | 1.35 | .45 | 1.10 | .35 | 44 |
| Outer Mongolia | 13 | [3]25 | [2].60 | .30 | ......... | ..... | 1.10 | .35 | 22 |
| Pakistan | 13 | 25 | .60 | .30 | 2.20 | .77 | 1.10 | .35 | 22 |
| Palestine | 13 | 25 | .60 | .30 | 1.86 | .57 | 1.10 | .35 | 11 |
| Panama | 13 | [4]15 | [2].40 | .10 | 1.58 | .28 | 1.00 | .30 | [4]70 |
| Papua | 13 | 25 | .60 | .30 | 1.73 | .84 | 1.10 | .35 | 22 |
| Paraguay | 13 | 15 | [2].50 | .20 | 1.57 | .43 | 1.10 | .35 | 44 |
| Peru | 13 | [4]15 | [2].50 | .20 | 1.83 | .37 | 1.10 | .35 | 44 |
| Philippines | 13 | 25 | .60 | .30 | 1.93 | .74 | 1.10 | .35 | [4]44 |
| Pitcairn Isl | 13 | 25 | .60 | .30 | 1.84 | .65 | 1.10 | .35 | 22 |
| Poland | 13 | 20 | .50 | .20 | 1.65 | .47 | 1.10 | .35 | 44 |
| Portugal | 13 | 20 | .50 | .20 | 1.30 | .40 | 1.10 | .35 | 44 |
| Portuguese E. Af. | 13 | 25 | .60 | .30 | 2.18 | .81 | 1.10 | .35 | 22 |
| Port. Timor | 13 | 25 | .60 | .30 | 2.31 | 1.09 | 1.10 | .35 | 22 |
| Port W. Africa | 13 | 25 | .60 | .30 | 1.86 | .64 | 1.10 | .35 | 22 |
| Qatar | 13 | 25 | .60 | .30 | 1.54 | .65 | 1.10 | .35 | 22 |
| Reunion | 13 | 25 | .60 | .30 | 1.84 | .80 | 1.10 | .35 | 44 |
| Rhodesia | 13 | 25 | .60 | .30 | 1.69 | .79 | 1.10 | .35 | 22 |
| Rio Muni | 13 | [3]25 | .60 | .30 | 1.79 | .77 | 1.10 | .35 | 44 |
| Rumania | 13 | [3]20 | [2].50 | .20 | 1.54 | .49 | 1.10 | .35 | 44 |
| Rwanda | 13 | 25 | .60 | .30 | 1.75 | .67 | 1.10 | .35 | 22 |
| Ryukyu Islands | 13 | [3]25 | .60 | .30 | 1.43 | .54 | 1.00 | .30 | 22 |
| Sabah | 13 | 15 | .40 | .10 | 1.33 | .28 | 1.00 | .30 | 44 |
| St. Christopher | 13 | 15 | .40 | .10 | 1.13 | .23 | 1.00 | .30 | 22 |
| St. Eustatius | 13 | 15 | .40 | .10 | 1.32 | .28 | 1.00 | .30 | 44 |
| St. Helena | 13 | 25 | .60 | .30 | 1.91 | .77 | 1.10 | .35 | 22 |
| St. Lucia | 13 | 15 | .40 | .10 | 1.52 | .30 | 1.00 | .30 | 22 |
| St. Pierre & Miquelon | 13 | 15 | .40 | .10 | 1.09 | .22 | 1.00 | .30 | 44 |
| St. Vincent | 13 | 15 | .40 | .10 | 1.52 | .30 | 1.00 | .30 | 22 |
| Santa Cruz Isl | 13 | 25 | .60 | .30 | 1.97 | .88 | 1.10 | .35 | 22 |
| Saudi Arabia | 13 | [3]25 | .60 | .30 | 1.97 | .63 | 1.10 | .35 | 22 |
| Senegal | 13 | 25 | .60 | .30 | 1.48 | .47 | 1.10 | .35 | 44 |
| Seychelles | 13 | 25 | .60 | .30 | 1.61 | 71 | 1.10 | .35 | 22 |
| Sierra Leone | 13 | 25 | .60 | .30 | 1.96 | .51 | 1.10 | .35 | 22 |
| Singapore | 13 | 25 | .60 | .30 | 2.05 | .90 | 1.10 | .35 | 22 |
| Solomon Isl | 13 | 25 | .60 | .30 | 1.98 | .88 | 1.10 | .35 | 22 |
| Somali Rep | 13 | 25 | .60 | .30 | [8]2.05 | .72 | 1.10 | .35 | 22 |
| South Africa[4] | 13 | 25 | [4].60 | .30 | 1.69 | .80 | 1.10 | .35 | [4]22 |
| Spain | 13 | 20 | .50 | .20 | 1.77 | .44 | 1.10 | .35 | [4]44 |
| Sp. W. Africa | 13 | [3]25 | .60 | .30 | 1.78 | .51 | 1.10 | .35 | 22 |
| Sudan | 13 | 25 | [2].60 | .30 | 1.99 | .64 | 1.10 | .35 | 44 |
| Surinam | 13 | 15 | .50 | .20 | 1.42 | .33 | 1.10 | .35 | 44 |
| Sweden | 13 | 20 | .50 | .20 | 1.35 | .45 | 1.10 | .35 | 44 |
| Switzerland | 13 | 20 | .50 | .20 | 1.52 | .43 | 1.10 | .35 | 44 |
| Syria | 13 | 25 | .60 | .30 | 1.57 | .58 | 1.10 | .35 | [4]44 |

# 1969 Edition
# THE WORLD ALMANAC ®
## and Book of Facts

---

*The Authority Since 1868*

---

LUMAN H. LONG, *Editor*

*Senior Assistants*

| | |
|---|---|
| VINCENT P. BANNAN | ALBERT C. AUMULLER |
| KENNETH C. JOHNSTON | THOMAS J. McGUIRE |
| JACK ROSENTHAL | FLORENCE BYRNES |

ELIZABETH LEDERLE LIPS

**230 Park Avenue, New York, N.Y. 10017**

---

The World Almanac is Published Annually by
**NEWSPAPER ENTERPRISE ASSOCIATION, INC.**
230 Park Avenue, New York, N.Y. 10017
1200 West Third Street, Cleveland, Ohio 44113

---

BOYD LEWIS, *President*
MEADE MONROE, *Vice President and General Manager*
EARL H. ANDERSON, *Vice President and Business Manager
Publisher for The World Almanac*
ROBERT ROY METZ, *Vice President and Editorial Director*
WILLIAM H. BORGLUND, *Vice President, Sales Development*
EDWARD R. KENNEDY, *Vice President, Client Services*
RICHARD W. JOHNSON, *Director Publications Division*

---

# QUICK REFERENCE INDEX

| | Page |
|---|---|
| ACTORS AND ACTRESSES | 673-685 |
| ADDENDA, CORRECTIONS | 64 |
| AGRICULTURE | 769-778 |
| AMBASSADORS AND MINISTERS | 170-171 |
| ANIMALS | 779-780 |
| ASS'NS. AND SOCIETIES | 449-464 or 469-484 |
| ASTRONOMICAL DATA, 1969 | 253-287 |
| AUTOMOBILE TRAVEL, HIGHWAYS | 108-115 |
| AVIATION | 246-252 |
| AWARDS, MEDALS, PRIZES | 64, 234-244 |
| BOOKS, BEST SELLERS | 155 |
| CABINETS, JUDICIARY, U. S. | 164-169 |
| CALENDARS | 233, 263, 279, 281 |
| CANADA | 55, 485-491 |
| PRIME MINISTER'S MESSAGE | 485 |
| CENSUS OF 1960 | 592-656 |
| CHRONOLOGY 1968 | 65-92 |
| CITIES OF NORTH AMERICA, GREAT | 390-448 |
| COLLEGES AND UNIVERSITIES | 319-348 |
| CONGRESS, NINETIETH, 2ND SESS. | 48 |
| CONGRESS, NINETY-FIRST, 1ST SESS. | 915-918 |
| CONSTITUTION OF THE U. S. | 199-206 |
| CORPORATIONS, STOCKS | 50-54 |
| COST OF LIVING | 142-143, 568 |
| DAMS, RESERV'RS, RIVERS | 61, 723-724, 728-736 |
| DEATH ROLL, 1968 | 56-58, 64 |
| DECLARATION OF INDEPENDENCE | 196-198 |
| DISASTERS | 64, 657-664 |
| ECONOMICS | 131-147 |
| EDUCATIONAL STATISTICS | 319-351 |
| ELECTION TABLES | 884-918 |
| FEDERAL CIVIL EMPLOYMENT | 145-146 |
| FISH AND GAME LAWS | 781-786 |
| FLAG, U. S. | 176-177 |
| FLAGS OF WORLD (COLOR) | 449-452 or 465-468 |
| FOREIGN AID | 574-575, 580 |
| FRATERNITIES AND SORORITIES | 339-342 |
| GOVERNORS AND STATE OFFICIALS | 919-923 |
| HEADS OF STATE | 576-577 |
| HOLIDAYS | 42, 590-591 |
| HYDROELECTRIC PLANTS | 732-735 |
| INCOME TAX, FEDERAL | 209-211 |
| INVENTIONS | 116-118 |
| LAWS AND DOCUMENTS | 196-208, 700-702 |
| MAGAZINES AND NEWSPAPERS | 352-353, 390-436 |
| MANUFACTURERS | 119-126 |
| MAPS | 453-468 or 469-484 |
| MAYORS, CITY MANAGERS | 924-926 |
| MEDICAL DEVELOPMENTS | 59-60 |
| MEMORABLE DATES | 295-318 |
| METEOROLOGICAL | 288-294 |
| MINERAL PRODUCTION | 127-130 |
| MISCELLANEOUS | 61-62 |
| NATIONAL DEFENSE | 739-756 |
| NATIONAL PARKS | 94, 388-389 |
| NATIONS OF THE WORLD | 485-567 |
| NEGROES IN AMERICAN HISTORY | 46-47 |
| NEWS, LATE | 63 |
| NEW YORK CITY | 415-416, 436-438 |
| NOTED PERSONALITIES | 665-699 |
| PAINTINGS, WHERE THEY ARE | 162 |
| PASSPORTS | 700, 703 |
| PATENTS, COPYRIGHT LAWS | 207-208 |
| POLITICAL COMMITTEES | 172-173 |
| POPULATION, NATIONS OF THE WORLD | 485-567 |
| POPULATION, U. S. | 64, 592-656 |
| POSTAL INFORMATION | 927-932 |
| PRESIDENTIAL ELECTIONS | 36-39, 884-918 |
| PRESIDENTS, U. S. | 37-39, 164, 183-195 |
| WIVES | 183-195 |
| RECORDINGS (PHONOGRAPHS) | 160 |
| RELIGIOUS INFORMATION | 219-233 |
| RULERS OF ANCIENT TIMES | 688-693 |
| SCULPTURES, WHERE YOU CAN SEE THEM | 163 |
| SOCIAL SECURITY WELFARE | 148-151 |
| SPACE DEVELOPMENTS | 43-44 |
| SPORTS | 794-883 |
| STATE GOVERNMENT OFFICIALS | 919-923 |
| STATES OF THE UNION | 354-380 |
| SUPREME COURT DECISIONS | 49 |
| SYMPHONY ORCHESTRAS | 161 |
| TAXATION | 209-218 |
| THEATER, OPERA, FILMS | 156-161 |
| TIDE TABLES | 786-793 |
| TRADE AND TRANSPORTATION | 95-115 |
| UNITED NATIONS | 569-572 |
| U. S. GOVERNMENT | 164-169, 178-182 |
| VETERANS ADMINISTRATION | 753 |
| VICE PRESIDENT, U. S. | 36-39, 164, 178 |
| VIETNAM, WAR IN | 40-42 |
| VITAL STATISTICS | 757-768 |
| WASHINGTON, THE NATION'S CAPITAL | 439-444 |
| WEIGHTS AND MEASURES | 581-589 |
| WORLD FACTS | 704-738 |
| ZIP CODES | 605-634, 655 |

## New Readers' Guide to the World Almanac

Every important subject covered in the World Almanac is listed in the comprehensive General Index, where it is cross-indexed under a number of headings, making it possible for a reader to quickly find the desired information.

The following hints are intended for the student or new reader so that he may use the General Index to best advantage.

When seeking any information, the reader would do well to check first the Quick Reference Index, which lists general subjects that experience has shown are popular topics often referred to by readers.

If the subject on which the reader is seeking information is not listed in the Quick Reference Index, he should ask the following questions of himself before consulting the General Index:

1. Is the subject famous? A noted personality, place. historical event etc.?

If so, chances are excellent it is specifically listed in the General Index and the reader will need to look no further. Such subjects as Babe Ruth, World War I, the Pentagon, the Alamo and hundreds of others, would fall into this category.

But if the information sought is not sufficiently noteworthy to have its own listing in the General Index, the reader should then ask himself:

2 Into what general category does the information sought fall?

If the reader was seeking information about a lesser known home run hitter than Babe Ruth, such as Al Kaline, he would not find a separate listing for Rosen, but under the listing "Baseball" would be guided to home run leaders of all time, including Kaline.

In the same way, if the Pentagon did not have its own listing, the reader could locate it in the book under "Washington, D. C." where he would find a sub-head "public buildings" which would lead him to the pages covering the Pentagon and other public buildings in the Capital. A check under "Buildings, office, world's largest," would also locate the information desired.

All of the subjects cited in these examples could be located by using the Quick Reference Index. Ruth's and Rosen's records come under "Sports Records" in the Quick Reference Index. The Pentagon's Quick Reference Index general listing is "Washington, the Nation's Capital." Information about the Alamo can be located under the Quick Reference Index heading of "Memorable Dates."

But if the Quick Reference Index should fail to turn up the information, a simple rule for using the General Index is:

Work from the specific subject to the more general subject.

Categorize the information wanted, historically, geographically or into any other logical subject heading to which it might reasonably belong.